Thomas Cook

EUROPEAN RAIL TIMETABLE

Winter 2009 / 10

Rail and ferry services
throughout Europe

An expanded edition of the monthly
European Rail Timetable
December 2009

Thomas Cook
Your travelling companion since 1873

Published by
Thomas Cook Publishing,
Unit 9, Thomas Cook Business Park
Coningsby Road
Peterborough PE3 8SB
United Kingdom

ISBN 978-1-84848-316-3

Director of Publishing : Chris Young
Head of Travel Books : Lisa Bass

Editor : Brendan Fox
Editorial team : John Potter, Reuben Turner
David Turpie, Chris Woodcock

Telephone (Sales) +44 (0)1733 416477 (Editorial) +44 (0)1733 416322
Fax +44 (0)1733 416688

e-mail (Sales): publishing-sales@thomascook.com
e-mail (Editorial): timetables@thomascook.com

Website and on-line bookshop : www.thomascookpublishing.com

Front cover photograph:
A Brennero to Bolzano train near Colle Isarco
© Phil Wormald

Printed in the UK by CPI William Clowes, Beccles NR34 7TL

INTRODUCTION

This **Winter 2009/10** edition is a specially enlarged version of the monthly **European Rail Timetable**, published by Thomas Cook for over 135 years and recognised throughout the world as the indispensable compendium of European rail schedules. This seasonal edition appears twice yearly in Summer and Winter versions based on the June and December monthly editions.

The much-loved **Thomas Cook European Rail Timetable** has for years been the travelling companion of the dedicated European rail-based tourist and business traveller. For travel further afield you need the **Thomas Cook Overseas Timetable** covering surface transport in North and South America, Asia, Africa and Australasia.

The intention of this special edition is to make the timetable more widely available to the increasing numbers of holidaymakers who are touring Europe by train, whether using InterRail, Eurail or one of the other popular European rail passes, or simply travelling point to point. It includes additional information of use to rail travellers, especially those trying this kind of holiday for the first time.

Our feature on **Rail Passes** (pages v to xi) includes full details of the InterRail Global Pass and InterRail One Country Pass schemes (for European residents), as well as latest details of the various Eurail passes for those resident outside Europe. Many other passes are also featured, including a selection of citywide tickets and visitor cards for those visiting major European cities.

The **Country-by-Country** section (pages xii to xxxii) is packed with useful information about each country, and there is a chart of visa requirements on page xxxii. In the main body of the timetable, **Newslines** on page 3 has information about the latest changes and about the particular contents of this edition. Pages 8 and 9 help you make vital preparations for your journey, whilst a little time spent reading the notes on pages 4 to 7, explaining how to read the timetable, will be amply repaid when you get down to the task of planning your travels.

Whether you intend to travel only in one or two countries, or are attempting a spectacular grand tour of Europe, the timetables in this book will cover most of the routes you will need and will enable you to pre-plan your journey, which is often half the fun. Rail timetables are, however, always liable to change and you are recommended to consult the latest monthly edition of the European Rail Timetable or local information before travelling.

£5 OFF

SPECIAL OFFER

The latest monthly edition for only £8.99

The Thomas Cook European Rail Timetable is published monthly throughout the year and contains the latest available information on European railway and ferry schedules, including advance information of forthcoming changes in many editions.

As a special offer to purchasers of this seasonal edition, a later edition of the regular monthly European Rail Timetable can be purchased at £5.00 off the normal cover price, making it only £8.99 plus postage and packing (which is £1.50 to UK addresses, £3.50 to Europe and £5.00 to the rest of the world).

Order your copy now using the order form at the back of this timetable, marking the form **'ITE W09 offer'**. Alternatively, phone +44 (0)1733 416477, quoting **'ITE W09 offer'**. The offer is valid for six months after purchasing this timetable.

ACCOMMODATION

Hotels:

Europe offers an excellent choice, from five-star hotels to room only. Your main problem may lie in finding something to suit your budget. Rooms in private houses are often a good, inexpensive and friendly option (local tourist offices often have lists), but you may be expected to stay for more than one night. The quality of cheaper hotels in Eastern Europe may still be less than inspiring and you may do better with a private room. Local tourist offices are almost always your best starting point if you haven't pre-booked. If they don't handle bookings themselves (there's usually a small charge), they will re-direct you to someone who does and/or supply you with the information to do it yourself – tell them your price horizons.

Hostels:

For those on a tight budget, the best bet is to join **HI** (Hostelling International); there's no age limit. Membership of a national association will entitle you to use over 5000 HI hostels in 60 different countries and, apart from camping, they often provide the cheapest accommodation. The norm is dormitory-style, but many hostels also have single and family rooms.

Many offer excellent-value dining and many have self-catering and/or laundry facilities. Some hostels are open 24 hours, but most have lock-out times and reception's hours are usually limited; advise them if you are arriving out of hours. Reservation is advisable – many hostels fill well in advance and even those with space are likely to limit your stay to three nights if you just turn up without booking. In winter (except around Christmas) you may be able to get special price deals.

Buy the HI's directory Europe, which lists hostel addresses, contact numbers, locations and facilities; the HI website is *www.iyhf.org.*

Camping:

This is obviously the cheapest accommodation if you're prepared to carry the equipment. There are campsites right across Europe, from basic (just toilets and showers) to luxury family-oriented sites with dining-rooms, swimming pools and complexes of permanent tents. The drawback is that sites are often miles from the city centres. There's no really good pan-European guide to campsites, but most tourist offices can provide a directory for their country.

WHAT TO TAKE WITH YOU

Luggage:

Backpack (not more than 50 litres for women or 60 litres for men) plus day sack; sort your luggage into see-through polythene bags (makes fishing out your socks from the backpack much easier), plus take plastic bags for dirty clothes etc, and elastic bands for sealing them.

Clothing:

Lightweight clothing, preferably of a type that doesn't need ironing; smart casual clothes for evening wear, swimsuit, sun hat, long-sleeved garment to cover shoulders (essential in some churches/temples; women may need head-scarves); non-slip foot-wear – and don't forget underwear! All-purpose hiking boots (useful for big walks around cities) or rubber sandals with chunky soles are good when it's hot; flip flops for the shower etc.

First Aid/Medical:

Insect repellent and antihistamine cream, sun-screen cream, after-sun lotion, water-sterilising tablets, something for headaches and tummy troubles, antiseptic spray or cream, medicated wet-wipes, plasters for blisters, bandage, contra-ceptives and tampons (especially if visiting Eastern Europe, where they can be sometimes difficult to get – or try the luxury shop in the city's biggest hotel). Spare spectacles/contact lenses and a copy of your prescription.

Overnight Equipment:

Lightweight sleeping-bag (optional), sheet liner (for hostelling), inflatable travel pillow, earplugs, and eyemask.

Documents:

Passport, tickets, photocopies of passport/visas (helps if you lose the passport itself) and travel insurance, travellers' cheques counterfoil, passport photos, student card, numbers of credit cards and where to phone if you lose them.

Other items:

A couple of lightweight towels, small bar of soap, water-bottle, pocket knife, torch (flashlight), sewing kit, padlock and chain (for anchoring your lug-gage), safety matches, mug and basic cutlery, toothbrush, travel wash, string (for a washing-line), travel adapter, universal bath plug (often missing from wash-basins), sunglasses, alarm clock, note-pad and pen, pocket calculator (to convert money), a money-belt and a good book/game (for long journeys).

EUROPEAN RAIL PASSES

Rail passes represent excellent value for train travellers who are touring around Europe (or parts of it) or making a number of journeys within a short period. They can offer substantial savings over point-to-point tickets, as well as greater flexibility. Passes may cover most of Europe (e.g. InterRail or Eurail), a specific group of countries, single countries, or just a certain area. InterRail passes are only available to European residents, whereas Eurail passes are only for non-European residents. Most passes cannot be used in your country of residence.

Passes either cover a specified number of consecutive days, or are of the *flexi* type where you get so many 'travel days' within a specified period (there are boxes on the pass where you write each date). Free travel requires the use of a travel day, whereas discounted travel does not.

With InterRail and Eurail *flexi* passes, direct night trains or ferries leaving after 1900 hrs can count as the next travel day (as long as it's not the first day of validity). Free overnight ferries count as either the day of departure or the next day. Passes generally cover the ordinary services of the national rail companies, but supplements often have to be paid for travel on high-speed services, night trains, and 'global price' trains. 'Private' railways may not accept passes but may give discounts to passholders. Extra charges always apply for travel in sleeping cars or couchettes.

Passes can be purchased from appointed agents and their websites, and some may be available from principal railway stations. Your passport may be required for identification, also one or two passport-size photos. In this feature USD = US dollars, € = euros, £ = pounds sterling.

InterRail

InterRail Global Pass

Area of validity

The *InterRail Global Pass* is valid for unlimited travel on the national railways of 30 European countries, namely Austria, Belgium, Bosnia-Herzegovina, Bulgaria, Croatia, Czech Republic, Denmark, Finland, France, Germany, Great Britain, Greece, Hungary, Ireland (including Northern Ireland), Italy, Luxembourg, FYRO Macedonia, Montenegro, the Netherlands, Norway, Poland, Portugal, Romania, Serbia, Slovakia, Slovenia, Spain, Sweden, Switzerland and Turkey. However, passes are **not** valid in the passholder's country of residence.

From January 1, 2010 there is a new 15 day pass, and a Global Pass Senior has been introduced. A further change is that passes valid in Ireland now also include Northern Ireland.

Who can buy the pass?

Any national of a European country (including Russia) with a valid passport, or anyone who has lived in Europe for at least six months. Passes can be purchased up to three months before travel begins.

Periods of validity and 2010 prices (in Euros)

- Any 5 days within 10 days (flexi): adult 1st class €374, adult 2nd class €249, youth 2nd class €159.
- Any 10 days within 22 days (flexi): adult 1st class €539, adult 2nd class €359, youth 2nd class €239.
- 15 days (continuous) NEW for 2010: adult 1st class €599, adult 2nd class €399, youth 2nd class €279.
- 22 days (continuous): adult 1st class €704, adult 2nd class €469, youth 2nd class €309.
- 1 month (continuous): adult 1st class €899, adult 2nd class €599, youth 2nd class €399.

Youth prices are available to those aged 25 or under on the first day for which the pass is valid. Child fares for ages 4 to 11 are approximately half the price of the adult pass. Children under four travel free.

A new Global Pass Senior from January 1, 2010 gives 10% discount on the first or second class Global passes for those aged 60+ (not available on One Country passes).

Day trains - supplements and reservation fees

Supplements or reservation fees are compulsory for certain types of high-speed or 'global price' train. The official website www.interrailnet.com gives full details. International examples (sample fees are 2nd class and subject to change): *Artesia* (France - Italy) €10; *Berlin - Warszawa Express* from €4; *Cisalpino* €5 - 15; *Eurostar* passholder fare from €75; *TGV* and *ICE* from / to France €3 - 5; *Thalys* passholder fare from €26; Talgo (France - Spain) €6.50; *X2000* Stockholm - København €7. Others include *EC* Milano - Nice €9; *EC* Venezia - Wien €7; *EC* Wien - Praha €7; *EC* München - Italy €5, *IC* Stockholm - Oslo €3. On other routes reservation is recommended, especially in July and August.

Domestic examples of compulsory reservation fees include: **Croatia** *IC* €1 - 5. **Czech Republic** *SC* €7. **Finland** *Pendolino* €3 - 5. **France** *TGV* €3 (peak €10), *Téoz* €3. **Germany** free on *ICE* (€11 on *ICE Sprinter*). **Greece** *ICity* €6 - 20, *IcityE* €9 - 33. **Hungary** *IC* €2.50. **Italy** *ES* and *ES City* €15, *AV* €20. **Norway** long-distance trains €6.30. **Poland** *IC / EC* €5.30, *Ex* €3. **Portugal** *AP* €8, *IC* €4. **Romania** *IC* €3 - 18. **Slovakia** *IC / EC* €3, *SC* €7. **Spain** *AVE, Avant, Talgo 200* €10, most other long-distance trains €6.50. **Sweden** *X2000* €7.

The number of seats allocated to InterRail Pass holders may be limited (e.g. on *TGV* and *Thalys* trains). If sold out, you may have to buy an ordinary ticket. The fold-out Travel Report inside the ticket cover must be filled in for all journeys taken and ticket inspectors may ask to see it.

Night trains - supplements

Many night trains are globally priced and fares for passholders vary widely. *Elipsos* night trains France / Italy - Spain give discounted fares. Passes do not include sleeping accommodation, which is typically €15 to €69 for a couchette, and €30 to €197 for a berth in a sleeping car.

Discount in country of residence

Although the pass is not valid in the country of residence, passholders can obtain a reduction for one return ticket to the border or nearest airport. This is usually 50% (Bosnia 30%, Germany 25%, Spain 35%) but there is no discount in Great Britain, Czech Republic, Poland or Romania.

Validity on private railways

InterRail passes are valid on the national railway companies in each country, plus many of the privately run railways (some give discounts). For full details see the InterRail Traveller's Guide or the official InterRail website www.interrailnet.com.

Selected details are as follows: **Berlin Night Express**: reduced fare if pass valid in Sweden. **Denmark**: free travel on Arriva and DSB-First, 50% discount on Hjørring - Hirtshals and Frederikshavn - Skagen. **France**: SNCF bus services free, 50% discount on CP (Nice - Digne), 50% on railways in Corsica. **Germany**: free on most regional services (not Züssow - Świnoujście). **Hungary**: GySEV services are included. **Netherlands**: Noordnet, Synthus, Veolia included. **Norway**: the Myrdal - Flåm line is treated as a private line and gives 30% discount. **Spain**: FEVE and FGC railways give 50% discount. **Sweden**: included are Arlanda Express, Arriva, DSB First, Inlandsbanan, MerResor, Skånetrafiken, Tågkompaniet, Västtrafik, Veolia. **Switzerland**: free travel on BLS, FART/SSIF, MOB, RhB, SOB, THURBO and ZB. Many others offer 50% discount, including AB, ASM, CJ, FB, Gornergratbahn, LEB, MBC, MVR, NStCM, Pilatusbahn, RA, Rigibahnen, RBS, SZU, TMR, TPC, TPF, TRN, WB, WSB. The MGB (Disentis - Brig - Zermatt and Göschenen - Andermatt) offer 50% to under-26s only. Discounted fare on William Tell Express (rail and boat tour). No discounts are available on the BRB or the narrow gauge railways in the Jungfrau area (BOB, JB, WAB).

Ferry and bus services

The pass includes free deck passage between Italy and Greece on SuperFast Ferries and Blue Star Ferries (you pay port taxes €7, fuel surcharge, also high-season surcharge €10 June / Sept, €20 July / Aug. Free dormitories for 1st class pass holders). Also free deck passage on Minoan Lines and Scandlines.

Many other ferry companies offer discounts (not on cabins), for example: Balearia 50%, Color Line 50%, DFDS 25%, Endeavor Lines (Patras - Brindisi) 30% - 50%, Fjord1 Fylkesbaatane 50%, Grimaldi 20%, Irish Ferries 30%, Sea France 50%, Stena Line 20% (30% on UK routes), Tallink Silja 30% - 50%, Viking Line 50%. Also valid on ÖBB Austrian lake services. Most Swiss lakes give 50% discount. DDSG offer 20% on Melk - Krems river cruises. Certain bus services in Scandinavia offer a 50% discount. Some railway museums offer free or discounted entry and a limited number of tourist attractions, hotels, hostels and cycle hire outlets offer discounts. Further details are given in the InterRail Traveller's Guide and on www.InterRailnet.com.

InterRail One Country Pass

Area of validity

The *InterRail One Country Pass* is valid for travel in any **one** of the participating countries above, with the exception of Bosnia-Herzegovina or Montenegro. It is **not** available for travel in the passholder's country of residence. Note that Benelux (Belgium, Luxembourg and the Netherlands) counts as one country. There are two passes for Greece - the *Greece Plus* variant includes ferry services between Italy and Greece operated by Attica (i.e. SuperFast Ferries and Blue Star Ferries). Eligibility / supplements / discounts are as for the *InterRail Global Pass*.

Periods of validity and prices

All passes are flexi passes, valid for 3, 4, 6 or 8 days within 1 month.

For full details of prices from January 1, 2010 see page 541 at the back of this edition.

Eurail

Eurail Global Pass

Area of validity

The *Eurail Global Pass* is valid for unlimited travel on the national railways of 21 European countries, namely Austria, Belgium, Croatia, Czech Republic, Denmark, Finland, France, Germany, Greece, Hungary, Ireland (including Northern Ireland), Italy, Luxembourg, the Netherlands, Norway, Portugal, Romania, Slovenia, Spain, Sweden and Switzerland. The addition of Northern Ireland is new for 2010. Additional countries participate in the *Eurail Select Pass*, *Eurail Regional Pass* and *Eurail National Pass* (see below).

Who can buy the pass?

The pass can be purchased by anyone resident outside Europe (but excluding residents of the former USSR or Turkey). Passes are sold through official Eurail Sales Agents (see www.eurailtravel.com) and can also be bought directly from Eurail through www.eurail.com.

The option exists to buy the passes after arrival in Europe but it is much cheaper to buy them beforehand, and since you can buy them up to six months in advance, there is no point in waiting until the last minute. Pass validity cannot be changed once in Europe, and passes must be validated before first use.

Periods of validity and prices

Adult *Eurail Global Passes* are valid for first class travel (naturally you can also travel in second class), wheras the under-26 Youth version is for 2nd class travel only. Prices in US dollars for 2010 are as follows:

- 15 days: adult 799 USD, youth 519 USD.
- 21 days: adult 1039 USD, youth 669 USD.
- 1 month: adult 1,289 USD, youth 839 USD.
- 2 months: adult 1,819 USD, youth 1,185 USD.
- 3 months: adult 2,245 USD, youth 1,459 USD.
- 10 days within 2 months: adult 945 USD, youth 615 USD.
- 15 days within 2 months: adult 1,239 USD, youth 805 USD.

Children aged 4 - 11 pay half fare, and children under 4 travel free (except if a reservation for a separate seat or bed is required).

Two or more people travelling together are eligible for the *Saver* rate, giving a reduction of 15% on the adult fare (there is no youth *Saver*, children aged 4 - 11 in the group pay half the *Saver* rate).

Supplements payable

Supplements are generally not required for *EC*, *IC*, *ICE* trains. *Thalys* charge a special passholder rate, as do other 'global price' trains (see the InterRail page for further details). French *TGV* and *Téoz* require the reservation fee only. In Spain most long-distance trains have a supplement/reservation fee (sample 2nd class rates: regional trains €4, long-distance €6.50, *AVE* Turista class €10; where meal provided in 1st/Preferente class €23.50). Supplements are also payable on *ICE Sprinter*, *Cisalpino* (€5-15), *Eurostar Italia* (€15 on *ES*, *ESc*, €20 on *AV*), *X2000* (€7-17) and *IcityE* in Greece (€9-33). As with all passes, sleeper/couchette supplements and seat reservations are extra.

Validity on other railways

Eurail passes are valid on the principal railway companies in each country, but may not be valid on 'private' or locally run railways (some give discounts). Selected details are as follows (some require reservations): **Denmark**: 50% discount on Hjørring - Hirtshals and Frederikshavn - Skagen. **France**: valid on RER in Paris (obtain a voucher), 50% discount on CP (Nice - Digne), 50% on railways in Corsica. **Hungary**: GySEV services are included, 50% discount on 'nostalgia' steam trips and the train to the railway museum. **Norway**: the Myrdal - Flåm line is treated as a 'private' line and gives 30% discount. **Spain**: FEVE and FGC railways give 50% discount. **Sweden**: most trains included (see under InterRail for a full list). **Switzerland**: free travel on many railways including BLS, CJ, FART/SSIF, MOB, RhB, SOB, SZU, THURBO, TMR, TPC, ZB. There is 50% discount on Vitznau-Rigi, the Pilatus line (and cable car) offers 30%, and there is a 25% discount on railways in the Jungfrau region (BOB, JB, WAB), the MGB (Disentis-Brig-Zermatt), and the Gornergratbahn. There are reductions on some cable cars as well. A list of bonuses is included in the Traveler's Guide issued with your pass. Note that *Eurostar* also offer special prices.

Ferry services

Free passage or fare reductions are available on various ferry services; the main ones are shown below. Ferry discounts usually exclude cabin accommodation, and other restrictions (such as compulsory reservation) may apply:

Balearia 20%; Color Line day sailings 50%; DFDS 25%; Grimaldi 20%, HML (Endeavor Lines) 30-50%; Irish Ferries 30%; Minoan Lines, free deck passage on Italy-Greece routes if pass valid in both countries (summer surcharges €16-26); Sea France 50%; Scanlines free; Stena Line 20-30%; Superfast/Blue Star free passage on Italy-Greece routes if pass valid in both countries (summer surcharge €10-20, port tax €7, also fuel surcharge); Tallink-Silja 30-50%, Viking Line 50%.

Most boat services on the Swiss lakes are included in the pass, as are Austrian lake services operated by ÖBB. Bodensee ferries operated by BSB, SBS, ÖBB give 50% discount. There are also reductions on some river cruises (e.g. certain DDSG sailings); KD Line give free travel on their scheduled Rhine and Mosel boats.

Other discounts

The Europabus services in our Table **927** give 60% reduction, and certain bus services in Norway offer a 50% discount. Some railway museums offer free or discounted entry and a limited number of tourist attractions, hotels and hostels offer discounts. If in doubt, ask!

Note regarding flexi passes: free travel requires the use of a 'travel day', wheras discounted travel does not, provided it is within the overall validity of the pass. For free overnight travel by ferry you can enter either the day of departure or day of arrival. A direct overnight train leaving after 1900 hrs requires only the following day to be used as a 'travel day'.

Eurail Select Pass

A *Eurail Select Pass* allows unlimited travel in 3, 4 or 5 adjoining countries from the following (some are grouped together and count as one):

- Austria • Bulgaria/Montenegro/Serbia
- Benelux (Belgium/Netherlands/Luxembourg) • Croatia/Slovenia
- Czech Republic • Denmark • Finland • France • Germany
- Greece • Hungary • Ireland (including NIR) • Italy • Norway
- Portugal • Romania • Spain • Sweden • Switzerland.

'Adjoining' means linked by a direct train (not through another country) or shipping line included in the Eurail scheme; for example Italy's links include Spain and Greece, and France can be linked with Ireland.

The Select Pass is available for 5, 6, 8 or 10 travel days within a two-month period (the 5-country pass is also available for 15 days). The 5-day adult pass costs 505/565/625 USD for 3/4/5 countries respectively; 6 days costs 559/619/679 USD, 8 days 665/725/786 USD, 10 days 769/825/885 USD, and the 5-country 15-day pass costs 1039 USD. The *Saver* pass for 2 or more people travelling together gives 15% reduction.

The Youth (under 26) pass is priced at 65% of the adult price and children aged 4 to 11 travel at half the adult fare. As with the *Eurail Global Pass*, the adult version gives 1st class travel, the youth version 2nd class.

Note: International ferry journeys using *Select*, *Regional* or *One Country* passes - the pass must be valid in both the country of departure and arrival to obtain free travel, but in only one of these for discounted travel.

Eurail Regional Pass

A *Eurail Regional Pass* allows unlimited travel in two European countries (or country combinations) as listed below. Conditions vary but all are available for 5, 6, 8 or 10 days within 2 months, and some also for 4, 7 or 9 days (Portugal-Spain also for 3 days). All are available in adult and saver 1st class versions (most also in 2nd class), and there is a youth 2nd class version for all except Portugal-Spain. Passes must be obtained before travelling to Europe, but those shown with the symbol § are also for sale in the countries where the pass is valid (but not to European residents). For current prices and further information see www.eurail.com. Eligibility, supplements, discounts etc are generally as for the *Global Pass* above.

- Austria-Croatia/Slovenia § • Austria-Czech Republic
- Austria-Germany • Austria-Hungary § • Austria-Switzerland
- Benelux-France • Benelux-Germany • Croatia/Slovenia-Hungary §
- Czech Republic-Germany • Denmark-Germany • France-Germany
- France-Italy • France-Spain • France-Switzerland
- Germany-Poland • Germany-Switzerland • Greece-Italy §
- Hungary-Romania § • Italy - Spain • Portugal - Spain
- Finland-Sweden • Denmark-Sweden • Norway-Sweden

Sample prices: France-Spain 4 days 1st/2nd 409/355 USD, 10 days 689/605 USD. Hungary-Romania 1st class 5/10 days 275/409 USD.

Eurail One Country Passes

A *Eurail One Country Pass* allows unlimited travel in a single European country (or country combination) as listed below. Each pass has its own characteristics regarding class of travel, number of travel days, and availability of saver, youth and child versions. A few also have discounts for seniors. For prices and further information see www.eurail.com.

- Austria • Benelux • Bulgaria • Croatia § • Czech Rep • Denmark
- Finland • Greece § • Hungary § • Ireland § • Italy § • Norway
- Poland • Portugal § • Romania § • Slovenia • Spain • Sweden
- Scandinavia (Denmark, Finland, Norway, Sweden. 2nd class only. Youth 25% off).

(§ - for sale in Europe)

Sample prices: Spain 3-10 days 299-609 USD 1st class, 239-489 USD 2nd class. Czech Rep 3-8 days 169-395 USD 1st, 125-295 USD 2nd.

BritRail

Britrail is a pass for overseas visitors to Great Britain, allowing unlimited travel on the national rail network in England, Scotland and Wales. It is not available to residents of Great Britain, Northern Ireland, the Isle of Man or the Channel Islands. It is best to buy the pass before arriving in Britain. Prices shown are the US prices for 2009. Further information: www.britrail.com.

BritRail Consecutive Pass
Allows travel for a certain number of consecutive days, in either first or standard class. Children (5-15) travel at half the adult fare.

(USD prices)	Adult 1st class	Adult Standard	Senior (60+) 1st class	Youth (16-25) Standard §
3 days	305	199	259	159
4 days	379	249	319	199
8 days	535	359	455	285
15 days	799	535	679	425
22 days	1015	675	859	539
1 month	1195	795	1015	635

BritRail FlexiPass
The FlexiPass version gives 3, 4, 8 or 15 days travel within a two-month period.

(USD prices)	Adult 1st class	Adult Standard	Senior (60+) 1st class	Youth (16-25) Standard §
3 days in 2 months	375	255	319	205
4 days in 2 months	465	315	399	249
8 days in 2 months	679	459	579	365
15 days in 2 months	1025	689	869	555

§ – First-class youth passes are also available (at 80% of the adult 1st rates).

Britrail England Pass
Excludes Wales and Scotland. Prices are 20% cheaper than those shown above. Available in both the Consecutive and Flexi versions.

Discounts
Reductions are available on adult passes as follows, but only one type of discount can be used (this includes youth and senior discounts):

Eurail Passholder Discount: Those aged 16 to 25 with valid Eurail passes pay about 50% of the normal adult fare.

Party Discount: for 3 to 9 adults travelling in a group. Passengers 3 to 9 receive a 50% discount on the cost of their passes. The passes must be of the same type and duration and the party must travel together.

Family Discount: if you purchase any adult or senior pass, one accompanying child (aged 5–15) receives a free pass of the same type and duration. Any further children travelling receive a 50% discount. All children under 5 travel free.

Guest Pass Discount: a friend or relative who is a UK resident may accompany the pass holder. Both get 25% off the adult fare and must travel together at all times. The guest must carry proof of UK residence.

Two additional passes are available covering larger or smaller areas:

BritRail + Ireland
Adds Northern Ireland and the Republic of Ireland, plus a return ferry crossing (Stena Line / Irish Ferries). 5 days within one month costs 699 USD first class, 469 USD standard. 10 days within one month: 1245 / 839 USD first / standard. Not available to residents of the Republic of Ireland.

BritRail London Plus Pass
This 'flexi' pass allows unlimited rail travel in London and the surrounding area. You can visit such places as Canterbury, Salisbury, Bristol, Oxford, Cambridge, Kings Lynn, the whole coast from Colchester to Weymouth, and even get as far as Worcester. Children aged 5–15 pay 50% of the adult fare. No youth or senior discount available.

(USD prices)	Adult 1st class	Adult Standard
2 days within 8 days	209	139
4 days within 8 days	289	225
7 days within 15 days	369	269

Other International Passes

BALKAN FLEXIPASS

Unlimited 1st class travel in Bulgaria, Greece, Macedonia, Montenegro, Romania, Serbia and Turkey for any 5 / 10 / 15 days in one month. Available in the countries above (but not for residents of those countries), also in the USA. Typical US prices : adults 256 / 447 / 539 USD, youth (12-25) 153 / 268 / 324 USD, senior (60+) 206 / 359 / 433 USD. Children half adult fare. Supplements for *IC* trains. Gives 30% discount on Attica Group ferries (Superfast / Bluestar). A 2nd class version is also available if purchased within the countries where it is valid (e.g. unconfirmed prices in Greece: €82 / 144 / 172 adult, €49 / 82 / 98 youth, €66 / 115 / 138 senior).

BENELUX TOURRAIL

A flexi pass for travel in Belgium, Netherlands and Luxembourg for 5 days within one month. Prices €219 1st class, €139 2nd class. Under 26 version (2nd class only) €99. Special pass price available on Thalys. Available from principal stations, also from International Rail in the UK, who call it the Benelux Pass.

EUREGIO - BODENSEE TAGESKARTE

One day's unlimited travel in border region Austria / Germany / Switzerland surrounding Lake Constance. Includes buses and ferries. In Germany valid only on DB local trains. Adult 37 CHF / €28, family 74 CHF / €56. Zonal versions also available for smaller areas.

EUREGIO MAAS-RHEIN

One days unlimited travel in border region Belgium / Netherlands / Germany by rail and bus (covers Liège, Hasselt, Maastricht, Heerlen, Aachen, Düren). In Germany covers only local trains and buses. Price €15. At weekends / public holidays valid as a family ticket (2 adults plus 3 children under 12). Further information: www.euregio-ticket.com

EUROPEAN EAST PASS

Available to non-European residents; offers unlimited rail travel throughout Austria, Czech Republic, Hungary, Poland and Slovakia for any 5 days within a month. 1st class 299 USD, 2nd class 209 USD (up to 5 extra days 36 / 28 USD per day 1st / 2nd class). Children aged 4 - 11 half price. Discounts available on river cruises, steam trips in Hungary, Children's Railway etc.

ÖRESUND RUNDT

Two days unlimited travel on trains in the København, Malmö and Helsingborg area, 199 SEK / 179 DKK. A larger area extending further into Sweden (Ystad, Kristianstad) is also available for 249 SEK / 229 DKK. Children 7-15 half price. The Öresund can only be crossed by rail in one direction; ferry (included) must be used in the other direction. Although some sources have quoted that this ticket is no longer available in Denmark, København Tourist Office have told us that they still sell it.

SAAR-LOR-LUX TICKET

One day's unlimited 2nd class travel on Saturday or Sunday throughout Saarland (i.e. Saarbrücken area of Germany, local trains only), Lorraine (i.e. Metz, Nancy, Épinal area of France) and all of Luxembourg. Price €20. For groups of 2 - 5 people add €10 per extra person.

Railplus

Railplus cards are valid for one year and offer a discount of 25% on cross-border rail travel (excluding supplements) between the participating countries, which are Austria, Belgium, Bulgaria, Croatia, Czech Republic, Denmark, Finland, France, Germany, Great Britain, Greece, Hungary, Italy, Latvia, Lithuania, Luxembourg, Macedonia, Montenegro, Netherlands, Norway, Poland, Portugal, Romania, Serbia, Slovakia, Slovenia, Spain, Sweden, Switzerland and Ukraine.

France, Norway, Spain and Sweden only grant discounts to youth (12-25) and seniors (60+), and Ireland only to seniors. Cards are not available for sale in all participating countries, and you may be required to hold a national railcard for the country where you buy the pass, in addition to the Railplus card. Note that Rail Europe in the UK, who used to sell the Railplus Senior Card, no longer do so, although they do sell the SNCF Carte Senior, giving 25% off cross-border journeys.

Passes for Domestic Travel

Every effort has been made to show latest prices, but some may have changed. Most cities offer day tickets valid on public transport (some include local trains), and larger cities often have Visitor Cards, available from airports and tourist information offices (often also hotels and online).

AUSTRIA

European residents: see InterRail Global Pass and One Country Pass. Non-European residents: see Eurail Global Pass, Eurail Select/ Regional/One Country Passes, European East Pass. See also Euregio -Bodensee Tageskarte.

Austria Pass: for non-Europeans, must be purchased outside Europe. 3 to 8 days within one month, 199/139 USD 1st/2nd class for 3 days plus 30/20 USD per extra day. Children aged 6-11 half price. Also valid on the private railway company Raab-Oedenburg Ebenfurter Eisenbahn. Discounts on selected river trips by DDSG, Wurm & Köck.

Einfach-Raus-Ticket: one day's 2nd class travel on regional trains for groups of 2 to 5 people, €28. On Mons to Fris not valid before 0900 hrs.

Discounts on ÖBB point to point tickets: **1-PLUS-Freizeitticket** discount of 25-40% for the 2nd to 5th people in a group travelling together, and bicycles may be taken free. **Gruppenticket** for groups of 6 or more, discounts of 30% up to 100km and 40% over 100km. **Vorteilscard** annual cards giving 50% discount; the *Classic* version is available to all but there are cheaper cards for families, seniors and those under 26.

Wien-Karte: unlimited travel on local transport in Vienna plus discounted museum entry, 72 hours €18.50. One child up to age 15 free.

Wien metro/tram/bus: 24 hours €5.70; 72 hours €13.60; 8 days €27.20; buy additional zone (€1.70) to include airport. Off-peak (after 0900 Mon-Fri) weekly ticket also available €14.00.

Other visitor cards giving local travel plus museum/sights discounts for 24/48/72 hours: **Salzburg Card** €24/32/37 (reduced by €2 outside May to Oct period); **Innsbruck Card** €25/30/35. Children half price.

BELARUS

There are no rail passes that we are aware of that are valid in Belarus.

Minsk: 10-day public transport passes are available from metro stations.

BELGIUM

European residents: see InterRail Global Pass and One Country Pass. Non-European residents: see Eurail Global Pass, Eurail Select/ Regional/One Country Passes. See also Benelux Tourrail, Euregio.

Discounts on SNCB point to point tickets: **Rail Pass** (age 26+) allows 10 single journeys between two specified stations for €73 2nd class, €112 1st class, valid 1 year. **Go Pass** is under 26 version, €50 (2nd class). Various discounts are available for return journeys at weekends.

Carte Jump d'un Jour valid on all public transport in greater Brussels (including SNCB rail services), 1 day €4.50. **Carte 3 Jours** gives 3 days on local transport (STIB only) for €9.50. Cards for 5 or 10 journeys also available. **Brussels Card** gives public transport (STIB) plus museums, 24 hrs €20, 48 hrs €28, 72 hrs, €33.

BOSNIA-HERZEGOVINA

European residents: see InterRail Global Pass.

BULGARIA

European residents: see InterRail Global Pass and One Country Pass. Non-European residents: see Eurail Select/ One Country Passes. See also Balkan Flexipass.

Sofiya: all SKGT local transport, 1 day 3 BGN, 5 days 12 BGN.

CROATIA

European residents: see InterRail Global Pass and One Country Pass. Non-European residents: see Eurail Select/Regional/One Country.

Zagreb: day ticket (dnevne karte) for all trams/buses (zone 1): 25 HRK. **Zagreb Card** with museum discounts etc, 24 hrs 60 HRK, 72 hrs 90 HRK.

CZECH REPUBLIC

European residents: see InterRail Global Pass and One Country Pass. Non-European residents: see Eurail Global Pass (from 2009), Eurail Regional/One Country Pass, European East.

Kilometrická banka 2000 (KMB): a prepaid card giving 2000 km of 2nd class travel within 6 months, 2000 CZK. The conductor deducts the appropriate distance (minimum 100 km) for each trip.

SONE+: one day's travel on Sat or Sun for up to 5 people (max 2 adults), 2nd class, 150 CZK local trains, 450 CZK all trains except *SC*. SONE+PKP variant includes local trains in border area of Poland (add 100 CZK). Smaller regional areas also available,

Network tickets: ČD Net ticket valid one day, 2nd class 450 CZK (900 CZK for group of 2-5 people); extra charge for *SC* travel (200 CZK each). Regional variants (Regionet) also available.

Praha: all public transport including ČD trains, extending up to 50 km from the centre: 24 hrs 100 CZK, 3 days 330 CZK, 5 days 500 CZK.

Prague Card: 4-day admission card with 3-day transport add-on as above costs 1120 CZK (children and students 860 CZK).

DENMARK

European residents: see InterRail Global Pass and One Country Pass. Non-European residents: see Eurail Global Pass, Eurail Select/ Regional/One Country Passes. See also Öresund Rundt.

Fares based on national zonal system. **Pendlerkort**: 30 day all-zone 2nd class ticket max fare 3,050 DKK, photocard required. 10-journey tickets also available. **DSB WildCard**: discount card for 16-25 year olds, giving up to 50% off tickets, 180 DKK.

København: **24-Hour Ticket** valid on bus, metro and DSB trains in greater København, 120 DKK. **Flexcard 7-Days** is a 7 day zonal card, from 205 DKK for 2 zones to 570 DKK for all 9 zones in København.

Copenhagen Card (CPH Card) gives public transport plus free entry to 60 attractions, 24 hrs 235 DKK (child 125), 72 hrs 460 DKK (child 235).

ESTONIA

There are no rail passes that we are aware of that are valid in Estonia.

Tallinn Card: free city transport, sightseeing tours, many museums etc; 6 hrs €12, 24 hrs €24, 48 hrs €28, 72 hrs €32. Under 14s half price.

FINLAND

European residents: see InterRail Global Pass and One Country Pass. Non-European residents: see Eurail Global Pass, Eurail Select/ Regional/One Country Passes.

Finnrailpass: unlimited rail travel for 3/5/10 days in any 1 month; 1st class €195/260/353, 2nd class €131/175/237. Ages 6-16 half price. Seat reservation fees required for Pendolino trains. Available to non-Finnish residents. Can be purchased at main stations in Finland.

Helsinki Tourist Ticket: bus/tram/metro/local trains 1/3/5 days for €6/12/18 (children 7-16 half price); regional area also available.
Helsinki Card: public transport plus free entry to over 50 attractions, €33/45/55 for 24/48/72 hours (children 7-16: €13/16/19).

FRANCE

European residents: see InterRail Global Pass and One Country Pass. Non-European residents: see Eurail Global Pass, Eurail Select/ Regional/One Country Passes.

France Railpass: only available to non-European residents, valid for 3 to 9 days within one month. Adult 3 days 293/250 USD 1st/2nd class plus 45/37 USD per extra day; Youth (12-25) 217/186 USD plus 33/28 USD per day; Senior (60+, 1st class only) 268 USD for 3 days plus 40 USD per day. Saver version for 2-5 people (must include at least 2 adults) gives around 15% discount. Children pay 50% of the adult (or Saver) fare. Special Passholder fare payable on *Eurostar*, *Thalys*, *Artesia*, night trains etc. Reservation fee payable on *TGV* and *Téoz*. 50% discount on CP, Corsica trains, Sea France. Further information: www.francerailpass.com

Discounts on point to point tickets: **Découverte Séjour**: 25% discount (15%-35% on *TGV* and *Corail Téoz*), blue periods only, min 200 km return trip, Sat night away. ***iDTGV*** are low-cost advance purchase tickets; book online for best deals.

Carte 12-25 and **Carte Sénior**: young person's railcard for those aged 12 - 25 (€49) and senior railcard for those over 60 (€56). Valid 1 year. Both give at least 25% discount (up to 50% for journeys purchased in advance). **Carte Escapades**: railcard for ages 26 - 59 giving at least 25% discount (min 200 km return, must spend Sat night away), €85.

Regional Tickets: several regions offer day tickets or discounted fares on TER (local) trains at weekends and holidays. Conditions vary and some only valid in Summer. Details generally available on TER website www.ter-sncf.com.

Paris Visite: public transport within greater Paris, plus free or discounted entry to 20 attractions: zones 1–3: €9/14.70/20/28.90 for 1/2/3/5 days. Zones 1–6 (includes airports): €18.90/28.90/40.50/49.40. Children 4-11 half price. **Mobilis**: Paris one-day ticket (not available on airport services), €5.80 (zones 1–2) to €16.40 (zones 1–6).

Lyon day ticket €4.50, covers all TCL tram/bus/metro/funicular.
Lille day ticket €3.50; similar tickets in most cities.

GERMANY

European residents: see InterRail Global Pass and One Country Pass. Non-European residents: see Eurail Global Pass, Eurail Select/Regional Passes. See also Euregio-Bodensee, Euregio Ticket, Sar-Lor-Lux Ticket.

German Rail Pass: for people resident outside Europe; 4 to 10 days unlimited travel within 1 month. 4 days €236/180 1st/2nd class; add €32/22 per extra day. Also **Youth Pass** for those under 26 (2nd class only) - 4 days €150, add €12 for each extra day. **Twin Pass** also available giving up to 50% for second adult. Available from Deutsche Bahn London and certain German stations, but not available to European residents. No supplements on *ICE*, *IC*, *EC*. 20% discount on Romantische Strasse and Burgenstrasse buses.

Passes for Domestic Travel

Schönes-Wochenende-Ticket: one day's unlimited travel on Saturday or Sunday (to 0300 following day) on local trains (IRE/RE/RB/S-Bahn), 2nd class. Price €37 from machines, €39 from ticket offices, €40.70 on train. Valid for up to 5 people, buy on the day. Also valid on trams / buses in certain areas, and on certain rail lines across the border into Poland.

Quer-Durchs-Land-Ticket from August 2009, local trains throughout Germany after 0900, from €34 (1 person) to €54 (5 people).

Regional tickets (Länder-Tickets): one day's unlimited travel for up to 5 people on DB local trains (not before 0900 on Mon-Fri, valid to 0300 next day). **Baden-Württemberg** €19 for one person, €28 for 2-5 people. **Bayern** €20 for one person, €28 for 2-5 people. **Brandenburg-Berlin** €26. **Hessen** (includes most buses) €30. **Mecklenburg-Vorpommern** €18 for one person, €25 for 2-5 people. **Niedersachsen** €20 for one person, €28 for 2-5 people. **Nordrhein-Westfalen** (SchönerTagTicket) one person €25, 2-5 people €34. **Rheinland-Pfalz** and **Saarland** €19 for one person, €27 for 2-5 people. **Sachsen**, **Sachsen-Anhalt** and **Thüringen** €19 for one person, €28 for 2-5 people. **Schleswig-Holstein** €30 (includes travel in Mecklenburg-Vorpommern and all public transport in Hamburg). Buy on the day from ticket machines (most cost €2 more if purchased from travel centres).

Bahncard 25 / 50: valid for 1 year, giving discounts of 25% or 50% on all national DB trains for €57 or €225, 2nd class, passport photo required (1st class €114 / 450). With Bahncard 50, travel companions get 50% and children under 15 travel free. Both cards entitle the holder to a 25% discount for international journeys between Germany and 29 European countries (discount not available where global fares are charged). Bahncards available at discounted prices to young people, families, seniors, disabled persons. **Mobility Bahncard 100** gives unlimited travel for 1 year, €3,650 (1st class €6,150). Bahncards also available from DB London.

Sparpreis 25 / 50: advance purchase tickets giving 25% or 50% discount, also 50% off for up to 4 travel companions. Weekend restrictions apply to 50% version. Group versions (6+) available giving 50% to 70% off.

Harz: HSB narrow gauge railway 3 / 5 days €42 / 47, child 6-11 50%.

Tageskarte (day ticket): most urban areas offer 24 / 48 / 72 hour tickets valid on most public transport; generally a zonal system operates.

Welcome Tickets: most public transport in selected cities, also includes free or reduced entry to many museums and visitor attractions. Buy from Tourist Information, main stations, some airports and hotels. Examples:

Berlin Welcome Card: one adult and up to 3 children under 14; 48 hours €18.50, 72 hours €25, 5 days €34.50. Covers zones A, B and C and includes DB trains.

Dresden City Card: 48 hours €21, includes some Elbe river trips.

Frankfurt Card: 1 day €8.90, 2 days €12.90; group ticket (up to 5) €18 (1 day)/€26 (2 days). Includes travel from / to the airport.

Hamburg Card: Day Ticket (valid from 1800 hrs previous day) €8.50. Also 3 days €18.90, 5 days €33.90. Group versions (up to 5) €12.50 / 31.50 / 54.90.

Hannover Card: 1 day €9.50, 3 days €16, group ticket (up to 5) €18 / 31.

Köln Welcome Card: 24 hours €9 (2 tickets €16, 3 tickets €23). Wider areas also available.

Leipzig Card: 1 day €8.90, 3 days €18.50, 3 day group (2 adults and up to 3 children under 14) €34.

Nürnberg Card: 2 days €19, children up to age 12 free.

GREAT BRITAIN

European residents: see InterRail Global Pass and One Country Pass. See also Britrail.

All-Line Rail Rover: covers whole National Rail network, 1st / standard class £650 / £430 (7 days), £990 / £650 (14 days). 34% discount for children aged 5-15 and holders of Senior and Disabled Persons railcards, and (standard class only) Young Persons railcard. Not valid on Eurostar, Heathrow Express, London Underground, private railways.

Freedom of Scotland Travelpass: all rail services in Scotland (includes Carlisle and Berwick) plus Caledonian MacBrayne ferry services and some buses. Standard class only. Valid 4 out of 8 days (£111) or 8 out of 15 days (£148); not before 0915 Mon to Fri (except on Glasgow - Oban / Mallaig services and north of Inverness). 34% discount with Young Persons / Senior / Disabled railcard; 50% discount for children (5-15). 20% discount on Northlink Ferries to Orkney and Shetland; 10% off sleeper fares to / from Scotland. Smaller areas also available: **Highland Rover**, 4 days out of 8 £72; **Central Scotland Rover** 3 days out of 7 £32.

Freedom of Wales Flexi Pass: gives 8 consecutive days travel on most buses in Wales, plus standard-class rail travel on any 4 days out of the 8 (not before 0915 Mon to Fri), price £74, children half price, railcard holders 34% discount. Includes Ffestiniog and Welsh Highland Railways, with discounts on other tourist railways and attractions. Tickets available online and at most staffed stations. Smaller areas also available: South Wales (£50), North and Mid Wales (£50).

A range of **Rover** tickets is available covering various areas, typically for 7 days, 3 in 7 days, 4 in 8 days, or 8 in 15 days. Most are not valid until after the morning peak on Monday to Friday. Examples: Anglia Plus, Coast and Peaks, Devon and Cornwall, East Midlands, Heart of England, Kent, North Country, North East, North West, Settle & Carlisle, Severn & Solent, Shakespeare Explorer, South West, Thames. **Ranger** day tickets also available, for example Cambrian Coast, Cheshire, Cornwall, Cumbrian Coast, Derbyshire, Devon, East Midlands, Lakes, Lancashire, Lincolnshire, North Downs, Oxfordshire, Settle & Carlisle line, South Pennines, Tyne & Tees, Valley Lines, West Midlands, West Yorkshire, Yorkshire Coast. Details: nationalrail.co.uk.

Railcards: annual cards giving 34% discount on most rail fares; 16-25 Railcard, Family, Senior, all £24. Disabled Persons £18, HM Forces £15. Network Railcard gives off-peak discount in South East England, £20.

London: Day Travelcards covers almost all transport (Underground / bus / rail) in the London area; peak version from £7.20 (central London, zones 1–2) to £14.80 (zones 1–6), off-peak version (not before 0930 Mon-Fri) from £5.60 to £7.50. 7 day tickets from £25.80 (central zones) to £47.60 (zones 1-6), no off-peak version. 3-day Travelcards are being withdrawn from January 2010. Children under 11 travel free with an Oyster photocard. Travelcard holders may take up to four children aged 11-15 for £1 each off-peak (otherwise half fare). Stored-value Oyster cards give best value; Visitor Oyster card preloaded with £10 credit costs £12 (also available online from www.visitlondon.com); can be topped up at numerous outlets.

All-day tickets (some off-peak) covering rail and bus are also available in Glasgow, Greater Manchester, Derbyshire, Merseyside, South Yorkshire, West Yorkshire, Tyneside and West Midlands. Most large bus companies have day and weekly tickets. 'Plus Bus' add-on tickets are available with many rail fares, giving bus travel in the specified city.

GREECE

European residents: see InterRail Global Pass and One Country Pass. Non-European residents: see Eurail Global Pass, Eurail Regional / One Country Passes. See also Balkan Flexipass.

Multiple journey card: unlimited journeys for 10 (€48.10), 20 (€72.20) or 30 (€96.30) days in 2nd class. Discounts available for up to 5 persons travelling together. Supplements not included. *Prices and availability are unconfirmed.*

Athens: 24-hour ticket valid on metro (including ISAP), trams and buses €3, but excludes airport (weekly ticket €10). A return to airport is €10.

HUNGARY

European residents: see InterRail Global Pass and One Country Pass. Non-European residents: see Eurail Global Pass, Eurail Select / Regional / One Country Passes, European East.

Turista Bérlet: MÁV 7 and 10 day tickets are available for HUF 22,000 and 28,000 (in 1st class HUF 27,500 and 35,000). GySEV tickets also available for HUF 12,000 and 16,000 (in 1st class 15,000 / 20,000). A day ticket for the Balaton area is available for HUF 3,000 (1st class 3,760).

Budapest: BKV tram / metro / bus, 1 day HUF 1,550, 3 days HUF 3,850, 7 day travelcard HUF 4,600. Weekend family ticket HUF 2,200. **Budapest Card** also includes museums and discounts: 48 hours HUF 6,300, 72 hours HUF 7,500; 1 child up to 14 years old goes free. The **BKSZ bérlet** includes local rail services and is aimed at commuters.

IRELAND

European residents: see InterRail Global Pass and One Country Pass. Non-European residents: see Eurail Global / Select / National Passes. InterRail and Eurail passes valid in the Republic of Ireland are also valid in Northern Ireland from January 1, 2010. See also Britrail + Ireland.

REPUBLIC OF IRELAND ONLY:

Irish Explorer: any 5 days in 15 on IÉ rail services, €160 (child €80), standard class. New **Trecker Ticket** gives 4 days on Irish Rail for €100.

Irish Explorer Rail and Bus: IÉ rail plus Bus Éireann services, any 8 days in 15, €245 (child €122).

Open Road passes; flexi passes giving 3 to 15 days travel on Bus Éireann services, €54 to €234.

Note that the Emerald Card and Irish Rover Rail Only are no longer available. There is, however, an **Irish Rover Bus Only** pass.

Dublin area: bus and suburban rail 'short hop' (excludes Airlink): 1 day €10.20, family (2 adults + 4 under 16s) €15.60, 3 days €20, 7 days €34.50. Medium / long / giant hop cover Dublin hinterland for 7 days, €52 to €80 (photo-card required). Rambler (bus only, includes Airlink): 1 day €6, family €10. Freedom ticket gives bus plus city tour, 3 days €25.

NORTHERN IRELAND ONLY:

The new **iLink** integrated smartcard gives unlimited bus and rail travel on Translink services (Northern Ireland Railways, Ulsterbus and Belfast Citybus). There are three zones; zone 3 covers the whole of Northern Ireland: 1 day £15, 7 days £55, 1 month £195. Zone 1 covering Belfast city starts at £5 for one day; zone 2 covers a wider area (1 day £9).

Passes for Domestic Travel

ITALY

European residents: see InterRail Global Pass and One Country Pass. Non-European residents: see Eurail Global Pass, Eurail Select/ Regional/One Country Passes.

Roma: Roma Pass is a 3-day transport pass (€23) with museum discounts; first two visited are free. Vatican and Rome card (1 day €19, 3 days €25) gives transport plus 'Open' bus tour operated by Roma Cristiana. Biglietto Integrato Giornaliero (BIG) covers rail/metro/bus in urban area for one day, €4 (excludes Fiumicino airport, restrictions on rail/metro). Biglietto Turistico Integrato (BTI) valid 3 days €11, weekly ticket (CIS) €16. Roma & Lazio day ticket (BIRG) covers wider area in 7 zones (max €10.50), also 3 day ticket (BTR) max €28.50.

Milano: 24 hour ticket (abbonamento) on ATM city services (including local rail) €3.00, 48 hrs €5.50.

Napoli: 'Campania > artecard' is a museum/transport visitors card, with two types of 3 day ticket. The standard card allows free entry to any two museums with 50% off all others. The higher priced card allows free entry to all museums. Various areas available, prices from €16.

Venice Card: *Transport* version - public transport (including waterbuses) with other discounts €48/68 for 3/7 days. *Transport & Culture* version adds museums €73/96. *Junior* discounts for those under 29; add-on available for Alilaguna boats. ACTV bus/boats: 12/24/48 hrs €16/18/28.

Day tickets available in other major cities.

LATVIA

There are no rail passes that we are aware of that are valid in Latvia.

Riga Card: unlimited travel on public transport, also free/discounted museum entry. 10/14/18 LVL for 24/48/72 hours.

LITHUANIA

There are no rail passes that we are aware of that are valid in Lithuania.

Vilnius: 24 hr ticket on local buses 6 LTL, 72 hrs 14 LTL, 10 days 27 LTL.

LUXEMBOURG

European residents: see InterRail Global Pass and One Country Pass. Non-European residents: see Eurail Global Pass, Eurail Select/Regional Passes. See also Benelux Tourrail, Sar-Lor-Lux Ticket.

Billet longue durée: day ticket €4.00, unlimited 2nd-class travel on all public transport throughout the country; not valid to border points; valid to 0800 hrs following morning. Carnet of 5 day tickets €16.00. Oeko Pass: valid one month €45 2nd class, €67.50 1st class; from CFL offices.

Luxembourg Card: unlimited travel on trains and buses throughout the country, plus free entry to 56 attractions. 1 day €10; any 2 days €17, any 3 days €24 (the 2/3 day tickets must be used within two weeks). Family pass for 2-5 people (max. 3 adults) at twice one person rate.

MACEDONIA

European residents: see InterRail Global Pass and One Country Pass. See also Balkan Flexipass.

MONTENEGRO

European residents: see InterRail Global Pass. Non-European residents: see Eurail Select Pass. See also Balkan Flexipass.

NETHERLANDS

European residents: see InterRail Global Pass and One Country Pass. Non-European residents: see Eurail Global Pass, Eurail Select/Regional Passes. See also Benelux Tourrail, Euregio Ticket.

NS Day Card (Dagkaart) allows unlimited travel on Netherlands Railways for one day: €74.80 1st class, €44 2nd class, available at stations. **OV Dagkaart** costs €5.50 extra and includes buses, trams and metro throughout the country. Five NS Day Cards can be purchased in one transaction as a 5-Dagkaart (price is five times the above). Monthly and yearly versions also available, with or without OV add-on. Available from booking offices and ticket automats.

Railrunner: Up to 3 children (aged 4–11) may accompany an adult (aged 19+) for a flat rate of €2 per day. Excludes *Thalys*.

Zomertoer: 2 days' unlimited travel within any 7 day period between July 1 and Sept. 6. 2nd class only, €65 for 2 people, €85 for 3 people. **Zomertoer Plus** includes bus / tram / metro: €75 for 2, €99 for 3.

Amsterdam: GVB tram/bus/metro tickets. 24 hrs €7, 48 hrs €11.50, 72 hrs €15, 96 hrs €18. **I amsterdam Card**: tram/bus/metro/canal boat tour, plus free museum admission and discounts at various tourist attractions, 24/48/72 hrs: €33/43/53.

NORWAY

European residents: see InterRail Global Pass and One Country Pass. Non-European residents: see Eurail Global Pass, Eurail Select/ Regional/One Country Passes.

Eurail Norway Pass: for non-Europeans: 3 to 8 days 2nd class travel within one month, 259 USD for 3 days, 395 USD for 8 days. Youth (under 26) get 25% reduction. 30% discount on Flåm Railway, various ferry discounts; not valid on Oslo Airport Express.

Oslo: 24 hour ticket for all public transport (Dagskort) 65 NOK, 7 days (Ukeskort) 200 NOK, children 4-16 half price. **Oslo Pass**: unlimited travel on buses, trams, underground and NSB local trains (up to Zone 4), free entry to attractions, discounts on sightseeing buses/boats: 24/48/72 hours 220/320/410 NOK (children 95/115/150 NOK).

Bergen Card: local bus travel plus free or discounted entry to various attractions, 24/48 hrs: 190/250 NOK (children aged 3-15, 75/100 NOK).

POLAND

European residents: see InterRail Global Pass and One Country Pass. Non-European residents: see Eurail Select/Regional/One Country Passes, European East.

Bilet Weekendowy (weekend ticket): unlimited travel on *Ex/IC/TLK* trains (except Berlin-Warszawa-Express) 1800 Fri to 2400 Sun and on public holidays, 149 PLZ 1st class, 99 PLZ 2nd class. Available from over 660 stations.

Bilet Turystyczny (tourist ticket): unlimited travel on PKP local trains 1800 Friday to 0600 Monday, 60 PLZ 2nd class, 80 PLZ 1st class. **Bilet Turystyczny + CD** adds border area of Czech Republic.

Tam, gdzie chcesz is a 2-day rover ticket valid 1000-2400 on Mon-Tues, Tues-Wed or Wed-Thurs, valid only on *IC*, *Ex*, *TLK* trains. Reservations compulsory (at 20% discount). Prices 157 PLN 2nd class, 217 PLN 1st.

Warsaw Tourist card: public transport within the city limits plus free or discounted entry to various attractions. 24/72 hours for 35/65 PLN.

PORTUGAL

European residents: see InterRail Global Pass and One Country Pass. Non-European residents: see Eurail Global Pass, Eurail Select/ Regional/One Country Passes.

Intra-Rail: zonal (4 zones) pass for ages 12-30, 3 days (Fri-Sun) €55 (€49 with Youth Card), 10 days (starting Mon-Thurs) €185/159. Includes nights at youth hostels. Not valid on Alfa. Buy at major stations.

Lisboa: Carris tram/bus and metro - one-day ticket (bilhete 1 dia) €3.70 in conjunction with 7 *Colinas* smartcard (€0.50). **Lisboa Card** (includes tourist attractions): 24/48/72 hrs for €16/27/33.50 (children 5-11 €9.50/14/17).

Train and Bus Tourist Ticket: day ticket valid on the CP Sintra and Cascais lines (also suburban trains Alcântara to Oriente), also on Scotturb bus network, €12. Buy from main stations in the area.

Coimbra: day ticket on local buses €3.20.

Porto: metro + STCP bus + local rail, all zones, 1 day €5, 3 days €11. **Porto Card** also includes free/discounted entry to tourist attractions, 1 day €7.50, 2 days €11.50, 3 days € 15.50.

ROMANIA

European residents: see InterRail Global Pass and One Country Pass. Non-European residents: see Eurail Global Pass, Eurail Select/ Regional/One Country Passes. See also Balkan Flexipass.

Bucureşti: day ticket for urban tram/bus network 8 RON, 7 days 17 RON, 15 days 25 RON.

RUSSIA

Moskva: bus/tram tickets available from kiosks in strips of 10/20. Separate 10-trip tickets available for metro. Monthly *yediniy bilyet* covers bus/tram/metro. No tourist tickets. **St Peterburg**: bus/tram tickets available in packs of 10; multi-journey cards can be bought for the metro.

SERBIA

European residents: see InterRail Global Pass and One Country Pass. Non-European residents: see Eurail Select Pass. See Balkan Flexipass.

Beograd: urban transport seems to use single tickets; no day tickets.

SLOVAKIA

European residents: see InterRail Global Pass and One Country Pass. Non-European residents: see European East.

Bratislava: urban tram/bus network, 24 hrs €3.50, 48 hrs €6.50, 3 days €8, 7 days €12. **Bratislava City Card** includes walking tour and many discounts, 1 day €6, 2 days €10, 3 days €12, available from tourist offices.

SLOVENIA

European residents: see InterRail Global Pass and One Country Pass. Non-European residents: see Eurail Global Pass, Eurail Select/ Regional/ One Country Passes.

Ljubljana Card: city buses, museums and discounts, 72 hrs €12.50.

Passes for Domestic Travel

SPAIN

European residents: see InterRail Global Pass and One Country Pass. Non-European residents: see Eurail Global Pass, Eurail Select/Regional/One Country Passes.

Eurail Spain Pass: this pass for people resident outside Europe gives unlimited travel on RENFE main-line services for 3 to 10 days within a period of 2 months. 3 days: 259 USD 1st class, 209 USD 2nd class. Each extra day 36-39 USD 1st class, 30 USD 2nd class. Children aged 4-11 half fare. No youth or group discounts. Reservation compulsory on all long distance trains.

Barcelona T-Dia ticket: valid 1 day on all public transport (TMB, FGC, tram, local rail), from €5.80 (1 zone) to €16.50 (all 6 zones). Zone 1 travelcards available for 2/3/4/5 days €10.70/15.20/19.50/23.10. **Barcelona Card**: various discounts 2/3/4/5 days €26/31.50/36/42.

Madrid: Abono Turístico gives all public transport in Zone A, 1/2/3 days €5.20/8.80/11.60, also 5/7 days €17.60/23.60, children 50%. Also available for wider area (zone T) at double the price. **Madrid Card** adds free or reduced entry to various attractions, 24/48/72 hrs €45/58/72.

Sevilla Card: public transport plus free entry to most museums, 24 hrs €50, 48 hrs €60, 72 hrs €65. Tourist cards also available for Burgos, Córdoba and Zaragoza.

SWEDEN

European residents: see InterRail Global Pass and One Country Pass. Non-European residents: see Eurail Global Pass, Eurail Select/Regional/One Country Passes. See also Öresund Rundt.

SJ Sommarkort: a pass giving 5 days 2nd class travel out of 30 days during the period mid-June to mid-August, 1750 SEK. Also valid to Oslo and København. Available from main stations. *Subject to confirmation.*

Stockholm: all SL public transport in Greater Stockholm, 24 hours 100 SEK, 72 hours 200 SEK, (72-timmarskort Plus adds various museums, summer only, 250 SEK). Also 7 days 260 SEK, 30 days 690 SEK; reductions of about 40% for under 20s and over 65s. Annual cards also available. **Stockholm Card** includes free entry to museums, 375/495/595 SEK for 24/48/72 hours (children aged 7-17 180/210/230 SEK).

SWITZERLAND

European residents: see InterRail Global Pass and One Country Pass. Non-European residents: see Eurail Global Pass, Eurail Select/Regional Passes. See also Euregio-Bodensee.

Swiss Pass: available to all non-Swiss residents. Consecutive days on Swiss Railways, boats and most alpine postbuses and city buses. Valid for 4, 8, 15, 22 days or 1 month. 1st class £229/332/402 for 4/8/15 days, £464/510 for 22 days/1 month. 2nd class £153/221/268 for 4/8/15 days, £309/340 for 22 days/1 month. Youth Pass gives 25% reduction for under 26s. All versions give 50% reduction on many funicular and mountain railways. Also acts as a Museum Pass - free entrance to 400 sites. Children aged 6-15 travel free with a Family Card (issued free by Switzerland Tourism, London) if accompanied by a parent (not other relatives), otherwise half fare.

Swiss Flexi Pass: as above but valid for 3, 4, 5 or 6 days within 1 month. Prices 1st/2nd class £220/146 (3 days), £266/178 (4 days), £308/205 (5 days), £351/234 (6 days). No Youth discount.

Saver Program: applies to the Swiss Pass or Flexi Pass (not Youth Pass) - 15% reduction per person for 2-5 adults travelling together.

Swiss Transfer Ticket: return ticket from any airport/border station to any other Swiss station; use within 1 month. Each journey must be completed on day of validation and on the most direct route. 1st class £113, 2nd class £75. Family Card valid, see above. Cannot be obtained in Switzerland.

Swiss Card: as Swiss Transfer Ticket but also offers unlimited half-fare tickets for 1 month and 50% reduction on many private railways. 1st class £150, 2nd class £107. Family card valid, see above under Swiss Pass.

Swiss Half Fare Card: 50% off most public transport, price £58, valid one month. Annual cards also available.

Note that the above passes are available from Switzerland Tourism, London, tel. 02074 204900, also online. Also available (except Swiss Transfer ticket) at major Swiss stations; Swiss Card only at border/airport stations. None of the above passes are available to Swiss residents.

Regional Passes: several areas available, e.g. Bernese Oberland for 7 days (3 days unlimited 2nd class travel plus 4 at 50% discount) 230 CHF, or 15 days (5 plus 10), 277 CHF, available May to October. Other passes include Adventure Card Wallis, and Graubünden Summer Holiday Pass. Not available from the UK, obtain locally in Switzerland.

Bern: day ticket, all transport in city (zones 10/11) 20/12 CHF 1st/2nd class, all zones in region 64/38 CHF.

Genève: Day ticket (Carte 24 Heures) includes buses, trams, trains and boats: 10 CHF (valid for 2 people at weekends). A version valid 0900 hrs until midnight costs 7 CHF.

Zürich: Tageskarte gives 24 hours on all transport including SBB trains, 13.20/8 CHF 1st/2nd class (central zone only); all zones in Canton 51.20/30.80 CHF. Off-peak version is 9-UhrPass, all zones, not before 0900 Mon-Fri, 38/23 CHF (also available for use on 6 different days 204/124 CHF; monthly version also available). **Zürich Card** includes visitor attractions: 24 hours 19 CHF, 72 hours 38 CHF (children 13/26 CHF), includes airport. **Zürich Card Plus** covers the whole Canton of Zürich with additional discounts: 24 hours 36 CHF (children 24 CHF).

TURKEY

European residents: see InterRail Global Pass and One Country Pass.

UKRAINE

There are no rail passes that we are aware of that are valid in Ukraine.

Kyїv: a monthly travelcard is available but there are no tourist tickets.

Where to Buy your Pass

Sources of rail passes include the following. Many can also provide point to point tickets and further information about rail travel.

IN THE UNITED KINGDOM

Rail Pass Direct
Chase House, Gilbert Street, Ropley, Hampshire SO24 0BY
✆ 08700 84 14 13   fax 0870 751 5005   www.railpassdirect.co.uk

Deutsche Bahn UK (German Railways)
UK Booking Centre, PO Box 687a, Surbiton KT6 6UB
✆ 08718 80 80 66 (8p per minute)   fax 08718 80 80 65
www.deutsche-bahn.co.uk

European Rail Ltd
Unit 25, Tileyard Studios, Tileyard Road, London N7 9AH
✆ 020 7619 1083   fax 020 7700 2164   www.europeanrail.co.uk

Ffestiniog Travel
Unit 6, Snowdonia Business Park, Minffordd, Gwynedd LL48 6LD
✆ 01766 772 050   fax 01766 772 056   www.festtravel.co.uk

Rail Canterbury
39 Palace Street, Canterbury, Kent CT1 2DZ
✆ 01227 450 088   fax 01227 470 072   www.rail-canterbury.co.uk

RailChoice - International Rail
Chase House, Gilbert Street, Ropley, Hampshire SO24 0BY
✆ 0870 165 7300   fax 0208 659 7466   www.railchoice.co.uk

Rail Europe
Britain Visitor Centre, 1 Regent Street, London SW1Y 4LR
✆ 08448 484 064   www.raileurope.co.uk

Stephen Walker Travel
Assembly Rooms, Market Place, Boston, Lincs PE21 6LY
✆ 01205 310000   www.stephenwalkertravel.co.uk

Trainseurope
4 Station Approach, March, Cambs PE15 8SJ
Also at St Pancras International, London, and Cambridge station
✆ 08717 00 77 22   fax 01354 660 444   www.trainseurope.co.uk

Ultima Travel
424 Chester Road, Little Sutton, South Wirral CH66 3RB
✆ 0151 339 6171   fax 0151 339 9199.

IN THE USA

Rail Europe Inc.
44 South Broadway, White Plains, NY 10601
✆ 1-800-622-8600   www.raileurope.com

IN CANADA

Rail Europe, Canada
✆ 1-800-361 7245   (1-800-361-RAIL)   www.raileurope.ca

See also **Rick Steve's** comprehensive website: www.ricksteves.com.

For a list of **Eurail** agents worldwide see www.eurailgroup.com.

Passes are sometimes available from the travel centres at major European stations.

AUSTRIA

CAPITAL
Vienna (Wien).

CLIMATE
Moderate Continental climate. Warm summer; high snowfall in winter.

CURRENCY
Euro (EUR / €). 1 euro = 100 cent. For exchange rates see page 11.

EMBASSIES IN VIENNA
Australia: Mattiellistraße 2, ✆ 01 506 740. **Canada**: Laurenzerberg 2, ✆ 01 383 000. **New Zealand** (Consulate): Salesianergasse 15/3, ✆ 01 318 8505. **UK**: Jaurèsgasse 12, ✆ 01 716 130. **USA**: Boltzmanngasse 16, ✆ 01 313 390.

EMBASSIES OVERSEAS
Australia: 12 Talbot St, Forrest, Canberra, ACT 2603, ✆ 2 6295 1533. **Canada**: 445 Wilbrod St, Ottawa ON, KIN 6M7, ✆ 613 789 1444. **UK**: 18 Belgrave Mews West, London SW1X 8HU, ✆ 020 7344 3250. **USA**: 3524 International Court NW, Washington DC 20008, ✆ 202 895 6700.

LANGUAGE
German; English is widely spoken in tourist areas.

OPENING HOURS
Banks: mostly Mon, Tues, Wed, Fri 0800–1230 and 1330–1500, Thur 0800–1230 and 1330–1730. **Shops**: Mon–Fri 0800–1830 (some closing for a 1- or 2-hour lunch), Sat 0800–1200/1300 (in larger towns often until 1700). **Museums**: check locally.

POST OFFICES
Indicated by golden horn symbol; all handle poste restante (*postlagernde Briefe*). Open mostly Mon–Fri 0800–1200 and 1400–1800. Main and station post offices in larger cities open 24 hrs. Stamps (*Briefmarke*) also sold at Tabak/Trafik shops.

PUBLIC HOLIDAYS
Jan 1, Jan 6 (Epiphany), Easter Mon, May 1, Ascension Day, Whit Mon, Corpus Christi, Aug 15 (Assumption), Oct 26 (National Day), Nov 1 (All Saints), Dec 8 (Immaculate Conception), Dec 25, 26. For dates of movable holidays see page 2.

PUBLIC TRANSPORT
Most long-distance travel is by rail (see below). Inter-urban buses operated by ÖBB-Postbus (www.postbus.at); usually based by rail stations or post offices. City transport is efficient with integrated ticketing; buy tickets from machines or Tabak/Trafik booths. Wien has an extensive metro and tram system; for day tickets see Passes section. Other cities with tram networks include Graz, Innsbruck and Linz. Taxis are metered; extra charges for luggage (fixed charges in smaller towns).

RAIL TRAVEL
See Tables **950 - 999**. Operated by Österreichische Bundesbahnen (ÖBB) (www.oebb.at). Mostly electrified; fast and reliable; ÖIC or IC trains every 1–2 hrs with connecting regional trains. Other fast trains, with stops only in larger cities: ICE, ÖEC, EC and the new Railjet (RJ) services; D (ordinary express trains); REX (semi-fast/local trains). Most overnight trains convey sleeping-cars (up to three berths), couchettes (four/six berths) and 2nd-class seats. Seat reservations available on long-distance services. Most stations have left luggage facilities.

TELEPHONES
Dial in: ✆ +43 then number (omit initial 0). Outgoing: ✆ 00. Phonecards are sold at post offices and tobacconists (Tabak Trafiken). Operator assistance / enquiries: ✆ 1611 (national); ✆ 1613 (rest of Europe); ✆ 1614 (rest of world). Emergency: ✆ 112. Police: ✆ 133. Fire: ✆ 122. Ambulance: ✆ 144.

TIPPING
Hotels, restaurants, cafés and bars: service charge of 10–15% but tip of around 10% still expected. Taxis 10%.

TOURIST INFORMATION
Austrian National Tourist Office (www.austria.info). Staff invariably speak some English. Tourist office opening times vary widely, particularly restricted at weekends in smaller places. Usually called *Fremdenverkehrsbüro*; look for green 'i' sign. Main tourist office in Vienna: Albertinaplatz / Maysedergasse, ✆ 01 24 555.

TOURIST OFFICES OVERSEAS
Australia: 36 Carrington St, 1st floor, Sydney NSW 2000, ✆ 02 9299 3621, info@antosyd.org.au. **Canada**: 2 Bloor St West, Suite 400, Toronto ON, M4W 3E2, ✆ 416 967 3381, travel@austria.info. **UK**: 9-11 Richmond Buildings, off Dean St., London W1D 3HF, ✆ 0845 101 18 18, holiday@austria.info. **USA**: 120 West 45th St, 9th floor, New York NY 10036, ✆ 212 944 6880, travel@austria.info.

VISAS
See page xxxii for visa requirements.

BELGIUM

CAPITAL
Brussels (Bruxelles/Brussel).

CLIMATE
Rain prevalent at any time; warm summers, cold winters (often with snow).

CURRENCY
Euro (EUR / €). 1 euro = 100 cent. For exchange rates see page 11.

EMBASSIES IN BRUSSELS
Australia: rue Guimard 6-8, ✆ 02 286 0500. **Canada**: Avenue de Tervueren 2, ✆ 02 741 0611. **New Zealand**: square de Meeûs 1, ✆ 02 512 1040. **UK**: rue d'Arlon 85, ✆ 02 287 6211. **USA**: Regentlaan 27 Boulevard du Régent, ✆ 02 508 2111.

EMBASSIES OVERSEAS
Australia: 19 Arkana St, Yarralumla, Canberra, ACT 2600, ✆ 2 6273 2501. **Canada**: 360 Albert St, Suite 820, Ottawa ON, K1R 7X7, ✆ 613 236 7267. **UK**: 17 Grosvenor Crescent, London SW1X 7EE, ✆ 020 7470 3700. **USA**: 3330 Garfield St NW, Washington DC 20008, ✆ 202 333 6900.

LANGUAGE
Dutch (north), French (south) and German (east). Many speak both French and Dutch, plus often English and/or German.

OPENING HOURS
Many establishments close 1200–1400. **Banks**: Mon–Fri 0900–1600. **Shops**: Mon–Sat 0900/1000–1800/1900 (often later Fri). **Museums**: vary, but most open six days a week: 1000–1700 (usually Tues–Sun, Wed–Mon or Thur–Tues).

POST OFFICES
Postes / Posterijen / De Post open Mon–Fri 0900–1700 (very few open Sat morning). Stamps are also sold at newsagents.

PUBLIC HOLIDAYS
Jan 1, Easter Mon, May 1, Ascension Day, Whit Mon, July 21 (National Day), Aug 15 (Assumption), Nov 1 (All Saints), Nov 11 (Armistice), Dec 25, 26. For dates of movable holidays see page 2. Transport and places that open usually keep Sunday times on public holidays.

PUBLIC TRANSPORT
National bus companies: De Lijn (Flanders), TEC (Wallonia, i.e. the French-speaking areas); few long-distance buses. Brussels has

extensive metro / tram / bus system operated by STIB with integrated ticketing; tickets can be purchased from tram / bus driver but it's cheaper to buy in advance from machines at metro stations or special kiosks (also offices labelled *Bootik*). For day tickets see Passes section. Some tram and bus stops are request stops – raise your hand. Taxis seldom stop in the street, so find a rank or phone; double rates outside city limits.

RAIL TRAVEL

See Tables **400 - 439**. Operated by NMBS (in Dutch) / SNCB (in French) (www.b-rail.be). Rail information offices: 'B' in an oval logo. Seat reservations available for international journeys only. Refreshments are not always available. Some platforms serve more than one train at a time; check carefully. Left luggage and cycle hire at many stations. Timetables usually in two sets: Mondays to Fridays and weekends/holidays.

TELEPHONES

Dial in: ✆ +32 then number (omit initial 0). Outgoing: ✆ 00. Phonecards are sold at post offices, newsagents and supermarkets. Some public phones accept credit cards. Emergency: ✆ 112. Police: ✆ 101. Fire, ambulance: ✆ 100.

TIPPING

Tipping in cafés, bars, restaurants and taxis is not the norm, as service is supposed to be included in the price, but is starting to be expected in places where staff are used to serving people from the international community (who often leave generous tips): 10 to 15%. Tip hairwashers in salons, delivery men, cloakroom / toilet attendants.

TOURIST INFORMATION

Toerisme Vlaanderen (www.toervl.be / www.visitflanders.co.uk). Office de Promotion du Tourisme de Wallonie et de Bruxelles (www.belgium-tourism.net). Dutch: *Dienst voor Toerisme*. French: *Office de Tourisme*. Brussels tourist office: Hôtel de Ville, Grand Place, ✆ 025 138 940. Most tourist offices have English-speaking staff and free English-language literature, but charge for walking itineraries and good street maps. Opening hours, especially in small places and off-season, are flexible.

TOURIST OFFICES OVERSEAS

UK: Tourism Flanders - Brussels, 1a Cavendish Square, London W1G 0LD. ✆ 020 7307 7738, info@visitflanders.co.uk; Belgian Tourist Office Brussels-Wallonia 217 Marsh Wall, London E14 9FJ. ✆ 020 7531 0390, ✆ 0800 954 5245 (to order brochures), info@belgiumtheplaceto.be. **USA / Canada**: 220 East 42nd St, Suite 3402, New York NY 10017, ✆ 212 758 8130, info@visitbelgium.com

VISAS

See page xxxii for visa requirements.

BULGARIA

CAPITAL

Sofia (Sofiya).

CLIMATE

Hot summers; wet spring and autumn; snow in winter (skiing popular).

CURRENCY

Lev (BGN or Lv.); 1 lev = 100 stotinki (st). Tied to euro. For exchange rates, see page 11. Credit cards are increasingly accepted.

EMBASSIES IN SOFIA

Australia (Consulate): ulitsa Trakia 37, ✆ 02 946 1334. **Canada**: (Consulate) ulitsa Moskovska 9, ✆ 02 969 9710. **New Zealand**: *refer to NZ Embassy in Belgium*. **UK**: ul. Moskovska 9, ✆ 02 933 9222. **USA**: ulitsa Kozyak 16, ✆ 02 937 5100.

EMBASSIES OVERSEAS

Australia: 33 Culgoa Circuit, O'Malley, Canberra, ACT 2606, ✆ 2 6286 9711. **Canada**: 325 Steward St, Ottawa ON, K1N 6K5, ✆ 613 789 3215. **UK**: 186–186 Queen's Gate, London SW7 5HL, ✆ 020 7584 9400. **USA**: 1621 22nd St NW, Washington DC 20008, ✆ 202 387 0174.

LANGUAGE

Bulgarian (written in the Cyrillic alphabet); English, German, Russian and French in tourist areas. Nodding the head indicates 'no' (*ne*); shaking it means 'yes' (*da*).

OPENING HOURS

Banks: Mon–Fri 0900–1500. Some exchange offices open longer hours and weekends. **Shops**: Mon–Fri 0800–2000, closed 1200–1400 outside major towns, Sat open 1000–1200. **Museums**: vary widely, but often 0800–1200, 1400–1830. Many close Mon or Tues.

POST OFFICES

Stamps (*marki*) are sold only at post offices (*poshta*), usually open Mon–Sat 0800–1730. Some close 1200–1400.

PUBLIC HOLIDAYS

Jan 1, Mar. 3 (National Day), Orthodox Easter Mon, May 1 (Labour Day), May 6, May 24 (Education and Culture), Sept 6 (Union), Sept 22 (Independence), Nov. 1 (Spiritual Leaders), Dec 24, 25, 26. For dates of movable holidays see page 2.

PUBLIC TRANSPORT

There is an extensive bus network but quality is variable. They are slightly more expensive than trains but both are very cheap for hard-currency travellers. In Sofia buses and trams use the same ticket; punch it at the machine after boarding, get a new ticket if you change. For day tickets see Passes section.

RAIL TRAVEL

See Tables **1500 - 1560**. Bulgarian State Railways (BDZ), (www.bdz.bg) run express, fast and stopping trains. Often crowded; reservations are recommended (obligatory for express trains). Most long-distance trains provide a limited buffet service; certain services also convey a restaurant car. Overnight trains convey 1st- and 2nd-class sleeping cars and seats (also 2nd-class couchettes on certain trains between Sofia and Black Sea resorts). One platform may serve two tracks, platforms and tracks are both numbered. Signs at stations are in Cyrillic.

TELEPHONES

Dial in: ✆ +359 then number (omit initial 0). Outgoing: ✆ 00. Tokens (for local calls) and phonecards are sold at post offices and tobacconists. Police: ✆ 166. Fire: ✆ 160. Ambulance: ✆ 150.

TIPPING

Waiters and taxi drivers expect a tip of about 10%.

TOURIST INFORMATION

Bulgarian Tourism Authority (www.bulgariatravel.org). Main tourist office: 1 Sveta Nedelia Sq., 1040 Sofia, ✆ 029 335 845. info@bulgariatravel.org. There are tourist offices in all main cities.

TOURIST OFFICES OVERSEAS

UK and **USA**: Tourist information available at the Bulgarian Embassies listed above.

VISAS

See page xxxii for visa requirements. Passports must have 3 months validity remaining. Visitors staying with friends or family (i.e. not in paid accommodation) need to register on arrival.

CROATIA

CAPITAL

Zagreb.

CLIMATE

Continental on the Adriatic coast, with very warm summers.

CURRENCY
Kuna (HRK or kn); 1 kuna = 100 lipa. For exchange rates, see page 11. Credit cards are widely accepted.

EMBASSIES IN ZAGREB
Australia: Centar Kaptol, 3rd Floor, Nova Ves 11, ✆ 014 891 200. **Canada**: Prilaz Gjure Dezelica 4, ✆ 014 881 200. **New Zealand** (Consulate): Vlaska ulica 50A, ✆ 014 612 060. **UK**: Ivana Lučića 4, ✆ 016 009 100. **USA**: Ulica Thomasa Jeffersona 2, ✆ 016 612 200.

EMBASSIES OVERSEAS
Australia: 14 Jindalee Crescent, O'Malley, Canberra, ACT 2606, ✆ 2 6286 6988. **Canada**: 229 Chapel St, Ottawa ON, K1N 7Y6, ✆ 613 562 7820. **New Zealand** (consulate): 291 Lincoln Rd, Henderson, PO Box 83-200, Edmonton, Auckland, ✆ 9 836 5581. **UK**: 21 Conway St, London, W1T 6BN, ✆ 020 7387 2022. **USA**: 2343 Massachusetts Ave. NW, Washington DC 20008-2803, ✆ 202 588 5899.

LANGUAGE
Croatian. English, German and Italian spoken in tourist areas.

OPENING HOURS
Banks: Mon–Fri 0700–1900, Sat 0700–1300, but may vary, some banks may open Sun in larger cities. Most **shops**: Mon–Fri 0800–2000, Sat 0800–1400/1500; many shops also open Sun, especially in summer. Some shops close 1200–1600. Most open-air **markets** daily, mornings only. **Museums**: vary.

POST OFFICES
Usual hours: Mon–Fri 0700–1900 (some post offices in larger cities open until 2200), Sat 0700–1300. Stamps (*markice*) are sold at newsstands and tobacconists (*trafika*), Post boxes are yellow.

PUBLIC HOLIDAYS
Jan 1, Jan 6 (Epiphany), Easter Mon, May 1, Corpus Christi, June 22 (Antifascist Struggle), June 25 (National Day), Aug. 5 (Nat. Thanksgiving), Aug. 15 (Assumption), Oct 8 (Independence), Nov 1 (All Saints), Dec. 25, 26. For dates of movable holidays see page 2. Many local Saints' holidays.

PUBLIC TRANSPORT
Buses and trams are cheap, regular and efficient. Zagreb and Osijek have tram networks. Jadrolinija maintains most domestic ferry lines; main office in Rijeka, ✆ +385 51 666 111.

RAIL TRAVEL
See Tables **1300 - 1359**. National railway company: Hrvatske željeznice (HŽ) (www.hznet.hr). Zagreb is a major hub for international trains. Efficient services but there is a limited network and services can be infrequent. Daytime trains on the Zagreb - Split line are operated by modern tilting diesel trains. Station amenities: generally left luggage, a bar, newsstand and WCs.

TELEPHONES
Dial in: ✆ +385 then number (omit initial 0). Outgoing: ✆ 00. Public phones accept phonecards only (sold at post offices, newsstands and tobacconists). Police: ✆ 92. Fire: ✆ 93. Ambulance: ✆ 94.

TIPPING
Leave 10% for good service in a restaurant. It's not necessary to tip in bars.

TOURIST INFORMATION
Croatian National Tourist Board (www.croatia.hr). Main office: Iblerov trg 10/IV, 10000 Zagreb, ✆ 014 699 333, info@htz.hr.

TOURIST OFFICES OVERSEAS
UK: Lanchesters, 162-164 Fulham Palace Rd, London, W6 9ER, ✆ 020 8563 7979, info@croatia-london.co.uk **USA**: 350 Fifth Ave., Suite 4003, New York NY 10118, ✆ 212 279 8672, cntony@earthlink.net

VISAS
See page xxxii for visa requirements.

CZECH REPUBLIC

CAPITAL
Prague (Praha).

CLIMATE
Mild summers and very cold winters.

CURRENCY
Czech crown or koruna (CZK or Kč); 1 koruna = 100 haléřu. For exchange rates, see page 11. Credit cards are widely accepted.

EMBASSIES IN PRAGUE
Australia (Consulate): 6th Floor, Solitaire Building, ulica Klimentska 10, ✆ 296 578 350. **Canada**: Muchova 6, ✆ 272 101 800. **New Zealand** (Consulate): Dykova 19, ✆ 222 514 672. **UK**: Thunovská 14, ✆ 257 402 111. **USA**: Tržíště 15, ✆ 257 022 000.

EMBASSIES OVERSEAS
Australia: 8 Culgoa Circuit, O'Malley, Canberra, ACT 2606, ✆ 2 6290 1386. **Canada**: 251 Cooper St., Ottawa ON, K2P 0G2, ✆ 613 562 3875. **UK**: 26–30 Kensington Palace Gardens, London W8 4QY, ✆ 020 7243 1115. **USA**: 3900 Spring of Freedom St NW, Washington DC 20008, ✆ 202 274 9100.

LANGUAGE
Czech. Czech and Slovak are closely related Slavic tongues. English, German and Russian are widely understood, but Russian is less popular.

OPENING HOURS
Banks: Mon–Fri 0800–1800. **Shops**: Mon–Fri 0900–1800, Sat 0900–1200 (often longer in Prague Sat–Sun). **Food shops**: usually open earlier plus on Sun. **Museums**: (usually) Tues–Sun 1000–1800. Most castles close Nov–Mar.

POST OFFICES
Usual opening hours are 0800–1900. Stamps also available from newsagents and tobacconists. Post boxes: orange and blue.

PUBLIC HOLIDAYS
Jan 1, Easter Mon, May 1, May 8 (Liberation), July 5 (Cyril & Methodius), July 6 (Jan Hus), Sept 28 (Statehood), Oct 28 (Founding), Nov. 17 (Freedom & Democracy), Dec 24, 25, 26. For dates of movable holidays see page 2.

PUBLIC TRANSPORT
Extensive long-distance bus network competing with the railways, run by ČSAD or increasingly by private companies. In Prague the long-distance bus station is close to Florenc metro station. If boarding at a bus station with a ticket window, buy your ticket in advance, otherwise pay the driver. Good urban networks with integrated ticketing. Prague (Praha) has metro and tram system - see Passes feature for day tickets. Other cities with trams include Brno, Ostrava, Plzeň, Olomouc, Liberec.

RAIL TRAVEL
See Tables **1100 - 1169**. National rail company is České Dráhy (ČD) (www.cd.cz). An extensive network with many branch lines and cheap fares, but sometimes crowded trains. The best mainline trains are classified *IC*, *EC* or *Ex*. The fastest Praha - Ostrava trains are classified *SC* meaning *SuperCity* and are operated by Pendolino tilting trains - a compulsory reservation fee of CZK 200 or €7.00 applies on these. Other fast (*R* for rychlík) trains are shown in our tables with just the train number. Semi-fast trains are *Sp* or spešný, local trains (very slow) are *Os* or osobný. Some branch lines are now operated by private companies. Many long-distance trains have dining or buffet cars. Seats for express trains may be reserved at least one hour before departure at the counter marked R at stations.

TELEPHONES
Dial in: ✆ +420 then number. Outgoing: ✆ 00. Payphones accept coins or phonecards (sold at post offices, tobacconists, newsstands, hotels and money exchange offices). Police: ✆ 158. Fire: ✆ 150. Ambulance: ✆ 155.

TIPPING
You should tip at pubs and restaurants, in hotels and taxis and hairdressers. In general, round up the nearest CZK 10 unless you are somewhere upmarket, when you should tip 10%.

TOURIST INFORMATION
Czech Tourism (www.czechtourism.com). Main office: Vinohradská 46, 120 41 Praha 2, Vinohrady, ✆ 221 580 111. Prague Information Service (www.pis.cz), Information centre, Old Town Hall, Staromestská námesti 1, Praha 1.

TOURIST OFFICES OVERSEAS
Canada: 2 Bloor Street West, Suite 1500, Toronto ON, M4W 3E2, ✆ 416 363 9928, info-ca@czechtourism.com **UK**: 13 Harley Street, London W1G 9QG, ✆ 020 7631 0427, info-uk@czechtourism.com **USA**: 1109 Madison Ave., New York NY 10028, ✆ 212 288 0830, info-usa@czechtourism.com

VISAS
See page xxxii for visa requirements.

DENMARK

CAPITAL
Copenhagen (København).

CLIMATE
Maritime climate. July–Aug is warmest, May–June often very pleasant, but rainier; Oct–Mar is wettest, with periods of frost.

CURRENCY
Danish crown or krone, DKK or kr; 1 krone = 100 øre. For exchange rates, see page 11.

EMBASSIES IN COPENHAGEN
Australia: Dampfaergevej 26, ✆ 70 26 36 76. **Canada**: Kristen Bernikowsgade 1, ✆ 33 48 32 00. **New Zealand** (Consulate): Store Strandstraede 21, ✆ 33 37 77 02. **UK**: Kastelsvej 36-40, ✆ 35 44 52 00. **USA**: Dag Hammarskjölds Allé 24, ✆ 33 41 71 00.

EMBASSIES OVERSEAS
Australia: 15 Hunter St, Yarralumla, Canberra, ACT 2600, ✆ 2 6270 5333. **Canada**: 47 Clarence St, Suite 450, Ottawa ON, K1N 9K1, ✆ 613 562 1811. **New Zealand** (Consulate): 273 Bleakhouse Rd, Howick, PO Box 619, Auckland 1015, ✆ 9 537 3099. **UK**: 55 Sloane St, London SW1X 9SR, ✆ 020 7333 0200. **USA**: 3200 Whitehaven St NW, Washington DC 20008-3683, ✆ 202 234 4300.

LANGUAGE
Danish. English is almost universally spoken.

OPENING HOURS
Banks (Copenhagen): Mon–Fri 0930–1600 (some until 1700; most until 1800 on Thur). Vary elsewhere. **Shops**: (mostly) Mon–Thur 0930–1730, Fri 0930–1900/2000, Sat 0900–1300/1400, though many in Copenhagen open until 1700 and may also open Sun. **Museums**: (mostly) daily 1000/1100–1600/1700. In winter, hours shorter and museums usually close Mon.

POST OFFICES
Mostly Mon–Fri 0900/1000–1700/1800, Sat 0900–1200 (but opening times vary greatly). Stamps also sold at newsagents.

PUBLIC HOLIDAYS
Jan 1, Maundy Thurs, Good Fri, Easter Sun/Mon, Common Prayer Day (4th Fri after Easter), Ascension, Whit Monday, June 5 (Constitution Day), Dec. 25, 26. For dates of movable holidays see page 2.

PUBLIC TRANSPORT
Long-distance travel is easiest by train (see below). Excellent regional and city bus services, many connecting with trains. Modern and efficient metro (www.m.dk) and suburban rail network in and around the capital; see Passes feature for day tickets. No trams in København; bus network can be tricky to fathom. Bridges or ferries link all the big islands. Taxis: green *Fri* sign when available; metered, and most accept major credit cards. Many cycle paths and bike hire shops; free use of City Bikes in Copenhagen central area (returnable coin required).

RAIL TRAVEL
See Tables **700 - 728**. Operator: Danske Statsbaner (DSB); (www.dsb.dk). Some independent lines, and certain former DSB services are now operated by private company ArrivaTog. *IC* trains reach up to 200 km/h. *Re* (regionaltog) trains are frequent, but slower. Refreshment trolley or vending machine available on most *IC* trains. Reservations are recommended (not compulsory) on *IC* and *Lyn* trains - DKK 20 in standard class; reservation included in business class. Reservations close 15 minutes before a train leaves its originating station. Nationwide reservations ✆ 70 13 14 15. Baggage lockers at most stations, usually DKK 20 per 24 hrs. Usually free trolleys, but you may need a (returnable) coin.

TELEPHONES
Dial in: ✆ +45 then number. Outgoing: ✆ 00. Most operators speak English. Phonecards are available from DSB kiosks, post offices and newsstands. Directory enquiries: ✆ 118. International operator/ directory: ✆ 14. Emergency services: ✆ 112.

TIPPING
At least DKK 20 in restaurants. Elsewhere (taxis, cafés, bars, hotels etc) tipping is not expected.

TOURIST INFORMATION
Danish Tourist Board (www.visitdenmark.com). Nearly every decent-sized town in Denmark has a tourist office (*turistbureau*), normally found in the town hall or central square; they distribute maps, information and advice. Some will also book accommodation for a small fee, and change money.

TOURIST OFFICES OVERSEAS
UK: 55 Sloane St, London SW1X 9SY, ✆ 020 7259 5958, london@visitdenmark.com **USA / Canada**: P.O.Box 4649, Grand Central Station New York NY 10163-4649, ✆ 212 885 9700, info@goscandinavia.com

VISAS
See page xxxii for visa requirements.

ESTONIA

CAPITAL
Tallinn.

CLIMATE
Warm summers, cold, snowy winters; rain all year, heaviest in August.

CURRENCY
Estonian crown or kroon (EEK or kr); 1 kroon = 100 senti. For exchange rates, see page 11. Currency exchange facilities are limited, though cash machines (ATMs) are plentiful, especially in Tallinn.

EMBASSIES IN TALLINN
Australia (Consulate): c/- Standard Ltd Marja 9, ✆ 6 509 308.
Canada (Consulate): Toom Kooli 13, ✆ 6 273 308.
New Zealand: *refer to NZ Embassy in Poland.*
UK: Wismari 6, ✆ 6 674 700.

USA: Kentmanni 20, ✆ 6 688 100.

EMBASSIES OVERSEAS

Australia (Consulate): 40 Nicholson St. Balmain East, Sydney, NSW 2041, ✆ 2 8014 8999. **Canada**: 260 Dalhousie St, Suite 210, Ottawa ON, K1N 7E4, ✆ 613 789 4222. **UK**: 16 Hyde Park Gate, London SW7 5DG, ✆ 020 7589 3428. **USA**: 2131 Massachusetts Ave. NW, Washington DC 20008, ✆ 202 588 0101.

LANGUAGE

Estonian. Some Finnish is useful, plus Russian in Tallinn and the north-east.

OPENING HOURS

Banks: Mon–Fri 0900–1600. **Shops**: Mon–Fri 0900/1000–1800/1900, Sat 0900/1000–1500/1700; many also open Sun. **Museums**: days vary (usually closed Mon and/or Tues); hours commonly 1100–1600.

POST OFFICES

Post offices *(Eesti Post)* are generally open 0900–1800 Mon–Fri, 0930–1500 Sat. The central post office in Tallinn is located at Narva 1. Stamps are also sold at large hotels, newsstands, and tourist offices.

PUBLIC HOLIDAYS

Jan 1, Feb 24 (Independence), Good Friday, Easter Mon (unofficial), May 1, June 23 (Victory), June 24 (Midsummer), Aug 20 (Restoration of Independence), Dec 25, 26. For dates of movable holidays see page 2.

PUBLIC TRANSPORT

Long-distance bus services are often quicker, cleaner, and more efficient than rail, but getting pricier. The main operator is Eurolines (www.eurolines.ee). Book international journeys in advance at bus stations; pay the driver on rural and local services. Tallinn has a tram network.

RAIL TRAVEL

See Tables **1800 - 1890**. Local rail services are operated by Edelaraudtee (www.edel.ee), international services by GoRail (www.gorail.ee). Comfortable overnight train to Moskva; best to take berth in 2nd-class coupé (4-berth compartments); 1st-class *luxe* compartments (2-berth) also available. Reservations are compulsory for all sleepers; entry visa to Russia may need to be shown when booking. Very little English spoken at stations.

TELEPHONES

Dial in: ✆ +372 then number. Outgoing: ✆ 00. Pay phones take phonecards (from hotels, tourist offices, post offices, newsstands). Police: ✆ 110. Fire, ambulance: ✆ 112.

TIPPING

Not necessary to tip at the bar or counter, but tip 10% if served at your table. Round up taxi fares to a maximum of 10%.

TOURIST INFORMATION

Estonian Tourist Board: www.visitestonia.com. tourism@eas.ee. Tallinn Tourist Information: Niguliste 2 / Kullassepa 4, 10146 Tallinn, ✆ 6457 777, turismiinfo@tallinnlv.ee. Ekspress Hotline (www.1182.ee), is an English-speaking information service covering all Estonian towns: ✆ 1182 (available only within Estonia).

TOURIST OFFICES OVERSEAS

UK: Tourism brochures available from the Estonian Embassy (see above) mon-fri 0900 - 1700. **Germany**: Baltikum Tourismus Zentrale, Katharinenstraße 19-20, 10711 Berlin, ✆ 030 89 00 90 91, info@baltikuminfo.de.

VISAS

See page xxxii for visa requirements.

FINLAND

CAPITAL

Helsinki (Helsingfors).

CLIMATE

Extremely long summer days; spring and autumn curtailed further north; continuous daylight for 70 days north of 70th parallel. Late June to mid-August best for far north, mid-May to September for south. Ski season: mid-January to mid-April.

CURRENCY

Euro (EUR / €). 1 euro = 100 cent. For exchange rates see page 11.

EMBASSIES IN HELSINKI

Australia (Consulate): c/- Tradimex Oy, museokatu 25B, ✆ 09 4777 6640. **Canada**: Pohjoisesplanadi 25B, ✆ 09 228 530.
New Zealand (Consulate): Johannesbrinken 2, ✆ 024 701 818.
UK: Itäinen Puistotie 17, ✆ 09 2286 5100.
USA: Itäinen Puistotie 14B, ✆ 09 616 250.

EMBASSIES OVERSEAS

Australia: 12 Darwin Ave., Yarralumla, Canberra, ACT 2600, ✆ 2 6273 3800. **Canada**: 55 Metcalfe St, Suite 850, Ottawa ON, K1P 6L5, ✆ 613 288 2233. **UK**: 38 Chesham Place, London SW1X 8HW, ✆ 020 7838 6200. **USA**: 3301 Massachusetts Ave. NW, Washington DC 20008, ✆ 202 298 5800.

LANGUAGE

Finnish, and, in the north, Lapp/Sami. Swedish, the second language, often appears on signs after the Finnish. English is widely spoken, especially in Helsinki. German is reasonably widespread.

OPENING HOURS

Banks: Mon–Fri 0915–1615, with regional variations. **Shops**: Mon–Fri 0900–2000, Sat 0900–1500, though many shops open Mon–Fri 0700–2100, Sat 0900–1800; many shops also open Sun, June–Aug. **Stores/food shops**: Mon–Sat 0900–1800/2000. **Museums**: usually close Mon, hours vary. Many close in winter.

POST OFFICES

Most *posti* open at least Mon–Fri 0900–1700. Stamps also sold at shops, hotels and bus and train stations. Yellow postboxes.

PUBLIC HOLIDAYS

Jan 1, Jan 6 (Epiphany), Good Friday, Easter Mon, May 1, Ascension, Midsummer (Sat falling June 20–26), All Saints (Sat falling Oct 31 - Nov 6), Dec 6 (Independence), Dec 25, 26. For dates of movable holidays see page 2.

PUBLIC TRANSPORT

The national timetable book *Aikataulut / Tidtabeller* (in Finnish and Swedish, from bookshops) covers trains, buses, and boats in detail. Bus stations (*Linja-autoasema*) have restaurants and shops. There are more than 300 bus services daily from Helsinki to all parts of the country. The main long-distance bus operators are Matkahuolto (www.matkahuolto.fi) and the Expressbus consortium (www.expressbus.com). It is usually cheaper to buy tickets in advance. Bus stop signs show a black bus on a yellow background (local services) or a white bus on a blue background (long distance). Helsinki has metro / tram / bus network with integrated ticketing. Taxis can be hailed in the street: they are for hire when the yellow *taksi* sign is lit.

RAIL TRAVEL

See Tables **790 - 799**. National rail company: VR (www.vr.fi); tilting Pendolinos (up to 220 km/h) run on certain lines. Fares depend upon train type - those for *S220* (Pendolino), *IC* (InterCity) and *P* (express) trains include a seat reservation. Sleeping-cars: two or three berths per compartment (2nd class), single compartment (1st class). In winter sleeping accommodation generally costs less on Mondays to Thursdays. Rail station: *Rautatieasema* or *Järnvägsstation*; virtually all have baggage lockers.

TELEPHONES

Dial in: ✆ +358 then number (omit initial 0). Outgoing: ✆ 00. Phonecards are sold by *R-kiosk* newsstands, tourist offices, *Tele* offices, and some post offices. There are no public telephone booths in Helsinki. Directory enquiries: ✆ 020202. Emergency services: ✆ 112.

TIPPING

Service charge included in hotel and restaurant bills but leave coins for good service. Hotel and restaurant porters and sauna attendants expect a euro or two. Taxi drivers and hairdressers do not expect a tip.

TOURIST INFORMATION

Finnish Tourist Board (www.visitfinland.com). PO Box 625, Töölönkatu 11, 00101 Helsinki, ✆ 010 60 58 000, mek@visitfinland.com. Every Finnish town has a tourist office *(Matkailutoimistot)* where staff speak English. English literature, mostly free.

TOURIST OFFICES OVERSEAS

Australia: P.O. Box 1427, North Sydney NSW 2059 ✆ 02 9929 6044. **UK**: 177-179 Hammersmith Road, London W6 8BS ✆ 020 8600 7283. **USA**: 297 York Street, Jersey City, NJ 07302 ✆ 917 863 5484.

VISAS

See page xxxii for visa requirements.

FRANCE

CAPITAL

Paris, divided into *arrondissements* 1 to 20 (1er, 2e etc).

CLIMATE

Cool–cold winters, mild–hot summers; south coast best Oct–Mar, Alps and Pyrenees, June and early July. Paris best spring and autumn.

CURRENCY

Euro (EUR / €). 1 euro = 100 cent. For exchange rates see page 11.

EMBASSIES IN PARIS

Australia: 4 rue Jean Rey, ✆ 01 40 59 33 00. **Canada**: 35 avenue Montaigne, ✆ 01 44 43 29 02. **New Zealand**: 7 ter rue Léonard de Vinci, ✆ 01 45 01 43 43. **UK**: 35 rue du Faubourg St Honoré, ✆ 01 44 51 31 00. **USA**: 2 avenue Gabriel, ✆ 01 43 12 22 22.

EMBASSIES OVERSEAS

Australia: 6 Perth Ave. Yarralumla, Canberra, ACT 2600, ✆ 2 6216 0100. **Canada**: 42 Sussex Drive, Ottawa ON, K1M 2C9, ✆ 613 789 1795. **New Zealand**: 34-42 Manners St, Wellington, ✆ 4 384 2555. **UK**: 58 Knightsbridge, London SW1X 7JT, ✆ 020 7258 6600. **USA**: 4101 Reservoir Rd, NW, Washington DC 20007, ✆ 202 944 6000.

LANGUAGE

French; many people can speak a little English, particularly in Paris.

OPENING HOURS

Paris and major towns: shops, banks and post offices are generally open 0900/1000–1700/1900 Mon-Fri, plus often Sat am / all day. Small shops can be open Sun am but closed Mon. **Provinces**: weekly closing is mostly Sun pm / all day and Mon; both shops and services generally close 1200–1400; services may have restricted opening times. Most **super/hypermarkets** open unti; 2100/2200. **Museums**: (mostly) 0900–1700, closing Mon and/or Tues; longer hours in summer; often free or discount rate on Sun. **Restaurants** serve 1200–1400 and 1900–2100 at least. Public holidays: services closed, food shops open am in general; check times with individual museums and tourist sights.

POST OFFICES

Called *La Poste*. Letter boxes are small, wall or pedestal-mounted, and yellow. Basic rate postage stamps (*timbres*) can also be bought from tobacconists (*Tabacs* or *Café-Tabacs*).

PUBLIC HOLIDAYS

Jan 1, Easter Mon, May 1, May 8 (Victory), Ascension Day, Whit Mon, July 14 (National Day), Aug 15 (Assumption), Nov 1 (All Saints), Nov 11 (Armistice), Dec 25. For dates of movable holidays see page 2. If a holiday falls on a Tuesday or Thursday, many businesses close additionally on the Monday or Friday.

PUBLIC TRANSPORT

In Paris, use the Métro where possible: clean, fast, cheap and easy. For urban and suburban transport, *carnets* (sets of 10 tickets) are cheaper than individual tickets; for day tickets see Passes feature. Bus and train timetable leaflets (free) are available from tourist offices, bus and rail stations. Many cities have modern tram / light rail networks; Lyon, Marseille and Toulouse also have metro systems. Bus services are infrequent after 2030 and on Sundays. Sparse public transport in rural areas, and few long-distance bus services. Licensed taxis (avoid others) are metered; white roof-lights when free; surcharges for luggage, extra passengers, and journeys beyond the centre.

RAIL TRAVEL

See Tables **250 - 399**. Société Nationale des Chemins de fer Français (SNCF) (www.sncf.com), ✆ 3635 (premium rate, in French), followed by 1 for traffic status, 2 for timetables, 3 for reservations and tickets, 4 for other services. Excellent network from Paris to major cities with *TGV* trains using dedicated high-speed lines (up to 320 km/h on the *Est Européen* line to eastern France) as well as conventional track. However, some cross-country journeys can be slow and infrequent. Trains can get very full at peak times, so to avoid having to spend the journey standing, book a seat. Prior reservation is compulsory on *TGV* high-speed trains and the charge is included in the ticket price; rail pass holders will have to pay at least the reservation fee. Tickets can cost more at busy times (known as 'white' periods). Long distance trains on several non-TGV routes are branded *Corail Téoz* using refurbished rolling stock - reservation is compulsory. Reservation is also compulsory on all overnight trains: most convey couchettes and reclining seats only (sleeping cars are only conveyed on international trains). A certain number of couchette compartments are reserved for women only or those with small children; otherwise, couchette accommodation is mixed. There is a minimal bar/trolley service on most long-distance trains. Larger stations have 24-hour coin-operated left-luggage lockers, and sometimes pay-showers.

TELEPHONES

Dial in: ✆ +33 then number (omit initial 0). Outgoing: ✆ 00. Most payphones have English instructions. Few accept coins; some take credit cards. Phonecards (*télécartes*) are sold by post offices, some tobacconists and certain tourist offices. Emergency: ✆ 112. Police: ✆ 17. Fire: ✆ 18. Ambulance: ✆ 15.

TIPPING

Not necessary to tip in bars or cafés although it is common practise to round up the price. In restaurants there is no obligation to tip, but if you wish to do so, leave €1–2.

TOURIST INFORMATION

Maison de la France (www.franceguide.com). 23 Place de Catalogne, 75685 Paris, ✆ 0 142 967 000. Local tourist offices: look for *Syndicat d'Initiative* or *Office de Tourisme*. Staff generally speak English. Many sell passes for local tourist sights or services and can organise accommodation (for a fee). Opening times are seasonal.

TOURIST OFFICES OVERSEAS

Australia: Level 13, 25 Bligh St, Sydney NSW 2000, ✆ 02 9231 5244, info.au@franceguide.com. **Canada**: 1800 avenue McGill College, Suite 1010, Montréal QC, H3A 3J6, ✆ 514 288 2026, canada@franceguide.com. **UK**: Lincoln House, 300 High Holborn, London WC1V 7JH, ✆ 0906 824 4123 (premium rate), info.uk@franceguide.com. **USA**: 825 Third Avenue, 29th floor, New York NY 10022, ✆ 514 288 1904, info.us@franceguide.com. Also in Los Angeles and Chicago.

VISAS

See page xxxii for visa requirements.

GERMANY

CAPITAL

Berlin.

CURRENCY

Euro (EUR / €). 1 euro = 100 cent. For exchange rates see page 11.

EMBASSIES IN BERLIN

Australia: Wallstraße 76-79, ✆ 030 88 00 880.
Canada: Leipziger Platz 17, ✆ 030 203 120.
New Zealand: Friedrichstraße 60, ✆ 030 206 210.
UK: Wilhelmstraße 70, ✆ 030 204 570.
USA: Pariser Platz 2, ✆ 030 830 50.

EMBASSIES OVERSEAS

Australia: 119 Empire Circuit, Yarralumla, Canberra, ACT 2600, ✆ 2 6270 1911. **Canada**: 1 Waverley St, Ottawa ON, K2P 0T8, ✆ 613 232 1101. **New Zealand**: 90-92 Hobson St, Thorndon, Wellington, ✆ 4 473 6063. **UK**: Embassy, 23 Belgrave Sq., London SW1X 8PZ, ✆ 020 7824 1300. **USA**: 4645 Reservoir Rd NW, Washington DC, 20007-1998, ✆ 202 298 4000.

LANGUAGE

German; English and French widely spoken in the west, especially by young people, less so in the east.

OPENING HOURS

Vary; rule of thumb: **Banks**: Mon–Fri 0830–1300 and 1430–1600 (until 1730 Thur). **Shops**: Mon–Fri 0900–1830 (large department stores may open 0830/0900–2000) and Sat 0900–1600. **Museums**: Tues–Sun 0900–1700 (until 2100 Thur).

POST OFFICES

Mon–Fri 0800–1800, Sat 0800–1200. Main post offices have poste restante (*Postlagernd*).

PUBLIC HOLIDAYS

Jan 1, Jan 6*, Good Fri, Easter Mon, May 1, Ascension Day, Whit Mon, Corpus Christi*, Aug 15*, Oct 3 (German Unity), Nov 1* (All Saints), Dec 25, 26. For dates of movable holidays see page 2.
* Catholic feastdays, celebrated only in the south (see p. 361 for other regional holidays).

PUBLIC TRANSPORT

Most large cities have U-Bahn (U) underground railway and S-Bahn (S) urban rail service, many have trams. City travel passes cover these and other public transport, including local ferries in some cities (e.g. Hamburg). International passes usually cover S-Bahn. Single fares are expensive; a day card (*Tagesnetzkarte*) or multi-ride ticket (*Mehrfahrkarte*) pays for itself if you take more than three rides (see Passes feature for selected day tickets). Long-distance buses are not common.

RAIL TRAVEL

See Tables **800 - 949**. Deutsche Bahn (DB) (www.bahn.de). ✆ 01805 99 66 33 (14ct/min) for timetable and fares information, ticket purchase and reservations. Timetable freephone (automated): ✆ 0800 1507090. UK booking centre ✆ 08718 80 80 66 (8p per minute). Discounts of 25% or 50% are available on long-distance tickets if purchased at least 3 days in advance - 50% tickets have restrictions. Long-distance trains: *ICE* (modern high-speed trains; up to 300km/h; higher fares but no extra charge for InterRail holders), *IC, EC, EN, CNL, D*. Regional trains: *IRE, RE, RB* (modern, comfortable, link with long-distance network). Frequent local S-Bahn services operate in major cities. Some local services now operated by private railways. Overnight services convey sleeping-cars (up to three berths) and/or couchettes (up to six berths), also reclining seats - reservation is generally compulsory. Most long-distance trains convey a bistro or restaurant car. Seat reservations possible on long-distance trains. Stations are well staffed, often with left luggage and bicycle hire. *Hbf.* (Hauptbahnhof) means main (central) station; *Bf.* (Bahnhof) means station.

TELEPHONES

Dial in: ✆ +49 then number (omit initial 0). Outgoing: ✆ 00. *Kartentelefon* boxes take phonecards only (available from news-agents, tobacconists and some kiosks). National directory enquiries: ✆ 11833 (11837 in English). International directory enquiries: ✆ 11834. Police: ✆ 110. Fire: ✆ 112. Ambulance: ✆ 112.

TIPPING

Not a must but customary for good service. Small sums are rounded up, while for larger sums you could add a tip of EUR 1, or up to 10% of the bill.

TOURIST INFORMATION

German National Tourist Office (www.germany-tourism.de). Main office: Beethovenstraße 69, 60325 Frankfurt am Main, ✆ 069 974 640, info@d-z-t.com Tourist offices are usually near rail stations. English is widely spoken; English-language maps and leaflets available. Most offer a room-finding service.

TOURIST OFFICES OVERSEAS

Australia: c/o Ink Publicity, Suite 502, Level 5, 5 Hunter St, Sydney NSW 2000, ✆ 02 9236 8982, germanytourism@smink.com.au. **Canada**: 480 University Avenue, Suite 1500, Toronto ON, M5G 1V2, ✆ 416 968 1685, info@-gnto.ca. **UK**: PO Box 2695, London W1A 3TN, ✆ 020 7317 0908, gntolon@d-z-t.com. **USA**: 122 East 42nd Street, New York NY 10168-0072, ✆ 212 661 7200, GermanyInfo@d-z-t.com. Also in Chicago (✆ 773 539 6303) and Los Angeles (✆ 310 545 1350).

VISAS

See page xxxii for visa requirements.

GREECE

CAPITAL

Athens (Athína).

CLIMATE

Uncomfortably hot in June–Aug; often better to travel in spring or autumn.

CURRENCY

Euro (EUR / €). 1 euro = 100 cent. For exchange rates see page 11.

EMBASSIES IN ATHENS

Australia: Level 6, Thon Building, Kifisias / Alexandras, Ambelokipi, ✆ 210 870 4000. **Canada**: Ioannou Ghennadiou 4, ✆ 210 727 3400. **New Zealand** (Consulate): Kifissias 76, Ambelokipi, ✆ 210 692 4136. **UK**: Ploutarchou 1, ✆ 210 727 2600. **USA**: Vassilissis Sophias 91, ✆ 210 721 2951.

EMBASSIES OVERSEAS

Australia: 9 Turrana St, Yarralumla, Canberra, ACT 2600, ✆ 2 6273 3011. **Canada**: 76-80 MacLaren St, Ottawa ON, K2P 0K6, ✆ 613 238 6271. **UK**: 1A Holland Park, London W11 3TP, ✆ 020 7221 6467. **USA**: 2217 Massachusetts Ave. NW, Washington DC 20008, ✆ 202 939 1300.

LANGUAGE

Greek; English widely spoken in Athens and tourist areas (some German, French or Italian), less so in remote mainland areas.

OPENING HOURS

Banks: (usually) Mon–Thur 0800–1400, Fri 0830–1330, longer hours in peak holiday season. **Shops**: vary; in summer most close midday and reopen in the evening (Tue, Thu, Fri) 1700–2000. **Sites and museums**: mostly 0830–1500; Athens sites and other major archaeological sites open until 1900 or open until sunset in summer.

POST OFFICES

Normally Mon–Fri 0800–1300, Sat 0800–1200; money exchange, travellers cheques, Eurocheques. Stamps sold from vending machines outside post offices, street kiosks.

PUBLIC HOLIDAYS

Jan 1, Jan 6 (Epiphany), Shrove Monday (48 days before Easter*), Mar 25 (Independence), Easter Monday*, May 1, Whit Monday*, Aug 15 (Assumption), Oct 28 (National Day), Dec 25, 26. Everything closes for Easter. Holidays related to Easter are according to the Orthodox calendar – dates usually differ from those of Western Easter (see page 2; same dates in 2010 and 2011).

PUBLIC TRANSPORT

KTEL buses: fast, punctual, fairly comfortable long-distance services; well-organised stations in most towns (tickets available from bus terminals), website: www.ktel.org. Islands connected by ferries and hydrofoils; see Thomas Cook guide *Greek Island Hopping* (order form at the back of this edition). City transport: bus or (in Athens) trolleybus, tram and metro; services may be crowded. Outside Athens, taxis are plentiful and good value.

RAIL TRAVEL

See Tables **1400 - 1499**. Operator: Hellenic Railways (Organismós Sidiródromon Éllados; OSE) (www.ose.gr). Call centre for reservations and information (24-hour, english spoken): ✆ 1110. Limited rail network, especially north of Athens. Reservations are essential on most express trains. *ICity* and *ICityE* trains are fast and fairly punctual, but supplements can be expensive (€6 to 20 on *ICity* and €9 to 33 on *ICityE*). Stations: often no left luggage or English-speaking staff, but many have bars.

TELEPHONES

Dial in: ✆+30 then number. Outgoing: ✆ 00. Payphones take phonecards only (on sale at most shops and street kiosks). Bars, restaurants, and kiosks often have privately owned metered phones: pay after making the call. Emergency: ✆ 112. Police: ✆ 100. Fire: ✆ 199. Ambulance: ✆ 166. Tourist police (24 hrs, English-speaking): ✆ 171.

TIPPING

Not necessary for restaurants or taxis.

TOURIST INFORMATION

Greek National Tourist Organisation (www.gnto.gr). Main office: Tsoha 7, 11521 Athens, ✆ 2 108 707 000. Athens information desk: Amalias 26, ✆ 2 103 310 392. Tourist offices provide sightseeing information, fact sheets, local and regional transport schedules.

TOURIST OFFICES OVERSEAS

Australia: 37-49 Pitt St, Sydney NSW 2000, ✆ 02 9241 1663, hto@tpg.com.au. **Canada**: 1500 Don Mills Road, Suite 102, Toronto ON, M3B 3K4, ✆ 416 968 2220, grnto.tor@on.aibn.com. **UK**: 4 Conduit St, London W1S 2DJ, ✆ 020 7495 9300, info@gnto.co.uk. **USA**: Olympic Tower, 645 Fifth Ave., Suite 903, New York NY 10022, ✆ 212 421 5777, info@greektourism.com.

VISAS

See page xxxii for visa requirements.

HUNGARY

CAPITAL

Budapest.

CURRENCY

Forint (HUF or Ft). For exchange rates see page 11. You can buy your currency at banks and official bureaux. Credit cards and small denomination travellers cheques are widely accepted. Euros are more useful than dollars or sterling.

EMBASSIES IN BUDAPEST

Australia: Királyhágó tér 8–9, ✆ 0 614 579 777. **Canada**: Ganz utca 12–14, ✆ 0 613 923 360. **New Zealand** (Consulate): Nagymazö utca 50, ✆ 013 022 484. **UK**: Harmincad utca 6, ✆ 012 662 888. **USA**: Szabadság tér 12, ✆ 01 475 4400.

EMBASSIES OVERSEAS

Australia: 17 Beale Crescent, Deakin, Canberra, ACT 2600, ✆ 2 6282 3226. **Canada**: 299 Waverley St, Ottawa ON, K2P 0V9, ✆ 613 230 2717. **UK**: 35 Eaton Place, London SW1X 8BY, ✆ 020 7201 3440. **USA**: 3910 Shoemaker St NW, Washington DC 20008, ✆ 202 362 6730.

LANGUAGE

Hungarian. English and German are both widely understood.

OPENING HOURS

Food/tourist shops, markets, malls open Sun. **Banks**: commercial banks Mon–Thur 0800–1500, Fri 0800–1300. **Food shops**: Mon–Fri 0700–1900, others: 1000–1800 (Thur until 1900); shops close for lunch and half-day on Sat (1300). **Museums**: usually Tues–Sun 1000–1800, free one day a week, closed public holidays.

POST OFFICES

Mostly 0800–1800 Mon–Fri, 0800–1200 Sat. Stamps also sold at tobacconists. Major post offices cash Eurocheques and change western currency; all give cash for Visa Eurocard/Mastercard, Visa Electron and Maestro cards.

PUBLIC HOLIDAYS

Jan 1, Mar 15 (Revolution), Easter Sun/Mon, May 1, Whit Monday, Aug 20 (Constitution), Oct 23 (Republic), Dec 25, 26. For dates of movable holidays see page 2.

PUBLIC TRANSPORT

Long-distance buses: *Volánbusz* (www.volanbusz.hu), ✆ +36 1 382 0888. Extensive metro / tram / bus system in Budapest with integrated tickets; for day tickets see Passes section. Debrecen, Miskolc and Szeged also have trams. Ferry and hydrofoil services operate on the Danube.

RAIL TRAVEL

See Tables **1200 - 1299**. A comprehensive network operated by Hungarian State Railways (MÁV) (www.mav.hu) connects most towns and cities. Express services link Budapest to major centres and Lake Balaton: *IC* trains require compulsory reservation and supplement. InterPici (*IP*) trains are fast railcars connecting with *IC* trains, also with compulsory reservation. Most *EC* trains require a supplement but not reservation (for exceptions see page 485). Other trains include *gyorsvonat* (fast trains) and *sebesvonat* (semi-fast). Local trains (*személyvonat*) are very slow. Book sleepers well in advance.

TELEPHONES

Dial in: ✆ +36 then number (omit initial 06). Outgoing: ✆ 00. Payphones take HUF 10, 20, 50 and 100 coins or phonecards (sold at hotels, newsstands, tobacconists and post offices). Directory enquiries: ✆ 198 (International ✆ 199). Emergency: ✆ 112. Police: ✆ 107. Fire: ✆ 105. Ambulance: ✆ 104.

TIPPING

Round up by 5–15% for restaurants and taxis. People do not generally leave coins on the table; instead the usual practise is to make it clear that you are rounding up the sum. Service is included in some upmarket restaurants.

TOURIST INFORMATION

Hungarian National Tourist Office (www.hungarytourism.hu). Tourinform ✆ 06 80 630 800, info@hungarytourism.hu *Tourinform* branches throughout Hungary. English-speaking staff. The *Hungarian Tourist Card* (www.hungarycard.hu), giving various discounts, costs HUF 7140.

TOURIST OFFICES OVERSEAS

UK: 46 Eaton Place, London SW1X 8AL, ✆ 020 7823 1032, htlondon@hungarytourism.hu **USA**: 350 Fifth Avenue, Suite 7107, New York NY 10118, ✆ 212 695 1221, info@gotohungary.com

VISAS

See page xxxii for visa requirements.

IRELAND

CAPITAL

Dublin. For Northern Ireland see under United Kingdom.

CLIMATE

Cool, wet winters, mild spring and autumn. Intermittent rain is a common feature of the Irish weather.

CURRENCY

Euro (EUR/€). 1 euro = 100 cent. For exchange rates see page 11.

EMBASSIES IN DUBLIN

Australia: Fitzwilton House, Wilton Terrace, ✆ 01 664 5300. **Canada**: 7–8 Wilton Terrace, ✆ 01 234 4000. **New Zealand** (Consulate): P.O. Box 9999, ✆ 01 660 4233. **UK**: 29 Merrion Road, Ballsbridge, ✆ 01 205 3700. **USA**: 42 Elgin Road, ✆ 01 668 8777.

EMBASSIES OVERSEAS

Australia: 20 Arkana St, Yarralumla, Canberra, ACT 2600 ✆ 2 6273 3022. **Canada**: Suite 1105, 130 Albert St, Ottawa ON, K1P 5G4, ✆ 613 233 6281. **UK**: 17 Grosvenor Place, London SW1X 7HR, ✆ 020 7235 2171. **USA**: 2234 Massachusetts Ave. NW, Washington DC 20008, ✆ 202 462 3939.

LANGUAGE

Most people speak English. The Irish language (Gaeilge) is spoken in several areas (known as the Gaeltacht) scattered over seven counties and four provinces, mostly along the western seaboard. Official documents use both languages.

OPENING HOURS

Shops generally open Mon - Sat 0900 - 1730; most shopping centres stay open until 2000 on Thurs and Fri. Some shops open on Sunday, 1200 - 1800.

POST OFFICES

Postal service: *An Post*, www.anpost.ie. Most communities have a post office, usually open Mon-Fri 0900 - 1730 or 1800, Sat 0900 - 1300; often closed one hour at lunchtime (except main offices). Sub post offices often close at 1300 one day per week.

PUBLIC HOLIDAYS

January 1 (New Year's Day), March 17 (St Patrick's Day), Good Friday (bank holiday only), Easter Monday, first Monday in May, first Monday in June, first Monday in August, last Monday in October, December 25 (Christmas Day), December 26 (St Stephen's Day). Holidays falling at the weekend are transferred to the next following weekday.

PUBLIC TRANSPORT

A modern tramway system in Dublin called *Luas* (www.luas.ie) has two unconnected lines; the red line is the most useful for visitors as it connects Connolly and Heuston stations. Dublin Bus operates an extensive network throughout the capital, but journeys can be very slow in rush-hour traffic. Almost all bus services outside Dublin are operated by Bus Éireann (www.buseireann.ie), ✆ 01 836 6111 (daily 0830–1900). Long distance services leave from the Dublin bus station (*Busáras*) in Store St, near Connolly rail station.

RAIL TRAVEL

See Tables **230 - 249**. Rail services are operated by Iarnród Éireann (IÉ) (www.irishrail.ie). Timetable and fares enquiries: ✆ 01 850 366 222 (0900–1800 Mon-Sat, 1000–1800 Sun). The *Enterprise* express service Dublin - Belfast is operated jointly with Northern Ireland Railways. Local IÉ north-south electric line in Dublin is called DART.

TELEPHONES

Dial in: ✆ +353 then number (omit initial 0). Outgoing: ✆ 00 (048 for Northern Ireland). Pay phones take coins, phonecards or credit cards. Directory enquiries: ✆ 11811/11850 (International ✆ 11818). Operator assistance: ✆ 10 (International ✆ 114). Emergency services: ✆ 112 or 999.

TIPPING

A tip of 12 - 15% is expected in restaurants. Taxis 10%.

TOURIST INFORMATION

Fáilte Ireland (www.discoverireland.ie). Main office: 5th Floor, Bishop's Square, Redmond's Hill, Dublin 2, ✆ 014 763 400. Tourist offices offer a wide range of information, also accommodation bookings.

TOURIST OFFICES OVERSEAS

Australia: Level 5, 36 Carrington St, Sydney NSW 2000, ✆ 02 9299 6177. **Canada**: 2 Bloor St West, Suite 3403, Toronto ON, M4W 3E2, ✆ 416 925 6368. **UK**: 103 Wigmore St, London W1U 1QS, ✆ 020 7518 0800. **USA**: 345 Park Avenue, 17th floor, New York NY 10154, ✆ 212 418 0800.

VISAS

See page xxxii for visa requirements.

ITALY

CAPITAL

Rome (Roma).

CLIMATE

Very hot in July and Aug. May, June, and Sept are best for sightseeing. Holiday season ends mid Sept or Oct. Rome is crowded at Easter.

CURRENCY

Euro (EUR/€). 1 euro = 100 cent. For exchange rates see page 11.

EMBASSIES IN ROME

Australia: Via Antonio Bosio 5, ✆ 06 852 721. **Canada**: Via Zara 30, ✆ 06 854 441. **New Zealand**: Via Clitunno 44, ✆ 06 853 7501. **UK**: Via XX Settembre 80a, ✆ 06 4220 0001. **USA**: Via Vittorio Veneto 121, ✆ 06 46 741.

EMBASSIES OVERSEAS

Australia: 12 Grey St, Deakin, Canberra ACT 2600, ✆ 2 6273 3333. **Canada**: 275 Slater St, Ottawa ON, K1P 5H9, ✆ 613 232 2401. **New Zealand**: 34-38 Grant Rd, Thorndon, Wellington, ✆ 4 473 5339. **UK**: 14 Three Kings Yard, London W1K 4EH, ✆ 020 7312 2200. **USA**: 3000 Whitehaven St NW, Washington DC 20008, ✆ 202 612 4400.

LANGUAGE

Italian; standard Italian is spoken across the country though there are marked regional pronunciation differences. Some dialects in more remote areas. Many speak English in cities and tourist areas. In the south and Sicily, French is often more useful than English.

OPENING HOURS

Banks: Mon–Fri 0830–1330, 1430–1630. **Shops**: (usually) Mon–Sat 0830/0900–1230, 1530/1600–1900/1930; closed Mon am/Sat pm July/Aug. **Museums/sites**: usually Tues–Sun 0930–1900; last Sun of month free; most refuse entry within an hour of closing. Churches often close at lunchtime.

POST OFFICES

Mostly Mon–Fri 0830–1330/1350, Sat 0830–1150. Some counters (registered mail and telegrams) may differ; in main cities some open in the afternoon. Send anything urgent via express. *Posta prioritaria* stamps also guarantee a faster delivery. Stamps (*francobolli*) are available from tobacconists (*tabacchi*). Poste restante (*Fermo posta*) at most post offices.

PUBLIC HOLIDAYS

All over the country: Jan 1, Jan 6 (Epiphany), Easter Mon, Apr 25 (Liberation), May 1, June 2 (Republic), Aug 15 (Assumption, virtually nothing opens), Nov 1 (All Saints), Dec 8 (Immaculate Conception), Dec 25, 26. For dates of movable holidays see page 2.
Regional Saints' days: Apr 25 in Venice, June 24 in Florence, Genoa and Turin, June 29 in Rome, July 11 in Palermo, Sept 19 in Naples, Oct 4 in Bologna, Dec 6 in Bari, Dec 7 in Milan.

PUBLIC TRANSPORT

Buses are often crowded, but regular, and serve many areas inaccessible by rail. Services may be drastically reduced at weekends; this is not always made clear in timetables. Roma, Milano and Napoli have metro systems; most major cities have trams. Taxis (metered) can be expensive; steer clear of unofficial ones.

RAIL TRAVEL

See Tables **580 - 648**. The national operator is Trenitalia, a division of Ferrovie dello Stato (FS) (website www.trenitalia.com). National rail information ✆ 89 20 21 (+39 06 68 47 54 75 from abroad). The trunk high-speed line from Torino to Salerno via Milano, Roma and Napoli is now complete, giving fast journey times between major cities. 'Alta Velocità' (*AV*) are premium fare services using high-speed lines; core services are branded *Frecciarossa*, whilst tilting *Frecciargento* trains divert off the high-speed lines to serve other cities. 'Eurostar Italia' (*ES*) and 'Eurostar City' (*ESc*) trains also require payment of a higher fare. InterCity Plus (*ICp*) uses refurbished *IC* stock. Reservation is compulsory on *AV*, *ES*, *ESc* and *ICp* trains. Reservation is also possible on *IC*, *EC* and *ICN* (InterCityNight) trains. Other services are classified *Espresso* (long-distance domestic train, stopping only at main stations) and *Regionale* (stops at most stations). Services are reasonably punctual. Some long-distance trains do not carry passengers short distances. Sleepers: single or double berths in 1st class, three (occasionally doubles) in 2nd. Couchettes: four berths in 1st class, six in 2nd. Refreshments on most long-distance trains. There are often long queues at stations; buy tickets and make reservations at travel agencies (look for FS symbol).

TELEPHONES

Dial in: ✆+39 then number. Outgoing: ✆ 00. Public phones take phonecards *(carta telefonica)* available from any newsstand, tobacconist or coffee shop. Some take coins or credit cards (mostly in tourist areas). Metered phones (*scatti*) are common in bars and restaurants; pay the attendant after use. Phone directory assistance: ✆ 12. International enquiries: ✆ 176. Carabinieri: ✆ 112. Police: ✆ 113. Fire: ✆ 115. Ambulance: ✆ 118.

TIPPING

In restaurants you need to look at the menu to see if service charge is included. If not, a tip of 10% is fine depending on how generous you feel like being. The same percentage applies to taxi drivers. A helpful porter can expect up to €2.50.

TOURIST INFORMATION

Italian State Tourist Board (www.enit.it). Main office: Via Marghera 2/6, 00185 Roma, ✆ 0 649 711, sedecentrale@enit.it. Most towns and resorts have an *Azienda Autonoma di Soggiorno e Turismo* (AAST), many with their own websites, or *Pro Loco* (local tourist board).

TOURIST OFFICES OVERSEAS

Australia: Level 4, 46 Market St, Sydney NSW 2000, ✆ 02 9262 1666, italia@italiantourism.com.au. **Canada**: 175 Bloor Street East, Suite 907, South Tower, Toronto ON, M4W 3R8, ✆ 416 925 4882, enitto@italiantourism.com. **UK**: 1 Princes St, London W1B 2AY, ✆ 020 7399 3562, italy@italiantouristboard.co.uk. **USA**: 630 Fifth Avenue, Suite 1565, New York NY 10111, ✆ 212 245 5618, enitny@italiantourism.com. Also in Chicago (✆ 312 644 0996) and Los Angeles (✆ 310 820 1898).

VISAS

See page xxxii for visa requirements.

LATVIA

CAPITAL

Riga.

CLIMATE

Warm summers, cold, snowy winters; rain all year, heaviest in August.

CURRENCY

Lats (LVL or Ls) 1 lats = 100 santimu. For exchange rates, see page 11.

EMBASSIES IN RIGA

Australia (Consulate): Tomsona iela 33–1, ✆ 6722 4251. **Canada**: Baznicas iela 20/22, ✆ 6781 3945. **New Zealand**: *refer to NZ Embassy in Poland.* **UK**: Alunana iela 5, ✆ 6777 4700. **USA**: Raiņa bulvaris 7, ✆ 6703 6200.

EMBASSIES OVERSEAS

Australia (Consulate): 2 Mackennel Street, Melbourne, VIC 3079, ✆ 3 9499 6920. **Canada**: 350 Sparks St, Suite 1200, Ottawa ON, K1R 7S8, ✆ 613 238 6014. **UK**: 45 Nottingham Place, London W1U 5LY, ✆ 020 7312 0040. **USA**: 2306 Massachusetts Ave. NW, Washington DC 20008, ✆ 202 328 2840.

LANGUAGE

Latvian is the majority language. Russian is the first language of around 30% and is widely understood. English and German can often be of use, especially in the larger towns.

OPENING HOURS

Banks: mainly Mon–Fri 0900–1700, some Sat 0900–1300. **Shops**: Mon–Fri 0900/1000–1800/1900 and Sat 0900/1000–1700. Many close on Mon. **Museums**: days vary, but usually open Tues/Wed–Sun 1100–1700.

POST OFFICES

Mon–Fri 0900–1800, Sat 0900–1300. The main post office in Riga, at Brivibas bulvaris 19, is open 24 hrs. Postboxes are yellow.

PUBLIC HOLIDAYS

Jan 1, Good Friday, Easter Mon, May 1, May 4 (Independence Day), June 23 (Ligo Day), June 24 (Saint John), Nov 18 (Republic), Dec 25, 26, 31. For dates of movable holidays see page 2.

PUBLIC TRANSPORT

Very cheap for Westerners. Taxis generally affordable (agree fare first if not metered). Beware of pickpockets on crowded buses and trams. Long-distance bus network preferred to slow domestic train service.

RAIL TRAVEL

See Table **1800 - 1899**. Comfortable overnight trains to Moscow and St Peterburg; best to take berth in 2nd-class coupé (4-berth compartment); 1st-class *luxe* compartments (2-berth) are also available. Reservation is compulsory for all sleepers; Russian-bound ones may require proof of entry visa when booking. Very little English spoken at stations.

TELEPHONES

Dial in: ✆ +371 then number. Outgoing: ✆ 00. Public phones take coins, phonecards or credit cards. Phonecards (LVL 2, 5, or 10) sold by shops, kiosks, hotels and post offices; look for the *Lattelekom* sign. Emergency: ✆ 112. Police: ✆ 02. Fire: ✆ 01. Ambulance: ✆ 03.

TIPPING

Not necessary to tip at the bar or counter, but tip 10% if served at your table. Round up taxi fares to a maximum of 10%.

TOURIST INFORMATION

Latvian Tourism Development Agency (www.latviatourism.lv). Pils Laukums 4, Riga 1050, ✆ 67 229 945, info@latviatourism.lv.

TOURIST OFFICES OVERSEAS

Germany: Baltikum Tourismus Zentrale, Katharinenstraße 19-20, 10711 Berlin, ✆ 030 89 00 90 91, info@baltikuminfo.de.
UK: Latvian Tourism Bureau, 72 Queensborough Terrace, London W2 3SH, ✆ 020 7229 8271, london@latviatourism.lv.

VISAS

See page xxxii for visa requirements. Applications may take up to 30 days; confirmed hotel reservations are required. Visas may also be valid for Estonia and Lithuania. Passports must be valid for at least 3 months following the stay. Visas issued on arrival at the airport (not train border crossings) are valid 10 days.

LITHUANIA

CAPITAL

Vilnius.

CLIMATE

Warm summers, cold, snowy winters; rain all year, heaviest in August.

CURRENCY

Litas (LTL or Lt); 1 litas = 100 centu (ct), singular centas. Travellers cheques and credit cards are widely accepted. For exchange rates see page 11.

EMBASSIES IN VILNIUS

Australia (Consulate): 23 Vilniaus St. ✆ 05 212 3369. **Canada** (Consulate): Jogailos St. 4, ✆ 05 249 0950. **New Zealand**: *refer to NZ Embassy in Poland.* **UK**: Antakalnio Str. 2, ✆ 05 246 2900. **USA**: Akmenu gatve 6, ✆ 05 266 5500.

EMBASSIES OVERSEAS

Australia (Consulate): 56 Somers St. Melbourne, VIC 3125, ✆ 3 9808 8300. **Canada**: 150 Metcalfe St. Suite 1600, Ottawa ON, K2P 1P1, ✆ 613 567 5458. **UK**: 84 Gloucester Pl., London W1U 6AU, ✆ 020 7486 6401. **USA**: 4590 MacArthur Blvd. NW, Suite 200, Washington DC 20007, ✆ 202 234 5860.

LANGUAGE

Lithuanian. Russian is the first language of around 10% of the population. English and German can often be of use, especially in the larger towns.

OPENING HOURS

Banks: mostly Mon–Thur 0900–1600, Fri 0900–1500. **Shops**: (large shops) Mon–Fri 1000/1100–1900; many also open Sat until 1600. Some close for lunch 1400–1500 and also on Sun and Mon. **Museums**: days vary, most close Mon and sometimes Tues and open at least Wed and Fri; often free on Wed; hours usually at least 1100–1700, check locally.

POST OFFICES

All towns have post offices *(Lietuvos Paštas)* with an international telephone service. Offices are generally open 0800–1830 Mon–Fri and 0800–1400 Sat. Smaller offices often close for an hour at midday.

PUBLIC HOLIDAYS

Jan 1, Feb 16 (Independence Day), Mar 11 (Restoration of Statehood), Easter Mon, May 1 (not banks), July 6 (King Mindaugas), Aug. 15 (Assumption), Nov 1 (All Saints), Dec 25, 26. For dates of movable holidays see page 2.

PUBLIC TRANSPORT

Similar to Latvia (see above).

RAIL TRAVEL

See Tables **1800 - 1899**. Major routes are to St Petersburg, Moscow, Kaliningrad, Warsaw, and Minsk. Warsaw trains have standard European couchettes and sleepers. Other overnight trains have 54-bunk open coaches (P), 4-bed compartments (K) and (on Moscow trains only) 2-bed compartments (M-2).

TELEPHONES

Dial in: ✆ +370 then number (omit initial 8). Outgoing: ✆ 00. Phonecards (*telefono kortelė*) are sold at newsstands and supermarkets. Emergency: ✆ 112. Police: ✆ 02. Fire: ✆ 01. Ambulance: ✆ 03.

TIPPING

Not necessary to tip at the bar or counter, but tip 10% if served at your table. Round up taxi fares to a maximum of 10%.

TOURIST INFORMATION

Lithuania State Department of Tourism (www.tourism.lt and www.travel.lt). Main tourist office in Vilnius: Vilniaus g. 22, LT-01119, Vilnius, ✆ 526 296 60, tic@vilnius.lt. There are tourist offices in most towns.

TOURIST OFFICES OVERSEAS

Germany: Baltikum Tourismus Zentrale, Katharinenstraße 19-20, 10711 Berlin, ✆ 030 89 00 90 91, info@baltikuminfo.de.

VISAS

See page xxxii for visa requirements.

LUXEMBOURG

CAPITAL

Luxembourg City (Ville de Luxembourg).

CLIMATE

Rain prevalent at any time; warm summers, cold winters (often with snow).

CURRENCY

Euro (EUR / €). 1 euro = 100 cent. For exchange rates see page 11.

EMBASSIES IN LUXEMBOURG

Australia: *refer to Australian Embassy in Belgium.* **Canada** (Consulate): 15, rue Guillaume Schneider, ✆ 27 05 70. **New Zealand**: *refer to NZ Embassy in Belgium.* **UK**: 5 Boulevard Joseph II, ✆ 22 98 64. **USA**: 22 Boulevard Emmanuel Servais, ✆ 46 01 23.

EMBASSIES OVERSEAS

Australia (Consulate): 6 Damour Ave, Sydney, NSW 2070, ✆ 2 9880 8002. **UK**: 27 Wilton Crescent, London SW1X 8SD, ✆ 020 7235 6961. **USA / Canada**: 2200 Massachusetts Ave. NW, Washington DC 20008, ✆ 202 265 4171.

LANGUAGE

Luxembourgish is the national tongue, but almost everybody also speaks fluent French and/or German, plus often at least some English.

OPENING HOURS

Many establishments take long lunch breaks. **Banks**: usually Mon–Fri 0830–1200 and 1400–1630 or later. **Shops**: Mon 1300/1400–1800; Tues–Sat 0800/0900–1800. **Museums**: most open six days a week (usually Tues–Sun).

POST OFFICES

Usually open Mon–Fri 0800–1200 and 1400–1700.

PUBLIC HOLIDAYS

Jan 1, Carnival (Monday before Shrove Tuesday), Easter Mon, May

1, Ascension, Whit Mon, Corpus Christi, June 23 (National Day), Aug 15 (Assumption), Nov 1 (All Saints), Dec 25, 26. For dates of movable holidays see page 2. When a holiday falls on a Sunday, the next working day becomes a substitute holiday.

PUBLIC TRANSPORT

Good bus network between most towns. Taxis not allowed to pick up passengers in the street; most stations have ranks.

RAIL TRAVEL

See Table **445** for local services. Operator: Société Nationale des Chemins de fer Luxembourgeois (CFL) (www.cfl.lu), ✆ +352 2489 2489. Frequent rail services converge on Luxembourg City. Inexpensive multi-ride passes (good for one hour or up to 24 hours) are valid on trains and local buses. Most rail stations are small with few facilities.

TELEPHONES

Dial in: ✆ +352 then number. Outgoing: ✆ 00. Phonecards (*Telekaarten*) are available from post offices and stations. Police: ✆ 113. Fire and ambulance: ✆ 112.

TIPPING

In restaurants, cafés and bars service charge is usually included (round up bill to the next euro). Taxi drivers EUR 2–5; porters EUR 1–2; hairdressers EUR 2; cloakroom attendants EUR 0.50; toilet attendants EUR 0.25.

TOURIST INFORMATION

Office National du Tourisme (www.ont.lu). Gare Centrale, P.O. Box 1001, L-1010 Luxembourg, ✆ 4 282 8220, info@visitluxembourg.lu. Information and hotel bookings: Luxembourg City Tourist Office, 30 Place Guillaume II, L-1648 Luxembourg, ✆ 222 809, touristinfo@lcto.lu (www.lcto.lu),

TOURIST OFFICES OVERSEAS

UK: Sicilian House, Sicilian Avenue, London WC1A 2QR, ✆ 020 7434 2800, tourism@luxembourg.co.uk. **USA**: 17 Beekman Place, New York NY 10022, ✆ 212 935 8888, info@visitluxembourg.com.

VISAS

See page xxxii for visa requirements.

NETHERLANDS

CAPITAL

Amsterdam is the capital city. The Hague (Den Haag) is the seat of government.

CLIMATE

Can be cold in winter; rain prevalent all year. Many attractions close Oct–Easter, while Apr–May is tulip time and the country is crowded; June–Sept can be pleasantly warm and is busy with tourists.

CURRENCY

Euro (EUR / €). 1 euro = 100 cent. For exchange rates see page 11.

EMBASSIES IN THE HAGUE

Australia: Carnegielaan 4, ✆ 0 70 31 08 200. **Canada**: Sophialaan 7, ✆ 0 70 31 11 600. **New Zealand**: Eisenhowerlaan 77, ✆ 0 70 34 69 324. **UK**: Lange Voorhout 10, ✆ 0 70 42 70 427. **USA**: Lange Voorhout 102, ✆ 0 70 31 02 209.

EMBASSIES OVERSEAS

Australia: 120 Empire Circuit, Yarralumla, Canberra, ACT 2600, ✆ 2 6220 9400. **Canada**: Constitution Square Building, 350 Albert St, Suite 2020, Ottawa ON, K1R 1A4, ✆ 613 237 5030. **New Zealand**: Investment House, cnr Ballance & Featherston Streets, Wellington, ✆ 4 471 6390. **UK**: 38 Hyde Park Gate, London SW7 5DP, ✆ 020 7590 3200. **USA**: 4200 Linnean Ave. NW, Washington DC 20008, ✆ 877 388 2443.

LANGUAGE

Dutch; English is very widely spoken.

OPENING HOURS

Banks: Mon–Fri 0900–1600/1700 (later Thur or Fri). **Shops**: Mon–Fri 0900/0930–1730/1800 (until 2100 Thur or Fri), Sat 0900/0930–1600/1700. Many close Mon morning. **Museums**: vary, but usually Mon–Sat 1000–1700, Sun 1100–1700 (some close Mon). In winter many have shorter hours.

POST OFFICES

Post offices *(TPG Post)* are generally open Mon–Fri 0830–1700; some also open on Sat 0830–1200. Many shops selling postcards also sell stamps. Post international mail in the left slot, marked *overige* (other), of the red *TPG* mailboxes.

PUBLIC HOLIDAYS

Jan 1, Good Fri, Easter Mon, Apr 30 (Queen's Birthday), May 5 (Liberation Day), Ascension Day, Whit Mon, Dec 25, 26. For dates of movable holidays see page 2.

PUBLIC TRANSPORT

Premium rate number for all rail and bus enquiries (computerised, fast and accurate): ✆ 09 009 292 (www.9292ov.nl). Taxis are best boarded at ranks or ordered by phone as they seldom stop in the street. In many cities (not Amsterdam), shared *Treintaxis* have ranks at stations and yellow roof signs (€4.20 for anywhere within city limits; tickets from rail ticket offices). *Strippenkaarten* (from stations, city transport offices, post offices and sometimes VVV) are strip tickets, valid nation-wide on metros, buses, trams and some trains (2nd class) within city limits; zones apply; validate on boarding; valid one hour; change of transport allowed.

RAIL TRAVEL

See Tables **450 - 499**. National rail company Nederlandse Spoorwegen (NS) (www.ns.nl) provides most services, though private operators run local train services in some parts of the north and east. Through tickets can be purchased between all stations in the Netherlands, regardless of operator. Credit cards are not accepted, though larger stations usually have ATM machines from which cash can be obtained. Cycle hire and cycle and baggage storage are usually available at larger stations. Smaller stations are usually unstaffed, but all stations have ticket vending machines. Undated tickets must be validated before travel in one of the ticket stamping machines located at platform entrances. Travellers found to have boarded a train without a valid ticket must pay a fine of €35 plus the cost of their fare. Seat reservations are not available except for international journeys. The fastest domestic trains, calling at principal stations only, are classified *Intercity*. *Stoptreinen* call at all stations. Between these two categories are *sneltreinen* (fast trains) which miss out the less important stations.

TELEPHONES

Dial in: ✆ +31 then number (omit initial 0). Outgoing: ✆ 00. Green booths take only phonecards (*telefoonkaarten*), available from post offices, tourist offices (VVV), rail stations (NS), telecom shops (Primafoon) and major department stores (some booths also take credit cards). Orange / grey booths take coins, credit cards and *Telfort* phonecards, available from Holland Welcome Service (GWK), Wizzl shops and NS rail stations. Most information-line numbers are prefixed 0900 and are at premium rates. Operator: ✆ 0800 0410. International enquiries: ✆ 09 008 418. National enquiries: ✆ 09 008 008. Emergency services: ✆ 112.

TIPPING

Although service charges are included, it is customary in restaurants, bars and cafés to leave a tip of 5–10% if you are satisfied. Taxi drivers expect a 10% tip.

TOURIST INFORMATION

Netherlands Board of Tourism (www.holland.com), Vlietweg 15, 2260 MG Leidschendam, ✆ 070 370 5705, info@holland.com. Vereniging voor Vreemdelingenverkeer (VVV: signs show a triangle with three Vs). Tourist bureaux are all open at least Mon–Fri 0900–1700, Sat 1000–1200. The *Museumkaart* (EUR 35, under 25s EUR 17.50) obtainable from VVV and participating museums, is valid for one year and gives free entry to over 400 museums nationwide.

TOURIST OFFICES OVERSEAS

UK: PO Box 30783, London WC2B 6DH, ✆ 020 7539 7950, info-uk@holland.com. **USA/Canada**: 355 Lexington Ave., 19th floor, New York NY 10017, ✆ 212 370 7360, information@holland.com.

VISAS

See page xxxii for visa requirements.

NORWAY

CAPITAL

Oslo.

CLIMATE

Surprisingly mild considering it's so far north; can be very warm in summer, particularly inland; the coast is appreciably cooler. May and June are driest months, but quite cool; summer gets warmer and wetter as it progresses, and the western fjords have high rainfall year-round. Days are very long in summer: the sun never sets in high summer in the far north. July and Aug is the busiest period; Sept can be delightful. Winter is the time to see the Northern Lights (*Aurora Borealis*). Excellent snow for skiing Dec–Apr.

CURRENCY

Norwegian crown or krone (NOK or kr); 1 krone = 100 øre. For exchange rates see page 11. On slot machines, *femkrone* means a NOK 5 coin and *tikrone* a NOK 10 coin.

EMBASSIES IN OSLO

Australia (Consulate): Wilh. Wilhelmsen ASA, Strandveien 20, Lysaker, ✆ 67 58 48 48. **Canada**: Wergelandsveien 7, ✆ 22 99 53 00. **New Zealand** (Consulate): c/o Halfdan Ditlev-Simonsen & Co AS, Strandveien 50, Lysaker. ✆ 67 11 00 33. **UK**: Thomas Heftyesgate 8, ✆ 23 13 27 00. **USA**: Henrik Ibsens gate 48, ✆ 21 30 85 40.

EMBASSIES OVERSEAS

Australia: 17 Hunter St, Yarralumla, Canberra, ACT 2600, ✆ 2 6273 3444. **Canada**: 150 Metcalfe St. Suite 1300, Ottawa ON, K2P 1P1, ✆ 613 238 6571. **UK**: 25 Belgrave Sq., London, SW1X 8QD, ✆ 020 7591 5500. **USA**: 2720 34th St NW, Washington D.C. 20008, ✆ 202 333 6000.

LANGUAGE

Norwegian, which has two official versions: *Nynorsk* and *Bokmål*. Norwegian has three additional vowels: æ, ø, å, which (in that order) follow z. Almost everyone speaks English; if not, try German.

OPENING HOURS

Banks: Mon–Wed and Fri 0815–1500 (1530 in winter), Thur 0815–1700. In Oslo, some open later, in the country some close earlier. Many have minibank machines that accept Visa, MasterCard (Eurocard) and Cirrus. **Shops**: Mon–Fri 0900–1600/1700 (Thur 0900–1800/2000), Sat 0900–1300/1500, many open later, especially in Oslo. **Museums**: usually Tues–Sun 1000–1500/1600. Some open Mon, longer in summer and/or close completely in winter.

POST OFFICES

Usually Mon–Fri 0800/0830–1700, Sat 0830–1300. Yellow postboxes with red crown-and-posthorn symbol are for local mail; red boxes with yellow symbol for all other destinations.

PUBLIC HOLIDAYS

Jan 1, Maundy Thur, Good Fri, Easter Mon, May 1, Ascension Day, May 17 (Constitution Day), Whit Mon, Dec 25, 26. For dates of movable holidays see page 2.

PUBLIC TRANSPORT

Train, boat and bus schedules are linked to provide good connections. It is often worth using buses or boats to connect two dead-end rail lines (e.g. Bergen and Stavanger), rather than retracing your route. Rail passes sometimes offer good discounts, even free travel, on linking services. NorWay Bussekspress (www.nor-way.no), Karl Johans gate 2, N-0154 Oslo, ✆ 82 021 300 (premium rate) has the largest bus network with routes going as far north as Kirkenes. Long-distance buses are comfortable, with reclining seats, ample leg room. Tickets: buy on board or reserve, ✆ 81 544 444 (premium-rate). Taxis: metered, can be picked up at ranks or by phoning; treat independent taxis with caution.

RAIL TRAVEL

See Tables **770 - 789**. Operated by: Norges Statsbaner (NSB) (www.nsb.no). All trains convey 2nd-class seating. Most medium- and long-distance trains also convey *NSB Komfort* accommodation, a dedicated area with complimentary tea/coffee and newspapers (supplement payable). Sleeping cars have one-, two and three-berth compartments (passengers may reserve a berth in any category with a 2nd-class ticket). Long-distance trains convey refreshments. Reservation possible on all long-distance trains, ✆ (within Norway) 81 500 888, then dial 4 for an english speaking operator. Reserved seats not marked, but your confirmation specifies carriage and seat/berth numbers. Carriage numbers shown by the doors, berth numbers outside compartments, seat numbers on seat-backs or luggage racks. Stations: most have baggage lockers, larger stations have baggage trolleys. Narvesen chain (at most stations; open long hours) sells English-language publications and a good range of snacks.

TELEPHONES

Dial in: ✆ +47 then number. Outgoing: ✆ 00. *Telekort* (phonecards) are available from Narvesen newsstands and post offices. Card phones are green; some accept credit cards. Coin and card phones are usually grouped together. Directory enquiries: ✆ 180 (Nordic countries), ✆ 181 (other countries). Local operator: ✆ 117. International operator: ✆ 115. Operators speak English. These are all premium-rate. Police: ✆ 112. Fire: ✆ 110. Ambulance: ✆ 113.

TIPPING

Tip 10% in restaurants (but not bars/cafés) if you are satisfied with the food, service etc. Not necessary for taxis.

TOURIST INFORMATION

Innovation Norway (www.visitnorway.com). Main office: P.O. Box 448, Sentrum 0158 Oslo, ✆ 2200 2500. Tourist offices (*Turistkontorer*) and bureaux (*Reiselivslag / Turistinformasjon*) exist in almost all towns and provide free maps, brochures, etc.

TOURIST OFFICES OVERSEAS

UK: Charles House, 5 Regent St, London SW1Y 4LR, ✆ 020 7389 8800, london@innovationnorway.no. **USA**: 655 Third Avenue, 18th floor, New York NY 10017, ✆ 212 885 9700, newyork@innovationnorway.no.

VISAS

See page xxxii for visa requirements.

POLAND

CAPITAL

Warsaw (Warszawa).

CLIMATE

Temperate, with warm summers and cold winters; rain falls throughout year.

CURRENCY

Złoty (PLN or zł), divided into 100 groszy. For exchange rates see page 11. British pounds, American dollars and (especially) euros are useful. *Kantor* exchange offices sometimes give better rates than banks and opening hours are longer. Credit cards are increasingly accepted but not universal.

EMBASSIES IN WARSAW

Australia: Ulica Nowogrodzka 11, ✆ 0 22 521 3444. **Canada**: Ulica Jana Matejki 1/5, ✆ 0 22 584 3100. **New Zealand**: Dom Dochodawy, Level 5, Aleje Ujazdowskie 51, ✆ 0 22 521 0500. **UK**: Aleje Róz 1,

✆ 0 22 311 0000. **USA**: Aleje Ujazdowskie 29/31, ✆ 0 22 504 2000.

EMBASSIES OVERSEAS

Australia: 7 Turrana St, Yarralumla, Canberra, ACT 2600, ✆ 2 6272 1000. **Canada**: 443 Daly Ave., Ottawa ON, K1N 6H3, ✆ 613 789 0468. **New Zealand**: 17 Upland Rd, Kelburn, Wellington, ✆ 4 475 9453. **UK**: 47 Portland Place, London W1B 1JH, ✆ 0870 774 2700. **USA**: 2640 16th St NW, Washington DC 20009, ✆ 202 234 3800.

LANGUAGE

Polish. Many older Poles speak German; younger Poles, particularly students, are likely to understand English. Russian is widely understood, but unpopular.

OPENING HOURS

Banks: Mon–Fri 0800–1600/1800, Sat 0800–1300. **Shops**: Mon–Fri 0800/1100–1900, Sat 0900–1300. **Food shops**: Mon–Fri 0600–1900, Sat 0600–1600. **Museums**: usually Tues–Sun 1000–1600; often closed public holidays and following day.

POST OFFICES

Known as *Poczta*; Mon–Fri 0700/0800–1800/2000, Sat 0800–1400 (main offices). City post offices are numbered (main office is always 1); number should be included in the post restante address. Post boxes: green (local mail), red (long-distance).

PUBLIC HOLIDAYS

Jan 1, Easter Mon, May 1, May 3 (Constitution), Corpus Christi, Aug 15 (Assumption), Nov 1 (All Saints), Nov 11 (Independence), Dec 25, 26. For dates of movable holidays see page 2.

PUBLIC TRANSPORT

PKS buses: cheap and sometimes more practical than trains. Main long-distance bus station in Warszawa is adjacent to the Zachodnia (western) station. Tickets normally include seat reservations (seat number is on back), bookable from bus station. In rural areas, bus drivers will often halt between official stops if you flag them down. Extensive tram networks in Warszawa and most other cities; Warszawa also has a modern north-south metro line.

RAIL TRAVEL

See Tables **1000 - 1099**. Cheap and punctual, run by Polskie Koleje Państwowe (PKP), www.pkp.pl. At stations, departures (*odjazdy*) are shown on yellow paper, arrivals (*przyjazdy*) on white. Intercity (IC), express (*ekspres* or Ex) and semi-express trains (*pospieszny*) are printed in red (all bookable). *Osobowy* trains are the slowest. Fares are about 50% higher for 1st class, but still cheap by western standards and probably worth it. Overnight trains usually have 1st/2nd-class sleepers, plus 2nd-class couchettes and seats. *TLK* are low cost, long distance trains on day and night services. Most long-distance trains have refreshments. Left luggage and refreshments in major stations. Few ticket clerks speak English.

TELEPHONES

Dial in: ✆ +48 then number (omit initial 0). Outgoing: ✆ 0*0 *(wait for tone after first 0)*. Older public phones take tokens (*żetony* – from post offices, hotels and Ruch kiosks). Newer phones accept phonecards. English-speaking operator: ✆ 903. Police: ✆ 997. Fire: ✆ 998. Ambulance: ✆ 999. Emergency (from mobile): ✆ 112.

TIPPING

An older system of rounding up has now been largely superseded by a flat rate 10% for table service in bars and restaurants, also for hairdressers, taxis and guides.

TOURIST INFORMATION

Polish National Tourist Office (www.poland.travel). IT tourist information office can usually help with accommodation. Also Orbis offices, for tourist information, excursions and accommodation.

TOURIST OFFICES OVERSEAS

UK: Level 3, Westgate House, West Gate, London W5 1YY, ✆ 08700 675 010, london@pot.gov.pl. **USA**: 5 Marine View Plaza, Hoboken NJ 07030-5722, ✆ 201 420 9910, info.na@poland.travel.

VISAS

See page xxxii for visa requirements.
For travellers in Germany, visas are obtainable from the Polish consulate in Berlin (www.berlin.polemb.net).

PORTUGAL

CAPITAL

Lisbon (Lisboa).

CLIMATE

Hotter and drier as you go south; southern inland parts very hot in summer; spring and autumn milder, but wetter. Mountains are very cold in winter.

CURRENCY

Euro (EUR / €). 1 euro = 100 cent. For exchange rates see page 11.

EMBASSIES IN LISBON

Australia: Avenida da Liberdade 200, ✆ 21 310 1500.
Canada: Avenida da Liberdade 196–200, ✆ 21 316 4600.
New Zealand: (Consulate) Rua do Periquito. Lote A-13, ✆ 21 370 5779. **UK**: Rua de São Bernado 33, ✆ 21 392 4000.
USA: Avenida das Forças Armadas, ✆ 21 727 3300.

EMBASSIES OVERSEAS

Australia: 23 Culgoa Circuit, O'Malley, Canberra, ACT 2606, ✆ 2 6290 1733. **Canada**: 645 Island Park Dr., Ottawa ON, K1Y OB8, ✆ 613 729 0883. **New Zealand**: (Consulate) 41 / 47 Dixon Street, Wellington, ✆ 4 382 7655. **UK**: 11 Belgrave Sq., London SW1X 8PP, ✆ 020 7235 5331. **USA**: 2125 Kalorama Rd. NW, Washington DC 20036, ✆ 202 328 8610.

LANGUAGE

Portuguese. Older people often speak French as second language, young people Spanish and/or English. English, French, and German in some tourist areas.

OPENING HOURS

Banks: Mon–Fri 0830–1445/1500. **Shops**: Mon–Fri 0900/1000–1300 and 1500–1900, Sat 0900–1300. City shopping centres often daily 1000–2300 or later. **Museums**: Tues–Sun 1000–1700/1800; some close for lunch and some are free on Sun. Palaces and castles usually close on Wed.

POST OFFICES

Post offices (*Correios*) are open Mon–Fri 0900–1800. The main offices in larger towns and at airports also open on Sat 0900–1300. Stamps (*selos*) can also be bought wherever you see the *Correios* symbol: a red-and-white horseback rider.

PUBLIC HOLIDAYS

Jan 1, Tues (47 days before Easter), Good Fri, Apr 25 (Freedom), May 1, Corpus Christi, June 10 (National Day), Aug 15 (Assumption), Oct 5 (Republic), Nov 1 (All Saints), Dec 1 (Independence), Dec 8 (Immaculate Conception), Dec 25. Many local saints' holidays. For dates of movable holidays see page 2.

PUBLIC TRANSPORT

Usually buy long-distance bus tickets before boarding. Bus stops: *paragem;* extend your arm to stop a bus. Taxis: black with green roofs or beige; illuminated signs; cheap, metered in cities, elsewhere fares negotiable; drivers may ask you to pay for their return journey; surcharges for luggage over 30 kg and night travel; 10% tip. City transport: single tickets can be bought as you board, but books of tickets or passes are cheaper; on boarding, insert 1–3 tickets (according to length of journey) in the machine behind the driver.

RAIL TRAVEL

See Tables **690 - 699**. Operator: Comboios de Portugal (CP) (www.cp.pt). Cheap and generally punctual; 1st/2nd class on long-distance. Fastest trains are *IC* and *AP* (Alfa Pendular), modern, fast; supplement payable; seat reservations compulsory, buffet cars. CP information line, ✆ 808 208 208. Left-luggage lockers in most stations.

TELEPHONES

Dial in: ✆ +351 then number. Outgoing: ✆ 00. Payphones take coins or phonecards (from Portugal Telecom shops, post offices, newsstands and hotels), and occasionally credit cards. International calls are best made at post offices; pay after the call. Operator: ✆ 118. Emergency services: ✆ 112.

TIPPING

Not necessary in hotels; customary to round up taxi fares and bills in cafés/bars, though not essential. Tip 10% in restaurants.

TOURIST INFORMATION

Portuguese National Tourist Office (www.portugal.org). Portuguese Tourism Institute (www.visitportugal.com). info@visitportugal.com, ✆ 211 205 050

TOURIST OFFICES OVERSEAS

Canada: 60 Bloor St West, Suite 1005, Toronto ON, M4W 3B8, ✆ 416 921 7376. **UK**: 11 Belgrave Square, London SW1X 8PP, ✆ 0845 355 1212, tourism@portugaloffice.org.uk. **USA**: 590 Fifth Avenue, 4th floor, New York NY 10036-4704, ✆ 212 354 4403, tourism@portugal.org.

VISAS

See page xxxii for visa requirements.

ROMANIA

CAPITAL

Bucharest (Bucureşti).

CLIMATE

Hot inland in summer, coast cooled by breezes; milder in winter, snow inland, especially in the mountains.

CURRENCY

Leu (plural: lei). 1 leu = 100 bani. For exchange rates see page 11. Carry pounds, euros or, ideally, dollars, in small denominations, plus traveller's cheques; change cash (commission-free) at exchange kiosks or banks; as rates can vary it's wise to check a few places first. Keep hold of your exchange vouchers; avoid black market exchange (risk of theft). Credit cards are needed for car rental, and are accepted in better hotels and restaurants. *Bancomats* (automatic cash dispensers; accept most cards at good rates) in most cities.

EMBASSIES IN BUCHAREST

Australia (Consulate): Str. Buzesti 14–18, ✆ 021 316 7558. **Canada**: 1-3 Tuberozelor St, ✆ 021 307 5000. **New Zealand**: *refer to NZ Embassy in Belgium.* **UK**: Jules Michelet 24, ✆ 021 201 7200. **USA**: Tudor Arghezi 7–9, ✆ 021 200 3300.

EMBASSIES OVERSEAS

Australia: 4 Dalman Crescent, O'Malley, Canberra ACT 2606, ✆ 2 6286 2343. **Canada**: 655 Rideau St, Ottawa ON, K1N 6A3, ✆ 613 789 3709. **UK**: Arundel House, 4 Palace Green, London W8 4QD, ✆ 020 7937 9666. **USA**: 1607 23rd St NW, Washington DC, 20008, ✆ 202 332 4846.

LANGUAGE

Romanian. English is understood by younger people, plus some German, and Hungarian throughout Transylvania.

OPENING HOURS

Banks: Mon–Fri 0900–1200/1300; private exchange counters open longer. **Shops**: usually 0800/0900–1800/2000, plus Sat morning or all day; often close 1300–1500. Local food shops often 0600–late. Few except in Bucharest open Sun. **Museums**: usually 0900/1000–1700/1800; open weekends, closed Mon (and maybe Tues).

POST OFFICES

There are post offices *(Posta Romana)* in all towns, open 0700-1900 Mon–Fri and until 1300 Sat. Postboxes are red. Mail usually takes five days to reach western Europe and up to two weeks to reach the US.

PUBLIC HOLIDAYS

Jan 1, Jan 2, Easter Mon (Orthodox), May 1, Dec 1 (National Unity Day), Dec 25, 26. For dates of movable holidays see page 2.

PUBLIC TRANSPORT

Buy bus/tram/metro tickets in advance from kiosks (as a rule) and cancel on entry. Taxis are inexpensive; if the meter not in use agree a price first and always pay in lei, not foreign currency. Trains are best for long-distance travel, although bus routes are expanding and connect important towns and cities.

RAIL TRAVEL

See Tables **1600 - 1699**. Societatea Naţională de Transport Feroviar de Călători (CFR) operates an extensive network linking all major towns (www.cfr.ro/călători). Most main lines are electrified and quite fast, but branch lines services are very slow. Trains are fairly punctual and very cheap. Except for local trains, reserve and pay a speed supplement in advance (tickets issued abroad include the supplement): cheapest are *tren de persoane* (very slow), then *accelerat* (still cheap), *rapid*, and finally *IC* trains (prices approaching Western levels). Food is normally available only on *IC* trains and some *rapids*; drinks are sold on some other trains. Couchette (*cuşeta*) or sleeper (*vagon de dormit*) accommodation is inexpensive. A number of local services are now operated by private operators, such as Regiotrans.

TELEPHONES

Dial in: ✆ +40 then number (omit initial 0). Outgoing: ✆ 00. Operator-connected calls from hotels and post offices: pay after making the call. Blue public phones accept coins only, Oranges' phones take phonecards available from post offices and newsstands. Emergency: ✆ 112. Police: ✆ 955. Fire: ✆ 981. Ambulance: ✆ 961.

TIPPING

Small tips are appreciated for good service at restaurants, hotels and in taxis. Only tip 10% at top-notch restaurants.

TOURIST INFORMATION

Romanian National Tourist Office (www.romaniatourism.com). Main office in Bucharest: ✆ 0 213 149 957. Regional tourist information offices in all major centres.

TOURIST OFFICES OVERSEAS

UK: 22 New Cavendish St, London W1M 7LHY, ✆ 020 7224 3692, romaniatravel@btconnect.com. **USA**: 355 Lexington Ave., 19th floor, New York NY 10017, ✆ 212 545 8484, info@romaniatourism.com.

VISAS

See page xxxii for visa requirements. Make sure you keep your visa papers when you enter – you'll pay a large fine if you don't have them when you leave Romania.

SLOVAKIA

CAPITAL

Bratislava.

CLIMATE

Mild summers and very cold winters.

CURRENCY

Euro (EUR/€). 1 euro = 100 cent. For exchange rates see page 11. Slovakia joined the Euro zone from January 1, 2009.

EMBASSIES IN BRATISLAVA

Australia: *refer to Australian Embassy in Austria.* **Canada**: Carlton Court Yard & Savoy Buildings, Mostova 2, ✆ 02 5920 4031. **New Zealand**: *refer to NZ Embassy in Germany.* **UK**: Panská 16, ✆ 02

5998 2000. **USA**: Hviezdoslavovo námestie 4, ✆ 02 5443 3338.

EMBASSIES OVERSEAS

Australia / New Zealand: 47 Culgoa Circuit, O'Malley, Canberra, ACT 2606, ✆ 2 6290 1516. **Canada**: 50 Rideau Terrace, Ottawa ON, K1M 2A1, ✆ 613 749 4442. **UK**: 25 Kensington Palace Gardens, London W8 4QY, ✆ 020 7243 0803. **USA**: 3523 International Court NW, Washington DC 20008, ✆ 202 237 1054.

LANGUAGE

Slovak, a Slavic tongue closely related to Czech. Some Russian (unpopular), German, Hungarian (especially in the south), plus a little English and French.

OPENING HOURS

Banks: Mon–Fri 0800–1800. **Shops**: Mon–Fri 0900–1800, Sat 0800–1200. **Food shops** usually open 0800 and Sun.
Museums: (usually) Tues–Sun 1000–1700. Most **castles** close on national holidays and Nov–Mar.

POST OFFICES

Usual post office hours: 0800–1900. Stamps are also available from newsagents and tobacconists. Post boxes are orange.

PUBLIC HOLIDAYS

Jan 1, Jan 6 (Epiphany), Good Fri, Easter Mon, May 1, May 8 (Victory Day), July 5 (Cyril & Methodius), Aug 29 (National Day), Sept 1 (Constitution), Sept 15 (Virgin Mary), Nov 1 (All Saints), Nov 17 (Freedom and Democracy), Dec 24, 25, 26. For dates of movable holidays, see page 2.

PUBLIC TRANSPORT

There is a comprehensive long-distance bus network, often more direct than rail in upland areas. Buy tickets from the driver; priority is given to those with bookings.

RAIL TRAVEL

See Tables **1170 - 1199**. The national rail operator is Železničná spoločnosť (ŽSSK), running on the network of ŽSR. Trains are cheap, but often crowded. Apart from a small number of *EC* and *IC* trains (for which higher fares apply), the fastest trains are *expresný* (*Ex*) and *Rýchlik* (*R*). Cheaper are *zrýchlený* (semi-fast) and *osobný* (very slow). At stations, departures (*odjezdy*) are shown on yellow posters, arrivals (*prijezdy*) on white. Sleeping cars/couchettes (reserve at all main stations, well in advance in summer) are provided on most overnight trains. Seat reservations (at station counters marked R) are recommended for express trains. Reservation agency: MTA, Páričkova 29, Bratislava, ✆ 0 255 969 343.

TELEPHONES

Dial in: ✆ +421 then number (omit initial 0). Outgoing: ✆ 00. Public phones take coins or phonecards, available from post offices and selected newsstands. Information: ✆ 120 (national), ✆ 0149 (international). Emergency: ✆ 112. Police: ✆ 158. Fire: ✆ 150. Ambulance: ✆ 155.

TIPPING

Tipping is expected at hotels, hairdressers, in eateries and taxis. In general, round up to the next SKK 10, unless you are somewhere very upmarket, where you should tip 10%.

TOURIST INFORMATION

Slovak Tourist Board (www.slovakia.travel). Main office: Námestie L'. Štúra 1, P.O. Box 35, 974 05 Banská Bystrica, ✆ 0 484 136 146, sacr@sacr.sk. Bratislava Information Service (www.bratislava.sk), Klobučnicka 2, 815 15 Bratislava, ✆ 0 254 433 715, info@bkis.sk. Staff speak English and can arrange accommodation.

TOURIST OFFICES OVERSEAS

Germany: Slowakische Zentrale für Tourismus, Zimmerstr. 27, D-10969, Berlin, ✆ +49 (0) 30 2594 2640, tourismus@botschaft-slowakei.de

VISAS

See page xxxii for visa requirements.

SLOVENIA

CAPITAL

Ljubljana.

CLIMATE

Warm summers, cold winters; Mediterranean climate along coast; snow in the mountains in winter.

CURRENCY

Euro (EUR / €). 1 euro = 100 cent. For exchange rates see page 11.

EMBASSIES IN LJUBLJANA

Australia (Consulate): Dunajska cesta 50, ✆ 01 425 4252. **Canada**: Trg Republike 3, ✆ 01 252 4444. **New Zealand**: (Consulate) Lek d.d., Verovskova 57, ✆ 01 580 2011. **UK**: Trg Republike 3, ✆ 01 200 3910. **USA**: Prešernova 31, ✆ 01 200 5500.

EMBASSIES OVERSEAS

Australia: 60 Marcus Clarke St, Canberra, ACT 2601, ✆ 2 6243 4830. **Canada**: 150 Metcalfe St. Suite 2101, Ottawa, ON, K2P 1P1, ✆ 613 565 5781. **UK**: 10 Little College St, London SW1P 3SH, ✆ 020 7222 5700. **USA**: 1525 New Hampshire Ave. NW, Washington DC 20036, ✆ 202 667 5363.

LANGUAGE

Slovenian. English, German and Italian are often spoken in tourist areas.

OPENING HOURS

Banks: vary, but mostly Mon–Fri 0830–1230 and 1400–1630, Sat 0830–1200. **Shops**: mostly Mon–Fri 0800–1900, Sat 0830–1200.
Museums: larger ones 1000–1800, many smaller ones 1000–1400; some close Mon.

POST OFFICES

Mon–Fri 0800–1800, Sat 0800–1200. Main post offices in larger centres may open evenings and on Sun. Ljubljana's main post office in Trg Osvobodilne Fronte 5, by the railway station, is open 24 hrs.

PUBLIC HOLIDAYS

Jan 1, 2, Feb 8 (Culture), Easter Sun/Mon, Apr 27 (Resistance), May 1, 2, June 25 (Statehood), Aug 15 (Assumption), Oct 31 (Reformation), Nov 1 (All Saints), Dec 25, 26. For dates of movable holidays, see page 2.

PUBLIC TRANSPORT

Long-distance bus services are frequent and inexpensive; normally, buy your ticket on boarding. Information: Trg Osvobodilne Fronte 5, next to Ljubljana station, ✆ 012 344 606. On city buses pay by dropping the exact flat fare or a cheaper token (available from newsstands and post offices) into the farebox next to the driver. Daily and weekly passes are available in the main cities.

RAIL TRAVEL

See Tables **1300 - 1359**. Operator: Slovenske železnice (SŽ) (www.slo-zeleznice.si). Information: ✆ 012 913 332 (+386 1 29 13 332 from abroad). Efficient network, but fewer services on Saturdays. Reserve for *ICS* trains; supplements are payable on other express services.

TELEPHONES

Dial in: ✆ +386 then number (omit initial 0). Outgoing: ✆ 00. Public phones take phonecards, available from post offices, newspaper kiosks and tobacconists. Police: ✆ 113. Fire and ambulance: ✆ 112.

TIPPING

No need to tip bar staff or taxi drivers, although you can round sums up as you wish. In restaurants add 10%.

TOURIST INFORMATION

Slovenian Tourist Board (www.slovenia.info). Main office: Krekov trg 10, SI-1000 Ljubljana, ✆ 01 306 45 75, stic@visitljubljana.si

TOURIST OFFICES OVERSEAS

UK: The Saltmarsh Partnership, 25d Copperfield Street, London SE1 0EN. ✆ 020 7928 6108, info@saltmarshpr.co.uk
USA: 2929 East Commercial Boulevard, Suite 201, Fort Lauderdale, FL 33308, ✆ 954 491 0112, info@slovenia.info

VISAS

See page xxxii for visa requirements.

SPAIN

CAPITAL

Madrid.

CURRENCY

Euro (EUR / €). 1 euro = 100 cent. For exchange rates see page 11.

EMBASSIES IN MADRID

Australia: Paseo de la Castellana, 259D, Planta 24, ✆ 913 536 600. **Canada:** Núñez de Balboa 35, ✆ 914 233 250. **New Zealand**: Pinar 7, ✆ 915 230 226. **UK**: Fernando el Santo 16, ✆ 917 008 200. **USA**: Serrano 75, ✆ 915 872 200.

EMBASSIES OVERSEAS

Australia: 15 Arkana St, Yarralumla, Canberra, ACT 2600, ✆ 2 6273 3555. **Canada**: 74 Stanley Avenue, Ottawa ON, K1M 1P4, ✆ 613 747 2252. **UK**: 39 Chesham Place, London SW1X 8SB, ✆ 020 7235 5555. **USA**: 2375 Pennsylvania Ave. NW, Washington DC 20037, ✆ 202 452 0100.

LANGUAGE

Castilian Spanish is the most widely spoken language. There are three other official languages: Catalan in the east; Galician (*Galego*) in the north-west, and Basque (*Euskera*) in the Basque country and parts of Navarre. English is fairly widely spoken in tourist areas. Note that in Spanish listings *Ch* often comes after the *C*'s, *Ll* after the *L*'s, and *Ñ* after the *N*'s.

OPENING HOURS

Banks: Mon–Thur 0930–1630; Fri 0830–1400; Sat 0830–1300 (winter); Mon–Fri 0830–1400 (summer). **Shops**: Mon–Sat 0930/1000–1400 and 1700–2000/2030; major stores do not close for lunch, food shops often open Sun. **Museums**: vary, mostly open 0900/1000, close any time from 1400 to 2030. Few open Mon and some also close (or open half day) Sun. Expect to find most places closed 1300–1500/1600, especially in the south.

POST OFFICES

Most *Oficinas de Correos* are open 0830–1430 Mon–Fri, 0930–1300 Sat, although the main offices in large cities often stay open until around 2100 on Mon–Fri. Main offices offer poste restante *(lista de correos)*. Stamps *(sellos)* are also sold at tobacconists (estancos). Post overseas mail in the slot marked *Extranjero*.

PUBLIC HOLIDAYS

Jan 1, Jan 6 (Epiphany), several days at Easter, May 1, July 25, Aug 15 (Assumption), Oct 12 (National Day); Nov 1 (All Saints), Dec 6 (Constitution), Dec 8 (Immaculate Conception) and several days at Christmas. Not all of these are official holidays, but many places close anyway. Each region has at least four more public holidays, usually local saints' days (e.g. Andalucia Feb 28, Galacia July 25, Catalonia Sept 11). For the dates of movable holidays, see page 2.

PUBLIC TRANSPORT

Numerous regional bus companies provide a fairly comprehensive and cheap (if sometimes confusing) service. The largest bus operating groups are ALSA (www.alsa.es) and Avanzabus (www.avanzabus.com). City buses are efficient and there are metro systems in Madrid, Barcelona, València and Bilbao.

RAIL TRAVEL

See Tables **650 - 689**. National rail company: Red Nacional de los Ferrocarriles Españoles (RENFE) (www.renfe.es). FEVE and a number of regionally-controlled railways operate lines in coastal regions. General information: RENFE ✆ 902 240 202; FEVE ✆ 902 100 818; AVE (high-speed): ✆ 915 066 329; Grandes Líneas (other long-distance): ✆ 902 105 205; international: ✆ 934 901 122. Spain's high-speed network has expanded considerably over the last few years and the Barcelona - Madrid service has some of the fastest trains in Europe. As well as *AVE* high-speed trains, other long-distance categories include *Altaria, Alaris, Euromed, Talgo* (light articulated trains) and IC expresses (see page 321 for further train categories). *Diurno*: ordinary long-distance day train. *Estrella*: night train (including sleeper and/or couchette cars). A pricier alternative for night travel is the *Trenhotel* (hotel train), offering sleeping compartments with their own shower and WC. All convey 1st- and 2nd-class accommodation (*Preferente* and *Turista*; AVE also have a 'super-first' class: *Club*) and require advance reservation. *Regionales*: local stopping service; *Cercanías*: suburban trains. In remoter parts of country, services may be very infrequent. Reservation is compulsory on all services for which a train category (*Talgo, IC* etc) is shown in the timing column of this timetable. RENFE offer money back if their AVE trains on the Sevilla line arrive more than 5 minutes late!

TELEPHONES

Dial in: ✆ +34 then number. Outgoing: ✆ 00. Public phones usually have English instructions and accept coins or phonecard (*Teletarjeta*; sold in tobacconists, post offices and some shops). Payphones in bars are usually more expensive. Emergency (police / fire / ambulance): ✆ 112.

TIPPING

Not necessary to tip in bars and taxis; tipping is more common in restaurants but by no means obligatory. If you want to tip for good service, add around 5%.

TOURIST INFORMATION

Spanish Tourist Office / Turespaña (USA: www.spain.info, UK: www.tourspain.co.uk). Local *Oficinas de Turismo* can provide maps and information on accommodation and sightseeing, and generally have English-speaking staff. Regional offices stock information for the whole region, municipal offices cover only that city; larger towns have both types of office.

TOURIST OFFICES OVERSEAS

Canada: 2 Bloor Street West, Suite 3402, Toronto ON M4W 3E2, ✆ 416 961 3131, toronto@tourspain.es. **UK**: PO Box 4009, London W1A 6NB, ✆ 020 7486 8077, londres@tourspain.es. **USA**: 666 Fifth Avenue, 35th Floor, New York NY 10103, ✆ 212 265 8822, nuevayork@tourspain.es. Also in Chicago ✆ 312 642 1992, Los Angeles ✆ 323 658 7195, and Miami ✆ 305 358 8223.

VISAS

See page xxxii for visa requirements.

SWEDEN

CAPITAL

Stockholm.

CLIMATE

Often warm (especially in summer; continuous daylight in far north). Huge range between north and south; it can be mild in Skåne (far south) in Feb, but spring comes late May in the north. Winter generally very cold everywhere.

CURRENCY

Swedish crown or krona (SEK, kr, or Skr); 1 krona = 100 öre. For exchange rates see page 11. *Växlare* machines give change. The best exchange rate is obtained from Forex, which has branches at many stations. Keep receipts so that you can reconvert at no extra cost.

EMBASSIES IN STOCKHOLM

Australia: Sergels Torg 12, ✆ 08 613 2900. **Canada**: Tegelbacken 4, ✆ 08 453 3000. **New Zealand**: Stureplan 4C, ✆ 08 463 3116. **UK**: Skarpögatan 6–8, ✆ 08 671 3000. **USA**: Dag Hammarskjölds Väg 31, ✆ 08 783 5300.

EMBASSIES OVERSEAS

Australia: 5 Turrana St, Yarralumla, Canberra, ACT 2600, ✆ 2 6270 2700. **Canada**: 377 Dalhousie St, Ottawa ON, K1N 9N8, ✆ 613 244 8200. **New Zealand** (Consulate): Molesworth House, 101 Molesworth Street, Wellington, ✆ 4 499 9895. **UK**: 11 Montagu Pl., London W1H 2AL, ✆ 020 7917 6400. **USA**: 901 30th. Street NW, Washington DC 20007, ✆ 202 467 2600.

LANGUAGE

Swedish. English is widely spoken. Useful rail / bus / ferry words include *daglig* (daily), *vardagar* (Mon–Sat), and *helgdagar* (Sundays and holidays).

OPENING HOURS

Banks: Mon–Fri 0930–1500 (Thur, and Mon–Fri in some cities, until 1730). Some, especially at transport terminals, have longer hours. **Shops**: mostly Mon–Fri 0900/0930–1700/1800, Sat 0900/0930–1300/1600. In larger towns department stores open until 2000/2200; also some on Sun 1200–1600. **Museums**: vary widely. In winter, many attractions close Mon and some close altogether.

POST OFFICES

Generally Mon–Fri 0900–1800, Sat 1000–1300, but there are local variations. Stamps are also sold at newsagents and tobacconists. Post boxes: yellow (overseas), blue (local).

PUBLIC HOLIDAYS

Jan 1, Jan 6 (Epiphany), Good Friday, Easter Mon, May 1, Ascension Day, Whit Sun, June 6 (National Day), Midsummer Day (Sat falling June 20–26) plus Midsummer Eve (previous day), All Saints Day (Sat falling Oct 31 - Nov 6), Dec 24, 25, 26. Many places close early the previous day, or Fri if it's a long weekend. For dates of movable holidays, see page 2.

PUBLIC TRANSPORT

The transport system is highly efficient; ferries are covered (in whole or part) by rail passes and city transport cards. Swebus (www.swebus.se), ✆ 08 410 653 00 is the biggest operator of long-distance buses. Advance booking is required on some routes and always advisable in summer; bus terminals usually adjoin rail stations.

RAIL TRAVEL

See Tables **730 - 769**. National rail company: Statens Järnvägar (SJ) (www.sj.se). Some local lines are run by regional authorities or private companies such as Veolia Transport (www.veolia.se), who also operate a service to the far north. SJ information and sales line, ✆ (0) 771 757575, Veolia ✆ (0) 771 260 000. Supplements are required on *X2000* trains (up to 200 km/h). Sleeping-cars: one or two berths in 2nd class; couchettes: six berths; female-only compartment available. 1st-class sleeping-cars (en-suite shower and WC) on many overnight services; 2nd-class have wash-basins, shower and WC are at the end of the carriage. Long-distance trains have a refreshment service. Many trains have a family coach with a playroom, and facilities for the disabled. Seat reservations are compulsory on *X2000* and night trains. *X2000* services operate between Sweden and Copenhagen via the Öresund bridge and tunnel but it is better to use the frequent local trains for short journeys. 'C' (for Central) in timetables etc. means the town's main station. Large, detailed timetables are displayed for long-distance trains: yellow for departures, white for arrivals. *Biljetter* indicates the station ticket office. *Pressbyrån* kiosks (at most stations) sell snacks and English-language publications.

TELEPHONES

Dial in: ✆ +46 then number (omit initial 0). Outgoing: ✆ 00. Coin-operated phones take krona or euro. Most card phones accept credit / debit cards and *Telia* phonecards (*telefonkor-ten*), available from most newsagents, tobacconists, and *Pressbyrån* kiosks). Emergency services (police / fire / ambulance): ✆ 112.

TIPPING

Restaurants include a service charge but a tip of 10–15% is appreciated. Taxis 10%. Tip hotel staff, porters, cloakroom attendants etc. at your discretion.

TOURIST INFORMATION

Swedish Travel & Tourism Council: www.visitsweden.com. info@visitsweden.com. Tourist offices, of which there are 400 throughout the country, are called *Turistbyråer*. Stockholm City Tourist Centre: Sverigehuset, Hamngatan 27, 10327 Stockholm, ✆ 085 0828508, info@svb.stockholm.se.

TOURIST OFFICES OVERSEAS

UK: 5 Upper Montagu St, London W1H 2AG, ✆ 020 7108 6168, uk@visitsweden.com. **USA**: P.O. Box 4649, Grand Central Station, New York NY 10163-4649, ✆ 212 885 9700, usa@visitsweden.com.

VISAS

See page xxxii for visa requirements.

SWITZERLAND

CAPITAL

Berne (Bern).

CLIMATE

Rainfall spread throughout the year. May–Sept are best in the mountains. June or early July best for the wild flowers. Snow at high altitudes even in midsummer. Season in the lakes: Apr–Oct. July and Aug get very busy.

CURRENCY

Swiss franc (CHF or Sfr.); 1 franc = 100 centimes. For exchange rates, see page 11.

EMBASSIES IN BERNE

Australia (Consulate in Geneva): 2 Chemin des Fins, Geneva, ✆ 0 22 799 9100. **Canada**: Kirchenfeldstrasse 88, ✆ 0 31 357 3200. **New Zealand** (Consulate in Geneva): 2 Chemin des Fins, Geneva, ✆ 0 22 929 0350. **UK**: Thunstrasse 50, ✆ 0 31 359 7700. **USA**: Sulgeneckstrasse 19, ✆ 0 31 357 7011.

EMBASSIES OVERSEAS

Australia: 7 Melbourne Avenue, Forrest, Canberra, ACT 2603, ✆ 2 6162 8400. **Canada**: 5 Marlborough Avenue, Ottawa ON, K1N 8E6, ✆ 613 235 1837. **UK**: 16-18 Montagu Place, London W1H 2BQ, ✆ 020 7616 6000. **USA**: 2900 Cathedral Ave. NW, Washington DC 20008, ✆ 202 745 7900.

LANGUAGE

German, French, Italian, and Romansch are all official languages. Most Swiss people are at least bilingual. English is widespread.

OPENING HOURS

Banks: Mon–Fri 0800–1200 and 1400–1700. Money change desks in most rail stations, open longer hours. **Shops**: Mon–Fri 0800–1200 and 1330–1830, Sat 0800–1200 and 1330–1600. Many close Mon morning. In stations, shops open longer hours and on Sun. **Museums**: usually close Mon. Hours vary.

POST OFFICES

Usually Mon–Fri 0730–1200 and 1345–1830, Sat 0730–1100; longer in cities. Poste restante (*Postlagernd*) facilities are available at most post offices.

PUBLIC HOLIDAYS

Jan 1, Jan. 2, Good Fri, Easter Mon, Ascension Day, Whit Mon, Aug 1 (National Day), Dec 25, 26. Also May 1 and Corpus Christi in some areas. For dates of movable holidays see page 2.

PUBLIC TRANSPORT

Swiss buses are famously punctual. Yellow postbuses call at rail stations; free timetables from post offices. Swiss Pass valid (see Passes feature), surcharge for some scenic routes. The best way to get around centres is often on foot. Most cities have efficient tram and bus networks with integrated ticketing.

RAIL TRAVEL

See Tables **500 - 579**. The principal rail carrier is Swiss Federal Railways (SBB / CFF / FFS) (www.sbb.ch). Information: ✆ 0 900 300 300 (English-speaking operator). There are also many local lines with independent operators. Services are fast and punctual, trains spotlessly clean. Some international trains have sleepers (3 berths) and/or couchettes (up to 6 people). Sleepers can be booked up to 3 months in advance, couchettes/seats up to 2 months ahead. Reservations are required on some sightseeing trains (e.g. Glacier Express, Bernina-Express). All main stations have information offices (and usually tourist offices), shopping and eating facilities. Bicycle hire at most stations.

TELEPHONES

Dial in: ✆ +41 then number (omit initial 0). Outgoing: ✆ 00. Phonecards (*taxcard*) are available from Swisscom offices, post offices, newsagents and most rail stations in denominations of CHF 5, 10, 20, and 50. Some payphones accept Euros. National enquiries: ✆ 111. International operator: ✆ 1141. All operators speak English. Emergency: ✆ 112. Police: ✆ 117. Fire: ✆ 118. Ambulance: ✆ 114.

TIPPING

Not necessary or expected in restaurants or taxis.

TOURIST INFORMATION

Switzerland Tourism (www.myswitzerland.com). Main office: Tödistrasse 7, CH-8027 Zürich. International toll-free ✆ 00800 100 200 30 (information, reservations, etc.). There are Tourist Offices in almost every town and village. The standard of information is excellent.

TOURIST OFFICES OVERSEAS

Canada: 926 The East Mall, Toronto ON, M9B 6K1, ✆ 800 794 7795 (toll-free), info.caen@myswitzerland.com.
UK: 30 Bedford Street, London WC2E 9ED, ✆ 00800 100 200 30 (free-phone), info.uk@myswitzerland.com.
USA: 608 Fifth Ave., New York NY 10020, ✆ 011800 100 200 30 (toll-free), info.usa@myswitzerland.com.

VISAS

See page xxxii for visa requirements.

TURKEY

CAPITAL

Ankara.

CLIMATE

Very hot summers, more manageable in spring or autumn. Cool Nov–Mar.

CURRENCY

New Turkish lira (TRY or YTL). 1 lira = 100 kuruş. For exchange rates, see page 11. Credit cards are widely accepted.

CONSULATES IN ISTANBUL

Australia: Ritz carlton residences, Askerocaği Caddesi No 15, Elmadağ 34367, ✆ 0 212 243 1333. **Canada**: Istiklal Caddesi No 189/5, Beyoglu, ✆ 0 212 251 9838. **New Zealand**: (Embassy in Ankara) Iran Caddesi 13, Kavaklidere, Ankara, ✆ 0 312 467 9054.
UK: Mesrutiyet Caddesi No 34, Tepebasi Beyoglu, ✆ 0 212 334 6400. **USA**: İstinye Mahallesi, Kaplıcalar Mekvii No 2, İstinye 34460, ✆ 0 212 335 9000.

EMBASSIES OVERSEAS

Australia: 6 Moonah Place, Yarralumla, Canberra, ACT 2600, ✆ 2 6234 0000. **Canada**: 197 Wurtemburg St., Ottawa ON, K1N 8L9, ✆ 613 789 4044. **UK**: 43 Belgrave Sq., London SW1X 8PA, ✆ 020 7393 0202. **USA**: 2525 Massachusetts Ave, NW, Washington, DC 20008, ✆ 202 612 6700.

LANGUAGE

Turkish, which is written using the Latin alphabet. English and German are often understood.

OPENING HOURS

Banks: 0830–1200, 1300–1700, Mon–Fri (some private banks are open at lunchtime). Shops 0930–1900; until around 2400 in tourist areas. **Government offices**: 0830–1230, 1300–1700 (closed Sat and Sun). In Aegean and Mediterranean regions, many establishments stay open very late in summer. **Museums**: many close on Mon.

POST OFFICES

Post offices have PTT signs. Major offices: Airport, Beyoğlu and Sirkeci open 24 hrs all week (limited services at night). Small offices: 0830–1700 (some close 1230–1300).

PUBLIC HOLIDAYS

Jan 1, Apr 23, May 1, 19, Aug 30, Oct 29. Religious festivals have movable dates and can affect travel arrangements and business opening times over an extended period. The main festival periods are *Kurban Bayrami* (Nov. 27 - 30 in 2009, Nov. 16 - 19 in 2010) and *Seker Bayrami* (Sept. 20 - 22 in 2009, Sept. 9 - 11 in 2010).

PUBLIC TRANSPORT

An excellent long-distance bus system, run by competing companies (amongst the best are Varan and Ulusoy), generally provides quicker journeys than rail. *Dolmuş* minibuses that pick up passengers like a taxi, but at much cheaper rates and operating along set routes, can be used for shorter journeys. Istanbul has a modern metro line, as well as a light-rail and tram route. TML (Turkish Maritime Lines) operates passenger ferries.

RAIL TRAVEL

See Table **1550** – for journeys in Asian Turkey beyond Istanbul, consult the *Thomas Cook Overseas Timetable*. Operator: TCDD (Turkish State Railways) (www.tcdd.gov.tr). Routes are tortuous and journeys slow, but a new high-speed route is now partially open between Istanbul and Ankara.

TELEPHONES

Dial in: ✆ +90 then number (omit initial 0). Outgoing: ✆ 00. Payphones take *Türk Telekom* phonecards (*Telekart*) available in 30, 60, and 100 units from post offices, shops, kiosks and some hotels. Hotels often charge very high rates. Directory enquiries: ✆ 118. International operator: ✆ 115. Emergency: ✆ 112. Police: ✆ 155. Fire: ✆ 110. Ambulance: ✆ 112.

TIPPING

A 10% tip is usual in restaurants, unless service is included. Do not tip barmen directly. 10–20% is customary at hair salons. Do not tip taxi drivers.

TOURIST INFORMATION

Turkish National Tourist Office (UK: www.gototurkey.co.uk, USA: www.tourismturkey.org). Ministry of Culture and Tourism: Atatürk Bulvarı 29, 06050 Opera, Ankara, ✆ 0312 309 0850.

TOURIST OFFICES OVERSEAS

UK: 4th Floor, 29-30 St James's Street, London SW1A 1HB, ✆ 020 7839 7778, info@gototurkey.co.uk. **USA**: 821 United Nations Plaza, New York NY 10017, ✆ 212 687 2194, info.ny@tourismturkey.org.

VISAS

See page xxxii for visa requirements.

UNITED KINGDOM

CAPITAL
London.

CLIMATE
Cool, wet winters, mild spring and autumn, winter can be more extreme. Wetter in the west. Aug and Bank Holiday weekends busiest in tourist areas.

CURRENCY
Pounds Sterling (GBP or £). £1 = 100 pence (p). For exchange rates, see page 11.

EMBASSIES IN LONDON
Australia (High Commission): Australia House, The Strand, ✆ 020 7379 4334. **Canada** (High Commission) Canada House, Trafalgar Square, ✆ 020 7258 6600. **New Zealand** (High Commission): New Zealand House, 80 Haymarket, ✆ 020 7930 8422. **USA**: 24 Grosvenor Square, ✆ 020 7499 9000.

EMBASSIES OVERSEAS
Australia (High Commission): Commonwealth Ave, Yarralumla, Canberra, ACT 2600, ✆ 2 6270 6666. **Canada** (High Commission): 80 Elgin St, Ottawa ON, K1P 5K7, ✆ 613 237 1530. **New Zealand** (High Commission): 44 Hill St, Wellington, ✆ 4 924 2888. **USA**: 3100 Massachusetts Ave. NW, Washington DC 20008, ✆ 202 588 6500.

LANGUAGE
English, plus Welsh in Wales and Gaelic in parts of Scotland.

OPENING HOURS
Banks: Mon–Fri 0930–1530 (or later); some open Sat morning. **Shops**: Mon–Sat 0900–1730. Many supermarkets and some small shops open longer, plus Sunday 1000–1600. **Museums**: usually Mon–Sat 0900/1000–1730/1800, half-day Sun.

POST OFFICES
Usually Mon–Fri 0930–1730, Sat 0930–1300; stamps sold in newsagents etc.

PUBLIC HOLIDAYS
Jan 1, Good Fri, Easter Mon *(not Scotland)*, Early May Bank Holiday (first Mon in May), Spring Bank Holiday (last Mon in May), Summer Bank Holiday (last Mon in August) *(not Scotland)*, Dec 25, 26. Scotland: *also* Jan 2, Summer Bank Holiday (first Monday in August). Northern Ireland: *also* Mar 17 (St Patrick), July 12 (Orangemen). Holidays falling at the weekend are transferred to the following weekday. For the dates of movable holidays, see page 2.

PUBLIC TRANSPORT
Intercity express bus services (coaches) are generally cheaper, but slower, than trains, and mostly require prebooking. The main long-distance coach operator in England and Wales is National Express (www.nationalexpress.com), or Citylink (www.citylink.co.uk) in Scotland. Comprehensive local bus network; most companies belong to large groups such as Stagecoach, First or Arriva. Bus stations are rarely adjacent to railway stations. Traveline (www.traveline.org.uk) is an on-line and telephone service for all UK timetables: ✆ 0871 200 22 23 (10p per minute). Extensive 'Underground' railway network in London operated by Transport for London (www.tfl.gov.uk) who also control the bus service using private companies.
In Northern Ireland, Ulsterbus (part of Translink) is the principal bus operator. (www.translink.co.uk)

RAIL TRAVEL
See Tables **100 - 234**. Passenger services in Great Britain are provided by a number of train operating companies, working together as National Rail (www.nationalrail.co.uk). Through tickets are available to all stations in the country. If asked, booking-office staff will quote the cheapest fare regardless of operator (time period restrictions apply to the very cheapest fares). National Rail enquiries: ✆ 08457 48 49 50. Fast trains, comfortable and frequent, have first and standard class. Other long- and medium-distance regional services are often standard-class only. Refreshments are often available on board. Sleepers: cabins are two-berth or (higher charge) single. Advance reservation (essential for sleepers) is available for most long-distance services - a fee may be charged. Travel between Saturday evening and Sunday afternoon is sometimes interrupted by engineering works and buses may replace trains.
In Northern Ireland, trains are operated by Northern Ireland Railways (NIR), part of Translink. NIR enquiries: ✆ 028 90 666 630.

TELEPHONES
Dial in: ✆ +44 then number (omit initial 0). Outgoing: ✆ 00. Payphones take coins, phonecards (sold at newsagents) or credit cards. Emergency services: ✆ 999 or 112.

TIPPING
Tip 10% in restaurants, except where service is included (becoming increasingly common), but not in pubs, self-service restaurants or bars. Tip taxis (10%) hailed in the street.

TOURIST INFORMATION
VisitBritain (www.visitbritain.com). Britain and London Visitor Centre: 1 Regent Street, London SW1Y 4XT, ✆ 0870 156 6366. There are local tourist offices in most towns and cities.

TOURIST OFFICES OVERSEAS
Australia: australia@visitbritain.org. **Canada**: 160 Bloor Street East, Suite 905, Toronto, ON, M4W 1B9 (not open to the public), britinfo@visitbritain.org. **New Zealand**: newzealand@visitbritain.org. **USA**: travelinfo@visitbritain.org, ✆ 1800 462 2748.

VISAS
See below for visa requirements.

VISA REQUIREMENTS

The table below shows whether nationals from selected countries (shown in columns) need visas to visit countries in Europe (shown in rows) - the symbol ▲ indicates that a visa **is** required. This information applies to tourist trips for up to 30 days - different requirements may apply for longer trips or for visits for other purposes, also if you are resident in a country other than your own. To enter certain countries you may need up to three months remaining validity on your passport.

The first row and column, labeled **Schengen area**, apply to the 25 European countries which have signed the Schengen Agreement whereby border controls between the member countries have been abolished. It is possible to obtain a single Schengen visa to cover all these countries, which are:

Austria, Belgium, Czech Republic, Denmark, Estonia, Finland, France, Germany, Greece, Hungary, Iceland, Italy, Latvia, Lithuania, Luxembourg, Malta, the Netherlands, Norway, Poland, Portugal, Slovakia, Slovenia, Spain, Sweden, Switzerland

Note that the Schengen area and the European Union (EU) differ in the following respects: Iceland, Norway and Switzerland are not in the EU but have implemented the Schengen agreement, whereas the United Kingdom and the Republic of Ireland are in the EU but have not implemented Schengen. Andorra is not included in the Schengen area.

Visas should generally be applied for in advance from an Embassy or Consulate of the country you are visiting, although sometimes they are available on arrival. Transit visas may be available for those travelling through a country in order to reach another, but these may also need to be purchased in advance. The information show below is given as a guide only - entry requirements may be subject to change.

NATIONALS OF →

▲ VISA REQUIRED

TRAVELLING TO ↓	Schengen area	Albania	Belarus	Bosnia-Herzegovina	Bulgaria	Croatia	Cyprus	Macedonia	Moldova	Montenegro	Romania	Russia	Serbia	Switzerland	Turkey	UK / Ireland	Ukraine	Australia	Canada	Japan	New Zealand	USA
Schengen area	–	▲	▲	▲	:	:	:	▲	▲	▲	:	▲	▲	:	▲	:	▲	:	:	:	:	:
Albania ◇	:	–	▲	▲	:	:	:	:	▲	:	:	▲	▲	:	:	:	▲	:	:	:	:	:
Belarus	▲	▲	–	▲	▲	▲	▲	:	:	:	▲	:	:	▲	▲	▲	:	▲	▲	▲	▲	▲
Bosnia-Herzegovina	:	▲	▲	–	:	:	:	:	▲	:	:	:	:	:	:	:	▲	:	:	:	:	:
Bulgaria	:	▲	▲	▲	–	:	:	▲	▲	▲	:	▲	▲	:	▲	:	▲	:	:	:	:	:
Croatia	:	▲	▲	:	:	–	:	:	▲	:	:	▲	:	:	:	:	▲	:	:	:	:	:
Cyprus	:	▲	▲	▲	:	:	–	▲	▲	▲	:	▲	▲	:	▲	:	▲	:	:	:	:	:
Macedonia	:	:	▲	:	:	:	:	–	▲	:	:	▲	:	:	:	:	▲[1]	:	:	:	:	:
Moldova	:	▲	:	▲	:	▲	:	▲	–	▲	:	:	▲	:	▲	:	:	▲	:	:	▲	:
Montenegro	:	:	:	:	:	:	:	:	▲	–	▲	:	:	:	▲	:	:	:	:	:	:	:
Romania	:	▲	▲	▲	:	:	:	▲	▲	▲	–	▲	▲	:	▲	:	▲	:	:	:	:	:
Russia	▲	▲	:	▲	▲	▲	▲	▲	:	▲	▲	–	▲	▲	▲	▲	:	▲	▲	▲	▲	▲
Serbia	:	▲	:	:	:	:	:	:	▲	:	:	:	–	:	▲	:	▲	:	:	:	:	:
Switzerland	:	▲	▲	▲	:	:	:	▲	▲	▲	:	▲	▲	–	▲	:	▲	:	:	:	:	:
Turkey	●[2]	●	●	:	:	:	●	:	●	:	●	●	●	:	–	●	●	●	●	:	:	●
UK / Ireland	:	▲	▲	▲	:	:	:	▲	▲	▲	:	▲	▲	:	▲	–	▲	:	:	:	:	:
Ukraine	:	▲	:	▲	▲	▲	:	▲	:	▲	▲	:	▲	:	▲	:	–	▲	:	:	▲	:

NOTES

▲ – Visa required (see also general notes above table).

▲[1] – Visa required except for organized tourist visits.

● – Sticker-type tourist visas must be purchased on entering the country (prices vary according to nationality, e.g. UK citizens pay GBP 10 per person, payable in £10 notes only).

●[2] – ● applies to nationals of Austria, Belgium, Hungary, Lithuania, Malta, Netherlands, Norway, Poland, Portugal, Slovakia, Slovenia and Spain.

◇ – Tax of 10 euro is payable on entry to Albania.

Thomas Cook

EUROPEAN RAIL TIMETABLE

DECEMBER 2009

GENERAL INFORMATION

SPECIAL FEATURES

The full version of these tables appears in alternate editions (Feb, Apr, June, Aug, Oct, Dec). Other editions contain a summary.

SPECIAL FEATURES *appear in the following editions:*

January	**Sample Fares**
March	**Cruise Trains and Rail Holidays**
May	**Rail Passes**
July	**Tourist Railways**
September	**High-Speed Trains**
November	**Night Trains**

TIMETABLES

ADVANCE INTERNATIONAL TIMINGS

International Summer Supplements with advance timings from June 13 will appear in editions from February to May 2010

CONTACT DETAILS

Editor	Brendan Fox	+44 (0)1733 416322
Editorial Team	John Potter	+44 (0)1733 417354
	Reuben Turner	+44 (0)1733 417478
	David Turpie	+44 (0)1733 417155
	Chris Woodcock	+44 (0)1733 416408
Head of Travel Books	Lisa Bass	+44 (0)1733 402003
Subscriptions / Sales	Gemma Slater	+44 (0)1733 402002
Advertising	Emma Foster	+44 (0)1733 417382
General enquiries	Mon-Fri 9am-5pm	+44 (0)1733 416477
Fax		+44 (0)1733 416688
e-mail (Sales)	publishing-sales@thomascook.com	
e-mail (Editorial)	timetables@thomascook.com	
Publishing website	www.thomascookpublishing.com	
Thomas Cook website	www.thomascook.com	

Cover picture (monthly edition): a Spanish Altaria train from Murcia del Carmen to Madrid passing Calasparra. © Phil Wormald

Every care has been taken to render the timetable correct in accordance with the latest advices, but changes are constantly being made by the administrations concerned and the publishers cannot hold themselves responsible for the consequences of either changes or inaccuracies.

ISSN 0952-620X Published monthly.
Printed in the UK by CPI William Clowes, Beccles NR34 7TL

Thomas Cook Publishing, Unit 9 Coningsby Road, Peterborough PE3 8SB, United Kingdom
Director of Publishing: Chris Young

A division of Thomas Cook Tour Operations Ltd
Company Registration No. 3772199 England

CALENDAR

CALENDRIER CALENDARIO KALENDER CALENDARIO

2009

JULY

M	T	W	T	F	S	S
①	②	③	④	⑤	⑥	⑦
–	–	1	2	3	4	5
6	7	8	9	10	11	12
13	14	15	16	17	18	19
20	21	22	23	24	25	26
27	28	29	30	31	–	–

AUGUST

M	T	W	T	F	S	S
①	②	③	④	⑤	⑥	⑦
31	–	–	–	–	1	2
3	4	5	6	7	8	9
10	11	12	13	14	15	16
17	18	19	20	21	22	23
24	25	26	27	28	29	30

SEPTEMBER

M	T	W	T	F	S	S
①	②	③	④	⑤	⑥	⑦
–	1	2	3	4	5	6
7	8	9	10	11	12	13
14	15	16	17	18	19	20
21	22	23	24	25	26	27
28	29	30	–	–	–	–

OCTOBER

M	T	W	T	F	S	S
①	②	③	④	⑤	⑥	⑦
–	–	–	1	2	3	4
5	6	7	8	9	10	11
12	13	14	15	16	17	18
19	20	21	22	23	24	25
26	27	28	29	30	31	–

NOVEMBER

M	T	W	T	F	S	S
①	②	③	④	⑤	⑥	⑦
30	–	–	–	–	–	1
2	3	4	5	6	7	8
9	10	11	12	13	14	15
16	17	18	19	20	21	22
23	24	25	26	27	28	29

DECEMBER

M	T	W	T	F	S	S
①	②	③	④	⑤	⑥	⑦
–	1	2	3	4	5	6
7	8	9	10	11	12	13
14	15	16	17	18	19	20
21	22	23	24	25	26	27
28	29	30	31	–	–	–

2009

2010

JANUARY

M	T	W	T	F	S	S
①	②	③	④	⑤	⑥	⑦
–	–	–	–	1	2	3
4	5	6	7	8	9	10
11	12	13	14	15	16	17
18	19	20	21	22	23	24
25	26	27	28	29	30	31

FEBRUARY

M	T	W	T	F	S	S
①	②	③	④	⑤	⑥	⑦
1	2	3	4	5	6	7
8	9	10	11	12	13	14
15	16	17	18	19	20	21
22	23	24	25	26	27	28
–	–	–	–	–	–	–

MARCH

M	T	W	T	F	S	S
①	②	③	④	⑤	⑥	⑦
1	2	3	4	5	6	7
8	9	10	11	12	13	14
15	16	17	18	19	20	21
22	23	24	25	26	27	28
29	30	31	–	–	–	–

APRIL

M	T	W	T	F	S	S
①	②	③	④	⑤	⑥	⑦
–	–	–	1	2	3	4
5	6	7	8	9	10	11
12	13	14	15	16	17	18
19	20	21	22	23	24	25
26	27	28	29	30	–	–

MAY

M	T	W	T	F	S	S
①	②	③	④	⑤	⑥	⑦
31	–	–	–	–	1	2
3	4	5	6	7	8	9
10	11	12	13	14	15	16
17	18	19	20	21	22	23
24	25	26	27	28	29	30

JUNE

M	T	W	T	F	S	S
①	②	③	④	⑤	⑥	⑦
–	1	2	3	4	5	6
7	8	9	10	11	12	13
14	15	16	17	18	19	20
21	22	23	24	25	26	27
28	29	30	–	–	–	–

JULY

M	T	W	T	F	S	S
①	②	③	④	⑤	⑥	⑦
–	–	–	1	2	3	4
5	6	7	8	9	10	11
12	13	14	15	16	17	18
19	20	21	22	23	24	25
26	27	28	29	30	31	–

AUGUST

M	T	W	T	F	S	S
①	②	③	④	⑤	⑥	⑦
30	31	–	–	–	–	1
2	3	4	5	6	7	8
9	10	11	12	13	14	15
16	17	18	19	20	21	22
23	24	25	26	27	28	29

SEPTEMBER

M	T	W	T	F	S	S
①	②	③	④	⑤	⑥	⑦
–	–	1	2	3	4	5
6	7	8	9	10	11	12
13	14	15	16	17	18	19
20	21	22	23	24	25	26
27	28	29	30	–	–	–

OCTOBER

M	T	W	T	F	S	S
①	②	③	④	⑤	⑥	⑦
–	–	–	–	1	2	3
4	5	6	7	8	9	10
11	12	13	14	15	16	17
18	19	20	21	22	23	24
25	26	27	28	29	30	31

NOVEMBER

M	T	W	T	F	S	S
①	②	③	④	⑤	⑥	⑦
1	2	3	4	5	6	7
8	9	10	11	12	13	14
15	16	17	18	19	20	21
22	23	24	25	26	27	28
29	30	–	–	–	–	–

DECEMBER

M	T	W	T	F	S	S
①	②	③	④	⑤	⑥	⑦
–	–	1	2	3	4	5
6	7	8	9	10	11	12
13	14	15	16	17	18	19
20	21	22	23	24	25	26
27	28	29	30	31	–	–

2010

PUBLIC HOLIDAYS 2010

JOURS FÉRIÉS GIORNI FESTIVI FEIERTAGE DÍAS FESTIVOS

The dates given below are those of national public holidays (those falling on a Sunday may not be shown). They do not include regional or half-day holidays. Passengers intending to travel on public holidays, or on days immediately preceding or following them, are strongly recommended to reserve seats and to confirm timings locally. Further information regarding special transport conditions applying on holiday dates may be found in the introduction to each country.

Austria : Jan. 1, 6, Apr. 5, May 1, 13, 24, June 3, Aug. 15, Oct. 26, Nov. 1, Dec. 8, 25, 26.

Belarus : Jan. 1, 7, Mar. 8, 15, Apr. 2, 5, May 1, 9, July 3, Nov. 2, Dec. 25.

Belgium : Jan. 1, Apr. 5, May 1, 13, 24, July 21, Aug. 15, Nov. 1, 11, Dec. 25, 26.

Bosnia-Herzegovina : Jan. 1, Mar. 1, Apr. 2, 5, May 1, Aug. 15, Nov. 1, 25, Dec. 25. *Other religious holidays are observed in certain areas.*

Bulgaria : Jan. 1, Mar. 3, Apr. 5, May 1, 6, 24, Sept. 6, 22, Nov. 1, Dec. 24, 25, 26.

Croatia : Jan. 1, 6, Apr. 5, May 1, June 3, 22, 25, Aug. 5, 15, Oct. 8, Nov. 1, Dec. 25, 26.

Czech Republic : Jan. 1, Apr. 5, May 1, 8, July 5, 6, Sept. 28, Oct. 28, Nov. 17, Dec. 24, 25, 26.

Denmark : Jan. 1, Apr. 1, 2, 5, 30, May 13, 24, June 5, Dec. 25, 26.

Estonia : Jan. 1, Feb. 24, Apr. 2, May 1, June 23, 24, Aug. 20, Dec. 25, 26.

Finland : Jan. 1, 6, Apr. 2, 5, May 1, 13, June 26, Nov. 6, Dec. 6, 25, 26.

France : Jan. 1, Apr. 5, May 1, 8, 13, 24, July 14, Aug. 15, Nov. 1, 11, Dec. 25.

Germany : Jan. 1, Apr. 2, 5, May 1, 13, 24, Oct. 3, Dec. 25, 26. *Regional holidays: see page 361.*

Great Britain : *England & Wales*: Jan. 1, Apr. 2, 5, May 3, 31, Aug. 30, Dec. 25, 26, 27, 28; *Scotland*: Jan. 1, 4, Apr. 2, May 3, 31, Aug. 2, Nov. 30, Dec. 25, 26, 27, 28.

Greece : Jan. 1, 6, Feb. 15, Mar. 25, Apr. 5, May 1, 24, Aug. 15, Oct. 28, Dec. 25, 26.

Hungary : Jan. 1, Mar. 15, Apr. 5, May 1, 24, Aug. 20, Oct. 23, Nov. 1, Dec. 25, 26.

Ireland (Northern) : Jan. 1, Mar. 17, Apr. 2, 5, May 3, 31, July 12, Aug. 30, Dec. 25, 26, 27, 28.

Ireland (Republic) : Jan. 1, Mar. 17, Apr. 5, May 3, June 7, Aug. 2, Oct. 25, Dec. 25, 26.

Italy : Jan. 1, 6, Apr. 5, 25, May 1, June 2, Aug. 15, Nov. 1, Dec. 8, 25, 26.

Latvia : Jan. 1, Apr. 2, 5, May 1, 4, June 23, 24, Nov. 18, Dec. 25, 26, 31.

Lithuania : Jan. 1, Feb. 16, Mar. 11, Apr. 5, May 1, June 24, July 6, Aug. 15, Nov. 1, Dec. 25, 26.

Luxembourg : Jan. 1, Apr. 5, May 1, 13, 24, June 23, Aug. 15, Nov. 1, Dec. 25, 26.

Macedonia : Jan. 1, 6, 7, Mar. 8, Apr. 5, May 1, Aug. 2, Sept. 8.

Moldova : Jan. 1, 8, Mar. 8, Apr. 5, May 1, 9, Aug. 27, 31.

Netherlands : Jan. 1, Apr. 2, 5, 30, May 5, 13, 24, Dec. 25, 26.

Norway : Jan. 1, Apr. 1, 2, 5, May 1, 13, 17, 24, Dec. 25, 26.

Poland : Jan. 1, Apr. 5, May 1, 3, June 3, Aug. 15, Nov. 1, 11, Dec. 25, 26.

Portugal : Jan. 1, Apr. 2, 25, May 1, June 3, 10, Aug. 15, Oct. 5, Nov. 1, Dec. 1, 8, 25.

Romania : Jan. 1, 2, Apr. 5, May 1, Dec. 1, 25, 26.

Russia : Jan. 1, 7, Feb. 23, Mar. 8, May 1, 3, 9, 10, June 12, 14, Nov. 4.

Serbia : Jan. 1, 7, Apr. 2, 5, 27, May 1, 9.

Slovakia : Jan. 1, 6, Apr. 2, 5, May 1, 8, July 5, Aug. 29, Sept. 1, 15, Nov. 1, 17, Dec. 24, 25, 26.

Slovenia : Jan. 1, 2, Feb. 8, Apr. 5, 27, May 1, 2, June 25, Aug. 15, Oct. 31, Nov. 1, Dec. 25, 26.

Spain : Jan. 1, 6*, Mar. 19*, Apr. 1*, 2, May 1, Aug. 15*, 16*, Oct. 12, Nov. 1, Dec. 6, 8, 25.
* *Regional.*

Sweden : Jan. 1, 6, Apr. 2, 5, May 1, 13, June 6, 26, Nov. 6, Dec. 25, 26.

Switzerland : Jan. 1, 2, Apr. 2, 5, May 13, 24, Aug. 1, Dec. 25, 26. Other regional holidays: Mar. 19, May 1, June 3, Aug. 15, Sept. 19, Nov. 1, Dec. 8.

Ukraine : Jan. 1, 7, Mar. 8, Apr. 2, 5, May 1, 2, 9, 24, June 28, Aug. 24.

MOVABLE HOLIDAYS

Fêtes mobiles – Feste mobile
Bewegliche Feste – Fiestas movibles

	2010	2011
Good Friday	Apr. 2	Apr. 22
Easter Monday	Apr. 5	Apr. 25
Ascension Day	May 13	June 2
Whit Monday (Pentecost)	May 24	June 13
Corpus Christi	June 3	June 23

TIME COMPARISON

COMPARAISON DES HEURES COMPARAZIONE DELLE ORE ZEITVERGLEICH COMPARACIÓN DE LAS HORAS

West European Time	*WINTER: GMT* *SUMMER: GMT +1*	Canaries, Faroes, Ireland, Portugal, United Kingdom; Iceland *(GMT all year)*
Central European Time	*WINTER: GMT +1* *SUMMER: GMT +2*	Albania, Austria, Belgium, Bosnia, Croatia, Czech Rep., Denmark, France, Germany, Hungary, Italy, Luxembourg, Macedonia, Malta, Montenegro, Netherlands, Norway, Poland, Serbia, Slovakia, Slovenia, Spain, Sweden, Switzerland
East European Time	*WINTER: GMT +2* *SUMMER: GMT +3*	Belarus, Bulgaria, Cyprus, Estonia, Finland, Greece, Kaliningrad, Latvia, Lithuania, Moldova, Romania, Turkey, Ukraine
Moskva Time	*WINTER: GMT +3* *SUMMER: GMT +4*	Western Russia *(except Kaliningrad)*

In 2010 clocks are advanced by one hour in all countries (except Iceland) between 0100 GMT on Mar. 28 and 0100 GMT on Oct. 31 *(GMT = Greenwich Mean Time = UTC)*

What's new this month

This edition shows, where possible, the new winter schedules from **December 13**. There are significant changes to both international and domestic rail services throughout Europe from this date. We have managed to obtain advance information from almost all European countries in time for this edition, but inevitably some railways were still making decisions about their services as we went to press, and our monthly editions will, of course, be updated as information is received.

Only partial information has been received from **Italy** and **Poland**, as shown under the relevant headings below, and details of local services in **FYRO Macedonia** and **Bosnia-Herzegovina** are still awaited. We also understand that changes in **Portugal** are expected from December 13, but no details were available as we went to press.

CAR-CARRYING TRAINS

Rail Europe has announced that the car-carrying services from Calais to the South of France will no longer operate. These ran once a week in summer to five different destinations. The nearest alternative for customers from the UK and the Benelux countries is 's-Hertogenbosch, with car-carrying services to Avignon, Fréjus, Livorno and Alessandria between June and September.

INTERNATIONAL

Most international trains are affected by the schedule change on December 13. For further details of the principal changes see pages 38 and 39.

GREAT BRITAIN

Highlight of the new timetable in Britain is the introduction of *Southeastern's* full high-speed service between London and destinations in Kent (Table **100**). *South West Trains* has a new timetable on the Waterloo to Exeter route (Table **113**) and no longer serves destinations west of Exeter.

Trains that formerly terminated at Derby operated by *East Midlands Trains* have been extended to Sheffield to give the 'steel city' a train from London every 30 minutes for most of the day.

Operation of long distance services on the East Coast Main Line was handed over to the Government appointed *Directly Operated Railways* on Friday November 13. Formerly operated by *National Express East Coast*, the new operator is trading as *East Coast*.

IRELAND

The Belfast to Dublin line reopened on November 16 ahead of schedule, following the reconstruction of the viaduct at Malahide.

Iarnród Éireann introduced its new timetable from November 29 with a mixture of cuts, additions and faster services. The 0630 Cork to Dublin service, stopping just at Mallow, now takes two and a half hours, a reduction of 15 minutes, but one evening service each way between Dublin and Cork has been withdrawn. The Dublin - Limerick service has less direct services but many more connections are available via Limerick Junction. All Dublin - Waterford services are now faster, including a new fast early morning Waterford - Dublin, which stops only at Carlow and takes two hours.

The new Limerick - Ennis - Athenry - Galway service, part of the Western Rail Corridor, is due to open in January (a date of January 10 has been mooted), and the timetable can be seen in new Table **242**. Passenger services last ran over this line between Ennis and Athenry in 1976. To make room, Table **238**, which showed the Bus Éireann service between Dublin and Tralee via Limerick, has been deleted.

Northern Ireland Railways issued a new timetable from December 13, with minor changes on the Belfast - Londonderry route.

FRANCE

Amongst the changes to TGV services are a new daily train between Paris and Calais Fréthun (Table **265**), and a new Montpellier - Nancy - Metz TGV (Table **379**) replacing a conventional Lyon - Metz train plus the summer dated Cerbère - Metz / Metz - Portbou **4240 / 4340**. There is a new early-morning train from Perpignan to Paris and an additional TGV from Paris to Montpellier (1020 weekdays, 1420 on Sundays). There are also later trains from Lille to Marseille on Fridays and Sundays from April, also northbound on Sundays.

In Table **390**, as well as the recasting of the Paris - Mulhouse - Basel - Zürich service (mentioned under the international heading), the remote TGV Meuse station sees an extra train to and from Paris (a Nancy train), whilst the Paris - Frankfurt train which used to call at Lorraine TGV no longer does so. There has been a major recast of the Toulouse - Tarbes - Bayonne service (Table **325**) with faster and more frequent trains. Paris to Amiens (Table **260**) has also been revised, with fewer fast services, particularly at weekends, but more regional trains.

Regarding night trains, the Metz - Portbou train is combined with the Luxembourg - Nice (Table **379**) joining at Dijon, giving a new facility from Luxembourg to Portbou. The weekend Strasbourg to Portbou and Nice portions are also combined with this train. The Nantes to Nice and Quimper - Nantes - Lyon night trains were expected to be withdrawn, but literally hours before our press deadline we learned of their reprieve, and have put basic details into a temporary table on page 211.

BELGIUM & NETHERLANDS

The *FYRA* high-speed shuttle service between Amsterdam and Rotterdam (included in Table **450**) has been retimed and now runs daily, as does the Antwerpen to Noorderkempen service (Table **410**).

ITALY

December 13 sees the completion of the core Italian high-speed line which now stretches from Torino to Salerno via Milano, Roma and Napoli. The main event is the opening of the difficult Bologna to Firenze stretch, the vast majority of which is in tunnel. Journey times over this portion of the line have reduced by 20 minutes to just 37 minutes. The other two new sections are Novara to Milano, and the final 19 km into Napoli from the north.

The headline journey time between Milano Centrale and Roma Termini (Table **642**) is now 2 hours and 59 minutes, a saving of 30 minutes on the current fastest timings. There are also a small number of Milano - Roma trains serving the suburban stations of Milano Rogoredo and Roma Tiburtina rather than the main stations - these take just 2 hours and 45 minutes.

Needless to say, there are huge changes to schedules throughout the country, with new services taking advantage of parts of the high-speed line. Advance schedules are difficult to obtain from Italy, but nevertheless we have managed to include in our tables timings for all *AV*, *ES*, *ESc*, *EC* and *EN* trains. No other timings were available as we went to press so the Italian tables should be used with caution, especially local trains.

SPAIN

Trenhotel **996/995** *Gibralfaro* Barcelona - Zaragoza - Córdoba - Málaga and **946/945** *Antonio Machado* Barcelona - Zaragoza - Sevilla - Cádiz both now call at Madrid Puerta de Atocha, with **995** and **945** departing Málaga 36 minutes and Cádiz 45 minutes earlier respectively.

In Table **650**, two pairs of *AVE* trains have been withdrawn between Madrid and Barcelona. In Table **670** a third service has been added between València and Zaragoza via Teruel; the compulsory reservation *Media Distancia* calls only at Teruel enroute, whilst other services have been retimed. Train **9386**, the 1805 Madrid - Huelva (Table **671**) now runs one hour later, and in Tables **681/682** - *Trenhotel* **752/751** *Atlántico* Madrid - Ferrol no longer runs on Mondays.

RENFE have introduced another new category *AVE-Lanzadera* which are regional high-speed gauge-changing trains. Contrary to some sources, we understand that **940/941** *Picasso* Bilbao - Málaga will continue running in 2010 on as yet unannounced dates. Further changes to services in Spain are expected from January 31, and we understand that certain domestic night trains will no longer run on Saturday nights.

PORTUGAL

Timetables changes were expected from December 13, but details were not available as we went to press.

DENMARK

The infrequent service to the port of Gedser ceases on December 12.

SWEDEN

During the reconstruction of Malmö Central station, certain services are calling at suburban stations instead. Malmö Syd / Svågertorp has been added to several tables to assist with connections.

CONTINUED ON PAGE 37

EXPLANATION OF STANDARD SYMBOLS

	EXPLANATION OF SYMBOLS	*EXPLICATION DES SIGNES*	*DELUCIDAZIONE DEI SEGNI*	*ZEICHENERKLÄRUNG*	*EXPLICACIÓN DE LOS SIGNOS*
	SERVICES	**SERVICES**	**SERVIZI**	**DIENSTE**	**SERVICIOS**
12	Through service (1st and 2nd class seats)	Relation directe (places assises 1re et 2e classe)	Relazione diretta (con posti di 1a e 2a classe)	Direkte Verbindung (Sitzplätze 1. und 2. Klasse)	Relación directa (con asientos de 1a y 2a clase)
🛏	Sleeping car	Voiture-lits	Carrozza letti	Schlafwagen	Coche-camas
	Couchette car	Voiture-couchettes	Carrozza cuccette	Liegewagen	Coche-literas
✕	Restaurant car	Voiture-restaurant	Carrozza ristorante	Speisewagen	Coche-restaurante
🍸	Snacks and drinks available *(see page 8)*	Voiture-bar ou vente ambulante *(voir page 8)*	Carrozza bar o servizio di buffet *(vedere pagina 8)*	Imbiss und Getränke im Zug *(siehe Seite 8)*	Servicio de cafetería o bar móvil *(véase pág. 8)*
2	Second class only	Uniquement deuxième classe	Sola seconda classe	Nur zweite Klasse	Sólo segunda clase
🚌	Bus or coach service	Service routier	Servizio automobilistico	Buslinie	Servicio de autobuses
🚢	Shipping service	Service maritime	Servizio marittimo	Schifffahrtslinie	Servicio marítimo
	DAYS OF RUNNING	**JOURS DE CIRCULATION**	**GIORNI DI EFFETTUAZIONE**	**VERKEHRSTAGE**	**DÍAS DE CIRCULACIÓN**
⚒	Mondays to Saturdays except holidays*	Du lundi au samedi, sauf les fêtes*	Dal lunedì al sabato, salvo i giorni festivi*	Montag bis Samstag außer Feiertage*	De lunes a sábado, excepto festivos*
Ⓐ	Mondays to Fridays except holidays*	Du lundi au vendredi, sauf les fêtes*	Dal lunedì al venerdì, salvo i giorni festivi*	Montag bis Freitag außer Feiertage*	De lunes a viernes, excepto festivos*
Ⓑ	Daily except Saturdays	Tous les jours sauf les samedis	Giornalmente, salvo il sabato	Täglich außer Samstag	Diario excepto sábados
Ⓒ	Saturdays, Sundays and holidays*	Les samedis, dimanches et fêtes*	Sabato, domenica e giorni festivi*	Samstage, Sonn- und Feiertage*	Sábados, domingos y festivos*
†	Sundays and holidays*	Les dimanches et fêtes*	Domenica e giorni festivi*	Sonn- und Feiertage*	Domingos y festivos*
①②	Mondays, Tuesdays	Les lundis, mardis	Lunedì, martedì	Montag, Dienstag	Lunes, martes
③④	Wednesdays, Thurdays	Les mercredis, jeudis	Mercoledì, giovedì	Mittwoch, Donnerstag	Miércoles, jueves
⑤⑥	Fridays, Saturdays	Les vendredis, samedis	Venerdì, sabato	Freitag, Samstag	Viernes, sábados
⑦	Sundays	Les dimanches	Domenica	Sonntag	Domingos
①–④	Mondays to Thursdays	Des lundis aux jeudis	Dal lunedì al giovedì	Montag bis Donnerstag	De lunes a jueves
	OTHER SYMBOLS	**AUTRES SIGNES**	**ALTRI SIMBOLI**	**SONSTIGE SYMBOLE**	**OTROS SÍMBOLOS**
IC **29**	Train number (**bold figures** above train times)	Numéro du train (en **caractères gras** au-dessus de l'horaire du train)	Numero del treno (in **neretto** sopra gli orari del treno)	Zugnummer (über den Fahrplanzeiten in **fetter Schrift** gesetzt)	Número del tren (figura en **negrita** encima del horario del tren)
◆	See footnotes (listed by train number)	Renvoi aux notes données en bas de page (dans l'ordre numérique des trains)	Vedi in calce alla pagina l'annotazione corrispondente al numero del treno	Siehe die nach Zugnummern geordneten Fußnoten	Véase al pie de la página la nota correspondiente al número del tren
R	Reservation compulsory	Réservation obligatoire	Prenotazione obbligatoria	Reservierung erforderlich	Reserva obligatoria
🏛	Frontier station	Gare frontalière	Stazione di frontiera	Grenzbahnhof	Estación fronteriza
✈	Airport	Aéroport	Aeroporto	Flughafen	Aeropuerto
|	Train does not stop	Sans arrêt	Il treno non ferma qui	Zug hält nicht	El tren no para aquí
—	Separates two trains in the same column between which no connection is possible	Sépare deux trains de la même colonne qui ne sont pas en correspondance	Separa due treni della stessa colonna che non sono in coincidenza	Trennt zwei in derselben Spalte angegebene Züge, zwischen denen kein Anschluß besteht	Separa dos trenes de la misma columna entre los cuales no hay enlace
→	Continued in later column	Suite dans une colonne à droite	Continuazione più avanti a destra	Fortsetzung weiter rechts	Continuación a la derecha
←	Continued from earlier column	Suite d'une colonne à gauche	Seguito di una colonna a sinistra	Fortsetzung von links	Continuación desde la izquierda
v.v.	Vice versa	Vice versa	Viceversa	Umgekehrt	A la inversa
	** Public holiday dates for each country are given on page 2.* *Other, special symbols are explained in table footnotes or in the introduction to each country.*	** Les dates des fêtes légales nationales sont données en page 2.* *D'autres signes particuliers sont expliqués dans les notes ou bien dans l'avant-propos relatif à chaque pays.*	** Per le date dei giorni festivi civili nei diversi paesi vedere pagina 2.* *Altri segni particolari vengono spiegati nelle note in calce ai quadri o nella introduzione attinente a ogni paese.*	** Gesetzlichen Feiertage der jeweiligen Länder finden Sie auf Seite 2.* *Besondere Symbole sind in den Fußnoten bzw. in der Einleitung zu den einzelnen Ländern erklärt.*	** Las fechas de los días festivos en cada país figuran en la página 2.* *La explicación de otros signos particulares se da en las notas o en el preámbulo correspondiente a cada país.*

What is the European Rail Timetable?

The Thomas Cook European Rail Timetable is a concise guide to rail and ferry schedules throughout Europe. Needless to say, it cannot be comprehensive (it would run into thousands of pages), but through our knowledge and experience, together with valuable feedback from our readers, we can select those services which we believe will satisfy the needs of most travellers.

When do the services change?

There is a major annual timetable change in mid-December affecting almost all European countries, with a second change in mid-June affecting most. There are, of course, exceptions. For example, the British summer timetable starts in late May, Sweden changes again in mid-August, and Russia and the other CIS countries have their main change at the end of May. Many holiday areas also have separate timetables for the high-summer period. In fact, changes can happen at any time of year, and railways issue amendments either on set dates or as and when necessary. Engineering work also causes frequent changes. Shipping schedules can change at any time.

Why do I need a subscription?

Apart from getting the latest available schedules, you will also be benefitting from advance information for the following season in relevant editions (see below) and also special features in alternate editions, covering the following topics: *January* **Sample Fares**, *March* **Cruise Trains and Rail Holidays**, *May* **Rail Passes**, *July* **Tourist Railways**, *September* **High-Speed Trains**, and *November* **Night Trains**. You may wish to keep a year's worth of timetables on your bookshelf so that you can refer to these features.

Note that the Rail Passes feature also appears in the *Independent Travellers Edition*, which is available from bookshops in Summer and Winter editions (based on the June and December monthly editions but with additional country by country information in a special section at the front).

What about forthcoming schedule changes?

A major benefit of a full subscription is obtaining the latest available details of forthcoming changes to International services. Advance summer timings start in our February edition with an 18-page Summer Supplement, which is expanded to 34 pages in March and the full 50 pages in April and May. Similarly, Winter Supplements appear in our September, October and November editions, leading up to the new schedules from mid-December.

How are the trains selected for inclusion?

People travel for many reasons, whether for leisure, business, sightseeing, visiting friends or relations, or just for the fun of it, and there are no hard and fast rules for selecting the services that we show. Naturally, major towns and inter-city services are shown as a matter of course, but the level of smaller places and local trains shown will depend on the country and even the area. It's surprising just how many minor lines we manage to squeeze in! Generally we will show a greater number of local trains in areas which are popular tourist destinations or where other services are sparse.

It is not possible to show suburban trains within cities or conurbations, or most outer-suburban routes to places close to large cities. However, where there are places of particular interest or importance in this category we do try to show brief details of frequency and journey time.

When should I use the International section?

The rail tables are divided into two sections - International (Tables **10** to **99**) and Country by Country (Tables **100** to **1999**). For some international services between adjacent countries (for example Stockholm - Oslo or Hamburg - Århus) it is necessary to use the relevant Country tables - the index or maps will guide you. Local trains which cross international frontiers will usually only be found in the Country sections.

Some international trains also carry passengers internally within each country and will therefore be found in the Country tables as well as the International section. Some services are primarily for international travel and will therefore only be found in the International section - this includes *Eurostar* trains (London - Paris / Brussels) and *Thalys* services between Paris and Brussels, as well as certain long-distance night trains.

What about places outside Europe?

No problem. Our sister publication, the **Thomas Cook Overseas Timetable**, is packed with rail, bus and ferry schedules for everywhere you can think of outside Europe, and plenty of other places you have probably never heard of! It is published six times per year and further details can be found at the back of this timetable, or on our website.

You can buy all our timetables, rail maps and guidebooks from our online bookstore at **www.thomascookpublishing.com**. There is a 10% discount for timetable orders.

HOW TO USE THE TIMETABLE

Using the index

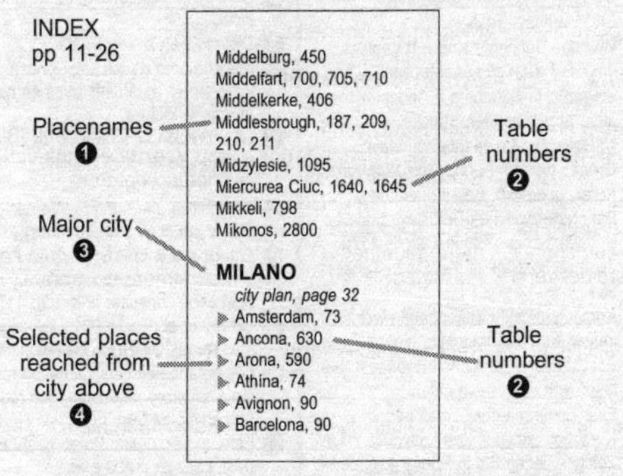

Look up the two places between which you are travelling. It can often be helpful to start your search from the *smaller* of the two locations. ❺

Using the maps

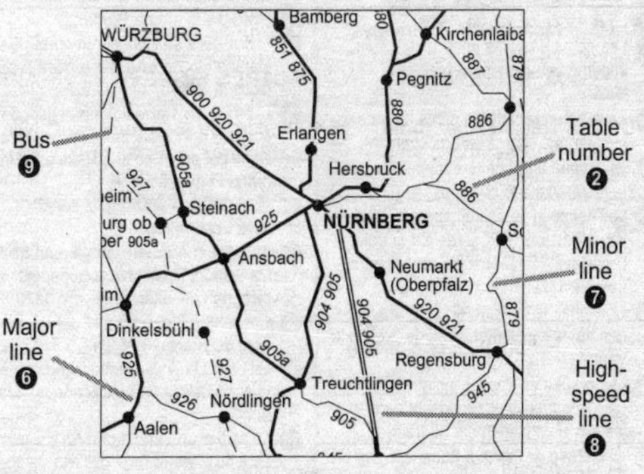

The maps can be the quickest way of finding the required table number, if you already know the geographical location of the places required. ❿

COMMENT TROUVER VOTRE TRAIN

❶ Localité.
❷ Numéros des tableaux.
❸ Grande ville.
❹ Localités sélectionnées à gagner de la grande ville en haut.
❺ Cherchez les deux bouts du parcours désiré sur la liste des villes. Commencer par la ville de moindre importance peut faciliter la recherche.
❻ Ligne principale.
❼ Ligne secondaire.
❽ Ligne à grande vitesse.
❾ Liaison en autocar.
❿ La consultation des cartes – si vous savez déjà la location géographique de vos points de départ et d'arrivée – est le moyen le plus rapide de repérer les numéros des tableaux relatifs à votre parcours.

COME TROVARE IL VOSTRO TRENO

❶ Località.
❷ Numeri dei quadri-orario.
❸ Grandi città.
❹ Principali destinazione raggiungibili dalla località in neretto sopra.
❺ Cercate le localita' tra le quali dovrete viaggiare; spesso può essere di aiuto iniziare la ricerca dalla località più piccola.
❻ Principale linea ferroviaria.
❼ Linea ferroviaria secondaria.
❽ Linea ad alta velocità.
❾ Autobus.
❿ Le mappe sono il metodo più rapido per trovare i numeri dei quadri-orario di cui avete bisogno, quando gia' siete a conoscenza della collocazione geografica delle localita' di partenza e arrivo del vostro viaggio.

WIE FINDE ICH MEINEN ZUG?

❶ Ortsname.
❷ Tabellennummer.
❸ Großstadt.
❹ Knotenpunkte erreichbar von der Großstadt oben.
❺ Suchen Sie Ihre Start- und Endbahnhof im Ortsverzeichnis. Dazu empfehlen wir, Ihre Suche aus der Richtung des *kleineren* Ortes aufzunehmen.
❻ Hauptstrecke.
❼ Nebenstrecke.
❽ Hochgeschwindigkeitsstrecke.
❾ Busverbindung.
❿ Kennen Sie die geographische Lage der Ausgangs- und Bestimmungsorte Ihrer Reise, dann empfehlen wir einen Blick in die im Kursbuch enthaltene Übersichtskarte.

COMO BUSCAR SU TREN

❶ Localidad.
❷ Números de los cuadros horarios.
❸ Gran ciudad.
❹ Principales destinos accesibles a través de esta localidad.
❺ Busque los dos lugares a través de los cuales viaja. Normalmente facilita la búsqueda empezar por la localidad más pequeña.
❻ Línea principal.
❼ Línea secundaria.
❽ Línea de alta velocidad.
❾ Línea de autobuses.
❿ Los mapas pueden ser la forma más rápida de encontrar los cuadros que debe consultar, si ya conoce el punto de inicio y conclusión de su viaje.

Numbers in circles refer to translations below

Reading the tables

Trains run daily unless otherwise shown by symbol or footnote ⓯

d. = depart, a. = arrive (the first time in a column is always a departure time, the last is an arrival). ⓮

Table number and route ❶

Station names in local language ❷

Distance from Praha in km ❸

Important stations are shown in **bold** for clarity ❹

Indented station: shows a branch off the main route of the table ❺

Train category (where shown) ⓭

Train number (where shown) ⓬

Standard symbols (e.g. Ⓐ, 🅁, ✕) are explained on page 4.

Other symbols (e.g. ⊖) and letters (**E**, **r**) are explained below the table.

◆ means footnotes are listed by train number. ⓫

1150 PRAHA - BRNO - WIEN / BRATISLAVA

km	*Sample table*		271	*EC* 71	*EC*• 131	*EC* 345	*SC** 15	*EC* 273	*EC* 73	475	*EC* 275	*EC* 103
				✕			🍷	✕	✕			✕
			Ⓐ		◆	◆	🅁		⊖	◆	E	◆
	Praha Holešovice	d.	...	...	...	...	...	0730	0830	...	0930	...
0	**Praha** hlavni ▷	d.	...	...	...	0528	0557	|	|	0918	|	...
62	Kolín ▷	d.	...	...	...	0613	|	0813	|	1013	1013	...
154	**Pardubice** ▷	d.	...	...	...	0636	0659	0836	0936	1036	1036	...
164	Česká Třebová ▷	d.	...	*0551*	...	0711	|	0911	|	1111	1111	...
255	**Brno** hlavní	a.	...	*0711*	...	0814	0825	1014	1114	1214	1214	...
255	**Brno** hlavní **1162**	d.	...	0716	...	0816	0827	1016	1116	1216	1216	...
314	**Břeclav** **1162**	a.	...	0751	...	0851	0900	1051	1151	1251	1251	...
314	**Břeclav** **991**	d.	0553	0802	0755	0855	0902	1055	1202	1255	1255	1302
	Wien Süd **991**	a.	|	0902	|	|	1002	|	1302	|	|	1402
332	Kúty 🏛	d.	0610	...	0810	0910	...	1110	...	1310	1310	...
396	**Bratislava** Hlavná	a.	0653**r**	...	0853	0947	...	1147	...	1347	1347	...
	Budapest Keleti **1170**	a.	...	...	...	1232	...	1432	...	...	...	...

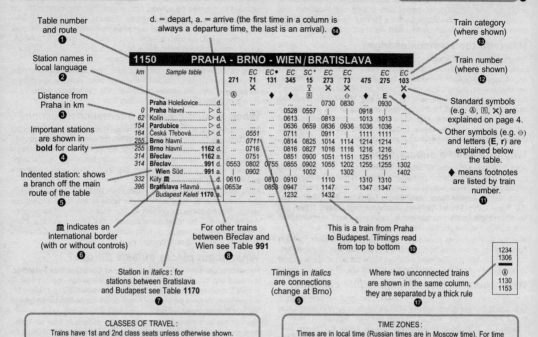

🏛 indicates an international border (with or without controls) ❻

Station in *italics*: for stations between Bratislava and Budapest see Table **1170** ❼

For other trains between Břeclav and Wien see Table **991** ❽

Timings in *italics* are connections (change at Brno) ❾

This is a train from Praha to Budapest. Timings read from top to bottom ❿

Where two unconnected trains are shown in the same column, they are separated by a thick rule ⓱

1234
1306
▬▬
Ⓐ
1130
1153

CLASSES OF TRAVEL:
Trains have 1st and 2nd class seats unless otherwise shown. However, local trains may only have 2nd class seats. ⓯

TIME ZONES:
Times are in local time (Russian times are in Moscow time). For time zones see page 2. Timings are given in 24 hour clock (see page 9). ⓰

COMMENT LIRE LES TABLEAUX

❶ Numéro et parcours du tableau.
❷ Nom de la gare en langue locale.
❸ La distance en km de Praha.
❹ Les noms de gares importantes sont imprimés en **gras** pour faciliter la lecture.
❺ La mise en retrait des noms de gares indique une ligne d'embranchement.
❻ 🏛 indique une frontière internationale (avec ou sans le contrôle).
❼ Les noms de gares imprimés en *italique*: vous trouverez des gares sur le trajet Bratislava - Budapest en consultant le tableau **1170**.
❽ Consultez le tableau **991** pour trouver des trains supplémentaires de Břeclav à Wien.
❾ Les heures en *italique* indiquent une *correspondance* et supposent dans tous les cas un changement de train.
❿ Ici un train de Praha à Budapest. Lire de haut en bas.
⓫ Les signes conventionnels sont expliqués à la page 4. Les autres signes et lettres sont expliqués en bas du tableau. Le symbole ◆ à l'en-tête d'une colonne signifie qu'il faut consulter le note qui porte le numéro du train concerné.
⓬ Le numéro du train (en cas échéant).
⓭ Indication de catégorie (en cas échéant).
⓮ d. = départ, a. = arrivée. Pour chaque train la *première* mention est toujours une heure de *départ*, la *dernière* toujours une heure d'*arrivée*.
⓯ Sauf indication contraire, les trains circulent *tous les jours* et y compris des places assises de 1ère et 2ème classe.
⓰ Toutes les indications horaires sont données en heures locales (voir page 2). En Russie c'est à l'heure Moskva.
⓱ Deux trains de la même colonne qui ne sont pas en correspondance sont separés par une règle épaisse.

COME SI CONSULTA UN QUADRO ORARIO

❶ Numero del quadro e percorso.
❷ Nome della stazione nella lingua locale.
❸ Distanze in km da Praha.
❹ I nomi delle stazioni piu' importante sono stampati in **neretto** per renderne più facile la lettura.
❺ I nomi delle stazioni rientrati rispetto alla colonna principale indicano una diramazione dal percorso principale del quadro-orario in questione.
❻ 🏛 indica una stazione di confine (con o senza controllo).
❼ Stazioni in *corsivo*: per gli orari tra le stazione di Bratislava e Budapest bisogna consultare il quadro **1170**.
❽ Consultare il quadro **991** per ulteriori treni da Břeclav a Wien.
❾ Gli orari *in corsivo* si riferiscono a servizi *in coincidenza* che implicano un cambio di treno.
❿ Questo e' un treno da Praha a Budapest. La lettura viene fatta dall'alto verso il basso.
⓫ I simboli convenzionali sono spiegate a pagina 4. Altri simboli e lettere sono spiegati sotto il quadro-orario in questione. Il simbolo ◆ all'inizio di una colonna-orario significa che bisogna fare riferimento alla nota corrispondente al numero del treno in questione.
⓬ Numero del treno (quando indicato).
⓭ Classificazione del treno (quando indicato).
⓮ d. = partenza, a. = arrivo. Notare che l'orario che compare per *primo* nel quadro-orario è sempre un l'orario di *partenza*, mentre quello che compare per *ultimo* è sempre l'orario di *arrivo*.
⓯ Se non ci sono altre indicazioni i treni si intendono giornalieri, con prima e seconda classe di viaggio.
⓰ Gli orari sono sempre espressi in ora locale (in Russia e' utilizzati l'ora di Mosca). Per informazioni sui fusi orari vedere a pagina 2.
⓱ Quando nella colonna-orario ci sono due treni che non sono in coincidenza tra loro, questo e' indicato dalla linea in grassetto che li separa.

WIE LESE ICH DIE FAHRPLÄNE

❶ Tabellennummer und Strecke.
❷ Bahnhof in der Landessprache.
❸ Entfernungsangabe.
❹ Wichtige Bahnhöfe sind **fett** gedruckt um das Lesen zu vereinfachen.
❺ Eingerückte Bahnhöfe befinden sich auf einer abzweigenden Strecke.
❻ 🏛 Bezeichnet eine internationale Grenze (mit oder ohne Grenzkontrolle).
❼ *Kursiv* gedruckte Bahnhofsnamen: Bahnhöfe zwischen Bratislava und Budapest finden Sie in Tabelle **1170**.
❽ Zusätzliche Züge finden Sie in Tabelle **991**.
❾ *Kursiv* gedruckte Zeitangaben weisen immer auf das Umsteigen hin.
❿ Ein Zug von Praha nach Budapest. Sie lesen von oben nach unten.
⓫ Eine Erklärung der überall in dem Kursbuch verwendeten konventionellen Zeichen finden Sie auf Seite 4. Anderen Zeichen und Buchstaben finden Sie unter der Fahrplantabelle. Das Zeichen ◆ im Kopf der Zugspalte bedeutet: Sehen Sie bei der Fußnote des Zuges mit der betreffenden Zugnummer nach.
⓬ Zugnummer (wo zutreffend).
⓭ Zuggattung (wo zutreffend).
⓮ d. = Abfahrt, a. = Ankunft. Es handelt sich stets bei der ersten für einen Zug angegebenen Zeit um eine Abfahrtzeit, bei der letzten um eine Ankunftzeit.
⓯ Sofern nicht anders angemeldet, verkehren die Züge *täglich*. Im Allgemeinen führen die Züge die 1. und 2. Wagenklasse.
⓰ Fahrzeiten sind immer in der jeweiligen Landeszeit angegeben (Seite 2). Russische Fahrzeiten sind auf Moskauer Zeit.
⓱ Im Falle von zwei Züge in der gleichen Spalte ohne Anschlussmöglichkeit, liegt das Zeichen ▬▬ zwischen den Zügen.

COMO LEER LOS CUADROS

❶ Número y línea del cuadro.
❷ Nombre de las estaciones en el idioma local.
❸ Distancia en km de Praga.
❹ Los nombres de las estaciones más importantes están impresas en **negrita** facilitar la lectura.
❺ La impresión sangrada de los nombres de estas estaciones significa un ramal de la línea principal.
❻ 🏛 significa una frontera internacional (con o sin control de aduanas).
❼ Estaciones impresas en *cursiva*: para las estaciones entre Bratislava y Budapest debe consultar el cuadro **1170**.
❽ Consultar el cuadro **991** para encontrar más trenes desde Břeclav hasta Viena.
❾ Los horarios en cursiva, hacen referencia a servicios de enlace, que requieren un cambio de tren.
❿ Esto un tren desde Praga hasta Budapest. Leer de arriba a abajo.
⓫ La explicación de los signos convencionales se da en la página 4. Ostros simbolos y letras se explican al pie del cuadro. El símbolo ◆ en el encabezamiento de la columna quiere decir: consulte la nota que lleva el número del tren interesado.
⓬ Número de tren (si se indica).
⓭ Tipo de tren (si se indica).
⓮ d. = salida, a. = llegada. Nótese que el primer horario indicado en las columnas es siempre un horario de salida, y el último un horario de llegada.
⓯ Salvo indicación contraria, los trenes circulan a *diario* y llevan plazas sentadas de primera y segunda clases.
⓰ Todas las indicaciones horarias son en horario local (Para Rusia se utiliza la hora local de Moscú). Para comprobar las franjas horarias mirar la página 2. Los horarios utilizan el sistema horario de 24h (ver página 9).
⓱ Cuando dos trenes que no tienen conexión aparecen en la misma columna, estos se encuentran separados por el símbolo ▬▬.

Reading the footnotes

These footnotes relate to the sample table on page 6 ❶

In certain tables, footnotes are listed by train number, shown by ♦ on relevant trains ❷

♦ – **NOTES** (LISTED BY TRAIN NUMBERS)

102/3 – POLONIA – 12 ✕ Warszawa - Ostrava - Břeclav - Wien and v.v.

131 – MORAVIA – 12 Bohumin - Ostrava - Břeclav - Bratislava.

345 – AVALA – 12 ✕ Praha - Bratislava - Budapest - Beograd. Conveys on ⑤ June 12 - Sept. 18 2 cl. Praha - Beograd (**335**) - Thessaloniki.

475 – JADRAN – June 19 - Sept. 4. 1, 2 cl., 2 cl., 2 Praha - Bratislava - Zagreb - Split (Table **92**); 12 Praha - Bratislava.

E – SLOVAN, not June 19 - Sept. 4.

r – 0659 on ©.

▷ – See also Table **1160**.

⊖ – Runs 10 mins later on Aug. 15.

• – *Ex* in Slovakia.

⁎ – Pendolino tilting train. Classified *EC* in Austria.

OTHER TRAIN NAMES:

71 – GUSTAV MAHLER

73 – FRANZ SCHUBERT

Letters and symbols may be found above the timings (e.g. **E**) or against individual times (e.g. **r**). Symbols may also appear in the station column (e.g. ▷). ❻

Train names are sometimes listed separately. ❺

Train **345** is named 'AVALA' and runs daily from Praha to Beograd with 1st and 2nd class seats and a restaurant car. On Fridays June 12 to September 18, a through couchette car runs from Praha to Thessaloniki, attached to train **335** between Beograd and Thessaloniki. ❸

Train **475** is named 'JADRAN' and runs only from June 19 to September 4. It has a sleeper, couchettes and second class seats from Praha to Split via Bratislava and Zagreb, as well as first and second class seats only going as far as Bratislava. Further details will be found in Table **92**. ❹

Always read the footnotes; they may contain important information. Standard symbols are explained on page 4. ❼

Dates shown are where a train **starts** its journey (unless otherwise noted). Some notes show both directions of the train (e.g. **102/3**) with "and v.v." ❽

FURTHER HINTS ON READING THE TIMETABLE

- Refer to the introduction to each country for important information such as train types, supplements, compulsory reservation, and the dates of validity of the timings. Exceptions are noted in individual tables.
- For dates of public holidays see page 2.
- Please allow adequate time for changing trains, especially at large stations. Connections are not guaranteed, especially when late running occurs (connecting trains are sometimes held for late running trains).
- A Glossary of common terms appears on page 10.

LES NOTES EN BAS DU TABLEAU

❶ Ces notes se rapportent au example de tableau à la page 6.

❷ Dans certains tableaux, le symbole ♦ à l'en-tête d'une colonne signifie qu'il faut consulter le note qui porte le numéro du train concerné.

❸ Le train **345** s'appelle AVALA et circule tous les jours de Praha à Beograd avec des places assises de 1ère et 2ème classe et une voiture-restaurant. Tous les vendredis du 12 juin jusqu'au 18 sept il y a aussi une voiture-couchettes de Praha à Thessaloniki, qui se joint au train **335** entre Beograd et Thessaloniki.

❹ Le train **475** s'appelle JADRAN et circule seulement entre le 19 juin et le 4 septembre. Il compris des voitures-lits, couchettes et places assises de 2ème classe à Split via Zagreb, et des places assises de 1ère et 2ème classe jusqu'à Bratislava. Voir le tableau **92**.

❺ Les noms des trains sont parfois indiqués séparément.

❻ Les lettres et signes sont situés à l'en-tête d'une colonne ou à côté d'une heure dans la colonne. Une signe peut sortir également à côté d'un nom de gare.

❼ Les notes peuvent vous donner des informations importantes. Les signes conventionnels sont expliqués à la page 4.

❽ Sauf indication contraire, les jours et dates de circulation mentionnés sont ceux applicables à la *gare d'origine* du train (mentionnée si elle ne figure pas sur le tableau même dans les notes). Les notes peuvent expliquer les deux sens d'un train (e.g. **102/3**) utilisant "and v.v." (et vice versa).

PLUS DE CONSEILS

- Il vous est fortement recommandé de consulter aussi l'introduction à chaque section nationale: vous y trouverez des précisions concernant la classification des trains, les prestations offertes à bord des trains, les suppléments, la réservation des places, etc.
- Jours fériés - voir page 2.
- Aucune correspondance n'est garantie pourtant. N'oubliez pas non plus que dans les grandes gares les changements peuvent entraîner une longue marche et l'emprunt d'escaliers.
- Lexique - voir page 10.

NOTE ALLA FINE DEL QUADRO-ORARIO

❶ Queste note si riferiscono all' esempio a pagina 6.

❷ In certi quadri-orario, il simbolo ♦ nelle note di testa significa che bisogna fare riferimento alla nota con il numero di treno corrispondente.

❸ Il treno **345** si chiama AVALA ed e' giornaliero tra Praha a Beograd con posti di 1ª e 2ª classe e carrozza ristorante. Il venerdì dal 12 giugno fino al 18 settembre e' aggiunta a Beograd una carrozza cuccette diretta a Thessaloniki, combinandosi con il treno **335** tra Beograd e Thessaloniki.

❹ Il treno **475** si chiama JADRAN ed e' operativo solo dal 19 giugno al 4 settembre. Il treno si compone di carrozze letti, carrozze cuccette, e posti di 2ª classe tra Praha e Split, via Bratislava e Zagrabria; inoltre ci sono anche posti di 1ª e 2ª classe fino a Bratislava. Consultare anche il quadro-orario **92** al riguardo

❺ I nomi dei treni sono talvolta indicati separatamente.

❻ Lettere e simboli possono essere sia alla testa di una colonna-orario, che accanto all'orario del treno stesso. Un simbolo potrebbe anche essere accanto al nome di una stazione.

❼ E' importante leggere sempre le note a le informazioni a fine quadro. I segni convenzionali sono elencati e spiegati a pagina 4.

❽ Salvo casi in cui sia diversamente indicato, le date di circolazione dei treni si riferiscono sempre alla stazione dove il treno inizia il suo viaggio (come viene riportato nelle note a fine quadro, e Inoltre nel quadro stesso).

ALTRI CONSIGLI UTILI

- Vi consigliamo vivamente di consultare anche l'introduzione dedicata ad ogni nazione. Troverete importanti informazioni riguardanti i servizi di trasporto di ciascun paese, così come le categorie dei treni, la ristorazione, il pagamento di supplementi, le necessità di prenotazione, ecc.
- I giorni festivi suddivisi per paese sono elencati a pagina 2.
- Le coincidenze indicate non sono garantite. Tenete presente che che nelle grandi stazioni il trasferimento tra due binari potrebbe significare un lungo tratto da percorrere a piedi e con l'uso di scale.
- Il glossario si trova a pagina 10.

FUSSNOTEN

❶ Fußnoten beziehen sich auf die Beispieltabelle auf Seite 6.

❷ ♦: Sehen Sie bei der Fußnote des Zuges mit der betreffenden Zugnummer nach.

❸ Zug **345** heißt AVALA und fährt täglich zwischen Praha und Beograd mit Sitzplätzen 1. und 2. Klasse. An Freitagen vom 12. Juni bis 18. September führt dieser Zug durchgehende Liegewagen von Praha nach Thessaloniki (mit Zug **335** vereinigt von Beograd nach Thessaloniki).

❹ Zug **475** heißt JADRAN und fährt nur von 19. Juni bis 4. September. Er führt Schlaf-, Liege und Sitzwagen 2. Klasse von Praha nach Split über Zagreb, auch Sitzwagen 1. und 2. Klasse, die nur bis Bratislava fahren. Auf Tabelle **92** finden Sie weitere Informationen.

❺ Zugnamen können besonders aufgeführt sein.

❻ Zeichen und Buchstaben finden sich im Kopf der Zugspalte oder neben einer bestimmten Zeitangabe. Zeichen sind auch in der Bahnhofsspalte möglich.

❼ In Fußnoten findet man wichtige Informationen. Standardzeichen sind auf Seite 4 erklärt.

❽ Die erwähnten Tage und Zeitabschnitte für Züge, die nicht täglich verkehren, gelten für den Ausgangsbahnhof des Zuges (wenn dieser nicht in der Tabelle steht, ist er in einer Fußnote erwähnt). Fußnoten dürfen beide Richtungen erklären (z.B. **102/3**), mit "and v.v." (und umgekehrt).

WEITERE HINWEISE

- Es ist zu empfehlen, die Einleitungen zu jedem einzelnen Land zu lesen. Darin werden Sie wichtige Informationen über die Besonderheiten jedes Landes finden: Zugcharakterisierung, Services an Bord der Züge, Zuschlagpflicht, Reservierungsbedingungen usw.
- Feiertage - siehe Seite 2.
- Anschlussversäumnisse durch Verspätung oder Ausfall von Zügen sind immer möglich. Bitte beachten Sie, dass auf Großstadtbahnhöfen häufig längere Fußwege zurückgelegt bzw. Treppen benutzen werden müssen.
- Glossar - siehe Seite 10.

LAS NOTAS AL PIE DEL CUADRO

❶ Estas notas hacen referencia al ejemplo de la página 6.

❷ El símbolo ♦ ciertas tablas horarias significa: que hay que consultar la nota a pie de página con el número correspondiente.

❸ El Tren **345** se llama AVALA y circula a diario entre Praga y Belgrado con plazas sentadas de 1ra y 2da clase, además de con coche-restaurante. Los Viernes del 12 de junio al 18 de septiembre el tren lleva coches litera desde Praga hasta Tesalónica que se combinan con el tren **335** entre Belgrado y Tesalónica.

❹ El Tren **475** se llama JADRAN y circula solamente del 19 de junio al 4 de septiembre. El Tren **475** se llama JADRAN y circula solamente del 19 de junio al 4 de sept. El tren dispone de lleva vagones de coches cama, litera, y plazas sentadas de 2da clase entre Praga y Split a través de Zagreb, también plazas sentadas de 1ra y 2da clase hasta Bratislava. Consulte el cuadro **92**.

❺ Los nombres de los Trenes a veces son enumerados por separado.

❻ Las letras y signos se encuentran en el encabezamiento de las distintas columnas horarias o adyacentes a horas de salida individuales. Los símbolos también pueden aparecer en la columna de la estación.

❼ Lea siempre las notas a pie de cuadro ya que pueden contener información importante. La explicación de los signos convencionales se da en la página 4.

❽ Salvo indicación contraria los días y fechas de circulación de los trenes son aquéllos mencionados en la estación de *origen* del tren. Algunas notas muestran ambas direcciones del tren mediante la nota "and v.v." (y viceversa).

INFORMACIÓN ADICIONAL

- Se recomienda vivamente que consulte también los preámbulos al comienzo de cada sección nacional: le proporcionarán datos importantes sobre las particularidades de cada país: tipos de trenes, restauración, pago de suplementos, y necesidades de reservación anticipada.
- Días festivos - cunsulte la página 2.
- Los trasbordos no se pueden garantizar, sobretodo en el caso de retrasos. Hay que ser consciente también que el trasbordo en las estaciones de grandes ciudades puede suponer un desplazamiento bastante largo a pie y el uso de escaleras.
- Glosario - cunsulte la página 10.

The following is designed to be a concise guide to travelling in Europe by train. For more details of accommodation available, catering, supplements etc., see the introduction to each country.

BUYING YOUR TICKET

Train tickets must be purchased before travelling, either from travel agents or at the station ticket office (or machine). Where a station has neither a ticket office nor a ticket machine, the ticket may usually be purchased on the train.

Tickets which are not dated when purchased (for example in France, Italy and the Netherlands) must be validated before travel in one of the machines at the entrance to the platform.

In certain Eastern European countries foreign nationals may have to buy international rail tickets at the office of the state tourist board concerned and not at the railway station. The tickets can sometimes only be purchased in Western currency and buying tickets can take a long time.

All countries in Europe (except Albania) offer two classes of rail accommodation, usually 1st and 2nd class. 1st class is more comfortable and therefore more expensive than 2nd class. Local trains are often 2nd class only. In Southern and Eastern Europe, 1st class travel is advisable for visitors as fares are reasonable and 2nd class can be very overcrowded.

RESERVATIONS

Many express trains in Europe are restricted to passengers holding advance seat reservations, particularly in France, Sweden and Spain. This is shown by the symbol Ⓡ in the tables, or by notes in the introduction to each country. All *TGV*, *Eurostar* and *Pendolino* trains require a reservation, as do all long-distance trains in Spain.

Reservations can usually be made up to two months in advance. A small fee is charged, but where a supplement is payable the reservation fee is often included. Reservations can often be made on other long-distance services and this is recommended at busy times.

SUPPLEMENTS

Many countries have faster or more luxurious train services for which an extra charge is made. This supplement is payable when the ticket is purchased and often includes the price of a seat reservation. The supplement can sometimes be paid on the train, but usually at extra cost. The introduction to each country gives further information. On certain high-speed services, the first class fare includes the provision of a meal.

RAIL PASSES

Passes are available which give unlimited travel on most trains in a given area. These range from InterRail and Eurail passes which cover most of Europe for up to one month, to local passes which cover limited areas for one day. Further details of InterRail and Eurail passes appear elsewhere in this edition, and a special feature on rail passes appears each year in our May edition as well as in the twice-yearly Independent Travellers Edition.

FINDING YOUR TRAIN

At most stations departures are listed on large paper sheets (often yellow), and/or on electronic departure indicators. These list trains by departure, giving principal stops, and indicate from which platform they leave.

On each platform of principal European stations, a display board can be found giving details of the main trains calling at that platform. This includes the location of individual coaches, together with their destinations and the type of accommodation provided.

A sign may be carried on the side of the carriage indicating the train name, principal stops and destination and a label or sign near the door will indicate the number allocated to the carriage, which is shown on reservation tickets. 1st class accommodation is usually indicated by a yellow band above the windows and doors and/or a figure 1 near the door or on the windows

A sign above the compartment door will indicate seat numbers and which seats are reserved. In non-compartment trains, reserved seats have labels on their headrests. In some countries, notably Sweden and Yugoslavia, reserved seats are not marked and occupants will be asked to move when the passenger who has reserved the seat boards the train.

🍴 CATERING 🍸

Many higher quality and long-distance trains in Europe have restaurant cars serving full meals, usually with waiter service, or serve meals at the passenger's seat. Such trains are identified with the symbol 🍴 in the tables. Full meals may only be available at set times, sometimes with separate sittings, and may only be available to passengers holding first class tickets. However, the restaurant car is often supplemented by a counter or trolley service offering light snacks and drinks.

Other types of catering are shown with the symbol 🍸. This varies from a self-service buffet car serving light meals (sometimes called bistro or café) to a trolley which is wheeled through the train, serving only drinks and sandwiches. Where possible, the introduction to each country gives further information on the level of catering to be expected on particular types of train.

The catering shown may not be available throughout the journey and may be suspended or altered at weekends or on holidays.

SLEEPING CARS 🛏

Sleeping cars are shown as 🛏 in the timetables. Standard sleeping car types have bedroom style compartments with limited washing facilities and full bedding. Toilets are located at one or both ends of the coach. An attendant travels with each car or pair of cars and will serve drinks and continental breakfast at an extra charge. 1st class sleeping compartments have one or two berths (in Britain and Norway, and in older Swedish sleeping cars, two berth compartments require only 2nd class tickets) and 2nd class compartments have three berths. Some trains convey special T2 cabins, shown as 🛏 (T2) in the tables, with one berth in 1st class and two berths in 2nd class.

Compartments are allocated for occupation exclusively by men or by women except when married couples or families occupy all berths. Children travelling alone, or who cannot be accommodated in the same compartment as their family, are placed in women's compartments. In Russia and other countries of the CIS, however, berths are allocated in strict order of booking and men and women often share the same compartments.

Some trains have communicating doors between sleeping compartments which can be opened to create a larger room if both compartments are occupied by the same family group. Berths can be reserved up to 2 months (3 months on certain trains) before the date of travel and early reservation is recommended as space is limited, especially on French ski trains and in Eastern Europe. Berths must be claimed within 15 minutes of boarding the train or they may be resold.

HOTEL TRAINS

A new generation of overnight trains known collectively as Hotel trains are now running on a selection of national and international routes. The facilities are of a higher standard than those offered in conventional sleeping cars, and special fares are payable. The trains fall into the following categories:

City Night Line: Most night trains radiating from Germany, as well as domestic overnight trains within Germany, now come under the *City Night Line* banner. They operate on 15 routes serving eight countries, and are shown as *CNL* in our tables. *Deluxe* class consists of one or two berth cabins, with one or two moveable armchairs, a table and an en suite washroom containing toilet, washbasin and shower. *Economy* compartments have two berths, the upper of which folds away against the cabin wall, and the lower becomes a seat for day use. There are also four berth family compartments as well as couchettes and reclining seats (sleeperettes). A first class ticket is required for *Deluxe* compartments (but no longer for single occupancy of a *Economy* compartment). Double deck cars, with *Deluxe* on the upper deck, are also available.

Trenhotel (Spain). These trains, of the *Talgo* type, run on the international routes from Madrid to Paris and Lisboa, and from Barcelona to Paris, Zürich and Milano. They also run on internal routes within Spain, from Barcelona to A Coruña, Vigo, Málaga and Sevilla and v.v., and Madrid to A Coruña and Vigo and v.v. The highest class of accommodation is known as *Gran Clase*, which has shower and toilet facilities in each compartment and can be used for single or double occupancy.

Compartments with showers can also now be found on a number of services in Sweden, Norway and Italy, and other international routes include Wien to Zürich and Roma, the Amsterdam - Warszawa *Jan Kiepura* and the *Berlin Night Express* running between Berlin and Malmö. Further details of sleeper services are shown in our Night Trains feature in the November edition.

COUCHETTES ▬

Couchettes (▬) are a more basic form of overnight accommodation consisting of simple bunk beds with a sheet, blanket and pillow. The couchettes are converted from ordinary seating cars for the night, and there are usually 4 berths per compartment in 1st class, 6 berths in 2nd class. On certain trains (e.g. in Austria and Italy), 4 berth compartments are available to 2nd class passengers, at a higher supplement. Washing and toilet facilities are provided at the ends of each coach. Men and women are booked into the same compartments and are expected to sleep in daytime clothes. A small number of trains in Germany, however, have women-only couchette compartments.

WHEELCHAIR ACCESS ♿

High-quality main line and international trains are now often equipped to accommodate passengers in wheelchairs. Access ramps are available at many stations and some trains are fitted with special lifts. The following trains have at least one wheelchair space, often with accessible toilets:

International: all Eurostar trains, many EC and other trains. CityNightLine trains have a special compartment. *Austria:* many IC/EC trains. *Denmark:* IC and Lyn trains. *France:* all TGV trains and many other long distance services. *Germany:* all EC, ICE, IC and IR trains. *Italy:* all Pendolino and many EC or IC trains. *Netherlands:* most trains. *Sweden:* X2000 and most IC and IR trains, some sleeping cars. *Switzerland:* All IC, most EC and some regional trains. *Austria, Great Britain, Ireland, Poland:* certain trains only.

Most of these railways publish guides to accessibility, and some countries, for example France, provide special staff to help disabled travellers. Wheelchair users normally need to reserve in advance, stating their requirements. The Editor would welcome information for countries not listed.

CAR-SLEEPERS

Trains which convey motor cars operate throughout much of Europe and are shown in Table **1** for international services and Table **2** for other services. The motor cars are conveyed in special wagons while passengers travel in sleeping cars or couchettes, usually (but not always) in the same train.

LUGGAGE & BICYCLES

Luggage may be registered at many larger stations and sent separately by rail to your destination. In some countries, bicycles may also be registered in advance and certain local and some express trains will convey bicycles (there may be a charge). The relevant railways will advise exact details on request.

HEALTH REQUIREMENTS

It is not mandatory for visitors to Europe to be vaccinated against infectious diseases unless they are travelling from areas where these are endemic. For travellers' peace of mind, however, protection against the following diseases should be considered:

AIDS	Cholera
Hepatitis A	Hepatitis B
Polio	Rabies
Tetanus	Typhoid

Full information is available from the manual published by the World Health Organisation, and travellers should seek advice from their Travel Agent.

DRINKING WATER

Tap water is usually safe to drink in most parts of Europe. The water in washrooms or toilets on trains is, however, not suitable for drinking. Those who doubt the purity of the tap water are recommended to boil it, to use sterilisation tablets, or to drink bottled water.

CLIMATE

Most of Europe lies within the temperate zone but there can be considerable differences between North and South, East and West, as illustrated in the table below. Local temperatures are also affected by altitude and the difference between summer and winter temperatures tends to be less marked in coastal regions than in areas far removed from the sea.

	Bucureşti	Dublin	Madrid	Moskva
JANUARY				
Highest	2°	8°	10°	– 6°
Lowest	– 6°	3°	3°	– 12°
Rain days	6	13	9	11
APRIL				
Highest	18°	11°	18°	10°
Lowest	6°	4°	7°	2°
Rain days	7	10	11	9
JULY				
Highest	29°	19°	31°	23°
Lowest	16°	11°	18°	14°
Rain days	7	9	3	12
OCTOBER				
Highest	18°	14°	19°	8°
Lowest	6°	8°	10°	2°
Rain days	5	11	9	10

Highest = Average highest daily temperature in °C
Lowest = Average lowest daily temperature in °C
Rain days = Average number of days with recorded precipitation

Source : World Weather Information Service

METRIC CONVERSION TABLES

The Celsius system of temperature measurement, the metric system of distance measurement and the twenty-four hour clock are used throughout this book. The tables below give Fahrenheit, mile and twelve-hour clock equivalents.

CURRENCY CONVERSION

The information shown below is intended to be indicative only. Rates fluctuate from day to day and commercial exchange rates normally include a commission element.

Country	unit	1 GBP =	1 USD =	1 EUR =	100 JPY =
Euro zone (‡)	**euro**	**1.11**	**0.67**	**1.00**	**0.76**
Albania	lek	152.58	92.34	137.17	103.86
Belarus	rubl	4513.14	2733.00	4057.55	3071.99
Bosnia	marka	2.18	1.32	1.96	1.48
Bulgaria	lev	2.18	1.32	1.96	1.48
Croatia	kuna	8.14	4.93	7.32	5.54
Czech Republic	koruna	28.84	17.47	25.93	19.63
Denmark	krone	8.28	5.01	7.44	5.63
Estonia	kroon	17.40	10.54	15.65	11.85
Hungary	forint	298.84	180.97	268.68	203.42
Iceland	krona	204.62	123.91	183.96	139.28
Latvia	lats	0.79	0.48	0.71	0.54
Lithuania	litas	3.84	2.33	3.45	2.61
Macedonia	denar	68.42	41.44	61.52	46.57
Moldova	leu	18.31	11.09	16.46	12.47
Norway	krone	9.37	5.67	8.42	6.37
Poland	złoty	4.62	2.80	4.15	3.14
Romania	leu nou	4.76	2.88	4.28	3.24
Russia	rubl	47.89	29.00	43.06	32.60
Serbia	dinar	104.97	63.57	94.37	71.45
Sweden	krona	11.50	6.96	10.34	7.83
Switzerland	franc	1.68	1.02	1.51	1.15
Turkey	yeni lira	2.47	1.50	2.22	1.68
Ukraine	hryvnya	13.39	8.11	12.04	9.12
United Kingdom	pound	1.00	0.61	0.90	0.68

‡ – Austria, Belgium, Cyprus, Finland, France, Germany, Greece, Ireland, Italy, Luxembourg, Malta, the Netherlands, Portugal, Slovakia, Slovenia, and Spain.

The euro is also legal tender in Andorra, Kosovo, Monaco, Montenegro, San Marino, and the Vatican City.

PASSPORTS AND VISAS

Nationals of one country intending to travel to or pass through another country normally require a valid passport and will also require a visa unless a special visa-abolition agreement has been made between the countries concerned. The limit of stay permitted in each country is usually 3 months.

Applications for visas should be made well in advance of the date of travel to the local consulate of the country concerned. Consuls usually make a charge for issuing a visa. Before issuing a transit visa, a consul normally requires to see the visa of the country of destination.

The possession of a valid passport or visa does not necessarily grant the holder automatic access to all areas of the country to be visited. Certain countries have zones which are restricted or prohibited to foreign nationals.

All border controls have been abolished, however, between those countries which have signed the **Schengen Agreement** (see list below), and a visa allowing entry to any of these countries is valid in all of them.

LIST OF SCHENGEN AREA COUNTRIES

Austria, Belgium, Czech Republic, Denmark, Estonia, Finland, France, Germany, Greece, Hungary, Iceland, Italy, Latvia, Lithuania, Luxembourg, Malta, Netherlands, Norway, Poland, Portugal, Slovakia, Slovenia, Spain, Sweden. Switzerland has also started to apply Schengen area rules.

TEMPERATURE

°C	°F
–20	–4
–15	5
–10	14
–5	23
0	32
5	41
10	50
15	59
20	68
25	77
30	86
35	95
40	104

Conversion formulae :
°C = (°F – 32) x 5 / 9
°F = (°C x 9 / 5) + 32

DISTANCE

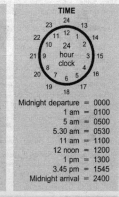

km	miles	km	miles	km	miles
1	0.62	45	27.96	300	186.41
2	1.24	50	31.07	400	248.55
3	1.86	55	34.18	500	310.69
4	2.49	60	37.28	600	372.82
5	3.11	65	40.39	700	434.96
6	3.73	70	43.50	800	497.10
7	4.35	75	46.60	900	559.23
8	4.97	80	49.71	1000	621.37
9	5.59	85	52.82	1100	683.51
10	6.21	90	55.92	1200	745.65
15	9.32	95	59.03	1300	807.78
20	12.43	100	62.14	1400	869.92
25	15.53	125	77.67	1500	932.06
30	18.64	150	93.21	2000	1242.74
35	21.75	175	108.74	3000	1864.11
40	24.85	200	124.27	4000	2485.48

TIME

Midnight departure	= 0000
1 am	= 0100
5 am	= 0500
5.30 am	= 0530
11 am	= 1100
12 noon	= 1200
1 pm	= 1300
3.45 pm	= 1545
Midnight arrival	= 2400

GLOSSARY

🔑	*FRANÇAIS*	*ITALIANO*	*DEUTSCH*	*ESPAÑOL*
additional trains	d'autres trains	ulteriori treni	weitere Züge	otros trenes
also	[circule] aussi	[si effettua] anche	[verkehrt] auch	[circula] también
alteration	modification	variazione	Änderung	modificación
approximately	environ	circa	ungefähr	aproximadamente
arrival, arrives (a.)	arrivée, arrive	arrivo, arriva	Ankunft, kommt an	llegada, llega
and at the same minutes past each hour until	puis toutes les heures aux mêmes minutes jusqu'à	poi ai stessi minuti di ogni ora fino a	und so weiter im Takt bis	luego a los mismos minutos de cada hora hasta
calls at	s'arrête à	ferma a	hält in	efectúa parada en
certain	déterminé	certo	bestimmt	determinado
change at	changer à	cambiare a	umsteigen in	cambiar en
composition	composition	composizione	Zugbildung	composición
confirmation	confirmation	conferma	Bestätigung	confirmación
connection	correspondance, relation	coincidenza, relazione	Anschluss, Verbindung	correspondencia, enlace
conveys	comporte, achemine	ha in composizione	befördert, führt	lleva
daily	tous les jours	giornalmente	täglich	diariamente
delay	retard	ritardo	Verspätung	retraso
departure, departs (d.)	départ, part	partenza, parte	Abfahrt, fährt ab	salida, sale
earlier	plus tôt	più presto	früher	más temprano
engineering work	travaux de voie	lavori sul binario	Bauarbeiten	obras de vía
even / uneven dates	jours pairs / impairs	giorni pari / dispari	gerade / ungerade Daten	fechas pares / impares
every 30 minutes	toutes les 30 minutes	ogni 30 minuti	alle 30 Minuten	cada 30 minutos
except	sauf	escluso	außer	excepto
fast(er)	(plus) rapide	(più) rapido	schnell(er)	(más) rápido
for	pour	per	für	para
from Rennes	(en provenance) de Rennes	(proviene) da Rennes	von Rennes	(procede) de Rennes
from Jan. 15	à partir du 15 janvier	dal 15 di gennaio	vom 15. Januar (an)	desde el 15 de enero
hourly	toutes les heures	ogni ora	stündlich	cada hora
hours (hrs)	heures	ore	Stunden	horas
journey	voyage, trajet	viaggio, percorso	Reise	viaje, trayecto
journey time	temps de parcours	tempo di tragitto	Reisezeit	duración del recorrido
later	plus tard	più tardi	später	más tarde
may	peut, peuvent	può, possono	kann, können	puede(n)
minutes (mins)	minutes	minuti	Minuten	minutos
not	ne [circule] pas	non [si effettua]	[verkehrt] nicht	no [circula]
not available	pas disponible	non disponibile	nicht erhältlich	no disponible
on the dates shown in Table **81**	les jours indiqués dans le tableau **81**	nei giorni indicati nel quadro **81**	an den in der Tabelle **81** angegebene Daten	los días indicados en el cuadro **81**
only	seulement	esclusivamente	nur	sólo
operator	entreprise de transports	azienda di trasporto	Verkehrsunternehmen	empresa de transportes
other	autre	altro	andere	otros
runs	circule	circola, si effettua	verkehrt	circula
sailing	traversée	traversata	Überfahrt	travesia
ship	bateau, navire	nave, battello	Schiff	barco
stopping trains	trains omnibus	treni regionali	Nahverkehrszüge	trenes regionales
stops	s'arrête	ferma	hält	efectúa parada
subject to	sous réserve de	soggetto a	vorbehaltlich	sujeto a
summer	été	estate	Sommer	verano
supplement payable	avec supplément	con pagamento di supplemento	zuschlagpflichtig	con pago de suplemento
then	puis	poi	dann	luego
through train	train direct	treno diretto	durchgehender Zug	tren directo
timings	horaires	orari	Zeitangaben	horarios
to York	vers, à destination de York	(diretto) a York	nach York	(continúa) a York
to / until July 23	jusqu'au 23 juillet	fino al 23 di luglio	bis zum 23. Juli	hasta el día 23 de julio
to pick up	pour laisser monter	per viaggiatori in partenza	zum Zusteigen	para recoger viajeros
to set down	pour laisser descendre	per viaggiatori in arrivo	zum Aussteigen	para dejar viajeros
unless otherwise shown	sauf indication contraire	salvo indicazione contraria	sofern nicht anders angezeigt	salvo indicación contraria
valid	valable	valido	gültig	válido
when train **44** runs	lors de la circulation du train **44**	quando circola il treno **44**	beim Verkehren des Zuges **44**	cuando circula el tren **44**
winter	hiver	inverno	Winter	invierno

PICTOGRAMS

Information
Information
Renseignements
Información

Ticket office
Fahrkartenschalter
Guichet
Despacho de billetes

Luggage office
Gepäckaufbewahrung
Consigne
Consigna

Luggage lockers
Gepäckschließfächer
Consigne automatique
Taquillas de equipaje

Ladies
Damen
Dames
Señoras

Gentlemen
Herren
Hommes
Caballeros

Lost property
Fundbüro
Objets trouvés
Objetos perdidos

Bureau de change
Geldwechsel
Bureau de change
Cambio

Post office
Postamt
Poste
Correos

Telephone
Telefon
Téléphone
Teléfono

Restaurant
Restaurant
Restaurant
Restaurante

Buffet
Buffet
Buffet
Comedor

Meeting point
Treffpunkt
Point de rencontre
Lugar de reunión

Entrance
Eingang
Entrée
Entrada

Exit
Ausgang
Sortie
Salida

Bus
Bus
Autobus
Autobús

Boat
Schiff
Bateau
Barco

Tram
Straßenbahn
Tramway
Tranvía

INDEX OF PLACES

by table number

🚆 Connection by train from the nearest station shown in this timetable.
⛴ Connection by boat from the nearest station shown in this timetable.
🚌 Connection by bus from the nearest station shown in this timetable.
10/355 Consult both indicated tables to find the best connecting services.

A

AMSTERDAM

ATHÍNA

B

BARCELONA

BASEL

PARIS ✈ CHARLES DE GAULLE

POZNAŃ

PRAHA

Q

R

CRUISE TRAINS

The services shown in the European Rail Timetable are the regular scheduled services of the railway companies concerned. However, a number of specialised operators also run luxurious cruise trains taking several days to complete their journey. Overnight accommodation is provided either on the train or in hotels. Cruise trains are bookable only through the operating company or its appointed agents and normal rail tickets are not valid on these trains. A selection of operators is shown below.

The Royal Scotsman: luxury tours of Scotland starting from Edinburgh. Operator: Orient-Express Hotels, Trains & Cruises, 20 Upper Ground, London SE1 9PF, UK; ✆ 0845 077 2222 or +44 (0) 20 7960 0500, fax +44 (0) 207 921 4708. Website: www.royalscotsman.com

El Transcantábrico: 1000-km 8-day rail cruise along Spain's northern coast. Operator: El Transcantábrico, Plaza de los Ferroviarios, s/n. 33012 Oviedo, Spain. ✆ +34 985 981 711, fax +34 985 981 710. Website: www.transcantabrico.feve.es

Trans-Siberian Express: Tours by private hotel train along the Trans-Siberian Railway. Operator: GW Travel Ltd, Denzell House, Denzell Gardens, Dunham Road, Altrincham WA14 4QF, UK. ✆ +44 (0)161 928 9410, fax +44 (0)161 941 6101. Website: www.gwtravel.co.uk. USA agent: MIR Corporation, 85 South Washington Street, Suite 210, Seattle, Washington 98104, USA; ✆ +1 (206) 624 7289, fax +1 (206) 624 7360. Website: www.mircorp.com

Venice Simplon-Orient-Express: This well-known luxury train runs once or twice weekly from late March to early November, mostly on its established London - Paris - Venezia route. Operator: Orient-Express Hotels, Trains & Cruises, 20 Upper Ground, London SE1 9PF, UK; ✆ 0845 077 2222 or +44 (0) 20 7960 0500, fax +44 (0) 207 921 4708. Website: www.orient-express.com

For further details of these and other operators, see our annual Cruise Trains and Rail Holidays feature in the March edition

LIST OF ADVERTISERS

CITY STATION LOCATION PLANS

Passenger railway	Main station
Metro	Local station
Bus / tram line	Bus station
Ferry	Airport

Only those metro, bus, and tram lines which provide inter-station links or connect outlying main stations to the city centre are shown.

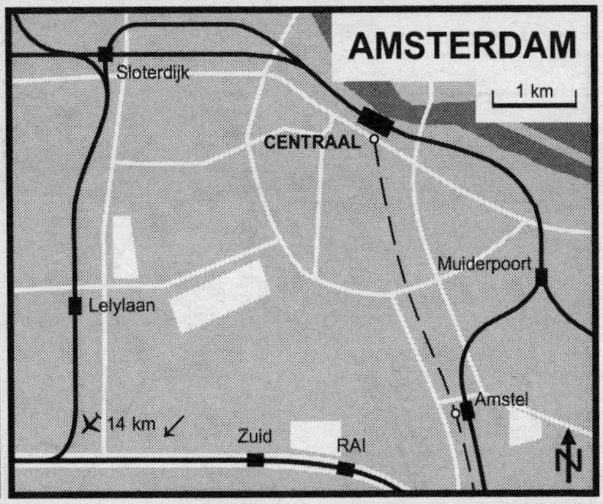

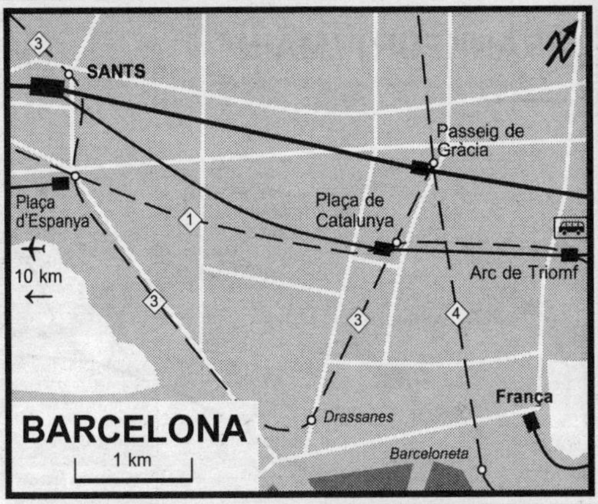

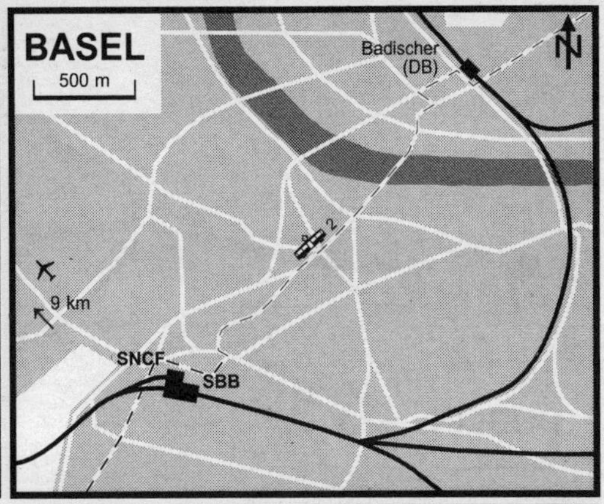

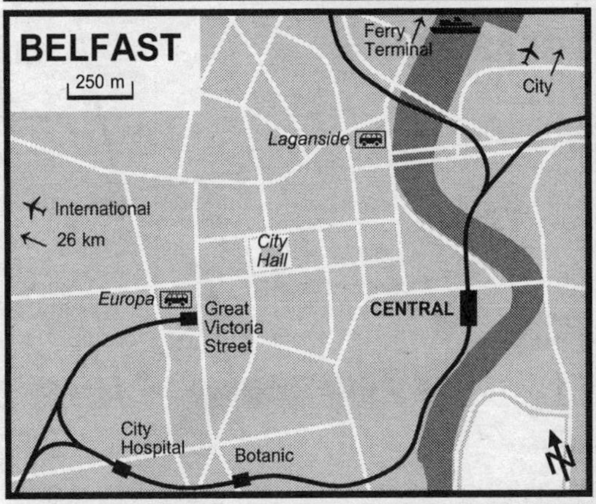

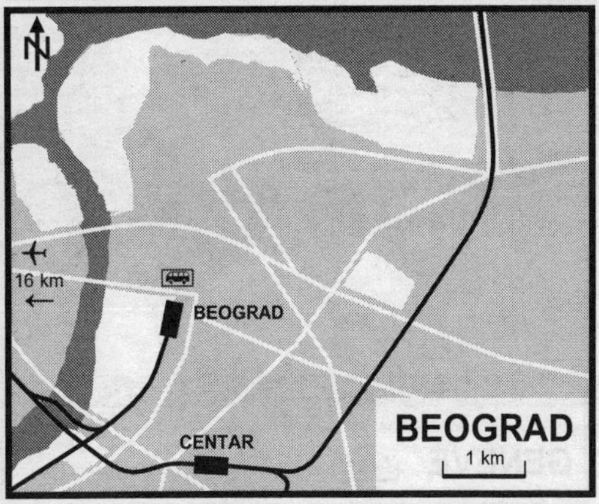

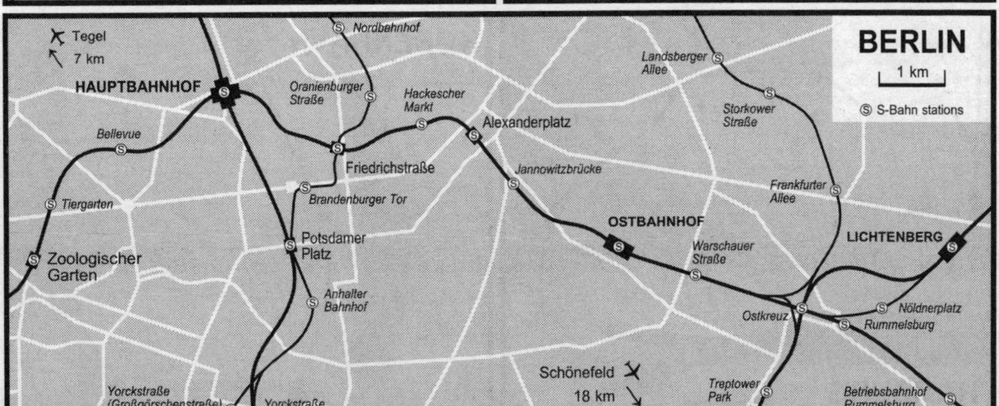

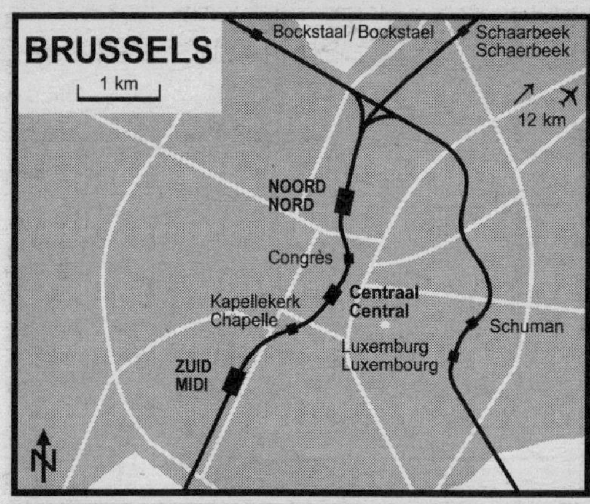
BRUSSELS
1 km
Bockstaal / Bockstael
Schaarbeek
Schaerbeek
12 km
NOORD
NORD
Congrès
Kapellekerk
Chapelle
Centraal
Central
Luxemburg
Luxembourg
Schuman
ZUID
MIDI
N

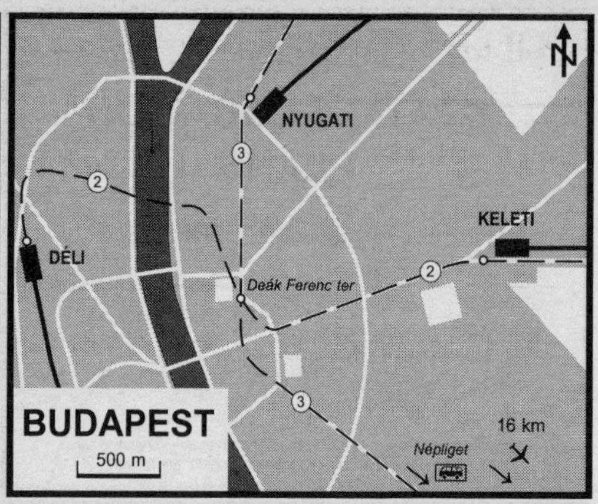
N
NYUGATI
KELETI
DÉLI
Deák Ferenc ter
BUDAPEST
500 m
16 km
Népliget

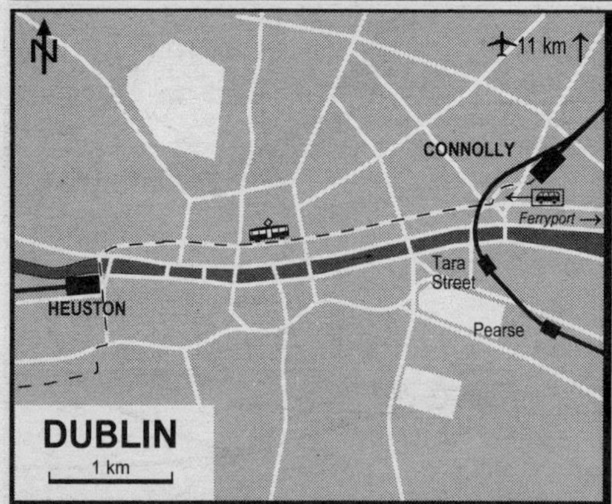
N
11 km
CONNOLLY
Ferryport
HEUSTON
Tara
Street
Pearse
DUBLIN
1 km

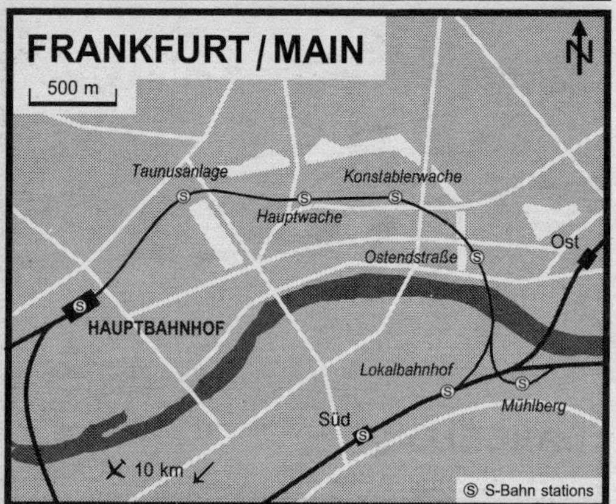
FRANKFURT / MAIN
500 m
N
Taunusanlage
Konstablerwache
Hauptwache
Ostendstraße
Ost
HAUPTBAHNHOF
Lokalbahnhof
Süd
Mühlberg
10 km
S-Bahn stations

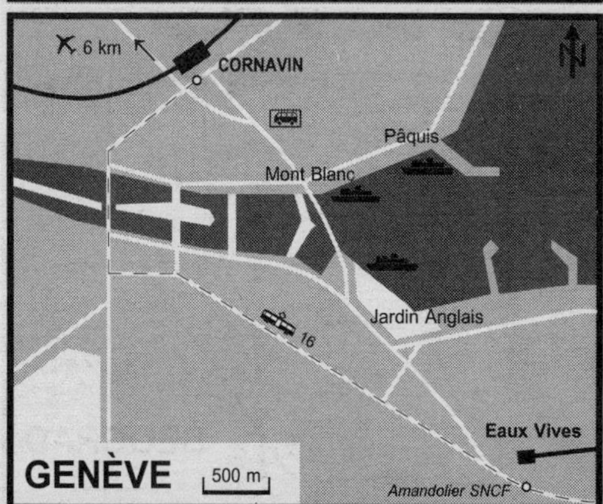
6 km
CORNAVIN
N
Pâquis
Mont Blanc
Jardin Anglais
16
Eaux Vives
GENÈVE
500 m
Amandolier SNCF

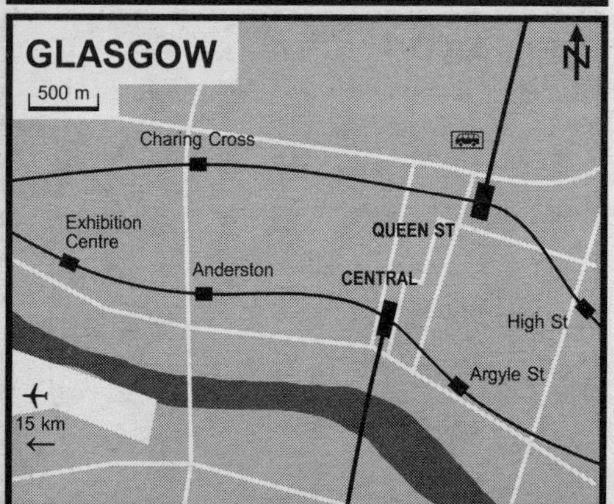
GLASGOW
500 m
N
Charing Cross
Exhibition
Centre
QUEEN ST
Anderston
CENTRAL
High St
Argyle St
15 km

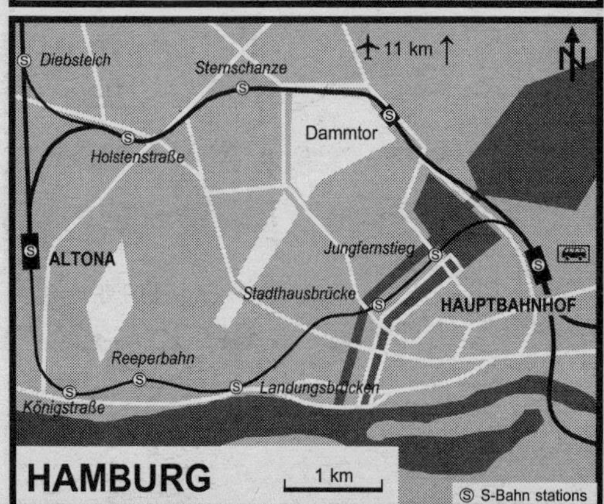
Diebsteich
Sternschanze
11 km
N
Dammtor
Holstenstraße
ALTONA
Jungfernstieg
Stadthausbrücke
HAUPTBAHNHOF
Reeperbahn
Königstraße
Landungsbrücken
HAMBURG
1 km
S-Bahn stations

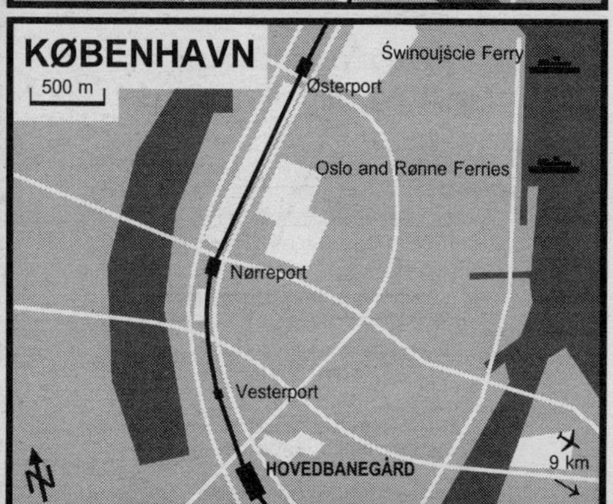
KØBENHAVN
500 m
Świnoujście Ferry
Østerport
Oslo and Rønne Ferries
Nørreport
Vesterport
HOVEDBANEGÅRD
9 km
N

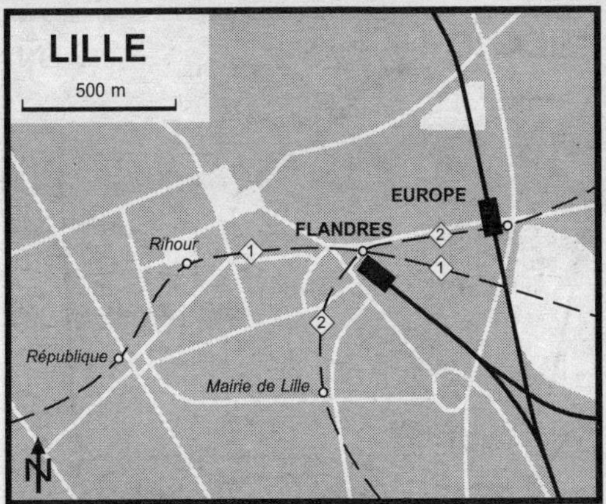
LILLE
500 m
EUROPE
FLANDRES
Rihour
République
Mairie de Lille
1
2

Entrecampos
Areeiro
Sete Rios
Roma-Areeiro
Sintra
Oriente
Roma
Campolide
Alameda
Oriente
Marquês de Pombal
Rato
Restauradores
Rossio
SANTA APOLÓNIA
Baixa-Chiado
Rossio
Cascais
Cais do Sodré
Terreiro do Paço
1 km
LISBOA
Barreiro

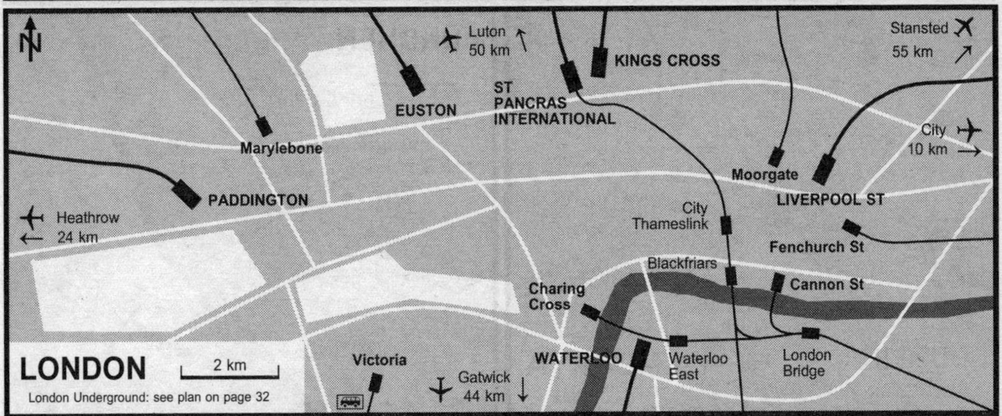
Luton 50 km
Stansted 55 km
KINGS CROSS
EUSTON
ST PANCRAS INTERNATIONAL
Marylebone
City 10 km
PADDINGTON
Moorgate
LIVERPOOL ST
Heathrow 24 km
City Thameslink
Fenchurch St
Blackfriars
Charing Cross
Cannon St
Victoria
WATERLOO
Waterloo East
London Bridge
LONDON
2 km
London Underground: see plan on page 32
Gatwick 44 km

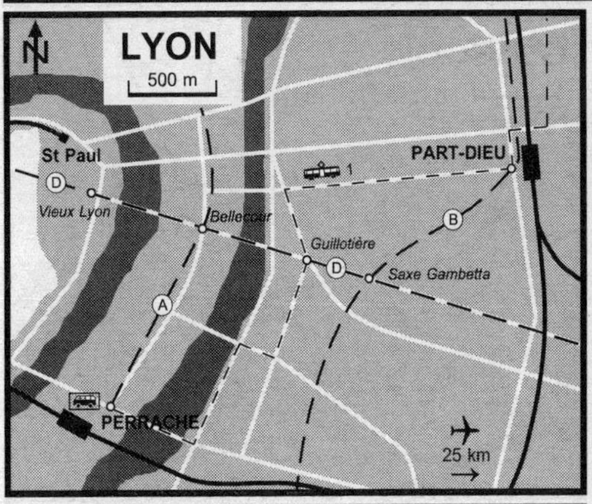
LYON
500 m
St Paul
PART-DIEU
1
D
Vieux Lyon
Bellecour
B
Guillotière
D
Saxe Gambetta
A
PERRACHE
25 km

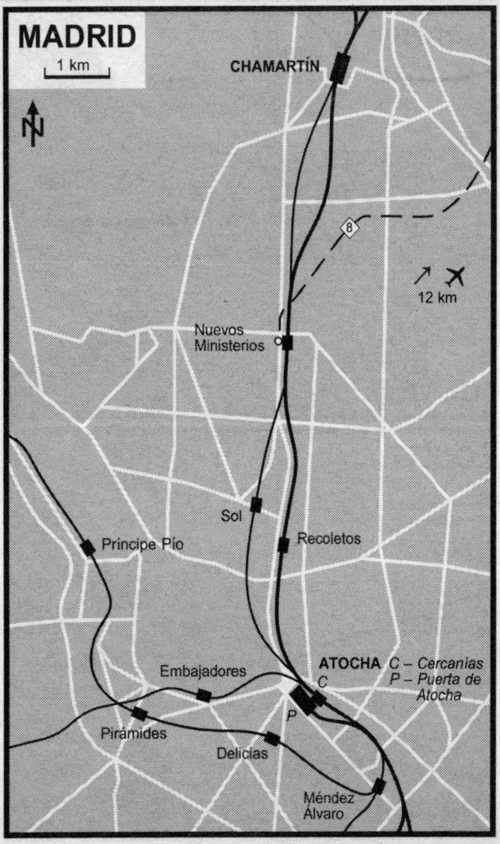
MADRID
1 km
CHAMARTÍN
8
12 km
Nuevos Ministerios
Sol
Príncipe Pío
Recoletos
Embajadores
ATOCHA
C
C – Cercanías
P – Puerta de Atocha
P
Pirámides
Delicias
Méndez Álvaro

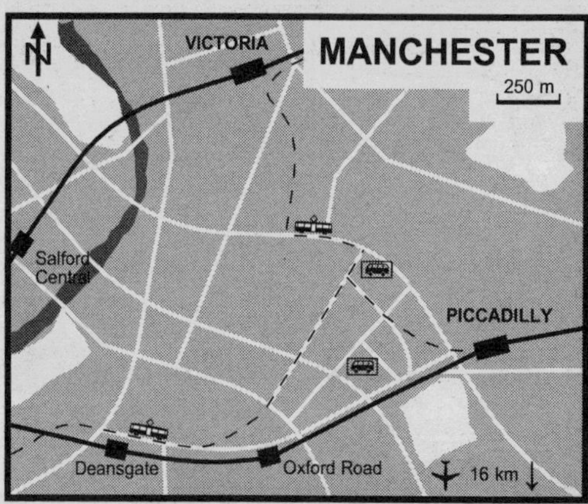
MANCHESTER
250 m
VICTORIA
Salford Central
PICCADILLY
Deansgate
Oxford Road
16 km

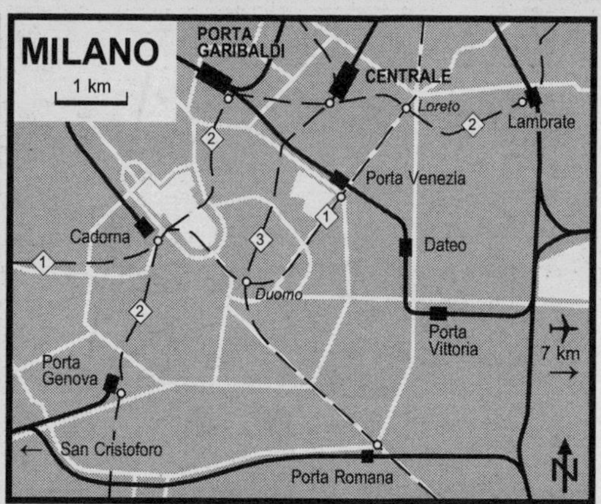
MILANO
1 km
PORTA GARIBALDI
CENTRALE
Loreto
Lambrate
Porta Venezia
Cadorna
Dateo
Duomo
Porta Vittoria
7 km
Porta Genova
San Cristoforo
Porta Romana

27 km
Savyolovsky
Rizhskaya
Yaroslavskaya
BELORUSSKAYA
(Smolenskaya)
OKTYABRSKAYA
(Leningradski vokzal)
Komsomolskaya
Kazanskaya
Kurskaya
KIYEVSKAYA
Paveletskaya
MOSKVA
1 km

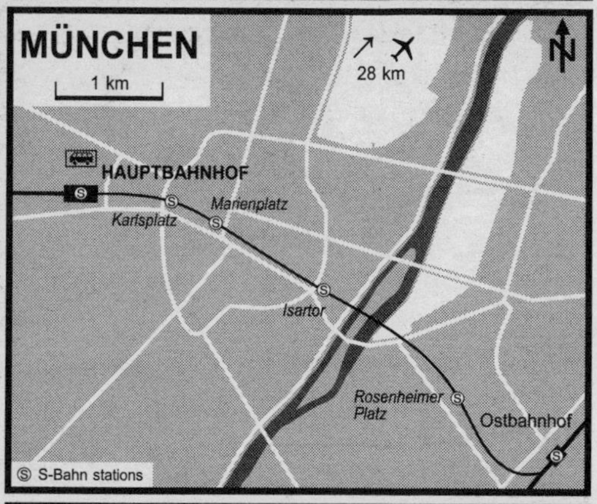
MÜNCHEN
1 km
28 km
HAUPTBAHNHOF
Marienplatz
Karlsplatz
Isartor
Rosenheimer Platz
Ostbahnhof
S S-Bahn stations

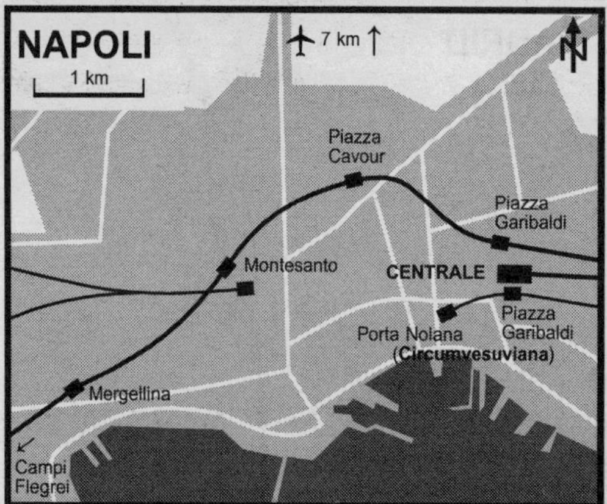
NAPOLI
1 km
7 km
Piazza Cavour
Piazza Garibaldi
Montesanto
CENTRALE
Porta Nolana
(Circumvesuviana)
Piazza Garibaldi
Mergellina
Campi Flegrei

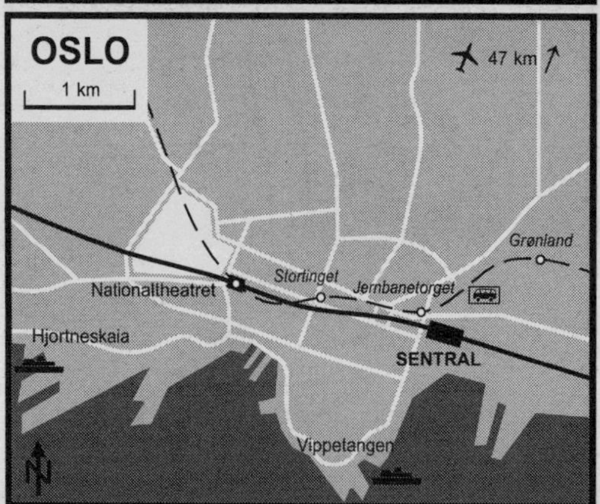
OSLO
1 km
47 km
Grønland
Stortinget
Jernbanetorget
Nationaltheatret
Hjortneskaia
SENTRAL
Vippetangen

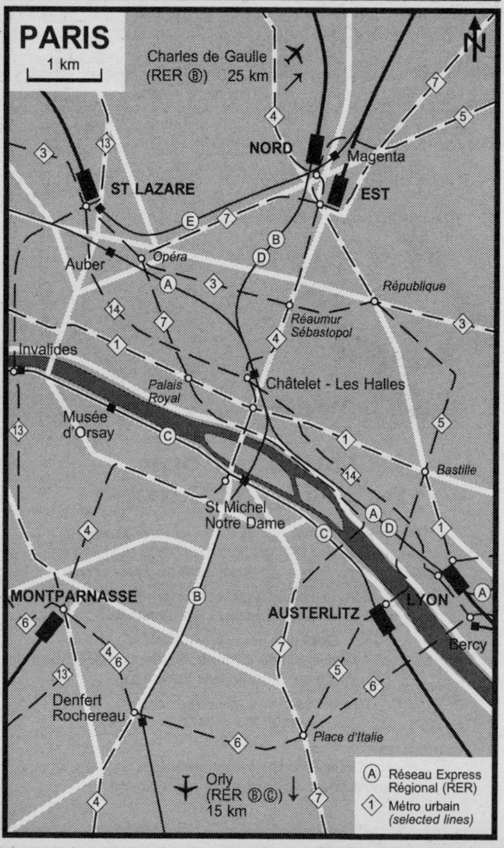
PARIS
1 km
Charles de Gaulle
(RER B) 25 km
NORD
Magenta
ST LAZARE
EST
Auber
Opéra
République
Réaumur Sébastopol
Invalides
Palais Royal
Châtelet - Les Halles
Musée d'Orsay
Bastille
St Michel Notre Dame
MONTPARNASSE
AUSTERLITZ
LYON
Bercy
Denfert Rochereau
Place d'Italie
Orly
(RER B C)
15 km
A Réseau Express Régional (RER)
1 Métro urbain
(selected lines)

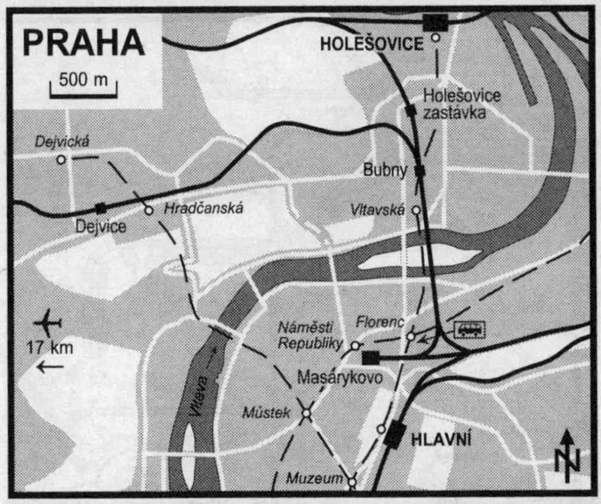
PRAHA
500 m
HOLEŠOVICE
Holešovice zastávka
Dejvická
Bubny
Hradčanská
Dejvice
Vltavská
Náměstí Republiky
Florenc
17 km
Vltava
Masarykovo
Můstek
HLAVNÍ
Muzeum

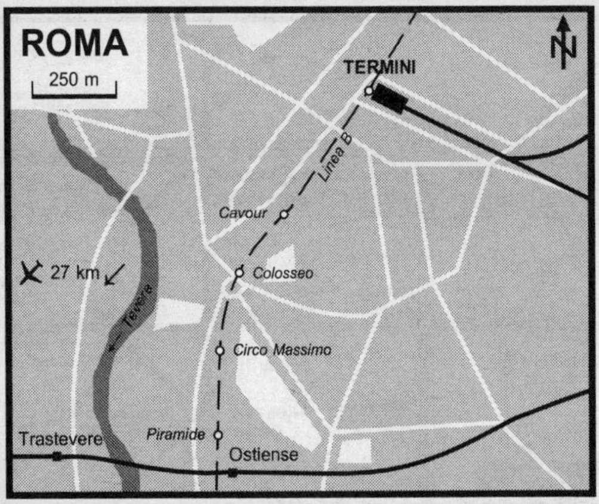
ROMA
250 m
TERMINI
Linea B
Cavour
27 km
Colosseo
Tevere
Circo Massimo
Trastevere
Piramide
Ostiense

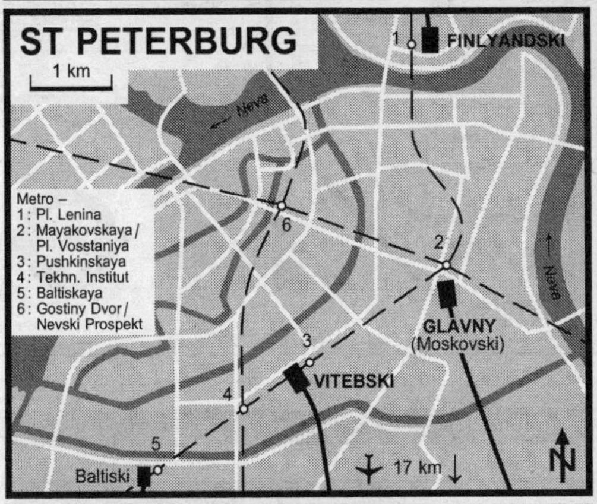
ST PETERBURG
1 km
1
FINLYANDSKI
Neva
Metro –
1 : Pl. Lenina
2 : Mayakovskaya / Pl. Vosstaniya
3 : Pushkinskaya
4 : Tekhn. Institut
5 : Baltiskaya
6 : Gostiny Dvor / Nevski Prospekt
6
2
Neva
GLAVNY (Moskovski)
3
VITEBSKI
4
5
Baltiski
17 km

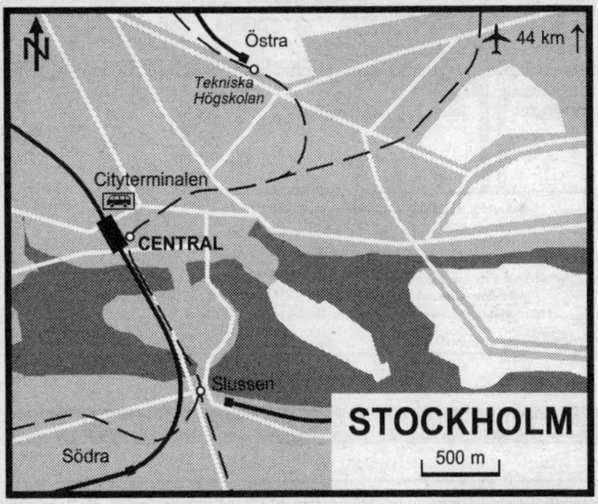
Östra
44 km
Tekniska Högskolan
Cityterminalen
CENTRAL
Slussen
STOCKHOLM
Södra
500 m

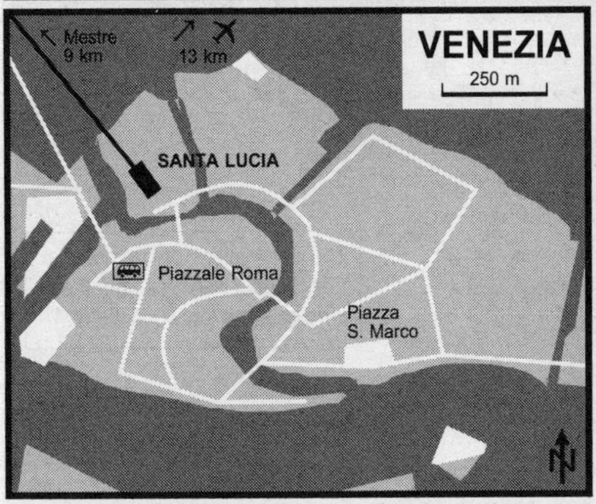
Mestre 9 km
13 km
VENEZIA
250 m
SANTA LUCIA
Piazzale Roma
Piazza S. Marco

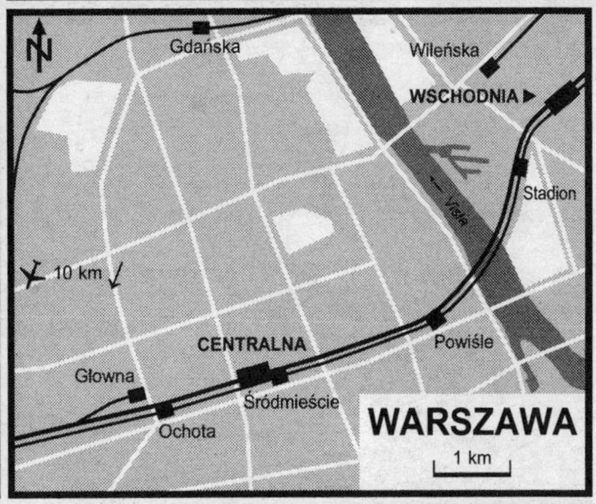
Gdańska
Wileńska
WSCHODNIA
Stadion
Wisła
10 km
CENTRALNA
Powiśle
Główna
Śródmieście
Ochota
WARSZAWA
1 km

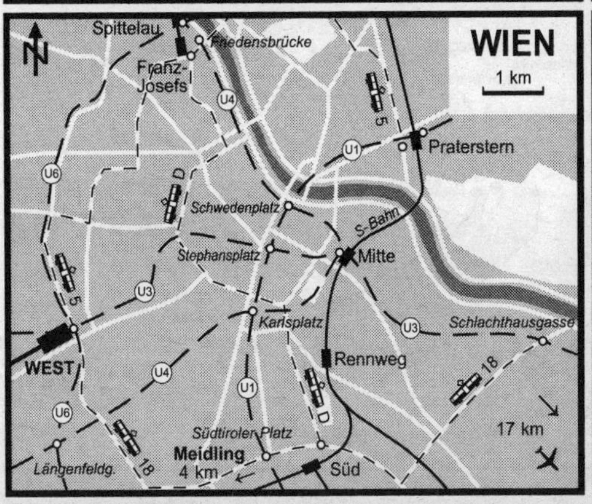
Spittelau
Friedensbrücke
WIEN
1 km
Franz-Josefs
U4
5
U1
Praterstern
U6
D
Schwedenplatz
S-Bahn
Stephansplatz
Mitte
5
U3
Karlsplatz
U3
Schlachthausgasse
WEST
U4
Rennweg
18
U1
D
U6
17 km
Südtiroler Platz
Längenfeldg.
18
Meidling 4 km
Süd

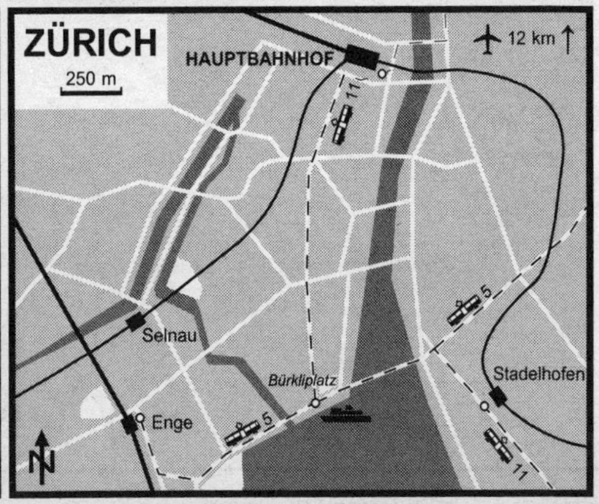
ZÜRICH
250 m
HAUPTBAHNHOF
12 km
11
5
Selnau
Stadelhofen
Bürkliplatz
Enge
5
11

LONDON UNDERGROUND

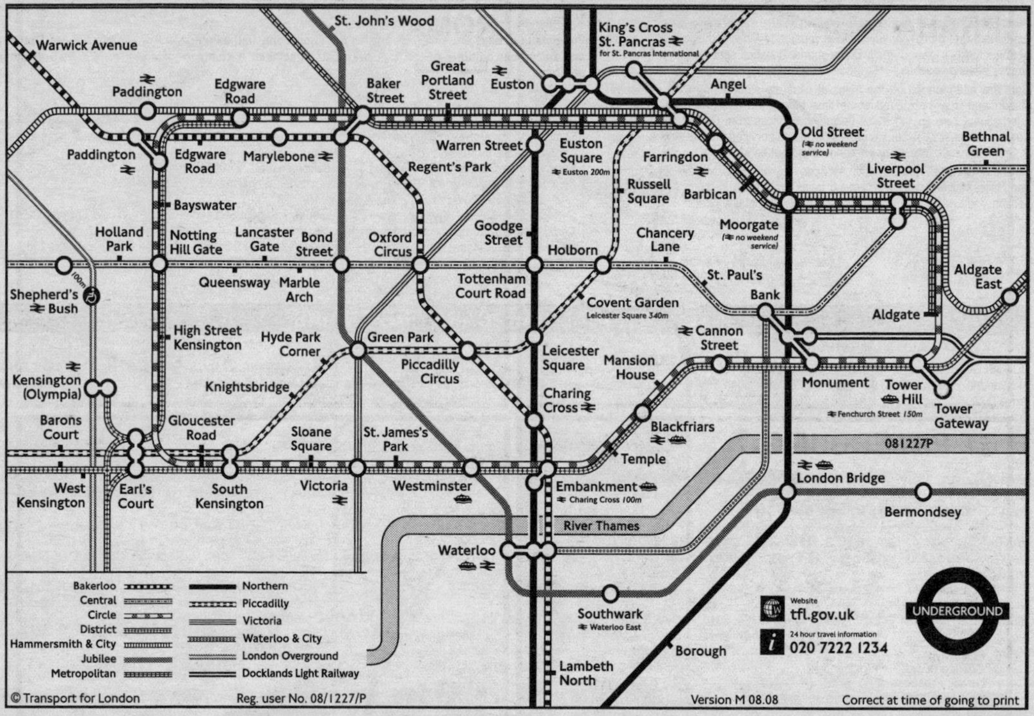

INTERNATIONAL CAR-CARRYING TRAIN TERMINALS

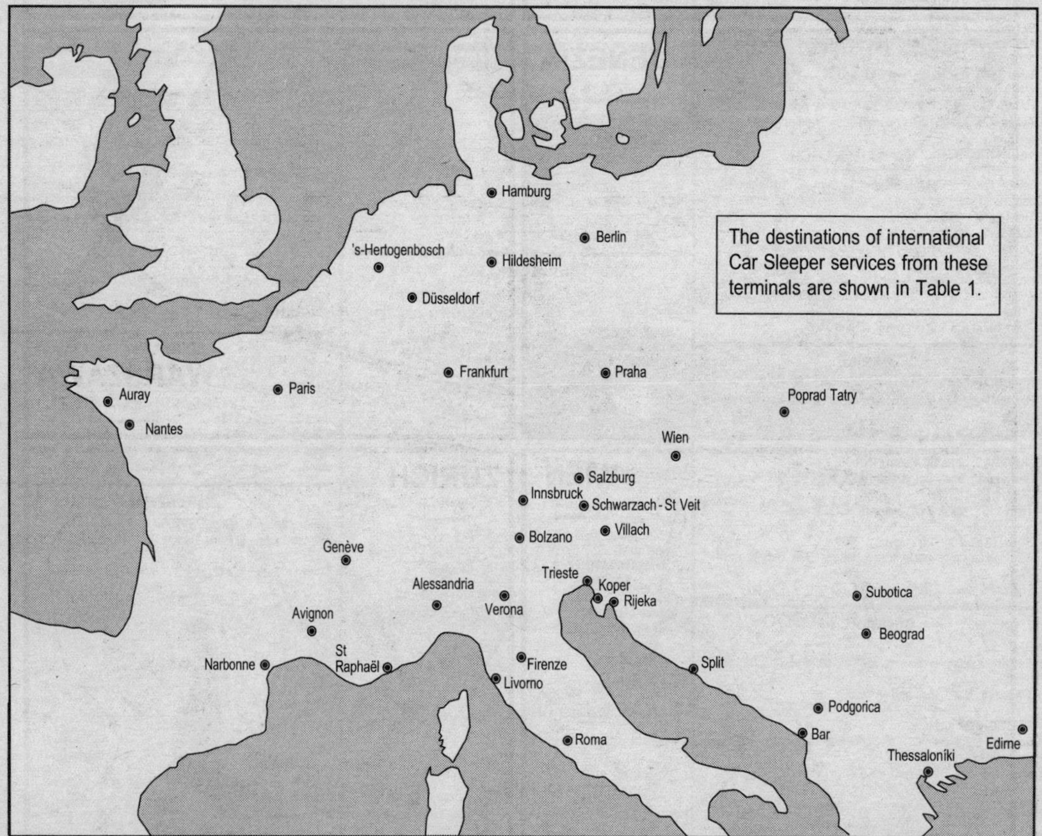

The destinations of international Car Sleeper services from these terminals are shown in Table 1.

Car-carrying trains are composed of special wagons or vans for the conveyance of motorcars usually with sleeping cars and couchettes enabling the driver and passengers to travel overnight in comfort in the same train. Some services (particularly in France) convey vehicles separately allowing passengers a choice of trains for their own journey. Some shorter distance services run by day and convey seating coaches.

Cars are often loaded on the trains at separate stations from the passenger station and may be loaded some time before the passenger train departs. International car-carrying trains (including services from Calais) are shown in Table **1**, Domestic car-carrying trains (including services from Genève) in Table **2**. Some services also carry passengers without cars.

Details of Channel Tunnel shuttle services may be found on page 44. Austrian and Swiss alpine tunnel car-carrying trains are shown in the relevant country section - see pages 451 and 258 respectively for details.

Readers should be careful to check that dates refer to current schedules, as old dates may be left in the table until such time as current information is received. Loading and train times may vary on some dates, but will be confirmed by the agent when booking.

Full details of days and dates of running are shown only in the February, April, June, August, October and December editions of the European Rail Timetable. A summary of services is shown in other editions.

Some services shown in Table **1** are operated by organisations other than national railway companies. Contact details for these are:
Services from Germany: DB AutoZug, (UK booking centre); ✆ 08718 80 80 66.
Services from Netherlands: Euro-Express-Traincharter, Singelstraat 1a, 2613 EM Delft; ✆ +31 (0)15 213 36 36.
Services from Calais: French Motorail (Rail Europe), 1 Regent St, London SW1Y 4XT; ✆ 0844 848 4041.
Certain Eastern European services (see table for details):
Optima Tours, Karlstrasse 56, 80333 D-München; ✆ +49 89 54880 - 111, fax +49 89 54880 - 155.

SEE MAP PAGE 34

INTERNATIONAL CAR-CARRYING TRAINS 1

ALESSANDRIA to

DÜSSELDORF: ① Apr. 6 - Oct. 26, 2009; ① Apr. 5 - 26, 2010.
Alessandria load 1530 - 1700, depart 1828, Düsseldorf Hbf arrive 0956.
Train **13372**: 🛏 1,2 cl., ▬ 2 cl. and ✕.

FRANKFURT: ①⑥ Apr. 4 - Oct. 31, 2009; ①⑥ Apr. 3 - 26, 2010.
Alessandria load 1530 - 1700, depart 1828, Frankfurt Neu Isenburg arrive 0603.
Train **13370/2/43370**: 🛏 1,2 cl., ▬ 2 cl. and ✕.

HAMBURG: ⑥ Apr. 4 - Oct. 31, 2009; ⑥ Apr. 3 - 24, 2010.
Alessandria load 1530 - 1700, depart 1828, Hamburg Altona arrive 1158.
Train **13370**: 🛏 1,2 cl., ▬ 2 cl. and ✕.

HILDESHEIM: ⑥ Apr. 4 - Oct. 31, 2009; ⑥ Apr. 3 - 24, 2010.
Alessandria load 1530 - 1700, depart 1828, Hildesheim arrive 0949.
Train **13370**: 🛏 1,2 cl., ▬ 2 cl. and ✕.

's-HERTOGENBOSCH: ⑥ June 5 - Sept. 4, 2010.
Timings not advised.
🛏 1,2 cl., ▬ 2 cl. and ✕.
Operator: Euro-Express-Traincharter (see table heading).

AVIGNON to

Loading at Avignon Sud (🚌 connection to Centre).

BERLIN: ① Apr. 6 - Oct. 26, 2009; ① Apr. 5 - 26, 2010.
Avignon load 1745 - 1845, depart 2001, Berlin Wannsee arrive 1502.
Train **1362**: 🛏 1,2 cl., ▬ 2 cl. and ✕.

HAMBURG: ④ Apr. 2 - Oct. 29, 2009; ④ Apr. 8 - 29, 2010.
Avignon load 1745 - 1845, depart 2000, Hamburg Altona arrive 1433.
Train **1372/6**: 🛏 1,2 cl., ▬ 2 cl. and ✕.

's-HERTOGENBOSCH: ⑥ June 5 - Sept. 4, 2010 (also ① July 12 - Aug. 16).
Timings not advised.
🛏 1,2 cl., ▬ 2 cl. and ✕.
Operator: Euro-Express-Traincharter (see table heading).

HILDESHEIM: ⑥ Apr. 4 - Oct. 31, 2009; ⑥ Apr. 3 - 24, 2010.
Avignon load 1745 - 1845, depart 2000, Hildesheim Hbf arrive 1152.
Train **1372**: 🛏 1,2 cl., ▬ 2 cl. and ✕.

BAR to

BEOGRAD: daily.
Bar loading times not advised, depart 2100, Beograd arrive 0632.
Train **434**: 🛏 1,2 cl. and ▬ 2 cl.

NOVI SAD: June 20 - Sept. 1, 2009.
Bar loading times not advised, depart 2010, Novi Sad arrive 0727.
Train **1138**: 🛏 1,2 cl., ▬ 2 cl., [2] and 🍷.

SUBOTICA: June 20 - Sept. 1, 2009.
Bar loading times not advised, depart 1800, Subotica arrive 0716.
Train **436**: 🛏 1,2 cl., ▬ 2 cl., [2] and 🍷.

BEOGRAD to

BAR: daily.
Beograd loading times not advised, depart 2210, Bar arrive 0800.
Train **435**: 🛏 1,2 cl. and ▬ 2 cl.

PODGORICA: daily.
Beograd loading times not advised, depart 2210, Podgorica arrive 0642.
Train **435**: 🛏 1,2 cl. and ▬ 2 cl.

BERLIN to

AVIGNON: ⑦ Apr. 5 - Oct. 25, 2009; ⑦ Apr. 4 - 25, 2010.
Berlin Wannsee load 1150 - 1220, depart 1311, Avignon arrive 0818.
Train **1360**: 🛏 1,2 cl., ▬ 2 cl. and ✕.

BOLZANO: ⑤ until Oct. 30; ⑤ Dec. 18, 2009 - Apr. 30, 2010.
Berlin Wannsee load 1640 - 1720 (1850 - 1910 from Dec. 18), depart 1803 (2020 from Dec. 18), Bolzano arrive 0645 (0940 from Dec. 19).
Train **13301/5**: 🛏 1,2 cl., ▬ 2 cl. and ✕.

INNSBRUCK: ⑤ Dec. 18, 2009 - Mar. 26, 2010.
Berlin Wannsee load 1910 - 1930, depart 2020, Innsbruck arrive 0711.
Train **43305**: 🛏 1,2 cl., ▬ 2 cl. and ✕.

NARBONNE: ⑦ Apr. 5 - Oct. 25, 2009; ⑦ Apr. 4 - 25, 2010.
Berlin Wannsee load 1120 - 1200, depart 1311, Narbonne arrive 1035.
Train **1360**: 🛏 1,2 cl., ▬ 2 cl. and ✕.

SCHWARZACH-ST VEIT: ⑤ Dec. 18, 2009 - Mar. 26, 2010.
Berlin Wannsee load 2000 - 2030, depart 2111, Schwarzach-St Veit arrive 0932.
Train **43395**: 🛏 1,2 cl., ▬ 2 cl. and ✕.

TRIESTE: ③ Apr. 1 - Oct. 28, 2009; ③ Apr. 7 - 28, 2010.
Berlin Wannsee load 1510 - 1540, depart 1703, Trieste arrive 1014.
Train **13307**: 🛏 1,2 cl., ▬ 2 cl. and ✕.

VERONA: ⑤ Apr. 3 - Oct. 30, 2009; ⑤ Apr. 2 - 30, 2010.
Berlin Wannsee load 1600 - 1630, depart 1803, Verona arrive 0903.
Train **13301**: 🛏 1,2 cl., ▬ 2 cl. and ✕.

VILLACH: ③ Apr. 7 - 28, 2010.
Timings not advised.
Train **13307**: 🛏 1,2 cl., ▬ 2 cl. and ✕.

WIEN: daily until Dec. 12, 2009.
Berlin Wannsee load 1620 - 1700, depart 1733, Wien Westbf arrive 0630.
Train **477/203**: 🛏 1,2 cl. and ▬ 2 cl.

BOLZANO to

German services may be bookable only in Germany.

BERLIN: ⑥ until Oct. 31; ⑥ Dec. 19, 2009 - Apr. 24, 2010.
Bolzano load 1830 - 1900, depart 2024 (1840 from Dec. 19), Berlin Wannsee arrive 0754 (0814 from Dec. 20).
Train **13300/4**: 🛏 1,2 cl., ▬ 2 cl. and ✕.

DÜSSELDORF: ④⑥ Apr. 30 - Oct. 17; ⑥ Dec. 19 , 2009 - Apr. 24, 2010 (also Oct. 24, 31).
Bolzano load 1830 - 1945, depart 2024 (2109⑥, 1655 from Dec. 19), Düsseldorf Hbf arrive 0840 (1025⑦, 0626 from Dec. 20).
Train **13316/20/24**: 🛏 1,2 cl., ▬ 2 cl. and ✕.

HAMBURG: ①④⑥ June 1 - Oct. 3; ⑥ Oct. 10 - 31; ⑥ Dec. 19, 2009 - Apr. 24, 2010 (also Oct. 1, 8, 15).
Bolzano load 1630 - 1900, depart 1740 - 2024, Hamburg Altona arrive 0935 (1034②, 1305⑤, 0759 from Dec. 20).
Train **13316/80/82/84**: 🛏 1,2 cl., ▬ 2 cl. and ✕.

HILDESHEIM: ⑥ Oct. 3 - 31, 2009; ⑥ Apr. 3 - 24, 2010.
Bolzano load 1630 - 1710, depart 1851, Bolzano arrive 0629.
Train **13380/2**: 🛏 1,2 cl., ▬ 2 cl. and ✕.

DÜSSELDORF to

ALESSANDRIA: ⑦ Apr. 5 - Oct. 25, 2009; ⑦ Apr. 4 - 29, 2010.
Düsseldorf Hbf load 1440 - 1510, depart 1554, Alessandria 0725.
Train **13373**: 🛏 1,2 cl., ▬ 2 cl. and ✕.

BOLZANO: ③⑤ Apr. 29 - Oct. 16; ⑤ Dec. 18, 2009 - Apr. 30, 2010 (also Oct. 23, 30).
Düsseldorf Hbf load 1645 - 1800 (2045 - 2110 from Dec. 18), depart 1735 (1854③, 2132 from Dec. 18), Bolzano arrive 0742 (0910④, 1117 from Dec. 19).
Train **13317/21/25**: 🛏 1,2 cl., ▬ 2 cl. and ✕.

INNSBRUCK: ③ Apr. 1 - Oct. 28; ②⑤ Dec. 18, 2009 - Mar. 30, 2010.
Düsseldorf load 2030 - 2050 (2100 - 2130②), depart 2155 (2132⑤, 2214②), Innsbruck arrive 0850 (0906 from Dec. 19).
Train **43325/9**: 🛏 1,2 cl., ▬ 2 cl. and ✕.

NARBONNE: ③ Apr. 1 - Oct. 28, 2009; ⑦ Feb. 28 - Mar. 28; ③ Apr. 7 - 28, 2010 (also Nov. 8, 22, Dec. 6, 20, Jan. 3, 17, 31, Feb. 14).
Düsseldorf Hbf load 1440 - 1510, depart 1554, Narbonne arrive 1004 (1035①).
Train **1311/54**: 🛏 1,2 cl., ▬ 2 cl. and ✕.

SALZBURG: ⑤ Dec. 19, 2008 - Mar. 27; ⑦ Apr. 5 - Oct. 25, 2009 (also Dec. 21, 28, Jan. 4).
Düsseldorf Hbf load 2050 - 2110, depart 2155, Salzburg Hbf arrive 0804.
Train **13315/23**: 🛏 1,2 cl., ▬ 2 cl. and ✕.

SCHWARZACH-ST VEIT: ⑤ Dec. 18, 2009 - Mar. 26; ⑦ Apr. 4 - 25, 2010.
Timings not advised.
Train **43315/23**: 🛏 1,2 cl., ▬ 2 cl. and ✕.

TRIESTE: ⑤ Apr. 3 - Oct. 30, 2009; ⑤ Apr. 2 - 30, 2010.
Düsseldorf Hbf load 1330 - 1350, depart 1501, Trieste arrive 1014.
Train **13311**: 🛏 1,2 cl., ▬ 2 cl. and ✕.

VERONA: ⑤ Apr. 3 - Oct. 30, 2009; ⑤ Apr. 2 - 30, 2010.
Düsseldorf Hbf load 1615 - 1645, depart 1735, Verona arrive 0955.
Train **13321**: 🛏 1,2 cl., ▬ 2 cl. and ✕.

VILLACH: ⑤ Apr. 2 - 30, 2010.
Timings not advised.
Train **13311**: 🛏 1,2 cl., ▬ 2 cl. and ✕.

EDIRNE to

VILLACH: ④ May 14 - June 18; ④⑦ June 21 - July 12; ①③④⑦ July 19 - Aug. 6; ①④⑤ Aug. 10 - 21; ①②③④⑤⑥ Aug. 22 - Sept. 11; ①④ Sept. 14 - Nov. 9, 2009 (also June 23, 29, Aug. 18).
Timings vary. ▬ 2 cl. (also 🛏 1,2 cl. on some services).
Contact operator for further details.
Operator: Optima Tours (see table heading).

FIRENZE to

WIEN: ⑥ Apr. 4 - Sept. 26, 2009.
Firenze Campo di Marte load 1845 - 1930, depart 2055, Wien Süd arrive 0838.
Train **1236**: 🛏 1,2 cl., ▬ 2 cl. and [12].

FRANKFURT (NEU ISENBURG) to

ALESSANDRIA: ⑤⑦ Apr. 3 - Oct. 30, 2009; ⑤⑦ Apr. 2-30, 2010.
Frankfurt Neu Isenburg load 1800 - 1900, depart 1943, Alessandria arrive 0725.
Train **13371/3/43371**: [sleeper] 1,2 cl., [couchette] 2 cl. and ✕.

NARBONNE: ③⑦ Apr. 1 - Oct. 28, 2009; ⑦ Feb. 28 - Mar. 28; ③⑦ Apr. 4-28, 2010 (also Nov. 8, 22, Dec. 6, 20, Jan. 3, 17, 31, Feb. 14).
Frankfurt Neu Isenburg load 1830 - 1930 (1910 - 2000⑦), depart 1953 (2020⑦), Narbonne arrive 1004 (1035①).
Train **1354/41360/91**: [sleeper] 1,2 cl., [couchette] 2 cl. and ✕.

TRIESTE: ⑤ Apr. 3 - Oct. 30, 2009; ⑤ Apr. 2-30, 2010.
Frankfurt Neu Isenburg load 1830 - 1900, depart 1921, Trieste arrive 1014.
Train **13311**: [sleeper] 1,2 cl., [couchette] 2 cl. and ✕.

VILLACH: ⑤ Apr. 3 - Oct. 30, 2009; ⑤ Apr. 2-30, 2010.
Frankfurt Neu Isenburg load 1800 - 1830, depart 1921, Villach Ost arrive 0643.
Train **13311**: [sleeper] 1,2 cl., [couchette] 2 cl. and ✕.

FRÉJUS ST. RAPHAEL – see St. Raphael

GENÈVE – see Table 2

HAMBURG to

ALESSANDRIA: ⑤ Apr. 3 - Oct. 30, 2009; ⑤ Apr. 2-30, 2010.
Hamburg Altona load 1110 - 1250, depart 1320, Alessandria arrive 0727 or 0745.
Train **13371**: [sleeper] 1,2 cl., [couchette] 2 cl. and ✕.

AVIGNON: ③ Apr. 1 - Oct. 28, 2009; ③ Apr. 7-28, 2010.
Hamburg Altona load 1210 - 1240, depart 1314, Avignon arrive 0820.
Train **1371/5**: [sleeper] 1,2 cl., [couchette] 2 cl. and ✕.

BOLZANO: ③⑤⑦ May 27 - Oct. 2; ⑤ Oct. 9-30; ⑤ Dec. 18, 2009 - Apr. 30, 2010 (also Oct. 7, 14).
Hamburg Altona load 1300 - 1735 (1750 - 1815 from Dec. 18), depart 1343③ (1734⑦, 1759⑤, 1915 from Dec. 18), Bolzano arrive 0910 (0949⑥, 1040 from Dec. 19).
Train **13317/81/83/85**: [sleeper] 1,2 cl., [couchette] 2 cl. and ✕.

INNSBRUCK: ②⑤ Dec. 18, 2009 - Mar. 30, 2010.
Hamburg Altona load 1620 - 1650 (1810 - 1840⑤), depart 1723 (1915⑤), Innsbruck arrive 0906 (0806⑥).
Train **13329/43385**: [sleeper] 1,2 cl., [couchette] 2 cl. and ✕.

NARBONNE: ③⑤ Apr. 1 - Oct. 30, 2009; ⑦ Feb. 28 - Mar. 28; ③⑤ Apr. 2-30, 2010 (also Nov. 8, 22, Dec. 6, 20, Jan. 3, 17, 31, Feb. 14).
Hamburg Altona load 1200 - 1230 (1225 - 1245⑦), depart 1314 (1323⑦), Narbonne arrive 1035.
Train **1371/5/91**: [sleeper] 1,2 cl., [couchette] 2 cl. and ✕.

SCHWARZACH-ST VEIT: ⑤ Dec. 18, 2009 - Mar. 26, 2010.
Hamburg Altona load 1600 - 1630, depart 1700, Schwarzach-St Veit arrive 0932.
Train **13395**: [sleeper] 1,2 cl., [couchette] 2 cl. and ✕.

TRIESTE: ⑦ Oct. 4-25, 2009; ⑦ Apr. 4-25, 2010.
Hamburg Altona load 1350 - 1420, depart 1454, Trieste arrive 1014.
Train **13393/97**: [sleeper] 1,2 cl., [couchette] 2 cl. and ✕.

VERONA: ③⑤⑦ May 27 - Oct. 2; ⑤ Oct. 9-30, 2009; ⑤ Apr. 2-30, 2010 (also Oct. 7, 14).
Hamburg Altona load 1240 - 1805, depart 1343 (1734⑦, 1759⑤), Verona arrive 1138 (1105①④).
Train **13317/81/3**: [sleeper] 1,2 cl., [couchette] 2 cl. and ✕.

VILLACH: ⑦ Oct. 4-25, 2009; ⑦ Apr. 4-25, 2010.
Hamburg Altona load 1400 - 1435, depart 1454, Villach Ost arrive 0643.
Train **13393/7**: [sleeper] 1,2 cl., [couchette] 2 cl. and ✕.

WIEN: daily until Dec. 12, 2009.
Hamburg Altona load 1915 - 1950, depart 2018, Wien Westbf arrive 0904.
Train **491**: [sleeper] 1,2 cl. and [couchette] 2 cl.

's-HERTOGENBOSCH to

ALESSANDRIA: ⑤ June 4 - Sept. 3, 2010.
Timings not advised.
[sleeper] 1,2 cl., [couchette] 2 cl. and ✕.
Operator: Euro-Express-Traincharter (see table heading).

AVIGNON: ⑤ June 4 - Sept. 3, 2010 (also ⑦ July 11 - Aug. 15).
Timings not advised.
[sleeper] 1,2 cl., [couchette] 2 cl. and ✕.
Operator: Euro-Express-Traincharter (see table heading).

LIVORNO: ⑤ June 2 - Aug. 20, 2010.
Timings not advised.
[sleeper] 1,2 cl., [couchette] 2 cl. and ✕.
Operator: Euro-Express-Traincharter (see table heading).

ST. RAPHAËL: ⑤ July 9 - Aug. 13, 2010.
Timings not advised.
[sleeper] 1,2 cl., [couchette] 2 cl. and ✕.
Operator: Euro-Express-Traincharter (see table heading).

HILDESHEIM to

ALESSANDRIA: ⑤ Apr. 3 - Oct. 30, 2009; ⑤ Apr. 2-30, 2010.
Hildesheim load 1450 - 1530, depart 1643, Alessandria arrive 0727.
Train **13371**: [sleeper] 1,2 cl., [couchette] 2 cl. and ✕.

AVIGNON: ⑤ Apr. 3 - Oct. 30, 2009; ⑤ Apr. 2-30, 2010.
Hildesheim load 1320 - 1350, depart 1500, Avignon arrive 0736.
Train **1371**: [sleeper] 1,2 cl., [couchette] 2 cl. and ✕.

BOLZANO: ⑤ Oct. 2-30, 2009; ⑤ Apr. 2-30, 2010.
Hildesheim load 1840 - 2010, depart 2134, Bolzano arrive 0949.
Train **13381/3**: [sleeper] 1,2 cl., [couchette] 2 cl. and ✕.

INNSBRUCK: ⑤ Dec. 18, 2009 - Mar. 26, 2010.
Hildesheim load 2020 - 2050, depart 2156, Innsbruck arrive 0806.
Train **43385**: [sleeper] 1,2 cl., [couchette] 2 cl. and ✕.

NARBONNE: ③⑤ Apr. 1 - Oct. 30, 2009; ⑦ Feb. 28 - Mar. 28; ③⑤ Apr. 2-30, 2010 (also Nov. 8, 22, Dec. 6, 20, Jan. 3, 17, 31, Feb. 14).
Hildesheim load 1410 - 1510, depart 1500 (1550⑦, 1600⑤), Narbonne arrive 1035 (0945⑥).
Train **1371/5/91**: [sleeper] 1,2 cl., [couchette] 2 cl. and ✕.

VILLACH: ⑦ Oct. 4-25, 2009; ⑦ Apr. 4-25, 2010.
Hildesheim load 1700 - 1745, depart 1827, Villach Ost arrive 0643.
Train **13393/7**: [sleeper] 1,2 cl., [couchette] 2 cl. and ✕.

INNSBRUCK to

BERLIN: ⑥ Dec. 19, 2009 - Mar. 27, 2010.
Loading time not advised, depart 2120, Berlin Wannsee arrive 0814.
Train **43304**: [sleeper] 1,2 cl., [couchette] 2 cl. and ✕.

DÜSSELDORF: ④ Apr. 2 - Oct. 29; ③⑥ Dec. 19, 2009 - Mar. 31, 2010.
Loading time not advised, depart 1938 (1918 from Dec. 19), Düsseldorf arrive 0626.
Train **43324/8**: [sleeper] 1,2 cl., [couchette] 2 cl. and ✕.

HAMBURG: ③⑥ Dec. 19, 2009 - Mar. 31, 2010.
Loading time not advised, depart 1918 (2017⑥), Hamburg Altona 1133 (0759⑦).
Train **13328/43384**: [sleeper] 1,2 cl., [couchette] 2 cl. and ✕.

HILDESHEIM: ⑥ Dec. 19, 2009 - Mar. 27, 2010.
Loading time not advised, depart 2017, Hildesheim arrive 0600.
Train **43384**: [sleeper] 1,2 cl., [couchette] 2 cl. and ✕.

KOPER to

WIEN: ⑥ June 6 - Aug. 29, 2009.
Koper load 1945 - 2130, depart 2215, Wien Sud arrive 0717.
Train **1458**: [couchette] 2 cl. and [2].

KOŠICE

PRAHA: daily except Dec. 24, 31.
Košice depart 2100, Praha Hlavní arrive 0709.
Train **424**: [sleeper] 1,2 cl., [couchette] 2 cl. and [2].

LIVORNO to

German services may be bookable only in Germany.

's-HERTOGENBOSCH: ⑥ July 3 - Aug. 21, 2010.
Timings not advised.
[sleeper] 1,2 cl., [couchette] 2 cl. and ✕.
Operator: Euro-Express-Traincharter (see table heading).

NARBONNE to

Loading at Gare auto/train ([bus] connection)

BERLIN: ① Apr. 6 - Oct. 26, 2009; ① Apr. 5-26, 2010.
Narbonne load 1500 - 1600, depart 1737, Berlin Wannsee arrive 1502.
Train **1362**: [sleeper] 1,2 cl., [couchette] 2 cl. and ✕.

DÜSSELDORF: ④ Apr. 2 - Oct. 29, 2009; ① Mar. 1-29; ④ Apr. 8-29, 2010 (also Nov. 9, 23, Dec. 7, 21, Jan. 4, 18, Feb. 1, 15).
Narbonne load 1400 - 1500 (1500 - 1540①), depart 1645 (1737①), Düsseldorf Hbf arrive 0956 (1228②).
Train **1356/51392**: [sleeper] 1,2 cl., [couchette] 2 cl. and ✕.

FRANKFURT: ①④ Apr. 2 - Oct. 29, 2009; ① Mar. 1-29; ①④ Apr. 5-29, 2010 (also Nov. 9, 23, Dec. 7, 21, Jan. 4, 18, Feb. 1, 15).
Narbonne load 1500 - 1600 (1400 - 1500④), depart 1737 (1645④), Frankfurt Neu Isenburg arrive 0753 (0603⑤).
Train **1356/41362/92**: [sleeper] 1,2 cl., [couchette] 2 cl. and ✕.

HAMBURG: ④⑥ Apr. 2 - Oct. 31, 2009; ① Mar. 1-29; ④⑥ Apr. 3-29, 2010 (also Nov. 9, 23, Dec. 7, 21, Jan. 4, 18, Feb. 1, 15).
Narbonne load 1500 - 1600, depart 1737, Hamburg Altona arrive 1433 or 1442.
Train **1372/6/92**: [sleeper] 1,2 cl., [couchette] 2 cl. and ✕.

HILDESHEIM: ④⑥ Apr. 2 - Oct. 31, 2009; ① Mar. 1-29; ④⑥ Apr. 3-29, 2010 (also Nov. 9, 23, Dec. 7, 21, Jan. 4, 18, Feb. 1, 15).
Narbonne load 1500 - 1600, depart 1737, Hildesheim Hbf arrive 1152 or 1210.
Train **1372/6/92**: [sleeper] 1,2 cl., [couchette] 2 cl. and ✕.

NOVI SAD to

BAR: June 19 - Aug. 31, 2009.
Novi Sad loading times not advised, depart 1940, Bar arrive 0705.
Train **1139**: [sleeper] 1,2 cl., [couchette] 2 cl., [2] and 🍷.

PODGORICA to

BEOGRAD: daily.
Podgorica loading times not advised, depart 2210, Beograd arrive 0632.
Train **434**: [sleeper] 1,2 cl. and [couchette] 2 cl.

POPRAD TATRY to

PRAHA: daily except Dec. 24, 31.
Poprad Tatry depart 2249, Praha Hlavni arrive 0709.
Train **424**: [sleeper] 1,2 cl., [couchette] 2 cl. and [2].

PRAHA to

KOŠICE: daily except Dec. 24, 31.
Praha Hlavní depart 2204, Košice arrive 0732.
Train **425**: [sleeper] 1,2 cl., [couchette] 2 cl. and [2].

POPRAD TATRY: daily except Dec. 24, 31.
Praha Hlavní depart 2204, Poprad Tatry arrive 0537
Train **425**: [sleeper] 1,2 cl., [couchette] 2 cl. and [2].

SPLIT: June 19 - Sept. 4, 2009.
Praha Hlavní depart 0918, Split arrive 0548.
Train **1475/1823**: [sleeper] 1,2 cl. and [couchette] 2 cl.

RIJEKA to

WIEN: ⑥ June 6 - Aug. 29, 2009.
Rijeka load 1900 - 2000, depart 2045, Wien Süd arrive 0717.
Train **480/1458**: [couchette] 2 cl. and [2].

ROMA to

WIEN: ⑥ Apr. 4 - Sept. 26, 2009 (also Apr. 5, 13, May 1, 22, June 1, 11).
Roma Termini load 1430 - 1545, depart 1650 or 1720, Wien Süd arrive 0838 or 0857.
Train **1236/8**: [sleeper] 1,2 cl., [couchette] 2 cl. and [12].

ST RAPHAËL to

's-HERTOGENBOSCH: ⑥ July 10 - Aug. 14, 2010.
Timings not advised.
[sleeper] 1,2 cl., [couchette] 2 cl. and ✕.
Operator: Euro-Express-Traincharter (see table heading).

SALZBURG to

DÜSSELDORF: ⑥ Dec. 20, 2008 - Mar. 28; ① Apr. 6 - Oct. 26, 2009 (also Dec. 22, 29, Jan. 5).
Salzburg Hbf load 1800 - 1850, depart 1850, Düsseldorf Hbf arrive 0625.
Train **13314/22**: 🛏 1, 2 cl., ▬ 2 cl. and ✕.

SCHWARZACH-ST VEIT to

BERLIN: ⑥ Dec. 19, 2009 - Mar. 27, 2010.
Loading time not advised, depart 1925, Berlin Wannsee arrive 0650.
Train **43394**: 🛏 1, 2 cl., ▬ 2 cl. and ✕.

DÜSSELDORF: ⑥ Dec. 19, 2009 - Mar. 27; ① Apr. 5-26, 2010.
Timings not advised.
Train **43314/22**: 🛏 1, 2 cl., ▬ 2 cl. and ✕.

HAMBURG: ⑥ Dec. 19, 2009 - Mar. 27, 2010.
Loading time not advised, depart 1925, Hamburg Altona arrive 1017.
Train **13394**: 🛏 1, 2 cl., ▬ 2 cl. and ✕.

SPLIT to

PRAHA: June 20 - Sept. 5, 2009.
Split depart 2050, Praha arrive 1840.
Train **1822/783/1474**: 🛏 1, 2 cl. and ▬ 2 cl.

WIEN: ⑥ June 6 - Aug. 29, 2009.
Split load 2015 - 2045, depart 2221, Wien Süd arrive 1405.
Train **824/158**: ▬ 2 cl.

SUBOTICA to

BAR: June 19 - Aug. 31, 2009.
Subotica loading times not advised, depart 1840, Bar arrive 0849.
Train **437**: 🛏 1, 2 cl., ▬ 2 cl., [2] and 🍸.

THESSALONÍKI to

VILLACH: ⑤ Aug. 15 - Sept. 5, 2008 (also July 27, Aug. 3).
Timings vary. ▬ 2 cl.
Contact operator for further details.
Operator: Optima Tours (see table heading).

TRIESTE to

BERLIN: ④ Apr. 2 - Oct. 29, 2009; ④ Apr. 8-29, 2010.
Trieste load 1400 - 1445, depart 1552, Berlin Wannsee arrive 0903.
Train **13306**: 🛏 1, 2 cl., ▬ 2 cl. and ✕.

DÜSSELDORF: ⑥ Apr. 4 - Oct. 31, 2009; ⑥ Apr. 3 - 24, 2010.
Trieste load 1400 - 1445, depart 1552, Düsseldorf Hbf arrive 0956.
Train **13310**: 🛏 1, 2 cl., ▬ 2 cl. and ✕.

FRANKFURT: ⑥ Apr. 4 - Oct. 31, 2009; ⑥ Apr. 3 - 24, 2010.
Trieste load 1400 - 1445, depart 1552, Frankfurt Neu Isenburg arrive 0600.
Train **13310**: 🛏 1, 2 cl., ▬ 2 cl. and ✕.

HAMBURG: ① Oct. 5-26, 2009; ① Apr. 5-26, 2010.
Trieste load 1400 - 1445, depart 1552, Düsseldorf Hbf arrive 1133.
Train **13392/96**: 🛏 1, 2 cl., ▬ 2 cl. and ✕.

VERONA to

German services may be bookable only in Germany.

BERLIN: ⑥ Apr. 4 - Oct. 31, 2009; ⑥ Apr. 3 - 24, 2010.
Verona load 1600 - 1645, depart 1755, Berlin Wannsee arrive 0754.
Train **13300**: 🛏 1, 2 cl., ▬ 2 cl. and ✕.

DÜSSELDORF: ⑥ Apr. 4 - Oct. 31, 2009; ⑥ Apr. 3 - 24, 2010.
Verona load 1700 - 1745, depart 1855, Düsseldorf Hbf arrive 1025.
Train **13320**: 🛏 1, 2 cl., ▬ 2 cl. and ✕.

HAMBURG: ①④⑥ June 1 - Oct. 3; ⑥ Oct. 10 - 31, 2009; ⑥ Apr. 3 - 24, 2010 (also Oct. 1, 8, 15).
Verona load 1400 - 1515 (1600 - 1645④), depart 1553 (1755④, 1638⑥), Hamburg Altona arrive 0934 (1034②, 1305⑤).
Train **13316/80/2**: 🛏 1, 2 cl., ▬ 2 cl. and ✕.

VILLACH to

BERLIN: ④ Apr. 8-29, 2010.
Timings not advised.
Train **13306**: 🛏 1, 2 cl., ▬ 2 cl. and ✕.

DÜSSELDORF: ⑥ Apr. 3-24, 2010.
Timings not advised.
Train **13310**: 🛏 1, 2 cl., ▬ 2 cl. and ✕.

EDIRNE: ②⑥ May 9 - June 30; ②③⑥ July 1 - 15; ①②③⑤⑥ July 17 - Aug. 8; ⑥ Aug. 15 - Oct. 10, 2009 (also Apr. 24, 27, 30, May 4, June 17, 25, 28, Oct. 24, Nov. 7).
Timings vary. ▬ 2 cl. (also 🛏 1, 2 cl. on some services).
Contact operator for further details.
Operator: Optima Tours (see table heading).

FRANKFURT: ⑥ Apr. 4 - Oct. 31, 2009; ⑥ Apr. 3 - 24, 2010.
Villach Ost load 1835 - 1920, depart 2009, Frankfurt Neu Isenburg arrive 0600.
Train **13310**: 🛏 1, 2 cl., ▬ 2 cl. and ✕.

HAMBURG: ① Oct. 5 - 26, 2009; ① Apr. 5 - 26, 2010.
Villach Ost load 1835 - 1920, depart 2009, Hamburg Altona arrive 1133.
Train **13392/6**: 🛏 1, 2 cl., ▬ 2 cl. and ✕.

HILDESHEIM: ① Oct. 5 - 26, 2009; ① Apr. 5 - 26, 2010.
Villach Ost load 1835 - 1920, depart 2009, Hildesheim Hbf arrive 0915.
Train **13392/6**: 🛏 1, 2 cl., ▬ 2 cl. and ✕.

THESSALONÍKI: ⑥ July 12 - Aug. 2, 2008 (also Aug. 14, 20).
Timings vary. ▬ 2 cl.
Contact operator for further details.
Operator: Optima Tours (see table heading).

WIEN to

BERLIN: daily until Dec. 12, 2009.
Wien Westbf load 2115 - 2150, depart 2212, Berlin Wannsee arrive 0943.
Train **202/476**: 🛏 1, 2 cl. and ▬ 2 cl.

FIRENZE: ⑤ Apr. 3 - Sept. 25, 2009.
Wien Süd load 1845 - 1905, depart 2023, Firenze Campo di Marte arrive 0705.
Train **1237**: 🛏 1, 2 cl., ▬ 2 cl. and [12].

HAMBURG: daily until Dec. 12, 2009.
Wien Westbf load 1925 - 1940, depart 1954, Hamburg Altona arrive 0804.
Train **490**: 🛏 1, 2 cl. and ▬ 2 cl.

KOPER: ⑤ June 5 - Aug. 28, 2009.
Wien Süd load 2130 - 2150, depart 2156, Koper arrive 0642.
Train **1459**: ▬ 2 cl. and [2].

RIJEKA: ⑤ June 5 - Aug. 28, 2009.
Wien Süd load 2110 - 2130, depart 2156, Rijeka arrive 0850.
Train **1459/481**: ▬ 2 cl. and [2].

ROMA: ⑤ Apr. 3 - Sept. 25, 2009 (also Apr. 4, 12, 30, May 20, 31, June 10).
Wien Süd load 1910 - 1930, depart 2023, Roma Termini arrive 1045.
Train **1237/9**: 🛏 1, 2 cl., ▬ 2 cl. and [12].

SPLIT: ⑤ June 5 - Aug. 28, 2009.
Wien Süd load 1500 - 1530, depart 1556, Split arrive 0655.
Train **159/825**: ▬ 2 cl.

AUSTRIA

to 12/12/09

Feldkirch - Graz: daily (day and overnight trains).
Feldkirch - Wien: daily (day and overnight trains).
Feldkirch - Villach: daily.
Graz - Feldkirch: daily (day and overnight trains).
Innsbruck - Wien: daily (day train).
Lienz - Wien: ⑥ until Apr. 11; ⑥ May 30 - Sept. 19 (also Apr. 13, 14, June 1, 2) (day train).
Villach - Feldkirch: daily.
Villach - Wien: daily (2 day trains).
Wien - Feldkirch: daily (day and overnight trains).
Wien - Innsbruck: daily (day train).
Wien - Lienz: ⑥ until Apr. 11; ⑥ May 30 - Sept. 19 (also Apr. 13, 14, June 1, 2) (day train).
Wien - Villach: daily (2 day trains).

CROATIA

to 11/12/10

Split - Zagreb: daily. Also additional train in summer.
Zagreb - Split: daily. Also additional train in summer.

FINLAND

to 12/12/09

Subject to alteration on and around holiday dates.

Helsinki - Kemijärvi: ⑤ May 29 - Dec. 11.
Helsinki - Kolari: ③⑤⑥ (also June 18; not June 19, 20).
Helsinki - Oulu: daily (not June 19).
Helsinki - Rovaniemi: daily.
Kemijärvi - Helsinki: ⑥ May 30 - Dec. 12.
Kolari - Helsinki: ④⑥⑦ (not June 20).
Kolari - Tampere: ④⑥⑦ (not June 20).
Kolari - Turku: *winter only.*
Oulu - Helsinki: daily (not June 20).
Rovaniemi - Helsinki: daily.
Rovaniemi - Tampere: daily (not June 19).
Rovaniemi - Turku: daily (not June 20).
Tampere - Kolari: ③⑤⑥ (also June 18; not June 19, 20).
Tampere - Rovaniemi: daily (not June 20).
Turku - Kolari: *winter only.*
Turku - Rovaniemi: daily (not June 19).

FRANCE

to 12/12/09

For services from Calais, see Table 1.

Auray - Genève: daily June 19 - Sept. 5 (not Aug. 14, 15).
Auray - Lyon: daily June 19 - Sept. 5.
Auray - Metz: ⑥ June 20 - Sept. 19.
Auray - Strasbourg: ⑥ June 20 - Sept. 19.
Avignon - Metz: ⑥ June 20 - Sept. 19.
Avignon - Paris▲: daily Apr. 25 - Oct. 3; ②④⑥ Oct. 6 - Dec. 12 (not Aug. 10, Sept. 20).
Avignon - Seclin (Lille)▲: ⑥ June 20 - Sept. 19.
Avignon - Strasbourg: ⑥ June 20 - Sept. 19.
Biarritz - Genève: ⑥ June 27 - Sept. 5 (not Aug. 15).
Biarritz - Metz: ⑥ June 20 - Sept. 19.
Biarritz - Paris: ②④⑥ May 21 - June 25; daily June 25 - Sept. 5; ②④⑥ Sept. 8 - Oct. 1.
Biarritz - Strasbourg: ⑥ June 20 - Sept. 19.
Bordeaux - Marseille: ⑤⑥⑦ June 12 - Sept. 13 (not June 13, Sept. 12).
Bordeaux - Metz: ⑥ June 20 - Sept. 19.
Bordeaux - Paris▲: ②④⑥ May 21 - June 25; daily June 26 - Sept. 5; ②④⑦ Sept. 8 - Oct. 1; ②⑥ Oct. 3 - Dec. 12.
Bordeaux - St. Raphaël▲: ⑤⑥⑦ June 12 - Sept. 13 (not June 13, Sept. 12).
Bordeaux - Strasbourg: ⑥ June 20 - Sept. 19.
Briançon - Paris: ②④⑥ June 16 - Sept. 19 (also June 21; not June 20, Aug. 11).
Brive - Paris▲: ②④⑥ May 21 - June 25; daily June 26 - Sept. 5; ②④⑥ Sept. 8 - Oct. 1 (not June 23).
Fréjus-St. Raphaël – see St. Raphaël.
Genève - Auray: daily June 20 - Sept. 6 (not Aug. 15, 16).
Genève - Biarritz: ⑤ June 26 - Sept. 4 (not Aug. 14).
Genève - Nantes: daily June 20 - Sept. 6 (not Aug. 15, 16).
Genève - Paris▲: ②④⑥ June 20 - Sept. 5 (not Aug. 11, 15).
Lille – see Seclin (Lille).
Lyon - Auray: daily June 20 - Sept. 6.
Lyon - Nantes: daily June 20 - Sept. 6.
Lyon - Paris▲: ②④⑥ Apr. 25 - Oct. 3; ⑥ Oct. 10 - Dec. 12 (not Aug. 11, Sept. 12, 19).
Marseille - Bordeaux▲: ⑤⑥⑦ June 12 - Sept. 13 (not June 13, Sept. 12).
Marseille - Paris▲: daily Apr. 25 - Oct. 3; ②④⑥ Oct. 6 - Dec. 12 (not Aug. 10, Sept. 20).
Metz - Auray: ⑤ June 19 - Sept. 18.
Metz - Avignon: ⑤ June 19 - Sept. 18.
Metz - Biarritz: ⑤ June 19 - Sept. 18.
Metz - Bordeaux: ⑤ June 19 - Sept. 18.
Metz - Nantes: ⑤ June 19 - Sept. 18.
Metz - Narbonne: ⑤ June 19 - Sept. 18.
Metz - St. Raphaël: ⑤ June 19 - Sept. 18.
Nantes - Genève: daily June 19 - Sept. 5 (not Aug. 14, 15).
Nantes - Lyon: daily June 19 - Sept. 5.
Nantes - Metz: ⑥ June 20 - Sept. 19.
Nantes - St. Raphaël: daily June 19 - Sept. 6 (also June 12, 14, Sept. 11, 13).
Nantes - Strasbourg: ⑥ June 20 - Sept. 19.
Narbonne - Metz: ⑥ June 20 - Sept. 19.
Narbonne - Paris: ②④⑥ May 21 - June 25; daily June 26 - Sept. 5; ②④⑥ Sept. 8 - Oct. 1; ②⑥ Oct. 3 - Dec. 12.
Narbonne - Seclin (Lille)▲: ⑥ June 20 - Sept. 19.
Narbonne - Strasbourg: ⑥ June 20 - Sept. 19.
Nice - Paris: daily Apr. 25 - Oct. 3; ②④⑥ Oct. 6 - Dec. 12 (not Aug. 10, Sept. 20).
Paris - Avignon▲: daily Apr. 25 - Oct. 2; ①③⑤ Oct. 5 - Dec. 11 (not Aug. 10, Sept. 20).
Paris - Biarritz: ①③⑤ May 20 - June 24; daily June 25 - Sept. 4; ①③⑤ Sept. 7 - 30.
Paris - Bordeaux▲: ①③⑤ May 20 - June 24; daily June 25 - Sept. 4; ①③⑤ Sept. 7 - 30; ①⑤ Oct. 2 - Dec. 11.
Paris - Briançon: ①③⑤ June 15 - Sept. 18 (not Aug. 10).
Paris - Brive▲: ①③⑤ May 20 - June 24; daily June 25 - Sept. 4; ①③⑤ Sept. 7 - 30 (not June 22).
Paris - Genève▲: ①③⑤ June 19 - Sept. 4 (not Aug. 10, 14).
Paris - Lyon▲: ①③⑤ Apr. 27 - Oct. 2; ⑤ Oct. 9 - Dec. 11 (not Aug. 10, Sept. 11, 18).
Paris - Marseille▲: daily Apr. 25 - Oct. 2; ①③⑤ Oct. 5 - Dec. 11 (not Aug. 8, Sept. 20).
Paris - Narbonne: ①③⑤ May 20 - June 24; daily June 25 - Sept. 4; ①③⑤ Sept. 7 - 30; ①⑤ Oct. 2 - Dec. 11.
Paris - Nice: daily Apr. 25 - Oct. 2; ①③⑤ Oct. 5 - Dec. 11 (not Aug. 10, Sept. 20).
Paris - St. Raphaël: daily Apr. 25 - Oct. 2; ①③⑤ Oct. 5 - Dec. 11 (not Aug. 10, Sept. 20).
Paris - Toulon: daily Apr. 25 - Sept. 30 (not Aug. 10, Sept. 20).
Paris - Toulouse: ①③⑤ May 20 - June 24; daily June 25 - Sept. 4; ①③⑤ Sept. 7 - 30; ①⑤ Oct. 2 - Dec. 11.
St. Raphaël - Bordeaux▲: ⑤⑥⑦ June 12 - Sept. 13 (not June 13, Sept. 12).
St. Raphaël - Metz: ⑥ June 20 - Sept. 19.
St. Raphaël - Nantes: daily June 19 - Sept. 6 (also June 12, 14, Sept. 11, 13).
St. Raphaël - Paris: daily Apr. 25 - Oct. 3; ②④⑥ Oct. 6 - Dec. 12 (not Aug. 10, Sept. 20).
St. Raphaël - Seclin (Lille)▲: ⑥ June 20 - Sept. 19.
St. Raphaël - Strasbourg: ⑥ June 20 - Sept. 19.
Seclin (Lille) - Avignon▲: ⑤ June 19 - Sept. 18.
Seclin (Lille) - Narbonne▲: ⑤ June 19 - Sept. 18.
Seclin (Lille) - St. Raphaël▲: ⑤ June 19 - Sept. 18.
Strasbourg - Auray: ⑤ June 19 - Sept. 18.
Strasbourg - Avignon: ⑤ June 19 - Sept. 18.
Strasbourg - Biarritz: ⑤ June 19 - Sept. 18.
Strasbourg - Bordeaux: ⑤ June 19 - Sept. 18.
Strasbourg - Nantes: ⑤ June 19 - Sept. 18.
Strasbourg - Narbonne: ⑤ June 19 - Sept. 18.
Strasbourg - St. Raphaël: ⑤ June 19 - Sept. 18.
Toulon - Paris: daily Apr. 25 - Oct. 1 (not Aug. 10, Sept. 20).
Toulouse - Paris: ②④⑥ May 21 - June 25; daily June 26 - Sept. 5; ②④⑥ Sept. 8 - Oct. 1; ②⑥ Oct. 3 - Dec. 12.

▲ – These services offer the passenger a choice of departure times, usually including day and night trains.

GERMANY

to 30/04/10

Basel (Lörrach) - Hamburg Altona: daily June 1 - Sept. 13; ①②④⑤⑥⑦ Sept. 14 - Oct. 18; ①⑤⑥⑦ Oct. 19 - 31; ⑥ Nov. 7 - Jan. 30; ①⑥ Feb. 6 - 13; ①④⑥ Feb. 15 - Apr. 29 (also Dec. 17, 18, 20, 21, 23, 25, 27, 28, 30, Jan. 1, 3, 4).
Basel (Lörrach) - Hildesheim: daily June 1 - Sept. 13; ①②④⑤⑥⑦ Sept. 14 - Oct. 18; ①⑤⑥⑦ Oct. 19 - 31; ⑥ Nov. 7 - Jan. 30; ①⑥ Feb. 6 - 13; ①④⑥ Feb. 15 - Apr. 29 (also Dec. 17, 18, 20, 21, 23, 25, 27, 28, 30, Jan. 1, 3, 4).
Berlin Wannsee - München Ost: daily. [*CNL* train].
Düsseldorf - München Ost: ③⑦ Apr. 1 - Oct. 28; ⑤ Nov. 6 - Mar. 26; ③⑦ Mar. 28 - Apr. 28 (also Dec. 20, 27, Jan. 3).
Hamburg Altona - Basel (Lörrach): daily June 1 - Sept. 13; ①③④⑤⑥⑦ Sept. 14 - Oct. 4; ③④⑤⑥⑦ Oct. 7 - 18; ④⑤⑥⑦ Oct. 22 - 30; ⑤ Nov. 6 - Jan. 29; ⑤⑦ Feb. 5 - 14; ③⑤⑦ Feb. 17 - Apr. 30 (also Dec. 16, 17, 19, 20, 22, 23, 26, 27, 29, 30, Jan. 2, 3).
Hamburg Altona - München Ost: ①③⑤⑦ June 1 - Oct. 4; ③⑤⑦ Oct. 7 - 18; ⑤⑦ Oct. 23 - 30; ⑤ Dec. 18 - Jan. 29; ⑤⑦ Feb. 5 - Apr. 4; ③⑤⑦ Apr. 7 - 30 (also Dec. 16, 17, 19, 20, 23, 26, 27, 29). Also daily *CNL* train.
Hildesheim - Basel (Lörrach): daily June 1 - Sept. 13; ①③④⑤⑥⑦ Sept. 14 - Oct. 4; ③④⑤⑥⑦ Oct. 7 - 18; ④⑤⑥⑦ Oct. 22 - 30; ⑤ Nov. 6 - Jan. 29; ⑤⑦ Feb. 5 - 14; ③⑤⑦ Feb. 17 - Apr. 30 (also Dec. 16, 17, 19, 20, 22, 23, 26, 27, 29, 30, Jan. 2, 3).
Hildesheim - München Ost: ①③⑤⑦ June 1 - Oct. 4; ③⑤⑦ Oct. 7 - 18; ⑤⑦ Oct. 23 - 30; ⑤ Dec. 18 - Jan. 29; ⑤⑦ Feb. 5 - Apr. 4; ③⑤⑦ Apr. 7 - 30 (also Dec. 16, 17, 19, 20, 23, 26, 27, 29).
München Ost - Berlin Wannsee: daily. [*CNL* train].
München Ost - Düsseldorf: ①④ Apr. 2 - Oct. 29; ⑥ Nov. 7 - Mar. 27; ①④ Mar. 29 - Apr. 29 (also Dec. 21, 28, Jan. 4).
München Ost - Hamburg Altona: ①②④⑥ June 1 - Oct. 3; ①④⑥ Oct. 5 - 17; ①⑥ Oct. 19 - 31; ⑥ Dec. 19 - Jan. 30; ①⑥ Feb. 6 - Mar. 29; ①④⑥ Apr. 3 - 29 (also Dec. 17, 18, 20, 21, 25, 27, 28, Jan. 1). Also daily *CNL* train.
München Ost - Hildesheim: ①②④⑥ June 1 - Oct. 3; ①④⑥ Oct. 5 - 17; ①⑥ Oct. 19 - 31; ⑥ Dec. 19 - Jan. 30; ①⑥ Feb. 6 - Mar. 29; ①④⑥ Apr. 3 - 29 (also Dec. 17, 18, 20, 21, 25, 27, 28, Jan. 1).
Niebüll - Westerland: Daily shuttle service; 18 - 28 per day in summer, 12 - 14 per day in winter.
Westerland - Niebüll: Daily shuttle service; 18 - 28 per day in summer, 12 - 14 per day in winter.

CNL – *DB City Night Line* (see page **8** for description).

GREECE

to 11/12/10

Athína - Thessaloníki: daily (day and night trains).
Thessaloníki - Athína: daily (day and night trains).

ITALY

to 12/12/09

Bari - Bolzano: ⑤ June 5 - Sept. 18.
Bari - Milano: ⑤⑦ until Sept. 13.
Bari - Torino: ⑦ (daily until Sept. 13; also Dec. 8, not Dec. 6).
Bologna - Catania: daily.
Bologna - Lamezia: ⑤ June 12 - Sept. 11.
Bologna - Villa San Giovanni: daily. Also ⑤ until Sept. 11.
Bolzano - Bari: ⑥ June 6 - Sept. 19.
Bolzano - Lamezia: ⑥ June 20 - Sept. 12.
Bolzano - Roma: ⑥⑦ June 20 - July 19; daily July 25 - Sept. 6 (not Aug. 3 - 22).
Bolzano - Villa San Giovanni: ⑥ June 20 - Sept. 12.
Calalzo - Roma: ⑥ June 20 - July 18; daily July 25 - Sept. 5.
Catania - Bologna: daily.
Catania - Milano: ② until Sept. 8.
Catania - Roma: ①④⑥ June 15 - Sept. 19 (also Sept. 25).
Catania - Torino: ⑤ until Sept. 11.
Genova - Lamezia: ⑤⑦ June 12 - July 5; ②⑤⑦ July 7 - Sept. 13. Also ①⑥ until Sept. 14.
Genova - Villa San Giovanni: ⑤⑦ June 12 - July 5; ②⑤⑦ July 7 - Sept. 13. Also ①⑥ until Sept. 14.
Lamezia - Bologna: ⑥ June 13 - Sept. 12.
Lamezia - Bolzano: ⑤ June 19 - Sept. 11.
Lamezia - Genova: ④⑥ June 11 - July 4; ①④⑥ July 6 - Sept. 12. Also ⑤⑦ until Sept. 13.
Lamezia - Milano: ⑤⑦ until Sept. 13.
Lamezia - Roma: ⑦ June 21 - Sept. 13.
Lamezia - Torino: ④⑥ until July 4; ①④⑥ July 6 - Sept. 12.
Milano - Bari: ①⑥ until Sept. 14.
Milano - Catania: ③ until Sept. 9.
Milano - Lamezia: ①⑥ until Sept. 14.
Milano - Milazzo: ③ until Sept. 9.
Milano - Palermo: ③ until Sept. 9.
Milano - Villa San Giovanni: ①⑥ until Sept. 14.
Milazzo - Milano: ② until Sept. 8.
Milazzo - Torino: ⑤ until Sept. 11.
Napoli - Torino: ⑦ June 14 - Dec. 12 (also Dec. 8; not Dec. 6).
Palermo - Milano: ② until Sept. 8.
Palermo - Roma: ④⑦ June 18 - Sept. 20.
Palermo - Torino: ⑤ until Sept. 11.
Roma - Bolzano: ⑤⑥ June 19 - July 18; daily July 24 - Sept. 5 (not Aug. 3 - 22).
Roma - Calalzo: ⑤ June 19 - July 17; daily July 24 - Sept. 4.
Roma - Catania: ③⑤⑦ June 17 - Sept. 20.
Roma - Lamezia: ⑤ until Sept. 4.
Roma - Palermo: ③⑤ June 17 - Sept. 18.
Roma - Torino: ⑦ June 14 - Dec. 12 (also Dec. 8; not Dec. 6).
Roma - Villa San Giovanni: ④⑥ June 14 - Dec. 12.
Torino - Bari: ⑤ (daily until Sept. 12).
Torino - Catania: ⑥ until Sept. 12.
Torino - Lamezia: ⑤⑦ until July 5; ②⑤⑦ July 7 - Sept. 13.
Torino - Milazzo: ⑥ until Sept. 12.
Torino - Napoli: ⑤ June 14 - Dec. 12.
Torino - Palermo: ⑥ until Sept. 12.
Torino - Roma: ⑤ June 14 - Dec. 12.
Torino - Villa San Giovanni: ⑤⑦ until July 5; ②⑤⑦ July 7 - Sept. 13. Also ①③⑤ until Sept. 18.
Venezia - Villa San Giovanni: ⑤ until Sept. 11.
Villa San Giovanni - Bologna: daily. Also ⑥ until Sept. 12.
Villa San Giovanni - Bolzano: ⑤ June 19 - Sept. 11.
Villa San Giovanni - Genova: ④⑥ June 11 - July 4; ①④⑥ July 6 - Sept. 12. Also ⑤⑦ until Sept. 13.
Villa San Giovanni - Milano: ⑤⑦ until Sept. 13.
Villa San Giovanni - Roma: ⑤⑦ June 14 - Dec. 12.
Villa San Giovanni - Torino: ④⑥ until July 4; ①④⑥ July 6 - Sept. 12. Also ②④⑦ until Sept. 20 (also Sept. 27).
Villa San Giovanni - Venezia: ⑥ until Sept. 12.

GERMANY

The overnight services from München to Berlin and Hamburg have been reorganised and are now combined between München and Hildesheim. As a result of this, journey times have been extended with some earlier evening departure times. For example, the northbound service now departs München Hbf 2051 (previously 2252 for Hamburg, 2304 for Berlin). The Talgo rolling stock which has been operating these trains for the past 15 years is being withdrawn and replaced by conventional stock.

The overnight trains summary which previously appeared on page 361 has been moved to the international section as Table **54**. A summary of the München to Berlin and Hamburg domestic overnight trains continues to be shown in a special panel on page 361.

Earlier this year, the journey times of tilting *ICE* trains on the routes München - Nürnberg - Jena - Leipzig - Hamburg and Wiesbaden - Frankfurt - Erfurt - Leipzig - Dresden were extended by approximately 10 minutes. These extra minutes, which are generally added at the end of the train's journey, will remain in force until mid-June (please be aware that minor delays may be experienced at intermediate stations).

IC services on the Karlsruhe - Heidelberg - Frankfurt - Gießen - Kassel - Hannover - Hamburg route are accelerated by approximately 30 minutes between Göttingen and Hannover by omitting stops at Northeim, Kreiensen, Alfeld and Elze. These trains are consequently re-timed between Karlsruhe and Hannover, one benefit of which is a regular hourly pattern for *IC* trains between Heidelberg and Frankfurt (Table **911**).

The regional service between Bad Harzburg and Kreiensen (Table **859**) has been improved and simplified with a train every two hours Bad Harzburg - Kreiensen - Holzminden, together with a new direct service (also operating every two hours) Bad Harzburg - Kreiensen - Göttingen.

The regional service between München and Passau has been improved with through trains now running every hour (Table **944**). A number of regional services have been taken over by private operators, particularly in the Nordrhein-Westfalen region. *eurobahn Keolis Deutschland* now operate routes RE3 (Düsseldorf - Duisburg - Gelsenkirchen - Dortmund) and RE13 (Venlo - Mönchengladbach - Düsseldorf - Wuppertal - Hamm) using modern *Flirt* electric multiple unit trains. Branch line services to Kleve and Xanten are now operated by *Nord West Bahn*.

AUSTRIA

Work to transform Wien Südbahnhof in to a new major through station – Wien Hauptbahnhof – has started and will take a number of years to complete. All but the S-Bahn platforms and some temporary platforms for services to / from Bratislava are now closed. Until the new station is ready, Wien Meidling will be the main terminus for services to / from Sopron, Wiener Neustadt, Graz, Klagenfurt and Villach. Most international services via Břeclav will also serve Wien Meidling and are routed via Wien Simmering (many services will run beyond Meidling to free up platform space). Services to Bratislava (also some local cross-border trains to Györ) use temporary platforms named Südbahnhof (Ostbahn) on the approaches to the east side of the old station.

All services via the Arlberg route have been retimed. Two of the three international trains in each direction to / from Zürich are now operated by *Railjet* trains, with the third being converted in June 2010. The early morning Bregenz to Wien train and evening return will be reclassified *Railjet* from Apr. 11. These particular services have been accelerated by approximately 40 minutes by omitting a number of intermediate stops. The Graz - Bregenz *ÖEC* train has been withdrawn.

The service between Salzburg and Innsbruck via Zell am See (Table **960**) has been completely recast with extra daily through services available.

The very scenic Kleinreifling to Selzthal route has seen all but one of its services withdrawn south of Weißenbach-St Gallen. The only through service is now the Saturdays and Sundays only Wien - Schladming train. Services on the narrow gauge route Waidhofen - Lunz am See continue to be replaced by bus between Gstadt and Lunz until further notice. This is due to flood damage inflicted earlier in 2009.

On a more positive note, services on the narrow gauge Zell am See - Krimml *Pinzgauer Lokalbahn* are now operated by train for an extra 10 kilometres between Mittersill and Bramberg (train services have not run beyond Mittersill since 2005). The final 14 kilometres remain closed with a replacement bus service in operation.

The summer only services between Wien and Linz via Krems have been withdrawn west of Emmersdorf. Unfortunately there are now no scheduled services running between Emmersdorf and Sarmingstein.

Following electrification of the cross-border Retz to Znojmo route, through journeys are now available between Wien and Znojmo (Table **982**). A number of early morning and late evening journeys between Wien and Bratislava (via Marchegg) have been withdrawn. On the route via Kittsee, the weekend service has been reduced from hourly to every two hours.

POLAND

Details of *IC* and many long-distance trains are included but all local trains remain subject to confirmation. Train **35/36** *Georgij Kirpa* Kraków - Kyïv has been withdrawn (Table **1056**). Warszawa to Katowice and Kraków services have been accelerated to below 2 hours 30 minutes. Additional *IR* services are running between Warszawa and Kraków and a few minutes have been shaved off the Warszawa - Łódź route.

The two Wrocław - Międzylesie - Lichkov - Praha trains have been cut back to one Wrocław - Międzylesie - Lichkov - Pardubice but with a good connection to and from Praha (Tables **1045** and **1095**). Also, additional cross border services to the Czech Republic are running between Międzylesie and Lichkov.

CZECH REPUBLIC

The Praha - Plzeň - Cheb trains (Table **1120**) no longer extend to Františkovy Lázně, leaving this tiny spa town to be served by existing local services. In Table **1135**, one of the Plzeň - České Budějovice - Brno trains has been reduced to three days per week (daily in summer), and train **660/1** no longer extends beyond Brno to Ostrava and Bohumín. This latter change means that the sleeping car from České Budějovice to Košice now runs via Praha (joining train **440/1**) instead of Brno, whilst a separate sleeper runs from Brno.

As mentioned under the International heading, all trains from Praha to Brno and beyond (Table **1150**) now serve the main station, Praha hlavní, using the newly built tracks into the north end of the station. There are additional trains from Praha to Žilina in Slovakia (Table **1160**), but a slight reduction in the Brno - Ostrava service (Table **1161**). Electrification of the line to Šumperk means that new through services have been introduced from Brno (Table **1164**). In Table **1145**, only one express train extends to and from Letohrad.

This year we are showing expanded details of Christmas and New Year cancellations in the Czech Republic, Slovakia and Hungary by the addition of a list of cancelled trains on page 539.

SLOVAKIA

The two Wien - Bratislava - Košice trains no longer run through from Wien and are replaced by Bratislava - Košice *IC* trains.

HUNGARY

There has been a major recast of services on the Budapest - Fonyód - Keszthely / Nagykanizsa line along the south shore of Lake Balaton (Table **1220**). Nagykanizsa to Dombóvár and Dombóvár to Kecskemet now runs as two separate services, now shown in Tables **1240** and **1242**. The Budapest to Wien trains (now *Railjet* operated) make additional stops at Tatabánya and Mosonmagyaróvár, previously served only by domestic trains. There are now only two trains a day between Miskolc and Košice (Table **1265**).

Trains from Budapest to Oradea and beyond have been reorganised (Table **1275**), whilst the Debrecen to Oradea and Baia Mare trains have been demoted to local status, no longer requiring reservations.

ROMANIA

There have been cutbacks on a number of routes.

LITHUANIA

Kaunas station reopened on November 17 following completion of work on the adjacent tunnel, which caused services to terminate in a temporary Kaunas-1 station (Table **1811**). Two of the five services between Vilnius and Turmantas have been withdrawn (Table **1820**).

RUSSIA

From December 18, Russian Railways are introducing new German built high-speed trains on the Moskva - St Peterburg route, running at speeds of up to 250 km/h. Branded *Sapsan*, meaning peregrine falcon (apparently the fastest bird in the world), there are initially three trains a day, the fastest two taking 3 hours 45 minutes (Table **1900**).

CONTINUED ON NEXT PAGE

Winter International Services from December 13

The new timetable from December 13 involves major changes to many international services. Highlights include the following:

Table **9** – *Snow Train* **27050 / 27052** Paris Nord to Bourg St Maurice has been withdrawn. This special charter train, run for Rail Europe and featuring a disco car, was designed for passengers travelling by Eurostar from London and Ebbsfleet International, and avoided the need to cross Paris.

Table **10** – For a five week period in January and February, two early morning Eurostar services from London to Paris, trains **9078** and **9004**, will be replaced on Tuesdays, Wednesdays and Thursdays by a single train numbered **9002**. In the reverse direction, one early morning service does not run on Tuesdays, Wednesdays and Thursdays in the same period. The new timetable includes various other minor changes.

Table **11** – Additional *TGV* services in this table are a Saturday Lille to Nantes train and a new Nantes / Rennes - Lille train on Sundays. A new Lille to Lyon train has also been introduced, leaving Lille at 1006 (train **5100**), with a northbound counterpart leaving Marseille at 0940 for Lille Flandres (train **5150**), which omits Marne la Vallée on Mondays to Fridays. Train **5261** Bordeaux - Lille Europe, which ran in a separate path on Sundays, has been retimed to run daily, albeit slightly later, and now terminates at Lille Flandres.

Table **16** – A pair of Sunday services between Paris and Oostende has been retimed.

Table **17a** – The direct Eurostar train from London St Pancras to Marne la Vallée - Chessy, the station for Disneyland Paris, does not run on Tuesdays and Saturdays except during school holidays, and does not call at Lille on the inbound journey. The Lille stop is taken up by a Brussels to St Pancras service.

Table **18** – Thalys services are running on the new high-speed line (*HSL Zuid*) between Antwerpen and Schiphol, reducing the journey time between Amsterdam and Brussels / Paris by around 50 minutes. Seven services (up from six) are now running daily between Paris and Amsterdam. We understand that trains are initially limited to 160 km/h between Rotterdam and Amsterdam.

Tables **20** and **21** – Thalys services are now running on the high-speed line between Liège and Aachen (used by *ICE* trains since June) with arrivals in Brussels generally 30 minutes earlier and departures 30 minutes later.

Table **24** – The couchette car has been withdrawn from the Basel - Warszawa service and replaced by a sleeping car Basel - Minsk.

Table **28** – The Amsterdam - Wien night train *Eridanus* is cut back to run between Köln and Wien (Dortmund - Köln - Wien on four days per week). It therefore no longer extends to Amsterdam (previously served on three days per week), but alternative connections are available between Köln and Amsterdam. This train, previously a *CNL*, is now a EuroNight service operated by Austrian Railways.

A new late evening Amsterdam to Köln *ICE* has been introduced running on Sundays, also Fridays from March. In the reverse direction, a new early morning Frankfurt to Amsterdam *ICE* is running on Mondays to Thursdays.

Table **32** – Night train **468/469** *Orient Express* Strasbourg - Wien has been withdrawn, bringing to an end the long and complex history of this once famous train, which many years ago plied between Paris and Istanbul (by 2001 it ran only between Paris and Wien, being cut back to Strasbourg - Wien in 2007). An overnight journey between Paris and Wien is still possible via München, but with a much later arrival in Wien. Another night train in this table which has been withdrawn is **409 / 408** *Danubius* Frankfurt - Salzburg - Wien - Budapest.

Table **40** – An increased *TGV* service between Paris and Zürich has been introduced, with five trains from Paris and four from Zürich (previously three each way).

Table **42** – The morning *TGV* **9281** from Paris to Bern and the evening return (*TGV* **9288**, with connections to and from Interlaken Ost) have been withdrawn. Alternative connections are available via Lausanne, or from Paris Est changing at Basel. *TGV* services between Paris and Lausanne have been speeded up by around 15 minutes due to the completion of track improvements.

Tables **43** and **73** – *City Night Line* **401/400** *Apus* Amsterdam / Dortmund - Milano has been withdrawn.

Table **44** – Train **9247/9242** Paris - Milano has been withdrawn, but is expected to return in the summer. Train **9249/9240** Paris - Milano has been cut back to Torino, where it terminates at Porta Nuova instead of Porta Susa. At the time of going to press Artesia were unable to confirm whether the other day train on this route, **9241/9248**, would be terminating at Milano or Torino.

Table **47** – The night trains from Luxembourg and Strasbourg to Nice are combined between Dijon and Nice, and continue to run daily. They convey dated portions from Luxembourg and Strasbourg to Port Bou, replacing the existing Metz and Strasbourg to Port Bou train.

Table **50** – Train *EC* **237/238** Hamburg - København, which previously ran only during the summer, is now running throughout the year, becoming an *ICE*. Furthermore, this connects with a new late-evening København - Göteborg train, arriving after midnight. Train *EC* **36/35** has also been converted to an *ICE*.

Due to the extensive building works at Malmö Central in connection with the new tunnel and through station, train *EN* **211/210** *Berlin Night Express* Berlin to Malmö has been temporarily diverted away from the station. Instead it calls at a suburban station, Malmö Persborg, continuing north to terminate at the university city of Lund, where connections are available to and from Stockholm, Göteborg and København.

Tables **53** and **60** – The *EC* trains on the Berlin - Praha - Wien / Bratislava axis have been recast, with all trains serving Praha hlavní station, thanks to the new lines and tunnel which have greatly enhanced capacity between hlavní and Holešovice / Libeň.

In Wien, long-term work has started on the future Hauptbahnhof (on the site of Südbahnhof) and the above *EC* trains now serve Wien Meidling, 4 km to the south-west (also calling at Wien Simmering). Most of these trains extend to Wiener Neustadt or Villach (one starts from Graz). Note that the first northbound train from Wien and the last southbound train serve Wien Praterstern instead (other stops are in Table **982**). The plan to run the *EC* trains via Wien Mitte, mentioned last month, did not go ahead.

Trains *EC* **177** Berlin - Wien and *EC* **378** Wien - Stralsund now convey through second class seating cars to and from Bratislava.

The *EC* Praha - Linz - Salzburg has been cut back to Linz, reclassified *IC* (although still *EC* in Austria) and renamed *Anton Bruckner*.

Tables **52** and **53** – The Praha - Linz - Zürich section of Table **53** has been split off to form new Table **52** to aid clarity. The Praha - Salzburg - Ljubljana - Zagreb sleeper in train **207/499** and **498/206** (summarised in a separate panel of Table **52**) now only operates from May to September.

Table **54** – The *Overnight Trains Summary* previously shown at the start of the German section has been moved to the International section as new Table **54**.

Table **56** – *EC* **46** Warszawa - Berlin departs one hour earlier to arrive Berlin Hbf at 1216.

Train **449/448** *Stanislaw Moniuszko* Berlin - Warszawa, with portions to Gdynia, Kaliningrad and Kraków has been withdrawn, but at the time of going to press, attempts were being made to retain the Berlin - Kaliningrad sleeping car formerly shown in atble **51**.

Table **60** – Train **336** *Olympus* Thessaloníki - Skopje - Beograd departs nearly four hours earlier from Thessaloníki at 0600.

Train **391/392** Beograd - Skopje *Bora Stankovic / Koco Racin* has been withdrawn, leaving one day service and one night service between the two capitals.

Train **343/342** Budapest - Beograd *Ivo Andrić*, which previously ran only in the summer, now runs all year. **375/374** Budapest - Braşov - Bucureşti *Pannonia* now only runs to and from Bucureşti until the end of February and again during the summer; at other times it runs only to and from Braşov.

The through sleeping car from Thessaloníki to Budapest in train **462** is attached to a later train at Bucureşti (train **360**), transferring to train *IC* **78** at Timişoara, and arrives in Budapest two hours later at 1047.

Table **62** – Train **419/418** Vinkovci - Šid - Beograd has been withdrawn and the München - Beograd seating cars in train **499/498** have been cut back to Vinkovci.

Table **65** – Additional *Railjet* services have been introduced, making five daily direct trains from München to Budapest via Wien and four in the reverse direction (the fifth terminates at Salzburg).

The couchettes cars that ran between München and Bucureşti have been withdrawn, whilst the sleeping car has been cut back to run during the summer only, plus the Christmas and New Year period.

Table **66** – As previously mentioned under Table **32**, the Frankfurt - Budapest night train *Danubius* has been withdrawn.

Table **70** – Train **85/84** *Michelangelo* München - Bologna - Rimini (which ran to Roma rather than Rimini prior to summer 2008) has been cut back to Bologna, whilst train **87/86** München - Verona - Venezia has been cut back to Verona.

Train **1281/1280** *Grossglockner* Zell am See - München continues to run on Winter Saturdays, with train **1281** extending to Schwarzach St Veit. A new train **1284** *Grossglockner* runs on Sundays from Schwarzach St Veit to München.

Table **73** – *City Night Line* **401/400** *Apus* Amsterdam / Dortmund - Milano has been withdrawn, but **418/419** Amsterdam - Mannheim - Basel - Zürich now runs daily. There is a new *ICE* **371** running on Mondays to Fridays from Karlsruhe (departing 0556) to Interlaken Ost.

Table **75** – With the Zürich to Berlin, Leipzig and Dresden *City Night Line* services now in new Table **54**, they have been moved out of Table **75**. In their place, additional stations have been added between München and Lindau, with all stopping points of the Zürich - München *EuroCity* services now shown.

Table **82** – Cisalpino, the company jointly owned by Swiss Railways (SBB) and Italian Railways (Trenitalia), has been dissolved with effect from December 13. Rolling stock has been divided between the parent companies, and we understand that Trenitalia has five **ETR 470** tilting trains and seven **ETR 610**, whilst SBB has four **ETR 470** and seven **ETR 610**. The Zürich - Milano service is operated by **ETR 470**, while the Basel - Bern - Milano and Genève - Milano (one extended to Venezia) is operated by **ETR 610** units. The *Cisalpino* name is no longer used, with all services being reclassified *EC*. The extensions to Firenze, Trieste and Genoa / La Spezia have been withdrawn.

Train **313/314** *Luna* Genève / Zürich - Roma has been withdrawn.

Table **86** – Trains *RJ* **169/160** and **362/363**, which ply the Zürich - Salzburg - Wien route, are now operated by new *Railjet* trains, and the schedule has been speeded up by around 40 minutes. Train *EC* **163/162** which previously ran from Basel to Wien has been modified to run between Zürich and Wien losing the Basel extension, and will become a *Railjet* train from June 13.

A third journey opportunity between Zürich and Wien is available through *IC* **166/165** providing connections at Feldkirch.

As there are now only two daily *IC* services between Innsbruck and Schwarzach St Veit via Zell am See, excellent connections from Zürich to Beograd, Graz and Klagenfurt have been provided via Salzburg.

Table **88** – The remaining through daytime train between Wien and Venezia (*EC* **30/31**) has been withdrawn. However, an increased service is now available by using *EC* trains between Wien and Villach, changing there to the Austrian Railways *InterCity* bus service to Venezia Piazzale Roma, close to Santa Lucia station. There are now four of these buses (five in the spring) each way, an increase from two. The buses run from Klagenfurt to Venezia, but connections from and to Wien are made at Villach.

Trains **1236/1237** and **1238/1239** Wien - Firenze - Roma now terminate at Firenze. At the time of going to press, Trenitalia were unable to confirm the running of trains **235+9702** and **9753+234** Wien - Venezia Mestre - Milano and v.v.

Table **89** – Night train **241/240** *Venezia* from Venezia to Budapest no longer carries through cars for Bucureşti. Train **204** *Maestral* Budapest - Zagreb runs one hour earlier. Train **246** *Citadella* Budapest - Hodoš - Murska Sobota - Ljubljana runs two hours later, whilst train **247** *Citadella* Ljubljana - Budapest runs two hours earlier.

Table **91** – Trains *IC* **253 / 254 / 350** Wien - Graz - Maribor have been cut back to Graz, thereby severing connections to Zidani Most and Ljubljana.

Table **92** – The second class couchettes have been withdrawn from train **399/398** Zagreb - Sarajevo leaving just second class seats.

A new Beograd - Doboj - Sarajevo train (**450/451**) has commenced, restoring a facility lost almost 20 years ago.

Table **94** – The Warszawa - St Peterburg sleeper now runs twice a week during the winter months instead of three times.

Table **95** – The St Peterburg - Zagreb sleeper now runs weekly only in the summer, instead of weekly all year.

Table **96** – The Wien - Lviv - Kyïv sleeping car is reduced to running twice weekly and now takes a completely different route, running from Wien in train **406/7** via Bohumín, where it combines with the Praha - Kyïv train continuing via Przemyśl. A separate sleeping car runs daily from Bratislava to Lviv (continuing five days per week to and from Kyïv) and this continues to run via Košice and Chop as before.

Train **36/35** *Georgij Kirpa* Kraków - Kyïv has been withdrawn, but connections are available by using the Wrocław - Kraków - Lviv sleeper service and changing at Lviv.

Table **99** – The daytime Kraków - Praha train, *EC* **118/119** *Comenius*, has been withdrawn, along with the Kraków - Wien portion of this train. Alternative connections are available via Katowice. Train *EC* **103/102** *Polonia* Warszawa - Wien has been extended to Villach, whilst train *EC* **105/104** *Sobieski* Warszawa - Wien has been retimed.

Advance information for the summer is that *Istria* **1459/1458** Wien - Koper / Rijeka (Table **91**) and *Jadran* **1474/1475** Praha - Split (Table **92**) will no longer run. The summer-weekend couchette car from Wien to Split is also withdrawn. Summer train **1381/1380** *Cracovia* will be renamed *Varsovia* and will be extended to run Warszawa - Kraków - Budapest - Keszthely, conveying once-weekly portions to Varna and Burgas (sleepers from Warszawa plus couchettes from Košice). These attach at Szolnok to new train *Nesebar* which will run once weekly from Budapest to Varna and three times a week to Burgas.

Rail Passes

From January 1 there are changes to the InterRail pass scheme. In particular a new 15 day pass has been added to the InterRail Global Pass, valid for 15 consecutive days. There is also a new Global Pass Senior giving a discount of 10% for those over 60.

The prices of the InterRail One Country passes have been revised, and there are now five price bands instead of four. Full details of the new 2010 prices for both InterRail and Eurail will be found on page 541.

Next Month

As well as updates to the latest schedules, the January edition will include our annual **Sample Fares** feature. Copies should be available from Thomas Cook Publishing from December 22.

The January-February edition of the Thomas Cook **Overseas Timetable**, covering North and South America, Africa, Asia and Australasia, will also be available from December 22.

Thomas Cook Publishing would like to wish all our readers a very

HAPPY CHRISTMAS

5 AIRPORT → CITY CENTRE LINKS

City Plans are on pages 27-31

Airport code	Airport name	City	Distance	Journey	Transport ‡	City terminal	Table
AAR	Aarhus	Århus	37 km	40 mins	🚌 flybus, connects with flights	Central train station	
ABZ	Aberdeen, Dyce	Aberdeen	11 km	40 mins	🚌 **27**, ①-⑥ every 30-40 mins, ⑦ 70-125 mins	Guild Street. Also taxis to Dyce rail station	
ALC	Alacant	Alacant	12 km	30 mins	🚌 **C6**, every 40 mins	Plaça del Mar	
AMS	Amsterdam, Schiphol	Amsterdam	17 km	20 mins	Train, every 10 mins (every hour 2400 - 0600)	Centraal rail station	**451, 454**
		Rotterdam	65 km	45 mins	Train, every 30 mins (every hour 2400 - 0600)	Centraal rail station	**450, 454**
		Den Haag	43 km	35 mins	Train, every 30 mins (every hour 2400 - 0600)	Centraal rail station	**450, 454**
AOI	Ancona, Falconara	Ancona	16 km	30 mins	1) 🚌 **9**, 2) Train hourly at peak times: 17 mins	Main rail station	
ATH	Athína, Elefthérios Venizélos	Athína	27 km	41 mins	Metro (line **3**), every 30 mins	Syntagma	
		Pireás	41 km	90 mins	🚌 **X96**, every 15-20 mins	Platía Karaiskáki	
SOB	Balaton, Sármellék	Keszthely	12 km	20 mins	🚌, connects with Ryanair flights	Rail station. Also 🚌 to Budapest Déli (190 mins), Siófok and Székesfehérvár	
BCN	Barcelona, Aeroport del Prat	Barcelona	14 km	22 mins	Train, every 30 mins: 0608 - 2338	Sants. Also calls at Passeig de Gràcia rail station.	**659**
BSL	Basel - Mulhouse - Freiburg	Basel	9 km	20 mins	🚌 **50**, ①-⑤ 8 per hour; ⑥⑦ 6 per hour	SBB rail station / Kannenfeldplatz	
		Freiburg	60 km	55 mins	🚌 ①-⑤ every 75-90 mins; ⑥⑦ every 2 hours	Rail station	
BHD	Belfast, City, George Best	Belfast	2 km	15 mins	🚌 *Airlink* **600**, ①-⑥ every 20 mins; ⑦ every 40 mins	Europa Buscentre. Also train from Sydenham rail station.	
BFS	Belfast, International	Belfast	26 km	40 mins	🚌 *Airbus* **300**, Ⓐ every 10 mins; ⑥ every 20; ⑦ every 30	Europa Buscentre (adjacent to Great Victoria St rail station)	
BEG	Beograd, Nikola Tesla	Beograd	16 km	30 mins	🚌 **72**, every 32 minutes	Rail station	
SXF	Berlin, Schönefeld	Berlin	24 km	27 mins	Train *AirportExpress* **RE7/ RB14** 2 per hour 0631 - 2331	Ost, Alexanderplatz, Hbf and Zoo rail stations	**847**
TXL	Berlin, Tegel	Berlin	7 km	40 mins	🚌 *JetExpressBus TXL*, Ⓐ every 10 mins, Ⓒ every 20 mins	Hauptbahnhof rail station	
BIQ	Biarritz - Anglet - Bayonne	Biarritz	3 km	22 mins	🚌 *STAB* **6**, every hour approx.	Town centre	
		Bayonne	7 km	28 mins	🚌 *STAB* **6**, every hour approx.	Rail station	
BIO	Bilbao, Sondika	Bilbao	10 km	45 mins	🚌 Bizkaibus **A-3247**, every 30 mins 0615 - 0000	Plaza Moyúa (Metro station Moyúa)	
BHX	Birmingham, International	Birmingham	12 km	11 mins	Train, ①-⑥ ± 7 per hour, ⑦ 5 per hour	New Street rail station from International	**129, 142, 143**
FRL	Bologna, Forlì	Bologna	66 km	85 mins	🚌, connects with Ryanair flights	Centrale rail station, also 🚌 to Forlì rail station every 20 minutes	
BLQ	Bologna, Guglielmo Marconi	Bologna	8 km	20 mins	🚌 *Aerobus* BLQ, every 15 mins 0600 - 2315	Centrale rail station	
BOD	Bordeaux, Mérignac	Bordeaux	12 km	45 mins	🚌 Jet' Bus, every 45 mins 0745 - 2245	St Jean rail station	
BOH	Bournemouth	Bournemouth	10 km	15 mins	🚌 **A 1** *Airport Shuttle*, hourly 0730 - 1830	Rail station, Bus station (Travel Interchange)	
BTS	Bratislava, Milan Rastislav Štefánika	Bratislava	10 km	20 mins	🚌 **61**, 3 per hour	Main rail station (Hlavná stanica)	
BRE	Bremen	Bremen	3 km	20 mins	Tram **6**, ①-⑥ every 10 mins, ⑦ every 20 mins	Main rail station	
VBS	Brescia, Montichiari, Verona	Verona	50 km	45 mins	🚌, connects with Ryanair flights	Main rail station	
		Brescia	18 km	20 mins	🚌, connects with Ryanair flights	Main rail station	
BRS	Bristol, International	Bristol	13 km	30 mins	🚌 *International Flyer*, ①-⑥ 2-4 per hour; ⑦ 2-4 per hour	Temple Meads rail station, also bus station	
BRU	Brussels, National / Zaventem	Brussels	12 km	25 mins	Train, every 20 mins	Midi / Zuid rail station (also calls at Central and Nord)	**402**
OTP	Bucureşti, Henri Coanda, Otopeni	Bucureşti	16 km	40 mins	🚌 **783**, ①-⑤ every 15 mins; ⑥⑦ every 30 mins	Piaţa Victoriei (800m from Nord station or 1 stop on subway)	
		Bucureşti	16 km	68 mins	🚌 to P.O. Aeroport H, then train; hourly 0556 - 2056	Nord station	
BUD	Budapest, Ferihegy	Budapest	16 km	40 mins	🚌 **200**, every 10 - 20 mins	Kőbánya-Kispest metro station (metro connection to city centre)	
	Terminal 1	Budapest	18 km	25 mins	Train, 2 - 6 per hour	Nyugati rail station. Ferihegy station is 200m from Terminal 1	
BZG	Bydgoszcz	Bydgoszcz	4 km	30 mins	🚌 **80**, 2 per hour	Main rail station	
CCF	Carcassonne, Salvaza	Carcassonne	5 km	10 mins	🚌, connects with Ryanair flights	Place Davilla and Carcassonne rail station	
CWL	Cardiff	Cardiff	19 km	40 mins	🚌 *Airbus Xpress* **X91**, ①-⑥ hourly, ⑦ every 2 hours	Central rail station, city centre	
		Cardiff	19 km	50 mins	🚌 to Rhoose then Train: ①-⑥ hourly, ⑦ every 2 hours	Central rail station	
CRL	Charleroi, Brussels	Brussels	55 km	60 mins	🚌, connects with Ryanair flights	Brussels Midi (corner of Rue de France / Rue de l'Instruction)	
		Charleroi		9 mins	🚌 *Line* **A**, ①-⑤ 2 per hour, ⑥⑦ hourly	Main rail station	
ORK	Cork	Cork	8 km	25 mins	🚌 **226**, hourly. Also SkyLink every 30 mins	Parnell Place Bus Station, then 🚌 **5** to rail station	
LDY	Derry (Londonderry)	Londonderry	11 km	30 mins	🚌 connects with flights	Foyle Street Bus Station	
DNR	Dinard - Pleurtuit - St-Malo	St Malo	14 km	20 mins	Taxis only. Dinard 6 km 10 mins		
DSA	Doncaster - Sheffield	Doncaster	10 km	25 mins	🚌 **91, 707, X19**, ①-⑥ 4 per hour; ⑦ 2 per hour	Rail station	
DTM	Dortmund, Wickede	Dortmund	10 km	25 mins	🚌 every hour, AirportExpress	Main rail station (Hbf). Also 🚌 to Holzwickede rail station.	
DRS	Dresden	Dresden	15 km	23 mins	Train (S-Bahn **S2**) every 30 mins	Main rail stations (Hauptbahnhof and Neustadt)	**857a**
DUB	Dublin	Dublin	11 km	35 mins	🚌 *Airlink* **747**, every 10 mins (15 - 20 mins on ⑦)	Bus station (Busaras), O'Connell Street	
		Dublin	11 km	45 mins	🚌 *Airlink* **748**, every 30 mins	Heuston rail station, Bus station (Busaras), Connolly rail station	
		Belfast	157 km	130 mins	🚌 **001 / 200**, hourly 24 hour service	Europa Buscentre (adjacent to Great Victoria St rail station)	
DBV	Dubrovnik, Čilipi	Dubrovnik	24 km	30 mins	🚌 *Atlas Bus*, connects with flights	Bus station	
DUS	Düsseldorf, International	Düsseldorf	7 km	12 mins	Train (S - Bahn **S7**) Ⓐ every 20 mins, Ⓒ every 30 mins	Main rail station (Hauptbahnhof)	**800, 802**
EMA	East Midlands, Nottingham - - Leicester - Derby	East Midlands	10 km	15 mins	🚌 every 30 min. 0700 - 2330	East Midlands Parkway rail station	
		Nottingham	21 km	45 mins	🚌 *Skylink*, every 30 min. 0405 - 2305; (60 mins 2305 - 0405)	Rail station, Market Square	
		Derby	19 km	40 mins	🚌 *Skylink* every 30 min. 0720 - 1820; (60 mins 2045 - 0645)	Bus station (also departures at 0615,1920)	
		Loughborough	8 km	30 mins	🚌 *Skylink* every 30 min. 0745 - 2045; (60 mins 2155 - 0645)	Rail station	
		Leicester	23 km	60 mins	🚌 *Skylink* hourly 0740, 0842 - 1545, 1650 - 1950, 2055 - 0655.	St Margaret's Bus station	
EDI	Edinburgh, Turnhouse	Edinburgh	11 km	25 mins	🚌 *Airlink* **100**, every 10 mins. **N22** 2400-0600 every 30mins.	Haymarket rail station; Waverley Bridge (next to Waverley station)	
ERF	Erfurt	Erfurt	6 km	22 mins	Tram, Line 4, Ⓐ every 10 mins, Ⓒ every 30 mins	Main rail station (Hauptbahnhof)	
EBJ	Esbjerg	Esbjerg	12 km	21 mins	🚌 **8**, hourly	*Bybusterminal*	
FAO	Faro	Faro	6 km	20 mins	🚌 *EVA*, **14, 16**, hourly	Bus station	
FLR	Firenze, Amerigo Vespucci	Firenze	7 km	20 mins	🚌 Ataf *Vola in bus* **62**, every 30 mins	Santa Maria Novella rail station	
HHN	Frankfurt, Hahn	Frankfurt	120 km	105 mins	🚌, connects with Ryanair flights	Mannheimer Straße, adjacent to main rail station (Hauptbahnhof)	
	Also 🚌 to Bingen, 60 mins; Heidelberg hbf, 140 mins; Koblenz, 70 mins; Köln hbf, 135 mins; Luxembourg, 105 mins; Mainz, 70 mins; Saarbrücken, 125 mins; Traben-Trarbach, 25 mins.						
FRA	Frankfurt	Frankfurt	10 km	15 mins	Train (S-Bahn **S8** or **S9**), 4-6 times hourly	Main rail station (Hauptbahnhof)	**917a**
FDH	Friedrichshafen	Friedrichshafen	4 km	7 mins	1-2 trains per hour	Main rail station (Stadt) or Harbour (Hafen)	**931**
GDN	Gdańsk, Lech Walesa	Gdańsk	10 km	26 mins	🚌 **110**, 1-2 per hour	Wrzeszcz rail station, then 3 stops (every 15 mins) to Głowny	
GVA	Genève	Genève	6 km	6 mins	Train, 5 times hourly	Cornavin rail station	**500, 570**
GOA	Genova, Cristoforo Colombo	Genova	7 km	20 mins	🚌 *Volabus* **100**, hourly	Principe rail station	
GRO	Girona	Girona	12 km	25 mins	🚌, hourly	Rail / Bus station (Estación autobuses)	
		Barcelona	102 km	70 mins	🚌, connects with Ryanair flights	Estacio del Nord, corner of carrer Ali Bei 80 / Sicilia	
GLA	Glasgow, International	Glasgow	15 km	25 mins	🚌 *GlasgowFlyer*, ①-⑥ every 10 mins, ⑦ every 15 mins.	Buchanan bus station	
PIK	Glasgow, Prestwick	Glasgow	61 km	50 mins	Train, ①-⑥ every 30 mins, ⑦ every 60 minutes	Central station	**216**
GSE	Göteborg, City	Göteborg	12 km	30 mins	🚌, connects with Ryanair, Air Berlin and WizzAir flights	Nils Ericson Terminalen (bus station) / Central rail station	
GOT	Göteborg, Landvetter	Göteborg	25 km	30 mins	🚌, ①-⑤ 3 per hour, ⑥⑦ 2-3 per hour	Nils Ericson Terminalen (bus station) / Central rail station	
GRZ	Graz	Graz	9 km	9 mins	Train ①-⑥ hourly, ⑦ every 2 hours	Main rail station (Hauptbahnhof)	
HAM	Hamburg, Fuhlsbüttel	Hamburg	11 km	24 mins	Train (S-Bahn **S1**), every 10 mins	Main rail station (Hauptbahnhof)	
HAJ	Hannover, Langenhagen	Hannover	15 km	17 mins	Train (S-Bahn **S5**), every 30 mins	Main rail station (Hauptbahnhof)	**809**
HEL	Helsinki, Vantaa	Helsinki	19 km	35 mins	🚌 **615**, ①-⑤ every 15 mins, ⑥⑦ every 20-30 mins	Rail station (stop 10)	
		Tikkurila	7 km	22 mins	🚌 **61**, ①-⑤ every 10 mins, ⑥ 10-15 mins, ⑦ 15-20 mins.	Rail station for trains to Helsinki (20 mins; 16 km)	
IOM	Isle of Man, Ronaldsway	Douglas	16 km	30 mins	🚌 **1**, hourly (every 30 mins in peak periods)	Lord street	
IST	İstanbul, Atatürk	İstanbul	24 km	40 mins	🚌, *Havaş Airport Shuttle* hourly 0400 - 2400	Taksim	
		İstanbul	24 km	60 mins	Metro to Zeytinburnu, then over bridge for Tram **T1**	Sirkeci rail station	
SAW	İstanbul, Sabiha Gökçen	İstanbul	32 km	60 mins	🚌, 1-2 per hour, 0540-2040	Bus station. Also Pendik rail station is 4km from airport.	
FKB	Karlsruhe - Baden-Baden	Baden-Baden	8 km	15 mins	🚌 **205**, connects with Ryanair flights	Rail station; also 🚌 **140** to Karlsruhe Hbf, 25min	
KTW	Katowice, Pyrzowice	Katowice	34 km	50 mins	🚌 hourly	Main rail station	
KUN	Kaunas	Kaunas	13 km	40 mins	🚌 **120, 29**	City centre	
		Vilnius	102 km	90 mins	🚌 connects with Ryanair flights	Hotel Panorama, close to bus and railway stations	
KLU	Klagenfurt	Klagenfurt	5 km	25 mins	🚌 **45**, to Annabichl rail station, then train or 🚌 **40**	Main rail station and bus station	
KOC	Knock	Charlestown	8 km	15 mins	🚌 **449A**, ①-⑥ 6 per day, ⑦ 5 per day	Rooney's public house.	
CPH	København, Kastrup	København	12 km	15 mins	Train, every 10 mins	Main rail station (Hovedbanegård)	**703**
		Malmö	36 km	22 mins	Train, every 20 mins	Central rail station	**703**
CGN	Köln / Bonn, Konrad Adenauer	Bonn	25 km	32 mins	🚌 **670**, ①-⑤ every 20-30 mins; ⑥⑦ every 30-60 mins	Main rail station (Hauptbahnhof)	
		Köln	15 km	16 mins	Train **S13**, ①-⑤ every 20 mins, ⑥⑦ every 30 mins	Main rail station (Hbf). Also to Mönchengladbach, Koblenz	**802**
KRK	Kraków, Balice	Kraków	12 km	15 mins	Train, 2 per hour	Kraków Główny. Balice rail station is 200m from air terminal	
KBP	Kyïv, Boryspil	Kyïv	34 km	60 mins	🚌 **322** *Polit*, 2-3 per hour	Main rail station	
LBA	Leeds - Bradford	Leeds	16 km	40 mins	🚌 **757**, ①-⑥ every 30 mins, ⑦ every 60 mins	Main rail station and bus station	
		Bradford	11 km	40 mins	🚌 **747**, ①-⑥ every 30 mins, ⑦ every 60 mins	Interchange rail station	
LEJ	Leipzig - Halle	Leipzig	20 km	14 mins	Train, every 30 mins	Main rail station (Hauptbahnhof)	**810**
		Halle	18 km	12 mins	Train, every 30 mins	Main rail station (Hauptbahnhof)	**810**
AOC	Leipzig, Altenburg-Nobitz	Leipzig	75 km	70 mins	🚌 **250** *ThüSac*, connects with Ryanair flights	Main rail station. Also stops at Altenburg rail station after 15 mins.	

‡ – The frequencies shown apply during daytime on weekdays and are from the airport to the city centre. There may be fewer journeys in the evenings, at weekends and during the winter months. Extended 🚌 journey times could apply during peak hours.

¶ – Graz Airport - Feldkirchen rail station is located about 300 metres away from the airport.

City Plans are on pages 27–31

AIRPORT → CITY CENTRE LINKS 5

Airport code	Airport name	City	Distance	Journey	Transport ‡	City terminal	Table
LNZ	Linz, Blue Danube	Linz	12 km	19 mins	🚌, connects with Ryanair flights	Main rail station. Also free 🚌 to Hörsching rail station, 3 mins.	
LIS	Lisboa, Portela	Lisboa	7 km	45 mins	🚌 *Aero-Bus* **91**, every 20 mins 0740–2040	Cais do Sodré, Rossio and Entrecampos rail stations	
LPL	Liverpool, John Lennon	Liverpool	11 km	35 mins	🚌 **500**, every 30 mins 0645–2345	Lime Street rail stn, Paradise St. Interchange; also 🚌 **700** to Manchester	
LJU	Ljubljana, Jože Pučnik, Brnik	Ljubljana	26 km	45 mins	🚌, Ⓐ hourly 0500–2000; Ⓒ 0700, every 2 hours 1000–2000	Bus station (Avtobusna postaja)	
LCJ	Łódź, Lublinek	Łódź	6 km	20 mins	🚌 **65**	Kaliska rail station	
LCY	London, City	London	12 km	23 mins	Train (Docklands Light Railway), every 8–10 mins	Bank underground (tube) station	**140**
LGW	London, Gatwick	London	44 km	30 mins	Train *Gatwick Express*, every 15 minutes	Victoria	**103, 140**
LHR	London, Heathrow	London	24 km	15 mins	Train *Heathrow Express*, every 15 minutes	Paddington	**140**
		London	24 km	58 mins	Underground train (tube), every 4–10 mins	King's Cross St Pancras	**140**
LTN	London, Luton	London	50 km	35 mins	6–7 per hour (🚌 between ✈ and Parkway rail station)	St Pancras International	**170, 140**
STN	London, Stansted	London	55 km	46 mins	Train *Stansted Express*, every 15 minutes	Liverpool Street rail station	**140**
LBC	Lübeck, Blankensee	Lübeck	8 km	30 mins	🚌 **6**, every 20 mins	Bus station (bus stop 5). Also train from Flughafen 300m walk	
		Hamburg	59 km	75 mins	🚌 *VHHAG*, connects with Ryanair flights	Corner Adenauerallee / Brockesstrasse (ZOB) near main rail station	
LUX	Luxembourg, Findel	Luxembourg	7 km	25 mins	🚌 **16**, every 15 mins ①–⑤, every 20 mins ⑥	Central rail station	
LWO	Lviv, Sknilov	Lvov	10 km		🚌, Taxi-bus *Marshrutka*	City Centre	
LYS	Lyon, St Exupéry	Grenoble	91 km	65 mins	🚌 Satobus, hourly 0730 - 2330	Bus station (gare routière), Place de la Résistance	
		Lyon	25 km	50 mins	🚌 *Navette Aéroport*, every 20 mins 0600 - 2340	Part Dieu (journey 35 mins) and Perrache (50 mins) rail stations	
		Chambéry	87 km	60 mins	🚌, 4–5 times daily	Bus station (gare routière)	
MAD	Madrid, Barajas	Madrid	12 km	45 mins	Metro (Line **8**) every 5 - 6 mins	Nuevos Ministerios rail / metro station (see city plans p31)	
AGP	Málaga	Málaga	8 km	12 mins	Train, every 30 mins	Centro-Alameda and RENFE rail stations	**662**
MMX	Malmö, Sturup	Malmö	30 km	45 mins	🚌 *flygbussarna*, connects with Sterling flights	Central rail station	
MAN	Manchester	Manchester	16 km	14 mins	Train, up to 8 per hour (houry through the night)	Piccadilly rail station	
MBX	Maribor, Orehova vas	Maribor	9 km	15 mins	🚌, connects with Ryanair flights	Bus station, stand 6	
MRS	Marseille, Provence	Marseille	28 km	25 mins	🚌, every 20 mins. See also rail / bus on Table **351**	St Charles rail station; also 🚌 to Aix TGV rail stn. every 30 mins.	
FMM	Memmingen	Memmingen	5 km	10 mins	🚌 **2, 810, 811**	Bus station. Train station is nearby; also 🚌 to München, 100 min.	
LIN	Milano, Linate	Milano	9 km	20 mins	1) 🚌 **73** every 10 mins; 2) 🚌 *Starfly*, every 30 mins	1) Piazza S. Babila, Metro line 1; 2) Centrale rail station	
MXP	Milano, Malpensa	Milano	45 km	40 mins	*Malpensa Express* train, every 30 mins	Cadorna and Bovisa rail stations	**583**
				50 mins	🚌 *Bus Express*, 2 per hour / *Shuttle Air* 3 per hour	Centrale rail station	
BGY	Milano, Orio al Serio, Bergamo	Milano	45 km	60 mins	🚌, every 30 - 60 mins	Centrale rail station (Air Terminal)	
		Bergamo	4 km	15 mins	🚌, 2 per hour	Rail station	
DME	Moskva, Domodedovo	Moskva	35 km	40 mins	Train, *Aeroekspress*, 1–2 per hour 0700 - 0000	Paveletskaya rail station	
SVO	Moskva, Sheremetyevo	Moskva	35 km	35 mins	Train, *Aeroekspress*, 1–2 per hour, approx	Belorusskaya rail station	
VKO	Moskva, Vnukovo	Moskva	28 km	35 mins	Train, *Aeroekspress*, every hour, approx	Kiyevskaya rail station	
MUC	München, International	München	37 km	40 mins	Train (S-Bahn **S1** for Hbf; **S8** for Ost), every 10 mins	Main rail stations (Hauptbahnhof, Ostbahnhof)	**892**
		Freising	6 km	24 mins	🚌 *MVV* **635**, every 20 mins	Rail station for connections to Regensburg, Passau	**878, 944**
NTE	Nantes, Atlantique	Nantes	9 km	30 mins	🚌 *Tan Air*, ± hourly	Main rail station	
NAP	Napoli, Capodichino	Napoli	7 km	20 mins	🚌 *ANM* **3S** line, every 30 mins	Piazza Garibaldi (Centrale rail station)	
NCL	Newcastle, International	Newcastle	9 km	23 mins	Metro train, every 7 - 12 mins	Main rail station	
NCE	Nice, Côte d'Azur	Nice	7 km	20 mins	🚌 **98**, ①–⑥ every 20 mins, ⑦ every 20–30 mins	SNCF rail station	
			8 km	6 mins	Train, from Nice St Augustin, 500m from Terminal 1	SNCF rail station	
NRN	Niederrhein	Düsseldorf	70 km	75 mins	🚌, connects with Ryanair flights	Main rail station (Hauptbahnhof) Worringer Street	
		Düsseldorf	74 km	82 mins	🚌 **SW1**, to Weeze rail station, then train, Table **802**	Main rail station (Hauptbahnhof)	
FNI	Nîmes - Arles - Camargue	Nîmes	12 km	20 mins	🚌, connects with Ryanair flights	Rail station	
NWI	Norwich, International	Norwich	6 km	38 mins	🚌 **27**, ①–⑥ every 20 mins, ⑦ every 60 mins	City centre	
NUE	Nürnberg	Nürnberg	6 km	12 mins	Train, U-bahn **U2**, 4–6 per hour	Main rail station (Hauptbahnhof)	
OSL	Oslo, Gardermoen	Oslo	49 km	19 mins	Train, 3–6 per hour	Central rail station	**771**
TRF	Oslo, Sandefjord Torp	Oslo	123 km	107 mins	🚌 to Sandefjord rail station for train to Oslo	Also 🚌 to Oslo Bus terminal	
RYG	Oslo, Rygge	Oslo	69 km	51 mins	🚌 connects with Ryanair flights, to Rygge rail station (4 km),	Sentral rail station (51 mins Rygge to Sentral)	
PMO	Palermo, Falcone-Borsellino	Palermo	24 km	45 mins	Train *Trinacria express*, ①–⑥ 2 per hour, ⑦ hourly	Centrale rail station	
PMI	Palma, Mallorca	Palma	11 km	30 mins	🚌 **1**, every 15 mins	Paseo de Mallorca, Plaça d'Espanya (for rail stations), the Port	
BVA	Paris, Beauvais	Paris	80 km	75 mins	🚌, connects with Ryanair and WizzAir flights	Porte Maillot, Metro (Line 1) for Châtelet Les Halles, Gare de Lyon	
CDG	Paris, Charles de Gaulle	Paris	25 km	35 mins	RER train, (Line B), every 7–15 mins	Nord, Châtelet Les Halles, and St Michel stations	**398**
		Disneyland	23 km	45 mins	🚌 **VEA** Navette / Shuttle, every 20 minutes	Disneyland Resort, Disneyland hotels	
ORY	Paris, Orly	Paris	15 km	35 mins	RER train, (Line C), every 15 mins	Austerlitz, St Michel, Musée d'Orsay, and Invalides stations	**398**
PGF	Perpignan, Rivesaltes	Perpignan	5 km	15 mins	🚌, connects with Ryanair, Bmibaby flights	Rail station, Bus station (gare routière)	
PSA	Pisa, Galileo Galilei	Pisa	2 km	5 mins	1) Train, 2 per hour 2) 🚌 *RedLAM*, every 10 mins	Central rail station (some trains continue to Firenze)	**614**
OPO	Porto	Porto	17 km	35 mins	Metro Train, 2 per hour	Campanhã rail station	
POZ	Poznań, Ławica	Poznań	6 km	20 mins	🚌 **L** *MPK*, every hour	Rail station	
PRG	Praha, Ruzyně	Praha	17 km	60 mins	🚌 **119**, every 10 mins	Dejvická metro station, then Metro line A to muzeum (see City Plans)	
		Praha	19 km	51 mins	🚌 **AE** *Airport Express*, every 30 mins	hlavní rail station	
PUY	Pula	Pula	6 km	15 mins	🚌, connects with Ryanair flights	Town centre	
REU	Reus	Reus	6 km	20 mins	🚌 **50**, *Hispano Igualadina* connects with Ryanair flights	Rail station	**652**
		Barcelona	90 km	80 mins	🚌 *Hispano Igualadina* connects with Ryanair flights	Sants rail station	
RZE	Rzeszów, Jasionka	Rzeszów	10 km	15 mins	🚌 **L**, departs 1150, 1505 Ⓑ, 2120 Ⓑ	Main rail station and bus station	
KEF	Reykjavík, Keflavík	Reykjavík	48 km	55 mins	🚌, connects with flights	Hótel Loftleidir	
RIX	Riga	Riga	13 km	30 mins	🚌 **22**, every 10–30 mins	Abrenes iela (street) next to rail station	
RJK	Rijeka	Rijeka	30 km	45 mins	🚌 Autotrolej, connects with flights	Bus station, Jelačić Square	
CIA	Roma, Ciampino	Roma	15 km	40 mins	🚌 *Terravision*	Termini rail station	**622**
FCO	Roma, Fiumicino	Roma	26 km	42 mins	Train, up to 4 per hour	Ostiense and Tiburtina rail stations	**622**
	(also known as Leonardo da Vinci)		26 km	31 mins	*Leonardo Express* rail service, every 30 mins	Roma Termini	**622**
RTM	Rotterdam	Rotterdam	5 km	20 mins	*Airport Shuttle* **33**, ①–⑤ every 10 mins, ⑥⑦ every 15 mins	Groot Handelsgebouw (adjacent to Centraal rail station)	
LED	St Peterburg, Pulkovo II	St Peterburg	17 km	60 mins	🚌 **T-13**	Moskovskaya Metro station, Line 2 for Nevski Pr. (see City Plans)	
SZG	Salzburg, W. A. Mozart	Salzburg	5 km	22 mins	🚌 **2**, ①–⑥ every 10 mins, ⑦ every 20 mins	Main rail station	
SOF	Sofiya, International	Sofiya	10 km	25 mins	🚌 **84**, every 10–20 mins	University	
SOU	Southampton	Southampton	8 km	8 mins	Train, 50 metres from terminal	Main rail station	**108, 126**
SPU	Split, Kaštela	Split	16 km	50 mins	🚌 **37**, ①–⑤ every 20 mins, ⑥⑦ every 30 mins	Bus station. Departs 200m from Airport terminal.	
SVG	Stavanger, Sola	Stavanger	14 km	30 mins	🚌, ①–⑤ every 20 mins, ⑥ 2 per hour, ⑦ hourly	Atlantic Hotel / Fiskepiren	
ARN	Stockholm, Arlanda	Stockholm	44 km	20 mins	*Arlanda Express* train, every 15 mins	Central rail station	**747**
NYO	Stockholm, Skavsta	Stockholm	103 km	80 mins	🚌, connects with Ryanair flights	Cityterminal (bus station), also 🚌 to Nyköping train station	
VST	Stockholm, Västerås	Stockholm	107 km	75 mins	🚌, connects with Ryanair flights	Cityterminal (bus station), also 🚌 **941** to Västerås train station	
SXB	Strasbourg, Entzheim	Strasbourg	12 km	20 mins	🚌, every 20–30 mins to Baggersee, then tram line **A**	Étoile / Homme de Fer / Gare Centrale (Central rail station)	
				12 mins	Train from Entzheim (5 mins walk) infrequent service	Strasbourg	
STR	Stuttgart, Echterdingen	Stuttgart	14 km	27 mins	Train (S-Bahn **S2**, **S3**), 2–4 times hourly 0508 - 0008	Main rail station (Hauptbahnhof)	**932**
SZZ	Szczecin, Goleniów	Szczecin	38 km	60 mins	🚌, connects with Ryanair flights	Szczecin Główny. Also 🚌, 7km, to Goleniów train station.	
TMP	Tampere, Pirkkala	Tampere	18 km	25 mins	🚌, connects with Ryanair flights	City Centre (Rautatieasema)	
TRN	Torino, Caselle	Torino	16 km	20 mins	*SATTI* train every 30 mins	Torino Dora rail station, Piazza Baldissera	
		Torino	16 km	40 mins	🚌, every 30–45 minutes	Torino Porta Nuova and Porta Susa	
TLS	Toulouse, Blagnac	Toulouse	8 km	20 mins	🚌, every 20 minutes	Place Jeanne d'Arc / Matabiau rail / Bus station (gare routière)	
TRS	Trieste, Ronchi dei Legionari	Trieste	33 km	50 mins	🚌 **51**, 2 per hour	Bus station, next to rail station	
		Monfalcone	4 km	17 mins	🚌 **10**, ①–⑥ 2–3 per hour; ⑦ hourly	Rail station	
TRD	Trondheim, Værnes	Trondheim	33 km	37 mins	Train, ①–⑤ hourly, ⑥⑦ every two hours	Rail station. Værnes rail station is 220m from Airport terminal	**787**
VLC	València	València	9 km	22 mins	Train, Lines **3**, **5**, Ⓐ every 6–9 mins; ⑥⑦ every 8–12 mins	Xátiva for Nord rail station	
VCE	Venezia, Marco Polo	Venezia	12 km	21 mins	🚌 **5**, ①–⑥ every 30 mins; ⑦ every 60 mins	Santa Lucia rail station	
		Venezia		60 mins	Waterbus ± every 60 mins	Lido / Piazza S. Marco	
TSF	Venezia, Treviso	Venezia	30 km	70 mins	🚌, connects with Ryanair flights	Mestre rail station, Piazzale Roma	
VRN	Verona, Villafranca	Verona	12 km	20 mins	🚌, every 20 mins 0635 - 2335	Rail station	
VNO	Vilnius	Vilnius	5 km	7 mins	Train, every 40 minutes	Rail station	
WAW	Warszawa, Frederic Chopin, Okęcie	Warszawa	10 km	30 mins	🚌 **175** *Airport-City*, ①–⑤ every 20 mins, ⑥⑦ every 30 mins	Centralna rail station	
VIE	Wien, Schwechat	Wien	21 km	16 mins	*CAT*, every 30 mins	Mitte rail station	**979**
		Wien	21 km	25 mins	S-bahn, every 30 mins	Mitte rail station	**979**
		Bratislava	45 km	70 mins	🚌 ÖBB-Bahn Bus / SAD Bratislava, hourly	AS Mlynské nivy (bus station)	**979**
WRO	Wrocław, Copernicus	Wrocław	10 km	30 mins	🚌 **406**, ①–⑥ 2–3 per hour; ⑦ every 40 mins	Rail station, bus station	
ZAG	Zagreb	Zagreb	17 km	25 mins	🚌, 1–2 per hour	Bus station (Autobusni kolodvor), Avenija Marina Drzica	
ZRH	Zürich	Zürich	10 km	13 mins	Train, 7–8 per hour	Main rail station (**HB**)	**529**
ZQW	Zweibrücken	Zweibrucken	4 km	10 mins	Taxi	Rail station. Also 🚌 to Saarbrücken.	

‡ – The frequencies shown apply during daytime on weekdays and are from the airport to the city centre. There may be fewer journeys in the evenings, at weekends and during the winter months. Extended 🚌 journey times could apply during peak hours.

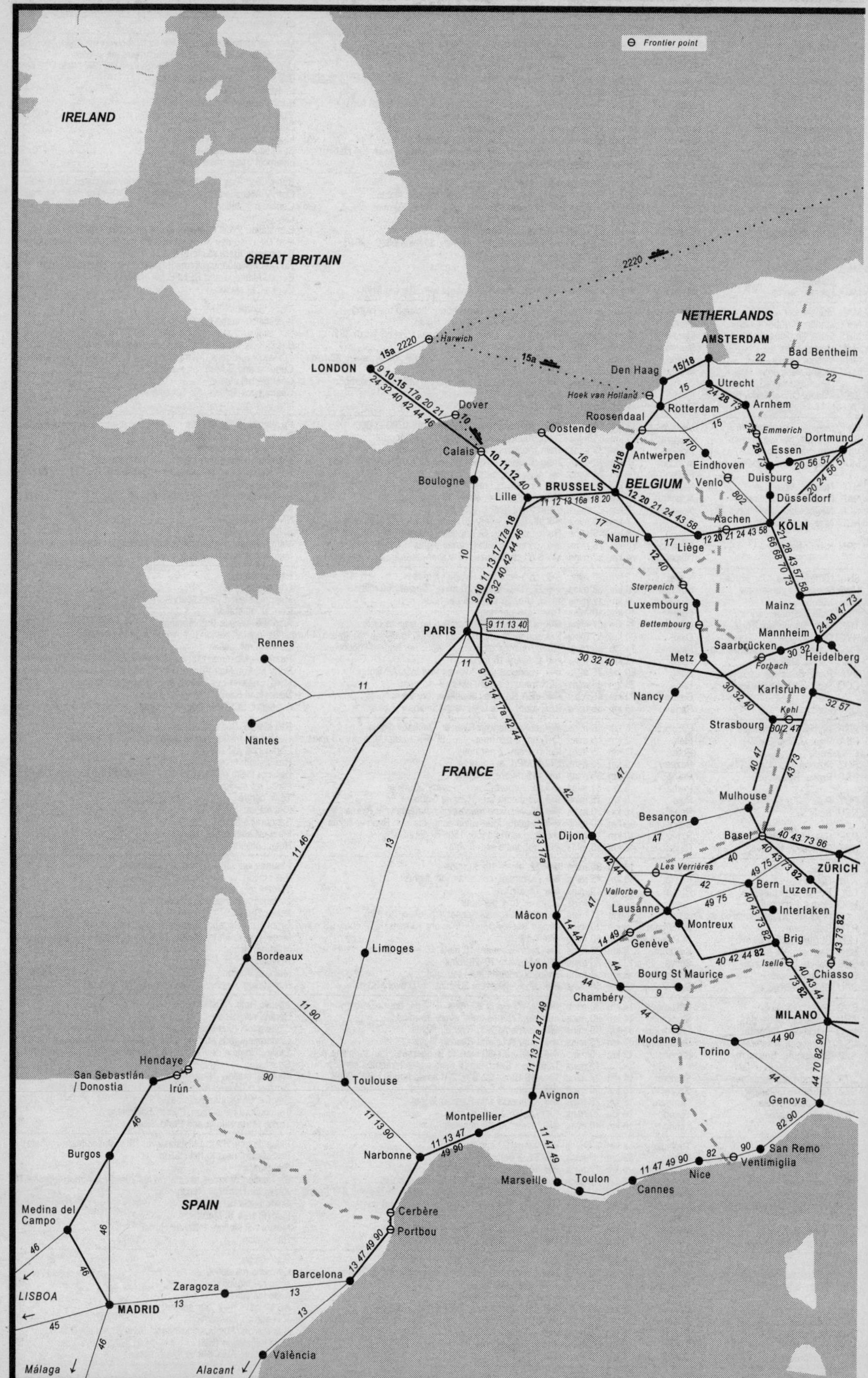
Frontier point
IRELAND
GREAT BRITAIN
NETHERLANDS
BELGIUM
FRANCE
SPAIN
LONDON
Harwich
Dover
Calais
Boulogne
Lille
BRUSSELS
Oostende
Antwerpen
Roosendaal
Rotterdam
Hoek van Holland
Den Haag
AMSTERDAM
Utrecht
Arnhem
Emmerich
Bad Bentheim
Eindhoven
Venlo
Duisburg
Essen
Dortmund
Düsseldorf
KÖLN
Aachen
Liège
Namur
Sterpenich
Luxembourg
Bettembourg
Metz
Saarbrücken
Forbach
Mainz
Mannheim
Heidelberg
Karlsruhe
Kehl
Strasbourg
Nancy
PARIS
Rennes
Nantes
Mulhouse
Besançon
Basel
ZÜRICH
Dijon
Les Verrières
Vallorbe
Lausanne
Bern
Luzern
Interlaken
Montreux
Genève
Brig
Iselle
Chiasso
Mâcon
Lyon
Bourg St Maurice
Chambéry
Modane
Torino
MILANO
Genova
San Remo
Ventimiglia
Nice
Cannes
Toulon
Marseille
Avignon
Montpellier
Narbonne
Cerbère
Portbou
Barcelona
Bordeaux
Limoges
Toulouse
Hendaye
Irún
San Sebastián / Donostia
Burgos
Medina del Campo
Zaragoza
MADRID
València
LISBOA
Málaga
Alacant
9 11 13 40

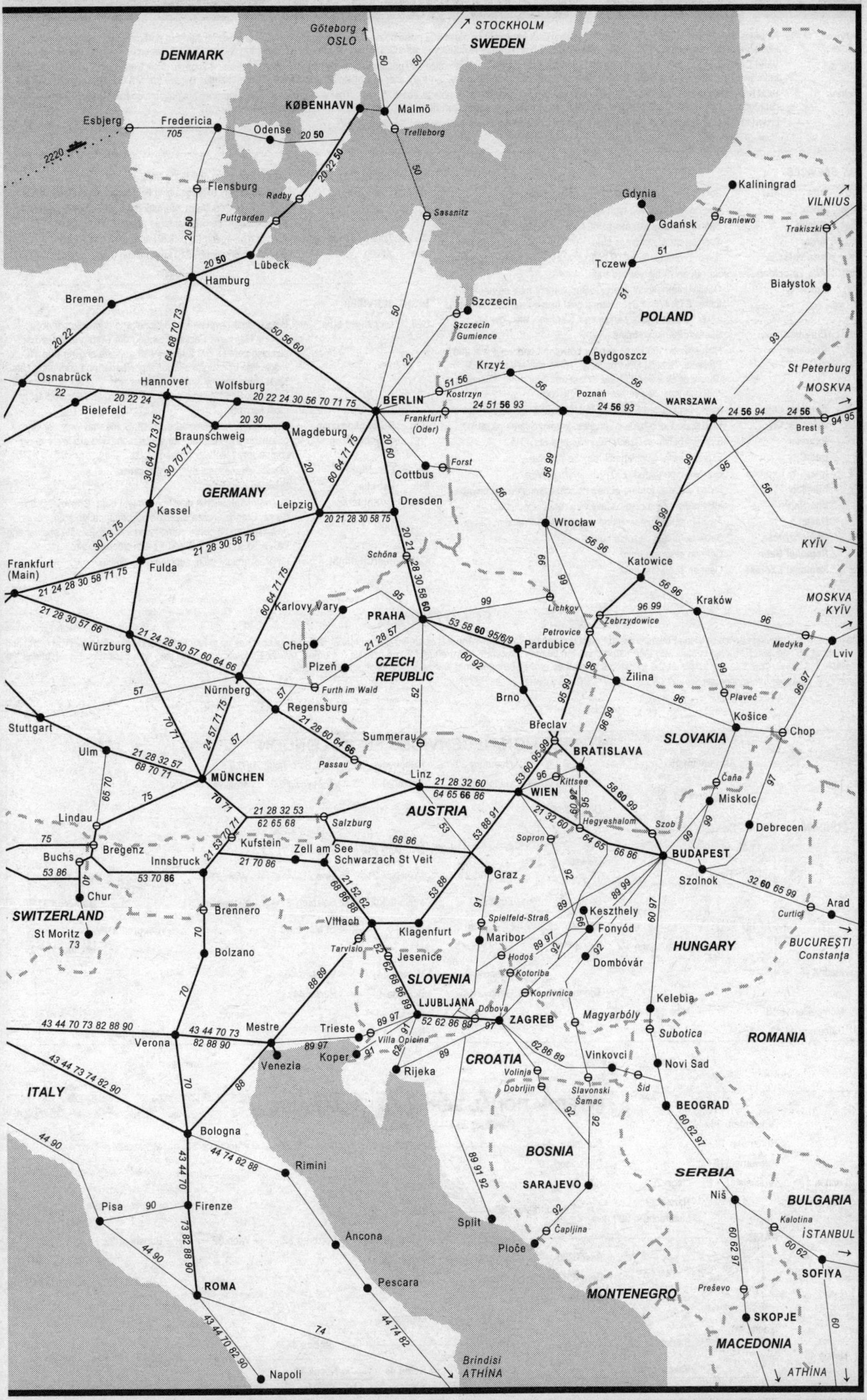
DENMARK
SWEDEN
Göteborg
OSLO
STOCKHOLM
KØBENHAVN
Malmö
Trelleborg
Esbjerg
Fredericia
Odense
Flensburg
Rødby
Puttgarden
Sassnitz
Lübeck
Hamburg
Bremen
Osnabrück
Hannover
Bielefeld
Wolfsburg
Braunschweig
Magdeburg
BERLIN
Frankfurt (Oder)
Kostrzyn
Szczecin
Szczecin Gumience
Krzyż
Bydgoszcz
Poznań
Gdynia
Gdańsk
Tczew
Kaliningrad
Braniewo
VILNIUS
Trakiszki
Białystok
POLAND
WARSZAWA
St Peterburg
MOSKVA
Brest
Cottbus
Forst
Dresden
Leipzig
GERMANY
Kassel
Fulda
Frankfurt (Main)
Würzburg
Wrocław
Katowice
KYÏV
Schöna
Karlovy Vary
PRAHA
Cheb
Plzeň
CZECH REPUBLIC
Furth im Wald
Nürnberg
Regensburg
Stuttgart
Ulm
MÜNCHEN
Lichkov
Petrovice
Zebrzydowice
Kraków
Medyka
Lviv
Pardubice
Brno
Žilina
Plaveč
Košice
Chop
Břeclav
BRATISLAVA
SLOVAKIA
Summerau
Passau
Linz
WIEN
Kittsee
Hegyeshalom
Szob
AUSTRIA
Salzburg
Lindau
Bregenz
Buchs
Chur
SWITZERLAND
St Moritz
Innsbruck
Kufstein
Zell am See
Schwarzach St Veit
Graz
Sopron
BUDAPEST
Szolnok
Čaňa
Miskolc
Debrecen
Arad
Curtici
BUCUREŞTI
Constanţa
Brennero
Bolzano
Villach
Tarvisio
Klagenfurt
Spielfeld-Straß
Maribor
Keszthely
Fonyód
Dombóvár
Hodoš
Kotoriba
Koprivnica
HUNGARY
Jesenice
SLOVENIA
LJUBLJANA
Dobova
ZAGREB
Magyarbóly
Kelebia
Subotica
ROMANIA
Verona
Mestre
Trieste
Villa Opicina
Koper
Venezia
Rijeka
CROATIA
Volinja
Dobrljin
Vinkovci
Slavonski Šamac
Šid
Novi Sad
BEOGRAD
ITALY
Bologna
BOSNIA
SARAJEVO
SERBIA
Niš
BULGARIA
Kalotina
İSTANBUL
Rimini
Pisa
Firenze
Split
Čapljina
Ploče
SOFIYA
Ancona
ROMA
Pescara
MONTENEGRO
Preševo
SKOPJE
MACEDONIA
Napoli
Brindisi
ATHÍNA

INTERNATIONAL SERVICES

Services All trains convey first and second classes of seating accommodation unless otherwise noted. For information on types of sleeping car (🛏) and couchette car (▬) see page 8. Restaurant (✕) and buffet (🍸) cars vary considerably from country to country in standard of service offered. The catering car may not be carried or open for the whole journey.

Timings **Valid December 13, 2009 - June 12, 2010.** Services can change at short notice and passengers are advised to consult the latest Thomas Cook European Rail Timetable before travelling. International trains are not normally affected by public holidays, but may alter at Christmas and Easter - these changes (where known) are shown in the tables.

Tickets **Seat reservations** are available for most international trains and are advisable as some trains can get very crowded. **Supplements** are payable on **EuroCity** (*EC*) trains in most countries and on most InterCity trains – consult the introduction at the start of each country to see which supplements apply.

Listed below is a selection of the different types of trains found in the International Section.

DAY SERVICES:

AP	**Alfa Pendular**	Portuguese high-quality tilting express train.
Alvia	**Alvia**	The newest Spanish high-speed trains.
Alta	**Altaria**	Spanish quality express using light, articulated stock.
Arco	**Arco**	Spanish quality express train.
AV	**Alta Velocità**	Italian premium fare **ETR 500** services using high-speed lines.
AVE	***Alta Velocidad Española***	Spanish high-speed train.
EC	**EuroCity**	Quality international express. Supplement may be payable. Italian **ETR 470** or **610** international high-speed (200 km/h) tilting train, previously known as *Cisalpino*, are now *EC*.
Em	***Euromed***	Spanish 200 km/h trains.
☆	**Eurostar**	High speed (300 km/h) service between London - Paris and Brussels. Special fares payable. Three classes of service: (Business Premier, Leisure Select and Standard). Minimum check-in time 30 minutes. Non–smoking.
ES	**Eurostar Italia**	Italian high speed **ETR 450 / 460 / 500** (250 - 300 km/h) service.
ESc	**Eurostar City**	High speed loco-hauled services, premium fares payable.
Ex	**Express**	Express between Czech Republic and Slovakia.
IC	**InterCity**	Express train. Supplement may be payable.
ICE	**InterCity Express**	German high speed (230 - 320 km/h) service.
ICp	**InterCity Plus**	Italian express formed of new coaches, supplement payable.
IR	**InterRegio**	Inter-regional express usually with refurbished coaches.
RJ	**Railjet**	Austrian quality international express with Premium Class.
RX	**RegioExpress**	Swiss semi-fast regional train.
RB	**Regional Bahn**	German stopping train.
RE	**Regional Express**	German semi-fast train.
SC	**Super City**	Czech Pendolino **680** tilting train, supplement payable.
Talgo	**Talgo**	Spanish quality express using light, articulated stock.
⇌	***Thalys***	High-speed (300 km/h) international train Paris - Brussels - Amsterdam/Köln. Special fares apply. Non–smoking.
TGV	**Train à Grande Vitesse**	French high-speed (270 - 320 km/h) train.
X2000	**X2000**	Swedish high speed (210 km/h) tilting trains.

NIGHT SERVICES:

CNL	**City Night Line**	Brand name covering international and domestic services serving Germany. Facilities range from *Comfortline Deluxe* sleeping cars (1 and 2 berth) with en-suite shower and WC, to modernised *Comfortline Economy* sleeper and couchette cars. Most trains convey shower facilities and 🍸 (also ✕ on certain services). Special fares apply and reservation is compulsory on most services.
D	**Durchgangszug** or **Schnellzug**	Overnight or international express. Some may only convey passengers to international destinations and are likely to be compulsory reservation, marked Ⓡ.
EN	**EuroNight**	Quality international overnight express.
Estr	**Estrella**	Spanish night train.
Hotel	**Trenhotel**	Spanish international quality overnight train. Conveys Gran Clase / Grande Classe sleeping accommodation comprising *de luxe* (1 and 2 berth) compartments with en-suite shower and WC. Also conveys 1, 2 and 4 berth sleeping cars.
ICN	**InterCityNight**	Italian overnight train, supplement payable.

EUROTUNNEL

The frequent car-carrying service between Folkestone and Calais through the **Channel Tunnel** is operated by Eurotunnel. The service operates up to four times hourly (less frequently at night) and takes about 35 minutes. Passengers stay with their cars during the journey. Separate less-frequent trains operate for lorries, coaches, motorcycles, and cars with caravans. Reservations are advisable but passengers can buy tickets at the toll booths when they arrive at the terminal and board the next available shuttle.

Freephone customer information service: ✆ 080 00 96 99 92. Reservations: ✆ 08705 35 35 35.

INTERNATIONAL SERVICES FROM LONDON

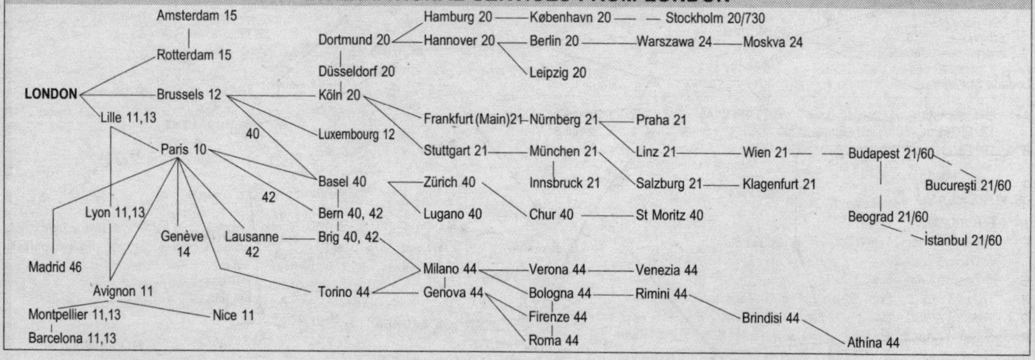

INTERNATIONAL SERVICES FROM PARIS

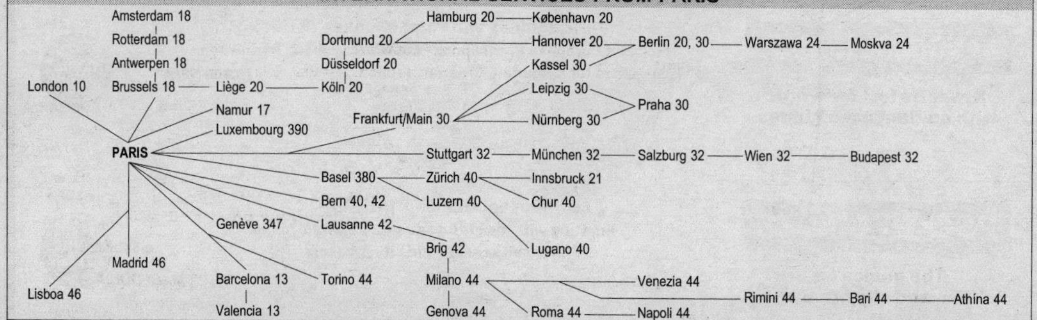

LONDON, BRUSSELS and LILLE - ST GERVAIS, BOURG ST MAURICE and BRIANÇON 9

Other connections are available by changing in Paris (or in Lille and Lyon). Supplements are payable on TGV trains

train type	*TGV*	*TGV*	*TGV*	⇌	⇌	*TGV*	*TGV*		☆	☆	*TGV*
train number	**962**	**964**	**5106**	**9904**	**9920**	**5108**	**762**		**9092**	**9096**	**5146**
train number	**963**	**965**	**5107**	**9905**	**9921**	**5109**	**763**		**9093**	**9097**	**5147**
notes	🅁🍷	🅁🍷	🅁🍷	🅁🍷	🅁🍷	🅁🍷	🅁🍷		🅁✕	🅁✕	🅁🍷
notes	**G**	**G**	**K**	**Q**	**A**	**K**	**G**		**M**	**R◐**	**H**
London St Pancras d.	...	...	...	...	...	...	...	...	1000	2031	...
Ashford International **11** d.	...	...	...	...	...	...	...	...	1047p	2115q	...
Amsterdam Centraal d.	...	...	...	...	0608	...	...	...	|	|	...
Schiphol ✈ d.	...	...	...	...	0626	...	...	...	|	|	...
Den Haag HS d.	...	...	...	...	|	...	...	...	|	|	...
Rotterdam CS d.	...	...	...	...	0658	...	...	...	|	|	...
Antwerpen Centraal d.	...	...	...	...	0730	...	...	...	|	|	...
Brussels Midi / Zuid d.	...	...	...	0724	0819	...	...	...	|	|	...
Dunkerque d.	...	...	...	|	|	...	...	...	|	|	2147
Lille Europe 11 d.	0532	0532	0651	|	|	0710	0725	...	|	|	2224
Douai **11** d.	|	0553	0717	|	|	|	0754	...	|	|	2250
Arras **11** d.	|	0610	0735	|	|	|	0817	...	|	|	2307
TGV Haute Picardie **11** d.	0601	|	0759	|	|	0739	|	...	|	|	2326
Paris Charles de Gaulle ✈ **11** d.	0634	|	0833	|	|	0812	|	...	|	|	2359
Marne la Valleé Chessy § **11** d.	|	|	0848	|	|	0827	0930	...	|	|	0017
Cluses (Haute Savoie) a.	|	|	|	|	|	1318	1446	...	|	|	|
Salanches Megève a.	|	|	|	|	|	1334	1502	...	|	|	|
St Gervais a.	|	|	|	|	|	1345	1511	1532	|	|	|
Chamonix a.	|	|	|	|	|	...	...	1611	|	|	|
Chambéry a.	|	1033	1146	1152	1236	...	...	...	|	|	0534
Albertville a.	1022	1112	1223	1238	1311	...	...	...	|	|	0613
Moûtiers-Salins a.	1058	1158	1252	1307	1348	...	...	...	1730	0537	0645
Aime la Plagne a.	...	1230	1309	...	1408	...	...	...	1802	0605	0708
Landry a.	...	1248	1319	...	1418	...	...	...	|	|	0723
Bourg St Maurice a.	...	1304	1328	...	1428	...	...	...	1820	0627	0736

train type	☆	*TGV*	⇌	*TGV*		*TGV*	*TGV*	*TGV*	*TGV*	⇌	☆
train number	**9094**	**5174**	**9963**	**764**		**5178**	**970**	**5182**	**972**	**9987**	**9098**
train number	**9095**	**5175**	**9962**	**765**	**18922**	**5196**	**971**	**5183**	**973**	**9986**	**9099**
notes	🅁✕	🅁🍷	🅁🍷	🅁🍷	2	🅁🍷	🅁🍷	🅁🍷	🅁🍷	🅁🍷	🅁✕
notes	**U**	**Y**	**N**	**J**		**K**	**J**	**K**	**J**	**B**	**S◧**
Bourg St Maurice d.	1004	1017	...	...	...	...	1410	1504	...	1532	2215
Landry d.	|	1028	...	...	...	...	1419	1515	...	1547	|
Aime la Plagne d.	|	1039	...	...	...	...	1428	1526	...	1555	|
Moûtiers-Salins d.	1045y	1101	1415	...	...	...	1445	1543	1550	1617	2309z
Albertville d.	|	1135	1444	...	...	...	1520	1619	1636	1658	|
Chambéry d.	|	|	1530	...	...	...	|	1652	|	1733	|
Chamonix d.	|	|	|	...	1439	...	|	|	|	|	|
St Gervais d.	|	|	|	1512	1520	1543	|	|	|	|	|
Salanches Megève d.	|	|	|	1521	...	1552	|	|	|	|	|
Cluses (Haute Savoie) d.	|	|	|	1537	...	1608	|	|	|	|	|
Marne la Vallée Chessy § **11** a.	|	1447	|	2010	...	2032	|	1944	2023	|	|
Paris Charles de Gaulle ✈ **11** a.	|	1505	|	2030	...	2048	|	2002	2038	|	|
TGV Haute Picardie **11** a.	|	|	|	|	...	2122	|	2042	2109	|	|
Arras **11** a.	|	|	|	2122	...	|	1953	2116j	|	|	|
Douai **11** a.	|	|	|	2139	...	|	2009	2132j	|	|	|
Lille Flandres a.	|	|	|	2201	...	|	2031	2155j	|	|	|
Lille Europe 11 a.	|	1602	|	...	...	2152	...	...	2138	|	|
Dunkerque a.	|	1642	|	...	...	...	...	...	...	|	|
Brussels Midi / Zuid a.	|	...	1951	...	...	...	...	...	...	2144	|
Antwerpen Centraal a.	|	...	...	...	...	...	...	...	...	2229	|
Rotterdam CS a.	|	...	...	...	...	...	...	...	...	2301	|
Den Haag HS a.	|	...	...	...	...	...	...	...	...	|	|
Schiphol ✈ a.	|	...	...	...	...	...	...	...	...	2333	|
Amsterdam Centraal a.	|	...	...	...	...	...	...	...	...	2353	|
Ashford International **11** a.	1536	...	...	...	...	...	...	...	...	...	0634
London St Pancras a.	1611	...	...	...	...	...	...	...	...	...	0716

A – THALYS NEIGE – ⑥ Dec. 19 - Mar. 20: [12] and 🍷 Amsterdam - Bourg St Maurice; ⑥ Dec. 19 - Apr. 17: [12] and 🍷 Brussels - Bourg St Maurice.
B – THALYS NEIGE – ⑥ Dec. 26 - Mar. 27: [12] and 🍷 Bourg St Maurice - Amsterdam; ⑥ Dec. 19 - Apr. 17: [12] and 🍷 Bourg St Maurice - Brussels.
G – Feb. 6, 13 only.
H – ⑤ Jan. 8 - Apr. 2 (also Dec. 18, 24, 31).
J – Feb. 13, 20 only.
K – ⑥ Dec. 19 - Apr. 24 (also Dec. 25, Jan. 1; not Apr. 5).
L – ⑥ Dec. 19 - Apr. 24.
M – ⑥ Dec. 19 - Apr. 10.
N – THALYS NEIGE – Dec. 26, Jan. 2, Feb. 20: [12] and 🍷 Moûtiers-Salins - Brussels.
Q – THALYS NEIGE – Dec. 19, 26, Feb. 13: [12] and 🍷 Brussels - Moûtiers-Salins.
R – ⑤ Jan. 1 - Apr. 2.
S – ⑥ Dec. 26 - Apr. 10.
U – ⑥ Jan 2 - Apr. 17.
Y – ⑥ Dec. 19 - Apr. 3 (also Dec. 25, Jan. 1).

j – On Dec. 25, Jan. 1 arrive Arras 2110, Douai 2126, Lille Flandres 2148.
p – Arrive 1028.
q – Arrive 2059.
y – Arrive 1032.
z – Arrive 2240.

◐ – 🍷 until 0100. ✕ after departure from Ashford. ✕ and 🍷 from 0500.
◧ – 🍷 until 0100. ✕ after departure from Moûtiers. ✕ and 🍷 from 0500.
§ – Station for Disneyland, Paris.
⇌ – *Thalys* high-speed train 🅁 🍷. Special fares payable.
☆ – Eurostar train. Special fares payable. Minimum check-in time 30 minutes.

10 LONDON - LILLE - PARIS and BRUSSELS *by Eurostar*

Minimum check-in time is 30 minutes. Not available for London - Ebbsfleet - Ashford or v.v. Special fares payable that include three classes of service.

All times shown are local times (France is one hour ahead of Great Britain). All Eurostar services are ®, non-smoking and convey ✕.

Service Dec. 13, 2009 - July 3, 2010. No service December 25.

km	km	train number	9078	9002	9108	9002	9004	9110	9006	9112	9114	9008	9010	9120	9012	9116	9012	9014	9014	9074	9018	9126	9020	9126	9022	9130	9024
		notes	①-⑤	②③④	①-⑤	⑥	①-⑥	⑥	①-⑥	①-④	⑥	①-⑥	⑦	①-⑤	①-⑤	⑥⑦	⑥	⑥	⑧			⑥		①-⑤	⑤⑥	⑦	
		notes	B	C	g	h	D	h	k	p		p	q	p	k	q	m	r	E	A			F	p		z	
0	0	**London St Pancras** .... d.	0525	0602	0620	0622	0655	0659	0727	0730	0757	0802	0826	0827	0855	0857	0900	0922	0932	0953	1025	1057	1100	1104	1132	1157	1229
35	35	Ebbsfleet International ..... d.	0542	0620	0637	|	|	0715	0745	|	|	|	0842	0845	0912	0915	|	0942	|	|	|	1115	|	|	|	1215	1245
90	90	Ashford International .... d.	|	0649	0657	|	0725	|	|	|	0828	|	|	|	|	|	|	|	|	1028	1055	|	|	|	|	|	|
166	166	Calais Fréthun .... a.	|	|	0829	|	|	|	0929	|	|	|	|	|	|	|	|	|	|	|	|	|	|	|	|	|	|
267	267	Lille Europe .... a.	|	|	0907	|	|	0924	|	|	1024	|	|	1054	|	1124	|	|	|	1224	|	1326	|	1326	|	1424	|
	373	**Brussels Midi / Zuid** .... a.	|	|	0944	|	|	1003	|	1028	1108	|	|	1133	|	1203	|	|	|	...	|	1405	|	1405	|	1503	|
492		**Paris Nord** .... a.	0850	0954	...	0947	1017	...	1056	...	...	1117	1147	...	1217	...	1217	1247	1247	...	1347o	...	1420	...	1447	...	1550

train number	9132	9026	9030	9138	9034	9036	9038	9144	9144	9144	9144	9040	9040	9042	9148	9148	9044	9150	9044	9044	9046	9154	9154	9050	9158	9054	9056
notes	①-⑥	⑦			⑧	⑥⑦	①-⑤	⑤	⑦	①-④	⑥	⑥⑦	⑤	①-⑤	⑦	⑥	⑥	①-⑤	①-⑤	⑦	⑧	⑦	①-⑤				⑦
notes	g	G		J	w	y	g		q	p	Q	y	w	g	q	L	r	p	b	q	f	q	c	j	j	v	q
London St Pancras .... d.	1257	1300	1404	1434	1502	1532	1602	1604	1604	1604	1604	1625	1632	1655	1657	1704	1725	1727	1730	1731	1755	1825	1835	1902	1934	2004	2032
Ebbsfleet International ..... d.	1315	|	|	|	|	|	|	|	|	|	|	|	|	|	1715	|	1742	1745	|	|	1812	|	|	|	|	|	|
Ashford International .... d.	|	|	|	|	|	|	|	|	|	|	|	1655	|	1727	|	|	|	|	|	|	|	1855	|	|	|	|	|
Calais Fréthun .... a.	|	|	|	|	|	|	|	|	1759	|	|	|	|	|	|	|	1926	|	|	1926	|	|	|	|	|	2159	|
Lille Europe .... a.	1524	|	1624	1654	|	|	|	|	|	1825	1826	|	|	|	1924	1924	|	1954	|	|	|	2051	|	|	2154	|	|
Brussels Midi / Zuid .... a.	1603	|	|	1733	|	|	|	1859	1903	1903	1908	|	|	|	2003	2003	|	2033	|	|	|	2130	2133	|	2233	|	|
Paris Nord .... a.	...	1617	1726	...	1817	1847	1917	...	...	...	...	1947	1947	2023	...	...	2053	...	2047	2053	2117	...	...	2217	...	2326	2347

train number	9109	9005	9007	9113	9113	9113	9011	9117	9119	9015	9019	9023	9181	9027	9031	9137	9139	9035	9141	9039	9039	9145	9043	9045	9149		
notes		①-⑤	①-⑥	⑤	⑥	①-④		⑦	①-⑥							⑥⑦	①-⑤	⑤⑥⑦	⑦	⑥⑦	①-⑤	⑤		⑦	⑧		
notes	K	B	x	d		P		M	p					H		z	g	t	q	q	p			q			
Paris Nord .... d.	...	0643	0713	...	...	...	0807	...	...	0913	1013	1113	...	1213	1304	...	...	1413	...	1507	1513	...	1613	1643	...	...	...
Brussels Midi / Zuid .... d.	0659	|	|	0759	0759	0805	|	0859	0929	|	|	|	1129	|	|	1359	1429	|	1459	|	|	1559	|	|	1659	...	...
Lille Europe .... d.	0735	|	|	0835	|	|	|	0935	1005	|	|	|	1205	|	1406	1435	1505	|	1535	|	|	|	|	|	1735	...	...
Calais Fréthun .... d.	|	|	|	|	0902	|	0934	|	|	|	|	|	|	|	|	|	|	|	|	1635	|	1702	|	|	|	...	...
Ashford International .... a.	|	|	|	|	|	|	0906	|	|	|	|	|	|	|	|	|	|	|	|	1606	1606	|	|	|	1733	...	...
Ebbsfleet International ..... a.	|	|	|	|	|	|	|	|	|	1018	|	|	1215	|	1415	1445	|	|	|	|	|	1645	1718	|	|	...	...
London St Pancras .... a.	0755	0758	0828	0856	0856	0856	0936	0956	1026	1034	1128	1229	1233	1328	1431	1503	1526	1529	1556	1636	1636	1703	1734	1759	1805	...	...

train number	9047	9047	9049	9153	9051	9051	9157	9053	9055	9161	9059	9163	9163	9059	9061	9063	9063										
notes	①-⑥	⑦	⑦		⑦	①-⑤	⑧	①-⑤		⑥	①-⑤	①-④	⑤⑦	⑥⑦	⑦	⑥⑦	①-⑤										
notes	p	q	q		q	p	j	c	j		c	c	q	q	e	n	c										
Paris Nord .... d.	1713	1713	1743	...	1813	1813	...	1843	1913	...	2013	...		2013	2043	2113	2113	...	...	...	...	...	...	...	...	...	...
Brussels Midi / Zuid .... d.	|	|	|	1759	|	|	1859	|	|	1959	|	2017	2029	|	|	|	|	...	...	...	...	...	...	...	...	...	...
Lille Europe .... d.	|	|	|	1835	|	|	1935	|	|	2035	|	2056	2105	|	|	|	|	...	...	...	...	...	...	...	...	...	...
Calais Fréthun .... d.	|	|	|	|	|	|	|	|	|	|	|	2132	|	|	|	|	|	...	...	...	...	...	...	...	...	...	...
Ashford International .... a.	|	|	|	|	|	|	|	1936	|	|	|	|	|	2106	|	|	|	...	...	...	...	...	...	...	...	...	...
Ebbsfleet International ...... a.	|	1818	|	1845	|	1918	|	|	2018	2045	|	2115	2115	|	|	|	2218	...	...	...	...	...	...	...	...	...	...
London St Pancras .... a.	1829	1834	1859	1903	1929	1934	1956	2006	2034	2103	2129	2133	2133	2136	2159	2229	2234	...	...	...	...	...	...	...	...	...	...

A – ①③④⑤⑦ (daily Dec. 13 - Jan. 4; Feb. 10–22; Mar. 31 - Apr. 19; also May 1; daily May 26 - June 7; July 21 - Sept. 3; Oct. 20 - Nov. 1). To Marne la Vallée - Chessy: (station for Disneyland). Table **17a**.
B – ①-⑤ (①⑤ Jan. 4 - Feb. 6) not Dec. 28, Jan. 1, Apr. 5, May 3, 13, 24, 31.
C – ②③④ Jan. 4 - Feb. 6.
D – ①-⑥ (①⑤⑥ Jan. 4 - Feb. 6) not Dec. 26, 28, Jan. 1, Apr. 5, May 3, 24, 31.
E – ⑧ (①⑤⑦ Jan. 4 - Feb. 6) not Jan. 1.
F – Dec. 13, 19, 20, 26, 27, 28, Jan. 1, 2, 3, Mar. 20, May 16, 29.
G – ⑦ (also Dec. 18, 28, Mar. 19, Apr. 2, 5, May 3, 24, 28, 31).
H – Daily Dec. 26 - Jan. 3; ①⑤⑦ Jan. 4 - Feb. 6; ⑧ Feb. 7 - July 3.
J – ⑤⑦ (also Dec. 19, 26, 28, Jan. 2, Apr. 5, May 3, 24, 31).
K – ①②③④⑥ (not Dec. 26, 28, Apr. 5, May 3, 13, 24, 31).
L – ⑥ Dec. 13 - Jan. 3.

M – ⑦ Dec. 13 - Jan. 3 (also Dec. 28).
P – ①-④ (not Dec. 28, Apr. 5, May 3, 13, 24, 31).
Q – ⑥ Jan. 4 - July 3.

b – Not Dec. 24, 28, 31, Jan. 1, Apr. 5, May 3, 24, 31.
c – Not Dec. 24, 28, 31, Apr. 5, May 3, 24, 31.
d – Also Dec. 26, May 13.
e – Also Dec. 26, 28, Apr. 5, May 3, 24, 31.
f – Not Dec. 24, 31, Jan. 1, Apr. 2.
g – Not Dec. 28, Jan. 1, Apr. 5, May 3, 24, 31.
h – Not Dec. 26.
j – Not Dec. 24, 31.
k – Not Dec. 26, 28, Jan. 1, Apr. 5, May 3, 24, 31.

m – Also Jan. 1, Apr. 5, May 24.
n – Also Dec. 28, Apr. 5, May 3, 24, 31; not Dec. 26.
o – 1350 on ⑥.
p – Not Dec. 28, Apr. 5, May 3, 24, 31.
q – Also Dec. 28, Apr. 5, May 3, 24, 31.
r – Also Jan. 1.
t – Also Dec. 28, Apr. 5, May 3, 24, 31; not Jan. 1.
v – Not Dec. 24, 31, May 23.
w – Not Jan. 1.
x – Not Dec. 26, 28, Jan. 1, Apr. 5, May 3, 13, 24, 31.
y – Also Dec. 28, Jan. 1, Apr. 5, May 3, 24, 31.
z – Also Apr. 5, May 24.

10 LONDON – PARIS *by rail – sea – rail*

Other services are available by taking normal service trains between London and Dover (Tables **100**, **101**), sailings between Dover and Calais (Table **2110**) and normal service trains between Calais and Paris, by changing at Boulogne (Tables **260** and **261**), passengers making their own way between stations and docks at Dover and Calais, allowing at least 1 hour for connections.

No service December 25.

French train number		ship	2	2032		ship	2	2036		ship	2	2038		ship	2	2	2042		ship	2	2044					
sea crossing (see below)	⑥	⑥	⑥	⑥⑦	①-⑤	①-⑤	①-⑤	①-⑤	⑦	⑦	⑦	⑦	①-⑥	①-⑥	①-⑤	⑥		⑦	⑦	⑦	⑦					
notes	j		g	h	z		f	q	x		h	y	z		f	h		x		h	k					
London Charing Cross ....d.	0600	...	...	...	0740	...	...	...	0908	...	...	...	1010	...	...	...	...	1108	...	...	...	...	...	...	...	...
Dover Priory ✣ ....a.	0801	...	...	...	0931	...	...	...	1101	...	...	...	1201	...	...	...	...	1301	...	...	...	...	...	...	...	...
Dover Eastern Docks 🚌 ✣d.	...	0915	...	...	...	1045	...	...	...	1215	...	...	...	1300	...	...	...	...	1430	...	...	...	...	...	...	...
Calais Port 🚌 ✣...................a.	...	1145	...	...	...	1315	...	...	...	1445	...	...	...	1530	...	...	...	...	1700	...	...	...	...	...	...	...
Calais Ville ✣ ....d.	...	...	1327	...	...	...	1433	...	...	...	1544	...	...	...	1644	1652	...	...	...	1746	...	...	...	...	...	...
Boulogne Ville.......................d.	...	...	1402	1438	...	...	1509	1536	...	...	1618	1635	...	...	1721	1726	1742	...	...	1818	1838	...	...	...	...	...
Amiens ....a.	...	...	...	1602	...	...	...	1704	...	...	...	1800	...	...	...	...	1859	...	...	...	2005	...	...	...	...	...
Paris Nord ....a.	...	...	...	1720	...	...	...	1823	...	...	...	1920	...	...	...	...	2020	...	...	...	2123	...	...	...	...	...

French train number	2003	2	ship		TGV 7229	ship		2015	2	2	2	ship		2025	2	ship		2	ship						
sea crossing (see below)	①-⑥	①-⑥	①-⑥	①-⑥			①-⑥		⑦	⑥	①-⑤				①-⑤	①-⑤	①-⑤	⑥⑦	⑥⑦	⑥⑦					
notes	p	f		z	® A		z		h	g	f				f		z	h		x					
Paris Nord ....d.	0707	...	...	...	0958	...	...	1004	...	...	...	...	...	1419	...	...	...	...	...	...	...	...	...	...	...
Amiens ....d.	0823	...	...	...	|	...	...	1123	...	...	...	...	...	1535	...	...	...	...	...	...					
Boulogne Ville.......................d.	0941	0957	...	...	|	...	...	1250	1258	1303	1305	...	...	1659	1707	...	...	1739	...	...					
Calais Ville ✣ ....a.	...	1031	...	...	1140	...	...	...	1333	1343	1342	...	...	...	1741	...	...	1816	...	...					
Calais Port 🚌 ✣....................d.	...	...	1140	...	...	1225	...	...	...	...	...	1525	...	...	...	1825	...	...	1955	...					
Dover Eastern Docks 🚌 ✣a.	...	...	1210	...	...	1255	...	...	...	...	...	1555	...	...	...	1855	...	...	2025	...					
Dover Priory ✣ ....d.	...	...	...	1324	...	...	1424	...	...	...	...	...	1724	...	...	...	2024	...	...	2124					
London Charing Cross ....a.	...	...	...	1522	...	...	1624	...	...	...	...	...	1922	...	...	...	2222	...	...	2323	...	...	...	...	...

RAIL – SEA – RAIL SERVICE
SEA CROSSING: Connections between Rail - Sea - Rail services are not guaranteed.

A – ①-⑥ (not Apr. 5, May 24).
f – Not Dec. 25, Jan. 1, Apr. 5, May 13, 24.
g – Not May 1, 8.
j – Not Dec. 26.
h – Also Dec. 25, Jan. 1, Apr. 5, May 13, 24.

k – Also Apr. 5, May 24; not Apr. 4, May 23.
p – Not Apr. 5, May 24.
q – Not Dec. 25, Jan. 1, Apr. 5, May 12, 13, 24.
x – Also Dec. 28, Jan. 1, Apr. 5, May 3, 31.
y – Also Apr. 5, May 24.
z – Not Dec. 28, Jan. 1, Apr. 5, May 3, 31.

ship – Ship service, operated by P & O Ferries. ✕ on ship. One class only on ship. For additional ferry services see Table **2110**.
✣ – 🚌 service between Dover Priory and Dover Eastern Docks and v.v. (every 20 minutes approx; 0715 – 1930; not a guaranteed connection). Calais Port - Calais Ville station 1100 – 1915; Calais Ville station - Calais Port 1030 – 1930.

LONDON / BRUSSELS - LILLE - CHARLES DE GAULLE ✈ - WESTERN / SOUTHERN FRANCE 11

DAY TRAINS (FOR NIGHT TRAINS SEE TABLE 13). Supplements are payable on *TGV* trains. Connections at Lille are not guaranteed. Other connections available via Paris.

km	train type	*TGV*	*TGV*	*TGV*	*TGV*	*TGV*	*TGV*	*TGV*	*TGV*	*TGV*	*TGV*	*TGV*	*TGV*	☆	☆	*TGV*	*TGV*	*TGV*	☆	☆	*TGV*	*TGV*	*TGV*	*TGV*	*TGV*
	train number	**5102**	**9804**	**5104**	**5200**	**5110**	**5148**	**9802**	**5212**	**8515**	**5112**	**5214**	**5214**	**9108**	**9110**	**5100**	**9826**	**5164**	**9120**	**9116**	**9832**	**5115**	**6818**	**5224**	**5227**
	train number	**5103**	**9805**	**5105**	**5201**	**5111**	**5149**	**9803**	R	R	**5113**	**5213**	**5215**	R ✕	R	R	**9827**	R	R ✕	R ✕	**9833**	R	**6819**	**5225**	R
	notes	R 🍷	R 🍷 A	R 🍷 B	R 🍷 r	R 🍷	R 🍷	R 🍷	🍷	🍷	R 🍷	R 🍷	R 🍷	①–⑤ b	✕ ⑥d	🍷	R 🍷	🍷	①–⑤ m	⑥⑦ w	R 🍷	🍷	R 🍷	R 🍷	🍷
	London St Pancras 12 .... d.	...	...	...	...	...	...	...	...	...	...	...	...	0620	0659	...	...	...	0827	0857	...	...	...	...	...
	Ebbsfleet International **12**.. d.	...	...	...	...	...	...	...	...	...	...	...	...	0637	0715	...	...	...	0845	0915	...	...	...	...	...
	Ashford International **12** .... d.	...	...	...	...	...	...	...	...	...	...	...	...	0657	|	...	...	...	|	|	...	...	...	...	...
	Brussels Midi / Zuid 12. d.	...	0540	...	...	...	...	0746	...	...	...	...	...	|	|	...	1021	...	|	|	1120	...	...	...	...
	Lille Europe 12 .... a.	...	0615	...	...	...	...	|	...	...	...	...	...	0907	0924	...	|	...	1054	1124	1156	...	...	...	...
0	**Lille Europe** .... d.	0559	0625	0625	0558	0643c	...	|	0814	...	0828	0846	0846	...	...	1006	|	1030	...	...	1206	1206	...	1210	1210
	Douai .... d.	|	|	|	0628	0709	...	|	|	...	|	0908	0908	...	...	|	|	|	...	...	|	|	...	|	|
	Arras .... d.	|	|	|	0647	0727	...	|	|	...	|	0927	0927	...	...	|	|	|	...	...	|	|	...	|	|
128	TGV Haute Picardie .... d.	|	0653	0653	0707	0746	...	|	|	...	|	0952	0952	...	...	|	|	1103	...	...	|	|	...	1244	1244
241	Paris Charles de Gaulle ✈ a.	0649	0720	0720	0735	0816	...	0902	0906	...	0921	1022	1022	...	...	1056	1137	1132	...	...	1256	1256	...	1312	1312
	Paris Charles de Gaulle ✈ d.	0654	0725	0725	0739	0821	...	0912	0912	...	0925	1027	1027	...	...	1100	1142	1142	...	...	1301	1301	...	1316	1316
264	Marne la Vallée § .... d.	0710	0740	0740	0756	0835	...	0927	0927	...	0940	1042	1042	...	...	1113	1156	1156	...	...	1314	1314	...	1329	1329
326	Massy TGV .... d.	|	|	|	0831	|	...	1000	1000	...	|	1117	1117	...	...	|	|	|	...	...	|	|	...	1401	1401
	Le Mans .... a.	|	|	|	|	|	...	|	|	...	|	1205	1205	...	...	|	|	|	...	...	|	|	...	1450	1450
	Rennes .... a.	|	|	|	|	|	...	|	|	...	|	|	1327	...	...	|	|	|	...	...	|	|	...	1607	|
	Angers St Laud .... a.	|	|	|	|	|	...	|	|	...	|	1250	...	...	...	|	|	|	...	...	|	|	...	...	1539
	Nantes .... a.	|	|	|	|	|	...	|	|	...	|	1333	...	...	...	|	|	|	...	...	|	|	...	...	1617
	St Pierre des Corps ...... a.	|	|	|	0922	|	...	1050	1050	...	|	...	...	...	...	|	|	|	...	...	|	|	...	...	...
	Poitiers .... a.	|	|	|	1011	|	...	1131	1131	...	|	...	...	...	...	|	|	|	...	...	|	|	...	...	...
	Angoulême .... a.	|	|	|	1057	|	...	1224	1224	...	|	...	...	...	...	|	|	|	...	...	|	|	...	...	...
	Bordeaux .... a.	|	|	|	1200	|	...	1327	1327	1318	|	...	...	...	...	|	|	|	...	...	|	|	...	...	...
	Irún .... a.	|	|	|	1433g	|	...	...	...	1549	|	...	...	...	...	|	|	|	...	...	|	|	...	...	...
558	Le Creusot TGV .... a.	|	|	|	...	|	...	...	...	...	|	...	...	...	...	|	|	|	...	...	|	|	...	...	...
682	**Lyon Part Dieu** .... a.	0901	0931	0931	...	1031	...	...	...	...	1131	...	...	...	...	1303	|	|	...	...	1501	1501	1537	...	...
	Lyon Perrache .... a.	|	|	|	...	|	...	...	...	...	|	...	...	...	...	1317	|	|	...	...	|	|	|	...	...
	Grenoble .... a.	|	|	|	...	|	...	...	...	...	|	...	...	...	...	...	|	|	...	...	|	|	|	...	...
	Valence TGV .... a.	|	1011	1011	...	1111	...	...	...	...	1213	...	...	...	...	...	1404	1404	...	...	1541	|	|	...	...
	Avignon TGV .... a.	1009	|	|	...	1145	...	...	...	...	|	...	...	...	...	...	1439	1439	...	...	|	|	1643	...	...
	Nîmes .... a.	|	1057	1057	...	|	...	...	...	...	1258	...	...	...	...	...	|	|	...	...	1629	|	|	...	...
	Montpellier .... a.	|	1128	1128	...	|	...	...	...	...	1330	...	...	...	...	...	|	|	...	...	1659	|	|	...	...
	Béziers .... a.	|	1213	1213	...	|	...	...	...	...	...	...	...	...	...	...	|	|	...	...	1751	|	|	...	...
	Narbonne .... a.	|	1235	1235	...	|	...	...	...	...	...	...	...	...	...	...	|	|	...	...	1807	|	|	...	...
	Toulouse Matabiau... a.	|	1355	1355	...	|	...	...	...	...	...	...	...	...	...	...	|	|	...	...	|	|	|	...	...
	Perpignan .... a.	|	...	...	...	|	...	...	...	...	...	...	...	...	...	...	|	|	...	...	1844	|	|	...	...
	Aix en Provence TGV .... a.	1033	...	...	...	1210	...	...	...	...	...	...	...	...	...	...	1502	1502	...	...	...	1633	|	...	...
	Marseille St Charles .... a.	1047	...	...	...	1225	1259	...	...	...	...	...	...	...	...	...	1516	1516	...	...	...	1647	1717	...	...
	Toulon .... a.	1143	...	...	...	...	1343	...	...	...	...	...	...	...	...	...	1611	1611	...	...	...	...	1814	...	...
	St Raphaël - Valescure ..... a.	1236	...	...	...	...	1437	...	...	...	...	...	...	...	...	...	1708	1708	...	...	...	...	1907	...	...
	Cannes .... a.	1300	...	...	...	...	1502	...	...	...	...	...	...	...	...	...	1732	1732	...	...	...	...	1932	...	...
	Nice .... a.	1332	...	...	...	...	1534	...	...	...	...	...	...	...	...	...	1803	1803	...	...	...	...	2004	...	...

train type	☆	☆	*TGV*	*TGV*	☆	*TGV*	*TGV*	☆	☆	☆	*TGV*	*TGV*	*TGV*	*TGV*	*TGV*	*TGV*	☆	*TGV*	*TGV*	☆	*TGV*	☆	*TGV*	*TGV*	
train number	**9120**	**9116**	**5218**	**5221**	**9074**	**9828**	**5117**	**9126**	**9126**	**9130**	**5232**	**5216**	**5216**	**5209**	**5118**	**5222**	**9132**	**9834**	**6181**	**9030**	**9836**	**9138**	**5236**	**5231**	
train number	R ✕	R ✕	**5219**	R 🍷	R	**9829**	**5116**	R	R ✕	R	**5233**	**5229**	**5217**	R	**5119**	**5223**	R ✕	**9835**	R	R	**9837**	R	**5238**	R	
notes	①–⑤ m	⑥⑦ w	R 🍷 z	⑦k z	✕ X	R 🍷	🍷 F	✕ ⑥	①–⑤ m	✕ ⑦k	R 🍷 C	R 🍷 ⑦k	R 🍷 ⑦k	🍷 ⑥p	R 🍷	R 🍷 y	①–⑥ b	R 🍷	🍷	✕	R 🍷	✕ J	R 🍷 ⑧h	🍷 ⑧q	
London St Pancras 12 ..... d.	0827	0857	...	...	0953	...	...	1057	1104	1157	...	...	...	...	...	...	1257	...	...	1404	...	1434	...	...	...
Ebbsfleet International **12**... d.	0845	0915	...	...	|	...	...	1115	|	1215	...	...	...	...	...	...	1315	...	...	|	...	|	...	...	...
Ashford International **12** ..... d.	|	|	...	...	1028	...	...	|	|	|	...	...	...	...	...	...	|	...	...	|	...	|	...	...	...
Brussels Midi / Zuid 12 . d.	|	|	...	...	|	1249	...	|	|	|	...	...	...	...	...	...	|	1520	...	|	1609	|	...	...	...
Lille Europe 12 .... a.	1054	1124	...	...	1224s	1323	...	1326	1326	1424	...	...	...	...	...	...	1524	1556	...	1624	1644	1654	...	...	...
Lille Europe .... d.	...	...	1238x	1238x	|	1333	...	...	...	...	1447	1447	1447	1447	1506	1540	...	1606	...	...	1654	...	1728	1728	...
Douai .... d.	...	...	|	|	|	|	...	...	...	...	|	|	|	|	|	|	...	|	...	...	|	...	|	|	...
Arras .... d.	...	...	|	|	|	|	...	...	...	...	|	|	|	|	|	|	...	|	...	...	|	...	|	|	...
TGV Haute Picardie .... d.	...	...	|	|	|	|	...	...	...	...	|	|	|	|	|	|	...	|	...	...	|	...	|	|	...
Paris Charles de Gaulle ✈. a.	...	...	1332	1332	|	1422	...	...	...	...	1538	1538	1538	1538	1556	1632	...	1656	...	...	1746	...	1820	1820	...
Paris Charles de Gaulle ✈. d.	...	...	1337	1337	|	1428	...	...	...	...	1542	1542	1542	1542	1601	1637	...	1701	...	...	1751	...	1825	1825	...
Marne la Vallée § .... d.	...	...	1351	1351	1331	1441	...	...	...	...	1557	1557	1557	1557	1614	1652	...	1714	...	...	1810	...	1840	1840	...
Massy TGV .... d.	...	...	1431	1431	...	|	...	...	...	...	1631	1631	1631	1631	|	1730	...	|	...	...	|	...	1917	1921	...
Le Mans .... a.	...	...	|	|	...	|	...	...	...	...	1719	|	|	1719	|	|	...	|	...	...	|	...	2005	|	...
Rennes .... a.	...	...	|	|	...	|	...	...	...	...	1836	|	|	|	|	|	...	|	...	...	|	...	2125	|	...
Angers St Laud .... a.	...	...	|	|	...	|	...	...	...	...	...	|	1812	1823	|	|	...	|	...	...	|	...	...	2105	...
Nantes .... a.	...	...	|	|	...	|	...	...	...	...	...	|	1854	1900	|	|	...	|	...	...	|	...	...	2147	...
St Pierre des Corps .... a.	...	...	1521	1521	...	|	...	...	...	...	...	1721	1721f	...	|	1821	...	|	...	...	|	...	...	2011f	...
Poitiers .... a.	...	...	1610	1610	...	|	...	...	...	...	...	1807	...	...	|	1902	...	|	...	...	|	...	...	...	...
Angoulême .... a.	...	...	1656	1655	...	|	...	...	...	...	...	...	...	...	|	1948	...	|	...	...	|	...	...	...	...
Bordeaux .... a.	...	...	1803	1803	...	|	...	...	...	...	...	...	...	...	|	2052	...	|	...	...	|	...	...	...	...
Irún .... a.	...	...	|	2047	...	|	...	...	...	...	...	...	...	...	|	...	...	|	...	...	|	...	...	...	...
Le Creusot TGV .... a.	...	...	|	...	...	|	...	...	...	...	...	...	...	...	|	...	...	|	...	...	|	...	...	...	...
Lyon Part Dieu .... a.	...	...	|	...	...	1631	1707	...	...	...	...	...	...	...	1801	...	...	1901	...	...	2001	...	...	...	...
Lyon Perrache .... a.	...	...	|	...	...	|	|	...	...	...	...	...	...	...	|	...	...	|	...	...	|	...	...	...	...
Grenoble .... a.	...	...	|	...	...	|	|	...	...	...	...	...	...	...	|	...	...	|	...	...	|	...	...	...	...
Valence TGV .... a.	...	...	|	...	...	1714	1742	...	...	...	...	...	...	...	|	...	...	|	...	...	2042	...	...	...	...
Avignon TGV .... a.	...	...	|	...	...	1748	|	...	...	...	...	...	...	...	|	...	...	2010	...	...	|	...	...	...	...
Nîmes .... a.	...	...	|	...	...	|	1830	...	...	...	...	...	...	...	1927	...	...	|	...	...	2128	...	...	...	...
Montpellier .... a.	...	...	|	...	...	|	1857	...	...	...	...	...	...	...	1958	...	...	|	...	...	2155	...	...	...	...
Béziers .... a.	...	...	|	...	...	|	1940	...	...	...	...	...	...	...	2048	...	...	|	...	...	2241t	...	...	...	...
Narbonne .... a.	...	...	|	...	...	|	1955	...	...	...	...	...	...	...	2104	...	...	|	...	...	2257t	...	...	...	...
Toulouse Matabiau.... a.	...	...	2015e	...	...	|	2110	...	...	...	...	...	...	...	|	...	...	|	...	...	|	...	...	...	...
Perpignan .... a.	...	...	...	...	...	|	...	...	...	...	...	...	...	...	2139	...	...	|	...	...	2332t	...	...	...	...
Aix en Provence TGV .... a.	...	...	...	...	...	1813	...	...	...	...	...	...	...	...	...	...	...	2033	2045	...	...	...	...	...	...
Marseille St Charles .... a.	...	...	...	...	...	1827	...	...	...	...	...	...	...	...	...	...	...	2047	|	...	...	...	...	...	...
Toulon .... a.	...	...	...	...	...	...	...	...	...	...	...	...	...	...	...	...	...	2146j	2137	...	...	...	...	...	...
St Raphaël - Valescure .... a.	...	...	...	...	...	...	...	...	...	...	...	...	...	...	...	...	...	...	2227	...	...	...	...	...	...
Cannes .... a.	...	...	...	...	...	...	...	...	...	...	...	...	...	...	...	...	...	...	2251	...	...	...	...	...	...
Nice .... a.	...	...	...	...	...	...	...	...	...	...	...	...	...	...	...	...	...	...	2324	...	...	...	...	...	...

A – ①–⑤ (not Dec. 25, Jan. 1, Apr. 5, May 13, 24).
B – ⑥⑦ (also Dec. 25, Jan. 1, Apr. 5, May 13, 24).
C – ①–⑥ (not Apr. 5, May 24).
F – ⑥⑦ (daily Dec. 19 - Feb. 14; not Dec. 13; daily Mar. 13 - Oct. 17).
J – ⑤⑦ (⑤⑥⑦ Dec. 13 - Feb. 6) also Dec. 28, Apr. 5, May 3, 24, 31.
X – ①③④⑤⑦ (daily Dec. 13 - Jan. 4; not Dec. 25; Feb. 10 – 22; Mar. 31 - Apr. 19; also May 1; daily May 26 - June 7; July 21 - Sept. 3; Oct. 20 - Nov. 1). To from Marne la Vallée - Chessy: (station for Disneyland). Table **17a**.

b – Not Dec. 28, Jan. 1, Apr. 5, May 3, 24, 31.
c – Lille **Flandres**, see note **x**. Departs 0647 on ⑥ (also Dec. 25, Jan. 1, May 13).
d – Not Dec. 26.
e – 2023 Jan. 4 - Mar. 12.
f – Runs Massy TGV - St Pierre des Corps - Angers St Laud - Nantes.
g – ⑥ (also Dec. 25, Jan. 1, May 13).
h – Not Dec. 25, Jan. 1, Apr. 5, May 13, 24.
j – ⑤⑦ (also Dec. 24, 31, Apr. 5, May 12, 24; not Dec. 25, Jan. 1).
k – Also Apr. 5, May 24.
m – Not Dec. 28, Apr. 5, May 3, 24, 31.
p – Also Dec. 25, Jan. 1, May 13.
q – Not Dec. 24, 25, 31, Jan. 1, Apr. 4, 30, May 7, 12, 13, 23.

r – Calls at Futuroscope 1004.
t – ⑤⑦ (also Apr. 5, May 24; not Dec. 25, Jan. 1).
w – Also Dec. 28, Apr. 5, May 3, 24, 31.
x – Lille **Flandres**, 500 metres from Lille Europe; see City Plan on page 31.
y – To Hendaye on ⑤⑥ (also Dec. 24, 31, May 12, 13) arrive 2324.
z – Calls at Futuroscope 1603.

☆ – Eurostar train. Special fares payable. Minimum check-in time 30 minutes. Valid Dec. 13, 2009 - July 3, 2010. No service Dec. 25.
§ – Marne la Vallée - Chessy (station for Disneyland).

11 LONDON / BRUSSELS - LILLE - CHARLES DE GAULLE ✈ - WESTERN / SOUTHERN FRANCE

DAY TRAINS (FOR NIGHT TRAINS SEE TABLE 13). Supplements payable on all *TGV* services. Connections at Lille are not guaranteed. Other connections available via Paris.

train type	☆	*TGV*	*TGV*	*TGV*	*TGV*	*TGV*	*TGV*	*TGV*	*TGV*	*TGV*	☆	*TGV*	*TGV*	*TGV*	*TGV*	☆	*TGV*	☆	*TGV*	*TGV*	*TGV*	*TGV*
train number	**9138**	**5123**	**5126**	**5124**	**5240**	**5242**	**5130**	**5132**	**5142**	**5142**	**9144**	**5136**	**5248**	**5248**	**5234**	**9148**	**5138**	**9150**	**5210**	**5210**	**5140**	**9846**
train number	Ⓡ	Ⓡ🍷	**5127**	**5125**	**5241**	**5243**	**5131**	**5133**	**5135**	**5143**	Ⓡ	**5137**	**5249**	**5245**	**5235**	Ⓡ	**5139**	Ⓡ	**5211**	**5247**	**5141**	Ⓡ
notes	✕	①–⑥	Ⓡ🍷	Ⓡ🍷	Ⓡ🍷	Ⓡ🍷	Ⓡ🍷	Ⓡ🍷	Ⓡ🍷	Ⓡ🍷	✕	Ⓡ🍷	Ⓡ🍷	Ⓡ🍷	Ⓡ🍷	✕	Ⓡ🍷	✕	Ⓡ🍷	Ⓡ🍷	Ⓡ🍷	🍷
	J	**k**	⑦**p**	**B**	⑧**y**	**C**	**m**	⑦**p**	⑦**p**	⑦**p**	**K**	①–⑥**k**	⑥**j**	⑥**j**	**F**	**M**	⑦**p**	**P**	⑤⑦**b**	⑤⑦**b**	**D**	
London St Pancras 12 d.	1434	...	...	...	...	...	...	...	...	...	1604	...	...	...	...	1657	...	1727	...	...	...	...
Ebbsfleet International **12** d.	|	...	...	...	...	...	...	...	...	...	|	...	...	...	...	1715**c**	...	1745	...	...	...	...
Ashford International **12** d.	|	...	...	...	...	...	...	...	...	...	|	...	...	...	...	|	...	|	...	...	...	...
Brussels Midi / Zuid 12 d.	|	...	...	...	...	...	...	...	...	...	|	...	...	...	...	|	...	|	...	...	...	2043
Lille Europe 12 a.	1654	...	...	...	...	...	...	...	...	...	1825	...	...	...	...	1924	...	1954	...	...	...	|
Lille Europe d.	...	1754	1754	1754	1809	1829**e**	1842**e**	1842**e**	1931	1931	...	1915	1939	1939	1940	...	2021**e**	...	2014	2014	2030**e**	|
Douai d.	...	|	|	|	|	|	|	|	|	|	...	1936	|	|	|	...	2043	...	|	|	|	|
Arras d.	...	|	|	|	|	|	|	|	|	|	...	1952	|	|	|	...	2059	...	|	|	|	|
TGV Haute Picardie d.	...	1829	1829	1829	1837	|	|	|	|	|	...	2015	|	|	|	...	2119	...	|	|	|	|
Paris Charles de Gaulle ✈ a.	...	1856	1856	1856	1907	1921	1936	1936	2022	2022	...	2043	2030	2030	2032	...	2146	...	2105	2105	2122	2157
Paris Charles de Gaulle ✈ d.	...	1900	1900	1900	1911	1926	1941	1941	2027	2027	...	2048	2034	2034	2036	...	2150	...	2110	2110	2127	2202
Marne la Vallée § d.	...	1913	1913	1913	1927	1942	1953	2008	2041	2041	...	2103	2050	2050	2050	...	2204	...	2124	2124	2143	2214
Massy TGV d.	...	|	|	|	2000	2017	...	|	|	|	...	|	2131	2131	2131	...	|	...	2201	2201	|	...
Le Mans a.	...	|	|	|	|	|	...	|	|	|	...	|	2223	2223	2219	...	|	...	2250	2250	|	...
Rennes a.	...	|	|	|	|	|	...	|	|	|	...	|	2340	|	|	...	|	...	|	0010	|	...
Angers St Laud a.	...	|	|	|	|	|	...	|	|	|	...	|	...	2303	2301	...	|	...	2328	...	|	...
Nantes a.	...	|	|	|	|	|	...	|	|	|	...	|	...	2340	2338	...	|	...	0007	...	|	...
St Pierre des Corps a.	...	|	|	|	|	2110	...	|	|	|	...	|	...	...	...	...	|	...	...	...	|	...
Poitiers a.	...	|	|	|	2122	2158	...	|	|	|	...	|	...	...	...	...	|	...	...	...	|	...
Angoulême a.	...	|	|	|	2211	2246	...	|	|	|	...	|	...	...	...	...	|	...	...	...	|	...
Bordeaux a.	...	|	|	|	2313	2348	...	|	|	|	...	|	...	...	...	...	|	...	...	...	|	...
Irún a.	...	|	|	|	...	...	...	|	|	|	...	|	...	...	...	...	|	...	...	...	|	...
Le Creusot TGV a.	...	|	|	|	...	...	...	|	|	|	...	2217	...	...	...	...	2318	...	...	...	|	...
Lyon Part Dieu a.	...	2101	|	2101	...	...	...	2201	2231	2231	...	2259	...	...	...	...	2359	...	...	...	2335	...
Lyon Perrache a.	...	|	|	|	...	...	...	|	|	|	...	|	...	...	...	...	0014	...	...	...	|	...
Grenoble a.	...	2225	|	|	...	...	...	2319	|	|	...	|	...	...	...	...	...	...	...	...	|	...
Valence TGV a.	...	...	2114	|	...	...	...	...	2316	|	...	2340**g**	...	...	...	...	...	...	...	...	0016	...
Avignon TGV a.	...	...	2148	2207	...	...	...	...	|	2343	...	0018**g**	...	...	...	...	...	...	...	...	|	...
Nîmes a.	...	...	|	|	...	...	...	...	0003	|	...	|	...	...	...	...	...	...	...	...	|	...
Montpellier a.	...	...	|	|	...	...	...	...	0030	|	...	|	...	...	...	...	...	...	...	...	|	...
Béziers a.	...	...	|	|	...	...	...	...	...	|	...	|	...	...	...	...	...	...	...	...	|	...
Narbonne a.	...	...	|	|	...	...	...	...	...	|	...	|	...	...	...	...	...	...	...	...	|	...
Toulouse Matabiau a.	...	...	|	|	...	...	...	...	...	|	...	|	...	...	...	...	...	...	...	...	|	...
Perpignan a.	...	...	|	|	...	...	...	...	...	|	...	|	...	...	...	...	...	...	...	...	|	...
Aix en Provence TGV a.	...	...	|	2232	...	...	...	...	...	0006	...	0041**g**	...	...	...	...	...	...	...	...	0111	...
Marseille St Charles a.	...	...	2221	2246	...	...	...	...	...	0020	...	0055**g**	...	...	...	...	...	...	...	...	0125	...
Toulon a.	...	...	...	...	...	...	...	...	...	...	...	...	...	...	...	...	...	...	...	...	...	...
St Raphaël - Valescure a.	...	...	...	...	...	...	...	...	...	...	...	...	...	...	...	...	...	...	...	...	...	...
Cannes a.	...	...	...	...	...	...	...	...	...	...	...	...	...	...	...	...	...	...	...	...	...	...
Nice a.	...	...	...	...	...	...	...	...	...	...	...	...	...	...	...	...	...	...	...	...	...	...
train type or number		*TGV*	*TGV*	*TGV*	*TGV*	☆		*TGV*	*TGV*	*TGV*	*TGV*		*TGV*	*TGV*	*TGV*	☆		*TGV*	☆			
train number		**9811**	**9807**	**5152**	**5154**	**9119**		**5158**	**5160**	**5254**	**5252**		**5156**	**9854**	**9856**	**9181**		**5261**	**9031**			
train number		Ⓡ	Ⓡ	**5153**	**5155**	Ⓡ		**5159**	**5161**	**5255**	Ⓡ		**5157**	**9855**	**9857**	Ⓡ		Ⓡ	Ⓡ			
notes		🍷	🍷	Ⓡ🍷	Ⓡ🍷	✕		Ⓡ🍷	Ⓡ🍷	Ⓡ🍷	🍷		Ⓡ🍷	Ⓡ🍷	Ⓡ🍷	✕		🍷	✕			
		G		**Gw**	**B**	**Q**		⑥**j**	⑦**p**	**B**	**B**		**Ax**	**G**	**A**							
Nice d.	...	...	...	...	...	...	...	...	...	...	...	...	...	...	...	...	...	...	...	...	...	...
Cannes d.	...	...	...	...	...	...	...	...	...	...	...	...	...	...	...	...	...	...	...	...	...	...
St Raphaël - Valescure d.	...	...	...	...	...	...	...	...	...	...	...	...	...	...	...	...	...	...	...	...	...	...
Toulon d.	...	...	...	...	...	...	...	...	...	...	...	...	...	...	0516**q**	...	...	...	...	...	...	...
Marseille St Charles d.	...	...	...	...	...	...	...	0539	...	...	...	...	...	0550	0610	...	...	...	...	...	...	...
Aix en Provence TGV d.	...	...	...	...	...	...	...	0554	...	...	...	...	...	0604	0624	...	...	...	...	...	...	...
Perpignan d.	...	...	...	...	...	...	...	|	...	...	...	...	...	|	|	...	...	...	...	...	...	...
Toulouse Matabiau d.	...	...	...	...	...	...	...	|	...	...	...	...	...	|	|	...	...	...	...	...	...	...
Narbonne d.	...	...	...	...	...	...	...	|	..	...	...	...	...	|	|	...	...	...	...	...	...	...
Béziers d.	...	...	...	...	...	...	...	|	...	...	...	...	...	|	|	...	...	...	...	...	...	...
Montpellier d.	...	...	...	...	...	...	...	|	...	...	...	...	...	|	|	...	...	...	...	...	...	...
Nîmes d.	...	...	...	...	...	...	...	|	...	...	...	...	...	|	|	...	...	...	...	...	...	...
Avignon TGV d.	...	...	...	...	...	...	...	0616	...	...	...	...	...	0629	0646	...	...	...	...	...	...	...
Valence TGV d.	...	...	...	...	...	...	...	0650	...	...	...	...	...	0713	|	...	...	...	...	...	...	...
Grenoble d.	...	...	...	...	0451	...	...	|	0540	...	...	...	...	|	|	...	...	...	...	...	...	...
Lyon Perrache d.	...	...	...	...	|	...	...	|	|	...	...	...	...	|	|	...	...	...	...	...	...	...
Lyon Part Dieu d.	...	...	...	...	0613	...	...	|	0659	...	...	...	...	0756	0756	...	...	...	...	...	...	...
Le Creusot TGV d.	...	...	...	...	0653	...	...	|	0741	...	...	...	...	|	|	...	...	...	...	...	...	...
Hendaye d.	...	...	...	...	|	...	...	|	|	...	...	...	...	|	|	...	...	...	...	...	...	...
Bordeaux d.	...	...	...	...	|	...	...	|	|	...	...	...	...	|	|	...	...	0633	...	...	...	...
Angoulême d.	...	...	...	...	|	...	...	|	|	...	...	...	...	|	|	...	...	1733	...	...	...	...
Poitiers d.	...	...	...	...	|	...	...	|	|	...	...	...	...	|	|	...	...	0819	...	...	...	...
St Pierre des Corps d.	...	...	...	...	|	...	...	|	|	...	...	...	...	|	|	...	...	0900	...	...	...	...
Nantes d.	...	...	...	...	|	...	...	|	|	...	0604	...	...	|	|	...	...	|	...	...	...	...
Angers St Laud d.	...	...	...	...	|	...	...	|	|	...	0643	...	...	|	|	...	...	|	...	...	...	...
Rennes d.	...	...	...	...	|	...	...	|	|	0610	|	...	...	|	|	...	...	|	...	...	...	...
Le Mans d.	...	...	...	...	|	...	...	|	|	0731	0731	...	...	|	|	...	...	|	...	...	...	...
Massy TGV d.	...	...	...	...	|	...	...	|	|	0821	0821	...	...	|	|	...	...	0953	...	...	...	...
Marne la Vallée § d.	...	...	0727	0810	0817	...	...	0908	0859	0904	0904	...	0922	0951	0951	...	...	1043	...	...	...	...
Paris Charles de Gaulle ✈ a.	...	...	0738	0820	0829	...	...	0918	0909	0914	0914	...	0932	1001	1002	...	...	1053	...	...	...	...
Paris Charles de Gaulle ✈ d.	...	...	0745	0825	0837	...	...	...	0913	0918	0918	...	0937	1010	1013	...	...	1057	...	...	...	...
TGV Haute Picardie d.	...	...	|	|	0909	...	...	...	0943	|	|	...	|	|	|	...	...	|	...	...	...	...
Arras a.	...	...	|	|	|	...	...	...	|	|	|	...	|	|	|	...	...	1137	...	...	...	...
Douai a.	...	...	|	|	|	...	...	...	|	|	|	...	|	|	|	...	...	1153	...	...	...	...
Lille Europe a.	...	...	|	0915	0937	...	...	...	1008	1008	1008	...	1027	1103	1103	...	...	1217**e**	...	...	...	...
Lille Europe 12 d.	...	0729	|	...	...	1005	...	...	...	...	...	...	...	1115	1114	1205	...	...	1406	...	...	...
Brussels Midi / Zuid 12 a.	...	0803	0859	...	...	|	...	...	...	...	...	...	...	1152	1150	|	...	...	|	...	...	...
Ashford International **12** a.	...	...	...	...	...	|	...	...	...	...	...	...	...	...	...	|	...	...	|	...	...	...
Ebbsfleet International **12** a.	...	...	...	...	...	|	...	...	...	...	...	...	...	...	...	1215	...	...	1415	...	...	...
London St Pancras 12 a.	...	...	...	...	...	1026	...	...	...	...	...	...	...	...	...	1233	...	...	1431	...	...	...

A – ⑥⑦ (also Dec. 25, Jan. 1, Apr. 5, May 13, 24).
B – ①–⑥ (not Apr. 5, May 24).
C – ⑤⑥⑦ (also Dec. 24, 31, Apr. 5, May 12, 13, 24).
D – ⑤ Apr. 9 - Aug. 27 (also May 12).
F – ①–④ (not Dec. 24, 25, 31, Jan. 1, Apr. 5, May 12, 13, 24).
G – ①–⑤ (not Dec. 25, Jan. 1, Apr. 5, May 13, 24).
J – ⑤⑦ (also Dec. 19, 26, 28, Jan. 2, Apr. 5, May 3, 24, 31.
K – ①②③④ (①②③④⑥ Jan. 4 - July 3) not Dec. 28, Apr. 5, May 3, 24, 31.
M – ⑦ (⑥⑦ Dec. 13 - Jan. 3) also Dec. 28, Apr. 5, May 3, 24, 31.
P – ①–⑤ (not Dec. 28, Apr. 5, May 3, 24, 31).
Q – ①–⑥ (not Dec. 28, Apr. 5, May 3, 24, 31).

b – Also Dec. 24, 31, Apr. 5, May 12, 24; not Dec. 25, Jan. 1.
c – ⑦ (also Dec. 28, Apr. 5, May 3, 24, 31).
e – Lille **Flandres**, 500 metres from Lille Europe; see City Plan on page 31.

g – ⑤⑥ (also Dec. 24, 31, May 12, 13).
h – Not Dec. 24, 31, May 12, 13.
j – Also Dec. 25, Jan. 1, May 13.
k – Not Apr. 5, May 24.
m – To Dijon (arrive 2139), and Besançon (2232) (Table **370**).
p – Also Apr. 5, May 24.
q – ⑥ (also Dec. 25, Jan. 1, May 13).
w – From Besançon (depart 0540), and Dijon (0632) (Table **370**).
x – From Besançon (depart 0652, and Dijon (0744).
y – Not Dec. 25, Jan. 1, May 13.

§ – Marne la Vallée - Chessy. Station for Disneyland Paris.
☆ – Eurostar train. Special fares payable. Minimum check-in time 30 minutes. Valid Dec. 13, 2009 - July 3, 2010. No service Dec. 25.

SOUTHERN / WESTERN FRANCE - CHARLES DE GAULLE ✈ - LILLE - BRUSSELS / LONDON 11

DAY TRAINS (FOR NIGHT TRAINS SEE TABLE 13). Supplements payable on all *TGV* services. Connections at Lille are not guaranteed. Other connections available via Paris.

train type or number	*TGV*	*TGV*	*TGV*	*TGV*	*TGV*	*TGV*	☆	*TGV*	*TGV*	☆	☆	*TGV*	*TGV*	☆	*TGV*	*TGV*	*TGV*	*TGV*	*TGV*	*TGV*	☆	*TGV*	☆	
train number	**5144**	**5162**	**5264**	**5268**	**9860**	**5166**	**9031**	**5270**	**5272**	**9137**	**9139**	**5150**	**5150**	**9071**	**5258**	**5256**	**5276**	**5368**	**5198**	**9862**	**9149**	**9864**	**9153**	
train number	🅁	**5163**	**5265**	🅁	🅁	🅁🍷	🅁	**5271**	🅁	🅁🍴	🅁🍴	**5151**	**5151**	🅁	🅁	🅁	**5277**	🅁	🅁	**9863**	🅁	**9865**	🅁	
notes	🍷	🅁🍷	🅁🍷	🍷	🍷		🍴	🅁🍷	🍷	⑥⑦	①–⑤	🅁🍷	🅁🍷	🍴	🍷	🍷	🅁🍷	🍷	🍷	🅁🍷	🍴	🅁	🍴	
			x	**W x**						**p**	**q**	**A**	**C**	**H**	⑦**h**	⑦**h**		**E**			⑧	🍷		
Nice d.	...	...	...	...	...	...	...	...	...	...	...	...	...	...	...	...	...	...	0925	...	...	1028	...	...
Cannes d.	...	...	...	...	...	...	...	...	...	...	...	...	...	...	...	...	...	...	0957	...	...	1058	...	...
St Raphaël - Valescure d.	...	...	...	...	...	...	...	...	...	...	...	...	...	...	...	...	...	...	1020	...	...	1123	...	...
Toulon d.	...	...	...	...	0745j	...	...	...	...	...	...	...	...	...	...	...	...	...	1113	...	...	1216	...	...
Marseille St Charles d.	0710	...	...	...	0841	...	...	...	...	...	...	0940	0940	...	...	...	...	1133	1210	...	...	1310	...	...
Aix en Provence TGV d.	0725	...	...	...	0855	...	...	...	...	...	...	0956	0956	...	...	...	...	1147	|	...	...	|	...	...
Perpignan d.	|	0505f	...	...	|	0642	...	...	...	...	...	|	|	...	...	...	...	|	|	...	...	|	...	...
Toulouse Matabiau d.	|	|	0527	...	|	|	...	...	...	...	...	|	|	...	...	...	...	|	|	...	...	|	...	...
Narbonne d.	|	0544f	|	...	|	0721	...	...	...	...	...	|	|	...	...	...	...	|	|	...	...	|	...	...
Béziers d.	|	0602f	|	...	|	0737	...	...	...	...	...	|	|	...	...	...	...	|	|	...	...	|	...	...
Montpellier d.	|	0651	|	...	|	0824	...	...	...	...	...	|	|	...	...	...	...	|	|	1157	...	|	...	...
Nîmes d.	|	0718	|	...	|	0853	...	...	...	...	...	|	|	...	...	...	...	|	|	1228	...	|	...	...
Avignon TGV d.	0747	|	|	...	0918	|	...	...	...	...	...	|	|	...	...	...	...	1210	1245	|	...	1341	...	...
Valence TGV d.	|	0810	|	...	|	0938	...	...	...	...	...	1046	1046	...	...	...	...	1245	|	|	...	1419	...	...
Grenoble d.	|	|	|	...	|	|	...	...	...	...	...	|	|	...	...	...	...	|	|	|	...	|	...	...
Lyon Perrache d.	|	|	|	...	|	|	...	...	...	...	...	|	|	...	...	...	...	|	|	|	...	|	...	...
Lyon Part Dieu d.	0856	0856	|	...	1026	1026	...	...	...	...	...	1126	1126	...	...	...	...	1320	1350	1356	...	|	...	...
Le Creusot TGV d.	|	|	|	...	|	|	...	...	...	...	...	|	|	...	...	...	...	...	...	|	...	|	...	...
Hendaye d.	|	|	|	0520	|	|	...	...	...	...	...	|	|	...	...	...	0834e	...	...	|	...	|	...	...
Bordeaux d.	|	|	0750	0750	|	|	...	...	...	...	...	|	|	...	...	...	1057	...	...	|	...	|	...	...
Angoulême d.	|	|	0850	0850	|	|	...	...	...	...	...	|	|	...	...	...	1201	...	...	|	...	|	...	...
Poitiers d.	|	|	0936	0936	|	|	...	...	...	...	...	|	|	...	...	...	1251	...	...	|	...	|	...	...
St Pierre des Corps d.	|	|	1023	1023	|	|	...	...	...	...	...	|	|	...	...	...	1332	...	...	|	...	|	...	...
Nantes d.	|	|	|	|	|	|	...	0910	...	...	...	|	|	...	1105	...	|	...	...	|	...	|	...	...
Angers St Laud d.	|	|	|	|	|	|	...	0949	...	...	...	|	|	...	1143	...	|	...	...	|	...	|	...	...
Rennes d.	|	|	|	|	|	|	...	|	0915	...	...	|	|	...	|	1100	|	...	...	|	...	|	...	...
Le Mans d.	|	|	|	|	|	|	...	1041	1041	...	...	|	|	...	1229	1229	|	...	...	|	...	|	...	...
Massy TGV d.	|	|	1116	1116	|	|	...	1141	1141	...	...	|	|	...	1321	1321	1427	...	...	|	...	|	...	...
Marne la Vallée § d.	1048	1048	1158	1158	1220	1220	...	1227	1227	...	...	|	1314	1540	1400	1400	1511	...	...	1549	...	1623	...	...
Paris Charles de Gaulle ✈ a.	1057	1057	1209	1209	1229	1229	...	1237	1237	...	...	1320	1328	|	1410	1410	1521	...	...	1558	...	1633	...	...
Paris Charles de Gaulle ✈ d.	1102	1102	1214	1214	1235	1235	...	1242	1242	...	...	1324	1332	|	1415	1415	1525	...	...	1603	...	1639	...	...
TGV Haute Picardie d.	|	|	|	|	|	|	...	1313	1313	...	...	|	|	|	1415	|	|	...	...	1639	...	1710	...	...
Arras a.	|	|	|	|	|	|	...	|	|	...	...	1403	1412	|	|	|	|	...	...	|	...	|	...	...
Douai a.	|	|	|	|	|	|	...	|	|	...	...	1419	1428	|	|	|	|	...	...	|	...	|	...	...
Lille Europe a.	1151	1151	1306	1306	1329	1329	...	1340	1340	...	...	1441c	1449c	|	1506	1506	1615	...	...	1707	...	1735	...	...
Lille Europe 12 d.	...	...	...	...	1340	...	1406	...	...	1435	1505	...	...	|	...	...	...	...	...	1721	1735	1745	1835	...
Brussels Midi / Zuid 12 a.	...	...	...	...	1414	...	|	...	...	|	|	...	...	|	...	...	...	...	...	1756	|	1820	|	...
Ashford International **12** a.	...	...	...	...	...	...	|	...	...	|	|	...	...	1636	...	...	...	...	...	...	1733	...	|	...
Ebbsfleet International **12** a.	...	...	...	...	...	...	1415	...	...	1445	|	...	...	|	...	...	...	...	...	...	|	...	1845	...
London St Pancras 12 a.	...	...	...	...	...	...	1431	...	...	1503	1526	...	...	1711	...	...	...	...	...	...	1805	...	1903	...

train type or number	*TGV*	*TGV*	*TGV*	☆	*TGV*	*TGV*	*TGV*	☆	☆	☆	☆	*TGV*	*TGV*	*TGV*	*TGV*	*TGV*	*TGV*	*TGV*	*TGV*	*TGV*	*TGV*	*TGV*	*TGV*	*TGV*
train number	**9866**	**5280**	**5278**	**9157**	**9868**	**9816**	**9816**	**9161**	**9057**	**9163**	**9163**	**9868**	**5180**	**5180**	**5284**	**5290**	**5288**	**5184**	**5187**	**5187**	**9886**	**5292/3**	**5294**	**5194**
train number	**9867**	**5281**	🅁	🅁🍴	**9869**	**9817**	**5279**	🅁	🅁	🅁🍴	🅁🍴	**9869**	**5181**	**5181**	**5285**	🅁	**5289**	**5185**	**5186**	**5186**	**9887**	🅁	**5295**	**5195**
notes	🅁🍷	🅁🍷	🍷	⑧	🅁🍷	🅁🍷	🅁🍷	🍴	🍴	①–④	⑤⑦	🅁🍷	🅁🍷	🅁🍷	🅁🍷	🍷	🅁	🅁	🅁🍷	🅁🍷	🅁🍷	🍷**y**	🅁🍷	🅁🍷
				w	**C**			⑥	**G**	**b**	**r**	**A**	**A**	**C**	**B z**		🍷	🍷	**P**	**Q**	⑥**k**	⑤⑥**g**	⑦**h**	**D**
Nice d.	...	...	...	...	...	...	...	...	...	...	...	...	...	...	...	...	...	1528	...	...	...	...	...	...
Cannes d.	...	...	...	...	...	...	...	...	...	...	...	...	...	...	...	...	...	1559	...	...	...	...	...	...
St Raphaël - Valescure d.	...	...	...	...	...	...	...	...	...	...	...	...	...	...	...	...	...	1623	...	...	...	...	...	...
Toulon d.	...	...	...	...	...	...	...	...	...	...	...	...	...	...	...	...	...	1715	...	...	...	...	...	...
Marseille St Charles d.	1339	...	...	...	...	...	...	...	...	...	...	...	1709	1709	...	...	...	1810	...	...	...	...	...	1941
Aix en Provence TGV d.	1353	...	...	...	...	...	...	...	...	...	...	...	1723	1723	...	...	...	1824	...	...	...	...	...	1958
Perpignan d.	|	...	...	...	1234	...	...	...	...	...	...	1410	|	|	...	...	...	|	...	...	...	...	...	|
Toulouse Matabiau d.	|	...	...	...	|	...	...	...	...	...	...	|	|	|	...	...	...	|	1609	1609	1644	...	...	|
Narbonne d.	|	...	...	...	1314	...	...	...	...	...	...	1449	|	|	...	...	...	|	1728	1728	1800	...	...	|
Béziers d.	|	...	...	...	1331	...	...	...	...	...	...	1507	|	|	...	...	...	|	1743	1744	1817	...	...	|
Montpellier d.	|	...	...	...	1430	...	...	...	...	...	...	1600	|	|	...	...	...	|	1832	1832	1900	...	...	|
Nîmes d.	|	...	...	...	1457	...	...	...	...	...	...	1627	|	|	...	...	...	|	1857	1857	1927	...	...	|
Avignon TGV d.	1416	...	...	...	|	...	...	...	...	...	...	|	|	|	...	...	...	1847	|	|	|	...	...	|
Valence TGV d.	|	...	...	...	1544	...	...	...	...	...	...	|	1815	1815	...	...	...	|	1945	1945	|	...	...	2050
Grenoble d.	|	...	...	...	|	...	...	...	...	...	...	|	|	|	...	...	...	|	|	|	|	...	...	|
Lyon Perrache d.	|	...	...	...	|	...	...	...	...	...	...	|	|	|	...	...	...	|	|	|	|	...	...	|
Lyon Part Dieu d.	1526	...	...	...	1626	...	...	...	...	...	...	1756	1856	1856	...	...	...	1956	2026	2030	2056	...	...	2130
Le Creusot TGV d.	|	...	...	...	|	...	...	...	...	...	...	|	|	|	...	...	...	|	|	|	|	...	...	|
Hendaye d.	|	...	...	...	|	...	...	...	...	...	...	|	|	|	...	...	...	|	|	|	|	1623j	...	|
Bordeaux d.	|	...	...	...	|	1422	1422	...	...	...	...	|	|	|	1643	...	...	|	|	|	|	1841	...	|
Angoulême d.	|	...	...	...	|	1526	1526	...	...	...	...	|	|	|	1745	...	...	|	|	|	|	1945	...	|
Poitiers d.	|	...	...	...	|	1614	1614	...	...	...	...	|	|	|	1833	...	...	|	|	|	|	2038	...	|
St Pierre des Corps d.	|	...	...	...	|	1655	1655	...	...	...	...	|	|	|	1928	...	...	|	|	|	|	2122	...	|
Nantes d.	|	...	1435	...	|	|	|	...	...	...	...	|	|	|	|	...	1835	|	|	|	|	|	...	|
Angers St Laud d.	|	...	1513	...	|	|	|	...	...	...	...	|	|	|	|	...	1912	|	|	|	|	|	...	|
Rennes d.	|	1435	|	...	|	|	|	...	...	...	...	|	|	|	|	1839	|	|	|	|	|	|	2020	|
Le Mans d.	|	1558	1558	...	|	|	|	...	...	...	...	|	|	|	|	2000	2000	|	|	|	|	|	2138	|
Massy TGV d.	|	1651	1651	...	|	1749	1749	...	...	...	...	|	|	|	2021	2050	2050	|	|	|	|	2217	2230	|
Marne la Vallée § d.	1723	1732	1732	...	1820	1831	1831	...	1937	...	...	1950	2048	2048	2102	2134	2134	2150	2219	2226	2249	2256	2306	2323
Paris Charles de Gaulle ✈ a.	1734	1742	1742	...	1830	1841	1841	...	|	...	...	1959	2057	2057	2112	2146	2146	2159	2229	2235	2258	2306	2316	2332
Paris Charles de Gaulle ✈ d.	1740	1754	1754	...	1840	1849	1845	...	|	...	...	2004	2102	2102	2116	2150	2150	2204	2234	2240	2302	2310	2320	2338
TGV Haute Picardie d.	1809	|	|	...	|	|	|	...	|	...	...	|	2138	2138	2150	2220	2220	|	|	2311	2335	2341	|	|
Arras a.	|	|	|	...	|	|	1925	...	|	...	...	|	|	2156	|	2238	2238	|	|	|	|	|	|	|
Douai a.	|	|	|	...	|	|	1942	...	|	...	...	|	|	2214	|	2254	2254	|	|	|	|	|	|	|
Lille Europe a.	1837	1849c	1849c	...	1937	|	2005c	...	|	...	...	2054	2205	2238	2220	2318	2318	2253	2323	2337	0001	0008	0010	0032c
Lille Europe 12 d.	1855	...	...	1935	1949	|	...	2035	|	2056	2105	2105	...	...	...	...	...	...	...	...	0011	...	...	...
Brussels Midi / Zuid 12 a.	1930	...	...	|	2027	2007	...	|	|	|	|	2143	...	...	...	...	...	...	...	...	0046	...	...	...
Ashford International **12** a.	...	...	...	|	...	...	...	|	2037	|	|	...	...	...	...	...	...	...	...	...	...	...	...	...
Ebbsfleet International **12** a.	...	...	...	|	...	...	...	2045	|	2115	2115	...	...	...	...	...	...	...	...	...	...	...	...	...
London St Pancras 12 a.	...	...	...	1956	...	...	...	2103	2112	2133	2133	...	...	...	...	...	...	...	...	...	...	...	...	...

A – ①–⑤ (not Dec. 25, Jan. 1, Apr. 5, May 13, 24).
B – ⑧ (not Dec. 25, Jan. 1, May 13).
C – ⑥⑦ (also Dec. 25, Jan. 1, Apr. 5, May 13, 24).
D – ⑦ Apr. 11 - Aug. 29 (also Apr. 5, May 24).
E – ①–⑥ (not Apr. 5, May 24).
G – ①③④⑤⑦ (daily Dec. 13 - Jan. 4; not Dec. 25, 31; Feb. 10 – 22; Mar. 31 - Apr. 19; also May 1; daily May 26 - June 7; July 21 - Sept. 3; Oct. 20 - Nov. 1). From Marne la Vallée - Chessy: (station for Disneyland).
H – Dec. 31.
P – ①②③④ (not Dec. 24, 31, Apr. 5, May 12, 13, 24).
Q – ⑤⑥⑦ (also Dec. 24, 31, Apr. 5, May 12, 13, 24).
W – ①⑥ (also Dec. 24, 31, Apr. 4, 6, 30, May 7, 12, 23, 25; not Apr. 5, May 24).

Z – Not Dec. 24, 25, 31.

b – Not Dec. 24, 28, 31, Apr. 5, May 3, 24, 31.
c – Lille **Flandres**, 500 metres from Lille Europe; see City Plan on page 31.
e – ⑦ (also Apr. 5, May 24; not May 16).
f – ①⑥ (also Dec. 24, 25, 31, Jan. 1, Apr. 4, 6, May 12, 13, 23, 25; not Apr. 5, May 24).
g – Also Dec. 24, 31, May 12, 13.
h – Also Apr. 5, May 24.
j – ⑥ (also Dec. 25, Jan. 1, May 13).
k – July 10 - Aug. 28.
p – Also Apr. 5, May 24.

q – Not Dec. 28, Jan. 1, Apr. 5, May 3, 24, 31.
r – Also Dec. 28, Apr. 5, May 3, 24, 31.
u – Stops to pick up only.
w – Not Dec. 24, 31.
x – Calls at Futuroscope 0947.
y – On ⑥ (also Dec. 25, Jan. 1, May 13) calls at Futuroscope 2050 and runs 3–5 minutes later to Lille.
z – Calls at Futuroscope 1849.

§ – Marne la Vallée - Chessy, Station for Disneyland Paris.
☆ – Eurostar train. Special fares payable. Minimum check-in time 30 minutes. Valid Dec. 13, 2009 - July 3, 2010. No service Dec. 25.

12 LONDON - LILLE - BRUSSELS *by Eurostar*

All times shown are local times (France and Belgium are one hour ahead of Great Britain).

For the complete service London - Lille see Table 10. For other services Lille - Brussels (by TGV) see Table 16a.

All Eurostar services are 🄁, non-smoking and convey ✕

Service Dec. 13, 2009 - July 3, 2010. No service December 25.

km	train type	☆		☆			☆	☆		☆		☆			☆	☆			☆	☆				*EC*
	train number	**9106**	①–⑤	**9110**	⑥⑦		**9112**	**9114**		**9120**		**9116**			**9126**	**9126**			**9130**	**9132**		⑥⑦	①–⑤	**295**
	notes	**B**	**t**	⑥**b**	**f**		**C**	⑥		**D**		⑥⑦**g**	❖		⑥	**D**	❖		⑦**c**	**E**	❖	**f**	**t**	**J**⑧
0	**London St Pancras** d.	0620	...	0659	...	...	0730	0757	...	0827	...	0857	...	...	1057	1104	...	...	1157	1257	...	...	...	...
35	Ebbsfleet International d.	0637	...	0715	...	...	|	|	...	0845	...	0915	...	...	1115	|	...	...	1215	1315	...	...	...	...
90	Ashford International d.	0657	...	|	...	...	|	0828	...	|	...	|	...	...	|	|	...	...	|	|	...	...	...	...
267	Lille Europe a.	0907	...	0924	...	...	|	1024	...	1054	...	1124	...	...	1326	1326	...	...	1424	1524	...	...	...	...
	Lille Europe d.	0910	...	0928	...	...	|	1028	...	1058	...	1128	...	...	1330	1330	...	...	1428	1528	...	...	...	...
373	**Brussels Midi / Zuid** a.	0944	1028	1003	1030	1033	1028	1108	1133	1133	1157	1203	1228	1233	1405	1405	1428	1433	1503	1603	1628	1633	1633	1727
	Brugge a.	*1104*	|	*1127*	|	|	*1204*	*1227*	|	*1304*	|	*1327*	|	|	*1527*	*1527*	|	|	*1627*	*1727*	|	|	|	|
	Leuven a.	...	1055	...	1058	|	...	...	|	...	1223	...	1255	|	...	...	1455	|	...	...	1655	|	|	|
	Liège Guillemins a.	...	1151	...	1156	|	...	...	|	...	1300	...	1351	|	...	...	1551	|	...	...	1751	|	|	|
	Namur a.	...	...	...	...	1139	...	...	1239	...	...	...	...	1339	...	...	...	1539	...	...	...	1739	1740	1832
	Luxembourg a.	...	...	...	...	1337	...	...	1445	...	...	...	...	1542	...	...	...	1742	...	...	...	1942	...	2016

train type	☆				☆	☆	☆	☆			☆	☆		☆			☆	☆			☆			
train number	**9138**		①–⑤		**9144**	**9144**	**9144**	**9144**			**9148**	**9148**		**9150**			**9154**	**9154**			**9158**		⑥⑦	
notes	**F**		**t**		⑤	**C**	⑦**gw**	**G**	❖		⑦**g**	**H**		**D**			⑦**g**	**K**			**j**		**f**	
London St Pancras d.	1434	...	...	...	1604	1604	1604	1604	...	...	1657	1704	...	1727	...	...	1825	1835	...	...	1934	...	...	...
Ebbsfleet International d.	|	...	...	...	|	|	|	|	...	...	1715	|	...	1745	...	...	|	|	...	...	|	...	...	...
Ashford International d.	|	...	...	...	|	|	|	|	...	...	|	|	...	|	...	...	1855	|	...	...	|	...	...	...
Lille Europe a.	1654	...	...	...	|	1825	|	1826	...	...	1924	1924	...	1954	...	...	2051	|	...	...	2154	...	...	...
Lille Europe d.	1658	...	...	...	|	1828	|	1832	...	...	1928	1928	...	1958	...	...	2055	|	...	...	2158	...	...	...
Brussels Midi / Zuid a.	1733	1757	1809	1833	1859	1903	1903	1908	1928	1933	2003	2003	2033	2033	2057	2133	2130	2133	2157	2203	2233	2257	2333	...
Brugge a.	*1904*	|	|	|	*2027*	*2027*	*2027*	*2027*	|	|	*2127*	*2127*	|	*2202*	|	|	*2302*	*2302*	|	|	*0002*	|	|	...
Leuven a.	...	1823	|	|	...	...	...	...	1955	|	...	...	|	...	2123	|	...	...	2223	|	...	2323	|	...
Liège Guillemins a.	...	1900	|	|	...	...	...	...	2051	|	...	...	|	...	2200	|	...	...	2300	|	...	0019	|	...
Namur a.	...	...	1912	1939	...	...	...	...	...	2039	...	...	2139	...	...	2239	...	...	...	2309	...	...	0046	...
Luxembourg a.	...	...	2103	2137	...	...	...	...	...	2237	...	...	2342	...	...	0040	...	...	...	...	...	...	...	...

train type				☆			☆	☆		☆		☆				☆			☆			*EC*	☆	
train number	⑥⑦		①–⑤	**9109**			**9113**	**9113**	①–④	**9113**	⑥⑦	**9117**	①–⑤			**9119**			**9181**			**296**	**9137**	
notes	**f**		**t**	**A**			⑥**m**	⑤**d**	**t**	**L**	**f**	**M**	**t**			**P**						**J**⑧	⑥⑦**p**	
Luxembourg d.	...	...	...	...	...	...	...	...	...	...	...	...	0520	...	...	...	0719	...	...	0920	...	1024	...	...
Namur d.	0436	...	0521	...	...	0620	...	...	...	...	0721	...	0720	0751	...	...	0921	...	...	1121	...	1221	...	...
Liège Guillemins d.	|	0443	|	...	0556	|	...	...	0639	...	|	...	|	|	0800	...	|	1000	...	|	1200	|	...	...
Leuven d.	|	0537	|	...	0637	|	...	...	|	...	|	...	|	|	0837	...	|	1035	...	|	1237	|	...	...
Brugge d.	|	|	|	*0524*	|	|	*0631*	*0631*	|	*0631*	|	*0731*	|	|	|	*0758*	|	|	*0958*	|	|	|	*1231*	...
Brussels Midi / Zuid d.	0546	0603	0627	0659	0703	0727	0759	0759	0736	0805	0827	0859	0827	0857	0903	0929	1027	1103	1129	1227	1303	1327	1359	...
Lille Europe a.	...	...	...	0732	...	...	|	0832	...	|	...	0932	...	...	...	1002	...	...	1202	...	...	...	1432	...
Lille Europe d.	...	...	...	0735	...	...	|	0835	...	|	...	0935	...	...	...	1005	...	...	1205	...	...	...	1435	...
Ashford International a.	...	...	...	|	...	...	|	|	...	|	...	|	...	...	...	|	...	...	|	...	...	...	|	...
Ebbsfleet International a.	...	...	...	|	...	...	|	|	...	|	...	|	...	...	...	|	...	...	1215	...	...	...	1445	...
London St Pancras a.	...	...	...	0755	...	...	0856	0856	...	0856	...	0956	...	...	...	1026	...	...	1233	...	...	...	1503	...

train type	*EC*		☆		☆			☆			☆			☆			☆			☆	*EC*	☆		☆
train number	**296**		**9139**		**9141**			**9145**			**9149**			**9153**			**9157**			**9161**	**90**	**9163**		**9163**
notes	**J**⑧		**B**		⑦**g**			⑤**k**			⑧						⑧**j**			⑥	**V**	**Q h**		⑤⑦**g**
Luxembourg d.	1024	...	...	1124	...	...	1224	...	...	1324	...	...	1420	...	...	1520	...	...	1620	...	1702	...	...	...
Namur d.	1221	...	...	1321	...	...	1421	...	...	1521	...	...	1621	...	...	1721	...	...	1821	...	1848	...	...	...
Liège Guillemins d.	|	1300	...	|	...	1400	|	...	1500	|	...	1600	|	...	1700	|	...	1800	|	...	|	...	1900	...
Leuven d.	|	1337	...	|	...	1437	|	...	1537	|	...	1635	|	...	1737	|	...	1837	|	...	|	...	1937	...
Brugge d.	|	|	*1258*	|	*1331*	|	|	*1431*	|	|	*1531*	|	|	*1631*	|	|	*1731*	|	|	*1831*	|	*1858*	|	*1858*
Brussels Midi / Zuid d.	1327	1403	1429	1427	1459	1503	1527	1559	1603	1627	1659	1703	1727	1759	1803	1827	1859	1903	1927	1959	1951	2017	2003	2029
Lille Europe a.	...	...	1502	...	1532	...	...	|	...	...	1732	...	...	1832	...	...	1932	...	...	2032	...	2050	...	2102
Lille Europe d.	...	...	1505	...	1535	...	...	|	...	...	1735	...	...	1835	...	...	1935	...	...	2035	...	2056	...	2105
Ashford International a.	...	...	|	...	|	...	...	|	...	...	1733	...	...	|	...	...	|	...	...	|	...	|	...	|
Ebbsfleet International a.	...	...	|	...	|	...	...	1645	...	...	|	...	...	1845	...	...	|	...	...	2045	...	2115	...	2115
London St Pancras a.	...	...	1526	...	1556	...	...	1703	...	...	1805	...	...	1903	...	...	1956	...	...	2103	...	2133	...	2133

A – ①②③④⑥ (not Dec. 26, 28, Apr. 5, May 3, 13, 24, 31).
B – ①–⑤ (not Dec. 28, Jan. 1, Apr. 5, May 3, 24, 31).
C – ①–④ (not Dec. 28, Apr. 5, May 3, 24, 31).
D – ①–⑤ (not Dec. 28, Apr. 5, May 3, 24, 31).
E – ①–⑥ (not Dec. 28, Jan. 1, Apr. 5, May 3, 24, 31).
F – ⑤⑦ (also Dec. 19, 26, 28, Jan. 2, Apr. 5, May 3, 24, 31).
G – ⑥ Jan. 4 - July 3.
H – ⑥ Dec. 13 - Jan. 3.
J – JEAN MONNET – ⑧: 🚃12 Brussels - Luxembourg - Basel and v.v.
K – ①–⑤ (not Dec. 24, 28, 31, Apr. 5, May 3, 24, 31).
L – ①–④ (not Dec. 28, Apr. 5, May 3, 13, 24, 31).
M – ⑦ Dec. 13 - Jan. 3 (also Dec. 28).

P – ①–⑥ (not Dec. 28, Apr. 5, May 3, 24, 31).
Q – ①–④ (not Dec. 24, 28, 31, Apr. 5, May 3, 24, 31).
V – VAUBAN – 🚃12 Basel - Brussels.

b – Not Dec. 26.
c – Also Apr. 5, May 24.
d – Also Dec. 26, May 13.
f – Also Dec. 25, Jan. 1, Apr. 5.
g – Also Dec. 28, Apr. 5, May 3, 24, 31.
h – Calls at Calais Fréthun 2132.
j – Not Dec. 24, 31.
k – Calls at Calais Fréthun 1702.

m – Calls at Calais Fréthun 0902.
p – Also Apr. 5, May 24.
t – Not Dec. 25, Jan. 1, Apr. 5.
w – Calls at Calais Fréthun 1759.

❖ – Timings may vary by a few minutes on ⑥⑦, see Tables **400**, **401**.

☆ – Eurostar train. Special fares payable. Minimum check-in time 30 minutes. Not available for London - Ebbsfleet - Ashford or v.v. journeys. Valid Dec. 13, 2009 - July 3, 2010.

INTERNATIONAL SERVICES FROM BRUSSELS

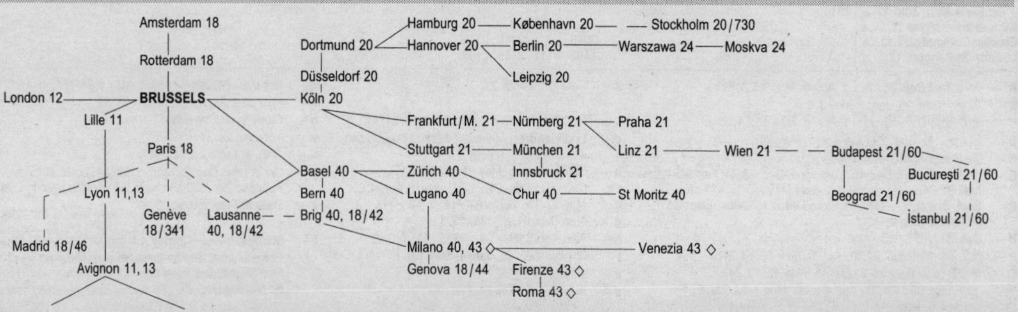

LONDON / BRUSSELS - LILLE / PARIS - BARCELONA - ALACANT 13

train type	TGV				TGV	☆	☆	TGV	Talgo	AVE				TGV	☆	☆	Hotel		AVE	☆	☆		Talgo	AVE	
train number	9804	2	2	2	5112	9002	9004	6209	70	3212		2	2	9832	9036	9038	477		3090	9040	9042	3731	463	3122	2
notes	5105			⑥⑦	5113	②③④	①–⑥		71			⑦	①–⑤	9833	⑥⑦	①–⑤	476		⑧	⑥⑦	①–⑤	🅁	462		
notes				q		S	R		K⁄		2	q	p		y	g	J			y	g	G	C⁄		
London St Pancras 10 .. d.	...	...	...	...	...	0602	0655	...	...	...	...	...	...	...	1532	1602	...	...	...	1625	1655	...	...	...	...
Brussels Midi / Zuid 12 d.	0540x	...	...	...	...	|	|	...	...	...	...	...	...	1120	|	|	...	...	...	|	|	...	...	...	...
Lille Europe 12 d.	0625	...	...	...	0828	|	|	...	...	...	...	...	...	1206	|	|	...	...	...	|	|	...	...	...	...
Paris Nord 10 a.	|	...	...	...	|	0954	1017	...	...	...	...	...	...	|	1847	1917	...	...	...	1947	2023	...	...	...	...
Paris Austerlitz d.	|	...	...	...	|	...	...	...	...	...	...	...	...	|	▬	▬	2034	...	...	▬	▬	2156	...	...	...
Paris Gare de Lyon d.	|	...	...	...	|	...	...	1120	...	...	...	...	...	|	...	...	|	...	...	...	...	|	...	...	...
Les Aubrais-Orléans d.	|	...	...	...	|	...	...	|	...	...	...	...	...	|	...	...	2136	...	...	...	...	2259	...	...	...
Limoges d.	|	...	...	...	|	...	...	|	...	...	...	...	...	|	...	...	2350	...	...	...	...	|	...	...	...
Lyon Part Dieu d.	0937	...	...	...	1137	...	...	|	...	...	...	...	...	1507	...	...	|	...	...	...	...	|	...	...	...
Montpellier d.	1128	1157	...	...	1330	...	...	1447	1509	...	...	...	...	1706	...	...	|	...	...	...	...	|	...	...	...
Narbonne d.	...	1257	...	...	▬	...	...	1550	1611	...	...	...	...	1810	2	...	|	...	...	...	...	0635	0820	...	...
Perpignan d.	...	1337	1346	...	⑧	...	...	1625	1654	...	1726	...	...	1844	1926	...	|	...	...	...	...	0724	0856	...	...
Cerbère 🏛 a.	...	...	1421	...	2	...	...	...	1719	...	1804	...	...	...	2001	2	|	...	...	...	...	0812	0921	...	...
Portbou 🏛 a.	...	...	1427	1526	1559	...	...	...	1748	...	1812	1829	1859	...	2009	2030e	|	...	...	...	...	0821	0948	...	1029
Figueres a.	...	...	...	1546	1623	...	...	...	1811	...	...	1854	1924	...	...	2057	0624	...	...	...	...	...	1012	...	1054
Girona a.	...	...	...	1615	1701	...	...	...	1837	...	...	1932	2002	...	...	2127	0654	...	...	*AVE*	*Em*	...	1040	...	1132
Barcelona França a.	...	...	...	|	|	...	...	...	1959	...	...	|	|	...	...	|	0824	0842	...	**3102**	**1101**	...	|	...	|
Barcelona Sants a.	...	...	...	1739	1839	...	...	...	...	2100	...	2109	2139	...	...	2256	...	0854	0930	1000	1000	...	1148	1200	1309
Zaragoza Delicias a.	...	...	...	...	...	...	...	...	...	2251	...	...	...	...	...	...	...	...	|	1151	|	...	|	1351	...
Madrid Puerta de Atocha .. a.	...	...	...	...	...	...	...	...	...	0017	...	...	...	...	...	...	...	...	1213	1323	|	...	|	1523	...
València Nord a.	...	...	...	...	...	...	...	...	...	...	...	...	...	...	...	...	...	...	...	...	1300	...	1515	...	...
Alacant Términal a.	...	...	...	...	...	...	...	...	...	...	...	...	...	...	...	...	...	...	...	...	1500	...	1724	...	...

train type			Talgo	TGV	☆	☆	TGV	☆	☆				TGV	AVE	Talgo	AVE			☆	AVE	Em	AVE	AVE	Hotel	☆
train number	2	2	73	6212	9059	9059	9868	9161	9057	2	2		9868	3123	460	3133	2	3730	9015	3163	1162	3171	3181	475	9023
notes	①–⑤	⑥⑦	72		①–⑤	⑥⑦	9869	⑥	⑦	⑥⑦	①–⑤		9869		461			🅁			⑧	⑧	⑧	474	
notes	p	q	T⁄		h	k	P			q	p	2	Q		D⁄			H						J	
Alacant Términal d.	...	...	...	...	...	...	...	...	...	...	...	...	...	...	1109	...	...	...	...	...	1420	...	...	...	...
València Nord d.	...	...	...	...	...	...	...	...	...	...	...	...	...	...	1308	...	...	...	...	...	1605	...	...	...	...
Madrid Puerta de Atocha .. d.	...	...	...	...	...	...	...	...	...	...	...	...	...	1230	|	1330	...	...	...	1630	|	1700	1800	...	...
Zaragoza Delicias d.	...	...	...	...	...	...	...	...	...	...	...	...	...	1349	|	1455	...	...	...	1749	|	|	|	...	...
Barcelona Sants d.	0716	0746	...	...	...	...	...	...	...	0846	0916	...	...	1527	1642	1654	1716	...	...	1927	1910	1938	2043	...	...
Barcelona França d.	|	|	0845	...	...	...	...	...	...	|	|	...	...	...	|	...	|	...	...	...	...	...	...	2105	...
Girona d.	0902	0911	0955	...	...	...	...	...	...	1025	1052	...	...	...	1748	...	1852	...	...	...	...	...	...	2217	...
Figueres d.	0940	0940	1025	...	...	...	...	...	...	1103	1130	...	...	...	1815	...	1930	...	...	...	...	...	...	2247	...
Portbou 🏛 d.	1005	1000	1053	...	...	...	...	...	...	1128	1155	...	...	...	1842	...	1956	...	...	...	...	...	...	|	...
Cerbère 🏛 d.	1010	...	1114	...	...	...	...	...	...	1133	1200	1228	...	...	1903	...	2000	2121	...	...	...	...	...	|	...
Perpignan d.	...	...	1144	...	...	...	1234	...	...	...	...	1303	1410	...	...	...	...	2210	...	...	...	...	...	|	...
Narbonne d.	...	...	1222	...	...	...	1314	...	...	...	...	...	1449	...	...	...	...	2304	...	...	...	...	...	|	...
Montpellier a.	...	...	1322	1421	...	...	1425	...	...	...	...	...	1554	...	...	...	...	|	...	...	...	...	...	|	...
Lyon Part Dieu a.	...	...	...	|	...	...	1620	...	...	...	...	...	1746	...	...	...	...	|	...	...	...	...	...	|	...
Limoges a.	...	...	...	|	...	...	|	...	...	...	...	...	|	...	...	...	...	|	...	...	...	...	...	0504	...
Les Aubrais-Orléans a.	...	...	...	|	...	...	|	...	...	...	...	...	|	...	...	...	...	0620	...	...	...	...	...	0737	...
Paris Gare de Lyon a.	...	...	...	1749	...	...	|	...	...	...	...	...	|	...	...	...	...	|	...	...	...	...	...	|	...
Paris Austerlitz a.	...	...	...	...	...	...	|	...	...	...	...	...	|	...	...	...	...	0727	...	...	...	...	...	0901	...
Paris Nord 10 d.	...	...	...	...	2013	2013	|	...	...	...	...	...	|	...	...	...	...	...	0913	...	...	...	...	...	1113
Lille Europe 12 a.	...	...	...	...	|	|	1937	2035	2038	...	...	...	2054	...	...	...	...	...	|	...	...	...	...	...	|
Brussels Midi / Zuid 12 a.	...	...	...	...	|	|	2027	|	|	...	...	...	2143	...	...	...	...	...	|	...	...	...	...	...	|
London St Pancras 10 a.	...	...	...	...	2129	2136	...	2103	2112	...	...	...	...	...	...	...	...	...	1034	...	...	...	...	...	1229

C – MARE NOSTRUM – ⟨12⟩ 🍷 Montpellier - Portbou - Barcelona - Alacant - Cartagena (arrive 1952), 🅁 ⁄ Special fares payable.
D – MARE NOSTRUM – ⟨12⟩ 🍷 Lorca (depart 0820) - Alacant - Barcelona - Portbou - Montpellier, 🅁 ⁄ Special fares payable.
G – *CORAIL LUNÉA* – ▬ 1, 2 cl., ⟨2⟩ (reclining), 🍷 Paris - Portbou (not Dec. 24, 31).
H – *CORAIL LUNÉA* – ▬ 1, 2 cl., ⟨2⟩ (reclining), 🍷 Cerbère - Paris (not Dec. 24, 31).
J – JOÁN MIRÓ *Trainhotel Elipsos* – 🛏 1, 2 cl., 🛏 2 cl. (T4), ⟨ ⟩ (reclining), ✕ Paris - Barcelona and v.v. 🅁 Special fares apply.
K – CATALÁN TALGO – ⟨12⟩ ✕ Montpellier - Portbou - Barcelona and v.v. 🅁 ⁄ Special fares payable.

P – ⑥⑦ (also Dec. 25, Jan. 1, Apr. 5, May 13, 24).
Q – ①–⑤ (not Dec. 25, Jan. 1, Apr. 5, May 13, 24).
R – ①–⑥ (①⑤⑥ Jan. 4 - Feb. 6) not Dec. 26, 28, Jan. 1, Apr. 5, May 3, 24, 31.
S – ②③④ Jan. 4 - Feb. 6.
e – 2036 on ①–⑤ (not Oct. 12, Dec. 8).
g – Not Dec. 28, Jan. 1, Apr. 5, May 3, 24, 31.
h – Not Dec. 24, 28, 31, Jan. 1, Apr. 5, May 3, 24, 31.
k – Also Dec. 28, Apr. 5, May 3, 24, 31.
p – Not Dec. 25, Jan. 1.
q – Also Dec. 25, Jan. 1.

x – ①–⑤ (not Dec. 25, Jan. 1, Apr. 5, May 13, 24).
y – Also Dec. 28, Jan. 1, Apr. 5, May 3, 24, 31.

⁄ – Supplement payable.
Em – *Euromed* train, 🅁 🍷 ⁄.
TGV – *Train à Grande Vitesse* 🅁 🍷 ⁄.
AVE – Alta Velocidad Española 🅁 🍷 ⁄.
Talgo – *Talgo* 🅁⁄🍷.
☆ – Eurostar train. Special fares payable. Minimum check-in time 30 minutes. Additional services are shown on Table 10. Valid Dec. 13, 2009 - July 3, 2010. No service Dec. 25.

LONDON - GENÈVE 14

For the full service Paris - Genève, see Table **341**. 90 minutes (including Eurostar check-in time of 30 minutes) has been allowed from Paris **Lyon** and Paris **Austerlitz** to Paris Nord; additional Eurostar services are available, see Table **10**.

train type	☆	☆	☆	TGV	☆	☆	TGV	☆	TGV	☆	☆	TGV	☆	TGV	☆	TGV	☆	☆			
train number	9078	9002	9002	6569	9008	9010	6573	9018	6577	9024	9026	6581	9030	6585	9034	6589	9044	9046	5705 5594		
notes	🅁✕	🅁✕	🅁✕	♥	🅁✕	🅁✕	♥	🅁	♥	🅁	🅁✕	♥	🅁	♥	🅁✕	♥	🅁	🅁	5591		
notes	①–⑤	②③④	⑥		①–⑥	⑦	⑧h	✕		✕	⑤⑦		✕		⑧	⑤f	✕	✕			
	E	G	y	D	p	q					j				w		⑥t	⑧g	A	B	
London St Pancras 10 d.	0525	0602	0622	...	0802	0826	...	1025	...	1229	1300	...	1404	...	1502	...	1725	1755	...	...	...
Paris Nord 10 a.	0850	0954	0947	...	1117	1147	...	1347n	...	1550	1617	...	1726	...	1817	...	2053	2117	...	...	...
Paris Gare de Lyon d.	...	...	...	1110	...	...	1310	...	1504	...	...	1810	...	1908	...	2010	...	...	...	...	...
Paris Austerlitz d.	...	...	...	|	...	...	|	...	|	...	...	|	...	|	...	|	...	...	2246z	...	...
La Roche sur Foron a.	...	...	...	|	...	...	|	...	|	...	...	|	...	|	...	|	...	...	0804	0820	...
Genève Cornavin a.	...	...	...	1435	...	...	1635	...	1835	...	...	2132	...	2245	...	2335	...	...	...	|	...
Genève Eaux Vives a.	...	...	...	...	...	...	...	...	...	...	...	...	...	...	...	...	...	...	...	0858	...

train type	TGV	☆	TGV	☆	TGV	☆	☆	TGV	☆	☆		5596	☆	
train number	6560	9023	6564	9031	6568	9039	9039	6572	9053	9055		5706	9011	
notes	♥	🅁	♥	🅁	♥	🅁✕	🅁✕	♥	🅁✕	🅁			🅁	
notes	①–⑤	✕		✕		⑥⑦	①–⑤		①–⑤	✕			✕	
	k					q	p		m	r	C	A		
Genève Eaux Vives d.	...	...	...	...	...	...	...	...	...	...	2032	...	...	...
Genève Cornavin d.	0535	...	0717	...	0917	...	...	1317	...	...	|	...	...	...
La Roche sur Foron a.	|	...	|	...	|	...	...	|	...	...	2137	2158	...	...
Paris Austerlitz a.	|	...	|	...	|	...	...	|	...	...	...	0621	...	...
Paris Gare de Lyon a.	0903	...	1051	...	1249	...	...	1649	...	...	...	...	...	...
Paris Nord 10 d.	...	1113	...	1304	...	1507	1513	...	1843	1913	...	...	0807	...
London St Pancras 10 a.	...	1229	...	1431	...	1636	1636	...	2006	2034	...	...	0936	...

TRAIN NAMES:

6577	EUROCITY VERSAILLES
6569/6572	EUROCITY VOLTAIRE
6581/6568	EUROCITY HENRY DUNANT
6585/6564	EUROCITY J J ROUSSEAU

A – *CORAIL LUNÉA* – 🅁 ▬ 1, 2 cl. and ⟨2⟩ (reclining) Paris - La Roche sur Foron - (St Gervais) and v.v. For days of running see Table **365**.
B – ①–⑥ (not Dec. 25, Jan. 1, Apr. 5, May 13, 24). Change at Annemasse (0839 / 0847).
C – ①–⑥ (not Dec. 25, Jan. 1, Apr. 5, May 13, 24). Change at Annemasse (2043 / 2118).
D – ⑥⑦ (daily Dec. 13 - Mar. 7; Mar. 13 - Apr. 4; Apr. 19 - May 2; May 22 - July 4).
E – ①–⑤ (①⑤ Jan. 4 - Feb. 6) not Dec. 28, Jan. 1, Apr. 5, May 3, 13, 24, 31.
G – ②③④ Jan. 4 - Feb. 6.
H – ⑦ (also Dec. 18, 28, Mar. 19, Apr. 2, 5, May 3, 24, 28, 31).

f – Also Dec. 24, 31, May 12; not Dec. 25, Jan. 1, Mar. 26, Apr. 2.
g – Not Dec. 24, 31, Jan. 1, Apr. 2.
h – Not Dec. 25, Jan. 1, May 13.
j – Also Dec. 18, 28, Mar. 19, Apr. 2, 5, May 3, 24, 28, 31.
k – Not Dec. 25, Jan. 1, Apr. 5, May 13, 24.
m – Not Dec. 24, 28, 31, Jan. 1, Apr. 5, May 3, 24, 31.
n – 1350 on ⑥.
p – Not Dec. 28, Apr. 5, May 3, 24, 31.
q – Also Dec. 28, Apr. 5, May 3, 24, 31.

r – Not Dec. 24, 31.
t – Also Jan. 1.
w – Not Jan. 1.
y – Not Dec. 26.
z – 2302 on certain days, see Table **365**.

☆ – Eurostar train. Minimum check-in time 30 minutes. Special fares payable. Valid Dec. 13, 2009 - July 3, 2010. No service Dec. 25. Connections across Paris between *TGV* and Eurostar services are not guaranteed. See Table **10**.
♥ – *TGV Lyria* service. 🅁 special fares payable. At-seat meal service in first class.

15 LONDON - ROTTERDAM - AMSTERDAM *by Eurostar*

train type	☆				⇌	☆	☆				☆	☆	⇌			☆	9229		⇌	☆	☆			☆	⇌
train number	9108	9217			9319	9110	9112	9221			9114	9120	9323	9225		9116	🍷		9331	9126	9126	9237		9130	9339
notes	E	①–⑤			⑤⑦t	⑥y	G	🍷			⑥	H		🍷		⑥⑦b	⑥			⑥	H	🍷		⑦g	⑤⑦t
London St Pancras 12 d.	0620	...	...	...	...	0659	0730	...	...	...	0757	0827	...	...	...	0857	...	...	...	1057	1104	...	...	1157	...
Ebbsfleet International **12** d.	0637	...	...	...	...	0715	|	...	...	...	|	0845	...	...	...	0915	...	...	...	1115	|	...	...	1215	...
Ashford International ..... d.	0657	...	...	...	...	|	|	...	...	...	0828	|	...	...	...	|	...	...	...	|	|	...	...	|	...
Lille Europe **12** .... d.	0910	...	...	...	...	0928	|	...	...	...	1033	1058	...	...	...	1128	...	...	...	1330	1330	...	...	1428	...
Brussels Midi / Zuid 12 a.	0944	...	...	...	...	1003	1028	...	...	...	1108	1133	...	...	...	1203	...	...	...	1405	1405	...	...	1503	...
Brussels Midi / Zuid ..... d.	...	1018	...	...	1050	...	...	1115x	...	...	...	...	1150	1215x	...	...	1315	...	1350	...	...	1515x	...	...	1550
Mechelen .... a.	...	1039	...	...	|	...	...	1139	...	...	...	...	|	1239	...	...	1339	...	|	...	...	1539	...	...	|
Antwerpen Berchem ..... a.	...	|	...	...	|	...	...	|	...	...	...	...	|	|	...	...	|	...	|	...	...	|	...	...	|
Antwerpen Centraal. a.	...	1057	...	...	1129	...	...	1157	...	...	...	...	1229	1257	...	...	1357	...	1429	...	...	1557	...	...	1629
Roosendaal 🏛 .... a.	...	1128	...	1151	|	...	...	1228	...	1251	...	...	|	1328	1351	...	1428	1451	|	...	...	1628	1651	...	|
Breda .... a.	...	|	...	1208	|	...	...	|	...	1308	...	...	|	|	1408	...	|	1508	|	...	...	|	1708	...	|
Tilburg .... a.	...	|	...	1223	|	...	...	|	...	1323	...	...	|	|	1423	...	|	1523	|	...	...	|	1723	...	|
's-Hertogenbosch ...... a.	...	|	...	1240	|	...	...	|	...	1340	...	...	|	|	1440	...	|	1540	|	...	...	|	1740	...	|
Nijmegen .... a.	...	|	...	1313	|	...	...	|	...	1413	...	...	|	|	1513	...	|	1613	|	...	...	|	1813	...	|
Arnhem .... a.	...	|	...	1336	|	...	...	|	...	1436	...	...	|	|	1536	...	|	1636	|	...	...	|	1836	...	|
Dordrecht .... a.	...	1153	...	...	|	...	...	1253	...	...	...	...	|	1353	▬	...	1453	▬	|	...	...	1653	▬	...	|
Rotterdam Centraal ..... a.	...	1206	1220	...	1201	...	...	1306	1320	...	...	...	1301	1406	1420	...	1506	1520	1501	...	...	1706	1720	...	1701
Utrecht Centraal .... a.	...	|	1258	...	|	...	...	|	1358	...	...	...	|	|	1458	...	|	1558	|	...	...	|	1758	...	|
Den Haag HS .... a.	...	1225	...	...	|	...	...	1325	...	...	...	...	|	1425	...	...	1525	...	|	...	...	1725	...	...	|
Schiphol ✈ .... a.	...	1249	...	...	1227	...	...	1349	...	...	...	...	1327	1449	...	...	1549	...	1527	...	...	1749	...	...	1727
Amsterdam Centraal ... a.	...	1306	...	...	1243	...	...	1406	...	...	...	...	1343	1506	...	...	1606	...	1543	...	...	1806	...	...	1743

train type	☆	⇌			☆		⇌	☆	9253	☆	☆	☆	⇌		☆	☆	☆	⇌		☆	☆		☆		
train number	9132	9343	9245		9138	9249	9351	9144	🍷	9144	9144	9144	9355	9257	9148	9148	9150	9359	9261	9154	9154	9265	9158	⑥⑦	①–⑤
notes	J		🍷		M	🍷		⑤	⑤	G	⑦b	⑥K		🍷p	⑦b	⑥F	H	⑦	🍷p	⑦b	L	p	j	h	q
London St Pancras 12 d.	1257		...	...	1434	...	...	1604	...	1604	1604	1604		...	1657	1704	1727		...	1825	1835	...	1934	...	...
Ebbsfleet International **12** d.	1315	...	...	...	|	...	...	|	...	|	|	|	...	...	1715	|	1745	...	...	|	|	...	|	...	...
Ashford International ..... d.	|	...	...	...	|	...	...	|	...	|	|	|	...	...	|	|	|	...	...	1855	|	...	|	...	...
Lille Europe **12** .... d.	1528	...	...	...	1658	...	...	|	...	1828	|	1832	...	...	1928	1928	1958	...	...	2055	|	...	2158	...	...
Brussels Midi / Zuid 12 a.	1603	...	...	...	1733	...	...	1859	...	1903	1903	1908	...	...	2003	2003	2033	...	...	2130	2133	...	2233	...	...
Brussels Midi / Zuid ..... d.	...	1650	1715x	...	...	1815x	1850	▬	1918	...	...	...	1950	2015x	▬	...	...	2050	2115x	▬	...	2215x	...	2333	2331
Mechelen .... a.	...	|	1739	...	...	1839	|	...	1939	...	...	...	|	2039	...	...	...	|	2139	...	...	2239	...	0000	0002
Antwerpen Berchem ..... a.	...	|	|	...	...	|	|	...	|	...	...	...	|	|	...	...	...	|	|	...	...	|	...	0016	0033
Antwerpen Centraal. a.	...	1729	1757	...	...	1857	1929	...	1957	...	...	...	2029	2057	...	...	...	2129	2157	...	...	2257	...	0022	0038
Roosendaal 🏛 .... a.	...	|	1828	1851	...	1928	|	1951	2029	...	...	...	|	2129	2151	...	...	|	2229	2251	...	2329	...	...	...
Breda .... a.	...	|	|	1908	...	|	|	2008	|	...	...	...	|	|	2208	...	...	|	|	2308	...	|	...	...	...
Tilburg .... a.	...	|	|	1923	...	|	|	2023	|	...	...	...	|	|	2223	...	...	|	|	2323	...	|	...	...	...
's-Hertogenbosch ...... a.	...	|	|	1940	...	|	|	2040	|	...	...	...	|	|	2240	...	...	|	|	2340	...	|	...	...	...
Nijmegen .... a.	...	|	|	2013	...	|	|	2113	|	...	...	...	|	|	2313	...	...	|	|	0013	...	|	...	...	...
Arnhem .... a.	...	|	|	2036	...	|	|	2136	|	...	...	...	|	|	2336	...	...	|	|	0036	...	|	...	...	...
Dordrecht .... a.	...	|	1853	▬	...	1953	|	▬	2053	...	...	...	|	2153	▬	...	...	|	2253	▬	...	2354	...	...	...
Rotterdam Centraal ..... a.	...	1801	1906	1920	...	2006	2001	2020	2106	...	...	...	2101	2206	2235	...	...	2201	2306	2335	...	0006	...	...	...
Utrecht Centraal .... a.	...	|	|	1958	...	|	|	2058	|	...	...	...	|	|	2313	...	...	|	|	0013	...	|	...	...	...
Den Haag HS .... a.	...	|	1925	...	...	2025p	|	...	2125	...	...	...	|	2225	...	...	...	|	2325	...	...	0025z	...	...	...
Schiphol ✈ .... a.	...	1827	1949	...	...	2049p	2027	...	2149	...	...	...	2127	2249	...	...	...	2227	2349	...	...	0049z	...	...	...
Amsterdam Centraal ... a.	...	1843	2006	...	...	2106p	2043	...	2206	...	...	...	2143	2306	...	...	...	2243	0006	...	...	0106z	...	...	...

train type			☆		☆	☆			☆			☆						9224		⇌	☆			☆	☆
train number	①–⑤	⑥⑦	9109	⑥⑦	9113	9113	①–⑤	①–⑤	9117	①–⑤	9212	9119	⑦	①–⑥	9220	⑦	①–⑥	🍷		9330	9137		9232	9139	9141
notes	q	h	A	h	⑤d	⑥	q	k	⑦P	k	D	R	h	k	🍷	h	k	⑥⑦		⑤⑥⑦	⑥⑦g		🍷	E	⑦b
Amsterdam Centraal ... d.	...	...	...	...	...	...	...	...	...	...	0554q	...	...	...	0754	...	...	0854	...	1116	...	...	1054	...	...
Schiphol ✈ .... △ d.	...	...	...	...	...	...	...	...	...	...	0609q	...	...	...	0809	...	...	0909	...	1131	...	...	1109	...	...
Den Haag HS .... d.	...	...	...	...	...	...	...	...	...	...	0635q	...	...	...	0835	...	...	0935	...	|	...	...	1135	...	...
Utrecht Centraal .... d.	...	...	...	...	...	...	...	0602	...	...	|	...	0743	0802	|	0847	0902	|	0917	|	...	1102	|	...	...
Rotterdam Centraal ..... d.	...	...	...	...	...	...	...	0640	...	...	0655	...	0835	0840	0855	0925	0940	0955	0955	1158	...	1140	1155	...	...
Dordrecht .... d.	...	...	...	...	...	...	...	▬	...	...	0709	...	...	▬	0909	▬	▬	1009	...	|	...	▬	1209	...	...
Arnhem .... d.	...	...	...	...	...	...	...	...	...	...	|	...	...	0720f	|	...	0820	|	...	|	...	1020	|	...	...
Nijmegen .... d.	...	...	...	...	...	...	...	...	...	...	|	...	...	0748f	|	...	0848	|	...	|	...	1048	|	...	...
's-Hertogenbosch ...... d.	...	...	...	...	...	...	...	...	...	0619	|	...	...	0819	|	...	0919	|	...	|	...	1119	|	...	...
Tilburg .... d.	...	...	...	...	...	...	...	...	...	0637	|	...	...	0837	|	...	0937	|	...	|	...	1137	|	...	...
Breda .... d.	...	...	...	...	...	...	...	...	...	0652	|	...	...	0852	|	...	0952	|	...	|	...	1152	|	...	...
Roosendaal 🏛 .... d.	...	...	...	...	...	...	...	...	...	0711	0734	...	...	0911	0934	...	1011	1034	...	|	...	1211	1234	...	...
Antwerpen Centraal. d.	0517	0538	...	0638	...	...	0645	☆	...	...	0803	...	...	...	1003	...	...	1103	...	1230	...	...	1303	...	...
Antwerpen Berchem ..... d.	0523	0544	...	0644	...	...	0651	**9113**	...	...	|	...	...	...	|	...	...	|	...	|	...	...	|	...	...
Mechelen .... d.	0540	0602	...	0702	...	...	0708	①–④	...	...	0821	...	...	...	1021	☆	...	1121	...	|	...	...	1321	...	...
Brussels Midi / Zuid ..... a.	0605	0627	...	0727	...	...	0732	m	...	...	0845v	...	...	...	1045v	**9181**	...	1145	...	1310	...	...	1345v	...	...
Brussels Midi / Zuid 12 d.	...	...	0659	...	0759	0759	...	0805	0859	...	...	0929	...	...	...	1129	...	...	...	...	1359	...	...	1429	1459
Lille Europe **12** .... a.	...	...	0732	...	0832	|	...	|	0932	...	...	1002	...	...	...	1202	...	...	...	...	1432	...	...	1502	1532
Ashford International ..... a.	...	...	|	...	|	|	...	|	|	...	...	|	...	...	...	|	...	...	...	...	|	...	...	|	|
Ebbsfleet International **12** a.	...	...	|	...	|	|	...	|	|	...	...	|	...	...	...	1215	...	...	...	...	1445	...	...	|	|
London St Pancras 12 a.	...	...	0755	...	0856	0856	...	0856	0956	...	...	1026	...	...	...	1233	...	...	...	...	1503	...	...	1526	1556

train type		9236		⇌	☆				☆				⇌		☆			⇌		☆	⇌			☆	☆
train number		🍷		9338	9145		9240		9149		9244		9346		9153		9248	9450		9157	9354		9256	9163	9163
notes		①–⑤		①–⑥	⑤		🍷	Q	⑧		🍷		C	Q			🍷	B	Q	⑧j	⑧t		🍷	S	⑤⑦b
Amsterdam Centraal ... d.	...	1154	...	1316	...	...	1254	...	...	...	1354	...	1516	...	...	...	1454	1616	...	...	1716	...	1654	...	...
Schiphol ✈ .... △ d.	...	1209	...	1331	...	...	1309	...	...	...	1409	...	1531	...	...	...	1509	1631	...	...	1731	...	1709	...	...
Den Haag HS .... d.	...	1235	...	|	...	...	1335	...	...	...	1435	...	|	...	...	...	1535	|	...	...	|	...	1735	...	...
Utrecht Centraal .... d.	1202	|	1232	|	...	1302	|	...	...	1402	|	1432	|	...	...	1502	|	|	...	...	|	1702	|	...	...
Rotterdam Centraal ..... d.	1240	1255	1310	1358	...	1340	1355	...	...	1440	1455	1510	1558	...	...	1540	1555	1658	...	...	1758	1740	1755	...	...
Dordrecht .... d.	▬	1309	...	|	...	▬	1409	...	...	▬	1509	...	|	...	...	▬	1609	|	...	...	|	▬	1809	...	...
Arnhem .... d.	1120	|	...	|	...	1220	|	...	...	1320	|	...	|	...	...	1420	|	|	...	...	|	1620	|	...	...
Nijmegen .... d.	1148	|	...	|	...	1248	|	...	...	1348	|	...	|	...	...	1448	|	|	...	...	|	1648	|	...	...
's-Hertogenbosch ...... d.	1219	|	...	|	...	1319	|	...	...	1419	|	...	|	...	...	1519	|	|	...	...	|	1719	|	...	...
Tilburg .... d.	1237	|	...	|	...	1337	|	...	...	1437	|	...	|	...	...	1537	|	|	...	...	|	1737	|	...	...
Breda .... d.	1252	|	...	|	...	1352	|	...	...	1452	|	...	|	...	...	1552	|	|	...	...	|	1752	|	...	...
Roosendaal 🏛 .... d.	1311	1334	...	|	...	1411	1434	...	...	1511	1534	...	|	...	...	1611	1634	|	...	...	|	1811	1834	...	...
Antwerpen Centraal. d.	...	1403	...	1430	...	...	1503	1538	...	...	1603	...	1630	1638	...	...	1703	1730	1738	...	1830	▬	1903	...	...
Antwerpen Berchem ..... d.	...	|	...	|	...	...	|	1544	...	...	|	...	|	1644	...	...	|	|	1744	...	|	☆	|	...	...
Mechelen .... d.	...	1421	...	|	...	...	1521	1602	...	...	1621	...	|	1657	...	...	1721	|	1757	...	|	**9161**	1921	...	...
Brussels Midi / Zuid ..... a.	...	1442	...	1510	...	...	1545v	1627	...	...	1645v	...	1710	1726	...	...	1745v	1810	1826	...	1910	⑥	1945v	...	...
Brussels Midi / Zuid 12 d.	...	...	...	...	1559	...	...	...	1659	...	...	...	...	...	1759	...	...	...	...	1859	...	1959	...	2017	2029
Lille Europe **12** .... a.	...	...	...	...	|	...	...	...	1732	...	...	...	...	...	1832	...	...	...	...	1932	...	2032	...	2050	2102
Ashford International ..... a.	...	...	...	...	|	...	...	...	1733	...	...	...	...	...	|	...	...	...	...	|	...	|	...	|	|
Ebbsfleet International **12** a.	...	...	...	...	1645	...	...	...	|	...	...	...	...	...	1845	...	...	...	...	|	...	2045	...	2115	2115
London St Pancras 12 a.	...	...	...	...	1703	...	...	...	1805	...	...	...	...	...	1903	...	...	...	...	1956	...	2103	...	2133	2133

A – ①②③④⑥ (not Dec. 26, 28, Apr. 5, May 3, 13, 24, 31).
B – ①⑤⑥⑦.
C – ①–⑤ (not Dec. 25).
D – ①–⑥ (also Dec. 27; not Jan. 1).
E – ①–⑤ (not Dec. 28, Jan. 1, Apr. 5, May 3, 24, 31).
F – ⑥ Dec. 13 - Jan. 3.
G – ①–④ (not Dec. 28, Apr. 5, May 3, 24, 31).
H – ①–⑤ (not Dec. 28, Apr. 5, May 3, 24, 31).
J – ①–⑥ (not Dec. 28, Jan. 1, Apr. 5, May 3, 24, 31).
K – ⑥ Jan. 4 - July 3.

L – ①–⑤ (not Dec. 24, 28, 31, Apr. 5, May 3, 24, 31).
M – ⑤⑦ (also Dec. 19, 26, 28, Jan. 2, Apr. 5, May 3, 24, 31).
P – ⑦ Dec. 13 - Jan. 3 (also Dec. 28).
Q – On ①–⑤ (not Dec. 25, Jan. 1, Apr. 5, May 5, 24) runs 5–7 minutes later.
R – ①–⑥ (not Dec. 28, Apr. 5, May 3, 24, 31).
S – ①–④ (not Dec. 24, 28, 31, Apr. 5, May 3, 24, 31).

b – Also Dec. 28, Apr. 5, May 3, 24, 31.
d – Also Dec. 26, May 13.
f – ①–⑥ (not Dec. 26).
g – Also Apr. 5, May 24.
h – Also Dec. 25, Jan. 1, Apr. 5, May 5, 24.
j – Not Dec. 24, 31.
k – Not Dec. 25, Jan. 1, Apr. 5, May 13, 24.
m – Not Dec. 28, Apr. 5, May 3, 13, 24, 31.
p – Not Dec. 31.
q – Not Dec. 25, 26, 27, Jan. 1, Apr. 5, 30, May 13, 24.

NOTES CONTINUED ON NEXT PAGE →

LONDON - AMSTERDAM *by rail–sea–rail via Harwich - Hoek van Holland* 15a

notes	⑥	①–⑤	①–⑥	⑥	①–⑤	①–⑤	⑦	⑦	⛴ Y					⑦
London Liverpool Street .. d.	...	...	...	0618	0625	...	...	...	...	...	...	...	...	...
Peterborough ... d.	...	...	...	|	|	...	...	...	...	...	...	...	...	1746
Cambridge ... d.	...	...	...	|	|	...	...	...	...	...	...	...	...	|
Norwich ... d.	0600	0610	...	|	|	...	0700	...	...	...	...	...	...	|
Ipswich ... d.	0640	0651	0700	|	|	...	0740	0745	...	...	...	...	...	1927
Manningtree ... d.	...	...	|	0726	0732	0735	...	|	...	...	...	...	...	...
Harwich International 🏢 ... d.	...	...	0725	0744	...	0751	...	0810	0900	...	...	...	...	...
Hoek van Holland Haven 🏢 . a.	...	...	...	...	...	...	...	...	1630	1707	...	...	...	...
Schiedam Centrum ... a.	...	...	...	...	...	...	...	...	...	1733	1746	...	...	...
Rotterdam Centraal ... a.	...	...	...	...	...	...	...	...	...	1738	|	1758	...	...
Den Haag HS ... a.	...	...	...	...	...	...	...	...	...	...	1802	1814	...	...
Schiphol ✈ ... a.	...	...	...	...	...	...	...	...	...	...	|	1845	...	...
Amsterdam Centraal ... a.	...	...	...	...	...	...	...	...	...	...	1852	1903	...	...

notes	⑦	⑦	⑦	①–⑥	①–⑥	①–⑥	①–⑥	⛴ X	①–⑤					
London Liverpool Street .. d.	...	...	2000	...	...	...	2038	...	...	...	...	...	...	...
Peterborough ... d.	...	...	|	...	...	1945	|	...	...	...	...	...	...	...
Cambridge ... d.	1912	...	|	...	1943	|	|	...	...	...	...	...	...	...
Norwich ... d.	|	2000	|	2000	|	|	|	...	...	...	...	...	...	...
Ipswich ... d.	2035	2042	|	2040	2104	2127	|	...	...	...	...	...	...	...
Manningtree ... d.	|	2052	2104	...	|	2136	2146	...	...	...	...	...	...	...
Harwich International 🏢 ... d.	2100	...	2122	...	2128	...	2202	2345	...	...	...	...	...	...
Hoek van Holland Haven 🏢 . a.	...	...	...	...	...	...	...	0745	0822	...	0837	...	...	...
Schiedam Centrum ... a.	...	...	...	...	...	...	...	...	0848	...	0903	0916	...	...
Rotterdam Centraal ... a.	...	...	...	...	...	...	...	...	0853	0908	0908	|	...	...
Den Haag HS ... a.	...	...	...	...	...	...	...	...	...	0925	...	0932	...	...
Schiphol ✈ ... a.	...	...	...	...	...	...	...	...	...	0951	...	|	...	...
Amsterdam Centraal ... a.	...	...	...	...	...	...	...	...	...	1006	...	1022	...	...

notes			⛴ Y	⑦	⑦	⑥	①–⑤	①–⑥	⑦	⑦	①–⑥	①–⑥		
Amsterdam Centraal ... d.	1154	...	...	...	...	...	...	...	...	...	...	...	1859	1910
Schiphol ✈ ... d.	1209	...	...	...	...	...	...	...	...	...	...	...	1913	|
Den Haag HS ... d.	1235	...	...	...	...	...	...	...	...	...	...	...	1946	2001
Rotterdam Centraal ... d.	1254	1313	...	...	...	...	...	...	...	...	...	...	2002	2020
Schiedam Centrum ... d.	...	1318	...	...	...	...	...	...	...	...	...	...	...	...
Hoek van Holland Haven 🏢 . d.	...	1342	1430	...	...	...	...	...	...	...	...	...	...	...
Harwich International 🏢 ... a.	...	...	2000	2058	...	2106	2106	...	2110	...	2134	...	...	...
Manningtree ... a.	...	...	...	2114	2118	2122	2122	2132	|	...	|	...	...	...
Ipswich ... a.	...	...	...	...	|	|	|	2142	2137	2144	2200	2243	...	...
Norwich ... a.	...	...	...	...	|	|	|	2228	...	2229	...	2329	...	...
Cambridge ... a.	...	...	...	...	|	|	|	...	...	...	...	...	...	...
Peterborough ... a.	...	...	...	...	|	|	|	...	...	...	...	...	...	...
London Liverpool Street .. a.	...	...	...	...	2242	2234	2236	...	...	...	...	...	...	...

notes		⛴ X	①–⑤	①–⑤	⑥	⑥	①–⑤	⑦	①–⑥	①–⑥	⑦	⑦	⑦	
Amsterdam Centraal ... d.	...	...	...	...	...	...	...	...	...	...	...	...	...	...
Schiphol ✈ ... d.	...	...	...	...	...	...	...	...	...	...	...	...	...	...
Den Haag HS ... d.	...	...	...	...	...	...	...	...	...	...	...	...	...	...
Rotterdam Centraal ... d.	2043	...	...	...	...	...	...	...	...	...	...	...	...	...
Schiedam Centrum ... d.	2048	...	...	...	...	...	...	...	...	...	...	...	...	...
Hoek van Holland Haven 🏢 . d.	2112	2200	...	...	...	...	...	...	...	...	...	...	...	...
Harwich International 🏢 ... a.	...	0630	0710	...	0715	...	...	0725	0747	...	0830	...	...	...
Manningtree ... a.	...	...	0722	0732	0728	0746	0750	0738	|	...	|	...	...	...
Ipswich ... a.	...	...	|	0741	|	0758	0759	|	0815	0842	0855	0944	0955	...
Norwich ... a.	...	...	|	0827	|	|	|	|	|	0927	|	1029	|	...
Cambridge ... a.	...	...	|	...	|	|	|	|	0939	...	1024	...	|	...
Peterborough ... a.	...	...	|	...	|	0938	0937	|	...	...	...	...	1136	...
London Liverpool Street .. a.	...	...	0848	...	0839	...	...	0859	...	...	...	...	...	...

X – Not Dec. 24, 25.
Y – Not Dec. 24, 25, 26.

SEA CROSSING (for rail / sea / rail journeys): ⛴ – Ship service, operated by Stena Line. R One class only on ship. ✕ on ship. A cabin berth is necessary on night sailings. Service Dec. 13, 2009 - Dec. 23, 2010

PARIS - BRUSSELS - OOSTENDE 16

For additional services change at Brussels Midi. Table 18 Paris - Brussels. Table 400 / 401 Brussels - Gent - Brugge. Table 400 Brussels - Oostende.

	⇌ 9313 ⑥ b	⇌ 9327 ⑦	⇌ 9355 ⑧ c	
Paris Nord 18 ... d.	0801	1125	1825	...
Brussels Midi / Zuid 18 ... a.	0923	1247	1947	...
Brussels Midi / Zuid ... d.	0940	1259	1959	...
Gent Sint-Pieters ... a.	1011	1329	2030	...
Brugge ... a.	1036	1354	2056	...
Oostende ... a.	1050	1409	2111	...

	⇌ 9308 ⑥ b	⇌ 9308 ①–⑤ c	⇌ 9350 ⑦	⇌ 9454 ⑥ b
Oostende ... d.	0610	0611	1650	1750
Brugge ... d.	0626	0626	1705	1805
Gent Sint-Pieters ... d.	0650	0653	1730	1830
Brussels Midi / Zuid ... a.	0721	0727	1801	1901
Brussels Midi / Zuid 18 ... d.	0737	0737	1815	1913
Paris Nord 18 ... a.	0859	0859	1935	2035

b – Also Dec. 25, Jan. 1.
c – Not Dec. 25, Jan. 1.

⇌ – *Thalys* high-speed train R 🍷 special fares payable.

LILLE - BRUSSELS (Summary Table) 16a

train type	*TGV*	☆	☆	*TGV*	*TGV*	☆	☆	☆	☆	*TGV*	☆	☆	☆	*TGV*	*TGV*	☆	☆	*TGV*	☆	*TGV*	☆	☆	*TGV*	☆	
train number	**9811**	**9106**	**9110**	**9856**	**9854**	**9114**	**9120**	**9116**	**9126**	**9860**	**9130**	**9132**	**9138**	**9862**	**9864**	**9144**	**9144**	**9866**	**9148**	**9868**	**9150**	**9154**	**9868**	**9158**	
train number				**9857**	**9855**					**9861**				**9863**	**9865**			**9867**		**9869**			**9869**		
notes	R 🍷	①–⑤	⑥	R 🍷	R 🍷	⑥	①–⑤	⑥⑦	①–⑥	R 🍷	⑦	①–⑥		R 🍷	R 🍷	①–④		R 🍷		R 🍷	①–⑤	⑦	R 🍷		
notes	A	g	h	B	A		p	q	p		r	g	J			p	K		D	B	p	q	A	j	
Lille Europe ... d.	0729	0910	0928	1114	1115	1033	1058	1128	1330	1340	1428	1528	1658	1721	1745	1828	1832	1855	1928	1949	1958	2055	2105	2158	...
Brussels Midi / Zuid ..... a.	0803	0944	1003	1150	1152	1108	1133	1203	1405	1414	1503	1603	1733	1756	1820	1903	1908	1930	2003	2027	2033	2130	2143	2233	...

train type	*TGV*	☆	☆	☆	☆		*TGV*	☆	*TGV*	☆		☆	☆	*TGV*		*TGV*	☆	☆	☆	☆	☆	☆			
train number	**9804**	**9109**	**9113**	**9117**	**9119**		**9832**	**9181**	**9828**	**9137**		**9139**	**9141**	**9834**		**9836**	**9149**	**9153**	**9157**	**9161**	**9163**	**9163**			
train number	**9805**						**9833**		**9829**					**9835**		**9837**									
notes	R 🍷		⑤	⑦	①–⑥		R 🍷		R 🍷	⑥⑦		①–⑤	⑦	R 🍷		R 🍷			⑧		①–④	⑤⑦			
notes	A	C	b	M	p					r		g	q				⑧		j	⑥	e	q			
Brussels Midi / Zuid ..... d.	0540	0659	0759	0859	0929	...	1120	1129	1249	1359	...	1429	1459	1520	...	1609	1659	1759	1859	1959	2017	2029	...	...	...
Lille Europe ... a.	0615	0732	0832	0932	1002	...	1156	1202	1323	1432	...	1502	1532	1556	...	1644	1732	1832	1932	2032	2050	2102	...	...	...

A – ①–⑤ (not Dec. 25, Jan. 1, Apr. 5, May 13, 24).
B – ⑥⑦ (also Dec. 25, Jan. 1, Apr. 5, May 13, 24).
C – ①②③④⑥ (not Dec. 26, 28, Apr. 5, May 3, 13, 24, 31).
D – ⑦ (⑥⑦ Dec. 13 - Jan. 3) also Dec. 28, Apr. 5, May 13, 24.
J – ⑤⑦ (also Dec. 19, 26, 28, Jan. 2, Apr. 5, May 3, 24, 31).
K – ⑥ Jan. 4 - July 3.
M – ⑦ Dec. 13 - Jan. 3 (also Dec. 28).

b – Not Dec. 26, May 13.
e – Not Dec. 24, 28, 31, Apr. 5, May 3, 24, 31.
g – Not Dec. 28, Jan. 1, Apr. 5, May 3, 24, 31.
h – Not Dec. 26.
j – Not Dec. 24, 31.
p – Not Dec. 28, Apr. 5, May 3, 24, 31.
q – Also Dec. 28, Apr. 5, May 3, 24, 31.

r – Also Apr. 5, May 28.

☆ – Eurostar train. Special fares payable. Minimum check-in time 30 minutes departing from Brussels. Valid Dec. 13, 2009 - July 3, 2010. No service Dec. 25.

PARIS - CHARLEROI - NAMUR - LIÈGE 17

km	*train type*	⇌	⇌
	train number	**9499**	**9499**
	notes	①–⑤	⑥⑦
	notes	p	q
0	**Paris Nord** ... ▲ d.	1943	2016
282	Mons ... a.	2101	2133
323	Charleroi Sud ... a.	2133	2201
359	**Namur** ... a.	2206	2234
419	**Liège Guillemins** ... ▲ a.	2245	2314

train type	⇌	⇌
train number	**9496**	**9496**
notes	①–⑤	⑥⑦
notes	p	q
Liège Guillemins .. ▲ d.	0640	0647
Namur ... d.	0720	0726
Charleroi Sud ... d.	0756	0759
Mons ... d.	0825	0826
Paris Nord ... ▲ a.	0944	0944

LONDON - ASHFORD - AVIGNON / MARNE LA VALLÉE 17a

train type	☆	☆	
train number	**9084**	**9074**	
train number	**9085**		
notes	P	A	
London St Pancras .... d.	0717	0953	...
Ashford International .... d.	0755	1028	...
Lille Europe ... a.	0952s	1224s	...
Marne la Vallée § ... a.	|	1331	...
Avignon Centre ... a.	1408	...	...

train type	☆	☆	☆
train number	**9071**	**9087**	**9057**
train number		**9086**	
notes	C	Q	B
Avignon Centre ... d.	...	1624	...
Marne la Vallée § ... d.	1540	|	1937
Lille Europe ... d.	|	2032u	|
Ashford International . a.	1636	2033	2037
London St Pancras . a.	1711	2109	2112

NOTES FOR TABLES 17 AND 17a

A – ①③④⑤⑦ (daily Dec. 13 - Jan. 4; not Dec. 25; Feb. 10–22; Mar. 31 - Apr. 19; also May 1; daily May 26 - June 7; July 21 - Sept. 3; Oct. 20 - Nov. 1).
B – ①③④⑤⑦ (daily Dec. 13 - Jan. 4; not Dec. 25, 31; Feb. 10–22; Mar. 31 - Apr. 19; also May 1; daily May 26 - June 7; July 21 - Sept. 3; Oct. 20 - Nov. 1).
C – Dec. 31.
P – ⑥ July 10, 2010 - Sept. 4.
Q – ⑥ July 17, 2010 - Sept. 11.

p – Not Dec. 25, Jan. 1.
q – Also Dec. 25, Jan. 1.
s – Stops to set down only.
u – Stops to pick up only.

⇌ – *Thalys* high-speed train. R 🍷. Special fares payable.
☆ – Eurostar train. Special fares payable. Minimum check-in time 30 minutes. Not available for London - Ashford or v.v. journeys.
▲ – For other trains Paris - Liège see Table **20**.
§ – Marne la Vallée - Chessy (station for Disneyland).

← **NOTES CONTINUED FROM PREVIOUS PAGE**

r – Not Dec. 25.
t – Not Dec. 25, Jan. 1.
v – On ①–⑤ (not Dec. 25, Jan. 1, Apr. 5, May 5, 24) arrive Brussels Midi / Zuid 3 minutes earlier.

x – On ①–⑤ (not Dec. 25, Jan. 1, Apr. 5, May 5, 24) depart Brussels Midi / Zuid 3 minutes later.
y – Not Dec. 26.
z – ⑦ (not Dec. 27).
△ – Trains stop to pick up only.

☆ – Eurostar train. Special fares payable. Minimum check-in time 30 minutes. Not available for London - Ebbsfleet - Ashford or v.v. journeys. Valid Dec. 13, 2009 - July 3, 2010. No service Dec. 25.
⇌ – *Thalys* high-speed train. R 🍷 Special fares payable.

18 AMSTERDAM - BRUSSELS - PARIS

Brussels - Disneyland: see Table 11

km	km	train number	9304	9306	9308	9208	9920/1	9310	9412	9212	9314	9314	9416	9216	9318	9320	9220	9322	9224	9326	9428	9228	9330	9330	
		train type	⇌	⇌	⇌		⇌	⇌	⇌		⇌	⇌	⇌		⇌	⇌		⇌		⇌	⇌		⇌	⇌	
		notes	①–④	①–⑤	①–⑥	①–⑥	A	①–⑤	9312	①–⑥	⑥	①–⑤		🍷		⑤g	🍷		🍷	⑧g		🍷	⑤⑥⑦		
			g	g		h	⊕	m		k	f														
0	0	**Amsterdam Centraal** d.	...	...	...	...	0608	0616	...	0554q	0716	...	...	0654c	0816	...	0754	...	0854	1016	...	0954	1116	...	...
17	17	Schiphol ✈ ⊕ d.	...	...	...	...	0626	0631	...	0609q	0731	...	...	0709c	0831	...	0809	...	0909	1031	...	1009	1131	...	...
60		Den Haag HS d.	...	...	...	...	|	|	...	0635q	|	...	...	0735c	|	...	0835	...	0935	|	...	1035	|	...	...
82	70	**Rotterdam Centraal** d.	...	...	...	0555	0658	0658	...	0655	0758	...	...	0755	0858	...	0855	...	0955	1058	...	1055	1158	...	...
102		Dordrecht d.	...	...	...	0609	|	|	...	0709	|	...	...	0809	|	...	0909	...	1009	|	...	1109	|	...	...
140		Roosendaal 🏛 d.	...	...	...	0634	|	|	...	0734	|	...	...	0834	|	...	0934	...	1034	|	...	1134	|	...	...
184	165	**Antwerpen Centraal** d.	...	...	...	0703	0730	0730	...	0803	0830	...	...	0903	0930	...	1003	...	1103	1130	...	1203	1230	...	...
208		Mechelen d.	...	...	...	0721	|	|	...	0821	|	...	...	0921	|	...	1021	...	1121	|	...	1221	|	...	...
229		Brussels Nord / Noord a.	...	...	...	0733v	|	|	...	0833v	|	...	...	0933v	|	...	1033v	...	1133v	|	...	1233v	|	...	...
235	212	**Brussels Midi / Zuid** a.	...	...	...	0742v	|	0810	...	0842v	0910	...	...	0942v	1010	...	1042v	...	1142v	1210	...	1242v	1310	...	...
235	212	**Brussels Midi / Zuid** d.	0637	0713	0737	...	0819	0813	0837	...	0913	0913	0937	...	1013	1037	...	1113	...	1213	1237	...	1313	1313	...
547	524	**Paris Nord** a.	0759	0835	0859	...	...	0935	0959	...	1035	1035	1059	...	1135	1159	...	1235	...	1335	1359	...	1435	1435	...

train number	9330	9232	9436	9236	9338	9338	9340	9240	9342	9342	9344	9244	9346	9346	9448	9248	9350	9350	9352	9252	9354	9454	9456	9256	9358
train type	⇌		⇌		⇌	⇌	⇌		⇌	⇌	⇌		⇌	⇌	⇌		⇌	⇌	⇌		⇌	⇌	⇌		⇌
notes		🍷		🍷	①–⑥		①⑤	🍷	⑥⑦		C	🍷	①–⑤			🍷			⑧	🍷	⑧			🍷	⑥⑦
									f				m				D		m		g				f
Amsterdam Centraal d.	...	1054	...	1154	1316	...	...	1254	1416	...	...	1354	1516	...	...	1454	1616	...	...	1554	1716	...	...	1654	1816
Schiphol ✈ ⊕ d.	...	1109	...	1209	1331	...	...	1309	1431	...	...	1409	1531	...	...	1509	1631	...	...	1609	1731	...	...	1709	1831
Den Haag HS d.	...	1135	...	1235	|	...	...	1335	|	...	...	1435	|	...	...	1535	|	...	...	1635	|	...	...	1735	|
Rotterdam Centraal d.	...	1155	...	1255	1358	...	...	1355	1458	...	...	1455	1558	...	...	1555	1658	...	...	1655	1758	...	...	1755	1858
Dordrecht d.	...	1209	...	1309	|	...	...	1409	|	...	...	1509	|	...	...	1609	|	...	...	1709	|	...	...	1809	|
Roosendaal 🏛 d.	...	1234	...	1334	|	...	...	1434	|	...	...	1534	|	...	...	1634	|	...	...	1734	|	...	...	1834	|
Antwerpen Centraal d.	...	1303	...	1403	1430	...	...	1503	1530	...	...	1603	1630	...	...	1703	1730	...	...	1803	1830	...	...	1903	1930
Mechelen d.	...	1321	...	1421	|	...	...	1521	|	...	...	1621	|	...	...	1721	|	...	...	1821	|	...	...	1921	|
Brussels Nord / Noord a.	...	1333v	...	1433v	|	...	...	1533v	|	...	...	1633v	|	...	...	1733v	|	...	...	1833v	|	...	...	1933v	|
Brussels Midi / Zuid a.	...	1342v	...	1442v	1510	...	...	1542v	1610	...	...	1642v	1710	...	...	1742v	1810	...	...	1842v	1910	...	...	1942v	2010
Brussels Midi / Zuid d.	1313	...	1437	...	1513	1513	1537	...	1613	1613	1637	...	1713	1713	1737	...	1813	1813	1837	...	1913	1913	1937	...	2013
Paris Nord a.	1435	...	1559	...	1635	1635	1659	...	1735	1735	1759	...	1835	1835	1859	...	1935	1935	1959	...	2035	2035	2059	...	2135

train number	9358	9360	9260	9362	9362	9464	9264	9366	9268	9272	9276		
train type	⇌	⇌		⇌	⇌	⇌		⇌					
notes	E	①⑦	🍷	⑧		⑤⑦	🍷	⑦	🍷	🍷	⑥		
		f		g		g	e		e	e	b		
Amsterdam Centraal d.	...	...	1754	1916	...	...	1854	...	1954	2054	2154	...	...
Schiphol ✈ ⊕ d.	...	...	1809	1931	...	...	1909	...	2009	2109	2209	...	...
Den Haag HS d.	...	...	1835	|	...	...	1935	...	2035	2135	2235	...	...
Rotterdam Centraal d.	...	...	1855	1958	...	...	1955	...	2055	2155	2255	...	...
Dordrecht d.	...	...	1909	|	...	...	2009	...	2109	2209	2309	...	...
Roosendaal 🏛 d.	...	...	1934	|	...	...	2034	...	2134	2234	2334	...	...
Antwerpen Centraal d.	...	...	2003	2030	...	...	2103	...	2203	2303	0003	...	...
Mechelen d.	...	...	2021	|	...	...	2121	...	2221	2321	0021	...	...
Brussels Nord / Noord a.	...	...	2033v	|	...	...	2133v	...	2233v	2333v	0033	...	...
Brussels Midi / Zuid a.	...	...	2042v	2110	...	...	2142v	...	2242v	2342v	0042	...	...
Brussels Midi / Zuid d.	2013	2037	...	2113	2113	2137	...	2213	...	...	...	...	...
Paris Nord a.	2135	2159	...	2235	2235	2259	...	2335	...	...	...	...	...

train number	9201	9205	9407	9307	9209	
train type			⇌	⇌		
notes	①–⑥	🍷	①–⑥	①–⑤	🍷	
	🍷 h			g		
Paris Nord d.	...	...	0625	0625	...	...
Brussels Midi / Zuid a.	...	...	0747	0747	...	...
Brussels Midi / Zuid d.	0618x	0715	...	0750	0816	...
Brussels Nord / Noord d.	0627x	0724y	...	|	0825y	...
Mechelen a.	0639	0739	...	|	0839	...
Antwerpen Centraal a.	0657	0757	...	0829	0857	...
Roosendaal 🏛 a.	0728	0828	...	|	0928	...
Dordrecht a.	0753	0853	...	|	0953	...
Rotterdam Centraal a.	0806	0906	...	0901	1006	...
Den Haag HS a.	0825	0925	...	|	1025	...
Schiphol ✈ a.	0851	0951	...	0927	1051	...
Amsterdam Centraal a.	0906	1006	...	0943	1106	...

train number	9309	9311	9311	9213	9413	9315	9217	9317	9319	9319	9221	9421	9323	9225	9325	9229	9327	9331	9233	9433	9237	9339	9339	9241	
train type	⇌	⇌	⇌		⇌	⇌		⇌	⇌	⇌		⇌	⇌		⇌		⇌	⇌		⇌		⇌	⇌		
notes	①–④	①–⑥	⑥	🍷		①–⑥	🍷		⑧	⑤⑦	🍷			🍷	⑤	🍷			🍷		🍷		⑤⑦	🍷	
	g		f						g	g					g								g		
Paris Nord d.	0701	0725	0725	...	0801	0825	...	0901	0925	0925	...	1001	1025	...	1101	...	1125	1225	...	1301	...	1425	1425	...	...
Brussels Midi / Zuid a.	0823	0847	0847	...	0923	0947	...	1023	1047	1047	...	1123	1147	...	1223	...	1247	1347	...	1423	...	1547	1547	...	...
Brussels Midi / Zuid d.	...	...	0850	0918x	...	0950	1018x	...	...	1050	1118x	...	1150	1218x	...	1318x	...	1350	1418x	...	1518x	...	1550	1618x	...
Brussels Nord / Noord d.	...	...	|	0927x	...	|	1027x	...	...	|	1127x	...	|	1227x	...	1327x	...	|	1427x	...	1527x	...	|	1627x	...
Mechelen a.	...	...	|	0939	...	|	1039	...	...	|	1139	...	|	1239	...	1339	...	|	1439	...	1539	...	|	1639	...
Antwerpen Centraal a.	...	...	0929	0957	...	1029	1057	...	...	1129	1157	...	1229	1257	...	1357	...	1429	1457	...	1557	...	1629	1657	...
Roosendaal 🏛 a.	...	...	|	1028	...	|	1128	...	...	|	1228	...	|	1328	...	1428	...	|	1528	...	1628	...	|	1728	...
Dordrecht a.	...	...	|	1053	...	|	1153	...	...	|	1253	...	|	1353	...	1453	...	|	1553	...	1653	...	|	1753	...
Rotterdam Centraal a.	...	...	1001	1106	...	1101	1206	...	...	1201	1306	...	1301	1406	...	1506	...	1501	1606	...	1706	...	1701	1806	...
Den Haag HS a.	...	...	|	1125	...	|	1225	...	...	|	1325	...	|	1425	...	1525	...	|	1625	...	1725	...	|	1825	...
Schiphol ✈ a.	...	...	1027	1151	...	1127	1251	...	...	1227	1351	...	1327	1451	...	1551	...	1527	1651	...	1751	...	1727	1851	...
Amsterdam Centraal a.	...	...	1043	1206	...	1143	1306	...	...	1243	1406	...	1343	1506	...	1606	...	1543	1706	...	1806	...	1743	1906	...

train number	9441	9343	9245	9445	9347	9249	9349	9351	9253	9453	9355	9257	9357	9359	9359	9261	9361	9986/7	9363	9265	9265	9365	9369	9371	
train type	⇌	⇌		⇌	⇌		⇌	⇌		⇌	⇌		⇌	⇌	⇌		⇌	⇌	⇌			⇌	⇌	⇌	
notes			🍷		①–④	🍷	⑧		🍷			🍷		⑧	⑦	🍷	①–⑥	B	⑤⑦	⑥	⑧			⑦	
							g		e			e				e		⊗	g	e					
Paris Nord d.	1501	1525	...	1601	1625	...	1701	1725	...	1801	1825	...	1901	1925	1925	...	2001	...	2025	...	...	2101	2201	2225	...
Brussels Midi / Zuid a.	1623	1647	...	1723	1747	...	1823	1847	...	1923	1947	...	2023	2047	2047	...	2123	2144	2147	...	...	2223	2323	2347	...
Brussels Midi / Zuid d.	...	1650	1718x	...	...	1818x	...	1850	1918x	...	1950	2018x	...	...	2050	2118x	...	|	...	2218	2218x	...	...	...	...
Brussels Nord / Noord d.	...	|	1727x	...	...	1827x	...	|	1927x	...	|	2027x	...	...	|	2127x	...	|	...	2227	2227x	...	...	...	...
Mechelen a.	...	|	1739	...	...	1839	...	|	1939	...	|	2039	...	...	|	2139	...	|	...	2239	2239	...	...	...	...
Antwerpen Centraal a.	...	1729	1757	...	...	1857	...	1929	1957	...	2029	2057	...	...	2129	2157	...	2229	...	2257	2257	...	...	...	...
Roosendaal 🏛 a.	...	|	1828	...	...	1928	...	|	2028	...	|	2128	...	...	|	2228	...	|	...	2328	2328	...	...	...	...
Dordrecht a.	...	|	1853	...	...	1953	...	|	2053	...	|	2153	...	...	|	2253	...	|	...	2353	2353	...	...	...	...
Rotterdam Centraal a.	...	1801	1906	...	...	2006	...	2001	2106	...	2101	2206	...	...	2201	2306	...	2301	...	0006	0006	...	...	...	...
Den Haag HS a.	...	|	1925	...	...	2025	...	|	2125	...	|	2225	...	...	|	2325	...	|	...	0025z	...	...	...	...	...
Schiphol ✈ a.	...	1827	1951	...	...	2051	...	2027	2151	...	2127	2251	...	...	2227	2351	...	2333	...	0049z	...	...	...	...	...
Amsterdam Centraal a.	...	1843	2006	...	...	2106	...	2043	2206	...	2143	2306	...	...	2243	0006	...	2353	...	0106z	...	...	...	...	...

A – THALYS NEIGE – ⑥ Dec. 19, 2009 - Mar. 20, 2010: [12] and 🍷 Amsterdam - Bourg St Maurice; ⑥ Dec. 19, 2009 - Apr. 17, 2010: [12] and 🍷 Brussels - Bourg St Maurice. (Table **9**).

B – THALYS NEIGE – ⑥ Dec. 26, 2010 - Mar. 27: [12] and 🍷 Bourg St Maurice - Amsterdam; ⑥ Dec. 19, 2009 - Apr. 17, 2010: [12] and 🍷 Bourg St Maurice - Brussels. (Table **9**).

C – ②③④⑤⑦ (not Dec. 25).

D – ①⑤⑥⑦.

E – ②③④⑤⑥⑦.

H – ②③④⑦.

b – Not Dec. 26.

c – Not Jan. 1.

e – Not Dec. 31.

f – Also Dec. 25, Jan. 1.

g – Not Dec. 25. Jan. 1.

h – Not Dec. 25, 26, Jan. 1, Apr. 5, May 13, 24.

k – Not Dec. 25, 26, Jan. 1, Apr. 5, 30, May 13, 24.

m – Not Dec. 25.

q – Not Dec. 25, 26, 27, Jan. 1, Apr. 5, 30, May 13, 24.

v – On ①–⑤ (not Dec. 25, Jan. 1, Apr. 5, May 5, 24) not call at Brussels Nord / Noord and arrive Brussels Midi / Zuid 3 minutes earlier.

x – On ①–⑤ (not Dec. 25, Jan. 1, Apr. 5, May 5, 24) depart Brussels Midi / Zuid 3 minutes later and not call at Brussels Nord / Noord.

y – Not ①–⑤ (not Dec. 25, Jan. 1, Apr. 5, May 5, 24).

z – ⑦ (not Dec. 27).

⇌ – *Thalys* high-speed train. R 🍷. Special fares payable.

⊗ – Calls to set down only.

⊕ – Calls to pick up only.

LONDON, PARIS and BRUSSELS - KÖLN, HAMBURG and BERLIN 20

For the full service London - Brussels and v.v. see Table **12**. For Paris - Brussels and v.v. see Table **18**. Connections at Brussels are not guaranteed.

train type	ICE	RE	IC	ICE	IC	RE	⇌	IC	ICE	RE	ICE	⇌	⇌	RE	IC	ICE	IC	ICE	EC	ICE	☆	☆	⇌	IC	ICE	IC
train number	**11**	**11010**	**231**	**857**	**2141**	**10115**	**9407**	**2028**	**614**	**11012**	**557**	**9413**	**9413**	**11014**	**333**	**859**	**2049**	**1641**	**179**	**1026**	**9112**	**9114**	**9421**	**335**	**951**	**2047**
notes	🍷		**331** 🍷	🍷	🍷		①–⑥	🍷	🍷		🍷		⑦		🍷	🍷	🍷	🍴	🍴	**1126** 🍷	🅁🍴 **P**	🅁🍴 ⑥		🍷	🍷	🍷 Ⓑf
London St Pancras .. d.	...	...	...	...	...	...	...	...	...	...	...	...	...	...	...	...	...	...	...	...	0730	0757	...	...	...	...
Ebbsfleet International d.	...	...	...	...	...	...	...	...	...	...	...	...	...	...	...	...	...	...	...	...	|	|	...	...	...	...
Ashford International .. d.	...	...	...	...	...	...	...	...	...	...	...	...	...	...	...	...	...	...	...	...	|	0828	...	...	...	...
Lille Europe .... d.	...	...	...	...	...	...	...	...	...	...	...	...	...	...	...	...	...	...	...	...	|	1033	...	...	...	...
Paris Nord .... d.	...	...	...	...	...	...	0625	...	...	...	...	0801	0801	...	...	...	...	...	...	...	|	|	1001	...	...	...
Brussels Midi/Zuid ... a.	...	...	...	...	...	...	0747	...	...	...	...	0923	0923	...	...	...	...	...	...	...	1028	1108	1123	...	...	...
Brussels Midi/Zuid ... d.	0725	...	...	...	...	...	0755	...	...	...	...	0928	0928	...	...	...	...	...	...	...	—	...	1128	...	...	...
Liège Guillemins .... a.	0812	...	...	...	...	...	0840	...	...	...	...	1011	1011	...	...	...	...	...	...	...	...	...	1211	...	...	...
Liège Guillemins .... d.	0814	...	...	...	...	...	0842	...	...	...	...	—	1013	...	...	...	...	...	...	...	...	...	1213	...	...	...
Aachen 🏛 .... a.	0836	...	...	...	...	...	0905	...	...	...	...	...	1036	...	...	...	...	...	...	...	...	...	1236	...	...	...
Köln Hbf .... a.	0915	...	...	...	...	...	0947	...	...	...	...	...	1115	...	...	...	...	...	...	...	...	...	1315	...	...	...
Köln Hbf .... d.	...	0931	0946	0948	...	0951	—	1010	1010	1031	1048	...	...	1131	1146	1148	...	...	...	1210	...	...	...	1346	1348	...
Wuppertal Hbf .... a.	...	|	|	1014	...	|	...	1041	|	|	1114	...	...	|	|	1214	...	...	...	1241	...	...	...	|	1414	...
Hagen Hbf .... a.	...	|	|	1032	...	|	...	1059	|	|	1132	...	...	|	|	1232	...	...	...	1259	...	...	...	|	1432	...
Düsseldorf Hbf .... a.	...	1000	1009	|	...	1021	...	|	1031	1100	|	...	...	1200	1209	|	...	...	...	|	...	...	...	1409	|	...
Duisburg Hbf .... a.	...	1018	1023	|	...	1037	...	|	1044	1118	|	...	...	1218	1223	|	...	...	...	|	...	...	...	1423	|	...
Oberhausen .... a.	...	1026	1031	|	...	|	...	|	|	1126	|	...	...	1226	1231	|	...	...	...	|	...	...	...	1431	|	...
Essen Hbf .... a.	...	...	|	|	...	1051	...	|	1057	...	|	...	...	...	|	|	...	...	...	|	...	...	...	|	|	...
Bochum Hbf .... a.	...	...	|	|	...	1103	...	|	1109	...	|	...	...	...	|	|	...	...	...	|	...	...	...	|	|	...
Dortmund Hbf .... a.	...	...	|	|	...	1115	...	1121	1121	...	|	...	...	...	|	|	...	...	...	1321	...	...	...	|	|	...
Hamm Hbf .... a.	...	...	|	1102	...	1145	...	|	—	...	1202	...	...	...	|	1302	...	...	...	|	...	...	...	|	1502	...
Bielefeld Hbf .... a.	...	...	|	1135	...	—	...	|	...	...	1236	...	...	...	|	1335	...	...	...	|	...	...	...	|	1535	...
Münster .... a.	...	...	1127	|	...	...	...	1154	*ICE*	...	|	*IC*	...	...	1327	|	...	...	...	1355	*ICE*	...	...	1527	|	...
Osnabrück Hbf ...... a.	...	...	...	|	...	...	...	1221	**237**	...	|	**2039**	...	...	...	|	...	...	...	1421	**37**	...	...	...	|	...
Bremen Hbf .... a.	...	...	...	|	...	...	...	1314	⚡	...	|	🍷	...	...	...	|	...	...	...	1514	⚡	...	...	...	|	...
Hannover Hbf .... a.	...	...	...	1228	1236	...	...	|	**D**	...	1328	1336	...	...	...	1428	1436	...	...	|	**D**	...	...	...	1628	1636
Hamburg Hbf .... a.	...	...	...	|	|	...	...	1412	1525	...	|	|	...	...	...	|	|	...	...	1612	1728	...	...	...	|	|
København H ⊙ a.	...	...	...	|	|	...	...	...	2011	...	|	|	...	...	...	|	|	...	...	...	2211	...	...	...	|	|
Wolfsburg .... a.	...	...	...	1303	|	...	...	...	...	...	|	|	...	...	...	1503	|	...	...	...	...	...	...	...	1703	|
Braunschweig Hbf...... a.	...	...	...	|	1309	*ICE*	...	...	...	...	|	1408	...	...	...	|	1509	...	...	...	...	...	...	...	|	1709
Magdeburg Hbf .... a.	...	...	...	|	1355	**1549**	*EC*	...	...	...	|	1457	...	...	...	|	1555	...	...	...	...	...	...	...	|	1755
Halle Hbf .... a.	...	...	...	|	1451	🍴	**379**	...	...	...	|	1553	...	...	...	|	1651	...	...	...	...	...	...	...	|	1851
Leipzig Hbf .... a.	...	...	...	|	1518	1551	🍴	...	...	...	|	1619	...	...	...	|	1718	1751	...	...	...	...	...	...	|	1918
Berlin Hbf .... a.	...	...	...	1411	...	|	1436	...	...	...	1508	...	...	...	...	1611	...	|	1636	...	...	...	...	...	1811	...
Berlin Ostbahnhof ... a.	...	...	...	1422	...	|	|	...	...	...	1519	...	...	...	...	1622	...	|	|	...	...	...	...	...	1822	...
Dresden Hbf .... a.	...	...	...	...	...	1704	1710**d**	...	...	...	...	...	...	...	...	...	...	1904	1910**d**	...	...	...	...	...	...	...
Bad Schandau 🏛 ... a.	...	...	...	...	...	...	1737	...	...	...	...	...	...	...	...	...	...	...	1937	...	...	...	...	...	...	...
Děčín .... a.	...	...	...	...	...	...	1755	...	...	...	...	...	...	...	...	...	...	...	1955	...	...	...	...	...	...	...
Praha Holešovice . a.	...	...	...	...	...	...	1916	...	...	...	...	...	...	...	...	...	...	...	2116	...	...	...	...	...	...	...
Praha hlavní .... a.	...	...	...	...	...	...	1927	...	...	...	...	...	...	...	...	...	...	...	2127	...	...	...	...	...	...	...

train type	☆	⇌	☆	ICE	RE	ICE	IC	ICE	RE	☆	☆	⇌	RE	ICE	IC	☆	☆	⇌	RE	ICE	IC	EC	⇌	RE	ICE	ICE
train number	**9120**	**9323**	**9116**	**15**	**11020**	**651**	**2133**	**1602**	**10125**	**9126**	**9126**	**9433**	**11024**	**653**	**2135**	**9130**	**9132**	**9441**	**11028**	**655**	**2137**	**6**	**9445**	**11030**	**957**	**514**
notes	🅁🍴 **Q**	🅁🍷	🅁🍴 **R**	🍷		🍷	🍷	🍷 Ⓑf		🅁🍴 ⑥	🅁🍴 **Q**			🍷	🍷	🅁🍴 ⑦c	🅁🍴 **S**			🍷	🍷 Ⓑf	🍷			🍷 Ⓑf	🍷
London St Pancras .. d.	0827	...	0857	...	...	...	...	...	...	1057	1104	...	...	...	...	1157	1257	...	...	...	...	...	...	...	...	...
Ebbsfleet International d.	0845	...	0915	...	...	...	...	...	...	1115	|	...	...	...	...	1215	1315	...	...	...	...	...	...	...	...	...
Ashford International .. d.	|	...	|	...	...	...	...	...	...	|	|	...	...	...	...	|	|	...	...	...	...	...	...	...	...	...
Lille Europe .... d.	1058	...	1128	...	...	...	...	...	...	1330	1330	...	...	...	...	1428	1528	...	...	...	...	...	...	...	...	...
Paris Nord .... d.	|	1025	|	...	...	...	...	...	...	|	|	1301	...	...	...	|	|	1501	...	...	...	...	1601	...	...	...
Brussels Midi/Zuid ... a.	1133	1147	1203	...	...	...	...	...	...	1405	1405	1423	...	...	...	1503	1603	1623	...	...	...	...	1723	...	...	...
Brussels Midi/Zuid ... d.	...	...	...	1225	...	...	...	...	...	—	...	1428	...	...	...	—	...	1628	...	...	...	...	1728	...	...	...
Liège Guillemins .... a.	...	...	...	1312	...	...	...	...	...	...	...	1511	...	...	...	*EC*	...	1711	...	...	...	...	1811	...	...	...
Liège Guillemins .... d.	...	...	...	1314	...	...	...	...	...	*IC*	...	1513	...	...	...	**100**	...	1713	...	...	...	...	1813	...	...	...
Aachen 🏛 .... a.	...	...	...	1336	...	...	...	...	...	**2112**	...	1536	...	...	...	**102**	...	1736	...	...	...	...	1836	...	...	...
Köln Hbf .... a.	...	...	...	1415	...	...	...	...	...	🍷	...	1615	...	...	...	**B**	...	1815	...	...	...	...	1915	...	...	...
Köln Hbf .... d.	...	...	...	...	1431	1448	...	...	1451	1510	...	...	1631	1648	...	1710	...	...	1831	1848	...	1910	...	1931	1948	2010
Wuppertal Hbf .... a.	...	...	...	...	|	1514	...	...	|	|	...	...	|	1714	...	|	...	...	|	1914	...	|	...	|	2014	|
Hagen .... a.	...	...	...	...	|	1532	...	...	|	|	...	...	|	1732	...	|	...	...	|	1932	...	|	...	|	2032	|
Düsseldorf Hbf .... a.	...	...	...	...	1500	|	...	...	1521	1531	...	...	1700	|	...	1731	...	...	1900	|	...	1931	...	2000	|	2031
Duisburg Hbf .... a.	...	...	...	...	1518	|	...	...	1537	1544	...	...	1718	|	...	1744	...	...	1918	|	...	1944	...	2018	|	2044
Oberhausen .... a.	...	...	...	...	1526	|	...	...	|	|	...	...	1726	|	...	|	...	...	1926	|	...	|	...	2026	|	|
Essen Hbf .... a.	...	...	...	...	...	|	...	...	1551	1557	...	...	...	|	...	1757	...	...	...	|	...	1957	...	...	|	2057
Bochum Hbf .... a.	...	...	...	...	...	|	...	...	1603	1609	...	...	...	|	...	1809	...	...	...	|	...	2009	...	...	|	2109
Dortmund Hbf .... a.	...	...	...	...	...	|	...	...	1615	1621	...	...	...	|	...	1821	...	...	...	|	...	2021	...	...	|	2121
Hamm .... a.	...	...	...	...	...	1602	...	...	1640	|	...	...	...	1802	...	|	...	...	...	2002	...	|	...	...	2102	|
Bielefeld .... a.	...	...	...	...	...	1636	...	...	...	|	...	...	...	1836	...	|	...	...	...	2036	...	|	...	...	2135	|
Münster .... a.	...	...	...	...	...	|	...	...	...	1654	...	...	...	|	...	1854	...	...	...	|	...	2054**e**	...	...	|	2156
Osnabrück .... a.	...	...	...	...	...	|	...	...	...	1721	...	...	...	|	...	1921	...	...	...	|	...	2121**e**	...	...	|	2225
Bremen Hbf .... a.	...	...	...	...	...	|	...	...	...	1814	...	...	...	|	...	2014	...	...	...	|	...	2218**e**	...	...	|	2320
Hannover Hbf .... a.	...	...	...	...	...	1728	1736	...	...	|	...	...	...	1928	1936	|	...	...	...	2128	2136	|	...	...	2228	|
Hamburg Hbf .... a.	...	...	...	...	...	|	|	...	...	1912	...	...	...	|	|	2112	...	...	...	|	|	2315**e**	...	...	|	0019
København H ⊙ a.	...	...	...	...	...	|	|	...	...	...	...	...	...	|	|	...	...	...	...	|	|	...	...	...	|	...
Wolfsburg .... a.	...	...	...	...	...	|	|	...	...	...	...	...	...	|	|	...	...	...	...	|	|	...	...	...	2303	...
Braunschweig Hbf ..... a.	...	...	...	...	...	|	1808	...	...	...	...	...	...	|	2008	...	...	...	...	|	2210	...	...	...	|	...
Magdeburg Hbf .... a.	...	...	...	...	...	|	1857	...	...	...	...	...	...	|	2057	...	...	...	...	|	2300	...	...	...	|	...
Halle .... a.	...	...	...	...	...	|	1953	...	...	...	...	...	...	|	2153	...	...	...	...	|	...	...	...	...	|	...
Leipzig Hbf .... a.	...	...	...	...	...	|	2019	2051	...	...	...	...	...	|	2219	...	...	...	...	|	...	...	...	...	|	...
Berlin Hbf .... a.	...	...	...	...	...	1908	...	|	...	...	...	...	...	2108	...	...	...	...	...	2308	...	...	...	...	0016	...
Berlin Ostbahnhof ... a.	...	...	...	...	...	1919	...	|	...	...	...	...	...	2120	...	...	...	...	...	2320	...	...	...	...	...	...
Dresden Hbf .... a.	...	...	...	...	...	...	...	2202	...	...	...	...	...	...	...	...	...	...	...	...	...	...	...	...	...	...
Bad Schandau 🏛 ... a.	...	...	...	...	...	...	...	...	...	...	...	...	...	...	...	...	...	...	...	...	...	...	...	...	...	...
Děčín .... a.	...	...	...	...	...	...	...	...	...	...	...	...	...	...	...	...	...	...	...	...	...	...	...	...	...	...
Praha Holešovice . a.	...	...	...	...	...	...	...	...	...	...	...	...	...	...	...	...	...	...	...	...	...	...	...	...	...	...
Praha hlavní .... a.	...	...	...	...	...	...	...	...	...	...	...	...	...	...	...	...	...	...	...	...	...	...	...	...	...	...

B – (1) (panorama car), (12) and 🍴 Chur - Basel - Köln - Dortmund - Hamburg (- Kiel ⑦ also Apr. 5, May 24; not Apr. 4, May 23).

D – (12) and 🍷 ⚡ Hamburg - København and v.v. (Table **50**).

P – ①–④ (not Dec. 28, Apr. 5, May 3, 24, 31).

Q – ①–⑤ (not Dec. 28, Apr. 5, May 3, 24, 31).

R – ⑥⑦ (also Dec. 28, Apr. 5, May 3, 24, 31).

S – ①–⑥ (not Dec. 28, Jan. 1, Apr. 5, May 3, 24, 31).

c – Also Apr. 5, May 24.

d – Departure time.

e – Ⓑ (Not Dec. 24, 25, 31, Apr. 2, 4, May 23).

f – Not Dec. 24, 25, 31, Apr. 2, 4, May 23.

p – Not Dec. 25, Jan. 1, Apr. 5, May 13, 24.

☆ – Eurostar train. Special fares payable. Minimum check-in time 30 minutes. Not available for London - Ebbsfleet - Ashford or v.v. journeys. Valid Dec. 13, 2009 - July 3, 2010. No service Dec. 25.

⊙ – 🏛 between Hamburg and København is Rødby, see Table **720**.

⇌ – *Thalys* high-speed train. 🅁 🍷. Special fares payable.

⚡ – Supplement payable.

For London - Esbjerg/København by rail and sea via Harwich, see DFDS Seaways Table 2220

20 LONDON, PARIS and BRUSSELS - KÖLN, HAMBURG and BERLIN

For the full service London - Brussels and v.v. see Table **12**. For Paris - Brussels and v.v. see Table **18**. Connections at Brussels are not guaranteed.

train type	☆	⇌	*ICE*	*RE*	*IC*	*ICE*	*IC*	☆	☆	☆	☆	⇌	*RE*	*RE*	*ICE*	*ICE*	*CNL*	*CNL*	*IC*	*IC*	*EC*	☆	☆	*CNL*	*ICE*	*ICE*
train number	**9138**	**9347**	**17**	**11032**	**2339**	**657**	**2318**	**9144**	**9144**	**9144**	**9144**	**9453**	**11034**	**10139**	**24**	**512**	**447**	**447**	**2020**	**2241**	**31**	**9036**	**9038**	**451**	**988**	**672**
notes	🅁✕		🍷	**11042**		🍷	🍷	🅁✕	🅁✕	🅁✕	🅁✕				🍷	🍷	**457**	**482**	🍷	🍷	**TK**	🅁✕	🅁✕	🅁	🍷	
	G				Ⓑp	⑦q	Ⓑ	⑤	⑦g	**H**	**J**						🅁**C**	🅁**E**		**P**		⑥⑦h	**L**	**A**	**P**	
London St Pancras .. d.	1434	...	...	...	...	...	...	1604	1604	1604	1604	...	...	...	...	...	...	...	...	...	...	1532	1602	...	...	...
Ebbsfleet International d.	|	...	...	...	...	...	...	|	|	|	|	...	...	...	...	...	...	...	...	...	...	|	|	...	...	...
Ashford International .. d.	|	...	...	...	...	...	...	|	|	|	|	...	...	...	...	...	...	...	...	...	...	|	|	...	...	...
Lille Europe .... d.	1658	...	...	...	...	...	...	|	|	1828	1832	...	...	...	...	...	...	...	...	...	...	|	|	...	...	...
Paris Nord .... d.	|	1625	...	...	...	...	...	|	|	|	|	1801	...	...	...	...	...	...	...	...	...	1847	1917	2020¶	...	...
Brussels Midi/Zuid ... a.	1733	1747	...	...	...	...	...	1859	1903	1903	1908	1923	...	...	...	...	...	...	...	...	...	▬	...	|	...	...
Brussels Midi/Zuid ... d.	...	...	1825	...	...	...	...	▬	▬	...	...	1928	...	...	...	...	...	...	...	...	...	...	...	|	...	...
Liège Guillemins ...... a.	...	...	1912	...	...	...	...	*ICE*	*ICE*	...	...	2011	...	...	...	...	...	...	...	...	...	...	...	|	...	...
Liège Guillemins ...... d.	...	...	1914	...	...	...	...	**1002**	**502**	...	...	2013	...	...	...	...	...	...	...	...	...	...	...	|	...	...
Aachen 🛃 .... a.	...	...	1936	...	...	...	...	🍷	🍷	...	...	2036	...	...	...	...	...	...	...	...	...	...	...	|	...	...
Köln Hbf .... a.	...	...	2015	...	...	...	...	⑥f	Ⓑp	...	...	2115	...	...	...	...	...	...	...	...	...	...	...	|	...	...
Köln Hbf .... d.	...	...	...	2031	2045	2048	2110	2110	2110	...	...	...	2131	2151	2210	2210	2228	2228	0210	...	...	...	...	|	...	...
Wuppertal Hbf .... a.	...	...	...	|	|	2114	|	|	2141	...	...	...	|	|	2241	|	2314u	2314u	|	...	...	...	...	|	...	...
Hagen Hbf .... a.	...	...	...	|	|	2132	|	|	2159	...	...	...	|	|	2259	|	2332u	2332u	|	...	...	...	...	|	...	...
Düsseldorf Hbf .... a.	...	...	...	2100	2107	|	2131	2131	|	...	...	...	2200	2221	|	2231	|	|	0232	...	...	...	...	|	...	...
Duisburg Hbf .... a.	...	...	...	2118	2128	|	2144	2144	|	...	...	...	2218	2237	|	2244	|	|	0250	...	...	...	...	|	...	...
Oberhausen .... a.	...	...	...	2126	|	|	|	|	|	...	...	...	2226	|	|	|	|	|	|	...	...	...	...	|	...	...
Essen Hbf .... a.	...	...	...	...	2143	|	2157	2157	|	...	...	...	...	2251	|	2257	|	|	0306	...	...	...	...	|	...	...
Bochum Hbf .... a.	...	...	...	...	2154	|	2209	2209	|	...	...	...	...	2303	|	2309	|	|	0316	...	...	...	...	|	...	...
Dortmund Hbf .... a.	...	...	...	...	2207	|	2221	2221	2220	...	...	...	...	2315	2320	2321	2356u	2356u	0329	...	...	...	...	|	...	...
Hamm .... a.	...	...	...	...	...	2202	|	2248	2248	...	...	...	...	2345	...	|	0014u	0014u	|	...	...	...	...	|	...	...
Bielefeld Hbf .... a.	...	...	...	...	...	2236	|	2318	2318	...	...	...	...	...	...	|	0043u	0043u	|	...	...	...	...	|	...	...
Münster .... a.	...	...	...	...	...	|	2254j	|	|	...	...	...	...	...	...	2357	|	|	0415	0538	...	...	...	|	...	...
Osnabrück Hbf ...... a.	...	...	...	...	...	|	...	|	|	...	...	...	...	...	...	...	|	|	0446	0602	...	*ICE*	...	|	...	...
Bremen Hbf .... a.	...	...	...	...	...	|	...	|	|	...	...	...	...	...	...	...	|	|	0552	|	...	**33**	...	|	...	...
Hannover Hbf .... a.	...	...	...	...	...	2328	...	0018	0018	...	...	...	...	...	...	...	|	|	|	0718	...	**K**	...	0702s	0736	0820
Hamburg Hbf .... a.	...	...	...	...	...	|	...	...	...	...	...	...	...	...	...	...	|	**b**	0651	|	0725	0928	...	|	0853	0934
København H ⊙ a.	...	...	...	...	...	|	...	...	...	...	...	...	...	...	...	...	|	0959	...	|	1211	1411	...	|	...	...
Wolfsburg .... a.	...	...	...	...	...	0003	...	...	...	...	...	...	...	...	...	...	|	...	...	0753	...	...	...	|	...	...
Braunschweig Hbf ...... a.	...	...	...	...	...	|	...	...	...	...	...	...	...	...	...	...	|	...	...	|	...	...	...	|	...	...
Magdeburg Hbf .... a.	...	...	...	...	...	|	...	...	...	...	...	...	...	...	...	...	|	...	...	|	...	...	...	|	...	...
Halle Hbf .... a.	...	...	...	...	...	|	...	...	...	...	...	...	...	...	...	...	|	...	...	|	...	...	...	|	...	...
Leipzig Hbf .... a.	...	...	...	...	...	|	...	...	...	...	...	...	...	...	...	...	|	...	...	|	...	...	...	|	...	...
Berlin Hbf .... a.	...	...	...	...	...	0112	...	...	...	...	...	...	...	...	...	...	|	...	...	0920	...	...	...	0859	...	...
Berlin Ostbahnhof ... a.	...	...	...	...	...	0122	...	...	...	...	...	...	...	...	...	...	|	...	...	0930	...	...	...	...	...	...
Dresden Hbf .... a.	...	...	...	...	...	...	...	...	...	...	...	...	...	...	...	...	0707	...	...	...	...	...	...	...	...	...
Bad Schandau 🛃 ... a.	...	...	...	...	...	...	...	...	...	...	...	...	...	...	...	...	0737	...	...	...	...	...	...	...	...	...
Děčín .... a.	...	...	...	...	...	...	...	...	...	...	...	...	...	...	...	...	0755	...	...	...	...	...	...	...	...	...
Praha Holešovice . a.	...	...	...	...	...	...	...	...	...	...	...	...	...	...	...	...	0916	...	...	...	...	...	...	...	...	...
Praha hlavní .... a.	...	...	...	...	...	...	...	...	...	...	...	...	...	...	...	...	0927	...	...	...	...	...	...	...	...	...

train type		*ICE*	*CNL*	☆		*ICE*	*IC*	*CNL*	*CNL*	*RE*	⇌	☆		*ICE*	*IC*	*RE*	*RE*	⇌	☆							
train number		**887**	**450**	**9023**		**32**	**2021**	**483**	**456**	**11003**	**9412**	**9119**		**501**	**2319**	**10104**	**11105**	**9416**	**9181**							
notes		**1087**	🅁	🅁			🍷	**446**	**446**	①–⑤	①–⑥	🅁✕		🍷	🍷				🅁							
			D	✕		**K**		🅁**E**	🅁**C**			**M**			**P**		**P**		✕							
Praha hlavní .... d.	...	...	...	...	...	...	...	...	1831	...	...	...	...	...	...	...	...	...	...	...	...	...	...	...	...	...
Praha Holešovice . d.	...	...	...	...	...	...	...	...	1840	...	...	...	...	...	...	...	...	...	...	...	...	...	...	...	...	...
Děčín .... d.	...	...	...	...	...	...	...	...	2002	...	...	...	...	...	...	...	...	...	...	...	...	...	...	...	...	...
Bad Schandau 🛃 ... d.	...	...	...	...	...	...	...	...	2019	...	...	...	...	...	...	...	...	...	...	...	...	...	...	...	...	...
Dresden Hbf .... d.	...	...	...	...	...	...	...	...	2053	...	...	...	...	...	...	...	...	...	...	...	...	...	...	...	...	...
Berlin Ostbahnhof ... d.	...	...	...	...	...	...	...	...	|	...	...	...	...	...	...	...	...	...	...	...	...	...	...	...	...	...
Berlin Hbf .... d.	...	...	1957	...	...	...	...	...	|	...	...	...	...	...	...	...	...	...	...	...	...	...	...	...	...	...
Leipzig Hbf .... d.	...	...	|	...	...	...	...	...	|	...	...	...	...	...	...	...	...	...	...	...	...	...	...	...	...	...
Halle Hbf .... d.	...	...	|	...	...	...	...	...	|	...	...	...	...	...	...	...	...	...	...	...	...	...	...	...	...	...
Magdeburg Hbf .... d.	...	...	|	...	...	...	...	...	|	...	...	...	...	...	...	...	...	...	...	...	...	...	...	...	...	...
Braunschweig Hbf ..... d.	...	...	|	...	...	...	...	...	|	...	...	...	...	...	...	...	...	...	...	...	...	...	...	...	...	...
Wolfsburg .... d.	...	...	|	...	...	...	...	...	|	...	...	...	...	...	...	...	...	...	...	...	...	...	...	...	...	...
København H ⊙ d.	...	...	|	...	...	1545	...	1853	|	...	...	...	...	...	...	...	...	...	...	...	...	...	...	...	...	...
Hamburg Hbf .... d.	...	2001	|	...	...	2016	2246	**k**	|	...	...	...	...	...	...	...	...	...	...	...	...	...	...	...	...	...
Hannover Hbf .... d.	...	2121	2216	...	...	...	|	|	|	...	...	...	...	...	...	...	...	...	...	...	...	...	...	...	...	...
Bremen Hbf .... d.	...	...	|	...	...	...	2347	|	|	...	...	...	...	...	...	...	...	...	...	...	...	...	...	...	...	...
Osnabrück Hbf ...... d.	...	...	|	...	...	...	0045	|	|	...	...	...	...	...	...	...	...	...	...	...	...	...	...	...	...	...
Münster .... d.	...	...	|	...	...	...	0113	|	|	...	...	...	...	...	0503**c**	...	...	...	...	...	...	...	...	...	...	...
Bielefeld Hbf .... d.	...	...	|	...	...	...	|	0356**s**	0356**s**	...	...	...	...	...	|	...	...	...	...	...	...	...	...	...	...	...
Hamm .... d.	...	...	|	...	...	...	0133	0429**s**	0429**s**	...	...	...	...	...	|	0516	...	...	...	...	...	...	...	...	...	...
Dortmund Hbf .... d.	...	...	|	...	...	...	0152	0450**s**	0450**s**	...	...	...	...	0537	0537	0545	...	...	...	...	...	...	...	...	...	...
Bochum Hbf .... d.	...	...	|	...	...	...	0203	|	|	...	...	...	...	|	0548	0556	...	...	...	...	...	...	...	...	...	...
Essen Hbf .... d.	...	...	|	...	...	...	0214	|	|	...	...	...	...	|	0559	0609	...	...	...	...	...	...	...	...	...	...
Oberhausen .... d.	...	...	|	...	...	...	|	|	|	0534	...	...	...	|	|	|	0634	...	...	...	...	...	...	...	...	...
Duisburg Hbf .... d.	...	...	|	...	...	...	0229	|	|	0542	...	...	...	|	0612	0624	0642	...	...	...	...	...	...	...	...	...
Düsseldorf Hbf .... d.	...	...	|	...	...	...	0247	|	|	0558	...	...	...	|	0627	0640	0658	...	...	...	...	...	...	...	...	...
Hagen Hbf .... d.	...	...	|	...	...	...	|	|	|	|	...	...	...	0557	|	|	|	...	...	...	...	...	...	...	...	...
Wuppertal Hbf .... d.	...	...	|	...	...	...	|	0538**s**	0538**s**	|	...	...	...	0614	|	|	|	...	...	...	...	...	...	...	...	...
Köln Hbf .... a.	...	...	|	...	...	...	0345	0614	0614	0629	...	...	...	0646	0650	0711	0729	...	...	...	...	...	...	...	...	...
Köln Hbf .... d.	...	...	|	...	...	...	...	...	...	...	0645	...	...	...	...	...	...	0745	...	...	...	...	...	...	...	...
Aachen 🛃 .... d.	...	...	|	...	...	...	...	...	...	...	0724	...	...	...	...	...	...	0824	...	...	...	...	...	...	...	...
Liège Guillemins ...... a.	...	...	|	...	...	...	...	...	...	...	0747	...	...	...	...	...	...	0847	...	...	...	...	...	...	...	...
Liège Guillemins ...... d.	...	...	|	...	...	...	...	...	...	...	0749	...	...	...	...	...	...	0849	...	...	...	...	...	...	...	...
Brussels Midi/Zuid ... a.	...	...	|	...	......	...	...	...	...	...	0832	...	...	...	...	...	...	0932	...	...	...	...	...	...	...	...
Brussels Midi/Zuid ... d.	...	...	|	...	...	...	...	...	...	...	0837	0929	...	...	...	...	...	0937	1129	...	...	...	...	...	...	...
Paris Nord .... a.	...	...	0923¶	1113	...	...	...	...	...	...	0959	|	...	...	...	...	...	1059	|	...	...	...	...	...	...	...
Lille Europe .... a.	...	...	...	|	...	...	...	...	...	...	...	1002	...	...	...	...	...	...	1202	...	...	...	...	...	...	...
Ashford International .. a.	...	...	...	|	...	...	...	...	...	...	...	|	...	...	...	...	...	...	|	...	...	...	...	...	...	...
Ebbsfleet International a.	...	...	...	|	...	...	...	...	...	...	...	|	...	...	...	...	...	...	1215	...	...	...	...	...	...	...
London St Pancras .. a.	...	...	...	1229	...	...	...	...	...	...	...	1026	...	...	...	...	...	...	1233	...	...	...	...	...	...	...

NOTES for this page and the following page

A – *City Night Line* PERSEUS ①⑤⑥⑦ (daily Mar. 28 - Oct. 30) – 🛏 1, 2 cl., 🛌 2 cl. (including ladies only berths), (2) (reclining) and ✕ Paris - Metz (depart 2353) - Forbach 🛃 - Saarbrücken (0059) - Göttingen (arrive 0611) - Hannover - Berlin Spandau (arrive 0849) - Berlin Hbf - Berlin Südkreuz (0907). 🅁 Special fares apply.

B – *ICE SPRINTER* – ①–④ Mar. 29 - Dec. 11 (also Dec. 14 – 17; not Apr. 5, May 24), supplement payable.

C – *City Night Line* PHOENIX – 🛏 1, 2 cl., 🛌 2 cl., (2) (reclining) and 🍷 Amsterdam - Köln - Berlin - Dresden - Praha and v.v. 🅁 Special fares apply.

D – *City Night Line* PERSEUS ④⑤⑥⑦ (daily Mar. 28 - Oct. 30) – 🛏 1, 2 cl., 🛌 2 cl. (including ladies only berths), (2) (reclining) and ✕ Berlin Südkreuz (depart 1948) - Berlin Hbf (1957) - Berlin Spandau (2007) - Hannover - Göttingen (2332) - Saarbrücken (arrive 0500) - Forbach 🛃 - Metz (0615) - Paris. 🅁 Special fares apply.

E – *City Night Line* BOREALIS – 🛏 1, 2 cl., 🛌 2 cl., (2) (reclining) and 🍷 Amsterdam - Köln - København and v.v. ✕ Hannover - København and v.v. 🅁 Special fares apply.

G – ⑤⑦ (also Dec. 19, 26, 28, Jan. 2, Apr. 5, May 3, 24, 31).

H – ①–④ (not Dec. 28, Apr. 5, May 3, 24, 31).

J – ⑥ Jan. 4 - July 3.

K – (12) and 🍷 ⁄ Hamburg - København and v.v. (Table **50**).

L – ①–⑤ (not Dec. 28, Jan. 1, Apr. 5, May 3, 24, 31).

M – ①–⑥ (not Dec. 28, Apr. 5, May 3, 24, 31).

P – ①–⑥ (not Dec. 25, 26, Jan. 1, Apr. 3, 5, May 24).

Q – ①–④ (not Dec. 24, 28, 31, Apr. 5, May 3, 24, 31).

S – Dec. 13 - Jan. 10 (not Dec. 24, 31); Mar. 12 - Oct. 24.

T – Dec. 14 - Jan. 11 (not Dec. 25, Jan. 1); Mar. 13 - Oct. 25.

NOTES CONTINUED ON NEXT PAGE →

For København/Esbjerg - London by rail and sea via Harwich, see DFDS Seaways Table 2220

BERLIN, HAMBURG and KÖLN - BRUSSELS, PARIS and LONDON 20

For the full service Brussels - London and v.v. see Table **12**. For Brussels - Paris and v.v. see Table **18**. Connections at Brussels are not guaranteed.

train type	ICE	RE	EC	ICE	⇌	ICE	ICE	RE	IC	⇌	ICE	IC	IC	ICE	RE	⇌	IC	ICE	IC	ICE	IC	ICE	☆	⇌	☆	
train number	25	10106	115	16	9322	515	1094	10112	2005	9428	654	2013	2023	517	11015	9436	2025	1642	2046	952	334	14	9149	9346	9153	
notes	✕		♀	♀		✕	[R] ♀				✕	♀	♀	✕		⑦	♀	♀	2246	✕	♀	♀	[R] ✕		[R]	
							B											P	P				⑧		✕	
Praha hlavní d.	...	...	...	...	...	...	...	...	...	...	...	...	...	...	...	...	...	...	...	...	...	...	...	...	...	...
Praha Holešovice d.	...	...	...	...	...	...	...	...	...	...	...	...	...	...	...	...	...	...	...	...	...	...	...	...	...	...
Děčín d.	...	...	...	...	...	...	...	...	...	...	...	...	...	...	...	...	...	...	...	...	...	...	...	...	...	...
Bad Schandau 🏛 d.	...	...	...	...	...	...	...	...	...	...	...	...	...	...	...	...	...	...	...	...	...	...	...	...	...	...
Dresden Hbf d.	...	...	...	...	...	...	...	...	...	...	...	...	...	...	...	...	...	0649	...	...	...	...	...	...	...	...
Berlin Ostbahnhof d.	...	...	...	...	...	...	...	...	...	...	0640	...	...	...	...	...	...	|	...	0938	...	...	...	...	...	...
Berlin Hauptbahnhof d.	...	...	...	...	...	...	...	...	...	...	0650	...	...	...	...	...	...	|	...	0948	...	...	...	...	...	...
Leipzig Hbf d.	...	...	...	...	...	...	...	...	...	...	|	...	...	...	...	...	...	0807	0840	|	...	...	...	...	...	...
Halle Hbf d.	...	...	...	...	...	...	...	...	...	...	|	...	...	...	...	...	...	▬	0907	|	...	...	...	...	...	...
Magdeburg Hbf d.	...	...	...	...	...	...	...	...	...	...	|	...	...	...	...	...	...	...	1002	|	...	...	...	...	...	...
Braunschweig Hbf d.	...	...	...	...	...	...	...	...	...	...	|	...	...	...	...	...	...	...	1051	|	...	...	...	...	...	...
Wolfsburg d.	...	...	...	...	...	...	...	...	...	...	|	...	...	...	...	...	...	...	|	1055	...	...	...	...	...	...
København H ⊙ d.	...	...	...	...	...	...	...	...	...	...	|	...	...	...	...	...	...	...	|	|	...	...	...	...	...	...
Hamburg Hbf d.	...	...	...	...	...	0538	0612	...	...	...	|	...	0746	...	...	...	0946	...	|	|	...	...	...	...	...	...
Hannover Hbf d.	...	...	...	...	...	|	|	...	...	...	0831	0740	|	...	...	...	|	...	1123	1131	...	...	...	...	...	...
Bremen Hbf d.	...	...	...	...	...	0637	|	...	...	...	|	|	0844	...	...	...	1044	...	...	|	...	...	...	...	...	...
Osnabrück Hbf d.	...	...	...	...	...	0732	|	...	...	...	|	|	0937	...	...	...	1137	...	...	|	...	...	...	...	...	...
Münster d.	...	...	0631	...	...	0801	|	...	0832	...	|	|	1003	...	...	...	1203	ICE	...	|	1232	...	...	...	...	...
Bielefeld Hbf d.	...	...	|	...	...	|	|	...	|	...	0922	0842	|	...	...	...	|	**519**	...	1222	|	...	...	...	...	...
Hamm d.	...	0616	|	...	...	|	|	0816	|	...	0954	0914	|	...	...	...	|	♀	...	1254	|	...	...	...	...	...
Dortmund Hbf d.	0636	0645	|	...	...	0837	|	0845	|	...	|	0952	1036	1037	...	...	1236	1237	...	|	|	...	...	...	...	...
Bochum Hbf d.	|	0656	|	...	...	|	|	0856	|	...	|	1003	|	1048	...	...	|	1248	...	|	|	...	...	...	...	...
Essen Hbf d.	|	0709	|	...	...	|	0853s	0909	|	...	|	1015	|	1059	...	...	|	1259	...	|	|	...	...	...	...	...
Oberhausen d.	|	|	0727	...	...	|	|	|	0928	...	|	|	|	|	1134	...	|	|	...	|	1328	...	...	...	...	...
Duisburg Hbf d.	|	0724	0735	...	...	|	|	0924	0935	...	|	1031	|	1112	1142	...	|	1312	...	|	1335	...	...	...	...	...
Düsseldorf Hbf d.	|	0740	0752	...	...	|	0916s	0940	0949	...	|	1051	|	1127	1158	...	|	1327	...	|	1349	...	...	...	...	...
Hagen Hbf d.	0657	|	|	...	...	0857	|	|	|	...	1024	|	1057	|	|	...	1257	|	...	1324	|	...	...	...	...	...
Wuppertal Hbf d.	0714	|	|	...	...	0914	|	|	|	...	1041	|	1114	|	|	...	1314	|	...	1341	|	...	...	...	...	...
Köln Hbf a.	0746	0811	0815	...	...	0946	0941	1011	1012	...	1109	1115	1146	1149	1229	...	1346	1349	...	1409	1412	...	...	...	...	...
Köln Hbf d.	...	...	...	0843	...	▬	...	...	...	1045	▬	▬	...	...	▬	1244	▬	▬	...	...	...	1443	...	...	...	...
Aachen 🏛 d.	...	...	...	0921	...	☆	...	...	...	1124	☆	☆	...	...	⇌	1324	☆	☆	...	...	...	1521	...	...	...	...
Liège Guillemins a.	...	...	...	0943	...	**9181**	...	...	...	1147	**9137**	**9139**	...	...	**9436**	1347	**9141**	**9145**	...	...	...	1543	...	...	...	...
Liège Guillemins d.	...	...	...	0946	...	[R]	...	...	...	1149	[R] ✕	[R] ✕	...	...	1349	1349	[R] ✕	[R] ✕	...	...	...	1546	...	...	...	...
Brussels Midi/Zuid a.	...	...	...	1035	...	✕	...	...	...	1232	⑥⑦r	L	...	...	1432	1432	⑦g	⑤	...	...	...	1635	...	...	...	...
Brussels Midi/Zuid d.	...	...	...	...	1113	1129	...	...	...	1237	1359	1429	...	...	1437	1437	1459	1559	...	...	...	...	1659	1713	1759	...
Paris Nord a.	...	...	...	...	1235	|	...	...	...	1359	|	|	...	...	1559	1559	|	|	...	...	...	...	|	1835	|	...
Lille Europe a.	...	...	...	...	...	1202	...	...	...	...	1432	1502	...	...	...	...	1532	|	...	...	...	...	1732	...	1832	...
Ashford International a.	...	...	...	...	...	|	...	...	...	...	|	|	...	...	...	...	|	|	...	...	...	...	1733	...	|	...
Ebbsfleet International a.	...	...	...	...	...	1215	...	...	...	...	1445	|	...	...	...	...	|	1645	...	...	...	...	|	...	1845	...
London St Pancras a.	...	...	...	...	...	1233	...	...	...	...	1503	1526	...	...	...	...	1556	1703	...	...	...	...	1805	...	1903	...

train type	IC	IC	ICE	RE	EC	ICE	ICE	IC	IC	ICE	RE	⇌	☆	☆	EC	ICE	ICE	IC	ICE	⇌	ICE	IC	ICE	RE	ICE	⇌
train number	2115	2130	650	11021	178	1640	38	2311	2038	558	11025	9456	9161	9163	176	858	1548	2140	2213	9462	1558	2036	556	11029	10	9366
notes	♀	♀	✕		✕	♀		♀	♀	✕			[R] ✕	[R] ✕	✕	✕	✕	♀	♀	♀	♀	♀	✕		♀	⑦
							K						⑥	Q												
Praha hlavní d.	...	...	...	...	0631	...	...	...	...	...	...	...	...	...	0831	...	...	...	...	...	...	...	...	...	...	...
Praha Holešovice d.	...	...	...	...	0640	...	...	...	...	...	...	...	...	...	0840	...	...	...	...	...	...	...	...	...	...	...
Děčín d.	...	...	...	...	0802	...	...	...	...	...	...	...	...	...	1002	...	...	...	...	...	...	...	...	...	...	...
Bad Schandau 🏛 d.	...	...	...	...	0820	...	...	...	...	...	...	...	...	...	1020	...	...	...	...	...	...	...	...	...	...	...
Dresden Hbf d.	...	...	...	...	0846	0854	...	...	...	...	...	...	...	...	1046	...	1054	...	...	...	1154	...	...	...	...	...
Berlin Ostbahnhof d.	...	...	1040	...	▬	|	...	...	...	1238	...	...	...	...	▬	1338	|	...	...	...	|	...	1440	...	...	...
Berlin Hauptbahnhof d.	...	...	1050	...	...	|	...	...	...	1249	...	...	...	...	...	1348	|	...	...	...	|	...	1450	...	...	...
Leipzig Hbf d.	...	0940	|	...	...	1007	...	...	1140	|	...	...	...	...	...	|	1207	1240	...	...	1307	1340	|	...	...	...
Halle Hbf d.	...	1007	|	...	...	▬	...	...	1207	|	...	...	...	...	...	|	▬	1307	...	...	▬	1407	|	...	...	...
Magdeburg Hbf d.	...	1100	|	...	...	...	...	...	1300	|	...	...	...	...	...	|	...	1402	...	...	...	1500	|	...	...	...
Braunschweig Hbf d.	...	1151	|	...	...	...	...	...	1351	|	...	...	...	...	...	|	...	1451	...	...	...	1551	|	...	...	...
Wolfsburg d.	...	|	|	...	...	...	...	...	|	|	...	...	...	...	...	1455	...	|	...	...	...	|	|	...	...	...
København H ⊙ d.	...	|	|	...	...	...	0745	...	|	|	...	...	...	...	...	|	...	|	...	...	...	|	|	...	...	...
Hamburg Hbf d.	1046	|	|	...	...	...	1216	1246	|	|	...	...	...	...	...	|	...	|	1446	...	...	|	|	...	...	...
Hannover Hbf d.	|	1223	1231	...	...	...	...	|	1423	1431	...	...	...	...	...	1531	...	1540	|	...	...	1623	1631	...	...	...
Bremen Hbf d.	1144	...	|	...	...	...	...	1344	...	|	...	...	...	...	...	|	...	|	1544	...	...	...	|	...	...	...
Osnabrück Hbf d.	1237	...	|	...	...	...	...	1437	...	|	...	...	...	...	...	|	...	|	1637	...	...	...	|	...	...	...
Münster d.	1303	...	|	...	...	...	...	1503	...	|	...	...	...	...	...	|	...	|	1703	...	RE	...	|	...	...	...
Bielefeld Hbf d.	|	...	1322	...	...	...	...	|	...	1522	...	...	...	...	...	1622	...	1642	|	...	**10130**	...	1722	...	...	...
Hamm d.	|	...	1354	...	...	...	...	|	...	1554	...	...	...	...	...	1654	...	1714	|	...	1720	...	1754	...	...	...
Dortmund Hbf d.	1337	...	|	...	...	...	...	1537	...	|	...	...	...	...	...	|	...	1737	1737	...	1745	...	|	...	...	...
Bochum Hbf d.	1348	...	|	...	...	...	...	1548	...	|	...	...	...	...	...	|	RE	|	1748	...	1756	...	|	...	...	...
Essen Hbf d.	1359	...	|	...	...	...	...	1559	...	|	...	...	...	...	...	|	**11027**	|	1759	...	1809	...	|	...	...	...
Oberhausen d.	|	...	|	1434	...	...	...	|	...	|	1634	...	...	...	...	|	1734	|	|	...	|	...	|	1834	...	...
Duisburg Hbf d.	1412	...	|	1442	...	...	...	1612	...	|	1642	...	...	...	...	|	1742	|	1812	...	1824	...	|	1842	...	...
Düsseldorf Hbf d.	1427	...	|	1458	...	...	...	1627	...	|	1658	...	...	...	...	|	1758	|	1827	...	1840	...	|	1858	...	...
Hagen Hbf d.	|	...	1424	|	⇌	...	...	|	...	1624	|	...	...	...	...	1724	|	1757	|	...	|	...	1824	|	...	...
Wuppertal Hbf d.	|	...	1441	|	**9448**	...	...	|	...	1641	|	...	...	...	...	1741	|	1814	|	...	|	...	1841	|	...	...
Köln Hbf a.	1450	...	1509	1529	♀	...	...	1650	...	1709	1729	...	...	...	...	1809	1829	1845	1850	...	1911	...	1909	1929	...	...
Köln Hbf d.	...	...	...	...	1545	...	...	...	...	...	...	1745	...	...	☆	...	...	...	...	1912	...	...	...	...	1943	...
Aachen 🏛 d.	...	...	...	...	1624	☆	...	...	...	...	...	1824	...	...	**9163**	...	...	...	...	1955	...	...	...	...	2021	...
Liège Guillemins a.	...	...	...	...	1647	**9153**	...	...	...	...	...	1847	...	...	[R] ✕	...	...	...	...	2018	...	...	...	...	2043	...
Liège Guillemins d.	...	...	...	...	1649	[R]	...	...	...	...	...	1849	...	...	⑤⑦	...	...	...	...	2020	...	...	...	...	2046	...
Brussels Midi/Zuid a.	...	...	...	...	1732	✕	...	...	...	...	...	1932	...	...	g	...	...	...	...	2103	...	...	...	...	2135	...
Brussels Midi/Zuid d.	...	...	...	...	1737	1759	...	...	...	...	...	1937	1959	2017	2029	...	...	...	...	2113	...	...	...	...	...	2213
Paris Nord a.	...	...	...	...	1859	|	...	...	...	...	...	2059	|	|	|	...	...	...	...	2235	...	...	...	...	...	2335
Lille Europe a.	...	...	...	...	...	1832	...	...	...	...	...	...	2032	2050	2102	...	...	...	...	...	...	...	...	...	...	...
Ashford International a.	...	...	...	...	...	|	...	...	...	...	...	...	|	|	|	...	...	...	...	...	...	...	...	...	...	...
Ebbsfleet International a.	...	...	...	...	...	1845	...	...	...	...	...	...	2045	2115	2115	...	...	...	...	...	...	...	...	...	...	...
London St Pancras a.	...	...	...	...	...	1903	...	...	...	...	...	...	2103	2133	2133	...	...	...	...	...	...	...	...	...	...	...

← **NOTES Continued from previous page**

b – Via Flensburg (0547**s**), Padborg (0600**s**) and Odense (0818**s**).
c – ① (also Apr. 6, May 25; not Apr. 5, May 24).
f – Also Dec. 24, 25, 31, Apr. 2, 4, May 23.
g – Also Dec. 28, Apr. 5, May 3, 24, 31.
h – Also Dec. 28, Jan. 1, Apr. 5, May 3, 24, 31
j – ⑦ (also Apr. 5, May 24; not Apr. 4, May 23).
k – Via Odense (2023**u**), Padborg (2218**u**) and Flensburg (2233**u**).
p – Not Dec. 24, 25, 31, Apr. 2, 4, May 23.
q – Also Apr. 5, May 24; not Apr. 4, May 23.
r – Also Apr. 5, May 24.
s – Stops to set down only.

u – Stops to pick up only.
y – ①–⑥.

☆ – Eurostar train. Special fares payable. Minimum check-in time 30 minutes. Not available for London - Ebbsfleet - Ashford or v.v. journeys. Valid Dec. 13, 2009 - July 3, 2010. No service Dec. 25. See Table **12**.
⇌ – *Thalys* high-speed train. [R] ♀. Special fares payable.
⊙ – 🏛 between Hamburg and København is Rødby (Table **720**).
⁄ – Supplement payable.
¶ – Paris **Est**.

For København/Esbjerg - London by rail and sea via Harwich, see DFDS Seaways Table 2220

21 LONDON and BRUSSELS - FRANKFURT, WIEN and MÜNCHEN

train type	ICE	ICE	ICE	IC	ALX	ICE	RE	ICE	⇌	ICE	EC	ICE	ICE	EC	EC	ICE	⇌	⇌	ICE	ICE	IC	☆	☆	⇌	ICE	ICE
train number	11	11	621	115	353	515	30021	27	9407	623	83	505	595	319	101	27	9413	9413	625	517	2023	9112	9114	9421	123	519
notes	🍷 ①–⑥	🍷 ⑦f	1121 🍷	♣		🍷		🍷 R	①–⑥	923 🍷	♣ P	🍷	🍷	🍷 g	🍷	🍷 R		⑦	🍷	🍷	🍷	🅁✕ A	🅁✕ ⑥		🍷	🍷
London St Pancras d.	...	...	...	...	...	...	...	...	...	...	...	...	...	...	...	...	...	...	...	...	...	0730	0757	...	...	...
Ebbsfleet International d.	...	...	...	...	...	...	...	...	...	...	...	...	...	...	...	...	...	...	...	...	...	|	|	...	...	...
Ashford International d.	...	...	...	...	...	...	...	...	...	...	...	...	...	...	...	...	...	...	...	...	...	|	0828	...	...	...
Lille Europe d.	...	...	...	...	...	...	...	...	...	...	...	...	...	...	...	...	...	...	...	...	...	|	1033	...	...	...
Paris Nord d.	...	...	...	...	...	...	...	...	0625	...	...	...	...	...	...	...	0801	0801	...	...	...	|	|	1001	...	...
Brussels Midi/Zuid a.	...	...	...	...	...	...	...	...	0747	...	...	...	...	...	...	...	0923	0923	...	...	...	1028	1108	1123	...	...
Brussels Midi/Zuid d.	0725	0725	...	...	...	...	...	...	0755	...	...	...	...	...	...	...	0928	0928	...	...	...	▬	...	1128	...	...
Liège Guillemins a.	0812	0812	...	...	...	...	...	...	0840	...	...	...	...	...	...	...	1011	1011	...	...	...	...	...	1211	...	...
Liège Guillemins d.	0814	0814	...	...	...	...	...	...	0842	...	...	...	...	...	...	...	▬	1013	...	...	...	...	...	1213	...	...
Aachen Hbf 🏛 a.	0836	0836	...	...	...	...	...	...	0905	...	...	...	...	...	...	...	...	1036	...	...	...	...	...	1236	...	...
Köln Hbf a.	0915	0915	...	...	...	...	...	...	0947	...	...	...	...	...	...	...	...	1115	...	...	...	...	...	1315	...	...
Köln Hbf d.	0928	0928	...	...	...	0955	...	0953	...	1019	...	1055	...	...	1053	...	...	...	1144x	1155	1153	...	...	...	1328	1355
Bonn Hbf a.	|	|	...	...	...	|	...	1012	...	|	...	|	...	...	1112	...	...	...	|	|	1212	ICE	...	...	|	|
Koblenz Hbf a.	⊖	⊖	...	...	...	⊖	...	1046	...	⊖	...	⊖	...	...	1146	←	...	...	⊖	⊖	1246	629	...	...	⊖	⊖
Mainz Hbf a.	|	|	...	...	...	|	...	1138	...	|	...	|	...	...	1237	1140	🚌	...	|	|	1338	🍷	...	...	|	|
Frankfurt Flughafen ✈ a.	1016	1027	...	...	...	1051	...	→	...	1126	...	1151	...	...	|	1159	1057	...	1234	1251	1359	⑧p	...	...	1416	1451
Frankfurt (Main) Hbf a.	1030	1041	1054	...	...	|	...	▬	...	1141	...	|	...	1220	|	1213	🅁	...	1248	|	1412	1454	...	...	1430	|
Würzburg Hbf a.	...	...	1203	...	...	|	...	...	...	1303	...	|	...	|	|	1331	🍷	...	1403	|	▬	1603	...	...	...	|
Nürnberg Hbf a.	...	...	1259	...	1405	|	...	...	...	1359	...	|	...	|	|	1428	1445	...	1459	|	...	1659	...	...	...	|
Regensburg Hbf a.	...	...	|	...	|	|	...	...	...	|	...	|	...	|	|	1522	|	...	|	|	...	...	...	...	...	|
Praha hlavní **57** a.	...	...	|	...	1858	|	...	...	...	|	...	|	...	|	|	|	1830	...	|	|	...	...	...	...	...	|
Mannheim Hbf a.	...	...	|	...	...	1124	...	...	...	|	...	1224	1230	|	1321	|	▬	...	|	1324	EC	...	...	...	...	1524
Stuttgart Hbf a.	...	...	|	...	...	1208	...	D	...	|	...	...	1308	1354	...	|	...	...	|	1408	189	...	...	...	...	1608
Ulm Hbf a.	...	...	|	...	...	1306	...	1281	...	|	...	...	1406	1453	...	|	...	...	|	1506	✕	...	...	...	...	1706
Augsburg Hbf a.	...	...	|	...	...	1352	...	G	...	|	...	...	1453	1540	...	|	...	...	|	1553	♣	...	...	...	...	1753
München Hbf a.	...	...	1405	1427	...	1433	1446	1511	...	1505	1531	...	1533	1617	...	|	...	...	1605	1633	1731	...	...	...	...	1832
Salzburg a.	...	...	...	1609	...	...	1642	|	...	...	|	...	...	1809	...	|	...	...	...	...	|	...	...	...	...	...
Kufstein 🏛 a.	...	...	...	|	...	...	...	1618	...	...	1633	...	...	...	...	|	...	...	...	...	1833	...	...	...	...	...
Wörgl a.	...	...	...	|	...	...	...	1633	...	...	1644	...	...	...	...	|	...	...	...	...	1844	...	...	...	...	...
Kitzbühel a.	...	...	...	|	...	...	...	1727	...	...	|	...	...	...	...	|	...	...	...	...	|	...	...	...	...	...
Zell am See a.	...	...	...	|	...	...	...	1824	...	...	|	...	...	...	...	|	...	...	...	...	|	...	...	...	...	...
Schwarzach St Veit a.	...	...	...	1709	...	...	...	1854	...	...	|	...	...	...	...	|	...	...	...	...	|	...	...	...	...	...
Innsbruck a.	...	...	...	|	...	...	...	...	...	...	1723	...	...	...	...	|	...	...	...	...	1923	...	...	...	...	...
Bad Gastein a.	...	...	...	1742	...	...	...	...	...	...	...	...	...	...	...	|	...	...	...	...	...	...	...	...	...	...
Villach a.	...	...	...	1843	...	...	...	...	...	...	...	...	...	...	...	|	...	...	...	...	...	...	...	...	...	...
Klagenfurt a.	...	...	...	1916	...	...	...	...	...	...	...	...	...	...	...	|	RJ	...	...	...	...	...	...	...	...	...
Passau 🏛 a.	...	...	...	...	...	...	...	...	...	...	...	...	...	...	...	1627	69	...	...	...	...	...	...	...	...	...
Linz a.	...	...	...	...	...	...	...	...	...	...	...	...	...	...	...	1743	🍷	...	...	...	...	...	...	...	...	...
Wien Westbahnhof a.	...	...	...	...	...	...	...	...	...	...	...	...	...	...	...	1922	1950	...	...	...	...	...	...	...	...	...
Budapest Keleti ▲ a.	...	...	...	...	...	...	...	...	...	...	...	...	...	...	...	...	2249	...	...	...	...	...	...	...	...	...

train type/number	☆	⇌	☆	ICE	ICE	ICE	ICE	ICE	🚌	EC	☆	☆	⇌	ICE	ICE	ICE	TGV	EN	D	☆	☆	⇌	ICE	ICE	ICE	ICE
train number	9120	9323	9120	15	721	509	599	229	1061	391	9126	9126	9433	725	601	691	9575	463	499	9130	9132	9441	729	603	1025	693
notes	🅁✕ C		🅁✕ E	🍷	921 🍷	🍷	🍷	🍷	🅁 🍷	🍷	🅁✕ ⑥	🅁✕ C		🍷	🍷	🍷		B	L	🅁✕ ⑦q	🅁✕ H		🍷	🍷	1125 🍷	🍷
London St Pancras d.	0827	...	0827	...	...	...	...	...	...	...	1057	1104	...	...	...	...	...	...	...	1157	1257	...	...	...	...	...
Ebbsfleet International d.	0845	...	0845	...	...	...	...	...	...	...	1115	|	...	...	...	...	...	...	...	1215	1315	...	...	...	...	...
Ashford International d.	|	...	|	...	...	...	...	...	...	...	|	|	...	...	...	...	...	...	...	|	|	...	...	...	...	...
Lille Europe d.	1058	...	1058	...	...	...	...	...	...	...	1330	1330	...	...	...	...	...	...	...	1428	1528	...	...	...	...	...
Paris Nord d.	|	1025	|	...	...	...	...	...	...	...	|	|	1301	...	...	...	...	...	...	|	|	1501	...	...	...	...
Brussels Midi/Zuid a.	1133	1147	1133	...	...	...	...	...	...	...	1405	1405	1423	...	...	...	...	...	...	1503	1603	1623	...	...	...	...
Brussels Midi/Zuid d.	...	...	...	1225	...	...	...	...	...	...	▬	▬	1428	...	...	...	...	...	...	▬	▬	1628	...	...	...	...
Liège Guillemins a.	...	...	...	1312	...	...	...	...	...	...	...	...	1511	...	...	...	...	...	...	...	...	1711	...	...	...	...
Liège Guillemins d.	...	...	...	1314	...	...	...	...	...	...	...	IC	1513	...	...	...	...	...	...	...	IC	1713	...	...	...	...
Aachen Hbf 🏛 a.	...	...	...	1336	...	...	...	...	...	...	...	2115	1536	...	...	...	...	...	...	...	2311	1736	...	...	...	...
Köln Hbf a.	...	...	...	1415	...	...	...	...	...	...	...	🍷	1615	...	...	...	...	...	...	...	🍷	1815	...	...	...	...
Köln Hbf d.	...	...	...	1420	...	1455	...	...	...	...	...	1453	...	1644x	1655	...	...	...	...	IC	1653	...	1844x	1855	...	...
Bonn Hbf a.	...	...	...	|	...	|	...	...	...	...	...	1512	...	|	|	...	...	...	...	2027	1712	...	|	|	...	...
Koblenz Hbf a.	...	...	...	⊖	...	⊖	...	...	...	...	...	1546	...	⊖	⊖	...	...	...	...	2327	1746	...	⊖	⊖	...	...
Mainz Hbf a.	...	...	...	|	...	|	...	...	...	...	...	1637	...	|	|	...	...	...	...	🍷	1837	...	|	|	...	...
Frankfurt Flughafen ✈ a.	...	...	...	1526	...	1551	...	...	...	...	...	|	...	1734	1751	...	..	..	..	1802	|	...	1934	1951	2002	...
Frankfurt (Main) Hbf a.	...	...	...	1540	1554	|	...	1621	...	1620	...	|	...	1748	|	...	...	...	...	1813	|	...	1948	|	2013	...
Würzburg Hbf a.	...	...	...	...	1703	|	...	1731	...	|	...	|	...	1903	|	...	...	...	...	1931	|	...	2103	|	2128	...
Nürnberg Hbf a.	...	...	...	...	1759	|	...	1828	1845	|	...	|	...	1959	|	...	...	...	...	2028	|	...	2159	|	2224	...
Regensburg Hbf a.	...	...	...	...	|	|	...	1922	|	|	...	|	...	|	|	...	...	...	...	2131	|	...	|	|	...	...
Praha hlavní **57** a.	...	...	...	...	|	|	...	|	2230	|	...	|	...	|	|	...	...	...	...	|	|	...	|	|	...	...
Mannheim Hbf a.	...	...	...	...	|	1624	1630	|	...	|	CNL	1721	...	|	1824	1830	...	...	...	|	1921	...	|	2024	...	2030
Stuttgart Hbf a.	...	...	...	...	|	...	1708	|	...	1754	485	1825	...	|	...	1908	1919	...	...	|	2023	...	|	...	...	2108
Ulm Hbf a.	...	...	...	...	|	...	1806	|	...	1853	363	...	...	|	...	2006j	2014	...	...	|	▬	...	|	...	...	2206
Augsburg Hbf a.	...	...	...	...	|	...	1853	|	...	1940	D	...	...	|	...	2052j	2059	...	...	|	...	...	|	...	...	2253
München Hbf a.	...	...	...	...	1905	...	1933	|	...	2017	2103	...	...	2105	...	2133j	2138	2340	2340	|	...	...	2308	...	...	2333
Salzburg a.	...	...	...	...	...	...	...	|	...	2212	|	...	...	...	...	...	...	0117	0117	|	...	...	...	...	...	...
Kufstein 🏛 a.	...	...	...	...	...	...	...	|	...	...	2207	...	...	...	...	...	...	|	|	|	...	...	...	...	...	...
Wörgl a.	...	...	...	...	...	...	...	|	...	...	2218	...	...	...	...	...	...	|	|	|	...	...	...	...	...	...
Kitzbühel a.	...						...	|	...	...	|	...	...	...	...	...	...	|	|	|	...	...	...	...	...	...
Zell am See a.	...						...	|	...	...	|	...	...	...	...	...	...	|	|	|	...	...	...	...	...	...
Schwarzach St Veit a.	...						...	|	...	...	|	...	...	...	...	...	...	|	0223	|	EN	...	...	...	...	...
Innsbruck a.	...						...	|	...	...	2256	...	...	...	...	...	...	|	|	|	234	...	...	...	...	...
Bad Gastein a.	...						...	|	...	...	...	...	...	...	...	...	...	|	|	|	2	...	...	...	...	...
Villach a.	...						...	|	...	...	...	...	...	...	...	...	...	|	0351	|	0417	...	...	...	...	...
Klagenfurt a.	...						...	|	...	...	...	...	...	...	...	...	...	|	...	|	0438	...	...	...	...	...
Passau 🏛 a.	...						...	2027	...	...	...	...	...	...	...	...	...	|	...	2242	...	...	...	...	...	...
Linz a.	...	...	...	...	...	...	...	2143	...	...	...	...	...	...	...	...	...	0340	...	...	...	...	...	...	...	...
Wien Westbahnhof a.	...	...	...	...	...	...	...	2322	...	...	...	...	...	...	...	...	...	0545h	...	...	...	...	...	...	...	...
Budapest Keleti ▲ a.	...	...	...	...	...	...	...	...	...	...	...	...	...	...	...	...	...	0849	...	...	...	...	...	...	...	...

OTHER TRAIN NAMES:

IC 83	GARDA
R 353	KAREL ČAPEK
R 357	FRANZ KAFKA

A – ①–④ (not Dec. 28, Apr. 5, May 3, 24, 31).
B – KÁLMÁN IMRE – 🛏 1,2 cl., 🛌 2 cl. and [2] München - Wien - Budapest. Conveys Dec. 13 - Jan. 11, June 17 - Sept. 17: 🛏 1,2 cl. München - Wien - Budapest (**375**) - Lökösháza - Bucureşti.
C – ①–⑤ (not Dec. 28, Apr. 5, May 3, 24, 31).
D – *CNL* LUPUS – 🛏 1,2 cl., 🛌 2 cl., [2] (reclining) and ✕ München - Innsbruck - Roma / Venezia. 🅁 Special fares apply (Table **70**).
E – ⑥⑦ (also Dec. 28, Apr. 5, May 3, 24, 31).
G – GROSSGLOCKNER – ⑥ Dec. 19 - Apr. 3 (also Dec. 23): [12] München - Kufstein 🏛 - Wörgl - Zell am See - Schwarzach St Veit.
H – ①–⑥ (not Dec. 28, Jan. 1, Apr. 5, May 3, 24, 31).
L – LISINSKI – 🛏 1,2 cl., 🛌 2 cl. and [2] München - Villach - Zagreb. [2] München - Beograd.
P – [12] and 🍷 München - Innsbruck - Verona (Table **70**).
R – [12] and ✕ Dortmund - Köln - Wien.
f – Also Apr. 5, May 24.
g – To Graz (Table **68**).
h – Wien **Hütteldorf**.
j – ⑧ (not Dec. 24, 25, 31, May 23).
p – Not Dec. 24, 25, 31, Apr. 2, 4, May 23.
q – Also Apr. 5, May 24.
x – Köln **Messe / Deutz** (Table **910**).
♣ – Special 'global' fares payable.
⊖ – Via Köln - Frankfurt high speed line.
▲ – 🏛 is at Hegyeshalom.
TGV – 🅁, supplement payable, 🍷.
⇌ – *Thalys* high-speed train. 🅁 🍷. Special fares payable.
🚌 – **DB / ČD** *ExpressBus*. 🅁 🍷. Rail tickets valid. 1st and 2nd class. 🏛 is Waidhaus (Germany) (Table **57**).
RJ – ÖBB *Railjet* service. [1] (premium class), [1] (first class), [2] (economy class) and 🍷. Classified *EC* in Hungary.
☆ – Eurostar train. Special fares payable. Minimum check-in time 30 minutes. Not available for London - Ebbsfleet - Ashford or v.v. journeys. Valid Dec. 13, 2009 - July 3, 2010. No service Dec. 25.

NOTES continued from Page 59
(on next page) →
r – Also Apr. 5, May 24.
s – Stops to set down only.
u – Stops to pick up only.
x – Köln **Messe / Deutz** (Table **910**).
▲ – 🏛 is at Hegyeshalom.
♣ – Special fares payable.
✣ – Subject to alteration on certain dates.
⇌ – *Thalys* high-speed train. 🅁 🍷. Special fares payable.
☆ – Eurostar train. Special fares payable. Min.check-in time 30 minutes. Not available for London - Ebbsfleet - Ashford or v.v. Valid Dec. 13, 2009 - July 3, 2010. No service Dec. 25.
RJ – ÖBB *Railjet* service. [1] (premium class), [1] (first class), [2] (economy class), 🍷.
⊖ – Via Köln - Frankfurt high speed line.

LONDON and BRUSSELS - FRANKFURT, WIEN and MÜNCHEN 21

train type	☆	⇌	*ICE*	*ICE*	*EN*	☆	*ICE*	*ICE*	*EN*	*RJ*	*CNL*	*IC*	☆	☆	☆	☆	⇌	*ICE*	*IC*	*IC*	*CNL*	*EC*	*EC*		
train number	**9132**	**9445**	**615**	**2029**	**421**	**9138**	**17**	**2029**	**421**	**43**	**459**	**2315**	**9144**	**9144**	**9144**	**9144**	**9453**	**617**	**2315**	**2321**	**419**	**81**	**111**	**13223**	**13221**
notes	🅁✕		🍷	🍷	🅁	🅁✕	🍷	🍷	**491**	🍷	🅁	**2215**	🅁✕	🅁✕	🅁✕	🅁✕		🍷	**2215**	**2121**	**429**	✕♣		🅁	🅁
	M				**B**	**P**			🅁**B**		**A**	🍷	⑤	⑦q	**Q**	**T**			🍷	🍷	**1319** 🅁**F**	**K**		**H** 2	**J** 2
London St Pancras .... d.	1257	...	...	...	...	1434	...	...	...	...	...	...	1604	1604	1604	1604	...	...	...	...	...	...	...	...	...
Ebbsfleet International .. d.	1315	...	...	...	...	|	...	...	...	...	...	...	|	|	|	|	...	...	...	...	...	...	...	...	...
Ashford International .... d.	|	...	...	...	...	|	...	...	...	...	...	...	|	|	|	|	...	...	...	...	...	...	...	...	...
Lille Europe .... d.	1528	...	...	...	...	1658	...	...	...	...	...	...	|	|	1828	1832	...	...	...	...	...	...	...	...	...
Paris Nord .... d.	|	1601	...	...	...	|	...	...	...	...	...	...	|	|	|	|	1801	...	...	...	...	...	...	...	...
Brussels Midi / Zuid .... a.	1603	1723	...	...	...	1733	...	...	...	...	...	...	1859	1903	1903	1908	1923	...	...	...	...	...	...	...	...
Brussels Midi / Zuid .... d.	...	1728	...	...	...	...	1825	...	...	...	...	...	...	...	...	...	1928	...	...	...	...	...	...	1959	2224
Liège Guillemins .... a.	...	1811	...	...	...	...	1912	...	...	...	...	...	...	...	...	...	2011	...	...	...	...	...	...	|	|
Liège Guillemins .... d.	...	1813	...	...	...	...	1914	...	...	...	...	...	...	...	...	...	2013	...	...	...	...	...	...	2120	2347
Aachen Hbf 🛃 .... a.	...	1836	...	...	...	...	1936	...	...	...	...	...	...	...	...	...	2036	...	...	...	...	...	...	|	|
Köln Hbf .... a.	...	1915	...	...	...	...	2015	...	...	...	...	...	...	...	...	...	2115	...	...	...	...	...	...	|	|
Köln Hbf .... d.	...	...	1957	1953	2005	...	2028	...	...	...	...	2053	...	...	...	...	...	2155	...	2153	2346	...	...	|	|
Bonn Hbf .... a.	...	...	|	2012	2034**d**	...	|	...	...	...	...	2112	...	...	...	...	...	|	...	2212	0007**u**	...	...	|	|
Koblenz Hbf .... a.	...	...	⊖	2046	2115**d**	...	⊖	...	...	...	...	2146	...	...	...	...	...	⊖	...	2246	0043**u**	...	...	|	|
Mainz Hbf .... a.	...	...	|	2141	2212**d**	...	|	...	...	...	...	2238	...	...	...	...	...	|	...	2338	|	...	...	|	|
Frankfurt Flughafen ✈ .... a.	...	...	2051	2159	|	...	2116	...	←	...	...	...	...	...	...	...	...	2255	2300	2359	|	...	...	|	|
Frankfurt (Main) Hbf .... a.	...	...	|	2213	2239	...	2130	2218	2321	...	0055**j**	...	...	...	...	...	...	|	2310	0013	|	...	...	|	|
Würzburg Hbf .... a.	...	...	|	2341	→	...	...	2341	|	...	|	...	...	...	...	...	...	|	...	...	|	...	...	|	|
Nürnberg Hbf .... a.	...	...	|	0038	...	...	...	0038	|	...	|	...	...	...	...	...	...	|	...	...	|	...	...	|	|
Regensburg Hbf .... a.	...	...	|	...	...	...	...	...	0427	...	|	...	...	...	...	...	...	|	...	...	|	...	...	|	|
Praha hlavní **57** .... a.	...	...	|	...	...	...	...	...	|	...	1051	...	...	...	...	...	...	|	...	...	|	...	...	|	|
Mannheim Hbf .... a.	...	...	2114	...	...	...	...	...	|	...	...	...	...	...	...	...	...	2337	...	...	|	...	...	|	|
Stuttgart Hbf .... a.	...	...	2208	...	...	...	...	...	|	...	...	...	...	...	...	...	...	0053	...	...	0417	...	...	|	|
Ulm Hbf .... a.	...	...	2306	...	...	...	...	...	|	...	...	...	...	...	...	...	...	...	...	...	0542	...	...	|	|
Augsburg Hbf .... a.	...	...	2353	...	...	...	...	...	|	...	...	...	...	...	...	...	...	...	...	...	0633	...	...	|	|
München Hbf .... a.	...	...	0034	...	...	...	...	...	|	...	...	...	...	...	...	...	...	...	...	...	0712	0731	0827	|	|
Salzburg .... a.	...	...	...	...	...	...	...	...	|	...	...	...	...	...	...	...	...	...	...	...	|	|	1009	|	|
Kufstein 🛃 .... a.	...	...	...	...	...	...	...	...	|	...	...	...	...	...	...	...	...	...	...	...	|	0833	|	0708	1027
Wörgl .... a.	...	...	...	...	...	...	...	...	|	...	...	...	...	...	...	...	...	...	...	...	0941**e**	0844	|	0730	1055
Kitzbühel .... a.	...	...	...	...	...	...	...	...	|	...	...	...	...	...	...	...	...	...	...	...	|	|	|	0804	1129
Zell am See .... a.	...	...	...	...	...	...	...	...	|	...	...	...	...	...	...	...	...	...	...	...	|	|	|	0900	1225
Schwarzach St Veit .... a.	...	...	...	...	...	...	...	...	|	...	...	...	...	...	...	...	...	...	...	...	|	|	1109	...	...
Innsbruck .... a.	...	...	...	...	...	...	...	...	|	...	...	...	...	...	...	...	...	...	...	...	1036**e**	0923	|	...	...
Bad Gastein .... a.	...	...	...	...	...	...	...	...	|	...	...	...	...	...	...	...	...	...	...	...	...	...	1142	...	...
Villach .... a.	...	...	...	...	...	...	...	...	|	...	...	...	...	...	...	...	...	...	...	...	...	...	1243	...	...
Klagenfurt .... a.	...	...	...	...	...	...	...	...	|	...	...	...	...	...	...	...	...	...	...	...	...	...	1316	...	...
Passau 🛃 .... a.	...	...	...	...	...	...	...	...	0532	...	...	...	...	...	...	...	...	...	...	...	...	...	...	...	...
Linz .... a.	...	...	...	...	...	...	...	...	0646	🍷	...	...	...	...	...	...	...	...	...	...	...	...	...	...	...
Wien Westbahnhof .... a.	...	...	...	...	...	...	...	...	0904	0950	...	...	...	...	...	...	...	...	...	...	...	...	...	...	...
Budapest Keleti ▲ .... a.	...	...	...	...	...	...	...	...	...	1249	...	...	...	...	...	...	...	...	...	...	...	...	...	...	...

train type		*EC*	*EC*	*RJ*	*CNL*	*ICE*	⇌	*CNL*	*EN*	*IC*	*ICE*	⇌		*IC*	*ICE*	*ICE*	⇌	*EN*	*ICE*	*ICE*	*ICE*	*ICE*	⇌	☆	☆
train number	**13222**	**110**	**188**	**68**	**418**	**608**	**9412**	**458**	**490**	**2212**	**826**	**9416**	**13220**	**2120**	**616**	**16**	**9322**	**490**	**2028**	**818**	**614**	**820**	**9428**	**9137**	**9139**
notes	🅁	✕	✕	🍷	**428**		①–⑥	🅁	**420**		🍷		🅁	**2320**	✣	🍷		**420**	🍷		🍷	①–⑤		🅁✕	🅁✕
notes	**D**				**1318** 🅁**G**			**A**	🅁**B**				**C**	🍷				🅁**B**				**p**		⑥⑦**r**	**R**
Budapest Keleti ▲ .... d.	...	...	...	1510		...	...	...	...	...	...	...	...	...	...	...	...	...	...	...	...	...	...	...	...
Wien Westbahnhof .. d.	...	...	...	1820	...	...	...	...	1954	...	...	...	...	...	...	...	...	...	...	...	...	...	...	...	...
Linz .... d.	...	...	...	1953	...	...	...	...	2157	...	...	...	...	...	...	...	...	...	...	...	...	...	...	...	...
Passau 🛃 .... d.	...	...	...	|	...	...	...	...	|	...	...	...	...	...	...	...	...	...	...	...	...	...	...	...	...
Klagenfurt .... d.	...	1631	...	|	...	...	...	...	|	...	...	...	...	...	...	...	...	...	...	...	...	...	...	...	...
Villach .... d.	...	1716	...	|	...	...	...	...	|	...	...	...	...	...	...	...	...	...	...	...	...	...	...	...	...
Bad Gastein .... d.	...	1819	...	|	...	...	...	...	|	...	...	...	...	...	...	...	...	...	...	...	...	...	...	...	...
Innsbruck .... d.	...	|	2036	|	1954**f**	...	...	...	|	...	...	...	...	...	...	...	...	...	...	...	...	...	...	...	...
Schwarzach St Veit .... d.	...	1851	|	|	|	...	...	...	|	...	...	...	...	...	...	...	...	...	...	...	...	...	...	...	...
Zell am See .... d.	1726	|	|	|	|	...	...	...	|	...	...	...	2122	...	...	...	...	...	...	...	...	...	...	...	...
Kitzbühel .... d.	1835	|	|	|	|	...	...	...	|	...	...	...	2216	...	...	...	...	...	...	...	...	...	...	...	...
Wörgl .... d.	1926	|	2113	|	2048	...	...	...	|	...	...	...	2304	...	...	...	...	...	...	...	...	...	...	...	...
Kufstein 🛃 .... d.	1938	|	2126	|	|	...	...	...	|	...	...	...	2316	...	...	...	...	...	...	...	...	...	...	...	...
Salzburg .... d.	|	1951	|	2102	|	...	...	...	|	...	...	...	|	...	...	...	...	...	...	...	...	...	...	...	...
München Hbf .... d.	|	2133	2225	2230	2243	...	...	...	|	...	0032**c**	...	|	...	0317	...	...	...	...	...	0523	0551	...	...	...
Augsburg Hbf .... d.	|	...	...	...	2320	...	...	...	|	...	0112**c**	...	|	...	0357	...	...	...	...	...	0604	|	...	...	...
Ulm Hbf .... d.	|	...	...	...	0010	...	...	...	|	...	0202**c**	...	|	...	0440	...	...	...	...	...	0651	|	...	...	...
Stuttgart Hbf .... d.	|	...	...	...	0125	...	...	...	|	...	0305	...	|	...	0551	...	...	...	...	...	0751	|	...	...	...
Mannheim Hbf .... d.	|	...	...	...	|	0224	...	...	|	...	0440	...	|	...	0635	...	...	...	...	...	0835	|	...	...	...
Praha hlavní **57** .... d.	|	...	...	...	|	|	...	1831	|	...	|	...	|	...	|	...	...	...	...	...	|	|	...	...	...
Regensburg Hbf .... d.	|	...	...	...	|	|	...	|	|	...	|	...	|	...	|	...	...	...	...	...	|	|	...	...	...
Nürnberg Hbf .... d.	|	...	...	...	|	|	...	|	|	...	|	...	|	...	|	...	...	...	0530	...	|	0700	...	...	...
Würzburg Hbf .... d.	|	...	...	...	|	|	...	|	|	...	|	...	|	...	|	...	...	←	0626	...	|	0756	...	...	...
Frankfurt (Main) Hbf .. d.	|	...	...	...	|	0315	...	0359**j**	0456	...	0544	...	|	0542	|	0729	...	0615	0742	0816	|	0910	...	...	...
Frankfurt Flughafen ✈ .. d.	|	...	...	...	|	0346	...	▬	→	...	0601	...	|	0558	0709	0743	...	|	0758	0832	0909	0924	...	...	...
Mainz Hbf .... d.	|	...	...	...	|	0408	...	...	...	...	|	...	|	0617	|	|	...	0646**s**	0820	|	|	|	...	...	...
Koblenz Hbf .... d.	|	...	...	...	0446**s**	0503	...	...	...	0606	⊖	...	|	0712	⊖	⊖	...	0744**s**	0912	⊖	⊖	⊖	...	...	...
Bonn Hbf .... d.	|	...	...	...	0519**s**	0544	...	...	...	0644	|	...	|	0744	|	|	...	0817**s**	0944	|	|	|	...	...	...
Köln Hbf .... a.	|	...	...	...	0542	0605	...	...	...	0705	0704**x**	...	|	0805	0805	0832	...	0842	1005	0939	1005	1014**x**	...	...	...
Köln Hbf .... d.	|	...	...	...	...	...	0645	☆	...	...	...	0745	|	...	...	0843	...	▬	...	...	...	...	1045	...	...
Aachen Hbf 🛃 .... d.	|	...	...	...	...	...	0724	**9119**	...	...	...	0824	|	...	...	0921	...	☆	...	...	...	...	1124	...	...
Liège Guillemins .... a.	0532	...	...	...	...	...	0747	🅁	...	...	...	0847	0909	...	...	0943	...	**9181**	...	...	...	...	1147	...	...
Liège Guillemins .... d.	|	...	...	...	...	...	0749	✕	...	...	...	0849	|	...	...	0946	...	🅁	...	...	...	...	1149	...	...
Brussels Midi / Zuid .... a.	0655	...	...	...	...	...	0832	**S**	...	...	...	0932	1033	...	...	1035	...	✕	...	...	...	...	1232	...	...
Brussels Midi / Zuid .... d.	...	...	...	...	...	...	0837	0929	...	...	...	0937	...	...	...	...	1113	1129	...	...	...	...	1237	1359	1429
Paris Nord .... d.	...	...	...	...	...	...	0959	|	...	...	...	1059	...	...	...	...	1235	|	...	...	...	...	1359	|	|
Lille Europe .... a.	...	...	...	...	...	...	...	1002	...	...	...	...	...	...	...	...	...	1202	...	...	...	...	...	1432	1502
Ashford International .... a.	...	...	...	...	...	...	...	|	...	...	...	...	...	...	...	...	...	|	...	...	...	...	...	|	|
Ebbsfleet International . a.	...	...	...	...	...	...	...	|	...	...	...	...	...	...	...	...	...	1215	...	...	...	...	...	1445	|
London St Pancras .... a.	...	...	...	...	...	...	...	1026	...	...	...	...	...	...	...	...	...	1233	...	...	...	...	...	1503	1526

A – *City Night Line* CANOPUS – 🛏 1,2 cl., ▬ 2 cl., (2) (reclining) and 🍷 Zürich - Basel - Frankfurt (Main) **Süd** - Děčín 🛃 - Praha and v.v. 🅁 Special fares apply.

B – 🛏 1, 2 cl., ▬ 2 cl. (4, 6 berth), (2) (reclining) and 🍷: Köln - Frankfurt - Passau 🛃 - Wien and v.v. 🅁 Special fares apply. For international journeys only.

C – TRESKI – Dec. 26, Jan. 2, Feb. 20: ▬ 2 cl. (6 berth), (2) Zell am See - Saalfelden (depart 2134) - St Johann in Tirol (2207) - Kitzbühel - Kirchberg in Tirol (2226) - Wörgl - Verviers (arrive 0841) - Leuven (0959) - Brussels. 🅁 special fares apply.

D – TRESKI – Feb. 20: ▬ 2 cl. (6 berth), (2) Zell am See - Saalfelden (depart 1738) - St Johann in Tirol (1825) - Kitzbühel - Kirchberg in Tirol (1845) - Wörgl - Verviers (arrive 0506) - Leuven (0616) - Brussels - Antwerpen Centraal (0741). 🅁 special fares apply.

F – *City Night Line* POLLUX – ①⑤⑥⑦ (daily Apr. 11 - July 24) also Mar 30, 31, Apr. 1, 6, 7, 8: 🛏 1,2 cl., 🛏 1,2 cl. (T4), ▬ 2 cl. (4, 6 berth), (2) (reclining) 🍷 Amsterdam - Köln - München (- Innsbruck ⑥ Dec. 26 - Apr. 10). 🅁 Special fares apply.

G – *City Night Line* POLLUX – ①⑤⑥⑦ (daily Apr. 11 - July 23) also Mar 30, 31, Apr. 1, 6, 7, 8: 🛏 1,2 cl., 🛏 1,2 cl. (T4), ▬ 2 cl. (4, 6 berth), (2) (reclining) and 🍷 (Innsbruck ⑥ Dec. 26 - Apr. 10 -) München - Amsterdam. 🅁 Special fares apply.

H – TRESKI – Dec. 18, 25, Feb. 12: ▬ 2 cl. (6 berth), and (2) Brussels - Leuven (depart 2030) - Verviers (2144) - Wörgl - Kirchberg in Tirol (arrive 0755) - Kitzbühel - St Johann in Tirol (0813) - Saalfelden (0849) - Zell am See. 🅁 special fares apply.

J – TRESKI – Feb. 12: ▬ 2 cl. (6 berth), (2) Antwerpen Centraal (depart 2111) - Brussels - Leuven (2252) - Verviers (0009) - Wörgl - Kirchberg in Tirol (arrive 1120) - Kitzbühel - St Johann in Tirol (1138) - Saalfelden (1214) - Zell am See. 🅁 special fares apply.

K – VAL GARDENA / GRÖDNERTAL – (12) and ✕ München - Innsbruck - Bolzano / Bozen.

M – ①–⑥ (not Dec. 28, Jan. 1, Apr. 5, May 3, 24, 31).

P – ⑤⑦ (also Dec. 19, 26, 28, Jan. 2, Apr. 5, May 3, 24, 31).

Q – ①–④ (not Dec. 28, Apr. 5, May 3, 24, 31).

R – ①–⑤ (not Dec. 28, Jan. 1, Apr. 5, May 3, 24, 31).

S – ①–⑥ (not Dec. 28, Apr. 5, May 3, 24, 31).

T – ⑥ Jan. 4 - July 3.

c – ① (also Apr. 6, May 25; not Apr. 5, May 24).

d – Departure time.

e – ⑥ Dec. 19 - Apr. 10.

f – ⑥ Dec. 26 - Apr. 10.

j – Frankfurt (Main) **Süd**.

p – Not Dec. 24, 25, 31, Jan. 1, Apr. 2, 5.

q – Also Dec. 28, Apr. 5, May 3, 24, 31.

NOTES continued on foot of previous page 58.

21 MÜNCHEN, WIEN and FRANKFURT - BRUSSELS and LONDON

train type	ICE	D	EN	CNL	ICE	ICE	⇌	⇌	☆	☆	IC	ICE	ICE	ALX	EC	ICE	ICE	☆	⇌	IC	ICE	IC	ICE	⇌	☆
train number	728	498	462	484	612	726	9436	9436	9141	9145	2024	108	610	350	390	722	14	9149	9346	2112	598	2026	508	9448	9153
notes	⊖			358	🍷	①–⑥	⑦		[R] ✕	[R] ✕	🍷	✕	🍷		①–⑥	🍷	🍷	[R] ✕	⑧	🍷	✕	🍷	🍷		[R] ✕
notes		L	K	♣C		f			⑦	⑤					f			⑧							
Budapest Keleti ▲ d.	...	...	2105	...	...	...	...	...	...	...	...	...	...	...	...	...	...	...	...	...	...	...	...	...	...
Wien Westbahnhof d.	...	...	0009h	...	...	...	...	...	...	...	...	...	...	...	...	...	...	...	...	...	...	...	...	...	...
Linz d.	...	...	0201	...	...	...	...	...	...	...	...	...	...	...	...	...	...	...	...	...	...	...	...	...	...
Passau 🛃 d.	...	...	|	...	...	...	...	...	...	...	0718	...	...	...	...	...	...	...	...	...	...	...	...	...	...
Klagenfurt d.	...	...	|	...	...	...	...	...	...	...	|	...	...	...	...	...	...	...	...	...	...	...	...	...	...
Villach d.	...	0146	|	...	...	...	...	...	...	...	|	...	...	...	...	...	...	...	...	...	...	...	...	...	...
Bad Gastein d.	...	|	|	...	...	...	...	...	...	...	|	...	...	...	...	...	...	...	...	...	...	...	...	...	...
Innsbruck d.	...	|	|	0436	...	...	...	...	...	...	|	0736	...	...	...	...	...	...	...	...	...	...	...	...	...
Schwarzach St Veit d.	...	0320	|	|	...	...	...	...	...	...	|	|	...	...	...	...	...	...	...	...	...	...	...	...	...
Zell am See d.	...	|	|	|	...	...	...	...	...	...	|	|	...	...	...	...	...	...	...	...	...	...	...	...	...
Kitzbühel d.	...	|	|	|	...	...	...	...	...	...	|	|	...	...	...	...	...	...	...	...	...	...	...	...	...
Wörgl d.	...	|	|	0518	...	...	...	...	...	...	|	0812	...	...	...	...	...	...	...	...	...	...	...	...	...
Kufstein 🛃 d.	...	|	|	0530	...	...	...	...	...	...	|	0821	...	...	...	...	...	...	...	...	...	...	...	...	...
Salzburg d.	...	0428	0428	|	...	...	...	...	...	...	|	|	...	...	0751	...	...	...	...	...	...	...	...	...	...
München Hbf d.	...	0615	0615	0630	0723	0755	...	...	...	...	|	0916	0923	...	0933	0955	...	...	...	...	1023	...	...	...	...
Augsburg Hbf d.	...	▬	...	...	0803	|	...	...	...	...	|	...	1003	...	...	|	...	...	...	...	1103	...	...	...	...
Ulm Hbf d.	...	...	...	...	0851	|	...	...	...	...	|	...	1051	...	...	|	...	...	...	...	1151	...	...	...	...
Stuttgart Hbf d.	...	...	...	...	0951	|	...	...	...	...	|	...	1151	...	...	|	...	...	...	1137	1251	...	...	...	...
Mannheim Hbf d.	...	...	...	...	1035	|	...	...	...	...	|	...	1235	...	...	|	...	...	...	1239	1329	...	1335	...	...
Praha hlavni **57** d.	...	...	...	...	|	|	...	...	...	...	|	...	|	0504	...	|	...	...	...	|	...	...	|	...	...
Regensburg Hbf d.	...	...	...	...	|	|	...	...	...	...	0827	...	|	|	...	|	...	...	...	|	...	...	|	...	...
Nürnberg Hbf d.	0800	...	...	...	|	0900	...	...	...	...	0928	...	|	0956	...	1100	...	...	...	|	...	...	|	...	...
Würzburg Hbf d.	0856	*ICE*	...	...	|	0956	...	...	...	...	1025	...	|	...	...	1156	...	...	...	|	...	...	|	...	...
Frankfurt (Main) Hbf d.	1010	**1126**	...	...	|	1110	...	...	...	...	1142	...	|	...	...	1305	1329	...	...	|	...	1344	|	...	...
Frankfurt Flughafen ✈ d.	1024	**1026**	...	...	1109	1124	...	...	...	...	1158	...	1309	...	...	...	1343	...	...	|	...	1355	1409	...	...
Mainz Hbf d.	|	1020	...	...	|	|	...	...	...	...	1220	...	|	...	...	...	|	...	...	1320	...	...	|	...	...
Koblenz Hbf d.	⊖	1112	...	...	⊖	⊖	...	...	...	...	1312	...	⊖	...	...	...	⊖	...	...	1412	...	...	⊖	...	...
Bonn Hbf d.	|	1144	...	...	|	|	...	...	...	...	1344	...	|	...	...	...	|	...	...	1444	...	...	|	...	...
Köln Hbf a.	1139	1205	...	...	1205	1212x	...	...	...	...	1405	...	1405	...	...	...	1432	...	...	1505	...	...	1505	...	...
Köln Hbf d.	...	...	...	...	...	...	1244	...	...	...	...	...	...	...	...	...	1443	...	...	...	...	...	...	1545	...
Aachen Hbf 🛃 d.	...	...	...	...	...	...	1324	...	...	...	...	...	...	...	...	...	1521	...	...	...	...	...	...	1624	...
Liège Guillemins a.	...	...	...	...	...	...	1347	...	...	...	...	...	...	...	...	...	1543	...	...	...	...	...	...	1647	...
Liège Guillemins d.	...	...	...	...	...	...	1349	1349	...	...	...	...	...	...	...	...	1546	...	...	...	...	...	...	1649	...
Brussels Midi/Zuid a.	...	...	...	...	...	...	1432	1432	...	...	...	...	...	...	...	...	1635	...	...	...	...	...	...	1732	...
Brussels Midi/Zuid d.	...	...	...	...	...	...	1437	1437	1459	1559	...	...	...	...	...	...	...	1659	1713	...	...	...	...	1737	1759
Paris Nord a.	...	...	...	...	...	...	1559	1559	|	|	...	...	...	...	...	...	...	|	1835	...	...	...	...	1859	|
Lille Europe a.	...	...	...	...	...	...	...	...	1532	|	...	...	...	...	...	...	...	1732	...	...	...	...	...	...	1832
Ashford International a.	...	...	...	...	...	...	...	...	|	|	...	...	...	...	...	...	...	1733	...	...	...	...	...	...	|
Ebbsfleet International a.	...	...	...	...	...	...	...	...	|	1645	...	...	...	...	...	...	...	|	...	...	...	...	...	...	1845
London St Pancras a.	...	...	...	...	...	...	...	...	1556	1703	...	...	...	...	...	...	...	1805	...	...	...	...	...	...	1903

train type	EC	ICE	ICE	🚌	ICE	EC	D	ICE	⇌	EC	ICE	ICE	IC	ALX	RJ	ICE	D	EC	ICE	IC	RJ	ICE	ICE	ICE	⇌
train number	100	596	506	1052	28	318	1280	626	9456	82	516	814	118	354	60	26	1284	114	1090	88	60	622	572	10	9366
notes	102	✕	🍷	[R] 🍷	✕	🍷		🍷		D	🍷	①–⑤	🍷		🍷	✕		🍷	594	♣	🍷	🍷	✕	🍷	⑦
notes						g	G	⑧j		♣		k				R	H		✕						
Budapest Keleti ▲ d.	...	...	...	...	...	...	...	...	...	...	...	...	...	...	0710	...	...	...	...	...	0710	...	...	...	...
Wien Westbahnhof d.	...	...	...	...	0840	...	...	...	...	...	...	...	...	...	1008	1040	...	...	...	...	1020	...	...	...	...
Linz d.	...	...	...	...	1016	...	...	...	...	...	...	...	...	...	▬	1216	...	...	...	...	1153	...	...	...	...
Passau 🛃 d.	...	...	...	...	1129	...	...	...	...	...	...	...	...	...	...	1329	...	...	...	...	|	...	...	...	...
Klagenfurt d.	...	...	...	...	|	...	...	...	...	...	...	...	...	...	...	|	...	0843	...	...	|	...	...	...	...
Villach d.	...	...	...	...	|	...	...	...	...	...	...	...	...	...	...	|	...	0916	...	...	|	...	...	...	...
Bad Gastein d.	...	...	...	...	|	...	...	...	...	...	...	...	...	...	...	|	...	1019	...	...	|	...	...	...	...
Innsbruck d.	...	...	...	...	|	...	...	...	...	1036	...	...	0856	...	...	|	...	|	...	1236	|	...	...	...	...
Schwarzach St Veit d.	...	...	...	...	|	...	...	...	...	|	...	...	|	...	...	|	0950	1051	...	|	|	...	...	...	...
Zell am See d.	...	...	...	...	|	...	0839	...	...	|	...	...	|	...	...	|	1020	|	...	|	|	...	...	...	...
Kitzbühel d.	...	...	...	...	|	...	0931	...	...	|	...	...	|	...	...	|	1112	|	...	|	|	...	...	...	...
Wörgl d.	...	...	...	...	|	...	1023	...	...	1114	...	...	|	...	...	|	1206	|	...	1314	|	...	...	...	...
Kufstein 🛃 d.	...	...	...	...	|	...	1034	...	...	1124	...	...	◐	...	...	|	1220	|	...	1324	|	...	...	...	...
Salzburg d.	...	...	...	...	|	0951	|	...	...	|	...	...	|	...	...	|	|	1151	...	|	1302	...	...	...	...
München Hbf d.	...	1223	...	...	|	1142	1150	1255	...	1225	1323	...	|	...	...	|	1322	1340	1423	1425	1430	1455	...	...	...
Augsburg Hbf d.	...	1303	...	...	|	1217	...	|	...	▬	1403	...	|	...	🚌	|	▬	1417	1503	...	...	|	...	...	...
Ulm Hbf d.	...	1351	...	...	|	1305	...	|	...	...	1451	...	1356	...	**1054**	|	...	1505	1551	...	...	|	...	...	...
Stuttgart Hbf d.	...	1451	...	...	|	1405	...	|	...	...	1551	...	1512	...	[R]	|	...	1610	1651	...	...	|	1727	...	...
Mannheim Hbf d.	1439	1529	1535	...	|	|	...	|	...	...	1635	...	1608	...	🍷	|	...	1656	1731	...	...	|	1806	...	...
Praha hlavní **57** d.	|	...	|	0930	|	|	...	|	...	...	|	...	|	0904	1130	|	...	...	|	...	...	|	|	...	...
Regensburg Hbf d.	|	...	|	|	1232	|	...	|	...	...	|	...	|	1331	|	1433	...	...	|	...	...	|	|	...	...
Nürnberg Hbf d.	|	...	|	1315	1328	|	...	1400	...	...	|	...	|	▬	1515	1528	...	...	|	...	...	1600	|	...	...
Würzburg Hbf d.	|	...	|	...	1427	|	...	1456	...	...	|	...	|	...	...	1627	*EC*	...	|	...	...	1656	|	...	...
Frankfurt (Main) Hbf d.	|	...	|	...	1536	1540	...	1610	...	...	|	1717	|	...	...	1736	**6**	...	1808	...	...	1805	|	1829	...
Frankfurt Flughafen ✈ d.	|	...	1609	...	...	...	...	1624	...	...	1709	1732	|	...	...	...	🍷	...	...	...	...	...	1838	1843	...
Mainz Hbf d.	1520	...	|	...	...	...	...	|	...	...	|	|	1648	...	...	...	1720	...	...	...	...	...	...	|	...
Koblenz Hbf d.	1612	...	⊖	...	...	...	...	⊖	...	...	⊖	⊖	1743	⇌	...	...	1812	...	...	...	...	...	...	⊖	...
Bonn Hbf d.	1644	...	|	...	...	...	...	|	...	...	|	|	1822	**9462**	...	...	1844	...	...	...	...	...	...	|	...
Köln Hbf a.	1705	...	1705	...	...	...	...	1732	...	...	1805	1839	1842	🍷	...	...	1905	...	...	...	...	...	...	1939	...
Köln Hbf d.	...	...	...	...	...	...	...	...	1745	...	▬	▬	...	1912	...	...	...	...	...	...	...	...	...	1943	...
Aachen Hbf 🛃 d.	...	...	...	...	...	...	...	...	1824	☆	☆	☆	...	1955	...	...	...	...	...	...	...	...	...	2021	...
Liège Guillemins a.	...	...	...	...	...	...	...	...	1847	**9161**	**9163**	**9163**	...	2018	...	...	...	...	...	...	...	...	...	2043	...
Liège Guillemins d.	...	...	...	...	...	...	...	...	1849	[R] ✕	[R] ✕	[R] ✕	...	2020	...	...	...	...	...	...	...	...	...	2046	...
Brussels Midi/Zuid a.	...	...	...	...	...	...	...	...	1932	⑥	①–④	⑤⑦	...	2103	...	...	...	...	...	...	...	...	...	2135	...
Brussels Midi/Zuid d.	...	...	...	...	...	...	...	...	1937	1959	2017	2029	...	2113	...	...	...	...	...	...	...	...	...	...	2213
Paris Nord d.	...	...	...	...	...	...	...	...	2059	|	|	|	...	2235	...	...	...	...	...	...	...	...	...	...	2335
Lille Europe a.	...	...	...	...	...	...	...	...	...	2032	2050	2102	...	...	...	...	...	...	...	...	...	...	...	...	...
Ashford International a.	...	...	...	...	...	...	...	...	...	|	|	|	...	...	...	...	...	...	...	...	...	...	...	...	...
Ebbsfleet International a.	...	...	...	...	...	...	...	...	...	2045	2115	2115	...	...	...	...	...	...	...	...	...	...	...	...	...
London St Pancras a.	...	...	...	...	...	...	...	...	...	2103	2133	2133	...	...	...	...	...	...	...	...	...	...	...	...	...

C – *CNL* LUPUS – 🛏 1,2 cl., 🛌 2 cl., [2] (reclining) and ✕ Roma/Venezia - Innsbruck - München. [R] Special fares apply. Table **70**.

D – GARDA – [12] Verona - Innsbruck - München.

G – ⑥ Dec. 26 - Apr. 10 (also Jan. 6): GROSSGLOCKNER – [12] Zell am See - Wörgl - Kufstein 🛃 - München.

H – ⑦ Dec. 20 - Mar. 28 (also Apr. 5): GROSSGLOCKNER – [12] Schwarzach St Veit - Zell am See - Wörgl - Kufstein 🛃 - München.

K – KÁLMÁN IMRE – 🛏 1,2 cl., 🛌 2 cl. and [2] Budapest - Wien - München. Conveys Dec. 13 - Jan. 9, June 15 - Sept. 15: 🛏 1,2 cl. București (**374**) - Budapest (**462**) - München.

L – LISINSKI – 🛏 1,2 cl., 🛌 2 cl. and [2] Zagreb - Villach - München. [2] Beograd - München.

M – LEONARDO DA VINCI – [12] Milano - Verona - Innsbruck - München.

R – [12] and ✕ Wien - Nürnberg - Frankfurt - Köln - Dortmund.

f – Not Dec. 25, 26, Jan. 1, Apr. 3, 5, May 24.

g – From Graz (Table **68**).

h – Wien **Hütteldorf**.

j – Not Dec. 24, 25, 31, Apr. 2, 4, May 23.

k – Not Dec. 24, 25, 31, Jan. 1, Apr. 2, 5, May 24.

🚌 – **DB/ČD** *ExpressBus*. [R] 🍷. Rail tickets valid. 1st and 2nd class. 🛃 is Waidhaus (Germany). (Table **57**).

☆ – Eurostar train. Special fares payable. Minimum check-in time 30 minutes. Not available for London - Ebbsfleet - Ashford or v.v. journeys. Valid Dec. 13, 2009 - July 3, 2010. No service Dec. 25. See Table **12**.

RJ – ÖBB *Railjet* service. [1] (premium class), [1] (first class), [2] (economy class) and 🍷. Classified *EC* in Hungary.

⇌ – *Thalys* high-speed train. [R] 🍷. Special fares payable.

▲ – 🛃 is at Hegyeshalom.

◐ – 🛃 is at Lindau and Bregenz.

♣ – Special 'global' fares payable.

⊖ – Via Köln - Frankfurt high speed line.

OTHER TRAIN NAMES:

R **350** KAREL ČAPEK
R **354** FRANZ KAFKA

AMSTERDAM - HAMBURG and BERLIN 22

train type		IC	IC		IC	IC		IC	IC	ICE		IC	IC		IC	ICE		IC	IC	IC	IC			IC
train number		141	2320		143	2028		245	145	1126		147	2024		149	2026		241	241	2022	241			243
notes	①–⑥	🍷	2120		🍷			⑥q	⑧p	1026		🍷			🍷			⑤⑦y	①–④		⑥q	⑥		🍷
	p	x						🍷	🍷A									🍷	p🍷		🍷			t
Schiphol ✈ ... a.	...	0649	...	...	0849	...	...	1049	1049	...	...	1249	...	...	1449	...	...	1649	1649	...	1649	...	...	1849
Amsterdam Centraal ... d.	0657	|	...	0857	|	...	1057	|	|	...	1257	|	...	1457	|	...	1657	|	|	...	|	...	1857	|
Amsterdam Zuid ... d.	|	0658	...	|	0858	...	|	1058	1058	...	|	1258	...	|	1458	...	|	1658	1658	...	1659	...	|	1858
Duivendrecht ... d.	|	0704	...	|	0904	...	|	1104	1104	...	|	1304	...	|	1504	...	|	1704	1704	...	1704	...	|	1904
Amersfoort ... d.	0731	0737	...	0931	0937	...	1131	1137	1137	...	1331	1337	...	1531	1537	...	1731	1737	1737	...	1737	...	1931	1937
Deventer ... d.	...	0819	...	...	1019	...	...	1219	1219	...	...	1419	...	...	1619	...	...	1819	1819	...	1819	...	▬	2019
Hengelo ... d.	...	0858	...	...	1058	...	...	1258	1258	...	...	1458	...	...	1658	...	...	1858	1858	...	1858	...	*RE*	2058
Bad Bentheim 🏛 ... a.	...	0918	...	...	1118	...	...	1318	1318	...	...	1518	...	...	1718	...	...	1918	1918	...	1918	1957	**14019**	2118
Rheine ... a.	...	0940	...	...	1140	...	...	1340	1340	...	...	1540	...	...	1740	...	...	1940	1940	...	...	2012	⑥	...
Osnabrück ... a.	...	1006	1023	...	1206	1223	...	1406	1406	1423	...	1606	1623	...	1806	1823	...	2006	2006	2023	...	2046	2116	...
Bremen Hbf ... a.	...	|	1114	...	|	1314	...	|	|	1514	...	|	1714	...	|	1914	...	|	|	2114	...	...	|	...
Hamburg Hbf ... a.	...	|	1211	...	|	1412	...	|	|	1612	...	|	1812	...	|	2012	...	|	|	2212	...	...	|	...
Minden ... a.	...	1047	...	...	1247	...	...	1447	1447	...	...	1647	...	...	1847	...	...	2047	2047	...	...	...	2206	...
Hannover Hbf ... a.	...	1118	...	...	1318	...	...	1518	1518	...	...	1718	...	...	1918	...	...	2118	2118	...	...	...	2250	...
Wolfsburg ... a.	...	1153	...	...	1353	...	...	1553	1553	...	...	1753	...	...	1953	...	...	2153	...	...	...	...	...	...
Stendal ... a.	...	1224	...	...	1424	...	...	1624	1624	...	...	1824	...	...	2024	...	...	2224	...	...	...	...	...	...
Berlin Hauptbahnhof ... a.	...	1320	...	...	1520	...	...	1720	1712	...	...	1920	...	...	2120	...	...	2320	...	...	...	...	...	...
Berlin Ostbahnhof ... a.	...	1331	...	...	1531	...	...	1730	|	...	...	1931	...	...	2130	...	...	2330	...	...	...	...	...	...
Szczecin Gł. ... a.	...	...	...	...	...	...	...	...	1933	...	...	...	...	...	...	...	...	...	...	...	...	...	...	...

train type	IC	ICE	IC		IC	IC	IC		ICE	IC	IC		IC	IC		ICE	IC		ICE	IC		IC	IC	
train number	242	515	242		240	2023	240		2025	148	248		2027	146		1125	144		2029	142		2321	140	
notes	⑦		①–⑥				①–⑥			①–⑥	⑦z		2327	🍷		1025	🍷			🍷		2121	🍷	
	🍷		r🍷				🍷e			Ae🍷	🍷												t	
Szczecin Gł. ... d.	...	...	...	...	...	...	...	...	...	0613	...	...	...	...	...	...	...	...	...	...	...	...	...	...
Berlin Ostbahnhof ... d.	...	...	...	...	...	...	0626	...	...	|	0826	...	...	1026	...	...	1226	...	...	1426	...	...	1626	...
Berlin Hauptbahnhof ... d.	...	...	...	...	...	...	0637	...	...	0837	0837	...	...	1037	...	...	1236	...	...	1437	...	...	1637	...
Stendal ... d.	...	...	...	...	...	...	0735	...	...	0935	0935	...	...	1135	...	...	1335	...	...	1535	...	...	1735	...
Wolfsburg ... d.	...	...	...	...	...	...	0805	...	...	1005	1005	...	...	1205	...	...	1405	...	...	1605	...	...	1805	...
Hannover Hbf ... d.	...	...	0640e	...	...	...	0840	...	...	1040	1040	...	...	1240	...	...	1440	...	...	1640	...	...	1840	...
Minden ... d.	...	...	0712e	...	...	...	0912	...	...	1112	1112	...	...	1312	...	...	1512	...	...	1712	...	...	1912	...
Hamburg Hbf ... d.	...	0537	|	...	...	0746	|	...	0946	|	|	...	1146	|	...	1346	|	...	1546	|	...	1746	|	...
Bremen Hbf ... d.	...	0637	|	...	...	0844	|	...	1044	|	|	...	1244	|	...	1444	|	...	1644	|	...	1844	|	...
Osnabrück ... d.	...	0730	0753e	...	...	0935	0953	...	1135	1153	1153	...	1335	1353	...	1535	1553	...	1735	1753	...	1935	1953	...
Rheine ... d.	...	...	0821e	...	...	...	1021	...	...	1221	1221	...	...	1421	...	...	1621	...	...	1821	...	...	2021	...
Bad Bentheim 🏛 ... d.	0844	...	0844	...	1044	...	1044	...	...	1244	1244	...	...	1444	...	...	1644	...	...	1844	...	...	2044	...
Hengelo ... a.	0904	...	0904	...	1104	...	1104	...	...	1304	1304	...	...	1504	...	...	1704	...	...	1904	...	...	2104	...
Deventer ... a.	0941	...	0941	...	1141	...	1141	...	...	1341	1341	...	...	1541	...	...	1741	...	...	1941	...	...	2141	...
Amersfoort ... a.	1022	...	1022	1029	1222	...	1222	1229	...	1422	1422	1429	...	1622	1629	...	1822	1829	...	2022	2029	...	2222	2229
Duivendrecht ... a.	1055	...	1055	|	1255	...	1255	|	...	1455	1455	|	...	1655	|	...	1855	|	...	2055	|	...	2255	|
Amsterdam Zuid ... a.	1102	...	1102	|	1302	...	1302	|	...	1502	1502	|	...	1702	|	...	1902	|	...	2102	|	...	2302	|
Amsterdam Centraal ... a.	|	...	|	1102	|	...	|	1302	...	|	|	1502	...	|	1702	...	|	1902	...	|	2102	...	|	2302
Schiphol ✈ ... a.	1109	...	1109	...	1309	...	1309	...	...	1509	1509	...	...	1709	...	...	1909	...	...	2109	...	...	2309	...

A – (12) and 🍷 Schiphol - Hannover - Berlin - 🏛 Tantow [ticket point] - 🏛 Szczecin Gumience - Szczecin and v.v.
e – Not Dec. 25, 26, Jan. 1, Apr. 3, 5, May 24.
p – Not Dec. 24, 25, 31, Apr. 2, 4, May 23.
q – Also Dec. 24, 25, 31, Apr. 2, 4, May 23.
r – Not Jan. 1.
x – Not Dec. 25, Jan. 1.
t – Not Dec. 24, 31.
y – Also Dec. 23, 30, Apr. 1, 5, May 12, 24; not Dec. 25, Jan. 1, Apr. 2, 4, May 14, 23.
z – Also Dec. 25, 26, Jan. 1, Apr. 3, 5, May 24.

LONDON, PARIS and BRUSSELS - WARSZAWA and MOSKVA 24

train type	☆	☆	☆	☆	⇌	EN	EN	EN	☆	☆	451
train number	9144	9144	9144	9144	9453	447	472	482	9036	9038	443
notes	[R]✕	[R]✕	[R]✕	[R]✕		A	C	E	[R]✕	[R]✕	①⑥
notes	⑤	⑦q	R	S		[R]	[R]	[R]	⑥⑦p	T	P
London St Pancras ... d.	1604	1604	1604	1604	...	...	...	...	1532	1602	...
Ebbsfleet International ... d.	|	|	|	|	...	...	...	...	|	|	...
Lille Europe **12** ... d.	|	|	1828	1832	...	...	...	...	|	|	...
Paris Nord ... d.	|	|	|	|	1801	...	...	...	1847	1917	2020h
Brussels Midi / Zuid ... d.	1859	1903	1903	1908	1928	...	...	...	...	...	|
Liège Guillemins ... d.	...	...	...	...	2013	...	...	...	...	...	|
Aachen 🏛 ... d.	...	...	...	...	2040	...	...	...	...	...	|
Amsterdam Centraal ... d.	...	...	...	...	|	1901	...	...	...	...	|
Köln Hbf ... d.	...	...	...	...	2115	2228	...	...	...	...	|
Dortmund Hbf ... d.	...	...	...	...	...	2356	...	...	...	...	|
Basel SBB ... d.	...	...	...	...	...	|	1804	...	...	...	|
Frankfurt (Main) Süd ... d.	...	...	...	...	...	|	2218	...	...	...	|
München Hbf ... d.	...	...	...	...	...	|	|	1900	...	...	|
Hannover ... d.	...	...	...	...	...	|	|	|	...	...	0713
Berlin Hbf ... a.	...	...	...	...	...	|	|	|	...	...	0859
Berlin Hbf ... d.	...	...	...	...	...	0423	0423	0423	...	...	1515
Berlin Ostbahnhof ... d.	...	...	...	...	...	0447	0447	0447	...	...	1532
Frankfurt (Oder) 🏛 ... d.	...	...	...	...	...	|	|	|	...	...	|
Rzepin ... a.	...	...	...	...	...	0602	0602	0602	...	...	1737
Poznań Gł. ... a.	...	...	...	...	...	0732	0732	0732	...	...	1943
Warszawa Centralna ... a.	...	...	...	...	...	1024	1024	1024	...	...	2255
Warszawa Wschodnia ... a.	...	...	...	...	...	1037	1037	1037	...	...	2307
Warszawa Wschodnia ... d.	...	...	...	...	...	1300	1300	1300	...	...	2353
Terespol ... a.	...	...	...	...	...	1525	1525	1525	...	...	0238
Terespol ... d.	...	...	...	...	...	1555	1555	1555	...	...	0330
Brest 🏛 ... a.	...	...	...	...	...	1741	1741	1741	...	...	0516
Brest 🏛 ... d.	...	...	...	...	...	1950	1950	1950	...	...	0720
Baranavichy ... a.	...	...	...	...	...	2154	2154	2154	...	...	0908
Minsk ... a.	...	...	...	...	...	2345	2345	2345	...	...	1046
Orsha Tsentralnaya ... § a.	...	...	...	...	...	0234	0234	0234	...	...	1332
Smolensk Tsentralny 🏛 ... § a.	...	...	...	...	...	0502	0502	0502	...	...	1601
Vyazma ... a.	...	...	...	...	...	0700	0700	0700	...	...	1745
Moskva Belorusskaya ... a.	...	...	...	...	...	1033	1033	1033	...	...	2035

train type	442	☆	EN	EN	EN	⇌	☆	⇌	☆
train number	450	9023	483	473	446	9412	9119	9416	9181
notes	④⑥	[R]✕	F	D	B	[R]✕	[R]✕	[R]✕	[R]
notes	Q		[R]	[R]	[R]	①–⑥	U		✕
Moskva Belorusskaya ... d.	0800	...	2109	2109	2109	...	...	...	...
Vyazma ... d.	1036	...	0035	0035	0035	...	...	...	...
Smolensk Tsentralny 🏛 § d.	1220	...	0231	0231	0231	...	...	...	...
Orsha Tsentralnaya ... § d.	1250	...	0311	0311	0311	...	...	...	...
Minsk ... d.	1529	...	0619	0619	0619	...	...	...	...
Baranavichy ... d.	1709	...	0804	0804	0804	...	...	...	...
Brest 🏛 ... a.	1855	...	1011	1011	1011	...	...	...	...
Brest 🏛 ... d.	2115	...	1223	1223	1223	...	...	...	...
Terespol ... a.	2033	...	1141	1141	1141	...	...	...	...
Terespol ... d.	2113	...	1248	1248	1248	...	...	...	...
Warszawa Wschodnia ... a.	2338	...	1514	1514	1514	...	...	...	...
Warszawa Wschodnia ... d.	0053	...	1753	1753	1753	...	...	...	...
Warszawa Centralna ... d.	0106	...	1810	1810	1810	...	...	...	...
Poznań Gł. ... d.	0436	...	2118	2118	2118	...	...	...	...
Rzepin ... d.	0627	...	2249	2249	2249	...	...	...	...
Frankfurt (Oder) 🏛 ... d.	|	...	|	|	|	...	...	...	...
Berlin Ostbahnhof ... d.	0823	...	0022	0022	0022	...	...	...	...
Berlin Hbf ... a.	0900	...	0032	0032	0032	...	...	...	...
Berlin Hbf ... d.	1957	...	|	|	|	...	...	...	...
Hannover ... d.	2216	...	|	|	|	...	...	...	...
München Hbf ... a.	|	...	0900	|	|	...	...	...	...
Frankfurt (Main) Süd ... a.	|	...	...	0654	|	...	...	...	...
Basel SBB ... a.	|	...	...	1037	|	...	...	...	...
Dortmund Hbf ... a.	|	...	...	...	0450	...	...	...	...
Köln Hbf ... a.	|	...	...	...	0614	0645	...	0745	...
Amsterdam Centraal ... d.	|	...	...	...	1024	|	...	|	...
Aachen 🏛 ... a.	|	...	...	...	...	0720	...	0820	...
Liège Guillemins ... a.	|	...	...	...	...	0747	...	0847	...
Brussels Midi / Zuid ... a.	|	...	...	...	...	0832	0929	0932	1129
Paris Nord ... a.	0920h	1113	...	...	...	0959	|	1059	|
Lille Europe **12** ... a.	...	|	...	...	...	...	1002	...	1202
Ebbsfleet International ... a.	...	|	...	...	...	...	|	...	1215
London St Pancras ... a.	...	1229	...	...	...	...	1026	...	1233

A – JAN KIEPURA – 🛏 1, 2 cl. Amsterdam (**447**) - Köln - Warszawa (**11013**) - Brest (**12**) - Moskva (journey 2 nights). 🛏 1, 2 cl., ▬ 2 cl. and (2) (reclining) Amsterdam - Warszawa. ✕ Rzepin - Warszawa and Brest - Moskva.

B – JAN KIEPURA – 🛏 1, 2 cl. Moskva (**11**) - Brest (**11014**) - Warszawa (**446**) - Köln - Amsterdam (journey 2 nights). 🛏 1, 2 cl., ▬ 2 cl. and (2) (reclining) Warszawa - Amsterdam. ✕ Moskva - Brest and Warszawa - Rzepin.

C – JAN KIEPURA – 🛏 1, 2 cl. Basel (**472**) - Frankfurt - Fulda (**482**) - Hannover (**447**) - Warszawa - Moskva (journey 2 nights). 🛏 1, 2 cl. Basel - Warszawa - Minsk. ✕ Basel - Fulda and Rzepin - Warszawa.

D – JAN KIEPURA – 🛏 1, 2 cl. Moskva (**11**) - Warszawa (**446**) - Hannover (**483**) - Fulda (**473**) - Frankfurt - Basel (journey 2 nights). 🛏 1, 2 cl. Minsk - Warszawa - Basel. ✕ Warszawa - Rzepin and Fulda - Basel.

E – JAN KIEPURA – 🛏 1, 2 cl. München (**482**) - Nürnberg - Fulda - Hannover (**447**) - Warszawa - Moskva (journey 2 nights). ▬ 2 cl. München - Warszawa. ✕ München - Fulda and Rzepin - Warszawa.

F – JAN KIEPURA – 🛏 1, 2 cl. Moskva (**11**) - Warszawa (**446**) - Hannover (**483**) - Fulda - Nürnberg - München (journey 2 nights). ▬ 2 cl. Warszawa - München. ✕ Warszawa - Rzepin and Fulda - München.

P – ①⑥ (①④⑥ June 3 - Oct. 18) 🛏 1, 2 cl. Paris (**451**) - Berlin (**443**) - Moskva (journey 2 nights with a 6 hour stay in Berlin).

Q – ④⑥ (②④⑥ June 1 - Oct. 16) 🛏 1, 2 cl. Moskva (**442**) - Berlin (**450**) - Paris (journey 2 nights with a 10 hour stay in Berlin).

R – ①–④ Not Dec. 28, Apr. 5, May 3, 24, 31.

S – ⑥ Jan. 4 - July 3.

T – ①–⑤ (not Dec. 28, Jan. 1, Apr. 5, May 3, 24, 31).

U – ①–⑥ (not Dec. 28, Apr. 5, May 3, 24, 31).

h – Paris **Est**.

p – Also Dec. 28, Jan. 1, Apr. 5, May 3, 24, 31.

q – Also Dec. 28, Apr. 5, May 3, 24, 31.

§ – 🏛: Osinovka (BY) / Krasnoye (RU).

⇌ – *Thalys* high-speed train. [R] 🍷. Special fares payable. For additional services see Tables **20**, **21**.

☆ – Eurostar train. Special fares payable. Minimum check-in time 30 minutes. Not available for London - Ebbsfleet - Ashford or v.v. journeys. Valid Dec. 13, 2009 - July 3, 2010. No service Dec. 25.

28 AMSTERDAM - FRANKFURT, WIEN and MÜNCHEN

train type		ICE	ICE		ICE	ICE	ICE	🚌		ICE	ICE	ICE	ICE	🚌		ICE	ICE	ICE		ICE	ICE	ICE		ICE	ICE	
train number		121	515		105	595	27	1057		123	629	519	229	1061		125	723	611		127 327	727	613		129	615	
notes	①–⑥ h	①–⑥ h	🍷		🍷 D	🍷	✕	Ⓡ 🍷		🍷	🍷 Ⓑb	🍷	✕	Ⓡ 🍷		🍷	🍷 Ⓑb	🍷		🍷 F	🍷 Ⓑb	🍷		🍷	🍷	
Amsterdam Centraal d.	...	0704j	...	...	0804g	...	...	...	...	1034x	...	...	...	...	...	1234x	...	...	...	1434x	...	...	...	1634x	...	...
Rotterdam Centraal d.	0635	|	...	0735	|	...	...	...	1005	|	...	...	...	...	1205	|	...	...	1405	|	...	...	1605	|	...	...
Utrecht Centraal d.	0713	0729	...	0813	0829f	...	...	...	1043	1059	...	...	...	...	1243	1259	...	...	1443	1459	...	...	1643	1659	...	...
Arnhem ◐ d.	...	0807	...	...	0907f	...	...	...	▬	1137	...	...	...	...	...	1337	...	...	...	1537	...	...	...	1737	...	...
Oberhausen ◐ a.	...	0858	...	...	0958f	...	...	...	...	1224	...	...	...	...	...	1424	...	...	...	1624	...	...	...	1824	...	...
Duisburg a.	...	0906	...	...	1006f	...	...	...	...	1232	...	...	...	...	...	1432	...	...	...	1632	...	...	...	1832	...	...
Düsseldorf Hbf a.	...	0920	...	...	1020f	...	...	...	...	1246	...	...	...	...	...	1446	...	...	...	1646	...	...	...	1846	...	...
Köln Hbf a.	...	0943t	...	...	1045f	...	...	...	...	1312	...	...	...	...	...	1512	...	...	...	1712	...	...	...	1912	...	...
Köln Hbf d.	...	0945t	...	...	1055	...	...	...	...	1328	...	...	...	...	...	1528	...	...	...	1720z	...	...	...	1920	...	...
Bonn Hbf a.	...	|	...	...	|	...	...	...	...	|	...	...	...	...	...	|	...	...	...	|	...	...	...	|	...	...
Koblenz a.	...	⊖	...	...	⊖	...	...	...	...	⊖	...	...	...	...	...	⊖	...	...	...	⊖	...	...	...	⊖	...	...
Mainz a.	...	|	...	...	|	...	...	...	...	|	...	...	...	...	...	|	...	...	...	|	...	...	...	|	...	...
Frankfurt Flughafen ✈ a.	...	1034	1054	...	1151	...	1202	...	...	1416	...	1454	...	...	...	1616	...	1654	...	1816	...	1854	...	2014	2054	...
Frankfurt (Main) Hbf a.	...	1050	|	...	|	...	1213	...	...	1430	1454	|	1621	...	...	1630	1654	|	...	1830	1854	|	...	2030	|	...
Würzburg a.	...	...	|	...	|	...	1331	...	ALX	...	1603	|	1731	...	...	...	1803	|	...	...	2003	|	...	...	|	...
Nürnberg a.	...	...	|	...	|	...	1428	1445	357	...	1659	|	1828	1845	...	...	1859	|	...	...	2058	|	...	...	|	...
Regensburg a.	...	...	|	...	|	...	1522	|	1839	...	|	|	1922	|	...	...	|	|	...	...	|	|	...	...	|	...
Praha hlavní 58 a.	...	...	|	...	|	...	|	1830	2258	...	|	|	|	2230	...	...	|	|	...	...	|	|	...	...	|	...
Mannheim a.	...	...	1124	...	1224	1231	|	...	...	...	|	1524	|	...	...	...	|	1724	...	...	|	1924	...	...	2124	...
Stuttgart a.	...	...	1208	...	...	1308	|	...	...	...	|	1608	|	...	...	...	|	1808	...	...	|	2008	...	...	2208	...
Ulm a.	...	...	1306	...	...	1406y	|	...	...	...	|	1706	|	...	...	...	|	1906	...	...	|	2106	...	...	2306	...
Augsburg a.	...	...	1352	...	...	1453y	|	...	...	...	|	1753	|	...	...	...	|	1953	...	...	|	2153	...	...	2353	...
München Hbf a.	...	...	1433	...	...	1533y	|	...	...	...	1805	1832	|	...	...	...	2005	2033	...	...	2205	2233	...	...	0034	...
Passau 🏛 a.	...	...	...	...	...	...	1627	...	...	...	...	...	2027	...	...	...	...	...	...	...	...	...	...	...	...	...
Linz a.	...	...	...	...	...	...	1743	...	...	...	...	...	2143	...	...	...	...	...	...	...	...	...	...	...	...	...
Wien Westbahnhof a.	...	...	...	...	...	...	1922	...	...	...	...	...	2322	...	...	...	...	...	...	...	...	...	...	...	...	...

train type	EN	ICE	EN	CNL		CNL	CNL	RJ	ICE	
train number	421	227	421 491	459		447 457	419	61	329	
notes	A	🍷	A	P		Ⓡ K	Ⓡ 🍷 B	🍷	🍷 S	
Amsterdam Centraal d.	...	1834x	...	...	...	1901x	2031	...	2104	...
Rotterdam Centraal d.	...	*1805*	...	...	1820	|	*1950*	...	*2035*	...
Utrecht Centraal d.	...	1859	...	...	1858	1929	2101	...	2132	...
Arnhem ◐ d.	...	1937	...	...	...	2007	2137	...	2207	...
Oberhausen ◐ a.	...	2024	...	...	...	2139d	2248d	...	2256	...
Duisburg a.	...	2032	...	...	...	2147d	2256d	...	2304	...
Düsseldorf Hbf a.	1935	2046	...	...	...	2202d	2312d	...	2318	...
Köln Hbf a.	2002	2112	...	...	...	|	|	...	2343	...
Köln Hbf d.	2005	2120	...	...	...	2228	2346	...	...	...
Bonn Hbf a.	2034d	|	...	...	...	|	0007d	...	...	...
Koblenz a.	2115d	⊖	...	...	...	|	0043d	...	...	...
Mainz a.	2212d	|	...	...	...	|	|	...	...	...
Frankfurt Flughafen ✈ a.	|	2214	←	...	...	|	|	...	...	...
Frankfurt (Main) Hbf a.	2239	2230	2321	0055k	...	|	|	...	...	...
Würzburg a.	→	...	|	|	...	|	|	...	...	...
Nürnberg a.	...	...	0212	|	...	|	|	...	...	...
Regensburg a.	...	...	0427	|	...	|	|	...	...	...
Praha hlavní 58 a.	...	...	|	1051	...	0927	|	...	...	...
Mannheim a.	...	...	|	...	...	...	|	...	...	...
Stuttgart a.	...	...	|	...	...	...	0417	...	...	...
Ulm a.	...	...	|	...	...	...	0542	...	...	...
Augsburg a.	...	...	|	...	...	...	0633	...	...	...
München Hbf a.	...	...	|	...	...	...	0716	0727	...	...
Passau 🏛 a.	...	...	0532	...	...	...	...	|	...	...
Linz a.	...	...	0646	...	...	...	...	1007	...	...
Wien Westbahnhof a.	...	...	0904	...	...	...	...	1140	...	...

train type	CNL	ICE	ICE	ICE	ICE	ICE	ICE	RE	ICE	ICE	ICE
train number	458	328	616	226	614	820	128	4242	612	726	126
notes	P	E	🍷 ❖	🍷	🍷	①–⑤ c	🍷		🍷	①–⑥ e	🍷 F
Wien Westbahnhof d.	...	...	...	...	...	...	...	...	...	...	...
Linz d.	...	...	...	...	...	...	...	...	...	...	...
Passau 🏛 d.	...	...	...	...	...	...	...	0549	...	...	...
München Hbf d.	...	...	0317	...	0523	0551	...	|	0723	0755	...
Augsburg d.	...	...	0357	...	0604	|	...	|	0803	|	...
Ulm d.	...	...	0440	...	0651	|	...	|	0851	|	...
Stuttgart d.	...	...	0551	...	0751	|	...	|	0951	|	...
Mannheim d.	...	...	0635	...	0835	|	...	|	1035	|	...
Praha hlavní 57 d.	1831	...	|	...	|	|	...	|	|	|	...
Regensburg d.	|	...	|	...	|	*0541*	...	0720	|	|	...
Nürnberg d.	|	...	|	...	|	0700	...	0825	|	0900	...
Würzburg d.	|	...	|	...	|	0756	...	▬	|	0956	...
Frankfurt (Main) Hbf d.	0359k	0510	|	0729	|	0905	0929	...	|	1105	1129
Frankfurt Flughafen ✈ d.	...	0524	0709	0743	0906	...	0943	...	1106	...	1143
Mainz d.	...	|	|	|	▬	...	|	...	...	...	|
Koblenz d.	...	|	⊖	⊖	...	...	⊖	...	...	...	⊖
Bonn Hbf d.	...	|	|	|	...	...	|	...	...	...	|
Köln Hbf a.	...	0639	0805	0832	...	...	1032	...	...	...	1232
Köln Hbf d.	...	0646	▬	0846	...	...	1046	...	...	...	1246
Düsseldorf Hbf d.	...	0713	...	0913	...	...	1113	...	...	...	1314
Duisburg d.	...	0726	...	0926	...	...	1126	...	...	...	1328
Oberhausen ◐ d.	...	0735	...	0935	...	...	1135	...	...	...	1335
Arnhem ◐ a.	...	0823	...	1024	...	...	1224	...	...	...	1424
Utrecht Centraal a.	...	0858	0917	1058	1117	...	1258	1317	...	...	1458
Rotterdam Centraal a.	...	|	0955	|	1155	...	|	1355	...	...	*1555*
Amsterdam Centraal a.	...	0925	...	1125x	...	...	1325x	...	...	...	1525x

train type	IC	ICE	ALX	ICE	ICE	EC	🚌	ICE	ICE	ICE	ICE	ALX	🚌	ICE	ICE	ICE	ICE	ICE	ICE	RJ	CNL	CNL	ICE	EN	ICE	
train number	2024	610	350	722	124	100 102	1052	28	596	626 1226	122	354	1054	26	1090 594	104	514	620 926 1220	120	68	418	456 446	616	490 420	226	
notes	🍷	🍷		🍷	🍷	🍷	Ⓡ 🍷	🍷	🍷	🍷	🍷		Ⓡ 🍷	🍷	🍷	🍷 D	🍷		R	🍷	🍷 C	Ⓡ K	🍷 ❖	A	🍷	
Wien Westbahnhof d.	...	...	...	...	...	...	...	0840	...	...	...	...	...	1040	...	...	...	...	...	1820	...	...	...	1954	...	...
Linz d.	...	...	...	...	...	...	...	1016	...	...	...	...	...	1216	...	...	...	...	...	1953	...	...	...	2157	...	...
Passau 🏛 d.	0718	...	...	...	...	...	...	1129	...	...	...	...	...	1329	...	...	...	...	...	|	...	...	...	2306	...	...
München Hbf d.	|	0923	...	0955	...	...	...	|	1223y	1255	...	...	...	|	1423	...	1523	1555	...	2230	2243	...	0317	|	...	...
Augsburg d.	|	1003	...	|	...	...	...	|	1303y	|	...	...	...	|	1503	...	1603	|	...	▬	2320	...	0357	|	...	...
Ulm d.	|	1051	...	|	...	...	...	|	1351y	|	...	...	...	|	1551	...	1651	|	...	...	0010	...	0440	|	...	...
Stuttgart d.	|	1151	...	|	...	...	...	|	1451	|	...	...	...	|	1651	...	1751	|	...	...	0125	...	0551	|	...	...
Mannheim d.	|	1235	...	|	...	1439	...	|	1531	|	...	...	...	|	1729	1735	1835	|	...	...	|	...	0635	|	...	...
Praha hlavní 58 d.	|	|	0504	|	...	|	0930	|	|	|	...	0904	1130	|	...	|	|	|	...	...	|	1831	|	|	...	...
Regensburg d.	0827	|	|	*0919*	...	|	|	1232	|	|	...	1331	|	1433	...	|	|	|	...	...	|	|	|	0014	...	...
Nürnberg d.	0928	|	0956	1100	...	|	1315	1328	|	1400	...	▬	1515	1528	...	|	|	1700	...	...	|	|	|	0240	...	...
Würzburg d.	1025	|	...	1156	...	|	...	1427	|	1456	...	...	...	1627	...	|	|	1756	...	...	|	|	|	|	...	...
Frankfurt (Main) Hbf d.	1142	|	...	1305	1329	|	...	1536	1608	1605	1629	...	...	1742	...	|	|	1905	1929	...	|	|	|	0456a	0729	...
Frankfurt Flughafen ✈ d.	1158	1306	...	...	1343	|	...	...	...	...	1643	...	...	1755	...	1809	1906	...	1943	...	|	|	0709	|	0743	...
Mainz d.	1220	...	...	...	|	1520	...	...	...	...	|	...	...	...	...	|	▬	...	|	...	|	|	|	0646a	|	...
Koblenz d.	1312	...	...	...	⊖	1612	...	...	...	...	⊖	...	...	...	...	⊖	...	...	⊖	...	0446a	|	⊖	0744a	⊖	...
Bonn Hbf d.	1344	...	...	...	|	1644	...	...	...	...	|	...	...	...	...	|	...	...	|	...	0519a	|	|	0817a	|	...
Köln Hbf a.	1405	...	...	...	1432	1705	...	...	...	...	1739	...	...	...	...	1905	...	...	2039	...	0542a	0614a	0805	0842	0832	...
Köln Hbf d.	...	...	...	...	1446	▬	...	...	...	...	1746	...	...	...	...	1917p	...	...	2046	...	|	|	...	0845	0846	...
Düsseldorf Hbf d.	...	...	...	...	1514	...	...	...	...	...	1813	...	...	...	...	1940p	...	...	2113	...	0608a	0654a	...	0911	0913	...
Duisburg d.	...	...	...	...	1528	...	...	...	...	...	1826	...	...	...	...	1953p	...	...	2126	...	0628a	0715a	...	...	0926	...
Oberhausen ◐ d.	...	...	...	...	1535	...	...	...	...	...	1835	...	...	...	...	2000p	...	...	2135	...	0637a	0737a	...	...	0935	...
Arnhem ◐ a.	...	...	...	...	1624	...	...	...	...	...	1924	...	...	...	...	2053p	...	...	2224	...	0753	0924	...	...	1024	...
Utrecht Centraal a.	...	...	...	...	1658	1717	...	...	...	...	1958	2017	...	...	...	2128p	2147	...	2258	2317	0828	0959	...	...	1058	1117
Rotterdam Centraal a.	...	...	...	...	|	1755	...	...	...	...	|	2055	...	...	...	|	2225	...	|	2355	|	|	...	...	|	1155
Amsterdam Centraal a.	...	...	...	...	1725x	...	...	...	...	...	2025x	...	...	...	...	2155p	...	...	2325x	...	0903x	1029x	...	...	1125x	...

A – 🛏 1, 2 cl., ▬ 2 cl. (4, 6 berth), [2] (reclining) and 🍷: (Dortmund ①–④ Dec. 13 - July 22) - Köln - Frankfurt - Passau 🏛 - Wien and v.v. Ⓡ Special fares apply. For international journeys only.
B – *City Night Line* POLLUX – ①⑤⑥⑦ (daily Apr. 11 - July 24) also Mar 30, 31, Apr. 1, 6, 7, 8: 🛏 1,2 cl., 🛏 1, 2 cl. (T4), ▬ 2 cl. (4, 6 berth), [2] (reclining) 🍷 Amsterdam - Köln - München - (- Innsbruck ⑥ Dec. 26 - Apr. 10, arrive 1036). Ⓡ Special fares apply.
C – *City Night Line* POLLUX – ①⑤⑥⑦ (daily Apr. 11 - July 23) also Mar 30, 31, Apr. 1, 6, 7, 8: 🛏 1,2 cl., 🛏 1, 2 cl. (T4), ▬ 2 cl. (4, 6 berth), [2] (reclining) and 🍷 (Innsbruck ⑥ Dec. 26 - Apr. 10, depart 1954 -) München - Amsterdam. Ⓡ Special fares apply.
D – [12] and 🍷 Amsterdam - Mannheim - Basel and v.v.
E – ①–④ (not Dec. 24, Apr. 5, May 24).
F – Mar. 26 - Nov. 7.
K – *City Night Line* PHOENIX – 🛏 1, 2 cl., ▬ 2 cl., [2] (reclining) and 🍷 Amsterdam - Köln - Berlin - Dresden - Praha and v.v. Ⓡ Special fares apply.
P – *City Night Line* CANOPUS – 🛏 1, 2 cl., ▬ 2 cl., [2] (reclining) and 🍷: Zürich - Basel - Frankfurt (Main) **Süd** - Děčín 🏛 - Praha and v.v. ✕ Basel - Frankfurt and v.v. Ⓡ Special fares apply.
R – ④⑤⑦ (also Dec. 23, Apr. 5, May 12, 24, June 2; not Dec. 24, 25, 31, Apr. 2, 4, May 23).
S – ⑦ (⑤⑦ Mar. 26 - Jul. 23; also Apr. 5, Mar. 24, June 1; not Apr. 2, 4, May 23).

a – Arrival time.
b – Not Dec. 24, 25, 31, Apr. 2, 4, May 23.
c – Not Dec. 24, 25, 31, Jan. 1, Apr. 2, 5, May 24.
d – Departure time.
e – Not Dec. 25, 26, Jan. 1, Apr. 3, 5, May 24.
f – Not Dec. 25, Jan. 1.
g – Not Dec. 25, Jan. 1, Apr. 30.
h – Not Dec. 25, 26, Jan. 1, Apr. 5, May 24.
j – Not Dec. 25, 26, Jan. 1, Apr. 5, 30, May 24.
k – Frankfurt (Main) **Süd**.
p – Not Dec. 24, 31.
q – Not Dec. 24, 31, Apr. 4, May 4, 23.
t – Köln **Messe / Deutz**.
x – Not Apr. 30.
y – Not Dec. 25, 27, Jan. 1.
z – 1728 on ⑥.

🚌 – **DB / ČD** *ExpressBus*. Ⓡ 🍷. Rail tickets valid. 1st and 2nd class. (Table **57**).
RJ – ÖBB *Railjet* service. [1] (premium class), [1] (first class), [2] (economy class) and 🍷.
◐ – 🏛 between Arnhem and Oberhausen is Emmerich.
⊖ – Via Köln - Frankfurt high speed line.
❖ – Subject to alteration on certain dates.

PARIS - FRANKFURT - BERLIN, LEIPZIG, DRESDEN and PRAHA 30

Alternative services Paris - Frankfurt are available via Brussels (Table **21**). Alternative services Paris - Berlin are available via Brussels (Table **20**).

train type	*ICE*	*ICE*	*ICE*	*EC*	*ICE*	*ICE*	*ICE*	*ICE*	*ICE*	*EC*	*ICE*	*ICE*	*ICE*	*ICE*	*ICE*	*ICE*	*ICE*	*ICE*	*IC*		*ICE*	*CNL*	*CNL*	
train number	**9551**	**278**	**1559**	**379**	**623**	**9553**	**9553**	**276**	**1651**	**179**	**627**	**9555**	**370**	**290**	**1655**	**725**	**9557**	**1659**	**2029**		**9559**	**459**	**451**	
notes	♣	🍷	🍷	🍴	923	♣	♣	🍷	🍷	🍴	927	♣	🍷	🍷		🍷	♣	Ⓑ f	🍷		♣		[R]	
notes	①–⑥	L		K	🍷	⑦	①–⑥	L		D	🍷		Ⓑ f	⑥ y	Ⓑ		Ⓑ	🍷				B	A	
	k					h	g						L	L	🍷		p							
Paris Est d.	0704	...	...	...	...	0909	0909	...	...	...	...	1309	...	...	...	...	1709	...	...	...	1905	...	2020	...
Metz d.	|	...	...	...	...	|	|	...	...	...	...	|	...	...	...	...	|	...	...	...	|	...	2353x	...
Forbach 🏛 d.	0849	...	...	...	...	1050	|	...	...	...	...	|	...	...	...	...	|	...	...	...	2049	...	|	...
Saarbrücken a.	0857	...	...	...	...	1058	1055	...	...	...	...	1457	...	...	...	...	1857	...	...	...	2057	...	0059u	...
Kaiserlautern a.	0934	...	...	...	...	1134	1134	...	...	...	...	1534	...	...	...	...	1934	...	...	...	2134	...	|	...
Karlsruhe Hbf a.	|	...	...	...	...	|	|	...	...	...	...	|	...	...	...	...	|	...	...	...	|	...	|	...
Mannheim a.	1016	...	...	...	...	1214	1214	...	...	...	...	1616	...	...	...	...	2016	...	...	...	2216	...	|	...
Frankfurt (Main) Hbf a.	1058	...	...	...	...	1258	1258	...	...	...	...	1658	...	...	...	...	2058	...	...	...	2258	...	|	...
Frankfurt (Main) Hbf d.	...	1113	1119	...	1154	...	...	1313	1319	...	1354	...	1713	1713	1720	1754	...	2119	2218	...	...	0055q	|	...
Würzburg a.	...	|	|	...	1303	...	...	|	|	...	1503	...	|	|	|	1903	...	|	2341	...	...	|	|	...
Nürnberg a.	...	|	|	...	1359	...	...	|	|	...	1559	...	|	|	|	1959	...	|	0038	...	...	|	|	...
Fulda a.	...	1209	1211	...	...	...	...	1409	1411	...	...	...	1809	1809	1811	...	...	2211	...	...	...	|	|	...
Erfurt a.	...	|	1332	...	...	...	...	|	1532	...	...	...	|	1932	1932	...	...	2331	...	...	...	0518	|	...
Leipzig Hbf a.	...	|	1441	...	...	...	...	|	1641	...	...	...	|	2046	2042	...	...	0048r	...	...	...	0641	|	...
Dresden Hbf a.	...	|	1604	1710	...	...	...	|	1804	1910	...	...	|	|	...	...	...	...	...	...	...	0804	|	...
Děčín (🏛 = Schöna) a.	...	|	...	1755	...	...	...	|	...	1955	...	...	|	|	...	...	...	...	...	...	...	0905	|	...
Praha Holešovice a.	...	|	...	1916	...	...	...	|	...	2116	...	...	|	|	...	...	...	...	...	...	...	1037	|	...
Praha hlavní a.	...	|	...	1927	...	...	...	|	...	2127	...	...	|	|	...	...	...	...	...	...	...	1051	|	...
Kassel Wilhelmshöhe a.	...	1241	...	...	...	...	...	1441	...	...	...	...	1841	|	...	...	...	...	...	...	..	...	|	...
Gottingen a.	...	1301	...	...	...	...	...	1501	...	...	...	...	1901	|	...	...	...	...	...	...	...	...	0611	...
Hannover Hbf a.	...	|	...	...	...	...	...	|	...	...	...	...	|	|	...	...	...	...	...	...	...	...	0702	...
Braunschweig a.	...	1358	...	...	...	...	...	1558	...	...	...	...	1958	|	...	...	...	...	...	...	...	...	|	...
Wolfsburg a.	...	1416	...	...	...	...	...	1616	...	...	...	...	2016	|	...	...	...	...	...	...	...	...	|	...
Berlin Hauptbahnhof a.	...	1525	...	...	...	...	...	1725	...	...	...	...	2126	2204	...	...	...	...	...	...	...	...	0859	...
Berlin Ostbahnhof a.	...	1536	...	...	...	...	...	1736	...	...	...	...	2137	...	...	...	...	...	...	...	...	...	...	...

train type	*CNL*	*ICE*	*ICE*	*ICE*	*ICE*	*ICE*	*ICE*	*ICE*	*ICE*	*ICE*	*ICE*	*ICE*	*ICE*	*EC*	*ICE*	*ICE*	*ICE*	*EC*	*ICE*	*ICE*	*ICE*		*CNL*	
train number	**458**	**9558**	**822**	**1656**	**373**	**9556**	**9556**	**724**	**1652**	**871**	**9554**	**626**	**279**	**176**	**1558**	**9552**	**622**	**378**	**1556**	**873**	**9550**		**450**	
notes		♣	🍷		🍷	♣	♣	🍷	🍷	🍷	♣	1226	🍷	🍴	🍷	♣	🍷	🍴	🍷	🍷	♣		[R]	
notes	B	①–⑥	①–⑥	①–⑥	①–⑤	①–⑥	⑦					🍷	L	G				E			Ⓑ		H	
		k	j	j	b	g	h														p			
Berlin Ostbahnhof d.	...	...	...	...	0421	...	...	...	...	0821	...	...	1221	...	...	...	...	...	...	1421	...	...	...	...
Berlin Hauptbahnhof d.	...	...	...	...	0432	...	...	...	...	0832	...	...	1232	...	...	...	...	...	...	1432	...	...	1957	...
Wolfsburg d.	...	...	...	...	0540	...	...	...	...	0940	...	...	1340	...	...	...	...	...	...	1540	...	...	|	...
Braunschweig d.	...	...	...	...	0558	...	...	...	...	0958	...	...	1358	...	...	...	...	...	...	1558	...	...	|	...
Hannover Hbf d.	...	...	...	...	|	...	...	...	...	|	...	...	|	...	...	...	...	...	...	|	...	...	2216	...
Gottingen d.	...	...	...	...	0655	...	...	...	...	1055	...	...	1455	...	...	...	...	...	...	1655	...	...	2332	...
Kassel Wilhelmshöhe d.	...	...	...	...	0716	...	...	...	...	1116	...	...	1516	...	...	...	...	...	...	1716	...	...	|	...
Praha hlavní d.	1831	...	...	...	|	...	...	...	...	|	...	...	|	0831	...	...	...	1031	..	|	...	...	|	...
Praha Holešovice d.	1840	...	...	...	|	...	...	...	...	|	...	...	|	0840	...	...	...	1040	...	|	...	...	|	...
Děčín (🏛 = Schöna) d.	2002	...	...	...	|	...	...	...	...	|	...	...	|	1002	...	...	...	1202	...	|	...	...	|	...
Dresden Hbf d.	2104	...	...	...	|	...	...	...	0754	|	...	...	|	1046	1154	...	...	1246	1354	|	...	...	|	...
Leipzig Hbf d.	2229	...	...	0458	|	...	...	...	0915	|	...	...	|	...	1315	...	...	...	1515	|	...	...	|	...
Erfurt d.	0123	...	...	0619	|	...	...	...	1024	|	...	...	|	...	1422	...	...	...	1624	|	...	...	|	...
Fulda d.	|	...	...	0744	0747	...	...	...	1144	1147	...	...	1547	...	1544	...	...	...	1744	1747	...	...	|	...
Nürnberg d.	|	...	0600	|	|	...	...	1000	|	|	...	1400	|	...	|	...	1600	...	|	|	...	...	|	...
Würzburg d.	|	...	0656	|	|	...	...	1056	|	|	...	1456	|	...	|	...	1656	...	|	|	...	...	|	...
Frankfurt (Main) Hbf a.	0359q	...	0805	0836	0844	...	...	1205	1236	1244	...	1605	1644	...	1636	...	1805	...	1836	1844	...	...	|	...
Frankfurt (Main) Hbf d.	...	0600	...	...	...	0901	0901	...	...	...	1301	...	...	...	...	1658	...	...	...	...	1901	...	|	...
Mannheim d.	...	0640	...	...	...	0941	0941	...	...	...	1341	...	...	...	...	1742	...	...	...	...	1941	...	|	...
Karlsruhe Hbf d.	...	|	...	...	...	|	|	...	...	...	|	...	...	...	...	|	...	...	...	...	|	...	|	...
Kaiserlautern d.	...	0722	...	...	...	1023	1023	...	...	...	1423	...	...	...	...	1825	...	...	...	...	2023	...	|	...
Saarbrücken d.	...	0800	...	...	...	1101	1101	...	...	...	1501	...	...	...	...	1902	...	...	...	...	2101	...	0500s	...
Forbach 🏛 a.	...	0808	...	...	...	|	1109	...	...	...	|	...	...	...	...	1911	...	...	...	...	2109	...	|	...
Metz a.	...	|	...	...	...	|	|	...	...	...	|	...	...	...	...	|	...	...	...	...	|	...	0615s	...
Paris Est a.	...	0949	...	...	...	1249	1253	...	...	...	1650	...	...	...	...	2053	...	...	...	...	2253	...	0920	...

A – *City Night Line* PERSEUS ①⑤⑥⑦ (daily Mar. 28 - Oct. 30): 🛏 1,2 cl., 🛏 2 cl. (including ladies only berths), (2) (reclining) and 🍴 Paris - Forbach 🏛 - Hannover - Berlin Spandau (arrive 0849) - Berlin Hbf - Berlin Südkreuz (0907). [R] Special fares apply. (Table **20**).

B – *City Night Line* CANOPUS – 🛏 1,2 cl., 🛏 2 cl., (2) (reclining) and 🍷 Zürich - Basel - Frankfurt (Main) **Süd** - Děčín 🏛 - Praha and v.v. [R] Special fares apply.

D – ALOIS NEGRELLI – (12) and 🍴 Berlin - Dresden - Praha.

E – CARL MARIA VON WEBER – (12) and 🍴 Wien - Praha - Dresden - Berlin - Stralsund. To Ostseebad Binz on dates in Table **60**.

G – ALOIS NEGRELLI – (12) and 🍴 Brno - Praha - Dresden - Berlin - Hamburg.

H – *City Night Line* PERSEUS ④⑤⑥⑦ (daily Mar. 28 - Oct. 30): 🛏 1,2 cl., 🛏 2 cl. (including ladies only berths), (2) (reclining) and 🍴 Berlin Südkreuz (depart 1948) - Berlin Hbf - Berlin Spandau (2007) - Hannover - Forbach 🏛 - Paris. [R] Special fares apply. (Table **20**).

K – CARL MARIA VON WEBER – (12) and 🍴 Stralsund - Berlin - Dresden - Praha - Brno. From Ostseebad Binz on dates in Table **60**.

L – (12) and 🍷 Interlaken Ost - Basel - Mannheim - Berlin and v.v.

b – Not Dec. 24, 25, 31, Jan. 1, Apr. 2, 5, May 24.

f – Not Dec. 24, 25, 31, Apr. 2, 4, May 23.

g – Not Apr. 5, May 24.

h – Also Apr. 5, May 24.

j – Not Dec. 25, 26, Jan. 1, Apr. 3, 5, May 24.

k – Not Dec. 25, Jan. 1, Apr. 5, May 24.

p – Not Dec. 24, 31, Apr. 4, May 23.

q – Frankfurt (Main) **Süd**.

r – ①⑥ (also Dec. 24, 31, Apr. 2, 6, May 13, 25; not Dec. 26, Jan. 2, Apr. 3, 5, May 15, 24).

s – Stops to set down only.

u – Stops to pick up only.

x – Stops to pick up only. Also departs 2328, 0030 on certain dates.

y – Also Dec. 24, 25, 31, Apr. 2, 4, May 23.

♣ – [R] (Paris - Saarbrücken and v.v.); supplement payable, 🍷.

32 LONDON - PARIS - MÜNCHEN - WIEN - BUDAPEST - BUCUREŞTI

Alternative services London - München and London - Wien - Budapest are available via Brussels (Table **21**)

train type	*EC*	*RJ*	*D*	*TGV*	*ICE*	*EC*	*RJ*	☆	☆	*TGV*	*ICE*	*EC*	*ICE*	☆	☆	*TGV*	*EN*	☆	☆	*TGV*	*ICE*
train number	**361**	**65**	**347**	**9571**	**1091**	**115**	**69**	**9002**	**9004**	**9573**	**597**	**117**	**661**	**9018**	**9020**	**9575**	**463**	**9024**	**9026**	**9577**	**693**
train number/notes	✕	🍷	✕		**593**	🍷	🍷	②③④	①–⑥		🍷	⑧y	🍷						⑦	⑧	🍷
notes			**M**		🍷			**A**	**B**			🍷			**C**		**J**		**D**	**p**	
London St Pancras 10 d.	...	...	...	...	...	...	...	0602	0655	...	...	...	...	1025	1100	...	...	1229	1300	...	...
Paris Nord 10 a.	...	...	...	...	...	...	...	0954	1017	...	...	...	...	1347r	1420	...	...	1550	1617	...	...
Paris Est d.	...	...	...	0724	...	...	...	...	...	1124	...	...	...	...	...	1524	...	...	...	1724	...
Strasbourg d.	0653f	...	...	0945f	...	...	...	...	...	1345f	...	...	...	...	...	1745	...	...	...	1946f	...
Kehl 🛃 d.	0705f	...	...	|	...	...	...	...	...	|	...	...	...	...	...	|	...	...	...	|	...
Baden Baden d.	0732f	...	...	|	...	...	...	...	...	|	...	...	...	...	...	|	...	...	...	|	...
Karlsruhe Hbf d.	0806	...	...	1028	...	...	...	...	...	1428	...	...	...	...	...	1828	...	...	...	2030	...
Stuttgart Hbf d.	0853	...	...	1104	1112	1158	...	...	...	1504	1512	1558	...	...	...	1919	...	...	...	2105	2112
Ulm Hbf d.	0955j	...	...	...	1208	1255	...	...	...	...	1608	1655	...	...	...	2017	...	...	...	...	2208
Augsburg Hbf d.	1038j	...	...	...	1255	1342	...	...	...	...	1655	1742	...	...	...	2102	...	...	...	...	2255
München Pasing a.	1106j	...	...	...	1323s	|	...	...	...	...	1723s	|	...	...	...	|	...	...	...	...	2323s
München Hbf a.	1117j	...	...	...	1333	1417	...	...	...	...	1733	1817	...	...	...	2138	...	...	...	...	2333
München Hbf d.	...	1127	...	...	...	1427	1527	...	...	...	...	1827	...	...	...	...	2340	...	...	...	...
Salzburg Hbf 🛃 a.	...	1258	...	...	...	1609	1656	...	...	...	...	2009	2102	...	...	...	0117	...	...	...	...
Linz Hbf a.	...	1407	...	...	...	...	1807	...	...	...	...	...	2207	...	...	...	0340	...	...	...	...
St Pölten Hbf a.	...	1458	...	...	...	...	1858	...	...	...	...	...	2258	...	...	...	0458	...	...	...	...
Wien Westbahnhof a.	...	1540	...	...	...	...	1940	...	...	...	...	...	2340	...	...	...	0545h	...	...	...	...
Wien Westbahnhof d.	...	1550	1850	...	...	...	1950	...	...	...	...	...	...	...	...	...	0600q	...	...	...	...
Hegyeshalom 🛃 a.	...	1654	1954	...	...	...	2054	...	...	...	...	...	...	...	...	...	0652	...	...	...	...
Győr a.	...	17121	2029	...	...	...	2121	...	...	...	...	...	...	...	...	...	0720	...	...	...	...
Budapest Keleti a.	...	1849	2220	...	...	...	2249	...	...	...	...	...	...	...	...	...	0849	...	...	...	...
Bucureşti Nord a.	...	...	1407	...	...	...	...	...	...	...	...	...	...	...	...	...	0035	...	...	...	...

train type	☆	☆	*CNL*	*RJ*	*EN*
train number	**9036**	**9038**	**40451**	**63**	**473**
train number/notes	⑥⑦	①–⑤	[R]	🍷	✕
notes	**m**	**w**	**G**		**R**
London St Pancras 10 d.	1532	1602	...	...	...
Paris Nord 10 a.	1847	1917	...	...	...
Paris Est d.	...	...	2020	...	...
Strasbourg d.	...	...	|	...	...
Kehl 🛃 d.	...	...	|	...	...
Baden Baden d.	...	...	|	...	...
Karlsruhe Hbf d.	...	...	|	...	...
Stuttgart Hbf d.	...	...	0417	...	...
Ulm Hbf d.	...	...	0542	...	...
Augsburg Hbf d.	...	...	0633	...	...
München Pasing a.	...	...	|	...	...
München Hbf a.	...	...	0716	...	...
München Hbf d.	...	...	...	0927	...
Salzburg Hbf 🛃 a.	...	...	...	1058	...
Linz Hbf a.	...	...	...	1207	...
St Pölten Hbf a.	...	...	...	1258	...
Wien Westbahnhof a.	...	...	...	1340	...
Wien Westbahnhof d.	...	...	...	1350	...
Hegyeshalom 🛃 a.	...	...	...	1454	...
Győr a.	...	...	...	1521	...
Budapest Keleti a.	...	...	...	1649	1913
Bucureşti Nord a.	...	...	...	...	1034

train type	*TGV*	☆	☆	*EN*	*TGV*	☆	☆
train number	**9578**	**9027**	**9031**	**462**	**9576**	**9035**	**9039**
train number/notes	①–⑥					⑤⑥⑦	①–⑤
notes	**k**	**E**		**K**		**t**	**e**
Bucureşti Nord d.	...	...	...	0530	...	...	...
Budapest Keleti d.	...	...	...	2105	...	...	...
Győr d.	...	...	...	2232	...	...	...
Hegyeshalom 🛃 d.	...	...	...	2301	...	...	...
Wien Westbahnhof a.	...	...	...	2354q	...	...	...
Wien Westbahnhof d.	...	...	...	0009h	...	...	...
St Pölten Hbf d.	...	...	...	0052	...	...	...
Linz Hbf d.	...	...	...	0201	...	...	...
Salzburg Hbf 🛃 d.	...	...	...	0428	...	...	...
München Hbf a.	...	...	...	0615	...	...	...
München Hbf d.	...	...	...	...	0621	...	...
München Pasing d.	...	...	...	...	|	...	...
Augsburg Hbf d.	...	...	...	...	0658	...	...
Ulm Hbf d.	...	...	...	...	0743	...	...
Stuttgart Hbf d.	0655	...	...	...	0855	...	...
Karlsruhe Hbf d.	0732	...	...	...	0932f	...	...
Baden Baden d.	|	...	...	...	|	...	...
Kehl 🛃 d.	|	...	...	...	|	...	...
Strasbourg a.	0813	...	...	...	1013f	...	...
Paris Est a.	1034	...	...	...	1234f	...	...
Paris Nord 10 d.	...	1213	1304	...	...	1413	1513
London St Pancras 10 a.	...	1328	1431	...	...	1529	1636

train type	*EC*	*ICE*	*TGV*	☆	☆	*RJ*	*EC*	*ICE*	*TGV*	*D*	*RJ*	*EC*	*ICE*	*TGV*	*EC*	*EN*	*RJ*	*CNL*	☆
train number	**390**	**598**	**9574**	**9049**	**9051**	**262**	**114**	**1090**	**9572**	**346**	**60**	**112**	**592**	**9570**	**360**	**472**	**66**	**40418**	**9023**
train number/notes	🍷	🍷		⑦	①–⑤	🍷	🍷	**594**	⑥⑦	✕	🍷	🍷	🍷	①–⑤	✕	✕	🍷	[R]	
notes				**d**	**e**			🍷	**g**	**M**				**b**		**R**		**H**	
Bucureşti Nord d.	...	...	...	...	...	...	...	...	...	1600	...	...	...	...	...	1910	...	...	...
Budapest Keleti d.	...	...	...	...	...	...	...	...	...	0600	0710	...	...	...	...	0847	1310	...	...
Győr d.	...	...	...	...	...	...	...	...	...	0727	0835	...	...	...	...	...	1435	...	...
Hegyeshalom 🛃 d.	...	...	...	...	...	...	...	...	...	0758	0906	...	...	...	...	...	1506	...	...
Wien Westbahnhof a.	...	...	...	...	...	...	...	...	...	0858	1008	...	...	...	...	...	1608	...	...
Wien Westbahnhof d.	...	...	...	...	...	0820	...	...	...	...	1020	...	...	...	...	...	1620	...	...
St Pölten Hbf d.	...	...	...	...	...	0902	...	...	...	...	1102	...	...	...	...	...	|	...	...
Linz Hbf d.	0624c	...	...	...	...	0953	...	...	...	...	1153	...	...	...	...	...	1753	...	...
Salzburg Hbf 🛃 d.	0751c	...	...	...	...	1102	1151	...	...	...	1302	1351	...	...	...	...	1902	...	...
München Hbf a.	0933c	...	...	...	...	1230	1333	...	...	...	1430	1533	...	...	...	...	2034	...	...
München Hbf d.	0940	1023	...	...	...	...	1340	1423	...	...	...	1541	1623	...	1643j	...	...	2243	...
München Pasing d.	|	1031u	...	...	...	...	|	1431u	...	...	...	|	1631u	...	1651j	...	...	|	...
Augsburg Hbf d.	1017	1103	...	...	...	...	1417	1503	...	...	...	1617	1703	...	1722j	...	...	2320u	...
Ulm Hbf d.	1105	1151	...	...	...	...	1505	1551	...	...	...	1705	1751	...	1805	...	...	0010u	...
Stuttgart Hbf d.	1201	1247	1255	...	...	...	1600	1647	1655	...	...	1801	1847	1855	1911	...	...	0125u	...
Karlsruhe Hbf d.	...	...	1332	...	...	...	...	...	1732	...	...	...	...	1932	2006f	...	...	|	...
Baden Baden d.	...	...	|	...	...	...	...	...	|	...	...	...	...	|	2024f	...	...	|	...
Kehl 🛃 d.	...	...	|	...	...	...	...	...	|	...	...	...	...	|	2051f	...	...	|	...
Strasbourg a.	...	...	1413	...	...	...	...	...	1813	...	...	...	...	2015	2101f	...	...	|	...
Paris Est a.	...	...	1634	...	...	...	...	...	2034	...	...	...	...	2237	...	...	...	0930	...
Paris Nord 10 d.	...	...	...	1743	1813	...	...	...	...	...	...	...	...	...	...	...	...	...	1113
London St Pancras 10 a.	...	...	...	1859	1934	...	...	...	...	...	...	...	...	...	...	...	...	...	1229

A – ②③④ Jan. 4 - Feb. 6.
B – ①–⑥ (①⑤⑥ Jan. 4 - Feb. 6) not Dec. 26, 28, Jan. 1, Apr. 5, May 3, 24, 31.
C – Dec. 13, 19, 20, 26, 27, 28, Jan. 1, 2, 3, Mar. 20, May 16, 29.
D – ⑦ (also Dec. 18, 28, Mar. 19, Apr. 2, 5, May 3, 24, 28, 31).
E – Daily Dec. 26 - Jan. 3; ①⑤⑦ Jan. 4 - Feb. 6; ⑧ Feb. 7 - July 3.
G – *City Night Line* CASSIOPEIA ①⑤⑥⑦ (daily Mar. 28 - Oct. 28): 🛏 1, 2 cl., ▬ 2 cl. (including ladies only compartment), [2] and ✕ Paris - Metz (depart 2353) - Forbach 🛃 - Saarbrücken (0059) - München (- Innsbruck ⑥ Dec. 26 - Apr. 10, arrive 1036). [R] Special fares apply.
H – *City Night Line* CASSIOPEIA ④⑤⑥⑦ (daily Mar. 28 - Oct. 27): 🛏 1, 2 cl., ▬ 2 cl. (including ladies only compartment), [2] and ✕ (Innsbruck ⑥ Dec. 26 - Apr. 10, depart 1954 -) München - Saarbrücken (arrive 0459) - Forbach 🛃 - Metz (0615) - Paris. [R] Special fares apply.
J – KÁLMÁN IMRE – 🛏 1, 2 cl., ▬ 2 cl. and [2] München - Wien - Budapest. Conveys Dec. 13 - Jan. 11, June 17 - Sept. 17: 🛏 1, 2 cl. München - Budapest (375) - Bucureşti and [12] and ✕ Budapest - Bucureşti.
K – KÁLMÁN IMRE – 🛏 1, 2 cl., ▬ 2 cl. and [2] Budapest - Wien - München. Conveys Dec. 13 - Jan. 9, June 15 - Sept. 15: 🛏 1, 2 cl. Bucureşti (**374**) - Budapest (**462**) - München. [12] and ✕ Bucureşti - Budapest.
M – DACIA – 🛏 1, 2 cl., ▬ 2 cl., and [2] Wien - Budapest - Bucureşti and v.v. [1] Wien - Budapest - Lökösháza and v.v. [12] and ✕ Budapest - Bucureşti and v.v.
R – *EuroNight* ISTER – 🛏 1, 2 cl., ▬ 1, 2 cl., [2] and 🍷 Budapest - Bucureşti and v.v. 🛏 1, 2 cl. Budapest - Bucureşti - Sofiya - Thessaloniki and v.v.
T – 🛏 1, 2 cl. and [2] Venezia - Budapest - Bucureşti and v.v.
b – Not Dec. 24, 25, 31, Jan. 1, Apr. 5, May 24.
c – ①–⑥ (not Dec. 25, 26, Jan. 1, Apr. 3, 5, May 10, 24).
d – Also Dec. 28, Apr. 5, May 3, 24, 31.
e – Not Dec. 28, Apr. 5, May 3, 24, 31.
f – Not Mar. 6, 7.
g – Also Dec. 24, 25, 31, Jan. 1, Apr. 5, May 24; not Mar. 6, 7.
h – Wien **Hütteldorf**.
j – Not Feb. 27 - May 16.
k – Not Dec. 25, Jan. 1, Mar. 6, Apr. 5, May 24.
m – Also Dec. 28, Jan. 1, Apr. 5, May 3, 24, 31.
p – Not Dec. 24, 31, Apr. 4, May 23.
q – Wien **Meidling**.
r – 1350 on ⑥.
s – Calls to set down only.
t – Also Dec. 28, Apr. 5, May 3, 24, 31; not Jan. 1.
u – Stops to pick up only.
w – Not Dec. 28, Jan. 1, Apr. 5, May 3, 24, 31.
y – Also Dec. 24, 25, 31, Apr. 2, 4, May 23.

TGV – [R], supplement payable, 🍷.
RJ – ÖBB *Railjet* service. [1] (premium class), [1] (first class), [2] (economy class) and 🍷. Classified *EC* in Hungary.
☆ – Eurostar train. [R], ✕. Special fares payable. Minimum check-in time 30 minutes. Valid Dec. 13, 2009 - July 3, 2010. No service Dec. 25. see Table **10**.

LONDON, PARIS and BRUSSELS - BASEL - ZÜRICH, INTERLAKEN, BRIG and MILANO 40

For Brussels - Köln - Basel - Milano services see Table **43**.

train type / number	*TGV*	*IC*		*IC*	*IR*	*IC*	*IC*	*ICN*	*ICN*	*ICN*	*TGV*	*IR*	*EC*		*ICN*	*ICN*	*ICN*	☆	*TGV*	*EC*	*ICN*	*ICN*	*IR*	*EC*	*IC*	
train number	**9205**	**1069**		**569**	**1771**	**969**	**820**	**620**	**1520**	**675**	**9211**	**1773**	**57**		**624**	**1524**	**679**	**9078**	**9215**	**7**	**1626**	**526**	**2177**	**21**	**1077**	
notes	**9207**	🍷		🍷		✕	✕	✕	✕	🍷	**9213**	🍷	[R]⊗		✕			①–⑤	♥	✕	✕	✕		[R]⊕	🍷	
	♥										♥k		✕					**B**						✕		
London St Pancras d.	...	...	...	...	...	...	...	...	...	...	...	...	...	...	...	...	...	0525	...	...	...	...	...	...	...	...
Paris Nord a.	...	...	...	...	...	...	...	...	...	...	...	...	...	...	...	...	...	0850	...	...	...	...	...	...	...	...
Paris Est d.	0624	...	...	...	...	...	...	...	...	...	0824	...	...	...	...	...	...	...	1024	...	...	...	...	...	...	...
Brussels Midi / Zuid § d.	|	...	...	...	...	...	...	...	...	...	|	...	...	...	...	...	...	...	|	...	...	...	...	...	...	...
Namur § d.	|	...	...	...	...	...	...	...	...	...	|	...	...	...	...	...	...	...	|	...	...	...	...	...	...	...
Luxembourg 🏛 § d.	|	...	...	...	...	...	...	...	...	...	|	...	...	...	...	...	...	...	|	...	...	...	...	...	...	...
Thionville d.	|	...	...	...	...	...	...	...	...	...	|	...	...	...	...	...	...	...	|	...	...	...	...	...	...	...
Metz d.	|	...	...	...	...	...	...	...	...	...	|	...	...	...	...	...	...	...	|	...	...	...	...	...	...	...
Strasbourg d.	0847	...	...	...	...	...	...	...	...	...	1047	...	...	...	...	...	...	...	1247	...	...	...	...	...	...	...
Mulhouse d.	0937	...	...	...	...	...	...	...	...	...	1138	...	...	...	...	...	...	...	1332	...	...	...	...	...	...	...
Basel SNCF 🏛 ▷ a.	0956	...	...	...	...	...	...	...	...	...	1156	...	...	...	...	...	...	...	1351	...	...	...	...	...	...	...
Basel SBB ▷ d.	1007	1028	...	1033	1047	1101	...	1103	...	1103	1207	...	1228	...	1303	...	1303	...	1407	...	1403	...	1403	...	1428	...
Zürich HB a.	1100	|	...	1126	1152	|	...	|	...	|	1300	1312	|	...	|	...	|	...	1500	1512	|	...	|	...	|	...
Sargans a.	...	|	...	1232	1319	|	...	|	...	|	...	1419	|	...	|	...	|	...	...	1619	|	...	|	...	|	...
Landquart a.	...	|	...	1241	1332	|	...	|	...	|	...	1432	|	...	|	...	|	...	...	1632	|	...	|	...	|	...
Davos Platz a.	...	|	...	*1355*	*1455*	|	...	|	...	|	...	*1555*	|	...	|	...	|	...	...	*1755*	|	...	|	...	|	...
Chur a.	...	|	...	1252	1343	|	...	|	...	|	...	1443	|	...	|	...	|	...	...	1643	|	...	|	...	|	...
St Moritz a.	...	|	...	*1458*	*1558*	|	...	|	...	|	...	*1658*	|	...	|	...	|	...	...	*1858*	|	...	|	...	|	...
Luzern a.	...	|	...	...	...	|	...	|	...	1205	...	...	|	...	|	...	1405	...	...	...	|	...	1505	...	|	...
Arth Goldau a.	...	|	...	...	...	|	...	|	...	1245	...	...	|	...	|	...	1445	...	...	...	|	...	1545	1550	|	...
Bellinzona a.	...	|	...	...	...	|	...	|	...	1423	...	...	|	...	|	...	1623	...	...	...	|	...	1753	1723	|	...
Locarno a.	...	|	...	...	...	|	...	|	...	*1457*	...	...	|	...	|	...	|	...	...	...	|	...	1813	|	|	...
Lugano a.	...	|	...	...	...	|	...	|	...	1446	...	...	|	...	|	...	1646	...	...	...	|	...	...	1746	|	...
Chiasso 🏛 a.	...	|	...	...	...	|	...	|	...	...	...	...	|	...	|	...	...	...	...	...	|	...	...	1808	|	...
Bern a.	...	1127	...	...	...	1156	1207	|	...	...	...	...	1327	...	|	...	...	...	...	...	|	...	...	|	1527	...
Thun a.	...	1152	...	...	...	1221	1224	|	...	...	...	...	1352	...	|	...	...	...	...	...	|	...	...	|	1552	...
Spiez a.	...	1202	1205	...	...	1231	1234	|	...	...	...	...	1402	1405	|	...	...	...	...	...	|	...	...	|	1602	1605
Interlaken West a.	...	|	1223	...	...	1251	|	|	...	...	...	...	|	1423	|	...	...	...	...	...	|	...	...	|	|	1623
Interlaken Ost a.	...	|	1228	...	...	1257	|	|	...	...	...	...	|	1428	|	...	...	...	...	...	|	...	...	|	|	1628
Biel/Bienne a.	...	|	...	...	...	...	|	1210	1216	...	...	...	|	...	1410	1416	...	...	...	...	1510	1519	...	|	|	...
Neuchâtel a.	...	|	...	...	...	...	|	1235	1232	...	...	...	|	...	1435	1432	...	...	...	...	1532	1535	...	|	|	...
Lausanne a.	...	|	...	...	...	...	|	|	1315	...	...	...	|	...	|	1515	...	...	...	...	1615	|	...	|	|	...
Genève a.	...	|	...	...	...	...	|	1346	...	...	...	...	|	...	1546	...	...	...	...	...	...	1646	...	|	|	...
Brig a.	...	1240	...	...	...	...	1311	...	...	...	...	...	1440	...	...	...	...	...	...	...	...	...	...	|	1640	...
Como San Giovanni a.	...	...	...	...	...	...	...	...	...	...	...	...	◧	...	...	...	...	...	...	...	...	...	...	1814	...	...
Milano a.	...	...	...	...	...	...	...	...	...	...	...	...	1640	...	...	...	...	...	...	...	...	...	...	1850	...	...

train type / number	*EC*	*IC*	*IC*	*ICN*	*ICN*	☆	☆	*TGV*	*IC*	*IC*	*IC*	*ICN*	*ICN*	*ICN*	☆	☆	*EC**	*ICE*	*ICN*	*IR*	*ICN*	*IC*	☆	*TGV*	☆	*EC*
train number	**91**	**977**	**828**	**628**	**683**	**9014**	**9014**	**9217**	**587**	**1085**	**838**	**638**	**1538**	**691**	**9120**	**9116**	**97**	**279**	**1640**	**2191**	**693**	**1091**	**9030**	**9219**	**9132**	**295**
notes		🍷	🍷	✕	🍷	⑥	Ⓑ	♥	🍷	🍷		✕	✕	🍷	①–⑤	⑥⑦		✕	✕			**1087**		♥	①–⑥	Ⓑ
	V					**r**	**C**								**p**	**q**	**A**								**g**	**J**
London St Pancras d.	...	...	...	...	...	0922	0932	...	...	...	...	...	...	...	0827	0857	...	...	...	...	...	...	1404	...	1257	...
Paris Nord a.	...	...	...	...	...	1247	1247	...	...	...	...	...	...	...	|	|	...	...	...	...	...	...	1726	...	|	...
Paris Est d.	...	...	...	...	...	▬	...	1424	...	...	...	...	...	...	|	|	...	...	...	...	...	...	▬	1824	|	...
Brussels Midi / Zuid § d.	0733	...	...	...	...	...	...	|	...	...	...	...	...	...	1133	1203	1309	...	...	...	...	...	...	|	1603	1715e
Namur § d.	0841	...	...	...	...	...	...	|	...	...	...	...	...	...	▬	▬	1414	...	...	...	...	...	...	|	▬	1834
Luxembourg 🏛 § d.	1046	...	...	...	...	...	...	|	...	...	...	...	...	...	...	...	1610	...	...	...	...	...	...	|	...	2027
Thionville d.	1111	...	...	...	...	...	...	|	...	...	...	...	...	...	...	...	1631	...	...	...	...	...	...	|	...	2051
Metz d.	1131	...	...	...	...	...	...	|	...	...	...	...	...	...	...	...	1653	...	...	...	...	...	...	|	...	2115
Strasbourg d.	1251	...	...	...	...	*EC*	...	1648	...	...	...	...	...	...	*IC*	...	1821	...	...	...	...	...	...	2047	...	2251
Mulhouse d.	1355	...	...	...	...	**23**	...	1730	...	...	...	...	...	...	**1085**	...	1923	...	...	...	...	...	*IR*	2132	...	2348
Basel SNCF 🏛 ▷ a.	1420	...	...	...	...	[R]🍷	...	1756	...	...	...	...	...	...	🍷	...	1947	...	...	...	...	...	**1793**	2151	*IR*	0013
Basel SBB ▷ d.	1447	1501	...	1503	1503	⊕	...	1809	...	1828	...	1903	...	1903	1828	...	2013	2001	2003	2003	...	2028	2047	2207	**1797**	...
Zürich HB a.	1552	|	...	|	|	1709	...	1914	1937	|	...	|	...	|	|	...	2124	|	|	|	...	|	2152	2300	2312	...
Sargans a.	1719	|	...	|	|	|	...	...	2032	|	...	|	...	|	|	...	...	|	|	|	...	|	2319	...	0024	...
Landquart a.	1732	|	...	|	|	|	...	...	2041	|	...	|	...	|	|	...	...	|	|	|	...	|	2334	...	0039	...
Davos Platz a.	*1855*	|	...	|	|	|	...	...	*2157*	|	...	|	...	|	|	...	...	|	|	|	...	|	|	...	|	...
Chur a.	1743	|	...	|	|	|	...	...	2052	|	...	|	...	|	|	...	...	|	|	|	...	|	2345	...	0049	...
St Moritz a.	*1958*	|	...	|	|	|	...	...	*2259*	|	...	|	...	|	|	...	...	|	|	|	...	|	...	...	...	...
Luzern a.	...	|	...	|	1605	|	...	...	...	|	...	|	...	2005	|	...	...	|	|	2105	...	|	...	...	...	...
Arth Goldau a.	...	|	...	|	1645	1748	...	...	...	|	...	|	...	2045	|	...	...	|	|	2145	2150	|	...	...	...	...
Bellinzona a.	...	|	...	|	1823	1923	...	...	...	|	...	|	...	2223	|	...	...	|	|	▬	2323	|	...	...	...	...
Locarno a.	...	|	...	|	*1857*	|	...	...	...	|	...	|	...	*2257*	|	...	...	|	|	...	*2357*	|	...	...	...	...
Lugano a.	...	|	...	|	1846	1946	...	...	...	|	...	|	...	2246	|	*IC*	...	|	|	...	2346	|	...	...	...	...
Chiasso 🏛 a.	...	|	...	|	1912	2008	...	...	...	|	...	|	...	2312	|	**838**	...	|	|	...	0012	|	...	...	...	...
Bern a.	...	1556	1607	|	▬	|	...	...	...	1927	2007	|	...	...	1927	2007	...	2056	|	...	...	2127	...	...	...	...
Thun a.	...	1621	1624	|	...	|	...	...	...	1952	2024	|	...	...	1952	2024	...	2124	|	...	...	2152	...	...	...	...
Spiez a.	...	1631	1634	|	*ICN*	|	...	...	...	2002	2034	|	...	...	2002	2034	...	2134	|	...	...	2202	...	...	...	...
Interlaken West a.	...	1651	|	|	**1528**	|	...	...	...	2022	|	|	...	...	2022	|	...	2151	|	...	...	|	...	...	...	...
Interlaken Ost a.	...	1657	|	|	✕	|	...	...	...	2028	|	|	...	...	2028	|	...	2157	|	*IR*	...	|	...	...	...	...
Biel/Bienne a.	...	...	|	1610	1616	|	...	...	...	...	|	2010	2016	...	...	|	...	...	2110	**2540**	...	|	...	...	...	...
Neuchâtel a.	...	...	|	1635	1632	|	...	...	...	...	|	2035	2032	...	...	|	...	...	2132	✕	...	|	...	...	...	...
Lausanne a.	...	...	|	|	1715	|	...	...	...	...	|	|	2115	...	...	|	...	...	2215	2220	...	|	...	...	...	...
Genève a.	...	...	|	1746	...	|	...	...	...	...	|	2146	...	...	...	|	...	...	...	2304	...	|	...	...	...	...
Brig a.	...	...	1711	...	...	|	...	...	...	...	2111	...	...	...	...	2111	...	...	...	...	...	2240v	...	...	...	...
Como San Giovanni a.	...	...	...	...	...	2014	...	...	...	...	...	...	...	...	...	...	...	...	...	...	...	...	...	...	...	...
Milano a.	...	...	...	...	...	2050	...	...	...	...	...	...	...	...	...	...	...	...	...	...	...	...	...	...	...	...

LONDON - LILLE - STRASBOURG - BASEL

			TGV	*TGV*			☆	☆	*TGV*					☆	☆	*TGV*	*EC*			
			5400	**9211**			**9114**	**9120**	**5402**	①–⑥	⑦			**9030**	**9138**	**5416**	**295**			
			D	**9213**			⑥	**E**							**G**		Ⓑ**J**			
London St Pancras d.	...	...	...	...	...	...	0757	0827	...	...	...	...	...	1404	1434	...	...	...	...	...
Lille Europe d.	...	...	0652	...	...	...	1024	1054	1121	...	...	...	...	1624	1654	1805	...	...	...	...
Strasbourg d.	...	...	1010	1047	...	...	...	...	1517	1553	1553	...	...	...	...	2131	2251	...	...	...
Basel SNCF a.	...	...	...	1156	...	...	...	...	...	1709	1716	...	...	...	...	...	0013	...	...	...

A – IRIS – [12] Brussels - Basel - Zürich.
B – ①–⑤ (①⑤ Jan. 4 - Feb. 6) not Dec. 28, Jan. 1, Apr. 5, May 3, 13, 24, 31.
C – Ⓑ (①⑤⑦ Jan. 4 - Feb. 6) not Jan. 1.
D – ①–⑥ (not Apr. 5, May 24).
E – ①–⑤ (not Dec. 28, Apr. 5, May 3, 24, 31).
G – ⑤⑦ (⑤⑥⑦ Dec. 13 - Feb. 6) also Dec. 28, Apr. 5, May 3, 24, 31.
J – JEAN MONNET – [12] Brussels - Basel.
V – VAUBAN – [12] Brussels - Basel - Zürich - Chur.

e – 1727 on ⑥.
g – Not Dec. 28, Jan. 1, Apr. 5, May 3, 24, 31.
k – Not Apr. 5, May 24.

p – Not Dec. 28, Apr. 5, May 3, 24, 31.
q – Also Dec. 28, Apr. 5, May 3, 24, 31.
r – Also Jan. 1.
v – 2301 on ⑦.
♥ – *TGV Lyria* service. [R] 🍷 special fares payable.
* – *IR* in Switzerland.
⊕ – **ETR 470**. Supplement payable for international journeys. *IC* supplement payable for internal journeys within Italy.
⊗ – **ETR 610**. Supplement payable for international journeys. *IC* supplement payable for internal journeys within Italy.
☆ – Eurostar train. [R] ✕ Special fares payable. Minimum check-in time 30 minutes. Valid Dec. 13, 2009 - July 3, 2010. No service Dec. 25.
▷ – Trains arrive at SNCF (French) platforms and depart from SBB (Swiss) platforms. Minimum connection time 10 minutes. Connections at Basel are not guaranteed.
◧ – 🏛 between Brig and Milano is Domodossola. Ticket point is **Iselle**.
§ – Additional services run Brussels - Namur - Luxembourg. (Table **430**).

40 MILANO, BRIG, INTERLAKEN and ZÜRICH - BASEL - BRUSSELS, PARIS and LONDON

For Milano - Basel - Köln - Brussels services see Table **43**.

train type	*IR*	*EC*	*ICN*	*IC*	*IR*	*IR*	*TGV*	☆	*ICN*	*IR*	*ICN*	*ICN*	*IC*		*IC*	*TGV*	☆	*EC*	*IC*	*IC*		*ICN*	*ICN*	*ICN*	*EC**	☆
train number	**1756**	**296**	**1609**	**1058**	**2454**	**1760**	**9210** **9212**	**9031**	**650**	**2164**	**515**	**1615**	**562**		**1064**	**9214**	**9039**	**50**	**570**	**1070**		**662**	**523**	**1623**	**90**	**9163**
notes		**B** Ⓑ	🍷				♥		🍷		🍴	🍴	🍷		🍷	♥	⑥⑦ **q**	🅁 ⊗ 🍷	🍷		2		🍴	🍴	**V**	Ⓑ **y**
Milano d.	...	...	...	...	...	...	...	...	...	...	...	...	...	...	...	...	...	0725	...	...	...	...	...	...	...	...
Como San Giovanni d.	...	...	...	...	...	...	...	...	...	...	...	...	...	...	...	...	...	◧	...	...	...	...	...	...	...	...
Brig d.	...	...	...	...	...	...	...	...	...	...	...	...	...	...	0720	...	...	0920	...	...	...	...	...	...	...	...
Genève d.	...	...	...	...	...	...	...	...	...	...	0614	...	...	...	|	...	...	|	...	...	...	...	1014	...	...	...
Lausanne d.	...	...	...	...	...	...	...	...	...	...	|	0645	...	...	|	...	...	|	...	...	...	...	|	1045	...	...
Neuchâtel d.	...	...	...	...	...	...	...	...	...	...	0724	0727	...	...	|	...	...	|	...	...	...	...	1124	1127	...	...
Biel/Bienne d.	...	...	0549	...	...	...	...	...	...	...	0741	0749	...	...	|	...	...	|	...	...	...	...	1141	1149	...	...
Interlaken Ost d.	...	...	|	0521	...	...	...	...	...	...	...	|	...	0729	|	...	...	|	...	1031	...	...	...	|	...	...
Interlaken West d.	...	...	|	0526	...	...	...	...	...	...	...	|	...	0731	|	...	...	|	...	1034	...	...	...	|	...	...
Spiez d.	...	...	|	0550	...	...	...	...	...	...	...	|	...	0750	0754	...	...	0954	...	1054	...	...	...	|	...	...
Thun d.	...	...	|	0601	...	...	...	...	...	...	...	|	...	...	0804	...	...	1004	...	1105	...	...	...	|	...	...
Bern d.	...	...	|	0634	...	...	...	...	...	...	...	|	...	...	0834	...	...	1034	...	1134	...	...	...	|	...	...
Chiasso 🏛 d.	...	...	|	|	...	...	...	...	0446	...	...	|	...	...	|	...	...	|	...	|	...	...	...	|	...	...
Lugano d.	...	...	|	|	...	...	...	...	0512	...	...	|	...	...	|	...	...	|	...	|	...	0912	...	|	...	...
Locarno d.	...	...	|	|	...	...	...	...	|	...	...	|	...	...	|	...	...	|	...	|	0903	|	...	|	...	...
Bellinzona d.	...	...	|	|	...	...	...	...	0536	...	...	|	...	...	|	...	...	|	...	|	0927	0936	...	|	...	...
Arth Goldau d.	...	...	|	|	...	...	...	...	0709	0714	...	|	...	...	|	...	...	|	...	|	...	1114	...	|	...	...
Luzern d.	...	...	|	|	0630	...	...	...	...	0754	...	|	...	...	|	...	...	|	...	|	...	1154	...	|	...	...
St Moritz d.	...	...	|	|	|	...	...	...	...	|	...	|	...	...	|	...	...	|	*0802*	|	...	|	...	|	...	...
Chur d.	...	...	|	|	|	0513	...	...	...	|	...	|	0709	...	|	...	...	|	1009	|	...	|	...	|	...	...
Davos Platz d.	...	...	|	|	|	|	...	...	...	|	...	|	*0550*	...	|	...	...	|	*0902*	|	...	|	...	|	...	...
Landquart d.	...	...	|	|	|	0523	...	...	...	|	...	|	0719	...	|	...	...	|	1019	|	...	|	...	|	...	...
Sargans d.	...	...	|	|	|	0539	...	...	...	|	...	|	0728	...	|	...	...	|	1028	|	...	|	...	|	...	...
Zürich HB d.	0508	...	|	|	|	0648	0702	...	...	|	...	|	0834	...	|	...	...	|	1134	|	...	|	...	|	1136	...
Basel SBB ◁ a.	0612	...	0653	0732	0744	...	0757	...	...	0853	...	0853	0927	...	0932	...	...	1132	1227	1232	...	1253	...	1253	1247	...
Basel SNCF 🏛 ◁ d.	...	0646	▬	▬	...	...	0802	...	...	...	...	...	...	...	...	1002	...	▬	...	...	...	...	...	...	1304	...
Mulhouse a.	...	0708	...	...	...	...	0824	...	...	...	...	...	...	...	...	1021	...	...	...	...	...	...	...	...	1332	...
Strasbourg a.	...	0803	...	...	...	...	0911	...	...	...	...	...	...	...	...	1110	...	...	...	...	...	...	...	...	1433	...
Metz a.	...	0926	☆	☆	...	...	|	...	...	...	...	...	...	...	...	|	...	...	...	...	...	...	...	...	1554	...
Thionville a.	...	0949	**9137**	**9139**	...	...	|	...	...	...	...	...	...	...	...	|	...	...	...	...	...	...	...	...	1615	...
Luxembourg 🏛 § a.	...	1014	⑥⑦	①–⑤	...	...	|	...	...	...	...	...	...	...	...	|	...	☆	...	...	...	...	...	...	1645	...
Namur § a.	...	1219	**h**	**g**	...	...	|	...	...	...	...	...	...	...	...	|	...	**9039**	...	...	...	...	...	...	1846	...
Brussels Midi/Zuid § a.	...	1327	1359	1429	...	...	|	...	...	...	...	...	...	...	...	|	...	①–⑤	...	...	...	...	...	...	1950	2017**e**
Paris Est a.	...	...	|	|	...	...	1134	...	...	...	...	...	...	...	...	1334	...	**p**	...	...	...	...	...	...	...	|
Paris Nord d.	...	...	|	|	...	...	...	1304	...	...	...	...	...	...	...	...	1507	1513	...	...	...	...	...	...	...	|
London St Pancras a.	...	...	1503	1526	...	...	...	1431	...	...	...	...	...	...	...	...	1636	1636	...	...	...	...	...	...	...	2133

train type	*ICN*	*ICN*		*ICN*		*IC*	*IC*	*TGV*	*ICN*	*ICN*		*EC*	*TGV*	*EC*	*IR*	*IC*	*EC**		*ICN*	*ICN*	*ICN*	*IC*		*IC*	*TGV*	
train number	**523**	**1623**		**662**	**5717**	**1072**	**572**	**9216**	**527**	**1627**	**5721**	**52**	**9218**	**16**	**2178**	**576**	**96**		**670**	**531**	**1631**	**580**	**5725**	**1080**	**9222** **9220**	
notes	🍴	🍴	2				🍷	♥	🍴	🍴		🅁 ⊗ 🍷	♥	🅁 ⊕ 🍷			**A**	2		🍴	🍴	**x**			♥	
Milano d.	...	...	...	...	...	...	...	...	...	...	...	1120	...	1110	...	...	...	...	...	...	...	...	...	...	...	...
Como San Giovanni d.	...	...	...	...	...	...	...	...	...	...	...	◧	...	1145	...	...	...	...	...	...	...	...	...	...	...	...
Brig d.	...	...	...	...	...	1120	...	...	...	...	...	1320	...	|	...	...	...	...	...	...	...	...	...	1520	...	...
Genève d.	1014	...	...	...	...	|	...	...	1214	...	...	|	...	|	...	...	...	...	...	1414	...	...	...	|	...	...
Lausanne d.	|	1045	...	...	...	|	...	...	|	1245	...	|	...	|	...	...	...	...	...	|	1445	...	...	|	...	...
Neuchâtel d.	1024	1127	...	...	...	|	...	...	1324	1327	...	|	...	|	...	...	...	...	...	1524	1527	...	...	|	...	...
Biel/Bienne d.	1141	1149	...	...	...	|	...	...	1341	1349	...	|	...	|	...	...	...	...	...	1541	1549	...	...	|	...	...
Interlaken Ost d.	...	|	...	...	1129	|	...	...	▬	|	1329	|	...	|	...	...	...	...	...	...	|	...	1529	|	...	...
Interlaken West d.	...	|	...	...	1131	|	...	...	...	|	1331	|	...	|	...	...	...	...	...	...	|	...	1531	|	...	...
Spiez d.	...	|	...	...	1150	1154	...	...	...	|	1350	1354	...	|	...	...	...	...	...	...	|	...	1550	1554	...	...
Thun d.	...	|	...	...	...	1204	...	...	...	|	...	1404	...	|	...	...	...	...	...	...	|	...	...	1604	...	...
Bern d.	...	|	...	...	...	1234	...	...	...	|	...	1434	...	|	...	...	...	...	...	...	|	...	...	1634	...	...
Chiasso 🏛 d.	...	|	...	...	...	|	...	...	...	|	...	|	...	1152	...	...	...	...	...	...	|	...	...	|	...	...
Lugano d.	...	|	...	0912	...	|	...	...	...	|	...	|	...	1212	...	...	...	...	1312	...	|	...	...	|	...	...
Locarno d.	...	|	0903	|	...	|	...	...	...	|	...	|	...	|	1145	...	...	1303	|	...	|	...	...	|	...	...
Bellinzona d.	...	|	0927	0936	...	|	...	...	...	|	...	|	...	1236	1206	...	...	1327	1336	...	|	...	...	|	...	...
Arth Goldau d.	...	|	...	1114	...	|	...	...	...	|	...	|	...	1409	1414	...	...	...	1514	...	|	...	...	|	...	...
Luzern d.	...	|	...	1154	...	|	...	...	...	|	...	|	...	▬	1454	...	...	...	1554	...	|	...	...	|	...	...
St Moritz d.	...	|	...	|	...	|	*0902*	...	...	|	...	|	...	...	|	*1102*	...	...	|	...	|	*1302*	...	|	...	...
Chur d.	...	|	...	|	...	|	1109	...	...	|	...	|	...	...	|	1309	...	...	|	...	|	1509	...	|	...	...
Davos Platz d.	...	|	...	|	...	|	*1002*	...	...	|	...	|	...	...	|	*1202*	...	...	|	...	|	*1402*	...	|	...	...
Landquart d.	...	|	...	|	...	|	1119	...	...	|	...	|	...	...	|	1319	...	...	|	...	|	1519	...	|	...	...
Sargans d.	...	|	...	|	...	|	1128	...	...	|	...	|	...	...	|	1328	...	...	|	...	|	1528	...	|	...	...
Zürich HB d.	...	|	...	|	...	|	1223	1302	...	|	...	|	1502	...	|	1423	1436	...	|	...	|	1623**x**	...	|	1627	...
Basel SBB ◁ a.	...	1253	...	1253	...	1332	...	1357	...	1453	...	1532	1557	...	1553	...	1547	...	1653	...	1653	1727	...	1732	1736	...
Basel SNCF 🏛 ◁ d.	...	...	...	...	...	...	...	1402	...	...	...	...	1602	...	...	...	1606	...	...	...	...	...	...	...	1802	...
Mulhouse a.	...	...	...	...	...	...	...	1423	...	...	...	...	1625	...	...	...	1631	...	...	...	...	...	...	...	1821	...
Strasbourg a.	...	...	...	...	...	...	...	1510	...	...	...	...	1711	...	...	...	1732	...	...	...	...	...	...	...	1910	...
Metz a.	...	...	...	...	...	...	...	|	...	...	...	...	|	...	...	...	1854	...	...	...	...	...	...	...	|	...
Thionville a.	...	...	...	...	...	...	...	|	...	...	...	...	|	...	...	...	1915	...	...	...	...	...	...	...	|	...
Luxembourg 🏛 § a.	...	...	...	...	...	...	...	|	...	...	...	...	|	...	...	...	1936	...	...	...	...	...	...	...	|	...
Namur § a.	...	...	...	...	...	...	...	|	☆	...	...	...	|	☆	...	...	2146	...	...	...	...	...	...	...	|	...
Brussels Midi/Zuid § a.	...	...	...	...	...	...	...	|	**9055**	...	...	...	|	**9063**	...	...	2250	...	...	...	...	...	...	...	|	...
Paris Est a.	...	...	...	...	...	...	...	1734	**y**	...	...	...	1934	**w**	...	...	...	...	...	...	...	...	...	...	2134	...
Paris Nord d.	...	...	...	...	...	...	...	...	1913	...	...	...	...	2113	...	...	...	...	...	...	...	...	...	...	...	...
London St Pancras a.	...	...	...	...	...	...	...	...	2034	...	...	...	...	2234	...	...	...	...	...	...	...	...	...	...	...	...

BASEL - STRASBOURG - LILLE - LONDON

		TGV	*TGV*	☆					*TGV*	☆	☆					*TGV*				
		5420	**5420**	**9181**			⑦	①–⑥	**5422**	**9149**	**9153**			①–⑤	⑥⑦	**5426**				
		D	**E**							Ⓑ						Ⓑ **f**				
Basel SNCF d.	...	...	...	...	...	...	1004	1018	...	...	...	...	...	1718	1718	...	...	...	...	...
Strasbourg d.	...	0611	0620	...	...	...	1134	1135	1206	...	...	...	...	1833	1842	1900	...	...	...	...
Lille Europe d.	...	0946	0946	1205	...	...	...	...	1559	1735	1835	...	...	...	...	2223	...	...	...	...
London St Pancras a.	...	...	...	1233	...	...	...	...	...	1805	1903	...	...	...	...	...	...	...	...	...

A – IRIS – 🚃12 Zürich - Basel - Brussels.
B – JEAN MONNET – 🚃12 Basel - Brussels.
D – ①–⑥ (not Apr. 5, May 24).
E – ⑦ (also Apr. 5, May 24).
V – VAUBAN – 🚃12 Zürich - Basel - Brussels.

e – 2029 on ⑤⑦.
f – Not Dec. 25, Jan. 1, May 13.
g – Not Dec. 28, Jan. 1, Apr. 5, May 3, 24, 31.
h – Also Apr. 5, May 24.
p – Not Dec. 28, Apr. 5, May 3, 24, 31.
q – Also Dec. 28, Apr. 5, May 3, 24, 31.
w – Not Dec. 24, 26, 31.

x – For trains **9220** and **9222** change at Basel SBB.
y – Not Dec. 24, 31.

♥ – *TGV Lyria* service. 🅁 🍷 special fares payable.
* – *IR* in Switzerland.
◧ – 🏛 between Brig and Milano is Domodossola. Ticket point is **Iselle**.
§ – Additional services run Luxembourg - Namur - Brussels. (Table **430**).
☆ – Eurostar train. 🅁 🍴 Special fares payable. Minimum check-in time 30 minutes. Valid Dec. 13, 2009 - Feb. 6, 2010. No service Dec. 25.
⊕ – **ETR 470**. Supplement payable for international journeys. *IC* supplement payable for internal journeys within Italy.
⊗ – **ETR 610**. Supplement payable for international journeys. *IC* supplement payable for internal journeys within Italy.
◁ – Trains arrive at SBB (Swiss) platforms and depart from SNCF (French) platforms. Minimum connection time 10 minutes. Connections at Basel are not guaranteed.

LONDON and PARIS - BERN, LAUSANNE and BRIG 42

train type	TGV	TGV		IR	IR	☆	☆	TGV	TGV	☆	☆	TGV	IR	☆	TGV	TGV	IR	IR	TGV	ICE	☆	TGV	IC	☆	TGV	EN
train number	9261	9261		1725	1427	9008	9010	9269	9269	9014	9014	9271	1739	9018	9273	9273	1743	1445	9285	279	9024	9287	991	9026	9277	311
notes	♥🍷	♥🍷				[R]🍴	[R]🍴	♥🍷	9267	[R]🍴	[R]🍴	♥🍷		[R]🍴	♥🍷	♥🍷			♥🍷	🍷	[R]🍴	♥🍷		[R]🍴	♥🍷	
		B	B			M	⑦q	E	L♥	⑥r	P	⑦j				C			⑤f			H		Q		
London St Pancras 10 d.	...	...	...	...	...	0802	0826	....	...	0922	0932	...	...	1025	...	...	...	...	...	...	1229	...	...	1300	...	...
Paris Nord 10 a.	...	...	...	...	...	1117	1147	...	...	1247	1247	...	...	1347e	...	...	...	...	...	...	1550	...	...	1617	...	...
Paris Gare de Lyon d.	0758	0758	...	...	...	...	...	1258	1258	▬	▬	1358	...	▬	1558	1558	...	...	1558	...	...	1658	...	...	1758	...
Dijon d.	0938	0938	...	...	...	...	...	1440	1440	...	...	1540	...	...	1738	1738	...	...	1738	...	...	1846	...	...	1938	...
Frasne a.	1046	1046	...	...	...	...	...	1547	1547	...	...	1647	...	...	1846	1846	...	...	1846	...	...	2003	...	...	2056	...
Pontarlier 🏛 a.	|	|	...	...	...	...	...	|	|	...	...	|	...	...	|	|	...	...	1904	...	...	2019	...	...	|	...
Neuchâtel a.	|	|	...	...	...	...	...	|	|	...	...	|	...	...	|	|	...	...	1947	...	...	2107	...	...	|	...
Bern a.	|	|	...	...	...	...	...	|	|	...	...	|	...	...	|	|	...	...	2036	2107	...	2140	2207	...	|	...
Thun a.	|	|	...	...	...	...	...	|	|	...	...	|	...	...	|	|	...	...	▬	2124	...	...	2224	...	|	...
Spiez a.	|	|	...	...	...	...	...	|	|	...	...	|	...	...	|	|	...	...	...	2134	...	...	2234	...	|	...
Interlaken West a.	|	|	...	...	...	...	...	|	|	...	...	|	...	...	|	|	...	...	...	2151	...	...	2251	...	|	...
Interlaken Ost a.	|	|	...	...	...	...	...	|	|	...	...	|	...	...	|	|	...	...	...	2157	...	...	2257	...	|	...
Vallorbe 🏛 a.	1102	1102	...	...	...	...	...	1602	1602	*IR*	*IR*	1702	...	*IR*	1902	1902	...	...	...	▬	...	...	...	...	2102	...
Lausanne a.	1137	1137	...	...	...	...	...	1637	1638	**1737**	**1439**	1737	...	**1441**	1940	1940	...	...	...	...	...	...	...	...	2137	...
Lausanne d.	...	1157	...	1220	1245	...	...	...	1657	1720	1745	...	1820	1850	...	1957	2020	2045	...	...	...	...	...	...	...	2220
Montreux a.	...	1215	...	1239	1304	...	...	...	1714	1739	1804	...	1839	1909	...	2015	2039	2104	...	...	...	...	...	...	...	2239
Aigle a.	...	1227	...	1250	1315	...	...	...	1727	1750	1815	...	1850	1920	...	2026	2050	2115	...	...	...	...	...	...	...	2250
Bex a.	...	|	...	|	1323	...	...	...	...	|	1823	...	|	1927	...	|	2058	2123	...	...	...	...	...	...	...	2258
St Maurice a.	...	|	...	|	1327	...	...	...	...	|	1827	...	|	1931	...	|	2102	2127	...	...	...	...	...	...	...	2302
Martigny a.	...	1247	...	1307	▬	...	...	...	...	1807	▬	...	1907	▬	...	2043	2112	2137	...	...	...	...	...	...	...	2313
Sion a.	...	1304	...	1322	...	...	...	...	...	1822	...	...	1922	...	...	2058	2127	2152	...	...	...	...	...	...	...	2327
Sierre a.	...	1315	...	1333	...	...	...	...	...	1833	...	...	1933	...	...	2113	...	2203	①–⑥	⑦	...	...	...	...	...	2338
Visp a.	...	1336	1343	1352	1410	...	...	...	...	1852	1910	...	1952	2010	...	2136	...	2222	2240	2323	...	...	...	...	...	2357
Zermatt a.	...	|	1452	|	1514	...	...	...	...	|	2014	...	|	2114	...	|	...	|	2344	0025	...	...	...	...	...	|
Brig a.	...	1345	...	1402	...	...	...	...	...	1902	...	...	2002	...	...	2147	...	2230	...	...	...	...	...	...	...	0005

train type	IR	IR	TGV	☆		EN	TGV	IC	TGV	☆		IR	TGV	TGV	☆	☆	IR		IR	TGV		TGV		IR	TGV	TGV
train number	1404	1706	9260	9031		316	9264	956	9284	9039		1720	9268	9268	9053	9055	1428		1730	9272		9272		1432	9274	9274
notes			♥🍷	[R]			♥🍷	🍷	♥🍷	[R]🍴			♥🍷	♥🍷	[R]🍴	[R]🍴				♥🍷		♥🍷			♥🍷	♥🍷
				🍴					D				F	A	R	t						A			G	J
Brig d.	0428	...	...	...	...	0657	...	...	...	...	...	1057	...	1101	...	...	...	...	1557	...	...	1541	...	1728	...	...
Zermatt d.	|	...	...	...	0539	|	...	...	...	...	0939	|	...	|	...	...	...	1439	|	...	1339	|	1613	|	...	...
Visp d.	0436	...	...	...	0647	0707	...	...	...	...	1047	1107	...	1111	...	...	...	1547	1607	...	1447	1549	1722	1736	...	...
Sierre d.	0455	...	...	...	▬	0726	...	...	...	...	▬	1126	...	1132	...	...	...	...	1626	...	...	1611	...	1755	...	...
Sion d.	0506	0537	...	...	*IR*	0737	...	...	...	...	*IR*	1137	...	1143	...	...	...	...	1637	...	...	1626	...	1806	...	...
Martigny d.	0520	0551	...	...	**1408**	0751	...	...	...	...	**1418**	1151	...	1205	...	...	...	...	1651	...	...	1642	...	1820	...	...
St Maurice d.	0531	|	...	...	0731	|	...	...	...	...	1126	|	...	|	...	...	1631	...	|	...	...	|	...	1831	...	...
Bex d.	0536	|	...	...	0736	|	...	...	...	...	1131	|	...	|	...	...	1636	...	|	...	...	|	...	1836	...	...
Aigle d.	0543	0608	...	...	0743	0808	...	...	...	...	1138	1208	...	1229	...	...	1643	...	1708	...	...	1714	...	1843	...	1835
Montreux d.	0554	0619	...	...	0754	0819	...	...	...	...	1149	1219	...	1248	...	...	1654	...	1719	...	...	1727	...	1854	...	1849
Lausanne a.	0615	0640	...	...	0815	0840	...	...	...	...	1210	1240	...	1308	...	...	1715	...	1740	...	...	1745	...	1915	...	1908
Lausanne d.	...	...	0722	...	...	...	0922	...	...	...	...	...	1322	1322	...	...	...	...	...	1803	...	1803	...	...	1922	1922
Vallorbe 🏛 d.	...	...	0757	...	...	...	0957	...	...	...	...	...	1357	1357	...	...	...	...	...	1840	...	1840	...	...	1957	1957
Interlaken Ost d.	...	...	|	...	...	...	|	0701	...	...	...	...	|	|	...	...	...	...	...	|	...	|	...	...	|	|
Interlaken West d.	...	...	|	...	...	...	|	0706	...	...	...	...	|	|	...	...	...	...	...	|	...	|	...	...	|	|
Spiez d.	...	...	|	...	...	...	|	0723	...	...	...	...	|	|	...	...	...	...	...	|	...	|	...	...	|	|
Thun d.	...	...	|	...	...	...	|	0733	...	...	...	...	|	|	...	...	...	...	...	|	...	|	...	...	|	|
Bern d.	...	...	|	...	...	...	|	0752	0831	...	...	...	|	|	...	...	...	...	...	|	...	|	...	...	|	|
Neuchâtel d.	...	...	|	...	...	...	|	...	0910	...	...	...	|	|	...	...	...	...	...	|	...	|	...	...	|	|
Pontarlier 🏛 d.	...	...	|	...	...	...	|	...	0954	...	...	...	|	|	...	...	...	...	...	|	...	|	...	...	|	|
Frasne d.	...	...	0814	...	...	...	1019	...	1019	...	...	...	1414	1414	...	...	...	...	...	1906	...	1906	...	...	2014	2014
Dijon d.	...	...	0925	...	...	...	1126	...	1126	...	...	...	1524	1524	...	...	...	...	...	2020	...	2020	...	...	2132	2132
Paris Gare de Lyon a.	...	...	1103	...	...	...	1303	...	1303	...	...	...	1703	1703	...	...	...	...	...	2159	...	2159	...	...	2315	2315
Paris Nord 10 d.	...	...	...	1304	...	...	...	...	...	1507c	...	...	...	...	1843	1913	...	...	...	...	...	...	...	...	...	...
London St Pancras 10 a.	...	...	...	1431	...	...	...	...	...	1636	...	...	...	...	2006	2034	...	...	...	...	...	...	...	...	...	...

A – ⑥ Dec. 19 - Apr. 3 (also Dec. 25, Jan. 1; not Dec. 26, Jan. 2).
B – ⑥ Dec. 19 - Apr. 3.
C – ⑤ Dec. 18 - Apr. 2 (also Dec. 24, 31).
D – Not ①–⑤ Apr. 6 – 23.
E – Not ①–⑤ Mar. 22 - Apr. 2.
F – Not ①–⑤ Apr. 5 – 16.
G – ⑤⑦ (also Dec. 24, 26, 31, Feb. 27, Mar. 6, Apr. 5, May 12, 24; not Dec. 25, Jan. 1).
H – ①②③④⑥⑦ (also Dec. 25, Jan 1; not Dec. 24, 31, May 12).

J – ⑦ Dec. 20 - Mar. 28 (also Apr. 5).
L – ⑦ Dec. 13 - Mar. 28 (also Apr. 5).
M – ①–⑥ (not Dec. 28, Apr. 5, May 3, 24, 31).
P – ⑧ (①⑤⑦ Jan. 4 - Feb. 6) not Jan. 1.
Q – ⑦ (also Dec. 18, 28, Mar. 19, Apr. 2, 5, May 3, 24, 28, 31).
R – ①–⑤ (not Dec. 24, 28, 31, Apr. 5, May 3, 24, 31).

c – 1513 on ①–⑤.
e – 1350 on ⑥.
f – Also Dec. 24, 31, May 12; not Dec. 25, Jan 1.

j – Also Feb. 20, 27, Apr. 5, May 24.
q – Also Dec. 28, Apr. 5, May 3, 24, 31.
r – Also Jan. 1.
t – Not Dec. 24, 31.

♥ – *TGV Lyria* service. [R]. Special fares payable. Supplement payable.
☆ – Eurostar train. Special fares payable. Minimum check-in time 30 minutes. Valid Dec. 13, 2009 - July 3, 2010. No service Dec. 25. Additional Eurostar services are available, see Table **10**.

BRUSSELS - KÖLN - MILANO, VENEZIA and ROMA 43

For Eurostar and rail/sea connections from London see Table **12**.

train type	ICE	EC	ICE	ICE	EC	AV	⇌	ICE	ICE	EC	E
train number	609	51	513	373	57	9529	9407	507	75	59	1911
notes	🍷	[R]🍷	🍷	🍷	[R]🍷	[R]🍴	①–⑥	🍷	🍷	[R]🍷	C
		⊗			⊗	⚡	🍷			⊗	
Brussels Midi / Zuid d.	...	...	...	...	...	...	0755	...	...	...	...
Aachen 🏛 d.	...	...	...	...	...	...	0909	...	...	...	...
Köln Hbf a.	...	...	...	...	...	...	0947	...	...	...	...
Köln Hbf d.	2353	...	0755	...	...	...	▬	1255	...	...	...
Frankfurt (Main) Hbf d.	0222	...	|	0850	...	...	...	|	1405	...	...
Mannheim Hbf d.	0302	...	0924	0936	...	...	...	1424	1444	...	...
Basel SNCF/SBB 🏛 d.	0547	0628	▬	1147	1228	...	...	...	1655	1728	...
Bern a.	...	0735	...	...	1335	...	...	...	...	1835	...
Domodossola 🏛 ¶ a.	...	0912	...	...	1512	...	...	...	...	2012	...
Milano Centrale a.	...	1035	...	...	1640	...	...	...	...	2135	...
		AV 9513 [R]🍴 ⚡	*ESc* 9715				*ESc* 9739 [R]🍴 ⚡				
Milano Centrale d.	...	1115	1135	...	...	1715	1735	...	...	...	2320
Verona a.	...	|	1257	...	...	|	1855	...	...	...	|
Padova a.	...	|	1341	...	...	|	1934	...	...	...	|
Venezia Santa Lucia a.	...	|	1410	...	...	|	2002	...	...	...	|
Bologna a.	...	1220	...	...	...	1820	...	...	...	...	|
Firenze SMN a.	...	1300	...	...	...	1900	...	...	...	...	|
Roma Termini a.	...	1445	...	...	...	2045	...	...	...	...	0723t
Napoli Centrale a.	...	1610	...	...	...	2210	...	...	...	...	1012

train number	EC	ICE	ICE	EC	ESc	ES	ES	ESc	EC	ICE	⇌
train number	50	374	518	100	9708	9506	9524	9732	56	608	9412
notes	[R]🍷	🍷	🍷	102	[R]🍴	[R]🍴	[R]🍴	[R]🍴	[R]🍷	🍷	①–⑥
	⊗			🍷	P	⚡	⚡		⊗		f
Napoli Centrale d.	...	...	...	...	...	...	1250	...	...	...	...
Roma Termini d.	...	...	...	...	...	0715	1415	...	...	...	...
Firenze SMN d.	...	...	...	...	...	0900	1600	...	...	...	...
Bologna d.	...	...	...	...	...	0940	1640	...	...	...	...
Venezia Santa Lucia d.	...	...	...	...	0750	|	|	1520	...	...	...
Padova d.	...	...	...	...	0818	|	|	1548	...	...	...
Verona d.	...	...	...	...	0902	|	|	1632	...	...	...
Milano Centrale d.	...	...	...	...	1025	1045	1745	1755	...	...	...
					▬	*EC* 52 [R]🍷 ⊗	▬	▬			
Milano Centrale d.	0725	...	...	...	...	1120	*ICE*	...	1825	...	...
Domodossola 🏛 ¶ d.	0848	...	...	...	...	1248	**870**	...	1948	...	...
Bern d.	1023	...	...	...	...	1423	🍷	*ICE*	2123	...	...
Basel SBB/SNCF 🏛 a.	1132	1212	...	1218	...	1532	1612	**514**	2232	2326	...
Mannheim Hbf a.	...	1422	1435	1437	⇌	...	1823	1835	...	0222	...
Frankfurt (Main) Hbf a.	...	1508	|	|	**9456**	...	1908	|	...	0308	...
Köln Hbf a.	...	...	1605	1705	🍷	...	...	2005	...	0605	...
Köln Hbf d.	...	...	...	...	1745	...	...	...	...	...	0645
Aachen 🏛 a.	...	...	...	...	1820	...	...	...	...	...	0720
Brussels Midi / Zuid a.	...	...	...	...	1932	...	...	...	...	...	0832

C – 🛏 1, 2 cl. (Excelsior), 🛏 1, 2 cl. (T2), 🛏 1, 2 cl., ▬ 2 cl. (4, 6 berth) and (12) Milano - Napoli.
P – ①–⑤ (not Dec. 25, Jan. 1, 6, Apr. 5.
f – Not Dec. 25, Jan. 1, Apr. 5, May 1, 13, 24.

t – Roma **Tiburtina**.
⚡ – Supplement payable.
¶ – Ticket point is **Iselle**.

⇌ – *Thalys* high-speed train. [R] 🍷. Special fares payable.
⊗ – **ETR 610**. Supplement payable for international journeys. *IC* supplement payable for internal journeys within Italy.

44 LONDON - PARIS - TORINO - MILANO - VENEZIA and ROMA

train type		TGV	EC	ESc	AV	ESc	ESc		☆		TGV	ICN			ICN	ICN			
train number	17983	9241	159	9771	9523	9819	9733		9018	17943	9249	799			785	1911	10601		
notes	①–⑥	R ✕	R 🍷	R 🍷	R ✕	R 🍷	R 🍷			①–⑤	R ✕	R ⚡			R ⚡	R ⚡			
notes	h	♣ ❖	⚡	⚡	⚡ ¶	⚡	⚡			y	♣x	E			C	H			
London St Pancras 10 12 d.	...	...	...	...	...	...	...	...	1025	...	...	...	...	...	...	...	...	...	...
Lille Europe 11 d.	...	...	...	...	...	...	...	...	|	...	...	...	...	...	...	...	...	...	...
Paris Nord 10 a.	...	...	...	...	...	...	...	...	1347n	...	...	...	...	...	...	...	...	...	...
Paris Gare de Lyon d.	...	0742	...	...	...	...	...	...	...	...	1524	...	...	...	...	...	...	...	...
Paris Gare de Bercy ◧ d.	...	|	...	...	...	...	...	...	...	...	|	...	...	...	...	...	...	...	...
Dijon d.	...	|	...	...	...	...	...	...	...	...	|	...	...	...	...	...	...	...	...
Lyon Perrache d.	...	|	...	...	...	...	...	...	...	...	|	...	...	...	...	...	...	...	...
Lyon Part Dieu d.	0841	|	...	...	...	...	...	...	...	1637	|	...	...	...	...	...	...	...	...
Aix les Bains d.	|	|	...	...	...	...	...	...	...	|	|	...	...	...	...	...	...	...	...
Chambéry d.	0955	1045	...	...	...	...	...	...	...	1755	1826	...	...	...	...	...	...	...	...
Modane 🛃 d.	...	1155	...	...	...	...	...	...	...	...	1930	...	...	...	...	...	...	...	...
Oulx ▲ a.	...	1228	...	...	...	...	...	...	...	...	2005	...	...	...	...	...	...	...	...
Torino Porta Nuova § a.	...	|	...	...	...	...	...	...	...	...	2100	2155	...	...	...	...	...	...	...
Torino Porta Susa § a.	...	1317	...	...	...	...	...	...	...	...	...	|	...	...	...	...	...	...	...
Novara a.	...	|	...	...	...	...	...	...	...	...	...	|	...	...	...	...	...	...	...
Milano Centrale a.	...	1455	1510	...	1515	1535	1605	...	...	...	...	|	...	...	2300	2320	0015	...	...
Alessandria a.	...	...	|	...	|	|	|	...	...	...	...	2257	...	...	|	|	|	...	...
Genova Piazza Principe a.	...	...	1642	1652	|	|	|	...	...	...	...	2350	...	...	|	|	|	...	...
La Spezia a.	...	...	...	1804	|	|	|	...	...	...	...	0124	...	...	|	|	|	...	...
Viareggio a.	...	..	...	1838	|	|	|	...	...	...	...	|	...	...	|	|	|	...	...
Pisa Centrale a.	...	...	...	1857	|	|	|	...	...	...	...	0214	...	...	|	|	|	...	...
Livorno a.	...	...	...	1914	|	|	|	...	...	...	...	0235	...	...	|	|	|	...	...
Grosseto a.	...	...	...	...	|	|	|	...	...	...	...	0356	...	...	|	|	|	...	...
Brescia a.	...	...	...	...	|	|	1651	...	...	...	...	|	...	...	|	|	0134	...	...
Verona Porta Nuova a.	...	...	...	...	|	|	1727	...	...	...	...	|	...	...	|	|	0223	...	...
Vicenza a.	...	...	...	...	|	|	1754	...	...	...	...	|	...	...	|	|	...	...	...
Padova a.	...	...	...	...	|	|	1811	...	...	...	...	|	...	...	|	|	...	...	...
Venezia Mestre a.	...	...	...	...	|	|	1828	...	...	...	...	|	...	...	|	|	...	...	...
Venezia Santa Lucia a.	...	...	...	...	|	|	1840	...	...	...	...	|	...	...	|	|	...	...	...
Piacenza a.	...	...	...	...	|	1620	...	...	...	...	...	|	...	...	2343	0008	...	...	...
Parma a.	...	...	...	...	|	1648	...	...	...	...	...	|	...	...	0016	0059	...	...	...
Reggio Emilia a.	...	...	...	...	|	1703	...	...	...	...	...	|	...	...	0036	|	...	...	...
Modena a.	...	...	...	...	|	1717	...	...	...	...	...	|	...	...	0053	|	...	...	...
Bologna Centrale a.	...	...	...	...	1620	1742	...	...	...	...	...	|	...	...	0124	|	...	...	...
Rimini a.	...	...	...	...	|	1845	...	...	...	...	...	|	...	...	0235	|	...	...	...
Ancona a.	...	...	...	...	|	1938	...	...	...	...	...	|	...	...	0333	|	...	...	...
Pescara Centrale a.	...	...	...	...	|	2049	...	...	...	...	...	|	...	...	0459	|	...	...	...
Bari Centrale a.	...	...	...	...	|	2335	...	...	...	...	...	|	...	...	0826	|	...	...	...
Athína ⊖ a.	...	...	...	...	|	...	...	...	...	...	...	|	...	...	⊖	|	...	...	...
Brindisi a.	...	...	...	...	|	...	...	...	...	...	...	|	...	...	...	|	...	...	...
Firenze SMN a.	...	...	...	...	1700	...	...	...	...	...	...	|	...	...	...	|	...	...	...
Roma Termini a.	...	...	...	...	1845c	...	...	...	...	...	...	0551	...	...	...	0730t	...	...	...
Napoli Centrale a.	...	...	...	...	2010	...	...	...	...	...	...	0911	...	...	...	1012	...	...	...

train type	☆	EN		IC	AV	IC	☆	☆	EN	AV		AV	AV	IC	IC	ESc	IC	ESc	IC	
train number	9030	227	2121	501	9505	727	9036	9038	221	9451	2004	9503	9601	645	515	9801	585	9803	553	
notes		⛝		R 🍷	R 🍷	R 🍷			⛝	R 🍷		R 🍷	R 🍷	R 🍷	R 🍷	R 🍷	R 🍷	R 🍷	R 🍷	
notes		A		①–⑥ g⚡	⚡	⚡	⑥⑦ b	①–⑤ e	B m	⚡		①–⑥ f⚡	①–⑤ f⚡	⚡	⚡	⚡	⚡	⚡	⚡	
London St Pancras 10 12 d.	1404	...	...	...	...	...	1532	1602	...	...	...	...	...	...	...	...	...	...	...	...
Lille Europe 11 d.	|	...	...	...	...	...	|	|	...	...	...	...	...	...	...	...	...	...	...	...
Paris Nord 10 a.	1726	...	...	...	...	...	1847	1917	...	...	...	...	...	...	...	...	...	...	...	...
Paris Gare de Bercy ◧ d.	...	1852	...	...	...	...	...	...	2033	...	...	...	...	...	...	...	...	...	...	...
Dijon d.	...	2137	...	...	...	...	...	...	2321	...	...	...	...	...	...	...	...	...	...	...
Modane 🛃 d.	...	⊙	...	...	...	...	...	...	⊙	...	...	...	...	...	...	...	...	...	...	...
Milano Centrale a.	...	|	...	...	...	...	...	...	0538	...	0600	0615	0630	0605	...	0635	0705	0735	0915	...
Novara a.	...	|	...	...	...	...	...	...	|	...	0643	|	|	|	...	|	|	|	|	...
Torino Porta Nuova a.	...	|	...	...	...	...	...	...	|	...	0800	|	|	|	...	|	|	|	|	...
Genova Piazza Principe a.	...	|	...	...	...	...	...	...	|	...	...	|	|	0744	0852	|	|	|	|	...
La Spezia a.	...	|	...	...	...	...	...	...	|	...	...	|	|	0917	1004	|	|	|	|	...
Viareggio a.	...	|	...	...	...	...	...	...	|	...	...	|	|	1000	1036	|	|	|	|	...
Pisa Centrale a.	...	|	...	...	...	...	...	...	|	...	...	|	|	1018	1057	|	|	|	|	...
Livorno a.	...	|	...	...	...	...	...	...	|	...	...	|	|	1038	1114	|	|	|	|	...
Grosseto a.	...	|	...	...	...	...	...	...	|	...	...	|	|	...	1226	|	|	|	|	...
Brescia a.	...	|	...	...	...	...	...	...	0643	0705	...	|	|	...	|	|	|	|	|	...
Verona Porta Nuova a.	...	|	...	...	...	...	...	...	0727	0739	...	|	|	...	|	|	|	|	|	...
Vicenza a.	...	|	...	...	...	...	...	...	0813	|	...	|	|	...	|	|	|	|	|	...
Padova a.	...	|	...	...	...	...	...	...	0851	|	...	|	|	...	|	|	|	|	|	...
Venezia Mestre a.	...	|	...	...	...	...	...	...	0921	|	...	|	|	...	|	|	|	|	|	...
Venezia Santa Lucia a.	...	|	...	...	...	...	...	...	0934	|	...	|	|	...	|	|	|	|	|	...
Piacenza a.	...	0444	...	...	...	...	...	...	...	|	...	|	|	...	|	0720	0748	0820	0954	...
Parma a.	...	0512	...	...	...	...	...	...	...	|	...	|	|	...	|	0748	0812	0848	1021	...
Reggio Emilia a.	...	|	...	...	...	...	...	...	...	|	...	|	|	...	|	0803	0827	0903	1036	...
Modena a.	...	|	...	...	...	...	...	...	...	|	...	|	|	...	|	0817	0840	0917	1051	...
Bologna Centrale a.	...	0558	0638	...	...	...	...	...	...	0844	...	0720	|	...	|	0842	0904	0942	1114	...
Rimini a.	...	|	0805	...	...	...	...	...	...	|	...	|	|	...	|	0956	|	1045	1234	...
Ancona a.	...	|	0924	...	...	...	...	...	...	|	...	|	|	...	|	1055	|	1138	1334	...
Pescara Centrale a.	...	|	...	...	...	...	...	...	...	|	...	|	|	...	|	...	|	1249	1509	...
Bari Centrale a.	...	|	...	...	...	...	...	...	...	|	...	|	|	...	|	...	|	1535	1841	...
Athína ⊖ a.	...	|	...	...	...	...	...	...	...	|	...	|	|	...	|	...	|	⊖	⊖	...
Brindisi a.	...	|	...	...	...	...	...	...	...	|	...	|	|	...	|	...	|	1640	...	...
Firenze SMN a.	...	0713	...	...	...	...	...	...	...	0924‡	...	0800	|	...	|	...	1024j	...	...	...
Roma Termini a.	...	1012	...	1027	1100	1128	...	...	...	1055	...	0945c	0929c	...	1414	...	1316	...	...	...
Napoli Centrale a.	...	...	...	1236	1210	1330	...	...	...	...	...	1110	1055	...	...	...	1550	...	...	...

NOTES for this page and the following page

A – PALATINO *Trainhotel Artesia* – 🛏 1, 2 cl., ▬ 2 cl. (6 berth, 4 berth and ladies only 4 berth) and ✕: Paris - Bologna - Firenze - Roma and v.v.

B – STENDHAL *Trainhotel Artesia* – 🛏 1, 2 cl., ▬ 2 cl. (6 berth, 4 berth and ladies only 4 berth) and ✕: Paris - Milano - Venezia and v.v. (not May 10–14, 17–21).

C – FRECCIA DEL LEVANTE – 🛏 1, 2 cl., 🛏 1, 2 cl. (T2), ▬ 2 cl. and (12) Milano - Bari - Taranto.

E – 🛏 1, 2 cl. (Excelsior), 🛏 1, 2 cl., ▬ 2 cl. (4 berth) and (2) Torino - Roma - Napoli and v.v. 🛏 1, 2 cl. and ▬ 2 cl. (2) Torino - Roma and v.v.

H – 🛏 1, 2 cl. (Excelsior), 🛏 1, 2 cl. (T2), 🛏 1, 2 cl., ▬ 2 cl. (4, 6 berth) and (2) Milano - Napoli and v.v.

O – FRECCIA ADRIATICA – 🛏 1, 2 cl. (T2), ▬ 2 cl. and (2) Torino - Brindisi - Lecce.

b – Also Dec. 28, Jan. 1, Apr. 5, May 3, 24, 31.

c – Departs 15–16 minutes later.

e – Not Dec. 28, Jan. 1, Apr. 5, May 3, 24, 31.

OTHER TRAIN NAMES:
9241 – ALESSANDRO MANZONI
9249 – CARAVAGGIO

f – Not Dec. 25, Jan. 1, 6, Apr. 5, 25, May 1.

g – Not Dec. 25, Jan. 1, Apr. 5.

h – Not Dec. 25, Jan. 1, Apr. 5, May 1, 8, 13, 24.

j – Firenze **Rifredi**.

k – Calls at Lyon St Exupéry TGV ✈, arrive 2124.

m – Calls at Dole, depart 2347.

n – 1350 on ⑥.

p – Not Dec. 25, Jan. 1, Apr. 5, May 13, 24.

q – Also Dec. 25, Jan. 1, Apr. 5, May 13, 24.

t – Roma **Tiburtina**.

v – Not Dec. 28, Apr. 5, May 3, 24, 31.

NOTES CONTINUED ON NEXT PAGE →

ROMA and VENEZIA - MILANO - TORINO - PARIS - LONDON 44

train type	*TGV*		☆			*IC*	*ESc*	*AV*	*ESc*	*AV*	*IC*	*IC*	*TGV*							
train number	**9240**	**17910**	**9043**			**582**	**9722**	**9516**	**9814**	**9520**	**606**	**516**	**9248**	**17928**						
notes	🅁✕		🅁			🅁🍷	🅁🍷	🅁✕	🅁🍷	🅁✕	🅁🍷	🅁🍷	🅁✕							
notes	♣		✕			⁄	⁄	⁄ ¶	⁄	⁄	⁄	⁄	♣k ❖	Ⓑ						
Napoli Centrale d.	...	...	...	...	...	0614		0950	...	1050	...	0730	...	...	...	...	...	...	...	...
Roma Termini d.	...	...	...	...	...	0841	...	1115	...	1215	...	0946	...	...	...	...	...	...	...	...
Firenze SMN d.	...	...	...	...	...	1136j	...	1300	...	1400	...	|	...	...	...	...	...	...	...	...
Brindisi d.	...	...	...	...	...	|	...	|	...	|	...	|	...	...	...	...	...	...	...	...
Athína ⊖ d.	...	...	...	...	...	|	...	|	⊖	|	...	|	...	...	...	...	...	...	...	...
Bari Centrale d.	...	...	...	...	...	|	...	|	0729	|	...	|	...	...	...	...	...	...	...	...
Pescara Centrale d.	...	...	...	...	...	|	...	|	1014	|	...	|	...	...	...	...	...	...	...	...
Ancona d.	...	...	...	...	...	|	...	|	1127	|	...	|	...	...	...	...	...	...	...	...
Rimini d.	...	...	...	...	...	|	...	|	1219	|	...	|	...	...	...	...	...	...	...	...
Bologna Centrale d.	...	...	...	...	...	1247	...	1340	1318	1440	...	|	...	...	...	...	...	...	...	...
Modena d.	...	...	...	...	...	1308	...	|	|	|	...	|	...	...	...	...	...	...	...	...
Reggio Emilia d.	...	...	...	...	...	1322	...	|	|	|	...	|	...	...	...	...	...	...	...	...
Parma d.	...	...	...	...	...	1337	...	|	|	|	...	|	...	...	...	...	...	...	...	...
Piacenza d.	...	...	...	...	...	1418	..	|	|	|	...	|	...	...	...	...	...	...	...	...
Venezia Santa Lucia d.	...	...	...	...	...	|	1250	|	|	|	...	|	...	...	...	...	...	...	...	...
Venezia Mestre d.	...	...	...	...	...	|	1302	|	|	|	...	|	...	...	...	...	...	...	...	...
Padova d.	...	...	...	...	...	|	1318	|	|	|	...	|	...	...	...	...	...	...	...	...
Vicenza d.	...	...	...	...	...	|	1335	|	|	|	...	|	...	...	...	...	...	...	...	...
Verona Porta Nuova d.	...	...	...	...	...	|	1402	|	|	|	...	|	...	...	...	...	...	...	...	...
Brescia d.	...	...	...	...	...	|	1439	|	|	|	...	|	...	...	...	...	...	...	...	...
Grosseto d.	...	...	...	...	...	|	|	|	|	|	...	1130	...	...	...	...	...	...	...	...
Livorno d.	...	...	...	...	...	|	|	|	|	|	1126	1242	...	...	...	...	...	...	...	...
Pisa Centrale d.	...	...	...	...	...	|	|	|	|	|	1144	1300	...	...	...	...	...	...	...	...
Viareggio d.	...	...	...	...	...	|	|	|	|	|	1202	|	...	...	...	...	...	...	...	...
La Spezia d.	...	...	...	...	...	|	|	|	|	|	1240	1353	...	...	...	...	...	...	...	...
Genova Piazza Principe d.	...	...	...	...	...	|	|	|	|	|	1419	1512	...	...	...	...	...	...	...	...
Alessandria d.	...	...	...	...	...	|	|	|	|	|	|	1557	...	...	...	...	...	...	...	...
Milano Centrale d.	...	...	...	...	...	1500	1525	1445	1530	1545	1555	|	1610	...	...	...	...	...	...	...
Novara d.	...	...	...	...	...	...	...	...	...	...	...	|	|	...	...	...	...	...	...	...
Torino Porta Susa § d.	...	...	...	...	...	...	...	...	...	...	...	|	1735	...	...	...	...	...	...	...
Torino Porta Nuova § d.	0805	...	...	...	...	...	...	...	...	...	...	1655	|	...	...	...	...	...	...	...
Oulx ▲ d.	0900	...	...	...	...	...	...	...	...	...	...	...	1825	...	...	...	...	...	...	...
Modane 🏛 a.	0938	1027	...	...	...	...	...	...	...	...	...	...	1905	...	...	...	...	...	...	...
Chambéry a.	1104	1152	...	...	...	...	...	...	...	...	...	...	2022	2101	...	...	...	...	...	...
Aix les Bains a.	|	|	...	...	...	...	...	...	...	...	...	...	|	|	...	...	...	...	...	...
Lyon Part Dieu a.	|	1316	...	...	...	...	...	...	...	...	...	...	|	2221	...	...	...	...	...	...
Lyon Perrache a.	|	...	...	...	...	...	...	...	...	...	...	...	|	...	...	...	...	...	...	...
Dijon a.	|	...	...	...	...	...	...	...	...	...	...	...	|	...	...	...	...	...	...	...
Paris Gare de Bercy ◧ a.	|	...	...	...	...	...	...	...	...	...	...	...	|	...	...	...	...	...	...	...
Paris Gare de Lyon a.	1403	...	...	...	...	...	...	...	...	...	...	...	2321	...	...	...	...	...	...	...
Paris Nord 10 d.	...	...	1613	...	...	...	...	...	...	...	...	...	...	...	...	...	...	...	...	...
Lille Europe 11 d.	...	...	|	...	...	...	...	...	...	...	...	...	...	...	...	...	...	...	...	...
London St Pancras 10 12 a.	...	...	1734	...	...	...	...	...	...	...	...	...	...	...	...	...	...	...	...	...

train type	*IC*	*ESc*	*IC*	*EC*	*AV*	*AV*		*ESc*	*IC*	*EN*	*TGV*	☆	☆		*AV*	*EN*	*TGV*	☆	☆	
train number	**568**	**9826**	**538**	**147 148**	**9534**	**9642**	**2029**	**9828**	**592**	**220**	**5152**	**9119**	**9019**		**9532**	**226**	**5156**	**9181**	**9023**	
notes	🅁🍷	🅁🍷	🅁🍷	🅁🍷	🅁✕	🅁✕		🅁🍷	🅁🍷	⊠	🅁🍷				🅁✕	⊠	🅁🍷			
notes	⁄	⁄	⁄	⁄	⁄	Ⓑ ⁄		⁄	⁄	B w	①–⑤ p⁄	①–⑥ v			⁄	A	⑥⑦ q⁄			
Napoli Centrale d.	...	...	1324	...	1750	...	...	...	1424	...	...	...	...	...	1650	...	...	...	...	...
Roma Termini d.	...	...	1546	...	1915	2000	...	...	1644	...	...	...	...	...	1800	1820	...	...	...	...
Firenze SMN d.	...	...	|	...	2100	|	...	...	1936j	...	...	...	...	...	...	2125	...	...	...	...
Brindisi d.	...	1224	|	...	|	|	...	...	|	...	...	...	...	...	...	|	...	...	...	...
Athína ⊖ d.	⊖	⊖	|	...	|	|	...	⊖	|	...	...	...	...	...	...	|	...	...	...	...
Bari Centrale d.	1113	1329	|	...	|	|	...	1405	|	...	...	...	...	...	...	|	...	...	...	...
Pescara Centrale d.	1435	1614	|	...	|	|	...	1700	|	...	...	...	...	...	...	|	...	...	...	...
Ancona d.	1620	1727	|	...	|	|	...	1813	|	...	...	...	...	...	...	|	...	...	...	...
Rimini d.	1726	1819	|	...	|	|	...	1905	|	...	...	...	...	...	...	|	...	...	...	...
Bologna Centrale d.	1856	1918	|	...	2140	|	...	2006	2056	...	...	...	...	...	...	2231	...	...	...	...
Modena d.	1915	|	|	...	|	|	...	2025	2115	...	...	...	...	...	...	|	...	...	...	...
Reggio Emilia d.	1929	|	|	...	|	|	...	|	2130	...	...	...	...	...	...	|	...	...	...	...
Parma d.	1945	|	|	...	|	|	...	|	2145	...	...	...	...	...	...	2314	...	...	...	...
Piacenza d.	2020	|	|	...	|	|	...	|	2220	...	...	...	...	...	...	2345	...	...	...	...
Venezia Santa Lucia d.	|	|	|	...	|	|	...	|	|	1957	...	...	...	...	...	|	...	...	...	...
Venezia Mestre d.	|	|	|	...	|	|	...	|	|	2009	...	...	...	...	...	|	...	...	...	...
Padova d.	|	|	|	...	|	|	...	|	|	2032	...	...	...	...	...	|	...	...	...	...
Vicenza d.	|	|	|	...	|	|	...	|	|	2052	...	...	...	...	...	|	...	...	...	...
Verona Porta Nuova d.	|	|	|	...	|	|	...	|	|	2124	...	...	...	...	...	|	...	...	...	...
Brescia d.	|	|	|	...	|	|	...	|	|	2206	...	...	...	...	...	|	...	...	...	...
Grosseto d.	|	|	1729	...	|	|	...	|	|	|	...	...	...	...	...	|	...	...	...	...
Livorno d.	|	|	1842	...	|	|	...	|	|	|	...	...	...	...	...	|	...	...	...	...
Pisa Centrale d.	|	|	1900	...	|	|	...	|	|	|	...	...	...	...	...	|	...	...	...	...
Viareggio d.	|	|	1917	...	|	|	...	|	|	|	...	...	...	...	...	|	...	...	...	...
La Spezia d.	|	|	1953	...	|	|	...	|	|	|	...	...	...	...	...	|	...	...	...	...
Genova Piazza Principe d.	|	|	2108	2119	|	|	...	|	|	|	...	...	...	...	...	|	...	...	...	...
Torino Porta Nuova d.	|	|	...	|	|	|	2055	|	|	|	...	...	...	...	...	|	...	...	...	...
Novara d.	|	|	...	|	|	|	2207	|	|	|	...	...	...	...	...	|	...	...	...	...
Milano Centrale d.	2105	2125	...	2250	2245	2259	2248	2230	2300	2335z	...	...	...	...	...	|	...	...	...	...
Modane 🏛 a.	...	...	...	...	...	...	...	...	...	⊙	...	...	...	...	...	⊙	...	...	...	...
Dijon a.	...	...	...	...	...	...	...	...	...	0536	0632	...	...	...	...	0633	0744	...	...	...
Paris Gare de Bercy ◧ a.	...	...	...	...	...	...	...	...	...	0819	|	...	...	...	...	0916	|	...	...	...
Paris Nord 10 d.	...	...	...	...	...	...	...	...	...	...	|	...	1013	...	...	...	|	...	1113	...
Lille Europe 11 d.	...	...	...	...	...	...	...	...	...	...	0915	1005	|	...	...	...	1027	1205	|	...
London St Pancras 10 12 a.	...	...	...	...	...	...	...	...	...	...	...	1026	1128	...	...	...	...	1233	1229	...

→ **NOTES continued from previous page**

- **q** – Also Dec. 25, Jan. 1, Apr. 5, May 13, 24.
- **t** – Roma **Tiburtina**.
- **v** – Not Dec. 28, Apr. 5, May 3, 24, 31.
- **w** – Calls at Dole, arrive 0509.
- **x** – Calls at Lyon St Exupéry TGV ✈, depart 1720.
- **y** – Not Dec. 25, Jan. 1, Apr. 5, May 13, 24.
- **z** – Arrive 2305.
- ‡ – Firenze Campo di Marte
- ¶ – To / from Salerno (Table **640**).
- ⁄ – Supplement payable.
- ♣ – *TGV Artesia* service. Special fares payable.
- ▲ – Station for the resorts of Cesana, Claviere and Sestriere.
- ◧ – Paris **Gare de Bercy**, 1km from **Gare de Lyon**; see City Plan of Paris page 30.
- ⊠ – For use by passengers making international journeys only. Special fares payable.
- ⊖ – For connections to Athína (by ⛴ Ancona / Bari - Pátra), see Tables **74, 2715, 2755**.
- ☆ – Eurostar train. Special fares payable. Minimum check-in time 30 minutes. Valid Dec. 13, 2009 - July 3, 2010. No service Dec. 25. Additional Eurostar services are available, see Table **10**.
- ⊙ – Frontier / ticketing points 🏛 are Vallorbe and Domodossola (via Switzerland, non–EU nationals may require transit visas). Ticket point for Domodossola is **Iselle**.
- § – Local train services (Tables **585 / 586**) and metro services run between Torino **Porta Susa** and Torino **Porta Nuova**.
- ❖ – Subject to confirmation. At the time of going to press Artesia were unable to confirm the running of trains **9241** and **9248**.

OTHER TRAIN NAMES: **9240** – CARAVAGGIO **9248** – ALESSANDRO MANZONI

45 MADRID - LISBOA

train number notes			Hotel 332 🅁✕ A		
Madrid Chamartín d.	...	...	2225	...	...
Talavera de La Reina d.	...	...	0008	...	...
Navalmoral de La Mata d.	...	...	0038	...	...
Cáceres d.	...	...	0153	...	...
San Vicente de Alcántara d.	...	...	0307	...	...
Valencia de Alcántara 🏛 ES d.	...	...	0415	...	...
Marvão Beirã 🏛 PT d.	...	...	0334	...	...
Abrantes a.	...	...	0531	...	...
Entroncamento a.	...	...	0554	...	...
Lisboa Oriente a.	...	...	0730	...	...
Lisboa Santa Apolónia a.	...	...	0741	...	...

train number notes			Hotel 335 🅁✕ A		
Lisboa Santa Apolónia d.	...	...	2230	...	...
Lisboa Oriente d.	...	...	2239	...	...
Entroncamento d.	...	...	2354	...	...
Abrantes d.	...	...	0020	...	...
Marvão Beirã 🏛 PT d.	...	...	0142	...	...
Valencia de Alcántara 🏛 ES d.	...	...	0340	...	...
San Vicente de Alcántara d.	...	...	0355	...	...
Cáceres a.	...	...	0505	...	...
Navalmoral de La Mata a.	...	...	0636	...	...
Talavera de La Reina a.	...	...	0713	...	...
Madrid Chamartín a.	...	...	0903	...	...

A – LUSITANIA *Hotel Train* – 🛏 *Gran Clase* (1, 2 berths), 🛏 *Preferente* (1, 2 berths), 🛏 2 cl. (4 berths), (12) and ✕ Madrid - Lisboa and v.v. Special fares apply. From Lisboa, passengers can board from 2130; ✕ from 2200. Not Dec. 24, 31.

ES – Spain (Central European Time).
PT – Portugal (West European Time).

46 LONDON - PARIS - LISBOA, PORTO and MADRID

train type / number	TGV	D	☆	TGV	Alvia		☆	TGV	312	IC	IC	Hotel	☆	☆	Hotel		AVE	AVE	☆	☆		Alvia	AVE		Arco
train number	8505	413	9078	8515	4166		9018	8543	313	521	523	752	9030	9034	409/8	18300	2102	2112	9044	9046	4053	4086	2162	18308	283
notes	🅁⁄ 🍸	🍸 2	🅁✕ K	🅁⁄ 🍸			🅁✕	🅁⁄ 🍸	🅁✕ A	①–⑥ 🅁🍸	🅁 🍸	🅁⁄ C	🅁✕	🅁✕ Ⓑj	🅁✕ G	2 ①–⑤	①–⑥		🅁✕ ⑥r	🅁✕ Ⓑf	🅁 F			2	E
London St Pancras 10 d.	...	...	0525	...	...	...	1025	...	...	...	...	...	1404	1502	...	...	...	...	1725	1755	...	...	...	...	...
Paris Nord 10 a.	...	...	0850	...	...	...	1347e	...	...	...	...	...	1726	1817	...	...	...	...	2053	2117	...	...	...	...	...
Paris Montparnasse d.	0715	...	...	1010	...	...	...	1550	...	...	...	...	▬	...	...	...	...	...	...	...	...	...	...	...	...
Paris Austerlitz d.	|	...	...	|	...	...	...	|	...	...	...	...	...	...	1947	...	...	...	...	...	2310	...	...	...	...
Les Aubrais-Orléans d.	|	...	...	|	...	...	...	|	...	...	...	...	...	...	2042	...	...	...	...	...	0019	...	...	...	...
Blois d.	|	...	...	|	...	...	...	|	...	...	...	...	...	...	2107	...	...	...	...	...	|	...	...	...	...
Poitiers d.	|	...	...	|	...	...	...	|	...	...	...	...	...	...	2208	...	...	...	...	...	|	...	...	...	...
Bordeaux St Jean d.	1030	...	...	1318	...	...	...	1903	...	...	...	...	...	...	|	...	...	...	...	...	|	...	...	...	...
Hendaye d.	1259	...	...	1544	...	...	...	2130	...	...	...	...	...	...	|	...	...	...	...	...	0730	...	...	...	...
Irún 🏛 d.	1304	1320	...	1549	1620	...	...	2136	2200	...	...	...	...	...	|	...	...	...	...	...	0736	0815	...	...	0845
San Sebastián / Donostia a.	...	1335	...	...	1637	...	...	...	2218	...	...	...	...	...	|	...	...	...	...	...	...	0830	...	...	0901
Vitoria / Gasteiz a.	...	1514	...	...	1815	...	...	...	0014	...	...	...	...	...	0405	...	...	...	...	...	...	1007	...	...	1039
Burgos Rosa de Lima a.	...	1703	...	...	1938	...	...	...	0157	...	...	...	...	...	0520	...	...	...	...	...	...	1125	...	...	1212
Valladolid Campo Grande a.	...	1811	...	...	2046	...	...	...	0318	...	...	0500	...	...	0622	0726	...	...	...	...	...	1235	...	1348	...
Medina del Campo a.	...	1843	...	...	|	...	...	...	0352	...	...	0526	...	...	|	0800	...	...	...	...	...	|	...	1416	...
Salamanca a.	...	1937	...	...	|	...	...	...	0448	...	...	|	...	...	|	0859	...	...	...	...	...	|	...	1515	...
Coimbra-B ⊙ a.	...	...	...	...	|	...	...	...	0849	0931	1134	|	...	...	|	...	...	...	...	...	...	|	...	...	...
Lisboa Santa Apolónia a.	...	...	...	...	|	...	...	...	1103	|	|	|	...	...	|	...	...	...	...	...	...	|	...	...	...
Porto Campanhã a.	...	...	...	...	|	...	...	...	...	1039	1239	|	AVE	...	|	...	...	...	...	...	...	|	...	...	...
Madrid Chamartín a.	...	...	...	...	2208	...	...	...	...	...	...	0805	2092	...	0910	...	...	...	...	...	...	1357	...	...	...
Madrid Puerta de Atocha a.	...	...	...	...	...	...	...	...	...	...	...	...	0935	...	...	...	1035	1130	...	...	...	...	1635	...	...
Málaga María Zambrano a.	...	...	...	...	...	...	...	...	...	...	...	...	1223	...	...	...	1315	1410	...	...	...	...	1915	...	...

train type / number	D	TGV		Arco	AVE		Alvia		☆		AVE		Hotel	☆		AVE	Hotel	IC	310	TGV	☆				
train number	410	8584		280	2123	18306	4167	4052	9015		2153	18316	406/7	9019		2183	751	528	311	8524	9043				
notes	🍸 2	🅁⁄		E		2		🅁 F	🅁 ✕			2 ⑦	🅁✕ H	🅁✕			🅁⁄ D	🅁 🍸	🅁✕ B	🅁⁄ 🍸	🅁 ✕				
Málaga María Zambrano d.	...	...	...	...	1200	...	...	...	...	...	1500	...	...	...	...	1805	...	...	...	...	...	...	...	...	...
Madrid Puerta de Atocha d.	...	...	...	...	1440	...	...	...	...	...	1740	...	...	...	...	2040	...	...	...	...	...	...	...	...	...
Madrid Chamartín d.	...	...	...	...	...	...	1610	...	...	...	...	...	1900	...	...	...	2230	...	...	...	...	...	...	...	...
Porto Campanhã d.	...	...	...	...	...	...	|	...	...	...	...	...	|	...	...	...	|	1652	...	...	...	...	...	...	...
Lisboa Santa Apolónia d.	...	...	...	...	...	...	|	...	...	...	...	...	|	...	...	...	|	|	1606	...	...	...	...	...	...
Coimbra-B ⊙ d.	...	...	...	...	...	...	|	...	...	...	...	...	|	...	...	...	|	1757	1824	...	...	...	...	...	...
Salamanca d.	1030	...	...	...	...	1350	|	...	...	...	...	1705	|	...	...	...	|	...	0005	...	...	...	...	...	...
Medina del Campo d.	1120	...	...	...	...	1448	|	...	...	...	...	1758	|	...	...	...	0051	...	0057	...	...	...	...	...	...
Valladolid Campo Grande d.	1151	...	...	...	...	1514	1734	...	...	...	...	1837	2120	...	...	...	0120	...	0130	...	...	...	...	...	...
Burgos Rosa de Lima d.	1304	...	...	1644	...	...	1837	...	...	...	...	...	2221	...	...	...	...	...	0258	...	...	...	...	...	...
Vitoria / Gasteiz d.	1503	...	...	1813	...	...	1956	...	...	...	...	...	2339	...	...	...	...	...	0424	...	...	...	...	...	...
San Sebastián / Donostia d.	1644	...	...	2005	...	...	2135	...	...	...	...	...	|	...	...	...	...	...	0634	...	...	...	...	...	...
Irún d.	1706s	...	...	2027s	...	...	2157s	...	...	...	...	...	|	...	...	...	...	...	0659s	...	...	...	...	...	...
Hendaye 🏛 a.	1713	1722	...	2035	...	...	2203	2218	...	...	...	...	|	...	...	...	...	...	0710	0753	...	...	...	...	...
Bordeaux St Jean a.	...	1947	...	...	...	...	...	|	...	...	...	...	|	...	...	...	...	...	...	1021	...	...	...	...	...
Poitiers a.	...	2138	...	...	...	...	...	|	...	...	...	...	0606	...	...	...	...	...	...	1211	...	...	...	...	...
Blois a.	...	|	...	...	...	...	...	|	...	...	...	...	0709	...	...	...	...	...	...	|	...	...	...	...	...
Les Aubrais-Orléans a.	...	|	...	...	...	...	...	0605	...	...	...	...	0735	...	...	...	...	...	...	|	...	...	...	...	...
Paris Austerlitz a.	...	|	...	...	...	...	...	0711	...	...	...	...	0831	...	...	...	...	...	...	|	...	...	...	...	...
Paris Montparnasse a.	...	2320	...	...	...	...	...	...	...	...	...	...	...	...	...	...	...	...	...	1345c	...	...	...	...	...
Paris Nord 10 d.	...	...	...	...	...	...	...	...	0913	...	...	...	...	1013	...	...	...	...	...	...	1613	...	...	...	...
London St Pancras 10 a.	...	...	...	...	...	...	...	...	1034	...	...	...	...	1128	...	...	...	...	...	...	1734	...	...	...	...

A – SUREX / SUD EXPRESSO – 🛏 1, 2 cl., 🛌 2 cl., (2) and ✕ Irún - Vilar Formoso (**313**) - Lisboa. Not Dec. 24. 31.
B – SUD EXPRESSO / SUREX – 🛏 1, 2 cl., 🛌 2 cl., (2) and ✕ Lisboa - Vilar Formoso (**311**) - Hendaye. Not Dec. 24, 31.
C – ATLÁNTICO *Hotel Train* – Ⓑ (①–⑥ from Valladolid): 🛏, 🛌 and (1) Ferrol - Valladolid - Madrid.
D – ATLÁNTICO *Hotel Train* – Ⓑ: 🛏, 🛌 and (1) Madrid - Valladolid - Ferrol.
E – CAMINO DE SANTIAGO – (12) and 🍸 Irún - Burgos - A Coruña and A Coruña - Burgos - Hendaye.
F – *CORAIL LUNÉA* – 🛌 1, 2 cl. and (2) (reclining) Paris - Irún and Hendaye - Paris. For timing variations, see Table **305**.
G – FRANCISCO DE GOYA *Trainhotel Elipsos* – ①④⑤⑥⑦ Dec. 13 - Mar. 21 (also Dec. 23, 30, Jan 6); daily Mar. 22 - Oct. 17: 🛏 1, 2 cl., 🛏 2 cl. (T4), (1) (reclining) and ✕ Paris - Madrid. 🅁 Special fares apply.
H – FRANCISCO DE GOYA *Trainhotel Elipsos* – ③④⑤⑥⑦ Dec. 13 - Mar. 21 (also Dec. 22, 29, Jan 5); daily Mar. 22 - Oct. 17: 🛏 1, 2 cl., 🛏 2 cl. (T4), (1) (reclining) and ✕ Madrid - Paris. 🅁 Special fares apply.
J – ①–⑤ June 14 - July 3; ⑤ Sept. 4 - Dec. 12.
K – ①–⑤ (①⑤ Jan. 4 - Feb. 6) not Dec. 28, Jan. 1, Apr. 5, May 3, 13, 24, 31.

c – On June 28 arrive Poitiers 0745, Blois 0846, Paris 1005.
e – 1350 on ⑥.
f – Not Dec. 24, 31, Jan. 1, Apr. 2.

j – Not Jan. 1.
s – Stops to set down only.
r – Also Jan. 1.

☆ – Eurostar train. Special fares payable. Minimum check-in time 30 minutes. Valid Dec. 13, 2009 - July 3, 2010. No service Dec. 25. Additional services are shown on Table **10**.
Alvia – *Alvia* 🅁 🍸⁄.
Arco – *Arco* 🅁⁄🍸.
Estr – *Estrella*. 🅁 🍸⁄.
AVE – *Alta Velocidad Española* 🅁 🍸 ⁄.
◐ – Via Pamplona.
⁄ – Supplement payable.
⊙ – 🏛 at Fuentes de Oñoro.

KÖLN and FRANKFURT - BARCELONA and NICE — 47

train type / number	IC	4248	4248	ICE	ICE	TGV	87460	4294	Talgo		4294
train number	334	4249	4295	601	79	9570	31966	4249	463		4295
notes	🍷	[R] J	[R] C	🍷	🍷	①-⑤ p	2	[R] P	462 A 🍷	2	[R] D
Köln Hbf d.	1418	...	...	1655	...	...	...	...	...	...	...
Luxembourg 🛂 d.	1743	1930	1930	|	...	...	...	...	...	...	...
Metz d.	...	2040	2040	|	...	...	...	...	...	...	...
Nancy d.	...	2159	2159	|	...	...	...	...	...	...	...
Frankfurt (Main) Hbf d.	...	|	|	|	1805	...	...	...	...	...	...
Mannheim d.	...	|	|	1826	1842	...	...	...	...	...	...
Karlsruhe d.	...	|	|	1850	1906	1932	...	...	...	...	...
Offenburg d.	...	|	|	...	...	|	2004	...	...	...	...
Kehl 🛂 d.	...	|	|	...	...	|	2022	...	...	...	...
Strasbourg d.	...	|	|	...	...	2015	2035	2058	...	...	2058
Mulhouse d.	...	|	|	...	...	...	...	2210	...	...	2210
Besançon d.	...	|	|	...	...	...	...	0007	...	...	0007
Dijon d.	...	|	|	...	...	...	...	|	...	...	|
Lyon Part Dieu a.	...	|	|	...	...	...	...	|	...	...	|
Avignon Centre a.	...	|	|	...	...	...	...	0449	...	...	0449
Arles a.	...	|	|	...	...	...	...	0511	...	...	0511
Nîmes a.	...	0553	|	...	...	...	...	0553	...	...	|
Montpellier a.	...	0627	|	...	...	...	...	0627	0727	...	|
Béziers a.	...	0720	|	...	...	...	...	0720	0802	...	|
Narbonne a.	...	0738	|	...	...	...	...	0738	0818	...	|
Perpignan a.	...	0824	|	...	...	...	...	0824	0854	...	|
Cerbère a.	...	0914	|	...	...	...	...	0914	0921	...	|
Portbou 🛂 a.	...	0923	|	...	...	...	...	0923	0948	1029	|
Figueres a.	...	...	|	...	...	...	...	...	1012	1054	|
Girona a.	...	...	|	...	...	...	...	...	1040	1132	|
Barcelona Sants a.	...	...	|	...	...	...	...	...	1146	1309	|
Marseille St Charles a.	...	...	0600	...	...	...	...	...	...	...	0600
Toulon a.	...	...	0712	...	...	...	...	...	...	...	0712
Les Arcs - Draguignan a.	...	...	0751	...	...	...	...	...	...	...	0751
St Raphaël - Valescure a.	...	...	0808	...	...	...	...	...	...	...	0808
Cannes a.	...	...	0833	...	...	...	...	...	...	...	0833
Antibes a.	...	...	0845	...	...	...	...	...	...	...	0845
Nice a.	...	...	0909	...	...	...	...	...	...	...	0909

train type / number	4394		4348	IC	4348	4394	87417	TGV	ICE	ICE
train number	4348		4349	335	4395	4395	31955	9571	76	600
notes	[R] C	2	[R] K	🍷	[R] S	[R] D	2			1008 🍷
Nice d.	2000	...	...	...	...	2000	...	...	...	...
Antibes d.	2020	...	...	...	...	2020	...	...	...	...
Cannes d.	2032	...	...	...	...	2032	...	...	...	...
St Raphaël - Valescure d.	2057	...	...	...	...	2057	...	...	...	...
Les Arcs - Draguignan d.	2115	...	...	...	...	2115	...	...	...	...
Toulon d.	2153	...	...	...	...	2153	...	...	...	...
Marseille St Charles d.	2252	...	...	...	...	2252	...	...	...	...
Barcelona Sants d.	|	1716	...	...	...	|	...	...	...	...
Girona d.	|	1852	...	...	...	|	...	...	...	...
Figueres d.	|	1930	...	...	...	|	...	...	...	...
Portbou d.	|	1956	...	...	...	|	...	...	...	...
Cerbère 🛂 d.	|	2000	2043	...	2043	|	...	...	...	...
Perpignan d.	|	...	2134	...	2134	|	...	...	...	...
Narbonne d.	|	...	2215	...	2215	|	...	...	...	...
Béziers d.	|	...	2231	...	2231	|	...	...	...	...
Montpellier d.	|	...	2321	...	2321	|	...	...	...	...
Nîmes d.	|	...	2350	...	2350	|	...	...	...	...
Arles d.	|	...	|	...	2335	2335	...	...	...	...
Avignon Centre d.	|	...	|	...	2356	2356	...	...	...	...
Lyon Part Dieu a.	|	...	|	...	|	|	...	...	...	...
Dijon a.	|	...	|	...	|	|	...	...	...	...
Besançon a.	|	...	|	...	0512	0512	...	...	...	...
Mulhouse a.	|	...	|	...	0720	0720	...	...	...	...
Strasbourg a.	|	...	|	...	0831	0831	0922	0945	...	...
Kehl 🛂 a.	|	...	|	...	...	...	0933	|	...	...
Offenburg a.	|	...	|	...	...	...	0952	|	...	...
Karlsruhe a.	|	...	|	...	...	...	...	1025	1051	1109
Mannheim a.	|	...	|	...	...	...	...	...	1114	1133
Frankfurt (Main) Hbf a.	|	...	|	...	...	...	...	...	1153	|
Nancy a.	0729	...	0729	...	...	...	...	...	...	|
Metz a.	0824	...	0824	...	...	...	...	...	...	|
Luxembourg 🛂 a.	0924	...	0924	1024	...	...	...	...	...	|
Köln Hbf a.	...	...	...	1342	...	...	...	...	...	1305

A – MARE NOSTRUM – [12] and 🍷 Montpellier - Barcelona - Alacant - Cartagena (arrive 1952), [R] ↗ Special fares payable.
C – *CORAIL LUNÉA* – 🛏 1, 2 cl. and [2] (reclining) Luxembourg - Metz - Nice and v.v. (not Dec. 24, 31, Jan. 9, 16, 23, 30).
D – *CORAIL LUNÉA* – 🛏 1, 2 cl. and [2] (reclining) Strasbourg - Nice and v.v. (not Dec. 24, 31, Jan. 9, 16, 23, 30).
J – *CORAIL LUNÉA* – ❖ 🛏 1, 2 cl. and [2] (reclining) Luxembourg - Metz - Portbou ❖.
K – *CORAIL LUNÉA* – ❖ 🛏 1, 2 cl. and [2] (reclining) Cerbère - Metz - Luxembourg ❖.
P – *CORAIL LUNÉA* – ❖ 🛏 1, 2 cl. and [2] (reclining) Strasbourg - Portbou ❖.
S – *CORAIL LUNÉA* – ❖ 🛏 1, 2 cl. and [2] (reclining) Cerbère - Strasbourg ❖.

p – Not Dec. 24, 25, 31, Jan. 1, Apr. 5, May 24.

❖ – Days of running: Dec. 13, 18 - 23, 25 - 30, Jan. 1 - 3; ⑤⑦ Jan. 8 - 31; ⑤⑥⑦ Feb. 5 - Mar. 7; ⑤⑦ Mar. 12 - 28; ⑤⑥⑦ from Apr. 2 (also Apr. 5, May 12, 13, 24).

BARCELONA - MARSEILLE, NICE, LYON, GENÈVE and ZÜRICH — 49

train type / number	Talgo	TGV	IC	4657	–	Talgo	–	Hotel EN 🍴	–
train number	73/2	6866/7	739	4656		460/1		273/2	
notes	[R] ↗ W 🍷	[R] ↗ 🍷	🍷	★		[R] ↗ P 🍷		[R] B	
Barcelona Sants d.	...	...	...	...	...	1642	...	...	...
Barcelona França d.	0845	...	...	...	...	|	...	1938	...
Girona d.	0955	...	...	...	...	1748	...	2057	...
Figueres d.	1025	...	...	...	...	1815	...	2125	...
Portbou d.	1053	...	...	...	...	1842	...	|	...
Cerbère 🛂 d.	1114	...	...	...	...	1907	...	|	...
Perpignan a.	1142	...	...	...	...	1934	...	2244d	...
Narbonne a.	1220	...	...	...	...	2015	...	|	...
Béziers a.	1237	...	...	...	...	2032	...	|	...
Montpellier a.	1322	1356	...	1416	...	2109	...	|	...
Nîmes a.	...	1422	...	|	...	...	...	|	...
Marseille St Charles a.	...	|	...	1542	...	...	...	|	...
Nice a.	...	|	...	1833	...	...	...	|	...
Valence Ville a.	...	1510v	...	...	...	...	...	|	...
Lyon Part Dieu a.	...	1550	...	...	...	...	...	|	...
Genève 🛂 a.	...	1735	1745	...	...	...	...	0545	...
Lausanne a.	...	...	1818	...	...	...	...	0654	...
Fribourg a.	...	...	1903	...	...	...	...	0747	...
Bern a.	...	...	1926	...	...	...	...	0849	...
Zürich HB a.	...	...	2028	...	...	...	...	1009	...

train type / number	Talgo	–	4758	IC	TGV	Talgo	–	Hotel EN 🍴	–
train number	463/2		4759	710	6816/7	70/71		274/5	
notes	[R] ↗ M 🍷		★	🍷	[R] ↗ 🍷	[R] ↗ W 🍷		[R] C	
Zürich HB d.	...	...	...	0732	...	...	...	1927	...
Bern d.	...	...	...	0834	...	...	...	2108	...
Fribourg d.	...	...	...	0855	...	...	...	2145	...
Lausanne d.	...	...	...	0942	...	...	...	2238	...
Genève 🛂 d.	...	...	...	1015	1117	...	...	2335	...
Lyon Part Dieu d.	...	...	...	...	1307	...	...	|	...
Valence Ville d.	...	...	...	...	1346v	...	...	|	...
Nice d.	...	...	0955	...	|	...	...	|	...
Marseille St Charles d.	...	...	1242	...	|	...	...	|	...
Nîmes d.	...	...	|	...	1425	...	...	|	...
Montpellier d.	0727	...	1409	...	1451	1509	...	|	...
Béziers d.	0804	...	...	...	...	1555	...	|	...
Narbonne d.	0820	...	...	...	...	1611	...	|	...
Perpignan d.	0856	...	...	...	...	1654	...	0614a	...
Cerbère d.	0931	...	...	...	...	1729	...	|	...
Portbou 🛂 a.	0948	...	...	...	...	1748	...	|	...
Figueres a.	1012	...	...	...	...	1811	...	0744	...
Girona a.	1040	...	...	...	...	1837	...	0818	...
Barcelona França a.	|	...	...	...	...	1959	...	0943	...
Barcelona Sants a.	1146	...	...	...	...	...	...	...	...

B – PAU CASALS *Trainhotel Elipsos* – ②④⑦: 🛏 1, 2 cl., 🛏 2 cl. (T4), [1] (reclining) and 🍴 Barcelona - Zürich.
C – PAU CASALS *Trainhotel Elipsos* – ①③⑤: 🛏 1, 2 cl., 🛏 2 cl. (T4), [1] (reclining) and 🍴 Zürich - Barcelona.
M – MARE NOSTRUM – [12] and 🍷 Montpellier - Barcelona - Alacant - Cartagena (arrive 1952). Special fares payable.
P – MARE NOSTRUM – [12] and 🍷 Lorca (depart 0820) - Alacant - Barcelona - Montpellier. Special fares payable.
W – CATALÁN TALGO – [12] and 🍴 Barcelona - Montpellier and v.v. Special fares payable.

a – Arrival time.
d – Departure time.
v – Valence **TGV**.

↗ – Supplement payable.
★ – CORAIL TÉOZ, [R], 🍷.

50 OSLO, STOCKHOLM and KØBENHAVN - HAMBURG - BERLIN

Day Trains (for night trains see below)

Services are subject to alteration around holidays, please refer to relevant countries for details.

train type/number		[R]		ICE				ICE	ICE			IC	X2000	ICE	IC							
train number		1		38				238	797			601	521	36	2071							
notes		G		🍷				🍷	🍷			①–⑤	①–⑥	🍷	🍷							
notes		⑧		c				c				f	m	c								
Oslo Sentral d.	...	...	...	...	...	...	...	...	...	...	...	...	...	...	...	...	...	...	...	...	...	...
Stockholm Central d.	...	2306	...	...	...	...	...	...	...	...	...	...	0621	...	...	...	...	...	...	...	...	...
Göteborg d.	...	|	...	...	...	...	...	...	...	...	...	0727	|	...	...	...	...	...	...	...	...	...
Malmö C d.	...	0627	0642	...	...	...	0842	...	...	...	...	1017s	1046s	...	...	...	...	...	...	...	...	...
København H. d.	...	...	0717	0745	...	...	0917	0945	...	...	...	1100	1133	1145	...	...	...	...	...	...	...	...
Rødby Ferry ⛴ d.	...	...	...	0935	...	...	...	1135	...	...	...	...	...	1335	...	...	...	...	...	...	...	...
Puttgarden ⛴ a.	...	...	...	1035	...	...	...	1235	...	...	...	...	...	1435	...	...	...	...	...	...	...	...
Lübeck Hbf a.	...	...	...	1136	...	...	...	1336	...	...	...	...	...	1536	...	...	...	...	...	...	...	...
Hamburg Hbf a.	...	...	...	1216	...	...	...	1416	1454	...	...	...	...	1616	1629	...	...	...	...	...	...	...
Berlin Hauptbahnhof a.	...	...	...	1427	...	...	...	...	1631	...	...	...	...	...	1833	...	...	...	...	...	...	...

train type		X2000	391	X2000	ICE	ICE			X2000	X2000		393	IC		EC							
train number		525	①–⑤	485	32	1005			529	531		⑥	603		30							
notes			🍷		🍷							p			🍷							
notes		y	g		c							🍷			S c							
Oslo Sentral d.	...	...	0700	...	...	...	...	...	...	...	...	0900	...	...	...	...	...	...	...	...	...	...
Stockholm Central d.	...	0821	|	...	...	...	...	...	1021	1121	...	|	...	...	...	...	...	...	...	...	...	...
Göteborg d.	...	|	1055	1132	...	...	...	...	|	|	...	1254	1327	...	...	...	...	...	...	...	...	...
Malmö C d.	...	1259	...	1415s	...	...	...	...	1459	1546	1602	...	1615s	1642	...	...	...	...	...	...	...	...
København H. d.	...	1333	...	1500	1545	...	...	...	1533	...	1637	...	1701	1717	1745	...	...	...	...	...	...	...
Rødby Ferry ⛴ d.	...	...	...	...	1735	...	...	...	...	...	...	...	...	...	1935	...	...	...	...	...	...	...
Puttgarden ⛴ a.	...	...	...	...	1835	...	...	...	...	...	...	...	...	...	2035	...	...	...	...	...	...	...
Lübeck Hbf a.	...	...	...	...	1936	...	...	...	...	...	...	...	...	...	2136	...	...	...	...	...	...	...
Hamburg Hbf a.	...	...	...	...	2016	2121	...	...	...	...	...	...	...	...	2216	...	...	...	...	...	...	...
Berlin Hauptbahnhof a.	...	...	...	...	...	2313	...	...	...	...	...	...	...	...	...	...	...	...	...	...	...	...

train type		ICE	EC		X2000	396	398					ICE	ICE		X2000							
train number		1006	31	1050	538	⑥	⑧					790	33	1062	542							
notes			🍷			q	j						🍷									
notes		🍷	T c		w	🍷	🍷					🍷	c		k							
Berlin Hauptbahnhof d.	...	0517	...	...	...	...	...	...	...	...	...	0713	...	...	...	...	...	...	...	...	...	...
Hamburg Hbf d.	...	0707	0725	...	...	...	...	...	...	...	...	0852	0928	...	...	...	...	...	...	...	...	...
Lübeck Hbf d.	...	...	0806	...	...	...	...	...	...	...	...	...	1006	...	...	...	...	...	...	...	...	...
Puttgarden ⛴ d.	...	...	0910	...	...	...	...	...	...	...	...	...	1110	...	...	...	...	...	...	...	...	...
Rødby Ferry ⛴ a.	...	...	1003	...	...	...	...	...	...	...	...	...	1205	...	...	...	...	...	...	...	...	...
København H. d.	...	...	1211	1223	...	...	...	...	...	...	...	...	1411	1423	...	...	...	...	...	...	...	...
Malmö C a.	...	...	...	1258	1314	...	...	...	...	...	...	...	...	1458	1514	...	...	...	...	...	...	...
Göteborg a.	...	...	...	1617	|	1639	1745	...	...	...	...	...	...	1817	|	...	...	...	...	...	...	...
Stockholm Central a.	...	...	...	...	1739	|	|	...	...	...	...	...	...	...	1939	...	...	...	...	...	...	...
Oslo Sentral a.	...	...	...	...	...	2045	2145	...	...	...	...	...	...	...	...	...	...	...	...	...	...	...

train type		ICE		X2000	[R]			ICE	ICE			ICE	ICE									
train number		35	1086	550	2			798	237	1098		890	37	1110								
notes		🍷		⑧	G				🍷				🍷									
notes		c		h	⑧			⑧	c				c									
Berlin Hauptbahnhof d.	...	1126	...	...	...	...	...	1316	...	...	...	1525	...	...	...	...	...	...	...	...	...	...
Hamburg Hbf d.	...	1328	...	...	...	...	...	1452	1525	...	...	1709	1728	...	...	...	...	...	...	...	...	...
Lübeck Hbf d.	...	1406	...	...	...	...	...	...	1606	...	...	...	1806	...	...	...	...	...	...	...	...	...
Puttgarden ⛴ d.	...	1510	...	...	...	...	...	...	1710	...	...	...	1910	...	...	...	...	...	...	...	...	...
Rødby Ferry ⛴ a.	...	1603	...	...	...	...	...	...	1803	...	...	...	2002	...	...	...	...	...	...	...	...	...
København H. d.	...	1811	1823	...	...	...	...	...	2011	2023	...	...	2211	2223	...	...	...	...	...	...	...	...
Malmö C a.	...	...	1858	1914	2248	...	...	...	...	2058	...	...	...	2258	...	...	...	...	...	...	...	...
Göteborg a.	...	...	2217	|	|	...	...	...	...	0017	...	...	...	...	...	...	...	...	...	...	...	...
Stockholm Central a.	...	...	...	2339	0556	...	...	...	...	...	...	...	...	...	...	...	...	...	...	...	...	...
Oslo Sentral a.	...	...	...	...	...	...	...	...	...	...	...	...	...	...	...	...	...	...	...	...	...	...

50 KØBENHAVN - KÖLN, AMSTERDAM, MÜNCHEN, BASEL and BERLIN

Night Trains (for day trains see above)

train type	391	393	X2000		CNL	CNL	CNL	X2000	395			EN
train number	①–⑤	⑥	533	1081	483	483	483	541	⑧	1105		211
notes	g	p			446	1383	473	k	r			[R]
notes	🍷	🍷			A	H	B		🍷			D b
Oslo Sentral d.	0700	0900	...	...	...	...	...	...	1300	...	...	...
Stockholm Central d.	|	|	1221	...	...	...	...	1615	|	...	...	...
Göteborg d.	1055	1254	|	1342	...	...	...	|	1659	1742	...	...
København H d.	...	...	|	|	...	...	...	|	...	|	1943	...
Lund d.	...	...	|	|	...	...	...	2031	...	2037	2043	2116
Malmö C d.	...	...	1659	1702	...	...	...	...	...	...	...	|
København H. d.	...	...	1733	1737	1842	1842	1842	...	...	...	...	|
Malmö Persborg d.	...	...	...	...	|	|	|	...	...	...	...	2133
Odense d.	...	...	...	...	2027	2027	2027	...	...	...	...	|
Padborg ⛴ d.	...	...	...	...	2218	2218	2218	...	...	...	...	|
Flensburg ⛴ d.	...	...	...	...	2233	2233	2233	...	...	...	...	|
Köln 20 800 a.	...	...	...	...	0614	|	|	...	...	...	...	|
Amsterdam 22 a.	...	...	...	...	1024	|	|	...	...	...	...	|
München Hbf 900 a.	...	...	...	...	...	0858	|	...	...	...	...	|
Kufstein ⛴ a.	...	...	...	...	...	1040x	|	...	...	...	...	|
Wörgl a.	...	...	...	...	...	1051x	|	...	...	...	...	|
Jenbach a.	...	...	...	...	...	1107x	|	...	...	...	...	|
Innsbruck a.	...	...	...	...	...	1136x	|	...	...	...	...	|
Basel SBB 912 a.	...	...	...	...	...	...	1037	...	...	...	...	|
Berlin Hbf d.	...	...	...	...	...	...	...	...	...	...	...	0604

train type	EN			394	X2000	CNL	CNL	CNL		X2000	396	398
train number	210	1031	1026	⑧	530	472	482	447	1038	534	⑥	⑧
notes	[R]			r		482	1382	482			q	j
notes	C b			🍷		B	H	A			🍷	🍷
Berlin Hbf d.	2301	...	...	...	...	...	...	...	...	...	...	...
Basel SBB 912 d.	|	...	...	...	...	1804	...	...	...	...	...	...
Innsbruck d.	|	...	...	...	...	|	1623z	...	...	...	...	...
Jenbach d.	|	...	...	...	...	|	1650z	...	...	...	...	...
Wörgl d.	|	...	...	...	...	|	1717z	...	...	...	...	...
Kufstein ⛴ d.	|	...	...	...	...	|	1730z	...	...	...	...	...
München Hbf 900 d.	|	...	...	...	...	|	1900e	...	...	...	...	...
Amsterdam 22 d.	|	...	...	...	...	|	|	1901	...	...	...	...
Köln 20 800 d.	|	...	...	...	...	|	|	2228	...	...	...	...
Flensburg ⛴ a.	|	...	...	...	...	0549	0549	0549	...	...	...	...
Padborg ⛴ a.	|	...	...	...	...	0602	0602	0602	...	...	...	...
Odense a.	|	...	...	...	...	0816	0816	0816	...	...	...	...
Malmö Persborg a.	0756	...	...	...	...	|	|	|	...	...	...	...
København H. a.	|	...	...	...	...	1006	1006	1006	1023	...	...	...
Malmö C a.	|	...	...	...	...	...	...	...	1058	1114	...	...
Lund a.	0811	0817	0922	...	0928	...	...	...	|	|	...	...
København H a.	...	0917	|	...	|	...	...	...	|	|	...	...
Göteborg a.	...	...	1217	1245	|	...	...	...	1417	|	1639	1745
Stockholm Central a.	...	...	...	|	1339	...	...	...	...	1539	|	|
Oslo Sentral a.	...	...	...	1645	...	...	...	...	...	...	2045	2145

A – *City Night Line* BOREALIS – 🛏 1, 2 cl., ━ 2 cl., (2) (reclining) and 🍷 København - Köln - Amsterdam and v.v. [R] Special fares apply.
B – *City Night Line* AURORA – 🛏 1, 2 cl., ━ 2 cl. (4, 6 berth), (2) (reclining) and ✕ København - Frankfurt - Basel and v.v. [R] Special fares apply.
C – BERLIN NIGHT EXPRESS – Dec. 25, 29, Jan. 1; ②④⑥ Mar. 23 - May 2 (also Apr. 5; not Apr. 3); daily May 3 - June 19: 🛏 1, 2 cl. and ━ 2 cl. Berlin - Malmö Persborg - Lund. [R] Special fares apply.
D – BERLIN NIGHT EXPRESS – Dec. 18, 28, 30; ③⑤⑦ Mar. 24 - May 2 (also Apr. 1; not Apr. 2); daily May 3 - June 19: 🛏 1, 2 cl. and ━ 2 cl. Lund - Malmö Persborg - Berlin. [R] Special fares apply.
G – ⑧ Dec. 13 – 22, Jan. 10 - June 19: 🛏 1, 2 cl., ━ 2 cl. and (2) Malmö - Stockholm and v.v. [R].
H – *City Night Line* HANS CHRISTIAN ANDERSEN – 🛏 1, 2 cl., ━ 2 cl., (2) (reclining) and ✕ København - München - (- Innsbruck ♥ and ♣) and v.v. [R] Special fares apply.
S – Dec. 13 - Jan. 10 (not Dec. 24, 31); daily Mar. 12 - Oct. 24.
T – Dec. 14 - Jan. 11 (not Dec. 25, Jan. 1); daily Mar. 13 - Oct. 25.

b – Train is conveyed by train-ferry Trelleborg ⛴ - Sassnitz Fährhafen ⛴ (Mukran) and v.v.
c – Passengers to / from Rødby or Puttgarden may be required to leave / board the train on board the ferry.
e – 1915 on ⑦ (also Dec. 19, 25, Jan. 1, Apr. 5, May 13, 24).
f – Not Dec. 25, Jan. 1, 6, Apr. 2, 5, May 13, 24, June 3.
g – Not Dec. 25, Jan. 1, Apr. 1, 2, 5, May 13, 17, 24, June 3.
h – Not Dec. 21 – Jan. 9, Apr. 4, May 1.
j – Also Apr. 3; not Dec. 25.
k – Not Dec. 24, 31.
m – Not Dec. 25, 26, Jan. 1, 6, Apr. 5, May 24, June 3.
p – Not Apr. 3.
q – Not Dec. 24, 31, Apr. 3.
r – Also Apr. 3
s – Stops to set down only.
u – Calls to pick up only.
w – Not Dec. 24.
x – See note ♥.
y – Not Dec. 25, Jan. 1.
z – See note ♣.

♥ – ⑤ Dec. 25 - Apr. 9 from København to Innsbruck, also calls at Kufstein ⛴ 1040**s**, Wörgl 1051**s**, Jenbach 1107**s**, arrives Innsbruck 1136.
♣ – ⑥ Dec. 26 - Apr. 10 from Innsbruck to København, departs 1623, also calls at Jenbach 1650**s**, Wörgl 1717**s**, Kufstein ⛴ 1730**s**.

X2000 – High speed train. [R] ✕.

PRAHA - ZÜRICH 52

train type	IC				CNL			
train number	101		207		458			
notes	✕		466		✕			
	A		B		C			
Praha hlavní d.	0716	...	1716	...	1831	...	...	...
Praha Holešovice d.	|	...	|	...	1840	...	...	...
Tábor d.	0856	...	1856	...	|	...	...	...
Veselí nad Lužnicí d.	0920	...	1920	...	|	...	...	...
České Budějovice d.	1007	...	2034	...	|	...	...	...
Summerau 🏛 d.	1113	...	2147	...	◧	...	...	...
Linz Hbf a.	1215	...	2244	...	|	...	...	...
Salzburg a.	...	...	0014	...	|	...	...	...
Zürich HB a.	...	...	0720	...	0917	...	...	...

train type	IC		CNL					
train number	100		459		467			
notes	✕		✕		206			
	A		C		B			
Zürich HB d.	...	...	1944	...	2240	...	...	...
Salzburg d.	...	...	|	...	0441	...	...	...
Linz Hbf d.	1535	...	|	...	0614	...	...	...
Summerau 🏛 a.	1633	...	◧	...	0714	...	...	...
České Budějovice a.	1748	...	|	...	0820	...	...	...
Veselí nad Lužnicí a.	1836	...	|	...	0936	...	...	...
Tábor a.	1901	...	|	...	1001	...	...	...
Praha Holešovice a.	|	...	1035	...	|	...	...	...
Praha hlavní a.	2040	...	1051	...	1140	...	...	...

A – ANTON BRUCKNER – 🚃12 and 🍷 Praha - Linz and v.v.
B – MATTHIAS BRAUN – 🛏 1, 2 cl. and ▬ 2 cl. Praha - Summerau 🏛 - Linz - Buchs 🏛 - Zürich and v.v. (Table **86**). 🚃12 Praha - Linz - Salzburg and v.v.
C – *City Night Line* CANOPUS – 🛏 1, 2 cl., ▬ 2 cl., 🚃2 (reclining) and ✕ Praha hlavní - Praha Holešovice - Bad Schandau 🏛 - Dresden - Leipzig - Frankfürt (Main) Süd - Basel Bad Bf 🏛 - Zürich and v.v. [R] Special fares apply.
◧ – 🏛 at Basel Bad Bf and Bad Schandau.

PRAHA - BŘECLAV - WIEN 53

train type	EC	SC*	EC	EC	EC	EC	EC	EC	EC	EC	EC		
train number	71	73	75	275	103	77	173	79	175	105	177	471	
notes	✕	🍷	🍷	🍷	🍷	✕	✕	✕	✕	🍷	✕	407	
		[R]					A				G	P	
Praha Holešovice d.	...	...	...	...	...	...	1317	...	1517	...	1717	...	...
Praha hlavní d.	0439e	0639	0839	0939	...	1039	1339	1439	1539	...	1739	2320	...
Brno Hlavní d.	0722	0924	1124	1224	...	1324	1624	1724	1824	...	2024	0244	...
Břeclav 🏛 d.	0802	1002	1202	1257	1302	1402	1702	1802	1857	1902	2102	0459	...
Wien Simmering a.	0906	1058	1258	...	1358	1458	1758	1910	...	1958	2204p	|	...
Wien Meidling a.	0923	1123	1323	...	1423	1523	1823	1929	...	2020	...	0608	...
Wien Westbahnhof a.	|	|	|	...	|	|	|	...	...	...	...	0622	...
Wiener Neustadt Hbf a.	0955	1155	1355	...	1455	1555	1855	...	...	...	...	...	...
Graz Hbf a.	...	...	...	...	|	...	|	...	...	...	...	...	...
Villach Hbf a.	...	...	...	...	1844	...	2235	...	...	...	...	...	...

train type	EC	EC	EC	EC	EC	EC	EC	EC	SC*	EC	EC		
train number	378	104	174	78	172	70	102	274	72	74	76	406	
notes	✕	🍷	✕	✕	✕	✕	🍷	🍷	🍷	🍷	✕	470	
	A				V				[R]			Q	
Villach Hbf d.	...	...	...	...	0527	...	0914	...	...	...	...	...	...
Graz Hbf d.	...	...	...	0540	|	...	|	...	...	...	...	...	...
Wiener Neustadt Hbf d.	...	...	...	0747	0904	1204	1304	...	1404	1604	1804	...	...
Wien Westbahnhof d.	...	...	...	|	|	|	|	...	|	|	|	2208	...
Wien Meidling d.	...	0733	...	0825	0932	1233	1333	...	1433	1633	1833	2223	...
Wien Simmering d.	0550p	0759	...	0857	0946	1257	1357	...	1457	1657	1857	|	...
Břeclav 🏛 d.	0702	0853	0902	1002	1102	1402	1453	1502	1602	1802	2002	0200	...
Brno Hlavní d.	0735	...	0935	1035	1135	1435	...	1535	1635	1835	2035	0259	...
Praha hlavní a.	1021	...	1221	1321	1421	1721	...	1821	1921	2121	2321	0615	...
Praha Holešovice a.	1039	...	1239	...	1439	...	...	...	...	...	...	...	...

A – VINDOBONA – 🚃12 and ✕ Hamburg - Berlin - Praha - Wien - Villach and v.v.
E – CARL MARIA VON WEBER – 🚃12 and ✕ Wien - Praha - Berlin - Stralsund. To Ostseebad Binz on dates in Table **844**.
G – JOHANNES BRAHMS – 🚃12 and ✕ Berlin - Dresden - Praha - Wien.
P – 🛏 1, 2 cl. Praha (**471**) - Přerov - Břeclav (**407**) - Wien.
Q – 🛏 1, 2 cl. Wien (**406**) - Břeclav (**470**) - Přerov - Praha.
e – ①–⑥ (not Dec. 25, 26, Jan. 1, 2, Apr. 5, July 5, 6).
p – Wien **Praterstern**.
x – ①–⑥ (not Dec. 24, 25, 26, Jan. 1, Apr. 5, May 1, 8).
* – Classified *EC* in Austria.

PRAHA - ZAGREB 52

train number	207 499	
notes	A	
Praha hlavní d.	1716	...
České Budějovice d.	2037	...
Summerau 🏛 d.	2147	...
Linz Hbf d.	2246	...
Wels d.	2303	...
Salzburg Hbf d.	0134	...
Ljubljana a.	0603	...
Zagreb a.	0839	...

train number	498 206	
notes		
Zagreb d.	2115	...
Ljubljana d.	2350	...
Salzburg Hbf d.	0441	...
Wels a.	0545	...
Linz Hbf a.	0602	...
Summerau 🏛 a.	0714	...
České Budějovice a.	0821	...
Praha hlavní a.	1140	...

A – MATTHIAS BRAUN – May 1 - Sept. 11 🛏 1, 2 cl., Praha (**207**) - Salzburg (**499**) - Ljubljana - Zagreb and May 2 - Sept. 12 🛏 1, 2 cl. Zagreb (**498**) - Ljubljana - Salzburg (**206**) - Praha. 🚃2 Praha - Linz - Salzburg and v.v. Conveys 🛏 1, 2 cl., ▬ 2 cl. Praha - Salzburg - Innsbruck - Zürich and v.v. (Table **86**).

MÜNCHEN, ZÜRICH, AMSTERDAM - KØBENHAVN, WARSZAWA, PRAHA, and BERLIN 54

	CNL	D	CNL	D	EN	CNL	CNL	CNL	CNL	CNL
	482	50482	472	50472	447	457	40447	1259	459	478
	[R] ✕	[R]	[R] 🍷	[R]	[R] 🍷	[R] 🍷	[R] 🍷	[R] ✕	[R] 🍷	[R] ✕
	H	M	A	N	J	K	B	S	C	⊖ L
München Hbf d.	1900y	1900y	...	...	...	...	...	...	...	...
Ingolstadt Hbf d.	1943y	1943y	...	...	...	...	...	...	...	...
Nürnberg Hbf d.	2135	2135	...	...	...	...	...	...	...	...
Würzburg Hbf d.	2233	2233	...	...	...	...	...	...	...	...
Zürich HB d.	|	|	...	...	...	...	...	1944	1944	2042
Basel SBB d.	|	|	1804	1804	...	...	...	2107	2107	2207
Karlsruhe Hbf d.	|	|	2018	2018	...	...	...	2305	2305	0018
Frankfurt (Main) Süd d.	|	|	2218	2218	...	...	...	0055	0055	|
Fulda d.	2343	2343	|	|	...	...	...	|	|	|
Erfurt Hbf a.	|	|	|	|	...	...	...	0413	0518	|
Weimar a.	|	|	|	|	...	...	...	0458	0538	|
Leipzig Hbf a.	|	|	|	|	...	...	...	|	0641	|
Amsterdam Centraal d.	|	|	|	|	1901	1901	1901	|	|	|
Köln Hbf d.	|	|	|	|	2228	2228	2228	|	|	|
Dortmund Hbf d.	|	|	|	|	2356	2356	2356	|	|	|
Hamm (Westf) d.	|	|	|	|	0014	0014	0014	|	|	|
Bielefeld Hbf d.	|	|	|	|	0043	0043	0043	|	|	|
Berlin Hbf a.	|	|	|	|	|	0421	|	0718	|	|
Berlin Ostbahnhof a.	|	|	|	|	|	0430	|	...	|	|
Warszawa Centralna a.	|	1000	|	1000	1000	|	|	...	|	|
Dresden Hbf a.	|	...	|	...	...	0707	|	...	0804	|
Praha hlavní a.	|	...	|	...	...	0927	|	...	1051	|
Hamburg Hbf a.	0356	...	0356	...	...	...	0356	...	...	0906e
Neumünster a.	0443	...	0443	...	...	...	0443	...	...	...
Flensburg a.	0559	...	0549	...	...	...	0549	...	...	...
København H a.	1006	...	1006	...	...	...	1006	...	...	...

	CNL	CNL	CNL	CNL	446	EN	CNL	CNL	446	CNL
	479	458	1258	483	483	446	456	40483	473	473
	[R] ✕	[R] 🍷	[R] ✕	[R] ✕	[R]	[R] 🍷	[R] 🍷	[R] 🍷	[R]	[R] 🍷
	⊖ L	C	S	H	M	J	K	B	N	A
København H d.	...	...	...	1842	...	...	...	1842	...	1842
Flensburg d.	...	...	...	2233	...	...	...	2233	...	2233
Neumünster d.	...	...	...	2335	...	...	...	2335	...	2335
Hamburg Hbf d.	1918c	...	...	0031	...	...	...	0031	...	0031
Praha hlavní d.	|	1831	...	|	...	...	1831	|	...	|
Dresden Hbf d.	|	2104	...	|	...	...	2053	|	...	|
Warszawa Centralna d.	|	|	...	|	1810	1810	|	|	1810	|
Berlin Ostbahnhof d.	|	|	...	|	|	|	0022	|	|	|
Berlin Hbf d.	|	|	2222	|	|	|	0032	|	|	|
Bielefeld Hbf a.	|	|	|	|	|	0356	0356	0356	|	|
Hamm (Westf) a.	|	|	|	|	|	0429	0429	0429	|	|
Dortmund Hbf a.	|	|	|	|	|	0450	0450	0450	|	|
Köln Hbf a.	|	|	|	|	|	0614	0614	0614	|	|
Amsterdam Centraal a.	|	|	|	|	|	1029	1029	1029	|	|
Leipzig Hbf d.	|	2229	|	|	|	...	...	...	|	|
Weimar d.	|	2333	0049	|	|	...	...	...	|	|
Erfurt Hbf d.	|	0123	0123	|	|	...	...	...	|	|
Fulda a.	|	|	|	0450r	0450r	...	...	...	|	|
Frankfurt (Main) Süd a.	|	0359	0359	|	|	...	...	...	0654	0654
Karlsruhe Hbf a.	0437	0540	0540	|	|	...	...	...	0818	0818
Basel SBB a.	0654	0755	0755	|	|	...	...	...	1037	1037
Zürich HB a.	0834	0917	0917	|	|	...	...	...	...	...
Würzburg Hbf a.	...	...	...	0534v	0534v	...	...	...	...	...
Nürnberg Hbf a.	...	...	...	0644x	0644x	...	...	...	...	...
Ingolstadt Hbf a.	...	...	...	0807	0807	...	...	...	...	...
München Hbf a.	...	...	...	0900	0900	...	...	...	...	...

A – *City Night Line* AURORA – 🛏 1, 2 cl., ▬ 2 cl. (4, 6 berth), 🚃2 (reclining) and ✕ Basel - Frankfurt - København and v.v. [R] Special fares apply.
B – *City Night Line* BOREALIS – 🛏 1, 2 cl., ▬ 2 cl., 🚃2 (reclining) and 🍷 Amsterdam - Köln - København and v.v. [R] Special fares apply.
C – *City Night Line* CANOPUS – 🛏 1, 2 cl., ▬ 2 cl., 🚃2 (reclining) and 🍷 Praha - Děčín 🏛 - Frankfurt (Main) Süd - Basel - Zürich and v.v. [R] Special fares apply.
H – *City Night Line* HANS CHRISTIAN ANDERSEN – 🛏 1, 2 cl., ▬ 2 cl., 🚃2 (reclining) and ✕ München - København and v.v. [R] Special fares apply.
J – JAN KIEPURA – 🛏 1, 2 cl., ▬ 2 cl., and 🚃2 (reclining) Amsterdam - Köln - Warszawa and v.v. 🛏 1, 2 cl. Amsterdam - Köln - Warszawa - Moskva and v.v. (Table **24**).
K – *City Night Line* KOPERNIKUS / PHOENIX – 🛏 1, 2 cl., ▬ 2 cl., 🚃2 (reclining) and 🍷 Amsterdam - Köln - Berlin - Dresden - Praha and v.v. [R] Special fares apply.
L – *City Night Line* KOMET – 🛏 1, 2 cl., 🛏 1, 2 cl. (T4), ▬ 2 cl. (4, 6 berth), 🚃2 (reclining) and ✕ Zürich - Basel - Hamburg. [R] Special fares apply.
M – ▬ 2 cl. München - Warszawa and v.v. 🛏 1, 2 cl. München - Warszawa - Moskva and v.v. ✕ München - Fulda and ✕ Rzepin - Warszawa and v.v.
N – JAN KIEPURA – 🛏 1, 2 cl. Basel - Warszawa - Minsk and v.v. 🛏 1, 2 cl. Basel - Warszawa - Moskva. ✕ Basel - Fulda; Rzepin - Warszawa and v.v.
S – *City Night Line* SIRIUS – 🛏 1, 2 cl., 🛏 1, 2 cl. (T4), ▬ 2 cl. (4, 6 berth), 🚃2 (reclining) and ✕ Zürich - Halle - Berlin and v.v. [R] Special fares apply.
c – 2024 on ⑥⑦.
e – 0829 on ⑥; 0836 on ⑦.
r – 0509 on ①⑦.
v – 0549 on ①⑦.
x – ②–⑦ from May 3 (also May 24; not May 25).
y – On ⑦ (also Dec. 19, 25, Jan. 1, Apr. 5, May 13, 24) München depart 1915, Ingolstadt depart 2013.
⊖ – ④⑤⑥⑦ Dec. 13 - Mar. 21; daily from Mar. 25.

56 KÖLN - BERLIN - WARSZAWA - MOSKVA

train type/number	*EC*				*ICE*	*EC*	*ICE*	*EC*		11011	*ICE*		443				441	441	*ICE*	*EC*	*ICE*			
train number	**41**	**12**	**10**	**12001**	**541**	**341**	**855**	**45**	**11011**	**116**	**857**	**443**	**14**	**1249**	**441**	**441**	**30**	**30**	**859**	**47**	**653**	**447**		
notes	✕	11013	11001	68	🍷	🅁⊡	🍷	✕	116	132	🍷	14	20	70	30	668	123	12	🍷	✕	🍷	🅁		
	Tp	Z	P	C	U	W	A	T	V	EE	A	M	L	D	K	AA	G	S	A	T	A	J		
Köln Hbf d.	...	...	...	...	0429	...	0748	...	...	...	0948	...	...	...	...	...	...	...	1148	...	1648	2228	...	...
Düsseldorf Hbf d.	...	...	...	...	0453	...	0753z	...	...	...	0953z	...	...	...	...	...	...	...	1153z	...	1653z	2202	...	...
Dortmund Hbf d.	...	...	...	...	0547	...	0848z	...	...	...	1048z	...	...	...	...	...	...	...	1248z	...	1748z	2356	...	...
Bielefeld Hbf d.	...	...	...	...	0640	...	0937	...	...	...	1137	...	...	...	...	...	...	...	1337	...	1838	0043	...	...
Hannover Hbf d.	...	...	...	...	0731	...	1031	...	...	...	1231	...	...	...	...	...	...	...	1431	...	1931	|	...	...
Hamburg Hbf d.	...	...	...	...	|	0705y	|	...	...	...	|	...	...	...	...	...	...	...	|	...	|	|	...	...
Berlin Zoo d.	...	...	...	...	|	|	|	...	...	...	|	1507	1507	1507	1507	1507	1507	1507	|	...	|	|	...	...
Berlin Hbf d.	0629	...	...	...	0912	0941t	1211	1229	...	...	1411	1515	1515	1515	1515	1515	1515	1515	1611	1629	2108	0423	...	...
Berlin Ostbahnhof d.	0640u	...	...	...	0919	0951v	1222	1240u	...	...	1422	1532	1532	1532	1532	1532	1532	1532	1622	1640u	2120	0447	...	...
Berlin Lichtenberg d.	|	...	...	...	...	|	...	|	...	...	...	|	|	|	|	|	|	|	...	|	...	|	...	...
Frankfurt (Oder) 🛃 d.	0733	...	...	...	...	|	...	1333	...	...	...	|	|	|	|	|	|	|	...	1733	...	|	...	...
Rzepin a.	0754	...	...	...	...	|	...	1354	...	...	...	1749u	1749u	1749u	1749u	1749u	1749u	1749u	...	1754	...	0602	...	...
Poznań Gł. a.	0925	...	...	...	...	|	...	1525	...	...	...	1946u	1946u	1946u	1946u	1946u	1946u	1946u	...	1925	...	0732	...	...
Wrocław Gł. a.	|	...	...	...	...	1518	...	|	...	...	...	|	|	|	|	|	|	|	...	|	...	|	...	...
Katowice a.	|	...	...	...	...	1754	...	|	...	...	...	|	|	|	|	|	|	|	...	|	...	|	...	...
Kraków Gł. a.	|	...	...	...	...	1935	...	|	...	...	...	|	|	|	|	|	|	|	...	|	...	|	...	...
Warszawa Centralna a.	1206	...	1555	1620	...	...	...	1806	2100	2100	...	2300u	2300u	2300u	2300u	2300u	2300u	2300u	...	2206	...	1024	...	...
Warszawa Wschodnia a.	1218	1300	1605d	1630d	...	...	...	1818	2110d	2110d	...	2353u	2353u	2353u	0017u	0017u	0017u	0017u	...	2218	...	1037	...	...
Terespol a.	...	1525	1842	|	...	...	...	...	0003	0003	...	0330u	0330u	0330u	|	|	|	|	...	...	...	1525	...	...
Brest 🛃 a.	...	1741	2058	|	...	...	...	...	0222	0222	...	0516r	0516r	0516r	|	|	|	|	...	...	...	1741	...	...
Yahodyn 🛃 a.	...	|	|	2255	...	...	...	...	|	|	...	|	|	|	0608	0608	0608	0608	...	...	...	|	...	...
Lviv a.	...	|	|	|	...	...	...	...	|	|	...	|	|	|	|	2255	|	|	...	...	...	|	...	...
Kyïv a.	...	|	|	1027	...	...	...	...	|	|	...	|	|	|	1648	...	1648	1648	...	...	...	|	...	...
Odesa a.	...	|	|	...	...	...	...	...	|	|	...	|	|	|	...	...	0541	|	...	...	...	|	...	...
Simferopol a.	...	|	|	...	...	...	...	...	|	|	...	|	|	|	...	...	...	0850	...	...	...	|	...	...
Minsk a.	...	2345	0158	...	...	...	...	...	0804	0837	...	1046	1046	1114	...	...	...	...	...	...	...	2345	...	...
Orsha Tsentralnaya § a.	...	0234	0424	...	...	...	...	...	...	1136	...	1332	1332n	1408c	...	...	...	...	...	...	...	0234	...	...
St Peterburg Vitebski a.	...	|	|	...	...	...	...	...	...	|	...	|	0615	|	...	...	...	...	...	...	...	|	...	...
Smolensk Tsentralny 🛃 § a.	...	0502	0643	...	...	...	...	...	...	1408	...	1601	...	1652	...	...	...	...	...	...	...	0502	...	...
Moskva Belorusskaya ‡ a.	...	1033	1145	...	...	...	...	...	...	1954	...	2035	...	...	...	...	...	...	...	...	...	1033	...	...

train type/number	25		*EC*	*ICE*			*EC*	*EC*	*ICE*		*EC*	*ICE*				19		40		106	134	*ICE*		
train number	**115**	**115**	**46**	**558**	**67**	**9**	**44**	**340**	**844**	**11**	**40**	**1502**	**446**		**70**	**13**	**13**	**29**	**29**	**29**	**84**	**652**		
notes	11008	11008	✕	🍷	21000	11002	✕	🅁⊡	🍷	11014	✕	700	🅁		1248	442	442	440	440	440	440	🍷		
	EE	V	T	A	C	P	T	W		Z	Tq	🍷	E		B	Q	F	O	R	H	BB	A		
Moskva Belorusskaya ‡ d.	1027	...	...	...	...	1650	...	...	...	2109	...	...	2109	...	...	...	0800	...	...	...	...	...	...	...
Smolensk Tsentralny 🛃 § d.	1620	...	...	...	...	2132	...	...	...	0231	...	...	0231	...	1117	...	1220	...	...	...	...	...	...	...
St Peterburg Vitebski d.	|	...	...	...	...	|	...	...	...	|	...	...	|	...	|	2355	|	...	...	...	...	...	...	...
Orsha Tsentralnaya § d.	1707	...	...	...	...	2153	...	...	...	0311	...	...	0311	...	1213	1250j	1250	...	...	...	...	...	...	...
Minsk d.	2040	2040	...	...	...	0019	...	...	...	0619	...	...	0619	...	1503	1529	1529	...	...	...	...	...	...	...
Simferopol d.	|	|	...	...	...	|	...	...	...	|	...	...	|	...	|	|	|	1537	...	...	...	...	...	...
Odesa d.	|	|	...	...	...	|	...	...	...	|	...	...	|	...	|	|	|	|	...	2257	...	...	...	...
Kyïv d.	|	|	...	...	1533	|	...	...	...	|	...	...	|	...	|	|	|	0924	0924	0924	...	...	...	...
Lviv d.	|	|	...	...	|	|	...	...	...	|	...	...	|	...	|	|	|	|	|	|	0108	...	...	...
Yahodyn 🛃 d.	|	|	...	...	0324	|	...	...	...	|	...	...	|	...	|	|	|	1930	1930	1930	1930	...	...	...
Brest 🛃 d.	0240	0240	...	...	|	0532	...	...	...	1223	...	...	1223	...	2115f	2115f	2115f	|	|	|	|	...	...	...
Terespol d.	0238	0238	...	...	|	0530	...	...	...	1248	...	...	1248	...	2113	2113	2113	|	|	|	|	...	...	...
Warszawa Wschodnia d.	0534a	0534a	0623	...	0835a	0814a	1123	...	...	1514	1624	...	1753e	...	2338s	2338s	2338s	2326s	2326s	2326s	2326s	...	...	...
Warszawa Centralna d.	0546	0546	0635	...	0845	0835	1135	...	...	...	1635	...	1810	...	0101s	0101s	0101s	0101s	0101s	0101s	0101s	...	...	...
Kraków Gł. d.	...	...	|	...	...	...	|	0724	...	...	|	...	|	...	|	|	|	|	|	|	|	...	...	...
Katowice d.	...	...	|	...	...	...	|	0907	...	...	|	...	|	...	|	|	|	|	|	|	|	...	...	...
Wrocław Gł. d.	...	...	|	...	...	...	|	1148	...	...	|	...	|	...	|	|	|	|	|	|	|	...	...	...
Poznań Gł. d.	...	...	0923	...	...	...	1423	|	...	...	1923	...	2118	...	0423s	0423s	0423s	0423s	0423s	0423s	0423s	...	...	...
Rzepin d.	...	...	1053	...	...	...	1553	|	...	...	2053	...	2249	...	0617s	0615s	0615s	0617s	0617s	0617s	0617s	...	...	...
Frankfurt (Oder) 🛃 a.	...	...	1112	...	...	...	1612	|	...	...	2112	...	|	...	|	|	|	|	|	|	|	...	...	...
Berlin Lichtenberg a.	...	...	|	...	...	...	|	|	...	...	|	...	|	...	|	|	|	|	|	|	|	...	...	...
Berlin Ostbahnhof a.	...	...	1205	1238	...	...	1715	1718v	1738	...	2215	...	0001	...	0823	0823	0823	0823	0823	0823	0823	0840	...	...
Berlin Hbf a.	...	...	1216	1249	...	...	1726	1733¶	1749	...	2227	2305	0029	...	0900	0900	0900	0900	0900	0900	0900	0850d	...	...
Berlin Zoo a.	...	...	...	|	...	...	...	|	|	...	...	|	|	...	0909	0909	0909	0909	0909	0909	0909	|	...	...
Hamburg Hbf a.	...	...	...	|	...	...	...	2021x	|	...	...	0043	|	...	...	...	...	...	...	...	...	|	...	...
Hannover Hbf a.	...	...	...	1428	...	...	...	...	1928	...	...	...	|	...	...	...	...	...	...	...	...	1028	...	...
Bielefeld Hbf a.	...	...	...	1520	...	...	...	...	2020	...	...	...	0356	...	...	...	...	...	...	...	...	1120	...	...
Dortmund Hbf a.	...	...	...	1609z	...	...	...	...	2109	...	...	...	0450	...	...	...	...	...	...	...	...	1209z	...	...
Düsseldorf Hbf a.	...	...	...	1705z	...	...	...	...	2207	...	...	...	0654	...	...	...	...	...	...	...	...	1305z	...	...
Köln Hbf a.	...	...	...	1709	...	...	...	...	2231	...	...	...	0614	...	...	...	...	...	...	...	...	1309	...	...

A – 🚃12 and ✕ Köln - Wuppertal - Hamm - Berlin and Düsseldorf - Hamm - Berlin and v.v. Table **810**.

B – SARATOV EXPRESS – ④ (④⑥ May 29 - Sept. 30): 🛏 1, 2 cl. (1, 2, 4 berth) Saratov (**69**) (depart 1129) - Smolensk (depart ⑤) - Orscha - Terespol (**1248**) - Warszawa - Berlin (arrive ⑥). ②: 🛏 2 cl. (3, 4 berth) Novosibirsk (**113**), also Rostov-na-Donu (**88**) (depart ④), Omsk ③ - Perm II ③ - Gorkii ④ - Orscha (**13**) (⑤) - Minsk - Terespol (**442**) - Berlin (arrive ⑥). (Table **1980**).

C – KYÏV EKSPRES / KIEV EXPRESS – 🛏 1, 2 cl. Warszawa - Kyïv and v.v.

D – SARATOV EXPRESS – ⑥ (①⑥ May 31 - Oct. 2): 🛏 1, 2 cl. (1, 2, 4 berth) Berlin (**1249**) - Warszawa - Brest 🛃 (**70**) (arrive ⑦) - Orsha - Smolensk - Saratov ① (arrive 1516). ⑥: 🛏 2 cl. (3, 4 berth) Berlin (**1249**) - Brest 🛃 (**70**) - Orscha (**64**) - Gorkii (arrive ①) - Perm II ② - Omsk ③ - Novosibirsk ③, also Rostov-na-Donu ② (Table **1980**).

E – JAN KIEPURA – 🛏 1, 2 cl. Moskva (**11**) - Brest (**11014**) - Warszawa (**446**) - Köln - Amsterdam (journey 2 nights). 🛏 1, 2 cl., ▬ 2 cl., and 🚃2 (reclining) Warszawa (*EN* **446**) - Köln - Amsterdam. Table **24**.

F – MOSKVA EXPRESS – ①④⑥ Dec. 13 - May 29 (not Dec. 31); ①②③④⑥ May 31 - Oct. 2; ①④⑥ Oct. 4 - Dec. 11: 🛏 1 cl. *Lux* and 🛏 1, 2 cl. Moskva (**13**) - Terespol (**442**) - Warszawa - Berlin. ✕ Moskva - Brest.

G – ①③④⑤: 🛏 2 cl. Berlin (**441**) - Dorohusk (**30**) - Kyïv (**123**) - Odesa (journey 2 nights).

H – ①②③⑥: 🛏 2 cl. Odesa (**106**) - Kyïv (**29**) - Dorohusk (**440**) - Berlin (journey 2 nights).

J – JAN KIEPURA – 🛏 1, 2 cl. Amsterdam (**447**) - Köln - Warszawa (**11013**) - Brest (**12**) - Moskva (journey 2 nights). 🛏 1, 2 cl., ▬ 2 cl., and 🚃2 (reclining) Amsterdam (*EN* **447**) - Köln - Warszawa. Table **24**.

K – 🛏 2 cl. Berlin (**441**) - Dorohusk (**30**) - Kyïv (not Jan. 1). ✕ Warszawa - Kyïv. Conveys on ④⑦: 🛏 2 cl. Berlin - Kyïv (**118**) - Kharkiv (journey 2 nights).

L – ⑤⑦: 🛏 2 cl. Berlin (**443**) - Warszawa - Brest 🛃 (**14**) - Orsha (**20**) - St Peterburg (journey 2 nights).

M – MOSKVA EXPRESS – ②⑤⑦ Dec. 13 - May 30 (not Jan. 1); ②③④⑤⑦ June 1 - Oct. 3; ②⑤⑦ Oct. 5 - Dec. 11: 🛏 1 cl. *Lux* and 🛏 1, 2 cl. Berlin (**443**) - Warszawa - Brest 🛃 (**14**) - Moskva. ✕ Brest - Moskva.

O – ④⑦ Dec. 13 - May 29: 🛏 2 cl. Simferopol (**40 / 39**) - Kyïv (**29**) - Dorohusk (**440**) - Berlin (journey 2 nights).

P – POLONEZ – 🛏 1, 2 cl., 🛏 1, 2 cl. (Lux) and 🍷 Warszawa - Moskva and v.v. ✕ Brest - Moskva and v.v.

Q – ③⑤: 🛏 2 cl. St Peterburg (**19**) - Orsha (**13**) - Terespol (**442**) - Warszawa - Berlin (journey 2 nights).

R – 🛏 2 cl. Kyïv (**29**) - Dorohusk (**440**) - Berlin (not Dec. 31). ✕ Kyïv - Warszawa. Conveys on ②⑤ 🛏 2 cl. Kharkiv (**343**) - Kyïv (**29**) - Dorohusk (**440**) - Berlin (journey 2 nights).

S – ②⑥ Dec. 12 - May 30: 🛏 2 cl. Berlin (**441**) - Dorohusk (**30**) - Kyïv (**12**) - Simferopol (journey 2 nights).

T – BERLIN WARSZAWA EXPRESS – 🚃12 and ✕ Berlin - Poznań - Warszawa and v.v. 🅁 Special fares apply. Supplement payable in Poland.

U – ①–⑥ (not Dec. 25, 26, Jan. 1, Apr. 2, 3, 5, May 24).

V – 🛏 1, 2 cl. Warszawa - Minsk and v.v.

W – WAWEL – 🚃12 and 🍷 (Hamburg ①–⑥ not Dec. 25, 26, 31, Jan. 1, Apr. 3, 5, May 24 -) Berlin - Cottbus - Forst 🛃 - Legnica - Wrocław - Kraków.

X – WAWEL – 🚃12 and 🍷 Kraków - Wrocław - Legnica - Forst 🛃 - Cottbus - Berlin (- Hamburg ⑧ not Dec. 24, 25, 30, 31, Apr. 2, 4, May 23).

Z – OST WEST – 🛏 1, 2 cl. Warszawa - Moskva and v.v.

AA – ① Dec. 13 - May 30: 🛏 2 cl. Berlin (**441**) - Dorohusk (**30**) - Kovel (**668**) - Lutsk - Lviv (journey 2 nights).

BB – ⑦ Dec. 13 - May 29: 🛏 2 cl. Lviv (**134**) - Zdolbunov (**84**) - Kovel (**29**) - Dorohusk (**440**) - Berlin (journey 2 nights).

EE – 🛏 1, 2 cl. Warszawa - Moskva and v.v.

- **a** – Arrival time.
- **c** – Depart 1426.
- **d** – Departure time.
- **e** – Arrive 1514.
- **f** – Arrive 1855.
- **j** – Arrive 1047.
- **n** – Depart 1637.
- **p** – Not Dec. 25.
- **q** – Not Dec. 24.
- **r** – Depart 0720.
- **s** – Stops to set down only.
- **t** – 0935 May 3 - Aug. 14.
- **u** – Stops to pick up only.
- **v** – Not May 3 - Aug. 14.
- **x** – ⑧ (not Dec. 24, 25, 30, 31, Apr. 2, 4, May 23).
- **y** – ①–⑥ (not Dec. 25, 26, 31, Jan. 1, Apr. 3, 5, May 24).
- **z** – For train number, days of running and possible earlier timings of Düsseldorf portion see Table **800**.

- ‡ – Also known as Moskva **Smolenskaya** station.
- ⊡ – Supplement payable in Poland.
- § – 🛃: Osinovka (BY) / Krasnoye (RU).
- ¶ – 1740 May 3 - Aug. 14.

Summary of Berlin - Lviv, Kyïv, Odesa, Simferopol service from May 31, 2010.

train number	**445**	**445**	**445**	**445**	*train number*	**444**	**444**	**444**	**444**
Berlin Licht. d.	2147	2147	2147	2147	Simferopol d.	1537	...	...	...
Warszawa C. d.	0440	0440	0440	0440	Odesa d.	|	...	1822	...
Warszawa W. d.	0502	0502	0502	0502	**Kyïv** d.	0924	0924	|	...
Yahodyn 🛃 a.	1050	1050	1050	1050	Lviv d.	|	|	|	0108
Lviv a.	|	2255	|	|	Yahodyn 🛃 d.	1930	1930	1930	1930
Kyïv a.	2112	...	|	2112	**Warszawa W.** a.	2326	2326	2326	2326
Odesa a.	...	...	0957	|	**Warszawa C.** a.	0005	0005	0005	0005
Simferopol a.	...	...	...	1330	**Berlin Licht** a.	0712	0712	0712	0712

DORTMUND - FRANKFURT - NÜRNBERG - PRAHA 57

train type	ALX¶	ICE	🚌	ICE	RE	RE	ALX¶	ICE	🚌	IC	ICE	🚌	ICE	ALX	ALX¶	ICE	🚌	IC	ICE	IC	ICE	RE	RE	ALX¶	ICE	IC	CNL
train number	**351**	**21**	**1051**	**523**	**19905**	**3583**	**355**	**23**	**1053**	**2065**	**25**	**1055**	**621**	**37978**	**353**	**27**	**1057**	**2069**	**29**	**2023**	**629**	**19919**	**3599**	**357**	**229**	**2215**	**459**
notes		🍷	[R]	**B**				🍷	[R]	🍷	🍷	[R]	🍷	🍷		🍷	[R]	🍷	🍷	🍷	Ⓑf	**19921**			🍷	**2315**	**A**
Dortmund Hbf d.	...	...	...	0406	...	...	...	0437j	...	...	0636	...	...	...	...	0837	...	...	...	1036	...	...	...	...	...	1937	...
Köln Hbf d.	...	...	...	0518t	...	...	...	0553	...	...	0753	...	0937t	...	...	0953	...	...	...	1153	1344t	...	...	...	...	2053	...
Bonn Hbf d.	...	...	...	|	...	...	...	0614	...	...	0814	...	|	...	...	1014	...	...	...	1214	|	...	...	...	...	2114	...
Koblenz d.	...	...	...	⊖	...	...	...	0648	...	...	0848	...	⊖	...	...	1048	...	...	...	1248	⊖	...	...	...	...	2148	...
Mainz d.	...	...	...	|	...	...	...	0740	...	...	0940	...	|	...	...	1140	...	...	...	1340	|	...	...	...	...	2240	...
Frankfurt Flughafen ✈ d.	...	...	...	0637	...	...	...	0802	...	...	1002	...	1029	...	...	1202	...	...	...	1401	1437	...	...	...	...	2300	...
Frankfurt (Main) Hbf d.	...	0622	...	0654	...	...	...	0819	...	...	1021	...	1054	...	...	1221	...	...	1416	1412	1454	...	...	...	1621	2310	0055k
Würzburg Hbf d.	...	0735	...	0805	...	...	...	0934	...	...	1134	...	1205	...	...	1334	...	...	1534	▬	1605	...	...	...	1734	▬	|
Karlsruhe Hbf d.	...	|	...	|	...	...	...	|	...	0906	|	...	|	...	...	|	...	1306	|	🚌	|	...	...	...	|	🚌	|
Stuttgart Hbf d.	...	|	...	|	0640	...	...	|	...	1007	|	...	|	...	...	|	...	1407	|	**1059**	|	1440	...	...	|	**1061**	|
München Hbf d.	...	|	...	|	|	...	0902	|	...	|	|	...	|	1244	...	|	...	|	|	[R]	|	|	...	1700	|	[R]	|
Nürnberg Hbf d.	0600	0831	0845	0859	0925	0936	|	1028	1045	1216	1228	1245	1259	|	1405	1428	1445	1616	1628	1645	1659	1725	1736	|	1828	1845	|
Regensburg d.	*0623*	0922	|	...	...	|	1031	...	|	...	...	|	...	1419	|	...	|	...	...	|	...	...	|	1839	...	|	|
Schwandorf d.	0704	...	|	...	...	1044	1108	...	|	...	...	|	...	1446	1508	...	|	...	...	|	...	...	1843	1909	...	|	|
Furth im Wald 🛃 d.	0750	...	◐	...	...	...	1150	...	◐	...	...	◐	...	...	1550	...	◐	...	...	◐	...	...	...	1952	...	◐	◧
Plzeň hlavní a.	0857	...	|	...	...	...	1257	...	|	...	...	|	...	...	1657	...	|	...	...	|	...	...	...	2059	...	|	|
Praha hlavní a.	1058	...	1230	...	...	...	1458	...	1430	...	...	1630	...	...	1858	...	1830	...	...	2030	...	...	...	2258	...	2230	1051

train type	ALX¶	ALX	ICE	🚌	ICE	IC	🚌	ICE	ALX¶	RE	ICE	🚌	ICE	IC	🚌	ICE	ALX¶	ALX	ICE	🚌	ICE	🚌	ICE	ALX¶	RE	CNL	IC
train number	**350**	**37977**	**722**	**1050**	**228**	**2100**	**1052**	**28**	**354**	**3558**	**624**	**1054**	**26**	**2104**	**1056**	**24**	**352**	**37985**	**526**	**1058**	**22**	**1060**	**20**	**356**	**3574**	**458**	**2320**
notes		🍷	🍷	[R]	🍷	🍷	[R]	🍷			🍷	[R]	🍷	🍷	[R]	🍷		🍷	Ⓑf	[R]	🍷	[R]	🍷			**A**	🍷
Praha hlavní d.	0504	...	...	0730	...	...	0930	...	0904	...	...	1130	...	...	1330	...	1304	...	...	1530	...	1730	...	1704	...	1831	...
Plzeň hlavní d.	0700	...	...	|	...	...	|	...	1100	...	...	|	...	...	|	...	1500	...	...	|	...	|	...	1900	...	|	...
Furth im Wald 🛃 a.	0810	...	...	◐	...	...	◐	...	1210	...	...	◐	...	...	◐	...	1610	...	...	◐	...	◐	...	2012	...	◧	...
Schwandorf a.	0853	0908	...	|	...	...	|	...	1256	1309	...	|	...	...	|	...	1653	1708	...	|	...	|	...	2105	2113	|	...
Regensburg a.	|	0937	...	|	...	...	|	...	1331	|	...	|	1433	...	|	...	|	1736	...	|	...	|	...	2133	|	|	...
Nürnberg Hbf a.	0956	|	1100	1115	1128	1141	1315	1328	|	1421	1500	1515	1524	1541	1715	1727	1756	|	1900	1915	1927	2115	2128	|	2223	|	...
München Hbf a.	|	1115	|	...	|	|	...	|	1502	|	|	...	|	|	...	|	|	1915	|	...	|	...	|	2306	...	|	...
Stuttgart Hbf a.	*1318*	...	|	...	|	1353	...	|	...	*1718*	|	...	|	1753	...	|	*2118*	...	|	...	|	...	|	...	...	|	...
Karlsruhe a.	...	...	|	...	|	1453	...	|	...	...	|	...	|	1853	...	|	...	...	|	...	|	...	|	...	...	|	...
Würzburg Hbf a.	...	...	1154	...	1225	...	...	1425	...	...	1554	...	1625	...	...	1825	...	...	1954	...	2025	...	2227	...	...	|	...
Frankfurt (Main) Hbf a.	...	...	1305	...	1340	...	...	1536	...	...	1705	...	1736	...	...	1936	...	...	2105	...	2136	...	2339	...	...	0359k	0542
Frankfurt Flughafen ✈ a.	...	...	1321	...	...	...	...	...	...	...	1721	...	1755	...	...	1955	...	...	2121	...	2157	...	...	...	...	...	0555
Mainz a.	...	...	|	...	...	...	...	...	...	...	|	...	1818	...	...	2018	...	...	|	...	2218	...	...	...	...	...	0615
Koblenz a.	...	...	⊖	...	...	...	...	...	...	...	⊖	...	1910	...	...	2110	...	...	⊖	...	2310	...	...	...	...	...	0710
Bonn Hbf a.	...	...	|	...	...	...	...	...	...	...	|	...	1942	...	...	2142	...	...	|	...	2342	...	...	...	...	...	0742
Köln Hbf a.	...	...	1414t	...	...	...	...	...	...	...	1814t	...	2005	...	...	2205	...	...	2219t	...	0005	...	...	...	...	...	0805
Dortmund Hbf a.	...	...	...	...	...	...	...	...	...	...	1929	...	2120	...	...	2320	...	...	2345	...	0121j	...	...	...	...	...	0921

A – *City Night Line* CANOPUS – 🛏 1, 2 cl., ▬ 2 cl., (2) (reclining) and 🍷 Zürich - Basel - Frankfurt (Main) **Süd** - Děčín 🛃 - Praha and v.v. [R] Special fares apply.
B – ①–⑥ (Not Dec. 25, 26, Jan. 1, Apr. 3, 5, May 24); Train **1123** on ⑥.
f – Not Dec. 24, 25, 31, Apr. 2, 4, May 23.
j – Not Dec. 25, Jan. 1.
k – Frankfurt (Main) **Süd**.
t – Köln **Messe / Deutz**.
¶ – *R* in the Czech Republic.
◐ – 🛃 is Waidhaus (Germany).
ALX – Arriva Länderbahn Express.
🚌 – **DB / ČD** *IC Bus*. [R] 🍷. Rail tickets valid. 1st and 2nd class.
⊖ – Via Köln - Frankfurt high speed line.
◧ – 🛃 is Děčín; Ticketing point is Schöna.

TRAIN NAMES				
	RE **351 / 352** JAN HUS	*RE* **353 / 350** KAREL ČAPEK	*ALX* **355 / 356** ALBERT EINSTEIN	*ALX* **357 / 354** FRANZ KAFKA

BRUSSELS - KÖLN - FRANKFURT - LEIPZIG - DRESDEN - PRAHA 58

train type	CNL	D	EC	ICE	EC	ICE	EC	ICE	ICE	ICE	EC	D	ICE	ICE	EC	⇌	ICE	ICE	EC	ICE	ICE	EN	EN
train number	**459**	**61459**	**171**	**1553**	**173**	**1555**	**175**	**813**	**1557**	**1597**	**177**	**277**	**11**	**1559**	**379**	**9407**	**105**	**1651**	**179**	**15**	**1643**	**477**	**60477**
notes			✕	🍷	✕	🍷	✕	🍷	🍷	🍷	✕	2	🍷	🍷	✕	①–⑥	🍷	🍷	✕	🍷	🍷		**407**
	A		**L**	①f	**C**	**U**	**H**	**X**	**U**	**V**	**S**	**R**			**D**				**Q**		**k**		
Brussels Midi / Zuid d.	...	...	...	...	...	...	...	...	...	...	...	...	0725	...	...	0755	...	...	...	1225	...	...	...
Köln Hbf d.	...	...	...	...	...	...	...	0720	...	...	...	...	0928	...	...	0947	1055	...	...	1420	...	...	...
Frankfurt Flughafen ✈ d.	...	...	...	...	...	...	...	0829	...	0901	...	...	1018e	...	...	...	1151	1302	...	1526	1611	...	...
Frankfurt (Main) Hbf d.	...	...	...	0517	...	0721	...	0841	0921	0921	...	...	1030e	1119	...	...	...	1319	...	...	|	...	...
Frankfurt (Main) Süd d.	0055	...	...	|	...	|	...	...	|	|	...	...	...	|	...	...	...	|	...	...	1622	...	...
Fulda d.	|	0341	...	0611	...	0814	...	...	1013	1013	...	...	...	1213	...	...	...	1413	...	...	1714	...	...
Erfurt Hbf d.	0518s	0523	...	0735	...	0934	...	...	1134	1134	...	...	...	1334	...	...	...	1534	...	...	1835	...	...
Weimar d.	0535s	0540	...	0752	...	0950	...	...	1150	1150	...	...	...	1350	...	...	...	1550	...	...	1853	...	...
Leipzig d.	0641s	0651	...	0851	...	1051	...	...	1251	1251	...	...	...	1451	...	...	...	1651	...	...	1951	...	...
Dresden Hbf d.	0804s	0816	0910	1004	1110	1204	1310	...	1404	1404	1510	1510	...	1604	1710	...	...	1804	1910	...	2104	2210	2210
Bad Schandau 🛃 ◧ d.	0855s	0857	0939	...	1139	...	1339	...	...	...	1539	1539	...	...	1739	...	...	...	1939	...	...	|	|
Děčín 🛃 ◧ d.	0915s	0917	0957	...	1157	...	1357	...	...	...	1557	1557	...	...	1757	...	...	...	1957	...	...	2257	2257
Praha Holešovice a.	1035s	1035	1116	...	1316	...	1516	...	...	...	1716	1716	...	...	1916	...	...	...	2116	...	...	0016	0017
Praha hlavní a.	1051	1051	1127	...	1327	...	1527	...	...	...	1727	1727	...	...	1927	...	...	...	2127	...	...	0027	0027
Wien Meidling a.	...	...	|	...	1823	...	|	...	...	...	2223	|	...	...	...	...	...	...	...	...	...	|	0608
Bratislava Hlavná a.	...	...	1551	...	...	...	1951	...	...	...	...	2202	...	...	...	...	...	...	...	...	...	0540	...
Budapest Keleti a.	...	...	1832	...	...	...	2232	...	...	...	...	...	...	...	...	...	...	...	...	...	...	0832	...

train type	EC	ICE	ICE	⇌	EC	ICE	ICE	⇌	D	EC	ICE	ICE	EC	ICE	ICE	EC	ICE	EC	ICE	RE	RE	D	CNL
train number	**178**	**1640**	**508**	**9448**	**176**	**1548**	**506**	**9456**	**278**	**378**	**1546**	**10**	**174**	**1744**	**1544**	**172**	**1542**	**170**	**1740**	**17470**	**17472**	**61458**	**458**
notes	✕	🍷	🍷	🍷	✕	🍷	🍷	🍷		✕	🍷	🍷	✕	🍷	🍷	✕	🍷	✕					
	T				**P**				**G**	**F**			**H**	⑦h	**X**	**C**	Ⓑg	**L**	**W**	Ⓑ			**A**
Budapest Keleti d.	...	...	...	...	...	...	...	...	...	...	...	...	0528	...	...	...	...	0928	...	...	...	...	...
Bratislava Hlavná d.	...	...	...	...	...	...	...	...	0605	...	...	...	0808	...	...	...	...	1208	...	...	...	...	...
Wien Meidling d.	...	...	...	...	...	...	...	...	|	0533	...	...	|	...	...	0933	...	|	...	...	...	...	...
Praha hlavní d.	0631	...	...	...	0831	...	...	...	1031	1031	...	...	1231	...	...	1431	...	1631	...	...	...	1831	1831
Praha Holešovice d.	0640	...	...	...	0840	...	...	...	1040	1040	...	...	1240	...	...	1440	...	1640	...	...	...	1840	1840u
Děčín 🛃 ◧ d.	0802	...	...	...	1002	...	...	...	1202	1202	...	...	1402	...	...	1602	...	1802	...	...	...	2002	2002u
Bad Schandau 🛃 ◧ a.	0817	...	...	...	1017	...	...	...	1217	1217	...	...	1417	...	...	1617	...	1817	...	...	...	2017	2019u
Dresden Hbf a.	0846	0854	...	...	1046	1054	...	...	1246	1246	1254	...	1446	1454	1454	1646	1654	1846	1854	1920	2020	2047	2104u
Leipzig a.	...	1007	...	...	...	1207	...	...	...	...	1407	...	...	1607	1607	...	1807	...	2005	2101	2201	2215	2229u
Weimar a.	...	1104	...	...	...	1304	...	...	...	...	1504	...	...	1704	1704	...	1904	...	...	...	...	2331	2333u
Erfurt Hbf a.	...	1120	...	...	...	1320	...	...	...	...	1520	...	...	1720	1720	...	1920	...	...	...	...	2350	0123u
Fulda a.	...	1242	...	...	...	1442	...	...	...	...	1642	...	...	1842	1842	...	2042	...	...	...	...	...	|
Frankfurt (Main) Süd a.	...	1335	...	...	...	1535	...	...	...	...	1735	...	...	1935	|	...	2138	...	...	...	...	...	0359
Frankfurt (Main) Hbf a.	...	|	...	...	...	|	...	...	...	...	|	...	...	|	1940	...	|	...	...	...	...	...	...
Frankfurt Flughafen ✈ a.	...	1348	1409	...	...	1548	1609	...	...	...	1748	1843	...	1948	...	...	2150	...	...	...	...	...	...
Köln Hbf a.	...	...	1505	1545	...	...	1705	1745	...	...	...	1939	...	...	...	...	...	...	...	...	...	...	...
Brussels Midi / Zuid a.	...	...	...	1732	...	...	...	1932	...	...	...	2135	...	...	...	...	...	...	...	...	...	...	...

A – *City Night Line* CANOPUS – 🛏 1, 2 cl., ▬ 2 cl., (2) (reclining) and 🍷: Zürich - Basel - Frankfurt (Main) **Süd** - Děčín 🛃 - Praha and v.v. [R] Special fares apply.
C – VINDOBONA – (12) and ✕ Hamburg - Berlin - Dresden - Praha - Wien - Villach and v.v.
D – (12) and ✕ Stralsund - Berlin - Dresden - Praha - Brno. From Ostseebad Binz on dates in Table **844**.
F – (12) and ✕ Wien - Praha - Dresden - Berlin - Stralsund. To Ostseebad Binz on dates in Table **844**.
G – (2) Bratislava - Praha - Dresden - Berlin - Stralsund. To Ostseebad Binz on dates in Table **844**.
H – JAN JESENIUS – (12) and ✕ Hamburg - Berlin - Dresden - Praha - Budapest and v.v.
L – HUNGARIA – (12) and ✕ Berlin - Dresden - Praha - Budapest and v.v.
P – (12) and ✕ Brno - Praha - Dresden - Berlin - Hamburg.
Q – (12) and ✕ Berlin - Dresden - Praha.
R – (2) Berlin - Dresden - Praha - Bratislava.
S – JOHANNES BRAHMS – (12) and ✕ Berlin - Dresden - Praha - Wien.
T – JOHANNES BRAHMS – (12) and ✕ Praha - Dresden - Berlin.
U – ①–⑥ (not Dec. 25, 26, Jan. 1, Apr. 3, 5, May 10, 24).
V – ⑦ (also Dec. 25, 26, Jan. 1, Apr. 3, 5, May 10, 24).
W – ①②③④⑦ (not Dec. 23, 24, 30, 31, Apr. 1, 4, May 23).
X – ①–⑤ (not Dec. 24, 25, 31, Jan. 1, Apr. 2, 5, May 24).
e – On ⑦ (also Apr. 5, May 24) departs Frankfurt Flughafen 1029, arrives Frankfurt (Main) Hbf 1041.
f – Also Apr. 6, May 25; not Apr. 5, May 24.
g – Not Dec. 24, 25, 31, Apr. 2, 4, May 23.
h – Also Apr. 5, May 24; not Apr. 4, May 23.
k – Not Dec. 24, 31.
j – Not Oct. 3.
s – Stops to set down only.
u – Stops to pick up only.
◧ – Ticketing point is Schöna.

60 HAMBURG - BERLIN - PRAHA / WIEN - BUDAPEST - BUCUREŞTI and İSTANBUL

train type	EC	377¶			IC	EC	EC		EC	EN	473	463	IC	463	EC	EC		EC	347¶	491				383		
train number	345	1822	293	335	55	273	275		171	473	463	[R]	51	491	173	137		175	341	81031	337	505	347¶	4663		
notes	✕				[R]⚡	✕	🍷		✕	🍷	[R]		[R]⚡	81031	✕	🍷		✕	491			UU				
	J	C	W	K	✕	P			Z	R	F	AA	✕	[R]	V				G	T	Y	[R]	E	LL		
Hamburg Hbf d.	...	...	...	...	...	...	...	...	...	...	...	...	...	KK	0628y	...	...	0831z	...	...	...	...	...	...	...	...
Berlin Hbf d.	...	...	...	...	...	...	...	...	0636	...	...	...	...	...	0836	...	...	1036	...	...	...	...	...	...	...	...
Dresden Hbf d.	...	...	...	...	...	...	...	...	0910	...	...	...	...	...	1110	...	...	1310	...	...	...	...	...	...	...	...
Bad Schandau 🏛 ⊖ d.	...	...	...	...	...	...	...	...	0939	...	...	...	...	...	1139	...	...	1339	...	...	...	...	...	...	...	...
Děčín d.	...	...	...	...	...	...	...	...	0957	...	...	...	...	...	1157	...	...	1357	...	...	...	...	...	...	...	...
Praha Holešovice d.	...	...	...	...	...	...	...	...	1117	...	...	...	...	...	1317	...	...	1517	...	...	...	...	...	...	...	...
Praha hlavní d.	0539	...	...	...	...	0739	0939	...	1139	...	...	...	...	...	1339	...	...	1539	...	...	...	...	...	...	...	...
Pardubice d.	0641	...	...	...	...	0841	1041	...	1241	...	...	...	...	...	1441	...	...	1641	...	...	...	...	...	...	...	...
Brno Hlavní d.	0824	...	...	...	...	1024	1224	...	1424	...	...	...	...	...	1624	...	...	1824	...	...	...	...	...	...	...	...
Břeclav d.	0900	...	...	...	...	1100	1300	...	1500	...	...	...	...	...	1702e	1700	...	1900	...	...	...	...	...	...	...	...
Wien Meidling a.	|	...	...	...	...	|	|	...	|	...	...	...	...	...	1823	|	...	|	...	...	...	...	...	...	...	...
Wien Westbahnhof d.	|	...	...	...	...	|	|	...	|	...	...	...	...	...	...	|	...	|	1850	...	...	...	1850	...	...	...
Kúty 🏛 d.	0914	...	...	...	...	1114	1314	...	1514	...	...	...	...	...	...	1714	...	1914	|	...	...	...	|	...	...	...
Bratislava Hlavná d.	0954	...	...	...	...	1154	1351	...	1554	...	...	...	...	...	...	1751	...	1954	|	...	...	...	|	...	...	...
Rajka 🏛 a.	|	...	...	...	...	|	...	...	|	...	...	...	...	...	...	...	...	|	|	...	...	...	|	...	...	...
Štúrovo 🏛 d.	1115	...	...	...	...	1315	...	...	1715	...	...	...	...	...	...	...	...	2115	|	...	...	...	|	...	...	...
Hegyeshalom 🏛 a.	|	...	...	...	...	|	...	...	|	...	...	...	...	...	...	...	...	|	1954	...	...	...	1954	...	...	...
Györ a.	|	...	...	...	...	|	...	...	|	...	...	...	...	...	...	...	...	|	2029	...	...	...	2029	...	...	...
Budapest Nyugati a.	|	...	...	...	...	|	...	...	|	...	...	...	...	...	...	...	...	|	|	...	...	...	|	...	...	...
Budapest Keleti a.	1232	...	...	...	...	1432	...	...	.1832	...	...	...	...	...	...	...	...	2232	2220	...	...	...	2220	...	...	...
Budapest Keleti d.	1300	1313	...	...	...	...	...	...	...	1913	1913	...	...	...	...	...	...	...	2300	...	...	...	2313	...	...	...
Lökösháza a.	|	1610	...	...	...	...	...	...	...	2203	2203	...	...	...	...	...	...	...	|	...	...	...	0155	...	...	...
Curtici 🏛 a.	|	1737	...	...	...	...	...	...	...	2330	2330	...	...	...	...	...	...	...	|	...	...	...	0322	...	...	...
Arad a.	|	1814	...	...	...	...	...	...	...	0007	0007	...	...	...	...	...	...	...	|	...	...	...	0359	...	...	...
Timişoara a.	|	|	...	...	...	...	...	...	...	|	|	...	...	...	...	...	...	...	|	...	...	...	|	...	...	...
Craiova a.	|	0158	...	...	...	...	...	...	...	|	|	...	...	...	...	...	...	...	|	...	...	...	|	...	...	...
Braşov a.	|	|	...	...	...	...	...	...	...	0726	0726	...	...	...	...	...	...	...	|	...	...	...	1110	...	...	...
Bucureşti Nord a.	|	0515	...	...	...	...	...	...	...	1034	1034	...	...	...	...	...	...	...	|	...	...	...	1407	...	...	...
Bucureşti Nord d.	|	...	...	...	...	...	...	...	...	...	1224	1224	...	1224	...	...	...	...	|	...	...	...	...	2002	...	...
Ruse 🏛 a.	|	...	...	...	...	...	...	...	...	...	1450	1450	...	1450	...	...	...	...	|	...	...	...	...	2230	...	...
Varna a.	|	...	...	...	...	...	...	...	...	...	|	|	...	|	...	...	...	...	|	...	...	...	...	|	...	...
Burgas a.	|	...	...	...	...	...	...	...	...	...	|	|	...	|	...	...	...	...	|	...	...	...	...	|	...	...
Subotica 🏛 a.	1631	...	...	...	...	...	...	...	...	...	|	|	...	|	...	...	...	...	0223	...	...	...	...	|	...	...
Novi Sad a.	1904	...	...	...	...	...	...	...	...	...	|	|	...	|	...	...	...	...	0456	...	...	...	...	|	...	...
Beograd a.	2036	...	2115	2150	...	...	...	...	...	...	|	|	...	|	...	...	...	...	0629	0750	0750	...	...	|	...	...
Niš a.	...	...	0124	0159	...	...	...	...	...	...	|	|	...	|	...	...	...	...	1200	1200	1200	...	...	|	...	...
Tabanovci 🏛 a.	...	...	|	0555	...	...	...	...	...	...	|	|	...	|	...	...	...	...	|	|	1550	...	...	|	...	...
Skopje a.	...	...	|	0706	...	...	...	...	...	...	|	|	...	|	...	...	...	...	|	|	1659	...	...	|	...	...
Idoméni 🏛 a.	...	...	|	1130	...	...	...	...	...	...	|	|	...	|	...	...	...	...	|	|	2115	...	...	|	...	...
Dimitrovgrad 🏛 a.	...	...	0432	|	...	...	...	...	...	...	|	|	...	|	...	...	...	...	1457	1457	|	...	...	|	...	...
Kalotina Zapad 🏛 a.	...	...	0545	|	...	...	...	...	...	...	|	|	...	|	...	...	...	...	1604	1604	|	...	...	|	...	...
Sofiya a.	...	...	0715	|	...	...	...	...	...	...	2130	2130	...	|	...	...	...	...	1737	1737	|	...	...	0555	...	...
Svilengrad a.	...	...	...	|	...	...	...	...	...	...	|	|	...	0010	...	...	...	...	...	0010	|	...	...	...	...	...
Kapikule 🏛 a.	...	...	...	|	...	...	...	...	...	...	|	|	...	0110	...	...	...	...	...	0110	|	...	...	...	...	...
İstanbul Sirkeci a.	...	...	...	|	...	...	...	...	...	...	|	|	...	0800	...	...	...	...	...	0750	|	...	...	...	...	...
Kulata 🏛 a.	...	...	...	|	...	...	...	...	...	...	0225	0225	...	...	...	...	...	...	...	...	|	...	...	...	...	...
Thessaloníki a.	...	...	...	1254	1454	...	...	...	...	...	0539	0539	0713	...	...	...	...	...	...	...	2237	2333	...	...	...	...
Athína Lárisa a.	...	...	...	...	1950	...	...	...	...	...	...	...	1140	...	...	...	...	...	...	...	...	0612	...	...	...	...

train type	EC	D	EC	EC	471	EN		463¶	D	EN	
train number	177	277	379	179	477	477	375	375	343	60477	
notes	✕	2	✕	✕	375			[R]		407	
			H		CC	A	B	L		M	
Hamburg Hbf d.	...	...	...	...	...	...	...	...	...	...	...
Berlin Hbf d.	1236	1236	1436	1636	...	1925	...	...	...	1925	...
Dresden Hbf d.	1510	1510	1710	1910	...	2210	...	...	...	2210	...
Bad Schandau 🏛 ⊖ d.	1539	1539	1739	1939	...	|	...	...	...	|	...
Děčín d.	1557	1557	1757	1957	...	2257	...	...	...	2257	...
Praha Holešovice d.	1717	1717	1917	2116	...	0017	...	...	...	0017	...
Praha hlavní d.	1739	1739	1939	2127	2311	0037	...	...	...	0037	...
Pardubice d.	1841	1841	2041	...	0023	|	...	...	...	|	...
Brno Hlavní d.	2024	2024	2222	...	0244	0324	...	...	...	0324	...
Břeclav d.	2102	2111	...	...	0335	0447	...	...	...	0459	...
Wien Meidling a.	2204p	|	...	...	|	|	...	0600	...	0608	...
Wien Westbahnhof d.	...	|	...	...	|	|	...	|	...	0622	...
Kúty 🏛 d.	...	2125	...	...	0350	0501	...	|	...	...	...
Bratislava Hlavná d.	...	2202	...	...	0553	0553	...	|	...	...	...
Rajka 🏛 a.	...	...	...	...	|	|	...	|	...	...	...
Štúrovo 🏛 d.	...	...	...	...	0718	0718	...	|	...	...	...
Hegyeshalom 🏛 a.	...	...	...	...	|	|	...	0652	...	...	...
Györ a.	...	...	...	...	|	|	...	0720	...	...	...
Budapest Nyugati a.	...	...	...	...	|	|	...	|	...	...	...
Budapest Keleti a.	...	...	...	...	0832	0832	...	0849	...	...	...
Budapest Keleti d.	...	...	...	...	0913	...	0913	0913	1005	...	...
Lökösháza a.	...	...	...	...	1210	...	1210	1210	|	...	...
Curtici 🏛 a.	...	...	...	...	1337	...	1337	1337	|	...	...
Arad a.	...	...	...	...	1414	...	1414	1414	|	...	...
Timişoara a.	...	...	...	...	|	...	|	|	|	...	...
Craiova a.	...	...	...	...	|	...	|	|	|	...	...
Braşov a.	...	...	...	...	2117	...	2117	2117	|	...	...
Bucureşti Nord a.	...	...	...	...	0035	...	0035	0035	|	...	...
Bucureşti Nord d.	...	...	...	...	...	...	...	...	|	...	...
Ruse 🏛 a.	...	...	...	...	...	...	...	...	|	...	...
Varna a.	...	...	...	...	...	...	...	...	|	...	...
Burgas a.	...	...	...	...	...	...	...	...	|	...	...
Subotica 🏛 a.	...	...	...	...	...	...	...	...	1352	...	...
Novi Sad a.	...	...	...	...	...	...	...	...	1621	...	...
Beograd a.	...	...	...	...	...	...	...	...	1750	...	...
Niš a.	...	...	...	...	...	...	...	...	...	...	...
Tabanovci 🏛 a.	...	...	...	...	...	...	...	...	...	...	...
Skopje a.	...	...	...	...	...	...	...	...	...	...	...
Idoméni 🏛 a.	...	...	...	...	...	...	...	...	...	...	...
Dimitrovgrad 🏛 a.	...	...	...	...	...	...	...	...	...	...	...
Kalotina Zapad 🏛 a.	...	...	...	...	...	...	...	...	...	...	...
Sofiya a.	...	...	...	...	...	...	...	...	...	...	...
Svilengrad a.	...	...	...	...	...	...	...	...	...	...	...
Kapikule 🏛 a.	...	...	...	...	...	...	...	...	...	...	...
İstanbul Sirkeci a.	...	...	...	...	...	...	...	...	...	...	...
Kulata 🏛 a.	...	...	...	...	...	...	...	...	...	...	...
Thessaloníki a.	...	...	...	...	...	...	...	...	...	...	...
Athína Lárisa a.	...	...	...	...	...	...	...	...	...	...	...

train type/number	EC	EC	D	EC		81032	490	EC			
train number	178	176	278	378	336	490	340	174			
notes	✕	✕	2	✕			346	✕			
			N	Q	Y	T	G [R]				
Athína Lárisa d.	...	...	...	...	...	...	...	...	...	...	...
Thessaloníki d.	...	...	...	...	0557	...	...	...	...	...	...
Kulata 🏛 d.	...	...	...	...	|	...	...	...	...	...	...
İstanbul Sirkeci d.	...	...	...	...	|	2200	...	...	...	...	...
Kapikule 🏛 d.	...	...	...	...	|	0405	...	...	...	...	...
Svilengrad d.	...	...	...	...	|	0508	...	...	...	...	...
Sofiya d.	...	...	...	...	|	1140	1140	...	...	...	...
Kalotina Zapad 🏛 d.	...	...	...	...	|	1303	1303	...	...	...	...
Dimitrovgrad 🏛 d.	...	...	...	...	|	1230	1230	...	...	...	...
Idomeni 🏛 d.	...	...	...	...	0712	|	|	...	...	...	...
Skopje d.	...	...	...	...	0900	|	|	...	...	...	...
Tabanovci 🏛 d.	...	...	...	...	1002	|	|	...	...	...	...
Niš d.	...	...	...	...	1400	1515	1515	...	...	...	...
Beograd d.	...	...	...	...	1806	1921	2125	...	...	...	...
Novi Sad d.	...	...	...	...	...	...	2254	...	...	...	...
Subotica 🏛 d.	...	...	...	...	...	...	0125	...	...	...	...
Burgas d.	...	...	...	...	...	...	|	...	...	...	...
Varna d.	...	...	...	...	...	...	|	...	...	...	...
Ruse 🏛 d.	...	...	...	...	...	...	|	...	...	...	...
Bucureşti Nord a.	...	...	...	...	...	...	|	...	...	...	...
Bucureşti Nord d.	...	...	...	...	...	...	|	...	...	...	...
Braşov d.	...	...	...	...	...	...	|	...	...	...	...
Craiova d.	...	...	...	...	...	...	|	...	...	...	...
Timişoara d.	...	...	...	...	...	...	|	...	...	...	...
Arad d.	...	...	...	...	...	...	|	...	...	...	...
Curtici 🏛 d.	...	...	...	...	...	...	|	...	...	...	...
Lököshaza d.	...	...	...	...	...	...	|	...	...	...	...
Budapest Keleti a.	...	...	...	...	...	...	0504	...	...	...	...
Budapest Keleti d.	...	...	...	...	...	...	0600	0528	...	...	...
Budapest Nyugati d.	...	...	...	...	...	...	|	|	...	...	...
Györ d.	...	...	...	...	...	...	0727	|	...	...	...
Hegyeshalom 🏛 d.	...	...	...	...	...	...	0758	|	...	...	...
Štúrovo 🏛 d.	...	...	...	...	...	...	|	0647	...	...	...
Rajka 🏛 d.	...	...	...	...	...	...	|	|	...	...	...
Bratislava Hlavná d.	...	...	0605	...	...	...	|	0808	...	...	...
Kúty 🏛 d.	...	...	0643	...	...	...	|	0847	...	...	...
Wien Westbahnhof a.	...	...	|	...	...	...	0858	|	...	...	...
Wien Meidling d.	...	...	|	0550p	...	...	...	|	...	...	...
Břeclav d.	...	...	0702	0702	...	...	...	0902	...	...	...
Brno Hlavní d.	...	0535	0735	0735	...	...	...	0935	...	...	...
Pardubice d.	...	0716	0916	0916	...	...	...	1116	...	...	...
Praha hlavní d.	0631	0831	1031	1031	...	...	...	1231	...	...	...
Praha Holešovice d.	0640	0840	1040	1040	...	...	...	1240	...	...	...
Děčín d.	0802	1002	1202	1202	...	...	...	1402	...	...	...
Bad Schandau 🏛 ⊖ a.	0817	1017	1217	1217	...	...	...	1417	...	...	...
Dresden Hbf a.	0846	1046	1246	1246	...	...	...	1446	...	...	...
Berlin Hbf a.	1117	1320	1520	1520	...	...	...	1720	...	...	...
Hamburg Hbf a.	...	1527f	...	...	...	...	...	1928f	...	...	...

CONTINUED ON NEXT PAGE

İSTANBUL - BUCUREŞTI - BUDAPEST - WIEN / PRAHA - BERLIN - HAMBURG 60

train type/number	4662		EC	EC		81032	462	462	EN	EC	EC	EC		IC		1821	EC	EN	D		EN	374	374		
train number	382	346¶	136	172	502	492	[R]	360	472	170	274	272	292	52	334	376¶	344	60406	342	374	476	476	462		
notes	[R]		🍷	V	🍷	462		[R]	🍷	✕		✕		[R]⟋			✕	476				470	[R]		
	LL	E				[R] KK	AA	F	R	Z		P	W	✕	K	D	J	X		B	U	DD	L		
Athína Lárisa d.	...	...	...	...	1453	...	...	...	...	...	...	...	...	1051	...	...	...	...	...	...	...	...	...	...	...
Thessaloníki d.	...	...	...	...	2051	...	0030	0030	...	...	...	...	...	1548	1705	...	...	...	...	...	...	...	...	...	...
Kulata 🏛 d.	...	...	...	...	...	...	0350	0350	...	...	...	...	...	...	|	...	...	...	...	...	...	...	...	...	...
İstanbul Sirkeci d.	...	...	...	...	...	2200	|	|	...	...	...	...	...	...	|	...	...	...	...	...	...	...	...	...	...
Kapikule 🏛 d.	...	...	...	...	...	0405	|	|	...	...	...	...	...	...	|	...	...	...	...	...	...	...	...	...	...
Svilengrad d.	...	...	...	...	...	0508	|	|	...	...	...	...	...	...	|	...	...	...	...	...	...	...	...	...	...
Sofiya d.	1940	...	...	...	...	|	0905	0905	...	...	...	...	2040	...	|	...	...	...	...	...	...	...	...	...	...
Kalotina Zapad 🏛 d.	|	...	...	...	...	|	|	|	...	...	...	...	2211	...	|	...	...	...	...	...	...	...	...	...	...
Dimitrovgrad 🏛 d.	|	...	...	...	...	|	|	|	...	...	...	...	2140	...	|	...	...	...	...	...	...	...	...	...	...
Idoméni 🏛 d.	|	...	...	...	...	|	|	|	...	...	...	...	|	...	1830	...	...	...	...	...	...	...	...	...	...
Skopje d.	|	...	...	...	...	|	|	|	...	...	...	...	|	...	2045	...	...	...	...	...	...	...	...	...	...
Tabanovci 🏛 d.	|	...	...	...	...	|	|	|	...	...	...	...	|	...	2155	...	...	...	...	...	...	...	...	...	...
Niš d.	|	...	...	...	...	|	|	|	...	...	...	...	0010	...	0152	...	...	...	...	...	...	...	...	...	...
Beograd d.	|	...	...	...	...	|	|	|	...	...	...	...	0425	...	0559	...	0720	...	1000	...	...	...	...	...	...
Novi Sad d.	|	...	...	...	...	|	|	|	...	...	...	...	...	...	...	...	0856	...	1135	...	...	...	...	...	...
Subotica 🏛 d.	|	...	...	...	...	|	|	|	...	...	...	...	...	...	...	...	1129	...	1401	...	...	...	...	...	...
Burgas d.	|	...	...	...	...	|	|	|	...	...	...	...	...	...	...	...	|	...	|	...	...	...	...	...	...
Varna d.	|	...	...	...	...	|	|	|	...	...	...	...	...	...	...	...	|	...	|	...	...	...	...	...	...
Ruse 🏛 d.	0315	...	...	...	...	1600	1600	1600	...	...	...	...	...	...	...	...	|	...	|	...	...	...	...	...	...
Bucureşti Nord a.	0544	...	...	...	...	1830	1830	1830	...	...	...	...	...	...	...	...	|	...	|	...	...	...	...	...	...
Bucureşti Nord d.	...	1600	...	...	...	...	...	2105	1910	...	...	...	...	...	...	2345	|	...	|	0530	...	0530	0530	...	...
Braşov d.	...	1856	...	...	...	...	...	|	2216	...	...	...	...	...	...	|	|	...	|	0832	...	0832	0832	...	...
Craiova d.	...	|	...	...	...	...	...	0015	|	...	...	...	...	...	...	0300	|	...	|	|	...	|	|	...	...
Timişoara d.	...	|	...	...	...	...	...	0654	|	...	...	...	...	...	...	|	|	...	|	|	...	|	|	...	...
Arad d.	...	0204	...	...	...	...	...	0743	0549	...	...	...	...	...	...	1149	|	...	|	1549	...	1549	1549	...	...
Curtici 🏛 d.	...	0238	...	...	...	...	...	0823	0623	...	...	...	...	...	...	1223	|	...	|	1623	...	1623	1623	...	...
Lököshaza d.	...	0213	...	...	...	...	...	0750	0555	...	...	...	...	...	...	1150	|	...	|	1550	...	1550	1550	...	...
Budapest Keleti a.	...	0517	...	...	...	...	...	1047	0847	...	...	...	...	...	...	1447	1455	...	1804	1847	...	1847	1847	...	...
Budapest Keleti d.	...	0600	...	...	...	...	...	...	...	0928	...	1328	...	...	...	...	1528	...	...	...	1958	1958	2105	...	...
Budapest Nyugati d.	...	|	...	...	...	...	...	...	...	|	...	|	...	...	...	...	|	...	...	...	|	|	|	...	...
Györ d.	...	0727	...	...	...	...	...	...	...	|	...	|	...	...	...	...	|	...	...	...	|	|	2232	...	...
Hegyeshalom 🏛 d.	...	0758	...	...	...	...	...	...	...	|	...	|	...	...	...	...	|	...	...	...	|	|	2301	...	...
Štúrovo 🏛 d.	...	|	...	...	...	...	...	...	...	1047	...	1447	...	...	...	...	1647	...	...	...	2112	2112	|	...	...
Rajka 🏛 d.	...	|	...	...	...	...	...	...	...	|	...	|	...	...	...	...	|	...	...	...	|	|	|	...	...
Bratislava Hlavná d.	...	|	1008	...	...	...	...	...	...	1208	1408	1608	...	...	...	...	1808	...	...	...	2250	2250	|	...	...
Kúty 🏛 d.	...	|	1047	...	...	...	...	...	...	1247	1447	1647	...	...	...	...	1847	...	...	...	2330	2330	|	...	...
Wien Westbahnhof a.	...	0858	|	...	...	...	...	...	...	|	|	|	...	...	...	...	|	2208	...	...	|	|	|	...	...
Wien Meidling d.	...	...	|	0932	...	...	...	...	...	|	|	|	...	...	...	...	|	2223	...	...	|	|	2354	...	...
Břeclav d.	...	...	1059	1102	...	...	...	...	...	1302	1502	1702	...	...	...	...	1902	0005	...	...	0005	0200	...	...	...
Brno Hlavní d.	...	...	...	1135	...	...	...	...	...	1335	1535	1735	...	...	...	...	1935	0038	...	...	0038	0259	...	...	...
Pardubice d.	...	...	...	1316	...	...	...	...	...	1516	1716	1916	...	...	...	...	2116	|	...	...	|	0458	...	...	...
Praha hlavní d.	...	...	...	1431	...	...	...	...	...	1631	1821	2021	...	...	...	...	2221	0333	...	...	0333	0615	...	...	...
Praha Holešovice d.	...	...	...	1440	...	...	...	...	...	1640	...	...	...	...	...	...	...	|	...	...	|	...	...	...	...
Děčín d.	...	...	...	1602	...	...	...	...	...	1802	...	...	...	...	...	...	...	0502	...	...	0502	...	...	...	...
Bad Schandau 🏛 ⊖ a.	...	...	...	1617	...	...	...	...	...	1817	...	...	...	...	...	...	...	|	...	...	|	...	...	...	...
Dresden Hbf a.	...	...	...	1646	...	...	...	...	...	1846	...	...	...	...	...	...	...	0546	...	...	0546	...	...	...	...
Berlin Hbf a.	...	...	...	1920	...	...	...	...	...	2120	...	...	...	...	...	...	...	0854	...	...	0854	...	...	...	...
Hamburg Hbf a.	...	...	...	2137**k**	...	...	...	...	...	...	...	...	...	...	...	...	...	...	...	...	...	...	...	...	...

A – METROPOL – 🛏 1, 2 cl., ━ 2 cl. and [2] Berlin **Hbf** - Berlin **Südkreuz** (depart 1937) - Praha - Budapest.

B – PANNONIA – Dec. 13 - Feb 28, May 31 - Sept. 19: [12] and ✕ [R] Budapest - Bucureşti and v.v.

C – MAROS / MUREŞ – [12] Budapest (**377**) - Arad - Targu Mureş. Conveys 🛏 1, 2 cl. and [2] Venezia (**241**) - Budapest (**377**) - Arad (**1822**) - Bucureşti (journey 2 nights) and conveys on May 31 - Sept. 20: ━ 1, 2 cl. Venezia - Budapest - Bucureşti.

D – MUREŞ / MAROS – [12] Targu Mureş - Arad (**354**) - Budapest. Conveys 🛏 1, 2 cl. and [2] Bucureşti (**1822**) - Arad (**354**) - Budapest (**240**) - Venezia (journey 2 nights) and conveys on May 29 - Sept. 19: ━ 1, 2 cl. Bucureşti - Budapest - Venezia.

E – DACIA – 🛏 1, 2 cl., ━ 2 cl., [2] and ✕ Wien - Budapest - Bucureşti and v.v. [1] Wien - Budapest - Lököshága and v.v. [12] Curtici - Bucureşti and v.v.

F – 🛏 1, 2 cl. Budapest (**473**) - Bucureşti (**463**) - Sofiya - Thessaloníki and Thessaloníki (**462**) - Sofiya - Bucureşti (**360**) - Timişoara (**78**) - Budapest (journey 2 nights).

G – BEOGRAD – 🛏 1, 2 cl. and ━ 2 cl. Wien - Budapest - Beograd and v.v. 🛏 1, 2 cl. Wien - Beograd - Sofiya and v.v. [2] Budapest - Beograd and v.v. [12] Beograd - Sofiya and v.v.

H – [12] and ✕ Stralsund (depart 1138) - Berlin - Praha - Brno (from Ostseebad Binz on dates shown in Table **844**).

J – AVALA – [12] and ✕ Praha - Budapest - Beograd and v.v. Conveys 🛏 2 cl. Moskva - Budapest - Beograd and v.v. (journey 2 nights, Table **97**).

K – HELLAS EXPRESS – 🛏 1, 2 cl., ━ 2 cl. and [12] Beograd - Thessaloníki and v.v. 🛏 1, 2 cl., ━ 2 cl. and [2] Beograd - Skopje and v.v.

L – KÁLMÁN IMRE – 🛏 1, 2 cl., ━ 2 cl. and [2] München - Wien - Budapest and v.v. 🛏 1, 2 cl. and ━ 1, 2 cl. München - Wien - Budapest (**375 / 374**) - Lököshága - Bucureşti and v.v.

M – METROPOL – 🛏 1, 2 cl., ━ 2 cl. and [2] Berlin **Hbf** (**60477**) - Berlin **Südkreuz** (depart 1937) - Praha - Wien.

N – [2] Bratislava - Praha - Berlin - Stralsund (arrive 1824). To Ostseebad Binz on dates shown in Table **844**.

P – JAROSLAV HAŠEK – [12] and ✕ Praha - Budapest and v.v.

Q – CARL MARIA VON WEBER – [12] and ✕ Wien - Praha - Berlin - Stralsund (arrive 1824). To Ostseebad Binz on dates shown in Table **844**.

R – *EuroNight* ISTER – 🛏 1, 2 cl., ━ 1, 2 cl., [2] and 🍷 Budapest - Bucureşti and v.v. [12] Budapest - Lököshága and v.v.

T – BALKAN EXPRESS – [12] Beograd - Sofiya and v.v. 🛏 1, 2 cl. Beograd - Sofia - İstanbul and v.v. 🛏 1, 2 cl. Sofia - İstanbul and v.v. Conveys June 2 - Oct. 30 from Sofia, June 3 - Oct. 31 from İstanbul: ━ 2 cl. Sofia - İstanbul and v.v.

U – METROPOL – 🛏 1, 2 cl., ━ 2 cl. and [2] Budapest - Praha - Berlin **Sudkreuz** (arrive 0847) - Berlin **Hbf**.

V – VINDOBONA – [12] and ✕ Hamburg Altona - Hamburg Hbf - Berlin - Praha - Wien - Villach and v.v.

W – 🛏 1, 2 cl., ━ 2 cl. and [2] Beograd - Sofiya and v.v.

X – METROPOL – 🛏 1, 2 cl., ━ 2 cl. and [2] Wien (**60406**) - Praha - Berlin **Sudkreuz** (arrive 0847) - Berlin **Hbf**.

Y – OLYMPUS – [12] and 🍷 Beograd - Skopje - Thessaloníki and v.v.

Z – HUNGARIA – [12] and ✕ Berlin - Praha - Budapest and v.v.

AA – ROMANIA – 🛏 1, 2 cl., ━ 1, 2 cl. and 🍷 Bucureşti - Sofiya - Thessaloníki and v.v. [2] Bucureşti - Sofiya and v.v.

CC – AMICUS – 🛏 1, 2 cl. and [2] Praha (**471**) - Břeclav (**477**) - Budapest. May 27 - Sept. 27: 🛏 1, 2 cl. Praha (**471**) - Břeclav (**477**) - Budapest (**375**) - Bucureşti.

DD – AMICUS – 🛏 1, 2 cl. and [2] Budapest (**476**) - Břeclav (**470**) - Praha. May 28 - Sept. 28: 🛏 1, 2 cl. Bucureşti (**374**) - Budapest (**476**) - Břeclav (**470**) - Praha.

KK – BOSPHOR – 🛏 1, 2 cl. and ━ 2 cl. Bucureşti - İstanbul and v.v.

LL – BULGARIA EXPRESS – 🛏 1, 2 cl. and [12] Bucureşti - Sofiya and v.v. Conveys 🛏 2 cl. Moskva, Lviv, Kyïv and Minsk - Sofiya and v.v. on dates shown in Table **98**.

UU – 🛏 1, 2 cl. Thessaloníki - Athína.

a – Arrival time.

e – Arrive 1657.

f – Arrive Hamburg **Altona** [13 – 15] minutes later.

k – Not Dec. 24, 31. Arrive Hamburg **Altona** 14 minutes later.

n – Arrive 0804.

p – Wien **Praterstern**.

q – Wien **Meidling**.

r – Depart 2020.

x – Depart 2300.

y – Not Dec. 25, Jan. 1. Depart Hamburg **Altona** 14 minutes earlier.

z – Depart Hamburg **Altona** 14 minutes earlier.

⟋ – Supplement payable.

¶ – Train number for international bookings.

§ – It is reported that ━ 2 cl. could replace the 🛏 1, 2 cl. on certain days.

⊖ – Routeing point for international tickets : Schöna.

OTHER TRAIN NAMES:

EC **174 / 175** –	JAN JESENIUS
EC **177** –	JOHANNES BRAHMS
EC **274 / 275** –	SLOVAN
D **342/343** –	IVO ANDRIĆ

62 MÜNCHEN - LJUBLJANA - ZAGREB - BEOGRAD - THESSALONÍKI

train type / number	IC	IC	EC 111		RJ	IC	IC	EC 113	EC	D				241	D	499		499				IC	
train number	592	313	EC 211	483	63	690	311	EC 213	115	315	491	337	505	413	413	741	481	481	415	293	335	55	
notes			🍷◧ G	A	🍷			🍷◧ M	✕ W	Y	D	K	🅁 P	R	✕	L		C	F	H	E	🅁✓ ✕	
München Hbf d.	...	...	0827	...	0927	...	...	1227	1427	...	...	...	...	...	...	2340	...	2340	...	...	...	...	...
Salzburg Hbf 🏛 d.	0812	...	1012	...	1058	1212	...	1412	1612	...	...	...	...	...	...	0134	...	0134	...	...	...	...	...
Bischofshofen d.	0854	...	1054	...	...	1254	...	1454	1654	...	...	...	...	...	...	|	...	|	...	...	...	...	...
Schwarzach St Veit d.	0911	...	1111	...	...	1311	...	1511	1711	...	...	...	...	...	...	0226	...	0226	0430	...	...	...	...
Bad Gastein d.	0942	...	1142	...	...	1342	...	1542	1742	...	...	...	...	...	...	|	...	|	0503	...	...	...	...
Villach Hbf d.	1043	1052	1254	...	...	1443	1452	1654	1843	1927	...	...	...	...	...	0407	...	0407	0626	...	...	...	...
Jesenice 🏛 a.	...	1132	1333	...	...	...	1532	1733	...	2007	...	...	...	...	...	0448	...	0444	0707	...	...	...	...
Ljubljana a.	...	1232	1431	1453	...	...	1633	1831	...	2110	...	...	...	0159	...	0603	0620	0603	0810	...	...	...	...
Rijeka a.	...	...	|	1725	...	...	|	|	...	|	...	...	...	|	...	|	0854	0854	|	...	...	...	...
Dobova 🏛 a.	...	...	1623	...	...	...	1811	2008	...	2250	...	...	...	0332	...	0754	...	...	0949	...	...	...	...
Zagreb a.	...	...	1710	...	...	...	1856	2055	...	2334	...	...	...	0418	...	0839	...	...	1034	...	...	...	...
Zagreb d.	...	...	1725	...	...	...	...	...	...	2355	...	...	...	0603	0603	0900	...	...	1058	...	...	...	...
Vinkovci a.	...	...	2032	...	...	...	...	...	...	0306	...	...	...	0916	0916	1209	...	...	1413	...	...	...	...
Šid 🏛 a.	...	...	2123	...	...	...	...	...	...	0401	...	...	...	1012	1012	...	...	...	1503	...	...	...	...
Beograd a.	...	...	2327	...	...	...	...	...	...	0619	0750	0750	...	1218	1218	...	...	...	1720	2115	2150	...	...
Niš a.	...	...	...	...	...	...	...	...	...	...	1200	1200	...	...	...	...	...	...	...	0124	0159	...	...
Dimitrovgrad 🏛 a.	...	...	...	...	...	...	...	...	...	...	1457	|	...	...	...	...	...	...	...	0432	|	...	...
Kalotina Zapad 🏛 a.	...	...	...	...	...	...	...	...	...	...	1604	|	...	...	...	...	...	...	...	0545	|	...	...
Sofiya a.	...	...	...	...	...	...	...	...	...	...	1737	|	...	...	...	...	...	...	...	0715	|	...	...
Tabanovci 🏛 a.	...	...	...	...	...	...	...	...	...	...	...	1550	...	...	...	...	...	...	...	...	0555	...	...
Skopje a.	...	...	...	...	...	...	...	...	...	...	...	1659	...	...	...	...	...	...	...	...	0706	...	...
Idoméni 🏛 a.	...	...	...	...	...	...	...	...	...	...	...	2115	...	...	...	...	...	...	...	...	1130	...	...
Thessaloníki a.	...	...	...	...	...	...	...	...	...	...	...	2237	2333	...	...	...	...	...	...	...	1254	1454	...
Athína Lárisa a.	...	...	...	...	...	...	...	...	...	...	...	...	0612	...	...	...	...	...	...	...	...	1950	...

train type	IC				748	480	D	412			D	EC	EC 212	IC	IC	RJ			EC 210	IC	IC		
train number	52	334	414	480	498	498	412	240	336	490	314	114	EC 112	310	691	64	292	482	EC 110	312	593		
notes	🅁✓ ✕	E	F		L	B	✕	R	K	D	Y	✕ W	🍷◧ M			🍷	H	A	🍷◧ G				
Athína Lárisa d.	1051	...	...	...	...	...	...	...	...	...	...	...	...	...	...	...	...	...	...	...	...	...	...
Thessaloníki d.	1548	1705	...	...	...	...	...	...	0557	...	...	...	...	...	...	...	...	...	...	...	...	...	...
Idoméni 🏛 d.	...	1830	...	...	...	...	...	...	0712	...	...	...	...	...	...	...	...	...	...	...	...	...	...
Skopje d.	...	2045	...	...	...	...	...	...	0900	...	...	...	...	...	...	...	...	...	...	...	...	...	...
Tabanovci 🏛 d.	...	2155	...	...	...	...	...	...	1002	...	...	...	...	...	...	...	...	...	...	...	...	...	...
Sofiya d.	...	|	...	...	...	...	...	...	|	1140	...	...	...	...	...	...	2040	...	...	...	...	...	...
Kalotina Zapad 🏛 d.	...	|	...	...	...	...	...	...	|	1303	...	...	...	...	...	...	2211	...	...	...	...	...	...
Dimitrovgrad 🏛 d.	...	|	...	...	...	...	...	...	|	1230	...	...	...	...	...	...	2140	...	...	...	...	...	...
Niš d.	...	0152	...	...	...	...	...	...	1400	1515	...	...	...	...	...	...	0010	...	...	...	...	...	...
Beograd d.	...	0559	1020	...	...	...	1525	1525	1806	1921	2140	...	...	...	...	...	0425	...	0545	...	...	...	...
Šid 🏛 d.	...	...	1338	...	...	...	1833	1833	...	...	0058	...	...	...	...	...	...	...	0853	...	...	...	...
Vinkovci d.	...	...	1445	...	1724	...	1930	1930	...	...	0144	...	...	...	...	...	...	...	0945	...	...	...	...
Zagreb a.	...	...	1755	...	2051	...	2244	2244	...	...	0453	...	...	...	...	...	...	...	1254	...	...	...	...
Zagreb d.	...	...	1814	...	2115	...	...	2335	...	...	0500	...	0700	0900	...	...	...	...	1300	...	...	...	...
Dobova 🏛 d.	...	...	1907	...	2200	...	...	0040	...	...	0550	...	0745	0945	...	...	...	...	1345	...	...	...	...
Rijeka d.	...	...	|	2045	|	2045	...	|	...	...	|	...	|	|	...	...	...	1250	|	...	...	...	...
Ljubljana d.	...	...	2048	2322	2350	2350	...	0210	...	...	0727	...	0927	1126	...	...	...	1518	1525	1655	...	...	...
Jesenice 🏛 d.	...	...	2153	...	0049	0054	...	...	...	...	0827	...	1024	1228	...	...	...	...	1627	1758	...	...	...
Villach Hbf a.	...	...	2232	...	0131	0131	...	...	...	...	0906	0916	1103	1306	1316	...	...	...	1703	1832	1916	...	...
Bad Gastein a.	...	...	0014	...	|	|	...	...	...	...	...	1019	1219	...	1419	...	...	...	1819	...	2019	...	...
Schwarzach St Veit a.	...	...	0042	...	0318	0318	...	...	...	...	...	1049	1249	...	1449	...	...	...	1849	...	2049	...	...
Bischofshofen a.	...	...	...	...	|	|	...	...	...	...	...	1106	1306	...	1506	...	...	...	1906	...	2106	...	...
Salzburg Hbf 🏛 a.	...	...	...	...	0409	0409	...	...	...	...	...	1148	1348	...	1548	1702	...	...	1948	...	2148	...	...
München Hbf a.	...	...	...	...	0615	0615	...	...	...	...	...	1333	1533	...	...	1833	...	...	2133	...	...	...	...

A – LJUBLJANA – [12] Ljubljana - Rijeka and v.v. Conveys [2] Wien - Ljubljana - Rijeka and v.v. Table **91**.
B – Dec. 14–18, Jan. 1–6, Mar. 26 - Apr. 16, May 2 - Sept. 18 ▬ 2 cl. (also June 20 - Sept. 19 🛏 1, 2 cl.) Rijeka - München.
C – Dec. 14–19, Jan. 2–7, Mar. 27 - Apr. 17, May 3 - Sept. 19 ▬ 2 cl. (also June 21 - Sept. 20 🛏 1, 2 cl.) München - Rijeka.
D – BALKAN – 🛏 1, 2 cl. Beograd - Sofiya - Svilengrad - İstanbul and v.v. [12] Beograd - Sofiya and v.v.
E – HELLAS EXPRESS – 🛏 1, 2 cl., ▬ 2 cl. and [12] Beograd - Thessaloníki and v.v.
F – [2] Zürich (**465**) - Schwarzach St Veit (**415**) - Zagreb - Beograd and Beograd (**414**) - Zagreb - Schwarzach St Veit (**464**) - Zürich. [12] and ✕ Villach - Beograd and v.v. Table **86**.
G – [12] München - Villach - Jesenice 🏛 - Beograd and v.v. [2] and ✕ Jesenice 🏛 - Beograd and v.v.
H – 🛏 1, 2 cl., ▬ 2 cl. and [2] Beograd - Sofiya and v.v.
K – OLYMPUS – [12] and 🍷 Beograd - Thessaloníki and v.v.
L – LISINSKI – 🛏 1, 2 cl., ▬ 2 cl. and [2] München - Zagreb and v.v. [2] München - Vinkovci and v.v. 🛏 1, 2 cl. Praha - Zagreb and v.v.

M – [12] Siegen - Frankfurt - Zagreb and v.v. ✕ München - Villach and v.v.
P – 🛏 1, 2 cl. Thessaloníki - Athína.
R – ▬ 2 cl. Venezia - Ljubljana - Beograd and v.v.
W – WÖRTHERSEE – [12] and ✕ Münster - Klagenfurt and Klagenfurt - Dortmund.
Y – 🛏 1, 2 cl., ▬ 2 cl. and [12] Villach - Beograd and v.v.

RJ – ÖBB *Railjet* service. [1] (premium class), [1] (first class), [2] (economy class) and 🍷
◧ – Supplement payable: Jesenice 🏛 - Ljubljana - Zagreb - Beograd and v.v.
✓ – Supplement payable.

64 HAMBURG and BERLIN - WIEN - BUDAPEST

train type	ICE	RJ	ICE	ICE	ICE	RJ	ICE	ICE	ICE	RJ	ICE	ICE	ICE	RJ	ICE	ICE	ICE	ICE	ICE	ICE		EN	RJ		
train number	21	63	1605	783	23	65	1727 1607	785	25	67	1609 1209	787	27	69	1611	789	29	1613	881	229		491	43		
notes	🍷	🍷 B	①–⑥ M	①–⑥ w	🍷	🍷 B	🍷	🍷	🍷	🍷 B	🍷	🍷	🍷	🍷	🍷	🍷	🍷	🍷	🍷	🍷		A	🍷		
Hamburg Hbf d.	...	...	...	0600	...	...	...	0803	...	...	...	1001	...	...	...	1201	...	...	1401	...	...	2033	...	...	...
Hannover Hbf d.	...	...	...	0726	...	...	...	0926	...	...	...	1126	...	...	...	1326	...	...	1526	...	...	2226	...	...	...
Berlin Hbf d.	...	...	...	|	...	...	0752	|	...	...	0952	|	...	...	1152	|	...	1352	|	...	...	|	...	...	...
Leipzig Hbf d.	...	...	0711	|	...	...	0911	|	...	...	1111	|	...	...	1311	|	...	1511	|	...	...	|	...	...	...
Nürnberg d.	0831	...	1020	1024	1031	...	1221	1224	1231	...	1420	1424	1431	...	1621	1624	1631	1821e	1824	1831	...	0324	...	...	...
Passau 🏛 d.	1033	...	...	...	1233	...	...	...	1433	...	...	...	1633	...	...	...	1833	...	...	2033	...	0532a	...	...	...
Linz Hbf a.	1143	1210	...	...	1343	1410	...	...	1543	1610	...	...	1743	1810	...	...	1943	...	...	2143	...	0646	...	...	...
Wien Westbahnhof a.	1322	1340	...	...	1522	1540	...	...	1722	1740	...	...	1922	1940	...	...	2122	...	...	2322	...	0904	0950	...	...
Budapest Keleti § a.	...	1649	...	...	...	1849	...	...	...	2049	...	...	...	2249	...	...	...	...	...	...	...	...	1249	...	...

train type	ICE	ICE	ICE	ICE	ICE	ICE	RJ	ICE	ICE	ICE	RJ	ICE	ICE	ICE	ICE	ICE	RJ	ICE	ICE	ICE	RJ	ICE	RJ	EN	
train number	228	880	1608	28	788	1606	60	26	786	1604 1704	62	24	784	1602	1655	1502	64	22	782	1600	66	20	68	490	
notes	🍷	🍷	🍷	🍷	🍷		🍷 B	🍷	🍷	🍷	🍷	🍷	🍷	🍷 ⑧f	🍷 ⑧f	e 🍷	🍷 B	🍷	🍷	⑤⑦ k	🍷 B	🍷	🍷 B	A	
Budapest Keleti § d.	...	...	...	...	...	...	0710	...	...	...	0910	...	...	...	...	...	1110	...	...	...	1310	...	1510	...	...
Wien Westbahnhof d.	0640	...	...	0840	...	...	1020	1040	...	...	1220	1240	...	...	...	...	1420	1440	...	...	1620	1640	1808	1954	...
Linz Hbf d.	0816	...	...	1016	...	...	1150	1216	...	...	1350	1416	...	...	...	...	1550	1616	...	...	1750	1816	...	2157	...
Passau 🏛 a.	0922	...	...	1122	...	...	...	1322	...	...	...	1522	...	...	...	...	...	1722	...	...	...	1922	...	2306d	...
Nürnberg a.	1124	1133	1137	1325	1333	1337	...	1524	1533	1537	...	1724	1733	1737	...	1833	...	1924	1933	1937	...	2124	...	0113	...
Leipzig Hbf a.	...	|	1446	...	|	1646	...	...	|	1846	...	...	|	2046	2051	2141	...	...	|	2251	...	...	...	|	...
Berlin Hbf a.	...	|	1605	...	|	1805	...	...	|	2005	...	...	|	...	2204	2256	...	...	|	0015	...	...	...	|	...
Hannover Hbf a.	...	1432	...	...	1632	...	...	...	1832	...	...	...	2032	...	...	...	...	...	2240	...	...	...	...	0613	...
Hamburg Hbf a.	...	1554	...	...	1754	...	...	...	1953	...	...	...	2154	...	...	...	...	...	0007	...	...	...	...	0750	...

A – HANS ALBERS – 🛏 1, 2 cl., ▬ 2 cl., [2] and 🍷 Hamburg - Passau 🏛 - Wien and v.v.
B – ÖBB *Railjet* service. [1] (premium class), [1] (first class), [2] (economy class) and 🍷 München - Wien - Budapest and v.v. Classified *EC* in Hungary.

a – Arrival time.
d – Departure time.
e – Not Dec. 24, 31.
f – Not Dec. 24, 25, 31, Apr. 2, 4, May 23.
k – Also Dec. 23, 30, Apr. 1, 5, May 24, June 2; not Dec. 25, Jan. 1, Apr. 2, 4, May 14, 23, June 4.

m – Not Dec. 25, 26, Jan. 1, Apr. 3, 5, May 24.
w – Not Dec. 25, 26, Jan. 1, Apr. 5, May 24.

§ – 🏛 is at Hegyeshalom.

MÜNCHEN - WIEN - BUDAPEST - BUCUREŞTI 65

train type	RJ	EN	RJ		RJ		RJ		RJ	EN		RJ	D	RJ	D	ICE		EC	IC	EC		EN	
train number	**41**	**467**	**43**	**377**	**61**		**63**		**65**	**473**		**67**	**347**	**69**	**347**	**261**		**117**	**847**	**391**		**463**	
notes	🍷	✕ W	🍷	1822	🍷		🍷		🍷	🍷 Y		🍷	✕ D	🍷	✕ D	🍷		H	🍷	H		A	
München Hbf d.	...	...	...	...	0727	...	0927	...	1127	...	...	1327	...	1527	...	1723	...	1827	...	2024	...	2340	...
Salzburg Hbf ▦ d.	...	0424	0702**c**	...	0902	...	1102	...	1302	...	...	1502	...	1700	...	1902	...	2009	2110	2215	...	0217	...
Linz Hbf d.	...	0543	0810**c**	...	1010	...	1210	...	1410	...	...	1610	...	1810	...	2010	...	...	2231	2342	...	0342	...
St Pölten Hbf d.	...	0650	|	...	1100	...	1300	...	1500	...	...	1700	...	1900	...	2100	...	...	2334	...	...	0500	...
Wien Westbahnhof a.	...	0736	0940**c**	...	1140	...	1340	...	1540	...	...	1740	...	1940	...	2140	...	...	0018	...	...	0545**h**	...
Wien Westbahnhof d.	0650	0758	0950	...	1150	...	1350	...	1550	...	...	1750	1850	1950	...	...	...	...	...	...	...	0600**q**	...
Hegyeshalom ▦ a.	0754	0854	1054	...	1254	...	1454	...	1654	...	...	1854	1954	2054	...	...	...	...	...	...	...	0652	...
Györ a.	0821	0921	1121	...	1321	...	1521	...	1721	...	...	1921	2029	2121	←	...	...	...	...	...	...	0720	...
Budapest Keleti a.	0949	1049	1249	1313	1449	...	1649	...	1849	1913	...	2049	2220	2249	2313	...	...	...	...	...	...	0849	...
Bucureşti Nord a.	...	...	...	0515	...	...	...	...	...	1034	...	...	→	...	1407	...	...	...	...	...	...	0035	...

train type	EC	ICE	RJ	D		RJ		EN	RJ	EC		RJ		RJ		RJ		RJ	RJ	EN		EN	
train number	**390**	**260**	**262**	**346**		**60**		**472**	**62**	**316**		**64**		**66**		**68**	**1821**	**42**	**40**	**466**		**462**	
notes	G	🍷	🍷	✕ D		🍷		🍷 Y	🍷			🍷		🍷		🍷	**376**	🍷	🍷	✕ W		B	
Bucureşti Nord d.	...	...	...	1600	...	...	...	1910	...	...	...	...	...	...	...	...	2345	...	...	...	...	0530	...
Budapest Keleti d.	...	...	...	0600	...	0710	...	0847	0910	...	...	1110	...	1310	...	1510	1447	1710	1810	1905	...	2105	...
Györ d.	...	...	...	0727	...	0835	...	...	1035	...	...	1235	...	1435	...	1635	...	1835	1935	2032	...	2232	...
Hegyeshalom ▦ d.	...	...	...	0758	...	0906	...	...	1106	...	...	1306	...	1506	...	1706	...	1906	2006	2103	...	2301	...
Wien Westbahnhof a.	...	...	...	0858	...	1008	...	...	1208	...	...	1408	...	1608	...	1808	...	2008	2108	2201	...	2354**q**	...
Wien Westbahnhof d.	...	0614	0820	...	...	1020	...	...	1220	...	...	1420	...	1620	...	1820	...	2020	...	2225	...	0009**h**	...
St Pölten Hbf d.	...	0655	0902	...	...	1102	...	...	1302	...	...	|	...	|	...	|	...	2102	...	2309	...	0052	...
Linz Hbf d.	0625	0747	0953	...	...	1153	...	...	1353	...	...	1553	...	1753	...	1953	...	2153	...	0010	...	0201	...
Salzburg Hbf ▦ d.	0751	0902	1102	...	...	1302	...	...	1459	1551	...	1702	...	1902	...	2102	...	2259	...	0126	...	0428	...
München Hbf a.	0933	1030	1230	...	...	1430	...	...	...	1735	...	1833	...	2034	...	2230	...	...	...	...	...	0615	...

A – KÁLMÁN IMRE – [sleeper] 1, 2 cl., [couchette] 2 cl. and [2] München - Wien - Budapest. Conveys Dec. 13 - Jan. 11, June 17 - Sept. 17: [sleeper] 1, 2 cl. München - Budapest (**375**) - Bucureşti and [12] and ✕ Budapest - Bucureşti.
B – KÁLMÁN IMRE – [sleeper] 1, 2 cl., [couchette] 2 cl. and [2] Budapest - Wien - München. Conveys Dec. 13 - Jan. 9, June 15 - Sept. 15: [sleeper] 1, 2 cl. Bucureşti (**374**) - Budapest (**462**) - München and [12] and ✕ Bucureşti - Wien.
D – DACIA – [sleeper] 1, 2 cl., [couchette] 2 cl., [2] and ✕ Wien - Budapest - Bucureşti and v.v. [1] Wien - Budapest - Lököshága and v.v.
G – ①–⑥ (not Dec. 25, 26, Jan. 1, Apr. 3, 5, May 24).
H – ⑧ (not Dec. 24, 25, 31, Apr. 2, 4, May 23).
W – WIENER WALZER – [sleeper] 1, 2 cl., [couchette] 2 cl., and [2] Zürich - Salzburg - Wien and v.v. [couchette] 2 cl. and [2] Zürich - Wien - Budapest and v.v. [12] and ✕ Wien - Budapest and v.v. [sleeper] 1, 2 cl. and [couchette] 2 cl. Zürich - Linz - Praha and v.v.
Y – *EuroNight* ISTER – [sleeper] 1, 2 cl., [couchette] 1, 2 cl., [2] and 🍷 Budapest - Bucureşti and v.v.

c – ①–⑥ (not Dec. 25, 26, Jan. 1, 2, 6, Apr. 5, May 24).
h – Wien **Hütteldorf**.
q – Wien **Meidling**.

RJ – ÖBB *Railjet* service. [1] (premium class), [1] (first class), [2] (economy class) and 🍷. Classified *EC* in Hungary.

DORTMUND - KÖLN - FRANKFURT - WIEN - BUDAPEST 66

train type	ICE	RJ	ICE	RJ	ICE	RJ	ICE	RJ	ICE	ICE	EN
train number	**21**	**63**	**23**	**65**	**25**	**67**	**27**	**69**	**29**	**229**	**421**
notes	🍷		🍷		🍷		🍷		🍷	🍷	A
Dortmund Hbf d.	...	...	0437**f**	...	0636	...	0837	...	...	...	1823**e**
Bochum Hbf d.	...	...	0448**f**	...	|	...	0848	...	...	...	|
Essen Hbf d.	...	...	0459**f**	...	⊙	...	0859	...	...	...	1903**e**
Duisburg Hbf d.	...	...	0512**f**	...	|	...	0912	...	...	...	|
Düsseldorf Hbf d.	...	...	0527**f**	...	|	...	0927	...	...	...	1935**e**
Köln Hbf d.	...	...	0553	...	0753	...	0953	...	...	...	2005
Bonn Hbf d.	...	...	0614	...	0814	...	1014	...	...	...	2034
Koblenz d.	...	...	0648	...	0848	...	1048	...	...	...	2115
Mainz d.	...	...	0740	...	0940	...	1140	...	...	...	2212
Frankfurt Flug. ✈ d.	...	...	0802	...	1002	...	1202	...	...	...	|
Frankfurt (M) Hbf d.	0622	...	0819	...	1021	...	1221	...	1416	1621	2321
Würzburg d.	0735	...	0934	...	1134	...	1334	...	1534	1734	|
Nürnberg d.	0831	...	1031	...	1231	...	1431	...	1631	1831	0324
Regensburg d.	0924	...	1124	...	1324	...	1524	...	1724	1924	0430
Passau ▦ d.	1033	...	1233	...	1433	...	1633	...	1833	2033	0535
Salzburg ▦ a.	|	...	|	...	|	...	|	...	|	|	|
Linz a.	1143	...	1343	...	1543	...	1743	...	1943	2143	0649
Wien Westbf a.	1322	1350	1522	1550	1722	1750	1922	1950	2122	2322	0904
Hegyeshalom ▦ a.	...	1454	...	1654	...	1854	...	2054	...	...	...
Budapest Keleti a.	...	1649	...	1849	...	2049	...	2249	...	...	...

train type	ICE	ICE	RJ	ICE	RJ	ICE	RJ	ICE	RJ	ICE	EN	
train number	**228**	**28**	**60**	**26**	**62**	**24**	**64**	**22**	**66**	**20**	**490**	
notes	🍷	🍷		🍷		🍷		🍷		🍷	A	
Budapest Keleti d.	...	...	0710	...	0910	...	1110	...	1310	...	...	...
Hegyeshalom ▦ d.	...	...	0906	...	1106	...	1306	...	1506	...	...	...
Wien Westbf d.	0640	0840	1008	1040	1208	1240	1408	1440	1608	1640	1954	...
Linz d.	0816	1016	...	1216	...	1416	...	1616	...	1816	2157	...
Salzburg ▦ d.	|	|	...	|	...	|	...	|	...	|	|	...
Passau ▦ a.	0922	1122	...	1322	...	1522	...	1722	...	1922	2306	...
Regensburg a.	1031	1230	...	1431	...	1631	...	1831	...	2031	0012	...
Nürnberg a.	1124	1325	...	1524	...	1724	...	1924	...	2124	0113	...
Würzburg a.	1225	1425	...	1625	...	1825	...	2025	...	2227	|	...
Frankfurt (M) Hbf a.	1340	1536	...	1736	...	1936	...	2136	...	2339	0456	...
Frankfurt Flug. ✈ a.	...	...	...	1755	...	1955	...	2157	...	...	|	...
Mainz a.	...	...	...	1818	...	2018	...	2218	...	...	0646	...
Koblenz a.	...	...	...	1910	...	2110	...	2310	...	...	0744	...
Bonn Hbf a.	...	...	...	1942	...	2142	...	2342	...	...	0817	...
Köln Hbf a.	...	...	...	2005	...	2205	...	0005	...	...	0842	...
Düsseldorf Hbf a.	...	...	...	|	...	|	...	0032**f**	...	...	0911**e**	...
Duisburg Hbf a.	...	...	...	|	...	|	...	0045**f**	...	...	0930**e**	...
Essen Hbf a.	...	...	...	⊙	...	⊙	...	0057**f**	...	...	0943**e**	...
Bochum Hbf a.	...	...	...	|	...	|	...	0109**f**	...	...	|	...
Dortmund Hbf a.	...	...	...	2120	...	2320	...	0121**f**	...	...	1006**e**	...

A – [sleeper] 1, 2 cl., [couchette] 2 cl. (4, 6 berth), [2] (reclining) and 🍷: (Dortmund ①–④ Dec. 13 - July 22 -) Köln - Frankfurt - Passau ▦ - Wien and v.v. Ⓡ Special fares apply. For international journeys only.

e – ①–④ Dec. 13 - July 22.
f – Not Dec. 25, Jan. 1.

RJ – ÖBB *RailJet* service. [1] (premium class), [1] (first class), [2] (economy class) and 🍷. Classified *EC* in Hungary.
⊙ – Via Hagen, Wuppertal (Table **800**).

DORTMUND - KÖLN - MÜNCHEN - GRAZ and KLAGENFURT 68

train type/number	EC	EC	EC	IC	IC	EC	EC	EC	EC	EC	ICE	
train number	**111**	**111**	**317**	**690**	**311**	**113**	**113**	**115**	**319**	**117**	**613**	**499**
notes	🍷	**211** H	🍷 G	🍷	🍷	🍷	**213** Z	✕ W	🍷	🍷 ⑧**f**	🍷	L
Hamburg Hbf d.	...	...	...	...	...	...	...	...	...	...	...	...
Dortmund Hbf d.	...	...	...	...	...	...	...	...	...	...	1637	...
Bochum Hbf d.	...	...	...	...	...	...	...	...	...	...	1648	...
Essen Hbf d.	...	...	...	...	...	...	...	...	...	...	1659	...
Duisburg Hbf d.	...	...	...	...	...	...	...	0735	...	...	1712	...
Düsseldorf Hbf d.	...	...	...	...	...	...	...	0752	...	...	1727	...
Köln Hbf d.	...	...	...	...	...	...	...	0818	...	...	1755	...
Bonn Hbf d.	...	...	...	...	...	...	...	0837	...	...	|	...
Koblenz Hbf d.	...	...	...	...	...	...	...	0917	...	...	|	...
Mainz Hbf d.	...	...	...	...	...	...	...	1015	...	...	|	...
Frankfurt (Main) Hbf d.	...	...	...	...	...	0820	0820	|	1220	1420	|	...
Mannheim d.	...	...	0712	...	...	|	|	1103	|	|	1932	...
Heidelberg d.	...	...	|	...	...	0914	0914	|	1314	1514	|	...
Stuttgart Hbf d.	...	...	0758	...	...	0958	0958	1158	1358	1558	2012	...
Ulm d.	...	...	0855	...	...	1055	1055	1255	1455	1655	2108	...
Augsburg d.	...	...	0942	...	...	1142	1142	1342	1542	1742	2155	...
München Hbf d.	0827	0827	1027	...	...	1227	1227	1427	1627	1827	2233	2340
Salzburg ▦ a.	1009	1009	1209	1212	...	1409	1409	1609	1809	2009	...	0117
Bischofshofen a.	1052	1052	1302	1252	...	1452	1452	1652	1902	2052	...	|
Selzthal a.	|	|	1440	|	...	|	|	|	2040	|	...	|
Graz a.	|	|	1622	|	...	|	|	|	2222	|	...	|
Schwarzach St Veit a.	1109	1109	...	1309	...	1509	1509	1709	...	2109	...	0223
Villach Hbf a.	1243	1243	...	1443	1452	1643	1643	1843	...	2245	...	0351
Klagenfurt a.	1316	|	...	...	|	1716	|	1916	...	2317	...	|
Ljubljana a.	...	1431	...	...	1633	...	1831	...	...	...	...	0603

train type/number	IC	EC	EC	EC	EC	EC	EC	EC	EC		ICE	
train number	**693**	**318**	**314**	**114**	**112**	**212**	**316**	**110**	**210**	**498**	**612**	
notes	🍷	🍷	🍷	✕ W	🍷	**112** Z	🍷 G	🍷	**110** H	L	🍷	
Ljubljana d.	...	...	0727	...	...	0927	...	...	1525	2350	...	...
Klagenfurt d.	0646	...	|	0843	1033	|	...	1631	|	|	...	...
Villach Hbf d.	0716	...	0906	0916	1116	1116	...	1716	1716	0146	...	...
Schwarzach St Veit d.	0851	...	...	1051	1251	1251	...	1851	1851	0320	...	...
Graz d.	|	0545	...	|	|	|	1138	|	|	|	...	...
Selzthal d.	|	0719	...	|	|	|	1319	|	|	|	...	...
Bischofshofen d.	0908	0857	...	1108	1308	1308	1457	1908	1908	|	...	...
Salzburg ▦ d.	0948	0951	...	1151	1351	1351	1551	1951	1951	0428	...	...
München Hbf a.	...	1133	...	1333	1533	1533	1735	2133	2133	0615	0723	...
Augsburg a.	...	1215	...	1413	1615	1615	1815	...	...	...	0801	...
Ulm a.	...	1303	...	1503	1703	1703	1903	...	...	...	0849	...
Stuttgart Hbf a.	...	1401	...	1600	1801	1801	2001	...	...	...	0947	...
Heidelberg a.	...	1444	...	|	1844	1844	|	...	...	...	|	...
Mannheim a.	...	|	...	1656	|	|	2048	...	...	...	1027	...
Frankfurt (Main) Hbf a.	...	1540	...	|	1940	1940	...	...	...	...	|	...
Mainz Hbf a.	...	...	...	1740	...	...	...	...	...	...	|	...
Koblenz Hbf a.	...	...	...	1841	...	...	...	...	...	...	|	...
Bonn Hbf a.	...	...	...	1920	...	...	...	...	...	...	|	...
Köln Hbf a.	...	...	...	1942	...	...	...	...	...	...	1205	...
Düsseldorf Hbf a.	...	...	...	2008	...	...	...	...	...	...	1231	...
Duisburg Hbf a.	...	...	...	2023	...	...	...	...	...	...	1244	...
Essen Hbf a.	...	...	...	2039	...	...	...	...	...	...	1257	...
Bochum Hbf a.	...	...	...	2049	...	...	...	...	...	...	1309	...
Dortmund Hbf a.	...	...	...	2102	...	...	...	...	...	...	1321	...
Hamburg Hbf a.	...	...	...	...	...	...	...	...	...	...	...	...

G – [12] and 🍷 Saarbrücken - Mannheim - Graz and v.v.
H – [12] and 🍷 München - Villach - Ljubljana - Zagreb - Beograd and v.v.
L – LISINSKI – [sleeper] 1, 2 cl., [couchette] 2 cl. and [2] München - Ljubljana - Zagreb and v.v.
W – WÖRTHERSEE – [12] and ✕ Münster - Klagenfurt and Klagenfurt - Dortmund.

Z – [12] and 🍷 Frankfurt - München - Villach - Ljubljana - Zagreb and v.v.
f – Not Dec. 24, 25, 31, Apr. 2, 4, May 23.

70 DORTMUND - MÜNCHEN - INNSBRUCK - VENEZIA and MILANO

train type	CNL	CNL	CNL	EC	IC	ICE	ICE	EC		IC	ICE	EC	EC		ES	ICE	EC 89	IC	EC	D	ICE	IC	EC		IC
train type / train number	1247	1287	419	81	515	699	521	85	1509	2021	525	361	87	1511	9735	529	EC 92‡	649	115	1281	623	2261	83	1515	119
train number	1245	ℝ	ℝ	♣	🍷	799	🍷	♣✕			925	✕	♣		ℝ✓	🍷	♣	🍷	✕	H	923	🍷	♣	2	🍷
notes	ℝP	A	L	✕		🍷		R			🍷	X	✕		✕		G		Q		🍷	X			K
Hamburg Hbf d.	...	2127	...	...	...	...	...	...	...	2246	...	...	...	...	...	...	...	...	...	...	...	...	...	...	...
Berlin Hbf d.	2103	|	...	...	...	...	...	...	...	|	...	...	...	...	...	...	...	...	...	...	...	...	...	...	...
Dortmund Hbf d.	|	|	...	...	...	...	...	...	...	0152	0523j	...	...	...	...	0723p	...	...	...	...	...	...	...	...	...
Bochum Hbf d.	|	|	...	...	...	...	...	...	...	0203	0535j	...	...	...	...	0735p	...	...	...	...	...	...	...	...	...
Essen Hbf d.	|	|	...	...	...	...	...	...	...	0214	0553j	...	...	...	...	0753	...	...	...	...	...	...	...	...	0823
Duisburg Hbf d.	|	|	2256	...	...	...	...	...	...	0229	0608j	...	...	...	...	0808	...	...	0735	...	...	...	...	...	0838
Dusseldorf Hbf d.	|	|	2312u	...	...	...	...	...	...	0247	0621j	...	...	...	...	0821	...	...	0752	...	...	...	...	...	0852
Köln Hbf d.	|	|	2346u	...	...	...	0422	...	...	0353	0644x	...	...	...	...	0844k	...	...	0818	...	1019	...	...	...	0918
Bonn Hbf d.	|	|	0007u	...	...	...	|	...	...	0416	|	...	...	...	...	|	...	...	0837	...	|	...	...	...	0937
Koblenz Hbf d.	|	|	0043u	...	...	...	⊖	...	...	0531	⊖	...	...	...	...	⊖	...	...	0917	...	⊖	...	...	...	1017
Mainz Hbf d.	|	|	|	...	...	...	|	...	...	0628	|	...	...	...	...	|	...	...	1015	...	|	...	...	...	1113
Frankfurt Flughafen ✈ d.	|	|	|	...	...	...	0535	...	...	0648	0737	...	...	...	...	0937	...	...	|	...	1137	...	...	...	|
Frankfurt (Main) Hbf d.	|	|	|	...	...	...	0551	...	...	0702	0754	...	...	...	...	0954	...	...	|	...	1154	...	...	...	|
Mannheim Hbf d.	|	|	|	...	...	...	|	...	...	▬	|	...	...	...	...	|	...	...	1103	...	|	...	...	...	1154
Heidelberg Hbf d.	|	|	|	...	...	...	|	...	...	...	|	...	...	...	...	|	...	...	|	...	|	...	...	...	1206
Stuttgart Hbf d.	|	|	0417a	...	...	0656	|	...	...	...	|	0853	...	...	...	|	...	...	1158	...	|	1253	...	...	1257
Ulm Hbf d.	|	|	0542a	...	...	0755	|	...	...	...	|	0955	...	...	...	|	...	...	1255	...	|	1355	...	...	1411
Lindau 🏛 a.	|	|	|	...	...	|	|	...	...	...	|	|	...	...	...	|	...	...	|	...	|	|	...	...	1554
Bregenz a.	|	|	|	...	...	|	|	...	...	...	|	|	...	...	...	|	...	...	|	...	|	|	...	...	1610
Bludenz a.	|	|	|	...	...	|	|	...	...	...	|	|	...	...	...	|	...	...	|	...	|	|	...	...	1654
Langen am Arlberg a.	|	|	|	...	...	|	|	...	...	...	|	|	...	...	...	|	...	...	|	...	|	|	...	...	1720
St Anton am Arlberg a.	|	|	|	...	...	|	|	...	...	...	|	|	...	...	...	|	...	...	|	...	|	|	...	...	1730
Landeck-Zams a.	|	|	|	...	...	|	|	...	...	...	|	|	...	...	...	|	...	...	|	...	|	|	...	...	1753
Augsburg Hbf d.	0622s	0622s	0633a	...	...	0839	|	...	...	...	|	1038	...	...	...	|	...	...	1342	...	|	1438	...	...	...
München Hbf d.	0705	0705	0716a	0731	...	0917	0906	0931	...	...	1106	1117	1131	...	...	1305	1331	...	1417	1511	1505	1516	1531	...	|
München Ost ▲ d.	...	...	|	0740	...	...	...	0940	...	...	▬	...	1140	...	...	▬	1340	...	...	|	...	...	1540	...	|
Kufstein 🏛 d.	...	...	0930z	0836	...	...	...	1036	...	...	...	...	1236	...	...	...	1436	...	...	1623	...	...	1636	...	|
Wörgl d.	...	...	0941z	0846	0902	...	...	1046	1137	...	...	...	1246	1337	...	...	1444a	1449	...	1645	...	...	1646	1737	|
Kitzbühel a.	...	...	|	|	0931	...	...	|	1217	...	...	...	|	1417	...	...	|	1519	...	1727	...	...	|	1817	|
St Johann in Tirol a.	...	...	|	|	0939	...	...	|	1226	...	...	...	|	1426	...	...	|	1527	...	1735	...	...	|	1826	|
Saalfelden a.	...	...	|	|	1007	...	...	|	1302	...	...	...	|	1502	...	...	|	1559	...	1811	...	...	|	1902	|
Zell am See a.	...	...	|	|	1019	...	...	|	1315	...	...	...	|	1515	...	...	|	1610	...	1824	...	...	|	1915	|
Jenbach a.	...	...	1001z	0900	...	...	...	1100	▬	...	...	...	1300	▬	...	...	1500	▬	...	...	...	...	1700	▬	|
Innsbruck Hbf a.	...	...	1036z	0923	...	...	...	1123	...	...	...	...	1323	...	...	...	1523	...	...	...	...	...	1723	...	1857
Innsbruck Hbf d.	...	...	...	0927	...	...	...	1127	...	*ESc*	*ESc*	...	1327	*EC*	...	*ES*	1527	...	...	...	...	...	1727	*ESc*	▬
Brennero/Brenner 🏛 a.	...	...	...	1002	...	...	...	1202	...	**9727**	**9730**	...	1402	**42**	...	**9457**	1602	...	...	...	...	...	1802	**9749**	...
Bolzano/Bozen a.	...	...	...	1128	...	...	...	1328	...	ℝ✓	ℝ	...	1528	ℝ🍷	...	ℝ✓	1728	**2107**	...	...	...	...	1928	ℝ	**2116**
Trento a.	...	...	...	...	...	...	...	1401	...	🍷	🍷✓	...	1601	⊗	...	✕	1801	...	...	...	...	...	2001	🍷✓	...
Verona a.	...	...	...	...	...	...	...	1457	*AV*	1559	1602	...	1657	1732	1757	1855	1901	1918	...	...	...	...	2057	2129	2140
Venezia Santa Lucia a.	...	...	...	...	...	...	...	|	**9523**	1710	|	...	...	|	1902	|	|	2051	...	...	...	...	...	2240	|
Milano Centrale a.	...	...	...	...	...	...	...	|	ℝ✓	...	1725	...	...	1855	...	|	2035	...	...	...	...	...	...	...	2335
Genova Piazza Principe a.	...	...	...	...	...	...	...	|	🍷	...	*1945*	...	...	*2148*	...	|	*2242*	...	...	...	...	...	...	...	...
Bologna Centrale a.	...	...	...	...	...	...	...	1611	1623	...	...	...	...	...	...	1944	...	...	...	...	...	...	...	...	...
Firenze SMN a.	...	...	...	...	...	...	...	...	1700	...	...	...	...	...	...	2024¶	...	...	...	...	...	...	...	...	...
Roma Termini a.	...	...	...	...	...	...	...	...	1845	...	...	...	...	...	...	2155	...	...	...	...	...	...	...	...	...
Napoli Centrale a.	...	...	...	...	...	...	...	...	2010	...	...	...	...	...	...	...	...	...	...	...	...	...	...	...	...
Rimini a.	...	...	...	...	...	...	...	...	...	...	...	...	...	...	...	...	...	...	...	...	...	...	...	...	...

train type/number	EC	ICE	ICE	EC	ICE	ICE	ICE	ICE	CNL	CNL
train number	101	517	627	189	519	109	723	611	485	40485
notes	🍷	🍷	927	✕	🍷	🍷	🍷	🍷	235	363
			🍷				⑧f		B	C
Hamburg Hbf d.	...	...	...	...	...	...	...	...	...	...
Berlin Hbf d.	...	...	...	...	...	...	...	...	...	...
Dortmund Hbf d.	...	1037	1100y	...	1237	...	...	1437	...	...
Bochum Hbf d.	...	1048	|	...	1248	...	...	1448	...	...
Essen Hbf d.	...	1059	|	...	1259	...	1453	1459	...	...
Duisburg Hbf d.	...	1112	|	...	1312	...	1508	1512	...	...
Dusseldorf Hbf d.	...	1127	|	...	1327	...	1521	1527	...	...
Köln Hbf d.	...	1155	1219	...	1355	...	1544k	1555	...	...
Bonn Hbf d.	1114	|	|	...	|	...	|	|	...	...
Koblenz Hbf d.	1148	⊖	⊖	...	⊖	...	⊖	⊖	...	...
Mainz Hbf d.	1239	|	|	...	|	...	|	|	...	...
Frankfurt Flughafen ✈ d.	|	1254	1329	...	1454	...	1637	1654	...	...
Frankfurt (Main) Hbf d.	|	|	1354	...	|	...	1654	|	...	...
Mannheim Hbf d.	1321	1332	|	...	1532	...	|	1732	...	...
Heidelberg Hbf d.	|	|	|	...	|	...	|	|	...	...
Stuttgart Hbf d.	...	1412	|	...	1612	...	|	1812	...	...
Ulm Hbf d.	...	1508	|	...	1708	...	|	1908	...	...
Lindau 🏛 a.	...	|	|	...	|	...	|	|	...	...
Bregenz a.	...	|	|	...	|	...	|	|	...	...
Bludenz a.	...	|	|	...	|	...	|	|	...	...
Langen am Arlberg a.	...	|	|	...	|	...	|	|	...	...
St Anton am Arlberg a.	...	|	|	...	|	...	|	|	...	...
Landeck-Zams a.	...	|	|	...	|	...	|	|	...	...
Augsburg Hbf d.	...	1555	|	...	1755	...	|	1955	...	...
München Hbf d.	...	1633	1705	1731	1832	1843	2005	2033	2103	2103
München Ost ▲ d.	...	...	...	1741	▬	|	▬	▬	|	|
Kufstein 🏛 d.	...	...	...	1836	E	1938	E	F	2209	2209
Wörgl d.	...	...	...	1846	1907	1948	2000	2037	2220	2220
Kitzbühel a.	...	...	...	|	1927	|	2033	2117	|	|
St Johann in Tirol a.	...	...	...	|	1935	|	2041	2126	|	|
Saalfelden a.	...	...	...	|	...	|	...	2202	|	|
Zell am See a.	...	...	...	|	...	|	...	2215	|	|
Jenbach a.	...	...	...	1900	...	2000	...	...	2234	2234
Innsbruck Hbf a.	...	...	...	1923	...	2023	...	...	2256	2256
Innsbruck Hbf d.	...	...	...	...	...	...	...	...	2305	2305
Brennero/Brenner 🏛 a.	...	...	...	...	...	...	...	...	2342	2342
Bolzano/Bozen a.	...	...	...	...	...	...	...	...	0107	0107
Trento a.	...	...	...	...	...	...	...	...	0140	0140
Verona a.	...	...	...	...	...	...	...	...	0237	0237
Venezia Santa Lucia a.	...	...	...	...	...	...	...	...	|	0638
Milano Centrale a.	...	...	...	...	...	...	...	...	|	...
Genova Piazza Principe a.	...	...	...	...	...	...	...	...	|	...
Bologna Centrale a.	...	...	...	...	...	...	...	...	0420	...
Firenze SMN a.	...	...	...	...	...	...	...	...	0618	...
Roma Termini a.	...	...	...	...	...	...	...	...	0905	...
Napoli Centrale a.	...	...	...	...	...	...	...	...	...	...
Rimini a.	...	...	...	...	...	...	...	...	...	...

train type		ICE	EC	D	ICE	IC	ESc	EC	ICE	D	EC
train number	1500	108	390	1280	596	118	9702	82	516	1284	114
notes	2	🍷	🍷		🍷	🍷	🍷✓	♣	🍷		🍷
				J	b	K	ℝ			D	
Rimini d.	...	...	...	...	...	...	...	...	...	...	...
Napoli Centrale d.	...	...	...	...	...	...	...	...	...	...	...
Roma Termini d.	...	...	...	...	...	...	...	...	...	...	...
Firenze SMN d.	...	...	...	...	...	...	...	...	...	...	...
Bologna Centrale d.	...	...	...	...	...	...	...	...	...	...	...
Genova Piazza Principe d.	...	...	...	...	...	...	...	...	...	...	...
Milano Centrale d.	...	...	...	...	...	...	...	...	...	...	...
Venezia Santa Lucia d.	...	...	...	...	...	...	0532q	...	...	...	...
Verona d.	...	...	...	...	...	...	0643	0659	...	...	...
Trento d.	...	...	...	...	...	...	▬	0758	...	...	...
Bolzano/Bozen d.	...	...	...	...	...	...	...	0832	...	...	...
Brennero/Brenner 🏛 d.	...	*0630*	...	...	...	...	...	1000	...	...	...
Innsbruck Hbf a.	...	*0708*	...	...	...	...	...	1032	...	...	...
Innsbruck Hbf d.	...	0736	...	...	...	0856	**1502**	1036	...	...	...
Jenbach d.	...	0757	...	...	...	|	2	1058	...	...	...
Zell am See d.	0630	|	...	0839	...	|	0847	|	...	1020	...
Saalfelden d.	0643	|	...	0850	...	|	0859	|	...	1031	...
St Johann in Tirol d.	0715	|	...	0923	...	|	0934	|	...	1103	...
Kitzbühel d.	0723	|	...	0931	...	|	0943	|	...	1112	...
Wörgl d.	0756	0812	...	1023	...	|	1023	1114	...	1206	...
Kufstein 🏛 a.	...	0820	...	1032	...	|	...	1122	...	1215	...
München Ost ▲ a.	...	|	...	|	...	|	...	1214	...	|	...
München Hbf a.	...	0915	0940	1150	1223	|	...	1225	1323	1322	1340
Augsburg Hbf a.	...	...	1015	...	1301	|	...	...	1401	...	1413
Landeck-Zams d.	...	...	|	...	|	0951	...	...	|	...	|
St Anton am Arlberg d.	...	...	|	...	|	1018	...	...	|	...	|
Langen am Arlberg d.	...	...	|	...	|	1029	...	...	|	...	|
Bludenz d.	...	...	|	...	|	1100	...	...	|	...	|
Bregenz d.	...	...	|	...	|	1144	...	...	|	...	|
Lindau 🏛 d.	...	...	|	...	|	1202	...	...	|	...	|
Ulm Hbf a.	...	...	1103	...	1349	1345	...	...	1449	...	1503
Stuttgart Hbf a.	...	...	1201	...	1447	1458	...	...	1547	...	1600
Heidelberg Hbf a.	...	...	1244	...	|	1553	...	...	|	...	|
Mannheim Hbf a.	...	...	|	...	1529	1606	...	...	1627	...	1656
Frankfurt (Main) Hbf a.	...	...	1340	...	1608	|	...	...	|	...	|
Frankfurt Flughafen ✈ a.	...	...	...	...	...	|	...	...	1706	...	|
Mainz Hbf a.	...	...	...	...	...	1646	...	...	|	...	1740
Koblenz Hbf a.	...	...	...	...	...	1741	...	...	⊖	...	1841
Bonn Hbf a.	...	...	...	...	...	1820	...	...	|	...	1920
Köln Hbf a.	...	...	...	...	...	1842	...	...	1805	...	1942
Dusseldorf Hbf a.	...	...	...	...	...	1909	...	...	|	...	2008
Duisburg Hbf a.	...	...	...	...	...	1922	...	...	|	...	2023
Essen Hbf a.	...	...	...	...	...	1934	...	...	|	...	2039
Bochum Hbf a.	...	...	...	...	...	...	...	...	|	...	2049
Dortmund Hbf a.	...	...	...	...	...	...	...	...	1920	...	2102
Berlin Hbf a.	...	...	...	...	...	...	...	...	...	...	...
Hamburg Hbf a.	...	...	...	...	...	...	...	...	...	...	...

FOR NOTES SEE NEXT PAGE

MILANO and VENEZIA - INNSBRUCK - MÜNCHEN - DORTMUND 70

train type / number	*EC* 93‡	*ICE*		*EC*	*ICE*	*EC*	*ESc*	*ESc*	*AV*	*EC*	*IC*	*ICE*	*ICE*	*IC*	*ESc*	*EC*	*ICE*	*CNL*	*CNL*		*EC*	*CNL*	*CNL*	*CNL*	*ICE*
train number	*EC* 88	**514**	**1506**	**80**	**528**	**360**	**9713**	**9714**	**9508**	**84**	**2092**	**524**	**510**	**2020**	**9719**	**86**	**990**	**1286**	**1246**	**1512**	**188**	**418**	**234**	**358**	**612**
notes	♣	🍷	2	♣	**924**	✖	🍷⚡	🍷⚡	Ⓡ⚡	♣✖	Ⓑf	🍷	**1010**		Ⓡ⚡	♣	✖	Ⓡ	**1244**	2	✖	Ⓡ	**484**		🍷
	G			✖	🍷	**X**	Ⓡ	Ⓡ	🍷e	**R**	🍷		**1110**		**W**	✖		**A**	Ⓡ**P**		**S**	**M**	**B**	**C**	
Rimini d.	...	...	...	...	...	...	...	...	...	...	...	...	...	...	...	...	...	...	...	...	...	...	...	...	...
Napoli Centrale d.	...	...	...	...	...	...	...	...	0650	...	...	...	...	...	...	...	...	...	...	...	...	...	...	...	...
Roma Termini d.	...	...	...	...	...	...	...	...	0815	...	...	...	...	...	...	...	...	...	...	...	...	...	1905	...	...
Firenze SMN d.	...	...	...	...	...	...	...	...	1010	...	...	...	...	...	...	...	...	...	...	...	...	...	2138	...	...
Bologna Centrale d.	...	...	...	...	...	...	...	...	1037	1117	...	...	...	...	...	...	...	...	...	...	...	...	2305	...	...
Genova Piazza Principe d.	...	...	...	...	...	...	...	...	▬	|	...	...	...	...	*0910*	...	...	...	...	...	...	...	|	...	...
Milano Centrale d.	0705	...	...	...	...	...	0935	...	...	|	...	...	...	...	1235	...	...	...	...	...	...	...	|	...	...
Venezia Santa Lucia d.	*0620*	...	...	...	...	...	|	1050	...	|	...	...	...	...	|	...	...	...	...	...	...	...	|	2251	...
Verona d.	0859	...	...	...	...	...	1057	1200	...	1259	...	...	...	...	1357	1459	...	...	...	...	...	...	0101	0101	...
Trento d.	0958	...	...	...	...	...	▬	▬	...	1358	...	...	...	...	▬	1558	...	...	...	...	...	...	0156	0156	...
Bolzano / Bozen d.	1032	...	...	1232	...	...	...	...	...	1432	...	...	...	...	...	1632	...	...	...	...	...	...	0230	0230	...
Brennero / Brenner 🏛 d.	1200	...	...	1400	...	...	...	...	...	1600	...	...	...	...	...	1800	...	...	...	...	...	...	0357	0357	...
Innsbruck Hbf a.	1232	...	...	1432	...	...	...	...	...	1632	...	...	...	...	...	1832	...	...	...	...	...	...	0431	0431	...
Innsbruck Hbf d.	1236	...	...	1436	...	...	...	...	**1508**	1636	...	...	...	...	*IC*	1836	...	...	...	...	2036	1954z	0436	0436	...
Jenbach d.	1258	...	...	1458	...	...	...	...	2	1658	...	...	...	...	**518**	1858	...	...	...	...	2058	2021z	0500	0500	...
Zell am See d.	|	...	1247	|	...	...	...	...	1447	|	...	...	...	...	1743	|	...	...	...	1847	|	|	|	|	...
Saalfelden d.	|	...	1259	|	...	...	...	...	1459	|	...	...	...	...	1753	|	...	...	...	1859	|	|	|	|	...
St Johann in Tirol d.	|	...	1334	|	...	...	...	...	1534	|	...	...	...	...	1820	|	...	...	...	1934	|	|	|	|	...
Kitzbühel d.	|	...	1343	|	...	...	...	...	1543	|	...	...	...	...	1828	|	...	...	...	1943	|	|	|	|	...
Wörgl d.	1314	...	1423	1514	...	...	...	*ICE*	1623	1714	...	...	...	...	1858	1914	...	...	...	2023	2114	2048z	0518	0518	...
Kufstein 🏛 a.	1322	...	...	1522	...	...	...	**512**	...	1722	...	...	...	...	...	1922	...	...	...	...	2122	2059z	0527	0527	...
München Ost ▲ a.	1414	...	...	1614	...	...	...	🍷	...	1814	...	...	...	...	...	2014	...	...	...	...	2214	|	|	|	...
München Hbf a.	1425	1523	...	1625	1650	1643	...	1723	...	1825	1844	1855	1923	...	...	2025	2040	2051	2051	...	2225	2243**d**	0630	0630	0723
Augsburg Hbf a.	...	1601	...	...	|	1720	...	1801	...	...	1917	|	2001	...	...	...	2114	|	|	...	...	2320**d**	...	...	0801
Landeck - Zams d.	...	|	...	...	|	|	...	|	...	...	|	|	|	...	...	...	|	|	|	...	...	|	...	...	|
St Anton am Arlberg d.	...	|	...	...	|	|	...	|	...	...	|	|	|	...	...	...	|	|	|	...	...	|	...	...	|
Langen am Arlberg d.	...	|	...	...	|	|	...	|	...	...	|	|	|	...	...	...	|	|	|	...	...	|	...	...	|
Bludenz d.	...	|	...	...	|	|	*IC*	|	...	...	|	|	|	...	...	...	|	|	|	...	...	|	...	...	|
Bregenz d.	...	|	...	...	|	|	**2110**	|	...	...	|	|	|	...	...	...	|	|	|	...	...	|	...	...	|
Lindau 🏛 a.	...	|	...	...	|	|	🍷	|	...	...	|	|	|	...	...	...	|	|	|	...	...	|	...	...	|
Ulm Hbf a.	...	1649	...	...	|	1803	Ⓑf	1849	...	...	2003	|	2049	...	...	...	2202	|	|	...	...	0010**d**	...	...	0849
Stuttgart Hbf a.	...	1747	...	...	|	1907	1937	1947	...	...	2107	|	2147	...	...	...	2300	|	|	...	...	0125**d**	...	...	0947
Heidelberg Hbf a.	...	|	...	...	|	...	2023	|	...	...	...	|	|	...	...	...	|	|	|	...	...	|	...	...	|
Mannheim Hbf a.	...	1827	...	...	|	...	2037	2027	...	...	...	|	2228	...	...	...	2342	|	|	...	...	|	...	...	1027
Frankfurt (Main) Hbf a.	...	|	...	...	2005	...	|	|	...	...	...	2205	2325t	...	...	...	0042r	|	|	...	...	|	...	...	|
Frankfurt Flughafen ✈ a.	...	1906	...	...	2021	...	|	2106	...	...	...	2221	2303r	2338	...	...	0023r	|	|	...	...	|	...	...	1106
Mainz Hbf a.	...	|	...	...	|	...	2118	|	...	...	...	|	...	2359	...	...	...	|	|	...	...	|	...	...	|
Koblenz Hbf a.	...	⊖	...	...	⊖	...	2210	⊖	...	...	...	⊖	...	0055	...	...	...	|	|	...	...	0446s	...	...	⊖
Bonn Hbf a.	...	|	...	...	|	...	2242	|	...	...	...	|	...	0133	...	...	...	|	|	...	...	0519s	...	...	|
Köln Hbf a.	...	2005	...	...	2114**k**	...	...	2205	...	...	...	2343**k**	...	...	...	...	...	|	|	...	...	0542s	...	...	1205
Dusseldorf Hbf a.	...	2031	...	...	2137	...	...	2231	...	...	...	0005	...	...	...	...	...	|	|	...	...	0608s	...	...	1231
Duisburg Hbf a.	...	2044	...	...	2149	...	...	2244	...	...	...	0018	...	...	...	...	...	|	|	...	...	0628	...	...	1244
Essen Hbf a.	...	2057	...	...	2202	...	...	2257	...	...	...	0030	...	...	...	...	...	|	|	...	...	...	...	...	1257
Bochum Hbf a.	...	2109	...	...	2214	...	...	2309	...	...	...	0041	...	...	...	...	...	|	|	...	...	...	...	...	1309
Dortmund Hbf a.	...	2121	...	...	2228	...	...	2321	...	...	...	0054	...	...	...	...	...	|	|	...	...	...	...	...	1321
Berlin Hbf a.	...	...	...	...	...	...	...	...	...	...	...	...	...	...	...	...	...	|	0828	...	...	...	...	...	...
Hamburg Hbf a.	...	...	...	...	...	...	...	...	...	...	...	...	...	...	...	...	...	0753	...	...	...	...	...	...	...

A – *CNL* PYXIS – 🛏 1, 2 cl., 🛏 1, 2 cl. (T4), ━ 2 cl. (6 berth), (2) (reclining) and ✖ Hamburg - München and v.v. Special fares payable.
B – *CNL* LUPUS – 🛏 1, 2 cl., ━ 2 cl., (2) and ✖ München - Innsbruck - Roma and v.v. Special fares apply. Ⓡ for journeys to / from Italy.
C – *CNL* PICTOR – 🛏 1, 2 cl., ━ 2 cl. and (2) München - Venezia and v.v. ✖ München - Innsbruck and v.v.
D – ⑦ Dec. 20 - Mar. 28 (also Apr. 5): GROSSGLOCKNER – (12) Schwarzach St Veit (depart 0950) - Zell am See - Wörgl - Kufstein 🏛 - München.
E – ①–⑤ (not Dec. 25, Jan. 1, Apr. 5).
F – ⑥⑦ (also Dec. 25, Jan. 1, Apr. 5).
G – LEONARDO DA VINCI – (12) München - Milano and v.v. 🍷 Brennero / Brenner - Milano and v.v.
H – ⑥ Dec. 19 - Apr. 3 (also Dec. 23): GROSSGLOCKNER – (12) München - Kufstein 🏛 - Wörgl - Zell am See - Schwarzach St Veit (arrive 1854).
J – ⑥ Dec. 26 - Apr. 10 (also Jan. 6): GROSSGLOCKNER – (12) Zell am See - Wörgl - Kufstein 🏛 - München.
K – (12) and 🍷 Munster - Köln - Stuttgart - Lindau 🏛 - Innsbruck and v.v.
L – *City Night Line* POLLUX – ①⑤⑥⑦ (daily Apr. 11 - July 24) also Mar 30, 31, Apr. 1, 6, 7, 8: 🛏 1, 2 cl., 🛏 1, 2 cl. (T4), ━ 2 cl. (4, 6 berth), (2) (reclining) 🍷 Amsterdam - Köln - München (- Innsbruck ⑥ Dec. 26 - Apr. 10). Ⓡ Special fares apply.
M – *City Night Line* POLLUX – ①⑤⑥⑦ (daily Apr. 11 - July 23) also Mar 30, 31, Apr. 1, 6, 7, 8: 🛏 1, 2 cl., 🛏 1, 2 cl. (T4), ━ 2 cl. (4, 6 berth), (2) (reclining) and 🍷 (Innsbruck ⑥ Dec. 26 - Apr. 10 -) München - Amsterdam. Ⓡ Special fares apply.
P – *CNL* CAPELLA – 🛏 1, 2 cl., 🛏 1, 2 cl. (T4), ━ 2 cl. (6 berth), (2) (reclining) and ✖ Berlin - München and v.v. Special fares payable.
Q – WÖRTHERSEE – (12) and ✖ Münster - Klagenfurt and Klagenfurt - Dortmund.
R – MICHELANGELO – (12) and ✖ München - Bologna and v.v.

W – ①–⑤ (not Dec. 25, Jan. 1, 6, Apr. 5).
X – Not Feb. 27 - May 16.
a – Arrival time.
b – Not Dec. 25, 27, Jan. 1.
d – Departure time.
e – From Salerno.
f – Not Dec. 24, 25, 31, Apr. 2, 4, May 23.
j – Depart 21 – 32 minutes earlier on ⑥⑦ (also Dec. 24, 25, 31, Jan 1, Apr. 2, 5, May 24).
k – Köln **Messe / Deutz.**
p – ⑥⑦ (also Dec. 24, 25, 31, Jan 1, Apr. 2, 5, May 24).
q – Venezia **Mestre**.
r – Train stops at Frankfurt Flughafen before Frankfurt (Main) Hbf.
s – Stops to set down only.
t – ①–⑥ (also Apr. 5, May 24; not Apr. 6, May 24).
u – Stops to pick up only.
x – Köln **Messe / Deutz.** Depart 0618 on ⑥⑦ (also Dec. 24, 25, 31, Jan 1, Apr. 2, 5, May 24).
y – ⑦ (also Dec. 25, 26, Jan 1, Apr. 3, 5, May 24).
z – ⑥ Dec. 26 - Apr. 10.
⊗ – **ETR 610.** Supplement payable for international journeys. *IC* supplement payable for internal journeys within Italy.
‡ – Train number Milano - Verona and v.v.
♣ – Special fares payable. Reservation compulsory for journeys to/from Italy.
⊖ – Via Köln - Frankfurt high speed line.
¶ – Firenze **Campo di Marte**.
⚡ – Supplement payable.
▲ – Change here for München Airport (Table **892**).

BERLIN - INNSBRUCK 71

For other services from Berlin to Innsbruck, change at München (Tables **850** and **70**); for Dresden - München connections see Table **880**.

train type	*CNL*	*ICE*	*ICE*	*ICE*	*ICE*	*ICE*	*ICE*	*ICE*	
train number	**1247**	**521**	**1603**	**1505**	**1507**	**1509**	**109**	**1213**	
notes	**1245**		①–⑥		**1707**		**A**		
	B		**p**						
Berlin Hbf d.	2103**x**	...	...	0652	0858**q**	1058	1258	1458	...
Leipzig Hbf d.	|	...	0456	0816	1016	1216	1416	1616	...
Nürnberg Hbf d.	|	0802	0823	1128	1328	1528	1728	1928	...
München Hbf a.	0705	0906	0938	1240	1440	1640	1838	2040	...
	EC	*EC*	*EC*	*EC*	*EC*	*EC*	|	*CNL*	
	81	**85**	**87**	**89**	**83**	**189**	|	**485**	
	E	**E**	**E**	**E**	**E**	**E**	|	**E**	
München Hbf d.	0731	0931	1131	1331	1531	1731	1843	2103	...
Kufstein 🏛 a.	0833	1033	1233	1433	1633	1833	1936	2207	...
Innsbruck a.	0923	1123	1323	1523	1723	1923	2023	2256	...

train type	*CNL*	*ICE*	*EC*	*EC*	*EC*	*EC*		*EC*	
train number	**484**	**108**	**82**	**88**	**80**	**84**		**86**	
notes	**E**	**A**	**E**	**E**	**E**	**E**		**E**	
Innsbruck d.	0436	0736	1036	1236	1436	1636	...	1836	...
Kufstein 🏛 d.	0530	0821	1124	1324	1524	1724	...	1924	...
München Hbf a.	0630	0915	1225	1425	1625	1825	...	2025	...
		|						*CNL*	
	ICE	|	*ICE*	*ICE*	*ICE*	*ICE*		**1246**	
	1512	|	**1206**	**1504**	**1502**	**1500**		**1244**	
		|			**t**	**t**		**C**	
München Hbf d.	0719	0920	1315	1519	1719	1919	...	2051	...
Nürnberg Hbf a.	0830	1030	1430	1630	1830	2030	...	|	...
Leipzig Hbf a.	1141	1341	1741	1941	2141	2349	...	|	...
Berlin Hbf a.	1300	1500	1900	2100	2256	...	...	0828**z**	...

A – (12) and ✖ Berlin - München - Kufstein 🏛 - Innsbruck and v.v.
B – *City Night Line* CAPELLA – 🛏 1, 2 cl., ━ 2 cl., (2) (reclining) and ✖ Berlin Lichtenberg (depart 2038) - Berlin Ostbahnhof (2053) - Berlin Hbf - Berlin Zoo (2114) - Berlin Wannsee (2154) - München. Ⓡ. Special fares payable.
C – *City Night Line* CAPELLA – 🛏 1, 2 cl., ━ 2 cl., (2) (reclining) and ✖ München - Berlin Wannsee (arrive 0747) - Berlin Zoo (0820) - Berlin Hbf - Berlin Ostbahnhof (0840) - Berlin Lichtenberg (0858). Special fares payable.
E – See notes in Table **70** for details of this train.
p – Not Dec. 24, 25, 31, Jan. 1, Apr. 2, 5, May 24.
q – ①–⑥ (not Dec. 25, 26, Jan. 1, Apr. 3, 5, May 24.

t – Not Dec. 24, 31.
x – Apr. 30 - Aug. 30 depart Berlin Lichtenberg 1940, Berlin Ostbahnhof (1955) - Berlin Hbf (2006), Berlin Zoo (2013) - Berlin Wannsee (2054).
z – Aug. 30 - Aug. 30 arrive Berlin Wannsee 0825, Berlin Zoo (0850), Berlin Hbf (0856), Berlin Ostbahnhof (0904) - Berlin Lichtenberg (0943).

73 AMSTERDAM, BERLIN, DORTMUND and KÖLN - BASEL - ZÜRICH, MILANO and ROMA

For other connections Basel - Luzern - Chiasso see Table **550**, for Basel - Bern - Interlaken and Brig see Table **560**.

train type	*ICE*	*ICE*	*IC*	*ICE*	*ICE*	*TGV*	*CNL*	*ICE*	*IC*	*ICE*	*ICE*	*IR*	*EC*	*ICE*	*ICE*	*IC*	*EC*	*ICE*	*ICE*	*ICE*	*ICE*	*ICE*	*EC*	*IC*	*ICN*
train number	**371**	**5**	**2021**	**511**	**271**	**9205**	**483**	**501**	**2319**	**513**	**373**	**2173**	**19**	**503**	**71**	**973**	**7**	**121**	**515**	**375**	**105**	**73**	**91**	**977**	**683**
notes	🍷	🍷 **M**		🍷	🍷	🍷	**1383 C**	🍷	①–⑥ **v**	🍷	🍷	¶	[R] 🍷 ⊕	🍷	🍷	🍷	✗ **B**	①–⑥ **g**	🍷	**291** 🍷	🍷	🍷	🍷	🍷	🍷
København H. d.	...	...	...	...	...	...	1842	...	...	...	...	...	...	...	...	...	...	...	...	...	...	...	...	...	...
Hamburg Hbf d.	...	0025e	2246	...	...	...	0031	...	...	...	...	...	...	...	0618	...	0442v	...	0538	...	...	0824	...	...	...
Bremen Hbf d.	...	|	2347	...	...	...	|	...	...	...	...	...	...	...	|	...	0540v	...	0637	...	...	|	...	...	...
Berlin Hauptbahnhof d.	...	|	|	...	...	...	|	...	...	...	0432p	...	...	...	|	...	|	...	|	0632o	...	|	...	...	...
Hannover Hbf d.	...	0150e	|	...	...	...	|	...	...	...	|	...	...	0540	0741	...	|	...	|	|	...	0941	...	...	...
Dortmund Hbf d.	...	|	0152	0437e	...	...	|	0537	...	0637	|	...	...	0737	|	...	0737	...	0837	|	...	|	...	...	...
Essen Hbf d.	...	|	0214	|	...	...	|	|	...	0659	|	...	...	|	|	...	0759	...	|	|	...	|	...	...	...
Amsterdam Centraal d.	...	|	|	|	...	...	|	|	...	|	|	...	...	|	|	...	|	0704	|	|	0804n	|	...	...	...
Utrecht Centraal d.	...	|	|	|	...	...	|	|	...	|	|	...	...	|	|	...	|	0729	|	|	0829n	|	...	...	...
Arnhem ⊙ d.	...	|	|	|	...	...	|	|	...	|	|	...	...	|	|	...	|	0807	|	|	0907n	|	...	...	...
Duisburg Hbf d.	...	|	0229	h	...	...	|	h	...	0712	|	...	...	h	|	...	0812	0908	h	|	1008n	|	...	...	...
Düsseldorf Hbf d.	...	|	0247	|	...	...	|	|	...	0727	|	...	...	|	|	...	0827	0923	|	|	1022n	|	...	...	...
Köln Hbf d.	...	|	0353	0555	...	...	|	0655	...	0755	|	...	...	0855	|	...	0853	0945x	0955	|	1055	|	...	...	...
Bonn Hbf d.	...	|	0416	|	...	...	|	|	0714	|	|	...	...	|	|	...	0914	|	|	|	|	|	...	...	...
Koblenz Hbf d.	...	|	0531	⊖	...	...	|	⊖	0748	⊖	|	...	...	⊖	|	...	0948	⊖	⊖	|	⊖	|	...	...	...
Mainz Hbf d.	...	|	0628	|	...	...	|	|	0839	|	|	...	...	|	|	...	1039	|	|	|	|	|	...	...	...
Frankfurt Flughafen ✈ d.	...	0555r	0645	0654	...	...	|	0754	|	0854	|	...	...	0954	|	...	|	1034	1054	|	1154	|	...	...	...
Frankfurt (Main) Hbf d.	...	0538r	▬	|	0650	...	0659j	|	|	|	0850	...	...	|	1005	...	|	▬	|	1050	|	1205	...	...	...
Mannheim Hbf d.	...	0627	...	0724	0736	...	0750s	0836	0921	0924	0936	...	...	1024	1044	...	1123	...	1124	1136	1236	1244	...	...	...
Karlsruhe Hbf d.	0556p	0656	...	▬	0800	...	0818s	0900	▬	▬	1000	...	...	▬	1108	...	1149	...	▬	1200	1300	1308	...	...	...
Freiburg (Brsg) Hbf d.	0702p	0802	...	...	0901	...	0939s	1002	...	...	1101	...	...	...	1211	...	1255	...	...	1301	1401	1411	...	...	...
Basel Bad Bf 🏛 a.	0737p	0837	...	...	0936	...	1027s	1037	...	...	1136	...	...	...	1247	...	1329	...	...	1336	1436	1447	...	...	...
Basel SBB a.	0747p	0847	...	...	0947	...	1037	1047	...	...	1147	...	...	...	1255	...	1337	...	...	1347y	1447	1455	...	...	...
	|	|		*ICN* **671** 🍷	|		▬	*IC* **969**	*ICN* **675** 🍷	*IC* **571** 🍷	|			*IC* **573**	▬ *EC* **57**⊗		|	*IR* **2177** ¶		|	▬ *IC* **577**	|			
Basel SBB ★ d.	0801	0907	...	0903	1001	1007	...	1101	1103	1133	1201	1203	...	1233	1228	1301	1347	1403	...	1401	1433	1507	...	1501	1503
Bern a.	0856	|	...	|	1056	|	...	1156	|	|	1256	|	...	|	1327	1356	|	|	...	1456	|	|	...	1556	|
Spiez a.	0931	|	...	|	*1131*	|	...	1231	|	|	1331	|	...	|	1402	1431	|	|	*CIS*	1531	|	|	...	1631	|
Interlaken Ost a.	0957	|	*IR*	|	*1157*	|	*IR*	1257	|	|	1357	|	...	|	|	1457	|	|	**21**	1557	|	|	...	1657	|
Brig a.	*1011*f	|	**1767**	|	*1211*f	|	**1769**	*1311*f	|	|	*1411*f	|	...	|	1440	*1511*f	|	|	⊡	*1611*f	|	|	...	*1711*f	|
Domodossola 🏛 § a.	...	|	🍷	|	...	|	🍷	...	|	|	...	|	...	|	1512	▬	|	|	🍷	▬	|	|	...	...	|
Zürich HB a.	...	1000	1012	|	...	1100	1112	...	|	1226	...	|	...	1326	|	...	1452	|	1509	...	1526	1600	1612	...	|
Landquart a.	...	...	1132	|	...	...	1232	...	|	1341	...	|	...	1441	|	...	1632	|	|	...	1641	...	1732	...	|
Davos Platz a.	...	...	*1255*	|	...	...	*1355*	...	|	*1455*	...	|	...	*1555*	|	...	*1755*	|	|	...	*1755*	...	*1855*	...	|
Chur a.	...	...	1143	|	...	...	1243	...	|	1352	...	|	...	1452	|	...	1643	|	|	...	1652	...	1743	...	|
St Moritz a.	...	...	*1358*	|	...	...	*1458*	...	|	*1558*	...	|	...	*1658*	|	...	*1858*	|	|	...	*1858*	...	*1958*	...	|
Luzern a.	...	...	...	1005	...	...	...	...	1205	...	...	1305	...	...	|	...	▬	1505	|	...	▬	...	...	...	1605
Arth-Goldau a.	...	...	...	1045	...	...	...	...	1245	...	...	1345	1350	...	|	...	...	1545	1546	...	...	...	...	...	1645
Bellinzona a.	...	...	...	1223	...	...	...	...	1423	...	...	1553	1523	...	|	*AV*	*ESc*	1753	1723	*ESc*	*AV*	...	...	...	1823
Lugano a.	...	...	...	1246	...	...	...	...	1446	...	...	...	1546	...	|	**9529**	**9739**	...	1746	**9745**	**9533**	...	...	...	1846
Chiasso 🏛 a.	...	...	...	...	...	...	...	...	...	...	...	...	1608	...	|	[R] ✗	[R] 🍷	...	1808	[R] 🍷	[R] ✗	...	...	...	1908
Como San Giovanni a.	...	...	...	...	...	...	...	...	...	...	...	...	1614	...	|	⚡	⚡	...	1814	⚡	⚡	...	...	...	...
Milano Centrale a.	...	...	...	...	...	...	...	...	...	...	...	...	1650	...	1640	1715	1735	...	1850	1905	1915	...	...	...	...
Venezia Santa Lucia a.	...	...	...	...	...	...	...	...	...	...	...	...	...	...	...	|	2002	...	...	2140	|	...	...	...	...
Bologna Centrale a.	...	...	...	...	...	...	...	...	...	...	...	...	...	...	...	1820	...	...	...	...	2020	...	...	...	...
Firenze SMN a.	...	...	...	...	...	...	...	...	...	...	...	...	...	...	...	1900	...	...	...	...	2100	...	...	...	...
Roma Termini a.	...	...	...	...	...	...	...	...	...	...	...	...	...	...	...	2045	...	...	...	...	2245	...	...	...	...

train type	*EC*	*ICE*	*ICE*	*EC*	*ICE*	*ICE*	*IR*	*IC*	*ICE*	*ICE*	*ICE*	*IR*	*ICE*	*ICE*	*ICE*	*ICN*	*ICE*	*IC*	*ICE*	*ICE*	*ICE*	*ICE*	*ICE*	*IC*	*IC*
train number	**101**	**517**	**871**	**101**	**507**	**75**	**1785**	**2113**	**123**	**519**	**277**	**2187**	**599**	**509**	**77**	**691**	**125**	**2115**	**611**	**279**	**601**	**691**	**79**	**1093**	**1095**
notes	✗ **D**	🍷	🍷	✗ **D**	🍷	🍷		🍷	🍷	🍷	🍷		🍷	🍷	🍷	🍷	🍷	🍷	🍷	🍷	🍷	🍷	🍷		
København H. d.	...	...	...	...	...	...	...	...	...	...	...	...	...	...	...	...	...	...	...	...	...	...	...	...	...
Hamburg Hbf d.	0646	...	...	...	...	1024	...	...	...	...	...	...	...	...	1224	...	...	...	...	...	...	...	1424	...	...
Bremen Hbf d.	0744	...	...	...	...	|	...	...	...	...	...	...	...	...	|	...	...	...	...	...	...	...	|	...	...
Berlin Hauptbahnhof d.	|	...	0832	...	...	|	...	...	...	...	1032	...	1137	...	|	...	...	...	...	1232	...	1337	|	...	...
Hannover Hbf d.	|	...	|	...	...	1141	...	...	...	...	|	...	|	...	1341	...	...	...	...	|	...	|	1541	...	...
Dortmund Hbf d.	0937	1037	|	...	...	|	...	...	...	1237	|	...	|	1337p	|	...	...	...	1437	|	...	|	|	...	...
Essen Hbf d.	0959	1059	|	...	...	|	...	...	...	1259	|	...	|	|	|	...	...	...	1459	|	...	|	|	...	...
Amsterdam Centraal d.	|	|	|	...	...	|	...	...	1034	|	|	...	|	|	|	...	1234	...	|	|	...	|	|	...	...
Utrecht Centraal d.	|	|	|	...	...	|	...	...	1059	|	|	...	|	|	|	...	1259	...	|	|	...	|	|	...	...
Arnhem ⊙ d.	|	|	|	...	...	|	...	...	1137	|	|	...	|	|	|	...	1337	...	|	|	...	|	|	...	...
Duisburg Hbf d.	1012	1112	|	...	...	|	...	...	1234	1312	|	...	|	h	|	...	1434	...	1512	|	...	|	|	...	...
Düsseldorf Hbf d.	1027	1127	|	...	...	|	...	...	1248	1327	|	...	|	|	|	...	1448	...	1527	|	...	|	|	...	...
Köln Hbf d.	1053	1155	|	...	1255	|	...	...	1328	1355	|	...	|	1455	|	...	1528	...	1555	|	1655	|	|	...	...
Bonn Hbf d.	1114	|	|	...	|	|	...	1314	|	|	|	...	|	|	|	...	|	1514	|	|	|	|	|	...	...
Koblenz Hbf d.	1148	⊖	|	...	⊖	|	...	1348	⊖	⊖	|	...	|	⊖	|	...	⊖	1548	⊖	|	⊖	|	|	...	...
Mainz Hbf d.	1239	|	|	...	|	|	...	1439	|	|	|	...	|	|	|	...	|	1639	|	|	|	|	|	...	...
Frankfurt Flughafen ✈ d.	|	1254	|	...	1354	|	...	|	1418	1454	|	...	|	1554	|	...	1618	|	1654	|	1754	|	|	...	...
Frankfurt (Main) Hbf d.	|	|	1250	...	|	1405	...	|	1430	|	1450	...	1550	|	1605	...	1630	|	|	1650	|	1750	1805	...	...
Mannheim Hbf d.	1323	1324	1336	...	1424	1444	...	1521	▬	1524	1536	...	1628	1636	1644	...	▬	1721	1724	1736	1824	1828	1844	...	...
Karlsruhe Hbf d.	1349	...	1400	...	▬	1508	...	▬	...	▬	1600	...	▬	1700	1708	...	...	▬	...	1800	▬	▬	1908	...	...
Freiburg (Brsg) Hbf d.	1455	...	1501	...	...	1611	...	...	...	...	1701	...	...	1801	1811	...	...	...	...	1901	...	...	2011	...	...
Basel Bad Bf 🏛 a.	1529	...	1536	←	...	1647	...	...	...	...	1736	...	...	1836	1847	...	...	...	...	1936	...	...	2047	...	...
Basel SBB a.	1537	...	1547	1537	...	1655	...	...	...	*EC*	1747	...	...	1847	1855	...	...	...	...	1947	...	...	2055	...	...
	|		*IC* **979**	|	*IR* **2181** ¶	|		*IC* **981** 🍷	*ICN* **687** 🍷	**59** [R] 🍷 ⊗	|			▬ *IC* **587**	|			*ICE* **987** 🍷		|	*IR* **2191**		|		
Basel SBB ★ d.	1607	...	1601	1607	1603	1707	...	1701	1703	1728	1801	1803	...	1833	1907	1903	...	1901	...	2001	2003	...	2107	2128	...
Bern a.	→	...	1656	|	|	|	...	1756	|	1827	1856	|	...	|	|	|	...	1956	...	2056	|	...	|	2227	2235
Spiez a.	...	...	1731	|	|	|	...	1831	|	1902	1931	|	...	|	|	|	...	2031	...	2134	|	...	|	...	2302
Interlaken Ost a.	...	...	1757	|	|	|	...	1857	|	|	1957	|	...	|	|	|	...	2054	...	2157	|	...	|	...	|
Brig a.	...	...	*1811*f	|	|	|	...	*1911*f	|	1940	*2011*f	|	...	|	|	|	*IR*	*2111*f	...	*2240*‡	|	...	|	...	2343
Domodossola 🏛 § a.	...	...	...	|	|	|	...	▬	|	2012	...	|	...	|	|	|	**1789**	...	...	...	|	...	|	...	...
Zürich HB a.	...	...	...	1700	|	1800	1812	...	|	|	...	|	...	1926	2000	|	2012	...	...	...	|	...	2200	...	...
Landquart a.	...	...	...	1832	|	▬	1932	...	|	|	...	|	...	2041	...	|	2134	...	...	...	|	...	...	...	...
Davos Platz a.	...	...	...	*1955*	|	*EC*	*2057*	...	|	|	...	|	*EC*	*2157*	...	|	*2257*	...	...	...	|	...	...	...	...
Chur a.	...	...	...	1843	|	**23**	1943	...	|	|	...	|	**25**	2052	...	|	2145	...	...	...	|	*ICN*	...	...	...
St Moritz a.	...	...	...	*2058*	|	[R] 🍷	*2159*	...	|	|	...	|	[R] 🍷	*2259*	...	|	⊠	...	...	...	|	**693**	...	...	...
Luzern a.	...	...	...	...	1705	⊕	▬	...	1805	|	...	1905	⊕	▬	...	2005	...	...	...	...	2105	🍷	...	...	...
Arth-Goldau a.	...	...	...	...	1745	1750	...	*ESc*	1845	|	...	1945	1950	...	...	2045	...	...	...	...	2145	2150	...	...	...
Bellinzona a.	...	...	...	...	1953	1923	*ESc*	**9537**	2023	|	...	2153	2123	*ICN*	...	2223	...	...	...	...	...	2323	...	...	...
Lugano a.	...	...	...	...	...	1946	**9753**	[R] 🍷	2046	|	...	2226	2146	**1911**	...	2246	...	...	...	...	...	2346	...	...	...
Chiasso 🏛 a.	...	...	...	...	...	2008	[R] 🍷	Ⓑ	...	|	...	2257	2208	[R]	...	2312	...	...	...	...	...	0012	...	...	...
Como San Giovanni a.	...	...	...	...	...	2014	⚡	⚡	...	|	...	...	2214	**E**	...	...	...	...	...	...	...	...	...	...	...
Milano Centrale a.	...	...	...	...	...	2050	2105	2145	...	2135	...	...	2250	2320	...	...	...	...	...	...	...	...	...	...	...
Venezia Santa Lucia a.	...	...	...	...	...	...	2356k	|	...	...	...	...	...	|	...	...	...	...	...	...	...	...	...	...	...
Bologna Centrale a.	...	...	...	...	...	...	...	2250	...	...	...	...	...	|	...	...	...	...	...	...	...	...	...	...	...
Firenze SMN a.	...	...	...	...	...	...	...	...	...	...	...	...	...	|	...	...	...	...	...	...	...	...	...	...	...
Roma Termini a.	...	...	...	...	...	...	...	...	...	...	...	...	...	0723t	...	...	...	...	...	...	...	...	...	...	...

CONTINUED ON NEXT PAGE

AMSTERDAM, BERLIN, DORTMUND and KÖLN - ZÜRICH, MILANO and ROMA 73

train type	IC	ICE	ICE	ICE	IR	IC		IR	ICE	IC	IC	ICE	CNL	CNL	IR	EC	IC	IC	CNL	IC	IR	IC	AV	ESc	
train number	2311	127	613	873	1797	993		2195	609	955	559	542	419	479	1765	15	959	458	1258	565	2165	1063	9517	9723	
notes	🍷	327	🍷	🍷					🍷	🍷	🍷	🍷		®	🍷	®🍷	🍷		®✕	🍷	¶	🍷	®✕	®🍷	
notes		T											A	K		⊕			G				⚡	⚡	
København H d.	...	...	...	...	...	...	...	...	...	...	...	...	...	...	...	...	...	...	...	...	...	...	...	...	...
Hamburg Hbf d.	...	...	...	...	...	...	...	...	1946	...	...	...	...	1918	...	...	...	...	...	...	...	...	...	...	...
Bremen Hbf d.	...	...	...	...	...	...	...	...	2044	...	...	...	...	|	...	...	...	...	...	...	...	...	...	...	...
Berlin Hauptbahnhof d.	...	...	...	1432	...	...	...	...	|	...	...	1850	...	|	...	...	...	...	2222	...	...	...	...	...	...
Hannover Hbf d.	...	...	...	|	...	...	...	...	|	...	...	2031	...	2216	...	...	...	...	|	...	...	...	...	...	...
Dortmund Hbf d.	...	...	1637	|	...	...	...	...	2237	...	...	2212	...	|	...	...	...	...	|	...	...	...	...	...	...
Essen Hbf d.	...	...	1659	|	...	...	...	...	2259	...	...	2236	...	|	...	...	...	...	|	...	...	...	...	...	...
Amsterdam Centraal d.	...	1434	|	|	...	...	...	...	|	...	...	|	2031	|	...	...	...	...	|	...	...	...	...	...	...
Utrecht Centraal d.	...	1459	|	|	...	...	...	...	|	...	...	|	2101u	|	...	...	...	...	|	...	...	...	...	...	...
Arnhem ⊙ d.	...	1537	|	|	...	...	...	...	|	...	...	|	2137u	|	...	...	...	...	|	...	...	...	...	...	...
Duisburg Hbf d.	...	1634	1712	|	...	...	...	...	2312	...	...	2249	2256u	|	...	...	...	...	|	...	...	...	...	...	...
Düsseldorf Hbf d.	...	1648	1727	|	...	...	...	...	2327	...	...	2308	2312u	|	...	...	...	...	|	...	...	...	...	...	...
Köln Hbf d.	...	1720	1755	|	...	...	...	...	2353	...	...	2330	2346u	|	...	...	...	...	|	...	...	...	...	...	...
Bonn Hbf d.	1714	|	|	|	...	...	...	...	0014	...	...	▬	0007u	|	...	...	...	...	|	...	...	...	...	...	...
Koblenz Hbf d.	1748	⊖	⊖	|	...	...	...	...	0048	...	...	...	0043u	|	...	...	...	...	|	...	...	...	...	...	...
Mainz Hbf d.	1839	|	|	|	...	...	...	...	0143	...	...	...	|	|	...	...	...	...	|	...	...	...	...	...	...
Frankfurt Flughafen ✈ d.	|	1817	1854	|	...	...	...	...	0205	...	...	...	|	|	...	...	...	...	|	...	...	...	...	...	...
Frankfurt (Main) Hbf d.	|	1830	|	1850	...	...	...	...	0222	...	...	...	|	|	...	...	...	0402j	0402j	...	...	...	...	...	...
Mannheim Hbf d.	1921	...	1924	1936	...	...	...	...	0302	...	...	...	|	|	...	...	...	0445	0445	...	...	...	...	...	...
Karlsruhe Hbf d.	...	...	...	2000	...	...	...	...	0347	...	...	...	0437s	0437s	...	...	...	0542	0542	...	...	...	...	...	...
Freiburg (Brsg) Hbf d.	...	...	...	2101	...	...	...	...	0452	...	...	...	0556s	0556s	...	...	...	0655	0655	...	...	...	...	...	...
Basel Bad Bf 🏛 a.	...	...	...	2136	...	...	...	...	0537	...	...	...	0644s	0644s	...	...	...	0746	0746s	...	...	...	...	...	...
Basel SBB a.	...	...	...	2147	...	...	...	...	0547	...	...	*EC*	0654s	0654s	...	...	...	0755	0755s	...	...	...	...	...	...
												51	|	|				▬	|						
				TGV								®🍷	|	|				*IC*	|						
				9219								⊗	|	|				810	|						
Basel SBB ★ d.	...	...	...	2207	...	2201	...	2203	...	0601	0633	0628	|	|	...	...	0701	🍷	|	...	0803	0828	...	...	...
Bern a.	...	...	...	|	...	2256	...	|	...	0656	|	0727	|	|	...	...	0756	0807	|	...	|	0927	...	...	...
Spiez a.	...	...	...	|	...	2335	0012	|	...	0731	|	0802	1047c	1047c	...	...	0831	0834	|	...	|	1002	...	...	...
Interlaken Ost a.	...	...	...	|	...	2359	|	|	...	0757	|	|	|	|	...	...	0857	|	|	...	|	|	...	...	...
Brig a.	...	...	...	|	...	...	0120	|	...	*0811*f	|	0840	1156c	1156c	...	...	...	0911	|	...	|	1040	...	...	...
Domodossola 🏛 § a.	...	...	...	|	...	...	...	|	...	...	|	0912	|	|	...	...	...	...	|	...	|	▬	...	...	...
Zürich HB a.	...	...	...	2300	2312	...	...	|	...	...	0726	|	0834	0834	0912	0909	...	...	0917	0937	|	...	...	...	...
Landquart a.	...	...	...	...	0039	...	...	|	...	...	0841	|	▬	▬	1032	|	...	...	...	1041	|	...	...	...	...
Davos Platz a.	...	...	...	...	|	...	...	|	...	...	*0955*	|	...	...	*1155*	|	...	...	...	*1155*	|	*EC*	...	...	...
Chur a.	...	...	...	...	0049	...	...	|	...	...	0852	|	...	...	1043	|	...	...	...	1052	|	15	...	...	...
St Moritz a.	...	...	...	...	...	...	...	|	...	...	*1058*	|	...	...	*1258*	|	...	...	...	*1258*	|	®🍷	...	...	...
Luzern a.	...	...	...	...	...	...	...	2305	...	...	...	|	...	...	...	|	...	...	...	...	0905	⊕	...	...	...
Arth-Goldau a.	...	...	...	...	...	...	...	*2345*	...	...	...	|	...	...	...	0948	...	...	...	...	0945	0950	...	...	...
Bellinzona a.	...	...	...	...	...	...	...	...	...	...	...	|	*AV*	*ESc*	...	1123	...	...	...	...	1153	1123	...	...	...
Lugano a.	...	...	...	...	...	...	...	...	...	...	...	|	9513	9715	...	1146	...	...	...	...	...	1146	...	...	...
Chiasso 🏛 a.	...	...	...	...	...	...	...	...	...	...	...	|	®✕	®🍷	...	1208	...	...	...	...	...	1208	...	...	...
Como San Giovanni a.	...	...	...	...	...	...	...	...	...	...	...	|	⚡	⚡	...	1214	...	...	...	...	...	1214	...	...	...
Milano Centrale a.	...	...	...	...	...	...	...	...	...	...	...	1035	1115	1135	...	1250	...	...	...	...	...	1250	1315	1335	...
Venezia Santa Lucia a.	...	...	...	...	...	...	...	...	...	...	...	...	|	1410	...	...	...	...	...	...	...	...	|	1610	...
Bologna Centrale a.	...	...	...	...	...	...	...	...	...	...	...	...	1220	...	...	...	...	...	...	...	...	...	1420	...	...
Firenze SMN a.	...	...	...	...	...	...	...	...	...	...	...	...	1300	...	...	...	...	...	...	...	...	...	1500	...	...
Roma Termini a.	...	...	...	...	...	...	...	...	...	...	...	...	1445	...	...	...	...	...	...	...	...	...	1645	...	...

A – *City Night Line* PEGASUS – 🛏 1, 2 cl., 🛏 1, 2 cl. (T4), ▬ 2 cl. (4, 6 berth), [2] (reclining) and 🍷 Amsterdam - Mannheim - Basel - Zürich (- Spiez - Brig ⑥ Dec. 26 - Apr. 10). ® Special fares apply.

B – [12] and ✕ (Hamburg ①–⑥ **v** -) Dortmund - Köln - Basel - Zürich - Chur.

C – *City Night Line* AURORA – 🛏 1, 2 cl., ▬ 2 cl. (4, 6 berth), [2] and ✕ København - Basel. ® Special fares apply.

D – [12] and ✕ Hamburg - Dortmund - Köln - Basel - Zürich - Chur.

E – 🛏 1, 2 cl., 🛏 1, 2 cl. (Excelsior), 🛏 1, 2 cl. (T2), ▬ 2 cl. and [2] Milano - Roma - Napoli.

G – *City Night Line* SIRIUS – 🛏 1, 2 cl., 🛏 1, 2 cl. (T4), ▬ 2 cl. (4, 6 berth), [2] (reclining) and ✕ Berlin - Basel - Zürich. ® Special fares apply. Conveys *City Night Line* **458** CANOPUS Praha - Dresden - Zürich (Table **75**).

K – *City Night Line* KOMET – ④⑤⑥⑦ (daily Mar. 28 - Oct. 30): 🛏 1, 2 cl., 🛏 1, 2 cl. (T4), ▬ 2 cl. (4, 6 berth), [2] (reclining) and ✕ Hamburg - Hannover - Mannheim - Basel - Zürich (- Spiez - Brig ⑥ Dec. 26 - Apr. 10). ® Special fares apply.

M – [12] and 🍷 (Hamburg ① **e**) - Frankfurt - Basel - Zürich.

T – Mar. 26 - Nov. 7.

c – ⑥ Dec. 26 - Apr. 10, Train **1179**. Note train calls in following order: Basel - Zürich - Spiez - Brig.

e – ① (also Apr. 6, May 25; not Apr. 5, May 24).

f – Change at Bern.

g – Not Dec. 25, 26, Jan. 1, Apr. 3, 5, May 24.

h – Via Hagen and Wuppertal.

j – Frankfurt (Main) **Süd**.

k – Venezia **Mestre**.

n – Not Dec. 25, Jan. 1.

o – 0549 on ⑦ (also Dec. 25, 26, Jan. 1, Apr. 3, 5, May 24).

p – ①–⑤ (not Dec. 24, 25, 31, Jan. 1, Apr. 2, 5, May 24).

r – Train stops at Frankfurt (Main) Hbf before Frankfurt Flughafen.

s – Stops to set down only.

t – Roma **Tiburtina**.

u – Stops to pick up only.

v – ①–⑥ (not Dec. 25, 26, Jan. 1, Apr. 3, 5, May 24).

x – Köln **Messe / Deutz**.

y – Connects with train in previous column.

¶ – To Locarno (Table **550**).

⊙ – 🏛 is at Emmerich.

§ – Ticket point is **Iselle**.

⚡ – Supplement payable.

★ – Connections at Basel are not guaranteed.

⊖ – Via Köln - Frankfurt high speed line.

‡ – Change at Bern. 2301 on ⑦.

⊡ – Supplement payable in Italy (except with international tickets).

⊕ – **ETR 470**. Supplement payable for international journeys. *IC* supplement payable for internal journeys within Italy.

⊗ – **ETR 610**. Supplement payable for international journeys. *IC* supplement payable for internal journeys within Italy.

⊠ – Change at Landquart for St Moritz. Landquart depart 2147, Klosters arrive 2228, change trains, depart 2230, St Moritz arrive 2346.

OTHER TRAIN NAMES:

EC **109** – TICINO
EC **111** – SAN MARCO
EC **115** – MEDIOLANUM
EC **117** – VERDI
EC **119** – TIZIANO
EC **177** – MONTE CENERI
EC **179** – INSUBRIA

MILANO and ROMA - PATRAS - ATHÍNAI 74

train type	*ESc*	*ES*				*ESc*				
train number	9803	9355			2320	9803				
notes	®✕ ⚡	®✕ ⚡	⛴ SF			®✕ ⚡	⛴ SF			
Milano Centrale d.	0735	...	...	...	...	0735	...	...	...	...
Bologna d.	0950	...	...	...	...	0950	...	...	...	...
Roma Termini d.	|	1445	...	...	0550	|	...	...	...	...
Foligno d.	|	|	...	...	0740	|	...	...	...	...
Ancona d.	1141	|	...	...	0955	1138	...	...	...	...
Ancona Marittima d.	|	|	...	...	...	...	1330	...	...	...
Pescara Centrale d.	1252	|	...	...	...	....	|	...	...	...
Caserta d.	|	1557	...	...	...	...	|	...	...	...
Foggia d.	1435	1742	...	...	...	...	|	...	...	...
Bari Centrale a.	1534	1844	...	...	...	...	|	...	...	...
Bari Marittima d.	...	...	2000	...	...	...	|	...	...	...
Patras a.	...	...	1230	...	...	...	1130	...	...	...
Athína Lárisa a.	...	...	❖	...	...	...	❖	...	...	...

train type		*ESc*	*ICp*	*ES*				*ES*	*ESc*	
train number		9822	568	9354			2327	9331	9816	
notes	⛴ SF	®✕ ⚡	®✕ ⚡	®✕ ⚡		⛴ SF		®✕ ⚡	®✕ ⚡	
Athína Lárisa d.	❖	...	...	...	...	❖	...	...	...	...
Patras d.	1800	...	...	...	...	1430	...	...	...	...
Bari Marittima a.	0830	...	...	...	...	|	...	...	...	...
Bari Centrale d.	...	1129	1113	1412	...	|	...	...	...	...
Foggia a.	...	1232	1224	1514	...	|	...	...	...	...
Caserta a.	...	|	|	1703	...	|	...	...	...	...
Pescara Centrale a.	...	1411	1432	|	...	|	...	...	...	...
Ancona Marittma a.	...	|	|	|	...	1030	...	...	...	...
Ancona a.	...	1524	1617	|	...	...	1408	1518	1227	...
Foligno a.	...	|	|	|	...	...	1610	1656	|	...
Roma Termini a.	...	|	|	1815	...	...	1803	1824	|	...
Bologna a.	...	1714	1846	...	...	...	...	...	1414	...
Milano Centrale a.	...	1925	2105	...	...	...	...	...	1625	...

❖ – For shipping operators' bus connections see Table **2770**; for rail service see Table **1450**.

SF – **Superfast Ferries**, for days of running see Tables **2715**, **2755**.

⚡ – Supplement payable.

73 ROMA, MILANO and ZÜRICH - KÖLN, DORTMUND, BERLIN and AMSTERDAM

For other connections Basel - Luzern - Chiasso see Table **550**, for Basel - Bern - Interlaken and Brig see Table **560**.

train type	*ICE*	*ICE*	*IR*	*TGV*	*ICN*	*IR*	*IC*	*IR*	*ICE*	*IC*	*IR*	*ICE*	*IC*	*ICN*	*IC*	*ICE*	*EC*	*IR*	*EC*	*EC*	*ICE*	*IC*	*ICN*	*ICE*	*IC*	*ICE*
train number	**78**	**602**	**1560**	**9210**	**650**	**2164**	**956**	**1562**	**76**	**562**	**2166**	**276**	**962**	**658**	**566**	**74**	**12**	**2170**	**100**	**50**	**374**	**570**	**662**	**72**	**968**	**122**
notes	🍷	🍷		**9212**					🍷			🍷		🍷		🍷	R 🍷		**102**	R 🍷	🍷	🍷	🍷	🍷		🍷
				🍷⚡													⊕		H ✕	⊗						
Roma Termini d.	...	...	...	...	...	...	...	...	...	...	...	...	...	...	...	...	...	...	...	...	...	...	...	...	...	...
Firenze SMN d.	...	...	...	...	...	...	...	...	...	...	...	...	...	...	...	...	...	...	...	...	...	...	...	...	...	...
Bologna Centrale d.	...	...	...	...	...	...	...	...	...	...	...	...	...	...	...	...	...	...	...	...	...	...	...	...	...	...
Venezia Santa Lucia d.	...	...	...	...	...	...	...	...	...	...	...	...	...	...	...	...	...	...	...	...	...	...	...	...	...	...
Milano Centrale d.	...	...	...	...	...	...	...	...	...	...	...	...	...	...	...	...	0710	...	...	0725	...	...	...	...	...	...
Como San Giovanni d.	...	...	...	...	...	...	...	...	...	...	...	...	...	...	...	...	0745	...	...	│	...	...	...	...	...	...
Chiasso 🏛 d.	...	...	...	...	0446	...	...	...	...	...	...	...	...	0641	...	...	0752	0711	...	│	...	...	...	...	...	...
Lugano d.	...	...	...	...	0512	...	...	...	...	...	...	...	...	0712	...	...	0812	0737	...	│	...	...	0912	...	...	...
Bellinzona d.	...	...	...	...	0536	...	...	...	...	...	0606	...	...	0736	...	...	0836	0806	...	│	...	...	0936	...	...	...
Arth-Goldau d.	...	...	...	...	0709	0714	...	...	...	...	0814	...	...	0914	...	...	1013	1014	...	│	...	...	1114	...	...	...
Luzern d.	...	...	...	...		0755	...	...	...	...	0855	...	...	0954	...	...	│	1054	...	│	...	...	1155	...	...	...
St Moritz d.	...	...	...	...	...	│	...	...	...	...	│	...	...	│	*0540*k	...	│	│	*0702*	│	...	*0802*	│	...	...	...
Chur d.	...	...	0513	...	...	│	...	0613	...	0709	│	...	...	│	0809	...	│	│	0916	│	...	1009	│	...	...	...
Davos Platz d.	...	...	│	...	...	│	...	│	...	*0550*	│	...	...	│	*0702*	...	│	│	*0802*	│	...	*0902*	│	...	...	...
Landquart d.	...	...	0523	...	*ICE*	│	...	0623	...	0719	│	...	...	│	0819	...	│	│	0926	│	...	1019	│	...	...	...
Zürich HB d.	0602	...	0648	0702	**278**	│	...	0748	0802	0834	│	...	...	│	0934	1002	1051	│	1102	│	...	1123	│	1202	...	...
Domodossola 🏛 § d.	│	...	...	│	🍷	│	...		│	│	│	...	...	│	│	│		│	│	0848	...		│	│	...	...
Brig d.	│	...	...	│	*0547*f	│	*0649*f	...	│	│	│	*0749*f	*0849*f	│	│	│	...	│	│	0920	...	*EC*	│	│	*1049*f	...
Interlaken Ost d.	│	...	...	│	0601	│	0701	...	│	│	│	0801	0901	│	│	│	...	│	│	│	...	**100/2**	│	│	1101	...
Spiez d.	│	...	...	│	0623	│	0723	...	│	│	│	0823	0923	│	│	│	...	│	│	0954	...	H ✕	│	│	1123	...
Bern d.	│	...	...	│	0704	│	0804	...	│	│	│	0904	1004	│	│	│	...	│	│	1034	1104	←	│	│	1204	...
Basel SBB ★ a.	0657	...	...	0757	0755	0853	0855	...	0857	0927	0953	0955	1055	1053	1027	1057	...	1153	1157	1132	1155	1157	1253	1257	1255	...
	│				│				│	*ICE*		│				│	*ICE* **508** 🍷		│		│	│		│		
Basel SBB d.	0704	0712c	...	...	0812	...	...	...	0904	**600**	...	1012	...	...	...	1104	1112	...	1218	...	1212	1218	...	1304	...	...
Basel Bad Bf 🏛 d.	0713	0721c	...	...	0822	*ICE*	*ICE*	*IC*	0913	**1008**	...	1022	*ICE*	...	*IC*	1113	1122	IC	→	...	1222	1227	...	1313	*ICE*	...
Freiburg (Brsg) Hbf d.	0749	0756c	...	...	0857	**612**	**126**	**2114**	0949	🍷	...	1057	**610**	*ICE*	**2112**	1149	1157	**2012**	...	...	1257	1304	...	1349	**506**	...
Karlsruhe Hbf d.	0851	0901	...	...	1000	🍷	🍷	🍷	1051	1109	...	1200	🍷	**124**	🍷	1251	1300	🍷	...	...	1400	1412	...	1451	🍷	...
Mannheim Hbf a.	0914	0924	...	...	1022	1035	T	1039	1114	1133	...	1222	1235	🍷	1239	1314	1323	1408	...	...	1422	1437	...	1514	1535	...
Frankfurt (Main) Hbf a.	0952	│	...	...	1108	│	1129	│	1153	│	...	1308	│	1329	│	1353	│	│	...	...	1508	│	...	1553	│	1629
Frankfurt Flughafen ✈ a.	│	1006	...	...	│	1106	1140	│	│	1206	...	│	1306	1340	│	│	1406	│	...	...	│	│	...	│	1606	1640
Mainz Hbf a.	│	│	...	...	│	│	│	1118	│	│	...	│	│	│	1318	│	│	1446	...	...	│	1518	...	│	│	│
Koblenz Hbf a.	│	⊖	...	...	│	⊖	⊖	1210	│	⊖	...	│	⊖	⊖	1410	│	⊖	1541	...	...	│	1610	...	│	⊖	⊖
Bonn Hbf a.	│	│	...	...	│	│	│	1242	│	│	...	│	│	│	1442	│	│	1620	...	...	│	1642	...	│	│	│
Köln Hbf a.	│	1105	...	...	│	1205	1232	1305	│	1305	...	│	1405	1432	1505	│	1505	1642	...	...	│	1705	...	│	1705	1739
Düsseldorf Hbf a.	│	...	...	...	│	1231	1312	1331	│	...	...	│	1431	1511	1531	│	│	1712	...	...	│	1731	...	│	│	1811
Duisburg Hbf a.	│	...	...	...	│	1244	1326	1344	│	...	...	│	1444	1526	1544	│	h	1725	...	...	│	1744	...	│	h	1824
Arnhem ⊙ a.	│	...	...	...	│	│	1424	│	│	...	...	│	│	1624	│	│	│	│	...	...	│	│	...	│	│	1924
Utrecht Centraal a.	│	...	...	...	│	│	1458	│	│	...	...	│	│	1658	│	│	│	│	...	...	│	│	...	│	│	1958
Amsterdam Centraal a.	│	...	...	...	│	│	1525	│	│	...	...	│	│	1725	│	│	│	│	...	...	│	│	...	│	│	2025
Essen Hbf a.	│	...	...	...	│	1257	...	1357	│	...	...	│	1457	...	1557	│	│	1740	...	...	│	1757	...	│	│	...
Dortmund Hbf a.	│	...	...	...	│	1321	...	1421	│	...	...	│	1521	...	1621	│	1620g	1805	...	...	│	1821	...	│	1820	...
Hannover Hbf a.	1217	...	...	...	│	...	...	│	1417	...	...	│	...	...	│	1617	...	2018	...	...	│	│	...	1817	...	...
Berlin Hauptbahnhof a.	│	...	...	...	1525	...	...	│	│	...	...	1725	...	...	│	│	...	...	...	...	1925	│	...	│	...	...
Bremen Hbf a.	│	...	...	...	...	...	...	1614	│	...	...	...	...	...	1814	│	...	...	...	...	...	2014	...	│	...	...
Hamburg Hbf a.	1334	...	...	...	...	...	...	1712	1534	...	...	...	...	...	1912	1734	...	...	...	...	...	2112	...	1934	...	...
København H. a.	...	...	...	...	...	...	...	...	...	...	...	...	...	...	...	...	...	...	...	...	...	...	...	...	...	...

train type	*EC*	*IR*	*EC*	*ICE*	*ICE*	*EC*	*IC*	*IC*	*ESc*	*AV*	*IC*	*EC*	*IR*	*IC*	*ICE*	*ICE*	*ES*	*ES*	*EC*	*ICE*	*ICE*	*ESc*	*ES*	*IR*	*EC*	*ICE*
train number	**14**	**2174**	**6**	**370**	**516**	**6**	**574**	**974**	**9708**	**9506**	**576**	**52**	**2178**	**978**	**514**	**120**	**9712**	**9508**	**34**	**376**	**592**	**9792**	**9512**	**2182**	**18**	**272**
notes	R 🍷	¶	✕	**290**	🍷	✕	🍷	🍷	R ✕	R 🍷	🍷	R 🍷	¶	🍷	🍷	**R**	R ✕	R 🍷	R 🍷	🍷	✕	R ✕	R 🍷	¶	R 🍷	**372**
	⊕		**G**	🍷		**G**			**W**	⚡		⊗					⚡	⚡	⊗			**X**	⚡		⊕	**292**
Roma Termini d.	...	...	...	...	...	...	...	...	...	0715	...	...	...	...	...	...	...	0815	...	...	...	...	0915	...	...	...
Firenze SMN d.	...	...	...	...	...	...	...	...	...	0900	...	...	...	...	...	...	...	1000	...	...	...	...	1100	...	...	...
Bologna Centrale d.	...	...	...	...	...	...	...	...	...	0940	...	...	...	...	...	...	...	1040	...	...	...	...	1140	...	...	...
Venezia Santa Lucia d.	*0514*	...	...	...	...	...	...	...	0750	│	...	...	...	...	...	...	0858	│	...	...	...	0950	│	...	...	...
Milano Centrale d.	0910	...	...	...	...	...	...	...	1025	1045	...	1120	...	...	...	...	1125	1145	1225	...	...	1225	1245	...	1310	...
Como San Giovanni d.	0945	...	...	...	...	...	...	...		...	...	│	...	...	...	...			│	...	...			...	1345	...
Chiasso 🏛 d.	0952	...	...	...	...	...	...	...	...	...	...	│	...	...	...	...	...	...	│	...	...	...	...	...	1352	...
Lugano d.	1012	...	...	...	...	...	...	...	...	...	...	│	...	...	...	...	...	...	│	...	...	...	...	...	1412	...
Bellinzona d.	1036	1006	...	...	...	...	...	...	...	...	...	│	1206	...	...	...	...	*IC*	│	...	...	*IC*	...	1406	1436	...
Arth-Goldau d.	1213	1214	...	...	...	...	...	...	...	...	...	│	1414	...	...	...	...	**578**	│	...	...	**580**	...	1614	1609	...
Luzern d.	│	1254	...	...	...	...	...	...	...	...	...	│	1454	...	...	...	...	🍷	│	...	...	🍷	...	1655	│	...
St Moritz d.	│	│	*0902*	...	...	...	*1002*	...	...	...	*1102*	│	│	...	...	...	...	*1202*	│	...	...	*1302*	...	│	│	...
Chur d.	│	│	1116	...	...	...	1209	...	...	...	1309	│	│	...	...	...	...	1409	│	...	...	1509	...	│	│	...
Davos Platz d.	│	│	*1002*	...	...	...	*1102*	...	...	...	*1202*	│	│	...	...	...	...	*1302*	│	...	...	*1402*	...	│	│	...
Landquart d.	│	│	1126	...	...	...	1219	...	...	...	1319	│	│	...	...	...	...	1419	│	...	...	1519	*IC*	│	│	...
Zürich HB d.	1251	│	1308	...	...	...	1334	...	...	...	1434	│	│	...	...	...	...	1534	│	...	...	1634	**1080**	│	1651	1702
Domodossola 🏛 § d.	...	│	│	...	...	...	│	...	...	...	│	1248	│	...	...	...	...	│	1348	...	...	│	🍷	│	...	│
Brig d.	...	│	│	*1149*f	...	...	│	*1249*f	...	...	│	1320	│	*1349*f	...	...	...	│	1416	*1449*f	...	│	1520	│	...	│
Interlaken Ost d.	...	│	│	1201	...	...	│	1301	...	...	│	│	│	1401	...	...	...	│	...	1501	...	│	*1529*	│	...	│
Spiez d.	...	│	│	1223	...	...	│	1323	...	...	│	1354	│	1423	...	...	...	│	...	1523	...	│	1554	│	...	│
Bern d.	...	│	│	1304	...	←	│	1404	...	...	│	1434	│	1504	...	...	...	│	...	1604	...	│	1634	│	...	│
Basel SBB ★ a.	...	1353	1412	1355	...	1412	1427	1455		...	1527	1532	1553	1555	...	...	...	1627	...	1655	...	1727	1732	1753	...	1757
			│	│		│		*ICE* **70** 🍷	*ICE* **104** 🍷					*ICE* **870** 🍷						│				*CNL* **472** **J**		│
Basel SBB d.	...	...	1420	1412	...	1420	...	1504	1512	...	...	...	...	1612	...	...	...	...	...	1704	...	*ICE*	...	1804	...	1812
Basel Bad Bf 🏛 d.	...	...	→	1422	...	1428	...	1513	1522	...	...	...	...	1621	...	...	*IC*	...	...	1713	...	**502**	...	1817u	...	1822
Freiburg (Brsg) Hbf d.	...	...	...	1457	...	1504	...	1549	1557	...	...	...	...	1656	...	...	**2318**	...	...	1749	...	**1002**	...	1904u	...	1857
Karlsruhe Hbf d.	...	...	...	1600	...	1612	...	1651	1700	...	...	...	...	1801	...	...	🍷	...	...	1851	...	✕	...	2018u	...	2000
Mannheim Hbf a.	...	...	...	1622	1635	1637	...	1714	1723	...	...	...	...	1823	1835	...	1839	...	...	1914	1931	1935	...	2116u	...	2022
Frankfurt (Main) Hbf a.	...	...	...	1708	│	│	...	1753	│	...	...	...	...	1908	│	1929	│	...	...	1953	2008	│	...	2218b	...	2108
Frankfurt Flughafen ✈ a.	...	...	...	│	1706	│	...	│	1806	...	...	...	...	│	1906	1940	│	...	...	│	│	2006	...	│	...	...
Mainz Hbf a.	...	...	...	│	│	1718	...	│	│	...	...	...	...	│	│	│	1918	...	...	│	│	│	...	│	...	...
Koblenz Hbf a.	...	...	...	│	⊖	1810	...	│	⊖	...	...	...	...	│	⊖	⊖	2010	...	...	│	│	⊖	...	│	...	...
Bonn Hbf a.	...	...	...	│	│	1842	...	│	│	...	...	...	...	│	│	│	2042	...	...	│	│	│	...	│	...	...
Köln Hbf a.	...	...	...	│	1805	1905	...	│	1905	...	...	...	...	│	2005	2039	...	...	...	│	│	2105	...	│	...	...
Düsseldorf Hbf a.	...	...	...	│	│	1931	...	│	1938p	...	...	...	...	│	2031	2111	...	...	...	│	│	│	...	│	...	...
Duisburg Hbf a.	...	...	...	│	h	1944	...	│	1950p	...	...	...	...	│	2044	2124	...	...	...	│	│	h	...	│	...	...
Arnhem ⊙ a.	...	...	...	│	│	│	...	│	2053p	...	...	...	...	│	│	2224	...	...	...	│	│	│	...	│	...	...
Utrecht Centraal a.	...	...	...	│	│	│	...	│	2128p	...	...	...	...	│	│	2258	...	...	...	│	│	│	...	│	...	...
Amsterdam Centraal a.	...	...	...	│	│	│	...	│	2155p	...	...	...	...	│	│	2325	...	...	...	│	│	│	...	│	...	...
Essen Hbf a.	...	...	...	│	│	1957	...	│	...	...	...	...	...	│	2057	...	...	...	...	│	│	│	...	│	...	...
Dortmund Hbf a.	...	...	...	│	1920	2021	...	│	...	...	...	...	...	│	2121	...	...	...	...	│	│	2221	...	│	...	...
Hannover Hbf a.	...	...	...	│	...	│	...	2017	...	...	...	...	...	│	│	...	...	...	...	2217j	│	...	...	│	...	...
Berlin Hauptbahnhof a.	...	...	...	2126n	...	│	...	│	...	...	...	...	...	2325	│	...	...	...	...	│	0023	...	...	│	...	...
Bremen Hbf a.	...	...	...	...	...	2218e	...	│	...	...	...	...	...	...	2320	...	...	...	...	│	...	...	...	│	...	...
Hamburg Hbf a.	...	...	...	...	...	2315e	...	2137	...	...	...	...	...	...	0019	...	...	...	...	2342j	...	...	...	0356	...	...
København H. a.	...	...	...	...	...	...	...	...	...	...	...	...	...	...	...	...	...	...	...	...	...	...	...	1006	...	...

CONTINUED ON NEXT PAGE

ROMA, MILANO and ZÜRICH - KÖLN, DORTMUND, BERLIN and AMSTERDAM 73

train type	*IC*	*ESc*	*ICN*	*AV*	*EC*	*IC*	*ICE*		*IC*	*IC*	*AV*	*ESc*	*EC*	*IR*	*IC*	*CNL*	*ESc*	*AV*	*IR*	*EC*	*ICE*	*ICE*			
train number	**582**	**9718**	**674**	**9516**	**20**	**586**	**270**		**588**	**990**	**9522**	**9726**	**22**	**2192**	**590**	**478**	**9732**	**9524**	**794**	**56**	**994**	**608**			
notes	🍷	[R]✕	🍷	[R]✕	[R]🍷	🍷	🍷		🍷		[R]🍷	[R]🍷	[R]🍷	¶		✕	[R]🍷	[R]✕	🍷	[R]🍷		🍷			
		⚡		⚡	⊕						⚡	⚡	⊕			K	⚡	⚡		⊗					
Roma Termini d.	...	...	...	1115	...	...	...	...	...	...	1315	...	...	...	...	...	...	1415	...	...	...	...	...	...	...
Firenze SMN d.	...	...	...	1300	...	...	...	...	...	...	1500	...	...	...	...	...	...	1600	...	...	...	...	...	...	...
Bologna Centrale d.	...	...	...	1340	...	...	...	...	...	...	1540	...	...	...	...	...	...	1640	...	...	...	...	...	...	...
Venezia Santa Lucia d.	...	1150	...	│	...	...	...	...	...	...	│	1350	...	...	...	...	1520	│	...	...	...	...	...	...	...
Milano Centrale d.	...	1425	...	1445	1510	...	...	...	...	...	1645	1625	1710	...	...	...	1755	1745	...	1825	...	...	...	...	...
Como San Giovanni d.	...	▬	...	▬	1545	...	...	...	...	...	▬	▬	1745	...	...	...	▬	...	...	│	...	...	...	...	...
Chiasso 🏛 d.	...	...	...	...	1552	...	...	...	...	...	...	...	1752	...	...	...	...	...	...	│	...	...	...	...	...
Lugano d.	...	...	1512	...	1612	...	...	...	...	...	...	...	1812	1746	...	...	...	...	...	│	...	...	...	...	...
Bellinzona d.	...	...	1536	...	1636	...	...	...	...	...	...	...	1836	1806	...	...	...	...	...	│	...	...	...	...	...
Arth-Goldau d.	...	...	1714	...	1813	...	...	...	...	...	...	...	2009	2014	...	...	...	...	...	│	...	...	...	...	...
Luzern d.	...	...	1755	*IC*	│	...	...	...	...	...	*CNL*	...	▬	2055	...	...	...	...	...	│	...	...	...	...	...
St Moritz d.	*1402*	...	│	**988**	│	*1502*	...	...	*1602*	...	**459**	...	...	│	*1702*	...	*CNL*	...	*1802*	│	...	...	...	...	...
Chur d.	1609	...	│	🍷	│	1709	...	...	1809	...	**1259**	...	...	│	1909	...	**418**	...	2013	│	...	...	...	...	...
Davos Platz d.	*1502*	...	│	*1749*f	│	*1602*	...	...	*1702*	...	✕	...	...	│	*1802*	...	✕	...	*1902*	│	...	...	...	...	...
Landquart d.	1619	*IC*	│	1801	│	1719	...	...	1819	...	**C**	...	...	│	1919	...	**A**	...	2023	│	...	...	...	...	...
Zürich HB d.	1734	**986**	│	1823	1851	1823	1902	...	1934	...	1944	...	*IC*	│	2023	2042	2042	...	2202	│	...	...	...	...	...
Domodossola 🏛 § d.	│	🍷	│	1904	...	...	│	...	│	...	│	...	**992**	│	...	│	│	...	│	1948	...	...	...	...	...
Brig d.	│	*1649*f	│	1955	...	...	│	...	│	*1849*f	│	...	*1949*f	│	...	1659r	1700r	...	│	2020	...	...	...	...	...
Interlaken Ost d.	│	1701	│		...	...	│	...	│	1901	│	...	2001	│	...	│	│	...	│	│	2101	...	...	...	...
Spiez d.	│	1723	│		...	...	│	...	│	1923	│	...	2023	│	...	1813r	1813r	...	│	2054	2123	...	...	...	...
Bern d.	│	1804	│		...	...	│	...	│	2004	│	...	2104	│	...	│	│	...	│	2134	2204	...	...	...	...
Basel SBB ★ a.	1827	1855	1853	...	...	...	1957	...	2027	2054	│	...	2155	2153	...	│	│	...	2257	2232	2255	...	...	...	...
			ICE	...			│				│		▬			│	│								
			500	...			│				│	*IC*				│	│								
			🍷	...			│				│	**60459**				│	│								
Basel SBB d.	...	...	1912	...	...	...	2012	...	...	...	2107u	2107	*ICE*	...	...	2207u	2207u	...	...	...	...	2326	...	...	...
Basel Bad Bf 🏛 d.	...	...	1921	...	...	...	2022	...	...	...	2121u	2121	**990**	...	...	2219u	2219u	...	...	...	...	2334	...	...	...
Freiburg (Brsg) Hbf d.	...	...	1956	...	...	...	2057	...	...	...	2158u	2158	🍷	...	...	2257u	2257u	...	...	...	...	0014	...	...	...
Karlsruhe Hbf d.	...	...	2101	...	...	...	2200	...	...	...	2305u	2305	**d**	...	...	0018u	0018u	...	...	...	...	0129	...	...	...
Mannheim Hbf a.	...	...	2124	...	...	...	2222	...	...	...	0005u	2346	2351	...	...	│	│	...	...	...	...	0222	...	...	...
Frankfurt (Main) Hbf a.	...	...	│	...	...	...	2315	...	...	...	0055b	...	0042	...	...	│	│	...	...	...	...	0308	...	...	...
Frankfurt Flughafen ✈ a.	...	...	2206	...	...	...	...	...	...	...	│	...	0023	...	...	│	│	...	...	...	...	0330	...	...	...
Mainz Hbf a.	...	...	│	...	...	...	...	...	...	...	│	...	...	...	...	│	│	...	...	...	...	0406	...	...	...
Koblenz Hbf a.	...	...	⊖	...	...	...	...	...	...	...	│	...	...	...	...	│	0446s	...	...	...	...	0501	...	...	...
Bonn Hbf a.	...	...	│	...	...	...	...	...	...	...	│	...	...	...	...	│	0519s	...	...	...	...	0535	...	...	...
Köln Hbf a.	...	...	2309	...	...	...	...	...	...	...	│	...	...	...	...	│	0542s	...	...	...	...	0605	...	...	...
Düsseldorf Hbf a.	...	...	2335	...	...	...	...	...	...	...	│	...	...	...	...	│	0608s	...	...	...	...	0631	...	...	...
Duisburg Hbf a.	...	...	2352	...	...	...	...	...	...	...	│	...	...	...	...	│	0628s	...	...	...	...	0644	...	...	...
Arnhem ⊙ a.	...	...	│	...	...	...	...	...	...	...	│	...	...	...	...	│	0753s	...	...	...	...	│	...	...	...
Utrecht Centraal a.	...	...	│	...	...	...	...	...	...	...	│	...	...	...	...	│	0828s	...	...	...	...	│	...	...	...
Amsterdam Centraal a.	...	...	│	...	...	...	...	...	...	...	│	...	...	...	...	│	0903	...	...	...	...	│	...	...	...
Essen Hbf a.	...	...	0005	...	...	...	...	...	...	...	│	...	...	...	...	│	...	...	...	...	...	0657	...	...	...
Dortmund Hbf a.	...	...	0028	...	...	...	...	...	...	...	│	...	...	...	...	│	...	...	...	...	...	0721	...	...	...
Hannover Hbf a.	...	...	...	...	...	...	...	...	...	...	│	...	...	...	...	0556s	...	...	...	...	...	│	...	...	...
Berlin Hauptbahnhof a.	...	...	...	...	...	...	...	...	...	...	0718	...	...	...	...	│	...	...	...	...	...	│	...	...	...
Bremen Hbf a.	...	...	...	...	...	...	...	...	...	...	...	...	...	...	...	│	...	...	...	...	...	0914	...	...	...
Hamburg Hbf a.	...	...	...	...	...	...	...	...	...	...	...	...	...	...	...	0820	...	...	...	...	...	1012	...	...	...
København H. a.	...	...	...	...	...	...	...	...	...	...	...	...	...	...	...	...	...	...	...	...	...	...	...	...	...

A – *City Night Line* PEGASUS – 🛏 1, 2 cl., 🛏 1, 2 cl. (T4), ▬ 2 cl. (4, 6 berth), [2] (reclining) and ✕ (Brig - Spiez ⑥ Dec 26 - Apr. 10 -) Zürich - Basel - Mannheim - Amsterdam. [R] Special fares apply.

C – *City Night Line* SIRIUS – 🛏 1, 2 cl., 🛏 1, 2 cl. (T4), ▬ 2 cl. (4, 6 berth), [2] (reclining) and ✕ Zürich - Basel - Berlin [R] Special fares apply. Conveys *City Night Line* **459** CANOPUS Zürich - Dresden - Praha, see Table **75**.

G – [12] and ✕ Chur - Basel - Köln - Dortmund (- Hamburg ⑧ **e**).

H – [12] and ✕ Chur - Basel - Köln - Dortmund - Hamburg.

J – *City Night Line* AURORA – 🛏 1, 2 cl., ▬ 2 cl. (4, 6 berth), [2] (reclining) and ✕ Basel (**472**) - Fulda (**482**) - København. [R] Special fares apply.

K – *City Night Line* KOMET – 🛏 1, 2 cl., 🛏 1, 2 cl. (T4), ▬ 2 cl. (4, 6 berth), [2] (reclining) and ✕ (Brig - Spiez ⑥ Dec 26 - Apr. 10 -) Zürich - Basel - Mannheim - Hannover - Hamburg. [R] Special fares apply.

R – ④⑤⑦ (also Apr. 5, May 24; not Dec. 24, 25, 31, Apr. 2, 4, May 23).

T – Mar. 26 - Nov. 7.

W – ①–⑤ (not Dec. 25, Jan. 1, 6, Apr. 5).

X – ⑥⑦ (also Dec. 25, Jan. 1, 6, Apr. 5).

b – Frankfurt (Main) **Süd**.

c – ①–⑥.

d – Note train calls in following order: Mannheim - Frankfurt Flughafen ✈ - Frankfurt (Main) Hbf.

e – ⑧ (not Dec. 24, 25, 31, Apr. 2, 4, May 23).

f – Change trains at Bern.

g – ⑥ (also Dec. 24, 25, 31, Apr. 2, 4, May 23).

h – Via Wuppertal, Hagen.

j – ⑤⑦ (also Dec. 23, 30, Apr. 1, 5, May 12, 24; not Dec. 25, Jan. 1, Apr. 2, 4, May 14, 23).

k – Depart 0557 on ⑦ (also holidays).

n – 2204 on ⑥ (also Dec. 24, 25, 31, Apr. 2, 4, May 23).

p – Not Dec. 24, 31.

r – ⑥ Dec 26 - Apr. 10, Train **1178**. Note train calls in following order: Brig - Spiez - Zürich - Basel.

s – Stops to set down only.

u – Stops to pick up only.

v – Not Dec. 24, 31, Apr. 4, May 4, 23.

⊕ – **ETR 470**. Supplement payable for international journeys. *IC* supplement payable for internal journeys within Italy.

⊗ – **ETR 610**. Supplement payable for international journeys. *IC* supplement payable for internal journeys within Italy.

★ – Connections at Basel are not guaranteed.

⊖ – Via Köln - Frankfurt high speed line.

§ – Ticket point is **Iselle**.

⚡ – Supplement payable.

⊙ – 🏛 is at Emmerich.

¶ – From Locarno (Table **550**).

For Table 74 see page 83

MÜNCHEN - ZÜRICH - BERN - GENÈVE 75

train type	*EC*	*ICN*	*IC*	*EC*	*ICN*	*IC*	*EC*	*IC*	*IR*	*EC*	*IC*
train number	**196**	**522**	**722**	**194**	**1532**	**732**	**192**	**842**	**2542**	**190**	**846**
notes	**Z**	🍷	✕	**Z**	🍷	🍷	**Z**			**Z**	
München Hbf d.	0713	...	...	1234	...	...	1634	...	...	1834	...
Buchloe d.	0758	...	...	1318	...	...	1717	...	...	1918	...
Memmingen d.	│	...	...	1346	...	...	1746	...	...	1946	...
Kempten Hbf d.	0843	...	...	│	...	...	│	...	...	│	...
Lindau 🏛 d.	0954	...	...	1454	...	...	1855	...	...	2055	...
Bregenz 🏛 d.	1006	...	...	1506	...	...	1906	...	...	2106	...
St Margrethen 🏛 a.	1018	...	...	1518	...	...	1918	...	...	2118	...
St Gallen a.	1041	...	...	1541	...	...	1941	...	...	2141	...
Winterthur a.	1117	...	...	1617	...	...	2017	...	...	2217	...
Zürich Flughafen ✈ a.	1132	...	...	1632	...	...	2032	...	...	2232	...
Zürich HB a.	1144	1204	1232	1644	1704	1732	2044	2100	...	2244	2300
Bern a.	...	│	1329	...	│	1829	...	2157	2204	...	0002
Lausanne a.	...	│	1440	...	1915	1940	...	...	2315	...	...
Genève a.	...	1446	1515	...	...	2015	...	...	0004	...	...
Genève Aéroport ✈ a.		1455	1524	...	...	2024	...	...	...	...	...

train type	*IC*	*EC*	*IR*	*IC*	*EC*	*IR*	*IC*	*EC*	*IC*	*IC*	*EC*
train number	**809**	**191**	**2515**	**815**	**193**	**2523**	**823**	**195**	**731**	**835**	**197**
notes	🍷	**Z**		✕	**Z**		✕	**Z**	🍷	🍷	**Z**
Genève Aéroport ✈ d.	...	...	...	...	...	1001	...	...	1436	...	...
Genève d.	...	...	0610	...	...	1010	...	...	1445	...	...
Lausanne d.	...	...	0645	...	...	1045	...	...	1520	...	...
Bern d.	0602	...	0756	0802	...	1156	1202	...	1632	1702	...
Zürich HB d.	0702	0716	...	0858	0916	...	1258	1316	1728	1758	1816
Zürich Flughafen ✈ d.	...	0728	...	...	0928	...	...	1328	...	...	1828
Winterthur d.	...	0742	...	...	0942	...	...	1342	...	...	1842
St Gallen d.	...	0819	...	...	1019	...	...	1419	...	...	1919
St Margrethen 🏛 d.	...	0842	...	...	1042	...	...	1442	...	...	1942
Bregenz 🏛 d.	...	0855	...	...	1055	...	...	1455	...	...	1955
Lindau 🏛 a.	...	0905	...	...	1105	...	...	1505	...	...	2005
Kempten Hbf a.	...	│	...	...	│	...	...	│	...	...	2120
Memmingen a.	...	1012	...	...	1212	...	...	1612	...	...	│
Buchloe a.	...	1041	...	...	1241	...	...	1641	...	...	2204
München Hbf a.	...	1128	...	...	1328	...	...	1728	...	...	2245

Z – [12] and ✕ München - Zürich and v.v.

82 GENÈVE, BASEL, ZÜRICH and LUZERN - MILANO - VENEZIA and ROMA

train type	EC	AV	ESc	IR	EC	IR	EC	AV	EC⚡	ESc	ESc		IC	IC	EC	AV	ESc		IR	EC	ESc	AV	ESc	
train number	35	9511	9791	1415	51	2159	13	9513	143 144	9811	9715		959	810	37	9515	9813		2165	15	9815	9517	9723	
notes	R 🍷 ⊗	✕⚡ R	R 🍷 A		R 🍷 ⊗		R 🍷 ⊕	✕⚡ R	R 🍷	R ✕ ⚡	R ✕ ⚡			🍷	R 🍷 ⊗	R ✕ ⚡	R ✕ ⚡			R 🍷 ⊕	R ✕ ⚡	R ✕ ⚡	R 🍷 ⚡	
Genève Aéroport ✈ d.	...	...	...	0547	...	...	...	...	...	...	...	...	...	...	...	...	...	...	...	...	...	...	...	...
Genève d.	0545	...	...	0556	...	...	...	...	...	...	...	...	...	...	0742	...	...	...	...	...	...	...	...	...
Lausanne d.	0620	...	...	0645	...	...	...	...	...	...	...	...	...	...	0820	...	...	...	...	...	...	...	...	...
Sion d.	0714	...	...	0754	...	...	...	...	...	...	...	...	...	...	0914	...	...	...	...	...	...	...	...	...
Zürich HB d.	│	...	...	│	...	...	0709	...	...	...	...	...	...	...	│	...	...	...	...	0909	...	...	...	...
Basel SBB d.	│	...	...	│	0628	...	│	...	...	...	...	...	0701	...	│	...	...	...	0803	│	...	...	...	...
Olten d.	│	...	...	│	0700	...	│	...	...	...	...	...	0729	...	│	...	...	...	0830	│	...	...	...	...
Bern d.	│	...	...	│	0735	...	│	...	...	...	...	...	0756	0807	│	...	...	...	│	│	...	...	...	...
Spiez d.	│	...	...	│	0805	...	│	...	...	...	...	...	...	0836	│	...	...	...	│	│	...	...	...	...
Luzern d.	│	...	...	│	│	0718	│	...	...	...	...	...	...	│	│	...	...	...	0918	│	...	...	...	...
Arth-Goldau d.	│	...	...	│	│	0745	0750	...	...	...	...	...	...	│	│	...	...	...	0945	0950	...	...	...	...
Bellinzona d.	│	...	...	│	│	...	0925	...	...	...	...	...	...	│	│	...	...	...	...	1125	...	...	...	...
Lugano d.	│	...	...	│	│	...	0948	...	...	...	...	...	...	│	│	...	...	...	...	1148	...	...	...	...
Chiasso 🏛 d.	│	...	...	│	│	...	1010	...	...	...	...	...	...	│	│	...	...	...	...	1210	...	...	...	...
Como San Giovanni a.	│	...	...	│	│	...	1014	...	...	...	...	...	...	│	│	...	...	...	...	1214	...	...	...	...
Visp d.	│	...	...	0824	0832	...	│	...	...	...	...	...	...	0903	│	...	...	...	...	│	...	...	...	...
Brig d.	0744	...	...	0830	0844	...	│	...	...	...	...	...	...	0911	0944	...	...	...	...	│	...	...	...	...
Domodossola 🏛 ¶ a.	0812	...	...	...	0912	...	│	...	...	...	...	...	...	...	1012	...	...	...	...	│	...	...	...	...
Stresa a.	0838	...	...	...	│	...	│	...	...	...	...	...	...	...	│	...	...	...	...	│	...	...	...	...
Arona a.	│	...	...	...	│	...	│	...	...	...	...	...	...	...	│	...	...	...	...	│	...	...	...	...
Milano Centrale a.	0935	...	...	...	1035	...	1050	...	...	...	...	...	...	...	1135	...	...	...	...	1250	...	...	...	...
Milano Centrale d.	...	1015	1035	...	...	...	...	1115	1110	1135	1135	...	...	...	1205	1215	1235	...	...	...	1335	1315	1335	...
Genova Piazza Principe a.	...	│	│	...	...	...	...	│	1242	│	│	...	...	...	│	│	│	...	...	...	│	│	│	...
Ventimiglia 🏛 a.	...	│	│	...	...	...	...	│	1507	│	│	...	...	...	│	│	│	...	...	...	│	│	│	...
Nice Ville a.	...	│	│	...	...	...	...	│	1610	│	│	...	...	...	│	│	│	...	...	...	│	│	│	...
Verona Porta Nuova a.	...	│	1157	...	...	...	...	│	...	│	1257	...	...	...	1327	│	│	...	...	...	│	│	1457	...
Venezia Santa Lucia a.	...	│	1310	...	...	...	...	│	...	│	1410	...	...	...	1440	│	│	...	...	...	│	│	1610	...
Bologna Centrale a.	...	1120	...	...	...	...	...	1220	...	1342	...	...	...	...	...	1320	1442	...	...	...	1542	1420	...	...
Rimini a.	...	│	...	...	...	...	...	│	...	1445	...	...	...	...	...	│	1556	...	...	...	1645	│	...	...
Ancona a.	...	│	...	...	...	...	...	│	...	1538	...	...	...	...	...	│	1655	...	...	...	1738	│	...	...
Pescara Centrale a.	...	│	...	...	...	...	...	│	...	1649	...	...	...	...	...	│	...	...	...	...	1849	│	...	...
Bari Centrale a.	...	│	...	...	...	...	...	│	...	1935	...	...	...	...	...	│	...	...	...	...	2135	│	...	...
Brindisi a.	...	│	...	...	...	...	...	│	...	2040	...	...	...	...	...	│	...	...	...	...	...	│	...	...
Lecce a.	...	│	...	...	...	...	...	│	...	2104	...	...	...	...	...	│	...	...	...	...	...	│	...	...
Firenze SMN a.	...	1200	...	...	...	...	...	1300	...	...	...	...	...	...	...	1400	...	...	...	...	...	1500	...	...
Roma Termini a.	...	1345	...	...	...	...	...	1445	...	...	...	...	...	...	...	1545	...	...	...	...	...	1645	...	...
Napoli Centrale a.	...	1510	...	...	...	...	...	1610	...	...	...	...	...	...	...	1710	...	...	...	...	...	1810	...	...

train type	IR	EC	ESc	ESc	EC⚡	AV	IR	EC	ICp	IR	EC	AV	ESc	ESc	EC	IC	ESc	AV	IR	EC	ICp	ESc	AV	E
train number	2169	17	9819	9729	159 160	9523	1427	57	659	2173	19	9529	9823	9739	39	661	9741	9531	2177	21	663	9745	9533	923
notes		R 🍷 ⊕	R ✕ ⚡	R ✕ ⚡	R 🍷	R ✕ f⚡		R 🍷 ⊗	R 🍷⚡		R 🍷 ⊕	R ✕ ⚡	R ✕ ⚡	R 🍷 ⚡	R 🍷 ⊗	R 🍷⚡	R 🍷 ⚡	R ✕ ⚡		R 🍷 ⊕	R 🍷⚡	R 🍷	R ✕ ⚡	T
Genève Aéroport ✈ d.	...	...	...	...	...	...	1147	...	...	...	...	...	...	...	...	...	...	...	...	...	...	...	...	...
Genève d.	...	...	...	...	...	...	1156	...	...	...	...	...	...	...	1342	...	...	...	...	...	...	...	...	...
Lausanne d.	...	...	...	...	...	...	1245	...	...	...	...	...	...	...	1420	...	...	...	...	...	...	...	...	...
Sion d.	...	...	...	...	...	...	1354	...	...	...	...	...	...	...	1514	...	...	...	...	...	...	...	...	...
Zürich HB d.	...	1109	...	...	...	...	│	...	...	...	1309	...	...	...	│	...	...	...	...	1509	...	...	...	...
Basel SBB d.	1003	│	...	...	...	...	│	1228	...	1203	│	...	...	...	│	...	...	...	1403	│	...	...	...	...
Olten d.	1031	│	...	...	...	...	│	1300	...	1231	│	...	...	...	│	...	...	...	1431	│	...	...	...	...
Bern d.	│	│	...	...	...	...	│	1335	...	│	│	...	...	...	│	...	...	...	│	│	...	...	...	...
Spiez d.	│	│	...	...	...	...	│	1405	...	│	│	...	...	...	│	...	...	...	│	│	...	...	...	...
Luzern d.	1118	│	...	...	...	...	│	│	...	1318	│	...	...	...	│	...	...	...	1518	│	...	...	...	...
Arth-Goldau d.	1145	1150	...	...	...	...	│	│	...	1345	1350	...	...	...	│	...	...	...	1545	1550	...	...	...	...
Bellinzona d.	...	1325	...	...	...	...	│	│	...	...	1525	...	...	...	│	...	...	...	▬	1725	...	...	...	...
Lugano d.	...	1348	...	...	...	...	│	│	...	...	1548	...	...	...	│	...	...	...	...	1748	...	...	...	...
Chiasso 🏛 d.	...	1410	...	...	...	...	│	│	...	...	1610	...	...	...	│	...	...	...	...	1810	...	...	...	...
Como San Giovanni a.	...	1414	...	...	...	...	│	│	...	...	1614	...	...	...	│	...	...	...	...	1814	...	...	...	...
Visp d.	...	│	...	...	...	...	1424	1432	...	...	│	...	...	...	│	...	...	...	...	│	...	...	...	...
Brig d.	...	│	...	...	...	...	1430	1444	...	...	│	...	...	...	1544	...	...	...	...	│	...	...	...	...
Domodossola 🏛 ¶ a.	...	│	...	...	...	...	...	1512	...	...	│	...	...	...	1612	...	...	...	...	│	...	...	...	...
Stresa a.	...	│	...	...	...	...	...	│	...	...	│	...	...	...	1638	...	...	...	...	│	...	...	...	...
Arona a.	...	│	...	...	...	...	...	│	...	...	│	...	...	...	│	...	...	...	...	│	...	...	...	...
Milano Centrale a.	...	1450	...	...	...	...	...	1640	...	...	1650	...	...	...	1735	...	...	...	...	1850	...	...	...	...
																			ESc 9825 R ✕ ⚡					
Milano Centrale d.	...	...	1535	1505	1510	1515	...	...	1700	...	...	1715	1735	1735	...	1800	1805	1815	1835	...	1905	1905	1915	2040
Genova Piazza Principe a.	...	...	│	│	1642	│	...	...	1842	...	...	│	│	│	...	1945	│	│	│	...	2042	│	│	│
Ventimiglia 🏛 a.	...	...	│	│	1907	│	...	...	2107	...	...	│	│	│	...	*2316*	│	│	│	...	*2316*	│	│	│
Nice Ville a.	...	...	│	│	2010	│	...	...	*0021*	...	...	│	│	│	...	...	│	│	│	...	...	│	│	│
Verona Porta Nuova a.	...	...	│	1627	...	│	...	...	...	...	...	│	│	1855	...	...	1927	│	│	...	...	2027	│	│
Venezia Santa Lucia a.	...	...	│	1740	...	│	...	...	...	...	...	│	│	2002	...	...	2028t	│	│	...	...	2140	│	│
Bologna Centrale a.	...	...	1742	...	...	1620	...	...	...	...	...	1820	1942	...	...	...	...	1920	2042	...	...	...	2020	2314
Rimini a.	...	...	1845	...	...	│	...	...	...	...	...	│	2056	...	...	...	...	│	2156	...	...	...	│	0027
Ancona a.	...	...	1938	...	...	│	...	...	...	...	...	│	2155	...	...	...	...	│	2255	...	...	...	│	0137
Pescara Centrale a.	...	...	2049	...	...	│	...	...	...	...	...	│	2330	...	...	...	...	│	...	...	...	...	│	0257
Bari Centrale a.	...	...	2335	...	...	│	...	...	...	...	...	│	...	...	...	...	...	│	...	...	...	...	│	0618
Brindisi a.	...	...	...	...	...	│	...	...	...	...	...	│	...	...	...	...	...	│	...	...	...	...	│	0738
Lecce a.	...	...	...	...	...	│	...	...	...	...	...	│	...	...	...	...	...	│	...	...	...	...	│	0810
Firenze SMN a.	...	...	...	...	...	1700	...	...	...	...	...	1900	...	...	...	...	...	2000	...	...	...	...	2100	...
Roma Termini a.	...	...	...	...	...	1845	...	...	...	...	...	2045	...	...	...	...	...	2145	...	...	...	...	2245	...
Napoli Centrale a.	...	...	...	...	...	2010	...	...	...	...	...	2210	...	...	...	...	...	...	...	...	...	...	...	...

A – ⑥⑦ (also Dec. 25, Jan. 1, 6, Apr. 5).
f – To Salerno.
r – Firenze **Rifredi**.

t – Venezia **Mestre**.
⚡ – Supplement payable.
¶ – Ticket point is **Iselle**.

⊕ – **ETR 470**. Supplement payable for international journeys. *IC* supplement payable for internal journeys within Italy.
⊗ – **ETR 610**. Supplement payable for international journeys. *IC* supplement payable for internal journeys within Italy.

GENÈVE, BASEL, ZÜRICH and LUZERN - MILANO - VENEZIA and ROMA 82

train type		*IR*	*EC*	*ESc*	*ICp*	*ESc*		*IR*	*EC*				*ICE*	*IC*	*EC*	*ICN*	*IR*	*EC*	*E*					
train number		**2181**	**23**	**9753**	**667**	**9537**		**1439**	**59**	**2199**			**277**	**836**	**41**	**785**	**2187**	**25**	**1911**					
notes			[R]🍸 ⊕	[R]🍴 ⚡	[R]⚡ Ⓑ	[R]🍴 Ⓑ⚡			[R]🍸 ⊗					🍸	[R]🍸 ⊗	[R]⚡ J		[R]🍸 ⊕	K					
Genève Aéroport ✈ d.	...	...	...	...	...	...	...	1647	...	...	...	...	...	...	...	...	...	...	...	...	...	...	...	...
Genève d.	...	...	...	...	...	...	...	1656	...	...	...	...	...	...	1842	...	...	...	...	...	...	...	...	...
Lausanne d.	...	...	...	...	...	...	...	1745	...	...	...	...	...	...	1917	...	...	...	...	...	...	...	...	...
Sion d.	...	...	...	...	...	...	...	1854	...	...	...	...	...	...	2014	...	...	...	...	...	...	...	...	...
Zürich HB d.	...	...	1709	...	...	...	...	|	...	...	...	...	...	1800	|	...	...	1909	...	...	...	...	...	...
Basel SBB d.	...	1603	|	...	...	...	...	|	1728	...	...	...	1801	|	|	...	1803	|	...	...	...	...	...	...
Olten d.	...	1631	|	...	...	...	...	|	1800	...	...	...	1829	|	|	...	1836	|	...	...	...	...	...	...
Bern d.	...	|	|	...	...	...	...	|	1835	...	...	...	1856	1907	|	...	|	|	...	...	...	...	...	...
Spiez d.	...	|	|	...	...	...	...	|	1905	...	...	...	...	1936	|	...	|	|	...	...	...	...	...	...
Luzern d.	...	1718	|	...	...	...	...	|	|	...	...	...	...	|	|	...	1918	|	...	...	...	...	...	...
Arth-Goldau d.	...	1745	1750	...	...	...	...	|	|	...	...	...	...	|	|	...	1945	1950	...	...	...	...	...	...
Bellinzona d.	...	...	1925	...	...	...	...	|	|	...	...	...	...	|	|	...	...	2125	...	...	...	...	...	...
Lugano d.	...	...	1948	...	...	...	...	|	|	...	...	...	...	|	|	...	...	2148	...	...	...	...	...	...
Chiasso 🏛 d.	...	...	2010	...	...	...	...	|	|	...	...	...	...	|	|	...	...	2210	...	...	...	...	...	...
Como San Giovanni a.	...	...	2014	...	...	...	...	|	|	...	...	...	...	|	|	...	...	2214	...	...	...	...	...	...
Visp d.	...	...	|	...	...	...	...	1924	1932	...	...	...	...	2003	|	...	...	|	...	...	...	...	...	...
Brig d.	...	...	|	...	...	...	...	1930	1944	...	...	...	...	2011	2044	...	...	|	...	...	...	...	...	...
Domodossola 🏛 ¶ a.	...	...	|	...	...	...	...	...	2012	...	...	...	...	...	2112	...	...	|	...	...	...	...	...	...
Stresa a.	...	...	|	...	...	...	...	...	|	...	...	...	...	...	|	...	...	|	...	...	...	...	...	...
Arona a.	...	...	|	...	...	...	...	...	|	...	...	...	...	...	|	...	...	|	...	...	...	...	...	...
Milano Centrale a.	...	...	2050	...	...	...	...	...	2135	...	...	...	...	...	2235	...	...	2250	...	...	...	...	...	...
Milano Centrale d.	...	...	...	2105	2105	2145	...	...	...	2225	2230	...	...	...	...	2300	...	...	2320	...	...	...	...	...
Genova Piazza Principe a.	...	...	...	|	2242	|	...	...	...	0020	|	...	...	...	...	|	...	...	|	...	...	...	...	...
Ventimiglia 🏛 a.	...	...	...	|	0107	|	...	...	...	...	|	...	...	...	...	|	...	...	|	...	...	...	...	...
Nice Ville a.	...	...	...	|	...	|	...	...	...	...	|	...	...	...	...	|	...	...	|	...	...	...	...	...
Verona Porta Nuova a.	...	...	...	2244	...	|	...	...	...	...	0020	...	...	...	...	|	...	...	|	...	...	...	...	...
Venezia Santa Lucia a.	...	...	...	2356q	...	|	...	...	...	...	...	...	...	...	...	|	...	...	|	...	...	...	...	...
Bologna Centrale a.	...	...	...	...	...	2250	...	...	...	...	...	...	...	...	...	0124	...	...	|	...	...	...	...	...
Rimini a.	...	...	...	...	...	...	...	...	...	...	...	...	...	...	...	0235	...	...	|	...	...	...	...	...
Ancona a.	...	...	...	...	...	...	...	...	...	...	...	...	...	...	...	0333	...	...	|	...	...	...	...	...
Pescara Centrale a.	...	...	...	...	...	...	...	...	...	...	...	...	...	...	...	0459	...	...	|	...	...	...	...	...
Bari Centrale a.	...	...	...	...	...	...	...	...	...	...	...	...	...	...	...	0826	...	...	|	...	...	...	...	...
Brindisi a.	...	...	...	...	...	...	...	...	...	...	...	...	...	...	...	*1104*	...	...	|	...	...	...	...	...
Lecce a.	...	...	...	...	...	...	...	...	...	...	...	...	...	...	...	*1205*	...	...	|	...	...	...	...	...
Firenze SMN a.	...	...	...	...	...	...	...	...	...	...	...	...	...	...	...	...	...	...	|	...	...	...	...	...
Roma Termini a.	...	...	...	...	...	...	...	...	...	...	...	...	...	...	...	...	...	...	0723t	...	...	...	...	...
Napoli Centrale a.	...	...	...	...	...	...	...	...	...	...	...	...	...	...	...	...	...	...	1012	...	...	...	...	...

train type	*EC*	*IR*	*EC*	*ICN*	*E*			*AV*⚡	*IC*	*ICN*	*AV*⚡	*ICp*	*ESc*	*EC*	*IR*	*E*	*AV*⚡	*AV*	*ESc*	*ICp*	*EC*	*IR*	*EC*	*IR*
train number	**12**	**2170**	**50**	**780**	**1910**	**2710**	**2178**	**9500**	**1072**	**784**	**9502**	**651**	**9702**	**14**	**2174**	**926**	**9604**	**9506**	**9710**	**656**	**16**	**2178**	**52**	**1424**
notes	[R]🍸 ⊕		[R]🍸 ⊗	[R]⚡ E	K			[R]🍴 W	🍸	[R]⚡ J	[R]🍴 W	[R]⚡ ⚒	[R]🍴 ⚡	[R]🍸 ⊕		T	[R]🍴 Y	[R]🍴 ⚡	[R]🍴 ⚡	[R] 🍸⚡	[R]🍸 ⊕		[R]🍸 ⊗	
Napoli Centrale d.	...	...	...	...	2030	...	...	...	...	...	...	...	...	...	...	...	0620	...	...	...	...	...	...	...
Roma Termini d.	...	...	...	...	2259t	...	...	...	...	...	...	...	...	...	...	...	0733t	0715	...	...	...	...	...	...
Firenze SMN d.	...	...	...	...	|	...	...	...	...	...	0700	...	...	...	...	...	|	0900	...	...	...	...	...	...
Lecce d.	...	...	...	1907	|	...	...	...	...	...	|	...	...	...	...	2205	|	|	...	...	...	...	...	...
Brindisi d.	...	...	...	1932	|	...	...	...	...	...	|	...	...	...	...	2236	|	|	...	...	...	...	...	...
Bari Centrale d.	...	...	...	2100	|	...	...	...	...	2259	|	...	...	...	...	2359	|	|	...	...	...	...	...	...
Pescara Centrale d.	...	...	...	0029	|	...	...	...	...	0204	|	...	...	...	...	0321	|	|	...	...	...	...	...	...
Ancona d.	...	...	...	0158	|	...	...	...	...	0330	|	...	...	...	...	0445	|	|	...	...	...	...	...	...
Rimini d.	...	...	...	0256	|	...	...	...	...	0427	|	...	...	...	...	0541	|	|	...	...	...	...	...	...
Bologna Centrale d.	...	...	...	0412	|	...	...	0640	...	0548	0740	...	...	...	...	0702	|	0940	...	...	...	...	...	...
Venezia Santa Lucia d.	...	...	...	|	|	...	...	|	...	|	|	...	0620	...	...	|	|	|	0832q	...	...	...	...	...
Verona Porta Nuova d.	...	...	...	|	|	0540	...	|	...	|	|	...	0732	...	...	|	|	|	0932	...	...	...	...	...
Nice Ville d.	...	...	...	|	|	|	...	|	...	|	|	...	|	...	...	|	|	|	|	*0525j*	...	...	...	...
Ventimiglia 🏛 d.	...	...	...	|	|	|	...	|	...	|	|	0445	|	...	...	|	|	|	|	*0633*	...	...	...	...
Genova Piazza Principe d.	...	...	...	|	|	|	0545	|	...	|	|	0719	|	...	...	|	|	|	|	0910	...	...	...	...
Milano Centrale a.	...	...	...	0705	0725	0735	0740	0745	...	0820	0845	0855	0855	...	...	0920	1030	1045	1055	1055	...	...	...	...
				▬				*EC* **32** [R]🍸 ⊗																
Milano Centrale d.	0710	...	0725	...	...	...	...	0825	...	...	...	...	...	0910	...	...	...	...	...	...	1110	...	1120	...
Arona d.	|	...	|	...	...	...	...	|	...	...	...	...	...	|	...	...	...	...	...	...	|	...	|	...
Stresa d.	|	...	|	*IR*	...	...	...	0920	...	...	...	...	...	|	...	...	...	...	...	...	|	...	1221	...
Domodossola 🏛 ¶ d.	|	...	0848	**1414**	...	...	...	0948	...	...	...	...	...	|	...	...	...	...	...	...	|	...	1248	...
Brig a.	|	...	0916	0928	...	...	...	1016	1120	...	...	...	...	|	...	...	...	...	...	...	|	...	1316	1328
Visp a.	|	...	0926	0934	...	...	...	|	1126	...	...	...	...	|	...	...	...	...	...	...	|	...	1326	1334
Como San Giovanni d.	0745	...	|	|	...	...	...	|	|	...	...	...	...	0945	...	...	...	...	...	...	1145	...	|	|
Chiasso 🏛 a.	0750	...	|	|	...	...	...	|	|	...	...	...	...	0950	...	...	...	...	...	...	1150	...	|	|
Lugano a.	0810	...	|	|	...	...	...	|	|	...	...	...	...	1010	...	...	...	...	...	...	1210	...	|	|
Bellinzona a.	0834	...	|	|	...	...	...	|	|	...	...	...	...	1034	...	...	...	...	...	...	1234	...	|	|
Arth-Goldau a.	1009	1014	|	|	...	...	...	|	|	...	...	...	...	1209	1214	...	...	...	...	...	1409	1414	|	|
Luzern a.	|	1041	|	|	...	...	...	|	|	...	...	...	...	|	1241	...	...	...	...	...	|	1441	|	|
Spiez a.	|	...	0953	|	...	...	...	|	1153	...	...	...	...	|	|	...	...	...	...	...	|	...	1353	|
Bern a.	|	...	1023	|	...	...	...	|	1223	...	...	...	...	|	|	...	...	...	...	...	|	...	1423	|
Olten a.	|	...	1100	|	...	...	...	|	1300	...	...	...	...	|	1328	...	...	...	...	...	|	...	1500	|
Basel SBB a.	|	...	1132	|	...	...	...	|	1332	...	...	...	...	|	1353	...	...	...	...	...	|	...	1532	|
Zürich HB a.	1051	...	...	|	...	...	...	|	...	...	...	...	...	1251	...	...	...	...	...	...	1451	...	...	|
Sion a.	...	...	...	1004	...	...	...	1049	...	...	...	...	...	...	...	...	...	...	...	...	...	...	...	1404
Lausanne a.	...	...	...	1115	...	...	...	1140	...	...	...	...	...	...	...	...	...	...	...	...	...	...	...	1515
Genève a.	...	...	...	1204	...	...	...	1218	...	...	...	...	...	...	...	...	...	...	...	...	...	...	...	1604
Genève Aéroport ✈ a.	...	...	...	1213	...	...	...	...	...	...	...	...	...	...	...	...	...	...	...	...	...	...	...	1613

E – FRECCIA SALENTINA – 🛏 1, 2 cl., 🛏 1, 2 cl. (T2), ▬ 2 cl. (4, 6 berth) and [12] Milano - Lecce.

J – FRECCIA DEL LEVANTE – 🛏 1, 2 cl., 🛏 1, 2 cl. (T2), ▬ 2 cl. and [12] Milano - Bari.

K – 🛏 1, 2 cl. (Excelsior), 🛏 1, 2 cl. (T2), 🛏 1, 2 cl., ▬ 2 cl. (4, 6 berth) and [12] Milano - Napoli.

T – 🛏 1, 2 cl. (T2), ▬ 2 cl. (4, 6 berth) and [2] Milano - Lecce.

W – ①–⑥ (not Dec. 25, 26, Jan. 1, 6, Apr. 5, May 1).

Y – ①–⑤ (not Dec. 25, Jan. 1, 6, Apr. 5).

j – ①–⑤ (not Dec. 25, Jan. 1, Apr. 5). Change at Ventimiglia and Genova.

q – Venezia **Mestre**.

t – Roma **Tiburtina**.

⚡ – Supplement payable.

¶ – Ticket point is **Iselle**.

⊕ – **ETR 470**. Supplement payable for international journeys. *IC* supplement payable for internal journeys within Italy.

⊗ – **ETR 610**. Supplement payable for international journeys. *IC* supplement payable for internal journeys within Italy.

82 ROMA, VENEZIA - MILANO - LUZERN, ZÜRICH, BASEL and GENÈVE

train type / train number / notes	ESc 9806 R Y ⚡	ESc 9712 R ✕ ⚡	AV 9508 R ✕ f⚡	AV⚡ 9610 R ✕ A	IC 1080 Y	ESc 9792 R ✕ ⑥⑦b	AV 9512 R ✕ ⚡	ICp 657/8 R ⚡Y	EC 18 R Y ⊕	IR 2182	ESc 9810 R ✕ ⚡	ESc 9718 R ✕ ⚡	AV 9516 R ✕ f⚡	EC⚡ 139 140 Y R	EC 20 R Y ⊕	IR 2188	ESc 9816 R ✕ ⚡	ESc 9726 R ✕ ⚡	AV 9522 R ✕ ⚡	IR 2192	AV⚡ 9618 R ✕ A	EC 36 R Y ⊗	IC 1092
Napoli Centrale d.	...	...	...	...	...	...	0750	...	...	...	...	...	0950	...	...	...	...	...	1150	...	...	...	...
Roma Termini d.	...	...	0815	0900	...	...	0915	...	...	...	...	...	1115	...	...	...	...	...	1315	...	1400	...	...
Firenze SMN d.	...	...	1000	|	...	...	1100	...	...	...	...	...	1300	...	...	...	...	...	1500	...	|	...	...
Lecce d.	...	...	|	|	...	...	|	...	...	...	...	...	|	...	...	...	0700	...	|	...	|	...	...
Brindisi d.	...	...	|	|	...	...	|	...	...	...	...	...	|	...	...	...	0725	...	|	...	|	...	...
Bari Centrale d.	...	...	|	|	...	...	|	...	...	...	...	...	|	...	...	...	0829	...	|	...	|	...	...
Pescara Centrale d.	...	...	|	|	...	...	|	...	...	...	0740	...	|	...	...	...	1114	...	|	...	|	...	...
Ancona d.	0710	...	|	|	...	...	|	...	...	...	0910	...	|	...	...	...	1227	...	|	...	|	...	...
Rimini d.	0808	...	|	|	...	...	|	...	...	...	1008	...	|	...	...	...	1319	...	|	...	|	...	...
Bologna Centrale d.	0918	...	1040	|	...	...	1140	...	...	...	1118	...	1340	...	...	...	1418	...	1540	...	|	...	...
Venezia Santa Lucia d.	|	0858	|	|	...	0950	|	...	...	...	|	1150	|	...	...	...	|	1350	|	...	|	...	...
Verona Porta Nuova d.	|	1005	|	|	...	1102	|	...	...	...	|	1302	|	...	...	...	|	1502	|	...	|	...	...
Nice Ville d.	|	|	|	|	...	|	|	*0751j*	...	...	|	|	|	0949	...	...	|	|	|	...	|	...	...
Ventimiglia 🛃 d.	|	|	|	|	...	|	|	0858	...	...	|	|	|	1058	...	...	|	|	|	...	|	...	...
Genova Piazza Principe d.	|	|	|	|	...	|	|	1119	...	...	|	|	|	1319	...	...	|	|	|	...	|	...	...
Milano Centrale a.	1125	1125	1145	1159	...	1225	1245	1255	...	...	1325	1425	1445	1450	...	...	1625	1625	1645	...	1659	...	...
				EC 34 R Y ⊗															EC 22 R Y ⊕				
Milano Centrale d.	...	...	...	1225	...	...	...	...	1310	...	...	...	...	...	1510	...	...	...	1710	...	...	1720	...
Arona d.	...	...	...	|	...	...	...	...	|	...	...	...	...	...	|	...	...	...	|	...	...	|	...
Stresa d.	...	...	...	1320	...	...	...	...	|	...	...	...	...	...	|	...	...	...	|	...	...	1821	...
Domodossola 🛃 ¶ d.	...	...	...	1348	...	...	...	...	|	...	...	...	...	...	|	...	...	...	|	...	...	1848	...
Brig a.	...	...	...	1416	1520	...	...	...	|	...	...	...	...	...	|	...	...	...	|	...	...	1916	1920
Visp a.	...	...	...	|	1526	...	...	...	|	...	...	...	...	...	|	...	...	...	|	...	...	|	1926
Como San Giovanni d.	...	...	...	|	|	...	...	...	1345	...	...	...	...	...	1545	...	...	...	1745	...	...	|	|
Chiasso 🛃 a.	...	...	...	|	|	...	...	...	1350	...	...	...	...	...	1550	...	...	...	1750	...	...	|	|
Lugano a.	...	...	...	|	|	...	...	...	1410	...	...	...	...	...	1610	...	...	...	1810	...	...	|	|
Bellinzona a.	...	...	...	|	|	...	...	...	1434	...	...	...	...	...	1634	...	...	...	1834	...	...	|	|
Arth-Goldau a.	...	...	...	|	|	...	...	...	1609	1614	...	...	...	...	1809	1814	...	...	2009	2014	...	|	|
Luzern a.	...	...	...	|	|	...	...	...	|	1641	...	...	...	...	|	1841	...	...	|	2041	...	|	|
Spiez a.	...	...	...	|	1553	...	...	...	|	...	...	...	...	...	|	...	...	...	|	...	...	|	1953
Bern a.	...	...	...	|	1623	...	...	...	|	...	...	...	...	...	|	...	...	...	|	...	...	|	2023
Olten a.	...	...	...	|	1700	...	...	...	|	1728	...	...	...	...	|	1928	...	...	|	2128	...	|	2100
Basel SBB a.	...	...	...	|	1732	...	...	...	|	1753	...	...	...	...	|	1953	...	...	|	2153	...	|	2132
Zürich HB a.	...	...	...	|	...	...	...	...	1651	...	...	...	...	...	1851	...	...	...	2051	...	...	|	...
Sion a.	...	...	...	1449	...	...	...	...	...	...	...	...	...	...	...	...	...	...	...	...	...	1949	...
Lausanne a.	...	...	...	1540	...	...	...	...	...	...	...	...	...	...	...	...	...	...	...	...	...	2040	...
Genève a.	...	...	...	1618	...	...	...	...	...	...	...	...	...	...	...	...	...	...	...	...	...	2118	...
Genève Aéroport ✈ a.	...	...	...	...	...	...	...	...	...	...	...	...	...	...	...	...	...	...	...	...	...	...	...

train type/number / train number / notes	ESc 9818 R ✕ ⚡	AV 9524 R ✕ ⚡	ESc 9732 R ✕ ⚡	ICp 664 R Y⚡	AV⚡ 9622 R ✕ Ⓑ	EC 56 R Y ⊗	IR 1440	ESc 9820 R ✕ ⚡	AV 9526 R ✕ ⚡	ICp 693 694 R⚡	EC 24 R Y ⊕	IR 2196	AV⚡ 9626 R ✕ Ⓑ	ICp 586 R ✕ ⚡	EC 42 R Y ⊗	IC 1096
Napoli Centrale d.	...	1250	...	...	...	...	...	...	1350	...	...	...	1435	1024	...	...
Roma Termini d.	...	1415	...	...	1500	...	...	...	1515	...	...	...	1600	1244t	...	...
Firenze SMN d.	...	1600	...	...	|	...	...	...	1700	...	...	...	|	1536g	...	...
Lecce d.	...	|	...	...	|	...	...	...	|	...	...	...	|	|	...	...
Brindisi d.	...	|	...	...	|	...	...	...	|	...	...	...	|	|	...	...
Bari Centrale d.	...	|	...	...	|	...	...	...	|	...	...	...	|	|	...	...
Pescara Centrale d.	...	|	...	...	|	...	...	...	|	...	...	...	|	|	...	...
Ancona d.	1310	|	...	...	|	...	...	1410	|	...	...	...	|	|	...	...
Rimini d.	1408	|	...	...	|	...	...	1508	|	...	...	...	|	|	...	...
Bologna Centrale d.	1518	1640	...	...	|	...	...	1618	1740	...	...	...	|	1703	...	...
Venezia Santa Lucia d.	|	|	1520	...	|	...	...	|	|	...	...	...	|	|	1620	...
Verona Porta Nuova d.	|	|	1632	...	|	...	...	|	|	...	...	...	|	|	1732	...
Nice Ville d.	|	|	|	...	|	...	...	|	|	*1335j*	...	...	|	|	|	...
Ventimiglia 🛃 d.	|	|	|	...	|	...	...	|	|	1458	...	...	|	|	|	...
Genova Piazza Principe d.	|	|	|	1619	|	...	...	|	|	1719	...	...	|	|	|	...
Milano Centrale a.	1730	1745	1755	1755	1759	...	...	1825	1845	1850	...	...	1859	1905	1855	...
Milano Centrale d.	...	...	...	...	...	1825	...	...	...	...	1910	...	...	...	1920	...
Arona d.	...	...	...	...	...	|	...	...	...	...	|	...	...	...	|	...
Stresa d.	...	...	...	...	...	1921	...	...	...	...	|	...	...	...	|	...
Domodossola 🛃 ¶ d.	...	...	...	...	...	1948	...	...	...	...	|	...	...	...	2048	...
Brig a.	...	...	...	...	...	2016	2028	...	...	...	|	...	...	...	2116	2120
Visp a.	...	...	...	...	...	2026	2034	...	...	...	|	...	...	...	|	2126
Como San Giovanni d.	...	...	...	...	...	|	|	...	...	...	1945	...	...	...	|	|
Chiasso 🛃 a.	...	...	...	...	...	|	|	...	...	...	1950	...	...	...	|	|
Lugano a.	...	...	...	...	...	|	|	...	...	...	2010	...	...	...	|	|
Bellinzona a.	...	...	...	...	...	|	|	...	...	...	2034	...	...	...	|	|
Arth-Goldau a.	...	...	...	...	...	|	|	...	...	...	2209	2214	...	...	|	|
Luzern a.	...	...	...	...	...	|	|	...	...	...	|	2241	...	...	|	|
Spiez a.	...	...	...	...	...	2053	|	...	...	...	|	|	...	...	|	2153
Bern a.	...	...	...	...	...	2123	|	...	...	...	|	|	...	...	|	2223
Olten a.	...	...	...	...	...	2200	|	...	...	...	|	2328	...	...	|	...
Basel SBB a.	...	...	...	...	...	2232	|	...	...	...	|	2353	...	...	|	...
Zürich HB a.	...	...	...	...	...	...	|	...	...	...	2251	...	...	...	|	...
Sion a.	...	...	...	...	...	...	2104	...	...	...	...	...	...	...	2149	...
Lausanne a.	...	...	...	...	...	...	2215	...	...	...	...	...	...	...	2240	...
Genève a.	...	...	...	...	...	...	*2304*	...	...	...	...	...	...	...	2315	...
Genève Aéroport ✈ a.	...	...	...	...	...	...	*2313*	...	...	...	...	...	...	...	...	...

A – ①–⑤ (not Dec. 25, Jan. 1, 6, Apr. 5).
b – Also Dec. 25, Jan. 1, 6, Apr. 5.
f – From Salerno.
g – Firenze **Rifredi**.
j – ①–⑥ (not Dec. 25, Jan. 1).
t – Roma **Tiburtina**.
⚡ – Supplement payable.
¶ – Ticket point is **Iselle**.
⊕ – **ETR 470**. Supplement payable for international journeys. *IC* supplement payable for internal journeys within Italy.
⊗ – **ETR 610**. Supplement payable for international journeys. *IC* supplement payable for internal journeys within Italy.

ZÜRICH - INNSBRUCK - WIEN, GRAZ, ZAGREB and BUDAPEST 86

train type/number	EC	IC	EC	EC	EC	EC	IC	EC	EC*	EC	EC	IC	IC	EC	EC	D	RJ	IC	IC	RJ	EC	RJ	EN	EN	EN	EN
train number	663	515	111	111	561	690	311	317	163	113	113	519	165	565	115	315	69	649	611	169	117	363	465	465	15465	467
				211						213														415	415	
notes	✕	🍷			✕	🍷		🍷	🍷 C	🍷	✕			✕	✕	A	🍷	🍷		🍷	✕ Ⓑf	🍷	Z	BT	BS	🍷 W
Zürich HB d.	...	...	...	...	...	...	...	...	0840	...	...	...	1006	...	...	...	...	...	...	1440	...	1640	2040	2040	2040	2240
Sargans d.	...	...	...	...	...	...	...	...	0937	...	...	...	|	...	...	...	...	...	...	1537	...	1737	2137	2137	2137	2337
Buchs 🛃 d.	...	...	...	...	...	...	...	...	0954	...	...	...	1122	...	...	...	...	...	...	1554	...	1754	2203	2203	2203	2358
Bregenz d.	0547	...	...	...	0713	...	...	...	|	...	...	...	|	1116	...	...	...	...	...	|	...	|	|	|	|	|
Feldkirch a.	0610	...	...	...	0743	...	...	...	1009	...	...	...	1137	1140	...	...	...	...	...	1609	...	1809	2219	2219	2219	0014
Bludenz a.	0624	...	...	...	0755	...	...	...	1024	...	...	...	...	1154	...	...	...	...	...	1626	...	1823	2255	2255	2334	0029
Langen am Arlberg a.	|	...	...	...	0822	...	...	...	1050	...	...	...	...	1221	...	...	...	...	...	|	...	|	2334	2334	0008	|
St Anton am Arlberg a.	0657	...	...	...	0832	...	...	...	1059	...	...	...	...	1230	...	...	...	...	...	1659	...	1857	2343	2343	0017	|
Landeck-Zams a.	0721	...	...	...	0856	...	...	...	1122	...	...	...	...	1258	...	...	...	...	...	1722	...	1922	0008	0008	0042	|
Ötztal a.	|	...	...	...	0922	...	...	...	|	...	...	...	...	1322	...	...	...	...	...	|	...	|	|	|	|	|
Innsbruck Hbf a.	0806	0824	...	...	0948	...	...	...	1206	...	...	...	...	1348	...	...	...	1413	...	1806	...	2006	0056	0056	0134	0215
Jenbach a.	|	0844	...	...	1012	...	...	...	|	...	...	...	...	1412	...	...	...	1433	...	|	...	|	|	|	|	|
Wörgl a.	|	0900	...	...	1028	...	...	...	|	...	...	...	...	1428	...	...	...	1448	...	|	...	|	0139	0139	0219	|
Kitzbühel a.	|	0931	...	...	|	...	...	...	|	...	...	...	...	|	...	...	...	1519	...	|	...	|	|	|	|	|
St Johann in Tirol a.	|	0939	...	...	|	...	...	...	|	...	...	...	...	|	...	...	...	1527	...	|	...	|	|	|	|	|
Saalfelden a.	|	1007	...	...	|	...	...	...	|	...	...	...	...	|	...	...	...	1559	...	|	...	|	|	|	|	|
Zell am See a.	|	1019	...	...	|	...	...	...	|	...	...	...	...	|	...	...	...	1610	...	|	...	|	|	|	|	|
Schwarzach St Veit a.	|	|	...	...	|	...	...	...	|	...	...	...	...	|	...	...	...	1639	...	|	...	|	0319	0319	0359	|
Salzburg Hbf a.	0959	|	1012	1012	1158	1212	...	1215	1359	1412	1412	1415	...	1558	1612	...	1700	|	...	1959	2012	2159	|	|	|	0412
Bischofshofen a.	|	|	1052	1052	|	1252	...	1302	|	1452	1452	1502	...	|	1652	...	|	1655	1713	|	2052	...	0336	|	|	|
Schwarzach St Veit a.	|	1048	1109	1109	|	1309	...	|	|	1509	1509	|	...	|	1709	...	|	...	|	|	2109	...	|	|	|	|
Selzthal a.	|	1240	|	|	|	|	...	1440	|	|	|	1640	...	|	|	...	|	...	1840	|	|	...	0504	|	|	|
Graz Hbf a.	|	1422	|	|	|	|	...	1622	|	|	|	1822	...	|	|	...	|	...	2022	|	|	...	0700	|	|	|
Villach Hbf a.	|	...	1243	1243	|	1443	1452	...	|	1643	1643	▬	...	|	1843	1927	|	...	...	|	2245	...	...	0608	0608	|
Klagenfurt a.	|	...	1316	|	|	▬	|	...	|	|	1716	...	...	|	1916	|	|	...	...	|	2317	...	...	|	|	|
Jesenice 🛃 a.	|	...	▬	1333	|	...	1532	...	|	1733	▬	...	...	|	...	2007	|	...	...	|	...	...	...	0707	0707	|
Ljubljana ⊙ a.	|	...	...	1431	|	...	1633	...	|	1831	...	...	...	|	...	2110	|	...	...	|	...	...	...	0810	0810	|
Zagreb ⊙ a.	|	...	...	1710	|	...	1856	...	|	2055	...	...	...	|	...	2334	|	...	...	|	...	...	...	1034	1034	|
Vinkovci ⊕ a.	|	...	...	2032	|	...	...	...	|	...	...	*D*	...	|	...	0306	|	...	...	|	...	...	...	1413	1413	|
Beograd ⊕ a.	|	...	*RJ*	2327	|	*RJ*	...	...	|	...	*RJ*	**347**	...	|	...	0619	|	...	...	|	...	...	...	1720	1720	|
Linz Hbf a.	1107	...	**63**	...	1307	**65**	...	...	1507	...	**67**	✕	...	1707	...	...	1807	...	...	2107	...	...	...	...	...	0542
St Pölten a.	1158	...	🍷	...	1358	🍷	...	...	1558	...	🍷	**D**	...	1758	...	...	1858	...	...	2158	...	...	...	...	...	0649
Wien Westbahnhof a.	1240	...	1350	...	1440	1550	...	...	1640	...	1750	1850	...	1840	...	...	1940	...	...	2240	...	...	...	...	...	0736
Hegyeshalom 🛃 a.	...	...	1454	...	...	1654	...	...	...	...	1854	1954	...	...	...	...	2054	...	...	...	...	...	...	...	...	0854
Győr a.	...	...	1521	...	...	1721	...	...	...	...	1921	2029	...	...	...	...	2119	...	...	...	...	...	...	...	...	0921
Budapest Keleti a.	...	...	1649	...	...	1849	...	...	...	...	2049	2220	...	...	...	...	2249	...	...	...	...	...	...	...	...	1049

train type/number	RJ	EC	IC	RJ	D	EC	IC	D	EC*	EC	EC	RJ	EC	IC	IC	RJ	EC	IC	RJ	EC	EC	EC	EN	EN	EN	EN
train number	362	318	693	160	314	114	542	346	162	212	112	60	564	310	691	62	566	518	66	210	110	662	466	414	414	464
										112										110				15464	464	
notes	🍷	🍷	🍷	🍷	A	✕	🍷	✕ D	🍷 C	✕	✕	🍷	✕			🍷	✕	🍷	🍷		🍷	✕	🍷 W	BS	BT	Z
Budapest Keleti d.	...	...	...	...	...	...	...	0600	...	...	...	0710	...	...	...	0910	...	...	1310	...	...	...	1905	...	...	...
Győr d.	...	...	...	...	...	...	...	0727	...	...	...	0835	...	...	...	1035	...	...	1435	...	...	...	2032	...	...	...
Hegyeshalom 🛃 d.	...	...	...	...	...	...	...	0758	...	...	...	0906	...	...	...	1106	...	...	1506	...	...	...	2103	...	...	...
Wien Westbahnhof d.	...	...	...	0720	...	...	...	0858	0920	...	...	1008	1120	...	...	1208	1320	...	1608	...	...	1720	2225	...	...	...
St Pölten d.	...	...	...	0802	...	...	...	▬	1002	...	...	▬	1202	...	...	▬	1402	...	...	...	...	1802	2309	...	...	...
Linz Hbf d.	...	...	...	0853	...	...	...	...	1053	...	...	...	1253	...	...	...	1453	...	...	...	...	1853	0010	...	...	...
Beograd ⊕ d.	...	...	...	|	2140	...	...	...	|	...	...	...	|	...	...	...	|	...	...	0545	...	|	|	1020	1020	...
Vinkovci ⊕ d.	...	...	...	|	0144	...	...	...	|	...	...	...	|	...	...	...	|	...	...	0945	...	|	|	1445	1445	...
Zagreb ⊙ d.	...	...	...	|	0500	...	...	...	|	0700	...	...	|	0900	...	...	|	...	...	1300	...	|	|	1814	1814	...
Ljubljana ⊙ d.	...	...	...	|	0727	...	...	...	|	0927	...	...	|	1126	...	...	|	...	...	1525	...	|	|	2048	2048	...
Jesenice 🛃 d.	...	...	...	|	0827	...	...	*IC*	|	1024	...	*IC*	|	1228	...	*EC*	|	...	...	1627	...	|	|	2153	2153	...
Klagenfurt d.	...	...	0646	|	|	0843	...	**512**	|	|	1033	**514**	|	|	1246	**316**	|	...	...	|	1631	|	|	|	|	...
Villach Hbf d.	...	...	0716	|	0906	0916	...	🍷	|	1116	1116	🍷	|	1306	1316	🍷	|	...	...	1716	1716	|	|	2300	2300	...
Graz Hbf d.	...	0545	|	|	...	|	...	0738	|	|	|	0938	|	▬	|	1138	|	1338	...	|	|	|	|	|	|	2228
Selzthal d.	...	0719	|	|	...	|	...	0919	|	|	|	1119	|	...	|	1319	|	1519	...	|	|	|	|	|	|	0029
Schwarzach St Veit d.	...	|	0851	|	...	1051	1121	|	|	1251	1251	|	|	...	1541	|	|	|	...	1851	1851	|	|	|	|	|
Bischofshofen d.	...	0857	0908	|	...	1108	|	1057	|	1308	1308	1257	|	...	1508	1457	|	1649	...	1906	1906	|	|	|	|	0158
Salzburg Hbf d.	0602	0944	0948	1002	...	1148	|	1144	1202	1348	1348	1344	1402	...	1548	1544	1602	|	...	1948	1948	2002	0140	|	|	|
Schwarzach St Veit d.	|	...	...	|	...	...	|	...	|	...	...	...	|	...	...	...	|	1712	...	...	...	|	|	0113	0235	0235
Zell am See d.	|	...	...	|	...	...	1150	...	|	...	...	...	|	...	...	...	|	1743	...	...	...	|	|	|	|	|
Saalfelden d.	|	...	...	|	...	...	1200	...	|	...	...	...	|	...	...	...	|	1753	...	...	...	|	|	|	|	|
St Johann in Tirol d.	|	...	...	|	...	...	1231	...	|	...	...	...	|	...	...	...	|	1820	...	...	...	|	|	|	|	|
Kitzbühel d.	|	...	...	|	...	...	1239	...	|	...	...	...	|	...	...	...	|	1828	...	...	...	|	|	|	|	|
Wörgl d.	|	...	...	|	...	...	1310	...	|	...	...	...	1532	...	...	...	1732	1900	...	...	...	|	|	0252	|	|
Jenbach d.	|	...	...	|	...	...	1325	...	|	...	...	...	1547	...	...	...	1747	1915	...	...	...	|	|	|	|	|
Innsbruck Hbf d.	0754	...	...	1154	...	...	1347	...	1354	...	...	...	1612	...	...	...	1812	1936	...	...	...	2154	0340	0356	0455	0455
Ötztal d.	|	...	...	|	...	...	...	...	|	...	...	...	1638	...	...	...	1838	▬	...	...	...	|	|	|	|	|
Landeck-Zams d.	0837	...	...	1237	...	...	...	...	1437	...	...	...	1701	...	...	...	1901	...	...	...	...	2238	|	0454	0546	0546
St Anton am Arlberg d.	0901	...	...	1301	...	...	...	...	1500	...	...	...	1730	...	...	...	1925	...	...	...	...	2302	|	0519	0613	0613
Langen am Arlberg d.	|	...	...	|	...	...	...	...	|	...	...	...	1741	...	...	...	1936	*IC*	...	...	...	|	|	0530	0625	0625
Bludenz d.	0935	...	...	1335	...	...	...	...	1534	...	...	...	1807	*EC*	...	...	2003	**166**	...	...	...	2336	0526	0614	0706	0706
Feldkirch d.	0948	...	...	1350	...	...	...	...	1548	...	...	...	1820	**192**	...	...	2018	2021	...	...	...	2349	0545	0738	0738	0738
Bregenz a.	|	...	...	|	...	...	...	...	|	...	...	...	1847	1906	...	...	2043	|	...	...	...	0012	|	|	|	|
Buchs 🛃 a.	1006	...	...	1406	...	...	...	...	1606	...	...	...	...	◧	...	...	...	2036	...	...	...	...	0601	0753	0753	0753
Sargans a.	1023	...	...	1423	...	...	...	...	1623	...	...	...	...	|	...	...	...	2015	...	...	...	...	0620	0823	0823	0823
Zürich HB a.	1120	...	...	1520	...	...	...	...	1720	...	...	...	...	2044	...	...	...	2224	...	...	...	...	0720	0920	0920	0920

A – 🛏 1, 2 cl., 🛌 2 cl. and [12] Villach - Beograd and v.v. Table **62**.

B – 🛏 1, 2 cl. and 🛌 2 cl. Zürich - Zagreb and v.v. [2] Zürich - Beograd and v.v. [12] and ✕ Villach - Beograd and v.v.

C – TRANSALPIN – [1] (panorama car), [12] and ✕ Zürich - Wien and v.v. *RJ* from June 13.

D – DACIA – 🛏 1, 2 cl., 🛌 2 cl., [2] and ✕ Wien - Budapest - Bucureşti and v.v. [1] Wien - Budapest - Lökösháza and v.v.

S – Daily Dec. 13 - Jan. 6 (also Feb. 13, 14, 20, 21) daily Apr. 2 – 14; ⑤⑥⑦ Apr. 17 - June 28 (also May 20, 21, June 1, 10, 11).

T – Daily except on dates in note **S**.

W – WIENER WALZER – 🛏 1, 2 cl., 🛌 2 cl., and [2] Zürich - Wien and v.v. Special fares payable. 🛌 2 cl. and [2] Zürich - Wien - Budapest and v.v. [12] and ✕ Wien - Budapest and v.v. 🛏 1, 2 cl. and 🛌 2 cl. Zürich - Linz - Praha and v.v. (see Table **52**).

Z – ZÜRICHSEE – 🛏 1,2 cl., 🛌 2 cl. and [2] Zürich - Graz and v.v.

d – Departure time, arrive 0910.

f – Not Dec. 24, 25, 31, Apr. 2, 4, May 23.

RJ – ÖBB *Railjet* service. [1] (premium class), [1] (first class), [2] (economy class) and 🍷. Classified *EC* in Hungary.

⊙ – 🛃 between Ljubljana and Zagreb is Dobova.

⊕ – 🛃 between Vinkovci and Beograd is Šid.

* – ÖBB *Railjet* service from June 13.

◧ – 🛃 is St Margrethen (Table **75**).

OTHER TRAIN NAMES: *EC* **960** – LISZT FERENC / FRANZ LISZT *EC* **962** – SEMMELWEIS IGNAC / IGNAZ SEMMELWEIS *EC* **967** – CSÁRDÁS

88 WIEN - VENEZIA, MILANO and ROMA

train type/number	🚌	AV	ESc	EC	🚌	AV	ESc	EC	🚌	EC	ES	EC	🚌	ESc	ES	EC	🚌	EN	EN	EN	EN	EN	ES	ESc
train number	831	9409	9714	731	833	9417	9730	531	835	42	9421	533	837	9746	9425	733	839	235	235	1237	1239	237	9405	9712
notes	Ⓡ	Ⓡ✕	Ⓡ🍷	✕	Ⓡ	Ⓡ✕	Ⓡ🍷	🍷	Ⓡ	Ⓡ🍷	Ⓡ✕	🍷	Ⓡ	Ⓡ🍷	Ⓡ✕	🍷	Ⓡ	R	9702	P	C	G	Ⓡ🍷	Ⓡ🍷
		⚡	⚡			⚡	⚡			⊗	⚡			⚡	⚡		B	⚡	V⚡	⚡	⚡	⚡	⚡	⚡
Wien Meidling d.	...	...	...	0630	...	...	...	0830	...	...	...	1030	...	...	...	1230	...	1930	1930	2030	2030	2040r	...	...
Bruck an der Mur d.	...	...	...	0815	...	...	...	1015	...	...	...	1215	...	...	...	1415	...	2125	2125	2222	2222	|	...	...
Klagenfurt Hbf d.	0605	...	...	1023	1010	...	...	1223	1210	...	...	1423	1410	...	...	1623	1610	2338	2338	0021	0021	|	...	...
Linz Hbf d.	|	...	...	|	|	...	...	|	|	...	...	|	|	...	...	|	|	|	|	|	|	2232	...	...
Salzburg Hbf d.	|	...	...	|	|	...	...	|	|	...	...	|	|	...	...	|	|	|	|	|	|	0134	...	...
Villach Hbf d.	0650	...	...	1044	1056	...	...	1246	1256	...	...	1446	1456	...	...	1644	1656	0003	0003	0045	0045	0445	...	...
Tarvisio 🛃 a.	|	...	...	...	|	...	...	1109	|	...	...	...	|	...	...	...	|	0029	0026	0108	0108	0508	...	...
Udine a.	0825	...	...	...	1230	...	...	...	1430	...	...	...	1630	...	...	...	1830	0135	|	|	|	0633	...	...
Venezia Mestre a.	1000	1039	1102	...	1405	1439	1502	...	1605	1632	1639	...	1805	1832	1839	...	2005	0252	0252h	0332	0332	0821	0839	0910
Venezia Santa Lucia a.	1020x	|	|	...	1425x	|	|	...	1625x	|	|	...	1825x	|	|	...	2025x	|	|	|	|	0834	|	|
Padova a.	...	1053	1116	...	...	1453	1516	...	...	1646	1653	...	...	1846	1853	...	...	|	0552	|	|	...	0853	0924
Verona Porta Nuova a.	...	|	1200	...	...	|	1600	...	...	1730	|	...	...	1930	|	...	...	|	0643	|	|	...	|	1003
Milano Centrale a.	...	|	1325	...	...	|	1725	...	...	1855	|	...	...	2055	|	...	...	|	0825	|	|	...	|	1125
Bologna Centrale a.	...	1150	...	...	...	1550	...	...	...	...	1750	...	...	...	1950	...	...	0448	...	|	|	...	0950	...
Firenze SMN a.	...	1230	...	...	...	1630	...	...	...	...	1830	...	...	...	2030	...	...	0618	...	0705	0705	...	1030	...
Roma Termini a.	...	1413	...	...	...	1813	...	...	...	...	2013	...	...	...	2213	...	...	0905	...	...	...	...	1213	...

train type/number	ESc	🚌	EC	AV	ESc	🚌	IC	ESc	AV	🚌	EC	ESc	AV	🚌	ESc	AV	🚌	AV	ESc	EN	EN	EN	EN	EN
train number	9701	830	732	9402	9711	832	630	9719	9410	834	730	9727	9414	836	9735	9418	838	9420	9741	236	1236	1238	234	9753
notes	Ⓡ🍷	Ⓡ	🍷	Ⓡ✕	Ⓡ🍷	Ⓡ	🍷	Ⓡ⚡	Ⓡ🍷	Ⓡ	✕	Ⓡ⚡	Ⓡ🍷	Ⓡ	Ⓡ🍷	Ⓡ🍷	Ⓡ	Ⓡ	Ⓡ	H	Q	D	R	234
	⚡			⚡	⚡			T	⚡				⚡	B	⚡	⚡		🍷⚡	⚡	⚡	⚡	⚡	⚡	W⚡
Roma Termini d.	...	...	...	0745	...	...	...	...	1145	...	...	...	1345	...	...	1545	...	1645	...	...	...	...	1905	...
Firenze SMN d.	...	...	...	0930	...	...	...	...	1330	...	...	...	1530	...	...	1730	...	1830	...	...	2055	2055	2138	...
Bologna Centrale d.	...	...	...	1010	...	...	...	...	1410	...	...	...	1610	...	...	1810	...	1910	...	...	|	|	2320	...
Milano Centrale d.	0635	...	...	|	0905	...	...	1235	|	...	...	1435	|	...	1635	|	...	|	1805	...	|	|	|	2105
Verona Porta Nuova d.	0759	...	...	|	1029	...	...	1359	|	...	...	1559	|	...	1757	|	...	|	1929	...	|	|	|	2247
Padova d.	0843	...	...	1107	1113	...	...	1443	1507	...	...	1643	1707	...	1836	1907	...	2007	2013	...	|	|	0041	2338
Venezia Santa Lucia d.	|	0920x	...	|	|	1120x	...	|	|	1520x	...	|	|	1720x	|	|	1920x	|	|	2105	|	|	|	|
Venezia Mestre d.	0858	0940	...	1121	1128	1140	...	1458	1521	1540	...	1658	1721	1740	1850	1921	1940	2021	2028	2118	0036	0036	0130	0130g
Udine d.	...	1115	...	...	...	1315	...	...	...	1715	...	...	...	1915	...	...	2115	...	...	2309	|	|	0246	|
Tarvisio 🛃 d.	...	|	...	...	...	|	...	...	...	|	...	...	...	|	...	...	|	...	...	0020	0319	0319	0352	0352
Villach Hbf a.	...	1250	1316	...	...	1450	1514	...	...	1850	1916	...	...	2050	...	...	2250	...	...	0042	0341	0341	0415	0415
Salzburg Hbf a.	...	|	|	...	...	|	|	...	...	|	|	...	...	|	...	...	|	...	...	0409	|	|	|	|
Linz Hbf a.	...	|	|	...	...	|	|	...	...	|	|	...	...	|	...	...	|	...	...	0627	|	|	|	|
Klagenfurt Hbf a.	...	1335	1339	...	...	1535	1537	...	...	1935	1937	...	...	2135	...	...	2335	...	...	|	0407	0407	0438	0438
Bruck an der Mur a.	...	...	1544	...	...	...	1744	...	...	...	2144	...	...	...	...	...	...	...	...	|	0622	0622	0639	0639
Wien Meidling a.	...	...	1728	...	...	...	1928	...	...	...	2328	...	...	...	...	...	...	...	...	0828r	0855	0855	0834	0834

B – Mar. 26 - Apr. 6; May 1 - Sept. 26.
C – Dec. 28, 29, 30, Jan. 1–5, Apr. 4, May 12, 23, June 2: 🛏 1, 2 cl. (T2), ▬ 2 cl. and [2] Ⓡ Wien - Firenze.
D – Dec. 29, 30, Jan. 1–6, Apr. 5, May 13, 24, June 3: 🛏 1, 2 cl. (T2), ▬ 2 cl. and [2] Ⓡ Firenze - Wien.
G – ALLEGRO DON GIOVANNI – 🛏 1, 2 cl., ▬ 2 cl. and [2] Wien (**744**) - Salzburg (**499**) - Villach (**237**) - Udine - Venezia.
H – ALLEGRO DON GIOVANNI – 🛏 1, 2 cl., ▬ 2 cl. and [2] Venezia (**236**) - Udine - Villach (**498**) - Salzburg (**745**) - Wien.
P – ALLEGRO ROSSINI ⑤ Mar. 26 - Sept. 24: 🛏 1, 2 cl. (T2), ▬ 2 cl. and [2] Wien - Firenze.
Q – ALLEGRO ROSSINI ⑥ Mar. 27 - Sept. 25: 🛏 1, 2 cl. (T2), ▬ 2 cl. and [2] Firenze - Wien.
R – ALLEGRO TOSCA – 🛏 1, 2 cl., 🛏 1, 2 cl. (Excelsior), ▬ 2 cl. and [2] Wien - Roma and v.v.
T – ①–⑤ (not Dec. 25, Jan. 1, 6, Apr. 5).
V – ❖ 🛏 1, 2 cl. and ▬ 2 cl. (4 berth) Wien (**235**) - Venezia Mestre (**9702**) - Milano ❖.
W – ❖ 🛏 1, 2 cl. and ▬ 2 cl. (4 berth) Milano (**9753**) - Venezia Mestre (**234**) - Wien ❖.

e – Firenze **Campo di Marte**.
g – Arrive 2356.
h – Depart 0532. Train **9700**.

j – Firenze **Rifredi**.
r – Wien **Westbahnhof**.
t – Roma **Tiburtina**.
x Venezia Piazzale Roma, see City Plan on page 31.

⊗ – **ETR 610**. Supplement payable for international journeys. *IC* supplement payable for internal journeys within Italy.
🚌 – ÖBB *IC Bus*. Ⓡ Rail tickets valid. 1st and 2nd class. 🍷 in first class. Connections to/from Wien are made at Villach.
⚡ – Supplement payable.
♣ – Special "global fares" payable.
❖ – Subject to confirmation. At the time of going to press Trenitalia were unable to confirm the running of trains **235+9702** and **9753+234** Wien - Milano and v.v.

89 VENEZIA - LJUBLJANA - ZAGREB - BUDAPEST and BEOGRAD

train type		703			IC	IC	IC	🚌	D	EN	EN
train number	703	205	247	520	284	284	501	834	315	241	241
notes	🍷			Ⓡ	201	✕	Ⓡ🍷	Ⓡ		Ⓡ	413
notes		MR	C	🍷	P	D			G	A♣	B♣
Venezia Santa Lucia d.	...	...	...	...	...	...	...	1520x	...	2120	2120
Venezia Mestre d.	...	...	...	...	...	...	...	1540	...	2132	2132
Villach Hbf d.	...	...	...	...	...	...	...	1850	1927	|	|
Monfalcone d.	...	...	...	...	...	...	...	...	|	2259	2259
Villa Opicina 🛃 d.	...	...	...	...	...	...	...	...	|	2348	2348
Ljubljana d.	...	...	0650	...	...	...	...	...	2115	0159	0159
Dobova 🛃 d.	...	...	|	...	...	...	...	...	2305	0349	0349
Split d.	...	...	|	0755	...	...	...	...	|	|	|
Rijeka d.	0545	...	|	|	...	...	1200	...	|	|	|
Zagreb a.	0938	...	|	1348	...	...	1551	...	2334	0418	0418
Zagreb d.	...	1000	|	...	1545	1545	...	...	2355	0456	0603
Vinkovci a.	...	|	|	...	|	|	...	...	0306	|	0916
Šid 🛃 a.	...	|	|	...	|	|	...	...	0401	|	1012
Beograd a.	...	|	|	...	|	|	...	...	0619	|	1218
Koprivnica 🛃 d.	...	1121	|	...	1700	1700	...	...	...	0611	...
Kotoriba 🛃 d.	...	|	|	...	|	|	...	...	...	|	...
Hodoš 🛃 d.	...	|	1114	...	|	|	...	...	...	|	...
Zalaegerszeg a.	...	|	1151	...	|	|	...	...	...	|	...
Gyékényes a.	...	1140	|	...	1714	1714	...	...	...	0625	...
Nagykanizsa a.	...	1235	|	...	1820	1802	...	...	...	0709	...
Fonyód a.	...	1408	|	...	1942	...	...	...	...	0810	...
Siófok a.	...	1458	|	...	2028	...	...	...	...	0857	...
Székesfehérvár a.	...	1538	1438	...	2111	...	...	...	...	0939	...
Budapest Déli a.	...	|	1545	...	|	...	...	...	...	|	...
Budapest Keleti a.	...	1654	...	...	2229	...	...	...	...	1059	...

train type	D	🚌	IC	IC					EN	EN
train number	314	833	200	285	525	702	246	204	412	240
notes		Ⓡ		✕	Ⓡ	🍷			240	Ⓡ
notes	G		P	D	🍷		C	MR	B♣	A♣
Budapest Keleti d.	...	...	0630	...	...	...	...	1305	...	1700
Budapest Déli d.	...	...	|	...	...	...	1411	|	...	|
Székesfehérvár d.	...	...	0746	...	...	...	1515	1416	...	1816
Siófok d.	...	...	0829	...	...	...	|	1458	...	1858
Fonyód d.	...	...	0922	...	...	...	|	1548	...	1944
Nagykanizsa d.	...	...	1025	1040	...	...	|	1707	...	2042
Gyékényes d.	...	...	1125	1125	...	...	|	1758	...	2134
Zalaegerszeg d.	...	...	|	|	...	...	1812	|	...	|
Hodoš 🛃 a.	...	...	|	|	...	...	1851	|	...	|
Kotoriba 🛃 a.	...	...	|	|	...	...	|	|	...	|
Koprivnica 🛃 a.	...	...	1139	1139	...	...	|	1812	...	2148
Beograd d.	2140	...	|	|	...	...	|	|	1525	|
Šid 🛃 d.	0058	...	|	|	...	...	|	|	1833	|
Vinkovci d.	0144	...	|	|	...	...	|	|	1930	|
Zagreb a.	0453	...	1259	1259	...	...	|	1936	2244	2307
Zagreb d.	0500	...	...	...	1519	1650	|	...	2335	2335
Rijeka a.	|	...	...	...	|	2034	|	...	|	|
Split a.	|	...	...	...	2052	...	|	...	|	|
Dobova 🛃 a.	0529	...	...	...	...	...	|	...	0004	0004
Ljubljana a.	0723	...	...	...	...	...	2305	...	0210	0210
Villa Opicina 🛃 a.	|	...	...	...	...	...	...	...	0516	0516
Monfalcone a.	|	...	...	...	...	...	...	...	0542	0542
Villach Hbf a.	0906	1056	...	...	...	...	...	...	|	|
Venezia Mestre a.	...	1405	...	...	...	...	...	...	0704	0704
Venezia Santa Lucia a.	...	1425x	...	...	...	...	...	...	0716	0716

A – VENEZIA – 🛏 1, 2 cl., ▬ 2 cl., [2] and ✕ Venezia - Budapest and v.v.
B – ♣ Ⓡ ▬ 2 cl. Venezia - Zagreb - Beograd and v.v. [12] and ✕ Zagreb - Beograd and v.v.
C – CITADELLA – [12] Ⓡ Budapest - Hodoš - Murska Sobota - Ljubljana and v.v.
D – ZAGREB – [12] and ✕ Wien - Sopron 🛃 - Szombathely - Nagykanizsa - Gyékényes 🛃 - Zagreb and v.v. Table **92**.
G – 🛏 1, 2 cl., ▬ 2 cl. and [12] Villach - Jesenice 🛃 - Ljubljana - Beograd and v.v.
M – Conveys on dates shown in Tables **95**/**97**: 🛏 1, 2 cl. Zagreb - Budapest - Kyïv/Moskva/St Peterburg and v.v.
P – KVARNER – [12] Ⓡ Budapest - Zagreb and v.v.
R – MAESTRAL – [12] Ⓡ Budapest - Zagreb and v.v.

x Venezia Piazzale Roma, see City Plan on page 31.

♣ – Special fares payable for journeys to or from Italy.
⚡ – Supplement payable.
🚌 – ÖBB *IC Bus*. Ⓡ Rail tickets valid. 1st and 2nd class. 🍷 in first class.

BARCELONA, MARSEILLE and NICE - MILANO, ROMA and VENEZIA 90

train type / number	4621	4620	EC	ESc	AV	ESc	TGV	TGV		IC	ESc	AV	IC	ESc	4652	EC	ICN	ICN		Hotel	AV	ESc	ESc
train number	4620	4621	139	9729	9523	9799	5301	5102		693	9745	9533	605	9773	4653	147	761	1911	10601	EN	9511	9791	9715
notes	R	R	140	R 🍷	R ✕	R ✕	R 🍷	5103	◇	694	9793	R ✕	R 🍷	R 🍷	R 🍷	148	R	R		272	R ✕	R 🍷	R 🍷
	G	C	D	⚡	⚡	⚡		R 🍷		R ⚡	🍷 ⚡	⚡	⚡	⚡	b	D	⚡	⚡		371	⚡	⑥⑦x	⚡
Hendaye d.	...	1911	...	...	...	...	...	...	...	...	...	...	...	...	...	...	...	...	...	11273	...	...	...
Bordeaux St Jean d.	2157	2157	...	...	...	...	...	...	...	...	...	...	...	...	0610	...	...	...	...	A	...	...	...
Toulouse d.	0025	0025	...	...	...	...	0654	...	...	...	...	...	...	...	0817	...	...	...	...	...	...	...	...
Barcelona França d.	|	|	...	...	...	...	|	...	...	...	...	...	...	...	|	...	...	...	...	1938	...	...	...
Girona d.	|	|	...	...	...	...	|	...	...	...	...	...	...	...	|	...	...	...	...	2057	...	...	...
Figueres d.	|	|	...	...	...	...	|	...	...	...	...	...	...	...	|	...	...	...	...	2125	...	...	...
Perpignan d.	|	|	...	...	...	...	|	...	...	...	...	...	...	...	|	...	...	...	...	2244	...	...	...
Montpellier d.	|	|	...	...	...	...	0915	...	...	...	...	...	...	...	1016	...	...	...	...	|	...	...	...
Marseille St Charles d.	0524	0524	...	...	...	...	1041	1059	...	...	...	...	...	...	1159	...	...	...	...	|	...	...	...
Toulon d.	0613	0613	...	...	...	...	...	1146	...	...	...	...	...	...	1247	...	...	...	...	|	...	...	...
Cannes d.	0736	0736	...	...	...	...	...	1304	...	...	...	...	...	...	1404	...	...	...	...	|	...	...	...
Nice d.	0807	0807	0949	...	...	...	...	1332	1356	...	...	...	...	...	1434	1749	...	...	...	|	...	...	...
Monaco - Monte Carlo d.	...	...	1010	...	...	...	...	...	1419	...	...	...	...	...	...	1810	...	...	...	|	...	...	...
Ventimiglia 🏛 d.	...	...	1058	...	...	...	...	...	1443	1458	...	...	...	...	...	1858	...	...	...	|	...	...	...
San Remo a.	...	...	1113	...	...	...	...	...	...	1513	...	...	...	...	...	1913	...	...	...	|	...	...	...
Genova Piazza Principe a.	...	...	1306	...	...	1452	...	...	...	1706	...	...	1748	1852	...	2106	2240	...	...	|	...	...	...
Torino Porta Susa a.	...	...	|	...	...	|	...	...	...	|	...	...	|	|	...	|	|	...	...	0812	...	...	...
Novara a.	...	...	|	...	...	|	...	...	...	|	...	...	|	|	...	|	|	...	...	0912	...	...	...
Milano Centrale a.	...	...	1450	1505	1515	|	...	...	...	1850	1905	1915	|	|	...	2250	|	2320	0015	0959	1015	1035	1135
Verona a.	...	...	...	1627	|	|	...	...	...	...	2027	|	|	|	...	...	|	|	0223	...	|	1157	1257
Venezia Santa Lucia a.	...	...	...	1740	|	|	...	...	...	...	2150h	|	|	|	...	...	|	|	...	...	|	1310	1410
La Spezia a.	...	...	...	...	|	1604	...	...	...	...	...	|	1917	2004	...	...	2355	|	...	...	|	...	...
Pisa Centrale a.	...	...	...	...	|	1657	...	...	...	...	...	|	2012	2055	...	...	0047	|	...	...	|	...	...
Firenze SMN a.	...	...	...	...	1700	|	...	...	...	...	...	2100	...	2155v	...	...	|	|	...	...	1200	...	...
Roma Termini a.	...	...	...	...	1845	1958	...	...	...	...	...	2245	...	...	...	...	|	0730t	...	...	1345	...	...
Napoli Centrale a.	...	...	...	...	2010	...	...	...	...	...	...	...	...	...	...	...	0558y	1012	...	...	1510	...	...

train type / number	ICN	IC	IC		4764	ESc	ESc	AV 🍷	CIS	EC	TGV		IC	IC	ESc	AV	EC	4730	4730	AV	ESc	Hotel	
train number	796	654	691		4765	9771	9708	9604	52	143	6876		516	664	9718	9518	159	4731	4731	9526	9738	EN	
notes	F	R 🍷	692	◇	R	R	R 🍷	R	R ✕	144	R		R 🍷	R 🍷	R 🍷	R ✕	160	R	R	R ⚡	R 🍷	372	
	R	⚡	R ⚡		🍷	🍷 ⚡	①–⑤p	①–⑤p	⚡	D	🍷		⚡	⚡	⚡	⚡	D	G	C	✕	⚡	274	
Napoli Centrale d.	2108	...	...	...	...	...	...	0620	...	...	...	...	0730	...	...	0950	...	...	...	1350	...	11274	...
Roma Termini d.	2350	...	...	...	...	...	...	0733	...	...	...	...	0946	...	...	1115	...	...	...	1515	...	A	...
Firenze SMN d.	|	...	...	...	...	0755v	...	|	...	...	...	...	|	...	...	1300	...	...	...	1700	...	...	...
Pisa Centrale d.	0328	0544	...	...	...	0859	...	|	...	...	...	...	1300	1344	...	|	...	...	...	|	...	...	...
La Spezia d.	0416	0640	...	...	...	0953	...	|	...	...	...	...	1353	1440	...	|	...	...	...	|	...	...	...
Venezia Santa Lucia d.	|	|	...	...	...	|	0750	|	0832q	...	...	...	|	|	1150	|	...	...	...	|	1650	...	...
Verona d.	|	|	...	...	...	|	0902	|	0932	...	...	...	|	|	1302	|	...	...	...	|	1802	...	...
Milano Centrale d.	|	|	0700	...	...	|	1025	1030	1055	1110	...	...	|	|	1425	1445	1510	...	...	1845	1925	1940	...
Novara a.	|	|	|	...	...	|	...	...	...	|	...	...	|	|	...	...	|	...	...	...	...	2018	...
Torino Porta Susa d.	|	|	|	...	...	|	...	...	...	|	...	...	|	|	...	...	|	...	...	...	...	2118	...
Genova Piazza Principe d.	0601	0816	0855	...	...	1108	...	...	...	1255	...	...	1508	1616	...	...	1655	...	...	...	...	|	...
San Remo d.	...	...	1050	...	...	...	...	...	...	1450	...	...	...	...	...	...	1850	...	...	...	...	|	...
Ventimiglia 🏛 a.	...	...	1107	1155	...	...	...	...	...	1507	...	...	...	...	...	...	1907	...	...	...	...	|	...
Monaco - Monte Carlo a.	...	...	...	1220	...	...	...	...	...	1548	...	...	...	...	...	...	1953	...	...	...	...	|	...
Nice a.	...	...	...	1242	1329	...	...	...	...	1610	1725	...	...	...	...	...	2010	2056	2056	...	...	|	...
Cannes a.	...	...	...	1322	1358	...	...	...	...	...	1754	...	...	...	...	...	...	2123	2123	...	...	|	...
Toulon a.	...	...	...	...	1516	...	...	...	...	...	1912	...	...	...	...	...	...	2242	2242	...	...	|	...
Marseille St Charles a.	...	...	...	...	1601	...	...	...	...	...	1959	...	...	...	...	...	...	2329	2329	...	...	|	...
Montpellier a.	...	...	...	...	1741	...	...	...	...	...	...	...	...	...	...	...	...	|	|	...	...	|	...
Perpignan a.	...	...	...	...	|	...	...	...	...	...	...	...	...	...	...	...	...	|	|	...	...	0614	...
Figueres a.	...	...	...	...	|	...	...	...	...	...	...	...	...	...	...	...	...	|	|	...	...	0744	...
Girona a.	...	...	...	...	|	...	...	...	...	...	...	...	...	...	...	...	...	|	|	...	...	0818	...
Barcelona França a.	...	...	...	...	|	...	...	...	...	...	...	...	...	...	...	...	...	|	|	...	...	0943	...
Toulouse a.	...	...	...	...	1944	...	...	...	...	...	...	...	...	...	...	...	...	0515	0515	...	...	...	...
Bordeaux St Jean a.	...	...	...	...	2150	...	...	...	...	...	...	...	...	...	...	...	...	0811	0811	...	...	...	...
Irún a.	...	...	...	...	...	...	...	...	...	...	...	...	...	...	...	...	...	...	1104	...	...	...	...

A – SALVADOR DALÍ *Train-hotel Elipsos* ②④⑦ from Barcelona; ①③⑤ from Milano: 🛏 1, 2 cl., 🛏 2 cl. (T4), (1) (reclining) and ✕ Barcelona - Milano and v.v. R special fares apply.

C – ⑤⑦ (daily Dec. 18 - Jan. 3; not Dec. 24, 31. Jan. 10, Feb. 5; daily Feb. 12 - Mar. 7; daily Apr. 2 - May 2; also May 12, 24; not May 14): *CORAIL LUNÉA* – 🛋 1, 2 cl. and (2) (reclining) Hendaye - Nice and Nice - Irún.

D – (12) and 🍷 R ⚡ Nice - Milano and v.v.

F – 🛏 1, 2 cl., 🛏 1, 2 cl. (Excelsior), 🛋 2 cl. (4 berth) and (2) Napoli - Genova - Torino.

G – *CORAIL LUNÉA* – 🛋 1, 2 cl. and (2) (reclining) Bordeaux - Nice and v.v.

b – Not Mar. 1–26.

h – 2140 on ⑥⑦ x.

p – Not Dec. 25, Jan. 1.

q – Venezia **Mestre**.

t – Roma **Tiburtina**.

v – Firenze **SMN**.

x – Also Dec. 28, Jan. 1.

y – Napoli **Campi Flegrei**.

◇ – Stopping train.

WIEN - LJUBLJANA and ZAGREB 91

train type	IC	ICS		IC		EC			EC				IC	ICS	IC	IC		IC			EC	ICS	
train number	251	13		285		151	2752		255	3915	2268		257	19	311	509		259	1615		159	23	
notes	🍷	R		🍷		483	2		🍷	2	2		🍷	R				🍷	2		✕	R	
				B		A													D		C ⚡		
Wien Meidling d.	...	...	...	0703	...	0803	...	...	1003	...	...	...	1203	...	...	...	...	1403	...	...	1603	...	...
Graz Hbf d.	0634	...	...	|	...	1036	...	...	1236	...	...	...	1436	...	...	...	...	1636	...	...	1836	...	...
Spielfeld-Straß 🏛 d.	0721	...	...	|	...	1121	...	...	1321	...	...	...	1521	...	...	...	...	1721	...	...	1921	...	...
Maribor a.	0739	0817	...	|	...	1138	...	...	1338	1415	...	...	1538	1545	...	...	...	1739	1800	...	1938	1945	...
Pragersko a.	...	0830	...	|	...	1201	...	...	...	1434	...	...	...	1558	...	...	...	...	1816	...	2010	1958	...
Zidani Most a.	...	0924	...	|	...	1306	...	...	...	1547	1600	...	...	1653	1729	...	...	...	1925	...	|	2053	...
Dobova 🏛 a.	...	|	...	|	...	|	...	...	...	...	|	...	...	|	1811	...	...	...	|	...	2151	|	...
Zagreb a.	...	|	...	1259	...	|	...	...	...	...	|	...	...	|	1856	...	...	...	|	...	2234	|	...
Ljubljana a.	...	1009	...	...	...	1406	1540	...	...	...	1703	...	...	1738	...	1810	...	...	2022	...	...	2138	...
Koper a.	...	...	...	...	...	|	1811	...	...	...	...	...	...	...	...	2033	...	...	...	...	...	...	...
Rijeka a.	...	...	...	...	...	1725	...	...	...	...	...	...	...	...	...	...	...	...	...	...	...	...	...
Split a.	...	...	...	...	...	...	...	...	...	...	...	...	...	...	...	...	...	...	...	...	...	...	...

train type / number	IC		ICS	IC		IC	ICS	EC		ICS	EC		IC		IC		IC		482				
train number	250		12	252		508	14	158		18	256		506	5000	258		284		EC				
notes	🍷		R	🍷			R	✕		R	🍷			2	🍷		🍷		150				
								C ⚡									B		A				
Split d.	...	...	...	...	...	...	...	...	...	...	...	...	...	...	...	...	...	...	...	...	...	...	...
Rijeka d.	...	...	...	...	...	...	...	...	...	...	...	...	...	...	...	...	...	...	1250	...	...	...	...
Koper d.	...	...	...	...	...	0523	...	...	...	...	...	...	...	...	...	...	...	...	|	...	...	...	...
Ljubljana d.	...	...	0545	...	...	0748	0805	...	...	1213	...	...	1235	...	...	...	...	...	1600	...	...	...	...
Zagreb d.	...	...	|	...	...	...	|	0725	...	|	...	...	|	...	...	...	1545	...	|	...	...	...	...
Dobova 🏛 d.	...	...	|	...	...	...	|	0813	...	|	...	...	|	...	...	...	|	...	|	...	...	...	...
Zidani Most d.	...	...	0630	...	...	...	0850	|	...	1259	...	...	1331	1400	...	...	|	...	1654	...	...	...	...
Pragersko d.	...	...	0722	...	...	...	0941	0959	...	1354	...	...	1444	1516	...	...	|	...	1758	...	...	...	...
Maribor d.	0619	...	0736	0821	...	...	0953	1022	...	1406	1422	...	1502	1541	1621	...	|	...	1821	...	...	...	...
Spielfeld-Straß 🏛 a.	0637	...	...	0839	...	...	...	1039	...	...	1439	...	...	...	1639	...	|	...	1839	...	...	...	...
Graz Hbf a.	0723	...	...	0923	...	...	...	1123	...	...	1523	...	...	...	1723	...	|	...	1923	...	...	...	...
Wien Meidling a.	0958	...	...	1158	...	...	...	1358	...	...	1758	...	...	...	1958	...	2125	...	2158	...	...	...	...

A – EMONA – (12) and ✕ Wien - Ljubljana and v.v. (2) Wien - Ljubljana - Rijeka and v.v. (12) Ljubljana - Rijeka and v.v.

B – ZAGREB – (12) and 🍷 Wien - Sopron 🏛 - Szombathely - Nagykanizsa - Gyékényes 🏛 - Zagreb and v.v. Table **92**.

C – CROATIA – (12) and ✕ Wien - Zagreb and v.v.

D – Daily (①–⑥ June 21 - Sept. 4) not Dec. 27, Feb. 7, Apr. 4, 25, Oct. 25.

⚡ – Supplement payable.

92 BUDAPEST / ZAGREB - SARAJEVO

train number	397	IC 537 259	399	391
notes	G		H	
Zagreb d.	0853	A	2126	...
Sunja d.	1015	...	2248	...
Volinja 🛃 d.	1101	...	2334	...
Dobrljin 🛃 d.	1127	...	2357	...
Novi Grad d.	1144	...	0011	...
Banja Luka d.	1315	...	0143	...
Budapest Keleti d.	|	0945	|	...
Dombóvár d.	|	1151	|	...
Pécs d.	|	1300	|	...
Magyarbóly 🛃 d.	|	1408	|	...
Beli Manastir 🛃 d.	|	1430	|	...
Osijek d.	|	1459	|	...
Slavonski Šamac 🛃 d.	|	1626	|	...
Šamac 🛃 d.	|	1645	|	...
Doboj d.	1512	1814	0345	...
Zenica d.	1647	1951	0521	...
Sarajevo a.	1805	2109	0639	...
Sarajevo d.	1818	...	...	0705
Mostar d.	2043	...	...	0926
Ploče d.	2217	...	...	1100

train number	IC 258 536	396	390	398
notes		G		H
Ploče d.	A	0600	1700	...
Mostar d.	...	0738	1840	...
Sarajevo a.	...	1002	2059	...
Sarajevo d.	0702	1027	...	2120
Zenica d.	0822	1147	...	2240
Doboj d.	1005	1329	...	0023
Šamac 🛃 d.	1131	|	...	|
Slavonski Šamac 🛃 d.	1145	|	...	|
Osijek d.	1258	|	...	|
Beli Manastir 🛃 d.	1342	|	...	|
Magyarbóly 🛃 a.	1355	|	...	|
Pécs a.	1457	|	...	|
Dombóvár a.	1610	|	...	|
Budapest Keleti a.	1814	|	...	|
Banja Luka d.	...	1529	...	0221
Novi Grad d.	...	1657	...	0348
Dobrljin 🛃 d.	...	1749	...	0420
Volinja 🛃 d.	...	1817	...	0452
Sunja d.	...	1844	...	0522
Zagreb a.	...	2005	...	0643

A – DRÁVA – [12] Budapest - Pécs - Magyarbóly - Sarajevo and v.v. ✕ Budapest - Pécs and v.v.
E – ZAGREB – [12] and 🍸 Wien - Zagreb and v.v.
G – [12] Zagreb - Sarajevo - Ploče and v.v.
H – [12] Zagreb - Sarajevo and v.v.
J – [12] Beograd - Sarajevo and v.v.

92 WIEN - ZAGREB

train number	IC 285
notes	E
Wien Meidling d.	0703
Sopron 🛃 d.	0814
Szombathely a.	0909
Nagykanizsa a.	1039
Gyékényes 🛃 a.	1104
Koprivnica 🛃 a.	1139
Zagreb a.	1259

train number	IC 284
notes	E
Zagreb d.	1545
Koprivnica 🛃 d.	1700
Gyékényes 🛃 d.	1737
Nagykanizsa d.	1803
Szombathely d.	1928
Sopron 🛃 a.	2026
Wien Meidling a.	2125

92 BEOGRAD - SARAJEVO

train number	451
notes	J
Beograd d.	0815
Šid 🛃 d.	1118
Vinkovci d.	1205
Strizivojna-Vrpolje **1345** d.	1226
Slavonski Šamac 🛃 d.	1300
Šamac 🛃 d.	1321
Doboj d.	1442
Zenica d.	1617
Sarajevo a.	1735

train number	450
notes	J
Sarajevo d.	1135
Zenica d.	1255
Doboj d.	1440
Šamac 🛃 d.	1606
Slavonski Šamac 🛃 d.	1640
Strizivojna-Vrpolje **1345** d.	1657
Vinkovci d.	1723
Šid 🛃 d.	1830
Beograd a.	2018

93 WARSZAWA - VILNIUS

train number	10011	394		🚌	
train number	910	91001		99928	
notes		2		D Ⓡ	
Berlin Hbf d.	...	...	...	...	...
Warszawa Centralna a.	...	...	...	...	...
Warszawa Centralna d.	0725	...	...	2300	...
Warszawa Wschodnia d.	0734	...	...	|	...
Białystok d.	1010	...	...	0140	...
Suwałki d.	1244	...	...	|	...
Šeštokai 🛃 § a.	1448	1503	...	|	...
Kaunas a.	...	1633	...	0610	...
Vilnius a.	...	1750	...	0750	...

train number	393	10012		🚌	
train number	10012	910		99927	
notes	2			E Ⓡ	
Vilnius d.	1200	...	...	2230	...
Kaunas d.	1317	...	...	0005	...
Šeštokai 🛃 § d.	1448	1508	...	|	...
Suwałki a.	...	1514	...	|	...
Białystok a.	...	1746	...	0230	...
Warszawa Wschodnia a.	...	2021	...	|	...
Warszawa Centralna a.	...	2030	...	0500	...
Warszawa Centralna d.	...	...	...	...	...
Berlin Hbf a.	...	...	...	...	...

D – ①③⑤ (also Dec. 20, 22, 27, 29, May 1, 8, 15, 22, 29, June 5, 12; not Dec. 21, 23, 28, 30) 🚌 run by PKP InterCity. Ⓡ.
E – ②④⑥ (also Dec. 21, 23, 28, 30, May 2, 9, 16, 23, 30, June 6, 13; not Dec. 22, 24, 29, 31) 🚌 run by PKP InterCity. Ⓡ.

§ – 🛃 at Trakiszki / Mockava.

94 MOSKVA / St PETERBURG - WARSZAWA

train number	19	13	19/25	25	115	9			11
notes	442	442	115	115	11008	11002		446	11014
	G	N	A	S	T	R		P	Q
Moskva Belorusskaya d.	...	0800	...	1027	...	1650	...	2109	2109
Smolensk Tsentralny 🛃 § d.	...	1220	...	1620	...	2132	...	0231	0231
St Peterburg Vitebski d.	2355	|	2355	|	...	|	...	|	|
Orsha Tsentralnaya § d.	1250j	1250	1707j	1707	...	2153	...	0311	0311
Minsk d.	1529	1529	2040	2040	2040	0019	...	0619	0619
Brest 🛃 d.	2115	2115	0240	0240	0240	0532	...	1223	1223
Terespol a.	2033	2033	0158	0158	0158	0450	...	1141	1141
Warszawa Wschodnia a.	2338	2338	0534	0534	0534	0814	...	1514	1514
Warszawa Centralna a.	0101	0101	0546	0546	0546	0835	...	1801	...

train number		12	10		11011	116	116	443	443
notes	447	11013	11001		116	132	14/20	14	20
	P	Q	R		T	S	B	M	H
Warszawa Centralna d.	1030	...	1555	...	2100	2100	2100	2300	2300
Warszawa Wschodnia d.	1300	1300	1605	...	2110	2110	2110	2353	2353
Terespol d.	1555	1555	1922	...	0036	0036	0036	0330	0330
Brest 🛃 a.	1741	1741	2058	...	0222	0222	0222f	0516f	0516f
Minsk a.	2345	2345	0158	...	0804	0837	1046	1046	1046
Orsha Tsentralnaya § a.	0234	0234	0424	...	...	1136	1332c	1332	1332c
St Peterburg Vitebski a.	|	|	|	...	...	|	0615	|	0615
Smolensk Tsentralny 🛃 § a.	0502	0502	0643	...	...	1408	...	1601	...
Moskva Belorusskaya a.	1033	1033	1145	...	...	1954	...	2035	...

A – ③⑤ Dec. 11 - May 28 (not Dec. 30); ①②③⑤⑦ May 30 - Oct. 3; ③⑤ Oct. 6 - Dec. 10: 🛏 2 cl. St Peterburg (**19**) - Orsha (**25**) - Minsk (**115**) - Brest 🛃 - Warszawa (journey 2 nights).
B – ⑤⑦ Dec. 13 - May 30 (not Jan. 1); ②③④⑤⑦ June 1 - Oct. 5; ③⑤⑦ Oct. 8 - Dec. 10: 🛏 2 cl. Warszawa (**116**) - Brest (**14**) - Orsha (**20**) - St Peterburg (journey 2 nights).
G – ③⑤: 🛏 2 cl. St Peterburg (**19**) - Orsha (**13**) - Terespol (**442**) - Warszawa - Berlin (journey 2 nights).
H – ⑤⑦: 🛏 2 cl. Berlin (**443**) - Warszawa - Brest 🛃 (**14**) - Orsha (**20**) - St Peterburg (journey 2 nights).
M – MOSKVA EXPRESS – ②⑤⑦ Dec. 13 - May 30 (not Jan. 1); ②③④⑤⑦ June 1 - Oct. 3; ②⑤⑦ Oct. 5 - Dec. 11: 🛏 1 cl. *Lux* and 🛏 1, 2 cl. Berlin (**443**) - Warszawa - Brest 🛃 (**14**) - Moskva.
N – MOSKVA EXPRESS – ①④⑥ Dec. 13 - May 29 (not Dec. 31); ①②③④⑥ May 31 - Oct. 2; ①④⑥ Oct. 4 - Dec. 11: 🛏 1 cl. *Lux* and 🛏 1, 2 cl. Moskva (**13**) - Terespol (**442**) - Warszawa - Berlin.
P – JAN KIEPURA – 🛏 1, 2 cl. Moskva - Warszawa - Köln - Amsterdam and v.v. (journey 2 nights; for timings of Basel, Amsterdam and München cars see Table **24**).
Q – OST–WEST – 🛏 1, 2 cl. Warszawa - Moskva and v.v.
R – POLONEZ – 🛏 1, 2 cl., 🛏 1, 2 cl. (Lux) and 🍸 Warszawa - Moskva and v.v. ✕ Brest - Moskva and v.v.
S – 🛏 1, 2 cl. Warszawa - Moskva and v.v.
T – 🛏 1, 2 cl. Minsk - Warszawa and v.v.

c – Depart 1637.
f – Depart 0720.
j – Arrive 1047.

§ – 🛃: Osinovka (BY) / Krasnoye (RU).

95 MOSKVA / St PETERBURG - WIEN, BRATISLAVA, BUDAPEST and PRAHA

train number	408	408	408	408	408	408	
notes	B	V	J	C	F	P	
Moskva Belorusskaya d.	...	2344	2344	2344	2344	...	...
Smolensk Tsentralny 🛃 § d.	...	0505	0505	0505	0505	...	...
St Peterburg Vitebski d.	1500	|	|	|	|	1500	...
Orsha Tsentralnaya § d.	0127	0542	0542	0542	0542	0127	...
Minsk d.	0408	0825	0825	0825	0825	0408	...
Brest 🛃 d.	1440x	1440z	1440z	1440z	1440z	1440x	...
Terespol a.	1358	1358	1358	1358	1358	1358	...
Łuków a.	1602	1602	1602	1602	1602	1602	...
Katowice a.	2153	2153	2153	2153	2153	2153	...
Bohumín 🛃 a.	2348	2348	2348	2348	2348	2348	...
Ostrava Hlavní a.	0050	0050	0050	0224	0224	0224	...
Břeclav a.	|	|	|	0411	0411	0411	...
Wien Westbahnhof a.	|	|	|	0622	|	|	...
Bratislava Hlavná a.	|	|	|	...	0540	0540	...
Budapest Keleti a.	|	|	|	...	0832	0832	...
Zagreb a.	|	|	|	...	...	1915	...
Olomouc a.	0202	0202	0202	...	...	...	...
Pardubice a.	0339	0339	0339	...	...	...	...
Praha hlavní a.	0505	0505	0505e	...	...	...	...
Karlovy Vary a.	...	...	1047	...	...	...	...
Cheb a.	...	...	1142	...	...	...	...

train number	409	409	409	409	409	409	
notes	Q	G	H	K	W	D	
Cheb d.	...	...	...	1614	...	...	...
Karlovy Vary d.	...	...	...	1706	...	...	...
Praha hlavní d.	...	...	...	2300f	2300	2300	...
Pardubice d.	...	...	...	0014	0014	0014	...
Olomouc d.	...	...	...	0152	0152	0152	...
Zagreb d.	0958	...	...	|	|	|	...
Budapest Keleti d.	1958	1958	...	|	|	|	...
Bratislava Hlavná d.	2250	2250	...	|	|	|	...
Wien Westbahnhof d.	|	|	2208	|	|	|	...
Břeclav d.	0012	0012	0012	|	|	|	...
Ostrava Hlavní d.	0159	0159	0159	0302	0302	0302	...
Bohumín 🛃 d.	0329	0329	0329	0329	0329	0329	...
Katowice d.	0512	0512	0512	0512	0512	0512	...
Łuków d.	1115	1115	1115	1115	1115	1115	...
Terespol d.	1318	1318	1318	1318	1318	1318	...
Brest 🛃 a.	1504c	1504c	1504c	1504c	1504c	1504c	...
Minsk a.	2102	2102	2102	2102	2102	2102	...
Orsha Tsentralnaya § a.	2344	2344	2344	2344	2344	2344	...
St Peterburg Vitebski a.	1243	|	|	|	|	1243	...
Smolensk Tsentralny 🛃 § a.	...	0214	0214	0214	0214	...	...
Moskva Belorusskaya a.	...	0805	0805	0805	0805	...	...

B – ③④ Dec. 13 - June 2; ①③④⑤⑥⑦ June 3 - Sept. 20; ③④ Sept. 21 - Dec. 11: 🛏 1, 2 cl. St Peterburg (**49**) - Brest (**408**) - Praha (journey 2 nights).
C – 🛏 1, 2 cl. Moskva (**21**) - Terespol (**408**) - Katowice - Bohumín (**407**) - Wien (journey 2 nights).
D – ⑤⑥ Dec. 13 - June 5; ①②③⑤⑥⑦ June 6 - Sept. 22; ⑤⑥ Sept. 23 - Dec. 11: 🛏 1, 2 cl. Praha (**409**) - Orsha (**62/61**) - St Peterburg (journey 2 nights).
F – 🛏 1, 2 cl. Moskva (**21**) - Terespol (**408**) - Katowice - Bohumín (**407**) - Břeclav (**477**) - Bratislava - Budapest (journey 2 nights).
G – 🛏 1, 2 cl. Budapest (**476**) - Bratislava - Břeclav (**406**) - Bohumín (**409**) - Katowice - Brest (**22**) - Moskva (journey 2 nights).
H – 🛏 1, 2 cl. Wien (**406**) - Bohumín (**409**) - Katowice - Brest (**22**) - Moskva (journey 2 nights).
J – 🛏 1, 2 cl. Moskva (**21**) - Terespol (**14012**) - Katowice - Bohumín (**408**) - Praha (**606**) - Cheb (journey 2 nights). ✕ Moskva - Brest.
K – 🛏 1, 2 cl. Cheb (**607**) - Praha (**409**) - Bohumín (**41012**) - Katowice - Brest (**22**) - Moskva (journey 2 nights). ✕ Brest - Moskva.
V – VLTAVA – 🛏 1, 2 cl. Moskva (**21**) - Terespol (**14012**) - Katowice - Bohumín (**408**) - Praha (journey 2 nights). ✕ Moskva - Brest.
W – VLTAVA – 🛏 1, 2 cl. Praha (**409**) - Bohumín (**41012**) - Katowice - Brest (**22**) - Moskva (journey 2 nights). ✕ Brest - Moskva.
P – ⑦ (May 30 - Sept. 12) 🛏 1, 2 cl. St Peterburg (**49**) - Brest (**408**) - Bohumín (**407**) - Břeclav (**477**) - Budapest (**204**) - Zagreb (journey 2 nights).
Q – ③ (June 2 - Sept. 15) 🛏 1, 2 cl. Zagreb (**205**) - Budapest (**476**) - Břeclav (**406**) - Bohumín (**409**) - Orsha (**61/62**) - St Peterburg (journey 2 nights).

c – Depart 1707.
e – Depart 0731.
f – Arrive 2027.
x – Arrive 0824.
z – Arrive 1226.

§ – 🛃: Osinovka (BY) / Krasnoye (RU).

PRAHA, WIEN and WROCŁAW - KYÏV 96

train number	EC	609	609		406		401	73102	83102	
train number	121	16	16	16	401	401	52/108	52	35	170
notes	✕	A	X		H	C	T	P	G	
Praha hlavní d.	1111	...	...	...	...	2132	2132	...	...	...
Pardubice d.	1226	...	...	...	...	2252	2252	...	...	...
Česká Třebová d.	1305	...	...	...	...	2342	2342	...	...	...
Olomouc d.	1354	...	...	...	...	0037	0037	...	...	...
Wien Westbahnhof d.	|	...	...	...	2208	|	|	...	...	...
Bratislava Hlavná d.	|	1410	1410	...	|	|	|	...	...	...
Žilina d.	1625	1654	1654	...	|	|	|	...	...	...
Košice a.	1918	2002	2002	...	|	|	|	...	...	...
Košice d.	...	2045	2045	...	|	|	|	...	...	...
Čierna nad Tisou 🏛 a.	...	2227	2227	...	|	|	|	...	...	...
Chop 🏛 a.	...	0050	0050	...	|	|	|	...	...	...
Bohumín 🏛 d.	...	|	|	...	0307	0307	0307	...	...	...
Zebrzydowice 🏛 d.	...	|	|	...	0327	0327	0327	...	...	...
Wrocław Główny d.	...	|	|	...	|	|	|	0808	1720	...
Katowice d.	...	|	|	...	|	|	|	1055	2025	...
Kraków Główny d.	...	|	|	...	1301e	1301e	1301e	1301	2234	...
Przemyśl a.	...	|	|	...	1705	1705	1705	1705	0207	...
Przemysl d.	...	|	|	...	1917	1917	1917	1917	0247	...
Mostiska II ◐ d.	...	|	|	...	2222	2222	2222	2222	0451	...
Lviv a.	...	1030	1030	1058	2344	2344	2344	2344	0603	0635
Ternopil a.	...	1305	...	1305	0221	0221	|	0221	...	|
Kozyatyn a.	...	1800	...	1800	0805	0805	|	0805	...	|
Kyïv a.	...	2000	...	2000	1018	1018	|	1018	...	1300
Odesa a.	...	...	...	...	...	...	1331	...	...	...

train number		36	51	51	51	108/51	7		7	
train number	169	38102	37102	400	407	400	422	7	422	442
notes		G	P	D	J	U	B		Y	E
Odesa d.	...	...	...	...	...	1813	...	...	...	...
Kyïv d.	1704	...	2042	2042	2042	|	2358	2358	...	...
Kozyatyn d.	|	...	2311	2311	2311	|	0215	0215	...	...
Ternopil d.	|	...	0437	0437	0437	|	0723	0723	...	...
Lviv d.	2329	2359	0719	0719	0719	0719	1001	0935	1001	...
Mostiska II ◐ d.	...	0145	0937	0937	0937	0937	|	...	|	...
Przemyśl a.	...	0117	0933	0933	0933	0933	|	...	|	...
Przemyśl d.	...	0154	1138	1138	1138	1138	|	...	|	...
Kraków Główny a.	...	0514	1527	1527c	1527c	1527c	|	...	|	...
Katowice a.	...	0725	1727	|	|	|	|	...	|	...
Wrocław Główny a.	...	1025	2022	|	|	|	|	...	|	...
Zebrzydowice 🏛 a.	...	...	...	0048	0048	0048	|	...	|	...
Bohumín 🏛 a.	...	...	...	0107	0107	0107	|	...	|	...
Chop 🏛 d.	...	...	...	|	|	|	1820	...	1820	...
Čierna nad Tisou 🏛 d.	...	...	...	|	|	|	1952	...	1952	...
Košice a.	...	...	...	|	|	|	2130	...	2130	...
Košice d.	...	...	...	|	|	|	2205	...	2205	2205
Žilina a.	...	...	...	|	|	|	0119	...	0119	0119
Bratislava Hlavná a.	...	...	...	|	|	|	0515	...	0515	|
Wien Westbahnhof a.	...	...	...	|	0622	|	...	...	...	|
Olomouc a.	...	...	...	0352	...	0352	...	...	...	0508
Česká Třebová a.	...	...	...	0446	...	0446	...	...	...	0609
Pardubice a.	...	...	...	0530	...	0530	...	...	...	0656
Praha hlavní a.	...	...	...	0651	...	0651	...	...	...	0815

A – ①②④⑤⑦: 🛏 1, 2 cl. Bratislava (**609**) - Košice (**8815**) - Čierna nad Tisou (**8860**) - Chop (**16**) - Kyïv.
B – ②③⑤⑥⑦: 🛏 1, 2 cl. Kyïv (**7**) - Chop (**8865**) - Čierna nad Tisou (**8814**) - Košice (**442**) - Žilina (**700**) - Bratislava (journey 2 nights).
C – 🛏 1, 2 cl. Praha (**401**) - Kraków (**73103**) - Przemyśl (**52**) - Kyïv (journey 2 nights). 🛏 1, 2 cl., ━ 2 cl. and (12) Praha - Kraków.
D – 🛏 1, 2 cl. Kyïv (**51**) - Przemyśl (**37102**) - Kraków (**400**) - Praha (journey 2 nights). 🛏 1, 2 cl., ━ 2 cl. and (12) Kraków - Praha.
E – SÍRAVA – 🛏 1, 2 cl., ━ 2 cl. and (12) Humenné - Košice - Praha.
G – 🛏 2 cl. Wrocław - Kraków - Lviv and v.v.
H – ④⑦: 🛏 1, 2 cl. Wien (**406**) - Bohumín (**401**) - Kraków (**73103**) - Przemyśl (**52**) - Kyïv (journey 2 nights).
J – ②⑤: 🛏 1, 2 cl. Kyïv (**51**) - Przemyśl (**37102**) - Kraków (**400**) - Bohumín (**407**) - Wien (journey 2 nights).
P – *TLK* 🛏 2 cl. Wrocław - Kraków - Przemyśl - Lviv - Kyïv and v.v. Conveys ━ 2 cl. Wrocław - Kraków - Odesa and v.v. on dates in Table **1056**.
T – ①②④⑤: 🛏 1, 2 cl. Praha - Odesa (journey 2 nights).
U – ②③⑥⑦: 🛏 1, 2 cl. Odesa - Praha (journey 2 nights).
X – ③⑥: 🛏 1, 2 cl. Bratislava - Lviv.
Y – ②⑤: 🛏 1, 2 cl. Lviv - Bratislava.

c – Depart 2211.
e – Arrive 0624.
◐ – 🏛 at Medyka / Mostiska **II** (Table **1056**).

MOSKVA - BUDAPEST, VENEZIA, BEOGRAD and ATHÍNAI 97

train type/number	15	204	*EN* 240	15	15	335	*IC* ⚡	15	15	15
notes	345	[R]	[R] ⚡	335	335		55			
notes	A		C	S	U	M	✕ [R]	K	Y	Q
Moskva Kiyevskaya d.	2213	...	...	2213	...	...	...	2213	...	2213
Minsk d.	|	...	...	|	...	...	...	|	...	|
Kyïv d.	1110	...	...	1110	1110	...	...	1110	1110	1110
Lviv d.	2120	...	...	2120	2120	...	...	2120	2120	2120
Chop 🏛 d.	0630	...	...	0630	0630	...	...	0630	0630	0630
Debrecen a.	0801	...	...	0801	0801	...	...	0801	0801	0801
Szolnok a.	0948	...	...	0948	0948	...	...	0948	0948	0948
Budapest Keleti a.	1117	...	...	1117	1117	...	...	1117	1117	1117
Budapest Keleti d.	1305	1305	1700	1305	1305	...	...	1305	1305	1700
Siófok a.	|	1456	1856	|	|	...	...	1456	1456	1856
Zagreb a.	|	1936	2307	|	|	...	...	1936	1936	2307
Ljubljana a.	|	...	0210	|	|	...	...	...	...	0210
Trieste Centrale a.	|	...	|	|	|	...	...	...	...	|
Venezia Santa Lucia a.	|	...	0716	|	|	...	...	...	...	0716
Subotica 🏛 a.	1631	...	...	1631	1631	...	...	...	...	...
Novi Sad a.	1904	...	...	1904	1904	...	...	...	...	...
Beograd a.	2036	...	...	2036	2036	2150	...	...	...	...
Niš a.	...	...	...	0159	0159	0159	...	...	...	...
Skopje ⊖ a.	...	...	...	0706	0706	0706	...	...	...	...
Thessaloníki ⊡ a.	...	...	...	1254	1254	1254	1454	...	...	...
Athína Lárisa a.	...	...	...	...	...	...	1950	...	...	...

train type/number	*IC* ⚡	334	*EN* 241	703	344	334	334	16	16	16
notes	52		[R] ⚡	205	16	16	16			
notes	✕ [R]	M	C	[R]	B	T	V	R	L	Z
Athína Lárisa d.	1051	...	...	...	...	...	...	...	...	...
Thessaloníki ⊡ d.	1548	1705	...	...	...	1705	1705	...	...	...
Skopje ⊖ d.	...	2045	...	...	...	2045	2045	...	...	...
Niš d.	...	0152	...	...	...	0152	0152	...	...	...
Beograd d.	...	0559	...	...	0720	0720	0720	...	...	...
Novi Sad d.	...	...	...	...	0856	0856	0856	...	...	...
Subotica 🏛 d.	...	...	...	...	1129	1129	1129	...	...	...
Venezia Santa Lucia d.	...	...	2120	...	|	|	|	2120	...	...
Trieste Centrale d.	...	...	|	...	|	|	|	|	...	...
Ljubljana d.	...	...	0159	...	|	|	|	0159	...	...
Zagreb d.	...	...	0456	1000	|	|	|	0456	1000	1000
Siófok d.	...	...	0900	1500	|	|	|	0900	1500	1500
Budapest Keleti a.	...	...	1059	1654	1455	1455	1455	1059	1654	1654
Budapest Keleti d.	...	...	...	...	1843	1843	1843	1843	1843	1843
Szolnok d.	...	...	...	...	2004	2004	2004	2004	2004	2004
Debrecen d.	...	...	...	...	2136	2136	2136	2136	2136	2136
Chop 🏛 a.	...	...	...	...	0113	0113	0113	0113	0113	0113
Lviv a.	...	...	...	...	1031	1031	1031	1031	1031	1031
Kyïv a.	...	...	...	...	2001	2001	2001	2001	2001	2001
Minsk a.	...	...	...	...	|	|	...	|	|	...
Moskva Kiyevskaya a.	...	...	...	...	0956	0956	...	0956	0956	...

A – TISZA – 🛏 2 cl. Moskva (**15**) - Budapest (**345**) - Beograd (journey 2 nights). Conveys on ② June 15 - Sept. 14: 🛏 1, 2 cl. Moskva - Bar; also from Kyïv on ⑦. (Table **1370**).
B – TISZA – 🛏 2 cl. Beograd (**344**) - Budapest (**16**) - Moskva (journey 2 nights). Conveys on ⑤ June 18 - Sept. 17: 🛏 2 cl. Bar - Moskva; also to Kyïv on ②. (Table **1370**).
C – VENEZIA – 🛏 1, 2 cl., ━ 2 cl., (2) and ✕ Budapest - Ljubljana - Venezia and v.v.
K – ②④⑥: 🛏 1, 2 cl. Moskva (**15**) - Kyïv - Budapest (**204**) - Zagreb (journey 2 nights).
L – ②⑤⑦: 🛏 1, 2 cl. Zagreb (**205**) - Budapest (**16**) - Kyïv - Moskva (journey 2 nights).
M – HELLAS EXPRESS – 🛏 1, 2 cl., ━ 2 cl. and (12) Beograd - Thessaloníki and v.v. 🛏 1, 2 cl., ━ 2 cl. and (2) Beograd - Skopje and v.v.
Q – ⑦: 🛏 1, 2 cl. Moskva (**15**) - Budapest (**240**) - Venezia (journey 3 nights).
R – ③: 🛏 1, 2 cl. Venezia (**241**) - Budapest (**16**) - Moskva (journey 3 nights).
S – ⑤ June 11 - Sept. 17: 🛏 2 cl. Moskva - Budapest (**345**) - Beograd (**335**) - Thessaloníki.
T – ① June 17 - Sept. 20: 🛏 2 cl. Thessaloníki (**334**) - Beograd (**344**) - Budapest (**16**) - Moskva.
U – ③ June 9 - Sept. 15: 🛏 2 cl. Kyïv - Thessaloníki.
V – ⑤ June 11 - Sept. 17: 🛏 2 cl. Thessaloníki - Kyïv.
Y – ④: 🛏 1, 2 cl. Kyïv - Zagreb.
Z – ⑥: 🛏 1, 2 cl. Zagreb - Kyïv.

⊖ – 🏛 at Preševo / Tabanovci.
⊡ – 🏛 at Gevgelija / Idomeni.
⚡ – [R] with supplement payable.

MOSKVA - BUCUREŞTI, SOFIYA and İSTANBUL 98

train number	463	101	1003	668	668	86	3	59	59	59
train number	491	1003	1005	59	1183	383	383	383	1181	1183
notes	M	R	Y	F	W	N	B	A	V	K
Moskva Kiyevskaya d.	...	...	...	...	...	...	2139	0025	0025	0025
St Peterburg Vit d.	...	1908	1908	...	...	...	|	|	|	|
Minsk d.	...	1729	1729	...	...	2050	|	|	|	|
Kyïv d.	...	|	|	...	...	1357	1540	1357	1357	1357
Lviv d.	...	0657	0657	2335	2335	|	|	|	|	|
Chernivtsi d.	...	1230	1230	0705	0705	0705	0705	0705	0705	0705
Vadul Siret 🏛 d.	...	1530	1530	1020	1020	1020	1020	1020	1020	1020
Bucureşti Nord a.	1216	0120	|	1930	1930	1930	1930	1930	1930	1930
Constanţa a.	|	|	0407	|	|	|	|	|	|	|
Ruse 🏛 a.	1450	0430	...	2230	2230	2230	2230	2230	2230	2230
Varna a.	|	0855	...	|	|	|	|	|	0655	|
Burgas a.	|	...	...	|	0913	|	|	|	...	0913
Sofiya a.	|	...	...	0555	...	0555	0555	0555	...	...
Kapikule 🏛 a.	0110	...	...	...	...	...	...	...	...	...
İstanbul Sirkeci a.	0800	...	...	...	...	...	...	...	...	...

train number	1180	1182			382	382	1182	1004	1006	492
train number	382	382	382	382	54	604	604	101	1004	462
notes	Q	S	C	D	P	T	U	X	Z	G
İstanbul Sirkeci d.	...	...	...	...	...	...	...	...	...	2200
Kapikule 🏛 d.	...	...	...	...	...	...	...	...	...	0405
Sofiya d.	...	...	1940	1940	1940	1940	...	...	...	|
Burgas d.	...	1925	|	|	|	|	1925	...	...	|
Varna d.	2200	|	|	|	|	|	|	2050	...	|
Ruse 🏛 d.	0315	0315	0315	0315	0315	0315	0315	0100	...	1600
Constanţa d.	|	|	|	|	|	|	|	|	0045	|
Bucureşti Nord d.	0620	0620	0620	0620	0620	0620	0620	0446	|	1831
Vadul Siret 🏛 a.	1510	1510	1510	1510	1510	1510	1510	1305	1305	...
Chernivtsi a.	1816	1816	1816	1816	1816	1816	1816	1613	1613	...
Lviv a.	|	|	|	|	|	0804	0804	2247	2247	...
Kyïv a.	0919	0919	0919	0919x	0919z	...	...	|	|	...
Minsk a.	|	|	|	|	2310	...	...	1150	1150	...
St Peterburg Vit a.	|	|	|	|	...	...	...	0853	0853	...
Moskva Kiyevskaya a.	2236	2236	2236	0452	...	...	...	...	...	...

A – BULGARIA EXPRESS – June 13 - Sept 3: 🛏 1, 2 cl. Moskva (**59**) - Vadul Siret (**383**) - Bucureşti - Sofiya.
B – BULGARIA EXPRESS – Dec. 13 - June 11, Sept. 3 - Dec. 8: 🛏 1, 2 cl. Moskva (**3**) - Kyïv (**59**) - Vadul Siret (**383**) - Bucureşti - Ruse - Sofiya.
C – BULGARIA EXPRESS – June 13 - Sept. 3: 🛏 1, 2 cl. Sofiya (**382**) - Bucureşti - Vadul Siret (**60**) - Moskva.
D – BULGARIA EXPRESS – Dec. 11 - June 12, Sept. 4 - Dec. 8: 🛏 1, 2 cl. Sofiya (**382**) - Ruse - Bucureşti - Vadul Siret (**60**) - Kyïv (**142**) - Moskva.
F – ①④⑥ Dec. 12 - June 12; Sept. 4 - Dec. 9: 🛏 2 cl. Lviv (**668**) - Chernivtsi (**59**) - Vadul Siret (**383**) - Bucureşti - Ruse 🏛 (**4665**) - Sofiya.
G – BOSPHOR – 🛏 1, 2 cl. and ━ 2 cl. İstanbul (**81032**) - Kapikule 🏛 (**492/464**) - Ruse 🏛 (**462**) - Bucureşti.
K – ④⑥ June 17 - Sept. 2: 🛏 2 cl. Moskva (**59**) - Vadul Siret (**383**) - Bucureşti - Ruse 🏛 (**1183**) - Burgas.
M – BOSPHOR – 🛏 1, 2 cl. and ━ 2 cl. Bucureşti (**463**) - Ruse 🏛 (**465/491**) - Kapikule 🏛 (**81031**) - İstanbul.
N – ⑥ (also ② June 12 - Aug. 31): 🛏 2 cl. Minsk (**86**) - Kyïv (**59**) - Sofiya.
P – ② (also ⑤ June 15 - Sept. 3): 🛏 2 cl. Sofiya (**382**) - Kyïv (**54**) - Homel (**615**) - Minsk.
Q – ②③④⑤⑦ June 15 - Sept. 8: 🛏 2 cl. Varna (**1180**) - Ruse 🏛 (**382**) - Bucureşti - Vadul Siret (**60**) - Moskva.
R – ② June 15 - Aug. 31: 🛏 2 cl. St Peterburg - Minsk - Varna.
S – ①⑥ June 19 - Sept. 4: 🛏 2 cl. Burgas (**1182**) - Ruse 🏛 (**382**) - Bucureşti - Vadul Siret (**60**) - Moskva.
T – ①③⑥ Dec. 14 - June 14; Sept. 6 - Dec. 11: 🛏 2 cl. Sofiya (**60**) - Ruse 🏛 (**382**) - Bucureşti - Vadul Siret (**60**) - Chernivtsi (**604**) - Lviv.
U – ①⑥ June 19 - Sept. 4: 🛏 2 cl. Burgas - Lviv.
V – ①②③⑤⑦ June 13 - Sept. 3: 🛏 2 cl. Moskva (**59**) - Vadul Siret (**383**) - Bucureşti - Ruse 🏛 (**1181**) - Varna.
W – ④⑥ June 17 - Sept. 2: 🛏 2 cl. Lviv - Burgas.
X – ⑤ June 18 - Sept. 3: 🛏 2 cl. Varna - Minsk - St Peterburg.
Y – ② June 15 - Aug. 31: 🛏 2 cl. St Peterburg - Minsk - Constanţa.
Z – ⑥ June 19 - Sept. 4. 🛏 2 cl. Constanţa - Minsk - St Peterburg.
x – Depart 1342 (Train **142**).
z – Depart 1030 (Train **54**).

99 WARSZAWA, WROCŁAW, KRAKÓW - PRAHA, WIEN, BUDAPEST and BUCUREŞTI

train type/number	EC	EC		EC			EC	EC	EC	EC			EC	EC	IC							
train number	340	103	275	144		38108	110	137	173	142		38106	105	175	540	400	400	400	407	407	407	
notes	Ⓡ⊡	Ⓡ	475	✕		38109	Ⓡ		✕	✕		38107	Ⓡ	✕	🍷	407	407		477		400	
notes	W	✕⊡					✕⊡	🍷					✕⊡			477			Ⓡ	Ⓡ	Ⓡ	
notes		R					X	T	Z				Y			A	D	S	B	C	Q	
Warszawa Wschodnia d.	...	0633	...	...	...	...	0923	...	...	...	...	...	1233	...	...	...	...	...	2057	2057	2057	...
Warszawa Centralna d.	...	0645	...	...	...	...	0945	...	...	...	...	...	1245	...	...	...	...	...	2110	2110	2110	...
Wrocław Główny d.	...	│	...	...	...	...	│	...	...	...	...	...	│	...	...	...	...	...	│	│	│	...
Lichkov 🏛 d.	...	│	...	...	...	...	│	...	...	...	...	...	│	...	...	...	...	...	│	│	│	...
Kraków Gł. d.	0724	│	...	...	...	0947	│	...	...	...	...	1247	│	...	...	2211	2211	2211	│	│	│	...
Tarnów d.	│	│	...	...	...	│	│	...	...	...	...	│	│	...	...	│	│	│	│	│	│	...
Katowice d.	0904	0913	...	...	...	1129	1214	...	...	...	...	1429	1511	...	...	│	│	│	2357	2357	2357	...
Zebrzydowice 🏛 d.	...	1015	...	...	...	...	1315	...	...	...	...	...	1613	...	...	0049	0049	0049	0105	0105	0105	...
Bohumín 🏛 a.	...	1033	...	...	...	...	1331	...	...	...	...	...	1633	...	...	0107	0107	0107	0128	0128	0128	...
Bohumín 🏛 d.	...	1045	...	...	...	...	1340	1445	...	...	...	...	1645	...	...	0217	0217	0210	0217	0217	0210	...
Ostrava Hlavní a.	...	1054	...	1157	...	...	1346	1452	...	1557	...	...	1652	...	1752	0224	0224	0218	0224	0224	0218	...
Přerov a.	...	1144	...	│	...	...	│	1544	...	│	...	...	1744	...	│	│	│	0313	│	│	0313	...
Olomouc a.	...	│	...	1305	...	...	1505	│	...	1705	...	...	│	...	1905	│	│	0352	│	│	0352	...
Pardubice a.	...	│	...	1435	...	...	1635	│	...	1835	...	...	│	...	2035	│	│	0530	│	│	0530	...
Praha hlavní a.	...	│	...	1551	...	...	1751	│	...	1951	...	...	│	...	2151	│	│	0651	│	│	0651	...
Břeclav a.	...	1251	1255	...	...	...	...	1651	1702	...	...	...	1851	1855	...	0411	0411	...	0411	0411	...	...
Wien Meidling a.	...	1423	│	...	...	...	...	│	1823	...	...	...	2020	│	...	│	0608	...	│	0608	...	...
Wien Westbahnhof a.	...	│	│	...	...	...	...	│	│	...	...	...	...	│	...	│	0622	...	│	0622	...	...
Wiener Neustadt Hbf a.	...	1457	│	...	...	...	...	│	1857	...	...	...	...	│	...	│	...	...	│	...	...	...
Villach Hbf a.	...	1844	│	...	...	...	...	│	2235	...	...	...	...	│	...	│	...	...	│	...	...	...
Kúty 🏛 a.	...	...	1312	...	...	...	...	1712	...	...	...	...	...	1912	...	0459	...	...	0459	...	...	...
Bratislava Hlavná a.	...	...	1351	...	...	...	...	1751	...	...	...	...	...	1951	...	0540	...	...	0540	...	...	...
Štúrovo 🏛 a.	...	...	...	...	...	...	...	...	...	...	...	...	...	2112	...	0715	...	...	0715	...	...	...
Plaveč 🏛 a.	...	...	...	...	...	...	...	...	...	...	...	...	...	│	...	│	...	...	│	...	...	...
Košice a.	...	...	...	...	...	...	...	...	...	...	...	...	...	│	...	│	...	...	│	...	...	...
Hidasnémeti 🏛 a.	...	...	...	...	...	...	...	...	...	...	...	...	...	│	...	│	...	...	│	...	...	...
Miskolc a.	...	...	...	...	...	...	...	...	...	...	...	...	...	│	...	│	...	...	│	...	...	...
Budapest Keleti a.	...	...	...	...	...	...	...	...	...	...	...	...	...	2232	...	0832	...	...	0832	...	...	...
Budapest Nyugati a.	...	...	...	...	...	...	...	...	...	...	...	...	...	...	...	...	...	...	...	...	...	...
Székesfehérvár a.	...	...	...	...	...	...	...	...	...	...	...	...	...	...	...	...	...	...	...	...	...	...
Siófok a.	...	...	...	...	...	...	...	...	...	...	...	...	...	...	...	...	...	...	...	...	...	...
Keszthely a.	...	...	...	...	...	...	...	...	...	...	...	...	...	...	...	...	...	...	...	...	...	...
Szolnok a.	...	...	...	...	...	...	...	...	...	...	...	...	...	...	...	...	...	...	...	...	...	...
Lökösháza 🏛 a.	...	...	...	...	...	...	...	...	...	...	...	...	...	...	...	...	...	...	...	...	...	...
Curtici 🏛 a.	...	...	...	...	...	...	...	...	...	...	...	...	...	...	...	...	...	...	...	...	...	...
Arad a.	...	...	...	...	...	...	...	...	...	...	...	...	...	...	...	...	...	...	...	...	...	...
Bucureşti Nord a.	...	...	...	...	...	...	...	...	...	...	...	...	...	...	...	...	...	...	...	...	...	...
Varna a.	...	...	...	...	...	...	...	...	...	...	...	...	...	...	...	...	...	...	...	...	...	...
Burgas a.	...	...	...	...	...	...	...	...	...	...	...	...	...	...	...	...	...	...	...	...	...	...

train type/number	EC	EC	EC			EC	SC	EC	EC			SC		EC								
train number	143	174	104	83100		172	503	136	111	83108		507	274	102	8310	401	401	406	406	476	476	
notes	✕	✕	Ⓡ	83101		Ⓡ	✕		Ⓡ	83109		✕	474	Ⓡ		406			401	406	406	
notes	⚡		✕⊡	🍷			⚡	🍷	✕⊡			⚡		✕⊡		Ⓡ		Ⓡ		Ⓡ	401	
notes			Y			Z		U	X					R		Q	S	C	E	B	F	
Burgas d.	...	...	...	...	...	...	...	...	...	...	...	...	...	...	...	...	...	...	...	...	...	...
Varna d.	...	...	...	...	...	...	...	...	...	...	...	...	...	...	...	...	...	...	...	...	...	...
Bucureşti Nord d.	...	...	...	...	...	...	...	...	...	...	...	...	...	...	...	...	...	...	...	...	...	...
Arad d.	...	...	...	...	...	...	...	...	...	...	...	...	...	...	...	...	...	...	...	...	...	...
Curtici 🏛 d.	...	...	...	...	...	...	...	...	...	...	...	...	...	...	...	...	...	...	...	...	...	...
Lökösháza 🏛 d.	...	...	...	...	...	...	...	...	...	...	...	...	...	...	...	...	...	...	...	...	...	...
Szolnok d.	...	...	...	...	...	...	...	...	...	...	...	...	...	...	...	...	...	...	...	...	...	...
Keszthely d.	...	...	...	...	...	...	...	...	...	...	...	...	...	...	...	...	...	...	...	...	...	...
Siófok d.	...	...	...	...	...	...	...	...	...	...	...	...	...	...	...	...	...	...	...	...	...	...
Székesfehérvár d.	...	...	...	...	...	...	...	...	...	...	...	...	...	...	...	...	...	...	...	...	...	...
Budapest Nyugati d.	...	...	...	...	...	...	...	...	...	...	...	...	...	...	...	...	...	...	...	...	...	...
Budapest Keleti d.	...	0528	...	...	...	...	...	...	...	...	...	...	...	...	...	...	...	...	...	1958	1958	...
Miskolc d.	...	│	...	...	...	...	...	...	...	...	...	...	...	...	...	...	...	...	...	│	│	...
Hidasnémeti 🏛 d.	...	│	...	...	...	...	...	...	...	...	...	...	...	...	...	...	...	...	...	│	│	...
Košice d.	...	│	...	...	...	...	...	...	...	...	...	...	...	...	...	...	...	...	...	│	│	...
Plaveč 🏛 d.	...	│	...	...	...	...	...	...	...	...	...	...	...	...	...	...	...	...	...	│	│	...
Štúrovo 🏛 d.	...	0647	...	...	...	...	...	...	...	...	...	...	...	...	...	...	...	...	...	2112	2112	...
Bratislava Hlavná d.	...	0808	...	...	...	...	...	1008	...	...	...	...	1408	...	...	...	...	...	...	2250	2250	...
Kúty 🏛 d.	...	0847	...	...	...	...	...	1047	...	...	...	...	1447	...	...	...	...	...	...	2330	2330	...
Villach Hbf d.	...	│	...	...	...	0527	...	│	...	...	...	...	│	0914	...	...	...	...	...	│	│	...
Wiener Neustadt Hbf d.	...	│	...	...	...	0847	...	│	...	...	...	...	│	1304	...	...	...	...	...	│	│	...
Wien Westbahnhof d.	...	│	...	...	...	│	...	│	...	...	...	...	│	│	...	...	...	2208	2208	│	│	...
Wien Meidling d.	...	│	0733	...	...	0932	...	│	...	...	...	...	│	1333	...	...	...	2223	2223	│	│	...
Břeclav d.	...	0854	0908	...	...	1053	...	1108	...	...	...	...	1454	1508	...	...	...	0012	0012	0012	0012	...
Praha hlavní d.	0611	...	│	...	...	...	0926	│	1011	...	...	1326	...	│	...	2132	2132	│	│	│	│	...
Pardubice d.	0721	...	│	...	...	...	1023	│	1121	...	...	1423	...	│	...	2252	2252	│	│	│	│	...
Olomouc d.	0854	...	│	...	...	...	1136	│	1254	...	...	1536	...	│	...	0037	0037	│	│	│	│	...
Přerov d.	│	...	1011	...	...	...	│	1211	│	...	...	│	...	1611	...	0116	0116	│	│	│	│	...
Ostrava Hlavní d.	1001	...	1105	...	...	...	1230	1305	1405	...	...	1630	...	1705	...	0211	0211	0159	0159	0159	0159	...
Bohumín 🏛 a.	...	...	1112	...	...	...	...	1312	1411	...	...	...	...	1712	...	0218	0218	0206	0206	0206	0206	...
Bohumín 🏛 d.	...	...	1126	...	...	...	...	...	1426	...	...	...	...	1726	...	0254	0307	0254	0307	0254	0307	...
Zebrzydowice 🏛 d.	...	...	1145	...	...	...	...	...	1445	...	...	...	...	1745	...	0314	0327	0314	0327	0314	0327	...
Katowice a.	...	...	1250	1430	...	...	...	...	1550	1630	...	...	...	1850	1941	0417	│	0417	│	0417	│	...
Tarnów a.	...	...	│	│	...	...	...	...	│	│	...	...	...	│	│	│	│	│	│	│	│	...
Kraków Gł. a.	...	...	│	1619	...	...	...	...	│	1819	...	...	...	│	2125	│	0624	│	0624	│	0624	...
Lichkov 🏛 a.	...	...	│	...	...	...	...	...	│	...	...	...	...	│	...	│	...	│	...	│	...	...
Wrocław Główny a.	...	...	│	...	...	...	...	...	│	...	...	...	...	│	...	│	...	│	...	│	...	...
Warszawa Centralna a.	...	...	1522	...	...	...	...	...	1824	...	...	...	...	2124	...	0710	...	0710	...	0710	...	...
Warszawa Wschodnia a.	...	...	1534	...	...	...	...	...	1837	...	...	...	...	2142	...	0722	...	0722	...	0722	...	...

A – 🛏 1, 2 cl. and ▬ 2 cl. Kraków (**400**) - Bohumín (**407**) - Břeclav (**477**) - Budapest.

B – 🛏 1, 2 cl., ▬ 2 cl. and [2] Warszawa - Bratislava - Budapest and v.v. Conveys 🛏 1, 2 cl. Moskva - Budapest and v.v.

C – CHOPIN – 🛏 1, 2 cl. (Lux), 🛏 1, 2 cl., ▬ 2 cl. and [2] Warszawa - Wien and v.v. Conveys 🛏 1, 2 cl. Moskva - Wien and v.v.

D – 🛏 1, 2 cl. (also ▬ 2 cl. Apr. 29 - Sept. 26) Kraków (**400**) - Bohumín (**407**) - Wien.

E – 🛏 1, 2 cl. (also ▬ 2 cl. Apr. 30 - Sept. 27) Wien (**406**) - Bohumín (**401**) - Kraków.

F – 🛏 1, 2 cl. and ▬ 2 cl. Budapest (**476**) - Břeclav (**406**) - Bohumín (**401**) - Kraków.

Q – 🛏 1, 2 cl., ▬ 2 cl. and [2] Warszawa - Praha and v.v.

R – POLONIA – [12] and ✕ Warszawa - Wien - Villach and v.v.

S – SILESIA – 🛏 1, 2 cl., ▬ 2 cl. and [12] Kraków - Praha and v.v.

T – MORAVIA – [12] and 🍷 Bohumín - Břeclav - Bratislava - Nové Zámky.

U – MORAVIA – [12] and 🍷 Bratislava - Břeclav - Bohumín.

W – WAWEL – [12] and 🍷 Kraków - Wrocław - Legnica - Forst 🏛 - Cottbus - Berlin - (- Hamburg Ⓡ not Dec. 24, 25, 30, 31, Apr. 2, 4, May 23).

X – PRAHA – [12] and ✕ Warszawa - Praha and v.v.

Y – SOBIESKI – [12] and ✕ Warszawa - Wien and v.v.

Z – VINDOBONA – [12] and ✕ Hamburg - Berlin - Praha - Wien - Villach and v.v.

z – Wien **Westbahnhof**.

⊡ – Supplement payable in Poland.

GREAT BRITAIN

SEE MAP PAGES 96/97

Operators: Passenger services are provided by a number of private passenger train companies operating the **National Rail** network on lines owned by the British national railway infrastructure company **Network Rail**. The following Network Rail codes are used in the table headings to indicate the operators of trains in each table:

AW	Arriva Trains Wales	GW	First Great Western	ME	Merseyrail	SW	South West Trains
CH	Chiltern Railways	HT	Hull Trains	NT	Northern Rail	TP	TransPennine Express
EM	East Midlands Trains	IL	Island Line	SE	Southeastern	VT	Virgin Trains
FC	First Capital Connect	LE	National Express East Anglia	SN	Southern	WS	Wrexham & Shropshire
GC	Grand Central Railway	LM	London Midland	SR	First ScotRail	XC	Arriva Cross Country
GR	East Coast	LT	c2c				

Timings: Except where indicated otherwise, timings are valid from **December 13, 2009** to **May 22, 2010**.
As service patterns at weekends (especially on ⑦) usually differ greatly from those applying on Mondays to Fridays, the timings in most tables are grouped by days of operation: Ⓐ = Mondays to Fridays; ⚒ = Mondays to Saturdays; ⑥ = Saturdays; ⑦ = Sundays. Track engineering work, affecting journey times, frequently takes place at weekends, so it is advisable to confirm your journey details locally if planning to travel in the period between the late evening of ⑥ and the late afternoon of ⑦. Confirm timings, too, if you intend travelling on public holidays (see page **2**) as there may be alterations to services at these times. Suburban and commuter services are the most likely to be affected; the majority of long-distance and cross-country trains marked Ⓐ and ⚒ run as normal on these dates. No trains (except limited Gatwick and Heathrow Express services) run on **December 25**, with only a limited service on certain routes on **December 26**. In Scotland only trains between Edinburgh/Glasgow and England run on **January 1**.

Services: Unless indicated otherwise (by '2' in the train column or '2nd class' in the table heading), trains convey both **first** (1st) and **standard** (2nd) classes of seated accommodation. Light refreshments (snacks, hot and cold drinks) are available from a **buffet car** or a **mobile trolley service** on board those trains marked 🍷 and ✖: the latter also convey a **restaurant car** or serve meals to passengers at their seats (this service is in some cases available to first-class ticket holders only). Note that catering facilities may not be available for the whole of a train's journey. **Sleeping-cars** (🛏) have one berth per compartment in first class and two in standard class.

Reservations: Seats on most long-distance trains and berths in sleeping-cars can be reserved in advance when purchasing travel tickets at rail stations or directly from train operating companies (quote the departure time of the train and your destination). Seat reservation is normally free of charge.

SE 2nd class — LONDON - THE SOUTH EAST via HS1 HIGH SPEED LINE — 100

Special fares payable for high-speed services. For slower services see Table **101**. For *Eurostar* services, see Table **10**.

LONDON - CHATHAM - FAVERSHAM

km																									
		Ⓐ	⚒	Ⓐ	Ⓐ		⚒		⚒		⚒		⚒												ⒶM
0	**London** St Pancras ..... 10 d.	0658	0722	0755	0822	...	0852	0925	0955	1028	1052	1125	1155	...	1225	1252	1325	1355	1428	1455	1525	1555	1625	1655	1725
	Stratford International ..... d.	0705	0728	0802	0829	...	0858	0932	1002	1035	1058	1132	1202	...	1236	1258	1332	1402	1435	1502	1532	1602	1632	1702	1738
35	Ebbsfleet International .... 10 d.	0716	0743	0813	0843	...	0913	0943	1013	1046	1113	1143	1213	...	1247	1313	1343	1413	1446	1513	1543	1613	1643	1713	1749
	Chatham ..... 101 d.	0738	0805	0835	0905	...	0935	1005	1035	1108	1135	1205	1235	...	1308	1335	1405	1435	1508	1535	1605	1635	1705	1738	1806
	Sittingbourne ..... 101 d.	0755	0823	0853	0923	...	0953	1023	1053	1125	1153	1223	1253	...	1325	1353	1423	1453	1525	1553	1623	1653	1723	1753	1823
	Faversham ..... 101 a.	0803	0831	0901	0931	...	1003	1034	1101	1134	1201	1231	1301	...	1334	1401	1431	1501	1534	1604	1633	1701	1734	1803	1831

	⑦		⑥	Ⓐ	ⒶM	⑥⑦		Ⓐ	ⒶM	⑥	⑦													⚒
London St Pancras ..... 10 d.	1725	...	1728	1744	1758	1758	...	1814	1825	1825	1828	...	1855	1925	1955	2025	2055	...	2125	2155	2225	2255	2325	...	2355
Stratford International ..... d.	1732	...	1735	1751	1805	1805	...	1821	1832	1832	1835	...	1902	1932	2002	2032	2102	...	2132	2202	2232	2302	2332	...	0002
Ebbsfleet International .... 10 d.	1743	...	1746	|	1816	1816	...	|	1843	1843	1846	...	1913	1943	2013	2043	2113	...	2143	2213	2243	2313	2343	...	0013
Chatham ..... 101 d.	1805	...	1808	1826	1840	1838	...	1853	1902	1905	1908	...	1935	2005	2035	2105	2135	...	2205	2235	2305	2335	0005	...	0035
Sittingbourne ..... 101 d.	1823	...	1825	1844	1853	1855	...	1910	1922	1923	1925	...	1952	2023	2053	2123	2153	...	2223	2253	2323	2353	0023	...	0053
Faversham ..... 101 a.	1831	...	1834	1854	1901	1904	...	1918	1930	1931	1933	...	2002	2034	2103	2133	2203	...	2233	2303	2333	0003	0033	...	0103

	Ⓐ	⚒	Ⓐ		⑥	ⒶM		ⒶM	⑥	ⒶM			⚒			⚒			⚒						
Faversham ..... 101 d.	0456	0528	0558	...	0628	0634	...	0704	0728	0734	...	0758	0828	0858	...	0928	0958	...	1028	1058	1128	1158	...	1228	1258
Sittingbourne ..... 101 d.	0507	0537	0606	...	0637	0643	...	0712	0737	0742	...	0806	0837	0907	...	0937	1007	...	1037	1107	1137	1207	...	1237	1307
Chatham ..... 101 d.	0524	0554	0624	...	0654	0701	...	0730	0754	0800	...	0824	0854	0924	...	0954	1024	...	1054	1124	1154	1224	...	1254	1324
Ebbsfleet International .... 10 d.	0548	0618	0648	...	0718	0718	...	0748	0818	0818	...	0848	0918	0948	...	1017	1048	...	1118	1148	1221	1248	...	1318	1348
Stratford International ..... a.	0559	0629	0659	...	0729	0729	...	0759	0830	0829	...	0859	0929	0959	...	1027	1059	...	1129	1159	1232	1259	...	1329	1359
London St Pancras ..... 10 a.	0606	0636	0707	...	0736	0736	...	0806	0836	0836	...	0907	0939	1006	...	1038	1106	...	1136	1206	1239	1306	...	1336	1406

Faversham ..... 101 d.	1328	...	1358	1428	...	1458	1528	1558	...	1628	1658	...	1728	1758	...	1828	1858	1928	1958	...	2028	2058	...	2128	2158
Sittingbourne ..... 101 d.	1337	...	1407	1437	...	1507	1537	1607	...	1637	1707	...	1737	1807	...	1837	1907	1937	2007	...	2037	2107	...	2137	2207
Chatham ..... 101 d.	1354	...	1424	1454	...	1524	1554	1624	...	1654	1724	...	1754	1824	...	1854	1924	1954	2024	...	2054	2124	...	2154	2224
Ebbsfleet International .... 10 d.	1421	...	1448	1518	...	1548	1618	1648	...	1717	1747	...	1817	1851	...	1917	1948	2017	2048	...	2121	2148	...	2217	2248
Stratford International ..... a.	1432	...	1502	1529	...	1559	1629	1702	...	1727	1802	...	1829	1902	...	1929	1959	2027	2102	...	2131	2159	...	2229	2259
London St Pancras ..... 10 a.	1439	...	1509	1536	...	1606	1640	1709	...	1738	1809	...	1838	1909	...	1938	2006	2038	2109	...	2142	2206	...	2238	2306

LONDON - ASHFORD - DOVER and MARGATE

km																									
		⚒	⚒	Ⓐ	Ⓐ																			Ⓐ	Ⓐ
0	**London** St Pancras ..... 10 d.	0640	0710	0740	0810	0840	0912	0940	1012	1042	1112	1142	1212	1242	1312	1342	1412	1442	1512	1542	1612	1642	...	1710	1710
	Stratford International ..... d.	0647	0717	0747	0817	0847	0919	0947	1019	1049	1119	1149	1219	1249	1319	1349	1419	1449	1519	1549	1619	1649	...	1717	1717
35	Ebbsfleet International .... 10 d.	0659	0730	0800	0830	0900	0931	0959	1031	1101	1131	1201	1231	1301	1331	1401	1431	1501	1531	1601	1631	1701	...	|	|
90	Ashford International ..... 10 d.	0722	0752	0822	0852	0922	0952	1022	1052	1122	1152	1222	1252	1322	1352	1422	1452	1522	1552	1622	1652	1722	...	1750	1752
	Folkestone Central ..... 101 a.	|	0810	|	0910	|	1010	|	1110	|	1210	|	1310	|	1410	|	1510	|	1610	|	1710	|	...	1806	|
	Dover Priory ..... 101 a.	|	0821	|	0921	|	1021	|	1121	|	1221	|	1321	|	1421	|	1521	|	1621	|	1721	|	...	1818	|
	Canterbury West ..... 101 d.	0740	...	0840	...	0940	...	1040	...	1140	...	1240	...	1340	...	1440	...	1540	...	1640	...	1740	...	...	1810
	Ramsgate ..... 101 a.	0802	...	0859	...	0959	...	1059	...	1159	...	1259	...	1359	...	1459	...	1559	...	1659	...	1759	...	...	1829
	Margate ..... 101 a.	0812	...	0910	...	1010	...	1110	...	1210	...	1310	...	1410	...	1510	...	1610	...	1710	...	1810	...	...	1840

	⑥⑦	ⒶF	Ⓐ	Ⓐ	⑥⑦	ⒶF	Ⓐ	Ⓐ		⑥⑦	ⒶF	Ⓐ	Ⓐ	⑥⑦											⑦
London St Pancras ..... 10 d.	1712	1725	1740	1740	1742	1758	1810	1810	...	1812	1825	1840	1840	1842	1912	1942	...	2012	2042	2112	2142	2212	2242	2312	2342
Stratford International ..... d.	1719	1738	1747	1747	1749	1805	1817	1817	...	1819	1832	1847	1847	1849	1919	1949	...	2019	2049	2119	2149	2219	2249	2319	2349
Ebbsfleet International .... 10 d.	1731	1749	|	|	1801	1816	|	|	...	1831	1843	|	|	1901	1931	2001	...	2031	2101	2131	2201	2231	2301	2331	2359
Ashford International ..... 10 d.	1752	|	1816	1822	1822	|	1850	1852	...	1852	|	1920	1922	1922	1952	2022	...	2052	2122	2152	2222	2252	2322	2352	0019
Folkestone Central ..... 101 a.	1810	|	1836	|	|	|	1906	|	...	1910	|	1936	|	|	2010	|	...	2110	|	2210	|	2310	|	0010	...
Dover Priory ..... 101 a.	1821	|	1848	|	|	|	1918	|	...	1921	|	1947	|	|	2021	|	...	2121	|	2221	|	2321	|	0021	...
Canterbury West ..... 101 d.	...	|	...	1840	1840	|	...	1910	...	...	|	...	1940	1940	...	2040	...	...	2140	...	2240	...	2340	...	...
Ramsgate ..... 101 a.	...	|	...	1859	1859	|	...	1929	...	...	|	...	1959	1959	...	2059	...	...	2159	...	2259	...	0001	...	...
Margate ..... 101 a.	...	1900	...	1910	1910	1930	...	1940	...	...	2001	...	2010	2010	...	2110	...	...	2210	...	2310	...	...	...	...

	Ⓐ	Ⓐ	⑥	⚒	⑥	Ⓐ	Ⓐ	ⒶF	Ⓐ	Ⓐ	⑥	ⒶF	Ⓐ	Ⓐ	ⒶF	Ⓐ	Ⓐ	⑦	Ⓐ	⑥⑦					
Margate ..... 101 d.	...	...	...	...	0543	...	0547	0605	...	...	...	0630	0644	...	0700	0726	...	...	0749	0753	...	0853	...	0953	...
Ramsgate ..... 101 d.	...	0500	0505	...	0555	...	0600	|	0626	...	...	|	0656	...	|	|	...	...	0801	0805	...	0905	...	1005	...
Canterbury West ..... 101 d.	...	0525	0525	...	0615	...	0620	|	0646	...	...	|	0716	...	|	0746	...	...	0825	0825	...	0925	...	1025	...
Dover Priory ..... 101 d.	...	|	|	0544	|	0612	|	|	|	0638	0644	|	|	0708	|	|	0738	0744	|	|	0844	|	0944	|	1044
Folkestone Central ..... 101 d.	...	|	|	0556	|	0624	|	|	|	0650	0656	|	|	0720	|	|	0750	0756	|	|	0856	|	0956	|	1056
Ashford International ..... 10 d.	0513	0543	0543	0613	0633	0643	0643	|	0712	0712	0713	|	0743	0743	|	0811	0811	0813	0843	0843	0913	0943	1013	1043	1113
Ebbsfleet International .... 10 d.	0533	0603	0603	0633	0653	|	|	0718	|	|	0733	0748	|	|	0818	|	|	0833	0903	0903	0933	1003	1033	1103	1133
Stratford International ..... a.	0544	0615	0615	0644	0704	0711	0711	0729	0740	0740	0744	0759	0811	0811	0829	0840	0840	0845	0914	0914	0944	1014	1044	1114	1144
London St Pancras ..... 10 a.	0551	0623	0623	0653	0710	0718	0718	0736	0748	0748	0750	0806	0819	0819	0836	0848	0848	0851	0921	0921	0951	1021	1051	1121	1151

																									⚒
Margate ..... 101 d.	1053	...	1153	...	1253	...	1353	...	1453	...	1553	...	1653	...	1753	...	1853	...	1953	...	2053	...	2153	...	...
Ramsgate ..... 101 d.	1105	...	1205	...	1305	...	1405	...	1505	...	1605	...	1705	...	1805	...	1905	...	2005	...	2105	...	2205	...	...
Canterbury West ..... 101 d.	1125	...	1225	...	1325	...	1425	...	1525	...	1625	...	1725	...	1825	...	1925	...	2025	...	2125	...	2225	...	...
Dover Priory ..... 101 d.	|	1144	|	1244	|	1344	|	1444	|	1544	|	1644	|	1744	|	1844	|	1944	|	2044	|	2144	|	...	2244
Folkestone Central ..... 101 d.	|	1156	|	1256	|	1356	|	1456	|	1556	|	1656	|	1756	|	1856	|	1956	|	2056	|	2156	|	...	2256
Ashford International ..... 10 d.	1143	1213	1243	1313	1343	1413	1443	1513	1543	1613	1643	1713	1743	1813	1843	1913	1943	2013	2047	2113	2143	2213	2243	...	2313
Ebbsfleet International .... 10 d.	1203	1233	1303	1333	1403	1433	1503	1533	1603	1633	1703	1733	1803	1833	1903	1933	2003	2033	2107	2133	2203	2233	2303	...	2333
Stratford International ..... a.	1214	1245	1314	1344	1414	1444	1514	1544	1614	1644	1714	1744	1814	1844	1914	1944	2014	2044	2119	2144	2214	2244	2314	...	2344
London St Pancras ..... 10 a.	1221	1254	1321	1351	1421	1451	1521	1551	1621	1651	1721	1751	1821	1851	1921	1951	2021	2051	2125	2151	2221	2251	2321	...	2351

F – Via Faversham. **M** – To/from Margate.

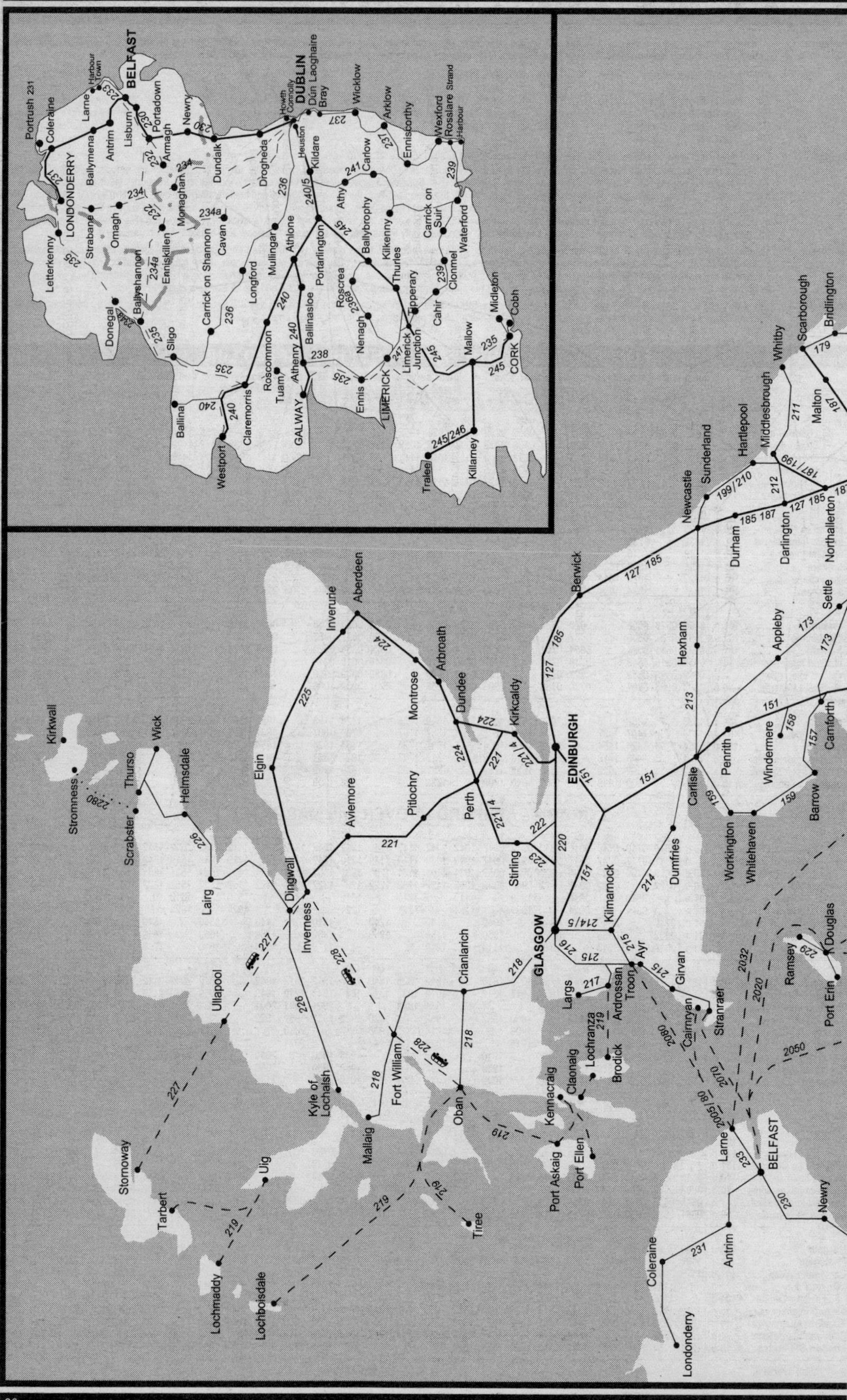

BELFAST
DUBLIN
Dún Laoghaire
Bray
Wicklow
Arklow
Enniscorthy
Wexford
Rosslare Strand
Rosslare Harbour
Howth
Connolly
Heuston
Kildare
Portrush 231
Coleraine
Larne
Larne Harbour
Larne Town
Ballymena
Antrim
Lisburn
Portadown
Armagh
Newry
Dundalk
Drogheda
LONDONDERRY
Letterkenny
Strabane
Omagh
Enniskillen
Monaghan
Cavan
Ballyshannon
Donegal
Sligo
Carrick on Shannon
Longford
Mullingar
Athlone
Portarlington
Athy
Carlow
Kilkenny
Ballybrophy
Thurles
Roscrea
Nenagh
Ballinasloe
Athenry
GALWAY
Tuam
Roscommon
Claremorris
Ballina
Westport
Ennis
LIMERICK
Limerick Junction
Tipperary
Cahir
Clonmel
Carrick on Suir
Waterford
Mallow
CORK
Cobh
Midleton
Killarney
Tralee
Kirkwall
Stromness
Thurso
Wick
Scrabster
Helmsdale
Lairg
Dingwall
Inverness
Elgin
Inverurie
Aberdeen
Aviemore
Pitlochry
Perth
Dundee
Arbroath
Montrose
Kirkcaldy
EDINBURGH
Stirling
GLASGOW
Crianlarich
Fort William
Mallaig
Kyle of Lochalsh
Ullapool
Oban
Stornoway
Tarbert
Uig
Lochmaddy
Lochboisdale
Tiree
Kennacraig
Claonaig
Lochranza
Brodick
Port Askaig
Port Ellen
Largs
Ardrossan
Troon
Ayr
Girvan
Kilmarnock
Stranraer
Cairnryan
Dumfries
Carlisle
Hexham
Berwick
Newcastle
Sunderland
Durham
Darlington
Hartlepool
Middlesbrough
Whitby
Scarborough
Bridlington
Malton
Northallerton
Appleby
Settle
Penrith
Windermere
Carnforth
Barrow
Workington
Whitehaven
Ramsey
Douglas
Port Erin
Larne
Antrim
Coleraine
Londonderry
Newry
127 185
185 187
187 / 199
199 / 210
211
212
179
181
173
151
158
157
159
213
214
214/5
215
216
217
218
219
220
221
221/4
222
223
224
225
226
227
228
229
230
231
232
233
234
234a
235
236
237
238
239
240
240/5
241
245
245/246
247
2368
2020
2032
2050
2070
2080
2005/80
2280

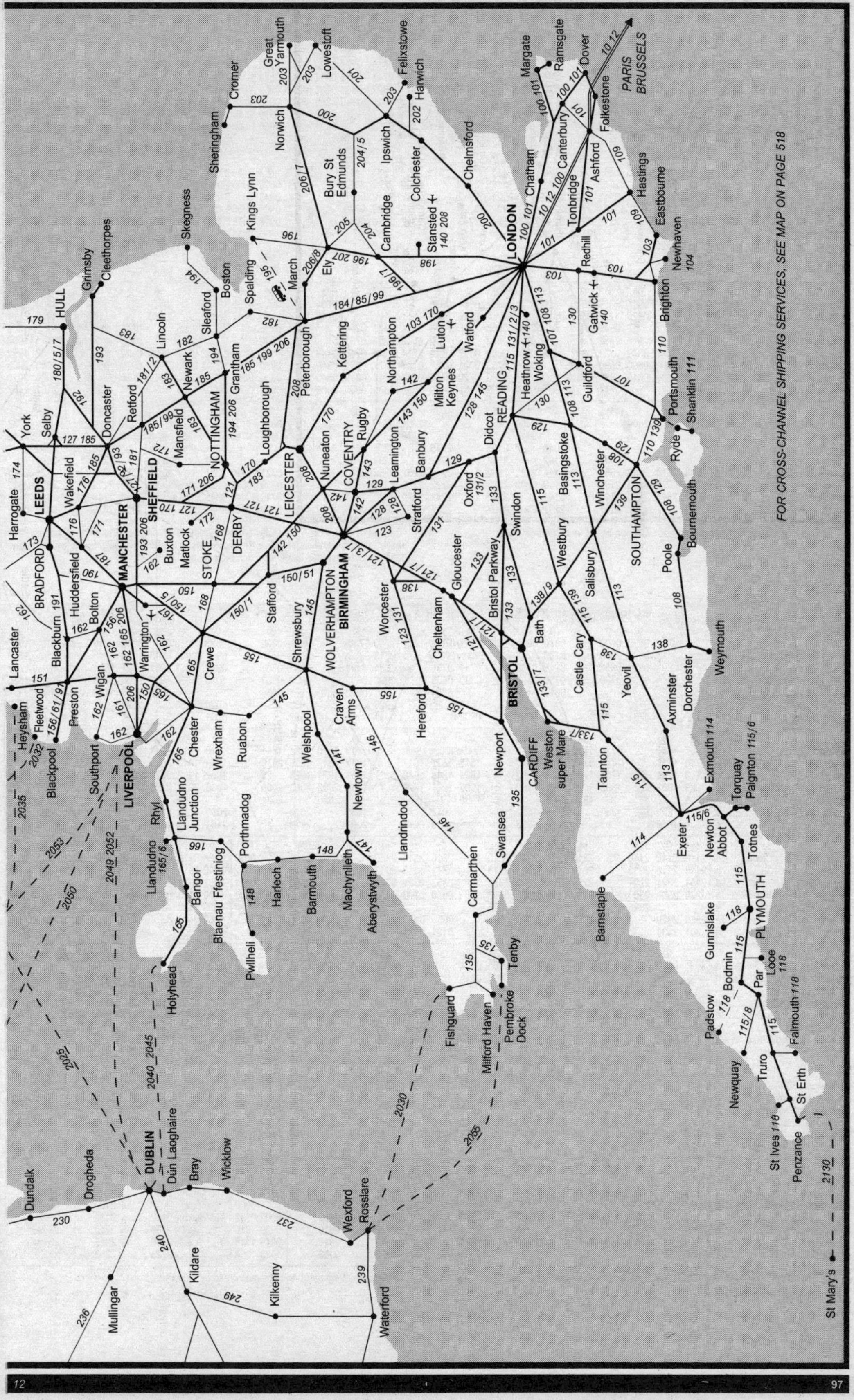
LONDON
BIRMINGHAM
MANCHESTER
LIVERPOOL
LEEDS
SHEFFIELD
BRADFORD
HULL
NOTTINGHAM
LEICESTER
COVENTRY
DERBY
STOKE
WOLVERHAMPTON
BRISTOL
CARDIFF
READING
SOUTHAMPTON
PLYMOUTH
DUBLIN
York
Selby
Harrogate
Wakefield
Huddersfield
Lancaster
Blackburn
Bolton
Preston
Wigan
Warrington
Blackpool
Fleetwood
Heysham
Southport
Doncaster
Retford
Lincoln
Grimsby
Cleethorpes
Skegness
Boston
Sleaford
Newark
Grantham
Mansfield
Buxton
Matlock
Loughborough
Peterborough
Spalding
Kings Lynn
March
Ely
Cambridge
Norwich
Cromer
Sheringham
Great Yarmouth
Lowestoft
Felixstowe
Harwich
Ipswich
Bury St Edmunds
Colchester
Chelmsford
Stansted
Kettering
Northampton
Luton
Watford
Milton Keynes
Nuneaton
Rugby
Leamington
Banbury
Stratford
Oxford
Didcot
Swindon
Heathrow
Woking
Guildford
Basingstoke
Winchester
Gatwick
Redhill
Tonbridge
Brighton
Newhaven
Eastbourne
Hastings
Ashford
Canterbury
Chatham
Margate
Ramsgate
Dover
Folkestone
PARIS
BRUSSELS
Portsmouth
Ryde
Shanklin
Bournemouth
Poole
Weymouth
Dorchester
Salisbury
Westbury
Bath
Bristol Parkway
Gloucester
Cheltenham
Worcester
Hereford
Shrewsbury
Stafford
Crewe
Chester
Wrexham
Ruabon
Welshpool
Newtown
Craven Arms
Llandrindod
Machynlleth
Aberystwyth
Barmouth
Harlech
Pwllheli
Porthmadog
Blaenau Ffestiniog
Llandudno
Llandudno Junction
Rhyl
Bangor
Holyhead
Newport
Swansea
Carmarthen
Tenby
Fishguard
Milford Haven
Pembroke Dock
Weston super Mare
Taunton
Castle Cary
Yeovil
Axminster
Exeter
Exmouth
Barnstaple
Newton Abbot
Torquay
Paignton
Totnes
Gunnislake
Looe
Bodmin
Par
Padstow
Newquay
Truro
Falmouth
St Ives
St Erth
Penzance
St Mary's
Dundalk
Drogheda
Dun Laoghaire
Bray
Wicklow
Wexford
Rosslare
Mullingar
Kildare
Kilkenny
Waterford
FOR CROSS-CHANNEL SHIPPING SERVICES, SEE MAP ON PAGE 518

101 LONDON - CANTERBURY, DOVER, RAMSGATE, ASHFORD and HASTINGS SE

For services to the south east via HS1 high-speed line see Table **100**.

LONDON VICTORIA - CHATHAM - DOVER and RAMSGATE

km		⚒	⚒	⑥		Ⓐ	Ⓐ		⚒	⚒		Ⓐ	⚒	⚒	⚒	⚒	and at the same minutes past each hour until ♠	⚒	⚒		⚒		①–⑤	⑥
0	**London** Victoria d.		0522	0522	...	0552	0552	...	0622	0622	...	0645	0722	0722	0752	0752		1922	1922	...	1952	...	1952	1952
55	Chatham 100 d.		0617	0617	...	0644	0644	...	0717	0717	...	0742	0813	0812	0842	0842		2012	2012	...	2042	...	2042	2042
72	Sittingbourne 100 d.		0636	0636	...	0702	0702	...	0738	0738	...	0802	0832	0831	0901	0901		2029	2029	...	2101	...	2101	2101
84	Faversham 100 d.		0647	0646	...	0713	0713	...	0749	0748	...	0813	0846	0848	0913	0915		2043	2045	...	2115	...	2115	2115
99	Canterbury East d.		|	*0704*	...	|	*0729*	...	|	*0804*	...	0827	|	0902	|	0929		|	2059	...	|	...	2126	2126
124	**Dover** 100 a.		|	*0731*	...	|	*0758*	...	|	*0831*	...	0854	|	0931	|	0950		|	2130	...	|	...	2152	...
119	Margate 100 d.		0719	...	...	0745	...	...	0820	...	...	...	0918	...	0941	...		2115	...	...	2141	...	...	...
128	**Ramsgate** 100 a.		0730	...	...	0756	...	...	0831	...	...	...	0929	...	0951	...		2127	...	...	2156	...	...	...

	⚒	⚒		Ⓐ	Ⓐ	⑥		⚒	⚒		⚒	⚒	⚒		⑦	⑦	⑦	⑦	⑦	and at the same minutes past each hour until ♠	⑦	⑦		⑦
London Victoria d.	2022	2022	...	2052	2052	2052	...	2122	2122	...	2222	2222	2322	...		0805	0805	0905	0905		2205	2205	...	2305
Chatham 100 d.	2112	2112	...	2142	2142	2147	...	2212	2212	...	2312	2312	0012	...		0848	0848	0948	0948		2248	2248	...	2348
Sittingbourne 100 d.	2129	2129	...	2201	2201	2206	...	2229	2229	...	2329	2329	0029	...		0905	0905	1005	1005		2305	2305	...	0005
Faversham 100 d.	2143	2145	...	2213	2215	2216	...	2243	2245	...	2343	2345	0043	...		0917	0919	1017	1019		2317	2319	...	0017
Canterbury East d.	|	2159	...	|	2229	2226	...	|	2259	...	|	2359	|	...		|	0933	|	1033		|	2333	...	|
Dover 100 a.	|	2226	...	|	2250	...	...	|	2326	...	|	0018	|	...		|	1001	|	1101		|	0001	...	|
Margate 100 d.	2215	...	...	2245	...	...	...	2315	...	...	0015	...	0115	...		0949	...	1049	...		2349	...	...	0049
Ramsgate 100 a.	2226	...	...	2256	...	...	...	2326	...	...	0026	...	0126	...		1000	...	1100	...		0001	...	...	0100

	⚒	Ⓐ	Ⓐ	⑥	⑥		Ⓐ	⑥	⚒	⚒	Ⓐ	⑥	⚒	⚒		⚒	⚒	⚒	⚒	⚒	⚒	and at the same minutes past each hour until ♠	⚒	⚒
Ramsgate 100 d.		...	0511	...	0540	...	...	...	0604	0632	...	...	...	0704	...	...	0736	0804	...	0840	...		1904	...
Margate 100 d.		...	0521	...	0550	...	...	...	0616	0643	...	...	...	0716	...	...	0747	0816	...	0850	...		1916	...
Dover 100 d.		*0505*	|	0545	|	...	0549	0605	|	|	*0619*	0645	0704	|	...	0735	|	|	0805	|	0845		|	1905
Canterbury East d.		*0532*	|	0602	|	...	0616	0632	|	|	*0646*	0702	0731	|	...	0802	|	|	0832	|	0902		|	1932
Faversham 100 d.		0549	0549	0622	0622	...	0638	0652	0652	0714	0714	0714	0749	0749	...	0822	0822	0852	0852	0922	0922		1952	1952
Sittingbourne 100 d.		0600	0600	0630	0630	...	0649	0703	0701	0727	0727	0727	0800	0800	...	0830	0830	0903	0903	0930	0930		2003	2003
Chatham 100 d.		0619	0619	0650	0650	...	0708	0720	0720	0746	0746	0746	0819	0819	...	0850	0850	0920	0920	0950	0950		2020	2020
London Victoria a.		0709	0709	0737	0737	...	0757c	0809	0809	0839	0839	0839	0909	0909	...	0943	0943	1007	1007	1037	1037		2107	2107

	Ⓐ	Ⓐ	⚒	⚒		Ⓐ	⚒	⚒		Ⓐ	⚒	⚒	Ⓐ		⑦	⑦	⑦	⑦	and at the same minutes past each hour until ♠	⑦	⑦		⑦	⑦
Ramsgate 100 d.	1924	...	2004	...	...	...	2104	...	...	...	2204	...	...	...		0634	0734	...		2134	...	...	...	2234
Margate 100 d.	1935	...	2016	...	...	...	2116	...	...	...	2216	...	...	...		0645	0745	...		2145	...	...	...	2245
Dover 100 d.	|	1940	|	2005	...	2045	|	2105	...	2145	|	*2205*	2245	...		|	|	0734		|	2134	...	*2234*	|
Canterbury East d.	|	1957	|	2032	...	2102	|	2132	...	2202	|	*2232*	2302	...		|	|	0801		|	2201	...	*2301*	|
Faversham 100 d.	2014	2014	2052	2052	...	2114	2152	2152	...	2214	2252	2252	2314	...		0721	0821	0821		2221	2221	...	2321	2321
Sittingbourne 100 d.	2022	2022	2103	2103	...	2122	2203	2303	...	2222	2303	2303	2322	...		0729	0829	0829		2229	2229	...	2329	2329
Chatham 100 d.	2041	2041	2120	2120	...	2141	2220	2220	...	2241	2320	2320	2341	...		0746	0846	0846		2246	2246	...	2346	2346
London Victoria a.	2137	2137	2207	2207	...	2237	2307	2307	...	2337	0007	0007	0038	...		0830	0929	0929		2329	2329	...	0029	0029

c – This train starts / terminates at London Cannon Street, not Charing Cross.

♠ – Timings may vary by ± 5 minutes on some journeys. During peak hours on Ⓐ certain trains leave London slightly later, leave Ramsgate, Margate and Dover slightly earlier, and may take up to 10 minutes longer to reach their destination.

LONDON CHARING CROSS - ASHFORD - CANTERBURY WEST and DOVER

km		⚒	Ⓐ	⑥		Ⓐ	Ⓐ		⚒	⚒		Ⓐ	⚒		⚒	⑥		Ⓐ	⚒	⚒	Ⓐ	⚒	and at the same minutes past each hour until ♣	Ⓐ
0	**London** Charing Cross d.		0530	0600	...	0630	0630	...	0700y	0700y	...	0740	0730y	...	0800y	0800	...	0833	0910	0910	0940	0940		1637
36	Sevenoaks d.		0609	0633	...	0703	0703	...	0733y	0733y	...	0813	0803y	...	0833y	0833	...	0907	0943	0943	1013	1013		1710
48	Tonbridge d.		0621	0651	...	0716	0716	...	0751	0751	...	0821	0821	...	0851	0851	...	0921	0951	0951	1021	1021		1718
90	**Ashford** International d.		0700	0730	...	0755	0800	...	0830	0833	...	0900	0903	...	0930	0933	...	1000	1030	1033	1100	1103		1800
113	**Canterbury** West a.		|	|	...	0817	|	...	|	0854	...	|	0922	...	|	0954	...	|	|	1056	|	1122		|
113	Folkestone Central a.		0720	0750	...	...	0820	...	0850	...	...	0920	...	...	0950	...	...	1020	1050	...	1120	...		1820
124	**Dover** a.		0731	0801	...	...	0831	...	0902	...	...	0931	...	...	1002	...	...	1031	1101	...	1131	...		1831

	Ⓐ	⑥		⚒	⚒	⑥	Ⓐ		Ⓐ	Ⓐ	Ⓐ		⑥	⑥	Ⓐ	Ⓐ		⚒	Ⓐ	Ⓐ	⚒		⚒	Ⓐ	⚒
London Charing Cross d.	1637	1640	...	1710	1710	1740	1741	...	1745c	1808c	1808c	...	1810	1840	1841	1841	...	1910	1910	1940	1940	...	2010	2040	2040
Sevenoaks d.	1710	1713	...	1743	1743	1813	1811	...	1815	1837	1837	...	1843	1913	1916	1916	...	1943	1943	2013	2013	...	2043	2113	2113
Tonbridge d.	1718	1721	...	1751	1751	1821	1820	...	1824	1848	1848	...	1851	1921	1925	1925	...	1952	1952	2021	2021	...	2051	2121	2121
Ashford International d.	1803	1803	...	1830	1833	1903	1902	...	1903	1927	1929	...	1930	2003	2003	2005	...	2030	2035	2100	2103	...	2130	2200	2203
Canterbury West a.	1825	|	...	|	1856	1925	|	...	1930	|	1952	...	|	2025	|	2024	...	|	2056	|	2125	...	|	|	2225
Folkestone Central a.	...	1822	...	1850	...	...	1922	...	...	1947	...	...	1950	...	2023	...	...	2050	...	2120	...	...	2150	2220	...
Dover a.	...	1826	...	1903	...	...	1933	...	...	1958	...	...	2001	...	2033	...	...	2101	...	2131	...	...	2201	2231	...

	⚒	Ⓐ	⚒		⚒		Ⓐ	⚒		⚒	⚒	⚒		⑦	⑦		⑦	⑦	⑦	and at the same minutes past each hour until	⑦	⑦		⑦
London Charing Cross d.	2110	2140	2140	...	2210	...	2240	2240	...	2310	2340	2340	...		0808	...	0838	0908	0938		2138	2208	...	2238
Sevenoaks d.	2143	2213	2213	...	2243	...	2313	2313	...	2344	0013	0013	...		0842	...	0912	0942	1012		2212	2242	...	2312
Tonbridge d.	2151	2221	2221	...	2251	...	2321	2321	...	2353	0021	0021	...		0853	...	0921	0953	1021		2221	2253	...	2321
Ashford International d.	2230	2301	2303	...	2330	...	0001	0003	...	0030	0100	0103	...		0930	...	1003	1030	1103		2303	2330	...	0001
Canterbury West a.	|	|	2325	...	|	...	|	0025	...	|	|	0124	...		|	...	1022	|	1122		2325	|	...	|
Folkestone Central a.	2250	2320	...	...	2350	...	0020	...	...	0050	0120	...	...		0950	...	...	1050	...		...	2350	...	0018
Dover a.	2301	2331	...	...	0001	...	0031	...	...	0101	0131	...	...		1001	...	...	1101	...		...	0001	...	0029

	⚒	Ⓐ		Ⓐ		⑥		⑥	Ⓐ		Ⓐ	⚒		Ⓐ	⑥		Ⓐ	⚒	⚒	Ⓐ	⚒	and at the same minutes past each hour until ♣		⚒
Dover d.		0526	...	...	...	...	...	0550	0604	...	...	0624	...	...	...	...	0700	0724	...	0756	...		...	1624
Folkestone Central d.		0538	...	...	...	...	...	0602	0616	...	...	0636	...	...	...	...	0712	0736	...	0808	...		...	1636
Canterbury West d.		|	...	0559	...	0555	...	|	|	...	0633	|	...	0703	0700	...	|	|	0735	|	0804		...	|
Ashford International d.		0602	...	0622	...	0625	...	0625	0637	...	0657	0702	...	0728	0732	...	0737	0802	0802	0832	0832		...	1702
Tonbridge d.		0640	...	0702	...	0702	...	0702	0715	...	0735	0740	...	0803	0810	...	0815	0840	0840	0910	0910		...	1740
Sevenoaks a.		0648	...	0710	...	0713	...	0713	0726	...	0746	0750	...	0811	0818	...	0826	0848	0848	0918	0918		...	1748
London Charing Cross a.		0725	...	0747	...	0748	...	0748	0759c	...	0820	0826	...	0846	0852	...	0902c	0925	0925	0954	0954		...	1825

	⚒		Ⓐ	⚒		⚒	⚒		Ⓐ	⚒		⚒	⚒		Ⓐ	⚒		⚒	⚒		Ⓐ	⚒		⚒	Ⓐ
Dover d.	...	...	1656	...	...	1724	...	...	1757	...	...	1824	...	...	1857	...	...	1924	...	...	1955	...	...	2024	...
Folkestone Central d.	...	...	1708	...	...	1736	...	...	1808	...	...	1836	...	...	1908	...	...	1936	...	...	2008	...	...	2036	...
Canterbury West d.	1635	...	|	1704	...	|	1735	...	|	1804	...	|	1835	...	|	1904	...	|	1935	...	|	2000	...	|	2035
Ashford International d.	1702	...	1732	1732	...	1802	1802	...	1832	1832	...	1902	1902	...	1932	1932	...	2002	2002	...	2032	2032	...	2102	2102
Tonbridge d.	1740	...	1810	1810	...	1840	1840	...	1910	1910	...	1940	1940	...	2010	2010	...	2040	2040	...	2110	2110	...	2140	2140
Sevenoaks a.	1748	...	1818	1818	...	1848	1848	...	1918	1918	...	1948	1948	...	2018	2018	...	2048	2048	...	2118	2118	...	2148	2148
London Charing Cross a.	1825	...	1852	1852	...	1922	1922	...	1952	1952	...	2022	2022	...	2051	2051	...	2122	2122	...	2152	2152	...	2222	2222

	Ⓐ		⚒		⚒		Ⓐ				⑦	⑦		⑦		⑦	⑦	and at the same minutes past each hour until	⑦		⑦		⑦	
Dover d.	2056	...	...	...	2124	...	...	...	2156	...		0724	...	...	...	0824	...		2024	...	...	...	2124	...
Folkestone Central d.	2108	...	...	...	2136	...	...	...	2208	...		0736	...	...	...	0836	...		2036	...	...	...	2136	...
Canterbury West d.	|	...	2100	...	|	...	2135	...	|	...		|	...	0800	...	|	0900		|	...	2100	...	|	...
Ashford International d.	2132	...	2132	...	2202	...	2202	...	2232	...		0802	...	0832	...	0902	0932		2102	...	2132	...	2202	...
Tonbridge d.	2210	...	2210	...	2240	...	2240	...	2314	...		0839	...	0910	...	0939	1010		2139	...	2210	...	2239	...
Sevenoaks a.	2218	...	2218	...	2248	...	2248	...	2324	...		0849	...	0918	...	0949	1018		2149	...	2218	...	2349	...
London Charing Cross a.	2252	...	2252	...	2322	...	2322	...	0001	...		0923	...	0953	...	1023	1053		2223	...	2253	...	2323	...

c – This train starts / terminates at London Cannon Street, not Charing Cross.
y – 10–13 minutes later on Ⓐ.

♣ – Timings may vary by up to 5 minutes on some journeys.

SE LONDON - CANTERBURY, DOVER, RAMSGATE, ASHFORD and HASTINGS 101

For services to the south east via HS1 high-speed line see Table **100**.

LONDON CHARING CROSS - TUNBRIDGE WELLS - HASTINGS

km			Ⓐ	Ⓐ		Ⓐ	Ⓐ		Ⓐ	Ⓐ		Ⓐ	Ⓐ		Ⓐ	Ⓐ		Ⓐ	Ⓐ	Ⓐ	Ⓐ		Ⓐ	Ⓐ
0	**London** Charing Cross d.	Ⓐ	0645	0715	...	0747c	0817	...	0842c	0920c	...	0945	1015	and at	1545	1615	...	1641	1702c	1701	1719	...	1723	1737c
36	Sevenoaks d.		0719	0749	...	0818	0852	...	0917	0951	...	1019	1049	the same	1619	1647	...	1714	1731	1737	|	...	1759	|
48	Tonbridge d.		0731	0759	...	0829	0900	...	0926	1000	...	1028	1058	minutes	1628	1655	...	1722	1741	1748	|	...	1811	|
55	**Tunbridge Wells** d.		0741	0813	...	0844	0914	...	0942	1013	...	1040	1112	past each	1639	1705	...	1737	1751	1800	1808	...	1822	1824
100	**Hastings** a.		0829	0900	...	0932	1002	...	1019	1059	...	1117	1159	hour until	1727	1755	...	1820	1841	...	1900	...	...	1911

	Ⓐ	Ⓐ		Ⓐ	Ⓐ	Ⓐ	Ⓐ		Ⓐ	Ⓐ	Ⓐ	Ⓐ		Ⓐ	Ⓐ	Ⓐ			⑥	⑥		⑥	⑥	
London Charing Cross d.	1745	1803	...	1807	1828c	1845	1904c	...	1915	1945	2015	2045	...	2145	2245	2345	...	⑥	0745	0815	...	0845	0915	and at
Sevenoaks d.	1821	|	...	1843	|	1920	1932	...	1949	2019	2049	2119	...	2219	2319	0019	...		0819	0849	...	0919	0949	the same
Tonbridge d.	1832	|	...	1854	|	1929	1942	...	1958	2028	2058	2128	...	2228	2328	0027	...		0828	0858	...	0928	0958	minutes
Tunbridge Wells d.	1844	1850	...	1906	1916	1940	1954	...	2009	2040	2110	2140	...	2240	2340	0039	...		0840	0910	...	0940	1010	past each
Hastings a.	...	1947	...	...	2005	2029	2039	...	2057	2122	2157	2227	...	2327	0027	0125	...		0927	0957	...	1017	1057	hour until

	⑥		⑥		⑥	⑥		⑥			⑦		⑦	⑦		⑦		⑦		⑦		⑦		⑦
London Charing Cross d.	1955	...	2055	...	2155	2255	...	2345	...	⑦	0823	...	0923	0953	and at	1923	...	2023	...	2123	...	2223	...	2331
Sevenoaks d.	2031	...	2131	...	2231	2328	...	0019	...		0856	...	0956	1026	the same	1956	...	2056	...	2156	...	2257	...	2357
Tonbridge d.	2040	...	2140	...	2240	2337	...	0027	...		0904	...	1004	1034	minutes	2004	...	2104	...	2204	...	2306	...	0006
Tunbridge Wells d.	2051	...	2151	...	2251	2348	...	0038	...		0915	...	1015	1045	past each	2015	...	2115	...	2215	...	2316	...	0016
Hastings a.	2138	...	2238	...	2339	0035	...	0125	...		1002	...	1102	1121	hour until	2102	...	2202	...	2302	...	0004	...	0104

		Ⓐ	Ⓐ	Ⓐ	Ⓐ		Ⓐ	Ⓐ	Ⓐ	Ⓐ		Ⓐ	Ⓐ	Ⓐ	Ⓐ		Ⓐ	Ⓐ		Ⓐ	Ⓐ	Ⓐ	Ⓐ	
Hastings d.	Ⓐ	0517	0548	0603	...	...	0630	...	0643	...	...	0703	...	0725	...	...	0745	0815	...	0847	0929	0950	1032	and at
Tunbridge Wells d.		0609	0634	0656	0700	...	0716	0720	0736	0740	...	0756	0800	0818	0822	...	0840	0909	...	0939	1009	1039	1109	the same
Tonbridge d.		0619	0644	|	0711	...	|	0730	|	0751	...	|	0811	|	0832	...	0850	0920	...	0950	1020	1050	1120	minutes
Sevenoaks d.		0630	0652	|	0722	...	|	0742	|	0802	...	|	0855	|	0842	...	0858	0928	...	0958	1028	1058	1128	past each
London Charing Cross a.		0705	0729c	0750	0801	...	0808	0820	0830c	0840	...	0850	0900	0910c	0922	...	0937	1003	...	1033	1103	1133	1203	hour until

	Ⓐ	Ⓐ		Ⓐ	Ⓐ	Ⓐ	Ⓐ		Ⓐ	Ⓐ	Ⓐ	Ⓐ		Ⓐ	Ⓐ			⑥	⑥		⑥	⑥		⑥	⑥
Hastings d.	1532	1545	...	1619	1650	1718	1750	...	1819	1846	1950	2050	...	2150	2210	...	⑥	0550	0620	...	0650	0720	...	0750	0820
Tunbridge Wells d.	1612	1639	...	1710	1739	1813	1839	...	1906	1939	2039	2139	...	2239	2259	...		0639	0709	...	0739	0809	...	0839	0909
Tonbridge d.	1620	1650	...	1720	1750	1823	1850	...	1920	1951	2050	2150	...	2250	2314	...		0650	0720	...	0750	0820	...	0850	0920
Sevenoaks d.	1628	1658	...	1728	1758	1831	1859	...	1928	1959	2058	2158	...	2258	2324	...		0658	0728	...	0758	0828	...	0858	0928
London Charing Cross a.	1704	1732c	...	1806	1835	1904	1933	...	2003	2033	2133	2233	...	2333	0001	...		0733	0803	...	0833	0903	...	0933	1003

	⑥	⑥			⑥	⑥	⑥	⑥		⑥	⑥			⑦	⑦	⑦		⑦		⑦	⑦	⑦	⑦
Hastings d.	0850	0932	and at	...	1750	1850	1958	2050	...	2150	2210	...	⑦	0728	0828	0908	and at	1828	...	1928	2028	2128	2228
Tunbridge Wells d.	0939	1009	the same	...	1839	1939	2039	2139	...	2239	2259	...		0815	0915	0945	the same	1915	...	2015	2115	2215	2315
Tonbridge d.	0950	1020	minutes	...	1850	1950	2050	2150	...	2250	2314	...		0825	0925	0955	minutes	1925	...	2025	2125	2225	2324
Sevenoaks d.	0958	1028	past each	...	1858	1958	2058	2158	...	2258	2324	...		0833	0933	1003	past each	1933	...	2033	2133	2233	...
London Charing Cross a.	1033	1103	hour until	...	1933	2033	2133	2233	...	2333	0001	...		0907	1007	1037	hour until	2007	...	2107	2207	2307	...

c – London Cannon Street.

LONDON VICTORIA - MAIDSTONE EAST - ASHFORD

km			Ⓐ	Ⓐ	Ⓐ	Ⓐ		Ⓐ	Ⓐ	Ⓐ	Ⓐ		Ⓐ	Ⓐ	Ⓐ	Ⓐ	Ⓐ	Ⓐ		Ⓐ	Ⓐ	Ⓐ	Ⓐ
0	**London** Victoria d.	Ⓐ	0607	0637	0707	0736	...	0807	0837	0907	0937	and at the same	1507	1537	1607	1637	1658	1712	...	1742	1803	1818	1842
76	Maidstone East d.		0709	0743	0809	0839	...	0909	0939	1002	1039	minutes past	1602	1639	1702	1739	1757	1815	...	1846	1903	1925	1946
95	**Ashford** International a.		0738	0811	0838	0908	...	0938	1008	1027	1108	each hour until	1630	1708	1732	1810	1827	1845	...	1916	1932	1955	2016

	Ⓐ	Ⓐ	Ⓐ		Ⓐ	Ⓐ	Ⓐ	Ⓐ	Ⓐ			⑥	⑥	⑥	⑥	⑥		⑥	⑥		⑥	⑥	⑥
London Victoria d.	1907	1937	2007	...	2037	2107	2207	2307	2358	...	⑥	0607	0707	0737	0807	0837	and at the same	2007	2107	...	2207	2307	2358
Maidstone East d.	2005	2039	2102	...	2139	2209	2309	0009	0106	...		0709	0809	0839	0902	0939	minutes past	2109	2209	...	2309	0009	0106
Ashford International a.	2033	2108	2130	...	2209	2238	2338	0038	0134	...		0738	0838	0908	0927	1008	each hour until	2138	2238	...	2338	0038	0134

		⑦	⑦		⑦		
London Victoria d.	⑦	0745	0845	and at the same	2245	...	...
Maidstone East d.		0845	0945	minutes past	2345	...	...
Ashford International a.		0913	1013	each hour until	0013	...	...

		Ⓐ	Ⓐ	Ⓐ	Ⓐ	Ⓐ	Ⓐ	Ⓐ	Ⓐ	Ⓐ
Ashford International d.	Ⓐ	0520	0550	0603	0616	0640	0658	0715	0747	0826
Maidstone East d.		0549	0620	0632	0645	0709	0727	0744	0818	0855
London Victoria a.		0651	0722	0743	0753	0823	0836	0853	0923	0951

	Ⓐ	Ⓐ			Ⓐ	Ⓐ	Ⓐ	Ⓐ		Ⓐ	Ⓐ	Ⓐ	Ⓐ		Ⓐ	Ⓐ	Ⓐ	Ⓐ				⑥	⑥
Ashford International d.	0817	0928	and at the same	...	1526	1547	1626	1647	...	1726	1747	1826	1847	...	1917	2017	2117	2217	...	...	⑥	0520	0547
Maidstone East d.	0918	0955	minutes past	...	1555	1618	1655	1718	...	1755	1818	1855	1918	...	1948	2048	2148	2248	...	...		0549	0618
London Victoria a.	1021	1051	each hour until	...	1651	1721	1753	1821	...	1853	1921	1951	2021	...	2051	2151	2251	2351	...	...		0651	0721

	⑥	⑥		⑥	⑥			⑥	⑥		⑥	⑥		⑥			⑦		⑦		⑦
Ashford International d.	0628	0647	...	0728	0747	and at the same	...	1828	1847	...	1947	2047	...	2200	...	⑦	0647	...	0747	and at the same	2147
Maidstone East d.	0655	0718	...	0755	0818	minutes past	...	1855	1918	...	2018	2118	...	2230	...		0716	...	0816	minutes past	2216
London Victoria a.	0751	0821	...	0851	0921	each hour until	...	1951	2021	...	2121	2221	...	2332	...		0818	...	0918	each hour until	2318

103 BEDFORD - LONDON - GATWICK ✈ - BRIGHTON and EASTBOURNE FC, SN

For details of the direct *Gatwick Express* service between London Victoria and Gatwick Airport, see Table **154**.

LONDON VICTORIA – BRIGHTON and EASTBOURNE

km		Ⓐ	Ⓐ	Ⓐ	Ⓐ	Ⓐ	Ⓐ	Ⓐ	Ⓐ	Ⓐ	Ⓐ	Ⓐ	Ⓐ	Ⓐ	Ⓐ	Ⓐ	Ⓐ		Ⓐ	Ⓐ	Ⓐ	Ⓐ	Ⓐ	Ⓐ
0	**London** Victoria ... **105** d.		0532	0621	0632	0647	0733**b**	0747	0753**b**	0817	0821	0836	0847	0906	0917	0936	0947	and at the same minutes past each hour until	1606	1617	1636	1647	1706	1730
17	East Croydon........ **105** d.		0549	0638	0649	0703	0749	0803	0806	0833	0839	0853	0903	0922	0933	0952	1003		1622	1633	1652	1703	1722	│
43	**Gatwick** Airport ✈ **105** d.		0620	0704	0720	0719	0805	0819	0829	0849	0856	│	0919	│	0949	│	1019		│	1649	│	1720	│	1800
61	Haywards Heath ... **105** d.		0634	0721	0740	0733	0819	0832	0843	0913	0910	│	0934	│	1007	│	1034		│	1710	1723	1736	1746	1812
82	**Brighton**........... **105** a.		│	0742	0802	│	0836	│	0904	│	0926	0930	│	0958	│	1027	│		1700	│	1739	│	1810	1834
81	Lewes........................a.		0649	...	...	0752	...	0851	...	0928	...	...	0952	...	1022	...	1051		...	1721	...	1756	...	...
106	**Eastbourne**.................a.		0715	...	...	0814	...	0913	...	0950	...	...	1013	...	1044	...	1113		...	1748	...	1818	...	...

	Ⓐ	Ⓐ	Ⓐ	Ⓐ	Ⓐ	Ⓐ	Ⓐ	Ⓐ		Ⓐ	Ⓐ	Ⓐ	Ⓐ	Ⓐ	Ⓐ		⑥	⑥	⑥	⑥	⑥	⑥	⑥	⑥
London Victoria ... **105** d.	1736	1800	1806	1830	1847	1906	1917	1936	and at the same minutes past each hour until	2147	2206	2236	2247	2306	2332	...		0706	0721	0747	0806	0817	0821	0847
East Croydon........ **105** d.	1752	│	1822	│	1903	1922	1933	1952		2203	2222	2252	2303	2322	2352	...		0722	0737	0803	0822	0833	0837	0903
Gatwick Airport ✈ **105** d.	1807	1835	1838	1905	1920	│	1949	│		2219	│	│	2319	│	0015	...		│	0758	0819	│	0849	0858	0919
Haywards Heath ... **105** d.	1818	1847	1850	1917	1934	1945	2007	2017		2234	2245	2315	2334	2345	0031	...		│	0817	0834	│	0907	0917	0934
Brighton........... **105** a.	│	1910	│	1939	│	2002	│	2033		│	2300	2230	│	2359	0052	...		0758	0840	│	0858	│	0940	│
Lewes........................a.	1838	...	1909	...	1953	...	2022	...		2251	...	...	2351	...	...	...		...	...	0848	...	0922	...	0951
Eastbourne.................a.	1900	...	1941	...	2014	...	2048	...		2314	...	...	0016	...	...	...		...	...	0913	...	0944	...	1013

		⑥	⑥	⑥	⑥	⑥	⑥	⑥	⑥	⑥	⑥	⑥	⑥	⑥	⑥	⑥	⑥	⑥		⑦	⑦	⑦	⑦	⑦
London Victoria ... **105** d.	and at the same minutes past each hour until	1906	1917	1921	1947	2006	2017	2021	2047	2106	2117	2136	2147	2206	2236	2247	2302	2332	...		0632	0732	0832	0847
East Croydon........ **105** d.		1922	1933	1937	2003	2022	2033	2037	2103	2122	2133	2152	2203	2222	2252	2303	2318	2352	...		0652	0751	0851	0907
Gatwick Airport ✈ **105** d.		│	1949	1958	2019	│	2049	2055	2119	│	2149	│	2219	│	│	2319	2339	0015	...		0719	0812	0912	0929
Haywards Heath ... **105** d.		│	2007	2017	2034	│	2107	2117	2134	2145	2208	2215	2234	2245	2315	2334	2353	0034	...		0736	0828	0928	0941
Brighton........... **105** a.		1958	│	2040	│	2058	│	2140	│	2200	│	2230	│	2300	2330	│	0015	0055	...		0758	0850	0950	│
Lewes........................a.		...	2022	...	2051	...	2122	...	2151	...	2223	...	2251	...	...	2351	...	...	...		...	...	...	0958
Eastbourne.................a.		...	2048	...	2113	...	2148	...	2215	...	2248	...	2314	...	...	0016	...	...	...		...	...	...	1019

	⑦	⑦	⑦		⑦	⑦	⑦	⑦	⑦	⑦
London Victoria ... **105** d.	0902	0932	0947	and at the same minutes past each hour until	2102	2132	2147	2232	2247	2332
East Croydon........ **105** d.	0922	0951	1007		2122	2151	2207	2251	2307	2353
Gatwick Airport ✈ **105** d.	0940	1012	1029		2140	2212	2229	2312	2329	0015
Haywards Heath ... **105** d.	│	1028	1041		│	2228	2241	2328	2341	0031
Brighton........... **105** a.	1003	1050	│		2203	2250	│	2350	│	0052
Lewes........................a.	...	...	1058		...	...	2259	...	2359	...
Eastbourne.................a.	...	...	1119		...	...	2319	...	0020	...

	Ⓐ	Ⓐ	Ⓐ	Ⓐ	Ⓐ	Ⓐ	Ⓐ	Ⓐ	Ⓐ
Eastbourne.........................d.		0508	0542	...	...	0624	...	...	0657
Lewes...................................d.		0529	0605	...	...	0650	...	...	0722
Brighton................. **105** d.		│	│	0617	0640	│	0656	0715	│
Haywards Heath .... **105** d.		0546	0622	0634	0703	0713	0720	0735	0743
Gatwick Airport ✈...... **105** d.		0558	0640	0653	0720	0729	0735	0750	│
East Croydon.............. **105** d.		0615	0656	0715	│	0747	│	│	0814
London Victoria.......... **105** a.		0632	0713**b**	0733	0750	0804**b**	0806	0820	0832

	Ⓐ	Ⓐ	Ⓐ	Ⓐ	Ⓐ	Ⓐ	Ⓐ	Ⓐ	Ⓐ	Ⓐ	Ⓐ	Ⓐ	Ⓐ	Ⓐ	Ⓐ		Ⓐ	Ⓐ	Ⓐ	Ⓐ	Ⓐ	Ⓐ	Ⓐ	Ⓐ
Eastbourne.................d.	...	0714	...	0732	0757	...	0818	...	0856	...	0930	...	0956	...	1031	and at the same minutes past each hour until	...	1858	...	1931	...	...	2031	...
Lewes........................d.	...	0742	...	0755	0823	...	0847	...	0917	...	0950	...	1019	...	1050		...	1921	...	1950	...	...	2050	...
Brighton........... **105** d.	0730	│	0744	│	│	0845	│	0919	│	0949	│	1019	│	1049	│		1919	│	1949	│	2019	2049	│	2119
Haywards Heath ... **105** d.	0751	0802	0806	0816	0844	0858	0904	│	0938	│	1009	│	1040	│	1105		│	1940	│	2010	│	│	2109	│
Gatwick Airport ✈ **105** d.	0805	│	0820	│	0855	0911	0922	│	0955	│	1024	│	1054	│	1124		│	1955	│	2025	│	│	2124	│
East Croydon........ **105** d.	│	0831	│	0846	0914	0926	0939	0955	1011	1024	1040	1056	1110	1124	1140		1954	2011	2024	2041	2054	2125	2140	2153
London Victoria ... **105** a.	0835	0850**b**	0852	0905	0932	0944	0958	1011	1028	1040	1057	1112	1127	1140	1157		2010	2028	2043	2058	2110	2141	2157	2210

	Ⓐ	Ⓐ	Ⓐ	Ⓐ	Ⓐ		⑥	⑥	⑥	⑥	⑥	⑥	⑥	⑥	⑥	⑥	⑥	⑥	⑥		⑥	⑥	⑥	⑥
Eastbourne.................d.	...	2131	...	2215	...	...		...	...	...	...	0624	...	...	0658	...	0731	...	0758	and at the same minutes past each hour until	...	1858	...	1932
Lewes........................d.	...	2150	...	2240	...	...		...	...	...	...	0650	...	...	0720	...	0750	...	0820		...	1920	...	1951
Brighton........... **105** d.	2149	│	2200	│	2302	...		0521	0550	0610	0649	│	0655	0719	│	0749	│	0819	│		1919	│	1949	│
Haywards Heath ... **105** d.	│	2206	2222	2258	2324	...		0537	0611	0640	│	0705	0716	│	0740	│	0805	│	0840		│	1940	│	2007
Gatwick Airport ✈ **105** d.	│	2224	2238	2312	2353	...		0553	0625	0655	│	0724	0738	│	0754	│	0824	│	0854		│	1954	│	2024
East Croydon........ **105** d.	2224	2240	2300	2330	0017	...		0611	0641	0711	0724	0740	0753	0756	0810	0824	0840	0856	0910		1956	2010	2024	2040
London Victoria ... **105** a.	2240	2257	2320	2352	0037	...		0630	0657	0727	0740	0757	0809	0812	0827	0840	0857	0912	0927		2012	2027	2040	2057

	⑥	⑥	⑥	⑥	⑥	⑥	⑥	⑥	⑥		⑦	⑦	⑦	⑦	⑦	⑦		⑦	⑦	⑦		⑦		⑦
Eastbourne.................d.	...	...	2031	...	...	2131	...	2218	...	...		...	0654	...	0755	...	and at the same minutes past each hour until	...	...	2055	...	...	...	...
Lewes........................d.	...	...	2050	...	...	2150	...	2240	...	...		...	0720	...	0816	...		...	...	2116	...	...	...	...
Brighton........... **105** d.	2019	2049	│	2119	2149	│	2200	│	2302	...		0700	│	0800	│	0844		2034	2100	│	...	2200	...	2302
Haywards Heath ... **105** d.	│	│	2106	│	│	2206	2222	2258	2324	...		0721	0736	0821	0836	│		│	2121	2135	...	2221	...	2324
Gatwick Airport ✈ **105** d.	│	│	2124	│	│	2223	2238	2312	2353	...		0738	0751	0838	0851	0856		2056	2138	2152	...	2238	...	2349
East Croydon........ **105** d.	2054	2124	2140	2154	2224	2240	2300	2330	0017	...		0759	0809	0859	0909	0913		2113	2159	2209	...	2259	...	0018
London Victoria ... **105** a.	2110	2140	2157	2210	2240	2258	2317	2352	0036	...		0818	0831	0918	0931	0935		2135	2218	2231	...	2320	...	0037

BEDFORD - LONDON ST. PANCRAS - BRIGHTON

Due to engineering work there are no through services between Bedford and Brighton on ©. On these days services between London and Brighton will start / terminate at **London Bridge**.
For more information please contact First Capital Connect (✆ 0845 026 4700 www.firstcapitalconnect.co.uk) or National Rail Enquiries (✆ 08457 484 950 www.nationalrail.co.uk).

	Ⓐ	Ⓐ	Ⓐ	Ⓐ	Ⓐ	Ⓐ	Ⓐ	Ⓐ	Ⓐ		Ⓐ	Ⓐ	Ⓐ	Ⓐ	Ⓐ	Ⓐ	Ⓐ	Ⓐ	Ⓐ	Ⓐ	Ⓐ	Ⓐ	Ⓐ	Ⓐ
Bedford .... **170** d.	0540	0558	0620	0700	0748	0824	0840	0854	0910	and at the same minutes past each hour until	1454	1510	1524	1610	1626	1708	1736	1810	1840	1854	1922	1952	2022	2052
Luton.................... **170** d.	0604	0621	0644	0724	0812	0848	0904	0918	0934		1518	1534	1548	1634	1650	1732	1800	1834	1904	1918	1946	2016	2046	2116
Luton Airport ✈ ... **170** d.	0606	0624	0646	0726	0814	0850	0906	0920	0936		1520	1536	1550	1636	1652	1734	1802	1836	1906	1920	1948	2018	2048	2118
St Albans City.............d.	0618	0636	0658	0738	0827	0903	0918	0934	0948		1534	1548	1604	1648	1704	1746	1814	1848	1918	1933	2000	2030	2100	2130
London St Pancras **170** d.	0638	0658	0720	0758	0848	0924	0940	0954	1010		1554	1610	1624	1710	1728	1808	1834	1910	1940	1954	2024	2054	2124	2154
London Bridge...........d.	0700	0716	0742	0818	0912	0942	0956	1012	1027		1612	1627	1643	1722	1740	1827	1857	1927	1957	2012	2042	2112	2142	2212
East Croydon....... **105** d.	0715	0731	0756	0837	0924	0954	1009	1024	1039		1624	1640	1700	1746	1809	1841	1910	1939	2009	2024	2054	2124	2154	2224
Gatwick Airport ... **105** d.	0732	0747	0812	0852	0941	1011	1026	1041	1056		1641	1656	1716	1810	1825	1856	1927	1956	2026	2041	2111	2141	2211	2241
Haywards Heath .. **105** d.	0746	0804	0828	0907	0957	1027	1038	1055	1108		1655	1712	1733	...	1836	1914	1941	2010	2038	2057	2126	2158	2226	2258
Brighton .... **105** a.	0805	0825	0849	0923	1019	1049	1054	1117	1124		1717	1729	1756	...	1904	1934	2000	2029	2057	2118	2147	2219	2247	2319

	Ⓐ	Ⓐ	Ⓐ	Ⓐ	Ⓐ	Ⓐ	Ⓐ	Ⓐ	Ⓐ		Ⓐ	Ⓐ	Ⓐ	Ⓐ	Ⓐ	Ⓐ	Ⓐ	Ⓐ	Ⓐ	Ⓐ	Ⓐ	Ⓐ	Ⓐ	Ⓐ
Brighton .... **105** d.	0549	0623	0700	0724	0802	0836	0907	0934	0937	and at the same minutes past each hour until	1507	1534	1607	1630	1703	1737	1807	1837	1907	1934	1937	2007	2034	2037
Haywards Heath ... **105** d.	0610	0646	0723	0746	0823	0900	0932	0948	0958		1532	1548	1626	1650	1718	1756	1832	1902	1932	1948	2002	2032	2048	2102
Gatwick Airport .... **105** d.	0624	0701	0738	0801	0838	0916	0946	1001	1016		1546	1601	1641	1708	1731	1816	1846	1916	1946	2001	2016	2046	2101	2116
East Croydon........ **105** d.	0644	0724	0754	0824	0854	0932	1002	1017	1032		1602	1617	1657	1723	1747	1832	1902	1932	2002	2017	2032	2102	2117	2132
London Bridge............a.	0658	│	│	│	0908	0946	1016	1030	1045		1616	│	│	│	1813	1846	1916	1945	2015	2030	2045	2115	2130	2145
London St Pancras. **170** a.	0715	0803	0831	0903	0932	1003	1033	1047	1103		1635	1701	1735	1801	1831	1905	1933	2003	2033	2047	2103	2133	2147	2203
St Albans City.............a.	0741	0823	0851	0925	0952	1024	1054	1110	1124		1656	1721	1756	1821	1851	1926	1955	2025	2055	2109	2125	2155	2209	2225
Luton Airport......... **170** a.	0753	0837	0900	0937	1001	1037	1106	1121	1137		1709	│	1809	│	│	1939	2007	2037	2107	2121	2137	2207	2221	2237
Luton.................... **170** a.	0756	0840	0904	0940	1004	1040	1109	1124	1140		1712	1734	1812	1834	1904	1943	2010	2040	2110	2124	2140	2210	2224	2240
Bedford .... **170** a.	0822	0906	0926	1008	1028	1106	1136	1150	1206		1738	1758	1838	1858	1926	2008	2036	2106	2136	2150	2206	2236	2250	2306

b – London Bridge.

104 BRIGHTON - NEWHAVEN - SEAFORD SN

FROM BRIGHTON:
Trains call at **Lewes** 15 minutes, and **Newhaven Town** (▲) 29 minutes later:

Ⓐ: 0545, 0639, 0652, 0710, 0740, 0813, 0845, 0910, 0940 and every 30 minutes until 1740; then 1808, 1817, 1838, 1908, 1940, 2010, 2040, 2104, 2140, 2204, 2234, 2334.

⑥: 0552, 0610, 0640 and every 30 minutes until until 2040; then 2104, 2140, 2204, 2234, 2334.

⑦: 0715, 0750, 0809, 0850, 0909, 0939 and then at 09 and 39 minutes past each hour until 2209; then 2239.

FROM SEAFORD:
Trains call at **Newhaven Town** (▲) 7 minutes, and **Lewes** 16 minutes later:

Ⓐ: 0509, 0545, 0630, 0716, 0733, 0758, 0857, 0925, 0958 and at 25 and 58 minutes past each hour until 1825; then 1844, 1902, 1919, 1937, 1958, 2028, 2058, 2128, 2158, 2220, 2258, 2325.

⑥: 0505, 0628, 0658, 0728, 0758, 0825, 0858 and at 25 and 58 minutes past each hour until 1958; then 2028, 2058, 2128, 2158, 2220, 2258, 2325.

⑦: 0753, 0828, 0853 and at 28 and 53 minutes past each hour until 2028; then 2051, 2128, 2153, 2228, 2253.

☛ For ⛴ services Newhaven – Dieppe and v.v., see Table **2125**.

▲ – ± 500m from **Newhaven Harbour**; most trains also call at the Harbour station.

SW Most trains 🍴 LONDON - GUILDFORD - PORTSMOUTH 107

km			Ⓐ	⑥	Ⓐ	Ⓐ	⑥	Ⓐ	⚒	⚒	⚒	⚒		⚒	⚒	⑥	Ⓐ	Ⓐ	⑥	Ⓐ	⑥	Ⓐ	⑥	Ⓐ
0	**London** Waterloo 113 d.	⚒	0500	0520	0520	0615	0645	0645	0730	0800	0830	0900	and at	1600	1630	1700	1700	1730	1800	1800	1830	1830	1900	1900
39	Woking 113 d.		0551	0613	0611	0643	0713	0713	0755	0825	0855	0925	the same	1625	1655	1725	1725	1756	1825	|	1855	1858	1925	1925
49	**Guildford** d.		0600	0625	0625	0655	0725	0725	0804	0834	0904	0934	minutes	1634	1704	1734	1737	1808	1834	1833	1904	1908	1934	1937
69	Haslemere d.		0625	0645	0655	0720	0745	0755	0821	0850	0921	0950	past	1650	1721	1750	1752	1826	1850	1852	1921	1926	1950	1953
107	Havant d.		0658	0720	0728	0752	0817	0827	0850	0916	0950	1016	each	1716	1750	1816	1820	1851	1916	1916	1950	1951	2016	2016
118	Portsmouth & Southsea a.		0716	0735	0746	0807	0832	0843	0902	0932	1002	1028	hour	1728	1802	1828	1832	1903	1928	1929	2002	2003	2028	2029
120	**Portsmouth** Harbour a.		0720	0740	...	0812	0837	0848	0907	0937	1007	1033	until	1735	1809	1833	1839	1910	1933	1936	2007	2010	2033	2034

	⚒	⑥	Ⓐ	⚒		⚒		⚒		⚒	⚒	⚒	⚒	⚒			⑦	⑦	⑦	⑦	⑦	⑦	⑦	
London Waterloo 113 d.	1930	2000	2000	2030	...	2100	...	2130	...	2200	2230	2245	2315	2345	...	⑦	...	0800	0830	0900	0930	1000	1030	and at
Woking 113 d.	1955	2025	2025	2055	...	2125	...	2155	...	2225	2255	2313	2343	0017	...		0732	0835	0904	0935	1004	1032	1102	the same
Guildford d.	2004	2034	2034	2104	...	2134	...	2204	...	2234	2304	2325	2352	0029	...		0741	0845	0914	0945	1014	1042	1112	minutes
Haslemere d.	2021	2050	2055	2121	...	2155	...	2225	...	2255	2325	2350	0013	0054	...		0807	0912	0929	1012	1029	1107	1127	past each
Havant d.	2049	2116	2119	2146	...	2219	...	2249	...	2319	2349	0022	0037	0126	...		0839	0945	0953	1045	1053	1139	1151	hour until
Portsmouth & Southsea a.	2102	2128	2132	2158	...	2232	...	2304	...	2332	0002	0038	0050	0142	...		0853	0959	1006	1059	1105	1153	1204	
Portsmouth Harbour a.	2107	2133	2137	2203	...	2237	...	2308	...	2337	0007	...	0055	...	...		0857	1004	1011	1104	1111	1158	1211	

	⑦	⑦	⑦	⑦	⑦	⑦			
London Waterloo 113 d.	2100	2130	2200	2230	2300	2330	...	...	...
Woking 113 d.	2132	2202	2232	2302	2332	0002	...	...	...
Guildford d.	2142	2212	2242	2312	2342	0012	...	...	...
Haslemere d.	2207	2227	2307	2327	0007	0027	...	...	...
Havant d.	2239	2251	2339	2351	0039	0051	...	...	...
Portsmouth & Southsea a.	2253	2304	2353	0004	0053	0104	...	...	...
Portsmouth Harbour a.	2258	2309	2358	0009	0058	0109	...	...	...

		Ⓐ	⑥	⚒	Ⓐ	Ⓐ	⑥	Ⓐ	⑥	Ⓐ
Portsmouth Harbour d.	Ⓐ	0430	0443	0519	0550	0615	0619	0642	0645	0713
Portsmouth & Southsea d.		0435	0448	0524	0555	0620	0624	0647	0650	0718
Havant d.		0451	0504	0540	0611	0634	0640	0700	0704	0732
Haslemere d.		0526	0539	0615	0647	0702	0715	0735	0732	0800
Guildford d.		0555	0602	0631	0707	0717	0734	0754	0747	0815
Woking 113 a.		0600	0611	0644	0715	0725	0744	|	0757	0826
London Waterloo 113 a.		0629	0640	0713	0745	0754	0813	0832	0823	0855

	⑥	⑥	Ⓐ	⑥	Ⓐ	⑥	Ⓐ	⚒	⚒		⑥	Ⓐ	⑥	Ⓐ	⑥	Ⓐ	Ⓐ	⑥	⑥	Ⓐ	⑥	Ⓐ	⚒	⚒
Portsmouth Harbour d.	0715	0745	0745	0815	0815	0845	0845	0915	0945	and at	1545	1545	1615	1615	1645	1645	1715	1718	1745	1745	1815	1815	1845	1915
Portsmouth & Southsea d.	0720	0750	0750	0820	0820	0850	0850	0920	0950	the same	1550	1550	1620	1620	1650	1650	1720	1724	1750	1750	1820	1820	1850	1920
Havant d.	0734	0804	0804	0834	0834	0904	0904	0934	1004	minutes	1604	1604	1634	1634	1704	1704	1734	1740	1804	1804	1834	1834	1904	1934
Haslemere d.	0802	0832	0832	0902	0902	0932	0932	1002	1032	past	1632	1637	1702	1702	1732	1737	1802	1815	1832	1832	1902	1902	1932	2002
Guildford d.	0817	0847	0854	0917	0917	0947	0947	1017	1047	each	1647	1700	1717	1717	1747	1800	1817	1834	1847	1855	1917	1921	1947	2017
Woking 113 a.	0826	0857	|	0925	0927	0957	0959	1025	1057	hour	1657	1711	1725	1725	1757	1811	|	1844	1857	1903	1925	1928	1957	2025
London Waterloo 113 a.	0851	0923	0931	0951	0955	1023	1027	1051	1124	until	1723	1743	1751	1754	1823	1843	1859	1913	1923	1929	1951	1959	2023	2050

	⚒	⚒	⚒	⚒	⚒	⚒			⑦		⑦	⑦		⑦	⑦		⑦	⑦	⑦	⑦		⑦		⑦
Portsmouth Harbour d.	1945	2015	2045	2118	2218	2319	...	⑦	0648	...	0732	0748	...	0832	0848	...	0932	0948	1032	1048	and at	2232	...	2248
Portsmouth & Southsea d.	1950	2020	2050	2124	2224	2324	...		0653	...	0737	0753	...	0837	0853	...	0937	0953	1037	1053	the same	2237	...	2253
Havant d.	2004	2034	2104	2140	2240	2340	...		0707	...	0750	0807	...	0850	0907	...	0950	1007	1050	1107	minutes	2250	...	2307
Haslemere d.	2032	2102	2132	2215	2315	0015	...		0742	...	0817	0842	...	0917	0942	...	1017	1042	1117	1142	past	2317	...	2342
Guildford d.	2047	2117	2147	2239	2339	0037	...		0805	...	0835	0905	...	0935	1005	...	1035	1105	1135	1205	each	2335	...	0005
Woking 113 a.	2057	2125	2157	2249	2349	...	...		0813	...	0842	0915	...	0942	1015	...	1042	1113	1142	1213	hour	2342	...	0013
London Waterloo 113 a.	2127	2150	2227	2319	0032	...	...		0849	...	0919	0949	...	1021	1049	...	1119	1149	1219	1249	until	0014	...	...

SW Most services 🍴 LONDON - SOUTHAMPTON - WEYMOUTH 108

km			Ⓐ	⚒	⚒	Ⓐ	⚒	⑥	Ⓐ	⚒	⚒		⚒	⚒	⑥	Ⓐ	⚒	Ⓐ	⑥	Ⓐ	⑥	Ⓐ	Ⓐ	⑥
0	**London** Waterloo 113 d.	⚒	...	0530	0630	0612	0735	0805	0805	0835	0905		1505	1535	1605	1605	1635	1705	1705	1735	1735	1748	1805	1805
39	Woking 113 d.		...	0601	0657	0650	0800	|	|	0900	|	and	|	1600	|	|	1700**b**	|	|	|	1800	1813	|	|
77	Basingstoke 129 d.		0540	0621	0718	0730	0820	0849	0849	|	0949	at	1549	|	1649	1649	|	|	1749	|	|	1833	|	1849
107	Winchester 129 d.		0559	0638	0734	0750	0837	0905	0905	0933	1005	the	1605	1633	1705	1705	1733	1800	1805	1830	1833	1850	1900	1905
120	**Southampton** Airport 129 d.		0613	0653	0748	0806	0851	0914	0914	0942	1014	same	1614	1642	1714	1714	1742	1809	1814	1839	1842	1903	1909	1914
128	**Southampton** Central 129 d.		0625	0701	0800	0819	0900	0924	0924	0951	1024	minutes	1624	1651	1724	1724	1751	1821	1824	1851	1851	1918	1919	1924
149	Brockenhurst 129 d.		0644	0718	0817	0844	0917	0938	0938	1005	1038	past	1638	1705	1738	1738	1805	|	1838	|	1905	...	1936	1938
174	**Bournemouth** 129 d.		0711	0746	0844	0911	0944	1004	1004	1024	1104	each	1704	1724	1804	1809	1824	1850	1904	1921	1924	...	2007	2004
183	Poole d.		0724	0758	0857	0924	0957	1014	1014	1037	1114	hour	1714	1737	1814	1819	1837	1903	1914	1934	1937	...	2019	2014
219	Dorchester South d.		0758	0833	0929	0958	1027	1049	1056	1105	1149	until	1749	1805	1849	1853	1905	1938	1949	2002	2005	...	2054	2049
230	**Weymouth** a.		0809	0845	0940	1009	1035	1100	1107	1113	1200		1802	1815	1900	1906	1917	1951	2000	2015	2013	...	2107	2100

	Ⓐ	⑥	⚒	⚒	⚒	⚒	⚒	⚒	⚒	⚒	⚒			⑦	⑦	⑦	⑦	⑦	⑦		⑦	⑦	⑦	⑦
London Waterloo 113 d.	1835	1835	1905	1935	2005	2035	2105	2135	2205	2235	2305	...	⑦	...	0754	0835	0854	0935	0954		2054	2135	2154	2254
Woking 113 d.	|	1900	|	2000	|	2100	2132	2200	2232	2300	2332	...		...	0828	0909	0928	1007	1028	and	2128	2207	2228	2328
Basingstoke 129 d.	|	|	1949	|	2049	|	2152	|	2252	|	2352	...		0748	0847	0929	0948	1029	1048	at	2148	2228	2248	2348
Winchester 129 d.	1930	1933	2005	2033	2105	2133	2209	2233	2309	2333	0012	...		0808	0908	0946	1008	1044	1108	the	2208	2244	2308	0008
Southampton Airport 129 d.	1939	1942	2014	2042	2114	2142	2222	2242	2322	2342	0025	...		0827	0927	0955	1027	1053	1127	same	2227	2253	2327	0027
Southampton Central 129 d.	1951	1951	2024	2051	2124	2151	2231	2251	2331	2351	0036	...		0835	0935	1003	1035	1103	1135	minutes	2235	2303	2335	0037
Brockenhurst 129 d.	|	2005	2038	2105	2143	2205	2250	2305	2350	0005	0052**s**	...		0857	0957	1018	1057	1117	1157	past	2257	2317	2354	0053**s**
Bournemouth 129 d.	2021	2024	2104	2124	2210	2224	2317	2329	0017	0024	0115	...		0925	1025	1040	1125	1140	1225	each	2325	2340	0022	0118
Poole d.	2034	2037	2114	2137	2223	2237	2329	2342	0029	0036	0130	...		0934	1034	1052	1134	1152	1234	hour	2334	2352	0035	0130
Dorchester South d.	2102	2105	2147	2209	...	2309	...	0014	...	...	...	...		*1025*	...	1125	...	1225	...	until	...	0025	...	...
Weymouth a.	2113	2113	2200	2223	...	2320	...	0026	...	...	...	...		*1036*	...	1136	...	1236	...		...	0036	...	...

		Ⓐ	⑥	Ⓐ	Ⓐ	Ⓐ	⑥	⑥	Ⓐ	⑥	Ⓐ	⚒	Ⓐ	⑥	Ⓐ	⑥	⚒	⚒	⚒	⚒		⚒	⚒	⚒
Weymouth d.	⚒	...	...	...	...	...	...	...	0555	...	0625	0655	...	0720	0755	0803	0820	0903	0920	1003		1520	1603	1620
Dorchester South d.		...	...	...	...	...	...	...	0607	...	0637	0707	...	0733	0807	0813	0833	0913	0933	1013	and	1533	1613	1633
Poole d.		0500	0528	0545	0611	...	...	0628	0641	0707	0711	0741	0755	0807	0841	0840	0907	0940	1007	1040	at	1607	1640	1707
Bournemouth 129 d.		0515	0542	0557	0625	...	...	0642	0656	0722	0726	0759	0810	0822	0859	0859	0918	0955	1022	1059	the	1622	1659	1722
Brockenhurst 129 d.		0538	0610	0614	|	...	...	0710	|	0745	|	0815	0841	0845	0915	0915	0941	1011	1045	1115	same	1645	1715	1745
Southampton Central 129 d.		0555	0630	0630	0700	0643	0700	0730	0730	0800	0800	0830	0900	0900	0930	0930	1000	1030	1100	1130	minutes	1700	1730	1800
Southampton Airport 129 d.		0603	0638	0638	0708	0654	0708	0738	0738	0808	0808	0838	0908	0908	0938	0938	1008	1038	1108	1138	past	1708	1738	1808
Winchester 129 d.		0618	0652	0648	0718	|	0724	0748	0748	0818	0818	0848	0918	0918	0948	0948	1018	1048	1118	1148	each	1718	1748	1818
Basingstoke 129 d.		0635	0709	|	|	0736	0742	|	|	0836	0835	|	0936	0936	|	|	1036	|	1136	|	hour	1736	|	1836
Woking 113 a.		0653	0727	|	|	0808	0807	0821	|	|	0853	0922	0954	|	1020	1019	|	1119	|	1219	until	|	1819	|
London Waterloo 113 a.		0724	0753	0747	0816	0839	0838	0849	0850	0920	0925	0953	1023	1020	1049	1049	1120	1149	1220	1249		1823	1849	1920

	⚒	⚒	⚒	⚒	⚒	⚒	⚒	⚒	⚒	⚒			⑦	⑦	⑦	⑦	⑦	⑦	⑦		⑦	⑦	⑦	⑦
Weymouth d.	1703	1720	1803	1820	1903	1920	...	2010	...	2110	...	⑦	...	...	0748	...	0848	...	0948		1848	...	1958	2058
Dorchester South d.	1713	1733	1813	1833	1913	1933	...	2022	...	2122	...		...	...	0800	...	0900	...	1000	and	1900	...	2010	2110
Poole d.	1740	1807	1840	1907	1940	2007	...	2054	...	2154	...		0650	0750	0832	0855	0932	0955	1032	at	1932	1955	2050	2150
Bournemouth 129 d.	1759	1822	1859	1922	1959	2022	...	2112	...	2212	...		0706	0806	0850	0906	0950	1006	1050	the	1950	2006	2106	2206
Brockenhurst 129 d.	1815	1845	1915	1945	2015	2045	...	2140	...	2240	...		0734	0834	0909	0934	1009	1034	1109	same	2009	2034	2134	2234
Southampton Central 129 d.	1830	1900	1930	2000	2030	2100	2130	2200	2230	2300	...		0755	0855	0925	0955	1025	1055	1125	minutes	2025	2055	2155	2255
Southampton Airport 129 d.	1838	1908	1938	2008	2038	2108	2138	2208	2238	2308	...		0803	0903	0933	1003	1033	1103	1133	past	2033	2103	2203	2303
Winchester 129 d.	1848	1918	1948	2018	2048	2118	2148	2218	2254	2324	...		0823	0923	0942	1023	1042	1123	1142	each	2042	2123	2223	2323
Basingstoke 129 d.	|	1936	|	2036	|	2136	|	2236	2313	2344	...		0844	0944	1000	1044	1100	1144	1200	hour	2100	2144	2244	2344
Woking 113 a.	1924	|	2019	|	2119	|	2219	2354	2333	0018	...		0902	1002	1019	1102	1118	1202	1218	until	2118	2202	2302	0002
London Waterloo 113 a.	1951	2020	2049	2124	2149	2222	2249	2323	0010	0102	...		0942	1042	1054	1140	1152	1240	1252		2149	2237	2337	0033

☛ For ⛴ services Poole – Jersey / Guernsey / St Malo and v.v., see Table **2100**.   **b** – Stops to pick up only on Ⓐ.   **s** – Stops to set down only.

109 ASHFORD - HASTINGS - BRIGHTON SN

km		⚒	⚒	⑦	⚒	⑦		⚒	⑦	⚒	
0	**Ashford** .... 100 101 d.	0623	0730	0816	0830	0921	and hourly until	2030	2121	2130	...
25	Rye .... d.	0648	0754	0841	0854	0946		2054	2146	2157	...
42	**Hastings** .... 101 d.	0711	0812	0904	0912	1004		2112	2204	2216	...
50	Bexhill .... d.	0722	0822	0914	0922	1014		2122	2214	2225	...
67	Eastbourne .... 102 a.	0737	0840	0929	0940	1029		2137	2229	2241	...
93	Lewes .... 102 a.	0807	0907	0959	1007	1059		2207	2259	2307	...
106	**Brighton** .... 102 a.	0820	0920	1012	1020	1112		2220	2312	2320	...

	⚒	⚒	⑦	⚒		⚒	⑦	⚒	⑦	⚒
Brighton .... 102 d.	0632	0732	0820	0832	and hourly until	1932	2020	2030	2120	2130
Lewes .... 102 d.	0644	0744	0832	0844		1944	2032	2044	2132	2144
Eastbourne .... 102 d.	0708	0808	0902	0908		2008	2102	2108	2202	2208
Bexhill .... d.	0723	0823	0916	0923		2023	2116	2123	2216	2223
Hastings .... 101 d.	0734	0834	0927	0934		2034	2127	2134	2226	2233
Rye .... d.	0754	0854	0946	0954		2054	2146	2157	...	...
Ashford ..... 100 101 a.	0816	0916	1008	1016		2116	2208	2219	...	...

☛ Additional trains operate Hastings - Eastbourne - Brighton and v.v.

110 BRIGHTON - PORTSMOUTH and SOUTHAMPTON SN

km			Ⓐ	Ⓐ	Ⓐ	Ⓐ	Ⓐ	Ⓐ	Ⓐ	Ⓐ	Ⓐ	Ⓐ	Ⓐ		Ⓐ	Ⓐ	Ⓐ	Ⓐ	Ⓐ	Ⓐ	Ⓐ	Ⓐ	Ⓐ	Ⓐ
0	**Brighton** .... 102 d.	Ⓐ	0530	0553	0627	0635	0706	0715	0730	0803	0839	0903	0933	and at the same minutes past each hour until ★	1503	1533	1603	1633	1703	1733	1800	1828	1900	1930
2	Hove .... d.		0534	0557	0631	0639	0710	0719	0734	0807	0843	0907	0937		1507	1537	1607	1637	1707	1737	1804	1832	1904	1934
17	Worthing .... d.		0555	0609	0643	0656	0723	0736	0752	0820	0856	0925	0955		1525	1555	1625	1655	1725	1755	1827	1854	1926	1956
36	Barnham .... d.		0618	0624	0705	0718	0744	0753	0814	0841	0916	0945	1017		1547	1617	1647	1717	1747	1817	1849	1912	1948	2018
46	**Chichester** .... d.		0626	0632	0713	0728	0752	0801	0822	0850	0924	0953	1025		1555	1625	1655	1725	1755	1825	1857	1920	1956	2026
60	Havant .... d.		0640	0653	0731	0741	0803	0822	0837	0901	0938	1007	1037		1609	1637	1709	1737	1813	1837	1908	1936	2007	2037
71	Portsmouth & Southsea a.		|	0708	|	0753	|	0837	|	0917	|	1019	|		1621	|	1722	|	1825	|	1921	|	2020	|
73	**Portsmouth Harbour** .... a.		|	0712	|	0758	|	0841	|	0921	|	1023	|		1626	|	...	|	1831	|	1926	|	...	|
76	Fareham .... a.		0659	...	0746	...	0818	...	0854	...	0953	...	1053		...	1653	...	1753	...	1852	...	1952	...	2053
100	**Southampton Central** ..... a.		0724	...	0813	...	0852	...	0919	...	1019	...	1119		...	1728	...	1819	...	1920	...	2018	...	2119

	Ⓐ	Ⓐ	Ⓐ	Ⓐ	Ⓐ	Ⓐ			⑥	⑥	⑥	⑥	⑥	⑥	⑥	⑥	⑥		⑥	⑥	⑥	⑥	⑥	⑥
Brighton .... 102 d.	2003	2030	2103	2133	2203	2233	...	⑥	0527	0601	0633	0703	0733	0803	0833	0903	0933	and at the same minutes past each hour until ★	1903	1929	1956	2030	2103	2133
Hove .... d.	2007	2034	2107	2137	2207	2237	...		0531	0605	0637	0707	0737	0807	0837	0907	0937		1907	1933	2000	2034	2107	2137
Worthing .... d.	2029	2056	2129	2159	2229	2259	...		0553	0623	0655	0725	0755	0826	0855	0925	0955		1929	1955	2022	2056	2129	2159
Barnham .... d.	2051	2118	2151	2221	2251	2332	...		0615	0645	0717	0741	0817	0841	0917	0945	1017		1951	2017	2044	2120	2151	2221
Chichester .... d.	2059	2126	2159	2229	2259	2339	...		0623	0653	0725	0749	0825	0849	0925	0953	1025		1959	2025	2052	2128	2159	2229
Havant .... d.	2110	2137	2210	2243	2311	...	...		0637	0704	0737	0804	0837	0904	0937	1007	1037		2010	2037	2110	2140	2210	2243
Portsmouth & Southsea a.	2122	|	2222	2255	2323	...	...		|	0716	|	0816	|	0916	|	1019	|		2022	|	2122	|	2222	2255
Portsmouth Harbour ..... a.	2126	|	2226	2259	2327	...	...		|	0720	|	0820	|	0920	|	1023	|		2026	|	2126	|	2226	2259
Fareham .... a.	...	2152	...	...	...	...	...		0653	...	0753	...	0853	...	0953	...	1053		...	2053	...	2154	...	...
Southampton Central ...... a.	...	2216	...	...	...	...	...		0718	...	0817	...	0919	...	1017	...	1119		...	2119	...	2220	...	...

	⑥	⑥			⑦	⑦	⑦	⑦	⑦	⑦		⑦	⑦	⑦	⑦	⑦	⑦	⑦		⑦	⑦	⑦	⑦	⑦	⑦
Brighton .... 102 d.	2203	2233	...	⑦	0714	0722	0814	0822	0917	1017	...	1117	1217	1317	1417	1517	1617	1717	...	1817	1917	2017	2117	2146	*2210*
Hove .... d.	2207	2237	...		0718	0726	0818	0826	0926	1026	...	1126	1226	1326	1426	1526	1626	1726	...	1826	1926	2026	2126	2150	2224
Worthing .... d.	2229	2259	...		0730	0747	0830	0847	0948	1048	...	1148	1248	1348	1448	1548	1648	1748	...	1848	1948	2048	2148	2203	2240
Barnham .... d.	2251	2332	...		0747	0820	0847	0920	1012	1112	...	1212	1312	1412	1512	1612	1712	1812	...	1812	2012	2112	2212	2218	2256
Chichester .... d.	2259	2339	...		0755	0828	0855	0928	1020	1120	...	1220	1320	1420	1520	1620	1720	1820	...	1920	2020	2120	2220	2226	2304
Havant .... d.	2310	...	...		0810	0849	0910	0949	1041	1144	...	1244	1344	1444	1544	1644	1744	1844	...	1944	2044	2144	2244	2247	2322
Portsmouth & Southsea a.	2322	...	...		0822	0903	0922	1003	1054	1157	...	1257	1357	1457	1557	1657	1757	1857	...	1957	2057	2157	2257	2300	2334
Portsmouth Harbour ..... a.	2326	...	...		0826	0907	0926	1007	1058	1201	...	1301	1401	1501	1601	1701	1801	1901	...	2001	2101	2201	2301	2304	2338
Fareham .... a.	...	...	...		...	...	...	...	...	...	...	...	...	...	...	...	...	...	...	...	...	...	...	...	...
Southampton Central ...... a.	...	...	...		...	...	...	...	...	...	...	...	...	...	...	...	...	...	...	...	...	...	...	...	...

		Ⓐ	Ⓐ	Ⓐ	Ⓐ	Ⓐ	Ⓐ	Ⓐ	Ⓐ		Ⓐ	Ⓐ	Ⓐ	Ⓐ	Ⓐ	Ⓐ	Ⓐ	Ⓐ	Ⓐ	Ⓐ	Ⓐ	Ⓐ	Ⓐ	Ⓐ
Southampton Central ...... d.	Ⓐ	...	...	0610	...	0733	...	0833	...	and at the same minutes past each hour until ★	1427	...	1533	...	1633	...	1733	...	1833	...	1933	...	2033	...
Fareham .... d.		...	...	0634	...	0758	...	0857	...		1500	...	1557	...	1657	...	1756	...	1856	...	1957	...	2057	...
Portsmouth Harbour ..... d.		0533	0604	|	0701	|	0829	|	0929		|	1529	|	1629	|	1729	|	1828	|	1932	|	...	|	...
Portsmouth & Southsea d.		0537	0608	|	0705	|	0833	|	0933		|	1533	|	1633	|	1733	|	1832	|	1936	|	2032	|	2115
Havant .... d.		0553	0620	0653	0720	0813	0846	0912	0946		1515	1546	1612	1646	1712	1746	1811	1844	1911	1944	2012	2044	2112	2131
Chichester .... d.		0614	0635	0708	0732	0828	0900	0925	1000		1529	1600	1625	1700	1725	1800	1825	1859	1922	1959	2025	2059	2125	2152
Barnham .... d.		0622	0643	0716	0740	0836	0908	0933	1008		1537	1608	1633	1708	1733	1808	1833	1907	1930	2007	2033	2107	2133	2200
Worthing .... d.		0644	0708	0738	0800	0856	0926	0956	1026		1559	1626	1656	1726	1756	1825	1852	1924	1952	2023	2052	2123	2155	2223
Hove .... d.		0705	0726	0756	0814	0914	0944	1014	1044		1617	1644	1714	1744	1814	1847	1914	1945	2014	2045	2114	2145	2216	2244
Brighton .... 102 a.		0709	0730	0800	0820	0918	0948	1018	1048		1621	1648	1718	1748	1818	1852	1918	1949	2018	2049	2118	2149	2221	2248

	Ⓐ	Ⓐ	Ⓐ	Ⓐ			⑥	⑥	⑥	⑥	⑥	⑥	⑥		⑥	⑥	⑥	⑥	⑥	⑥	⑥	⑥	⑥	⑥
Southampton Central ...... d.	2113	...	2213	...	...	⑥	...	0633	...	0733	...	0833	...	and at the same minutes past each hour until ★	1427	...	1533	...	1633	...	1733	...	1833	...
Fareham .... d.	2140	...	2237	...	...		...	0656	...	0756	...	0856	...		1500	...	1556	...	1656	...	1756	...	1856	...
Portsmouth Harbour ..... d.	|	2215	|	2244	...		0629	|	0729	|	0829	|	0929		|	1529	|	1629	|	1729	|	1829	|	1929
Portsmouth & Southsea d.	|	2219	|	2248	...		0633	|	0733	|	0833	|	0933		|	1533	|	1633	|	1733	|	1833	|	1933
Havant .... d.	2156	2235	2257	2305	...		0646	0711	0746	0811	0846	0911	0946		1514	1546	1611	1646	1711	1746	1811	1846	1911	1946
Chichester .... d.	2207	2252	2311	2317	...		0700	0725	0800	0825	0900	0925	1000		1525	1600	1625	1700	1725	1800	1825	1900	1925	1959
Barnham .... d.	2215	2300	2319	2325	...		0708	0733	0808	0833	0908	0933	1008		1533	1608	1633	1708	1733	1808	1833	1908	1933	2007
Worthing .... d.	2252	2322	...	2359	...		0726	0756	0826	0856	0926	0956	1026		1556	1626	1656	1726	1756	1826	1856	1926	1953	2023
Hove .... d.	2314	2344	...	0020	...		0744	0814	0844	0914	0944	1014	1044		1614	1644	1714	1744	1814	1844	1914	1944	2015	2045
Brighton .... 102 a.	2318	2348	...	0025	...		0748	0818	0848	0918	0948	1018	1048		1618	1648	1718	1748	1881	1848	1918	1948	2019	2049

	⑥	⑥	⑥	⑥	⑥	⑥	⑥	⑥		⑦	⑦		⑦	⑦		⑦	⑦	⑦	⑦	⑦		⑦	⑦
Southampton Central ...... d.	1933	...	2033	...	2113	...	2213	...	⑦	...	...	...	...	...	and at the same minutes past each hour until	...	...	...	...	...	...	...	...
Fareham .... d.	1956	...	2056	...	2140	...	2239	...		...	...	...	...	...		...	...	...	...	...	...	...	...
Portsmouth Harbour ..... d.	|	2028	|	2111	|	2215	|	2244		0714	0814	...	0914	1014		1714	1814	1914	2014	2043	...	2114	2143
Portsmouth & Southsea d.	|	2032	|	2115	|	2219	|	2248		0718	0818	...	0918	1018		1718	1818	1918	2018	2047	...	2118	2147
Havant .... d.	2011	2044	2111	2131	2156	2235	2255	2305		0733	0833	...	0933	1033		1733	1833	1933	2033	2100	...	2133	2200
Chichester .... d.	2025	2059	2125	2152	2207	2252	2309	2318		0753	0853	...	0953	1053		1753	1853	1953	2053	2114	...	2153	2214
Barnham .... d.	2033	2107	2133	2200	2215	2300	2317	2326		0808	0908	...	1008	1108		1808	1908	2008	2108	2122	...	2208	2222
Worthing .... d.	2052	2123	2155	2223	2252	2322	...	2359		0830	0930	...	1030	1130		1830	1930	2030	2130	2200	...	2230	2300
Hove .... d.	2114	2145	2216	2244	2314	2344	...	0021		0856	0956	...	1056	1156		1856	1956	2056	2151	2221	...	2251	2321
Brighton .... 102 a.	2118	2149	2221	2248	2318	2348	...	0025		0900	1000	...	1100	1200		1900	2000	2100	2155	2226	...	2256	2325

★ – Timings may vary by up to 5 minutes.

111 PORTSMOUTH - RYDE - SHANKLIN 2nd class IL

PORTSMOUTH Harbour – **RYDE** Pierhead *Valid until December 20.* ⛴ (*Wightlink*)

0015, 0140⑥, 0415⚒, 0515⚒, 0540Ⓐ, 0615, 0640Ⓐ, 0715, 0740Ⓐ, 0815, 0840⚒, 0915⑥⑦, 0940⚒, 1015, 1040⑥, 1115, 1140⑥, 1215⑧, 1240⑥⑦, 1315⚒, 1340⑦, 1415⚒, 1440, 1515⑥⑦, 1540, 1615, 1640, 1715, 1740⚒, 1815, 1845Ⓐ, 1915, 2015, 2115, 2215, 2315.

RYDE Pierhead – **PORTSMOUTH** Harbour Journey time: ± 18 minutes

0045, 0210⑥, 0445⚒, 0545⚒, 0610Ⓐ, 0645, 0710Ⓐ, 0745, 0810Ⓐ, 0845, 0910⚒, 0945⑥⑦, 1010⚒, 1045, 1110⑥, 1145, 1210⑥, 1245⑧, 1310⑥⑦, 1345⚒, 1410⑦, 1445⚒, 1510, 1545⑥⑦, 1610, 1645, 1710, 1745, 1810, 1845, 1915Ⓐ, 1945, 2045, 2145, 2245, 2345.

RYDE Pierhead – **SHANKLIN** *14 km*

0549⚒, 0608⚒, 0649, 0708⚒ and then at 49 and 08⚒ minutes past each hour until 1849, 1908, 1949, 2008⚒, 2049⑦, 2108⚒, 2149⑦, 2208⚒.

SHANKLIN – **RYDE** Pierhead Journey time: ± 24 minutes

0617⚒, 0636⚒, 0717, 0736 then at 17 and 36⚒ minutes past each hour until 2928, 1836, 1917, 1936, 2017⑥, 2036⚒, 2117⑦, 2136⚒, 2217⑦, 2236⚒.

☛ Through fares including ferry travel are available. Allow at least 10 minutes for connections between trains and ferries. Ferry operator: Wightlink. ✆ 0871 376 4342. www.wightlink.co.uk

SW Most trains 🍸 LONDON - SALISBURY - EXETER 113

For *First Great Western* services London Paddington - Exeter and v.v., see Table **120**.

km			Ⓐ	⑥	Ⓐ	⑥	⚒	⚒	⚒ B	⚒	⚒	⚒ B	⚒	Ⓐ	⚒	⚒	Ⓐ	⑥	Ⓐ	Ⓐ	⑥	Ⓐ	Ⓐ	⑥	Ⓐ
0	**London** Waterloo .... **108** d.	⚒	...	...	...	...	0710	0820	0920	1020	1120	1220	1320	1350	1420	1520	1550	1620	1620	1650	1720	1720	1750	1820	1820
39	Woking .... **108** d.		...	...	...	...	0736	0846	0946	1046	1146	1246	1346	1416	1446	1546	1616	1646	1646	1716**u**	1746	1746**u**	|	1846	1846
77	Basingstoke .... **108** d.		...	...	...	...	0757	0907	1007	1107	1207	1307	1407	1437	1507	1607	1637	1707	1707	1737	1807	1815	1838	1907	1907
107	Andover .... d.		...	...	...	...	0819	0924	1024	1124	1224	1324	1424	1459	1524	1624	1659	1724	1729	1759	1824	1829	1900	1924	1929
134	**Salisbury** .... **139** a.		...	...	...	...	0842	0943	1042	1142	1242	1343	1442	1520	1542	1642	1718	1742	1748	1818	1843	1848	1920	1943	1948
134	**Salisbury** .... d.		0608	0615	0740	0745	0847	0947	1047	1147	1247	1347	1447	1523	1547	1647	1723	1747	1753	1823	1847	1853	1923	1947	1953
169	Gillingham .... d.		0642	0642	0811	0811	0918	1018	1118	1218	1318	1418	1518	1547	1618	1718	1747	1818	1819	1851	1918	1919	1951	2018	2019
190	Sherborne .... d.		0657	0657	0826	0826	0933	1033	1133	1233	1333	1433	1533	...	1633	1733	...	1833	1834	1906	1933	1934	2006	2033	2034
197	**Yeovil** Junction .... a.		0703	0703	0832	0832	0938	1038	1138	1238	1338	1438	1538	...	1638	1738	...	1838	1840	1914	1938	1940	2014	2038	2040
197	**Yeovil** Junction .... d.		0707	0707	0840	0840	0940	1040	1140	1240	1340	1440	1540	...	1640	1740	...	1840	1841	...	1940	1941	...	2040	2041
211	Crewkerne .... d.		0716	0716	0849	0849	0949	1049	1149	1249	1349	1449	1549	...	1649	1749	...	1849	1851	...	1949	1951	...	2049	2051
233	Axminster .... d.		0736	0738	0904	0904	1004	1104	1204	1304	1404	1504	1604	...	1704	1804	...	1904	1905	...	2004	2005	...	2104	2105
249	Honiton .... d.		0749	0752	0916	0916	1016	1116	1216	1316	1416	1516	1616	...	1716	1816	...	1916	1917	...	2016	2017	...	2116	2117
276	**Exeter** Central .... a.		0811	0813	0937	0937	1037	1137	1237	1337	1437	1537	1635	...	1737	1838	...	1937	1938	...	2039	2038	...	2137	2137
277	**Exeter** St Davids ... **115 116** a.		0816	0818	0942	0912	1042	1142	1242	1342	1442	1542	1642	...	1742	1842	...	1942	1945	...	2043	2044	...	2142	2144

	⑥ B	Ⓐ B	⑥	Ⓐ	⚒	⚒			⑦	⑦	⑦	⑦	⑦	⑦	⑦ B	⑦	⑦	⑦	⑦	⑦	⑦ B	⑦	⑦	⑦	⑦
London Waterloo .... **108** d.	1920	1920	2020	2020	2120	2220	...	⑦	...	...	0815	0915	1015	1115	1215	1315	1415	1515	1615	1715	1815	1915	2015	2115	2215
Woking .... **108** d.	1946	1946	2046	2046	2149	2249	...		...	...	0847	0947	1046	1146	1246	1346	1446	1546	1646	1746	1846	1946	2046	2146	2246
Basingstoke .... **108** d.	2007	2007	2107	2107	2210	2310	...		...	0805	0908	1008	1107	1207	1307	1407	1507	1607	1707	1807	1907	2007	2107	2207	2307
Andover .... d.	2024	2029	2129	2129	2232	2332	...		...	0827	0930	1025	1129	1224	1329	1424	1520	1624	1729	1824	1929	2024	2129	2226	2329
Salisbury .... **139** a.	2042	2049	2148	2148	2255	2353	...		...	0846	0946	1045	1145	1245	1345	1445	1545	1645	1745	1845	1945	2045	2145	2245	2348
Salisbury .... d.	2047	2053	2153	2206	2310	...	...		0710	0851	0951	1051	1151	1251	1351	1451	1551	1551	1751	1851	1951	2051	2151	2251	...
Gillingham .... d.	2118	2119	2218	2235	2337**s**	...	...		0735	0921	1021	1121	1221	1321	1421	1521	1621	1721	1821	1921	2021	2121	2221	2321	...
Sherborne .... d.	2133	2134	2233	2250	2352**s**	...	...		0750	0936	1036	1136	1236	1336	1436	1536	1636	1736	1836	1936	2036	2136	2236	2336	...
Yeovil Junction .... a.	2138	2140	2240	2255	2359	...	...		0755	0941	1041	1141	1241	1341	1441	1541	1641	1741	1841	1941	2041	2141	2242	2341	...
Yeovil Junction .... d.	2140	2141	...	2257	...	...	...		0757	0943	1043	1143	1243	1343	1443	1543	1643	1743	1843	1943	2043	2143	...	2343	...
Crewkerne .... d.	2149	2151	...	2306	...	...	...		0806	0952	1052	1152	1252	1352	1452	1552	1652	1752	1852	1952	2052	2152	...	2352	...
Axminster .... d.	2204	2205	...	2320	...	...	...		0820	1006	1106	1206	1306	1406	1506	1606	1706	1806	1906	2006	2106	2206	...	0006	...
Honiton .... d.	2216	2217	...	2332	...	...	...		0835	1019	1119	1219	1319	1419	1519	1619	1719	1819	1919	2019	2119	2219	...	0019	...
Exeter Central .... a.	2237	2240	...	2356	...	...	...		0856	1040	1140	1240	1340	1440	1540	1640	1740	1840	1940	2040	2140	2241	...	|	...
Exeter St Davids .... **115 116** a.	2242	2245	...	0001	...	...	...		0901	1045	1145	1245	1345	1445	1545	1645	1745	1845	1945	2045	2145	2245	...	0040	...

		Ⓐ	Ⓐ	Ⓐ	⑥	⚒	Ⓐ	⚒	Ⓐ	⑥	Ⓐ	⚒ B	⚒	⚒	⚒	⚒	⚒ B	⚒	Ⓐ	⚒ B	⑥	Ⓐ	⑥	Ⓐ	⚒
Exeter St Davids .... **115 116** d.	⚒	...	...	0510	0510	...	...	0640	0724	0726	...	0826	0926	1026	1126	1226	1326	1426	...	1526	1626	1626	1726	1726	1826
Exeter Central .... d.		...	...	0514	0514	...	...	0644	0728	0730	...	0830	0930	1030	1130	1230	1330	1430	...	1530	1630	1630	1730	1730	1830
Honiton .... d.		...	...	0539	0539	0619	...	0711	0748	0753	...	0855	0953	1053	1153	1253	1353	1453	...	1553	1653	1653	1753	1753	1853
Axminster .... d.		...	...	0552	0552	0630	...	0722	0759	0806	...	0906	1006	1106	1206	1306	1406	1506	...	1606	1706	1706	1806	1806	1906
Crewkerne .... d.		...	...	0605	0605	0643	...	0735	0812	0819	...	0919	1019	1119	1219	1319	1419	1519	...	1619	1719	1719	1819	1819	1919
Yeovil Junction .... a.		...	...	0614	0614	0652	...	0745	0821	0827	...	0927	1027	1127	1227	1327	1427	1527	...	1627	1727	1727	1827	1827	1927
Yeovil Junction .... d.		0515	0550	0620	0620	0653	0722	0750	0829	0829	...	0929	1029	1129	1229	1329	1429	1529	...	1629	1729	1729	1829	1829	1929
Sherborne .... d.		0521	0556	0626	0626	0700	0728	0756	0836	0836	...	0936	1036	1136	1236	1336	1436	1536	...	1636	1736	1736	1836	1836	1936
Gillingham .... d.		0537	0612	0642	0642	0715	0744	0812	0851	0851	0918	0951	1051	1151	1251	1351	1451	1551	1618	1651	1751	1751	1851	1851	1951
Salisbury .... a.		0602	0639	0707	0707	0740	0809	0837	0916	0916	0942	1016	1116	1216	1316	1416	1516	1616	1643	1716	1816	1821	1916	1923	2021
Salisbury .... **139** d.		0606	0645	0715	0721	0745	0815	0845	0921	0921	0945	1021	1121	1221	1321	1421	1521	1621	1648	1721	1821	1826	1926	1926	2026
Andover .... d.		0626	0705	0735	0738	0804	0835	0904	0938	0938	1004	1038	1138	1238	1338	1438	1538	1638	1707	1738	1838	1843	1945	1945	2045
Basingstoke .... **108** a.		0649	0728	0758	0755	0828	0858	0927	0955	0955	1027	1055	1155	1255	1355	1455	1555	1655	1729	1755	1855	1900	2008	2008	2108
Woking .... **108** a.		|	|	0818	0817	0849	0918	0949	1015	1015	1049	1115	1215	1315	1415	1515	1615	1715	1749	1815	1915	1920	2029	2029	2129
London Waterloo .... **108** a.		0739	0814	0846	0849	0919	0951	1019	1049	1049	1119	1149	1249	1349	1449	1549	1649	1749	1821	1849	1949	1950	2104	2100	2204

	⚒	⚒	⚒	⚒			⑦	⑦	⑦	⑦	⑦	⑦	⑦	⑦	⑦	⑦ B	⑦	⑦	⑦	⑦	⑦	⑦	⑦	⑦	⑦
Exeter St Davids .... **115 116** d.	1926	2026	2123	2257	...	⑦	...	...	...	0926	1026	1126	1226	1326	1426	1526	1626	1726	1826	1926	2026	2126	2315	...	...
Exeter Central .... d.	1930	2030	2129	2301	...		...	...	...	0930	1030	1130	1230	1330	1430	1530	1630	1730	1830	1930	2030	2130	2319	...	...
Honiton .... d.	1953	2053	2153	2332	...		...	...	0858	0955	1053	1153	1253	1353	1453	1553	1653	1753	1853	1953	2053	2155	2334**s**	...	...
Axminster .... d.	2006	2106	2206	2343	...		...	...	0909	1009	1109	1209	1309	1409	1509	1609	1709	1809	1909	2009	2109	2209	2345**s**	...	...
Crewkerne .... d.	2019	2119	2219	2356	...		...	...	0922	1022	1122	1222	1322	1422	1522	1622	1722	1822	1922	2022	2122	2222	0011**s**	...	...
Yeovil Junction .... a.	2027	2127	2227	0004	...		...	...	0930	1030	1130	1230	1330	1430	1530	1630	1730	1830	1930	2030	2130	2230	0020**s**	...	...
Yeovil Junction .... d.	2029	2129	2229	0006	...		0732	...	0932	1032	1132	1232	1332	1432	1532	1632	1732	1832	1932	2032	2132	2232	|	...	...
Sherborne .... d.	2036	2136	2236	|	...		0739	...	0939	1039	1139	1239	1339	1439	1539	1639	1739	1839	1939	2039	2139	2238	|	...	...
Gillingham .... d.	2051	2151	2251	|	...		0754	0854	0954	1054	1154	1254	1354	1454	1554	1654	1754	1854	1954	2054	2154	2254	|	...	...
Salisbury .... a.	2121	2221	2319	0041	...		0820	0920	1020	1120	1220	1320	1420	1520	1620	1720	1820	1920	2020	2120	2220	2318	0056	...	...
Salisbury .... **139** d.	2126	2226	...	...	...		0827	0927	1027	1127	1227	1327	1427	1527	1627	1727	1827	1927	2027	2127	2227	...	...	...	...
Andover .... d.	2145	2245	...	...	...		0846	0946	1044	1146	1244	1346	1744	1546	1644	1746	1844	1946	2044	2146	2246	...	...	...	...
Basingstoke .... **108** a.	2207	2307	...	...	...		0908	1002	1106	1202	1306	1402	1506	1602	1706	1802	1906	2002	2106	2202	2308	...	...	...	...
Woking .... **108** a.	2228	*2333*	...	...	...		0928	1028	1128	1228	1328	1428	1528	1628	1728	1828	1928	2028	2128	2228	*2350*	...	...	...	...
London Waterloo .... **108** a.	2258	*0010*	...	...	...		1008	1109	1203	1303	1359	1459	1559	1659	1759	1859	1959	2059	2159	2259	*0033*	...	...	...	...

☛ **Full service London Waterloo – Salisbury and v.v.**

From London Waterloo:

⚒: 0710, 0750, 0820, 0850 and every 30 minutes until 2020; then 2120, 2220, 2335.

⑦: 0815 and hourly until 2215; then 2335.

From Salisbury:

⚒: 0606Ⓐ, 0621⑥, 0645, 0715Ⓐ, 0721⑥, 0745, 0815Ⓐ, 0821⑥, 0845, 0921, 0945 and then at 21 and 45 minutes past each hour until 1745; then 1821⑥, 1826Ⓐ, 1845, 1926, 2026, 2126, 2226.

⑦: 0645, 0727 and hourly until 2227.

B – Conveys 🍴12 London - Salisbury - Bristol and v.v.
s – Stops to set down only.
u – Stops to pick up only.

GW 2nd class BARNSTAPLE - EXETER - EXMOUTH 114

BARNSTAPLE – EXETER ST DAVIDS

km			⚒	⚒	⚒	⚒	⚒	⚒	⚒	⚒	⚒	⚒	⚒	⑥	⚒	Ⓐ	⑥			⑦	⑦	⑦	⑦	⑦	⑦
0	**Barnstaple** .... d.	⚒	0708	0843	0943	1043	1143	1243	1343	1443	1543	1710	1813	1916	2023	2218	2218	...	⑦	1110	1317	1514	1720	1917	2130
28	Eggesford .... d.		0738	0907	1007	1107	1207	1307	1407	1507	1607	1737	1840	1940	2048	2247	2247	...		1141	1342	1544	1750	1948	2155
51	Crediton .... d.		0804	0937	1037	1137	1237	1337	1437	1537	1637	1813	1911	2006	2116	2313	2313	...		1208	1409	1614	1818	2014	2218
63	**Exeter** St Davids ... **115 116** a.		0816	0948	1048	1148	1248	1348	1448	1548	1648	1830	1925	2019	2134	2326	2326	...		1222	1426	1627	1833	2030	2229

		⚒	⚒	⚒	⚒	⚒	⚒		⚒	⚒	⚒	⚒	⚒	⚒	⚒		⚒			⑦	⑦	⑦	⑦	⑦	⑦
Exeter St Davids .... **115 116** d.	⚒	0556	0650	0831	0927	1027	1127	...	1227	1327	1427	1527	1657	1757	1857	...	2100	...	⑦	0940	1158	1355	1601	1800	1959
Crediton .... d.		0607	0701	0842	0938	1038	1138	...	1238	1338	1438	1538	1708	1811	1911	...	2114	...		1000	1210	1411	1616	1816	2016
Eggesford .... d.		0632	0739	0911	1008	1108	1208	...	1308	1408	1508	1608	1738	1841	1942	...	2143	...		1028	1237	1439	1642	1845	2044
Barnstaple .... a.		0659	0808	0939	1035	1135	1235	...	1337	1437	1535	1635	1807	1913	2008	...	2213	...		1058	1303	1509	1714	1912	2115

EXETER ST DAVIDS – EXMOUTH

Journey time ± 37–40 minutes *18 km*

From Exeter St Davids:

Ⓐ: 0606, 0629, 0711, 0736, 0816, 0848, 0918, 0948 and then at 18 and 48 minutes past the hour until 1618; then 1650, 1718, 1752, 1820, 1850, 1932, 2030, 2130, 2236, 2327.

⑥: 0629, 0711, 0736, 0816, 0848, 0918, 0948 and then at 18 and 48 minutes past the hour until 1650; then 1718, 1750, 1820, 1850, 1932, 2030, 2130, 2236, 2306.

⑦: 0930, 1036, 1135, 1233, 1333, 1433, 1532, 1633, 1733, 1833, 1933, 2039, 2133, 2233, 2326

From Exmouth:

Ⓐ: 0612, 0646, 0715, 0753, 0823, 0853 and then at 23 and 53 minutes past the hour until 1553; then 1625, 1655, 1725, 1755, 1828, 1855, 1935, 2008, 2104, 2204, 2310.

⑥: 0612, 0715, 0753, 0823, 0853 and then at 23 and 53 minutes past the hour until 1553; then 1625, 1655, 1725, 1755, 1827, 1855, 1938, 2008, 2104, 2204, 2310.

⑦: 1003, 1110, 1210, 1310, 1410, 1510, 1610, 1710, 1810, 1910, 2010, 2120, 2210, 2308.

115 LONDON and BRISTOL - EXETER - PLYMOUTH - PENZANCE GW, XC

Services on ⑦ valid until March 28.

km	Operator		XC ①	GW ②–⑤ 🍷 Z	XC ②–⑤	GW ① 🍷 Z	GW Ⓐ 🍷	GW Ⓐ 2	XC Ⓐ 🍷	GW Ⓐ 2	XC Ⓐ 🍷	GW Ⓐ 2	XC Ⓐ 🍷	GW Ⓐ 🍷	GW Ⓐ 2C	XC Ⓐ 🍷	GW Ⓐ 🍷	GW Ⓐ 🍷	GW Ⓐ 2C	XC Ⓐ 🍷	GW Ⓐ 🍷	XC Ⓐ 🍷	XC Ⓐ 🍷	GW Ⓐ 🍷	GW Ⓐ 2
0	**London** Paddington 133 d.	Ⓐ	...	2345b	...	2350d	...	...	...	...	...	...	...	0730	...	...	0818	0906	...	...	1006	...	...	1000	...
58	Reading 133 d.		...	0037u	...	0037u	...	...	...	...	...	...	...	0757	...	...	0848	0932	...	...	1032	...	...	1027	...
85	Newbury d.		...	│	...	│	...	...	...	...	...	...	...	│	...	...	0912	│	...	...	│	...	...	│	...
154	Westbury 138 d.		...	│	...	│	...	...	...	...	...	...	...	Y	...	...	1000	│	...	...	│	...	...	Y	...
186	Castle Cary 138 d.		...	│	...	│	...	...	...	...	...	...	...	│	...	...	1017	│	...	...	│	...	...	│	...
	Birmingham New St 127 d.		...	│	...	│	...	...	...	...	0642	...	0712	│	...	0812	│	│	...	0912	│	0942	1012	│	...
	Bristol Temple Meads 133 d.		...	│	...	│	...	0524e	0634	0626	0811	...	0844	0913	0855	0944	│	│	0955	1044	│	1115	1144	1147	...
230	Taunton 137 d.		...	0235	...	│	...	0622	0708	0729	0843	...	0917	0946	1002	1018	1040	1048	1058	1118	│	1202	1217	1229	...
253	Tiverton Parkway d.		...	│	...	│	...	0638	0720	0744	0855	...	0929	│	│	1030	1053	1101	1113	1130	│	1214	1229	│	...
279	**Exeter** St Davids 116 a.		...	0305	...	0405	...	0657	0734	0803	0910	...	0943	1012	1033	1046	1110	1118	1133	1146	1209	1230	1243	1255	...
279	**Exeter** St Davids 116 d.		...	0412	...	0435	...	0659	0736	0804	0911	0934	0945	1014	1035	1048	—	1119	1134	1148	1209	1232	1245	1256	...
299	Dawlish 116 d.		...	│	...	│	...	0720	│	0820	│	│	│	│	1051	│	...	│	│	│	│	1244	│	1309	...
303	Teignmouth 116 d.		...	│	...	│	...	0725	│	0825	│	│	│	│	1057	│	...	│	│	│	│	1249	│	1315	...
311	**Newton Abbot** 116 d.		...	0434	...	0456	...	0732	0757	0832	│	0955	1004	1035	1105	1109	...	1139	1155	1208	1230	1256	1304	1323	...
321	Torquay 116 d.		...	│	...	│	...	│	│	│	0941	│	│	│	1118	│	GW	│	│	│	│	1308	│	1335	...
324	**Paignton** 116 a.		...	│	...	│	...	│	│	│	0946	│	│	│	1127	│	Ⓐ	│	│	│	│	1314	│	1343	...
325	Totnes d.		...	│	...	│	...	0746	0809	0846	...	1008	1017	1049	...	1123	2	1153	1209	1222	│	...	1317	...	...
363	**Plymouth** 118 a.		...	0513	...	0535	...	0818	0837	0916	...	1039	1046	1117	...	1151		1222	1242	1251	1306	...	1343	...	...
363	**Plymouth** d.		0550	0550	0628	0640	0702	0819	...	0920	...	1042	...	1120	...	...	1239	...	...	...	1312	...	...	...	1354
370	Saltash d.		│	│	│	│	0715	0830	...	0931	...	1053	...	│	...	...	1248	...	...	...	│	...	...	...	1403
392	Liskeard 118 d.		0615	0615	0651	0709	0734	0851	...	0950	...	1112	...	1143	...	...	1307	...	...	...	1335	...	...	...	1422
406	Bodmin Parkway d.		0629	0629	0703	0723	0746	0903	...	1002	...	1124	...	1156	...	...	1319	...	...	...	1348	...	...	...	1434
419	Par 118 d.		0642	0642	0715	0737	0759	0915	...	1014	...	1136	...	1207	...	...	1331	...	...	...	1359	...	...	...	1446
452	**Newquay** 118 a.		│	│	│	│	│	│	...	│	...	│	...	│	...	...	│	...	...	...	│	...	...	...	│
426	St Austell d.		0650	0650	0722	0745	0807	0922	...	1022	...	1143	...	1215	...	...	1338	...	...	...	1407	...	...	...	1453
449	**Truro** 118 d.		0709	0709	0739	0805	0826	0940	...	1040	...	1201	...	1232	...	...	1356	...	...	...	1424	...	...	...	1511
464	Redruth d.		0723	0723	0750	0819	0838	0954	...	1053	...	1214	...	1245	...	...	1409	...	...	...	1437	...	...	...	1524
470	Camborne d.		0730	0730	0757	0826	0845	1000	...	1059	...	1220	...	1252	...	...	1415	...	...	...	1445	...	...	...	1530
482	St Erth 118 d.		0744	0744	0812	0843	0858	1011	...	1112	...	1230	...	1303	...	...	1426	...	...	...	1459	...	...	...	1542
491	**Penzance** a.		0757	0800	0819	0859	0911	1025	...	1125	...	1242	...	1316	...	...	1439	...	...	...	1512	...	...	...	1554

Operator	GW Ⓐ 🍷	XC Ⓐ 🍷	GW Ⓐ 🍷	XC Ⓐ 🍷	GW Ⓐ 🍷	GW Ⓐ 🍷	XC Ⓐ 🍷	XC Ⓐ 🍷	GW Ⓐ 🍷	XC Ⓐ 🍷	GW Ⓐ 2	GW Ⓐ 🍷	XC Ⓐ 🍷	XC Ⓐ 🍷	GW Ⓐ 🍷	XC Ⓐ 🍷	GW ①–④ 🍷	GW ⑤ 🍷	GW Ⓐ 🍷	XC Ⓐ 🍷	GW Ⓐ 🍷	GW Ⓐ 🍷	XC Ⓐ 🍷	GW ①–④ 🍷	GW ⑤ 🍷
London Paddington 133 d.	1106	...	1206	...	1218	1306	...	...	1406	...	...	1506	...	...	1606	...	1636	1636	1703	...	1733	1803	...	1836	1836
Reading 133 d.	1132	...	1232	...	1248	1332	...	...	1432	...	...	1532	...	...	1632	...	1703	1703	1731	...	1801	1832	...	1903	1903
Newbury d.	│	...	│	...	1312	│	...	...	│	...	...	│	...	...	│	...	1719	1719	1748	...	1817	│	...	1919	1919
Westbury 138 d.	1222	...	│	...	1359	│	...	...	│	...	...	1623	...	...	│	...	1803	1803	│	...	1901	│	...	2005	2005
Castle Cary 138 d.	1239	...	│	...	1435	│	...	...	│	...	...	1641	...	...	│	...	1821	1821	│	...	1919	│	...	2022	2022
Birmingham New St 127 d.	│	1112	│	1212	│	│	1312	1342	│	1412	...	│	1512	1542	│	1612	│	│	│	1712	│	│	1812	│	│
Bristol Temple Meads 133 d.	│	1244	│	1344	│	│	1444	1513	│	1544	...	│	1644	1714	│	1744	│	│	│	1844	│	│	1944	│	│
Taunton 137 d.	1302	1318	│	1417	1459	1448	1518	1546	1550	1617	...	1705	1717	1746	1750	1818	1843	1843	1852	1917	1941	1948	2017	2045	2045
Tiverton Parkway d.	1315	1330	│	1429	—	1501	1530	1558	1603	1629	...	1718	1729	1758	1803	1830	1856	1856	1905	1929	1954	│	2030	2058	2058
Exeter St Davids 116 a.	1332	1346	1409	1443	...	1517	1546	1613	1619	1643	...	1734	1743	1813	1820	1844	1914	1913	1921	1943	2010	2013	2044	2115	2115
Exeter St Davids 116 d.	1333	1348	1409	1445	...	1519	1548	—	1621	1645	...	1736	1745	1815	1821	1847	...	1914	1922	1945	2019	2016	2045	...	2116
Dawlish 116 d.	│	│	│	│	...	│	│	...	│	│	...	│	│	1827	│	│	...	│	│	│	2041	│	│	...	│
Teignmouth 116 d.	│	│	│	│	...	│	│	...	│	│	...	│	│	1832	│	│	...	│	│	│	2047	│	│	...	│
Newton Abbot 116 d.	1354	1408	1430	1504	...	1540	1608	...	1642	1704	...	1757	1812	1839	1844	1907	...	1935	1943	2006	2055	2036	2104	...	2137
Torquay 116 d.	│	│	│	│	GW	│	│	GW	│	│	...	│	│	1851	│	│	...	│	│	│	2109	│	│	...	│
Paignton 116 a.	│	│	│	│	Ⓐ	│	│	Ⓐ	│	│	...	│	│	1857	│	│	...	│	│	│	2117	│	│	...	│
Totnes d.	1407	1422	│	1517	2	1553	1622	2	1655	1717	...	1810	1824	...	1857	1920	...	│	1957	2018	...	2049	2117	...	2215
Plymouth 118 a.	1436	1450	1506	1543		1622	1650		1723	1743	...	1838	1851	...	1927	1945	...	2013	2025	2045	...	2117	2150	...	...
Plymouth d.	...	...	1512	...	1557	...	...	1706	1726	...	1755	1843	1900	...	1931	1950	...	...	2029	2050	...	2120	...	...	...
Saltash d.	...	...	│	...	1611	...	...	1720	1736	...	1803	│	│	...	1941	│	...	...	2039	│	...	│	...	...	...
Liskeard 118 d.	...	...	1535	...	1632	...	...	1742	1755	...	1820	1907	1923	...	1957	2013	...	...	2057	2113	...	2144	...	...	...
Bodmin Parkway d.	...	...	1548	...	1644	...	...	...	1807	...	1832	1919	1935	...	2009	2026	...	...	2109	2126	...	2158	...	...	...
Par 118 d.	...	...	1559	...	1656	...	...	...	1820	...	1844	1930	1945	...	2020	2036	...	...	2120	2138	...	2209	...	...	...
Newquay 118 a.	...	...	│	...	│	...	...	...	│	...	│	│	│	...	│	│	...	...	│	│	...	│	...	...	...
St Austell d.	...	...	1607	...	1705	...	...	...	1828	...	1851	1938	1952	...	2028	2043	...	...	2128	2145	...	2217	...	...	...
Truro 118 d.	...	...	1624	...	1724	...	...	...	1846	...	1909	1956	2010	...	2046	2100	...	...	2145	2203	...	2235	...	...	...
Redruth d.	...	...	1637	...	1737	...	...	...	1858	...	1922	2008	2025	...	2058	2115	...	...	2158	2214	...	2247	...	...	...
Camborne d.	...	...	1645	...	1743	...	...	...	1907	...	1928	2017	2033	...	2107	2122	...	...	2210	2223	...	│	...	...	...
St Erth 118 d.	...	...	1656	...	1754	...	...	...	1920	...	1940	2027	2044	...	2117	2133	...	...	2217	2235	...	│	...	...	...
Penzance a.	...	...	1709	...	1807	...	...	...	1934	...	1953	2041	2054	...	2131	2142	...	...	2230	2245	...	2312	...	...	...

Operator	GW ①–④ 🍷	GW ⑤ 🍷	GW ①–④	XC Ⓐ	XC Ⓐ	GW Ⓐ 🍷	XC Ⓐ	GW Ⓐ 🍷	GW Ⓐ 🍷 B	GW Ⓐ 🍷 D			GW ⑥	GW ⑥ 🍷 Z	XC ⑥ 🍷	GW ⑥ 2	XC ⑥ 🍷	GW ⑥ 2	GW ⑥ 2	XC ⑥ 🍷	GW ⑥ 2	XC ⑥ 🍷	GW ⑥ 🍷	XC ⑥ 🍷	GW ⑥ 🍷
London Paddington 133 d.	1903	1903	...	...	...	1945	...	2035	2145	2145	...	⑥	...	2345c	...	...	...	...	...	...	...	...	0730	...	0818
Reading 133 d.	1932	1932	...	...	...	2011	...	2101	2211	2211	...		...	0037	...	...	...	...	...	...	...	...	0757	...	0849
Newbury d.	1948	1948	...	...	...	2027	...	2118	│	│	...		...	│	...	...	...	...	...	...	...	...	│	...	0914
Westbury 138 d.	│	│	...	...	...	2105	...	2157	Y	Y	...		...	│	...	...	...	...	...	...	...	...	Y	...	1000
Castle Cary 138 d.	│	│	...	...	...	2127	...	2215	│	│	...		...	│	...	...	...	...	...	...	...	...	│	...	1018
Birmingham New St 127 d.	│	│	...	1912	1942	│	2012	│	│	│	...		...	│	...	...	...	...	...	0642	...	0712	│	0812	│
Bristol Temple Meads 133 d.	│	│	...	2047	2113	│	2144	│	2335	2335	...		...	│	...	0528f	0608	0636	...	0811	...	0844	0917	0944	│
Taunton 137 d.	2053	2053	...	2119	2146	2149	2217	2237	0037s	0134	...		...	0225	...	0622	0717	0724	...	0843	...	0917	0951	1017	1040
Tiverton Parkway d.	│	│	...	2132	2158	2202	2229	2250	0050s	0147	...		...	│	...	0638	0729	0741	...	0855	...	0929	│	1029	1053
Exeter St Davids 116 a.	2121	2121	...	2146	2213	2219	2244	2306	0107	0204	...		...	0257	...	0656	0743	0759	...	0910	...	0943	1017	1046	1110
Exeter St Davids 116 d.	2122	2122	...	2148	2215	2220	2245	2308	...	...	...		...	0300	...	0658	0745	0805	...	0911	0928	0945	1018	1048	—
Dawlish 116 d.	│	│	...	│	│	│	│	│	...	...	...		...	│	...	0718	│	0820	...	│	│	│	│	│	...
Teignmouth 116 d.	│	│	...	│	│	│	│	│	...	...	...		...	│	...	0723	│	0825	...	│	│	│	│	│	...
Newton Abbot 116 d.	2143	2143	...	2207	2234	2241	2305	2329	...	...	...		...	0322	...	0731	0804	0833	...	│	0949	1005	1039	1108	...
Torquay 116 d.	│	│	...	│	│	│	│	│	...	...	...		...	│	...	│	│	│	...	0939	│	│	│	│	GW
Paignton 116 a.	│	│	...	│	│	│	│	│	...	...	...		...	│	...	│	│	│	...	0946	│	│	│	│	⑥
Totnes d.	2157	2157	...	2220	2247	2255	2318	2343	...	...	...		...	│	...	0744	0817	0846	...	...	1002	1017	1052	1122	2
Plymouth 118 a.	2225	2225	...	2246	2312	2327	2344	0012	...	...	...		...	0401	...	0815	0843	0917	...	...	1032	1044	1120	1151	
Plymouth d.	...	2228	2230	...	...	...	...	...	...	...	...		...	0550	0628	0816	...	0920	0951	...	1033	...	1124	...	1230
Saltash d.	...	2238	2238	...	...	...	...	...	...	...	...		...	│	│	0827	...	0930	1001	...	1044	...	│	...	1239
Liskeard 118 d.	...	2257	2257	...	...	...	...	...	...	...	...		...	0615	0651	0848	...	0949	1022	...	1103	...	1147	...	1258
Bodmin Parkway d.	...	2311	2311	...	...	...	...	...	...	...	...		...	0629	0703	0900	...	1001	1034	...	1115	...	1159	...	1310
Par 118 d.	...	2323	2323	...	...	...	...	...	...	...	...		0609	0642	0715	0912	...	1014	1046	...	1127	...	1210	...	1322
Newquay 118 a.	...	│	│	...	...	...	...	...	...	...	...		│	│	│	│	...	│	│	...	│	...	│	...	│
St Austell d.	...	2331	2331	...	...	...	...	...	...	...	...		0616	0650	0722	0919	...	1022	1054	...	1137	...	1218	...	1329
Truro 118 d.	...	2349	2349	...	...	...	...	...	...	...	...		0641	0709	0739	0938	...	1041	1111	...	1155	...	1236	...	1354
Redruth d.	...	0002	0002	...	...	...	...	...	...	...	...		0654	0723	0750	0951	...	1054	1124	...	1208	...	1248	...	1407
Camborne d.	...	0009	0009	...	...	...	...	...	...	...	...		0700	0730	0757	0957	...	1100	1130	...	1214	...	1256	...	1413
St Erth 118 d.	...	0020	0020	...	...	...	...	...	...	...	...		0710	0744	0812	1008	...	1110	1144	...	1224	...	1306	...	1424
Penzance a.	...	0038	0038	...	...	...	...	...	...	...	...		0723	0800	0819	1021	...	1124	1158	...	1237	...	1320	...	1435

A – Feb. 7 – May 16, London d. 1142, Reading d. 1216.
B – Dec. 14 – Jan. 29.
C – From / to Cardiff, Table **132**.
D – Feb. 1 – May 21.
E – Dec. 13 – Jan. 31.
F – Feb. 7 – May 16.

Y – Via Swindon, Table **130**.

Z – THE NIGHT RIVIERA – 🛏 1, 2 cl. and (2).

b – From London on ①–④.
c – From London on ⑤.

d – From London on ⑦.
e – ①–⑤ Dec. 14 – Jan. 29; ① Feb. 1 – May 21.
f – ⑥ Dec. 19 – Jan. 30.
g – Dec. 14 – Mar. 26, a. 2344.
s – Stops to set down only.
u – Stops to pick up only.

GW, XC — LONDON and BRISTOL - EXETER - PLYMOUTH - PENZANCE — 115

Services on ⑦ valid until March 28.

Operator	GW	XC	GW	XC	XC	GW	GW	XC	GW	XC	GW	GW	XC	GW	XC	GW	GW	XC	GW	XC	GW	XC	GW	GW	XC
	⑥	⑥	⑥	⑥	⑥	⑥	⑥	⑥	⑥	⑥	⑥	⑥	⑥	⑥	⑥	⑥	⑥	⑥	⑥	⑥	⑥	⑥	⑥	⑥	⑥
	🍷	🍷	🍷	🍷	🍷	2	🍷	🍷	🍷	🍷	🍷	🍷	🍷	🍷	🍷	2	🍷	🍷		🍷	🍷	🍷	🍷	🍷	🍷
London Paddington...... **133** d.	0906	...	1006	...	...	...	1106	...	1206	...	1218	1306	...	1406	...	...	1506	...	...	...	1606	...	1706	1630	...
Reading...................... **133** d.	0932	...	1032	...	...	...	1132	...	1232	...	1249	1332	...	1432	...	...	1532	...	...	...	1632	...	1732	1657	...
Newbury .... d.	|	...	|	...	...	...	|	...	|	...	1314	|	...	|	...	...	|	...	...	...	|	...	|	|	...
Westbury..................... **138** d.	|	...	|	...	...	...	1222	...	|	...	1359	|	...	|	...	...	1623	...	...	...	|	...	1822	|	...
Castle Cary.................. **138** d.	|	...	|	...	...	...	1240	...	|	...	1435	|	...	|	...	...	1641	...	...	...	|	...	1841	Y	...
Birmingham New St **127**.... d.	|	0912	|	0942	1012	...	|	1112	|	1212	|	|	1312	|	1412	...	|	1512	...	1542	|	1612	|	|	1712
Bristol Temple Meads **133** d.	|	1044	|	1114	1144	...	|	1244	|	1344	|	|	1444	|	1544	...	|	1644	...	1711	|	1744	|	1817	1844
Taunton...................... **137** d.	1048	1117	|	1201	1217	...	1302	1317	|	1417	1500	1448	1518	1548	1617	...	1703	1718	...	1743	1749	1817	1902	1906	1917
Tiverton Parkway................ d.	1101	1129	|	1213	1229	...	1315	1329	|	1429	—	1501	1530	1601	1629	...	1716	1731	...	1755	1802	1829	1915	1921	1929
Exeter St Davids .... **116** a.	1118	1143	1210	1227	1243	...	1332	1343	1410	1443	...	1518	1546	1618	1643	...	1733	1747	...	1810	1819	1843	1932	1937	1943
Exeter St Davids .... **116** d.	1120	1145	1210	1229	1245	...	1333	1345	1411	1445	...	1519	1548	1620	1645	...	1735	1748	1753	1811	1820	1846	1934	1938	1945
Dawlish...................... **116** d.	|	|	|	1241	|	...	|	|	|	|	...	|	|	|	|	...	|	|	1808	1823	|	|	|	|	|
Teignmouth.................. **116** d.	|	|	|	1246	|	...	|	|	|	|	...	|	|	|	|	...	|	|	1813	1828	|	|	|	|	|
Newton Abbot............ **116** d.	1139	1205	1231	1253	1305	...	1354	1405	1432	1505	...	1540	1608	1641	1705	...	1757	1811	1821	1836	1841	1905	1954	1959	2005
Torquay...................... **116** d.	|	|	|	1305	|	...	|	|	|	|	GW	|	|	|	|	...	|	|	|	1847	|	|	|	2012	|
Paignton.................. **116** a.	|	|	|	1311	|	...	|	|	|	|	⑥	|	|	|	|	...	|	|	|	1854	|	|	|	2021	|
Totnes .... d.	1153	1217	|	...	1317	...	1406	1417	|	1517	2	1554	1622	1653	1717	...	1810	1824	1834	...	1854	1918	2007	...	2017
Plymouth................... **118** a.	1225	1244	1311	...	1344	...	1436	1444	1509	1544		1621	1650	1724	1744	...	1838	1851	1904	...	1926	1943	2035	...	2043
Plymouth............................ d.	...	...	1313	...	...	1358	...	...	1511	...	1603	1628	...	1728	...	1752	1842	1901	1911	...	...	1948	2039	...	2058
Saltash .... d.	...	...	|	...	...	1407	...	...	|	...	1612	|	...	|	...	1806	|	|	1920	...	...	|	2049	...	|
Liskeard...................... **118** d.	...	...	1337	...	...	1426	...	...	1535	...	1633	1651	...	1752	...	1826	1906	1925	1939	...	...	2011	2108	...	2125
Bodmin Parkway................. d.	...	...	1350	...	...	1438	...	...	1548	...	1645	1704	...	1803	...	1838	1919	1937	1951	...	...	2024	2120	...	2138
Par .... **118** d.	...	...	1401	...	...	1450	...	...	1558	...	1657	|	...	1815	...	1851	1930	1948	2003	...	...	2036	2131	...	2148
Newquay .... **118** a.	...	...	|	...	...	|	...	...	|	...	|	|	...	|	...	|	|	|	|	...	...	|	|	...	|
St Austell............................ d.	...	...	1409	...	...	1458	...	...	1606	...	1705	1719	...	1822	...	1858	1938	1956	2010	...	...	2043	2142	...	2155
Truro......................... **118** d.	...	...	1426	...	...	1524	...	...	1624	...	1724	1737	...	1840	...	1916	1958	2014	2029	...	...	2100	2202	...	2219
Redruth .... d.	...	...	1439	...	...	1536	...	...	1636	...	1737	1751	...	1852	...	1929	2008	2027	2042	...	...	2112	2212	...	2230
Camborne........................... d.	...	...	1447	...	...	1542	...	...	1645	...	1743	1759	...	1901	...	1935	2017	2034	2048	...	...	2118	|	...	2236
St Erth........................ **118** d.	...	...	1501	...	...	1552	...	...	1655	...	1754	1813	...	1911	...	1946	2027	2045	2058	...	...	2130	2228	...	2246
Penzance.......................... a.	...	...	1514	...	...	1607	...	...	1709	...	1807	1826	...	1924	...	1957	2041	2056	2109	...	...	2143	2242	...	2257

Operator	GW	XC	GW	XC	XC	GW	XC	GW			XC	GW	GW	GW	XC	GW	GW	XC	GW	XC	GW	XC	GW		GW
	⑥	⑥	⑥	⑥	⑥	⑥	⑥	⑥			⑦	⑦	⑦	⑦	⑦	⑦	⑦	⑦	⑦	⑦	⑦	⑦	⑦		⑦
	🍷	🍷	🍷	🍷	🍷	🍷	🍷	2C				2🍷	2	2	🍷	🍷	🍷	🍷	🍷	🍷	🍷	🍷	🍷A		🍷
London Paddington...... **133** d.	1806	...	1906	...	...	2006	...	...	...	⑦	...	...	...	...	...	0757	0857	...	0957	...	1057	...	1127	...	1157
Reading...................... **133** d.	1832	...	1932	...	...	2032	...	...	...		...	...	...	...	...	0834	0932	...	1032	...	1132	...	1202	...	1232
Newbury .... d.	|	...	1949	...	...	2046	...	...	...		...	...	...	...	...	|	0948	...	|	...	|	...	|	...	1248
Westbury..................... **138** d.	|	...	2028	...	...	2125	...	...	...		...	...	...	...	...	Y	1023	...	|	...	|	...	1307	...	|
Castle Cary.................. **138** d.	|	...	2045	...	...	2143	...	...	...		...	...	...	...	...	|	|	...	1134	...	|	...	1324	...	|
Birmingham New St **127**.... d.	|	1812	|	1912	1942	|	2012	...	...		...	...	...	...	...	|	|	0912	|	1012	|	1112	|	...	|
Bristol Temple Meads **133** d.	|	1944	|	2044	2113	|	2144	2155	...		...	...	0745	0828	0948	0953	|	1044	|	1144	|	1244	|	...	|
Taunton...................... **137** d.	1947	2017	2108	2117	2145	2206	2217	2259	...		...	...	0839	0930	1021	1027	1059	1121	1156	1216	1247	1316	1346	...	1354
Tiverton Parkway................ d.	|	2029	2121	2129	2157	2219	2229	2314	...		...	...	0854	0945	1033	1041	1112	1134	|	1228	|	1329	1359	...	|
Exeter St Davids .... **116** a.	2014	2043	2138	2143	2212	2236	2244	2333	...		...	...	0912	1004	1047	1058	1129	1148	1226	1246	1314	1346	1416	...	1422
Exeter St Davids .... **116** d.	2015	2045	2138	2146	2213	2237	2246	...	...		...	...	0914	1005	1049	1100	1130	1150	1228	1248	1315	1348	1417	...	1423
Dawlish...................... **116** d.	|	|	|	|	|	2249	|	...	...		...	...	0930	1018	|	1114	|	|	|	|	|	|	1430	...	|
Teignmouth.................. **116** d.	|	|	|	|	|	2255	|	...	...		...	...	0935	1023	|	1120	|	|	|	|	|	|	1436	...	|
Newton Abbot............ **116** d.	2037	2105	2159	2210	2233	2303	2312	...	...		...	...	0943	1031	1109	1127	1152	1209	1249	1311	1337	1409	1444	...	1449
Torquay...................... **116** d.	|	|	|	|	|	|	|	...	...		...	...	|	|	|	|	|	|	|	|	|	|	1456	...	|
Paignton.................. **116** a.	|	|	|	|	|	|	|	...	...		...	...	|	|	|	|	|	|	|	|	|	|	1504	...	|
Totnes .... d.	2051	2117	2213	2223	2245	2317	2328	...	...		...	...	0956	1044	1121	1141	1204	1223	1302	1324	|	1422	...	...	1502
Plymouth................... **118** a.	2119	2144	2242	2249	2312	2348	2354	...	...		...	...	1026	1112	1148	1209	1232	1249	1331	1352	1414	1450	...	...	1531
Plymouth............................ d.	2121	...	...	...	...	...	...	...	...		0905	0925	1030	1114	...	1211	1236	1255	...	...	1420	...	...	...	...
Saltash .... d.	|	...	...	...	...	...	...	...	...		|	|	1041	1123	...	|	|	|	...	...	|	...	...	...	...
Liskeard...................... **118** d.	2145	...	...	...	...	...	...	...	...		0930	0949	1105	1144	...	1235	1258	1318	...	...	1443	...	...	...	...
Bodmin Parkway................. d.	2200	...	...	...	...	...	...	...	...		0943	1001	1120	1156	...	1248	1311	1330	...	...	1457	...	...	...	...
Par .... **118** d.	2210	...	...	...	...	...	...	...	...		0953	1014	1132	1208	...	1259	1322	1340	...	...	|	...	...	...	...
Newquay .... **118** a.	|	...	...	...	...	...	...	...	...		|	|	|	|	...	|	|	|	...	...	|	...	...	...	...
St Austell............................ d.	2218	...	...	...	...	...	...	...	...		0959	1021	1140	1216	...	1306	1329	1347	...	...	1512	...	...	...	...
Truro......................... **118** d.	2236	...	...	...	...	...	...	...	...		1017	1040	1158	1234	...	1324	1348	1404	...	...	1531	...	...	...	...
Redruth .... d.	2248	...	...	...	...	...	...	...	...		1028	1053	1212	1247	...	1336	1400	1416	...	...	1541	...	...	...	...
Camborne........................... d.	2257	...	...	...	...	...	...	...	...		1034	1059	1218	1253	...	1345	1409	1423	...	...	1550	...	...	...	...
St Erth........................ **118** d.	2309	...	...	...	...	...	...	...	...		1044	1110	1231	1304	...	1357	1421	1433	...	...	1600	...	...	...	...
Penzance.......................... a.	2324	...	...	...	...	...	...	...	...		1055	1124	1245	1318	...	1409	1432	1443	...	...	1621	...	...	...	...

Operator	GW	XC	GW	XC	GW	GW	GW	XC	XC	GW	XC	GW	GW	XC	GW	XC	GW	XC	GW	XC	XC	GW	GW	XC	GW
	⑦	⑦	⑦	⑦	⑦	⑦	⑦	⑦	⑦	⑦	⑦	⑦	⑦	⑦	⑦	⑦	⑦	⑦	⑦	⑦	⑦	⑦	⑦	⑦	⑦
	2🍷	🍷	🍷	🍷	🍷	2	🍷	🍷	🍷	🍷	🍷	🍷	2	🍷	🍷	🍷	🍷	🍷	🍷	🍷	🍷	🍷	🍷	🍷	🍷
London Paddington...... **133** d.	...	...	1257	...	1303	...	1357	...	...	1457	...	1557	...	...	1657	...	1757	...	1859	...	...	1903	1957	...	2057
Reading...................... **133** d.	...	...	1332	...	1337	...	1432	...	...	1532	...	1632	...	...	1732	...	1832	...	1932	...	...	1937	2032	...	2132
Newbury .... d.	...	...	|	...	|	...	1448	...	...	|	...	1648	...	...	|	...	1848	...	|	...	...	|	2049	...	|
Westbury..................... **138** d.	...	...	1419	...	Y	...	|	...	...	|	...	1724	...	...	|	...	1928	...	|	...	...	Y	2128	...	|
Castle Cary.................. **138** d.	...	...	|	...	|	...	1535	...	...	|	...	1741	...	...	|	...	|	...	2029	...	...	|	2146	...	|
Birmingham New St **127**.... d.	...	1212	|	1312	|	...	|	1412	1442	|	1512	|	...	1612	|	1712	|	1812	|	1842	1912	|	|	2012	|
Bristol Temple Meads **133** d.	...	1344	|	1444	1455	...	|	1544	1614	|	1644	|	...	1744	|	1844	|	1944	|	2019	2044	2055	|	2144	|
Taunton...................... **137** d.	...	1417	1455	1517	1529	...	1555	1617	1646	1651	1717	1806	...	1821	1849	1917	2002	2018	2051	2059	2117	2150	2206	2217	2248s
Tiverton Parkway................ d.	...	1429	1508	1529	|	...	|	1628	1658	1704	1729	1819	...	1833	1901	1929	2016	2030	2104	2112	2129	2203	2219	2229	2302s
Exeter St Davids .... **116** a.	...	1444	1524	1544	1555	...	1622	1647	1713	1720	1744	1835	...	1848	1918	1948	2033	2045	2121	2126	2144	2219	2237	2244	2319
Exeter St Davids .... **116** d.	...	1445	1525	1545	1556	1605	1623	1648	1714	1722	1745	1836	...	1849	1920	1949	2033	2046	2122	2130	2145	...	2237	2245	...
Dawlish...................... **116** d.	...	|	|	|	|	1620	|	|	1726	|	|	|	...	|	|	|	|	|	2136	2143	|	...	|	|	...
Teignmouth.................. **116** d.	...	|	|	|	|	1625	|	|	1731	|	|	|	...	|	|	|	|	|	2142	2148	|	...	|	|	...
Newton Abbot............ **116** d.	...	1504	1546	1604	1619	1631	1642	1709	1739	1741	1804	1858	...	1909	1940	2009	2055	2106	2149	2156	2204	...	2258	2306	...
Torquay...................... **116** d.	...	|	|	|	|	|	|	|	1750	|	|	|	...	|	|	|	|	|	|	|	|	...	|	|	...
Paignton.................. **116** a.	...	|	|	|	|	|	|	|	1758	|	|	|	...	|	|	|	|	|	|	|	|	...	|	|	...
Totnes .... d.	...	1517	1600	1617	|	1647	1658	1722	...	1756	1817	|	...	1921	1953	2021	2110	2118	2203	|	2217	...	2311	2321	...
Plymouth................... **118** a.	...	1544	1629	1644	1658	1717	1726	1750	...	1823	1844	1936	...	1948	2021	2048	2137	2145	2231	2238	2246	...	2341	2349	...
Plymouth............................ d.	1536	...	1635	...	...	1735	...	...	...	1825	1855	...	1943	...	2024	2050	2140	...	...	...	...	...	...	...	...
Saltash .... d.	1545	...	|	...	...	1744	...	...	...	|	|	...	1952	...	|	|	|	...	...	...	...	...	...	...	...
Liskeard...................... **118** d.	1604	...	1657	...	...	1806	...	...	...	1849	1918	...	2011	...	2048	2113	2203	...	...	...	...	...	...	...	...
Bodmin Parkway................. d.	1617	...	1709	...	...	1818	...	...	...	1902	1930	...	2023	...	2100	2125	2217	...	...	...	...	...	...	...	...
Par .... **118** d.	1630	...	1722	...	...	1830	...	...	...	1913	1940	...	2035	...	2112	2135	2229	...	...	...	...	...	...	...	...
Newquay .... **118** a.	|	...	|	...	...	|	...	...	...	|	|	...	|	...	|	|	|	...	...	...	...	...	...	...	...
St Austell............................ d.	1637	...	1728	...	...	1837	...	...	...	1920	1951	...	2043	...	2119	2142	2237	...	...	...	...	...	...	...	...
Truro......................... **118** d.	1656	...	1747	...	...	1855	...	...	...	1938	2008	...	2101	...	2136	2200	2254	...	...	...	...	...	...	...	...
Redruth .... d.	1709	...	1759	...	...	1908	...	...	...	1950	2019	...	2114	...	2149	2211	2307	...	...	...	...	...	...	...	...
Camborne........................... d.	1715	...	1806	...	...	1914	...	...	...	2100	2027	...	2120	...	2157	2221	2315	...	...	...	...	...	...	...	...
St Erth........................ **118** d.	1726	...	1820	...	...	1925	...	...	...	2014	2037	...	2131	...	2210	2231	2326	...	...	...	...	...	...	...	...
Penzance.......................... a.	1738	...	1831	...	...	1938	...	...	...	2024	2047	...	2144	...	2221	2241	2339	...	...	...	...	...	...	...	...

For notes see page 104.

115 PENZANCE - PLYMOUTH - EXETER - BRISTOL and LONDON GW, XC

Services on ⑦ valid until March 28.

Operator		GW	GW	XC	GW	GW	GW	GW	XC	XC	GW	GW	GW	GW	GW	XC	GW	XC	GW	XC	GW	GW	XC	XC	GW
		Ⓐ	Ⓐ	Ⓐ	Ⓐ	Ⓐ	Ⓐ	Ⓐ	Ⓐ	Ⓐ	Ⓐ	Ⓐ	Ⓐ	Ⓐ	Ⓐ	Ⓐ	Ⓐ	Ⓐ	Ⓐ	Ⓐ	Ⓐ	Ⓐ	Ⓐ	Ⓐ	Ⓐ
		🍷	2	🍷	🍷	🍷	🍷	🍷	🍷	🍷	🍷	2	🍷	🍷	2	🍷	🍷	🍷	🍷	🍷	🍷	🍷	🍷	🍷	🍷
Penzance d.	Ⓐ	...	...	...	...	...	...	...	...	...	0505	0521	...	0541	0600	0628	0648	...	0739	0828	0844	...	...	0940	1000
St Erth 118 d.		...	...	...	...	...	...	...	...	...	|	|	...	|	0608	0636	0659	...	0749	0836	0855	...	...	0948	1011
Camborne d.		...	...	...	...	...	...	...	...	...	|	0540	...	0600	0622	0646	0710	...	0803	0846	0907	...	...	1001	1022
Redruth d.		...	...	...	...	...	...	...	...	...	0526	|	...	0607	0628	0652	0717	...	0810	0852	0914	...	...	1008	1029
Truro 118 d.		...	...	...	...	...	...	...	...	...	0539	0556	...	0619	0640	0704	0729	...	0823	0904	0926	...	...	1019	1041
St Austell d.		...	...	...	...	...	...	...	...	...	0556	—	...	0637	0657	0720	0747	...	0840	0920	0944	...	...	1035	1059
Newquay 118 d.		...	...	...	...	...	...	...	...	...	|	...	...	|	|	|	|	...	|	|	|	...	...	|	|
Par 118 d.		...	...	...	...	...	...	...	...	...	|	...	...	0644	0704	0728	0755	...	0848	0928	0951	...	...	1043	1107
Bodmin Parkway d.		...	...	...	...	...	...	...	...	...	0612	XC	...	0658	0717	0739	0808	...	0901	0939	1003	...	...	1057	1118
Liskeard 118 d.		...	...	...	...	...	...	...	...	...	0624	Ⓐ	...	0711	0730	0751	0821	...	0914	0951	1016	...	...	1109	1131
Saltash d.		...	...	...	...	...	...	...	...	...	|	🍷	...	0729	0749	|	0839	...	0932	|	|	...	...	|	|
Plymouth a.		...	...	...	...	...	...	...	...	...	0649		...	0740	0805	0820	0851	...	0944	1015	1041	...	...	1139	1156
Plymouth 118 d.		...	...	0520	...	0530	0540	0553	0625	...	0655	0725	...	0748	0807	0825	0855	...	0947	1025	1044	...	1125	1150	1200
Totnes d.		...	...	0545	...	0557	|	|	0650	...	|	0750	...	0815	0836	0850	0922	...	1017	1050	|	...	1150	1215	1229
Paignton 116 d.		...	...	|	...	|	|	|	|	0701	|	|	0740	|	|	|	|	1006	|	|	|	...	|	|	|
Torquay 116 d.		...	...	|	...	|	|	|	|	0707	|	|	0746	|	|	|	|	1012	|	|	|	...	|	|	|
Newton Abbot 116 d.		...	...	0603	...	0610	0617	0630	0703	0718	0731	0803	0806	0828	0850	0903	0935	1023	1030	1103	|	...	1203	1228	1242
Teignmouth 116 d.		...	...	|	...	|	0625	|	|	0725	|	|	0813	|	0857	|	|	1030	|	|	|	...	|	|	|
Dawlish 116 d.		...	...	|	...	0620	|	|	|	0730	|	|	0819	|	0902	|	|	1035	|	|	|	...	|	|	|
Exeter St Davids 116 a.		...	...	0621	...	0633	0641	0650	0721	0742	0751	0821	0839	0848	0921	0922	0955	1047	1054	1121	1138	...	1221	1246	1302
Exeter St Davids d.		0546	0600	0623	0630	0635	0643	0651	0723	0744	0752	0823	0840	0850	...	0924	0957	1049	1056	1123	1140	1155	1223	1248	1304
Tiverton Parkway d.		0602	0618	0637	|	0650	0658	|	0737	0757	|	0837	|	0905	...	0938	1012	1102	1111	1137	|	1209	1237	1302	1319
Taunton 137 d.		0617	0635	0651	0654	0705	0713	0717	0751	0812	0818	0851	0905	0920	...	0952	1027	1117	1126	1151	|	1224	1251	1316	1334
Bristol Temple Meads 13... a.		|	0743	0726	0758	|	0825	|	0827	0855	|	0927	0958	|	...	1026	|	1153	1159	1224	|	|	1324	1356	|
Birmingham New St 127 a.		|	...	0856	|	|	|	|	0956	1026	|	1056	|	|	...	1158	|	1326	|	1356	|	|	1456	1526	|
Castle Cary 138 d.		0638	...	...	|	0727	|	|	...	...	|	...	|	0941	...	...	|	...	|	...	|	1245	...	...	|
Westbury 138 d.		0705	...	...	Y	0751	Y	|	...	...	|	...	Y	1000	...	...	1103	...	Y	...	|	1305	...	...	|
Newbury a.		0746	...	...	|	0829	|	|	...	...	|	...	|	|	...	...	|	...	|	...	|	1349	...	...	|
Reading 133 a.		0807	...	...	0913	0850	0944	0832	...	...	0932	...	1109	1050	...	...	1150	...	1309	...	1315	1415	...	...	1450
London Paddington 133 a.		0838	...	...	0944	0921	1014	0900	...	...	1002	...	1137	1124	...	...	1225	...	1340	...	1344	1444	...	...	1524

Operator	XC	GW	GW	GW	XC	XC	GW	GW	XC	GW	GW	XC	XC	GW	XC	GW	GW	XC	GW	XC	GW	GW	GW	GW	GW
	Ⓐ	Ⓐ	Ⓐ	Ⓐ	Ⓐ	Ⓐ	Ⓐ	Ⓐ	Ⓐ	Ⓐ	Ⓐ	Ⓐ	Ⓐ	Ⓐ	Ⓐ	Ⓐ	Ⓐ	Ⓐ	Ⓐ	Ⓐ	①–④	⑤	①–④	⑤	Ⓐ
	🍷	2	2**C**	🍷	🍷	🍷	2	🍷	🍷	2	🍷	🍷	🍷	🍷	🍷	2	🍷	🍷	🍷	🍷	2	2	🍷	🍷	🍷
Penzance d.	...	1046	...	...	...	...	1143	...	...	1254	...	...	...	1400	...	1449	...	...	1600	...	1644	1644	...	...	1739
St Erth 118 d.	...	1054	...	...	...	...	1151	...	...	1302	...	...	...	1411	...	1457	...	...	1611	...	1652	1652	...	...	1749
Camborne d.	...	1107	...	...	...	...	1204	...	...	1315	...	...	...	1422	...	1510	...	...	1623	...	1705	1705	...	...	1804
Redruth d.	...	1113	...	...	...	...	1210	...	...	1321	...	...	...	1429	...	1516	...	...	1630	...	1711	1711	...	...	1811
Truro 118 d.	...	1125	...	...	...	...	1222	...	...	1333	...	...	...	1441	...	1527	...	...	1642	...	1724	1724	...	...	1824
St Austell d.	...	1142	...	...	...	...	1239	...	...	1350	...	...	...	1459	...	1544	...	...	1700	...	1741	1741	...	...	1841
Newquay 118 d.	...	|	...	...	...	...	|	...	...	|	...	...	...	|	...	|	...	...	|	...	|	|	...	...	|
Par 118 d.	...	1150	...	...	...	...	1246	...	...	1357	...	...	...	1506	...	1552	...	...	1708	...	1748	1748	...	...	1849
Bodmin Parkway d.	...	1202	...	...	...	...	1259	...	...	1410	...	...	...	1518	...	1604	...	...	1722	...	1801	1801	...	...	1900
Liskeard 118 d.	...	1215	...	...	...	...	1312	...	...	1423	...	...	...	1532	...	1617	...	...	1735	*1749*	1814	1814	...	...	1913
Saltash d.	...	1234	...	...	...	...	1331	...	...	1441	...	...	...	|	...	1637	...	...	|	*1807*	1832	1832	...	...	|
Plymouth a.	...	1246	...	...	...	...	1342	...	...	1451	...	...	...	1557	...	1652	...	...	1758	*1819*	1842	1842	...	...	1938
Plymouth 118 d.	1223	...	...	1255	1323	...	1343	...	1425	...	1500	1523	...	1600	1625	...	1657	1723	1800	1825	1843	1843	...	...	1942
Totnes d.	1249	...	...	1322	1349	...	1413	...	1450	...	1527	1549	...	1627	1650	...	1727	1749	1830	1850	1913	1913	...	...	2009
Paignton 116 d.	|	...	1247	|	|	1401	|	1415	|	...	|	|	...	|	|	...	|	|	|	|	|	|	...	...	|
Torquay 116 d.	|	...	1252	|	|	1407	|	1421	|	...	|	|	...	|	|	...	|	|	|	|	|	|	...	...	|
Newton Abbot 116 d.	1303	...	1305	1335	1403	1418	1428	1433	1503	...	1540	1603	...	1640	1703	...	1740	1803	1843	1903	1925	1925	...	...	2022
Teignmouth 116 d.	|	...	1313	|	|	1425	—	1440	|	...	|	|	...	|	|	...	|	|	|	|	|	|	...	...	|
Dawlish 116 d.	|	...	1319	|	|	1430	GW	1446	|	...	|	|	...	|	|	...	|	|	|	|	|	|	...	...	|
Exeter St Davids 116 a.	1323	...	1333	1355	1423	1442	Ⓐ	1459	1521	...	1600	1623	...	1700	1721	...	1800	1823	1903	1921	1948	1948	...	...	2042
Exeter St Davids d.	1325	...	1334	1357	1425	1444	🍷	1500	1523	...	1600	1625	1653	1700	1723	...	1800	1825	1905	1923	...	1948	1954	...	2044
Tiverton Parkway d.	1339	...	1353	|	1439	1457		1516	1537	...	1616	1639	1707	1717	1737	...	1816	1839	1920	1937	...	2005	2009	...	2059
Taunton 137 d.	1354	...	1411	1423	1454	1512	1519	1530	1551	...	1630	1654	1721	1731	1751	...	1830	1854	1935	1951	...	2021	2024	2026	2114
Bristol Temple Meads 13... a.	1427	...	1517	|	1527	1557	|	|	1627	...	|	1727	1754	|	1824	...	|	1927	|	2024	...	...	|	|	2147
Birmingham New St 127 a.	1556	...	...	|	1658	1726	|	|	1756	...	|	1855	1926	|	1956	...	|	2052	|	2209	...	...	|	|	|
Castle Cary 138 d.	...	...	...	1444	...	...	1541	|	...	...	|	...	...	|	...	...	1853	...	|	...	...	...	2045	2045	|
Westbury 138 d.	...	...	...	1503	...	...	1609	|	...	...	|	...	...	|	...	...	1911	...	|	...	...	...	2104	2104	Y
Newbury a.	...	...	...	|	...	...	1649	|	...	...	|	...	...	|	...	...	1945	...	|	...	...	...	2142	2142	|
Reading 133 a.	...	...	...	1550	...	...	1715	1650	...	...	1750	...	...	1849	...	...	2006	...	2050	...	...	...	2159	2159	2306
London Paddington 133 a.	...	...	...	1621	...	...	1754	1724	...	...	1821	...	...	1924	...	...	2039	...	2121	...	...	...	2230	2230	2350

Operator	XC	GW	GW	GW	GW	GW	GW	XC	
	Ⓐ	Ⓐ	Ⓐ	Ⓐ	Ⓐ	⑤	①–④	Ⓐ	
		2	2		2**D**	🍷**Z**	🍷**Z**		
Penzance d.	...	1916	...	2016	...	2145	2145	2208	...
St Erth 118 d.	...	1924	...	2026	...	2155	2155	2216	...
Camborne d.	...	1937	...	2040	...	2207	2207	2230	...
Redruth d.	...	1943	...	2047	...	2214	2214	2236	...
Truro 118 d.	...	1955	...	2100	...	2227	2227	2248	...
St Austell d.	...	2012	...	2117	...	2245	2245	2304	...
Newquay 118 d.	...	|	...	|	...	|	|	|	...
Par 118 d.	...	2019	...	2125	...	2253	2253	2312	...
Bodmin Parkway d.	...	2032	...	2138	...	2305	2305	2326	...
Liskeard 118 d.	...	2045	...	2151	...	2320	2320	2339	...
Saltash d.	...	2105	...	2209	...	|	|	|	...
Plymouth a.	...	2120	...	2221	...	2347	2347	0003	...
Plymouth 118 d.	...	—	2125	—	...	2351	2351	...	...
Totnes d.	...	...	2154	...	...	0019	0019	...	...
Paignton 116 d.	2012	...	|	...	...	|	|	...	...
Torquay 116 d.	2018	...	|	...	...	|	|	...	...
Newton Abbot 116 d.	2029	...	2206	GW	...	0032	0032	...	...
Teignmouth 116 d.	|	...	2213	Ⓐ	...	|	|	...	...
Dawlish 116 d.	|	...	2218	2**B**	...	|	|	...	...
Exeter St Davids 116 a.	2048	GW	2240		...	0054	0054	...	...
Exeter St Davids d.	2050	Ⓐ	...	2125	2156	0202	0202	...	...
Tiverton Parkway d.	2103		...	2142	2213	|	|	...	...
Taunton 137 d.	2118	2123	...	2159	2230	0235	0235	...	...
Bristol Temple Meads 13... a.	2151	2213	...	2313	2352	|	|	...	...
Birmingham New St 127 a.	0025**g**	|	...	...	...	|	|	...	...
Castle Cary 138 d.	...	|	...	...	...	|	|	...	...
Westbury 138 d.	...	Y	...	...	...	|	|	...	...
Newbury a.	...	|	...	...	...	|	|	...	...
Reading 133 a.	...	2354	...	...	...	0417**s**	0427**s**	...	...
London Paddington 133 a.	...	0033	...	...	...	0543	0543	...	...

Operator		XC	GW	XC	XC	GW	GW	GW	XC	GW	GW	XC	GW	XC	GW	XC
		⑥	⑥	⑥	⑥	⑥	⑥	⑥	⑥	⑥	⑥	⑥	⑥	⑥	⑥	⑥
		🍷	2	🍷	🍷	🍷	🍷	🍷	🍷	🍷	2	🍷	🍷	🍷	2	🍷
Penzance d.	⑥	...	0522	...	...	...	...	...	...	...	0601	0630	0650	...	0735	...
St Erth 118 d.		...	|	...	...	...	...	...	...	...	0608	0638	0701	...	0747	...
Camborne d.		...	0539	...	...	...	...	...	...	...	0621	0651	0712	...	0801	...
Redruth d.		...	0545	...	...	...	...	...	...	...	0627	0657	0719	...	0808	...
Truro 118 d.		...	0556	...	...	...	...	...	...	...	0639	0709	0731	...	0821	...
St Austell d.		...	—	...	...	...	...	...	...	...	0656	0725	0749	...	0836	...
Newquay 118 d.		...	...	...	...	...	...	...	...	...	|	|	|	...	|	...
Par 118 d.		...	...	...	...	...	...	...	...	...	0703	0732	0756	...	0845	...
Bodmin Parkway d.		...	GW	...	...	...	...	...	...	...	0716	0746	0810	...	0858	...
Liskeard 118 d.		...	⑥	...	...	...	...	...	...	...	0730	0758	0823	...	0911	...
Saltash d.		...	🍷	...	...	...	...	...	...	...	0749	|	|	...	0930	...
Plymouth a.		...	...	...	...	...	...	...	...	...	0805	0822	0848	...	0941	...
Plymouth 118 d.		0525	0540	0625	...	...	0655	...	0725	0747	0806	0825	0852	0925	...	...
Totnes d.		0550	0607	0650	...	...	|	...	0750	0814	0835	0850	0919	0950	...	...
Paignton 116 d.		|	|	|	0700	...	|	0720	|	|	|	|	|	|	...	1006
Torquay 116 d.		|	|	|	0706	...	|	0726	|	|	|	|	|	|	...	1012
Newton Abbot 116 d.		0603	0620	0703	0718	...	0731	0740	0803	0827	0848	0903	0932	1003	...	1023
Teignmouth 116 d.		|	|	|	0725	...	|	0748	|	|	0855	|	|	|	...	1030
Dawlish 116 d.		|	|	|	0730	...	|	0754	|	|	0900	|	|	|	...	1035
Exeter St Davids 116 a.		0621	0640	0721	0746	...	0751	0806	0821	0847	0916	0921	0952	1021	...	1047
Exeter St Davids d.		0623	0641	0723	0748	0728	0753	0808	0823	0849	...	0923	0954	1023	...	1049
Tiverton Parkway d.		0637	0656	0737	|	0743	|	0823	0837	0904	...	0937	1009	1037	...	1102
Taunton 137 d.		0651	0711	0751	0812	0758	0819	0838	0851	0919	...	0951	1024	1051	...	1117
Bristol Temple Meads 13... a.		0725	|	0824	0849	0857	|	0923	0926	|	...	1026	|	1126	...	1155
Birmingham New St 127 a.		0856	|	0956	1026	|	|	|	1056	|	...	1156	|	1256	...	1326
Castle Cary 138 d.		...	0733	...	...	Y	|	Y	...	0940	...	...	|	...	...	...
Westbury 138 d.		...	0756	...	...	|	|	|	...	0959	...	...	1102	...	...	...
Newbury a.		...	0833	...	...	|	|	|	...	|	...	...	|	...	...	...
Reading 133 a.		...	0852	...	...	1008	0935	1045	...	1051	...	...	1151	...	...	...
London Paddington 133 a.		...	0921	...	...	1038	1008	1114	...	1124	...	...	1223	...	...	...

For notes see page 104.

GW, XC — PENZANCE - PLYMOUTH - EXETER - BRISTOL and LONDON — 115

Services on ⑦ valid until March 28.

Operator	GW	XC	GW	GW	XC	XC	GW	XC	GW	GW	XC	XC	GW	GW	GW	XC	GW	GW	XC	GW	XC	GW	GW	XC	GW
	⑥	⑥	⑥	⑥	⑥	⑥	⑥	⑥	⑥	⑥	⑥	⑥	⑥	⑥	⑥	⑥	⑥	⑥	⑥	⑥	⑥	⑥	⑥	⑥	⑥
	🍷	🍷	🍷	🍷	🍷	🍷	🍷	🍷	2	🍷	🍷	🍷	2	🍷	🍷	🍷	2	🍷	🍷	🍷	🍷	2	🍷	🍷	🍷
Penzance d.	0759	0828	0845	...	...	0943	1000	...	1036	1059	...	...	1149	...	...	...	1300	...	...	1400	...	1449	...	...	1551
St Erth **118** d.	0809	0836	0856	...	...	0951	1011	...	1044	1109	...	...	1157	...	...	...	1308	...	...	1411	...	1457	...	...	1602
Camborne d.	0823	0846	0907	...	...	1001	1022	...	1057	1120	...	...	1210	...	...	...	1321	...	...	1422	...	1510	...	...	1614
Redruth d.	0830	0852	0914	...	...	1007	1029	...	1103	1127	...	...	1216	...	...	...	1327	...	...	1429	...	1516	...	...	1621
Truro **118** d.	0843	0904	0926	...	...	1019	1041	...	1115	1140	...	...	1228	...	...	...	1339	...	...	1441	...	1528	...	...	1633
St Austell d.	0900	0920	0944	...	...	1035	1059	...	1132	1157	...	...	1245	...	...	...	1355	...	...	1459	...	1545	...	...	1651
Newquay **118** d.	|	|	|	...	...	|	|	...	|	|	...	...	|	...	...	...	|	...	...	|	...	|	...	...	|
Par **118** d.	0908	0928	0951	...	...	1042	1107	...	1139	|	...	...	1253	...	...	...	1404	...	...	1506	...	1553	...	...	1658
Bodmin Parkway d.	0919	0939	1003	...	...	1056	1118	...	1152	1214	...	...	1305	...	...	...	1415	...	...	1518	...	1605	...	...	1712
Liskeard **118** d.	0932	0951	1016	...	...	1108	1131	...	1205	1227	...	...	1318	...	...	...	1428	...	...	1532	...	1618	...	...	1725
Saltash d.	|	|	|	...	...	|	|	...	1224	|	...	...	1340	...	...	...	1546	...	...	|	...	1638	...	...	|
Plymouth a.	0957	1015	1040	...	...	1132	1158	...	1237	1252	...	...	1349	...	...	...	1459	...	...	1556	...	1648	...	...	1750
Plymouth **118** d.	1001	1025	1044	...	1125	1148	1200	1223	...	1254	1325	...	...	1400	...	1425	...	1504	1525	1600	1625	...	1657	1723	1754
Totnes d.	1030	1050	|	...	1150	1213	1229	1249	...	1321	1350	...	...	|	...	1450	...	1531	1550	1627	1650	...	1727	1749	1821
Paignton **116** d.	|	|	|	...	|	|	|	|	...	|	|	1353	...	|	...	|	...	|	|	|	|	...	|	|	|
Torquay **116** d.	|	|	|	...	|	|	|	|	...	|	|	1359	...	|	...	|	...	|	|	|	|	...	|	|	|
Newton Abbot **116** d.	1043	1103	|	...	1203	1225	1242	1303	...	1335	1403	1410	...	1436	...	1503	...	1544	1603	1640	1703	...	1740	1803	1834
Teignmouth **116** d.	|	|	|	...	|	|	|	|	...	|	|	1417	...	|	...	|	...	|	|	|	|	...	|	|	|
Dawlish **116** d.	|	|	|	...	|	|	|	|	...	|	|	1422	...	|	...	|	...	|	|	|	|	...	|	|	|
Exeter St Davids **116** a.	1104	1121	1138	...	1221	1244	1302	1323	...	1354	1421	1434	...	1456	...	1521	...	1604	1621	1700	1721	...	1800	1823	1854
Exeter St Davids d.	1106	1123	1140	1154	1223	1248	1304	1325	...	1356	1424	1436	...	1458	...	1523	...	1606	1623	1702	1723	...	1802	1825	1856
Tiverton Parkway d.	1121	1137	|	1209	1237	1302	1319	1339	...	|	1437	1449	...	1513	...	1537	...	1621	1637	1716	1737	...	1817	1839	1911
Taunton **137** d.	1136	1151	|	1224	1251	1316	1334	1354	...	1423	1452	1504	...	1528	1534	1551	...	1636	1651	1731	1751	...	1832	1854	1926
Bristol Temple Meads **13** a.	|	1225	|	|	1324	1356	|	1427	...	|	1525	1549	...	|	|	1625	...	|	1725	|	1825	...	|	1927	|
Birmingham New St **127** a.	|	1356	|	|	1456	1526	|	1555	...	|	1656	1726	...	|	|	1756	...	|	1856	|	1956	...	|	2053	|
Castle Cary **138** d.	|	...	|	1245	...	...	|	...	...	1444	...	...	...	|	1600	...	...	|	...	|	...	...	1853	...	1947
Westbury **138** d.	|	...	|	1305	...	...	|	...	...	1503	...	...	...	|	1625	...	...	|	...	|	...	...	1912	...	2006
Newbury a.	|	...	|	1349	...	...	|	...	...	|	...	...	...	|	1709	...	...	|	...	|	...	...	1949	...	|
Reading **133** a.	1252	...	1317	1419	...	...	1451	...	...	1551	...	...	...	1650	1739	...	...	1753	...	1849	...	...	2007	...	2058
London Paddington **133** a.	1321	...	1346	1445	...	...	1522	...	...	1623	...	...	...	1721	1808	...	...	1821	...	1922	...	...	2037	...	2132

Operator	XC	GW	GW	GW	GW	GW	XC	
	⑥	⑥	⑥	⑥	⑥	⑥	⑥	
	🍷	2	🍷	🍷	2	2	🍷	
Penzance d.	...	1643	1739	...	1906	...	2132	...
St Erth **118** d.	...	1651	1749	...	1914	...	2142	...
Camborne d.	...	1704	1804	...	1927	...	2153	...
Redruth d.	...	1710	1811	...	1933	...	2200	...
Truro **118** d.	...	1724	1824	...	1945	...	2213	...
St Austell d.	...	1739	1841	...	2003	...	2230	...
Newquay **118** d.	...	|	|	...	|	2115	|	...
Par **118** d.	...	1746	1849	...	2011	2206	2338	...
Bodmin Parkway d.	...	1758	1900	...	2023	2221	2249	...
Liskeard **118** d.	...	1811	1913	...	2036	2234	2302	...
Saltash d.	...	1832	|	...	2057	2253	|	...
Plymouth a.	...	1842	1938	...	2112	2309	2327	...
Plymouth **118** d.	1825	1844	1942	...	2115	...	...	...
Totnes d.	1850	1913	2009	...	2144	...	...	...
Paignton **116** d.	|	|	|	...	|	...	...	...
Torquay **116** d.	|	|	|	...	|	...	...	...
Newton Abbot **116** d.	1903	1926	2022	...	2156	...	...	...
Teignmouth **116** d.	|	1933	|	...	2203	...	...	...
Dawlish **116** d.	|	1938	|	...	2208	...	...	...
Exeter St Davids **116** a.	1921	1950	2042	...	2230	...	...	...
Exeter St Davids d.	1923	...	2044	...	...	...	...	...
Tiverton Parkway d.	1937	...	2059	...	...	...	...	...
Taunton **137** d.	1951	...	2114	2129	...	...	...	...
Bristol Temple Meads **13** a.	2025	...	2147	2230	...	...	...	...
Birmingham New St **127** a.	2152	...	|	|	...	...	...	...
Castle Cary **138** d.	...	...	Y	Y	...	...	...	...
Westbury **138** d.	...	...	|	|	...	...	...	...
Newbury a.	...	...	|	|	...	...	...	...
Reading **133** a.	...	...	2304	2352	...	...	...	...
London Paddington **133** a.	...	...	2336	0033	...	...	...	...

⑦

Operator	GW	GW	GW	XC	GW	XC	XC	XC	GW	XC	GW	XC	XC	XC	GW	XC
	⑦	⑦	⑦	⑦	⑦	⑦	⑦	⑦	⑦	⑦	⑦	⑦	⑦	⑦	⑦	⑦
	C	🍷	🍷	🍷	🍷	🍷	🍷E	🍷F	🍷	🍷	🍷	🍷E	🍷F	🍷	🍷	🍷
Penzance d.	...	...	...	...	...	...	...	...	0835	0930	0947	...	...	...	1100	1125
St Erth **118** d.	...	...	...	...	...	...	...	...	0845	0938	0958	...	...	...	1110	1136
Camborne d.	...	...	...	...	...	...	...	...	0901	0948	1010	...	...	...	1123	1146
Redruth d.	...	...	...	...	...	...	...	...	0907	0954	1016	...	...	...	1129	1153
Truro **118** d.	...	...	...	...	...	...	...	...	0920	1006	1029	...	...	...	1142	1206
St Austell d.	...	...	...	...	...	...	...	...	0937	1024	1046	...	...	...	1159	1225
Newquay **118** d.	...	...	...	...	...	...	...	...	|	|	|	...	...	...	|	|
Par **118** d.	...	...	...	...	...	...	...	...	0945	1031	1054	...	...	...	1206	1232
Bodmin Parkway d.	...	...	...	...	...	...	...	...	0957	1042	1106	...	...	...	1219	1244
Liskeard **118** d.	...	...	...	...	...	...	...	...	1010	1054	1119	...	...	...	1232	1257
Saltash d.	...	...	...	...	...	...	...	...	1030	|	|	...	...	...	|	|
Plymouth a.	...	...	...	...	...	...	...	...	1039	1117	1142	...	...	...	1257	1320
Plymouth **118** d.	...	...	0840	0925	1010	1025	...	...	1040	1125	1145	1200	1200	1225	1300	1323
Totnes d.	...	...	0908	0950	1040	1050	...	...	1110	1150	1214	|	|	1250	1329	1349
Paignton **116** d.	...	...	|	|	|	|	1050	1050	|	|	|	|	|	|	|	|
Torquay **116** d.	...	...	|	|	|	|	1056	1056	|	|	|	|	|	|	|	|
Newton Abbot **116** d.	...	...	0921	1003	1054	1103	1108	1108	1123	1203	1228	1236	1236	1303	1342	1403
Teignmouth **116** d.	...	...	0928	|	|	|	1115	1115	|	|	|	|	|	|	|	|
Dawlish **116** d.	...	...	0934	|	|	|	1120	1120	|	|	|	|	|	|	|	|
Exeter St Davids **116** a.	...	...	0948	1021	1114	1121	1130	1130	1143	1221	1248	1255	1255	1321	1402	1423
Exeter St Davids d.	0804	0845	0949	1023	1116	1123	1132	1132	1145	1223	1250	1257	1257	1323	1404	1425
Tiverton Parkway d.	0819	0900	|	1037	1131	1137	1146	1146	1200	1237	|	1310	1310	1337	1418	1439
Taunton **137** d.	0835	0914	1015	1051	1146	1151	1200	1200	1215	1251	1315	1325	1325	1351	1433	1454
Bristol Temple Meads **13** a.	0938	|	|	1127	1222	1226	1245	1245	|	1324	|	1357	1357	1424	|	1527
Birmingham New St **127** a.	...	|	|	1250	|	1350	1420	1426	|	1450	|	1520	1527	1550	|	1650
Castle Cary **138** d.	...	0936	|	...	Y	...	...	...	1236	...	|	...	...	...	|	...
Westbury **138** d.	...	0956	1053	...	|	...	...	...	1256	...	1355	...	...	...	|	...
Newbury a.	...	1033	1126	...	|	...	...	...	1333	...	|	...	...	...	|	...
Reading **133** a.	...	1051	1148	...	1343	...	...	...	1351	...	1449	...	...	...	1549	...
London Paddington **133** a.	...	1129	1229	...	1421	...	...	...	1429	...	1529	...	...	...	1629	...

Operator	GW	GW	XC	XC	XC	GW	GW	XC	GW	GW	GW	GW	XC	GW	GW	XC	GW	XC	GW	XC	GW	GW	GW	GW	GW
	⑦	⑦	⑦	⑦	⑦	⑦	⑦	⑦	⑦	⑦	⑦	⑦	⑦	⑦	⑦	⑦	⑦	⑦	⑦	⑦	⑦	⑦	⑦	⑦	⑦
	🍷	2	🍷	🍷E	🍷F	🍷	🍷	🍷	🍷	🍷		🍷	🍷	🍷	2	🍷	🍷	🍷	🍷	🍷	🍷	🍷	2	2🍷	🍷Z
Penzance d.	...	1215	...	1230	1230	1254	...	...	...	...	1350	...	...	1445	1508	1530	...	...	1610	...	1720	...	1900	2005	2115
St Erth **118** d.	...	1222	...	1240	1240	1306	...	...	...	...	1400	...	...	1455	1517	1538	...	...	1621	...	1730	...	1909	2014	2125
Camborne d.	...	1234	...	1255	1255	1317	...	...	...	...	1413	...	...	1507	1530	1551	...	...	1633	...	1743	...	1920	2026	2138
Redruth d.	...	1240	...	1301	1301	1323	...	...	...	...	1419	...	...	1514	1536	1557	...	...	1640	...	1750	...	1926	2032	2145
Truro **118** d.	...	1252	...	1313	1313	1335	...	...	...	...	1432	...	...	1527	1548	1609	...	...	1652	...	1801	...	1938	2044	2200
St Austell d.	...	1310	...	1330	1330	1354	...	...	...	...	1449	...	...	1544	1605	1625	...	...	1710	...	1820	...	1955	2101	2218
Newquay **118** d.	...	|	...	|	|	|	...	...	...	...	|	...	...	|	|	|	...	...	|	...	|	...	|	|	|
Par **118** d.	...	1318	...	1337	1337	1400	...	...	...	...	1457	...	...	1552	1612	1633	...	...	1716	...	1827	...	2002	2109	|
Bodmin Parkway d.	...	1332	...	1351	1351	1413	...	...	...	...	1510	...	...	1603	1625	1644	...	...	1728	...	1839	...	2015	2121	2235
Liskeard **118** d.	...	1346	...	1403	1403	1426	...	...	...	...	1524	...	...	1616	1638	1656	...	...	1741	...	1852	...	2028	2135	2250
Saltash d.	...	1406	...	|	|	|	...	...	...	...	|	...	...	|	1659	|	...	...	|	...	|	...	2047	|	|
Plymouth a.	...	1415	...	1427	1427	1451	...	...	...	...	1555	...	...	1641	1708	1720	...	...	1807	...	1916	...	2059	2200	2315
Plymouth **118** d.	1344	...	1423	1435	1435	1455	1505	1523	1543	...	1602	1610	1625	1645	1709	1726	1745	...	1810	1823	1920	1955	2115	...	2320
Totnes d.	1411	...	1449	1500	1500	1522	1533	1549	1611	...	1631	1642	1650	1712	1739	1752	1813	...	1838	1849	1948	|	2142	...	2348
Paignton **116** d.	|	...	|	|	|	|	|	|	|	1545	|	|	|	|	|	|	|	1817	|	|	|	|	|	...	|
Torquay **116** d.	|	...	|	|	|	|	|	|	|	1551	|	|	|	|	|	|	|	1824	|	|	|	|	|	...	|
Newton Abbot **116** d.	1425	...	1503	1512	1512	1535	1546	1603	1624	1605	1644	1655	1703	1725	1752	1804	1826	1835	1850	1903	2001	2032	2154	...	0001
Teignmouth **116** d.	|	...	|	|	|	|	|	|	|	1613	|	|	|	|	1759	|	|	|	|	|	|	|	2202	...	|
Dawlish **116** d.	|	...	|	|	|	|	|	|	|	1618	|	|	|	|	1804	|	|	|	|	|	|	|	2207	...	|
Exeter St Davids **116** a.	1445	...	1523	1531	1531	1555	1606	1623	1644	1632	1707	1715	1721	1745	1818	1821	1847	1854	1914	1923	2021	2053	2221	...	0036
Exeter St Davids d.	1446	...	1525	1533	1533	1558	1608	1625	1645	1634	...	1717	1723	1747	1833	1823	1849	1856	1916	1925	2022	2055	...	...	0127
Tiverton Parkway d.	|	...	1538	1546	1546	1613	1623	1638	1701	1649	...	1732	1737	1802	|	1838	|	1909	1931	1938	2038	2110	...	...	|
Taunton **137** d.	1511	...	1554	1601	1601	1628	1638	1654	1715	1703	...	1746	1751	1817	1904	1851	1912	1923	1945	1954	2051	2123	...	...	|
Bristol Temple Meads **13** a.	|	...	1627	1653	1653	|	1721	1728	|	1754	...	1825	1827	|	2010	1927	|	1955	|	2027	|	2201	...	...	|
Birmingham New St **127** a.	|	...	1749	1819	1827	|	|	1855	|	|	...	|	1950	|	...	2050	|	2120	|	2155	|	|	...	...	|
Castle Cary **138** d.	1533	...	...	...	...	|	Y	...	1737	Y	...	Y	...	|	...	...	|	...	2007	...	2115	Y	...	...	|
Westbury **138** d.	1551	...	...	...	...	|	|	...	1757	|	...	|	...	1858	...	...	|	...	2027	...	2133	|	...	...	|
Newbury a.	1630	...	...	...	...	|	|	...	1834	|	...	|	...	|	...	...	2023	...	|	...	2211	|	...	...	|
Reading **133** a.	1649	...	...	...	...	1744	1844	...	1852	1915	...	1943	...	1944	...	...	2043	...	2112	...	2229	2329	...	...	0417s
London Paddington **133** a.	1729	...	...	...	...	1829	1921	...	1929	1959	...	2021	...	2029	...	...	2127	...	2159	...	2316	0013	...	...	0505

For notes see page 104.

116 EXMOUTH - EXETER - BARNSTAPLE and PAIGNTON — 2nd class GW

Local trains.

km			⚒	Ⓐ	⚒	⑥	Ⓐ	⑥	Ⓐ	⚒	⑥	Ⓐ	⑥	Ⓐ	⚒	⑥	Ⓐ	⚒	Ⓐ	⑥	⚒	⚒	⑥	Ⓐ	⑥
0	**Exeter** St Davids ... 115 d.	⚒	0611	0720	0750	0856	0916	0956	0956	1056	1156	1156	1256	1303	1356	1430	1456	1556	1626	1656	1726	1826	1916	1928	2007
20	Dawlish ... 115 d.		0631	0740	0810	0928	0936	1016	1016	1116	1216	1228	1316	1324	1427	1445	1516	1616	1646	1716	1753	1846	1936	1948	2036
24	Teignmouth ... 115 d.		0636	0745	0815	0933	0941	1021	1021	1121	1221	1233	1321	1329	1432	1450	1521	1621	1651	1721	1758	1851	1941	1953	2041
32	**Newton Abbot** ... 115 d.		0645	0754	0824	0942	0950	1031	1036	1130	1230	1241	1330	1337	1441	1459	1530	1630	1700	1730	1809	1910	1920	2009	2049
42	Torquay ... 115 d.		0656	0805	0835	0953	1001	1042	1050	1141	1241	1253	1341	1349	1452	1510	1541	1641	1711	1741	1820	1921	2001	2020	2100
45	**Paignton** ... 🚂 115 a.		0706	0814	0844	1003	1010	1052	1059	1151	1251	1300	1351	1358	1500	1518	1551	1651	1720	1751	1830	1931	2009	2029	2108

	⑥	Ⓐ	Ⓐ			⑦	⑦	⑦	⑦		⑦	⑦	⑦	⑦		⑦	⑦	⑦	⑦		⑦	⑦	⑦		⑦
Exeter St Davids ... 115 d.	2056	2129	2237	...	⑦	0905	0953	1105	1135	...	1208	1254	1338	1405	...	1454	1549	1654	1754	...	1854	1959	2058	...	2154
Dawlish ... 115 d.	2116	2149	2303	...		0925	1013	1125	1148	...	1228	1315	1351	1424	...	1513	1615	1714	1814	...	1814	2019	2118	...	2214
Teignmouth ... 115 d.	2121	2154	2308	...		0930	1018	1130	1153	...	1233	1320	1356	1429	...	1518	1620	1719	1819	...	1919	2024	2123	...	2219
Newton Abbot ... 115 d.	2130	2202	2316	...		0947	1035	1139	1201	...	1241	1328	1404	1438	...	1527	1629	1728	1828	...	1928	2033	2132	...	2228
Torquay ... 115 d.	2141	2213	2327	...		0958	1046	1150	1212	...	1252	1339	1416	1449	...	1538	1640	1739	1836	...	1939	2044	2143	...	2239
Paignton ... 🚂 115 a.	2148	2222	2337	...		1005	1055	1157	1219	...	1259	1346	1423	1457	...	1546	1647	1746	1846	...	1946	2051	2150	...	2246

		⚒	⚒	Ⓐ	⑥	Ⓐ	⚒	Ⓐ	⑥	⑥	Ⓐ	⚒	⚒	⑥	Ⓐ	⚒	⚒	Ⓐ	⑥	Ⓐ	⚒	Ⓐ	⑥	⚒	⑥
Paignton ... 🚂 115 d.	⚒	0609	0634	0707	0806	0823	0911	1020	1023	1113	1123	1213	1313	1413	1422	1513	1613	1655	1713	1725	1752	1835	1853	1931	2013
Torquay ... 115 d.		0614	0639	0714	0811	0828	0916	1025	1028	1118	1128	1218	1318	1418	1427	1518	1618	1700	1718	1730	1757	1840	1858	1936	2018
Newton Abbot ... 115 d.		0631	0652	0734	0834	0841	0936	1037	1047	1141	1141	1232	1341	1440	1440	1531	1631	1713	1743	1743	1810	1853	1912	1949	2031
Teignmouth ... 115 d.		0638	0659	0741	0841	0848	0943	1044	1054	1148	1148	1239	1348	1447	1447	1538	1638	1720	1750	1750	1817	1900	1919	1957	2038
Dawlish ... 115 d.		0643	0704	0746	0846	0853	0948	1049	1059	1153	1153	1244	1353	1452	1452	1543	1643	1725	1755	1455	1822	1905	1924	2002	2043
Exeter St Davids ... 115 a.		0708	0733	0810	0909	0915	1014	1113	1115	1216	1216	1313	1416	1515	1515	1618	1713	1750	1818	1818	1846	1933	1945	2026	2105

	Ⓐ	⑥	Ⓐ	⑥	Ⓐ			⑦	⑦	⑦	⑦		⑦	⑦	⑦	⑦		⑦	⑦	⑦	⑦		⑦	⑦	⑦
Paignton ... 🚂 115 d.	2032	2113	2131	2153	2240	...	⑦	1010	1101	1201	1305	...	1404	1434	1508	1610	...	1704	1825	1855	1955	...	2055	2155	2300
Torquay ... 115 d.	2037	2118	2137	2158	2245	...		1015	1106	1206	1310	...	1409	1439	1513	1615	...	1709	1830	1900	2000	...	2100	2200	2305
Newton Abbot ... 115 d.	2050	2131	2152	2211	2258	...		1035	1128	1219	1323	...	1428	1452	1525	1628	...	1729	1841	1913	2013	...	2113	2213	2318
Teignmouth ... 115 d.	2057	2138	*2213*	2218	2305	...		1042	1136	1226	1330	...	1435	1459	1532	1635	...	1736	1849	1920	2020	...	2120	2220	2325
Dawlish ... 115 d.	2102	2143	*2218*	2223	2310	...		1047	1141	1231	1335	...	1440	1504	1537	1640	...	1741	1854	1925	2025	...	2125	2225	2330
Exeter St Davids ... 115 a.	2127	2205	*2240*	2245	2334	...		1110	1203	1307	1357	...	1502	1517	1551	1703	...	1803	1910	1947	2047	...	2147	2247	2352

🚂 – **Paignton – Kingswear** and v.v. (*Paignton and Dartmouth Steam Railway*). *10 km.* ②④⑥⑦ Apr. 1 – Oct. 31 (daily Jun. – Sept.). Paignton station is shared with National Rail services. Connection at Kingswear with ⛴ to Dartmouth, combined ####/⛴ tickets available. Operator: Paignton & Dartmouth Steam Railway. ✆ (0)1803 555872. www.pdsr.co.uk

118 CORNISH BRANCH LINES and BUS CONNECTIONS — 2nd class GW

Rail tickets are generally **not** valid on 🚌 services shown in this table.

PLYMOUTH – GUNNISLAKE #### Journey time ± 45 minutes. *24 km.*

From Plymouth:

⚒: 0512Ⓐ, 0644, 0850⑥, 0857Ⓐ, 1046, 1255, 1447⑥, 1455Ⓐ, 1642, 1823, 2130.

⑦: 0930, 1140, 1345, 1540, 1745.

From Gunnislake:

⚒: 0556Ⓐ, 0732, 0945, 1135, 1345, 1545, 1730, 1915, 2219.

⑦: 1025, 1245, 1445, 1654, 1839.

LISKEARD – LOOE #### Journey time ± 29 minutes. *14 km.*

From Liskeard:

Ⓐ: 0605, 0712, 0837, 1000, 1116, 1214, 1319, 1428, 1540, 1640, 1802, 1917.

⑥: 0604, 0710, 0837, 1000, 1108, 1212, 1324, 1429, 1541, 1657, 1802, 1918.

⑦: *No service.*

From Looe:

Ⓐ: 0637, 0747, 0915, 1032, 1145, 1246, 1351, 1458, 1612, 1715, 1834, 1951.

⑥: 0637, 0744, 0915, 1032, 1137, 1244, 1356, 1458, 1614, 1729, 1834, 1952.

⑦: *No service.*

PAR – NEWQUAY #### Journey time ± 55 minutes. *33 km.*

From Par:

Ⓐ: 0601, 0919, 1211, 1403, 1610, 1829, 2028.

⑥: 0652, 0919, 1215, 1408, 1610, 1821, 2015.

⑦: *No service.*

From Newquay:

Ⓐ: 0657, 1013, 1303, 1458, 1722, 1925, 2126.

⑥: 0748, 1013, 1309, 1459, 1721, 1921, 2115.

⑦: *No service.*

TRURO – FALMOUTH DOCKS #### Journey time ± 23 minutes. *20 km.*

From Truro:

Ⓐ: 0610, 0637, 0716, 0748, 0820, 0850 and every 30 minutes until 1650; then 1727, 1758, 1829, 1900, 2001, 2103, 2206.

⑥: 0610, 0637, 0717, 0748, 0820, 0850 and every 30 minutes until 1650; then 1727, 1758, 1829, 1900, 2001, 2103, 2206.

⑦: 1045, 1215, 1337, 1431, 1535, 1700, 1806, 1948, 2105, 2204.

From Falmouth Docks:

Ⓐ: 0637, 0717, 0748, 0820, 0850 and every 30 minutes until 1650; then 1727, 1758, 1829, 1900, 1927, 2029, 2130, 2233.

⑥: 0637, 0717, 0748, 0820, 0850 and every 30 minutes until 1650; then 1727, 1758, 1829, 1900, 1927, 2029, 2130, 2233.

⑦: 1112, 1244, 1403, 1457, 1600, 1730, 1837, 2015, 2131, 2235.

ST ERTH – ST IVES #### Journey time ± 14 minutes. *7 km.*

From St Erth:

Ⓐ: 0645**p**, 0714, 0805, 0905**p**, 0938, 1011 and every 30 minutes until 2041; then 2138.

⑥: 0645**p**, 0714, 0801, 0905**p**, 0938, 1011 and every 30 minutes until 1711; then 1759, 1858**p**, 1950, 2046, 2146.

⑦: 1155**p**, 1234, 1311 and every 30 minutes until 1741; then 1830, 1930.

From St Ives:

Ⓐ: 0659, 0728, 0819**q**, 0922, 0953, 1025 and every 30 minutes until 2055; then 2154**q**.

⑥: 0659, 0728, 0815**q**, 0922, 0953, 1025 and every 30 minutes until 1625; then 1657, 1727, 1817, 1928, 2010, 2112, 2202**q**.

⑦: 1211, 1249, 1325 and every 30 minutes until 1725; then 1757, 1850, 1950.

p – (2) Penzance - St Ives (departs Penzance 8 minutes earlier).

q – (2) St Ives - Penzance (journey time St Ives - Penzance: ± 25 minutes).

BODMIN PARKWAY – PADSTOW 🚌 service 555 Journey time ± 62 minutes. Operator: Western Greyhound.

From Bodmin Parkway. Buses call at **Wadebridge** 30 minutes later:

⚒: 0725, 0830 and hourly until 1930; then 2200.

⑦: 0930, 1130, 1330, 1530, 1730, 1930.

From Padstow. Buses call at **Wadebridge** 25 minutes later:

⚒: 0630 and hourly until 1830; then 2030.

⑦: 0830, 1030, 1230, 1430, 1630, 1830.

ST AUSTELL – EDEN PROJECT 🚌 service T9 Journey time ± 20 minutes. Operator: First Truronian.

From St Austell Railway Station:

Ⓐ: 0835, 0850, 0930, 0935, 1030, 1035, 1055, 1135, 1140, 1235, 1240, 1310, 1335, 1350, 1435, 1515, 1535, 1550, 1635, 1650, 1730.

⑥: 0850, 0930, 1030, 1140, 1240, 1250, 1350, 1535, 1550, 1635, 1650, 1720, 1730.

⑦: 0850, 1000, 1040, 1135, 1230, 1335, 1500, 1520, 1540, 1630, 1635, 1720, 1735.

From Eden Project:

Ⓐ: 0900, 0910, 0950, 1000, 1100, 1200, 1210, 1300, 1310, 1400, 1500, 1505, 1600, 1630, 1700, 1710, 1800.

⑥: 0910, 0950, 1100, 1210, 1310, 1420, 1505, 1630, 1700, 1710, 1800.

⑦: 1010, 1020, 1100, 1155, 1250, 1440, 1520, 1615, 1635, 1700, 1710, 1750, 1800.

XC CARDIFF - GLOUCESTER - BIRMINGHAM - NOTTINGHAM 121

Services on ⑦ valid until March 28. For faster services Birmingham – Derby and v.v. see Table 127.

km			⚒	⚒	⚒	⚒		⑥	Ⓐ	⚒	⚒		⚒ A	⚒	⚒	⚒		⚒	⚒	⚒	⚒		⚒		⚒
0	**Cardiff** Central .... 133 d.	⚒	...	...	...	...	...	...	...	0640	...	...	0700	0745	...	0845	...	...	0945	...	1045	...	...	...	1145
19	Newport .... 133 d.		...	...	...	...	...	...	...	0655	...	...	0715	0800	...	0902	...	...	1000	...	1100	...	...	...	1200
91	**Gloucester** .... 133 d.		...	...	...	...	...	0706	0710	0746	...	...	|	0846	...	0946	...	...	1046	...	1146	...	...	...	1246
101	Cheltenham .... 133 d.		...	...	...	...	...	0718	0721	0757	...	...	0842	0857	...	0957	...	...	1057	...	1157	...	...	...	1357
174	**Birmingham** New St .... a.		...	...	...	...	...	0808	0816	0845	...	...	0926	0945	...	1045	...	...	1145	...	1245	...	...	...	1345
174	**Birmingham** New St .... 127 d.		0619	0649	0719	0749	...	0819	0819	0849	0919	...	...	0949	1019	1049	...	1119	1149	1219	1249	...	1319	...	1349
202	Tamworth .... 127 d.		0639	0707	0738	0807	...	0837	0837	0907	0939	...	...	1007	1037	1107	...	1139	1207	1237	1307	...	1339	...	1407
222	Burton on Trent .... 127 d.		0651	0719	0750	0819	...	0849	0849	0919	0951	...	...	1019	1049	1119	...	1151	1219	1249	1319	...	1351	...	1419
241	Derby .... 127 170 a.		0706	0737	0805	0834	...	0905	0905	0934	1006	...	...	1036	1105	1134	...	1205	1236	1305	1335	...	1405	...	1435
267	**Nottingham** .... 170 a.		0741	0808	0834	0905	...	0936	0935	1005	1033	...	...	1105	1133	1205	...	1233	1305	1335	1405	...	1435	...	1505

	⚒	⚒		⚒	⚒	⚒	⚒		⚒	⚒	⚒		⚒	⚒	⚒	⑥	Ⓐ	Ⓐ		Ⓐ	⑥	Ⓐ		⑥	Ⓐ
Cardiff Central .... 133 d.	...	1245	...	...	1345	...	1445	...	...	1545	...	...	1645	...	1745	1945	1845	1950	...	...	2000	...	...	2050	2105
Newport .... 133 d.	...	1301	...	...	1400	...	1501	...	...	1600	...	...	1700	...	1800	1901	1901	2005	...	...	2015	...	...	2105	2120
Gloucester .... 133 d.	...	1346	...	...	1446	...	1546	...	...	1646	...	...	1746	...	1846	1946	1946	2058	...	...	2107	...	...	2149	2206
Cheltenham .... 133 d.	...	1357	...	...	1457	...	1557	...	...	1657	...	...	1757	...	1857	1957	1957	2109	...	...	2118	...	...	2200	2217
Birmingham New St .... a.	...	1445	...	...	1545	...	1645	...	...	1745	...	...	1845	...	1945	2040	2045	2153	...	...	2207	...	...	2242	2327
Birmingham New St .... 127 d.	1419	1449	...	1519	1549	1619	1649	...	1719	1749	1819	...	1849	1919	1949	2049	2049	...	...	2202	2210	2309	...	...	...
Tamworth .... 127 d.	1437	1507	...	1539	1607	1637	1707	...	1739	1807	1837	...	1907	1939	2007	2108	2109	...	...	2228	2228	2328	...	...	...
Burton on Trent .... 127 d.	1449	1519	...	1551	1619	1649	1719	...	1751	1819	1849	...	1919	1951	2019	2120	2121	...	...	2240	2239	2340	...	...	...
Derby .... 127 170 a.	1505	1534	...	1605	1634	1705	1734	...	1805	1835	1905	...	1934	2005	2034	2135	2136	...	...	2254	2255	2355	...	...	...
Nottingham .... 170 a.	1533	1605	...	1633	1705	1733	1805	...	1833	1905	1935	...	2005	2035	2106	2208	2208	...	...	2327	2328	0018	...	...	...

		⑦		⑦		⑦		⑦		⑦		⑦		⑦		⑦		⑦		⑦		⑦		⑦	
Cardiff Central .... 133 d.	⑦	...	...	1045	...	1145	...	1245	...	1345	...	1445	...	1545	...	1645	...	1745	...	1845	...	1945	...	2045	...
Newport .... 133 d.		...	...	1059	...	1159	...	1259	...	1359	...	1459	...	1559	...	1659	...	1759	...	1859	...	2000	...	2059	...
Gloucester .... 133 d.		...	...	1152	...	1247	...	1351	...	1447	...	1547	...	1647	...	1747	...	1847	...	1950	...	2050	...	2147	...
Cheltenham .... 133 d.		...	...	1203	...	1258	...	1402	...	1458	...	1558	...	1658	...	1758	...	1858	...	2000	...	2100	...	2158	...
Birmingham New St .... a.		...	...	1245	...	1341	...	1445	...	1541	...	1641	...	1741	...	1841	...	1941	...	2042	...	2145	...	2241	...
Birmingham New St .... 127 d.		1149	...	1249	...	1349	...	1449	...	1549	...	1649	...	1749	...	1849	...	1949	...	...	...	...	...	...	...
Tamworth .... 127 d.		1207	...	1307	...	1407	...	1509	...	1607	...	1707	...	1807	...	1909	...	2007	...	...	...	...	...	...	...
Burton on Trent .... 127 d.		1219	...	1319	...	1419	...	1521	...	1619	...	1719	...	1819	...	1921	...	2019	...	...	...	...	...	...	...
Derby .... 127 170 a.		1234	...	1338	...	1434	...	1534	...	1635	...	1735	...	1834	...	1934	...	2034	...	...	...	...	...	...	...
Nottingham .... 170 a.		1302	...	1404	...	1507	...	1608	...	1703	...	1802	...	1909	...	2003	...	2101	...	...	...	...	...	...	...

		Ⓐ	⑥ y	⑥ Az	⑥ y	Ⓐ	⚒ B		⑥	Ⓐ	⚒	⑥	Ⓐ	⚒		⑥ y	Ⓐ	⚒	⑥	Ⓐ	⚒		Ⓐ	⑥	⚒
Nottingham .... 170 d.	⚒	...	...	...	0557	0600	0637	...	0656	0656	0735	0808	0808	0837	...	0908	0911	0937	1008	1011	1037	...	1108	1111	1137
Derby .... 127 170 d.		...	...	...	0636	0636	0706	...	0736	0736	0803	0835	0836	0906	...	0936	0936	1006	1036	1037	1106	...	1136	1136	1206
Burton on Trent .... 127 d.		...	...	...	0648	0648	0718	...	0749	0749	0818	0848	0849	0918	...	0948	0949	1018	1048	1049	1118	...	1149	1148	1218
Tamworth .... 127 d.		...	...	0649	0700	0700	0730	...	0801	0801	0830	0900	0901	0930	...	1000	1001	1030	1100	1101	1130	...	1201	1200	1230
Birmingham New St .... 127 a.		...	...	0707	0724	0724	0755	...	0824	0824	0854	0924	0924	0954	...	1024	1024	1054	1124	1124	1154	...	1224	1224	1254
Birmingham New St .... d.		0542	0542	0719	0730	0730	...	...	0830	0830	...	0930	0930	...	...	1030	1030	...	1130	1130	...	...	1230	1230	...
Cheltenham .... 133 d.		0643	0643	0739	0811	0816	...	...	0911	0911	...	1011	1011	...	...	1112	1111	...	1211	1211	...	...	1311	1311	...
Gloucester .... 133 a.		0654	0654	0744	0822	0827	...	...	0922	0922	...	1022	1022	...	...	1123	1122	...	1222	1222	...	...	1322	1322	...
Newport .... 133 a.		0752	0752	0802	0907	0912	...	...	1005	1009	...	1105	1111	...	...	1206	1211	...	1306	1311	...	...	1409	1405	...
Cardiff Central .... 133 a.		0808	0808	0808	0923	0930	...	...	1021	1025	...	1123	1127	...	...	1222	1229	...	1322	1329	...	...	1427	1421	...

	⑥	Ⓐ	⚒	⑥	Ⓐ		⚒	⑥	Ⓐ	⚒	⑥	Ⓐ	⚒	⑥	Ⓐ		⚒	⑥	Ⓐ	Ⓐ A	⚒	⚒	⚒		Ⓐ
Nottingham .... 170 d.	1208	1208	1237	1308	1311	...	1337	1408	1408	1437	1508	1511	1537	1608	1608	...	1637	1708	1708	...	1737	1808	1837	...	1908
Derby .... 127 170 d.	1236	1237	1306	1336	1336	...	1406	1436	1436	1506	1536	1536	1606	1636	1636	...	1706	1736	1736	...	1805	1837	1906	...	1936
Burton on Trent .... 127 d.	1248	1249	1320	1348	1349	...	1418	1448	1449	1518	1548	1549	1618	1648	1649	...	1718	1748	1749	...	1820	1849	1918	...	1949
Tamworth .... 127 d.	1300	1301	1333	1400	1401	...	1430	1500	1501	1530	1600	1601	1630	1700	1701	...	1730	1800	1804	...	1833	1900	1930	...	2001
Birmingham New St .... 127 a.	1324	1324	1354	1424	1424	...	1454	1524	1524	1554	1624	1624	1654	1724	1725	...	1754	1824	1825	...	1857	1924	1954	...	2024
Birmingham New St .... d.	1330	1330	...	1430	1430	...	...	1530	1530	...	1630	1630	...	1730	1730	...	...	1830	1830	1842	...	1930	...	...	2030
Cheltenham .... 133 d.	1411	1411	...	1511	1511	...	...	1611	1611	...	1711	1715	...	1818	1818	...	...	1911	1915	1925	...	2011	...	...	2111
Gloucester .... 133 a.	1422	1422	...	1522	1522	...	...	1622	1622	...	1722	1726	...	1829	1830	...	...	1922	1927	|	...	2022	...	...	2122
Newport .... 133 a.	1506	1512	...	1606	1610	...	...	1706	1711	...	1805	1810	...	1912	1916	...	...	2005	2012	2047	...	2110	...	...	2215
Cardiff Central .... 133 a.	1522	1529	...	1622	1629	...	...	1724	1728	...	1821	1827	...	1929	1933	...	...	2021	2031	2102	...	2128	...	...	2235

	⑥		⚒	⚒	⚒			⑦	⑦		⑦	⑦	⑦	⑦		⑦	⑦	⑦	⑦		⑦		⑦		⑦
Nottingham .... 170 d.	1908	...	1937	2036	2137	...	⑦	...	...	...	1110	1210	1303	1410	...	1505	1605	1710	1805	...	1910	...	2010	...	2108
Derby .... 127 170 d.	1936	...	2005	2106	2210	...		...	...	...	1136	1235	1356	1435	...	1535	1635	1735	1834	...	1933	...	2035	...	2135
Burton on Trent .... 127 d.	1948	...	2018	2120	2221	...		...	...	...	1148	1248	1348	1448	...	1548	1648	1748	1848	...	1948	...	2048	...	2148
Tamworth .... 127 d.	2000	...	2030	2133	2233	...		...	...	...	1200	1300	1400	1500	...	1600	1700	1800	1900	...	2000	...	2100	...	2200
Birmingham New St .... 127 a.	2024	...	2057	2158	2302	...		...	...	...	1226	1322	1422	1521	...	1623	1721	1821	1921	...	2023	...	2118	...	2223
Birmingham New St .... d.	2030	...	...	...	...	...		1030	1130	...	1230	1330	1430	1530	...	1630	1730	1830	1930	...	...	...	...	...	...
Cheltenham .... 133 d.	2111	...	...	...	...	...		1111	1211	...	1311	1412	1511	1611	...	1711	1811	1912	2011	...	...	...	...	...	...
Gloucester .... 133 a.	2122	...	...	...	...	...		1121	1221	...	1321	1422	1522	1621	...	1721	1821	1922	2021	...	...	...	...	...	...
Newport .... 133 a.	2221	...	...	...	...	...		1206	1306	...	1406	1507	1610	1706	...	1806	1906	2007	2106	...	...	...	...	...	...
Cardiff Central .... 133 a.	2244	...	...	...	...	...		1226	1326	...	1426	1528	1631	1726	...	1828	1926	2027	2126	...	...	...	...	...	...

CARDIFF – GLOUCESTER – CHELTENHAM

2nd class AW

km	Operator		⚒	⚒	⚒	⚒	⚒	⚒	⚒	Ⓐ F	⑥	⚒	⚒	Ⓐ	Ⓐ			⑦	⑦	⑦	⑦	⑦	⑦		⑦
0	**Cardiff** Central .... 133 d.	⚒	0612	0712	0912	1012	1212	1312	1512	1605	1612	1712	1812	2112	2320	...	⑦	1024	1224	1424	1624	1824	2024	...	2230
19	Newport .... 133 d.		0627	0727	0927	1027	1227	1327	1527	1621	1627	1727	1827	2127	2340	...		1039	1239	1439	1639	1839	2039	...	2249
36	Caldicot .... d.		0640	0740	0940	1040	1240	1340	1540	1633	1640	1740	1840	2140	2359	...		1059	1259	1459	1659	1859	2059	...	2309
47	Chepstow .... d.		0649	0749	0949	1049	1249	1349	1549	1642	1649	1749	1849	2149	0008	...		1108	1308	1508	1708	1908	2108	...	2318
59	Lydney Junction .... 🚂 d.		0658	0758	0958	1058	1258	1358	1558	1651	1658	1758	1858	2158	0017	...		1117	1317	1517	1717	1917	2117	...	2327
91	**Gloucester** .... 133 a.		0720	0820	1020	1120	1320	1420	1620	1716	1720	1820	1920	2221	0042	...		1138	1338	1538	1738	1938	2138	...	2351
101	**Cheltenham** .... 133 a.		0734	0834	1034	1134	1334	1434	1634	1734	1734	1834	1934	2236	...	...		1159	1357	1552	1752	1952	...	...	...

Operator		Ⓐ	⑥	⚒	⚒	⚒	⚒	⚒	⚒	⚒	⚒	⚒	⚒	⑥	Ⓐ			⑦	⑦	⑦		⑦	⑦	⑦	⑦
Cheltenham .... 133 d.	⚒	0537	...	0745	0845	1045	1145	1345	1445	1645	1745	1845	1945	...	2300	...	⑦	...	1218	1418	...	1618	1818	2018	...
Gloucester .... 133 d.		0550	0550	0758	0858	1058	1158	1358	1458	1658	1758	1858	1958	2309	2313	...		1033	1233	1433	...	1637	1833	2033	2233
Lydney Junction .... 🚂 d.		0609	0609	0817	0917	1117	1217	1417	1517	1717	1817	1917	2017	2328	2333	...		1052	1252	1452	...	1656	1852	2052	2252
Chepstow .... d.		0619	0619	0827	0927	1127	1227	1427	1527	1727	1827	1927	2027	2338	2342	...		1102	1302	1502	...	1706	1902	2102	2302
Caldicot .... d.		0626	0626	0835	0935	1135	1235	1435	1535	1735	1835	1935	2035	2346	2351	...		1110	1310	1510	...	1713	1909	2110	2312
Newport .... 133 a.		0642	0642	0850	0950	1150	1250	1450	1550	1750	1850	1950	2051	0009	0012	...		1131	1332	1531	...	1735	1931	2131	2331
Cardiff Central .... 133 a.		0700	0700	0907	1007	1207	1307	1507	1610	1810	1910	2010	2110	0034	0034	...		1148	1350	1549	...	1755	1948	2148	2354

A – Via Bristol, Table **127**.
B – To Bournemouth, Table **129**.
F – From Fishguard, Table **135**.

y – ⑥ Dec. 12 – Jan. 30 and Apr. 3 – May 16.
z – ⑥ Feb. 6 – Mar. 27.

🚂 – **Lydney Junction – Parkend** (*Dean Forest Railway*). *7 km.* ③⑥⑦ Jun. 3 – Sept. 30 and certain other dates throughout the year. Lydney Junction station is shared with National Rail services. Operator: Dean Forest Railway. ✆ 01594 845840. www.deanforestrailway.co.uk

123 STRATFORD UPON AVON - BIRMINGHAM - WORCESTER - HEREFORD 2nd class LM

For additional services Worcester Shrub Hill – Hereford and v.v., see Table **131**.

BIRMINGHAM - BROMSGROVE - WORCESTER - HEREFORD

km		Ⓐ	Ⓐ	Ⓐ	Ⓐ	Ⓐ	Ⓐ	Ⓐ	Ⓐ	Ⓐ	Ⓐ	Ⓐ	Ⓐ	Ⓐ	Ⓐ	Ⓐ	Ⓐ	Ⓐ	Ⓐ	Ⓐ	Ⓐ	Ⓐ		⑥	⑥
0	**Birmingham** New St ... d.		...	0659	0759	0849	0949	1049	1149	1249	1349	1449	1549	1649	1719	1749	1819	1919	1949	2059	2200	2300	...		...
21	Bromsgrove ... d.		...	0723	0821	0911	1011	1111	1211	1311	1413	1511	1611	1711	1745	|	1846	1940	2009	2123	2223	2320	...		...
32	Droitwich ... d.		...	0733	0831	0921	1023	1122	1221	1322	1423	1521	1621	1722	1755	1819	1856	1950	2025	2133	2234	2330	...		...
41	Worcester Shrub Hill ... a.		0600	|	|	|	|	|	|	|	|	|	|	1729	1804	1828	1911	2001	2034	|	2248	2339	...		0630
41	Worcester Foregate St ... a.		0602	0741	0839	0929	1031	1131	1230	1330	1431	1531	1631	1735	1811	1834	*1948*	2014	*2045*	2141	*2307*	...	...		0632
54	Great Malvern ... a.		0615	0754	0852	0942	1045	1144	1242	1343	1445	1544	1644	1747	1824	1847	*2002*	2026	*2058*	2154	*2319*	...	...		0644
65	Ledbury ... a.		0627	0813	0906	0956	1058	1158	1256	1357	1457	1558	1658	1801	1836	1901	*2016*	2040	*2112*	2210	...	...	...		0657
87	**Hereford** ... a.		0650	0834	0930	1019	1120	1222	1318	1422	1519	1622	1720	1823	1857	1926	*2034*	2100	*2133*	2232	...	...	...		0714

	⑥	⑥	⑥	⑥	⑥	⑥	⑥	⑥	⑥	⑥	⑥	⑥	⑥	⑥	⑥		⑦	⑦		⑦		⑦	⑦		⑦
Birmingham New St ... d.	0649	0749	0849	0949	1049	1149	1249	1349	1449	1549	1649	1749	1849	1919	2059	...		1324	...	1600	...	1800	1900	...	2100
Bromsgrove ... d.	0711	0811	0911	1011	1111	1211	1311	1411	1511	1611	1711	1811	1911	1942	2121	...		1342	...	1621	...	1821	1921	...	2121
Droitwich ... d.	0721	0821	0921	1021	1121	1221	1321	1421	1521	1621	1721	1819	1921	1957	2131	...		1352	...	1630	...	1830	1931	...	2131
Worcester Shrub Hill ... a.	|	|	|	|	|	|	|	|	|	|	|	1827	1928	|	|	...		1359	...	1641	...	1838	1941	...	2138
Worcester Foregate St ... a.	0729	0829	0929	1029	1129	1229	1329	1429	1529	1629	1729	1833	1935	2005	2139	...		1423	...	1646	...	1844	...	...	2144
Great Malvern ... a.	0741	0842	0942	1042	1142	1242	1342	1442	1542	1642	1742	1846	1950	2018	2154	...		1435	...	1701	...	1856	...	...	2157
Ledbury ... a.	0755	0856	0956	1056	1156	1257	1356	1456	1556	1656	1755	1859	...	2038	2213	...		1448	...	*1742*	...	1910	...	...	2210
Hereford ... a.	0821	0920	1021	1120	1221	1320	1421	1518	1619	1720	1821	1920	...	2103	2234	...		1510	...	*1801*	...	1931	...	...	2230

	Ⓐ	Ⓐ	Ⓐ	Ⓐ	Ⓐ	Ⓐ	Ⓐ	Ⓐ	Ⓐ	Ⓐ	Ⓐ	Ⓐ	Ⓐ	Ⓐ	Ⓐ	Ⓐ	Ⓐ	Ⓐ	Ⓐ	Ⓐ		⑥	⑥	⑥	⑥
Hereford ... d.		...	...	...	0708	0734	...	0849	0940	1040	1140	1239	1341	1440	1540	1640	1740	1848	1950	2130	...		...	...	0740
Ledbury ... d.		...	...	...	0724	0751	...	0908	0958	1059	1157	1300	1359	1459	1600	1659	1801	1904	2018	2147	...		...	...	0758
Great Malvern ... d.		0550	0648	0705	0739	0803	0838	0919	1010	1110	1211	1311	1411	1510	1611	1710	1813	1915	2029	2158	...		0620	...	0810
Worcester Foregate St ... d.		0602	0659	0717	0751	0819	0851	0931	1023	1123	1223	1323	1423	1523	1623	1724	1825	1927	2042	2210	...		0631	...	0822
Worcester Shrub Hill ... d.		|	0706	0724	0757	|	|	0937	|	|	|	|	|	|	|	|	|	|	|	|	...		|	0733	|
Droitwich ... d.		0612	0714	0732	0805	0830	0900	0945	1033	1133	1233	1332	1432	1533	1633	1733	1834	1936	2049	2217	...		0640	0740	0831
Bromsgrove ... d.		0621	0725	|	|	0841	0909	0954	1042	1142	1242	1342	1442	1542	1642	1743	1842	1946	2059	2228	...		0650	0750	0840
Birmingham New St ... a.		0645	0745	0809	0837	0907	0942	1024	1113	1213	1313	1413	1513	1613	1713	1813	1912	2020	2123	2252	...		0716	0816	0911

	⑥	⑥	⑥	⑥	⑥	⑥	⑥	⑥	⑥	⑥	⑥	⑥	⑥	⑥		⑦	⑦		⑦		⑦		⑦		⑦
Hereford ... d.	0840	0936	1040	1140	1240	1340	1440	1540	1640	1740	1911	2000	2133	2243	...		...	...	1530	...	*1633*	...	*1830*	...	2005
Ledbury ... d.	0858	0958	1058	1158	1258	1358	1457	1558	1658	1758	1928	2016	2149	2302	...		...	...	1551	...	*1652*	...	*1848*	...	2021
Great Malvern ... d.	0910	1010	1110	1210	1310	1410	1510	1610	1710	1810	1940	2028	2200	2314	...		1435	...	1603	...	1716	...	*1911*	...	2032
Worcester Foregate St ... d.	0922	1022	1122	1222	1322	1422	1522	1622	1722	1824	1951	2042	2218	2325	...		1445	...	1615	...	1728	...	*1823*	...	2044
Worcester Shrub Hill ... d.	|	|	|	|	|	|	|	|	|	|	...	|	2220	2331	...		1451	...	1633	...	1734	...	1953	...	2050
Droitwich ... d.	0931	1033	1133	1233	1333	1433	1533	1633	1734	1835	...	2049	...	...	...		1459	...	1641	...	1742	...	2001	...	2058
Bromsgrove ... d.	0940	1042	1142	1242	1342	1442	1542	1642	1743	1844	...	2059	...	...	...		1509	...	1651	...	1752	...	2010	...	2108
Birmingham New St ... a.	1011	1111	1211	1311	1411	1511	1611	1711	1811	1911	...	2122	...	...	...		1537	...	1717	...	1813	...	2036	...	2142

STRATFORD UPON AVON - BIRMINGHAM - KIDDERMINSTER - WORCESTER

km		⚒	Ⓐ	⑥	Ⓐ	⑥	Ⓐ	Ⓐ	⑥	Ⓐ	⑥	Ⓐ	⑥	Ⓐ	⑥	⚒	⚒	⚒	⚒	⚒	⚒	⚒	⚒	⑥	Ⓐ
	Stratford upon Avon ... d.		...	...	...	...	...	0631	...	0654	0700	0723	0745	0745	...	...	0827	...	0927	...	1027	...	1127	...	...
	Henley in Arden ... d.		...	...	...	...	...	0645	...	0709	0714	0734	0759	0759	...	...	0841	...	0941	...	1041	...	1141	...	...
	Birmingham Moor St ... d.		0616	0631	0648	0701	0719	0723	0750	0748	0755	0807	0838	0839	0844	0909	0917	1009	1017	1109	1117	1209	1217	1309	1309
0	**Birmingham** Snow Hill ... d.		0620	0635	0653	0705	0723	0727	0753	0753	0757	0811	0842	0843	0853	0913	0920	1013	1020	1113	1120	1213	1220	1313	1313
30	Kidderminster ... d.		0700	0716	0735	0746	0803	...	0829	0831	...	...	...	0920	0929	0949	...	1049	...	1149	...	1249	...	1349	1351
45	Droitwich ... d.		0712	0729	0747	0758	0817	...	0840	0844	...	...	...	0932	0940	1001	...	1101	...	1201	...	1301	...	1401	1403
54	**Worcester** Shrub Hill ... a.		|	0739	|	0806	0824	...	|	|	...	...	...	0942	0949	|	...	|	...	|	...	|	...	|	1411
54	**Worcester** Foregate St ... a.		0722	...	0757	0812	0830	...	0849	0859	...	...	...	...	...	1011	...	1110	...	1211	...	1310	...	1409	...

	⚒	⚒	⚒	Ⓐ	⑥	⚒	⚒	⚒	⑥	Ⓐ	Ⓐ	⑥	Ⓐ	Ⓐ	⑥		Ⓐ	⑥	⑥	Ⓐ	⚒	⑥	Ⓐ	⑥	Ⓐ
Stratford upon Avon ... d.	1227	...	1327	...	...	1427	...	1527	...	...	1623	1627	...	1727	1727	...	1758	...	1808	1826	...	1847	1850	...	...
Henley in Arden ... d.	1241	...	1341	...	...	1441	...	1541	...	...	1638	1641	...	1741	1741	...	1808	...	1822	1840	...	1901	1904	...	...
Birmingham Moor St ... d.	1317	1409	1417	1509	1509	1517	1609	1617	1709	1709	1717	1717	1750	1817	1817	...	1839	1851	1902	1917	1923	1940	1932	1951	1953
Birmingham Snow Hill ... d.	1320	1413	1421	1513	1513	1521	1613	1621	1713	1713	1721	1721	1753	1823	1823	...	1843	1857	1904	1919	1927	1943	1935	1955	1957
Kidderminster 🚂 ... d.	...	1449	...	1551	1549	...	1649	...	1749	1754	...	...	1832	1906	1859	...	1920	1937	...	...	2007	...	...	2035	2037
Droitwich ... d.	...	1501	...	1603	1601	...	1701	...	1803	1806	...	...	1846	...	1913	...	1932	1949	...	...	2019	...	...	2047	2050
Worcester Shrub Hill ... a.	...	|	...	1611	|	...	|	...	1814	1818	...	...	1858	...	|	...	|	1957	...	...	2029	...	...	2054	2100
Worcester Foregate St ... a.	...	1509	...	...	1609	...	1712	...	...	...	...	...	...	...	1921	...	1941	...	...	...	...	...	...	2100	...

	⚒	⚒	⚒	⑥	Ⓐ	⑥	Ⓐ		⑦	⑦		⑦	⑦	⑦	⑦	⑦	⑦	⑦	⑦	⑦	⑦	⑦	⑦		⑦
Stratford upon Avon ... d.	1927	...	2027	...	...	...	...	...		...	...	0928	1028	1128	1230	1328	1428	1528	1628	1728	1828	1928	...	...	...
Henley in Arden ... d.	1941	...	2041	...	...	...	...	...		...	...	0940	1040	1140	1242	1340	1440	1540	1640	1740	1840	1940	...	...	...
Birmingham Moor St ... d.	2017	2051	2117	2151	2154	2251	2256	...		0926	...	1013	1113	1213	1315	1413	1513	1613	1713	1813	1913	2013	2135	...	2252
Birmingham Snow Hill ... d.	2020	2055	2120	2155	2157	2256	2300	...		0930	...	1018	1118	1218	1320	1418	1518	1618	1720	1818	1918	2018	2145	...	2255
Kidderminster 🚂 ... d.	...	2136	...	2235	2238	2337	2340	...		1004	...	1052	1155	1254	1355	1454	1552	1652	1754	1855	1952	2053	2218	...	2329
Droitwich ... d.	...	2147	...	2246	2249	2348	2352	...		1015	...	1104	1206	1306	1407	1506	1604	1704	1806	1906	2008	2105	2230	...	2340
Worcester Shrub Hill ... a.	...	2158	...	2255	2257	2356	0001	...		1023	...	1111	1214	1313	|	|	|	|	1813	1914	2015	2125	2237	...	2348
Worcester Foregate St ... a.	...	...	...	2300	2307	...	...	...		1029	...	1127	...	1331	1420	1514	1612	1712	...	...	...	2131	2243	...	...

	⚒	Ⓐ	⑥	Ⓐ	Ⓐ	⑥	Ⓐ	⑥	Ⓐ	⑥	Ⓐ	⑥	⚒	Ⓐ	⑥	⚒	⚒	⚒	⚒	⚒	⑥	Ⓐ	⚒	⚒	⚒
Worcester Foregate St ... d.		...	...	...	...	...	...	...	...	0743	0804	...	...	0835	0856	...	...	...	...	...	1147	1150	...	1246	...
Worcester Shrub Hill ... d.		0530	...	0615	0647	0658	0715	...	...	|	|	0814	...	0843	|	...	0947	...	1047	...	|	|	...	|	...
Droitwich ... d.		0538	...	0623	0655	0706	0723	...	...	0752	0811	0822	...	0851	0905	...	0955	...	1055	...	1156	1158	...	1255	...
Kidderminster 🚂 ... d.		0548	...	0638	0709	0722	0737	0746	...	0806	0822	0836	...	0906	0916	...	1006	...	1106	...	1206	1210	...	1306	...
Birmingham Snow Hill ... d.		0629	0720	0725	0750	0807	0817	0827	0827	0847	0907	0917	0927	0947	0957	1027	1047	1127	1147	1227	1247	1247	1327	1347	1427
Birmingham Moor St ... d.		0632	0723	0728	0753	0810	0820	0830	0830	0850	0910	0920	0930	0950	1000	1030	1050	1130	1150	1230	1250	1250	1330	1350	1430
Henley in Arden ... d.		0703	0801	0806	...	...	...	0905	0905	...	...	...	1005	...	...	1105	...	1205	...	1305	...	...	1405	...	1505
Stratford upon Avon ... a.		0715	0817	0820	...	...	...	0921	0919	...	...	...	1021	...	...	1121	...	1221	...	1321	...	...	1421	...	1521

	Ⓐ	⑥	⚒	⚒	⚒	Ⓐ	⑥	Ⓐ	⑥	Ⓐ	Ⓐ	⑥	⚒	⑥	Ⓐ	⚒	Ⓐ	⑥	Ⓐ	⑥	Ⓐ	⑥	⑥	Ⓐ	Ⓐ
Worcester Foregate St ... d.	...	1347	...	...	...	1540	1546	...	...	...	1647	...	...	1748	1755	...	1847	1849	...	...	1945	1952	...	...	...
Worcester Shrub Hill ... d.	1347	|	...	1443	...	1547	|	...	...	...	|	1647	...	|	|	...	|	|	...	...	|	|	2052	2053	2152
Droitwich ... d.	1355	1356	...	1455	...	1555	1555	...	...	...	1656	1655	...	1757	1804	...	1856	1858	...	...	1954	2001	2100	2101	2200
Kidderminster 🚂 ... d.	1406	1406	...	1506	...	1606	1606	1623	1626	...	1706	1706	...	1807	1817	...	1910	1911	...	1940	2010	2011	2111	2111	2210
Birmingham Snow Hill ... d.	1447	1447	1525	1547	1627	1647	1647	1702	1707	1727	1747	1747	1827	1847	1857	1927	1955	1955	2027	2023	2055	2054	2155	2155	2257
Birmingham Moor St ... d.	1450	1450	1528	1550	1630	1650	1650	1705	1710	1730	1750	1750	1830	1850	1900	1930	1958	1958	2030	2030	2058	2058	2158	2158	2300
Henley in Arden ... d.	...	...	1604	...	1706	...	...	1735	1748	1806	1828	1828	1905	...	...	2008	...	...	2108	2108	...	...	...	...	...
Stratford upon Avon ... a.	...	...	1621	...	1722	...	...	1749	1803	1822	1845	1843	1923	...	...	2023	...	...	2123	2123	...	...	...	...	...

	⑥	Ⓐ	⑥		⑦	⑦	⑦		⑦	⑦	⑦	⑦		⑦	⑦	⑦	⑦		⑦	⑦	⑦	⑦		⑦	⑦
Worcester Foregate St ... d.	2142	2217	...	...		...	...	...	1016	1120	1216	1320	...	1420	1520	...	1620	...	1720	1820	...	...	...	...	2217
Worcester Shrub Hill ... d.	2152	2227	2248	...		...	0921	...	1022	|	1224	|	...	|	|	1546	|	...	|	|	1938	2034	...	2122	2226
Droitwich ... d.	2200	2235	2256	...		...	0932	...	1030	1129	1232	1329	...	1429	1529	1554	1629	...	1729	1829	1946	2042	...	2130	2234
Kidderminster 🚂 ... d.	2210	2245	2306	...		...	0942	...	1040	1139	1242	1339	...	1439	1539	1604	1639	...	1739	1839	1956	2052	...	2141	2244
Birmingham Snow Hill ... d.	2255	2325	2338	...		0919	1022	...	1118	1219	1322	1419	...	1519	1619	1645	1719	...	1819	1921	2033	2128	...	2218	2321
Birmingham Moor St ... d.	2258	2328	2341	...		0922	1025	...	1122	1222	1325	1422	...	1522	1622	1647	1722	...	1822	1923	2036	2131	...	2221	...
Henley in Arden ... d.	...	...	...	...		0953	1056	...	1153	1253	1356	1452	...	1553	1653	...	1753	...	1853	...	...	...	...	...	...
Stratford upon Avon ... a.	...	...	...	...		1008	1111	...	1208	1308	1411	1506	...	1608	1708	...	1808	...	1908	...	...	...	...	...	...

S – From / to Stratford upon Avon.
j – 6 minutes earlier on ⑥.
‡ – Birmingham Snow Hill.

🚂 – **Kidderminster** – **Bridgnorth** and v.v. (*Severn Valley Railway*). *26 km.* Daily May – Sept. and on certain other dates throughout the year. Kidderminster station is 100 metres from the National Rail station. Operator: Severn Valley Railway. ✆ 01299 403816. www.svr.co.uk

XC Most trains 🍸

BRISTOL - BIRMINGHAM - YORK - NEWCASTLE - EDINBURGH 127

Services on ⑦ valid until January 31. For Cardiff - Birmingham - Nottingham and v.v., see Table **121**.

km			Ⓐ	Ⓐ	Ⓐ	Ⓐ	Ⓐ	Ⓐ	Ⓐ	Ⓐ	Ⓐ	Ⓐ C	Ⓐ	Ⓐ	Ⓐ T	Ⓐ	Ⓐ	Ⓐ	Ⓐ Z	Ⓐ	Ⓐ	Ⓐ A	Ⓐ	Ⓐ T	Ⓐ ZP
	Plymouth **115** d.	Ⓐ	...	...	...	...	...	...	...	0520	...	...	0625	...	...	0725	...	...	0825	...	...	0925	...	...	1025
	Exeter **115** d.		...	...	...	...	...	...	...	0623	...	...	0723	...	0744	0823	...	...	0924	...	...	1023	...	1049	1123
0	**Bristol** T Meads **133** d.		...	...	...	...	0615	...	0700	0730	...	0800	0830	...	0900	0930	...	1000	1030	...	1100	1130	...	1200	1230
10	**Bristol** Parkway **133** d.		...	...	...	...	0625	...	0710	0740	...	0810	0840	...	0910	0940	...	1010	1040	...	1110	1140	...	1210	1240
72	Cheltenham Spa **133** d.		...	...	...	...	0712	...	0742	0812	...	0842	0912	...	0942	1012	...	1042	1112	...	1142	1212	...	1242	1312
	Reading **129** d.		...	...	...	...	|	0641	|	|	0741	|	|	0841	|	|	0941	|	|	1041	|	|	1141	|	|
145	**Birmingham** New St **142** a.		...	...	...	...	0756	0816	0826	0856	0918	0926	0956	1018	1026	1056	1118	1126	1158	1218	1226	1256	1318	1326	1356
145	**Birmingham** New St **150** d.		0600	0630	0703	0730	0803	0830	0831	0903	0930	0931	1003	1030	1031	1103	1130	1131	1203	1230	1231	1303	1330	1343	1403
	Manchester Piccadilly **150** a.		|	|	|	|	|	|	0959	|	|	1059	|	|	1159	|	|	1259	|	|	1359	|	|	1459	|
173	Tamworth **121** d.		|	|	0719	|	0819	|	...	|	|	...	1019	|	...	|	|	...	1219	|	...	|	|	...	1419
193	Burton on Trent **121** d.		|	|	0729	|	0829	|	...	0926	|	...	|	|	...	1126	|	...	|	|	...	1328	|	...	|
212	**Derby** **121 170** a.		0632	0711	0742	0811	0842	0911	...	0939	1008	...	1039	1108	...	1139	1208	...	1241	1309	...	1340	1408	...	1439
250	Chesterfield **170** a.		0652	0731	0802	0832	0902	|	...	1002	|	...	1102	|	...	1202	|	...	1302	|	...	1402	|	...	1502
270	**Sheffield** **170** a.		0706	0748	0817	0846	0917	0946	...	1017	1046	...	1117	1146	...	1218	1246	...	1317	1346	...	1417	1446	...	1517
299	Doncaster **185** a.		|	0825	|	0920	|	1015	...	|	1115	...	|	1215	...	|	1320	...	|	1417	...	|	1516	...	|
316	Wakefield Westgate **185** a.		0736	|	0848	|	0946	|	...	1046	|	...	1146	|	...	1246	|	...	1346	|	...	1446	|	...	1546
332	**Leeds** **185 187** a.		0752	|	0903	|	1002	|	...	1102	|	...	1201	|	...	1302	|	...	1402	|	...	1504	|	...	1602
344	**York** **185 187** a.		0823	0847	0933	0948	1027	1040	...	1128	1145	...	1229	1245	...	1329	1346	...	1429	1443	...	1529	1540	...	1629
415	Darlington **185 187** a.		0855	0920	1004	1017	1059	1112	...	1158	1220	...	1300	1313	...	1400	1416	...	1458	1516	...	1606	1611	...	1657
450	Durham **185 187** a.		0913	0937	1021	1034	1117	1219	...	1222	1238	...	1318	1330	...	1418	1434	...	1515	1534	...	1624	1629	...	1714
473	**Newcastle** **185 187** a.		0926	0955	1036	1052	1132	1149	...	1236	1301	...	1333	1346	...	1437	1451	...	1531	1553	...	1637	1646	...	1734
529	Alnmouth **185** a.		0955	...	|	...	1200	...	...	|	...	...	1400	...	...	|	...	...	1601	...	...	|	...	...	1801
581	Berwick upon Tweed **185** a.		|	...	1120	...	|	...	...	1321	...	...	|	...	...	1521	...	...	|	...	...	1725	...	...	|
673	**Edinburgh** Waverley **185** a.		1057	...	1211	...	1305	...	...	1414	...	...	1510	...	...	1616	...	...	1704	...	...	1813	...	...	1903

	Ⓐ	Ⓐ	Ⓐ D	Ⓐ	Ⓐ Z	Ⓐ Q	Ⓐ	Ⓐ	Ⓐ	Ⓐ	Ⓐ T	Ⓐ	Ⓐ	Ⓐ	Ⓐ	Ⓐ	Ⓐ E	Ⓐ	Ⓐ	Ⓐ	Ⓐ E	Ⓐ	Ⓐ	Ⓐ E	Ⓐ
Plymouth **115** d.	...	...	1125	...	1150	1223	...	...	1323	...	...	1425	...	...	1523	...	...	...	1625	...	...	...	1723	...	...
Exeter **115** d.	...	...	1223	...	1248	1325	...	...	1425	...	1444	1523	...	...	1625	...	...	1653	1723	...	...	...	1825	...	...
Bristol T Meads **133** d.	...	1300	1330	...	1400	1430	...	1500	1530	...	1600	1630	...	1700	1730	...	...	1800	1830	...	...	1900	1930	...	2000
Bristol Parkway **133** d.	...	1310	1340	...	1410	1440	...	1510	1540	...	1610	1640	...	1710	1740	...	...	1810	1840	...	...	1910	1940	...	2010
Cheltenham Spa **133** d.	...	1342	1412	...	1442	1512	...	1542	1612	...	1642	1712	...	1742	1812	...	...	1842	1912	...	...	1942	2012	...	2042
Reading **129** d.	1241	|	|	1341	|	|	1441	|	|	1541	|	|	1641	|	|	1741	...	|	|	1841	...	|	|	...	|
Birmingham New St **142** a.	1418	1426	1456	1518	1526	1556	1618	1626	1658	1718	1726	1756	1818	1826	1855	1918	...	1926	1956	2018	...	2028	2052	...	2145
Birmingham New St **150** d.	1430	1431	1503	1530	1531	1603	1630	1631	1703	1730	1731	1803	1830	1831	1903	1930	...	1931	2003	2030	...	2031	2103	...	...
Manchester Piccadilly **150** a.	|	1549	|	|	1659	|	|	1759	|	|	1859	|	|	2000	|	|	...	2058	|	|	...	2200	|	...	...
Tamworth **121** d.	|	...	|	|	...	1619	|	...	|	|	...	1819	|	...	|	|	...	...	2019	|	...	...	2119	...	...
Burton on Trent **121** d.	|	...	1526	|	...	|	|	...	1726	|	...	|	|	...	1926	|	...	...	|	|	...	...	2130	...	...
Derby **121 170** a.	1508	...	1539	1608	...	1640	1708	...	1740	1808	...	1842	1908	...	1939	2008	...	...	2042	2111	2134	...	2144	...	...
Chesterfield **170** a.	|	...	1602	|	...	1702	|	...	1801	|	...	1902	1929	...	2002	|	2052	...	2102	2133	2153	...	2205	2220	...
Sheffield **170** a.	1546	...	1617	1646	...	1719	1745	...	1818	1849	...	1920	1947	...	2019	2049	2114	...	2118	2148	2216	...	2224	2237	...
Doncaster **185** a.	1615	...	|	1715	...	|	|	...	|	1917	...	|	2020	...	|	2121	|	...	|	2229	|	...	|	|	...
Wakefield Westgate **185** a.	|	...	1647	|	...	1747	1812	...	1847	|	...	1949	|	...	2053	|	2154	...	2150	|	2246	...	2257	2321	...
Leeds **185 187** a.	|	...	1702	|	...	1803	1830	...	1902	|	...	2005	|	...	2108	|	2212	...	2204	|	2305	...	2316	2338	...
York **185 187** a.	1640	...	1730	1740	...	1831	1858	...	1930	1944	...	2031	2046	...	...	2145	...	...	...	2254	...	...	...	...	...
Darlington **185 187** a.	1708	...	1759	1815	...	1900	1938	...	2004	2012	...	2107	2120	...	...	2213	...	...	...	...	...	...	...	...	...
Durham **185 187** a.	1725	...	1817	1833	...	1918	1955	...	2022	2030	...	2125	2139	...	...	2230	...	...	...	...	...	...	...	...	...
Newcastle **185 187** a.	1751	...	1836	1850	...	1934	2013	...	2038	2048	...	2139	2155	...	...	2251	...	...	...	...	...	...	...	...	...
Alnmouth **185** a.	...	...	|	...	...	2004	...	...	|	2127	...	2211	...	...	...	...	...	...	...	...	...	...	...	...	...
Berwick upon Tweed **185** a.	...	...	1924	...	...	|	...	...	2127	2147	...	2232	...	...	...	...	...	...	...	...	...	...	...	...	...
Edinburgh Waverley **185** a.	...	...	2012	...	...	2108	...	...	2217	2235	...	2323	...	...	...	...	...	...	...	...	...	...	...	...	...

	Ⓐ	Ⓐ Tv	Ⓐ Tw			⑥	⑥	⑥	⑥	⑥ E	⑥	⑥	⑥	⑥	⑥ B	⑥ C	⑥	⑥	⑥ T	⑥	⑥	⑥	⑥ Z	⑥	⑥
Plymouth **115** d.	1825	...	...	...	⑥	...	...	...	...	...	...	...	...	0525	...	...	0625	...	...	0725	...	...	0825	...	...
Exeter **115** d.	1923	2050	2050	...		...	...	...	...	...	...	...	...	0623	...	...	0723	...	0748	0823	...	...	0923	...	...
Bristol T Meads **133** d.	2030	2200	2200	...		...	...	...	...	...	0615	...	0700	0730	...	0800	0830	...	0900	0930	...	1000	1030	...	1100
Bristol Parkway **133** d.	2040	2210	2215	...		...	...	...	...	...	0625	...	0710	0740	...	0810	0840	...	0910	0940	...	1010	1040	...	1110
Cheltenham Spa **133** d.	2117	2242	2327	...		...	...	...	...	...	0712	...	0742	0812	...	0842	0912	...	0942	1012	...	1042	1112	...	1142
Reading **129** d.	|	|	|	...		...	...	...	...	...	|	0646	|	|	0747	|	|	0840	|	|	0940	|	|	1040	|
Birmingham New St **142** a.	2209	2344	0025	...		...	...	...	...	...	0756	0817	0826	0856	0919	0926	0956	1017	1026	1056	1117	1126	1156	1217	1226
Birmingham New St **150** d.	...	...	...	...		0555	0630	0703	0730	...	0803	0830	0831	0903	0930	0931	1003	1030	1031	1103	1130	1131	1203	1230	1231
Manchester Piccadilly **150** a.	...	...	...	...		|	|	|	|	...	|	|	0959	|	|	1059	|	|	1159	|	|	1259	|	|	1359
Tamworth **121** d.	...	...	...	...		0612	0646	0719	0746	...	0819	|	...	|	|	...	1019	|	...	|	|	...	1219	|	...
Burton on Trent **121** d.	...	...	...	...		0622	0656	0729	0756	...	0829	|	...	0926	|	...	|	|	...	1126	|	...	|	|	...
Derby **121 170** a.	...	...	...	...		0635	0709	0743	0809	0828	0842	0908	...	0941	1009	...	1041	1109	...	1141	1209	...	1241	1309	...
Chesterfield **170** a.	...	...	...	...		0655	0729	0802	0829	0846	0902	|	...	1002	|	...	1102	|	...	1202	|	...	1302	|	...
Sheffield **170** a.	...	...	...	...		0709	0748	0817	0846	0907	0917	0946	...	1017	1046	...	1117	1146	...	1217	1246	...	1317	1346	...
Doncaster **185** a.	...	...	...	...		|	0823	|	0921	0953	|	1018	...	|	1116	...	|	1216	...	|	1319	...	|	1416	...
Wakefield Westgate **185** a.	...	...	...	...		0736	|	0846	|	|	0946	|	...	1046	|	...	1146	|	...	1246	|	...	1346	|	...
Leeds **185 187** a.	...	...	...	...		0752	|	0902	|	|	1002	|	...	1102	|	...	1202	|	...	1302	|	...	1402	|	...
York **185 187** a.	...	...	...	...		0825	0849	0930	0945	1016	1030	1044	...	1130	1144	...	1230	1244	...	1332	1344	...	1430	1444	...
Darlington **185 187** a.	...	...	...	...		0854	0918	0959	1013	...	1059	1116	...	1159	1214	...	1301	1312	...	1359	1416	...	1459	1515	...
Durham **185 187** a.	...	...	...	...		0911	0935	1016	1030	...	1116	1133	...	1216	1234	...	1318	1329	...	1416	1434	...	1516	1532	...
Newcastle **185 187** a.	...	...	...	...		0926	0954	1033	1046	...	1132	1149	...	1233	1250	...	1333	1345	...	1432	1450	...	1532	1546	...
Alnmouth **185** a.	...	...	...	...		0955	...	|	...	...	1159	...	...	|	...	...	1359	...	...	|	...	...	1602	...	...
Berwick upon Tweed **185** a.	...	...	...	...		|	...	1117	...	...	|	...	...	1317	...	...	|	...	...	1517	...	...	|	...	...
Edinburgh Waverley **185** a.	...	...	...	...		1057	...	1207	...	...	1301	...	...	1407	...	...	1504	...	...	1605	...	...	1705	...	...

	⑥ A	⑥	⑥ T	⑥ Z	⑥ R	⑥	⑥ D	⑥	⑥ Z	⑥	⑥ S	⑥	⑥	⑥	⑥ T	⑥	⑥	⑥	⑥	⑥	⑥	⑥	⑥ E	⑥	⑥
Plymouth **115** d.	0925	...	...	1025	...	...	1125	...	1148	1223	...	...	1325	...	...	1425	...	...	1525	...	...	1625	...	...	...
Exeter **115** d.	1023	...	1049	1123	...	...	1223	...	1248	1325	...	...	1424	...	1436	1523	...	...	1623	...	...	1723	...	...	...
Bristol T Meads **133** d.	1130	...	1200	1230	...	1300	1330	...	1400	1430	...	1500	1530	...	1600	1630	...	1700	1730	...	1800	1830	...	...	1900
Bristol Parkway **133** d.	1140	...	1210	1240	...	1310	1340	...	1410	1440	...	1510	1540	...	1610	1640	...	1710	1740	...	1810	1840	...	...	1910
Cheltenham Spa **133** d.	1212	...	1242	1312	...	1342	1412	...	1442	1512	...	1542	1612	...	1642	1712	...	1742	1812	...	1842	1912	...	...	1942
Reading **129** d.	|	1140	|	|	1240	|	|	1340	|	|	1440	|	|	1540	|	|	1640	|	|	1740	|	|	...	1840	|
Birmingham New St **142** a.	1256	1317	1326	1356	1417	1426	1456	1517	1526	1555	1617	1626	1656	1717	1726	1756	1817	1826	1856	1917	1926	1956	...	2018	2026
Birmingham New St **150** d.	1303	1330	1331	1403	1430	1431	1503	1530	1531	1603	1630	1631	1703	1730	1731	1803	1830	1831	1903	1930	1931	2003	...	2030	2031
Manchester Piccadilly **150** a.	|	|	1459	|	|	1559	|	|	1659	|	|	1759	|	|	1859	|	|	1959	|	|	2059	|	...	|	2204
Tamworth **121** d.	|	|	...	1419	|	...	|	|	...	1617	|	...	|	|	...	1819	|	...	|	|	...	2019	...	2046	...
Burton on Trent **121** d.	1326	|	...	|	|	...	1526	|	...	|	|	...	1726	|	...	|	|	...	1926	|	...	|	...	2056	...
Derby **121 170** a.	1341	1409	...	1441	1508	...	1541	1608	...	1640	1708	...	1741	1808	...	1841	1908	...	1941	2008	...	2042	...	2109	...
Chesterfield **170** a.	1402	|	...	1502	|	...	1602	|	...	1700	|	...	1802	|	...	1902	1929	...	2002	2029	...	2102	2052	2129	...
Sheffield **170** a.	1417	1446	...	1517	1546	...	1618	1646	...	1718	1744	...	1818	1847	...	1918	1951	...	2018	2049	...	2118	2114	2144	...
Doncaster **185** a.	|	1516	...	|	1615	...	|	1719	...	|	|	...	|	1918	...	|	2016	...	|	2125	...	|	|	2219	...
Wakefield Westgate **185** a.	1446	|	...	1546	|	...	1649	|	...	1747	1814	...	1846	|	...	1946	|	...	2048	|	...	2146	2151	|	...
Leeds **185 187** a.	1502	|	...	1502	|	...	1704	|	...	1802	1832	...	1901	|	...	2002	|	...	2104	|	...	2202	2210	|	...
York **185 187** a.	1532	1544	...	1630	1644	...	1729	1744	...	1831	1859	...	1931	1944	...	2031	2040	...	2158	2148	...	...	...	2243	...
Darlington **185 187** a.	1559	1613	...	1659	1712	...	1759	1812	...	1901	1937	...	2003	2012	...	2104	2114	...	...	2221	...	...	...	...	...
Durham **185 187** a.	1616	1632	...	1716	1729	...	1816	1829	...	1919	1954	...	2021	2029	...	2121	2132	...	...	2241	...	...	...	...	...
Newcastle **185 187** a.	1632	1646	...	1732	1748	...	1837	1845	...	1935	2013	...	2033	2045	...	2133	2150	...	...	2305	...	...	...	...	...
Alnmouth **185** a.	|	...	...	1801	...	...	|	...	...	2003	...	...	|	2116	...	2159	...	...	...	...	...	...	...	...	...
Berwick upon Tweed **185** a.	1717	...	...	|	...	...	1925	...	...	|	...	...	2119	2137	...	2220	...	...	...	...	...	...	...	...	...
Edinburgh Waverley **185** a.	1805	...	...	1907	...	...	2015	...	...	2106	...	...	2210	2223	...	2304	...	...	...	...	...	...	...	...	...

A – To Aberdeen, Table **224**.
B – From Bournemouth, Table **115**.
C – From Cardiff, Table **135**.
D – To Dundee, Table **224**.
E – Operated by *EM*, see Table **170**.
G – From Glasgow (d. 0601).
H – From Glasgow (d. 0900).

Notes continue on next page ▶ ▶ ▶.

127 BRISTOL - BIRMINGHAM - YORK - NEWCASTLE - EDINBURGH

Most trains 🍴 XC

Services on ⑦ valid until January 31. For Cardiff - Birmingham - Nottingham and v.v., see Table **121**.

	⑥	⑥ E	⑥	⑥		⑦	⑦ E	⑦	⑦	⑦	⑦	⑦ A	⑦	⑦	⑦ T	⑦	⑦ ZV	⑦	⑦	⑦ X	⑦	⑦ E	⑦	⑦ Z	⑦
Plymouth 115 d.	1723	...	...	1825	...		...	...	...	...	...	0925	...	1025	...	...	1125	1200	...	1225	...	...	...	1323	...
Exeter 115 d.	1825	...	...	1923	...		...	...	...	...	...	1023	...	1123	1132	...	1223	1257	...	1323	...	...	...	1425	...
Bristol T Meads 133 d.	1930	...	2000	2030	...		...	...	0915	1030	...	1130	...	1230	1300	...	1330	1400	...	1430	1500	...	...	1530	1600
Bristol Parkway 133 d.	1940	...	2010	2040	...		...	...	0925	1040	...	1140	...	1240	1310	...	1340	1410	...	1440	1510	...	...	1540	1610
Cheltenham Spa 133 d.	2012	...	2042	2112	...		...	...	1012	1112	...	1212	...	1312	1342	...	1412	1442	...	1512	1542	...	...	1611	1642
Reading 129 d.	|	...	|	|	...		...	...	|	|	...	|	...	|	|	1254	|	|	1340	|	|	...	1440	|	|
Birmingham New St 142 a.	2053	...	2138	2152	...		...	...	1050	1150	...	1250	...	1350	1420	1419	1450	1520	1510	1550	1620	...	1609	1650	1719
Birmingham New St 150 d.	2103	...	...	...	...		...	1003	1103	1203	1230	1303	1330	1403	1427	1430	1503	1527	1530	1603	1627	...	1630	1703	1727
Manchester Piccadilly 150 a.	|	...	...	...	...		...	|	|	|	|	|	|	|	1620	|	|	1719	|	|	1819	...	|	|	1919
Tamworth 121 d.	2119	...	...	...	...		...	1019	|	1219	|	|	|	1419	...	|	|	...	|	1619	...	...	|	|	...
Burton on Trent 121 d.	2130	...	...	...	...		...	1029	1126	|	|	1326	|	|	...	|	1526	...	|	|	...	...	|	1729	...
Derby 121 170 a.	2144	2134	...	...	...		1048	1042	1142	1242	1309	1344	1409	1442	...	1505	1542	...	1605	1642	...	1656	1705	1742	...
Chesterfield 170 a.	2205	2155	...	...	...		1108	1102	1202	1302	1329	1402	1429	1502	...	|	1602	...	|	1702	...	1716	|	1803	...
Sheffield 170 a.	2223	2216	...	...	...		1128	1117	1218	1317	1343	1417	1444	1517	...	1547	1618	...	1648	1717	...	1732	1748	1819	...
Doncaster 185 a.	2247	|	...	...	...		1152	|	|	|	1413	|	1513	|	...	1615	|	...	1713	|	...	|	1813	|	...
Wakefield Westgate 185 a.	2309	2244	...	...	...		|	1144	1244	1344	|	1444	|	1544	...	|	1644	...	|	1745	...	1806	1833	1847	...
Leeds 185 187 a.	2224	2304	...	...	...		|	1202	1302	1402	|	1502	|	1602	...	|	1702	...	|	1802	...	1824	1853	1904	...
York 185 187 a.	...	...	...	...	...		1215	1232	1332	1432	1443	1532	1540	1632	...	1640	1732	...	1742	1832	...	...	1921	1932	...
Darlington 185 187 a.	...	...	...	...	...		...	1308	1402	1507	1515	1601	1612	1701	...	1714	1801	...	1810	1901	...	...	1951	2003	...
Durham 185 187 a.	...	...	...	...	...		...	1325	1419	1524	1532	1618	1630	1718	...	1732	1818	...	1827	1918	...	...	2008	2021	...
Newcastle 185 187 a.	...	...	...	...	...		...	1341	1435	1538	1546	1634	1645	1734	...	1748	1834	...	1847	1934	...	...	2026	2037	...
Alnmouth 185 a.	...	...	...	...	...		...	1407	|	1607	...	|	...	1801	...	...	|	...	...	2004	...	...	...	|	...
Berwick upon Tweed 185 a.	...	...	...	...	...		...	|	1519	|	...	1719	...	|	...	...	1919	...	...	|	...	...	...	2123	...
Edinburgh Waverley 185 a.	...	...	...	...	...		...	1509	1607	1709	...	1807	...	1903	...	...	2007	...	...	2106	...	...	...	2215	...

	⑦		⑦		⑦ Z	⑦		⑦	⑦		⑦		⑦ E		⑦	⑦		⑦ Z	⑦ T		⑦		⑦ E		⑦
Plymouth 115 d.	...	...	1423	...	1435	...	...	1523	...	...	...	...	...	...	1625	...	...	1726	...	...	1823	...	...	...	...
Exeter 115 d.	...	...	1525	...	1533	...	...	1625	...	...	...	...	...	...	1723	...	...	1823	1856	...	1925	...	...	...	...
Bristol T Meads 133 d.	...	...	1630	...	1700	...	...	1730	1800	...	...	...	...	...	1830	1900	...	1930	2000	...	2030	...	...	...	2210
Bristol Parkway 133 d.	...	...	1640	...	1710	...	...	1740	1810	...	...	...	...	...	1840	1910	...	1940	2010	...	2040	...	...	...	2220
Cheltenham Spa 133 d.	...	...	1711	...	1742	...	...	1811	1842	...	...	...	...	...	1912	1942	...	2012	2042	...	2111	...	...	...	2252
Reading 129 d.	1540	...	|	...	|	1640	...	|	|	...	1740	...	...	...	|	|	...	|	|	...	|	...	...	...	|
Birmingham New St 142 a.	1709	...	1749	...	1819	1809	...	1855	1919	...	1909	...	...	...	1950	2020	...	2050	2120	...	2155	...	...	...	2339
Birmingham New St 150 d.	1730	...	1803	...	1827	1830	...	1903	1927	...	1930	...	...	...	2003	2027	...	2103	...	...	2203	...	...	...	...
Manchester Piccadilly 150 a.	|	...	|	...	2018	|	...	|	2122	...	|	...	...	...	|	2216	...	|	...	...	|	...	...	...	...
Tamworth 121 d.	|	...	1819	...	...	|	...	|	...	...	|	...	...	...	2019	...	...	2119	...	...	2219	...	...	...	...
Burton on Trent 121 d.	|	...	|	...	...	|	...	1926	...	...	|	...	...	...	|	...	...	2129	...	...	|	...	...	...	...
Derby 121 170 a.	1805	...	1842	...	...	1904	...	1941	...	...	2005	...	2022	...	2042	...	...	2142	...	...	2245	...	2251	...	...
Chesterfield 170 a.	|	...	1904	...	...	|	...	2001	...	...	|	...	2041	...	2102	...	...	2202	...	...	2306	...	2311	...	...
Sheffield 170 a.	1846	...	1920	...	...	1936	...	2017	...	...	2038	...	2058	...	2116	...	...	2218	...	...	2322	...	2328	...	...
Doncaster 185 a.	1913	...	|	...	...	2016	...	|	...	...	2119	...	|	...	|	...	...	|	...	...	|	...	|	...	...
Wakefield Westgate 185 a.	|	...	1948	...	...	|	...	2046	...	...	|	...	2132	...	2144	...	...	2245	...	...	|	...	2355	...	...
Leeds 185 187 a.	|	...	2005	...	...	|	...	2103	...	...	|	...	2149	...	2201	...	...	2304	...	...	0033	...	0032	...	...
York 185 187 a.	1942	...	2032	...	...	2044	...	2132	...	...	2142	...	...	...	...	...	...	...	...	...	...	...	...	...	...
Darlington 185 187 a.	2010	...	2103	...	...	2118	...	...	...	...	2222	...	...	...	...	...	...	...	...	...	...	...	...	...	...
Durham 185 187 a.	2027	...	2121	...	...	2136	...	...	...	...	2239	...	...	...	...	...	...	...	...	...	...	...	...	...	...
Newcastle 185 187 a.	2043	...	2137	...	...	2154	...	...	...	...	2307	...	...	...	...	...	...	...	...	...	...	...	...	...	...
Alnmouth 185 a.	2115	...	2205	...	...	...	...	...	...	...	...	...	...	...	...	...	...	...	...	...	...	...	...	...	...
Berwick upon Tweed 185 a.	2136	...	2228	...	...	...	...	...	...	...	...	...	...	...	...	...	...	...	...	...	...	...	...	...	...
Edinburgh Waverley 185 a.	2220	...	2314	...	...	...	...	...	...	...	...	...	...	...	...	...	...	...	...	...	...	...	...	...	...

	Ⓐ	Ⓐ T	Ⓐ	Ⓐ	Ⓐ	Ⓐ E	Ⓐ NB	Ⓐ	Ⓐ	Ⓐ	Ⓐ E	Ⓐ	Ⓐ	Ⓐ T	Ⓐ	Ⓐ	Ⓐ	Ⓐ	Ⓐ	Ⓐ	Ⓐ G	Ⓐ	Ⓐ	Ⓐ D	Ⓐ
Edinburgh Waverley 185 d.		...	...	...	...	...	...	...	...	...	...	...	...	...	...	...	...	0608	0644	...	0708	...	...	0811	...
Berwick upon Tweed 185 d.		...	...	...	...	...	...	...	...	...	...	...	...	...	...	...	...	0649	0723	...	0751	...	...	0852	...
Alnmouth 185 d.		...	...	...	...	...	...	...	...	...	...	...	...	...	...	...	...	0710	0747	...	|	...	...	|	...
Newcastle 185 187 d.		...	...	...	...	...	...	...	...	...	...	...	0621	...	0644	0723	...	0745	0824	...	0843	0935	...	0943	1025
Durham 185 187 d.		...	...	...	...	...	...	...	...	...	...	...	0639	...	0656	0737	...	|	0840	...	0855	0948	...	0956	1037
Darlington 185 187 d.		...	...	...	...	...	...	...	...	...	...	...	0656	...	0714	0755	...	0813	0857	...	0912	1005	...	1013	1054
York 185 187 d.		...	...	...	...	...	...	...	...	...	...	0632	0727	...	0744	0827	...	0845	0927	...	0944	1034	...	1044	1127
Leeds 185 187 d.		...	...	...	...	0525	...	0600	0615	...	0634	0705	|	...	0811	|	...	0911	|	...	1011	|	...	1111	|
Wakefield Westgate 185 d.		...	...	...	...	0537	...	0612	0627	...	0646	0718	|	...	0824	|	...	0924	|	...	1024	|	...	1124	|
Doncaster 185 d.		...	...	...	...	0557	...	|	0645	...	|	|	0752	...	|	0851	...	|	0956	...	|	1058	...	|	1154
Sheffield 170 d.		...	...	0601	...	0627	...	0650	0718	...	0732	0753	0820	...	0854	0923	...	0954	1023	...	1054	1123	...	1154	1223
Chesterfield 170 d.		...	...	0627	...	0639	...	0704	0730	...	0745	0806	0832	...	0906	|	...	1006	|	...	1106	|	...	1206	|
Derby 121 170 d.		...	0610	0648	...	0703	0706	0726	0750	...	...	0828	0853	...	0928	0953	...	1028	1053	...	1128	1153	...	1228	1253
Burton on Trent 121 d.		...	0620	0658	...	...	0718	0737	0800	...	...	0838	|	...	0938	|	...	|	|	...	|	|	...	|	|
Tamworth 121 d.		...	0631	0709	...	...	0730	0749	0811	...	...	0849	|	...	|	|	...	1048	|	...	|	|	...	1248	|
Manchester Piccadilly 150 d.		...	|	|	0600	...	|	|	|	0706	...	|	|	0807	|	|	0907	|	|	1007	|	|	1107	|	|
Birmingham New St 150 a.		...	0652	0727	0731	...	0755	0809	0829	0831	...	0909	0927	0939	1007	1027	1031	1109	1127	1139	1207	1227	1239	1309	1327
Birmingham New St 142 d.		0642	0712	0733	0742	...	0803	0812	0833	0842	...	0912	0933	0942	1012	1033	1042	1112	1133	1142	1212	1233	1242	1312	1333
Reading 129 a.		|	|	0908	|	...	0939	|	1008	|	...	|	1108	|	|	1208	|	|	1308	|	|	1408	|	|	1508
Cheltenham Spa 133 a.		0720	0751	...	0823	...	...	0851	...	0923	...	0951	...	1023	1050	...	1123	1151	...	1223	1250	...	1323	1355	...
Bristol Parkway 133 a.		0756	0825	...	0856	...	...	0924	...	0956	...	1026	...	1056	1126	...	1156	1228	...	1256	1324	...	1357	1427	...
Bristol T Meads 133 a.		0808	0840	...	0914	...	...	0939	...	1008	...	1041	...	1112	1138	...	1208	1241	...	1310	1339	...	1409	1441	...
Exeter 115 a.		0910	0943	...	...	...	...	1046	...	...	...	1146	...	1230	1243	...	...	1346	...	...	1443	...	...	1546	...
Plymouth 115 a.		...	1046	...	...	...	...	1151	...	...	...	1251	...	...	1313	...	...	1450	...	...	1543	...	...	1650	...

	Ⓐ	Ⓐ D	Ⓐ	Ⓐ	Ⓐ HZ	Ⓐ	Ⓐ T	Ⓐ AZ	Ⓐ	Ⓐ	Ⓐ Z	Ⓐ	Ⓐ	Ⓐ	Ⓐ	Ⓐ C	Ⓐ	Ⓐ	Ⓐ	Ⓐ	Ⓐ	Ⓐ	Ⓐ v	Ⓐ w	Ⓐ
Edinburgh Waverley 185 d.	...	0907	...	...	1008	...	...	1108	...	...	1205	...	...	1306	...	...	1408	...	...	1508	...	...	1608	1608	...
Berwick upon Tweed 185 d.	...	0951	...	...	|	...	...	1151	...	...	|	...	...	1351	...	...	|	...	...	1551	...	...	|	|	...
Alnmouth 185 d.	...	|	...	...	1105	...	...	|	...	...	1305	...	...	|	...	...	1505	...	...	|	...	...	1709	1709	...
Newcastle 185 187 d.	...	1044	1127	...	1140	1219	...	1244	1334	...	1344	1426	...	1440	1522	...	1542	1632	...	1640	1717	...	1744	1744	1820
Durham 185 187 d.	...	1056	1139	...	1152	1235	...	1256	1346	...	1356	1440	...	1452	1534	...	1554	1648	...	1652	1733	...	1757	1757	1836
Darlington 185 187 d.	...	1113	1156	...	1211	1253	...	1313	1403	...	1413	1457	...	1512	1551	...	1612	1705	...	1712	1750	...	1814	1814	1856
York 185 187 d.	...	1145	1227	...	1245	1326	...	1344	1432	...	1444	1529	...	1544	1625	...	1644	1734	...	1744	1824	...	1845	1845	1929
Leeds 185 187 d.	...	1211	|	...	1311	|	...	1412	|	...	1511	|	...	1611	|	...	1711	|	...	1811	|	...	1912	1912	|
Wakefield Westgate 185 d.	...	1224	|	...	1324	|	...	1424	|	...	1524	|	...	1623	|	...	1724	|	...	1823	|	...	1924	1924	|
Doncaster 185 d.	...	|	1255	...	|	1355	...	|	1457	...	|	1555	...	|	1653	...	|	1758	...	|	1852	...	|	|	1957
Sheffield 170 d.	...	1254	1323	...	1354	1423	...	1454	1523	...	1554	1623	...	1654	1723	...	1754	1823	...	1854	1923	...	1954	1954	2023
Chesterfield 170 d.	...	1306	|	...	1406	|	...	1506	|	...	1606	|	...	1706	|	...	1807	|	...	1906	|	...	2006	2006	|
Derby 121 170 d.	...	1328	1353	...	1428	1453	...	1528	1553	...	1628	1653	...	1728	1753	...	1828	1853	...	1928	1954	...	2028	2028	2054
Burton on Trent 121 d.	...	1338	|	...	|	|	...	1538	|	...	|	|	...	1738	|	...	|	|	...	1938	|	...	|	|	|
Tamworth 121 d.	...	|	|	...	1448	|	...	|	|	...	1648	|	...	|	|	...	1848	|	...	|	|	...	2048	2048	|
Manchester Piccadilly 150 d.	1207	|	|	1307	|	|	1407	|	|	1507	|	|	1607	|	|	1706	|	|	1805	|	|	1907	|	|	|
Birmingham New St 150 a.	1331	1407	1427	1431	1507	1527	1539	1608	1627	1631	1709	1728	1739	1807	1828	1838	1908	1928	1931	2009	2027	2033	2107	2107	2135
Birmingham New St 142 d.	1342	1412	1433	1442	1512	1533	1542	1612	1633	1642	1712	1733	1842	1812	1833	1842	1912	1933	1942	2012	2033	2042	2112	2112	...
Reading 129 a.	|	|	1608	|	|	1708	|	|	1808	|	|	1908	|	|	2008	|	|	2107	|	|	2216		|	|	...
Cheltenham Spa 133 a.	1423	1450	...	1523	1550	...	1623	1651	...	1723	1750	...	1823	1851	...	1923	1950	...	2023	2051	...	2125	2150	2150	...
Bristol Parkway 133 a.	1456	1524	...	1556	1626	...	1656	1724	...	1758	1827	...	1907	1926	...	1956	2027	...	2056	2125	...	2202	2223	2245	...
Bristol T Meads 133 a.	1510	1540	...	1608	1641	...	1711	1740	...	1810	1840	...	1922	1939	...	2013	2041	...	2108	2138	...	2215	2236	2257	...
Exeter 115 a.	1613	1643	...	...	1743	...	1813	1844	...	...	1943	...	...	2043	...	...	2146	...	2213	2244	...	...	...	...	...
Plymouth 115 a.	...	1743	...	...	1851	...	...	1945	...	...	2045	...	...	2150	...	...	2246	...	2312	2344					

J – From Glasgow (d. 0700).
K – From Glasgow (d. 1137).
L – From Glasgow (d. 1345).
N – From Nottingham, Table **135**.
P – To Glasgow (a. 2025).
Q – To Glasgow (a. 2230).
R – To Glasgow (a. 2024).

Notes continue on next page ▶ ▶ ▶.

XC Most trains 🍸

EDINBURGH - NEWCASTLE - YORK - BIRMINGHAM - BRISTOL 127

Services on ⑥⑦ valid until January 31. For Cardiff - Birmingham - Nottingham and v.v., see Table **121**.

	Ⓐ v	Ⓐ w	Ⓐ	Ⓐ		⑥	⑥ T	⑥	⑥	⑥	⑥ NB	⑥	⑥	⑥ E	⑥	⑥	⑥	⑥ E	⑥ T	⑥	⑥	⑥	⑥	⑥	⑥
Edinburgh Waverley 185 d.	1708	1708	...	1808	...		...	...	...	...	...	...	...	...	...	...	...	...	...	...	...	...	0612	0655	...
Berwick upon Tweed 185 d.	1751	1751	...	1851	...		...	...	...	...	...	...	...	...	...	...	...	...	...	...	...	...	0651	0735	...
Alnmouth 185 d.	|	|	...	1911	...		...	...	...	...	...	...	...	...	...	...	...	...	...	...	...	...	0711	0755	...
Newcastle 185 187 d.	1840	1840	1925	1943	...		...	...	...	...	...	...	...	...	...	...	0621	...	...	0642	0725	...	0744	0830	...
Durham 185 187 d.	1852	1852	1944	1955	...		...	...	...	...	...	...	...	...	...	...	0639	...	...	0656	0738	...	0756	0842	...
Darlington 185 187 d.	1912	1912	2004	2012	...		...	...	...	...	...	...	...	...	...	...	0656	...	...	0713	0755	...	0813	0859	...
York 185 187 d.	1944	1944	2032	2044	...		...	...	...	...	...	...	...	...	...	0609	0725	...	...	0744	0827	...	0844	0928	...
Leeds 185 187 d.	2011	2011	|	2111	...		...	...	...	...	...	0600	0615	0634	...	0705	|	0734	...	0811	|	...	0911	|	...
Wakefield Westgate 185 d.	2023	2023	|	2123	...		...	...	...	...	...	0612	0629	0646	...	0718	|	0746	...	0824	|	...	0924	|	...
Doncaster 185 d.	|	|	2057	|	...		...	...	...	...	...	|	0647	|	...	|	0752	|	...	|	0853	...	|	0953	...
Sheffield 170 d.	2054	2054	2127	2200	...		...	...	...	...	...	0650	0718	0732	...	0754	0820	0832	...	0854	0923	...	0954	1023	...
Chesterfield 170 d.	2106	2106	2139	2224	...		...	...	...	...	...	0703	0730	0745	...	0806	0832	0845	...	0906	|	...	1006	|	...
Derby 121 170 d.	2128	2128	2200	2245	...		...	0610	0647	...	0706	0725	0750	...	...	0828	0853	...	...	0928	0953	...	1028	1053	...
Burton on Trent 121 d.	2138	2138	|	2255	...		...	0620	0657	...	0718	0736	0800	...	...	0838	|	...	...	0938	|	...	|	|	...
Tamworth 121 d.	2149	2149	|	2306	...		...	0631	0708	...	0730	0748	0811	...	...	0850	|	...	...	|	|	...	1048	|	...
Manchester Piccadilly 150 d.	|	|	|	|	...		...	|	|	0600	|	|	|	...	0707	|	|	...	0807	|	|	0907	|	|	1007
Birmingham New St 150 a.	2207	2207	2254	2334	...		...	0650	0727	0731	0755	0808	0829	...	0838	0907	0929	...	0939	1007	1027	1039	1107	1127	1139
Birmingham New St 142 d.	2212	2212	...	...	...		0642	0712	0733	0742	0803	0812	0833	...	0842	0912	0933	...	0942	1012	1033	1042	1112	1133	1142
Reading 129 a.	|	|	...	...	...		|	|	0908	|	0939	|	1008	...	|	|	1109	...	|	|	1208	|	|	1308	|
Cheltenham Spa 133 a.	2250	2250	...	...	...		0723	0750	...	0823	...	0851	...	...	0923	0950	...	...	1023	1050	...	1123	1150	...	1223
Bristol Parkway 133 a.	2320	2331	...	...	...		0756	0824	...	0856	...	0924	...	...	0956	1029	...	...	1057	1124	...	1156	1229	...	1256
Bristol T Meads 133 a.	2340	2348	...	...	...		0808	0838	...	0908	...	0938	...	...	1008	1042	...	...	1110	1138	...	1208	1242	...	1308
Exeter 115 a.	...	...	...	...	...		0910	0943	...	...	...	1046	...	...	...	1143	...	...	1227	1243	...	...	1343	...	...
Plymouth 115 a.	...	...	...	...	...		...	1044	...	...	...	1151	...	...	...	1244	...	...	...	1344	...	...	1444	...	...

	⑥	⑥	⑥	⑥ J	⑥	⑥	⑥ D	⑥	⑥	⑥ HZ	⑥	⑥ T	⑥ AZ	⑥	⑥	⑥ Z	⑥	⑥	⑥	⑥	⑥ C	⑥	⑥	⑥	⑥ E
Edinburgh Waverley 185 d.	0707	...	...	0806	...	...	0905	...	...	1005	...	...	1105	...	...	1205	...	...	1305	...	...	1405	...	...	...
Berwick upon Tweed 185 d.	0750	...	...	0847	...	...	0949	...	...	|	...	...	1148	...	...	|	...	...	1348	...	...	|	...	...	...
Alnmouth 185 d.	|	...	...	0909	...	...	|	...	...	1104	...	...	|	...	...	1305	...	...	|	...	...	1505	...	...	...
Newcastle 185 187 d.	0840	0925	...	0941	1025	...	1044	1125	...	1141	1222	...	1244	1327	...	1344	1422	...	1444	1525	...	1544	1622	...	...
Durham 185 187 d.	0856	0937	...	0955	1038	...	1056	1137	...	1155	1238	...	1256	1339	...	1356	1434	...	1456	1538	...	1556	1638	...	...
Darlington 185 187 d.	0913	0956	...	1012	1056	...	1113	1156	...	1212	1255	...	1313	1358	...	1413	1452	...	1513	1556	...	1613	1656	...	...
York 185 187 d.	0944	1025	...	1045	1127	...	1145	1225	...	1245	1327	...	1344	1427	...	1444	1526	...	1545	1625	...	1645	1725	...	1749
Leeds 185 187 d.	1011	|	...	1111	|	...	1211	|	...	1311	|	...	1411	|	...	1511	|	...	1611	|	...	1711	|	...	|
Wakefield Westgate 185 d.	1024	|	...	1124	|	...	1224	|	...	1323	|	...	1424	|	...	1524	|	...	1624	|	...	1724	|	...	|
Doncaster 185 d.	|	1053	...	|	1155	...	|	1252	...	|	1354	...	|	1456	...	|	1555	...	|	1653	...	|	1755	...	1818
Sheffield 170 d.	1054	1123	...	1154	1223	...	1254	1323	...	1354	1423	...	1454	1523	...	1554	1623	...	1654	1723	...	1754	1823	...	1847
Chesterfield 170 d.	1106	|	...	1207	|	...	1306	|	...	1407	|	...	1506	|	...	1607	|	...	1706	|	...	1806	|	...	|
Derby 121 170 d.	1128	1153	...	1229	1253	...	1328	1353	...	1429	1453	...	1528	1553	...	1628	1653	...	1728	1753	...	1828	1853	...	1919
Burton on Trent 121 d.	1138	|	...	|	|	...	1338	|	...	|	|	...	1538	|	...	|	|	...	1738	|	...	|	|	...	...
Tamworth 121 d.	|	|	...	1249	|	...	|	|	...	1448	|	...	|	|	...	1648	|	...	|	|	...	1848	|	...	...
Manchester Piccadilly 150 d.	|	|	1107	|	|	1207	|	|	1307	|	|	1407	|	|	1507	|	|	1607	|	|	1706	|	|	1805	...
Birmingham New St 150 a.	1207	1227	1239	1309	1327	1339	1407	1427	1439	1508	1527	1539	1607	1627	1639	1707	1727	1739	1807	1827	1831	1907	1927	1933	...
Birmingham New St 142 d.	1212	1233	1242	1312	1333	1342	1412	1433	1442	1512	1533	1542	1612	1633	1642	1712	1733	1742	1812	1833	1842	1912	1933	1942	...
Reading 129 a.	|	1408	|	|	1508	|	|	1608	|	|	1708	|	|	1808	|	|	1908	|	|	2008	|	|	2108	|	...
Cheltenham Spa 133 a.	1250	...	1325	1351	...	1423	1450	...	1523	1550	...	1623	1650	...	1723	1750	...	1823	1850	...	1923	1950	...	2023	...
Bristol Parkway 133 a.	1324	...	1358	1426	...	1457	1524	...	1556	1629	...	1656	1724	...	1756	1829	...	1908	1927	...	1956	2029	...	2056	...
Bristol T Meads 133 a.	1338	...	1410	1441	...	1510	1538	...	1609	1642	...	1708	1738	...	1808	1842	...	1922	1941	...	2008	2042	...	2108	...
Exeter 115 a.	1443	...	...	1546	...	...	1643	...	...	1747	...	1810	1843	...	...	1943	...	...	2043	...	...	2143	...	2212	...
Plymouth 115 a.	1544	...	...	1650	...	...	1744	...	...	1851	...	...	1943	...	...	2043	...	...	2144	...	...	2249	...	2312	...

	⑥	⑥	⑥	⑥	⑥	⑥	⑥	⑥		⑦	⑦ Z	⑦	⑦	⑦ E	⑦	⑦ E	⑦	⑦	⑦	⑦	⑦ T	⑦ Z	⑦	⑦	⑦
Edinburgh Waverley 185 d.	1505	...	...	1605	...	1705	...	1805	...		...	...	...	...	...	...	...	...	0850	...	...	0950	...	...	1050
Berwick upon Tweed 185 d.	1548	...	...	|	...	1748	...	1848	...		...	...	...	...	...	...	...	...	0933	...	...	|	...	...	1133
Alnmouth 185 d.	|	...	...	1705	...	|	...	1908	...		...	...	...	...	...	...	...	...	|	...	...	1047	...	...	|
Newcastle 185 187 d.	1644	1722	...	1744	1822	1844	1925	1943	...		...	...	...	...	...	...	0925	...	1025	...	...	1125	...	...	1225
Durham 185 187 d.	1656	1738	...	1756	1838	1856	1937	1956	...		...	...	...	...	...	...	0938	...	1037	...	...	1137	...	...	1237
Darlington 185 187 d.	1713	1755	...	1813	1856	1913	1954	2013	...		...	...	...	...	...	...	0955	...	1054	...	...	1154	...	...	1254
York 185 187 d.	1745	1825	...	1844	1925	1944	2023	2044	...		...	...	...	...	0928	...	1028	...	1128	...	...	1228	...	...	1328
Leeds 185 187 d.	1811	|	...	1911	|	2011	|	2111	...		...	0810	0900	0944	1000	1020	1100	...	1200	...	...	1300	...	...	1400
Wakefield Westgate 185 d.	1824	|	...	1924	|	2023	|	2123	...		...	0822	0911	0958	1012	1032	1112	...	1212	...	...	1312	...	...	1412
Doncaster 185 d.	|	1854	...	|	1953	|	|	|	...		...	|	0932	|	1030	|	1130	...	1230	...	...	1330	...	...	|
Sheffield 170 d.	1854	1924	...	1954	2023	2054	2123	2154	...		...	0854	0957	1028	1057	1106	1157	...	1257	...	...	1357	1420	...	1450
Chesterfield 170 d.	1906	|	...	2006	|	2106	2135	2206	...		...	0907	1009	1041	1109	1125	1209	...	1309	...	...	1409	1432	...	1502
Derby 121 170 d.	1928	1954	...	2028	2053	2128	2157	2227	...		...	0930	1033	...	1130	1147	1230	...	1332	1352	...	1430	1453	...	1523
Burton on Trent 121 d.	1938	|	...	|	|	2138	2207	2237	...		...	|	|	...	1141	...	|	...	1343	|	...	|	|	...	1535
Tamworth 121 d.	|	|	...	2049	|	2149	2218	2248	...		...	0948	|	...	|	...	1248	...	|	|	...	1449	|	...	|
Manchester Piccadilly 150 d.	|	|	1907	|	|	|	|	|	...		...	|	|	...	|	...	|	...	|	|	1241	|	|	1342	|
Birmingham New St 150 a.	2007	2027	2033	2107	2127	2207	2245	2306	...		...	1010	1109	...	1207	...	1307	...	1410	1427	1430	1507	1527	1530	1600
Birmingham New St 142 d.	2012	2033	2042	2112	...	...	...	...	...		0912	1012	1112	...	1212	...	1312	1342	1412	1433	1442	1512	1533	1542	1612
Reading 129 a.	|	2210	|	|	...	...	...	...	...		|	|	|	...	|	...	|	|	|	1609	|	|	1709	|	|
Cheltenham Spa 133 a.	2050	...	2123	2150	...	...	...	...	...		0949	1055	1150	...	1250	...	1350	1423	1451	...	1524	1550	...	1624	1650
Bristol Parkway 133 a.	2123	...	2158	2223	...	...	...	...	...		1023	1128	1223	...	1323	...	1423	1456	1525	...	1600	1623	...	1657	1723
Bristol T Meads 133 a.	2135	...	2212	2236	...	...	...	...	...		1035	1141	1236	...	1335	...	1439	1508	1538	...	1611	1635	...	1709	1735
Exeter 115 a.	2244	...	...	...	...	...	...	...	...		1148	1246	1346	...	1444	...	1544	...	1647	...	1713	1744	...	...	1848
Plymouth 115 a.	2354	...	...	...	...	...	...	...	...		1249	1352	1450	...	1544	...	1644	...	1750	...	...	1844	...	...	1948

	⑦ E	⑦	⑦	⑦ Z		⑦	⑦	⑦ K	⑦		⑦	⑦ A	⑦	⑦		⑦ E	⑦ L	⑦	⑦		⑦	⑦	⑦	⑦	⑦
Edinburgh Waverley 185 d.	...	...	...	1150	...	...	...	1250	1333	...	...	1350	...	...	...	...	1450	...	...	...	1550	...	1650	...	1750
Berwick upon Tweed 185 d.	...	...	...	|	...	...	...	1333	1418	...	...	|	...	...	...	...	1533	...	...	...	|	...	1733	...	|
Alnmouth 185 d.	...	...	...	1247	...	...	...	|	1438	...	...	1447	...	...	...	...	|	...	...	...	1647	...	|	...	1851
Newcastle 185 187 d.	...	1318	...	1325	...	1418	...	1425	1518	...	...	1525	1618	...	...	...	1625	1718	...	...	1725	1818	1825	1918	1925
Durham 185 187 d.	...	1334	...	1337	...	1430	...	1437	1530	...	...	1537	1630	...	...	...	1637	1733	...	...	1737	1833	1838	1933	1939
Darlington 185 187 d.	...	1352	...	1354	...	1447	...	1454	1547	...	...	1554	1647	...	...	...	1654	1750	...	...	1755	1850	1854	1950	1956
York 185 187 d.	...	1422	...	1428	...	1520	...	1528	1620	...	...	1628	1721	...	...	1740	1728	1820	...	...	1828	1920	1928	2020	2028
Leeds 185 187 d.	1405	|	...	1500	...	|	...	1600	|	...	...	1700	|	...	...	|	1800	|	...	...	1900	|	2000	|	2100
Wakefield Westgate 185 d.	1418	|	...	1512	...	|	...	1612	|	...	...	1712	|	...	...	|	1812	|	...	...	1912	|	2012	|	2112
Doncaster 185 d.	|	1450	...	|	...	1550	...	|	1650	...	...	|	1750	...	...	1806	|	1850	...	...	|	1950	|	2050	|
Sheffield 170 d.	1502	1520	...	1550	...	1620	...	1650	1720	...	...	1750	1820	...	...	1832	1850	1920	...	...	1950	2020	2050	2120	2150
Chesterfield 170 d.	1515	|	...	1602	...	|	...	1702	|	...	...	1802	|	...	...	1844	1902	|	...	...	2002	|	2102	2132	2202
Derby 121 170 d.	1535	1551	...	1623	...	1651	...	1725	1751	...	...	1823	1851	...	...	1908	1923	1951	...	...	2023	2051	2123	2153	2223
Burton on Trent 121 d.	...	|	...	|	...	|	...	1735	|	...	...	|	|	...	...	...	1935	|	...	...	|	|	2135	2204	2235
Tamworth 121 d.	...	|	...	1642	...	|	...	|	|	...	...	1843	|	...	...	...	|	|	...	...	2043	|	2146	2214	2246
Manchester Piccadilly 150 d.	...	|	1442	|	...	|	1542	|	|	...	1642	|	|	1742	...	...	|	|	1842	...	|	|	|	|	|
Birmingham New St 150 a.	...	1627	1630	1702	...	1727	1730	1800	1827	...	1830	1902	1927	1930	...	...	2000	2027	2032	...	2102	2124	2204	2233	2304
Birmingham New St 142 d.	...	1633	1642	1712	...	1733	1742	1812	1833	...	1842	1912	1933	1942	...	...	2012	2033	2042	...	2112	...	2212	...	...
Reading 129 a.	...	1809	|	|	...	1909	|	|	2009	...	|	|	2109	|	...	...	|	2210	|	...	|	...	|	...	...
Cheltenham Spa 133 a.	...	...	1724	1750	...	...	1824	1850	...	...	1924	1950	...	2024	...	...	2050	...	2124	...	2150	...	2250	...	...
Bristol Parkway 133 a.	...	...	1802	1823	...	...	1908	1923	...	...	2002	2023	...	2057	...	...	2123	...	2159	...	2224	...	2324	...	...
Bristol T Meads 133 a.	...	...	1814	1837	...	...	1920	1935	...	...	2016	2035	...	2109	...	...	2135	...	2221	...	2236	...	2336	...	...
Exeter 115 a.	...	...	...	1948	...	...	...	2045	...	...	2126	2144	...	...	...	...	2244	...	...	...	...	...	...	...	...
Plymouth 115 a.	...	...	...	2048	...	...	...	2145	...	...	2238	2246	...	...	...	...	2349	...	...	...	...	...	...	...	...

S – To Glasgow (a. 2218).
T – From Paignton, Table **120**.
V – To Glasgow (a. 2112).
X – To Glasgow (a. 2214).
Z – From Penzance, Tabe **120**.

128 LONDON - AYLESBURY, STRATFORD and BIRMINGHAM

2nd class CH

LONDON - STRATFORD UPON AVON and BIRMINGHAM

km		⚒	Ⓐ	⚒	Ⓐ	⑥	Ⓐ	⚒	Ⓐ	Ⓐ	⑥	Ⓐ	⚒	⑥	Ⓐ	⑥	Ⓐ	⑥	Ⓐ	⑥	Ⓐ	⚒	⚒	⚒	⚒
0	**London** Marylebone ... d.		...	...	0610	0624	0650	...	0715	0723	0724	0750	0818	0845	0850	0912	0917	0915	0920	0945	0950	1018	1050	1053	1120
45	High Wycombe ... d.		...	0610	0650	0710	0720	...	0750	0800	0810	|	0851	0915	0920	|	|	0942	0950	1015	1020	1048	|	1127	1150
111	Banbury ... **129** d.		...	0702	0744	0801	0805	...	0834	0845	0858	0858	0935	0958	0957	1020	|	1038	1035	1058	1057	1135	1157	1217	1235
143	**Leamington Spa** ... **129** d.		0655	0721	...	0821	0824	0830	0852	0903	0917	0915	0954	1017	1015	1038	1049	1058	1054	1117	1115	1154	1215	1238	1254
146	Warwick ... d.		0659	0725	...	0824	0828	0834	0857	0908	0921	0919	0958	1021	1019	1042	1053	1102	1059	1121	1119	1159	1219	1242	1259
167	**Stratford upon Avon** ... a.		0730	|	...	|	|	0906	|	0940	|	|	|	|	|	1111	1116	|	|	|	|	|	|	1311	|
169	Solihull ... a.		...	0750	...	0850	0848	...	0920	...	0941	0938	1022	1045	1038	...	...	1123	1118	1142	1138	1222	1238	...	1319
180	**Birmingham** Snow Hill ... a.		...	0811	...	0908	0907	...	0941	...	1002	1001	1041	1104	1101	...	...	1141	1141	1201	1201	1242	1302	...	1341

	⚒	⚒	⚒	⚒	⚒	⚒	⚒	⚒	⚒	⑥	Ⓐ	⑥	Ⓐ	Ⓐ	⑥	⑥	Ⓐ	⑥	Ⓐ	Ⓐ	Ⓐ	⑥	Ⓐ	⑥	Ⓐ
London Marylebone ... d.	1150	1220	1250	1320	1350	1353	1420	1450	1520	1550	1600	1620	1630	1636	1650	1653	1700	1720	1730	...	1738	1750	1800	1820	1830
High Wycombe ... d.	|	1249	|	1350	|	1428	1450	|	1550	|	|	1650	|	1705	|	1727	|	1749	|	...	1815	|	|	1850	|
Banbury ... **129** d.	1257	1332	1357	1435	1457	1513	1535	1557	1635	1658	1703	1735	1733	1752	1758	1819	1803	1832	1839	...	1904	1903	1905	1935	1936
Leamington Spa ... **129** d.	1315	1351	1415	1454	1515	1533	1554	1615	1654	1717	1722	1754	1750	...	1817	1838	1823	1851	1858	1906	...	1923	1922	1954	1954
Warwick ... d.	1319	1358	1419	1459	1519	1538	1559	1619	1659	1721	1727	1759	1756	...	1821	1842	1829p	1858	1903	1910	...	1927	1928p	1959	1959
Stratford upon Avon ... a.	|	|	|	|	|	1611	|	|	|	|	|	|	|	...	|	1913	|	|	|	1939	...	|	|	|	|
Solihull ... a.	1342	1422	1441	1519	1541	...	1622	1642	1722	1742	1748	1822	1817	...	1841	...	1845	1922	1927	...	...	1948	1944	2022	2022
Birmingham Snow Hill ... a.	1401	1442	1502	1541	1601	...	1642	1702	1741	1802	1812	1841	1841	...	1904	...	1901	1941	1947	...	...	2006	2001	2042	2044

	⑥	⑥	Ⓐ	Ⓐ	⑥	Ⓐ	Ⓐ	Ⓐ	⑥	Ⓐ	Ⓐ	⑥	Ⓐ	Ⓐ	⑥	Ⓐ	Ⓐ	⑥		⑦	⑦	⑦	⑦	⑦	⑦
London Marylebone ... d.	1850	1853	1900	1903	1920	1930	1933	2000	2000	2030	...	2050	2100	2133	2200	2220	2240	2245	...		0810	0915	...	1015	1050
High Wycombe ... d.	|	1927	|	1933	1949	|	2004	|	2030	2100	...	2121	|	|	|	|	2321	2320	...		0840	0949	...	1049	|
Banbury ... **129** d.	2003	2019	2003	2026	2032	2038	2049	2106	2119	2147	...	2207	2210	2243	2306	2330	0014	0014	...		0927	1041	1100	1138	1202
Leamington Spa ... **129** d.	2023	2038	2023	...	2051	2056	2107	2125	2138	2205	2220	2227	2230	2300	2324	2348	...	...	...		0946	1101	1120	1158	1222
Warwick ... d.	2027	2042	2029p	...	2058	2100	2112	2131p	2142	2210	2224	2231	2235p	2305	2328	2353	...	...	...		0951	1105	1124	1202	1227p
Stratford upon Avon ... a.	|	2110	|	...	|	|	2143	|	|	|	2250	|	|	|	|	|	...	...	...		|	|	1154	|	|
Solihull ... a.	2047	...	2045	...	2122	2124	...	2147	2203	2235	...	2251	2251	2323	2349	0012	...	...	...		1014	1126	...	1225	1244
Birmingham Snow Hill ... a.	2106	...	2103	...	2141	2147	...	2204	2226	2258	...	2310	2305	2345	0010	0032	...	...	...		1039	1145	...	1244	1303

	⑦	⑦	⑦	⑦	⑦	⑦	⑦	⑦	⑦	⑦	⑦	⑦	⑦	⑦	⑦	⑦	⑦	⑦	⑦	⑦	⑦	⑦	⑦	⑦	⑦
London Marylebone ... d.	1120	...	1150	1220	...	1250	1320	1350	1420	1433	1450	1520	1557	1622	1657	1720	1736	1757	1820	1857	1922	1957	2020	2050	2200
High Wycombe ... d.	1154	...	|	1254	...	|	1354	|	1454	1508	|	1554	|	1656	|	1754	1811	|	1854	|	1956	|	2054	2124	|
Banbury ... **129** d.	1241	1245	1305	1341	...	1402	1441	1502	1540	1600	1605	1641	1706	1743	1809	1841	1901	1909	1946	2009	2044	2109	2141	2211	2306
Leamington Spa ... **129** d.	1301	1305	1325	1401	1420	1425	1501	1522	1559	1620	1625	1701	1725	1803	1829	1901	1921	1929	2005	2029	2103	2129	2201	2231	2324
Warwick ... d.	1305	1309	1331p	1405	1424	1431p	1505	1527p	1603	1624	1630p	1705	1731p	1807	1834p	1905	1925	1934p	2009	2034p	2108	2134p	2205	2235	2328
Stratford upon Avon ... a.	|	1339	|	|	1454	|	|	|	|	1654	|	|	|	|	|	|	1954	|	|	|	|	|	|	|	|
Solihull ... a.	1325	...	1347	1426	...	1447	1525	1544	1626	...	1647	1725	1748	1831	1851	1927	...	1951	2032	2051	2129	2151	2225	2259	2347
Birmingham Snow Hill ... a.	1346	...	1408	1445	...	1506	1549	1602	1649	...	1704	1746	1807	1849	1910	1946	...	2010	2053	2110	2148	2210	2245	2318	0008

	⚒	Ⓐ	Ⓐ	⑥	Ⓐ	Ⓐ	Ⓐ	Ⓐ	⑥	⑥	Ⓐ	Ⓐ	Ⓐ	Ⓐ	⑥	⑥	Ⓐ	Ⓐ	⑥	Ⓐ	⑥	Ⓐ	⑥	⚒	⑥
Birmingham Snow Hill ... d.		...	...	...	...	0543	...	0614	0612	0636	...	0648	...	0714	0712	...	...	0745	0752	0812	0812	0852	0852	0912	...
Solihull ... d.		...	...	...	...	0556	...	0627	0625	0649	...	0703	...	0725	0725	...	...	0758	0805	0825	0825	0905	0905	0925	...
Stratford upon Avon ... d.		...	...	...	...	|	0610	|	|	|	0646	|	...	|	|	0735	0736	|	|	|	|	|	|	|	0938
Warwick ... d.		...	0540p	...	...	0615	0638	0644p	0645	0708	0713	0719p	...	0750	0748	0804	0805	0823	0825	0844	0849	0924	0925	0947	1004
Leamington Spa ... **115** d.		...	0545	...	...	0620	0645	0649	0649	0713	0718	0724	...	0854	0753	0809	0811	0827	0830	0849	0853	0929	0930	0953	1009
Banbury ... **115** d.		0524	0603	0605	0625	0638	...	0707	0707	0733	0736	0742	0752	0812	0813	0829	...	0845	0849	0910	0913	0947	0949	1012	1029
High Wycombe ... d.		0612	|	0653	0713	|	...	|	0753	|	|	|	0838	|	0857	0918	...	|	|	0951	0957	|	|	1057	1118
London Marylebone ... a.		0651	0718	0731	0750	0753	...	0816	0829	0849	0851	0854	0920	0927	0930	0955	...	0959	1001	1026	1034	1058	1102	1132	1156

	Ⓐ	⚒	⚒	⚒	⚒	⑥	Ⓐ	⚒	⚒	⚒	Ⓐ	⑥	⚒	Ⓐ	⑥	⑥	⚒	⚒	⚒	⚒	⑥	Ⓐ	⑥	Ⓐ	⑥
Birmingham Snow Hill ... d.	...	0952	1012	1052	1112	...	...	1152	1212	1252	1312	1312	1352	1412	1412	...	1452	1512	1552	1612	1652	1652	1712	1710	...
Solihull ... d.	...	1005	1025	1105	1125	...	...	1205	1225	1305	1325	1325	1405	1425	1425	...	1505	1525	1605	1625	1705	1705	1825	1723	...
Stratford upon Avon ... d.	0942	|	|	|	|	1138	1140	|	|	|	|	|	|	|	|	1436	|	|	|	|	|	|	|	|	1740
Warwick ... d.	1010	1024	1048	1124	1145	1204	1203	1224	1248	1324	1345	1345	1424	1449	1448	1504	1524	1544	1624	1648	1725	1723	1748	1749	1802
Leamington Spa ... **129** d.	1014	1029	1053	1129	1149	1209	1209	1229	1253	1329	1352	1353	1429	1454	1453	1509	1529	1549	1629	1653	1730	1728	1753	1754	1806
Banbury ... **129** d.	1032	1047	1112	1147	1207	1229	1228	1247	1312	1347	1409	1413	1447	1512	1513	1529	1547	1607	1647	1712	1749	1746	1813	1812	1824
High Wycombe ... d.	1117	|	1157	|	1253	1318	1317	|	1357	|	1453	1457	|	1557	1557	1618	|	1653	1726	1756	1828	1831	1857	1857	|
London Marylebone ... a.	1157	1202	1230	1301	1329	1358	1356	1402	1432	1501	1528	1531	1601	1631	1637	1656	1702	1731	1805	1833	1902	1908	1930	1934	1937

	Ⓐ	Ⓐ	⚒	⚒	Ⓐ	⑥	Ⓐ	⑥	Ⓐ	⑥	⑥	Ⓐ	Ⓐ		⑦	⑦	⑦	⑦	⑦	⑦	⑦	⑦	⑦	⑦	⑦
Birmingham Snow Hill ... d.	...	...	1752	1812	1912	1910	...	...	2012	2010	2111	2115	...	...		0840	0910	0940	...	1010	1040	1110	1140	...	1210
Solihull ... d.	...	...	1805	1825	1925	1923	...	...	2025	2023	2123	2127	...	...		0852	0922	0952	...	1022	1052	1122	1152	...	1222
Stratford upon Avon ... d.	1740	1740	|	|	|	|	1940	1948	|	|	|	|	2300	...		|	|	|	1000	|	|	|	|	1200	|
Warwick ... d.	1804p	1808	1825	1849	1950	1947	2009	2019	2050	2047	2147	2151	2321	...		0912	0941	1009p	1025	1041	1112p	1141	1209p	1225	1241
Leamington Spa ... **129** d.	1808	1812	1830	1853	1954	1952	2014	2023	2054	2052	2152	2155	2325	...		0917	0947	1016	1029	1047	1118	1147	1216	1229	1247
Banbury ... **129** d.	1826	1832	1848	1912	2012	2013	2032	2042	2112	2115	2215	2215	2343	...		0936	1006	1035	1048	1106	1137	1206	1235	1248	1306
High Wycombe ... d.	|	1920	1928	1959	2056	2100	2120	2134	2156	2202	2304	2259	...	...		|	|	1122	1136	|	1225	|	1322	1336	|
London Marylebone ... a.	1939	1958	2006	2037	2132	2137	2157	2222	2232	2240	2340	2334	...	...		1051	1123	1158	1217	1222	1301	1322	1358	1416	1422

	⑦	⑦	⑦		⑦	⑦	⑦		⑦	⑦		⑦	⑦	⑦		⑦	⑦		⑦	⑦	⑦	⑦		⑦	⑦
Birmingham Snow Hill ... d.	1240	1310	1340	...	1410	1440	...	...	1510	1540	...	1610	1640	1710	...	1740	...	...	1810	1840	1910	...	...	2015	2115
Solihull ... d.	1252	1322	1352	...	1422	1452	...	...	1522	1552	...	1622	1652	1722	...	1752	...	...	1822	1852	1921	...	...	2028	2128
Stratford upon Avon ... d.	|	|	|	...	|	|	1500	...	|	|	...	|	|	|	...	|	1800	...	|	|	|	1957	...	|	|
Warwick ... d.	1309p	1341	1412p	...	1442	1509p	1525	...	1544	1612p	...	1641	1709p	1741	...	1812p	1825	...	1841	1909p	1946	2022	...	2049	2149
Leamington Spa ... **129** d.	1316	1347	1418	...	1447	1516	1529	...	1549	1618	...	1647	1716	1747	...	1818	1829	...	1847	1916	1950	2026	...	2054	2154
Banbury ... **129** d.	1335	1406	1437	...	1506	1535	1548	...	1608	1637	...	1706	1735	1806	...	1837	1848	...	1906	1935	2010	2050	...	2113	2215
High Wycombe ... d.	1422	|	1525	...	|	1622	1641	...	|	1725	...	|	1822	|	...	1925	1936	...	|	2022	2104	...	...	2203	2307
London Marylebone ... a.	1500	1523	1602	...	1622	1658	1720	...	1723	1802	...	1821	1859	1922	...	2002	2016	...	2021	2058	2153	...	...	2252	2354

LONDON - AYLESBURY

FROM LONDON MARYLEBONE:

Ⓐ: 0632, 0704, 0726, 0756, 0827, 0857 and every 30 minutes until 1557; then 1627, 1657, 1727, 1803, 1836, 1851, 1925, 1957, 2027, 2057, 2127, 2157, 2227, 2257, 2327, 2357.

⑥: 0727, 0757 and every 30 minutes until 1957; then 2057, 2157, 2257, 2357.

⑦: 0827 and hourly until 2327.

FROM AYLESBURY:

Journey time: ± 55–60 minutes. *61 km.*

Ⓐ: 0531, 0608, 0626, 0647, 0700, 0732, 0750, 0806, 0835, 0910, 0935, 1005 and every 30 minutes until 1735; then 1755, 1825, 1845, 1915, 1935, 2005, 2035, 2105, 2135, 2235.

⑥: 0605, 0705, 0735 and every 30 minutes until 1905; then 2005, 2105, 2205.

⑦: 0735, 0835, 0905 and hourly until 2105; then 2235.

p – Warwick Parkway.

XC All services 🍸 **BOURNEMOUTH - READING - BIRMINGHAM** 129

Services on ⑦ valid until January 31.

km		Ⓐ	Ⓐ	Ⓐ	Ⓐ	Ⓐ	Ⓐ	Ⓐ	Ⓐ	Ⓐ	Ⓐ	Ⓐ	Ⓐ	Ⓐ	Ⓐ	Ⓐ	Ⓐ	Ⓐ	Ⓐ	Ⓐ	Ⓐ	Ⓐ	Ⓐ
																					E		
0	**Bournemouth** 108 d.	...	...	...	...	0630	...	0730	...	0845	...	0945	...	1045	...	1145	...	1245	...	1345	...	1445	...
25	Brockenhurst 108 d.	...	...	...	...	0649	...	0749	...	0900	...	1000	...	1100	...	1200	...	1300	...	1400	...	1500	...
46	**Southampton** Central 108 d.	0515	...	0615	...	0715	...	0815	...	0915	...	1015	...	1115	...	1215	...	1315	...	1415	...	1515	...
54	**Southampton** Airport ✈ 108 d.	0522	...	0622	...	0722	...	0822	...	0922	...	1022	...	1122	...	1222	...	1322	...	1422	...	1522	...
67	Winchester 108 d.	0531	...	0631	...	0731	...	0831	...	0931	...	1031	...	1131	...	1231	...	1331	...	1431	...	1531	...
97	Basingstoke 108 d.	0547	...	0647	...	0747	...	0847	...	0947	...	1047	...	1147	...	1247	...	1347	...	1447	...	1547	...
122	**Reading** 132 d.	0611	0641	0711	0741	0811	0841	0911	0941	1010	1041	1111	1141	1211	1241	1311	1341	1411	1441	1511	1541	1611	1641
166	Oxford 132 d.	0636	0707	0736	0807	0836	0905	0936	1007	1036	1107	1136	1207	1236	1307	1336	1407	1436	1507	1536	1607	1636	1707
203	Banbury 128 d.	0654	0726	0755	0827	0854	0926	0954	1025	1054	1125	1156	1227	1254	1325	1354	1428	1456	1525	1554	1630	1655	1728
235	**Leamington Spa** 128 d.	0712	0743	0812	0844	0912	0943	1012	1045	1112	1143	1213	1245	1312	1343	1412	1445	1514	1543	1612	1649	1713	1745
250	Coventry 142 143 d.	0727	|	0827	|	0927	|	1027	|	1127	|	1227	|	1327	|	1427	|	1527	|	1627	|	1727	|
267	Birmingham Intl. ✈ 142 143 d.	0738	|	0838	|	0938	|	1038	|	1138	|	1238	|	1338	|	1438	|	1538	|	1638	|	1738	|
280	**Birmingham** New St. 142 143 a.	0748	0816	0848	0918	0948	1018	1048	1118	1148	1218	1248	1318	1348	1418	1448	1518	1548	1618	1648	1718	1748	1818
	Manchester Piccadilly 150 a.	0939	|	1039	|	1139	|	1239	|	1339	|	1439	|	1539	|	1639	|	1739	|	1839	|	1939	|
	York 127 a.	...	1040	...	1145	...	1246	...	1346	...	1443	...	1540	...	1640	...	1740	...	1858	...	1944	...	2046
	Newcastle 127 a.	...	1149	...	1301	...	1346	...	1451	...	1553	...	1646	...	1751	...	1850	...	2013	...	2048	...	2155

	Ⓐ	Ⓐ	Ⓐ	Ⓐ	Ⓐ	Ⓐ	Ⓐ	Ⓐ	Ⓐ	Ⓐ		⑥	⑥	⑥	⑥	⑥	⑥	⑥	⑥	⑥	⑥	⑥	⑥	⑥
Bournemouth 108 d.	1545	...	1645	...	1745	...	1845	...	1945	...	...	⑥	...	...	...	0625	0637	...	0745	...	0845	...	0945	...
Brockenhurst 108 d.	1600	...	1700	...	1800	...	1900	...	2000	...	...		...	...	...	0639	0655	...	0800	...	0900	...	1000	...
Southampton Central 108 d.	1615	...	1715	...	1815	...	1915	...	2015	...	...		0509	...	0615	0653	0712	...	0815	...	0915	...	1015	...
Southampton Airport ✈ 108 d.	1622	...	1722	...	1822	...	1922	...	2022	...	...		0516	...	0622	0701	0722	...	0822	...	0922	...	1022	...
Winchester 108 d.	1631	...	1731	...	1831	...	1931	...	2031	...	...		0525	...	0631	0709	0731	...	0831	...	0931	...	1031	...
Basingstoke 108 d.	1647	...	1747	...	1847	...	1947	...	2047	...	...		0541	...	0647	0725	0747	...	0847	...	0947	...	1047	...
Reading 132 d.	1711	1741	1811	1841	1911	1941	2011	2041	2111	2146	...		0610	0646	0711	0747	0811	0840	0911	0940	1011	1040	1111	1140
Oxford 132 d.	1736	1807	1836	1910	1936	2007	2036	2118	2136	2230	...		0638	0712	0736	0815	0836	0907	0936	1007	1036	1107	1136	1207
Banbury 128 d.	1755	1827	1855	1928	1954	2028	2054	2141	2154	2253	...		0656	0733	0754	0835	0854	0925	0954	1025	1054	1125	1154	1225
Leamington Spa 128 d.	1812	1845	1912	1945	2012	2046	2112	2200	2212	2313	...		0714	0751	0812	0855	0912	0943	1012	1043	1112	1143	1212	1245
Coventry 142 143 d.	1827	|	1927	|	2027	|	2127	|	2224	2327	...		0727	|	0827	|	0927	|	1027	|	1127	|	1227	|
Birmingham Intl. ✈ 142 143 d.	1838	|	1938	|	2038	|	2138	|	2234	2337	...		0740	|	0838	|	0938	|	1038	|	1138	|	1238	|
Birmingham New St 142 143 a.	1848	1918	1948	2018	2048	2122	2148	2230	2245	2349	...		0751	0817	0848	0919	0949	1017	1048	1117	1148	1217	1248	1317
Manchester Piccadilly 150 a.	2039	|	2140	|	2235	...	2337	...	...	...	...		0939	|	1039	|	1139	|	1239	|	1339	|	1439	|
York 127 a.	...	2145	...	2254	...	...	...	...	...	...	...		...	1044	...	1144	...	1244	...	1344	...	1444	...	1544
Newcastle 127 a.	...	2251	...	...	...	...	...	...	...	...	...		...	1149	...	1250	...	1345	...	1450	...	1546	...	1646

	⑥	⑥	⑥	⑥	⑥		⑥	⑥	⑥	⑥	⑥		⑥	⑥	⑥	⑥	⑥		⑥	⑥	⑥	⑥		⑥
									E															
Bournemouth 108 d.	1045	...	1145	...	1245	...	...	1345	...	1445	...	...	1545	...	1645	...	1745	...	...	1845	...	1945	...	...
Brockenhurst 108 d.	1100	...	1200	...	1300	...	...	1400	...	1500	...	...	1600	...	1700	...	1800	...	...	1900	...	2000	...	...
Southampton Central 108 d.	1115	...	1215	...	1315	...	...	1415	...	1515	...	...	1615	...	1715	...	1815	...	...	1915	...	2015	...	...
Southampton Airport ✈ 108 d.	1122	...	1222	...	1322	...	...	1422	...	1522	...	...	1622	...	1722	...	1822	...	...	1922	...	2022	...	...
Winchester 108 d.	1131	...	1231	...	1331	...	...	1431	...	1531	...	...	1631	...	1731	...	1831	...	...	1931	...	2031	...	...
Basingstoke 108 d.	1147	...	1247	...	1347	...	...	1447	...	1547	...	...	1647	...	1747	...	1847	...	...	1947	...	2047	...	...
Reading 132 d.	1211	1240	1311	1340	1411	...	1440	1511	1540	1611	1640	...	1711	1740	1811	1840	1911	...	1940	2011	2040	2111	...	2140
Oxford 132 d.	1236	1307	1336	1407	1436	...	1507	1536	1607	1636	1707	...	1736	1807	1836	1907	1936	...	2007	2036	2107	2136	...	2207
Banbury 128 d.	1254	1325	1354	1425	1454	...	1525	1554	1625	1654	1725	...	1754	1825	1853	1925	1954	...	2030	2054	2125	2153	...	2225
Leamington Spa 128 d.	1312	1343	1412	1445	1512	...	1543	1612	1648	1712	1743	...	1812	1845	1912	1943	2012	...	2047	2112	2145	2212	...	2243
Coventry 142 143 d.	1327	|	1427	|	1527	...	|	1627	|	1727	|	...	1827	|	1927	|	2027	...	|	2127	2156	2227	...	|
Birmingham Intl. ✈ 142 143 d.	1338	|	1438	|	1538	...	|	1638	|	1738	|	...	1838	|	1938	|	2039	...	|	2138	2213	2239	...	|
Birmingham New St 142 143 a.	1348	1417	1448	1517	1548	...	1617	1648	1717	1748	1817	...	1848	1917	1948	2018	2048	...	2116	2148	2225	2248	...	2309
Manchester Piccadilly 150 a.	1539	|	1639	|	1739	...	|	1839	|	1940	|	...	2039	|	2141	|	2241	...	...	2334	...	...	...	...
York 127 a.	...	1644	...	1744	...	...	1859	...	1944	...	2040	...	...	2148	...	2243	...	...	...	...	...	...	...	...
Newcastle 127 a.	...	1748	...	1845	...	...	2013	...	2045	...	2150	...	...	2305	...	...	...	...	...	...	...	...	...	...

		⑦	⑦	⑦	⑦	⑦	⑦	⑦	⑦	⑦	⑦	⑦	⑦	⑦	⑦	⑦	⑦	⑦	⑦	⑦	⑦	⑦	⑦	⑦
												E												
Bournemouth 108 d.	⑦	...	...	0940	1040	...	1140	...	1240	...	1340	...	1440	...	1540	...	1640	...	1740	...	1840	...	1940	...
Brockenhurst 108 d.		...	...	0957	1057	...	1157	...	1257	...	1357	...	1457	...	1557	...	1657	...	1757	...	1857	...	1957	...
Southampton Central 108 d.		...	0915	1015	1115	...	1215	...	1315	...	1415	...	1515	...	1615	...	1715	...	1815	...	1915	...	2015	...
Southampton Airport ✈ 108 d.		...	0922	1022	1122	...	1222	...	1322	...	1422	...	1522	...	1622	...	1722	...	1822	...	1922	...	2022	...
Winchester 108 d.		...	0931	1031	1131	...	1231	...	1331	...	1431	...	1531	...	1631	...	1731	...	1831	...	1931	...	2031	...
Basingstoke 108 d.		...	0947	1047	1147	...	1247	...	1347	...	1447	...	1547	...	1647	...	1747	...	1847	...	1947	...	2047	...
Reading 132 d.		0911	1011	1111	1211	1254	1311	1340	1411	1440	1511	1540	1611	1640	1711	1740	1811	1840	1911	1940	2011	2040	2111	2140
Oxford 132 d.		0937	1037	1136	1237	1317	1337	1406	1437	1506	1537	1606	1637	1706	1737	1806	1836	1906	1937	2006	2037	2106	2136	2206
Banbury 128 d.		0953	1053	1153	1253	1335	1353	1425	1453	1525	1553	1625	1653	1725	1753	1825	1853	1925	1953	2025	2053	2125	2153	2225
Leamington Spa 128 d.		1011	1111	1211	1311	1353	1411	1443	1511	1543	1611	1643	1711	1743	1811	1843	1911	1943	2011	2043	2111	2143	2211	2243
Coventry 142 143 d.		1028	1128	1228	1326	|	1426	|	1526	|	1626	|	1726	|	1826	|	1926	1954	2026	2054	2126	2154	2223	2254
Birmingham Intl. ✈ 142 143 d.		1040	1140	1240	1338	|	1438	|	1538	|	1638	|	1738	|	1838	|	1938	2004	2038	2104	2138	2204	2233	2304
Birmingham New St 142 143 a.		1050	1150	1250	1348	1419	1448	1510	1548	1609	1648	1709	1748	1809	1848	1909	1948	2015	2048	2115	2148	2215	2242	2314
Manchester Piccadilly 150 a.		1246	1348	1442	1540	|	1640	|	1740	|	1840	|	1940	|	2040	|	2140	...	2244	...	2342	...	...	...
York 127 a.		...	...	...	...	1640	...	1742	...	1921	...	1942	...	2044	...	2142	...	...	...	...	...	...	...	...
Newcastle 127 a.		...	...	...	...	1748	...	1847	...	2026	...	2043	...	2154	...	2307	...	...	...	...	...	...	...	...

E – To / from Edinburgh.

L – To / from Leeds.

129 BIRMINGHAM - READING - BOURNEMOUTH

All services 🍸 XC

Services on ⑦ valid until January 31.

		Ⓐ	Ⓐ	Ⓐ	Ⓐ	Ⓐ	Ⓐ	Ⓐ	Ⓐ	Ⓐ	Ⓐ	Ⓐ	Ⓐ	Ⓐ	Ⓐ	Ⓐ	Ⓐ	Ⓐ	Ⓐ	Ⓐ	Ⓐ	Ⓐ	Ⓐ
					S	N	L						E										
Newcastle **127** d.	Ⓐ	...	...	...	...	...	...	...	0621	...	0723	...	0824	...	0935	...	1025	...	1127	...	1219	...	1334
York **127** d.		...	...	...	...	...	...	...	0727	...	0827	...	0927	...	1034	...	1127	...	1227	...	1326	...	1432
Manchester Piccadilly **150** d.		...	...	0500b	...	...	...	0726	|	0827	|	0927	|	1027	|	1127	|	1227	|	1327	|	1427	|
Birmingham New St **142 143** d.		0603	0633	0703	0733	0803	0833	0903	0933	1003	1033	1103	1133	1203	1233	1303	1333	1403	1433	1503	1533	1603	1633
Birmingham Intl. ✈ **142 143** d.		0614	|	0714	|	0814	|	0914	|	1014	|	1114	|	1214	|	1314	|	1414	|	1514	|	1614	|
Coventry **142 143** d.		0625	|	0725	|	0825	|	0925	|	1025	|	1125	|	1225	|	1325	|	1425	|	1525	|	1625	|
Leamington Spa **128** d.		0638	0700	0738	0804	0838	0900	0938	1000	1038	1100	1138	1200	1238	1300	1338	1400	1438	1500	1538	1600	1638	1700
Banbury **128** a.		0656	0721	0754	0820	0854	0918	0954	1017	1054	1117	1154	1217	1254	1317	1354	1417	1454	1517	1554	1617	1654	1717
Oxford **132** a.		0714	0741	0814	0840	0914	0941	1014	1041	1114	1140	1214	1240	1314	1340	1414	1440	1514	1541	1614	1640	1714	1741
Reading **132** a.		0739	0808	0840	0908	0939	1008	1039	1108	1139	1208	1239	1308	1339	1408	1439	1508	1539	1608	1639	1708	1739	1808
Basingstoke **108** a.		0808	...	0908	...	1008	...	1108	...	1208	...	1308	...	1408	...	1508	...	1608	...	1708	...	1808	...
Winchester **108** a.		0824	...	0924	...	1024	...	1124	...	1224	...	1324	...	1424	...	1524	...	1624	...	1724	...	1824	...
Southampton Airport ✈ **108** a.		0832	...	0932	...	1032	...	1132	...	1232	...	1332	...	1434	...	1532	...	1632	...	1732	...	1833	...
Southampton Central **108** a.		0844	...	0941	...	1043	...	1143	...	1241	...	1341	...	1442	...	1541	...	1641	...	1741	...	1844	...
Brockenhurst **108** a.		0859	...	0956	...	1058	...	1158	...	1256	...	1356	...	1456	...	1556	...	1656	...	1756	...	1858	...
Bournemouth **108** a.		0915	...	1012	...	1112	...	1212	...	1310	...	1410	...	1511	...	1610	...	1710	...	1815	...	1913	...

	Ⓐ	Ⓐ	Ⓐ	Ⓐ	Ⓐ	Ⓐ	Ⓐ	Ⓐ	Ⓐ	Ⓐ			⑥	⑥	⑥	⑥	⑥	⑥	⑥	⑥	⑥	⑥	⑥
																D	N	L					
Newcastle **127** d.	...	1426	...	1522	...	1632	...	1717	...	...	...	⑥	...	...	...	...	...	...	...	0621	...	0725	...
York **127** d.	...	1529	...	1625	...	1734	...	1824	...	...	...		...	...	...	...	...	...	...	0725	...	0827	...
Manchester Piccadilly **150** d.	1527	|	1627	|	1727	|	1827	|	1927	...	...		...	...	0511	...	...	...	0727	|	0827	|	0927
Birmingham New St **142 143** d.	1703	1733	1803	1833	1903	1933	2003	2033	2103	2203			0603	0633	0703	0733	0803	0833	0903	0933	1003	1033	1103
Birmingham Intl. ✈ **142 143** d.	1714	|	1814	|	1914	|	2014	|	2114	2214	...		0614	|	0715	|	0814	|	0914	|	1014	|	1114
Coventry **142 143** d.	1725	|	1825	|	1925	|	2025	|	2125	2225	...		0625	|	0725	|	0825	|	0925	|	1025	|	1125
Leamington Spa **128** d.	1738	1800	1838	1900	1938	2005	2038	2100	2138	2238	...		0638	0700	0738	0800	0838	0900	0938	1000	1038	1100	1138
Banbury **128** a.	1754	1818	1854	1917	1954	2021	2054	2117	2154	2254	...		0654	0717	0754	0817	0854	0917	0954	1017	1054	1117	1154
Oxford **132** a.	1814	1840	1914	1941	2014	2041	2114	2140	2214	2314	...		0714	0740	0814	0840	0914	0940	1014	1040	1114	1140	1214
Reading **132** a.	1839	1908	1939	2008	2039	2107	2140	2216	2242	2352	...		0739	0808	0839	0908	0939	1008	1039	1109	1139	1208	1239
Basingstoke **108** a.	1908	...	2009	...	2109	...	2209	...	2212	...	...		0808	...	0908	...	1008	...	1108	...	1208	...	1308
Winchester **108** a.	1924	...	2024	...	2124	...	2224	...	2228	...	...		0824	...	0924	...	1024	...	1124	...	1224	...	1324
Southampton Airport ✈ **108** a.	1933	...	2033	...	2133	...	2233	...	2337	...	...		0832	...	0932	...	1032	...	1132	...	1232	...	1332
Southampton Central **108** a.	1941	...	2041	...	2141	...	2242	...	0047	...	...		0841	...	0940	...	1043	...	1141	...	1241	...	1341
Brockenhurst **108** a.	1956	...	2058	...	2156	...	2356	...	...	...	...		0856	...	0957	...	1058	...	1157	...	1257	...	1357
Bournemouth **108** a.	2012	...	2115	...	2216	...	2321	...	...	...	...		0914	...	1011	...	1112	...	1211	...	1311	...	1411

	⑥	⑥	⑥	⑥	⑥	⑥	⑥	⑥	⑥	⑥	⑥	⑥	⑥	⑥	⑥	⑥	⑥	⑥	⑥	⑥			⑦
	E																						
Newcastle **127** d.	0830	...	0925	...	1025	...	1125	...	1222	...	1327	...	1422	...	1525	...	1622	...	1722	...	...	⑦	...
York **127** d.	0928	...	1025	...	1127	...	1225	...	1327	...	1427	...	1526	...	1625	...	1725	...	1825	...	...		...
Manchester Piccadilly **150** d.	|	1027	|	1127	|	1227	|	1327	|	1427	|	1527	|	1627	|	1727	|	1827	|	1927	...		...
Birmingham New St **142 143** d.	1133	1203	1233	1303	1333	1403	1433	1503	1533	1603	1633	1703	1733	1803	1833	1903	1933	2003	2033	2103	...		0903
Birmingham Intl. ✈ **142 143** d.	|	1214	|	1315	|	1414	|	1514	|	1614	|	1714	|	1814	|	1914	|	2014	|	2114	...		0914
Coventry **142 143** d.	|	1225	|	1325	|	1425	|	1525	|	1625	|	1725	|	1825	|	1925	|	2025	|	2125	...		0925
Leamington Spa **128** d.	1200	1238	1302	1338	1400	1438	1500	1538	1602	1638	1700	1738	1800	1838	1900	1938	2003	2038	2100	2138	...		0938
Banbury **128** a.	1217	1254	1319	1354	1417	1454	1519	1554	1618	1654	1717	1754	1817	1854	1917	1954	2019	2054	2119	2154	...		0954
Oxford **132** a.	1240	1314	1340	1414	1440	1514	1541	1614	1640	1714	1741	1814	1840	1914	1940	2014	2040	2114	2141	2216	...		1014
Reading **132** a.	1308	1339	1408	1439	1508	1539	1608	1639	1708	1739	1808	1839	1908	1939	2008	2039	2108	2139	2210	2241	...		1042
Basingstoke **108** a.	...	1408	...	1508	...	1608	...	1708	...	1808	...	1908	...	2008	...	2108	...	2208	...	2311	...		1109
Winchester **108** a.	...	1424	...	1524	...	1624	...	1724	...	1824	...	1924	...	2024	...	2124	...	2224	...	2327	...		1124
Southampton Airport ✈ **108** a.	...	1433	...	1532	...	1632	...	1732	...	1832	...	1932	...	2032	...	2133	...	2232	...	2335	...		1133
Southampton Central **108** a.	...	1441	...	1541	...	1641	...	1741	...	1840	...	1941	...	2041	...	2141	...	2241	...	2343	...		1142
Brockenhurst **108** a.	...	1457	...	1557	...	1657	...	1757	...	1857	...	1957	...	2057	...	2157	...	2257	...	...	...		1201
Bournemouth **108** a.	...	1511	...	1611	...	1711	...	1811	...	1911	...	2011	...	2111	...	2215	...	2321	...	...	...		1227

	⑦	⑦	⑦	⑦	⑦	⑦	⑦	⑦	⑦	⑦	⑦	⑦	⑦	⑦	⑦	⑦	⑦	⑦	⑦	⑦	⑦		⑦
									D		S						E						
Newcastle **127** d.	...	...	...	...	...	...	...	...	...	...	...	...	1318	...	1418	...	1518	...	1618	...	1718	...	...
York **127** d.	...	...	...	...	...	...	...	...	...	...	...	...	1422	...	1520	...	1620	...	1721	...	1820	...	...
Manchester Piccadilly **150** d.	0810	0911	...	1006	...	1105	...	1206	...	1303	...	1405	|	1502	|	1602	|	1702	|	1802	|	...	1902
Birmingham New St **142 143** d.	1003	1103	1133	1203	1233	1303	1333	1403	1433	1503	1533	1603	1633	1703	1733	1803	1833	1903	1933	2003	2033	...	2103
Birmingham Intl. ✈ **142 143** d.	1014	1114	|	1214	|	1314	|	1414	|	1514	|	1613	|	1714	|	1814	|	1914	|	2014	|	...	2114
Coventry **142 143** d.	1025	1125	|	1225	|	1325	|	1425	|	1525	|	1624	|	1725	|	1825	|	1925	|	2025	|	...	2124
Leamington Spa **128** d.	1038	1138	1200	1238	1300	1338	1400	1438	1500	1538	1600	1637	1700	1738	1800	1838	1900	1938	2000	2038	2100	...	2135
Banbury **128** a.	1054	1154	1218	1254	1318	1354	1418	1454	1518	1554	1618	1654	1718	1754	1818	1854	1918	1954	2018	2054	2118	...	|
Oxford **132** a.	1114	1214	1239	1314	1341	1414	1437	1514	1541	1614	1641	1714	1741	1814	1839	1914	1941	2014	2041	2114	2138	...	2208
Reading **132** a.	1142	1242	1309	1342	1410	1442	1509	1542	1609	1642	1709	1742	1809	1842	1909	1942	2009	2042	2109	2142	2210	...	2235
Basingstoke **108** a.	1209	1309	...	1409	...	1509	...	1609	...	1709	...	1809	...	1909	...	2009	...	2109	...	2211	...	...	...
Winchester **108** a.	1224	1324	...	1424	...	1524	...	1624	...	1724	...	1824	...	1924	...	2024	...	2124	...	2226	...	...	...
Southampton Airport ✈ **108** a.	1233	1333	...	1433	...	1533	...	1633	...	1733	...	1833	...	1933	...	2033	...	2133	...	2235	...	...	...
Southampton Central **108** a.	1242	1342	...	1442	...	1542	...	1642	...	1740	...	1842	...	1940	...	2043	...	2143	...	2243	...	...	...
Brockenhurst **108** a.	1301	1401	...	1501	...	1601	...	1701	...	1801	...	1901	...	2001	...	2101	...	2201	...	...	...	...	...
Bournemouth **108** a.	1327	1427	...	1527	...	1627	...	1727	...	1827	...	1927	...	2027	...	2127	...	2227	...	...	...	...	...

A – To / from Aberdeen.
D – To / from Derby.
E – To / from Edinburgh.
G – To / from Glasgow.
L – To / from Leeds.
N – To / from Nottingham.
S – To / from Sheffield.
b – ③④⑤ only.

130 GATWICK AIRPORT ✈ - READING

GW

km			Ⓐ	Ⓐ	Ⓐ	Ⓐ	Ⓐ	Ⓐ		Ⓐ	Ⓐ	Ⓐ	Ⓐ	Ⓐ	Ⓐ	Ⓐ			⑥	⑥		⑥	⑥	⑥
0	**Gatwick** Airport **102** d.	Ⓐ	0531	0556	0700	0758	0907	1003	and at	1703	1803	1916	2003	2103	2222	2318	...	⑥	0531	0603	and at	2103	2222	2318
10	Redhill d.		0543	0613	0710	0808	0923	1013	the same	1713	1813	1926	2013	2113	2233	2328	...		0541	0613	the same	2113	2233	2328
43	Guildford **107** d.		0612	0642	0742	0837	0954	1043	minutes past each	1745	1849	1955	2043	2143	2314	0001	...		0612	0643	minutes past each	2143	2314	0001
84	**Reading** **129 133** a.		0658	0729	0830	0917	1023	1119	hour until	1824	1925	2032	2119	2219	0001	0039	...		0703	0719	hour until	2219	2359	0038

		⑦	⑦	⑦		⑦	⑦	⑦
Gatwick Airport **102** d.	⑦	0608	0708	0808	and at	2108	2207	2307
Redhill d.		0619	0719	0819	the same	2119	2220	2320
Guildford **107** d.		0649	0751	0858	minutes past each	2151	2258	2351
Reading **129 133** a.		0724	0835	0935	hour until	2237	2337	0037

		Ⓐ	Ⓐ	Ⓐ	Ⓐ	Ⓐ	Ⓐ		Ⓐ	Ⓐ	Ⓐ
Reading **129 133** d.	Ⓐ	0434	0534	0634	0734	0834	0934	and at	1528	1634	1734
Guildford **107** d.		0510	0610	0710	0818	0913	1010	the same	1610	1710	1818
Redhill a.		0540	0639	0738	0846	0942	1038	minutes past each	1642	1738	1847
Gatwick Airport **102** a.		0554	0656	0750	0901	0959	1050	hour until	1659	1754	1900

	Ⓐ	Ⓐ	Ⓐ	Ⓐ	Ⓐ	Ⓐ			⑥	⑥		⑥	⑥	⑥	⑥			⑦	⑦	⑦		⑦	⑦	⑦
Reading **129 133** d.	1834	1934	2034	2134	2234	2334	...	⑥	0434	0534	and at	2034	2134	2234	2334	...	⑦	0603	0703	0803	and at	2103	2203	2315
Guildford **107** d.	1910	2010	2110	2218	2318	0021	...		0510	0610	the same	2110	2208	2318	0021	...		0640	0747	0839	the same	2147	2239	2359
Redhill a.	1938	2038	2149	2248	2358	0049	...		0539	0639	minutes past each	2144	2256	2358	0049	...		0709	0818	0918	minutes past each	2218	2318	0030
Gatwick Airport **102** a.	1953	2050	2206	2306	0012	0103	...		0558	0650	hour until	2159	2305	0010	0102	...		0727	0831	0931	hour until	2231	2331	0041

LONDON - WORCESTER - HEREFORD 131

GW Most trains 🍸

Services on ⑦ valid until January 31.

km			Ⓐ	Ⓐ	Ⓐ	Ⓐ	Ⓐ	Ⓐ	Ⓐ	Ⓐ	Ⓐ	Ⓐ	Ⓐ	Ⓐ	Ⓐ	Ⓐ	Ⓐ	Ⓐ 🚌	Ⓐ 🚌			⑥	⑥	⑥	⑥
0	**London** Paddington ..... 132 d.	Ⓐ	...	0548	0648	0822	0921	1022	1121	1321	1421	1551	...	1722	1750	1822	1922	...	...	...	⑥	0518	0621	0721	0821
58	Reading ..... 132 d.		...	0621	0722	0852	0952	1052	1152	1352	1452	1622	...	1750	1821	1850	1952	...	...	...		0549	0654	0753	0854
103	**Oxford** ..... 132 d.		...	0656	0804	0921	1025	1119	1219	1419	1519	1647	1731	1816	1854	1919	2022	2131	2301	...		0624	0721	0821	0921
148	Moreton in Marsh ..... d.		0537	0732	0834	0959	1100	1157	1257	1458	1556	1725	1814	1855	1935	1959	2100	2301	0040	...		0702	0800	0900	1000
172	Evesham ..... a.		0551	0750	0853	1019	1116	1217	1317	1516	...	1745	1833	1915	1952	2019	2120	2351	0130	...		0721	0822	0922	1021
172	Evesham ..... d.		0606	0757	0854	1029	1118	1229	1319	1519	...	1747	1841	1921	1957	2020	2125	2351	0130	...		0723	0824	0924	1024
194	**Worcester** Shrub Hill ..... 123 a.		0630	0817	0916	1051	1135	1250	1339	1539	...	1807	1911	1944	2023	2041	2145	0036s	0215	...		0742	0843	0944	1044
195	**Worcester** Foregate St. 123 a.		0636	0821	0919	1055	1139	1254	1343	1547	...	...	1917	1948	...	2045	2152	0046s	...	...		0746	0847	0947	1048
208	Great Malvern ..... 123 a.		...	0834	0931	1109	...	1307	1357	1600	...	...	...	2002	...	2058	2208	0116	...	...		0801	0904	1004	1104
219	Ledbury ..... 123 a.		...	...	...	1123	...	1323	...	...	...	...	...	2016	...	2112	2236	...	...	...		...	...	...	1121
241	**Hereford** ..... 123 a.		...	...	...	1144	...	1345	...	...	...	...	...	2034	...	2133	2257	...	...	...		...	...	...	1142

	⑥	⑥	⑥	⑥	⑥	⑥	⑥	⑥	⑥	⑥			⑦	⑦	⑦	⑦	⑦	⑦	⑦	⑦	⑦		⑦	⑦	⑦
London Paddington ..... 132 d.	1021	1121	1321	1421	1521	1621	1721	1821	1950	2150	...	⑦	0800	0935	1042	1242	1342	1442	1542	1642	1742	...	1842	1942	2127
Reading ..... 132 d.	1054	1156	1355	1454	1555	1654	1755	1854	2022	2222	...		0844	1011	1120	1320	1420	1520	1621	1720	1820	...	1920	2020	2208
Oxford ..... 132 d.	1121	1223	1421	1521	1621	1721	1821	1921	2049	2250	...		0916	1043	1150	1350	1450	1550	1650	1750	1850	...	1950	2050	2240
Moreton in Marsh ..... d.	1200	1302	1500	1600	1700	1800	1900	2000	2128	2329	...		0957	1123	1230	1429	1526	1629	1724	1829	1929	...	2029	2130	2323
Evesham ..... a.	1219	1321	1521	1618	1722	1822	1919	2019	2146	2347	...		1015	1142	1249	1445	1547	1648	1740	1846	1948	...	2049	2149	2341
Evesham ..... d.	1224	1324	1524	1624	1724	1824	1922	2027	2149	2349	...		1017	1144	1252	1448	1549	1650	1748	1853	1951	...	2055	2151	2344
Worcester Shrub Hill ..... 123 a.	1243	1344	1543	1644	1743	1844	1941	2046	2208	0011	...		1036	1203	1311	1509	1608	1710	1808	1913	2009	...	2114	2210	0003
Worcester Foregate St. 123 a.	1248	1347	1547	1648	1747	1854	1945	2050	2211	...	...		1039	1207	1315	1513	...	1714	1811	1917	2015	...	2118	2223	...
Great Malvern ..... 123 a.	1304	1404	1604	1704	1804	1907	...	2104	2227	...	...		1054	1221	1329	1526	...	1727	...	1930	2029	...	2132	2237	...
Ledbury ..... 123 a.	1321	...	...	...	...	1921	...	2118	...	...	...		...	1235	1343	1541	...	1742	...	...	...	...	2146	...	...
Hereford ..... 123 a.	1342	...	...	...	...	1945	...	2136	...	...	...		...	1255	1405	1606	...	1801	...	...	...	...	2205	...	...

		Ⓐ	Ⓐ	Ⓐ	Ⓐ	Ⓐ	Ⓐ	Ⓐ	Ⓐ	Ⓐ	Ⓐ	Ⓐ	Ⓐ	Ⓐ	Ⓐ	Ⓐ	Ⓐ 🚌	Ⓐ 🚌					⑥	⑥	⑥
Hereford ..... 123 d.	Ⓐ	...	...	0535	...	0643	...	...	...	1311	...	...	1511	...	...	...	...	...	...	...	...	⑥	...	...	0710
Ledbury ..... 123 d.		...	...	0552	...	0659	...	...	...	1330	...	...	1527	...	...	...	...	...	...	...	...		...	...	0730
Great Malvern ..... 123 d.		...	0517	0605	...	0714	0858	0954	...	1347	1434	...	1540	1700	...	...	...	...	...	...	...		0539	0635	0743
Worcester Foregate St. 123 d.		...	0531	0620	0651	0730	0909	1005	1206	1402	1452	...	1602	1720	1849	1927	2049	...	...	...	...		0554	0650	0757
Worcester Shrub Hill ..... 123 d.		0502	0535	0626	0653	0735	0912	1008	1208	1406	1456	...	1606	1724	1853	1929	2059	2250	...	...	...		0559	0654	0802
Evesham ..... a.		0516	0553	0644	0710	0753	0929	1026	1226	1424	1514	...	1625	1742	1917	1954	2144	2335	...	...	...		0616	0711	0820
Evesham ..... d.		0518	0555	0645	0711	0754	0930	1027	1227	1426	1522	...	1630	1751	1919	2022	2144	2335	...	...	...		0625	0725	0827
Moreton in Marsh ..... d.		0548	0616	0706	0727	0815	0950	1047	1247	1447	1543	1614	1651	1812	1936	2043	2234	0025	...	...	...		0646	0745	0848
Oxford ..... 132 a.		0625	0653	0746	0812	0849	1026	1128	1325	1525	1627	1646	1736	1901	2023	2120	0009	0148	...	...	...		0723	0828	0928
Reading ..... 132 a.		0654	0725	0821	...	0914	1054	1154	1354	1554	1654	...	1801	1925	2054	...	...	...	...	...	...		0752	0854	0954
London Paddington ..... 132 a.		0727	0759	0853	...	0947	1129	1229	1429	1627	1727	...	1830	2000	2129	...	...	...	...	...	...		0824	0929	1029

	⑥	⑥	⑥	⑥	⑥	⑥	⑥	⑥	⑥	⑥	⑥	⑥		⑦	⑦	⑦	⑦	⑦	⑦	⑦	⑦	⑦	⑦	⑦
Hereford ..... 123 d.	...	...	...	1213	...	1510	...	...	...	...	2020	...	⑦	...	...	...	1328	1430	...	1633	...	1830	...	...
Ledbury ..... 123 d.	...	...	...	1231	...	1529	...	...	...	...	2040	...		...	...	...	1346	1455	...	1652	...	1848	...	...
Great Malvern ..... 123 d.	0843	0943	1032	1243	1432	1543	1632	1743	1829	...	2053	2240		0900	1107	1310	1359	1508	...	1705	...	1911	2010	2055
Worcester Foregate St. 123 d.	0857	0957	1057	1257	1457	1557	1657	1757	1842	2002	2110	2251		0912	1119	1323	1414	1523	...	1723	1824	1924	2024	2110
Worcester Shrub Hill ..... 123 d.	0902	1002	1102	1302	1502	1602	1702	1802	1900	2006	2125	2254		0917	1123	1327	1419	1526	1628	1728	1828	1928	2028	2118
Evesham ..... a.	0920	1019	1119	1321	1519	1620	1719	1820	1917	2023	2142	2312		0934	1140	1344	1436	1544	1645	1745	1848	1945	2046	2136
Evesham ..... d.	0927	1027	1127	1327	1527	1627	1727	1827	1927	2037	2154	...		0936	1146	1347	1450	1551	1651	1751	1851	1951	2051	2151
Moreton in Marsh ..... d.	0948	1048	1148	1348	1548	1648	1748	1848	1948	2058	2215	...		0956	1207	1407	1507	1612	1712	1812	1912	2012	2112	2212
Oxford ..... 132 a.	1028	1128	1228	1428	1628	1728	1828	1928	2028	2136	2256	...		1034	1248	1450	1548	1650	1750	1849	1949	2049	2149	2248
Reading ..... 132 a.	1054	1154	1254	1454	1654	1754	1854	1954	2054	2204	2330	...		1120	1320	1520	1619	1721	1821	1919	2022	2119	2221	...
London Paddington ..... 132 a.	1129	1229	1329	1529	1729	1829	1929	2029	2129	2239	0010	...		1159	1359	1558	1659	1805	1902	2002	2102	2205	2313	...

s – Stops to set down only.

LONDON - OXFORD 132

GW

Services on ⑦ valid until February 7. Frequent additional, but slower, services operate London Paddington - Reading - Oxford and v.v.

km			Ⓐ	Ⓐ	Ⓐ	Ⓐ	Ⓐ	Ⓐ	Ⓐ	Ⓐ	Ⓐ	Ⓐ	Ⓐ	Ⓐ	Ⓐ	Ⓐ	Ⓐ	Ⓐ	Ⓐ	Ⓐ	Ⓐ	Ⓐ	Ⓐ	Ⓐ
0	**London** Paddington. 129 133 d.	Ⓐ	0548	0648	0722	0750	0822	0851	0921	0950	1022	1050	1121	1150	1222	1250	1321	1350	1421	1450	1522	1551	1622	1648
58	Reading ..... 129 133 d.		0621	0722	0752	0822	0852	0922	0952	1022	1052	1122	1152	1222	1252	1322	1352	1422	1452	1522	1552	1622	1652	1720
102	**Oxford** ..... 129 a.		0656	0802	0819	0848	0920	0952	1018	1048	1118	1150	1218	1248	1319	1351	1418	1447	1518	1550	1618	1647	1723	1750

	Ⓐ	Ⓐ	Ⓐ	Ⓐ	Ⓐ	Ⓐ	Ⓐ	Ⓐ	Ⓐ	Ⓐ	⑤	①–④	⑤	①–④	⑤	①–④			⑥	⑥	⑥	⑥	⑥	⑥
London Paddington 129 133 d.	1722	1750	1822	1851	1922	1950	2020	2051	2121	2148	2221	2221	2248	2248	2320	2320	...	⑥	0550	0621	0650	0721	0750	0821
Reading ..... 129 133 d.	1750	1822	1850	1922	1952	2022	2052	2122	2152	2222	2252	2306	2322	2334	2354	0004	...		0622	0654	0722	0753	0822	0854
Oxford ..... 129 a.	1815	1847	1918	1950	2021	2048	2121	2153	2224	2252	2326	2338	2348	0013	0028	0033	...		0652	0719	0748	0819	0848	0918

	⑥	⑥	⑥	⑥	⑥	⑥	⑥	⑥	⑥	⑥	⑥	⑥	⑥	⑥	⑥	⑥	⑥	⑥	⑥	⑥	⑥	⑥	⑥	⑥
London Paddington 129 133 d.	0850	0921	0950	1021	1050	1121	1150	1221	1250	1321	1350	1421	1450	1521	1550	1621	1650	1721	1750	1821	1850	1921	1950	2021
Reading ..... 129 133 d.	0922	0954	1022	1054	1122	1156	1222	1254	1322	1355	1422	1454	1522	1555	1622	1654	1722	1755	1822	1854	1922	1952	2022	2052
Oxford ..... 129 a.	0948	1019	1048	1119	1148	1221	1248	1319	1348	1419	1448	1518	1548	1619	1648	1718	1747	1818	1848	1918	1948	2020	2047	2119

	⑥	⑥	⑥	⑥					⑦	⑦	⑦	⑦	⑦	⑦	⑦	⑦	⑦	⑦	⑦	⑦	⑦	⑦	⑦	⑦
London Paddington 129 133 d.	2050	2117	2150	2206	...	...	...	⑦	0800	0842	0935	1042	1142	1242	1342	1442	1542	1642	1742	1842	1942	2042	2127	2242
Reading ..... 129 133 d.	2122	2152	2222	2241	...	...	...		0844	0922	1011	1120	1222	1320	1420	1520	1621	1720	1820	1920	2020	2122	2208	2320
Oxford ..... 129 a.	2153	2220	2249	2309	...	...	...		0916	0951	1041	1149	1250	1349	1449	1550	1650	1749	1849	1950	2048	2151	2237	*0010**

		Ⓐ	Ⓐ	Ⓐ	Ⓐ	Ⓐ	Ⓐ	Ⓐ	Ⓐ	Ⓐ	Ⓐ	Ⓐ	Ⓐ	Ⓐ	Ⓐ	Ⓐ	Ⓐ	Ⓐ	Ⓐ	Ⓐ	Ⓐ	Ⓐ	Ⓐ	Ⓐ
Oxford ..... 129 d.	Ⓐ	0559	0627	0656	0709	0733	0751	0805	0851	0901	0931	1001	1031	1101	1131	1201	1231	1301	1331	1401	1431	1501	1531	1601
Reading ..... 129 133 a.		0629	0654	0725	|	0758	0821	0836	0914	0932	0955	1025	1054	1124	1154	1225	1254	1324	1354	1424	1454	1524	1554	1624
London Paddington 129 133 a.		0709	0729	0759	0824	0830	0853	0906	0947	1009	1029	1059	1129	1157	1229	1300	1329	1359	1429	1501	1528	1600	1627	1700

	Ⓐ	Ⓐ	Ⓐ	Ⓐ	Ⓐ	Ⓐ	Ⓐ	Ⓐ	Ⓐ	Ⓐ	Ⓐ		⑤	①–④	Ⓐ			⑥	⑥	⑥	⑥	⑥	⑥	⑥
Oxford ..... 129 d.	1631	1701	1736	1801	1831	1901	1931	2001	2031	2101	2131	...	2234	2234	2305	...	⑥	0631	0701	0731	0801	0831	0901	0931
Reading ..... 129 133 a.	1654	1724	1801	1824	1854	1925	1954	2024	2054	2124	2206	...	2258	2258	2334	...		0700	0727	0752	0825	0854	0924	0954
London Paddington 129 133 a.	1727	1759	1830	1859	1929	2000	2029	2101	2129	2158	2243	...	2330	2337	0022	...		0737	0759	0824	0859	0929	0959	1029

	⑥	⑥	⑥	⑥	⑥	⑥	⑥	⑥	⑥	⑥	⑥	⑥	⑥	⑥	⑥	⑥	⑥	⑥	⑥	⑥	⑥	⑥	⑥	⑥
Oxford ..... 129 d.	1001	1031	1101	1131	1201	1231	1301	1331	1401	1431	1501	1531	1601	1631	1701	1731	1801	1831	1901	1931	2001	2031	2101	2136
Reading ..... 129 133 a.	1025	1054	1124	1154	1225	1254	1325	1354	1425	1454	1525	1554	1624	1654	1725	1754	1825	1854	1925	1954	2025	2054	2125	2204
London Paddington 129 133 a.	1059	1129	1159	1229	1259	1329	1359	1429	1459	1529	1559	1629	1659	1729	1759	1829	1859	1929	1959	2029	2059	2129	2159	2239

	⑥	⑥	⑥			⑦	⑦	⑦	⑦		⑦	⑦	⑦	⑦	⑦	⑦	⑦	⑦	⑦	⑦	⑦	⑦		
Oxford ..... 129 d.	2208	2231	2301	...	⑦	*0745**	0901	1050	1150	...	1250	1350	1450	1550	1650	1750	1850	1950	2050	2150	2221	*2300**	...	...
Reading ..... 129 133 a.	2235	2254	2330	...		0847	0942	1120	1218	...	1320	1419	1520	1619	1721	1821	1919	2022	2119	2221	2300	2355	...	...
London Paddington 129 133 a.	2309	2331	0010	...		0951	1050	1159	1259	...	1359	1458	1558	1659	1805	1902	2002	2102	2205	2313	2354	0038	...	...

* – By 🚌, change at Didcot Parkway.

133 LONDON - BRISTOL - CARDIFF - SWANSEA

Most trains 🍸 GW

Services on ⑦ valid until January 31. For Cardiff – Swansea – South West Wales services, see Table **135**.

km			Ⓐ	Ⓐ	⑥ 2	⚒	Ⓐ	Ⓐ 2	⑥	Ⓐ	Ⓐ	Ⓐ Z	⑥	⚒	Ⓐ	⑥	Ⓐ	⑥	Ⓐ	⚒	⚒	Ⓐ 2	⚒	⑥ 2	Ⓐ
0	**London** Paddington ...... **115** d.	⚒	0530	0535	...	0630	0645	...	0700	0700	0715	0730	0730	0745	0748	0800	0800	0815	0815	0830	0845	...	0900	...	0915
58	Reading ...... **115** d.		0556	0606	...	0656	0711	...	0727	0726	0741	0757	0757	0811	0816	0827	0827	0841	0841	0857	0911	...	0927	...	0941
85	Didcot ...... d.		|	0620	...	0712	|	...	|	0742	0756	|	0812	|	0833	|	0842	0855	0856	0912	|	...	|	...	0956
124	**Swindon** ...... d.		0625	0650	0716	0730	0738	0754	0755	0800	0813	0827	0830	0838	0854	0855	0900	0915	0913	0930	0938	0954	0955	1014	1013
164	Stroud ...... d.		|	0722	0745	|	|	0822	|	|	|	|	|	|	0922	|	|	0945	|	|	|	1022	|	1043	|
183	Gloucester ...... **121** d.		|	0745	0806	|	|	0850	|	|	|	|	|	|	0944	|	|	1006	|	|	|	1050	|	1107	|
194	**Cheltenham** ...... **121** a.		|	0801	0824	|	|	0903	|	|	|	|	|	|	1001	|	|	1022	|	|	|	1103	|	1122	|
151	Chippenham ...... d.		0640	...	...	0745	|	...	0810	0815	|	0841	0845	|	...	0910	0915	...	|	0945	|	...	1010	...	|
172	Bath ...... **138 139** a.		0652	...	...	0757	|	...	0824	0827	|	0855	0900	|	...	0924	0929	...	|	0959	|	...	1023	...	|
180	**Bristol** Parkway ...... d.		|	...	...	|	0807	...	|	|	0840	|	|	0907	...	|	|	...	0940	|	1007	...	|	...	1040
190	**Bristol** T. Meads ...... **139** a.		0707	...	...	0817	|	...	0839	0844	|	0910	0915	|	...	0939	0944	...	|	1015	|	...	1039	...	|
221	Weston super Mare .... **137** a.		|	...	...	...	|	...	...	...	|	|	|	|	...	...	...	...	|	...	|	...	...	...	|
	Taunton ...... **137** a.		|	...	...	...	|	...	...	...	|	0945	0950	|	...	...	...	...	|	...	|	...	...	...	|
215	Newport ...... **139** a.		0744	...	...	...	0831	...	...	...	0907	...	...	0931	...	...	...	...	1004	...	1031	...	...	...	1104
234	**Cardiff** Central ...... **139** a.		0800	...	...	...	0849	...	...	...	0924	...	...	0947	...	...	...	...	1021	...	1046	...	...	...	1123
307	**Swansea** ...... **135** a.		0857	...	...	...	0946	...	...	...	...	...	...	1044	...	...	...	...	...	...	1143	...	...	...	...

	⚒	⚒	Ⓐ	Ⓐ	⑥	Ⓐ	⑥	⚒	⚒	Ⓐ 2	⚒	Ⓐ	⑥ 2	⚒	⚒	Ⓐ	⚒	Ⓐ	⑥	⚒	⚒	Ⓐ 2	⚒	Ⓐ	⑥ 2
London Paddington ...... **115** d.	0930	0945	0948	1000	1000	1015	1015	1030	1045	...	1100	1115	...	1130	1145	1148	1200	1215	1215	1230	1245	...	1300	1315	...
Reading ...... **115** d.	0957	1011	1016	1027	1027	1041	1041	1057	1111	...	1127	1141	...	1157	1211	1216	1227	1241	1241	1257	1311	...	1327	1341	...
Didcot ...... d.	1012	|	1033	|	|	1056	1055	1112	|	...	|	1156	...	1212	|	1233	|	1256	1255	1312	|	...	|	1356	...
Swindon ...... d.	1030	1038	1054	1055	1055	1113	1115	1130	1138	1154	1155	1213	1214	1230	1238	1254	1255	1313	1315	1330	1338	1354	1355	1413	1414
Stroud ...... d.	|	|	1122	|	|	|	1145	|	|	1222	|	|	1243	|	|	1322	|	|	1345	|	|	1422	|	|	1443
Gloucester ...... **121** d.	|	|	1144	|	|	|	1207	|	|	1250	|	|	1303	|	|	1344	|	|	1406	|	|	1450	|	|	1503
Cheltenham ...... **121** a.	|	|	1201	|	|	|	1222	|	|	1303	|	|	1322	|	|	1401	|	|	1422	|	|	1503	|	|	1525
Chippenham ...... d.	1045	|	...	1110	1110	|	...	1145	|	...	1210	|	...	1245	|	...	1310	|	...	1345	|	...	1410	|	...
Bath ...... **138 139** a.	1100	|	...	1124	1124	|	...	1159	|	...	1223	|	...	1259	|	...	1324	|	...	1359	|	...	1423	|	...
Bristol Parkway ...... d.	|	1107	...	|	|	1140	...	|	1207	...	|	1240	...	|	1307	...	|	1340	...	|	1407	...	|	1440	...
Bristol T. Meads ...... **139** a.	1115	|	...	1140	1139	|	...	1215	|	...	1239	|	...	1315	|	...	1342	|	...	1415	|	...	1439	|	...
Weston super Mare .... **137** a.	...	|	...	1206	...	|	...	...	|	...	...	|	...	...	|	...	...	|	...	...	|	...	...	|	...
Taunton ...... **137** a.	...	|	...	1229	...	|	...	...	|	...	...	|	...	...	|	...	...	|	...	...	|	...	...	|	...
Newport ...... **139** a.	...	1131	...	...	...	1204	...	...	1231	...	...	1304	...	...	1331	...	...	1404	...	...	1431	...	...	1504	...
Cardiff Central ...... **139** a.	...	1146	...	...	...	1221	...	...	1246	...	...	1322	...	...	1347	...	...	1422	...	...	1446	...	...	1523	...
Swansea ...... **135** a.	...	1243	...	...	...	...	...	...	1343	...	...	...	...	...	1443	...	...	...	...	...	1543	...	...	...	...

	⚒	⚒	Ⓐ	⚒	Ⓐ	⑥	Ⓐ	⑥	⚒	Ⓐ 2	⚒	Ⓐ	⑥ 2	Ⓐ	⑥	⚒	Ⓐ	⚒	Ⓐ	⑥	Ⓐ	⑥ T	⚒	Ⓐ 2	⑥
London Paddington ...... **115** d.	1330	1345	1348	1400	1415	1415	1430	1430	1445	...	1500	1515	...	1530	1530	1545	1548	1600	1615	1615	1630	1630	1645	...	1700
Reading ...... **115** d.	1357	1411	1416	1427	1441	1441	1457	1457	1511	...	1527	1541	...	1557	1559	1611	1616	1627	1641	1641	1657	1657	1711	...	1727
Didcot ...... d.	1412	|	1433	|	1456	1455	1512	1512	|	...	|	1556	...	1612	1612	1638	1633	|	1656	1655	1712	1712	|	...	|
Swindon ...... d.	1430	1438	1454	1455	1513	1515	1530	1530	1538	1554	1555	1613	1614	1630	1632	|	1654	1655	1713	1715	1730	1730	1738	1754	1755
Stroud ...... d.	|	|	1522	|	|	1545	|	|	|	1622	|	|	1643	|	|	|	1722	|	|	1745	|	|	|	1822	|
Gloucester ...... **121** d.	|	|	1544	|	|	1606	|	|	|	1650	|	|	1703	|	|	|	1746	|	|	1806	|	|	|	1849	|
Cheltenham ...... **121** a.	|	|	1601	|	|	1622	|	|	|	1703	|	|	1725	|	|	|	1801	|	|	1822	|	|	|	1903	|
Chippenham ...... d.	1445	|	...	1510	|	...	1545	1545	|	...	1610	|	...	1645	1647	|	...	1710	|	...	1745	1745	|	...	1810
Bath ...... **138 139** a.	1459	|	...	1524	|	...	1559	1559	|	...	1624	|	...	1659	1700	|	...	1724	|	...	1800	1800	|	...	1824
Bristol Parkway ...... d.	|	1507	...	|	1540	...	|	|	1607	...	|	1640	...	|	|	1707	...	|	1740	...	|	|	1807	...	|
Bristol T. Meads ...... **139** a.	1515	|	...	1541	|	...	1615	1615	|	...	1639	|	...	1715	1715	|	...	1741	|	...	1815	1815	|	...	1839
Weston super Mare .... **137** a.	...	|	...	...	|	...	1650	...	|	...	...	|	...	1749	...	|	...	...	|	...	1855	1836	|	...	...
Taunton ...... **137** a.	...	|	...	...	|	...	...	...	|	...	...	|	...	...	...	|	...	...	|	...	1928	1906	|	...	...
Newport ...... **139** a.	...	1531	...	...	1604	...	...	...	1631	...	...	1704	...	...	...	1731	...	...	1804	...	...	...	1831	...	...
Cardiff Central ...... **139** a.	...	1546	...	...	1622	...	...	...	1646	...	...	1722	...	...	...	1746	...	...	1820	...	...	...	1848	...	...
Swansea ...... **135** a.	...	1643	...	...	...	...	...	...	1743	...	...	...	...	...	...	1848	...	...	1919	...	...	...	1945	...	...

	Ⓐ	Ⓐ	⑥ 2	Ⓐ	⑥	⚒ C	Ⓐ	⑥	Ⓐ	Ⓐ	⑥	Ⓐ	⑥	①–④	⑤	⑥	Ⓐ	⑥	Ⓐ	⑥ 2	⚒	Ⓐ 2	Ⓐ	⑥	⑥
London Paddington ...... **115** d.	1700	1715	...	1730	1730	1745	1748	1800	1800	1815	1815	1830	1830	1845	1845	1845	1848	1900	1900	...	1915	...	1930	1930	1945
Reading ...... **115** d.	1726	1741	...	1753	1757	1811	1816	1827	1827	1841	1841	1856	1857	1911	1911	1911	1916	1927	1927	...	1941	...	1957	1957	2011
Didcot ...... d.	1742	1756	...	1812	1812	|	1833	|	1842	1856	1855	1912	1912	|	|	|	1933	|	1942	...	1955	...	2012	2012	|
Swindon ...... d.	1800	1813	1814	1830	1830	1838	1854	1855	1900	1913	1915	1930	1930	1938	1938	1939	1954	1955	2000	2000	2013	2024	2030	2030	2039
Stroud ...... d.	|	|	1843	|	|	|	1922	|	|	|	1945	|	|	|	|	|	2022	|	|	2030	|	2052	|	|	|
Gloucester ...... **121** d.	|	|	1903	|	|	|	1945	|	|	|	2006	|	|	|	|	|	2044	|	|	2051	|	2114	|	|	|
Cheltenham ...... **121** a.	|	|	1925	|	|	|	2001	|	|	|	2022	|	|	|	|	|	2101	|	|	2105	|	2129	|	|	|
Chippenham ...... d.	1815	|	...	1845	1845	|	...	1910	1915	|	...	1945	1945	|	|	|	...	2010	2015	...	|	...	2045	2045	|
Bath ...... **138 139** a.	1827	|	...	1857	1900	|	...	1924	1928	|	...	1957	1959	|	|	|	...	2024	2028	...	|	...	2059	2100	|
Bristol Parkway ...... d.	|	1840	...	|	|	1911	...	|	|	1940	...	|	|	2007	2007	2006	...	|	|	...	2040	...	|	|	2107
Bristol T. Meads ...... **139** a.	1844	|	...	1912	1915	|	...	1939	1943	|	...	2013	2015	|	|	|	...	2040	2044	...	|	...	2115	2115	|
Weston super Mare .... **137** a.	...	|	...	1948	1950	|	...	...	...	|	...	2053	2036	|	|	|	...	2126	...	...	|	...	2148	...	|
Taunton ...... **137** a.	...	|	...	2021	...	|	...	...	...	|	...	...	2103	|	|	|	...	2158	...	...	|	...	...	...	|
Newport ...... **139** a.	...	1911	...	...	...	1937	...	...	...	2007	...	...	...	2031	2035	2031	...	...	...	...	2104	...	...	...	2130
Cardiff Central ...... **139** a.	...	1926	...	...	...	1952	...	...	...	2022	...	...	...	2045	2051	2055	...	...	...	...	2122	...	...	...	2146
Swansea ...... **135** a.	...	2023	...	...	...	2049	...	...	...	2119	...	...	...	2143	2149	2143	...	...	...	...	2219	...	...	...	2243

	Ⓐ	⚒	Ⓐ	⑥	⑥ E	⑥		Ⓐ 2	Ⓐ	⑥	⑥	Ⓐ Ev	Ⓐ Ew	⑥		⑤	①–④	Ⓐ 2	⑥	⑤	①–④		⑥	⑤	①–④
London Paddington ...... **115** d.	1948	2000	2015	2015	2030	2045	...	...	2115	2130	...	2145	2145	2200	...	2215	2215	...	2235	2245	2245	...	2330	2330	2330
Reading ...... **115** d.	2016	2027	2041	2041	2057	2111	...	...	2141	2157	...	2211	2211	2227	...	2241	2250	...	2302	2311	2321	...	2359	0005	0008
Didcot ...... d.	2033	2042	2056	2055	2112	|	...	...	2200	2212	...	2230	2230	2241	...	2301	2308	...	2322	2330	2339	...	0018	0025	0025
Swindon ...... d.	2054	2100	2113	2015	2130	2145	...	2154	2219	2230	2235	2249	2249	2259	...	2320	2325	2333	2341	2319	2358	...	0036	0042	0045
Stroud ...... d.	2126	|	|	2145	|	|	...	2222	|	|	2304	|	|	|	...	|	|	0002	|	|	|	...	|	|	|
Gloucester ...... **121** d.	2146	|	|	2205	|	|	...	2245	|	|	2325	|	|	|	...	|	|	0024	|	|	|	...	|	|	|
Cheltenham ...... **121** a.	2202	|	|	2220	|	|	...	2303	|	|	...	|	|	|	...	|	|	...	|	|	|	...	|	|	|
Chippenham ...... d.	...	2115	|	...	2145	|	...	...	|	2245	...	2304	2304	2327	...	2334	2340	...	2356	|	|	...	0052	0057	0100
Bath ...... **138 139** a.	...	2128	|	...	2158	|	...	...	|	2259	...	2317	2317	2328	...	2347	2354	...	0010	|	|	...	0107	0111	0113
Bristol Parkway ...... d.	...	|	2140	...	|	2211	...	...	2245	|	...	|	|	|	...	|	|	...	|	0016	0024	...	|	|	|
Bristol T. Meads ...... **139** a.	...	2145	|	...	2215	|	...	...	|	2315	...	2333	2333	|	...	0003	0010	...	0025	|	|	...	0121	0127	0129
Weston super Mare .... **137** a.	...	...	|	...	2248s	|	...	...	|	...	...	0006s	0103	|	...	...	...	...	...	|	|	...	...	|	|
Taunton ...... **137** a.	...	...	|	...	2318	|	...	...	|	...	...	0037s	0134	|	...	...	...	...	...	|	|	...	...	|	|
Newport ...... **139** a.	...	...	2203	...	...	2246	...	...	2318	...	...	...	...	2358	...	...	...	...	...	0038	0052	...	...	0202s	0210s
Cardiff Central ...... **139** a.	...	...	2223	...	...	2306	...	...	2339	...	...	...	...	0019	...	...	...	...	...	0053	0112	...	...	0218	0231
Swansea ...... **135** a.	...	...	2320	...	...	0002	...	...	0037	...	...	...	...	...	...	...	...	...	...	0153	0213	...	...	...	...

C – To / from Carmarthen, Table **135**.
E – To / from Exeter, Table **115**.
P – To / from Plymouth, Table **115**.
Q – From Carmarthen on ⑥, Table **135**.
R – From Carmarthen on Ⓐ, Table **135**.

T – To / from Paignton, Table **115**.
Z – To / from Penzance, Table **115**.

s – Stops to set down only.
u – Stops to pick up only.

v – Ⓐ, Dec. 14 – Jan. 29.
w – Ⓐ, Feb. 1 – May 21.

♀ – Calling order: Newport - Bristol Parkway - Bristol Temple Meads - Bath.

GW Most trains 🍸 — LONDON - BRISTOL - CARDIFF - SWANSEA — 133

Services on ⑦ valid until January 31. For Cardiff – Swansea – South West Wales services, see Table **135**.

		⑦	⑦	⑦	⑦	⑦	⑦	⑦	⑦	⑦	⑦	⑦	⑦	⑦	⑦	⑦	⑦	⑦	⑦	⑦	⑦	⑦	⑦	⑦	⑦
		Z					2		C						C	P	2				C				
London Paddington 115 d.	⑦	0757	0830	...	0903	0930	...	1003	1037	...	1103	1137	1203	...	1237	1303	...	1337	1403	...	1437	1503	1537	1603	1627
Reading 115 d.		0834	0905	...	0937	1005	...	1037	1111	...	1137	1211	1237	...	1311	1337	...	1411	1437	...	1511	1537	1611	1637	1705
Didcot d.		0848	0922	...	0953	1019	...	1051	1126	...	1151	1225	1251	...	1325	1351	...	1425	1451	...	1525	1551	1625	1651	|
Swindon d.		0908	0941	0950	1010	1038	1047	1109	1145	1156	1209	1244	1309	1340	1345	1409	1421	1444	1509	1535	1545	1609	1642	1709	1735
Stroud d.		|	|	1018	|	|	1116	|	|	1222	|	|	|	1409	|	|	1451	|	|	1603	|	|	|	|	1804
Gloucester 121 d.		|	|	1040	|	|	1137	|	|	1245	|	|	|	1432	|	|	1518	|	|	1624	|	|	|	|	1824
Cheltenham 121 a.		|	|	1056	|	|	1150	|	|	1302	|	|	|	1448	|	|	1533	|	|	1646	|	|	|	|	1847
Chippenham d.		0924	|	...	1027	|	...	1125	|	...	1225	|	1325	...	|	1425	...	|	1525	...	|	1625	|	1725	...
Bath 138 139 a.		0937	|	...	1042	|	...	1239	|	...	1239	|	1339	...	|	1439	...	|	1539	...	|	1639	|	1741	...
Bristol Parkway d.		|	1008	...	|	1105	...	|	1211	...	|	1311	|	...	1411	|	...	1511	|	...	1612	|	1712	|	...
Bristol T. Meads 139 a.		0951	|	...	1056	|	...	1155	|	...	1253	|	1354	...	|	1455	...	|	1553	...	|	1654	|	1756	...
Weston super Mare 137 a.		|	|	...	...	|	...	1231	|	...	...	|	1425	...	|	|	...	|	...	...	|	1736	|	...	...
Taunton 137 a.		1027	|	...	...	|	...	...	|	...	...	|	...	...	|	1528	...	|	...	...	|	1800	|	...	...
Newport 139 a.		...	1033	...	...	1134	...	...	1236	...	...	1336	...	...	1436	...	...	1536	...	...	1636	...	1740	...	...
Cardiff Central 139 a.		...	1052	...	...	1153	...	...	1255	...	...	1355	...	...	1455	...	...	1555	...	...	1656	...	1759	...	...
Swansea 135 a.		...	1148	...	...	1250	...	...	1356	...	...	1451	...	...	15451	...	...	1651	...	...	17527	...	1855	...	...

	⑦	⑦	⑦	⑦	⑦		⑦	⑦	⑦	⑦	⑦	⑦	⑦		⑦	⑦	⑦	⑦	⑦		⑦	⑦	⑦	⑦	⑦
			2							E	2										2				
London Paddington 115 d.	1637	1703	...	1730	1737	...	1803	1827	1837	1903	...	1930	1937	...	2003	2030	2037	2103	2137	...	...	2203	2237	2303	2337
Reading 115 d.	1711	1737	...	1804	1811	...	1837	1905	1911	1937	...	2005	2011	...	2037	2105	2111	2137	2214	...	...	2250	2314	2346	0015
Didcot d.	1725	1751	...	|	1825	...	1851	|	1925	1951	...	|	2025	...	2051	|	2125	2152	2230	...	...	2305	|	|	|
Swindon d.	1744	1809	1822	1833	1845	...	1909	1935	1944	2009	2028	2033	2044	...	2109	2135	2144	2214	2251	...	2257	2325	2348s	0021s	0052s
Stroud d.	|	|	1850	|	|	...	|	2004	|	|	2057	|	|	...	|	2204	|	|	|	...	2326	|	|	|	|
Gloucester 121 d.	|	|	1918	|	|	...	|	2028	|	|	2117	|	|	...	|	2224	|	|	|	...	2347	|	|	|	|
Cheltenham 121 a.	|	|	*1947*	|	|	...	|	2048	|	|	2134	|	|	...	|	2245	|	|	|	...	0005	|	|	|	|
Chippenham d.	|	1825	...	1849	|	...	1925	...	|	2025	...	2048	|	...	2125	...	|	2227	|	...	...	2341	|	0037s	0107s
Bath 138 139 a.	|	1839	...	1908	|	...	1939	...	|	2039	...	2102	|	...	2139	...	|	2242	|	...	...	2355	|	0052s	0122s
Bristol Parkway d.	1811	|	...	|	1913	...	|	...	2011	|	...	|	2111	...	|	...	2211	|	2318	...	...	|	0016s	|	|
Bristol T. Meads 139 a.	|	1853	...	1924	|	...	1953	...	|	2054	...	2116	|	...	2153	...	|	2256	|	...	...	0009	0030	0105	0136
Weston super Mare 137 a.	|	...	...	1956	|	...	...	...	|	2125	...	...	|	...	2226	...	|	...	|	...	...	...	...	...	...
Taunton 137 a.	|	...	...	...	|	...	...	...	|	2149	...	...	|	...	...	...	|	...	|	...	...	...	...	...	...
Newport 139 a.	1836	...	...	...	1941	...	...	...	2036	...	...	...	2136	...	...	...	2240	...	2345	...	...	...	...	...	...
Cardiff Central 139 a.	1855	...	...	...	2000	...	...	...	2055	...	...	...	2259	...	...	...	2302	...	0007	...	...	...	...	...	...
Swansea 135 a.	1954	...	...	...	2056	...	...	...	2152	...	...	...	2255	...	...	...	2358	...	0103	...	...	...	...	...	...

		Ⓐ	Ⓐ	⚒	⑥	Ⓐ	⑥	Ⓐ	Ⓐ	⑥	Ⓐ	⚒	Ⓐ	⚒	Ⓐ	⚒	Ⓐ	⑥	Ⓐ	⑥	⚒	⚒	Ⓐ	⑥	Ⓐ
			2		♀		2																E		
Swansea 135 d.	⚒	...	...	...	0358	0358	...	...	0458	0458	...	...	...	0527	...	...	0558	0558	...	...	0628	...	...	...	0658
Cardiff Central 139 d.		...	...	...	0455	0515	...	...	0555	0555	...	...	...	0624	...	...	0655	0655	...	...	0725	...	...	...	0755
Newport 139 d.		...	...	...	0509	0533	...	...	0609	0609	...	...	...	0638	...	...	0709	0709	...	...	0739	...	...	...	0809
Taunton 137 d.		...	...	...	|	|	...	...	|	|	...	...	...	|	...	...	|	|	...	...	|	...	0654	0655	|
Weston super Mare 137 d.		...	...	...	|	|	...	...	|	|	...	...	...	|	...	0620	|	|	0649	...	|	...	0724	0725	|
Bristol T. Meads 139 d.		0447	...	0530	0600	|	...	0600	|	|	...	0630	0640	|	...	0700	|	|	0730	0730	|	...	0800	0800	|
Bristol Parkway d.		0457u	...	|	0542	0601	...	|	0631	0631	...	|	|	0701	...	|	0731	0731	|	|	0801	...	|	|	0831
Bath 138 139 d.		|	...	0543	0613	|	...	0613	|	|	...	0643	0652	|	...	0713	|	|	0743	0743	|	...	0813	0813	|
Chippenham d.		|	...	0555	0625	|	...	0625	|	|	...	0655	0705	|	...	0725	|	|	0755	0755	|	...	0825	0825	|
Cheltenham 121 d.		|	...	|	|	|	0530	|	|	|	0553	|	|	|	0630	|	|	|	|	...	|	0729	|	|	|
Gloucester 121 d.		|	0519	|	|	|	0544	|	|	|	0610	|	|	|	0647	|	|	|	|	...	|	0745	|	|	|
Stroud d.		|	0536	|	|	|	0601	|	|	|	0629	|	|	|	0705	|	|	|	|	...	|	0803	|	|	|
Swindon d.		0523	0606	0611	0641	0628	0632	0641	0658	0659	0701	0711	0720	0728	0735	0741	0758	0758	0811	0811	0828	0835	0841	0841	0859
Didcot a.		0541	...	0628	0658	0646	...	0658	|	0716	0719	0728	|	0745	0753	0800	|	0816	0828	0828	0846	0852	0858	0858	|
Reading 115 a.		0556	...	0643	0714	0700	...	0713	0728	0731	0734	0743	|	0800	0812	0816	|	0832	0844	0844	0901	0907	0913	0914	0925
London Paddington 115 a.		0624	...	0716	0744	0732	...	0744	0802	0802	0807	0814	0815	0833	0840	0844	0856	0902	0913	0914	0932	0939	0944	0944	0959

	⑥	Ⓐ	⑥	Ⓐ	⑥	Ⓐ	Ⓐ	⑥	⚒	⑥	Ⓐ	⑥	Ⓐ	Ⓐ	⑥	Ⓐ	⑥	Ⓐ	⚒	Ⓐ	⑥	Ⓐ	⚒	⑥	Ⓐ
		P						E				T	R	T		2	2								
Swansea 135 d.	0658	...	...	0728	0728	...	...	...	0758	...	...	...	0828	...	...	...	...	...	...	0928	0928	...	...	...	...
Cardiff Central 139 d.	0755	...	...	0825	0825	...	...	...	0855	...	...	...	0925	...	...	...	...	0955	...	1025	1025	...	...	...	1055
Newport 139 d.	0809	...	...	0839	0839	...	...	...	0909	...	...	...	0939	...	...	...	...	1009	...	1039	1039	...	...	...	1109
Taunton 137 d.	|	0713	...	|	|	...	...	0758	|	...	...	0838	|	0905	...	...	...	|	...	|	|	...	...	...	|
Weston super Mare 137 d.	|	0749	...	|	|	...	...	0829	|	...	...	0902	|	0929	...	...	...	|	...	|	|	...	...	...	|
Bristol T. Meads 139 d.	|	0830	0830	|	|	...	0900	0900	|	...	0930	0930	|	1000	1000	...	...	|	1030	|	|	...	1100	...	|
Bristol Parkway d.	0831	|	|	0901	0901	...	|	|	0931	...	|	|	1001	|	|	...	...	1031	|	1101	1101	...	|	...	1131
Bath 138 139 d.	|	0843	0843	|	|	...	0913	0913	|	...	0943	0943	|	1013	1013	...	...	|	1043	|	|	...	1113	...	|
Chippenham d.	|	0855	0855	|	|	...	0925	0925	|	...	0955	0955	|	1025	1025	...	...	|	1055	|	|	...	1125	...	|
Cheltenham 121 d.	|	|	|	|	|	0831	|	|	|	0900	|	|	|	|	|	0940	1001	|	|	|	|	1031	|	1100	|
Gloucester 121 d.	|	|	|	|	|	0846	|	|	|	0916	|	|	|	|	|	0954	1015	|	|	|	|	1046	|	1116	|
Stroud d.	|	|	|	|	|	0905	|	|	|	0934	|	|	|	|	|	1011	1032	|	|	|	|	1105	|	1134	|
Swindon d.	0859	0911	0811	0928	0929	0935	0941	0941	0959	1004	1011	1011	1028	1041	1041	1042	1102	1059	1111	1128	1129	1135	1141	1204	1159
Didcot a.	0916	0928	0928	|	0946	0952	|	|	1016	1021	1028	1028	1046	|	|	...	...	1116	1128	|	1146	1152	|	1221	1216
Reading 115 a.	0932	0944	0944	0959	1000	1006	1010	1008	1032	1036	1044	1045	1100	1109	1111	...	...	1130	1144	1159	1200	1206	1210	1236	1230
London Paddington 115 a.	1002	1014	1014	1032	1032	1037	1039	1038	1102	1108	1114	1114	1132	1137	1140	...	...	1200	1214	1232	1232	1237	1240	1306	1309

	⚒	⚒	Ⓐ	⑥	Ⓐ	⑥	Ⓐ	⚒	Ⓐ	⑥	Ⓐ	⚒	⑥	Ⓐ	⚒	⚒	⚒	Ⓐ	⑥	Ⓐ	⚒	Ⓐ	⑥	Ⓐ	⚒
		Q	Z		2	2												2	2						
Swansea 135 d.	...	1028	...	...	...	...	...	...	1128	1128	...	...	...	...	...	1228	...	...	...	...	...	1328	1328	...	...
Cardiff Central 139 d.	...	1125	...	...	...	...	1155	...	1225	1225	...	...	...	1255	...	1325	...	...	...	1355	...	1425	1425	...	...
Newport 139 d.	...	1139	...	...	...	...	1209	...	1239	1239	...	...	...	1309	...	1339	...	...	...	1409	...	1439	1439	...	...
Taunton 137 d.	...	|	1126	...	...	...	|	...	|	|	...	...	...	|	...	|	...	...	...	|	...	|	|	...	...
Weston super Mare 137 d.	...	|	|	...	...	...	|	...	|	|	...	...	...	|	...	|	...	...	...	|	...	|	|	...	...
Bristol T. Meads 139 d.	1130	|	1200	1200	...	...	|	1230	|	|	...	1300	...	|	1330	|	1400	...	...	|	1430	|	|	...	1500
Bristol Parkway d.	|	1201	|	|	...	...	1231	|	1301	1301	...	|	...	1331	|	1401	|	...	...	1431	|	1501	1501	...	|
Bath 138 139 d.	1143	|	1213	1213	...	...	|	1243	|	|	...	1313	...	|	1343	|	1413	...	...	|	1443	|	|	...	1513
Chippenham d.	1155	|	1225	1225	...	...	|	1255	|	|	...	1325	...	|	1355	|	1425	...	...	|	1455	|	|	...	1525
Cheltenham 121 d.	|	|	|	|	1140	1201	|	|	|	|	1231	|	1300	|	|	|	|	1340	1401	|	|	|	|	1431	|
Gloucester 121 d.	|	|	|	|	1154	1215	|	|	|	|	1246	|	1316	|	|	|	|	1354	1415	|	|	|	|	1446	|
Stroud d.	|	|	|	|	1211	1232	|	|	|	|	1305	|	1334	|	|	|	|	1411	1432	|	|	|	|	1505	|
Swindon d.	1211	1228	1241	1241	1242	1302	1259	1311	1328	1329	1335	1341	1404	1359	1411	1428	1441	1442	1502	1458	1511	1528	1529	1535	1541
Didcot a.	1228	1246	|	|	...	...	1316	1328	|	1346	1352	|	1421	1415	1428	1446	|	...	...	1515	1528	|	1546	1552	|
Reading 115 a.	1244	1300	1309	1310	...	...	1330	1344	1359	1400	1406	1410	1436	1432	1443	1500	1509	...	...	1531	1544	1600	1600	1606	1610
London Paddington 115 a.	1314	1332	1340	1341	...	...	1406	1414	1432	1432	1437	1440	1509	1507	1514	1532	1539	...	...	1609	1614	1630	1632	1639	1644

C – To / from Carmarthen, Table **135**.
E – To / from Exeter, Table **115**.
P – To / from Plymouth, Table **115**.
Q – From Carmarthen on ⑥, Table **135**.
R – From Carmarthen on Ⓐ, Table **135**.
T – To / from Paignton, Table **115**.
Z – To / from Penzance, Table **115**.
s – Stops to set down only.
u – Stops to pick up only.
v – Ⓐ, Dec. 14 – Jan. 29.
w – Ⓐ, Feb. 1 – May 21.
♀ – Calling order: Newport - Bristol Parkway - Bristol Temple Meads - Bath.

133 SWANSEA - CARDIFF - BRISTOL - LONDON

Most trains 🍷 GW

Services on ⑦ valid until January 31. For South West Wales – Swansea – Cardiff services, see Table 135.

	⑥	Ⓐ	⚒	⚒	⚒	Ⓐ	⑥	Ⓐ	⚒	Ⓐ	⑥	Ⓐ	⚒	Ⓐ	⑥	Ⓐ	⑥	⚒	⚒	Ⓐ	⑥	Ⓐ	Ⓐ	⑥	⚒
						2	2													2	2				
Swansea 135 d.	...	...	...	1428	...	...	...	...	...	1528	1528	...	...	...	...	...	...	1628	...	...	...	...	...	...	1728
Cardiff Central 139 d.	...	1455	...	1425	...	...	...	1555	...	1625	1625	...	...	1655	...	...	...	1725	...	...	...	1755	...	...	1825
Newport 139 d.	...	1509	...	1539	...	...	...	1609	...	1639	1639	...	...	1709	...	...	...	1739	...	...	...	1809	...	...	1839
Taunton 137 d.	...	|	...	|	...	...	...	|	...	|	|	...	...	|	...	...	...	|	...	...	...	|	...	...	|
Weston super Mare 137 d.	...	|	...	|	...	...	...	|	...	|	|	...	...	|	...	1710	...	|	...	...	...	|	1810	...	|
Bristol T. Meads 139 d.	...	|	1530	|	1600	...	...	|	1630	|	|	...	1700	|	...	1730	1730	|	1800	...	...	|	1830	1830	|
Bristol Parkway d.	...	1531	|	1601	|	...	...	1631	|	1701	1701	...	|	1731	...	|	|	1801	|	...	...	1831	|	|	1901
Bath 138 139 d.	...	|	1543	|	1613	...	...	|	1643	|	|	...	1713	|	...	1743	1743	|	1813	...	...	|	1843	1843	|
Chippenham d.	...	|	1555	|	1625	...	...	|	1655	|	|	...	1725	|	...	1755	1755	|	1825	...	...	|	1855	1855	|
Cheltenham 121 d.	1500	|	|	|	|	1540	1601	|	|	|	|	1631	|	|	1700	|	|	|	|	1740	1801	|	|	|	|
Gloucester 121 d.	1516	|	|	|	|	1554	1615	|	|	|	|	1646	|	|	1716	|	|	|	|	1754	1815	|	|	|	|
Stroud d.	1534	|	|	|	|	1611	1632	|	|	|	|	1705	|	|	1734	|	|	|	|	1811	1832	|	|	|	|
Swindon d.	1640	1559	1611	1628	1641	1642	1702	1659	1711	1728	1729	1735	1741	1759	1804	1811	1811	1828	1841	1841	1902	1859	1911	1911	1928
Didcot a.	1621	1616	1628	1646	|	...	...	1716	1728	|	1746	1752	|	1816	1821	1828	1828	1846	|	...	...	1916	1928	1928	|
Reading 115 a.	1636	1631	1644	1700	1709	...	...	1731	1744	1755	1800	1806	1812	1831	1836	1844	1844	1901	1909	...	...	1931	1945	1944	1959
London Paddington 115 a.	1706	1706	1714	1732	1739	...	...	1802	1814	1824	1832	1839	1844	1902	1908	1914	1914	1932	1938	...	...	2007	2014	2014	2032

	Ⓐ	⑥	⚒	Ⓐ	⑥		⚒	Ⓐ	⑥	⑥	Ⓐ		Ⓐ	⑥	⑤	①–④		⑥	⑤	①–④	Ⓐ		⑥	⑤	①–④
							2						2	2				Z	Z	Z	2			y	x
Swansea 135 d.	...	...	...	1828	1828	...	...	...	...	1928	1929	...	...	...	2028	2028	...	...	...	...	...	...	...	...	...
Cardiff Central 139 d.	...	...	...	1925	1925	...	...	...	...	2025	2025	...	...	...	2125	2125	...	...	...	...	...	...	...	...	...
Newport 139 d.	...	...	...	1939	1939	...	...	...	...	2039	2039	...	...	...	2139	2139	...	...	...	...	...	...	...	...	...
Taunton 137 d.	...	...	...	|	|	...	...	...	...	|	|	...	...	...	|	|	...	2114	2114	2114	...	...	2129	2123	2123
Weston super Mare 137 d.	...	...	...	|	|	...	...	...	2010	|	|	...	...	...	|	|	...	|	|	|	...	...	|	2153	2153
Bristol T. Meads 139 d.	...	...	1930	|	|	...	...	2030	2033	|	|	...	...	...	|	|	...	2147	2150	2150	...	...	2233	2235	2235
Bristol Parkway d.	...	...	|	2001	2001	...	...	|	|	2101	2101	...	...	...	2201	2201	...	|	|	|	...	...	|	|	|
Bath 138 139 d.	...	...	1943	|	|	...	...	2043	2046	|	|	...	...	...	|	|	...	2202	2202	2202	...	...	2246	2247	2247
Chippenham d.	...	...	1955	|	|	...	...	2055	2058	|	|	...	...	...	|	|	...	2215	2215	2215	...	...	2258	2300	2300
Cheltenham 121 d.	1834	1900	|	|	|	...	2000	|	|	|	|	...	2048	2119	|	|	...	|	|	|	2200	...	|	|	|
Gloucester 121 d.	1852	1916	|	|	|	...	2013	|	|	|	|	...	2105	2135	|	|	...	|	|	|	2213	...	|	|	|
Stroud d.	1910	1934	|	|	|	...	2030	|	|	|	|	...	2123	2152	|	|	...	|	|	|	2230	...	|	|	|
Swindon d.	1941	2004	2011	2028	2029	...	2103	2111	2114	2129	2128	...	2151	2222	2228	2228	...	2231	2234	2234	2302	...	2314	2316	2316
Didcot a.	1958	2021	2028	2046	2046		...	2128	2131	2147	2149	...	...	...	|	|	...	2248	2250	2250	...	...	2331	2333	2333
Reading 115 a.	2013	2036	2044	2100	2106	...	...	2143	2148	2159	2209	...	...	...	2303	2303	...	2304	2306	2306	...	...	2352	2354	2354
London Paddington 115 a.	2046	2107	2114	2132	2136	...	...	2214	2216	2230	2245	...	...	...	2336	2340	...	2336	2342	2350	...	...	0033	0027	0033

		⑦	⑦	⑦	⑦	⑦	⑦	⑦	⑦	⑦	⑦	⑦	⑦	⑦	⑦	⑦	⑦	⑦	⑦	⑦	⑦	⑦	⑦	⑦	⑦
							2							P	2										
Swansea 135 d.	⑦	...	...	...	...	0807	...	...	...	0921	...	...	1021	...	...	1121	...	1221	...	...	1321	...	1421	...	...
Cardiff Central 139 d.		...	...	0755	...	0905	...	...	...	1015	...	...	1115	...	...	1215	...	1315	...	...	1415	...	1515	...	...
Newport 139 d.		...	...	0813	...	0919	...	...	...	1032	...	...	1132	...	...	1232	...	1332	...	...	1432	...	1533	...	...
Taunton 137 d.		...	...	|	...	|	...	...	...	|	...	...	|	1146	...	|	...	|	...	...	|	...	|	...	...
Weston super Mare 137 d.		...	...	|	0811	|	...	...	0956	|	...	...	|	|	...	|	1251	|	...	...	|	1452	|	...	...
Bristol T. Meads 139 d.		0745	0820	|	0845	|	...	0948	1030	|	1130	...	|	1230	...	|	1330	|	...	1430	|	1530	|	...	1630
Bristol Parkway d.		|	|	0844	|	0949	...	|	|	1102	|	...	1202	|	...	1302	|	1402	...	|	1502	|	1602	...	|
Bath 138 139 d.		0758	0833	|	0858	|	...	1000	1043	|	1143	...	|	1243	...	|	1343	|	...	1443	|	1543	|	...	1643
Chippenham d.		0810	0845	|	0910	|	...	1012	1055	|	1155	...	|	1255	...	|	1355	|	...	1455	|	1555	|	...	1655
Cheltenham 121 d.		|	|	|	|	|	0924	|	|	|	|	1120	|	|	1224	|	|	|	1346	|	|	|	|	1546	|
Gloucester 121 d.		|	|	|	|	|	0938	|	|	|	|	1137	|	|	1238	|	|	|	1404	|	|	|	|	1604	|
Stroud d.		|	|	|	|	|	0955	|	|	|	|	1155	|	|	1255	|	|	|	1423	|	|	|	|	1622	|
Swindon d.		0826	0900	0910	0926	1014	1024	1029	1111	1129	1211	1223	1229	1311	1324	1329	1411	1429	1452	1511	1529	1611	1629	1651	1711
Didcot a.		0844	...	|	0944	|	...	1045	1128	1146	1228	...	1246	1328	...	1346	1428	1446	...	1528	1546	1628	1646	|	1728
Reading 115 a.		0902	...	0945	0959	1043	...	1101	1143	1201	1243	...	1301	1343	...	1401	1444	1501	...	1544	1601	1644	1701	1719	1744
London Paddington 115 a.		0939	...	1021	1039	1121	...	1139	1221	1239	1321	...	1339	1421	...	1439	1521	1539	...	1621	1639	1722	1739	1759	1821

	⑦		⑦	⑦	⑦	⑦		⑦	⑦	⑦	⑦	⑦	⑦		⑦	⑦	⑦	⑦		⑦	⑦	⑦		⑦	⑦
			2		P			T		C	P					2		C				C		2	P
Swansea 135 d.	1521	...	...	...	...	1621	...	...	...	1651	...	...	1751	...	...	...	...	1851	...	...	...	1959	...	...	...
Cardiff Central 139 d.	1615	...	...	...	...	1715	...	...	...	1748	...	...	1848	...	...	...	...	1948	...	...	...	2055	...	...	...
Newport 139 d.	1632	...	...	...	...	1733	...	...	...	1804	...	...	1904	...	...	...	...	2004	...	...	...	2109	...	...	...
Taunton 137 d.	|	...	...	...	1638	|	...	1703	...	|	1746	...	|	...	1823	...	...	|	...	...	...	|	...	...	2123
Weston super Mare 137 d.	|	...	...	...	1700	|	...	1725	...	|	|	...	|	...	1853	...	...	|	...	...	2038	|	...	...	|
Bristol T. Meads 139 d.	|	...	...	1700	1730	|	...	1800	...	|	1830	1900	|	...	1930	...	2000	|	...	...	2100	|	...	...	2205
Bristol Parkway d.	1702	...	...	|	|	1802	...	|	...	1834	|	|	1934	...	|	...	|	2034	...	...	|	2139	...	...	|
Bath 138 139 d.	|	...	...	1713	1743	|	...	1813	...	|	1843	1913	|	...	1943	...	2013	|	...	...	2113	|	...	...	2219
Chippenham d.	|	...	...	1725	1755	|	...	1825	...	|	1855	1925	|	...	1955	...	2025	|	...	...	2125	|	...	...	2231
Cheltenham 121 d.	|	...	1633	|	|	|	...	|	1746	|	|	|	|	...	|	*1912*	|	|	...	2005	|	|	...	2146	|
Gloucester 121 d.	|	...	1647	|	|	|	...	|	1805	|	|	|	|	...	|	1934	|	|	...	2023	|	|	...	2159	|
Stroud d.	|	...	1704	|	|	|	...	|	1823	|	|	|	|	...	|	1953	|	|	...	2042	|	|	...	2217	|
Swindon d.	1729	...	1734	1741	1811	1829	...	1841	1853	1901	1911	1941	2001	...	2011	2023	2041	2101	...	2111	2141	2206	...	2247	2252
Didcot a.	1746	...	...	1758	|	1846	...	1859	|	1918	|	1958	2018	...	|	...	2059	2118	...	2130	2200	|	...	...	2310
Reading 115 a.	1801	...	...	1814	1844	1901	...	1915	1922	1933	1943	2014	2033	...	2042	...	2116	2133	...	2146	2217	2238	...	...	2329
London Paddington 115 a.	1839	...	...	1859	1921	1939	...	1959	2005	2009	2021	2059	2109	...	2121	...	2202	2209	...	2229	2308	2320	...	...	0013

C – To / from Carmarthen, Table **135**.
E – To / from Exeter, Table **115**.
P – To / from Plymouth, Table **115**.
Q – From Carmarthen on ⑥, Table **135**.
R – From Carmarthen on Ⓐ, Table **135**.

T – To / from Paignton, Table **115**.
Z – To / from Penzance, Table **115**.

s – Stops to set down only.
u – Stops to pick up only.

v – Ⓐ, Dec. 14 – Jan. 29.
w – Ⓐ, Feb. 1 – May 21.

♀ – Calling order: Newport - Bristol Parkway - Bristol Temple Meads - Bath.

AW, GW Most services 🍸

CARDIFF - SWANSEA - SOUTH WEST WALES

For ⛴ services to Ireland, see Table 2030.

km		⚒	⚒ 2	⚒ 2	⚒ 2	⚒ 2K	⑥	⑥	Ⓐ 2R	⑥ 2R	Ⓐ	Ⓐ 2S	Ⓐ	⑥	Ⓐ 2R	Ⓐ 2	⑥ 2R	⚒	⚒ 2	⚒	⚒ 2	⚒ 2	⚒ 2	⚒	⚒ 2
	London Paddington 133 d.		...	...	...	...	...	...	...	...	0530	...	0645	...	...	...	...	0745	...	0845	...	...	...	0945	...
	Manchester Piccadilly 155 d.		...	...	...	...	...	...	...	...	|	...	|	...	...	...	...	|	0630	|	...	0730	...	|	0830
0	**Cardiff** Central d.		...	...	0539	0642	...	0750	0758	0804	0802	0809	0851	...	0904	...	0904	0948	1004	1048	1054	1104	...	1148	1204
32	Bridgend d.		...	...	0607	0702	...	0809	0817	0823	0823	0829	0909	...	0923	...	0923	1009	1023	1109	|	1123	...	1209	1223
52	Port Talbot d.		...	...	0623	0718	...	0822	0830	0836	0836	0845	0922	...	0936	...	0936	1022	1036	1122	|	1136	...	1222	1236
61	Neath d.		...	...	0634	0729	...	0830	0837	0843	0844	0856	0930	...	0943	...	0943	1030	1043	1130	|	1143	...	1230	1243
73	**Swansea** ■ a.		...	...	0651	0745	...	0845	0849	0855	0857	0912	0946	...	0956	...	0956	1044	1055	1143	|	1155	...	1243	1255
73	**Swansea** d.		...	0550	0653	0750	0815	...	0902	0900	...	0916	...	0948	1000	1005	1005	...	1100	...	|	1200	1205	...	1300
91	Llanelli d.		...	0609	0709	0808	0836	...	0924	0924	...	0932	...	1007	1016	1025	1028	...	1117	...	1158	1216	1225	...	1318
124	**Carmarthen** a.		...	0642	0741	0840	0908	...	0954	0954	...	...	...	1040	1047	1058	1050	...	1143	...	|	1247	1258	...	1344
124	**Carmarthen** d.		0600	0645	0744	0855	...	...	0957	0957	...	...	...	1056	...	1100	...	...	1147	...	|	...	1300	...	1347
147	Whitland d.		0613	0700	0758	0909	...	...	1012	1012	...	...	...	1110	...	1115	...	...	1200	...	1234	...	1315	...	1400
172	Tenby d.		|	0742	|	0943	...	...	|	|	...	...	...	1141	...	1145	...	...	|	...	|	...	1345	...	|
191	**Pembroke Dock** a.		|	0817	|	1017	...	...	|	|	...	...	...	1216	...	1219	...	...	|	...	|	...	1419	...	|
174	Haverfordwest d.		0635	...	0821	...	...	...	1034	1034	...	...	...	...	...	...	...	...	1222	...	|	...	...	...	1422
188	**Milford Haven** a.		0658	...	0846	...	...	...	1059	1059	...	...	...	...	...	...	...	...	1247	...	|	...	...	...	1445
191	**Fishguard** a.		...	...	...	...	...	...	...	...	...	...	...	...	...	...	...	...	...	...	1315	...	...	...	...

	⚒	⚒ 2	⚒ 2	⚒	Ⓐ 2	⑥ 2	Ⓐ	⚒ 2	⚒ 2	⚒	⚒ 2	⚒	⚒ 2	⚒ 2	⚒	⚒ 2	Ⓐ	⚒	⚒ 2	Ⓐ	⚒	⚒ 2	Ⓐ	①-④	⑥
London Paddington 133 d.	1045	...	...	1145	...	...	1245	...	...	1345	...	1445	...	...	1545	...	1615	1645	...	1715	1745	...	1815	1845	1845
Manchester Piccadilly 155 d.	|	0930	...	|	1030	1030	|	1130	...	|	1230	|	...	1330	|	1430	|	|	1530	|	|	1630	|	|	|
Cardiff Central d.	1248	1304	...	1348	1404	1404	1448	1504	...	1548	1604	1648	...	1704	1748	1804	1822	1850	1904	1928	1955	1959	2024	2049	2049
Bridgend d.	1309	1323	...	1409	1423	1423	1509	1523	...	1609	1623	1709	...	1725	1809	1823	1845	1909	1923	1949	2015	2020	2045	2109	2109
Port Talbot d.	1322	1336	...	1422	1436	1436	1522	1536	...	1622	1639	1722	...	1739	1822	1839	1858	1922	1938	2002	2028	2033	2058	2122	2122
Neath d.	1330	1343	...	1430	1443	1443	1530	1543	...	1630	1646	1730	...	1749	1830	1846	1905	1930	1948	2010	2036	|	2105	2130	2130
Swansea ■ a.	1343	1355	...	1443	1455	1455	1543	1555	...	1643	1658	1743	...	1805	1848	1858	1919	1945	2004	2023	2049	|	2119	2143	2143
Swansea d.	...	1400	1405	...	1500	1500	...	1600	1605	...	1705	...	1750	1809	...	1905	...	...	2010	...	2100	|	...	...	...
Llanelli d.	...	1416	1424	...	1518	1521	...	1616	1624	...	1725	...	1810	1827	...	1925	...	...	2026	...	2116	2104	...	...	...
Carmarthen a.	...	1447	1457	...	1544	1547	...	1647	1657	...	1755	...	1843	1900	...	1951	...	...	2056	...	2145	2131	...	...	...
Carmarthen d.	...	...	1500	...	1547	1549	...	...	1700	...	1758	...	1905	...	...	1955	...	...	2100	...	...	2204	...	...	...
Whitland d.	...	...	1514	...	1600	1602	...	...	1714	...	1814	...	1919	...	...	2008	...	...	2113	...	...	2219	...	...	...
Tenby d.	...	...	1545	...	|	|	...	...	1745	...	|	...	1952	...	...	|	...	...	2143	...	...	|	...	...	...
Pembroke Dock a.	...	...	1619	...	|	|	...	...	1819	...	|	...	2022	...	...	|	...	...	2218	...	...	|	...	...	...
Haverfordwest d.	...	...	...	...	1622	1625	...	...	...	...	1837	...	...	...	...	2030	...	...	...	...	...	2241	...	...	...
Milford Haven a.	...	...	...	...	1645	1650	...	...	...	...	1900	...	...	...	...	2055	...	...	...	...	...	2306	...	...	...
Fishguard a.	...	...	...	...	...	...	...	...	...	...	...	...	...	...	...	...	...	...	...	...	...	...	...	...	...

	⑤	⑥ 2	Ⓐ 2	⚒	⑥	⑥ 2	Ⓐ 2	Ⓐ	⚒ 2	⑥ 2	⑥	Ⓐ 2	Ⓐ	⑤	①-④		⑦	⑦ 2	⑦ 2	⑦ 2	⑦	⑦ 2H	⑦	⑦ 2	⑦ 2
London Paddington 133 d.	1845	...	...	1915	1945	...	...	2015	...	...	2045	...	2115	2245	2245	...		...	...	...	0830	...	0930	...	...
Manchester Piccadilly 155 d.	|	1730	1730	|	|	1830	1830	|	...	...	|	...	|	|	|	...		...	...	...	|	...	|	...	...
Cardiff Central d.	2055	2106	2106	2122	2148	2212	2212	2226	...	2243	2307	2315	2342	0055	0115	...		...	...	0950	1054	1118	1155	1205	...
Bridgend d.	2116	2125	2128	2145	2209	2233	2241	2246	...	2310	2328	2345	0001	0119	0138	...		...	...	1020	1115	1139	1216	1226	...
Port Talbot d.	2129	2140	2141	2158	2222	2247	2255	2259	...	2327	2341	0001	0014	0132	0151	...		...	...	1037	1128	1153	1229	1243	...
Neath d.	2137	2147	2152	2206	2230	2255	2303	2307	...	2338	2349	0012	0022	0139	0158	...		...	...	1045	1135	1201	1236	1251	...
Swansea ■ a.	2149	2200	2207	2219	2243	2307	2315	2320	...	2353	0002	0028	0037	0153	0213	...		...	...	1058	1148	1213	1249	1303	...
Swansea d.	...	2226	2226	...	...	2311	2320	...	2345	0008	...	0045	...	...	...	...		...	...	1100	...	1216	...	1306	1346
Llanelli d.	...	2244	2244	...	...	2330	2339	...	0001	0025s	...	0102s	...	...	...	...		...	...	1117	...	1235	...	1322	1406
Carmarthen a.	...	2318	2314	...	...	0007	0016	...	0028	0103	...	0140	...	...	...	...		...	...	1150	...	1307	...	1352	1438
Carmarthen d.	...	...	2317	...	...	...	...	...	0031	...	...	...	...	...	...	...		0955	1026	1155	...	1310	...	1359	1504
Whitland d.	...	...	2330	...	...	...	...	...	0046	...	...	...	...	...	...	...		1011	1041	1211	...	1326	...	1415	1520
Tenby d.	...	...	|	...	...	...	...	...	|	...	...	...	...	...	...	...		|	1112	|	...	|	...	|	1551
Pembroke Dock a.	...	...	|	...	...	...	...	...	|	...	...	...	...	...	...	...		|	1145	|	...	|	...	|	1624
Haverfordwest d.	...	...	2353	...	...	...	...	...	|	...	...	...	...	...	...	...		1035	...	1235	...	|	...	1439	...
Milford Haven a.	...	...	0018	...	...	...	...	...	|	...	...	...	...	...	...	...		1058	...	1258	...	|	...	1502	...
Fishguard a.	...	...	...	...	...	...	...	...	0127	...	...	...	...	...	...	...		...	...	...	...	1400	...	...	...

	⑦	⑦	⑦ 2	⑦	⑦ 2	⑦	⑦ 2	⑦	⑦ 2	⑦	⑦ 2	⑦ 2	⑦ y	⑦ z	⑦ y	⑦ z	⑦ 2	⑦ y	⑦ z	⑦ y	⑦ z	⑦ 2	⑦ y	⑦ z	⑦
London Paddington 133 d.	1037	1137	...	1237	...	1337	...	1437	...	1537	...	...	1637	1642	1737	1742	...	1837	1842	1937	1942	...	2037	2042	2137
Manchester Piccadilly 155 d.	|	|	1030	|	...	|	1230	|	...	|	1430	1430	|	|	|	|	...	|	|	|	|	...	|	|	|
Cardiff Central d.	1302	1357	1401	1457	...	1558	1616	1700	...	1801	1805	1805	1901	1902	2003	2003	2015	2055	2101	2200	2207	2230	2304	2309	0010
Bridgend d.	1322	1431	1431	1517	...	1617	1637	1721	...	1822	1836	1836	1920	1923	2022	2022	2037	2118	2123	2222	2230	2251	2324	2329	0030
Port Talbot d.	1336	1437	1448	1531	...	1631	1654	1734	...	1835	1852	1852	1933	1936	2035	2035	2054	2130	2135	2234	2242	2305	2338	2343	0043
Neath d.	1342	1451	1456	1537	...	1638	1702	1742	...	1842	1900	1900	1942	1945	2043	2043	2102	2138	2144	2243	2250	2313	2346	2351	0051
Swansea ■ a.	1356	...	1508	1551	...	1651	1714	1757	...	1855	1913	1913	1954	1957	2056	2056	2114	2152	2156	2255	2303	2325	2358	0003	0103
Swansea d.	1404	...	1511	1557	1605	...	1722	1803	1824	...	1921	1921	...	*2006*	...	...	2118	...	...	...	...	2332	...	...	...
Llanelli d.	1421	...	1528	1614	1624	...	1739	1821	1843	...	1939	1939	...	*2025*	...	...	2135	...	...	...	...	2351	...	...	...
Carmarthen a.	1450	...	1603	1643	1657	...	1808	1849	1917	...	2007	2007	...	*2102*	...	...	2204	...	...	...	...	0024	...	...	...
Carmarthen d.	...	...	1604	...	1700	...	1810	...	1919	...	2010	2010	...	...	...	...	2207	...	...	...	...	0027	...	...	...
Whitland d.	...	...	1622	...	1723	...	1826	...	1941	...	2026	2032	...	...	...	...	2224	...	...	...	...	0044	...	...	...
Tenby d.	...	...	|	...	1751	...	|	...	|	...	|	2103	...	...	...	...	|	...	...	...	...	|	...	...	...
Pembroke Dock a.	...	...	|	...	1830	...	|	...	|	...	|	2135	...	...	...	...	|	...	...	...	...	|	...	...	...
Haverfordwest d.	...	...	1646	...	...	...	1850	...	2006	...	2050	...	...	...	...	...	2248	...	...	...	...	|	...	...	...
Milford Haven a.	...	...	1707	...	...	...	1913	...	...	...	2112	...	...	...	...	...	2310	...	...	...	...	|	...	...	...
Fishguard a.	...	...	...	...	...	...	...	...	...	...	...	...	...	...	...	...	...	...	...	...	...	0126	...	...	...

	⚒	⚒ 2	Ⓐ	⑥	⚒	⚒	⚒ 2	Ⓐ	⑥	⚒	⚒ 2	Ⓐ	⑥	⚒ 2	⚒	⚒ 2	⚒	⑥	Ⓐ	⚒ 2	⚒ 2S	⑥ 2	⚒	Ⓐ 2	⑥ 2
Fishguard d.		0150	...	...	...	...	...	...	...	...	...	...	...	...	...	...	...	...	...	...	...	...	...	...	...
Milford Haven d.		|	...	...	...	...	...	...	...	...	...	...	...	...	...	0600	...	...	...	0703	...	...	...	...	...
Haverfordwest d.		|	...	...	...	...	...	...	...	...	...	...	...	...	...	0615	...	...	...	0718	...	...	...	...	...
Pembroke Dock d.		|	...	...	...	...	...	...	...	...	...	...	...	...	...	|	...	...	...	|	...	...	...	0709	0709
Tenby d.		|	...	...	...	...	...	...	...	...	...	...	...	...	...	|	...	...	...	|	...	...	...	0737	0737
Whitland d.		0222	...	...	...	...	...	...	...	...	...	...	...	...	...	0638	...	...	...	0741	...	...	...	0807	0807
Carmarthen a.		0239	...	...	...	...	...	...	...	...	...	...	...	...	...	0654	...	...	...	0757	...	...	...	0825	0824
Carmarthen d.		0244	...	...	...	...	0504	...	...	...	0550	...	...	0616	...	0657	...	...	0730	0801	...	0830	...	0830	0900
Llanelli d.		0305	...	...	...	...	0528	...	...	...	0618	...	...	0644	...	0721	...	...	0804	0829	0845	0900	...	0859	0927
Swansea ■ a.		0326	...	...	...	...	|	...	...	...	0638	...	...	0705	...	0741	...	...	0821	0849	0908	0923	...	0923	0947
Swansea d.		...	0358	0358	0458	0527	|	0558	0558	0628	0645	0658	0658	0709	0728	0745	0758	0828	0828	0855	0910	...	0928	0955	0955
Neath d.		...	0410	0410	0510	0539	|	0610	0610	0640	0656	0710	0710	0724	0740	0756	0809	0840	0840	0906	0926	...	0940	1006	1006
Port Talbot d.		...	0418	0418	0518	0547	0601	0618	0618	0648	0703	0718	0718	0735	0748	0803	0917	0848	0848	0913	0937	...	0948	1013	1013
Bridgend d.		...	0430	0430	0530	0559	0613	0630	0630	0700	0717	0730	0730	0750	0800	0817	0829	0900	0900	0925	0953	...	1000	1025	1025
Cardiff Central a.		...	0456	0452	0552	0622	0643	0652	0652	0722	0740	0752	0752	0834	0822	0844	0852	0922	0922	0947	1017	...	1022	1048	1047
Manchester Piccadilly 155 a.		...	|	|	|	|	1015	|	|	|	1115	|	|	...	|	1215	|	|	|	1315	...	...	|	1415	1415
London Paddington 133 a.		...	0732	0744	0802	0833	...	0856	0902	0932	...	0959	1002	...	1032	...	1102	1132	1132	...	...	...	1232	...	...

B – From Bristol.
C – To / from Chester.
E – To Cheltenham on Ⓐ.
H – To / from Hereford.
K – From Hereford on Ⓐ.
L – To Hereford on ⑥.
R – To / from Crewe.
S – To / from Shrewsbury.

s – Stops to set down only.
v – ⑥ until Jan. 30, arrives Manchester Piccadilly 2219.
y – Dec. 12 – Jan. 31 and Apr. 4 – May 16.
z – Feb. 7 – Mar. 28.

■ – Minimum official connecting time at Swansea is 7 minutes.

135 SOUTH WEST WALES - SWANSEA - CARDIFF

Most trains 🍸 AW, GW

For ⛴ services to Ireland, see Table **2030**.

	Ⓐ 2	Ⓐ	⑥	⚒ 2	⚒ 2	⚒	⚒ 2	⚒	⚒ 2	⚒ 2S	⚒ 2	Ⓐ	⑥	⚒ 2	⚒	⚒ 2	⚒ 2E	⚒ 2	Ⓐ	⑥	⚒ 2	⚒	⚒ 2	⚒ 2	⚒
Fishguard d.	...	...	...	...	...	...	...	...	...	...	...	...	...	...	...	...	1327	...	...	...	...	...	...	...	...
Milford Haven d.	...	...	...	0908	...	...	...	...	1108	...	...	...	...	...	...	1308	|	...	...	...	...	...	1508	...	...
Haverfordwest d.	...	...	...	0923	...	...	...	...	1123	...	...	...	...	...	...	1323	|	...	...	...	...	...	1523	...	...
Pembroke Dock d.	...	...	...	|	0905	...	...	...	|	...	1105	...	...	...	...	|	|	1305	...	...	...	...	|	1505	...
Tenby d.	...	...	...	|	0938	...	...	...	|	...	1139	...	...	...	...	|	|	1342	...	...	...	...	|	1542	...
Whitland d.	...	...	...	0946	1009	...	...	...	1146	...	1210	...	...	...	...	1346	1359	1411	...	...	...	...	1546	1611	...
Carmarthen a.	...	...	...	1003	1026	...	...	...	1202	...	1229	...	...	...	...	1402	1416	1429	...	...	...	...	1602	1628	...
Carmarthen d.	0900	...	0935	1006	1029	...	1101	...	1205	...	1231	...	...	1304	...	1405	1419	1431	...	...	1505	...	1605	1631	...
Llanelli d.	0930	...	1003	1029	1055	...	1129	...	1229	1237	1257	...	...	1331	...	1429	1443	1501	...	...	1529	...	1629	1701	...
Swansea ■ a.	0950	...	1021	1047	1123	...	1151	...	1247	1301	1323	...	...	1349	...	1449	|	1523	...	...	1547	...	1649	1723	...
Swansea d.	...	1028	1028	1055	...	1128	1155	1228	1255	1310	...	1328	1328	1355	1428	1455	|	...	1528	1528	1555	1628	1655	...	1728
Neath d.	...	1040	1040	1106	...	1140	1206	1240	1306	1325	...	1340	1340	1406	1440	1506	|	...	1540	1540	1606	1640	1706	...	1740
Port Talbot d.	...	1048	1048	1113	...	1148	1213	1248	1313	1336	...	1348	1348	1413	1448	1513	|	...	1548	1548	1613	1648	1713	...	1748
Bridgend d.	...	1100	1100	1125	...	1200	1225	1300	1325	1352	...	1400	1400	1425	1500	1525	|	...	1600	1600	1625	1700	1725	...	1800
Cardiff Central a.	...	1122	1122	1147	...	1222	1247	1322	1347	1415	...	1422	1422	1447	1522	1547	1603	...	1622	1622	1647	1722	1747	...	1822
Manchester Piccadilly **155** a.	...	|	|	1515	...	|	1615	|	1715	...	...	|	|	1815	...	1915	...	...	|	|	2015	...	2115	...	|
London Paddington **133** a.	...	1332	1332	...	...	1432	...	1532	...	...	...	1630	1632	...	1732	...	...	...	1824	1832	...	1932	...	...	2032

	⚒ 2v	Ⓐ	⑥	⚒ 2	⚒ 2	⑥	Ⓐ	⚒ 2C	⑤	①–④	⚒ 2L	⚒ 2	⚒ 2	Ⓐ 2	⚒ 2	⚒ 2	⚒ 2		⑦	⑦ 2	⑦	⑦	⑦	⑦ 2	⑦
Fishguard d.	...	...	...	...	...	...	...	...	...	...	...	...	...	...	...	...	...	...		0150	...	...	...	...	...
Milford Haven d.	...	...	...	1708	...	...	...	...	...	...	1908	...	2118	...	...	...	2319	...		|	...	...	...	...	...
Haverfordwest d.	...	...	...	1723	...	...	...	...	...	...	1923	...	2133	...	...	...	2334	...		|	...	...	...	...	...
Pembroke Dock d.	...	...	...	|	1705	...	...	...	...	...	|	1916	|	...	2111	2223	|	...		|	...	...	...	...	...
Tenby d.	...	...	...	|	1742	...	...	...	...	...	|	1948	|	...	2144	2250	|	...		|	...	...	...	...	...
Whitland d.	...	...	...	1747	1811	...	...	...	...	...	1946	2017	2156	...	2214	2320	2357	...		0222	...	...	...	...	...
Carmarthen a.	...	...	...	1805	1828	...	...	...	...	...	2002	2036	2216	...	2232	2339	0018	...		0240	...	...	...	...	...
Carmarthen d.	1704	...	...	1807	1831	...	...	1908	...	...	2005	2038	▬	...	2235	...	...	...		0243	...	...	...	0938	...
Llanelli d.	1731	...	...	1836	1901	...	...	1932	...	...	2029	2109	⑥	...	2305	...	...	...		0307	...	...	...	1008	...
Swansea ■ a.	1749	...	...	1854	1923	...	...	1950	...	...	2050	2133	2	...	2330	...	...	...		0326	...	...	...	1030	...
Swansea d.	1755	1828	1828	1910	...	1928	1929	2000	2028	2028	2055	2135	2220	2232	...	...	...	...		0335	0807	0921	1021	...	1121
Neath d.	1806	1840	1840	1925	...	1940	1941	2011	2040	2040	2106	2150	2235	2247	...	...	...	...		0346	0819	0933	1033	...	1133
Port Talbot d.	1813	1848	1848	1936	...	1948	1948	2018	2048	2048	2113	2201	2246	2258	...	...	...	...		0353	0826	0940	1040	...	1140
Bridgend d.	1825	1900	1900	1951	...	2000	2000	2030	2100	2100	2125	2216	2301	2313	...	...	...	...		0406	0838	0952	1052	...	1152
Cardiff Central a.	1847	1922	1922	2016	...	2023	2022	2051	2122	2122	2148	2239	2326	2338	...	...	...	...		0435	0901	1015	1115	...	1215
Manchester Piccadilly **155** a.	2215	|	|	...	...	|	|	...	|	|	...	...	...	...	...	...	...	...		...	|	|	|	...	|
London Paddington **133** a.	...	2132	2136	...	...	2230	2245	...	2336	2340	...	...	...	...	...	...	...	...		...	1121	1239	1339	...	1439

	⑦ 2	⑦ 2	⑦	⑦	⑦ 2	⑦ 2	⑦	⑦	⑦ 2	⑦ 2	⑦	⑦	⑦ 2	⑦	⑦	⑦ 2	⑦ 2	⑦	⑦ 2S	⑦ 2	⑦ 2	⑦ 2H	⑦ 2	⑦ 2	⑦ 2
Fishguard d.	...	...	...	...	...	...	...	...	...	1408	...	...	...	...	...	...	...	...	...	...	...	...	...	...	...
Milford Haven d.	...	...	...	...	1128	...	...	...	1321	|	...	...	1528	...	...	...	1728	...	...	...	1928	...	2128	...	2313
Haverfordwest d.	...	...	...	...	1143	...	...	...	1336	|	...	...	1543	...	...	...	1743	...	...	...	1943	...	2147	...	2328
Pembroke Dock d.	...	...	...	...	|	1146	...	...	|	|	...	...	|	...	...	1625	|	...	...	1840	|	...	|	2145	|
Tenby d.	...	...	...	...	|	1214	...	...	|	|	...	...	|	...	...	1653	|	...	...	1908	|	...	|	2213	|
Whitland d.	...	...	...	...	1208	1245	...	...	1402	1440	...	...	1608	...	...	1724	1808	...	...	1940	2007	...	2212	2244	2353
Carmarthen a.	...	...	...	...	1226	1303	...	...	1420	1500	...	...	1626	...	...	1742	1830	...	...	1958	2025	...	2229	2302	0015
Carmarthen d.	1030	1120	...	...	1230	1310	...	...	1423	1500	...	1555	1629	...	1755	1810	...	1909	...	2000	...	2050	2232	...	...
Llanelli d.	1056	1150	...	...	1256	1340	...	...	1449	1531	...	1622	1700	...	1822	1841	...	1936	1951	2030	...	2116	2302	...	...
Swansea ■ a.	1115	1215	...	...	1315	1405	...	...	1508	1555	...	1639	1719	...	1839	1905	...	1953	2013	2055	...	2135	2325	...	...
Swansea d.	1132	...	1221	1321	1341	...	1421	1521	1533	...	1621	1651	1731	1751	1851	...	...	1959	2035	...	...	2140	2327	...	...
Neath d.	1143	...	1233	1333	1352	...	1433	1533	1544	...	1633	1703	1742	1803	1903	...	...	2011	2046	...	...	2151	2338	...	...
Port Talbot d.	1150	...	1240	1340	1359	...	1440	1540	1551	...	1640	1710	1749	1810	1910	...	...	2018	2053	...	...	2158	2345	...	...
Bridgend d.	1205	...	1252	1352	1414	...	1452	1552	1606	...	1652	1722	1804	1822	1922	...	...	2030	2106	...	...	2213	0001	...	...
Cardiff Central a.	1234	...	1315	1415	1438	...	1515	1615	1636	...	1715	1745	1833	1845	1945	...	...	2053	2131	...	...	2237	0024	...	...
Manchester Piccadilly **155** a.	1615	...	|	|	1815	...	|	|	2015	...	|	|	2215	|	|	...	...	|	...	...	...	...	...	...	...
London Paddington **133** a.	...	...	1539	1539	...	...	1739	1839	...	...	1939	2009	...	2109	2209	...	...	2320	...	...	...	...	...	...	...

For footnotes see previous page.

137 CARDIFF - BRISTOL - TAUNTON

2nd class GW

km		⚒	Ⓐ Zy	① Zz	⑥ Zy	②–⑤ Zz	⑥ Zz	⑥	Ⓐ Z	⚒ G	Ⓐ	Ⓐ T	⑥	Ⓐ	⑥	⚒	Ⓐ ◇T	⚒	⚒	Ⓐ	⑥	⚒	⚒	⚒	⑥
0	**Cardiff** Central **133** d.		...	...	...	...	...	...	...	...	...	0800	0800	0900	0900	1000	...	1100	1200	1300	1300	1400	1500	1600	1700
	Newport **133** d.		...	...	...	...	...	...	...	...	...	0815	0815	0915	0915	1015	...	1115	1215	1315	1315	1415	1515	1615	1715
	London Paddington **133** d.		...	...	...	...	...	...	...	...	...	|	|	|	|	|	1000	|	|	|	|	|	|	|	|
	Bristol Temple Meads **133** d.		0524	0528	0528	...	...	0618	0626	0718	0825	0855	0855	0955	0955	1053	1147	1153	1253	1353	1353	1451	1553	1653	1753
	Weston super Mare d.		0549	0549	0549	0549	0549	0647	0651	0750	0900	0929	0930	1023	1022	1122	1207	1221	1323	1423	1423	1523	1623	1727	1823
	Highbridge & Burnham d.		0600	0600	0600	0600	0600	0658	0702	0801	0911	0940	0941	1034	1033	1133	|	1232	1334	1434	1434	1534	1634	1738	1834
	Bridgwater d.		0608	0608	0608	0608	0608	0706	0710	0809	0919	0948	0949	1042	1041	1141	|	1240	1342	1442	1442	1543	1642	1746	1842
	Taunton 115 a.		0621	0621	0621	0621	0621	0720	0723	0825	0933	1001	1006	1057	1059	1200	1229	1259	1359	1455	1459	1604	1700	1801	1859
	Exeter St Davids **115** a.		0657	0657	0656	0657	0656	...	0803	...	...	...	...	1133	...	...	1255	...	...	1530	...	...	...	...	...
	Plymouth **115** a.		0818	0818	0815	0818	0815	...	0916	...	...	...	...	1242	...	...	...	...	...	...	...	...	...	...	...

	Ⓐ	⑥ ◇T	Ⓐ ◇	⑥	Ⓐ	Ⓐ ◇	⑥	Ⓐ	⑥ ◇	⑥	⑥ ◇	Ⓐ	Ⓐ y	Ⓐ z	⑥	⑥ ◇	Ⓐ	⑥	Ⓐ y	Ⓐ y	Ⓐ z		⑦	⑦ Z	⑦ Z
Cardiff Central **133** d.	1700	...	...	1800	1800	...	1900	1900	...	1950	...	2000	...	...	2100	...	2130	2200	2200	...	...	...		...	...
Newport **133** d.	1715	...	...	1815	1815	...	1915	1915	...	2005	...	2015	...	...	2115	...	2144	2217	2217	...	...	...		...	...
London Paddington **133** d.	|	1630	1630	|	|	1730	|	|	1830	|	1900	|	...	...	|	2030	|	|	|	2145	2145	...		...	...
Bristol Temple Meads **133** d.	1753	1817	1821	1853	1855	1915	1953	1955	2015	2048	2055	2055	2155	2155	2155	2217	2227	2301	2311	2335	2335	...		0745	0828
Weston super Mare d.	1829	1840	1855	1923	1929	1957	2023	2030	2038	...	2126	2133	2229	2303	2227	2248s	...	...	2345	0006s	0104	...		0808	0856
Highbridge & Burnham d.	1840	|	1907	1934	1940	|	2034	2041	|	...	2139	2144	2240	2314	2238	2259s	...	...	2356	0017s	0114	...		|	0907
Bridgwater d.	1848	|	1915	1942	1948	|	2042	2049	|	...	2146	2152	2248	2322	2246	2306s	...	...	0004	0025s	0122	...		0824	0915
Taunton 115 a.	1909	1906	1928	1958	2003	2021	2059	2110	2103	...	2158	2207	2303	2337	2259	2318	...	...	0017s	0037	0134	...		0837	0928
Exeter St Davids **115** a.	...	1937	...	...	...	...	...	...	...	...	...	...	...	0012	2333	...	...	...	0053	0107	0204	...		0912	1004
Plymouth **115** a.	...	...	...	...	...	...	...	...	...	...	...	...	...	...	...	...	...	...	...	...	...	...		1026	1112

	⑦	⑦ G	⑦	⑦	⑦ ◇	⑦	⑦	⑦	⑦ ◇
Cardiff Central **133** d.	...	...	...	...	...	...	...	...	...
Newport **133** d.	...	...	...	...	...	...	...	...	...
London Paddington **133** d.	...	...	...	...	1503	...	...	...	1903
Bristol Temple Meads **133** d.	1005	1110	1305	1555	1702	1807	1905	2025	2055
Weston super Mare d.	1034	1139	1333	1628	1737	1836	1939	2058	2127
Highbridge & Burnham d.	1045	1149	1344	1640	|	1847	1950	2109	|
Bridgwater d.	1053	1159	1352	1648	|	1855	1958	2117	|
Taunton 115 a.	1106	1211	1406	1703	1800	1909	2012	2133	2149
Exeter St Davids **115** a.	...	...	...	...	...	1944	...	...	2219
Plymouth **115** a.	...	...	...	...	...	...	...	...	...

	⚒	⚒	⑥	Ⓐ	Ⓐ	Ⓐ ◇	⑥ ◇	⚒	Ⓐ ◇	Ⓐ
Plymouth **115** d.		...	...	...	...	...	...	...	0540	...
Exeter St Davids **115** d.		...	0525	...	0600	0630	...	...	0643	...
Taunton 115 d.		0528	0600	0602	0635	0654	0655	...	0713	0728
Bridgwater d.		0540	0613	0614	0648	0705	0706	...	0723	0740
Highbridge & Burnham d.		0548	0620	0621	0655	0712	0713	...	0731	0748
Weston super Mare d.		0601	0633	0636	0708	0724	0725	0737	0749	0806
Bristol Temple Meads **133** a.		0634	0710	0710	0743	0758	0758	0810	0825	0846
London Paddington **133** a.		...	...	|	...	0944	0944	|	1014	...
Newport **133** a.		...	...	0808	...	...	...	0859	...	...
Cardiff Central **133** a.		...	...	0825	...	...	...	0924	...	...

A – To Gloucester (Dec. 12 – Mar. 28 to Worcester).
G – To / from Gloucester.
T – To / from Paignton.
W – To / from Worcester.
Z – To / from Penzance.

s – Stops to set down only.
y – Dec. 14 – Jan. 30.
z – Feb. 1 – May 21.
◇ – Conveys 🛏12 and 🍸.

Table continues on next page.

GW 2nd class — TAUNTON - BRISTOL - CARDIFF — 137

	⑥	⑥ ◇	⚒	Ⓐ	⑥ ◇	⑥	Ⓐ T◇	Ⓐ	Ⓐ	Ⓐ	⑥	Ⓐ	⑥	⚒	⚒	⑥	Ⓐ T	⑥	Ⓐ	⑥	Ⓐ	Ⓐ	⑥	⑥	Ⓐ
Plymouth 115 d.	...	...	...	...	...	...	...	...	...	...	...	...	...	...	...	...	...	...	...	...	...	...	...	...	...
Exeter St Davids 115 d.	...	0728	...	...	...	...	0840	...	...	0933	...	...	...	...	...	...	...	...	...	...	...	...	...	...	...
Taunton 115 d.	0732	0758	...	0836	0838	0858	0905	...	0937	1007	1011	1102	1107	1207	1307	1407	1411	1507	1515	1607	1616	1705	1707	1807	1808
Bridgwater d.	0744	0809	...	0848	|	0910	|	...	0949	1019	1023	1114	1119	1219	1319	1419	1423	1519	1527	1619	1628	1717	1717	1819	1819
Highbridge & Burnham d.	0752	0816	...	0856	|	0918	|	...	0956	1027	1031	1122	1127	1227	1327	1427	1431	1527	1534	1627	1636	1725	1725	1827	1827
Weston super Mare d.	0808	0829	0840	0910	0902	0940	0929	0945	1010	1040	1042	1145	1139	1239	1340	1439	1445	1539	1546	1639	1651	1738	1737	1839	1842
Bristol Temple Meads **133** a.	0841	0857	0916	0944	0923	1009	0958	1018	1043	1113	1112	1217	1210	1310	1412	1509	1517	1609	1617	1709	1714	1815	1811	1908	1918
London Paddington 133 a.	...	1038	|	...	1114	|	1137	|	...	|	|	|	|	|	|	|	|	|	|	|	|	|	|	|	|
Newport **133** a.	...	...	0959	...	...	1059	...	1059	...	1159	1159	1259	1259	1359	1459	1559	1606	1659	1659	1759	1759	1906	1906	1959	1959
Cardiff Central **133** a.	...	...	1018	...	...	1122	...	1122	...	1218	1218	1322	1322	1418	1523	1618	1629	1721	1725	1818	1818	1923	1923	2018	2019

	⑥	Ⓐ	⑥	Ⓐ	⑤ ◇	①–④ ◇	⑥ ◇	⑥	Ⓐ y	Ⓐ z	Ⓐ y		⑦	⑦	⑦	⑦ A	⑦	⑦	⑦ ◇	⑦ T◇	⑦	⑦ ◇	⑦ Z	⑦	⑦
Plymouth 115 d.	...	...	...	...	...	...	...	...	...	...	...	...	⑦	...	...	...	...	...	...	...	...	...	1709	...	...
Exeter St Davids 115 d.	...	...	...	...	...	...	...	...	2125	2156	...	...		0804	0934	...	...	...	...	1634	...	...	1833	...	...
Taunton 115 d.	1907	1917	2018	2030	2123	2123	2129	2135	2159	2230	2245	...		0835	1020	1117	1311	1518	1638	1703	1719	1823	1904	2020	2135
Bridgwater d.	1919	1930	2030	2042	2133	2133	2140	2147	2211	2242	2257	...		0846	1032	1129	1323	1530	|	|	1730	1834	1916	2032	2148
Highbridge & Burnham d.	1927	1938	2038	2050	2140	2140	2148	2155	2219	2250	2305	...		0853	1039	1136	1330	1547	|	|	1737	1841	1924	2040	2155
Weston super Mare d.	1939	2007	2052	2102	2153	2153	2159	2207	2231	2311	2317	...		0907	1051	1149	1343	1549	1700	1725	1750	1853	1941	2055	2207
Bristol Temple Meads **133** a.	2008	2045	2127	2135	2213	2213	2230	2244	2313	2352	2353	...		0938	1120	1221	1414	1620	1721	1754	1820	1925	2010	2129	2238
London Paddington 133 a.	...	...	|	...	0027	0033	0033	...	...	...	...	...		|	...	...	...	...	1921	1959	...	2121	...	...	...
Newport **133** a.	...	...	2208	...	...	...	...	...	...	...	...	...		1027	...	...	...	...	...	...	...	...	...	...	...
Cardiff Central **133** a.	...	...	2229	...	...	...	...	...	...	...	...	...		1043	...	...	...	...	...	...	...	...	...	...	...

For footnotes and return services, see previous page.

GW 2nd class — WORCESTER - GLOUCESTER - BRISTOL - WEYMOUTH — 138

Services on ⑦ valid until March 28.

km			⑥	Ⓐ	⚒	⚒ T	⚒	⑥	Ⓐ	⑥	Ⓐ	⚒	Ⓐ	⑥	⚒	Ⓐ B	⑥ B	⚒	⑥	Ⓐ	Ⓐ	⑥	Ⓐ		⑥
0	**Worcester** Shrub Hill □ d.	⚒	...	...	...	...	...	...	...	0647	0647	...	0857	0908	...	1106	1106	...	1254	1306	...	...	1506	...	1506
24	Ashchurch for Tewkesbury d.		...	...	...	...	...	...	...	0703	0703	...	0921	0925	...	1121	1121	...	1310	1321	...	...	1521	...	1521
36	Cheltenham Spa **121** d.		...	...	...	...	...	0648	0657	0713	0713	...	0931	0935	...	1131	1131	...	1320	1331	...	...	1531	...	1531
46	**Gloucester** **121** d.		...	...	...	0620	...	0702	0711	0740	0740	0842	0945	0946	1042	1145	1146	1242	1342	1342	1442	1442	1545	...	1545
97	Bristol Parkway a.		...	...	...	0658	...	0739	0748	0819	0819	0919	1024	1024	1119	1222	1224	1320	1420	1422	1520	1518	1622	...	1622
108	**Bristol** Temple Meads a.		...	...	...	0714	...	0754	0801	0836	0836	0935	1039	1039	1135	1235	1239	1336	1440	1440	1537	1534	1638	...	1638
108	**Bristol** Temple Meads **139** d.		...	0544	0644	...	0749	...	...	0840	0840	0949	1049	1049	1149	1239	1243	1349	1449	1449	1543	1538	1649	...	1649
127	Bath **139** d.		...	0602	0702	...	0807	...	...	0858	0858	1007	1107	1107	1207	1257	1300	1407	1507	1507	1601	1556	1707	...	1707
142	Bradford on Avon **139** d.		...	0618	0718	...	0822	...	...	0913	0913	1022	1122	1122	1222	1312	1313	1422	1522	1522	1616	1612	1722	...	1722
147	Trowbridge **139** d.		...	0625	0724	...	0828	...	...	0919	0919	1028	1128	1128	1228	1318	1319	1428	1528	1528	1622	1618	1728	...	1728
157	**Westbury** **139** d.		0647	0647	0735	...	0836	...	...	0927	0931	1037	1136	1135	1237	1325	1326	1436	1537	1537	1629	1628	1738	...	1738
166	Frome d.		0656	0656	...	...	...	...	...	0936	0940	1046	...	...	1247	...	...	...	1546	1546	...	...	1747	...	1747
189	Castle Cary d.		0715	0714	...	...	...	...	...	0953	0957	1103	...	...	1304	...	...	...	1609	1609	...	...	1805	...	1805
208	Yeovil Pen Mill d.		0731	0735	...	...	...	...	...	1017	1012	1117	...	...	1317	...	...	...	1624	1624	...	...	1821	...	1821
241	Dorchester West d.		0805	0809	...	...	...	...	...	1038	1045	1154	...	...	1354	...	...	...	1658	1658	...	...	1858	...	1854
252	**Weymouth** a.		0818	0823	...	...	...	...	...	1056	1102	1208	...	...	1409	...	...	...	1709	1709	...	...	1913	...	1909

	⚒	Ⓐ	⑥	Ⓐ S	⚒	⚒	⚒	Ⓐ	⑥	⑥	Ⓐ	Ⓐ y	Ⓐ z	Ⓐ			⑦ T	⑦	⑦	⑦	⑦	⑦	⑦	⑦	⑦
Worcester Shrub Hill □ d.	...	...	1708	1706	...	1907	...	2131	2131	...	...	...	...	2235	...	⑦	...	...	...	1436	...	1640	1840	...	2036
Ashchurch for Tewkesbury d.	...	...	1721	1721	...	1921	...	2152	2151	...	...	...	...	2251	...		...	...	...	1451	...	1658	1855	...	2053
Cheltenham Spa **121** d.	...	1730	1731	1740	...	1931	2100	2205	2201	...	...	2231	2231	2305	...		1005	1200	...	1501	...	1708	1906	...	2103
Gloucester **121** d.	1642	1742	1746	1754	1842	1945	2115	2221	2210	...	...	2249	2249	2318	...		1019	1214	...	1513	...	1720	1920	...	2115
Bristol Parkway a.	1720	1820	1824	|	1920	2022	2153	...	...	...	...	2316	|	...	...		1055	1251	...	1549	...	1757	1957	...	2153
Bristol Temple Meads a.	1737	1837	1839	|	1938	2039	2210	...	...	...	...	2337	0015	...	...		1108	1309	...	1609	...	1810	2010	...	2207
Bristol Temple Meads **139** d.	1749	1849	1849	|	1949	2049	...	...	...	2311	2317	...	...	...	...		...	...	1340	...	1744	...	...	2050	...
Bath **139** d.	1807	1907	1907	|	2007	2107	...	...	...	2329	2335	...	...	...	...		...	...	1357	...	1801	...	...	2107	...
Bradford on Avon **139** d.	1822	1922	1922	|	2022	2122	...	...	...	2344	2350	...	...	...	...		...	...	1414	...	1817	...	...	2124	...
Trowbridge **139** d.	1828	1928	1928	1920	2028	2128	...	...	...	2350	2356	...	...	...	...		...	...	1420	...	1823	...	...	2130	...
Westbury **139** d.	1839	1936	1935	1940	2036	2138	...	...	...	2357	0004	...	...	...	...		...	...	1430	...	1830	...	...	2138	...
Frome d.	1849	...	...	...	2047	2149	...	...	...	0007	0015	...	...	...	...		...	...	1449	...	1839	...	...	2148	...
Castle Cary d.	1906	...	...	...	...	2206	...	...	...	...	...	...	...	...	...		...	...	1506	...	1858	...	...	2205	...
Yeovil Pen Mill d.	1919	...	...	...	...	2220	...	...	...	...	...	...	...	...	...		...	...	1520	...	1912	...	...	2219	...
Dorchester West d.	1954	...	...	...	...	2254	...	...	...	...	...	...	...	...	...		...	...	1600	...	1947	...	...	2253	...
Weymouth a.	2008	...	...	...	...	2309	...	...	...	...	...	...	...	...	...		...	...	1614	...	2001	...	...	2306	...

		⑥	Ⓐ	⚒	Ⓐ A	⑥ A	Ⓐ	⚒	⚒	Ⓐ	⑥	⚒ S	⚒	⚒ B	⚒	Ⓐ S	⑥ S	⚒	⚒	⚒	Ⓐ	⑥	⚒	⚒	Ⓐ B
Weymouth d.	⚒	...	...	...	...	...	0533	...	0640	...	...	...	0850	...	1110	...	...	1310	...	1508	...	...	...	1730	...
Dorchester West d.		...	...	...	...	...	0545	...	0653	...	...	...	0903	...	1123	...	...	1323	...	1521	...	...	...	1743	...
Yeovil Pen Mill d.		...	...	...	...	...	0620	...	0730	...	...	...	0938	...	1205	...	...	1406	...	1556	...	...	...	1823	...
Castle Cary d.		...	...	...	...	...	0645	...	0744	...	...	...	0952	...	1222	...	...	1420	...	1610	...	...	...	1837	...
Frome d.		...	...	...	...	...	0704	...	0802	...	...	...	1014	...	1239	...	...	1439	...	1629	...	...	...	1905	...
Westbury **139** d.		...	...	...	0634	0638	0718	0738	0817	0845	...	0938	1038	1138	1249	1344	1338	1448	1538	1638	1738	1738	1838	1917	1941
Trowbridge **139** d.		...	...	...	0640	0644	0724	0744	0823	0851	...	0944	1044	1144	1255	1350	1344	1454	1544	1644	1744	1744	1844	1923	1947
Bradford on Avon **139** d.		...	...	...	0646	0649	0730	0750	0829	0857	...	0950	1050	1150	1301	1357	1350	1500	1550	1650	1750	1750	1850	1929	1953
Bath **139** d.		...	...	...	0702	0706	0747	0806	0845	0913	...	1006	1106	1205	1317	1413	1405	1517	1605	1706	1806	1806	1906	1946	2010
Bristol Temple Meads **139** a.		...	...	...	0725	0729	0806	0829	0905	0935	...	1029	1129	1229	1336	1435	1429	1536	1629	1729	1828	1829	1929	2005	2029
Bristol Temple Meads d.		...	...	...	0734	0741	...	0841	...	0941	0941	1041	1141	1241	1341	1441	1441	1541	1641	1741	1841	1841	1941	...	2041
Bristol Parkway d.		...	...	...	0748	0752	...	0852	...	0952	0952	1052	1152	1252	1352	1452	1452	1552	1652	1752	1852	1852	1952	...	2052
Gloucester **121** d.		0550	0601	0715	0829	0832	...	0938	...	1032	1032	1136	1231	1338	1433	1537	1538	1632	1738	1832	1938	1938	2036	...	2135
Cheltenham Spa **121** d.		0600	0612	0725	...	...	...	0948	...	...	...	1148	...	1348	...	1548	1548	...	1748	...	1948	1948	2048	...	2146
Ashchurch for Tewkesbury d.		0609	0620	0734	...	...	...	0956	...	...	...	1156	...	1356	...	1556	1556	...	1756	...	1956	1956	...	...	2154
Worcester Shrub Hull a.		0633	0640	0754	...	...	...	1014	...	...	...	1215	...	1415	...	1621	1614	...	1819	...	2015	2015	...	...	2213

	⑥ B	⚒	Ⓐ	⑥	Ⓐ y	Ⓐ z	⚒			⑦	⑦		⑦ T	⑦		⑦		⑦	⑦		⑦		⑦		⑦
Weymouth d.	...	...	...	...	...	...	2021	...	⑦	...	...	...	...	...	...	1400	...	...	...	...	1756	...	...	...	2009
Dorchester West d.	...	...	...	...	...	...	2034	...		...	...	...	...	...	...	1413	...	...	...	...	1809	...	...	...	2022
Yeovil Pen Mill d.	...	...	...	...	...	...	2109	...		...	...	...	...	...	...	1448	...	...	...	...	1844	...	...	...	2057
Castle Cary d.	...	...	...	...	...	...	2123	...		...	...	...	...	...	...	1503	...	...	...	...	1859	...	...	...	2119
Frome d.	...	...	...	...	...	...	2142	...		...	0940	...	...	...	...	1521	...	...	...	...	1918	...	...	...	2138
Westbury **139** d.	1948	2038	...	...	...	...	2155	...		...	0958	...	...	...	...	1531	...	...	...	...	1930	...	...	...	2149
Trowbridge **139** d.	1954	2044	...	...	...	...	2201	...		...	1004	...	...	...	...	1537	...	...	...	...	1936	...	...	...	2155
Bradford on Avon **139** d.	2000	2050	...	...	...	...	2207	...		...	1009	...	...	...	...	1543	...	...	...	...	1942	...	...	...	2201
Bath **139** d.	2016	2106	...	...	...	...	2224	...		...	1026	...	...	...	...	1600	...	...	...	...	1959	...	...	...	2218
Bristol Temple Meads **139** a.	2035	2129	...	...	...	...	2245	...		...	1045	...	...	...	...	1623	...	...	...	...	2018	...	...	...	2237
Bristol Temple Meads d.	2041	...	...	2206	2211	2211	...	...		0941	...	...	1241	1441	...	...	...	1641	1841	...	...	...	2041	...	...
Bristol Parkway d.	2052	...	...	2218	2222	2222	...	...		0954	...	...	1252	1453	...	...	...	1652	1852	...	...	...	2052	...	...
Gloucester **121** d.	2140	...	2254	2301	2302	2333	...	...		1037	...	...	1335	1552	...	...	...	1735	1938	...	...	...	2138	...	...
Cheltenham Spa **121** d.	2149	...	2303	...	...	...	...	...		1048	...	...	1348	1603	...	...	...	1747	1948	...	...	...	2146	...	...
Ashchurch for Tewkesbury d.	...	...	|	...	...	...	...	...		...	...	...	1357	1611	...	...	...	1755	1957	...	...	...	...	...	...
Worcester Shrub Hull a.	...	...	2330	...	...	...	...	...		...	...	...	1424	1634	...	...	...	1815	2018	...	...	...	...	...	...

A – From Salisbury.
B – To/from Brighton.
S – To/from Southampton.
T – To/from Taunton.
W – To/from Weston super Mare.
y – Dec. 14 – Mar. 28.
z – Mar. 29 – May 21.

139 CARDIFF - BRISTOL - SOUTHAMPTON - PORTSMOUTH

2nd class GW

km			Ⓐ	⑥	Ⓐ	⑥		⚒	⚒	⚒ ◇L	Ⓐ	⑥		⚒	⚒	⚒	⚒ WB	Ⓐ ◇L	⑥ ◇L		⚒	⚒	⚒	⚒ ◇L	Ⓐ
0	**Cardiff** Central .... **133 138** d.	⚒	...	...	...	...	...	0628	0730	...	0830	0830	...	0930	1030	1130	...	...	...	...	1230	1330	1430	...	1530
19	Newport .... **133 138** d.		...	...	...	...	...	0642	0744	...	0844	0844	...	0944	1044	1144	...	...	...	...	1244	1344	1444	...	1544
61	**Bristol** T Meads .... **133 138** d.		...	...	0544	0549	...	0723	0823	0851	0923	0923	...	1023	1123	1223	1239	1310	1315	...	1323	1423	1523	1554	1623
80	Bath .... **133 138** d.		...	...	0602	0607	...	0736	0836	0907	0936	0936	...	1036	1136	1236	1257	1323	1328	...	1336	1436	1536	1607	1636
95	Bradford on Avon .... **138** d.		...	...	0618	0622	...	0747	0847	0920	|	0947	...	1047	1147	1247	1312	1335	1340	...	1347	1447	1547	1622	1647
100	Trowbridge .... **138** d.		...	...	0625	0628	...	0753	0853	0927	0951	0953	...	1053	1153	1253	1318	1342	1347	...	1353	1453	1553	1628	1653
107	**Westbury** .... **138** d.		0549	0601	0637	0643	...	0801	0901	0939	0958	1003	...	1101	1201	1301	1327	1353	1354	...	1401	1501	1601	1639	1701
114	Warminster .... d.		0556	0608	0643	0650	...	0808	0908	0946	1006	1008	...	1108	1208	1308	1336	1400	1402	...	1408	1508	1608	1647	1708
146	**Salisbury** .... **113** d.		0620	0632	0711	0724	...	0832	0932	1009	1030	1032	...	1132	1232	1332	1359	1425	1425	...	1432	1532	1632	1709	1732
173	Romsey .... d.		0638	0650	0730	0744	...	0850	0950	...	1050	1050	...	1150	1250	1350	1419	...	...	...	1450	1550	1650	...	1750
184	**Southampton** Central .. **110** a.		0649	0702	0741	0802	...	0904	1004	...	1104	1102	...	1202	1304	1404	1432	...	...	...	1504	1604	1704	...	1804
208	Fareham .... **110** a.		0714	0727	0805	0827	...	0927	1027	...	1127	1127	...	1227	1327	1427	1455	...	...	...	1527	1627	1727	...	1827
225	Portsmouth & Southsea **110** a.		0738	0746	0824	0846	...	0946	1046	...	1145	1146	...	1246	1346	1446	...	...	...	...	1546	1646	1746	...	1852
226	**Portsmouth** Harbour .... **110** a.		0745	0752	0830	0852	...	0954	1054	...	1154	1152	...	1254	1354	1454	...	...	...	...	1554	1654	1754	...	1858

	⑥	⚒	⚒	Ⓐ W	⚒	⑥	Ⓐ	⚒	⚒ ◇			⑦	⑦	⑦ B	⑦	⑦ B	⑦	⑦	⑦ ◇L	⑦	⑦	⑦ B	⑦		⑦
Cardiff Central .... **133 138** d.	1530	1630	1730	...	1830	1930	1930	2030	...	...	⑦	0805	0915	1008	1108	1208	1308	1408	...	1508	1608	1635	1708	...	1740
Newport .... **133 138** d.	1544	1643	1744	...	1844	1944	1944	2044	...	...		0823	0929	1022	1122	1222	1322	1422	...	1522	1622	1659	1722	...	1754
Bristol T Meads ..... **133 138** d.	1623	1723	1823	...	1923	2023	2023	2123	2223	...		0910	1015	1110	1210	1310	1410	1510	1604	1610	1710	1740	1810	...	1850
Bath .... **133 138** d.	1636	1736	1836	...	1936	2036	2037	2136	2236	...		0927	1029	1127	1222	1327	1424	1527	1620	1624	1727	1752	1827	...	1902
Bradford on Avon .... **138** d.	1647	1747	1847	...	1947	2047	2047	2147	2247	...		0939	1045	1139	1238	1339	1439	1539	1631	1641	1739	1804	1839	...	1914
Trowbridge .... **138** d.	1653	1753	1853	1920	1953	2053	2053	2153	2253	...		0945	1051	1146	1244	1346	1445	1545	1637	1647	1745	1811	1845	...	1920
Westbury .... **138** d.	1701	1801	1901	1940	2001	2101	2101	2201	2304	...		0958	1100	1203	1300	1403	1500	1558	1646	1658	1800	1819	1858	...	1929
Warminster .... d.	1708	1808	1908	1949	2008	2108	2108	2208	2311	...		1007	1107	1212	1307	1412	1507	1607	1653	1707	1807	1828	1905	...	1938
Salisbury .... **113** d.	1732	1832	1932	2013	2032	2132	2132	2232	2334	...		1031	1131	1236	1331	1448	1531	1631	1716	1731	1831	1857	1930	...	2000
Romsey .... d.	1750	1850	1950	2035	2050	2150	2150	2250	...	...		1050	1149	1254	1349	1510	1551	1649	...	1749	1849	1915	1948	...	2019
Southampton Central .. **110** a.	1802	1904	2004	2048	2104	2202	2202	2303	...	...		1100	1204	1306	1400	1520	1605	1704	...	1804	1904	1926	1958	...	2029
Fareham .... **110** a.	1827	1927	2027	...	2127	2226	2242	2327	...	...		1125	1228	1333	1422	1550	1628	1728	...	1828	1928	1948	2024	...	2054
Portsmouth & Southsea **110** a.	1847	1946	2046	...	2146	2244	2259	2348	...	...		1144	1247	...	1441	...	1647	1747	...	1847	1947	...	2043	...	2115
Portsmouth Harbour .... **110** a.	1852	1954	2054	...	2152	2252	2304	2354	...	...		1153	1253	...	1448	...	1653	1753	...	1853	1953	...	2049	...	2126

	⑦	⑦		⑦	⑦ ◇		⑦		⑦	
Cardiff Central .... **133 138** d.	1808	1908	...	2018	...	...	...	...	2200	...
Newport .... **133 138** d.	1822	1922	...	2031	...	...	...	...	2218	...
Bristol T Meads ..... **133 138** d.	1910	2010	...	2122	2135	...	2215	...	2310	...
Bath .... **133 138** d.	1927	2022	...	2135	2149	...	2232	...	2322	...
Bradford on Avon .... **138** d.	1939	2038	...	2146	2200	...	2249	...	2334	...
Trowbridge .... **138** d.	1945	2044	...	2152	2206	...	2255	...	2340	...
Westbury .... **138** d.	1953	2055	...	2200	2215	...	2302	...	2350	...
Warminster .... d.	2002	2102	...	2208	2222	...	...	...	2359	...
Salisbury .... **113** d.	2030	2129	...	2231	2246	...	...	...	...	...
Romsey .... d.	2048	2148	...	2250	...	...	...	...	...	...
Southampton Central .. **110** a.	2059	2159	...	2300	...	...	...	...	...	...
Fareham .... **110** a.	2122	2222	...	2323	...	...	...	...	...	...
Portsmouth & Southsea **110** a.	2140	2240	...	2341	...	...	...	...	...	...
Portsmouth Harbour .... **110** a.	2148	2248	...	2349	...	...	...	...	...	...

		Ⓐ	Ⓐ G	⑥ G	⑥	Ⓐ	⚒ ◇	⚒ W	Ⓐ
Portsmouth Harbour .... **110** d.	⚒	...	...	...	...	...	...	...	0600
Portsmouth & Southsea ...... **110** d.		...	...	...	...	...	...	...	0604
Fareham .... **110** d.		...	...	...	...	...	...	...	0624
Southampton Central .... **110** d.		...	...	...	...	...	...	...	0646
Romsey .... d.		...	...	...	...	...	...	...	0700
Salisbury .... **113** d.		...	0604	0603	...	...	0640	...	0719
Warminster .... d.		...	0625	0623	...	...	0700	0723	0739
Westbury .... **138** d.		0558	0634	0638	0651	0655	0707	0738	0754
Trowbridge .... **138** d.		0604	0640	0644	0657	0701	0713	0744	0800
Bradford on Avon .... **138** d.		0610	0646	0649	0703	0707	0719	0750	0806
Bath .... **133 138** d.		0626	0702	0706	0720	0724	0732	0806	0821
Bristol T Meads .... **133 138** a.		0645	0725	0729	0739	0745	0752	0829	0839
Newport .... **133 138** a.		0726	...	...	0825	0827	...	...	0925
Cardiff Central .... **133 138** a.		0744	...	...	0843	0846	...	...	0943

	⑥	Ⓐ	⑥	⚒ W	⚒	⚒	⚒ ◇L	⚒ BW	⚒	⚒	Ⓐ W	⑥ W	⚒	⚒ ◇L	⚒	⚒	⚒	⚒	①–④	⑥	⑤	Ⓐ BW	⑥ B	⚒	⚒
Portsmouth Harbour .... **110** d.	0600	0651	0705	...	0823	0923	...	...	1023	1123	...	...	1223	...	1323	1423	1523	1622	1723	1723	1723	...	...	1823	1923
Portsmouth & Southsea **110** d.	0604	0655	0709	...	0827	0927	...	...	1027	1127	...	...	1227	...	1327	1427	1527	1627	1727	1727	1727	...	...	1827	1927
Fareham .... **110** d.	0628	0718	0730	...	0847	0947	...	1014	1047	1147	...	...	1247	...	1347	1447	1547	1647	1747	1747	1747	1813	1815	1847	1947
Southampton Central .. **110** d.	0653	0747	0754	0823	0910	1010	...	1042	1110	1210	1226	1227	1310	...	1410	1510	1610	1710	1810	1810	1810	1842	1845	1910	2010
Romsey .... d.	0711	0800	0812	0835	0921	1021	...	1053	1121	1221	1239	1238	1321	...	1421	1521	1621	1721	1821	1821	1821	1854	1856	1921	2021
Salisbury .... **113** d.	0730	0821	0834	0903	0941	1041	1052	1113	1141	1241	1306	1304	1341	1352	1441	1541	1641	1741	1841	1841	1841	1913	1916	1941	2041
Warminster .... d.	0750	0841	0854	0923	1001	1101	1112	1133	1201	1301	1333	1335	1401	1412	1501	1601	1701	1801	1901	1901	1901	1932	1937	2001	2101
Westbury .... **138** d.	0802	0854	0908	0938	1008	1108	1119	1138	1208	1308	1344	1338	1408	1419	1508	1607	1708	1808	1908	1908	1908	1941	1948	2008	2108
Trowbridge .... **138** d.	0808	0900	0914	0944	1014	1114	1125	1144	1214	1314	1350	1344	1414	1425	1514	1614	1714	1814	1914	1914	1914	1947	1954	2014	2114
Bradford on Avon .... **138** d.	0814	0906	0920	0950	1020	1120	1131	1150	1220	1320	1402	1450	1420	1431	1520	1620	1720	1820	1920	1920	1920	1953	2000	2020	2120
Bath .... **133 138** d.	0831	0920	0933	1006	1033	1133	1145	1206	1233	1333	1413	1406	1433	1445	1533	1633	1733	1833	1935	1933	1935	2010	2016	2033	2135
Bristol T Meads ..... **133 138** a.	0845	0939	0947	1029	1048	1147	1205	1229	1247	1347	1435	1429	1447	1505	1549	1647	1747	1849	1949	1947	1949	2029	2035	2050	2151
Newport .... **133 138** a.	0925	1025	1025	...	1125	1225	...	...	1325	1425	...	...	1525	...	1625	1725	1825	1925	...	2025	2030	...	...	2127	2237
Cardiff Central .... **133 138** a.	0943	1042	1043	...	1143	1243	...	...	1343	1443	...	...	1543	...	1643	1743	1843	1943	...	2043	2047	...	...	2145	2300

	⚒ ◇L	A	Ⓐ	Ⓐ	⑥	Ⓐ			⑦	⑦	⑦ B	⑦ ◇L	⑦	⑦	⑦	⑦	⑦ B	⑦	⑦	⑦ ◇L	⑦ B	⑦	⑦		⑦
Portsmouth Harbour .... **110** d.	...	2023	...	...	...	2123	...	⑦	0908	1108	...	...	1308	1408	1508	1608	...	1708	1808	...	...	1908	2008	...	2203
Portsmouth & Southsea **110** d.	...	2027	...	...	...	2127	...		0912	1112	...	...	1312	1412	1512	1616	...	1712	1812	...	...	1912	2012	...	2212
Fareham .... **110** d.	...	2047	...	...	...	2147	...		0932	1132	1232	...	1332	1432	1532	1632	1703	1732	1832	...	1903	1932	2032	...	2232
Southampton Central .. **110** d.	...	2110	2120	...	2127	2222	...		0954	1154	1254	...	1354	1454	1554	1654	1726	1754	1854	...	1930	1954	2054	...	2257
Romsey .... d.	...	2121	2131	...	2138	2233	...		1005	1206	1306	...	1406	1506	1606	1706	1739	1806	1906	...	1942	2006	2106	...	2309
Salisbury .... **113** d.	2057	2141	2153	...	2154	2300	...		1030	1228	1328	1355	1428	1528	1628	1728	1802	1828	1925	1955	2003	2028	2128	...	2328
Warminster .... d.	2117	2201	2215	...	2225	2320	...		1050	1248	1347	1415	1448	1548	1648	1748	1822	1848	1948	2015	2028	2048	2148	...	2353
Westbury .... **138** d.	2124	2208	2225	2232	2238	2330	...		1058	1255	1355	1422	1501	1558	1659	1801	1831	1901	2001	2022	2039	2101	2201	...	0002
Trowbridge .... **138** d.	2130	2214	...	2238	2244	...	...		1104	1301	1401	1428	1507	1604	1705	1807	1837	1907	2007	2028	2045	2107	2207	...	...
Bradford on Avon .... **138** d.	2136	2220	...	2244	2250	...	...		1110	1307	1407	1434	1513	1610	1711	|	1843	1913	2013	2034	2052	2113	2213	...	...
Bath .... **133 138** d.	2150	2233	...	2300	2306	...	...		1125	1325	1423	1448	1527	1628	1725	1825	1859	1927	2027	2048	2112	2127	2228	...	...
Bristol T Meads ..... **133 138** a.	2206	2249	...	2322	2329	...	...		1143	1343	1442	1502	1540	1641	1743	1838	1918	1940	2040	2104	2131	2140	2241	...	...
Newport .... **133 138** a.	...	2334	...	...	...	...	...		1230	1428	1527	...	1627	1730	1827	1927	...	2029	2127	...	...	2232	2328	...	...
Cardiff Central .... **133 138** a.	...	2357	...	...	...	...	...		1245	1449	1542	...	1645	1747	1845	1943	...	2047	2143	...	...	2254	2349	...	...

SOUTHAMPTON – BRIGHTON

	Ⓐ	⑥	⑦	⑦	⑦				
Cardiff Central .... d.	...	...	1008	1208	1635	...	...	...	...
Worcester Shrub Hill .... d.	1106	1106	|	|	|	...	...	...	...
Bristol Temple Meads .... d.	1239	1243	1110	1310	1740	...	...	...	...
Southampton Central ... **110** d.	1432	1432	1306	1520	1926	...	...	...	...
Fareham .... **110** d.	1456	1455	1334	1551	1949	...	...	...	...
Havant .... **110** d.	1510	1510	1403	1611	2010	...	...	...	...
Chichester .... **110** d.	1521	1521	1419	1622	2021	...	...	...	...
Barnham .... **110** d.	1529	1529	1427	1630	2029	...	...	...	...
Worthing .... **110** d.	1545	1544	1444	1645	2051	...	...	...	...
Hove .... **110** d.	1607	1607	1459	1658	2104	...	...	...	...
Brighton .... **110** a.	1614	1614	1506	1705	2110	...	...	...	...

	⚒	Ⓐ	⑥	⑦	⑦	⑦			
Brighton .... **110** d.	0900	1700	1700	1110	1547	1747	...	...	...
Hove .... **110** d.	0904	1704	1704	1114	1551	1751	...	...	...
Worthing .... **110** d.	0922	1722	1722	1129	1608	1808	...	...	...
Barnham .... **110** d.	0938	1739	1738	1146	1625	1825	...	...	...
Chichester .... **110** d.	0947	1747	1746	1158	1634	1834	...	...	...
Havant .... **110** d.	0959	1758	1800	1210	1648	1848	...	...	...
Fareham .... **110** a.	1014	1813	1814	1231	1702	1902	...	...	...
Southampton Central .... **110** a.	1042	1842	1845	1254	1726	1930	...	...	...
Bristol Temple Meads .... a.	1229	2029	2035	1442	1918	2131	...	...	...
Worcester Shrub Hill .... a.	1415	2213	...	|	...	...	...	...	...
Cardiff Central .... a.	...	...	...	1542	...	...	...	...	...

A – ①–⑤ Dec. 14 – Feb. 5; ①–⑥ Feb. 6 – May 22.
B – To/from Brighton.
G – To/from Gloucester.
L – To/from London Waterloo.
W – To/from Worcester.

◇ – Operated by *SW*. Conveys (12).

LONDON AIRPORT LINKS 140

Gatwick ✈

GATWICK EXPRESS daily non-stop rail service from / to **London Victoria**. Journey time: 30 minutes (35 minutes on ⑦). ✆ +44 (0) 845 850 1530.

From Victoria:
0001, 0030, 0330, 0430; then every 15 minutes 0500–2345.

From Gatwick:
0005, 0020, 0035, 0050, 0135, 0435 ⚒, 0450 ⑦, 0520 ⚒, 0525 ⑦; then every 15 minutes 0550–2350.

Other rail services:
Table **103** – London Victoria - Gatwick - Brighton; and Bedford (***A***) - Luton (***A***) - London St Pancras (***A B***) - Gatwick - Brighton.
Table **130** – Reading (***C***) - Gatwick.

A – Connections from / to Leicester, Nottingham, Derby and Sheffield (Table **170**).
B – Connections from / to Paris and Brussels (Table **10**).
C – Connections from / to Exeter and the South West (Table **115**), Birmingham (Table **129**), Worcester (Table **131**), Bristol and South Wales (Table **133**).

Heathrow ✈

HEATHROW EXPRESS daily non-stop rail service from / to **London Paddington**. Journey times: 15 mins to Heathrow Central ★ (Terminals 1 / 2 / 3), 21 mins to Heathrow Terminal 5.
From Paddington: Every 15 minutes 0510–2325. From Heathrow Terminal 5: Every 15 minutes 0503–2342 (6 minutes later from Heathrow Central).
★ – Free rail transfer services operate every 15 minutes Heathrow Central to Heathrow Terminal 4 and v.v.

HEATHROW CONNECT daily rail service from / to **London Paddington**. Journey times: 26 mins to Heathrow Central ♣ (Terminals 1 / 2 / 3), 37 mins to Heathrow Terminal 4.
From Paddington: Every 30 minutes 0503–2303 on ①–⑥. Hourly on ⑦ 0612–2312. **From Heathrow** Terminal 4: Every 30 minutes 0521–2321 on ①–⑥. Hourly on ⑦ 0607–2307 (5 minutes later from Heathrow Central).
♣ – Free rail transfer services operate every 15 minutes Heathrow Central to Heathrow Terminal 5 and v.v.

PICCADILLY LINE (London Underground) service.
Frequent trains (every 4–10 mins) 0530 – 2300 on ①–⑥, 0730 – 2330 on ⑦, between King's Cross St Pancras and all Heathrow terminals via Central London. Journey time: 50–58 minutes.

RAILAIR LINK 🚌 service from / to **Reading** rail station.

From Reading:
Ⓐ: 0400, 0500, 0530, 0555, 0608, 0620, 0640 and every 20 minutes until 0840; then 0905, 0925 and every 20 minutes until 1805; then 1835, 1905, 1935, 2005, 2035, 2105, 2205, 2305.
Ⓒ: 0400, 0500, 0545, 0615 and every 30 minutes until 1945; then 2025, 2055, 2205, 2305.

From Heathrow Central Bus Station (8–10 minutes later from Terminal 5):
Ⓐ: 0005, 0500, 0600, 0630, 0657, 0720, 0740 and every 20 minutes until 1000; then 1015, 1035 and every 20 minutes until 1915; then 1940, 2010, 2040, 2110, 2140, 2215, 2305.
Ⓒ: 0005, 0500, 0600, 0700, 0730 and every 30 minutes until 1900; then 1920, 1950, 2020, 2050, 2130, 2200, 2305.

Approximate journey times in minutes from Reading: 39 to Terminal 5, 48 to Terminal 1, 51 to Terminal 2, 54 to Terminal 3. Approximate journey time Heathrow Central to Reading: 49 minutes.

RAILAIR LINK 🚌 from / to **Woking** rail station.

From Woking: Journey time to Heathrow Central Bus Station: 50–70 minutes △
0530 Ⓐ, 0600 Ⓐ, 0630, 0700 and every 30 minutes until 2100; then 2200.
△ – 30–50 minutes to Terminal 4.

From Heathrow Central Bus Station ▽: Journey time to Woking: 50–70 minutes
0545 Ⓐ, 0615 Ⓐ, 0645, 0715 and every 30 minutes until 2015, then 2100, 2200, 2300.
▽ – 15 minutes later from Terminal 4.

Luton ✈

Frequent *First Capital Connect* trains from / to **London Kings Cross Thameslink**, **London Blackfriars**, **Gatwick** and **Brighton** serve Luton Airport Parkway station ★.
East Midlands Trains express services (Table **170**) from / to **London St Pancras**, **Leicester**, **Nottingham**, **Derby** and **Sheffield** serve both Luton main rail station and Airport station ★.
★ – A frequent shuttle 🚌 service operates between each of the rail stations and the airport terminal.

🚌 service **Milton Keynes - Luton** ✈ (journey time 55 minutes) for train connections from / to **Birmingham** (Table **143**), **Liverpool** and **Manchester** (Table **150**).

From Milton Keynes rail station:
⚒: 0640, 0740, 0840, 0955, 1055 and hourly until 2055, then 2155 Ⓐ.
⑦: 0920, 1120, 1220 and hourly until 2120.

From Luton ✈:
⚒: 0550, 0650, 0750, 0905, 1005 and hourly until 2005; then 2105 Ⓐ.
⑦: 0820, 1020, 1220, 1320 and hourly until 2020.

Stansted ✈

STANSTED EXPRESS rail link service from / to **London Liverpool St**. Journey time: ± 45 minutes. Operating company: *one* ✆ +44 (0) 845 600 7245.

From London Liverpool St:
⚒: 0410 ⑥, 0440, 0510, 0525 and every 15 minutes until 2255; then 2325.
⑦: 0410, 0440, 0510, 0540, 0610, 0625 and every 15 minutes until 2255; then 2325.

From Stansted ✈:
⚒: 0030, 0100 ⑥, 0130 ⑥, 0530 ⑥, 0600, 0615 and every 15 minutes until 2345; then 2359.
⑦: 0030, 0530, 0600, 0630, 0700, 0715 and every 15 minutes until 2345; then 2359.

Trains call at **Tottenham Hale** for London Underground (Victoria Line) connections to / from Kings Cross, Euston, and Victoria stations.
For *Arriva Cross Country* services to / from **Cambridge**, **Peterborough** and **Birmingham**, see Table **208**.

City ✈

DOCKLANDS LIGHT RAILWAY from / to **Bank** (interchange with London Underground: Central, Circle, District, Northern, and Waterloo & City Lines).
Trains run every 7–10 minutes 0530–0030 on ⚒, 0700–2330 on ⑦. Journey time: ± 22 minutes.

Inter - Airport 🚌 links

From **Gatwick** to **Heathrow** *Journey 70 minutes*
0050, 0250, 0420, 0520, 0605, 0635, 0705, 0750, 0820 and every 30 minutes until 2350.

From **Gatwick** to **Luton** *Journey 150 minutes*
0250, 0450, 0635, 0850, 1050 and every 2 hours until 1850, then 2150.

From **Gatwick** to **Stansted** *Journey 165 minutes*
0420, 0520, 0605, 0705, 0820, 0920 and hourly until 1920, then 2120, 2220.

From **Heathrow** to **Gatwick** *Journey 70 minutes*
0005, 0205, 0435, 0505 and every 30 minutes until 2205, then 2305.

From **Heathrow** to **Luton** *Journey 70 minutes*
0410, 0520 and at 10 mins past even hours, 20 mins past uneven hours until 2010, 2120, then 2310.

From **Heathrow** to **Stansted** *Journey 85 minutes*
0540, 0640 and hourly until 2040, then 2240, 2340.

From **Luton** to **Gatwick** *Journey 145 minutes*
0050, 0450, 0630 Ⓐ, 0650 Ⓒ, 0850, 1050 and every 2 hours until 2250.

From **Luton** to **Heathrow** *Journey 65 minutes*
0050, 0450, 0535, 0630 Ⓐ, 0650 Ⓒ, 0735, 0850 and at 35 mins past uneven hours, 50 mins past even hours until 2135, 2250.

From **Stansted** to **Heathrow** *(80 mins)* and **Gatwick** *(160 mins)*
0305, 0405, 0605, 0650 Ⓐ, 0705 Ⓒ, 0805, 0905 and hourly until 2005.

SN EAST CROYDON - MILTON KEYNES 141

km		⚒	Ⓐ	⑥	⑥	Ⓐ	⑥	Ⓐ	⑥	Ⓐ	⑥	Ⓐ	⑥	⚒		Ⓐ	⑥	Ⓐ	⑥	⑥	Ⓐ	Ⓐ	⑥	⑥	Ⓐ
0	**East Croydon** .... d.		...	...	...	...	0610	...	0710	...	0810	...	0910	1010	and	1808	1810	1907	1907	...	...	...	...	...	...
12	Clapham Junction .... d.		0530	0538	0608	0638	0638	0738	0738	0838	0838	0938	0938	1038	hourly	1838	1838	1938	1938	2025	2038	2138	2138	2238	2238
18	Kensington Olympia ..... d.		0544	0549	0622	0649	0650	0750	0750	0850	0850	0950	0950	1050	until	1850	1850	1950	1950	2036	2050	2150	2157	2250	2250
40	Watford Junction... **142** d.		0614	0619	0650	0719	0719	0820	0819	0920	0919	1020	1019	1120	★	1921	1921	2020	2015	2106	2120	2223	2227	2319	2323
88	**Milton Keynes** ..... **142** a.		0655	0700	...	0803	0800	0901	0900	1001	1000	1102	1100	1201		2006	...	2101	...	...	2204	...	...	...	...

	⑦	⑦	⑦	⑦	⑦	⑦		⑦	⑦	
East Croydon .... d.		...	...	...	...	...	and	...	...	...
Clapham Junction .... d.		0815	0915	1015	1115	1205	hourly	2115	2215	...
Kensington Olympia ..... d.		0826	0926	1026	1126	1216	until	2126	2226	...
Watford Junction... **142** d.		0858	0958	1058	1158	1246		2157	2258	...
Milton Keynes ..... **142** a.		...	...	...	...	...		...	...	...

	⚒	Ⓐ	⑥	Ⓐ	⑥	Ⓐ	⑥	⚒		⚒
Milton Keynes .... **142** d.		...	...	...	...	0701	0713	0813	and	1713
Watford Junction .... **142** d.		0554	0552	0653	0655	0738	0752	0851	hourly	1751
Kensington Olympia .... d.		0621	0622	0721	0722	0806	0822	0921	until	1821
Clapham Junction .... a.		0632	0633	0732	0733	0817	0833	0933	★	1833
East Croydon .... a.		...	0657	...	0757	...	0857	0957		1902

	Ⓐ	⑥	Ⓐ	⑥	⑥	Ⓐ	⑥	Ⓐ	Ⓐ	⑥	Ⓐ	⑥	Ⓐ		⑦	⑦	⑦	⑦	⑦		⑦	⑦	⑦		⑦
Milton Keynes ..... **142** d.	1813	1813	1915	1913	...	2013	...	2113	...	...	2211	...	...	...		...	...	...	...	and	...	...	...	...	...
Watford Junction... **142** d.	1851	1852	1954	1951	2043	2051	2143	2151	2227	2248	2253	2325	2329	...		0917	1017	1117	1222	hourly	2022	2117	2217	...	2317
Kensington Olympia ..... d.	1920	1922	2023	2022	2108	2124	2210	2225	2252	2315	2324	2351	2356	...		0947	1047	1147	1247	until	2047	2147	2247	...	2347
Clapham Junction .... a.	1932	1933	2033	2033	2121	2134	2221	2234	2302	2326	2334	0002	0007	...		0958	1058	1158	1258		2058	2158	2258	...	2358
East Croydon .... a.	...	1957	...	2057	...	...	...	...	...	...	...	...	...	...		...	...	...	...		...	...	...	...	0022

★ – Timings may vary by up to 5 minutes.

142 LONDON - NORTHAMPTON - BIRMINGHAM and CREWE LM

LONDON - NORTHAMPTON - BIRMINGHAM

Selected through and connecting services. For full services London - Northampton and v.v., and Northampton - Birmingham and v.v., see below.

km		Ⓐ	Ⓐ	Ⓐ	Ⓐ		Ⓐ	Ⓐ	Ⓐ	Ⓐ	Ⓐ	Ⓐ	Ⓐ	Ⓐ	Ⓐ	Ⓐ		⑥	⑥	⑥	⑥	⑥	⑥	
0	**London** Euston .. 150 d.		0530	0653	0754	and	1554	1648	1724	1746	1813	1849	1954	2046	2054	2146	...		0534	0624	0746	0846	0946	and
27	Watford Junction . 150 d.		0550	0710	0811	at	1611	|	1743	|	|	|	2011	|	2111	|	...		0553	0641	0801	|	1001	at
78	Milton Keynes ..... 150 d.		0637	0749	0849	the	1649	1731	1821	1832	1852	1934	2049	2131	2149	2236	...		0640	0723	0825	0923	1024	the
104	**Northampton** .... a.		0654	0806	0909	same	1706	1749	1837	1850	1910	1949	2106	2150	2206	2251	...		0657	0740	0841	0939	1041	same
			|	|	|	minutes	|	Ⓐ	|	Ⓐ	|	|	|	|	Ⓐ	Ⓐ	...		⑥	⑥	⑥	|	|	minutes
104	**Northampton** .... d.		0656	0817	0917	past	1717	1756	1841	1856	1917	1956	2117	2156	2217	2256	...		0717	0756	0856	0956	1056	past
	Rugby .... 150 d.		0716	0837	0937	each	1737	1816	1903	1916	1937	2016	2137	2216	2239	2316	...		0737	0816	0916	1016	1116	each
	Coventry .... 150 d.		0729	0849	0949	hour	1749	1829	...	1929	1949	2029	2149	2229	2250	2329	...		0749	0829	0929	1029	1129	hour
	Birmingham Int'l 150 d.		0745	0904	1004	until	1804	1845	...	1945	2004	2045	2204	2245	2306	2347	...		0804	0845	0945	1045	1145	until
	Birmingham NS. 150 a.		0803	0916	1017		1817	1901	...	2001	2016	2101	2216	2303	2319	0004	...		0816	0901	1001	1101	1201	

	⑥	⑥	⑥	⑥	⑥	⑥	⑥		⑦	⑦	⑦	⑦	⑦		⑦	⑦	⑦	⑦	⑦	⑦	⑦		⑦	⑦	⑦	⑦
London Euston ... 150 d.	1646	1746	1846	1854	1944	2034	2128	...		0750	0823	0923	1023	...	1123	1234	1334	1434	1534	1634	1734	...	1834	1934	2034	2102
Watford Junction .. 150 d.	1701	1801	1901	1911	2001	2051	2145	...		0808	0842	0942	1042	...	1142	1251	1351	1451	1551	1651	1751	...	1851	1951	2051	2123
Milton Keynes ...... 150 d.	1725	1825	1927	1948	2044	2133	2225	...		0851	0927	1027	1127	...	1227	1329	1429	1529	1629	1729	1829	...	1929	2029	2129	2204
Northampton .... a.	1741	1840	1941	2006	2103	2159	2247	...		0909	0945	1045	1145	...	1245	1346	1446	1546	1646	1746	1846	...	1946	2046	2146	2222
	|	⑥	⑥	⑥	⑥	⑥	⑥	...		⑦	⑦	⑦	⑦	...	⑦	⑦	⑦	⑦	⑦	⑦	⑦	...	⑦	⑦	⑦	⑦
Northampton .... d.	1756	1856	1956	2017	2117	2217	2256	...		0930	1000	1100	1200	...	1253	1351	1453	1551	1653	1751	1853	...	1951	2053	2153	2253
Rugby .... 150 d.	1816	1616	2016	2043	2137	2237	2316	...		0950	1020	1120	1221	...	1315	1415	1515	1615	1715	1815	1915	...	2015	2115	2215	2315
Coventry .... 150 d.	1829	1929	2029	2054	2149	2249	2329	...		1004	1034	1134	1234	...	1329	1429	1529	1629	1729	1829	1929	...	2029	2129	2229	2329
Birmingham Int'l .150 d.	1845	1945	2045	2112	2204	2304	2347	...		1013	1052	1152	1252	...	1347	1447	1547	1647	1747	1847	1947	...	2047	2147	2247	2347
Birmingham NS .. 150 a.	1901	2001	2101	2125	2216	2316	0004	...		1030	1103	1203	1303	...	1358	1458	1558	1658	1759	1858	1958	...	2058	2158	2258	2358

	Ⓐ	Ⓐ	Ⓐ	Ⓐ	Ⓐ	Ⓐ	Ⓐ	Ⓐ		Ⓐ	Ⓐ	Ⓐ	Ⓐ	Ⓐ	Ⓐ	Ⓐ	Ⓐ		⑥	⑥	⑥	⑥		⑥
Birmingham NS .... d.		...	0553	...	0653	0753	0853	0953	and	1553	1653	1753	1853	1953	2053	2133	2153	...		0653	0733	0833	and	1533
Birmingham Int'l .... d.		...	0605	...	0705	0805	0905	1005	at	1605	1705	1805	1905	2005	2105	2145	2205	...		0705	0745	0845	at	1545
Coventry .... d.		...	0621	...	0721	0821	0921	1021	the	1621	1721	1821	1921	2021	2121	2201	2221	...		0721	0801	0901	the	1601
Rugby .... d.		0608	0633	0704	0733	0833	0933	1033	same	1633	1733	1833	1933	2033	2133	2213	2233	...		0733	0813	0913	same	1613
Northampton .... a.		0633	0654	0725	0754	0855	0954	1054	minutes	1654	1754	1854	1955	2054	2154	2234	2255	...		0754	0834	0935	minutes	1634
		|	|	|	|	|	|	|	past	|	|	|	|	|	|	|	②–⑤			⑥	|	|	past	|
Northampton .... d.		0637	0700	0732	0805	0905	1005	1105	each	1705	1805	1905	2005	2105	2205	2252	2346	...		0805	0850	0950	each	1650
Milton Keynes .... d.		0653	0716	0746	0821	0921	1021	1121	hour	1721	1821	1921	2021	2121	2222	2313	0004	...		0921	0903	1004	hour	1704
Watford Junction .... d.		|	|	0827	|	0957	1057	1157	until	1757	1857	1959	2057	2157	2301	2358	0046	...		0857	0934	1029	until	1729
London Euston .... a.		0743	0802	0848	0911	1020	1118	1218		1820	1918	2020	2118	2220	2325	0020	0108	...		0918	0950	1048		1749

	⑥	⑥	⑥	⑥	⑥	⑥	⑥		⑦	⑦	⑦	⑦	⑦		⑦	⑦	⑦	⑦		⑦	⑦	⑦	⑦		⑦	⑦
Birmingham NS .... d.	1633	1733	1753	1853	1953	2053	2133	...		0914	1014	1114	1214	...	1314	1414	1514	1614	...	1714	1814	1914	2014	...	2114	2214
Birmingham Int'l .... d.	1645	1745	1805	1905	2005	2105	2145	...		0925	1025	1125	1225	...	1325	1425	1525	1625	...	1425	1825	1925	2025	...	2125	2225
Coventry .... d.	1701	1801	1821	1921	2021	2121	2201	...		0944	1044	1144	1244	...	1344	1444	1544	1644	...	1744	1844	1944	2044	...	2144	2244
Rugby .... d.	1713	1813	1833	1933	2033	2133	2213	...		0956	1056	1156	1256	...	1356	1456	1556	1656	...	1756	1856	1956	2056	...	2156	2256
Northampton .... a.	1734	1834	1854	1954	2054	2154	2234	...		1017	1117	1217	1317	...	1417	1517	1617	1717	...	1817	1917	2017	2117	...	2217	2317
	|	|	⑥	⑥	⑥	⑥	⑥	...		⑦	⑦	⑦	⑦	...	⑦	⑦	⑦	⑦	...	⑦	⑦	⑦	⑦	...	⑦	
Northampton .... d.	1750	1850	1905	2000	2100	2205	2255	...		1037	1125	1225	1325	...	1425	1525	1625	1725	...	1825	1925	2025	2125	...	2225	...
Milton Keynes .... d.	1804	1904	1921	2016	2116	2224	2311	...		1055	1142	1241	1341	...	1441	1541	1641	1741	...	1841	1941	2041	2144	...	2242	...
Watford Junction .... d.	1829	1929	1959	2051	2150	2307	2357	...		1137	1218	1317	1417	...	1517	1617	1717	1817	...	1917	2017	2126	2227	...	2324	...
London Euston .... a.	1848	1948	2019	2109	2211	2327	0017	...		1157	1237	1337	1437	...	1537	1637	1737	1837	...	1937	2037	2146	2247	...	2346	...

Full service **LONDON EUSTON – NORTHAMPTON** and v.v. :

From London Euston :

Ⓐ: 0530, 0624, 0653, 0713**w**, 0746, 0754, 0846, 0854, 0913**w**, 0946, 0954 and then at 13**w**, 46 and 54 minutes past each hour until 1613**w**; then 1648**w**, 1713**w**, 1724, 1746, 1813**w**, 1751, 1805, 1829, 1849, 1913**w**, 1946, 1954, 2013**w**, 2046, 2054, 2113**w**, 2146, 2154, 2224, 2254, 2324.

⑥: 0534, 0624, 0704, 0746, 0754, 0846**w**, 0854, 0913**w**, 0946, 0954 and then at 13**w**, 46, and 54 minutes past each hour until 1913**w**: then 1944, 2034, 2107, 2128, 2154, 2234, 2304, 2348.

⑦: 0653, 0723, 0750, 0823, 0853 and every 30 minutes until 1153; then 1234, 1250, 1334, 1350 and then at 34 and 50 minutes past each hour until 2034; then 2102, 2128, 2158, 2228, 2258, 2334.

w – Train does not call at Watford Junction.

From Northampton :

Ⓐ: 0415, 0448, 0505, 0545, 0617, 0637**w**, 0700**w**, 0713**w**, 0732, 0738**w**, 0805**w**, 0825**w**, 0847, 0905, 0937, 0950 and then at 05, 25**w**, and 50 minutes past each hour until 2025**w**; then 2105, 2132, 2205, 2252, 2330①, 2346②–⑤.

⑥: 0516, 0605, 0705, 0733, 0805, 0825**w**, 0850, 0905, 0925**w**, 0950 and then at 05, 25**w**, and 50 minutes past each hour until 1805; then 1831, 1850, 1905, 1931, 2000, 2030, 2100, 2114, 2205, 2255, 2330.

⑦: 0753, 0823, 0853, 0930, 1007, 1037, 1107, 1125, 1225, 1250 and then at 25 and 50 minutes past each hour until 2025; then 2045, 2125, 2153, 2225, 2255.

Full service **NORTHAMPTON – BIRMINGHAM NEW STREET** and v.v. :

From Northampton :

Ⓐ: 0517, 0556, 0617, 0656, 0717, 0756, 0817, 0856 and then at 17 and 56 minutes past each hour until 2217; then 2256.

⑥: 0556, 0617, 0656, 0717, 0756, 0817, 0856 and then at 17 and 56 minutes past each hour until 2217; then 2256.

⑦: 0930, 1000, 1100, 1200, 1253, 1351, 1453, 1551, 1653, 1751, 1853, 1951, 2053, 2153, 2253.

From Birmingham New Street :

Ⓐ: 0553, 0633, 0653, 0733, 0753, 0833, 0853 and then at 33 and 53 minutes past each hour until 2153; then 2253.

⑥: 0633, 0653, 0733, 0753, 0833, 0853 and then at 33 and 53 minutes past each hour until 2153; then 2253.

⑦: 0914, 1014, 1114, 1214, 1314, 1414, 1514, 1614, 1714, 1814, 1914, 2014, 2114, 2214.

LONDON - NORTHAMPTON - STAFFORD - CREWE

km		Ⓐ	Ⓐ	Ⓐ	Ⓐ	Ⓐ	Ⓐ	Ⓐ	Ⓐ	Ⓐ		Ⓐ	Ⓐ	Ⓐ	Ⓐ	Ⓐ		⑥	⑥	⑥	⑥	⑥	⑥	⑥	⑥
0	**London** Euston .... 150 d.		...	...	0624	0746	0846	0946	1046	1146	...	1246	1346	1446	1546	1829	...		...	...	0624	0746	0846	0946	1046
27	Watford Junction .... 150 d.		...	...	0641	0801	0901	1001	1101	1201	...	1301	1401	1501	1601	1845	...		...	...	0641	0801	|	1001	1101
78	Milton Keynes .... 150 d.		0521	...	0723	0831	0925	1025	1125	1225	...	1325	1425	1525	1625	1923	...		0521	...	0723	0825	0923	1024	1125
104	**Northampton** .... d.		0542	0638	0745	0845	0945	1045	1145	1245	...	1345	1445	1545	1645	1945	...		0542	0638	0745	0845	0945	1045	1145
	Rugby .... 150 d.		0605	0659	0803	0903	1003	1103	1203	1303	...	1403	1503	1603	1703	2003	...		0605	0656	0804	0903	1003	1103	1203
	Nuneaton .... 150 d.		0617	0712	0817	0916	1016	1116	1216	1316	...	1416	1516	1616	1716	2018	...		0617	0710	0817	0916	1016	1116	1216
	Tamworth .... d.		0631	0729	0831	0930	1030	1131	1231	1330	...	1430	1530	1630	1730	2032	...		0631	0728	0831	0931	1031	1131	1231
	Lichfield Trent Valley .... d.		0637	0735	0837	0936	1036	1137	1237	1336	...	1436	1536	1636	1736	2038	...		0637	0734	0837	0937	1037	1137	1237
	Stafford .... 150 d.		0658	0754	0854	0954	1054	1154	1254	1354	...	1454	1554	1654	1820	|	...		0654	0754	0854	0954	1054	1154	1254
	Stoke on Trent .... 150 d.		0726	0813	0913	1013	1113	1213	1313	1413	...	1513	1613	1713	1841	2105	...		0713	0813	0913	1013	1113	1213	1313
	Crewe .... 150 a.		0749	0838	0939	1038	1138	1238	1338	1438	...	1539	1638	1738	1905	2127	...		0736	0837	0938	1038	1138	1238	1338

	⑥		⑥	⑥	⑥	⑥	⑥	⑥	⑥	⑥	⑥		⑦	⑦	⑦	⑦	⑦		⑦		⑦		⑦		⑦
London Euston .... 150 d.	1146	...	1246	1346	1446	1546	1646	1746	...	1754	...	...		...	0953	...	...	...	1250	...	1450	...	1650	...	1850
Watford Junction .... 150 d.	1201	...	1301	1401	1501	1601	1701	1801	...	1811	...	...		...	1012	...	...	...	1306	...	1506	...	|	...	|
Milton Keynes .... 150 d.	1225	...	1325	1425	1524	1625	1725	1825	...	1849	...	...		...	1058	...	...	...	1136	...	1536	...	1736	...	1936
Northampton .... d.	1245	...	1345	1445	1545	1645	1745	1840	1845	1909	1945	...		...	1116	1136	...	...	1356	...	1556	...	1756	...	1956
Rugby .... 150 d.	1303	...	1403	1503	1603	1703	1803	...	1903	...	2003	...		...	...	1201	...	...	1416	...	1616	...	1816	...	2016
Nuneaton .... 150 d.	1316	...	1416	1516	1616	1716	1816	...	1916	...	2016	...		...	...	1216	...	...	1430	...	1630	...	1830	...	2030
Tamworth .... d.	1331	...	1431	1531	1631	1731	1831	...	1930	...	2030	...		...	...	1230	...	...	1445	...	1645	...	1845	...	2045
Lichfield Trent Valley .... d.	1337	...	1437	1537	1637	1737	1837	...	1936	...	2036	...		...	...	1136	...	...	1451	...	1651	...	1851	...	2051
Stafford .... 150 d.	1354	...	1454	1554	1654	1820	1854	...	1953	...	2055	...		1141	...	1300	1310	...	1516	...	1716	...	1916	...	2116
Stoke on Trent .... 150 d.	1413	...	1513	1613	1713	1841	1913	...	2013	...	2116	...		1159	...	...	|	...	1541	...	1741	...	1941	...	2143
Crewe .... 150 a.	1438	...	1538	1638	1738	1905	1936	...	2035	...	2138	...		1224	...	...	1331	...	1607	...	1809	...	2008	...	2212

For return service see next page

LM LONDON - NORTHAMPTON - BIRMINGHAM and CREWE 142

CREWE - STAFFORD - NORTHAMPTON - LONDON

		Ⓐ	Ⓐ	Ⓐ	Ⓐ	Ⓐ	Ⓐ		Ⓐ	Ⓐ	Ⓐ	Ⓐ	Ⓐ	Ⓐ	Ⓐ	Ⓐ			⑥	⑥	⑥	⑥	⑥		⑥
Crewe 150 d.	Ⓐ	0634	0733	0833	0933	1033	1133	...	1233	1333	1433	1533	1633	1733	1833	...	...	⑥	0638	0738	0833	0933	1033	...	1133
Stoke on Trent 150 d.		0656	0754	0854	0955	1054	1155	...	1254	1354	1454	1554	1654	1754	1854	...	...		0700	0759	0854	0954	1054	...	1154
Stafford 150 d.		0722	0821	0921	1021	1121	1221	...	1321	1421	1521	1621	1721	1821	1921	...	...		0726	0823	0921	1021	1121	...	1221
Lichfield Trent Valley d.		0740	0840	0940	1039	1139	1239	...	1339	1439	1539	1639	1739	1840	1940	...	...		0741	0840	0939	1039	1139	...	1239
Tamworth d.		0747	0847	0947	1046	1146	1246	...	1346	1446	1546	1646	1746	1847	1947	...	...		0748	0847	0946	1046	1146	...	1246
Nuneaton 150 d.		0802	0903	1002	1102	1202	1302	...	1402	1502	1602	1702	1802	1902	2002	...	...		0804	0904	1002	1103	1202	...	1303
Rugby 150 a.		0818	0918	1018	1117	1217	1317	...	1417	1517	1617	1717	1817	1918	2018	...	...		0819	0920	1017	1119	1217	...	1319
Northampton a.		0841	0942	1042	1142	1243	1348	...	1442	1542	1643	1742	1842	1944	2044	2105	...		0840	0941	1038	1140	1238	...	1340
Milton Keynes 150 a.		0900	1005	1104	1204	1304	1404	...	1504	1604	1704	1804	1904	2004	...	2120	...		0903	1004	1104	1204	1304	...	1404
Watford Junction 150 a.		0927	1030	1129	1229	1329	1429	...	1529	1629	1729	1829	1929	2029	...	2157	...		0933	1029	1129	1229	1329	...	1429
London Euston 150 a.		0944	1049	1149	1249	1349	1449	...	1549	1649	1749	1849	1949	2049	...	2220	...		0950	1048	1148	1248	1348	...	1448

	⑥	⑥		⑥	⑥	⑥		⑥	⑥		⑥	⑥			⑦		⑦		⑦		⑦		⑦		⑦
Crewe 150 d.	1233	1333	...	1433	1533	1633	...	1733	...	...	1833	...	...	⑦	1037	...	1138	...	1338	...	1538	...	1738	...	1936
Stoke on Trent 150 d.	1254	1354	...	1454	1554	1654	...	1754	...	...	1854	...	...		1058	...	1159	...	1359	...	1559	...	1759	...	1957
Stafford 150 d.	1321	1421	...	1521	1621	1721	...	1821	...	...	1921	...	...		1117	...	1218	...	1419	...	1618	...	1818	...	2016
Lichfield Trent Valley d.	1339	1439	...	1539	1639	1739	...	1839	...	...	1939	...	...		...	...	1235	...	1436	...	1635	...	1835	...	2035
Tamworth d.	1346	1446	...	1546	1646	1746	...	1946	...	...	1946	...	...		...	...	1242	...	1443	...	1642	...	1842	...	2042
Nuneaton 150 d.	1402	1502	...	1602	1703	1802	...	1902	...	...	2002	...	...		...	...	1258	...	1458	...	1658	...	1858	...	2058
Rugby 150 a.	1417	1517	...	1617	1719	1817	...	1918	...	...	2017	...	...		...	...	1317	...	1517	...	1717	...	1917	...	2117
Northampton a.	1438	1539	...	1638	1740	1838	...	1938	2000	...	2038	2100	...		...	...	1339	...	1539	...	1739	...	1939	...	2139
Milton Keynes 150 a.	1504	1604	...	1704	1804	1904	...	...	2015	...	...	2115	...		...	...	1404	...	1604	...	1804	...	2006	...	2210
Watford Junction 150 a.	1529	1629	...	1729	1829	1929	...	...	2050	...	...	2150	...		...	...	1434	...	1634	...	1833	...	2033	...	2252
London Euston 150 a.	1548	1648	...	1749	1848	1948	...	...	2109	...	...	2211	...		...	...	1453	...	1653	...	1853	...	2053	...	2313

NUNEATON - COVENTRY

From Nuneaton: *16 km*

Ⓐ: 0637, 0737, 0828, 0930, 1110 and hourly until 2110; then 2220.

⑥: 0647, 0814, 0915 and hourly until 1815; then 1946, 2115, 2215.

⑦: 1230, 1411, 1511, 1611, 1711, 1811, 2011, 2200.

From Coventry: *Journey time:* ± 18 minutes

Ⓐ: 0612, 0706, 0804, 0906, 1045 and houry until 2045; then 2144.

⑥: 0616, 0716, 0845 and hourly until 1845; then 2015, 2145.

⑦: 1155, 1346, 1446, 1546, 1646, 1746, 1946, 2135.

VT Most trains 🍸 LONDON - BIRMINGHAM - WOLVERHAMPTON 143

Services on ⑦ valid until January 31.

km			Ⓐ	⚒	Ⓐ	⚒	⚒	⚒		⚒	⚒	Ⓐ	⑥	⚒	⚒	Ⓐ	⑥	Ⓐ	Ⓐ	⑥	Ⓐ	Ⓐ	⑥	Ⓐ	⑥
0	**London** Euston d.	⚒	0603	0623	0643	0703	0723	0743		1803	1823	1843	1843	1903	1923	1943	1943	2003	2023	2023	2043	2103	2103	2143	2143
28	Watford Junction △ d.		|	0637	|	|	0737	|	and at	|	1837	|	|	|	1937	|	|	|	2037	2038	|	|	2118	2158	2158
80	Milton Keynes d.		|	|	0713	|	|	0813	the same	|	|	1913u	1913	|	|	2013	2020	|	|	|	2113	2134	2150	2217	2230
133	Rugby d.		0651	|	|	0751	|	|	minutes	1851	|	|	|	1951	|	|	|	2051	|	|	|	2157	2212	|	2252
151	**Coventry** a.		0702	0722	0742	0802	0822	0842	past each	1902	1922	1942	1942	2002	2022	2042	2049	2101	2122	2135	2142	2206	2222	2246	2302
168	Birmingham Int'l ✈ a.		0713	0733	0753	0813	0833	0853	hour until	1913	1933	1953	1953	2013	2033	2053	2100	2113	2133	2153	2153	2218	2233	2300	2313
182	**Birmingham** New St. a.		0727	0745	0808	0827	0845	0908	▼	1927	1945	2008	2008	2027	2045	2106	2112	2125	2146	2205	2206	2229	2245	2316	2325
190	Sandwell & Dudley a.		...	0757	...	...	0857	...		1953t	1958	|	...	2053t	2058	2123	|	|	2158	2224	2223	2240	2256	2333	2337
202	**Wolverhampton** a.		...	0811	...	...	0911	...		2008t	2012	2037	...	2108t	2112	2138	2138	2156	2212	2238	2238	2256	2310	2347	2351

	Ⓐ	Ⓐ			⑦	⑦	⑦	⑦	⑦	⑦	⑦		⑦	⑦	⑦	⑦	⑦	⑦	⑦	⑦	⑦	⑦	⑦	⑦	⑦
London Euston d.	2230	2330	...	⑦	0850	0950	1050	1145	1218	1238	1258		1758	1818	1838	1858	1918	1938	1958	2018	2038	2054	2155	2225	2325
Watford Junction △ d.	2245	|	...		0904	1004	1104	1201	1232	|	|	and at	|	1832	|	|	1932	|	|	2032	|	2111	2209	2239	2340
Milton Keynes d.	2329	0026	...		0939	1037	1137	1227	|	1311	|	the same	|	|	1911	|	|	2011	|	|	2116	2145	2244	2312	0012
Rugby d.	0001s	0105s	...		1014	1112	1212	1248	|	|	1349	minutes	1849	|	|	1949	|	|	2049	|	|	2207	2323	2349	0047s
Coventry a.	0010s	0118s	...		1023	1121	1221	1256	1320	1340	1400	past each	1900	1920	1940	2000	2020	2040	2100	2120	2146	2216	2333	2358	0058s
Birmingham Int'l ✈ a.	0021s	0129s	...		1034	1134	1234	1307	1331	1351	1411	hour until	1911	1931	1951	2011	2031	2051	2111	2131	2157	2227	2351	0009	0109s
Birmingham New St. a.	0032s	0141s	...		1047	1145	1247	1325	1344	1406	1425		1923	1944	2006	2023	2044	2104	2124	2144	2209	2239	0004	0022	0122s
Sandwell & Dudley a.	|	|	...		1117	1215	...	1356	...	...	1456		1956	...	...	2056	2114	2137	2214	2226	2248	2313	|	|	|
Wolverhampton a.	0103	0210	...		1134	1231	...	1410	...	...	1510		2010	...	...	2110	2128	2151	2231	2240	2302	2327	0047	0103	0203

		Ⓐ	⑥	Ⓐ	Ⓐ	⑥	⚒	Ⓐ	⑥	Ⓐ	⑥	Ⓐ	⑥	⚒	⚒ M	⚒	⚒	⚒	⚒		⚒	Ⓐ	⑥	Ⓐ	Ⓐ
Wolverhampton d.	⚒	0500	...	0524	0545	0545	0604	0627	0627	0645	0645	0704	0704	...	0744	0806t	...	0845	...		...	1845	1845	...	...
Sandwell & Dudley d.		|	...	0534	0556	0556	0615	0637	0637	0656	0656	0715	0715	...	0756	|	...	0856	...	and at	...	1856	1856	...	...
Birmingham New St. d.		0529	0550	0550	0610	0610	0630	0650	0650	0710	0710	0730	0730	0750	0810	0830	0850	0910	0930	the same	1850	1910	1910	1930	1950
Birmingham Int'l ✈ d.		0539	0600	0600	0620	0620	0639	0700	0700	0720	0720	|	0740	0800	0820	0839	0900	0920	0939	minutes	1900	1920	1920	1939	2000
Coventry d.		0550	0610	0611	0631	0631	0651	0711	0711	0731	0731	|	0752	0811	0831	0851	0911	0931	0951	past each	1911	1931	1931	1951	2011
Rugby d.		0603	0624	|	|	|	|	|	0723	|	|	|	|	0823	|	|	0923	|	|	hour until	1923	|	1944	|	2023
Milton Keynes a.		0623	|	0638	0659	0659	|	0740s	|	|	|	|	0819	|	|	0919	|	|	1019		|	|	2007	2019	|
Watford Junction ▽ a.		0643	|	|	|	0719	0736	|	|	|	0815	|	|	|	0917	|	|	1015	|		|	2015	2034	|	|
London Euston a.		0702	0716	0713	0734	0738	0755	0816	0814	0830	0834	0842	0854	0914	0935	0954	1014	1034	1054		2017	2034	2056	2054	2114

	Ⓐ	⑥	Ⓐ	Ⓐ	⑥	⑥	Ⓐ	Ⓐ			⑦	⑦	⑦	⑦	⑦	⑦	⑦		⑦	⑦	⑦	⑦	⑦	⑦	⑦
Wolverhampton d.	1945	1945	...	2047	2045	2145	2145	2245	...	⑦	0749	0842	0945	1045	...	...	1138		...	1838	...	1938	2038	2138	2215
Sandwell & Dudley d.	1956	1956	...	2057	2056	2157	2156	2255	...		0800	0853	0956	1056	...	...	1153	and at	...	1853	...	1953	2053	2153	2226
Birmingham New St. d.	2010	2010	2050	2110	2110	2210	2210	2310	...		0830	0930	1030	1130	1150	1210	1230	the same	1910	1930	2010	2030	2130	2230	2300
Birmingham Int'l ✈ d.	2020	2020	2100	2120	2120	2220	2220	2320	...		0840	0940	1040	1140	1200	1220	1239	minutes	1920	1939	2020	2040	2140	2240	2310
Coventry d.	2031	2031	2111	2131	2131	2231	2231	2331	...		0851	0951	1051	1151	1211	1231	1251	past each	1931	1951	2031	2051	2151	2251	2321
Rugby d.	|	2043	2123	|	2143	2243	2243	2344	...		0904	1004	1104	1205	1224	|	|	hour until	|	|	|	2105	2204	2304	2355
Milton Keynes a.	2059	2105	|	2159	2205	2305s	2305s	0023s	...		0939	1039	1137	1226	|	|	1319		|	2019	|	2128	2239	2327	0012s
Watford Junction ▽ a.	2119	2134	|	2220	2234	2334	2337	0052	...		1007	1108	1207	|	|	1318	|		2016	|	2130	2203	2308	0001	0042
London Euston a.	2138	2156	2216	2243	2255	2357	0005	0113	...		1028	1130	1227	1304	1319	1339	1359		2036	2059	2152	2224	2328	0022	0106

M – From Manchester Piccadilly on Ⓐ.

t – ⑥ only.

w – Also calls at Watford Junction 20–25 minutes after / before London Euston.

△ – Trains stop here to pick up only.

▽ – Trains stop here to set down only.

▼ – On Ⓐ, the 1620, 1720 and 1820 trains from London call at Milton Keynes to pick up only.

145 LONDON and BIRMINGHAM - SHREWSBURY - CHESTER

2nd class AW, LM, WS

Services on ⑦ valid until January 31.

km			Ⓐ	⑥	Ⓐ V	Ⓐ	⑥		⚒	⚒	⚒	⚒	⑥	Ⓐ		Ⓐ W	⚒	⚒ B	⑥ W	⚒	⚒	⚒ B	⚒	Ⓐ W	Ⓐ
	London Marylebone ... **128** d.	⚒	...	...	...	...	...	...	...	...	...	...	...	...	...	0733	...	...	0814	...	...	...	...	1120	...
	Banbury ... **128** d.		...	...	...	...	...	...	...	...	...	...	...	...	...	0837u	...	...	0930u	...	...	...	...	1230u	...
	Tame Bridge Parkway ... d.		...	...	...	...	...	...	...	...	...	...	...	...	...	0942	...	...	1044	...	...	...	...	|	...
0	**Birmingham** International ... d.		...	...	...	...	...	...	...	0709	...	0809	0909	0909	...	|	...	1009	|	1109	...	1209	1309	|	...
13	**Birmingham** New St ... ◇ d.		...	...	...	...	...	...	0624	0722	...	0824	0924	0924	...	|	...	1024	|	1124	...	1224	1323	|	...
34	Wolverhampton ... ◇ d.		...	...	...	...	...	...	0642	0741	...	0843	0943	0943	...	|	...	1043	1059u	1143	...	1243	1343	|	...
59	Telford Central ... ◇ d.		...	...	...	...	...	...	0659	0758	...	0859	0959	1003	...	1019	...	1059	1119	1159	...	1259	1359	1419	...
65	Wellington ... ◇ d.		...	...	...	...	...	...	0705	0804	...	0906	1006	1010	...	|	...	1106	1125	1206	...	1306	1406	|	...
	Cardiff Central **155** ... d.		...	...	...	0510	0520	...	|	|	0720	|	|	|	...	|	0920	|	|	|	1120	|	|	|	...
81	**Shrewsbury** ... ◇ a.		...	...	...	0720	0722	...	0718	0818	0915	0919	1019	1023	...	1040	1115	1119	1140	1219	1315	1319	1419	1436	...
81	**Shrewsbury** ... d.		0610	0610	...	0724	0724	...	0727	0824	0924	0927	1022	1026	...	1041	1124	1127	1144	1222	1324	1327	1422	1438	1524
	Aberystwyth **147** ... a.		|	|	...	|	|	...	0925	|	|	1125	|	|	...	|	|	1325	|	|	|	1525	|	|	|
110	Gobowen ... d.		0630	0630	...	0743	0743	...	...	0843	0943	...	1042	1046	...	1102	1143	...	1205	1242	1343	...	1442	1459	1543
122	Ruabon ... d.		0642	0642	...	0754	0754	...	...	0855	0954	...	1054	1057	...	|	1154	...	1217	1254	1354	...	1454	|	1554
129	Wrexham General ... d.		0649	0649	0700	0802	0801	...	...	0903	1002	...	1100	1104	...	1119	1202	...	1226	1300	1402	...	1500	1516	1602
149	**Chester** ... a.		...	0707	0716	0820	0819	...	...	0920	1020	...	1119	1121	...	...	1219	...	...	1319	1420	...	1521	...	1620
	Holyhead **165** ... a.		...	...	...	1005	1005	...	...	1119	1213	...	1319	1319	...	...	1414	...	...	1511	1614	...	1711	...	1819

	⑥	⚒ B	⑥ W	⚒	⚒		⚒	Ⓐ f	⚒	⑥	⚒	⚒	Ⓐ W		⚒	⑥ W	⑥ L	Ⓐ	⚒	Ⓐ W	⚒	⑥ W		⑥	Ⓐ
London Marylebone ... **128** d.	...	...	1224	...	...	...	...	...	...	...	...	...	1630	...	...	1724	...	...	...	1833	...	1924	...	...	...
Banbury ... **128** d.	...	...	1337u	...	...	...	...	...	...	...	...	...	1733u	...	...	1837u	...	...	...	1937u	...	2037u	...	...	...
Tame Bridge Parkway ... d.	...	...	1441	...	...	...	...	...	...	...	...	...	1840	...	...	1943	...	...	...	2040	...	2140	...	...	...
Birmingham International ... d.	...	1409	|	1509	...	...	1609	...	1709	...	...	1809	|	...	1909	|	...	...	2009	|	2109	|	...	...	...
Birmingham New St ... ◇ d.	...	1424	|	1524	...	...	1624	...	1724	...	...	1824	|	...	1924	|	...	...	2024	|	2124	|	...	...	...
Wolverhampton ... ◇ d.	...	1443	1455u	1543	...	...	1643	...	1743	...	...	1843	1858u	...	1943	2000u	...	...	2043	2104u	2142	2200u	...	...	...
Telford Central ... ◇ d.	...	1459	1515	1559	...	...	1659	...	1759	...	...	1859	1915	...	1959	2020	...	...	2059	2124	2159	2220	...	...	...
Wellington ... ◇ d.	...	1506	1521	1606	...	...	1706	...	1806	...	...	1906	1921	...	2006	2027	...	...	2106	|	2205	2226	...	...	...
Cardiff Central **155** ... d.	1320	|	|	|	1520	...	|	1615	|	...	1720	|	|	...	|	|	1934	1934	|	|	|	|	...	...	...
Shrewsbury ... ◇ a.	1515	1519	1534	1620	1715	...	1719	1805	1820	...	1918	1919	1934	...	2019	2040	2135	2137	2123	2146	2222	2239	...	...	...
Shrewsbury ... d.	1524	1527	1538	1622	1724	...	1727	1806	1824	...	1924	1930	1939	...	2024	2044	2137	2139	2142	2151	2223	2243	...	2333	2337
Aberystwyth **147** ... a.	|	1725	|	|	|	...	1925	|	|	...	|	2126	|	...	|	|	|	|	2342	|	|	|	...	|	|
Gobowen ... d.	1543	...	1602	1642	1743	...	...	b	1843	...	1943	...	2003	...	2043	2105	2156	2158	...	2216	2243	2305	...	2352	2356
Ruabon ... d.	1554	...	1614	1654	1754	...	...	|	1855	...	1954	...	2015	...	2055	2110	2207	2209	...	2228	2254	2317	...	0004	0008
Wrexham General ... d.	1602	...	1623	1702	1801	...	...	|	1902	1946	2002	...	2023	...	2102	2126	2213	2215	...	2236	2302	2325	...	0014	0014
Chester ... a.	1620	...	...	1722	1820	...	...	1909	1920	2006	2020	...	...	...	2121	...	2231	2234	...	...	2321	...	...	0034	0035
Holyhead **165** ... a.	1819	...	...	1916	2016	...	...	2049	2121	...	2212	...	...	...	...	...	...	0055	...	...	...	...	...	...	...

		⑦	⑦ y	⑦ W		⑦ y	⑦ y	⑦ y		⑦ y	⑦ B y	⑦		⑦ y	⑦ y	⑦		⑦ W y	⑦ y	⑦ y		⑦ y	⑦ W		⑦
London Marylebone ... **128** d.	⑦	...	...	0933	...	...	...	...	...	...	...	...	...	...	...	...	...	1605	...	...	...	...	1833	...	...
Banbury ... **128** d.		...	...	1037u	...	...	...	...	...	...	...	...	...	...	...	...	...	1716u	...	...	...	...	1943u	...	...
Tame Bridge Parkway ... d.		...	...	1146	...	...	...	...	...	...	...	...	...	...	...	...	...	1827	...	...	...	...	2047	...	...
Birmingham International ... d.		...	...	|	...	...	...	...	...	...	...	...	...	...	...	...	...	|	...	...	...	2007	|	...	...
Birmingham New St ... ◇ d.		...	1050	|	...	1207	1307	1407	...	1507	1607	...	...	1707	1807	...	...	|	1907	2007	...	2024	|	...	...
Wolverhampton ... ◇ d.		...	1123	1203u	...	1242	1342	1443	...	1543	1643	...	...	1743	1843	...	...	1844u	1943	2043	...	2043	2101u	...	...
Telford Central ... ◇ d.		...	1153	1223	...	1259	1409	1459	...	1609	1659	...	...	1809	1859	...	...	1905	2009	2059	...	2059	2121	...	...
Wellington ... ◇ d.		...	1201	1229	...	1305	1415	1506	...	1617	1706	...	...	1816	1906	...	...	1912	2017	2106	...	2106	2127	...	...
Cardiff Central **155** ... d.		...	|	|	...	|	|	|	...	|	|	1514	...	|	|	1714	...	|	|	|	...	|	|	...	...
Shrewsbury ... ◇ a.		...	1214	1245	...	1318	1429	1519	...	1630	1719	1721	...	1830	1919	1911	...	1930	2030	2119	...	2119	2140	...	...
Shrewsbury ... d.		1016	1217	1247	...	1327	1431	1527	...	1632	1727	1730	...	1831	1927	1932	...	1943	2034	2127	...	2127	2143	...	...
Aberystwyth **147** ... a.		|	|	|	...	1525	|	1725	...	|	1925	|	...	|	2125	|	...	|	|	2323	...	2323	|	...	...
Gobowen ... d.		1035	1237	1308	...	...	1450	...	...	1651	...	1749	...	1851	...	1951	...	2011	2053	...	...	...	2204	...	...
Ruabon ... d.		1047	1249	1320	...	...	1502	...	...	1703	...	1801	...	1903	...	2003	...	2023	2105	...	...	...	2216	...	...
Wrexham General ... d.		1054	1256	1330	...	...	1509	...	...	1710	...	1808	...	1909	...	2010	...	2031	2113	...	...	...	2226	...	2235
Chester ... a.		1112	1320	...	...	...	1529	...	...	1730	...	1825	...	1930	...	2031	...	...	2131	...	...	...	...	...	2253
Holyhead **165** ... a.		...	...	...	...	...	...	...	...	...	...	2020	...	2130	...	2238	...	...	...	...	...	...	..	....	...

		Ⓐ W	Ⓐ	⑥	Ⓐ	⚒	Ⓐ W	⑥ W	Ⓐ f	Ⓐ	⑥	Ⓐ	⑥	⚒ C		Ⓐ	⑥	Ⓐ	⑥	⚒ B	⑥ W	Ⓐ W	⚒	⚒	⚒ B
Holyhead **165** ... d.	⚒	...	...	0425	0425	...	...	...	0532	0511	0522	0629	0635	...	...	0715	0715	0805	0820	...	...	...	0923	1033	...
Chester ... d.		...	0515	0612	0622	...	...	...	0708	0722	0722	0822	0822	...	...	0930	0930	1022	1022	...	...	...	1122	1222	...
Wrexham General ... d.		0510	0531	0638	0638	...	0723	0723	|	0744	0744	0838	0838	...	...	0946	0946	1038	1038	...	1123	1127	1144	1238	...
Ruabon ... d.		|	0538	0645	0645	...	0731	0731	c	0751	0751	0845	0845	...	...	0953	0953	1045	1045	...	1131	|	1151	1245	...
Gobowen ... d.		0525	0550	0657	0657	...	0743	0743	|	0803	0803	0857	0857	...	...	1005	1005	1057	1057	...	1143	1144	1203	1257	...
Aberystwyth **147** ... d.		|	|	|	|	0514	|	|	|	|	|	|	|	0730	...	|	|	|	|	0930	|	|	|	|	1130
Shrewsbury ... a.		0550	0610	0717	0717	0711	0805	0806	0809	0823	0823	0917	0917	0925	...	1031	1027	1117	1117	1125	1206	1205	1227	1319	1325
Shrewsbury ... □ d.		0552	0613	0719	0719	0731	0807	0807	0810	0831	0831	0921	0921	0931	...	1035	1031	1121	1121	1131	1207	1207	1231	1321	1331
Cardiff Central **155** ... a.		|	0817	0922	0922	|	|	|	0958	|	|	1114	1120	|	...	|	|	1320	1320	|	|	|	|	1521	|
Wellington ... □ d.		|	...	...	...	0745	0821	0821	...	0845	0845	...	...	0945	...	1050	1045	...	...	1145	1221	1221	1245	...	1345
Telford Central ... □ d.		0609	...	...	...	0751	0827	0827	...	0851	0851	...	...	0951	...	1056	1051	...	...	1151	1227	1227	1251	...	1351
Wolverhampton ... □ a.		|	...	...	...	0808	|	0847s	...	0908	0908	...	...	1008	...	1113	1108	...	...	1208	1247s	1247s	1308	...	1408
Birmingham New St ... □ a.		|	...	...	...	0827	|	|	...	0927	0928	...	...	1026	...	1130	1128	...	...	1226	|	|	1326	...	1426
Birmingham International ... a.		|	...	...	...	0850	|	|	...	0950	0950	...	...	1050	...	1150	1150	...	...	1250	|	|	1350	...	1450
Tame Bridge Parkway ... a.		0641	...	...	...	...	0902	0901	...	...	...	...	...	...	...	...	...	...	...	...	1301	1302	...	...	...
Banbury ... **128** d.		0747s	...	...	...	...	1004s	1007s	...	...	...	...	...	...	...	...	...	...	...	...	1407s	1406s	...	...	...
London Marylebone ... **128** a.		0857	...	...	...	...	1115	1115	...	...	...	...	...	...	...	...	...	...	...	...	1515	1515	...	...	...

	⚒	⑥ W	⚒	⚒ B		Ⓐ W	⚒	Ⓐ	⑥	⚒ B	⑥ W	⚒	Ⓐ	⑥	⚒	Ⓐ	⑥		Ⓐ V	⑥	Ⓐ	⚒	Ⓐ	⑥	⚒
Holyhead **165** ... d.	1123	...	1238	...	...	...	1323	1432	1423	...	...	1523	1636	1638	...	1721	1721	...	...	...	...	...	1921	1921	...
Chester ... d.	1322	...	1422	...	...	...	1522	1622	1622	...	...	1722	1820	1822	...	1927	1927	...	2022	2027	...	...	2121	2122	2228
Wrexham General ... d.	1344	1418	1438	...	...	1525	1544	1638	1638	...	1723	1744	1836	1838	...	1943	1943	...	2038	2043	2049	...	2137	2139	2244
Ruabon ... d.	1351	1426	1445	...	...	|	1551	1645	1645	...	1731	1751	1843	1845	...	1950	1950	...	...	2051	2057	...	2144	2147	2251
Gobowen ... d.	1403	1437	1457	...	...	1543	1603	1657	1657	...	1743	1803	1855	1857	...	2002	2002	...	...	2102	2108	...	2156	2201	2303
Aberystwyth **147** ... d.	|	|	|	1330	...	|	|	|	|	1530	|	|	|	|	1730	|	|	...	...	|	|	1930	|	|	|
Shrewsbury ... a.	1427	1500	1517	1525	...	1606	1628	1717	1717	1725	1806	1825	1915	1918	1925	2025	2025	...	...	2122	2128	2128	2216	2223	2323
Shrewsbury ... □ d.	1431	1507	1521	1531	...	1607	1631	1721	1721	1731	1807	1831	1917	1920	1933	...	...	...	...	...	...	2133	2218	2231	2326
Cardiff Central **155** ... a.	|	|	1717	|	...	|	|	1921	1921	|	|	|	2119	2121	|	...	...	...	...	...	...	|	|	|	|
Wellington ... □ d.	1445	1521	...	1545	...	1621	1645	...	...	1745	1821	1845	...	...	1947	...	...	...	...	...	...	2147	2232	2245	2340
Telford Central ... □ d.	1451	1527	...	1551	...	1627	1651	...	...	1751	1827	1851	...	...	1953	...	...	...	...	...	...	2153	2238	2251	2347
Wolverhampton ... □ a.	1508	1547s	...	1608	...	1647s	1710	...	...	1808	1849s	1908	...	...	2010	...	...	...	...	...	...	2210	2255	2308	0020
Birmingham New St ... □ a.	1526	|	...	1626	...	|	1727	...	...	1826	|	1926	...	...	2027	...	...	...	...	...	...	2235	2326	2329	...
Birmingham International ... a.	1550	|	...	1650	...	|	1750	...	...	1850	|	1950	...	...	2050	...	...	...	...	...	...	...	...	...	...
Tame Bridge Parkway ... a.	...	1601	...	...	...	1702	...	...	...	...	1902	...	...	...	...	...	...	...	...	...	...	...	...	...	...
Banbury ... **128** d.	...	1707s	...	...	...	1805s	...	...	...	...	2005s	...	...	...	...	...	...	...	...	...	...	...	...	...	...
London Marylebone ... **128** a.	...	1815	...	...	...	1919	...	...	...	...	2115	...	...	...	...	...	...	...	...	...	...	...	...	...	...

B – To / from Pwllheli and v.v., Table **148**.
C – From Barmouth, Table **148**.
L – To / from Llandudno Junction.
V – Operated by *VT*. To / from London Euston, Table **150**. Conveys (12).
W – Operated by *WS*. Conveys (12) and 🍷 (✕ in 1st class).

b – Via Crewe (a. 1845).
c – Via Crewe (d. 0735).
f – Conveys (12) and 🍷 (✕ in 1st cl.).
s – Stops to set down only.
u – Stops to pick up only.

◇ – Additional trains **Birmingham New St - Shrewsbury** (±70 minutes. Operator *LM*): 0551Ⓐ, 0705⑥, 0727Ⓐ, 0805⚒ and hourly until 2105⚒; then 2205⑥, 2221Ⓐ.

□ – Additional trains **Shrewsbury - Birmingham New St** (±70 minutes. Operator *LM*): 0528Ⓐ, 0558Ⓐ, 0647⑥, 0655Ⓐ, 0714Ⓐ, 0747⚒ and hourly until 2147⚒.

AW, LM, WS 2nd class — CHESTER - SHREWSBURY - BIRMINGHAM and LONDON — 145

		⑦	⑦	⑦ W	⑦	⑦	⑦		⑦	⑦ W	⑦	⑦		⑦	⑦	⑦ W	⑦	⑦		⑦	⑦	⑦	⑦	⑦
Holyhead **165** d.	⑦	...	...	...	...	...	1020	...	...	...	...	...	...	...	...	...	...	1625	...	...	...	...	...	...
Chester d.		0808	0911	...	...	1122	1222	...	...	...	1322	...	...	1531	...	...	1722	1824	...	...	1926	...	2124	2204
Wrexham General d.		0826	0928	1047	...	1139	1238	...	...	1311	1339	...	...	1548	...	1702	1739	1840	...	...	1942	...	2142	2222
Ruabon d.		...	0935	1055	...	1146	1245	...	...	1319	1346	...	...	1555	...	1710	1746	1847	...	...	1949	...	2149	...
Gobowen d.		...	0947	1107	...	1158	1257	...	...	1331	1358	...	...	1607	...	1722	1758	1859	...	...	2001	...	2201	...
Aberystwyth **147** d.		...	|	|	0930	|	|	...	1130	|	|	1330	...	|	1530	|	|	|	...	1730	|	1930	|	...
Shrewsbury a.		...	1007	1130	1125	1218	1318	...	1325	1354	1418	1525	...	1627	1725	1745	1818	1920	...	1925	2022	2125	2221	...
Shrewsbury □ d.		...	1009	1131	1140	1220	1319	...	1331	1357	1420	1533	...	1629	1733	1755	1820	1921	...	1931	2023	2131	2223	...
Cardiff Central **155** a.		...	|	|	|	|	1527	...	|	|	|	|	...	|	|	|	|	2136	...	|	|	|	|	...
Wellington □ d.		...	1023	1144	1154	1234	...	...	1345	1410	1434	1547	...	1643	1747	1809	1834	...	...	1945	2037	2145	2237	...
Telford Central □ d.		...	1030	1150	1200	1241	...	...	1351	1416	1441	1533	...	1650	1753	1815	1841	...	...	1951	2045	2151	2245	...
Wolverhampton □ a.		...	1057	1210s	1223	1308	...	...	1408	1438s	1508	1610	...	1717	1810	1835s	1908	...	...	2008	2113	2208	2317	...
Birmingham New St □ a.		...	1130	|	1257	1334	...	...	1437	|	1537	1637	...	1753	1837	|	1937	...	...	2037	2138	2233	...	...
Birmingham International a.		...	...	|	...	...	...	...	...	|	...	...	...	...	...	|	...	...	...	...	...	...	...	...
Tame Bridge Parkway a.		...	...	1226	...	...	...	...	...	1455	...	...	...	...	...	1854	...	...	...	...	...	...	...	...
Banbury **128** d.		...	...	1330s	...	...	...	...	...	1625s	...	...	...	...	...	2025s	...	...	...	...	...	...	...	...
London Marylebone **128** a.		...	...	1436	...	...	...	...	...	1740	...	...	...	...	...	2140	...	...	...	...	...	...	...	...

For footnotes, see previous page.

AW 2nd class — SHREWSBURY - LLANDRINDOD - SWANSEA — 146

km			⚒ C	⚒ C		⚒	⚒			⑦	⑦
0	**Shrewsbury** 155 d.	⚒	0519	0905	...	1405	1805	...	⑦	1206	1618
20	Church Stretton .. 155 d.		0536	0922	...	1423	1823	...		1223	1635
32	Craven Arms 155 d.		0550	0934	...	1436	1835	...		1234	1647
52	Knighton d.		0612	0956	...	1458	1857	...		1258	1711
84	**Llandrindod** a.		0648	1033	...	1534	1933	...		1336	1749
84	**Llandrindod** d.		0652	1033	...	1536	1934	...		1339	1751
110	Llanwrtyd d.		0721	1106	...	1607	2010	...		1410	1822
128	**Llandovery** d.		0745	1132	...	1633	2035	...		1435	1848
146	Llandeilo d.		0806	1153	...	1654	2057	...		1505	1909
159	Pantyffynnon d.		0823	1210	...	1712	2114	...		1520	1927
178	**Llanelli** 135 a.		0842	1229	...	1732	2134	...		1540	1947
196	**Swansea** 135 a.		0908	1301	...	1806	2210	...		1613	2013

		⚒	⚒ C	⚒	⚒				⑦	⑦
Swansea 133 d.	⚒	0436	0916	1315	1821	...	...	⑦	1106	1517
Llanelli 133 d.		0453	0934	1335	1839	...	...		1129	1536
Pantyffynnon d.		0513	0955	1355	1859	...	...		1150	1557
Llandeilo d.		0532	1015	1415	1918	...	...		1210	1617
Llandovery d.		0554	1037	1437	1940	...	...		1232	1639
Llanwrtyd d.		0619	1105	1501	2007	...	...		1257	1704
Llandrindod a.		0647	1134	1531	2036	...	...		1328	1735
Llandrindod d.		0655	1138	1539	2040	...	...		1341	1757
Knighton d.		0732	1216	1615	2117	...	...		1420	1835
Craven Arms 155 d.		0753	1235	1636	2138	...	...		1442	1857
Church Stretton 155 d.		0806	1247	1649	2151	...	...		1455	1911
Shrewsbury 155 a.		0822	1308	1710	2208	...	...		1513	1929

C – From / to Cardiff.

AW 2nd class — SHREWSBURY - MACHYNLLETH - ABERYSTWYTH — 147

km			⚒	⚒	Ⓐ	⚒	⚒	⚒	⚒	⚒	⚒	⚒	⚒			⑦	⑦	⑦	⑦	⑦	⑦	⑦		⑦
	Birmingham New St **145** d.	⚒	...	...	...	0624	0824	1024	1224	1424	1624	1824	2024	...	⑦	...	...	...	1207	1407	1607	1807	...	2007
0	**Shrewsbury 145** d.		...	...	...	0727	0927	1127	1327	1527	1727	1930	2142	...		...	...	1127	1327	1527	1727	1927	...	2127
32	Welshpool 🚂 d.		...	...	...	0749	0949	1149	1349	1549	1749	1952	2204	...		...	...	1149	1349	1549	1749	1949	...	2149
54	Newtown d.		...	...	...	0804	1004	1204	1404	1604	1804	2007	2219	...	★	...	...	1204	1404	1604	1804	2004	...	2204
63	Caersws d.		...	...	...	0813	1013	1213	1413	1613	1813	2016	2229	...		...	...	1213	1413	1613	1813	2013	...	2213
98	**Machynlleth 148** d.		0435	0630	0807	0848	1048	1248	1448	1648	1848	2049	2305	...		0850	1050	1248	1448	1648	1848	2048	...	2246
104	Dovey Junction d.		0442	0637	0814	0855	1055	1255	1455	1655	1855	2056	2312	...		0857	1057	1255	1455	1655	1855	2055	...	2253
118	Borth d.		0453	0648	0825	0906	1106	1306	1506	1706	1906	2107	2323	...		0908	1108	1306	1506	1706	1906	2106	...	2304
131	**Aberystwyth** 🚂 a.		0512	0707	0844	0925	1125	1325	1525	1725	1925	2126	2342	...		0927	1127	1325	1525	1725	1925	2125	...	2323

		⚒		⚒	⚒	⚒	⚒	⚒	⚒	⚒	⚒	⑥	Ⓐ			⑦	⑦		⑦	⑦	⑦	⑦	⑦	⑦
Aberystwyth 🚂 d.	⚒	0514	...	0730	0930	1130	1330	1530	1730	1930	2136	2346	2353	...	⑦	0930	1130	...	1330	1530	1730	1930	2130	2330
Borth d.		0527	...	0743	0943	1143	1343	1543	1743	1943	2149	2359	0006	...		0943	1143	...	1343	1543	1743	1943	2143	2343
Dovey Junction d.		0538	...	0754	0954	1154	1354	1554	1754	1954	2200	0010	0017	...		0954	1154	...	1354	1554	1754	1954	2154	2354
Machynlleth 148 d.		0547	...	0807	1007	1207	1407	1607	1807	2007	2210	0017	0027	...	★	1007	1207	...	1407	1607	1807	2007	2204	0004
Caersws d.		0615	...	0835	1035	1235	1435	1635	1835	2038	...	...	...	...		1035	1235	...	1435	1635	1835	2035	...	...
Newtown d.		0625	...	0845	1045	1245	1445	1645	1845	2048	...	...	...	...		1045	1245	...	1445	1645	1845	2045	...	...
Welshpool 🚂 d.		0641	...	0901	1101	1301	1501	1701	1901	2104	...	...	...	...		1101	1301	...	1501	1701	1901	2101	...	...
Shrewsbury 145 a.		0711	...	0925	1125	1325	1525	1725	1925	2128	...	...	...	...		1125	1325	...	1525	1725	1925	2125	...	...
Birmingham New St **145** a.		0827	...	1026	1226	1426	1626	1826	2027	2235	...	...	...	...		1257	1437	...	1637	1837	2037	2233	...	...

★ – Services on ⑦ valid until January 31.

🚂 – See page **141** for details of Heritage and Tourist railways in North and Mid Wales.

AW 2nd class — MACHYNLLETH - PWLLHELI — 148

km			⚒	⚒		⚒	⚒		⚒	⚒		⚒	⑤		⚒			⑦						
	Birmingham New St **145** d.	⚒	...	...	...	...	...	...	1024	1224	...	1424	...	...	...	...	⑦	1607	...	...	...	...	...	...
	Shrewsbury **146** d.		...	...	...	...	...	...	1127	1327	...	1527	...	...	...	...		1727	...	...	...	...	...	...
0	**Machynlleth** d.		0515	0649	...	0903	1100	...	1256	1456	...	1659	1850	...	2115	...		1855	...	...	...	...	...	...
6	Dovey Junction d.		0521	0655	...	0910	1107	...	1303	1503	...	1705	1907	...	2122	...	★	1902	...	...	...	...	...	...
16	Aberdovey d.		0534	0708	...	0922	1120	...	1315	1515	...	1719	1919	...	2134	...		1914	...	...	...	...	...	...
22	Tywyn 🚂 d.		0541	0715	...	0929	1126	...	1323	1526	...	1727	1926	...	2141	...		1921	...	...	...	...	...	...
37	Fairbourne 🚂 d.		0559	0733	...	0947	1144	...	1341	1544	...	1745	1944	...	2158	...		1939	...	...	...	...	...	...
41	**Barmouth** a.		0607	0741	...	0955	1153	...	1349	1553	...	1753	1955	...	2206	...		1948	...	...	...	...	...	...
	Barmouth d.		0611	0747	...	0957	1156	...	1352	1556	...	1757	...	...	2208	...		1949	...	...	...	...	...	...
58	Harlech a.		0631	0809	...	1021	1220	...	1416	1620	...	1821	...	...	2232	...		2015	...	...	...	...	...	...
	Harlech d.		0631	0821	...	1024	1226	...	1431	1622	...	1826	...	...	2234	...		2018	...	...	...	...	...	...
67	Penrhyndeudraeth d.		|	0834	...	1037	1239	...	1444	1635	...	1839	...	...	2247	...		2031	...	...	...	...	...	...
69	Minffordd 166 🚂 d.		|	0837	...	1040	1242	...	1447	1639	...	1842	...	...	2251	...		2035	...	...	...	...	...	...
72	Porthmadog 🚂 d.		0650	0843	...	1046	1248	...	1453	1644	...	1848	...	...	2256	...		2041	...	...	...	...	...	...
80	Criccieth d.		|	0851	...	1054	1256	...	1501	1652	...	1856	...	...	2304	...		2048	...	...	...	...	...	...
93	**Pwllheli** a.		0710	0906	...	1109	1314	...	1518	1709	...	1913	...	...	2319	...		2104	...	...	...	...	...	...

		⚒		⚒	⚒		⚒	⚒		⚒	⚒		⚒	⚒	⑤			⑦						
Pwllheli d.	⚒	...	...	0625	0724	...	0936	1138	...	1342	1534	...	1738	2000	...	...	⑦	1348	...	...	...	...	...	...
Criccieth d.		...	...	0639	0739	...	0950	1152	...	1356	1548	...	1752	2014	...	...		1402	...	...	...	...	...	...
Porthmadog 🚂 d.		...	...	0652	0749	...	1000	1202	...	1406	1558	...	1802	2024	...	...		1412	...	...	...	...	...	...
Minffordd 166 🚂 d.		...	...	0656	0753	...	1004	1206	...	1410	1602	...	1806	2028	...	...	★	1416	...	...	...	...	...	...
Penrhyndeudraeth d.		...	...	0700	0757	...	1008	1210	...	1414	1606	...	1810	2032	...	...		1420	...	...	...	...	...	...
Harlech a.		...	...	0712	0809	...	1020	1222	...	1426	1618	...	1822	2044	...	...		1432	...	...	...	...	...	...
Harlech d.		...	...	0716	0830	...	1025	1225	...	1430	1623	...	1824	2046	...	...		1434	...	...	...	...	...	...
Barmouth a.		...	...	0740	0854	...	1049	1249	...	1454	1648	...	1849	2111	...	...		1459	...	...	...	...	...	...
Barmouth d.		0646	...	0749	0900	...	1052	1253	...	1457	1653	...	1851	2113	2210	...		1501	...	...	...	...	...	...
Fairbourne 🚂 d.		0654	...	0757	0908	...	1100	1301	...	1505	1701	...	1859	2121	2218	...		1509	...	...	...	...	...	...
Tywyn 🚂 d.		0716	...	0818	0930	...	1127	1324	...	1524	1728	...	1927	2146	2236	...		1527	...	...	...	...	...	...
Aberdovey d.		0722	...	0824	0936	...	1133	1330	...	1530	1734	...	1933	2152	2242	...		1535	...	...	...	...	...	...
Dovey Junction d.		0737	...	0838	0950	...	1148	1344	...	1544	1748	...	1948	2206	2256	...		1549	...	...	...	...	...	...
Machynlleth a.		0807	...	0848	1007	...	1207	1407	...	1607	1758	...	1957	2216	2304	...		1556	...	...	...	...	...	...
Shrewsbury **146** a.		0925	...	...	1125	...	1325	1525	...	1725	...	...	...	...	...	...		...	...	...	...	...	...	...
Birmingham New St **145** a.		1026	...	...	1226	...	1426	1626	...	1826	...	...	...	...	...	...		...	...	...	...	...	...	...

★ – Services on ⑦ valid until January 31.

🚂 – See page **141** for details of Heritage and Tourist railways in North and Mid Wales.

150 LONDON and BIRMINGHAM - CHESTER, MANCHESTER and LIVERPOOL

AW, LM, VT, XC

Services on ⑦ valid until January 31. For services to Scotland see Table **151**. For slower services London - Crewe see Table **142**.

km	Operator		LM Ⓐ	VT ⚒H	XC ⚒	LM ⚒	LM ⚒	XC Ⓐ	XC ⑥	VT Ⓐw	LM ⚒	VT Ⓐ	XC ⚒	LM ⚒	VT ⚒w	LM Ⓐ	XC Ⓐ	XC ⑥	VT ⚒	LM ⑥	VT Ⓐ	VT ⑥	VT Ⓐ	VT ⚒	XC ⚒S	LM ⚒
0	**London** Euston d.	⚒	...	...	...	...	...	...	...	0527	...	0617	...	...	0636	...	...	...	0655	...	0707	0707	0710	0720	...	...
80	Milton Keynes d.		...	...	...	...	...	...	...	0610	...	0647	...	...	│	...	...	...	0727	...	│	│	0740	0750	...	...
131	Rugby d.		...	...	...	...	...	...	...	│	...	│	...	...	│	...	...	...	│	...	│	│	│	│	...	...
155	Nuneaton d.		...	...	...	...	...	...	...	0639	...	│	...	...	│	...	...	...	│	...	│	│	│	│	...	...
	Birmingham New St d.		...	0530	0557	...	0601	0620	0631	│	0636	│	0657	0701	│	0718	0731	0731	│	0736	│	│	│	│	0757	0801
	Wolverhampton d.		...	0548	0616	...	0618	0640	0649	│	0651	│	0714	0718	│	0736	0749	0749	│	0753	│	│	│	│	0815	0819
215	**Stafford** d.		...	0601	0630	...	0636	0654	0701	0703	0705	│	0729	0738	│	0809	│	0801	│	0809	0823	0823	│	│	0830	0836
235	Stoke on Trent d.		...	│	0650	...	│	0712	0718	│	│	0745	│	│	│	│	0818	0819	0824	│	│	│	│	0848	0854	│
267	Macclesfield d.		...	│	0711	...	│	0730	0736	│	│	0801	│	│	│	│	0835	0836	0851	│	│	│	│	│	0911	│
254	**Crewe** 165 d.		0602	0623	│	0632	0657	│	│	0724	0731	│	0752	0758	0811	0831	│	│	│	0831	│	0843	0849	│	│	0858
288	**Chester** 165 a.		│	0644	│	│	│	│	│	│	│	│	│	│	│	│	│	│	│	│	│	│	0912	│	│	│
	Stockport a.		│	...	0727	│	│	0745	0749	│	│	0816	0820	│	0837	│	0849	0849	0850	│	│	│	...	0916	0927	│
□	**Manchester** P'dilly a.		│	...	0738	│	│	0800	0759	│	│	0828	0835	│	0849	│	0859	0859	0907	│	│	│	...	0928	0939	│
290	Runcorn a.		0627	...	...	0659	0723	...	...	0741	0802	...	...	0824	...	0850	...	...	...	0850	0855	0900	...	...	...	0922
312	**Liverpool** Lime St a.		0649	...	...	0722	0742	...	...	0801	0824	...	...	0846	...	0910	...	...	...	0912	0915	0921	...	...	...	0943

Operator	VT ⚒	XC ⚒B	VT ⚒	LM ⚒	VT ⚒	VT ⚒A	VT ⚒	XC ⚒S	LM ⚒	VT ⚒	XC ⚒C	VT ⚒	LM ⚒	VT ⑥Hw	VT ⚒	VT ⒶH	VT ⚒	VT ⚒U	LM ⚒	VT ⚒	XC ⚒G	VT ⚒	LM ⚒	VT ⚒	VT ⚒	VT ⚒
London Euston d.	0735	...	0800	...	0807	0810	0820	...	...	0840	...	0900	...	0850	0907	0910	0920	...	...	0940	...	1000	...	1007	1010	1020
Milton Keynes d.	0806	...	│	...	│	0840	0850	...	...	│	...	│	...	0925	│	0940	0950	...	...	│	...	│	...	│	1040	1050
Rugby d.	│	...	│	...	│	│	│	...	...	│	...	│	...	│	│	│	│	...	...	│	...	│	...	│	│	│
Nuneaton d.	│	...	│	...	│	│	│	...	...	│	...	│	...	│	│	│	│	...	...	│	...	│	...	│	│	│
Birmingham New St d.	│	0831	│	0836	│	│	│	0857	0901	│	0931	│	0936	│	│	│	│	0957	1001	│	1031	│	1036	│	│	│
Wolverhampton d.	│	0849	│	0853	│	│	│	0915	0919	│	0949	│	0953	│	│	│	│	1015	1019	│	1049	│	1053	│	│	│
Stafford d.	│	0901	│	0909	0923	│	│	0930	0935	│	1001	│	1009	│	1023	│	│	1030	1035	│	1101	│	1109	1123	│	│
Stoke on Trent d.	│	0919	0924	│	│	│	0948	0954	│	│	1019	1024	│	│	│	│	1048	1054	│	│	1119	1124	│	│	│	1148
Macclesfield d.	│	│	0941	│	│	│	│	1011	│	│	│	1041	│	│	│	│	│	1111	│	│	│	1141	│	│	│	│
Crewe 165 d.	0911	│	│	0931	│	0949	│	│	0957	1011	│	│	1031	1045	│	1049	│	│	1057	1111	│	│	1131	│	1149	│
Chester 165 a.	│	│	│	│	│	1012	│	│	│	│	│	│	│	1112	│	1109	│	│	│	│	│	│	│	│	1312	│
Stockport a.	0936	0949	0955	│	│	...	1016	1027	│	1036	1049	1055	│	...	│	...	1116	1127	│	1136	1149	1155	│	│	...	1216
Manchester P'dilly a.	0949	0959	1007	│	│	...	1028	1039	│	1049	1059	1107	│	...	│	...	1128	1139	│	1149	1159	1207	│	│	...	1228
Runcorn a.	...	...	...	0950	0955	...	...	...	1022	...	...	...	1050	...	1055	...	...	...	1121	...	...	...	1150	1155	...	...
Liverpool Lime St a.	...	...	...	1010	1015	...	...	...	1044	...	...	...	1110	...	1116	...	...	...	1143	...	...	...	1210	1215	...	...

Operator	XC ⚒U	LM ⚒	VT ⚒	XC ⚒B	VT ⚒	LM ⚒	VT ⚒	VT ⚒	VT ⚒	XC ⚒U	LM ⚒	VT ⚒	XC ⚒B	VT ⚒	LM ⚒	VT ⚒	VT ⚒	VT ⚒	XC ⚒U	LM ⚒	VT ⚒	XC ⚒G	VT ⚒	LM ⚒	VT ⚒	VT ⚒
London Euston d.	...	...	1040	...	1100	...	1107	1110	1120	...	...	1140	...	1200	...	1207	1210	1220	...	...	1240	...	1300	...	1307	1310
Milton Keynes d.	...	...	│	...	│	...	│	1140	1150	...	...	│	...	│	...	│	1240	1250	...	...	│	...	│	...	│	1340
Rugby d.	...	...	│	...	│	...	│	│	│	...	...	│	...	│	...	│	│	│	...	...	│	...	│	...	│	│
Nuneaton d.	...	...	│	...	│	...	│	│	│	...	...	│	...	│	...	│	│	│	...	...	│	...	│	...	│	│
Birmingham New St d.	1057	1101	│	1131	│	1136	│	│	│	1157	1201	│	1231	│	1236	│	│	│	1257	1301	│	1331	│	1336	│	│
Wolverhampton d.	1115	1119	│	1149	│	1153	│	│	│	1215	1219	│	1249	│	1253	│	│	│	1315	1319	│	1349	│	1353	│	│
Stafford d.	1130	1135	│	1201	│	1209	1223	│	│	1230	1235	│	1301	│	1309	1323	│	│	1330	1335	│	1401	│	1409	1423	│
Stoke on Trent d.	1154	│	│	1219	1224	│	│	│	1248	1254	│	│	1319	1324	│	│	│	1348	1354	│	│	1419	1424	│	│	│
Macclesfield d.	1211	│	│	│	1241	│	│	│	│	1311	│	│	│	1341	│	│	│	│	1411	│	│	│	1441	│	│	│
Crewe 165 d.	│	1157	1211	│	│	1231	│	1249	│	│	1257	1311	│	│	1331	│	1349	│	│	1357	1411	│	│	1431	│	1449
Chester 165 a.	│	│	│	│	│	│	│	1312	│	│	│	│	│	│	│	│	1412	│	│	│	│	│	│	│	│	1512
Stockport a.	1227	│	1236	1249	1255	│	│	...	1316	1327	│	1336	1349	1355	│	│	...	1416	1427	│	1436	1449	1455	│	│	...
Manchester P'dilly a.	1239	│	1249	1259	1307	│	│	...	1328	1339	│	1349	1359	1407	│	│	...	1428	1439	│	1449	1459	1507	│	│	...
Runcorn a.	...	1222	...	...	...	1250	1255	...	...	...	1321	...	...	...	1350	1355	...	...	...	1421	...	...	...	1450	1455	...
Liverpool Lime St a.	...	1244	...	...	...	1310	1315	...	...	...	1343	...	...	...	1410	1415	...	...	...	1443	...	...	...	1510	1515	...

Operator	VT ⚒	XC ⚒U	LM ⚒	VT ⚒	XC ⚒B	VT ⚒	LM ⚒	VT ⚒	VT ⚒J	VT ⚒	XC ⚒U	LM ⚒	VT ⚒	XC ⒶZ	XC ⑥Z	VT ⚒	LM ⚒	VT ⚒	VT ⚒	VT ⚒	XC ⚒U	LM ⚒	VT ⚒	XC ⚒B	VT ⚒	LM ⚒
London Euston d.	1320	...	...	1340	...	1400	...	1407	1410	1420	...	...	1440	...	...	1500	...	1507	1510	1520	...	...	1540	...	1600	...
Milton Keynes d.	1350	...	...	│	...	│	...	│	1440	1450	...	...	│	...	...	│	...	│	1540	1550	...	...	│	...	│	...
Rugby d.	│	...	...	│	...	│	...	│	│	│	...	...	│	...	...	│	...	│	│	│	...	...	│	...	│	...
Nuneaton d.	│	...	...	│	...	│	...	│	│	│	...	...	│	...	...	│	...	│	│	│	...	...	│	...	│	...
Birmingham New St d.	│	1357	1401	│	1431	│	1436	│	│	│	1457	1501	│	1531	1531	│	1536	│	│	│	1557	1601	│	1631	│	1636
Wolverhampton d.	│	1415	1419	│	1449	│	1453	│	│	│	1515	1519	│	1550	1549	│	1553	│	│	│	1615	1619	│	1649	│	1653
Stafford d.	│	1430	1435	│	1501	│	1509	1523	│	│	1530	1535	│	│	1601	│	1609	1623	│	│	1630	1635	│	1701	│	1709
Stoke on Trent d.	1448	1454	│	│	1519	1524	│	│	│	1548	1554	│	│	1618	1619	1624	1631	│	│	1648	1654	│	│	1719	1724	│
Macclesfield d.	│	1511	│	│	│	1541	│	│	│	│	1611	│	│	│	│	1641	│	│	│	│	1711	│	│	│	1741	│
Crewe 165 d.	│	│	1457	1511	│	│	1531	│	1549	│	│	1557	1612	│	│	│	│	│	1649	│	│	1657	1711	│	│	1731
Chester 165 a.	│	│	│	│	│	│	│	│	1612	│	│	│	│	│	│	│	│	│	1712	│	│	│	│	│	│	│
Stockport a.	1516	1527	│	1536	1549	1555	│	│	...	1616	1627	│	1636	1648	1649	1654	│	│	...	1716	1727	│	1736	1749	1755	│
Manchester P'dilly a.	1528	1539	│	1549	1559	1607	│	│	...	1628	1639	│	1649	1659	1659	1707	│	│	...	1728	1739	│	1749	1759	1807	│
Runcorn a.	...	...	1521	...	...	...	1550	1555	...	...	...	1623	...	...	...	...	1650	1655	...	...	...	1721	...	...	...	1750
Liverpool Lime St a.	...	...	1543	...	...	...	1610	1615	...	...	...	1645	...	...	...	...	1710	1715	...	...	...	1743	...	...	...	1810

Operator	VT ⚒	VT ⚒D	VT ⚒	XC ⚒U	LM ⚒	VT ⑥	VT ⚒	XC ⚒G	LM ⚒	VT ⚒	VT ⑥	VT Ⓐ	VT ⑥H	VT ⒶH	VT ⚒	XC ⚒U	LM ⚒	VT Ⓐ	VT ⚒	XC ⑥B	XC ⒶB	LM ⑥	LM Ⓐ	VT ⚒	VT ⑥	VT Ⓐ
London Euston d.	1607	1610	1620	...	...	1633	1640	...	...	1700	1707	1707	1710	1710	1720	...	...	1733	1740	...	...	...	...	1800	1807	1807
Milton Keynes d.	│	1640v	1650v	...	...	│	│	...	...	│	│	│	1740	1740u	1750v	...	...	│	│	...	...	...	...	│	│	│
Rugby d.	│	│	│	...	...	│	│	...	...	│	│	│	│	│	│	...	...	1823	│	...	...	...	...	│	│	│
Nuneaton d.	│	│	│	...	...	│	│	...	...	│	1803	│	│	1812	│	...	...	│	│	...	...	...	...	│	│	│
Birmingham New St d.	│	│	│	1657	1701	│	│	1731	1736	│	│	│	│	│	│	1757	1801	│	│	1831	1831	1836	1836	│	│	│
Wolverhampton d.	│	│	│	1715	1719	│	│	1749	1753	│	│	│	│	│	│	1815	1819	│	│	1849	1849	1853	1853	│	│	│
Stafford d.	1723	│	│	1730	1736	1758	│	1801	1809	│	1827	1825	│	│	│	1830	1835	1856	│	1901	│	1909	1909	│	1923	1925
Stoke on Trent d.	│	│	1748	1754	│	│	│	1819	│	1824	│	│	│	│	1848	1854	│	│	│	1919	1918	│	│	1924	│	│
Macclesfield d.	│	│	│	1811	│	│	│	│	│	1841	│	│	│	│	│	1911	│	│	│	│	│	│	│	1941	│	│
Crewe d.	│	1749	│	│	1800	│	1811	│	1831	│	│	1843	1850	1856	│	│	1859	1917	1911	│	│	1930	1931	│	│	1945
Chester a.	│	1809	│	│	│	│	│	│	│	│	│	│	1910	1915	│	│	│	│	│	│	│	...	│	│	│	│
Stockport a.	│	...	1816	1827	│	│	1837	1849	│	1855	│	│	...	...	1916	1927	│	│	1936	1949	1947	...	│	1955	│	│
Manchester P'dilly a.	│	...	1828	1839	│	│	1849	1859	│	1907	│	│	...	...	1928	1940	│	│	1949	1959	2000	...	│	2007	│	│
Runcorn a.	1755	...	...	...	1823	1831	...	...	1858	...	1859	1903	...	...	...	...	1923	1934	...	...	...	...	1957	...	1955	2002
Liverpool Lime St a.	1815	...	...	...	1844	1854	...	...	1918	...	1919	1923	...	...	...	...	1944	1955	...	...	...	...	2018	...	2015	2021

Operator	VT ⑥	VT ⒶX	VT ⚒	XC ⚒U	LM ⑥	LM Ⓐ	VT ⑥	VT Ⓐ	VT ⚒	XC ⒶE	XC ⑥B	LM Ⓐ	VT Ⓐ	VT ⚒	VT Ⓐ	VT ⑥	VT ⒶH	VT ⚒	XC ⚒U	LM ⑥	VT ⑥	VT Ⓐ	VT ⑥	XC ⒶU	XC ⑥B	VT Ⓐ
London Euston d.	1810	1810	1820	...	...	...	1833	1833	1840	...	...	...	1843	1900	1907	1907	1910	1920	...	...	...	1940	1940	...	...	2000
Milton Keynes d.	1840	1840u	1850v	...	...	...	│	│	│	...	...	...	1913u	│	│	│	1940u	1950	...	...	...	│	│	...	...	│
Rugby d.	│	│	│	...	...	...	│	1923	│	...	...	...	│	│	│	│	│	│	...	...	...	│	│	...	...	│
Nuneaton d.	│	1913	│	...	...	...	│	│	│	...	...	...	│	│	2003	2003	│	│	...	...	...	│	│	...	...	│
Birmingham New St d.	│	│	│	1857	1901	1901	│	│	│	1931	1931	1936	2020	│	│	│	│	│	1957	2001	2020	│	│	2031	2031	│
Wolverhampton d.	│	│	│	1915	1919	1919	│	│	│	1949	1949	1953	2037	│	│	│	│	│	2016	2020	2037	│	│	2049	2049	│
Stafford d.	│	│	│	1929	1936	1936	1959	1956	│	2001	2001	2009	2053	│	2027	2027	│	│	2030	2036	2050	2104	│	│	2101	│
Stoke on Trent d.	│	│	1948	1954	│	│	│	│	│	2019	2019	│	│	2024	│	│	│	2048	2054	│	│	│	│	2118	2120	2123
Macclesfield d.	│	│	│	2011	│	│	│	│	│	│	2036	│	│	2041	│	│	│	│	2111	│	│	│	│	│	2138	2140
Crewe 165 d.	1950	1956	│	│	1958	2001	│	2017	2011	│	│	2031	2116	│	│	2047	2050	│	│	2105	2109	2123	2119	│	│	│
Chester 165 a.	2012	2015	│	│	│	...	│	│	│	│	│	│	...	│	│	│	2110	│	│	│	...	│	│	│	│	│
Stockport a.	...	...	2016	2027	│	...	│	│	2036	2048	2049	│	...	2055	│	│	...	2116	2127	│	...	│	2144	2147	2153	2155
Manchester P'dilly a.	...	...	2028	2039	│	...	│	│	2049	2058	2059	│	...	2107	│	│	...	2128	2141	│	...	2157	2158	2200	2204	2207
Runcorn a.	...	...	...	...	2024	...	2032	2034	...	...	...	2056	...	...	2101	2105	...	...	...	2129	...	...	...	...	...	...
Liverpool Lime St a.	...	...	...	...	2046	...	2053	2055	...	...	...	2116	...	...	2121	2125	...	...	...	2150	...	...	...	...	...	...

FOR NOTES SEE NEXT PAGE ▶ ▶ ▶

AW, LM, VT, XC — LONDON and BIRMINGHAM - CHESTER, MANCHESTER and LIVERPOOL — 150

Services on ⑦ valid until January 31. For services to Scotland see Table **151**. For slower services London - Crewe see Table **142**.

Operator	LM ⑥	LM Ⓐ	VT Ⓐ	VT Ⓐ	XC Ⓐ**U**	XC ⑥**U**		VT ⑥	VT ⑥	VT Ⓐ	VT Ⓐ	LM Ⓐ	LM ⑥	XC ⑥**V**	XC Ⓐ**U**	VT ⑥	VT Ⓐ	VT Ⓐ	XC Ⓐ		XC ⑥	LM ⚒	AW Ⓐ2**H**	AW ⑥2	VT Ⓐ	LM Ⓐ
London Euston d.	...	...	2207	2010	...	...	...	2011	2020	2040	2100	...	...	...	...	2100	2107	2140	...	...	...	...	...	...	2200	...
Milton Keynes d.	...	...	|	2040	...	...	...	|	2105	|	2131	...	...	...	...	2145	2138	|	...	...	...	...	...	...	2231	...
Rugby d.	...	...	|	|	...	...	...	2118	2133	|	|	...	...	...	...	|	|	|	...	...	...	...	...	...	2254	...
Nuneaton d.	...	...	2103	|	...	...	...	|	|	|	|	...	...	...	...	|	2208	|	...	...	...	...	...	...	2304	...
Birmingham New St d.	2036	2036	|	|	2058	2057	...	|	|	|	|	2136	2136	2157	2157	|	|	|	2228	...	2231	2236	2255	2255	|	2309
Wolverhampton d.	2053	2053	|	|	2117	2117	...	|	|	|	|	2153	2153	2216	2216	|	|	|	2246	...	2249	2256	2313	2313	|	2336
Stafford d.	2109	2109	2127	|	2130	2130	...	2149	|	|	|	2209	2209	2230	2230	2236	|	|	2259	...	2303	2313	2330	|	2338**s**	2353
Stoke on Trent d.	|	|	|	|	2154	2154	...	|	2205	|	2228	|	|	2250	2253	|	|	2306**s**	2320	...	2320	|	|	|	|	|
Macclesfield d.	|	|	|	|	2211	2211	...	|	2221	|	2244	|	|	2307	2311	|	|	2323**s**	|	...	2338	|	|	|	|	|
Crewe 165 d.	2130	2131	|	2150	|	|	...	2216	|	2213	|	2231	2234	|	|	2301	2248	|	|	...	|	2343	2359	0035	0003**s**	0016
Chester 165 a.	...	|	|	2215	|	|	...	|	|	|	|	|	...	|	|	|	|	|	|	...	|	...	0020	...	|	...
Stockport a.	...	|	|	...	2225	2227	...	|	2235	2238	2258	|	...	2321	2325	2326	|	2337**s**	|	...	2353	...	...	...	0026**s**	...
Manchester P'dilly a.	...	|	|	...	2235	2241	...	|	2253	2248	2311	|	...	2334	2337	2341	|	2348	0012**y**	...	0010	...	...	...	0035	...
Runcorn d.	...	2154	2159	...	...	...	...	2234	...	...	...	2256	...	...	...	...	2308	...	...	...	...	...	...	...	...	...
Liverpool Lime St a.	...	2215	2220	...	...	...	...	2252	...	...	...	2323	...	...	...	...	2332	...	...	...	...	...	...	...	...	...

Operator		XC ⑦	VT ⑦	VT ⑦	LM ⑦	VT ⑦	XC ⑦		VT ⑦	LM ⑦	VT ⑦	XC ⑦**R**	VT ⑦	LM ⑦	VT ⑦	XC ⑦**S**	VT ⑦	LM ⑦		VT ⑦	VT ⑦	XC ⑦**U**	VT ⑦	LM ⑦	VT ⑦	VT ⑦
London Euston d.	⑦	...	0810	0815	...	0820	...	...	0915	...	0920	...	1015	...	1020	...	1120	...	...	1202	1215	...	1235	...	1255	1302
Milton Keynes d.		...	0855	|	...	0905	...	...	|	...	1007	...	|	...	1107	...	1208	...	...	|	1248	...	|	...	|	|
Rugby d.		...	|	|	...	|	...	...	|	...	|	...	|	...	|	...	|	...	...	|	|	...	|	...	|	|
Nuneaton d.		...	|	0942	...	|	...	...	1045	...	|	...	1146	...	|	...	|	...	...	|	|	...	|	...	|	|
Birmingham New St d.		0901	|	|	0927	|	1001	...	|	1027	|	1101	|	1127	|	1158	|	1217	...	|	|	1258	|	1317	|	|
Wolverhampton d.		0928	|	|	0959	|	1029	...	|	1059	|	1130	|	1159	|	1229	|	1252	...	|	|	1326	|	1351	|	|
Stafford d.		0943	|	1008	1017	|	1045	...	1111	1117	|	1145	1212	1216	|	1245	|	1310	...	1325	|	1340	|	1410	|	1422
Stoke on Trent d.		|	|	|	|	1018	1102	...	|	|	1122	1203	|	|	1222	1302	1307	|	...	|	1350	1358	|	|	1426	|
Macclesfield d.		|	|	|	|	1036	1120	...	|	|	1138	1221	|	|	1239	1320	1324	|	...	|	|	1416	|	|	1442	|
Crewe 165 d.		1008	1018	1029	1038	|	|	...	1132	1138	|	|	1234	1238	|	|	|	1331	...	1345	|	|	1413	1431	|	1442
Chester 165 a.		|	|	|	|	|	|	...	|	|	|	|	|	|	|	|	|	|	...	|	|	|	|	|	|	|
Stockport a.		1037	1042	|	|	1051	1134	...	|	|	1153	1235	|	|	1253	1337	1341	|	...	|	1418	1432	1438	|	1456	|
Manchester P'dilly a.		1048	1057	|	|	1105	1146	...	|	|	1208	1246	|	|	1308	1348	1353	|	...	|	1430	1442	1451	|	1509	|
Runcorn d.		...	...	1046	1101	...	...	...	1149	1201	...	...	1251	1301	...	...	...	1354	...	1402	...	...	...	1454	...	1459
Liverpool Lime St a.		...	...	1107	1121	...	...	...	1205	1221	...	...	1311	1321	...	...	...	1414	...	1423	...	...	...	1514	...	1520

Operator	XC ⑦	VT ⑦	XC ⑦**U**	VT ⑦	LM ⑦	VT ⑦		VT ⑦	XC ⑦**G**	VT ⑦	XC ⑦**U**	VT ⑦	LM ⑦	VT ⑦	VT ⑦	VT ⑦	XC ⑦**P**	VT ⑦	XC ⑦**U**		VT ⑦	KM ⑦	VT ⑦	VT ⑦	VT ⑦	XC ⑦**B**
London Euston d.	...	1315	...	1335	...	1355	...	1402	...	1415	...	1435	...	1455	1502	1505	...	1515	...	...	1535	...	1555	1602	1605	...
Milton Keynes d.	...	1348	...	|	...	|	...	|	...	1448	...	|	...	|	|	1538	...	1548	...	...	|	...	|	|	1639	...
Rugby d.	...	|	...	|	...	|	...	|	...	|	...	|	...	|	|	|	...	|	...	...	|	...	|	|	|	...
Nuneaton d.	...	|	...	|	...	|	...	|	...	|	...	|	...	|	|	|	...	|	...	...	|	...	|	|	|	...
Birmingham New St d.	1327	|	1358	|	1417	|	...	|	1427	|	1458	|	1517	|	|	|	1527	|	1558	...	|	1617	|	|	|	1627
Wolverhampton d.	1401	|	1426	|	1452	|	...	|	1501	|	1526	|	1552	|	|	|	1601	|	1626	...	|	1652	|	|	|	1650
Stafford d.	|	|	1440	|	1510	|	...	1525	|	|	1540	|	1610	|	1621	|	|	|	1640	...	|	1710	|	1725	|	|
Stoke on Trent d.	1431	1450	1457	|	|	1525	...	|	1534	1550	1557	|	|	1624	|	|	1634	1650	1657	...	|	|	1725	|	|	1734
Macclesfield d.	1448	|	1515	|	|	1542	...	|	1554	|	1615	|	|	1642	|	|	1654	|	1715	...	|	|	1742	|	|	1754
Crewe 165 d.	|	|	|	1513	1531	|	...	1545	|	|	|	1613	1634	|	|	1652	|	|	|	...	1713	1731	|	|	1752	|
Chester 165 a.	|	|	|	|	|	|	...	|	|	|	|	|	|	|	|	1714	|	|	|	...	|	|	|	|	1814	|
Stockport a.	1502	1518	1529	1538	|	1556	...	|	1607	1618	1629	1638	|	1656	|	...	1707	1718	1729	...	1738	|	1756	|	...	1807
Manchester P'dilly a.	1519	1530	1540	1551	|	1609	...	|	1620	1630	1640	1651	|	1709	|	...	1719	1730	1740	...	1751	|	1809	|	...	1819
Runcorn d.	...	...	...	...	1554	...	...	1602	...	...	...	...	1656	...	1659	...	...	...	...	...	...	1754	...	1757	...	...
Liverpool Lime St a.	...	...	...	...	1614	...	...	1622	...	...	...	...	1717	...	1722	...	...	...	...	...	...	1814	...	1519	...	...

Operator	VT ⑦	XC ⑦**U**	VT ⑦	LM ⑦	VT ⑦		VT ⑦	VT ⑦**H**	XC ⑦**B**	VT ⑦	XC ⑦**U**	VT ⑦	LM ⑦	VT ⑦	VT ⑦	XC ⑦**Z**	VT ⑦**H**	VT ⑦	XC ⑦**U**	VT ⑦		VT ⑦	LM ⑦	XC ⑦**B**	VT ⑦	VT ⑦**H**
London Euston d.	1615	...	1635	...	1655	...	1702	1705	...	1715	...	1735	...	1755	1802	...	1805	1815	...	1835	...	1855	...	...	1902	1905
Milton Keynes d.	1648	...	|	...	|	...	|	1738	...	1748	...	|	...	|	|	...	1838	1848	...	|	...	|	...	...	|	1938
Rugby d.	|	...	|	...	|	...	|	|	...	|	...	|	...	|	|	...	|	|	...	|	...	|	...	...	|	|
Nuneaton d.	|	...	|	...	|	...	|	1810	...	|	...	|	...	|	|	...	|	|	...	|	...	|	...	...	2001	|
Birmingham New St d.	|	1658	|	1717	|	...	|	|	1727	|	1758	|	1817	|	|	1827	|	|	1858	|	...	|	1917	1927	|	|
Wolverhampton d.	|	1726	|	1752	|	...	|	|	1801	|	1826	|	1852	|	|	1901	|	|	1926	|	...	|	1952	2001	|	|
Stafford d.	|	1710	|	1810	|	...	1825	|	|	|	1840	|	1910	|	1925	|	|	|	1940	|	...	|	2010	|	2030	|
Stoke on Trent d.	1750	1757	|	|	1825	...	|	|	1830	1850	1857	|	|	1925	|	1930	|	1950	1957	|	...	2025	|	2036	|	|
Macclesfield d.	|	1815	|	|	1842	...	|	|	1849	|	1915	|	|	1942	|	1949	|	|	2015	|	...	2042	|	2057	|	|
Crewe 165 d.	|	|	1813	1831	|	...	|	1856	|	|	|	1913	1931	|	|	|	1952	|	|	2013	...	|	2031	|	2050	2055
Chester 165 a.	|	|	|	|	|	...	|	1914	|	|	|	|	|	|	|	|	2011	|	|	|	...	|	|	|	|	2114
Stockport a.	1818	1829	1838	|	1856	...	|	...	1904	1918	1929	1938	|	1956	|	2002	...	2018	2029	2038	...	2056	|	2109	|	...
Manchester P'dilly a.	1830	1840	1851	|	1909	...	|	...	1919	1930	1940	1951	|	2009	|	2018	...	2030	2040	2051	...	2109	|	2122	|	...
Runcorn d.	...	...	...	1854	...	...	1857	...	...	...	...	...	1954	...	1958	...	...	...	...	...	...	...	2054	...	2107	...
Liverpool Lime St a.	...	...	...	1914	...	...	1919	...	...	...	...	...	2014	...	2019	...	...	...	...	...	...	...	2114	...	2127	...

Operator	VT ⑦		XC ⑦**U**	VT ⑦		VT ⑦	VT ⑦	XC ⑦**B**		VT ⑦	VT ⑦	VT ⑦			XC ⑦**U**	VT ⑦	LM ⑦		AW ⑦2	XC ⑦**U**	VT ⑦		VT ⑦	AW ⑦2**H**		VT ⑦
London Euston d.	1915	...	...	...	...	1935	1955	...	...	2002	2005	2015	...	...	...	2035	...	...	...	...	2121	...	2114	...	...	2150
Milton Keynes d.	1948	...	...	...	...	|	|	...	...	|	2038	2048	...	...	...	|	...	...	...	...	|	...	2213	...	...	2238
Rugby d.	|	...	...	...	...	|	|	...	...	|	|	|	...	...	...	|	...	...	...	...	2254	...	|	...	...	2319
Nuneaton d.	|	...	...	...	...	|	|	...	...	2101	|	|	...	...	...	|	...	...	...	...	|	...	|	...	...	2329
Birmingham New St d.	|	...	1958	2001	...	|	|	2027	...	|	|	|	...	...	2058	|	2140	...	2107	2158	|	...	|	2246	...	|
Wolverhampton d.	|	...	2026	2038	...	|	|	2057	...	|	|	|	...	...	2130	|	2208	...	2143	2226	|	...	|	2313	...	|
Stafford d.	|	...	2039	2052	...	|	|	|	...	|	2133	|	...	...	2144	2204	2226	...	|	2240	2319	...	|	2331	...	2354**s**
Stoke on Trent d.	2050	...	2057	|	...	|	2125	2130	...	|	|	2150	...	...	2203	|	|	...	|	2258	|	...	2329	|	...	|
Macclesfield d.	|	...	2115	|	...	|	2142	2148	...	|	|	|	...	...	2221	|	|	...	|	2315	|	...	2345	|	...	|
Crewe 165 d.	|	...	|	2110	...	2114	|	|	...	2146	2155	|	...	...	|	2223	2249	...	2306	|	2341	...	|	0010	...	0012**s**
Chester 165 a.	|	...	|	...	...	|	|	|	...	|	|	|	...	...	|	|	...	...	2330	|	|	...	|	0031	...	|
Stockport a.	2118	...	2129	...	...	2139	2156	2202	...	|	|	2218	...	...	2234	2248	...	...	...	2329	|	...	2359	...	...	0041**s**
Manchester P'dilly a.	2130	...	2140	...	...	2152	2209	2216	...	|	|	2230	...	...	2244	2300	...	...	...	2342	|	...	0013	...	...	0053
Runcorn d.	...	...	...	...	...	...	...	...	...	2203	2212	...	...	...	...	...	...	...	...	...	0004	...	...	...	...	...
Liverpool Lime St a.	...	...	...	...	...	...	...	...	...	2223	2232	...	...	...	...	...	...	...	...	...	0031	...	...	...	...	...

A – To Bangor on Ⓐ.
B – From Bristol.
C – From Cardiff.
D – To Bangor on Ⓐ, to Holyhead on ⑥.
E – From Exeter.
G – From Paignton.
H – To Holyhead.
J – To Holyhead on ⑥.
P – From Plymouth.
R – From Reading.

S – From Southampton.
U – From Bournemouth.
V – Dec. 19 – Mar. 27. From Bournemouth.
X – To Holyhead. Conveys [12] London Euston - Chester - Wrexham.
Z – From Penzance.

s – Stops to set down only.
u – Stops to pick up only.

w – Also calls at Watford Junction 13–18 minutes after London Euston to pick up only.
v – Stops to pick up only on Ⓐ.
y – Arrives 0032 on ②③.

□ – London Euston - Manchester: *296* km via Stoke on Trent, *304* km via Crewe.

150 LIVERPOOL, MANCHESTER and CHESTER - BIRMINGHAM and LONDON AW, LM, VT, XC

Services on ⑦ valid until January 31. For services from Scotland see Table **151**. For slower services Crewe - London see Table **142**.

⚒

Operator	AW ⚒2	VT Ⓐ	VT ⑥w	XC ⒶU	XC ⑥U	VT Ⓐ	VT ⑥w	LM ⚒	VT ⑥	VT Ⓐ	XC ⒶB	XC ⑥B	VT Ⓐ	VT Ⓐ	VT ⑥	LM ⚒	VT ⒶD	VT Ⓐw	VT ⚒	VT Ⓐ	VT ⑥	LM ⚒	VT Ⓐ	VT Ⓐ	VT ⑥
Liverpool Lime St ..... d.	...	...	...	...	...	0527	0547	...	...	...	...	...	...	0605	...	...	...	...	...	...	0645	0630	...	0700	...
Runcorn .... d.	...	...	...	...	...	0543	0603	...	...	...	...	...	...	0621	...	...	...	...	...	...	0701	0648	...	0715u	...
Manchester P'dilly .. d.	...	0505	0525	0500	0511	|	|	...	0555	0555	0600	0600	0610	|	0610	...	...	0627	0635	0643	|	|	0700	|	0655
Stockport .... d.	...	0513	0534	|	|	|	|	...	0603	0603	0608	0608	0618	|	0618	...	...	0635	0643	0651	|	|	0707u	|	0704
Chester .... 165 d.	0423	|	|	|	|	|	|	...	|	|	|	|	|	|	|	...	0626	|	|	|	|	|	|	|	|
Crewe .... 165 d.	0500	0536	0600	0547	0547	0602	|	0620	0629	0629	0638	|	|	|	|	0647	0653	|	|	0717	0720	0716	|	|	0729
Macclesfield .... d.	|	|	|	|	|	|	|	|	|	|	|	0621	0631	|	0631	|	|	0648	0655	|	|	|	|	|	|
Stoke on Trent .... d.	|	|	|	0607	0608	|	|	|	|	|	|	0639	0648	|	0648	|	|	0706	0712	|	|	|	|	|	|
Stafford .... d.	0524	0555	0619	0625	0626	0621	0635	0641	|	|	0658	0658	|	0653	|	0712	|	0728	|	0735	0739	0741	|	|	|
Wolverhampton .... a.	0538	|	|	0639	0639	|	|	0657	|	|	0712	0712	|	|	|	0728	|	0743	|	|	|	0757	|	|	|
Birmingham New St a.	0600	|	|	0658	0657	|	|	0718	|	|	0731	0731	|	|	|	0748	|	0805	|	|	|	0817	|	|	|
Nuneaton .... d.	...	0617	|	...	...	|	0657	...	|	0706	...	...	|	|	|	...	0732	|	|	|	|	...	|	|	|
Rugby .... a.	...	0630	0649	...	...	0652	|	...	|	|	...	...	0728	|	|	...	|	|	0752	|	|	...	|	|	|
Milton Keynes .... a.	...	0651	0711	...	...	0712	|	...	0731	|	...	...	|	|	|	...	|	|	|	|	|	...	|	|	|
London Euston .... a.	...	0728	0752	...	...	0750	0805	...	0809	0811	...	...	0822	0822	0827	...	0835	0934	0846	0855	0859	...	0858	0901	0904

Operator	XC ⒶB	XC ⑥B	VT ⚒	VT ⑥	LM ⚒	VT ⒶV	VT ⑥	VT ⑥	XC ⚒U	VT Ⓐw	VT Ⓐ	VT ⑥	LM ⚒	VT ⚒	XC ⚒G	LM ⚒	VT ⚒	VT ⚒H	XC ⚒U	VT ⚒	VT ⑥	LM ⚒	VT Ⓐ	VT ⚒	XC ⒶB	XC ⑥B
Liverpool Lime St ..... d.	...	...	...	...	0704	...	...	0719	...	...	0748	0748	0734	...	...	0804	...	...	...	...	0848	0834	0848	...	...	...
Runcorn .... d.	...	...	...	...	0722	...	...	0736	...	...	0804	0804	0752	...	...	0824	...	...	...	...	0904	0852	0904	...	...	...
Manchester P'dilly .. d.	0706	0707	0715	...	|	...	0735	|	0726	0735	|	|	|	0755	0807	|	0815	...	0827	0835	|	|	|	0855	0907	0907
Stockport .... d.	0716	0716	0723	...	|	...	0743	|	0735	0743	|	|	|	0804	0816	|	0823	...	0835	0842	|	|	|	0904	0916	0916
Chester .... 165 d.	|	|	|	0717	|	0735	|	|	|	|	|	|	|	|	|	|	|	0835	|	|	|	|	|	|	|	|
Crewe .... 165 d.	|	|	|	0739	0749	0757	|	0755	|	|	|	|	0822	0829	|	0849	|	0856	|	|	|	0922	|	0929	|	|
Macclesfield .... d.	|	|	|	|	|	|	0756	|	0749	0756	|	|	|	|	|	|	|	|	0849	0855	|	|	|	|	|	|
Stoke on Trent .... d.	0744	0744	0750	|	|	|	0812	|	0807	0812	|	|	|	|	0844	|	0850	|	0907	0912	|	|	|	|	0944	0944
Stafford .... d.	|	0803	|	|	0810	|	|	0816	0825	|	0836	0836	0843	|	|	0910	|	|	0925	|	0936	0943	0936	|	|	1003
Wolverhampton .... a.	0813	0816	|	|	0828	|	|	|	0839	|	|	|	0858	|	0915	0927	|	|	0939	|	|	0956	|	|	1013	1015
Birmingham New St a.	0831	0838	|	|	0847	|	|	|	0858	|	|	|	0918	|	0939	0947	|	|	0958	|	|	1017	|	|	1031	1039
Nuneaton .... d.	...	...	|	|	...	|	|	|	...	0844	|	0858	...	|	...	...	|	|	...	|	0958	...	|	|	...	...
Rugby .... a.	...	...	|	|	...	0845	|	|	...	|	|	|	...	|	...	...	|	|	...	|	|	...	|	|	...	...
Milton Keynes .... a.	...	...	0846v	|	...	|	|	|	...	|	|	|	...	|	...	...	0946	1001	...	|	|	...	|	|	...	...
London Euston .... a.	...	...	0923	0930	...	0938	0942	0946	...	0952	0956	1001	...	1004	...	...	1023	1038	...	1042	1101	...	1056	1104	...	...

Operator	LM ⚒	VT ⚒	VT ⚒J	XC ⚒U	VT ⚒	VT ⚒	LM ⚒	VT ⚒	XC ⒶB	XC ⑥B	LM ⚒	VT ⚒	VT ⚒H	XC ⚒U	VT ⚒	VT ⚒	LM ⚒	VT ⚒	XC ⚒B	LM ⚒	VT ⚒	VT ⚒	XC ⚒U	VT ⚒	VT ⚒	LM ⚒
Liverpool Lime St ..... d.	0904	...	...	...	...	0948	0934	...	...	...	1004	...	...	...	...	1048	1034	...	...	1104	...	...	...	...	1148	1134
Runcorn .... d.	0924	...	...	...	...	1004	0952	...	...	...	1025	...	...	...	...	1104	1052	...	...	1125	...	...	...	...	1204	1152
Manchester P'dilly .. d.	|	0915	...	0927	0935	|	|	0955	1007	1007	|	1015	...	1027	1035	|	|	1055	1107	|	1115	...	1127	1135	|	|
Stockport .... d.	|	0923	...	0935	0942	|	|	1004	1016	1016	|	1023	...	1035	1042	|	|	1104	1116	|	1123	...	1135	1142	|	|
Chester .... 165 d.	|	|	0935	|	|	|	|	|	|	|	|	|	1035	|	|	|	|	|	|	|	|	1135	|	|	|	|
Crewe .... 165 d.	0949	|	0956	|	|	|	1022	1029	|	|	1049	|	1056	|	|	|	1122	1129	|	1149	|	1156	|	|	|	1222
Macclesfield .... d.	|	|	|	0949	0955	|	|	|	|	|	|	|	|	1049	1055	|	|	|	|	|	|	|	1149	1155	|	|
Stoke on Trent .... d.	|	0950	|	1007	1011	|	|	|	1044	1044	|	1050	|	1107	1111	|	|	|	1144	|	1150	|	1207	1211	|	|
Stafford .... d.	1010	|	|	1025	|	1036	1043	|	|	1103	1110	|	|	1125	|	1136	1143	|	1203	1210	|	|	1225	|	1236	1243
Wolverhampton .... a.	1027	|	|	1039	|	|	1056	|	1116	1116	1127	|	|	1139	|	|	1156	|	1216	1227	|	|	1239	|	|	1256
Birmingham New St a.	1047	|	|	1058	|	|	1118	|	1139	1139	1147	|	|	1158	|	|	1217	|	1239	1247	|	|	1258	|	|	1317
Nuneaton .... d.	...	|	|	...	|	|	...	|	...	...	...	|	|	...	|	|	...	|	...	...	|	|	...	|	|	...
Rugby .... a.	...	|	|	...	|	|	...	|	...	...	...	|	|	...	|	|	...	|	...	...	|	|	...	|	|	...
Milton Keynes .... a.	...	1046	1101	...	|	|	...	|	...	...	...	1146	1201	...	|	|	...	|	...	...	1246	1301	...	|	|	...
London Euston .... a.	...	1123	1138	...	1142	1156	...	1204	...	...	...	1223	1238	...	1242	1256	...	1304	...	...	1323	1338	...	1342	1356	...

Operator	VT ⚒	XC ⒶE	XC ⑥B	LM ⚒	VT ⚒	XC ⚒U	VT ⚒	VT ⚒	VT ⚒	LM ⚒	VT ⚒	XC ⒶB	XC ⑥B	LM ⚒	VT ⚒	VT ⚒A	XC ⚒U	VT ⚒	VT ⚒	LM ⚒	VT ⚒	XC ⒶG	XC ⑥G	LM ⚒	VT ⚒	VT ⚒
Liverpool Lime St ..... d.	...	...	...	1204	...	...	...	...	1248	1234	...	...	...	1304	...	...	...	...	1348	1334	...	...	...	1404	...	...
Runcorn .... d.	...	...	...	1225	...	...	...	...	1304	1252	...	...	...	1325	...	...	...	...	1404	1352	...	...	...	1425	...	...
Manchester P'dilly .. d.	1155	1207	1207	|	1215	1227	...	1235	|	|	1255	1307	1307	|	1315	...	1327	1335	|	|	1355	1407	1407	|	1415	...
Stockport .... d.	1204	1216	1216	|	1223	1235	...	1242	|	|	1304	1316	1316	|	1323	...	1335	1342	|	|	1404	1416	1416	|	1423	...
Chester .... 165 d.	|	|	|	|	|	|	1235	|	|	|	|	|	|	|	|	1335	|	|	|	|	|	|	|	|	|	1435
Crewe .... 165 d.	1229	|	|	1249	|	|	1256	|	|	1322	1329	|	|	1349	|	1356	|	|	|	1422	1429	|	|	1449	|	1456
Macclesfield .... d.	|	|	|	|	|	1249	|	1255	|	|	|	|	|	|	|	|	1349	1355	|	|	|	|	|	|	|	|
Stoke on Trent .... d.	|	1244	1244	|	1250	1307	|	1311	|	|	|	1344	1344	|	1350	|	1407	1411	|	|	|	1444	1444	|	1450	|
Stafford .... d.	|	|	1303	1310	|	1325	|	|	1336	1343	|	|	1403	1410	|	|	1425	|	1436	1446	|	|	1503	1510	|	|
Wolverhampton .... a.	|	1313	1315	1327	|	1339	|	|	|	1356	|	1413	1416	1427	|	|	1439	|	|	1459	|	1515	1516	1527	|	|
Birmingham New St a.	|	1331	1339	1347	|	1358	|	|	|	1417	|	1431	1439	1447	|	|	1458	|	|	1520	|	1539	1539	1547	|	|
Nuneaton .... d.	|	...	...	...	|	...	|	|	|	...	|	...	...	...	|	|	...	|	|	...	|	...	...	...	|	|
Rugby .... a.	|	...	...	...	|	...	|	|	|	...	|	...	...	...	|	|	...	|	|	...	|	...	...	...	|	|
Milton Keynes .... a.	|	...	...	...	1346	...	1401	|	|	...	|	...	...	...	1446	1501	...	|	|	...	|	...	...	...	1546	1601
London Euston .... a.	1404	...	...	...	1424	...	1438	1442	1457	...	1504	...	...	...	1523	1538	...	1542	1556	...	1604	...	...	...	1623	1638

Operator	XC ⚒U	VT ⚒	VT ⚒	LM ⚒	VT ⚒	XC ⒶB	XC ⑥B	LM ⚒	VT ⚒	VT ⚒J	XC ⚒U	VT ⚒	VT ⚒	LM ⚒	VT ⚒	VT ⚒B	LM ⚒	VT ⚒	VT ⑥H	VT Ⓐ	XC ⚒U	VT ⚒	VT ⑥	VT Ⓐ	LM ⚒	VT ⑥
Liverpool Lime St ..... d.	...	...	1448	1434	...	...	...	1504	...	...	...	...	1548	1534	...	...	1604	...	...	...	...	...	1648	1648	1634	...
Runcorn .... d.	...	...	1504	1452	...	...	...	1525	...	...	...	...	1604	1552	...	...	1625	...	...	...	...	...	1704	1704	1652	...
Manchester P'dilly .. d.	1427	1435	|	|	1455	1507	1507	|	1515	...	1527	1535	|	|	1555	1607	|	1615	...	...	1627	1635	|	|	|	1655
Stockport .... d.	1435	1442	|	|	1504	1516	1516	|	1523	...	1535	1542	|	|	1604	1616	|	1623	...	...	1635	1642	|	|	|	1704
Chester .... 165 d.	|	|	|	|	|	|	|	|	|	1535	|	|	|	|	|	|	|	|	1620	1635	|	|	|	|	|	|
Crewe .... 165 d.	|	|	|	1522	1529	|	|	1549	|	1556	|	|	|	1622	1629	|	1649	|	1656	1656	|	|	|	|	1722	1729
Macclesfield .... d.	1449	1455	|	|	|	|	|	|	|	|	1549	1555	|	|	|	|	|	|	|	|	1649	1656	|	|	|	|
Stoke on Trent .... d.	1507	1511	|	|	|	1544	1544	|	1550	|	1607	1611	|	|	|	1644	|	1650	|	|	1707	1712	|	|	|	|
Stafford .... d.	1525	|	1536	1543	|	|	1603	1610	|	|	1625	|	1636	1646	|	1703	1710	|	|	|	1725	|	1736	1736	1743	|
Wolverhampton .... a.	1539	|	|	1556	|	1613	1616	1627	|	|	1639	|	|	1659	|	1716	1727	|	|	|	1739	|	|	|	1756	|
Birmingham New St a.	1558	|	|	1617	|	1631	1639	1647	|	|	1658	|	|	1720	|	1739	1747	|	|	|	1758	|	|	|	1817	|
Nuneaton .... d.	...	|	|	...	|	...	...	...	|	|	...	|	|	...	|	...	...	|	|	|	...	|	|	|	...	|
Rugby .... a.	...	|	|	...	|	...	...	...	|	|	...	|	|	...	|	...	...	|	|	|	...	|	|	|	...	|
Milton Keynes .... a.	...	|	|	...	|	...	...	...	1646	1701	...	|	|	...	|	...	...	1746	1801	1801	...	|	|	1823	...	|
London Euston .... a.	...	1642	1656	...	1704	...	...	...	1723	1738	...	1742	1757	...	1804	...	...	1823	1838	1838	...	1842	1856	1859	...	1904

Operator	VT Ⓐw	XC ⑥C	XC ⒶC	LM ⚒	VT ⚒	VT Ⓐ	XC ⒶU	XC ⑥U	VT ⚒	VT ⑥	VT Ⓐw	LM ⚒	VT ⑥	VT Ⓐ	XC ⒶP	XC ⑥P	LM ⚒	VT Ⓐ	VT ⑥	XC ⚒U	VT Ⓐ	VT ⑥	LM ⚒	VT Ⓐw	VT ⑥	VT Ⓐ
Liverpool Lime St ..... d.	...	...	...	1704	...	...	...	...	...	1748	1748	1734	...	...	...	...	1804	...	...	...	...	...	1834	1848	1848	...
Runcorn .... d.	...	...	...	1725	...	...	...	...	...	1804	1804	1752	...	...	...	...	1824	...	...	...	...	...	1852	1904	1904	...
Manchester P'dilly .. d.	1655	1706	1706	|	1715	...	1727	1727	1735	|	|	|	1755	1755	1805	1805	|	1815	1815	1827	1835	1835	|	|	|	1855
Stockport .... d.	1704	|	|	|	1723	...	1735	1735	1743	|	|	|	1804	1804	1813	1813	|	1823	1823	1835	1842	1842	|	|	|	1904
Chester .... 165 d.	|	|	|	|	|	1735	|	|	|	|	|	|	|	|	|	|	|	|	|	|	|	|	|	|	|	|
Crewe .... 165 d.	1729	|	|	1749	|	1756	1807	|	|	|	|	1822	1829	1829	|	|	1849	|	|	|	|	|	1918	1923	|	1929
Macclesfield .... d.	|	1727	1727	|	|	|	|	1754	1755	|	|	|	|	|	1826	1826	|	|	|	|	1855	1855	|	|	|	|
Stoke on Trent .... d.	|	1744	1744	|	1750	|	|	1808	1813	|	|	|	|	|	1844	1844	|	1850	1850	1907	1912	1912	|	|	|	|
Stafford .... d.	|	|	1804	1810	|	|	1828	1827	|	1836	1836	1843	|	|	|	1903	1910	|	|	1925	|	|	1942	1943	1936	|
Wolverhampton .... a.	|	1813	1815	1827	|	|	1839	1840	|	|	|	1856	|	|	1913	1916	1927	|	|	1939	|	|	1957	|	|	|
Birmingham New St a.	|	1831	1838	1848	|	|	1858	1858	|	|	|	1917	|	|	1931	1933	1947	|	|	1958	|	|	2017	|	|	|
Nuneaton .... d.	|	...	...	...	|	|	...	...	|	|	|	...	|	|	...	...	...	|	|	...	|	|	...	|	|	|
Rugby .... a.	|	...	...	...	|	|	...	...	|	|	|	...	|	|	...	...	...	|	|	...	|	|	...	|	|	|
Milton Keynes .... a.	|	...	...	...	1847	1901	...	...	|	|	|	...	|	1931	...	...	...	1946	1946	...	|	|	...	|	|	2032
London Euston .... a.	1908	...	...	...	1923	1938	...	...	1942	1956	2002	...	2004	2007	...	...	...	2023	2028	...	2042	2101	...	2106	2116	2107

FOR NOTES SEE NEXT PAGE ▶ ▶ ▶

AW, LM, VT, XC

LIVERPOOL, MANCHESTER and CHESTER - BIRMINGHAM and LONDON 150

Services on ⑦ valid until January 31. For services from Scotland see Table **151**. For slower services Crewe - London see Table **142**.

Operator	VT	XC	LM	LM	VT	VT	XC	VT	LM	VT	VT	VT	XC	XC	LM	VT	XC	VT	LM	XC	VT	VT	VT	XC	XC	LM
	⑥	⚒B	⑥	Ⓐ	Ⓐ	Ⓐ	⚒S	⑥	⚒	Ⓐw	Ⓐ	⑥	Ⓐ	⑥	Ⓐ	Ⓐw	⚒	⑥w	⚒	⑥	Ⓐw	Ⓐw	ⒶA	Ⓐ	⑥	Ⓐ
Liverpool Lime St ..... d.	...	...	1904	1911	...	...	...	...	1934	1948	...	1948	...	...	2004	...	...	...	2034	...	...	2048	...	...	...	2134
Runcorn ..... d.	...	...	1923	1929	...	...	...	...	1952	2004	...	2004	...	...	2024	...	...	...	2052	...	...	2104	...	...	...	2152
Manchester P'dilly .. d.	1855	1907	|	|	1915	...	1927	1935	|	|	1955	|	2007	2007	|	2015	2027	2035	|	2107	2115	|	...	2128	2128	|
Stockport ..... d.	1904	1916	|	|	1923	...	1935	1942	|	|	2004	|	2016	2016	|	2023	2035	2043	|	|	2123	|	...	2136	2136	|
Chester ..... **165** d.	|	|	|	|	|	1935	|	|	|	|	|	|	|	|	|	|	|	|	|	|	|	|	2135	|	|	|
Crewe ..... **165** d.	1929	|	1951	1955	|	1956	|	|	2018	2023	2029	|	|	|	2047	|	|	|	2117	|	|	2124	2156	|	|	2220
Macclesfield ..... d.	|	|	|	|	1936	|	1949	1955	|	|	|	|	|	|	|	2036	2049	2056	|	|	2136	|	|	2150	2150	|
Stoke on Trent ..... d.	|	1944	|	|	1952	|	2007	2012	|	|	|	|	2044	2044	|	2053	2107	2113	|	2145	2153	|	|	2208	2208	|
Stafford ..... d.	|	2003	2012	2016	|	|	2026	|	2042	|	2048	2036	|	2103	2110	|	2125	|	2141	2203	|	2144	|	2226	2234	2241
Wolverhampton ..... a.	|	2016	2028	2029	|	|	2040	|	2057	|	|	|	2113	2115	2126	|	2139	|	2158	2214	|	|	2227	2239	2250	2257
Birmingham New St a.	|	2033	2047	2047	|	|	2100	|	2118	|	|	|	2131	2132	2147	|	2200	|	2220	2232	|	|	2250	2258	2317	2318
Nuneaton ..... d.	|	...	...	...	|	|	...	|	...	2102	|	|	...	...	...	|	...	|	...	...	|	2216	...	...	...	...
Rugby ..... a.	|	...	...	...	|	|	...	|	...	|	|	|	...	...	...	|	...	|	...	...	|	2230	...	...	...	...
Milton Keynes ..... a.	|	...	...	...	2048	2103	...	2110	...	|	2135	|	...	...	...	2150	...	2212	...	...	2252	2258	...	...	...	...
London Euston ..... a.	2120	...	...	...	2126	2142	...	2200	...	2209	2212	2217	...	...	...	2233	...	2304	...	...	2348	2358	...	...	...	...

Operator	LM	LM	XC	LM			VT	XC	VT	VT	VT	XC	VT	VT	LM	XC	VT	VT	VT	XC	VT	VT	VT	VT	LM	VT
	⑥	⑥	Ⓐ	Ⓐ		⑦	⑦w	⑦U	⑦w	⑦	⑦w	⑦U	⑦	⑦	⑦	⑦U	⑦w	⑦	⑦w	⑦U	⑦	⑦	⑦	⑦	⑦	⑦
Liverpool Lime St ..... d.	2134	2204	...	2234	...		...	...	...	0815	0838	...	...	0938	...	...	...	...	1038	...	...	...	...	1148	1134	...
Runcorn ..... d.	2152	2221	...	2252	...		...	...	...	0835	0854	...	...	0954	...	...	...	...	1054	...	...	...	...	1204	1152	...
Manchester P'dilly .. d.	|	|	2207	|	...		0805	0810	0820	|	|	0911	0920	|	...	1006	1020	1035	|	1105	1115	...	1135	|	|	1155
Stockport ..... d.	|	|	2216	|	...		0814	0819	0828	|	|	0919	0927	|	...	1016	1029	1042	|	1114	1123	...	1143	|	|	1205
Chester ..... **165** d.	|	|	|	|	...		|	|	|	|	|	|	|	|	...	|	|	|	|	|	|	1128	|	|	|	|
Crewe ..... **165** d.	2223	2248	|	2322	...		0843	0847	|	0853	0913	|	|	1014	1020	|	1055	|	1114	|	|	1149	|	|	1222	1230
Macclesfield ..... d.	|	...	2229	...	...		|	|	0842	|	|	0932	0940	|	|	1029	|	1055	|	1127	|	|	1156	|	|	|
Stoke on Trent ..... d.	|	...	2247	...	...		|	|	0859	|	|	0950	0957	|	|	1047	|	1112	|	1145	1151	|	1213	|	|	|
Stafford ..... d.	2247	...	2307	...	...		0902	0908	|	|	0932	1011	|	1033	1042	1105	|	|	1133	1204	|	|	|	1236	1242	|
Wolverhampton ..... a.	2303	...	2319	...	...		|	0926	|	|	|	1025	|	|	1100	1124	|	|	|	1218	|	|	|	|	1259	|
Birmingham New St a.	2321	...	2338	...	...		|	0955	|	|	|	1054	|	|	1133	1152	|	|	|	1249	|	|	|	|	1330	|
Nuneaton ..... d.	...	...	...	...	...		|	...	|	|	0954	...	|	1055	...	...	|	|	1204	...	|	1230	|	|	...	|
Rugby ..... a.	...	...	...	...	...		|	...	|	|	|	...	|	|	...	...	|	|	|	...	|	|	|	|	...	|
Milton Keynes ..... a.	...	...	...	...	...		|	...	|	1017	|	...	1112	1149	...	...	|	1218	|	...	1250	1303	|	|	...	|
London Euston ..... a.	...	...	...	...	...		1056	...	1100	1107	1135	...	1208	1237	...	...	1256	1259	1315	...	1331	1344	1349	1403	...	1412

Operator	XC	VT	VT	VT	VT	LM	XC	VT	XC	VT	VT	VT	VT	LM	VT	XC	VT	VT	VT	VT	XC	LM	VT	XC	VT	VT
	⑦U	⑦	⑦H	⑦	⑦	⑦	⑦G	⑦	⑦U	⑦	⑦H	⑦	⑦	⑦	⑦	⑦U	⑦	⑦H	⑦	⑦	⑦B	⑦	⑦	⑦U	⑦	⑦H
Liverpool Lime St ..... d.	...	...	...	...	1248	1234	...	...	...	...	...	...	1348	1334	...	...	...	...	...	1448	...	1434	...	...	...	...
Runcorn ..... d.	...	...	...	...	1304	1252	...	...	...	...	...	...	1404	1352	...	...	...	...	...	1504	...	1452	...	...	...	...
Manchester P'dilly .. d.	1206	1215	...	1235	|	|	1241	1255	1303	1315	...	1335	|	|	1355	1405	1415	...	1435	|	1442	|	1455	1502	1515	...
Stockport ..... d.	1215	1223	...	1244	|	|	1251	1305	1313	1322	...	1342	|	|	1404	1414	1422	...	1442	|	1451	|	1504	1511	1522	...
Chester ..... **165** d.	|	|	1233	|	|	|	|	|	|	|	1330	|	|	|	|	|	|	1433	|	|	|	|	|	|	|	1533
Crewe ..... **165** d.	|	|	1254	|	|	1322	|	1330	|	|	1351	|	|	1422	1429	|	|	1454	|	|	|	1522	1529	|	|	1554
Macclesfield ..... d.	1228	|	|	1257	|	|	1304	|	1326	|	|	1355	|	|	|	1427	|	|	1455	|	1505	|	|	1524	|	|
Stoke on Trent ..... d.	1247	1251	|	1314	|	|	1322	|	1344	1350	|	1412	|	|	|	1445	1450	|	1512	|	1523	|	|	1545	1550	|
Stafford ..... d.	1307	|	|	|	1336	1343	|	|	1402	|	|	|	1436	1443	|	1506	|	|	|	1536	|	1543	|	1606	|	|
Wolverhampton ..... a.	1320	|	|	|	|	1359	1353	|	1420	|	|	|	|	1458	|	1519	|	|	|	|	1553	1558	|	1620	|	|
Birmingham New St a.	1352	|	|	|	|	1433	1430	|	1452	|	|	|	|	1533	|	1552	|	|	|	|	1630	1633	|	1652	|	|
Nuneaton ..... d.	...	|	|	|	|	...	...	|	...	|	1431	|	|	...	|	...	|	|	|	|	...	...	|	...	|	|
Rugby ..... a.	...	|	|	|	|	...	...	|	...	|	|	|	|	...	|	...	|	|	|	|	...	...	|	...	|	|
Milton Keynes ..... a.	...	1350	1402	|	|	...	...	|	...	1449	1504	|	|	...	|	...	1549	1604	|	|	...	...	|	...	1649	1703
London Euston ..... a.	...	1430	1443	1450	1503	...	...	1511	...	1530	1545	1548	1603	...	1611	...	1630	1644	1648	1703	...	...	1711	...	1730	1744

Operator	VT	XC	LM	VT	XC	VT	VT	VT	VT	XC	VT	VT	XC	VT	VT	VT	VT	XC	VT	XC	VT	VT	VT	VT	XC	LM
	⑦	⑦B	⑦	⑦	⑦U	⑦	⑦	⑦	⑦	⑦P	⑦	⑦	⑦U	⑦	⑦	⑦	⑦	⑦B	⑦	⑦S	⑦	⑦	⑦	⑦	⑦B	⑦
Liverpool Lime St ..... d.	1548	...	1534	...	...	...	1618	...	1648	...	1634	...	...	...	...	...	1748	...	1734	...	...	...	...	1848	...	1834
Runcorn ..... d.	1604	...	1552	...	...	...	1634	...	1704	...	1652	...	...	...	...	...	1804	...	1752	...	...	...	...	1904	...	1852
Manchester P'dilly .. d.	|	1542	|	1555	1602	1615	|	1635	|	1642	|	1655	1702	1715	...	1735	|	1742	|	1802	1815	...	1835	|	1842	|
Stockport ..... d.	|	1551	|	1604	1611	1623	|	1642	|	1651	|	1704	1711	1722	...	1742	|	1751	|	1811	1822	...	1842	|	1951	|
Chester ..... **165** d.	|	|	|	|	|	|	|	|	|	|	|	|	|	|	1735	|	|	|	|	|	|	1835	|	|	|	|
Crewe ..... **165** d.	|	|	1622	1629	|	|	1654	|	|	|	1722	1729	|	|	1755	|	|	|	1822	|	|	1855	|	|	|	1922
Macclesfield ..... d.	|	1605	|	|	1624	|	|	1655	|	1705	|	|	1724	|	|	1755	|	1805	|	1824	|	|	1855	|	1905	|
Stoke on Trent ..... d.	|	1623	|	|	1645	1650	|	1712	|	1723	|	|	1745	1750	|	1812	|	1823	|	1845	1850	|	1912	|	1923	|
Stafford ..... d.	1637	|	1643	|	1706	|	|	|	1736	|	1743	|	1806	|	|	|	1836	|	1843	1906	|	|	|	1936	|	1943
Wolverhampton ..... a.	|	1653	1658	|	1720	|	|	|	|	1753	1758	|	1819	|	|	|	|	1853	1858	1919	|	|	|	|	1953	1958
Birmingham New St a.	|	1730	1733	|	1756	|	|	|	|	1830	1833	|	1852	|	|	|	|	1930	1933	1952	|	|	|	|	2032	2033
Nuneaton ..... d.	|	...	...	|	...	|	|	|	|	...	...	|	...	|	|	|	|	...	...	...	|	|	|	|	...	...
Rugby ..... a.	|	...	...	|	...	|	|	|	|	...	...	|	...	|	|	|	|	...	...	...	|	|	|	|	...	...
Milton Keynes ..... a.	|	...	...	|	...	1749	1804	|	|	...	...	|	...	1849	1903	|	|	...	...	...	1949	2003	|	|	...	...
London Euston ..... a.	1804	...	...	1811	...	1830	1844	1848	1903	...	...	1911	...	1930	1944	1948	2003	...	...	...	2030	2044	2048	2104	...	...

Operator	VT		XC		VT	VT		LM	VT		XC		VT		AW	VT		LM	VT		VT	VT		LM		XC
	⑦		⑦R		⑦	⑦		⑦	⑦		⑦B		⑦		⑦2H	⑦		⑦	⑦w		⑦w	⑦		⑦		⑦
Liverpool Lime St ..... d.	...	...	...	...	...	...	...	1934	1948	...	...	...	...	...	...	...	...	2034	...	...	2048	...	...	2134	...	...
Runcorn ..... d.	...	...	...	...	...	...	...	1952	2004	...	...	...	...	...	...	...	...	2052	...	...	2104	...	...	2152	...	...
Manchester P'dilly .. d.	1855	...	1902	...	1915	1935	...	|	|	...	1942	...	2002	...	...	2020	...	|	2055	...	|	2102	...	|	...	2202
Stockport ..... d.	1904	...	1911	...	1922	1942	...	|	|	...	1951	...	2011	...	...	2027	...	|	2103	...	|	2111	...	|	...	2211
Chester ..... **165** d.	|	...	|	...	|	|	...	|	|	...	|	...	|	...	2027	|	...	|	|	...	|	|	...	|	...	|
Crewe ..... **165** d.	1929	...	|	...	|	|	...	2018	2024	...	|	...	|	...	2054	|	...	2117	|	...	2124	|	...	2222	...	|
Macclesfield ..... d.	|	...	1924	...	|	1955	...	|	|	...	2005	...	2024	...	|	2040	...	|	2115	...	|	2124	...	|	...	2224
Stoke on Trent ..... d.	|	...	1945	...	1950	2012	...	|	|	...	2023	...	2043	...	|	2057	...	|	2133	...	|	2147	...	|	...	2243
Stafford ..... d.	|	...	2006	...	|	|	...	2038	2043	...	2047	...	2101	...	2116	|	...	2138	|	...	2144	2207	...	2244	...	2301
Wolverhampton ..... a.	|	...	2019	...	|	|	...	2055	|	...	2059	...	2116	...	2134	|	...	2155	|	...	|	2220	...	2300	...	2317
Birmingham New St a.	|	...	2052	...	|	|	...	2130	|	...	2133	...	2152	...	2201	|	...	2230	|	...	|	2301	...	2330	...	2348
Nuneaton ..... d.	|	...	...	...	|	|	...	...	|	...	...	...	...	...	...	|	...	...	|	...	2215	...	...	...	...	...
Rugby ..... a.	|	...	...	...	|	|	...	...	|	...	...	...	...	...	...	|	...	...	|	...	2229	...	...	...	...	...
Milton Keynes ..... a.	|	...	...	...	2048	|	...	...	2136	...	...	...	...	...	...	2203	...	...	2250	...	2304	...	...	...	...	...
London Euston ..... a.	2114	...	...	...	2132	2204	...	...	2229	...	...	...	...	...	...	2256	...	...	2353	...	2357	...	...	...	...	...

A – From Bangor on Ⓐ.
B – To Bristol.
C – To Cardiff.
D – From Holyhead. Conveys [12] Lancaster - Crewe - London Euston.
E – To Exeter.
G – To Paignton.
H – From Holyhead.
J – From Holyhead on ⑥.
P – To Plymouth.
R – To Reading.
S – To Southampton.
U – To Bournemouth.
V – From Holyhead. Conveys [12] Wrexham - Chester - London Euston.
Z – To Penzance.

s – Stops to set down only.
u – Stops to pick up only.
v – Stops to set down only on Ⓐ.
w – Also calls at Watford Junction 13–18 minutes before London Euston to set down only.

151 LONDON and BIRMINGHAM - PRESTON - EDINBURGH and GLASGOW

Most trains 🍸 VT

Services on ⑥⑦ valid until January 31.

km			⚒	Ⓐ T	Ⓐ T	⑥ T	Ⓐ	⑥	Ⓐ w	Ⓐ T	⑥ T	⑥	⚒	⚒	⚒	Ⓐ T	⑥ T	⚒	⚒	Ⓐ T	⑥ T	⚒	⚒
0	**London Euston** 150 d.	⚒	...	...	...	...	...	...	0539	...	...	0605	...	0730	...	...	...	0830	...	...	...	0930	...
80	Milton Keynes 150 d.		...	...	...	...	...	...	0622	...	...	0641	...	|	...	...	...	|	...	...	...	|	...
132	Rugby 150 d.		...	...	...	...	...	...	0645	...	...	0703	...	|	...	...	...	|	...	...	...	|	...
	Birmingham New St 150 d.		...	...	...	...	0617	0620	|	...	...	|	0719	|	0820	...	...	|	0920	...	...	|	1020
	Wolverhampton 150 d.		...	...	...	...	0634	0637	|	...	...	|	0736	|	0837	...	...	|	0937	...	...	|	1037
214	Stafford 150 d.		...	...	...	...	|	|	|	...	...	0734	|	|	|	...	...	|	|	...	...	|	|
253	**Crewe** 150 d.		0557	...	...	...	0709	0709	0732	...	...	0755	0809	|	0909	...	...	|	1009	...	...	|	1109
291	Warrington Bank Quay d.		0614	...	...	...	0727	0727	0749	...	...	0812	0827	0914	0927	...	...	1014	1027	...	...	1114	1127
310	Wigan North Western d.		0625	...	...	...	0738	0738	0800	...	...	0823	0838	0925	0938	...	...	1025	1038	...	...	1125	1138
	Manchester Piccadilly **160** d.		|	0603	0633	0633	|	|	|	0745	0745	|	|	|	|	0916	0916	|	|	1016	1016	|	|
334	**Preston** d.		0640	0644	0714	0714	0753	0753	0815	0824	0824	0837	0853	0941	0953	0958	0958	1041	1053	1058	1058	1141	1153
368	Lancaster d.		0654	0700	0730	0730	0808	0809	0830	0840	0840	0852	0908	0955	1008	1014	1014	1055	1108	1114	1114	1155	1208
398	Oxenholme d.		0710	0715	|	|	0822	0823	0843	0854	0854	0906	|	|	1023	|	|	1108	|	1128	1128	|	1224
450	Penrith d.		0735	|	0807	0807	|	|	|	0920	0920	0932	0945	1031	|	|	1053	|	1145	1154	1154	1230	|
478	**Carlisle** d.		0751	0756	0825	0825	0901	0903	0922	0836	0936	0948	1002	1047	1104	1106	1109	1147	1202	1211	1211	1247	1303
519	Lockerbie d.		0810	0816	|	|	|	|	|	0955	0955	|	|	|	|	1127	1130	|	|	|	1230	|	|
683	**Edinburgh** a.		|	0922	|	|	1020	1022	|	1103	1110	|	|	|	1222	|	|	|	|	1339	1339	|	1422
683	**Glasgow** Central a.		0914	...	0945	0945	...	...	1036	...	...	1103	1117	1201	...	1228	1232	1301	1318	...	...	1401	...

km		Ⓐ	⑥	⚒	Ⓐ T	⑥ T	⚒	⚒	Ⓐ T	⑥ T	Ⓐ	⑥	⚒	Ⓐ T	⑥ T	Ⓐ	⑥	⚒	⑤	⑥	①-④	⑤	Ⓐ
	London Euston 150 d.	1030	1030	...	...	...	1130	...	...	...	1230	1230	...	...	...	1330	1330	...	1333	1430	1430	1430	...
	Milton Keynes 150 d.	|	|	...	...	...	|	...	...	...	|	|	...	...	...	|	|	...	|	|	|	|	...
	Rugby 150 d.	|	|	...	...	...	|	...	...	...	|	|	...	...	...	|	|	...	|	|	|	|	...
0	**Birmingham** New St 150 d.	|	|	1120	...	...	|	1220	...	...	|	|	1320	...	...	|	|	1420	|	|	|	|	1520
19	Wolverhampton 150 d.	|	|	1137	...	...	|	1237	...	...	|	|	1337	...	...	|	|	1437	|	|	|	|	1537
43	Stafford 150 d.	|	|	|	...	...	|	|	...	...	|	|	|	...	...	|	|	|	|	|	|	|	|
82	**Crewe** 150 d.	|	|	1209	...	...	|	1309	...	...	1414	1414	1409	...	...	|	|	1509	1519	|	|	|	1609
120	Warrington Bank Quay d.	1214	1214	1227	...	...	1314	1327	...	...	1425	1425	1427	...	...	1514	1514	1527	1540	1614	1617	1617	1627
139	Wigan North Western d.	1225	1225	1238	...	...	1325	1338	...	...	1441	1441	1438	...	...	1525	1525	1538	1551	1625	1629	1629	1638
	Manchester Piccadilly **160** d.	|	|	|	1216	1216	|	|	1316	1316	|	|	|	1416	1416	|	|	|	|	|	|	|	|
163	**Preston** d.	1241	1241	1253	1258	1258	1341	1353	1358	1358	1500	1455	1453	1458	1458	1541	1541	1553	1610	1641	1644	1644	1653
197	Lancaster d.	1300	1255	1308	1314	1314	1355	1408	1414	1414	...	|	1509	1514	1514	|	1556	1608	1632	1655	1700	1700	1710
227	Oxenholme d.	...	1309	1324	1328	1328	1408	|	|	1428	...	1530	1524	1528	1528	1606	1609	|	...	|	...	1716	1725
279	Penrith d.	...	|	|	1354	1354	|	1445	|	1454	...	1547	|	1554	1554	1631	|	1645	...	1730	...	1742	1751
307	**Carlisle** d.	...	1347	1403	1411	1411	1447	1502	1508	1514	...	|	1603	1611	1611	1647	1647	1702	...	1747	...	1800	1807
348	Lockerbie d.	...	|	|	1430	1430	|	|	1529	1533	...	|	|	1630	1630	|	|	|	...	|	...	|	|
512	**Edinburgh** a.	...	|	|	1542	1542	|	1622	|	|	...	|	|	1739	1739	|	|	1822	...	|	...	|	|
512	**Glasgow** Central a.	...	1501	1517	...	...	1601	...	1630	1642	...	1701	1715	...	...	1801	1801	...	...	1901	...	1914	1919

	⑥	Ⓐ T	⑥ T	⚒	⚒	Ⓐ T	Ⓐ	⑥	⚒	Ⓐ T	⑥ T	Ⓐ	Ⓐ	Ⓐ	⑥	Ⓐ	⑥	Ⓐ	⚒	Ⓐ	⑥	⑤	Ⓐ
London Euston 150 d.	...	...	...	1530	...	...	1630	1630	...	...	...	1633	1657	1730	1730	...	...	1757	1830	...	...	1846	1843
Milton Keynes 150 d.	...	...	...	|	...	...	|	|	...	...	...	|	|	|	|	...	...	|	|	...	...	|	1913u
Rugby 150 d.	...	...	...	|	...	...	|	|	...	...	...	1722	|	|	|	...	...	|	|	...	...	|	|
Birmingham New St 150 d.	1520	...	...	|	1620	...	|	|	1720	...	...	|	|	|	|	1820	1820	|	|	1920	1920	|	2020
Wolverhampton 150 d.	1537	...	...	|	1637	...	|	|	1737	...	...	|	|	|	|	1837	1837	|	|	1937	2037	|	2037
Stafford 150 d.	|	...	...	|	|	...	|	|	|	...	...	1756	|	|	|	|	|	|	|	|	|	2035s	2053
Crewe 150 d.	1609	...	...	|	1709	...	|	|	1809	...	...	1818	|	|	|	1909	1909	|	|	2009	2009	2103s	2116
Warrington Bank Quay d.	1627	...	...	1714	1727	...	|	1814	1827	...	...	1836	1850	1914	1914	1927	1927	1950	2014	2027	2028	2126s	...
Wigan North Western d.	1638	...	...	1725	1738	...	|	1825	1838	...	...	1847	1901	1925	1925	1938	1938	2001	2025	2038	2039	2138s	...
Manchester Piccadilly **160** d.	|	1616	1616	|	|	1715	|	|	|	1816	1816	|	|	|	|	|	|	|	|	|	|	|	...
Preston d.	1653	1700	1700	1741	1753	1800	1832	1841	1853	1900	1900	1901	1915	1941	1941	1953	1959	2015	2041	2053	2100	2155	...
Lancaster d.	1710	1716	1716	1755	1808	1816	|	1855	1909	1916	1916	...	1930	1955	1955	2008	...	2030	2055	2108	...	...	...
Oxenholme d.	1725	1730	1730	1808	1823	|	|	1909	1924	1932	1930	...	1945	2008	2008	|	...	|	2109	2124	...	...	...
Penrith d.	|	|	|	|	1849	1854	|	1934	|	1956	1956	...	2010	|	2034	2045	...	|	2134	|	...	...	...
Carlisle d.	1804	1811	1811	1847	1903	1911	|	1951	2003	2013	2012	...	2025	2047	2050	2102	...	2118	2150	2203	...	...	...
Lockerbie d.	|	1830	1830	|	|	|	|	|	|	|	2031	...	2044	|	|	|	...	2137	|	|	...	...	...
Edinburgh a.	|	1939	1939	|	2022	|	|	|	|	2139	|	...	|	|	|	2222	...	|	|	|	...	...	...
Glasgow Central a.	1917	...	...	2001	...	2033	2040	2101	2117	...	2132	...	2147	2201	2201	...	...	2239	2304	2317	...	...	...

	⑥	Ⓐ		⑥	Ⓐ	⑥ w	Ⓐ	Ⓐ w	...		⑦ T	⑦	⑦		⑦ T	⑦	⑦	⑦	⑦	⑦ T	⑦	⑦	⑦ T
London Euston 150 d.	...	1930	...	1930	2030	2030	...	2110	...	⑦	...	...	...	...	...	0845	...	0945	...	...	1045	...	...
Milton Keynes 150 d.	...	|	...	|	|	|	...	|	...		...	...	...	...	...	0933	...	1032	...	...	1132	...	...
Rugby 150 d.	...	|	...	|	|	2136	...	2204	...		...	...	...	...	...	1008	...	1107	...	...	1207	...	...
Birmingham New St 150 d.	2020	|	...	|	|	|	2120	|	...		...	...	0911	...	...	|	1011	|	1111	...	|	1201	...
Wolverhampton 150 d.	2037	|	...	|	|	|	2141	|	...		...	0904	0937	...	...	|	1037	|	1137	...	|	1236	...
Stafford 150 d.	2050	|	...	|	|	|	2155	2235	...		...	0919	|	...	...	|	|	|	|	...	|	|	...
Crewe 150 d.	2109	|	...	2103	|	2240	2219	2254	...		...	0945	1008	...	...	1057	1109	1156	1209	...	1300	1309	...
Warrington Bank Quay d.	...	2120	...	2120	2223	2257	2237	2312	...		...	1002	1026	...	...	1114	1127	1213	1227	...	1317	1327	...
Wigan North Western d.	...	2131	...	2132	2234	2309	2247	2323	...		...	1013	1037	...	...	1125	1138	1224	1238	...	1328	1338	...
Manchester Piccadilly **160** d.	...	|	...	|	|	|	|	|	...		0916	|	|	...	1016	|	|	|	|	1216	|	|	1316
Preston d.	...	2145	...	2148	2253	2322	2304	2341	...		1000	1030	1052	...	1058	1140	1153	1239	1253	1258	1343	1353	1400
Lancaster d.	...	2200	...	...	...	...	...	...	...		1016	...	1108	...	1114	1155	1208	1254	1308	1314	1358	1408	1416
Oxenholme d.	...	2213	...	...	...	...	...	...	...		1030	...	1123	...	1128	1208	1224	1307	1324	1328	1411	|	1430
Penrith d.	...	2239	...	...	...	...	...	...	...		1056	...	|	...	1154	1234	|	1333	|	1354	1437	1445	1455
Carlisle d.	...	2255	...	...	...	...	...	...	...		1114	...	1206	...	1211	1250	1303	1349	1403	1411	1453	1503	1517
Lockerbie d.	...	|	...	...	...	...	...	...	...		1133	...	|	...	1230	|	|	|	|	1430	|	|	|
Edinburgh a.	...	|	...	...	...	...	...	...	...		1241	...	|	...	|	|	1422	|	|	1535	|	1622	|
Glasgow Central a.	...	0009	...	...	...	...	...	...	...		...	...	1320	...	1336	1401	...	1504	1516	...	1606	...	1635

	⑦	⑦	⑦ T	⑦	⑦	⑦	⑦	⑦ T	⑦	⑦	⑦ T	⑦	⑦	⑦ T	⑦	⑦	⑦	⑦	⑦	⑦	⑦	⑦	⑦
London Euston 150 d.	1225	...	...	1325	...	1425	...	...	1525	...	...	1625	...	...	1725	...	1825	...	...	1925	2025	...	2050
Milton Keynes 150 d.	|	...	...	|	...	|	...	...	|	...	...	|	...	...	|	...	|	...	...	|	|	...	2139
Rugby 150 d.	|	...	...	|	...	|	...	...	|	...	...	|	...	...	|	...	|	...	...	|	|	...	2201
Birmingham New St 150 d.	|	1301	...	|	1401	|	1501	...	|	1600	...	|	1701	...	|	1801	|	1901	2001	|	|	2101	|
Wolverhampton 150 d.	|	1336	...	|	1437	|	1537	...	|	1637u	...	|	1737u	...	|	1837	|	1937	2038	|	|	2137	|
Stafford 150 d.	|	|	...	|	|	|	|	...	|	|	...	|	|	...	|	|	|	|	2052	|	|	2159	|
Crewe 150 d.	|	1411	...	|	1511	|	1611	...	|	1711	...	|	1811	...	|	1911	|	2011	2110	|	2213	2218	2251
Warrington Bank Quay d.	1416	1429	...	1516	1529	1616	1629	...	1716	1729	...	1817	1829	...	1916	1929	2016	2029	...	2116	2230	2239	2308
Wigan North Western d.	1427	1440	...	1527	1540	1627	1640	...	1727	1740	...	1828	1840	...	1927	1940	2027	2040	...	2127	2241	2250	2319
Manchester Piccadilly **160** d.	|	|	1416	|	|	|	|	1616	|	|	1716	|	|	1816	|	|	|	|	...	|	|	|	|
Preston d.	1442	1455	1500	1542	1555	1642	1655	1700	1742	1755	1802	1842	1855	1900	1942	1955	2042	2055	...	2142	2258	2309	2339
Lancaster d.	1458	1511	1516	1558	1610	1657	1710	1716	1757	1810	1818	1858	1910	1916	1957	2010	2057	2110	...	2157	...	...	...
Oxenholme d.	|	1525	1530	1611	|	|	1725	1730	1810	1825	1832	1911	1926	1930	2010	|	2111	2126	...	2211	...	...	...
Penrith d.	1532	|	1555	|	1647	1732	|	1756	|	1851	1858	1936	|	1955	2036	2047	2136	|	...	2236	...	...	...
Carlisle d.	1548	1605	1611	1649	1704	1748	1805	1813	1849	1906	1918	1953	2005	2011	2052	2104	2152	2205	...	2253	...	...	...
Lockerbie d.	|	|	1630	|	|	|	|	|	|	|	1937	|	|	2030	|	|	|	2223	...	|	...	...	...
Edinburgh a.	|	|	1739	|	1822	|	|	1937	|	2022	|	|	|	2139	|	2223	|	|	...	|	...	...	...
Glasgow Central a.	1700	1718	...	1803	...	1900	1918	...	2003	...	2045	2108	2118	...	2207	...	2309	2322	...	0002	...	...	...

T – 12 (Manchester Airport -) Manchester Piccadilly - Preston - Edinburgh or Glasgow and v.v. Operated by *TP*.

s – Stops to set down only.

u – Stops to pick up only.

w – Also calls at Watford Junction 20–25 minutes after / before London Euston.

VT Most trains 🍸 GLASGOW and EDINBURGH - PRESTON - BIRMINGHAM and LONDON 151

Services on ⑥⑦ valid until January 31.

		Ⓐ	Ⓐ	Ⓐ	⑥	Ⓐ	⑥	Ⓐ	⑥	⚒	Ⓐ	⚒	⚒	⚒	Ⓐ	⑥	⚒	Ⓐ	⚒	⚒	⚒	⚒	⑥
											T				T	T		T					T
Glasgow Central d.	⚒	...	...	...	...	0428	0426	...	...	0540	...	0550	0630	...	0710	0710	0735	...	0800	0840	...	0940	0922
Edinburgh d.		...	...	...	...	|	|	...	...	|	0536	|	|	0652	|	|	|	0742	|	|	0852	|	|
Lockerbie d.		...	...	...	...	|	|	...	...	|	|	|	0726	|	0807	0807	|	|	|	|	|	|	1024
Carlisle d.		...	...	...	...	0543	0544	...	...	0649	0658	0704	0746	0807	0831	0831	0849	0859	0910	0949	1007	1048	1052
Penrith d.		...	...	...	...	0557	0559	...	...	|	|	0719	0800	0822	0845	0845	|	|	|	1003	|	|	1107
Oxenholme d.		...	...	...	...	0620	0622	...	...	0724	|	0742	0823	|	0911	0911	0923	|	|	|	1042	1123	1131
Lancaster d.		...	0535	...	...	0635	0637	0658	0658	0738	0747	0757	0838	0857	0926	0926	0938	|	0957	1038	1057	1138	1146
Preston d.		0530	0600	0616	0617	0656	0658	0717	0717	0758	0812	0817	0858	0917	0947	0947	0958	1012	1017	1058	1117	1158	1210
Manchester Piccadilly **160** a.		|	|	|	|	|	|	|	|	|	0856	|	|	|	1027	1027	|	1056	|	|	|	|	1256
Wigan North Western d.		0545	0611	0627	0628	0708	0710	0728	0728	0809	...	0828	0909	0928	...	...	1009	...	1028	1109	1128	1209	...
Warrington Bank Quay d.		0556	0622	0638	0639	0718	0720	0739	0739	0820	...	0839	0920	0939	...	...	1020	...	1039	1120	1139	1220	...
Crewe 150 d.		|	0653	0701	0701	|	|	0801	0801	|	...	0901	|	1001	...	...	|	...	1101	|	1201	|	...
Stafford 150 d.		|	|	|	|	|	|	|	|	|	...	|	|	|	...	...	|	...	|	|	|	|	...
Wolverhampton 150 a.		|	|	0731	0732	|	|	0831	0831	|	...	0931	|	1031	...	...	|	...	1131	|	1231	|	...
Birmingham NS 150 a.		|	|	0755	0755	|	|	0856	0855	|	...	0956	|	1055	...	...	|	...	1156	|	1255	|	...
Rugby 150 a.		0706	|	...	...	|	|	...	...	|	...	...	|	...	...	...	|	...	...	|	...	|	...
Milton Keynes 150 a.		|	|	...	...	|	|	...	...	|	...	...	|	...	...	...	|	...	...	|	...	|	...
London Euston 150 a.		0757	0835	...	...	0906	0912	...	...	1012	...	...	1112	...	...	...	1212	...	...	1312	...	1412	...

	⚒	⑥	Ⓐ	Ⓐ	⚒	⚒	Ⓐ	⑥	Ⓐ	⚒	Ⓐ	⑥	⚒	⚒	Ⓐ	⑥	Ⓐ	⑥	Ⓐ	⚒	Ⓐ	⑥	⚒
		T	T	T							T	T			T	T					T	T	
Glasgow Central d.	1000	1010	...	1010	1040	...	1140	1140	...	1200	...	...	1240	...	1254	1300	1340	1340	...	1400	...	...	1440
Edinburgh d.	|	|	0953	|	|	1052	|	|	...	|	1208	1208	|	1252	|	|	|	|	...	|	1408	1408	|
Lockerbie d.	|	|	1100	|	|	|	|	|	...	|	1306	1306	|	|	1357	1357	|	|	...	|	|	1505	|
Carlisle d.	1109	1128	1131	1131	1149	1207	1249	1249	...	1309	1329	1329	1349	1407	1420	1430	1449	1449	...	1509	1530	1530	1549
Penrith d.	1124	1142	1145	1145	|	|	1303	1303	...	|	|	|	|	1422	1434	1445	|	|	...	|	1544	1544	|
Oxenholme d.	|	1207	1210	1210	1223	1243	|	|	...	|	1410	1406	1424	|	1458	1509	1524	1523	...	1544	1608	1608	1624
Lancaster d.	|	1223	1226	1226	1238	1257	|	1338	1339	1358	1426	1422	1438	1457	1513	1526	|	1538	1539	|	1623	1626	1638
Preston d.	1217	1247	1247	1247	1258	1317	1353	1358	1359	1417	1447	1447	1458	1517	1547	1547	1553	1558	1559	1617	1647	1647	1658
Manchester Piccadilly **160** a.	|	1327	1327	1327	|	|	|	|	|	|	1527	1527	|	|	1627	1627	|	|	|	|	1727	1727	|
Wigan North Western d.	1228	...	...	...	1309	1328	|	1409	1410	1428	...	...	1509	1528	...	...	|	1609	1610	1628	...	...	1709
Warrington Bank Quay d.	1239	...	...	...	1320	1339	|	1420	1421	1439	...	...	1520	1539	...	...	|	1620	1621	1639	...	...	1720
Crewe 150 d.	1301	...	...	...	|	1401	|	|	|	1501	...	...	|	1601	...	...	|	|	|	1701	...	...	|
Stafford 150 d.	|	...	...	...	|	|	|	|	|	|	...	...	|	|	...	...	|	|	|	|	...	...	|
Wolverhampton 150 a.	1331	...	...	...	|	1431	|	|	|	1531	...	...	|	1631	...	...	|	|	|	1731	...	...	|
Birmingham NS 150 a.	1356	...	...	...	|	1455	|	|	|	1556	...	...	|	1655	...	...	|	|	|	1756	...	...	|
Rugby 150 a.	...	...	...	...	|	...	|	|	|	...	...	...	|	...	...	...	|	|	|	...	...	...	|
Milton Keynes 150 a.	...	...	...	...	|	...	|	|	|	...	...	...	|	...	...	...	|	|	|	...	...	...	|
London Euston 150 a.	...	...	...	...	1512	...	1603	1612	1611	...	...	...	1712	...	...	...	1801	1812	1808	...	...	...	1913

	⚒	Ⓐ	⑥	⚒	Ⓐ	⑥	Ⓐ	⑥	⚒	Ⓐ	Ⓐ	⑥	Ⓐ	⑥	⑥	Ⓐ	⑥	⑥	Ⓐ	Ⓐ	⑥	Ⓐ	⑤
					T	T		w			T	T				T	T		w				T
Glasgow Central d.	...	...	1540	1600	...	...	1640	1640	...	...	1706	1706	1740	1740	1800	...	...	1840	1840	...	...	2010	...
Edinburgh d.	1452	...	|	|	1611	1611	|	|	1652	...	|	|	|	|	|	1812	1812	|	|	1852	1852	|	2011
Lockerbie d.	|	...	|	|	1710	1710	|	|	|	...	1806	1806	1833	1832	|	1912	1912	|	|	|	|	2102	2112
Carlisle d.	1607	...	1649	1709	1733	1733	1751	1752	1807	...	1829	1829	1854	1852	1910	1934	1934	1948	1949	2008	2007	2126	2136
Penrith d.	1622	...	1703	|	1748	1748	1805	|	|	...	1844	1844	1909	1906	|	1948	1948	2002	|	|	2022	2141	|
Oxenholme d.	|	...	|	1744	|	|	1829	1826	1842	...	1908	1908	1932	1929	|	2012	2012	2025	2024	2042	2045	2205	2212
Lancaster d.	1657	1736	1738	|	1826	1826	1844	1841	1857	...	1926	1926	1947	1944	1956	2026	2026	2040	2038	2057	2100	2220	2226
Preston d.	1717	1756	1758	1817	1847	1847	1904	1901	1916	1958	1947	1947	2008	2004	2017	2047	2047	2100	2058	2117	2120	2240	2247
Manchester Piccadilly **160** a.	|	|	|	|	1927	1927	|	|	|	|	2027	2027	|	|	|	2127	2127	|	|	|	|	|	2330
Wigan North Western d.	1728	1808	1809	1828	...	...	1916	1912	1929	2009	...	...	2019	2015	2028	...	...	2111	2109	2128	2131	2252	...
Warrington Bank Quay d.	1739	1819	1820	1839	...	...	1927	1923	1939	2020	...	...	2031	2026	2039	...	...	2122	2120	2139	2142	2303	...
Crewe 150 d.	1801	|	|	1901	...	...	|	|	2001	2041	...	...	2053	2047	2101	...	...	2143	|	2201	2204	2327	...
Stafford 150 d.	|	|	|	|	...	...	|	|	|	|	...	...	2113	|	|	...	...	2208	|	|	2229	...	...
Wolverhampton 150 a.	1831	|	|	1931	...	...	|	|	2033	|	...	...	2129	|	2131	...	...	2222	|	2232	2240	...	...
Birmingham NS 150 a.	1855	|	|	1956	...	...	|	|	2055	|	...	...	2150	|	2154	...	...	2246	|	2255	2259	...	...
Rugby 150 a.	...	|	|	...	...	...	|	|	...	2127	...	...	...	|	...	...	...	...	|	...	...	...	...
Milton Keynes 150 a.	...	|	|	...	...	...	2045	2041	...	2147	...	...	...	2152	...	...	...	...	2239	...	...	...	...
London Euston 150 a.	...	2014	2015	...	...	...	2124	2136	...	2222	...	...	...	2244	...	...	...	...	2338	...	...	...	...

		⑦	⑦		⑦	⑦		⑦	⑦		⑦	⑦		⑦	⑦	⑦	⑦	⑦		⑦	⑦		⑦
		w													T						T		
Glasgow Central d.	⑦	...	...	...	...	...	...	...	0937	...	...	1032	...	...	...	1132	1152	1242	...	...	...	...	1334
Edinburgh d.		...	...	...	...	...	...	...	|	...	...	|	...	1052	1110	|	|	|	...	1252	1309	...	|
Lockerbie d.		...	...	...	...	...	...	...	|	...	...	|	...	|	1209	|	|	|	...	|	1408	...	|
Carlisle d.		...	...	...	...	...	...	...	1046	...	...	1146	...	1207	1232	1249	1310	1354	...	1407	1431	...	1449
Penrith d.		...	...	...	...	...	...	...	1100	...	...	1200	...	|	1246	|	|	|	...	1422	1446	...	|
Oxenholme d.		...	...	...	...	...	...	...	1123	...	...	1224	...	1243	1310	1323	|	1428	...	|	1510	...	1523
Lancaster d.		...	...	...	...	...	...	...	1138	...	1200	1238	...	1257	1326	1338	1358	1443	...	1457	1525	...	1538
Preston d.		0900	1000	...	1017	1058	...	1117	1158	...	1217	1258	...	1317	1347	1358	1417	1503	...	1517	1547	...	1558
Manchester Piccadilly **160** a.		|	|	...	|	|	...	|	|	...	|	|	...	|	1427	|	|	|	...	|	1627	...	|
Wigan North Western d.		0911	1011	...	1028	1109	...	1128	1209	...	1228	1309	...	1328	...	1409	1428	1514	...	1528	...	...	1609
Warrington Bank Quay d.		0922	1022	...	1039	1120	...	1139	1220	...	1239	1320	...	1339	...	1420	1439	1525	...	1539	...	...	1620
Crewe 150 d.		0943	1043	...	1102	|	...	1201	|	...	1301	|	...	1401	...	|	1501	|	...	1601	...	...	|
Stafford 150 d.		|	|	...	|	|	...	|	|	...	|	|	...	|	...	|	|	|	...	|	...	...	|
Wolverhampton 150 a.		|	|	...	1134	|	...	1232	|	...	1331	|	...	1432	...	|	1531	|	...	1632	...	...	|
Birmingham NS 150 a.		|	|	...	1203	|	...	1305	|	...	1406	|	...	1506	...	|	1606	|	...	1706	...	...	|
Rugby 150 a.		1031	1131	...	...	|	...	...	|	...	...	|	...	...	...	|	...	|	...	...	...	...	|
Milton Keynes 150 a.		1106	1205	...	...	|	...	...	|	...	...	|	...	...	...	|	...	|	...	...	...	...	|
London Euston 150 a.		1204	1244	...	...	1323	...	...	1417	...	...	1515	...	...	...	1617	...	1723	...	...	...	...	1817

	⑦	⑦		⑦	⑦		⑦	⑦		⑦	⑦		⑦	⑦		⑦	⑦		⑦	⑦		⑦	⑦
					T					T				T		w	T					T	
Glasgow Central d.	1355	1435	...	...	1506	...	1536	1554	...	...	1638	...	...	1706	...	1736	...	...	1830	...	...	...	2005
Edinburgh d.	|	|	...	1452	|	...	|	|	...	1610	|	...	1652	|	...	|	1810	...	|	1852	...	1957	|
Lockerbie d.	|	|	...	|	1607	...	|	|	...	1709	|	...	|	|	...	1832	1909	...	|	|	...	|	2059
Carlisle d.	1509	1549	...	1607	1630	...	1649	1709	...	1732	1751	...	1807	1828	...	1852	1932	...	1944	2007	...	2115	2124
Penrith d.	|	|	...	1622	1644	...	1703	|	...	1746	1805	...	|	1842	...	1906	1946	...	|	2022	...	|	2139
Oxenholme d.	1544	1623	...	|	1708	...	|	1744	...	1811	1828	...	1842	1907	...	1929	2011	...	2019	|	...	|	2203
Lancaster d.	|	1638	...	1657	1723	...	1738	|	...	1826	1843	...	1857	1922	...	1944	2026	...	2034	2057	...	2203	2218
Preston d.	1617	1658	...	1717	1747	...	1758	1817	...	1847	1903	...	1917	1947	...	2004	2047	...	2055	2117	...	2229	2238
Manchester Piccadilly **160** a.	|	|	...	|	1827	...	|	|	...	1927	|	...	|	2027	...	|	2127	...	|	|	...	2314	|
Wigan North Western d.	1628	1709	...	1728	...	...	1809	1828	...	...	1914	...	1928	...	...	2015	...	...	2107	2128	...	...	2250
Warrington Bank Quay d.	1639	1720	...	1739	...	...	1820	1839	...	...	1925	...	1939	...	...	2026	...	...	2118	2139	...	...	2301
Crewe 150 d.	1701	|	...	1801	...	...	|	1901	...	...	|	...	2001	...	...	2047	...	...	2140	2201	...	...	2320
Stafford 150 d.	|	|	...	|	...	...	|	|	...	...	|	...	|	...	...	|	...	...	2202	|	...	...	...
Wolverhampton 150 a.	1731	|	...	1831	...	...	|	1931	...	...	|	...	2032	...	...	|	...	...	2217	2231	...	...	...
Birmingham NS 150 a.	1807	|	...	1906	...	...	|	2006	...	...	|	...	2106	...	...	|	...	...	2259	2309	...	...	...
Rugby 150 a.	...	|	...	...	...	...	|	...	...	...	|	...	...	...	...	|	...	...	...	...	...	...	...
Milton Keynes 150 a.	...	|	...	...	...	...	|	...	...	...	|	...	...	...	...	2155	...	...	...	...	...	...	...
London Euston 150 a.	...	1917	...	...	...	...	2017	...	...	...	2121	...	...	...	...	2253	...	...	...	...	...	...	...

For notes and return service see previous page.

155 CARDIFF - HEREFORD - CREWE - MANCHESTER

2nd class Most trains 🍸 AW

Services on ⑦ valid until March 28.

km			Ⓐ	⑥	Ⓐ	⑥	⚒	⚒ C	⚒	⚒ C	⚒ N	⚒	⚒ M	⚒ P	⚒	Ⓐ M	⑥ M	⚒ C	⚒	⚒ M	Ⓐ C	⑥ C	⚒	⚒ M	Ⓐ f
0	**Cardiff** Central 133 d.	⚒	0435	0440	0510	0520	0540	0650	0720	0750	0850	0920	0950	1050	1120	1150	1150	1250	1320	1350	1450	1450	1520	1550	1615
19	Newport 133 d.		0453	0457	0528	0535	0554	0704	0734	0805	0905	0934	1005	1105	1134	1205	1205	1305	1334	1405	1505	1505	1534	1605	1629
30	Cwmbrân d.		0504	0507	0538	0545	0604	0715	0745	0815	0915	0945	1015	1115	1145	1215	1215	1315	1345	1415	1515	1515	1544	1615	1640
35	Pontypool & New Inn d.		0510	0513	0544	0551	0610	|	0749	|	|	0949	|	|	1149	|	|	|	1349	|	|	|	1549	1621	|
50	Abergavenny d.		0519	0522	0553	0600	0619	0728	0800	0828	0928	1000	1028	1128	1200	1228	1232	1328	1400	1428	1528	1528	1559	1630	1654
89	**Hereford** 131 d.		0548	0548	0624	0626	0648	0755	0828	0855	0955	1028	1055	1155	1228	1255	1258	1355	1428	1455	1555	1555	1628	1656	|
109	Leominster d.		0602	0602	0638	0640	0701	0808	|	0908	1008	|	1108	1208	|	1308	1311	1408	|	1508	1608	1608	|	1708	|
127	Ludlow d.		0613	0613	0649	0651	0712	0819	0849	0919	1019	1049	1119	1219	1249	1319	1322	1419	1449	1519	1619	1619	1649	1719	|
138	Craven Arms 146 d.		0621	0621	0657	0659	0721	0828	|	0928	1028	|	1128	1228	|	1328	1328	1428	|	1528	1628	1628	|	1728	|
150	Church Stretton 146 d.		0630	0630	0706	0708	0730	0837	|	0937	1037	|	1137	1237	|	1337	1347	1437	|	1537	|	|	|	1738	|
170	**Shrewsbury** 146 a.		0644	0644	0720	0722	0745	0851	0915	0951	1051	1115	1151	1251	1315	1351	1354	1451	1515	1551	1650	1648	1715	1754	1805
170	**Shrewsbury** d.		0646	0646	0724	0724	0745	0853	0924	0953	1053	1124	1153	1253	1324	1353	1355	1453	1524	1553	1652	1650	1724	1754	1806
	Whitchurch d.		0706	0706	|	|	0806	|	|	|	|	|	|	|	|	|	|	|	|	|	|	1710	|	|	|
223	**Crewe** 150 151 a.		0725	0725	|	|	0826	0925	|	1026	1125	|	1225	1326	|	1426	1426	1525	|	1626	1726	1726	|	1826	1845
	Chester 165 a.		|	|	0820	0819	|	|	1020	|	|	1219	|	|	1420	|	|	|	1621	|	|	|	1820	|	1909
	Holyhead 165 a.		|	|	1005	1005	|	|	1213	|	|	1414	|	|	1614	|	|	|	1819	|	|	|	2016	|	2049
263	Stockport 150 a.		0754	0754	...	...	0858	0958	...	1058	1158	...	1258	1358	...	1458	1458	1558	...	1658	1758	1758	...	1858	...
273	**Manchester** Piccadilly 150 a.		0808	0808	...	...	0915	1015	...	1115	1215	...	1315	1415	...	1515	1515	1615	...	1715	1815	1815	...	1915	...

	⚒ C	⚒	⚒ M	Ⓐ C	⑥ C	Ⓐ	⑥ L	⚒	Ⓐ C	⑥	⑥	Ⓐ	
Cardiff Central 133 d.	1650	1720	1750	1850	1850	1934	1934	2010	2053	2053	2149	2155	...
Newport 133 d.	1705	1734	1805	1905	1905	1948	1948	2026	2110	2110	2207	2211	...
Cwmbrân d.	1715	1745	1815	1915	1915	1958	1958	2036	2121	2121	2219	2223	...
Pontypool & New Inn d.	|	1749	1821	|	|	2003	2003	2042	|	|	2224	2229	...
Abergavenny d.	1728	1800	1830	1928	1928	2012	2013	2051	2134	2134	2134	2239	...
Hereford 131 d.	1755	1828	1856	1955	1955	2039	2039	2117	2200	2200	2258	2307	...
Leominster d.	1808	1841	1908	2009	2008	2052	2052	2131	2214	2214	...	2320	...
Ludlow d.	1819	1852	1919	2019	2019	2103	2103	2142	2225	2225	...	2332	...
Craven Arms 146 d.	1828	|	1928	2028	2028	2112	2112	2150	2233	2233	...	2341	...
Church Stretton 146 d.	1837	|	1937	2037	2037	2121	2121	2203	2242	2242	...	2351	...
Shrewsbury 146 a.	1851	1918	1953	2051	2051	2137	2137	2218	2257	2257	...	0006	...
Shrewsbury d.	1853	1924	1954	2053	2053	2139	2137	2219	2301	2306	...	0007	...
Whitchurch d.	|	|	|	|	|	|	|	2243	2325	2330	...	0034	...
Crewe 150 151 a.	1925	|	2026	2126	2127	|	|	2304	2348	2353	...	0102	...
Chester 165 a.	|	2020	|	|	|	2234	2231	|	0033	0024	...	...	...
Holyhead 165 a.	|	2223	|	|	|	0055	...	|	...	...	...	...	...
Stockport 150 a.	1958	...	2058	2158	2158	...	...	2332	...	...	...	...	...
Manchester Piccadilly 150 a.	2015	...	2115	2215	2219	...	...	2348	...	...	...	...	...

⑦	⑦	⑦	⑦	⑦	⑦	⑦ C	⑦	⑦ M	⑦		⑦
Cardiff Central 133 d.	...	0830	0930	1030	1135	1240	1340	1455	1514	...	1555
Newport 133 d.	...	0849	0950	1050	1154	1254	1354	1514	1528	...	1614
Cwmbrân d.	...	0859	1000	1100	1204	1309	1409	1525	1543	...	1624
Pontypool & New Inn d.	...	0905	1006	1106	1210	|	1415	|	1548	...	|
Abergavenny d.	...	0914	1016	1117	1220	1322	1424	1538	1558	...	1637
Hereford 131 d.	...	0943	1043	1144	1257	1355	1450	1604	1624	...	1704
Leominster d.	...	0957	1056	1158	1310	1408	1504	|	1638	...	|
Ludlow d.	...	1008	1107	1209	1321	1419	1515	1625	1649	...	1726
Craven Arms 146 d.	...	1016	|	1219	|	1428	|	|	1654	...	|
Church Stretton 146 d.	...	1025	|	1228	|	1437	|	|	1706	...	|
Shrewsbury 146 a.	...	1039	1136	1243	1347	1451	1541	1651	1721	...	1752
Shrewsbury d.	0955	1041	1137	1252	1350	1453	1542	1653	1730	...	1754
Whitchurch d.	|	1102	1203	|	|	|	1608	|	|	...	|
Crewe 150 151 a.	1025	1121	1225	1327	1422	1525	1629	1725	|	...	1825
Chester 165 a.	|	|	|	|	|	|	|	|	1825	...	|
Holyhead 165 a.	|	|	|	|	|	|	|	|	2020y	...	|
Stockport 150 a.	1058	|	1258	1401	1458	1558	1658	1758	...	...	1858
Manchester Piccadilly 150 a.	1117	1205	1315	1418	1515	1615	1715	1815	...	...	1915

	⑦ M	⑦	⑦	⑦ M	⑦	⑦	⑦	⑦ C	
Cardiff Central 133 d.	1640	1714	1735	1840	1940	...	2035	2250	...
Newport 133 d.	1654	1728	1749	1854	1955	...	2055	2310	...
Cwmbrân d.	1709	1743	1804	1909	2010	...	2105	2319	...
Pontypool & New Inn d.	1715	|	1810	|	2016	...	2111	2325	...
Abergavenny d.	1724	1756	1820	1922	2026	...	2121	2335	...
Hereford 131 d.	1753	1824	1849	1949	2054	...	2149	0004	...
Leominster d.	1807	|	1903	2003	2108	...	2202	...	...
Ludlow d.	1818	1845	1914	2014	2119	...	2214	...	...
Craven Arms 146 d.	1826	|	|	2022	2129	...	2223	...	...
Church Stretton 146 d.	1835	|	|	2031	2138	...	2233	...	...
Shrewsbury 146 a.	1849	1911	1940	2045	2155	...	2248	...	...
Shrewsbury d.	1851	1932	1941	2048	...	2232	2254	...	...
Whitchurch d.	|	|	2006	|	...	|	2321	...	...
Crewe 150 151 a.	1922	|	2027	2121	...	2303	2349	...	...
Chester 165 a.	|	2031	|	|	...	2330	...	...	...
Holyhead 165 a.	|	2238y	|	|	...	...	...	...	...
Stockport 150 a.	1958	...	2057	2158	...	...	...	...	...
Manchester Piccadilly 150 a.	2015	...	2114	2215	...	...	...	...	...

		Ⓐ M	Ⓐ M	Ⓐ	⚒ C	⑥	Ⓐ	⑥ M	Ⓐ M	Ⓐ f
Manchester Piccadilly 150 d.	⚒	...	...	...	...	...	...	0630	0630	...
Stockport 150 d.		...	...	...	...	...	...	0639	0639	...
Holyhead 165 d.		...	...	...	...	0425	0425	|	|	0532
Chester 165 d.		...	...	0515	...	0612	0622	|	|	0708
Crewe 150 151 d.		0454	0454	|	0555	|	|	0708	0708	0733
Whitchurch d.		0512	0512	|	0615	|	|	|	|	|
Shrewsbury a.		0533	0533	0610	0642	0717	0717	0738	0738	0809
Shrewsbury 146 d.		0540	0540	0613	0644	0719	0719	0739	0743	0810
Church Stretton 146 d.		0555	0555	0629	0659	|	|	0755	0758	|
Craven Arms 146 d.		0603	0603	0637	0707	|	|	0803	0806	|
Ludlow d.		0611	0611	0645	0715	0747	0747	0811	0814	|
Leominster d.		0622	0622	0656	0726	0758	0758	0821	0825	|
Hereford 131 d.		0642	0642	0713	0742	0814	0814	0838	0842	|
Abergavenny d.		0705	0705	0736	0805	0837	0837	0901	0905	|
Pontypool & New Inn d.		0715	0715	0746	|	0846	0846	|	|	|
Cwmbrân d.		0720	0720	0751	0818	0852	0852	0914	0917	|
Newport 133 a.		0733	0737	0801	0834	0902	0902	0934	0934	0940
Cardiff Central 133 a.		0751	0755	0817	0855	0922	0922	0953	0953	0958

	⚒ C	Ⓐ	⑥	⚒ M	⚒ C	Ⓐ	⑥	Ⓐ M	⑥ M	⚒ C	⚒	⚒ M	⚒ C	⚒	⚒ M	⚒ P	⑥	Ⓐ	⑥ M	Ⓐ M	⚒ D	Ⓐ	⑥	⑥ C	Ⓐ C
Manchester Piccadilly 150 d.	0730	...	...	0830	0930	...	...	1030	1030	1130	...	1230	1330	...	1430	1530	...	...	1630	1630	1730	...	...	1830	1830
Stockport 150 d.	0739	...	...	0839	0939	...	...	1039	1039	1139	...	1239	1339	...	1439	1539	...	...	1639	1639	1740	...	...	1839	1839
Holyhead 165 d.	|	0629	0635	|	|	0805	0820	|	|	|	1033	|	|	1238	|	|	1423	1432	|	|	|	1636	1638	|	|
Chester 165 d.	|	0822	0822	|	|	1022	1022	|	|	|	1222	|	|	1422	|	|	1622	1622	|	|	|	1820	1822	|	|
Crewe 150 151 d.	0808	|	|	0908	1008	|	|	1108	1108	1208	|	1308	1408	|	1508	1608	|	|	1708	1708	1812	|	|	1910	1910
Whitchurch d.	0827	|	|	|	|	|	|	|	|	|	|	|	|	|	|	1627	|	|	|	|	1831	|	|	1930	1930
Shrewsbury a.	0848	0917	0917	0938	1038	1117	1117	1138	1138	1238	1319	1338	1438	1517	1538	1648	1717	1717	1738	1739	1852	1915	1918	1956	1956
Shrewsbury 146 d.	0850	0921	0921	0939	1039	1121	1121	1139	1139	1239	1321	1339	1439	1521	1539	1650	1721	1721	1739	1741	1854	1917	1920	1958	1958
Church Stretton 146 d.	|	|	|	0955	1055	|	|	1155	1155	1255	|	1355	1455	|	1555	1705	|	|	1755	1759	1909	|	|	2013	2013
Craven Arms 146 d.	|	|	|	1003	1103	|	|	1203	1203	1303	|	1403	1503	|	1603	1713	|	|	1803	1807	1917	|	|	2021	2021
Ludlow d.	0917	0947	0947	1011	1111	1147	1147	1211	1211	1311	1347	1411	1511	1547	1611	1721	1747	1747	1811	1815	1925	1945	1948	2029	2029
Leominster d.	0928	|	|	1021	1121	|	|	1221	1221	1321	|	1421	1521	|	1621	1732	|	|	1821	1826	1936	|	|	2040	2040
Hereford 131 d.	0944	1012	1012	1038	1138	1212	1212	1238	1238	1338	1412	1438	1538	1612	1638	1751	1812	1812	1838	1843	1952	2010	2012	2057	2101
Abergavenny d.	1007	1035	1034	1101	1201	1234	1234	1312	1301	1401	1434	1501	1601	1635	1701	1814	1835	1835	1901	1906	2015	2033	2035	2120	2124
Pontypool & New Inn d.	1018	|	|	|	|	1245	1245	|	|	|	1445	|	|	1645	|	|	1845	1845	|	|	|	2043	2045	|	|
Cwmbrân d.	1022	1048	1047	1114	1214	1250	1250	1324	1314	1414	1450	1514	1614	1650	1714	1826	1850	1850	1914	1918	2027	2048	2050	2132	2136
Newport 133 a.	1034	1057	1057	1136	1234	1300	1300	1334	1334	1434	1500	1534	1638	1700	1734	1838	1900	1900	1929	1932	2040	2057	2100	2143	2148
Cardiff Central 133 a.	1053	1114	1120	1153	1253	1320	1320	1353	1353	1455	1521	1553	1653	1717	1754	1856	1921	1921	1946	1949	2056	2119	2121	2203	2206

	⚒	⑥	Ⓐ	⑥	Ⓐ	Ⓐ	Ⓐ	
Manchester Piccadilly 150 d.	1930	2030	2030	2130	2135	...	2235	...
Stockport 150 d.	1939	2039	2039	2139	2144	...	2244	...
Holyhead 165 d.	|	|	|	|	|	...	|	...
Chester 165 d.	|	|	|	|	|	...	|	...
Crewe 150 151 d.	2010	2111	2112	2213	2212	...	2314	...
Whitchurch d.	2030	2130	2133	2234	2233	...	2334	...
Shrewsbury a.	2050	2156	2159	2304	2302	...	0004	...
Shrewsbury 146 d.	2052	2156	2201	...	...	2308	...	...
Church Stretton 146 d.	2107	2212	2216	...	...	2324	...	...
Craven Arms 146 d.	2115	2220	2224	...	...	2332	...	...
Ludlow d.	2123	2228	2232	...	...	2341	...	...
Leominster d.	2134	2238	2243	...	...	2352	...	...
Hereford 131 d.	2150	2256	2304	...	...	0008	...	...
Abergavenny d.	2213	2319	2327	...	...	0032	...	...
Pontypool & New Inn d.	2223	2329	|	...	...	0042	...	...
Cwmbrân d.	2228	2334	2339	...	...	0047	...	...
Newport 133 a.	2242	2347	2350	...	...	0057	...	...
Cardiff Central 133 a.	2305	0012	0015	...	...	0120	...	...

	⑦ F	⑦	⑦ M	⑦	⑦	⑦ M	⑦	⑦ MP	⑦	⑦	⑦	⑦	⑦	⑦	⑦	⑦
Manchester Piccadilly 150 d.	...	0930	1030	1124	...	1230	1330	1430	1530	1630	1730	...	1830	1930	2030	...
Stockport 150 d.	...	0939	1039	1140	...	1240	1339	1439	1539	1639	1739	...	1839	1939	2039	...
Holyhead 165 d.	...	|	|	|	1020y	|	|	|	|	|	|	1625y	|	|	|	...
Chester 165 d.	...	|	|	|	1222	|	|	|	|	|	|	1824	|	|	|	...
Crewe 150 151 d.	...	1011	1113	1213	|	1313	1413	1510	1613	1713	1813	|	1913	2013	2113	2320
Whitchurch d.	...	1035	|	|	|	1334	|	|	|	1734	|	|	1934	|	2135	2342
Shrewsbury a.	...	1101	1143	1243	1318	1359	1443	1545	1643	1800	1843	1920	2000	2043	2203	0011
Shrewsbury 146 d.	*0750**	1103	1144	1244	1319	1401	1444	1547	1644	1801	1844	1921	2001	2044	2204	...
Church Stretton 146 d.	*0815**	1119	|	|	1335	|	1500	|	1700	|	|	1937	|	2100	2220	...
Craven Arms 146 d.	*0835**	1127	|	|	1343	|	1508	|	1708	|	|	1845	|	2108	2229	...
Ludlow d.	*0855**	1136	1212	1312	1351	1428	1516	1617	1716	1829	1912	1953	2029	2116	2237	...
Leominster d.	*0920**	1147	1222	1322	1402	1439	1526	1628	1726	1839	|	2004	2039	2126	2249	...
Hereford 131 d.	1009	1203	1238	1339	1419	1456	1543	1642	1743	1857	1936	2021	2055	2143	2305	...
Abergavenny d.	1032	1227	1301	1402	1442	1519	1606	1707	1806	1920	1959	2046	2118	2206	2328	...
Pontypool & New Inn d.	1043	|	1311	|	1452	|	1616	|	1816	|	|	2056	|	2216	2339	...
Cwmbrân d.	1048	1240	1316	1414	1457	1531	1621	1720	1821	1933	2011	2101	2131	2221	2344	...
Newport 133 a.	1058	1250	1327	1427	1507	1544	1631	1732	1831	1948	2022	2114	2143	2236	2354	...
Cardiff Central 133 a.	1115	1312	1343	1454	1527	1601	1652	1751	1850	2009	2043	2136	2205	2302	0020	...

C – To / from Carmarthen.
D – To Milford Haven on Ⓐ, to Carmarthen on ⑥.
F – To Fishguard Harbour.
L – To / from Llandudno Junction.
M – To / from Milford Haven.
N – From Milford Haven on Ⓐ.
P – To / from Pembroke Dock.
f – Conveys 🛏12 and 🍸 (✕ in 1 cl.).
y – ⑦ Dec. 12 – Jan. 31.
* – By 🚌.

TP MANCHESTER - PRESTON - BLACKPOOL 156

Services on ⑥⑦ valid until January 31.

km		⚒	Ⓐ	⚒	⚒	Ⓐ	⑥	⚒	Ⓐ	⑥	Ⓐ	⑥	⑥	Ⓐ	⚒	Ⓐ	⚒	⚒	⚒	⚒	⑥	Ⓐ	⚒	Ⓐ	⑥
0	**Manchester** Airport d.		0545	0618	0700	0728	0728	0758	0825	0825	0900	0900	0900	0900	0929	0929	1000	1029	1100	1129	1200	1200	1229	1300	1300
16	**Manchester** Piccadilly d.		0603	0633	0715	0745	0745	0815	0846	0846	0916	0916	0916	0916	0946	0946	1016	1046	1116	1146	1216	1216	1246	1316	1316
34	Bolton d.		0619	0650	0731	0759	0729	0832	0907	0907	0933	0933	0933	0933	1007	1007	1033	1107	1133	1207	1233	1233	1307	1333	1333
66	**Preston** 151 d.		0642	0711	0757	0822	0822	0858	0933	0930	0955	0944	0944	0955	1033	1033	1055	1133	1155	1233	1255	1255	1333	1355	1355
66	**Preston** 151 a.		0644	0714	0759	0824	0824	0859	0938	0932	0958	0945	1008	1007	1038	1045	1058	1138	1158	1238	1258	1258	1338	1358	1358
94	**Blackpool** North a.		|	|	0829	|	|	0925	1005	|	|	0958	|	|	1105	|	|	1205	|	1305	|	|	1405	|	|
	Barrow in Furness 157 a.		|	|	...	|	|	...	...	|	|	|	1036	1120	...	...	|	|	1310	...	...	|	...	|	|
	Windermere 158 a.		|	|	...	|	|	...	...	1026	|	|	...	...	...	1139	|	...	...	...	|	|	...	|	|
	Edinburgh Waverley 151 a.		0955	|	...	1103	1110	...	...	...	|	|	...	...	...	...	1339	...	...	...	1542	1252	...	|	|
	Glasgow Central 151 a.		...	0945	...	...	...	...	...	...	1228	1232	...	...	...	...	...	...	...	...	...	...	...	1630	1642

	Ⓐ	⚒	⑥	⚒	⚒	⚒	⚒	⚒	⑥	Ⓐ	⚒	Ⓐ	⑥	Ⓐ	⚒	Ⓐ	⑥	Ⓐ	⚒	Ⓐ	⑥	⚒	Ⓐ	⑥	⚒
Manchester Airport d.	1300	1329	1329	1400	1429	1500	1529	1600	1600	1600	1629	1700	1700	1700	1729	1800	1800	1800	1829	1900	1900	1929	2000	2000	2029
Manchester Piccadilly d.	1316	1346	1346	1416	1446	1516	1546	1616	1616	1616	1646	1715	1715	1715	1746	1816	1816	1816	1846	1916	1916	1946	2016	2016	2046
Bolton d.	1333	1407	1407	1433	1507	1533	1607	1633	1633	1633	1706	1732	1732	1732	1807	1833	1833	1833	1907	1933	1933	2007	2033	2033	2107
Preston 151 d.	1355	1433	1433	1455	1533	1555	1635	1655	1655	1655	1730	1755	1755	1755	1838	1855	1855	1855	1933	1955	1958	2033	2057	2059	2133
Preston 151 a.	1404	1438	1445	1458	1538	1558	1638	1700	1704	1705	1732	1800	1758	1808	1840	1900	1900	1904	1938	1958	2002	2038	2059	2102	2138
Blackpool North a.	|	1505	|	|	1605	|	1707	|	|	|	1802	|	|	|	1909	|	|	|	2005	|	|	2106	|	|	2206
Barrow in Furness 157 a.	1515	...	1556	|	...	1718	...	|	|	|	...	|	1919	1930	...	|	|	2024	...	2117	2120	...	2218	2220	...
Windermere 158 a.	...	...	...	|	...	...	...	|	1800	1808	...	|	...	...	...	|	|	...	...	...	...	...	...	...	...
Edinburgh Waverley 151 a.	...	...	...	1739	...	...	...	1939	...	...	...	|	...	...	...	2139	|	...	...	...	...	...	...	...	...
Glasgow Central 151 a.	...	...	...	...	...	...	...	...	...	...	...	2033	...	...	...	...	2132	...	...	...	...	...	...	...	...

	⚒	⑥	Ⓐ	⚒		⑦	⑦	⑦	⑦	⑦	⑦	⑦	⑦	⑦	⑦	⑦	⑦	⑦	⑦	⑦	⑦	⑦	⑦	⑦	⑦
Manchester Airport d.	2128	2200	2200	2227	...	...	...	...	...	0958	1029	1127	1158	1226	1226	...	1330	1400	1430	1500	1530	1600	1630	1700
Manchester Piccadilly d.	2146	2216	2216	2246	...	0746	0906v	0916	0946	1016	1046	1146	1216	1246	1246	1316	1346	1416	1446	1516	1546	1616	1646	1716
Bolton d.	2207	2233	2233	2307	...	0806	0923	0933	1005	1033	1105	1205	1233	1305	1305	1333	1405	1433	1505	1533	1605	1633	1705	1733
Preston 151 d.	2233	2254	2309	2333	...	0831	0949	0957	1032	1057	1132	1232	1257	1332	1332	1357	1432	1457	1532	1557	1632	1657	1732	1757
Preston 151 a.	2235	2255	2313	2335	...	0832	0951	1000	1034	1058	1134	1234	1258	1336	1347	1400	1434	1500	1534	1600	1634	1700	1734	1802
Blackpool North a.	2301	|	|	0001	...	0858	1017	|	1100	|	1200	1300	|	1402	|	|	1500	|	1600	|	1700	|	1800	|
Barrow in Furness 157 a.	...	0015	0032	...	...	...	...	|	...	|	...	...	|	...	1506	|	...	|	...	1719	...	|	...	|
Windermere 158 a.	...	...	...	...	...	...	...	|	...	|	...	...	|	...	...	|	...	|	...	...	...	|	...	|
Edinburgh Waverley 151 a.	...	...	...	...	...	...	...	1241	...	|	...	...	1535	...	...	|	...	1739	...	...	...	1937	...	|
Glasgow Central 151 a.	...	...	...	...	...	...	...	...	...	1336	...	...	...	...	...	1635	...	...	...	...	...	...	...	2045

	⑦	⑦	⑦	⑦	⑦	⑦	⑦	⑦	⑦
Manchester Airport d.	1700	1730	1800	1830	1900	1930	2030	2130	2230
Manchester Piccadilly d.	1716	1746	1816	1846	1916	1946	2046	2146	2246
Bolton d.	1733	1805	1833	1905	1633	2005	2105	2205	2305
Preston 151 d.	1757	1832	1857	1932	1957	2032	2132	2232	2342
Preston 151 a.	1806	1834	1900	1934	2000	2034	2134	2234	2347
Blackpool North a.	|	1900	|	2000	|	2100	2200	2300	0014
Barrow in Furness 157 a.	1926	...	|	...	2119	...	...	...	...
Windermere 158 a.	...	...	|	...	...	...	...	...	...
Edinburgh Waverley 151 a.	...	...	2139	...	...	...	...	...	...
Glasgow Central 151 a.	...	...	...	...	...	...	...	...	...

	Ⓐ	⚒	⚒	⚒	Ⓐ	Ⓐ	⑥	Ⓐ	⑥	Ⓐ
Glasgow Central 151 d.		...	...	...	...	...	...	...	...	...
Edinburgh Waverley 151 d.		...	...	...	...	...	...	...	...	0536
Windermere 158 d.		...	...	...	...	...	...	...	...	|
Barrow in Furness 157 d.		...	0531	...	...	0619	0619	...	...	|
Blackpool North d.		0545	|	0634	0710	|	|	0736	0744	|
Preston 151 a.		0608	0645	0701	0737	0741	0741	0803	0811	0807
Preston 151 d.		0610	0647	0703	0747	0747	0747	0812	0812	0812
Bolton d.		0635	0708	0735	0808	0808	0808	0835	0835	0835
Manchester Piccadilly a.		0656	0727	0756	0827	0827	0835	0856	0856	0856
Manchester Airport a.		0717	0747	0817	0847	0847	0853	0919	0919	0919

	⚒	⚒	⚒	Ⓐ	⑥	Ⓐ	⚒	⚒	⚒	⑥	⑥	Ⓐ	Ⓐ	⑥	Ⓐ	⚒	⚒	⚒	⑥	⑥	Ⓐ	⚒	Ⓐ	⑥	⚒
Glasgow Central 151 d.	...	...	0710	...	...	...	...	...	...	...	...	...	...	1010	1010	...	...	...	...	...	...	...	1254	1300	...
Edinburgh Waverley 151 d.	...	...	|	...	...	0742	...	...	...	...	0922	...	0953	|	|	...	...	...	...	1208	1208	...	|	|	...
Windermere 158 d.	...	...	|	...	...	|	...	...	1049	...	|	...	|	|	|	...	1251	...	...	|	|	...	|	|	...
Barrow in Furness 157 d.	0728	...	|	...	...	|	0922	...	|	...	|	...	|	|	|	...	|	...	1325	|	|	...	|	|	...
Blackpool North d.	|	0845	|	0943	0945	|	|	1045	|	1132	|	1145	|	|	|	1245	|	1345	|	|	|	1445	|	|	1545
Preston 151 a.	0845	0909	0945	1007	1009	1011	1045	1109	1145	1158	1205	1209	1245	1241	1245	1309	1345	1409	1437	1441	1445	1509	1534	1545	1609
Preston 151 d.	0847	0910	0947	1012	1010	1012	1047	1110	1147	1210	1210	1210	1247	1247	1247	1310	1347	1410	1447	1447	1447	1510	1547	1547	1610
Bolton d.	0908	0935	1008	1035	1035	1035	1108	1135	1208	1235	1235	1235	1308	1308	1308	1335	1408	1435	1508	1508	1508	1535	1608	1608	1635
Manchester Piccadilly a.	0927	0956	1027	1056	1056	1056	1127	1156	1227	1256	1256	1256	1327	1327	1327	1356	1427	1456	1527	1527	1527	1556	1627	1627	1656
Manchester Airport a.	0947	1017	1047	1117	1117	1117	1150	1217	1247	1317	1317	1317	1347	1347	1347	1417	1447	1517	1547	1547	1547	1617	1647	1647	1717

	Ⓐ	Ⓐ	⑥	⚒	⑥	Ⓐ	⚒	Ⓐ	⑥	⚒	⚒	⚒	Ⓐ	⑥	⑥	⚒	Ⓐ	⚒	⑤	⚒	⑦	⑦	⑦	⑦
Glasgow Central 151 d.	...	...	...	...	...	...	...	...	...	...	1706	...	...	...	...	...	...	...	...	...		...	...	...
Edinburgh Waverley 151 d.	...	1408	1408	...	...	...	...	1611	1611	...	|	...	1812	1812	...	...	...	...	2011	...		...	...	...
Windermere 158 d.	...	|	|	...	...	...	1706	|	|	...	|	...	|	|	...	...	...	...	|	...		...	...	...
Barrow in Furness 157 d.	1525	|	|	...	...	...	|	|	|	...	|	...	|	|	1942	...	2007	...	|	...		...	...	...
Blackpool North d.	|	|	|	1641	1711	1720	|	|	|	1845	|	1945	|	|	|	2045	|	2145	|	2245		0814	0844	0944
Preston 151 a.	1637	1642	1644	1709	1739	1745	1806	1845	1845	1909	1945	2009	2045	2045	2105	2109	2129	2209	2245	2309		0838	0908	1008
Preston 151 d.	1647	1647	1647	1710	1747	1747	1808	1847	1847	1910	1947	2010	2047	2047	2115	2110	2131	2210	2247	2310		0842	0910	1010
Bolton d.	1708	1708	1708	1735	1808	1808	1835	1908	1908	1935	2008	2035	2108	2108	2139	2135	|	2235	2306	2335		0906	0935	1035
Manchester Piccadilly a.	1727	1727	1727	1756	1827	1827	1856	1927	1927	1956	2027	2056	2127	2127	2202	2156	2230	2256	2330	2353		0932	0957	1057
Manchester Airport a.	1748	1748	1748	1817	1847	1847	1917	1947	1950	2017	2047	2117	2147	*2157*	*2257*	2217	2247	2317	...	0022		0949	1017	1117

	⑦	⑦	⑦	⑦	⑦	⑦	⑦	⑦	⑦	⑦	⑦	⑦	⑦	⑦	⑦	⑦	⑦	⑦	⑦	⑦	⑦	⑦	⑦		⑦
Glasgow Central 151 d.	...	...	...	...	...	...	...	...	...	...	...	...	1506	...	...	...	...	1706	...	...	...	...	...	...	...
Edinburgh Waverley 151 d.	...	...	...	...	1110	...	...	...	1309	...	...	...	|	...	1610	...	...	|	...	1810	...	...	1957	...	...
Windermere 158 d.	...	...	...	...	|	...	...	...	|	...	...	...	|	...	|	...	...	|	...	|	...	...	|	...	...
Barrow in Furness 157 d.	...	...	1123	...	|	...	1323	...	|	...	1523	...	|	...	|	...	1815	|	...	|	...	...	|	...	...
Blackpool North d.	1044	1144	|	1244	|	1344	|	1444	|	1544	|	1644	|	1744	|	1844	|	|	1944	|	2044	2156	|	...	2300
Preston 151 a.	1108	1208	1245	1308	1345	1408	1445	1508	1545	1608	1646	1708	1742	1808	1845	1908	1936	1941	2008	2045	2108	2220	2223	...	2326
Preston 151 d.	1110	1210	1247	1310	1347	1410	1447	1510	1547	1610	1647	1710	1747	1810	1847	1910	1947	1947	2010	2047	2110	2229	2229	...	2328
Bolton d.	1135	1235	1308	1335	1408	1435	1508	1535	1608	1635	1708	1735	1808	1835	1908	1935	2008	2008	2035	2108	2135	2251	2251	...	2359
Manchester Piccadilly a.	1157	1257	1327	1357	1427	1457	1527	1557	1627	1657	1727	1757	1827	1857	1927	1957	2027	2027	2057	2127	2157	2314	2314	...	0015
Manchester Airport a.	1217	1317	1347	1417	1447	1517	1547	1617	1647	1717	1747	1817	1847	1917	1947	2017	2047	2047	2117	2147	2217	2330	2330	...	0030

v – Manchester Victoria.

NT, TP MANCHESTER - PRESTON - BARROW IN FURNESS 157

Services on ⑥⑦ valid until January 31. Trains conveying 2nd class only are operated by *NT*.

km		⚒	Ⓐ2C	⚒	Ⓐ2C	⑥2C	Ⓐ2	⑥2B		Ⓐ	⑥2C	Ⓐ2	⚒	⑥2C	Ⓐ2	Ⓐ	⑥2C	⑥	Ⓐ2C	⚒		Ⓐ2M	⑥2M	Ⓐ2	⑥2
	Manchester Piccadilly 156 d.		...	...	...	...	...	...	...	0916	...	...	1116	...	...	1316	...	1346	...	1516	...	...	...	...	...
0	**Preston** 151 d.		0522	0720	0838	0842	...	0945	...	1007	...	...	1158	...	...	1404	...	1445	...	1558	...	...	...	...	...
34	Lancaster 151 d.		0542	0736	0858	0902	0939	1001	...	1023	1128	1132	1214	1332	1332	1420	1422	1501	1533	1614	...	1655	1700	1719	1733
44	Carnforth d.		0552	0745	0908	0912	0949	1009	...	1033	1137	1142	1223	1341	1342	1428	1432	1509	1543	1622	...	1705	1710	1728	1743
53	Arnside d.		0603	0755	0919	0923	1000	1019	...	1042	1148	1153	1231	1352	1352	1437	1442	1518	1554	1632	...	1716	1721	1740	1752
58	Grange over Sands d.		0609	0800	0925	0929	1006	1025	...	1047	1154	1159	1237	1358	1358	1442	1448	1523	1600	1638	...	1722	1727	1746	1759
74	Ulverston d.		0625	0816	0941	0945	1023	1041	...	1100	1210	1216	1249	1414	1415	1455	1505	1536	1617	1654	...	1739	1744	1802	1816
90	**Barrow in Furness** 159 a.		0647	0839	1003	1007	1047	1103	...	1120	1232	1240	1310	1436	1438	1515	1526	1556	1639	1718	...	1802	1807	1825	1838

	Ⓐ2	⑥	Ⓐ	Ⓐ	⑥2		Ⓐ	⑥	Ⓐ	⑥	Ⓐ2	⑥2	⑥	Ⓐ		⑦	⑦	⑦	⑦	⑦2	⑦	⑦	⑦W		⑦2
Manchester Piccadilly 156 d.	1627	1715	1718	1819	...	...	1919	1919	2019	2016	...	...	2216	2219	...		...	1246	1616	...	1716	1916	...	...	...
Preston 151 d.	1649	1758	1808	1904	1904	...	1958	2002	2059	2102	2151	2159	2255	2313	...		1118	1347	1600	...	1806	2000	...	...	...
Lancaster 151 d.	1728	1814	1825	1920	1920	...	2014	2018	2115	2118	2211	2219	2311	2329	...		1134	1403	1616	1704	1822	2016	2123	...	2205
Carnforth d.	1748	1824	1835	1929	1929	...	2022	2026	2123	2126	2221	2229	2320	2337	...		1142	1412	1624	1714	1831	2024	2131	...	2215
Arnside d.	1800	1834	1845	1939	1939	...	2032	2036	2133	2136	2232	2240	2335	2347	...		1152	1422	1634	1725	1841	2034	2142	...	2226
Grange over Sands d.	1811	1840	1851	1944	1944	...	2038	2042	2139	2142	2238	2246	2339	2353	...		1158	1427	1640	1731	1846	2040	2147	...	2232
Ulverston d.	1819	1856	1907	2000	2000	...	2054	2058	2155	2158	2254	2302	2351	0009	...		1214	1443	1656	1747	1902	2056	2203	...	2248
Barrow in Furness 159 a.	1859	1919	1930	2024	2024	...	2117	2120	2218	2220	2316	2324	0015	0032	...		1237	1506	1719	1809	1926	2119	2225	...	2310

B – To Blackpool, Table **156**. C – To Carlisle, Table **159**. M – To Millom, Table **159**. W – To / from Windermere, Table **158**.

157 MANCHESTER - PRESTON - BARROW IN FURNESS NT, TP

Services on ⑥⑦ valid until January 31. Trains conveying 2nd class only are operated by *NT*.

		⚒	⚒		⚒		Ⓐ2M	⚒		Ⓐ2	⑥2		⑥	Ⓐ		⚒2	⚒	⚒2C		Ⓐ	⑥		⚒2	⑥2C	Ⓐ
Barrow in Furness 159 d.	⚒	0435	0531	...	0619	...	0700	0728	...	0800	0825	...	0922	0922	...	1016	1125	1211	...	1325	1325	...	1416	1518	1525
Ulverston d.		0451	0547	...	0638	...	0719	0745	...	0819	0844	...	0941	0941	...	1035	1141	1229	...	1341	1341	...	1435	1536	1541
Grange over Sands d.		0503	0559	...	0654	...	0736	0800	...	0836	0902	...	0957	0957	...	1051	1153	1245	...	1353	1353	...	1451	1553	1553
Arnside d.		0509	0605	...	0700	...	0743	0806	...	0843	0908	...	1003	1003	...	1027	1159	1251	...	1359	1359	...	1457	1559	1559
Carnforth d.		0519	0615	...	0712	...	0754	0818	...	0854	0920	...	1016	1016	...	1108	1208	1302	...	1408	1408	...	1508	1610	1608
Lancaster 151 d.		0528	0626	...	0722	...	0804	0826	...	0907	0933	...	1026	1026	...	1120	1218	1315	...	1418	1418	...	1520	1623	1618
Preston 151 a.		...	0647	...	0747	...	0829	0847	...	...	...	...	1047	1047	...	...	1237	...	...	1437	1447	...	...	...	1647
Manchester Piccadilly 156 a.		...	0727	...	0827	...	...	0927	...	...	...	...	1127	1127	...	...	...	...	...	...	1527	...	...	...	1727

	⑥	Ⓐ2		⑥		ⒶW	Ⓐ2		⚒2C	⑥	Ⓐ		⚒2			⑦	⑦		⑦2	⑦		⑦		⑦	⑦2
Barrow in Furness 159 d.	1617	1620	...	1721	...	1721	1743	...	1803	1942	2007	...	2143	...	⑦	0925	1123	...	1245	1323	...	1523	...	1815	2002
Ulverston d.	1634	1638	...	1738	...	1738	1759	...	1821	2001	2026	...	2201	...		0941	1142	...	1304	1342	...	1542	...	1834	2021
Grange over Sands d.	1649	1654	...	1753	...	1753	|	...	1837	2017	2042	...	2217	...		0953	1158	...	1320	1358	...	1558	...	1850	2037
Arnside d.	1655	1700	...	1759	...	1759	|	...	1843	2023	2048	...	2223	...		0959	1204	...	1326	1404	...	1604	...	1856	2043
Carnforth d.	1706	1711	...	1809	...	1809	1823	...	1854	2036	2101	...	2234	...		1008	1216	...	1337	1416	...	1616	...	1907	2054
Lancaster 151 d.	1715	1725	...	1817	...	1820	1838	...	1905	2045	2110	...	2245	...		1021	1226	...	1350	1426	...	1626	...	1917	2107
Preston 151 a.	1734	...	...	1836	...	...	...	...	1930	2115	2131	...	2310	...		1040	1247	...	...	1447	...	1647	...	1947	...
Manchester Piccadilly 156 a.	...	...	...	...	...	...	...	...	...	2202	2230	...	...	...		...	1327	...	...	1527	...	1727	...	2027	...

For notes and return service see previous page.

158 PRESTON - OXENHOLME - WINDERMERE TP

Services on ⑥⑦ valid until January 31.

km			Ⓐ	Ⓐ	Ⓐ	Ⓐ	Ⓐ	Ⓐ	Ⓐ	Ⓐ	Ⓐ	Ⓐ	Ⓐ	Ⓐ	Ⓐ	Ⓐ	Ⓐ	Ⓐ	Ⓐ			⑥	⑥	⑥	⑥
	Manchester Piccadilly 156 d.	Ⓐ	...	...	...	...	...	0946	...	...	...	...	...	1616	...	...	...	...	...	...	⑥	...	...	...	...
0	**Preston** 151 d.		...	...	...	...	...	1045	...	1304	...	...	...	1705	...	...	...	...	...	...		...	...	...	...
34	Lancaster 151 d.		0546	...	...	...	...	1101	...	1320	...	...	...	1725	1829	...	...	...	...	...		0546	...	...	...
68	**Oxenholme** 151 d.		0621	0721	0827	0914	1027	1118	1228	1337	1427	1538	1628	1749	1846	1937	2027	2115	2220	...		0621	0721	0827	0911
72	Kendal d.		0626	0725	0831	0918	1031	1122	1232	1341	1431	1543	1632	1753	1850	1941	2031	2119	2224	...		0626	0725	0831	0915
84	**Windermere** a.		0641	0740	0846	0933	1044	1139	1247	1356	1446	1559	1648	1808	1908	1956	2046	2134	2239	...		0641	0740	0846	0930

	⑥	⑥	⑥	⑥	⑥	⑥	⑥	⑥	⑥	⑥	⑥	⑥			⑦	⑦	⑦	⑦	⑦	⑦	⑦	⑦	⑦	⑦	⑦
Manchester Piccadilly 156 d.	0846	...	...	...	...	...	...	1616	...	...	...	...	...	⑦	...	...	...	...	...	...	...	...	...	...	...
Preston 151 d.	0932	1045	...	1304	...	...	...	1704	...	...	...	...	...		...	...	...	...	...	...	...	...	...	...	...
Lancaster 151 d.	0948	1101	...	1320	...	...	...	1721	...	...	...	...	...		1023	...	...	...	...	...	...	...	...	...	...
Oxenholme 151 d.	1005	1118	1228	1337	1433	1538	1628	1738	1830	1937	2023	2115	...		1040	1135	1229	1335	1437	1539	1633	1737	1837	1929	2016
Kendal d.	1009	1122	1232	1341	1437	1542	1632	1742	1834	1941	2027	2119	...		1044	1139	1233	1339	1441	1543	1637	1741	1841	1933	2020
Windermere a.	1026	1139	1247	1356	1452	1559	1648	1800	1849	1956	2042	2134	...		1058	1154	1248	1354	1456	1556	1652	1856	1856	1945	2035

		Ⓐ	Ⓐ	Ⓐ	Ⓐ	Ⓐ	Ⓐ	Ⓐ	Ⓐ	Ⓐ	Ⓐ	Ⓐ	Ⓐ	Ⓐ	Ⓐ	Ⓐ	Ⓐ	Ⓐ			⑥	⑥	⑥	⑥	⑥
Windermere d.	Ⓐ	0650	0757	0850	0959	1049	1159	1251	1400	1459	1602	1706	1815	1910	2000	2050	2140	2245	...	⑥	0657	0757	0850	0938	1049
Kendal d.		0704	0811	0901	1013	1103	1213	1302	1414	1513	1614	1720	1829	1921	2014	2104	2154	2259	...		0711	0811	0901	0952	1103
Oxenholme 151 a.		0709	0816	0906	1018	1108	1218	1307	1419	1518	1619	1725	1834	1927	2019	2109	2219	2304	...		0716	0816	0906	0957	1108
Lancaster 151 a.		...	...	...	...	1126	...	1326	...	...	...	1747	1852	...	...	...	...	2323	...		...	...	...	1016	1126
Preston 151 a.		...	...	...	...	1145	...	1345	...	...	...	1806	1911	...	...	...	...	2345	...		...	...	...	1035	1145
Manchester Piccadilly 156 a.		...	...	...	...	1227	...	1427	...	...	...	1856	2001	...	...	...	...	...	...		...	...	...	...	1227

	⑥	⑥	⑥	⑥	⑥	⑥	⑥	⑥	⑥	⑥	⑥			⑦	⑦	⑦	⑦	⑦	⑦	⑦	⑦	⑦	⑦		⑦B
Windermere d.	1159	1251	1400	1459	1602	1706	1802	1900	2000	2047	2140	...	⑦	1101	1158	1258	1358	1500	1559	1658	1804	1900	1950	...	2040
Kendal d.	1213	1302	1414	1513	1614	1720	1816	1914	2014	2058	2154	...		1113	1212	1312	1412	1512	1613	1711	1818	1914	2001	...	2054
Oxenholme 151 a.	1218	1307	1419	1518	1619	1725	1821	1919	2019	2104	2159	...		1118	1218	1317	1417	1517	1618	1717	1823	1919	2006	...	2101
Lancaster 151 a.	...	1326	...	...	...	1747	...	...	...	...	2217	...		...	...	...	...	...	...	...	...	...	...	...	2118
Preston 151 a.	...	1345	...	...	...	1806	...	...	...	...	2238	...		...	...	...	...	...	...	...	...	...	...	...	...
Manchester Piccadilly 156 a.	...	1427	...	...	...	1856	...	...	...	...	...	...		...	...	...	...	...	...	...	...	...	...	...	...

B – To Barrow in Furness, Table **159**.

159 BARROW - WHITEHAVEN - CARLISLE 2nd class NT

km		⚒	⑥	Ⓐ	ⒶP	⑥	⚒	Ⓐ	⑥	⑥	Ⓐ	⚒P	Ⓐ	⑥	⑥	⑦	Ⓐ	Ⓐ	⑥	Ⓐ	⑥	⑥	Ⓐ	⑦	⑥
	Lancaster 151 d.	...	...	...	0542	...	...	...	...	...	...	0858	...	...	...	...	...	...	1128	...	...	1332	...	...	1422p
0	**Barrow in Furness** 157 d.	...	0600	0600	0650	0705	0801	...	...	0907	0910	1011	1119	1122	...	...	...	1231	1234	1331	1350	1450	1454	...	1533
26	Millom d.	...	0626	0629	0719	0734	0829	...	...	0935	0938	1039	1147	1150	...	...	...	1259	1302	1358	1418	1518	1522	...	1601
47	Ravenglass ‡ 🚂 d.	...	0642	0647	0737	0752	0844	...	...	0952	0955	1056	1204	1207	...	...	...	1315	1319	1415	1435	1535	1539	...	1618
56	Sellafield d.	...	0655	0702	0751	0806	0858	...	...	1004	1010	1106	1215	1219	...	...	...	1328	1331	1427	1447	1551	1551	...	1630
74	**Whitehaven** d.	0630	0719	0725	0811	0826	...	0902	0915	1024	1028	1129	1235	1241	1254	1257	1305	1347	1351	1448	1506	1611	1611	1628	1656
85	Workington d.	0648	0737	0743	0829	0844	...	0920	0933	1042	1046	1147	1253	...	1312	1315	1322	1405	1409	1506	1524	1629	1629	1646	1714
92	Maryport d.	0656	0745	0751	0837	0852	...	0928	0941	1050	1054	1155	1301	...	1320	1323	1330	1413	1417	1514	1532	1637	1637	1654	1722
119	Wigton d.	0715	0805	0811	0857	0912	...	0947	1000	1109	1113	1214	1321	...	1339	1342	1350	1432	1436	1533	1552	1657	1657	1713	1742
138	**Carlisle** 151 a.	0738	0827	0835	0921	0936	...	1013	1024	1134	1137	1239	1345	...	1404	1407	1411	1457	1501	1558	1616	1721	1721	1737	1806

	Ⓐ	⑥	Ⓐ	Ⓐ	⑦	⑥	⚒	⑥	Ⓐ	⚒
Lancaster 151 d.	1533	...	...	1655	...	1700	...	...	...	...
Barrow in Furness 157 d.	1641	1725	1728	1805	...	1810	...	1930	1935	2125
Millom d.	1709	1753	1758	1835	...	1840	...	2000	2005	2155
Ravenglass ‡ 🚂 d.	1726	1810	1815	▬	...	...	...	...	...	▬
Sellafield d.	1739	1822	1827	⚒	...	...	...	...	...	Ⓐ
Whitehaven d.	1758	1843	1855	1931	2028	...	2030	...	...	2150
Workington d.	1816	1901	1912	1949	2046	...	2048	...	...	2210
Maryport d.	1826	1909	1920	1957	2054	...	2056	...	...	...
Wigton d.	1846	1928	1940	2016	2113	...	2115	...	...	...
Carlisle 151 a.	1908	1953	2004	2041	2138	...	2139	...	...	...

	ⒶP	⑥	Ⓐ	⑥	Ⓐ	⚒	⚒		⑥	Ⓐ
Carlisle 151 d.	...	...	...	...	...	0744	...	...	0837	0844
Wigton d.	...	...	...	...	...	0801	...	...	0854	0901
Maryport d.	...	...	0600	0626	...	0821	...	...	0914	0921
Workington d.	...	...	0609	0637	...	0833	...	...	0926	0933
Whitehaven d.	...	...	0628	0657	0728	0854	...	...	0945	0951
Sellafield d.	...	...	0648	0722	0748	...	0907	...	1003	1009
Ravenglass ‡ 🚂 d.	...	...	0657	0732	0757	...	0916	...	1013	1020
Millom d.	0610	0610	0717	0751	0815	...	0936	...	1032	1040
Barrow in Furness 157 a.	0642	0642	0749	0824	0849	...	1007	...	1107	1114
Lancaster 151 a.	0803	...	0907	0933	...	...	1120	...	...	...

	⚒	⚒		⑥	⑥	Ⓐ	Ⓐ	⑥	Ⓐ	⑥	⑦	ⒶP	⑥Q	⑥	Ⓐ		Ⓐ	⑥	⚒	⑥⑦	Ⓐ	⑥	Ⓐ	⑥	Ⓑ
Carlisle 151 d.	0940	1043	...	1139	...	1149	1247	1248	1420	1421	1500	1512	1525	1630	1631	...	1727	1740	1811	1900	1915	2005	2033	2145	2150
Wigton d.	0957	1100	...	1156	...	1206	1304	1305	1437	1438	1517	1529	1542	1647	1648	...	1744	1757	1828	1917	1932	2022	2050	2202	2207
Maryport d.	1017	1120	...	1216	...	1226	1324	1325	1457	1458	1537	1549	1602	1707	1708	...	1804	1817	1848	1937	1952	2042	2110	2222	2227
Workington d.	1029	1132	...	1228	...	1238	1336	1337	1509	1510	1549	1601	1614	1719	1720	...	1816	1829	1900	1949	2004	2054	2122	2234	2239
Whitehaven d.	1048	1151	...	1249	1254	1259	1356	1357	1528	1530	1610	1620	1634	1739	1739	...	1835	1848	1923	2010	2025	2115	2143	2255	2300
Sellafield d.	1108	1210	...	...	1312	...	1414	1415	1554	1550	...	1642	1653	1759	1803	...	1854	1906	▬	...	...	...	▬	...	...
Ravenglass ‡ 🚂 d.	1118	1220	...	...	1321	...	1423	1424	1604	1559	...	1652	1703	1808	1814	...	1903	1916	⚒	...	...	...	⚒	...	...
Millom d.	1137	1239	...	...	1341	...	1443	1444	1625	1619	...	1713	1722	1828	1834	...	1923	1936	2010	...	...	...	2202	...	...
Barrow in Furness 157 a.	1209	1314	...	...	1413	...	1517	1516	1659	1653	...	1747	1755	1902	1910	...	1957	2010	2045	...	...	...	2235	...	...
Lancaster 151 a.	1315	...	...	...	1521	...	...	1623p	...	...	...	1904	1906	...	...	...	...	...	...	...	...	...	...	...	...

P – From / to Preston, Table **157**.
Q – Dec. 19 – Jan. 30 and Apr. 3 – May 22 to Preston; Feb. 6 – Mar. 27 to Lancaster.
p – Dec. 19 – Jan. 30 and Apr. 3 – May 22.
‡ – Ravenglass for Eskdale.

🚂 – **Ravenglass - Dalegarth** and v.v. (*Ravenglass and Eskdale Railway*). *11 km.* Daily Mar. 21 - Oct. 25. Ravenglass station is adjacent to main line station. Operator: Ravenglass and Eskdale Railway. ✆ 01229 717171. www.ravenglass-railway.co.uk

SR 🛏 Sleeper trains LONDON - SCOTLAND 🛏 160

km		⑦	Ⓐ	⑦	⑤	①–④				
0	**London** Euston **150** d.	2055	2115	2327	2350	2350	...	...	...	...
28	Watford Junction **150** d.	2117	2133	2347	0010	0010	...	...	...	...
254	Crewe **150 151** d.	2337	2354	|	|	|	...	...	...	...
336	Preston **151** d.	0030	0052	|	|	|	...	...	...	...
481	Carlisle **151** a.	|	|	0504	0518	0511	...	...	...	...
625	Motherwell a.	|	|	0701	0659	0701	...	...	...	...
646	**Glasgow** Central **151** ◧ a.	|	|	0719	0621	0719	...	...	...	...
646	**Edinburgh 151** ◧ a.	|	|	0720	0713	0720	...	...	...	...
	Perth **221** a.	0539	0539	...	...	...	...	...	...	...
	Dundee **224** a.	0608	0608	...	...	...	...	...	...	...
	Aberdeen **224** ◧ a.	0735	0735	...	...	...	...	...	...	...
	Inverness **221** a.	0830	0830	...	...	...	...	...	...	...
	Fort William **218** a.	0954	0954	...	...	...	...	...	...	...

	①–④	⑤	⑦	⑦	①–④	⑤			
Fort William **218** d.	...	...	...	1900	1950	1950	...	...	...
Inverness **221** d.	...	...	...	2025	2046	2046	...	...	...
Aberdeen **224** d.	...	...	...	2140	2140	2140	...	...	...
Dundee **224** d.	...	...	...	2306	2306	2306	...	...	...
Perth **221** d.	...	...	...	2300	2321	2321	...	...	...
Edinburgh 151 d.	2340	2340	2315	|	|	|	...	...	...
Glasgow Central **151** d.	2340	2340	2315	|	|	|	...	...	...
Motherwell d.	2356	2356	2331	|	|	|	...	...	...
Carlisle **151** d.	0140	0140	0108	|	|	|	...	...	...
Preston **151** a.	|	|	|	0432	0432	0441	...	...	...
Crewe **150 151** a.	|	|	|	0532	0534	0537	...	...	...
Watford Junction **150** a.	0620	0627	0623	|	|	|	...	...	...
London Euston **150** ◧ a.	0643	0650	0646	0747	0748	0747	...	...	...

☛ All trains in this table convey 🛏 1, 2 cl., (2) (reservation compulsory) and 🍷.

◧ – Sleeping-car passengers may occupy their cabins until 0800 following arrival at these stations.

NT 2nd class BLACKPOOL - PRESTON - LIVERPOOL 161

Services on ⑦ valid until January 31.

km		⚒	⚒	⚒	Ⓐ	⑥	⚒		⚒	⚒	⚒	Ⓐ	⑥		⚒			⑦	⑦		⑦		⑦
	Blackpool North **156** d.	...	0702	...	*0829*	0838	0937	and at	1837	1937	2038	...	...	...	2214	...	⑦	0850	0950	and at	2150	...	2244
0	**Preston** **156** d.	*0616*	0730	*0758*	0904	0904	1004	the same	1904	2004	2104	*2131*	*2120*	...	2243	...		0915	1015	the same	2215	...	2309
24	Wigan North Western d.	0638	0750	0828	0924	0924	1024	minutes past	1924	2024	2123	2225	2225	...	2303	...		0936	1036	minutes past	2236	...	2330
38	St Helens Central d.	0656	0806	0846	0939	0939	1039	each hour	1939	2039	2141	2243	2243	...	2321	...		0953	1053	each hour	2253	...	2347
57	**Liverpool** Lime St **150** a.	0728	0835	0918	1002	1002	1102	until	2002	2102	2214	2315	2315	...	2354	...		1024	1124	until	2324	...	0018

		⚒	⚒		⚒		⚒	⚒	⚒	⚒	⚒	⚒	⚒	⚒	⚒			⑦	⑦		⑦		⑦
Liverpool Lime St **150** d.	⚒	0657	0757	...	0857	and at	1557	1657	1727	1744	1801	1923	2025	2142	2302	...	⑦	0831	0931	and at	2131	...	2231
St Helens Central d.		0715	0815	...	0915	the same	1615	1715	1751	1811	1830	1941	2043	2211	2331	...		0858	0958	the same	2158	...	2258
Wigan North Western d.		0731	0831	...	0931	minutes past	1631	1731	1805	1831	1849	1955	2057	2228	2348	...		0914	1014	minutes past	2214	...	2314
Preston **156** a.		0756	0855	...	0954	each hour	1656	1754	1831	1854	1915	2018	2122	2254	0013	...		0937	1037	each hour	2237	...	2335
Blackpool North **156** a.		*0829*t	*0925*t	...	1020	until	1723	1823	*1909*	1922	*2000*	2044	2153	2321	...	...		1007	1107	until	2307	...	0005

t – Through train on ⑥, arrives 4 – 8 minutes earlier.

ME, NT 2nd class MANCHESTER and LIVERPOOL local services 162

MANCHESTER - CLITHEROE
Journey time: ± 77 – 85 minutes *57 km* NT

From Manchester Victoria:

Trains call at **Bolton** ± 20 minutes and **Blackburn** ± 50 minutes later.

⚒: 0555, 0654**p**, 0800 and hourly until 1500; then 1540, 1623, 1700 and hourly until 2200.

⑦: 0801, 0900 and hourly until 2100.

From Clitheroe:

Trains call at **Blackburn** ± 21 minutes and **Bolton** ± 50 minutes later.

⚒: 0640Ⓐ, 0707, 0740, 0826, 0940 and hourly until 1440; then 1526, 1640, 1709, 1809, 1840, 1940, 2040, 2140, 2240Ⓐ, 2246⑥.

⑦: 0940 and hourly until 2240.

p – From Manchester Piccadilly.

MANCHESTER - BUXTON
Journey time: ± 56 minutes *41 km* NT

From Manchester Piccadilly:

Trains call at **Stockport** ± 11 minutes and **New Mills Newtown** ± 31 minutes later.

⚒: 0649, 0752, 0852, 0952, 1052, 1152, 1252, 1352, 1452, 1552, 1621Ⓐ, 1651, 1721, 1752, 1821Ⓐ, 1852, 1951, 2051, 2152, 2310.

⑦: 0855**d**, 0917**c**, 0951**d**, 1052, 1151, 1252 and hourly until 2252.

From Buxton:

Trains call at New Mills Newtown ± 21 minutes and at Stockport ± 46 minutes later.

⚒: 0559, 0623, 0650Ⓐ, 0724, 0748Ⓐ, 0756⑥, 0827, 0927, 1030, 1127, 1230, 1325, 1430, 1527, 1630, 1659Ⓐ, 1727, 1759Ⓐ, 1827, 1927, 2027, 2127, 2256.

⑦: 0823**d**, 0919, 1023, 1121, 1226, 1327 and hourly until 2227.

c – ⑦ Dec. 13 – Jan. 31.

d – ⑦ Feb. 7 – May 16.

MANCHESTER - NORTHWICH - CHESTER
Journey time: ± 87 minutes *73 km* NT

From Manchester Piccadilly:

Trains call at **Stockport** ± 9 mins., **Altrincham** ± 26 mins., and **Northwich** ± 53 mins. later.

Ⓐ: 0617, 0717 and hourly until 1617; then 1709, 1817, 1917, 2017, 2117, 2217, 2317.

⑥: 0617, 0717 and hourly until 2017; then 2116, 2217, 2317.

⑦: 0922, 1121, 1321, 1522, 1722, 1922, 2122.

From Chester:

Trains call at **Northwich** 28 mins., **Altrincham** ± 55 mins, and **Stockport** ± 73 mins later.

Ⓐ: 0605, 0635, 0703, 0735, 0807 and hourly until 2107; then 2248.

⑥: 0605, 0703, 0807 and hourly until 1907; then 2005, 2133, 2249.

⑦: 0858, 1107, 1307, 1507, 1707, 1907, 2107.

MANCHESTER - ST HELENS - LIVERPOOL
Journey time: ± 63 minutes *51 km* NT

From Manchester Victoria:

Trains call at **St Helens Junction** ± 29 minutes later.

⚒: 0539, 0609, 0709, 0739, 0809, 0839 and hourly until 1639; then 1709, 1737, 1839, 1939, 2039, 2139, 2239, 2309.

⑦: 0850**bp**, 0853**a**, 0950**p**, 1050**p**, 1150**dp**, 1153**cr**, 1250**dp**, 1253**cr**, 1350**dp**, 1353**cr**, 1450**p** and hourly (note '**p**' applies to all trains) until 2250**p**.

From Liverpool Lime Street:

Trains call at **St Helens Junction** ± 28 minutes later.

⚒: 0546, 0646, 0716, 0746, 0844, 0946 and hourly until 1546; then 1616, 1646, 1710, 1735, 1748, 1846, 1912, 2012, 2112, 2212, 2316.

⑦: 0805**bp**, 0819**ar**, 0901**p**, 1001**cr**, 1001**dp**, 1101**cr**, 1101**dp**, 1201**cr**, 1201**dp**, 1301**p** and hourly (note '**p**' applies to all trains) until 2301**p**.

a – ⑦ Dec. 13 – Mar. 28.
b – ⑦ Apr. 4 – May 16.
c – ⑦ Dec. 13 – Jan. 31.
d – ⑦ Feb. 7 – May 16.
p – On ⑦ this train starts / terminates at Manchester Piccadilly, not Victoria.
r – On ⑦ this train starts / terminates at Manchester Oxford Road, not Victoria.

MANCHESTER - WIGAN - SOUTHPORT
Journey time: ± 71 minutes *62 km* NT

From Manchester Piccadilly:

Trains call at **Bolton** ± 20 minutes and **Wigan Wallgate** ± 39 minutes later.

⚒: 0706Ⓐ**v**, 0710⑥**v**, 0747Ⓐ**v**, 0822 and hourly until 1822; then 1920, 2020, 2120, 2239**r**.

⑦: 0835**b**, 0839**av**, 0935, 1026, 1133, 1235**d**, 1238**ar**, 1335, and hourly until 2035.

From Southport:

Trains call at **Wigan Wallgate** ± 30 minutes and **Bolton** ± 48 minutes later.

⚒: 0623, 0721, 0825, 0924 and hourly until 1724; then 1817, 1923, 2023**r**, 2123**v**, 2218.

⑦: 0909, 1005, 1105**cr**, 1105**d**, 1205 and hourly until 2205.

a – ⑦ Dec. 13 – Mar. 28.
b – ⑦ Apr. 4 – May 16.
c – ⑦ Dec. 13 – Jan. 31.
d – ⑦ Feb. 7 – May 16.
r – This trains starts / terminates at Manchester Oxford Road.
v – This trains starts / terminates at Manchester Victoria.

LIVERPOOL - BIRKENHEAD - CHESTER
Journey time: 43 minutes *29 km* ME

From Liverpool Lime Street:

Trains call at **Birkenhead Central** ± 9 minutes later.

⚒: 0536, 0606, 0641 and every 30 minutes until 1611; then 1633Ⓐ, 1641⑥, 1648Ⓐ, 1703Ⓐ, 1711⑥, 1718Ⓐ, 1733Ⓐ, 1741⑥, 1748Ⓐ, 1811, 1841 and every 30 minutes until 2341.

⑦: 0811, 0841 and every 30 minutes until 2341.

From Chester:

Trains call at **Birkenhead Central** ± 34 minutes later.

⚒: 0600, 0630, 0700, 0722Ⓐ, 0730⑥, 0737Ⓐ, 0752Ⓐ, 0800⑥, 0807Ⓐ, 0830, 0900 and every 30 minutes until 2300.

⑦: 0800, 0830 and every 30 minutes until 2300.

LIVERPOOL – SOUTHPORT
Journey time: 44 minutes *30 km* ME

From Liverpool Central:

⚒: 0608, 0623 and every 15 minutes until 2308; then 2323, 2338 (also 1713Ⓐ).

⑦: 0808, 0823, 0853 and every 30 minutes until 2253; then 2338.

From Southport:

⚒: 0543, 0558 and every 15 minutes until 2258, then 2316 (also 0748Ⓐ, 0803Ⓐ).

⑦: 0758, 0828 and every 30 minutes until 2258; then 2316.

165 HOLYHEAD - CREWE and MANCHESTER

Most services 🍷 2nd class AW, VT

Services on ⑦ valid until January 31. For ⛴ connections to / from **Dublin** see Table **2040**.

km		⚒	⚒	⚒	⚒ C	⚒	Ⓐ ◇	⑥	Ⓐ	Ⓐ B	⚒	⑥ B	Ⓐ C□	Ⓐ ◇	⚒	⑥ C	Ⓐ C	⑥ ◇	Ⓐ ◇	⚒	⚒ B	⑥ ◇	⚒	Ⓐ C
0	**Holyhead** d.	⚒	...	...	0425	...	0448	...	...	0511	...	0522	0532	0553	...	0635	0629	0653	0655	...	0715	0755	...	0805
40	Bangor d.		...	...	0457	...	0514	...	...	0540	...	0601	0602	0620	...	0707	0707	0720	0722	...	0802	0822	...	0902
	Llandudno ‡ d.		...	...	|	...	|	...	...	|	...	|	|	|	0634	|	|	|	|	0745	|	|	0845	|
64	Llandudno Junction ‡ d.		0438	...	0515	...	0532	0537	0546	0607	...	0624	0621	0638	0644	0725	0725	0738	0740	0754	0825	0840	0854	0925
71	Colwyn Bay d.		0444	...	0521	...	0538	0543	0552	0613	...	0630	|	0644	0650	0731	0731	0744	0747	0800	0831	0847	0900	0931
81	Abergele & Pensarn d.		0451	...	|	...	|	0550	|	|	...	|	|	|	0657	|	|	|	|	0807	|	|	0907	|
88	Rhyl d.		0457	...	0531	...	0549	0556	0602	0623	...	0640	0636	0655	0703	0741	0741	0755	0758	0813	0841	0858	0913	0941
94	Prestatyn d.		0502	...	0537	...	|	0602	0608	0629	...	0646	|	0700	0708	0747	0747	0801	0804	0819	0847	0904	0919	0947
116	Flint d.		0516	...	0550	...	|	0616	0621	0642	...	0659	0652	|	0721	0800	0800	0815	0817	0832	0900	0918	0932	1000
136	**Chester 150** ▼ a.		0533	0538	0605	0613	0617	0634	0638	0700	0712	0715	0707	0725	0738	0815	0815	0828	0831	0850	0915	0931	0950	1015
170	**Crewe 150** ▼ a.		0558	|	...	|	0647	0659	|	...	|	...	0732	0754	|	...	...	0854	0854	|	...	0954	|	...
	London Euston **150** a.		...	|	...	|	0835	...	|	...	|	...	...	0938	|	...	...	1038	1038	|	...	1138	|	...
165	Warrington Bank Quay a.		...	0605	...	0639	...	...	0706	...	0738	...	...	...	0806	...	...	...	...	0918	...	...	1018	...
201	**Manchester** Piccadilly a.		...	0646	...	0718	...	...	0750	...	0818	...	...	...	0850	...	...	...	...	0957	...	...	1057	...

	⑥ C	Ⓐ ◇	⑥ ◇	⚒	⚒ B	⚒	⚒ C	⚒	⚒ B	Ⓐ ◇	⚒	⚒ C	⚒	⚒ B	Ⓐ ◇	⚒	Ⓐ	⑥ C	Ⓐ C	⑥ ◇	⑥	Ⓐ	Ⓐ B	⑥ B
Holyhead d.	0820	0855	0855	...	0923	...	1033	...	1123	...	...	1238	...	1323	1358	...	...	1423	1432	1436	...	...	1523	1523
Bangor d.	0902	0922	0922	...	1002	...	1105	...	1202	1224	...	1307	...	1402	1425	...	...	1454	1502	1506	...	...	1602	1602
Llandudno ‡ d.	|	|	|	0945	|	1044	|	1144	|	|	1244	|	1344	|	|	1440	1508	|	|	|	1544	1608	|	|
Llandudno Junction ‡ d.	0925	0940	0940	0954	1025	1053	1125	1153	1225	1242	1253	1325	1353	1425	1443	1449	1517	1517	1525	1525	1553	1617	1625	1625
Colwyn Bay d.	0931	0947	0947	1000	1031	1059	1131	1159	1231	1248	1259	1331	1359	1431	1450	1455	1523	1523	1531	1533	1559	1623	1631	1631
Abergele & Pensarn d.	|	|	|	1007	|	1106	|	1206	|	|	1306	|	1406	|	|	1502	|	|	1538	|	1606	|	1638	|
Rhyl d.	0941	0958	0958	1013	1041	1112	1141	1212	1241	1259	1312	1341	1412	1441	1500	1508	1534	1534	1544	1546	1612	1634	1644	1641
Prestatyn d.	0947	1004	1003	1019	1047	1118	1147	1218	1247	1305	1318	1347	1418	1447	|	1514	1539	1539	1549	|	1618	1639	1650	1647
Flint d.	1000	1017	|	1032	1100	1131	1200	1231	1300	1318	1331	1400	1431	1500	|	1527	1553	1553	1603	|	1631	1653	1703	1700
Chester 150 ▼ a.	1015	1031	1028	1050	1115	1149	1215	1249	1315	1332	1349	1415	1449	1517	1527	1546	1610	1607	1616	1617	1649	1710	1717	1714
Crewe 150 ▼ a.	...	1054	1054	|	...	|	...	|	...	1354	|	...	|	...	1554	|	|	...	...	1643	|	|	...	...
London Euston **150** a.	...	1238	1238	|	...	|	...	|	...	1538	|	...	|	...	1738	|	|	...	...	1838	|	|	...	...
Warrington Bank Quay a.	...	...	...	1118	...	1218	...	1318	...	...	1418	...	1518	...	...	1616	1651	...	...	...	1718	1749	...	...
Manchester Piccadilly a.	...	...	...	1157	...	1257	...	1357	...	...	1457	...	1557	...	...	1657	1730	...	...	...	1757	1828	...	...

	⑥	Ⓐ	Ⓐ C	⑥ C	⑥	Ⓐ	⚒	⚒	⚒	⚒	⚒ B	Ⓐ B◇	⚒	⚒	⚒	⚒	⚒			⑦	⑦	⑦	⑦	⑦
Holyhead d.	...	...	1636	1638	...	...	1721	...	1823	...	1921	...	...	...	2037	...	...	...	⑦	...	...	0845	...	...
Bangor d.	...	...	1704	1707	...	...	1800	...	1902	...	2000	2020	...	...	2106	...	...	...		...	...	0913	...	...
Llandudno ‡ d.	1644	1707	|	|	1744	...	|	1844	|	1942	|	|	2042	...	|	2145	...	...		...	...	|	...	...
Llandudno Junction ‡ d.	1653	1716	1722	1725	1753	...	1823	1853	1925	1951	2023	2038	2051	...	2129	2155	...	...		...	...	0935	...	...
Colwyn Bay d.	1659	1722	1728	1731	1759	...	1829	1859	1931	1957	2029	2044	2057	...	2135	2201	...	...		...	...	0941	...	...
Abergele & Pensarn d.	1706	|	1735	|	1806	...	|	1906	|	2004	|	|	2104	...	2142	2209	...	...		...	...	0948	...	...
Rhyl d.	1712	1733	1741	1741	1812	...	1839	1912	1941	2010	2039	2055	2110	...	2148	2216	...	...		...	...	0954	...	...
Prestatyn d.	1718	1738	1747	1747	1818	...	1845	1918	1947	2016	2045	2101	2116	...	2153	2222	...	...		...	...	0959	...	...
Flint d.	1731	1752	1802	1800	1831	...	1858	1931	2000	2029	2058	2114	2129	...	2207	2237	...	...		...	...	1013	...	...
Chester 50 ▼ a.	1749	1811	1816	1815	1849	1850	1913	1949	2015	2047	2115	2128	2147	2152	2224	2255	2322	...		0841	0942	1030	1036	1136
Crewe 150 ▼ a.	|	|	...	...	|	|	...	|	2041	|	...	2154	...	|	2250	2329	|	...		|	|	1101	|	|
London Euston **150** a.	|	|	...	...	|	|	...	|	...	|	...	...	...	|	...	...	|	...		|	|	...	|	|
Warrington Bank Quay a.	1818	1845	...	...	1918	1918	...	2018	...	2116	...	...	...	2218	...	...	2350	...		0910	1007	...	1103	1203
Manchester Piccadilly a.	1857	1929	...	...	1952	1952	...	2057	...	2157	...	...	...	2258	...	...	0028	...		0949	1050	...	1141	1241

	⑦ C	⑦ ◇	⑦	⑦ ◇	⑦	⑦ ◇	⑦	⑦ ◇	⑦	⑦		⑦	⑦	⑦ C	⑦	⑦	⑦	⑦ B	⑦	⑦	⑦	⑦	⑦	⑦
Holyhead d.	1020	1055	...	1150	...	1250	...	1355	...	1430	...	1530	...	1625	...	1730	...	1825	...	1940	...	...	2035	2140
Bangor d.	1059	1122	...	1217	...	1318	...	1422	...	1508	...	1559	...	1704	...	1759	...	1904	...	2009	...	...	2114	2211
Llandudno ‡ d.	|	|	...	|	...	|	...	|	...	|	...	|	...	|	...	|	...	|	...	|	...	...	|	|
Llandudno Junction ‡ d.	1122	1140	...	1235	...	1336	...	1440	...	1526	...	1625	...	1725	...	1824	...	1924	...	2037	...	...	2137	2229
Colwyn Bay d.	1128	1147	...	1242	...	1342	...	1446	...	1532	...	1631	...	1731	...	1830	...	1930	...	2043	...	...	2143	2235
Abergele & Pensarn d.	1135	|	...	|	...	|	...	|	...	1539	...	1638	...	1738	...	1837	...	1937	...	2050	...	...	2150	|
Rhyl d.	1141	1158	...	1253	...	1353	...	1457	...	1545	...	1644	...	1744	...	1843	...	1943	...	2056	...	...	2156	2245
Prestatyn d.	1146	1203	...	1259	...	1359	...	1503	...	1551	...	1649	...	1749	...	1848	...	1948	...	2101	...	...	2201	2251
Flint d.	1200	1217	...	|	...	1413	...	|	...	1604	...	1703	...	1803	...	1902	...	2002	...	2115	...	...	2215	2304
Chester 50 ▼ a.	1218	1230	1236	1323	1336	1426	1436	1531	1536	1621	...	1720	1736	1820	1836	1919	1936	2019	2036	2133	2136	2209	2232	2320
Crewe 150 ▼ a.	...	1252	|	1349	|	1452	|	1552	|	|	...	1745	|	...	|	1944	|	2048	|	2159	|	|	2259	...
London Euston **150** a.	...	1443	|	1545	|	1644	|	1744	|	|	...	...	|	...	|	...	|	...	|	...	|	|	...	...
Warrington Bank Quay a.	...	...	1303	...	1403	...	1503	...	1603	1703	...	...	1803	...	1903	...	2003	...	2103	...	2203	2234	...	...
Manchester Piccadilly a.	...	...	1341	...	1441	...	1541	...	1641	1741	...	...	1841	...	1941	...	2041	...	2141	...	2241	2315	...	...

		⚒ B◇	⚒	Ⓐ	⑥	⚒	Ⓐ C	⑥ C	⚒	⚒ B	⚒	Ⓐ ◇	⑥ C	Ⓐ C	⚒	Ⓐ ◇	⑥ ◇	⚒ B	⚒	⚒ C	⚒	⚒ B	⚒	⚒ C
Manchester Piccadilly d.	⚒	...	0550	...	...	0650	...	...	0750	...	0850	...	...	...	0950	...	...	...	1050	...	1150	...	1250	...
Warrington Bank Quay d.		...	0626	...	...	0722	...	...	0824	...	0926	...	...	...	1026	...	...	...	1126	...	1226	...	1326	...
London Euston **150** d.		...	|	...	...	|	...	...	|	...	|	0810	...	...	|	0910	0850	...	|	...	|	...	|	...
Crewe 150 ▼ d.		0623	|	0654	0703	|	...	...	|	...	|	0949	...	...	|	1049	1045	...	|	...	|	...	|	...
Chester 150 ▼ d.		0644	0655	0725	0725	0755	0820	0825	0855	0925	0955	1016	1025	1025	1055	1116	1115	1125	1155	1225	1255	1325	1355	1425
Flint d.		0657	0710	0739	0739	0810	0839	0839	0910	0939	1010	1029	1039	1039	1110	|	|	1139	1210	1239	1310	1339	1410	1439
Prestatyn d.		0710	0723	0752	0752	0823	0852	0852	0923	0952	1023	1042	1052	1052	1123	|	|	1152	1223	1252	1323	1352	1423	1452
Rhyl d.		0716	0729	0758	0758	0829	0858	0858	0929	0958	1029	1048	1058	1058	1129	1143	1144	1158	1229	1258	1329	1358	1429	1458
Abergele & Pensarn d.		|	0735	|	|	0835	|	|	0935	|	1035	|	|	|	1135	|	|	|	1235	|	1335	|	1435	|
Colwyn Bay d.		0727	0743	0809	0809	0843	0909	0909	0943	1009	1043	1059	1109	1109	1143	1154	1157	1209	1243	1309	1343	1409	1443	1509
Llandudno Junction ‡ d.		0733	0750	0815	0815	0850	0915	0915	0950	1015	1050	1106	1115	1115	1150	1201	1204	1215	1250	1315	1350	1415	1450	1515
Llandudno ‡ a.		|	0806	|	|	0906	|	|	1006	|	1106	|	|	|	1206	|	|	|	1306	|	1406	|	1506	|
Bangor d.		0750	...	0838	0838	...	0932	0932	...	1038	...	1127	1138	1140	...	1217	1223	1238	...	1332	...	1438	...	1532
Holyhead a.		0823	...	0919	0919	...	1005	1005	...	1119	...	...	1211	1213	...	1250	1258	1319	...	1414	...	1511	...	1614

	⚒	⚒ B	⚒	⚒ C	⚒	⚒ S	⚒	Ⓐ ◇	⑥ ◇	⑥ C	Ⓐ	Ⓐ C	⚒	Ⓐ C□	⑥ ◇	Ⓐ ◇	⚒ S	⚒	Ⓐ ◇	⚒ C	⚒	Ⓐ ◇	⑥	Ⓐ
Manchester Piccadilly d.	1350	...	1450	...	1550	...	1650	...	...	...	1719	...	1750	...	...	...	...	1850	...	...	1950	...	...	...
Warrington Bank Quay d.	1426	...	1526	...	1626	...	1726	...	...	...	1753	...	1824	...	...	...	...	1926	...	...	2026	...	...	...
London Euston **150** d.	|	...	|	...	|	...	|	1610	1610	...	|	...	|	...	1710	1710	...	|	1810	...	|	1910	...	...
Crewe 150 ▼ d.	|	...	|	...	|	...	|	1749	1749	...	|	...	|	1843	1850	1856	...	|	1956	...	|	2050	2100	2100
Chester 150 ▼ d.	1455	1525	1555	1625	1655	1725	1755	1810	1816	1825	1823	1828	1855	1907	1917	1921	1931	1955	2026	2035	2057	2117	2126	2130
Flint d.	1510	1539	1610	1639	1710	1741	1810	1823	1829	1839	...	1841	1910	1921	1930	1935	1946	...	|	2048	...	2130	2141	2145
Prestatyn d.	1523	1552	1623	1652	1723	1754	1823	1836	1842	1852	...	1854	1923	|	1943	1948	1959	...	|	2102	...	2143	2154	2159
Rhyl d.	1529	1558	1629	1658	1729	1800	1829	1842	1849	1858	...	1900	1929	1939	1950	1954	2005	...	2053	2108	...	2150	2200	2205
Abergele & Pensarn d.	1535	|	1635	|	1735	1806	1835	|	|	|	...	|	1935	|	|	|	2011	...	|	|	...	|	2206	2211
Colwyn Bay d.	1543	1609	1643	1709	1743	1814	1843	1853	1900	1909	...	1911	1943	|	2001	2005	2019	...	2104	2119	...	2201	2214	2219
Llandudno Junction ‡ d.	1550	1615	1650	1715	1750	1821	1850	1900	1906	1915	...	1917	1950	1953	2007	2012	2026	...	2110	2126	...	2207	2221	2226
Llandudno ‡ a.	1606	|	1706	|	1806	|	1906	|	|	|	...	|	2006	|	|	|	|	...	|	|	...	|	|	|
Bangor d.	...	1638	...	1738	...	1843	...	1921	1923	1932	...	1934	...	2011	2024	2028	2048	...	2127	2143	...	2224	2243	2248
Holyhead a.	...	1711	...	1819	...	1916	...	...	1955	2016	...	2014	...	2049	2056	2059	2121	...	2159	2223	...	2256	2315	2321

‡ – All trains Llandudno Junction - Llandudno. Journey time ± 10 minutes.

⚒ : 0613, 0651, 0731, 0750, 0825, 0850, 0926, 0950, 1000, 1026, 1050, 1126, 1150, 1226, 1250, 1300, 1326, 1350, 1426, 1450, 1526⑥, 1550, 1600⑥, 1604Ⓐ, 1626⑥, 1650, 1726⑥, 1750, 1826, 1841, 1850, 1926, 1950, 2024, 2132.

⑦ : By 🚌 : 1300, 1610, 1900.

‡ – All trains Llandudno - Llandudno Junction. Journey time ± 10 minutes.

⚒ : 0634, 0710, 0745, 0810, 0845, 0910, 0945, 1010, 1020, 1044, 1110, 1144, 1210, 1244, 1310, 1320, 1344, 1410, 1440, 1508, 1544⑥, 1608, 1620, 1644⑥, 1707, 1744⑥, 1808, 1844, 1903, 1910, 1942, 2008, 2042, 2145.

⑦ : By 🚌 : 1015, 1310, 1600.

AW, VT 2nd class Most services 🍷 MANCHESTER and CREWE - HOLYHEAD 165

Services on ⑦ valid until January 31. For ⛴ connections to / from **Dublin** see Table **2040**.

	⚒	Ⓐ C	⑥ C	⚒	Ⓐ	⑥	⚒	Ⓐ B		⑦	⑦ 🚌	⑦	⑦	⑦ ◇	⑦	⑦		⑦	⑦	⑦	⑦	⑦	⑦	⑦
Manchester Piccadilly d.	2050	...	...	2150	2212	2226	2314	...	...		0728	...	0953	...	1055	...	...	1156	...	1256	...	1356	...	1456
Warrington Bank Quay d.	2126	...	...	2224	2259	2259	2348	...	...		0838	...	1028	...	1130	...	...	1228	...	1329	...	1428	...	1529
London Euston **150** d.	│	...	...	│	│	│	│	...	...		│	...	│	...	│	...	...	│	...	│	...	│	...	│
Crewe 150 ▼ d.	│	...	...	│	│	│	│	2359	...		│	0924	│	1042	│	1127	...	│	1227	│	1327	│	1427	│
Chester 150 ▼ d.	2154	2256	2236	2251	2326	2326	0015	0040	...		0938	0948	1057	1106	1157	1203	...	1255	1302	1356	1402	1455	1502	1556
Flint d.	...	2311	2251	...	...	...	...	0053	...		...	1003	...	│	...	1218	...	...	1317	...	1417	...	1517	...
Prestatyn d.	...	2324	2305	...	...	...	...	0106	...		...	1016	...	1130	...	1231	...	...	1330	...	1430	...	1530	...
Rhyl d.	...	2330	2311	...	...	...	...	0112	...		...	1022	...	1136	...	1237	...	...	1336	...	1436	...	1536	...
Abergele & Pensarn d.	...	2336	2317	...	...	...	...	│	...		...	1028	...	│	...	│	...	...	1342	...	1442	...	1542	...
Colwyn Bay d.	...	2344	2325	...	...	...	...	0123	...		...	1036	...	1147	...	1248	...	...	1350	...	1450	...	1550	...
Llandudno Junction ‡ d.	...	2351	2333	...	...	...	...	0129	...		...	1043	...	1154	...	1254	...	...	1357	...	1457	...	1557	...
Llandudno ‡ a.	...	│	│	...	...	...	...	│	...		...	│	...	│	...	│	...	...	│	...	│	...	│	...
Bangor d.	...	0013	*0038**	...	...	...	...	0145	...		...	1105	...	1210	...	1311	...	...	1419	...	1514	...	1619	...
Holyhead a.	...	0055	*0202**	...	...	...	...	0215	...		...	1147	...	1243	...	1345	...	...	1455	...	1555	...	1654	...

	⑦	⑦	⑦	⑦	⑦	⑦ C	⑦	⑦	⑦ ◇	⑦ B	⑦	⑦ ◇	⑦ C	⑦	⑦ ◇		⑦	⑦	⑦	⑦	⑦	⑦		⑦ B
Manchester Piccadilly d.	...	1556	...	1656	...	...	1756	...	...	...	1856	...	...	1956	...	...	2056	...	2156	...	2256	2325	...	...
Warrington Bank Quay d.	...	1628	...	1728	...	...	1828	...	...	...	1929	...	...	2030	...	...	2128	...	2228	...	2328	2356	...	...
London Euston **150** d.	...	│	...	│	...	...	│	...	1705	...	│	1805	...	│	1905	...	│	...	│	...	│	│	...	...
Crewe 150 ▼ d.	1527	│	1627	│	1727	...	│	...	1856	...	│	1952	...	│	2055	...	│	2127	│	2232	│	│	...	0010
Chester 150 ▼ d.	1602	1655	1702	1755	1802	1829	1855	1855	1922	1938	1956	2018	2036	2057	2117	...	2155	2200	2255	2300	2355	0025	...	0035
Flint d.	1617	...	1717	...	1817	1844	...	1910	1935	1953	...	2031	2051	...	2130	...	...	2215	...	2315	...	...	...	0048
Prestatyn d.	1630	...	1730	...	1830	1857	...	1923	1948	2006	...	2044	2104	...	2143	...	...	2228	...	2328	...	...	...	0101
Rhyl d.	1636	...	1736	...	1836	1903	...	1929	1954	2012	...	2051	2110	...	2150	...	...	2234	...	2334	...	...	...	0107
Abergele & Pensarn d.	1642	...	1742	...	1842	1909	...	1935	│	2018	...	│	2116	...	│	...	...	2240	...	│	...	...	...	│
Colwyn Bay d.	1650	...	1750	...	1850	1917	...	1943	2004	2026	...	2102	2124	...	2201	...	...	2248	...	2345	...	...	...	0118
Llandudno Junction ‡ d.	1657	...	1757	...	1857	1924	...	1950	2011	2033	...	2108	2131	...	2207	...	...	2255	...	2351	...	...	...	0125
Llandudno ‡ a.	│	...	│	...	│	│	...	│	│	│	...	│	│	...	│	...	...	│	...	│	...	...	...	│
Bangor d.	1714	...	1819	...	1914	1945	...	2012	2027	2055	...	2125	2154	...	2224	...	...	2312	...	0014	...	...	...	0141
Holyhead a.	1755	...	1855	...	1955	2018	...	2047	2059	2130	...	2157	2238	...	2256	...	...	2352	...	0049	...	...	...	0215

▼ – Additional trains Chester - Crewe. Journey time ± 24 minutes.
⚒: 0455, 0551, 0643Ⓐ, 0755 and hourly until 2055.
⑦: 0840, 0940, 1223, 1319, 1422, 1627, 1856, 1951, 2051, 2148, 2300.

▼ – Additional trains Cewe - Chester. Journey time ± 24 minutes.
⚒: 0723, 0823 and hourly until 2323.
⑦: 1105, 1156, 1254, 1357, 1457, 1652, 1752, 1924, 2024, 2200, 2306, 2338.

B – To / from Birmingham, Table **145** or **152**.
C – To / from Cardiff, Table **131**.
S – From Shrewsbury on Ⓐ, from Birmingham on ⑥, Table **145**.

▼ – For additional trains Crewe - Chester and v.v. see above.

‡ – For full service Llandudno Junction - Llandudno and v.v. see previous page.
◇ – Operated by *VT*. Conveys 🛏12.
□ – Also conveys 🛏1.

AW 2nd class LLANDUDNO - BLAENAU FFESTINIOG - PORTHMADOG 166

km		⚒	⚒		⚒	🚂 F		⑦ 🚌	⚒		⑦ 🚌	🚂 F		Ⓐ 🚌	⚒		⚒						
0	**Llandudno** 165 d.	...	*0710*	...	1020	...	...	1015	1320	...	1310	...	...	1600	1620	...	1903	...	...	...	...	...	...
5	**Llandudno** Junction 165 d.	0535	0739	...	1033	...	...	1035	1333	...	1335	...	...	1620	1633	...	1921	...	...	...	...	...	...
18	Llanrwst d.	0553	0802	...	1055	...	...	1100	1355	...	1400	...	...	1645	1655	...	1943	...	...	...	...	...	...
24	Betws y Coed d.	0559	0808	...	1101	...	...	1110	1401	...	1410	...	...	1655	1701	...	1949	...	...	...	...	...	...
44	**Blaenau Ffestiniog** d.	0626	0840	...	1133	1145	...	1145	1433	...	1445	1510	...	1730	1733	...	2020	...	...	...	...	...	...
63	Minffordd 148 a.	...	...	...	...	1240	...	...	...	...	...	1610	...	...	...	...	...	...	...	...	...	...	...
66	**Porthmadog** Harbour a.	...	...	...	...	1255	...	...	...	...	...	1620	...	...	...	...	...	...	...	...	...	...	...

		⚒	⚒		🚂 F	⚒		⑦ 🚌	🚂 F		⚒	⑦ 🚌		⚒	⑦ 🚌		⚒						
Porthmadog Harbour d.	...	...	...	...	1015	...	...	...	1335	...	...	...	...	...	...	...	...	...	...	...	...	...	...
Minffordd 148 d.	...	...	...	...	1025	...	...	...	1345	...	...	...	...	...	...	...	...	...	...	...	...	...	...
Blaenau Ffestiniog d.	...	0630	0852	...	1125	1152	...	1150	1445	...	1452	1500	...	1737	1750	...	2023	...	...	...	...	...	...
Betws y Coed d.	...	0656	0919	...	...	1219	...	1220	...	...	1519	1530	...	1804	1820	...	2050	...	...	...	...	...	...
Llanrwst d.	...	0702	0925	...	...	1225	...	1230	...	...	1525	1540	...	1810	1830	...	2056	...	...	...	...	...	...
Llandudno Junction 165 a.	...	0726	0951	...	...	1251	...	1300	...	...	1551	1610	...	1835	1900	...	2121	...	...	...	...	...	...
Llandudno 165 a.	...	*0741*	1008	...	...	1309	...	1320	...	...	1613	1630	...	1849	1920	...	2142	...	...	...	...	...	...

F – Ffestiniog Railway (www.festrail.co.uk ✆ +44 (0) 1766 516 000). Running dates: Dec. 2, 3, 9, 10, 16, 17, 26 - 31.

NT 2nd class CREWE - MANCHESTER AIRPORT ✈ 167

From CREWE *37 km*
⚒: 0633, 0730⑥, 0831, 0933 and hourly until 1833.
⑦: *No direct trains. Connections available by changing at* ***Wilmslow***.
1018, 1228, 1428, 1631, 1828, 2028, 2223.

From MANCHESTER AIRPORT ✈ Journey: ± 33 minutes (50 - 60 minutes on ⑦)
⚒: 0605, 0711, 0811, 0911 and hourly until 1811.
⑦: *No direct trains. Connections available by changing at* ***Wilmslow***.
1108, 1306, 1506, 1706, 1906, 2106.

EM 2nd class CREWE - STOKE - DERBY 168

km		⚒	⚒	Ⓐ	⑥	⚒		⚒	Ⓐ	⑥		⑦	⑦		⑦		⑦	⑦		⑦	⑦		⑦	⑦
0	**Crewe** 150 d.		0607	0658	0707	0807		1907	2045	2045	...		1404	...	1505	...	1609	1708	...	1810	1908	...	2010	2116
24	Stoke on Trent 150 d.		0633	0724	0733	0833	and	1933	2118	2119	...		1429	...	1532	...	1635	1735	...	1837	1935	...	2040	2142
33	Blythe Bridge d.		0645	0736	0745	0845	hourly	1945	2129	2131	...		1441	...	1544	...	1647	1747	...	1849	1947	...	2052	2159
51	Uttoxeter d.		0658	0749	0758	0858	until	1958	2142	2144	...		1453	...	1556	...	1700	1759	...	1901	1959	...	2104	2212
82	**Derby** 170 a.		0724	0816	0822	0924		2024	2210	2211	...		1521	...	1624	...	1732	1822	...	1924	2027	...	2133	2240

	⚒	⚒		⚒	⚒	Ⓐ		⚒		⚒		⑦	⑦		⑦		⑦	⑦		⑦		⑦		⑦
Derby 170 d.		0640	...	0740	0840	0940		1940	...	2040	...		1438	...	1538	...	1638	1739	...	1839	...	1938	...	2040
Uttoxeter d.		0705	...	0807	0907	1007	and	2007	...	2107	...		1503	...	1603	...	1703	1806	...	1907	...	2005	...	2105
Blythe Bridge d.		0719	...	0821	0921	1021	hourly	2021	...	2121	...		1517	...	1617	...	1717	1820	...	1921	...	2019	...	2119
Stoke on Trent 150 a.		0734	...	0833	0934	1034	until	2034	...	2134	...		1531	...	1629	...	1730	1835	...	1933	...	2032	...	2136
Crewe 150 a.		0801	...	0859	0959	1059		2059	...	2159	...		1603	...	1658	...	1757	1903	...	2001	...	2105	...	2205

HERITAGE and TOURIST RAILWAYS IN NORTH and MID WALES

ABERYSTWYTH – DEVIL'S BRIDGE. (*Vale of Rheidol Steam Railway*)
Narrow gauge. Trains run May to October. Most trains steam hauled. Aberystwyth station is adjacent to the main-line station.
Operator: Vale of Rheidol Railway. ✆ 01970 625819. www.rheidolrailway.co.uk.

FAIRBOURNE – BARMOUTH FERRY. (*Fairbourne and Barmouth Railway*)
Miniature railway. Trains run April to October. Most trains steam hauled. Fairbourne station is a short walk from the main-line station.
Operator: Fairbourne Railway. ✆ 01341 250362. www.fairbournerailway.co.uk.

PORTHMADOG – MINFFORDD – BLAENAU FFESTINIOG. (*Ffestiniog Railway*)
Narrow gauge. Trains run May to October. Most trains steam hauled. See Table **157**.
Porthmadog Station is at least 20 minutes walk from main-line station. Minffordd and Blaenau Ffestiniog stations are adjacent to main-line stations.
Operator: Ffestiniog Railway. ✆ 01766 516000. www.festrail.co.uk.

PORTHMADOG – PEN-Y-MOUNT Junction. (*Welsh Highland Heritage Railway*)
Narrow gauge. Trains run April to October. Most trains steam hauled. Porthmadog station is opposite the main-line station.
Operator: Welsh Highland Heritage Railway. ✆ 01766 513402. www.whr.co.uk.

TYWYN Wharf – **NANT GWERNOL**. (*Talyllyn Railway*)
Narrow gauge. Trains run May to October. Most trains steam hauled. Tywyn Wharf station is 10 minutes walk from the main-line station.
Operator: Talyllyn Railway. ✆ 01654 710472. www.talyllyn.co.uk.

WELSHPOOL Raven Square – **LLANFAIR** Caereinion. (*Welshpool and Llanfair Railway*)
Narrow gauge. Trains run April to September. Most trains steam hauled. Welshpool Raven Square station is approximately 1 mile from the main-line station.
Operator: Welshpool and Llanfair Light Railway. ✆ 01938 810441. www.wllr.org.uk.

170 LONDON - LEICESTER - NOTTINGHAM, DERBY and SHEFFIELD

Most trains 🍸 EM

Services on ⑦ valid until January 31.

km			Ⓐ	⑥	Ⓐ	⑥	⚒	⚒	Ⓐ	⑥	⚒	⚒	⚒	⚒	⚒	⚒	⚒	⚒	⚒	⚒	⚒	⚒	⚒	⚒	⚒
						Y							Ca										Ca		
0	**London** St Pancras ..... **102** d.	⚒	0610	0610	0637	0637	0655	0700	0725	...	0730	0755	0800	0815	0825	0830	0855	0900	0915	0925	0930	0955	1000	1015	1025
47	Luton ✈ Parkway .... **102** d.		|	|	|	|	0716	|	|	...	0751	|	|	|	|	0851	|	|	|	|	0951	|	|	|	|
49	Luton .... **102** d.		0633	0633	0659	0659	|	0723	|	...	|	|	0823	|	|	|	|	0923	|	|	|	|	1023	|	|
80	Bedford .... **102** d.		0648	0648	|	|	|	0738	|	...	0807	|	0838	|	|	0907	|	0938	|	|	1007	|	1038	|	|
105	Wellingborough ....d.		0701	0701	|	|	|	0751	|	...	0820	|	0851	|	|	0920	|	0951	|	|	1020	|	1051	|	|
116	Kettering ....d.		0708	0708	0728	0728	|	0801	|	...	0827	|	0900	|	|	0927	|	1000	|	|	1027	|	1100	|	|
133	Market Harborough ....d.		0718	0718	0738	0738	|	0812	0821	...	0837	|	...	0912	|	0937	|	...	1012	|	1037	|	...	1112	|
159	**Leicester** .... **171** d.		0736	0736	0757	0755	0806	0830	0838	0838	0854	0904	...	0930	0935	0954	1004	...	1030	1035	1054	1104	...	1130	1135
180	Loughborough .... **171** d.		0747	0747	0807	0805	0817	0841	0848	0849	0904	|	...	|	0945	1004	|	...	|	1045	1104	|	...	|	1145
	East Midlands Parkway **171** d.		0754	|	|	|	|	0850	0856	0856	|	|	...	0946	0952	|	|	...	1046	1053	|	|	...	1146	1153
204	**Nottingham** .... **171** a.		|	|	|	|	0842	0903	|	|	0926	|	...	0959	|	1026	|	...	1059	|	1126	|	...	1159	|
207	**Derby** .... **127** a.		0809	0809	0824	0826	...	...	0914	0914	...	0926	...	...	1009	...	1026	...	...	1109	...	1126	...	...	1209
246	Chesterfield .... **127** d.		0838	0837	0847	0847	...	...	0937	0937	...	0947	...	...	1037	...	1047	...	...	1137	...	1147	...	...	1237
265	**Sheffield** .... **127** a.		0852	0852	0904	0907	...	...	0952	0952	...	1004	...	...	1052	...	1104	...	...	1152	...	1204	...	...	1252

	⚒	⚒	⚒	⚒	⚒	⚒	⚒	⚒	⚒	⚒	⚒	⚒	⚒	⚒	⚒	⚒	⚒	⚒	⚒	⚒	⚒	⚒	⚒	⚒	⚒
			Ca					Ca					Ca					C					C		
London St Pancras ..... **102** d.	1030	1055	1100	1115	1125	1130	1155	1200	1215	1225	1230	1255	1300	1315	1325	1330	1355	1400	1415	1425	1430	1455	1500	1515	1525
Luton ✈ Parkway .... **102** d.	1051	|	|	|	|	1151	|	|	|	|	1251	|	|	|	|	1351	|	|	|	|	1451	|	|	|	|
Luton .... **102** d.	|	|	1123	|	|	|	|	1223	|	|	|	|	1323	|	|	|	|	1423	|	|	|	|	1523	|	|
Bedford .... **102** d.	1107	|	1138	|	|	1207	|	1238	|	|	1307	|	1338	|	|	1407	|	1438	|	|	1507	|	1538	|	|
Wellingborough ....d.	1120	|	1151	|	|	1220	|	1251	|	|	1320	|	1351	|	|	1420	|	1451	|	|	1520	|	1551	|	|
Kettering ....d.	1127	|	1200	|	|	1227	|	1303	|	|	1327	|	1400	|	|	1427	|	1500	|	|	1527	|	1601	|	|
Market Harborough ....d.	1137	|	...	1212	|	1237	|	...	1312	|	1337	|	...	1412	|	1437	|	...	1512	|	1537	|	...	1612	|
Leicester .... **171** d.	1154	1204	...	1230	1235	1254	1304	...	1330	1335	1354	1404	...	1430	1435	1454	1504	...	1530	1535	1554	1604	...	1630	1635
Loughborough .... **171** d.	1204	|	...	|	1245	1304	|	...	|	1345	1404	|	...	|	1445	1504	|	...	|	1545	1604	|	...	|	1645
East Midlands Parkway **171** d.	|	|	...	1246	1253	|	|	...	1345	1353	|	|	...	1446	1453	|	|	...	1546	1553	|	|	...	1645	1653
Nottingham .... **171** a.	1226	|	...	1259	|	1327	|	...	1359	|	1426	|	...	1459	|	1526	|	...	1559	|	1626	|	...	1659	|
Derby .... **127** a.	...	1226	...	...	1309	...	1326	...	...	1409	...	1426	...	...	1513	...	1526	...	...	1609	...	1626	...	...	1709
Chesterfield .... **127** d.	...	1247	...	...	1337	...	1347	...	...	1437	...	1447	...	...	1534	...	1547	...	...	1636	...	1647	...	...	1737
Sheffield .... **127** a.	...	1304	...	...	1352	...	1404	...	...	1452	...	1504	...	...	1552	...	1604	...	...	1652	...	1704	...	...	1752

	⚒	⚒	⚒	⚒	⚒	⚒	⚒	Ⓐ	⑥	⑥	Ⓐ	⑥	Ⓐ	⑥	⚒	Ⓐ	Ⓐ	⑥	⑥	Ⓐ	Ⓐ	⑥	⑥	Ⓐ	⑥
			C					A	C					P			M	C			L	L		P	
London St Pancras ..... **102** d.	1530	1555	1600	1615	1625	1630	1655	1700	1700	1715	1715	1725	1730	1730	1755	1745	1800	1800	1825	1825	1815	1815	1830	1830	1855
Luton ✈ Parkway .... **102** d.	1551	|	|	|	|	1651	|	|	|	|	|	|	|	1751	|	1810	|	|	|	|	|	|	1851	1854	|
Luton .... **102** d.	|	|	1623	|	|	|	|	|	1723	|	1741	|	|	|	|	|	1823	1823	|	1851	|	|	|	|	|
Bedford .... **102** d.	1607	|	1638	|	|	1707	|	1735	1738	|	|	|	|	1807	|	|	1838	1838	|	|	|	|	1907	1911	|
Wellingborough ....d.	1620	|	1651	|	|	1720	|	1748	1751	|	|	|	1818	1820	|	1834	1851	1851	|	|	1902	|	1920	1924	|
Kettering ....d.	1627	|	1700	|	|	1727	|	1804	1801	|	|	|	1826	1827	|	1845	1910	1900	|	|	1910	|	1927	1932	|
Market Harborough ....d.	1637	|	...	1712	|	1737	|	|	...	1812	1819	|	1836	1837	|	1900	...	...	|	1928	|	1912	1937	|	|
Leicester .... **171** d.	1654	1704	...	1730	1735	1754	1804	1832	...	1830	1837	1835	1855	1854	1904	1925	...	...	1935	1946	1936	1930	1954	1957	2004
Loughborough .... **171** d.	1704	|	...	|	1745	1804	|	1843	...	|	1853	1845	1905	1904	|	1936	...	...	1945	1957	1947	|	2004	|	|
East Midlands Parkway **171** d.	|	|	...	1746	1752	|	|	1850	...	1846	|	1853	1912	|	|	1944	...	...	1953	|	1955	1946	|	2012	|
Nottingham .... **171** a.	1726	|	...	1759	|	1830	|	|	...	1859	1910	|	1927	1926	|	1958	...	...	|	|	2008	1959	2026	2028	|
Derby .... **127** a.	...	1726	...	...	1814	...	1826	1909	...	...	...	1909	...	...	1928	2035	...	...	2009	2019	|	|	...	...	2026
Chesterfield .... **127** d.	...	1747	...	...	1839	...	1847	1937	...	...	...	1937	...	...	1947	...	...	...	2037	2041	2053	2053	...	...	2047
Sheffield .... **127** a.	...	1804	...	...	1859	...	1904	1952	...	...	...	1955	...	...	2006	...	...	...	2054	2058	2114	2114	...	...	2100

	Ⓐ	⚒	⑥	Ⓐ	⑥	Ⓐ	⑥	⚒	Ⓐ	⚒	Ⓐ	⑥	⚒	⚒	⑥	Ⓐ	Ⓐ	⑥	⑥	Ⓐ	⑥	Ⓐ	Ⓐ	⑥	⑥
		C						L	L	C														b	c
London St Pancras ..... **102** d.	1855	1900	1915	1915	1925	1925	1930	1955	1930	2000	2015	2015	2025	2030	2055	2055	2100	2100	2125	2125	2130	2130	2200	2200	2200
Luton ✈ Parkway .... **102** d.	|	|	|	|	|	|	1951	|	1951	|	|	|	|	2051	|	|	|	|	|	|	2151	2153	|	|	|
Luton .... **102** d.	|	1923	|	|	|	|	|	|	|	2023	|	|	|	|	|	|	2123	2123	|	|	|	|	2224	2236	2236
Bedford .... **102** d.	|	1938	|	|	|	|	2007	|	2007	2038	|	|	|	2107	|	|	2138	2138	|	|	2210	2209	2240	2258	2258
Wellingborough ....d.	|	1951	|	|	|	|	2020	|	2020	2051	|	|	|	2120	|	|	2151	2151	|	|	2222	2222	2253	2311	2311
Kettering ....d.	|	2001	|	|	|	2017	2027	|	|	2101	|	|	|	2127	|	|	2158	2201	|	|	2230	2231	2301	2320	2320
Market Harborough ....d.	1954	...	2012	2012	|	2027	2037	|	2037	...	2111	2112	|	2137	|	|	2208	2212	2220	2223	2240	2242	2312	2331	2331
Leicester .... **171** d.	2013	...	2030	2030	2035	2043	2054	2104	2054	...	2126	2130	2135	2154	2204	2204	2228	2230	2237	2241	2254	2302	2330	2349	2349
Loughborough .... **171** d.	2023	...	|	|	2045	2054	2104	|	2104	...	|	|	2145	2204	|	|	|	2241	2248	2252	2307	2313	2341	0002	0002
East Midlands Parkway **171** d.	2031	...	2046	2045	2053	2101	|	|	|	...	2143	2146	2153	2227	|	|	2246	|	2255	2301	2314	2324	2350	0010	0011
Nottingham .... **171** a.	|	...	2059	2107	|	|	2126	|	2129	...	2158	2201	|	...	|	|	|	|	2306	2312	|	|	0014	...	0027
Derby .... **127** a.	2046	...	...	...	2110	2116	...	2132	|	...	...	...	2212	...	2226	2226	2259	2302	...	...	2329	2350	...	...	...
Chesterfield .... **127** d.	2109	...	...	...	...	...	...	2155	2221	...	...	...	...	...	2247	2247	...	...	...	...	...	...	...	...	...
Sheffield .... **127** a.	2125	...	...	...	...	...	...	2216	2237	...	...	...	...	...	2300	2304	...	...	...	...	...	...	...	...	...

	Ⓐ	⑥	Ⓐ			⑦	⑦	⑦	⑦	⑦	⑦	⑦	⑦	⑦	⑦	⑦	⑦	⑦	⑦	⑦	⑦	⑦	⑦	⑦	⑦
		d				Y												L							
London St Pancras ..... **102** d.	2225	2225	2315	...	⑦	...	0900	0930	1000	1030	1000	1130	1200	1230	1300	1330	1400	1430	1500	1530	1600	1625	1630	1655	1700
Luton ✈ Parkway .... **102** d.	2248	2303	|	...		...	0923	|	1027	|	1129	1156	1227	1257	1329	1402	1429	|	1529	|	1629	|	|	|	1721
Luton .... **102** d.	|	|	2346	...		...	|	0955	|	1059	1132	1159	1230	1300	1333	1406	|	1501	|	1601	|	|	1652	|	|
Bedford .... **102** d.	2304	2328	0010	...		...	0952	1021	1050	1125	1155	1225	1256	1326	1356	1421	1447	1517	1547	1617	1647	|	1715	|	1745
Wellingborough ....d.	2317	2341	0023	...		...	1006	1037	1104	1139	1209	1240	1310	1340	1410	1435	1500	1531	1601	1631	1700	|	1728	|	1758
Kettering ....d.	2326	2350	0040	...		...	1015	1044	1113	1146	1216	1248	1317	1349	1417	1443	1508	1539	1609	1639	1708	|	1736	|	1806
Market Harborough ....d.	2337	0001	0050	...		...	1026	1054	1124	1156	1226	1258	1327	1400	1427	1454	1518	1550	1620	1650	1718	|	1746	|	1816
Leicester .... **171** d.	2355	0019	0105	...		1010	1048	1116	1146	1219	1247	1319	1348	1422	1448	1518	1539	1619	1643	1712	1739	1749	1810	1822	1837
Loughborough .... **171** d.	0006	0030	0115	...		1021	1059	1126	1157	1229	1357	1330	1358	1433	1458	1529	1549	1630	1654	1724	1749	|	1820	|	1847
East Midlands Parkway **171** d.	0014	0038	0123	...		|	1107	1134	1205	1237	1305	1337	1406	1441	1506	1537	1557	1638	1702	1732	1757	1805	1828	1836	1855
Nottingham .... **171** a.	|	|	0144	...		|	1122	|	1219	|	1319	|	1422	|	1520	|	1612	|	1714	|	1814	|	1848	1852	1911
Derby .... **127** a.	0034	0052	0210	...		1046	...	1149	...	1251	...	1352	...	1500	...	1556	...	1655	...	1753	...	1817	...	...	...
Chesterfield .... **127** d.	0058	...	...	...		1109	...	1210	...	1312	...	1413	...	1522	...	1618	...	1717	...	|	...	1840	...	...	...
Sheffield .... **127** a.	0113	...	...	...		1128	...	1228	...	1328	...	1428	...	1541	...	1633	...	1732	...	1829	...	1857	...	...	...

	⑦		⑦	⑦		⑦	⑦	⑦		⑦	⑦	⑦		⑦	⑦	⑦		⑦	⑦	⑦		⑦	⑦		⑦
London St Pancras ..... **102** d.	1725	...	1730	1755	...	1800	1825	1830	...	1855	1900	1925	...	1930	1955	2000	...	2025	2030	2100	...	2130	2230	...	2300
Luton ✈ Parkway .... **102** d.	|	...	|	|	...	1821	|	|	...	|	1921	|	...	|	|	2023	...	|	|	2123	...	|	2253	...	2328
Luton .... **102** d.	|	...	1752	|	...	|	|	1852	...	|	|	|	...	1952	|	|	...	|	2054	|	...	2154	|	...	|
Bedford .... **102** d.	|	...	1815	|	...	1845	|	1915	...	|	1945	|	...	2015	|	2048	...	|	2118	2147	...	2217	2317	...	2352
Wellingborough ....d.	|	...	1828	|	...	1858	|	1928	...	|	1958	|	...	2028	|	2100	...	|	2131	2200	...	2230	2331	...	0016
Kettering ....d.	|	...	1836	|	...	1906	|	1936	...	|	2006	|	...	2036	|	2108	...	|	2139	2208	...	2238	2338	...	0013
Market Harborough ....d.	|	...	1846	|	...	1916	|	1946	...	|	2016	|	...	2046	|	2118	...	|	2150	2218	...	2248	2348	...	0023
Leicester .... **171** d.	1846	...	1911	1921	...	1937	1949	2007	...	2020	2037	2049	...	2107	2119	2139	...	2149	2213	2239	...	2309	0009	...	0044
Loughborough .... **171** d.	|	...	1921	|	...	1947	|	2017	...	|	2047	|	...	2117	2130	2149	...	2201	|	2249	...	2319	0019	...	0054
East Midlands Parkway **171** d.	1900	...	1929	1935	...	1955	2008	2025	...	2034	2055	2105	...	2125	2139	2157	...	2209	2229	2257	...	2327	0027	...	0102
Nottingham .... **171** a.	|	...	|	1951	...	2008	|	|	...	|	2112	|	...	|	2152	2211	...	|	|	2318	...	|	0048	...	|
Derby .... **127** a.	1914	...	1945	...	...	...	2020	2045	...	2048	...	2117	...	2140	...	...	...	2221	2243	...	...	2349	...	...	0121
Chesterfield .... **127** d.	1935	...	...	...	...	...	2043	...	...	...	...	2140	...	...	...	...	...	...	2313	...	...	0010	...	...	...
Sheffield .... **127** a.	1950	...	...	...	...	...	2058	...	...	...	...	2155	...	...	...	...	...	...	2328	...	...	0024	...	...	...

KETTERING - CORBY. *Journey 9 minutes.*

From **Kettering**:

⚒: 0738, 0832Ⓐ, 0928**S**, 1131**S**, 1231**S**, 1331**S**, 1415**S**, 1501**S**, 1601**S**, 1701**S**, 1801⑥**S**, 1808Ⓐ**S**, 1901⑥**S**, 1910Ⓐ**S**, 2001**S**, 2101**S**, 2205, 2300⑥, 2305Ⓐ.

⑦: 0955, 1055, 1155, 1255, 1355, 1455, 1545, 1645, 1750, 1850, 1945, 2046, 2155.

From **Corby**:

⚒: 0634Ⓐ**S**, 0708, 0803Ⓐ, 0815⑥**S**, 0915**S**, 1115**S**, 1215**S**, 1315**S**, 1405**S**, 1443**S**, 1543**S**, 1643**S**, 1743**S**, 1843Ⓐ**S**, 1848Ⓐ**S**, 1943**S**, 2043**S**, 2143, 2243.

⑦: 0937, 1037, 1138, 1236, 1343, 1440, 1532, 1629, 1732, 1830, 2136.

FOR FOOTNOTES AND RETURN SERVICE SEE NEXT PAGE.

EM Most trains 🍸 SHEFFIELD, DERBY and NOTTINGHAM - LEICESTER - LONDON 170

Services on ⑦ valid until January 31.

	⚒	⚒	Ⓐ	Ⓐ	⑥	Ⓐ	Ⓐ N	⑥	⑥	Ⓐ	Ⓐ	⑥	⑥	Ⓐ	Ⓐ	⑥	Ⓐ L	⑥	Ⓐ	⑥	Ⓐ	⑥	⑥ C	Ⓐ	Ⓐ
Sheffield 127 d.		...	...	...	...	...	...	0527	...	0527	...	...	...	0556	...	0625	0627	...	...	...	0647	...	...	...	...
Chesterfield 127 d.		...	...	...	...	...	...	0539	...	0539	...	...	...	0609	...	0637	0639	...	...	...	0659	...	...	...	...
Derby 127 d.		...	0455	0517	0525	...	...	0601	...	0603	...	0618	...	0632	...	0701	0705	...	...	0718	0720	...	...	0726	...
Nottingham 171 d.		...	|	|	|	0532	...	|	0602	|	0628	|	0628	|	0648	|	|	0702	0710	|	|	0728	...	|	0750
East Midlands Parkway 171 d.		...	0506	|	0539	0543	...	|	|	0616	0640	0632	0639	|	0701	|	|	|	0725	0732	0734	0739	...	|	0801
Loughborough 171 d.		...	0514	|	0547	0551	...	|	0620	0624	|	0640	|	0652	|	|	0722	0720	|	0740	0742	|	...	0747	|
Leicester 171 d.		0440	0526	0544	0559	0605	...	0625	0633	0638	0657	0653	0657	0706	0716	0725	0735	0733	0742	0753	0755	0757	...	0801	0818
Market Harborough d.		|	0541	0558	0614	0620	...	|	0647	0653	0712	|	0712	|	0731	|	|	0747	0758	|	|	0812	...	0816	|
Kettering d.		0501	0551	0609	0626	0631	0644	|	0656	0705	0722	0726	|	0729	0741	|	0759	0756	0809	|	0817	|	0826	0828	|
Wellingborough d.		0509	0559	0617	0634	0639	0653	|	0704	0713	0730	0734	|	0738	0749	|	0807	0804	|	|	0825	|	0834	0839	|
Bedford 102 d.		0532	|	0632	0649	|	0708	|	0719	|	|	0749	|	0755	|	|	|	0819	0829	|	|	|	0849	0902	|
Luton 102 d.		|	0624	|	0705	|	0724	|	|	|	0756	0805	|	|	0815	|	|	|	|	|	|	|	0905	0919	|
Luton ✈ Parkway 102 d.		0555	|	|	|	0705	|	|	0735	0740	|	|	|	0812	|	|	|	0835	|	|	|	|	|	|	|
London St Pancras 102 a.		0621	0653	0713	0731	0736	0753	0734	0800	0809	0826	0831	0812	0838	0844	0834	0857	0901	0908	0906	0913	0912	0929	0947	0930

	⚒	⚒ P	Ⓐ	⑥	⚒ L	⚒ C	⚒	⚒	⚒	⑥ L	Ⓐ	⚒	⚒	⚒	Ⓐ	⑥	⚒	⚒ C	⚒	⚒	⚒	⚒	⚒ C	⚒	⚒
Sheffield 127 d.	0727	...	0741	...	0732	...	0827	...	0847	0832	...	...	0927	...	0935	0947	...	...	1027	...	1047	...	...	1127	...
Chesterfield 127 d.	0739	...	|	...	0745	...	0839	...	|	0845	...	...	0939	...	0947	|	...	...	1039	...	|	...	...	1139	...
Derby 127 d.	0801	...	0816	0818	|	...	0901	...	0918	|	...	...	1001	...	1018	1018	...	...	1101	...	1118	...	...	1201	...
Nottingham 171 d.	|	0802	|	|	0828	...	|	0902	|	0928	0928	...	|	1002	|	|	1028	...	|	1102	|	1128	...	|	1202
East Midlands Parkway 171 d.	|	|	0832	0832	0839	...	|	|	0932	0939	0939	...	|	|	1032	1032	1039	...	|	|	1132	1139	...	|	|
Loughborough 171 d.	|	0820	0840	0840	|	...	|	0920	0940	|	|	...	|	1020	1040	1040	|	...	|	1120	1140	|	...	|	1220
Leicester 171 d.	0825	0833	0852	0853	0857	...	0925	0933	0953	0957	0957	...	1025	1033	1053	1053	1057	...	1125	1133	1153	1157	...	1225	1233
Market Harborough d.	|	0847	|	|	0912	...	|	0947	|	1012	1012	...	|	1047	|	|	1112	...	|	1147	|	1212	...	|	1247
Kettering d.	|	0856	|	|	|	0926	|	0956	|	|	|	1024	|	1056	|	|	|	1126	|	1156	|	|	1226	|	1256
Wellingborough d.	|	0904	|	|	|	0934	|	1004	|	|	|	1032	|	1104	|	|	|	1134	|	1204	|	|	1234	|	1304
Bedford 102 d.	|	0919	|	|	|	0949	|	1019	|	|	|	1049	|	1119	|	|	|	1149	|	1219	|	|	1249	|	1319
Luton 102 d.	|	|	|	|	|	1004	|	|	|	|	|	1105	|	|	|	|	|	1205	|	|	|	|	1305	|	|
Luton ✈ Parkway 102 d.	|	0934	|	|	|	|	|	1034	|	|	|	|	|	1135	|	|	|	|	|	1235	|	|	|	|	1335
London St Pancras 102 a.	0937	1000	1005	1006	1019	1030	1034	1101	1106	1112	1118	1129	1134	1202	1206	1206	1212	1229	1234	1301	1307	1312	1329	1334	1402

	⚒	⚒	⚒ C	⚒	⚒	Ⓐ	⑥	⚒	⚒ C	⚒	⚒	⚒	⚒	⚒ Ca	⚒	⚒	Ⓐ	⑥	⚒	⚒ Ca	⚒	⚒	⑥	Ⓐ	⑥
Sheffield 127 d.	1147	...	...	1227	...	1235	1247	...	...	1327	...	1347	...	...	1427	...	1435	1447	...	...	1527	...	1547	1547	...
Chesterfield 127 d.	|	...	...	1239	...	|	|	...	...	1339	...	|	...	...	1439	...	1447	|	...	...	1539	...	|	|	...
Derby 127 d.	1218	...	...	1301	...	1318	1318	...	...	1401	...	1418	...	...	1501	...	1518	1518	...	...	1601	...	1618	1618	...
Nottingham 171 d.	|	1228	...	|	1302	|	|	1328	...	|	1402	|	1428	...	|	1502	|	|	1528	...	|	1602	|	|	1628
East Midlands Parkway 171 d.	1232	1239	...	|	|	1332	1332	1339	...	|	|	1432	1439	...	|	|	1532	1532	1539	...	|	|	1632	1632	1639
Loughborough 171 d.	1240	|	...	|	1320	1340	1340	|	...	|	1420	1440	|	...	|	1520	1540	1540	|	...	|	1620	1640	1640	|
Leicester 171 d.	1253	1257	...	1325	1333	1353	1353	1357	...	1425	1433	1453	1457	...	1525	1533	1553	1553	1557	...	1625	1633	1653	1653	1657
Market Harborough d.	|	1312	...	|	1347	|	|	1412	...	|	1447	|	1512	...	|	1547	|	|	1612	...	|	1647	|	|	1712
Kettering d.	|	|	1326	|	1356	|	|	|	1426	|	1456	|	|	1526	|	1556	|	|	|	1626	|	1656	|	1715	|
Wellingborough d.	|	|	1334	|	1404	|	|	|	1434	|	1504	|	|	1534	|	1604	|	|	|	1634	|	1704	|	|	|
Bedford 102 d.	|	|	1349	|	1419	|	|	|	1449	|	1519	|	|	1549	|	1619	|	|	|	1649	|	1717	|	|	|
Luton 102 d.	|	|	1405	|	|	|	|	|	1505	|	|	|	|	1605	|	|	|	|	|	1705	|	|	|	|	|
Luton ✈ Parkway 102 d.	|	|	|	|	1435	|	|	|	|	|	1535	|	|	|	|	1635	|	|	|	|	|	1730	|	|	|
London St Pancras 102 a.	1407	1414	1429	1438	1501	1507	1506	1513	1529	1534	1601	1606	1613	1629	1634	1701	1707	1706	1720	1729	1734	1806	1806	1811	1812

	Ⓐ	⚒ Ca	⑥	Ⓐ	⚒	Ⓐ	⑥	⚒	⚒ Ca	⚒	⚒	⚒	⚒	⚒ Ca	⚒	⚒	⑥ Y	Ⓐ	⚒	⚒ Ca	⚒	⚒	Ⓐ Ca	⑥ Ca	⑥
Sheffield 127 d.	...	...	1627	1627	...	1635	1635	...	...	1727	...	1735	...	...	1827	...	1847	1835	...	...	1927	...	...	...	...
Chesterfield 127 d.	...	...	1639	1639	...	1650	1647	...	...	1739	...	1750	...	...	1839	...	|	|	...	...	1939	...	...	...	...
Derby 127 d.	...	...	1701	1701	...	1718	1718	...	...	1801	...	1818	...	...	1901	...	1921	1918	...	...	2001	...	...	...	...
Nottingham 171 d.	1628	...	|	|	1702	|	|	1728	...	|	1802	|	1828	...	|	1902	|	|	1928	...	|	2002	...	...	2043
East Midlands Parkway 171 d.	1639	...	|	|	|	1732	1732	1739	...	|	|	1832	1839	...	|	|	1935	1932	1939	...	|	2016	...	...	2055
Loughborough 171 d.	|	...	|	|	1720	1740	1740	|	...	|	1820	1840	|	...	|	1920	1941	1940	|	...	|	2024	...	...	2103
Leicester 171 d.	1657	...	1725	1725	1733	1753	1753	1757	...	1825	1833	1853	1857	...	1925	1933	1955	1953	1957	...	2025	2036	...	...	2115
Market Harborough d.	1712	...	|	|	1747	|	|	1812	...	|	1847	|	1912	...	|	1947	|	|	2012	...	|	2050	...	...	2129
Kettering d.	|	1726	|	|	1756	1815	|	|	1826	|	1856	|	|	1924	|	1956	|	|	|	2026	|	2059	2117	2124	2138
Wellingborough d.	|	1734	|	|	1804	|	|	|	1834	|	1904	|	|	1932	|	2004	|	|	|	2034	|	2107	2126	2132	2147
Bedford 102 d.	|	1749	|	|	1819	|	|	|	1849	|	1919	|	|	1943	|	2017	|	|	|	2049	|	2120	2149	2145	2202
Luton 102 d.	1750	1805	|	1815	|	|	|	|	1905	|	|	|	|	2004	|	|	|	|	|	2105	|	|	2209	2204	2220
Luton ✈ Parkway 102 d.	|	|	|	|	1835	|	|	|	|	|	1930	|	|	|	|	2030	|	|	|	|	|	2136	|	|	2223
London St Pancras 102 a.	1819	1829	1834	1839	1901	1907	1909	1918	1931	1935	2002	2007	2012	2029	2034	2106	2106	2110	2115	2134	2138	2206	2235	2244	2259

	Ⓐ	⑥	⑥	Ⓐ	Ⓐ		⑦	⑦	⑦	⑦	⑦	⑦	⑦	⑦	⑦	⑦	⑦ L	⑦ L	⑦	⑦	⑦	⑦	⑦	⑦	⑦
Sheffield 127 d.	...	2027	...	2039	...	...	...	...	...	...	...	...	0917	...	1017	1028	1106	...	1224	...	1320	...	1407	...
Chesterfield 127 d.	...	2039	...	2053	...	...	...	...	...	...	...	...	0929	...	1029	1041	1125	...	1237	...	1333	...	1420	...
Derby 127 d.	...	2100	...	2120	...	...	0650	...	0752	...	0847	...	0951	...	1052	|	1148	...	1302	...	1354	...	1449	...
Nottingham 171 d.	2102	|	2118	|	2128	...	|	*0658**	|	*0731**	|	*0846**	|	1015	|	1119	|	1215	|	1314	|	1430	|	1510
East Midlands Parkway 171 d.	2115	2114	|	2133	|	...	0702	0738	0803	0832	0902	0926	1005	1030	1106	1130	1201	1230	1316	1330	1409	1443	1508	1523
Loughborough 171 d.	2122	2123	2132	2141	2147	...	|	|	0811	0839	0910	0934	1013	1038	1114	1138	1209	1238	1324	1338	1417	1451	1515	1530
Leicester 171 d.	2133	2139	2145	2155	2200	...	0720	0754	0823	0852	0922	0949	1025	1053	1126	1153	1223	1253	1336	1353	1429	1504	1527	1544
Market Harborough d.	2147	...	2159	|	2214	...	0738	0811	0840	0909	0939	1007	1039	1108	1140	1208	1238	1308	1350	1408	1443	1518	|	1601
Kettering d.	2157	...	2215	|	2224	...	0749	0821	0850	0919	0951	1018	1051	1119	1150	1219	1249	1319	1400	1419	1453	1528	|	1611
Wellingborough d.	2205	...	2222	|	2232	...	0801	0832	0902	0930	1004	1026	1059	1127	1158	1227	1257	1327	1407	1429	1500	1535	|	1618
Bedford 102 d.	2219	...	2237	|	2246	...	0815	0845	0914	0945	1016	1045	1116	1145	1215	1246	1315	1346	1425	1454	1525	1555	|	1635
Luton 102 d.	2234	...	2259	|	2305	...	0834	|	0939	|	1041	|	1139	|	1240	|	1339	|	1449	|	1542	|	1625	|
Luton ✈ Parkway 102 d.	2238	...	|	|	|	...	|	0911	|	1010	|	1110	|	1209	|	1310	|	1410	|	1511	|	1614	|	1653
London St Pancras 102 a.	2304	...	2335	2307	2338	...	0916	0950	1020	1049	1120	1149	1220	1250	1320	1350	1419	1444	1522	1545	1615	1645	1655	1727

	⑦	⑦	⑦		⑦	⑦	⑦		⑦	⑦	⑦		⑦	⑦	⑦		⑦	⑦ Y	⑦		⑦	⑦	⑦		⑦
Sheffield 127 d.	...	1502	1532	...	...	...	...	...	1629	...	...	...	...	1729	...	...	...	1832	...	...	1931	2024	...	...	2213
Chesterfield 127 d.	...	1515	1544	...	...	...	...	...	1643	...	...	...	...	1743	...	...	...	1844	...	...	1944	2038	...	...	2227
Derby 127 d.	...	1538	1614	...	...	...	1647	...	1709	...	...	...	1747	1807	...	...	...	1909	...	...	2006	2059	...	...	2304
Nottingham 171 d.	1536	|	|	...	1618	1645	|	...	|	1720	1734	...	|	|	1810	...	1844	|	1946	...	|	|	2113	...	...
East Midlands Parkway 171 d.	1546	1552	1625	...	1631	1655	1701	...	1721	1732	1749	...	1801	1820	1825	...	1854	1926	1958	...	2021	2111	2123	...	...
Loughborough 171 d.	|	1601	|	...	1639	|	1709	...	|	1740	|	...	1809	|	1833	...	1902	1933	2006	...	2030	|	2131	...	...
Leicester 171 d.	1603	1615	1641	...	1652	1713	1722	...	1740	1752	1808	...	1821	1840	1845	...	1915	1945	2018	...	2044	2130	2143	...	...
Market Harborough d.	|	1630	|	...	1706	|	1736	...	|	1806	|	...	1835	|	1905	...	1931	2003	2032	...	2059	2145	2157	...	...
Kettering d.	|	1641	|	...	1716	|	1746	...	|	1816	|	...	1845	|	1915	...	1941	2013	2042	...	2110	2156	2207	...	...
Wellingborough d.	|	1649	|	...	1723	|	1753	...	|	1823	|	...	1852	|	1922	...	1948	2021	2049	...	2118	2204	2214	...	...
Bedford 102 d.	|	1707	|	...	1740	|	1811	...	|	1840	|	...	1910	|	1940	...	2007	2040	2108	...	2137	2224	2232	...	...
Luton 102 d.	|	1725	|	...	|	|	1829	...	|	|	|	...	1929	|	|	...	2026	|	2123	...	2152	2240	2250	...	...
Luton ✈ Parkway 102 d.	|	|	|	...	1759	|	|	...	|	1859	|	...	|	|	1959	...	|	2055	|	...	|	|	|	...	...
London St Pancras 102 a.	1731	1759	1804	...	1829	1834	1859	...	1904	1929	1934	...	1959	2004	2029	...	2057	2127	2157	...	2227	2313	2327	...	...

A – Conveys (12) London St Pancras - Corby.
C – To / from Corby.
L – To / from Leeds, Table **127**.
M – To Corby, Oakham (a. 1943) and Melton Mowbray (a. 1955).
N – From Melton Mowbray (d. 0559) Oakham (d. 0610) and Corby.
P – To / from Lincoln, Table **171**.

S – To / from London St Pancras.
Y – To / from York, Table **125**.
a – Waits at Kettering for up to 31 minutes before departing for Corby / London.
b – ⑥ Dec. 19 – Jan. 30.
c – ⑥ Feb. 6 – May 22.
d – ⑥ Dec. 19 – Jan. 30 and Apr. 3 – May 22.

* – By 🚌.

FOR SERVICES KETTERING – CORBY AND V.V., SEE PREVIOUS PAGE.

171 NOTTINGHAM - SHEFFIELD - BARNSLEY - LEEDS

2nd class NT

Services on ⑦ valid until March 28.

km			⚒	Ⓐ	⑥	Ⓐ	⚒	⚒	⚒	⚒	⚒	⚒		⚒	⚒	⚒	⚒	⚒	⚒	⚒	⚒E	Ⓐ	①-④	⑥
0	**Nottingham** 170 206 d.	⚒	...	...	...	0623	...	0713	...	0811	...	0915	and at the same minutes past each hour until ◇	...	1715	...	1815	...	1915	...	2015	2045	...	2115
18	Langley Mill d.		...	...	...	0638	...	0729	...	0831	...	0932		...	1731	...	1832	...	1932	...	2033	|	...	2131
29	Alfreton 206 d.		...	...	...	0646	...	0737	...	0839	...	0940		...	1739	...	1840	...	1940	...	2041	|	...	2139
45	Chesterfield 170 206 d.		...	0626	...	0658	...	0750	...	0851	...	0952		...	1752	...	1852	...	1952	...	2053	2128	...	2150
64	**Sheffield** 170 206 a.		...	0646	...	0718	...	0808	...	0915	...	1015		...	1815	...	1915	...	2015	...	2114	2154	...	2213
64	**Sheffield** 192 193 d.		0606	0649	0706	0720	0751	0818	0851	0918	0951	1018		1751	1818	1851	1918	1951	2018	2106	2124	...	2206	...
70	Meadowhall 192 193 d.		0612	0655	0712	0726	0757	0824	0857	0924	0957	1024		1757	1824	1857	1924	1957	2024	2112	|	...	2212	...
90	Barnsley d.		0633	0712	0733	0742	0812	0842	0912	0942	1012	1042		1812	1842	1912	1942	2012	2042	2133	|	...	2233	...
107	Wakefield Kirkgate d.		0650	0728	0750	0758	0828	0858	0928	0958	1028	1058		1832	1858	1932	1958	2028	2058	2152	2152g	...	2250	...
130	**Leeds** 127 185 187 a.		0728	0751	0825	0821	0849	0919	0949	1018	1048	1118		1851	1923	1955	2019	2048	2122	2228	2212	...	2328	...

	⚒E	ⒶE			⑦	⑦	⑦		⑦	⑦	⑦	⑦	⑦	⑦	⑦	⑦E	⑦	⑦	⑦	⑦	⑦E	⑦	⑦	⑦	⑦E
Nottingham 170 206 d.	...	2143	...	⑦	...	...	...	...	1006	1115	1219	1309	1419	1512	1614	...	1714	1814	1919	...	...	2013	2120	...	...
Langley Mill d.	...	2201	...		...	...	...	...	1027	1131	1235	1327	1435	1534	1630	...	1730	1830	1935	...	...	2029	2141	...	...
Alfreton 206 d.	...	2209	...		...	...	...	...	1035	1139	1243	1335	1443	1542	1638	...	1738	1838	1943	...	...	2037	2149	...	...
Chesterfield 170 206 d.	2155	2221	...		...	...	...	...	1054	1151	1254	1351	1454	1553	1650	1717	1749	1849	1954	...	2043	2048	2208	...	2313
Sheffield 170 206 a.	2216	2237	...		...	...	...	...	1115	1215	1315	1415	1515	1615	1715	1732	1815	1915	2015	...	2058	2114	2232	...	2328
Sheffield 192 193 d.	2219	2248	...		0839	0917	1039	...	1117	1216	1317	1417	1517	1617	1717	1734	1817	1916	2017	2039	2103	...	...	2239	2330
Meadowhall 192 193 d.	|	|	...		0845	0923	1045	...	1123	1223	1323	1423	1523	1623	1723	|	1823	1923	2023	2045	|	...	...	2245	|
Barnsley d.	|	|	...		0910	0937	1110	...	1137	1237	1337	1437	1537	1637	1737	|	1837	1937	2037	2110	|	...	...	2310	|
Wakefield Kirkgate d.	2245g	2322g	...		0930	0955	1130	...	1153	1253	1353	1453	1553	1653	1753	1807g	1853	1953	2053	2130	2133g	...	...	2330	2356g
Leeds 127 185 187 a.	2305	2338	...		1014	1015	1205	...	1218	1318	1418	1518	1618	1718	1818	1824	1918	2018	2116	2204	2149	...	...	0004	0032

		Ⓐ	⑥	Ⓐ	ⒶE	⑥	Ⓐ	⚒E	⚒	⑥E		⚒	⚒	⚒	⚒	⚒		⚒	⚒	⚒	⚒	⚒	⑥	Ⓐ
Leeds 127 185 187 d.	⚒	...	...	...	0525	...	0605	0634	0705	0734	...	0735	0802	0837	0905	0937	and at the same minutes past each hour until ◇	1605	1637	1705	1737	1805	1837	1843
Wakefield Kirkgate d.		...	...	...	0537g	...	0621	0646g	0725	0746g	...	0755	0823	0855	0923	0955		1623	1655	1723	1755	1823	1855	1859
Barnsley d.		...	...	...	|	0621	0638	|	0740	|	...	0814	0840	0914	0940	1014		1640	1714	1740	1814	1840	1914	1918
Meadowhall 192 193 d.		...	...	...	|	0642	0649	|	0754	|	...	0831	0852	0928	0952	1028		1652	1726	1752	1827	1852	1928	1934
Sheffield 192 193 a.		...	...	...	0618	0655	0700	0725	0805	0821	...	0839	0902	0937	1002	1037		1702	1737	1802	1838	1903	1937	1943
Sheffield 170 206 d.		0505	0554	0600	0627	0703	0703	0732	0805	0832	...	...	0905	...	1005	...		1705	...	1805	...	1905	...	...
Chesterfield 170 206 d.		0520	0620	0616	0639	0720	0720	0745	0822	0845	...	...	0922	...	1022	...		1722	...	1822	...	1922	...	...
Alfreton 206 d.		|	0630	0630	...	0733	0733	0756	0835	0856	...	...	0933	...	1033	...		1733	...	1833	...	1933	...	...
Langley Mill d.		|	0638	0637	...	0740	0740	0804	0842	|	...	...	0940	...	1040	...		1740	...	1840	...	1940	...	...
Nottingham 170 206 a.		0612	0704	0708	...	0802	0802	0823	0901	0921	...	...	1000	...	1100	...		1800	...	1900	...	2000	...	...

	⚒	⚒	⚒	⚒	⚒	Ⓐ			⑦	⑦	⑦	⑦E	⑦	⑦	⑦	⑦	⑦	⑦	⑦	⑦	⑦	⑦	⑦		⑦
Leeds 127 185 187 d.	1905	1943	2030	2037	2137	2237	...	⑦	...	0834	0905	0935	1002	1057	1129	1229	1405	1505	1605	1705	1805	1904	2017	...	2217
Wakefield Kirkgate d.	1923	2000	2046	2107	2207	2310	...		...	0903	0921	0947g	1018	1113	1146	1246	1421	1522	1622	1721	1822	1920	2046	...	2246
Barnsley d.	1940	2016	2103	2124	2225	2331	...		...	0924	0941	|	1038	1133	1206	1306	1441	1542	1642	1741	1842	1940	2112	...	2312
Meadowhall 192 193 d.	1952	2032	2119	2146	2247	2351	...		...	0944	0955	|	1051	1146	1217	1318	1456	1556	1656	1756	1856	1954	2133	...	2332
Sheffield 192 193 a.	2003	2044	2130	2158	2258	0002	...		...	0955	1004	1021	1100	1156	1229	1329	1506	1605	1705	1805	1905	2004	2142	...	2343
Sheffield 170 206 d.	2005	...	...	...	...	...	...		0900	...	1007	1028	1103	1200	1231	1331	1507	1607	1707	1807	1907	2006	...	...	...
Chesterfield 170 206 d.	2022	...	...	...	...	...	...		0917	...	1023	1041	1120	1218	1249	1348	1525	1625	1724	1825	1925	2022	...	...	...
Alfreton 206 d.	2033	...	...	...	...	...	...		0928	...	1035	...	1131	1229	1259	1359	1536	1636	1735	1836	1936	2033	...	...	...
Langley Mill d.	2040	...	...	...	...	...	...		0935	...	1042	...	1138	1236	1307	1406	1543	1643	1743	1843	1943	2040	...	...	...
Nottingham 170 206 a.	2100	...	...	...	...	...	...		0957	...	1102	...	1158	1256	1326	1426	1603	1703	1803	1903	2003	2101	...	...	...

SHEFFIELD - BARNSLEY - HUDDERSFIELD

km			Ⓐ	⚒	⚒	⚒		⚒	⚒	⚒	⚒	⚒	⚒	⚒			⑦	⑦	⑦	⑦	⑦	⑦	⑦	⑦
0	**Sheffield** d.	⚒	0536	0636	0736	0836	and hourly until	1636	1736	1836	1936	2041	2141	2241	...	⑦	0939	1149	1235	1339	1539	1654	1739	1939
6	Meadowhall d.		0542	0642	0742	0842		1642	1742	1842	1942	2047	2147	2247	...		0945	1155	1241	1345	1543	1700	1746	1945
26	Barnsley d.		0601	0701	0801	0901		1703	1803	1908r	2008	2108	2208	2308	...		1006	1216	1306	1406	1604	1715	1810	2006
59	**Huddersfield** a.		0649	0749	0849	0949		1750	1857r	1956r	2055	2156	2256	2356	...		1053	1303	1353	1453	1653	1805	1858	2053

		⚒	⚒	⚒	⚒		⚒	Ⓐ	⑥	Ⓐ	⚒	⚒	⚒	⚒			⑦	⑦	⑦	⑦	⑦	⑦	⑦	⑦
Huddersfield d.	⚒	0610	0710	0810	0913	and hourly until	1713	1756	1813	1822	1918	2018	2118	2218	...	⑦	0919	1015	1129	1319	1415	1519	1719	1919
Barnsley d.		0658	0758	0858	1001		1801	1855	1901	1910	2006	2111	2206	2306	...		1012	1103	1217	1412	1503	1612	1812	2012
Meadowhall d.		0720	0818	0921	1019		1820	1916	1920	1930	2024	2129	2225	2326	...		1033	1120	1235	1433	1521	1634	1833	2034
Sheffield a.		0729	0829	0930	1030		1830	1927	1930	1940	2036	2141	2236	2336	...		1043	1128	1247	1448	1528	1644	1844	2043

E – London St Pancras – Leeds and v.v. Operated by *East Midlands Trains*. Conveys (12).
g – Wakefield Westgate.
r – 5–6 minutes earlier on ⑥.
◇ – Timings may vary by up to 3 minutes.

172 NOTTINGHAM - WORKSOP and MATLOCK

2nd class EM

NOTTINGHAM - WORKSOP

km			⚒	⚒	⚒	⚒	⚒		⚒	⚒	⚒	⚒	⚒	⚒			⑦A		⑦B		⑦	⑦		⑦
0	**Nottingham** 170 d.	⚒	0540	0605	0659	0825	0925	and hourly until	1725	1755	1855	1955	2055	2205	...	⑦	0730	...	0825	...	0925	1425	...	1725
	Mansfield d.		0613	0638	0740	0900	0957		1803	1835	1929	2035	2135	2242	...		0857	...	0858	...	0958	1459	...	1759
	Worksop a.		0648	0720	0818	0935	1034		1837	1909	2004	2109	2208	2316	...		0959	...	0932	...	1030	1532	...	1836

		⚒	⚒		⚒	⚒		⚒	⚒	⚒	⚒	⚒	⚒	⚒			⑦B		⑦		⑦		⑦	
Worksop d.	⚒	0550	0656	...	0738	0838	and hourly until	1642	1745	1841	1921	2015	2119	2220	...	⑦	0938	...	1038	...	1538	...	1840	...
Mansfield d.		0622	0729	...	0810	0910		1714	1818	1913	1952	2050	2152	2252	...		1010	...	1110	...	1610	...	1812	...
Nottingham 170 a.		0658	0805	...	0844	0944		1748	1851	1947	2036	2126	2228	2326	...		1042	...	1142	...	1641	...	1944	...

NOTTINGHAM - DERBY - MATLOCK

Services on ⑦ valid until March 28.

km			⚒	⑥	Ⓐ	⚒	⚒	⚒		⚒	⑥	Ⓐ	⑥	Ⓐ			⑦	⑦	⑦	⑦	⑦	⑦		⑦
0	**Nottingham** 170 d.	⚒	...	0610	0618	0718	0815	0918	and hourly until	1918	2009	2011	*2108*	*2137*	...	⑦	0928	1123	1320	1453	1723	1923	...	2123
26	**Derby** 170 d.		0538	0648	0650	0750	0850	0950		1950	2050	2056	2150	2216	...		0958	1157	1357	1528	1754	1953	...	2155
50	Cromford d.		0605	0715	0717	0817	0917	1017		2017	2117	2123	2218	2243	...		1023	1224	1424	1555	1822	2021	...	2223
53	**Matlock** a.		0614	0722	0724	0824	0924	1024		2024	2124	2130	2224	2250	...		1032	1231	1431	1606	1831	2027	...	2229

		⚒		⚒		⚒	⚒		⚒		⚒		⑥	Ⓐ			⑦	⑦	⑦	⑦		⑦	⑦	⑦
Matlock d.	⚒	0621	...	0736	...	0836	0936	and hourly until	2036	...	2136	...	2255	2255	...	⑦	1042	1238	1437	1642	...	1842	2042	2244
Cromford d.		0626	...	0741	...	0841	0941		2041	...	2141	...	2300	2300	...		1047	1243	1442	1647	...	1847	2047	2249
Derby 170 a.		0656	...	0810	...	0910	1010		2110	...	2212	...	2329	2329	...		1116	1312	1510	1716	...	1916	2115	2320
Nottingham 170 a.		*0741*	...	0853	...	0953	1053		2154	...	*2328*	...	2357	0002	...		1146	1347	1540	1746	...	1947	2145	...

A – Dec. 13 – Jan. 31. By 🚌.

B – Feb. 7 – May 16.

NT 2nd class — LEEDS - LANCASTER and CARLISLE — 173

km		Ⓐ	⑥	Ⓐ	⑥	⚒	⚒	⑦	⚒	⚒A	⚒	⑥	Ⓐ	⑦	⑥	Ⓐ	⚒	⑦	⑥	Ⓐ	⑦	⑦	⑥	Ⓐ	⚒	
0	**Leeds** 176 d.	...	0555	...	0619	0819	0849	0900	0947	1019	1049	1249	1249	1315	1349	1349	1449	1457	1639	1639	1721	1733	1750	1756	1919	...
17	Shipley d.	...	0608	...	0632	0832	0902	0914	1002	1032	1102	1302	1302	1329	1403	1403	1502	1510	1655	1655	1734	1746	1803	1808	1932	...
27	Keighley 🚂 176 d.	...	0621	...	0642	0843	0912	0928	1012	1042	1112	1312	1312	1339	1414	1414	1512	1520	1710	1710	1744	1756	1814	1824	1942	...
42	**Skipton** 176 d.	0540	0640	...	0656	0900	0926	0946	1026	1100	1126	1326	1326	1354	1434	1434	1526	1536	1725	1724	1800	1811	1835	1841	2000	...
58	Hellifield d.	0555	0654	...	0708	0914	0940	0957	|	1114	1137	1340	1340	1408	1448	1448	1537	1550	1740	1739	1814	1822	1849	1855	2015	...
66	Giggleswick d.	0608	0707	...	|	0925	|	|	|	1125	|	|	|	|	1459	1459	|	1600	1750	1749	1825	|	|	|	|	...
103	Carnforth 157 a.	0643	0742	...	|	1000	|	|	|	1200	|	|	|	|	1534	1534	|	1636	1826	1829	1900	|	|	|	|	...
113	**Lancaster** 157 a.	0653	0752	...	|	1012	|	|	|	1211	|	|	|	|	1547	1547	|	1646	1838	1842	1913	|	|	|	|	...
120	Morecambe a.	*0736*	*0846*	...	|	1032	|	|	|	1239	|	|	|	|	1602	1613	|	1703	1859	1901	1935	|	|	|	|	...
66	Settle d.	...	...	...	0715	...	0950	1006	1044	...	1146	1348	1348	1417	...	...	1545	...	...	...	...	1830	1857	1903	2024	...
76	Horton in Ribblesdale d.	...	...	...	0724	...	0958	1015	|	...	1154	1357	1357	1426	...	...	1553	...	...	...	...	1839	1906	1912	2032	...
84	Ribblehead d.	...	...	...	0732	...	1006	1023	|	...	1202	1405	1405	1434	...	...	1601	...	...	...	...	1847	1914	1920	2042	...
99	Garsdale d.	...	...	...	0747	...	1021	1039	|	...	1217	1420	1420	1450	...	...	1616	...	...	...	...	1902	1929	1935	...	...
115	Kirkby Stephen d.	...	...	0728	0759	...	1034	1052	1122	...	1230	1432	1432	1503	...	...	1629	...	...	...	...	1915	1941	1947	...	...
132	Appleby d.	...	...	0740	0812	...	1047	1105	1136	...	1243	1445	1445	1515	...	...	1641	...	...	...	...	1928	1954	2000	...	...
166	Armathwaite d.	...	...	0808	0839	...	1115	1133	|	...	1311	1512	1512	1543	...	...	1709	...	...	...	...	1956	2021	2027	...	...
182	**Carlisle** a.	...	...	0824	0858	...	1134	1149	1217	...	1329	1527	1532	1600	...	...	1728	...	...	...	...	2013	2041	2048	...	...

	⚒	Ⓐ	⑥	⑥	Ⓐ	⑦	⑥	⚒	⚒	⚒B	⑦	Ⓐ	⑥	Ⓐ	⑥	⑥	⚒	⑦	⑦	⑥	Ⓐ	⚒	⑦	⚒	⚒	
Carlisle d.	...	0620	...	0752	0853	0925	0926	...	1151	...	1351	1400	1426	1503	1549	...	1618	1637	...	1800	1807	...	...	...	...	...
Armathwaite d.	...	0634	...	0806	0907	0939	0940	...	1205	...	1405	1414	1440	|	|	...	1632	1651	...	1814	1821	...	...	...	...	...
Appleby d.	...	0702	...	0834	0935	1007	1008	...	1233	...	1433	1443	1509	1550	1626	...	1701	1720	...	1842	1849	...	...	...	...	...
Kirkby Stephen d.	...	0717	...	0847	0948	1021	1021	...	1246	...	1447	1456	1522	1533	1639	...	1714	1734	...	1856	1902	...	...	...	...	...
Garsdale d.	...	▬	...	0900	1002	1034	1035	...	1259	...	1500	1509	1535	|	|	...	1727	1747	...	1909	1915	...	...	...	...	...
Ribblehead d.	0714	...	...	0915	1017	1049	1049	...	1314	...	1515	1523	1549	|	|	...	1742	1802	...	1924	1930	...	...	2100	...	...
Horton in Ribblesdale d.	0821	...	...	0921	1024	1056	1056	...	1320	...	1522	1530	1556	|	|	...	1748	1809	...	1931	1936	...	...	2106	...	...
Settle d.	0829	Ⓐ	...	0929	1032	1104	1104	...	1328	...	1530	1539	1604	1635	1716	...	1757	1819	...	1939	1944	...	...	2114	...	...
Morecambe d.	|	*0619*	*0738*	|	|	|	|	1034	|	1329	|	|	|	|	|	1619	|	|	1745	|	|	1908	2000	|	...	...
Lancaster 157 d.	|	0710	0824	|	|	|	|	1049	|	1348	|	|	|	|	|	1640	|	|	1804	|	|	1924	2020	|	...	...
Carnforth 157 d.	|	0720	0834	|	|	|	|	1109	|	1358	|	|	|	|	|	1650	|	|	1814	|	|	1934	2030	|	...	...
Giggleswick d.	|	0754	0908	|	|	|	|	1144	|	1433	|	|	|	|	|	1725	|	|	1849	|	|	2009	2105	|	...	...
Hellifield d.	0737	0806	0920	0937	1039	1113	1111	1156	1337	1444	1539	1548	1611	|	|	1736	1806	1826	1900	1947	1952	2021	2116	2123	...	...
Skipton 176 d.	0756	0827	0942	0957	1059	1130	1128	1213	1358	1510	1557	1612	1628	1658	1741	1758	1828	1843	1918	2007	2007	2038	2133	2140	2148	...
Keighley 🚂 176 d.	0809	0837	0952	1008	1109	1140	1138	1223	1409	1520	1607	1622	1638	1708	1751	1808	1838	1853	1928	2017	2017	2048	2143	...	2201	...
Shipley d.	0819	0847	1002	1019	1118	1149	1149	1233	1418	1530	1616	1631	1649	1720	1800	1819	1848	1903	1938	2028	2028	2057	2154	...	2214	...
Leeds 176 a.	0837	0904	1022	1034	1136	1206	1207	1255	1437	1547	1633	1651	1707	1740	1817	1839	1907	1920	1956	2044	2044	2117	2210	...	2232	...

A – To Heysham Port (a. 1257).
B – From Heysham Port (d. 1315).

🚂 – **Keighley – Haworth – Oxenhope** and v.v. (*Keighley and Worth Valley Railway*). *8* km. ⑥⑦ Jan. – Dec. (daily in July and Aug.) and on certain other dates throughout the year. Keighley station is shared with National Rail services. Operator: Keighley and Worth Valley Railway. ✆ 01535 645214. www.kwvr.co.uk

NT 2nd class — LEEDS - HARROGATE - YORK — 174

km		⚒	⚒	Ⓐ	⑥	⚒	⑥	Ⓐ	⑥	Ⓐ	⚒	⚒	⚒	⚒	⚒	⚒		⚒	⚒	⚒	⚒	Ⓐ	⚒
0	**Leeds** 127 185 187 d.	⚒	0607	0629	0637	0713	0739	0743	0754	0759	0829	0859	0929	0959	1029	1059	and at	1629	1659	1713	1729	1744	1759
29	**Harrogate** d.		0645	0705	0714	0749	0816	0816	0829	0834	0905	0935	1005	1035	1105	1135	the same minutes	1708	1735	1749	1805	1816	1835
36	Knaresborough d.		0655	0719	0723	0759	0828	0828	0840	0845	0915	0945	1014	1045	1114	1145	past each	1721	1745	1800	1814	1826	1845
62	**York** 127 185 187 a.		0721	0748	0751	0828	0859	0858	...	...	0947	...	1046	...	1145	...	hour until	1748	...	...	1846	...	...

	⚒	Ⓐ	⚒	⚒		⑥	Ⓐ	⚒	⑥	Ⓐ			⑦	⑦	⑦	⑦	⑦	⑦	⑦	⑦	⑦	⑦	⑦	⑦
Leeds 127 185 187 d.	1829	1859	1929	2029	...	2120	2129	2229	2321	2329	...	⑦	0954	1054	1254	1454	1554	1654	1754	1854	1954	2116	2223	2322
Harrogate d.	1905	1935	2005	2105	...	2156	2205	2308	2358	0006	...		1031	1130	1330	1530	1630	1730	1830	1930	2030	2153	2300	2359
Knaresborough d.	1914	1945	2014	2114	...	2206	2215	...	...	...	...		...	1140	1340	1540	1645	1744	1844	1944	2045	2203	...	...
York 127 185 187 a.	1945	...	2045	2148	...	...	...	...	...	...	...		...	1207	1408	1608	1710	1810	1912	2012	2115	...	...	...

	⚒	Ⓐ	⑥	Ⓐ	ⒶA	⑥	Ⓐ	⑥A	Ⓐ	⑥	Ⓐ	Ⓐ	⚒	⑥	Ⓐ	⑥	Ⓐ	⚒	⚒	⚒		⚒	⑥
York 127 185 187 d.	...	...	...	...	...	0653	0652	...	...	...	...	...	0757	...	...	0845	0845	0910	...	1011	and at	...	1654
Knaresborough d.	...	...	0647	0700	...	0721	0724	...	0742	0751	0756	...	0821	0851	0856	0909	0910	0935	1005	1035	the same minutes	1705	1718
Harrogate d.	0606	0630	0656	0711	0728	0731	0740	0744	0751	0800	0806	0814	0830	0900	0905	0918	0919	0944	1014	1044	past each	1714	1730
Leeds 127 185 187 a.	0644	0708	0734	0748	0757	0808	0817	0810	0829	0838	0840	0852	0908	0937	0937	0955	0956	1022	1052	1122	hour until	1755	1807

	Ⓐ	⚒	⚒	⚒	Ⓐ	⚒	⚒	Ⓐ	⑥	Ⓐ			⑦	⑦	⑦	⑦	⑦	⑦	⑦	⑦	⑦	⑦	⑦	⑦
York 127 185 187 d.	1654	1717	...	1811	...	1911	2011	2111	2157	2211	...	⑦	...	...	...	1218	1420	1618	1717	1817	1917	2018	2126	...
Knaresborough d.	1718	1741	1805	1835	1905	1935	2035	2135	2221	2236	...		...	...	1142	1242	1444	1642	1742	1842	1942	2042	2150	...
Harrogate d.	1737	1750	1818	1844	1914	1944	2044	2145	2237	2247	...		0953	1053	1153	1253	1453	1653	1753	1853	1953	2053	2202	2305
Leeds 127 185 187 a.	1817	1828	1855	1922	1952	2022	2122	2223	2314	2324	...		1030	1130	1230	1330	1530	1730	1830	1930	2030	2130	2240	2343

A – [12] and 🍸 Harrogate - Leeds - London Kings Cross. Operated by *GR*. See Table **185**.

NT 2nd class — WEST YORKSHIRE local services — 176

LEEDS - BRADFORD FORSTER SQUARE
Journey: ± 21 minutes *22 km*

From Leeds:
Ⓐ : 0649, 0739, 0810, 0840 and every 30 minutes until 1610; then 1635, 1710, 1736, 1810, 1840, 1910, 1959.
⑥ : 0710, 0810, 0840 and every 30 minutes until 1610; then 1635, 1710, 1740, 1810, 1840, 1910, 2043.
⑦: 0834 and hourly until 1534; then 1635, 1737, 1834, 1934, 2034, 2134, 2234.

From Bradford Forster Square:
Ⓐ : 0601, 0630, 0655, 0759, 0826, 0901, 0931 and every 30 minutes until 1801; then 1827, 1901, 1931.
⑥ : 0601, 0701, 0733, 0759, 0831, 0901 and every 30 minutes until 1931.
⑦: 0902 and houry until 2302.

LEEDS - BRADFORD INTERCHANGE
Journey: ± 20 minutes *15 km*

From Leeds:
Ⓐ : 0508, 0551, 0603, 0622, 0637, 0651, 0708, 0722, 0737, 0751 and at 08, 22, 37 and 51 minutes past each hour until 2008; then 2037, 2108, 2137, 2208, 2237, 2308.
⑥ : 0537, 0551, 0616, 0637, 0651, 0708, 0722, 0737, 0751 and at 08, 22, 37 and 51 minutes past each hour until 2008; then 2037, 2108, 2137, 2208, 2237, 2300.
⑦: 0802, 0821, 0902, 0918, 0935, 0954, 1012, 1035, 1053 and at 12, 35 and 53 minutes past each hour until 1812; then 1835, 1903, 1935, 2012, 2035, 2104, 2135, 2205, 2235, 2322.

From Bradford Interchange:
Ⓐ : 0618, 0648, 0705, 0720, 0734, 0750 and at 04, 19, 34 and 50 minutes past each hour until 2019; then 2037, 2104, 2137, 2204, 2219, 2237, 2304, 2346
⑥ : 0626, 0705, 0720, 0734, 0750, and at 04, 19, 34 and 50 minutes past each hour until 2019; then 2037, 2104, 2137, 2204, 2219, 2237, 2306.
⑦: 0831, 0920, 1002, 1025, 1102, 1125, 1144, 1202, 1225, 1244 and at 02, 25 and 44 minutes past each hour until 1725; then 1800, 1825, 1844, 1902, 1925, 1944, 2002, 2025, 2102, 2126, 2144, 2202, 2226, 2301, 2347.

BRADFORD FORSTER SQUARE - ILKLEY
Journey: ± 31 minutes *22 km*

From Bradford Forster Square:
⚒ : 0615, 0644Ⓐ, 0711Ⓐ, 0715⑥, 0746Ⓐ, 0816, 0846 and every 30 minutes until 1616; then 1644, 1716, 1746, 1816, 1846, 1941, 2038, 2138, 2238, 2320.
⑦ : 1038, 1238, 1438, 1638, 1838, 2038, 2238.

From Ilkley:
⚒ : 0617, 0650Ⓐ, 0722, 0750Ⓐ, 0821, 0851, 0921, 0951 and every 30 minutes until 1921; then 2005, 2040, 2140, 2240.
⑦ : 0953, 1153, 1353, 1553, 1753, 1953, 2153.

FOR NOTES AND CONTINUATION OF TABLE SEE NEXT PAGE ▶ ▶ ▶

176 WEST YORKSHIRE local services — 2nd class NT

BRADFORD FORSTER SQUARE - SKIPTON
Journey: ± 38 minutes *30 km*

From Bradford Forster Square: Trains call at **Keighley** (🚂) ± 21 minutes later.

Ⓐ: 0610, 0640, 0715, 0742, 0811 and every 30 minutes until 1611; then 1640, 1711, 1738, 1811, 1841, 1907, 1936, 2007, 2105, 2205, 2309.

⑥: 0610, 0711, 0811, 0841 and every 30 minutes until 1841; then 1907, 1936, 2007, 2105, 2205, 2305.

⑦: 1048, 1248, 1448, 1648, 1848, 2048, 2248.

From Skipton: Trains call at **Keighley** (🚂) ± 13 minutes later.

Ⓐ: 0602, 0627, 0701, 0732, 0801, 0832, 0902 and every 30 minutes until 1602; then 1636, 1702, 1728, 1802, 1832, 1900, 1932, 1954, 2054, 2154.

⑥: 0602, 0701, 0732, 0801, 0832, 0902 and every 30 minutes until 1702; then 1730, 1802, 1832, 1900, 1932, 1954, 2054, 2154.

⑦: 0936, 1137, 1337, 1537, 1737, 1937, 2139.

HUDDERSFIELD - WAKEFIELD WESTGATE
Journey: ± 33 minutes *25 km*

From Huddersfield:

⚒: 0532Ⓐ, 0637⑥, 0641Ⓐ, 0732⑥, 0749Ⓐ, 0837, 0935 and hourly until 1735; then 1835⑥, 1840Ⓐ, 1935, 2035, 2135.

From Wakefield Westgate:

⚒: 0630 Ⓐ, 0729, 0829 and hourly (see note **B**) until 2129; then 2242.

LEEDS - DONCASTER
Journey: ± 48 minutes *48 km*

Stopping trains. For faster trains see Table **185.**

From Leeds:

Ⓐ: 0619, 0727, 0819, 0919 and hourly until 1919; then 2021, 2128, 2239.

⑥: 0619, 0726, 0819, 0919 and hourly until 1819; then 1922, 2021, 2134, 2216.

⑦: 1009, 1209, 1409, 1609, 1809, 2020, 2109.

From Doncaster:

Ⓐ: 0625, 0714, 0758, 0826, 0914, 1014, 1126, 1225, 1327, 1427, 1514, 1614, 1727, 1827, 1927, 2038, 2138, 2238.

⑥: 0625, 0714, 0826, 0914 and hourly until 1514; then 1627, 1727, 1827, 1927, 2045, 2128, 2252.

⑦: 0910, 1110, 1310, 1510, 1710, 1930, 2149.

LEEDS - ILKLEY
Journey: ± 30 minutes *26 km*

From Leeds:

⚒: 0602, 0627Ⓐ, 0702, 0729Ⓐ, 0735Ⓐ, 0802, 0832 and every 30 minutes until 1702; then 1715Ⓐ, 1732, 1802, 1832, 1902, 1932, 2002, 2106, 2206, 2315.

⑦: 0912 and hourly until 2212; then 2314.

From Ilkley:

⚒: 0609, 0640Ⓐ, 0710, 0740Ⓐ, 0805Ⓐ, 0810⑥, 0817Ⓐ, 0840, 0910 and every 30 minutes until 1640; then 1710⑥, 1714Ⓐ, 1740, 1804Ⓐ, 1810, 1840, 1910, 1940, 2021, 2121, 2221, 2321.

⑦: 0930, 1021 and hourly until 2321.

LEEDS - SKIPTON
Journey: ± 45 minutes *42 km*

See Table **173** for additional services.

From Leeds: Trains call at **Keighley** (🚂) ± 24 minutes later.

Ⓐ: 0555, 0621, 0656, 0725, 0751, 0825, 0856, 0926 and every 30 minutes until 1626; then 1656, 1726, 1750, 1826, 1850, 1925, 1956, 2026, 2055, 2126, 2156, 2226, 2256, 2318.

⑥: 0555, 0619, 0656, 0756, 0825, 0849, 0856, 0926 and every 30 minutes until 1856; then 1925, 2006, 2026, 2055, 2126, 2156, 2226, 2256, 2318.

⑦: 0900, 1008, 1108 and hourly until 2208; then 2310.

From Skipton: Trains call at **Keighley** (🚂) ± 13 minutes later.

Ⓐ: 0618, 0642, 0708, 0724, 0747, 0815, 0843, 0918, 0948 and every 30 minutes until 1618; then 1649, 1719, 1749, 1816, 1848, 1918, 1948, 2018, 2048, 2118, 2148, 2218.

⑥: 0647, 0747, 0756, 0818, 0848 and every 30 mins until 1618; then 1649, 1719, 1749, 1816, 1848, 1918, 1948, 2007, 2018, 2048, 2118, 2148, 2218.

⑦: 0835, 0915, 1015 and hourly until 1815; then 1924, 2015, 2115, 2215, 2315.

B – 14xx service departs 1438 on ⑥.

🚂 – *Keighley and Worth Valley Railway*. For details see Table **173**.

179 HULL - BRIDLINGTON - SCARBOROUGH — 2nd class NT

km		⚒	⚒	⚒		⚒	⚒	⚒		⚒	⚒	Ⓐ		⑥		⑦	⑦		⑦	⑦		⑦	⑦
0	**Hull** 185 187 d.	0654	0814	0947	...	1114	1314	1444	...	1619	1738	1914	...	1920	...	0925	1025	...	1200	1405	...	1605	1800
13	Beverley d.	0707	0827	1000	...	1127	1327	1457	...	1632	1751	1927	...	1933	...	0938	1038	...	1213	1418	...	1618	1813
31	Driffield d.	0724	0842	1015	...	1139	1339	1512	...	1646	1808	1941	...	1947	...	0955	1053	...	1228	1433	...	1633	1825
50	**Bridlington** a.	0740	0857	1030	...	1153	1353	1527	...	1701	1824	1957	...	2003	...	1011	1108	...	1243	1448	...	1648	1839
50	**Bridlington** d.	0749	0900	1037	...	1205	1405	1531	...	1704	1830	2000	...	2006	...	1013	1111	...	1246	1451	...	1653	1845
71	Filey d.	0811	0922	1059	...	1227	1427	1553	...	1725	1852	2022	...	2028	...	1035	1133	...	1308	1513	...	1715	1907
87	**Scarborough** 187 a.	0829	0939	1117	...	1244	1445	1610	...	1743	1909	2039	...	2045	...	1054	1150	...	1328	1530	...	1732	1927

	⚒		⚒	⚒		⚒		⚒	⚒		⚒		⚒	⚒		⑦	⑦		⑦	⑦		⑦	⑦
Scarborough 187 d.	0650	...	0902	1000	...	1128	...	1328	1454	...	1622	...	1753	2006	...	1112	1208	...	1408	1608	...	1808	1937
Filey d.	0704	...	0916	1014	...	1142	...	1342	1508	...	1636	...	1807	2020	...	1126	1222	...	1422	1622	...	1822	1951
Bridlington a.	0727	...	0938	1036	...	1204	...	1404	1530	...	1658	...	1829	2043	...	1148	1244	...	1444	1644	...	1844	2013
Bridlington d.	0734	...	0941	1041	...	1211	...	1411	1538	...	1706	...	1841	2045	...	1151	1251	...	1451	1651	...	1851	2017
Driffield d.	0749	...	0956	1056	...	1224	...	1424	1553	...	1719	...	1856	2101	...	1206	1304	...	1504	1704	...	1906	2030
Beverley d.	0807	...	1011	1111	...	1237	...	1437	1608	...	1732	...	1911	2115	...	1220	1317	...	1517	1717	...	1923	2043
Hull 185 187 a.	0823	...	1027	1127	...	1254	...	1553	1624	...	1749	...	1927	2131	...	1235	1333	...	1533	1734	...	1939	2059

☛ Additional trains **Hull - Bridlington**:

⚒: 0623, 0714, 0752, 0917, 1014, 1044, 1144, 1214, 1244, 1344, 1414, 1514, 1544, 1644, 1714.

⑦: 0900, 1125, 1300, 1505, 1655, 1715, 1900.

☛ Additional trains **Bridlington - Hull**:

⚒: 0646, 0714, 0808, 0905, 1011, 1111, 1141, 1241, 1311, 1341, 1441, 1511, 1609, 1641, 1734, 1815, 1910, 2128, 2242.

⑦: 0951, 1351, 1551, 1721, 1751, 1811, 1955.

180 HULL - YORK — 2nd class NT

km		⑥	Ⓐ		⚒	⚒	⚒	⑥		Ⓐ	⚒	⚒	⑥		Ⓐ		⑦	⑦	⑦A	⑦	⑦A	⑦	⑦A	⑦
0	**Hull** 185 187 d.	0657	0707	...	0902	1105	1312	1451	...	1502	1610	1718	1846	...	1910	...	0854	1153	1324	1428	1600	1723	1904	2022
50	Selby 185 187 d.	0740	0748	...	0938	1139	1354	1525	...	1538	1647	1806	1922	...	1947	...	0928	1227	1358	1502	1634	1757	1938	2056
84	**York** 185 187 a.	0815	0821	...	1011	1209	1425	1554	...	1605	1713	1836	1956	...	2016	...	0956	1251	1422	1527	1658	1823	2002	2120

	⚒	⚒	⑥	Ⓐ	⑥	Ⓐ	Ⓐ	⑥	⚒	⑥	Ⓐ	⑥	Ⓐ	⑥	Ⓐ		⑦	⑦A	⑦	⑦A	⑦	⑦A	⑦	⑦
York 185 187 d.	0730	0953	1150	1153	1338	1344	1459	1505	1612	1718	1727	1813	1820	2017	2203	...	1040	1205	1323	1442	1543	1710	1910	2141
Selby 185 187 d.	0750	1012	1209	1218	1404	1408	1518	1524	1639	1737	1746	1842	1846	2036	2222	...	1059	1224	1342	1501	1602	1731	1930	2200
Hull 185 187 a.	0846	1056	1254	1302	1445	1449	1559	1603	1727	1822	1829	1928	1932	2123	2309	...	1138	1303	1423	1542	1642	1812	2010	2241

A – Apr.4 – May 16.

181 LINCOLN - SHEFFIELD — 2nd class NT

km		⚒	⚒	⚒	⚒		⚒	⚒	⚒	⚒	⚒	⚒	⑥	Ⓐ	⚒		⑦	⑦	⑦	⑦	⑦	⑦
0	**Lincoln** 171 d.	...	...	0704	0827	and at	1627	1722	...	1824	1943	2027	2124	2127	...	...	...	1515	1735	1935	2115	...
26	Gainsborough Lea Road d.	...	...	0726	0849	the same	1649	1744	...	1846	2005	2049	2146	2149	...	...	...	1537	1757	1957	2137	...
40	Retford d.	...	0703	0740	0903	minutes	1703	1758	1814	1904	2019	2103	2200	2203	2245	...	1450	1551	1811	2011	2151	2224
52	Worksop 172 d.	0630	0716	0752	0915	past each	1715	1810	1825	1916	2031	2115	2212	2215	2258	...	1501	1603	1823	2023	2203	2235
78	**Sheffield** 170 a.	0702	0748	0826	0949	hour until	1749	1835	1857	1955	2105	2146	2246	2250	2333	...	1533	1636	1855	2056	2234	2307

	⚒	⚒		⚒	⚒	⚒		⚒	⚒	⚒	⚒	⚒	⚒	⚒	⚒		⑦	⑦	⑦	⑦	⑦	⑦
Sheffield 170 d.	0539	0546	...	0643	0730	0844	and at	1644	1724	1744	1845	1948	2044	2144	2244	...	1342	1357	1602	1802	1926	2106
Worksop 172 d.	0601	0623	...	0714	0759	0913	the same	1713	1752	1813	1914	2017	2123	2214	2322	...	1402	1426	1630	1830	1954	2134
Retford d.	0610	0638	...	0724	0809	0923	minutes	1723	1807	1823	1924	2027	...	2228	...	...	1412	1439	1640	1840	2004	2149
Gainsborough Lea Road d.	0625	...	...	0738	0824	0938	past each	1738	...	1838	1939	2042	...	...	...	...	1426	...	1654	1854	2018	...
Lincoln 171 a.	0653	...	...	0806	0852	1006	hour until	1806	...	1907	2006	2110	...	...	...	...	1454	...	1721	1922	2045	...

EM 2nd class — PETERBOROUGH - LINCOLN - DONCASTER — 182

km		⚒L	⚒N	⚒	⚒	Ⓐ	⚒	⚒	⚒	Ⓐ	Ⓐ	⑥	⚒E	⑥	Ⓐ	⑥	⚒	⚒	Ⓐ	⑥	⚒	⚒	⚒	⚒	⚒
0	**Peterborough** .... 184 185 d.	...	0630	...	0730	...	0833	0933	...	1038	1148	1148	1241	...	1340	...	1510	1625	...	...	1730	...	1836	...	2028
27	Spalding .... d.	...	0656	...	0756	...	0857	0957	...	1101	1210	1210	1303	...	1402	...	1532	1649	...	...	1758	...	1902	...	2054
57	Sleaford .... 194 d.	0650	...	0742	—	0846	0925	1025	...	1130	1242	1242	1332	...	1432	...	1614	1718	1754	1754	...	1900	...	2007	...
91	**Lincoln** .... a.	0721	...	0812	⑥	0916	0959	1059	...	1204	1314	1314	1405	...	1505	...	1648	1751	1827	1827	...	1932	...	2041	...
91	**Lincoln** .... 181 d.	...	...	...	0915	0918	...	...	1154	...	1317	...	...	1410	...	1510	...	...	1829	...	...	1932	...	...	...
117	Gainsborough Lea Rd ... 181 d.	...	...	...	0937	0940	...	...	1217	...	1339	...	...	1432	...	1532	...	...	1857	...	...	1953	...	...	...
151	**Doncaster** .... 185 a.	...	...	...	1007	1008	...	...	1247	...	1415	...	...	1501	...	1602	...	...	1925	...	...	2023	...	...	...

	⚒	⚒	⚒	⚒N	Ⓐ	⚒	⚒	⚒	Ⓐ	⚒E	⚒	⚒	Ⓐ	Ⓐ	⑥	⚒E	⚒	⑥	⚒	⚒	⚒	⚒	Ⓐ	⚒	⚒
Doncaster .... 185 d.	...	...	...	...	...	...	...	1026	...	...	1304	...	...	1427	1507	...	...	1627	...	...	...	...	1934	...	2033
Gainsborough Lea Road 181 d.	...	...	...	...	...	...	...	1052	...	...	1330	...	...	1454	1533	...	...	1656	...	...	...	...	2000	...	2100
Lincoln .... 181 a.	...	...	...	...	...	...	...	1116	...	...	1354	...	...	1518	1557	...	...	1720	...	...	...	...	2026	...	2126
Lincoln .... d.	...	0705	...	0800	0910	1015	1110	...	1210	1330	...	1441	1512	...	...	1603	1715	...	...	1810	1910	...	—	2048	...
Sleaford .... 194 d.	...	0736	...	0834	0942	1050	1142	...	1242	1402	...	1516	1543	...	...	1634	1747	...	...	1841	1941	...	⚒N	2119	...
Spalding .... d.	0700	...	0800	0902	1007	1115	1207	...	1307	1427	...	1541	...	...	...	1659	...	...	1802	...	...	1956	2058	...	...
Peterborough .... 184 185 a.	0725	...	0825	0927	1031	1141	1234	...	1332	1453	...	1609	...	...	...	1724	...	...	1827	...	...	2021	2126	...	...

E – To / from Newark Northgate. L – To / from Leicester. N – To / from Nottingham.

EM 2nd class — GRIMSBY - LINCOLN - NEWARK - NOTTINGHAM - LEICESTER — 183

km		⚒	⚒	⚒	ⒶC	⚒L	⚒	⚒	⚒	⚒		⚒	⚒	⚒	⚒	⚒	⚒	⚒		⚒	⚒	⚒	⚒	⚒	⚒
0	**Grimsby** Town .... 193 d.		...	...	0556	...	...	0703	...	...	...	...	0928	...	...	1128	...	...	...	...	...	1352	...	...	1603
47	Market Rasen .... d.		...	...	0632	...	...	0739	...	...	...	...	1003	...	...	1203	...	...	...	...	...	1427	...	...	1636
71	**Lincoln** .... 182 d.		0526	...	0653	0708	0726	0759	0835	0911	...	0931	1023	1036	1142	1223	1230	1340	...	1405	1435	1448	1530	1635	1657
97	Newark North Gate ..... 185 d.		0559	...	0722	|	|	0825	|	0936	...	|	1052	|	|	1252	|	|	...	1433	|	1514	|	|	1725
98	Newark Castle .... d.		0609	...	...	0733	0756	...	0904	...	...	0954	...	1103	1204	...	1257	1405	...	...	1459	...	1557	1703	...
126	**Nottingham** .... a.		0645	...	...	0758	0830	...	0932	...	...	1030	...	1129	1230	...	1330	1430	...	...	1530	...	1630	1730	...
126	**Nottingham** .... 170 d.		...	0731	...	0802	0832	...	0932	...	...	1032	...	1132	1232	...	1332	1432	...	...	1532	...	1632	1732	...
	East Midlands Parkway . 170 d.		...	0746	...	|	0843	...	0943	...	...	1043	...	1143	1243	...	1343	1443	...	...	1543	...	1646	1746	...
150	Loughborough .... 170 d.		...	0756	...	0820	0854	...	0954	...	...	1054	...	1154	1254	...	1354	1454	...	...	1554	...	1656	1756	...
170	**Leicester** .... 170 a.		...	0821	...	0832	0921	...	1021	...	...	1122	...	1221	1321	...	1421	1521	...	...	1621	...	1722	1822	...

	⚒	Ⓐ	⚒		⚒	⚒	⑥	⚒	⑥	⚒	Ⓐ	⚒	ⒶC	Ⓐ		⑦	⑦	⑦	⑦	⑦	⑦	⑦	⑦		⑦
Grimsby Town .... 193 d.	...	...	...	...	...	1828	...	...	1945	...	...	...	2122	...	...		...	...	...	...	...	...	...	...	...
Market Rasen .... d.	...	...	...	...	...	1904	...	...	2018	...	...	...	2155	...	...		...	...	...	...	...	...	...	...	...
Lincoln .... 182 d.	1728	1818	1835	...	...	1925	1935	...	2037	2045	2140	...	2218	2238	...		1105	1300	1500	1810	1910	2010	2100	...	2210
Newark North Gate ..... 185 d.	|	1844	|	...	...	1954	|	...	...	|	|	...	...	|	...		1130	1325	1532	|	|	|	2131	...	|
Newark Castle .... d.	1756	...	1902	...	...	...	2003	...	...	2110	2205	...	...	2257	...		...	...	1542	1839	1940	2040	2140	...	2239
Nottingham .... a.	1831	...	1929	...	...	...	2030	...	...	2139	2234	...	...	2333	...		...	...	1611	1917	2008	2108	2209	...	2317
Nottingham .... 170 d.	1832	...	1932	...	2032	...	...	2132	...	...	...	2310	...	...	...		...	...	...	...	...	...	...	...	...
East Midlands Parkway . 170 d.	1843	...	1946	...	2046	...	...	2143	...	...	...	2321	...	...	...		...	...	...	...	...	...	...	...	...
Loughborough .... 170 d.	1854	...	1956	...	2056	...	...	2154	...	...	...	2329	...	...	...		...	...	...	...	...	...	...	...	...
Leicester .... 170 a.	1921	...	2022	...	2122	...	...	2221	...	...	...	2355	...	...	...		...	...	...	...	...	...	...	...	...

	⚒	⚒	⚒	⚒	Ⓐ	⚒	⚒	⑥	Ⓐ	⚒	⚒	⚒	⚒	⚒	⚒	⚒	⚒	⚒	⚒	⚒	⚒	⚒	⚒	⚒	Ⓐ
Leicester .... 170 d.		...	...	...	...	0633	...	...	...	0725	0825	...	0925	1025	...	1125	...	1225	...	1325	...	1425	1525	...	...
Loughborough .... 170 d.		...	...	...	...	0657	...	...	...	0746	0847	...	0947	1047	...	1147	...	1247	...	1347	...	1447	1547	...	...
East Midlands Parkway . 170 d.		...	...	...	...	0708	...	...	...	0757	0857	...	0957	1057	...	1157	...	1257	...	1357	...	1457	1557	...	...
Nottingham .... 170 a.		...	...	...	...	0727	...	...	...	0815	0913	...	1013	1114	...	1213	...	1314	...	1413	...	1513	1613	...	...
Nottingham .... d.		...	0555	0655	...	—	...	0801	0805	...	0923	...	1029	1117	...	1227	...	1317	...	1429	...	1527	1614	...	...
Newark Castle .... d.		...	0630	0729	...	...	...	0837	0841	...	0950	...	1058	1151	...	1253	...	1351	...	1455	...	1553	1648	...	...
Newark Northgate .... 185 d.		...	|	|	0745	⑥	0831	|	|	...	|	0957	|	|	1204	|	1302	|	1436	|	1536	|	|	...	1734
Lincoln .... 182 d.		0557	0704	0758	0817	0817	0902	0908	0908	...	1017	1023	1130	1221	1237	1320	1330	1423	1501	1522	1603	1625	1714	1721	1803
Market Rasen .... d.		0613	...	...	0834	0834	...	...	...	...	...	1040	...	...	1254	...	...	...	1517	...	...	...	...	1737	...
Grimsby Town .... 193 a.		0656	...	...	0915	0915	...	...	...	...	...	1121	...	...	1336	...	...	...	1557	...	...	...	...	1817	...

	⚒	⑥	Ⓐ	⚒	ⒶC	Ⓐ	⑥L	Ⓐ	Ⓐ	⑥	ⒶL	Ⓐ	⑥	⚒	Ⓐ		⑦	⑦	⑦	⑦	⑦	⑦	⑦	⑦	⑦
Leicester .... 170 d.	1625	...	...	1725	...	1825	1854	...	1925	1925	1957	2025	2025	2125	...	...		...	...	...	...	...	...	...	...
Loughborough .... 170 d.	1647	...	...	1747	...	1846	1904	...	1946	1947	|	2047	2047	2146	...	...		...	...	...	...	...	...	...	...
East Midlands Parkway . 170 d.	1657	...	...	1757	...	1857	|	...	1957	1957	2012	2057	2057	2157	...	...		...	...	...	...	...	...	...	...
Nottingham .... 170 a.	1713	...	...	1813	...	1915	1926	...	2020	2015	2028	2115	2115	2216	...	...		...	...	...	...	...	...	...	...
Nottingham .... d.	1717	...	1750	1815	...	...	1929	...	—	2029	2029	...	2125	...	2225	...		...	...	1635	1730	1837	1937	2037	2226
Newark Castle .... d.	1753	...	1814	1850	...	...	1959	...	⑥	2057	2057	...	2157	...	2256	...		...	...	1700	1805	1902	2002	2102	2301
Newark Northgate .... 185 d.	|	1805	|	|	1924	...	|	2030	2030	|	|	...	2209	...	2308	...		1135	1335	|	|	1917	|	|	2315
Lincoln .... 182 d.	1826	1833	1848	1922	1955	...	2026	2056	2058	2124	2124	...	2240	...	2340	...		1202	1402	1732	1838	1948	2034	2134	2346
Market Rasen .... d.	...	1849	...	...	2012	...	...	...	2115	...	...	...	...	...	...	...		...	...	...	...	...	...	...	...
Grimsby Town .... 1+3 a.	...	1929	...	...	2052	...	...	...	...	...	...	...	...	...	...	...		...	...	...	...	...	...	...	...

C – Fro, / to Cleethorpes. Journey Cleethorpes – Grimsby 6–8 minutes. L – (12) Lincoln - London St Pancras and v.v., see Table **170**.

FC — LONDON - PETERBOROUGH — 184

Stopping trains. For faster trains see Table **185**.

km		Ⓐ	Ⓐ	Ⓐ	Ⓐ	Ⓐ	Ⓐ		Ⓐ	Ⓐ	Ⓐ	Ⓐ	Ⓐ	Ⓐ	Ⓐ	Ⓐ	Ⓐ	Ⓐ	Ⓐ	Ⓐ	Ⓐ	Ⓐ	Ⓐ
0	**London** Kings Cross .... 185 d.		0036	0136	0522	0622	0636	and at the same	1522	1536	1640	1650	1710	1714	1740	1744	1810	1814	1840	1844	1910	1922	2007
44	Stevenage .... 185 d.		0112	0218	0558	0646	0712	minutes past	1546	1612	|	1717	|	1740	|	1809	|	1839	|	1910	|	1947	|
95	Huntingdon .... a.		0155s	0256s	0635	0720	0747	each hour until	1620	1647	1725	1753	1758	1816	1828	1846	1858	1916	1926	1946	2000	2023	2049
123	**Peterborough** .... 185 a.		0217	0314	0654	0738	0809	❖	1637	1704	1743	1812	1822	1833	1850	1903	1914	1933	1943	2003	2024	2040	2105

	Ⓐ	Ⓐ	Ⓐ	Ⓐ	Ⓐ	Ⓐ	Ⓐ		⑥	⑥	⑥	⑥	⑥	⑥	⑥		⑥	⑥	⑥	⑥	⑥		⑥
London Kings Cross .... 185 d.	2022	2107	2122	2207	2222	2301	2322	...		0001	0036	0136	0522	0622	0636	and at the same	2122	2136	2222	2252	2322	...	2352
Stevenage .... 185 d.	2047	|	2147	|	2247	|	2346	...		0020s	0112	0218	0558	0646	0712	minutes past	2146	2212	2246	2316	2356	...	|
Huntingdon .... a.	2123	2151	2223	2251	2322	2346	0026	...		0104s	0152s	0256s	0635	0720	0747	each hour until	2220	2247	2323	2353	0033	...	0102s
Peterborough .... 185 a.	2140	2207	2240	2307	2343	0012	0042	...		0124	0213	0314	0656	0736	0804	❖	2236	2305	2343	0013	0053	...	0121

	⑦	⑦j	⑦k		⑦k	⑦k	⑦j	⑦j	⑦	⑦	⑦	⑦	⑦	⑦	⑦	⑦	⑦	⑦	⑦	⑦	⑦	⑦		⑦	⑦
London Kings Cross .... 185 d.		0036	0036	...	0606	0706	0722	0822	0922	1022	1122	1222	1322	1422	1522	1622	1722	1736	1822	1922	2022	2122	...	2222	2322
Stevenage .... 185 d.		0116	0118	...	0649	0749	0750	0846	0946	1046	1146	1246	1346	1446	1546	1646	1746	1812	1846	1946	2042	2146	...	2246	2346
Huntingdon .... a.		0124s	0321*	...	0809*	0955*	0829	0920	1020	1120	1220	1320	1420	1520	1620	1720	1820	1847	1820	2020	2120	2220	...	2320	0023
Peterborough .... 185 a.		0216	0401*	...	0849*	1035*	0850	0939	1036	1136	1236	1336	1436	1536	1638	1736	1838	1905	1936	2036	2136	2236	...	2340	0042

	Ⓐ	Ⓐ	Ⓐ	Ⓐ	Ⓐ	Ⓐ	Ⓐ	Ⓐ	Ⓐ	Ⓐ	Ⓐ	Ⓐ	Ⓐ	Ⓐ	Ⓐ	Ⓐ	Ⓐ	Ⓐ	Ⓐ	Ⓐ		Ⓐ	Ⓐ
Peterborough .... 186 d.		0325	0412	0512	0540	0600	0621	0632	0653	0714	0704	0726	0733	0758	0816	0845	0915	0923	0944	1015	and at the same	1645	1720
Huntingdon .... d.		0339	0426	0526	0554	0614	0636	0647	0709	0732	0718	0740	0750	0812	0831	0900	0930	0941	0959	1033	minutes past	1659	1741
Stevenage .... 185 d.		0413	0504	0603	0625	0652	|	0724	0736	0759	0801	|	0827	0839	0905	0934	0956	1018	1033	1109	each hour until	1733	1817
London Kings Cross .... 185 a.		0459	0555	0630	0652	0725	0728	0750	0759	0822	0829	0831	0856	0903	0932	1002	1022	1045	1102	1149	❖	1801	1858

	Ⓐ	Ⓐ	Ⓐ	Ⓐ	Ⓐ	Ⓐ	Ⓐ	Ⓐ	Ⓐ		⑥	⑥	⑥	⑥	⑥	⑥		⑥	⑥	⑥	⑥		⑥
Peterborough .... 185 d.	1756	1820	1844	1915	1941	2016	2055	2128	2230	...		0325	0412	0514	0545	0618	and at the same	2045	2118	2145	2218	...	2245
Huntingdon .... d.	1812	1841	1859	1933	1959	2033	2112	2142	2244	...		0339	0426	0528	0559	0633	minutes past	2059	2133	2159	2233	...	2259
Stevenage .... 185 d.	1848	1917	1933	2009	2033	2109	2147	2217	2322	...		0413	0505	0609	0633	0709	each hour until	2133	2209	2233	2309	...	2334
London Kings Cross .... 185 a.	1915	1958	2003	2049	2100	2148	2214	2256	0001	...		0459	0556	0649	0701	0749	❖	2201	2249	2301	2352	...	0009

	⑦	⑦j	⑦j		⑦k	⑦j	⑦k	⑦	⑦	⑦	⑦	⑦	⑦		⑦	⑦	⑦	⑦	⑦	⑦	⑦	⑦		⑦	⑦
Peterborough .... 185 d.		0545	0645	...	0527*	0745	0627*	0845	0914	0945	1045	1142	1242	...	1342	1445	1544	1645	1745	1845	1942	2045	...	2145	2251
Huntingdon .... d.		0559	0659	...	0607*	0759	0707*	0859	0928	0959	1059	1159	1259	...	1359	1459	1559	1659	1759	1859	1959	2059	...	2159	2305
Stevenage .... 185 d.		0636	0733	...	0810	0833	0915	0933	|	1033	1133	1233	1333	...	1433	1533	1634	1733	1833	1833	2033	2133	...	2233	2339
London Kings Cross .... 185 a.		0716	0818	...	0849	0900	0951	1000	1015	1100	1200	1300	1400	...	1500	1600	1700	1800	1900	2000	2100	2200	...	2300	0014

j – ⑦ Dec. 13 – Jan. 31 and Apr. 4 – May 16.
K – ⑦ Feb. 7 – Mar. 28.
s – Stops to set down only.
* – By 🚌.
❖ – Timings may vary by up to 5 minutes on some journeys.

185 LONDON - YORKSHIRE, THE NORTH EAST and SCOTLAND

All trains 🍸 GC, GR, HT

km			Ⓐ am	Ⓐ am	Ⓐ A	Ⓐ	Ⓐ	Ⓐ	Ⓐ m	Ⓐ	Ⓐ H	Ⓐ	Ⓐ	Ⓐ	Ⓐ	Ⓐ	Ⓐ	Ⓐ	Ⓐ am	Ⓐ	Ⓐ n	Ⓐ	Ⓐ H	Ⓐ	Ⓐ
0	**London** Kings Cross 184 d.	Ⓐ	...	...	...	0600	0615	0635	0700	0710	0720	0730	0735	0800	0800	0810	0830	0840	0900	0910	0930	0935	0948	1000	1010
44	Stevenage 184 d.		...	...	...	0619	0634	|	0719	0729	0744u	0750	0756	|	|	|	0849	|	|	|	0949	0954	1009u	|	|
123	**Peterborough** 184 206 d.		...	...	...	0651	0707	0721	0751	0801	|	0826	|	0846	|	0901	0921	0927	0947	0957	1021	1027	|	1045	1056
170	Grantham 206 d.		...	...	...	0710	0726	0740	|	|	0830	0845	|	|	|	|	|	0946	|	|	|	1046	1055	|	1116
193	Newark Northgate d.		...	...	...	0722	0738	|	|	0828	|	|	|	|	|	|	0948	|	|	|	1048	|	|	|	1128
223	Retford d.		...	...	...	0737	0753	|	|	|	0851	|	|	|	|	|	|	1008	|	|	|	|	1117	|	1143
251	**Doncaster** 127 176 d.		...	0615	...	0751	0808	0812	|	0900	0806	0917	|	|	|	|	|	1030	1035	|	1112	1119	1136	|	1159
283	Wakefield Westgate 176 a.		...	|	...	0810	|	0831	|	0917	|	|	0930	|	|	1003	|	1050	|	1057	|	1136	|	|	1216
299	**Leeds** 127 187 a.		...	|	0710	0832	|	0850	|	0935	|	|	0946	|	|	1023	|	1109	|	1118	|	1155	|	|	1236
	Selby 187 a.		...	|	|	...	|	...	|	...	0921	|	...	|	|	...	|	...	|	...	|	...	1151	|	...
	Hull 187 a.		...	|	|	...	|	...	|	...	1003	|	...	|	|	...	|	...	|	...	|	...	1232	|	...
303	**York** 127 187 d.		...	0637	0737	...	0833	...	0858	...	...	0944	...	0955	1002	...	1036	...	1105	...	1141	...	...	1155	...
374	Darlington 127 187 d.		...	0706	0805	...	0903	...	0928	...	...	1012	...	1023	...	...	1106	...	1133	...	1213	...	...	1226	...
409	Durham 127 187 d.		...	0723	0823	...	0920	...	|	...	...	|	...	1040	...	...	1123	...	|	...	1231	...	...	|	...
432	**Newcastle** 127 187 d.		0625	0741	0841	...	0938	...	1004	...	...	1044	...	1059	...	...	1142	...	1205	...	1250	...	...	1257	...
540	Berwick upon Tweed 127 d.		0714	0829	0930	...	1021	...	1047	...	...	...	...	1142	...	...	...	...	1253	...	...	...	...	|	...
632	**Edinburgh** Waverley 127 a.		0805	0919	1020	...	1108	...	1132	...	...	...	...	1231	...	...	...	...	1337	...	...	...	...	1425	...
725	**Glasgow** Central a.		0922	1030	...	...	...	...	1247	...	...	...	...	...	...	...	...	...	1447	...	...	...	...	...	...

	Ⓐ A	Ⓐ	Ⓐ m	Ⓐ	Ⓐ G	Ⓐ	Ⓐ	Ⓐ H	Ⓐ B	Ⓐ	Ⓐ n	Ⓐ	Ⓐ m	Ⓐ	Ⓐ a	Ⓐ H	Ⓐ	Ⓐ A	Ⓐ	Ⓐ	Ⓐ	Ⓐ m	Ⓐ	Ⓐ an	Ⓐ
London Kings Cross 184 d.	1030	1035	1100	1110	1127	1130	1135	1148	1200	1210	1230	1235	1300	1310	1330	1333	1335	1400	1410	1430	1435	1500	1510	1530	1535
Stevenage 184 d.	|	|	|	|	|	1150	1154	|	|	1229	|	1254	|	|	|	|	|	|	|	|	1454	|	|	|	1554
Peterborough 184 206 d.	1117	1123	1146	1156	|	1221	1227	|	1247	1301	1317	|	1346	1358	|	|	1425	|	1456	1517	|	|	1557	1617	1626
Grantham 206 d.	|	1142	|	1215	|	|	1246	1254	|	1320	|	1341	|	1417	|	1435	1444	|	1515	|	|	|	1618	|	1645
Newark Northgate d.	|	1155	|	1227	|	1250	1258	|	|	|	|	1355	|	1429	|	|	1458	|	1527	|	|	|	1629	|	|
Retford d.	|	|	|	|	|	|	|	1316	|	1342	|	|	|	|	1448	1456	|	|	|	|	|	|	1645	|	|
Doncaster 127 176 d.	|	1219	|	1258	|	1315	|	1329	|	1357	1407	1421	1434	1453	1503	1511	1529	1530	1555	|	1610	|	1701	1709	1719
Wakefield Westgate 176 a.	|	1236	|	1317	|	|	1337	|	|	1414	|	1439	|	1514	|	|	1551	|	1615	|	1630	|	1718	|	1736
Leeds 127 187 a.	|	1254	|	1341	|	|	1355	|	|	1435	|	1501	|	1535	|	|	1609	|	1635	|	1648	|	1736	|	1756
Selby 187 a.	|	...	|	...	|	|	...	1344	|	...	|	...	|	...	|	1527	...	|	...	|	...	|	...	|	...
Hull 187 a.	|	...	|	...	|	|	...	1425	|	...	|	...	|	...	|	1610	...	|	...	|	...	|	...	|	...
York 127 187 d.	1229	...	1252	...	1319	1342	...	...	1404	...	1436	...	1500	...	1528	...	...	1555	...	1623	...	1646	...	1736	...
Darlington 127 187 d.	|	...	1320	...	...	1410	...	...	|	...	1511	...	1528	...	1601	...	...	1623	...	1651	...	1715	...	1809	...
Durham 127 187 d.	|	...	|	...	...	1428	...	...	|	...	1529	...	|	...	|	...	...	|	...	1708	...	|	...	1826	...
Newcastle 127 187 d.	1324	...	1351	...	...	1446	...	...	1500	...	1547	...	1559	...	1632	...	...	1654	...	1726	...	1746	...	1850	...
Berwick upon Tweed 127 d.	|	...	1434	...	...	...	...	...	|	...	...	...	1642	...	|	...	...	1738	...	...	...	1829	...	|	...
Edinburgh Waverley 127 a.	1453	...	1519	...	...	...	...	...	1627	...	...	...	1733	...	1803	...	...	1826	...	...	...	1913	...	2026	...
Glasgow Central a.	...	...	1627	...	...	...	...	...	...	...	...	...	1841	...	...	...	...	...	...	...	...	2020	...	...	...

	Ⓐ A	Ⓐ H	Ⓐ	Ⓐ ✕b	Ⓐ	Ⓐ G	Ⓐ ✕	Ⓐ	Ⓐ	Ⓐ ✕a	Ⓐ C	Ⓐ ✕m	Ⓐ	Ⓐ D	Ⓐ ✕	Ⓐ ✕n	Ⓐ	Ⓐ H	Ⓐ ✕b	Ⓐ ✕	Ⓐ G	⑤ ✕	Ⓐ ✕	Ⓐ n	Ⓐ
London Kings Cross 184 d.	1600	1605	1610	1630	1635	1650	1700	1703	1719	1730	1733	1800	1749	1803	1819	1830	1835	1850	1900	1903	1918	1930	1933	2000	2003
Stevenage 184 d.	|	|	|	1649	|	|	|	|	|	|	1752	|	|	|	|	1850	|	|	|	|	|	|	|	|	|
Peterborough 184 206 d.	|	|	1656	|	1725	|	|	1751	1807	1817	|	|	1839	1854	1907	|	1925	|	1947	1953	|	|	2021	2046	2053
Grantham 206 d.	|	1707	1715	1734	|	|	|	1810	|	|	1840	|	1905	1915	|	1935	|	1956	2006	|	|	|	2040	|	2112
Newark Northgate d.	|	|	1727	1746	|	|	|	|	1835	|	|	|	1917	|	1934	|	1954	|	|	2022	|	|	2052	|	2124
Retford d.	|	1728	|	|	1804	|	|	|	|	|	1902	|	|	|	|	1957	|	2018	|	|	|	|	|	2123	|
Doncaster 127 176 d.	1730	1741	|	1810	1819	|	|	1843	1904	|	1917	1928	1942	1948	|	2015	2019	2031	2038	2054	|	|	2120	2139	2155
Wakefield Westgate 176 a.	|	|	1804	|	1836	|	|	1900	|	|	1934	|	2001	2007	|	|	2036	|	|	2113	|	|	2137	|	2213
Leeds 127 187 a.	|	|	1823	|	1855	|	|	1920	|	|	1952	|	2021	2024	|	|	2055	|	|	2135	|	|	2155	|	2233
Selby 187 a.	|	1759	...	|	...	|	|	...	1920	|	...	|	...	...	|	|	...	2046	|	...	|	|	...	|	...
Hull 187 a.	|	1840	...	|	...	|	|	...	2000	|	...	|	...	...	|	|	...	2127	|	...	|	|	...	|	...
York 127 187 d.	1758	...	...	1839	...	1844	1853	...	...	1925	...	1953	...	...	2023	2044	...	...	2103	...	2115	2123	...	2203	...
Darlington 127 187 d.	1827	...	...	1913	...	...	1921	...	...	1953	...	2023	...	...	2051	2116	...	...	2131	...	...	2154	...	2236	...
Durham 127 187 d.	|	...	...	1931	...	...	|	...	...	2010	...	|	...	...	2109	2134	...	...	2149	...	...	2211	...	2253	...
Newcastle 127 187 d.	1859	...	...	1949	...	...	1954	...	...	2029	...	2054	...	...	2127	2152	...	...	2207	...	...	2229	...	2313	...
Berwick upon Tweed 127 d.	1943	...	...	|	...	...	|	...	...	2122	...	2137	...	...	...	2237f	...	...	2300f	...	...	...	...	...	...
Edinburgh Waverley 127 a.	2032	...	...	2115f	...	...	2120	...	...	2214	...	2223	...	...	...	2330f	...	...	2353f	...	...	...	...	...	...
Glasgow Central a.	...	...	...	...	...	...	...	...	...	...	...	2332	...	...	...	...	...	...	...	...	...	...	...	...	...

	Ⓐ	Ⓐ	Ⓐ	Ⓐ	Ⓐ	Ⓐ		⑥ am	⑥ amn	⑥ A	⑥	⑥ m	⑥	⑥ H	⑥ a	⑥ G	⑥	⑥	⑥ m	⑥	⑥	⑥ n	⑥	⑥ A	⑥
London Kings Cross 184 d.	2030	2033	2100	2130	2200	2330	⑥	...	...	...	0615	0700	0710	0736	0800	0757	0810	0830	0900	0910	0930	1000	1010	1030	1040
Stevenage 184 d.	|	|	2120	|	|	|		...	...	...	0634	|	|	0756u	0820	|	|	0849	|	0929	0949	|	|	|	|
Peterborough 184 206 d.	|	2120	2154	2217	2247	0023s		...	...	...	0706	0746	0756	|	0851	|	0857	0921	0946	|	1021	1046	1056	1117	1127
Grantham 206 d.	2132	2139	|	2238	2308	0044s		...	...	...	0726	0805	0815	0838	|	|	0916	0940	|	|	1040	|	1115	|	1148
Newark Northgate d.	|	2151	2223	2249	2319	0056s		...	...	...	0738	0817	0827	|	|	|	0928	|	|	1022	|	|	1127	|	|
Retford d.	2153	|	|	2305	|	|		...	...	...	0753	|	0842	0859	|	|	|	|	1023	|	|	|	|	|	|
Doncaster 127 176 d.	2207	2218	2248	2324	2349	0124s		...	0620	...	0808	0842	0858	0914	0937	|	0957	1012	1040	1048	1114	1132	1159	|	1221
Wakefield Westgate 176 a.	|	2235	|	2342	|	|		...	|	...	|	|	0915	|	|	|	1014	|	|	1111	|	|	1216	|	|
Leeds 127 187 a.	|	2253	|	2359	|	0237		...	|	0710	|	|	0935	|	|	|	1035	|	|	1135	|	|	1235	|	|
Selby 187 a.	2229	...	|	...	|	...		...	|	|	|	|	...	0932	|	|	...	|	|	...	|	|	...	|	|
Hull 187 a.	2313	...	|	...	|	...		...	|	|	|	|	...	1016	|	|	...	|	|	...	|	|	...	|	|
York 127 187 d.	...	...	2314	...	0041	...		...	0642	0735	0833	0906	...	...	1003	1013	...	1042	1104	...	1141	1159	...	1229	1249
Darlington 127 187 d.	...	...	2350	...	...	...		...	0715	0805	0901	0936	...	...	1031	...	...	1111	1132	...	1209	1233	...	|	1317
Durham 127 187 d.	...	...	0007	...	...	...		...	0733	0822	0918	|	...	...	1048	...	...	|	|	...	1227	|	...	|	1335
Newcastle 127 187 d.	...	...	0041	...	...	...		0630	0752	0845	0939	1007	...	...	1108	...	...	1143	1203	...	1245	1305	...	1326	1353
Berwick upon Tweed 127 d.	...	...	...	...	...	...		0719	0842	0929	1022	1050	...	...	|	...	...	1226	|	...	1328	|	...	|	...
Edinburgh Waverley 127 a.	...	...	...	...	...	...		0809	0931	1021	1108	1135	...	...	1239	...	...	1313	1327	...	1415	1431	...	1453	...
Glasgow Central a.	...	...	...	...	...	...		0916	1047	...	...	1247	...	...	...	...	...	...	1447	...	...	...	...	...	...

	⑥ m	⑥	⑥ G	⑥	⑥ H	⑥ B	⑥	⑥ n	⑥ am	⑥	⑥	⑥ A	⑥	⑥ m	⑥ H	⑥	⑥ An	⑥	⑥ G	⑥ m	⑥ H	⑥ E	⑥	⑥ a	⑥
London Kings Cross 184 d.	1100	1110	1127	1130	1148	1200	1210	1230	1300	1310	1330	1400	1430	1500	1508	1530	1600	1630	1650	1700	1704	1730	1740	1800	1803
Stevenage 184 d.	|	|	|	1150	|	|	|	|	|	|	1349	|	|	|	1528u	1549	|	|	|	|	1724u	1750	|	|	|
Peterborough 184 206 d.	1146	1156	|	1221	|	1247	1256	1316	1346	1356	1421	1447	1516	1546	|	1621	1646	1716	|	1746	|	1821	1827	1846	1852
Grantham 206 d.	|	1216	|	1242	1249	|	1315	1335	|	1416	1440	|	1535	|	1610	1640	|	1735	|	|	1810	1842	1848	|	|
Newark Northgate d.	|	1228	|	|	|	|	1327	|	|	1428	1452	|	1547	|	|	1652	|	1747	|	|	|	1854	1900	|	1920
Retford d.	|	1243	|	|	1313	|	|	|	|	1443	|	|	1602	|	1630	|	|	1802	|	|	1831	|	|	|	|
Doncaster 127 176 d.	1234	1259	|	1315	1326	|	1359	1407	1434	1458	|	1536	1621	1633	1647	1716	1735	1818	|	1834	1846	1918	1928	1934	|
Wakefield Westgate 176 a.	|	1317	|	|	|	|	1416	|	|	1515	|	|	1638	|	|	1733	|	1835	|	|	|	1935	|	|	2000
Leeds 127 187 a.	|	1335	|	|	|	|	1435	|	|	1535	|	|	1701	|	|	1753	|	1853	|	|	|	1951	|	|	2022
Selby 187 a.	|	...	|	|	1342	|	...	|	|	...	|	|	...	|	1705	...	|	...	|	|	1907	...	|	|	...
Hull 187 a.	|	...	|	|	1422	|	...	|	|	...	|	|	...	|	1747	...	|	...	|	|	1947	...	|	|	...
York 127 187 d.	1258	...	1325	1341	...	1359	...	1436	1500	...	1541	1601	...	1657	...	...	1802	...	1845	1858	...	...	1955	2003	...
Darlington 127 187 d.	1326	...	...	1409	...	|	...	1508	1528	...	1609	1629	...	1727	...	...	1834	...	...	1926	...	...	2023	2032	...
Durham 127 187 d.	|	...	...	1427	...	|	...	1526	1545	...	1626	|	...	1745	...	...	|	...	...	1943	...	...	2040	|	...
Newcastle 127 187 d.	1359	...	...	1445	...	1459	...	1547	1603	...	1644	1701	...	1806	...	...	1906	...	...	2001	...	...	2059	2103	...
Berwick upon Tweed 127 d.	1442	...	...	|	...	1543	...	|	1652	...	|	|	...	1849	...	...	1949	...	...	|	...	...	...	2157	...
Edinburgh Waverley 127 a.	1527	...	...	1618	...	1629	...	1714	1737	...	1811	1827	...	1934	...	...	2035	...	...	2130	...	...	...	2243	...
Glasgow Central a.	1652	...	...	...	...	...	...	...	1850	...	...	...	...	2045	...	...	...	...	...	2246	...	...	...	...	...

A – To/ from Aberdeen.
B – To/ from Inverness.
C – To Bradford Forster Square (a. 2022Ⓐ/2106⑥).
D – To Keighley (a. 2057**s**) and Skipton (a. 2113).
E – To Keighley (a. 2017**s**) and Skipton (a. 2031).
G – [12] and 🍸 (✕ in 1st class on Ⓐ) London Kings Cross - York - Sunderland and v.v. Operated by *GC*.
H – Operated by *HT*.
J – From Skipton (d. 0655) and Keighley (d. 0705**u**).
K – From Harrogate (d. 0728).
L – From Bradford Forster Square (d. 0630Ⓐ/0733⑥).
M – From Skipton (d. 0655) and Keighley (d. 0707**u**).
N – From Harrogate (d. 0744).

GC, GR, HT. All trains 🍷

LONDON - YORKSHIRE, THE NORTH EAST and SCOTLAND

185

	⑥	⑥	⑥	⑥	⑥	⑥	⑥	⑥	⑥	⑦	⑦	⑦	⑦	⑦	⑦	⑦	⑦	1010	⑦	⑦	⑦	⑦	⑦	⑦	⑦
	C			n	G		H				amn	m		G				|	m	H	A		n		B
London Kings Cross .... **184** d.	1830	1835	1840	1900	1907	1930	1937	2000	2030		...	...	0900	0907	0910	0930	1000	1054	1030	1041	1100	1110	1200	1210	1230
Stevenage .... **184** d.	|	|	|	1919	|	|	1957u	|	|		...	...	0920	|	|	|	|	1116	1049	1101u	|	|	|	1229	|
Peterborough .... **184 206** d.	|	1921	1927	1951	|	2016	|	2046	2117		...	...	0949	|	0957	1014	1046	|	1119	|	1145	1154	1244	1259	1315
Grantham .... **206** d.	1930	|	|	|	|	2035	2043	2105	2138		...	...	1011	|	|	|	|	1138	|	1146	|	1216	|	1321	|
Newark Northgate .... d.	|	|	1955	|	|	2047	|	2117	2149		...	...	|	|	1031	|	1116	1156	|	|	|	1228	1314	|	|
Retford .... d.	|	|	2011	|	|	|	2105	2132	|		...	...	|	|	1046	|	|	1213	|	1207	|	1243	|	1343	|
Doncaster .... **127 176** d.	2002	2008	2027	2038	|	2112	2120	2148	2214		...	0943	1044	|	1103	1106	1141	1232	1210	1223	1238	1300	1342	1359	1409
Wakefield Westgate .... **176** a.	2019	|	|	|	|	|	|	2205	|		...	|	|	|	1120	|	|	...	|	|	|	1317	|	1416	|
Leeds .... **127 187** a.	2035	|	|	|	|	|	|	2224	|		...	|	|	|	1139	|	|	...	|	|	|	1336	|	1436	|
Selby .... **187** a.	...	|	2043	|	|	|	2135	...	|		...	|	|	|	...	|	|	...	|	1241	|	...	|	...	|
Hull .... **187** a.	...	|	2127	|	|	|	2216	...	|		...	|	|	|	...	|	|	...	|	1323	|	...	|	...	|
York .... **127 187** d.	...	2041	...	2104	2115	2142	...	...	2239		0900	1006	1109	1114	...	1130	1206	...	1235	...	1309	...	1406	...	1435
Darlington .... **127 187** d.	...	2109	...	2137	...	2210	...	...	2308		0932	1034	1137	...	...	1158	1234	...	1303	...	1337	...	1438	...	1503
Durham .... **127 187** d.	...	2127	...	2156	...	2227	...	...	2325		0950	1052	1154	...	...	|	1252	...	|	...	1355	...	1456	...	|
Newcastle .... **127 187** d.	...	2145	...	2214	...	2245	...	...	2346		1015	1111	1215	...	...	1231	1309	...	1334	...	1414	...	1514	...	1534
Berwick upon Tweed ..... **127** d.	...	...	...	...	...	...	...	...	...		1108	1154	1258	...	...	|	|	...	1417	...	|	...	1557	...	|
Edinburgh Waverley .... **127** a.	...	...	...	...	...	...	...	...	...		1157	1238	1346	...	...	1402	1435		1501	...	1540	...	1643	...	1700
Glasgow Central .... a.	...	...	...	...	...	...	...	...	...		1307	1355	...	...	...	...	...		1614	...	...	...	...	...	...

	⑦	⑦	⑦	⑦	⑦	⑦	⑦	⑦	⑦	⑦	⑦	⑦	⑦	⑦	⑦	⑦	⑦	⑦	⑦	⑦	⑦	⑦	⑦	⑦	⑦
	H	m		a	G	A			m			H			n		m		n	H	a		G	n	
London Kings Cross .... **184** d.	1240	1300	1310	1330	1345	1400	1410	1430	1500	1510	1530	1544	1600	1610	1630	1640	1700	1710	1730	1744	1800	1810	1820	1830	1840
Stevenage .... **184** d.	1300u	1319	|	1349	|	|	|	|	1519	|	|	1604u	|	1629	1649	|	|	|	1749	1801u	|	|	|	1850	|
Peterborough .... **184 206** d.	|	1351	1357	1419	|	1445	1454	1514	1549	1555	1615	|	1647	1659	1719	1725	1744	1754	1819	|	1845	1855	|	1919	1925
Grantham .... **206** d.	13456	|	1419	|	|	|	1516	|	|	1618	1639	1649	|	|	|	1747	|	1817	|	1846	1906	|	|	|	1947
Newark Northgate .... d.	|	|	1431	|	|	|	1528	|	|	1631	1650	|	|	|	|	|	1814	|	1849	|	|	1926	|	|	|
Retford .... d.	1406	|	|	|	|	|	1543	|	|	|	|	1710	|	1739	|	|	|	|	|	1907	|	1942	|	|	|
Doncaster .... **127 176** d.	1420	1442	1456	1510	|	1539	1600	1609	|	1657	1720	1725	1740	1755	1811	|	1843	1850	1920	1923	1942	1959	|	2012	2020
Wakefield Westgate .... **176** a.	|	|	1513	|	|	|	1617	|	|	1714	|	|	|	1812	|	1838	|	1907	|	|	|	2016	|	|	2038
Leeds .... **127 187** a.	|	|	1533	|	|	|	1636	|	|	1734	|	|	|	1832	|	1859	|	1927	|	|	|	2039	|	|	2059
Selby .... **187** a.	1436	|	...	|	|	|	...	|	|	...	|	1750	|	...	|	...	|	...	|	1940	|	...	|	|	...
Hull .... **187** a.	1516	|	...	|	|	|	...	|	|	...	|	1832	|	...	|	...	|	...	|	2022	|	...	|	|	...
York .... **127 187** d.	...	1507	...	1538	1544	1606	...	1642	1705	...	1747	...	1807	...	1842	...	1907	...	1947	...	2008	...	2023	2040	...
Darlington .... **127 187** d.	...	1535	...	1608	...	1634	...	1710	1733	...	1816	...	1836	...	1915	...	1936	...	2021	...	2036	...	...	2113	...
Durham .... **127 187** d.	...	1554	...	1625	...	|	...	|	|	...	1833	...	|	...	1933	...	1953	...	2038	...	|	...	...	2131	...
Newcastle .... **127 187** d.	...	1611	...	1644	...	1707	...	1745	1805	...	1852	...	1907	...	1951	...	2011	...	2056	...	2107	...	...	2153	...
Berwick upon Tweed ..... **127** d.	...	|	...	1737	...	|	...	1828	1848	...	...	...	|	...	...	...	2054	...	...	...	2157	...	...	2237	...
Edinburgh Waverley .... **127** a.	...	1737	...	1825	...	1833	...	1914	1933	...	...	...	2035	...	...	...	2138	...	...	...	2244	...	...	2329	...
Glasgow Central .... a.	...	1845	...	...	...	...	...	...	2038	...	...	...	...	...	...	...	2245	...	...	...	...	...	...	...	...

	⑦	⑦	⑦	⑦	⑦	⑦	⑦	⑦	⑦	⑦	⑦	⑦
		G					H		n			
London Kings Cross .... **184** d.	1900	1910	1930	1935	2000	2003	2010	2030	2100	2130	2200	2210
Stevenage .... **184** d.	|	|	1950	1954	|	|	2030u	|	|	|	|	|
Peterborough .... **184 206** d.	1944	1956	2019	2024	2044	2050	|	2114	2146	2215	2245	2259s
Grantham .... **206** d.	|	2019	|	|	|	|	2119	2136	|	2239	|	2331s
Newark Northgate .... d.	|	2030	|	|	|	|	|	2148	|	2250	|	2342s
Retford .... d.	|	|	|	|	|	|	2140	2203	|	2306	|	|
Doncaster .... **127 176** d.	2035	2056	2110	2123	2136	|	2154	2220	2243	2327	2345	0012s
Wakefield Westgate .... **176** a.	|	...	2127	|	|	2157	|	2237	|	|	|	|
Leeds .... **127 187** a.	|	...	2147	|	|	2216	|	2300	|	0024	|	0118
Selby .... **187** a.	|	...	...	|	|	...	2209s	...	|	...	|	...
Hull .... **187** a.	|	...	...	|	|	...	2250	...	|	...	|	...
York .... **127 187** d.	2102	...	...	2148	2202	...	...	...	2311	...	0039	...
Darlington .... **127 187** d.	2130	...	...	2229	2243	...	...	...	2359	...	...	...
Durham .... **127 187** d.	|	...	...	2246	2301	...	...	...	0017	...	...	...
Newcastle .... **127 187** d.	2202	...	...	2316	2334	...	...	...	0050	...	...	...
Berwick upon Tweed ..... **127** d.	...	...	...	...	...	...	...	...	...	...	...	...
Edinburgh Waverley .... **127** a.	...	...	...	...	...	...	...	...	...	...	...	...
Glasgow Central .... a.	...	...	...	...	...	...	...	...	...	...	...	...

	Ⓐ	Ⓐ	Ⓐ	Ⓐ	Ⓐ	Ⓐ	Ⓐ	Ⓐ
					n		n	
Glasgow Central .... d.		...	...	...	...	...	...	...
Edinburgh Waverley . **127** d.		...	...	...	...	...	...	...
Berwick upon Tweed . **127** d.		...	...	...	...	...	...	...
Newcastle .... **127 187** d.		...	...	...	0420t	...	0525	...
Durham .... **127 187** d.		...	...	...	0434t	...	0538	...
Darlington .... **127 187** d.		...	...	...	0452t	...	0556	...
York .... **127 187** d.		...	...	...	0600	...	0630	...
Hull .... **187** d.		...	...	...	|	...	|	...
Selby .... **187** d.		...	...	...	|	...	|	...
Leeds .... **127 187** d.		...	0505	0530	|	0605	|	0640
Wakefield Westgate **176** d.		...	0517	0542	|	0618	|	0652
Doncaster .... **127 176** d.		...	0535	0600	0623	|	0654	|
Retford .... d.		...	0550	|	|	0648	|	|
Newark North Gate .... d.		...	0605	0624	0646	0704	|	0729
Grantham .... **206** d.		...	0618	0637	0659	0717	0725	|
Peterborough .... **184 206** a.		0610	0637	0658	0718	0737	0745	|
Stevenage .... **184** a.		|	|	|	|	|	|	|
London K Cross .... **184** a.		0700	0730	0753	0813	0833	0843	0846

	Ⓐ	Ⓐ	Ⓐ	Ⓐ	Ⓐ	Ⓐ	Ⓐ	Ⓐ	Ⓐ	Ⓐ	Ⓐ	Ⓐ	Ⓐ	Ⓐ	Ⓐ	Ⓐ	Ⓐ	Ⓐ	Ⓐ	Ⓐ	Ⓐ	Ⓐ	Ⓐ	Ⓐ	Ⓐ
	✕	✕L	H		✕n		J		✕	K	G	a	H						n		am	H	G		
Glasgow Central .... d.	...	...	...	...	...	...	...	...	...	...	...	...	...	...	...	...	...	...	...	...	0650	...	...	...	...
Edinburgh Waverley .... **127** d.	...	...	...	...	...	...	...	...	0550	...	...	0600	...	...	...	...	0700	...	...	...	0800	...	...	...	...
Berwick upon Tweed ..... **127** d.	...	...	...	...	...	...	...	...	0629	...	...	0643	...	...	...	...	0742	...	...	...	|	...	...	...	...
Newcastle .... **127 187** d.	0600	...	...	...	0630	...	...	0700	0720	...	...	0740	...	...	0752	...	0832	...	0900	...	0930	...	...	...	...
Durham .... **127 187** d.	0612	...	...	...	0644	...	...	0712	|	...	...	|	...	...	0804	...	0845	...	0912	...	|	...	...	...	...
Darlington .... **127 187** d.	0630	...	...	...	0702	...	...	0730	|	...	...	|	...	...	0822	...	0905	...	0932	...	0958	...	...	...	...
York .... **127 187** d.	0700	...	...	...	0736	...	...	0800	0811	...	0820	0836	...	...	0852	...	0935	...	1006	...	1029	...	1053	...	...
Hull .... **187** d.	|	...	0625	...	|	...	...	|	|	...	|	|	0805	...	|	...	|	...	|	...	|	1012	|	...	...
Selby .... **187** d.	|	...	0700	...	|	...	...	|	|	...	|	|	0845	...	|	...	|	...	|	...	|	1047	|	...	...
Leeds .... **127 187** d.	|	0700	|	0720	|	...	0740	|	|	0805	|	|	|	0840	|	0905	|	0940	|	1005	|	|	|	1040	1105
Wakefield Westgate .... **176** d.	|	0712	|	0732	|	...	0752	|	|	0817	|	|	|	0852	|	0918	|	0952	|	1018	|	|	|	1052	1117
Doncaster .... **127 176** d.	|	0730	0718	|	|	0755	|	|	|	0837	|	|	0902	0912	0921	0936	1004	1011	1030	1035	1053	1105	|	1118	1137
Retford .... d.	|	|	0732	|	|	|	0819	|	|	|	|	|	0916	|	|	0951	|	|	|	|	1108	1120	|	|	|
Newark North Gate .... d.	|	|	|	|	|	|	0834	|	|	|	|	|	|	0937	0946	1006	|	1035	|	1059	|	|	|	1141	|
Grantham .... **206** d.	|	|	0757	|	|	0829	|	|	0902	|	|	0928	0942	|	0958	|	1038	|	|	1111	|	1140	|	1154	1209
Peterborough .... **184 206** a.	0803	|	|	0832	|	0850	|	|	|	0926	|	0947	|	1005	1018	1035	1057	1103	1116	1131	1148	|	|	1213	1228
Stevenage .... **184** a.	|	|	|	|	0906	|	|	|	|	0957	|	|	|	|	|	1105	|	|	1147	|	|	|	|	1243	|
London K Cross .... **184** a.	0859	0907	0917	0926	0935	0945	0951	0955	1011	1025	1031	1040	1051	1058	1114	1134	1151	1156	1215	1225	1242	1247	1249	1310	1322

	Ⓐ	Ⓐ	Ⓐ	Ⓐ	Ⓐ	Ⓐ	Ⓐ	Ⓐ	Ⓐ	Ⓐ	Ⓐ	Ⓐ	Ⓐ	Ⓐ	Ⓐ	Ⓐ	Ⓐ	Ⓐ	Ⓐ	Ⓐ	Ⓐ	Ⓐ	Ⓐ	Ⓐ	Ⓐ
	m					A		H		am	B		G			A			n	m			H		
Glasgow Central .... d.	0750	...	...	...	...	...	...	...	...	0950	...	...	...	...	...	...	...	...	...	1150	...	...	...	...	...
Edinburgh Waverley .... **127** d.	0900	...	0930	...	...	1030	...	...	...	1100	1130	...	...	...	1200	1230	...	...	...	1300	...	...	...	...	1400
Berwick upon Tweed ..... **127** d.	0939	...	1010	...	...	|	...	...	...	1139	|	...	...	...	1239	|	...	...	...	1339	...	...	...	...	1439
Newcastle .... **127 187** d.	1034	...	1101	...	1130	1159	...	...	...	1235	1301	...	...	...	1329	1400	...	...	1405	1434	...	1455	...	...	1530
Durham .... **127 187** d.	1047	...	|	...	1144	|	...	...	...	1248	|	...	...	...	|	|	...	...	1417	|	...	1507	...	...	|
Darlington .... **127 187** d.	1105	...	1129	...	1202	|	...	...	...	1306	|	...	...	...	1356	|	...	...	1435	1502	...	1525	...	...	1602
York .... **127 187** d.	1135	...	1200	...	1232	1253	...	...	...	1336	1354	...	1408	...	1426	1453	...	...	1511	1535	...	1554	...	...	1632
Hull .... **187** d.	|	...	|	...	|	|	...	1245	...	|	|	...	|	...	|	|	...	...	|	|	...	|	1518	...	|
Selby .... **187** d.	|	...	|	...	|	|	...	1320	...	|	|	...	|	...	|	|	...	...	|	|	...	|	1557	...	|
Leeds .... **127 187** d.	|	1140	|	1205	|	|	1240	|	1305	|	|	1340	|	1405	|	|	1440	1505	|	|	1540	|	|	1605	|
Wakefield Westgate .... **176** d.	|	1152	|	1217	|	|	1252	|	1318	|	|	1353	|	1418	|	|	1452	1517	|	|	1552	|	|	1617	|
Doncaster .... **127 176** d.	1200	1212	|	1236	1255	|	1314	1337	1339	1403	|	1417	|	|	1450	|	1515	|	1536	1600	|	|	1615	1636	|
Retford .... d.	|	|	|	1251	|	|	|	|	1355	|	|	|	|	|	|	|	|	|	1551	|	|	|	1634	|	|
Newark North Gate .... d.	|	1237	|	|	|	|	1342	|	1410	|	|	|	|	|	1513	|	1541	|	1606	|	|	|	|	1700	|
Grantham .... **206** d.	|	|	|	1314	|	|	|	1409	1423	|	|	|	|	1503	1526	|	1554	|	1619	|	|	1644	1655	|	|
Peterborough .... **184 206** a.	1246	1305	1311	|	1342	1402	1409	|	1442	1449	|	1505	|	1522	1545	1601	|	1618	|	1647	1651	1704	|	1727	|
Stevenage .... **184** a.	1316	|	|	|	1417	|	|	|	1512	|	|	|	|	1552	1618	|	|	1648	|	|	|	1734	1746s	|	|
London K Cross .... **184** a.	1343	1402	1410	1420	1444	1457	1505	1520	1540	1544	1550	1558	1605	1622	1645	1657	1704	1715	1728	1741	1746	1804	1813	1824	1827

a – Also calls at Alnmouth (25 minutes after Newcastle / 55 minutes after Edinburgh).
b – Also calls at Alnmouth on ⑤.
f – ⑤ only.
m – Also calls at Motherwell (40 minutes after Edinburgh / 14 minutes after Glasgow).
n – Also calls at Northallerton (18 minutes after / 21 minutes before York).

s – Stops to set down only.
t – 10 minutes earlier on ①.
u – Stops to pick up only.

185 SCOTLAND, THE NORTH EAST and YORKSHIRE - LONDON

All trains 🍸 GC, GR, HT

	Ⓐ	Ⓐ	Ⓐ m	Ⓐ	Ⓐ H	Ⓐ	Ⓐ	Ⓐ	Ⓐ	Ⓐ	Ⓐ G	Ⓐ	Ⓐ n	Ⓐ am	Ⓐ H	Ⓐ	Ⓐ A	Ⓐ a	Ⓐ m	Ⓐ amn		⑥	⑥ n	⑥	⑥
Glasgow Central ... d.	...	...	1350	...	...	...	...	...	...	...	...	...	...	1550	...	...	...	...	1750	1950	⑥	...	...	...	...
Edinburgh Waverley ... **127** d.	...	...	1500	...	...	...	...	...	1600	...	...	...	...	1700	...	...	1730	1835	1900	2100		...	...	...	...
Berwick upon Tweed ... **127** d.	...	...	|	...	...	...	...	...	1643	...	...	...	...	|	...	...	1817	1918	1943	2143		...	...	...	...
Newcastle ... **127 187** d.	...	1555	1628	...	...	...	1655	...	1732	...	...	...	1810	1835	...	...	1908	2018	2038	2245		...	0430	...	0600
Durham ... **127 187** d.	...	1608	|	...	...	...	1707	...	|	...	...	...	1822	|	...	...	|	—	2051	2300		...	0445	...	0612
Darlington ... **127 187** d.	...	1626	|	...	...	...	1725	...	1759	...	...	...	1840	1904	...	...	1936	...	2109	2318		...	0503	...	0630
York ... **127 187** d.	...	1656	1721	...	...	...	1755	...	1831	...	1908	...	1913	1935	...	...	2009	...	2140	0016		...	0600	...	0700
Hull ... **187** d.	...	|	|	...	1706	...	|	...	|	...	|	...	|	|	1918	...	|	Ⓐ	|	...		...	|	...	|
Selby ... **187** d.	...	|	|	...	1743	...	|	...	|	...	|	...	|	|	1953	...	|		|	...		...	|	...	|
Leeds ... **127 187** d.	1640	|	|	1705	|	1740	|	1805	|	1840	|	1905	|	|	|	1940	|	2040	|	...		0505	|	0610	|
Wakefield Westgate ... **176** d.	1652	|	|	1717	|	1752	|	1817	|	1852	|	1917	|	|	|	1952	|	2055	|	...		0517	|	0622	|
Doncaster ... **127 176** d.	1710	1720	|	1737	1803	1811	1821	1835	1854	1913	|	1935	1939	2000	2010	2014	2032	2112	2203	...		0535	0623	0640	0723
Retford ... d.	|	|	|	1757	1817	|	1836	|	|	|	|	|	|	|	|	|	|	2127	|	...		0550	|	0655	|
Newark North Gate ... d.	1733	1744	|	|	|	1834	1851	|	1917	1938	|	|	2003	|	|	2037	|	2142	2226	...		0605	|	0710	|
Grantham ... **206** d.	|	1757	|	|	1837	1847	|	|	|	1951	|	2006	|	|	2041	2050	|	2155	2239	...		0617	|	0723	|
Peterborough ... **184 206** a.	1801	|	1826	|	|	1906	1919	1925	1945	|	|	2027	2032	2046	|	2109	2120	2214	2258	...		0637	0709	0742	0809
Stevenage ... **184** a.	|	1842	|	1902	1924s	|	1950	|	2016	2035	|	|	|	2117	2130s	|	2152	2246s	2333s	...		|	|	|	|
London K Cross ... **184** a.	1854	1912	1919	1930	1949	1959	2018	2021	2044	2103	2109	2120	2125	2144	2158	2204	2220	2311	0005	...		0729	0804	0840	0903

	⑥	⑥	⑥ M	⑥ n	⑥ L	⑥ N	⑥	⑥ G	⑥ H	⑥ a	⑥	⑥	⑥ n	⑥	⑥ am	⑥ H	⑥ G	⑥	⑥	⑥ m	⑥	⑥	⑥ m	⑥	⑥ A
Glasgow Central ... d.	...	...	...	...	...	...	...	...	...	...	...	...	...	...	0650	...	...	...	...	0750	...	...	0850	...	...
Edinburgh Waverley ... **127** d.	...	...	...	...	...	...	...	...	...	0615	...	0700	0730	...	0800	...	...	0835	...	0900	0930	...	1000	...	1030
Berwick upon Tweed ... **127** d.	...	...	...	...	...	...	...	...	...	0658	...	0740	0809	...	|	...	...	0914	...	0941	1010	...	|	...	|
Newcastle ... **127 187** d.	...	0635	...	0700	...	...	0730	...	...	0754	...	0833	0900	...	0932	...	...	1005	...	1032	1100	...	1129	...	1200
Durham ... **127 187** d.	...	0648	...	0712	...	...	0742	...	...	|	...	0846	0913	...	|	...	...	|	...	1045	|	...	1142	...	1213
Darlington ... **127 187** d.	...	0706	...	0730	...	...	0800	...	...	0821	...	0904	0931	...	1001	...	...	1035	...	1103	1127	...	1201	...	1231
York ... **127 187** d.	...	0736	...	0803	...	...	0830	0847	...	0851	...	0935	1005	...	1031	...	1104	1107	...	1133	1159	...	1231	...	1302
Hull ... **187** d.	0650	|	...	|	...	...	|	|	0802	|	...	|	|	...	|	1006	|	|	...	|	|	...	|	...	|
Selby ... **187** d.	0723	|	...	|	...	...	|	|	0837	|	...	|	|	...	|	1041	|	|	...	|	|	...	|	...	|
Leeds ... **127 187** d.	|	|	0740	|	0805	0815	|	|	|	|	0905	|	|	1005	|	|	|	|	1105	|	|	1205	|	0700	|
Wakefield Westgate ... **176** d.	|	|	0752	|	0818	|	|	|	|	|	0917	|	|	1018	|	|	|	|	1117	|	|	1217	|	0712	|
Doncaster ... **127 176** d.	0743	0800	|	|	|	0845	0855	|	0901	0915	0935	1001	1029	1036	1055	1102	|	1129	1139	1157	1221	1235	1257	0730	|
Retford ... d.	|	|	0820	|	|	|	0910	|	0921	|	|	|	|	|	1110	1117	|	|	|	|	|	1250	|	|	|
Newark North Gate ... d.	|	0824	0834	|	0854	|	|	|	|	|	1000	|	|	1100	|	|	|	|	1201	|	|	1305	|	0753	|
Grantham ... **206** d.	|	0837	0846	|	0906	|	|	|	0942	|	1012	|	|	1112	|	1138	|	1200	1214	1228	|	1317	|	0806	|
Peterborough ... **184 206** a.	0831	0857	0906	0912	0926	0932	0951	|	|	1006	1032	1050	1115	1132	1149	|	|	1219	1233	1248	1307	|	1343	0825	1409
Stevenage ... **184** a.	|	|	|	0945	|	|	|	|	|	|	1103	|	1150	|	|	1225s	|	|	1303	|	|	|	1416	|	|
London K Cross ... **184** a.	0925	0951	1000	1013	1020	1026	1044	1048	1052	1058	1133	1144	1217	1224	1242	1252	1255	1312	1333	1341	1359	1427	1443	0918	1510

	⑥	⑥ m	⑥ H	⑥ Ba	⑥ G	⑥	⑥ n	⑥ A	⑥	⑥ m	⑥ H	⑥	⑥	⑥	⑥ m	⑥	⑥	⑥ H	⑥	⑥ G	⑥ am	⑥ A	⑥	⑥ amn	
Glasgow Central ... d.	...	0950	...	...	...	...	...	...	...	1150	...	...	...	...	1350	...	...	...	...	...	1550	...	...	1750	...
Edinburgh Waverley ... **127** d.	...	1100	...	1130	...	...	1200	1230	...	1300	...	1330	...	1400	1500	...	1600	...	...	...	1700	1730	...	1900	...
Berwick upon Tweed ... **127** d.	...	1139	...	|	...	...	1239	|	...	|	...	1409	...	1439	|	...	1639	...	...	...	|	1813	...	1944	...
Newcastle ... **127 187** d.	...	1233	...	1303	...	...	1331	1359	...	1429	...	1459	...	1528	1629	...	1730	...	...	...	1833	1906	...	2047	...
Durham ... **127 187** d.	...	1246	...	|	...	...	1344	1412	...	1442	...	1526	...	1542	1642	...	|	...	...	...	1846	|	...	2100	...
Darlington ... **127 187** d.	...	1304	...	|	...	...	1402	1430	...	1500	...	|	...	1604	1700	...	1759	...	...	...	1905	1934	...	2118	...
York ... **127 187** d.	...	1334	...	1357	1405	...	1437	1501	...	1530	...	1557	...	1634	1731	...	1829	...	...	1915	1936	2006	...	2152	...
Hull ... **187** d.	...	|	1305	|	|	...	|	|	...	|	1506	|	...	|	|	...	|	1812	...	|	|	|	...	|	...
Selby ... **187** d.	...	|	1340	|	|	...	|	|	...	|	1542	|	...	|	|	...	|	1847	...	|	|	|	...	|	...
Leeds ... **127 187** d.	1305	|	|	|	|	1405	|	|	1505	|	|	|	1605	|	|	1740	|	|	1840	|	|	|	2015	|	...
Wakefield Westgate ... **176** d.	1317	|	|	|	|	1417	|	|	1517	|	|	|	1617	|	|	1752	|	|	1854	|	|	|	2031	|	...
Doncaster ... **127 176** d.	1338	1358	1404	|	|	1435	1504	|	1535	1555	1602	1621	1639	1659	1755	1810	1852	1905	1914	|	2000	2030	2048	2217	...
Retford ... d.	|	|	1419	|	|	1450	|	|	|	|	1617	|	1654	|	|	1825	|	1920	1929	|	|	|	2103	...	...
Newark North Gate ... d.	1401	|	|	|	|	1505	|	|	1602	|	|	|	1709	|	1818	1840	|	|	1944	|	|	|	2118	...	...
Grantham ... **206** d.	|	1429	1439	|	|	1518	|	|	1615	|	1637	1652	|	1730	|	1852	|	1940	1956	|	|	|	2131	...	...
Peterborough ... **184 206** a.	1429	1449	|	1504	|	1538	1550	|	1634	1642	|	1711	1736	1749	1846	1912	1938	|	2016	|	2046	2118	2150	...	...
Stevenage ... **184** a.	|	|	1526s	|	|	|	1621	|	1706	1716	1725s	|	|	1819	|	1943	2007	2025s	2048	|	2118	2154	2220	...	...
London K Cross ... **184** a.	1521	1542	1552	1603	1607	1634	1647	1658	1733	1743	1752	1810	1828	1846	1940	2010	2035	2052	2115	2130	2145	2220	2247	...	...

		⑦	⑦	⑦ H	⑦	⑦ n	⑦	⑦ G	⑦	⑦	⑦	⑦	⑦	⑦ H	⑦	⑦	⑦	⑦	⑦	⑦ n	⑦ m	⑦ H	⑦ Aa	⑦	⑦ G
Glasgow Central ... d.	⑦	...	...	...	...	...	...	...	...	...	...	...	...	...	...	...	...	...	...	...	1050	...	...	...	...
Edinburgh Waverley ... **127** d.		...	...	...	...	...	...	...	...	0900	...	0930	1000	...	1030	...	1100	...	1130	...	1200	...	1230	...	...
Berwick upon Tweed ... **127** d.		...	...	...	...	...	...	...	...	0939	...	|	1039	...	1109	...	|	...	|	...	1239	...	|	...	...
Newcastle ... **127 187** d.		...	0800	...	...	0900	0930	...	...	1032	...	1055	1134	...	1158	...	1229	...	1301	1310	1338	...	1402	...	...
Durham ... **127 187** d.		...	0812	...	...	0912	|	...	...	|	...	1108	|	...	|	...	1242	...	|	1323	|	...	|	...	...
Darlington ... **127 187** d.		...	0830	...	...	0930	0959	...	...	1059	...	|	|	...	1225	...	1300	...	1328	1341	1405	...	1430	...	...
York ... **127 187** d.		...	0900	...	...	1004	1028	1049	...	1129	...	1153	1229	...	1255	...	1337	...	1400	1414	1436	...	1502	...	1531
Hull ... **187** d.		...	|	0910	...	|	|	|	...	|	...	|	|	1212	|	...	|	...	|	|	|	1410	|	...	|
Selby ... **187** d.		...	|	|	...	|	|	|	...	|	...	|	|	1247	|	...	|	...	|	|	|	1445	|	...	|
Leeds ... **127 187** d.		0825	|	|	0940	|	|	|	1040	|	1140	|	|	|	|	1240	|	1340	|	|	|	|	|	1440	|
Wakefield Westgate ... **176** d.		0837	|	|	0952	|	|	|	1052	|	1152	|	|	|	|	1252	|	1352	|	|	|	|	|	1452	|
Doncaster ... **127 176** d.		0855	0925	0957	1010	1028	1053	|	1113	1153	1210	|	1254	1306	1319	1311	1401	1410	1424	1438	1500	1505	|	1510	|
Retford ... d.		|	0940	1012	|	|	|	|	1128	|	|	|	|	1321	|	1334	|	|	|	|	|	1520	|	1525	|
Newark North Gate ... d.		0918	|	|	1032	1051	|	|	1142	|	|	1236	|	|	|	1348	|	1433	|	|	|	|	|	1539	|
Grantham ... **206** d.		0931	1002	1032	|	1103	|	|	1154	|	1240	|	1326	1340	|	1400	|	|	1454	|	|	1540	|	1552	|
Peterborough ... **184 206** a.		0953	1024	|	1102	1125	1143	|	1216	1240	|	1306	|	|	1406	1422	1448	|	|	1525	1547	|	|	1613	|
Stevenage ... **184** a.		|	1055	1121s	|	1155	|	|	|	|	|	1336	1416	1429s	|	|	|	1528	|	|	1618	1629s	|	1648	|
London K Cross ... **184** a.		1048	1123	1147	1155	1223	1240	1251	1314	1339	1350	1404	1444	1455	1504	1516	1542	1555	1604	1618	1646	1655	1710	1717	1724

	⑦ n	⑦	⑦ B	⑦ m	⑦	⑦ H	⑦ n	⑦ A	⑦	⑦	⑦	⑦ n	⑦	⑦	⑦ m	⑦	⑦ Aa	⑦ H	⑦ m	⑦ n	⑦ G	⑦	⑦ a	⑦ m	⑦ n
Glasgow Central ... d.	...	...	...	1250	...	...	...	...	...	...	...	...	...	...	1450	...	...	...	1550	...	...	...	...	1750	...
Edinburgh Waverley ... **127** d.	1300	...	1330	1400	...	...	...	1430	...	1500	...	1530	...	...	1600	...	1630	...	1700	1730	...	...	1800	1900	2000
Berwick upon Tweed ... **127** d.	1339	...	1409	|	...	...	...	|	...	1539	...	1609	...	...	|	...	1709	...	|	|	...	...	1839	|	2043
Newcastle ... **127 187** d.	1432	...	1459	1530	...	...	1550	1603	...	1626	...	1704	...	1710	1732	...	1810	...	1829	1855	...	...	1935	2031	2140
Durham ... **127 187** d.	|	...	1513	|	...	...	1602	|	...	1646	...	|	...	1722	|	...	|	...	1843	1908	...	...	1948	|	2153
Darlington ... **127 187** d.	1459	...	1531	1557	...	...	1620	1631	...	1704	...	1731	...	1740	1759	...	|	...	1901	1926	...	...	2006	2058	2211
York ... **127 187** d.	1534	...	1603	1628	...	...	1653	1701	...	1736	...	1805	...	1814	1829	...	1903	...	1931	2002	2015	...	2036	2128	2319
Hull ... **187** d.	|	...	|	|	...	1623	|	|	...	|	...	|	1730	|	|	...	|	1848	|	|	|	...	|	|	...
Selby ... **187** d.	|	...	|	|	...	1658	|	|	...	|	...	|	1805	|	|	...	|	1923	|	|	|	...	|	|	...
Leeds ... **127 187** d.	|	1540	|	|	1640	|	|	|	1705	|	1740	|	|	|	|	1840	|	|	|	|	|	2015	|	|	...
Wakefield Westgate ... **176** d.	|	1552	|	|	1652	|	|	|	1718	|	1752	|	|	|	|	1852	|	|	|	|	|	2028	|	|	...
Doncaster ... **127 176** d.	1558	1610	1628	1652	1710	1715	1722	1730	1736	1803	|	1831	1823	1839	1853	1910	1929	1943	1955	2026	|	2047	2100	2152	...
Retford ... d.	|	|	|	|	|	1730	|	|	1751	|	|	|	1844	|	|	|	|	1958	|	|	|	|	2115	|	...
Newark North Gate ... d.	1620	|	|	|	|	|	1746	|	1805	|	|	|	|	1903	|	|	|	|	2017	|	|	|	2134	|	...
Grantham ... **206** d.	|	1640	|	|	1740	1749	|	|	|	|	1837	|	1906	|	|	1940	|	2018	|	2056	|	|	|	2222	...
Peterborough ... **184 206** a.	1651	1701	1718	1739	1802	|	|	1821	|	1850	1859	1918	1928	1933	1942	2001	2019	|	2047	2117	|	2135	2203	2243	...
Stevenage ... **184** a.	1721	|	|	1810	|	|	1842	|	1902	1921	|	|	|	2008	2018	2032	2052	2109s	2120	2148	|	2209	2234	|	...
London K Cross ... **184** a.	1749	1755	1814	1837	1855	1906	1914	1917	1933	1948	1952	2014	2023	2034	2043	2101	2120	2135	2147	2216	2217	2237	2304	2337	...

For footnotes see page 148 and 149.

TP NEWCASTLE and MIDDLESBROUGH - LEEDS - MANCHESTER and LIVERPOOL 187

Services on ⑦ valid until January 31. For other services Newcastle - York and v.v., see Tables **127** and **185**.

km		⚒	⚒	⚒	⚒	⚒	Ⓐ	Ⓐ	⑥	⚒	⚒	⚒	⚒	Ⓐ	⑥	Ⓐ	⑥	⚒	⚒	⚒	⚒	⚒	⚒	⚒	⚒	⚒
170	**Newcastle** .... 127 185 d.		...	...	...	...	...	...	...	0613	...	...	...	...	...	0726	0733	...	...	...	...	...	0912	...	...	...
147	Durham .... 127 185 d.		...	...	...	...	...	...	...	0629	...	...	...	...	...	0743	0748	...	...	...	...	...	0927	...	...	...
136	**Middlesbrough** .... d.		...	...	...	0557	...	...	...	|	...	...	0721	...	...	|	|	...	...	...	0900	...	|	...	0959	...
112	Darlington............ 127 185 d.		...	...	...	|	...	...	...	0646	...	...	|	...	...	0800	0806	...	...	...	|	...	0944	...	|	...
89	Northallerton........ 127 185 d.		...	...	...	0625	...	...	...	0658	...	...	0748	...	...	0812	0818	...	...	...	0927	...	0956	...	1027	...
77	Thirsk........................ d.		...	...	...	0633	...	...	...	0706	...	...	0756	...	...	0820	0826	...	...	...	0935	...	|	...	1035	...
108	**Scarborough**................ d.		...	...	...	|	...	0630	0634	|	0700	...	|	0738	0747	|	|	...	...	0847	|	...	|	0947	|	...
74	Malton........................ d.		...	...	...	|	...	0653	0657	|	0723	...	|	0801	0810	|	|	...	...	0910	|	...	|	1010	|	...
41	**York**.................. 127 185 d.		0557	0628	...	0654	...	0723	0728	0740f	0754	...	0824f	0840f	0840	0858	0858	...	0928	0940	0958	...	1028f	1040	1058	...
83	**Hull** .... 127 185 d.		|	|	0600	|	0635	|	|	|	|	0733	|	|	|	|	|	0840	|	|	|	0940	|	|	|	1038
34	Selby .... 127 185 d.		|	|	0636	|	0707	|	|	|	|	0807	|	|	|	|	|	0911	|	|	|	1011	|	|	|	1109
0	**Leeds** .... 127 185 d.		0625	0655	0708	0723	0738	0755	0755	0808	0825	0840	0855	0908	0908	0925	0925	0940	0955	1008	1025	1040	1055	1108	1125	1140
15	Dewsbury.................... d.		0636	0706	|	0734	|	0806	0806	|	0836	|	0906	|	|	0936	0936	|	1006	|	1036	|	1106	|	1136	|
28	**Huddersfield**............... d.		0645	0716	0726	0744	0757	0816	0816	0826	0845	0859	0916	0926	0926	0946	0946	0959	1016	1026	1046	1059	1116	1126	1146	1159
57	Stalybridge .... d.		0704	0734	0744	0802	0817	|	|	0844	|	|	|	0944	0944	|	|	|	|	1044	|	|	|	1144	|	|
69	**Manchester** Piccadilly 206 a.		0719	0751	0805	0819	0836	0851	0851	0905	0919	0936	0949	1005	1005	1019	1019	1036	1049	1105	1119	1136	1149	1205	1219	1236
85	**Manchester** Airport ✈ .... a.		0742	0812	|	0842	...	0912	0912	|	0942	...	1012	|	|	1042	1042	...	1112	|	1145	...	1212	|	1242	...
95	Warrington Central ..... 206 a.		...	...	0829	...	...	...	...	0929	...	...	...	1029	1029	...	...	...	...	1129	...	...	...	1229	...	...
125	**Liverpool** Lime St...... 206 a.		...	...	0857	...	...	...	...	0957	...	...	...	1057	1057	...	...	...	...	1157	...	...	...	1257	...	...

	⚒	⚒	⚒	⚒	⚒	⚒	⚒	⚒	⚒	⚒	⚒	⚒	⚒	⚒	Ⓐ	⑥	⚒	⚒	⚒	⑥	①–④	⑤	⑤	⚒	⚒	⚒
Newcastle........... 127 185 d.	1012	...	...	...	1115	...	...	...	1215	...	...	...	1315	...	...	...	...	1412	...	...	...	...	...	...	1512	...
Durham .... 127 185 d.	1027	...	...	...	1127	...	...	...	1227	...	...	...	1327	...	...	...	...	1424	...	...	...	...	...	...	1527	...
Middlesbrough...............d.	|	...	1100	...	|	...	1200	...	|	...	1250	...	|	...	1350	1400	...	|	...	1450	1450	1450	...	...	|	...
Darlington............ 127 185 d.	1044	...	|	...	1144	...	|	...	1244	...	|	...	1344	...	|	|	...	1444	...	|	|	|	...	...	1544	...
Northallerton......... 127 185 d.	1056	...	1127	...	1156	...	1227	...	1256	...	1317	...	1356	...	1417	1437	...	1456	...	1517	1517	1517	...	...	1556	...
Thirsk ....d.	|	...	1135	...	|	...	1235	...	|	...	1325	...	|	...	1425	1435	...	|	...	1525	1525	1525	...	...	|	...
Scarborough..................d.	|	1047	|	...	|	1147	|	...	|	1247	|	...	|	1347	|	|	...	|	1447	|	|	|	...	...	|	1547
Malton...........................d.	|	1110	|	...	|	1210	|	...	|	1310	|	...	|	1410	|	|	...	|	1510	|	|	|	...	...	|	1610
York.................. 127 185 d.	1128f	1140	1158	...	1228f	1239	1258	...	1328f	1340	1358f	...	1428f	1440	1458f	1458	...	1528f	1540	1558f	1558f	1550	1558	...	1628f	1640
Hull.................. 127 185 d.	|	|	|	1138	|	|	|	1238	|	|	|	1338	|	|	|	|	1438	|	|	|	|	...	|	1538	|	|
Selby.................. 127 185 d.	|	|	|	1209	|	|	|	1309	|	|	|	1409	|	|	|	|	1509	|	|	|	|	...	|	1609	|	|
Leeds.................. 127 185 d.	1155	1208	1225	1240	1255	1308	1325	1340	1355	1408	1425	1437	1455	1508	1525	1525	1540	1555	1608	1625	1625	...	1625	1640	1655	1708
Dewsbury ....d.	1236	|	1236	|	1306	|	1336	|	1406	|	1436	|	1506	|	1536	1536	|	1606	|	1636	1636	...	1636	|	1706	|
Huddersfield...................d.	1216	1226	1246	1258	1316	1326	1346	1359	1416	1426	1446	1456	1516	1526	1546	1546	1559	1616	1626	1646	1646	...	1646	1659	1716	1726
Stalybridge ....d.	|	1244	|	|	|	1344	|	|	|	1444	|	|	|	1544	|	|	|	|	1644	|	|	...	|	1718	|	1744
Manchester Piccadilly .206 a.	1249	1305	1319	1336	1349	1405	1419	1436	1449	1505	1519	1536	1549	1605	1619	1619	1636	1649	1705	1721	1725	...	1725	1737	1749	1805
Manchester Airport ✈......a.	1312	|	1342	...	1412	|	1442	...	1512	|	1542	...	1612	|	1642	1642	...	1712	|	...	...	...	...	...	1812	|
Warrington Central.......206 a.	...	1329	...	...	...	1429	...	...	...	1529	...	...	...	1629	...	...	...	...	1729	...	...	...	...	...	...	1829
Liverpool Lime St ....206 a.	...	1357	...	...	...	1457	...	...	...	1557	...	...	...	1657	...	...	...	...	1800	...	...	...	...	...	...	1859

	⚒	⚒	⚒	⑥	Ⓐ	⚒	Ⓐ	⑥	⚒	Ⓐ	⑥	⑥	Ⓐ	Ⓐ	⑥	⚒	⚒	⚒	⑥	Ⓐ	⑥	⚒	⑤	①–④	⑤	⑥
Newcastle........... 127 185 d.	...	...	1606	...	...	...	...	...	1701	...	...	...	...	...	...	...	...	...	1852	1858	...	...	...	...	...	...
Durham .... 127 185 d.	...	...	1621	...	...	...	...	...	1713	...	...	...	...	...	...	...	...	...	1904	1910	...	...	...	...	...	...
Middlesbrough...............d.	1550	...	|	...	...	...	1650	1700	|	...	...	...	...	1750	1807	...	...	1900	|	|	...	...	2000	2000	...	2010
Darlington............ 127 185 d.	|	...	1639	...	...	...	|	|	1730	...	...	...	...	|	|	...	...	|	1922	1927	...	...	2031	2031	...	|
Northallerton......... 127 185 d.	1617	...	1650	...	...	...	1717	1727	1742	...	...	...	...	1817	1835	...	...	1927	1936	1938	...	...	2042	2042	...	2037
Thirsk ....d.	1625	...	1658	...	...	...	1725	1735	|	...	...	...	...	1825	1843	...	...	1935	|	|	...	...	2050	2050	...	2045
Scarborough..................d.	|	...	|	...	...	1647	|	|	|	...	...	1745	1747	|	|	...	1847	|	|	|	...	1947	|	|	...	|
Malton...........................d.	|	...	|	...	...	1710	|	|	|	...	...	1808	1810	|	|	...	1910	|	|	|	...	2010	|	|	...	|
York.................. 127 185 d.	1658f	...	1728	...	...	1740	1758f	1758	1809	...	...	1838	1840	1910t	1910f	...	1939	1958	2010f	2010f	...	2040	2110	2110	...	2110
Hull.................. 127 185 d.	|	1640	|	1701	1701	|	|	|	|	1758	1803	|	|	|	|	1859	|	...	|	|	1956	|	...	|	2035	|
Selby.................. 127 185 d.	|	1711	|	1732	1732	|	|	|	|	1831	1834	|	|	|	|	1930	|	...	|	|	2027	|	...	|	2106	|
Leeds.................. 127 185 d.	1726	1740	1755	1729	1802	1808	1825	1825	1840	1855	1908	1904	1908	1940	1940	1956	2008	...	2040	2040	2056	2108	...	2140	2140	2140
Dewsbury ....d.	1736	|	1806	...	1813	|	1836	1836	|	1906	|	...	|	1951	1951	...	|	...	2051	2051	...	|	...	2151	2151	2151
Huddersfield...................d.	1746	1759	1816	...	1824	1826	1846	1846	1859	1916	1926	...	1926	2000	2000	...	2026	...	2100	2100	...	2126	...	2200	2200	2200
Stalybridge ....d.	|	1818	|	...	...	1844	|	|	|	|	1944	...	1944	|	|	...	2044	...	|	|	...	2144	...	|	|	|
Manchester Piccadilly .206 a.	1819	1837	1849	...	...	1905	1921	1921	1933	1957	2005	...	2005	2033	2033	...	2105	...	2133	2133	...	2205	...	2233	2233	2233
Manchester Airport ✈......a.	1842	...	1913	...	...	|	...	...	1959	...	|	...	|	2057	2057	...	|	...	2157	2157	...	|	...	2257	2257	2257
Warrington Central.......206 a.	...	...	...	...	...	1929	...	...	...	...	2029	...	2029	...	...	...	2129	...	...	...	...	2229	...	...	...	...
Liverpool Lime St ....206 a.	...	...	...	...	...	1957	...	...	...	...	2059	...	2059	...	...	...	2157	...	...	...	...	2258	...	...	...	...

	①–④	Ⓐ	⑥	Ⓐ	⚒	Ⓐ	⚒	Ⓐ	⑥B	⑥C		⑦	⑦	⑦	⑦	⑦	⑦	⑦	⑦	⑦	⑦	⑦	⑦	⑦	⑦	⑦
Newcastle........... 127 185 d.	...	...	...	...	...	...	...	2147	...	...	...		...	0806	...	...	...	0933	...	...	...	1103	...	...	1205	...
Durham .... 127 185 d.	...	...	...	...	...	...	...	2200	...	...	...		...	0818	...	...	...	0948	...	...	...	1115	...	...	1217	...
Middlesbrough...............d.	...	...	2050	2050	...	2140	...	|	2150	2150	...		...	|	...	...	...	|	1015	...	...	|	...	...	|	...
Darlington............ 127 185 d.	...	...	|	|	...	2208	...	2217	2219	2219	...		...	0835	...	...	...	1005	|	...	...	1132	...	...	1234	...
Northallerton......... 127 185 d.	...	...	2117	2119	...	2219	...	2228	2230	2330	...		...	0847	...	...	...	1016	1042	...	...	1144	...	...	|	...
Thirsk ....d.	...	...	|	|	...	2227	...	|	2338	2238	...		...	|	...	...	...	|	1051	...	...	|	...	...	|	...
Scarborough..................d.	...	2037	|	|	...	|	2207	|	|	|	...		...	|	...	...	0920	|	|	...	1050	|	...	1150	|	...
Malton...........................d.	...	2100	|	|	...	|	2230	|	|	|	...		...	|	...	...	0943	|	|	...	1113	|	...	1213	|	...
York.................. 127 185 d.	...	2128	2142	2145	...	2254	2257	2307f	2307f	2307f	...		0840	0915	...	...	1015f	1043	1115f	...	1143	1215f	...	1245f	1315f	...
Hull.................. 127 185 d.	2045	...	|	|	2133	...	...	|	|	|	...		|	|	0900	...	|	|	|	1058	|	|	1200	|	|	1258
Selby.................. 127 185 d.	2116	...	|	|	2207	...	...	|	|	|	...		|	|	0933	...	|	|	|	1129	|	|	1233	|	|	1329
Leeds.................. 127 185 d.	2144	...	2208	2208	2240	...	...	2335	2333	2335	...		0915	0940	1006	...	1040	1108	1140	1159	1208	1240	1259	1310	1340	1359
Dewsbury ....d.	...	...	|	|	2251	...	...	2346	|	2346	...		0925	0951	|	...	1051	|	1151	|	|	1251	|	|	1351	|
Huddersfield...................d.	...	...	2226	2226	2300	...	...	2356	*0020**	2356	...		0934	1001	1026	...	1100	1126	1201	1217	1226	1301	1317	1328	1401	1417
Stalybridge ....d.	...	...	2244	2244	|	...	...	|	|	|	...		0953	|	1046	...	|	1144	|	|	1244	|	|	1346	|	|
Manchester Piccadilly .206 a.	...	...	2305	2305	2337	...	...	0054	*0120**	0041	...		1010	1034	1105	1107	1134	1208	1234	1254	1303	1334	1354	1405	1434	1454
Manchester Airport ✈......a.	...	...	...	...	...	...	...	0110	...	0100	...		|	1055	...	|	1155	|	1306	...	|	1355	...	|	1455	...
Warrington Central.......206 a.	...	...	...	...	...	...	...	...	...	...	...		1034	...	...	1129	...	1129	...	...	1329	...	...	1429	...	...
Liverpool Lime St ....206 a.	...	...	...	...	...	...	...	...	...	...	...		1059	...	...	1157	...	1257	...	...	1357	...	...	1457	...	...

	⑦	⑦	⑦	⑦	⑦	⑦	⑦	⑦	⑦	⑦	⑦	⑦	⑦	⑦	⑦	⑦	⑦	⑦	⑦	⑦	⑦	⑦	⑦	⑦	⑦	⑦
Newcastle........... 127 185 d.	...	1306	...	...	1408	...	...	1507	...	...	1608	...	...	1652	...	...	1757	...	...	1906	...	...	2007	...	...	...
Durham .... 127 185 d.	...	1318	...	...	1420	...	...	1522	...	...	1620	...	...	1708	...	...	1809	...	...	1917	...	...	2019	...	...	...
Middlesbrough...............d.	1245	|	...	...	|	...	1445	|	...	...	|	...	1645	|	...	...	|	...	1845	|	...	2007	|	...	...	2207
Darlington............ 127 185 d.	|	1335	...	...	1437	...	|	1540	...	...	1637	...	|	1726	...	...	1826	...	|	1935	...	|	2036	...	...	|
Northallerton......... 127 185 d.	1312	|	...	...	1448	...	1512	|	...	...	1648	...	1712	1738	...	...	|	...	1914	|	...	2034	2048	...	...	2234
Thirsk ....d.	1321	|	...	...	|	...	1521	|	...	...	|	...	1721	|	...	...	|	...	1923	|	...	2042	|	...	...	2242
Scarborough..................d.	|	|	...	1350	|	...	|	|	...	1550	|	...	|	|	...	1750	|	...	|	|	1950	|	|	...	2120	|
Malton...........................d.	|	|	...	1413	|	...	|	|	...	1613	|	...	|	|	...	1813	|	...	|	|	2013	|	|	...	2143	|
York.................. 127 185 d.	1345	1415f	1433	1445f	1515	...	1545	1615	1633	1645f	1715	...	1745	1815t	1833	1845f	1915f	...	1945	2015f	2045f	2102	2115	...	2212	2312
Hull.................. 127 185 d.	|	|	|	|	|	1458	|	|	|	|	|	1658	|	|	|	|	|	1858	|	|	|	...	|	2100	|	|
Selby.................. 127 185 d.	|	|	|	|	|	1529	|	|	|	|	|	1729	|	|	|	|	|	1929	|	|	|	...	|	2131	|	|
Leeds.................. 127 185 d.	1410	1440	1459	1510	1540	1559	1610	1640	1659	1710	1740	1759	1810	1840	1859	1910	1940	1959	2010	2040	2110	...	2140	2159	2240	2340
Dewsbury ....d.	|	1451	|	|	1551	|	|	1651	|	|	1751	|	|	1851	|	|	1951	|	|	2051	|	...	2151	...	|	2351
Huddersfield...................d.	1428	1501	1517	1528	1601	1617	1628	1701	1717	1728	1801	1817	1828	1901	1917	1928	2001	2017	2028	2101	2128	...	2201	...	2258	0001
Stalybridge ....d.	1446	|	|	1546	|	|	1646	|	|	1746	|	|	1846	|	|	1946	|	|	2046	2119	|	...	2219	...	2319	|
Manchester Piccadilly .206 a.	1505	1534	1554	1650	1634	1654	1705	1734	1754	1805	1835	1854	1905	1934	1954	2005	2034	2054	2105	2136	2205	...	2234	...	2336	0043
Manchester Airport ✈......a.	|	1555	...	|	1655	...	|	1755	...	|	1855	...	|	1955	...	|	2055	...	|	...	|	...	2255	...	...	0100
Warrington Central.......206 a.	1529	...	...	1629	...	...	1729	...	...	1829	...	...	1929	...	...	2029	...	...	2129	...	2229	...	...	...	...	...
Liverpool Lime St ....206 a.	1557	...	...	1657	...	...	1757	...	...	1857	...	...	1957	...	...	2057	...	...	2157	...	2257	...	...	...	...	...

A – On ⑥, arrives York at 1718.
B – ⑥ Dec. 19 – Jan. 30.
C – ⑥ Feb. 6 – May 22.
f – Arrives 5 – 10 minutes earlier.
t – Arrives 11 – 16 minutes earlier.

187 NEWCASTLE and MIDDLESBROUGH - LEEDS - MANCHESTER and LIVERPOOL TP

Services on ⑦ valid until January 31. For other services York - Newcastle and v.v., see Tables **127** and **185**.

	⚒	⚒	⚒	⚒	⚒	⚒	Ⓐ	⑥	⚒	Ⓐ	⑥	⑥	Ⓐ	⚒	⚒	⚒	⚒	⚒	⚒	⚒	⚒	⚒	⚒	⚒	⑥	Ⓐ
Liverpool Lime St 206 d.		...	...	...	...	...	...	...	0616	0616	...	...	...	...	...	0716	...	...	...	0822	...	...	...	0922	...	...
Warrington Central 206 d.		...	...	...	...	...	...	...	0638	0638	...	...	...	...	...	0740	...	...	...	0844	...	...	...	0944	...	...
Manchester Airport ✈ d.		...	...	0537	...	...	0623	0623	|	|	...	0705	0705	...	0733	|	0805	...	0835	|	0905	...	0935	|	1005	1005
Manchester Piccadilly 206 d.		...	0539	0557	0621	...	0654	0654	0711	0711	...	0726	0726	0736	0755	0810	0826	0842	0855	0911	0926	0942	0957	1011	1027	1027
Stalybridge d.		...	0552	|	|	...	0707	0707	0726	0726	...	|	|	0749	0809	0826	|	|	|	0926	|	|	|	1026	|	|
Huddersfield d.		...	0611	0627	0656	...	0726	0726	0745	0745	...	0757	0757	0810	0830	0845	0857	0916	0927	0945	0957	1016	1027	1045	1057	1057
Dewsbury d.		...	|	0637	0706	...	|	|	0755	0755	...	0807	0807	0820	0839	|	0907	|	0937	|	1007	|	1037	|	1107	1107
Leeds 127 185 d.		...	0635	0655	0723	...	0750	0750	0812	0812	...	0827	0827	0838	0857	0912	0927	0938	0957	1012	1027	1038	1057	1112	1127	1127
Selby 127 185 d.		...	|	|	0743	...	|	|	|	|	...	|	|	0858	|	|	|	0957	|	|	|	1057	|	|	|	|
Hull 127 185 a.		...	|	|	0820	...	|	|	|	|	...	|	|	0931	|	|	|	1034	|	|	|	1134	|	|	|	|
York 127 185 d.		0640	0706f	0725	...	0732	0823	0823	0838f	0842f	0842	0857	0903f	...	0926	0938	0956	...	1026	1038	1054	...	1126	1138	1154	1201f
Malton d.		0704	|	0749	...	|	|	|	0902	|	|	|	|	...	|	1002	|	...	|	1102	|	...	|	1202	|	|
Scarborough a.		0730	|	0815	...	|	|	|	0930	|	|	|	|	...	|	1030	|	...	|	1130	|	...	|	1230	|	|
Thirsk d.		...	0722	...	...	0754	0839	0845	...	|	|	|	|	...	0945	...	|	...	1045	...	|	...	1142	...	|	|
Northallerton 127 185 d.		...	0730	...	...	0802	0849	0856	...	0902	0902	0917	0924	...	0957	...	1021	...	1055	...	1115	...	1155	...	1215	1221
Darlington 127 185 d.		...	0741	...	...	|	|	|	...	0914	0914	0929	0936	...	|	...	1032	...	|	...	1127	...	|	...	1227	1233
Middlesbrough a.		...	|	...	...	0834	0921	0932	...	|	|	|	|	...	1030	...	|	...	1131	...	|	...	1230	...	|	|
Durham 127 185 a.		...	0758	...	...	...	...	...	...	0931	0931	0946	0953	...	...	...	1050	...	...	...	1144	...	...	...	1245	1250
Newcastle 127 185 a.		...	0818	...	...	...	...	...	...	0949	0949	1004	1010	...	...	...	1114	...	...	...	1200	...	...	...	1300	1308

	⚒	⚒	⚒	⚒	⚒	⚒	⚒	⚒	⚒	Ⓐ	⑥	⚒	⚒	⚒	⚒	⚒	⚒	⚒	⚒	⚒	⚒	⚒	Ⓐ	⑥	Ⓐ	⑥
Liverpool Lime St 206 d.	...	...	1022	...	...	...	1122	...	...	...	...	1222	...	...	...	1322	...	...	...	1422	...	...	...	...	1522	1522
Warrington Central 206 d.	...	...	1044	...	...	...	1144	...	...	...	...	1244	...	...	...	1344	...	...	...	1444	...	...	...	...	1544	1544
Manchester Airport ✈ d.	...	1035	|	1105	...	1135	|	1205	...	1235	1235	|	1305	...	1335	|	1405	...	1435	|	1505	...	1535	1535	|	|
Manchester Piccadilly 206 d.	1042	1057	1111	1127	1142	1157	1211	1227	1242	1257	1257	1311	1327	1342	1357	1411	1427	1442	1457	1511	1527	1542	1557	1557	1611	1611
Stalybridge d.	|	|	1126	|	|	|	1226	|	|	|	|	1326	|	|	|	1426	|	|	|	1526	|	|	|	|	1626	1626
Huddersfield d.	1116	1127	1145	1157	1216	1227	1245	1257	1316	1327	1327	1345	1357	1416	1427	1445	1457	1516	1527	1545	1557	1616	1627	1627	1645	1645
Dewsbury d.	|	1137	|	1207	|	1237	|	1307	|	1337	1337	|	1407	|	1437	|	1507	|	1537	|	1607	|	1637	1637	|	|
Leeds 127 185 d.	1138	1157	1212	1227	1238	1257	1312	1327	1338	1357	1357	1412	1427	1438	1457	1512	1527	1538	1557	1612	1627	1638	1657	1647	1712	1712
Selby 127 185 d.	1157	|	|	|	1257	|	|	|	1357	|	|	|	|	1457	|	|	|	1557	|	|	|	1700	|	|	|	|
Hull 127 185 a.	1236	|	|	|	1334	|	|	|	1434	|	|	|	|	1534	|	|	|	1634	|	|	|	1737	|	|	|	|
York 127 185 d.	...	1226	1238	1254	...	1326	1338	1354	...	1426	1426	1438	1454	...	1526	1538	1554	...	1626	1638	1702	...	1726	1726	1743f	1738
Malton d.	...	|	1302	|	...	|	1402	|	...	|	|	1502	|	...	|	1602	...	...	|	1702	|	...	1750	|	|	1802
Scarborough a.	...	|	1330	|	...	|	1430	|	...	|	|	1530	|	...	|	1630	...	...	|	1730	|	...	1817	|	|	1830
Thirsk d.	...	1246	...	|	...	1343	...	|	...	1442	1445	...	|	...	1546	...	...	...	1644	...	1714	...	...	1742	1802	...
Northallerton 127 185 d.	...	1255	...	1319	...	1355	...	1415	...	1453	1500	...	1522	...	1555	...	...	...	1655	...	1722	...	...	1752	1809	...
Darlington 127 185 d.	...	|	...	1331	...	|	...	1427	...	|	|	...	1534	...	|	...	...	...	|	...	1736	...	...	|	|	...
Middlesbrough a.	...	1330	...	|	...	1430	...	|	...	1530	1535	...	|	...	1630	...	...	...	1733	...	|	...	...	1832	1842	...
Durham 127 185 a.	...	...	...	1351	...	...	...	1450	...	...	...	...	1551	...	...	...	...	...	...	...	1756	...	...	...	...	...
Newcastle 127 185 a.	...	...	...	1412	...	...	...	1506	...	...	...	...	1612	...	...	...	...	...	...	...	1817	...	...	...	...	...

	⑥	Ⓐ	⑥	Ⓐ	Ⓐ	⑥	Ⓐ	⚒	⚒	⑥	Ⓐ	⚒	Ⓐ	⚒	⚒	⚒	⚒	⑥	⑥	Ⓐ	⚒	⑥	Ⓐ	Ⓐ	⑥	Ⓐ
Liverpool Lime St 206 d.	...	...	...	...	...	1622	1622	...	...	...	...	1722	...	...	...	1822	...	...	1922	1922	...	2022	2022	...	...	...
Warrington Central 206 d.	...	...	...	...	...	1644	1644	...	...	...	...	1744	...	...	...	1844	...	...	1944	1944	...	2044	2044	...	...	...
Manchester Airport ✈ d.	1605	1605	...	...	1635	|	|	1705	...	1735	1735	|	...	...	1835	|	1919	...	|	|	2020	|	|	...	2120	2120
Manchester Piccadilly 206 d.	1627	1627	1642	1642	1656	1711	1711	1726	1742	1756	1756	1811	1827	1842	1857	1911	1942	...	2011	2011	2042	2111	2111	...	2142	2142
Stalybridge d.	|	|	|	|	1709	1726	1726	1739	|	1809	1809	1826	|	|	|	1926	|	...	2026	2026	|	2126	2126	...	2155	2155
Huddersfield d.	1657	1657	1716	1716	1728	1745	1745	1757	1816	1828	1828	1845	1857	1916	1927	1945	2016	...	2045	2045	2116	2145	2145	...	2216	2216
Dewsbury d.	1707	1707	|	|	1737	|	|	1807	|	1837	1837	|	1907	|	1937	|	2026	...	|	|	2126	|	|	...	2226	2226
Leeds 127 185 d.	1724	1724	1738	1738	1757	1812	1812	1827	1838	1857	1857	1912	1927	1938	1957	2012	2045	2105	2112	2112	2142	2222	2212	2222	2242	2242
Selby 127 185 d.	|	|	1757	1804	|	|	|	|	1900	|	|	|	|	2000	|	|	|	2127	|	2134	|	2244	|	2244	|	|
Hull 127 185 a.	|	|	1837	1846	|	|	|	|	1937	|	|	|	|	2040	|	|	|	2205	|	2212	|	2321	|	2321	|	|
York 127 185 d.	1757	1802f	...	...	1826	1838	1843f	1856	...	1926	1931f	1938	1955	...	2026	2038	2111	...	2140	...	2211	...	2237	...	2308	2321f
Malton d.	...	1826	...	...	|	1902	1907	|	...	|	|	2002	...	...	|	2102	|	...	...	...	2235	...	...	...	...	|
Scarborough a.	...	1852	...	...	|	1930	1933	|	...	|	|	2030	...	...	|	2130	|	...	...	...	2305	...	...	...	...	|
Thirsk d.	...	...	...	...	1844	...	...	|	...	1942	1947	...	...	...	2043	...	2128	...	...	...	...	...	...	...	...	2335
Northallerton 127 185 d.	...	...	...	...	1855	...	...	1920	...	1950	1958	...	...	...	2051	...	2136	...	...	...	...	...	...	...	...	2355
Darlington 127 185 d.	...	...	...	...	|	...	...	1933	...	|	|	...	...	...	|	...	2147	...	...	...	...	...	...	...	...	0006
Middlesbrough a.	...	...	...	...	1930	...	...	|	...	2023	2030	...	...	...	2125	...	|	...	...	...	...	...	...	...	...	|
Durham 127 185 a.	...	...	...	...	...	...	...	1950	...	...	...	...	...	...	...	...	2207	...	...	...	...	...	...	...	...	0024
Newcastle 127 185 a.	...	...	...	...	...	...	...	2009	...	...	...	...	...	...	...	...	2223	...	...	...	...	...	...	...	...	0056

	⚒	⑥C	⑥B	Ⓐ	⑥B	⑤	①–④	⑥C	⑥B		⑦	⑦	⑦	⑦	⑦	⑦	⑦	⑦	⑦	⑦	⑦	⑦	⑦	⑦	⑦	⑦
Liverpool Lime St 206 d.	...	2230	2230	2230	...	...	...	...	...	...		...	...	...	0822	...	...	0922	...	1022	...	...	1122	...	...	1222
Warrington Central 206 d.	...	2252	2252	2252	...	...	...	...	...	...		...	...	...	0844	...	...	0944	...	1044	...	...	1144	...	...	1244
Manchester Airport ✈ d.	2222	|	|	|	...	2318	2318	2324	2324*	...		...	...	...	|	...	...	|	1019	|	1117	...	|	1202	...	|
Manchester Piccadilly 206 d.	2242	2321	2321	2321	...	2338	2338	2341	2349*	...		...	...	0842	0911	...	0929	1011	1042	1111	1142	1155	1210	1242	1302	1311
Stalybridge d.	2255	2334	2334	2334	...	|	|	|	|	...		...	...	0855	0924	...	|	1024	|	1124	|	|	1224	|	|	1324
Huddersfield d.	2316	2353	2352	2353	...	0008	0026	0026	0049*	...		...	...	0914	0943	...	1012	1043	1112	1143	1212	1233	1243	1312	1333	1343
Dewsbury d.	2326	|	*0019**	|	...	0018s	0035s	0035s	|	...		...	...	0922	|	...	1021	|	1121	|	1221	|	|	1322	|	|
Leeds 127 185 d.	2342	0016	*0044**	0036	0054	0042	0054	0054	0124*	...		...	0912	0940	1020	...	1040	1112	1140	1212	1240	1300	1312	1340	1357	1412
Selby 127 185 d.	|	|	...	|	|	|	|	|	|	...		...	|	|	1043	...	|	|	|	|	|	1323	|	|	|	|
Hull 127 185 a.	|	|	...	|	|	|	|	|	|	...		...	|	|	1118	...	|	|	|	|	|	1400	|	|	|	|
York 127 185 d.	0010	0044	...	0118	0120	0125	0143	0131	0209*	...		0821	0940	1013f	...	1045	1115f	1143f	1215f	1244f	1215f	...	1340	1415f	1424	1440
Malton d.	...	...	...	...	...	...	...	...	...	...		|	1004	|	...	|	|	1208	|	|	|	...	1404	|	...	|
Scarborough a.	...	...	...	...	...	...	...	...	...	...		|	1032	|	...	|	|	1232	|	|	|	...	1432	|	...	|
Thirsk d.	...	...	...	...	...	...	...	...	...	...		0836	...	|	...	1104	|	...	|	1301	|	...	...	|	...	1502
Northallerton 127 185 d.	...	...	...	...	...	...	...	...	...	...		0844	...	1035	...	1112	1135	...	1235	1310	1335	...	...	1435	...	1510
Darlington 127 185 d.	...	...	...	...	...	...	...	...	...	...		0856	...	1046	...	|	1147	...	1246	|	1346	...	...	1446	...	|
Middlesbrough a.	...	...	...	...	...	...	...	...	...	...		0926	...	|	...	1148	|	...	|	1344	|	...	...	|	...	1552
Durham 127 185 a.	...	...	...	...	...	...	...	...	...	...		...	...	1108	...	...	1203	...	1303	...	1403	...	...	1503	...	...
Newcastle 127 185 a.	...	...	...	...	...	...	...	...	...	...		...	...	1124	...	...	1220	...	1320	...	1422	...	...	1520	...	...

	⑦	⑦	⑦	⑦	⑦	⑦	⑦	⑦	⑦	⑦	⑦	⑦	⑦	⑦	⑦	⑦	⑦	⑦	⑦	⑦	⑦	⑦	⑦	⑦	⑦	⑦
Liverpool Lime St 206 d.	...	...	1322	...	...	1422	...	...	1522	...	1622	...	...	1722	...	...	1822	...	...	1922	...	2022	...	...	2152	...
Warrington Central 206 d.	...	...	1344	...	...	1444	...	...	1544	...	1644	...	...	1744	...	...	1844	...	...	1944	...	2044	...	...	2214	...
Manchester Airport ✈ d.	1320	...	|	1420	...	|	1520	...	|	1620	|	1720	...	|	1820	...	|	1920	...	|	2020	|	...	2120	|	2320
Manchester Piccadilly 206 d.	1342	1402	1411	1442	1502	1511	1542	1602	1611	1642	1711	1742	1802	1811	1842	1902	1911	1942	2006	2011	2042	2111	...	2142	2242	2342
Stalybridge d.	|	|	1424	|	|	1524	|	|	1624	|	1724	|	|	1824	|	|	1924	|	|	2024	|	2124	...	|	2255	|
Huddersfield d.	1412	1433	1443	1512	1533	1543	1612	1633	1643	1712	1743	1812	1833	1843	1912	1933	1943	2012	2037	2043	2112	2143	...	2212	2314	0012
Dewsbury d.	1421	|	|	1521	|	|	1621	|	|	1721	|	1821	|	|	1921	|	|	2021	|	|	2121	|	...	2221	2323	|
Leeds 127 185 d.	1440	1500	1512	1540	1557	1612	1640	1700	1712	1740	1812	1840	1900	1912	1940	1957	2012	2040	2104	2112	2140	2212	2220	2240	2340	0053
Selby 127 185 d.	|	1523	|	|	|	|	|	1723	|	|	|	|	1923	|	|	2016	|	|	2138	|	|	|	2242	|	|	|
Hull 127 185 a.	|	1600	|	|	|	|	|	1800	|	|	|	|	2000	|	|	2053	|	|	2215	|	|	|	2318	|	|	|
York 127 185 d.	1515f	...	1540	1615f	1624	1640	1714f	...	1740	1814f	1840	1914f	...	1940	2013f	...	2040	2108	...	2137	2210	2242	...	2311	0010	0122
Malton d.	|	...	1604	|	...	|	|	...	1804	|	|	|	...	2004	|	...	2104	|	...	...	2234	|	...	...	...	...
Scarborough a.	|	...	1632	|	...	|	|	...	1832	|	|	|	...	2032	|	...	2132	|	...	...	2302	|	...	...	...	...
Thirsk d.	|	...	...	|	...	1702	|	...	...	|	1859	|	...	...	2030	...	...	2126	...	...	...	2306	...	...	...	...
Northallerton 127 185 d.	1535	...	...	1635	...	1710	1735	...	...	1835	1907	1935	...	...	2038	...	...	2134	...	...	...	2316	...	...	...	...
Darlington 127 185 d.	1546	...	...	1646	...	|	1746	...	...	1846	|	1946	...	...	|	...	...	2146	...	...	...	2332	...	...	...	...
Middlesbrough a.	|	...	...	|	...	1743	|	...	...	|	1940	|	...	...	2112	...	...	|	...	...	...	|	...	...	...	...
Durham 127 185 a.	1603	...	...	1703	...	...	1803	...	...	1903	...	2003	...	...	...	...	...	2203	...	...	...	2349	...	...	...	...
Newcastle 127 185 a.	1620	...	...	1720	...	...	1822	...	...	1920	...	2022	...	...	...	...	...	2220	...	...	...	0021	...	...	...	...

For footnotes see previous page.

NT 2nd class — LEEDS - HALIFAX - MANCHESTER — 190

Services on ⑦ valid until January 31.

km			Ⓐ	⑥	Ⓐ	Ⓐ	⑥	⚒	⚒	⚒	⚒	⚒		⚒	⚒	⚒	⚒	⑥	Ⓐ	⚒			⑦	⑦
0	**Leeds** 127 185 d.	⚒	0508	0537	0603	0613	0616	0637	0708	0713	0737	0808	and at	1837	1908	1937	2037	2137	2137	2237	...	⑦	0821	0902
15	Bradford Interchange 176 d.		0532	0600	0624	|	0640	0700	0731	|	0800	0832	the same	1900	1932	2000	2100	2200	2200	2300	...		0845	0925
28	**Halifax** 191 d.		0544	0612	0636	|	0652	0712	0744	|	0812	0844	minutes	1912	1944	2012	2112	2212	2212	2312	...		0901	0937
	Dewsbury d.		|	|	|	0629	|	|	|	0729	|	|	past each	|	|	|	|	|	|	|	...		|	|
42	Hebden Bridge 191 d.		0600	0628	0652	0708	0708	0728	0756	0808	0828	0856	hour until	1928	1956	2028	2128	2228	2228	2328	...		0917	0953
49	Todmorden d.		0608	0635	0659	0715	0715	0736	0804	0815	0836	0904		1936	2004	2036	2136	2236	2236	2336	...		0924	1000
63	Rochdale d.		0624	0655	0716	0730	0730	0752	0814	0830	0851	0914	❖	1952	2014	2052	2152	2252	2352	2352	...		0941	1017
81	**Manchester** Victoria a.		0648	0717	0737	0753	0753	0814	0838	0853	0908	0932		2015	2032	2114	2214	2308	2314	0008	...		1002	1038

	⑦		⑦	⑦		⑦	⑦		⑦
Leeds 127 185 d.	0954	and at	1754	1903	...	1954	2104	...	2135
Bradford Interchange 176 d.	1017	the same	1817	1927	...	2019	2128	...	2158
Halifax 191 d.	1029	minutes	1829	1939	...	2031	2141	...	2211
Dewsbury d.	|	past each	|	|	...	|	|	...	|
Hebden Bridge 191 d.	1045	hour until	1845	1955	...	2047	2157	...	2227
Todmorden d.	1052		1851	2002	...	2054	...	...	2234
Rochdale d.	1109	❖	1909	2019	...	2111	...	...	2251
Manchester Victoria a.	1130		1930	2041	...	2133	...	...	2312

		Ⓐ	⑥	⚒	⚒	⚒	⚒	⚒	⚒	⚒
Manchester Victoria d.	⚒	0617	0621	0643	0658	0717	0748	0800	0821	0848
Rochdale d.		0637	0635	0656	0718	0737	0801	0820	0835	0902
Todmorden d.		0654	0652	0708	0735	0754	0813	0834	0852	0914
Hebden Bridge 191 d.		0700	0700	0716	0741	0800	0821	0841	0900	0921
Dewsbury d.		|	|	|	0811	|	|	0912	|	|
Halifax 191 d.		0716	0716	0733	|	0816	0833	|	0916	0933
Bradford Interchange 176 d.		0734	0734	0750	|	0834	0850	|	0934	0950
Leeds 127 185 a.		0757	0757	0812	0833	0856	0912	0931	0958	1012

		⚒	⚒	⚒	⚒	⚒	⚒	⚒	⚒	⚒	⚒	Ⓐ	⑥	Ⓐ			⑦	⑦		⑦	⑦		⑦
Manchester Victoria d.	and at	1700	1718	1743	1800	1821	1848	1900	1921	2021	2121	2228	2254	2320	...	⑦	0908	1008	and at	2008	2108	...	2208
Rochdale d.	the same	1720	1738	1803	1818	1836	1901	1919	1941	2041	2141	2248	2307	2341	...		0928	1028	the same	2028	2128	...	2228
Todmorden d.	minutes	1734	1755	1816	1935	1853	1913	1934	1958	2058	2158	2305	2324	2358	...		0945	1045	minutes	2045	2145	...	2245
Hebden Bridge 191 d.	past each	1741	1801	1823	1842	1900	1920	1941	2005	2105	2205	2311	2331	0004	...		0952	1052	past each	2052	2152	...	2252
Dewsbury d.	hour until	1812	|	|	1913	|	|	2012	|	|	|	|	|	|	...		|	|	hour until	|	|	...	|
Halifax 191 d.		|	1817	1835	|	1916	1932	|	2021	2121	2221	2329	2347	0020	...		1008	1108		2108	2210	...	2308
Bradford Interchange 176 d.	❖	|	1834	1850	|	1934	1950	|	2037	2137	2237	2346	0003	0037	...		1025	1125	❖	2126	2226	...	2325
Leeds 127 185 a.		1833	1856	1913	1933	1958	2015	2034	2101	2201	2301	0009	0027	0055	...		1046	1148		2148	2247	...	2346

❖ – Timings may vary by ± 3 minutes.

NT 2nd class — YORK - LEEDS - HALIFAX - BLACKPOOL — 191

Services on ⑦ valid until January 31.

km			⚒	⚒	⚒	⚒	⚒		⚒	⚒	⚒	⚒	⚒			⑦	⑦	⑦		⑦	⑦		⑦
	York 127 185 d.	⚒	...	0613	0706	0809j	0909		1508	1613	1708	1812j	1904	...	⑦	0850	1057	1252		1652	1752	...	1852
0	**Leeds** 127 185 d.		0551	0651	0751	0851	0951		1551	1651	1751	1851	1951	...		0935	1135	1335		1735	1835	...	1835
15	Bradford Interchange 176 d.		0614	0714	0812	0912	1012	and at	1613	1712	1812	1912	2013	...		0955	1155	1355	and at	1755	1855	...	1955
28	**Halifax** 190 d.		0626	0726	0824	0924	1024	the same	1625	1724	1824	1924	2025	...		1007	1207	1407	the same	1807	1807	...	2007
42	Hebden Bridge 190 d.		0638	0738	0836	0936	1036	minutes	1638	1738	1838	1936	2037	...		1020	1220	1420	minutes	1820	1919	...	2020
63	Burnley Manchester Rd d.		0657	0757	0857	0956	1057	past each	1657	1757	1857	1956	2056	...		1038	1238	1438	past each	1838	...	...	2038
72	Accrington d.		0706	0806	0906	1006	1106	hour until	1706	1806	1906	2005	2105	...		1047	1247	1447	hour until	1847	...	...	2047
81	Blackburn d.		0716	0814	0914	1014	1114		1714	1814	1914	2014	2114	...		1056	1255	1455		1855	...	...	2055
100	**Preston** 156 a.		0736	0838	0932	1032	1132	❖	1732	1833	1932	2032	2132	...		1113	1313	1513	❖	1913	...	...	2113
129	**Blackpool** North 156 a.		0805	0905	1000	1100	1200		1806	1900	2000	2100	2200	...		1139	1338	1539		1938	...	...	2138

			⚒	⚒	⚒	⚒	⚒		⚒	⚒	⚒	⚒				⑦	⑦		⑦	⑦		⑦	⑦
Blackpool North 156 d.	⚒	...	0529	0628	0729	0829	0929		1629	1714	1829	2029	...	...	⑦	...	...	...	...	1111		1913	2113
Preston 156 d.		...	0554	0654	0754	0854	0954	and at	1654	1744	1854	2054	...	...		...	...	...	...	1137	and at	1937	2139
Blackburn d.		...	0610	0710	0810	0910	1010	the same	1710	1811	1910	2110	...	...		...	...	...	...	1154	the same	1954	2155
Accrington d.		...	0617	0717	0817	0917	1017	minutes	1717	1819	1917	2117	...	...		...	...	...	...	1201	minutes	2001	2202
Burnley Manchester Rd d.		...	0626	0726	0826	0926	1026	past each	1726	1828	1926	2128	...	...		...	...	...	...	1210	past each	2010	2212
Hebden Bridge 190 d.		...	0650	0750	0850	0950	1050	hour until	1750	1850	1950	2151	...	...		...	1032	...	1132	1232	hour until	2032	2234
Halifax 190 d.		...	0703	0803	0903	1003	1103		1803	1903	2003	2203	...	...		0906	1045	...	1145	1245		2045	2247
Bradford Interchange 176 d.		...	0720	0820	0920	1019	1120	❖	1819	1919	2019	2219	...	...		0920	1102	...	1202	1302	❖	2102	2304
Leeds 127 185 a.		...	0739	0839	0939	1039	1139		1839	1939	2041	2241	...	...		0942	1121	...	1222	1322		2122	2323
York 127 185 a.		...	0821	0921	1021	1119	1221		1921	2021	2131	2336	...	...		1028	1159	...	1302	1402		2159	...

j – ⑥ only.
❖ – Timings may vary by ± 5 minutes.

NT 2nd class — HULL - DONCASTER - SHEFFIELD — 192

km			⚒	⚒	⚒	Ⓐ		⑥	⚒	⚒	⚒		⚒	⚒	⚒	⚒		⚒	⚒	⚒	⑥		Ⓐ	⚒		⚒
0	**Hull** 185 d.	⚒	0520	0640	0736	0804	...	0808	0855	0956	1057	...	1155	1257	1357	1456	...	1557	1654	1752	1740	...	1742	1853	...	1925
38	Goole d.		0547	0715	0813	0830	...	0834	0922	1022	1123	...	1222	1323	1423	1523	...	1623	1722	|	1819	...	1819	1919	...	1958
66	**Doncaster** 185 a.		0616	0745	0843	0855	...	0857	0946	1046	1146	...	1246	1346	1446	1546	...	1646	1747	1845	1851	...	1851	1946	...	2030
66	**Doncaster** 193 d.		0625	0746	...	0856	...	0859	0948	1048	1148	...	1248	1348	1448	1548	...	1647	1748	1847	...	...	1855	1949	...	...
90	Meadowhall 193 d.		0654	0822	...	0915	...	0919	1006	1106	1206	...	1306	1406	1506	1607	...	1706	1806	1906	...	...	1925	2007	...	...
96	**Sheffield** 170 193 a.		0707	0832	...	0926	...	0928	1020	1120	1220	...	1320	1420	1520	1620	...	1719	1819	1917	...	...	1935	2018	...	...

	⚒	⑥	Ⓐ		⑥	Ⓐ			⑦	⑦	⑦	⑦		⑦	⑦		⑦		⑦	⑦	⑦		⑦		⑦	⑦
Hull 185 d.	2003	2051	2056	...	2217	2220	...	⑦	0842	0941	1041	1141	...	1241	1335	...	1441	...	1541	1641	1741	...	1838	...	2030	2115
Goole d.	2036	2117	2122	...	2248	2251	...		0915	1009	1109	1209	...	1309	1408	...	1509	...	1609	1709	1809	...	1906	...	2058	2148
Doncaster 185 a.	2105	2146	2145	...	2318	2321	...		0938	1036	1132	1232	...	1332	1431	...	1532	...	1632	1731	1833	...	1935	...	2121	2217
Doncaster 193 d.	2107	2148	2148	...	2319	2322	...		0939	...	1133	...	...	1334	1433	...	1533	...	1633	1732	1834	...	1937	...	2123	2220
Meadowhall 193 d.	2135	2209	2209	...	2349	2354	...		1000	...	1152	...	...	1353	1452	...	1552	...	1653	1753	1853	...	1957	...	2145	2250
Sheffield 170 193 a.	2147	2221	2221	...	2359	0004	...		1009	...	1203	...	...	1404	1503	...	1601	...	1703	1801	1903	...	2006	...	2156	2258

		⚒		⚒	⚒	⚒		Ⓐ	⑥	⚒	Ⓐ		Ⓐ	Ⓐ	Ⓐ	⑥		Ⓐ	Ⓐ	⑥	Ⓐ		⑥	Ⓐ	⑥	⚒
Sheffield 170 193 d.	⚒	0529	...	...	0741	0841	...	0941	0941	1041	1141	...	1241	1341	1441	1541	...	1541	1641	1641	1741	...	1741	1841	1841	1944
Meadowhall 193 d.		0535	...	...	0747	0847	...	0947	0947	1047	1147	...	1247	1346	1447	1547	...	1547	1647	1647	1747	...	1747	1847	1847	1950
Doncaster 193 a.		0606	...	...	0820	0912	...	1011	1011	1109	1211	...	1311	1413	1511	1612	...	1612	1712	1712	1814	...	1814	1911	1911	2011
Doncaster 185 d.		0614	...	0728	0822	0916	...	1016	1022	1117	1214	...	1318	1417	1514	1614	...	1618	1714	1714	1816	...	1824	1913	1913	2014
Goole d.		0639	...	0753	0842	0939	...	1035	1041	1137	1235	...	1337	1437	1533	1636	...	1636	1735	1735	1836	...	1844	1934	|	2033
Hull 185 a.		0722	...	0836	0912	1010	...	1106	1112	1209	1306	...	1408	1510	1607	1705	...	1711	1806	1810	1909	...	1916	2007	2011	2106

	Ⓐ	⑥	Ⓐ		Ⓐ	⑥			⑦		⑦	⑦		⑦	⑦	⑦		⑦	⑦	⑦		⑦	⑦	⑦		⑦
Sheffield 170 193 d.	...	...	2015	...	2115	2115	...	⑦	0800	...	0845	1026	...	1228	1324	1428	...	1528	1628	1728	...	1828	2002	2124	...	2226
Meadowhall 193 d.	...	...	2021	...	2121	2121	...		0806	...	0851	1032	...	1234	1330	1434	...	1534	1634	1734	...	1835	2009	2130	...	2232
Doncaster 193 a.	...	...	2056	...	2152	2155	...		0838	...	0922	1051	...	1254	1402	1456	...	1555	1654	1757	...	1854	2030	2203	...	2304
Doncaster 185 d.	2044	2046	2057	...	2154	2157	...		...	...	0926	1053	...	1255	1404	1459	...	1556	1656	1803	...	1855	2030	2204	...	2307
Goole d.	|	2111	2123	...	2222	2222	...		...	...	0947	1113	...	1315	1425	1519	...	1617	1715	1822	...	1921	2049	2223	...	2328
Hull 185 a.	2145	2145	...	...	2258	2258	...		...	...	1021	1147	...	1348	1459	1557	...	1650	1749	1857	...	1955	2123	2257	...	0002

193 CLEETHORPES - DONCASTER - SHEFFIELD - MANCHESTER TP

Services on ⑦ valid until January 31.

km			⚒	⚒	⑥	Ⓐ	⚒	⚒	⚒	Ⓐ	⑥	⚒	⚒	⚒	⚒	⚒	⚒	⚒	⚒	⚒	Ⓐ	⑥			⑦	⑦
0	**Cleethorpes** d.	⚒	...	0518	0618	0618	0718	0828	0928	1028	1028	1128	1228	1328	1428	1528	1628	1728	1828	1928	2028	2028	...	⑦	...	0928
5	Grimsby Town d.		...	0526	0626	0626	0726	0836	0936	1036	1036	1136	1236	1336	1436	1536	1636	1736	1836	1936	2036	2036	...		...	0936
48	Scunthorpe d.		...	0600	0700	0700	0800	0910	1010	1110	1110	1210	1310	1410	1510	1610	1710	1810	1910	2010	2110	2110	...		...	1010
85	**Doncaster** 185 a.		...	0638	0733	0733	0830	0940	1040	1140	1140	1240	1340	1440	1540	1640	1740	1840	1940	2040	2140	2140	...		...	1040
85	**Doncaster** 192 d.		0540	0639	0735	0735	0841	0942	1042	1142	1142	1242	1342	1442	1542	1642	1742	1842	1942	2042	2142	2142	...		...	1042
109	Meadowhall 192 d.		0558	0658	0753	0753	0901	1001	1101	1201	1159	1301	1401	1501	1558	1701	1801	1901	2001	2107	2158	2158	...		0900	1100
115	**Sheffield** 192 a.		0608	0706	0800	0800	0908	1008	1108	1208	1208	1308	1408	1508	1608	1708	1808	1908	2010	2119	2208	2210	...		0907	1107
115	**Sheffield** 206 d.		0611	0709	0805	0805	0911	1011	1111	1211	1211	1311	1411	1511	1610	1711	1810	1911	2011	...	2211	...	...		0910	1110
175	Stockport 206 a.		0653	0753	0853	0853	0953	1053	1153	1253	1253	1353	1453	1553	1653	1753	1853	1953	2053	...	2253	...	...		|	1155
184	**Manchester** P'dilly a.		0702	0802	0902	0902	1002	1102	1202	1302	1302	1402	1502	1602	1702	1802	1902	2002	2102	...	2302	...	...		1015	1209
200	**Manchester** Airport a.		0726	0826	0926	0933	1026	1126	1226	1326	1333	1426	1526	1626	1732	1826	1928	2037	2136	...	2326	...	...		*1041*	1237

	⑦	⑦	⑦	⑦	⑦	⑦	⑦	⑦	⑦	⑦	⑦
Cleethorpes d.	1028	1128	...	1328	1428	1528	1628	1728	1828	1928	2028
Grimsby Town d.	1036	1136	...	1336	1436	1536	1636	1736	1836	1936	2036
Scunthorpe d.	1110	1210	...	1410	1510	1610	1710	1810	1910	2010	2110
Doncaster 185 a.	1140	1240	...	1440	1540	1640	1740	1840	1940	2040	2140
Doncaster 192 d.	1142	1242	1342	1442	1542	1642	1742	1842	1942	2042	2145
Meadowhall 192 d.	1200	1300	1400	1500	1600	1700	1800	1900	2000	2100	2204
Sheffield 192 a.	1207	1307	1408	1507	1607	1707	1807	1907	2007	2107	2215
Sheffield 206 d.	1210	1310	1411	1511	1611	1711	1811	1911	2011	2111	...
Stockport 206 a.	1253**d**	1353	1453	1553	1656	1753	1853	1953	2053	2153	...
Manchester P'dilly a.	1306	1406	1506	1606	1706	1806	1906	2006	2106	2206	...
Manchester Airport a.	1329	1429	1529	1629	1729	1829	1929	2029	2129	2229	...

		⚒	Ⓐ	⑥	⚒	⚒	⚒	⚒	⚒	⚒
Manchester Airport d.	⚒	0515	0655	0655	0754	0855	0955	1055	1155	1255
Manchester P'dilly d.		0544	0720	0720	0820	0920	1020	1120	1220	1320
Stockport 206 d.		0552	0728	0728	0828	0928	1028	1128	1228	1328
Sheffield 206 a.		0649	0810	0810	0908	1008	1108	1208	1308	1408
Sheffield 192 d.		0655	0811	0811	0911	1011	1111	1211	1311	1411
Meadowhall 192 d.		0701	0817	0817	0917	1017	1117	1217	1317	1417
Doncaster 192 a.		0722	0840	0840	0940	1040	1140	1240	1340	1440
Doncaster 185 d.		0724	0842	0842	0942	1042	1142	1242	1342	1442
Scunthorpe d.		0750	0908	0908	1008	1108	1208	1308	1408	1508
Grimsby Town a.		0826	0942	0944	1044	1142	1245	1342	1445	1542
Cleethorpes a.		0846	0954	0959	1059	1154	1257	1354	1457	1554

	⚒	⚒	⚒	⚒	⚒		⚒	Ⓐ	⑥F	⑥	Ⓐ			⑦	⑦	⑦	⑦		⑦	⑦	⑦	⑦		⑦	⑦	⑦
Manchester Airport d.	1355	1455	1555	1655	1755	...	1855	1955	...	2047	2047	...	⑦	...	1044	1253	1355	...	1455	1555	1655	1755	...	1855	1955	...
Manchester P'dilly d.	1420	1520	1620	1720	1820	...	1918	2020	...	2120	2120	...		...	1118	1317	1420	...	1520	1620	1720	1820	...	1920	2016	...
Stockport 206 d.	1428	1528	1628	1728	1828	...	1926	2028	...	2128	2128	...		...	1127	1328	1428	...	1528	1628	1728	1828	...	1928	2027	...
Sheffield 206 a.	1508	1608	1708	1815	1910	...	2008	2109	...	2208	2208	...		...	1208	1408	1508	...	1608	1708	1808	1908	...	2008	2108	...
Sheffield 192 d.	1511	1611	1711	1824	1911	...	2011	2111	2134	2211	2211	...		0952	1211	1411	1511	...	1611	1711	1811	1911	...	2011	2111	2230
Meadowhall 192 d.	1517	1617	1717	1829	1917	...	2017	2117	2140	2217	2217	...		0957	1216	1416	1516	...	1616	1716	1816	1916	...	2016	2116	2236
Doncaster 192 a.	1540	1640	1740	1853	1940	...	2040	2140	2203	2236	2240	...		1026	1239	1435	1539	...	1635	1736	1839	1939	...	2039	2137	2256
Doncaster 185 d.	1542	1642	1742	1855	1942	...	2042	2142	2211	2238	2242	...		1028	1242	1442	1542	...	1642	1742	1842	1942	...	2042	2142	2258
Scunthorpe d.	1608	1708	1808	1923	2008	...	2108	2208	2237	2312	2317	...		1055	1310	1510	1610	...	1710	1810	1910	2010	...	2110	2210	2324
Grimsby Town d.	1646	1742	1844	1958	2042	...	2144	2246	2318	2348	2356	...		1129	1345	1545	1645	...	1745	1845	1945	2045	...	2145	2245	2358
Cleethorpes a.	1657	1754	1859	2009	2055	...	2159	2259	2329	0001	0009	...		1144	1358	1558	1658	...	1758	1858	1958	2058	...	2158	2258	0010

SHEFFIELD – MANCHESTER Local Trains — 2nd class NT

km			⚒E	⚒	⚒	⚒	⚒	⚒	⚒	⚒		⚒	⚒	⑥	Ⓐ			⑦	⑦	⑦	⑦	⑦	⑦		⑦
0	**Sheffield** ⊙ d.	⚒	0620	0712	0914	1014	1214	1414	1614	1714	...	1914	2035	2224	2247	...	⑦	0926	1114	1313	1514	1714	1914	...	2217
16	Grindleford d.		0635	0729	0929	1029	1229	1429	1629	1729	...	1929	2050	2238	2301	...		0941	1129	1328	1529	1729	1929	...	2232
18	Hathersage d.		0639	0732	0932	1032	1232	1432	1632	1732	...	1932	2053	2241	2305	...		0944	1132	1331	1532	1732	1932	...	2235
24	Hope d.		0647	0739	0939	1039	1239	1439	1639	1739	...	1939	2100	2248	2312	...		0951	1139	1338	1539	1739	1939	...	2242
32	Edale d.		0655	0747	0947	1047	1247	1447	1647	1747	...	1947	2108	2256	2319	...		0959	1147	1346	1547	1747	1947	...	2250
41	Chinley d.		0703	0755	0955	1055	1255	1455	1655	1755	...	1955	2116	2304	2327	...		1007	1155	1354	1555	1755	1955	...	2258
67	**Manchester** Piccadilly ⊙ a.		0734	0833	1032	1132	1332	1532	1732	1832	...	2032	2205	2343	0002	...		1047	1231	1431	1631	1831	2031	...	2329

		⚒	⑥	Ⓐ	⚒	⚒	⚒	⚒	⚒	Ⓐ	⑥	⚒	⚒	⑥T	ⒶE			⑦	⑦	⑦	⑦	⑦	⑦	⑦	⑦E
Manchester Piccadilly ⊙ d.	⚒	0550	0635	0706	0845	1045	1245	1445	1545	1718	1745	1845	2045	2220	2228	...	⑦	0800	0922	1145	1345	1545	1745	1945	2211
Chinley d.		0618	0712	0747	0919	1119	1319	1519	1621	1751	1821	1919	2119	2245	2253	...		0826	0959	1223	1423	1623	1823	2023	2243
Edale d.		0626	0721	0755	0928	1128	1328	1528	1630	1806	1830	1928	2128	2253	2302	...		0835	1008	1232	1432	1632	1832	2032	2251
Hope d.		0632	0727	0801	0934	1134	1334	1534	1636	1809	1836	1934	2134	2258	2308	...		0841	1014	1238	1438	1638	1838	2038	2257
Hathersage d.		0639	0733	0809	0940	1140	1340	1540	1642	1816	1842	1940	2140	2304	2315	...		0847	1020	1245	1445	1645	1845	2045	2303
Grindleford d.		0642	0737	0811	0944	1144	1344	1544	1646	1825	1846	1944	2144	2308	2319	...		0851	1024	1248	1448	1648	1848	2048	2307
Sheffield ⊙ a.		0701	0757	0832	1003	1203	1403	1603	1703	1836	1903	2003	2203	2327	2335	...		0908	1043	1306	1506	1706	1906	2106	2325

E – (2) Nottingham – Liverpool and v.v., operated by *EM*.
F – Dec. 19 – Jan. 30 and Apr. 3 – May 22.
T – (12) Manchester Airport – Sheffield and v.v., operated by *TP*.

⊙ – Additional trains Sheffield – Manchester Piccadilly on ⑥.
From Sheffield at 0814, 1114, 1314, 1514, 1814.
From Manchester at 0744, 0945, 1145, 1345, 1645.

194 SKEGNESS - NOTTINGHAM 2nd class EM

km			⚒	⚒	⚒	Ⓐ	⑥		Ⓐ	⑥	⚒	⚒	⚒	⚒	⚒		⚒	⚒	⚒	⚒	Ⓐ	⑥		⚒	⚒
0	**Skegness** d.	⚒	...	...	0708	0810	0815	...	0906	0915	1015	1115	1215	1315	1415	...	1509	1610	1730	1814	1914	1919	...	2015	2102
38	Boston d.		...	0614	0745	0845	0850	...	0941	0950	1050	1150	1250	1350	1450	...	1544	1648	1805	1849	1949	1954	...	2050	2137
66	Sleaford d.		...	0636	0811	0907	0912	...	1003	1014	1112	1212	1312	1413	1512	...	1610	1713	1827	1913	2013	2018	...	2112	2200
89	Grantham 185 a.		...	0706	0842	0935	0941	...	1031	1043	1141	1242	1341	1442	1541	...	1641	1742	|	1941	2040	2045	...	2143	|
89	Grantham 206 d.		0610	0710	0845	0940	0945	...	1036	1045	1145	1245	1345	1445	1545	...	1645	1745	|	1945	2044	2048	...	2147	|
126	**Nottingham** 206 a.		0654	0753	0923	1018	1022	...	1114	1124	1223	1323	1422	1523	1622	...	1722	1825	1922	2028	2121	2124	...	2225	2254

		⑦	⑦		⑦	⑦		⑦		⑦
Skegness d.	⑦	...	1410	...	1617	1807	...	1915	...	...
Boston d.		1213	1445	...	1652	1842	...	1950	...	...
Sleaford d.		1235	1507	...	1714	1904	...	2012	...	2141
Grantham 185 a.		1307	1535	...	1743	1933	...	2041	...	2210
Grantham 206 d.		...	1540	...	1747	1937	...	2045	...	2213
Nottingham 206 a.		...	1617	...	1823	2014	...	2121	...	2249

		⚒	⚒	⚒	⚒	⑥	Ⓐ	⑥	Ⓐ	⚒
Nottingham 206 d.	⚒	0510	...	0550	0645	0728	0731	0845	0845	0955
Grantham 206 a.		0549	...	0627	0722	0807	0812	0927	0926	|
Grantham 185 d.		...	...	0631	0726	0816	0816	0930	0936	|
Sleaford d.		...	...	0657	0752	0845	0845	0956	1004	1044
Boston d.		...	0625	0724	0820	0912	0912	1022	1029	1111
Skegness a.		...	0703	0806	0859	0951	0951	1101	1108	1150

	⚒	⚒	Ⓐ	⑥		⚒	⚒	⚒	⚒	⚒		⚒	⚒			⑦	⑦		⑦	⑦		⑦	⑦		⑦
Nottingham 206 d.	1045	1145	1245	1245	...	1345	1445	1545	1645	1745	...	1845	2051	...	⑦	1155	1239	...	...	1456	...	1621	1831	...	1948
Grantham 206 a.	1123	1219	1323	1325	...	1421	1522	1625	1728	1825	...	1923	2132	...		1229	1313	...	...	1531	...	1703	1908	...	2022
Grantham 185 d.	1127	1223	1327	1329	...	1425	1526	1629	1732	1829	...	1926	2136	...		1235	...	...	1350	1536	...	1707	1913	...	2026
Sleaford d.	1153	1249	1355	1355	...	1451	1552	1655	1801	1855	...	1955	2201	...		1301	...	...	1416	1604	...	1736	1941	...	2054
Boston d.	1219	1315	1421	1421	...	1517	1620	1721	1826	1921	...	2019	2229	...		1327	...	...	1444	1631	...	1802	2010	...	...
Skegness a.	1258	1354	1500	1500	...	1556	1659	1803	1905	2000	...	2057	...	...		1406	...	...	1523	1710	...	1841	...	...	...

195 PETERBOROUGH - KINGS LYNN - HUNSTANTON First Excel service X1

Rail Link service – through rail tickets are available.

		Ⓐ	Ⓐ	⑥	⚒	⚒		⚒	⚒	⚒	⚒	⚒	⚒	⚒	⚒	⚒	⚒			⑦	⑦		⑦
Peterborough rail station d.	⚒	0700	0730	0735	0805	0835	and every	1635	1710	1740	1810	1840	1910	2010	2110	2210	2310	...	⑦	0810	0910	and every	2310
Wisbech bus station a.		0751	0821	0826	0856	0926	30 minutes	1726	1800	1730	1900	1930	2000	2100	2200	2300	0001	...		0900	1000	60 minutes	0001
Kings Lynn bus station a.		0832	0902	0902	0932	1002	until	1802	1835	1858	1935	1958	2035	2135	2228	2328	0028	...		0935	1035	until	0028

		Ⓐ	Ⓐ		⚒	⚒	⚒	⚒		⚒	⚒		⚒	⚒			⚒			⑦	⑦		⑦
Kings Lynn bus station d.	⚒	0540	0610	...	0645	0715	0745	0815	and every	1745	1850	...	1950	2050	...	...	2150	...	⑦	0650	0750	and every	2150
Wisbech bus station d.		0613	0643	...	0718	0748	0818	0848	30 minutes	1818	1922	...	2022	2122	...	...	2222	...		0722	0822	60 minutes	2222
Peterborough rail station a.		0654	0724	...	0759	0829	0859	0929	until	1859	2001	...	2101	2201	...	...	2301	...		0801	0901	until	2301

FC LONDON - ELY - KINGS LYNN 196

km		Ⓐ	Ⓐ	Ⓐ	Ⓐ	Ⓐ	Ⓐ		Ⓐ	Ⓐ		Ⓐ	Ⓐ	Ⓐ	Ⓐ	Ⓐ	Ⓐ	Ⓐ	Ⓐ	⑤	Ⓐ	Ⓐ	Ⓐ
0	**London** Kings Cross .... **197** d.	...	0545	0645	0715	0745	0845	and	1545	1644	...	1658**p**	1744	1814	1758**p**	1844	1858**p**	1945	2015	2045	2115	2215	2315
93	Cambridge .... **197** d.	0618	0658	0735	0804	0838	0935	hourly	1635	1739	...	1814	1839	1905	1919	1939	2015	2040	2110	2135	2208	2308	0013
117	**Ely** .... **197** a.	0633	0713	0751	0819	0853	0950	until	1650	1755	...	1830	1855	1918	1934	1955	2030	2055	2125	2152	2223	2323	0029
142	Downham Market .... a.	0654	0729	0807	0837	0910	1006	★	1706	1812	...	1847	1912	1938	1952	2012	2047	2111	2141	2209	2239	2339	0045
160	**Kings Lynn** .... a.	0710	0745	0823	0853	0925	1021		1721	1828	...	1905	1928	1953	2010	2028	2105	2126	2156	2224	2254	2354	0100

	⑥	⑥	⑥		⑥	⑥	⑥		⑥	⑥	⑥	⑥		⑦y	⑦		⑦		⑦		⑦
London Kings Cross .... **197** d.	...	0645	0745	and	1645	1745	1845	...	1945	2045	2215	2315	...	0752	0915	and	2115	...	2215	...	2315
Cambridge .... **197** d.	0632	0735	0835	hourly	1735	1840	1940	...	2040	2140	2311	0013	...	0907	1005	hourly	2205	...	2305	...	0013
Ely .... **197** a.	0647	0750	0850	until	1750	1855	1955	...	2055	2155	2326	0029	...	0922	1019	until	2219	...	2319	...	0029
Downham Market .... a.	0703	0806	0906	★	1806	1911	2011	...	2111	2211	2343	0045	...	0938	1035	★	2235	...	2335	...	...
Kings Lynn .... a.	0720	0821	0921		1821	1927	2027	...	2127	2227	2358	0059	...	0952	1050		2250	...	2350	...	...

	Ⓐ	Ⓐ	Ⓐ	Ⓐ	Ⓐ	Ⓐ		Ⓐ	Ⓐ	Ⓐ	Ⓐ	Ⓐ		Ⓐ	Ⓐ	Ⓐ	Ⓐ	Ⓐ		Ⓐ	Ⓐ	Ⓐ	Ⓐ
Kings Lynn .... d.	...	0519	0552	0618	0652	0723	...	0755	0827	0859	0959	1056	and	1456	1556	1654	1736	1836	...	1936	2036	2136	2228
Downham Market .... d.	...	0533	0605	0632	0705	0736	...	0808	0840	0912	1012	1109	hourly	1509	1609	1707	1749	1849	...	1949	2049	2149	2241
Ely .... **197** d.	0526	0552	0622	0650	0722	0754	...	0825	0857	0929	1029	1126	until	1526	1626	1724	1806	1906	...	2008	2108	2208	2258
Cambridge .... **197** a.	0544	0610	0640	0708	0740	0814	...	0844	0916	0947	1047	1144	★	1544	1644	1743	1822	1922	...	2026	2126	2224	2314
London Kings Cross .... **197** a.	0638	0734**p**	0739	0834**p**	0839	0912	...	0942	1013	1046	1139	1233		1633	1738	1838	1935	2033	...	2130	2230	2330	0042

	⑥	⑥	⑥	⑥	⑥	⑥		⑥	⑥	⑥	⑥	⑥	⑥		⑦	⑦		⑦	⑦	⑦	⑦
Kings Lynn .... d.	0556	0656	0756	0856	0930	0956	and	1756	1835	1935	2035	2135	2310	...	0828	0928	and	1928	2028	2128	2228
Downham Market .... d.	0609	0709	0809	0909	0941	1009	hourly	1809	1848	1948	2048	2148	2323	...	0841	0941	hourly	1941	2041	2141	2241
Ely .... **197** d.	0626	0726	0826	0926	0958	1026	until	1826	1905	2005	2105	2205	2343	...	0858	0958	until	1958	2058	2158	2258
Cambridge .... **197** a.	0644	0744	0844	0944	1013	1044	★	1844	1921	2021	2121	2221	2359	...	0916	1016	★	2016	2116	2216	2315
London Kings Cross .... **197** a.	0734	0834	0934	1034	1104	1134		1934	2031	2131	2231	2331	...	...	1008	1108		2108	2208	2308	0032

p – London Liverpool Street. **y** – Dec. 13 – Jan. 31 and Apr. 4 – May 16. ★ – Timings may vary by up to 4 minutes.

FC, LE LONDON - CAMBRIDGE 197

LONDON KINGS CROSS - CAMBRIDGE

Journey time: ± 55 - 62 minutes. *93 km.* FC

From London Kings Cross:

Ⓐ: 0004, 0545, 0606, 0645, 0715, 0745 and every 30 minutes until 1615, then 1644, 1714, 1744, 1814, 1844, 1915, 1945, 2015, 2045, 2115, 2152, 2215, 2252, 2315.

⑥: 0004, 0031, 0545, 0606, 0645, 0706, 0745, 0815 and every 30 minutes until 1945; then 1952, 2006, 2045, 2152, 2215, 2315.

⑦: 0004, 0652, 0652**A**, 0752**A**, 0852, 0915, 0952, and at 15 and 52 minutes past each hour until 2315.

From Cambridge:

Ⓐ: 0545, 0615 and every 30 minutes until 0845; then 0920, 0950, 1020, 1050, 1115, 1145 and every 30 minutes until 1945; then 2028, 2045, 2128, 2145, 2228, 2315.

⑥: 0545, 0628, 0645, 0728, 0745, 0815 and every 30 minutes until 1945; then 2028, 2045, 2128, 2145, 2228, 2310.

⑦: 0628**A**, 0728**A**, 0828**A**, 0920, 0928 and then at 20 and 28 minutes past each hour until 2220, 2241, 2315.

A – Dec. 13 – Jan. 31 and Apr. 4 – May 16.

LONDON LIVERPOOL STREET - CAMBRIDGE

Journey time: ± 80 minutes. *90 km.* LE

From London Liverpool Street:

Ⓐ: 0528, 0558, 0628 and every 30 minutes until 1628; then 1643, 1658, 1713, 1728, 1743, 1813, 1828, 1843, 1858, 1913, 1928, 1958, 2028, 2058, 2128, 2158, 2228, 2258, 2328, 2358⑤.

⑥: 0558, 0628 and every 30 minutes until 2358.

⑦: 0743, 0828, 0928 and hourly until 2228.

From Cambridge:

Ⓐ: 0448, 0521, 0541, 0551, 0618, 0621, 0648, 0651, 0718, 0721, 0748, 0751, 0818, 0821, 0851, 0932, 0948, 1032, 1048, 1132, 1151, 1232, 1251, 1332, 1351, 1432, 1451, 1521, 1551 and every 30 minutes until 1951; then 2032, 2051, 2132, 2151, 2232, 2251.

⑥: 0425, 0521, 0551, 0632, 0651 and at 32 and 51 minutes past each hour until 2251.

⑦: 0732, 0832 and hourly until 2232.

LE, LT LONDON - SOUTHEND 198

LONDON FENCHURCH STREET - SOUTHEND CENTRAL

Journey time ± 56 minutes. *56km.* LT

From London: Trains call at **Basildon** ± 35 minutes later.

Ⓐ: 0610, 0640, 0700, 0709, 0730, 0740 and then at 00, 10, 30 and 40 minutes past each hour until 1610; then 1628, 1645, 1705, 1720, 1735, 1750, 1800, 1806, 1820, 1840, 1910, 1930, 1940, 2000, 2010, 2030, 2040, 2100, 2110, 2130, 2140, 2200, 2210, 2240, 2300, 2310, 2340.

⑥: 0610, 0640, 0710, 0740, 0810, 0840 and then at 00, 10, 30 and 40 minutes past each hour until 2010; then 2040, 2100, 2110, 2140, 2200, 2210, 2240, 2310, 2340.

⑦: 0640 and every 30 minutes until 2340.

Services continue to **Shoeburyness**, arriving 12 minutes after Southend Central.

From Southend: Trains call at **Basildon** ± 19 minutes later.

Ⓐ: 0534, 0555, 0608, 0614, 0623, 0638, 0656, 0715, 0734, 0749, 0804, 0820, 0834, 0850, 0915, 0930, 0945 and then at 00, 15, 30 and 45 minutes past each hour until 1615; then 1625, 1638, 1659, 1706, 1719, 1740, 1755, 1815, 1830, 1845, 1900, 1915, 1930, 1945, 2000, 2015, 2030, 2045, 2115, 2130, 2145, 2215, 2245, 2315.

⑥: 0544, 0614, 0644, 0714, 0744, 0759 and then at 14, 29, 44 and 59 minutes past each hour until 2014; then 2044, 2059, 2114, 2144, 2214, 2244, 2314.

⑦: 0544 and every 30 minutes until 2244.

Services start at **Shoeburyness**, departing 10 minutes before Southend Central.

LONDON LIVERPOOL STREET - SOUTHEND VICTORIA

Journey time ± 57 minutes. *66km.* LE

From London: Trains call at **Rayleigh** ± 40 minutes later.

Ⓐ: 0615, 0634, 0655, 0715, 0734, 0755, 0814, 0835, 0855 and then at 15, 34 and 55 minutes past each hour until 1555; then 1610, 1625, 1640, 1655, 1704, 1717, 1725, 1734, 1745, 1749, 1756, 1804, 1815, 1825, 1835, 1845, 1855, 1915, 1935, 1955, 2015, 2034, 2055, 2115, 2134, 2155, 2215, 2245, 2315, 2345.

⑥: 0604, 0634, 0655, 0715, 0734, 0755 and then at 15, 34 and 55 minutes past each hour until 2115; then 2145, 2215, 2245, 2315, 2345.

⑦: 0715, 0745 and every 30 minutes until 2345.

From Southend: Trains call at **Rayleigh** ± 14 minutes later.

Ⓐ: 0601, 0616, 0629, 0640, 0656, 0709, 0717, 0721, 0725, 0733, 0740, 0753, 0803, 0811, 0826, 0846 and then at 06, 26 and 46 minutes past each hour until 1606; then 1621, 1635, 1651, 1706, 1721, 1736, 1751, 1806, 1826, 1846, 1906, 1926, 1946, 2006, 2026, 2046, 2106, 2136, 2206, 2236, 2306.

⑥: 0606, 0626, 0646 and then at 06, 26 and 46 minutes past each hour until 2006; then 2036, 2106, 2136, 2206, 2236, 2306.

⑦: 0618, 0648, 0718, 0752, 0822, 0852 and every 30 minutes until 2252.

GC LONDON - YORK - SUNDERLAND 199

km		Ⓐ ✕	Ⓐ ✕	Ⓐ ✕	Ⓐ ✕				⑥ 🍷	⑥ 🍷	⑥ 🍷	⑥ 🍷				⑦ 🍷	⑦ 🍷	⑦ 🍷				
0	**London** Kings Cross .... **180** d.	0804	1127	1650	1918	...	...	...	0757	1127	1650	1907	...	...	...	0907	1345	1820	...	...	...	...
29	**York** .... **180** a.	1002	1319	1844	2115	...	...	...	1013	1325	1845	2115	...	...	...	1114	1544	2023	...	...	...	...
53	**York** .... d.	1014	1322	1847	2118	...	...	...	1017	1330	1846	2117	...	...	...	1118	1550	2025	...	...	...	...
76	Thirsk .... d.	1030	1338	1905	2138	...	...	...	1039	1351	1903	2136	...	...	...	1135	1606	2042	...	...	...	...
89	Northallerton .... **180** d.	1039	1347	1915	2147	...	...	...	1046	1409	1910	2146	...	...	...	1144	1616	2050	...	...	...	...
124	Eaglescliffe .... a.	1058	1405	1932	2205	...	...	...	1106	1427	1928	2206	...	...	...	1203	1636	2113	...	...	...	...
124	Hartlepool .... a.	1122	1424	2000	2227	...	...	...	1125	1446	1956	2225	...	...	...	1222	1655	2133	...	...	...	...
428	**Sunderland** .... a.	1152	1453	2037	2254	...	...	...	1152	1517	2035	2254	...	...	...	1252	1726	2205	...	...	...	...

		Ⓐ ✕	Ⓐ ✕	Ⓐ ✕	Ⓐ ✕				⑥ 🍷	⑥ 🍷	⑥ 🍷	⑥ 🍷				⑦ 🍷	⑦ 🍷	⑦ 🍷				
Sunderland .... d.	...	0641	0918	1230	1730	...	...	...	0653	0929	1230	1730	...	...	...	0910	1342	1842	...	...	...	...
Hartlepool .... d.	...	0708	0942	1254	1756	...	...	...	0717	0953	1254	1756	...	...	...	0934	1406	1906	...	...	...	...
Eaglescliffe .... d.	...	0728	1001	1316	1815	...	...	...	0745	1015	1313	1828	...	...	...	0955	1434	1925	...	...	...	...
Northallerton .... **180** d.	...	0746	1020	1339	1837	...	...	...	0805	1035	1332	1846	...	...	...	1013	1454	1947	...	...	...	...
Thirsk .... d.	...	0757	1029	1348	1846	...	...	...	0816	1044	1343	1855	...	...	...	1027	1506	1956	...	...	...	...
York .... a.	...	0817	1051	1406	1905	...	...	...	0844	1102	1403	1913	...	...	...	1046	1528	2013	...	...	...	...
York .... **180** d.	...	0820	1053	1408	1908	...	...	...	0847	1104	1405	1915	...	...	...	1049	1531	2015	...	...	...	...
London Kings Cross .... **180** a.	...	1031	1249	1605	2109	...	...	...	1048	1255	1607	2130	...	...	...	1251	1724	2217	...	...	...	...

200 LONDON - IPSWICH - NORWICH

Most trains 🍴 LE

For London - Lowestoft and v.v. see Table 201. For London - Harwich and v.v. see Table 202.

km		⚒	Ⓐ P	⑥ P	Ⓐ	⑥	⑥	Ⓐ	Ⓐ	⑥	⚒ P	⑥	Ⓐ	⚒	⚒ L	⚒	⚒	⑥ P	⚒	⚒	⚒ L	⚒	⚒	⚒ P	⚒
0	**London** Liverpool St .... d.		...	...	...	0530	...	0600	0625	0630	0638	0700	0700	0730	0738	0800	0830	0838	0900	0930	0938	1000	1030	1038	1100
48	Chelmsford .... d.		...	...	...	0607	...	|	0657	0702	0712	|	|	0802	0812	|	0902	0912	|	1002	1012	|	1102	1112	|
84	**Colchester** .... d.		0535	0538	...	0637	...	0650	0722	0722	0738	0750	0750	0822	0838	0850	0922	0938	0950	1022	1038	1050	1122	1138	1150
97	Manningtree .... 202 d.		0544	0546	...	0645	...	0659	0732	0731	0746	0759	0759	0831	|	0859	0931	0946	0959	1031	|	1059	1131	|	1159
111	**Ipswich** .... 201 204 205 d.		0601	0600	0642	0656	0709	0709	0742	0742	0802	0809	0809	0842	0856	0909	0942	1002	1009	1043	1056	1109	1142	1202	1209
130	Stowmarket .... d.		0612	0611	0653	...	0720	0720	0753	0753	0813	|	0820	0853	...	|	0953	1013	|	1052	...	|	1153	1213	|
153	Diss .... d.		...	...	0705	...	0732	0732	0805	0805	...	0830	0832	0905	...	0930	1005	...	1030	1105	...	1130	1205	...	1230
185	**Norwich** .... 206 a.		...	...	0727	...	0752	0754	0827	0827	...	0852	0854	0927	...	0952	1027	...	1052	1127	...	1152	1227	...	1252

	⚒	⚒ L	⚒	⚒	⚒ P	⚒	⚒	⚒ L	⚒	⚒	⚒ P	⚒	⚒	⑥ L	Ⓐ L	⑥	Ⓐ	Ⓐ	⑥	Ⓐ P	⑥ P	Ⓐ	⑥	Ⓐ	⑥
London Liverpool St .... d.	1130	1138	1200	1230	1238	1300	1330	1338	1400	1430	1438	1500	1530	1538	1538	1600	1600	1630	1630	1632	1638	1700	1700	1730	1730
Chelmsford .... d.	1202	1212	|	1302	1312	|	1402	1412	|	1502	1512	|	1559	1612	1612u	|	1631	|	1702	|	1712	|	|	|	1802
Colchester .... d.	1222	1238	1250	1322	1338	1350	1422	1438	1450	1522	1538	1550	1622	1638	1641	1650	1650	1718	1722	1726	1738	|	1750	|	1822
Manningtree .... 202 d.	1231	|	1259	1331	|	1359	1431	|	1459	1531	|	1559	1631	|	|	1659	1659	|	1731	1735	|	|	1759	1827	1831
Ipswich .... 201 204 205 d.	1242	1256	1309	1342	1402	1409	1442	1456	1509	1542	1602	1609	1642	1656	1658	1709	1709	1734	1742	1749	1802	1759	1809	1837	1842
Stowmarket .... d.	1253	...	|	1353	1413	|	1453	...	|	1553	1613	|	1653	...	...	1720	1720	1745	1753	1803	1813	|	|	1848	1853
Diss .... d.	1305	...	1330	1405	...	1430	1505	...	1530	1605	...	1630	1705	...	...	1732	1732	1757	1805	...	...	1820	1830	1900	1905
Norwich .... 206 a.	1327	...	1352	1427	...	1452	1527	...	1552	1627	...	1652	1727	...	...	1752	1755	1820	1827	...	...	1842	1852	1923	1927

	⑥ L	Ⓐ	⑥	Ⓐ	Ⓐ	Ⓐ	⑥	⑥ P	⑥	Ⓐ	⚒	Ⓐ L	⑥ L	⑥	Ⓐ	⚒	⚒ L	⚒	Ⓐ	⑥	⑥	Ⓐ	⚒	⑥	Ⓐ
London Liverpool St .... d.	1746	1750	1800	1800	1820	1830	1830	1846	1900	1900	1930	1932	1938	2000	2000	2030	2100	2130	2200	2200	2230	2230	2300	2330	2330
Chelmsford .... d.	1816u	|	|	|	|	|	1902	1916u	|	|	2000	|	2012	|	|	2103	|	2203	2231	2233	2303	2303	2333	0003	0003
Colchester .... d.	1840	1843	1850	1853	1912	1923	1922	1940	1950	1953	2021	2026	2038	2050	2050	2123	2150	2223	2254	2256	2323	2323	2357	0023	0023
Manningtree .... 202 d.	|	1852	1859	1902	1921	|	1931	|	1959	2002	2030	|	|	2059	2059	2132	2158	2232	2302	2304	2332	2332	0004	0032	0032
Ipswich .... 201 204 205 d.	1856	1903	1909	1912	1932	1940	1942	2002	2009	2012	2041	2044	2056	2109	2109	2143	2209	2243	2314	2315	2343	2343	0020	0044	0044
Stowmarket .... d.	...	|	|	1923	|	1951	1953	2013	|	2023	2052	...	...	|	2120	2154	...	2254	...	...	2354	2354	...	0055	0055
Diss .... d.	...	|	1930	1935	|	2003	2005	...	2030	2035	2104	...	...	2130	2132	2206	...	2307	...	...	0007	0007	...	0108	0108
Norwich .... 206 a.	...	1944	1952	1958	2014	2026	2027	...	2052	2057	2128	...	...	2152	2154	2228	...	2329	...	...	0032	0045	...	0134	0145

	⑦	⑦	⑦	⑦	⑦	⑦	⑦	⑦	⑦	⑦	⑦	⑦	⑦		⑦	⑦	⑦	⑦	⑦	⑦	⑦	⑦	⑦	⑦
London Liverpool St .... d.		...	...	0802	0830	0902	0930	1002	1030	1102	1130	1202	1230	and at the same minutes past each hour until	1902	1930	2002	2030	2102	2130	2202	2230	2302	2330
Chelmsford .... d.		...	...	0842	|	0942	|	1042	|	1142	|	1242	|		1942	|	2042	|	2142	|	2242	|	2342	|
Colchester .... d.		0740	0812	0912	0924	1012	1024	1112	1124	1212	1224	1312	1324		2012	2024	2112	2124	2212	2224	2312	2324	0012	0028
Manningtree .... 202 d.		0748	0820	0920	0933	1020	1033	1120	1133	1220	1233	1320	1333		2020	2033	2120	2133	2220	2233	2320	2333	0020	0037
Ipswich .... 201 204 205 d.		0800	0832	0932	0944	1032	1044	1132	1144	1232	1244	1332	1344		2032	2044	2132	2144	2232	2244	2332	2344	0036	0048
Stowmarket .... d.		...	...	...	0955	...	1055	...	1155	...	1255	...	1355		...	2055	...	2155	...	2255	...	2355	...	0059
Diss .... d.		...	...	...	1007	...	1107	...	1207	...	1307	...	1407		...	2107	...	2207	...	2307	...	0007	...	0111
Norwich .... 206 a.		...	...	...	1029	...	1129	...	1229	...	1329	...	1429		...	2129	...	2229	...	2329	...	0039	...	0143

	⚒	⑥	Ⓐ	⑥	Ⓐ	⑥	Ⓐ	⑥	Ⓐ	Ⓐ	⑥	Ⓐ	⑥ L	Ⓐ	⑥	Ⓐ	⑥	Ⓐ Y	Ⓐ	⑥ L	⚒	⚒	⑥ P	Ⓐ P	⚒
Norwich .... 206 d.		0500	0510	0530	0540	...	...	0600	0610	0625	0630	0640	...	0655	0700	0710	0730	0730	0740	...	0800	0830	...	...	0900
Diss .... d.		0517	0528	0547	0558	...	...	0617	0628	0643	0647	0658	...	0713	0717	0728	0747	|	0758	...	0817	0847	...	...	0917
Stowmarket .... d.		0529	0540	|	0610	...	...	0629	0640	0655	|	0710	...	0725	0729	0740	|	|	0810	...	0829	|	0912	0912	0929
Ipswich .... 201 204 205 d.		0542	0553	0608	0623	0630	0638	0642	0653	0708	0708	0723	0730	0738	0742	0753	0808	0818	0823	0830	0842	0908	0930	0930	0942
Manningtree .... 202 d.		0552	0603	0618	0633	|	0648	0652	0703	0718	0718	0733	|	0748	0752	0803	0818	|	0833	|	0852	0918	|	|	0952
Colchester .... d.		0603	0615	0629	0645	0649	0659	0703	0715	0730	0729	0745	0749	0800	0803	0815	0829	|	0845	0849	0903	0929	0949	0949	1003
Chelmsford .... d.		|	|	0646	|	0711	0711	|	|	|	0746	|	0811	|	|	|	0846	|	0902	0906s	|	0944	1006s	1010s	|
London Liverpool St .... a.		0654	0710	0724	0737	0745	0759	0754	0809	0823	0824	0839	0845	0855	0854	0910	0924	0925	0940	0938	0956	1024	1038	1046	1054

	⚒	⑥ L	Ⓐ L	⚒	⚒	⚒ P	⚒	⚒	⚒ L	⚒	⚒	⚒ P	⚒	⚒	⚒ L	⚒	⚒	⑥ P	Ⓐ P	Ⓐ	⚒	⚒	⑥ L	⚒	⚒
Norwich .... 206 d.	0930	...	...	1000	1030	...	1100	1130	...	1200	1230	...	1300	1330	...	1400	1430	...	...	...	1500	1530	...	1600	1630
Diss .... d.	0947	...	...	1017	1047	...	1117	1147	...	1217	1247	...	1317	1347	...	1417	1447	...	...	...	1517	1547	...	1617	1647
Stowmarket .... d.	|	...	...	1029	|	1112	1129	|	...	1229	|	1312	1329	|	...	1429	|	1512	1512	...	1529	|	...	1629	|
Ipswich .... 201 204 205 d.	1008	1030	1030	1042	1108	1130	1142	1208	1230	1242	1308	1330	1342	1408	1430	1442	1508	1530	1526	...	1542	1608	1630	1642	1708
Manningtree .... 202 d.	1018	|	|	1052	1118	|	1152	1218	|	1252	1318	|	1352	1418	|	1452	1518	|	|	...	1552	1618	|	1652	1718
Colchester .... d.	1029	1049	1049	1103	1129	1149	1203	1229	1249	1303	1329	1349	1403	1429	1449	1503	1529	1549	1543	1547	1603	1629	1649	1703	1729
Chelmsford .... d.	1046	1106s	1111	|	1146	1211	|	1246	1311	|	1346	1411	|	1446	1511	|	1546	1611	...	1614	|	1646	1711	|	1746
London Liverpool St .... a.	1124	1142	1145	1154	1224	1245	1254	1324	1345	1354	1424	1445	1454	1524	1545	1554	1624	1645	...	1649	1654	1724	1745	1754	1824

	⑥ P	Ⓐ P	⚒	⚒	⑥ L	Ⓐ L	⚒	⚒	⚒ P	⚒	⚒	⑥ L	Ⓐ L	⚒	⚒	Ⓐ P	⑥ P	⚒	⚒	⚒	⚒	⑥ P	Ⓐ P	Ⓐ	⑥
Norwich .... 206 d.	...	...	1700	1730	...	...	1800	1830	...	1900	...	...	...	2000	...	...	...	2100	...	2200	...	...	...	2305	2305
Diss .... d.	...	...	1717	1747	...	...	1817	1847	...	1917	...	...	...	2017	...	...	...	2117	...	2217	...	...	...	2322	2322
Stowmarket .... d.	1712	1712	1729	1759	...	...	1829	|	1912	1929	...	...	...	2029	...	2108	2112	2129	...	2229	...	2317	2324	2334	2334
Ipswich .... 201 204 205 d.	1730	1730	1742	1811	1830	1830	1842	1908	1927	1942	2008	2030	2030	2042	2108	2127	2127	2142	2208	2242	2322	2335	2338	2348	2350
Manningtree .... 202 d.	|	|	1752	1821	|	|	1852	1918	1937	1952	2018	|	|	2052	2118	2137	2137	2152	2218	2252	2331	2345	2348	...	...
Colchester .... d.	1749	1749	1803	1832	1849	1849	1903	1929	1947	2003	2029	2049	2049	2103	2129	2149	2149	2203	2229	2303	2341	2356	2358	...	...
Chelmsford .... d.	1811	1813	|	1849	1911	1913	|	1946	2011	|	2046	2111	2111	|	2146	2211	2211	|	2256	2324	...	...	...	...	...
London Liverpool St .... a.	1845	1851	1854	1927	1945	1947	1954	2024	2046	2054	2121	2145	2149	2154	2223	2246	2245	2254	2334	0003	...	...	...	...	...

	⑦	⑦	⑦	⑦	⑦	⑦	⑦	⑦	⑦	⑦	⑦		⑦	⑦	⑦	⑦	⑦	⑦	⑦	⑦	⑦	⑦	⑦	⑦
Norwich .... 206 d.		0700	...	0800	...	0900	...	1000	...	1100	...	and at the same minutes past each hour until	1700	...	1800	...	1900	...	2000	...	2100	...	2200	2305
Diss .... d.		0717	...	0817	...	0917	...	1017	...	1117	...		1717	...	1817	...	1917	...	2017	...	2117	...	2217	2322
Stowmarket .... d.		0729	...	0829	...	0929	...	1029	...	1129	...		1729	...	1829	...	1929	...	2029	...	2129	...	2229	2334
Ipswich .... 201 204 205 d.		0742	0808	0842	0908	0942	1008	1042	1108	1142	1208		1742	1808	1842	1908	1942	2008	2042	2108	2142	2208	2242	2348
Manningtree .... 202 d.		0752	0818	0852	0918	0952	1018	1052	1118	1152	1218		1752	1818	1852	1918	1952	2018	2052	2118	2152	2218	2252	...
Colchester .... d.		0803	0830	0903	0930	1003	1030	1103	1130	1203	1230		1803	1830	1903	1930	2003	2030	2103	2130	2203	2230	2303	...
Chelmsford .... d.		|	0857	|	0957	|	1057	|	1157	|	1257		|	1857	|	1957	|	2057	|	2157	|	2257	2324	...
London Liverpool St .... a.		0903	0942	1001	1042	1101	1142	1201	1242	1301	1342		1901	1942	2001	2042	2101	2142	2201	2242	2301	2342	0007	...

L – To / from Lowestoft, Table 201.
P – To / from Peterborough, Table 205.
Y – To / from Great Yarmouth, Table 203.
s – Stops to set down only.
u – Stops to pick up only.

201 IPSWICH - LOWESTOFT

LE

km		⚒	Ⓐ	⑥	Ⓐ2	⚒	⚒	⚒	⚒	⚒	Ⓐ2	Ⓐ2	⑥	Ⓐ	⑥	⚒		⑦	⑦	⑦2	⑦	⑦2	⑦	⑦	⑦2
	London L'pool St 200 d.		...	...	...	0738	0938	1138	1338	1538	...	...	1746	1932	1938	2100	...		...	...	...	...	...	...	...
0	**Ipswich** .... 200 d.		0647	0650	0732	0902	1102	1302	1502	1702	1813	1855	1902	2052	2102	2215	...		1000	1200	1400	1600	1800	2000	2200
17	Woodbridge .... d.		0706	0709	0755	0921	1121	1321	1521	1721	1832	1914	1921	2111	2121	2234	...		1019	1219	1419	1619	1819	2019	2219
36	Saxmundham .... d.		0727	0730	0817	0942	1142	1342	1542	1742	1853	1935	1942	2132	2142	2255	...		1040	1240	1440	1640	1840	2040	2240
65	Beccles .... d.		0758	0801	...	1013	1213	1413	1613	1813	1931	2006	2013	2203	2213	2326	...		1111	1311	1511	1711	1911	2111	2311
79	**Lowestoft** .... 203 a.		0817	0820	...	1032	1232	1432	1632	1833	1950	2025	2032	2222	2232	2345	...		1130	1330	1530	1730	1930	2130	2330

	⚒	Ⓐ2	⑥	Ⓐ	⑥	Ⓐ2	⑥	Ⓐ	⚒	⚒	⑥	Ⓐ2	⚒	Ⓐ	⑥	⚒2			⑦	⑦2	⑦	⑦2	⑦	⑦	⑦2
Lowestoft .... 203 d.		0531	0558	0644	0658	...	0858	0858	1058	1258	1458	1458	1658	1843	1858	2058	...		0805	1005	1205	1405	1605	1805	2005
Beccles .... d.		0547	0614	0700	0714	...	0914	0914	1114	1314	1514	1514	1714	1859	1914	2114	...		0821	1021	1221	1421	1621	1821	2021
Saxmundham .... d.		0619	0646	0732	0746	0821	0946	0946	1146	1346	1546	1546	1746	1936	1946	2146	...		0853	1053	1253	1453	1653	1853	2053
Woodbridge .... d.		0640	0707	0753	0807	0842	1007	1007	1207	1407	1607	1607	1807	1957	2007	2207	...		0914	1114	1314	1514	1714	1914	2114
Ipswich .... 200 a.		0659	0726	0812	0826	0901	1026	1026	1226	1426	1626	1626	1826	2016	2026	2226	...		0933	1133	1333	1533	1733	1933	2133
London L'pool St 200 a.		...	0845	0925	0938	...	1142	1145	1345	1545	1745	...	1947z	2146	2145	...	...		...	...	...	...	...	...	...

z – 1945 on ⑥.

LE (LONDON -) MANNINGTREE - HARWICH 202

For boat trains London - Harwich International and v.v., see Table **15a.**

km			Ⓐ	Ⓐ	Ⓐ	Ⓐ	Ⓐ	Ⓐ	Ⓐ		Ⓐ	Ⓐ	Ⓐ	Ⓐ	Ⓐ	Ⓐ	Ⓐ		Ⓐ	Ⓐ	Ⓐ		Ⓐ	
	London Liverpool St... **200** d.	Ⓐ	...	...	...	0718	...	0918	1018	and	1518	1615	1645	...	...	...	...	...	1918	2018	...	...	...	...
0	**Manningtree** .... **200** d.		0538	0636	0735	0829	0922	1029	1126	hourly	1626	1721	1755	1823	1857	1927	2007	...	2025	2125	2238	...	2338	...
15	Harwich International..........d.		0556	0652	0751	0846	0939	1047	1144	until	1644	1738	1712	1839	1913	1943	2023	...	2042	2142	2254	...	2354	...
18	**Harwich Town** ....a.		0601	0657	0756	0851	0944	1052	1149		1649	1745	1819	1846	1918	1948	2028	...	2047	2147	2259	...	2359	...

		⑥	⑥	⑥		⑥		⑥		⑥		⑥			⑦		⑦		⑦		⑦		⑦
London Liverpool St.... **200** d.	⑥	...	...	0618	...	0718	and	2018	...	...	...	...	...	⑦	...	...	...	...	...	and	...	...	...
Manningtree .... **200** d.		0526	0626	0726	...	0826	hourly	2126	...	2238	...	2338	...		0826	...	0926	...	1026	hourly	2126	...	2226
Harwich International ....d.		0544	0644	0744	...	0844	until	2144	...	2254	...	2354	...		0842	...	0942	...	1042	until	2142	...	2242
Harwich Town ....a.		0549	0649	0749	...	0849		2149	...	2259	...	2359	...		0847	...	0947	...	1047		2147	...	2247

		Ⓐ	Ⓐ	Ⓐ	Ⓐ	Ⓐ		Ⓐ	Ⓐ	Ⓐ	Ⓐ		Ⓐ	Ⓐ	Ⓐ		Ⓐ	Ⓐ	Ⓐ		Ⓐ	Ⓐ	Ⓐ	
Harwich Town ....d.	Ⓐ	0537	0622	0708	0800	0900	and	1400	1500	1605	1700	...	1753	1825	1853	...	1928	2000	2033	...	2100	2154	2305	...
Harwich International ....d.		0542	0627	0713	0806	0906	hourly	1406	1506	1611	1706	...	1758	1830	1858	...	1933	2006	2038	...	2106	2159	2310	...
Manningtree .... **200** a.		0558	0643	0729	0822	0922	until	1422	1522	1627	1722	...	1814	1846	1914	...	1949	2022	2056	...	2122	2215	2326	...
London Liverpool St.... **200** a.		...	...	...	0935	1033		1534	1635	...	1838	...	...	...	...	...	...	2133	...	...	2236	...	...	...

		⑥	⑥	⑥		⑥	⑥	⑥	⑥	⑥	⑥	⑥			⑦		⑦		⑦		⑦		⑦
Harwich Town ....d.	⑥	0600	0700	0800	and	1700	1803	1900	2000	2100	2154	2305	...	⑦	0853	...	0953	...	1053	and	2153	...	2253
Harwich International ....d.		0606	0706	0806	hourly	1706	1809	1906	2006	2106	2159	2310	...		0858	...	0958	...	1058	hourly	2158	...	2258
Manningtree .... **200** a.		0622	0722	0822	until	1722	1825	1922	2022	2122	2215	2326	...		0914	...	1014	...	1114	until	2214	...	2314
London Liverpool St.... **200** a.		0733	0833	0933		1833	1937	2033	2134	2234	...	...	...		...	...	...	...	...		...	...	...

LE 2nd class NORWICH and IPSWICH local services 203

NORWICH - GREAT YARMOUTH

Journey time: ± 32 mins. *30 km (33 km via Reedham)*

From Norwich : Trains noted '**r**' call at **Reedham** 18–21 minutes later.

Ⓐ: 0515, 0634, 0705, 0736 **r**, 0836, 0936, 1036 **r**, 1136, 1236, 1336, 1436, 1536, 1640, 1705, 1736, 1840, 1936, 2040, 2140, 2300.

⑥: 0536 **r**, 0636, 0705, 0736 **r**, 0836, 0936, 1036 **r**, 1136, 1236, 1336, 1436, 1536, 1640, 1705, 1736, 1840, 1936, 2040, 2140, 2300.

⑦: 0736 **r**, 0845, 0936 **r**, 1045, 1136 **r**, 1245, 1336 **r**, 1445, 1536 **r**, 1645, 1736 **r**, 1845, 1936 **r**, 2045, 2136 **r**, 2236.

From Great Yarmouth : Trains noted '**r**' call at **Reedham** 12–14 minutes later.

Ⓐ: 0555, 0640 **L**, 0717, 0744, 0817, 0917, 1017, 1117, 1217, 1317, 1412 **r**, 1517, 1617, 1717, 1747 **r**, 1817, 1917, 2017, 2117, 2217, 2333 **r**.

⑥: 0617, 0717, 0744, 0817, 0917, 1017, 1117, 1217, 1317, 1412 **r**, 1517, 1617, 1717, 1747 **r**, 1817, 1917, 2017, 21117, 2217, 2333 **r**.

⑦: 0820 **r**, 0922, 1018 **r**, 1122, 1218 **r**, 1322, 1420 **r**, 1522, 1618 **r**, 1722, 1818 **r**, 1922, 2022 **r**, 2122, 2222 **r**, 2320 **r**.

NORWICH - LOWESTOFT

Journey time: ± 38 mins. *38 km*

From Norwich : Trains noted '**r**' call at **Reedham** 18–21 minutes later.

Ⓐ: 0545 **r**, 0624, 0657 **r**, 0754 **r**, 0857, 0957 **r**, 1057, 1157 **r**, 1257, 1357 **r**, 1457, 1557 **r**, 1657 **r**, 1757 **r**, 1857 **r**, 1957 **r**, 2057 **r**, 2157 **r**, 2240 **r**.

⑥: 0549 **r**, 0655 **r**, 0754 **r**, 0957 **r**, 1057, 1157 **r**, 1257, 1357 **r**, 1457 **r**, 1557 **r**, 1657 **r**, 1757 **r**, 1857 **r**, 1957 **r**, 2057 **r**, 2157 **r**, 2240 **r**.

⑦: 0725, 0857 **r**, 1057 **r**, 1257 **r**, 1457 **r**, 1657 **r**, 1857 **r**, 2057 **r**.

From Lowestoft : Trains noted '**r**' call at **Reedham** 18–21 minutes later.

Ⓐ: 0536 **r**, 0638 **r**, 0840 **r**, 0755 **r**, 0842 **r**, 0942 **r**, 1050, 1142 **r**, 1250, 1342 **r**, 1450, 1542 **r**, 1647 **r**, 1747 **r**, 1847 **r**, 1947 **r**, 2050, 2142 **r**, 2245 **r**, 2330 **r**.

⑥: 0640 **r**, 0742 **r**, 0842 **r**, 0942 **r**, 1050, 1142 **r**, 1250, 1342 **r**, 1450, 1542 **r**, 1647 **r**, 1747 **r**, 1847 **r**, 1947 **r**, 2050, 2142 **r**, 2245 **r**, 2330 **r**.

⑦: 0950 **r**, 1150 **r**, 1350 **r**, 1550 **r**, 1750 **r**, 1950 **r**, 2150 **r**, 2335 **r**.

NORWICH - SHERINGHAM (🚂)

Journey time: ± 57 mins. *49 km*

From Norwich : Trains call at **Cromer** ± 45 minutes later.

Ⓐ: 0520, 0550, 0715, 0823, 0945 and hourly until 1745; then 1847, 1945, 2115, 2245.

⑥: 0520, 0545, 0715, 0823, 0945 and hourly until 1745; then 1847, 1945, 2115, 2245.

⑦: 0836, 1036, 1236, 1436, 1636, 1836, 2036.

From Sheringham : Trains call at **Cromer** ± 11 minutes later.

Ⓐ: 0632, 0717, 0825, 0946 and hourly until 1546, 1649, 1748, 1748, 1849, 1948, 2049, 2216, 2346.

⑥: 0622, 0717, 0825, 0946 and hourly until 1546, 1649, 1748, 1748, 1849, 1948, 2049, 2216, 2346.

⑦: 0943, 1143, 1343, 1543, 1743, 1943, 2143.

IPSWICH - FELIXSTOWE

Journey time: ± 25 mins. *25 km*

From Ipswich :

⚒: 0504, 0604, 0713, 0827 and hourly until 2027; then 2227.

⑥: 0627, 0727, 0827, 0927 and hourly until 2027; then 2227.

⑦: 1155 and hourly until 1955.

From Felixstowe :

Ⓐ: 0534, 0638, 0750, 0856 and hourly until 2056; then 2256.

⑥: 0656, 0756, 0856, 0959 and hourly until 2056; then 2256.

⑦: 1225 and hourly until 2025.

L – (12) Great Yarmouth - London Liverpool St and v.v., Table **190**.

🚂 – **Sheringham – Holt** and v.v. (*North Norfolk Railway*). *8* km. ②③④⑥⑦ mid Apr. – Oct. (daily May – Sept.) and on certain other dates throughout the year. Sheringham station is opposite the National Rail station. Operator: North Norfolk Railway. ✆ 01263 820800. www.nnrailway.co.uk

LE 2nd class IPSWICH - CAMBRIDGE 204

km			⚒	⚒	Ⓐ	⑥	⚒		⚒	⑥	Ⓐ	⚒			⑦	⑦	⑦	⑦	⑦	⑦	⑦	⑦	
0	**Ipswich** .... **200 205** d.	⚒	0510	0613	0652	0716	0816		1916	2016	2116	2216	...	⑦	0845	0902	1102	1302	1502	1702	1902	2102	...
19	Stowmarket .... **200 205** d.		0526	0629	0708	0732	0832	and	1932	2032	2132	2232	...		0859	0918	1118	1318	1518	1718	1918	2118	...
42	Bury St. Edmunds.................d.		0549	0651	0730	0755	0855	hourly	1955	2055	2155	2255	...		0917	0940	1140	1340	1540	1740	1940	2140	...
65	Newmarket ....d.		0610	0713	0751	0817	0915	until	2017	2115	2215	...	...		...	1000	1200	1400	1600	1800	2000	2200	...
88	**Cambridge** .... **196 197** a.		0636	0739	0819	0839	0939		2039	2139	2239	...	...		...	1024	1224	1424	1624	1824	2024	2224	...

		Ⓐ	⚒		⚒	⚒		⚒		⑥		Ⓐ			⑦	⑦	⑦	⑦	⑦	⑦	⑦	⑦	
Cambridge .... **196 197** d.	⚒	...	...	...	0641	0743		2043	...	2143	...	2243	...	⑦	...	1112	1312	1512	1712	1912	2112	2300	...
Newmarket ....d.		...	...	...	0701	0803	and	2103	...	2204	...	2304	...		...	1134	1334	1534	1734	1934	2134	2321	...
Bury St. Edmunds.................d.		0536	0622	...	0723	0823	hourly	2123	...	2225	...	2325	...		0955	1155	1355	1555	1755	1955	2155	2342	...
Stowmarket............. **200 205** d.		0557	0644	...	0745	0845	until	2145	...	2246	...	2346	...		1017	1217	1417	1617	1817	2017	2217	0004	...
Ipswich .... **200 205** a.		0615	0703	...	0803	0903		2203	...	2303	...	0003	...		1034	1234	1434	1634	1834	2034	2234	0021	...

LE IPSWICH - PETERBOROUGH 205

km			⑥	Ⓐ	⚒	⚒		⚒	⚒	⚒	Ⓐ		⑥	⑥	Ⓐ			⑦	⑦		⑦	⑦		⑦
	London Liverpool St **200**......d.	⚒	...	...	0638	0838j	...	1038	1238	1438	1632	...	1638	1846	*1900*	...	⑦	...	...	...	...	...	...	...
0	**Ipswich** .... **204** d.		0600	0601	0802	1002	...	1202	1402	1602	1749	...	1802	2002	2016	...		0955	1155	...	1355	1555	...	1755
19	Stowmarket .... **204** d.		0611	0612	0813	1013	...	1213	1413	1613	1803	...	1813	2013	2030	...		1007	1207	...	1407	1607	...	1807
42	Bury St. Edmunds........... **204** d.		0627	0628	0829	1029	...	1229	1429	1629	1823	...	1829	2029	2050	...		1023	1223	...	1423	1623	...	1823
82	Ely.................................. **208** d.		0657	0700	0858	1058	...	1258	1458	1658	1901	...	1858	2058	2119	...		1052	1252	...	1452	1652	...	1852
108	March .... **208** d.		0714	0716	0915	1115	...	1315	1515	1715	1917	...	1915	2115	2136	...		1109	1309	...	1509	1709	...	1909
132	**Peterborough** .... **208** a.		0737	0738	0938	1137	...	1337	1537	1737	1942	...	1938	2137	2158	...		1136	1331	...	1531	1731	...	1932

		⑥	Ⓐ	Ⓐ	⑥	⚒	Ⓐ	⑥	⑥	Ⓐ	⚒	Ⓐ	⑥	⑥	Ⓐ			⑦	⑦		⑦	⑦		⑦
Peterborough .... **208** d.	⚒	0745	0746	0945	0955	1145	1345	1345	1545	1545	1745	1946	1945	2145	2205	...	⑦	1146	1346	...	1546	1746	...	1944
March .... **208** a.		0804	0805	1004	1014	1204	1404	1404	1604	1604	1804	2005	2004	2204	2224	...		1205	1405	...	1605	1805	...	2003
Ely.................................. **208** a.		0830	0830	1026	1032	1230	1430	1430	1630	1630	1830	2027	2030	2230	2242	...		1230	1430	...	1630	1830	...	2022
Bury St. Edmunds........... **204** d.		0856	0856	1056	1058	1256	1456	1456	1656	1656	1856	2052	2056	2258	2308	...		1256	1456	...	1656	1856	...	2047
Stowmarket..................... **204** d.		0912	0912	1112	1114	1312	1512	1512	1712	1712	1912	2108	2112	2317	2324	...		1312	1512	...	1712	1912	...	2105
Ipswich .... **204** a.		0925	0926	1125	1127	1327	1525	1525	1727	1727	1925	2125	2127	2332	2337	...		1325	1527	...	1725	1927	...	2118
London Liverpool St **200**......a.		1038	1046	1245	1245	1445	*1649*	1645	1845	1851	2046	2246	2245	...	...	...		...	...	...	...	...	...	...

j – Connection on Ⓐ.

206 NORWICH - NOTTINGHAM - SHEFFIELD - MANCHESTER - LIVERPOOL

2nd class EM

Services on ⑦ valid until March 28.

km			⚒	⚒	⚒	⚒ m	Ⓐ m	⑥ m	Ⓐ m	⑥ m	⑥	Ⓐ	⚒	⚒	⚒	⚒	⚒	⚒	Ⓐ	⑥	⚒	⚒ m	⚒	⑥	Ⓐ A
0	**Norwich** 200 207 d.	⚒	...	...	...	0550	0652	0652	0757	0757	0857	0857	0957	1057	1157	1257	1357	1457	1552	1552	1657	1754	1857	...	...
49	Thetford 207 d.		...	...	...	0623	0720	0720	0824	0824	0924	0924	1024	1124	1224	1324	1424	1524	1627	1623	1727	1827	1924	...	...
86	Ely 207 d.		...	...	...	0651	0745	0744	0850	0854	0951	0952	1052	1152	1252	1352	1452	1552	1652	1652	1752	1852	1952	...	...
135	**Peterborough** a.		...	...	...	0725	0824	0826	0925	0928	1025	1026	1124	1224	1326	1425	1525	1625	1726	1726	1825	1930	2026	...	...
135	**Peterborough** 185 d.		...	...	...	0727	0827	0830	0927	0930	1028	1030	1125	1225	1326	1426	1526	1627	1727	1727	1826	1930	2027	2127	2130
181	Grantham 185 d.		...	...	...	0758	0858	0858	0958	0958	1058	1113	1156	1258	1358	1458	1558	1658	1758	1803	1858	2003	2058	2202	|
218	**Nottingham** 170 a.		...	...	...	0838	0936	0936	1036	1036	1135	1143	1236	1336	1436	1536	1636	1736	1836	1836	1936	2037	2135	2232	2250
218	**Nottingham** 171 d.		0518	0640	0745	0845	0945	0945	1045	1045	1145	1145	1245	1345	1445	1545	1645	1745	1845	1845	1940	...	...	...	...
	Alfreton 171 d.		|	0702	0807	0907	1007	1007	1107	1107	1207	1207	1307	1407	1507	1607	1707	1808	1907	1907	2001	...	...	...	...
264	Chesterfield 127 170 171 d.		0549	0713	0818	0918	1018	1018	1118	1118	1218	1218	1318	1418	1518	1618	1718	1818	1918	1918	2011	...	...	...	...
283	**Sheffield** 127 170 171 a.		0615	0731	0838	0938	1038	1038	1138	1138	1238	1238	1338	1438	1538	1638	1734	1839	1939	1939	2027	...	...	...	...
283	**Sheffield** 193 d.		0620	0735	0842	0942	1042	1042	1142	1142	1242	1242	1342	1442	1542	1642	1740	1842	1942	1942	2031	...	...	...	...
343	Stockport 193 a.		0722	0824	0925	1025	1125	1125	1225	1225	1325	1325	1425	1525	1625	1725	1825	1925	2025	2025	2120k	...	...	...	...
352	**Manchester** Piccadilly 193 a.		0734	0836	0936	1036	1136	1136	1236	1236	1336	1336	1436	1536	1636	1737	1836	1936	2036	2037	2132	...	...	...	...
378	Warrington 187 a.		0753	0857	0957	1057	1157	1157	1257	1257	1357	1357	1457	1557	1657	1803	1857	1957	2057	...	...	...	...	...	...
389	Widnes a.		0801	0905	1005	1105	1205	1205	1305	1305	1405	1405	1505	1605	1705	1811	1905	2005	2105	...	...	...	...	...	...
408	**Liverpool** Lime St. 187 a.		0831	0931	1031	1131	1231	1231	1331	1331	1431	1431	1531	1631	1731	1835	1935	2035	2135	...	...	...	...	...	...

		⑦	⑦		⑦	⑦		⑦	⑦		⑦	⑦		⑦	⑦		⑦	⑦		⑦	⑦				
Norwich 200 207 d.	⑦	...	...	...	...	...	...	1047	...	...	...	1349	...	1449	1553	...	1657	1756	...	1857	2052	...	...	...	...
Thetford 207 d.		...	...	...	...	...	...	1114	...	...	...	1416	...	1516	1620	...	1724	1823	...	1924	2119	...	...	...	...
Ely 207 d.		...	...	...	...	...	...	1139	...	...	...	1445	...	1548	|	...	1748	1848	...	1949	2144	...	...	...	...
Peterborough a.		...	...	...	...	...	...	1216	...	...	...	1524	...	1622	1710	...	1825	1924	...	2029	2220	...	...	...	...
Peterborough 185 d.		...	...	...	...	...	...	1218	...	...	...	1526	...	1624	1714	...	1830	1926	...	2031	2222	...	...	...	...
Grantham 185 d.		...	...	...	...	...	...	1247	...	...	...	1559	...	1656	1755	...	1901	1957	...	2103	2250	...	...	...	...
Nottingham 170 a.		...	...	...	...	...	...	1326	...	...	...	1628	...	1725	1829	...	1930	2031	...	2135	2326	...	...	...	...
Nottingham 171 d.		0931	1041	...	1146	1239	...	1338	1437	...	1544	1641	...	1737	1837	...	1938	...	...	...	...	...	...	...	...
Alfreton 171 d.		0953	1103	...	1208	1304	...	1403	1502	...	1604	1708	...	1802	1902	...	2000	...	...	...	...	...	...	...	...
Chesterfield 127 170 171 d.		1008	1114	...	1218	1317	...	1418	1513	...	1623	1720	...	1817	1913	...	2010	...	...	...	...	...	...	...	...
Sheffield 127 170 171 a.		1032	1135	...	1235	1333	...	1436	1531	...	1639	1740	...	1834	1931	...	2031	...	...	...	...	...	...	...	...
Sheffield 193 d.		1041	1138	...	1241	1338	...	1439	1537	...	1644	1744	...	1837	1935	...	2035	...	...	...	...	...	...	...	...
Stockport 193 a.		1125	1225	...	1325	1425	...	1525	1625	...	1727	1825	...	1925	2025	...	2124	...	...	...	...	...	...	...	...
Manchester Piccadilly 193 a.		1137	1237	...	1337	1437	...	1537	1637	...	1737	1837	...	1937	2038	...	2136	...	...	...	...	...	...	...	...
Warrington 187 a.		1158	1258	...	1358	1458	...	1558	1658	...	1758	1858	...	1958	...	...	...	...	...	...	...	...	...	...	...
Widnes a.		1206	1306	...	1406	1506	...	1606	1706	...	1806	1906	...	2006	...	...	...	...	...	...	...	...	...	...	...
Liverpool Lime St. 187 a.		1230	1330	...	1430	1530	...	1630	1730	...	1830	1930	...	2030	...	...	...	...	...	...	...	...	...	...	...

		Ⓐ Am	⑥ Am	Ⓐ	⑥ Am	Ⓐ	⑥	Ⓐ	Ⓐ	⑥	Ⓐ	⑥	⚒	Ⓐ	⑥	⚒	⚒	⚒	Ⓐ	⑥	⚒	⑥ m	Ⓐ m	⚒	⑥
Liverpool Lime St. 187 d.	⚒	...	...	...	...	...	...	...	...	...	0647	0649	0742	0852	0852	0952	1052	1152	1252	1252	1352	1452	1452	1552	1652
Widnes d.		...	...	...	...	...	...	...	...	...	0707	0707	0805	0911	0911	1011	1111	1211	1311	1311	1411	1511	1511	1611	1711
Warrington 187 d.		...	...	...	...	...	...	...	...	...	0715	0715	0813	0919	0919	1019	1119	1219	1319	1319	1419	1519	1519	1619	1719
Manchester Piccadilly 193 d.		...	...	...	...	...	...	...	...	...	0742	0742	0843	0943	0943	1043	1143	1243	1343	1343	1443	1543	1543	1643	1743
Stockport 193 d.		...	...	...	...	...	...	...	...	...	0754	0754	0854	0954	0954	1054	1154	1254	1354	1354	1454	1554	1554	1654	1754
Sheffield 193 a.		...	...	...	...	...	...	...	...	...	0834	0834	0935	1033	1034	1134	1234	1334	1435	1434	1534	1635	1634	1737	1834
Sheffield 127 170 171 d.		...	...	...	...	...	...	...	...	...	0838	0838	0938	1038	1038	1138	1238	1338	1438	1438	1538	1638	1638	1744	1838
Chesterfield 127 170 171 d.		...	...	...	...	...	...	...	...	...	0853	0853	0953	1052	1053	1153	1253	1352	1453	1453	1553	1653	1656	1758	1853
Alfreton 171 d.		...	...	...	...	...	...	...	...	...	0903	0903	1003	1103	1103	1203	1303	1403	1507	1504	1603	1704	1706	1808	1903
Nottingham 171 a.		...	...	...	...	...	...	...	...	...	0930	0930	1030	1130	1129	1230	1330	1431	1530	1529	1633	1729	1731	1834	1933
Nottingham 170 d.		0451	0504	0510	0554	0556	0745	0752	0834	0834	0934	0934	1034	1134	1134	1234	1334	1434	1534	1534	...	1734	1734	1834	...
Grantham 185 d.		|	|	0551	|	|	0816	0825	0911	0911	1008	1008	1107	1207	1207	1306	1407	1507	1607	1607	...	1815	1812	1905	...
Peterborough 185 a.		0617	0619	0625	0733	0733	0844	0857	0938	0943	1042	1037	1136	1242	1238	1338	1439	1534	1634	1638	...	1842	1841	1936	...
Peterborough d.		0627	0627	...	0735	0735	0846	0859	0940	0946	1044	1044	1138	1243	1240	1338	1440	1535	1636	1640	...	1842	1842	1937	...
Ely 207 a.		0701	0701	...	0811	0811	0919	0941	1013	1019	1116	1117	1211	1316	1313	1413	1514	1609	1709	1713	...	1919	1924	2013	...
Thetford 207 a.		0728	0730	...	0836	0836	0944	1005	1038	1044	1141	1144	1236	1340	1339	1437	1538	1634	1733	1737	...	1944	1949	2036	...
Norwich 207 a.		0813	0813	...	0915	0913	1019	1043	1113	1118	1213	1218	1313	1413	1413	1513	1613	1713	1813	1818	...	2018	2022	2113	...

	Ⓐ	⚒	⑥	Ⓐ	Ⓐ	Ⓐ	⑥	Ⓐ			⑦	⑦	⑦	⑦	⑦ m	⑦	⑦	⑦	⑦	⑦		⑦	⑦		
Liverpool Lime St. 187 d.	1652	1752	1852	1852	1952	1952	2052	2137	...	⑦	...	...	...	1252	1352	1452	1552	1652	1752	1852	...	1952	2122	...	...
Widnes d.	1711	1811	1911	1911	2011	2011	2111	2155	...		...	...	...	1311	1411	1511	1611	1711	1811	1911	...	2011	2139	...	...
Warrington 187 d.	1719	1819	1919	1919	2019	2019	2119	2203	...		...	...	...	1319	1419	1519	1619	1719	1819	1919	...	2019	2147	...	...
Manchester Piccadilly 193 d.	1743	1843	1943	1943	2043	2043	2143	2228	...		...	...	1244	1344	1444	1544	1644	1744	1844	1944	...	2044	2211	...	...
Stockport 193 d.	1754	1854	1954	1954	2054	2054	2152	2237	...		...	...	1255	1354	1454	1554	1654	1754	1854	1954	...	2054	2228	...	...
Sheffield 193 a.	1841	1935	2035	2036	2134	2135	2231	2335	...		...	...	1337	1439	1537	1636	1736	1837	1934	2034	...	2136	2325	...	...
Sheffield 127 170 171 d.	1845	1938	2041	2041	2138	2139	2235	2337	...		...	1249	1349	1453	1543	1640	1739	1841	1940	2040	...	2140	2329	...	...
Chesterfield 127 170 171 d.	1901	1953	2059	2058	2154	2155	2251	0002	...		...	1303	1403	1507	1557	1656	1754	1856	1955	2055	...	2154	2343	...	...
Alfreton 171 d.	1911	2004	2109	2109	2205	2205	|	|	...		...	1314	1414	1519	1608	1707	1804	1906	2006	2106	...	2205	2354	...	...
Nottingham 171 a.	1938	2031	2133	2138	2233	2238	2330	0041	...		...	1339	1438	1544	1633	1732	1829	1935	2031	2136	...	2235	0030	...	...
Nottingham 170 d.	...	2034	...	...	...	...	...	...	...		1239	1349	1443	1552	1645	1736	1847	...	2044	...	...	...	...	...	...
Grantham 185 d.	...	2107	...	...	...	...	...	...	...		1314	1422	|	1625	1723	1818	1923	...	2119	...	...	...	...	...	...
Peterborough 185 a.	...	2135	...	...	...	...	...	...	...		1341	1452	1604	1656	1753	1845	1956	...	2146	...	...	...	...	...	...
Peterborough d.	...	2136	...	...	...	...	...	...	...		1343	1452	1605	1658	1756	1847	1958	...	2148	...	...	...	...	...	...
Ely 207 a.	...	2210	...	...	...	...	...	...	...		1416	1529	1638	1731	1831	1920	2031	...	2221	...	...	...	...	...	...
Thetford 207 a.	...	2234	...	...	...	...	...	...	...		1450	1553	1702	1756	1855	1948	2055	...	2245	...	...	...	...	...	...
Norwich 207 a.	...	2318	...	...	...	...	...	...	...		1531	1635	1735	1829	1929	2028	2135	...	2325	...	...	...	...	...	...

A – Via Melton Mowbray, Table **208**.

k – ⑥ Dec. 20 – Jan. 30 arrives Stockport 2113.

m – Also calls at March (± 15 minutes from Peterborough and Ely).

207 CAMBRIDGE - NORWICH

2nd class LE

km			Ⓐ	⑥	⑥	Ⓐ	⚒	⚒		⚒	Ⓐ	⑥	⑥	Ⓐ	⑥	Ⓐ	⑥	Ⓐ	⑥	Ⓐ			⑦	⑦
0	**Cambridge** d.	⚒	0605	0608	0700	0704	0812	0912	and at the	1712	1809	1812	1912	1925	2012	2020	2112	2113	2230	2255	...	⑦	1046	1246
24	Ely 206 d.		0620	0623	0715	0719	0827	0927	same	1727	1824	1827	1929	1940	2027	2036	2127	2131	2245	2310	...		1102	1302
63	Thetford 206 d.		0645	0648	0742	0747	0852	0952	minutes	1752	1848	1852	1954	2004	2052	2100	2152	2156	2309	2334	...		1129	1329
	Wymondham 🚂 d.		0710	0713	0809	0814	0913	1013	past each	1813	1910	1913	2015	2025	2113	2123	2213	2217	2330	2355	...		1150	1350
110	**Norwich** 206 a.		0730	0729	0824	0830	0930	1030	hour until	1830	1925	1930	2030	2042	2130	2138	2230	2231	2345	0012	...		1209	1409

	⑦	⑦	⑦	⑦	⑦	⑦	⑦	⑦	
Cambridge d.	1346	1446	1546	1646	1746	1846	1948	2148	...
Ely 206 d.	1402	1502	1602	1702	1802	1902	2003	2203	...
Thetford 206 d.	1415	1526	1629	1726	1826	1926	2027	2227	...
Wymondham 🚂 d.	1447	1547	1650	1747	1847	1947	2048	2248	...
Norwich 206 a.	1509	1609	1709	1809	1909	2009	2109	2305	...

		Ⓐ	⑥	Ⓐ	⑥	Ⓐ	⑥	⚒	
Norwich 206 d.	⚒	0533	0538	0633	0640	0737	0740	0840	and at the
Wymondham 🚂 d.		0545	0550	0645	0652	0749	0752	0852	same
Thetford 206 d.		0605	0610	0705	0712	0809	0812	0912	minutes
Ely 206 a.		0630	0635	0730	0737	0837	0837	0938	past each
Cambridge a.		0651	0655	0751	0758	0857	0858	0958	hour until

	⚒	⑥	Ⓐ	⚒	⚒	⚒	⑥	Ⓐ	⑥	Ⓐ	⑥	Ⓐ			⑦	⑦	⑦	⑦	⑦	⑦	⑦	⑦	⑦		⑦
Norwich 206 d.	1440	1535	1540	1638	1735	1840	1940	1945	2040	2115	2240	2240	...	⑦	0915	1115	1215	1315	1415	1515	1615	1715	1815	...	2015
Wymondham 🚂 d.	1452	1547	1552	1650	1747	1852	1952	1957	2052	2127	2252	2252	...		0927	1127	1227	1327	1427	1527	1627	1727	1827	...	2027
Thetford 206 d.	1512	1612	1612	1712	1812	1912	2012	2017	2112	2147	2312	2312	...		0947	1147	1247	1347	1447	1546	1647	1747	1847	...	2047
Ely 206 a.	1537	1637	1637	1737	1839	1937	2037	2044	2137	2214	2337	2338	...		1019	1219	1312	1412	1512	1614	1712	1812	1912	...	2112
Cambridge a.	1558	1658	1658	1758	1858	1958	2058	2104	2158	2233	2359	0002	...		1036	1236	1332	1432	1532	1632	1732	1832	1932	...	2132

🚂 – **Wymondham Abbey – Dereham** and v.v. (*Mid Norfolk Railway*). *17*km. ⑥⑦ mid Mar. – mid Oct. (also ③ May – Sept.) and on certain other dates throughout the year. Wymondham Abbey station is 20 minutes walk from the National Rail station. Operator: Mid Norfolk Railway. ✆ 01362 690633. www.mnr.org.uk

XC STANSTED AIRPORT - CAMBRIDGE - PETERBOROUGH - LEICESTER - BIRMINGHAM 208

Services on ⑥⑦ valid until January 31.

km			Ⓐ	Ⓐ	Ⓐ	Ⓐ	Ⓐ	Ⓐ	Ⓐ	Ⓐ		Ⓐ	Ⓐ	Ⓐ	Ⓐ	Ⓐ	Ⓐ	Ⓐ	Ⓐ	ⒶA	Ⓐ			⑥	⑥	⑥
0	**Stansted Airport** d.	Ⓐ	...	0515	0606	0721	0821	0921	1021	1125	...	1225	1325	1425	1520	1625	1718	1821	1921	...	2021	...	⑥	...	0525	0625
40	**Cambridge** 205 d.		0515	0555	0652	0800	0900	1000	1100	1200	...	1300	1400	1500	1600	1700	1751	1900	2000	...	2100	...		0515	0555	0656
64	Ely 205 d.		0530	0610	0708	0815	0915	1015	1115	1215	...	1315	1415	1515	1615	1715	1806	1915	2015	...	2115	...		0530	0610	0711
89	March d.		0546	0628	0726	0831	0931	1031	1131	1231	...	1331	1431	1531	1631	1731	1825	1931	2031	...	2131	...		0546	0628	0729
113	**Peterborough** 205 a.		0608	0650	0750	0850	0950	1050	1150	1250	...	1350	1450	1550	1650	1750	1850	1950	2050	...	2150	...		0608	0650	0750
113	**Peterborough** d.		0610	0652	0750	0852	0952	1052	1152	1252	...	1352	1452	1552	1652	1752	1852	1952	2052	2130	2152	...		0610	0652	0752
131	Stamford d.		0623	0705	0805	0905	1005	1105	1205	1305	...	1405	1505	1605	1705	1805	1905	2005	2105	2143	2205	...		0623	0705	0805
154	Oakham d.		0639	0721	0821	0921	1021	1121	1221	1321	...	1421	1521	1621	1721	1821	1921	2021	2121	2158	2221	...		0639	0721	0821
174	Melton Mowbray d.		0650	0733	0833	0933	1033	1133	1233	1333	...	1433	1533	1633	1733	1833	1933	2033	2133	2211	2233	...		0650	0733	0833
197	**Leicester** d.		0710	0749	0849	0949	1049	1149	1249	1349	...	1449	1549	1649	1749	1849	1949	2049	2149	...	2249	...		0716	0749	0849
227	Nuneaton a.		0729	0815	0908	1008	1108	1208	1308	1408	...	1508	1608	1708	1816	1908	2008	2108	2208	...	2308	...		0735	0808	0908
	Coleshill Parkway ▶ a.		0745	0832	0925	1025	1125	1225	1325	1425	...	1525	1625	1725	1832	1925	2025	2125	2225	...	2325	...		0751	0824	0925
259	**Birmingham** New St. a.		0800	0845	0938	1038	1138	1239	1339	1444	...	1544	1639	1738	1845	1939	2038	2139	2245	...	2339	...		0804	0838	0938

	⑥	⑥	⑥	⑥	⑥		⑥	⑥	⑥	⑥	⑥	⑥	⑥	⑥			⑦	⑦	⑦	⑦	⑦	⑦	⑦	⑦	⑦	⑦
Stansted Airport d.	0725	0825	0925	1025	1125	...	1225	1325	1425	1525	1625	1725	1825	1925	...	⑦	1025	1125	1225	1325	1425	1525	1625	1725	1825	1925
Cambridge 205 d.	0800	0900	1000	1100	1200	...	1300	1400	1500	1600	1700	1800	1900	2000	...		1056	1157	1257	1357	1457	1557	1656	1757	1857	1957
Ely 205 d.	0815	0915	1015	1115	1215	...	1315	1415	1515	1615	1715	1815	1915	2015	...		1111	1215	1315	1415	1515	1615	1715	1815	1915	2015
March d.	0831	0931	1031	1131	1231	...	1331	1431	1531	1631	1731	1833	1931	2031	...		1127	1231	1331	1431	1531	1631	1731	1831	1931	2031
Peterborough 205 a.	0850	0950	1050	1150	1250	...	1350	1450	1550	1650	1750	1850	1950	2050	...		1150	1250	1350	1450	1550	1650	1750	1850	1950	2050
Peterborough d.	0852	0952	1052	1152	1252	...	1352	1452	1552	1652	1752	1852	1952	2052	...		1152	1252	1352	1452	1552	1652	1752	1852	1952	2052
Stamford d.	0905	1005	1105	1205	1305	...	1405	1505	1605	1705	1805	1905	2005	2105	...		1205	1305	1405	1505	1605	1705	1805	1905	2005	2105
Oakham d.	0921	1021	1121	1221	1321	...	1421	1521	1621	1721	1821	1921	2021	2121	...		1221	1321	1421	1521	1621	1721	1821	1921	2021	2121
Melton Mowbray d.	0933	1033	1133	1233	1333	...	1433	1533	1633	1733	1833	1933	2033	2133	...		1233	1333	1433	1533	1632	1732	1833	1933	2033	2133
Leicester d.	0949	1049	1149	1249	1349	...	1449	1549	1649	1749	1849	1949	2049	2149	...		1249	1349	1449	1549	1648	1748	1849	1949	2049	2149
Nuneaton a.	1008	1108	1208	1308	1408	...	1508	1608	1708	1808	1908	2008	2108	2208	...		1308	1408	1508	1608	1708	1808	1908	2008	2108	2208
Coleshill Parkway ▶ a.	1025	1125	1225	1325	1425	...	1525	1625	1725	1825	1925	2025	2125	2225	...		1324	1424	1524	1624	1724	1824	1924	2024	2124	2224
Birmingham New St a.	1038	1138	1238	1338	1438	...	1538	1638	1738	1838	1938	2038	2138	2238	...		1339	1437	1539	1639	1737	1839	1937	2039	2137	2238

		ⒶA	Ⓐ	ⒶA	Ⓐ	Ⓐ	Ⓐ	Ⓐ	Ⓐ	Ⓐ	Ⓐ	Ⓐ	Ⓐ	Ⓐ	Ⓐ	Ⓐ	Ⓐ	Ⓐ	Ⓐ	Ⓐ			⑥A	⑥	⑥A	⑥
Birmingham New St. d.	Ⓐ	...	0522	...	0622	0722	0822	0922	1022	1122	1222	1322	1422	1522	1622	1652	1722	1822	1922	2022	...	⑥	...	0522	...	0622
Coleshill Parkway ▶ d.		...	|	...	0635	0735	0835	0935	1035	1135	1235	1335	1435	1535	1635	1705	1735	1835	1935	2035	...		...	0535	...	0635
Nuneaton d.		...	0550	...	0652	0751	0851	0952	1052	1152	1252	1352	1452	1552	1652	1722	1752	1852	1952	2052	...		...	0552	...	0652
Leicester d.		...	0611	...	0717	0817	0917	1017	1117	1217	1317	1417	1517	1617	1717	1750	1817	1917	2017	2117	...		...	0613	...	0715
Melton Mowbray d.		0529	0627	0652	0733	0833	0933	1033	1133	1233	1333	1433	1533	1633	1733	1807	1833	1933	2033	2133	...		0537	0631	0652	0731
Oakham d.		0541	0640	0704	0745	0845	0945	1045	1145	1245	1345	1445	1545	1645	1745	1819	1845	1945	2045	2145	...		0549	0643	0704	0743
Stamford d.		0602	0654	0718	0801	0901	1001	1101	1201	1301	1401	1501	1601	1701	1801	1840	1901	2001	2101	2201	...		0606	0657	0718	0759
Peterborough a.		0617	0707	0733	0816	0916	1016	1116	1216	1316	1416	1516	1616	1716	1816	1857	1916	2016	2116	2216	...		0619	0711	0733	0816
Peterborough 205 d.		0627	0709	0735	0818	0918	1018	1116	1218	1316	1418	1516	1618	1718	1818	1859	1918	2018	2116	2218	...		0627	0713	0735	0818
March a.		0642	0728	0750	0833	0934	1033	1134	1233	1334	1433	1534	1633	1736	1833	1915	1933	2033	2134	2233	...		0642	0731	0750	0833
Ely 205 a.		0701	0751	0811	0852	0952	1052	1152	1252	1352	1452	1552	1652	1758	1852	1933	1952	2052	2152	2252	...		0701	0752	0811	0852
Cambridge 205 a.		...	0807	...	0908	1008	1108	1208	1308	1408	1508	1608	1708	1816	1908	1950	2008	2108	2208	2311	...		...	0808	...	0908
Stansted Airport a.		...	0838	...	0945	1045	1145	1245	1345	1445	1545	1645	1739	1845	1942	...	2045	2145	2255	...	...		...	0845	...	0945

	⑥	⑥	⑥	⑥	⑥	⑥	⑥	⑥	⑥	⑥	⑥	⑥	⑥	⑥			⑦	⑦	⑦	⑦	⑦	⑦	⑦	⑦	⑦	⑦
Birmingham New St. d.	0722	0822	0922	1022	1122	1222	1322	1422	1522	1622	1722	1822	1922	2022	...	⑦	1122	1222	1322	1422	1522	1622	1722	1822	1922	2022
Coleshill Parkway ▶ d.	0735	0835	0935	1035	1135	1235	1335	1435	1535	1635	1735	1835	1935	2035	...		1135	1235	1335	1435	1535	1635	1735	1835	1935	2035
Nuneaton d.	0752	0852	0952	1052	1152	1252	1352	1452	1552	1652	1752	1852	1952	2052	...		1152	1252	1352	1452	1552	1652	1752	1852	1952	2051
Leicester d.	0815	0915	1015	1115	1215	1315	1415	1515	1615	1715	1815	1915	2015	2115	...		1215	1315	1415	1515	1615	1715	1815	1915	2015	2115
Melton Mowbray d.	0831	0931	1031	1131	1231	1331	1431	1531	1631	1731	1831	1931	2031	2131	...		1233	1333	1433	1533	1631	1733	1831	1931	2031	2131
Oakham d.	0843	0943	1043	1143	1243	1343	1443	1543	1643	1743	1843	1943	2043	2143	...		1245	1345	1445	1545	1643	1745	1843	1943	2043	2143
Stamford d.	0859	0959	1059	1159	1259	1359	1459	1559	1659	1759	1859	1959	2059	2159	...		1301	1401	1501	1601	1659	1801	1859	1959	2059	2159
Peterborough a.	0916	1014	1116	1214	1316	1416	1516	1616	1716	1814	1916	2014	2116	2216	...		1316	1416	1516	1616	1714	1816	1914	2014	2114	2214
Peterborough 205 d.	0918	1018	1116	1218	1318	1418	1518	1618	1718	1818	1918	2018	2118	2218	...		1318	1418	1518	1618	1718	1818	1918	2018	2118	2218
March a.	0933	1033	1134	1233	1334	1433	1534	1633	1737	1833	1933	2033	2134	2233	...		1333	1433	1533	1633	1733	1833	1933	2033	2133	2233
Ely 205 a.	0952	1052	1152	1252	1352	1452	1552	1652	1759	1852	1952	2052	2152	2253	...		1352	1452	1552	1652	1752	1852	1952	2052	2152	2252
Cambridge 205 a.	1008	1108	1208	1308	1408	1508	1608	1708	1816	1908	2008	2108	2208	2310	...		1408	1508	1608	1707	1807	1907	2007	2107	2207	2307
Stansted Airport a.	1045	1145	1245	1345	1445	1545	1645	1745	1853	1945	2045	2145	2245	...	...		1440	1540	1640	1740	1840	1943	2043	2143	2243	...

Additional trains LEICESTER - BIRMINGHAM and v.v.

km			Ⓐ	⑥	Ⓐ	⑥	Ⓐ	⚒		⚒	⚒	⚒	⑥	Ⓐ			⑦	⑦		⑦	⑦	⑦	⑦	⑦
0	**Leicester** d.	⚒	0616	0649	0643	0716	0724	0816		1916	2016	2116	2216	2227	...	⑦	1119	1216		1816	1919	2008	2119	2319
	Hinckley d.		0635	0708	0702	|	0742	0834	and	1935	2035	2135	2235	2246	...		1136	1236	and	1833	1938	2029	2138	2338
	Nuneaton d.		0642	0715	0710	0736	0750	0841	hourly	1942	2042	2142	2243	2254	...		1144	1246	hourly	1841	1945	2036	2146	2346
	Coleshill Parkway ▶ d.		0659	0731	0726	0752	0805	0857	until	1959	2059	2159	2259	2310	...		1159	1301	until	1857	2001	2052	2201	0001
	Birmingham New St. a.		0715	0747	0744	0804	0819	0915		2015	2115	2214	2315	2323	...		1215	1315		1915	2015	2106	2218	0014

		⚒	⚒	⚒		Ⓐ	⚒	Ⓐ	⚒	⚒	⚒	⑥	Ⓐ	Ⓐ			⑦	⑦	⑦		⑦	⑦	⑦	⑦
Birmingham New St. d.	⚒	0552	0652	0752		1609	1652	1709	1752	1852	1952	2052	2052	2222	...	⑦	0952	1052	1152		1852	1952	2052	2152
Coleshill Parkway ▶ d.		0605	0705	0805	and	1623	1705	1727	1807	1905	2007	2105	2105	2235	...		1005	1105	1205	and	1905	2005	2105	2205
Nuneaton d.		0622	0722	0822	hourly	1639	1722	1744	1823	1922	2023	2122	2122	2252	...		1022	1122	1222	hourly	1922	2022	2122	2226
Hinckley d.		0629	0729	0829	until	1646	1729	1751	1830	1929	2030	2129	2129	2259	...		1029	1129	1229	until	1929	2029	2129	2233
Leicester a.		0650	0748	0850		1706	1750	1809	1850	1950	2050	2149	2158	2320	...		1050	1149	1250		1950	2050	2152	2253

A – 🚃2 Nottingham - Norwich and v.v., Table **196**. Operated by *EM*.

▶ – 🚌 connections available to the National Exhibition Centre (NEC) and Birmingham International Airport.

NT 2nd class MIDDLESBROUGH - NEWCASTLE 210

km			Ⓐ	⚒	⚒S	⚒	⚒	⚒S	⚒		⚒	⚒	⚒	⚒			⑦	⑦		⑦	⑦	⑦			⑦
0	**Middlesbrough 212** d.	⚒	0545	...	0649	0656	0732	0742	0832	and at	1730	1830	1920	2030	...	⑦	0930	1130	...	1330	1530	1730	...	...	1930
25	Darlington **212** d.		0614	...	0720	|	|	0815	|	the same	|	|	|	|	...		|	|	...	|	|	|	...	...	|
9	Stockton d.		|	...	|	0708	0743	|	0843	minutes	1741	1841	1931	2041	...		0941	1141	...	1341	1541	1741	...	...	1941
28	Hartlepool d.		|	0703	|	0727	0802	|	0902	past each	1802	1900	1949	2100	...		1000	1200	...	1400	1600	1800	...	...	2000
57	Sunderland d.		|	0730	|	0755	0828	|	0929	hour until	1830	1927	2027	2127	...		1028	1228	...	1428	1628	1828	...	...	2028
77	**Newcastle** a.		0655	0753	0802	0817	0852	0900	0953		1853	1948	2049	2148	...		1050	1248	...	1448	1649	1848	...	...	2047

		⚒	⚒	⚒		⚒	⚒	⚒	⚒	⚒	Ⓐ	⑥	⑥	Ⓐ			⑦	⑦		⑦	⑦	⑦		⑦	⑦S
Newcastle d.	⚒	0600	0700	0730	and at	1630	1653	1730	1830	1930	2045	2100	2150	2200	...	⑦	1000	1200	...	1359	1600	1800	...	2000	2106
Sunderland d.		0620	0720	0750	the same	1650	1715	1750	1850	1950	2105	2120	|	|	...		1020	1221	...	1421	1621	1821	...	2021	|
Hartlepool d.		0646	0745	0815	minutes	1715	1739	1815	1915	2015	2129	2145	|	|	...		1045	1245	...	1445	1645	1845	...	2045	|
Stockton d.		...	0804	0833	past each	1733	1757	1833	1933	2033	2147	2203	|	|	...		1103	1304	...	1504	1704	1904	...	2104	|
Darlington 212 d.		...	|	|	hour until	|	|	|	|	|	|	|	2230	2242	...		|	|	...	|	|	|	...	|	2145
Middlesbrough 212 a.		...	0820	0848		1749	1815	1848	1948	2050	2202	2218	2257	2310	...		1118	1320	...	1519	1725	1918	...	2120	2207

S – To/from Saltburn, Table **212**.

NT 2nd class MIDDLESBROUGH - WHITBY 211

km			Ⓐ	Ⓐ		Ⓐ	Ⓐ			⑥	⑥		⑥	⑥										
0	**Middlesbrough** 209 212 d.	Ⓐ	0706	1038	...	1416	1740	...	⑥	0706	1038	...	1416	1740	...	⑦	...	...	...	...	...	...	...	...
46	Grosmont 🚂 d.		0820	1144	...	1522	1846	...		0820	1144	...	1522	1846	...		...	...	...	...	...	...	...	...
56	**Whitby** 🚂 a.		0841	1205	...	1543	1907	...		0841	1205	...	1543	1907	...		...	...	...	...	...	...	...	...

		Ⓐ	Ⓐ		Ⓐ	Ⓐ			⑥	⑥		⑥	⑥										
Whitby 🚂 d.	Ⓐ	0852	1241	...	1605	1915	...	⑥	0852	1241	...	1605	1915	...	⑦	...	...	...	...	...	...	...	...
Grosmont 🚂 d.		0909	1258	...	1622	1932	...		0909	1258	...	1622	1932	...		...	...	...	...	...	...	...	...
Middlesbrough 209 212 a.		1018	1407	...	1735	2041	...		1018	1407	...	1735	2041	...		...	...	...	...	...	...	...	...

🚂 – The *North Yorkshire Moors Railway* also operates 🚂 services to Whitby during the summer. Operator: North Yorkshire Moors Railway. ✆ 01751 472508. www.nymr.co.uk

212 BISHOP AUCKLAND - MIDDLESBROUGH - SALTBURN

2nd class NT

Services on ⑦ valid until January 31.

km		Ⓐ	Ⓐ	Ⓐ	Ⓐ	Ⓐ	Ⓐ	Ⓐ	Ⓐ	Ⓐ	Ⓐ	Ⓐ	Ⓐ	Ⓐ	⑥	⑥	⑥	⑥	⑥	⑥	⑥	⑥	⑥	⑥	⑥	⑥
0	**Bishop Auckland** d.		0721	...	0925	1003	1140	1340	1530	1630	1803	1903	2115	...		0735	0923	0953	1140	1326	1532	1700	1800	1859	2117	...
4	Shildon d.		0726	...	0930	1008	1145	1345	1535	1635	1808	1908	2120	...		0740	0928	0958	1145	1331	1537	1705	1805	1904	2122	...
	Newcastle **210** d.		|	...	|	|	|	|	|	|	|	|	|	2200		|	|	|	|	|	|	|	|	|	|	2150
19	**Darlington** ▶ d.		0748	0810	0953	1030	1207	1408	1557	1659	1833	1931	2144	2242		0809	0951	1020	1206	1353	1600	1727	1830	1927	2144	2230
43	**Middlesbrough** ▶ d.		0812	0839	1024	1055	1232	1433	1624	1724	1859	1956	2209	2310		0839	1020	1054	1233	1421	1623	1754	1901	1954	2209	2257
55	Redcar Central ▶ d.		...	0851	1035	1105	1242	1443	1636	1735	1909	2006	2220	...		0851	1030	1104	1243	1431	1635	1806	1911	2004	2220	...
63	**Saltburn** ▶ a.		...	0907	1052	1122	1258	1459	1655	1752	1926	2023	2237	...		0908	1047	1120	1259	1448	1652	1823	1928	2021	2237	...

	⑦	⑦	⑦	⑦	⑦	⑦	⑦	⑦	⑦	⑦	⑦
Bishop Auckland d.		...	1029	1240	1449	1656	...	1849	...	...	...
Shildon d.		...	1034	1245	1454	1701	...	1854	...	...	...
Newcastle **210** d.		...	|	|	|	|	...	|	...	...	2106
Darlington ▶ d.		1003	1104	1310	1516	1724	1831	1916	1932	2032	2145
Middlesbrough ▶ d.		|	1130	1335	1542	1750	1854	...	1958	2058	2208
Redcar Central ▶ d.		1040	1141	1346	1552	1801	1904	...	2008	2108	2218
Saltburn ▶ a.		1055	1157	1402	1608	1817	1919	...	2023	2124	2234

	Ⓐ	Ⓐ	Ⓐ	Ⓐ	Ⓐ	Ⓐ	Ⓐ	Ⓐ	Ⓐ	Ⓐ
Saltburn ▷ d.		...	...	0624	0717	0738	0830	1000	1200	1400
Redcar Central ▷ d.		...	...	0637	0730	0751	0843	1013	1213	1413
Middlesbrough ▷ d.		0545	...	0649	0742	0802	0855	1024	1224	1424
Darlington ▷ d.		0614	0647	0720	0815	0833	0926	1055	1255	1454
Newcastle **210** a.		0655	|	0802	0900	|	|	|	|	|
Shildon d.		...	0706	...	...	0852	0945	1114	1314	1513
Bishop Auckland a.		...	0718	...	...	0859	0952	1121	1321	1519

	Ⓐ	Ⓐ	Ⓐ	Ⓐ	⑥	⑥	⑥	⑥	⑥	⑥	⑥	⑥	⑥	⑥	⑥	⑥	⑥	⑥		⑦	⑦	⑦	⑦	⑦	⑦	⑦
Saltburn ▷ d.	1503	1630	1730	1930		...	...	0624	0717	0738	0830	1000	1156	1358	1530	1630	1728	1935	...		...	...	1100	1300	1520	1720
Redcar Central ▷ d.	1516	1643	1743	1943		...	...	0637	0730	0751	0843	1013	1209	1411	1543	1643	1741	1948	...		...	...	1113	1313	1533	1733
Middlesbrough ▷ d.	1527	1657	1755	1955		0550	...	0649	0742	0802	0855	1024	1220	1423	1555	1655	1756	1959	...		0845	0915	1124	1325	1550	1749
Darlington ▷ d.	1557	1728	1832	2030		0618	0648	0720	0815	0838	0924	1057	1250	1453	1625	1730	1826	2036	...		0915	0951	1154	1406	1622	1820
Newcastle **210** a.	|	|	|	|		...	|	0802	0900	|	|	|	|	|	|	|	|	|	...		...	|	|	|	|	|
Shildon d.	1616	1747	1851	2049		...	0707	...	...	0857	0943	1116	1309	1512	1644	1749	1845	2055	...		...	1010	1213	1425	1641	1839
Bishop Auckland a.	1624	1755	1858	2056		...	0719	...	...	0904	0950	1123	1316	1520	1652	1758	1853	2102	...		...	1020	1219	1431	1646	1844

▶ – Additional trains Darlington - Middlesbrough - Redcar - Saltburn:

Ⓐ: 0640, 0705, 0724, 0900, 0936, 1100, 1135, 1230, 1256, 1330, 1432, 1500, 1530, 1630, 1734, 1803, 2030.

⑥: 0640, 0658, 0719, 0856, 0923, 1047, 1130, 1235, 1258, 1331, 1435, 1504, 1532, 1627, 1704, 1802, 2030.

⑦: 0920, 1202, 1410, 1542, 1619.

▷ – Additional trains Saltburn - Redcar - Middlesbrough - Darlington:

Ⓐ: 0800, 0921, 1030, 1100, 1130, 1230, 1300, 1330, 1430, 1530, 1555, 1700, 1800, 1830, 1900, 2030, 2130, 2240.

⑥: 0800, 0913, 1030, 1100, 1130, 1230, 1300, 1330, 1430, 1500, 1600, 1659, 1800, 1828, 1900, 2030, 2130, 2240.

⑦: 1028, 1201, 1414, 1625, 1648, 1827, 1923, 2031, 2130, 2238.

213 NEWCASTLE - CARLISLE

2nd class NT

km		⚒	⑥	Ⓐ	⚒	⚒	⚒	⚒	⚒	⚒	⚒	⚒	⚒W	Ⓐ	⑥	⚒	⚒	⚒	⚒		⑦	⑦	⑦	⑦	⑦
0	**Newcastle** 127 185 d.		0634	0649	0824	0923	1024	1124	1239	1324	1424	1524	1626	1712	1712	1754	1824	1910	2122	...		0910	1010	1110	1210
6	MetroCentre d.		|	|	0832	0932	1032	1133	1247	1332	1432	1532	1634	1720	1720	1802	1832	1918	2130	...		0918	1018	1118	1218
36	Hexham d.		0711	0717	0859	0955	1055	1156	1311	1401	1457	1555	1705	1747	1747	1832	1903	1949	2201	...		0949	1049	1149	1249
62	Haltwhistle d.		0733	0740	0921	1016	1114	1219	1329	1419	1517	1618	1725	1809	1809	1855	1921	2009	2223	...		1011	1111	1208	1311
99	**Carlisle** 151 a.		0807	0813	0956	1046	1146	1253	1400	1456	1549	1655	1759	1845	1854	1928	1957	2042	2258	...		1045	1145	1238	1345
	Stranraer **215** a.		|	|	...	...	...	...	...	|	...	...	...	|	|	...	...	...	...	...		...	...	...	...
	Glasgow **214** a.		1037	1037	...	...	...	...	...	1735	...	...	...	2135	2135	...	...	...	...	...		...	...	...	...

	⑦	⑦	⑦	⑦	⑦	⑦	⑦		
Newcastle 127 185 d.	1310	1410	1510	1610	1710	1810	2015	...	...
MetroCentre d.	1318	1418	1518	1620	1718	1818	2023	...	...
Hexham d.	1349	1449	1549	1651	1749	1849	2054	...	...
Haltwhistle d.	1408	1508	1611	1710	1808	1911	2116	...	...
Carlisle 151 a.	1438	1540	1645	1740	1838	1945	2150	...	...
Stranraer **215** a.	...	...	...	...	...	...	...	...	...
Glasgow **214** a.	...	...	...	...	...	...	...	...	...

	⚒	⚒	⚒	⚒D	⚒	⑥	Ⓐ	⚒	⑥	Ⓐ
Glasgow **214** d.		...	...	...	...	0708	0709	...	...	...
Stranraer **215** d.		...	...	...	...	|	|	...	...	...
Carlisle 151 d.		...	0625	0713	0830	0937	0937	1033	1134	1134
Haltwhistle d.		...	0656	0745	0901	1005	1010	1102	1202	1202
Hexham d.		0613	0718	0807	0923	1023	1028	1122	1223	1223
MetroCentre d.		|	0748	0840	0947	1046	1051	1145	1245	1245
Newcastle 127 185 a.		0652	0804	0854	1000	1101	1101	1159	1257	1303

	⚒	⚒	⚒	⚒	⚒	⚒	⚒	⚒	⚒		⑦	⑦	⑦	⑦		⑦	⑦	⑦	⑦		⑦	⑦		⑦	⑦
Glasgow **214** d.	...	...	1212	...	...	...	1612	...	...	...		...	...	...	...	...	...	...	...	...	...	...	...	...	...
Stranraer **215** d.	...	...	|	...	...	...	|	...	...	...		...	...	...	...	...	...	...	...	...	...	...	...	...	...
Carlisle 151 d.	1230	1335	1435	1526	1637	1720	1837	1945	2120	...		0905	1005	1112	...	1205	1312	1412	1505	...	1612	1712	...	1805	2015
Haltwhistle d.	1301	1403	1504	1556	1708	1752	1908	2013	2152	...		0936	1036	1140	...	1236	1340	1440	1536	...	1640	1740	...	1836	2043
Hexham d.	1323	1421	1521	1616	1731	1814	1926	2031	2214	...		0959	1059	1159	...	1259	1359	1459	1559	...	1659	1759	...	1859	2059
MetroCentre d.	1347	1444	1545	1640	1755	1844	1956	2102	2245	...		1030	1130	1230	...	1330	1430	1530	1630	...	1730	1830	...	1930	2130
Newcastle 127 185 a.	1400	1457	1559	1650	1808	1856	2011	2114	2259	...		1040	1140	1240	...	1340	1440	1540	1640	...	1740	1840	...	1940	2143

214 CARLISLE - DUMFRIES - GLASGOW

2nd class SR

km		⚒	⚒	⚒	⚒		⑥	Ⓐ	⚒		⚒	⚒	⚒		⚒	⚒		⚒		⑦	⑦	⑦		⑦	⑦
	Newcastle **213** d.		...	...	...	...	0634	0649	...	...	...	1324	...	...	...	1712	...	...	...		...	...	...	...	...
0	**Carlisle** 151 d.		...	0527	0608	...	0815	0815	1112	...	1312	1508	1617	...	1755	1917	...	2301	...		1312	1512	...	1912	2122
28	Annan d.		...	0547	0627	...	0834	0834	1131	...	1331	1527	1636	...	1814	1936	...	2320	...		1331	1531	...	1931	2141
53	**Dumfries** d.		0541	0604	0646	...	0853	0853	1153	...	1348	1550	1654	...	1833	1955	...	2338	...		1350	1549	...	1950	2159
124	Auchinleck d.		0629	...	0734	...	0941	0941	1241	...	1438	1638	...	...	1938	2043	...	...	...		1438	...	...	2038	...
146	**Kilmarnock 215** d.		0653	...	0753	...	0959	0959	1300	...	1500	1657	...	...	2000	2101	...	...	...		1457	...	...	2057	...
185	**Glasgow** Central 151 a.		0733	...	0835	...	1037	1037	1333	...	1533	1735	...	...	2034	2135	...	...	...		1536	...	...	2135	...

	⚒	⚒	⚒	⚒	⚒		⚒	⚒	⚒		⚒	⚒	⚒		⚒	⚒	⚒	Ⓐ		⑦	⑦	⑦	⑦	⑦	⑦
Glasgow Central 151 d.		...	...	...	0708	...	0837	1012	1212	...	1312	...	1612	...	1742	2012	2212	2312	...		...	...	1512	...	2212
Kilmarnock 215 d.		...	...	...	0748	...	0917	1049	1248	...	1349	...	1649	...	1826	2051	2249	2359	...		...	...	1553	...	2249
Auchinleck d.		...	...	...	0805	...	0934	1106	1305	...	1406	...	1706	...	1842	2106	2306	0016	...		...	...	1610	...	2306
Dumfries d.		0456	0617	0745	0856	...	1022	1156	1355	...	1456	1707	1756	...	1933	2156	2356	0115	...		1300	1501	1700	1901	2356
Annan d.		0511	0632	0800	0911	...	1038	1211	1410	...	1511	1722	1811	...	1948	2211	0011	...	...		1315	1516	1715	1916	0011
Carlisle 151 a.		0533	0654	0822	0937	...	1102	1235	1434	...	1534	1744	1835	...	2011	2236	0035	...	...		1337	1538	1737	1638	0035
Newcastle **213** a.		...	0854	...	1101	...	...	...	1559	...	...	...	2011	...	...	...	...	...	...		...	...	...	...	...

☛ Additional trains Carlisle - Dumfries and v.v. on ⑥. From Carlisle at 0942, 1220, 1422, 1712, 2022; From Dumfries at 1102, 1314, 1604, 1849, 2113.

215 GLASGOW and KILMARNOCK - STRANRAER

2nd class SR

km		⚒	⚒	⚒	⚒		⚒	⚒	⚒		⚒	⚒	⚒		⚒	⚒	⚒			⑦	⑦		⑦	
0	**Glasgow** Central 216 d.		...	0630	0912	...	...	1142	...	...	1512	...	1712	...	...	...	...	...	...		1137	...	1625	...
12	Paisley Gilmour St 216 d.		...	|	|	...	...	1153	...	...	|	...	|	...	...	...	...	...	...		1148	...	1639	...
43	Kilwinning 216 d.		...	|	|	...	...	1210	...	...	|	...	|	...	...	...	...	...	...		1205	...	1656	...
	Kilmarnock a.		...	0720	0948	...	...	|	...	...	1549	...	1751	...	...	...	...	...	...		|	...	|	...
	Kilmarnock 214 d.		...	0732	1005	...	1105	|	1334	...	1604	1704	1809	...	1902	2110	2310	...	...		|	...	|	...
56	Troon 216 d.		...	0745	1018	...	1117	|	1346	...	1616	1716	1821	...	1916	2122	2322	...	...		|	...	|	...
61	Prestwick Airport ✈ 216 d.		...	0750	1022	...	1122	|	1351	...	1621	1721	1826	...	1922	2127	2327	...	...		|	...	|	...
67	**Ayr** 216 a.		...	0759	1032	...	1131	1229	1406	...	1630	1730	1836	...	1930	2136	2236	...	...		|	...	|	...
	Ayr d.		0545	0800	1032	...	1132	1232	1407	...	1631	1731	1838	...	1931	2137	2338	...	...		1230	...	1719	...
101	Girvan d.		0612	0826	1102	...	1159	1258	1434	...	1658	1757	1905	...	1957	2207	0005	...	...		1256	...	1747	...
121	Barrhill d.		...	0845	1121	...	...	1318	...	...	...	1816	...	...	2018	2226	0024	...	...		1314	...	1806	...
163	**Stranraer** a.		...	0921	1157	...	...	1354	...	...	...	1852	...	...	2054	2302	0100	...	...		1351	...	1842	...
	Belfast Port ⛴ **2070** a.		...	...	...	...	...	*1630*	...	...	...	*2205*	...	...	...	...	*0600*	...	...		*1630*	...	*2205*	...

j – ②–⑥ only.

SR 2nd class — STRANRAER - KILMARNOCK and GLASGOW — 215

km		⑥	⚒	⚒		⚒	⚒	⚒		⚒	⚒	⚒		⚒	⚒	Ⓐ			⑦	⑦	⑦	
	Belfast Port 🚢 **2070** d.	...	*0320j*	...	...	...	*0730*	...	...	*1145*	...	...	...	...	*1705*	...	...	...	*0730*	*1145*	...	...
0	**Stranraer** d.	...	0709	1007	...	...	1240	...	...	1443	...	...	...	1940	2112	2312	...	...	1040	1440	1940	...
42	Barrhill d.	...	0743	1042	...	...	1319	...	...	1517	...	...	...	2019	2146	2348	...	...	1114	1514	2015	...
61	Girvan d.	0620	0801	1101	...	1206	1337	1440	...	1536	1733	1933	...	2037	2206	0006	...	...	1132	1532	2033	...
96	**Ayr** a.	0648	0825	1129	...	1234	1405	1508	...	1604	1808	2008	...	2105	2235	0034	...	...	1200	1559	2059	...
96	**Ayr** **216** d.	0650	0836	1131	...	1236	1418	1518	...	1606	1817	2018	...	2106	2236	...	...	...	1200	1559	2100	...
102	Prestwick Airport ✈ **216** d.	0657	0843	|	...	1243	1425	1525	...	1613	1825	2025	...	2113	|	...	...	...	|	|	|	...
106	Troon **216** d.	0702	0848	|	...	1248	1430	1630	...	1618	1830	2030	...	2218	2246	...	...	...	|	|	|	...
120	**Kilmarnock 214** a.	0716	|	|	...	1304	1453	1546	...	1634	1846	2046	...	2137	|	...	...	...	|	|	|	...
	Kilmarnock 214 d.	0723	|	|	...	...	...	1600	...	...	...	...	...	2200	|	...	...	...	|	|	|	...
	Kilwinning **216** d.	|	|	1149	...	...	...	|	...	...	...	...	...	|	2255	...	...	...	1215	1614	2115	...
	Paisley Gilmour St **216** a.	|	|	1215	...	...	...	|	...	...	...	...	...	|	2314	...	...	...	1236	1637	2136	...
	Glasgow Central **216** a.	0809	1005	1233	...	...	...	1633	...	...	...	...	...	2234	2325	...	...	...	1251	1649	2148	...

j – ②–⑥ only.

SR 2nd class — GLASGOW - AYR — 216

km		②–⑥	⚒	⚒	⚒	⚒	⚒		⚒	⚒	⚒	⚒		⑦	⑦		⑦	⑦	⑦	⑦	⑦
0	**Glasgow** Central **215** d.	0600	0630	0700	0730	0800	0830	and at	2200	2230	2300	2330	...	0900	1000	and at	1900	2000	2100	2200	2300
12	Paisley Gilmour St **215** d.	0611	0641	0711	0741	0811	0841	the same	2211	2241	2311	2341	...	0911	1011	the same	1911	2011	2111	2211	2311
43	Kilwinning **215** d.	0627	0659	0729	0800	0833	0903	minutes	2229	2259	2327	2359	...	0929	1029	minutes	1929	2029	2129	2229	2329
48	Irvine d.	0631	0703	0733	0804	0837	0907	past each	2233	2303	2333	0003	...	0933	1033	past each	1933	2033	2133	2233	2333
56	Troon **215** d.	0637	0710	0739	0812	0845	0915	hour until	2239	2311	2339	0011	...	0941	1041	hour until	1941	2041	2141	2241	2341
61	Prestwick Airport ✈ **215** d.	0641	0714	0743	0816	0849	0919	✣ ⊡	2243	2315	2343	0015	...	0945	1045	✣♠	1945	2045	2145	2245	2345
67	**Ayr** **215** a.	0652	0724	0754	0826	0858	0930		2252	2324	2352	0025	...	1001	1101		1954	2054	2154	2254	2354

	⚒	⚒	⚒	Ⓐ	⑥	⚒	⚒		⚒	⚒	⚒	⚒		⑦	⑦		⑦	⑦	⑦	⑦	⑦
Ayr **215** d.	0540	0613	0643	0713	0713	0743	0813	and at	2113	2143	2213	2300	...	0943	1043	and at	1843	1943	2043	2143	2300
Prestwick Airport ✈ **215** d.	0548	0621	0651	0721	0721	0750	0821	the same	2121	2150	2221	2308	...	0950	1050	the same	1850	1950	2050	2150	2307
Troon **215** d.	0552	0625	0655	0725	0725	0754	0825	minutes	2125	2154	2225	2312	...	0954	1054	minutes	1854	1954	2054	2154	2311
Irvine d.	0559	0632	0702	0732	0732	0759	0832	past each	2132	2159	2232	2319	...	1001	1101	past each	1901	2001	2101	2201	2318
Kilwinning **215** d.	0604	0637	0707	0737	0737	0804	0834	hour until	2137	2204	2237	2324	...	1006	1106	hour until	1906	2006	2106	2206	2323
Paisley Gilmour St **215** d.	0632	0655	0725	0757	0805	0823	0856	✣	2157	2225	2257	2345	...	1024	1124	✣♣	1924	2024	2124	2224	2341
Glasgow Central **215** a.	0643	0707	0738	0809	0816	0834	0907		2209	2236	2309	0001	...	1043	1143		1936	2036	2136	2236	2353

⊡ – The 1730 Ⓐ service from Glasgow stops at Paisley to pick up only and does not call at Kilwinning.
♠ – The 1600, 1700 and 1800 trains from Glasgow Central arrive Ayr at 54 minutes past the hour.
♣ – The 1643 and 1743 trains from Ayr arrives Glasgow Central at 36 minutes past the hour.
✣ – Timings may vary by up to 8 minutes.

SR 2nd class — GLASGOW - ARDROSSAN - LARGS — 217

km		⚒	⚒	⚒	⚒		⚒	⚒	⚒	⚒	⚒		⚒	①–④	⑤		⑦	⑦		⑦	
0	**Glasgow** Central **215** d.	0615	0715	0845	0945	and at	1545	1618	1720	1745	1845	and at	2245	2315	2345	...	0840	0940		2240	...
12	Paisley Gilmour St **215** d.	0626	0726	0856	0956	the same	1556	1628	1732	1756	1856	the same	2256	2326	2356	...	0851	0951	and	2251	...
43	Kilwinning **215** d.	0654	0752	0918	1020	minutes	1618	1656	1754	1820	1918	minutes	2318	2354	0023	...	0915	1019	hourly	2318	...
50	**Ardrossan** Sth Beach d.	0702	0803	0926	1028	past each	1626	1711	1802	1828	1926	past each	2326	0002	0031	...	0923	1027	until	2327	...
54	Fairlie d.	0713	0814	0935	1039	hour until	1637	1722	1813	1839	1939	hour until	2337	0014	0043	...	...	1039	♣	2339	...
69	**Largs** a.	0720	0822	0944	1047	✣	1644	1728	1820	1848	1944	✣	2344	0019	0049	...	...	1052		2345	...

	⚒	Ⓐ	⚒	Ⓐ	⑥	⚒		⚒	⚒	⚒	⚒		⚒	⚒	⚒		⑦	⑦		⑦	
Largs d.	0641	0725	0742	0828	0851	0953	and at	1553	1650	1735	1853	and at	2053	2153	2253	...	0958	1058		2258	...
Fairlie d.	0646	0730	0747	0833	0856	0958	the same	1558	1655	1740	1858	the same	2058	2158	2258	...	1003	1103	and	2303	...
Ardrossan Sth Beach d.	0657	0741	0758	0844	0907	1009	minutes	1609	1706	1751	1909	minutes	2109	2209	2309	...	1014	1114	hourly	2314	...
Kilwinning **215** d.	0710	0750	0808	0853	0916	1018	past each	1618	1715	1800	1918	past each	2118	2218	2318	...	1023	1123	until	2327	...
Paisley Gilmour St **215** a.	0734	0814	0834	0917	0940	1040	hour until	1641	1741	1823	1940	hour until	2140	2242	2342	...	1052	1152	♠	2355	...
Glasgow Central **215** a.	0747	0824	0846	0930	0953	1052	✣	1652	1755	1834	1953	✣|	2252	2254	2354	...	1110	1210		0005	...

♣ – The 1642 to 2140 trains from Glasgow Central arrives Largs at 45 minutes past the hour.
♠ – The 1658 to 2158 trains from Largs arrive Glasgow Central at 03 minutes past the hour.
✣ – Timings may vary by up to 5 minutes.

SR 2nd class Most services 🍷 — GLASGOW - OBAN, FORT WILLIAM and MALLAIG — 218

km		⚒	⚒ A	⚒ B	⑦ E	⑥ ND	⚒ BC	B			
	Edinburgh **220** d.	...	0450	*0715*	...	*0930*	*1100*	*1700*	...	...	...
0	**Glasgow** Queen St d.	...	*0530*	0821	...	1037	1220	1820	...	...	...
10	Westerton d.	...	0556	|	...	|	|	|	...	...	...
16	Dalmuir d.	...	0604	0839	...	1050	1242	1834	...	...	...
26	Dumbarton Central d.	...	|	0848	...	1104	1248	1843	...	...	...
40	Helensburgh Upper d.	...	0629	0906	...	1123	1306	1858	...	...	...
51	Garelochhead d.	...	0642	0917	...	1134	1317	1910	...	...	...
68	Arrochar & Tarbet d.	...	0708	0937	...	1154	1337	1930	...	...	...
81	Ardlui d.	...	0722r	0953	...	1208	1353	1950	...	...	...
95	**Crianlarich** a.	...	0743	1009	...	1224	1409	2006	...	...	...
95	**Crianlarich** d.	...	0745	1021	...	...	1421	2018	...	...	...
115	Bridge of Orchy d.	...	0815	1046	...	...	1446	2046	...	...	...
140	Rannoch d.	...	0845	1108	...	...	1508	2108	...	...	...
177	Roy Bridge d.	...	0929r	1146	...	...	1546	2146	...	...	...
183	Spean Bridge d.	...	0937	1154	...	...	1553	2153	...	...	...
197	**Fort William** a.	...	0954	1207	...	...	1606	2206	...	...	...
197	**Fort William** d.	0830	...	1212	1212	...	1619	2215	...	...	...
223	Glenfinnan d.	0903	...	1245	1245	...	1654	2248	...	...	...
251	Arisaig d.	0936	...	1318	1318	...	1727	2320	...	...	...
259	Morar d.	0944	...	1326	1326	...	1735	2328	...	...	...
264	**Mallaig** a.	0952	...	1335	1335	...	1743	2335	...	...	...

	①–⑤	⚒ B	BC	①–⑤ NF	⑥ ND	⑦ B	⚒ B	⑦ A	C	①–⑤ A
Mallaig d.	...	0603	1010	...	...	1605	1605	...	1815	...
Morar d.	...	0610	1017	...	...	1612	1612	...	1822	...
Arisaig d.	...	0619	1026	...	...	1621	1621	...	1831	...
Glenfinnan d.	...	0652	1059	...	...	1654	1654	...	1904	...
Fort William a.	...	0726	1133	...	...	1727	1727	...	1937	...
Fort William d.	...	0742	1140	...	...	1737	1737	1900	...	1950
Spean Bridge d.	...	0755	1153	...	...	1750	1750	1919	...	2010
Roy Bridge d.	...	0802	1200	...	...	1757	1757	1927r	...	2017r
Rannoch d.	...	0842	1242	...	...	1836	1836	2015	...	2105
Bridge of Orchy d.	...	0902	1302	...	...	1856	1856	2047	...	2134
Crianlarich a.	...	0930	1333	...	...	1926	1926	2116	...	2204
Crianlarich d.	...	0936	1336	1412	1730	1932	1932	2119	...	2205
Ardlui d.	...	0952	1352	1428	1747	1949	1949	2139r	...	2226r
Arrochar & Tarbet d.	0708	1007	1407	1443	1801	2003	2003	2157	...	2244
Garelochhead d.	0730	1029	1427	1503	1822	2024	2024	2223	...	2310
Helensburgh Upper d.	0742	1041	1439	1515	1834	2036	2036	2237	...	2324
Dumbarton Central a.	0757	1058	1452	1528	1847	2049	2049	|	...	|
Dalmuir a.	|	1108	1504	1537	1856	2058	2104	2302	...	2349
Westerton a.	|	|	|	|	|	|	|	2311	...	2356
Glasgow Queen St a.	0837	1120	1531	1556	1918	2114	2129	*2346*	...	*0020*
Edinburgh **220** a.	*0948*	*1235*	*1639*z	*1706*	*2021*	*2224*	*2250*	0015	...	0050

km		⚒	⑥ D	C							
	Edinburgh **220** d.	*0715*	*0930*	*1100*	*1700*	...	...	...	...	...	...
	Glasgow Queen St d.	0821	1037	1220	1820	...	...	...	...	...	...
0	**Crianlarich** d.	1015	1227	1414	2012	...	...	...	...	...	...
28	Dalmally d.	1042	1257	1442	2039	...	...	...	...	...	...
47	Taynuilt d.	1103	1318	1502	2100	...	...	...	...	...	...
67	**Oban** a.	1127	1343	1527	2126	...	...	...	...	...	...

	⚒	C	①–⑤ F	⑥ D	⑦	⚒				
Oban d.	0811	1211	1256	1611	1810	1810	...	...	...	...
Taynuilt d.	0835	1235	1320	1638	1834	1834	...	...	...	...
Dalmally d.	0856	1256	1341	1700	1855	1855	...	...	...	...
Crianlarich a.	0915	1315	1400	1728	1927	1914	...	...	...	...
Glasgow Queen St a.	1130	1531	1556	1918	2114	2129	...	...	...	...
Edinburgh **220** a.	*1235*	*1639*z	*1706*	*2021*	*2224*	*2250*	...	...	...	...

A – Ⓡ. (12) (limited accommodation), 🛏 1,2 cl. and 🍷 London - Fort William and v.v. (Table **151**).
B – Conveys (2) Glasgow Queen St - Crianlarich - Oban and v.v.
C – ⚒ Dec. 14 – Mar. 27; Daily Mar. 28 – May 22.
D – ⑥ Mar. 27 - May 22.
E – ⑦ Mar. 28 - May 16.
F – ①–⑤ Mar. 29 - May 21.
N – To / from Oban.
r – Stops on request.
z – 1655 on ⑦.

219 SCOTTISH ISLAND FERRIES

Caledonian MacBrayne Ltd operates numerous ferry services linking the Western Isles of Scotland to the mainland and to each other. Principal routes – some of which are seasonal – are listed below (see also the map on page **98**). Service frequencies, sailing-times and reservations: ✆ +44 (0)1475 650 100 ; fax +44 (0)1475 637 607 ; www.calmac.co.uk

Ardrossan – Brodick (Arran)
Claonaig – Lochranza (Arran)
Kennacraig – Port Askaig (Islay)
Kennacraig – Port Ellen (Islay)
Kilchoan – Tobermory (Mull)
Leverburgh (Harris) – Otternish (North Uist)
Mallaig – Armadale (Skye)
Mallaig – Eigg, Muck, Rum and Canna
Oban – Castlebay (Barra) and Lochboisdale (South Uist)
Oban – Coll and Tiree
Oban – Colonsay, Port Askaig (Islay) and Kennacraig
Oban – Craignure (Mull)
Uig (Skye) – Lochmaddy (North Uist)
Uig (Skye) – Tarbert (Harris)
Ullapool – Stornaway (Lewis)
Wemyss Bay – Rothesay (Bute)

220 EDINBURGH - GLASGOW — SR

From Edinburgh: *76 km*
Trains call at **Falkirk High** ± 27 minutes later.
⚒: 0555, 0630, 0645Ⓐ, 0700 and every 15 minutes until 1930; then 2000 and every 30 minutes until 2330.
⑦: 0800, 0900, 1000, 1100, 1200, 1230 and every 30 minutes until 2100; then 2200, 2300, 2330.

From Glasgow Queen St: Journey time: ± 51 minutes
Trains call at **Falkirk High** ± 21 minutes later.
⚒: 0600, 0630, 0645Ⓐ, 0700 and every 15 minutes until 1930; then 2000 and every 30 minutes until 2330.
⑦: 0750, 0830, 0930, 1030, 1130, 1230, 1300 and every 30 minutes until 2130; then 2230, 2330.

221 EDINBURGH and GLASGOW - INVERNESS — Most trains 🍷 SR

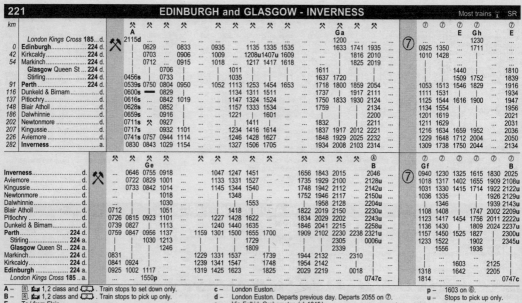

km		⚒ A	⚒	⚒	⚒		⚒	⚒	⚒	⚒	⚒		⚒	⚒ Ga	⚒	⚒		⑦	⑦	⑦ E	⑦ Gh		⑦ E
	London Kings Cross **185** ... d.	2115d	...	...	...	...	...	...	...	...	...	...	...	1200	...	...	...	...	...	...	1230	...	...
0	**Edinburgh** **224** d.	|	0629	...	0833	...	0935	...	1135	1335	1535	...	...	1633	1741	1935	...	0925	1350	...	1711	...	...
42	Kirkcaldy **224** d.	|	0703	...	0906	...	1009	...	1208u	1407u	1609	...	...	|	1816	2010	...	1010	1428	...	|	...	...
54	Markinch **224** d.	|	0712	...	0915	...	1018	...	1217	1417	1618	...	...	|	1825	2019	...	|	|	...	|	...	...
	Glasgow Queen St ... **224** d.	|	|	0706	|	...	|	1011	|	|	|	...	1611	|	|	|	...	|	|	1440	|	...	1810
	Stirling **224** d.	0456s	|	0733	|	...	|	1035	|	|	|	...	1637	1720	|	|	...	|	|	1509	1752	...	1839
91	**Perth** **224** d.	0539s	0750	0804	0950	...	1052	1113	1253	1454	1653	...	1718	1800	1859	2054	...	1053	1513	1546	1829	...	1916
116	Dunkeld & Birnam d.	0600s	—	0829	|	...	...	1134	1311	1511	...	...	1737	|	1917	2111	...	1111	1531	|	|	...	1934
137	Pitlochry d.	0616s	...	0842	1019	...	...	1147	1324	1524	...	...	1750	1833	1930	2124	...	1125	1544	1616	1900	...	1947
148	Blair Atholl d.	0628s	...	0852	|	...	...	1157	1333	1534	...	...	1759	|	|	2134	...	1134	1554	|	|	...	1956
186	Dalwhinnie d.	0659s	...	0916	|	...	...	1221	|	1601	...	...	|	|	|	2200	...	1201	1619	|	|	...	2021
202	Newtonmore d.	0711s	⚒	0927	|	...	...	|	1411	|	...	...	1832	|	|	2211	...	1211	1629	|	|	...	2031
207	Kingussie d.	0717s		0932	1101	...	...	1234	1416	1614	...	...	1837	1917	2012	2221	...	1216	1634	1659	1952	...	2036
226	Aviemore d.	0741s	0757	0944	1114	...	...	1246	1428	1627	...	...	1848	1929	2025	2232	...	1229	1648	1712	2004	...	2050
282	**Inverness** a.	0830	0843	1029	1154	...	...	1327	1506	1705	...	...	1934	2008	2103	2314	...	1309	1738	1750	2044	...	2134

	⚒	⚒	⚒ Ge	⚒		⚒	⚒	⚒	⚒	⚒		⚒	⚒	⚒	⚒	Ⓐ B		⑦ Gf	⑦	⑦	⑦	⑦	⑦ B
Inverness d.	...	0646	0755	0918	...	...	1047	1247	1451	...	...	1656	1843	2015	...	2046	...	0940	1230	1325	1615	1830	2025
Aviemore d.	...	0722	0829	1001	...	...	1133	1331	1527	...	...	1735	1929	2100	...	2128u	...	1018	1317	1402	1655	1909	2108u
Kingussie d.	...	0733	0842	1014	...	...	1145	1344	1540	...	...	1748	1942	2112	...	2142u	...	1031	1330	1415	1714	1922	2122u
Newtonmore d.	...	|	|	1018	...	...	|	1348	|	...	...	1752	1946	2117	...	2150u	...	1036	1335	|	|	1926	2129u
Dalwhinnie d.	...	|	|	1030	...	...	|	|	1553	...	...	|	1958	2128	...	2204u	...	|	1346	|	|	1939	2143u
Blair Atholl d.	0712	|	|	1051	...	...	|	1418	|	...	...	1822	2019	2150	...	2230u	...	1108	1408	|	1747	2002	2209u
Pitlochry d.	0726	0815	0923	1101	...	...	1227	1428	1622	...	...	1834	2029	2202	...	2243u	...	1123	1417	1454	1756	2011	2222u
Dunkeld & Birnam d.	0739	0827	|	1113	...	...	1240	1440	1635	...	...	1846	2041	2215	...	2258u	...	1136	1430	|	1809	2024	2237u
Perth **224** d.	0759	0847	0956	1137	...	1159	1301	1500	1655	1700	...	1909	2102	2230	2238	2321u	...	1157	1450	1525	1827	|	2300u
Stirling **224** a.	|	|	1030	1213	...	|	|	|	1729	|	...	|	|	2305	|	0006u	...	1233	1522	|	1902	|	2345u
Glasgow Queen St ... **224** a.	|	|	|	1246	...	|	|	|	1809	|	...	|	|	2339	|	|	...	|	1556	|	1936	|	|
Markinch **224** d.	0831	|	|	...	...	1229	1331	1537	...	1739	...	1944	2132	...	2310	|	...	|	...	|	...	|	|
Kirkcaldy **224** d.	0841	0924	|	...	...	1239	1341	1547	...	1748	...	1954	2142	...	|	|	...	|	...	1603	...	2125	|
Edinburgh **224** a.	0925	1002	1117	...	...	1319	1425	1623	...	1825	...	2029	2219	...	0018	|	...	1318	...	1642	...	2205	|
London Kings Cross **185** .. a.	...	...	1550p	...	...	...	...	...	...	...	...	...	...	...	...	0747c	...	1814	...	...	...	...	0747c

A – 🅁. 🛏 1,2 class and 🚃2. Train stops to set down only.
B – 🅁. 🛏 1,2 class and 🚃2. Train stops to pick up only.
E – To / from Elgin.
G – Operated by *GR*.
a – Via Falkirk Grahamston (d. 1705).
c – London Euston.
d – London Euston. Departs previous day. Departs 2055 on ⑦.
e – Via Falkirk Grahamston (d. 1045).
f – Via Falkirk Grahamston (d. 1249).
h – Via Falkirk Grahamston (d. 1737).
p – 1603 on ⑥.
u – Stops to pick up only.

222 EDINBURGH - STIRLING — SR

From Edinburgh: *75 km*
Ⓐ: 0518, 0633, 0703, 0733 and every 30 minutes until 2033; then 2133, 2233, 2333.
⑥: 0518, 0633, 0703, 0733 and every 30 minutes until 2033; then 2133, 2233, 2333.
⑦: 0934, 1033, 1133, 1233, 1338, 1433, 1533, 1633, 1733, 1833, 1933, 2033, 2133, 2236.

From Stirling: Journey time: ± 50 minutes
Ⓐ: 0530, 0636, 0716, 0729, 0749, 0805 and every 30 minutes until 2105; then 2206, 2314.
⑥: 0530, 0636, 0716, 0805 and every 30 minutes until 2106; then 2206, 2314.
⑦: 0905, 1002, 1106 and hourly until 1806 (also 1233); then 1906, 2006, 2106, 2206.

☛ All trains (except the 0729Ⓐ from Stirling) call at **Falkirk Grahamston**: *41 km* (± 30 minutes) from Edinburgh; *34 km* (± 20 minutes) from Stirling.

Timings may vary by up to 4 minutes

223 GLASGOW - STIRLING — SR

From Glasgow Queen St: *47 km*
Ⓐ: 0555, 0613, 0648, 0706, 0718, 0741, 0748 and at 18, 41 and 48 minutes past each hour until 2218 (also 1611; not 1641); then 2248, 2318, 2348.
⑥: 0555, 0613, 0648, 0706, 0718, 0741, 0748 and at 18, 41 and 48 minutes past each hour until 2218; then 2248, 2318, 2348.
⑦: 0938, 1015, 1115, 1145, 1215, 1315, 1345, 1415, 1440, 1515, 1545, 1615, 1715, 1745, 1810, 1815, 1915, 1945, 2015, 2115, 2145, 2215, 2335.

From Stirling: Journey time: ± 35 minutes
Ⓐ: 0553, 0621, 0654, 0722, 0740, 0753, 0810, 0821, 0844, 0851, 0921, 0944, 0951 and at 21, 43 and 51 minutes past each hour until 2251; then 2305.
⑥: 0553, 0621, 0654, 0722, 0740, 0753, 0810, 0821, 0844, 0851, 0913, 0921, 0944, 0951 and at 21, 43 and 51 minutes past each hour until 2251; then 2305.
⑦: 0928, 0938, 1028, 1125, 1138, 1225, 1325, 1338, 1425, 1522, 1526, 1545, 1625, 1725, 1738, 1828, 1902, 1924, 1955, 2025, 2125, 2138.

Timings may vary by up to 3 minutes

224 EDINBURGH and GLASGOW - ABERDEEN — Most services 🍷 GR, SR, XC

km		⚒ N	⚒ Y	⚒ V	⚒ x	⚒	⚒ x	⚒ D	⚒	⚒	⚒ V	⚒	⚒	⚒ V	⚒	⚒	Ⓐ	⑥	⑥	Ⓐ	⚒	⚒ Lg	⚒	⚒
	London Kings Cross **185** ... d.	...	2115q	...	...	...	...	...	...	...	...	...	...	...	...	...	...	...	...	...	...	...	...	...
0	**Edinburgh** **221** d.	...	|	...	...	0530	0533	...	0629	0700	0730	...	0800	0829	...	0857	0930	0930	...	...	1000	1027	...	1100
42	Kirkcaldy **221** d.	...	0517s	...	...	0602	|	...	0703	0736	0802	...	0833	|	...	0933	|	|	...	...	1034	1104	...	1133
54	Markinch **221** d.	...	|	...	...	0611	0639	...	0712	0745	|	...	0842	|	...	0942	|	|	...	...	1043	|	...	1142
82	Leuchars d.	...	0546s	...	...	0632	0658	...	|	0806	0825	...	0906	0923	...	1003	|	1023	...	...	1104	1129	...	1203
	Glasgow Queen St ... **221** d.	...	|	...	...	|	|	0555	|	|	|	0741	|	|	0841	|	|	|	0942	0942	|	|	1041	|
	Stirling **221** d.	...	|	...	...	|	|	0624	|	|	|	0807	|	|	0907	|	|	|	1007	1007	|	|	1107	|
	Perth **221** d.	...	|	0601	...	|	|	0700	0750	|	|	0841	|	|	0936	|	|	|	1036	1036	|	|	1138	|
95	**Dundee** d.	...	0608s	0624	0640	0651	0713	0723	0816	0823	0841	0904	0921	0937	1000	1018	1033	1036	1100	1100	1120	1144	1200	1218
123	Arbroath d.	...	0631s	0641	0656	0710	...	0742	...	...	0857	0923	...	0953	1017	...	1050	1053	1118	1118	...	1201	1217	...
145	Montrose d.	0625	0647s	0657	0711	0723	...	0758	...	...	0913	0938	...	|	1031	...	1104	1107	1134	1134	...	1217	1232	...
184	Stonehaven d.	0649	0713s	0722	0732	0748	...	0822	...	...	0934	|	...	1029	1053	...	1126	1129	|	1204	...	1242	|	...
210	**Aberdeen** a.	0713	0735s	0744	0755	0813	...	0844	...	...	0952	1016	...	1053	1117	...	1145	1148	1214	1233	...	1307	1314	...

A – Dec. 12 – Mar. 28 from Plymouth; Apr. 4 – May 16 from Birmingham New Street.
B – Dec. 12 – Mar. 28 to Plymouth; Apr. 4 – May 16 to Birmingham New Street .
D – To / from Dyce.
E – To / from Penzance.
L – To / from Leeds.
N – To / from Inverness.
P – To / from Plymouth.
V – To / from Inverurie.
Y – 🅁. 🛏 1,2 class and 🚃2. Train stops to set down only.
Z – 🅁. 🛏 1,2 class and 🚃2. Train stops to pick up only.
a – 1510 on ⑥.
g – Operated by *GR*.
j – London Euston.
q – London Euston. Previous day. 2055 on ⑦.
x – Operated by *XC*.

SR EDINBURGH and GLASGOW - ABERDEEN 224

	⚒	⚒	⚒	⚒ V	⚒	⚒	⚒ V	⚒	⚒	⚒	⚒	⚒ g	⚒	⚒ V		⚒	⚒	⚒ V	⑥	Ⓐ	⚒ 2	⚒	⑥	Ⓐ	Ⓐ
London Kings Cross **185** .. d.	...	...	...	...	...	...	...	...	...	...	...	1030	...	...	...	...	...	...	...	...	...	...	...	...	...
Edinburgh 221 d.	1130	...	1200	1230	...	1300	1330	...	1400	1430	...	1500	1503	1530	...	...	1600	1629	...	...	1703	1735	...	...	1800
Kirkcaldy 221 d.	|	...	1235	|	...	1333	|	...	1433	|	...	1536	1542	|	...	...	1633	|	...	...	1739	|	...	...	1840
Markinch 221 d.	|	...	1242	|	...	1342	|	...	1442	|	...	|	1551	|	...	...	1642	|	...	...	1748	|	...	...	1851
Leuchars d.	1223	...	1303	1323	...	1403	1423	...	1503	1523	...	1600	1612	1623	...	...	1703	1724	...	...	1812	1835	...	...	1912
Glasgow Queen St 221 d.	|	1141	|	|	1241	|	|	1341	|	|	1441	|	|	|	...	1541	|	|	1641	1641	|	|	1741	1740	|
Stirling 221 d.	|	1207	|	|	1307	|	|	1407	|	|	1507	|	|	|	...	1607	|	|	1707	|	|	|	1807	1815	|
Perth 221 d.	|	1237	|	|	1336	|	|	1436	|	|	1536	|	|	|	...	1636	|	|	1737	1737	|	|	1844	1853	|
Dundee d.	1237	1300	1318	1336	1400	1418	1436	1500	1518	1537	1600	1619	1628	1636	...	1700	1720	1739	1800	1800	1834	1848	1915	1916	1927
Arbroath d.	1253	1319	...	1353	1418	...	1453	1519	...	1554	1617	1637	...	1654	...	1720	...	1802	1820	1820	...	1904	1934	1935	...
Montrose d.	|	1333	...	1407	1432	...	|	1538	...	1608	1631	1653	...	1708	...	1733	...	1816	|	|	...	1922	1948	1949	...
Stonehaven d.	1327	|	...	1429	1454	...	1527	|	...	1630	|	1716	...	1733	...	1755	...	1841	1853	1853	...	1943	2010	2011	...
Aberdeen a.	1346	1412	...	1453	1513	...	1546	1619	...	1650	1711	1738	...	1752	...	1815	...	1900	1913	1913	...	2009	2029	2032	...

	⑥ Px	Ⓐ Px	⚒ g		⚒	⚒	⚒ N	⚒	⚒ 2	Ⓐ Px	⑥ Px	Ⓐ g	⚒	⑥ 2	Ⓐ 2	⑥	Ⓐ	⑥	Ⓐ	⚒ 2	⚒		⑦	⑦ x	⑦ g
London Kings Cross **185** .. d.	...	...	1400	...	...	...	...	...	...	...	...	1600	...	...	...	...	...	...	...	...	...	...		...	...
Edinburgh 221 d.	1808	1816	1830	...	...	1900	1930	...	2000	2015	2022	2032	...	2100	2109	2132	2140	...	...	2209	2309	...		0804	0910
Kirkcaldy 221 d.	1842	1900	1911	...	...	1933	|	...	2045	2051	2100	2109	...	2145	2154	2204	2212	...	...	2254	2354	...		0840	0949
Markinch 221 d.	1851	1909	|	...	...	1942	|	...	2054	2100	2110	|	...	2154	2203	|	|	...	...	2303	0003	...		|	|
Leuchars d.	1912	1930	1938	...	...	2003	2028	...	2115	2122	2132	2133	...	2215	2224	2228	2234	...	...	2329	0024	...		|	1013
Glasgow Queen St 221 d.	|	|	|	...	1841	|	|	1941	|	|	|	|	2041	|	|	|	|	2141	2141	|	|	...		|	|
Stirling 221 d.	|	|	|	...	1907	|	|	2007	|	|	|	|	2107	|	|	|	|	2207	2207	|	|	...		|	|
Perth 221 d.	|	|	|	...	1943	|	|	2036	|	|	|	|	2143	|	|	|	|	2237	2235	|	|	...		|	|
Dundee d.	1925	1946	1953	...	2009	2020	2041	2100	2130	2140	2147	2148	2208	2230	2239	2243	2249	2258	2303	2344	0039	...		0917	1028
Arbroath d.	1942	2002	2010	...	2025	...	2058	2117	...	...	...	2205	2225	...	...	2300	2305	2317	2325	...	...	...		0933	1045
Montrose d.	2002	2016	2026	...	2040	...	2112	|	...	...	...	2222	2239	...	...	2314	2324	2333	2341	...	...	...		0947	1101
Stonehaven d.	2023	2036	2049	...	|	...	2134	2154	...	...	...	2245	2301	...	...	2339	2346	2355	0006	...	...	...		1008	1124
Aberdeen a.	2041	2055	2112	...	2118	...	2153	2213	...	...	...	2307	2320	...	...	2358	0008	0018	0026	...	...	...		1026	1147

	⑦ 2		⑦	⑦	⑦ 2	⑦	⑦	⑦ 2	⑦	⑦ 2	⑦	⑦ g	⑦	⑦ 2	⑦	⑦ Ax	⑦ g	⑦ 2	⑦	⑦	⑦	⑦ 2	⑦ 2		⑦
London Kings Cross **185** .. d.	...	...	...	...	...	...	...	...	...	...	...	1100	...	...	...	...	1400	...	...	...	...	...	...	...	...
Edinburgh 221 d.	0915	...	...	1055	1115	...	1240	1315	...	1515	...	1600	1705	1715	...	1810	1842	1915	...	2100	...	2225	2236	...	...
Kirkcaldy **221** d.	1003	...	...	1131	1203	...	1316	1405	...	1603	...	1641	1738	1800	...	1844	1919	2000	...	2134	...	2310	|	...	...
Markinch **221** d.	1012	...	...	|	1212	...	|	1414	...	1612	...	|	|	1809	...	1853	|	2009	...	2143	...	2319	|	...	...
Leuchars (for St Andrews) d.	1033	...	...	1155	1233	...	1340	1435	...	1633	...	1706	1802	1830	...	1914	1943	2030	...	2205	...	2340	|	...	...
Glasgow Queen St **221** d.	|	...	0938	|	|	1145	|	|	1345	|	1545	|	|	|	1745	|	|	|	1945	|	2145	|	|	...	2335
Stirling **221** d.	|	...	1012	|	|	1212	|	|	1412	|	1612	|	|	|	1812	|	|	|	2012	|	2211	|	2327	...	0014
Perth 221 d.	|	...	1048	|	|	1247	|	|	1448	|	1647	|	|	|	1845	|	|	|	2047	|	2246	|	0008	...	0056
Dundee d.	1050	...	1113	1208	1248	1311	1353	1450	1511	1648	1711	1724	1815	1846	1909	1930	1958	2045	2111	2218	2309	2356	...	...	...
Arbroath d.	...	...	1129	1225	...	1327	1410	...	1527	...	1727	1742	1832	...	1927	1946	2015	...	2127	2235	2326	...	...	...	...
Montrose d.	...	...	1146	1237	...	1342	1424	...	1542	...	1742	1800	1846	...	1942	2000	2031	...	2142	2249	2341	...	...	...	...
Stonehaven d.	...	...	1210	1259	...	1403	1446	...	1606	...	1803	1823	1908	...	2006	2023	2054	...	2203	2311	0002	...	...	...	...
Aberdeen a.	...	...	1235	1323	...	1423	1505	...	1626	...	1823	1846	1930	...	2029	2042	2117	...	2224	2333	0025	...	...	...	...

km		⚒	Ⓐ 2	⚒ 2	⑥ 2	⚒ 2	Ⓐ 2	Ⓐ 2	Ⓐ Px	⚒	⚒	⚒ 2		⚒ Px	⚒	⚒	⚒ N	⚒ 2	⚒ V	⚒ g	⚒ Ex	⚒ 2	⚒	⚒	⚒ 2
0	**Aberdeen** d.		...	...	...	...	...	...	...	0533	0556	...	...	...	0633	...	0706	...	0740	0752	0820	...	0842	0907	...
26	Stonehaven d.		...	...	...	...	...	...	...	0552	0612	...	...	...	0652	...	0722	...	0756	0809	0838	...	|	|	...
65	Montrose d.		...	...	...	...	...	...	...	0617	0634	...	...	...	0713	...	0747	...	0818	0832	0859	...	0918	0946	...
87	Arbroath d.		...	...	...	...	...	...	...	0631	0648	...	...	...	0727	...	0801	...	0832	0848	0915	...	0932	1000	...
115	**Dundee** d.		...	...	...	0605	...	...	0632	0652	0708	0720	...	0735	0752	0818	0822	0828	0853	0906	0933	0942	0952	1017	1034
149	**Perth** 221 d.		0510	0516	0535	|	0609	0614	|	0715	|	|	...	|	0812	0841	|	|	0915	|	|	|	1014	|	|
202	Stirling 221 d.		|	0553	|	|	0654	|	|	0753	|	|	...	|	0843	0913	|	|	0944	|	|	|	1043	|	|
249	**Glasgow** Queen St 221 a.		|	0634	|	|	0734	|	|	0834	|	|	...	|	0915	0945	|	|	1014	|	|	|	1114	|	|
	Leuchars d.		|	...	|	0617	...	|	0646	...	0720	0732	...	0748	...	...	|	0842	...	0920	0947	0955	...	1029	1046
	Markinch 221 d.		0544	...	0607	0640	...	0646	0711	...	|	0756	...	0811	...	...	|	0904	...	|	1009	1017	...	|	1108
	Kirkcaldy 221 d.		0553	...	0616	0649	...	|	0721	...	0748	0806	...	0820	...	...	|	0913	...	0944	1017	1027	...	|	1118
	Edinburgh 221 a.		0646	...	0706	0738	...	0757	0805	...	0826	0855	...	0858	...	...	0930	0956	...	1027	1101	1109	...	1129	1201
	London Kings Cross **185** a.		...	...	...	...	...	...	...	...	...	...	...	...	...	...	...	...	...	1457a	...	...	...	...	...

	⚒ D	⚒ g	⚒ 2	⚒	⚒ V	⚒	⚒		⚒ V	⚒	⚒	⚒	⚒ 2	⚒		⚒	⚒ 2	⚒	⚒ g		⚒	⚒ 2	⚒ V	⚒ 2	⚒
Aberdeen d.	0937	0952	...	1038	1105	...	1142	...	1207	...	1242	1306	...	1342	...	1407	...	1439	1450	...	1533	...	1601	...	1637
Stonehaven d.	0953	1009	...	|	1121	...	|	...	1226	...	1258	1322	...	|	...	1423	...	|	1507	...	1549	...	1618	...	1653
Montrose d.	1015	1032	...	1114	1146	...	1217	...	|	...	1317	1344	...	1417	...	|	...	1512	1530	...	1611	...	|	...	1713
Arbroath d.	1029	1049	...	1128	1200	...	1231	...	1300	...	1331	1358	...	1431	...	1500	...	1526	1546	...	1625	...	1655	...	1729
Dundee d.	1052	1106	1130	1149	1217	1234	1252	...	1317	1334	1350	1417	1434	1452	...	1517	1535	1549	1604	...	1645	1650	1717	1726	1751
Perth 221 d.	1114	|	|	1211	|	|	1314	...	|	|	1411	|	|	1514	...	|	|	1611	|	...	1711	|	|	|	1812
Stirling 221 d.	1143	|	|	1243	|	|	1343	...	|	|	1440	|	|	1543	...	|	|	1643	|	...	1742	|	|	|	1842
Glasgow Queen St 221 a.	1215	|	|	1314	|	|	1414	...	|	|	1515	|	|	1615	...	|	|	1717	|	...	1815	|	|	|	1914
Leuchars d.	...	1120	1145	...	1229	1246	...	...	1329	1346	...	1429	1446	...	...	1529	1547	...	1618	...	...	1702	1729	1739	...
Markinch 221 d.	...	|	1208	...	|	1308	...	...	|	1408	...	|	1508	...	...	|	1608	...	|	...	...	1723	|	1804	...
Kirkcaldy 221 d.	...	1144	1217	...	|	1318	...	...	|	1418	...	|	1518	...	...	|	1619	...	1645	...	...	1733	|	1813	...
Edinburgh 221 a.	...	1225	1255	...	1327	1357	...	...	1428	1455	...	1527	1555	...	...	1631	1656	...	1727	...	...	1822	1832	1850	...
London Kings Cross **180** .. a.	...	1658	...	...	...	...	...	...	...	...	...	...	...	...	...	...	...	...	2220	...	...	...	...	...	...

	⚒ V	⚒ 2	⚒	⑥		Ⓐ g	⚒	⚒ V	⚒ 2	⚒	⚒ 2V	⚒	⚒	⑥ x	Ⓐ x	⚒	Ⓐ Z	①–④	⑤		⑦	⑦ 2	⑦	⑦ 2	⑦
Aberdeen d.	1707	...	1736	1816	...	1816	1830	1909	...	1946	2005	2042	2106	2117	2132	...	2140	2230	2322	...		...	...	...	0927
Stonehaven d.	|	...	1752	1833	...	1833	1849	1926	...	2005	2021	2058	2122	2134	2149	...	2200u	2249	2341	...		...	...	...	0943
Montrose d.	1749	...	1817	1856	...	1856	1910	1951	...	2023	2043	2120	2144	2155	2210	...	2225u	2313	0005	...		...	...	...	1008
Arbroath d.	1803	...	1831	1912	...	1912	1924	2005	...	2037	2057	2134	2158	2211	2226	...	2243u	2328	0020	...		...	...	...	1022
Dundee d.	1819	1846	1852	1930	...	1930	1946	2021	2042	2056	2116	2152	2215	2229	2243	...	2306u	2351	0043	...		0725	0845	0925	1043
Perth 221 d.	|	|	1914	|	...	|	2011	|	|	2117	|	2214	|	|	|	2238	|	0015	0107	...		|	0903	|	1105
Stirling 221 d.	|	|	1943	|	...	|	2040	|	|	2145	|	2243	|	|	|	|	|	...	...	...		|	0938	|	1138
Glasgow Queen St 221 a.	|	|	2015	|	...	|	2114	|	|	2219	|	2315	|	|	|	|	|	...	...	...		|	1015	|	1211
Leuchars d.	1831	1856	...	1944	...	1944	...	2033	2054	...	2128	...	2227	2242	2256	|	2325u	...	...	...		0737	...	0937	...
Markinch 221 d.	|	1919	...	|	...	|	...	|	2116	...	2151	...	2252	2305	2318	2310	|	...	...	...		0759	...	0959	...
Kirkcaldy 221 d.	|	1928	...	2008	...	2008	...	|	2126	...	2159	...	2301	2314	2326	|	2353u	...	...	...		0808	...	1008	...
Edinburgh 221 a.	1934	2013	...	2048	...	2050	...	2132	2216	...	2250	...	2352	2355	0005	0018	|	...	...	...		0900	...	1106	...
London Kings Cross **185** .. a.	...	...	...	...	...	...	...	...	...	...	...	...	...	...	...	...	0748j	...	...	...		...	...	...	...

	⑦ g	⑦ 2	⑦ Bx	⑦	⑦ g	⑦ 2	⑦		⑦ g	⑦ 2	⑦	⑦	⑦ 2	⑦	⑦ N	⑦ 2	⑦	⑦		⑦	⑦ x		⑦ Z	⑦	
Aberdeen d.	0948	...	1112	1129	1147	...	1327	...	1350	...	1510	1530	...	1710	1747	...	1910	1935	...	2010	2128	...	2140	2229	...
Stonehaven d.	1005	...	1129	1145	1204	...	1343	...	1407	...	1526	1546	...	1726	1804	...	1926	1951	...	2026	2145	...	2200u	2248	...
Montrose d.	1028	...	1150	1207	1227	...	1407	...	1430	...	1548	1608	...	1748	1828	...	1948	2013	...	2048	2206	...	2225u	2311	...
Arbroath d.	1044	...	1206	1221	1243	...	1422	...	1446	...	1602	1622	...	1802	1842	...	2002	2027	...	2102	2222	...	2243u	2325	...
Dundee d.	1102	1125	1225	1243	1301	1325	1445	...	1504	1525	1625	1643	1725	1819	1904	1927	2020	2043	...	2121	2239	...	2306u	2347	...
Perth 221 d.	|	|	|	1305	|	|	1508	...	|	|	|	1705	|	|	1927	|	|	2105	...	|	|	...	|	0009	...
Stirling 221 d.	|	|	|	1338	|	|	1545	...	|	|	|	1738	|	|	1955	|	|	2138	...	|	|	...	|	...	...
Glasgow Queen St 221 a.	|	|	|	1411	|	|	1628	...	|	|	|	1812	|	|	2031	|	|	2215	...	|	|	...	|	...	...
Leuchars d.	1116	1137	1238	...	1315	1337	...	...	1518	1537	1637	...	1737	1831	...	1939	2032	...	...	2133	2252	...	2325u	...	...
Markinch 221 d.	|	1159	|	...	|	1359	...	...	|	1559	|	...	1759	|	...	2001	|	...	...	2154	2314	...	|	...	...
Kirkcaldy 221 d.	1140	1208	1303	...	1339	1408	...	...	1542	1608	1702	...	1807	1856	...	2010	2059	...	...	2205	2322	...	2353u	...	...
Edinburgh 221 a.	1224	1306	1342	...	1424	1506	...	...	1625	1659	1741	...	1900	1935	...	2101	2136	...	...	2243	2358	...	|	...	...
London Kings Cross **185** .. a.	1710	...	...	...	1917	...	...	...	2120	...	...	...	...	...	...	...	...	...	...	...	...	...	0747j	...	...

225 INVERNESS - ELGIN - ABERDEEN SR

km		⚒ 🍷E	⚒ 🍷	⚒ G	⚒	⚒ 🍷	⚒ 🍷	⚒ 🍷	⚒ 🍷	⚒	⚒ 🍷	⚒ 🍷	⚒	⚒	⚒	
0	**Inverness** 221 d.	0451	0558	...	0710	0903	1058	1242	1427	...	1521	1711	1810	1957	2120	...
24	Nairn d.	0508	0615	...	0728	0921	1115	1259	1444	...	1540	1728	1827	2014	2137	...
40	Forres d.	0519	0626	...	0739	0937	1126	1310	1455	...	1551	1739	1838	2025	2148	...
59	**Elgin** d.	0534	0642	...	0800	0955	1142	1328	1512	...	1607	1758	1855	2041	2206	...
89	Keith d.	0556	0703	...	0821	1014	1203	1347	1532	...	1628	1819	1916	...	2227	...
109	Huntly d.	0610	0719	...	0845	1030	1217	1401	1546	...	1647	1840	1937	...	2247	...
130	Insch d.	0626	0735	...	0903	1049	1235	1419	1604	...	1704	1856	1953	...	2303	...
147	**Inverurie** d.	0639	0749	...	0915	1101	1247	1431	1618	...	1716	1909	2005	...	2316	...
164	Dyce ✈ d.	0652	0803	0908	0927	1115	1302	1443	1631	1705	1730	1921	2019	...	2328	...
174	**Aberdeen** 224 a.	0704	0814	0919	0938	1126	1313	1454	1641	1716	1741	1932	2030	...	2339	...

	⑦ 🍷	⑦ 🍷	⑦ 🍷G	⑦ 🍷	⑦ G🍷	⑦ 🍷	⑦ G🍷
Inverness 221 d.	0955	1230	1527	1712	1800	2100	2142
Nairn d.	1012	1247	1544	1730	1817	2117	2159
Forres d.	1023	1258	1555	1741	1828	2128	2210
Elgin d.	1038	1313	1610	1756	1844	2144	2226
Keith d.	1059	1335	1632	1818	...	2205	...
Huntly d.	1118	1352	1646	1837	...	2219	...
Insch d.	1134	1408	1702	1853	...	2235	...
Inverurie d.	1147	1420	1714	1905	...	2247	...
Dyce ✈ d.	1159	1432	1730	1917	...	2259	...
Aberdeen 224 a.	1210	1443	1741	1928	...	2310	...

	⚒	⚒	⚒ M	⚒	⚒ G	⚒ 🍷	⚒ 🍷		⚒ 🍷	⚒ 🍷	⚒	⚒ 🍷	⚒ 🍷	⚒ 🍷	⚒ 🍷E	
Aberdeen 224 d.	...	0614	0714	0823	0850	1014	1159	...	1340	1525	1643	1718	1820	2007	2155	...
Dyce ✈ d.	...	0624	0731	0836	0859	1023	1208	...	1353	1538	1652	1729	1829	2020	2205	...
Inverurie d.	...	0646	0749	0848	...	1035	1220	...	1405	1550	...	1741	1841	2032	2217	...
Insch d.	...	0658	0801	0903	...	1047	1233	...	1417	1602	...	1753	1853	2044	2229	...
Huntly d.	...	0719	0817	0919	...	1103	1249	...	1433	1618	...	1809	1909	2100	2246	...
Keith d.	...	0733	0831	0933	...	1120	1305	...	1447	1634	...	1826	1924	2114	2300	...
Elgin d.	0700	0759	0853	0955	...	1142	1327	...	1511	1656	...	1854	1946	2136	2322	...
Forres d.	0714	0813	0907	1011	...	1156	1341	...	1525	1710	...	1908	2000	2155	2336	...
Nairn d.	0727	0824	0922	1022	...	1207	1352	...	1541	1729	...	1919	2015	2206	2347	...
Inverness 221 a.	0748	0841	0940	1040	...	1225	1410	...	1559	1747	...	1938	2033	2224	0005	...

	⑦ 🍷	⑦ 🍷		⑦ 🍷	⑦ 🍷		⑦ 🍷
Aberdeen 224 d.	1000	1300	...	1525	1718	...	2100
Dyce ✈ d.	1009	1309	...	1534	1729	...	2109
Inverurie d.	1021	1321	...	1547	1741	...	2121
Insch d.	1033	1333	...	1559	1753	...	2133
Huntly d.	1049	1351	...	1615	1809	...	2149
Keith d.	1105	1404	...	1635	1824	...	2209
Elgin d.	1127	1426	...	1658	1846	...	2231
Forres d.	1141	1440	...	1712	1900	...	2245
Nairn d.	1152	1451	...	1732	1911	...	2256
Inverness 221 a.	1210	1510	...	1750	1929	...	2314

Other trains on ⚒:
Inverurie – Aberdeen at 0714 **G**, 0822, 1038 **E**, 1135 **E**, 1338, 1524 **E**, 1638 **E**, 1843 **E**, 1940 **E**, 2124.
Aberdeen – Inverurie at 0750 **P**, 1000 **E**, 1104 **E**, 1250, 1456 **E**, 1555 **E**, 1756 **E**, 1907 **E**, 2056, 2250.

E – To/from Edinburgh.
G – To/from Glasgow.
M – From Montrose.
P – From Perth.

226 NORTH HIGHLAND BRANCHES 2nd class SR

INVERNESS - THURSO and WICK

km		⚒ 🍷	⚒ 🍷	⚒ 🍷	⚒ 🍷	⑦ 🍷	
0	**Inverness** 221 ‡ d.	0706	1038	1359	1752	1800	...
16	Beauly ‡ d.	0720	1052	|	1806	1814	...
21	Muir of Ord ‡ d.	0729	1058	1416	1812	1820	...
30	Dingwall ‡ d.	0743	1107	1428	1829	1829	...
51	Invergordon ‡ d.	0800	1126	1446	1847	1847	...
71	Tain ‡ d.	0818	1145	1504	1905	1905	...
93	Ardgay ‡ d.	0833	1200	1521	1924	1924	...
108	Lairg d.	0852	1219	1544	1944	1944	...
136	Golspie d.	0916	1243	1608	2007	2007	...
146	Brora d.	0930	1254	1618	2018	2018	...
163	Helmsdale d.	0946	1309	1633	2033	2033	...
237	Georgemas Jcn a.	1050	1412	1733	2133	2133	...
248	**Thurso** a.	1102	1424	1745	2145	2145	...
248	**Thurso** d.	1104	1426	1747	2147	2147	...
237	Georgemas Jcn d.	1114	1437	1758	2157	2157	...
260	**Wick** a.	1132	1455	1815	2214	2214	...

	⚒	⚒ 🍷	⚒ 🍷	⑦ 🍷	⚒ 🍷	⚒ 🍷
Wick d.	...	0620	0812	1153	1236	1600
Georgemas Jcn d.	...	0637	0829	1210	1253	1617
Thurso a.	...	0646	0838	1219	1302	1626
Thurso d.	...	0648	0841	1222	1305	1629
Georgemas Jcn d.	...	0700	0853	1234	1317	1641
Helmsdale d.	...	0801	0947	1333	1418	1740
Brora d.	...	0816	1003	1348	1433	1755
Golspie d.	...	0826	1011	1358	1442	1804
Lairg d.	0634	0853	1038	1424	1508	1830
Ardgay ‡ d.	0651	0911	1051	1440	1525	1848
Tain ‡ d.	0706	0926	1107	1455	1541	1905
Invergordon ‡ d.	0724	0944	1126	1512	1558	1922
Dingwall ‡ d.	0742	1004	1145	1530	1619	1941
Muir of Ord ‡ d.	0752	1013	1155	1542	1629	1950
Beauly ‡ d.	0757	1019	|	1547	1634r	1956
Inverness 221 ‡ a.	0812	1035	1213	1602	1648	2010

‡ – Additional trains operate Inverness - Invergordon (- Tain - Ardgay) and v.v.:
From Inverness: 1000†**T**, 1249†**T**, 1439⚒**N**, 1521†**N**, 1715⚒**A**, 2109**T**, 2320⑤⑥**T**.
From Invergordon: 0658⚒**A**, 1126†**T**, 1416†**T**, 1619†**N**, 1538⚒**N**, 1958⚒**A**, 2236**T**.

A – From/to Ardgay.
N – From/to Invergordon.
T – From/to Tain.
r – Request stop.

INVERNESS - KYLE OF LOCHALSH

km		⚒	⚒	⑦	⚒ 🍷	⚒	
0	**Inverness** 221 d.	0900	1101	1111	1334	1752	...
16	Beauly d.	0914	|	1125	1348	1806	...
21	Muir of Ord d.	0920	1118	1131	1354	1812	...
30	Dingwall d.	0931	1129	1144	1403	1826	...
49	Garve d.	0953	1151	1205	1425	1849	...
75	Achnasheen d.	1019	1216	1231	1450	1917	...
104	Strathcarron d.	1046	1243	1258	1517	1946	...
116	Stromeferry d.	1104	1301	1316	1535	2004	...
124	Plockton d.	1116	1313	1328	1546	2015	...
133	**Kyle of Lochalsh** a.	1128	1326	1340	1559	2029	...

	⚒		⚒	⚒ 🍷	⑦	⚒	
Kyle of Lochalsh d.	0621	...	1203	1435	1522	1715	...
Plockton d.	0633	...	1214	1447	1534	1727	...
Stromeferry d.	0644	...	1226	1458	1545	1738	...
Strathcarron d.	0702	...	1245	1520	1603	1756	...
Achnasheen d.	0729	...	1313	1548	1630	1824	...
Garve d.	0755	...	1339	1614	1656	1850	...
Dingwall d.	0816	...	1404	1637	1718	1913	...
Muir of Ord d.	0829	...	1416	1646	1729	1925	...
Beauly d.	0835	...	1421	|	1734	1930	...
Inverness 221 a.	0853	...	1437	1706	1749	1949	...

227 🚌 / ⛴ INVERNESS - ULLAPOOL - STORNOWAY

Valid until May 23, 2010.

	⚒	⚒	⑥⑦							
Inverness 🚌 d.	0810	1500	1540	...	...	...	...	...	...	...
Ullapool 🚌 a.	0930	1620	1700	...	...	...	...	...	...	...
Ullapool ⛴ d.	1025	1735	1815	...	...	...	...	...	...	...
Stornoway ⛴ a.	1310	2020	2100	...	...	...	...	...	...	...

	⚒	⚒	⑥⑦							
Stornoway ⛴ d.	0700	1350	1430	...	...	...	...	...	...	...
Ullapool ⛴ a.	0945	1635	1715	...	...	...	...	...	...	...
Ullapool 🚌 d.	0950	1640	1720	...	...	...	...	...	...	...
Inverness 🚌 a.	1110	1800	1840	...	...	...	...	...	...	...

🚌 Operated by Scottish Citylink (service **961**) www.citylink.co.uk, ✆ +44 (0) 8705 50 50 50. Runs in conjunction with Ullapool - Stornoway ferry.

⛴ Operated by Caledonian MacBrayne Ltd. Latest passenger check-in : 30 minutes before departure.

228 🚌 INVERNESS - FORT WILLIAM - OBAN

Valid until May 23, 2010.

Service number	919 ⚒	918 ⚒	919 ⚒	919	918 ⚒	919 ⚒	919	918 ⚒	19 ⚒	919 ⚒	
Inverness d.	0845	...	1045	1245	...	1445	1645	...	1745	2015	...
Fort Augustus d.	0943	...	1143	1343	...	1543	1743	...	1848	2120	...
Fort William d.	1035	1100	1235	1435	1500	1635	1835	1900	1937	2209	...
Ballachulish d.	...	1125	...	...	1527	...	...	1927	...	...	...
Oban a.	...	1225	...	...	1627	...	...	2027	...	...	...

Service number	19 ⚒	919 ⚒	918 ⚒	919 ⚒	919	918 ⚒	919 ⚒	919 Ⓐ	919 ⑥⑦	918 ⚒	919
Oban d.	...	...	0840	...	...	1240	...	...	...	1640	...
Ballachulish d.	...	...	0939	...	...	1339	...	...	...	1739	...
Fort William d.	0730	0815	1008	1030	1215	1408	1415	1520	1530	1808	1815
Fort Augustus d.	0819	0903	...	1118	1303	...	1503	1632	1619	...	1903
Inverness a.	0920	1001	...	1216	1401	...	1601	1733	1720	...	2001

☛ Operated by Highland Country Buses / Scottish Citylink: www.citylink.co.uk, ✆ +44 (0) 8705 50 50 50.

229 ISLE OF MAN RAILWAYS ✆ +44 (0)1624 663366

km	*Manx Electric Railway*	A	C	B	D	B	A	C	B	B	D	C	C				
0	**Douglas** Derby Castle ‡ d.	0940	1010	1040	1110	1140	1240	1340	1410	1510	1540	1610	1640	...	...	...	...
4	Groudle d.	0952	1022	1052	1122	1152	1252	1352	1422	1522	1552	1622	1652	...	...	...	...
11	Laxey ▲ d.	1010	1040	1110	1140	1210	1310	1410	1440	1540	1610	1640	1710	...	...	...	...
29	**Ramsey** a.	1055	1125	1155	1225	1255	1355	1455	1525	1625	1655	...	1755	...	...	...	...

		B	A	C	B	D	B	A	C	B	C	C	D				
Ramsey d.	...	1010	1110	1140	1210	1240	1340	1440	1510	1540	...	1640	1710	...	...	...	...
Laxey ▲ d.	...	1055	1155	1225	1255	1325	1425	1525	1555	1625	1655	1725	1755	...	...	...	...
Groudle d.	...	1113	1213	1243	1313	1343	1443	1543	1613	1643	1713	1743	1813	...	...	...	...
Douglas Derby Castle ‡ a.	...	1125	1225	1255	1325	1355	1455	1555	1625	1655	1725	1755	1825	...	...	...	...

A – Daily Apr. 6 - Nov. 1.
B – Daily Apr. 6 - Sept. 27.
C – Daily May 25 - Sept. 6.
D – Daily Jun. 29 - Aug. 28.

‡ – 🚌 services **23, 24, 25, 26** connect Derby Castle and the Steam Railway Station.

▲ – **Snaefell Mountain Railway** operates daily until Nov. 1, subject to weather conditions. First departure from Laxey 1015, last departure 1545. Journey time to summit: 30 mins.

km	*Isle of Man Steam Railway*	Service Apr. 6 - Nov. 1 (★ until Sept. 27)		★				★		
0	**Douglas** Railway Station ‡ d.	1020	...	1220	...	1420	...	1620	...	...
9	Santon (request stop) d.	1041	...	1241	...	1441	...	1641	...	...
16	**Castletown** d.	1057	...	1257	...	1457	...	1657	...	...
25	Port Erin a.	1117	...	1317	...	1517	...	1717	...	...

	Service Apr. 6 - Nov. 1 (★ until Sept. 27) ★				★				
Port Erin d.	1020	...	1220	...	1420	...	1620	...	...
Castletown d.	1042	...	1242	...	1442	...	1642	...	...
Santon (request stop) d.	1058	...	1258	...	1458	...	1658	...	...
Douglas Railway Station ‡ a.	1117	...	1317	...	1517	...	1717	...	...

IRELAND

SEE MAP PAGE 96

Operators: Iarnród Éireann (**IÉ**) and Northern Ireland Railways (**NIR**), Bus Éireann, Ulsterbus and Dublin Area Rapid Transit (**DART**). Most cross-border services are jointly operated.

Timings: Rail: **NIR** services are valid from **December 13, 2009** until further notice.
IÉ and **DART** services are valid from **November 29, 2009** until further notice.
Bus: **Ulsterbus** services are valid from **May 5, 2009** until further notice.
Bus Éireann services are valid until **May 10, 2010**.

Rail services: Except for *Enterprise* cross-border expresses (for details, see Table **230** below), **all trains** convey *Standard* (2nd) class seating. Most express trains in the Republic of Ireland, as noted in the tables, also have first class accommodation.
On public holiday dates in the **Republic of Ireland**, DART trains run as on Sundays; outer-suburban services to or from Drogheda and Dundalk do not run. Other services may be amended, though most main-line trains run normally. All services are subject to alteration during the Christmas, New Year and Easter holiday periods.

Bus services: **Bus Éireann** and **Ulsterbus**: services are shown in detail where there is no comparable rail service; only basic information is given for other routes. Buses do not always call at the rail station, but usually stop nearby. Where possible the stop details are given in the station bank or as a footnote. On longer routes, a change of bus may be required – please check with the driver. At holiday times bus travellers should consult detailed leaflets or seek further information from the operator. **Bus Éireann**: ✆ +353 1 836 6111 (Dublin) or + 353 21 450 8188 (Cork); **Ulsterbus**: ✆ + 028 9033 3000 (Translink, Belfast). **Dublin Busaras** (bus station) is a 5 minute walk from Dublin Connolly station.

The Dublin Tram service (Luas) connects Dublin Connolly and Heuston stations at frequent intervals. Journey time is 14 minutes, depending on traffic conditions. See Dublin City Plan on page 28.

NIR, IÉ BELFAST - DUNDALK - DUBLIN 230

Enterprise express trains (*E*) convey Standard (2nd) class and Premium (1st) class seating, 🍸 (Café Bar and trolley service) and ✕ (at-seat meal service in Premium)

km		Ⓐ	Ⓐ	⑥	Ⓐ	⚒	⚒ E	⑥	⚒	⚒ E	⚒	⚒	⚒	⚒ E	⚒	⚒	⚒ E	⚒	⚒ E	⚒	⑤	⚒	⚒ E	⚒	⚒	⑥	Ⓐ
0	**Belfast Central** § d.	...	...	...	...	...	0650	...	0750x	0800	...	...	0945c	1035	...	1159	1235	1329	1410	...	...	1529	1610	...	...	1659	1710
13	Lisburn § d.	...	...	...	...	...	|	...	0801z	|	...	...	1032	|	...	1232	|	1402	|	...	...	1602	|	...	...	1732	1732
42	Portadown § d.	...	...	...	...	...	0721	...	0826z	0831	...	...	1058	1106	...	1258	1306	1428	1441	...	...	1630	1641	...	...	1800	1800
71	Newry d.	...	...	...	...	...	0742	...	▬	0852	...	...	▬	1127	...	▬	1327	▬	1502	...	...	▬	1703	...	...	1825	1825
95	**Dundalk** d.	0540	0630	0700	0700	...	0800	0815	Ⓐ	|	0950	1045	⚒	1145	...	⚒	1345	⚒	1520	...	1605	⚒	1720	...	...	...	...
131	Drogheda d.	0604	0654	0724	0724	0800	0822	0840	0830	|	1015	1109	1135	1206	1220	1305	1406	1415	1541	1555	1630	1655	1741	1748	1800	...	...
148	Balbriggan d.	0619	0711	0741	0741	0815	|	0855	0845	|	1030	1123	1150	|	1235	1320	|	1430	|	1610	|	1710	|	|	1815	...	...
154	Skerries d.	0625	0718	0747	0747	0821	|	0901	0851	|	1036	1129	1156	|	1241	1326	|	1436	|	1616	|	1716	|	|	1821	...	...
168	Malahide d.	0640	0734	0804	|	0837	|	0916	0908	|	1051	1144	1211	|	1256	1341	|	1451	|	1635	|	1735	|	|	1838	...	...
183	**Dublin Connolly** a.	0658	0757	0828	0828	0858	0904	0943	0928	1000	1115	1200	1229	1244	1316	1403	1444	1518	1617	1700	1715	1758	1815	1829	1857	...	...

	Ⓐ	⚒ E	⚒	⚒ E	⚒	⑦	⑦ E	⑦ E	⑦ E	⑦ E	⑦ E
Belfast Central § d.	1750	1810	1859	2010	...	...	1000	1300	1500	1600	1900
Lisburn § d.	1812	|	1932	|	...	...	1015	*1302*	*1502*	*1602*	*1902*
Portadown § d.	1837	1843	1958	2041	...	...	1042	1334	1534	1634	1934
Newry d.	▬	1903	▬	2102	...	...	1103	1356	1556	1656	1956
Dundalk d.	⚒	1920	⚒	2120	...	0920	1121	1415	1615	1715	2015
Drogheda d.	1845	1941	2000	2141	2205	0945	1142	1436	1636	1736	2036
Balbriggan d.	1900	|	2015	|	2220	1000	|	|	|	|	|
Skerries d.	1906	|	2021	|	2226	1006	|	|	|	|	|
Malahide d.	1923	|	2038	|	2241	1021	|	|	|	|	|
Dublin Connolly a.	1946	2015	2101	2215	2301	1040	1213	1513	1715	1815	2105

	Ⓐ	⑥	Ⓐ	⚒ E	⚒	⚒ E	⚒	⚒	⚒ E	⚒	⚒	⚒ E
Dublin Connolly d.	...	...	0708	0735	0849	0935	1000	1035	1100	1104	1234	1320
Malahide d.	...	...	0727	|	0909	|	1026	1056	|	1131	1300	|
Skerries d.	...	...	0741	|	0923	|	1040	1110	|	1145	1314	|
Balbriggan d.	...	...	0747	|	0929	|	1046	1116	|	1151	1320	|
Drogheda d.	...	...	0803	0807	0946	1006	1103	1132	1136	1208	1337	1350
Dundalk d.	...	...	...	0830	1010	1030	▬	...	1158	▬	...	1415
Newry d.	0650	0720	...	0848	...	1048	⚒	...	1216	⚒	...	1433
Portadown § d.	0720	0745	...	0909	...	1109	1115	...	1237	1245	...	1456
Lisburn § a.	0745	0808	...	*0938*	...	|	1138	...	|	1308	...	|
Belfast Central § a.	0804	0842	...	0945	...	1145	1212	...	1315	1342	...	1535

	⚒	⚒ E	⚒	⚒	⚒ E	⚒	⑥	Ⓐ	Ⓐ	⑥	⚒	⑥	⚒	⚒ E	⚒	⚒	⚒ E	⚒	⚒	Ⓐ	⚒	⑦ E	⑦ E	⑦ E	⑦ E	⑦ E	⑦
Dublin Connolly d.	1335	1520	1549	1621	1650	1651	...	...	1721	1721	1803	...	1840	1900	1920	2020	2050	...	2132	2232	2320	1000	1300	1600	1800	1900	2122
Malahide d.	1356	|	1609	1639	|	1712	...	...	|	1740	1827	...	|	|	1939	2038	|	...	2157	2257	2339	|	|	|	|	|	2140
Skerries d.	1411	|	1623	1654	|	1726	...	...	1751	1756	1841	...	1907	|	1953	2053	|	...	2211	2311	2353	|	|	|	|	|	2155
Balbriggan d.	1416	|	1629	1649	|	1732	...	...	1756	1801	1847	...	1913	|	1959	2058	|	...	2217	2317	2359	|	|	|	|	|	2200
Drogheda d.	1433	1550g	1646	1716	|	1749	...	...	1813	1818	1903	...	1928	1932	2016	2115	2120	...	2233	2334	0018	1032	1332	1632	1832	1932	2220
Dundalk d.	...	1612g	▬	▬	1743	▬	...	...	1837	1845	1928f	...	...	1955	▬	...	2142	...	2258e	2358	0042	1054	1354	1654	1854	1954	2243
Newry d.	...	1630g	Ⓐ	⑥	1801	Ⓐ	...	1935	...	...	...	...	...	2013	⚒	...	2200	...	...	...	...	1112	1412	1712	1912	2012	...
Portadown § d.	...	1651g	1705	1715	1822	1830	1832	2000	...	...	...	2000	...	2034	2045	...	2221	2230	...	...	...	1134	1434	1734	1934	2034	...
Lisburn § a.	...	|	1728	1738	|	1853	1855	2023	...	...	...	2023	...	|	2108	...	|	2253	...	...	...	1203	*1510*	*1810*	*2010*	*2110*	...
Belfast Central § a.	...	1727t	1737j	1812	1857	1902j	1927	2055	...	...	...	2057	...	2110	2142	...	2257	2325	...	...	...	1216	1507	1807	2007	2107	...

c – 1000 on ⑥.
e – ⑤ only.
f – Not ⑥.
g – 3–9 minutes later on ⑥.
j – Belfast **G V Street**.
t – 1735 on ⑥.
x – Belfast **Great Victoria Street**. On ⑥ depart Belfast **Central** 0729, arrive Portadown 0828.
z – On ⑥ depart Lisburn 0802, arrive Portadown 0828.
§ – Other local trains run Belfast - Lisburn - Portadown and v.v.

NIR BELFAST - LONDONDERRY and PORTRUSH 231

km		Ⓐ	⑥	Ⓐ	⑥	⑥	Ⓐ	⑥	Ⓐ	⑥	Ⓐ	⑥	Ⓐ	Ⓐ	Ⓐ	⑥	Ⓐ	Ⓐ	⑥	Ⓐ	⑥	Ⓐ	⑦	⑦	⑦	⑦	⑦
	Belfast GVSt. ★ d.	...	0710	0830	0910	1015	1028	1110	1228	1310	1410	1510	1600	1628	1658	1710	1730	...	1910	1943	2110	2115	0943	1243	1543	1843	2143
0	**Belfast Central** d.	0650	0720	0840	0920	1027	1040	1120	1240	1320	1420	1520	1610	1640	1710	1720	1740	1810	1920	1953	2120	2125	0953	1253	1553	1853	2153
33	Antrim d.	0716	0746	0906	0946	1055	1106	1146	1306	1346	1447	1546	1637	1706	1737	1746	1806	1836	1946	2019	2146	2151	1019	1319	1619	1919	2219
52	Ballymena d.	0732	0800	0920	1000	1115	1120	1200	1320	1400	1501	1600	1651	1720	1751	1800	1820	1850	2000	2033	2200	2205	1033	1333	1633	1933	2233
97	**Coleraine** ▲ d.	0815	0838	0958	1038	1154	1158	1238	1358	1438	1542	1638	1735	...	1828	1838	1858	1927	2038	2110	2240	2241	1111	1411	1711	2011	2311
107	Portrush ▲ a.	|	|	|	|	1205	|	|	|	|	|	|	|	...	1838	|	|	1937	|	|	2250	|	|	|	|	|	|
151	**Londonderry** a.	0902	0925	1045	1125	...	1245	1325	1445	1525	1629	1725	1822	...	...	1925	1945	...	2125	2157	*2325*	2328	1158	1458	1758	2058	2358

	Ⓐ	Ⓐ	Ⓐ	⑥	Ⓐ	Ⓐ	⑥	Ⓐ	⑥	Ⓐ	⑥	Ⓐ	⑥	Ⓐ	⑥	⑥	Ⓐ	⑥	Ⓐ	⑥	Ⓐ		⑦	⑦	⑦	⑦	⑦
Londonderry d.	...	...	...	0635	0638	0727	0751	0910	0951	1110	1151	1310	1351	1455	1551	...	1705	1751	1828	1951	2023	...	0723	1023	1323	1623	1923
Portrush ▲ d.	...	0613	0643	|	|	|	|	|	|	|	|	|	|	|	|	1707	|	|	|	|	|	...	|	|	|	|	|
Coleraine ▲ d.	...	0626	0656	0722	0726	0815	0838	0957	1038	1157	1238	1357	1438	1543	1638	1720	1802	1838	1930	2038	2110	...	0810	1110	1410	1710	2010
Ballymena d.	0630	0702	0732	0800	0802	0851	0914	1033	1114	1233	1314	1433	1514	1619	1714	1800	1850	1914	2006	2114	2146	...	0846	1146	1446	1746	2046
Antrim d.	0643	0716	0746	0813	0816	0905	0927	1047	1127	1247	1327	1447	1527	1635	1727	1813	1903	1927	2020	2127	2206	...	0859	1159	1459	1759	2059
Belfast Central a.	0708	0743	0813	0838	0841	0930	1000	1120	1200	1320	1400	1512	1600	1700	1800	1838	1927	2000	2045	2200	2232	...	0924	1224	1524	1824	2124
Belfast GVSt. ★ a.	0718	...	0824	0849	0852	0940	1012	1132	1212	1332	1412	1524	1612	1711	1812	1849	1936	2012	2056	2212	2243	...	0934	1234	1534	1834	2134

km		⑥	Ⓐ	⑥	Ⓐ	Ⓐ	⑥	Ⓐ	⑥	Ⓐ	⑥y	Ⓐ	⑥	Ⓐ	Ⓐ	⑥	⑥	Ⓐ	Ⓐ	⑥	⚒	⚒	Ⓐy	⑥	Ⓐ	Ⓐy	⑥	Ⓐ	
0	Coleraine d.	0725	0730	0845	0820	0915	1000	1000	1045	1115	1154	1200	1245	1315	1400	1400	1445	1455	1545	1600	1645	1730	1828	1845	1900	1927	2000	2033	...
10	Portrush a.	0735	0743	0855	0833	0928	1010	1013	1055	1128	1205	1213	1255	1328	1413	1410	1455	1508	1558	1610	1658	1743	1838	1855	1910	1937	2010	2043	...

		⑥	Ⓐ	⑥	Ⓐ	⑥y	Ⓐ						
Coleraine d.	...	2045	2115	2200	2214	2240	2245	...	...	...	...	...	...
Portrush a.	...	2055	2125	2210	2224	2250	2255	...	...	...	...	...	...

	Ⓐy	Ⓐy	⑥	Ⓐ	Ⓐ	⑥	Ⓐ	⑥	Ⓐ	⑥	Ⓐ	⑥	Ⓐ
Portrush d.	0613	0643	0705	0708	0750	0815	0837	0915	0933	1015	1025	1115	1133
Coleraine a.	0623	0653	0715	0721	0803	0825	0850	0925	0946	1025	1038	1125	1146

		⑥	Ⓐ	⑥	Ⓐ	Ⓐ	⑥	⑥	Ⓐ	⑥	Ⓐ	⑥y	Ⓐ	Ⓐ	⑥	Ⓐ	⑥	Ⓐ	Ⓐ	⑥	Ⓐ	⑥	Ⓐ	⑥	Ⓐ				
Portrush d.	...	1215	1225	1315	1333	1425	1415	1515	1513	1615	1610	1707	1710	1746	1815	1843	1915	1915	1945	2015	2048	2115	2128	2215	2227	...	...	...	...
Coleraine a.	...	1225	1238	1325	1346	1438	1425	1525	1526	1625	1623	1717	1723	1759	1825	1853	1925	1926	1955	2025	2058	2125	2138	2225	2237	...	...	...	...

	⑦	⑦	⑦		⑦	⑦	⑦	⑦		⑦	⑦	⑦	⑦
Coleraine d.	0815	1035	1120	...	1335	1420	1635	1720	...	1935	2020	2235	2315
Portrush a.	0825	1045	1130	...	1345	1430	1645	1730	...	1945	2030	2245	2325

	⑦	⑦	⑦	⑦		⑦	⑦	⑦	⑦	⑦	⑦	⑦	
Portrush d.	0750	0850	1050	1150	...	1350	1450	1650	1750	1950	2050	2250	...
Coleraine a.	0800	0900	1100	1200	...	1400	1500	1700	1800	2000	2100	2300	...

y – Through train to / from Belfast.
★ – Belfast GVSt. (Belfast Great Victoria St.) is the nearest station to Belfast City Centre and the Europa Buscentre is adjacent.
▲ – **COLERAINE - PORTRUSH** (for all trains see panel).

Ulsterbus 212 express 🚌 service, Belfast - Londonderry. Journey time: 1 hour 40 minutes.
Ⓐ: 0645, 0800, 0830, 0900, 0930 and every 30 minutes until 1900, 1930 then 2030, 2130, 2300; also 1545, 1745. ⑥: 0645, 0930, 1030, 1130, 1230, 1330, 1400 and every 30 minutes to 1800, 1830 then 1930, 2030, 2130, 2300.
⑦: 0830, 1000, 1130, 1330, 1430, 1600, 1730, 1930, 2030, 2130, 2215.

Ulsterbus 212 express 🚌 service, Londonderry - Belfast. Journey time: 1 hour 40 minutes.
Ⓐ: 0530, 0545, 0600, 0630, 0700, 0730, 0745, 0800, 0830 and every 30 minutes until 1630, 1700 then 1800, 1930, 2100. ⑥: 0700, 0800, 0830, 0900, 0930, 1000, 1030, 1100, 1130, 1200, 1230, 1300, 1400, 1500, 1600, 1700, 1800, 1930, 2100.
⑦: 0800, 0900, 1030, 1200, 1330, 1500, 1600, 1700, 1800, 1900.

232 BELFAST - ENNISKILLEN and ARMAGH

Ulsterbus 251, 261

From Belfast★ to Enniskillen (Bus Stn) (journey time 2 hours 15 mins)

Ⓐ: 0805, 0905 and hourly until 1905, 2005.
⑥: 0905, 1005, 1105, 1205, 1305, 1505, 1605, 1805, 2005.
⑦: 1605, 2005.

From Enniskillen (Bus Stn) to Belfast★

Ⓐ: 0725, 0825, and hourly until 1625, 1725, 1825◧.
⑥: 0725, 0925, 1025, 1225, 1325, 1525, 1725.
⑦: 1225, 1525, 1725, 1825.

From Belfast★ to Armagh (Bus Stn) (journey time 1 hour 25 mins)

Ⓐ: 0800, 0935, 1035, 1135, 1235, 1335, 1435, 1645, 1715, 1735, 1835, 1935, 2115.
⑥: 1035, 1235, 1435, 1735, 1835, 2005.
⑦: 1335, 1735, 2015, 2200.

From Armagh (Bus Stn) to Belfast★

Ⓐ: 0630, 0715, 0800, 0900, 1000, 1100, 1200, 1300, 1500, 1600, 1700, 1800.
⑥: 0730, 0900, 1100, 1300, 1600, 1700.
⑦: 1210, 1410, 1610, 1830, 2015.

Buses call at **Portadown (Market Street)** 40–75 minutes from Belfast and **Portadown (Northern Bank)** 20–30 minutes from Armagh (Bus Stn).

◧ – Change at Dungannon; arrive Europa Buscentre 2140.

★ – Europa Buscentre / Great Victoria St. Rail Station.

233 BELFAST - LARNE

NIR

From Belfast Central – Ⓐ: 0553**H**, 0652, 0729**H**, 0842**H**, and hourly until 1342**H**, 1442, 1512**H**, 1612, 1642, 1716**H**, 1735, 1812, 1850, 1930**H**, 2030**H**, 2130**H**, 2230**H**, 2330**H**.
⑥: 0629**H**, 0729**H**, and hourly until 2229**H**, 2329**H**. ⑦: 0850**H**, 1020**H**, 1150**H**, 1320**H**, 1450**H**, 1620**H**, 1750**H**, 1920**H**, 2050**H**, 2220**H**.

From Larne Town – Ⓐ: 0600, 0625**S**, 0653**S**, 0727**S**, 0756, 0810**S**, 0857**S**, 0957**S** and hourly until 1457**S**, 1545, 1630**S**, 1715, 1743, 1821, 1845, 1915, 1950, 2030**S**, 2130**S**, 2230**S**.
⑥: 0545**S**, 0644**S**, 0744**S**, 0844**S** and hourly until 2044**S**, 2144**S**, 2240**S**. ⑦: 0820**S**, 0950**S**, 1120**S**, 1250**S**, 1420**S**, 1550**S**, 1720**S**, 1850**S**, 2020**S**, 2150**S**.

Trains call at: **Carrickfergus** 27–29 minutes from Belfast and 28–31 minutes from Larne and **Whitehead** 38–40 minutes from Belfast, 18–21 minutes from Larne.

Trains marked **H** arrive Larne **Harbour** 4 minutes after Larne **Town**. Trains marked **S** depart Larne **Harbour** 3 minutes before Larne **Town**. Journey time Belfast Central - Larne Harbour 57–65 mins.

234 DUBLIN - LONDONDERRY

Bus Éireann 33 / Ulsterbus 274

Dublin ● d.	0400	0715	0915	1000	1145	1345	1545	1745	1945	2145	2300
Dublin Airport ✈ △ d.	0420	0735	0935	1020	1205	1405	1605	1805	2005	2205	2320
Monaghan a.	0545	0910	1110	1155	1340	1540	1740	1940	2140	2340	0055
Monaghan d.	0600	0925	1125	1210	1355	1555	1755	1955	2155	2340	0055
Omagh ▽ a.	0650	1010	1210	1255	1440	1640	1840	2040	2240	0025	0140
Strabane ▽ a.	0720	1045	1245	1330	1515	1715	1915	2115	2315	0100	0215
Londonderry a.	0745	1115	1315	1400	1545	1745	1945	2145	2345	0130	0245

Londonderry d.	0045	0415	0615	0815	1015	1115	1215	1415	1615	1815	2045
Strabane △ d.	0105	0445	0645	0845	1045	1145	1245	1445	1645	1845	2115
Omagh △ d.	0130	0520	0720	0920	1120	1220	1320	1520	1720	1920	2150
Monaghan a.	0210	0605	0805	1005	1205	1305	1405	1605	1805	2005	2235
Monaghan d.	0210	0605	0820	1020	1220	1320	1420	1620	1820	2020	2250
Dublin Airport ✈ ▽ a.	0350	0755	0955	1155	1350	1455	1555	1755	1955	2155	0025
Dublin ● a.	0410	0815	1015	1215	1410	1515	1615	1815	2015	2215	0045

△ – Buses stop here to pick up only. ▽ – Buses stop here to set down only. ● – Dublin **Busaras**. ☛ The calling point in each town is the bus station unless otherwise indicated.

234a DUBLIN - DONEGAL

Bus Éireann 30

				⑤					⑦		
Dublin ● d.	0700	0930	1130	1300	1300	1500	1700	1900	2100	2200	2400
Dublin Airport ✈ △ d.	0720	0950	1150	|	1320	1520	1720	1920	|	2220	0020
Navan ◧ d.	0810	1040	1240	|	1410	1610	1810	2010	|	2250	0050
Cavan d.	0925**c**	1155**c**	1355**c**	1450	1525**c**	1725**u**	1925**u**	2125**u**	2250	0005**c**	0150
Enniskillen d.	1010	1240	1440	1555	1610	1810	2010	2210	2335	0055	0240
Ballyshannon d.	1055	1325	1525	|	1655	1855	2055	2255	|	0140	0325
Donegal ⊡ a.	1120	1350	1550	1700	1720	1920	2120	2320	0030	0205	0350

							⑦			
Donegal ⊡ d.	0200	0500	0700	0900	1100	1300	1500	1500	1645	1830
Ballyshannon d.	0225	0525	0725	0925	1125	1325	|	1525	1710	1855
Enniskillen d.	0305	0605	0810	1010	1210	1410	1600	1610	1755	1940
Cavan d.	0350	0650	0910**c**	1110**c**	1310**c**	1510**c**	1645**u**	1710**c**	1840**s**	2040**c**
Navan ◐ d.	0445	0745	1010	1210	1410	1610	|	1810	1955	2140
Dublin Airport ✈ ▽ a.	0535	0835	1100	1300	1500	1700	|	1900	2045	2230
Dublin ● a.	0555	0855	1120	1320	1520	1720	1840	1920	2105	2250

c – Arrive 15 minutes earlier.
s – Stops to set down only.
u – Stops to pick up only.
● – Dublin **Busaras**.
◐ – Navan **Bypass**.
◧ – Navan **Mercy Convent**.
⊡ – Donegal **Abbey Hotel**.
△ – Buses stop here to pick up only.
▽ – Buses stop here to set down only.

235 LONDONDERRY - GALWAY and GALWAY - CORK

Bus Éireann 51, 64

	⚒	⚒	⚒	⚒	⚒	⚒	⑦	⑦	⑦	⑦
Londonderry d.	...	0720	0830	1200	1600	1830	...	1130	1440	1715
Letterkenny d.	...	0755	0905	1235	1635	1905	...	1205	1515	1750
Donegal (Abbey Hotel) d.	...	0845	0955	1330	1730	1955	...	1255	1605	1840
Ballyshannon d.	...	0905	1015	1350	1750	2015	...	1315	1625	1900
Sligo d.	0815	1000	1115	1500	1900	2100	1115	1415	1720	2000
Knock d.	0925	1110	1225	1610	2010	...	1220	1525	1830	2110
Claremorris (Dalton St.) d.	|	1122	|	1622	|	...	1232	|	|	2122
Galway (Bus Station) ❖ a.	1045	1230	1345	1730	2130	...	1345	1645	1950	2230

Cork d.	...	...	0725	0825	and hourly until	1725	1825	1925	2055
Mallow (Town Park) d.	...	...	0800	0900		1800	1900	2000	2130
Charleville d.	...	...	0830	0930		1830	1930	2030	2200
Limerick (Rail Station) a.	...	...	0910	1010		1910	2010	2110	2240
Limerick (Rail Station) d.	0725	0825	0925	1025		1925	2025	...	...
Shannon Airport ✈ d.	0755	0855	0955	1055		1955	2055	...	...
Ennis d.	0825	0925	1025	1125		2025	2125	...	...
Galway (Bus Station) ❖ a.	0945	1045	1145	1245		2145	2245	...	...

	⚒	⚒	⚒	⚒	⚒	⑤	⑦	⑦	⑦	⑦
Galway (Bus Station) ❖ d.	0900	1200	1400	1600	1815	...	1000	1400	1600	2100
Claremorris (Dalton St.) d.	|	1308	|	|	1923	...	|	|	|	2208
Knock d.	1020	1320	1520	1720	1935	...	1120	1520	1720	2220
Sligo d.	1145	1445	1645	1845	2045	2050	1245	1645	1900	2330
Ballyshannon d.	1225	1525	1725	1925	...	2130	1325	1725	1940	...
Donegal (Abbey Hotel) d.	1250	1550	1750	1950	...	2155	1350	1750	2005	...
Letterkenny d.	1340	1640	1840	2040	...	2245	1440	1840	2055	...
Londonderry a.	1415	1715	1915	2115	...	2325	1515	1915	2130	...

Galway (Bus Station) ❖ d.	...	...	0705	0805	and hourly until	1705	1805	1905	2005
Ennis d.	...	...	0820	0920		1820	1920	2020	2120
Shannon Airport ✈ d.	...	...	0850	0950		1850	1950	2050	2150
Limerick (Rail Station) a.	...	...	0920	1020		1920	2020	2120	2220
Limerick (Rail Station) d.	0725	0835	0935	1035		1935	2035	...	...
Charleville d.	0800	0910	1010	1110		2010	2110	...	...
Mallow (Town Park) d.	0830	0940	1040	1140		2040	2140	...	...
Cork a.	0915	1025	1125	1225		2125	2225	...	...

❖ – Change buses at Galway. Minimum connection time 45 minutes.

☛ The calling point in each town is the bus station unless otherwise indicated.

236 DUBLIN - SLIGO

IÉ

km		Ⓐ 🍷	⚒ 🍷	⚒ 🍷	⚒ 🍷	⚒ 🍷	⚒ 🍷	⚒ 🍷	Ⓐ	Ⓐ	Ⓐ	⚒ 🍷	
0	**Dublin Connolly** d.	0705	0905	1105	1305	1505	1600	1705	1715	1805	1817	1905	...
26	Maynooth d.	0732	0937	1136	1335	1535	1629	1734	1757	1833	1859	1937	...
83	Mullingar d.	0817	1017	1216	1415	1615	1714	1814	1851	1916	1948	2017	...
125	**Longford** d.	0848	1047	1246	1444	1645	1744	1845	1923	1948	2019	2047	...
143	Dromod d.	0900	1100	1259	1457	1658	1801	1858	...	...	...	2059	...
159	Carrick on Shannon d.	0916	1116	1314	1513	1713	1816	1915	...	...	...	2116	...
173	Boyle d.	0933	1135	1334	1534	1734	1828	1935	...	...	...	2129	...
219	**Sligo** a.	1009	1210	1410	1610	1810	1907	2010	...	...	...	2205	...

km		⑦ 🍷		⑦ 🍷		⑦ 🍷	⑦ 🍷	⑦ 🍷		⑦ 🍷	
0	**Dublin Connolly** d.	0905	...	1305	...	1505	1600	1705	...	1905	...
26	Maynooth d.	0932	...	1333	...	1534	1629	1731	...	1933	...
83	Mullingar d.	1012	...	1413	...	1614	1714	1811	...	2015	...
125	**Longford** d.	1043	...	1442	...	1643	1743	1843	...	2045	...
143	Dromod d.	1056	...	1456	...	1656	1801	1857	...	2057	...
159	Carrick on Shannon d.	1113	...	1512	...	1712	1816	1913	...	2114	...
173	Boyle d.	1134	...	1534	...	1734	1828	1935	...	2127	...
219	**Sligo** a.	1210	...	1610	...	1810	1909	2010	...	2204	...

	Ⓐ	Ⓐ	Ⓐ 🍷	⚒ 🍷	⚒ 🍷	⚒ 🍷	⚒ 🍷	⚒ 🍷	⚒ 🍷	⚒ 🍷	Ⓐ	
Sligo d.	...	...	0545	0700	0900	1100	1300	1500	1700	1900	...	...
Boyle d.	...	...	0617	0733	0934	1133	1333	1533	1733	1934	...	...
Carrick on Shannon d.	...	...	0628	0745	0947	1146	1346	1546	1746	1945	...	...
Dromod d.	...	...	0644	0800	1002	1201	1401	1601	1800	2000	...	...
Longford d.	0545	0615	0658	0815	1017	1216	1416	1616	1815	2021	2105	...
Mullingar d.	0618	0648	0727	0855	1054	1253	1453	1652	1852	2055	2138	...
Maynooth d.	0658	0729	0810	0936	1135	1334	1534	1733	1934	2136	2217	...
Dublin Connolly a.	0736	0818	0848	1005	1201	1400	1559	1800	2002	2202	2250	...

	⑦ 🍷		⑦ 🍷		⑦ 🍷		⑦ 🍷		⑦ 🍷		⑦ 🍷
Sligo d.	0900	...	1100	...	1300	...	1500	...	1700	...	1900
Boyle d.	0933	...	1133	...	1333	...	1533	...	1733	...	1934
Carrick on Shannon d.	0945	...	1145	...	1345	...	1545	...	1745	...	1945
Dromod d.	1000	...	1200	...	1400	...	1600	...	1800	...	2000
Longford d.	1015	...	1215	...	1415	...	1615	...	1817	...	2015
Mullingar d.	1051	...	1246	...	1452	...	1652	...	1852	...	2054
Maynooth d.	1131	...	1320	...	1531	...	1730	...	1931	...	2135
Dublin Connolly a.	1203	...	1355	...	1606	...	1759	...	2004	...	2209

236a BALLYBROPHY - ROSCREA - LIMERICK

IÉ

km		Ⓐ	⚒ 🍷	⚒		⚒ ◇🍷	⚒		⑦ ◇🍷	⑦	
0	Dublin Heuston d.	...	0900	...	...	1725	...	...	1825	...	...
107	Ballybrophy d.	...	1007	1015	...	1849	1855	...	1947	1955	...
123	Roscrea d.	...	...	1034	...	...	1914	...	...	2014	...
154	Nenagh d.	0740	...	1109	...	...	1949	...	...	2049	...
199	**Limerick** a.	0842	...	1207	...	...	2047	...	...	2143	...

	⚒	⚒h ◇✕		⚒	⚒h ◇✕	Ⓐ		⑦	⑦ ◇🍷	
Limerick d.	0630	...	...	1645	...	1745	...	1735	...	...
Nenagh d.	0728	...	...	1742	...	1846	...	1832	...	...
Roscrea d.	0808	...	...	1818	...	...	...	1908	...	...
Ballybrophy a.	0828	0836	...	1838	1910	...	...	1928	1937	...
Dublin Heuston a.	...	0950	...	...	2025	...	...	...	2100	...

h – ✕ on Ⓐ, 🍷 on ⑥.

◇ – Also conveys 1st class.

IÉ — DUBLIN - ROSSLARE — 237

km		Ⓐ	⚒	⚒	⚒🍷	Ⓐ	Ⓐ	⚒🍷§		⑦	⑦🍷	⑦🍷§
0	**Dublin Connolly** ▲ d.	...	0732	1205	1330	1630	1730	1830	...	1025	1345	1830
11	Dún Laoghaire ▲ d.	...	0757	1226	1356	1655	1756	1856	...	1044	1402	1847
21	Bray ▲ d.	...	0818	1248	1417	1717	1817	1917	...	1102	1423	1904
47	Wicklow d.	...	0840	1315	1441	1742	1844	1944	...	1127	1446	1929
80	Arklow d.	...	0908	1346	1510	1810	1915	2012	...	1155	1514	1957
97	Gorey d.	...	0924	...	1523	1823	1931	2024	...	1207	1526	2009
126	Enniscorthy d.	0625	0943	...	1542	1842	1952	2044	...	1227	1546	2029
150	**Wexford** d.	0647	1005	...	1604	1904	2013	2106	...	1249	1608	2051
160	Rosslare Strand d.	0705	1023	...	1622	...	...	2123	...	1306	1625	2108
166	**Rosslare** Europort a.	0710	1030	...	1628	...	...	2130	...	1314	1632	2115

	Ⓐ	Ⓐ	⚒	⚒🍷§	⚒🍷	⚒	⚒	Ⓐ		⑦🍷	⑦🍷	⑦	
Rosslare Europort d.	...	0535	...	0750	1255	...	1755	...	...	0940	1420	1740	...
Rosslare Strand d.	...	0540	...	0756	1301	...	1801	...	...	0946	1426	1745	...
Wexford d.	...	0559	...	0815	1320	...	1820	1930	...	1005	1445	1805	...
Enniscorthy d.	...	0619	0623f	0835	1340	...	1840	1950	...	1025	1505	1827	...
Gorey d.	0600	...	0645	0856	1401	...	1904	2027	...	1046	1528	1847	...
Arklow d.	0612	...	0700	0911	1413	1435	1915	2039	...	1058	1540	1900	...
Wicklow d.	0640	...	0733	0939	1441	1509	1942	2107	...	1126	1608	1928	...
Bray ▲ d.	0704	...	0801	1001	1503	1534	2004	2132	...	1148	1631	1953	...
Dún Laoghaire ▲ d.	0722	...	0820	1020	1521	1552	2023	2151	...	1208	1648	2011	...
Dublin Connolly ▲ a.	0749	...	0847	1044	1545	1616	2048	2215	...	1230	1710	2035	...

f – Ⓐ only.
§ – Does not connect with Ferry: Rosslare - Fishguard and v.v.
▲ – Additional surburban trains (*DART*) run Howth - Dublin Connolly - Dún Laoghaire - Bray. Trains run every 10–15 minutes on ⚒, every 20–30 minutes on ⑦.

IÉ; Bus Éireann 40, 55, 372 — LIMERICK - WATERFORD - ROSSLARE — 239

km		⚒	⚒	⚒	⚒		🚌	🚌 ⚒	🚌	🚌 ⚒	🚌 x
0	**Limerick** d.	*0755*	*1355*	...	*1800*	...	0825	1230	1615	1730	2030
35	**Limerick Jct.** d.	0850	1510	...	1845	...	0855	1300	1645	1800	2100
40	Tipperary d.	0859	1520	...	1854	...	0900	1305	1650	1805	2105
62	Cahir d.	0923	1545	...	1918	...	0930	1335	1720	1835	2135
79	Clonmel d.	0942	1605	...	1937	...	0950	1355	1740	1855	2155
101	Carrick on Suir d.	1006	1640	...	2001	...	1010	1415	1800	1915	2215
124	**Waterford** a.	1032	1705	...	2027	...	1055	1455	1840	1955	2255
	Waterford d.	...	...	1720	...	...	*1130*c	*1630*	*1930*	...	...
	Wexford d.	...	...	|	...	...	*1230*c	*1730*	*2030*	...	...
186	**Rosslare** Europort a.	...	...	1835	...	...	*1255*c	*1830*e	*2050*	...	...

	⚒	⚒	⚒	⚒	⚒	🚌	🚌	🚌	🚌	🚌
Rosslare Europort d.	...	0700	...	...	...	*0700*x	*0900*c	*1300*	*1440*	*1900*
Wexford d.	...	|	...	...	...	*0725*x	*0925*c	*1325*	*1505*	*1925*
Waterford a.	...	0820	...	...	...	*0845*	*1025*	*1425*	*1605*	*2020*
Waterford d.	0630	...	...	1230	1615	0850	1050	1450	1650	2030
Carrick on Suir d.	0655	...	...	1255	1641	0920	1120	1520	1720	2100
Clonmel d.	0718	...	...	1318	1706	0945	1145	1545	1745	2125
Cahir d.	0737	...	...	1337	1726	1010	1210	1610	1810	2150
Tipperary d.	0800	...	...	1400	1750	1035	1235	1635	1835	2215
Limerick Jct. a.	0812	...	...	1412	1801	1040	1240	1640	1840	2220
Limerick a.	*0916*	...	...	*1526*	*1911*	1115	1315	1715	1915	2300

c – ⚒ only. e – Change additionally at Wexford. x – 10–15 minutes later on ⑦.

Additional journeys: –
Limerick - Waterford 🚌 0930 ⚒, 1130, 1430, 1840 ⑦.
Waterford - Limerick 🚌 0750 ⚒, 1250 ⚒, 1750 ⚒, 1830 ⑦.
Waterford - Wexford 🚌 0700, 0900 ⚒.
Wexford - Waterford 🚌: 1720 Ⓐ; 1745 ⑦; 1840 Ⓐ.

Buses call at rail stations **except**: Limerick (Bus Station), Limerick Junction (Bit and Bridle Pub), Tipperary (Abbey St), Cahir (Castle St), Carrick (Greenside), Waterford (Bus Station).

IÉ — DUBLIN - GALWAY, BALLINA and WESTPORT — 240

km		⚒	⚒🍷	⚒🍷	⚒🍷	⚒🍷	⚒🍷	⚒🍷	⚒🍷	⚒🍷	⚒h ◇🍴	⚒	⚒ ◇🍷	⚒ ◇🍷	⚒🍷	⑦🍷	⑦	⑦ ◇🍷	⑦🍷	⑦	⑦🍷	⑦🍷	⑦🍷	⑦🍷	⑦ ◇🍷	⑦ ◇
0	**Dublin Heuston** 245 d.	...	0730	0730	0930	1130	1230	1430	1530	1530	1630	1710	1745	1830	1915	0830	...	1130	1330	...	1430	1530	1630	1830	1845	2030
48	Kildare 245 d.	...	|	|	1003	1203	1303	|	|	|	|	1745	|	|	1950	0903	...	1203	1405	...	|	|	|	1911	1922	|
67	Portarlington 245 d.	...	0815	0815	1019	|	1319	1517	|	|	|	1802	1836	|	2006	0918	...	1218	1422	...	1516	|	1716	1926	1937	2117
93	Tullamore d.	...	0833	0833	1037	1234	1337	1538	1636	1636	1735	1820	1854	1933	2029	0936	...	1236	1439	...	1535	1636	1734	1943	2002	2135
129	**Athlone** d.	0705	0907	0910	1109	1304	1408	1604	1708	1711	1802	1853	1935	1959	2055	1008	1015	1306	1509	...	1604	1706	1804	2014	2028	2204
152	Ballinasloe d.	0719	0922	|	1124	1320	|	1621	1723	|	1818	...	1951	|	2112	1024	|	1322	|	...	1621	|	1821	|	2045	2221
187	Athenry d.	0749	0957	|	1149	1347	|	1648	1747	|	1847	...	2015	|	2138	1053	|	1347	|	...	1648	|	1852	|	2112	2245
208	**Galway** a.	0807	1015	|	1208	1407	|	1705	1810	|	1905	...	2033	|	2155	1113	|	1406	|	...	1712	|	1910	|	2130	2305
160	Roscommon d.	...	...	0932	▬	...	1439	▬	...	1733	▬	...	...	2024	▬	...	1036	▬	1532	...	...	1729	▬	2037	▬	...
186	Castlerea d.	...	...	0950	...	...	1458	...	...	1752	...	...	...	2043	...	...	1055	...	1551	...	...	1748	...	2056	...	...
204	Ballyhaunis d.	...	...	1004	⚒	...	1511	...	...	1808	...	...	...	2057	...	...	1109	...	1605	...	...	1802	...	2110	...	...
222	Claremorris d.	...	...	1018	q	...	1524	⚒	...	1823	⚒	...	...	2112	⚒	...	1124	⑦	1620	...	...	1819	⑦	2125	⑦	...
240	Manulla Junction § d.	...	...	1033	1036	...	1538	1540	...	1837	1840	...	...	2126	2129	...	1138	1141	1634	1637	...	1833	1836	2139	2142	...
273	**Ballina** a.	...	...	|	1104	...	|	1608	...	|	1908	...	...	|	2157	...	|	1209	|	1705	...	|	1904	|	2210	...
246	Castlebar d.	...	...	1041	...	...	1545	...	...	1844	...	...	...	2134	...	...	1146	...	1642	...	...	1841	...	2147	...	...
264	**Westport** a.	...	...	1100	...	...	1600	...	...	1900	...	...	...	2155	...	...	1205	...	1700	...	...	1900	...	2205	...	...

	Ⓐ	Ⓐ ◇	⚒🍷	Ⓐ	⚒h ◇🍴	⚒	⚒ ◇🍷	⚒🍷	⚒🍷	⚒ q	⚒🍷	⚒🍷	⚒	⚒🍷	Ⓐ	⑦	⑦🍷	⑦🍷	⑦	⑦ ◇🍷	⑦	⑦🍷	⑦ ◇🍷	⑦	⑦🍷	⑦
Westport d.	...	...	...	0515	...	...	0715	...	...	...	1315	...	...	1745	...	...	0745	...	...	1315	...	1545	...	...	1745	...
Castlebar d.	...	...	...	0527	...	...	0727	...	...	...	1327	...	...	1757	...	...	0757	...	...	1327	...	1557	...	...	1757	...
Ballina d.	...	...	...	|	...	0705	|	...	...	1305	|	...	1735	|	...	0735	|	...	1305	|	1535	|	...	1735	|	...
Manulla Junction § d.	...	...	...	|	...	0733	0735	...	...	1333	1335	...	1803	1805	...	0803	0805	...	1333	1335	1603	1605	...	1803	1805	...
Claremorris d.	...	...	...	0547	...	...	0750	...	...	▬	1352	...	▬	1822	...	▬	0820	...	▬	1350	▬	1621	...	▬	1820	...
Ballyhaunis d.	...	...	...	0600	...	...	0803	...	...	...	1405	...	...	1835	...	...	0833	...	...	1403	...	1634	...	...	1833	...
Castlerea d.	...	...	...	0615	...	...	0818	...	...	⚒	1420	...	⚒	1850	...	⑦	0847	...	⑦	1418	⑦	1649	...	⑦	1848	...
Roscommon d.	...	...	...	0635	...	...	0838	...	...	🍷	1440	...	🍷	1910	...	◇🍷	0906	...	🍷	1438	◇🍷	1709	...	🍷	1908	...
Galway d.	...	0505	0605	|	0705	...	|	0905	1105	1305	|	1505	1805	|	2215	0805	|	1105	1305	|	1505	|	1705	1805	|	1930
Athenry d.	...	0518	0618	|	0718	...	|	0918	1118	1318	|	1518	1818	|	2228	0818	|	1123	1318	|	1518	|	1718	1818	|	1943
Ballinasloe d.	...	0543	0640	|	0741	...	|	0944	1146	1345	|	1543	1845	|	2252	0843	|	1148	1346	|	1543	|	1743	1846	|	2007
Athlone d.	0515	0601	0705	0705	0759	...	0903	1002	1204	1406	1506	1603	1903	1935	2310	0901	0930	1206	1404	1508	1603	1740	1803	1905	1933	2027
Tullamore d.	0541	0629	0731	0731	0832	...	0931	1036	1233	1434	1539	1635	1934	2008	...	0935	0956	1235	1438	1536	1635	1814	1831	1942	2003	...
Portarlington 245 d.	0600	0649	0754	0754	|	...	0951	1056	1253	1456	1559	1654	1953	2028	...	0955	1015	1255	1458	1555	1656	1833	1851	2001	2022	...
Kildare 245 d.	0615	0703	0810	0810	|	...	|	|	|	|	1612	|	2008	|	...	1009	|	1309	|	|	|	1848	1905	2015	|	...
Dublin Heuston 245 a.	0700	0753	0850	0850	0935	...	1045	1147	1340	1542	1650	1742	2045	2120	...	1047	1110	1345	1545	1645	1747	1925	1947	2050	2110	...

h – 🍴 on Ⓐ, 🍷 on ⑥. q – 🚌 on ⑥. ◇ – Also conveys [1]. § – Passenger transfer point only.

IÉ — DUBLIN - KILKENNY - WATERFORD — 241

km		⚒🍷	⚒🍷	⚒🍷	⚒🍷	⚒🍷	⚒	⚒ ◇🍷	Ⓐ	⑦🍷	⑦🍷	⑦🍷	⑦ ◇🍷
0	**Dublin Heuston** △ d.	0720	0910	1110	1510	1635	1735	1835	2010	0910	1410	1740	1840
48	Kildare △ d.	0755	0945	1143	1546	1715	|	|	2055	0946	1446	1816	1916
72	Athy d.	0817	1002	1201	1604	1732	1830	1923	2109	1004	1504	1834	1933
90	Carlow d.	0830	1015	1214	1617	1745	1845	1936	2123	1017	1517	1847	1946
106	Muine Bheag d.	0843	1028	1227	1630	1758	...	1950	...	1030	1530	1902	1959
130	**Kilkenny** a.	0903	1047	1246	1649	1818	...	2009	...	1049	1549	1923	2018
	Kilkenny d.	0907	1052	1251	1654	1822	...	2014	...	1054	1554	1927	2023
147	Thomastown d.	0919	1104	1303	1706	1834	...	2026	...	1106	1606	1939	2035
179	**Waterford** a.	0945	1137	1337	1733	1900	...	2050	...	1133	1633	2005	2103

	Ⓐ	⚒ ◇🍷	⚒🍷	⚒🍷	⚒🍷	⚒🍷	⚒🍷	⚒🍷	⑦🍷	⑦🍷	⑦ ◇🍷	⑦🍷
Waterford d.	...	0610	0710	0740	1100	1300	1500	1820	0905	1305	1505	1805
Thomastown d.	...	0633	|	0803	1123	1323	1523	1849	0928	1328	1528	1828
Kilkenny a.	...	0648	|	0818	1138	1338	1538	1904	0943	1343	1543	1843
Kilkenny d.	...	0653	|	0823	1143	1343	1543	1909	0948	1348	1550	1848
Muine Bheag d.	...	0708	|	0843	1158	1358	1558	1925	1003	1403	1605	1903
Carlow d.	0625	0720	0806	0855	1213	1410	1616	1939	1016	1415	1617	1915
Athy d.	0636	0733	|	0908	1226	1423	1629	1953	1029	1428	1630	1932
Kildare △ d.	0654	0751	|	0926	1246	1445	1647	2013	1047	1448	1648	1950
Dublin Heuston △ a.	0747	0840	0910	1010	1330	1530	1730	2055	1130	1530	1730	2032

h – 🍴 on Ⓐ, 🍷 on ⑥. ◇ – Also conveys [1]. △ – For additional trains Dublin - Kildare and v.v, see Tables **240**, **245**.

IÉ — LIMERICK - GALWAY — 242

Service due to start January 2010

km		⚒	⚒	⚒	⚒	⚒		⑦	⑦	⑦	⑦	
0	**Limerick** d.	0600	0935	1155	1415	1805	...	0900	1240	1610	1830	...
39	Ennis d.	0705x	1014	1234	1454	1844	...	0941	1321	1649	1909	...
68	Gort d.	0733	1041	1301	1521	1911	...	1009	1349	1716	1936	...
97	Athenry d.	0808	1119	1335	1556	1945	...	1042	1422	1750	2010	...
117	**Galway** a.	0825	1134	1351	1613	2000	...	1059	1439	1809	2025	...

	⚒	⚒	⚒	⚒	⚒		⑦	⑦	⑦	⑦	
Galway d.	0640	0945	1210	1430	1725	...	0825	1205	1625	1840	...
Athenry d.	0656	1003	1226	1446	1741	...	0841	1221	1641	1857	...
Gort d.	0732	1041	1301	1521	1814	...	0914	1254	1716	1936	...
Ennis d.	0800	1108	1328	1548	1844	...	0941	1321	1743	2003	...
Limerick a.	0839	1148	1408	1628	1924	...	1023	1402	1824	2043	...

x – Arrive 0640.

245 DUBLIN - LIMERICK, TRALEE and CORK IE

km		⚒h ◇✕	⚒	⚒ 🍷	⚒	⚒ 🍷	⚒	⚒ ◇🍷	⚒	⚒ ◇🍷	⚒	⚒h ◇✕	⚒	⚒h ◇✕	⚒	⚒ ◇🍷	⚒	⚒ ◇🍷	⚒ 🍷	⚒h ◇✕	⚒	⚒h ◇✕	⚒h ◇✕	⚒	⚒h ◇✕
0	**Dublin Heuston** .. **240** d.	0700	...	0800	...	0900	...	1000	...	1100	...	1200	...	1300	...	1400	...	1500	1525	1600	...	1625	1700	...	1705
48	Kildare **240** d.	|	...	|	...	|	...	|	...	1130	...	|	...	1330	...	|	...	|	1557	|	...	|	|	...	|
67	Portarlington **240** d.	|	...	|	...	|	...	|	...	1144	...	|	...	1344	...	|	...	|	1613	|	...	|	|	...	|
82	Portlaoise d.	0752	...	|	...	0954	...	1052	...	1156	...	|	...	1356	...	|	...	|	1625	|	...	|	|	...	|
107	Ballybrophy d.	|	...	|	...	1007	...	|	...	|	...	|	...	1409	...	|	...	|	1640	|	...	|	|	...	|
127	Templemore d.	|	...	0914	...	1018	...	|	...	1218	...	|	...	1420	...	|	...	|	1654	|	...	1739	|	...	1820
139	Thurles d.	0821	...	0922	...	1026	...	1121	...	1226	...	1318	...	1428	...	1518	...	|	1701	1718	...	1746	1818	...	1828
172	**Limerick Junction** .. § d.	0846x	0847	0947x	0947	1050x	1050	1147x	1147	1250x	1253	1343x	1344	1452x	1454	1543x	1544	|	|	1743x	1744	|	1841x	1842	|
208	**Limerick** § a.	|	0916	|	1016	|	1119	|	1216	|	1327	|	1410	|	1526	|	1613	|	1748	|	1813	1835	|	1911	|
**	Ennis a.	|	*1014*	|	...	|	*1234*	|	*1320*	|	...	|	*1454*	|	...	|	*1710*	|	*1844*	|	...	...	|	*2010*	|
208	Charleville d.	|	...	|	...	1107	...	|	...	1309	...	|	...	1511	...	|	...	1656	...	|	...	...	|	...	1906
232	**Mallow** **246** d.	0918	...	1017	...	1122	...	1219	...	1324	...	1415	...	1526	...	1615	...	1712	...	1815	...	...	1912	...	1923
	Tralee **246** a.	|	...	|	...	|	...	|	...	|	...	|	...	|	...	|	...	|	...	|	...	...	|	...	2100
266	**Cork** **246** a.	0953	...	1052	...	1150	...	1253	...	1355	...	1450	...	1555	...	1650	...	1745	...	1850	...	...	1948	...	...

	⚒	⚒ ◇🍷	⚒h ◇✕	⚒	⚒	⚒ ◇🍷	⚒	⚒ ◇	⚒	⑦ 🍷	⑦	⑦	⑦ ◇🍷	⑦	⑦ ◇🍷	⑦ ◇🍷	⑦	⑦ ◇🍷	⑦ 🍷	⑦ ◇🍷	⑦ ◇🍷	⑦ 🍷	⑦ ◇🍷	⑦ ◇🍷	⑦ ◇🍷
Dublin Heuston ... **240** d.	...	1725	1800	...	1840	1900	...	2100	...	0825	...	...	1000	...	1125	1200	...	1300	1325	1400	1500	1525	1600	1700	1800
Kildare **240** d.	...	1806	|	...	1918	|	...	|	...	|	...	...	|	...	1157	|	...	|	1357	|	|	1557	|	|	|
Portarlington **240** d.	...	1822	|	...	1934	|	...	2142	...	|	...	...	|	...	1213	|	...	|	1413	|	|	1613	|	|	|
Portlaoise d.	...	1834	|	...	1945	1957	...	2155	...	0919	...	...	1052	...	1225	|	...	|	1425	|	|	1625	|	|	|
Ballybrophy d.	...	1849	|	...	1959	|	...	|	...	|	...	...	|	...	1240	|	...	|	1440	|	|	1640	|	|	|
Templemore d.	...	1901	|	...	2010	|	...	|	...	|	...	...	|	...	1252	|	...	|	1452	|	|	1652	|	|	|
Thurles d.	...	1910	1918	...	2020	2026	...	2224	...	0948	...	...	1121	...	1301	1318	...	1418	1501	1518	1618	1701	1718	1818	1918
Limerick Junction ... § d.	...	|	1943x	1944	...	2051x	2052	2249x	2250	1010x	1013	...	1146x	1147	|	1343x	1344	|	|	1543x	|	|	1743x	|	1943
Limerick § a.	...	1955	|	2013	...	|	2125	|	2319	|	1042	...	|	1215	1348	|	1413	|	1548	*1613*	|	1748	*1813*	|	*2025*
Ennis a.	...	...	|	*2100*	...	|	...	|	...	|	*1140*	...	|	*1319*	...	|	*1500*	|	*1649*	|	|	...	*1909*	|	|
Charleville d.	...	...	|	...	...	2110	...	|	...	1029	...	...	|	...	...	|	...	1459	...	|	|	...	|	|	|
Mallow **246** d.	2000	...	2015	...	...	2126	...	2321	...	1045	...	1050	1218	...	...	1415	...	1515	...	1615	1712	...	1815	1912	2015
Tralee **246** a.	|	...	|	...	...	|	...	|	...	1222	...	|	|	...	...	|	...	|	...	|	|	...	|	|	|
Cork **246** a.	2024	...	2050	...	...	2158	...	2355	...	...	...	1115	1253	...	...	1450	...	1550	...	1650	1745	...	1850	1945	2050

	⑦ 🍷	⑦	⑦ ◇🍷	⑦ ◇🍷	⑦	⑦ ◇🍷	⑦ ◇	⑦ 🍷
Dublin Heuston .. **240** d.	1825	...	1900	1910	...	1925	2100	2125
Kildare **240** d.	1904	...	|	|	...	1957	|	2200
Portarlington **240** d.	1920	...	|	1955	...	2013	2142	2216
Portlaoise d.	1932	...	|	|	...	2025	|	2228
Ballybrophy d.	1947	...	|	|	...	2040	|	|
Templemore d.	1959	...	|	|	...	2052	|	|
Thurles d.	2008	...	2021	2033	...	2101	2221	2258
Limerick Junction .. § d.	|	...	|	2057x	2057	|	2246	|
Limerick § a.	2055	2100	|	|	2125	2148	|	2345
Ennis a.	...	2140	|	|	—	...	|	...
Charleville d.	...	...	|	2114	⑦	...	|	...
Mallow **246** d.	...	...	2115	2130	2135	...	2318	...
Tralee **246** a.	...	...	|	2305	|	...	|	...
Cork **246** a.	...	...	2145	...	2200	...	2355	...

	⚒	⚒ ◇	⚒h ◇✕	⚒ ◇🍷	⚒	⚒h ◇✕	⚒	⚒h ◇✕	⚒	⚒	⚒	⚒h ◇✕
Cork **246** d.	...	0505	0630	...	...	...	...	0730	0830	...	...	...
Tralee **246** d.	...	|	|	...	...	...	...	|	|	...	...	0720
Mallow **246** d.	...	0527	0652	...	...	...	...	0752	0855	...	...	0857
Charleville d.	...	0542	|	...	...	...	...	|	...	...	...	0909
Ennis d.	...	|	|	...	0645	...	...	|	...	0800	...	|
Limerick § d.	0535	|	|	0655	0725	0735	0755	|	...	0839	0900	|
Limerick Junction § d.	|	0606	|	0730	...	|	0827	0831	...	...	0928	0934
Thurles d.	0617	0625	|	0748	...	0817	...	0849	...	...	...	0952
Templemore d.	0625	0634	|	0755	...	0825	...	|	...	...	...	|
Ballybrophy d.	|	0647	|	0806	...	0836	...	|	...	...	...	|
Portlaoise d.	0649	0710	|	0820	...	0850	...	|	...	...	...	|
Portarlington **240** d.	0701	0722	|	|	...	|	...	|	...	...	...	|
Kildare **240** d.	0718	|	|	|	...	|	...	|	...	...	...	|
Dublin Heuston **240** a.	0800	0823	0900	0915	...	0950	...	1020	...	...	...	1115

	⚒	⚒ ◇🍷	⚒	⚒ ◇🍷	⚒	⚒ 🍷	⚒	⚒ 🍷	⚒	⚒h ◇✕	⚒	⚒	⚒ ◇🍷	⚒	⚒ ◇🍷	⚒	⚒	⚒h ◇✕	⚒	⚒h ◇✕	⚒	⚒ ◇🍷	⚒	⚒	⚒ ◇🍷
Cork **246** d.	...	0930	...	1030	...	1130	...	1230	...	1330	...	...	1430	...	1530	...	...	1630	...	1730	...	1830	...	...	2030
Tralee **246** d.	...	|	...	|	...	|	...	|	...	|	...	...	|	...	|	...	...	|	...	|	...	|	...	...	|
Mallow **246** d.	...	0952	...	1052	...	1151	...	1251	...	1352	...	...	1452	...	1552	...	...	1652	...	1754	...	1852	...	...	2052
Charleville d.	...	|	...	1108	...	|	...	|	...	|	...	...	1507	...	|	...	...	1707	...	|	...	1907	...	...	|
Ennis d.	...	|	*1015*	|	*1108*	|	...	|	...	|	1328	...	|	*1500*	|	1548	...	|	*1715*	|	...	|	1844	...	|
Limerick § d.	1000	|	1100	|	1200	|	1255	|	1355	|	1408	1455	|	1555	|	1628	1655	|	1800	|	1855	|	1924	2055	|
Limerick Junction § d.	1027	1031	1130	1134	1227	1231	1322	1328	1425	1430	...	1522	1533	1624	1630	...	1722	1732	1831	1834	1925	1933	...	2122	2130
Thurles d.	...	1049	...	|	...	1249	...	|	...	1448	...	...	1551	...	1648	...	...	1750	...	1852	...	1951	...	...	2148
Templemore d.	...	|	...	1157	...	1256	...	|	...	1455	...	...	|	...	|	...	...	1757	...	1859	...	1959	...	...	|
Ballybrophy d.	...	|	...	|	...	1307	...	|	...	|	...	...	|	...	|	...	...	1808	...	1910	...	|	...	...	|
Portlaoise d.	...	1118	...	|	...	1321	...	1412	...	1518	...	...	|	...	1717	...	...	1822	...	1924	...	2022	...	...	2217
Portarlington **240** d.	...	|	...	|	...	1332	...	|	...	1530	...	...	|	...	|	...	...	1834	...	|	...	2035	...	...	2229
Kildare **240** d.	...	|	...	|	...	1345	...	|	...	1543	...	...	|	...	1741	...	...	1847	...	|	...	2049	...	...	2242
Dublin Heuston ... **240** a.	...	1225	...	1323	...	1425	...	1515	...	1625	...	...	1720	...	1823	...	...	1930	...	2025	...	2125	...	...	2323

	⑦ ◇🍷	⑦ ◇🍷	⑦ ◇🍷	⑦ ◇🍷	⑦ ◇🍷	⑦ ◇🍷	⑦	⑦ ◇🍷	⑦ ◇🍷	⑦ ◇🍷	⑦ ◇🍷	⑦	⑦ ◇🍷	⑦ ◇🍷	⑦ ◇🍷	⑦	⑦ ◇🍷	⑦ ◇🍷	⑦	⑦ ◇🍷	⑦ 🍷	⑦	⑦	⑦ ◇🍷	
Cork **246** d.	0830	...	...	1030	...	1230	...	1330	...	1430	...	...	1530	...	1630	...	1730	...	...	1830	...	...	...	1930	...
Tralee **246** d.	|	...	...	|	...	|	...	|	...	|	1345	...	|	...	|	...	|	...	...	|	1745	...	...	|	...
Mallow **246** d.	0852	...	...	1052	...	1252	...	1352	...	1452	1512	...	1552	...	1652	...	1752	...	...	1852	1920	...	...	1952	...
Charleville d.	0907	...	...	1107	...	1307	...	|	...	1507	1527	...	|	...	1707	...	|	...	...	1907	|	...	...	|	...
Ennis d.	|	*0750*	*0941*	|	*1150*	|	...	|	*1321*	|	|	...	|	*1525*	|	...	|	*1743*	...	|	|	1910	...	|	...
Limerick § d.	|	0835	1035	|	1235	|	1355	|	1435	|	|	1555	|	1635	|	1755	|	1835	1855	|	|	1950	1955	|	...
Limerick Junction ... § d.	0933	|	|	1133	|	|	1424	1430	|	|	|	1624	1630	|	|	1824	1830	|	1923	1933	1956	...	2023	2030	...
Thurles d.	|	0917	1117	|	1317	1348	...	1448	1517	1548	1607	...	1648	1717	1748	...	1848	1917	...	1951	2014	...	...	2048	...
Templemore d.	|	0925	1125	|	1325	|	...	|	1525	|	|	...	|	1725	|	...	|	1925	...	|	|	...	...	|	...
Ballybrophy d.	|	0937	1137	|	1337	|	...	|	1537	|	|	...	|	1737	|	...	|	1937	...	|	|	...	...	|	...
Portlaoise d.	|	0952	1152	|	1352	|	...	|	1552	|	|	...	|	1752	|	...	|	1954	...	|	|	...	...	|	...
Portarlington **240** d.	|	1004	1204	|	1404	|	...	|	1604	|	|	...	|	1804	|	...	|	2006	...	|	|	...	...	|	...
Kildare **240** d.	|	1018	1218	|	1418	|	...	|	1618	|	|	...	|	1818	|	...	|	2020	...	|	|	...	...	|	...
Dublin Heuston ... **240** a.	1120	1058	1258	1320	1458	1520	...	1620	1658	1720	1735	...	1820	1858	1920	...	2020	2100	...	2125	2140	...	...	2220	...

h – ✕ on Ⓐ, 🍷 on ⑥. x – Arrives 1–2 minutes earlier. ◇ – Also conveys [1]. § – See also Table **247**. ** – Limerick - Ennis: *40 km.*

246 (DUBLIN -) CORK - MALLOW - TRALEE IE

km		Ⓐ	⚒	⚒	⚒	⚒	⚒	⚒h ◇✕	⚒	⑦	⑦ 🍷	⑦	⑦	⑦	⑦	⑦	⑦ ◇🍷	
	Dublin **245** d.	...	*0700*	*0900*	*1100*	*1300*	*1500*	1705	*1900*	...	0828	*1000*	*1200*	*1300*	*1500*	*1700*	1910	...
0	**Cork** **245** d.	0620	0900	*1030*	*1230*	*1430*	*1655*	*1830*	2100	*0830*	*1015*	1210	1405	*1430*	*1630*	1850	*2055*	...
34	**Mallow** **245** d.	0700	0930	1130	1330	1530	1725	1923	2135	0925	1045	1245	1440	1525	1725	1925	2130	...
66	Millstreet d.	0723	0953	1153	1353	1553	1748	1949	2258	0948	1112	1308	1508	1548	1748	1948	2157	...
100	Killarney d.	0754	1023	1223	1423	1623	1823	2023	2225	1015	1141	1336	1544	1624	1824	2026	2226	...
134	**Tralee** a.	0829	1058	1258	1458	1658	1858	2100	2300	1050	1222	1412	1618	1658	1858	2102	2305	...

	Ⓐ	⚒h ◇✕	⚒	⚒	⚒	⚒	⚒	⚒		⑦	⑦	⑦	⑦ ◇🍷	⑦	⑦	⑦ 🍷	⑦	
Tralee d.	0520	0720	0915	1115	1315	1515	1715	1915	...	0715	1115	1305	1345	1515	1715	1750	1915	...
Killarney d.	0549	0755	0946	1146	1346	1546	1746	1946	...	0746	1146	1340	1421	1546	1746	1825	1946	...
Millstreet d.	0613	0823	1012	1212	1412	1612	1812	2013	...	0812	1212	1406	1446	1612	1812	1852	2012	...
Mallow **245** d.	0655	0852	1040	1240	1440	1640	1844	2044	...	0840	1255	1433	1512	1640	1845	1920	2045	...
Cork **245** a.	0720	*0925*	*1150*	*1355*	*1555*	*1745*	1910	2110	...	*0920*	1320	|	*1550*	*1745*	1910	*2050*	2110	...
Dublin **245** a.	*0900*	1115	*1323*	*1515*	*1720*	*1930*	*2125*	*2323*	...	*1120*	*1520*	*1720*	1735	*1920*	*2125*	2140	...	...

h – ✕ on Ⓐ, 🍷 on ⑥. ◇ – Also conveys [1].

CORK - COBH Journey time: 24 minutes *19 km.*

⚒ 0530 Ⓐ, 0600 ⑥, 0630 Ⓐ, 0700, 0730, 0800, 0830 Ⓐ, 0900, 1000, then hourly until 1600, 1630, 1700, 1730, 1800, 1830, 1900 Ⓐ, 1930 Ⓐ, 2000, 2130, 2230.

† 0800, 0900, 1100, 1200, 1300, 1430, 1600, 1700, 1830, 2000, 2100, 2200.

COBH - CORK

⚒ 0600 Ⓐ, 0630 ⑥, 0700 Ⓐ, 0730, 0800 Ⓐ, 0830, 0900 Ⓐ, 0930, 1030, then hourly until 1630, 1700, 1730, 1800, 1830, 1900, 1930 Ⓐ, 2000 Ⓐ, 2030, 2200, 2300.

† 0830, 0930, 1130, 1230, 1330, 1500, 1630, 1730, 1900, 2030, 2130, 2230.

CORK - MIDLETON Journey time: 24 minutes *19 km.*

⚒ 0615, 0645, 0715, 0745 Ⓐ, 0815, 0845 Ⓐ, 0915, 1015, then hourly until 1715, 1745,Ⓐ, 1815, 1915, 2015, 2115, 2215.

† 0815, 1015, 1215, 1415, 1615, 1715, 1815, 2015.

MIDLETON - CORK

⚒ 0645, 0715 Ⓐ, 0745, 0815 Ⓐ, 0845, 0915 Ⓐ, 0945, 1045, then hourly until 1745, 1815 Ⓐ, 1845, 1945, 2045, 2145, 2245.

† 0845, 1045, 1245, 1445, 1645, 1745, 1845, 2045.

247 LIMERICK JUNCTION - LIMERICK IE

Shuttle service connecting with main-line trains. *35 km.* Journey time: 25–40 minutes. For through services to or from Dublin Heuston see Table **245** above. For notes see Table **246**.

From Limerick Junction ⚒: 0800, 0847, 0947, 1050, 1147, 1253, 1344, 1454, 1544, 1635, 1744, 1842, 1944, 2052, 2250. ⑦: 1013, 1147, 1344, 1430, 1544, 1631, 1744, 1831, 1950, 2057.

From Limerick ⚒: 0655, 0755, 0900, 1000, 1100, 1200, 1255, 1355, 1455, 1555, 1655, 1800, 1855, 2010, 2055. ⑦: 0935, 1055, 1255, 1355, 1455, 1555, 1655, 1755, 1855, 1955.

FRANCE

SEE MAP PAGES 170/1

Operator: Société Nationale des Chemins de Fer Français (SNCF), unless otherwise shown.

Services: Most trains convey first and second classes of accommodation; many purely local services are second class only (it is not possible to show classes in the tables). *TGV* (*train à grande vitesse*) trains have a bar car in the centre of the train selling drinks and light refreshments. Selected *TGV* trains have an at-seat meal service in first class. On *Téoz* services refreshments are available from a trolley wheeled through the train. Certain other long-distance trains also have refreshments available (sometimes seasonal or on certain days of the week), but it is not possible to identify these in the tables as this information is no longer supplied. Regional and local trains (outside Paris) are classified *TER* (*Train Express Regional*). Domestic night trains are classified *Lunéa* - sleeping accommodation consists of modern four-berth couchettes (first class) or six-berth couchettes (second class). Women-only compartments are available on request. There are no sleeping cars on domestic trains in France. Note that all luggage placed on luggage racks must be labelled.

Timings: Valid **December 13, 2009 - June 12, 2010**. Amended services operate on and around public holidays and, whilst we try to show holiday variations, passengers are advised to confirm their train times locally before travelling during these periods. Public holidays in 2010 are Jan. 1, Easter Monday (Apr. 5), May 1, 8, Ascension Day (May 13), Whit Monday (May 24), July 14, Aug. 15, Nov. 1, 11, Dec. 25. **Engineering work** can often affect schedules; major changes are shown in the tables where possible but other changes may occur at short notice. Where a train is shown *subject to alteration* on certain dates this often means that part of the journey may be provided by bus, often with earlier departure or later arrival times.

Tickets: **Seat reservations** are compulsory for travel by all *TGV*, *Téoz* and *Lunéa* trains, and are also available for a small fee on most other long distance trains. Advance reservations are recommended for travel to ski resorts during the winter sports season. **Supplements** (which include the cost of seat reservation) are payable for travel in *TGV*, *Téoz* and *Lunéa* trains. Rail tickets must be date-stamped by the holder before boarding the train using the self-service validating machines (composteurs) at the platform entrances – this applies to all tickets except passes and hand-written tickets. Note that where two *TGV* units are coupled together, they will often carry different train numbers for reservation purposes.

Note: The *TGV* services **Lille Europe - Charles de Gaulle ✈ - Marne-la-Vallée - Lyon / Bordeaux / Rennes / Nantes** are shown in the International section (Table **11**).

PARIS - LILLE - TOURCOING — 250

TGV Nord high-speed trains

For slower trains via Douai see Table **256**. For **Charles de Gaulle ✈ - Lille** see Table **11**. Certain trains continue to Dunkerque, Calais or Boulogne - see Table **265**.

km		TGV 7001	TGV 7005	TGV 7207	TGV 7211	TGV 7015	TGV 7021	TGV 7229*	TGV 7033	TGV 7235	TGV 7043		TGV 7245	TGV 7049	TGV 7053	TGV 7059	TGV 7061	TGV 7065	TGV 7275	TGV 7277	TGV 7281	TGV 7079	TGV 7285	TGV 7087
		①	Ⓐ	Ⓐ		①–⑥								Ⓐ	⑤		Ⓐ		Ⓐ		Ⓐ	⑤		Ⓐ
		g				n									f							f	‡	
0	**Paris Nord** d.	0628	0658	0728	0758	0828	0858	0958	1058	1158	1258	...	1428	1458	1528	1558	1628	1658	1728	1758	1828	1849	1858	1928
227	**Lille Europe** a.	|	|	0827	|	|	|	1057	|	|	|	...	1526	|	|	|	|	|	1827	|	1926	|	1956	|
227	**Lille Flandres** a.	0730	0800	...	0900	0930	1000	...	1200	1303	1400	...	...	1600	1630	1700	1730	1800	...	1900	...	1951	...	2030
227	**Lille Flandres 405** d.	...	...	...	0912	...	...	...	...	1313	...	...	...	...	...	...	...	...	...	1910	...	...	...	...
237	Roubaix **405** a.	...	...	...	0926	...	...	...	...	1327	...	...	...	...	...	...	...	...	...	1924	...	...	...	...
240	**Tourcoing 405** a.	...	...	...	0932	...	...	...	...	1333	...	...	...	...	...	...	...	...	...	1930	...	...	...	...

	TGV 7091	TGV 7291	TGV 7093	TGV 7089	TGV 7293	TGV 7097	TGV 7097	TGV 7099	
	⑦	①–⑥	⑥	Ⓐ	⑦	⑤	⑦	u	
	e	n	t	⊡	e	f	e	⊡	
Paris Nord d.	1958	1958	2058	2058	2058	2158	2158	2258	...
Lille Europe a.	|	|	|	|	|	|	|	|	...
Lille Flandres a.	2100	2100	2200	2219	2200	2300	2300	0018	...
Lille Flandres 405 d.	...	2112	...	...	2212	...	...	...	...
Roubaix **405** a.	...	2126	...	...	2225	...	...	...	...
Tourcoing 405 a.	...	2132	...	...	2232	...	...	...	...

	TGV 7000	TGV 7002	TGV 7206	TGV 7022	TGV 7214	TGV 7220	TGV 7222	TGV 7028	
	Ⓐ	Ⓐ	①–⑥	①–⑥	Ⓐ	①–⑥	⑦	Ⓐ	
			n	n		n	e		
Tourcoing 405 d.	...	...	0630	...	...	...	0747	...	...
Roubaix **405** d.	...	...	0636	...	...	...	0753	...	...
Lille Flandres 405 a.	...	...	0650	...	...	...	0807	...	...
Lille Flandres d.	0600	0630	0700	0703	...	...	0817	0830	...
Lille Europe d.	|	|	|	|	0732	0802	|	|	...
Paris Nord a.	0702	0732	0802	0808	0832	0902	0920	0932	...

	TGV 7030	TGV 7036	TGV 7040	TGV 7246	TGV 7050	TGV 7254		TGV 7256	TGV 7058	TGV 7062	TGV 7066	TGV 7270	TGV 7072	TGV 7074	TGV 7082	TGV 7288	TGV 7088	TGV 7092	TGV 7292	TGV 7294	TGV 7294	TGV 7098	TGV 7298	TGV 7096	
						①–⑥			⑤		Ⓐ		Ⓐ		Ⓐ	Ⓑ	⑥	Ⓒ	Ⓐ	⑤	⑦	⑥	⑦	Ⓐ	
						n			f							h	t			f	e	t	e	⊡	
Tourcoing 405 d.	...	...	...	1130	...	...	...	1430	...	...	...	...	...	...	...	...	...	...	...	2030	2030	...	...	...	...
Roubaix **405** d.	...	...	...	1136	...	...	...	1436	...	...	...	...	...	...	...	...	...	...	...	2036	2036	...	...	...	...
Lille Flandres 405 a.	...	...	...	1150	...	...	...	1450	...	...	...	...	...	...	...	...	...	...	...	2050	2050	...	...	...	...
Lille Flandres d.	...	1000	1100	1200	1300	...	...	1500	1530	1600	1630	...	1730	1800	1830	...	1900	...	...	2100	2100	...	...	...	...
Lille Europe d.	0902	|	|	|	|	1324	...	|	|	|	|	1702	|	|	|	1902	|	2002	2010	|	|	2202	2202	2209	...
Paris Nord a.	1002	1102	1202	1302	1402	1426	...	1602	1632	1702	1732	1802	1832	1902	1932	2002	2002	2102	2111	2202	2202	2302	2302	2323	...

e – Also Apr. 5, May 24.
f – Also Dec. 24, 31, May 12; not Dec. 25, Jan. 1.
g – Also Apr. 6, May 25; not Apr. 5, May 24.
h – Not Dec. 25, Jan. 1, May 13.
n – Not Apr. 5, May 24.
t – Also Dec. 25, Jan. 1, May 13.
u – Not May 9 - 13, 16 - 20.
TGV – Ⓡ, supplement payable.
⊡ – Via Arras (Table **256**).
‡ – Also runs as **7289** on ⑦.
* – Runs as **7029** on ⑦.

PARIS - LAON — 251

km		⚒	⚒	†	⑥t	Ⓐ			Ⓐ	†	⑥t	Ⓐ		Ⓐ	⑥t	Ⓐ	Ⓒ	Ⓐ	Ⓐ	Ⓒ	Ⓐ			Ⓐ	
0	**Paris Nord** d.	0558	0712	0806	0806	0831	0957	...	1202	1246	1326	1326	...	1448	1448	1530	1600	1631	1745	1752	1847	...	2005	2118	...
61	Crépy-en-Valois d.	0651	0744	0840	0856	0908	1038	...	1244	1322	1402	1403	...	1536	1536	1612	1642	1706	1831	1832	1927	...	2043	2153	...
105	Soissons d.	0730	0814	0912	0928	0938	1110	...	1316	1355	1431	1434	...	1614	1615	1645	1711	1735	1903	1901	1958	...	2113	2223	...
140	**Laon** a.	0755	0838	0939	0954	1004	1136	...	1340	1425	1456	1501	...	1652	1648	1709	1735	1804	1931	1926	2023	...	2139	2248	...

	Ⓐ	Ⓐ	Ⓐ	⑥t	†	⚒	†	⚒	Ⓒ	Ⓐ	⚒	†	Ⓐ	⑥t	†	Ⓐ	†	Ⓐ	⑥t	Ⓑh	Ⓐ	⚒	†	Ⓐ	†
Laon d.	0506	0532	0640	0640	0710	0753	0848	0933	1118	1119	1222	1231	1405	1554	1602	1621	1718	1718	1739	1803	1907	2013	2029	2114	2107
Soissons d.	0533	0600	0710	0708	0737	0822	0916	1001	1144	1148	1254	1258	1432	1625	1626	1649	1743	1751	1806	1831	1935	2041	2054	2143	2134
Crépy-en-Valois d.	0601	0630	0741	0740	0806	0852	0947	1031	1213	1220	1329	1330	1502	1657	1702	1724	1816	1821	1841	1900	2006	2112	2122	2215	2208
Paris Nord a.	0637	0706	0826	0818	0853	0927	1022	1110	1253	1253	1417	1420	1539	1749	1753	1802	1855	1902	1918	1937	2039	2158	2201	2256	2305

h – Also May 1, 8.
t – Not May 1, 8.

AMIENS - LAON - REIMS — 252

km		⑥t	Ⓐ	Ⓐv	†	⚒u	⚒s	†	⑥t	Ⓐ	Ⓑh‡	⑥t	Ⓐ‡	Ⓐ	Ⓐ	Ⓒ	Ⓒ	Ⓐ	†	Ⓒ	Ⓐ	⚒	Ⓐ		†
0	**Amiens** d.	0602	0611	0724	0800	0830	...	...	...	*1107*	1226	1247	1453	...	1611	1612	...	...	...	1805	1806	1847	...	*1927*a	2125
	Cambrai **257** d.	|	|	|	|	|	0858	...	...	|	|	|	|	...	|	|	...	...	...	|	|	|	...	|	|
	St Quentin **255/7** d.	|	|	|	|	|	0941	...	...	|	|	|	|	1637	|	|	1716	1730	...	|	|	|	1940	|	|
80	Tergnier **255/7** a.	0710	0720	0831	0907	0932	0958	...	...	*1209*	1334	1355	1550	1656	1714	1717	1735	1751	...	1908	1911	1955	1959	*2027*a	2228
80	Tergnier d.	0724	0735	0832	0912	...	1000	...	...	1233	1346	1357	1551	1658	1722	...	1749	1806	...	1922	1924	...	2001	2037	2230
108	Laon a.	0753	0801	0859	0935	...	1023	...	...	1300	1411	1423	1613	1722	1745	...	1816	1831	...	1949	1950	...	2029	2102	2252
108	Laon d.	...	0802	...	...	...	1027	1211	1256	1301	...	...	*1703*	*1732*	...	...	*1840*r	1833	1925	1950	...	...	2031	...	...
160	**Reims** a.	...	0844	...	...	...	1103	1257	1343	1354	...	...	*1740*	*1808*	...	...	*1928*r	1925	2012	2026	...	...	2105	...	...

	Ⓐ	⚒	Ⓐ	⚒	†	⚒	Ⓐ	†n	Ⓐ	Ⓒy	Ⓐ	Ⓐ	⑥t	Ⓐ	⑥t	Ⓐ	Ⓒ	Ⓐ	Ⓐ	†	Ⓐ	Ⓐ	†	⚒	
Reims d.	...	...	...	0627	...	...	0734	1100	1119	...	1222	...	1222	1505	1509	...	...	...	1652	1705	1733	...	1830	1845	...
Laon a.	...	...	...	0708	...	...	0811	1150	1154	...	1309	...	1309	1540	1546	...	...	...	1737	1742	1820	...	1916	1933	...
Laon d.	0553	0628	0654	0710	0720	0741	0813	...	1158	1202	...	1313	1310	1541	...	1627	1706	*1723*	1739	1744	1826	...	...	*1945*a	2005
Tergnier a.	0615	0653	0720	0731	0745	0808	0836	...	1222	1225	...	1339	1333	1604	...	1651	1732	*1748*	1757	1805	1850	...	...	*2011*a	2032
Tergnier **255/7** d.	0624	0655	0722	0736	0747	0811	...	...	1233	1233	...	1341	...	1610	...	1652	1742	1807	1758	...	1852	1858	...	...	2039
St Quentin **255/7** a.	0643	|	|	0752	|	|	...	...	|	|	...	|	...	1623	...	|	|	|	1816	...	|	1916	...	...	|
Cambrai **257** a.	...	|	|	0841	|	|	...	...	|	|	...	|	...	...	...	|	|	|	...	...	|	...	...	...	|
Amiens a.	...	0801	0825	...	0843	0910	...	...	1337z	1339	...	1444	...	...	...	1753	1848	1913	...	...	1956	...	...	...	2144

a – Ⓐ only.
h – Also May 1, 8.
n – Subject to alteration on May 13, 16.
r – ⑥ (not May 1, 8).
s – Subject to alteration on Ⓐ Apr. 6 - 16, Apr. 26 - May 7.
t – Not May 1, 8.
u – Subject to alteration on Ⓐ May 3 - 21.
v – Subject to alteration Apr. 26 - May 7.
y – Not May 13.
z – By 🚌 Chaulnes - Amiens.
‡ – Subject to alteration on Ⓐ Mar. 8 - 19.

Additional journey on ⚒: Laon d. 0636 - Reims a. 0725.

🚌 AMIENS - TGV HAUTE-PICARDIE — 253

SNCF 🚌 service

All *TGV* departures and arrivals at TGV Haute-Picardie (Table 11) have 🚌 connections from / to Amiens and St Quentin. Departs 50 - 60 mins before the train; journey 40 minutes. Reservations for the 🚌 should be made at the same time as for the *TGV* service.

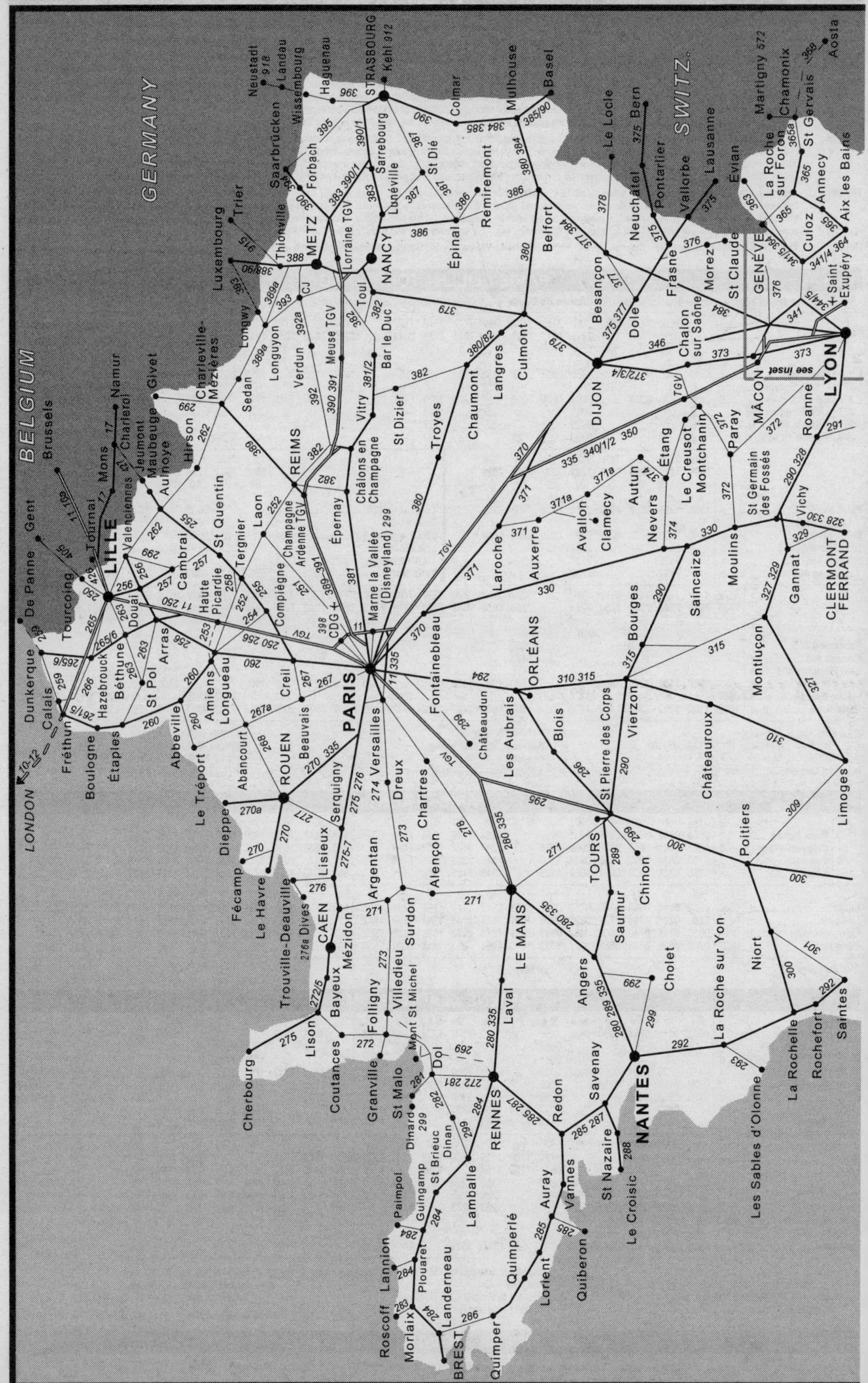
LONDON
Dunkerque
De Panne
Gent
Brussels
BELGIUM
Namur
Charleroi
Mons
Tournai
Tourcoing
LILLE
Calais
Fréthun
Boulogne
Étaples
Hazebrouck
Béthune
St Pol
Arras
Douai
Valenciennes
Cambrai
Jeumont
Maubeuge
Aulnoye
Hirson
Givet
Charleville-Mézières
Sedan
Longwy
Luxembourg
Trier
GERMANY
Saarbrücken
Neustadt
Landau
Wissembourg
Haguenau
STRASBOURG
Kehl
Forbach
Thionville
METZ
Sarrebourg
Lunéville
NANCY
St Dié
Épinal
Remiremont
Colmar
Mulhouse
Basel
Belfort
Besançon
Le Locle
Bern
Neuchâtel
Pontarlier
Vallorbe
Lausanne
SWITZ.
Frasne
Morez
St Claude
Évian
Martigny
Chamonix
St Gervais
Aosta
La Roche sur Foron
Annecy
Aix les Bains
Culoz
GENÈVE
Saint Exupéry
LYON
see inset
Dole
Chalon sur Saône
DIJON
MÂCON
Roanne
Paray
Le Creusot Montchanin
Étang
Autun
Nevers
Clamecy
Avallon
Auxerre
Laroche
Langres
Culmont
Chaumont
Troyes
St Dizier
Vitry
Bar le Duc
Toul
Verdun
Longuyon
Meuse TGV
Lorraine TGV
REIMS
Châlons en Champagne
Épernay
Champagne Ardenne TGV
Laon
Tergnier
St Quentin
Haute Picardie
Compiègne
Amiens
Longueau
Abbeville
Le Tréport
Creil
Beauvais
Abancourt
ROUEN
Dieppe
Fécamp
Le Havre
PARIS
CDG
Marne la Vallée (Disneyland)
Fontainebleau
Versailles
Serquigny
Lisieux
Trouville-Deauville
Dives
CAEN
Bayeux
Lison
Cherbourg
Coutances
Granville
Folligny
Villedieu
Mont St Michel
Argentan
Surdon
Mézidon
Dreux
Chartres
Alençon
LE MANS
Laval
RENNES
Dol
St Malo
Dinard
Dinan
St Brieuc
Lamballe
Guingamp
Paimpol
Lannion
Plouaret
Morlaix
Roscoff
Landerneau
BREST
Quimper
Quimperlé
Lorient
Auray
Quiberon
Vannes
Redon
Savenay
St Nazaire
Le Croisic
NANTES
Angers
Saumur
Cholet
TOURS
Chinon
St Pierre des Corps
Blois
ORLÉANS
Les Aubrais
Châteaudun
Vierzon
Bourges
Saincaize
Moulins
Châteauroux
Montluçon
Limoges
Poitiers
Niort
La Rochelle
Rochefort
Saintes
La Roche sur Yon
Les Sables d'Olonne
St Germain des Fossés
Vichy
Gannat
CLERMONT FERRAND

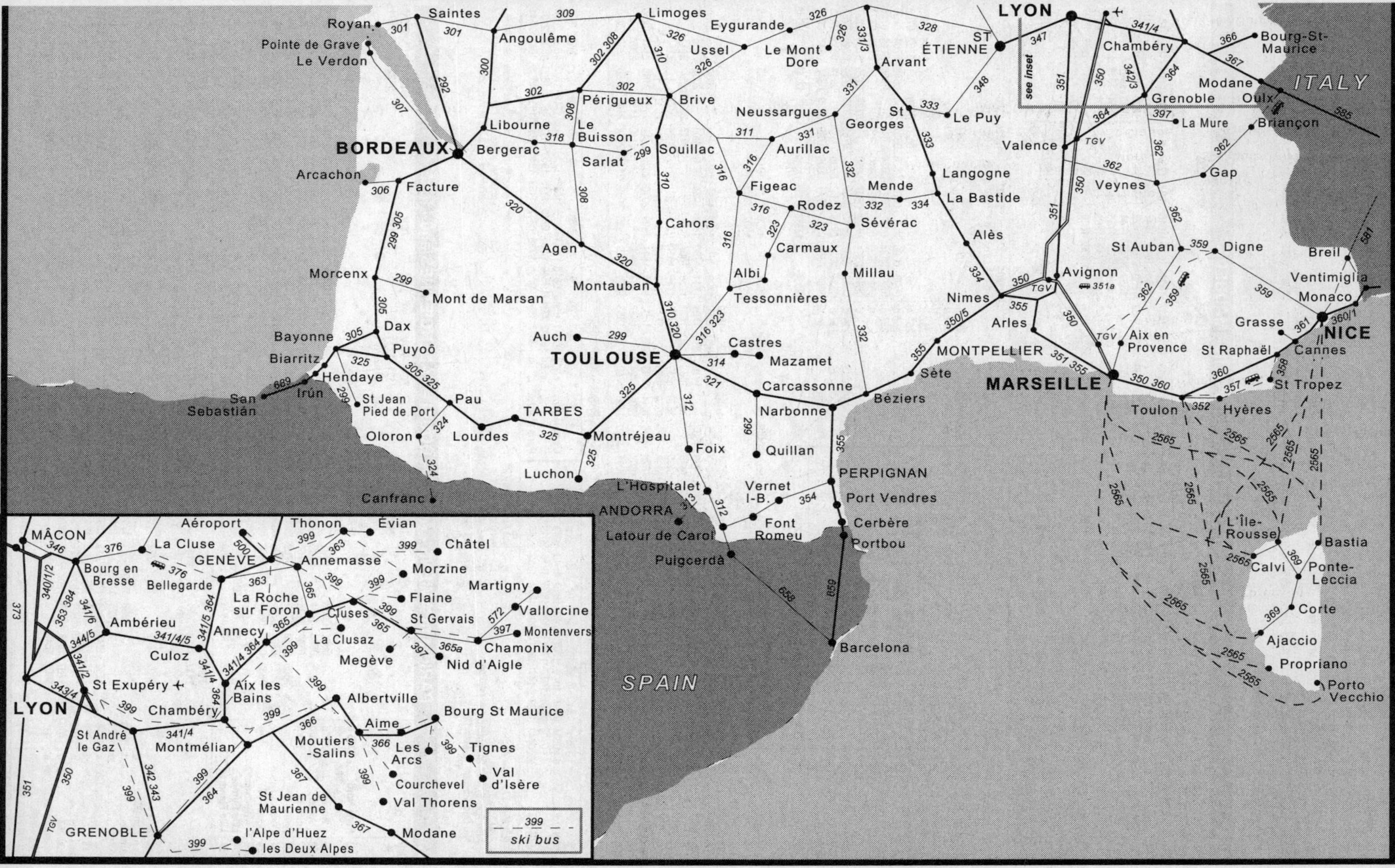
LYON
ST ÉTIENNE
see inset
ITALY
Bourg-St-Maurice
Modane
Oulx
Briançon
Chambéry
Grenoble
La Mure
Valence
Gap
Veynes
St Auban
Digne
Breil
Ventimiglia
Monaco
NICE
Grasse
Cannes
St Raphaël
St Tropez
Avignon
Aix en Provence
MARSEILLE
Toulon
Hyères
Arles
Nimes
MONTPELLIER
Sète
Alès
La Bastide
Langogne
Mende
Le Puy
St Georges
Arvant
Neussargues
Aurillac
Figeac
Rodez
Sévérac
Millau
Carmaux
Albi
Tessonnières
Castres
Mazamet
Béziers
Carcassonne
Narbonne
Quillan
PERPIGNAN
Port Vendres
Cerbère
Portbou
Barcelona
Vernet I-B.
Font Romeu
L'Hospitalet
ANDORRA
Latour de Carol
Puigcerdà
Foix
TOULOUSE
Auch
Montauban
Cahors
Souillac
Brive
Ussel
Le Mont Dore
Eygurande
Limoges
Périgueux
Le Buisson
Sarlat
Bergerac
Libourne
Angoulême
Saintes
Royan
Pointe de Grave
Le Verdon
BORDEAUX
Arcachon
Facture
Agen
Morcenx
Mont de Marsan
Dax
Bayonne
Biarritz
Hendaye
Irún
San Sebastián
Puyoô
St Jean Pied de Port
Pau
Oloron
Lourdes
TARBES
Montréjeau
Luchon
Canfranc
SPAIN
Bastia
L'Île-Rousse
Calvi
Ponte-Leccia
Corte
Ajaccio
Propriano
Porto Vecchio
MÂCON
Aéroport
La Cluse
Bourg en Bresse
Bellegarde
GENÈVE
Thonon
Évian
Annemasse
Châtel
Morzine
Flaine
Martigny
Vallorcine
Montenvers
Chamonix
Nid d'Aigle
St Gervais
Megève
La Clusaz
Cluses
La Roche sur Foron
Annecy
Ambérieu
Culoz
St Exupéry
Aix les Bains
Albertville
Bourg St Maurice
Aime
Les Arcs
Tignes
Val d'Isère
Moutiers -Salins
Courchevel
Val Thorens
St Jean de Maurienne
Modane
St André le Gaz
Montmélian
GRENOBLE
l'Alpe d'Huez
les Deux Alpes
ski bus
TGV

254 AMIENS - COMPIÈGNE

km			Ⓐ	Ⓐ	Ⓐ	Ⓐn	Ⓐn	Ⓐ	Ⓐn	Ⓐ	Ⓐ	Ⓐ	Ⓐ	Ⓐ		⑥t	Ⓒ	Ⓒ	Ⓒ	⑥t	†	Ⓒ	Ⓒ	Ⓒ	Ⓒ
0	**Amiens** d.	Ⓐ	0557	0626	0743	0909	1100	1232	1440	1642	1704	1751	1829	1951	Ⓒ	0620	0745	0926	1130	1245	1330	1630	1740	1912	2021
5	Longueau d.		|	0632	0751	|	|	1238	|	|	1710	1758	1835	1957		0626	|	0933	|	1251	1336	|	1746	|	2027
76	**Compiègne** a.		0658	0746	0907	1012	1158	1347	1538	1740	1822	1909	1944	2111		0735	0846	1045	1231	1400	1445	1731	1900	2011	2136

		Ⓐ	Ⓐ	Ⓐ	Ⓐ	Ⓐn	Ⓐn	Ⓐn	Ⓐ	Ⓐn	Ⓐ	Ⓐ	Ⓐ	Ⓐ		⑥t	Ⓒ	Ⓒ	Ⓒ	⑥t	†	Ⓒ	Ⓒ	Ⓒ	Ⓒ
Compiègne d.	Ⓐ	0552	0636	0717	0759	0836	0914	1100	1232	1440	1642	1753	1842	1918	Ⓒ	0620	0745	0930	1130	1245	1330	1630	1745	1910	2021
Longueau a.		0705	0733	0825	|	0945	|	|	1341	|	|	1904	1937	2031		0729	|	1039	|	1354	1440	|	1854	|	2130
Amiens a.		0712	0739	0831	0856	0951	1012	1158	1347	1538	1744	1911	1943	2038		0735	0846	1045	1231	1400	1446	1731	1900	2013	2136

n – Subject to alteration May 25 - June 4.

t – Not May 1, 8.

255 PARIS - COMPIÈGNE - ST QUENTIN - MAUBEUGE

km				12305		12309		12313		12321				12327	12325				12331	2335			12337	12339	
		Ⓐ	†	①–⑥ n	Ⓐ §	Ⓐ §	⑦	§	⑥ t	⚒	⑥ t	Ⓐ	†	Ⓒ	Ⓐ	Ⓐ	Ⓒ	Ⓐ			Ⓒ	Ⓐ	Ⓐ	Ⓑ h	†
0	**Paris Nord** ▶ d.	0640	0640	0734	0746	0837	0907	1037	1207	1237	...	1207	1243	1437	1437	1422	1616	1616	1637	1737	...	1740	1804	1837	1840
51	Creil ▶ d.	0706	0713	|	0823	|	0944	|	1236	|	←	1239	1317	|	|	1458	1643	1643	|	|	...	1807	|	|	1914
84	**Compiègne** ▶ d.	0753	0752	0816	0846	0917	1018	1118	1312	1319	1322	1326	1339	1518	1532	1539	1706	1722	1718	1819	...	1830	1852	1925	1936
108	Noyon d.	0807	0812	|	0900	|	1030	|	→	|	1347	1351	1352	|	|	1552	1719	1744	|	|	...	1843	1907	|	1949
124	Chauny d.	0819	0824	|	0911	|	1041	|	...	|	1400	1404	1402	|	|	1604	1731	1755	|	|	...	1854	1919	|	1959
131	Tergnier 257 d.	0827	0831	|	0918	|	1047	|	...	|	1408	1413	1409	|	|	1610	1743	1803	|	|	...	1901	1927	|	2010
154	**St Quentin** 257 a.	0841	0845	0848	...	0952	1100	1153	...	1352	1426	1429	1422	1551	1605	...	1802	1820	1752	1852	...	...	1940	1957	2027
154	**St Quentin** 257 d.	...	...	0850	...	...	...	1153	...	1354	...	1430	...	1553	1607	...	...	...	1754	1854	...	...	...	1959	...
181	Busigny 257 d.	...	...	|	...	...	...	|	...	|	...	1447	...	|	|	...	...	...	|	1912	1920	...	...	|	...
207	*Cambrai* 257 a.	...	...	|	...	...	...	|	...	|	...	...	...	|	|	...	...	...	|	1937	|	...	...	|	...
217	Aulnoye Aymeries 262 d.	...	...	0924	...	...	...	1228	...	1427	...	...	...	1626	1638	...	...	...	1827	...	1946	...	...	2034	...
229	**Maubeuge** 262 d.	...	...	0934	...	...	...	1242	...	1437	...	...	...	1637	1649	...	...	...	1837	...	2001	...	...	2045	...

			12343			12349				
	Ⓐ	⑥ t		†	Ⓐ	⑦ e	Ⓐ	⑥ t	Ⓑ u	
Paris Nord ▶ d.	1907	1907	1937	1943	2010	2104	2104	2134	2237	...
Creil ▶ d.	1934	1934	|	2020	2044	|	2131	2208	2315	...
Compiègne ▶ d.	1958	1957	2019	2056	2122	2145	2155	2246	2337	...
Noyon d.	2013	2020	|	2117	2144	2200	2209	2300	2349	...
Chauny d.	2025	2032	|	2128	2155	2213	2221	2311	2359	...
Tergnier 257 d.	2033	2045	|	2135	2201	2221	2229	2318	0006	...
St Quentin 257 a.	2048	2059	2053	...	...	2234	2242	2332	0020	...
St Quentin 257 d.	...	...	2055	...	...	2236	...	...	...	...
Busigny 257 d.	...	...	|	...	...	|	...	...	...	...
Cambrai 257 a.	...	...	|	...	...	|	...	...	...	...
Aulnoye Aymeries 262 d.	...	...	2127	...	...	2315	...	...	...	...
Maubeuge 262 d.	...	...	2137	...	...	...	...	...	...	...

	12300			12302		12304	2306			
	Ⓐ	⑥ t	†	Ⓐ	⑥ t	Ⓐ	Ⓐ	⑥ t	Ⓐ	†
Maubeuge 262 d.	...	...	...	...	...	0547	...	...	...	...
Aulnoye Aymeries 262 d.	...	...	...	...	...	0559	...	...	...	...
Cambrai 257 d.	...	...	...	...	...	|	0611	...	...	...
Busigny 257 d.	...	...	...	...	...	|	0641	...	0645	0645
St Quentin 257 a.	...	...	...	...	...	0630	0656	...	0702	0703
St Quentin 257 d.	0508	0508	...	0600	0620	0632	0658	0648	0704	0705
Tergnier 257 d.	0523	0523	0611	0617	0634	|	|	0708	0718	0720
Chauny d.	0531	0530	0618	0625	0640	|	|	0715	0725	0727
Noyon d.	0544	0541	0629	0637	0650	|	0724	0726	0735	0737
Compiègne ▶ d.	0559	0555	0651	0652	0703	0709	0739	0750	0749	0751
Creil ▶ d.	0624	0624	0715	|	0735	|	|	0813	0821	0813
Paris Nord ▶ a.	0650	0659	0741	0741	0805	0750	0820	0847	0847	0847

	12308		2312			12318		12320			12326			12330		12334		12336	12338	12340			12342		12346
		Ⓐ	Ⓒ	Ⓐ	Ⓐ		⑥ t	Ⓐ b	† w	⑦		Ⓐ	†	Ⓐ	Ⓐ	†	⑥ t	Ⓑ h	Ⓒ	Ⓐ	Ⓐ	†	⑦ e	†	⑦ e
Maubeuge 262 d.	0647	...	...	...	...	1048	...	1134	...	...	1449	...	...	1549	...	1628	...	1750	1847	1913	...	...	1945	...	2048
Aulnoye Aymeries 262 d.	0659	...	...	...	...	1100	...	1146	...	...	1502	...	...	1601	...	1640	...	1802	1859	1925	...	...	1957	...	2101
Cambrai 257 d.	|	...	0727	...	...	|	...	|	...	...	|	...	...	|	...	|	...	|	|	|	...	...	|	...	|
Busigny 257 d.	|	...	0757	...	...	|	...	|	...	...	|	...	...	|	1640	|	...	|	|	|	...	...	|	...	|
St Quentin 257 a.	0730	...	0811	...	...	1129	...	1215	...	...	1531	...	...	1630	1659	1709	...	1832	1932	1954	...	...	2030	...	2131
St Quentin 257 d.	0732	0812	0813	1003	1114	1131	1212	1217	1218	1429	1533	...	1616	1632	1701	1711	1750	1834	1934	1956	2003	...	2032	2055	2133
Tergnier 257 d.	|	0828	0828	1018	1130	|	1228	1232	1232	1448	|	1613	1633	|	1721	1728	1804	|	|	|	2017	2021	|	2111	|
Chauny d.	|	0835	0837	1026	1136	|	1236	1240	1238	1455	|	1620	1639	|	1729	1736	1810	|	|	|	2024	2027	|	2117	|
Noyon d.	|	0847	0849	1038	1148	|	1248	1253	1248	1506	|	1630	1650	|	1741	1749	1820	|	|	|	2034	2037	|	2128	|
Compiègne ▶ d.	0808	0901	0905	1052	1201	1208	1303	1309	1301	1528	1610	1644	1703	1709	1808	1804	1841	1909	2010	2032	2047	2050	2108	2141	2208
Creil ▶ d.	|	0924	0924	1116	1224	|	1328	|	1321	1607	|	1706	1724	|	1827	1823	1902	|	|	|	2110	2111	|	2207	|
Paris Nord ▶ a.	0853	0950	0950	1150	1250	1250	1353	1350	1350	1641	1650	1738	1750	1750	1853	1853	1929	1950	2050	2114	2144	2141	2150	2238	2250

ADDITIONAL LOCAL TRAINS PARIS - COMPIÈGNE

	⑥t	⑥t	Ⓐ§	Ⓐ	Ⓒ	Ⓐ	Ⓐ	⑥t	†	
Paris Nord d.	0634	0907	1040	1707	1749	1819	1840	1943	2134	...
Creil d.	0708	0944	1112	1741	1824	1853	1915	2019	2208	...
Compiègne a.	0742	1023	1147	1811	1908	1920	1952	2055	2247	...

	Ⓐ	Ⓐ	Ⓐ	⑥t	Ⓐ	Ⓒ	Ⓒ	Ⓐ	Ⓑd	⑥t	Ⓑd	⑥t
Compiègne d.	0504	0548	0618	0621	0655	1047	1226	1242	1719	1723	1822	2024
Creil d.	0542	0613	0649	0704	0746	1117	1307	1307	1804	1803	1906	2107
Paris Nord a.	0617	0647	0726	0738	0817	1153	1341	1341	1838	1838	1941	2141

b – Not May 17 - June 4.
d – Also May 1, 8.
e – Also Apr. 5, May 24; not Apr. 4, May 23.
h – Not Dec. 25, Jan. 1, May 13.
n – Not Apr. 5, May 24.
t – Not May 1, 8.
u – Also May 1, 8; not May 3-6.
w – Not May 24.
▶ – For additional local trains see panel below main table. Additional suburban trains run Paris - Creil and v.v.
§ – Subject to alteration on ①–⑤ May 3-21.

256 PARIS and AMIENS - ARRAS - DOUAI - VALENCIENNES and LILLE

km ★						◇		TGV 7101	TGV 7105				TGV 7111	TGV 7113				TGV 7121					TGV 5422		TGV 7131
		Ⓐ	⚒	Ⓐ	Ⓐ	Ⓐ	⑥ t	① g	①–⑥ n§	Ⓐ	⑦ v	⑥	Ⓒ	Ⓐ §		Ⓒ	Ⓐ	⑤⑥ u	Ⓐ ⊖	†	⑥ t	Ⓐ ⊖	S		
0	**Paris Nord** 265 d.	...	...	...	...	...	...	0722	0752	...	...	...	0952	1022	...	...	...	1222	...	...	...	...	...	...	1452
	Rouen 268 d.	...	...	...	...	...	...	|	|	0704	...	0814	|	|	...	...	1038*	|	...	...	...	...	...	...	|
131	**Amiens** d.	...	...	0601	0653	...	0705	|	|	0818	0932	0935	|	|	1050	1155	1208	|	1337	...	1359	1410	...	...	|
162	Albert d.	...	...	0625	0714	...	0728	|	|	0840	0957	0956	|	|	1119	1220	1228	|	1359	...	1420	1429	...	...	|
199	Arras 265 a.	...	...	0647	0735	...	0750	0812	0842	0900	1020	1014	1042	1112	1142	1246	1248	1312	1419	...	1444	1452	...	...	1542
199	Arras d.	0526	0609	0649	0739	0747	0752	0815	0845	0901	1022	1016	1045	1115	1147	1248	1250	1315	1420	1417	1446	1454	1523	1539	1548
224	Douai a.	0550	0637	0704	0754	|	0806	0830	0900	0915	1036	1030	1059	1129	1202	1304	1304	1330	1437	1437	1500	1508	1538	1556	1602
224	Douai 257 ▶ d.	0557	0639	0706	0804	|	0808	0838	0910	0916	1038	1032	1109	1137	1204	1306	1306	1338	1439	1439	1502	1510	1541	1558	1612
260	Valenciennes ▶ a.	|	|	|	|	|	|	0904	0937	|	|	|	1135	1202	|	|	|	1404	|	|	|	|	|	|	1639
257	**Lille Europe** a.	|	|	|	|	0807	|	...	...	|	|	|	...	...	|	|	|	...	|	|	|	|	1559	|	...
257	**Lille Flandres 257** a.	0636	0716	0730	0826	...	0830	...	...	0937	1059	1053	...	...	1231	1328	1327	...	1508	1508	1523	1529	...	1621	...

			TGV 7137	TGV 7139			TGV 7141		TGV 7343		TGV 7145	TGV 5192	TGV 5279	TGV 7347			TGV 7149		TGV 7151	TGV 7089	TGV 7155	TGV 5181	TGV 5288	TGV 7159	TGV 7099
	Ⓐ ⊖	⑥	⑤ f	①–④ m	Ⓐ	Ⓒ	Ⓑ h	†	Ⓐ	Ⓐ		Ⓐ Y	Y	Ⓑ h	Ⓐ	Ⓐ	①–④ m		⑤–⑦ w	Ⓐ	Ⓐ	Ⓒ Y	Y	⑦ e	b
Paris Nord 265 d.	...	...	1622	1652	...	...	1722	...	1752	...	1822	...	...	1852	...	...	1922	...	1952	2058	2058	...	...	2152	2258
Rouen 268 d.	...	...	|	|	...	...	|	...	|	...	|	...	...	|	...	...	|	1814	|	|	|	...	...	|	|
Amiens d.	1600z	...	|	|	1658	1700	|	1751	|	1803	|	...	...	|	1852	...	|	1939	|	|	|	...	...	|	|
Albert d.	1623	...	|	|	1725	1723	|	1814	|	1826	|	...	...	|	1919	...	|	2001	|	|	|	...	...	|	|
Arras 265 a.	1648	...	1712	1741	1748	1749	1812	1839	1842	1845	1912	...	...	1941	1946	...	2012	2019	2042	2149	2149	...	...	2242	2348
Arras d.	1650	1650	1715	1744	1750	1751	1815	1841	...	1847	1915	1922	1928	...	...	1951	2015	2021	2048	2153	2156	2159	2240	2245	2354
Douai a.	1704	1704	1729	1758	1804	1805	1829	1854	...	1910	1929	1937	1942	...	...	2007	2029	2035	2103	|	2211	2214	2254	2300	|
Douai 257 ▶ d.	1706	1706	1737	1806	1806	1807	1837	1856	...	1912	1937	1939	1945	...	...	2009	2037	2037	2111	|	2219	2217	2257	2310	|
Valenciennes ▶ a.	|	|	1802	1840	|	|	1904	|	...	|	2003	|	|	...	...	|	2104	|	2137	|	2246	|	|	2337	|
Lille Europe a.	|	|	...	...	|	|	...	|	...	|	...	2003	|	...	...	|	...	|	...	|	...	2238	2318	...	|
Lille Flandres 257 a.	1734	1727	...	...	1832	1831	...	1914	...	1941	...	...	2005	...	...	2031	...	2058	...	2219	...	...	...	...	0018

LILLE and VALENCIENNES - DOUAI - ARRAS - AMIENS and PARIS 256

	TGV 7100 Ⓐ	TGV 5200 Y	TGV 7102 Ⓐ	⑥ t	Ⓐ	TGV 5110 Y	TGV 7104 Ⓐ	⑥ t	Ⓐ	TGV 7108 ①–⑥ n	⑥ t	†	Ⓐ	TGV 7110 ⑦ e	TGV 5214 Y	⚒	Ⓐ	Ⓒ	TGV 7118 L	Ⓐ E	Ⓐ F	TGV 5402 S	⑥ t	Ⓐ △	†	TGV 7124 ①–⑥ n
Lille Flandres 257 d.	...	...	...	0620	0620	0643	...	0704	0705	...	0805	0805	0805	...	...	0910	1010	1010	...	1037	1103	...	1203	1202	1202	...
Lille Europe d.	...	0558	...	|	|	|	...	|	|	...	|	|	|	...	0846	|	|	|	...	|	|	1121	|	|	|	...
Valenciennes ▶ d.	0533	|	0600	|	|	|	0638	|	|	0733	|	|	|	0813	|	|	|	|	1006	|	|	|	|	|	|	1156
Douai **257** ▶ a.	0558	0625	0625	0638	0641	0706	0704	0727	0726	0759	0827	0824	0830	0841	0906	0934	1035	1035	1032	1055	1121	1139	1224	1224	1224	1222
Douai d.	0606	0628	0633	0640	0643	0709	0712	0728	0727	0810	0829	0826	0832	0849	0908	0936	1037	1037	1042	1057	1123	1142	1226	1226	1226	1232
Arras a.	0620	0644	0649	0653	0658	0724	0728	0744	0740	0825	0843	0839	0846	0903	0925	0954	1054	1052	1059	1110	1136	1155	1241	1241	1242	1246
Arras **265** d.	0623	...	0656	0655	0701	...	0735	0746	0742	0835	0845	0841	0848	0906	...	...	...	1054	1106	1119	1138	...	1243	1243	...	1249
Albert d.	|	...	|	0714	0720	...	|	0809	0806	|	0906	0903	0916	|	...	...	...	1118	|	1137	1156	...	1310	1311	...	|
Amiens a.	|	...	|	0735	0741	...	|	0840	0829	|	0925	0923	0936	|	...	...	...	1139	|	1158	1216	...	...	1341	...	|
Rouen **268** a.	|	...	|	...	0908	...	|	...	...	|	1050	...	...	|	...	...	...	...	|	...	1344	...	...	...	...	|
Paris Nord 265 a.	0714	...	0747	...	...	...	0827	...	...	0926	...	...	...	0956	...	...	...	...	1156	...	...	...	...	...	...	1338

	Ⓐ △	Ⓒ	⑥ t	TGV 7136 ⑤–⑦ w		Ⓐ	TGV 7342	Ⓐ	⑥ t	TGV 7144 Ⓑ h	Ⓐ	TGV 7148 Ⓑ h	Ⓒ	Ⓐ	◇ Ⓐ	TGV 7152 ⑤⑥ d	Ⓐ	TGV 5136 ①–⑥ Yn	TGV 7156 ⑦ e	TGV 7154 ①–④ m	Ⓐ	TGV 7158 ⑤ f	TGV 5138 ⑦ Ye	TGV 7160 ⑦ e		TGV 7096 Ⓐ
Lille Flandres 257 d.	1256	1301	1410	...	1540	1605	...	1634	1638	...	1702	...	1805	1804	...	...	1909	...	...	...	2014	...	2021	...	2110	2209
Lille Europe d.	|	|	|	...	|	|	...	|	|	...	|	...	|	|	1839	...	|	1915	...	...	|	...	|	...	|	|
Valenciennes ▶ d.	|	|	|	1438	|	|	...	|	|	1640	|	1739	|	|	|	1845	|	|	1938	1942	|	2008	|	2038	|	|
Douai **257** ▶ a.	1321	1322	1439	1504	1607	1630	...	1656	1701	1707	1726	1805	1827	1829	|	1910	1928	1933	2004	2008	2037	2034	2040	2106	2136	|
Douai d.	1323	1324	1441	1512	1609	1632	...	1658	1703	1717	1730	1813	1829	1831	|	1918	1930	1936	2012	2016	2040	2043	2043	2116	2138	|
Arras a.	1338	1340	1500	1528	1629	1650	...	1713	1719	1733	1744	1829	1844	1850	1900	1933	1943	1949	2028	2032	2054	2058	2056	2132	2156	2229
Arras **265** d.	1340	1342	...	1535	1632	...	1706	*1725*	...	1736	1746	1836	1846	1852	...	1940	1945	...	2035	2035	2055	2105	...	2135	...	2232
Albert d.	1406	1408	...	|	1656	...	|	*1755*	...	|	1808	|	1906	1919	...	|	2007	...	|	|	2119	|	...	|	...	|
Amiens a.	1428	1428	...	|	1721	...	|	*1817*	...	|	1828	|	1927	1941	...	|	2028	...	|	|	2141	|	...	|	...	|
Rouen **268** a.	...	...	...	|	...	...	|	...	...	|	1943	|	2056	...	...	|	...	...	|	|	...	|	...	|	...	|
Paris Nord 265 a.	...	...	...	1626	...	...	1756	...	...	1826	...	1926	...	...	...	2032	...	...	2126	2126	...	2156	...	2226	...	2323

E – Dec. 14 - Apr. 30.
F – May 3 - Dec. 10.
L – ①⑥⑦ (also Dec. 25, Jan. 1, Apr. 6, May 13, 25).
S – To/from Strasbourg (Table **391**).
Y – For origin/destination see Table **11**.

b – Not May 9 - 13, 16 - 20.
d – Also Dec. 24, 31, May 12, 13.
e – Also Apr. 5, May 24.
f – Also Dec. 24, 31, May 12; not Dec. 25, Jan. 1.
g – Also Apr. 6, May 25; not Apr. 5, May 24.
h – Not Dec. 25, Jan. 1, May 13.
m – Not Dec. 24, 25, 31, Jan. 1, Apr. 5, May 12, 13, 24.
n – Not Apr. 5, May 24.

t – Not May 1, 8.
u – Also Dec. 24, 31, May 12, 13.
v – Also May 1, 8.
w – Also Dec. 24, 31, Apr. 5, May 12, 13, 24.
z – 1556 on ⑤.

TGV – Ⓡ, supplement payable.

◇ – TER à Grande Vitesse (via high-speed line). Supplement *Côte d'Opale* is payable (€3 per day).
⊖ – Subject to alteration Apr. 12 - 16.
△ – Subject to alteration Apr. 19 - 30.
§ – Subject to alteration Douai - Valenciennes Feb. 8, 11, 12.
* – From May 25.

★ – Paris - Arras via high-speed line is *179 km*.

▶ – Local trains Douai - Valenciennes (journey 30 - 35 mins):
From Douai: 0600 ⚒, 0658 ⚒, 0725 Ⓐ, 0753 ⚒, 0814 Ⓐ, 0854 ⑥, 0855 Ⓑ, 0953 ⚒, 1048 †, 1155 Ⓐ, 1216, 1248 Ⓐ, 1312 ⚒, 1350, 1623 ⚒, 1650, 1724 Ⓐ, 1754 ⑥, 1755 Ⓑ, 1822 Ⓐ, 1856 Ⓐ, 1914 †, 1921 Ⓐ, 1958 ⚒, 2046 Ⓐ, 2123 ⑥ **t**, 2142 Ⓐ, 2214 †.
From Valenciennes: 0508 Ⓐ, 0545 ⚒, 0624 ⚒, 0654 ⚒, 0753 ⚒, 0803 Ⓑ, 0839 Ⓐ, 0934 Ⓐ, 0946 Ⓒ, 1120 †, 1148 ⑥ **t**, 1201 Ⓐ, 1223 ⑥ **t**, 1224 Ⓐ, 1301, 1401 ⚒, 1455 ⚒, 1601, 1644 Ⓐ, 1650 ⑥ **t**, 1721 Ⓑ, 1751 ⚒, 1819 Ⓑ, 1856 ⑥ **t**, 1859 Ⓐ, 1928 Ⓑ, 2143 Ⓐ.

LILLE - CAMBRAI - ST QUENTIN 257

km		Ⓐ	Ⓐ p	Ⓐ	Ⓒ p	⚒	Ⓐ	Ⓐ	⚒	⚒ ⊕r	b	† u	Ⓐ c	⚒ ⊗	†	⚒ s	⚒ d	⚒ d	Ⓐ c	⑥ t	⑦	⑥ t	⑥ t	Ⓑ ▽	⑥ t
0	**Lille Flandres 256** d.	...	...	0531	...	*0620*	...	*0647*	0733	...	0850	...	*0910*	...	1108	...	1130	*1202*	...	*1301*	*1301*	...	1505	*1540*	*1540*
34	Douai **256** a.	...	...	0607	...	*0641*	...	*0723*	0757	...	0917	...	*0934*	...	1131	...	1200	*1224*	...	*1322*	*1322*	...	1529	*1607*	*1607*
34	Douai d.	...	...	0609	...	0649	...	0728	0759	...	0919	...	0944	...	1133	...	1202	1238	1342	1342	1342	...	1531	1618	1627
66	**Cambrai Ville** a.	...	...	0643	...	0723	...	0757	0830	...	0948	...	1014	...	1201	...	1235	1315	1413	1413	1414	...	1559	1647	1658
66	**Cambrai Ville** d.	0520	0611	...	0727	...	0743	...	...	0858	...	1000	...	1020	...	1216	...	1317	...	...	1416	1431	...	...	1700
82	Caudry d.	0534	0626	...	0743	...	0756	...	...	0911	...	1013	...	1033	...	1234	...	1330	...	...	1429	1445	...	...	1714
92	Busigny **255** d.	0546	0641	...	0757	...	0806	...	...	0923	...	1023	...	1043	...	1246	...	1339	...	...	1438	1454	...	...	1724
119	**St Quentin 255** d.	0607	0656	...	0813	...	0828	...	...	0941	...	1043	...	1103	...	1309	...	...	...	...	...	1515	...	...	1744
142	Tergnier **255** a.	...	...	...	0826	...	...	...	...	0958	...	...	...	...	...	...	...	...	...	...	...	...	...	...	...

	Ⓐ	Ⓐ	Ⓒ	Ⓐ	Ⓐ	†	⑥ t	Ⓐ	Ⓐ	⑥ t	Ⓐ	Ⓐ
Lille Flandres 256 d.	...	*1634*	1705	*1702*	1738	1818	*1805*	*1804*	1838	1920	*1909*	*2014*
Douai **256** a.	...	*1656*	1729	*1726*	1802	1840	*1827*	*1829*	1903	1942	*1928*	*2037*
Douai d.	...	1705	1731	1734	1810	1842	1844	1849	1909	1944	1950	2050
Cambrai Ville a.	...	1740	1801	1810	1840	1912	1913	1920	1949	2014	2018	2115
Cambrai Ville d.	1715	...	1805	1812	1842	1916	...	...	1950	2016	...	...
Caudry d.	1734	...	1820	1830	1857	1929	...	...	2003	2029	...	...
Busigny **255** d.	1747	...	1829	1842	1911	1939	...	...	2013	2037	...	...
St Quentin 255 d.	1807	...	1846	1900	1930	1958	...	...	2033	...	...	...
Tergnier **255** a.	...	...	1906	1915	...	...	...	...	...	...	...	...

	Ⓐ	Ⓐ	Ⓐ	⚒	Ⓐ	Ⓐ	⑥ t	Ⓐ
Tergnier **255** d.	...	...	0527	...	...	...	...	...
St Quentin 255 d.	...	0515	0541	0617	...	0649	0650	...
Busigny **255** d.	...	0534	0559	0634	...	0710	0714	...
Caudry d.	...	0544	0608	0643	...	0722	0724	...
Cambrai Ville a.	...	0555	0620	0655	...	0736	0737	...
Cambrai Ville d.	0513	0557	0625	0657	0710	0804	0805	0834
Douai a.	0543	0628	0652	0731	0755	0833	0835	0903
Douai **256** d.	*0557*	0630	*0706*	0733	*0804*	0835	0837	*0916*
Lille Flandres 256 a.	*0636*	0659	*0730*	0759	*0826*	0902	0902	*0937*

	⚒ r	⚒	†	⚒ △	⚒ c	⑦ v	⚒ d	⚒ k	Ⓑ c	Ⓐ	⑥ t	⑦	Ⓐ	⑥ t	Ⓐ	Ⓒ	Ⓐ	⑥ t	†	Ⓐ	Ⓐ	†	⑥ t	p	
Tergnier **255** d.	0736	...	...	...	...	...	...	...	...	...	...	...	...	...	...	...	...	...	...	...	...	1811	...	...	...
St Quentin 255 d.	0755	...	...	0858	...	1120	...	1202	...	1402	1402	...	...	1602	...	...	...	...	1722	1720	1830	1828	1832	1854	2103
Busigny **255** d.	0818	...	...	0920	...	1141	...	1225	...	1423	1422	1421	...	1624	1638	...	...	...	1741	1745	1852	1851	1854	1912	2126
Caudry d.	0828	...	...	0928	...	1151	...	1235	...	1434	1432	1431	...	1634	1648	...	...	...	1751	1756	1902	1902	1903	1924	2137
Cambrai Ville a.	0841	...	...	0941	...	1203	...	1247	...	1446	1444	1444	...	1646	1701	...	...	...	1803	1808	1914	1913	1914	1937	2150
Cambrai Ville d.	...	0855	0852	...	1128	1205	1210	1249	1319	...	1446	1446	1622	...	1703	1703	1741	1809	1809	1814	1924	1916	1917	...	...
Douai a.	...	0918	0919	...	1157	1234	1236	1320	1345	...	1515	1515	1655	...	1731	1731	1816	1833	1833	1849	1949	1947	1947	...	...
Douai **256** d.	...	0920	0921	...	*1204*	*1244*	1237	...	1347	...	*1558*	*1558*	1706*	...	1733	1733	*1829*	1835	1835	*1912*	1951	1949	1949	...	...
Lille Flandres 256 a.	...	0941	0947	...	*1231*	*1322*	1304	...	1410	...	*1621*	*1621*	1734*	...	1801	1758	*1858*	1858	1858	*1941*	2014	2012	2014	...	...

b – Not Mar. 22 - Apr. 2.
c – Not on Ⓐ Mar. 22 - Apr. 2.
d – Not Mar. 22 - 26, Mar. 29 - Apr. 2.
k – Not on Ⓐ Mar. 22 - Apr. 2, May 3 - 21.
p – To/from Paris (Table **255**).

r – To/from Reims (Table **252**).
s – To May 14/from June 7.
t – Not May 1, 8.
u – Not Apr. 5.
v – Also Apr. 5, May 1, 8, 24; not Apr. 4

△ – Subject to alteration on Ⓐ Apr. 19 - 30.
▽ – On † runs 6 - 7 mins later Douai - Cambrai.
⊕ – Subject to alteration on Ⓐ Apr. 6 - 16, Apr. 26 - May 7.
⊗ – Subject to alteration on Ⓐ Apr. 6 - 16.
* – Subject to alteration Apr. 12 - 16.

AMIENS - ST QUENTIN 258

km		Ⓐ	⑥t	Ⓐ	⚒⊖	†	⚒	Ⓐv	Ⓐ	⚒	†	Ⓐ
0	Amiens d.	0638	0650	0747	0830	1025	1212	1442	1718	1826	1851	2035
76	St Quentin a.	0734	0747	0844	1001	1121	1310	1539	1811	1926	1945	2133

	⑥t	Ⓐ	Ⓐ	†	⚒§	Ⓐ§	Ⓐ	Ⓐ	⑥t	†
St Quentin d.	0629	0637	0745	0755	1220	1311	1716	1841	1851	2017
Amiens a.	0724	0736	0841	0853	1317	1408	1813	1937	1951	2116

t – Not May 1, 8. **v** – Subject to alteration on Mar. 8 - 19. ⊖ – Not on Ⓐ May 3 - 21. Via Tergnier (d. 0941). § – Subject to alteration May 17 - June 5.

CALAIS - DUNKERQUE - DE PANNE 259

km		Ⓐ	⚒		⚒	Ⓐ	
0	**Calais Ville** d.	0534	0638	...	1222	1719	...
23	Gravelines d.	0553	0701	...	1249	1742	...
46	**Dunkerque** a.	0616	0731	...	1316	1810	...

	⚒	🚌 Ⓐ		⚒	⑥t	Ⓐ	Ⓐ	Ⓐ
Dunkerque d.	0629	0734	...	1217	1328	1542	1711	1827
Gravelines d.	0701	0825	...	1247	1352	1609	1743	1855
Calais Ville a.	0724	0855	...	1309	1412	1627	1806	1918

Additional 🚌 service (Ligne BCD): 10 journeys on Ⓐ, 3 on ⑥ (4 journeys run from/to Boulogne on Ⓐ, 2 on ⑥). ✆ 0800 62 00 59. Rail tickets not valid.

t – Not May 1, 8.

🚌 **DUNKERQUE GARE - ADINKERKE (DE PANNE STATION)** Operator DK'BUS Marine (route 2). Journey 50 minutes. Connects at De Panne station with coastal tram service (Table **404**). From Dunkerque Gare: ⚒: 0702 and approx hourly to 2006. †: 0754 and approx hourly to 1956. From Adinkerke: ⚒: 0704, 0807 and approx hourly to 2106. †: 0910 and hourly to 2010, 2105.

260 PARIS - AMIENS - BOULOGNE

For *TGV* service Paris - Boulogne / Calais (and connections via Hazebrouck) see Table **265**; other services are available by changing at Lille (Tables **250** and **266**).

km		Ⓐ	⚒	Ⓐ	2003 ①–⑥ n	🚌 ①–⑥	12007 ①–⑤ u	2007 ⑦ e	🚌 †	2015	🚌	⚒		🚌	Ⓐ	2025 ⊕	🚌 ⚒	Ⓐ	Ⓒ	Ⓐ	Ⓒ ▷	12031 Ⓐ b	Ⓐ	2033	Ⓐ
0	**Paris Nord** ▶ d.	...	...	...	0707	...	0804	0804	...	1004*	...	...	...	...	...	1419	...	...	...	...	...	1610	...	1704	...
51	Creil ▶ d.	...	...	...	|	...	0831	0831	...	|	...	...	...	...	...	|	...	...	...	...	...	|	...	|	...
126	Longueau ▶ d.	...	...	...	0807	...	0909	0909	...	1107	...	...	...	...	...	1519	...	...	...	...	...	1710	...	1804	...
131	**Amiens** ▶ a.	...	...	...	0812	...	0914	0914	...	1112	...	...	...	...	...	1524	...	...	...	...	...	1716	...	1809	...
131	**Amiens** d.	...	...	0630	0823	...	...	0925	...	1123	...	...	1230	...	1430	1535	...	...	*1630z*	*1640*	...	...	1730	1820	...
176	Abbeville d.	...	...	0704	0849	0907	...	0950	1000	1148	1158	...	1303	1322	1504	1601	1608	...	1708	1742	...	...	1805	1846	1854
213	Le Treport a.	...	...	|	|	1015	...	|	1106	|	1306	...	...	1430	|	|	1715	...	1757	1835	...	...	|	|	1941
216	Rang du Fliers ⊙ d.	0611	0656	0734	0913	...	...	1023	...	1222	...	1303	...	...	1535	1631	...	...	...	...	1817	...	1839	1916	...
227	Étaples-Le Touquet § d.	0619	0704	0743	0923	...	...	1033	...	1232	...	1311	...	...	1543	1641	...	1729	...	...	1826	...	1848	1925	...
254	**Boulogne Ville** § a.	0642	0723	0805	0941	...	...	1050	...	1250	...	1334	...	...	1559	1659	...	1752	...	...	1843	...	1904	1942	...
	Calais Ville **261** a.	0718	0808	...	...	...	...	...	...	...	...	1414	...	...	...	...	...	...	...	...	1921	...	1949	...	...

	12035 Ⓐ		⑥ t	12037 Ⓐ	2041	🚌 ⑤⑥ w	2045 ⑤ f	12045 ①–④ m	2049 ⑦ e	①–⑥ n
Paris Nord ▶ d.	1734	...	...	1807	1904	...	2004	2007	2107	...
Creil ▶ d.	|	...	...	|	|	...	|	|	|	...
Longueau ▶ d.	1834	...	...	1911	2004	...	2109	2109	2207	...
Amiens ▶ a.	1840	...	...	1917	2008	...	2114	2114	2212	...
Amiens d.	...	1900	...	...	2019	...	2125	...	2223	...
Abbeville d.	...	1943	1952	...	2046	2054	2150	...	2248	0641
Le Treport a.	...	...	2039	...	|	2202	|	...	|	0745
Rang du Fliers ⊙ d.	...	...	...	...	2119	...	2223	...	2321	...
Étaples-Le Touquet § d.	...	...	...	...	2129	...	2233	...	2331	...
Boulogne Ville § a.	...	...	...	...	2148	...	2250	...	2348	...
Calais Ville **261** a.	...	...	...	...	...	...	...	...	...	...

	2004 ① g	12004 ②–⑤ y	12006 Ⓐ	2008 ①–⑥ n	12010 Ⓐ	⚒	Ⓐ	⑥ t	12012 Ⓐ	⚒
Calais Ville **261** d.	...	...	...	...	...	...	0548	0601	...	...
Boulogne Ville § d.	0429	...	...	0538	...	...	0628	0636	...	...
Étaples-Le Touquet § d.	0447	...	...	0556	...	...	0644	0652	...	...
Rang du Fliers ⊙ d.	0457	...	...	0606	...	...	0653	0701	...	...
Le Treport d.	|	...	...	|	...	0632	|	|	...	0732
Abbeville d.	0530	...	*0600*	0638	...	0719	0724	0731	...	0814
Amiens a.	0554	...	*0643*	0701	...	...	0759	0806	...	...
Amiens ▶ d.	0605	0605	0646	0715	0747	...	...	...	0830	...
Longueau ▶ d.	0613	0613	0654	0723	0755	...	...	...	0838	...
Creil ▶ a.	|	|	|	|	|	...	...	...	|	...
Paris Nord ▶ a.	0723	0723	0753	0823	0856	...	...	...	0938	...

	2014 ⑥ a	2014 Ⓑ h	🚌 Ⓐ	①–⑥	🚌 Ⓒ	2022	⚒	🚌		Ⓐ	⑥ t	🚌	2032 Ⓒ	2036 ①–⑤ q	†	🚌 Ⓑ	Ⓐ	12038 Ⓐ	2038 ⑦ e	🚌 x	2042	Ⓐ	2044 ⑦ e	†	Ⓐ	2048 ⑦ e ‡
Calais Ville **261** d.	...	...	...	...	...	...	...	...	...	1240	1246	...	...	...	...	...	...	...	...	...	...	...	...	...	...	...
Boulogne Ville § d.	0738	0746	...	...	...	1046	1220	...	...	1325	1329	...	1438	1536	1557	...	1630	...	1635	...	1742	1826	1838	...	2015	2048
Étaples-Le Touquet § d.	0758	0803	...	...	...	1104	1238	...	...	1341	1344	...	1456	1554	1613	...	1649	...	1653	...	1800	1852	1856	...	2031	2106
Rang du Fliers ⊙ d.	0809	0812	...	...	...	1115	1247	...	...	1350	1353	...	1506	1604	1622	...	1657	...	1703	...	1811	1900	1907	...	2039	2117
Le Treport d.	|	|	0746	...	1020	|	...	1202	...	|	|	1437c	|	|	|	1600	|	...	|	1720	|	|	|	...	...	|
Abbeville d.	0835	0838	0853	1000	1128	1139	...	1310	1320	1420	1422	1523	1539	1637	1653	1708	1727	...	1736	1823	1834	1931	1941	2035	...	2140
Amiens a.	0902	0902	...	1043	...	1202	...	...	1403	1452	1503	...	1602	1704	1724	...	1758	...	1800	...	1859	2002	2005	2108	...	2205
Amiens ▶ d.	0913	0913	...	...	...	1213	...	...	...	...	...	...	1613	1712	...	...	...	1809	1811	...	1909	...	2016	...	...	2216
Longueau ▶ d.	0921	0921	...	...	...	1221	...	...	...	...	...	...	1620	1719	...	...	...	1816	1818	...	1916	...	2023	...	...	2224
Creil ▶ a.	|	|	...	...	...	|	...	...	...	...	...	...	|	1755	...	...	...	1852	1853	...	1953	...	|	...	...	|
Paris Nord ▶ a.	1020	1020	...	...	...	1320	...	...	...	...	...	...	1720	1823	...	...	...	1920	1920	...	2020	...	2123	...	...	2323

ADDITIONAL TRAINS PARIS - AMIENS

	Ⓐ	⑥ t	Ⓐ	⑥ t	Ⓐ	⑥ t	Ⓐ	†		⚒ ⊡	† d	⑥ t	⑥ t	Ⓒ	Ⓐ	†	⑥ t	Ⓐ	†	Ⓐ	⑥ t	⑥ t	Ⓐ	Ⓒ	Ⓐ
Paris Nord d.	0631	0710	0740	0804	0819	0904	0907	0919	1137	1231	1231	1337	1610	1719	1749	1807	1807	1834	1910	1910	1940	2010	2107	2149	2234
Creil d.	0657	0744	0807	0833	0853	0939	0937	0953	1211	1257	1258	1413	1637	1753	1823	1834	1836	|	1939	1944	2012	2040	2136	2219	2304
Clermont-de-l'Oise d.	0709	0800	0825	0845	0903	0949	0952	1009	1228	1309	1317	1430	1651	1810	1833	1845	1852	1908	1955	2001	2028	2049	2153	2235	2315
Longueau d.	0754	0846	0859	0923	0950	1032	1024	1048	1321	1346	1405	1529	1730	1859	1927	1919	1933	1948	2040	2051	2108	2126	2236	2317	2350
Amiens a.	0759	0852	0905	0929	0956	1037	1029	1053	1327	1353	1411	1534	1735	1905	1933	1925	1938	1953	2045	2057	2113	2131	2241	2323	2356

	Ⓐ	⑥ t	†	⑥ t	Ⓐ	†	Ⓒ	Ⓐ	⑥ t	Ⓐ		Ⓐ	⑥ t	Ⓑ ⊗	Ⓒ	Ⓐ ⊗	Ⓐ ⊗	†	⑥ t	Ⓒ	†	Ⓐ	Ⓐ	†	Ⓐ ☆
Amiens d.	0520	0547	0620	0638	0654	0736	0930	0931	1045	1105	1218	1300	1405	1457	1523	1538	1625	1653	1744	1825	1932	1943	2040	2102	2200
Longueau d.	0526	0552	0625	0643	0700	0743	0936	0936	1052	1111	1226	1305	1410	1505	1529	1544	1631	1659	1750	1831	1939	1950	2050	2108	2206
Clermont-de-l'Oise d.	0616	0636	0706	0725	0753	0820	1019	1019	1129	1144	1318	1340	1444	1543	1616	1621	1718	1741	1843	1919	2022	2029	2128	2149	2238
Creil d.	0634	0652	0722	0740	0809	0831	1037	1037	1142	1155	1335	1352	1455	1555	1634	1636	1733	1753	1854	1937	2038	2053	2139	2202	2250
Paris Nord a.	0708	0723	0753	0817	0841	0856	1111	1111	1208	1220	1411	1423	1520	1620	1708	1708	1808	1820	1920	2011	2114	2120	2208	2229	2317

a – Also Dec. 25, Jan. 1, May 13.
b – Subject to alteration Mar. 3 - Apr. 16.
c – 1413 on ⑥.
d – Not Apr. 5.
e – Also Apr. 5, May 24; not Apr. 4, May 23.
f – Also Dec. 24, 31; not Dec. 25, Jan. 1, May 14.
g – Also Apr. 6, May 25; not Apr. 5, May 24.
h – Not Dec. 25, Jan. 1, May 13.
m – Also May 14; not Dec. 24, 31, Apr. 5, May 12, 13, 24.
n – Not Apr. 5, May 24.
q – Not Dec. 25, Jan. 1, Apr. 5, May 12, 13, 24.
t – Not May 1, 8.
u – Also Apr. 4, May 23; not Dec. 25, Jan. 1, Apr. 5, May 13, 24.
v – Also Apr. 5, May 24.
w – Not Dec. 25, Jan. 1, May 1, 8.
x – Runs 10 minutes earlier on †.
y – Not Dec. 25, Jan. 1, Apr. 6, May 13, 25.
z – 1559 on ⑥.
▶ – For additional trains see below main table.
⊙ – Rang du Fliers-Verton-Berck.
⊡ – Not on Ⓐ Apr. 6 - 16.
⊕ – Subject to alteration on Apr. 5 - 9, 12 - 16.
⊗ – Subject to alteration on Ⓐ Apr. 19 - 30.
☆ – Subject to alteration on May 10 - 12, 17 - 20.
▷ – To Lille Flandres (Table **261**).
§ – See also Table **263**.
‡ – Subject to alteration Amiens - Paris on May 2, 9, 16.
* – 1007 on ⑤–⑦.

261 BOULOGNE - CALAIS

km		Ⓐ	Ⓐ	⚒	⚒	⊗	⚒	①–④ m ⊗	†	⑤ f	Ⓐ	⑥ t	⚒	†	⑥ t	Ⓐ	Ⓐ	⑥ t	† △ u	Ⓒ	⑥ △ t	Ⓐ	Ⓒ	Ⓐ
0	**Boulogne Ville** d.	0602	0644	0702	0725	0828	0957	1036	1057	1138	1157	1157	1221	1258	1303	1305	1336	1335	1346	1444	1517	1613	1644	1707
7	Wimille-Wimereux d.	0609	0651	0711	0733	0836	1006	1043	1104	1146	1204	1205	1230	1307	1311	1312	1344	1344	|	1451	1524	1622	1652	1715
17	Marquise-Rinxent d.	0617	0659	0718	0740	0844	1014	1051	1112	1154	1212	1212	1239	1315	1320	1320	1352	1353	1358	1459	1532	1630	1700	1723
34	Calais Fréthun **265** d.	0629	0710	0733	0755	0856	|	|	|	|	1223	1223	1251	|	1334	1332	1407	1409	1410	|	1544	1642	|	1734
42	**Calais Ville 265** a.	0637	0718	0741	0808	0903	1031	1108	1128	1211	1230	1230	1258	1333	1343	1342	1414	1416	1417	1517	1551	1649	1716	1741
	Lille Flandres **266** a.	0759	...	0858	...	1033	...	1238	1250	...	1403	1403	...	1508	1511	...	...	...	...	1643	...	...	1840	...

	Ⓐ	Ⓒ	Ⓐ	Ⓒ	Ⓐ ⊖ §	Ⓐ ▷	Ⓒ	Ⓐ
Boulogne Ville d.	1731	1739	1818	1845	1842	1911	1951	1952
Wimille-Wimereux d.	1740	1747	1827	1854	1850	1920	1959	1958
Marquise-Rinxent d.	1751	1755	1835	1903	1857	1929	2006	2005
Calais Fréthun **265** d.	1808	|	1853	|	1908	1942	2017	2016
Calais Ville 265 a.	1817	1816	1901	1921	1915	1949	2024	2023
Lille Flandres **266** a.	2002	1948	...	2100	...	...	...	2158

	Ⓐ ▷	⑥ ▷ t	Ⓐ	⑥ t	Ⓐ	Ⓐ	⑥ t	Ⓐ	⑥ t	Ⓐ	†
Lille Flandres **266** d.	...	...	...	...	...	0627	...	0700	0727	0800	...
Calais Ville 265 d.	0548	0601	0642	0647	0739	0800	0804	0822	0904	0916	0953
Calais Fréthun **265** d.	|	|	0650	0656	|	0812	0811	0829	0911	0925	1000
Marquise-Rinxent d.	0611	0618	0707	0714	0755	0825	0824	0840	0922	0937	1011
Wimille-Wimereux d.	0619	0626	0716	0723	0803	0832	0831	0847	0929	0947	1020
Boulogne Ville a.	0626	0634	0724	0732	0809	0839	0839	0854	0936	0954	1027

	Ⓐ ⊕	Ⓒ	Ⓐ ▷	⑥ ▷ t	Ⓒ	⑥ t	Ⓐ	Ⓐ	⑥ t	Ⓐ	⑥ t	Ⓐ	Ⓒ	Ⓐ ▽	Ⓒ ⊖	Ⓐ	Ⓒ	Ⓐ	Ⓐ	Ⓐ	Ⓐ	Ⓒ	Ⓐ	Ⓒ
Lille Flandres **266** d.	0815	0922	...	...	1124	...	...	...	...	...	1338	1403	1416	...	...	1600	1621	...	1700	...	1810	1821	1915	2020
Calais Ville 265 d.	0953	1046	1240	1246	1306	1327	1328	1351	1433	1433	1503	1529	1544	1644	1652	1728	1746	1754	1821	1909	1931	1953	2041	2154
Calais Fréthun **265** d.	1000	|	1248	1254	|	1334	|	1358	1442	1441	1511	|	|	1653	1659	1737	|	1805	1828	1917	1940	|	2049	|
Marquise-Rinxent d.	1012	1104	1306	1312	1323	1347	1349	1409	1452	1453	1523	1546	1602	1707	1711	1755	1803	1818	1839	1932	1952	2009	2101	2212
Wimille-Wimereux d.	1020	1112	1315	1320	1331	1355	1357	1417	1459	1501	1532	1553	1610	1714	1719	1803	1811	1827	1846	1940	1959	2016	2108	2220
Boulogne Ville a.	1027	1119	1323	1327	1338	1402	1405	1424	1505	1509	1540	1600	1618	1721	1726	1810	1818	1834	1852	1948	2007	2022	2115	2228

f – Not Dec. 25, Jan. 1.
m – Not Apr. 5, May 13, 24.
t – Not May 1, 8.
u – Not May 13.
△ – From Lille via Bethune and St Pol (Table **263**).
▽ – To Lille via St Pol and Bethune (Table **263**).
▷ – To / from Amiens (Table **260**).
⊖ – To / from Arras (Table **263**).
⊕ – Subject to alteration on Ⓐ Feb. 1 - 18.
⊗ – Subject to alteration on Ⓐ Feb. 22 - Mar. 12.
§ – Subject to alteration on Ⓐ Apr. 6 - 16.

LILLE - VALENCIENNES - MAUBEUGE and CHARLEVILLE MÉZIÈRES 262

km		Ⓐ	⚒	Ⓐ	Ⓐ	⑥ t	⚒	Ⓐ	Ⓐ	Ⓐ	⑥ t	⚒	Ⓐ ⊕	⊕	⑥ t	†	Ⓐ ⊕	†	†	⚒ ⊕	Ⓐ ⊕	⑥ t	⚒			⚒
0	**Lille Flandres** ▷ d.	0554	*0554*	0655	...	0655	...	0750	...	0815	0817	...	0850	0917	...	...	...	1117	...	1200	1219	1219	...	1318	...	1415
48	Valenciennes ▷ d.	0635	*0635*	0736	...	0736	...	0832	...	0856	0856	...	0931	0955	...	...	...	1157	...	1233	1257	1257	...	1357	...	1453
82	Aulnoye Aymeries a.	0704	*0704*	0802	...	0803	...	0901	...	0925	0925	...	0957	1022	...	...	...	1227	...	1301	1324	1324	...	1423	...	1520
82	Aulnoye Aymeries d.	0706	0717	0810	0812	0813	0835	0909	0909	0928	0928	0938	1005	1027	1039	1041	1044	1235	1235	1303	1334	1333	1332	1430	1437	1522
94	**Maubeuge** a.	0718	|	0822	|	|	0848	|	0922	0941	0941	|	|	1038	|	|	|	|	1249	1315	|	|	1347	1443	|	1534
104	Jeumont a.	0727	|	0832	|	|	0901	|	0932	0951	0949	|	|	1046	|	|	|	|	1257	1324	|	|	1359	1451	|	1543
94	Avesnes d.	...	0733	...	0828	0828	...	0921	...	...	...	0950	1018	...	1050	1058	1057	1246	...	...	1345	1344	...	...	1448	...
123	Hirson a.	...	0759	...	0854	0854	...	0946	...	...	...	1013	1042	...	1114	1124	1121	1310	...	...	1407	1408	...	...	1512	...
184	**Charleville-Mézières** a.	...	...	...	0936	0935	...	...	...	...	...	...	1120	...	...	1202	...	...	...	...	...	1450	...	...	...	...

	⚒	Ⓐ	Ⓐ	Ⓐ			Ⓐ	Ⓐ	Ⓐ	Ⓐ	Ⓐ	Ⓐ	Ⓐ	Ⓒ	Ⓐ	Ⓒ	Ⓐ	Ⓐ	Ⓐ	Ⓐ	Ⓐ	Ⓐ	Ⓒ		Ⓐ	Ⓐ
Lille Flandres ▷ d.	...	1515	1550	1550	1616	...	1650	1716	1716	1727	...	1808	...	1813	1816	...	1846	1850	...	1930	...	2016	2018	...	2116	...
Valenciennes ▷ d.	...	1555	1628	1628	1658	...	1729	1752	1756	1808	...	1838	1842	1856	1859	...	1921	1932	...	2008	...	2056	2057	...	2153	...
Aulnoye Aymeries a.	...	1621	1654	1654	1728	...	1756	1813	|	1837	...	1902	|	1925	1928	...	|	1958	...	2036	...	2124	2125	...	2220	...
Aulnoye Aymeries d.	1540	1623	1703	1707	1730	1740	1802	1814	|	1839	1847	1904	|	1935	1933	1946	|	2005	2007	2038	2047	2131	2132	2136	2222	2235
Maubeuge a.	|	1634	1718	|	1742	|	1815	1823	|	1854	|	1912	|	|	1945	2001	|	|	2019	2049	|	2143	2144	|	2232	|
Jeumont a.	|	1641	1730	|	1751	|	1826	1832	|	1905	|	1920	|	|	1955	2012	|	|	2028	2058	|	2152	2155	|	2240	|
Avesnes d.	1552	...	...	1718	...	1756	...	...	1822	...	1903	...	1916	1946	...	...	1948	2016	...	...	2059	...	...	2149	...	2246
Hirson a.	1622	...	...	1740	...	1821	...	...	1841	...	1927	...	1938	2011	...	...	2009	2040	...	...	2124	...	...	2217	...	2310
Charleville-Mézières a.	...	...	...	...	...	1900v	...	...	1919	...	...	...	...	2052	...	...	2050	...	...	...	...	...	...	...	...	...

	Ⓐ	Ⓐ	⚒	⚒	Ⓐ	Ⓐ	⚒	⚒		Ⓐ	Ⓐ	⚒	⚒	Ⓐ	Ⓒ		Ⓐ	Ⓐ	Ⓐ	Ⓒ		Ⓐ	⚒	⚒	⚒	⑥
Charleville-Mézières d.	...	...	...	...	...	0600	...	...	...	...	...	...	...	...	...	...	...	...	0956	1013	...	...	...	...	...	1150
Hirson d.	...	0518	0545	...	...	0637	0614	0640	...	...	0720	0752	...	0824	0832	...	0936	...	1031	1055	...	1115	1149	...	...	1228
Avesnes d.	...	0542	0607	...	...	0658	0640	0707	...	...	0744	0815	...	0847	0856	...	1000	...	1053	1120	...	1143	1215	...	...	1255
Jeumont d.	0501	*0527*r	|	0611	0635	|	|	|	0708	0738	|	|	0815	|	|	0912	|	1003	|	|	1114	|	|	1215	1232	|
Maubeuge d.	0508	*0535*r	|	0619	0644	|	|	|	0716	0746	|	|	0823	|	|	0920	|	1011	|	|	1122	|	|	1223	1244	|
Aulnoye Aymeries a.	0519	0551	0623	0630	0652	|	0651	0723	0729	0757	0753	0831	0833	0857	0911	0932	1011	1021	|	1129	1134	1154	1229	1235	1302	1306
Aulnoye Aymeries d.	0521	0600	...	0632	0655	|	0706	...	0731	0759	0804	...	0835	...	...	0934	...	1023	|	...	1136	1204	...	1237	...	1316
Valenciennes ▷ d.	0552	0627	...	0704	0717	0724	0738	...	0800	0821	0831	...	0906	...	...	1003	...	1052	1121	...	1206	1232	...	1307	...	1344
Lille Flandres ▷ a.	0630	0700	...	0742	0746	0751	0817	...	0838	0850	0907	...	0944	...	...	1042	...	1132	1148	...	1245	1306	...	1346	...	1428

	Ⓐ ⊗	†	†	Ⓐ ⊗	Ⓐ ⊗	†	†	⑥ t	⚒ ⊗	Ⓐ	Ⓐ	Ⓐ	Ⓐ	Ⓐ	Ⓐ	†	†	⚒	⚒	Ⓐ	†	Ⓐ	†	†	⚒	⚒ b
Charleville-Mézières d.	1153	1309	...	...	...	...	...	...	...	...	...	...	...	...	...	...	...	...	...	...	...	...	...	1921	...	2045
Hirson d.	1233	1347	...	1421	...	1534	...	1540	...	...	1616	1645	...	...	1719	1737	...	1749	...	...	1855	1951	...	2000	...	2127
Avesnes d.	1258	1410	...	1444	...	1601	...	1605	...	...	1639	1710	...	...	1741	1803	...	1815	...	...	1919	2015	...	2026	...	2149
Jeumont d.	|	|	1404	|	1500	|	1555	|	1610	1626	|	|	1706	1727	|	|	1803	|	1812	1857	*1901*r	|	2020	|	2123	|
Maubeuge d.	|	|	1413	|	1508	|	1604	|	1617	1638	|	|	1714	1736	|	|	1812	|	1820	1906	*1912*r	|	2028	|	2130	|
Aulnoye Aymeries a.	1308	1420	1425	1454	1521	1615	1616	1615	1627	1652	1649	1724	1725	1749	1752	1816	1824	1829	1831	1919	1929	2027	2038	2035	2141	2200
Aulnoye Aymeries d.	1319	...	1427	...	1523	...	1624	...	1629	...	1703	...	1736	...	1759	...	1826	...	1833	1921	1938	...	...	2047	...	2210
Valenciennes ▷ d.	1348	...	1500	...	1550	...	1655	...	1700	...	1730	...	1805	...	1824	...	1859	...	1902	1953	2005	...	...	2113	...	2235
Lille Flandres ▷ a.	1427	...	1542	...	1627	...	1737	...	1739	...	1805	...	1842	...	1903	...	1942	...	1942	2035	2045	...	...	2149	...	2312

LOCAL TRAINS LILLE - VALENCIENNES

	Ⓐ	⚒	⚒	Ⓐ	Ⓐ	⑥t	†	Ⓐ	†	⚒	Ⓐ	⑥t	Ⓐ	Ⓐ	Ⓐ	⑥t	†	Ⓐ	Ⓐ	Ⓐ	†	⑥t	Ⓐ	Ⓐ	Ⓒ	Ⓐ
Lille Flandres d.	0537	0634	0737	0838	0945	1011	1011	1137	1224	1235	1337	1342	1535	1638	1655	1721	1721	1733	1750	1832	1911	1921	1942	2037	2120	2216
Valenciennes a.	0620	0721	0824	0923	1031	1055	1059	1223	1308	1328	1425	1425	1622	1724	1735	1807	1805	1820	1827	1915	1958	2007	2027	2121	2205	2305

	Ⓐ	⑥t	Ⓐ	⚒	Ⓐ	Ⓐ	⑥t	⚒	†	Ⓐ	Ⓐ	⑥t	Ⓐ	⑥t	†	Ⓒ	Ⓐ	Ⓐ	†	⑥t	Ⓐ	Ⓐ	⑥t	Ⓐ		
Valenciennes d.	0435	0439	0537	0635	0650	0742	0748	0835	1123	1139	1235	1235	1334	1352	1354	1553	1633	1736	1814	1815	1836	1935	2017	2035	...	...
Lille Flandres a.	0524	0526	0623	0724	0734	0830	0832	0924	1213	1225	1323	1323	1423	1440	1440	1642	1722	1822	1903	1903	1918	2023	2104	2123	...	...

b – Not May 3-6, 10-12.
r – Change at Aulnoye Aymeries.
t – Not May 1, 8.

v – † only.
▷ – For local trains see panel below main table.

⊕ – Subject to alteration on Ⓐ Feb. 22 - Mar. 12.
⊗ – Subject to alteration on Ⓐ Mar. 15 - Apr. 2.

BOULOGNE - ST POL - ARRAS and LILLE 263

km		Ⓐ	Ⓐ	⚒ ⊕	Ⓐ	⑥ t	Ⓐ	Ⓐ	⚒ ⊙	Ⓐ	⑥ t	Ⓐ ⊕	† z	† u	Ⓐ	⑥ t	Ⓐ		Ⓐ ⊗	⚒ ⊗	Ⓐ	† z	Ⓐ d	Ⓐ	Ⓐ ⊕	†
	Calais Ville **260** d.	...	...	...	...	...	...	...	...	...	...	...	...	...	...	...	...	...	...	...	...	...	...	...	...	...
0	**Boulogne Ville** § d.	...	...	0519	...	...	...	...	0652	...	...	0850	0857	...	...	...	...	...	...	1229	...	1346	...	...	1527	1537
27	Étaples Le Touquet § d.	...	...	0553	...	...	...	...	0711	...	...	0940	0933	...	...	...	...	...	...	1300	...	1404	...	...	1545	1556
39	Montreuil sur Mer d.	...	...	0603	...	...	...	...	0721	...	...	0952	0944	...	...	...	...	...	...	1310	...	1415	...	...	1556	1606
88	St Pol sur Ternoise a.	...	...	0646	...	...	...	...	0802	...	...	1030	1021	...	...	...	...	...	...	1357	...	1453	...	...	1640	1645
88	St Pol sur Ternoise d.	0543	0618	0648	0658	0716	...	0727	0811	0813	0816	...	1029	1047	1116	1116	1216	...	1323	1404	...	1455	1505	...	1648	1647
127	**Arras** a.	|	|	0725	|	|	...	0759	0845	|	|	...	1101	|	|	|	|	...	1359	1438	...	1522	|	...	1724	1718
120	Béthune a.	0614	0648	...	0729	0746	...	...	...	0846	0846	...	...	1117	1148	1146	1248	...	...	...	...	...	1540	...	...	...
120	Béthune ▶ d.	0616	0650	...	0731	0748	0750	...	...	0848	0848	...	...	1119	1150	1148	1251	1319	...	...	1501	...	1550	1719	...	...
162	**Lille Flandres** ▶ a.	0658	0725	...	0818	0824	0825	...	...	0925	0924	...	...	1158	1225	1224	1325	1358	...	...	1547	...	1625	1758	...	...

	Ⓐ	Ⓒ	Ⓒ	Ⓐ	Ⓐ	Ⓐ	Ⓒ	Ⓒ	Ⓐ	†
Calais Ville **260** d.	...	...	...	...	...	1644	1652	...	1754	...
Boulogne Ville § d.	...	1646	...	...	...	1723	1728	...	1842	...
Étaples Le Touquet § d.	...	1705	...	...	...	1803	1807	...	1909	...
Montreuil sur Mer d.	...	1716	...	...	...	1813	1817	...	1919	...
St Pol sur Ternoise a.	...	1759	...	...	...	1904	1855	...	2004	...
St Pol sur Ternoise d.	1737	1808	1810	...	1826	1906	1857	1921	...	...
Arras a.	1816	|	1841	...	1906	|	1924	|	...	...
Béthune a.	...	1838	...	...	...	1937	...	1947	...	...
Béthune ▶ d.	...	1847	...	1850	...	*1950*	...	1948	...	2019
Lille Flandres ▶ a.	...	1924	...	1925	...	*2025*	...	2025	...	2058

	⚒ ⊕	⚒ ⊕	Ⓐ	Ⓐ	Ⓐ	⑥ t	Ⓐ	Ⓐ ⊗	†	† z
Lille Flandres ▷ d.	...	...	...	0642	0735	0802	0835	...	0902	...
Béthune ▷ a.	...	...	...	0730	0811	0842	0908	...	0942	...
Béthune d.	...	...	...	0732	...	...	0909	...	0944	...
Arras d.	...	...	0640	|	...	...	|	0909	|	0942
St Pol sur Ternoise a.	...	...	0723	0802	...	...	0937	0943	1015	1017
St Pol sur Ternoise d.	0554	0712	...	...	...	...	...	0945	...	1026
Montreuil sur Mer d.	0647	0803	...	...	...	...	...	1031	...	1105
Étaples Le Touquet § d.	0712	0813	...	...	...	...	...	1040	...	1115
Boulogne Ville § a.	0737	0835	...	...	...	...	...	1102	...	1132
Calais Ville **260** a.	...	...	...	...	...	...	...	...	...	...

	⑥ t	⑥ q	†	† v	Ⓐ ⊗	⑥ q	Ⓐ	⚒ ⊗	Ⓐ ⊕	⑥ q		Ⓐ	Ⓐ	Ⓐ ⊕	Ⓐ	Ⓒ	Ⓐ	Ⓐ	Ⓐ	Ⓐ	Ⓒ	Ⓒ		Ⓐ	⑥ t	Ⓐ
Lille Flandres ▷ d.	0902	...	...	1133	...	...	1235	...	...	1236	1402	...	1533	...	1635	...	...	1735	...	...	1802	...	...	*1902*	1902	1940
Béthune ▷ a.	0948	...	...	1209	...	...	1310	...	...	1312	1442	...	1610	...	1710	...	...	1810	...	...	1841	...	...	*1939*	1942	2020
Béthune d.	0950	...	...	1211	...	...	1312	...	...	1314	...	...	1622	...	1712	...	...	1812	...	...	1842	...	...	1947	1948	2022
Arras d.	|	0942	1143	|	1223	1223	|	1319	...	|	...	1608	|	1645	|	1736	1736	|	1822	1842	|	1849	1935	|	|	|
St Pol sur Ternoise a.	1020	1017	1215	1242	1259	1259	1343	1355	...	1348	...	1644	1652	1721	1743	1803	1813	1843	1859	1913	1912	1924	2006	2017	2018	2052
St Pol sur Ternoise d.	...	1028	...	1244	...	1301	...	...	1406	1406	...	...	...	1724	...	1808	1815	...	...	1914	...	1926	...	2019	2020	...
Montreuil sur Mer d.	...	1106	...	1319	...	1353	...	...	1448	1449	...	...	...	1816	...	1856	1857	...	...	2002	...	2004	...	2101	2100	...
Étaples Le Touquet § d.	...	1115	...	1328	...	1402	...	...	1456	1458	...	...	...	1826	...	1906	1908	...	...	2013	...	2015	...	2111	2110	...
Boulogne Ville § a.	...	1135	...	1344	...	1419	...	...	...	1516	...	...	...	1841	...	1921	1926	...	...	2029	...	2032	...	2127	2127	...
Calais Ville **260** a.	...	...	...	1417	...	...	...	...	...	1551	...	...	...	1915	...	...	...	...	...	...	...	...	...	...	...	...

▶ – **Additional trains** Béthune - Lille (journey 35-52 minutes):
Ⓐ: 0531, 0600, 0631, 0700, 0719, 0819, 1231, 1300, 1631, 1700, 1731, 1750, 1818, 1833, 1900, 2027. ⑥: 0646, 0726, 0819, 1019, 1226, 1419, 1626, 1719.
†: 0826, 0919, 1226, 1626, 1719, 1819, 1926.

▷ – **Additional trains** Lille - Béthune (journey 35-52 minutes):
Ⓐ: 0542, 0607, 0702, 1202, 1242, 1602, 1642, 1702, 1742, 1802, 1835, 1910, 2042.
⑥: 0642, 1002, 1202, 1242, 1602, 1742, 1942, 2102.
†: 1002, 1142, 1602, 1742, 1942, 2102.

d – Not Apr. 2.
q – Not Apr. 10, May 1, 8.
t – Not May 1, 8.

u – Also Dec. 25, Jan. 1, Apr. 5, May 1, 8, 13; not May 2, 9.
v – Not May 13.
z – Not Apr. 5.

⊕ – Subject to alteration Apr. 3-18.
⊗ – Subject to alteration on Ⓐ Mar. 29 - Apr. 16.
⊙ – Subject to alteration Apr. 6-16.

§ – See also Table **260**.

265 PARIS and LILLE - DUNKERQUE and CALAIS *Fast trains*

Alternative connections are available by using *TGV* trains between Paris and Lille Flandres (Table **250**) and local trains between Lille Flandres and Dunkerque / Calais (Table **266**)

km		◇	◇		TGV	TGV	◇	🚌	TGV	TGV	◇	TGV		◇		◇		TGV		TGV		◇	🚌	TGV	
					7207	7301			7303	7229		7311						7321		7245				7331	
		Ⓐ	Ⓐ		Ⓐ	Ⓐ			⑥	①–⑥	⑦	Ⓒ	Ⓒ	⚒	⚒	⚒		①–⑥	⑥			†	†		Ⓒ
									v ‡	n	d	§				⊕		n	t						
0	**Paris Nord** 256 d.	...	...	...	0728	0722	...	...	0822	0958	...	0952	...	...	...	...	...	1222	...	1428	...	...	...	1452	...
199	Arras 256 d.	...	...	...	|	0818	...	...	0915	|	...	1048	...	...	...	...	...	1318	...	|	...	...	...	1545	...
219	Lens d.	...	...	...	|	0832	...	...	0928	|	...	1102	...	...	...	...	...	1332	...	|	...	...	...	1600	...
238	Béthune d.	...	...	...	|	0845	...	...	0941	|	...	1115	...	...	...	...	...	1345	...	|	...	...	...	1618	...
	Lille Europe d.	0722	0822	...	0832	|	0912	...	|	1101	1119	|	...	1247	...	1300	...	|	...	1529	...	1554	...	|	...
272	Hazebrouck d.	|	|	...	|	0908	|	...	1006	|	|	1138	1201	|	...	|	...	1408	1414	|	...	|	...	1641	1656
∆312	**Dunkerque** a.	0757	|	...	0905	0929	|	...	1028	|	1151	1200	|	|	...	1336	...	1429	|	|	...	|	...	1702	|
293	St Omer d.	...	|	...	...	...	|	...	...	|	...	...	1216	|	...	...	...	...	1428	|	...	|	...	...	1709
	Calais Fréthun a.	...	0850	0856	...	...	0940	0950	...	1131	...	...	|	1315	1332	...	...	...	|	1558	...	1626	1639	...	|
336	**Calais Ville** a.	...	|	0903	...	...	|	1007	...	1140	...	...	1248	|	1343	...	...	...	1453	...	...	|	1654	...	1738
	Boulogne 260 a.	...	0925	...	...	...	1009	...	...	...	...	...	1338	1344	...	...	...	...	1540	...	...	1654	...	...	1818

	◇	◇	🚌	◇	🚌	TGV	TGV	◇	🚌	TGV		◇	TGV	TGV	TGV	🚌	TGV	TGV			TGV	◇	🚌	TGV	
						7337	7339			7275			7343	7281	7285		7289	7347			7351			7357	
	Ⓐ	Ⓐ	Ⓐ	⑥	⑥	⑤–⑦	①–④	†	⑦	Ⓐ	Ⓐ	⑥	Ⓐ	Ⓐ			⑦	Ⓑ	Ⓐ	Ⓒ	⑤–⑦	†	†	⑤	
				t		w	m					t					e	h			w	u		f	
Paris Nord 256 d.	...	...	...	...	...	1622	1652	...	...	1728	...	...	1752	1828	1858	...	1858	1852	...	...	1952	...	...	2131	...
Arras 256 d.	...	...	...	...	...	1718	1747	...	...	|	...	...	1845	|	|	...	|	1944	...	...	2045	...	...	2224	...
Lens d.	...	...	...	...	...	1733	1801	...	...	|	...	...	1858	|	|	...	|	1957	...	...	2059	...	...	2238	...
Béthune d.	...	...	...	...	...	1746	1818	...	...	|	...	...	1911	|	|	...	|	2009	...	...	2112	...	...	2251	...
Lille Europe d.	1715	1721	...	1731	...	|	|	1825	...	1830	...	1905	|	1930	2000	...	2003	|	...	...	|	2213	...	|	...
Hazebrouck d.	|	|	...	|	...	1809	1841	|	...	|	...	|	1933	|	|	...	|	2032	2049	2059	2135	|	...	2313	...
Dunkerque a.	1749	|	...	|	...	1830	1904	|	...	|	...	1937	|	2001	|	...	2035	2053	|	|	2156	|	...	2335	...
St Omer d.	...	|	...	|	...	...	...	|	...	|	...	...	1946	...	|	...	...	...	2102	2114	...	|	...	...	...
Calais Fréthun a.	...	1749	1757	1759	1807	...	...	1854	1910	1858	1908	...	...	...	2031	2039	...	...	|	|	...	2241	2249	...	...
Calais Ville a.	...	|	1812	|	1822	...	...	|	1925	|	1915	...	...	...	|	2054	...	...	2132	2144	...	|	2304	...	...
Boulogne 260 a.	...	1817	...	1829	...	...	...	1922	...	1927	...	...	...	...	2101	...	...	...	...	2228	...	2309	...	...	...

	TGV		TGV	◇	TGV	🚌	TGV	TGV	🚌	◇	◇		TGV		◇	◇	🚌	◇	🚌	◇	🚌	◇	TGV		TGV
	7302		7304		7214		7220	7308					7318										7254		7336
	Ⓐ	Ⓐ	Ⓐ	Ⓐ	Ⓐ	Ⓐ	①–⑥	①⑥	⚒	⚒	Ⓐ			Ⓐ	Ⓐ	†	†	†	Ⓐ	Ⓐ	⑥	⑥	①–⑥	†	
							n	y				☆		⊗		s						t	n		
Boulogne 260 d.	...	...	...	...	...	...	0657	...	...	0744	...	0828	...	...	0940	...	...	1042	...	1133	...	1139	...	1258	...
Calais Ville d.	...	0542	...	...	...	0706	|	...	0750	|	...	0913	...	0953	|	...	1048	|	1139	|	1145	|	1235	1343	...
Calais Fréthun d.	...	|	...	...	...	0721	0729	...	0805	0813	...	|	...	1000	1011	...	1103	1111	1154	1202	1200	1208	1244	|	...
St Omer d.	...	0611	0623	...	...	...	|	...	...	|	...	0946	...	...	|	...	...	|	...	|	...	|	|	1415	...
Dunkerque d.	0535	|	|	0642	0646	...	|	0717	...	|	0814	|	0944	...	|	1035	...	|	...	|	...	|	|	|	1413
Hazebrouck d.	0559	0624	0638	|	|	...	|	0741	...	|	|	0959	1008	...	|	|	...	|	...	|	...	|	|	1429	1437
Lille Europe a.	|	...	|	0712	0719	...	0758	|	...	0843	0847	...	|	...	1043	1107	...	1142	...	1232	...	1238	1314	...	|
Béthune d.	0621	...	0700	...	|	...	|	0802	...	...	...	...	1030	...	...	...	...	...	...	...	...	...	|	...	1459
Lens d.	0634	...	0712	...	|	...	|	0815	...	...	...	...	1043	...	...	...	...	...	...	...	...	...	|	...	1512
Arras 256 d.	0656	...	0735	...	|	...	|	0835	...	...	...	...	1106	...	...	...	...	...	...	...	...	...	|	...	1535
Paris Nord 256 a.	0747	...	0827	...	0832	...	0902	0926	...	...	...	...	1156	...	...	...	...	...	...	...	...	...	1426	...	1626

			TGV	TGV	◇	🚌	◇	TGV	🚌	◇	◇	◇	TGV	TGV		TGV		TGV	🚌	◇	TGV	🚌	◇	TGV	
			7342	7270				7348					7288	7352		7356		7292			7358			7298	
	Ⓐ	Ⓒ			Ⓐ	⚒	⚒		†	†	Ⓐ	⑥	Ⓑ	⑦	Ⓒ	⑦	Ⓐ	Ⓐ	⑥	⑥	⑤	†	†	⑦	
												t	h	e		e				t	f			e	
Boulogne 260 d.	...	1444	...	...	...	...	1600	...	...	1716	...	...	...	...	1739	...	...	1904	...	1906	...	...	1946	...	...
Calais Ville d.	1525	1527	...	...	...	1609	|	...	1721	|	...	...	...	...	1826	...	1909	|	1906	|	...	1953	|	...	...
Calais Fréthun d.	|	|	...	1617	...	1624	1632	...	1736	1745	...	...	...	...	|	...	1917	1933	1921	1936	...	2008	2016	...	...
St Omer d.	1553	1556	...	|	...	...	|	...	...	|	...	...	...	1832	1859	...	...	|	...	|	...	...	|	...	...
Dunkerque d.	|	|	1552	|	1623	...	|	1711	...	|	1801	1816	1825	|	|	1912	...	|	...	|	1943	...	|	2115	...
Hazebrouck d.	1606	1608	1615	|	|	...	|	1737	...	|	|	|	|	1844	1913	1937	...	|	...	|	2007	...	|	|	...
Lille Europe a.	...	...	|	1646	1658	...	1703	|	...	1815	1834	1847	1859	|	...	|	...	2003	...	2006	|	...	2045	2147	...
Béthune d.	...	...	1639	|	...	...	...	1800	...	...	...	...	|	1906	...	2000	...	|	...	...	2029	...	...	|	...
Lens d.	...	...	1651	|	...	...	...	1813	...	...	...	...	|	1920	...	2013	...	|	...	...	2042	...	...	|	...
Arras 256 d.	...	...	1706	|	...	...	...	1836	...	...	...	...	|	1936	...	2035	...	|	...	...	2105	...	...	|	...
Paris Nord 256 a.	...	...	1756	1802	...	...	...	1926	...	...	...	...	2002	2026	...	2126	...	2111	...	...	2156	...	...	2302	...

FOR NOTES SEE BELOW TABLE 266 ON NEXT PAGE →

Note: 🚌 connections between Calais Ville and Calais Fréthun are subject to confirmation

266 ARRAS and LILLE - DUNKERQUE and CALAIS *Local trains*

km	*See also Table 265*	⚒	Ⓐ	Ⓐ	⚒	Ⓐ	⚒	Ⓐ	Ⓐ	⑥	Ⓐ	Ⓐ	Ⓒ	Ⓐ	†	Ⓐ	⑥	Ⓐ	Ⓐ	Ⓐ	†	Ⓒ	†	Ⓐ	⚒	Ⓐ
										t				⊗			t		⊗		§		§	▷	▷	⊗
0	**Arras** d.	...	...	0605	...	...	0634	...	...	...	0721	...	...	...	...	...	0805	0805	...	0845	0852	...	...	...	0920	...
20	Lens d.	...	...	0621	...	...	0650	...	...	...	0739	...	...	...	...	...	0822	0822	...	0901	0908	...	...	...	0937	...
39	Béthune d.	0603a	...	0638	...	...	0710	...	...	...	0800	...	...	...	...	...	0850	0853	...	0918	0926	...	...	...	0955	...
•46	**Lille Flandres** d.	|	0627	|	0641	0700	|	0715	0732	0727	|	0800	0813	0815	...	0841	|	|	0900	|	|	0922	...	0932	|	0958
•25	Armentières d.	|	0642	|	0655	0715	|	0730	|	0747	|	|	0828	0830	...	0857	|	|	0917	|	|	0939	...	0947	|	1012
73	Hazebrouck a.	0632a	0658	0705	0719	0729	0738	0754	0801	0803	0825	0831	0848	0854	...	0914	0917	0920	0938	0943	0952	0955	←	1004	1019	1028
73	Hazebrouck d.	0634	0700	0707	0721	0731	0739	0756	0803	0805	...	0833	0850	0856	0900	0916	0919	...	0940	...	→	0957	1009	1006	1021	1030
113	**Dunkerque** a.	|	|	0734	0753	|	0804	|	0833	|	...	|	0921	|	|	0943	0945	...	|	...	...	|	1041	1031	1044	|
94	St Omer d.	0652	0720	...	...	0749	...	0811	...	0821	...	0845	...	0911	0914	...	...	...	0953	...	...	1009	...	...	...	1043
137	**Calais Ville** a.	0730	0748	...	...	0812	...	0842	...	0848	...	0907	...	0943	0940	...	...	...	1018	...	...	1037	...	...	...	1113
	Boulogne 260 a.	...	0839	...	...	0854	...	...	...	0936	...	0954	...	1027	...	...	...	...	...	...	...	1119	...	...	...	...

	Ⓒ	Ⓒ	Ⓒ	Ⓐ	⚒	Ⓐ	⑥	⚒	Ⓐ	⚒	†	⑥	Ⓐ	⑥	Ⓐ	Ⓐ	Ⓒ	†	Ⓐ		Ⓐ	Ⓐ	Ⓒ	Ⓒ	Ⓐ	Ⓐ
		§		▽	▷	▷	t	g		▷		t		t						b						
Arras d.	...	1052	...	...	...	1215	...	...	...	1220	...	...	...	1324	1324	...	...	1402	1442	...	...	1537	...	1548	...	...
Lens d.	...	1110	...	...	...	1230	...	...	...	1243	...	...	...	1341	1341	...	...	1419	1500	...	...	1603	...	1606	...	...
Béthune d.	...	1128	...	...	...	1247	...	...	...	1306	...	...	...	1357	1359	...	...	1436	1520	...	...	1625	...	1624	...	1648
Lille Flandres d.	1017	|	1124	1200	1232	|	...	1241	1300	|	1316	1338	1339	|	|	1403	1416	|	|	1532	1600	|	1621	|	1632	|
Armentières d.	1035	|	1139	1217	|	|	...	1302	|	|	1334	1354	1354	|	|	1418	1431	|	|	1549	|	|	1636	|	|	|
Hazebrouck a.	1053	1156	1159	1236	1306	1311	...	1318	1326	1336	1356	1412	1414	1420	1425	1436	1449	1500	1547	1607	1628	1650	1654	1650	1704	1718
Hazebrouck d.	1055	1209	1201	1238	1308	1313	1316	1320	1328	1338	1357	1414	1416	1422	1449	1438	1451	1502	...	1612	1630	1652	1656	1705	1706	1719
Dunkerque a.	1124	1245	*1245*	|	1333	|	|	1356	|	1406	1421	|	1440	1447	1522	*1522*	|	1528	...	1646	|	1717	|	1733	1730	|
St Omer d.	...	...	1216	1251	...	1331	1334	...	1344	...	...	1428	...	...	...	1451	1504	...	...	...	1646	...	1709	...	...	1735
Calais Ville a.	...	...	1248	1316	...	1359	1407	...	1407	...	...	1453	...	...	...	1520	1534	...	...	...	1712	...	1738	...	...	1802
Boulogne 260 a.	...	...	1338	...	...	...	1505	...	...	...	...	1540	...	...	...	1600	1618	...	...	...	1810	...	1818	...	...	...

	Ⓐ	Ⓐ	Ⓒ	Ⓐ		Ⓐ	Ⓐ	Ⓐ	Ⓒ	Ⓐ	Ⓐ	Ⓐ	Ⓐ	Ⓐ	Ⓒ	Ⓐ	†	⑥	Ⓐ	Ⓒ	Ⓐ	Ⓒ		Ⓐ		⑦
																		t					q		x	p
Arras d.	...	1644	...	...	1722	...	...	1727	...	...	1806	...	...	1851	...	...	1926	1936	...	...	2020	2029	...	...	2151	...
Lens d.	...	1700	...	...	1738	...	...	1749	...	...	1823	...	...	1906	...	...	1942	1953	...	...	2039	2045	...	...	2206	...
Béthune d.	...	1720	...	...	1756	...	...	1824r	...	...	1844	...	...	1923	...	...	2000	2012	...	...	2059	2102	...	...	2225	...
Lille Flandres d.	1700	|	1718	1729	|	1745	1810	|	1821	1832	|	1841	1915	|	1921	1930	|	|	2015	2020	|	|	2108	2208	|	2223
Armentières d.	|	|	1736	|	|	1803	|	|	1839	|	|	1856	|	|	1938	1944	|	|	2030	2036	|	|	2126	2224	|	2238
Hazebrouck a.	1730	1749	1753	1759	1820	1822	1844	1851	1857	1901	1909	1914	1945	1951	1956	2001	2025	2036	2047	2057	2128	2126	2147	2245	2250	2257
Hazebrouck d.	1732	1751	1755	1801	1822a	1825	1846	1853	1859	1903	1911	1916	1947	...	1958	2003	...	2038	2049	2059	...	2128	2151	2247	...	2259
Dunkerque a.	|	1823	1826	|	1848a	1857	|	1915	|	1925	|	1949	|	...	2032	2037	...	2103	*2123*	|	...	2153	2223	2311	...	|
St Omer d.	1746	...	...	1819	...	...	1859	...	1912	...	1931	...	2000	...	...	...	...	...	2102	2114	...	...	...	...	...	2312
Calais Ville a.	1812	...	...	1848	...	...	1921	...	1943	...	2001	...	2028	...	...	...	...	...	2132	2144	...	...	...	...	...	2342
Boulogne 260 a.	1852	...	...	...	...	...	2007	...	2022	...	...	...	2115	...	...	...	...	...	...	2228	...	...	...	...	...	...

CALAIS and DUNKERQUE - LILLE and ARRAS — 266

Local trains

	Ⓐ	⚒	Ⓐ	⚒	Ⓐ	Ⓐ	⚒	†	Ⓐ	⑥ t	⑥ t	Ⓐ	Ⓐ	⑥ t	Ⓐ	⚒	Ⓐ	⚒	Ⓒ	Ⓐ ☆	Ⓐ		☆	Ⓐ ⊡	Ⓐ ⊡	Ⓐ
Boulogne **260** d.	...	...	...	...	...	...	...	...	0602	...	...	...	...	...	...	0702	...	...	...	...	...	...	0828	...	...	...
Calais Ville 260 d.	0503	...	0542	...	0558	...	...	...	0647	0643	...	...	0705	0705	...	0749	...	...	...	0838	...	...	0913	...	...	...
St Omer d.	0529	...	0611	...	0629	...	...	...	0712	0715	...	...	0740	0743	...	0815	...	...	...	0909	...	...	0946	...	...	...
Dunkerque d.	*0507*	0541a	|	0559	|	0619	0636	...	|	|	0655	0701	|	|	0737	*0748*	0821	...	0842	|	0910	0911c	|	1023	1044	...
Hazebrouck a.	0542	0607a	0624	0633	0642	0652	0704	...	0725	0733	0730	0736	0754	0755	0802	0830	0845	...	0910	0921	0935	0944c	0959	1047	1112	...
Hazebrouck d.	0544	0609	0626	0639	0644	0654	0706	0724	0727	0735	0737	0738	0756	0757	0804	0832	0847	0854	0912	0923	0937	0945	1001	1049	1114	...
Armentières d.	0601	|	|	0704	|	0716	|	|	|	|	0804	0805	|	0823	|	|	0903	|	0932	0946	1002	|	1018	1111	|	...
Lille Flandres a.	0617	|	0658	0721	|	0731	|	|	0759	0802	0819	0821	|	0842	0831	0858	0917	|	0947	1003	1019	|	1033	1125	|	←
Béthune d.	...	0637	...	...	0715	...	0743	0750	...	...	...	...	0824	...	...	...	...	0923	...	...	...	1012	...	...	1139	1220
Lens d.	...	0655	...	...	0734	...	0759	0807	...	...	...	...	0841	...	...	...	...	0941	...	...	...	1030	...	...	→	1239
Arras a.	...	0714	...	...	0746	...	0821	0820	...	...	...	...	0855	...	...	...	...	0959	...	...	...	1049	...	...	...	1259

	Ⓐ ☆	Ⓒ	Ⓐ ⊡	⑥ t	Ⓐ ☆	⑥ t	†	⚒ ⊡	⚒ ⊡	⚒ ⊡	Ⓐ	⑥ t	Ⓐ	Ⓒ	⑥⑦ k	†	⑥ t	Ⓐ	⑥ t	Ⓐ	Ⓐ	Ⓐ	Ⓐ	Ⓐ	Ⓒ	Ⓒ
Boulogne **260** d.	...	...	...	...	1036z	...	1057	...	...	...	...	1157	1157	...	...	1258	1303	...	...	...	...	...	...	...	1444	...
Calais Ville 260 d.	1038	...	...	...	1118	1120	1136	...	...	...	1231	1240	1245	...	...	1343	1353	...	...	1441	...	...	...	1525	1527	...
St Omer d.	1107	...	...	...	1146	1150	1202	...	...	...	1256	1312	1314	...	...	1415	1425	...	...	1509	...	...	...	1553	1556	...
Dunkerque d.	|	1057	1106	1118	|	|	|	1157	...	1210	|	|	|	1307	1343	|	|	...	1438	|	...	1512	1534	|	*1531*	1531
Hazebrouck a.	1120	1121	1143	1146	1202	1202	1213	1224	...	1243	1314	1323	1327	1335	1417	1429	1438	...	1506	1520	...	1545	1602	1606	1608	1603
Hazebrouck d.	1122	1123	1145	1148	1204	1204	1215	1226	1229	1243	1316	1330	1329	1337	1419	1431	1440	1454	1508	1522	1541	1547	1604	1608	1610	1626
Armentières d.	1143	1141	1204	|	1224	1225	1236	|	|	1309	|	1347	1350	1356	|	1453	1457	|	1528	1544	|	1609	|	1629	1627	|
Lille Flandres a.	1158	1157	1220	|	1238	1240	1250	1259	|	1330	1348	1403	1403	1411	|	1508	1511	|	1542	1558	|	1622	|	1645	1643	|
Béthune d.	...	...	...	1216	...	...	...	...	1302	...	...	...	...	...	1446	...	...	1522	...	...	1606	...	1644	...	...	1652
Lens d.	...	...	...	1234	...	...	...	...	1320	...	...	...	...	...	1505	...	...	1540	...	...	1626	...	1702	...	...	1710
Arras a.	...	...	...	1253	...	...	...	...	1335	...	...	...	...	...	1522	...	...	1555	...	...	1642	...	1718	...	...	1724

	Ⓐ	Ⓐ	Ⓒ	Ⓐ		Ⓐ	Ⓐ	Ⓐ	Ⓐ	Ⓒ	Ⓐ	Ⓒ	Ⓐ	Ⓒ	Ⓐ	Ⓐ	Ⓒ	Ⓐ		Ⓒ	Ⓐ	Ⓐ	Ⓒ	Ⓐ	Ⓒ	Ⓐ
Boulogne **260** d.	...	...	...	...	...	...	...	...	...	1644	...	...	...	...	...	...	1739	1731	...	...	...	...	1845	...	...	1952
Calais Ville 260 d.	...	...	...	1617	...	...	...	1715	...	1726	...	...	1746	...	...	...	1826	1827	...	...	1914	...	1932	...	...	2036
St Omer d.	...	...	...	1646	...	...	...	1744	...	1755	...	...	1815	...	...	...	1859	1856	...	...	1942	...	2005	...	...	2108
Dunkerque d.	1614	...	1633	|	1639a	1715	1726	|	...	*1725*	...	...	|	1807	1810	1836	|	*1845*	1845	1917	|	1930	|	...	2050	|
Hazebrouck a.	1644	...	1659	1659	1713a	1740	1758	1801	...	1806	...	...	1827	1835	1843	1858	1913	1912	1917	1945	1956	1959	2018	...	2115	2120
Hazebrouck d.	1646	1649	1701	1701	1715	1742	1800	1803	1806	1808	1815	1824	1829	1837	1845	1900	1915	1922	1918	1947	...	2001	2020	2037	2117	2122
Armentières d.	1707	|	1722	1727	|	1806	|	|	1832	1825	|	|	|	1900	1909	|	1933	1946	|	2004	...	2023	2045	|	2135	2142
Lille Flandres a.	1721	|	1739	1744	|	1821	1831	|	1846	1840	|	|	1858	1915	1923	1930	1948	2002	|	2020	...	2038	2100	|	2150	2158
Béthune d.	...	1723	...	...	1744	...	...	1829	...	...	1845	1853	...	...	...	...	...	...	1943	...	...	...	...	2105	...	...
Lens d.	...	1742	...	...	1803	...	...	1851	...	...	1903	1912	...	...	...	...	...	...	2004	...	...	...	...	2123	...	...
Arras a.	...	1759	...	...	1817	...	...	1902	...	...	1918	1929	...	...	...	...	...	...	2020	...	...	...	...	2138	...	...

NOTES FOR TABLES 265 AND 266

- **a** – Ⓐ only.
- **b** – On Ⓒ Lille 1535, Hazebrouck d. 1610, Dunkerque 1638.
- **c** – Ⓒ only.
- **d** – Also May 1, 8.
- **e** – Also Apr. 5, May 24.
- **f** – Also Dec. 24, 31, May 12; not Dec. 25, Jan. 1.
- **g** – Depart Lille 1246 on Ⓐ.
- **h** – Not Dec. 25, Jan. 1, May 13.
- **k** – Not May 1, 8.
- **m** – Not Dec. 24, 31, Apr. 5, May 12, 13, 24.
- **n** – Not Apr. 5, May 24.
- **p** – Also Dec. 25, Jan. 1, May 1, 8.
- **q** – On Ⓒ depart Lille 2118.
- **r** – Arrive 1807.
- **s** – Not May 24.
- **t** – Not May 1, 8.
- **u** – Not Jan. 10 - 31.
- **v** – Also Dec. 25, Jan. 1, May 13.
- **w** – Also Dec. 24, 31, Apr. 5, May 12, 13, 24.
- **x** – Runs 6 - 12 minutes later on Ⓐ.
- **y** – Also Dec. 25, Jan. 1, Apr. 6, May 13, 25.
- **z** – ①–④ (not holidays).

TGV –🅁, supplement payable.

- ▵ – *303 km* by *TGV* via Lille Europe.
- ▷ – Subject to alteration Apr. 26 - May 14.
- ▽ – Subject to alteration on Feb. 5, 12, 19.
- ◇ – TER à Grande Vitesse (TER GV) via high-speed line (1, 2 class), operated by *TGV* unit. Supplement *Côte d'Opale* payable (€3, valid all day). Reservation not necessary.
- ⊕ – Not on ①–⑤ Apr. 26 - May 14.
- ⊗ – Subject to alteration on Ⓐ Feb. 1 - 19.
- ⊡ – Subject to alteration on Ⓐ May 17 - June 4.
- ☆ – Subject to alteration on Ⓐ Feb. 22 - Mar. 12.
- ‡ – On May 13 by 🚌 Hazebrouck - Dunkerque.
- § – Subject to alteration on May 13.
- • – Distance from Hazebrouck.
- 🚌 – Connecting SNCF bus service.

PARIS - BEAUVAIS — 267

km		Ⓐ	⑥t	Ⓐ	Ⓐ	⑥t	†v	†	Ⓐ	⑥t	Ⓐ			⚒	Ⓐ	Ⓒ	Ⓐ	⑥t	Ⓐ	Ⓐ	Ⓒ	Ⓐ	⑥t	Ⓐ	Ⓐ	Ⓒ
0	**Paris Nord** d.	0615	0632	0656	0741	0748	0801	0903	0929	0933	1018	1118	1218	1318	1418	1433	1618	1630	1649	1718	1733	1748	1801	1818	1836*	1901
80	**Beauvais** a.	0730	0739	0807	0853	0902	0908	1011	1042	1050	1131	1235	1337	1439	1537	1549	1730	1740	1759	1833	1844	1906	1913	1927	1959	2011

	Ⓐ	Ⓐ	⑥t	Ⓑh	Ⓒ
Paris Nord d.	1918	1949	1948	2048	2148
Beauvais a.	2030	2100	2105	2202	2300

	Ⓐ	⑥t	Ⓐ	⑥t	†	Ⓐ	Ⓐ	⑥t	†	Ⓐ	⑥t	Ⓐ	†		⚒	⚒	†
Beauvais d.	0508	0511	0614	0621	0633	0642	0717	0719	0742	0759	0845	0847	0922	1031	1144	1239	1253
Paris Nord a.	0630	0624	0725	0731	0745	0757	0829	0831	0855	0914	1000	0958	1029	1145	1300	1400	1401

	⚒		Ⓐ	⑥t	Ⓒ	Ⓐ	Ⓐ	†	⑥t	Ⓐ	⑥t	†	⑥t	†	Ⓐ	†
Beauvais d.	1349	1428	1558	1613	1717	1740	1814	1824	1826	1908	1918	1924	2004	2008	2010	2111
Paris Nord a.	1500	1546	1716	1730	1831	1849	1933	1931	1932	2018	2032	2031	2108	2129	2117	2217

Most trains call at Persan-Beaumont (30 minutes from Paris). Trains also run Creil - Beavais and v.v. (11 trains each way on Ⓐ, 7 on ⑥, 4 on †).

- **h** – Also May 1, 8.
- **t** – Not May 1, 8.
- **v** – Not Apr. 5.
- ***** – From suburban platforms.

BEAUVAIS - LE TRÉPORT — ↄ 267a

km		Ⓐ ⊕	①⑥ b	† v	⚒ ⊗	⑤ f	Ⓐ	⑥ t	†	†	⑥ t	⑤ z
	Paris Nord **267** d.	...	...	0801	...	...	...	...	...	...	...	...
0	**Beauvais** d.	0734	0907	0910	1243	1453	1844	1900	1902	2027	2032	2041
49	Abancourt d.	0829	0952	0955	1335	1538	1936	1945	1956	2115	2115	2125
103	Eu d.	0913	1039	1041	1420	1629	2021	2031	2041	2159	2201	2210
106	**Le Tréport** a.	0917	1044	1046	1425	1633	2025	2035	2046	2203	2205	2215

	Ⓐ	⑥ t	†	① d	⚒ ⊗	†	⑤ f	†	⚒	†
Le Tréport d.	0613	0650	0740	0951	1205	1247	1545	1648	1720	1835
Eu d.	0618	0655	0745	0956	1210	1252	1550	1653	1724	1840
Abancourt d.	0706	0740	0832	1047	1259	1335	1647	1738	1815	1924
Beauvais a.	0749	0826	0916	1132	1344	1422	1731	1822	1903	2006
Paris Nord **267** a.	...	...	...	...	...	...	...	1931	...	2129

- **b** – Also May 14, 25; not Mar. 22, 27, 29, Apr. 3, 5, May 1, 8, 24.
- **d** – Also May 14, 25; not Mar. 22, 29, Apr. 5, May 24.
- **f** – Not Dec. 25, Jan. 1, Mar. 26, June 11.
- **t** – Not May 1, 8.
- **v** – Not Apr. 5.
- **z** – Not Dec. 25, Jan. 1.
- ⊕ – Subject to alteration Mar. 22 - Apr. 9.
- ⊗ – Subject to alteration on ②–⑤ Mar. 2 - 26.

AMIENS - ROUEN — 268

km		① g	Ⓐ	Ⓐ	⑥ t	⑦ d	Ⓐ E ‡	Ⓐ E 🚌	Ⓐ D	⑥ t	†		⑤ z	①–④ §		Ⓐ	†	⑥ t		Ⓐ	Ⓐ		Ⓒ	
	Lille Flandres **256** d.	...	...	0620	0805	...	...	...	1103	...	...	...	...	...	...	...	...	...	...	1702	...	...	1805	...
0	**Amiens** d.	0543	...	0751	0933	0952	1217	...	1227	1234	1450	...	1610	1613	...	1716	1721	1733	...	1830	1848	...	1935	...
31	Poix de Picardie d.	0602	...	0811	0952	1011	1235	...	1250	1258	1509	...	1632	1636	...	1738	1744	1754	...	1847	1913	...	1955	...
52	Abancourt d.	0619	0722	0825	1005	1025	1248	...	1301	1312	1522	...	1650	1648	...	1750	1800	1807	...	1859	1934	...	2009	...
73	Serqueux d.	0639	0738	0837	1018	1040	1300	1322	1313	1327	1539	...	1705	1703	...	1807	1816	1827	...	1911	1949	...	2023	...
121	**Rouen Rive-Droite** a.	0722	0826	0908	1050	1115	...	1412	1344	1408	1625	...	1740	...	...	1841	1850	1907	...	1943	...	...	2056	...

	Ⓐ	Ⓐ		⑥ t	† v		Ⓐ E 🚌	Ⓐ E	Ⓐ F		Ⓐ E 🚌	Ⓐ A	Ⓐ B	⑥ t		L 🚌	①–④ G§	⑤	Ⓐ H			Ⓐ	⑤ z	†
Rouen Rive-Droite d.	...	0704	...	0814	0916	...	1012	...	1038	...	1120	...	1230	1230	...	1600	...	1635	1635	...	1814	1835	1917	1927
Serqueux d.	0622	0735	...	0848	0949	...	1102	1112	1110	...	1300	1311	1311	1311	...	1710	1715	1708	1708	...	1846	1916	1950	2001
Abancourt d.	0637	0748	...	0902	1004	...	...	1126	1125	...	...	1327	1327	1327	...	...	1731	1722	1722	...	1859	1929	2006	2015
Poix de Picardie d.	0655	0800	...	0915	1016	...	...	1139	1138	...	...	1342	1342	1342	...	...	1743	1734	1734	...	1912	...	2018	2028
Amiens a.	0719	0817	...	0933	1033	...	...	1158	1155	...	...	1407	1407	1407	...	...	1801	1753	1753	...	1929	...	2037	2048
Lille Flandres **256** a.	...	0937	...	1053	...	...	...	1327	1327	...	...	...	...	...	...	...	...	...	...	...	2058	...	...	...

- **A** – To Apr. 16.
- **B** – From Apr. 19.
- **D** – From May 3.
- **E** – To Apr. 30.
- **F** – From May 25.
- **G** – To Apr. 15.
- **H** – From Apr. 16.
- **L** – ①–④ to Apr. 29 (not Apr. 5).
- **d** – Also May 1, 8.
- **g** – Also Apr. 6, May 14, 25.
- **t** – Not May 1, 8.
- **v** – Not May 13.
- **z** – Not Dec. 25, Jan. 1.
- § – Not holidays.
- ‡ – Subject to alteration Apr. 12 - 30.

269 RENNES / DOL / ST MALO - MONT ST MICHEL

By Keolis Emeraude

km		⚒		Ⓐ	Ⓒ					
0	Rennes (Gare SNCF) d.	0930	...	...	...	...	1130	1245	1640	...
	Dol (Gare SNCF) d.	|	...	1032	1107	...	|	|	|	...
68	Mont St Michel a.	1050	...	1102	1137	...	1250	1405	1800	...

Mont St Michel d.	0930	1110	...	1430	...	1600	...	1725	...
Dol (Gare SNCF) a.	|	|	...	|	...	1635	...	|	...
Rennes (Gare SNCF) a.	1050	1235	...	1550	...	...	...	1845	...

Service Dec. 13, 2009 - July 3, 2010

Connections (not guaranteed) are available at Rennes with *TGV* services to / from Paris.
Combined rail / bus tickets are available from rail stations. Rail passes not valid.
Operator: Keolis Emeraude, St Malo, ✆ 02 99 19 70 70.

St Malo - Mont St Michel: *service to July 2, 2010.* Tickets may be purchased from the station. Take route 17 from St Malo Gare SNCF (direction Fougères); change at Pontorson to route 6:
Depart St Malo 0940 and 1630 (arrive Mont St Michel 1138 and 1813).
Depart Mont St Michel 0920 Ⓐ and 1545 (arrive St Malo 1110 Ⓐ and 1740).

270 PARIS - ROUEN - LE HAVRE

km							3101		13101	3103	3103		13103	3105	3105	13105	3191	3107	3193				13107	3109	3143
		Ⓐ	⑥ t	⚒	Ⓐ	⚒	Ⓐ	⑥ t	Ⓐ	⑥	Ⓐ	⑦ d		Ⓒ	Ⓐ	⚒	⑦ Dd	Ⓐ	⑥ Du	⑥ t	†	⚒		①–⑥ s	R
0	**Paris St Lazare** § d.	...	...	...	...	0611	0653	...	0720	0750	0753	...	0820	0850	0853	1020	1036	1050	1050	...	...	...	1220	1250	1350
57	Mantes la Jolie § d.	...	...	...	0627	0644	|	0737	0752	|	|	...	0853	|	|	1052	1108	|	|	...	...	...	1252	|	|
79	Vernon (Eure) d.	...	...	...	0645	0708	|	0750	0806	|	|	...	0907	|	|	1106	1126	|	|	...	...	...	1306	|	|
111	Val de Reuil d.	...	...	...	0706	0729	|	0812	0828	|	|	...	0928	|	|	1128	1147	|	|	...	...	...	1328	|	|
126	Oissel d.	...	...	...	0717	0739	|	0824	0838	|	|	...	0938	|	|	1138	1157	|	|	...	...	...	1339	|	|
140	**Rouen** Rive-Droite a.	...	...	...	0727	0750	0801	0838	0849	0901	0901	...	0949	1001	1001	1149	1207	1201	1201	...	...	...	1349	1401	1457
140	**Rouen** Rive-Droite d.	0632	0634	0700	*0735*	...	0804	...	...	0904	0904	0904	...	1004	1004	...	...	1204	...	1204	1219	1249	...	1404	1500
178	Yvetot d.	0654	0656	0731	*0807*	...	0825	...	...	0925	0925	0925	...	1025	1025	...	...	1225	...	1225	1240	1320	...	1425	1521
203	Bréauté-Beuzeville ▲ d.	0707	0708	0750	*0823*	...	0840	...	...	0941	0940	0940	...	1040	1040	...	...	1240	...	1240	1255	1339	...	1440	1537
228	**Le Havre** a.	0724	0723	0813	*0839*	...	0855	...	...	0956	0955	0955	...	1055	1055	...	...	1255	...	1255	1310	1402	...	1455	1552

	3111	3113	13109	3115	3117		3119	13111	3121			3123	13113	13115	3125		13117	3127	3129	13119	3131			13121	13123
	⑤ q	⑥ u			Ⓐ	⑥ t	⑥ v	Ⓑ h	Ⓐ	†	Ⓐ	Ⓐ	Ⓒ t	Ⓐ		Ⓐ	Ⓒ	①–④ m	⑤ b	Ⓐ	Ⓐ	Ⓒ	Ⓐ	⑦ e	Ⓐ
Paris St Lazare § d.	1350	1350	1420	1450	1550	...	1620	1620	1650	...	1653	1725	1720	1730	1750	1753	1820	1825	1825	1830	1850	...	1853	1920	1930
Mantes la Jolie § d.	|	|	1452	|	|	...	1652	1652	|	...	1725	|	1752	|	|	1825	1852	|	|	|	|	...	1925	1952	|
Vernon (Eure) d.	|	|	1506	|	|	...	1707	1706	|	...	1747	|	1806	1811	|	1847	1906	|	|	1911	|	...	1947	2007	2011
Val de Reuil d.	|	|	1528	|	|	...	1728	1728	|	...	1809	|	1828	1833	|	1909	1928	|	|	1933	|	...	2008	2028	2033
Oissel d.	|	|	1538	|	|	...	1738	1738	|	...	1819	|	1838	1844	|	1919	1938	|	|	1944	|	...	2019	2038	2044
Rouen Rive-Droite a.	1501	1501	1549	1601	1701	...	1749	1750	1801	...	...	1836	1849	1855	1901	...	1949	1936	1936	1955	2001	...	2031	2049	2055
Rouen Rive-Droite d.	...	1504	...	1604	1704	1704	1752	...	1804	1804	...	1839	...	...	1904	...	...	...	1939	...	2004	2004	...	...	...
Yvetot d.	...	1525	...	1625	1725	1725	1813	...	1825	1827	...	1900	...	...	1925	...	...	...	2000	...	2025	2027	...	...	...
Bréauté-Beuzeville ▲ d.	...	1540	...	1640	1740	1740	1829	...	1840	1841	...	1915	...	...	1940	...	...	...	2015	...	2040	2040	...	...	...
Le Havre a.	...	1555	...	1655	1755	1755	1843	...	1855	1855	...	1930	...	...	1955	...	...	...	2030	...	2055	2056	...	...	...

	3133	5376	5438	13125	3135	3137	13127	3137	3139	13129	3141	13131
		TGV ♥	*TGV* ♠ y	Ⓐ	⑥ v	①–④ c	⑤ b	⑦	⑤ a	N	⑤⑦ x	⑥
Paris St Lazare § d.	1950	...	...	2020	2020	2120	2120	2120	2150	2320	2350	2350
Mantes la Jolie § d.	|	2030	2110	2052	2052	2152	2151	2152	|	2352	0022	0022
Vernon (Eure) d.	|	|	|	2106	2107	2207	2206	2207	|	0006	0037	0037
Val de Reuil d.	|	|	|	2128	2128	2228	2228	2228	|	0028	0059	0100
Oissel d.	|	|	|	2138	2138	2238	2238	2238	|	0038	0110	0110
Rouen Rive-Droite a.	2101	2114	2155	2149	2147	2249	2249	2249	2301	0049	0119	0119
Rouen Rive-Droite d.	2104	2118	2158	...	2150	2252	...	2252	2304	...	0122	...
Yvetot d.	2125	|	|	...	2211	2313	...	2313	2325	...	0143	...
Bréauté-Beuzeville ▲ d.	2140	|	|	...	2226	2328	...	2328	2340	...	0158	...
Le Havre a.	2155	2200	2240	...	2241	2343	...	2343	2355	...	0213	...

		13100	13102	3100		13104	13106	3104
	Ⓐ	Ⓐ	⑥ u	Ⓐ	Ⓐ	Ⓐ	Ⓐ	⑥ u
Le Havre d.	...	...	...	0531	...	...	...	0613
Bréauté-Beuzeville ▲ d.	...	...	...	0548	...	...	...	0628
Yvetot d.	...	...	...	0603	...	...	...	0643
Rouen Rive-Droite a.	...	...	...	0623	...	...	...	0705
Rouen Rive-Droite d.	0526	0559	0609	0626	...	0649	0659	0709
Oissel d.	0538	0609	0620	|	0638	|	0709	0719
Val de Reuil d.	0548	0619	0630	|	0648	0706	0719	0730
Vernon (Eure) d.	0611	0641	0653	|	0711	0724	0742	0753
Mantes la Jolie § a.	0631	0656	0706	|	0731	|	0756	0806
Paris St Lazare § a.	0708	0735	0740	0738	0808	0815	0835	0840

	13108	3102			3106	13110		5436	5316	3108	13112		13114	3110		3112	13116	3114	13118	3116		3118	13120	3120	3122
	⑦ e	Ⓐ	Ⓐ	⑥ t	Ⓐ	①–⑥ s	Ⓐ	*TGV* ♠	*TGV* ♥		①–⑥ n	Ⓐ	Ⓑ h	⑥ v		①–⑥ s	⑥ u	⑦ e		①–⑥ n	⑥ t	Ⓐ			⑤ p
Le Havre d.	...	0631	...	0645	0703	...	0725	0743	0755	0803	...	0903	...	0913	...	1003	...	1103	...	1203	1245	1303	...	1403	...
Bréauté-Beuzeville ▲ d.	...	0648	...	0709	0719	...	0740	|	|	0819	...	0919	...	0928	...	1019	...	1119	...	1219	1309	1320	...	1419	...
Yvetot d.	...	0703	...	0728	0734	...	0753	|	|	0834	...	0934	...	0943	...	1034	...	1134	...	1234	1327	1334	...	1434	...
Rouen Rive-Droite a.	...	0723	...	0759	0756	...	0825	0830	0840	0856	...	0956	...	1005	...	1056	...	1156	...	1256	1359	1356	...	1456	...
Rouen Rive-Droite d.	0709	0726	...	...	0759	0809	...	0833	0845	0859	0909	...	1009	1009	...	1059	1109	1159	1209	1259	...	1359	1409	1459	1559
Oissel d.	0719	|	0738	...	|	0819	...	|	|	|	0919	...	1020	1019	...	|	1120	|	1219	|	...	|	1420	|	|
Val de Reuil d.	0729	|	0748	...	|	0830	...	|	|	|	0929	...	1030	1030	...	|	1130	|	1230	|	...	|	1430	|	|
Vernon (Eure) d.	0752	|	0811	...	|	0853	...	|	|	|	0952	...	1053	1053	...	|	1152	|	1253	|	...	|	1453	|	|
Mantes la Jolie § a.	0805	|	0831	...	|	0906	...	0914	0930	|	1005	...	1106	1106	...	|	1206	|	1306	|	...	|	1506	|	|
Paris St Lazare § a.	0840	0838	0908	...	0915	0940	...	...	...	1010	1040	...	1140	1140	...	1210	1240	1310	1340	1410	...	1510	1540	1610	1710

	3138		13122	3124	3190	3192	13124	3126		3128		13126		3130		13128	3194	3132		3134		13130		3136	
	Y	Ⓐ	⑦ d	Ⓐ	⑦ Dd	⑥ Du	Ⓐ	⑦ d			Ⓐ	⑦ d	⑥ t	Ⓑ h	⑥ t	Ⓐ	⑦ De			Ⓑ h	⑥ t	⑦ d		⑦ z	
Le Havre d.	1503	...	...	1603	...	...	...	1613	...	1703	...	...	...	1803	1803	...	...	1913	...	2003	2003	...	...	2113	...
Bréauté-Beuzeville ▲ d.	1519	...	...	1620	...	...	...	1628	...	1720	...	...	...	1819	1819	...	...	1929	...	2019	2020	...	...	2129	...
Yvetot d.	1534	...	...	1634	...	...	...	1643	...	1734	...	...	...	1834	1834	...	...	1944	...	2034	2035	...	...	2144	...
Rouen Rive-Droite a.	1556	...	...	1656	...	...	...	1705	...	1756	...	...	...	1856	1856	...	...	2005	...	2056	2056	...	...	2205	...
Rouen Rive-Droite d.	1559	1609	1609	1659	1659	1709	1709	1709	...	1759	1809	1809	1825	1859	...	1912	1959	2009	...	2059	...	2109	...	2209	...
Oissel d.	|	1619	1620	|	|	1719	1719	1719	...	|	1819	1820	1839	|	...	|	|	2020	...	|	...	2119	...	2219	...
Val de Reuil d.	|	1630	1630	|	|	1730	1729	1730	...	|	1830	1830	1850	|	...	1930	|	2030	...	|	...	2130	...	2230	...
Vernon (Eure) d.	|	1653	1653	|	|	1753	1752	1753	...	|	1852	1853	1912	|	...	1953	|	2053	...	|	...	2153	...	2253	...
Mantes la Jolie § a.	|	1706	1706	|	|	1806	1806	1806	...	|	1906	1906	1925	|	...	2006	|	2108	...	|	...	2206	...	2308	...
Paris St Lazare § a.	1710	1740	1740	1810	1810	1840	1840	1840	...	1910	1940	1940	...	2010	...	2040	2110	2140	...	2210	...	2240	...	2340	...

D – 🚌12 Paris - Rouen - Dieppe and v.v. (Table **270a**).
N – ①②③④⑥ (not May 1, 8, 13). Will not run on ①–④ Mar. 29 - Apr. 29, May 17 - 27.
R – Dec. 18, 24, 31, Apr. 2, 16, 23, May 12, 21 only.
Y – Dec. 27, Jan. 3, May 16 only.
a – Also Dec. 24, 31, May 12.
b – Also May 12; not Dec. 25, Jan. 1.
c – Not Dec. 24, 31, May 12, 13.
d – Also Dec. 25, Jan. 1, Apr. 5, May 24.
e – Also Apr. 5, May 24.
h – Not Dec. 25, Jan. 1, May 13.
m – Not Dec. 24, 31, Apr. 5, May 12, 13, 24.
n – Not Apr. 5, May 24.
p – Also Dec. 24, 31, May 12; not Dec. 25, Jan. 1.
q – Not Dec. 25, Jan. 1, Apr. 2, 16, 23, May 21.
s – Not Dec. 25, Jan. 1, Apr. 5, May 24.
t – Not May 1, 8.
u – Also May 13.
v – Also Dec. 25, Jan. 1, May 13.
x – Also Apr. 5; not Dec. 25, Jan. 1, Apr. 9, 16, 23, 30.
y – On ⑥ **v** arrive Le Havre 2245. On ⑦ **e** Rouen a. 2149 / d. 2152, arrive Le Havre 2234.
z – Also Dec. 25, Jan. 1, Apr. 5.
TGV – Ⓡ, supplement payable, 🍸.
♥ – To/from Lyon and Marseille (Table **335**).
♠ – To / from Strasbourg via Charles de Gaulle ✈ (Table **391**).
▲ – Trains run 6 - 8 times per day from either Le Havre or Bréauté-Beuzeville to Fécamp.
§ – Frequent suburban trains run Paris - Mantes-la-Jolie and v.v.

270a ROUEN - DIEPPE

km		⚒	Ⓐ	Ⓐ	†	⚒		Ⓐ	⑦ d	⑥ u	⑥ t	Ⓐ	⑥ t	⑥ t	Ⓐ	Ⓐ		Ⓐ	Ⓐ		Ⓐ	⚒	†	
	Paris St Lazare **270** d.	...	...	...	...	...	...	...	1036	1050	...	...	...	...	...	...	...	...	...	...	...	...	...	...
0	**Rouen** Rive-Droite d.	0640	0714	0730	0841	0914	1014	1214	1224	1216	1241	1341	1414	1514	1641	1714	1741	1814	1844	1914	2014	2124	2124	...
63	**Dieppe** a.	0742	0758	0843	0940	0958	1059	1258	1306	1258	1343	1440	1459	1559	1746	1800	1844	1859	1941	1958	2058	2206	2210	...

	Ⓐ	⚒	Ⓐ	Ⓐ	Ⓒ	Ⓐ	⚒		⚒	⑥ t	†	Ⓐ	Ⓐ	⑦ d	Ⓐ	⑥ u	Ⓐ	†	⚒	⑦ e	Ⓐ	⚒	†	
Dieppe d.	0534	0619	0701	0714	0751	0801	0814	1001	1201	1314	1314	1314	1401	1559	1601	1609	1714	1801	1813	1859	1901	2001	2014	...
Rouen Rive-Droite a.	0618	0718	0746	0819	0835	0846	0919	1046	1246	1419	1413	1419	1446	1644	1647	1654	1819	1846	1919	1944	1946	2046	2113	...
Paris St Lazare **270** a.	...	...	...	...	...	...	...	...	...	...	...	...	...	1810	...	1840	...	...	...	2110	...	...	...	...

FOR NOTES SEE TABLE 270

CAEN - LE MANS - TOURS 271

km		⚒	Ⓐ	Ⓐ	⚒		⑥	⚒	Ⓑ	⑥	⑤	P		⑥	†	①-④	⑤	⚒	⑥t	⑦	Ⓐ	⑦	Ⓐ	⑥	Ⓐ	⑦
						▷	t	⊡	h	t	d			t		m	f		🚌	q		b		t		e
0	**Caen** 275 d.	...	0527z	0600	0727	0832	...	1035	...	...	1300	1300	...	...	1617	1622	1622	...	...	...	1731	1748	1819	1830	1952	2135
23	Mézidon 275 d.	...	0544z	0616	0741	0852	...	1052	...	...	1317	1317	...	...	1634	1637	1637	...	...	...	1747	1806	1834	1845	2006	2150
67	Argentan 273 d.	...	0612	0647	0810	0918	...	1113	...	...	1347	1347	...	...	1704	1707	1707	...	...	...	1822	1834	1905	1910	2031	2212
82	Surdon 273 d.	...	|	0659	0820	|	...	1123	...	...	1357	1357	...	...	|	|	|	...	...	...	1832	1846	1916	1919	2041	|
91	Sées d.	...	0627	0707	0827	|	...	1129	...	...	1404	1404	...	...	1719	1721	1722	...	...	...	1840	1855	1923	1926	2048	2227
111	Alençon d.	...	0641	0722	0840	0944	...	1142	...	...	1419	1419	...	1644	1733	1736	1736	...	...	...	1853	1911	1937	1939	2100	2240
166	**Le Mans** a.	...	0730	0809	0909	1012	...	1218	...	...	1447	1447	...	1715	1808	1809	1809	...	...	...	...	1941	2008	2008	...	2308
166	**Le Mans** d.	0627	0734	...	...	1016	1212	...	1242	1309	1450	1450	1643	...	1811	1820	1824	1840	...	1911	...	2003	2019	...	...	...
215	Château du Loir d.	0656	0805	...	...	1047	1255	...	1312	1339	1518	1518	1719	...	1842	1847	1854	1922	1950	1950	...	2035	2053	...	...	...
262	St Pierre des Corps a.	|	|	...	...	1117	|	...	|	|	|	1545	|	...	|	|	1923	...	|	|	...	|	|	...	...	...
265	**Tours** a.	0735	0834	...	...	1136	1332	...	1340	1407	1548	1555	1747	...	1911	1915	1933	...	2035	2024	...	2105	2127	...	...	...

	Ⓐ	①	⚒	①	Ⓐ	⚒	†	⚒	†	⚒	⚒	⑥	Ⓐ	①-④	⑤	†	⚒	⑥	①-④	⑤	Ⓑ	⑤	†	①-④	⑦	⑤⑦
		z		z				⊗		⊕	△	t	▽	m	f			t	m	f		f		m	b	v
Tours d.	...	0545	...	0600	0644	0756	0900	0919	1040	...	1149	1225	1405	...	1530	1651	1701	...	...	...	1831	...	...	...	2005	2144
St Pierre des Corps d.	...	|	...	|	|	|	0911	0929	1050	...	|	|	|	...	|	|	|	...	...	...	|	...	...	...	2017	2153
Château du Loir d.	...	0614	...	0637	0719	0826	0940	1000	1119	...	1219	1305	1434	...	1603	1723	1734	...	...	...	1902	...	...	...	2048	2222
Le Mans a.	...	0650	...	0718	0804	0856	1009	1031	1149	...	1250	1348	1504	...	1630	1751	1801	...	...	...	1934	...	...	...	2118	2252
Le Mans d.	0628z	...	0705	...	0849	...	1030	1037	1214	1236	...	...	1513	...	1633	1805	1806	1858	1914	1914	...	1957	2012	2031	2120	...
Alençon d.	0700	...	0749	...	0931	...	1059	1107	1250	1322	...	...	1548	1722	1722	1837	1837	1927	1952	1957	...	2030	2044	2111	2152	...
Sées d.	0712	...	0801	...	...	...	1112	1120	...	1334	...	...	1601	1734	1736	1852	1853	1939	2004	2010	...	2043	2058	2124	2206	...
Surdon 273 d.	0718	...	0809	...	...	...	1119	1127	...	1341	...	...	|	1740	1744	1901	1901	1946	2011	2018	...	2051	2105	2132	|	...
Argentan 273 d.	0728	...	0819	...	...	...	1128	1139	...	1350	...	...	1614	1750	1756	1912	1914	1956	2020	2028	...	2101	2116	2142	2221	...
Mézidon 275 d.	0753	...	0846	...	...	...	1152	1203	...	1416	...	...	1638	1819	1829	1942	1949	2021	2046	2056	...	2129	2144	...	|	...
Caen 275 a.	0808	...	0901	...	...	...	1206	1217	...	1430	...	...	1652	1833	1844	1957	2005	2035	2100	2112	...	2145	2200	...	2259	...

P – Daily except ⑤ (not Dec. 24, 31, May 12).
b – Also Dec. 25, Jan. 1, Apr. 5, May 13, 24; not Apr. 4, May 23.
d – Also Dec. 24, 31, May 12.
e – Also Apr. 5, May 24; not Apr. 4, May 23.
f – Also Dec. 24, 31, May 12; not Dec. 25, Jan. 1.
h – Also May 1, 8.
m – Not Dec. 24, 31, Apr. 5, May 12, 13, 24.
q – Also Apr. 5, May 13, 24; not Apr. 4, May 23.
t – Not May 1, 8.
v – Also Dec. 24, 31, Apr. 5, May 12, 24; not Dec. 25, Jan. 1, Apr. 4, May 23.
z – ① (also Apr. 6, May 25; not Apr. 5, May 24).
⊡ – Not on Ⓐ Jan. 18 - Feb. 5, Apr. 26 - 30, May 17 - June 4.
△ – Subject to alteration May 17 - 21.
▽ – Subject to alteration Jan. 11 - 22, Apr. 26 - May 14.
▷ – Not Jan. 18 - 22, Apr. 26 - May 14.
⊕ – Subject to alteration Apr. 26 - May 14.
⊗ – Not Jan. 11 - 15, Apr. 19 - May 21.

CAEN - COUTANCES - RENNES 272

km		①	⚒	⑥	Ⓐ	Ⓐ	⑥	Ⓐ		Ⓐ		Ⓒ	Ⓐ			⚒	⑤		Ⓐ	⑤f	⚒	Ⓐ		⑤	†
		g		t			t					🚌	▷	E	F	▷	f⊕	P		🚌				f	
0	**Caen** 275 d.	0542	0625	0713	0713	0833	0913	0913	1113	1213	1233	...	1333	1413	1413	1605	1643	1713	1733	...	1805	1833	1905	1905	1905
30	Bayeux 275 d.	0558	0649	0730	0730	0856	0930	0930	1130	1231	1258	...	1356	1430	1430	1627	1700	1730	1756	...	1829	1858	1928	1928	1928
57	Lison 275 d.	0613	0709	0747	0747	0914	0946	0946	1146	1248	1318	...	1415	1446	1446	1646	1716	1746	1815	...	1849	1918	1946	1946	1946
75	St Lô 275 d.	0628	0722	0800	0800	0927	1000	1000	1200	1300	1333	1339	1430	1501	1500	1659	1730	1800	1828	1834	1902	1934	1959	1959	2000
105	**Coutances** d.	0654	0741	0821	0822	...	1025	1020	1220	1323	...	1416	...	1521	1520	...	1801	1831	...	1911	1925	...	2020	2021	2028
	Granville ▲ a.	0743n	0821a	0900	|	...	|	...	1303c	1404	...	1449	...	1559	1557	...	1831	1904	...	1944	...	...	...	2059	2059
132	Folligny d.	0719	...	...	0843	...	1045	...	...	...	...	...	...	1541	...	...	1822	1852	...	...	...	...	...	2041	2049
151	Avranches d.	0736	...	...	0859	...	1100	...	...	...	...	...	...	1556	...	...	1839	1908	...	...	...	...	...	2056	2104
173	Pontorson ⊡ d.	0757	...	...	0916	...	1116	...	...	...	...	...	...	1613	...	...	1859	1925	...	...	...	...	...	2112	2120
194	Dol 281 d.	0818	...	...	0934	...	1133	...	...	...	...	...	...	1630	...	...	1917	1943	...	...	...	...	...	2129	2137
252	**Rennes** 281 a.	0850	...	...	1007	...	1205	...	...	...	...	...	...	1705	...	...	1952	2015	...	...	...	...	...	2200	2208

	⚒	⚒	①	②-⑤		⑥	Ⓐ	Ⓐ	⚒	Ⓐ	Ⓐ	⑦			⑤	Ⓐ		⑤	①-④	①-④	Ⓒ	⑤	⑤	†	†
			g	🚌§		t	⊗	▽		⊙	▷	v	Y	▷	f⊕		P	f	m	m		f	f		
Rennes 281 d.	...	...	0550	...	...	0838	0906	...	...	...	...	1251	1414	...	1451	...	...	1615	...	1643	1645	...	1821	1842	2045
Dol 281 d.	...	...	0625	...	...	0911	0938	...	...	...	...	1323	1446	...	1522	...	...	1647	...	1716	1717	...	1858	1913	2116
Pontorson ⊡ d.	...	...	0641	...	...	0928	0956	...	...	...	...	1340	1503	...	1539	...	...	1704	...	1733	1734	...	1915	1929	2133
Avranches d.	...	...	0703	...	...	0949	1020	...	...	...	...	1400	1524	...	1602	...	...	1725	...	1754	1755	...	1937	1950	2154
Folligny d.	...	...	0718	...	...	1003	1035	...	...	...	...	1415	1542	...	1618	...	...	1739	...	1809	1809	...	1952	2004	2209
Granville ▲ d.	...	0608r	0648n	0646	0747c	0943	1015	...	1151	1252z	...	1345n	1511n	...	1554	...	1651s	1719	1712*	1752	1752	...	1937	1946	2139n
Coutances d.	0603	0641*	0742	0720	0830	1026	1058	...	1236	1335	...	1437	1602	1542*	1639	1642x	1734	1803	1746*	1837	1837	1837	2020	2029	2231
St Lô 275 d.	0627	0728	0803	0757	0853	1047	1120	1229	1301	1358	1500	1500	1621	1629	1700	1729	1759	1829	1833	1901	1901	1901	2041	2050	2252
Lison 275 d.	0643	0743	0816	0817	0910	1101	1136	1244	1314	1411	1513	1513	1634	1642	1712	1742	1811	1841	1845	1914	1914	1914	2053	2103	2306
Bayeux 275 d.	0700	0800	0830	...	0925	1116	1151	1301	1329	1427	1528	1528	1649	1700	1728	1800	1827	1856	1902	1929	1929	1929	2108	2118	2321
Caen 275 a.	0723	0822	0846	...	0943	1132	1207	1323	1347	1445	1545	1545	1705	1722	1745	1822	1845	1913	1923	1945	1945	1946	2124	2135	2337

E – ①⑤⑥⑦ (also Dec. 24, 31, May 12, 13, 25; not Mar. 15, 19, 22, 26, 29, Apr. 2).
F – ②③④ (not Dec. 24, 31, Apr. 6, May 12, 13, 25).
P – Daily except ⑤ (also runs Dec. 25, Jan. 1; not Dec. 24, 31, May 12).
Y – Dec. 25, Jan. 1, Apr. 5, May 13, 24 only.
a – Ⓐ only.
c – Ⓒ only.
f – Also Dec. 24, 31, May 12; not Dec. 25, Jan. 1.
g – Also Apr. 6, May 25; not Apr. 5, May 24.
m – Not Dec. 24, 31, Apr. 5, May 12, 13, 24.
n – 🚌 Folligny - Granville and v.v.
r – ⑥ (not May 1, 8).
s – ①②③④⑦ (not holidays).
t – Not May 1, 8.
v – Also May 1, 8.
x – ①-④ m. By 🚌.
z – ⑤ (also Dec. 24, 31, May 12; not Dec. 25, Jan. 1).
▲ – Connection by 🚌.
⊡ – 10 km from Mont St Michel.
⊙ – Subject to alteration on Ⓐ Mar. 15 - Apr. 22.
⊕ – Subject to alteration Mar. 19 - Apr. 2.
⊗ – Subject to alteration Dec. 14 - 18, Feb. 15 - Mar. 19, Apr. 6 - 23.
▽ – Subject to alteration Dec. 14 - 18, Apr. 6 - 23.
▷ – Subject to alteration Ⓐ Mar. 15 - Apr. 2, ②-④ Apr. 6 - 22.
§ – Not Dec. 25, Jan. 1, Apr. 6, May 13, 25.
* – By 🚌.

PARIS - DREUX - GRANVILLE 273

km			3411	3413	16511		3421	3423	3431	3433	3435		3441	3443	3445		3453	3451	
		Ⓐ	Ⓐ	Ⓒ	⑦	Ⓐ	⚒	†	⚒	†	⑤	⑥	Ⓐ	Ⓒ	⑤	Ⓐ	Ⓒ	Ⓐ	
				§	e		⊕		▽		f	t			f				
0	**Paris Montparnasse** ⊖ d.	...	0710	0837	0925	0920	1024	1030	1316	1322	1515	1520	1629	1638	1726	1829	1930	1959	...
17	Versailles Chantiers ▲ d.	...	|	0849	|	|	|	|	|	|	|	|	|	|	|	1841	1944	|	...
82	**Dreux** ▶ d.	0456	0756	0925	1012	1008	1111	1116	|	|	|	1607	1720	1725	|	1924	2025	2051	...
118	Verneuil sur Avre d.	0528	|	0944	1042	1031	|	|	1420	1425	|	1637	1740	1745	|	1947	2044	2111	...
142	L'Aigle d.	0546	0826	0959	1059	1045	1140	1146	1433	1439	1627	1655	1754	1758	1847	2001	2058	2124	...
183	Surdon 271 d.	0616	0847	1019	1133	1113	|	|	1454	1459	|	1720	1815	1819	1910	2027	2119	2145	...
198	Argentan 271 d.	0627	0857	1030	1144	1124	1211	1214	1504	1510	1658	1730	1825	1830	1922	2037	2129	2155	...
226	Briouze d.	0650	0914	1046	1200	...	|	|	1521	1526	|	...	|	|	1941	...	2145	2211	...
243	Flers d.	0701	0925	1057	1211	...	1234	1237	1531	1537	1723	...	1847	1852	1954	...	2155	2222	...
272	Vire d.	0719	0942	1112	1227	...	1251	1253	1548	1555	1739	...	1905	1908	2010	...	2211	2238	...
298	Villedieu d.	0739	0956	1127	1242	...	1306	1307	1602	1609	1754	...	1921	1924	2025	...	2226	2252	...
313	Folligny 272 d.	0750	1006	1138	1254	...	|	|	|	|	|	...	|	|	2035	...	|	|	...
328	**Granville** 272 a.	0800	1016	1148	1304	...	1324	1328	1620	1626	1812	...	1938	1944	2045	...	2245	2311	...

	16510			3410	3410	3412	3420		3430		3432	3440	3442			3444	13272	3450	3454
	①	Ⓐ	Ⓒ	⑥	Ⓐ	†		⑥	⚒	Ⓐ	†	⚒	†	⑤	①-④	⑦	⑦		⑦
	g			t			△	t	⊕		▷	▽		f	m▽	e	e	☆	v
Granville 272 d.	0444	...	...	0553	0558	0658	0907	...	1218	...	1351	1516	1519	1621	1637	1658	...	1859	1955
Folligny 272 d.	|	...	...	|	|	|	|	...	|	...	|	|	|	1633	1649	|	...	1909	2006
Villedieu d.	0502	...	...	0610	0615	0717	0925	...	1235	...	1410	1533	1539	1644	1700	1717	...	1921	2016
Vire d.	0517	...	...	0625	0630	0732	0941	...	1252	...	1425	1548	1555	1703	1720	1732	...	1936	2032
Flers d.	0535	...	...	0642	0647	0749	0959	...	1309	...	1443	1606	1611	1722	1738	1749	...	1954	2049
Briouze d.	0546	...	...	0653	0658	0800	|	...	1321	...	1454	|	|	1734	1750	1800	...	2006	2100
Argentan 271 d.	0604	0604	0624	0710	0715	0817	1025	1150	1339	1421	1511	1634	1636	1755	1811	1817	1920	2023	2117
Surdon 271 d.	0614	0614	0634	0720	0725	0828	1035	1200	1349	1431	1521	|	|	...	...	|	1931	2032	|
L'Aigle d.	0639	0639	0700	0740	0745	0849	1056	1225	1410	1500	1542	1701	1702	...	...	1845	2000	2052	2144
Verneuil sur Avre d.	0653	0653	0713	0754	0758	0903	1109	1243	|	1514	1555	|	|	...	...	|	2013	2106	|
Dreux ▶ d.	0716	0716	0736	0814	0818	0923	|	1314	|	1538	|	1733	1734	...	...	|	2037	2126	2216
Versailles Chantiers ▲ a.	0759	0759	|	|	|	|	|	|	|	|	|	|	|	...	...	|	2113	|	2250
Paris Montparnasse ⊖ a.	0811	0811	0823r	0908	0911	1008	1215	1405	1523	1625	1704	1819	1819	...	...	1959	2125	2219	2303

e – Also Apr. 5, May 24; not Apr. 4, May 23.
f – Also Dec. 24, 31, May 12; not Dec. 25, Jan. 1, May 14.
g – Also Apr. 6, May 25; not Apr. 5, May 24.
m – Not Dec. 24, 31, Apr. 5, May 12, 13, 24.
r – 0830 on †.
t – Not May 1, 8.
v – Also Apr. 5, May 24; not Mar. 28, Apr. 4, May 23.
⊖ – Most trains use **Vaugirard** platforms (5 - 10 mins walk).
▲ – Local travel to / from Paris not permitted on some trains (see Table **274** for local services).
▶ – Suburban trains run Paris - Versailles - Dreux approx hourly.
△ – Subject to alteration Jan. 25 - Feb. 7.
▽ – Subject to alteration on ②-④ Mar. 16 - Apr. 1.
▷ – On Dec. 25, Jan. 1, May 13, 24 runs up to 16 mins earlier.
☆ – Subject to alteration Jan. 8, Ⓐ Jan. 15 - Feb. 12, Mar. 1 - May 21.
⊕ – Subject to alteration on Ⓐ Feb. 15 - Apr. 2.
§ – On Dec. 25, Jan. 1, Apr. 4, May 13, 24 runs up to 50 mins later Argentan - Granville.

274 PARIS - VERSAILLES

RER (express Métro) Line C: **Paris Austerlitz** - St Michel Notre Dame - **Versailles Rive Gauche** (for Château). Every 15 - 30 minutes. Journey 40 minutes.
Alternative service: RER Line C: Paris Austerlitz - St Michel Notre Dame - Versailles Chantiers. Journey 39 minutes.
SNCF suburban services: Paris St Lazare - Versailles Rive Droite (journey 28 - 35 minutes); Paris Montparnasse - Versailles Chantiers (journey 12 - 28 minutes). See also Table **278**.

275 PARIS - CAEN - CHERBOURG

For other trains Paris - Lisieux (- Trouville-Deauville) see Table **276**. Many fast trains have 🍷

km		3325 ① g	⚒	Ⓐ	Ⓐ	①⑥ u	②–⑤ w	⚒	3331 Ⓐ	3301 Ⓐ	Ⓐ		3333 ⑥ v	⑥ t	3327 T	Ⓐ	3335 Ⓐ	Ⓐ	3303 Ⓒ	3337 ⑥ v	3339 ⑦ z	Ⓒ	3305 Ⓐ	Ⓐ	3341 Ⓒ	Ⓒ
0	**Paris St Lazare** ▷ d.	0025	...	...	...	...	...	...	0645	0707	...	...	0745	...	0802	...	0845	...	0910	0945	0945	...	1010	...	1145	...
57	Mantes la Jolie ▷ d.	|	...	...	...	...	...	...	|	|	...	...	|	...	|	...	|	...	|	|	|	...	|	...	|	...
108	Evreux ▷ d.	0132	...	...	0609	...	...	...	0741	|	...	...	0841	...	|	...	0941	...	|	1041	1041	...	|	...	1241	...
160	Bernay d.	0210	...	...	0647	...	...	...	0807	|	...	...	0907	...	|	...	1007	...	|	1107	1107	...	|	...	1307	...
191	Lisieux **277** d.	0240	...	*0609*	0702	...	...	0744	0826	|	...	0844	0926	...	|	0944	1026	...	|	1126	1126	...	|	...	1326	...
216	Mézidon **271 277** d.	|	...	*0624*	0715	...	...	0759	|	|	...	0859	|	...	|	0959	|	...	|	|	|	...	|	...	|	...
239	**Caen** **271 277** a.	0317	...	*0644*	0734	...	...	0819	0851	0855	...	0919	0951	...	1002	1019	1051	...	1057	1151	1151	...	1157	...	1351	...
239	**Caen** **272** d.	0320	0559	0659	...	0759	0814	...	...	0857	0913	...	...	0959	1004	...	...	1059	1059	1153	...	1159	1159	1259	...	1359
269	Bayeux **272** d.	0349	0615	0715	...	0815	0830	...	...	|	0930	...	...	1015	1023	...	...	1115	1116	1210	...	1216	1216	1315	...	1415
296	Lison **272** d.	0411	0630	0730	...	0830	0845	...	...	|	0946	...	...	1030	1039	...	...	1130	1130	1225	...	1230	1230	1330	...	1430
314	St Lô **272** a.	|	|	|	...	|	|	...	...	|	0959	...	...	|	|	...	...	|	|	1240	...	|	|	|	...	|
314	Carentan d.	0424	0640	0740	...	0840	0855	...	...	0930	...	...	...	1040	1052	...	...	1140	1141	...	...	1240	1241	1340	...	1440
343	Valognes d.	0444	0656	0756	...	0856	0911	...	...	0946	...	...	...	1056	1109	...	...	1156	1155	...	...	1256	1255	1356	...	1456
371	**Cherbourg** a.	0500	0711	0811	...	0911	0926	...	...	1000	...	...	...	1111	1124	...	...	1211	1209	...	...	1311	1309	1411	...	1511

	3307 Ⓐ ⊗	3309 ⑥ ⊡	Ⓐ ◧	3343 Ⓐ ◧	Ⓐ ⊙	3345 ⑤ x	3347 Ⓒ k	3311 Ⓐ ◧	Ⓐ ◧	3313 Ⓒ	Ⓐ ◧		3349 Ⓐ	3315 Ⓐ	Ⓐ	3351	3317 Ⓐ	Ⓒ	3353 Ⓐ	3319 ⑤ f	3321 Ⓒ	*TGV* 5348 ▽ ♠	3361	3323 Ⓑ h	3357 ⑥ v	3359 Ⓐ
Paris St Lazare ▷ d.	1210	1310	...	1345	...	1410	1445	1510	...	1610	...	...	1645	1710	...	1745	1810	...	1845	1905	1910	...	1959	2045	2045	2145
Mantes la Jolie ▷ d.	|	|	...	|	...	|	|	|	...	|	...	...	|	|	...	|	|	...	|	|	|	2019	2038	|	|	|
Evreux ▷ d.	|	|	...	1441	...	1505	1541	|	...	|	...	...	1741	|	...	1841	|	...	1941	|	|	2049	2107	2141	2141	2241
Bernay d.	|	|	...	1507	...	1532	1607	|	...	|	...	...	1807	|	...	1907	|	...	2007	|	|	|	2133	2207	2207	2307
Lisieux **277** d.	|	|	1444	1526	...	1551	1626	|	1644	|	1725	1744	1826	|	1844	1926	|	...	2026	|	|	2134	2152	2224	2226	2325
Mézidon **271 277** d.	|	|	1459	|	...	|	|	|	1659	|	1740	1759	|	|	1859	|	|	...	|	|	|	|	|	|	|	|
Caen **271 277** a.	1357	1457	1519	1551	...	1616	1651	1657	1719	1757	1757	1818	1851	1857	1919	1951	1957	...	2051	2057	2057	2201	2217	2245	2251	2351
Caen **272** d.	1359	1459	...	...	1559	...	...	1659	...	1759	1759	1821	...	1859	...	...	1959	1959	2054	2101	2059	2204	...	2247	...	...
Bayeux **272** d.	1416	1516	...	...	1615	...	...	1716	...	1816	1815	1839	...	1916	...	...	2016	2015	2111	2118	2116	|	...	2302	...	...
Lison **272** d.	1430	1530	...	...	1630	...	...	1730	...	1833	1830	1855	...	1930	...	...	2030	2030	2127	2133	2130	|	...	2317	...	...
St Lô **272** a.	|	|	...	...	|	...	...	|	...	|	|	|	...	|	...	...	|	|	2140	|	|	|	...	|	...	...
Carentan d.	1441	1541	...	...	1640	...	...	1741	...	1844	1840	1905	...	1941	...	...	2041	2040	...	2143	2141	|	...	2327	...	...
Valognes d.	1455	1555	...	...	1656	...	...	1755	...	1858	1856	1920	...	1955	...	...	2055	2056	...	2157	2155	|	...	2341	...	...
Cherbourg a.	1509	1609	...	...	1711	...	...	1809	...	1912	1911	1935	...	2009	...	...	2109	2111	...	2212	2209	2309	...	2356	...	...

	3330 Ⓐ	3332 ①–⑥ n	Ⓐ	3300 Ⓐ	3334 Ⓐ	3336 Ⓒ	⚒	*TGV* 5330 m ♠	Ⓐ	Ⓒ	3302		3338 ☆	⚒ §	☆	3340 ⑤ y	3304 H	†		3306 ⑤ f⊕	3342 Ⓒ	Ⓐ	⚒	3344 Ⓐ	3324 Y	3308
Cherbourg d.	...	...	...	0556	...	...	0630	0655	0724	...	0746	...	...	0946	...	...	1046	1146	...	1200	...	...	1246	...	1315	1346
Valognes d.	...	...	...	0612	...	...	0645	|	0739	...	0802	...	...	1001	...	...	1102	1201	...	1217	...	...	1301	...	1333	1402
Carentan d.	...	...	...	0626	...	...	0701	|	0755	...	0816	...	...	1017	...	...	1116	1217	...	1232	...	...	1317	...	1349	1416
St Lô **272** d.	...	...	...	|	0651	...	|	|	|	...	|	0853	...	|	...	...	|	|	...	|	...	...	|	...	|	|
Lison **272** d.	...	...	...	0637	0705	...	0712	|	0806	...	0827	0910	...	1028	...	...	1127	1228	...	|	...	...	1328	...	1401	1427
Bayeux **272** d.	...	...	...	0651	0721	...	0729	|	0820	...	0841	0925	...	1042	...	...	1141	1242	...	|	...	...	1342	...	1416	1441
Caen **272** a.	...	...	...	0706	0738	...	0750	0801	0836	...	0856	0943	...	1058	...	...	1156	1258	...	1306	...	...	1358	...	1433	1456
Caen **271 277** d.	0508	0608	0642	0708	0742	0742	0752	0804	0842	0842	0858	...	1008	...	1112	1155	1158	...	...	1308	1308	1312	...	1408	1435	1458
Mézidon **271 277** d.	|	|	0702	|	|	|	0812	|	0901	0901	|	...	|	...	1132	|	|	...	...	|	|	1331	...	|	|	|
Lisieux **277** d.	0535	0636	0716	|	0810	0810	0825	0833	0915	0915	|	...	1036	...	1146	|	|	...	...	1337	1336	1346	...	1436	1500	|
Bernay d.	0553	0654	...	|	0829	0829	...	|	...	...	|	...	1054	...	...	|	|	...	...	1354	1354	...	...	1454	1518	|
Evreux ▷ d.	0620	0721	...	|	0855	0856	...	0920	...	...	|	...	1121	...	...	|	|	...	...	1421	1421	...	...	1521	1543	|
Mantes la Jolie ▷ a.	|	|	...	|	0921	0921	...	0947	...	...	|	...	|	...	...	|	|	...	...	|	|	...	...	|	|	|
Paris St Lazare ▷ a.	0716	0818	...	0858	0957	0957	...	...	...	...	1046	...	1216	...	...	1345	1345	...	...	1516	1516	...	...	1616	1640	1645

	3326 Y	Ⓐ	3346 Ⓒ	Ⓐ		3348	Ⓐ	⚒	3312 ⑦ e	3310 Ⓐ	Ⓐ		Ⓐ	†	3314 ①–⑤ b	3316 ⑥ c	3350 ⑦ e	Ⓐ	⑥ t		3318 ⑦ e	3352 ⑦ d	3320 Ⓐ	Ⓐ	3322 ⑦ d	
Cherbourg d.	1355	...	...	...	1546	...	...	1624	1646	1700	...	...	...	1739	1746	1755	...	1824	1824	...	1846	...	1912	1946	2016	...
Valognes d.	1413	...	...	...	1601	...	...	1639	1702	|	...	...	...	1754	1802	1811	...	1839	1839	...	1902	...	1928	2001	2032	...
Carentan d.	1430	...	...	...	1617	...	...	1655	1716	|	...	...	...	1810	1816	1825	...	1855	1855	...	1916	...	1942	2017	2046	...
St Lô **272** d.	|	1500	...	...	|	...	...	|	|	|	...	...	...	|	|	|	1819	|	|	...	|	...	|	|	|	...
Lison **272** d.	1442	1513	...	...	1628	...	...	1706	1727	|	...	...	...	1821	1827	1836	1832	1906	1906	...	1927	...	1953	2028	2057	...
Bayeux **272** d.	1459	1528	...	...	1642	...	...	1720	1741	|	...	...	...	1835	1841	1851	1848	1920	1920	...	1941	...	2007	2042	2111	...
Caen **272** a.	1516	1545	...	...	1658	...	...	1736	1756	1756	...	...	...	1851	1856	1905	1905	1936	1936	...	1956	...	2022	2058	2126	...
Caen **271 277** d.	1523	1547	1608	1642	...	1708	1722	1742	1758	1758	1824	...	1842	...	1858	1908	1908	1938	...	...	1958	2008	2024	...	2128	...
Mézidon **271 277** d.	|	1601	|	1702	...	|	1742	1801	|	|	1843	...	1901	...	|	|	|	1957	...	...	|	|	|	...	|	...
Lisieux **277** d.	|	1616	1636	1716	...	1736	1756	1815	|	|	1855	...	1914	...	|	1935	1935	2011	...	...	|	2035	2049	...	|	...
Bernay d.	|	...	1654	...	...	1754	...	...	|	|	1910	...	...	...	|	1953	1953	...	...	...	|	2053	|	...	|	...
Evreux ▷ d.	|	...	1720	...	...	1821	...	...	|	|	1948	...	...	...	|	2020	2020	...	...	...	|	2120	|	...	|	...
Mantes la Jolie ▷ a.	|	...	|	...	...	|	...	...	|	|	...	...	...	...	|	|	|	...	...	...	|	|	|	...	|	...
Paris St Lazare ▷ a.	1715	...	1816	...	...	1916	...	...	1945	1946	...	...	...	...	2045	2116	2116	...	...	...	2145	2216	2216	...	2316	...

LOCAL TRAINS PARIS - EVREUX △

	Ⓐ	Ⓐ	Ⓐ◧	Ⓐ	Ⓐ	Ⓐ	Ⓐ	Ⓐ	
Paris St Lazare d.	0907	1110	1310	1610	1713	1813	1913	2013	...
Mantes la Jolie d.	0941	1144	1344	1644	1747	1847	1947	2047	...
Evreux a.	1017	1220	1417	1715	1820	1920	2022	2120	...

	Ⓐ	Ⓐ	Ⓐ	Ⓐ		Ⓐ☆	Ⓐ☆	Ⓐ	
Evreux d.	0539	0639	0739	0841	...	1139	1339	1740	...
Mantes la Jolie a.	0616	0716	0816	0916	...	1213	1413	1813	...
Paris St Lazare a.	0652	0755	0855	0954	...	1248	1448	1849	...

TGV CHERBOURG - CAEN - DIJON

See above for other stations	*TGV* 5330 m
Cherbourg d.	0655
Caen d.	0804
Charles de Gaulle ✈ a.	1113
Marne la Vallée-Chessy a.	1131
Montbard a.	1241
Dijon a.	1318

	TGV 5348 ▽
Dijon d.	1709
Montbard d.	1745
Marne la Vallée-Chessy d.	1848
Charles de Gaulle ✈ d.	1904
Caen a.	2201
Cherbourg a.	2309

H – ①②③④⑥ (not Dec. 24, 31, May 12). Will not run on ①–④ Dec. 14 - 17, Apr. 5 - 22, May 17 - June 3.
T – Dec. 19, 26, Apr. 3, 10, 17, 24, May 13, 22 only.
Y – Dec. 27, Jan. 3, Apr. 5, May 16, 24 only.
b – Also Dec. 27, Jan. 3, May 16; not Dec. 25, Jan. 1, May 13.
c – Also Dec. 25, Jan. 1, May 13.
d – Also Dec. 25, Jan. 1, Apr. 5, May 24.
e – Also Apr. 5, May 24.
f – Also Dec. 24, 31, May 12; not Dec. 25, Jan. 1.
g – Also Apr. 6; not Apr. 5, May 24.
h – Not Dec. 25, Jan. 1, May 13.
k – Not May 13.
m – Not on ①–⑤ Apr. 26 - May 7.
n – Not Dec. 25, Jan. 1, Apr. 5, May 24.
t – Not May 1, 8.
u – Also Apr. 6, May 25; not Apr. 5, May 1, 8, 24.
v – Also May 13.
w – Not Dec. 25, Jan. 1, Apr. 6, May 13, 25.
x – Also Dec. 19, 24, 31, Apr. 3, 10, 17, 24, May 22; not Dec. 25, Jan. 1, Apr. 30, May 7, 14.
y – Also Dec. 24, 31, May 12; not Dec. 25, Jan. 1, May 21, 28, June 4.
z – Not Dec. 25, Jan. 1, Apr. 5, May 24.
♠ – To/from Dijon (see panel below table).
◧ – Subject to alteration Apr. 26 - May 14.
▷ – For additional trains see panel below main table (also Table **276**).
△ – Frequent suburban trains run Paris - Mantes-la-Jolie. Additional local trains run Mantes la Jolie - Evreux.
▽ – On † arrive Caen 2208, Cherbourg 2315.
☆ – Subject to alteration on ①–⑤ May 17 - June 4.
⊡ – Also runs Dec. 25, Jan. 1 (arrive Cherbourg 1705).
⊙ – Subject to alteration Mar. 15 - Apr. 2.
⊖ – Subject to alteration Ⓐ Mar. 15 - Apr. 2, ②–④ Apr. 6 - 22.
⊕ – Will not run on Dec. 18, Apr. 9, 16, 23.
⊗ – Subject to alteration Mar. 15 - Apr. 2.
§ – Not on ①–⑤ Dec. 14 - 18, Apr. 5 - 23.

PARIS - LISIEUX - TROUVILLE DEAUVILLE — 276

km		3371	3373	3377	3379	3395	3381	3383	3393	
		Ⓐ	Ⓒ	⑥	Ⓐ		⑥	⑤	Ⓐ	
		☆	u	S		U	T	z		
0	**Paris St Lazare** ▷ d.	0745	0845	1010	1145	1212	1345	1545	1910	...
108	Evreux ▷ d.	0841	0941	1106	1241	|	1441	1641	2007	...
160	Bernay ▷ d.	0907	1007	1131	1307	|	1507	1707	2032	...
191	Lisieux ▷ d.	0927	1026	1150	1326	|	1526	1726	2050	...
221	**Trouville-Deauville** a.	0948	1046	1212	1346	1408	1546	1746	2112	...

	3370	3372	3374	3390	3378	3380	3382	3384	3388
	Ⓐ	Ⓐ			⑦	Ⓒ	⑦	Ⓐ	⑦
		☆	X	Y	d		W		W
Trouville-Deauville d.	0712	1108	1409	1550	1638	1811	1853	1911	2058
Lisieux ▷ d.	0735	1135	1436	|	1705	1835	|	1935	2121
Bernay ▷ d.	0753	1153	1453	|	1723	1853	|	1953	2140
Evreux ▷ d.	0820	1220	1520	|	1750	1920	|	2020	2205
Paris St Lazare ▷ a.	0918	1316	1616	1756	1846	2016	2046	2116	2305

	⚒		Ⓑh		⑥v		Ⓐ		⚒		Ⓒ		Ⓐ		⚒	†		Ⓐ						
Lisieux d.	0734	...	0835	...	0935	...	1034	...	1235	...	1335	...	1535	...	1635	1635	...	1834	...	1934	...	...	...	...
Trouville-Deauville a.	0756	...	0857	...	0957	...	1056	...	1257	...	1357	...	1557	...	1657	1658	...	1856	...	1954	...	...	...	...
	⚒	†		Ⓐ		Ⓒ	Ⓐ		⑥t	Ⓐ		⑤f	Ⓒ		Ⓐ					Ⓐ		†	Ⓐ	
Trouville-Deauville d.	0700	0738	...	0804	...	1004	1004	...	1149	1204	...	1302	1304	...	1404	...	1604	...	1702	1804	...	2004	2017	...
Lisieux a.	0722	0800	...	0826	...	1024	1026	...	1219	1226	...	1324	1326	...	1426	...	1626	...	1726	1826	...	2026	2039	...

S – ⑥ from Apr. 3 (also Dec. 19, 26, May 13; not May 1, 8, 15, 29).
T – ⑥ from Apr. 3 (also Dec. 19, 26; not May 1, 8, 15, 29).
U – Dec. 19, 26, Apr. 3, 17, 24, May 22 only.
W – ⑦ June 6 - Sept. 26.
X – Apr. 5, May 24 only.
Y – Dec. 27, Jan. 3, Apr. 5, May 16, 24 only.
d – Also Dec. 25, Jan. 1, Apr. 5, May 24.
f – Also Dec. 24, 31, May 12; not Dec. 25, Jan. 1.
h – Not Dec. 25, Jan. 1, May 13.
t – Not May 1, 8.
u – Not May 24.
v – Also Dec. 25, Jan. 1, May 13.
z – Also Dec. 24, 31; not Apr. 30, May 7, 14.
▷ – For other trains see Table **275**.
☆ – Subject to alteration on ①–⑤ May 17 - June 4.

TROUVILLE DEAUVILLE - DIVES CABOURG — 276a

km										
		Ⓒ		Ⓒ	⑥	⑦		④	⑤	
			E		S	d		u	f	
0	Trouville-Deauville d.	1102	1223	1416	1557	1645	...	2126	2126	...
24	Dives Cabourg a.	1131	1252	1445	1626	1714	...	2155	2155	...

	①				⑦		⑥	⑦	Ⓒ
	g		E	F		E	S	d	
Dives Cabourg d.	0620	...	1138	1222	1222	1321	1511	1558	1731
Trouville-Deauville a.	0650	...	1207	1252	1252	1351	1541	1628	1801

E – Dec. 19, 26, Apr. 3, 10, 17, 24, May 13 and ⑥ from June 5.
F – ⑥ to May 29 (not Dec. 19, 26, Apr. 3, 10, 17, 24, May 13).
S – ⑥ from Apr. 3 (also Dec. 19, 26, May 13; not May 1, 8, 15, 29
d – Also Dec. 25, Jan. 1, Apr. 5, May 24.
f – Also May 12; not Dec. 25, Jan. 1.
g – Also Apr. 6, May 25; not Apr. 5, May 24.
u – Not May 13.

ROUEN - LISIEUX - CAEN — 277

km																								
		Ⓐ	⑥	Ⓐ		Ⓐ	⑥	†		①	②–⑤	†	⑥		⑤	⑤	†		⑥	Ⓐ			Ⓐ	†
			t				t			g	w		t		b	b	v		t					
0	**Rouen Rive Droite** d.	0610	0704	0710	...	1004	1004	1004	...	1204	1202	1204	1304	...	1504	1604	1604	...	1704	1704	1804	...	1904	1904
23	Elbeuf-St Aubin d.	0625	0720	0725	...	1019	1020	1019	...	1220	1218	1220	1320	...	1520	1620	1620	...	1720	1720	1820	...	1920	1920
73	Serquigny d.	0654	|	|	...	|	1049	|	...	1249	1251	1248	1349	...	|	1648	1650	...	1745	1747	1853	...	|	|
83	Bernay ▷ d.	0702	0751	0759	...	1052	1058	1053	...	1258	1259	1256	1358	...	1551	1656	1659	...	1753	1756	1901	...	1952	1953
114	Lisieux ▷ d.	0718	0807	0815	...	1108	1113	1109	...	1313	1319	1312	1414	...	1607	1712	1714	...	1809	1811	1917	...	2008	2010
139	Mézidon **271** ▷ d.	0733	0822	0829	...	1122	1127	1122	...	1327	1336	1326	1428	...	1621	1726	1728	...	1823	1825	1931	...	2022	2024
162	**Caen 271** ▷ a.	0748	0836	0843	...	1136	1141	1136	...	1340	1352	1340	1442	...	1636	1740	1741	...	1838	1838	1946	...	2036	2038

	Ⓐ		⑥	Ⓐ				①–④	⑤	Ⓒ		Ⓐ	Ⓒ		Ⓐ	⑥	†		Ⓐ		⑤	⑥	†	
			t			⊕		m	u	z						t					f	S		
Caen 271 ▷ d.	0552	...	0717	0720	...	1020	...	1205	1215	1215	...	1715	1721	...	1812	1817	1817	...	1915	...	2001	2028	2028	...
Mézidon **271** ▷ d.	0606	...	0732	0735	...	1034	...	1221	1229	1230	...	1729	1736	...	1826	1832	1831	...	1929	...	2015	2042	2042	...
Lisieux ▷ d.	0620	...	0746	0749	...	1048	...	1238	1243	1246	...	1743	1750	...	1840	1846	1844	...	1943	...	2029	2056	2056	...
Bernay ▷ d.	0638	...	0803	0806	...	1105	...	1258	1300	1303	...	1800	1808	...	1857	1903	1902	...	2001	...	2046	2113	2114	...
Serquigny d.	0645	...	0811	0814	...	|	...	1307	1307	1310	...	|	|	...	1904	1911	1910	...	|	...	|	|	|	...
Elbeuf-St Aubin d.	0720	...	0839	0839	...	1139	...	1339	1339	1339	...	1832	1839	...	1932	1939	1939	...	2032	...	2118	2145	2145	...
Rouen Rive Droite a.	0736	...	0855	0855	...	1155	...	1355	1355	1355	...	1848	1855	...	1948	1955	1955	...	2048	...	2134	2200	2200	...

S – ⑥ Apr. 3 - Sept. 25 (not May 1, 8).
b – Also Dec. 24, 31; not Dec. 25, Jan. 1, Apr. 30, May 7, 14.
f – Also Dec. 24, 31, May 12; not Dec. 25, Jan. 1.
g – Also Apr. 6, May 25; not Apr. 5, May 24.
m – Not Dec. 24, 31, Apr. 5, May 12, 13, 24.
t – Not May 1, 8.
u – Also Dec. 24, 31, May 12; not Dec. 25, Jan. 1, May 21, 28, June 4.
v – Not May 13.
w – Not Dec. 25, Jan. 1, Apr. 6, May 13, 25.
z – Not May 24.
▷ – See also Table **275**.
⊕ – Subject to alteration Feb. 1 - 12, Mar. 1 - 12, May 17 - June 4.

PARIS - CHARTRES - LE MANS — 278

For TGV trains Paris - Le Mans see Table 280

km																									
		Ⓐ	Ⓐ	⚒	⚒	⚒	Ⓐ	Ⓐ	Ⓒ				Ⓐ	⚒	†	Ⓐ				Ⓐ	⑥t	†	Ⓐ	Ⓐ	
0	**Paris Montparnasse 274** d.	...	0533	0618	0643	0718	0748	0818	0818	0933	1033	1133	1203	1233	1233	1303	1333	...	1433	1533	1533	1533	1603	1624	1633
17	Versailles Chantiers **274** d.	...	0547	0631	0657	0732	0802	0832	0832	0947	1047	1147	1217	1247	1247	1317	1347	...	1447	1547	1547	1547	1617	1639	1647
48	Rambouillet d.	...	|	0648	|	0754	|	0854	0849	1004	1104	1204	|	1304	1304	|	1404	...	1504	1604	1604	1604	1634	|	1707
88	**Chartres** d.	0610	0645	0726	0740	0833	0858	0925	0920	1043	1135	1245	1313	1335	1335	1415	1443	...	1535	1644	1645	1645	1713	1722	1745
149	Nogent le Rotrou d.	0659	0731	...	0814	...	...	1002	0956	...	1209	1335	...	1410	1410	1500	...	...	1610	1732	1742	1731	...	1759	1830
211	**Le Mans** a.	0745	...	...	0849	...	...	1040	1035	...	1246	...	...	1444	...	...	...	...	1650	1819	1837	1817	...	1840	1915

	Ⓐ	Ⓐ	Ⓒ	Ⓐ		Ⓐ		Ⓐ	Ⓐ	Ⓐ	Ⓐ	Ⓒ	Ⓐ	Ⓐ			L	Ⓐ			Ⓑ				
Paris Montparnasse 274 d.	1703	1718	1718	1728	1733	1748	...	1803	1818	1824	1833	1833	1848	1903	...	1933	1933	2003	2033	...	2133	2233	...	0025	...
Versailles Chantiers **274** d.	1717	1732	1732	1742	1747	1802	...	1817	1832	1838	1847	1847	1902	1917	...	1947	1947	2017	2047	...	2147	2247	...	0039	...
Rambouillet d.	1734	1749	|	|	1805	1819	...	1834	1849	|	1905	1904	1919	1934	...	2004	2004	2034	2104	...	2204	2304	...	0056	...
Chartres d.	1813	1818	1810	1825	1843	1850	...	1913	1918	1925	1945	1945	1948	2013	...	2035	2035	2113	2143	...	2235	2343	...	0134	...
Nogent le Rotrou d.	...	...	1855	1905	...	1942	...	...	...	2004	2036	2037	...	...	...	2115	2116	...	...	...	2312	...	...	...	...
Le Mans a.	...	...	1935	1945	...	...	...	...	...	2044	...	2122	...	...	...	...	2207	...	...	...	2349	...	...	...	...

	Ⓐ	⑥t	Ⓐ	Ⓐ	⑥t	Ⓐ	Ⓒ	Ⓐ	Ⓐ	⑥t	Ⓐ	Ⓐ	Ⓐ	Ⓒ	Ⓐ	⑥t	Ⓐ	†	⚒		Ⓐ	Ⓒ		y	y
Le Mans d.	...	...	0400	...	...	...	...	...	0535	...	...	...	...	...	...	...	...	...	0656	...	0748	...	...	0920	...
Nogent le Rotrou d.	...	...	0436	...	...	...	...	0548	0614	...	...	...	0638	0641	0655	...	...	...	0756	...	0837	0827	...	0959	...
Chartres d.	0427	0454	0511	0534	0554	0604	0624	0628	0653	0657	0658	0726	0731	0734	0749	0757	0810	0835	0835	...	0927	0922	...	1035	1124
Rambouillet d.	|	0535	0536	0614	0635	0644	0705	0659	|	0736	0729	|	0800	0803	0829	0836	0839	0906	0906	...	1004	1003	...	1106	1204
Versailles Chantiers **274** d.	0523	0552	0553	0633	0652	0703	0722	0718	0736	0753	0748	0806	0818	0822	0848	0853	0903	0922	0923	...	1022	1022	...	1123	1222
Paris Montparnasse 274 a.	0534	0605	0604	0645	0705	0715	0735	0730	0750	0804	0800	0820	0830	0834	0900	0904	0915	0935	0935	...	1034	1034	...	1134	1234
	Ⓐy	Ⓒ	Ⓐy	⚒y	†	†	⚒y			Ⓐ		Ⓐ		Ⓐ	Ⓐ			Ⓐ	Ⓒ	†		Ⓑ		Ⓐ	†
Le Mans d.	1115	1117	...	...	...	1258	1324	...	...	...	1524	...	...	...	1645	1730	...	1745	...	1845	1930	...	...	...	2124
Nogent le Rotrou d.	1157	1157	...	...	...	1346	1359	...	...	...	1559	...	1631	...	1737	1805	...	1837	1837	1934	2005	...	...	...	2201
Chartres d.	1236	1236	1257	1322	1327	1435	1435	...	1527	1557	1635	1657	1725	1757	1827	1840	...	1927	1927	...	2041	2125	...	2235	2240
Rambouillet d.	1305	1305	|	1403	1405	1506	1506	...	1606	|	1705	|	1804	|	|	1905	...	2005	2005	...	2105	2205	...	2305	2309
Versailles Chantiers **274** d.	1322	1322	1353	1422	1422	1522	1522	...	1622	1652	1722	1752	1822	1852	1918	1922	...	2022	2022	...	2122	2222	...	2322	2326
Paris Montparnasse 274 a.	1334	1334	1404	1434	1434	1534	1534	...	1634	1704	1734	1804	1834	1904	1930	1934	...	2034	2034	...	2134	2234	...	2334	2338

L – ⑤–⑦ (also Dec. 24, 31, Apr. 5, May 12, 13, 24).
t – Not May 1, 8.
y – Subject to alteration on Ⓐ Mar. 29 - Apr. 16.

280 PARIS - LE MANS - RENNES and NANTES

TGV Atlantique

TGV trains convey 🍷. Many trains continue to destinations in Tables **281**, **284**, **285**, **288** and **293**. For other trains Massy - Nantes via St Pierre des Corps see Table **335**.

km		⚒	Ⓐ	TGV 8801 Ⓐ	TGV 8001 Ⓐ	TGV 8603* ①–⑥ n	TGV 8805 ①–⑥ n	Ⓐ	TGV 8081 Ⓐ	TGV 8807 ①–⑥ q	TGV 8009*	TGV 8909 ⊕	TGV 8611	TGV 5486 ☆	TGV 5471 Ⓐ ☆	TGV 8913	TGV 8715	†		TGV 8921* ①–⑥ n	TGV 8619 Ⓒ	TGV 8617 Ⓐ	TGV 5214	TGV 5213
	Lille Europe **11** d.	...	...	...	...	...	...	...	...	...	...	...	...	...	...	...	...	...	...	...	...	...	0846	0846
	Charles de Gaulle ✈ d.	...	...	...	...	...	...	...	...	...	...	...	...	...	...	...	...	...	...	...	...	...	1027	1027
	Marne la Vallée - Chessy § d.	...	...	...	...	...	...	...	...	...	...	...	...	0900	0900	...	...	...	...	...	...	...	1042	1042
0	**Paris Montparnasse** d.	...	...	0630	0635	0705	0730	...	0735	0800	0805	0900	0905	|	|	1000	1005	...	...	1100	1105	1105	|	|
14	Massy TGV d.	...	...	|	|	|	0741	...	0747	|	|	|	|	0933	0933	|	|	...	...	|	|	|	1117	1117
202	**Le Mans** d.	0625r	0650	0727	0733	|	0832	0838	|	|	0902	|	|	1023	1028	1057	|	1104	1104	|	1202	1202	1209	1213
292	Laval d.	0728	|	|	0815	|	|	|	|	|	0943	|	|	|	1109	|	|	1150	|	|	1244	1244	|	|
327	Vitré d.	0754	|	|	|	|	|	|	|	|	|	|	|	|	|	|	|	1214	|	|	|	1304	|	|
365	**Rennes** a.	0815	|	|	0852	0908	|	|	0947	|	1020	|	1108	|	1145	|	1208	1245	|	|	1321	1323	1327	|
251	Sablé d.	...	0713	|	...	...	0852	0859	...	|	...	|	...	|	...	|	...	...	1124	|	...	...	...	|
299	Angers St Laud **289** d.	...	0738	0806	...	...	0916	0922	...	0933	...	1033	...	1102	...	1137	...	...	1145	|	...	...	...	1253
387	**Nantes 289** a.	...	0818	0842	...	...	0952	1001	...	1008	...	1108	...	1140	...	1213	...	...	1226	1259	...	...	...	1333

	TGV 5350 Ⓑ ♠h	TGV 5361 ⑥ ♣u	TGV 5365 ⑥ ♣u	TGV 8823	TGV 5476 Ⓒ ☆	TGV 8717	TGV 8929 ⑤ f	TGV 8621 ⑤ f	TGV 5224	TGV 5227	TGV 8933*	TGV 8623* Ⓐ	TGV 8625 Ⓒ	TGV 8835 ⑤ f	TGV 8837*	TGV 8729*	TGV 5375 ⑦ ♠e	TGV 5371 ⑦ ♠e	TGV 8843 p	TGV 8033* Ⓑ h	TGV 8031 ⑥ u	⚒	TGV 5232 ①–⑥ n	TGV 5209 ⑥ u	TGV 5216 ⑦ e
Lille Europe **11** d.	...	...	...	...	...	...	...	...	1210	1210	...	...	...	...	...	...	...	...	...	...	...	...	1447	1447	1447
Charles de Gaulle ✈ d.	...	...	...	...	...	...	...	...	1316	1316	...	...	...	...	...	...	...	...	...	...	...	...	1542	1542	1542
Marne la Vallée - Chessy § d.	...	...	...	...	1122	...	...	...	1329	1329	...	...	...	...	...	...	...	...	...	...	...	...	1557	1557	1557
Paris Montparnasse d.	...	...	...	1200	|	1205	1300	1305	|	|	1400	1405	1405	1430	1500	1505	...	...	1600	1605	1605	...	|	|	|
Massy TGV d.	1131	1131	1131	|	1200	|	|	|	1401	1401	|	|	|	|	|	|	1532	1532	|	|	|	...	1631	1631	1631
Le Mans d.	1222	1221	1225	|	1252	1302	|	1402	1453	1502	1457	|	|	1524	|	|	1622	1626	|	|	1702	1706	1722	1727	|
Laval d.	|	|	|	|	1334	|	|	|	|	|	|	1539	1539	...	|	|	|	1709	|	|	1744	|	|	|	|
Vitré d.	|	|	|	|	|	|	|	|	|	|	|	|	1558	...	|	|	|	|	|	|	|	|	|	|	◐
Rennes a.	1340	1333	|	|	1410	1414	|	1515	1607	|	|	1615	1619	...	|	1708	|	1743	|	1808	1820	|	1836	|	|
Sablé d.	...	...	|	|	...	...	1414	...	...	|	|	...	...	...	|	...	|	...	|	...	...	1726	...	|	|
Angers St Laud **289** d.	...	...	1306	1339	...	...	1436	...	...	1542	1538	...	...	...	1632	...	1702	...	1733	...	...	1749	...	1825	1815
Nantes 289 a.	...	...	1342	1414	...	...	1511	...	...	1617	1612	...	...	...	1707	...	1736	...	1808	...	...	1830	...	1900	1854

	TGV 8737* Ⓐ	Ⓐ	†	TGV 8845 Ⓐ	TGV 8847 Ⓐ	TGV 8747* ①–⑥ n	Ⓐ	TGV 8743 ⑦ e	TGV 8953*	TGV 8645 ①–④ m	TGV 8649* ⑤ f	TGV 8957 Ⓒ	TGV 8955 Ⓐ	TGV 8861 Ⓐ	TGV 8655* Ⓐ	TGV 8659 ⑦ e	TGV 8653 ⑥ u	TGV 8965 ①–⑥ n	TGV 8095 Ⓐ	TGV 8873 Ⓒ	TGV 8867 ①–④ m	TGV 8869 ⑤ f	TGV 8871 Ⓐ	TGV 5373 ①–⑥ ♠n	TGV 5363 ①–⑥ ♠n
Lille Europe **11** d.	...	...	...	...	...	...	...	...	...	...	...	...	...	...	...	...	...	...	...	...	...	...	...	...	...
Charles de Gaulle ✈ d.	...	...	...	...	...	...	...	...	...	...	...	...	...	...	...	...	...	...	...	...	...	...	...	...	...
Marne la Vallée - Chessy § d.	...	...	...	...	...	...	...	...	...	...	...	...	...	...	...	...	...	...	...	...	...	...	...	...	...
Paris Montparnasse d.	1635	...	...	1650	1700	1705	...	1705	1730	1735	1735	1750	1750	1800	1805	1805	1805	1830	1835	1845	1845	1845	1900	...	...
Massy TGV d.	|	...	...	|	|	|	...	|	|	|	|	|	|	|	|	|	|	|	|	|	|	|	|	1901	1901
Le Mans d.	1732	1738	1745	1747	|	|	1800	1801	|	|	1832	1847	1847	|	|	1902	1902	|	|	1942	1942	1942	|	1952	1957
Laval d.	1813	1824	|	|	|	|	|	1843	|	1910	1914	|	|	|	|	|	1943	|	2012	|	|	|	|	2034	|
Vitré d.	|	1841	|	|	|	|	|	|	|	|	|	|	|	|	|	|	2003	|	2030	|	|	|	|	|	|
Rennes a.	1850	1904	|	|	|	1908	|	1920	|	1946	1950	|	|	|	2008	2015	2024	|	2049	|	|	|	|	2110	|
Sablé d.	...	...	1805	|	|	...	1820	...	|	...	...	|	|	|	...	...	...	|	...	2002	2002	2002	|	...	|
Angers St Laud **289** d.	...	...	1828	1826	1832	...	1843	...	|	...	...	1927	1931	|	...	...	...	|	...	2025	2031	2031	|	...	2038
Nantes 289 a.	...	...	1908	1906	1910	...	1923	...	1931	...	...	2003	2008	2002	...	...	...	2033	...	2102	2106	2112	2102	...	2116

	TGV 8665 ①–⑥ n	TGV 8669 ⑦ e	TGV 5236* Ⓑ h	Ⓑ	TGV 5231 Ⓑ c	TGV 8761* ①–⑥ n	TGV 8879* Ⓑ k	TGV 8071*	TGV 5387 ①–④ ♣m	TGV 8777 ⑤ f	TGV 8887*	TGV 5488 ☆	TGV 8077 ①–④ m	TGV 8679 ⑤ f	TGV 8069 ⑦ e	TGV 5234 ①–④ m	TGV 5248 ⑥ u	TGV 5245 ⑥ u	TGV 5390 ⑤⑦ ♣w	TGV 5210 ⑤⑦ w	TGV 5247 ⑤⑦ w	TGV 8893* E	TGV 8779* ⑤ f	TGV 8045* ⑦ b	
Lille Europe **11** d.	...	...	1728	...	1728	...	...	...	...	...	...	...	...	...	...	1940	1939	1939	...	2014	2014	...	...	...	...
Charles de Gaulle ✈ d.	...	...	1825	...	1825	...	...	...	...	...	...	...	...	...	...	2036	2034	2034	...	2110	2110	...	...	...	...
Marne la Vallée - Chessy § d.	...	...	1840	...	1840	...	...	...	...	...	...	2024	...	...	...	2050	2050	2050	...	2124	2124	...	...	...	...
Paris Montparnasse d.	1905	1905	|	...	|	1935	2000	2005	...	2035	2100	|	2105	2105	2105	|	|	|	...	|	|	2200	2205	2205	...
Massy TGV d.	|	|	1917	...	1921	|	|	|	2032	|	|	2101	|	|	|	2131	2131	2131	2137	2201	2201	|	|	|	...
Le Mans d.	2002	|	2008	2015	|	|	|	2102	2122	2132	|	2158	|	2202	2202	2222	2223	2226	2227	2253	2257	2257	|	|	...
Laval d.	|	2039	2048	|	|	|	|	2143	|	|	|	|	|	|	2245	|	2304	|	|	|	|	|	2340	2343	...
Vitré d.	|	2058	|	|	◐	|	|	|	|	|	|	|	|	2258	|	|	|	|	|	|	|	|	|	|	...
Rennes a.	2115	2119	2125	|	|	2138	|	2220	2234	2243	|	|	2308	2317	2323	|	2340	|	2339	|	0010	|	0018	0019	...
Sablé d.	...	...	...	2040	|	...	|	...	...	...	|	|	...	...	...	|	...	|	...	|	...	|	...	...	...
Angers St Laud **289** d.	...	...	...	2103	2108	...	2133	...	...	...	2231	2239	...	...	...	2304	...	2306	...	2331	...	2337	...	...	...
Nantes 289 a.	...	...	...	2143	2147	...	2208	...	...	...	2308	2314	...	...	...	2338	...	2340	...	0007	...	0013	...	...	...

	TGV 8800 ① g	TGV 8802 Ⓐ	TGV 8002 Ⓐ d	TGV 8804 Ⓐ	TGV 8690 Ⓐ a	TGV 5252 ①–⑥ n	TGV 5254 ①–⑥ n	TGV 8904* Ⓐ	TGV 8706* ①–⑥ j	TGV 8808 Ⓐ	TGV 8806 ⑥ u	Ⓐ	TGV 8910 Ⓐ	TGV 8608 ⑥ v	TGV 8610 Ⓐ	Ⓐ	TGV 8820 Ⓐ	TGV 8812 Ⓒ	TGV 8712 Ⓐ	TGV 5312 ♠	Ⓐ	TGV 8814 Ⓐ	TGV 8012 Ⓐ	TGV 8014 Ⓒ	TGV 8816 Ⓐ
Nantes 289 d.	0500	0530	...	0600	...	0604	...	0630	...	...	0634	0634	0700	...	...	...	0730	0730	...	0735	0739	0800	...	...	0830
Angers St Laud **289** d.	0542	0608	...	0639	...	0643	...	|	...	0715	0715	0719	|	...	...	...	0809	0809	...	0813	0820	|	...	...	0907
Sablé d.	|	0630	...	|	...	|	...	|	...	|	|	0744	|	...	...	...	|	|	...	|	0841	|	...	...	|
Rennes d.	|	|	0535	|	0605	|	0610	|	0635	|	|	|	|	0705	0705	0710	|	|	0735	|	|	|	0805	0805	|
Vitré d.	|	|	0556	|	|	|	|	|	|	|	|	|	|	|	|	0728	|	|	|	|	|	|	|	|	|
Laval d.	|	|	0616	|	0639	|	|	|	|	|	|	|	|	|	|	0748	|	|	|	|	|	|	0841	0841	|
Le Mans d.	0623	0652	0703	|	|	0731	0731	|	|	0759	0759	0805	|	|	0819	0835	|	0849	0849	0854	0903	|	0925	0929	|
Massy TGV a.	|	|	|	|	|	0818	0818	|	|	|	|	...	|	|	|	...	|	|	|	0943	...	|	|	|	|
Paris Montparnasse a.	0720	0750	0800	0810	0820	|	|	0835	0840	0855	0855	...	0905	0910	0915	...	0940	0945	0945	...	...	1005	1020	1025	1040
Marne la Vallée - Chessy § a.	...	...	...	...	...	0900	0900	...	...	...	...	...	...	...	...	...	...	...	...	...	...	...	...	...	...
Charles de Gaulle ✈ a.	...	...	...	...	...	0914	0914	...	...	...	...	...	...	...	...	...	...	...	...	...	...	...	...	...	...
Lille Europe **11** a.	...	...	...	...	...	1008	1008	...	...	...	...	...	...	...	...	...	...	...	...	...	...	...	...	...	...

	TGV 5478 ☆	TGV 8618*	TGV 8818	TGV 5318 ♠	TGV 5272	TGV 5270	TGV 8824 G	TGV 8922 ⊗	TGV 5256 ⑦ e	TGV 5258 ⑦ e	TGV 8620*	TGV 8082 ① g	▽	TGV 8828 Ⓐ	TGV 8022 Ⓐ	TGV 8926 ⑥ u	TGV 5324 H ♣	TGV 8932 ⑦ e	TGV 8834 Ⓐ	TGV 8084	TGV 8730*	TGV 8836	TGV 5326 ⑤⑥ ♠o	TGV 5278	TGV 5280
Nantes 289 d.	0834	...	0900	...	...	0910	0955	1100	...	1105	...	...	1144	1200	...	1200	...	1300	1300	...	...	1400	...	1435	...
Angers St Laud **289** d.	0913	...	0937	...	...	0949	1034	1138	...	1143	...	...	1227	1237	...	1238	...	|	|	...	...	1438	...	1513	...
Sablé d.	|	...	|	...	...	|	|	|	...	|	...	...	1248	|	...	|	...	|	|	...	...	|	...	|	...
Rennes d.	|	0905	|	0910	0915	|	|	|	1100	|	1105	1140	|	|	1205	|	1230	|	|	1305	1405	|	1414	|	1435
Vitré d.	|	|	|	|	|	|	|	|	|	|	|	|	|	|	|	|	|	|	|	|	|	|	|	|	|
Laval d.	|	|	|	0944	0952	|	|	|	|	|	1141	1217	|	|	|	|	|	|	|	1340	|	|	|	|	|
Le Mans d.	0956	|	1019	1029	1041	1041	|	|	1229	1229	1224	|	1309	|	1319	1319	1351	|	1414	|	|	1519	1529	1558	1558
Massy TGV a.	1047	|	|	1118	1133	1133	|	|	1318	1318	|	|	...	|	|	|	1438	|	|	|	|	|	1618	1647	1647
Paris Montparnasse a.	|	1110	1115	...	|	|	1205	1310	|	|	1325	1350	...	1410	1415	1415	...	1505	1510	1515	1610	1615	...	|	|
Marne la Vallée - Chessy § a.	1123	...	...	...	1223	1223	...	...	1355	1355	...	...	...	...	...	...	...	...	...	...	...	...	...	1728	1728
Charles de Gaulle ✈ a.	...	...	...	...	1237	1237	...	...	1410	1410	...	...	...	...	...	...	...	...	...	...	...	...	...	1742	1742
Lille Europe **11** a.	...	...	...	...	1340	1340	...	...	1506	1506	...	...	...	...	...	...	...	...	...	...	...	...	...	1849z	1849z

E – Ⓑ to Apr. 4 (not Dec. 25, Jan. 1), ①②③④⑦ from Apr. 6 (not May 12, 13).
G – Daily to Mar. 14; ①⑦ Mar. 15 - Apr. 26 (also Apr. 6); ①⑥⑦ May 1 - 30 (also May 13, 25); daily from May 31.
H – ①②③④⑦ (not Dec. 24, 31, May 12, 13).
R – ⑦ to Apr. 4.
S – ⑦ from Apr. 11 (also Apr. 5, May 24).

a – Not Dec. 31.
b – Also Apr. 5, May 24; not May 23.
c – Not Dec. 24, 25, 31, Jan. 1, Apr. 4, 30, May 7, 12, 13, 23.
d – Not May 14.
e – Also Apr. 5, May 24.
f – Also Dec. 24, 31, May 12; not Dec. 25, Jan. 1.
g – Also Apr. 6, May 25; not Apr. 5, May 24.
h – Not Dec. 25, Jan. 1, May 13.

j – Not Dec. 25, 31, Jan. 1, Apr. 5, May 24.
k – Not Dec. 25, Jan. 1, Apr. 6, May 13, 17.
m – Not Dec. 24, 31, Apr. 5, May 12, 13, 24.
n – Not Apr. 5, May 24.
o – Also Dec. 24, 31, May 12, 13.
p – Not Dec. 25, Jan. 1, Apr. 4, May 23.

NOTES CONTINUED ON NEXT PAGE →

NANTES and RENNES - LE MANS - PARIS 280

	TGV 8844	TGV 8942	TGV 8040	TGV 8042	TGV 5346	TGV 5460	TGV 5480			TGV 8848	TGV 8646	TGV 8752	TGV 8950	TGV 5334	TGV 5466		TGV 8956*	TGV 8090		TGV 8088	TGV 8660	TGV 8862*	TGV 8864*	TGV 8762
	⑤		⑤⑦	①–④	①–④	Ⓐ		Ⓑ	⑥	Ⓑ				⑦	Ⓒ	†	Ⓐ	⑥	Ⓐ	Ⓑ	Ⓑ		Ⓐ	
	f	⊖	y	m	♠m	☆	☆		t	h			⊖	♣e	☆			u		h	h			
Nantes 289 d.	...	1500	...	...	...	...	1520	1527	1527	1600	...	...	1700	1708	...	1724	1730	...	1734	...	...	1800	1830	...
Angers St Laud **289** d.	...	1537	...	...	...	...	1556	1609	1610	1637	...	...	1739	1745	...	1806	|	...	1816	...	...	1838	|	...
Sablé d.	...	|	...	...	...	...	|	1631	1633	|	...	...	|	|	...	1827	|	...	1838	...	...	1858	|	...
Rennes d.	...	|	1505	1505	1510	1515	|	|	|	|	1605	1705	|	|	1710	|	|	1735	|	1735	1805	|	|	1835
Vitré d.	...	|	|	|	|	|	|	|	|	|	|	|	|	|	|	|	|	|	|	1758	|	|	|	|
Laval d.	...	|	|	|	|	1551	|	|	|	|	1641	|	|	|	1748	|	|	1812	|	1819	|	|	|	|
Le Mans d.	1609	|	|	1619	1630	1640	1640	1652	1703	|	1725	|	1819	1825	1835	1848	|	1859	1859	1904	|	|	|	|
Massy TGV a.	|	|	|	|	1717	1727	1727	...	...	|	|	|	|	1912	1922	...	|	|	...	|	|	|	|	|
Paris Montparnasse a.	1705	1710	1715	1715	...	|	|	...	...	1810	1820	1910	1915	...	|	...	1935	1955	...	2000	2010	2020	2035	2040
Marne la Vallée - Chessy § a.	...	...	...	...	...	1803	1803	...	...	...	...	...	...	...	2003	...	...	...	...	...	...	...	...	...
Charles de Gaulle ✈ a.	...	...	...	...	...	...	...	...	...	...	...	...	...	...	...	...	...	...	...	...	...	...	...	...
Lille Europe **11** a.	...	...	...	...	...	...	...	...	...	...	...	...	...	...	...	...	...	...	...	...	...	...	...	...

	TGV 8864	TGV 5338	TGV 5290	TGV 5288	TGV 8668*	TGV 8866*	TGV 5344	TGV 5342	TGV 8986	TGV 8774*	TGV 8980*	TGV 8782	TGV 8096		TGV 5294	TGV 8688	TGV 8894	TGV 8682*	TGV 8890*	TGV 8896	TGV 8996	TGV 8686	TGV 8998	TGV 8796
	⑦	⑦					⑤	⑤	⑦	⑦		⑤	Ⓒ	†	⑦	⑦	①–④	Ⓑ	⑤	⑦	⑦	⑦	⑦	⑦
	e	♣e					♣f	♣f	e	e		f			e	e	m	h	f	R	e	x	S	S
Nantes 289 d.	1830	...	...	1835	...	1900	...	1904	1930	...	2000	...	...	1934	...	...	2045	...	2100	2100	2200	...	2225	...
Angers St Laud **289** d.	|	...	...	1912	...	1939	...	1943	|	...	2039	...	...	2048	...	...	2122	...	2139	2143	|	...	2307	...
Sablé d.	|	...	...	|	...	|	...	|	|	...	|	...	...	2111	...	...	|	...	|	|	|	...	|	...
Rennes d.	|	1825	1839	|	1905	|	1909	|	|	1935	|	2005	2005	|	2020	2035	|	2105	|	|	|	2205	|	2235
Vitré d.	|	|	|	|	|	|	|	|	|	|	|	|	2026	|	|	|	|	|	|	|	|	|	|	|
Laval d.	|	|	|	|	|	|	|	|	|	|	|	2044	2046	|	|	|	|	|	|	|	|	|	|	2312
Le Mans d.	1948	1952	2000	2000	|	2019	2030	2030	|	|	|	2129	2132	2135	2138	|	|	|	2219	2225	|	|	|	|
Massy TGV a.	|	2042	2048	2048	|	|	2118	2118	|	|	|	|	|	...	2227	|	|	|	|	|	|	|	|	|
Paris Montparnasse a.	2045	...	|	|	2110	2115	...	...	2135	2140	2210	2225	2230	...	|	2240	2255	2310	2315	2325	0005	0010	0040	0045
Marne la Vallée - Chessy § a.	...	...	2129	2129	...	...	...	...	...	...	...	...	...	...	2301	...	...	...	...	...	...	...	...	...
Charles de Gaulle ✈ a.	...	...	2146	2146	...	...	...	...	...	...	...	...	...	...	2316	...	...	...	...	...	...	...	...	...
Lille Europe **11** a.	...	...	2318	2318	...	...	...	...	...	...	...	...	...	...	0010	...	...	...	...	...	...	...	...	...

NOTES - CONTINUED FROM PREVIOUS PAGE

q – Not Jan. 1, Apr. 5, May 24.
r – 0637 on ⑥.
t – Not May 1, 8.
u – Also Dec. 25, Jan. 1, May 13.
v – Also May 13.
w – Also Dec. 24, 31, Apr. 5, May 12, 24; not Dec. 25, Jan. 1.
x – Also Apr. 5, May 24; not Dec. 20.
y – Also Apr. 5, May 12, 24; not Dec. 25, Jan. 1.
z – Lille **Flandres**.

TGV – 🄱, supplement payable, 🍸.

♣ – From/to Lyon (Table **335**).
♠ – From/to Lyon and Marseille (Table **335**).
◐ – Via St Pierre des Corps (Table **335**).
☆ – From/to Strasbourg (Table **391**).
▽ – Not Mar. 20, 27, Apr. 3, 10, 17, 24.

⊕ – Not Jan. 25 - 29.
⊗ – Not Jan. 18 - 22.
⊖ – Not Jan. 11 - 15.
⊖ – Not on Ⓐ Feb. 1 - 19.
§ – Station for Disneyland Paris.

*** – The train number shown is altered as below:**

5236 runs as 5238 on ⑤.
8009 runs as 8711 on Ⓒ.
8033 runs as 8633 on ⑤⑦.
8045 runs as 8075 to Apr. 4.
8071 runs as 8773 on ⑦.
8603 also runs as 8705 on Ⓐ.
8618 runs as 8016 on ⑦.
8620 runs as 8622 on Ⓒ. Also runs as 8722 ①–⑥, 8724 ⑦.
8623 runs as 8023 on ⑤.
8649 also runs as 8691.
8655 runs as 8657 on ⑤ (also runs as 8759 on ①–④).
8668 runs as 8670 on Ⓒ.
8682 runs as 8696/8794 on ⑦ (also as 8790 on ⑤).
8706 runs as 8704 on ①.
8729 runs as 8027 on ⑤.
8730 runs as 8734 on ⑦, also as 8634 on Ⓐ, 8636 on ⑦.
8737 runs as 8739 on ⑤.
8747 runs as 8741 on ⑥; also runs as 8643 on ①–④.
8761 runs as 8763 on ⑤.
8774 also runs as 8676.
8779 runs as 8073 to Apr. 4.
8837 runs as 8937 on ⑥.
8862 runs as 8860 on Ⓒ.
8864 runs as 8964 on ⑤.
8866 runs as 8966 on ⑦.
8879 runs as 8979 on ⑤.
8887 runs as 8987 on ⑤.
8890 runs as 8892 to Apr. 2.
8893 runs as 8895 on certain days.
8904 runs as 8902 on ①.
8921 runs as 8819 on ⑤, 8919 on ⑥ (arrive 1304 on ⑥).
8933 runs as 8833 on ⑤⑥.
8953 runs as 8951 on ⑤.
8956 runs as 8856 on ⑤.
8980 runs as 8880 on ⑤.

For the winter Saturday train Nantes/Rennes - Bourg St Maurice see Table **335**.

RENNES - ST MALO 281

km	*TGV trains*, 🄱	TGV 8081		TGV 8083		TGV 8089	TGV 8095	TGV 8099	TGV 8097	
		Ⓐ				Ⓒ	Ⓐ	⑦	⑤	
								e	f	
	Paris Montparnasse **280** d.	0735	...	1005	...	1505	1835	1905	2035	...
0	**Rennes 272** d.	0952	...	1215	...	1715	2058	2126	2251	...
58	Dol **272** d.	1027	...	|	...	|	2130	|	2321	...
81	**St Malo** a.	1040	...	1258	...	1758	2145	2210	2337	...

TGV trains, 🄱	TGV 8080	TGV 8080		TGV 8082	TGV 8084	TGV 8088	TGV 8090		TGV 8096
	Ⓐ	⑥		①		Ⓑ	⑥		Ⓒ
		t		g		h	u		
St Malo d.	0605	0605	...	1053	1213	1640	1643	...	1917
Dol **272** d.	0621	0622	...	|	|	1657	1659	...	|
Rennes 272 a.	0655	0655	...	1135	1300	1730	1730	...	2000
Paris Montparnasse **280** a.	0915	0910	...	1350	1515	2000	1955	...	2230

	⚒	⚒	Ⓐ	Ⓒ	Ⓒ	Ⓐ	③⑥ t	⚒	†	⚒	⑤ f	Ⓒ	Ⓐ	Ⓐ	Ⓐ	⑦ e	Ⓐ	Ⓑ	⑥ t	Ⓐ	Ⓒ	①–④ m	⑤ f	†	①–⑥ n	⑤ f
Rennes 272 d.	0630	0730	0920	0930	1130	1230	1300	1340	1350	1430	1530	1630	1630	1700	1730	1730	1800	1830	1830	1900	1930	2000	2020	2030	2150	2256
Dol 272 d.	0709	0809	0956	1006	1208	1310	1342	1414	1426	1506	1606	1705	1710	1736	1809	1808	1844	1905	1910	1938	2006	2037	2058	2105	2228	2330
St Malo a.	0730	0825	1010	1020	1222	1328	1400	1430	1440	1520	1620	1719	1727	1750	1828	1822	1903	1920	1928	1952	2022	2051	2112	2119	2241	2344

	⚒	Ⓐ	⚒	Ⓐ	Ⓒ	Ⓐ	⚒	†	⑥ t	③	†	⚒ ⊕		Ⓐ	†	⑤ f	Ⓒ	Ⓐ	Ⓐ	†	Ⓐ	⑥ t	†	Ⓐ		⑦ x
St Malo d.	0550	0620	0650	0720	0750	0750	0950	0950	1050	1220	1250	1250	1450	1550	1550	1650	1720	1720	1750	1750	1820	1820	1830	1850	1950	2050
Dol 272 d.	0604	0638	0703	0737	0805	0805	1004	1005	1109	1239	1303	1309	1505	1604	1604	1704	1734	1739	1809	1809	1835	1839	1844	1906	2004	2104
Rennes 272 a.	0641	0718	0744	0816	0840	0845	1039	1043	1148	1320	1341	1350	1537	1636	1642	1736	1808	1817	1849	1850	1914	1918	1916	1948	2038	2136

e – Also Apr. 5, May 24.
f – Also Dec. 24, 31, May 12; not Dec. 25, Jan. 1.
g – Also Apr. 6, May 25; not Apr. 5, May 24.
h – Not Dec. 25, Jan. 1, May 13.
m – Not Dec. 24, 31, Apr. 5, May 12, 13, 24.
n – Not Apr. 5, May 24.
t – Not May 1, 8.
u – Also Dec. 25, Jan. 1, May 13.
x – Also Dec. 25, Jan. 1, Apr. 5, May 13, 24; not Apr. 4, May 23.
⊕ – Runs up to 20 mins earlier on Ⓐ Feb. 1 - 11.

DOL - DINAN 282

km		Ⓐ	⑥ t	Ⓐ ⊙v	Ⓒ ⊙	⑥ t	Ⓐ	†	⑥ t	Ⓒ	Ⓐ	Ⓐ	†	①–④ m	⑤ f	⑦ u	⑤⑥ c
0	Dol d.	0702	0818	1032	1108	1350	1420	1433	1511	1725	1730	1814	1920	2045	2105	2110	2235
28	Dinan a.	0725	0841	1055	1130	1413	1443	1456	1542	1806	1801	1842	1943	2108	2128	2133	2258

	Ⓐ	⚒	⑥ t		Ⓒ	Ⓐ	⑥ t	⑤ f	E	Ⓐ		† ⊙	⑤	①–④ m	⑥ t	†	
Dinan d.	0630	0732	0927	...	1230	1232	1432	1617	1624	1657	...	1816	1849	1910	1936	2034	...
Dol a.	0657	0800	0957	...	1255	1300	1455	1640	1647	1720	...	1839	1912	1933	1959	2057	...

E – Daily except ⑤ (also runs Dec. 25, Jan. 1; not Dec. 24, 31, May 12).
c – Also Dec. 24, 31, May 12; not May 1, 8.
f – Also Dec. 24, 31, May 12; not Dec. 25, Jan. 1.
m – Not Dec. 24, 31, Apr. 5, May 12, 13, 24.
t – Not May 1, 8.
u – Also Dec. 25, Jan. 1, Apr. 5, May 13, 24; not Apr. 4, May 23.

v – Subject to alteration Apr. 26 - May 7.
⊙ – To/from St Brieuc (Table **299**).
Most journeys will be replaced by 🚌 *Mar. 15 - 26.*

MORLAIX - ROSCOFF 283

km		🚌 Ⓐ	🚌 ⚒	Ⓐ	⑥ v	⑦ e	⚒	†	🚌 ⑥	🚌 ①–④ b	🚌 ⑤	🚌 ①–④ m	🚌 Ⓒ	🚌 ⑤	🚌 †	🚌 ①–④ m	🚌 ⑤
0	**Morlaix** d.	0803	0929	1057	1057	1159	1303	1519	1515	1640	1705	1756	1806	1950	2010	2057	2122
28	**Roscoff** a.	0833	1004	1126	1125	1228	1331	1548	1545	1710	1735	1831	1841	2025	2040	2132	2157

	🚌 Ⓐ	🚌 ⑥	🚌 Ⓐ		⚒	🚌 †	🚌 ⚒	†	⑥ t	Ⓐ	🚌 ⑥	†	🚌 ①–④ m		🚌 Ⓐ	🚌 †	🚌 ⑤
Roscoff d.	0643	0830	0835	...	1132	1135	1330	1336	1431	1529	1630	1632	1712	...	1839	1925	2030
Morlaix a.	0713	0905	0910	...	1200	1210	1405	1403	1459	1557	1705	1700	1742	...	1914	2000	2105

b – Schooldays only.
e – Also Apr. 5, May 24.
m – Not Dec. 24, 31, Apr. 5, May 12, 13, 24.
t – Not May 1, 8.
v – Also Dec. 25, Jan. 1, May 13.

All services call at St Pol de Léon (*21 km*/15 mins from Morlaix). 🚌 call at Roscoff port on days of sailings.

🚌 services are subject to confirmation

284 RENNES - ST BRIEUC - MORLAIX - BREST

km	TGV trains convey 🍷								55803				TGV 8603						TGV 8611						TGV 8617
		Ⓐ	Ⓐ	Ⓐ	⑥	Ⓐ	Ⓐ	⑥	Ⓐ	Ⓐ	⑥		①–⑥	⚒	Ⓐ	†	⑥	Ⓐ		⚒	Ⓑ	⑥	③	⑥	Ⓐ
					t	u		t			t		n		▽		t	E		△▽		t		t	
	Paris ⊡ **280** d.	...	...	...	...	...	...	...	...	...	...	...	0705	...	...	...	...	...	0905	...	...	...	...	...	1105
0	**Rennes** d.	...	...	0605	...	...	0620	0640	0700	0720	0830	...	0911	...	...	1006	1035	1032	1111	...	...	...	...	1236	1326
80	Lamballe **299** d.	...	...	0647	...	0701	0724	0742	|	0806	0913	...	|	...	...	1049	1115	1112	1154	...	...	...	...	1315	|
101	**St Brieuc 299** d.	...	...	0701	0708	0723	0741	0759	0753	0824	0927	...	1007	...	...	1103	1132	1126	1212	...	...	1221	1235	1332	1422
132	Guingamp d.	...	...	0719	0726	0746	...	...	|	...	0945	...	1024	1033	...	1120	1151	...	1230	...	1237	1241	1302	1351	1440
158	Plouaret-Trégor d.	...	...	0733	0742	0802	...	...	|	...	0959	...	|	1051	...	1135	1205	...	|	...	1254	1259	1322	1405	1456
175	Lannion a.	...	...	|	|	0818	...	...	|	...	|	...	|	1107	...	*1157*	*1227*	...	|	...	1310	1316	1338	|	*1522*
189	Morlaix d.	0616	0637	0758	0804	...	...	...	0835	...	1017	...	1054	...	1102	1155	1223	...	1300	1310	...	...	...	1423	1515
215	Landivisiau d.	0631	0701	0813	0821	...	...	...	|	...	1032	...	|	...	1119	1210	1238	...	|	1334	...	...	...	1438	|
230	Landerneau **286** d.	0641	0714	0826	0835	...	...	...	|	...	1042	...	|	...	1129	1220	1248	...	|	1346	...	...	...	1448	1539
248	**Brest 286** a.	0658	0733	0842	0851	...	...	...	0912	...	1058	...	1130	...	1143	1235	1304	...	1336	1406	...	...	...	1504	1555

	TGV 8619		TGV 8627					TGV 8621					TGV 8623	TGV 8625									TGV 8633	55845	
	Ⓒ		①–④	⑤	Ⓒ	Ⓐ	①–④	⑤	⑤	①–④	⑦	⑤	①–④	Ⓒ	Ⓐ	Ⓒ	⑥	①–④	⑤	†	Ⓐ	Ⓐ	⑤⑦	①–④	†
			m	f			m	f	f	m	⊖	f	m				t	m	f		△		w	m △	
Paris ⊡ **280** d.	1105	...	1205	...	...	...	...	1305	...	...	...	...	1405	1405	...	...	...	...	...	...	...	...	1605	...	...
Rennes d.	1324	1333	1420	1426	1426	...	...	1518	...	...	...	1603	1618	1622	...	...	...	...	1650	1723	1746	...	1812	1821	...
Lamballe **299** d.	|	1435	|	1505	1505	...	...	1601	...	...	...	1646	|	1705	...	...	...	1713	1732	1806	1829	...	|	1904	...
St Brieuc 299 d.	1420	1450	1515	1522	1522	...	...	1619	...	...	...	1700	1714	1723	...	...	1731	1736	1745	1820	1842	...	1907	1917	...
Guingamp d.	1439	...	1533	1540	1540	...	...	1637	...	...	...	1718	1732	1741	...	...	1759	1802	1802	1838	1900	...	1924	|	...
Plouaret-Trégor d.	1455	...	|	1554	1554	...	1630	|	...	...	1656	1733	|	|	...	...	1820	1821	1816	1853	1915	1932	|	|	2005
Lannion a.	*1519*	...	|	*1625*r	|	...	1647	|	...	...	1713	*1754*	|	|	...	...	1837	1837	*1846*	*1938*	|	1952	|	|	2022
Morlaix d.	1514	...	1604	1612	1612	1630	...	1707	1714	1722	...	1751	1801	1811	1809	1816	...	...	1835	1910	1933	...	1952	|	...
Landivisiau d.	|	...	|	|	1627	1646	...	|	1738	1747	...	1806	|	|	1829	1835	...	...	1851	1925	1948	...	|	|	...
Landerneau **286** d.	1538	...	|	1635	1637	1656	...	|	1750	1800	...	1816	|	|	1839	1845	...	...	1901	1935	1958	...	2017	|	...
Brest 286 a.	1553	...	1640	1652	1654	1711	...	1743	1810	1818	...	1832	1838	1847	1855	1902	...	...	1916	1952	2014	...	2033	2033	...

			TGV 8647		TGV 8643		🚌				TGV 8645	TGV 8691	TGV 8649	TGV 8655	TGV 8657	TGV 8659			TGV 8653	TGV 8665	TGV 8669		TGV 5238	TGV 8679	TGV 8689
	⑥	Ⓑ	⑤	⑤	①–④	①–④	①–④	Ⓐ	†	†	①–④	⑤	⑤	①–④	⑤	⑦	⑦	Ⓐ	⑥	①–⑥	⑦		⑤	⑤	⑦
	t		q	f	m	m	m				m	f	f	m	f	e	e		y	n	e		♥f	f	k
Paris ⊡ **280** d.	...	...	1710	...	1705	...	...	...	...	...	1735	1735	1735	1805	1805	1805	...	...	1805	1905	1905	...	...	2105	2355
Rennes d.	1846	1838	|	1920	1914	...	...	1925	1935	...	1949	2001	1953	2011	2011	2018	...	2025	2027	2120	2122	...	2130	2320	|
Lamballe **299** d.	1929	1939	|	2003	|	...	...	2021	2018	...	2031	2043	|	|	|	|	...	|	|	2203	2205	...	2212	|	|
St Brieuc 299 d.	1942	1954	2006	2018	2010	...	...	2033	2032	...	2046	2101	|	2105	2108	2115	...	2127	2123	2220	2222	...	2229	0016	0425
Guingamp d.	1959	...	|	2035	2027	2035	...	...	2050	...	...	2120	|	|	2127	2133	2141	...	2141	2240	2239	...	2250	0034	0442
Plouaret-Trégor d.	2014	...	|	2049	|	2053	...	...	2104	2125	...	|	|	|	|	|	2158	...	|	2255	2254	2259	|	|	|
Lannion a.	*2036*	...	|	*2109*	|	2109	...	...	|	2142	...	2150	|	|	|	|	2214	...	|	|	|	2316	|	|	|
Morlaix d.	2031	...	|	2108	2057	...	2100	...	2121	...	...	...	2126	|	2157	2203	...	...	2211	2314	2313	...	2322	0104	0512
Landivisiau d.	2046	...	|	|	|	...	2118	...	2136	...	...	...	|	|	|	|	...	...	|	|	|	...	|	|	|
Landerneau **286** d.	2056	...	|	2131	|	...	2138	...	2145	...	...	...	|	|	|	|	...	...	|	2337	|	...	|	|	0537
Brest 286 a.	2113	...	2122	2147	2132	...	...	...	2202	...	...	...	2203	2217	2233	2239	...	...	2247	2353	2349	...	2358	0141	0552

	TGV 8690	TGV 8608		TGV 8610					55802					TGV 8618						TGV 8622	TGV 8620				
	Ⓐ	⑥	①	Ⓐ	Ⓐ	⑥	Ⓐ	Ⓐ	Ⓐ	Ⓐ	†	Ⓐ	⑥	①–⑥	Ⓐ	Ⓐ	⑥	Ⓐ	Ⓒ	Ⓒ	Ⓐ	⑥	†	†	Ⓐ
	z	v	g			t	△	u	△				t	n			t				⊗	t	▷		⊗
Brest 286 d.	...	0438	...	0442	...	...	0519	...	0534	...	...	...	...	0637	0700	0747	0807	...	...	0834	0839	1009	...	1023	1124
Landerneau **286** d.	...	|	...	|	...	...	0533	...	|	...	...	...	...	0650	0718	0800	0822	...	...	|	|	1021	...	1037	1136
Landivisiau d.	...	|	...	|	...	...	0543	...	|	...	...	...	...	|	0730	0810	0833	...	...	|	|	|	...	1047	1146
Morlaix d.	...	0511	...	0515	...	...	0558	...	0607	...	...	...	...	0714	0755	0827	0857	...	...	0906	0912	1044	...	1101	1204
Lannion d.	...	|	0503	|	...	...	...	...	*0605*	...	...	0652	0656	|	...	—	—	0859	0901	|	|	|	1056	|	—
Plouaret-Trégor d.	...	|	0518	|	...	...	...	...	0626	...	...	0707	0711	|	...	...	⚒	0914	0918	0925	|	|	1113	1119	...
Guingamp d.	...	0541	0535	0545	...	...	...	0631	0639	0706	0721	0727	0731	0744	...	†	⊗	0931	...	0941	0942	1114	...	1133	Ⓐ
St Brieuc 299 d.	0504	0604	...	0606	0613	0633	...	0648	0700	0728	0739	0748	0753	0806	...	0932	0936	...	...	1005	1005	1135	...	1154	1240
Lamballe **299** d.	0518	0618	...	|	0624	0644	...	0704	0712	0741	0751	...	...	|	...	0943	0947	...	...	|	|	1147	...	1206	1251
Rennes a.	0600	0700	...	0700	0725	0748	...	...	0755	0840	0850	...	...	0900	...	1040	1045	...	...	1056	1056	1230	...	1250	1345
Paris ⊡ **280** a.	0820	0910	...	0915	...	...	...	...	...	...	...	...	...	1110	...	...	...	...	...	1320	1325	...	...	...	...

		TGV 8634	TGV 8636					TGV 8646							TGV 8660				TGV 5290				TGV 8670	TGV 8668	
	⑥	Ⓐ	⑦	⑤	⚒		†		⑥		①–④	⑤–⑦	①–④	Ⓑ	Ⓑ	⑦	⑤	①–④	⑦	⑤	①–④	⑥	Ⓒ	Ⓐ	⑥
	t		e	f	△				y		m	s	m	h	h	⊖	f	m	♠e	f	m				t
Brest 286 d.	1127	1138	1141	1153	1225	...	1303	1335	...	...	1426	1427	1512	...	1531	1549	...	...	1604	1624	...	...	1634	1651	...
Landerneau **286** d.	1139	|	|	1205	1243	...	1321	|	...	...	1438	1439	1527	...	|	1601	...	...	|	1637	...	...	|	|	...
Landivisiau d.	1149	|	|	1215	1256	...	1332	|	...	...	1448	1449	1537	...	|	1611	...	...	|	1647	...	...	|	|	...
Morlaix d.	1206	1210	1214	1231	1321	...	1356	1409	...	...	1505	1505	1553	...	1603	1628	...	...	1639	1703	...	...	1707	|	...
Lannion d.	*1143*	*1203*	|	|	...	1356	...	|	1444	...	|	|	...	1557	|	*1623*	...	...	|	*1650*	1702	1655	|	|	...
Plouaret-Trégor d.	1224	1229	|	1249	...	1413	...	|	1500	...	1522	1523	...	1614	1622	1646	...	...	|	1720	1717	1712	|	|	...
Guingamp d.	1238	1245	1244	1303	...	1430	...	1439	...	...	1537	1538	...	...	1638	1702	...	...	1712	1736	1734	1727	1737	|	...
St Brieuc 299 d.	1259	1307	1307	1325	...	1450	...	1504	...	...	1558	1558	...	...	1704	1721	1725	1731	1733	1758	1755	...	1804	1808	1823
Lamballe **299** d.	1311	|	|	1337	...	...	...	1518	...	...	1610	1611	...	...	1718	1734	1739	1744	1749	1811	...	...	1818	|	1837
Rennes a.	1355	1400	1400	1420	...	...	...	1600	...	...	1653	1655	...	...	1800	1817	1839	1825	1832	1852	...	...	1900	1900	1944
Paris ⊡ **280** a.	...	1610	1610	...	...	...	...	1820	...	...	...	...	...	...	2010	...	...	...	...	...	...	...	2110	2110	...

			TGV 8676						TGV 8688						TGV 8696		TGV 8682				TGV 8686				
	①–④	⚒	⑦	Ⓐ	†	⑤	Ⓐ	⑦	⑦	†	Ⓐ	⑤	⑥	⑤⑥	⑦	①–④	Ⓐ	†	①–④	⑤	⑦	⑤	†	⑦	
	m		e			f		e	e			f	t	z	e	m	b		m	f	d	f		c	
Brest 286 d.	...	1705	1707	...	1720	...	1734	...	1808	...	1803	...	...	1825	...	...	1842	1853	1917	1933	1940	...	...	2046	...
Landerneau **286** d.	...	1721	|	...	1733	...	1746	...	|	...	1820	...	...	1837	...	...	|	1905	1935	1951	1952	...	...	2058	...
Landivisiau d.	...	1731	|	...	1743	...	|	...	|	...	1832	...	...	1847	...	...	|	1916	1948	2004	|	...	...	|	...
Morlaix d.	...	1749	1740	...	1801	...	1809	...	1841	...	1855	...	...	1903	...	...	1915	1931	2003	2020	2016	...	...	2121	...
Lannion d.	1733	|	|	...	*1757*	1759	|	1819	|	...	...	1853	1858	|	1902	1902	|	|	...	...	|	2020	2029	*2103*	...
Plouaret-Trégor d.	1750	1815	|	...	1820	1816	|	1836	|	...	...	1910	1914	1920	|	1918	|	1948	...	...	|	2037	2046	2139	...
Guingamp d.	1805	...	1811	...	1834	1832	1840	1853	1911	...	...	...	...	1935	1939	1935	1945	2003	...	...	|	...	...	2154	...
St Brieuc 299 d.	1827	...	1834	1834	1850	...	1900	1913	1937	1944	...	...	...	1955	2004	...	2008	2023	...	...	2103	...	...	2215	...
Lamballe **299** d.	...	...	|	1849	1902	...	1912	...	|	1958	...	...	...	2007	2018	...	|	2034	...	...	|	...	...	2228	...
Rennes a.	...	...	1926	1945	1945	...	1955	...	2030	2055	...	...	...	2050	2100	...	2100	2115	...	...	2156	...	...	2310	...
Paris ⊡ **280** a.	...	...	2140	...	...	...	...	...	2240	...	...	...	...	...	2310	...	2310	...	...	...	0010	...	...	...	...

E – Not Apr. 26 - May 7.

b – Not Dec. 24, 31.
c – Also Apr. 5, May 24; not Apr. 4, May 23.
d – Also Apr. 5, May 24; not Dec. 20.
e – Also Apr. 4, May 24.
f – Also Dec. 24, 31, May 12; not Dec. 25, Jan. 1.
g – Also Apr. 6, May 25; not Apr. 5, May 24.
h – Not Dec. 25, Jan. 1, May 13.
k – Also Apr. 5, May 24; not Jan. 24 - Feb. 28, May 23.
m – Not Dec. 24, 31, Apr. 5, May 12, 13, 24.
n – Not Apr. 5, May 24.
q – Also Dec. 24, 31, May 12; not Dec. 25, Jan. 1, May 14.
r – By 🚌.
s – Also Dec. 24, 31, Apr. 5, May 12, 13, 24.

t – Not May 1, 8.
u – From/to Dinan, Table **299**.
v – Also May 13.
w – Also Dec. 24, 31, Apr. 5, May 12, 24; not Dec. 25, Jan. 1.
x – Also Dec. 24, 31, May 2; not Dec. 25, Jan. 1, May 1, 8.
y – Also Dec. 25, Jan. 1, May 13.
z – Not Dec. 31.
TGV – Ⓡ, supplement payable, 🍷.
⊡ – Paris Montparnasse.
⊗ – Not on Ⓐ May 10 - 21.
⊖ – Also Dec. 25, Jan. 1, Apr. 5, May 13, 24; not Apr. 4, May 23.
△ – Subject to alteration Dec. 14 - 18, 21, 22.
▽ – Not on Ⓐ Apr. 25 - May 7.
▷ – Depart 1042 on Dec. 25, Jan. 1, May 1, 8.

♥ – From Lille Europe, depart 1728 (Table **11**).
♠ – To Lille Europe, arrive 2318 (Table **11**). Runs 5 - 8 minutes later Brest - Rennes to Mar. 21.

Lannion - Plouaret-Trégor may be by 🚌 on Ⓐ in May.

GUINGAMP - PONTRIEUX - PAIMPOL

Trains operate 4 - 5 times per day.
47 km. Journey 45 minutes.

A steam train operates between Guingamp and Pontrieux on ③–⑦ early May to late Sept. (also certain ② in July/Aug). www.vapeurdutrieux.com

RENNES and NANTES - QUIMPER 285

km													TGV 8705						TGV 8711					TGV 8715	
		Ⓐ	Ⓐ	⑥	Ⓐ	Ⓐ	⑥	Ⓐ	Ⓐ	Ⓐ	Ⓒ		Ⓐ	⑥	⑥	†	†	⑥	Ⓒ	Ⓐ	Ⓐ		⑥		⑥
				p			t						⊖	t	t			t		§	§		t		t
0	*Paris* ⊡ **280** d.	...	...	...	...	...	...	...	...	...	...	...	0705	...	...	...	...	...	0805	...	...	...	...	1005	...
365	**Rennes 287** d.	...	...	...	0626	...	0625	0645	...	0723	0830	...	0914	0925	...	0930	...	...	1023	1030	...	...	1118	1211	...
	Nantes ◧ d.	...	...	...	|	0612	|	|	0651	|	|	...	|	|	0910	|	1003	1008	|	|	1019	...	|	|	1227
	Savenay ◧ d.	...	...	...	|	0636	|	|	0715	|	|	...	|	|	|	|	1026	1030	|	|	1041	...	|	|	1249
437	Redon **287** ◧ d.	...	...	...	0712	0712	0711	0737	0744	0759	0908	...	|	1007	1007	1005	1053	1056	1101	1117	1117	...	1153	1249	1316
492	Vannes d.	...	0639	0642	0742	0742	...	0808	...	0825	...	...	1014	1033	1033	1030	...	...	1128	1147	1147	...	1223	1316	1345
511	Auray d.	...	0653	0657	0754	0754	...	0819	...	|	...	...	1027	1044	1044	1043	...	...	1141	1200	1200	...	1236	1329	1357
545	Lorient d.	0645	0727	0724	0815	0815	...	0843	...	0852	...	...	1047	1103	1103	1102	...	...	1200	1221	1221	...	1258	1350	1419
565	Quimperlé d.	0657	0742	...	0827	0827	...	...	...	|	...	...	|	1115	1115	1114	...	...	|	1233	1233	...	1310	1403	1431
612	**Quimper** a.	0728	0809	...	0853	0853	...	...	...	0926	...	...	1123	1142	1142	1142	...	...	1235	1259	1259	...	1336	1431	1457

			TGV 8717			13895	TGV 8723										TGV 8729								3854 3855
	⑥	Ⓐ					⑤	①-④	⑤	①-④	①-④	⑥	⑥	†	⑤	⑤		①-④	⑤	Ⓐ	⑦	Ⓑ	⑤	⑥	♠
	t				◇		f	m	f	m	m	t	t		f	f	A	m	f	u	z	s	f	t	⊗
Paris ⊡ **280** d.	...	...	1205	...	...	...	1345	...	...	...	...	...	...	...	...	...	1505	...	...	...	...	...	...	...	...
Rennes 287 d.	...	1341	1417	...	1426	...	|	...	1610	1639	...	1637	...	...	...	1654	1711	...	1727	...	...	1745	...	1815	...
Nantes ◧ d.	1312	|	|	...	|	1450	|	...	|	|	1622	|	1622	1622	1624	|	|	...	|	1705	1723	|	1809	|	1818
Savenay ◧ d.	1336	|	|	...	|	|	|	...	|	|	1644	|	1643	1644	1645	|	|	...	|	1749	1748	|	|	|	1841
Redon **287** ◧ d.	1403	1417	|	...	1503	1535	|	...	1648	1723	1723	1723	1723	1712	1716	1733	|	1755	1804	1821	1813	1828	1853	1855	1910
Vannes d.	...	1444	1518	...	...	1605	1647	1710	1718	1748	1748	1753	1753	...	...	1800	1812	1826	1830	...	...	1857	1922	...	1942
Auray d.	...	1457	1531	...	...	1618	1700	1722	1731	1801	1801	1805	1805	...	...	1813	1826	1840	...	...	...	1910	1935	...	1957
Lorient d.	...	1514	1551	1600	...	1640	1720	1755	1753	1820	1820	1826	1826	...	...	1834	1847	1905	...	...	...	1931	1957	...	2018
Quimperlé d.	...	...	|	1611	...	1652	|	1810	1805	|	|	1838	1838	...	...	1846	|	...	...	...	...	1943	2008	...	|
Quimper a.	...	...	1626	1642	...	1719	1754	1840	1832	1854	1854	1904	1904	...	...	1913	1924	...	...	...	...	2009	2035	...	2056

	TGV 5232		TGV 8737	TGV 8739	TGV 8747	TGV 8741	TGV 8743	TGV 8759	TGV 8757							TGV 5236	TGV 5236	3856	TGV 8763		TGV 8761	TGV 8773	TGV 8777	TGV 8779	TGV 8799
	⑤	⑦	①-④	⑤	Ⓐ	⑥	⑦	①-④	⑤	⑦	Ⓐ	①-④	†	⑥	⑦	①-④	⑦	⑤⑦	⑤			⑦	⑤	⑤	⑦
	♥f	d	m	f		v	e	m	f	z		m		t	z	♥m	♥e	♠w	f	L	L	e	f	D	q
Paris ⊡ **280** d.	...	...	1635	1635	1705	1705	1705	1805	1810	...	...	...	...	...	...	...	...	...	1935	...	1935	2005	2035	2205	2355
Rennes 287 d.	1844	...	1853	1855	1911	1911	1923	2014	|	...	...	2020	2030	2034	...	2129	2129	...	2141	...	2141	2223	2246	0022	|
Nantes ◧ d.	|	...	|	|	|	|	|	|	|	1940	1944	|	|	|	2043	|	|	2116	|	2126	|	|	|	|	|
Savenay ◧ d.	|	...	|	|	|	|	|	|	|	2002	2015	|	|	|	2104	|	|	2141	|	2147	|	|	|	|	|
Redon **287** ◧ d.	1928	1924	1931	1936	|	1949	|	|	|	2030	2044	2108	2106	2111	2135	2206	2206	2207	2219	2212	2218	2300	2323	|	|
Vannes d.	1955	1953	1959	2004	2016	2016	2025	2114	2115	...	...	2137	2132	...	...	2233	2233	...	2246	...	2246	2327	2350	0123	0449
Auray d.	2009	2008	...	2017	2029	2029	2039	|	2128	...	...	...	2145	...	...	2246	2246	...	2259	...	2258	2341	0003	0136	0505
Lorient d.	2028	2030	...	2036	2049	2050	2059	2142	2148	...	...	...	2204	...	...	2303	2305	...	2320	...	2318	0001	0023	0154	0525
Quimperlé d.	2040	2041	...	|	2102	2103	|	|	|	...	...	...	2215	...	...	...	2319	...	|	...	2332	0014	0036	...	|
Quimper a.	2107	2107	...	2114	2128	2130	2132	2216	2222	...	...	...	2242	...	...	...	2346	...	2354	...	2359	0041	0104	...	0600

	TGV 8704	TGV 8706	TGV 8712						TGV 8718	TGV 5272	TGV 5272			3832 3833		TGV 8724	TGV 8722		13894	TGV 8730	TGV 8734				
	①	②-⑤	Ⓐ	Ⓐ	Ⓐ	Ⓒ	Ⓐ	Ⓐ	①-⑥	①⑥	①-⑥	⑥	Ⓐ	♠	Ⓐ	⑦	①-⑥	Ⓒ		①-⑥	⑦	①-④	①-④	⑤	⑤
	g	y							n	♣r	♣n	t		b	⊖	e	n⊖		⊕	n	e	m	m	k	f
Quimper d.	0418	...	0525	...	0532	...	0613	0613	0635	0646	...	0705	0725	0739	0800	0839	0842	1007	1112	1144	1147	1234	1234	1240	1320
Quimperlé d.	|	...	|	...	0559	...	|	|	0704	0715	...	0734	0752	|	0827	0908	0912	1035	1139	|	|	1301	1301	1308	1348
Lorient d.	0452	0457	0601	...	0611	...	0647	0647	0718	0729	0729	0748	0805	0820	0838	0922	0926	1049	1153	1220	1222	1314	1314	1321	1401
Auray d.	0511	|	|	...	0632	...	0704	0704	0738	0749	0749	...	0826	0842	...	0942	0945	1107	1218	1240	1242	1333	1333	1341	1418
Vannes d.	0524	0524	0630	...	0645	...	0717	0717	0751	0803	0803	...	0838	0857	...	0956	0959	1120	1233	1254	1255	1347	1347	1354	1431
Redon **287** d.	0553	0553	|	0650	0716	0734	0747	0750	0821	0829	0829	...	0909	0929	...	1025	|	1147	1303	1324	|	1420	1423	1420	1508
Savenay ◧ d.	|	|	|	0734	|	|	|	0817	|	|	|	...	|	|	...	|	|	|	1327	|	|	|	1446	|	1530
Nantes ◧ a.	|	|	|	0810	|	|	|	0840	|	|	|	...	|	1012	...	|	|	|	1350	|	|	|	1507	|	1550
Rennes 287 ◧ a.	0630	0630	0730	...	0755	0814	0826	...	0857	0904	0904	...	0943	...	...	1100	1100	1220	...	1357	1357	1455	...	1455	...
Paris ⊡ **280** a.	0840	0840	0945	...	...	...	...	...	1110	...	...	...	...	...	...	1325	1325	...	...	1610	1610	...	...	...	...

						TGV 8752											TGV 8762							TGV 8774	
	⑥	⑥	†	†	Ⓐ		Ⓐ	⑦	⑦	①-④	①-④	①-④	†	⑤	⑤	†		⚒	⑦	Ⓐ	⑥	①-④	⑦	⑦	⑥
	t	t						z	d	m	m	m		f	f				d		t	m	z	e	t
Quimper d.	1333	1333	1337	...	...	1437	1512	...	...	...	...	...	1547	1547	...	...	1617	...	1633	...	...	1715	...	1717	...
Quimperlé d.	1400	1400	1404	...	...	1505	1539	...	...	...	...	...	1614	1614	...	...	|	...	1700	...	...	|	...	|	...
Lorient d.	1412	1412	1417	...	...	1523	1552	...	...	...	1630	...	1627	1632	...	...	1653	...	1712	1714	1740	1750	...	1753	...
Auray d.	1434	1434	1439	...	...	1542	1614	...	...	...	1651	...	1649	1654	...	...	1713	...	1734	1739	1808	|	...	1812	...
Vannes d.	1446	1446	1451	...	...	1556	1627	...	1645	...	1703	...	1703	1707	...	...	1728	...	1746	1750	1820	1821	...	1825	...
Redon **287** d.	1520	1526	1522	1526	1538	1626	1658	1658	1717	1719	1730	1744	1736	1737	1745	1749	|	1809	1818	...	1850	1847	1851	1854	1901
Savenay ◧ d.	|	1549	|	1549	|	|	1722	1729	|	|	...	1814	|	|	1816	1815	|	|	|	...	...	|	1919	|	1928
Nantes ◧ a.	|	1610	|	1610	|	|	1745	1750	|	|	...	1835	|	|	1840	1836	|	|	|	...	...	|	1941	|	1950
Rennes 287 ◧ a.	1555	...	1555	...	1616	1700	...	...	1750	1807	...	...	1811	1811	...	...	1829	1906	1855	...	...	1920	...	1930	...
Paris ⊡ **280** a.	...	...	...	...	...	1910	...	...	...	...	...	...	...	...	...	...	2040	...	...	...	...	...	...	2140	...

						TGV 8776	TGV 8782						TGV 8794				TGV 8790			TGV 8798			TGV 8796		
	①-④	①-④	⑤	Ⓐ	⑥	⑦	⑤	⑦	†	①-④	⑤		⑦	①-④	①-④	⑤	⑤	†	⑦	⑦	①-④	⑤	⑦	⑦	
	m	m	f		v	e	f	e		m	f		e	m	m	f	f		z	x	m	f	E	c	
Quimper d.	...	1730	1735	...	1740	1746	1750	1757	...	...	1757	...	1836	1838	1838	...	1846	1918	...	1950	2000	2003	...	2025	...
Quimperlé d.	...	1800	1803	...	1808	|	|	1825	...	←	1830	...	1905	1905	1905	...	|	1945	...	|	2027	2030	...	2053	...
Lorient d.	1755	1815	1815	...	1820	1822	1827	1838	...	1834	1847	...	1919	1918	1918	...	1922	1958	...	2026	2039	2042	2055	2107	...
Auray d.	1820	→	1833	...	1839	1842	1847	1857	...	1903	1918	...	1939	1935	1935	...	1942	2021	...	2046	2100	2102	2114	2127	...
Vannes d.	1834	...	1845	...	1851	1857	1901	1910	...	1915	1930	...	1953	1948	1948	...	1955	2034	...	2059	2111	2114	2128	2140	...
Redon **287** d.	1904	...	1918	1921	1922	|	|	1937	1951	...	...	...	2020	2021	2026	2028	|	2105	2130	|	2141	2144	|	2207	...
Savenay ◧ d.	...	...	|	1949	|	|	|	|	2019	...	...	...	|	|	2052	2055	|	|	2155	|	...	2211	|	|	...
Nantes ◧ a.	...	...	|	2012	|	|	|	|	2039	...	...	...	|	|	2115	2116	|	|	2216	|	...	2233	|	|	...
Rennes 287 ◧ a.	...	...	1950	...	1955	|	2000	2010	...	...	...	...	2056	2055	...	...	2056	2139	...	2200	...	...	2230	2240	...
Paris ⊡ **280** a.	...	...	...	...	...	2200	2225	...	...	...	...	...	2310	...	...	...	2310	...	...	0010	...	...	0045	...	...

A – Daily except ⑤ (also runs Dec. 25, Jan. 1; not Dec. 24, 31, May 12).
D – ⑤ from Apr. 9 (also May 12).
E – ⑦ from Apr. 11 (also Apr. 5, May 24).
L – ①②③④⑥ (also Dec. 25, Jan. 1; not Dec. 24, 31, Apr. 5, May 12, 24).

b – Not Jan. 18-22, May 13-16.
c – Also Apr. 5, May 24; not Apr. 4, 25, May 23.
d – Also Apr. 5, May 24; not Apr. 4, May 23.
e – Also Apr. 5, May 24.
f – Also Dec. 24, 31, May 12; not Dec. 25, Jan. 1.
g – Also Apr. 6, May 25; not Apr. 5, May 24.
k – Also Dec. 24, 31; not Dec. 25, Jan. 1.
m – Not Dec. 24, 31, Apr. 5, May 12, 13, 24.
n – Not Apr. 5, May 24.
p – Not Mar. 13, Apr. 10, May 1, 8.
q – Not Apr. 4, May 23.
r – Also Dec. 25, Jan. 1, Apr. 6, May 13, 25; not Apr. 5, May 24.
s – Also May 1, 8.
t – Not May 1, 8.
u – On ⑤ **f** Nantes d. 1725, Savenay d. 1748, Redon a. 1817.
v – Also Dec. 25, Jan. 1, May 13.
w – Also Dec. 24, 31, May 12; not Dec. 25, Jan. 1, Apr. 4, May 14, 16, 23.
x – Also Apr. 5, 24; not Dec. 20.
y – Not Dec. 25, Jan. 1, Apr. 6, May 25.
z – Also Dec. 25, Jan. 1, Apr. 5, May 13, 24; not Apr. 4, May 23.

TGV – Ⓡ, supplement payable, 🍸.

⊡ – Paris Montparnasse.
◇ – On Ⓒ depart 1430, arrive 1510.
◧ – See also **287** Nantes - Redon, **287/8** Nantes - Savenay.
♥ – From Lille Europe (**5232** departs 1447, **5236** departs 1728, Table **11**).
♣ – To Lille Europe (arrive 1340, Table **11**).
♠ – To/from Bordeaux (Table **292**).
⊕ – Not on Ⓐ Apr. 12-23.
⊗ – Subject to alteration on May 13-16.
⊖ – Not Mar. 29 - Apr. 9.
⊖ – Not Apr. 10-24.
§ – Subject to alteration on Mar. 29 - Apr. 9 (also Nantes - Redon Jan. 25-29.

AURAY - QUIBERON

⑥⑦ **June 12-20**, ⑥⑦ **Sept. 4-12**:

From Auray: 1050, 1345, 1545, 1830.
From Quiberon: 1145, 1440, 1730, 1945.
Journey 45 minutes.

A daily service operates **June 26 - Aug. 29**.

🚐 operates 4-5 times daily all year.

286 BREST - QUIMPER

km		Ⓐ	Ⓐ	⑥ t	⚒	†		⑤ f	Ⓒ	Ⓐ	†	①–④ m	⑤ f	⑥ t	⑤ f	⑦ d
0	**Brest 284** d.	0553*	0716	0719	0920	1019	1203r	1539	1659	1713	1834	1836	1846	1920	2006	2006
18	Landerneau **284** d.	0606	0728	0732	0931	1033	1216	1551	1712	1725	1849	1855	│	1935	2022	2021
72	Châteaulin d.	0644	0804	0812	1009	1109	1250	1627	1749	1803	1923	1927	1929	2013	2057	2058
102	**Quimper** a.	0705	0825	0832	1029	1130	1311	1649	1810	1823	1944	1948	1951	2033	2118	2119

	Ⓐ	Ⓐ	⑥ t	†	⚒			⑤ f	Ⓒ	Ⓐ		†	①–④ m	⑤ f	⑤ f	⑦ e
Quimper d.	0621	0741	0749	0925	0946	...	1445	1604	1727	1740	...	1900	1905	1907	2034	2035
Châteaulin d.	0646	0806	0814	0946	1011	...	1506	1629	1751	1805	...	1925	1929	1931	2059	2100
Landerneau **284** d.	0725	0841	0852	1021	1047	...	1543	1706	1830	1843	...	2000	│	2005	2140	2141
Brest 284 a.	0737	0854	0904	1034	1101	...	1558	1722	1843	1859	...	2013	2017	2021	2154	2153

CAT 🚌, journey 90 minutes:

From Brest: 0700 Ⓐ, 0930 †, 1000 ⚒, 1415 †, 1440 ⚒, 1610 ⑤, 1800 Ⓐ.

From Quimper: 0713 Ⓐ, 1135 ⑤, 1247 †, 1255 ⚒, 1639 Ⓐ, 1730 Ⓐ, 1740 †.

d – Also Apr. 5, May 24; not Apr. 4, May 23.
e – Also Apr. 5, May 24.
f – Also Dec. 24, 31, May 12; not Dec. 25, Jan. 1.
m – Not Dec. 24, 31, Apr. 5, May 12, 13, 24.
r – Subject to alteration Apr. 26 - 30, May 3 - 7.
t – Not May 1, 8.

* – Subject to alteration Dec. 15 - 18, 22, 23.

287 RENNES - REDON - NANTES

km		⑥ t	⚒	Ⓐ	Ⓒ	3832 ▽	Ⓐ	Ⓒ	Ⓐ	8715 ☆		⑥ t	⑤ f	Ⓒ	⑤ f	⑤ f	Ⓐ	⑤ f	①–④ m	⑤ f	⑤ t	†	Ⓐ	Ⓐ	Ⓐ	⑦ z	†
0	**Rennes** § d.	0625	...	0710	0830	...	0847	1130	1223	1211	...	1245	1426	1430	1537	1610	...	1647	1644	...	1658	1729	1736	...	1750	...	1803
72	Redon § a.	0711	...	│	0908	...	│	1222	│	1247	...	│	1503	1510	│	1646	...	│	1736	...	1753	│	│	...	1846	...	1859
72	Redon ◇ d.	...	0750	│	...	0929	│	...	│	...	1303	│	1508	1526	│	...	1658	│	1744	1745	...	│	│	1832	...	1851	...
106	Savenay ◇ d.	...	0817	│	...	│	│	...	│	...	1327	│	1530	1549	│	...	1722	│	1814	1816	...	│	│	1904	...	1919	...
145	**Nantes** ◇ a.	...	0840	0826	...	1012	1001	...	1337	...	1350	1359	1550	1610	1652	...	1745	1808	1835	1840	...	1848	1852	1932	...	1941	...

	⑥ t	①–④ m	⑤ f	†	①–④ m	⑤ f	①–④ m	Ⓐ	⑥ t	† ⊖	⑤ f
Rennes § d.	1815	1831	1835	1858	1920	1921	1925	2020	2034	2047	...
Redon § a.	1855	1916	1916	1939	│	2019	2024	2107	2111	2125	...
Redon ◇ d.	1901	1921	1921	1951	│	2028	2026	...	...	2130	2144
Savenay ◇ d.	1928	1950	1949	2019	│	2055	2052	...	...	2155	2211
Nantes ◇ a.	1950	2012	2012	2039	2034	2116	2115	...	...	2216	2233

	Ⓐ	Ⓒ	Ⓐ	Ⓐ a	Ⓐ ⊕	†	⑥ t	⊗	⑥ t	8730 R☆	Ⓐ	⑥ t	†
Nantes ◇ d.	0612	...	0651	0725	0920	1003	1008	...	1227	...	1231	1312	...
Savenay ◇ d.	0636	...	0715	│	0941	1026	1030	...	1249	...	│	1336	...
Redon ◇ a.	0701	..	0744	│	1010	1053	1056	...	1314	...	│	1403	...
Redon § d.	0716	0734	0754	│	1015	1102	1102	1236	...	1324	│	...	1408
Rennes § a.	0755	0814	0834	0843	1052	1151	1151	1340	...	1357	1347	...	1455

	Ⓐ		Ⓐ	⑥ t	⑥ t	†	⑤ f	①–④ m	†	①–④ m	⑥ t	†	⑤ f	†	⑤ f	Ⓐ	⑥ t⊖	①–④ m	3854 △	⑥ v	⑤ t	①–④ m	⑤⑦ w	⑥ t	⑤ f	⑤⑦ b	L
Nantes ◇ d.	1441	1450	...	1500	...	...	1600	1602	...	1622	1622	1622	1624	1723	1725	1758	1802	...	1818	...	...	1903	1918	...	2022	2116	2126
Savenay ◇ d.	│	│	...	│	...	...	│	│	...	1644	1643	1644	1645	1748	1748	│	│	...	1841	...	...	│	│	...	2045	2141	2147
Redon ◇ a.	│	1532	...	│	...	...	│	│	...	1712	1712	1712	1716	1813	1817	│	│	...	1908	...	...	│	│	...	2114	2207	2212
Redon § d.	│	...	1538	│	1548	1540	│	│	1646	1719	...	1736	1737	1818	...	│	│	1847	...	1922	1936	│	│	2025	2119	2228	2227
Rennes § a.	1555	...	1616	1616	1626	1617	1715	1718	1742	1807	...	1811	1811	1855	...	1912	1916	1920	...	1955	2015	2024	2035	2105	2155	2307	2305

L – ①②③④⑥ (also Dec. 25, Jan. 1, Apr. 4, May 14, 23; not Dec. 24, 31, Apr. 5, May 12, 24).
R – ①–⑥ (not Apr. 5, May 24).
a – From Angers (depart 0618).
b – From Bordeaux (train **3856**). Also Dec. 24, 31, May 12; not Dec. 25, Jan. 1, Apr. 4, May 14, 16, 23.
f – Also Dec. 24, 31, May 12; not Dec. 25, Jan. 1.
m – Not Dec. 24, 31, Apr. 5, May 12, 13, 24.
t – Not May 1, 8.
v – Also Dec. 25, Jan. 1, May 13.
w – Also Dec. 24, 31, Apr. 5, May 12, 13, 24.
z – Also Dec. 25, Jan. 1, Apr. 5, May 13, 24; not Apr. 4, May 23.
☆ – *TGV* train, Ⓡ. Supplement payable.
⊖ – To/from Tours (Table **289**).
§ – For other trains Rennes - Redon see Table **285**.
◇ – For other trains Redon - Nantes see Table **285**, for Savenay - Nantes see Tables **285** and **288**.
⊕ – Not Jan. 25 - 29, Apr. 12 - 16, 19 - 23.
⊗ – Not Apr. 12 - 16, 19 - 23.
△ – Not May 13 - 16.
▽ – Not Jan. 18 - 22, May 13 - 16.

288 NANTES - ST NAZAIRE - LE CROISIC

TGV trains convey 🍷

km		⑥ ⊙	Ⓐ	Ⓐ	⑥ t	Ⓐ	Ⓐ △	⑥ Ot	† O	TGV 8909 Ⓒ	TGV 8909 Ⓐ	Ⓐ	▷	TGV 8919 ⑥ v	TGV 8921 ①–④ m	⑤ f	①–④ m	Ⓐ O	⑥	TGV 8929 ⑤ f	⑤ f	TGV 8933 L	Ⓐ	TGV 8937 ⑥ v	①–④ m
	Paris ⊡ **280** d.	...	...	...	...	...	...	...	...	0900	0900	...	...	1100	1100	...	...	...	...	1300	...	1400	...	1500	...
0	**Nantes 285/7** d.	0656	0656	0753	0800	0800	1005	1003	1007	1112	1114	1200	1222	1307	1303	1309	1312	1355	1504	1515	1605	1616	1643	1710	1721
39	Savenay **285/7** d.	0722	0720	0821	0832	0834	1026	1026	1040	│	│	1233	1243	│	│	1330	1334	1429	1539	│	1640	│	1704	│	1745
64	**St Nazaire** d.	0741	0739	0835	0850	0858	1041	1042	1055	1148	1154	1248	1258	1344	1344	1344	1348	1445	1556	1550	1659	1652	1728	1747	1803
79	Pornichet d.	...	0752	...	0901	0910	1051	1054	1105	│	│	...	1309	1356	│	1355	...	...	1608	│	1711	│	1739	│	1814
83	La Baule Escoublac d.	...	0800	...	0908	0918	1058	1102	1113	1204	1210	...	1319	1403	1403	1402	...	...	1615	1606	1719	1709	1747	1802	1821
90	**Le Croisic** a.	...	0815	...	0918	0930	1111	1116	1126	1213	1219	...	1332	1416	1412	1414	...	...	1627	1615	1730	1717	1800	1811	1835

	⑤ f	⑥	Ⓐ T	† T	①–④ m	TGV 5216 ⑦ ♥e	⑤⑥ Oft	⑦ d	①–④ m	TGV 8953 A	TGV 8951 ⑤ f	①–④ m	⑥ t	⑤ f	⑦ d	TGV 8965 ①–⑥ n	①–④ m	TGV 5231 ⑤ ♥f	⑤ f	TGV 8979 ⑤ f	L	TGV 8987 ⑤ f	†	⑤⑥ z	①–④ m
Paris ⊡ **280** d.	...	...	...	...	...	...	...	...	...	1730	1730	...	...	...	...	1830	...	...	...	2000	...	2100	...	...	...
Nantes 285/7 d.	1730	1735	1802	1807	1834	1858	1900	1906	1927	1935	1936	...	...	1927	2018	2037	2132	2150	2157	2212	2220	2310	2322	2323	2325
Savenay **285/7** d.	1753	1801	│	1832	1911	│	│	1928	2001	│	│	...	...	2005	2044	│	2154	│	2218	│	2251	│	2345	2354	2353
St Nazaire d.	1810	1818	1843	1847	1925	1934	1934	1943	2016	2009	2012	2021	2021	2025	2113	2112	2209	2225	2233	2248	2307	2347	0001	0008	0006
Pornichet d.	1823	1829	1857	1858	1936	1946	1945	1955	...	...	2024	2032	2032	2035	2124	│	2219	2237	2246	2300	...	│	0012	0019	...
La Baule Escoublac d.	1831	1838	1906	1907	1943	1952	1952	2002	...	...	2031	2040	2040	2044	2131	2128	2224	2244	2253	2307	...	0003	0021	0025	...
Le Croisic a.	1844	1851	1919	1922	1956	2004	2006	2015	...	...	2043	2053	2053	2056	2144	2137	2235	2257	2306	2319	...	0012	0035	0036	...

	① ⊖	TGV 8902 ① g	TGV 8904 ②–⑤ w	Ⓐ	⑥ N	Ⓐ	⚒	Ⓐ	Ⓐ		Ⓐ	Ⓒ O	TGV 5270 ①⑥ ♥u	Ⓒ	Ⓐ ▽	Ⓐ ▽	TGV 8922 ▽		Ⓐ	TGV 8932 ⑦ e	Ⓐ	Ⓒ	Ⓐ	TGV 8942 ▷	①–④ m
Le Croisic d.	0456	...	...	...	0547	0610	...	0634	...	...	0730	0730	0800	0851	0852	0939	0954	...	1127	1146	...	1219	...	1352	...
La Baule Escoublac d.	0509	...	...	...	0557	0624	...	0647	...	...	0744	0744	0813	0906	0905	0952	1005	...	1137	1202	...	1231	...	1403	...
Pornichet d.	0516	...	...	...	0602	0632	...	0653	...	...	0751	0751	0820	0911	0912	0959	│	...	1142	1210	...	1238	...	│	...
St Nazaire d.	0527	0547	0551	0600	0613	0644	0649	0705	0745	...	0803	0803	0833	0922	0925	1010	1021	...	1153	1222	1237	1249	1402	1419	1453
Savenay **285/7** d.	0541	0603	│	0618	0627	0659	0709	0729	0759	...	0821	0822	│	0936	0946	1024	│	...	│	│	1258	1307	1418	│	1508
Nantes 285/7 a.	0605	0625	0625	0650	0648	0720	0743	0750	0820	...	0848	0846	0906	0957	1006	1045	1055	...	1227	1255	1333	1335	1450	1455	1540
Paris ⊡ **280** a.	...	0835	0835	...	...	...	...	...	...	...	...	...	...	...	...	...	1310	...	...	1505	...	...	...	1710	...

	⑤ f	Ⓑ ◧	TGV 8952 ①–④ m	Ⓐ	TGV 8956 ①–④ m	⑥	Ⓐ O	†	Ⓐ	TGV 8964 ⑤ f	TGV 8966 ⑦ e	①–④ m	Ⓐ	⑥ Ot	TGV 8980 B	† O	Ⓐ		①–④ m	⑤ f	†	TGV 8996 ⑦ e	Ⓐ	TGV 8998 ⑦ E	⑤ f
Le Croisic d.	1424	1509	1546	...	...	1641	...	1652	...	1717	1748	...	1816	1823	1855	1902	...	...	1931	1939	2019	2040	...	2120	...
La Baule Escoublac d.	1435	1522	1557	...	...	1653	...	1707	...	1732	1802	...	1830	1836	1906	1917	...	...	1944	1951	2031	2054	...	2131	...
Pornichet d.	1442	1529	│	...	...	1659	...	1714	...	1739	1808	...	1835	1843	│	1923	...	...	1950	1956	2037	2100	...	│	...
St Nazaire d.	1453	1539	1614	1632	1650	1710	1704	1727	1736	1751	1821	1823	1847	1856	1921	1935	1939	...	2003	2007	2049	2115	2120	2147	2214
Savenay **285/7** d.	1508	1557	│	1650	│	1723	1727	1744	1754	│	│	1839	1909	1912	│	│	1954	...	2022	2022	2108	│	2136	│	2232
Nantes 285/7 a.	1540	1619	1648	1714	1725	1750	1800	1816	1818	1825	1855	1910	1940	1939	1955	2009	2020	...	2043	2045	2135	2150	2205	2220	2252
Paris ⊡ **280** a.	...	...	1915	...	1935	...	...	...	...	2035	2115	...	...	...	2210	...	...	...	...	...	...	0005	...	0040	...

A – Daily except ⑤ (also runs Dec. 25, Jan. 1; not Dec. 24, 31, May 12, 13).
B – Daily except ⑤ (also runs Dec. 25, Jan. 1; not Dec. 24, 31, May 12).
E – ⑦ from Apr. 11 (also Apr. 5, May 24).
L – ①②③④⑦ (not Dec. 24, 31, May 12, 13).
N – ⑥ to Feb. 20/from May 22.
O – To/from Orléans (Table **289**).
T – [12] Le Croisic - Nantes - Tours and v.v.
d – Also Dec. 25, Jan. 1, Apr. 5, May 13, 24; not May 23.
e – Also Apr. 5, May 24.
f – Also Dec. 24, 31, May 12; not Dec. 25, Jan. 1.
g – Also Apr. 6, May 25; not Apr. 5, May 24.
m – Not Dec. 24, 31, Apr. 5, May 12, 13, 24.
n – Not Apr. 5, May 24.
t – Not May 1, 8.
u – Also Dec. 25, Jan. 1, Apr. 6, May 13, 25; not Apr. 5, May 24.
v – Also Dec. 25, Jan. 1, May 13.
w – Not Dec. 25, Jan. 1, Apr. 6, May 25.
z – Also Dec. 24, 31, Apr. 24; not Dec. 25, Jan. 1.
TGV – Ⓡ, supplement payable, 🍷.
♥ – To/from Lille Europe (Table **11**).
◧ – On Jan. 11 - 15 by 🚌 Le Croisic - St Nazaire.
⊡ – Paris Montparnasse.
⊙ – Additional journeys on Ⓐ depart Nantes at 0616, 0645.
⊖ – Also May 25; not Mar. 15 - Apr. 19, May 24.
△ – Subject to alteration Jan. 25 - 29.
▽ – Subject to alteration Jan. 18 - 22.
▷ – Not Jan. 11 - 15.

Subject to alteration Mar. 15 - Apr. 21

NANTES - ANGERS - TOURS 289

For other *TGV* trains Nantes - Lyon (via Massy) see Table **335**. *Timings Nantes - Le Croisic and v.v. are subject to altertation Mar. 15 - Apr. 21*

km		*TGV* 5302		*TGV* 5304	4402							*TGV* 5322	4406	*TGV* 5328												
		①–④	Ⓐ	⑥	⑥	Ⓐ	Ⓐ	Ⓒ	Ⓐ	Ⓐ		♠	⑦	Ⓐ	⑤	Ⓐ	⑦	①–④	⑤	†	⑥	Ⓐ	⑦	⑥	†	⑦
		m		t			d		d				G	b	f		H	m	f		v		E	v		⊖j
	Le Croisic **288** d.	...	...	...	...	...	...	0730	...	...	...	...	...	...	...	...	...	...	...	...	...	...	...	1823	1902	...
0	**Nantes 280** d.	0455	...	0630	0658	0706	0837	0849	...	1123	...	1252	1505	1555	...	1630	1630	1636	1636	...	...	1818	1854	1945	2012	2218
88	Angers St Laud **280** d.	0536	0655	0708	0739	0743	0921	0931	1100	1201	1231	1337	1548	1633	1640	1710	1711	1750	1750	1749	1810	1859	1934	2029	2051	2301
132	Saumur d.	0559	0720	0733	0802	0805	0944	0953	1121	1222	1304	|	1610	1655	1710	1732	1732	1815	1815	1822	1842	1920	1958	2056	2112	2322
196	St Pierre des Corps a.	0628	|	0804	|	0837	1022	1031	|	1255	|	1426	|	1724	|	|	1802	|	1852	1858	1920	1952	|	2134	2141	2352
199	**Tours** a.	*0639*	0759	*0814*	0834	*0847*	1032	*1045*	1158	*1305*	1355	*1437*	1643	*1734*	1750	1804	1812	1854	1902	1911	1931	*2010*	2035	*2144*	*2154*	0002
202	St Pierre des Corps a.	|	...	|	0850	|	...	|	...	|	...	|	1710	|	...	1816	...	...	...	...	...	|	...	|	|	...
	Orléans **296** a.	◐	...	◐	|	0935	...	1130	...	1349	...	◐	|	◐	...	1910	...	...	...	...	...	2050	...	2226	2232	...
	Lyon Part Dieu **290** a.	0935	...	1103	1324	...	...	...	...	...	...	1731	2149	2031	...	...	...	...	...	...	...	...	...	...	...	...

					TGV 5352									*TGV* 5368							*TGV* 5378	*TGV* 5231	4506 4507		*TGV* 5380
	Ⓐ	Ⓐ	⑥	†	Ⓐ	Ⓐ	Ⓐ	⚒	Ⓐ			Ⓐ	⑥	†	①–⑥	⑤⑥	Ⓐ	①–④	⚒	⑤	†	⑦	Ⓑ	⑤–⑦		
			v		y		△						⊖v		♠n	F		m		f		♠e	♥u	x		k
Lyon Part Dieu **290** d.	...	...	...	...	...	0656	...	...	...	...	...	...	...	...	1326	...	...	...	...	...	...	1656	...	1526	...	1826
Orléans **296** d.	...	0641	0727	0727	...	◐	1108	...	...	...	...	...	...	...	◐	1630	...	1727	...	...	1759	◐	...	|	...	◐
St Pierre des Corps d.	...	|	|	|	...	|	|	...	...	...	...	...	...	...	|	|	...	|	...	...	|	|	...	2005	...	|
Tours d.	0639	*0728*	*0809*	*0809*	0914	*0943*	*1151*	1228	1325	1432	...	1611	1611	1618	*1611*	*1709*	1732	*1759*	1837	1837	*1845*	*1939*	*1957*	2021	2042	*2112*
St Pierre des Corps d.	|	0738	0820	0820	|	0954	1201	|	1336	|	...	|	|	|	1626	1723	|	1819	|	|	1855	1955	2014	|	2053	2132
Saumur d.	0716	0810	0856	0856	0955	|	1232	1318	1412	1505	...	1649	1648	1656	|	1755	1822	1851	1929	1929	1927	|	|	2053	2131	2204
Angers St Laud **280** d.	0744	0833	0921	0921	1023	1049	1257	1349	...	1528	...	1714	1713	1720	1722	1817	1845	1914	...	1954	1950	2049	2108	2117	2206c	2228
Nantes 280 a.	0826	0910	1001	1001	...	1125	1337	...	...	1608	...	1759	1759	1804	1803	1857	...	1956	...	...	2029	2127	2147	2158	...	2303
Le Croisic **288** a.	...	...	1116	1126	...	...	...	...	...	...	...	1919	...	1922	...	2006	...	...	...	...	...	...	2257f	...	...	...

FOR NOTES SEE BELOW

Additional trains: Saumur - Tours 0635⚒, 0813Ⓐ, 0836Ⓒ, 1623⑤**f**, 1626⑦**e**, 1657⑥, 1704①–④, 1710†, 1850†.
Tours - Saumur 0719Ⓐ, 1202†, 1450⑤**f**, 1450⑥, 1933Ⓑ, 2315⑦**q**.

TOURS - BOURGES - LYON 290

For faster *TGV* trains Nantes / Tours - Massy - Lyon and v.v. see Table **335**. For additional trains Bourges - Nevers see below main table

km			16831		4402	4402	4402				16834			4406			4406							
		Ⓐ		⚒	①	⑥	⚒	⚒	⑦	⚒		⑤⑥		①–⑥	⑤	†	⑦	⚒	Ⓐ	Ⓑ			Ⓐ	⑦
				⊡z	g		⊕	⊗	s		M	J		B	f		G			⊡p				w
	Nantes **289** d.	...	...	...	...	0658	...	...	...	...	...	...	...	...	...	...	1505	...	...	...	...	...	...	...
0	**Tours** d.	0617	...	0703	0845	0845	...	1008	1008	...	1213	1241	1331	1505	1608	1627	1705	1706	...	1817	1838	1928	2050	2050
3	St Pierre des Corps d.	0624	...	0710	0852	0852	...	1015	1015	...	1220	1248	1338	1512	1614	1633	1712	1713	...	1824	1845	1935	2057	2057
	Orléans **315** d.	|	0707	|	|	|	...	|	|	...	|	|	|	|	|	|	|	|	...	|	|	|	|	|
113	Vierzon **315** d.	0737	0748	0824	0951	0951	...	1128	1138	...	1328	1400	1456	1616	1727	1759	1814	1820	...	1938	2011	2102	2211	2213
145	**Bourges 315** d.	0755	0806	0842	1011	1011	...	1145	1157	1217	1348	1418	1515	1636	1749	...	1835	1838	1845	1958	...	2128	...	2233
	Nevers ▷ d.	...	*0820*	|	|	|	...	...	|	|	*1400*	...	|	*1652*a	|	...	*1847*	...	|	|	...	|	...	|
203	Saincaize d.	...	0836	|	1043	1043	...	...	|	|	1418	...	|	1709	|	...	1907	...	|	|	...	|	...	|
214	**Nevers 330** ▶ a.	...	*0856*	0918	|	|	...	...	1233	1308	*1440*	...	1550	*1727*a	1828	...	*1928*	...	1935	2034	...	2210	...	*2338*
252	Moulins-sur-Allier **330** d.	...	0901	...	1112	1112	...	...	...	...	1444	...	...	1735	...	...	1936	...	...	...	...	...	...	...
293	St Germain des Fossés **328** d.	...	|	...	1135	1135	1135	...	...	...	|	...	...	1758	...	...	2000	...	...	...	...	...	...	...
360	Roanne **328** d.	...	⊙	...	1216	1216	1216	...	...	...	⊙	...	...	1839	...	...	2041	...	...	...	...	...	...	...
457	**Lyon Part Dieu 328** a.	...	1143	...	1324	1324	1324	...	...	...	|	...	...	1947	...	...	2149	...	...	...	...	...	...	...
461	**Lyon Perrache 328** a.	...	1158	...	1339	1339	1339	...	...	...	1727	...	...	2001	...	...	2205	...	...	...	...	...	...	...

									4504	4504			16842				4506						16846	
	⚒	⚒	Ⓐ	⚒	⚒		⊡	⚒	⚒	①⑥		⑤								Ⓑ	⑤⑦			
						▽	▽	▽	⊕	g		f	D							⊡p	L			
Lyon Perrache 328 d.	...	...	...	...	...	...	...	...	0904	0904	...	...	1226	...	...	...	1511	...	...	...	...	...	1751	...
Lyon Part Dieu 328 d.	...	...	...	...	...	...	...	...	0918	0918	...	...	1239	...	...	...	1526	...	...	...	...	...	1804	...
Roanne **328** d.	...	...	...	...	...	...	...	...	1032	1032	...	...	⊙	...	...	...	1637	...	...	...	...	...	⊙	...
St Germain des Fossés **328** d.	...	...	...	...	...	...	...	...	1112	1114	...	...	|	...	...	...	1718	...	...	...	...	...	|	...
Moulins-sur-Allier **330** d.	...	...	...	...	...	...	...	...	...	1138	...	...	1521	...	...	...	1742	...	...	...	...	...	2055	...
Nevers 330 ▷ d.	...	...	0549	0658	0736	...	0923	...	...	|	...	...	*1528*	...	1643	...	*1751*r	...	...	1923	...	...	*2104*	...
Saincaize d.	...	...	|	|	|	...	|	...	...	1206	...	...	1545	...	|	...	1808	...	...	|	...	...	2120	...
Nevers ▶ a.	...	...	|	|	|	...	|	...	...	|	...	...	*1611*	...	|	...	*1825*r	...	...	|	...	...	*2138*	...
Bourges 315 d.	...	...	0636	0740	0826	0858	1000	1215	...	1238	...	1532	1616	...	1724	...	1841	1848	...	2010	2135	...	2151	...
Vierzon **315** d.	0602	0633	0656	0801	...	0916	1019	1236	...	1300	...	1550	1638	...	1747	...	1902	1915	...	2029	2157	...	2211	...
Orléans **315** a.	|	|	|	|	...	|	|	|	...	|	...	|	|	...	|	...	|	|	...	|	|	...	2249	...
St Pierre des Corps a.	0724	0759	0807	0915	...	1028	1129	1348	...	1402	...	1658	1748	...	1901	...	2003	2031	...	2144	2255	...	...	...
Tours a.	0731	0806	0814	0922	...	1035	1136	1355	...	1409	...	1705	1755	...	1908	...	2010	2038	...	2151	2302	...	...	...
Nantes **289** a.	...	...	...	...	...	...	...	...	...	...	...	...	...	...	...	...	2158x	...	...	...	...	...	...	...

also:	⚒	⚒	⚒		Ⓐ	⚒	†	⚒	
Bourges d.	0640	0741	0911	...	1622	1725	1753	1933	...
Nevers a.	0730	0831	1001	...	1715	1817	1843	2026	...

	⚒	⚒	Ⓐ	⑥v		Ⓐ	⚒	Ⓐ	†
Nevers d.	0633	0906	1230	1315	1625	1737	1830	2005	2120
Bourges a.	0723	0955	1319	1404	1716	1826	1920	2054	2209

NOTES FOR TABLES 289 AND 290

B – Not Dec. 25, Jan. 1, Apr. 5, May 13, 24.
D – Not on Mar. 1-5, 8-12.
E – Also Apr. 5, May 13, 24; not Apr. 4, May 23.
F – Also Dec. 24, 31, May 12; not Dec. 25, Jan. 1, May 1, 8.
G – Also Dec. 25, Jan. 1, Apr. 5, May 13, 24.
H – Also Dec. 25, Jan. 1, Apr. 5, May 13, 24; not Apr. 4, May 23.
J – Also Dec. 24, 31, May 12; not Dec. 25, Jan. 1, Feb. 19, 26, May 1, 8.
L – Also Dec. 24, 31, Apr. 5, May 12, 24; not Dec. 25, Jan. 1, Apr. 4, May 23.
M – Not Feb. 15-19, 22-26, Apr. 19-30.

a – Ⓐ only.
b – To Grenoble on ⑤**f** (train **5332**), a. 2153.
c – ⑤⑦ (also Dec. 24, 31, Apr. 5, May 12, 24; not Dec. 25, Jan. 1, Apr. 4, May 23).
d – Not Feb. 22 - Mar. 5.
e – Also Apr. 5, May 24.
f – ⑤ (also Dec. 24, 31, May 12; not Dec. 25, Jan. 1).
g – Also Dec. 22-24, 29-31, May 25; not Mar. 1, 8, 15, Apr. 5, 12, 19, 26, May 24.
j – Also Dec. 25, Jan. 1, Apr. 5, May 24; not Mar. 14 - Apr. 4, May 23.
k – From Montpellier (Table **350**).
m – Not Dec. 24, 31, Apr. 5, May 12, 13, 24.
n – Not Apr. 5, May 24.
p – Not Apr. 4, May 23.
q – Also Apr. 5, May 24; not Apr. 4, May 23.
r – Daily except ⑥.
s – Also Dec. 25, Jan. 1.
t – Also Dec. 25, Jan. 1, May 13.
u – Not Dec. 24, 25, 31, Jan. 1, Apr. 4, May 12, 13, 23.
v – Not May 1, 8.
w – Also Apr. 5, May 13, 24; not Apr. 4, May 23.
x – ⑤⑥⑦ (also Dec. 24, 31, Apr. 5, May 12, 24).
y – Not Feb. 8-19.
z – Not on ①–⑤ Feb. 1-26.

TGV – Ⓡ, supplement payable, 🍸.

⊙ – Via Paray le Monial (Table **372**).
⊡ – Tours - Nevers - Dijon and v.v. (Table **374**).
⊖ – To / from Rennes (Table **287**).
⊕ – Not on ①–⑤ Apr. 12-30.
⊗ – Not on ①–⑤ Feb. 15 - Mar. 19.
♥ – From Lille (Table **11**).
♠ – To / from Marseille (Table **335**).
◐ – Via Massy (Table **335**).
▶ – Timings in *Italics*: connections from Saincaize to Nevers.
▷ – Timings in *Italics*: connections from Nevers to Saincaize.
△ – Departs Orléans up to 22 minutes earlier Jan. 11 - Mar. 26.
▽ – Subject to alteration on ①–⑤ Feb. 8-26.

ROANNE - ST ÉTIENNE 291

km		Ⓐ	Ⓐ	⚒	Ⓐ	⚒		Ⓐ		Ⓐ				Ⓐ	Ⓐ		Ⓑ			Ⓐ				†
0	**Roanne** d.	0527	0547	0612	0641	0715	...	0818	0841	0941	1041	...	1237	1343	1445	...	1541	1641	...	1719	1818	1925	...	2047
80	**St Étienne** Châteaucreux a.	0647	0707	0731	0803	0838	...	0938	1003	1103	1204	...	1403	1503	1603	...	1703	1803	...	1843	1938	2044	...	2203

		Ⓐ	⚒	⚒			Ⓐ	⚒		Ⓐ				Ⓐ			Ⓐ	⚒			Ⓐ			
St Étienne Châteaucreux d.	...	0550	0621	0714	...	0815	0850	0950	...	1150	1233	...	1450	1550	1650	...	1715	1750	1822	...	1850	1950	2050	...
Roanne a.	...	0704	0743	0829	...	0929	1004	1104	...	1304	1341	...	1604	1704	1804	...	1823	1905	1936	...	2005	2104	2204	...

292 NANTES - LA ROCHELLE - BORDEAUX

km			13899								3832 3833			3835							3837	3839		
		Ⓐ	①-⑥ n	Ⓐ ◇	Ⓐ	†	① g	⚒		⚒	⊕	Ⓐ ⊗	⚒ ⊗	b	⑤ f	①-④ m◇		⑤ f	A	⑤ f		⑤⑦ u	†	①-④ m
	Quimper 285 d.	...	...	...	...	...	...	...	...	...	0739	...	...	...	...	...	...	...	...	...	...	...	...	...
0	**Nantes 293** d.	...	...	...	...	...	...	...	...	...	1016	...	...	1409	...	...	...	...	...	...	1728	1903	...	1935
77	La Roche sur Yon **293** d.	...	...	...	...	...	...	...	...	...	1101	...	...	1455	...	...	...	...	...	...	1812	1947	...	2030
	La Rochelle Pte Dauphine d.	...	...	...	0708	...	...	0807	...	...	|	1225	1358	|	...	...	...	...	1759	1817	|	|	2114	|
180	**La Rochelle** d.	...	0606	0642	0715	0750	0750	0814	...	1122	1206	1232	1405	1558	1638	1649	...	1753	1807	1824	1917	2053	2122	2132
209	Rochefort d.	...	0632	0705	0743	0815	0816	0842	...	1144	1226	1300	1433	1619	1700	1712	...	1817	1836	1851	1937	2113	2150	...
253	Saintes d.	0613	0702	0741	...	0844	0846	...	...	1218	1257	...	...	1648	1737	1747	1755	1858	1913	...	2007	2143	...	...
376	**Bordeaux St Jean** a.	0750	0837	...	...	1016	1015	...	...	1351	1419	...	...	1816	...	...	1935	2046	...	...	2135	2305	...	...
	Toulouse 320 a.	...	...	...	...	...	...	...	...	...	...	...	...	2058	...	...	...	...	...	...	...	...	...	...

							3852	3852			3854 3855				3856					3858	3888	13898	
	②-⑤ w	Ⓐ	Ⓐ	Ⓐ ◇	Ⓐ	Ⓒ	⑥ t	①-⑤ k	⑥⑦ d	Ⓐ △	⚒		⚒	Ⓐ	◇		⑤ f	Ⓐ	Ⓑ h	⑥ t	⑤⑦ s	①-④ m	⑤⑦ v	⑤ f
Toulouse 320 d.	...	...	...	...	...	...	...	...	0754	...	...	...	...	...	...	...	...	...	...	...	...	...	...	...
Bordeaux St Jean d.	...	...	...	...	...	0821	...	1034	1104	...	1205	1403	...	...	...	1703	...	1719	1757	1818	1851	1908	2004	2140
Saintes d.	...	0631	...	0736	...	0952	...	1155	1225	...	1339	1525	...	...	1742	1827	...	1905	1946	2010	2014	2039	2144	2316
Rochefort d.	...	0709	0753	0814	1009	1024	1130	1223	1253	1312	1409	1554	1714	1757	1820	1859	1924	...	...	...	2044	2108	2215	2346
La Rochelle d.	0650	0738	0822	0836	1038	1046	1200	1244	1314	1341	1433	1615	1744	1826	1845	1922	1953	...	...	...	2105	2127	2240	0008
La Rochelle Pte Dauphine a.	|	0744	0828	...	1044	...	1206	|	|	1347	...	|	1750	1832	...	|	1959	...	...	...	|	...	...	...
La Roche sur Yon **293** d.	0752	...	...	...	...	...	...	1349	1419	...	...	1721	...	...	...	2028	...	...	...	...	2208	...	...	...
Nantes 293 a.	0846	...	...	...	...	...	...	1435	1506	...	...	1810	...	...	...	2113	...	...	...	...	2252	...	...	...
Quimper 285 a.	...	...	...	...	...	...	...	...	...	...	...	2056	...	...	...	...	...	...	...	...	...	...	...	...

A – Daily except ⑤ (also runs Dec. 25, Jan. 1, May 14; not Dec. 24, 31, May 12).
b – Not on ①-⑤ Feb. 1 - 19, May 3 - 7.
d – Also Dec. 25, Jan. 1, May 24; not May 15, 16.
f – Also Dec. 24, 31, May 12; not Dec. 25, Jan. 1.
g – Also Apr. 6, May 25; not Apr. 5, May 24.
h – Also May 1, 8.
k – Not Dec. 25, Jan. 1, 11 - 29, Apr. 5, May 10, 13, 14, 24.
m – Not Dec. 24, 31, Apr. 5, May 12, 13, 24.
n – Not Apr. 5, May 13, 14, 15, 24.
s – Also Dec. 24, 31, Apr. 5, May 12, 24; not Dec. 25, Jan. 1, Apr. 4, May 14, 16, 23.
t – Not May 1, 8.
u – Also Dec. 24, 31, Apr. 5, May 12; not Dec. 25, Jan. 1, Apr. 4, May 14, 23.
v – Also Dec. 24, 31, May 12, 13, 24; not Apr. 4, May 14, 23.
w – Not Dec. 25, Jan. 1, Apr. 6, May 13, 14, 25.
◇ – To / from Angoulême (Table **301**).
△ – Subject to alteration on Ⓐ Jan. 11 - 29.
⊖ – Extended to Rennes on ⑤⑦.
⊕ – Subject to alteration on Jan. 18 - 22, May 13 - 16.
⊗ – Subject to alteration on Ⓐ Feb. 1 - 19.

Services to Bordeaux are subject to alteration on May 13 - 16

293 NANTES - LES SABLES D'OLONNE

For TGV trains see below

Local trains

km		Ⓐ	⚒	Ⓐ	Ⓐ	⑥ v	†	†	Ⓐ ⊕	Ⓒ	⑤ f⊕	Ⓐ	⑥ v	Ⓐ	Ⓐ	Ⓐ ⊕	Ⓒ	Ⓐ	⑥ v	①-④ m	①-④ m	⑤⑦ u	†	⑤ f	⑤⑦ u
0	**Nantes 292** d.	...	0706	0857	...	0922	0926	1030	1233	1232	...	1424	1424	1635	1644	1735	1738	1815	1926	1955	2043	2043	2129	2132	2230
77	La Roche sur Yon **292**. d.	0735	0830	0943	0948	1011	1031	1119	1325	1338	1357	1511	1510	1722	1808	1843	1840	1907	2018	2042	2135	2137	2223	2223	2316
114	**Les Sables d'Olonne** . a.	0808	0900	...	1015	1038	1058	1146	1353	1405	1427	1540r	...	1751	1842	1912	1911	1933	2047	...	...	2205	2251	2249	...

	Ⓐ	⑥ v	Ⓐ	Ⓐ	Ⓒ	Ⓐ	Ⓐ 🚌	⚒		⑥ v	Ⓐ ⊗	Ⓐ	Ⓒ	Ⓐ	Ⓒ	Ⓐ	Ⓐ	†	Ⓐ	⑥ v	Ⓐ	†	Ⓐ	Ⓐ	†
Les Sables d'Olonne .. d.	0524	...	0637	0701	0728	0735	0755	...	0917	1129	1130	1226	1223	1359r	1415	1511r	1639r	1716	1721	1810	1810	1934	1950	...	...
La Roche sur Yon **292**.. d.	0552	0602	0703	0730	0756	0806	0840	0852	0945	1154	1156	1254	1253	1426	1442	1540	1708	1744	1756	1838	1841	2002	2017	2028	2124
Nantes 292 a.	0641	0648	0748	0820	0850	...	...	0953	1038	1240	1242	1345	1345	1510	...	1625	1801	1843	1847	1938	1942	2050	...	2113	2208

TGV trains

TGV trains, 🄁	*TGV* 8913 R		*TGV* 8955 Ⓐ	*TGV* 8957 Ⓒ
Paris M'parnasse 280 d.	1000	...	1750	1750
Nantes d.	1224	...	2020	2015
La Roche sur Yon d.	1307	...	2102	2057
Les Sables d'Olonne a.	1333	...	2127	2123

TGV trains, 🄁	*TGV* 8910 Ⓐ		*TGV* 8926 ⑥ t	*TGV* 8950		*TGV* 8986 ⑦ e
Les Sables d'Olonne d.	0543	...	1043	1547r	...	1812
La Roche sur Yon d.	0610	...	1110	1613	...	1838
Nantes a.	0651	...	1151	1655	...	1920
Paris M'parnasse 280 a.	0905	...	1415	1915	...	2135

R – Not on ①-⑤ Feb. 1 - 19, May 3 - 7.
e – Also Apr. 5, May 24.
f – Also Dec. 24, 31, May 12; not Dec. 25, Jan. 1.
m – Not Dec. 24, 31, Apr. 5, May 12, 13, 24.
r – Subject to alteration on ①-⑤ Feb. 1 - 19.
t – Also Dec. 25, Jan. 1, May 13.
u – Also Dec. 25, Jan. 1, Apr. 5, May 13, 24; not May 23.
v – Not May 1, 8.
TGV – 🄁, supplement payable, 🍷.
⊕ – Subject to alteration Feb. 1 - 19, May 3 - 7.
⊗ – Subject to alteration Jan. 11 - Feb. 19, May 10 - 14.

294 PARIS - LES AUBRAIS - ORLÉANS

Selected trains

km		⚒	Ⓐ	⚒	⚒	⚒		⚒		⚒	†		b	⚒	⚒		⑤f		Ⓐ	z		Ⓑh	⚒	†	H
0	**Paris Austerlitz** § d.	0555	0626	0656	0648	0656	0725	0807	0921	1048	1048	1141	1210	1206	1239	1335	1454	1548	1632	1706	1720	1736	1805	1805	1817
56	Étampes § d.	0624	|	|	0719	|	|	|	|	|	|	|	|	1237	|	|	|	|	|	|	1750	|	|	|	|
119	Les Aubrais-Orléans a.	0716	0723	0750	0816	0750	0821	0905	1017	1146	1204	1239	1302	1328	1336	1433	1552	1646	1730	1803	1843	1830	1903	1903	1928
121	**Orléans** a.	0721	0729	*0800*	0822	*0800*	*0834*	0911	*1030*	1152	1210	1244	*1312*	1335	*1346*	1439	*1601*	*1655*	1736	1809	1848	*1839*	1909	*1914*	1934

	Ⓑ	⑤f			H	⑤⑦v	⑤⑦x	s	s	
Paris Austerlitz § d.	1836	1849	1903	1956	2048	2048	2152	2252	2339	...
Étampes § d.	|	|	|	|	|	|	|	|	|	...
Les Aubrais-Orléans a.	1934	1947	1955	2053	2146	2146	2253	2352	0041	...
Orléans a.	1940	1955	*2005*	2059	2152	*2156*	2259	*0001*	0047	...

	⚒	R	⚒	⚒	Ⓐ	⚒	⚒	⚒	†	⚒	
Orléans d.	0500	0608	*0621*	0618	*0650*	0705	*0723*	*0734*	0742	0750	0841
Les Aubrais-Orléans d.	0505	0615	0629	0624	0700	0711	0732	0744	0748	0755	0846
Étampes § a.	|	|	|	0722	|	|	|	|	|	0839	|
Paris Austerlitz § a.	0608	0715	0731	0800	0803	0812	0827	0842	0846	0914	0945

	†	⚒	u		⚒u	⚒d		⚒b	Ⓐ	Ⓒ	†		⚒		†	⚒	⚒		Ⓑ		†	Ⓐ	⑦e		
Orléans d.	0857	0939	1037	*1123*	1140	1227	1231	*1317*	*1356*	1434	1559	1633	1719	*1751*	1812	1816	*1822*	1854	1925	*1957*	2043	2100	*2124*	2217	...
Les Aubrais-Orléans d.	0902	0944	1042	1133	1145	1232	1238	1328	1406	1439	1604	1638	1724	1800	1817	1821	1837	1859	1931	2006	2049	2106	2134	2222	...
Étampes § a.	|	|	|	|	|	1324	|	|	|	|	|	1704	|	|	1918	1922	|	|	|	|	2119	|	|	|	...
Paris Austerlitz § a.	1022	1044	1142	1229	1244	1357	1338	1423	1506	1538	1703	1737	1838	1858	1950	1954	1935	1958	2050	2105	2150	2206	2231	2321	...

H – ①-④ (not Dec. 24, 31, Apr. 5, May 12, 13, 24).
R – ②-⑤ (not Dec. 25, Jan. 1, Apr. 6, May 13, 25).
b – Not on ①-⑤ Mar. 22 - Apr. 23.
d – Not on ①-⑤ Mar. 1 - 26.
e – Also Apr. 5, May 24; not Apr. 4, May 23.
f – Also Dec. 24, 31, May 12; not Dec. 25, Jan. 1.
h – Not Dec. 25, Jan. 1, May 13.
s – Not Dec. 14, Jan. 18 - 21, 25 - 28.
u – Not on ①-⑤ Jan. 11 - Mar. 26.
v – Also Dec. 24, 31, Apr. 5, May 12, 24; not Dec. 25, Jan. 1.
x – Also Dec. 24, 31, Apr. 5, May 1, 8, 12, 13, 24.
z – Not Apr. 4, May 23.
§ – Suburban trains run Paris Austerlitz - Étampes and v.v. approximately every 30 minutes (journey 55 minutes).

PARIS - TOURS 295

TGV trains

<table>
<tr><th>km</th><th>TGV trains convey 🍷</th><th>TGV 8405</th><th>TGV 8315</th><th>TGV 5200</th><th>TGV 8317</th><th>TGV 5212</th><th>TGV 8417</th><th>TGV 8323</th><th>TGV 8333</th><th>TGV 5218</th><th>TGV 8441</th><th>TGV 8343</th><th>TGV 8345</th><th>TGV 8349</th><th>TGV 5216</th><th>TGV 8347</th><th>TGV 8353</th><th>TGV 8451</th><th>TGV 5222</th><th>TGV 8363</th><th>TGV 8357</th><th>TGV 8365</th><th>TGV 8367</th><th>TGV 8469</th></tr>
<tr><td></td><td></td><td></td><td>①–⑥</td><td></td><td></td><td>9802</td><td></td><td></td><td>‡</td><td></td><td>‡</td><td>⑤</td><td>⑤</td><td>①–④</td><td>⑦</td><td>⑤</td><td>⑤</td><td></td><td></td><td>①–④</td><td>⑤</td><td>D</td><td>Ⓐ</td><td></td></tr>
<tr><td></td><td></td><td>⊖</td><td>d</td><td></td><td></td><td>b</td><td>▽</td><td></td><td></td><td></td><td></td><td>f</td><td>f</td><td>m</td><td>e</td><td>f</td><td>f</td><td></td><td></td><td>m</td><td>f</td><td></td><td>¶</td><td></td></tr>
<tr><td></td><td>Lille Europe 11 d.</td><td>...</td><td>...</td><td>0558</td><td>...</td><td>0814</td><td>...</td><td>...</td><td>...</td><td>1238v</td><td>...</td><td>...</td><td>...</td><td>...</td><td>1447</td><td>...</td><td>...</td><td>...</td><td>1540</td><td>...</td><td>...</td><td>...</td><td>...</td><td>...</td></tr>
<tr><td></td><td>Charles de Gaulle ✈ d.</td><td>...</td><td>...</td><td>0739</td><td>...</td><td>0912</td><td>...</td><td>...</td><td>...</td><td>1337</td><td>...</td><td>...</td><td>...</td><td>...</td><td>1542</td><td>...</td><td>...</td><td>...</td><td>1636</td><td>...</td><td>...</td><td>...</td><td>...</td><td>...</td></tr>
<tr><td></td><td>Marne la Vallée - Chessy d.</td><td>...</td><td>...</td><td>0756</td><td>...</td><td>0927</td><td>...</td><td>...</td><td>...</td><td>1351</td><td>...</td><td>...</td><td>...</td><td>...</td><td>1557</td><td>...</td><td>...</td><td>...</td><td>1656</td><td>...</td><td>...</td><td>...</td><td>...</td><td>...</td></tr>
<tr><td>0</td><td>Paris Montparnasse d.</td><td>0650</td><td>0750</td><td>|</td><td>0910</td><td>|</td><td>1050</td><td>1225</td><td>1350</td><td>|</td><td>1515</td><td>1535</td><td>1610</td><td>1615</td><td>|</td><td>1645</td><td>1655</td><td>1715</td><td>|</td><td>1740</td><td>1755</td><td>1810</td><td>1840</td><td>1850</td></tr>
<tr><td>14</td><td>Massy-TGV d.</td><td>0702</td><td>|</td><td>0831</td><td>|</td><td>1000</td><td>|</td><td>|</td><td>|</td><td>1431</td><td>|</td><td>|</td><td>|</td><td>|</td><td>1631</td><td>|</td><td>|</td><td>|</td><td>1731</td><td>|</td><td>|</td><td>|</td><td>|</td><td>|</td></tr>
<tr><td>162</td><td>Vendôme-Villiers TGV d.</td><td>|</td><td>0835</td><td>|</td><td>|</td><td>|</td><td>|</td><td>1309</td><td>|</td><td>|</td><td>|</td><td>|</td><td>1653</td><td>|</td><td>|</td><td>|</td><td>|</td><td>|</td><td>|</td><td>|</td><td>1839</td><td>1855</td><td>1923</td><td>|</td></tr>
<tr><td>221</td><td>St Pierre des Corps a.</td><td>0752</td><td>0853</td><td>0922</td><td>1006</td><td>1050</td><td>1146</td><td>1327</td><td>1447</td><td>1521</td><td>1611</td><td>1631</td><td>1712</td><td>1712</td><td>1721</td><td>1740</td><td>1751</td><td>1811</td><td>1821</td><td>1834</td><td>1858</td><td>1913</td><td>1942</td><td>1946</td></tr>
<tr><td>221</td><td>St Pierre des Corps d.</td><td>0757</td><td>0855</td><td>0927</td><td>1011</td><td>1056</td><td>1158</td><td>1330</td><td>1456</td><td>1526</td><td>1616</td><td>1633</td><td>1714</td><td>1714</td><td>1729</td><td>1743</td><td>1757</td><td>1816</td><td>1829</td><td>1836</td><td>1900</td><td>1916</td><td>1945</td><td>1952</td></tr>
<tr><td>224</td><td>Tours a.</td><td>0802</td><td>0900</td><td>0932</td><td>1016</td><td>1101</td><td>1203</td><td>1335</td><td>1501</td><td>1531</td><td>1621</td><td>1639</td><td>1719</td><td>1719</td><td>1734</td><td>1748</td><td>1802</td><td>1821</td><td>1834</td><td>1841</td><td>1905</td><td>1921</td><td>1950</td><td>1957</td></tr>
</table>

<table>
<tr><th>TGV trains convey 🍷</th><th>TGV 5231</th><th>TGV 8375</th><th>TGV 8377</th><th>TGV 5242</th><th>TGV 8483</th><th>TGV 8383</th><th>TGV 8489</th><th>TGV 8497</th></tr>
<tr><td></td><td>Ⓑ</td><td>①–⑥</td><td>⑦</td><td>⑤–⑦</td><td>①–④</td><td>⑤⑦</td><td>⑦</td><td>⑤</td></tr>
<tr><td></td><td>s</td><td>n</td><td>e</td><td>y</td><td>m</td><td>w</td><td>c</td><td>f</td></tr>
<tr><td>Lille Europe 11 d.</td><td>1728</td><td>...</td><td>...</td><td>1829</td><td>...</td><td>...</td><td>...</td><td>...</td></tr>
<tr><td>Charles de Gaulle ✈ d.</td><td>1825</td><td>...</td><td>...</td><td>1926</td><td>...</td><td>...</td><td>...</td><td>...</td></tr>
<tr><td>Marne la Vallée - Chessy d.</td><td>1840</td><td>...</td><td>...</td><td>1942</td><td>...</td><td>...</td><td>...</td><td>...</td></tr>
<tr><td>Paris Montparnasse d.</td><td>|</td><td>1930</td><td>1930</td><td>|</td><td>2020</td><td>2030</td><td>2110</td><td>2135</td></tr>
<tr><td>Massy-TGV d.</td><td>1921</td><td>|</td><td>|</td><td>2017</td><td>|</td><td>|</td><td>|</td><td>|</td></tr>
<tr><td>Vendôme-Villiers TGV d.</td><td>|</td><td>2015</td><td>|</td><td>|</td><td>2104</td><td>2114</td><td>|</td><td>|</td></tr>
<tr><td>St Pierre des Corps a.</td><td>2011</td><td>2033</td><td>2025</td><td>2110</td><td>2125</td><td>2132</td><td>2206</td><td>2231</td></tr>
<tr><td>St Pierre des Corps d.</td><td>2017</td><td>2036</td><td>2030</td><td>2115</td><td>2134</td><td>2134</td><td>2212</td><td>2236</td></tr>
<tr><td>Tours a.</td><td>2022</td><td>2041</td><td>2035</td><td>2120</td><td>2139</td><td>2139</td><td>2217</td><td>2241</td></tr>
</table>

<table>
<tr><th></th><th>TGV 8300</th><th>TGV 8320</th><th>TGV 8302</th><th>TGV 8304</th><th>TGV 8310</th><th>TGV 8312</th><th>TGV 5261</th><th>TGV 8414</th><th>TGV 5264</th></tr>
<tr><td></td><td>①–④</td><td>⑤</td><td>①–⑥</td><td>Ⓐ</td><td>①–⑥</td><td>⑦</td><td></td><td></td><td></td></tr>
<tr><td></td><td>m</td><td>f</td><td>n</td><td></td><td>n</td><td>e</td><td></td><td></td><td></td></tr>
<tr><td>Tours d.</td><td>0610</td><td>0623</td><td>0652</td><td>0740</td><td>0806</td><td>0809</td><td>0850</td><td>0925</td><td>1012*</td></tr>
<tr><td>St Pierre des Corps a.</td><td>0615</td><td>0628</td><td>0657</td><td>0745</td><td>0811</td><td>0814</td><td>0855</td><td>0930</td><td>1017*</td></tr>
<tr><td>St Pierre des Corps d.</td><td>0618</td><td>0631</td><td>0700</td><td>0747</td><td>0815</td><td>0823</td><td>0902</td><td>0937</td><td>1023</td></tr>
<tr><td>Vendôme-Villiers TGV d.</td><td>0640</td><td>0652</td><td>0722</td><td>|</td><td>0837</td><td>|</td><td>|</td><td>|</td><td>|</td></tr>
<tr><td>Massy-TGV a.</td><td>|</td><td>0728</td><td>|</td><td>|</td><td>|</td><td>|</td><td>0952</td><td>|</td><td>1113</td></tr>
<tr><td>Paris Montparnasse a.</td><td>0725</td><td>0740</td><td>0805</td><td>0845</td><td>0920</td><td>0920</td><td>|</td><td>1035</td><td>|</td></tr>
<tr><td>Marne la Vallée - Chessy a.</td><td>...</td><td>...</td><td>...</td><td>...</td><td>...</td><td>...</td><td>1035</td><td>...</td><td>1154</td></tr>
<tr><td>Charles de Gaulle ✈ a.</td><td>...</td><td>...</td><td>...</td><td>...</td><td>...</td><td>...</td><td>1053</td><td>...</td><td>1209</td></tr>
<tr><td>Lille Europe 11 a.</td><td>...</td><td>...</td><td>...</td><td>...</td><td>...</td><td>...</td><td>1217v</td><td>...</td><td>1306</td></tr>
</table>

<table>
<tr><th></th><th>TGV 8318</th><th>TGV 8420</th><th>TGV 8322</th><th>TGV 8324</th><th>TGV 5276</th><th>TGV 8328</th><th>TGV 8436</th><th>TGV 8540</th><th>TGV 5279</th><th>TGV 8346</th><th>TGV 8548</th><th>TGV 8350</th><th>TGV 8358</th><th>TGV 8364</th><th>TGV 8362</th><th>TGV 5284</th><th>TGV 8466</th><th>TGV 8472</th><th>TGV 8474</th><th>TGV 8378</th><th>TGV 5292</th><th>TGV 8584</th><th>TGV 8386</th><th>TGV 8390</th></tr>
<tr><td></td><td>①–④</td><td>◇</td><td></td><td></td><td></td><td>⑤</td><td></td><td></td><td>9816</td><td>Ⓑ</td><td></td><td>⑤</td><td>⑤</td><td>⑤–⑦</td><td>①–④</td><td>Ⓑ</td><td>⑦</td><td>①–⑥</td><td>⑦</td><td>⑦</td><td>⑤⑥</td><td></td><td>⑤</td><td>⑦</td></tr>
<tr><td></td><td>m</td><td></td><td></td><td>△</td><td>a</td><td>f</td><td>☆</td><td></td><td>b</td><td>h</td><td></td><td>k</td><td>f</td><td>z</td><td>m</td><td>h</td><td>e</td><td>x</td><td>e</td><td>e</td><td>g</td><td>▷</td><td>q</td><td>e</td></tr>
<tr><td>Tours d.</td><td>1020</td><td>1023</td><td>1202</td><td>1251</td><td>1320</td><td>1412</td><td>1441</td><td>1611</td><td>1643</td><td>1712</td><td>1742</td><td>1755</td><td>1829</td><td>1855</td><td>1911</td><td>1914</td><td>1957</td><td>2020</td><td>2035</td><td>2054</td><td>2112</td><td>2208</td><td>2236</td><td>2307</td></tr>
<tr><td>St Pierre des Corps a.</td><td>1025</td><td>1028</td><td>1206</td><td>1256</td><td>1325</td><td>1417</td><td>1446</td><td>1616</td><td>1648</td><td>1717</td><td>1747</td><td>1800</td><td>1834</td><td>1900</td><td>1916</td><td>1919</td><td>2002</td><td>2025</td><td>2040</td><td>2059</td><td>2117</td><td>2213</td><td>2241</td><td>2312</td></tr>
<tr><td>St Pierre des Corps d.</td><td>1038</td><td>1038</td><td>1209</td><td>1302</td><td>1332</td><td>1422</td><td>1452</td><td>1622</td><td>1655</td><td>1720</td><td>1753</td><td>1805</td><td>1836</td><td>1908</td><td>1923</td><td>1928</td><td>2008</td><td>2037</td><td>2047</td><td>2101</td><td>2122</td><td>2222</td><td>2252</td><td>2319</td></tr>
<tr><td>Vendôme-Villiers TGV d.</td><td>|</td><td>|</td><td>1232</td><td>|</td><td>|</td><td>|</td><td>|</td><td>|</td><td>|</td><td>1748</td><td>|</td><td>|</td><td>1857</td><td>|</td><td>|</td><td>|</td><td>|</td><td>|</td><td>|</td><td>2122</td><td>|</td><td>|</td><td>|</td><td>|</td></tr>
<tr><td>Massy-TGV a.</td><td>|</td><td>|</td><td>|</td><td>|</td><td>1423</td><td>|</td><td>|</td><td>|</td><td>1747</td><td>|</td><td>|</td><td>|</td><td>|</td><td>|</td><td>|</td><td>2018</td><td>|</td><td>|</td><td>2137</td><td>|</td><td>2213</td><td>|</td><td>|</td><td>|</td></tr>
<tr><td>Paris Montparnasse a.</td><td>1135</td><td>1135</td><td>1315</td><td>1400</td><td>|</td><td>1520</td><td>1550</td><td>1720</td><td>|</td><td>1835</td><td>1850</td><td>1905</td><td>1940</td><td>2005</td><td>2020</td><td>|</td><td>2105</td><td>2135</td><td>2150</td><td>2205</td><td>|</td><td>2320</td><td>2350</td><td>0015</td></tr>
<tr><td>Marne la Vallée - Chessy a.</td><td>...</td><td>...</td><td>...</td><td>...</td><td>1506</td><td>...</td><td>...</td><td>...</td><td>1827</td><td>...</td><td>...</td><td>...</td><td>...</td><td>...</td><td>...</td><td>2057</td><td>...</td><td>...</td><td>...</td><td>...</td><td>2251</td><td>...</td><td>...</td><td>...</td></tr>
<tr><td>Charles de Gaulle ✈ a.</td><td>...</td><td>...</td><td>...</td><td>...</td><td>1521</td><td>...</td><td>...</td><td>...</td><td>1841</td><td>...</td><td>...</td><td>...</td><td>...</td><td>...</td><td>...</td><td>2112</td><td>...</td><td>...</td><td>...</td><td>...</td><td>2306</td><td>...</td><td>...</td><td>...</td></tr>
<tr><td>Lille Europe 11 a.</td><td>...</td><td>...</td><td>...</td><td>...</td><td>1615</td><td>...</td><td>...</td><td>...</td><td>2005v</td><td>...</td><td>...</td><td>...</td><td>...</td><td>...</td><td>...</td><td>2220</td><td>...</td><td>...</td><td>...</td><td>...</td><td>0011</td><td>...</td><td>...</td><td>...</td></tr>
</table>

D – Daily except ⑤ (also runs Dec. 25, Jan. 1; not Dec. 24, 31, May 12).
a – Connection departs Tours 1317 on Ⓐ Feb. 8 - Mar. 26.
b – To / from Lille Europe and Brussels (Table **11**).
c – Also Apr. 5; not Mar. 28, Apr. 11, 18, 25, May 23, 30, June 6.
d – Not Dec. 25, Jan. 1, Apr. 5, May 24.
e – Also Apr. 5, May 24.
f – Also Dec. 24, 31, May 12; not Dec. 25, Jan. 1.
g – Also Dec. 24, 31, May 12, 13.
h – Not Dec. 25, Jan. 1, May 13.
k – Also Dec. 31, May 12; not Dec. 25, Jan. 1.
m – Not Dec. 24, 31, Apr. 5, May 12, 13, 24.
n – Not Apr. 5, May 24.
q – Also May 12; not Dec. 25, Jan. 1.
s – Not Dec. 24, 25, 31, Jan. 1, May 13
v – Lille **Flandres**.
w – Also Dec. 24, 31, Apr. 5, May 12, 24; not Dec. 25, Jan. 1.
x – Not Dec. 24, Apr. 5, May 24.
y – Also Dec. 24, 31, Apr. 5, May 12, 24. Depart Lille Europe 1824 on Dec. 24, 31, May 12.
z – Also Dec. 24, 31, Apr. 5, May 12, 13, 24.
TGV –🅁, supplement payable, 🍷.
◇ – Train number **8422** on ⑦.
△ – Runs up to 25 minutes later on Ⓐ Feb. 8 - Mar. 26.
▽ – Depart Paris 5 minutes earlier on Jan. 14, 18 - 21.
▷ – Arrive Paris 5 - 15 min later on Dec. 14 - 17, Jan. 11 - 21.
⊖ – Depart Paris 5 minutes earlier on Ⓐ Jan. 4 - Feb. 5, Feb. 15 - 26.
☆ – Arrive Paris 1605 on Feb. 21, Mar. 28.
¶ – Train number **8371** on ⑤.
‡ – On ⑦ **8333** is numbered **8331**, **8441** is **8547**.
* – Subject to alteration Jan. 11, 12, 18, 19, Feb. 1, 2, 8, 9.

ORLÉANS - BLOIS - TOURS 296

For fast *TGV* services Paris - Tours and v.v. see Table **295**

<table>
<tr><th>km</th><th></th><th>⚒</th><th>Ⓐ</th><th>Ⓐ</th><th>⚒</th><th>Ⓒ</th><th>Ⓐ</th><th>Ⓐ</th><th>⚒</th><th></th><th>†</th><th></th><th>▽</th><th>Ⓐ</th><th>Ⓐ △</th><th>⚒</th><th>⚒</th><th></th><th>⚒</th><th></th><th></th><th>⑤ f</th><th>⑤ f</th><th></th></tr>
<tr><td></td><td>Paris Austerlitz 294 d.</td><td>...</td><td>...</td><td>...</td><td>...</td><td>...</td><td>...</td><td>0626</td><td>...</td><td>0725</td><td>...</td><td>...</td><td>0921</td><td>...</td><td>...</td><td>1048</td><td>...</td><td>1141</td><td>1239</td><td>...</td><td>1335</td><td>...</td><td>1454</td><td>...</td></tr>
<tr><td>0</td><td>Orléans d.</td><td>...</td><td>0641</td><td>0623</td><td>0702</td><td>0727</td><td>0727</td><td>0739</td><td>0743</td><td>0813</td><td>0851</td><td>...</td><td>1010</td><td>1019</td><td>1108</td><td>1202</td><td>1222</td><td>1254</td><td>1328</td><td>...</td><td>1449</td><td>1540</td><td>1545</td><td>...</td></tr>
<tr><td>2</td><td>Les Aubrais-Orléans d.</td><td>...</td><td>|</td><td>|</td><td>|</td><td>|</td><td>|</td><td>0725x</td><td>|</td><td>0823</td><td>|</td><td>...</td><td>1019</td><td>1028</td><td>|</td><td>1148x</td><td>|</td><td>1240x</td><td>1338</td><td>...</td><td>1435x</td><td>|</td><td>1554</td><td>...</td></tr>
<tr><td>30</td><td>Beaugency d.</td><td>...</td><td>|</td><td>0642</td><td>0722</td><td>|</td><td>|</td><td>0801</td><td>0810</td><td>0840</td><td>0918</td><td>...</td><td>1037</td><td>1053</td><td>|</td><td>1224</td><td>1247</td><td>1315</td><td>|</td><td>...</td><td>1510</td><td>1557</td><td>|</td><td>...</td></tr>
<tr><td>61</td><td>Blois d.</td><td>0637</td><td>0708</td><td>0712</td><td>0742</td><td>0755</td><td>0755</td><td>0825</td><td>0834</td><td>0901</td><td>0943</td><td>...</td><td>1059</td><td>1111</td><td>1137</td><td>1246</td><td>1312</td><td>1336</td><td>1408</td><td>...</td><td>1531</td><td>1616</td><td>1625</td><td>...</td></tr>
<tr><td>93</td><td>Amboise d.</td><td>0704</td><td>|</td><td>0733</td><td>0801</td><td>|</td><td>|</td><td>0847</td><td>...</td><td>0923</td><td>1008</td><td>...</td><td>1120</td><td>...</td><td>|</td><td>1308</td><td>1338</td><td>1357</td><td>|</td><td>...</td><td>1552</td><td>1634</td><td>|</td><td>...</td></tr>
<tr><td>115</td><td>St Pierre des Corps a.</td><td>0720</td><td>0733</td><td>0744</td><td>0814</td><td>0818</td><td>0818</td><td>0859</td><td>...</td><td>0936</td><td>1023</td><td>...</td><td>1132</td><td>...</td><td>1159</td><td>1320</td><td>1353</td><td>1408</td><td>1433</td><td>...</td><td>1603</td><td>1647</td><td>1650</td><td>...</td></tr>
<tr><td>118</td><td>Tours a.</td><td>0726</td><td>0745</td><td>0751</td><td>0820</td><td>0829</td><td>0825</td><td>0906</td><td>...</td><td>0943</td><td>1030</td><td>...</td><td>1139</td><td>...</td><td>1210</td><td>1327</td><td>1400</td><td>1414</td><td>1440</td><td>...</td><td>1610</td><td>1652</td><td>1659</td><td>...</td></tr>
<tr><td></td><td>Nantes 289 a.</td><td>...</td><td>0910</td><td>...</td><td>...</td><td>1001</td><td>...</td><td>...</td><td>...</td><td>...</td><td>...</td><td>...</td><td>...</td><td>...</td><td>1337</td><td>...</td><td>...</td><td>...</td><td>...</td><td>...</td><td>...</td><td>...</td><td>...</td><td>...</td></tr>
</table>

<table>
<tr><th></th><th>①–④ m</th><th>⑤⑥ u</th><th>①–④ m</th><th></th><th></th><th>①–④ m</th><th>†</th><th>⚒</th><th>†</th><th>Ⓐ</th><th>⚒</th><th>z</th><th>⑥ b</th><th></th><th>Ⓑ h</th><th>Ⓐ</th><th>†</th><th>⚒</th><th>Ⓑ</th><th>Ⓐ</th><th></th><th>Ⓑ</th><th></th><th>⊖</th></tr>
<tr><td>Paris Austerlitz 294 d.</td><td>...</td><td>...</td><td>...</td><td>1548</td><td>...</td><td>...</td><td>...</td><td>...</td><td>...</td><td>1632</td><td>...</td><td>1706</td><td>1706</td><td>...</td><td>1736</td><td>...</td><td>1805</td><td>1805</td><td>1836</td><td>...</td><td>1956</td><td>...</td><td>...</td><td>2252</td></tr>
<tr><td>Orléans d.</td><td>1558</td><td>1630</td><td>1607</td><td>1640</td><td>...</td><td>1727</td><td>1713</td><td>1735</td><td>1759</td><td>1746</td><td>...</td><td>1819</td><td>1819</td><td>...</td><td>1822</td><td>1850</td><td>1858</td><td>1919</td><td>1950</td><td>1954</td><td>2109</td><td>2141</td><td>...</td><td>2344</td></tr>
<tr><td>Les Aubrais-Orléans d.</td><td>|</td><td>|</td><td>|</td><td>1648</td><td>...</td><td>|</td><td>|</td><td>|</td><td>|</td><td>1732x</td><td>...</td><td>1805x</td><td>1805x</td><td>...</td><td>1832</td><td>|</td><td>1906</td><td>1905x</td><td>1936x</td><td>|</td><td>2055x</td><td>2153</td><td>...</td><td>2354</td></tr>
<tr><td>Beaugency d.</td><td>1616</td><td>|</td><td>1634</td><td>1706</td><td>...</td><td>|</td><td>1738</td><td>1802</td><td>|</td><td>1808</td><td>...</td><td>1840</td><td>1840</td><td>...</td><td>|</td><td>1917</td><td>1925</td><td>1940</td><td>|</td><td>2021</td><td>2130</td><td>2211</td><td>...</td><td>|</td></tr>
<tr><td>Blois d.</td><td>1635</td><td>1658</td><td>1701</td><td>1728</td><td>...</td><td>1754</td><td>1804</td><td>1826</td><td>1825</td><td>1832</td><td>1842</td><td>1900</td><td>1902</td><td>...</td><td>1906</td><td>1942</td><td>1946</td><td>2003</td><td>2020</td><td>2039</td><td>2151</td><td>2232</td><td>...</td><td>0023</td></tr>
<tr><td>Amboise d.</td><td>1653</td><td>|</td><td>1728</td><td>1749</td><td>...</td><td>|</td><td>1830</td><td>...</td><td>1840</td><td>1852</td><td>1908</td><td>...</td><td>1923</td><td>...</td><td>|</td><td>2007</td><td>2007</td><td>2025</td><td>...</td><td>...</td><td>2212</td><td>2251</td><td>...</td><td>|</td></tr>
<tr><td>St Pierre des Corps a.</td><td>1704</td><td>1721</td><td>1744</td><td>1801</td><td>...</td><td>1817</td><td>1845</td><td>...</td><td>1853</td><td>1904</td><td>1923</td><td>...</td><td>1935</td><td>...</td><td>1929</td><td>2022</td><td>2019</td><td>2037</td><td>...</td><td>...</td><td>2224</td><td>2302</td><td>...</td><td>0049</td></tr>
<tr><td>Tours a.</td><td>1711</td><td>1731</td><td>1751</td><td>1808</td><td>...</td><td>1828</td><td>1853</td><td>...</td><td>1903</td><td>1911</td><td>1930</td><td>...</td><td>1941</td><td>...</td><td>1936</td><td>2029</td><td>2026</td><td>2044</td><td>...</td><td>...</td><td>2230</td><td>2308</td><td>...</td><td>0055</td></tr>
<tr><td>Nantes 289 a.</td><td>...</td><td>1857</td><td>...</td><td>...</td><td>...</td><td>1956</td><td>...</td><td>...</td><td>2029</td><td>...</td><td>...</td><td>...</td><td>...</td><td>...</td><td>...</td><td>...</td><td>...</td><td>...</td><td>...</td><td>...</td><td>...</td><td>...</td><td>...</td><td>...</td></tr>
</table>

<table>
<tr><th></th><th>⚒</th><th>⚒</th><th>Ⓐ</th><th>⚒</th><th>⚒</th><th>Ⓐ</th><th>⚒</th><th></th><th>⚒</th><th>Ⓐ</th><th>⚒</th><th>Ⓐ</th><th>Ⓐ</th><th></th><th>†</th><th>Ⓒ</th><th>Ⓐ</th><th></th><th>▽</th><th>⚒ ▽</th><th>⑥ t</th><th>Ⓐ ▷</th><th>Ⓐ</th><th>Ⓒ</th></tr>
<tr><td>Nantes 289 d.</td><td>...</td><td>...</td><td>...</td><td>...</td><td>...</td><td>...</td><td>...</td><td>...</td><td>...</td><td>...</td><td>...</td><td>0706</td><td>...</td><td>...</td><td>...</td><td>0849</td><td>...</td><td>...</td><td>...</td><td>...</td><td>...</td><td>...</td><td>1123</td><td>...</td></tr>
<tr><td>Tours d.</td><td>...</td><td>0532</td><td>...</td><td>...</td><td>0627</td><td>...</td><td>0647</td><td>0708</td><td>...</td><td>0802</td><td>0812</td><td>0829</td><td>...</td><td>0904</td><td>0940</td><td>1023</td><td>1026r</td><td>...</td><td>1101</td><td>...</td><td>1229</td><td>1229</td><td>1247</td><td>1304</td></tr>
<tr><td>St Pierre des Corps d.</td><td>...</td><td>0539</td><td>...</td><td>...</td><td>0634</td><td>...</td><td>0653</td><td>0715</td><td>...</td><td>0809</td><td>0819</td><td>0839</td><td>...</td><td>0911</td><td>0947</td><td>1033</td><td>1033</td><td>...</td><td>1108</td><td>...</td><td>1236</td><td>1237</td><td>1257</td><td>1310</td></tr>
<tr><td>Amboise d.</td><td>...</td><td>0551</td><td>...</td><td>...</td><td>0646</td><td>...</td><td>0710</td><td>0727</td><td>...</td><td>|</td><td>0830</td><td>|</td><td>...</td><td>0924</td><td>1005</td><td>1046</td><td>|</td><td>...</td><td>1120</td><td>...</td><td>1251</td><td>1254</td><td>|</td><td>1323</td></tr>
<tr><td>Blois d.</td><td>0549</td><td>0613</td><td>0628</td><td>0632</td><td>0705</td><td>0715</td><td>0737</td><td>0749</td><td>0753</td><td>0836</td><td>0851</td><td>0906</td><td>0923</td><td>0946</td><td>1030</td><td>1101</td><td>1101</td><td>...</td><td>1141</td><td>1227</td><td>1316</td><td>1325</td><td>1322</td><td>1344</td></tr>
<tr><td>Beaugency d.</td><td>0610</td><td>0634</td><td>|</td><td>0652</td><td>|</td><td>0734</td><td>...</td><td>0811</td><td>0818</td><td>|</td><td>0910</td><td>|</td><td>0949</td><td>1007</td><td>1055</td><td>|</td><td>|</td><td>...</td><td>1201</td><td>1253</td><td>...</td><td>1346</td><td>|</td><td>1404</td></tr>
<tr><td>Les Aubrais-Orléans a.</td><td>0627</td><td>0709v</td><td>0658</td><td>|</td><td>0730</td><td>|</td><td>...</td><td>0844v</td><td>|</td><td>|</td><td>0942v</td><td>|</td><td>|</td><td>1040v</td><td>|</td><td>|</td><td>1143v</td><td>...</td><td>1234v</td><td>1319</td><td>...</td><td>1404</td><td>|</td><td>1437v</td></tr>
<tr><td>Orléans a.</td><td>0637</td><td>0655</td><td>0707</td><td>0719</td><td>0743</td><td>0801</td><td>...</td><td>0831</td><td>0845</td><td>0905</td><td>0929</td><td>0935</td><td>1021</td><td>1027</td><td>1121</td><td>1130</td><td>1130</td><td>...</td><td>1221</td><td>1328</td><td>...</td><td>1413</td><td>1349*</td><td>1424</td></tr>
<tr><td>Paris Austerlitz 294 a.</td><td>0731</td><td>0812</td><td>0803</td><td>...</td><td>0827</td><td>...</td><td>...</td><td>0945</td><td>...</td><td>...</td><td>1044</td><td>...</td><td>...</td><td>1142</td><td>...</td><td>...</td><td>1244</td><td>...</td><td>1338</td><td>...</td><td>...</td><td>1506</td><td>...</td><td>1538</td></tr>
</table>

<table>
<tr><th></th><th></th><th>Ⓐ</th><th>Ⓐ</th><th></th><th>Ⓐ</th><th></th><th></th><th>Ⓐ</th><th></th><th></th><th>Ⓐ</th><th>†</th><th>Ⓐ</th><th></th><th>Ⓐ</th><th>⑥ t</th><th></th><th></th><th>⑥ t</th><th>†</th><th></th><th>†</th><th>Ⓐ</th><th></th></tr>
<tr><td>Nantes 289 d.</td><td>...</td><td>...</td><td>...</td><td>...</td><td>...</td><td>...</td><td>...</td><td>1630</td><td>...</td><td>...</td><td>...</td><td>...</td><td>...</td><td>...</td><td>1818</td><td>...</td><td>...</td><td>...</td><td>1945</td><td>2012</td><td>...</td><td>...</td><td>...</td><td>...</td></tr>
<tr><td>Tours d.</td><td>1500</td><td>1550</td><td>1630</td><td>1656</td><td>...</td><td>1723</td><td>1735</td><td>1811</td><td>...</td><td>1842</td><td>1852</td><td>1911</td><td>1911</td><td>...</td><td>1938</td><td>1947</td><td>2046</td><td>...</td><td>2126</td><td>2133</td><td>...</td><td>2223</td><td>2223</td><td>...</td></tr>
<tr><td>St Pierre des Corps d.</td><td>1508</td><td>1557</td><td>1636</td><td>1703</td><td>...</td><td>1730</td><td>1740</td><td>1818</td><td>...</td><td>1849</td><td>1858</td><td>1918</td><td>1918</td><td>...</td><td>1954</td><td>1954</td><td>2052</td><td>...</td><td>2136</td><td>2143</td><td>...</td><td>2230</td><td>2230</td><td>...</td></tr>
<tr><td>Amboise d.</td><td>1521</td><td>1611</td><td>1653</td><td>|</td><td>...</td><td>1743</td><td>1756</td><td>|</td><td>...</td><td>1901</td><td>1914</td><td>1931</td><td>1930</td><td>...</td><td>|</td><td>2006</td><td>2105</td><td>...</td><td>|</td><td>|</td><td>...</td><td>2241</td><td>2241</td><td>...</td></tr>
<tr><td>Blois d.</td><td>1542</td><td>1631</td><td>1718</td><td>1730</td><td>1735</td><td>1804</td><td>1820</td><td>1843</td><td>...</td><td>1924</td><td>1938</td><td>1953</td><td>1953</td><td>...</td><td>2024</td><td>2025</td><td>2126</td><td>...</td><td>2200</td><td>2207</td><td>...</td><td>2300</td><td>2300</td><td>...</td></tr>
<tr><td>Beaugency d.</td><td>1603</td><td>1657</td><td>...</td><td>|</td><td>1801</td><td>1825</td><td>1839</td><td>|</td><td>...</td><td>1945</td><td>...</td><td>2013</td><td>2012</td><td>...</td><td>|</td><td>2043</td><td>2147</td><td>...</td><td>|</td><td>|</td><td>...</td><td>2319</td><td>2319</td><td>...</td></tr>
<tr><td>Les Aubrais-Orléans a.</td><td>1636v</td><td>|</td><td>...</td><td>1757</td><td>|</td><td>1858v</td><td>|</td><td>|</td><td>...</td><td>2004</td><td>...</td><td>2047v</td><td>|</td><td>...</td><td>|</td><td>|</td><td>2220v</td><td>...</td><td>|</td><td>|</td><td>...</td><td>|</td><td>|</td><td>...</td></tr>
<tr><td>Orléans a.</td><td>1623</td><td>1724</td><td>...</td><td>1806</td><td>1827</td><td>1844</td><td>1905</td><td>1910</td><td>...</td><td>2014</td><td>...</td><td>2033</td><td>2029</td><td>...</td><td>2050</td><td>2101</td><td>2207</td><td>...</td><td>2226</td><td>2232</td><td>...</td><td>2337</td><td>2337</td><td>...</td></tr>
<tr><td>Paris Austerlitz 294 a.</td><td>1737</td><td>...</td><td>...</td><td>1858</td><td>...</td><td>1958</td><td>...</td><td>...</td><td>...</td><td>2105</td><td>...</td><td>2150</td><td>...</td><td>...</td><td>...</td><td>...</td><td>2321</td><td>...</td><td>...</td><td>...</td><td>...</td><td>...</td><td>...</td><td>...</td></tr>
</table>

b – Also Dec. 25, Jan. 1, May 13.
f – Also Dec. 24, 31, May 12; not Dec. 25, Jan. 1.
h – Not Dec. 25, Jan. 1, May 13.
m – Not Dec. 24, 31, Apr. 5, May 12, 13, 24.
r – Also Jan. 11, 12, 18, 19, Feb. 1, 2, 8, 9.
t – Not May 1, 8.
u – Also Dec. 24, 31, May 12; not Dec. 25, Jan. 1, May 1, 8.
v – Calls after Orléans.
x – Calls before Orléans.
z – Not Apr. 4, May 23.
△ – Runs up to 22 minutes earlier Jan. 11 - Mar. 26.
▽ – Subject to alteration on ①–⑤ Jan. 11 - Mar. 26.
▷ – Runs up to 12 minutes earlier on ①–⑤ Jan. 11 - Mar. 26.
⊖ – Not Dec. 14, Jan. 18 - 21, 25 - 28.
* – 1400 Jan. 11 - Mar. 26.

299 OTHER LOCAL SERVICES

Subject to alteration on holidays

ANGERS - CHOLET: *60 km* Journey 50-65 minutes

Angers depart: 0645Ⓐ, 0722Ⓐ, 0756⚒, 0937⚒, 1151, 1303Ⓐ, 1310⑥, 1553, 1638⑥, 1725Ⓐ, 1741Ⓐ, 1847⚒, 1935Ⓑ, 2043, 2140⑤**f**, 2247Ⓑ**z**.

Cholet depart: 0615Ⓐ, 0635⚒, 0655Ⓐ, 0718⑥, 0742Ⓐ, 0844†, 0847⚒, 0944Ⓐ, 1052⑥, 1241⚒, 1352†, 1353Ⓐ, 1357⑥, 1643Ⓑ, 1737, 1840⑦, 1842Ⓐ, 1942⑥, 1944Ⓑ, 2206⑦.

BAYONNE - ST JEAN PIED DE PORT *50 km*

To Jan. 31 △	① g	M	⚒				⚒		⑤⑦	
Bayonne .... d.	0745	0822	1157	...	1510	...	1811	...	2106	...
St Jean Pied de Port.... a.	0900	0937	1312	...	1625	...	1933	...	2219	...

To Jan. 31 △	Ⓐ		⑥						†	
St Jean Pied de Port.... d.	0618	...	0653	0942	...	1318	...	1635	1836	...
Bayonne .... a.	0740	...	0815	1056	...	1432	...	1749	1950	...

BORDEAUX - MONT DE MARSAN *147 km*

	⚒	Ⓐ	▽	▽	⚒	†	⚒			Q	⑤f
Bordeaux 305 ... d.	...	0636	0836	1036	1236	1336	1436	1726	...	2136	2156
Morcenx **305** ...... d.	0658	0735	0935	1135	1335	1435	1535	1825	1935	2235	2255
Mont de Marsan a.	0727	0801	0956	1158	1358	1456	1556	1848	1959	2256	2316

	Ⓐ	⚒	⚒		⚒▽				Ⓑ	Ⓒ	
Mont de Marsan d.	0550	0624	0804	1004	1204	1404	1613	1754	1858	2004	...
Morcenx **305** ...... d.	0611	0650	0827	1027	1227	1427	1634	1824	1919	2026	...
Bordeaux 305 ... a.	0716	...	0925	1128	1325	1525	1734	...	2025	...	...

CARCASSONNE - LIMOUX - QUILLAN

		🚌	⚒	🚌 †	⚒	⚒	🚌 †	⚒	⚒	⚒	🚌 †
0	Carcassonne .... d.	0610	0717	0915	1050	1300	1326	1604	1729	1845	1839
26	Limoux .... a.	0643	0747	0948	1120	1331	1359	1634	1759	1916	1912
54	Quillan.............. a.	0723	...	1028	*1210*r	1407	1439	*1735*r	...	1951	1952

	⚒	⚒	🚌 †	⚒	🚌 †	⚒	⚒	🚌 †	⚒	🚌 ⚒	🚌 †
Quillan.............. d.	0602	...	0736	*1035*r	1040	1419	*1555*r	1606	...	1750	2007
Limoux.............. d.	0637	0755	0816	1127	1122	1454	1646	1650	1808	1833	2047
Carcassonne ..... a.	0708	0826	0849	1157	1200	1525	1717	1727	1840	1910	2120

CHARLEVILLE MÉZIÈRES - GIVET: *64 km* Journey 65-75 minutes

Charleville Mézières depart: 0605⚒, 0650⚒, 0743Ⓐ, 0955⚒, 1115, 1220⚒, 1259⑥, 1330, 1440, 1615, 1635Ⓐ, 1730⚒, 1819Ⓐ, 1837Ⓐ, 1908Ⓐ, 1915⑥, 1932Ⓑ, 2040**y**.

Givet depart: 0450Ⓐ, 0520Ⓐ, 0553Ⓐ, 0608⚒, 0649Ⓐ, 0653Ⓒ, 0743Ⓐ, 0748⑥, 1021, 1215⑥, 1233⚒, 1349Ⓐ, 1358⑥, 1500Ⓑ, 1604Ⓑ, 1721⚒, 1748†, 1756⚒, 1821Ⓐ, 1905Ⓑ.

DINARD - ST MALO

🚌: 7-10 times per day (3-5 on †), journey 24 minutes. Operator: TIV. *11 km*

⛴: *Le Bus de Mer* passenger ferry operates 10-15 times daily from April to October. Journey time 10 minutes.

LILLE - LENS: *39 km* Journey 31-48 minutes

Lille Flandres depart: 0548Ⓐ, 0700⚒, 0724Ⓐ, 0756⑥, 0759Ⓐ, 0827Ⓐ, 0902⚒, 1003⑦, 1142⑥, 1156Ⓑ, 1242⚒, 1329, 1558, 1624Ⓐ, 1658, 1723Ⓐ, 1758, 1827Ⓐ, 1858Ⓐ, 1934⑥, 1942Ⓑ, 2026.

Lens depart: 0453Ⓐ, 0524⚒, 0626⚒, 0650⚒, 0724⑥, 0727Ⓐ, 0800⚒, 0827Ⓐ, 0851, 0958⑥, 1054Ⓒ, 1119⚒, 1230⚒, 1255Ⓐ, 1258†, 1342⑥, 1431Ⓒ, 1555⚒, 1630Ⓑ, 1658⚒, 1730†, 1737Ⓐ, 1758⚒, 1852⚒, 1900†, 2002.

NANTES - CHOLET: *65 km* Journey 51-65 minutes

Nantes dep: 0628Ⓐ, 0726⑥, 0805Ⓐ🚌, 0915①🚌, 0930⑥🚌, 1237‡, 1635⚒🚌, 1709Ⓐ, 1800Ⓐ, 1844.

Cholet depart: 0606⚒, 0635Ⓐ🚌, 0737Ⓐ, 1019🚌, 1218†, 1240⚒🚌, 1653Ⓐ, 1825Ⓐ, 2043†.

PARIS - CHÂTEAUDUN - VENDÔME

Certain journeys continue to Tours

			†	⚒		⑤f	Ⓐ	⚒	⑦u	⑤f	⑦v
0	Paris Austerlitz . d.	0825	0825	1152	1348	1618	1748	1854	1916	2212	2239
134	Châteaudun...... a.	0958	0958	1319	1519	1749	1926	2026	2043	2339	0006
178	Vendôme.......... a.	...	1038	...	1601	1829	...	2107	2122	...	...

	⚒	⚒			⑤f	⚒		⑦u	⑤f	⑦u	
Vendôme........... d.	0537	...	...	...	1437	...	1616	1742	...	2001	...
Châteaudun....... d.	0617	0721	1023	...	1525	1525	1656	1821	2033	2047	...
Paris Austerlitz... a.	0757	0857	1154	...	1656	1656	1830	1954	2202	2216	...

PARIS - DISNEYLAND (Marne la Vallée - Chessy): *32 km* Journey 39 minutes

Trains run approximately every 15 minutes 0500 - 2400 on RER Line A:
Paris Châtelet les Halles - Paris Gare de Lyon - Marne la Vallée Chessy (for Disneyland).
Operator: RATP. For *TGV* services serving Marne la Vallée see Tables **11**, **391**.

ST BRIEUC - DINAN

km		Ⓐ	⑥ t		†	⚒ ▽	⑥ t	Ⓐ	† ◇	
0	St Brieuc **284**............. d.	0647	0717	...	1231	1313	1713	1716	1711	...
21	Lamballe **284**............. d.	0706	0735	...	1248	1329	1730	1734	1728	...
62	Dinan......................... a.	0739	0809	...	1323	1405	1805	1808	1812	...

	Ⓐ	⑥ t	Ⓐ	Ⓐ§ ◇	Ⓒ ◇		⑥ t	Ⓐ	†	
Dinan.......................... d.	0624	0657	0749	1058	1134	...	1820	1838	1916	...
Lamballe **284**............... a.	0659	0730	0821	1128	1207	...	1854	1912	1950	...
St Brieuc **284**.............. a.	0719	0747	0835	1148	1224	...	1912	1930	2008	...

SOUILLAC - SARLAT 🚌: *30 km* Journey 41 minutes Rail tickets not valid

Souillac (rail station) depart: 0645Ⓐ**s**, 0910⑥, 1501, 1843⑤**s**, 1843⑦**s**.

Sarlat (rail station) depart: 0802①**s**, 1219, 1310③**s**, 1552†, 1638①②④⑤**s**, 1737⑥**x**, 1815Ⓐ**s**, 1858†. Most journeys continue to/from the town centres of Sarlat and Souillac.

TOULOUSE - AUCH: *88 km* Journey 90-100 minutes

🚌 *serves Toulouse gare routière.*

Toulouse Matabiau depart: 0626Ⓐ, 0726, 1040**a**, 1226, 1426Ⓐ, 1615⚒🚌, 1627Ⓐ, 1726, 1827, 2026, 2120🚌.

Auch depart: 0607Ⓐ, 0707, 0747⚒🚌, 0807Ⓐ, 0907, 1107, 1407Ⓐ**a**, 1407Ⓒ, 1500🚌, 1707, 1807, 1907.

TOURS - CHINON: *49 km* Journey 45-50 minutes (70 minutes by 🚌)

Tours depart: 0534Ⓐ, 0640⚒🚌, 0735Ⓐ, 0800†🚌, 0909⑥, 0915Ⓐ🚌, 1145†🚌, 1220⚒, 1410, 1633⚒, 1719Ⓐ, 1750Ⓐ🚌, 1832, 1929Ⓐ, 2058⑦.

Chinon depart: 0635Ⓐ, 0639⑥, 0714Ⓐ, 0745⚒, 0837Ⓐ, 0919🚌, 1100Ⓐ🚌, 1116⑥, 1314⚒, 1335†🚌, 1516⑥, 1615Ⓑ, 1728⚒, 1816Ⓐ, 1915Ⓐ🚌, 1934⑥, 1949†, 2010⑤🚌.

VALENCIENNES - CAMBRAI: *40 km* Journey 36-44 minutes

Valenciennes depart: 0631⚒, 0725⚒, 0809⚒, 1013Ⓐ, 1217Ⓐ, 1220⑥, 1308⚒, 1717, 1743Ⓐ, 1840Ⓐ, 1929Ⓐ, 2010†.

Cambrai depart: 0606Ⓐ, 0644⑥, 0648Ⓐ, 0744⚒, 0759Ⓐ, 0957⑥, 1102Ⓐ, 1209Ⓐ, 1211⑥, 1314Ⓐ, 1352⑥, 1712Ⓐ, 1812Ⓒ, 1836Ⓐ, 1921†, 1942Ⓐ.

M – ②–⑦ (also Dec. 21, 28).
Q – ①②③④⑦ (also Dec. 25, Jan. 1, May 1, 8; not Dec. 24, 31, May 12).

a – Depart/arrive Toulouse Arènes (connection by métro with main station).
f – Also Dec. 24, 31, May 12; not Dec. 25, Jan. 1.
g – Not Dec. 21, 28.
r – By 🚌.
s – School term only.
t – Not May 1, 8.
u – Also Apr. 5, May 13, 24; not Apr. 4, May 23.
v – Also Apr. 5, May 13, 24; not Jan. 3, 10, Mar. 14, 21, Apr. 4, 11, 18, May 23.
x – Also Ⓐ in school holidays.
y – 2100 on ⑤.
z – Not Apr. 4, May 23.

◇ – To/from Dol (Table **282**).
△ – Service Feb. 1 - June 30 is by 🚌.
▽ – Timings may vary.
§ – Subject to alteration Mar. 15-26.
‡ – Subject to alteration on Ⓐ Feb. 1-19, May 3-7.

300 NOTES FOR TABLE 300 (on next page) →

A – Daily except ⑤ (also runs Dec. 25, Jan. 1; not Dec. 24, 31, May 12).
M – ①②③④⑦ (not Dec. 24, 31, May 12, 13).
N – ①②③④⑥ (also Dec. 25, Jan. 1; not Dec. 24, 31, Apr. 5, May 12, 24).
Q – ①②③④⑥ (also Dec. 25, Jan. 1, May 14; not Dec. 24, 31, Apr. 5, May 12, 24).

b – Depart Paris 0700 on Ⓐ Jan. 4 - Feb. 2, Feb. 15-19; 0710 on Feb. 20, 22-26, Mar. 27.
c – Ⓒ only.
d – Also Apr. 5; not Mar. 28, Apr. 11, 18, 24, May 23, 30, June 6.
e – Also Apr. 5, May 24.
f – Also Dec. 24, 31, May 12; not Dec. 25, Jan. 1.
g – Also Apr. 6, May 25; not Apr. 5, May 24.
h – Not Dec. 25, Jan. 1, May 13.
k – Also May 12; not Dec. 25, Jan. 1. Arrive Bordeaux 0110 night of ⑤ Jan. 8 - Apr. 9.
m – Not Dec. 24, 31, Apr. 5, May 12, 13, 24.
n – Not Apr. 5, May 24.
p – Not holidays.
q – On ⑥ Poitiers d. 0722, Niort 0814, La Rochelle 0851.
s – Depart Tours 1212 on Jan. 14, 18-21.
t – Also Dec. 25, Jan. 1, May 13.
u – Also Dec. 24, 31, May 12.
v – Also Dec. 24, 31, May 12, 13.
w – Also Dec. 24, 31, Apr. 5, May 12, 24.
x – Arrive 1028.
y – Also Dec. 31, Apr. 5, May 12; not Dec. 25, Jan. 1, Mar. 28, Apr. 11, 18, 24, May 23, 30, June 6.
z – Lille **Flandres**.

TGV – Ⓡ, supplement payable, 🍷.

♥ – From Lyon (Table **335**).
♣ – [12] Brussels (d. 0746) - Bordeaux (Table **11**); [12] Lille Europe (train **5212**) - Charles de Gaulle ✈ - Bordeaux.
◧ – Runs 6 minutes earlier on ⑤**f**.
◐ – Runs up to 14 minutes earlier Feb. 15-19. Timings vary Jan. 4-15, Feb. 8-12, 22-26.
☆ – From Strasbourg (Table **391**).
△ – Depart Paris 1040 on Jan. 14, 18-21.
▽ – Depart Paris 1120 on Jan. 14, 18-21.
⊕ – On Ⓐ Jan. 4 - Feb. 5, Feb. 15-19 depart Paris 0755, Futuroscope 0930.
⊗ – Depart Paris 0945 on Jan. 12-14.
⊖ – Not for journeys to/from Poitiers or Châtellerault.

PARIS - POITIERS - LA ROCHELLE and BORDEAUX 300

km	*TGV* trains convey 🍸							*TGV* 8501		*TGV* 8405	*TGV* 8305		*TGV* 8505	*TGV* 8507	*TGV* 8411	*TGV* 8511	*TGV* 8513	*TGV* 5200	*TGV* 5200	*TGV* 5356	*TGV* 8317	*TGV* 8415	*TGV* 8515	*TGV* 8516
		Ⓐ	Ⓐ	⚒	⚒	①	②–⑤	①–⑤	②–⑤		①–⑥	†		①–⑥	⑦	Ⓐ	Ⓒ		⑥	⑥		①–⑥		
			◐	q		g	p		p				b	n	e	⊕			t	♥t		n	⊗	⊗
	Lille Europe **11** d.	...	...	...	...	...	...	...	...	...	...	...	...	...	...	...	...	0558	0558	...	...	...	...	...
	Charles de Gaulle ✈ d.	...	...	...	...	...	...	...	...	...	...	...	...	...	...	...	...	0739	0739	...	...	...	...	...
	Marne la Vallee - Chessy d.	...	...	...	...	...	...	...	...	...	...	...	...	...	...	...	...	0756	0756	...	...	...	...	...
0	**Paris Montparnasse 295** d.	...	...	...	...	...	...	0610	...	0650	0720	...	0715	0745	0755	0810	0810	|	|	...	0910	0915	1010	1010
14	Massy TGV **295** d.	...	...	...	...	...	...	|	...	0702	|	...	|	|	|	|	|	0831	0831	0901	|	|	|	|
	Tours d.	...	...	...	0601	0642	0647	|	...	*0745*	|	...	|	|	|	|	|	*0913*	*0913*	*0943*	*0956*	|	|	|
221	St Pierre des Corps **295** d.	...	...	...	|	|	|	|	...	0755	|	...	|	|	|	|	|	0926	0926	0954	1009	|	|	|
289	Châtellerault d.	...	...	...	0655	0715	0719	|	...	0823	|	...	|	|	|	|	|	|	|	|	|	|	|	|
311	Futuroscope ⊖ d.	...	...	...	|	|	|	|	...	|	|	...	|	|	|	0936	0936	1004	1004	1045x	|	|	|	|
321	**Poitiers** a.	...	...	...	0726	0731	0735	0740	←	0838	0848	...	|	0914	0922	|	|	1011	1011	1052	1047	|	|	|
321	**Poitiers** d.	0620	0624	0719	...	0733	→	0743	0752	0845	0851	0901	|	0917	0925	|	|	1014	1014	...	1050	|	|	|
401	Niort d.	0723	|	0802	...	0826	...	|	0846	|	0936	0946	|	|	|	|	|	|	|	...	1136	|	|	|
468	**La Rochelle** a.	0804	|	0840	...	0907	...	|	0926	|	1023	1032	|	|	|	|	|	|	|	...	1217	|	|	|
434	Angoulême d.	...	0730	...	...	...	...	|	...	0935	...	...	|	1003	1013	|	|	1059	1059	...	...	|	|	|
517	Coutras **302** d.	...	0818	...	...	...	...	|	...	|	...	...	|	|	|	|	|	|	|	...	...	|	|	|
533	Libourne **302** d.	...	0829	...	...	...	...	|	...	|	...	...	|	1046	1053	|	|	|	|	...	...	|	|	|
570	**Bordeaux St Jean 302** a.	...	0854	...	...	...	...	0927	...	1036c	...	...	1025	1111	1118	1124	1124	1201	1201	...	...	1225	1314	1314
	Hendaye **305** a.	...	...	...	...	...	...	|	...	...	...	...	1256	|	...	|	|	...	1426	...	...	...	1541	|
	Irún **305** a.	...	...	...	...	...	...	|	...	...	...	...	1304	|	...	|	|	...	1435	...	...	...	1549	|
	Tarbes **305** a.	...	...	...	...	...	...	|	...	...	...	...	...	1353	...	|	|	...	...	...	...	...	...	1609
	Toulouse **320** a.	...	...	...	...	...	...	1138	...	...	...	...	...	...	...	1326	1338	...	...	...	...	...	...	...

	TGV 9802		*TGV* 8319	*TGV* 8417	*TGV* 5450		*TGV* 8519		*TGV* 8525	*TGV* 8321	*TGV* 8429	*TGV* 8329	*TGV* 8333	*TGV* 8331	*TGV* 8535	*TGV* 8335		*TGV* 8539	*TGV* 5218	*TGV* 5221	*TGV* 8339		*TGV* 5452	
	♣					⚒			①–⑥	①–④	⑤	⑤⑥	①–⑥	⑦		⑤	⑤			⑦		⑦	⑤–⑦	Ⓐ
			△		☆		▽	s	n	m	f	u	n	e		f	f			e	N	e	☆w	
Lille Europe **11** d.	0814	...	...	...	...	...	...	...	...	...	...	...	...	...	...	...	...	...	1238z	1238z	...	...	...	...
Charles de Gaulle ✈ d.	0912	...	...	...	...	...	...	...	...	...	...	...	...	...	...	...	...	...	1337	1337	...	...	...	...
Marne la Vallee - Chessy d.	0927	...	...	...	1023	...	...	...	...	...	...	...	...	...	...	...	...	...	1351	1351	...	...	1421	...
Paris Montparnasse 295 d.	|	...	1045	1050	|	...	1130	...	1210	1215	1310	1310	1350	1350	1410	1420	...	1440	|	|	1445	...	|	...
Massy TGV **295** d.	1000	...	|	|	1101	...	|	...	|	|	|	|	|	|	|	|	...	|	1431	1431	|	...	1501	...
Tours d.	*1043*	...	|	*1138*	*1138*	...	|	1223	|	|	|	|	*1441*	*1441*	|	|	...	|	*1512*	*1512*	|	...	*1542*	...
St Pierre des Corps **295** d.	1053	...	|	1149	1156	...	|	|	|	|	|	|	1457	1457	|	|	...	|	1524	1524	|	...	1555	...
Châtellerault d.	|	...	|	|	|	...	|	1310	|	|	|	|	1532	1532	|	|	...	|	|	|	|	...	|	...
Futuroscope ⊖ d.	|	...	|	|	1233	...	|	|	|	|	|	|	|	|	|	|	...	|	1603	1603	|	...	|	...
Poitiers a.	1131	...	1212	|	1240	...	|	1334	|	1343	1437	1437	1547	1546	|	|	...	|	1610	1610	1616	...	1633	...
Poitiers d.	1138	...	1215	|	1242	1259	|	...	|	1346	1440	1445	...	1549	|	|	1601	|	1612	1612	1619	1619	1636	1645
Niort d.	|	...	1258	|	|	1401	|	...	|	1428	|	1529	...	1639	|	1636	1649	|	|	|	1702	1706	|	1735
La Rochelle a.	|	...	1343	|	|	1446	|	...	|	1506	|	1617	...	1723	|	1725	1729	|	|	|	1749	1746	|	1819
Angoulême d.	1227	1231	...	1313	1329	...	|	...	1422	...	1527	...	...	...	1624	...	...	|	1658	1658	...	...	1721	...
Coutras **302** d.	|	1322	...	|	|	...	|	...	|	...	|	...	...	...	|	...	...	|	|	|	...	...	|	...
Libourne **302** d.	|	1334	...	1359	|	...	|	...	|	...	|	...	...	...	|	...	...	|	1739	1739	...	...	|	...
Bordeaux St Jean 302 a.	1327	1403	...	1424	1428	...	1435	...	1522	...	1628	...	...	...	1723	...	...	1740	1803	1803	...	...	1828	...
Hendaye **305** a.	...	...	...	...	...	...	|	...	1745	...	...	...	...	...	|	...	...	|	|	2031	...	...	...	...
Irún **305** a.	...	...	...	...	...	...	|	...	...	...	...	...	...	...	|	...	...	|	|	2047	...	...	...	...
Tarbes **305** a.	...	...	...	...	...	...	|	...	...	...	...	...	...	...	|	...	...	2039	|	...	...	...	...	...
Toulouse **320** a.	...	...	...	...	...	...	1645	...	...	...	...	...	...	...	1936	...	...	...	2015	...	...	...	...	...

	TGV 8441	*TGV* 8547	*TGV* 8341			*TGV* 8543	*TGV* 8551	*TGV* 8545		*TGV* 5229			*TGV* 8353			*TGV* 5222	*TGV* 5222	*TGV* 5452	*TGV* 8451	*TGV* 8355	*TGV* 8549	*TGV* 8557	*TGV* 8361	
	①–⑥	⑦	⑦	⑥	Ⓑ		①–④	⑤	①–④	⑦	⑤	①–④	⑤			⑤⑥		①–④		⑦				⚒
	n	e	e	t	h		m	f	m	e	f	m	f	A		v	M	☆m					M	◧
Lille Europe **11** d.	...	...	...	...	...	...	...	...	...	1447	...	...	...	...	...	1540	1540	...	...	...	...	...	...	...
Charles de Gaulle ✈ d.	...	...	...	...	...	...	...	...	...	1542	...	...	...	...	...	1637	1636	...	...	...	...	...	...	...
Marne la Vallee - Chessy d.	...	...	...	...	...	...	...	...	...	1557	...	...	...	...	...	1652	1656	1656	...	...	...	...	...	...
Paris Montparnasse 295 d.	1515	1515	1535	...	...	1550	1610	1620	...	|	...	...	1655	...	...	|	|	|	1715	1715	1720	1745	1755	...
Massy TGV **295** d.	|	|	|	...	...	|	|	|	...	1631	...	...	|	...	...	1730	1731	1731	|	|	|	|	|	...
Tours d.	*1602*	*1602*	|	...	...	|	|	|	1642	*1715*	1712	...	*1742*	1736	...	*1814*	*1814*	*1814*	*1759*	*1759*	|	|	|	1848
St Pierre des Corps **295** d.	1614	1614	|	...	...	|	|	|	|	1730	|	...	1754	|	...	1824	1824	1824	1814	1814	|	|	|	|
Châtellerault d.	|	|	|	...	...	|	|	|	1739	|	1758	...	|	1824	...	|	|	|	1843	1843	|	|	|	1932
Futuroscope ⊖ d.	|	|	|	...	...	|	|	|	|	|	|	...	|	|	...	|	|	|	1901	1901	|	|	|	|
Poitiers a.	1653	1652	|	...	...	|	1738	|	1805	1807	1814	...	1833	1840	...	1902	1902	1902	1908	1908	|	|	1922	1946
Poitiers d.	1656	1655	|	1708	1722	|	1741	|	...	...	*1822*	1831	1836	...	...	1905	1905	1905	1915	1920	|	|	1927	...
Niort d.	|	|	1749	1755	1818	|	|	|	...	...	|	1923	1923	...	...	|	|	|	|	2002	|	|	2014	...
La Rochelle a.	|	|	1822	1840	1913	|	|	|	...	...	|	2007	2006	...	...	|	|	|	|	2041	|	|	2057	...
Angoulême d.	1744	1745	...	...	...	|	|	|	...	...	*1942*	...	...	...	...	1951	1950	1950	2008	...	|	1958	...	...
Coutras **302** d.	|	|	...	...	...	|	|	|	...	...	...	...	...	...	...	|	|	|	|	...	|	|	...	...
Libourne **302** d.	1825	1825	...	...	...	|	|	|	...	...	...	...	...	...	...	|	|	|	2049	...	|	|	...	...
Bordeaux St Jean 302 a.	1850	1850	...	...	...	1859	1922	1922	...	...	...	...	...	...	...	2052	2053	2053	2113	...	2025	2058	...	...
Hendaye **305** a.	...	|	...	...	...	2125	|	|	...	...	...	...	...	...	...	2324	...	...	...	...	|	|	...	...
Irún **305** a.	...	|	...	...	...	2136	|	|	...	...	...	...	...	...	...	...	...	...	...	...	|	|	...	...
Tarbes **305** a.	...	2206	...	...	...	...	2214	2213	...	...	...	...	...	...	...	...	...	...	...	...	|	2349	...	...
Toulouse **320** a.	...	...	...	...	...	...	...	...	...	...	...	...	...	...	...	...	...	...	...	...	2243	...	...	...

	TGV 8359	*TGV* 8565	*TGV* 8469	*TGV* 8369		*TGV* 8477	*TGV* 8577	*TGV* 8579	*TGV* 8377	*TGV* 8479	*TGV* 5240	*TGV* 5454				*TGV* 8379	*TGV* 5242	*TGV* 8483	*TGV* 8495	*TGV* 8489	*TGV* 8491	*TGV* 8391	*TGV* 8497	*TGV* 8589
	⑤	Ⓑ			⑤	①–④	⑤	⑤	⑦		Ⓑ			⑦	†	⑤	⑤⑦	①–④	⑤	⑦	⑤	⑤	⑤	⑤⑦
	f	h		N	f	m	f	f	e		h	☆	Q	e		f	w	m	f	d	k	f	f	y
Lille Europe **11** d.	...	...	...	...	...	...	...	...	...	...	1809	...	...	...	...	...	1829	...	...	...	...	...	...	...
Charles de Gaulle ✈ d.	...	...	...	...	...	...	...	...	...	...	1911	...	...	...	...	...	1926	...	...	...	...	...	...	...
Marne la Vallee - Chessy d.	...	...	...	...	...	...	...	...	...	...	1927	1908	...	...	...	...	1942	...	...	...	...	...	...	...
Paris Montparnasse 295 d.	1820	1825	1850	1850	...	1925	1925	1925	1930	1950	|	|	...	...	...	2020	|	2020	2110	2110	2115	2120	2135	2250
Massy TGV **295** d.	|	|	|	|	...	|	|	|	|	|	2000	1951	...	...	...	|	2017	|	|	|	|	|	|	|
Tours d.	|	|	*1938*	*1938*	...	|	|	|	*2016*	|	|	*2035*	...	2039	...	|	*2101*	*2112*	|	*2158*	|	*2208*	*2208*	*2345*
St Pierre des Corps **295** d.	|	|	1949	1949	...	|	|	|	2028	|	|	2047	...	2050	...	|	2113	2128	|	2209	|	2219	2233	2356
Châtellerault d.	|	|	2018	2018	...	|	|	|	|	|	|	|	...	2130	...	2138	|	2200	|	2239	2233	|	|	|
Futuroscope ⊖ d.	|	|	|	|	...	|	|	|	|	|	|	|	...	|	...	|	|	|	|	|	|	|	|	|
Poitiers a.	1947	|	2033	2033	...	|	|	|	2108	2118	2122	2127	...	2145	...	2153	2158	2215	|	2254	2248	|	2312	0048
Poitiers d.	1958	|	2036	2040	2041	|	|	|	2111	2120	2126	2130	2146	...	2155	2156	2201	2218	|	2257	2251	|	2315	0056
Niort d.	2046	|	|	2121	2125	|	|	|	2157	|	|	|	2231	...	2251	2241	|	|	|	|	|	2342	|	|
La Rochelle a.	2128	|	|	2200	2207	|	|	|	2244	|	|	|	2314	...	2333	2324	|	|	|	|	|	0026	|	|
Angoulême d.	...	|	2122	...	...	|	|	|	...	2209	2213	2219	...	...	...	...	2248	2304	|	2345	2344	...	0001	|
Coutras **302** d.	...	|	|	...	...	|	|	|	...	|	|	|	...	...	...	...	|	|	|	|	|	...	|	|
Libourne **302** d.	...	|	2203	...	...	|	|	|	...	|	|	|	...	...	...	...	|	|	|	|	0025	...	|	|
Bordeaux St Jean 302 a.	...	2128	2227	...	...	2236	2233	2233	...	2309	2313	2319	...	...	...	...	2353	0006	0017	0048	0050	...	0115	|
Hendaye **305** a.	...	2345	...	...	...	...	0054	|	...	...	...	...	...	...	...	...	...	...	...	...	...	...	...	|
Irún **305** a.	...	...	...	...	...	...	...	|	...	...	...	...	...	...	...	...	...	...	...	...	...	...	...	|
Tarbes **305** a.	...	...	...	...	...	...	...	|	...	...	...	...	...	...	...	...	...	...	...	...	...	...	...	0703
Toulouse **320** a.	...	...	...	...	...	...	...	0043	...	...	...	...	...	...	...	...	...	...	...	...	...	...	...	...

← **FOR NOTES SEE FOOT OF PREVIOUS PAGE**

For overnight trains Paris - Irún / Tarbes see Table **305**. *For overnight TGV Paris - Toulouse see Table* **320**.

Engineering work – timings may vary (especially Toulouse arrival times); please enquire when reserving.
On May 13 - 16 many *TGV* journeys are replaced by 🚌 between Libourne and Bordeaux.

300 BORDEAUX and LA ROCHELLE - POITIERS - PARIS

TGV trains convey 🍸	TGV 8308 ① g	TGV 8406 Ⓐ	⑥ p	Ⓐ	TGV 8408 Ⓐ y	TGV 8306 ①–⑥ n	TGV 8312 ⑦ e	Ⓐ	TGV 8410 ①–⑥ n	TGV 8412 Ⓐ	⑥ p	TGV 5440 ☆	TGV 5261	Ⓐ	†	TGV 8414	TGV 8314 Ⓑ h	TGV 8416 Ⓐ	⚒	TGV 5264	TGV 5268 ①⑥ u		TGV 8518 ①–⑥ n	TGV 8523 Ⓐ
Toulouse **320** d.	...	...	...	...	...	...	...	...	...	...	...	...	...	...	...	...	...	...	...	0529	...	...	0608	...
Tarbes **305** d.	...	...	...	...	...	...	...	...	...	...	...	...	...	...	...	...	...	...	...	|	...	...	|	0530
Hendaye **305** d.	...	...	...	...	...	...	...	...	...	...	...	...	...	...	...	...	...	...	...	|	0520	...	|	|
Bordeaux St Jean 302 d.	...	0440	...	...	0512	...	...	...	0552	0621	...	0633	0633	...	...	0656	...	0722	...	0750	0750	...	0827	0827
Libourne **302** d.	...	0506	...	...	|	...	...	...	0618	|	...	|	|	...	...	0723	...	|	...	|	|	...	|	|
Coutras **302** d.	...	|	...	...	|	...	...	...	|	|	...	|	|	...	...	|	...	|	...	|	|	...	|	|
Angoulême d.	...	0547	...	...	0612	...	...	...	0700	|	...	0733	0733	...	...	0806	...	|	...	0850	0850	...	|	|
La Rochelle d.	...	|	...	...	|	0535	...	...	|	|	0631	|	|	0654	0701	|	0722	|	0733	|	|	...	|	|
Niort d.	...	|	...	...	|	0625	...	...	|	|	0721	|	|	0738	0751	|	0807	|	0832	|	|	...	|	|
Poitiers a.	...	0633	...	...	|	0714	...	...	0746	|	0805	0817	0817	0823	0837	0851	0846	|	0916	0933	0933	...	|	|
Poitiers d.	0506	0636	0641	0641	|	0717	0733	0736	0749	|	...	0819	0819	...	...	0856	0856	|	...	0936	0936	...	|	|
Futuroscope ⊖ d.	|	|	|	|	|	|	|	|	|	|	...	|	|	...	...	|	|	|	...	0947	0947	...	|	|
Châtellerault d.	|	0654	0659	0659	|	|	0752	0753	0806	|	...	|	|	...	...	|	|	|	...	|	|	...	|	|
St Pierre-des-Corps **295** a.	0546	|	|	|	|	|	0818	|	|	|	...	0859	0859	...	...	0934	0934	|	...	1020	1020	...	|	|
Tours a.	*0556*	|	0747	0753	|	|	*0829*	0830	|	|	...	*0910*	*0910*	...	...	*0946*	*0946*	|	...	*1030*	*1030*	...	|	|
Massy TGV **295** a.	0637	|	...	...	|	|	|	...	|	|	...	0952	0952	...	...	|	|	|	...	1113	1113	...	|	|
Paris Austerlitz **296** a.	|	|	...	...	|	|	|	...	|	|	...	|	|	...	...	|	|	|	...	|	|	...	|	|
Paris Montparnasse 295 a.	0650	0815	...	...	0830	0850	0920	...	0925	0930	...	|	|	...	...	1035	1035	1030	...	|	|	...	1145	1145
Marne la Vallee - Chessy a.	...	...	...	...	...	...	...	...	...	...	...	1035	1035	...	...	...	...	...	...	1154	1154	...	...	...
Charles de Gaulle ✈ a.	...	...	...	...	...	...	...	...	...	...	...	...	1053	...	...	...	...	...	...	1209	1209	...	...	...
Lille Europe **11** a.	...	...	...	...	...	...	...	...	...	...	...	...	1217c	...	...	...	...	...	...	1306	1306	...	...	...

	TGV 8420 ①–⑥ n	TGV 8422 ⑦ e	TGV 5442 Ⓒ ☆	TGV 8524	TGV 8527	TGV 8324	TGV 5442 Ⓐ ☆		TGV 5276	TGV 8528 ⊕	TGV 8530 S	TGV 8330 ⑤ f	Ⓐ	TGV 8436	TGV 8334	TGV 8534	Ⓐ	TGV 8541	TGV 8542 Ⓐ k	TGV 8438 Ⓐ §	TGV 8338	TGV 9816 ♣	TGV 8444	TGV 8548
Toulouse **320** d.	...	...	...	...	...	...	...	...	...	0922	...	...	...	...	...	...	...	...	...	...	...	...	...	1314
Tarbes **305** d.	...	...	...	...	0726	...	...	...	...	|	...	...	...	...	...	...	...	1052r	...	...	...	...	...	|
Hendaye **305** d.	...	...	...	0748	|	...	...	...	0834x	|	0847	...	...	...	...	1026z	...	|	1113	...	...	...	...	|
Bordeaux St Jean 302 d.	...	0755	1022	1026	1026	...	1030	...	1043	1125	1133	...	...	1201	...	1251	...	1355	1355	1416	...	1422	1450	1525
Libourne **302** d.	...	|	|	|	|	...	|	...	|	|	|	...	...	1227	...	|	...	|	|	|	...	1446	|	|
Coutras **302** d.	...	|	|	|	|	...	|	...	|	|	|	...	...	|	...	|	...	|	|	|	...	|	|	|
Angoulême d.	0856	0856	1121	1128	1128	...	1135	...	1201	|	|	...	...	1311	...	|	...	1457	1457	|	...	1526	|	1625
La Rochelle d.	|	|	|	|	|	1040	|	...	|	|	|	...	1152*	|	1220	|	1309*	|	|	|	1447v	|	|	|
Niort d.	|	|	|	|	|	1138	|	...	|	|	|	...	1241	|	1309	|	1357	|	|	|	1524	|	|	|
Poitiers a.	0947	0947	1206	1211	1211	1217	1223	...	1248	|	|	...	1326	1358	1358	|	1447	|	|	1558	1604	1611	|	1709
Poitiers d.	0950	0950	1209	1214	1214	1220	1226	1232	1251	|	|	1327	...	1403	1403	|	...	|	|	1601	1607	1614	|	1712
Futuroscope ⊖ d.	|	|	|	|	|	|	|	|	|	|	|	|	...	|	|	|	...	|	|	|	|	|	|	|
Châtellerault d.	1006	1008	|	|	|	|	|	1308	|	|	|	|	...	1422	1422	|	...	|	|	|	|	|	|	|
St Pierre-des-Corps **295** a.	1033	1035	1248	|	|	1259	1304	|	1328	|	|	1412	...	1449	1449	|	...	1619	1619	|	|	1652	|	1750
Tours a.	*1045*	*1045*	*1259*	|	|	*1314*	*1314*	1406	*1339*	|	|	|	...	*1501*	*1501*	|	...	*1632*	*1632*	|	|	*1702*	|	*1802*
Massy TGV **295** a.	|	|	1342	|	|	|	1358	...	1423	|	|	|	...	|	|	|	...	|	|	|	|	1747	|	|
Paris Austerlitz **296** a.	|	|	|	|	|	|	|	...	|	|	|	|	...	|	|	|	...	|	|	|	|	|	|	|
Paris Montparnasse 295 a.	1135	1135	|	1345	1345	1400	|	...	|	1440	1500	1520	...	1550	1550	1600	...	1720	1720	1730	1740	|	1800	1850
Marne la Vallee - Chessy a.	...	...	1422	...	...	...	1438	...	1506	...	...	...	...	...	...	...	...	...	...	...	...	1827	...	...
Charles de Gaulle ✈ a.	...	...	...	...	...	...	...	...	1521	...	...	...	...	...	...	...	...	...	...	...	...	1841	...	...
Lille Europe **11** a.	...	...	...	...	...	...	...	...	1615	...	...	...	...	...	...	...	...	...	...	...	...	2005c	...	...

	TGV 8348 ⑤ f	⚒	†	TGV 5444 ⑦ ☆e	TGV 8558	Ⓐ	TGV 8354 ①–④ m◇	TGV 8364 ⑤–⑦ w	TGV 5284 Ⓑ h	TGV 8456 ⑤–⑦ w		TGV 8362 ①–④ m	TGV 5446 ①–⑥ ☆n	TGV 8563	Ⓑ	TGV 8466 ⑦ e	TGV 5336 ⑦ ♥e	TGV 8370 ⑤ f	TGV 8372 ⑦ e	TGV 8472 ①–⑥ q	†	TGV 8474 ⑦ e	⑤ f	⑥
Toulouse **320** d.	...	...	...	...	...	...	...	...	...	...	...	...	...	...	...	...	...	...	...	...	...	...	...	...
Tarbes **305** d.	...	...	...	...	...	...	...	...	...	...	...	...	...	1430	...	...	...	...	...	...	...	...	...	...
Hendaye **305** d.	...	...	...	...	1357	...	...	...	...	...	...	...	...	|	...	...	...	...	...	...	...	...	...	...
Bordeaux St Jean 302 d.	...	...	...	1613	1632	...	...	...	1643	1647	...	...	1708	1725	...	1733	...	...	...	1749	...	1803	...	1753
Libourne **302** d.	...	...	...	|	|	...	...	...	|	|	...	...	|	|	...	|	...	...	...	1822	...	1829	...	1829
Coutras **302** d.	...	...	...	|	|	...	...	...	|	|	...	...	|	|	...	|	...	...	...	|	...	|	...	1841
Angoulême d.	...	...	...	1714	1734	...	...	...	1745	1751	...	...	1812	|	...	1835	...	...	...	1904	...	1910	...	1929
La Rochelle d.	1540	...	...	|	|	1620	...	1645	|	|	...	1659	|	|	1730	|	...	...	1741	|	1754	|	1801	...
Niort d.	1629	...	...	|	|	1707	...	1728	|	|	...	1748	|	|	1818	|	...	...	1831	|	1850	|	1851	...
Poitiers a.	1714	...	...	1802	|	1758	...	1813	1830	1838	...	1837	1857	|	1910	1924	...	...	1937	1951	1945	1957	1947	...
Poitiers d.	1717	1735	1735	1805	|	...	1821	1821	1833	1841	...	1840	1904	|	1912	1927	1932	1941	1941	1954	...	2006	...	...
Futuroscope ⊖ d.	|	|	|	1815	|	...	|	|	1849	|	...	|	1915	|	|	|	1944	1952	1952	|	...	|	...	...
Châtellerault d.	|	1807	1801	|	|	...	1840	1840	|	|	...	|	|	|	1930	|	|	|	|	|	...	|	...	...
St Pierre-des-Corps **295** a.	1755	|	|	1851	|	...	|	1905	1925	|	...	1920	1947	|	|	2005	2018	|	|	2033	...	2044	...	...
Tours a.	*1808*	1858	1848	*1903*	|	...	|	*1915*	*1941*	|	...	*1930*	*1957*	|	2002	*2015*	*2035*	|	|	*2044*	...	*2055*	...	...
Massy TGV **295** a.	|	...	...	1943	|	...	|	|	2018	|	...	|	2042	|	...	|	2118	|	|	|	...	2137	...	...
Paris Austerlitz **296** a.	|	...	...	|	|	...	|	|	|	|	...	|	|	|	...	|	...	|	|	|	...	|	...	...
Paris Montparnasse 295 a.	1905	...	...	|	1945	...	2005	2005	|	2015	...	2020	|	2030	...	2105	...	2120	2120	2135	...	2150	...	...
Marne la Vallee - Chessy a.	...	...	...	2025	...	...	...	...	2057	...	...	...	2120	...	...	...	...	...	...	...	...	...	...	...
Charles de Gaulle ✈ a.	...	...	...	...	...	...	...	...	2112	...	...	...	...	...	...	...	...	...	...	...	...	...	...	...
Lille Europe **11** a.	...	...	...	...	...	...	...	...	2220	...	...	...	...	...	...	...	...	...	...	...	...	...	...	...

	Ⓐ	TGV 8568 Ⓑ h	TGV 8374 L	TGV 8570 ⑥ t	TGV 8382 ⑤ f	† △	①–④ m	TGV 5292 ⑥ t	TGV 5292 ⑤ f	†	TGV 8384 ⑦ e	TGV 8580 Ⓑ h	⚒	TGV 8584	TGV 8583		TGV 8494 ⑦ e	TGV 8496 ⑤ d	TGV 8586 ⑦ e	TGV 8590 ⑦ e		TGV 8386 ⑤ f	TGV 8390 ⑦ e	TGV 8498 ⑦ e
Toulouse **320** d.	...	1608	...	1631	...	...	...	...	...	...	...	1736	...	...	...	...	...	...	1825	...	...	...	...	...
Tarbes **305** d.	...	|	...	|	...	...	...	...	...	...	...	|	...	...	1650	...	...	...	|	...	...	...	...	...
Hendaye **305** d.	...	|	...	|	...	...	...	1616	...	...	...	|	...	1718	|	...	...	...	|	1815	...	...	...	...
Bordeaux St Jean 302 d.	1753	1823	...	1846	...	1831	...	1841	1841	...	...	1947	...	1951	1951	...	2017	2030	2041	2041	...	...	...	2119
Libourne **302** d.	1829	|	...	|	...	1909	...	|	|	...	...	|	...	|	|	...	2042	|	|	|	...	...	...	|
Coutras **302** d.	1853	|	...	|	...	1918	...	|	|	...	...	|	...	|	|	...	|	|	|	|	...	...	...	|
Angoulême d.	1943	|	...	|	...	2004	...	1945	1951	...	...	|	...	2053	2053	...	2123	2130	|	|	...	...	...	2219
La Rochelle d.	...	|	1819	|	1846	...	1833	|	|	1857	1922	|	1940	|	|	...	|	|	|	|	...	2041	2103	|
Niort d.	...	|	1908	|	1932	...	1922	|	|	1948	2007	|	2030	|	|	...	|	|	|	|	...	2129	2153	|
Poitiers a.	...	|	1955	|	2012	...	2018	2031	2037	2038	2045	|	2123	2138	2138	...	2214	2214	|	|	...	|	2236	2302
Poitiers d.	...	|	1958	|	2017	...	...	2038	2041	...	2049	|	...	2141	2141	...	2217	2217	|	|	...	|	2239	2305
Futuroscope ⊖ d.	...	|	2013	|	|	...	...	2050	|	...	|	|	...	|	|	...	|	|	|	|	...	|	|	|
Châtellerault d.	...	|	|	|	|	...	...	|	|	...	|	|	...	|	|	...	2241	|	|	|	...	|	|	|
St Pierre-des-Corps **295** a.	...	|	|	|	|	...	...	2124	2119	...	|	|	...	2219	2219	...	|	|	|	|	...	2249	2316	|
Tours a.	...	|	|	|	|	...	...	*2136*	*2132*	...	|	|	...	*2230*	*2230*	...	|	|	|	|	...	*2308*	*2326*	|
Massy TGV **295** a.	...	|	|	|	|	...	...	2217	2213	...	|	|	...	|	|	...	|	|	|	|	...	|	|	|
Paris Austerlitz **296** a.	...	|	|	|	|	...	...	|	|	...	|	|	...	|	|	...	|	|	|	|	...	|	|	|
Paris Montparnasse 295 a.	...	2130	2140	2205	2150	...	...	|	|	...	2220	2300s	...	2320s	2320s	...	0000	2345	2355	2355	...	2350	0015	0035
Marne la Vallee - Chessy a.	...	...	...	...	...	...	...	2254	2251	...	...	...	...	...	...	...	...	...	...	...	...	...	...	...
Charles de Gaulle ✈ a.	...	...	...	...	...	...	...	2309	2306	...	...	...	...	...	...	...	...	...	...	...	...	...	...	...
Lille Europe **11** a.	...	...	...	...	...	...	...	0011	0008	...	...	...	...	...	...	...	...	...	...	...	...	...	...	...

Engineering work – timings may vary (especially Toulouse arrival times); please enquire when reserving.
On May 13 - 16 many *TGV* journeys are replaced by 🚌 between Libourne and Bordeaux.

FOR NOTES SEE FOOT OF NEXT PAGE →

ANGOULÊME - SAINTES - ROYAN — 301

Some trains 2nd class

km		① g	Ⓐ ◇	Ⓐ	Ⓐ	Ⓐ	Ⓐ ▷	Ⓒ		△	Ⓐ	⊗	⚒ ▷		◇	⑤⑦ d	①–④ m		M	⑤ f	⚒	⑤⑥ u	†	①–④ m	⑤ f	Ⓐ
	Paris Austerlitz ◐ ... d.	...	...	...	...	...	...	...	...	...	...	...	...	...	...	...	...	...	...	...	...	...	...	...	...	...
0	**Angoulême** ... d.	...	0613	...	...	0721	0939	1017	...	...	1236	...	1437	...	1639	...	...	...	...	...	1750	1750	...	...	...	1907
49	Cognac ... d.	...	0702	...	...	0803	1017	1059	...	...	1315	...	1516	...	1719	...	...	...	...	...	1831	1831	...	...	...	1945
•77	Niort ... d.	0557	|	...	0655	|	|	|	...	1148	|	1323	|	...	|	1652	...	...	1720	1742	|	|	1827	1834	1844	|
75	**Saintes** ... a.	0657	0722	...	0758	0822	1035	1117	...	1247	1333	1415	1534	...	1739	1746	...	...	1820	1841	1850	1850	1936	1946	1957	2004
75	**Saintes** ... d.	...	...	0733	0800	...	1043	1122	...	1303	...	1417	1541	...	...	1748	1752	...	1838	...	...	1902	...	...	...	2019
111	**Royan** ... a.	...	...	0802	0831	...	1112	1155	...	1332	...	1446	1614	...	...	1817	1821	...	1910	...	...	1932	...	...	...	2048

	⑥ t	⑤⑦ d	N		†	⑤ f	⑤ u	†	Ⓐ	
Paris Austerlitz ◐ ... d.	...	...	...	...	...	...	...	...	...	...
Angoulême ... d.	1905	2016	2024	...	...	...	2127	2223	2224	...
Cognac ... d.	1944	2058	2101	...	...	...	2204	2304	2302	...
Niort ... d.	|	|	|	...	2029	2054	|	|	|	...
Saintes ... a.	2002	2116	2120	...	2126	2150	2223	2323	2321	...
Saintes ... d.	...	...	2127	...	2137	2154	2230	2328	2333	...
Royan ... a.	...	...	2156	...	2207	2223	2259	2357	0003	...

	Ⓐ	Ⓐ	Ⓐ	① §g	②–⑥ ▽	R	Ⓐ ◇	⑥ t	⚒		Ⓐ	Ⓒ
Royan ... d.	...	...	0601	0628	0628	0656	...	0708	0814	...	...	...
Saintes ... a.	...	...	0629	0657	0657	0724	...	0736	0842	...	...	...
Saintes ... d.	0542	0615	0640	0711	0713	...	0743	0743	...	...	0957	0959
Niort ... a.	|	0730	|	0812	0826	...	|	|	...	...	|	|
Cognac ... d.	0600	...	0701	...	...	...	0802	0802	...	...	1018	1017
Angoulême ... a.	0641	...	0746	...	...	...	0839	0839	...	...	1055	1054
Paris Austerlitz ◐ a.	...	...	...	...	...	...	...	...	...	...	...	...

	⊕		Ⓐ	▷		Ⓐ ⊗		①–④ m	⑥ t	⑤⑦ d	⑤	†		☆	†	⑤ f	M	⑤ f		①–④ m	⑤ f		⑤⑦ d	†	†	
Royan ... d.	0956	...	...	1222	...	1338	...	...	1555	1555	...	...	...	1706	1822	1822	...	...	...	1852	...	...	1934	2106	...	...
Saintes ... a.	1024	...	...	1250	...	1407	...	...	1623	1624	...	...	...	1734	1851	1850	...	...	...	1920	...	...	2002	2134	...	...
Saintes ... d.	1036	...	1233	...	1345	1418	...	1614	1634	1626	1637	1637	...	1747	1853	...	1900	1913	...	1925	1925	...	2013	2158	2200	...
Niort ... a.	1130	...	|	...	|	1510	...	|	|	1722	|	|	...	|	1958	...	2005	2014	...	|	|	...	|	|	2258	...
Cognac ... d.	...	...	1251	...	1404	...	...	1632	1654	...	1655	1655	...	1809	...	...	...	...	...	1946	1946	...	2032	2218	...	...
Angoulême ... a.	...	...	1335	...	1440	...	...	1714	1737	...	1737	1737	...	1850	...	...	...	...	...	2023	2023	...	2113	2259	...	...
Paris Austerlitz ◐ ... a.	...	...	...	...	...	...	...	...	...	...	...	...	...	...	...	...	...	...	...	...	...	...	...	...	...	...

M – ①②③④⑥ (also May 14; not Dec. 24, 31, Apr. 5, May 1, 8, 12, 13, 24).
N – ①②③④⑥ (not Dec. 24, 31, Apr. 5, May 1, 8, 12, 13, 24).
R – ②–⑤ (not Dec. 25, Jan. 1, Apr. 6, May 25).
d – Also Dec. 24, 31, Apr. 5, May 12, 13, 24; not May 14.
f – Also Dec. 24, 31, May 12; not Dec. 25, Jan. 1.
g – Also Apr. 6, May 25; not Apr. 5, May 24.
m – Not Dec. 24, 31, Apr. 5, May 12, 13, 24.
t – Not May 1, 8.
u – Also Dec. 24, 31; not Dec. 25, Jan. 1.
◐ – See Table **300** for *TGV* connections at Niort or Angoulême.
◇ – To/from La Rochelle (Table **292**).
△ – Subject to alteration Niort - Saintes on Ⓐ Mar. 15 - Apr. 9 and Saintes - Royan on Mar. 1 - 4, 8 - 11.
▽ – Subject to alteration.
▷ – Subject to alteration on Mar. 1 - 4, 8 - 11.
⊕ – Subject to alteration Saintes - Niort on Mar. 19, 26, Apr. 2, 9.
⊗ – Subject to alteration Royan - Saintes and v.v. on Mar. 1 - 4, 8 - 11; subject to alteration Saintes - Niort and v.v. on ①–④ Mar. 15 - Apr. 8.
☆ – Change at Saintes on ①–④ **m**.
§ – To Poitiers (arrive 0859).
• – Distance from Saintes.

BORDEAUX - PÉRIGUEUX - BRIVE and LIMOGES — 302

km		Ⓐ	⚒	4490 ⑤ ◇v	R	⑥	Ⓐ	4492 ⑥ ⊖	4480 B	4484 C	4486 D	Ⓐ b	⑥ t		①–④ m	⑤ f	†	Ⓐ	⑥	Ⓑ h	Ⓑ ⊡	Ⓑ h	⚒	Ⓑ	⑤⑦ f	†
0	**Bordeaux 300** ... d.	0612	0645	0734	0734	...	0813	0908	1047	1047	1047	1226	1226	1359	1558	1558	1621	1658	1658	1738	1807	...	1856	2009	2009	2155
37	Libourne **300** ... d.	0634	0716	0800	0800	...	|	|	1113	1113	1113	1252	1252	1425	|	1623	1646	1726	1726	1809	1834	...	1929	2036	2036	2220
53	Coutras **300** ... d.	0645	0726	0812	0814	...	|	|	1123	1123	1123	1302	1304	1436	|	1633	|	1735	1735	1821	|	...	1943	2046	2046	2230
93	Mussidan ... d.	0711	0752	0840	0837	...	|	|	1143	1143	1143	1331	1333	1504	|	1700	1713	1803	1803	1850	1905	...	2010	2112	2112	2253
129	Périgueux ... a.	0735	0822	0902	0858	...	0920	1022	1202	1203	1203	1352	1358	1528	1707	1720	1735	1824	1824	1911	1925	...	2032	2133	2133	2314
129	Périgueux **308** ... d.	*0740*	...	0904	0900	0925	0925	1024	1208	1208	...	...	...	...	1715	...	1740	1834	*1840*	...	1932	1942	...	...	2141	...
203	**Brive la Gaillarde** ... a.	|	...	0958	0953	|	|	1109	|	|	...	...	...	...	|	...	|	|	|	...	|	2035	...	...	|	...
228	**Limoges 308** ... a.	*0839*	...	...	...	1024	1024	...	1306	1306	...	...	...	...	1820	...	1855	2000	*1951*	...	2048	...	...	...	2253	...
639	*Lyon Part Dieu* **327** .. a.	...	...	...	...	...	...	...	1816	...	...	...	...	...	...	...	...	...	...	...	...	...	...	...	...	...
643	*Lyon Perrache* **327** .. a.	...	...	...	...	...	...	...	1829	...	...	...	...	...	...	...	...	...	...	...	...	...	...	...	...	...

	⚒	Ⓐ	Ⓐ	⚒	Ⓐ	Ⓒ		⚒	⑥ t	Ⓑ	⑤ f		Ⓑ h	①–④ m	§	⑤ f		Ⓐ	4590 ⑤ ◇v	4595 ⑦ ⊖d	⑥ t	4580 G	Ⓐ	†	
Lyon Perrache **327** ... d.	...	...	...	...	...	...	...	...	...	...	...	...	...	...	...	...	...	...	...	...	...	1251	...	...	...
Lyon Part Dieu **327** ... d.	...	...	...	...	...	...	...	...	...	...	...	...	...	...	...	...	...	...	...	...	...	1305	...	...	...
Limoges 308 ... d.	...	...	0611	...	...	0718	...	1021**r**	*1110***r**	*1110***r**	...	1455	...	1705	1705	...	...	1735	...	...	...	1809	1835	...	2200
Brive la Gaillarde ... d.	...	...	|	...	...	|	0730	|	|	|	...	|	*1557***c**	|	|	*1708*	...	|	1801	1801	1803	|	|	...	|
Périgueux **308** ... a.	...	...	0722	...	...	0825	0821	1119**r**	*1206***r**	*1206***r**	...	1559	*1647***c**	1815	1815	*1806*	...	1852	1856	1855	1858	1906	2005	...	2302
Périgueux ... d.	0606	0652	0734	0734	0800	...	0833	1125	1215	1218	1437	1606	1658	1821	...	1820	1836	...	1859	1858	...	1912	...	2031	...
Mussidan ... d.	0629	0714	0755	0755	|	...	0854	1146	1240	1240	1458	1627	1723	|	...	1841	1905	...	|	|	...	1931	...	2053	...
Coutras **300** ... d.	0701	0742	0822	0822	|	...	0921	1210	1310	1310	1522	1657	1756	|	...	1905	1936	...	|	|	...	1956	...	2117	...
Libourne **300** ... d.	0716	0754	0833	0833	|	...	0931	1222	1320	1320	1532	1707	1808	|	...	1916	1947	...	1952	1951	...	2009	...	2128	...
Bordeaux St Jean 300 . a.	0742	0821	0859	0859	0915	...	0957	1257	1347	1347	1558	1734	1837	1930	...	1942	2013	...	2018	2017	...	2037	...	2154	...

ADDITIONAL TRAINS PÉRIGUEUX - BRIVE / LIMOGES

	Ⓐ	Ⓐ		⚒			†		⑤ f	Ⓑ ⊙	Ⓒ	⑤⑥ u
Périgueux ... d.	0629	0735	0740	1222	1319	1428	1454	1602	1652	1657	1840	1846
Brive la G. ... a.	0726	0831	|	1313	|	|	1545	|	|	1755	|	1950
Limoges ... a.	...	...	0839	...	1430	1535	...	1709	1801	...	1951	...

	Ⓐ	Ⓐ		⚒	①–④ m	①–④ m	⑤ f	Ⓑ	†	Ⓐ	
Limoges ... d.	...	...	1248	...	...	...	...	2035	...	2304	...
Brive la G. ... d.	0620	1045	|	1349	1619	1822	2037	|	2115	|	...
Périgueux ... a.	0726	1136	1355	1451	1716	1923	2127	2136	2205	2359	...

B – Dec. 13 - Jan. 17; ⑤–⑦ Jan. 22 - Feb. 28; daily Mar. 5 - Apr. 25.
C – ① Jan. 18 - Feb. 15; ①–④ Feb. 22 - Mar. 4.
D – ①–⑤ Apr. 26 - May 3 (also May 10, 17, 25, 31).
G – Dec. 13 - Jan. 17; ⑤–⑦ Jan. 22 - Feb. 28; daily Mar. 5 - Apr. 11, also Apr. 17, 18, 24, 25.
R – ①②③④⑥ from Jan. 4.
b – Not Apr. 12, May 20, 31.
c – † only.
d – Also Apr. 5, May 24; not Apr. 4, May 23.
f – Also Dec. 24, 31, May 12; not Dec. 25, Jan. 1.
h – Also May 1, 8.
m – Not Dec. 24, 31, Apr. 5, May 12, 13, 24.
r – Subject to alteration Mar. 1 - 19, Apr. 12 - June 18.
t – Not May 1, 8.
u – Also Dec. 24, 31, May 12; not Dec. 25, Jan. 1, May 1, 8, 14.
v – Also Dec. 21 - 24, 28 - 31; not Dec. 25, Jan. 1.
⊖ – To/from Clermont Ferrand (Table **326**).
◇ – To/from Ussel (Table **326**).
⊡ – On ⑤ depart Périgueux 1946.
⊙ – On ①–④ **m** depart 1802, arrive 1908.
§ – Through train to Bordeaux on ⑤ (next column).

Engineering Work

Limoges - Périgueux is subject to alteration Apr. 27 - June 4

← NOTES FOR TABLE 300 (previous page) — 300

← NOTES FOR TABLE 300 (previous page)

L – ①②③④⑥ (also Dec. 25, Jan. 1; not Dec. 24, 31, Apr. 5, May 12, 24).
S – June 7 - Sept. 26. On Ⓒ depart Hendaye 0920, Bordeaux 1151.
b – Also May 12; not Dec. 25, Jan. 1.
c – Lille **Flandres**.
d – Also Dec. 24, May 12; not Dec. 25, Jan. 1.
e – Also Apr. 5, May 24.
f – Also Dec. 24, 31, May 12; not Dec. 25, Jan. 1.
g – Also Apr. 6, May 25; not Apr. 5, May 24.
h – Not Dec. 25, Jan. 1, May 13.
k – Not Hendaye - Bordeaux on Feb. 8 - Mar. 5.
m – Not Dec. 24, 31, Apr. 5, May 12, 13, 24.
n – Not Apr. 5, May 24.
p – Not May 1, 8.
q – Not Dec. 24, Apr. 5, May 24.
r – ⑥⑦ (daily Dec. 25 - Jan. 3, Jan. 9 - Feb. 7, also Apr. 5, May 13, 14).
s – Arrive 20 mins later on Dec. 14 - 17, arrive 15 mins later on ①–④ Jan. 11 - 21.
t – Also Dec. 25, Jan. 1, May 13.
u – Also Dec. 25, Jan. 1, Apr. 6, May 13, 25; not Apr. 5, May 24.
v – 1417 on Ⓐ Mar. 29 - May 20 (not May 12); 1439 on Ⓒ Mar. 27 - May 16 (also Mar. 26, May 12).
w – Also Dec. 24, 31, Apr. 5, May 12, 13, 24.
x – ⑦ (also Apr. 5, May 24). Depart 0810 on Feb. 21, Mar. 28.
y – Not Dec. 31, May 14.
z – Not on ①–⑤ Feb. 8 - Mar. 5.
TGV – Ⓡ, supplement payable, 🍸.
♥ – To Lyon (Table **335**).
♣ – (12) Bordeaux - Brussels (Table **11**); (12) Bordeaux - Charles de Gaulle ✈ (**5279**) - Lille Flandres.
☆ – To Strasbourg (Table **391**).
⊖ – Not for journeys to/from Poitiers or Châtellerault.
△ – On Dec. 25, Jan. 1, May 1, 8 depart Bordeaux 1822.
⊕ – Depart Toulouse 0840 Jan. 4 - Mar. 26. Will not run Toulouse - Bordeaux on Ⓐ Mar. 29 - May 7.
◇ – Also calls at Vendôme-Villers TGV station, depart 1922.
§ – Train number **8442** on ⑤.
* – Subject to alteration from Feb. 6.

305 BORDEAUX - TARBES and IRÚN

km	All *TGV* convey 🍷	Ⓐ	Ⓐ	Ⓐ	Ⓐ	⑤ q	Ⓒ		†	4730 Ⓡ U	4778 4779 Ⓡ ♥	⊙		*TGV* 8505 ⊕	Ⓐ	*TGV* 8507 ①–⑥ n	Ⓐ	*TGV* 5200 ⑥ t	⑥ p	Ⓐ	Ⓐ		*TGV* 8515 ⊗	*TGV* 8516 ⊗
	Lille Europe **11** d.	...	...	...	...	...	...	...	...	...	...	...	...	...	...	...	...	0558	...	...	...	...	...	...
	Charles de Gaulle ✈ d.	...	...	...	...	...	...	...	...	...	...	...	...	...	...	...	...	0739	...	...	...	...	...	...
	Paris M'parnasse **300** d.	...	...	...	...	...	...	...	...	...	...	...	...	0715	...	0745	...	|	...	...	...	...	1010	1010
	Paris Austerlitz **300** d.	...	...	...	...	...	...	...	...	...	...	...	...	|	...	|	...	|	...	...	...	...	|	|
0	**Bordeaux St Jean** d.	...	...	0627	0627	0627	0727	...	...	0825	...	...	...	1030	...	1116	...	1205	...	1217	1217	...	1318	1318
109	Morcenx d.	...	...	0727	0727	0727	0823	...	...	|	...	...	...	|	...	|	...	|	...	1313	1313	...	|	|
148	Dax a.	...	...	0747	0747	0747	0842	...	...	0939	...	...	...	1137	...	|	...	1310	...	1333	1333	...	1427	1427
148	Dax d.	0615r	0650	0752	0800	0800	0847	0902	0902	0942	0952	1055	...	1140	1200	|	1245	1313	1325	1338	1358	...	1430	1434
179	Puyoô **325** d.	|	|	|	0818	0818	|	0921	0921	|	|	|	...	|	1217	|	|	|	|	|	1419	...	|	|
193	Orthez **325** d.	|	|	|	0829	0829	|	0932	0932	|	|	|	...	|	1228	|	|	|	|	|	1430	...	|	1503
233	Pau **325** d.	|	|	|	0853	0854	|	0959	1004	|	|	|	...	|	1253	1312	|	|	|	|	1454	...	|	1528
272	Lourdes **325** d.	|	|	|	...	0921	|	...	1032	|	|	|	...	|	...	1338	|	|	|	|	...	...	|	1555
293	**Tarbes 325** a.	|	|	|	...	0935	|	...	1047	|	|	|	...	|	...	1353	|	|	|	|	...	...	|	1609
199	**Bayonne 325** d.	0706	0739	0833	...	...	0925	...	...	1020	1032	1146	...	1217	...	...	1336	1349	1416	1416	...	...	1506	...
209	Biarritz **325** d.	0716	0749	0843	...	...	0935	...	...	1032	1044	1156	...	1232	...	...	1346	1401	1426	1426	...	...	1518	...
222	St Jean de Luz **325** d.	0728	0801	0856	...	...	0948	...	...	1045	1056	1208	...	1246	...	...	1358	1414	1439	1439	...	...	1532	...
235	Hendaye **325** a.	0739	0813	0907	...	...	1000	...	...	1054	1105	1219	...	1256	...	...	1409	1424	1450	1450	...	...	1541	...
237	**Irún 325** a.	...	...	...	...	...	...	...	...	1104	1115	...	...	1304	...	...	...	1433	...	...	...	...	1549	...

	Ⓐ ⊖	Ⓐ	*TGV* 8525 ①–⑥ n	Ⓐ	Ⓐ	⑤–⑦ v	⑤–⑦ v		⚒	*TGV* 8539	Ⓐ	*TGV* 5221 ⑦ e	⊡		4678 4679 Ⓡ ♣	*TGV* 8547 ⑦ e	*TGV* 8543	*TGV* 8551 ①–④ m	*TGV* 8545 ⑤ f		*TGV* 5222 ⑤⑥ w	*TGV* 8557	Ⓑ x	
Lille Europe **11** d.	...	...	...	...	...	...	...	...	...	...	...	1238z	...	...	...	...	...	...	...	...	1540	...	...	...
Charles de Gaulle ✈ d.	...	...	...	...	...	...	...	...	...	...	...	1337	...	...	...	...	...	...	...	...	1637	...	...	...
Paris M'parnasse **300** d.	...	...	1210	...	...	...	...	...	...	1440	...	|	...	...	...	1515	1550	1610	1620	...	|	1745	...	...
Paris Austerlitz **300** d.	...	...	|	...	...	...	...	...	...	|	...	|	...	...	...	|	|	|	|	...	|	|	...	...
Bordeaux St Jean d.	1427	...	1527	...	...	1637	...	...	...	1743	1747	1813	1827	...	...	1900	1903	1926	1926	...	2056	2102	...	...
Morcenx d.	1522	...	|	...	...	1732	...	...	...	|	1853	|	1923	...	...	|	|	|	|	...	|	|	...	...
Dax a.	1542	...	1632	...	...	1751	...	...	...	1858	1911	1917	1943	...	...	2007	2012	2036	2033	...	2203	2210	...	...
Dax d.	1547	1555	1635	1645	1705	1756	1805	...	1825	1901	1916	1920	1948	...	1958	2010	2015	2039	2036	...	2206	2213	2215	...
Puyoô **325** d.	|	1614	|	|	|	|	1823	...	|	|	|	|	2007	...	|	|	|	|	|	...	|	|	|	...
Orthez **325** d.	|	1625	|	|	|	|	1833	...	|	|	|	|	2018	...	2030	2042	|	2109	2106	...	|	2243	|	...
Pau **325** d.	|	1650	|	|	|	|	1858	...	|	1951	|	|	2045	...	2100	2124	|	2133	2131	...	|	2307	|	...
Lourdes **325** d.	|	...	|	|	|	|	...	...	|	2024	|	|	2112	...	2134	2151	|	2200	2158	...	|	2334	|	...
Tarbes 325 a.	|	...	|	|	|	|	...	...	|	2039	|	|	2128	...	2149	2206	|	2214	2213	...	|	2349	|	...
Bayonne 325 d.	1626	...	1710	1736	1753	1835	...	...	1914	...	1954	1956	...	...	...	...	2050	...	...	...	2249	...	2256	...
Biarritz **325** d.	1637	...	1723	1746	1803	1845	...	...	1924	...	2005	2009	...	...	...	...	2103	...	...	...	2301	...	2306	...
St Jean de Luz **325** d.	1650	...	1736	1758	1816	1858	...	...	1937	...	2018	2022	...	...	...	...	2116	...	...	...	2314	...	2319	...
Hendaye **325** a.	1702	...	1745	1809	1828	1910	...	...	1949	...	2030	2031	...	...	...	...	2125	...	...	...	2324	...	2331	...
Irún 325 a.	...	...	...	...	...	...	...	...	...	...	...	2041	...	...	...	...	2136	...	...	...	...	...	...	...

	TGV 8565 Ⓑ h	Ⓒ ...	*TGV* 8577 ⑤ f	⑤ q	*TGV* 8589 ⑤⑦ y		4053 Ⓡ W	4054 Ⓡ W	
Lille Europe **11** d.	...	...	...	...	...	...	...	...	...
Charles de Gaulle ✈ d.	...	...	...	...	...	...	...	...	...
Paris M'parnasse **300** d.	1825	...	1925	...	2250	...	...	...	...
Paris Austerlitz **300** d.	|	...	|	...	|	...	2310	2310	...
Bordeaux St Jean d.	2132	2227	2237	...	|	...	|	|	...
Morcenx d.	|	2323	|	...	|	...	0532	0532	...
Dax a.	|	2343	2343	...	0507	...	0554	0554	...
Dax d.	|	2348	2346	2350	0510	...	0606	0626	...
Puyoô **325** d.	|	|	|	0008	|	...	|	|	...
Orthez **325** d.	|	|	|	0019	0546	...	|	0655	...
Pau **325** d.	|	|	|	0044	0620	...	|	0722	...
Lourdes **325** d.	|	|	|	0112	0648	...	|	0749	...
Tarbes 325 a.	|	|	|	0127	0703	...	|	0806	...
Bayonne 325 d.	2312	0026	0020	...	...	...	0643	...	...
Biarritz **325** d.	2324	0036	0032	...	...	...	0657	...	...
St Jean de Luz **325** d.	2336	0049	0045	...	...	...	0713	...	...
Hendaye **325** a.	2345	0101	0054	...	...	...	0725	...	...
Irún 325 a.	...	...	...	...	...	...	0736	...	...

	① g	②–⑤ H	⑥	① g	Ⓐ	*TGV* 5268 ①⑥ u		*TGV* 8523 Ⓐ	Ⓐ
Hendaye 325 d.	0502	0519	...	...	...	0520	...	...	...
St Jean de Luz **325** d.	0516	0533	...	...	...	0532	...	...	...
Biarritz **325** d.	0528	0545	...	...	...	0546	...	...	...
Bayonne 325 d.	0540	0558	...	...	...	0557	...	...	0634
Tarbes 325 d.	|	|	0444	0449	...	|	...	0530	|
Lourdes **325** d.	|	|	0500	0505	...	|	...	0548	|
Pau **325** d.	|	|	0530	0535	0535	|	...	0615	|
Orthez **325** d.	|	|	0557	0601	0601	|	...	0639	|
Puyoô **325** d.	|	|	0608	0612	0612	|	...	|	|
Dax a.	0617	0635	0630	0630	0630	0629	...	0705	0720
Dax d.	0640	0640	0640	...	...	0632	...	0708	...
Morcenx d.	0700	0700	0700	...	...	|	...	|	...
Bordeaux St Jean a.	0806	0806	0806	...	...	0743	...	0822	...
Paris Austerlitz **300** a.	...	...	...	...	...	|	...	|	...
Paris Montparnasse a.	...	...	...	...	...	|	...	1145	...
Charles de Gaulle ✈ a.	...	...	...	...	...	1209	...	...	...
Lille Europe **11** a.	...	...	...	...	...	1306	...	...	...

	Ⓐ	Ⓐ	⚒	*TGV* 8527	*TGV* 8524	4778 4779 Ⓡ ♥	*TGV* 5276 ⑦ △e	*TGV* 8530 Ⓐ S	Ⓐ		*TGV* 8530 Ⓒ S	Ⓐ ▷	*TGV* 8534 b		*TGV* 8542 Ⓐ b	*TGV* 8541 E	◇	Ⓐ ◇	*TGV* 8558	Ⓐ ▽	⑤⑦ v	*TGV* 8563	†	Ⓑ
Hendaye 325 d.	...	0632	0725	...	0748	...	0834	0847	0905	...	0920	...	1026	...	1113	...	1235	1258	1357	...	...	...	...	1557
St Jean de Luz **325** d.	...	0646	0738	...	0807	...	0848	0902	0918	...	0935	...	1039	...	1132	...	1248	1312	1416	...	...	...	...	1611
Biarritz **325** d.	...	0658	0751	...	0820	...	0900	0915	0931	...	0949	...	1052	...	1145	...	1301	1325	1430	...	...	...	...	1624
Bayonne 325 d.	...	0710	0804	...	0832	...	0912	0928	0943	...	1002	...	1103	...	1157	...	1313	1338	1443	...	1530	...	...	1636
Tarbes 325 d.	...	|	|	0726	|	0746	|	|	|	0846	|	...	|	...	|	1052	|	|	|	...	|	1430	1524	|
Lourdes **325** d.	...	|	|	0746	|	0803	|	|	|	0902	|	...	|	...	|	1111	|	|	|	...	|	1454	1540	|
Pau **325** d.	0647	|	|	0813	|	0833	|	|	|	0930	|	1026	|	...	|	1138	|	|	|	1432	|	1521	1609	|
Orthez **325** d.	0712	|	|	0838	|	0859	|	|	|	0954	|	1050	|	...	|	|	|	|	|	1457	|	|	1636	|
Puyoô **325** d.	0722	|	|	|	|	|	|	|	|	1005	|	1101	|	...	|	|	|	|	|	1508	|	|	1647	|
Dax a.	0739	0744	0839	0904	0909	0925	0944	1002	1016	1021	1035	1117	1134	...	1229	1234	1402	1414	1517	1527	1607	1608	1704	1712
Dax d.	0749	0749	...	0914	0914	...	0947	1005	...	1026	1038	1122	1137	...	1239	1239	...	1416	1520	1532	...	1611	1709	1714
Morcenx d.	0809	0809	...	|	|	...	|	|	...	1046	|	1142	|	...	|	|	...	1437	|	1552	...	|	1730	1734
Bordeaux St Jean a.	0905	0905	...	1021	1021	...	1052	1128	...	1143	1146	1236	1246	...	1350	1350	...	1535	1627	1646	...	1720	1826	1833
Paris Austerlitz **300** a.	...	...	...	|	|	...	|	|	...	...	|	...	|	...	|	|	...	...	|	...	...	|	...	...
Paris M'parnasse **300** a.	...	...	...	1345	1345	...	|	1500	...	...	1500	...	1600	...	1720	1720	...	...	1945	...	...	2030	...	...
Charles de Gaulle ✈ a.	...	...	...	...	...	...	1521	...	...	...	...	...	...	...	...	...	...	...	...	...	...	...	...	...
Lille Europe **11** a.	...	...	...	...	...	...	1615	...	...	...	...	...	...	...	...	...	...	...	...	...	...	...	...	...

	TGV 5292 ⑥ c	Ⓐ	①–④ m	⑤⑦ v	*TGV* 8584	*TGV* 8583	†	⚒		4678 4679 Ⓡ ♣	*TGV* 8590 ⑦ e	Ⓐ	①–④ a	⑤⑥	⚒	4630 Ⓡ T	†	†		*TGV* 8595 ⑦ d		4052 Ⓡ Y	4051 Ⓡ Z	*TGV* 8595 ⑤ k
Hendaye 325 d.	1616	...	1635	1659	1718	...	...	1735	...	1807	1815	1832	...	...	1858	1911	...	1858	...	...	...	2218	...	...
St Jean de Luz **325** d.	1630	...	1648	1713	1736	...	...	1748	...	1820	1828	1846	...	...	1912	1923	...	1912	...	...	...	2236	...	...
Biarritz **325** d.	1643	...	1702	1725	1748	...	...	1800	...	1850	1840	1858	...	...	1924	1937	...	1924	...	...	...	2253	...	...
Bayonne 325 d.	1655	...	1715	1737	1759	...	...	1811	...	1902	1852	1910	...	...	1937	1950	...	1937	...	...	...	2306	...	...
Tarbes 325 d.	|	...	|	|	|	1650	...	|	...	|	|	|	...	1830	|	|	1830	|	...	2115	...	|	2202	2243
Lourdes **325** d.	|	...	|	|	|	1710	...	|	...	|	|	|	...	1845	|	|	1845	|	...	2134	...	|	2219	2302
Pau **325** d.	|	1700	|	|	|	1737	1745	|	...	|	|	|	1912	1915	|	|	1915	|	...	2209	...	|	2247	2330
Orthez **325** d.	|	1728	|	|	|	1803	1813	|	...	|	|	|	1937	1942	|	|	1942	|	...	2239	...	|	2314	2356
Puyoô **325** d.	|	1738	|	|	|	|	1823	|	...	|	|	|	1948	1952	|	|	1952	|	...	|	...	|	|	|
Dax a.	1727	1756	1800	1819	1834	1829	1841	1859	...	1938	|	1957	2013	2013	2013	2025	2010	2013	...	2313	...	2339	2344	0022
Dax d.	1730	1801	...	1821	1839	1839	1843	...	...	...	|	...	2018	2018	2018	2027	...	2033	...	2316	...	0005	0005	0025
Morcenx d.	|	1823	...	1844	|	|	1904	...	...	...	|	...	2036	2036	2036	|	...	2053	...	|	...	0032	0032	|
Bordeaux St Jean a.	1837	1922	...	1943	1947	1947	1959	...	...	...	2036	...	2135	2135	2135	2139	...	2157	...	|	...	|	|	|
Paris Austerlitz **300** a.	|	...	...	...	|	|	...	...	...	...	|	...	...	...	...	...	...	...	...	|	...	0711	0711	|
Paris M'parnasse **300** a.	|	...	...	...	2320s	2320s	...	...	...	...	2355	...	...	...	...	...	...	...	...	0555	...	...	...	0715
Charles de Gaulle ✈ a.	2309	...	...	...	...	...	...	...	...	...	...	...	...	...	...	...	...	...	...	...	...	...	...	...
Lille Europe **11** a.	0011	...	...	...	...	...	...	...	...	...	...	...	...	...	...	...	...	...	...	...	...	...	...	...

BORDEAUX - TARBES and IRÚN 305

E – ⑥⑦ (daily Dec. 25 - Jan. 3, Jan. 9 - Feb. 7, also Apr. 5, May 13, 14).
H – Not Dec. 25, Jan. 1, Apr. 6, May 13, 25.
S – June 7 - Sept. 26.
T – ⑤⑦ (daily Dec. 18 - 23, 25 - 30, Jan. 2, Feb. 8 - Mar. 7, Apr. 2 - May 2), also May 12, 24; not May 14, 23. 🛏 2 cl. and (2) (reclining) Hendaye - Bordeaux - Nice.
U – Runs from Nice on ⑤ (also Dec. 13, 19, 20, 26 - 30, Jan. 2, 3, Feb. 8 - 13, 15 - 21, 27, 28, Mar. 6, 7, 14, 21, 28, ⑥⑦ Apr. 3 - May 9, also May 16, 24, 30, June 6; not May 14). 🛏 2 cl. and (2) (reclining) Nice - Bordeaux - Irún.
W – *CORAIL LUNÉA* – 🛏 1, 2 cl. and (2) (reclining). Subject to alteration on Mar. 27, Apr. 10, 17, 24, May 22, 23, 29 (train **4063** Paris d. 2055). Not Dec. 24, 31 Paris - Tarbes.
Y – *CORAIL LUNÉA* – 🛏 1, 2 cl. and (2) (reclining). Not Dec. 24, 31. On Jan. 16 arrive Paris 0731. On Feb. 6 depart Hendaye 1939, arrive Paris 0750 (train **4056**). On Mar. 27 depart Hendaye 1939, arrive Paris 0923; on Apr. 10, 17, 24, May 22, 23, 29, June 5 depart Hendaye 1939, arrive Paris 0808 (train **4066**). Subject to alteration on May 8, 12 - 15, June 12.
Z – *CORAIL LUNÉA* – 🛏 1, 2 cl. and (2) (reclining). Not Dec. 24, 31. On Apr. 10, 17, 24, May 22, 23, 29, June 5 depart Tarbes 1918, arrive Paris 0808 (train **4061**).

a – Not Apr. 5, May 13, 24.
b – Not on ①–⑤ Feb. 8 - Mar. 5.
c – Also Dec. 25, Jan. 1, May 8, 13.
d – Also Dec. 24, Apr. 5; not Mar. 28, Apr. 11, 18, 25, May 23, 30, June 6.
e – Also Apr. 5, May 24.
f – Also Dec. 24, 31, May 12; not Dec. 25, Jan. 1.
g – Also Apr. 6, May 25; not Apr. 5, May 24.
h – Not Dec. 25, Jan. 1, May 13.
k – Not Dec. 25, Jan. 1, May 14.
m – Not Dec. 24, 31, Apr. 5, May 12, 13, 24.
n – Not Apr. 5, May 24.
p – Not May 1, 8.
q – Also Dec. 24, 31, May 12; not Dec. 25, Jan. 1, May 14.
r – Not Jan. 4 - Feb. 5.
s – Arrive 20 mins later on Dec. 14 - 17; arrive 15 mins later on ①–④ Jan. 11 - 21.
t – Also Dec. 25, Jan. 1, May 13.
u – Also Dec. 25, Jan. 1, Apr. 6, May 13, 25; not Apr. 5, May 24.
v – Also Dec. 24, 31, Apr. 5, May 12, 13, 24; not May 14.
w – Also Dec. 24, 31, May 12, 13.
x – Also May 1, 8.
y – Also Dec. 31, Apr. 5, May 12; not Dec. 25, Jan. 1, Mar. 28, Apr. 11, 18, 24, May 23, 30, June 6.
z – Lille Flandres.

TGV – Ⓡ, supplement payable, 🍸.

♥ – *CORAIL LUNÉA* – for days of running see Table **325**. 🛏 1, 2 cl. and (2) (reclining) Genève - Bayonne - Irún.
♣ – *CORAIL LUNÉA* – for days of running see Table **325**. 🛏 1, 2 cl. and (2) (reclining) Hendaye - Genève.
◇ – Not on ①–⑤ Feb. 8 - Mar. 5.
△ – Runs up to 25 minutes earlier on Feb. 21, Mar. 28.
▷ – Will not run Dax - Bordeaux on ①–⑤ Feb. 8 - Mar. 5.
▽ – Subject to alteration Pau - Dax on ①–⑤ Feb. 8 - 19.
⊡ – Depart Bordeaux 1824 on ⑥ Mar. 13 - Apr. 24.
⊖ – Depart Bordeaux 1427 to Mar. 5 / from May 10.
⊕ – Depart Paris 0700 on Ⓐ Jan. 4 - Feb. 2, Feb. 15 - 19; 0710 on Feb. 20, 22 - 26, Mar. 27.
⊗ – Depart Paris 0945 on Jan. 12 - 14.
⊙ – Not on ①–⑤ Jan. 11 - Feb. 5.

Note: where a change of train is shown at Dax, certain trains may have a through car to / from Bordeaux. Check before boarding.

*On May 13 - 16 many TGV journeys are replaced by 🚌 between Libourne and Bordeaux (Libourne is 37km north of Bordeaux, Table **300**).*

BORDEAUX - ARCACHON 306

Local services

	⚒	Ⓐ	⚒§	Ⓐ‡	§	△			Ⓐ				Ⓐ		Ⓐ	Ⓐ		Ⓐ		Ⓐ			Ⓑ	⑤⑦r	⑥t
Bordeaux St Jean ......d.	0641	0711	0741	0811	0841	1041	1141	1241	1322	1341	1441	1541	1611	1641	1711	1731	1751	1811	1841	1911	1941	2041	2141	2241	0001
Facture Biganos..........d.	0711	0741	0811	0841	0911	1111	1211	1311	1356	1411	1511	1611	1641	1711	1741	1806	1821	1841	1911	1941	2011	2111	2211	2311	0032
Arcachon .... ⊖ a.	0733	0803	0833	0903	0933	1133	1233	1333	1416	1433	1533	1633	1703	1733	1803	1827	1843	1903	1933	2003	2033	2133	2233	2333	0055

	Ⓐ	Ⓐ	⚒	Ⓐ	Ⓐ	Ⓐ	⚒	Ⓐ	⚒			▽	▽	z	Ⓒ		Ⓐ		Ⓐ		Ⓐ		Ⓑ	⚒	†
Arcachon .... ⊖ d.	0526	0556	0616	0635	0646	0710	0726	0756	0826	0926	1026	1126	1226	1254	1426	1526	1606	1621	1656	1726	1756	1826	1926	2026	2126
Facture-Biganos..........d.	0548	0618	0638	0657	0705	0732	0748	0818	0848	0948	1048	1148	1248	1316	1448	1548	1628	1644	1718	1748	1818	1848	1948	2048	2148
Bordeaux St Jean ......a.	0615	0647	0707	0720	0737	0758	0817	0847	0917	1017	1117	1217	1317	1345	1517	1617	1657	1714	1751	1817	1847	1917	2017	2117	2217

TGV Trains

km	*TGV services,* Ⓡ	*TGV* **8411** ⑦ e	*TGV* **8415** ①–⑥ n		*TGV* **8467** ⑤ f
	Paris M. ◐ **300** ... d.	0755	0915	...	1825
0	**Bordeaux St Jean** d.	1122	1230	...	2136
40	Facture-Biganos..... d.	1143	1253	...	2158
56	La Teste .... a.	|	|	...	2209
59	**Arcachon** .... a.	1159	1307	...	2216

TGV services, Ⓡ	*TGV* **8438** Y	*TGV* **8456** ⑤–⑦ u		*TGV* **8482** ⑦ e	
Arcachon ....d.	1333	1557	...	1849	...
La Teste.................d.	|	|	...	1857	...
Facture-Biganos .....d.	1349	1616	...	1911	...
Bordeaux St Jean .a.	1411	1642	...	1935	...
Paris M. ◐ **300**....a.	1730	2015	...	2300	...

Y – ①–④ Dec. 28 - 30, Jan. 11 - Feb. 4, May 31 - June 10.
e – Also Apr. 5, May 24.
f – Also Dec. 24, 31, May 12; not Dec. 25, Jan. 1.
n – Not Apr. 5, May 24.
r – Also Dec. 24, 31, Apr. 5, May 1, 8, 12, 13, 24.
t – Also Dec. 25, Jan. 1, May 13; not Dec. 26, Jan. 2.
u – Also Dec. 24, 31, Apr. 5, May 12, 13, 24.
z – Dec. 28 - 31, Ⓐ Jan. 11 - Feb. 5, Ⓐ from May 31.
TGV – Ⓡ, supplement, 🍸.

⊖ – Trains also call at La Teste, 5 minutes from Arcachon.
◐ – Paris Montparnasse.
△ – Not on ①–⑤ Jan. 11 - Feb. 5.
▽ – Not on ①–⑤ Feb. 8 - Mar. 5.
‡ – Subject to alteration Dec. 15 - 18, 22 - 24, Jan. 5 - Feb. 5, May 11, 12, 18 - 21, 26 - 28.
§ – Subject to alteration Dec. 15 - 18, 22 - 24, Jan. 5 - Feb. 5, ②–⑤ Mar. 9 - Apr. 30, also May 11, 12, 18 - 21, 26 - 28.

Timings may vary by a few minutes Mar. 8 - May 7

BORDEAUX - LE VERDON - POINTE DE GRAVE 307

km		Ⓐ	⚒ △	Ⓐ	Ⓒ z	⚒ △	Ⓐ △	🚌 Ⓐ	Ⓐ	Ⓒ z	🚌 ⑥		🚌 Ⓐ	Ⓐ	b	⑤⑦ v	①–④ m
0	**Bordeaux** St Jean......d.	0631	0705	0805	0905	1105	1205	...	1305	1305	...	1605	...	1700	1805	1930	1935
23	Blanquefort.................d.	0710	0748	0848	0948	1148	1248	...	1348	1348	...	1648	...	1748	1848	2014	2014
39	Margaux......................d.	0730	0808	0908	1008	1208	1308	...	1408	1408	...	1708	...	1808	1908	2038	2038
61	Pauillac.......................d.	0751	0832	0932	1032	1232	1332	...	1432	1432	...	1732	...	1832	1932	2102	2101
80	Lesparre.......................d.	0805	0847	0946	1047	1246	1347	1415	1446	1447	1500	1746	1805	1847	1947	2116	...
106	Soulac sur Mer...........d.	...	0906	...	1106	...	1406	1453	...	1506	1538	...	1842	1906	2006	...	...
113	**Le Verdon**..................d.	...	0913	...	1113	...	1413	1505*	...	1513	1550*	...	1851*	1913	2013	...	...
116	Pointe de Grave ....a.	...	...	...	...	...	...	1510	...	...	1555	...	1855	...	...	...	...

	Ⓐ	Ⓐ	⑥ t	Ⓐ	Ⓐ	Ⓒ z	⑥ t	Ⓐ △	🚌 ⚒	△	Ⓐ		Ⓐ	🚌 †	Ⓐ	Ⓒ x	
Pointe de Grave...........d.	...	...	...	...	...	...	...	...	1055	...	...	...	...	1655	...	...	...
Le Verdon..................d.	...	...	...	0626	...	0748	0948	...	1102*	1148	...	1548	...	1701*	...	1748	...
Soulac sur Mer ....d.	...	...	...	0633	...	0756	0956	...	1111	1156	...	1556	...	1712	...	1756	...
Lesparre.......................d.	...	0554	0615	0652	0815	0815	1015	1115	1200	1215	1415	1615	1715	1800	1815	1815	...
Pauillac.......................d.	0537	0609	0633	0707	0833	0833	1033	1133	...	1233	1433	1633	1733	...	1833	1833	...
Margaux.......................d.	0556	0628	0654	0729	0854	0854	1054	1154	...	1254	1454	1654	1754	...	1854	1854	...
Blanquefort..................d.	0615	0647	0715	0749	0915	0915	1115	1215	...	1315	1515	1715	1815	...	1915	1915	...
Bordeaux St Jean.......a.	0654	0729	0754	0827	0954	0954	1154	1254	...	1354	1554	1755	1854	...	1954	1954	...

⛴ **POINTE DE GRAVE - ROYAN**:
Sailing time approx 20 minutes
Nov. 3, 2009 - Mar. 25, 2010:
From Pointe de Grave: 0715 Ⓐ, 0800 Ⓒ, 0930 Ⓐ, 0945 Ⓒ, 1130, 1430, 1645, 1845.
From Royan: 0745 Ⓐ, 0830 Ⓒ, 1000 Ⓐ, 1015 Ⓒ, 1200, 1500, 1715, 1915.
Mar. 27 - June 25, Sept. 1 - 21: *2009 timings*
From Pointe de Grave: 0715, 0855, 1025, 1155, 1325, 1510, 1640, 1825, 1955.
From Royan: 0750, 0930, 1100, 1230, 1400, 1545, 1715, 1900, 2030.
June 26 - Aug. 31: every 30 - 45 minutes. (0630 - 2030 from Pointe de Grave, 0715 - 2115 from Royan).
Sept. 22 - Nov. 2: 6 - 7 sailings per day.
✆ 05 56 73 37 73. www.gironde.fr

b – Not May 15.
m – Not Dec. 24, 31, Apr. 5, May 12, 13, 24.
t – Not May 1, 8.
v – Also Dec. 24, 31, Apr. 5, May 12, 13, 24; not May 14.
x – Not May 15.
z – Not May 16.
△ – Subject to alteration ①–⑤ Apr. 5 - May 14.
* – Serves village centre, not rail station.
🚌 services are subject to confirmation

308 LIMOGES - PÉRIGUEUX - AGEN

2nd class

km		Ⓐd	Ⓒ	⚒u	†	Ⓐb	⚒	⚒	Ⓐ§	⑤§	†
0	**Limoges 302** d.	...	...	1110	...	...	...	...	1735	1735	...
99	Périgueux **302** a.	...	...	1206	...	...	...	...	1852	1852	...
99	Périgueux d.	0720	0951	1208	1405	1602	1722	1820	1914	1913	1914
139	Les Eyzies d.	0750	1021	1243	1436	1634	1759	1857	1947	1947	1947
156	Le Buisson a.	0805	1036	1258	1451	1649	1814	1912	2002	2002	2002
156	Le Buisson d.	0806	1037	1259	1452	1650	1815	...	...	2004	2004
251	**Agen** a.	0928	1216	1416	1617	1813	1942	...	...	2123	2123

	⚒	Ⓐ	†	v	Ⓑb	⑥t	†	⑥	Ⓑ	⑤f
Agen d.	...	0641	...	1107	1503	1625	...	1828	1828	2043
Le Buisson a.	...	0800	...	1223	1616	1739	...	1951	1951	2200
Le Buisson d.	0733	0815	0845	1224	1617	1740	1815	1953	2003	2201
Les Eyzies d.	0751	0831	0900	1244	1635	1800	1831	2008	2018	2217
Périgueux a.	0835	0905	0935	1314	1705	1830	1907	2039	2049	2248
Périgueux **302** d.	...	...	...	1319	...	...	...	...	...	...
Limoges 302 a.	...	...	...	1430	...	...	...	...	...	...

b – Subject to alteration on ①–④ Mar. 29 - Apr. 29.
d – Subject to alteration on Ⓐ Mar. 29 - Apr. 30.
f – Also Dec. 24, 31, May 12; not Dec. 25, Jan. 1.
t – Not May 1, 8.
u – Subject to alteration Limoges - Périgueux on Ⓐ Mar. 1 - 19 and from Apr. 12. Note **v** also applies.
v – Subject to alteration Périgueux - Agen and v.v. on Ⓐ Feb. 1 - Apr. 30.
§ – Subject to alteration Limoges - Périgueux and v.v. on Apr. 26 - June 3.

309 LIMOGES - ANGOULÊME and POITIERS

km		①g	⑥t	Ⓐ	⑥t		u			⑤	†	⑤f
0	**Limoges** d.	0530	0530	0635	0821	...	1226	...	1707	1836	1836	2042
122	**Angoulême** a.	0722	0722	0842	1006	...	1424	...	1856	2029	2029	2235

	⚒	H		⚒	†	⑤f		H	G	⑤f
Angoulême d.	0550	0754	...	1229	1510	1632	...	1837	1900	2011
Limoges a.	0758	0941	...	1416	1653	1825	...	2039	2100	2201

km	*To Apr. 5* ◐	Ⓐ			⚒z	†	⑤f			⑤	†	
0	**Limoges** d.	0525	0635	...	1342	1504	1606	...	1725	1834	1834	...
139	**Poitiers** a.	0731	0834	...	1548	1659	1809	...	1931	2053	2053	...

To Apr. 5 ◐	Ⓐ		z			⚒		⑤	†	
Poitiers d.	0615	1055	1236	...	1817	1942	...	2150	2150	...
Limoges a.	0822	1255	1436	...	2026	2143	...	2353	2353	...

G – ⑤⑥⑦ (also Apr. 5, May 12, 13, 24).
H – ①–④ (not Dec. 24, 31, Apr. 5, May 12, 13, 24).
f – Also Dec. 24, 31, May 12; not Dec. 25, Jan. 1.
g – Also Apr. 6, May 25; not Apr. 5, May 24.
t – Not May 1, 8.
u – Subject to alteration on Ⓐ Mar. 1 - 26.
z – Subject to alteration on Dec. 14 - 17, Mar. 29 - 31.
◐ – An enhanced service will operate from Apr. 6.

310 PARIS - LIMOGES - TOULOUSE

For faster TGV services Paris - Agen - Toulouse and v.v. see Table 320. Additional relief trains run on peak dates.

km									★ 3601			★ 3611		★ 3621				★ 3631	★ 3701			★ 3635		★ 3637
		⚒	Ⓐ		⑦ W	⑥ t	⚒	⚒	Ⓐ s	Ⓐ ⊕	Ⓐ	⊗	†	k	⚒	Ⓐ ⊡	Ⓒ	Yk	G	⑥ t	Ⓐ	⑤⑦ q	⑤⑦ b	y
	Lille Europe d.	...	...	...	...	...	...	...	...	...	...	...	...	...	...	...	...	...	...	...	...	...	...	...
0	**Paris Austerlitz 294 315** d.	...	...	...	...	...	...	...	0635	...	...	0740	...	0855	...	...	...	1019	0951	...	...	1252	...	1256
	Orléans 315 d.	...	...	...	...	...	...	0630	|	...	0800	*0826*	...	|	...	1014	1014	|	*1045*	1214	1307	|	...	|
119	Les Aubrais-Orléans **294 315** d.	...	...	...	...	...	...	|	|	...	0808	0835	...	|	...	1024	1024	|	1055	|	1316	|	...	|
200	Vierzon **315** d.	...	...	...	...	...	0634	0730	|	...	0904	|	...	1026	...	1114	1114	|	|	1313	1410	|	...	1426
236	Issoudun d.	...	...	...	...	...	0657	0751	0815	...	0921	|	...	|	...	1132	1132	|	|	1334	1431	|	...	1445
263	Châteauroux d.	...	...	...	...	...	0715	0806a	0830	...	0935	0942	...	1057	...	1146	1145	|	1217	1349	1444	1450	...	1501
294	Argenton sur Creuse d.	...	...	...	...	...	0734	0822a	|	...	0952	|	...	1114	...	1203	...	|	|	1405	▬	|	...	|
341	La Souterraine d.	...	...	...	...	...	0801	0849a	|	...	...	1019	...	1139	...	1229	...	|	|	1434	...	|	...	1538
400	**Limoges** a.	...	...	...	...	...	0837	▬	0937	...	...	1052	...	1212	...	1307	...	1315	1329	1512	...	1557	...	1610
400	**Limoges** d.	...	...	0621	0645	0734	▬	...	0940	...	...	1055	...	1215	1225	...	...	1318	1339	...	...	1600	...	...
459	Uzerche d.	...	...	0659	|	0814	...	...	|	...	...	1131	...	1252	1315	...	...	|	|	...	...	1638	...	...
499	**Brive la Gaillarde** a.	...	...	0729	0744	0843	...	...	1039	...	...	1156	...	1318	1342	...	...	1418	1438	...	...	1703	...	...
499	**Brive la Gaillarde** d.	...	0601	0735	...	...	...	...	...	1108	...	1159	1205	...	...	...	...	1421	1441	...	...	...	1717	...
536	Souillac d.	...	0627	0759	...	...	...	⚒	...	1131	...	|	1228	...	...	...	...	1447	|	...	...	...	1743	...
559	Gourdon d.	...	0642	0814	...	...	...	△	...	1147	...	|	1244	...	...	...	...	1502	|	...	Ⓑ	...	1759	...
600	Cahors d.	0621	0710	0840	...	...	Ⓐ	1035	...	1213	...	1300	1310	...	...	...	...	1530	1547	...	1830	...	1830	...
639	Caussade d.	0649	0738	0907	...	...		1101	...	1238	...	|	1335	...	...	...	...	1556	|	...	1858	...	1858	...
662	Montauban **320** d.	0707	0757	0924	...	...	1043	1118	...	1254	...	1341	1352	...	...	...	...	1614	1630	...	1915	...	1915	...
713	**Toulouse Matabiau 320** a.	0736	0834	0950	...	...	1121	1145	...	1320	...	1409	1418	...	...	...	...	1640	1657	...	1953	...	1953	...
	Portbou **355** a.	...	...	...	...	...	...	...	...	...	...	...	...	...	...	...	...	...	...	...	...	...	...	...

	★ 3641	★ 3641					★ 3651				★ 3657	★ 3661			★ 3665	★ 3667		*TGV* 5298	★ 3673	★ 3681	*TGV* 5298		3731	3751
	Ⓐ	Ⓒ u	⚒	Ⓐ	Ⓐ	Ⓐ	Ⓐ	Ⓒ	†	Ⓐ	Ⓐ s	Ⓑ	Ⓐ	†	⑤–⑦ w		Ⓐ	⑦ ♠e	⑤ f		①–⑥ ♣n		♦ Ⓡ	♦ Ⓡ
Lille Europe d.	...	...	...	...	...	...	...	...	...	...	...	...	...	...	...	...	...	1740	...	...	1821	...	...	...
Paris Austerlitz 294 315 d.	1352	1352	...	...	...	...	1605	...	...	...	1702	1732	...	...	1817	1832	...	|	1916	1951	|	...	2156	2256
Orléans 315 d.	|	|	...	...	...	...	|	1655	1655	1710	|	|	...	...	|	|	1928	*1957*	|	|	*2042*	...	*2249*	*2344*
Les Aubrais-Orléans **294 315** d.	|	|	...	...	...	...	|	1704	1704	|	|	|	...	...	|	|	|	2009	|	|	2051	...	2259	0000
Vierzon **315** d.	|	|	...	...	1636	...	1734	1801	1801	1801	|	|	1903	...	1947	2003	2025	2044	|	2119	2127	...	2344	|
Issoudun d.	|	|	...	...	1657	...	|	1821	1821	1821	|	|	1924	...	|	2022	2043	|	|	|	|	...	|	|
Châteauroux d.	1548	1548	1558	1636	1714	...	1806	1838	1840	1840	1859	1929	1938	1938	2019	2038	2057	2115	|	2149	2157	...	|	|
Argenton sur Creuse d.	|	|	1617	1653	▬	...	|	...	1855	1855	|	|	1955	1954	|	2055	...	|	|	|	|	...	|	|
La Souterraine d.	|	|	▬	1722	...	...	1842	...	1924	1924	1935	|	2023	2023	|	2120	...	2153	|	|	2235	...	|	|
Limoges a.	1656	1656	Ⓐ	1800	†	...	1916	...	2002	2002	2010	2035	2058	2058	2124	2153	...	2225	2212	2257	2308	...	0122	|
Limoges d.	1700	1700	1730	...	1827	1827	1919	...	...	...	...	2038	...	...	2127	...	...	2228	...	2300	2311	...	0125	|
Uzerche d.	|	|	1817	...	1916	1916	|	...	...	...	...	2115	...	...	2203	...	...	|	...	|	|	...	|	|
Brive la Gaillarde a.	1800	1800	1845	...	1945	1945	2019	...	...	...	...	2140	...	...	2228	...	...	2326	...	2359	0010	...	|	|
Brive la Gaillarde d.	1803	1803	...	...	1949	...	...	...	...	...	...	2143	...	...	2231	...	...	...	...	...	...	...	|	|
Souillac d.	1828	|	...	...	2013	...	...	...	...	...	...	2208	...	...	2257	...	...	...	...	...	...	...	|	0443x
Gourdon d.	1844	|	...	...	2028	...	...	...	...	...	...	2224	...	...	2313	...	...	...	...	...	...	...	|	0500x
Cahors d.	1911	1905	...	...	2055	...	...	...	...	...	...	2252	...	...	2341	...	...	...	...	...	...	...	|	0529
Caussade d.	|	|	...	...	2121	...	...	...	...	...	...	...	...	...	|	...	...	...	...	...	...	...	|	0557x
Montauban **320** d.	|	|	...	...	2138	...	...	...	...	...	...	...	...	...	|	...	...	...	...	...	...	...	|	0615
Toulouse Matabiau 320 a.	2019	2011	...	...	2204	...	...	...	...	...	...	...	...	...	0049	...	...	...	...	...	...	...	|	0643
Portbou **355** a.	...	...	...	...	...	...	...	...	...	...	...	...	...	...	...	...	...	...	...	...	...	...	0821	...

		★ 3600	★ 3604		★ 3606		*TGV* 5296		★ 3610	★ 3612			★ 3620				★ 3624		★ 3626	★ 3700	★ 3630		★ 3640	
	⚒	Ⓐ		⚒	Ⓐ s	⚒	♥	Ⓐ	①–⑥ n	⑦ e	①	⚒	①–⑥ kn	⚒	†	Ⓐ	▽	Ⓐ	⑦ d	H		⚒		⑥
Cerbère **355** d.	...	...	...	...	...	...	...	...	...	...	...	...	...	...	...	...	...	...	...	...	0750	...	...	...
Toulouse Matabiau 320 d.	...	...	...	...	...	...	...	...	...	...	0632	0654	0717	...	0724	0734	...	0950	...	1022	1117	...	...	1222
Montauban **320** d.	...	...	...	...	...	...	...	...	...	...	0700	0732	0745	...	0751	0811	...	1026	...	1050	1145	...	...	1303
Caussade d.	...	...	...	...	...	...	...	...	...	...	0713	0747	|	...	0807	▬	...	▬	...	|	1200	...	...	1320
Cahors d.	...	...	...	...	...	...	...	...	0633	...	0741	0818	0825	...	0837	...	...	...	...	1130	1227	...	...	1346
Gourdon d.	...	...	...	...	...	...	...	...	0701	...	0809	0843	|	...	0903	...	...	...	...	|	1253	...	...	▬
Souillac d.	...	...	...	...	...	...	...	...	0718	...	0825	0858	|	...	0919	...	...	...	...	|	1310	...	...	...
Brive la Gaillarde a.	...	...	...	...	...	...	...	...	0742	...	0849	0923	0927	...	0942	...	...	Ⓒ	...	1231	1338	...	...	...
Brive la Gaillarde d.	...	0442	...	...	...	0615	0636	0728	0745	0745	▬	▬	0930	...	▬	...	...	1240	1300	1233	1341	...	1438	...
Uzerche d.	...	0507	...	...	...	0644	|	0755	|	|	...	...	|	...	...	...	...	1310	1326	|	|	...	1503	...
Limoges a.	...	0544	...	...	...	0730	0735	0835	0844	0844	...	Ⓐ	1029	...	...	⚒	...	1357	1403	1335	1440	...	1540	...
Limoges d.	0522	0547	0602	0606	0657	0741a	0738	▬	0848	0848	Ⓐ	1014	1032	...	...	1250	1345	...	1406	1338	1443	...	1544	...
La Souterraine d.	0554	|	0633	0639	0728	0815a	0810	...	|	|	0902	1048	1102	...	⚒	1331	1416	...	|	|	|	...	|	⚒
Argenton sur Creuse d.	0622	|	|	0707	|	...	|	...	|	|	0927	1116	|	←	⊡	1358	1439	...	|	|	|	1625	|	←
Châteauroux d.	0640	0651	0711	0731	0806	...	0847	0857	0952	0952	0956*	1134	1140	1145	1224	1419	1458	...	1511	1449	|	1642	1650	1654
Issoudun d.	0654	|	0726	0749	|	...	|	0911	|	|	1009	→	|	1159	1241	...	1514	...	|	|	|	→	|	1712
Vierzon **315** d.	0724	|	0749	0815	|	...	0921	0933	|	|	1032	...	|	1222	1305	...	1538	...	|	|	|	...	|	1735
Les Aubrais-Orléans **294 315** a.	|	|	|	|	|	...	0955	|	|	|	|	...	|	1316	1352	...	|	...	|	1602	|	...	|	...
Orléans 315 a.	0820	|	|	0903	|	...	*1004*	1021	|	|	1120	...	|	1325	1400	...	|	...	|	*1619*	|	...	|	...
Paris Austerlitz 294 315 a.	...	0846	0918	...	1005	...	|	...	1150	1150	...	...	1342	...	...	...	1707	...	1711	1720	1741r	...	1850	...
Lille Europe a.	...	...	...	...	...	...	1226	...	...	...	...	...	...	...	...	...	...	...	...	...	...	...	...	...

TOULOUSE - LIMOGES - PARIS 310

	⚒ j	⚒	★ 3652 ⑦ e	★ 3654 ⑤ f	⚒	⚒ ▷	★ 3660 ①–⑥ n	★ 3664 ⑦ e	Ⓑ p	★ 3672 ⑦ e	†	★ 3680 Ⓑ h	Ⓑ z	Ⓐ	⑥	★ 3690 E	★ 3690 F	⑦ W	⑤ g	①–④ m	⑤ g	Ⓐ	Ⓒ	3750 ◆ 🅁	3730 ◆ 🅁
Cerbère **355** d.	...	...	...	...	...	...	...	...	...	...	...	...	...	...	...	...	...	...	...	...	...	...	...	...	2121
Toulouse Matabiau 320 d.	...	...	1346	...	...	1346	...	...	...	1506	...	...	...	...	...	1652	1701	...	1713	1753	1801	1858	1934	2235	0049
Montauban **320** d.	...	...	|	...	...	1412	...	...	...	|	...	...	...	...	1709	|	|	...	1755	1828	1828	1945	2000	2305	|
Caussade d.	...	...	|	...	...	1425	...	...	...	|	...	...	...	...	1724	|	|	...	1811	1841	1841	2002	2015	2322c	|
Cahors d.	...	...	1450	...	...	1452	...	...	...	1612	1644	...	...	1730	1753	1756	1806	...	1839	1909	1909	2030	2044	2350	|
Gourdon d.	...	...	1517	...	...	1517	...	...	...	1640	1711	...	...	1759	1820	1824	|	...	1906	1936	1936	▬	2111	0018c	|
Souillac d.	...	...	1534	...	...	1533	...	...	...	1657	1727	...	...	1815	1836	1841	|	...	1922	1952	1952	①–④	2128	0036c	|
Brive la Gaillarde a.	...	...	1600	...	...	1600	...	...	...	1721	1751	...	...	1841	1900	1907	1907	...	1945	2017	2016	m	2153	|	|
Brive la Gaillarde d.	...	...	1603	...	...	▬	1617	...	...	1724	▬	1804	1833	...	...	1910	1910	1920	...	...	2018	2041	2155	|	|
Uzerche d.	...	...	|	...	...	...	|	...	...	|		1829	1902	...	...	|	|	|	...	...	2044	2107	2221	|	|
Limoges a.	...	...	1703	...	...	...	1717	...	...	1822	⑤f	1906	1943	...	...	2009	2009	2019	...	...	2121	2145	2259	|	|
Limoges d.	...	1638	1706	1706	...	...	1720	1720	1740	1825	1831	1909	▬	...	...	2012	2012	...	...	...	...	...	...	|	|
La Souterraine d.	...	1717	|	|	...	†	1750	1750	1821	|	1921	1939	⑤f	...	...	|	|	...	...	...	...	...	...	|	|
Argenton sur Creuse d.	...	1742	|	|	←	1742	1814	1814	1849	|	1952	|	←	...	...	|	|	...	...	...	...	...	...	|	|
Châteauroux d.	...	1802	1810	1810	1813	1813	1832	1832	1908	1930	2010	2017	2025	...	...	2119	2119	...	...	...	...	...	...	|	|
Issoudun d.	...	→	|	|	1830	1830	1848	1848	...	|	→	|	2044	...	...	|	|	...	...	...	...	...	...	|	|
Vierzon **315** d.	1801	...	1845	1845	1914	1914	1911	1911	...	|	...	2052	2106	...	...	2153	2153	...	...	...	...	...	...	|	0539
Les Aubrais-Orléans **294 315** a.	1854	...	|	|	2000	2000	|	|	...	|	...	|	...	...	...	2226	2226	...	...	...	...	...	...	0549	0620
Orléans 315 a.	1903	...	|	|	2009	2009	|	|	...	|	...	|	...	...	...	*2237*	*2237*	...	...	...	...	...	...	*0558*	*0630*
Paris Austerlitz 294 315 a.	...	...	2013	2013	...	...	2039	2039	...	2128	...	2220	...	...	...	2325	2325	...	...	...	...	...	...	0657	0727
Lille Europe a.	...	...	...	...	...	...	...	...	...	...	...	...	...	...	...	...	...	...	...	...	...	...	...	...	...

◆ – **NOTES** (LISTED BY TRAIN NUMBER):

3730 – *CORAIL LUNÉA* – 🛏 1,2 cl., 💺 (reclining) Cerbère - Paris and Latour de Carol (**3970**) - Toulouse - Paris. Not Dec. 24, 31.

3731 – *CORAIL LUNÉA* – 🛏 1,2 cl., 💺 (reclining) Paris - Portbou; 🛏 1,2 cl. and 💺 (reclining) Paris - Latour de Carol (train **3971**). Not Dec. 24, 31.

3750 – *CORAIL LUNÉA* – 🛏 1,2 cl., 💺 (reclining) Toulouse - Paris. Train **3752** on dates in note **c**. Conveys (from Brive) portions from Rodez and Albi on dates in Table **316**.

3751 – *CORAIL LUNÉA* – 🛏 1,2 cl. and 💺 (reclining) Paris - Toulouse. Train **3753** on dates in note **x**. Conveys (to Brive) portions for Rodez and Albi on dates in Table **316**.

E – ①⑤⑦ (also Dec. 24, 31, Apr. 6, May 12, 25; not Dec. 25, Jan. 1).
F – Daily except dates in note **E**
G – ①⑤⑥⑦ (also Dec. 24, 31, May 12, 13; not Jan. 4, 8, 11, 15 or ①⑤ Mar. 22 - Apr. 23).
H – ①⑤⑥⑦ to Mar. 21 / from Apr. 24 (also Dec. 24, 31, May 25; not Dec. 14, Jan. 18, 22, 25, 29, May 10, 14). Timings vary on Jan. 11 (depart Toulouse 1013) and Jan. 15 (Toulouse depart 0953).
W – ⑦ Dec. 13 - Mar. 7.
Y – To Cerbère (Table **355**). Depart Paris 0951 on Mar. 2, 3, 11. Additional relief train **3629** runs on Dec. 19, 20, 24, 26, Feb. 20, 27, Apr. 3, 17, 24, May 13, 22 (Paris 1023, Toulouse 1648).

a – Ⓐ only.
b – Also Apr. 5, May 1, 8, 13, 24.
c – Calls on night of ⑤⑥⑦ (also Apr. 5, May 12, 13, 24).
d – Also Apr. 5, May 24; not Apr. 4, May 23.
e – Also Apr. 5, May 24.
f – Also Dec. 24, 31, May 12; not Dec. 25, Jan. 1, May 14.
g – Not Dec. 25, Jan. 1.
h – Not Dec. 25, Jan. 1, May 13, 14.
j – 15 minutes later on Ⓐ.
k – Will not run on ①–⑤ Mar. 22 - Apr. 23.
m – Not Apr. 5, May 13, 24.
n – Not Apr. 5, May 24.
p – 15 minutes later on †.
q – Also Dec. 24, 31, Apr. 5, May 12, 24; not Dec. 25, Jan. 1, Apr. 4.
r – Arrive 1815 on Dec. 14, 15.
s – Not May 14.
t – Not May 1, 8.
u – Arrive Toulouse 2019 on ⑦.
w – Also Dec. 24, 31, Apr. 5, May 12, 13, 24.
x – Calls on morning of ①⑥⑦ (also Apr. 6, May 13, 14, 25).
y – Not June 4, 5.
z – Runs 12 minutes later on †.
TGV – 🅁, supplement payable, 🍷.

⊕ – Subject to alteration Jan. 4 - 15.
⊗ – Arrives up to 30 minutes later on Dec. 16 - 18.
⊡ – Subject to alteration Mar. 22 - Apr. 23.
△ – Arrive Toulouse 1158 Jan. 4 - 8, 1206 Jan. 11 - 13.
▽ – Not Jan. 18 - 22.
▷ – Depart Toulouse 1331 on Jan. 11 - 13.
★ – CORAIL TÉOZ. 🅁. 🍷.
♥ – Not Apr. 12, 19, 26. Also calls at Marne la Vallée (a. 1117), Charles de Gaulle ✈ (a. 1131).
♠ – Also calls at Charles de Gaulle ✈ (1835), Marne la Vallée (1853).
♣ – Also calls at Charles de Gaulle ✈ (1917), Marne la Vallée (1933).
* – Arrive 0945.

A revised service operates on June 5, 6

BRIVE - AURILLAC 311

km		W	Ⓐ ⊕		⑥	⊗			Ⓑ	⑥ t
0	**Brive la Gaillarde 316** d.	0758	1050	...	1205	1430	...	1806	2151	2235
27	St Denis-près-Martel **316** d.	0822	1113	...	1228	1455	...	1832	2213	2259
102	**Aurillac** a.	0934	1231	...	1340	1623	...	1950	2324	0009

	⚒	⚒		⊕	†	⑤ f		◇	
Aurillac d.	0545	0737	...	1144	1415	1545	...	1718	...
St Denis-près-Martel **316** d.	0700	0859	...	1302	1532	1706	...	1832	...
Brive la Gaillarde 316 a.	0724	0921	...	1326	1553	1727	...	1855	...

W – Dec. 13 - Mar. 7 (not Dec. 14, 15, Jan. 25, 26). To Le Lioran (a. 1010).
f – ⑤ to Mar. 26, ⑤ Apr. 16 - 30.
t – Not May 1, 8.

◇ – From Neussargues on dates in Table **331**.
⊕ – Subject to alteration Feb. 22 - 26, Mar. 1 - 5.
⊗ – Subject to alteration Feb. 22 - 26, Mar. 1 - 5, 29 - 31, Apr. 1, 2, 5 - 9.

A revised service will operate May 3 - June 11

TOULOUSE - LATOUR DE CAROL 312

km		3971 ◇ 🅁		⊕	⊕	⊕					
	Paris Austerlitz **310** d.	2156	...	...	...	...	...	...	...	...	...
0	**Toulouse Matabiau** d.	|	0650	0750	0850	1050	1450	1650	1750	1850	1950
65	Pamiers d.	0545	0750	0850	0950	1150	1550	1750	1850	1950	2050
83	Foix a.	0555	0800	0905	1000	1200	1600	1800	1905	2000	2105
83	Foix d.	0558	0801	0906	1001	1201	1601	1801	1906	2001	2106
123	Ax les Thermes d.	0647	0849	0945	1049	1249	1649	1849	1945	2049	2145
144	L'Hospitalet ⊖ a.	0720	0920	...	1120	1320	1720	1920	...	2120	...
163	**Latour de Carol** a.	0751	0952	...	1152	1352	1752	1952	...	2152	...

	Ⓐ		Ⓒ	Ⓐ ‡		Ⓐ	d			3970 ◇ 🅁
Latour de Carol d.	0521	0721	0921	*0903**	1321	*1530**	...	1721	1921	2021
L'Hospitalet ⊖ d.	0552	0752	0952	*0930**	1352	*1600**	...	1752	1952	2049
Ax les Thermes d.	0620	0820	1020	1020	1420	*1625**	1716	1820	2020	2120
Foix a.	0704	0904	1104	1104	1504	*1720**	1759	1904	2104	2210
Foix d.	0705	0907	1107	1107	1507	1734	1802	1907	2107	2220
Pamiers d.	0721	0921	1121	1121	1521	1751	1821	1921	2121	2237
Toulouse Matabiau a.	0816	1016	1216	1216	1616	1846	1916	2016	2216	|
Paris Austerlitz **310** a.	...	...	...	...	...	...	...	...	...	0727

d – Runs 30 minutes later on Ⓒ to Apr. 5.
◇ – 🛏 1,2 cl. and 💺 (reclining). Not Dec. 24, 31, Apr. 26 - 28, May 3 - 5.
⊕ – Subject to alteration Feb. 8 - 12, 15 - 19.

⊖ – Full name: Andorre-L'Hospitalet. For 🚌 connections to / from Andorra see Table **313**.
‡ – Subject to alteration Feb. 22 - 26, Mar. 1 - 5, 8 - 12.
* – By 🚌.

Subject to alteration Apr. 27 - 29, May 4 - 6. From May 10 departures from Toulouse are 4 minutes earlier.

ANDORRA 🚌 313

Subject to cancellation when mountain passes are closed by snow

🚌		☆			⊖			
Andorre-L'Hospitalet (Gare) d.	0735	0935	1945	...	and	...	...	...
Pas de la Casa d.	0815	1001	2000	0845	hourly	2145	...	...
Soldeu ⊙ d.	0840	...	2025	0855	until	2155	...	...
Andorra la Vella a.	0905	...	2105	0940	...	2240	...	...

🚌		☆			⊖			
Andorra la Vella d.	0545	...	1700	0745	and	2045	...	...
Soldeu ⊙ d.	0610	...	1735	0825	hourly	2125	...	...
Pas de la Casa d.	0640	1245	1815	0840	until	2140	...	...
Andorre-L'Hospitalet (Gare) a.	0710	1310	1930	...	...	...	...	...

⊙ – Also calls at Canillo, Encamp and Escaldes.
⊖ – Additional journeys operated by Cooperativa Interurbana run from Andorra hourly 0720 - 2020, from Pas de la Casa hourly 0820 - 2120.

☆ – Operated by SNCF. Terminates on French side of the border, 100 metre walk from central bus stop in Pas de la Casa.
Operator: La Hispano Andorrana, Av. Santa Coloma, entre 85 - 87, Andorra la Vella, ✆ + 376 821 372. www.andorrabus.com
Additional service: approx hourly (5 per day on ⑦) Escaldes - Andorra la Vella - Sant Julià de Lòria - Seu d'Urgell (Spain).

TOULOUSE - CASTRES - MAZAMET 314

Castres - Mazamet and v.v. is by 🚌 Dec. 13 - Jan. 29

km		Ⓐ		◇	◇	Ⓐ	Ⓐ	Ⓐ			
0	**Toulouse Matabiau** d.	0645	0746	1145	1346	1546	1642	1724	1742	1846	2046
86	Castres a.	0753	0853	1255	1453	1653	1753	1834	1854	1953	2155
105	**Mazamet** a.	0820	0924	1320	1520	1720	1818	1903	1927	2020	2220

	Ⓐ	Ⓐ		Ⓐ ◇	Ⓐ ◇	◇	◇	Ⓐ		
Mazamet d.	0556	0631	0731	...	0931	1126	1431	1731	1822	1931
Castres d.	0625	0655	0756	0908	0956	1153	1456	1756	1857	1957
Toulouse Matabiau d.	0737	0804	0905	1016	1104	1304	1603	1903	2004	2104

◇ – Subject to alteration Feb. 15 - 19, 22 - 26.

315 PARIS - VIERZON - BOURGES - MONTLUÇON

km		⚒	♥	3903 Ⓐ	3905 ⑥	⚒	†		▽	3909 △		Ⓐ	Ⓐ	⚒	Ⓐ	3913 Ⓑ h	3913 ⑤ f	†	①–④ m	⚒	†	3917	3923 ⑦ e	†	3921 ⑤ f
0	**Paris Austerlitz** 310 d.	...	...	0656	0656	...	...	...	...	1210	...	...	...	...	...	1716	1716	...	...	...	...	1903	2048	...	2048
	Orléans 310 d.	...	0707	*0734*	*0734*	...	...	0902	...	*1253*	1448	...	1634	...	1756	|	|	...	...	1828	...	*1947*	*2137*	...	*2137*
119	Les Aubrais-Orléans 310 d.	...	|	0752	0752	...	...	0910	...	1304	|	...	|	...	|	|	|	...	...	1837	...	1957	2148	...	2148
200	Vierzon 310 a.	...	0746	0829	0831	...	...	0959	...	1339	1538	...	1727	...	1841	1846	1846	...	...	1927	...	2037	2223	...	2223
200	Vierzon ▷ d.	...	0748	0834	0834	0842	...	1004	1050	1341	1540	*1646*	1740	...	1843	1848	1848	1852	1852	1929	...	2039	2230	2235	2227
	Bourges ▷ a.	...	0804	0852	0852	|	...	1029	|	1357	1601	*1712*	1806	...	1900	1904	1904	|	|	1952	...	2056	2249	|	2244
	Bourges d.	0530	...	...	...	|	1025	...	|	1414	...	1747	...	1822	...	...	1921	|	|	...	2004	2113	...	|	...
291	St Amand-Montrond-Orval d.	0653	...	...	...	0937	1111	...	1144	1456	...	1840	...	1913	...	...	2005	1940	1948	...	2048	2159	...	2329	...
341	**Montluçon** a.	0734	...	...	...	1010	...	...	1218	1528	...	1916	...	...	...	...	2040	2015	2022	...	2130	2236	...	0002	...

	⚒	⚒	3904 ①–⑥ n	⚒	Ⓐ	Ⓐ	3908	⚒ ▽	3914 ①–⑥ u	†	⚒ ▽	Ⓐ §	Ⓑ §	Ⓑ h	§	3918 ⚒	3920 †	Ⓐ	†	Ⓐ	Ⓐ	Ⓐ	3924 ⑦ b	♥	
Montluçon d.	...	0508	...	0615	...	...	0856	1108	...	...	...	...	...	...	...	1558	1630	1726	1755	...	...	1843	1902	...	...
St Amand-Montrond-Orval d.	...	0543	...	0650	...	...	0936	1146	...	1150	1310	...	...	...	...	1633	1705	1810	1838	...	...	1921	1941	...	...
Bourges a.	...	0630	...	|	...	...	1020	|	...	1231	1355	...	...	...	...	1723	1751	1907	1925	...	...	|	2025	...	...
Bourges ▷ d.	0607	...	0646	|	0734	0808	1037	|	1232	...	...	1512	1605	...	1630	1740	1808	...	...	1936	...	|	2042	2151	...
Vierzon ▷ a.	0627	...	0702	0740	0752	0835	1055	1242	1249	...	...	1532	1624	...	1653	1756	1825	...	...	1956	...	2023	2058	2209	...
Vierzon 310 d.	0630	...	0704	...	0754	0841	1057	...	1252	...	...	1543	...	1632	1656	1758	1827	...	...	...	2008	...	2100	2211	...
Les Aubrais-Orléans 310 a.	0719	...	0742	...	|	|	1131	...	1326	...	...	1631	...	1709	1748	1835	1905	...	...	...	2056	...	2132	|	...
Orléans 310 a.	0732	...	*0800*	...	0828	0932	*1145*	...	*1338*	...	...	1640	...	*1719*	1756	*1903*	*1914*	...	...	...	2104	...	*2145*	2249	...
Paris Austerlitz 310 a.	...	...	0842	...	...	...	1229	...	1423	...	...	...	...	1811	...	1935	2005	...	...	...	...	...	2231	...	...

LOCAL TRAINS VIERZON - BOURGES (see also Table **290**)

	Ⓐ	⚒	Ⓐ	Ⓒ		⑥t	⚒‡	⚒‡	Ⓐ	
Vierzon d.	0626	0659	0801	0907	1054	1215	1347	1432	1646	1832
Bourges a.	0650	0725	0827	0930	1113	1241	1411	1452	1712	1857

	⚒	†			⚒§	Ⓑ§		Ⓐ	Ⓐ	†	
Bourges d.	0702	0720	0840	...	1246	1605	1743	1818	1936	1954	...
Vierzon a.	0728	0740	0906	...	1311	1624	1811	1837	1956	2021	...

b – Also Apr. 5, May 24; not Apr. 4, May 23.
e – Also Apr. 5, May 24.
f – Also Dec. 24, 31, May 12; not Dec. 25, Jan. 1.
h – Not Dec. 25, Jan. 1, May 13.
m – Not Dec. 24, 31, Apr. 5, May 12, 13, 24.
n – Not Apr. 5, May 24.
t – Not May 1, 8.
u – Not on ①–⑤ Mar. 22 - Apr. 23, May 24.
♥ – To/from Lyon (Table **290**). Not Apr. 6-23 from Lyon.
▷ – See also panel below table (also Table **290**).
△ – Not on ①–⑤ Mar. 22 - Apr. 23.
▽ – Subject to alteration on ①–⑤ Mar. 29 - Apr. 23.
§ – Subject to alteration on Mar. 1-5, 8-12.
‡ – Subject to alteration on Feb. 15-19, 22-26.

316 BRIVE and AURILLAC - FIGEAC - TOULOUSE

km		♣ R	♣ Y R		Ⓐ			Ⓐ	Ⓐ	⚒			Ⓐ	Ⓐ			Ⓐ				⑥		⑤ f	
	Paris Austerlitz 310 d.	2256	2256	...	...	...	...	...	...	...	...	...	...	...	...	...	...	...	...	...	...	...	...	...
0	**Brive la Gaillarde 311** d.	|	|	...	...	0556	...	...	0830	...	...	...	1102	...	...	1330	1611	...	...	1827	...	...	...	2145
27	St Denis-près-Martel 311 d.	0423	0423	...	...	0618	...	...	0856	...	...	...	1123	...	...	1351	1632	...	...	1859	...	...	...	2207
45	Rocamadour-Padirac d.	0443	0443	...	...	0637	...	...	0915	...	...	...	1141	...	...	1410	1651	...	...	1918	...	...	...	2226
	Clermont Ferrand 331 d.	|	|	...	...	|	...	...	|	0636	...	...	|	...	...	|	|	...	...	|	...	...	...	|
◧	**Aurillac** d.	|	|	...	...	|	0655r	...	|	0904	...	...	|	...	1305	|	|	1652	1830	|	1830	...	2119	|
88	Figeac d.	0526	0526	...	0614	0710	0809	0908	0954	1015	1015	...	1214	1207	1416	1444	1725	1812	1948	1953	1959	...	2231	2259
94	Capdenac a.	0533	0533	...	0621	0717	0815	0914	1000	1021	1021	...	1220	1213	1422	1450	1731	1819	...	1959	2006	...	2238	2305
94	Capdenac d.	0535	0535	...	0623	0722	0822	0915	...	1023	1023	...	1221	1223	1424	1453	1733	1821	...	2000	...	...	...	2306
161	**Rodez 323** a.	0644	0644	...	|	0826	|	1019	...	|	|	...	1325	|	|	1557	1836	|	...	2101	...	...	...	0006
	Carmaux 323 a.	...	0804	...	|	...	|	...	...	|	|	...	...	|	|	...	...	|	...	...	...	...	...	...
	Albi 323 a.	...	0824	...	|	...	|	...	...	|	|	...	...	|	|	...	...	|	...	...	...	...	...	...
123	Villefranche de Rouergue d.	...	...	...	0650	...	0851	...	...	1052	1052	...	...	1251	1452	...	...	1851	...	...	...	...	...	...
140	Najac d.	...	...	...	0705	...	0905	...	...	1107	1107	...	...	1305	1507	...	...	1905	...	...	...	...	...	...
193	Gaillac 323 a.	...	...	...	0751	...	0950	...	...	1150	1150	...	...	1352	1552	...	...	1950	...	...	...	...	...	...
247	**Toulouse Matabiau 323** a.	...	...	...	0834	...	1033	...	...	1233	1233	...	...	1434	1633	...	...	2034	...	...	...	...	...	...

	⚒	⚒	†	Ⓐ ⊕	Ⓐ	Ⓐ			Ⓐ						⑤	Ⓐ 🚌	Ⓐ	⑤ f			Ⓐ		♠ R	♠ Z R
Toulouse Matabiau 323 d.	...	...	...	...	0634	...	...	0839	...	...	1240	...	...	1637	1637	...	...	...	1838	...	1947	...	...	...
Gaillac 323 d.	...	...	...	...	0717	...	...	0915	...	...	1318	...	...	1717	1717	...	...	...	1915	...	2030	...	...	...
Najac d.	...	...	...	...	0804	...	...	1005	...	...	1406	...	...	1803	1803	...	...	...	2004	...	2115	...	...	...
Villefranche de Rouergue d.	...	...	...	...	0819	...	...	1020	...	...	1421	...	...	1819	1819	...	...	...	2019	...	2130	...	...	...
Albi 323 d.	...	...	...	...	|	...	...	|	...	...	|	...	...	|	|	...	...	...	|	...	|	...	...	2038
Carmaux 323 d.	...	...	...	...	|	...	...	|	...	...	|	...	...	|	|	...	...	...	|	...	|	...	...	2058
Rodez 323 d.	...	0648	...	...	|	0840	...	|	...	1146	|	1421	1631	|	|	1730	...	...	|	2005	|	...	2233	2233
Capdenac a.	...	0752	...	...	0848	0945	...	1049	...	1250	1449	1524	1730	1849	1849	1849	...	...	2046	2108	2156	...	2336	2336
Capdenac d.	0555	0753	0753	...	0849	0946	...	1059	1110	1251	1451	1526	1732	1854	1854	1849	...	1912	2049	2110	2157	...	2338	2338
Figeac d.	0603	0800	0800	0838	0856	0953	...	1107	1117	1258	1459	1534	1739	1900	1906	1904	1920	1920	2057	2117	2204	...	2347	2347
Aurillac a.	0722	|	|	0958	...	...	...	1215r	|	|	1609	|	|	...	2018	...	|	|	2210	|	*2322s*	...	|	|
Clermont Ferrand 331 a.	...	|	|	...	...	...	...	...	|	|	1859	|	|	...	...	...	|	|	...	|	...	...	|	|
Rocamadour-Padirac d.	...	0834	0834	...	...	...	...	...	1156	1331	...	1613	1813	...	...	...	1956	1956	...	|	...	...	0028	0028
St Denis-près-Martel 311 d.	...	0853	0853	...	...	...	...	...	1214	1352	...	1634	1839	...	...	...	2014	2014	...	2212	...	...	0048	0048
Brive la Gaillarde 311 a.	...	0914	0914	...	...	...	...	...	1234	1417	...	1655	1901	...	...	...	2036	2036	...	2233	...	...	|	|
Paris Austerlitz 310 a.	...	...	...	...	...	...	...	...	...	...	...	...	...	...	...	...	...	...	...	...	...	...	0657	0657

Y – From Paris on ⑤ to Apr. 23.
Z – ⑦ to Apr. 25 (also Apr. 5; not Apr. 4).
f – Not Dec. 25, Jan. 1.
r – ⚒ only.
s – ⑤ (also Dec. 24, 31, May 12; not Dec. 25, Jan. 1). By 🚌.
◧ – Aurillac is *65* km from Figeac.
⊕ – Subject to alteration on May 4-6.
♣ – 🛏 1,2 cl. and (2) (reclining). Train **3751/3/5/7**.
♠ – 🛏 1,2 cl., (2) (reclining). Not Dec. 24, 31. Train **3756/4/0/2**.

Capdenac - Toulouse: subject to alteration from Mar. 1 with 🚌 substitution. Rodez - Capdenac: subject to alteration from Apr. 26.

318 BORDEAUX - LIBOURNE - BERGERAC - SARLAT

km		① g	Ⓐ	⚒ z		⚒	⑦ e		Ⓐ b	Ⓒ		Ⓐ	Ⓐ ▽	▽			Ⓐ		Ⓐ			⚒	⑤ d		Ⓑ h
0	**Bordeaux St Jean 300/2** d.	...	0556	0706	...	0800	0833	...	...	1042	...	1226	...	1333	...	1603	1651	...	1729	1811	...	1919	2036	...	2145
37	Libourne 300/2 d.	...	0625	0745	...	0829	0911	...	1116	1116	...	1251	1257	1403	...	1630	1722	...	1813	1845	...	1949	2108	...	2215
99	Bergerac d.	0550	0727	0849	...	0915	1006	...	1209	1209	...	...	1356	1450	...	1724	1818	...	1920	1935	...	2040	2203	...	2300
135	Le Buisson a.	0630	0805	0922	...	...	1040	...	1243	1243	...	...	...	1522	...	1803	...	...	...	2008	...	...	2236	...	...
135	Le Buisson d.	0631	0816	...	...	...	1048	...	1244	1244	...	...	...	...	...	1805x	...	...	...	2013	...	...	2237	...	...
168	**Sarlat** a.	0715	0900	...	...	...	1130	...	1326	1326	...	...	...	...	...	1848x	...	...	...	2055	...	...	2319	...	...

	① g	⚒		Ⓐ	① g	②–⑤ w	⑥ t				†	Ⓐ ▽	Ⓒ	Ⓐ b	Ⓐ		Ⓐ ▽	▷			Ⓑ h				⑤⑦ u
Sarlat d.	...	...	...	...	0527	0601	...	...	0729	...	...	...	...	...	...	...	...	1201	...	...	...	...	1735	...	1940
Le Buisson a.	...	...	...	...	0611	0644	...	...	0810	...	...	...	...	...	...	...	...	1244	...	...	...	...	1818	...	2021
Le Buisson d.	...	...	...	...	0645	0645	...	...	0813	...	...	...	1057	1057	...	...	...	1247	...	1650	...	...	1819	...	2022
Bergerac d.	0519	0604	...	0642	0725	0725	0725	...	0852	...	1013	1013	1131	1131	...	...	1213	1329	...	1721	1819	...	1857	...	2056
Libourne 300/2 a.	0607	0653	...	0741	0816	0816	0816	...	0939	...	1102	1102	1217	1217	1222	...	1312	1419	...	1812	1917	...	1948	...	2140
Bordeaux St Jean 300/2 a.	0636	0725	...	0813	0849	0848	0846	...	1010	...	1132	...	1253	...	1257	...	1342	1449	...	1841	1953	...	2033	...	2213

b – Subject to alteration on ①–⑤ Jan. 4 - Apr. 15 (also ⑤ Feb. 19 - Apr. 2).
d – Also Dec. 24, 31, May 12; not Dec. 25, Jan. 1, May 14.
e – Also Dec. 25, Jan. 1, May 1, 8.
g – Also Apr. 6, May 25; not Apr. 5, May 24.
h – Also May 1, 8.
t – Not May 1, 8.
u – Also Dec. 24, 31, Apr. 5, May 1, 8, 12, 13, 24; not May 14.
w – Not Dec. 25, jan. 1, Apr. 6, May 13, 25.
x – On ⑤ **d** Le Buisson d. 1828, Sarlat a. 1911.
z – Depart Bordeaux 0702 Feb. 1-5. Subject to alteration Bergerac - Le Buisson on ①–⑤ Jan. 4 - Feb. 12, Apr. 5-16.
▽ – Subject to alteration on Ⓐ Feb. 15 - Apr. 2.
▷ – Subject to alteration Bergerac - Libourne on ①–④ Feb. 15 - Apr. 1; Sarlat - Bergerac on Ⓐ Jan. 4 - Apr. 16 (runs ⑤ Feb. 19 - Apr. 2).

BORDEAUX - TOULOUSE 320

km		TGV 5171 ♦	4652 4653 ★ ♠	⚒	4654 4655 ★ ♣	TGV 8501 Ⓐ d	†	4656 4657 ★ ♥	TGV 8511 Ⓐ ⊕	TGV 8513 Ⓒ g	4660 4661 ★ ▽	TGV 8519 ◇	N	4662 4663 ★ ◧	4664 4665 ★	TGV 8535	R	TGV 5218 ♦	3835	14109 Ⓐ §	14111 ⑦ x§	⑥ t	TGV 8549	4620 4621 Ⓡ ♦	TGV 8579 ⑤ f	TGV 7993 ⑤⑦ w
	Paris M'parnasse **300** d.	...	...	...	...	0610	...	...	0810	0810	...	1130	...	...	...	1410	...	...	...	...	...	...	1720	...	1925	2250
	Nantes **292** d.	...	...	...	...	|	...	...	|	|	...	|	...	...	...	|	...	...	1409	...	...	...	|	...	|	|
0	**Bordeaux St Jean** d.	0533	0610	0727	0829	0930	1014	1010	1128	1128	1238	1439	1447	1459	1638r	1727	1722	1807	1833	1930	1930	1939	2029	2157	2237	|
79	Marmande d.	|	|	0809	0908	|	1100	|	|	|	|	|	1548	|	|	|	1815	|	1924	1958	2019	2028	|	2236	|	|
136	Agen d.	0646	|	0847	0938	1037	1137	|	|	1232	1345	1541	1626	|	1743	1832	1855	1912	1955	2038	2100	2103	2138	2311	2340	0544
206	Montauban d.	|	|	0933	1014	1113	1221	|	|	1309	|	1618	...	|	1821	1909	1942	1949	2032	2119	2146	...	2215	2348	0018	|
257	**Toulouse Matabiau** a.	0744	0812	0958	1039	1138	1246	1212	1326	1338	1445	1645	...	1659	1846	1936	2008	2015	2058	2145	2212	...	2243	0013	0043	0646
	Narbonne **321** a.	0857	|	...	1201	...	...	|	...	...	1602	...	...	|	2004	...	...	...	...	...	...	...	...	|	...	...
	Marseille **355** a.	...	1142	...	1442	...	...	1542	...	...	1842	...	...	2042	2242	...	...	...	...	...	...	...	...	0509	...	...
	Nice **360** a.	...	1434	...	...	...	...	1833	...	...	...	...	...	...	...	...	...	...	...	...	...	...	...	0807	...	...

	⑥ t	Ⓐ	TGV 5264 ♦	4720 4721 Ⓡ ♦	TGV 8518 ①-⑥ n	14100 Ⓐ	14102 Ⓐ B	3852 Ⓒ z	E	TGV 8528 ⊗	4752 4753 ★ D	4754 4755 ★ q	4756 4757 ★ ⊙	TGV 8548 k		TGV 8568 Ⓑ h	4758 4759 ★ ⊡	TGV 8570 ⑥ v		TGV 8580 Ⓑ h	4762 4763 ★	TGV 8586 ⑦ e	4764 4765 ★	TGV 5116 ♦	TGV 7992 ⑤⑦ w	4766 ★ ⑤⑦ p
Nice **360** d.	...	...	...	2056	...	...	...	...	...	...	...	...	...	...	...	...	0955	...	...	...	...	...	1329	...	...	...
Marseille **355** d.	...	...	...	0010	...	...	...	...	...	...	0614	0714	0914	...	...	...	1242	...	...	...	1414	...	1615	...	...	1841
Narbonne **321** d.	...	...	...	|	...	...	...	...	...	...	|	0952	1151	...	...	...	|	...	...	...	1652	...	|	1958	...	2126
Toulouse Matabiau d.	...	...	0529	0536	0608	0649	0748	0754	...	0922	0947	1115	1310	1314	...	1608	1621	1631	1656	1736	1811	1825	1950	2115	2218	2253
Montauban d.	...	...	0556	0609	0636	0718	0816	0822	...	|	|	1142	|	1342	...	1636	|	1701	1723	1803	1838	1853	|	|	|	2325
Agen d.	0525	0614	0632	0646	0714	0754	0853	0859	0947	|	|	1219	1411	1419	1439	1713	|	1740	1809	1840	1915	1930	|	2219	2339	|
Marmande d.	0556	0647	|	0717	|	0827	0923	0929	1024	|	|	1250	|	|	1514	|	|	|	1849	|	1945	|	|	|	|	|
Bordeaux St Jean a.	0642	0729	0737	0810	0817	0904	1007	1007	1114	1119	1147	1327	1513	1520	1554	1818	1823	1841	1933	1942	2022	2032	2150	2320	|	0101
Nantes **292** a.	...	...	...	...	|	...	...	1438	...	|	...	...	...	|	...	|	...	|	...	|	...	|	...	...	|	...
Paris M'parnasse **300** a.	...	...	...	...	1145	...	...	...	...	1440	...	...	...	1850	...	2130	...	2205	...	2300s	...	2355	...	...	0715c	...

FOR NOTES SEE TABLE 321 BELOW *For Paris - Toulouse via Limoges see Table* **310**.

TOULOUSE - NARBONNE 321

Other night trains: Hendaye / Bordeaux - Marseille - Nice see Table **355**; Hendaye - Genève see Table **355**

km		3731 Ⓡ ♦	Ⓐ	TGV 5301		TGV 5171 ♦	4652 4653 ★ ♠	TGV 5307 △	4654 4655 ★ ♣	a	4656 4657 ★ ♥	Ⓐ	4660 4661 ★ ▽	TGV 5315 Ⓑ h	⚒	TGV 5186 L	4658 4659 ★ H		3631 ★ m	4662 4663 ★ ◧	Ⓐ			4664 4665 ★	4666 4667 ★ ⑤⑦ y
	Paris Austerlitz **310** d.	2156	...	...	...	...	...	...	...	...	...	...	...	...	...	...	...	...	1019	...	...	...	...	...	
	Bordeaux **320** d.	|	...	...	...	0533	0610	...	0829	...	1010	...	1238	...	...	...	...	...	|	1459	...	...	...	1638r	...
0	**Toulouse Matabiau** ▷ d.	|	0617	0654	0701	0749	0817	1040	1044	1142	1217	1221	1450	1545	...	1609	1613	...	1648	1704	...	1747	1838	1851	1951
55	Castelnaudary ▷ d.	0517	0711	|	0745	|	|	|	1112	1217	|	1255	|	|	1551	|	1641	1645	1716	|	1735	1838	1906	|	|
91	Carcassonne ▷ d.	0538	0733	0742	0810	|	|	1127	1133	1242	|	1315	1534	1629	1614	1655	1701	1709	1737	|	1757	1859	1925	1936	2035
128	Lézignan d.	0601	0752	|	0831	|	|	|	|	1303	|	...	|	|	1632	|	|	1727	|	|	1815	...	1945	|	|
150	**Narbonne** a.	0615	0805	0809	0843	0857	|	1155	1201	1316	|	...	1602	1656	1643	1724	1730	1739	1805	|	1827	...	1958	2004	2104
	Marseille **355** a.	|	...	1041	...	|	1142	|	1442	...	1542	...	1842	|	...	|	2014	2038	|	2042	...	...	|	2242	2342
	Nice **360** a.	|	...	...	...	|	1434	|	...	...	1833	...	...	|	...	|	2304	...	|	...	...	...	|	...	...
	Lyon Part Dieu **350/1** a.	|	...	...	...	1149	...	1450	...	...	...	...	...	1946	...	2020	...	...	|	...	...	...	|	...	...
	Perpignan **355** a.	0720	...	...	...	...	...	...	...	...	...	...	...	...	...	...	...	...	1903	...	...	...	2108	...	...
	Cerbère **355** a.	0812	...	...	...	...	...	...	...	...	...	...	...	...	...	...	...	...	1951	...	...	...	...	...	...
	Portbou **355** a.	0821	...	...	...	...	...	...	...	...	...	...	...	...	...	...	...	...	...	...	...	...	...	...	...

	Ⓐ ◐	⚒	Ⓐ b	4752 4753 ★ D	Ⓐ	3630 ★	4754 4755 ★ q	TGV 5355 Ⓑ h	4756 4757 ★ ⊙		TGV 5104 L‡	4768 ★ F	4758 4759 ★ ⊡	Ub	4762 4763 ★	Ⓐ		Ⓐ	4764 4765 ★		TGV 5116 ♦	4766 ★ ⑤⑦ p	TGV 5385 u	TGV 5398	3730 Ⓡ ♦
Cerbère **355** d.	...	...	...	...	...	0750	...	...	...	1039	...	...	...	...	...	...	...	...	...	...	...	...	...	...	2121
Perpignan **355** d.	...	...	...	...	...	0840	...	...	...	1118	...	...	...	...	...	...	...	...	...	...	...	...	...	...	2210
Lyon Part Dieu **350/1** d.	...	...	...	...	...	|	...	0711	...	|	0937	...	...	...	...	...	...	...	...	...	1707	...	1911	...	|
Nice **360** d.	...	...	...	...	...	|	...	|	...	|	|	0827	0955	...	...	...	...	...	1329	...	|	...	|	...	|
Marseille **355** d.	...	...	...	0614	...	|	0714	|	0914	|	|	1114	1242	...	1414	...	...	...	1615	...	|	1841	|	1933	|
Narbonne d.	0649	0745	0815	|	0930	0938	0952	1002	|	1210	1238	1359	|	1533	1652	1745	...	1824	|	1847	1958	2126	2158	2204	2304
Lézignan d.	0702	0758	0828	|	0944	|	|	|	|	1223	|	|	|	1546	|	1759	...	1838	|	1900	|	|	|	|	2319
Carcassonne ▷ d.	0721	0819	0845	|	1005	1011	1023	1034	|	1244	1312	1430	|	1608	1723	1820	1842	1904	|	1920	2028	2157	|	2236	2341
Castelnaudary ▷ d.	0742	0841	0906	|	...	1032	1043	|	|	1305	|	1450	|	1630	|	...	1904	1926	|	1941	|	|	|	|	0001
Toulouse Matabiau ▷ a.	0819	0912	...	0942	...	1101	1110	1121	1305	1342	1355	1517	1612	1700	1806	...	1938	...	1944	2015	2110	2248	2309	2317	0029
Bordeaux **320** a.	...	...	...	1147	...	|	1327	...	1513	...	...	...	1823	...	2022	...	...	...	2150	...	2320	0101	...	...	|
Paris Austerlitz **310** a.	...	...	...	...	...	1741*	...	...	...	...	...	...	...	...	...	...	...	...	...	...	...	...	...	...	0727

♦ – **NOTES FOR TABLES 320/1** (LISTED BY TRAIN NUMBER):

3730 – *CORAIL LUNÉA* – 1,2 cl. and (2) (reclining) Cerbère - Paris. Not Dec. 24, 31.
3731 – *CORAIL LUNÉA* – 1,2 cl. and (2) (reclining) Paris - Portbou. Not Dec. 24, 31.
4620/1 – *CORAIL LUNÉA* – 1,2 cl. and (2) (reclining) Bordeaux - Nice. Not Dec. 24, 31. Starts from Hendaye on dates in Table **305** (numbered **4630/1**).
4720/1 – *CORAIL LUNÉA* – 1,2 cl. and (2) (reclining) Nice - Bordeaux. Not Dec. 24, 31. To Irún on dates in Table **305** (numbered **4730/1**).
5116 – (12) 🍷 Dijon - Lyon - Bordeaux.
5171 – (12) 🍷 Bordeaux - Toulouse - Lyon - Dijon.
5218 – (12) 🍷 Lille Flandres - Charles de Gaulle ✈ - Bordeaux - Toulouse (Table **11**).
5264 – (12) 🍷 Toulouse - Bordeaux - Charles de Gaulle ✈ - Lille Europe (Table **11**).

B – To Mar. 26 / from May 10.
D – Runs Marseille - Toulouse to Mar. 28 / from May 8, also ⑥⑦ Apr. 3 - May 2. Runs Marseille - Bordeaux to Jan. 3 / from May 8, also ⑥⑦ Mar. 27 - May 2.
E – Not on ①–⑤ Mar. 29 - May 7.
F – Dec. 18 - 20, 24, 26, 27, 31, Jan. 2, 3, Feb. 12 - 14, 19 - 21, 26 - 28, Mar. 6, 7, Apr. 5, 17, 24, May 2, 12, 16, 24.
H – Dec. 19, 20, 24, 26, 27, Jan. 1 - 3, Feb. 12 - 14, 19 - 21, 26, 28, Mar. 5, 7, Apr. 2, 5, 10, 16 - 18, May 2, 12, 21.
L – (12) Toulouse - Lyon - Charles de Gaulle ✈ - Lille Europe and v.v. (Table **11**).
N – Not on ①–⑤ Mar. 29 - May 7. On Jan. 4 - Mar. 26 runs only to Marmande.
R – Daily to Agen, Ⓑ to Toulouse.
U – Daily to Carcassonne, Ⓑ to Toulouse. Will not run on ①–⑤ Mar. 1 - 26.

a – To Montpellier (also Avignon Centre on Ⓐ), Table **355**.
b – To / from Montpellier and Avignon Centre.
c – 0555 on morning of ① (also Dec. 25, Apr. 6).
d – Toulouse times vary (arrive 1202 Jan. 4 - 8, 11 - 13; 1148 on Ⓐ Jan. 14 - 22, Feb. 1 - 12, Feb. 22 - Mar. 12). On Feb. 15 - 19 Bordeaux d. 1012, Toulouse a. 1251.
e – Also Apr. 5, May 24.
f – Also Dec. 24, 31, May 12; not Dec. 25, Jan. 1.
g – Arrive Toulouse 1412 on Feb. 20, Mar. 27.
h – Not Dec. 25, Jan. 1, May 13.
k – On Dec. 16, 17 depart Toulouse 1213.
m – Depart Paris 0951 on Mar. 2, 3, 11. Will not run on ①–⑤ Mar. 22 - Apr. 23.
n – Not Apr. 5, May 24.
p – Also Dec. 24, 26, 31, Jan. 2, Apr. 5, May 12, 24; not Dec. 25, Jan. 1, Apr. 4, May 14.
q – On Ⓑ Jan. 4 - Mar. 26 runs 17 - 20 minutes later Toulouse - Bordeaux.
r – 1625 Jan. 4 - Mar. 12.
s – Arrive 20 minutes later on Dec. 14 - 17, arrive 15 minutes later on ①–④ Jan. 11 - 21.
t – Not May 1, 8.
u – From Dijon on dates in Table **355**.
v – Also Dec. 25, Jan. 1, May 13.
w – Also Apr. 5, May 24; not Dec. 25, Jan. 1, Apr. 4, May 14.
x – Also Apr. 5, May 24; not Apr. 4, May 23.
y – Also Jan. 2, Apr. 5, May 24; not Dec. 20, 25, Jan. 1, Apr. 4, May 14, 23.
z – Not Apr. 5, May 13, 15, 16.

TGV – Ⓡ, supplement payable, 🍷.

★ – *CORAIL TÉOZ*, Ⓡ, 🍷.
♠ – Not on ①–⑤ Mar. 1 - 26. Depart Bordeaux 0600 on Jan. 4 - Feb. 28 (also Mar. 6, 7, 13).
♣ – Not on ①–⑤ Mar. 1 - 26. Depart Bordeaux 0817 on Jan. 4 - Feb. 28 (also Mar. 6, 7).
♥ – Not on ①–⑤ Mar. 8 - 26. Depart Bordeaux 1000 Jan. 4 - Mar. 7.
◧ – Not on ①–⑤ Mar. 29 - May 7. Runs earlier Jan. 4 - Mar. 12 (Bordeaux 1423, Toulouse 1638, Marseille 2016).
◐ – From Nimes, Table **355**.
⊙ – Not on ①–⑤ Mar. 29 - Apr. 9. On ①–⑤ Jan. 11 - 21 depart Marseille 0821. Subject to alteration Toulouse - Bordeaux Dec. 14 - 17, Apr. 19 - 23, May 13 - 15.
⊡ – Not on ①–⑤ Mar. 1 - 26.
◇ – Depart Paris 1120 on Jan. 14, 18 - 21.
△ – On ①–⑤ Mar. 1 - 26 runs 25 - 40 minutes later. Continues to Dijon on dates in Table **355**.
▽ – Not on ①–⑤ Mar. 29 - May 7. Not Bordeaux - Toulouse on Dec. 16, 17.
⊕ – On Ⓐ Jan. 4 - Feb. 5, Feb. 15 - 19 depart Paris 0755. Arrive Toulouse 1348 on Ⓐ Jan. 4 - Feb. 5, Feb. 15 - Mar. 12. On Feb. 8 - 12 Bordeaux d. 1150, Toulouse a. 1418.
⊗ – On Jan. 4 - Mar. 26 Toulouse d. 0840, Bordeaux a. 1054. Will not run Ⓐ Mar. 29 - May 7.
§ – Depart Bordeaux and Marmande 10 minutes earlier Jan. 4 - Mar. 12.
‡ – Train **9804** on Ⓐ (from Brussels).
* – 1815 on Dec. 14, 15.

▷ – Additional trains Toulouse - Carcassonne (journey approx 70 minutes):
From Toulouse: 0820, 0950, 1313, 1510, 1617 Ⓐ, 1710 Ⓐ, 1959.
From Carcassonne: 0607 Ⓐ, 0649, 1135, 1319, 1434 Ⓐ, 1537, 1646 Ⓐ, 1735 Ⓐ.

323 TOULOUSE - ALBI - RODEZ - MILLAU

km		Ⓐ	n			Ⓐ		⑥🚌	Ⓐu				Ⓑ🚌		Ⓐ		⚒🚌	Ⓐ			Ⓐ		PⓇ	Ⓐ	
0	**Toulouse Matabiau 316** d.	0619	...	0721	0902	1017	1120	...	...	1158	1300	1419	...	1600	1656	1710	...	1730	1800	...	1815	1900	...	1928	2120
54	Gaillac **316** d.	0701	...	0806	0953	1104	1205	...	...	1244	1353	1501	...	1652	1741	1756	...	1820	1853	...	1905	1939	...	2021	2214
58	Tessonnières **316** d.	|	...	|	1001	|	|	...	...	1249	1358	|	...	1657	1746	|	...	1824	|	...	1911	|	...	2027	2222
75	**Albi Ville** d.	0715	...	0826	1016	1117	1224	...	...	1305	1412	1515	...	1711	1804	1815	...	1841	1909	...	1925	2001	2038	2045	2237
92	Carmaux d.	0732	...	0845	1032	1132	1243	...	...	1320	1429	1532	...	1728	...	1831	...	1903	1925	...	...	2018	2058	2101	2253
158	**Rodez** d.	0830	0852	0947	...	1230	1345	1410	1427	...	...	1628	1636	...	...	1937	1942	...	2025	2106	...	2119	2207	...	...
202	Sévérac-le-Château **332** d.	...	0936	...	...	...	...	1454	1511	...	...	...	1717	...	...	...	2023	...	...	2147	...	...	...	...	...
232	**Millau 332** a.	...	1005	...	...	...	...	1530	1538	...	...	...	1751	...	...	...	2053	...	...	2214	...	...	...	...	...

	Ⓐ	Ⓐ			Ⓐ	PⓇ				Ⓐ🚌			Ⓒ🚌	Ⓐn	Ⓐ	Ⓐ				Ⓐu	Ⓐ	†🚌		Ⓒ	
Millau 332 d.	...	...	...	...	...	...	0618	...	...	0900	...	...	1005	1027	...	...	...	...	...	1605	...	1650	...	1917	...
Sévérac-le-Château **332** d.	...	...	...	...	...	...	0648	...	...	0930	...	...	1040	1057	...	...	...	...	...	1636	...	1725	...	1951	...
Rodez d.	...	...	...	...	0633	0708	0729	0744	0833	1014	1024	...	1130	1138	1233	...	1433	...	1634	1716	1731	1808	1824	2033	2058
Carmaux d.	0510	0555	0624	0654	0733	0806	...	0846	0933	...	1133	1205	...	...	1330	1455	1533	1654	1731	...	1832	...	1926	...	2153
Albi Ville d.	0526	0614	0642	0716	0750	0824	...	0904	0949	...	1150	1223	...	...	1346	1516	1550	1720	1748	...	1849	...	1943	...	2209
Tessonnières **316** d.	0540	0630	0657	0732	|	...	...	|	|	...	|	1237	...	...	|	1532	|	1734	|	...	|	...	|	...	|
Gaillac **316** d.	0545	0635	0701	0737	0806	...	...	0925	1005	...	1205	1243	...	...	1405	1537	1604	1740	1806	...	1915	...	2002	...	2226
Toulouse Matabiau 316 a.	0635	0725	0749	0830	0843	...	...	1008	1043	...	1244	1329	...	...	1449	1625	1641	1833	1842	...	1950	...	2043	...	2304

P – 🛏 1, 2 cl. and 💺 (reclining) Paris - Rodez - Albi and v.v. For days of running see Table **316**.

n – Not Apr. 30, May 7, 14.

u – Subject to alteration on Apr. 26-29, May 3-6, 10-12.

324 PAU - OLORON - CANFRANC

km		Ⓐ‡	§	§		Ⓑh	⚒	†	⚒	
0	**Pau** d.	0730	0905	1220	1345	1533	1705	1747	1830	1957
36	Oloron-Ste-Marie a.	0807	0942	1257	1422	1610	1742	1824	1907	2034
36	Oloron-Ste-Marie 🚌 d.	*0816*	*0950*	...	*1440*	...	*1749*r	*1835*	*1914*	...
58	Bedous (Gare) 🚌 d.	*0841*	*1015*	...	*1505*	...	*1814*r	*1900*	*1939*	...
73	Urdos 🏛 🚌 d.	*0901*	*1035*	...	*1525*	...	*1834*r	*1920*	*1959*	...
90	**Canfranc** (Gare) 🚌 a.	*0937*	*1111*	...	*1601*	...	...	...	...	...

	Ⓐn	Ⓒ	Ⓐ‡	§	Ⓐ§	Ⓒ		⚒	†	⚒◇
Canfranc (Gare) 🚌 d.	...	...	...	...	*1120*	...	*1257*	*1612*	*1654*	...
Urdos 🏛 🚌 d.	...	...	...	...	*1152*	...	*1329*	*1644*	*1726*	...
Bedous (Gare) 🚌 d.	...	...	...	...	*1212*	...	*1349*	*1704*	*1746*	...
Oloron-Ste-Marie 🚌 a.	...	...	...	...	*1241*	...	*1418*	*1733*	*1815*	...
Oloron-Ste-Marie d.	0648	0725	0812	1053	1303	1303	1428	1748	1829	1915
Pau a.	0725	0802	0849	1130	1340	1340	1505	1825	1906	1952

h – Also May 1, 8; not Mar. 2.

n – On ① (also Apr. 6, May 25; not Apr. 5, May 24) d. 0630, a. 0707.

r – ⑤ only.

◇ – Additional journeys: 1616 Ⓐ, 1650 †, 2123 †.

§ – Subject to alteration on ①–⑤ Jan. 11-22, Apr. 12-23.

‡ – Subject to alteration on ①–⑤ Apr. 12-23.

🚌 – By SNCF bus Oloron - Canfranc and v.v. (timings subject to confirmation)

325 HENDAYE - BAYONNE - TARBES - TOULOUSE

km				⚒	‡	Ⓐ	14140	14142 ▽	⊗‡	Ⓐ ⊗	14144 ⊙			Ⓐ ⊙	14146 ⊙	14148 Ⓐ	14150 Ⓒ	Ⓐ	Ⓑ	†	⚒	14152 ⑤⑦ u	4678 4679 Ⓡ G	†
0	**Hendaye 305** d.	...	...	...	...	...	0607	0745	...	...	1145x	...	...	...	...	...	...	...	...	...	...	1824	1807	...
13	St Jean de Luz **305** d.	...	...	...	...	...	0620	0757	...	...	1156x	...	...	...	...	...	...	...	...	...	...	1835	1820	...
26	Biarritz **305** § d.	...	...	...	...	...	0632	0809	...	...	1207x	...	...	...	...	...	...	...	...	...	...	1846	1850	...
36	**Bayonne 305** § a.	...	...	...	...	...	0641	0819	...	...	1217x	...	...	...	...	...	...	...	...	...	...	1856	1900	...
36	**Bayonne 305** § d.	...	...	0545c	...	0608	0700	0839	...	...	1238	...	...	1437	1515	1627	1659	1717	...	1805	1819	1918	1902	2016
	Dax **305** d.	...	...	|	...	|	|	|	...	...	|	...	...	|	|	|	|	|	...	|	|	|	1958	|
87	Puyoô **305** d.	...	...	0616c	...	0654	0736	|	...	...	1315	...	...	1519	|	1708	1733	1755	...	1843	1858	|	|	2104
101	Orthez **305** d.	...	...	0627c	...	0704	0748	|	...	...	1326	...	...	1530	|	1719	1744	1806	...	1853	1910	|	2030	2114
141	**Pau 305** d.	...	0600	0653	...	0736	0814	0946	...	1227	1354	...	1550z	1558	1620	1743	1808	1832	1858	1917	1938	2028	2100	2139
180	Lourdes **305** d.	0601	0629	0722	...	0805	0843	1012	...	1256	1423	...	|	...	1646	1811	1836	1907	1926	1950	...	2054	2134	2210
201	**Tarbes 305** d.	0617	0646	0736	0807	0820	0859	1029	1112	1315	1439	1540	1628	...	1702	1828	1853	1923	1945	2006	...	2110	2156	2225
238	Lannemezan d.	0645	0714	...	0835	...	0922	|	1140	1343	|	1607	1657	...	|	1852	1917	...	2013	...	...	|	2220	...
255	Montréjeau d.	0657	0726	...	0848	...	0933	|	1152	1354	|	1618	1709	...	|	1904	1929	...	2024	...	...	|	|	...
268	St Gaudens d.	0706	0736	...	0857	...	0943	|	1202	1404	|	1627	1718	...	|	1914	1939	...	2034	...	...	|	2240	...
293	Boussens d.	0720	0751	...	0912	...	|	|	1216	1418	|	1640	1734	...	|	|	|	...	2048	...	...	|	|	...
359	**Toulouse Matabiau** a.	0759r	0842	...	1012	...	1028*	1153	1259	1458	1600	1738	1820	...	1826	2000	2024	...	2129	...	...	2236	2324	...

	Ⓐ	⚒	4778 4779 Ⓡ H	Ⓐ		Ⓑ h	14141 ⚒ △	▷‡	14143 ⊡	14145 14165 ⊙	⊕	⑤ ⊕v	14147 Ⓐ	14149 Ⓒ	⚒	Ⓐ	14151 14153 b		†		Ⓐ	14155 ⑤⑦ u		
Toulouse Matabiau d.	...	...	0609	0613	0714	...	0810	0908	0958	1151	1205	1205	1330	1330	1435	...	1636	1704	1704	...	1808	1906	1936	2106
Boussens d.	...	...	|	0712	0754	...	|	0947	|	|	1305	1305	|	|	1532	...	|	1748	1748	...	1853	|	2031	2201
St Gaudens d.	...	...	0659	0735	0808	...	|	1001	1042	|	1319	1319	1413	1413	1545	...	|	1804	1804	...	1908	|	2045	2215
Montréjeau d.	...	...	|	0746	0818	...	|	1011	1052	|	1329	1329	1423	1423	1555	...	|	1814	1814	...	1918	|	2054	2225
Lannemezan d.	...	...	0720	0758	0830	...	|	1023	1104	|	1341	1341	1436	1436	1606	...	|	1826	1826	...	1930	|	2106	2237
Tarbes 305 d.	...	0632	0746	0825	0857	...	0935	1048	1129	1316	1408	1411	1500	1500	1630	1713	1800	1855	1855	...	1958	2034	2133	2304
Lourdes **305** d.	...	0649	0803	...	...	...	0951	...	1145	1331	...	1427	1516	1516	1647	1728	1818	1914	1914	...	...	2050	2152	2321
Pau 305 d.	0633	0721	0833	...	...	0920	1018	...	1214	1358	...	1456	1545	1545	1715	1756	1846	1941	1943	1952	...	2117	2220	...
Orthez **305** d.	0657	0744	0859	...	...	0944	|	...	1238	|	...	...	1611	1611	...	1822	|	...	2005	2018	...	|	...	...
Puyoô **305** d.	0709	0757	|	...	...	0955	|	...	1249	|	...	...	1622	1621	...	1833	|	...	2016	2028	...	|	...	...
Dax d.	|	|	0952	...	...	|	|	...	|	|	...	...	|	|	...	|	|	...	|	|	...	|	...	...
Bayonne 305 § a.	0749	0834	1029	...	...	1035	1123	...	1328	1507	...	...	1657	1656	...	1913	1954	...	2053	2106	...	2223	...	...
Bayonne 305 § d.	0759	...	1032	...	...	...	...	...	...	...	...	...	1721	1717	...	...	2015	...	2113	2116	...	2243	...	...
Biarritz **305** § d.	0809	...	1044	...	...	...	...	...	...	...	...	...	1732	1728	...	...	2025	...	2123	2126	...	2254	...	...
St Jean de Luz **305** d.	0822	...	1056	...	...	...	...	...	...	...	...	...	1744	1740	...	...	2037	...	2134	2139	...	2305	...	...
Hendaye **305** a.	0834	...	1105	...	...	...	...	...	...	...	...	...	1753	1749	...	...	2046	...	2143	2151	...	2314	...	...
Irún 305 a.	...	...	1115	...	...	...	...	...	...	...	...	...	...	...	...	...	...	...	...	...	...	...	...	...

	🚌 ⚒	🚌 ⚒	🚌	▽	🚌 †	🚌 ⚒	🚌 ⚒	Ⓒ	🚌 ⚒	🚌 †	3992 ⓇZ	3990 ⓇY
Luchon ◐ d.	0620	0830	0950	1058	1317	1455	1606	1700	1755	1945	2042	2136
Montréjeau d.	0713	0922	1038	1215	1405	1540	1656	1812	1840	2037	2200	2254
St Gaudens d.	...	...	...	1225	...	...	...	1822	...	...	2212	2306
Boussens d.	...	...	...	1246	...	...	...	1838	...	...	2227	2320
Toulouse M a.	...	...	...	1342	...	...	...	1927	...	...	2307	0001

	3991 ⓇW	🚌 ⚒	🚌 ⚒	q	🚌	🚌 ⚒	🚌 †	🚌 ⚒	🚌	🚌
Toulouse M d.	0542	...	...	0730	...	...	...	...	...	...
Boussens d.	0622	...	...	0821	...	...	...	...	...	...
St Gaudens d.	0637	...	...	0837	...	...	...	...	...	...
Montréjeau d.	0707	0720	0805	0904	1100	1405	1430	1625	1825	2100
Luchon a.	0805	0813	0853	0956	1153	1454	1518	1713	1913	2145

G – *CORAIL LUNÉA* – ⑤⑦ (daily Dec. 18-23, 25-30, Jan. 1-3, Feb. 12 - Mar. 7, Apr. 1 - May 2), also May 12, 24; not May 14, 23. 🛏 1, 2 cl., 💺 (reclining) Hendaye - Lyon - Genève.

H – *CORAIL LUNÉA* – from Genève (next day from Toulouse) on ⑤⑦ (daily Dec. 18-23, 25-30, Jan. 1-3, Feb. 12 - Mar. 7, Apr. 1 - May 2), also May 12, 24; not May 14, 23. 🛏 1, 2 cl. and 💺 (reclining) Genève - Lyon - Irún. Train number **14778** on certain dates.

W – From Paris on ⑤ (also ⑥ Dec. 19 - Mar. 6), also May 12; not May 14. 🛏 1, 2 cl. Paris Austerlitz (d. 2156) - Luchon.

Y – ⑥ Dec. 19 - Mar. 6 (also Apr. 5, May 24). 🛏 1, 2 cl. Luchon - Paris Austerlitz (arrive 0727).

Z – ⑦ (not Apr. 4, May 23). 🛏 1, 2 cl. Luchon - Paris Austerlitz (arrive 0727).

b – On ⑤⑦ and holidays arrive Bayonne 2006 and runs 11 minutes later Bayonne - Hendaye.

c – ① (also Apr. 6, May 25; not Apr. 5, May 24).

h – Also May 1, 8.

q – Subject to alteration on June 1-3, 8-10.

r – 0816 on Ⓒ.

u – Also Dec. 25, Jan. 1, Apr. 5, May 1, 8, 13, 24.

v – Not Feb. 12, 19.

x – † only.

z – ⑤ only.

◐ – Luchon - Montréjeau is *35* km.

▽ – Not on ①–⑤ Feb. 22 - Mar. 12, June 7-18.

△ – Not on ①–⑤ Feb. 8-19, May 24 - June 4.

▷ – Not on ①–⑤ Feb. 8-19.

⊡ – Not on ①–⑤ Feb. 8 - Mar. 5, May 24 - June 4.

⊙ – Not on ①–⑤ Feb. 8 - Mar. 5.

⊕ – Subject to alteration Boussens - Tarbes Apr. 12-23.

⊗ – Not on ①–⑤ Feb. 22 - Mar. 12.

§ – 🚌 services available to / from Biarritz town.

‡ – Subject to alteration Montrejeau - Boussens and v.v. on ①–⑤ Apr. 12-23.

* – Arrive 1038 from May 10.

From May 10 departures from Toulouse are 5-6 minutes earlier and arrivals may be 3-4 minutes later

BRIVE / LIMOGES - USSEL - CLERMONT FERRAND — 326

km			4490	🚌	4492					
		⚒‡	⑤v	Ⓐ	⑥		⑤f	⑤f	⚒	⑦d
	Bordeaux **302** d.	...	0734	...	0908	...	...	...	...	...
0	**Brive la Gaillarde** d.	0625	1001	1050	1111	1316	1539	1617	1734	1815
26	Tulle d.	0654	1037	1130	1146	1344	1609	1647	1809	1844
79	Meymac d.	0747	1135	1238	1244	1433	1705	1743	1857	1942
92	**Ussel** a.	0801	1149	1302	1258	1446	1718	1755	1910	1955
	Clermont Ferrand § a.	1012a	...	...	1453	...	1923	1950	...	2202

				4595	4591					
	①g		△	⑦d	⑤v		⑤f	†	⑦d	⑦d
Clermont Ferrand § d.	...	...	1009	1409	...	...	1730	...	1847	2042
Ussel d.	0541	0847	1227	1612	1612	1612	1928	1928	2040	2242
Meymac d.	0554	0900	1245	1627	1627	1627	1944	1944	2053	2255
Tulle d.	0650	0954	1343	1734	1734	1734	2037	2037	2155	2349
Brive la Gaillarde a.	0716	1021	1409	1756	1756	1757	2100	2100	2221	0010
Bordeaux **302** a.	...	...	...	2017	2018	...	...	...	...	...

km				🚌	🚌		4492		🚌	🚌	🚌	🚌			🚌	🚌		🚌			🚌			🚌	
		⚒	Ⓐ‡	⑥t		▽	⑥	Ⓐ	⑥t	⑤	⑦d	⚒	⚒z	†	Ⓒ	⑥t	†	H	⑤f	⑤f	⑤f	⑤f	H	⑦d	⑦d
	Brive la Gaillarde § d.	...	0625	...	...	...	1111	...	...	...	...	...	...	...	...	...	...	...	1539	1617	...	...	...	...	1815
	Limoges § d.	...	|	...	...	...	|	...	...	...	...	...	1322	1322	...	...	...	...	|	|	...	1701	1714	...	|
0	**Ussel** d.	...	0811	...	1032	...	1302	...	...	...	...	...	1520	1529	1620	...	...	...	1721	1759	...	1930	1930	...	1958
18	Eygurande-Merlines d.	...	0828	...	1052	...	1320	...	...	...	...	...	1539	1547	1636	...	...	...	1739	1818	...	1949	1948	...	2020
*13	**Le Mont Dore** d.	0558	*0822*c	0850	|	1103	|	1426	1432	1444	1449	1534	|	*1543*c	|	1655	1653	1730	*1734*c	|	1943	|	|	2016	|
*8	La Bourboule d.	0605	*0830*c	0858	|	1111	|	1433	1440	1452	1457	1540	|	*1549*c	|	1703	1700	1738	*1742*c	|	1951	|	|	2024	|
40	Laqueuille d.	0616	0853	0910	1112	1122	1345	1444	1453	1505	1510	1553	1603	1612	1705	1715	1718	1750	1804	1846	2003	2014	2013	2036	2047
100	Royat-Chamalières d.	0725	1003	|	...	1225	1445	1547	1600	...	...	...	|	|	...	|	1823	|	|	|	...	2126	2112	...	2153
105	**Clermont Ferrand** a.	0735	1012	1010	...	1234	1453	1557	1615	...	...	...	1710	1720	...	1815	1832	1855	1923	1950	...	2133	2119	...	2202

		🚌	🚌		🚌	🚌		🚌	4595	🚌	🚌		🚌	🚌		🚌			🚌		🚌		🚌		🚌
	⚒‡	⚒	①n	△	⑤	⑥t	Ⓑ		⑦d	⚒	†	S	⑥t	⑥t	⑤f	⑦d	†	Ⓐ	H	⑦d	H	⑤x	⑤f	⑦d	⑤f
Clermont Ferrand d.	0610	...	...	1009	...	1240	1248	...	1409	...	...	1645	1737	...	1730	1750	1758	1803	...	1847	1935	2012	...	2042	*2136*
Royat-Chamalières d.	0619	...	...	1018	...	|	1256	...	1417	...	...	1653	|	...	1738	|	1807	1812	...	1856	|	2019	...	2050	|
Laqueuille d.	0726	0730	0903	1127	1249	1353	1402	1407	1520	1607	1616	1759	1837	1842	1845	|	1913	1927	1931	1954	2038	2127	2134	2157	2236
La Bourboule a.	|	0743	0916	*1135*c	1300	1406	1413	|	*1538*c	1620	1629	1810	1849	|	|	|	1924	1937	|	|	2050	2138	|	*2212*c	2248
Le Mont Dore a.	|	0751	0924	*1141*c	1309	1414	1420	|	*1543*c	1628	1637	1817	1857	|	|	|	1931	1945	|	|	2058	2145	|	*2220*c	2256
Eygurande-Merlines d.	0752	...	...	1152	...	...	...	1427	1546	...	...	...	...	1900	1911	|	...	...	1951	2021	...	...	2152	2222	...
Ussel a.	0808	...	...	1209	...	...	...	1447	1603	...	...	...	...	1920	1927	1918	...	...	2011	2037	...	...	2212	2238	...
Limoges § a.	1009	...	...	|	...	...	...	...	|	...	...	...	...	...	|	...	...	...	...	|	...	...	...	|	...
Brive la Gaillarde § a.	...	...	...	1409	...	...	...	...	1756	...	...	...	...	...	2100	...	...	...	...	2221	...	...	...	0010	...

LIMOGES - USSEL

km		Ⓐ	Ⓐ	⑥		⑤f	⑥t	H	†	⑤f	
0	**Limoges** d.	0537	1023	1119	1322	1701	1701	1714	1714	1835	2034
98	Meymac d.	0721	1205	1301	1502	1913	1913	1913	1902	2019	2216
111	**Ussel** a.	0733	1218	1313	1515	1925	1925	1925	1914	2032	2228

	⚒	⚒‡	⑥	Ⓑ		⑦b	⑦u	⑤	⑥t	Ⓑ	
Ussel d.	0617	0817	*1227*	1245	...	1518	1557	*1612*	*1612*	1801	...
Meymac d.	0630	0831	1258	1258	...	1531	1616	1636	1636	1814	...
Limoges a.	0816	1009	1442	1442	...	1710	1800	1823	1822	1958	...

H – ①–④ (not Dec. 24, 31, Apr. 5, May 12, 13, 24).
S – June 12 - July 4 (also Feb. 13, 20, 27).
a – Ⓐ only.
b – Also Dec. 25, Jan. 1, May 1, 8.
c – Connection by 🚌.
d – Also Apr. 5, May 24; not Apr. 4, May 23.
f – Also Dec. 24, 31, May 12; not Dec. 25, Jan. 1.
g – Also Apr. 6, May 25; not Dec. 26, Jan. 2, Apr. 5, May 2, 9, 24.
n – Also Apr. 6, May 25; not Apr. 5, May 24.
t – Not May 1, 8.
u – Also Dec. 25, Jan. 1, Apr. 5, May 13, 24.
v – Also Dec. 21 - 24, 28 - 31; not Dec. 25, Jan. 1.
x – Also May 12; not Dec. 25, Jan. 1.
z – Subject to alteration on ①–⑤ Apr. 5 - 30, May 24 - June 4.
△ – Not Dec. 22, 24, Feb. 16, 18, ①–⑤ Apr. 12 - 30, May 25 - June 4, June 8, 10.
▽ – Not Feb. 14, 21, 28, Apr. 19 - 23.
§ – See other part of this table.
‡ – Subject to alteration on Ⓐ Apr. 19 - 30.
* – Distance from Laqueuille.

LIMOGES - MONTLUÇON - LYON — 327

km		🚌		🚌		4403	4480	🚌		
		⚒	①g	Ⓐ	⑥t	⚒z	B	Ⓐ	△	⑤f
	Bordeaux **302** d.	...	...	...	...	...	1047	...	...	...
0	**Limoges** d.	...	0556	...	0805	...	1313	...	1553	1840
78	Guéret d.	...	0701	...	0908	...	1416	...	1705	1944
156	**Montluçon 329** d.	0730	0758	1000	1007	...	1515	1745	1804	2045
224	Gannat **329** d.	0850	▬	|	1108	...	1620	1903	▬	...
247	**St Germain des Fossés** d.	|	h	1124	1121	1135	|	|	Ⓐ§	...
	Vichy **330** a.	0919	0929	...	...	|	|	1924	1938	...
314	Roanne **328** d.	...	1014	...	...	1216	1713	...	2021	...
411	**Lyon Part Dieu 328** a.	...	1117	...	...	1324	1816	...	2125	...
411	**Lyon Perrache 328** a.	...	1129	...	...	1339	1829	...	2137	...

			4504	🚌	4580			🚌		
	①g	⚒d	⚒z	Ⓐ	G	⑤⑦r		⑤⑦		⑤⑦r
Lyon Perrache 328 d.	...	...	0904	...	1251	...	1620	...	1720	...
Lyon Part Dieu 328 d.	...	...	0918	...	1305	...	1634	...	1734	...
Roanne 328 d.	...	...	1032	...	1414	...	1739	...	1839	...
Vichy **330** d.	...	...	|	...	|	...	1822	1826	1921	...
St Germain des Fossés d.	...	...	1112	1135	|	...	...	|	|	...
Gannat **329** d.	...	...	...	|	1508	...	...	|	*1953*c	...
Montluçon 329 d.	0617	0800	...	1301	1605	1912	...	1953	*2111*c	2146
Guéret d.	0738	0910	...	...	1704	2012	...	...	...	2243
Limoges a.	0842	1015	...	...	1804	2110	...	...	...	2343
Bordeaux **302** a.	...	...	...	...	2037	...	...	...	...	...

B – Dec. 13 - Jan. 17; ⑤–⑦ Jan. 22 - Feb. 28; daily Mar. 5 - Apr. 25.
G – Dec. 13 - Jan. 17; ⑤–⑦ Jan. 22 - Feb. 28; daily Mar. 5 - Apr. 11, also Apr. 17, 18, 24, 25.
c – Connection by 🚌.
d – Subject to alteration on ②–⑤ Jan. 19 - Mar. 5, also May 29.
f – Also Dec. 24, 31, May 12; not Dec. 25, Jan. 1.
g – Also Apr. 6, May 25; not Apr. 5, May 24.
h – Not on ①–⑤ Apr. 12 - May 7.
r – Also Dec. 24, 25, Apr. 5, May 12, 13, 24; not May 30.
t – Not May 1, 8, 22, 29, June 5, 12.
z – Not on ①–⑤ Apr. 12 - 30.
△ – Subject to alteration on ①–④ Jan. 18 - Mar. 4, also May 29, 30.
§ – Not June 7 - 9.

CLERMONT FERRAND - LYON — 328

km		⚒		⚒	⚒					Ⓐ	⑦
			h	s	z	k	b	n		§	
0	**Clermont Ferrand** ▷ d.	0633	0858	1036	...	1158	1406	1504	1755	1906	1958
14	Riom-Châtel-Guyon ▷ d.	0643	0907	1049	...	1207	1415	1513	1804	1915	2007
55	Vichy **330** d.	0705	0929	|	...	1229	1436	1535	1826	1938	2028
65	St Germain des Fossés d.	|	|	1128	1135	|	|	|	|	|	|
132	Roanne **290** ▶ d.	0751	1014	...	1216	1314	1522	1620	1912	2021	2114
229	**Lyon Part Dieu 290** ▶ a.	0856	1117	...	1324	1417	1625	1724	2017	2125	2217
229	**Lyon Perrache 290** a.	0908	1129	...	1339	1429	1637	1736	2029	2137	2229

	⚒				Ⓐ				
		d							
Lyon Perrache 290 d.	0620	1120	1420	1511	...	1620	1720	1820	2020
Lyon Part Dieu 290 ▶ d.	0634	1134	1434	1526	...	1634	1734	1834	2034
Roanne **290** ▶ d.	0739	1239	1539	1637	...	1739	1839	1942	2139
St Germain des Fossés d.	|	|	|	1717	1739	|	|	|	|
Vichy **330** d.	0823	1322	1625	...	1747	1822	1922	2025	2222
Riom-Châtel-Guyon ▷ d.	0844	1343	1647	...	1811	1843	1944	2048	2244
Clermont Ferrand ▷ a.	0853	1353	1657	...	1822	1852	1952	2057	2252

CLERMONT FERRAND - ST ÉTIENNE

km		Ⓐ	⚒			u				
0	**Clermont Ferrand** d.	...	0749	0903	...	1121	...	1613	1823	...
112	Montbrison d.	0749	0933	1046	...	1301	...	1801	2016	...
145	**St Étienne** Châteaucreux a.	0829	1008	1124	...	1336	...	1839	2049	...

	⚒	Ⓐ		u					
St Étienne Châteaucreux d.	0608	0807	...	1228	1404	...	1729	1915	...
Montbrison d.	0653	0846	...	1259	1435	...	1803	1944	...
Clermont Ferrand a.	0849	...	...	1436	1608	...	1940	2119	...

b – Not on Feb. 15 - 20, 22 - 26. Train **5528** on certain dates.
d – Not on ①–⑤ Feb. 15 - 26, Apr. 5, 12 - 30, May 24. Train **5526** on certain dates.
h – Not on ①–⑤ Apr. 12 - May 7.
k – Not Dec. 13 - 18, Feb. 15 - 26, May 3 - 7.
n – Not Feb. 15 - 26, May 3 - 7.
s – Not on ①–⑤ Apr. 5 - 16, May 3 - 7.
u – Subject to alteration on Apr. 19 - 23.
z – Not on ①–⑤ Apr. 12 - 30.
▷ – See also Tables **329** and **330**.
▶ – Local trains Roanne - Lyon Part Dieu (journey 90 minutes):
From Roanne: 0522 Ⓐ, 0559, 0627 Ⓐ, 0711 ⚒, 0729, 0829 ⚒, 0929, 1123 ⚒,
From Lyon Part Dieu: 0808 ⚒, 1008, 1208, 1508, 1608, 1708, 1800, 1908 Ⓐ, 2008 Ⓑ, 2108.
§ – Not June 7 - 9.

MONTLUÇON - CLERMONT FERRAND — 329

km		⚒	Ⓐ	⑦	Ⓐc		Ⓒ	Ⓑr		†
0	**Montluçon 327** d.	0600	0715	0840	0937	1230	*1515*z	1710	1821	1925
68	Gannat **327** d.	0705	0817	0936	1034	1333	1642	1814	1929	2023
96	Riom-Châtel-Guyon d.	0730	0836	0953	1051	1355	1708	1831	1947	2040
110	**Clermont Ferrand** a.	0744	0845	1002	1101	1404	1719	1841	1956	2049

	Ⓐ	⚒	Ⓐ	†	⚒	x	Ⓐ	Ⓑ	⑥t	Ⓑ	⑤†
Clermont Ferrand d.	0555	0654	0744	1035	1303	*1418*	1615	1733	1808	1820	2003
Riom-Châtel-Guyon d.	0609	0704	0757	1044	1313	*1431*	1624	1745	1821	1831	2015
Gannat **327** d.	0626	0723	0818	1105	1334	1508	1643	1811	1849	1849	2039
Montluçon 327 a.	0727	0828	0918	1205	1436	1605	1740	1906	1953	1953	2136

c – Subject to alteration Mar. 29 - Apr. 16.
r – Not Dec. 24, 31, Apr. 4.
t – Not May 1, 8.
x – See Table **327** note **G**.
z – See Table **327** note **B**.

Subject to alteration from Apr. 6

330 PARIS - NEVERS - CLERMONT FERRAND

km							5951	5953	5955		5957		5959	5963		5967	5971	5975			5979	5981	5983	5985
							🅁★	🅁★	🅁★		🅁★		🅁★	🅁★		🅁★	🅁★	🅁★			🅁★	🅁★	🅁★	🅁★
		⚒	Ⓐ	⚒	†	Ⓐ	⚒			⚒		Ⓐ				⑤		①-⑤	⚒	†	Ⓑ	⑤		
							⊗	R	⊗	⊡	T	⊡			△	d			▽		k	f	A	X
0	**Paris Gare de Lyon** ▶ d.	...	...	...	...	...	0701	0801	0901	...	1101	...	1301	1401	...	1456	1601	1701	...	...	1801	1901	1901	2101
254	**Nevers** ▶ d.	...	...	0640	...	...	0858	0958	1058	...	1257	...	1458	1558	...	1656	1757	|	...	...	1958	2057	2057	2258
	Dijon 372 d.	...	...	|	...	...	|	|	|	...	|	...	|	|	...	|	|	|	1716	*1716*	|	|	|	|
314	Moulins sur Allier d.	0625	0713	0727	0805	0810	0927	1030	1127	1231	1328	1431	1528	1628	1652	1727	1827	|	1958	2006	2027	2126	2127	2330
355	St Germain des Fossés d.	0648	0740	0804	0830	0834	|	|	|	1259	|	1454	|	|	1722	|	|	|	2022	2031	|	2147	|	|
365	Vichy ▷ d.	0656	0749	0813	0839	0842	0955	1059	1155	1307	1358	1502	1555	1655	1730	1755	1854	|	2031	2040	2055	2157	2154	2359
406	Riom-Châtel-Guyon ▷ d.	0717	0813	0839	0901	0904	1019	1124	1219	1330	1423	1523	1618	1718	1753	1818	1918	|	2053	2102	2118	2221	2218	0024
420	**Clermont Ferrand** ▷ a.	0725	0822	0848	0910	0912	1027	1132	1227	1342	1431	1532	1626	1726	1801	1826	1926	2000	2101	2110	2126	2229	2226	0032

	5948	5950	5954		5958			5962		5966		5968		5970	5974		5978		5982		5986		5990	
	🅁★	🅁★	🅁★		🅁★			🅁★		🅁★		🅁★		🅁★	🅁★		🅁★		🅁★		🅁★		🅁★	
	①	②-⑤	Ⓐ	Ⓐ	⑥	Ⓐ	⚒		⑥⑦	①-⑥	⚒		⚒		⑦	Ⓐ			Ⓑ	⚒	⑦	Ⓐ		
	g	w	b	▽	t				▽	u	⊙	V	y		e				h		q			
Clermont Ferrand ▷ d.	0526	0529	0601	0616	0629	0650	0740	0829	0834	1029	1036	1216	1220	1329	1429	1530	1629	1659	1724	1800	1824	1830	1924	2030
Riom-Châtel-Guyon ▷ d.	0537	0539	|	0626	0639	0700	0749	0839	0844	1039	1049	1227	1233	1340	1440	1539	1640	1709	1735	1809	1835	1839	1935	2039
Vichy ▷ d.	0559	0602	|	0649	0701	0723	0809	0902	0907	1101	|	1251	1258	1402	1502	1603	1702	1730	1758	1833	1858	1902	1958	2104
St Germain des Fossés d.	0609	|	|	0658	|	0732	0817	|	0916	|	1130	|	1307	|	|	1611	|	1738	|	1841	|	1911	|	2113
Moulins sur Allier d.	0631	0629	|	0734	0727	0802	0841	0928	0942	1126	1157	1319	1332	1428	1529	1637	1729	1801	1826	1904	1925	1935	2025	2140
Dijon 372 a.	|	|	|	1010	|	...	|	|	1221	|	...	|	...	|	|	...	|	...	|	...	|	...	|	...
Nevers ▶ d.	0700	0658	|	...	0757	...	0912	0957	...	1156	...	1352	...	1457	1558	...	1759	...	1856	...	1954	...	2054	...
Paris Gare de Lyon ▶ a.	0853	0854	0900	...	0952	...	...	1152	...	1352	...	1552	...	1652	1752	...	1952	...	2052	...	2152	...	2252	...

STOPPING TRAINS PARIS (BERCY) - NEVERS

km			5901	5905		5909		5911	5915	5917	5919	5921
		⚒	Ⓐ			⚒	Ⓑ	Ⓐ	Ⓐ	Ⓒ	Ⓐ	†
				⊡	⊡							
0	**Paris Bercy** d.	...	0703	0903	...	1403	...	1635	1759	1803	1931	2003
119	Montargis d.	...	0804	1003	...	1503	...	1801	1903	1903	2050	2103
155	Gien d.	...	0826	1027	...	1525	...	1826	1927	1928	2113	2126
196	Cosne d.	0721	0850	1051	1243	1549	1743	1850	1951	1952	2138	2150
228	La Charité d.	0753	0910	1111	1313	1608	1813	1906	2010	2009	2154	2210
254	**Nevers** d.	0825	0931	1132	1346	1627	1843	1926	2029	2029	2216	2230

	5900	5904	5906	5908	5910	5912		5914	5916	5918	
	Ⓐ	Ⓐ	⑥	Ⓐ		Ⓐ	⚒	† ⊕	⚒	†	Ⓐ
Nevers d.	0500	0600	0621	0725	1025	1425	1524	1636	1821	1823	2009
La Charité d.	0522	0621	0642	0745	1045	1445	1554	1652	1842	1844	2040
Cosne d.	0539	0638	0702	0804	1104	1504	1623	1710	1902	1901	2109
Gien d.	0603	0702	0726	0827	1127	1527	...	1733	1926	1925	...
Montargis d.	0626	0726	0750	0850	1150	1550	...	1756	1950	1950	...
Paris Bercy a.	0733	0833	0849	0949	1250	1649	...	1853	2049	2049	...

A – Daily except ⑤ (will not run Dec. 24, 31, May 12).
R – Feb. 20, 27, Apr. 17 only.
T – Dec. 19, 24 only.
V – Dec. 26, 27, Jan. 2 only.
X – Apr. 2 only.

b – Not Dec. 31.
d – Also Dec. 24, 31, May 12; not Dec. 25, Jan. 1, May 14.
e – Also Apr. 5, May 24.
f – Also Dec. 24, 31, May 12.
g – Also Apr. 6, May 25; not Apr. 5, May 24.
h – Not Dec. 25, Jan. 1, May 13.
k – Not Dec. 25, Jan. 1, Apr. 4, May 13, 25.
q – Also Apr. 5, May 24; not Apr. 4, May 23.
t – Also May 13.
u – Not Apr. 5 - 9, 12 - 16, May 1 - 8, 24.
w – Not Dec. 25, Jan. 1, Apr. 6, May 13, 25.
y – Not Mar. 22 - 26.

★ – *CORAIL TÉOZ* service, 🅁, 🍷.

▶ – For additional trains see below main table.
▷ – See also Tables **328** and **329**.
△ – Not Dec. 19 - Jan. 3.
▽ – Not Mar. 16 - Apr. 2.
⊕ – On Apr. 5, May 2, 16 runs up to 25 minutes later.
⊗ – Not Apr. 26 - 30.
⊡ – Not on ①-⑤ Apr. 19 - 30.
⊙ – Not on ①-⑤ Apr. 5 - 16, May 3 - 7.

331 CLERMONT FERRAND - NEUSSARGUES - AURILLAC

km		⚒	⑦					Ⓑ	⚒	Ⓑ	⑤⑦
		△	W	b	n	F	b	△	△	△	e
0	**Clermont Ferrand** ▷ d.	0636	0710	1038	1242	...	1637	1738	1840	1942	2141
36	Issoire ▷ d.	0702	0736	1104	1309	...	1705	1806	1907	2008	2206
61	Arvant ▷ d.	0727	0757	1124	1330	...	1723	1823	1927	2025	2226
85	Massiac-Blesle d.	0749	0819	1148	1352	...	1745	1846	1948	2045	2248
111	**Neussargues** a.	0808	|	1208	1415	...	1805	1907	2010	2107	2308
111	**Neussargues** d.	0809	|	1209	*1443*	1609	1806	1908	2012	2113	2309
120	Murat (Cantal) d.	0818	0848	1218	*1452*	1618	1817	1918	2022	2122	2318
131	Le Lioran d.	0831	0858	1230	*1503*	1629	1828	1929	2036	2136	2329
168	**Aurillac** a.	0902	...	1259	*1535*	1702	1858	1959	2105	2204	2359
476	*Toulouse 316* a.	1233	...	...	...	...	...	...	...	...	...

	⚒	Ⓐ					Ⓐ	Ⓑ	⑦	⑤
	⊕	⊕	d		n	▽	⊗	⊙	z	f
Toulouse 316 d.	...	...	...	...	...	1237	...	...	...	...
Aurillac d.	0552	0737	1034	1331	...	1631	1731	1828	2017	2036
Le Lioran d.	0623	|	1106	1403	...	1702	1803	1904	2049	2110
Murat (Cantal) d.	0635	0820	1117	1414	...	1714	1816	1917	2101	2124
Neussargues a.	0643	0829	1126	1423	...	1722	1824	1925	2108	2134
Neussargues d.	0644	0830	1127	...	1433	1723	1825	1926	2111	2135
Massiac-Blesle d.	0706	0850	1151	...	1456	1747	1848	1949	2131	2156
Arvant ▷ d.	0726	|	1213	...	1518	1814	1909	2010	2153	2218
Issoire ▷ d.	0745	0925	1231	...	1538	1834	1927	2028	2211	2237
Clermont Ferrand ▷ a.	0813	0954	1258	...	1603	1859	1953	2056	2239	2302

F – Daily to Mar. 7; ⑤ Mar. 12 - June 6. To Brive (Table 317).
W – ⑦ Dec. 13 - Mar. 7.
b – Daily to Mar. 14; Ⓒ Apr. 24 - May 30; daily from June 5.
d – Daily to Mar. 14; Ⓒ Mar. 20 - Apr. 25; daily from June 5.
e – ⑤⑦ to Mar. 14 / from Apr. 23 (also May 12, 13, 24; not May 23).
f – ⑤ to Apr. 23 / from June 4 (not Dec. 25, Jan. 1).
n – Subject to alteration Clermont - Neussargues and v.v. Mar. 15 - Apr. 18 (also ①-⑤ Apr. 19 - June 4).
z – ⑦ Dec. 13 - Apr. 25 (also Dec. 25, Jan. 1, Apr. 5, June 6, 13).
▷ – See also Table **333**.
△ – Subject to alteration Mar. 15 - Apr. 23.
▽ – Subject to alteration Mar. 26 - June 3.
⊕ – Subject to alteration on ①-⑤ Apr. 27 - June 4.
⊗ – Subject to alteration on ①-⑤ Apr. 26 - June 3.
⊙ – Subject to alteration Apr. 26 - June 5.
◇ – Additional journeys:
Aurillac d. 0754 - Le Lioran a. 0826 on ⑥ Dec. 19 - Jan. 30, daily Feb. 6 - 21 (also Feb. 27, Mar. 6).
(Brive d. 0758) - Aurillac d. 0939 - Le Lioran a. 1010 daily Dec. 13 - Mar. 7 (not Dec. 14, 15, Jan. 25, 26).

332 CLERMONT FERRAND - MILLAU - BÉZIERS

km						15941	15941			
		⚒	①	⚒		†	⚒	⑤	†	⑤
			g	b	⊡	n	n	v		v
0	**Clermont Ferrand** ▷ d.	...	...	...	...	1242	1242	...	...	...
85	Massiac-Blesle ▷ d.	...	...	...	...	1352	1352	...	...	...
111	**Neussargues** ▷ d.	...	...	...	...	1437	1437	...	1728	2140
130	St Flour d.	...	...	...	...	1459	1503	...	1750	2202
168	St Chély d'Apcher d.	...	...	1147	...	1539	1548	1645	1828	2240
201	Marvejols d.	...	...	1226	1242	1616	1629	1720	1903	2316
236	**Mende** a.	...	...	|	1329	|	|	|	|	|
243	Sévérac le Château d.	...	...	1310	...	1704	1716	1810	1947	2357
273	Millau ⊙ d.	0542	0848	1350	...	1733	1746	1843	2016	0024
352	Bédarieux ▶ d.	0656	1008	1508	...	1851	1903	2002	2132	...
394	**Béziers** ▶ a.	0730	1040	1540	...	1925	1936	2035	2205	...

		15940							🚌		
	⚒		†	⑤	①-④	Ⓐ	†	⚒	Ⓐ	⑦	⑤
	u	n		f	m§					q	v
Béziers ▶ d.	...	0910	...	1238	1300	...	1817	1828	...	1857	2055
Bédarieux ▶ d.	...	0943	...	1311	1334	...	1850	1904	...	1936	2128
Millau ⊙ d.	0853	1103	1415	1427	1455	1842	2007	2021	2033	2100	2245
Sévérac le Château d.	0920	1133	1443	1456	...	1910	...	...	2102	2128	...
Mende d.	|	*1125r*	|	|	...	|	...	...	|	|	...
Marvejols d.	1010	1223	1526	1538	...	1954	...	...	2212	2216	...
St Chély d'Apcher d.	1044	1301	1603	1612	...	2029	...	...	2242	2250	...
St Flour d.	...	1342	1641	...	...	2108**c**	...	...	...	...	...
Neussargues ▷ a.	...	1402	1700	...	...	2128**c**	...	...	...	...	...
Massiac-Blesle ▷ a.	...	1455	...	...	...	...	...	...	...	...	...
Clermont Ferrand ▷ a.	...	1603	...	...	...	...	...	...	...	...	...

SNCF 🚌 service	🚌	🚌	🚌	🚌	🚌	🚌	🚌	🚌	
	⚒				Ⓑ	⑤z	⑤f	Ⓑ	
Clermont Ferrand ▷ d.	...	...	1640	...	...	1940	...	2145	...
Massiac-Blesle ▷ d.	0805	1155	|	1750	1849	|	2051	|	...
St Flour - Chaudes Aigues d.	0830	1219	|	1815	1918	|	2116	2303	...
St Chély d'Apcher d.	...	...	1815	...	...	2115	...	2324	...
Marvejols d.	...	...	1853	...	...	2151	...	2358	...
Mende a.	...	...	1930	...	...	2230	...	0037	...

SNCF 🚌 service	🚌	🚌	🚌	🚌	🚌	🚌	🚌	🚌	🚌
	⚒	Ⓐ			†	d	⑤z	Ⓐ	†
Mende d.	...	0700	...	1000	1507	...	1552	...	...
Marvejols d.	...	0740	...	1050	1549	...	1634	...	1815
St Chély d'Apcher d.	...	0816	...	1128	1625	...	1710	...	1854
St Flour - Chaudes Aigues d.	0631	0843	1116	|	1653	1713	1738	1813	1918
Massiac-Blesle ▷ a.	0656	|	1140	|	|	1737	|	1838	|
Clermont Ferrand ▷ a.	...	1000	...	1300	1811	...	1856	...	2040

b – Arrive Millau 1338. Runs 12 - 14 minutes later Millau - Béziers on ⑤⑥.
c – St Chély d'Apcher - Neussargues runs on ⑤**v** only.
d – On ⑤**f** runs to Arvant, arrive 1753 (not calling at Massiac-Blesle).
f – Also Dec. 24, 31, May 12; not Dec. 25, Jan. 1.
g – Also Apr. 6, May 25; not Dec. 21, 28, Feb. 15, 22, Apr. 5, 12, 19, May 24.
m – Also May 14; not Dec. 24, 31, May 12.
n – Subject to alteration Clermont - Neussargues and v.v. Mar. 15 - Apr. 18 (also ①-⑤ Apr. 19 - June 4).
q – Also Apr. 5, May 24; not Dec. 20, 27, Feb. 14, 21, Apr. 4, 11, 18, May 23. From Montpellier (d. 1802).
r – ⚒ only. Subject to alteration on Ⓐ May 17 - June 4.
u – Runs 14 - 30 mins later on ①-⑤ Apr. 6 - 23.
v – Also Dec. 24, 31, May 12; not Dec. 25, Jan. 1, May 14.
z – Also Dec. 24, 31; not Dec. 25, Jan. 1.
▷ – For connections see Table **331**.
⊡ – Subject to alteration on Ⓐ May 17 - June 4.
§ – Subject to alteration Jan. 25 - Feb. 4, Mar. 8 - 25.
▶ – Additional trains Bédarieux - Béziers and v.v.:
From Bédarieux: 0615 ⚒, 0658 †, 0750 ⚒, 1202, 1508 †, 1651 Ⓐ, 1739.
From Béziers: 0702 ⚒, 0757, 1300 Ⓒ, 1600 Ⓐ, 1746 Ⓐ.
⊙ – Additional SNCF 🚌 service Millau - Montpellier:
From Millau 0520, 0700 ⚒, 0710 †, 1500, 1716.
From Montpellier 0710, 0955, 1715 ⚒, 2115 ⑤, 2210.
Journey 90 - 120 minutes.

CLERMONT FERRAND - LE PUY EN VELAY 333

km																								
				🚌			🚌				🚌		🚌		🚌			🚌		🚌			🚌	
		Ⓐ	①–⑥		Ⓐ		Ⓒ	⑥	Ⓐ	Ⓒ	Ⓒ	Ⓐ	Ⓐ	Ⓐ	Ⓐ	Ⓐ	Ⓒ	⑥	Ⓑ	⑤	Ⓐ	Ⓑ	⑤	⑦
		§	▽		§	§		t §	▽	▽		§		▽		▽	▽	§	§	f	§	§	f	e §
0	**Clermont Ferrand** .... **331** d.	0600	0646	...	0929	1038	...	1207	1203	1227	...	1242	...	1642	...	...	1715	...	1738	...	1900	1942	...	2115
36	Issoire .... **331** d.	0626	0712	...	0955	1104	...	1235	1235	1258	...	1309	...	1714	...	...	1743	...	1806	...	1930	2008	...	2139
61	Arvant .... **331** d.	0645	0732	...	1014	1123	1128	1255	1255	1317	...	1329	1335	1735	...	←	1803	...	1822	1830	1951	2024	2029	2158
71	Brioude .... d.	0654	0741	...	1022	...	1139	1304	1304	1326	1335	...	1348	1744	1750	1758	1814	1817	...	1843	2001	...	2040	2210
95	St Georges d'Aurac .... d.	0718	|	...	1044	...	|	1323	|	|	|	...	|	→	|	1819	1836	|	...	1911	2022	...	|	2231
103	Langeac .... d.	|	0808	0815	|	...	1207	|	1331	1353	|	...	|	...	|	1828	1844	|	...	1920	|	...	2107	|
147	**Le Puy en Velay** .... a.	0807	...	0901	1133	...	1252	1414	...	...	1442	...	1455	...	1850	...	...	1917	...	2003	2111	...	2150	2319

				🚌		🚌				🚌		🚌				🚌			🚌	🚌				
	①	②–⑤	⑥	Ⓐ	Ⓐ	†		⚒		Ⓐ	Ⓐ	Ⓒ	Ⓒ	Ⓐ	†	⑥	⑥		Ⓐ	⑦	Ⓑ	Ⓐ	†	⑦
	g §	w §	§		§		▽	§			▽		▽	§	§	t	t			e		▽	▽	e §
Le Puy en Velay .... d.	0545	0628	0801	0755	...	1130	...	1156	...	1644	...	1702	...	1725	1743	1748	...	...	1843	1859	...	...	...	2020
Langeac .... d.	|	|	|	|	...	|	1214	|	...	|	1728	|	1745	|	|	1835	...	...	|	|	...	2135	2138	|
St Georges d'Aurac .... d.	0632	0716	0848	|	...	|	|	1244	...	|	1738	|	1754	1820	1837	|	...	...	|	|	...	|	|	2110
Brioude .... d.	0700	0743	0909	0856	0909	1230	1240	1305	...	1744	1757	1802	1816	1838	1857	1912	1922	...	1946	1945	...	2200	2209	2130
Arvant .... **331** d.	0710	0751	0917	...	0917	...	|	1314	...	...	1808	...	1828	|	|	...	1930	...	1956	1958	2010	2210	2217	2139
Issoire .... **331** d.	0732	0813	0938	...	0937	...	1308	1335	...	...	1829	...	1848	1901	1919	...	1951	...	...	...	2028	2229	2236	2200
Clermont Ferrand .... **331** a.	0801	0841	1006	...	1007	...	1336	1407	...	...	1856	...	1914	1929	1950	...	2029	...	...	...	2056	2254	2301	2227

e – Not Apr. 4, May 23.
f – Also Dec. 24, 31, May 12; not Dec. 25, Jan. 1.
g – Not Dec. 21, 28.
t – Not May 1, 8.
w – Not Dec. 25, Jan. 1, Apr. 6.
▽ – Through train to Nimes or beyond (see Table **334**).
§ – Subject to alteration from Mar. 15.

From Mar. 15 certain journeys will be replaced by 🚌

CLERMONT FERRAND and MENDE - NIMES - MONTPELLIER 334

km											
					🚌		**15947**	**15957**			
		⚒	⑦	①–⑥	⑤⑥	①–⑥					
		c	c	▽		c	Ⓐ	Ⓒ	◇	Ⓐ	Ⓒ
0	*Clermont Ferrand* **333** . d.	...	...	0646	...	...	1203	1227	...	1642	1715
103	**Langeac** .... d.	...	...	0809	...	...	1332	1354	...	1829	1845
170	Langogne .... d.	...	...	1018	...	1230	1535	1550	...	2050	2050
*47	**Mende** .... d.	0510	0835	|	1130	|	*1350*x	*1350*x	1650	|	|
188	La Bastide-St Laurent ..... d.	0628	0957	1038	1240	1249	1554	1609	1808	2112	2112
241	Grand Combe la Pise ..... d.	0720	1051	1135	...	1342	1649	1704	1908	2205	2205
254	Alès .... ▶ d.	0740	1115	1203	...	1406	1707	1721	1930	2221	2221
303	**Nimes 355** .... ▶ a.	0817	1152	1243	...	1442	1746	1759	2009	2259	2259
	Marseille **355** .... a.	|	|	...	...	...	1914	1947	|	...	...
353	**Montpellier 355** .... a.	0845	1224	...	...	...	...	...	2039	...	...

				15942	**15952**	🚌			
	⚒		Ⓐ	Ⓐ	Ⓒ		Ⓐ	†	
	b c	△							◇
Montpellier 355 .... d.	0643	...	...	...	...	...	1624	1624	1739
Marseille **355** .... d.	|	...	...	1128	1128	...	|	|	|
Nimes 355 .... ▶ d.	0722	0802	1245z	1312	1312	...	1714	1714	1808
Alès .... ▶ d.	0806	0842	1327	1356	1356	...	1803	1803	1852
Grand Combe la Pise ..... d.	0821	0858	1343	1412	1412	...	1819	1819	1909
La Bastide-St Laurent .... d.	0914	0955	1440	1514	1525	1600	1915	1915	2020
Mende .... a.	|	*1123*r	1555	|	|	1710	|	|	2135v
Langogne .... d.	0932	1014	...	1534	1551	...	1935	1935	...
Langeac .... a.	...	1213	...	1727	1744	...	2134	2137	...
Clermont Ferrand **333**. a.	...	1336	...	1856	1914	...	2254	2301	...

b – From Narbonne (Table **355**).
c – Change at Alès.
r – ⚒ only.
v – 2116 on ⑦.
x – Connection by 🚌 (arrive La Bastide 1500).
z – 1233 on Ⓒ.
◇ – Change at Alès on certain dates.

△ – Subject to alteration Alès - Langogne on ①–⑤ Apr. 9 - 30.
▽ – Arrive Nimes 1302 on ①–⑤ Feb. 22 - Mar. 12. Subject to alteration Brioude - Langogne on Mar. 16 - 26 and Langogne - Alès on ①–⑤ Apr. 19 - 30.
* – Distance from La Bastide.

▶ – Additional services Alès - Nimes and v.v.:
From Alès 0600 ⚒, 0637 Ⓐ, 0704, 0809 Ⓐ, 0841, 0920 Ⓐ, 1113 Ⓐ, 1254, 1515, 1615 🚌, 1805 Ⓑ, 1845 🚌, 2050 🚌.
From Nimes 0626 Ⓐ, 0655 Ⓐ, 0856 Ⓐ, 1022 Ⓐ, 1104, 1225 Ⓐ, 1520 🚌, 1639, 1900 Ⓐ, 1945 🚌, 2055, 2145 🚌.

TGV services LYON - MASSY - TOURS, RENNES and NANTES 335

For slower services via Bourges see Table **290**. For Lille - Massy - Rennes / Nantes see Table **11**. For Strasbourg - Massy - Rennes / Nantes see Table **391**.

	TGV	*TGV*	*TGV*		*TGV*	*TGV*	*TGV*		*TGV*	*TGV*	*TGV*	*TGV*		*TGV*	*TGV*	*TGV*	*TGV*		*TGV*	*TGV*		*TGV*	*TGV*	*TGV*
	5352	**5352**	**5356**		**5350**	**5361**	**5364**		**5374**	**5371**	**5368**	**5233**		**5372**	**5363**	**5378**	**5236**		**5380**	**5387**		**5394**	**5394**	**5390**
	①	Ⓐ	⑥		Ⓑ	⑥	⑥		⑦	⑦	①–⑥	①–⑥		①–⑥	①–⑥	⑦	⑦			①–④		⑥	⑥	⑤⑦
	g ⊖	⊖	t		h	t	t		e	e	n	♥n		n	n	e	♥e		◇	◇m		F	F	w
Bourg St Maurice **366** ..... d.	...	...	...	...	...	...	...	...	...	...	...	...	...	...	...	...	...	...	...	...	...	1644	1644	...
Chambéry **366** .... d.	...	...	...	...	...	...	...	...	...	...	...	...	...	...	...	...	...	...	...	...	...	1832	1832	...
Grenoble **343** .... d.	0532	...	...	...	...	0811	0811	...	...	...	...	...	...	...	...	...	...	...	...	...	...	|	|	...
Marseille **350** .... d.	|	...	...	...	0739	|	|	...	1133	1133	1133	...	...	1507	1507	1507	...	...	...	...	...	|	|	...
Avignon TGV **350** .... d.	|	...	...	...	|	|	|	...	1209	1209	1210	...	...	1546	1546	1546	...	...	...	...	...	|	|	...
Lyon Perrache .... d.	|	...	...	...	|	|	|	...	|	|	|	...	...	|	|	|	...	...	...	...	...	|	|	1907
Lyon Part Dieu .... d.	0656	0656	0656	...	0926	0926	0926	...	1326	1326	1326	...	...	1656	1656	1656	...	...	1826	1826	...	|	|	1926
Massy TGV .... d.	0901	0901	0901	...	1131	1131	1131	...	1532	1532	1533	1631	...	1901	1901	1901	1917	...	2032	2032	...	2137	2137	2137
St Pierre des Corps .... a.	0951	0951	0951	...	|	|	|	...	|	|	1622	|	...	|	|	1953	|	...	2129	|	...	|	|	|
Futuroscope **300** .... a.	|	|	1028	...	|	|	|	...	|	|	|	|	...	|	|	|	|	...	|	|	...	|	|	|
Poitiers 300 .... a.	|	|	1052	...	|	|	|	...	|	|	|	|	...	|	|	|	|	...	|	|	...	|	|	|
Le Mans **280** .... a.	|	|	...	...	1219	1217	1217	...	1619	1619	|	1719	...	1949	1949	|	2005	...	|	2119	...	2225	2225	2224
Rennes 280 .... a.	|	|	...	...	1340	1333	|	...	|	1743	|	1836	...	2110	|	|	2125	...	|	2234	...	|	2346	2339
Angers St Laud **280** .... a.	1046	1046	...	...	...	...	1303	...	1659	...	1719	...	...	...	2035	2046	...	...	2225	...	...	2308	...	...
Nantes 280 .... a.	1125	1125	...	...	...	...	1342	...	1736	...	1803	...	...	...	2116	2127	...	...	2303	...	...	2345	...	...

	TGV	*TGV*	*TGV*	*TGV*	*TGV*	*TGV*	*TGV*	*TGV*	*TGV*		*TGV*	*TGV*	*TGV*	*TGV*	*TGV*	*TGV*	*TGV*		*TGV*	*TGV*	*TGV*	*TGV*	*TGV*	*TGV*
	5302	**5308**	**5310**	**5304**	**8712**	**5312**	**5311**	**8818**	**5318**		**5324**	**5322**	**8836**	**5326**	**5346**	**5332**	**5328**		**5334**	**5338**	**5344**	**5342**	**5336**	**5340**
	①–④	⑥	⑥	⑥	Ⓐ									⑤⑥	①–④	⑤	①–④		⑦	⑦	⑤	⑤	⑦	⑦
	m	F	F	t			△				G		⊕	y	m	f	m		e	e	f	f	e	e
Nantes 280 .... d.	0455	0621	...	0630	...	0735	0735	0900	...	...	...	1252	1400	...	...	1555	1555	...	1707	...	...	1904	...	1849
Angers St Laud **280** .... d.	0536	0701	...	0708	...	0813	0813	0937	...	...	...	1337	1438	...	...	1633	1633	...	1745	...	...	1943	...	1927
Rennes 280 .... d.	|	|	0629	|	0735	|	|	|	0910	...	1230	|	|	1414	1510	|	|	...	|	1825	1909	|	...	|
Le Mans **280** .... d.	|	0748	0748	|	0846	0854	0854	1016	1029	...	1351	|	1516	1529	1630	|	|	...	1825	1952	2030	2030	...	|
Poitiers 300 .... d.	|	|	|	|	...	|	|	...	|	...	|	|	...	|	|	|	|	...	|	|	|	|	1932	|
Futuroscope **300** .... a.	|	|	|	|	...	|	|	...	|	...	|	|	...	|	|	|	|	...	|	|	|	|	1944	|
St Pierre des Corps .... d.	0631	|	|	0807	...	|	|	...	|	...	|	1430	...	|	|	1727	1727	...	|	|	|	|	2028	2028
Massy TGV .... d.	0723	0841	0841	0900	...	0949	0949	...	1121	...	1446	1521	...	1621	1720	1821	1821	...	1915	2045	2121	2121	2126	2126
Lyon Part Dieu .... a.	0935	|	|	1103	...	1201	1201	...	1331	...	1655	1731	...	1831	1931	2031	2031	...	2131	2255	2331	2331	2331	2331
Lyon Perrache .... a.	0950	|	|	1115	...	|	...	...	|	...	1710e	|	...	|	|	|	2046	...	|	|	2346	2346	2347	2347
Avignon TGV **350** .... a.	...	|	|	...	...	1309	...	...	1446	...	...	1846	...	1945	2046	|	...	...	|	0016	...	...	...	...
Marseille **350** .... a.	...	|	|	...	...	1349	...	...	1523	...	...	1918	...	2024	2117	|	...	...	|	0055	...	...	...	...
Grenoble **343** .... a.	...	|	|	...	...	...	...	...	...	...	...	...	...	...	...	2153	...	...	2253	...	...	...	...	...
Chambéry **366** .... a.	...	1215	1215	...	...	...	...	...	...	...	...	...	...	...	...	...	...	...	...	...	...	...	...	...
Bourg St Maurice **366** ..... a.	...	1410	1410	...	...	...	...	...	...	...	...	...	...	...	...	...	...	...	...	...	...	...	...	...

LYON - ROUEN	*TGV*	*TGV*
	5366	**5376**
	⑥K	
Marseille **350** .... d.	...	1539
Avignon TGV **350**. d.	...	1610
Lyon Perrache .... d.	1212	|
Lyon Part Dieu .... d.	1226	1726
Massy-Palaiseau .... d.	1458	1940
Versailles Chantiers . d.	1518	1956
Mantes la Jolie .... a.	|	2027
Rouen Rive Droite.. a.	1636	2114
Le Havre **270** .... a.	...	2200

ROUEN - LYON	*TGV*	*TGV*
	5316	**5320**
		⑦K
Le Havre **270** ...... d.	0755	...
Rouen Rive Droite d.	0845	1243
Mantes la Jolie .... d.	0933	|
Versailles Chantiers d.	1006	1400
Massy-Palaiseau .... d.	1022	1417
Lyon Part Dieu ...... a.	1231	1621
Lyon Perrache .... a.	|	1641
Avignon TGV **350** a.	1347	...
Marseille **350** ...... a.	1418	...

F – ⑥ Dec. 19 - Apr. 3 (also Dec. 25, Jan. 1).
G – ①②③④⑦ (not Dec. 24, 31, May 12, 13).
K – July 3 - Aug. 29.

e – ⑦ (also Apr. 5, May 24).
f – Also Dec. 24, 31, May 12; not Dec. 25, Jan. 1.
g – Also Apr. 6, May 25; not Apr. 5, May 24.
h – Not Dec. 25, Jan. 1, May 13.
m – Not Dec. 24, 31, Apr. 5, May 12, 13, 24.
n – Not Apr. 5, May 24.
t – Also Dec. 25, Jan. 1, May 13.

w – Also Dec. 24, 31, Apr. 5, May 12, 24; not Dec. 25, Jan. 1.
y – Also Dec. 24, 31, May 12, 13.

TGV – Ⓡ, supplement payable, 🍷.

♥ – To / from Lille (Table **11**).
◇ – From Montpellier (depart 1628, Table **350**).
△ – To Montpellier (arrive 1356, Table **350**).
⊖ – Not via St Pierre des Corps on Ⓐ Feb. 8 - 19.
⊕ – Not Mar. 15 - Apr. 20.

340 PARIS - LYON *TGV Sud-Est*

For Charles de Gaulle ✈ - Marne la Vallée - Lyon see Table **11**. For Paris - Lyon St Exupéry ✈ see Table **342**. Trains not serving Lyon Perrache continue to/from other destinations.

km	*TGV* trains convey 🍸	*TGV* 6601	*TGV* 6641	*TGV* 6681	*TGV* 6603		*TGV* 6643	*TGV* 6605		*TGV* 6645	*TGV* 6607		*TGV* 6609	*TGV* 6609	*TGV* 6611	*TGV* 6613	*TGV* 6685	*TGV* 6615		*TGV* 6657	*TGV* 6617		*TGV* 6619	*TGV* 6621
		Ⓐ	Ⓐ	①-⑥	①-⑥					①-④	①-⑥									⑤				
			b	n	a		k			m	n		E	F				p		f				
0	**Paris Gare de Lyon** ▷ d.	0554	0624	0654	0654	...	0724	0754	...	0824	0854	...	0954	0958	1053	1154	1254	1254	...	1324	1354	...	1452	1554
303	Le Creusot TGV d.	0718	|	|	|	...	|	0918	...	|	|	...	1118	|	|	|	|	|	...	|	1518	...	|	1716
363	Mâcon Loché TGV ▷ a.	|	|	|	|	...	0901	|	...	|	|	...	|	|	|	|	|	|	...	|	|	...	|	|
427	**Lyon Part-Dieu** a.	0757	0821	0851	0851	...	0924	0957	...	1021	1051	...	1157	1157	1251	1351	1451	1451	...	1521	1557	...	1651	1757
431	**Lyon Perrache** a.	0809	0833	...	0903	...	0936	1009	...	1033	1103	...	1209	1209	1303	1403	...	1503	...	1533	1609	...	1703	1809

	TGV 6659	*TGV* 6687	*TGV* 6623		*TGV* 6663	*TGV* 6627		*TGV* 6665	*TGV* 6689	*TGV* 6629		*TGV* 6669	*TGV* 6631		*TGV* 6671	*TGV* 6633		*TGV* 6673	*TGV* 6635*		*TGV* 5139	*TGV* 6675		
	Ⓐ				Ⓐ			Ⓑ				⑤			⑦	Ⓑ		⑤	Ⓑ		⑦	⑦		
	d	L	H		d			z		M		f			e	h		f	v		e⊡	u		
Paris Gare de Lyon ▷ d.	1624	1654	1654	...	1724	1754	...	1824	1854	1854	...	1924	1954	...	2024	2054	...	2124	2154	...	...	2224	...	...
Le Creusot TGV d.	|	|	|	...	|	1919	...	|	|	|	...	|	2117	...	|	|	...	|	|	...	2320	|	...	...
Mâcon Loché TGV ▷ a.	|	|	|	...	|	|	...	|	|	|	...	|	|	...	|	|	...	|	|	...	|	|	...	...
Lyon Part-Dieu a.	1821	1853	1853	...	1921	1957	...	2021	2051	2051	...	2121	2157	...	2221	2251	...	2321	2351	...	2359	0021	...	...
Lyon Perrache a.	1833	...	1905	...	1933	2009	...	2033	...	2103	...	2133	2209	...	2233	2303	...	2333	0003	...	0014	0033	...	...

	TGV 6640	*TGV* 6602		*TGV* 5154		*TGV* 6642	*TGV* 6604	*TGV* 6690		*TGV* 6648	*TGV* 6644		*TGV* 6608	*TGV* 6608		*TGV* 6610	*TGV* 6612	*TGV* 6692	*TGV* 6614	*TGV* 6616	*TGV* 6616		*TGV* 6618	*TGV* 6694
	①	Ⓐ		①-⑥		Ⓐ	①-⑥	①-⑥			①		Ⓐ	Ⓒ						Ⓑ	⑥			
	g			n⊙		d	x	n		q	g							L	r				J	
Lyon Perrache d.	0516	0546	...	...	...	0616	0641	...	...	0716	0731	...	0746	0746	...	0846	0946	...	1040	1130	1146	...	1240	...
Lyon Part-Dieu d.	0530	0600	...	0613	...	0630	0700	0700	...	0730	0745	...	0800	0800	...	0900	1000	1100	1100	1144	1200	...	1300	1300
Mâcon Loché TGV ▷ d.	|	0626	...	|	...	|	|	|	...	|	|	...	|	0827	...	|	|	|	|	|	|	...	|	|
Le Creusot TGV d.	|	0646	...	0651	...	|	|	|	...	|	|	...	0841	0848	...	|	1041	|	|	|	|	...	1344	1344
Paris Gare de Lyon ▷ a.	0727	0807	...	...	...	0827	0857	0857	...	0927	0943	...	1003	1009	...	1057	1203	1257	1257	1344	1359	...	1503	1503

	TGV 6620	*TGV* 6620		*TGV* 6622	*TGV* 6624		*TGV* 6664	*TGV* 6626	*TGV* 6668	*TGV* 6628	*TGV* 6638		*TGV* 6696	*TGV* 6630	*TGV* 6632	*TGV* 6674	*TGV* 6634	*TGV* 6636		*TGV* 6588	*TGV* 6676	*TGV* 6676		*TGV* 6678
		⑤					⑤		Ⓐ		Ⓑ					⑦		⑤		⑦	⑤	⑦		⑦
	A	f					f		z		y			G		s	N	f		e△	c	e		u
Lyon Perrache d.	1346	1346	...	1446	1546	...	1616	1646	1716	1746	1816	...	...	1841	1946	2012	2046	2046	...	...	2146	2146	...	2242
Lyon Part-Dieu d.	1400	1400	...	1500	1600	...	1630	1700	1730	1800	1830	...	1900	1900	2000	2026	2100	2100	...	...	2200	2200	...	2300
Mâcon Loché TGV ▷ d.	|	|	...	|	|	...	|	|	|	|	|	...	|	|	|	|	|	|	...	...	|	2226	...	|
Le Creusot TGV d.	|	1441	...	|	1641	...	|	|	|	1841	|	...	|	|	2041	|	|	2140	...	2236	|	|	...	|
Paris Gare de Lyon ▷ a.	1559	1603	...	1656	1803	...	1827	1857	1926	2001	2027	...	2057	2057	2203	2223	2257	2303	...	2359	2359	0003	...	0059

A – Daily except ⑤ (also runs Dec. 25, Jan. 1; not Dec. 24, 31, May 12).
E – Daily except dates in note **F**.
F – Feb. 20, 21, 27, 28, Mar. 6, 7 only.
G – Not Feb. 15-18, 22-25, Mar. 2, 3.
H – Not Dec. 28, Feb. 15, 16, 22, Mar. 1, Apr. 4, May 15, 23.
J – Not Feb. 21, 27, 28, Mar. 1-4, 6-11, Apr. 4, May 15.
L – Not Feb. 21, 28, Mar. 7.
M – Not Feb. 15, 20, 22-24, 27, Mar. 1, 2, 6, May 14, 23.
N – ①②③④⑦ (not Dec. 24, 31, May 12, 13).
a – Not Dec. 28-30, Apr. 5, May 14, 15, 24.
b – Not Feb. 22-24, Mar. 1-4, May 14.
c – Not Dec. 25, Jan. 1, May 14.
d – Not May 14.
e – Also Apr. 5, May 24.
f – Also Dec. 24, 31, May 12; not Dec. 25, Jan. 1.
g – Also Apr. 6, May 25; not Apr. 5, May 24.
h – Not Dec. 25, Jan. 1, May 13.
k – Not Feb. 27, Mar. 6.
m – Not Dec. 24, 31, Apr. 5, May 12, 13, 24.
n – Not Apr. 5, May 24.
p – Not Feb. 15-17, Mar. 2, 3, Apr. 4, May 14, 23.
q – Not May 14, 15.
r – Not Apr. 4, May 15, 23.
s – Also Apr. 5, May 24; not Apr. 4.
u – Also Apr. 5, May 24; not Apr. 4, May 23.
v – Not Dec. 24, 25, 31, Jan. 1, May 12, 13.
x – Not Apr. 5, May 14, 15, 24.
y – Not Dec. 25, Jan. 1, Apr. 4, May 13, 14, 23.
z – Not Dec. 25, Jan. 1, Apr. 4, May 13.

TGV –Ⓡ, supplement payable, 🍸.

▷ – For other trains Paris - Mâcon Loché TGV and v.v. see Table **341**.
△ – From Genève (Table **341**).
⊙ – Grenoble - Lyon - Lille Europe (Table **11**).
⊡ – Lille Flandres - Lyon (Table **11**).
* – Train number **6637** on ⑤.

341 PARIS - GENÈVE, CHAMBÉRY and ANNECY *TGV trains*

For the night trains Paris Austerlitz - Aix les Bains - Chambéry - Bourg St Maurice / Modane see Tables **365** and **366** (Paris - Annecy see Table **365**).

km	All trains convey 🍸	*TGV* 6931	*TGV* 6561	*TGV* 9241		*TGV* 6565	*TGV* 6937	*TGV* 6939	*TGV* 6569		*TGV* 6573	*TGV* 9247	*TGV* 6941		*TGV* 6577	*TGV* 9249	*TGV* 6947	*TGV* 6949	*TGV* 6581	*TGV* 6951	*TGV* 6585	*TGV* 6953	*TGV* 6589
				△		Ⓐ					Ⓑ	△				△		Ⓑ				⑤	⑤
				M					G		h	M				M		h				E	f
0	**Paris Gare de Lyon** 340 d.	0650	0710	0742	...	0910	0950	1050	1110	...	1310	1350	1350	...	1504	1524	1650	1750	1810	1850	1908	1950	2010
365	Mâcon Loché TGV 340 d.	|	|	|	...	|	1128	|	|	...	|	1528	1528	...	1641	|	|	1927	|	|	2046	2128	|
406	Bourg-en-Bresse d.	|	0903	|	...	|	|	|	1303	...	1504	|	|	...	1703	|	|	1949	|	|	2109	|	|
	Lyon St Exupéry TGV ✈ 342 d.	0846	|	|	...	|	|	1247	|	...	|	|	|	...	|	1720	1846	|	|	2046	|	|	|
489	Culoz 345 d.	|	|	|	...	|	|	|	|	...	|	|	|	...	|	|	|	|	|	|	2156	|	|
522	Bellegarde ▲ 345 a.	|	1007	|	...	1204	|	|	1407	...	1607	|	|	...	1807	|	|	|	2103	|	2216	|	2306
555	**Genève** 345 a.	|	1035	|	...	1232	|	|	1435	...	1635	|	|	...	1835	|	|	|	2132	|	2245	|	2335
*532	Chambéry a.	0942	...	1040	...	...	|	1343	...	...	...	1705	|	...	...	1821	1943	|	...	2143	...	2300	...
*532	Chambéry 344 364 d.	0951	...	...	...	...	|	1352	...	...	...	|	|	...	...	...	1952	|	...	2152	...	|	...
*546	Aix les Bains 344 364 a.	1001	...	...	...	...	1250	1401	...	...	...	1649z	1649	...	...	...	2001	2050	...	2201	...	2245z	...
*585	**Annecy** 344 364 a.	1032	...	...	...	...	1330	1432	...	...	...	...	1730	...	...	...	2032	2129	...	2232	...	...	...

All trains convey 🍸	*TGV* 6560	*TGV* 6960	*TGV* 6962	*TGV* 6564	*TGV* 6964	*TGV* 6568	*TGV* 6968	*TGV* 9240	*TGV* 9240		*TGV* 9242	*TGV* 6972	*TGV* 6572	*TGV* 6976	*TGV* 6576	*TGV* 6576		*TGV* 6580	*TGV* 6980	*TGV* 6984	*TGV* 6584	*TGV* 9248	*TGV* 6588
	Ⓐ	①-⑥	Ⓐ		Ⓒ			①-⑤	⑥⑦		△							Ⓐ		Ⓑ		△	⑦
		n						M△	M△		M				P	Q			B	h		M	e⊖
Annecy 344 364 d.	...	0532	0632	...	0830	...	0935	...	...	...	...	1232	...	1535	...	...	...	...	1735	1832	...	...	...
Aix les Bains 344 364 d.	...	0601	0709	...	0907	...	1004	...	...	...	...	1309	...	1604	...	...	...	...	1804	1910	...	...	...
Chambéry 344 364 a.	...	0612	|	...	|	...	1014	...	...	...	...	|	...	1614	...	...	...	...	1815	|	...	...	...
Chambéry 348 d.	...	0622	|	...	|	...	1024	1104	1110	...	1225	|	...	1624	...	...	...	...	1826	|	...	2027	...
Genève 345 d.	0535	|	|	0717	|	0917	|	|	|	...	|	|	1317	|	1613	1613	...	1717	|	|	1917	|	2017
Bellegarde ▲ 345 d.	0603	|	|	0749	|	0948	|	|	|	...	|	|	1348	|	1641	1641	...	1748	|	|	1948	|	2049
Culoz 345 d.	|	|	|	|	|	|	|	|	|	...	|	|	|	|	|	|	...	1810	|	|	|	|	|
Lyon St Exupéry TGV ✈ 342 a.	|	|	|	|	|	|	|	|	|	...	|	|	|	|	|	|	...	|	|	|	|	2124	|
Bourg-en-Bresse d.	0710	|	|	0856	|	1056	|	|	|	...	|	|	1454	|	|	1748	...	1856	|	|	2056	|	2158
Mâcon Loché TGV 340 d.	|	|	0829	|	1030	|	|	|	|	...	|	1430	|	|	1807	1816	...	|	|	2029	|	|	|
Paris Gare de Lyon 340 a.	0903	0915	1007	1051	1207	1249	1320	1359	1403	...	1515	1607	1649	1915	1943	1955	...	2049	2115	2207	2249	2321	2359

B – Daily to Apr. 3, Ⓑ from Apr. 4 (not May 13).
E – ⑤ from Apr. 30 (also May 12).
G – Will not run on ①-⑤ Mar. 8-12, Apr. 5-16, May 3-21.
M – 🚃 Paris - Modane - Torino - Milano and v.v. (Table **44**).
P – Daily to Apr. 25, Ⓐ Apr. 26 - July 2.
Q – Ⓒ May 1 - July 3.
e – Also Apr. 5, May 24.
f – Also Dec. 24, 31, May 12; not Dec. 25, Jan. 1, Mar. 26, Apr. 2.
h – Not Dec. 25, Jan. 1, May 13.
n – Not Apr. 5, May 24.
z – Calls before Chambéry.

TGV –Ⓡ, supplement payable, 🍸.

△ – Special 'global' fares payable.
▲ – Additional trains operate Paris - Bellegarde - (Évian les Bains) and v.v. at weekends – see Table **363**.
⊖ – Also calls at Le Creusot TGV (d. 2236).
* – Via Lyon St Exupéry TGV (Paris - Aix les Bains via Bourg en Bresse = *511* km).

PARIS - LYON ST EXUPÉRY ✈ - GRENOBLE 342

Shows complete service Paris - Lyon St Exupéry ✈ and v.v. Journeys not serving Grenoble continue to destinations in other tables

km	All trains convey 🍷	TGV	TGV	TGV	TGV	TGV	TGV	TGV	TGV	TGV		TGV	TGV	TGV	TGV	TGV	TGV	TGV	TGV	TGV	TGV	TGV	TGV	TGV	TGV
		6901	6931	6191	6905	6193	6911	6939	6917	6917		6919	6919	9249	6921	6947	6195	6923	6923	6925	6951	6927	6197	6927	6929
		Ⓐ		①–⑥						⑤		①–④	⑤–⑦					①–④	⑤⑦	Ⓐ		⑤			⑤⑦
		v		n	E		b		A‡	f		m	w				⊙	m	z			f		A	y
0	Paris Gare de Lyon ... d.	0638	0650	0750	0750	0946	0946	1050	1138	1138	...	1338	1338	1524	1638	1650	1745	1745	1746	1838	1850	1938	1945	1945	2038
441	Lyon St Exupéry ✈ ..... a.	|	0843	0943	0943	1139	1139	1244	|	1333	...	1531	|	1717	|	1843	1939	1939	1939	|	2043	|	2139	2139	|
441	Lyon St Exupéry ✈ ..... d.	|	...	...	0947	...	1146	...	|	1345	...	1533	|	...	|	...	...	1947	1947	|	...	|	...	2146	|
553	Grenoble ..... a.	0933	...	...	1050	...	1249	...	1433	1446	...	1634	1634	...	1933	...	...	2050	2050	2133	...	2236	...	2248	2333

	TGV	TGV	TGV		TGV	TGV		TGV	TGV		TGV	TGV		TGV	TGV		TGV	TGV		TGV	TGV	TGV		TGV	TGV
	6900	6192	6902		6904	6194		6908	6910		6196	6916		6920	6198		6922	6924		6926	6918	9248		6928	6928
	①–④	Ⓐ	Ⓐ		①–⑥												Ⓐ			⑤	⑦			⑦	⑦
	q		u		x							d						A		f	G			R	S
Grenoble ..... d.	0521	...	0601	...	0725	...	...	1005	1205	...	...	1322	...	1605	...	...	1805	1921	...	2005	2005	...	...	2122	2158
Lyon St Exupéry ✈ ..... a.	|	...	0710	...	0830	...	...	1109	1314	...	...	|	...	1710	...	...	1910	|	...	2110	2109	...	...	|	|
Lyon St Exupéry ✈ ..... d.	|	0647	0713	...	0833	0933	...	1112	1317	...	1417	|	...	1713	1816	...	1913	|	...	2113	2112	2127	...	|	|
Paris Gare de Lyon ..... a.	0820	0841	0907	...	1027	1127	...	1316	1511	...	1611	1619	...	1907	2015	...	2107	2219	...	2307	2307	2323	...	0022	0052

A – Daily except ⑤ (also runs Dec. 25, Jan. 1; not Dec. 24, 31, May 12).
E – Daily to Apr. 4, ①–⑥ from Apr. 6 (not May 24). On Feb. 20, 27, Mar. 6 depart Paris 0738 (⊖).
G – ⑦ from Apr. 11 (also Apr. 5, May 24).
R – ⑦ to Apr. 4 (also Apr. 5, May 24).
S – ⑦ from Apr. 11.
b – On ⑥ Feb. 6 - Mar. 6 Paris 1038, Grenoble 1334 (⊖); on Feb. 21, 28, Mar. 7 Paris 0938, Grenoble 1234 (⊖).
d – Not Apr. 4, May 14. On Feb. 20, 27, Mar. 6 Paris 1405, Grenoble 1711.
f – Also Dec. 24, 31, May 12; not Dec. 25, Jan. 1.
m – Not Dec. 24, 31, Apr. 5, May 12, 13, 24.
n – Not Apr. 5, May 24.
q – Not Dec. 29, 30, Apr. 5, May 13, 24.
u – Not Dec. 31.
v – Not May 14.
w – Also Dec. 24, 31, Apr. 5, May 12, 13, 24; not May 15.
x – Also Feb. 28, Mar. 7; not Apr. 5, May 24.
y – Also Dec. 24, Apr. 5, May 12, 24; not Dec. 25, Jan. 1, Apr. 4, May 14, 23.
z – Also Dec. 24, 31, Apr. 5, May 12, 24; not Dec. 25, Jan. 1.
TGV – Ⓡ, supplement payable, 🍷.
⊙ – Not on ⑤⑦ **z**.
⊖ – Not calling at Lyon St Exupéry.
‡ – On Feb. 6, 13 runs one hour later.

LYON - GRENOBLE 343

km																										
		⚒		⚒		Ⓐ				Ⓐ		Ⓐ		Ⓐ		Ⓐ	B	Ⓐ				B			Ⓐ	
							◇		◇		◇		◇		◇		◇		◇	◇		◇		◇		◇
0	Lyon Part-Dieu . 344 d.	0557	0645	0703	0745	0815	0845	0945	1045	1115	1145	1215	1245	1315	1345	1415	1445	1515	1545	1603	...	1647	1715	1745	1811	1845
41	Bourgoin-Jallieu . 344 d.	0627	0715	0732	0813	|	0913	1013	1115	|	1214	|	1314	|	1413	|	1513	|	1613	1632	...	1716	1745	1815	1836	1912
56	La Tour du Pin ... 344 d.	0637	0726	0742	0825	|	0924	1025	1126	|	1224	|	1325	|	1424	|	1525	|	1625	1643	...	1727	1755	1825	|	1924
104	Voiron ..... d.	0713	0755	0815	0855	|	0954	1054	1155	|	1254	|	1354	|	1454	|	1555	|	1654	1714	...	1755	1824	1854	|	1954
129	Grenoble ..... a.	0734	0811	0831	0911	0930	1011	1111	1211	1229	1311	1329	1411	1429	1511	1529	1611	1629	1711	1731	...	1811	1846	1911	1929	2011

			TGV		TGV	TGV		TGV		🚌
			5333		5123	5335		5132		
	Ⓐ		⑤		①–⑥	⑦		⑦	⑤–⑦	Ⓐ
			Nf		Ln	Ne		Le	u	
Lyon Part-Dieu .... 344 d.	1915	1945	2037	2045	2111	2137	2145	2211	2245	2310*
Bourgoin-Jallieu .... 344 d.	1943	2014	|	2116	|	|	2217	|	2315	2355
La Tour du Pin ...... 344 d.	1954	2023	|	2126	|	|	2228	|	2325	|
Voiron ..... d.	2028	2056	|	2154	|	|	2257	|	2355	|
Grenoble ..... a.	2045	2111	2153	2211	2225	2253	2313	2319	0011	0055

	TGV		TGV	TGV						TGV
	5154		5352	5160						5364
	①–⑥	⚒	①	⑦		Ⓐ	⚒	Ⓐ		⑥
	Ln		Ng	Le			◇		◇	Nt
Grenoble ..... d.	0451	0458	0532	0540	0544	0615	0644	0711	0744	0811
Voiron ..... d.	|	0515	|	|	0601	0634	0701	|	0801	|
La Tour du Pin ..... 344 d.	|	0545	|	|	0631	0706	0731	0759	0831	|
Bourgoin-Jallieu ..... 344 d.	|	0557	|	|	0643	0717	0743	0809	0843	|
Lyon Part-Dieu ..... 344 a.	0604	0629	0650	0653	0712	0746	0812	0842	0912	0920

																							🚌			
	Ⓐ		Ⓐ		Ⓐ		Ⓐ		Ⓐ		Ⓐ				Ⓐ		Ⓐ		Ⓐ		Ⓐ		Ⓐ			
		◇		◇		◇		◇		◇		◇						◇		◇		◇				
Grenoble ..... d.	0826	0844	0926	0944	1026	1044	1126	1144	1226	1244	1326	1344	1444	1544	1625	1644	1725	1744	1825	1844	1926	1944	2015	2044	2144	...
Voiron ..... d.	|	0900	|	1001	|	1101	|	1201	|	1301	|	1401	1502	1600	1642	1701	1742	1801	|	1901	|	2001	|	2102	2159	...
La Tour du Pin ..... 344 d.	|	0930	|	1031	|	1132	|	1231	|	1331	|	1431	1532	1630	1713	1730	1814	1831	|	1931	|	2031	|	2132	2229	...
Bourgoin-Jallieu ... 344 d.	|	0942	|	1043	|	1143	|	1243	|	1343	|	1443	1544	1642	1725	1741	1824	1843	1918	1943	|	2043	|	2142	2240	...
Lyon Part-Dieu ... 344 a.	0942	1012	1042	1112	1142	1212	1242	1312	1342	1412	1442	1512	1612	1712	1759	1812	1859	1912	1942	2012	2042	2112	2145*	2212	2312	...

B – Dec. 14 - 18, ①–⑤ Feb. 1 - Mar. 12.
L – [12] Grenoble - Charles de Gaulle ✈ - Lille Europe and v.v. (Table **11**).
N – [12] Grenoble - Massy - Nantes and v.v. (Table **335**).
e – Also Apr. 5, May 24.
f – Also Dec. 24, 31, May 12; not Dec. 25, Jan. 1.
g – Also Apr. 6, May 25; not Apr. 5, May 24.
n – Not Apr. 5, May 24.
t – Also Dec. 25, Jan. 1, May 13.
u – Also Apr. 5, May 13, 24; not on ⑤⑥ Mar. 5 - Apr. 3.
TGV – Ⓡ, supplement payable, 🍷.
◇ – To/from Dijon (Table **373**).
* – Bus station on eastern side of station (Rue de la Villette).

LYON - CHAMBÉRY - ANNECY 344

km																								
			🚌			⚒	⚒			🚌				🚌	Ⓒ		⑥⑦	⚒	⑥					
		b△	⚒						◇				F		Y	z	Y		E	§	u	△		△
	Lyon Perrache ..... d.	...	...	...	...	...	...	...	...	...	...	...	...	...	...	...	...	1316	...	...	...	...	...	...
0	Lyon Part Dieu ..... 343 d.	0631	0638*	...	0738	0741	0841	...	0941	0938*	1038	1038	1138	1138*	1230	1241	1313	1338	1425	1441	1445	1541	1638	1637
41	Bourgoin-Jallieu ..... 343 d.	0658	|	...	|	0807	0906	...	|	|	|	|	|	|	|	1305	|	|	|	1506	|	|	|	1706
56	La Tour du Pin ..... 343 d.	0708	|	...	|	|	|	...	|	|	|	|	|	|	|	|	|	|	|	|	|	|	|	|
50	Ambérieu ..... ▷ d.	|	|	...	0809	|	|	...	|	|	1109	1109	1212	|	|	|	|	|	|	|	1510	|	1709	|
•106	Chambéry ..... a.	0756	|	...	|	0901	0955	...	1057	|	|	1220r	1311r	|	1401	1356	1455	1450	1602r	1559	|	1658	|	1757
•106	Chambéry ..... 341 364 d.	...	|	0814	|	...	...	1013	...	|	|	|	|	|	...	1405	...	1456	|	...	|	*1713*	|	...
•120	Aix les Bains ..... 341 364 a.	...	|	0825	0855	...	...	1024	...	|	1159	1159	1256	|	...	1416	...	1507	1549	...	1557	*1724*	1756	...
•159	Annecy ..... 341 364 a.	...	0830	0909	0933	...	...	1107	...	1130	1245	...	...	1330	...	1457	...	1556	...	...	1642	*1814*	1852	...

						⚒		🚌
	⊖	B§		§				⑤f
Lyon Perrache ..... d.	...	...	...	...	...	...	...	...
Lyon Part Dieu ..... 343 d.	1738	1741	1841	1941	...	2041	2141	...
Bourgoin-Jallieu ..... 343 d.	|	|	|	|	...	|	2208	...
La Tour du Pin ..... 343 d.	|	|	1913	|	...	|	|	...
Ambérieu ..... ▷ d.	1808	|	|	|	...	|	|	...
Chambéry ..... a.	|	1859	1956	2059	...	2157	2300	...
Chambéry ..... 341 364 d.	|	...	2004	...	2120	2205	...	2305
Aix les Bains ..... 341 364 a.	1854	...	2015	...	2132	2216	...	|
Annecy ..... 341 364 a.	1929	...	2055	...	2204	2249	...	2357

		⚒		Ⓒ							🚌
				Y	D§	△			§	⚒	⚒
Annecy ..... 341 364 d.	...	0523	0609	...	...	...	...	0730	...	...	0925
Aix les Bains ..... 341 364 d.	...	0601	0644	...	...	...	0814	0814	0914	...	|
Chambéry ..... 341 364 a.	...	|	0655	...	...	...	|	|	|	...	|
Chambéry ..... d.	0557	|	0701	0734	0735	0801	0750r	|	0858r	1001	|
Ambérieu ..... ▷ d.	|	0654	|	|	|	|	0901	0901	0959	|	|
La Tour du Pin ..... 343 d.	|	|	|	0817	0817	|	|	|	|	|	|
Bourgoin-Jallieu ..... 343 d.	0651	|	0752	0828	0828	0851	|	|	|	1053	|
Lyon Part Dieu ..... 343 a.	0716	0727	0816	0856	0854	0916	0926	0926	1028	1116	1115*
Lyon Perrache ..... a.	...	...	...	...	...	...	...	...	...	...	...

					🚌	⚒	🚌	⑥⑦		⑥	①–⑤			Ⓒ					🚌		Ⓑ			Ⓑ
	c	c	△	d	Ⓐ					H	v			Y	▽◇	◇		§				△		
Annecy ..... 341 364 d.	...	1039	...	...	1135	...	1235	...	1333	...	...	1435	...	...	...	...	1629	...	1735	1815	...	...	1931	...
Aix les Bains ..... 341 364 d.	1115	1115	...	1215	|	...	|	...	1408	...	...	1516	1516	1555	...	...	1712	...	|	1849	...	...	2013	...
Chambéry ..... 341 364 a.	|	|	...	|	|	...	|	...	|	...	...	|	|	|	...	...	|	...	|	|	...	...	|	...
Chambéry ..... d.	1101r	|	1200	1203r	|	1301	|	1401	|	1450	1459	|	1501r	1541r	1601	1701	|	1801	|	|	1901	2000	|	2101
Ambérieu ..... ▷ d.	1201	1201	|	1300	|	|	|	|	1453	|	|	1601	1601	|	|	|	1800	|	|	1940	|	|	2101	|
La Tour du Pin ..... 343 d.	|	|	|	|	|	|	|	|	|	|	|	|	|	|	|	|	|	|	|	|	|	2045	|	|
Bourgoin-Jallieu ..... 343 d.	|	|	1251	|	|	|	|	1452	|	|	1554	|	|	|	1652	|	|	1852	|	|	|	|	|	|
Lyon Part Dieu ..... 343 a.	1228	1228	1316	1325	1330*	1416	1430*	1516	1518	1612	1624	1626	1626	1729	1716	1816	1826	1921	1930*	2006	2016	2116	2126	2221
Lyon Perrache ..... a.	1247	1247	...	...	...	...	...	...	...	1625	...	...	...	...	...	...	...	...	...	...	...	...	...	...

B – Daily to May 7; Ⓑ May 9 - June 18.
D – Ⓐ to May 12 (not Jan. 12, 13); ⚒ from May 14.
E – ⑥ Dec. 19 - Apr. 17.
F – ⚒ to Apr. 10; ⑥ Apr. 17 - 24; daily from May 3.
G – Ⓑ to Apr. 16; daily from Apr. 18.
H – ⑥ Dec. 26 - Apr. 24.
Y – Dec. 13 - May 2.
b – Not Feb. 23, May 9, 13, 16, 23, 24, 30, June 6, 13.
c – Subject to alteration on ①–⑤ Jan. 19 - 29, Apr. 5 - 16.
d – Not on ①–⑤ Apr. 6 - 16.
f – Also Dec. 24, 31, May 12; not Dec. 25, Jan. 1.
r – Via Aix les Bains.
u – Not on ①–⑤ Apr. 12 - 30.
v – Not Dec. 25, Jan. 1, Apr. 5.
z – Subject to alteration Chambéry - Aix ①–⑤ Mar. 1 - 26.
◇ – To/from Dijon (Table **373**).
△ – To/from Modane (Table **367**).
▽ – From Modane on dates in Table **367**.
▷ – Lyon - Ambérieu: see also Table **345**.
⊖ – To Annemasse and Évian les Bains (Tables **365**/**363**).
§ – To/from Bourg St Maurice (Table **365**).
• – Distances via Ambérieu: Chambéry *138 km*, Aix les Bains *124 km*, Annecy *163 km*.
* – Eastern side of station (Rue de la Villette).

345 LYON - BELLEGARDE - GENÈVE

Certain trains convey through portions Lyon - Bellegarde - Annemasse - St Gervais (see Table 365)

km																								
		Ⓐ	Ⓐ	⚒	4678 4679 🅁Z		Ⓐ	⚒		d	Ⓐn	Ⓐn	b		TGV 6866 M	Ⓐ	⊖ Ⓐ	⊖ Ⓒ	Ⓒ	Ⓐ	TGV 6886 N			TGV 6874 L
0	**Lyon Part Dieu** .... **344** d.	...	...	...	0651	0704	...	0804	0904	1104	...	...	1304	1504	1556	...	1704	1704	...	...	1804	1904	2004	2056
50	Ambérieu .... **344** d.	...	...	...	|	0730	...	0830	0929	1130	...	...	1329	1530	|	...	1731	1730	...	...	|	1930	2032	|
102	Culoz .... d.	...	...	...	|	0804	...	0902	1002	1202	...	...	1402	1602	|	...	1805	1806	...	...	|	2003	2106	|
135	Bellegarde .... **341 364** d.	0619	0645	0726	|	0830	0845	0929	1028	1228	1244	1345	1428	1628	1710	1745	1830	1827	1830	1845	1917	2028	2132	2207
168	**Genève** .... **341 364** a.	0654	0726	0803	0845	0857	0926	0957	1057	1257	1326	1426	1457	1657	1735	1826	1857	...	1857	1926	1942	2057	2157	2233

	⚒	Ⓐ		Ⓐ	TGV 6806 L	Ⓐ	Ⓒ	Ⓒ	k	TGV 6816 Mh	Ⓐn	Ⓐn	k	TGV 6818 N			Ⓐ		Ⓐ	Ⓐ	Ⓐ			4778 4779 🅁Y
Genève .... **341 364** d.	0558	0635	0658	0735	0817	0858	0858	...	1058	1117	1142	1205	1258	1344	1358	1416	1635	1658	1735	1817	1835	1858	1958	2044
Bellegarde .... **341 364** d.	0628	0713	0730	0812	0848	0930	0926	0928	1126	1145	1222	1250	1328	1411	1425	1446	1715	1730	1812	1843	1914	1930	2028	|
Culoz .... d.	0649	...	0753	...	|	0955	...	0956	1147	|	...	...	1351	|	1451	...	...	1751	...	...	...	1951	2051	|
Ambérieu .... **344** d.	0724	...	0823	...	|	1036	...	1036	1223	|	...	...	1423	|	1523	...	...	1823	...	...	...	2023	2123	|
Lyon Part Dieu .... **344** a.	0751	...	0847	...	1001	1102	...	1107	1247	1259	...	...	1447	1531	1550	...	...	1847	...	...	...	2047	2147	2245

L – [12] Genève - Lyon - Marseille and v.v. (Table **350**).
M – [12] Genève - Lyon - Montpellier and v.v. (Table **350**).
N – [12] Genève - Lyon - Marseille - Nice and v.v. (Table **350**).
Y – 🛏 1, 2 cl. and [2] (reclining) Genève - Lyon - Toulouse - Irún. For days of running see Table **355**.
Z – 🛏 1, 2 cl. and [2] (reclining) Hendaye - Toulouse - Lyon - Genève. For days of running see Table **355**.

b – Subject to alteration on Dec. 19, 20, 25 - 27, Jan. 1 - 3; ⑥⑦ Feb. 6 - Mar. 7, also Mar. 8 - 12, ①–⑤ Apr. 5 - 30.
d – Subject to alteration on Mar. 8 - 12 and ①–⑤ Apr. 5 - 30.
h – Subject to alteration Mar. 15 - 19, Apr. 5 - 9, 12 - 16, June 7 - 11.
k – Subject to alteration Mar. 15 - 19, Ⓐ Apr. 5 - 16, June 7 - 11.
n – Subject to alteration Apr. 2 - 16.

TGV – 🅁, supplement payable, 🍷.
⊖ – From Lyon Perrache, depart 1650.

***Note:** early-morning and late-evening services are subject to alteration on Jan. 9, 10.*

346 MÂCON - BOURG EN BRESSE - AMBÉRIEU - (LYON)

km																										
		②–⑤	🚌	Ⓐ	🚌	🚌 Ⓐ	Ⓐ	🚌 ⑥t	Ⓐ	🚌 ⚒	🚌	🚌	Ⓐr	🚌	🚌 ⑥t	Ⓐ	🚌	🚌	Ⓐ	🚌 ⑥t	🚌 Ⓐ	🚌	Ⓐ	🚌	🚌	🚌
0	**Mâcon Ville** .... d.	...	...	*0654*	0710	0725	...	...	0810	...	0925	...	1156	...	1255	1310	1455	...	1650	1655	...	...	1755	1855	...	2055
37	Bourg en Bresse ... ▷ d.	0653	0707	0730	0815	0805	0827	0827	0840	0927	1025	1027	1225	1312	1350	1340	1555	1627	1721	1750	1820	1827	1826	1955	2027	2150
68	Ambérieu .... ▷ a.	0711	0750	0750	...	...	0851	0905	...	1005	...	1105	1249	1350	...	...	...	1707	1748	...	1855	1905	...	...	2105	...
118	**Lyon Part-Dieu** .... ▷ a.	0747	...	0826	...	...	...	...	...	...	...	...	...	...	...	...	...	...	...	...	...	...	...	...	...	...

	🚌 Ⓐ	△	Ⓐ	🚌 ⑥t	🚌	△	Ⓐ	🚌 ⑥t	Ⓐn	🚌 ⑥t	🚌	🚌	Ⓐz	🚌	🚌 ⑥t	Ⓐ	Ⓐ	🚌	🚌	Ⓐ	Ⓐ	H	🚌	🚌	🚌	⚒
Lyon Part-Dieu ..... ▷ d.	...	...	...	...	...	...	...	...	...	...	...	...	...	...	...	...	...	...	...	...	...	1838	...	...	...	2112
Ambérieu .... ▷ d.	...	...	0656	0700	0800	...	0916	0917	...	...	1217	...	1317	1417	...	...	...	...	1717	...	1817	1908	...	1917	2117	2154
Bourg en Bresse .... ▷ d.	0635	0731	0721	0740	0842	0932	0940	0957	1231	1232	1257	1332	1341	1457	1532	1612	1713	1732	1802	1833	1841	1927	1932	1957	2157	2212
Mâcon Ville .... a.	0715	0804	...	...	...	1004	...	...	1303	1335	...	1435	...	...	1635	1644	1746	1835	...	1905	...	...	2030	...	...	...

H – ①–④ (not Dec. 24, 31, Apr. 5, May 12, 13, 24).
a – Ⓐ only.
c – Runs 30 minutes later on ①–⑤ May 3 - 21.
n – Subject to alteration Feb. 22 - 26.
r – Subject to alteration Mar. 1 - 5.
t – Not Dec. 26, Jan. 2, May 1, 8.
x – ①–④ only (not holidays).
z – Subject to alteration Apr. 19 - 30.

km		⚒		⚒c	Ⓐ	Ⓐ	
0	Dijon .... d.	0630	0830	1230	1630	1800	1931
86	Louhans .... d.	0740	0941	1345	1745	1904	2045
140	Bourg en Bresse .... a.	0815	1016	1418	1818	1936	2118
171	Ambérieu .... a.	...	...	...	...	2004x	...

	⚒		⚒z	Ⓑ		Ⓑ
Ambérieu .... d.	...	0656a	...	...	...	...
Bourg en Bresse .. d.	0530	0728	1129	1630	1742	1830
Louhans .... d.	0605	0801	1203	1701	1815	1905
Dijon .... a.	0718	0914	1315	1815	1916	2010

▷ – Lyon - Ambérieu: see also Tables **344** / **345**. Lyon - Bourg en Bresse: see also Tables **353** and **384**.
△ – By 🚌 on Ⓒ (arrive Mâcon Ville 30 minutes later).

347 LYON - ST ÉTIENNE

km	*TGV* trains convey 🍷																									
			⚒	⚒ y	⚒	⚒		⚒	Ⓐ	Ⓐ		Ⓐ	TGV 6681 P		Ⓐ	b	Ⓐ b	b	Ⓐ b	b	b	Ⓐ d	b	⚒ k		Ⓐ k
	Paris ▽ **340** .... d.	...	...	...	...	...	...	...	...	...	...	...	0654	...	...	...	...	...	...	...	...	...	...	...	...	...
0	**Lyon Part-Dieu** .... d.	0019	0619	...	0649	...	0719	...	0749	...	0819	0849	0858	0919	0949	1019	1049	1119	1149	1219	...	1249	1319	1349	1419	1449
	Lyon Perrache .... d.	|	|	0636	|	0706	|	0733	|	0806	|	|	|	|	|	|	|	|	|	|	1236	|	|	|	|	|
22	Givors Ville .... d.	0039	0638	0654	0708	0724	0739	0754	0808	0825	0838	0909	|	0938	1009	1038	1108	1138	1208	1238	1256	1308	1339	1409	1439	1508
47	St Chamond .... d.	0059	0658	0715	0728	0745	0758	0815	0828	0845	0858	0928	|	0958	1028	1058	1128	1158	1228	1258	1319	1328	1359	1428	1459	1528
59	**St Étienne** ⊙ .... a.	0108	0708	0724	0738	0754	0808	0824	0838	0854	0908	0938	0941	1008	1038	1108	1138	1208	1238	1310	1329	1338	1408	1438	1508	1538

	TGV 6685 u		Ⓐ	Ⓐ			Ⓑ	Ⓑ			Ⓐ	Ⓐ			Ⓐ	TGV 6687 v	Ⓐ ◇			Ⓐ		Ⓑ	TGV 6689		Ⓑ	
Paris ▽ **340** .... d.	1254	...	...	...	...	...	...	...	...	...	...	...	...	...	...	1654	...	...	...	...	...	...	1854	...	...	...
Lyon Part-Dieu .... d.	1458	1519	1549	...	1619	...	1649	...	1719	...	1749	...	1819	...	1849	1900	...	1919	...	1949	2019	2049	2058	2119	2219	2319
Lyon Perrache .... d.	|	|	|	1606	|	1636	|	1706	|	1736	|	1806	|	1836	|	|	1906	|	1936	|	|	|	|	|	|	|
Givors Ville .... d.	|	1539	1609	1625	1638	1657	1709	1724	1739	1754	1808	1824	1839	1854	1908	|	1925	1939	1954	2008	2038	2108	|	2139	2238	2338
St Chamond .... d.	|	1559	1629	1649	1659	1721	1729	1745	1759	1815	1828	1845	1859	1915	1928	|	1945	1959	2015	2028	2058	2128	|	2159	2258	2357
St Étienne ⊙ .... a.	1541	1608	1638	1700	1708	1731	1738	1754	1808	1824	1838	1854	1908	1924	1938	1941	1954	2008	2024	2038	2108	2138	2141	2208	2308	0007

	⚒		TGV 6691 Q	⚒	Ⓐ z		⚒	⚒	Ⓐ	⚒		⚒	Ⓐ	⚒		⚒	Ⓐ		TGV 6693 u	Ⓐ n		k		TGV 6695 v	⚒	b
St Étienne ⊙ .... d.	0518	0548	0614	0618	0631	0648	0701	0718	0731	0734	0748	0801	0818	0831	0848	0901	0918	0948	1014	1018	1048	1118	1148	1214	1218	1248
St Chamond .... d.	0528	0559	|	0629	0641	0659	0710	0729	0740	0746	0759	0810	0830	0841	0857	0910	0929	0959	|	1029	1057	1129	1157	|	1228	1259
Givors Ville .... d.	0550	0620	|	0650	0703	0719	0732	0750	0802	0807	0820	0832	0850	0902	0919	0932	0950	1020	|	1050	1119	1150	1219	|	1250	1320
Lyon Perrache .... a.	|	|	|	|	0723	|	0750	|	0820	|	|	0850	|	0920	|	0950	|	|	|	|	|	|	|	|	|	|
Lyon Part-Dieu .... a.	0608	0638	0654	0708	...	0738	...	0808	...	0826	0838	...	0908	...	0938	...	1008	1038	1054	1108	1138	1208	1238	1254	1308	1338
Paris ▽ **340** .... a.	...	...	0857	...	...	...	...	...	...	...	...	...	...	...	...	...	...	...	1257	...	...	...	...	1505	...	...

	b	Ⓐ b	◇ d	Ⓐ b	b	Ⓐ b	Ⓐ b	Ⓐ	Ⓐ				Ⓐ			TGV 6697 u	Ⓐ		Ⓑ		Ⓑ		Ⓑ			
St Étienne ⊙ .... d.	1301	1318	1348	1418	1448	1548	1613	1618	1631	1648	1701	1718	1731	1748	1801	1814	1818	1831	1848	1901	1918	1948	2018	2048	2118	2218
St Chamond .... d.	1310	1329	1359	1428	1459	1559	|	1629	1640	1658	1710	1729	1740	1759	1810	|	1829	1840	1858	1910	1928	1959	2029	2059	2129	2229
Givors Ville .... d.	1332	1348	1420	1450	1520	1620	|	1650	1702	1720	1732	1750	1802	1820	1832	|	1850	1902	1920	1932	1950	2020	2048	2120	2150	2250
Lyon Perrache .... a.	1350	|	|	|	|	|	|	|	1720	|	1750	|	1820	|	1850	|	|	1920	|	1950	|	|	|	|	|	|
Lyon Part-Dieu .... a.	...	1408	1438	1508	1538	1638	1654	1708	...	1738	...	1808	...	1838	...	1854	1908	...	1938	...	2008	2038	2108	2138	2208	2308
Paris ▽ **340** .... a.	...	...	...	...	...	...	...	...	...	...	...	...	...	...	...	2057	...	...	...	...	...	...	...	...	...	...

P – ①–⑥ (not Feb. 6, 13, 20, 27, Mar. 6, Apr. 5, May 24).
Q – ①–⑥ (not Apr. 5, May 24).
b – Subject to alteration on Ⓐ Mar. 22 - Apr. 2.
d – Subject to alteration Ⓐ Mar. 22 - Apr. 2, Apr. 12 - 30.
k – Subject to alteration Apr. 6 - 9, 12 - 16.
n – Subject to alteration on Ⓐ Apr. 12 - 30.
u – Not Feb. 6, 13, 20, 21, 27, 28, Mar. 6, 7.
v – Not Feb. 6, 13, 20, 27, Mar. 6.
y – Additional journey runs at 0536 Ⓐ.
z – Additional journeys run at 0531 ⚒, 0601 ⚒.

TGV – 🅁, supplement payable, 🍷.
◇ – To / from Le Puy en Velay (Table **348**).
▽ – Paris Gare de Lyon.
⊙ – St Étienne Châteaucreux.

348 ST ÉTIENNE - LE PUY

km		⚒		⚒c	c				Ⓐ	b	
	Lyon Part Dieu **347** .. d.	...	...	...	...	...	...	...	...	...	...
0	**St Étienne** ⊙ .... d.	0612	0813	0953	1222	1553	1713	1818	1919	1957	2152
15	Firminy .... d.	0629	0830	1011	1244	1611	1735	1834	1935	2019	2214
88	**Le Puy en Velay** .... a.	0739	0937	1114	1354	1714	1838	1943	2038	2121	2315

	⚒	Ⓐ	†	⚒	c	d		Ⓑ		†
Le Puy en Velay .... d.	0605	0748	0808	0839	1039	1211	1618	1736	1841	1909
Firminy .... d.	0713	0852	0913	0943	1141	1322	1725	1853	1954	2014
St Étienne ⊙ .... a.	0738	0909	0929	1000	1201	1343	1743	1914	2010	2030
Lyon Part Dieu **347** a.	...	...	...	...	...	1438	...	...	...	2138

b – From Lyon Perrache on Ⓐ (depart 1906).
c – Subject to alteration Apr. 12 - 16, 19 - 23.
d – Subject to alteration on Ⓐ Mar. 22 - Apr. 2, Apr. 12 - 23.
⊙ – St Étienne Châteaucreux.

Additional journeys: Le Puy - St Étienne 0436 Ⓐ, 2046 †.

TGV Méditerranée — PARIS and LYON - MONTPELLIER, MARSEILLE and NICE via high-speed line — 350

km	All TGV trains are 🅁	TGV 6831 ① g	TGV 6815 Ⓐ F	TGV 6815 Ⓐ E	TGV 5355 Ⓑ h	TGV 6803 ⑥ d	TGV 6801 Ⓐ	TGV 6805 Ⓒ	TGV 6101 Ⓐ	TGV 6201 Ⓐ	TGV 6813	TGV 6151 Ⓐ E	TGV 6151 Ⓐ F	TGV 6811 Ⓒ	TGV 6103	TGV 5301 A	TGV 6203	TGV 5102	TGV 6171	TGV 9804 Ⓐ	TGV 5104 Ⓒ	TGV 6105	TGV 6205	TGV 6807
	Brussels Midi **11** d.	...	...	...	...	...	...	...	...	...	...	...	...	...	...	...	...	...	...	0540	...	...	...	...
	Lille Europe **11** d.	...	...	...	...	...	...	...	...	...	...	...	...	...	...	...	...	0559	...	0625	0625	...	...	...
	Charles de Gaulle ✈ **11** d.	...	...	...	...	...	...	...	...	...	...	...	...	...	...	...	...	0654	...	0725	0725	...	...	...
	Marne la Vallée-Chessy § d.	...	...	...	...	...	...	...	...	...	...	...	...	...	...	...	...	0710	...	0740	0740	...	...	...
0	**Paris Gare de Lyon** d.	...	...	...	...	...	...	...	0615	0620	...	0642	0642	...	0715	...	0719	|	0746	|	|	0816	0820	...
	Genève **345** d.	...	...	...	...	...	...	...	|	|	...	|	|	...	|	...	|	|	|	|	|	|	|	0817
	Dijon **373** d.	...	...	...	...	...	0549	...	|	|	0616x	|	|	0645	|	...	|	|	|	|	|	|	|	|
**	**Lyon Part Dieu** d.	0050p	0635	0635	0711	0711	0737	0735	|	|	0811	|	|	0837	|	...	|	0907	|	0937	0937	|	|	1007
527	Valence TGV d.	|	|	|	|	|	0815	0816	|	0834	|	|	|	0915	|	...	|	|	|	1014	1014	|	1034	1045
657	**Avignon TGV** d.	|	0741	0741	|	|	0851	|	0859	|	|	|	|	0951	0958	1005	|	1012	1027	|	|	|	|	|
686	Nîmes **355** d.	|	|	|	0831	0831	|	|	|	0920	0930	|	|	|	|	|	1014	|	|	1100	1100	|	1120	|
736	**Montpellier 355** a.	|	|	|	0855	0855	|	|	|	0949	1002	|	|	|	|	|	1038	|	|	1128	1128	|	1147	|
	Sète **355** a.	|	|	|	|	|	|	|	|	...	...	|	|	|	|	|	1057	|	|	|	|	|	...	|
	Agde **355** a.	|	|	|	|	|	|	|	|	...	...	|	|	|	|	|	1113	|	|	|	|	|	...	|
	Béziers **355** a.	|	|	|	0941	0941	|	|	|	...	...	|	|	|	|	|	1127	|	|	1213	1213	|	...	|
	Narbonne **355** a.	|	|	|	0959	0959	|	|	|	...	...	|	|	|	|	|	1144	|	|	1235	1235	|	...	|
	Toulouse **321** a.	|	|	|	1121	|	|	|	|	...	...	|	|	|	|	|	|	|	|	1355	1355	|	...	|
	Perpignan 355 a.	|	|	|	...	1037	|	|	|	...	...	|	|	|	|	|	1220	|	|	...	...	|	...	|
731	Aix en Provence TGV d.	|	0805	0805	...	...	|	|	0922	...	...	0943	0943	|	1021	1030	...	1036	|	...	...	|	...	1136
750	**Marseille St Charles** a.	|	0817	0817	...	...	0920	0917	0933	...	...	|	0957	1021	1035	1041	...	1047	|	...	...	1118	...	1147
750	**Marseille St Charles 360** d.	|	...	0829	...	...	...	0929	...	...	...	|	...	...	...	...	...	1059	|	...	...	...	...	...
817	**Toulon 360** a.	0541	...	0913	...	...	...	1013	...	...	...	1037	...	...	...	...	...	1143	1137	...	...	...	...	...
885	Les Arcs-Draguignan **360** a.	0619	...	|	...	...	...	|	...	...	...	...	...	...	...	...	...	1218	|	...	...	...	...	...
911	St Raphaël-Valescure **360** a.	0637	...	1006	...	...	...	1107	...	...	...	...	...	...	...	...	...	1236	1227	...	...	...	...	...
944	Cannes **360** a.	0700	...	1031	...	...	...	1132	...	...	...	...	...	...	...	...	...	1300	1251	...	...	...	...	...
955	Antibes **360** a.	0711	...	1043	...	...	...	1144	...	...	...	...	...	...	...	...	...	1312	1302	...	...	...	...	...
975	**Nice 360** a.	0739	...	1103	...	...	...	1204	...	...	...	...	...	...	...	...	...	1332	1324	...	...	...	...	...

	TGV 6809 ①⑥ ⊡	TGV 5110	TGV 6107 ①–⑥ n	TGV 6207	TGV 6173	TGV 5148 M	TGV 5112	TGV 6109 ◇	TGV 6233 ①–⑥ q	TGV 5312 N	TGV 5311 N	TGV 5316 H	TGV 6111	TGV 6209	TGV 6816 ⊗	TGV 5462 ⊙	TGV 6175 w	TGV 5405 S	TGV 9826	TGV 5164	TGV 5318 R	TGV 6113	TGV 6211	TGV 6211 ⑤ D
Brussels Midi **11** d.	...	...	...	...	...	...	...	...	...	...	...	...	...	...	...	...	...	...	1021	...	...	...	...	...
Lille Europe **11** d.	...	0643c	...	...	...	...	0828	...	...	...	...	...	...	...	...	...	...	...	|	1030	...	...	...	...
Charles de Gaulle ✈ **11** d.	...	0821	...	...	...	...	0925	...	...	...	...	...	...	...	...	...	...	...	1142	1142	...	...	...	...
Marne la Vallée-Chessy § d.	...	0835	...	...	...	...	0940	...	...	...	...	...	...	...	...	...	...	...	1156	1156	...	...	...	...
Paris Gare de Lyon d.	...	|	0916	0920	0942	...	|	1015	1020	...	...	...	1116	1120	...	...	1146	...	|	|	...	1315	1319	1319
Genève **345** d.	...	|	|	|	|	...	|	|	|	...	...	...	|	|	1117	...	|	...	|	|	...	|	|	|
Dijon **373** d.	...	|	|	|	|	0916	|	|	|	...	...	...	|	|	|	1124	|	...	|	|	...	|	|	|
Lyon Part Dieu d.	1011	1037	|	|	|	1107	1137	|	|	1207	1211	1237	|	|	1307	1311	|	1323	|	|	1337	|	|	|
Valence TGV d.	1052	1114	|	|	|	|	1216	|	1234	|	|	1314	|	1334	|	|	|	|	1407	1407	1414	|	1534	1534
Avignon TGV d.	1130	1148	1159	|	|	1216	|	|	|	1312	|	1350	1359	|	|	|	|	1433	1442	1442	1449	1559	|	|
Nîmes **355** d.	|	|	|	1220	|	|	1301	|	1320	|	1328	|	|	1419	1425	1430	|	|	|	|	|	|	1620	1620
Montpellier 355 a.	|	|	|	1247	|	|	1330	|	1346	|	1356	|	|	1442	1451	1455	|	|	|	|	|	|	1644	1644
Sète **355** a.	|	|	|	...	|	|	...	|	...	|	...	|	|	1501	...	...	|	|	|	|	|	|	...	1705
Agde **355** a.	|	|	|	...	|	|	...	|	...	|	...	|	|	1517	...	...	|	|	|	|	|	|	...	1720
Béziers **355** a.	|	|	|	...	|	|	...	|	...	|	...	|	|	1531	...	...	|	|	|	|	|	|	...	1735
Narbonne **355** a.	|	|	|	...	|	|	...	|	...	|	...	|	|	1547	...	...	|	|	|	|	|	|	...	1751
Toulouse **321** a.	|	|	|	...	|	|	...	|	...	|	...	|	|	|	...	...	|	|	|	|	|	|	...	|
Perpignan 355 a.	|	|	|	...	|	|	...	|	...	|	...	|	|	1625	...	...	|	|	|	|	|	|	...	1830
Aix en Provence TGV d.	1156	1213	1222	...	1246	|	...	|	...	1335	...	|	1422	...	...	...	1446	1457	1505	1505	1512	1622	...	...
Marseille St Charles a.	1208	1225	1235	...	|	1247	...	1321	...	1349	...	1418	1435	...	...	...	|	1513	1516	1516	1523	1634	...	...
Marseille St Charles 360 d.	...	...	...	...	|	1259	...	1333	...	...	...	...	...	...	...	...	|	...	1527	1527	...	...	...	...
Toulon 360 a.	...	...	...	...	|	1343	...	1416	...	...	...	...	...	...	...	...	1537	...	1611	1611	...	...	...	...
Les Arcs-Draguignan **360** a.	...	...	...	...	1411	|	...	...	...	...	...	...	...	...	...	...	|	...	1652	1652	...	...	...	...
St Raphaël-Valescure **360** a.	...	...	...	...	1428	1437	...	...	...	...	...	...	...	...	...	...	1627	...	1708	1708	...	...	...	...
Cannes **360** a.	...	...	...	...	1453	1502	...	...	...	...	...	...	...	...	...	...	1651	...	1732	1732	...	...	...	...
Antibes **360** a.	...	...	...	...	1505	1514	...	...	...	...	...	...	...	...	...	...	1703	...	1743	1743	...	...	...	...
Nice 360 a.	...	...	...	...	1524	1534	...	...	...	...	...	...	...	...	...	...	1724	...	1803	1803	...	...	...	...

	TGV 9832	TGV 5115	TGV 6177	TGV 6115	TGV 6235 ⑦ e	TGV 6818		TGV 6145	TGV 9828	TGV 6117	TGV 6213	TGV 5117 B	TGV 6179 L	TGV 5322 N	TGV 6119 △	TGV 6231 Ⓐ	TGV 6829	TGV 5118		TGV 6121	TGV 6821 Q	TGV 5326 ⑤⑥ Rb	TGV 6123	TGV 6215
Brussels Midi **11** d.	1120	...	...	...	...	...	...	...	1249	...	...	...	...	...	...	...	...	...	...	...	...	...	...	...
Lille Europe **11** d.	1206	1206	...	...	...	...	...	...	1333	...	...	...	...	...	...	...	...	1506	...	...	...	...	...	...
Charles de Gaulle ✈ **11** d.	1301	1301	...	...	...	...	...	...	1428	...	...	...	...	...	...	...	...	1601	...	...	...	...	...	...
Marne la Vallée-Chessy § d.	1314	1314	...	...	...	...	...	...	1441	...	...	...	...	...	...	...	...	1614	...	...	...	...	...	...
Paris Gare de Lyon d.	|	|	1346	1415	1420	...	...	1446	|	1515	1520	...	1546	...	1615	1620	...	|	...	1646	...	...	1716	1719
Genève **345** d.	|	|	|	|	|	1344	...	|	|	|	|	...	|	...	|	|	...	|	...	|	...	...	|	|
Dijon **373** d.	|	|	|	|	|	|	...	|	|	|	|	1516	|	...	|	|	1616	|	...	|	...	...	|	|
Lyon Part Dieu d.	1507	1511	|	|	|	1537	...	|	1641	|	|	1707	|	1737	|	|	1803	1807	...	|	1837	1837	|	|
Valence TGV d.	1546	|	|	|	1634	|	...	|	1717	|	|	1745	|	1814	|	1834	1844	|	...	|	1915	1914	|	1935
Avignon TGV d.	|	|	1630	|	|	1646	...	|	1751	1759	|	|	|	1849	|	|	|	|	...	1929	|	1948	1959	|
Nîmes **355** d.	1632	|	|	|	1723	|	...	|	|	|	1813	1833	|	|	|	1921	|	1930	...	|	|	|	|	2020
Montpellier 355 a.	1659	|	|	|	1747	|	...	|	|	|	1838	1857	|	|	|	1949	|	1958	...	|	|	|	|	2046
Sète **355** a.	1721	|	|	|	...	|	...	|	|	|	1858	|	|	|	|	...	|	2017	...	|	|	|	|	2105
Agde **355** a.	1737	|	|	|	...	|	...	|	|	|	1913	|	|	|	|	...	|	2033	...	|	|	|	|	2120
Béziers **355** a.	1751	|	|	|	...	|	...	|	|	|	1928	1940	|	|	|	...	|	2048	...	|	|	|	|	2133
Narbonne **355** a.	1807	|	|	|	...	|	...	|	|	|	1944	1955	|	|	|	...	|	2104	...	|	|	|	|	2149
Toulouse **321** a.	|	|	|	|	...	|	...	|	|	|	|	2110	|	|	|	...	|	|	...	|	|	|	|	|
Perpignan 355 a.	1844	|	|	|	...	|	...	|	|	|	2021	...	|	|	|	...	|	2139	...	|	|	|	|	2223
Aix en Provence TGV d.	...	1636	|	|	...	|	...	1747	1816	1822	...	...	1845	|	|	...	|	...	...	|	2011	2011	2022	...
Marseille St Charles a.	...	1647	|	1721	...	1717	...	1758	1827	1834	...	...	|	1918	1922	...	1942	...	...	1958	2024	2024	2034	...
Marseille St Charles 360 d.	...	...	|	...	...	1729	...	...	...	...	...	...	|	...	1933	...	1959	...	...	...	...	...	...	...
Toulon 360 a.	...	...	1737	...	...	1814	...	...	...	...	...	...	|	...	2016	...	2043	...	...	...	...	...	...	...
Les Arcs-Draguignan **360** a.	...	...	1812	...	...	|	...	...	...	...	...	...	2018	...	...	...	|	...	...	...	...	...	...	...
St Raphaël-Valescure **360** a.	...	...	1830	...	...	1907	...	...	...	...	...	...	2036	...	...	...	2137	...	...	...	...	...	...	...
Cannes **360** a.	...	...	1854	...	...	1932	...	...	...	...	...	...	2100	...	...	...	2202	...	...	...	...	...	...	...
Antibes **360** a.	...	...	1905	...	...	1943	...	...	...	...	...	...	2112	...	...	...	2214	...	...	...	...	...	...	...
Nice 360 a.	...	...	1924	...	...	2004	...	...	...	...	...	...	2131	...	...	...	2237	...	...	...	...	...	...	...

A – [12] Toulouse - Montpellier - Marseille (Table **355**).
B – [12] Dijon - Lyon - Toulouse - Bordeaux. Will not run on Dec. 13 - 18 or Ⓐ Feb. 15 - Mar. 12.
D – ⑤ from Apr. 9 (also May 12).
E – Ⓐ Dec. 21 - Jan. 22, Ⓐ Apr. 12 - May 28.
F – Ⓐ Dec. 14 - 18, Jan. 25 - Apr. 9, from May 31.
H – [12] Le Havre - Rouen - Lyon - Marseille (Table **335**).
L – Daily Apr. 5 - Sept. 16.
M – From Metz d. 0611, Nancy d. 0651 (Table **379**).
N – From Nantes via Massy TGV (Table **335**).
Q – ①②③④⑦ (not Dec. 24, 31, May 12, 13).
R – From Rennes via Massy TGV (Table **335**).
S – From Strasbourg (Table **384**).

b – Also Dec. 24, 31, May 12, 13.
c – Lille **Flandres**. Depart 0647 on ⑥ **d**.
d – Also Dec. 25, Jan. 1, May 13.
e – Also Apr. 5, May 24.
g – Also Apr. 6, May 25; not Apr. 5, May 24.
h – Not Dec. 25, Jan. 1, May 13.
n – Not Apr. 5, May 24.
p – Lyon **Perrache**.
q – Not Feb. 13, 20, Apr. 5, May 24.
w – To Ventimiglia (Table **360**).
x – ①⑥ (also Dec. 25, Jan. 1, Apr. 6, May 13, 25; not Apr. 5, May 24).

TGV – 🅁, supplement payable, 🍷.
◇ – To Hyères (Table **352**).
△ – To Hyères on dates in Table **352**.
⊡ – Also Dec. 25, Jan. 1, Apr. 6, May 13, 25; not Apr. 5, May 24. From Melun (Table **370**).
⊙ – From Metz (Table **379**).
⊗ – Not Mar. 15 - 19, Apr. 5 - 9, 12 - 16, June 7 - 11, 14 - 18.
§ – Station for Disneyland Paris.
** – Distance Lyon Part Dieu - Valence TGV = *104 km*.

350 PARIS and LYON - MONTPELLIER, MARSEILLE and NICE via high-speed line *TGV Méditerranée*

All *TGV* trains are Ⓡ	*TGV* 9834	*TGV* 5385	*TGV* 5398	*TGV* 6181	*TGV* 5346	*TGV* 6821	*TGV* 6127	*TGV* 6187	*TGV* 6217	*TGV* 9836	*TGV* 9836	*TGV* 6183	*TGV* 6157	*TGV* 6135	*TGV* 5126	*TGV* 6129	*TGV* 5124	*TGV* 6219	*TGV* 6219	*TGV* 6219	*TGV* 6131	*TGV* 6221	*TGV* 5142	*TGV* 5135
					①-④	⑤⑥		⑤			⑤⑦	⑤		Ⓑ	⑦		①-⑥		①-④	⑤⑦			⑦	⑦
			A		**Rm**	**z**	**Y**	**D**			**u**	**D**	**Y**	**h**	**e**		**n**		**m**	**u**			**e**	**e**
Brussels Midi **11** d.	1520	...	...	...	...	...	...	...	...	1609	1609	...	...	...	...	...	...	...	...	...	...	...	...	...
Lille Europe **11** d.	1606	...	...	...	...	...	...	...	...	1654	1654	...	...	...	1754	...	1754	...	...	...	...	...	1931	1931
Charles de Gaulle ✈ **11** d.	1701	...	...	...	...	...	...	...	...	1751	1751	...	...	...	1900	...	1900	...	...	...	...	...	2027	2027
Marne la Vallée-Chessy § d.	1714	...	...	...	...	...	...	...	...	1810	1810	...	...	...	1913	...	1913	...	...	...	...	...	2041	2041
Paris Gare de Lyon d.	|	...	...	1742	...	...	1814	1815	1819	|	|	1842	1842	1846	|	1916	|	1920	1920	1920	2015	2019	|	|
Genève **345** d.	|	...	...	|	...	...	|	|	|	|	|	|	|	|	|	|	|	|	|	|	|	|	|	|
Dijon **373** d.	|	1717c	...	|	...	...	|	|	|	|	|	|	|	|	|	|	|	|	|	|	|	|	|	|
Lyon Part Dieu d.	1907	1911	...	|	1937	1937	|	|	|	2007	2007	|	|	|	|	|	2107	|	|	|	|	|	2237	2241
Valence TGV d.	|	|	...	|	2014	2014	|	|	2034	2045	2045	|	|	|	2117	|	|	|	|	|	|	2234	|	2319
Avignon TGV d.	2013	|	2013	|	2049	|	|	|	|	|	|	|	|	2129	2151	2159	2210	|	|	|	2258	|	2346	|
Nîmes **355** d.	|	2030	2034	|	|	|	|	|	2120	2131	2131	|	|	|	|	|	|	2214	2214	2214	|	2320	|	0006
Montpellier 355 a.	|	2057	2101	|	|	|	|	|	2146	2155	2155	|	|	|	|	|	|	2238	2238	2238	|	2355	|	0030
Sète **355** a.	|	|	2119	|	|	|	|	|	2205	...	2213	|	|	|	|	|	|	...	|	2258	|	...	|	...
Agde **355** a.	|	|	|	|	|	|	|	|	2222	...	2228	|	|	|	|	|	|	...	|	2314	|	...	|	...
Béziers **355** a.	|	2138	2144	|	|	|	|	|	2236	...	2241	|	|	|	|	|	|	...	2320	2329	|	...	|	...
Narbonne **355** a.	|	2155	2201	|	|	|	|	|	...	...	2257	|	|	|	|	|	|	...	2337	2345	|	...	|	...
Toulouse **321** a.	|	2309	2317	|	|	|	|	|	...	...	|	|	|	|	|	|	|	...	|	|	|	...	|	...
Perpignan 355 a.	|	...	...	|	|	|	|	|	...	...	2332	|	|	|	|	|	|	...	0012	0021	|	...	|	...
Aix en Provence TGV d.	2036	...	...	2045	|	2106	|	|	...	...	...	2151	2151	|	|	2222	2235	...	...	...	|	...	0009	...
Marseille St Charles a.	2047	...	...	|	2117	2118	2122	2121	...	...	...	|	|	2158	2221	2234	2246	...	...	...	2326	...	0020	...
Marseille St Charles 360 d.	2059r	...	...	|	...	...	...	2133	...	...	...	|	|	...	...	...	...	...	...	...	2338	...	...	...
Toulon 360 a.	2146r	...	...	2137	...	...	...	2216	...	...	...	2241	2241	...	...	...	...	...	...	...	0022	...	...	...
Les Arcs-Draguignan **360** a.	...	...	...	|	...	...	...	|	...	...	...	|	...	...	...	...	...	...	...	...	...	...	...	...
St Raphaël-Valescure **360** a.	...	...	...	2227	...	...	...	2305	...	...	...	2330	...	...	...	...	...	...	...	...	...	...	...	...
Cannes **360** a.	...	...	...	2251	...	...	...	2329	...	...	...	2355	...	...	...	...	...	...	...	...	...	...	...	...
Antibes **360** a.	...	...	...	2303	...	...	...	2341	...	...	...	0006	...	...	...	...	...	...	...	...	...	...	...	...
Nice 360 a.	...	...	...	2324	...	...	...	0001	...	...	...	0026	...	...	...	...	...	...	...	...	...	...	...	...

	TGV 6137	*TGV* 6225	*TGV* 5136	*TGV* 5338	*TGV* 5140		*TGV* 7989	*TGV* 7995	
	⑤⑦	⑤⑦	⑤⑥	⑦	⑤		⑤-⑦	⑤-⑦	
	u	**y**▽	**b**	**Re**	**D**		**E**⊗	**E**⊗	
Brussels Midi **11** d.	...	...	...	...	...	...	...	...	...
Lille Europe **11** d.	...	...	1915	...	2030v	...	...	...	...
Charles de Gaulle ✈ **11** d.	...	...	2048	...	2127	...	...	...	...
Marne la Vallée-Chessy § d.	...	...	2103	...	2143	...	...	...	...
Paris Gare de Lyon d.	2116	2120	|	...	|	...	2220	2220	...
Genève **345** d.	|	|	|	...	|	...	|	|	...
Dijon **373** d.	|	|	|	...	|	...	|	|	...
Lyon Part Dieu d.	|	|	2305	2305	2341	...	|	|	...
Valence TGV d.	|	2334	2344	2343	0019	...	|	|	...
Avignon TGV d.	0000	|	0021	0019	|	...	|	|	...
Nîmes **355** d.	|	0019	|	|	|	...	|	0510	...
Montpellier 355 a.	|	0045	|	|	|	...	|	0538	...
Sète **355** a.	|	...	|	|	|	...	|	|	...
Agde **355** a.	|	...	|	|	|	...	|	|	...
Béziers **355** a.	|	...	|	|	|	...	|	0627	...
Narbonne **355** a.	|	...	|	|	|	...	|	0645	...
Toulouse **321** a.	|	...	|	|	|	...	|	|	...
Perpignan 355 a.	|	...	|	|	|	...	|	0733	...
Aix en Provence TGV d.	0023	...	0044	0044	0114	...	|	...	...
Marseille St Charles a.	0035	...	0055	0055	0125	...	0514	...	...
Marseille St Charles 360 d.	...	...	...	...	...	...	0528	...	...
Toulon 360 a.	...	...	...	...	...	...	0619	...	...
Les Arcs-Draguignan **360** a.	...	...	...	...	...	...	|	...	...
St Raphaël-Valescure **360** a.	...	...	...	...	...	...	0720	...	...
Cannes **360** a.	...	...	...	...	...	...	0753	...	...
Antibes **360** a.	...	...	...	...	...	...	0807	...	...
Nice 360 a.	...	...	...	...	...	...	0829	...	...

	TGV 6102	*TGV* 5158		*TGV* 6202	*TGV* 9854	*TGV* 6150	*TGV* 9856	*TGV* 9856	
	Ⓐ	⑥		Ⓐ	Ⓐ	Ⓐ	⑥	⑦	
		d					**d**	**e**	
Nice 360 d.	...	...	...	...	...	...	...	...	...
Antibes **360** d.	...	...	...	...	...	...	...	...	...
Cannes **360** d.	...	...	...	...	...	...	...	...	...
St Raphaël-Valescure **360** d.	...	...	...	...	...	...	...	...	...
Les Arcs-Draguignan **360** d.	...	...	...	...	...	...	...	...	...
Toulon 360 d.	...	...	...	...	...	0519	0516	...	...
Marseille St Charles 360 a.	...	...	...	...	...	|	0559	...	...
Marseille St Charles d.	0528	0539	...	...	0550	|	0610	0610	...
Aix en Provence TGV d.	0542	0554	...	...	0604	0617	0624	0624	...
Perpignan 355 d.	|	|	...	...	|	|	|	|	...
Toulouse **321** d.	|	|	...	...	|	|	|	|	...
Narbonne **355** d.	|	|	...	...	|	|	|	|	...
Béziers **355** d.	|	|	...	0447	|	|	|	|	...
Agde **355** d.	|	|	...	0501	|	|	|	|	...
Sète **355** d.	|	|	...	0517	|	|	|	|	...
Montpellier 355 d.	|	|	...	0539	|	|	|	|	...
Nîmes **355** d.	|	|	...	0605	|	|	|	|	...
Avignon TGV d.	0604	0616	...	|	0629	0640	0646	0646	...
Valence TGV d.	|	0650	...	0656	0713	|	|	|	...
Lyon Part Dieu a.	|	|	...	|	0750	|	0750	0750	...
Dijon **373** a.	|	|	...	|	|	|	|	|	...
Genève **345** a.	|	|	...	|	|	|	|	|	...
Paris Gare de Lyon a.	0845	|	...	0911	|	0918	|	|	...
Marne la Vallée-Chessy § a.	...	0857	...	...	0946	...	0945	0945	...
Charles de Gaulle ✈ **11** a.	...	0918	...	...	1001	...	1002	1002	...
Lille Europe **11** a.	...	...	...	...	1103	...	1103	1103	...
Brussels Midi **11** a.	...	...	...	...	1152	...	1150	1150	...

	TGV 6136	*TGV* 6136	*TGV* 6230		*TGV* 5162	*TGV* 5162	*TGV* 5144	*TGV* 6204	*TGV* 6204	*TGV* 6106	*TGV* 5350	*TGV* 6850	*TGV* 6108		*TGV* 5166	*TGV* 9860	*TGV* 9860	*TGV* 6172	*TGV* 6206	*TGV* 6112	*TGV* 5301	*TGV* 5150	*TGV* 5150	*TGV* 5170
		Ⓒ	Ⓐ			①⑥			⑥		Ⓑ	Ⓒ	①-⑥				⑥					Ⓐ	Ⓒ	⊕
						k			**d**		**Rh**		**n**				**d**				**A**			**B**
Nice 360 d.	...	...	...	...	...	...	...	...	...	...	...	...	...	...	...	...	...	0635	...	...	...	...	...	...
Antibes **360** d.	...	...	...	...	...	...	...	...	...	...	...	...	...	...	...	...	...	0654	...	...	...	...	...	...
Cannes **360** d.	...	...	...	...	...	...	...	...	...	...	...	...	...	...	...	...	...	0705	...	...	...	...	...	...
St Raphaël-Valescure **360** d.	...	...	...	...	...	...	...	...	...	...	...	...	...	...	...	...	...	0729	...	...	...	...	...	...
Les Arcs-Draguignan **360** d.	...	...	...	...	...	...	...	...	...	...	...	...	...	...	...	...	...	|	...	...	...	...	...	...
Toulon 360 d.	...	0533	...	...	...	...	...	...	...	...	...	...	0719	...	...	...	0745	0818	...	...	...	...	...	...
Marseille St Charles 360 a.	...	0616	...	...	...	...	...	...	...	...	...	...	0809	...	...	...	0829	|	...	...	...	...	...	...
Marseille St Charles d.	0628	0628	...	...	...	...	0710	...	...	0728	0739	0810	0828	...	...	0841	0841	|	...	0928	...	0940	0940	...
Aix en Provence TGV d.	|	|	...	...	...	...	0725	...	...	0743	0754	0824	|	...	...	0855	0855	|	...	0943	...	0956	0956	...
Perpignan 355 d.	|	|	0423	...	...	0505	|	...	0531	|	|	|	|	...	0642	|	|	|	0732	|	...	|	|	...
Toulouse **321** d.	|	|	|	...	...	|	|	...	|	|	|	|	|	...	|	|	|	|	|	|	0654	|	|	0749
Narbonne **355** d.	|	|	0512	...	...	0544	|	...	0610	|	|	|	|	...	0721	|	|	|	0816	|	0812	|	|	0859
Béziers **355** d.	|	|	0534	...	...	0602	|	...	0627	|	|	|	|	...	0737	|	|	|	0832	|	0827	|	|	0916
Agde **355** d.	|	|	0548	...	...	0615	|	...	0642	|	|	|	|	...	0751	|	|	|	0846	|	|	|	|	|
Sète **355** d.	|	|	0603	...	...	0630	|	...	0658	|	|	|	|	...	0806	|	|	|	0902	|	0855	|	|	|
Montpellier 355 d.	|	|	0623	...	0651	0651	|	0720	0720	|	|	|	|	...	0824	|	|	|	0922	|	0915	|	|	0958
Nîmes **355** d.	|	|	0650	...	0718	0718	|	0750	0750	|	|	|	|	...	0853	|	|	|	0950	|	0943	|	|	1026
Avignon TGV d.	|	|	|	...	|	|	0747	|	|	0805	|	|	|	...	|	0918	0918	0931	|	1005	1002	|	|	|
Valence TGV d.	|	|	0736	...	0810	0810	|	|	|	|	0846	|	|	...	0938	|	|	|	|	|	...	1046	1046	1112
Lyon Part Dieu a.	|	|	|	...	0846	0846	0850	|	|	|	0920	0950	|	...	1016	1020	1020	|	|	|	...	1120	1120	1149
Dijon **373** a.	|	|	|	...	|	|	|	|	|	|	...	1143	|	...	|	|	|	|	|	|	...	|	|	1354
Genève **345** a.	|	|	|	...	|	|	|	|	|	|	...	...	|	...	|	|	|	|	|	|	...	|	|	...
Paris Gare de Lyon a.	0931	0931	0949	...	|	|	|	1041	1041	1045	...	...	1131	...	|	|	|	1210	1241	1245	...	|	|	...
Marne la Vallée-Chessy § a.	...	...	...	...	1044	1044	1044	...	...	...	...	...	...	...	1216	1216	1216	...	...	...	...	|	1314	...
Charles de Gaulle ✈ **11** a.	...	...	...	...	1057	1057	1057	...	...	...	...	...	...	...	1229	1229	1229	...	...	...	...	1320	1328	...
Lille Europe **11** a.	...	...	...	...	1151	1151	1151	...	...	...	...	...	...	...	1329	1329	1329	...	...	...	...	1441v	1449v	...
Brussels Midi **11** a.	...	...	...	...	...	...	...	...	...	...	...	...	...	...	...	1414	1414	...	...	...	...	...	...	...

NOTES FOR PAGES 208/209

A – [12] Toulouse - Montpellier - Marseille and v.v. (Table **355**).
B – [12] Bordeaux - Toulouse - Lyon - Dijon.
D – ⑤ from Apr. 9 (also May 12).
E – ⑤⑥⑦ (also Dec. 24, 31, Apr. 5, May 12, 13, 24; not Feb. 19, 20, 26, 27, Mar. 5, 6).
F – ⑦ from Apr. 4 (also Apr. 5, May 24).
G – Daily from Apr. 5.
H – [12] Marseille - Lyon - Rouen - Le Havre.
M – To Metz (Table **379**), arrive Nancy 1759, Metz 1849.
N – To Nantes via Massy TGV (Table **335**).
P – ⑦ from Apr. 11 (also Apr. 5, May 24).
R – To / from Rennes via Massy TGV (Table **335**).
S – To Strasbourg (Table **384**).
T – ①②③④⑥ (also Dec. 25, Jan. 1; not Dec. 24, 31, Apr. 5, May 12, 24).
Y – Daily to Apr. 2; not on ⑤ from Apr. 3 (not May 12).
b – Also Dec. 24, 31, May 12, 13.
c – ①⑤⑥⑦ from Apr. 5 (also Apr. 6, May 12, 13, 25).
d – Also Dec. 25, Jan. 1, May 13.
e – Also Apr. 5, May 24.
f – Also Dec. 24, 31, May 12; not Dec. 25, Jan. 1.
h – Not Dec. 25, Jan. 1, May 13.
k – Also Dec. 25, Jan. 1, Apr. 6, May 13, 25; not Apr. 5, May 24.
m – Not Dec. 24, 31, Apr. 5, May 12, 13, 24.
n – Not Apr. 5, May 24.
r – ⑤⑦ (also Dec. 24, 31, Apr. 5, May 12, 24; not Dec. 25, Jan. 1).
u – Also Dec. 24, 31, Apr. 5, May 12, 24; not Dec. 25, Jan. 1.
v – Lille **Flandres**.
w – From Ventimiglia (Table **360**).
x – Arrive 2238 on Ⓒ.
y – Also Dec. 24, 31, Apr. 5, May 24; not Dec. 25, Jan. 1.
z – Also Dec. 24, 31, May 12, 13. On ⑤ starts from Lyon Perrache at 1921 (train **6822**).

NOTES CONTINUED ON NEXT PAGE →

TGV Méditerranée NICE, MARSEILLE and MONTPELLIER - LYON and PARIS via high-speed line 350

All *TGV* trains are 🅁	*TGV* 6854	*TGV* 6114	*TGV* 6208	*TGV* 5368	*TGV* 5374	*TGV* 9862	*TGV* 5198	*TGV* 6174	*TGV* 6116	*TGV* 6232	*TGV* 5430		*TGV* 5307	*TGV* 9864	*TGV* 6176	*TGV* 6210	*TGV* 6118	*TGV* 6866	*TGV* 9866	*TGV* 6120	*TGV* 6212	*TGV* 9868	*TGV* 5372	
				①–⑥	⑦																	Ⓒ	①–⑥	
				Nn	Ne		M	w	△		S		◧										Rn	
Nice 360 d.	0723	...	...	...	...	...	0925	0935	...	...	...	...	...	1028	1035	...	...	...	...	...	...	...	...	...
Antibes **360** d.	0745	...	...	...	...	...	0945	0955	...	...	...	...	...	1047	1054	...	...	...	...	...	...	...	...	...
Cannes **360** d.	0800	...	...	...	...	...	0957	1006	...	...	...	...	...	1058	1105	...	...	...	...	...	...	...	...	...
St Raphaël-Valescure **360** d.	0826	...	...	...	...	...	1020	1030	...	...	...	...	...	1123	1130	...	...	...	...	...	...	...	...	...
Les Arcs-Draguignan **360** d.	|	...	...	...	...	...	|	1046	...	...	...	...	...	1139	1147	...	...	...	...	...	...	...	...	...
Toulon 360 d.	0919	...	...	...	...	...	1113	|	1132	...	...	...	...	1216	|	...	...	...	...	1319	...	...	...	...
Marseille St Charles 360 a.	1001	...	...	...	...	...	1159	|	1216	...	...	...	...	1259	|	...	...	...	...	1409	...	...	...	...
Marseille St Charles d.	1012	1028	...	1133	1133	...	1210	|	1228	...	1246	...	...	1310	|	...	1328	...	1339	1428	...	...	1507	...
Aix en Provence TGV d.	1027	1042	...	1147	1147	...	|	1213	|	...	1300	...	...	|	|	...	1343	...	1353	1443	...	...	1523	...
Perpignan 355 d.	|	|	...	|	|	...	|	|	|	...	|	...	...	|	|	1135	|	...	|	|	...	1234	|	...
Toulouse **321** d.	|	|	...	|	|	...	|	|	|	...	|	...	1040	|	|	|	|	...	|	|	...	|	|	...
Narbonne **355** d.	|	|	...	|	|	...	|	|	|	...	|	...	1158	|	|	1210	|	...	|	|	...	1314	|	...
Béziers **355** d.	|	|	...	|	|	...	|	|	|	...	|	...	1215	|	|	1226	|	...	|	|	...	1331	|	...
Agde **355** d.	|	|	...	|	|	...	|	|	|	...	|	...	|	|	|	1241	|	...	|	|	...	1351	|	...
Sète **355** d.	|	|	...	|	|	...	|	|	|	...	|	...	|	|	|	1255	|	...	|	|	...	1407	|	...
Montpellier 355 d.	|	|	1021	|	|	1157	|	|	|	1221	|	...	1256	|	|	1318	|	1356	|	|	1421	1430	|	...
Nîmes **355** d.	|	|	1050	|	|	1228	|	|	|	1250	|	...	1325	|	|	1348	|	1425	|	|	1450	1457	|	...
Avignon TGV d.	1052	|	|	1210	1209	|	1245	1238	|	|	1324	...	|	1341	1332	|	1405	|	1416	|	|	|	1546	...
Valence TGV d.	|	|	1136	1245	1243	|	|	|	|	1336	|	...	1412	1419	|	|	|	1513	|	|	1537	1544	|	...
Lyon Part Dieu a.	1155	|	|	1320	1320	1346	1350	|	|	|	1430	...	1450	|	|	|	|	1550	1520	|	|	1620	1650	...
Dijon **373** a.	...	|	|	...	...	|	1539	|	|	|	...	...	1630c	|	|	|	|	|	|	|	|	|	...	...
Genève **345** a.	...	|	|	...	...	|	...	|	|	|	...	...	...	|	|	|	|	1735	|	|	|	|	...	...
Paris Gare de Lyon a.	...	1337	1348	...	...	|	...	1519	1531	1549	...	...	...	|	1615	1641	1645	...	|	1737	1749	|	...	...
Marne la Vallée-Chessy § a.	...	...	...	...	...	1545	...	...	...	...	...	...	...	1619	...	...	...	...	1717	...	...	1816	...	...
Charles de Gaulle ✈ **11** a.	...	...	...	...	...	1558	...	...	...	...	...	...	...	1633	...	...	...	...	1734	...	...	1830	...	...
Lille Europe **11** a.	...	...	...	...	...	1707	...	...	...	...	...	...	...	1735	...	...	...	...	1837	...	...	1937	...	...
Brussels Midi **11** a.	...	...	...	...	...	1756	...	...	...	...	...	...	...	1820	...	...	...	...	1930	...	...	2027	...	...

	TGV 5378	*TGV* 6122	*TGV* 6214	*TGV* 5376	*TGV* 6124		*TGV* 9868	*TGV* 6886	*TGV* 6178	*TGV* 6126	*TGV* 6216	*TGV* 5380	*TGV* 6168	*TGV* 5464	*TGV* 5180	*TGV* 6218	*TGV* 6128	*TGV* 6872	*TGV* 6130		*TGV* 6868	*TGV* 5314	*TGV* 5184	*TGV* 5186
	⑦						Ⓐ			Ⓑ			⑦								⑥	Ⓑ		
	Ne			H					G	h		N	F	⊙				⊡			d	h		
Nice 360 d.	...	...	...	...	...	...	...	1323	1335	...	...	...	1435	...	...	...	...	...	...	...	...	...	1528	...
Antibes **360** d.	...	...	...	...	...	...	...	1343	1356	...	...	...	1455	...	...	...	...	...	...	...	...	...	1548	...
Cannes **360** d.	...	...	...	...	...	...	...	1354	1408	...	...	...	1506	...	...	...	...	...	...	...	...	...	1559	...
St Raphaël-Valescure **360** d.	...	...	...	...	...	...	...	1418	1434	...	...	...	1530	...	...	...	...	...	...	...	...	...	1623	...
Les Arcs-Draguignan **360** d.	...	...	...	...	...	...	...	|	1451	...	...	...	|	...	...	...	...	...	...	...	...	...	1640	...
Toulon 360 d.	...	...	...	...	...	...	...	1512	|	...	...	...	1619	...	...	...	...	...	...	...	...	...	1715	...
Marseille St Charles 360 a.	...	...	...	...	...	...	...	1557	|	...	...	...	|	...	...	...	...	...	...	...	...	...	1759	...
Marseille St Charles d.	1507	1528	...	1539	1558	...	...	1610	|	1628	...	...	|	...	1709	...	1728	1735	1758	...	...	...	1810	...
Aix en Provence TGV d.	1523	|	...	|	|	...	...	|	1619	|	...	...	|	...	1723	...	1743	1749	|	...	...	...	1824	...
Perpignan 355 d.	|	|	...	|	|	...	1410	|	|	|	...	...	|	...	|	1531	|	|	|	...	1619	...	|	...
Toulouse **321** d.	|	|	...	|	|	...	|	|	|	|	...	...	|	...	|	|	|	|	|	...	|	1545	|	1609
Narbonne **355** d.	|	|	...	|	|	...	1449	|	|	|	...	...	|	...	|	1610	|	|	|	...	1659	1659	|	1728
Béziers **355** d.	|	|	...	|	|	...	1507	|	|	|	...	...	|	...	|	1627	|	|	|	...	1714	1714	|	1743
Agde **355** d.	|	|	...	|	|	...	1521	|	|	|	...	...	|	...	|	|	|	|	|	...	|	|	|	|
Sète **355** d.	|	|	...	|	|	...	1537	|	|	|	...	...	|	...	|	|	|	|	|	...	1737	1739	|	|
Montpellier 355 d.	|	|	1525	|	|	...	1600	|	|	|	1620	1627	|	1648	|	1716	|	|	|	...	1759	1800	|	1832
Nîmes **355** d.	|	|	1554	|	|	...	1627	|	|	|	1650	1700	|	1720	|	1744	|	|	|	...	1830	1830	|	1857
Avignon TGV d.	1546	1600	|	1610	1630	...	|	1645	|	|	|	|	1728	|	|	|	1804	1813	1830	...	|	|	1847	|
Valence TGV d.	|	|	|	1645	|	...	|	|	|	|	1736	1745	|	|	1815	1828	|	1849	|	...	|	|	|	1945
Lyon Part Dieu a.	1650	|	|	1720	|	...	1746	1750	|	|	|	1820	|	1846	1850	|	|	1927	|	...	1946	1946	1950	2020
Dijon **373** a.	...	|	|	...	|	...	|	|	|	|	|	...	|	2044	|	|	|	...	|	...	...	...	|	|
Genève **345** a.	...	|	|	...	|	...	|	1942	|	|	|	...	|	...	|	|	|	...	|	...	...	...	|	|
Paris Gare de Lyon a.	...	1841	1845	...	1911	...	|	...	1921	1931	1949	...	2011	...	|	2041	2045	...	2111	...	...	...	|	|
Marne la Vallée-Chessy § a.	...	...	...	...	...	...	1946	...	...	...	...	...	...	...	2044	...	...	...	...	...	...	...	2146	2215*
Charles de Gaulle ✈ **11** a.	...	...	...	...	...	...	1959	...	...	...	...	...	...	...	2057	...	...	...	...	...	...	...	2159	2229*
Lille Europe **11** a.	...	...	...	...	...	...	2054	...	...	...	...	...	...	...	2205x	...	...	...	...	...	...	...	2253	2323*
Brussels Midi **11** a.	...	...	...	...	...	...	2143	...	...	...	...	...	...	...	...	...	...	...	...	...	...	...	...	...

	TGV 6156	*TGV* 6138	*TGV* 6220	*TGV* 6184	*TGV* 6874	*TGV* 6222	*TGV* 6880	*TGV* 6132	*TGV* 5398	*TGV* 5194	*TGV* 6876	*TGV* 6180	*TGV* 6134	*TGV* 6134	*TGV* 6226	*TGV* 6224	*TGV* 6140	*TGV* 6186	*TGV* 6228	*TGV* 6142	*TGV* 6144		*TGV* 7994	*TGV* 7988
										⑦				⑤⑦	⑤	⑦	⑤	⑦	⑦	⑦	⑦		⑤–⑦	⑤–⑦
	◇					☆		⊖	A	P		▷	T‡	u‡	◐	e	f	P	e	e	P		E♠	E
Nice 360 d.	...	...	...	1635	...	...	...	...	...	...	1725	1735	...	...	...	...	...	1835	...	...	...	...	...	2035
Antibes **360** d.	...	...	...	1654	...	...	...	...	...	...	1745	1754	...	...	...	...	...	1854	...	...	...	...	...	2100
Cannes **360** d.	...	...	...	1705	...	...	...	...	...	...	1757	1805	...	...	...	...	...	1905	...	...	...	...	...	2115
St Raphaël-Valescure **360** d.	...	...	...	1730	...	...	...	...	...	...	1823	1830	...	...	...	...	...	1931	...	...	...	...	...	2143
Les Arcs-Draguignan **360** d.	...	...	...	|	...	...	...	...	...	...	|	|	...	...	...	...	...	|	...	...	...	...	...	|
Toulon 360 d.	1719	...	...	1820	...	...	...	...	...	...	1915	1919	...	...	...	...	...	2019	...	...	...	...	...	2234
Marseille St Charles 360 a.	|	...	...	|	...	...	...	...	...	...	1959	|	...	...	...	...	...	|	...	...	...	...	...	2318
Marseille St Charles d.	|	1828	...	|	1909	...	...	1928	1933	1941	2010	|	2021	2028	...	...	2058	|	...	2128	2138	...	...	2333
Aix en Provence TGV d.	1818	|	...	1914	1924	...	...	1943	1951	1958	|	2013	2036	|	...	...	2112	2119	...	2143	2152	...	...	|
Perpignan 355 d.	|	|	...	|	|	1737	...	|	|	|	|	|	|	|	...	1837	|	|	...	|	|	...	2150	|
Toulouse **321** d.	|	|	...	|	|	|	...	|	|	|	|	|	|	|	...	|	|	|	...	|	|	...	|	|
Narbonne **355** d.	|	|	...	|	|	1818	...	|	|	|	|	|	|	|	...	1914	|	|	...	|	|	...	2239	|
Béziers **355** d.	|	|	...	|	|	1834	...	|	|	|	|	|	|	|	...	1931	|	|	...	|	|	...	2256	|
Agde **355** d.	|	|	...	|	|	1848	...	|	|	|	|	|	|	|	...	1945	|	|	...	|	|	...	|	|
Sète **355** d.	|	|	...	|	|	1903	...	|	|	|	|	|	|	|	...	2000	|	|	...	|	|	...	|	|
Montpellier 355 d.	|	|	1821	|	|	1923	1927	|	|	|	|	|	|	|	2021	2023	|	|	2117	|	|	...	2347	|
Nîmes **355** d.	|	|	1851	|	|	1950	1956	|	|	|	|	|	|	|	2050	2050	|	|	2144	|	|	...	0015	|
Avignon TGV d.	|	|	|	|	1946	|	|	2005	2010	|	|	|	2058	2059	|	|	2135	|	|	2205	|	...	|	|
Valence TGV d.	|	|	1936	|	|	|	2044	|	...	2050	2110	|	|	|	2136	2136	|	|	2229	|	|	...	|	|
Lyon Part Dieu a.	|	|	|	|	2050	|	2120	|	...	2126	2150	|	|	|	|	|	|	|	|	|	|	...	|	|
Dijon **373** a.	|	|	|	|	|	|	2305r	|	...	|	2340	|	|	|	|	|	|	|	|	|	|	...	|	|
Genève **345** a.	|	|	|	|	2233	|	...	|	...	|	...	|	|	|	|	|	|	|	|	|	|	...	|	|
Paris Gare de Lyon a.	2121	2131	2149	2211	...	2241	...	2245	...	|	...	2311	2337	2337	2347	2347	0016	0011	0039	0045	0049	...	0720	0720
Marne la Vallée-Chessy § a.	...	...	...	...	...	...	...	...	...	2319	...	...	...	...	...	...	...	...	...	...	...	...	...	...
Charles de Gaulle ✈ **11** a.	...	...	...	...	...	...	...	...	...	2332	...	...	...	...	...	...	...	...	...	...	...	...	...	...
Lille Europe **11** a.	...	...	...	...	...	...	...	...	...	0032v	...	...	...	...	...	...	...	...	...	...	...	...	...	...
Brussels Midi **11** a.	...	...	...	...	...	...	...	...	...	...	...	...	...	...	...	...	...	...	...	...	...	...	...	...

← ***FOR OTHER NOTES SEE PREVIOUS PAGE***

TGV –🅁, supplement payable, 🍷.

◐ – Also Dec. 24, 31, May 12. On night of Dec. 25, Jan. 1 arrive Paris 0003. On ⑤ Jan. 8 - Feb. 26 arrive Paris 2355.
◧ – On ①–⑤ Mar. 1 - 26 runs 25 - 40 minutes later.
♠ – On ⑦ depart Narbonne 2227, Béziers 2246, Montpellier 2330, Nimes 2359.
⊡ – On ⑦ (also Apr. 5, May 24) train is numbered **6870** and continues to Melun (Table **370**).
⊙ – To Nancy on ①–⑥, Nancy and Metz on ⑦ (Table **379**).
⊕ – Depart Bordeaux 0533 on certain dates. On ①–⑤ Feb. 1 - 26 arrive Dijon 1436.
⊗ – Depart Paris 2209 on ⑤ Jan. 8 - Feb. 12.

◇ – To/from Hyères (Table **352**).
⊖ – Arrive Paris 10 minutes later on ①–④ Jan. 4 - Feb. 25.
△ – To/from Hyères on dates in Table **352**.
▽ – On night of Jan. 22, 29 arrive Nimes/Montpellier 21 minutes later. Additional train **6223** runs on Feb. 19, Apr. 2, 16, May 21 (Paris d. 2110, Nimes d. 0006, Montpellier a. 0040).
▷ – Arrive Paris 2316 on ①–⑤ Jan. 4 - Feb. 26 (also Mar. 5).
☆ – Arrive Paris 2254 on ①–④ Jan. 4 - 21, Feb. 8 - 25.
§ – Station for Disneyland Paris.
‡ – Arrives Paris up to 15 minutes later on certain dates Jan. - Mar.
* – On ⑤–⑦ (also Dec. 24, 31, Apr. 5, May 12, 13, 24) arrive Marne la Vallée 2222, Charles de Gaulle 2235, Lille Europe 2337.

351 LYON - VALENCE - AVIGNON - MARSEILLE

Via 'classic' line. For *TGV* trains via high-speed line see Table **350**. For night train Strasbourg / Luxembourg - Avignon - Arles - Marseille - Nice see Tables **379** and **384**.

km	All *TGV* trains are 🅁	⚒	⚒		17705		*TGV* 6191 ①–⑥ n	17709	⚒ ▷	*TGV* 6199 ⑥ W	*TGV* 6193 △	17713 ▷	★	17717	17721		⚒	17725		*TGV* 6295 ⑤⑦ u		*TGV* 6195 N	17729	*TGV* 6197
	Paris Gare de Lyon ▲ d.	...	...	...	...	...	0750	...	...	0924	0946	...	...	...	...	...	...	...	...	1710	...	1745	...	1945
	Lyon St Exupéry TGV ✈ d.	...	...	...	...	...	0951	...	...	|	1143	...	...	...	...	...	...	...	...	|	...	1942	...	2143
0	**Lyon Perrache** ▶ d.	...	...	...	...	...	|	...	...	|	|	...	...	...	...	...	...	...	1738	|	...	|	...	|
0	**Lyon Part-Dieu** ▶ d.	...	...	...	0725	...	|	0925	1025	|	|	1125	1225	1327	1525	...	1625	1725	|	|	1825	|	1925	|
32	Vienne ▶ d.	...	...	...	0744	...	|	0944	1045	|	|	1145	1245	1348	1544	...	1643	1745	1800	|	1845	|	1945	|
87	Tain-Hermitage-Tournon ▶ d.	...	...	...	0819	...	|	1018	1124	|	|	1217	1324	1425	1617	...	1724	1817	1841	|	1924	|	2017	|
105	**Valence Ville** ▶ a.	...	...	...	0829	...	1020	1029	1135	1152	1212	1228	1333	1435	1628	...	1735	1829	1851	1928	1935	2012	2028	2213
105	**Valence Ville** d.	0555	0645	0715	0832	0945	1023	1032	1145	...	1215	1231	1335	1438	1631	1715	1745	1832	1913	1931	1939	2015	2031	2216
150	Montélimar d.	0619	0713	0743	0857	1014	1046	1056	1214	...	1237	1257	1359	1458	1656	1743	1814	1854	1945	1956	2007	2037	2056	2237
202	Orange d.	0651	0748	0819	0932	1049	|	1133	1249	...	1303	1332	1431	1533	1732	1819	1849	1931	2019	2031	2043	2103	2132	|
230	**Avignon Centre** a.	0714	0810	0843	0946	1113	1120	1146	1313	...	1317	1346	1446	1547	1746	1843	1913	1946	2043	2049	2100	2117	2146	2312
230	**Avignon Centre** ▶ d.	0720	...	...	0949	...	...	1149	...	...	1321	1349	...	1550	1749	...	...	1949	...	2053	...	2121	2149	...
265	Arles § ▶ d.	0738	...	...	1008	...	...	1208	...	...	1342	1408	...	1610	1809	...	...	2009	...	2112	...	2139	2209	...
299	Miramas § ▶ d.	0800	...	...	1026	...	...	1226	...	...	1400	1426	...	1629	1826	...	...	2026	...	2130	...	2158	2227	...
328	Vitrolles (for ✈) ⊖ § ▶ d.	0820	...	...	|	...	...	|	...	...	...	|	...	|	|	...	...	|	...	...	...	...	|	...
351	**Marseille** St Charles § ▶ a.	0837	...	...	1054	...	...	1254	...	...	...	1454	...	1655	1854	...	...	2054	...	...	...	...	2258	...

	TGV 6192 Ⓐ	⚒	17702 ⚒	D	⚒		*TGV* 6194	17706	17704 ▽	◧	17714 ☆	*TGV* 6196		*TGV* 6190 ⑥ W	17716	17718	*TGV* 6198 ①–⑥ n	*TGV* 6198 ⑦ e		Ⓐ	17724		E	Ⓑ
Marseille St Charles § ▶ d.	...	...	0503	...	...	...	...	0703	0903	...	1101	...	...	...	1403	1503	...	...	...	...	1703	...	...	1903
Vitrolles (for ✈) ⊖ § ▶ d.	...	...	|	...	...	...	...	|	|	...	1119	...	...	...	|	|	...	...	...	...	|	...	...	1917
Miramas § ▶ d.	...	...	0533	...	...	...	0715	0734	0933	...	1135	...	...	...	1433	1533	1558	1554	...	...	1733	...	...	1934
Arles § ▶ d.	...	...	0552	...	...	...	0736	0752	0951	...	1152	...	...	...	1452	1552	1618	1615	...	...	1752	...	...	1953
Avignon Centre ▶ a.	...	...	0609	...	...	...	0752	0809	1009	...	1209	...	...	...	1511	1609	1634	1630	...	...	1810	...	...	2013
Avignon Centre d.	0511	0524	0612	0616	0646	0716	0755	0812	1012	1146	1212	1239	1316	...	1514	1612	1637	1637	1646	1716	1813	1846	1940	2016
Orange d.	|	0540	0628	0641	0710	0741	0810	0828	1028	1211	1229	|	1340	...	1530	1628	1652	1653	1711	1740	1829	1911	2003	2034
Montélimar d.	0550	0616	0704	0716	0746	0817	0836	0903	1104	1247	1305	1320	1414	...	1605	1704	1719	1719	1747	1816	1904	1947	2038	2110
Valence Ville a.	0612	0644	0725	0744	0814	0844	0858	0925	1125	1314	1326	1341	1441	...	1625	1725	1741	1741	1814	1844	1925	2014	2105	2135
Valence Ville ▶ d.	0615	0707	0728	0807	0822	...	0901	0928	1128	...	1329	1344	...	1550	1628	1728	1744	1744	1822	...	1928	2022	2122	...
Tain-Hermitage-Tournon ▶ d.	|	0717	0741	0818	0834	...	|	0939	1139	...	1340	|	...	|	1640	1740	|	|	1833	...	1942	2033	2133	...
Vienne ▶ d.	|	0758	0813	0859	0914	...	|	1012	1212	...	1414	|	...	|	1714	1814	|	|	1915	...	2023	2113	2213	...
Lyon Part-Dieu ▶ a.	|	|	0834	|	0934	...	|	1034	1234	...	1434	|	...	|	1734	1834	|	|	1934	...	2046	2134	2234	...
Lyon Perrache ▶ a.	|	0814	...	0919	...	...	|	...	...	...	...	|	...	|	...	...	|	|	...	...	...	...	...	...
Lyon St Exupéry TGV ✈ a.	0644	...	...	...	...	...	0930	...	...	...	...	1414	...	|	...	...	1813	1815	...	...	...	...	...	...
Paris Gare de Lyon ▲ a.	0841	...	...	...	...	...	1127	...	...	...	...	1611	...	1811	...	...	2011	2015	...	...	...	...	...	...

ADDITIONAL TRAINS LYON - VALENCE

		⚒	⚒		Ⓐ	Ⓐ	Ⓐ		⚒◐			Ⓐ◐		Ⓐ		Ⓐ	Ⓑ	Ⓐ						
Lyon Perrache d.	...	0538	...	...	0638	0738	...	...	1338	...	...	1538	1638	1708	...	1810	1838	1908	1942	...	...	...	...	...
Lyon Part Dieu d.	...	|	0625	...	|	|	0825	...	|	1425	...	|	|	|	...	|	|	|	|	...	2025	...	2125	...
Vienne d.	...	0600	0645	...	0700	0800	0845	...	1400	1444	...	1600	1700	1731	...	1831	1900	1930	2000	...	2045	...	2144	...
Tain-Hermitage-Tournon d.	...	0640	0724	...	0740	0840	0924	...	1440	1525	...	1640	1740	1811	...	1910	1940	2010	2040	...	2124	...	2224	...
Valence Ville a.	...	0651	0734	...	0751	0851	0935	...	1451	1535	...	1651	1751	1821	...	1921	1951	2021	2051	...	2135	...	2235	...

		Ⓐ	Ⓐ	⚒	⚒		⚒		Ⓐ⊡		⊙		⚒‡	Ⓑ		⚒	Ⓑ				Ⓑ	⑦d	†	
Valence Ville d.	...	0537	0606	0622	0637	...	0737	...	1022	...	1222	...	1422	1507	...	1607	1707	...	1807	...	1905	1921	2145	...
Tain-Hermitage-Tournon d.	...	0548	0618	0633	0649	...	0748	...	1033	...	1233	...	1432	1518	...	1618	1718	...	1818	...	1916	1933	2156	...
Vienne d.	...	0628	0657	0713	0728	...	0827	...	1113	...	1313	...	1513	1558	...	1658	1758	...	1857	...	1957	2008	2236	...
Lyon Part Dieu a.	...	|	|	0734	|	...	|	...	1134	...	1334	...	1534	|	...	|	|	...	|	...	|	2030	2254	...
Lyon Perrache a.	...	0649	0719	...	0749	...	0850	...	...	...	...	...	...	1619	...	1719	1819	...	1919	...	2019	...	...	...

ADDITIONAL TRAINS AVIGNON - MARSEILLE

	Ⓐ	Ⓐ	⚒	Ⓐ	Ⓐ			⚒	Ⓐ	Ⓐ	s	⚒s	sx	sx	Ⓐx		Ⓐ		Ⓐ			Ⓐ		
Avignon Centre d.	...	0549	0551	0620	0621	0644	0644	0721	0751	0820	...	1220	1221	1357	1620	1621	1720	1721	1751	1820	1851	1920	1933	2110
Arles 355 d.	...	0609	|	0640	|	0704	|	|	|	0840	...	1239	|	|	1640	|	1739	|	|	1839	|	1940	|	2129
Salon de Provence d.	...	|	0634	|	0719	|	0734	0819	0841	|	...	...	1319	1449	|	1719	|	1819	1848	|	1943	|	2030	|
Miramas d.	0542	0630	0645	0701	0730	0727	0745	0832	0850	0901	1245	...	1330	1500	1701	1730	1801	1830	1857	1901	1952	1959	2039	2151
Vitrolles (for ✈) ⊖ 355 d.	0606	0649	0709	0720	0749	|	0809	0853	...	0920	1309	...	1350	1518	1720	1754	1820	1849	...	1920	...	...	...	2212
Marseille St Charles 355 a.	0623	0706	0733	0738	0806	0756	0832	0910	...	0938	1333	...	1408	1534	1738	1814	1838	1911	...	1939	...	...	...	2230

	⚒			⚒z	⚒	Ⓐ◧	v		b	⚒		y	Ⓐ			Ⓐ	Ⓐ			Ⓐ	Ⓐ			
Marseille St Charles 355 d.	...	0618	0636	0718	...	0748	0818	...	...	...	1218	1318	1418	...	1546	1619	...	1646	...	1722	1746	1846	...	2045
Vitrolles (for ✈) ⊖ 355 d.	...	0635	0659	0735	...	0808	0837	...	...	...	1242	1335	1443	...	1603	1636	...	1704	...	1746	1803	1903	...	2103
Miramas d.	0625	0655	0725	0755	0802	0825	0857	...	1125	...	1307	1355	1506	...	1625	1700	1702	1729	...	1810	1827	1925	...	2123
Salon de Provence d.	0634	|	0734	|	0811	...	|	...	1134	...	1316	|	...	...	1634	|	1711	1738	...	|	1836	1934	...	|
Arles 355 d.	|	0717	|	0817	|	...	0918	...	|	1315	|	1416	...	...	|	1725	|	|	...	1832	|	|	...	2145
Avignon Centre a.	0730	0734	0830	0834	0900	...	0936	...	1231	1334	1411	1433	...	...	1730	1742	1800	1835	...	1849	1929	2030	...	2201

D – Daily to Valence, Ⓐ to Lyon.
E – Daily to Valence, ⚒ to Lyon.
N – ①②③④⑥ (also Dec. 25, Jan. 1; not Dec. 24, 31, Apr. 5, May 12, 24).
W – ⑥ Dec. 19 - Apr. 3 (also Dec. 25, Jan. 1).

b – Subject to alteration on Ⓐ Feb. 22 - Mar. 5.
d – Also Apr. 5, May 24; not Apr. 4, May 23.
e – Also Apr. 5, May 24.
n – Not Apr. 5, May 24.
s – Subject to alteration on Ⓐ Mar. 8 - 26.
u – Also Dec. 24, 31, Apr. 5, May 12, 24; not Dec. 25, Jan. 1.
v – Not on Ⓐ Mar. 29 - Apr. 9. On Ⓐ Jan. 11 - 21 will not call at Arles (Marseille d. 0815).
x – Subject to alteration Feb. 15 - 19.
y – Subject to alteration June 2 - 19.
z – Subject to alteration from Mar. 29. On Ⓐ Jan. 11 - 21 will not call at Arles (Avignon a. 0848).

TGV – 🅁, supplement payable, 🍷.

▲ – For *TGV* services via high-speed line see Table **340** Paris - Lyon, Table **350** Paris - Marseille / Montpellier.
▶ – For additional trains Lyon - Valence Ville and Avignon - Marseille see separate panel.
★ – Subject to alteration on Ⓐ Mar. 8 - 26, Apr. 12 - May 7.
◐ – Subject to alteration on Ⓐ Jan. 4 - 22.
◧ – Subject to alteration on Ⓐ Mar. 29 - Apr. 9.
△ – On ①–⑤ Mar. 8 - 26 diverted after St Exupéry to Valence **TGV** (a. 1206) and Avignon **TGV** (a. 1244) only.
▽ – Not Mar. 29 - 31, Apr. 1, 2, 5 - 9, 26 - 30, May 3 - 7. On Jan. 11 - 15, 18 - 21 Lyon a. 1258.
▷ – Not on ①–⑤ Mar. 8 - 26, Apr. 12 - 23.
⊡ – Subject to alteration Jan. 4 - 22, Apr. 26 - May 7.
⊙ – Subject to alteration on Ⓐ Mar. 1 - 19, Apr. 26 - May 7.
☆ – On Jan. 11 - 15, 18 - 21 Marseille d. 1023, Vitrolles d. 1042, Miramas d. 1109, not calling at Arles or Avignon.
⊖ – Full station name is Vitrolles Aéroport Marseille-Provence. A shuttle bus runs to the airport terminal (journey 5 minutes) connecting with trains.
§ – See also Table **355**.
‡ – Subject to alteration on Ⓐ Mar. 1 - 19.

351a 🚐 AVIGNON CENTRE - AVIGNON TGV

City 🚐 service *Navette TGV* operated by TCRA ✆ 04 32 74 18 32. Journey time 13 minutes (10 minutes Gare TGV - Avignon Centre). Rail tickets not valid. *Valid to Dec. 12, 2009*

Avignon Centre (Poste) ▲ depart: 0544 Ⓐ, 0614 Ⓐ, 0623 Ⓒ, 0643, 0716, 0737, 0828, 0850, 0903, 0923, 0940, 0955, 1018, 1045, 1059, 1120, 1131, 1146, 1210, 1237, 1304, 1322, 1337, 1405, 1415, 1433, 1456, 1520, 1533, 1603, 1619, 1634, 1650, 1725, 1742, 1802, 1823, 1901, 1918, 1931, 1949, 2004, 2026, 2101, 2121, 2137, 2158, 2235.

Avignon TGV depart: 0618 Ⓐ, 0653, 0714, 0754, 0812, 0847, 0910, 0925, 0940, 1005, 1020, 1036, 1100, 1120, 1135, 1150, 1206, 1226, 1252, 1319, 1347, 1357, 1420, 1440, 1456, 1516, 1553, 1607, 1617, 1637, 1652, 1719, 1742, 1803, 1837, 1856, 1915, 1936, 1953, 2006, 2021, 2106, 2115, 2145, 2206, 2218, 2305.

▲ – Cross road in front of station, through city 'gate', turn first left, first bus stop. On ⑦ (until approx 1300) departs from Cité Administrative (cross road, through ramparts, first stop on the right).

TOULON - HYÈRES 352

km						TGV 6109			TGV 6119	
		①-⑥	Ⓐ	⑥⑦					⑤⑦ w	
	Paris Gare de Lyon 350 d.	...	...	...	...	1016	...	...	1615	...
	Marseille 360 d.	...	...	...	...	1333	...	1703	1933	...
0	**Toulon** d.	0627	0730	0852	...	1420	1720	1806	2020	...
20	**Hyères** a.	0648	0751	0913	...	1435	1741	1828	2036	...

						TGV 6116		TGV 6156	
	①-④ m		Ⓐ		⑥⑦	Ⓒ			
Hyères d.	0617	0700	0803	...	1026	1100	...	1651	...
Toulon a.	0635	0721	0823	...	1047	1117	...	1708	...
Marseille 360 a.	0736	0826	0926	...	1155	1216	...	|	...
Paris Gare de Lyon 350 a.	...	...	...	...	...	1531	...	2121	...

m – Not Dec. 24, 31, Apr. 5, May 12, 24.
w – Also Dec. 24, 31, Apr. 5, May 12, 24; not Dec. 25, Jan. 1.

TGV – Ⓡ, supplement payable, 🍷.

LYON - BOURG EN BRESSE 353

Most trains 2nd class only

For long-distance trains see Table **384**. For local trains via Ambérieu see Table **346**

km		Ⓐ	⚒	Ⓐ			Ⓐ	Ⓑ	⚒			Ⓐ			Ⓐ	Ⓐ	Ⓐ			⚒		Ⓐ		
0	Lyon Perrache d.	0604	0703	0852	...	0952	...	1211	1256	...	1404	1518	1604	...	...	1704	...	1804	...	1852	2004	2104	...	...
5	Lyon Part Dieu d.	0626	0716	0904	...	1004	1056	1226	1308	...	1416	1530	1616	...	1704	1716	1811	1816	...	1904	2016	2116	...	...
65	Bourg en Bresse a.	0734	0826	0957	...	1101	1202	1328	1358	...	1516	1634	1723	...	1753	1836	1901	1927	...	1957	2117	2214	...	...

	⚒	Ⓐ	⚒	Ⓐ			Ⓐ		Ⓐ		Ⓐ			Ⓐ	Ⓒ				⚒		Ⓐ	Ⓒ	⚒	
Bourg en Bresse d.	0536	0611	0636	0709	...	0736	0804	...	0932	1036	1136	1236	...	1404	1429	...	1636	1729	1812	...	1904	1936	2004	...
Lyon Part Dieu a.	0639	0713	0739	0801	...	0839	0855	...	1039	1139	1239	1339	...	1456	1539	...	1739	1825	1906	...	1953	2039	2055	...
Lyon Perrache a.	0651	0725	0751	0813	...	0851	0912	...	...	1154	1251	1351	...	1508	1551	...	1751	1837	...	...	2005	2051	...	...

PERPIGNAN - VILLEFRANCHE - LATOUR DE CAROL 354

km		⚒		§		Ⓐ§		Ⓑ		
0	**Perpignan** d.	0630	0747	0850	1226	1505	1711	1837	1958	...
40	Prades-Molitg les Bains d.	0712	0829	0929	1308	1544	1753	1919	2040	...
46	**Villefranche-Vernet les Bains** a.	0719	0836	0936	1315	1551	1800	1926	2047	...

	⚒		§		Ⓐ§			Ⓑ
Villefranche-Vernet les Bains d.	0629	0746	1105	1225	1345	1710	1836	1957
Prades-Molitg les Bains d.	0636	0753	1112	1232	1352	1717	1843	2004
Perpignan a.	0714	0831	1150	1310	1430	1755	1921	2042

Villefranche - Latour de Carol is narrow gauge, 2nd class only ('Petit Train Jaune'). In summer most trains include open sightseeing carriages.

		P	T	H	S	▽	R	H	▽									
Villefranche-Vernet les Bains d.	**Dec. 13 - July 3** →	0905	0905	0905	1005	1330	1610	1725	1825	**July 4 - Aug. 29** →	0710	0900	1000	1120	1345	1545	1730	1830
Mont Louis la Cabanasse d.		1018	1040	1040	1133	1446	1746	1842	1936		0820	1028	1124	1257	1502	1702	1847	1936
Font Romeu-Odeillo-Via a.		1038	1056	1059	1149	1503	1802	1858	1952		0836	1047	1140	1313	1518	1718	1906	1955
Font Romeu-Odeillo-Via d.		1041	1059	1102	1154	...	1805	1901	1954		...	1052	1145	...	1523	...	1908	1956
Bourg Madame d.		1138	1145	1159	1245	...	1852	1945	2039		...	1151	1236	...	1607	...	1959	2050
Latour de Carol a.		1152	1200	1212	1300	...	1906	2001	2053		...	1204	1249	...	1620	...	2016	2103

km			①G	▽	S	T	▽	▽	H									
0	**Latour de Carol** d.	**Dec. 13 - July 3** →	0525	0810	0905	...	...	1527	1620	**July 4 - Aug. 29** →	...	0900	1025	...	1335	1457	...	1730
7	Bourg Madame d.		0539	0827	0922	...	...	1542	1635		...	0917	1041	...	1354	1512	...	1744
28	Font Romeu-Odeillo-Via a.		0620	0912	1015	...	...	1635	1730		...	1003	1141	...	1439	1610	...	1825
28	Font Romeu-Odeillo-Via d.		0622	0917	1021	1247	1520	1638	1734		0917	1008	1146	1340	1444	1637	1740	1828
35	Mont Louis la Cabanasse d.		0638	0935	1040	1304	1540	1659	1756		0936	1030	1210	1404	1509	1702	1759	1851
63	**Villefranche-Vernet les Bains** a.		0737	1051	1155	1406	1650	1809	1908		1047	1200	1319	1520	1627	1812	1913	2000

G – ① Dec. 14 - May 17 (also Apr. 6, May 25; not Apr. 5).
H – May 31 - July 3.
P – ①–⑤ Dec. 14 - Mar. 26; Ⓒ Mar. 27 - Apr. 11; daily Apr. 17 - May 30.
R – ⑤⑥⑦ Dec. 13 - Mar. 20; ⑦ Mar. 21 - May 16 (also Apr. 5, May 24; not Apr. 4).
S – ⑥⑦ Dec. 13 - Mar. 21; daily May 31 - July 3.
T – ⑥⑦ Dec. 13 - Mar. 21.
▽ – No rail service on Ⓐ Mar. 29 - Apr. 16 (runs Apr. 5).
§ – Subject to alteration on Ⓐ Apr. 26 - May 21.

STOP PRESS

The following night trains were to have been withdrawn and were removed from our tables.
They appear to have been reprieved, and the following details were received as we went to press:

CORAIL LUNÉA NICE - NANTES

	4724 4725 Ⓡ N		4624 4625 Ⓡ N◇
Nice Ville d.	1828	**Nantes** d.	2034
Antibes d.	1858	La Roche sur Yon d.	2119
Cannes d.	1913	**La Rochelle** d.	2219
St Raphaël-Valescure d.	1942	Rochefort d.	2240
Fréjus d.	1947	Saintes d.	2310
Les Arcs-Draguignan d.	2005	Bordeaux d.	0051
Toulon d.	2043	**Montpellier** a.	0620
Marseille St Charles d.	2124	Nimes a.	0654
Nimes d.	2233	**Marseille St Charles** a.	0821
Montpellier d.	2303	**Toulon** a.	0907
Bordeaux a.	0437	Les Arcs-Draguignan a.	0944
Saintes a.	0614	Fréjus a.	1000
Rochefort a.	0644	St Raphaël-Valescure a.	1005
La Rochelle a.	0705	**Cannes** a.	1030
La Roche sur Yon a.	0825	Antibes a.	1040
Nantes a.	0918	**Nice Ville** a.	1100

N – ⑤⑦ (also Dec. 19, 24, 26, 31, Jan. 2, Feb. 6, 11, 13, 18, 20, 25, Mar. 4, Apr. 3, 8, 10, 15, 17, 22, 24, 29, May 1; not Mar. 28, May 14, 23). 🛏 2 cl. and (2) (reclining) Nice - Nantes and v.v.

◇ – Arrival times may vary approx 30 minutes earlier or later.

CORAIL LUNÉA LYON - NANTES - QUIMPER

	4548 4549 Ⓡ P◐		4448 4449 Ⓡ P◧
Lyon Perrache d.	2129	**Quimper** d.	1820
Lyon Part Dieu d.	2143	Rosporden d.	1835
St Pierre des Corps a.	0507	Quimperlé d.	1852
Saumur a.	0542	Lorient d.	1907
Angers a.	0604	Auray d.	1927
Nantes a.	0704	Vannes d.	1941
Redon a.	0758	Redon d.	2010
Vannes a.	0835	**Nantes** d.	2105
Auray a.	0850	Angers d.	2151
Lorient a.	0908	Saumur d.	2213
Quimperlé a.	0923	St Pierre des Corps d.	2247
Rosporden a.	0940	**Lyon Part Dieu** a.	0631
Quimper a.	0955	**Lyon Perrache** a.	0645

P – ⑤ (also Dec. 19, 20, 24, 26, 27, 31, Jan. 2, 3, 31, Feb. 6, 7, 11 - 14, 18, 21, 25, 27, Mar. 4, 6, 7, 14, 21, 28, Apr. 3, 4, 18, 25, May 1, 2, 9, 16, 23; not Mar. 26, June 4). 🛏 2 cl. and (2) (reclining) Lyon - Quimper and v.v.

◐ – On ⑥⑦ Dec. 19 - Jan. 3 (also Feb. 6, 7, 13, 14, 21, 27, Mar. 6, 7) starts from Chambéry (d. 1937) via Aix les Bains (d. 1952), departing Lyon Part Diau at 2113, Lyon Perrache at 2127.

◧ – On morning of ⑥⑦ Dec. 19 - Jan. 3 (also Feb. 6, 7, 13, 14, 21, 27, Mar. 6, 7) arrive Lyon Perrache 0626, Lyon Part Dieu 0639 and extends to Aix les Bains (a. 0753) and Chambéry (a. 0807).

355 MARSEILLE and AVIGNON - NARBONNE - PORTBOU

km			3731				TGV 7995			4248 4249	4295 4248		463		4752 4753						4754 4755	TGV 5355	TGV 6803	
		Ⓐ	♦ 🄁	R	Ⓐ	Ⓐ	⑤–⑦ N	Ⓐ	⑥⑦ W	P 🄁	Q 🄁	Ⓐ	🄁✕ ♦✓	Ⓐ	★ D	Ⓐ	⚒	⚒	⚒		★	Ⓑ h	⑥ t	Ⓑ
	Paris Gare de Lyon **350** d.	...	...	...	...	...	2220	...	...	...	...	...	...	...	...	...	...	...	...	...	...	...	...	...
	Paris Austerlitz **310** d.	...	2156	...	...	...	|	...	...	...	...	...	...	...	...	...	...	...	...	...	...	...	...	...
	Brussels Midi **11** d.	...	|	...	...	...	|	...	...	...	...	...	...	...	...	...	...	...	...	...	...	...	...	...
	Lille Europe **11** d.	...	|	...	...	...	|	...	...	...	...	...	...	...	...	...	...	...	...	...	...	...	...	...
	Charles de Gaulle ✈ **350** d.	...	|	...	...	...	|	...	...	...	...	...	...	...	...	...	...	...	...	...	...	...	...	...
	Metz **379** d.	...	|	...	...	...	|	...	...	2040	...	...	...	...	...	...	...	...	...	...	...	...	...	...
	Strasbourg **384** d.	...	|	...	...	...	|	...	...	|	2058	...	...	...	...	...	...	...	...	...	...	...	...	...
	Dijon **373** d.	...	|	...	...	...	|	...	...	|	|	...	...	...	...	...	...	...	...	...	...	...	...	...
	Genève **345** d.	...	|	...	...	...	|	...	...	|	|	...	...	...	...	...	...	...	...	...	...	...	...	...
	Lyon Part Dieu **350** d.	...	|	...	...	...	|	...	...	|	|	...	...	...	...	...	...	...	...	...	...	0711	0711	...
	Nice **360** d.	...	|	...	...	...	|	...	...	|	|	...	...	...	...	...	...	...	...	...	...	|	|	...
▵	**Marseille St Charles** d.	...	|	...	...	...	|	...	...	|	|	...	...	...	0614	...	...	...	0624	...	0714	|	|	...
	Vitrolles Aéroport Marseille ‡ d.	...	|	...	...	...	|	...	...	|	|	...	...	...	|	...	...	...	0641	...	|	|	|	...
	Arles d.	...	|	...	...	...	|	...	...	|	|	...	...	...	|	...	...	...	0721	...	0758	|	|	...
0	**Avignon Centre** d.	...	|	...	...	...	|	...	...	|	|	0603	...	...	|	...	...	0638	|	0730	|	|	|	...
21	Tarascon-sur-Rhône d.	...	|	...	...	...	|	...	...	|	|	0615	...	...	|	...	...	0651	0731	0742	|	|	|	...
49	Nimes a.	...	|	...	...	...	0506	...	...	0554	0554	0629	...	...	|	...	...	0712	0752	0756	0822	0828	0828	...
49	Nimes d.	...	|	...	...	0515	0510	...	...	0557	0557	0631	...	0635	|	0704	...	0720	...	0759	0825	0831	0831	...
99	**Montpellier** a.	...	|	...	...	0546	0538	...	...	0627	0627	0700	...	0717	0740	0735	...	0752	...	0829	0849	0855	0855	...
99	**Montpellier** d.	...	|	...	...	0549	0542	0620	0625	0631	0631	0703	0727	0731	0744	0748	...	0800	...	0832	0853	0859	0859	...
126	Sète d.	...	|	...	...	0609	|	0644	0644	0652	0652	0722	|	0748	|	0806	...	0821	...	0852	0910	|	|	...
149	Agde d.	...	|	...	...	0622	|	0700	0700	0708	0708	0737	|	0801	|	0820	...	0838	...	0907	|	|	|	...
170	Béziers d.	...	|	...	...	0635	0630	0716	0716	0722	0722	0752	0804	0813	|	0833	...	0850	...	0921	0935	0943	0943	...
196	**Narbonne** a.	...	0615	...	...	0647	0645	0734	0729	0738	0738	0807	0818	0826	|	0846	...	0904	...	0936	0949	0959	0959	...
196	**Narbonne 321** d.	...	0635	0640	...	0649	0656	0737	0732	0742	0742	0815	0820	...	|	...	0851	...	...	0938	0952	1002	1002	...
	Carcassonne **321** a.	...	|	|	...	0719	|	|	|	|	|	0844	|	...	|	...	|	...	...	|	1021	1032	|	...
	Toulouse **321** a.	...	|	|	...	0819	|	|	|	|	|	...	|	...	0942	...	|	...	...	|	1110	1121	|	...
	Irún **325** a.	...	|	|	...	...	|	|	|	|	|	...	|	...	|	...	|	...	...	|	|	...	|	...
	Bordeaux **320** a.	...	|	|	...	...	|	|	|	|	|	...	|	...	1147	...	|	...	...	|	1327s	...	|	...
259	**Perpignan** a.	...	0720	0726	...	...	0733	0818	0817	0824	0824	...	0854	...	...	...	0932	...	...	1022	...	...	1037	...
259	**Perpignan** d.	0620	0724	...	0745	...	...	...	...	0828	0828	...	0856	...	...	...	0934	...	...	...	...	...	...	1047
281	Argelès sur Mer d.	0636	0746	...	0800	...	...	...	...	0848	0848	...	|	...	...	...	0950	...	...	...	...	...	...	1103
286	Collioure d.	0641	0753	...	0805	...	...	...	...	0855	0855	...	|	...	...	...	0955	...	...	...	...	...	...	1108
289	Port Vendres d.	0645	0758	...	0809	...	...	...	...	0900	0900	...	|	...	...	...	0958	...	...	...	...	...	...	1112
294	Banyuls sur Mer d.	0650	0805	...	0814	...	...	...	...	0907	0907	...	|	...	...	...	1003	...	...	...	...	...	...	1116
301	Cerbère a.	0656	0812	...	0819	...	...	...	...	0914	0914	...	0921	...	...	...	1009	...	...	...	...	...	...	1122
303	**Portbou** a.	...	0821	...	...	...	...	...	...	0923	0923	...	0948	...	...	...	...	...	...	...	...	...	...	...

		TGV 6201		TGV 6813		TGV 6203	4756 4757			TGV 5104	TGV 9804		TGV 6205			TGV 6207	4768 4769		15942 15952	TGV 5112		TGV 6233	TGV 5311	
	⚒	Ⓐ	▽				★ ⊙			Ⓒ	Ⓐ				⑦		★ F	⚒ u	C		Ⓑ d	①–⑥ q	△	⚒
Paris Gare de Lyon **350** d.	...	0620	...	...	...	0719	...	...	...	...	...	...	0820	...	...	0920	...	...	...	...	...	1020	...	...
Paris Austerlitz **310** d.	...	|	...	...	...	|	...	...	...	...	...	...	|	...	...	|	...	...	...	...	...	|	...	...
Brussels Midi **11** d.	...	|	...	...	...	|	...	...	...	...	0540	...	|	...	...	|	...	...	...	...	...	|	...	...
Lille Europe **11** d.	...	|	...	...	...	|	...	...	...	0625	0625	...	|	...	...	|	...	...	...	0828	...	|	...	...
Charles de Gaulle ✈ **350** d.	...	|	...	...	...	|	...	...	...	0725	0725	...	|	...	...	|	...	...	...	0925	...	|	...	...
Metz **379** d.	...	|	...	...	...	|	...	...	...	|	|	...	|	...	...	|	...	...	...	|	...	|	...	...
Strasbourg **384** d.	...	|	...	...	...	|	...	...	...	|	|	...	|	...	...	|	...	...	...	|	...	|	...	...
Dijon **373** d.	...	|	...	0616x	...	|	...	...	...	|	|	...	|	...	...	|	...	...	...	|	...	|	...	...
Genève **345** d.	...	|	...	|	...	|	...	...	...	|	|	...	|	...	...	|	...	...	...	|	...	|	...	...
Lyon Part Dieu **350** d.	...	|	...	0811	...	|	...	...	...	0937	0937	...	|	...	...	|	...	...	...	1137	...	|	1211	...
Nice **360** d.	...	|	...	|	...	|	...	...	...	|	|	...	|	...	...	|	0827	...	...	|	...	|	|	...
Marseille St Charles d.	...	|	0806	|	...	|	0914	...	...	|	|	...	|	...	...	|	1114	...	1128	|	...	|	|	...
Vitrolles Aéroport Marseille ‡ d.	...	|	0821	|	...	|	|	...	...	|	|	...	|	...	...	|	|	...	|	|	...	|	|	...
Arles d.	...	|	0857	|	...	|	0959	...	...	|	|	...	|	...	...	|	1157	...	1226	|	...	|	|	...
Avignon Centre d.	...	|	|	|	0915	|	|	...	1025	|	|	...	|	...	...	|	|	1157	|	|	...	|	|	...
Tarascon-sur-Rhône d.	...	|	0907	|	0927	|	|	...	1037	|	|	...	|	...	...	|	|	1209	1237	|	...	|	|	...
Nimes a.	...	0917	0923	0927	0943	1011	1023	...	1051	1057	1057	...	1117	...	...	1217	1223	1231	1254	1258	...	1317	1325	...
Nimes d.	0842a	0920	0925	0930	0946	1014	1026	...	1054	1100	1100	1115	1120	...	1155	1220	1226	1234	...	1301	...	1320	1328	1338
Montpellier a.	0911a	0949	0955	1002	1021	1038	1051	...	1120	1128	1128	1143	1147	←	1224	1247	1251	1305	...	1330	...	1346	1356	1404
Montpellier d.	0914	...	...	...	1024	1043	1055	1100	▬	1132	1132	→	...	1157	▬	▬	1255	1308	...	▬	1337	...	...	1407
Sète d.	0933	...	...	...	1044	1100	|	1118	...	|	|	...	...	1216	...	...	1312	1329	...	...	1357	...	...	1432
Agde d.	0947	...	...	...	1100	1116	|	1131	...	|	|	...	...	1230	...	...	1328	1345	...	...	1411	...	...	1447
Béziers d.	0959	...	...	...	1115	1130	1134	1143	...	1216	1216	...	...	1243	...	...	1342	1402	...	...	1424	...	...	1500
Narbonne a.	1015	...	...	...	1130	1144	1148	1156	...	1235	1235	...	...	1255	...	...	1356	1417	...	...	1438	...	...	1513
Narbonne 321 d.	...	...	...	...	1132	1147	1151	▬	1220	1238	1238	...	...	1257	...	...	1359	1420	...	...	1446	...	...	...
Carcassonne **321** a.	...	...	...	...	|	|	1220	...	|	1309	1309	...	...	|	...	...	1428	|	...	...	1517	...	...	...
Toulouse **321** a.	...	...	...	...	|	|	1305	...	|	1355	1355	...	...	|	...	...	1517	|	...	...	...	...	...	...
Irún **325** a.	...	...	...	...	|	|	|	...	|	...	...	...	...	|	...	...	...	|	...	...	...	...	...	...
Bordeaux **320** a.	...	...	...	...	|	|	1513	...	|	...	...	...	...	|	...	⑥⑦	...	|	...	...	...	...	...	...
Perpignan a.	...	...	...	...	1209	1220	...	...	1304	...	...	...	...	1337	...	W	...	1455	...	⚒	...	...	...	...
Perpignan d.	...	...	...	...	...	...	...	1224	...	...	...	...	...	...	1346	1350	...	...	...	1540	...	...	...	...
Argelès sur Mer d.	...	...	...	...	...	...	...	1243	...	...	...	...	...	...	1402	1405	...	...	...	1555	...	...	...	...
Collioure d.	...	...	...	...	...	...	...	1247	...	...	...	...	...	...	1407	1410	...	...	...	1601	...	...	...	...
Port Vendres d.	...	...	...	...	...	...	...	1251	...	...	...	...	...	...	1411	1414	...	...	...	1604	...	...	...	...
Banyuls sur Mer d.	...	...	...	...	...	...	...	1256	...	...	...	...	...	...	1416	1419	...	...	...	1609	...	...	...	...
Cerbère a.	...	...	...	...	...	...	...	1301	...	...	...	...	...	...	1421	1424	...	...	...	1615	...	...	...	...
Portbou a.	...	...	...	...	...	...	...	1308	...	...	...	...	...	...	1427	1430	...	...	...	1621	...	...	...	...

♦ – **NOTES** (LISTED BY TRAIN NUMBER)

463 – MARE NOSTRUM – [12] and ✕ Montpellier - Barcelona - Alacant - Murcia - Cartagena. In France calls to pick up only.

3731 – *CORAIL LUNÉA* – 🛏 1,2 cl. and [2] (reclining) Paris - Toulouse - Narbonne - Portbou. Not Dec. 24, 31.

C – [12] Marseille - Clermont Ferrand (Table **334**).

D – Runs Marseille - Toulouse to Mar. 28 / from May 8, also ⑥⑦ Apr. 3 - May 2. Runs Marseille - Bordeaux to Jan. 3 / from May 8, also ⑥⑦ Mar. 27 - May 2 (subject to alteration Marmande - Bordeaux on May 13 - 16).

F – Dec. 18 - 20, 24, 26, 27, 31, Jan. 2, 3, Feb. 12 - 14, 19 - 21, 26 - 28, Mar. 6, 7, Apr. 5, 17, 24, May 2, 12, 16, 24.

N – ⑤⑥⑦ (also Dec. 24, 31, Apr. 5, May 12, 13, 24; not Feb. 19, 20, 26, 27, Mar. 5, 6).

P – *CORAIL LUNÉA* – Dec. 13, 18 - 23, 25 - 30, Jan. 1 - 3; ⑤⑦ Jan. 8 - 31; ⑤⑥⑦ Feb. 5 - Mar. 7; ⑤⑦ Mar. 12 - 28; ⑤⑥⑦ from Apr. 2 (also Apr. 5, May 12, 13, 24). 🛏 1,2 cl. and [2] (reclining) Luxembourg (depart 1930) Metz - Portbou.

Q – *CORAIL LUNÉA* – Dec. 13, 18 - 23, 25 - 30, Jan. 1 - 3; ⑤⑦ Jan. 8 - 31; ⑤⑥⑦ Feb. 5 - Mar. 7; ⑤⑦ Mar. 12 - 28; ⑤⑥⑦ from Apr. 2 (also Apr. 5, May 12, 13, 24). 🛏 1,2 cl., [2] (reclining) Strasbourg - Portbou. Subject to confirmation.

R – Ⓐ (also ⑥⑦ Dec. 13 - Mar. 21).

W – ⑥⑦ Dec. 13 - Mar. 21.

a – Ⓐ only.

d – Not on ①–⑤ Mar. 1 - 26.

h – Not Dec. 25, Jan. 1, May 13.

q – Not Feb. 13, 20, Apr. 5, May 24.

s – 1347 on Ⓑ Jan. 4 - Mar. 26. Subject to alteration May 13 - 16.

t – Also Dec. 25, Jan. 1, May 13.

u – Will not call at Tarascon on ①–⑤ Mar. 8 - 26.

x – ①⑥ (also Dec. 25, Jan. 1, Apr. 6, May 13, 25; not Apr. 5, May 24).

TGV – 🄁, supplement payable, 🍷.

✓ – Special 'global' fares payable.

△ – From Nantes (Table **335**).

▽ – On ①–⑤ Jan. 11 - 21 runs 30 minutes later Tarascon - Montpellier.

⊙ – Not on ①–⑤ Mar. 29 - Apr. 9. On ①–⑤ Jan. 11 - 21 depart Marseille 0821. Subject to alteration Toulouse - Bordeaux Dec. 14 - 17, Apr. 19 - 23, May 13 - 15.

★ – *CORAIL TÉOZ*, 🄁, 🍷.

▵ – *135 km* from Nîmes via Avignon TGV, *128 km* via Arles.

‡ – Vitrolles Aéroport Marseille-Provence. A shuttle bus runs to the airport terminal (journey 5 mins).

MARSEILLE and AVIGNON - NARBONNE - PORTBOU 355

	4758 4759 ★ ⊡	b	TGV 6209	TGV 6816 ⊗	TGV 5462	70 71 ♦⁄ R✕		⚒	4762 4763 ★	⚒ d	TGV 6211	Ⓐ	TGV 9833	3631 ★ L		4764 4765 ★	Ⓐ	TGV 6235 ⑦ e		TGV 6213		TGV 5117	Ⓑ	◇	⚒
Paris Gare de Lyon **350** d.	...	...	1120	...	...	...	...	...	...	...	1319	...	...	...	...	...	...	1420	...	1520	...	...	...	...	...
Paris Austerlitz **310** d.	...	...	|	...	...	...	...	...	...	...	|	...	...	1019	...	...	...	|	...	|	...	...	...	...	...
Brussels Midi **11** d.	...	...	|	...	...	...	...	...	...	...	|	...	1120	|	...	...	...	|	...	|	...	...	...	...	...
Lille Europe **11** d.	...	...	|	...	...	...	...	...	...	...	|	...	1206	|	...	...	...	|	...	|	...	...	...	...	...
Charles de Gaulle ✈ **350** d.	...	...	|	...	...	...	...	...	...	...	|	...	1301	|	...	...	...	|	...	|	...	...	...	...	...
Metz **379** d.	...	...	|	...	0811	...	...	...	...	...	|	...	|	|	...	...	...	|	...	|	...	...	...	...	...
Strasbourg **384** d.	...	...	|	...	|	...	...	...	...	...	|	...	|	|	...	...	...	|	...	|	...	...	...	...	...
Dijon **373** d.	...	...	|	...	1124	...	...	...	...	...	|	...	|	|	...	...	...	|	...	|	...	1516n	...	...	...
Genève **345** d.	...	...	|	1117	|	...	...	...	...	...	|	...	|	|	...	...	...	|	...	|	...	|	...	...	...
Lyon Part Dieu **350** d.	...	...	|	1307	1311	...	...	...	...	...	|	...	1507	|	...	...	...	|	...	|	...	1707	...	...	...
Nice **360** d.	0955	...	|	|	|	...	...	...	...	...	|	...	|	|	...	1329	...	|	...	|	...	|	...	...	...
Marseille St Charles d.	1242	...	|	|	|	...	...	...	1414	...	|	...	|	|	...	1615	...	|	...	|	...	|	1714	...	...
Vitrolles Aéroport Marseille ‡ d.	|	...	|	|	|	...	...	...	|	...	|	...	|	|	...	|	...	|	...	|	...	|	1732	...	...
Arles d.	|	...	|	|	|	...	...	...	1458	...	|	...	|	|	...	|	...	|	...	|	...	|	1814	...	...
Avignon Centre d.	|	1327	|	|	|	...	...	...	|	1514	|	...	|	|	1606	|	...	|	1702	|	1735	|	|	...	1805
Tarascon-sur-Rhône d.	|	1340	|	|	|	...	...	...	|	1526	|	...	|	|	1619	|	...	|	1715	|	1748	|	1825	...	1818
Nimes a.	|	1353	1416	1422	1427	...	...	...	1522	1545	1617	...	1629	|	1634	|	...	1720	1729	|	1803	1830	1839	...	1834
Nimes d.	|	1356	1419	1425	1430	...	...	1455	1525	1554	1620	1624	1632	|	1636	|	1654	1723	1731	|	1806	1833	1842	...	1847
Montpellier a.	1409	1423	1442	1451	1455	...	...	1525	1549	1623	1644	1653	1659	|	1707	1741	1736	1747	1803	1838	1835	1857	1913	...	1928
Montpellier d.	1413	1426	1447	...	...	1509	...	1528	1553	1626	▬	1656	1706	|	1710	1745	1749	...	1806	1844	1848	1901	1916	...	1931
Sète d.	|	1445	1504	...	...	|	...	1550	1610	1646	...	1715	1723	|	1730	|	1812	...	1831	1900	1907	|	1935	...	1949
Agde d.	|	1500	1519	...	...	|	...	1606	|	1702	...	1729	1740	|	1745	|	1828	...	1847	1916	1922	|	1949	...	2002
Béziers d.	|	1513	1534	...	...	1555	...	1621	1635	1716	...	1742	1754	|	1758	|	1842	...	1905	1930	1936	1943	2002	...	2014
Narbonne a.	|	1526	1547	...	...	1609	...	1639	1649	1733	...	1755	1807	1805	1812	|	1858	...	1920	1944	1948	1955	2015	...	2027
Narbonne 321 d.	|	1533	1550	...	...	1611	1618	▬	1652	1736	...	▬	1810	1825	1815	|	...	...	...	1947	...	1958	...	2027	...
Carcassonne **321** a.	|	1604	|	...	...	|	|	...	1721	|	...	...	|	|	|	|	...	...	...	|	...	2026	...	|	...
Toulouse **321** a.	1612	1700z	|	...	...	|	|	...	1806	|	...	...	|	|	|	1944	...	...	...	|	...	2110	...	|	...
Irún **325** a.	|	...	|	...	...	|	|	...	|	|	...	...	|	|	|	|	...	...	...	|	...	|	...	|	...
Bordeaux **320** a.	1823	...	|	...	...	|	|	...	2022*	|	⑥⑦	...	|	|	|	2150*	...	...	...	|	...	2320	...	|	...
Perpignan a.	...	...	1625	...	...	1652	1701	...	...	1817	W	Ⓐ	1844	1903	1859	...	...	...	...	2021	...	...	...	2108	...
Perpignan d.	...	...	...	...	...	1654	1703	1753	...	...	1832	1835	...	1906	1913	...	...	...	...	...	...	...	...	...	...
Argelès sur Mer d.	...	...	...	...	...	|	1718	1810	...	...	1848	1850	...	1926	1936	...	...	...	...	...	...	...	...	...	...
Collioure d.	...	...	...	...	...	|	1723	1815	...	...	1853	1855	...	1933	1942	...	...	...	...	...	...	...	...	...	...
Port Vendres d.	...	...	...	...	...	|	1727	1818	...	...	1856	1859	...	1938	1946	...	...	...	...	...	...	...	...	...	...
Banyuls sur Mer d.	...	...	...	...	...	|	1732	1823	...	...	1901	1904	...	1944	1953	...	...	...	...	...	...	...	...	...	...
Cerbère a.	...	...	...	...	...	1719	1737	1829	...	...	1907	1909	...	1951	2001	...	...	...	...	...	...	...	...	...	...
Portbou a.	...	...	...	...	...	1748	...	1837	...	...	...	...	...	...	2009	...	...	...	...	...	...	...	...	...	...

	⚒	TGV 6231 Ⓐ	TGV 5118			4766 ★ ⑤⑦ p			TGV 6215	TGV 5385	TGV 5398			TGV 6217	TGV 9836	TGV 9836 ⑤⑦ u	TGV 6219	TGV 6219 ①–④ m	TGV 6219 ⑤ u		TGV 6221	TGV 5135 ⑦ e	TGV 6225 ⑤⑦ y	4778 4779 ♦ R	4720 4721 ♦ R
Paris Gare de Lyon **350** d.	...	1620	...	...	...	...	...	...	1719	...	...	...	...	1819	...	...	1920	1920	1920	...	2019	...	2120	...	...
Paris Austerlitz **310** d.	...	|	...	...	...	...	...	...	|	...	...	...	...	|	...	...	|	|	|	...	|	...	|	...	...
Brussels Midi **11** d.	...	|	...	...	...	...	...	...	|	...	...	...	...	|	1609	1609	|	|	|	...	|	...	|	...	...
Lille Europe **11** d.	...	|	1506	...	...	...	...	...	|	...	...	...	...	|	1654	1654	|	|	|	...	|	1931	|	...	...
Charles de Gaulle ✈ **350** d.	...	|	1601	...	...	...	...	...	|	...	...	...	...	|	1751	1751	|	|	|	...	|	2027	|	...	...
Metz **379** d.	...	|	|	...	...	...	...	...	|	...	...	...	...	|	|	|	|	|	|	...	|	|	|	...	...
Strasbourg **384** d.	...	|	|	...	...	...	...	...	|	...	...	...	...	|	|	|	|	|	|	...	|	|	|	...	...
Dijon **373** d.	...	|	|	...	...	...	...	...	|	1717c	...	...	...	|	|	|	|	|	|	...	|	|	|	...	...
Genève **345** d.	...	|	|	...	...	...	...	...	|	|	...	...	...	|	|	|	|	|	|	...	|	|	|	2044	...
Lyon Part Dieu **350** d.	...	|	1807	...	...	...	...	...	|	1911	...	...	...	|	2007	2007	|	|	|	...	|	2241	|	2250	...
Nice **360** d.	...	|	|	...	...	...	...	...	|	|	...	...	...	|	|	|	|	|	|	...	|	|	|	|	2056
Marseille St Charles d.	...	|	|	1818	...	1841	...	...	|	|	1933	...	1914	|	|	|	|	|	|	...	|	|	|	|	0010
Vitrolles Aéroport Marseille ‡ d.	...	|	|	1836	...	|	...	...	|	|	|	...	1933	|	|	|	|	|	|	...	|	|	|	|	|
Arles d.	...	|	|	1917	...	1929	...	...	|	|	|	...	2016	|	|	|	|	|	|	...	|	|	|	|	|
Avignon Centre d.	1846	|	|	|	...	|	...	1928	|	|	2013v	2009	|	|	|	|	|	|	|	...	|	|	|	|	|
Tarascon-sur-Rhône d.	1858	|	|	1927	...	|	...	1941	|	|	|	2021	2026	|	|	|	|	|	|	...	|	|	|	|	|
Nimes a.	1913	1918	1927	1941	...	1953	...	1957	2017	2027	2031	2036	2039	2117	2128	2128	2211	2211	2211	...	2317	0003	0016	|	|
Nimes d.	...	1921	1930	1943	...	1956	2012	...	2020	2030	2034	...	2042	2120	2131	2131	2214	2214	2214	2221	2320	0006	0019	|	|
Montpellier a.	...	1949	1958	2014	...	2021	2039	...	2046	2057	2101	...	2109	2146	2155	2155	2238	2238	2238	2250	2355	0030	0045	|	|
Montpellier d.	...	...	2002	2017	...	2025	2042	...	2051	2101	2105	...	2112	2151	...	2159	...	2244	2244	2253	...	...	...	|	|
Sète d.	...	...	2020	2037	...	2043	2059	...	2107	|	2122	...	2130	2207	...	2215	...	|	2301	2311	...	...	...	|	|
Agde d.	...	...	2036	2051	...	|	2113	...	2122	|	|	...	2144	2224	...	2230	...	|	2317	2325	...	...	...	|	|
Béziers d.	...	...	2050	2104	...	2109	2125	...	2136	2140	2147	...	2157	2236	...	2244	...	2323	2331	2340	...	...	...	|	|
Narbonne a.	...	...	2104	2117	...	2123	2138	...	2149	2155	2201	...	2210	...	...	2257	...	2337	2345	2353	...	...	...	|	|
Narbonne 321 d.	...	...	2107	...	2127	2126	...	...	2152	2158	2204	...	*2219*	...	...	2300	...	2340	2347	...	...	...	...	|	|
Carcassonne **321** a.	...	...	|	...	|	2155	...	...	|	|	2233	...	|	...	...	|	...	|	|	...	...	...	...	|	|
Toulouse **321** a.	...	...	|	...	|	2248	...	...	|	2309	2317	...	|	...	...	|	...	|	|	...	...	...	...	0500	0515
Irún **325** a.	...	...	|	...	|	|	...	...	|	...	...	...	|	...	...	|	...	|	|	...	...	...	...	1115	|
Bordeaux **320** a.	...	...	|	...	|	0101	...	...	|	...	...	...	|	...	...	|	...	|	|	...	...	...	...	...	0811
Perpignan a.	...	...	2139	...	2203	...	...	...	2223	...	...	...	*2255*	...	...	2332	...	0012	0021	...	...	...	...	...	...
Perpignan d.	...	...	...	...	2205	...	...	...	...	...	...	...	...	...	...	...	...	...	...	...	...	...	...	...	...
Argelès sur Mer d.	...	...	...	...	2220	...	...	...	...	...	...	...	...	...	...	...	...	...	...	...	...	...	...	...	...
Collioure d.	...	...	...	...	2225	...	...	...	...	...	...	...	...	...	...	...	...	...	...	...	...	...	...	...	...
Port Vendres d.	...	...	...	...	2228	...	...	...	...	...	...	...	...	...	...	...	...	...	...	...	...	...	...	...	...
Banyuls sur Mer d.	...	...	...	...	2233	...	...	...	...	...	...	...	...	...	...	...	...	...	...	...	...	...	...	...	...
Cerbère a.	...	...	...	...	2239	...	...	...	...	...	...	...	...	...	...	...	...	...	...	...	...	...	...	...	...
Portbou a.	...	...	...	...	...	...	...	...	...	...	...	...	...	...	...	...	...	...	...	...	...	...	...	...	...

♦ – **NOTES** (LISTED BY TRAIN NUMBER)

70/1 – CATALAN TALGO – (12) and ✕ Montpellier - Barcelona. In France calls to pick up only.

4720/1 – *CORAIL LUNÉA* – 🛏 1,2 cl. and (2) (reclining) Nice - Bordeaux. To Irún (numbered **4730/1**) on dates in Table **305**.

4778/9 – *CORAIL LUNÉA* – ⑤⑦ (daily Dec. 18 - 23, 25 - 30, Jan. 1 - 3, Feb. 12 - Mar. 7, Apr. 1 - May 2), also May 12, 24; not May 14, 23. 🛏 1,2 cl. and (2) (reclining) Genève - Lyon - Irún. Train number **14778** on certain dates.

L – Daily to Mar. 21; ⑥⑦ Mar. 27 - Apr. 18; daily from Apr. 24. Depart Paris 0951 on Mar. 2, 3, 11. On June 5, 6 starts from Limoges.

W – ⑥⑦ Dec. 13 - Mar. 21.

b – Not on ①–⑤ Mar. 1 - 26.

c – ①⑤⑥⑦ from Apr. 5 (also Apr. 6, May 12, 13, 25).

d – Will not call at Tarascon on ①–⑥ Mar. 6 - 27.

e – Also Apr. 5, May 24.

m – Not Dec. 24, 31, Apr. 5, May 12, 13, 24.

n – 1436 on Dec. 14 - 18 and ①–⑤ Feb. 15 - Mar. 12.

p – Also Dec. 24, 26, 31, Jan. 2, Apr. 5, May 12, 24; not Dec. 25, Jan. 1, Apr. 4, May 14.

u – Also Dec. 24, 31, Apr. 5, May 12, 24; not Dec. 25, Jan. 1.

v – Avignon **TGV** station.

y – Also Dec. 24, 31, Apr. 5, May 24; not Dec. 25, Jan. 1.

z – Ⓑ only.

TGV – R, supplement payable, 🍸.

⁄ – Special 'global' fares payable.

★ – *CORAIL TÉOZ*, R, 🍸.

◇ – From Toulouse (Table **321**).

⊡ – Not on ①–⑤ Mar. 1 - 26. Not Toulouse - Bordeaux on May 13 - 15.

⊗ – Not Mar. 15 - 19, Apr. 5 - 9, 12 - 16, June 7 - 11, 14 - 18.

‡ – Vitrolles Aéroport Marseille-Provence. A shuttle bus runs to the airport terminal (journey 5 mins).

* – Subject to alteration May 13 - 15 Marmande - Bordeaux.

355 CERBÈRE - NARBONNE - AVIGNON and MARSEILLE

	Ⓐ	Ⓐ	TGV 6202 Ⓐ	Ⓐ	Ⓐ	⚒	TGV 6230 Ⓐ	⚒	TGV 5162	TGV 5162 ①⑥ k		TGV 6204	TGV 6204 ⑥ t	Ⓐ m	Ⓐ	⚒ m			TGV 5166	Ⓐ		⚒	⑦ W	TGV 5301	TGV 6206
Cerbère d.	...	...	...	...	...	...	...	...	...	...	...	...	...	...	...	...	0540	...	...	...	...	0641	0641	...	...
Banyuls sur Mer d.	...	...	...	...	...	...	...	...	...	...	...	...	...	...	...	...	0547	...	...	...	...	0648	0648	...	...
Port Vendres d.	...	...	...	...	...	...	...	...	...	...	...	...	...	...	...	...	0552	...	...	...	...	0653	0653	...	...
Collioure d.	...	...	...	...	...	...	...	...	...	...	...	...	...	...	...	...	0556	...	...	...	...	0657	0657	...	...
Argelès sur Mer d.	...	...	...	...	...	...	...	...	...	...	...	...	...	...	...	...	0602	...	...	...	...	0702	0702	...	...
Perpignan a.	...	...	...	...	...	...	...	...	...	...	...	...	...	...	...	...	0618	...	...	...	...	0717	0717	...	...
Perpignan d.	...	...	...	...	...	...	0423	...	...	0505	...	...	0531	...	0600	...	...	0624	0642	...	...	0719	0719	...	0728
Bordeaux **320** d.	...	...	...	...	...	...	|	...	...	|	...	...	|	...	|	...	...	|	|	...	...	|	|	...	|
Hendaye **325** d.	...	...	...	...	...	...	|	...	...	|	...	...	|	...	|	...	...	|	|	...	...	|	|	...	|
Toulouse **321** d.	...	...	...	...	...	...	|	...	...	|	...	...	|	...	|	...	...	|	|	...	...	|	|	0654	|
Carcassonne **321** d.	...	...	...	...	...	...	|	...	...	|	...	...	|	...	|	...	...	|	|	...	0714	|	|	0742	|
Narbonne a.	...	...	...	...	...	...	0509	...	...	0541	...	...	0607	...	0645	...	...	0709	0718	...	0746	0801	0806	0809	0811
Narbonne d.	...	0428	...	...	...	...	0512	0540	...	0544	0556	...	0610	...	0647	0653	...	0724	0721	0745	0801	...	...	0812	0816
Béziers d.	...	0443	0447	...	0521	...	0534	0554	...	0602	0611	...	0627	...	0702	0707	...	0744	0737	0803	0816	...	...	0827	0832
Agde d.	...	0455	0501	...	0534	...	0548	0608	...	0615	0626	...	0642	...	0716	0722	...	0756	0751	0817	0830	...	...	|	0846
Sète d.	...	0509	0517	...	0550	...	0603	0622	...	0630	0644	...	0658	...	0730	0739	...	0809	0806	0832	0844	...	...	0855	0902
Montpellier a.	...	0527	0534	←	0611	...	0617	0640	...	0645	0708	...	0714	...	0748	0802	...	0826	0820	0851	0902	...	...	0910	0916
Montpellier d.	...	→	0539	0602	0614	0614	0623	0643	0651	0651	0710	0720	0720	...	0751	0805	...	0830r	0824	0853	0906	...	...	0915	0922
Nimes a.	...	...	0602	0629	0706	0706	0647	0710	0715	0715	0740	0747	0747	...	0825	0836	...	0905r	0851	0926	0936	...	...	0940	0947
Nimes d.	0530	...	0605	0631	0708	0708	0650	...	0718	0718	0742	0750	0750	0806	...	0842	...	...	0853	...	0938	...	...	0943	0950
Tarascon-sur-Rhône d.	0545	...	|	0647	0731	0731	|	...	|	|	0758	|	|	0829	...	0900	...	...	|	...	0952	...	...	|	|
Avignon Centre a.	0557	...	|	|	0743	0743	|	...	|	|	|	|	|	0840	...	0912	...	...	|	...	1004	...	...	1002v	|
Arles d.	...	...	|	0658	...	...	|	...	|	|	0810	|	|	...	...	...	...	...	|	...	...	...	...	|	|
Vitrolles Aéroport Marseille ‡ d.	...	...	|	|	...	...	|	...	|	|	|	|	|	...	...	...	...	...	|	...	...	...	...	|	|
Marseille St Charles a.	...	...	|	0751	...	...	|	...	|	|	0856	|	|	...	...	...	...	...	|	...	...	...	...	1041	|
Nice **360** a.	...	...	|	...	...	...	|	...	|	|	...	|	|	...	...	...	...	...	|	...	...	...	...	...	|
Lyon Part Dieu **350** a.	...	...	|	...	...	...	|	...	0846	0846	...	|	|	...	...	...	...	...	1016	...	...	...	...	...	|
Genève **345** a.	...	...	|	...	...	...	|	...	|	|	...	|	|	...	...	...	...	...	|	...	...	...	...	...	|
Dijon **373** a.	...	...	|	...	...	...	|	...	|	|	...	|	|	...	...	...	...	...	|	...	...	...	...	...	|
Strasbourg **384** a.	...	...	|	...	...	...	|	...	|	|	...	|	|	...	...	...	...	...	|	...	...	...	...	...	|
Metz **392** a.	...	...	|	...	...	...	|	...	|	|	...	|	|	...	...	...	...	...	|	...	...	...	...	...	|
Charles de Gaulle ✈ **350** a.	...	...	|	...	...	...	|	...	1057	1057	...	|	|	...	...	...	...	...	1229	...	...	...	...	...	|
Lille Europe **11** a.	...	...	|	...	...	...	|	...	1151	1151	...	|	|	...	...	...	...	...	1329	...	...	...	...	...	|
Brussels Midi **11** a.	...	...	|	...	...	...	|	...	...	...	...	|	|	...	...	...	...	...	...	...	...	...	...	...	|
Paris Austerlitz **310** a.	...	...	|	...	...	...	|	...	...	...	...	|	|	...	...	...	...	...	...	...	...	...	...	...	|
Paris Gare de Lyon **350** a.	...	...	0911	...	...	...	0949	...	...	...	...	1041	1041	...	...	...	...	...	...	...	...	...	...	...	1241

			TGV 5170 ⊕	4652 4653 ★ ♠	TGV 6208	3630 ★			TGV 9862	g		TGV 6232		TGV 5307 ⊗	⊡	4654 4655 ★ ♣	TGV 6210	72 73 ♦⚡ 🄁✕		TGV 6866	⑦ W	⚒	4656 4657 ★ ♥	TGV 6212	TGV 9868 ©
Cerbère d.	...	0727	...	...	...	0750	...	...	...	...	...	...	...	...	1039	...	...	1114	...	...	1120	1125	...	...	...
Banyuls sur Mer d.	...	0734	...	...	...	0759	...	...	...	...	...	...	...	...	1045	...	...	|	...	...	1127	1132	...	...	...
Port Vendres d.	...	0738	...	...	...	0806	...	...	...	...	...	...	...	...	1050	...	...	|	...	...	1132	1137	...	...	...
Collioure d.	...	0742	...	...	...	0811	...	...	...	...	...	...	...	...	1054	...	...	|	...	...	1136	1140	...	...	...
Argelès sur Mer d.	...	0747	...	...	...	0819	...	...	...	...	...	...	...	...	1059	...	...	|	...	...	1141	1146	...	...	...
Perpignan a.	...	0802	...	...	...	0837	...	...	...	...	...	...	...	...	1116	...	...	1142	...	...	1157	1203	...	...	...
Perpignan d.	...	0805	...	...	...	0840	...	...	...	...	1027	...	...	...	1118	...	1135	1144	...	...	1159	1205	...	...	1234
Bordeaux **320** d.	...	|	0543	0610	...	|	...	...	...	...	|	...	...	...	|	0829	|	|	...	...	|	|	1010	...	|
Hendaye **325** d.	...	|	|	|	...	|	...	...	...	...	|	...	...	...	|	|	|	|	...	...	|	|	|	...	|
Toulouse **321** d.	...	|	0749	0817	...	|	...	...	...	...	|	...	...	1040	|	1044	|	|	...	...	|	|	1217	...	|
Carcassonne **321** d.	...	|	|	|	...	|	...	...	...	...	|	...	...	1127	|	1133	|	|	1209	...	|	|	|	...	|
Narbonne a.	...	0844	0857	|	...	0916	...	...	...	...	1109	...	...	1155	1158	1201	1207	1220	1240	...	1245	1250	|	...	1311
Narbonne d.	0821	0848	0859	|	...	0938	...	1050	...	...	1111	...	...	1158	...	1204	1210	1222	1243	...	...	...	|	...	1314
Béziers d.	0838	0903	0916	|	...	|	...	1105	...	...	1126	...	...	1215	...	1220	1226	1239	1256	...	...	...	|	...	1331
Agde d.	0852	0914	|	|	...	|	...	1117	...	...	1139	...	...	|	...	|	1241	|	1311	...	...	...	|	...	1351
Sète d.	0908	0929	|	|	...	|	...	1131	...	...	1153	...	...	|	...	1245	1255	|	1328	...	...	...	|	...	1407
Montpellier a.	0923	0945	0951	1012	...	|	...	1150	...	←	1213	...	←	1253	...	1300	1312	1322	1346	...	...	...	1412	...	1425
Montpellier d.	0926	0948	0958	1016	1021	|	...	→	1157	1204	→	1221	1237	1256	...	1304	1318	...	1349	1356	...	...	1416	1421	1430
Nimes a.	0953	1016	1023	|	1047	|	...	...	1225	1233	...	1247	1313	1322	...	1329	1345	...	1417	1422	...	...	|	1447	1454
Nimes d.	...	1019	1026	|	1050	|	1215	...	1228	...	...	1250	1317	1325	...	1332	1348	...	...	1425	...	...	|	1450	1457
Tarascon-sur-Rhône d.	...	1034	|	|	|	|	1231	...	|	...	...	|	1333	|	...	|	|	...	...	|	...	...	|	|	|
Avignon Centre a.	...	|	|	|	|	|	1243	...	|	...	...	|	1345	|	...	|	|	...	...	|	...	...	|	|	|
Arles d.	...	1044	|	|	|	|	...	...	|	...	...	|	...	|	...	1357	|	...	...	|	...	...	|	|	|
Vitrolles Aéroport Marseille ‡ d.	...	1121	|	|	|	|	...	...	|	...	...	|	...	|	...	|	|	...	...	|	...	...	|	|	|
Marseille St Charles a.	...	1138	|	1142	|	|	...	...	|	...	...	|	...	|	...	1442	|	...	...	|	...	...	1542	|	|
Nice **360** a.	...	...	|	1434	|	|	...	...	|	...	...	|	...	|	...	...	|	...	...	|	...	...	1833	|	|
Lyon Part Dieu **350** a.	...	...	1149	...	|	|	...	...	1346	...	...	|	...	1450	...	...	|	...	...	1550	...	...	...	|	1620
Genève **345** a.	...	...	|	...	|	|	...	...	|	...	...	|	...	|	...	...	|	...	...	1735	...	...	...	|	|
Dijon **373** a.	...	...	1354	...	|	|	...	...	|	...	...	|	...	1630c	...	...	|	...	...	...	...	...	...	|	|
Strasbourg **384** a.	...	...	...	...	|	|	...	...	|	...	...	|	...	...	...	...	|	...	...	...	...	...	...	|	|
Metz **392** a.	...	...	...	...	|	|	...	...	|	...	...	|	...	...	...	...	|	...	...	...	...	...	...	|	|
Charles de Gaulle ✈ **350** a.	...	...	...	...	|	|	...	...	1557	...	...	|	...	...	...	...	|	...	...	...	...	...	...	|	1830
Lille Europe **11** a.	...	...	...	...	|	|	...	...	1707	...	...	|	...	...	...	...	|	...	...	...	...	...	...	|	1937
Brussels Midi **11** a.	...	...	...	...	|	|	...	...	1756	...	...	|	...	...	...	...	|	...	...	...	...	...	...	|	2027
Paris Austerlitz **310** a.	...	...	...	...	|	1741n	...	...	...	...	...	|	...	...	...	...	|	...	...	...	...	...	...	|	...
Paris Gare de Lyon **350** a.	...	...	...	...	1348	...	...	...	...	...	...	1549	...	...	...	...	1641	...	...	...	...	...	...	1749	...

♦ – **NOTES FOR PAGES 216/217** (LISTED BY TRAIN NUMBER)

72/3 – CATALAN TALGO – [12] and ✕ Barcelona - Montpellier.

460 – MARE NOSTRUM – [12] and ✕ Lorca - Murcia - Alacant - Barcelona - Montpellier. After Cerbère calls to set down only.

3730 – *CORAIL LUNÉA* – 🛏 1,2 cl. and [2] (reclining) Cerbère - Paris. Not Dec. 24, 31.

4620/1 – *CORAIL LUNÉA* – 🛏 1,2 cl. and [2] (reclining) Bordeaux - Nice. From Hendaye (numbered **4630/1**) on dates in Table **305**.

4678/9 – CORAIL LUNÉA – ⑤⑦ (daily Dec. 18 - 23, 25 - 30, Jan. 1 - 3, Feb. 12 - Mar. 7, Apr. 1 - May 2), also May 12, 24; not May 14, 23. 🛏 1,2 cl., [2] (reclining) Hendaye - Lyon - Genève.

C – [12] Clermont Ferrand - Marseille (Table **334**).

D – ①–⑤ Dec. 14 - Mar. 19; daily from Mar. 22.

N – ⑤⑥⑦ (also Dec. 24, 31, Apr. 5, May 12, 13, 24; not Feb. 19, 20, 26, 27, Mar. 5, 6). On ⑦ depart Narbonne 2227, Béziers 2246, Montpellier 2330, Nimes 2359.

P – Dec. 13, 18 - 23, 25 - 30, Jan. 1 - 3; ⑤⑦ Jan. 8 - 31; ⑤⑥⑦ Feb. 5 - Mar. 7; ⑤⑦ Mar. 12 - 28; ⑤⑥⑦ from Apr. 2 (also Apr. 5, May 12, 13, 24). 🛏 1, 2 cl. and [2] (reclining) Cerbère - Metz - Luxembourg (arrive 0924).

Q – Dec. 13, 18 - 23, 25 - 30, Jan. 1 - 3; ⑤⑦ Jan. 8 - 31; ⑤⑥⑦ Feb. 5 - Mar. 7; ⑤⑦ Mar. 12 - 28; ⑤⑥⑦ from Apr. 2 (also Apr. 5, May 12, 13, 24). 🛏 1, 2 cl. and [2] (reclining) Cerbère - Strasbourg.

R – Dec. 19, 20, 24, 26, 27, Jan. 1 - 3, Feb. 12 - 14, 19 - 21, 26, 28, Mar. 5, 7, Apr. 2, 5, 10, 16 - 18, May 2, 12, 21.

W – Dec. 13 - Mar. 21.

b – Also Jan. 2, Apr. 5, May 24; not Dec. 20, 25, Jan. 1, Apr. 4, May 14, 23.

c – ①⑤⑥⑦ from Apr. 5 (also Apr. 6, May 12, 13, 25).

d – Also Dec. 24, 31, May 12. On night of Dec. 25, Jan. 1 arrive Paris 0003. On ⑤ Jan. 8 - Feb. 26 arrive Paris 2355.

e – Also Apr. 5, May 24.

g – On © Montpellier d. 1151, Nimes a. 1220.

h – Not Dec. 25, Jan. 1, May 13.

k – Also Dec. 25, Jan. 1, Apr. 6, May 13, 25; not Apr. 5, May 24.

m – Subject to alteration Mar. 29 - Apr. 9.

n – 1815 on Dec. 14, 15.

r – ⚒ only.

s – 1950 on ⑥⑦ Dec. 13 - Mar. 21.

t – Also Dec. 25, Jan. 1, May 13.

u – 1625 Jan. 4 - Mar. 12. Subject to alteration May 13 - 15.

v – Avignon **TGV** station.

y – Terminates at Nancy on ①–⑥ (arrive 2312). On night of Feb. 1 - 4, Mar. 29 - Apr. 1 arrive Metz 0035.

z – ⑤⑦ (also Dec. 24, 31, Apr. 5, May 12, 24; not Dec. 25, Jan. 1).

TGV – 🄁, supplement payable.

♠ – Not on ①–⑤ Mar. 1 - 26. Depart Bordeaux 0600 on Jan. 4 - Feb. 28 (also Mar. 6, 7, 13). Subject to alteration Bordeaux - Marmande on May 13 - 16.

♣ – Not on ①–⑤ Mar. 1 - 26. Depart Bordeaux 0817 on Jan. 4 - Feb. 28 (also Mar. 6, 7). Subject to alteration Bordeaux - Marmande on May 13 - 16.

♥ – Not on ①–⑤ Mar. 8 - 26. Depart Bordeaux 1000 Jan. 4 - Mar. 7. Subject to alteration Bordeaux - Toulouse on May 13 - 16.

NOTES CONTINUED ON NEXT PAGE →

CERBÈRE - NARBONNE - AVIGNON and MARSEILLE 355

	Ⓐ	Ⓒ			TGV 6214		TGV 9868 Ⓐ		TGV 6216	TGV 5380 △		TGV 5464	4660 4661 ★ ▽		TGV 6218	15947 C ⊙	Ⓐ	Ⓐ	Ⓐ	TGV 6868 ⑥ t	TGV 5314 Ⓑ h			TGV 6220	TGV 5186
Cerbère d.	...	...	1228	...	...	...	...	...	...	...	1409	...	...	...	...	...	...	1503	...	...	...	1544	...	...	...
Banyuls sur Mer d.	...	...	1234	...	...	...	...	...	...	...	1416	...	...	...	...	...	...	1510	...	...	...	1551	...	...	...
Port Vendres d.	...	...	1239	...	...	...	...	...	...	...	1420	...	...	...	...	...	...	1514	...	...	...	1556	...	...	...
Collioure d.	...	...	1243	...	...	...	...	...	...	...	1424	...	...	...	...	...	...	1518	...	...	...	1600	...	...	...
Argelès sur Mer d.	...	...	1248	...	...	...	...	...	...	...	1429	...	...	...	...	...	...	1523	...	...	...	1605	...	...	...
Perpignan a.	...	...	1303	...	...	...	...	...	...	...	1444	...	...	...	...	...	...	1538	...	...	...	1620	...	...	...
Perpignan d.	...	...	...	1326	...	...	1410	...	...	...	1446	...	...	...	1531	...	...	▬	1548	1619	...	...	1630	...	...
Bordeaux **320** d.	...	...	...	|	...	...	|	...	...	...	|	...	1238	...	|	...	...	...	|	|	...	...	|	...	...
Hendaye **325** d.	...	...	...	|	...	...	|	...	...	...	|	...	|	...	|	...	...	...	|	|	...	...	|	...	...
Toulouse **321** d.	1142	1142	...	|	...	...	|	...	...	...	|	...	1450	...	|	...	...	...	|	|	1545	...	|	...	1609
Carcassonne **321** d.	1242	1242	...	|	...	...	|	...	...	...	|	...	1534	...	|	...	...	...	|	|	1629	...	|	...	1655
Narbonne a.	1316	1316	...	1409	...	...	1446	...	...	...	1528	...	1602	...	1607	...	...	...	1631	1652	1656	...	1706	...	1724
Narbonne d.	1336	1336	...	1411	...	1425	1449	1455	...	...	▬	...	1605	1555	1610	...	1617	1629	1633	1659	1659	...	1708	...	1728
Béziers d.	1352	1352	...	1426	...	1445	1507	1513	...	...	...	...	1621	1609	1627	...	1633	1646	1653	1714	1714	...	1724	...	1743
Agde d.	1405	1405	...	1439	...	1457	1521	1527	...	...	...	...	|	1620	|	...	1647	1659	1707	|	|	...	1735	...	|
Sète d.	1420	1420	...	1455	...	1512	1537	1543	...	...	...	...	1645	1634	|	...	1701	1716	1720	1739	1739	...	1749	...	|
Montpellier a.	1438	1438	...	1513	...	1527	1554	1601	...	...	...	...	1700	1651	1709	...	1719	1736	1740	1754	1754	...	1806	...	1826
Montpellier d.	1441	...	...	1516	1525	1530	1600	1604	1620	1628	...	1648	1704	1654	1716	...	1722	1739	1742	1800	1800	...	1809	1821	1832
Nimes a.	1507	...	...	1543	1551	1558	1624	1632	1647	1657	...	1717	1729	1734	1741	...	1800	1805	1823	1827	1827	...	1838	1848	1854
Nimes d.	1510	...	...	...	1554	1601	1627	1635	1650	1700	1704	1720	1732	1736	1744	1758	1803	...	...	1830	1830	...	1841	1851	1857
Tarascon-sur-Rhône d.	1524	...	...	...	|	1616	|	1657	|	|	1726	|	|	1751	|	1816	1826	...	...	|	|	...	1858	|	|
Avignon Centre a.	1542	...	...	...	|	|	|	1708	|	|	1738	|	|	1802	|	|	1837	...	...	|	|	...	1909	|	|
Arles d.	...	...	...	...	|	1626	|	...	|	|	...	|	1756	...	|	1827	...	...	...	|	|	...	...	|	|
Vitrolles Aéroport Marseille ‡ d.	...	...	...	...	|	1710	|	...	|	|	...	|	|	...	|	|	...	...	...	|	|	...	...	|	|
Marseille St Charles a.	...	...	...	...	|	1734	|	...	|	|	...	|	1842	...	|	1914	...	...	...	|	|	...	...	|	|
Nice **360** a.	...	...	...	...	|	...	|	...	|	|	...	|	...	...	|	...	...	...	...	|	|	...	...	|	|
Lyon Part Dieu **350** a.	...	...	...	...	|	...	1746	...	|	1820	...	1846	...	...	|	...	...	...	...	1946	1946	...	...	|	2020
Genève **345** a.	...	...	...	...	|	...	|	...	|	...	...	|	...	...	|	...	...	...	...	...	...	...	...	|	|
Dijon **373** a.	...	...	...	...	|	...	|	...	|	...	...	2044	...	...	|	...	...	...	...	...	...	...	...	|	|
Strasbourg **384** a.	...	...	...	...	|	...	|	...	|	...	...	|	...	...	|	...	...	...	...	...	...	...	...	|	|
Metz **392** a.	...	...	...	...	|	...	|	...	|	...	...	2354y	...	...	|	...	...	...	...	...	...	...	...	|	|
Charles de Gaulle ✈ **350** a.	...	...	...	...	|	...	1959	...	|	...	...	...	...	...	|	...	...	...	...	...	...	...	...	|	2229*
Lille Europe **11** a.	...	...	...	...	|	...	2054	...	|	...	...	...	...	...	|	...	...	...	...	...	...	...	...	|	2323*
Brussels Midi **11** a.	...	...	...	...	|	...	2143	...	|	...	...	...	...	...	|	...	...	...	...	...	...	...	...	|	...
Paris Austerlitz **310** a.	...	...	...	...	|	...	...	...	|	...	...	...	...	...	|	...	...	...	...	...	...	...	...	|	...
Paris Gare de Lyon **350** a.	...	...	...	...	1845	...	...	...	1949	...	...	...	...	...	2041	...	...	...	...	...	...	...	...	2149	...

	4658 4659 ★ R		4662 4663 ★ ◧	Ⓐ	TGV 6222 ☆	TGV 6880	⚒	Ⓑ	Ⓑ	⑥ W	TGV 6226 ⑤ d	TGV 6224 ⑦ e	⚒		4664 4665 ★	TGV 6228 ⑦ e	460 [R] ✕ ♦ ⁄		4666 4667 ⑤⑦ ★b	4348 4349 P [R]	4348 4392 Q [R]	TGV 7994 ⑤–⑦ N	3730 ♦ [R]	4620 4621 ♦ [R]	4678 4679 ♦ [R]
Cerbère d.	...	...	...	1653	...	...	...	1722	...	...	...	...	...	1825	...	...	1907	...	...	2043	2043	...	2121	...	...
Banyuls sur Mer d.	...	...	...	1700	...	...	...	1729	...	...	...	...	...	1832	...	...	|	...	...	2052	2052	...	2129	...	...
Port Vendres d.	...	...	...	1705	...	...	...	1734	...	...	...	...	...	1837	...	...	|	...	...	2059	2059	...	2136	...	...
Collioure d.	...	...	...	1708	...	...	...	1738	...	...	...	...	...	1840	...	...	|	...	...	2104	2104	...	2141	...	...
Argelès sur Mer d.	...	...	...	1713	...	...	...	1743	...	...	...	...	...	1845	...	...	|	...	...	2111	2111	...	2148	...	...
Perpignan a.	...	...	...	1728	...	...	...	1800	...	...	...	...	...	1900	...	...	1934	...	...	2130	2130	...	2206	...	...
Perpignan d.	...	...	...	...	1737	...	1745	...	1810	1813	...	1837	...	1902	...	...	1937	1957s	...	2134	2134	2150	2210	...	...
Bordeaux **320** d.	...	...	1459	...	|	...	|	...	|	|	...	|	...	|	1638u	...	|	|	...	|	|	|	|	2157	...
Hendaye **325** d.	...	...	|	...	|	...	|	...	|	|	...	|	...	|	|	...	|	|	...	|	|	|	|	|	1807
Toulouse **321** d.	1613	...	1704	...	|	...	|	...	|	|	...	|	...	|	1851	...	|	|	1951	|	|	|	|	0025	0029
Carcassonne **321** d.	1701	1709	|	...	|	...	|	...	|	|	...	|	...	|	1936	...	|	|	2035	|	|	|	|	|	|
Narbonne a.	1730	1739	|	...	1815	...	1829	...	1853	1856	...	1911	...	1945	2004	...	2015	2032	2104	2211	2211	2235	2244	|	|
Narbonne d.	1733	1741	|	...	1818	...	1833	...	1856	1859	...	1914	1934	...	2007	...	2018	2034	2107	2215	2215	2239	2304	|	|
Béziers d.	1748	1801	|	...	1834	...	1850	...	1912	1914	...	1931	1950	...	2023	...	2034	2049	2122	2231	2231	2256	|	|	|
Agde d.	1802	1815	|	...	1848	...	1902	...	1926	1926	...	1945	2002	...	|	...	|	2101	|	2246	2246	|	|	|	|
Sète d.	1818	1830	|	...	1903	...	1916	...	1941	1940	...	2000	2017	...	2047	...	|	2115	2147	2303	2303	|	|	|	|
Montpellier a.	1833	1845	1900	...	1917	...	1935	...	1958	1958	...	2017	2032	...	2101	...	2109	2133	2202	2318	2318	2343	|	|	|
Montpellier d.	1837	1848	1904	...	1923	1927	1938	...	2001	...	2023	2023	2034	...	2105	2117	...	2135	2206	2321	2321	2347	|	|	|
Nimes a.	1902	1916	|	...	1947	1953	2007	...	2030	...	2047	2047	2106	...	2129	2141	...	2203	2230	2347	2347	0012	|	|	|
Nimes d.	1905	1919	|	...	1950	1956	...	...	2033	...	2050	2050	...	...	2132	2144	...	...	2233	2350	2350	0015	|	|	|
Tarascon-sur-Rhône d.	|	1935	|	...	|	|	...	...	2049	...	|	|	...	...	|	|	...	...	|	|	|	|	|	|	|
Avignon Centre a.	|	|	|	...	|	|	...	...	2101	...	|	|	...	...	|	|	...	...	|	|	|	|	|	|	|
Arles d.	1930	1946	|	...	|	|	...	...	...	...	|	|	...	...	2157	|	...	...	2258	|	|	|	|	|	|
Vitrolles Aéroport Marseille ‡ d.	|	2024	|	...	|	|	...	...	...	...	|	|	...	...	|	|	...	...	|	|	|	|	|	|	|
Marseille St Charles a.	2014	2038	2042	...	|	|	...	...	...	...	|	|	...	...	2242	|	...	...	2342	|	|	|	|	0509	|
Nice **360** a.	2304	...	...	...	|	|	...	...	...	...	|	|	...	...	...	|	...	...	...	|	|	|	|	0807	|
Lyon Part Dieu **350** a.	...	...	...	...	|	2120	...	...	...	...	|	|	...	...	...	|	...	...	...	|	|	|	|	...	0644
Genève **345** a.	...	...	...	...	|	|	...	...	...	...	|	|	...	...	...	|	...	...	...	|	|	|	|	...	0845
Dijon **373** a.	...	...	...	...	|	2305z	...	...	...	...	|	|	...	...	...	|	...	...	...	|	|	|	|	...	...
Strasbourg **384** a.	...	...	...	...	|	...	...	...	...	...	|	|	...	...	...	|	...	...	...	|	0831	|	|	...	...
Metz **392** a.	...	...	...	...	|	...	...	...	...	...	|	|	...	...	...	|	...	...	...	0824	...	|	|	...	...
Charles de Gaulle ✈ **350** a.	...	...	...	...	|	...	...	...	...	...	|	|	...	...	...	|	...	...	...	...	...	|	|	...	...
Lille Europe **11** a.	...	...	...	...	|	...	...	...	...	...	|	|	...	...	...	|	...	...	...	...	...	|	|	...	...
Brussels Midi **11** a.	...	...	...	...	|	...	...	...	...	...	|	|	...	...	...	|	...	...	...	...	...	|	|	...	...
Paris Austerlitz **310** a.	...	...	...	...	|	...	...	...	...	...	|	|	...	...	...	|	...	...	...	...	...	|	0727	...	...
Paris Gare de Lyon **350** a.	...	...	...	...	2241	...	...	...	...	...	2347	2347	...	...	...	0039	...	...	...	...	...	0720	...	...	...

NOTES (CONTINUED FROM PREVIOUS PAGE)

⁄ – Special 'global' fares payable.
★ – *CORAIL TÉOZ* [R], 🍷.
◧ – Not on ①–⑤ Mar. 29 - May 7. Runs earlier Jan. 4 - Mar. 12 (Bordeaux 1423, Toulouse 1638, Montpellier 1838, Marseille 2016). Subject to alteration Bordeaux - Marmande on May 13 - 15.
⊡ – To Toulouse (Table **321**).
⊙ – On Ⓒ Nimes 1805, Tarascon 1824, Arles 1844, Marseille 1947 (train **15957**).
▽ – Not on ①–⑤ Mar. 29 - May 7. Not Bordeaux - Toulouse on Dec. 16, 17. Subject to alteration Bordeaux - Marmande on May 13 - 16.
△ – To Nantes (Table **335**).
⊕ – Depart Bordeaux 0533 on certain dates. On ①–⑤ Feb. 1 - 26 arrive Dijon 1436.
⊗ – On ①–⑤ Mar. 1 - 26 runs 25 - 40 minutes later.
☆ – Arrive Paris 2254 on ①–④ Jan. 4 - 21, Feb. 8 - 25.
‡ – Vitrolles Aéroport Marseille-Provence. A shuttle bus runs to the airport terminal (journey 5 mins).
* – On ⑤–⑦ (also Dec. 24, 31, Apr. 5, May 12, 13, 24) arrive Charles de Gaulle 2235, Lille Europe 2337.

🚌 routes 7801/2 — 🚌 TOULON - ST TROPEZ 357

km		⚒	⚒	⚒					⚒				
0	**Toulon** Gare Routière d.	0550	0620	0650	0810	1210	1245	1345	1530	1615	1715	1815	...
23	Hyères, Gare Routière d.	0630	0650	0730	0850	1240	1325	1425	1600	1655	1815	1845	...
46	Le Lavandou, Gare Routière d.	0705	|	0805	0925	|	1400	1500	|	1730	1850	|	...
78	La Foux a.	0750	0750	0850	1010	1340	1445	1545	1700	1815	1935	1945	...
84	**St Tropez** Gare Routière a.	0800	0800	0900	1020	1350	1455	1555	1710	1825	1945	1955	...

	⚒	⚒				⚒				⚒			
St Tropez Gare Routière d.	0615	0640	0845	1040	1210	1230	...	1500	1630	1730	...	1920	...
La Foux d.	0625	0645	0855	1050	1220	1240	...	1510	1640	1740	...	1930	...
Le Lavandou, Gare Routière d.	|	0730	0940	1135	1305	|	...	1555	|	|	...	2015	...
Hyères, Gare Routière d.	0715	0810	1015	1210	1340	1340	...	1630	1740	1840	...	2050	...
Toulon Gare Routière a.	0745	0845	1055	1250	1420	1410	...	1710	1810	1910	...	2130	...

Operator: Groupement SUMA, 13340 Rognac
✆ 06 66 44 08 24 www.transports.var.fr

Note: Toulon Gare Routière (bus station) is situated adjacent to the railway station.

Buses serving Le Lavandou also serve Cavalaire (buses from Toulon call 30 minutes after Le Lavandou; buses from St Tropez call 30 minutes before Le Lavandou).

358 🚌 ST RAPHAEL - ST TROPEZ

🚌 route 7601/7201

km											W												
0	**St Raphael** Gare Routière d.	0600	...	...	...	...	0745	...	0915	...	...	1230	...	1335	...	1515	1615	...	...	1815	...	2015	...
9	St Aygulf, La Poste d.	0620	...	...	...	...	0805	...	0935	...	...	1250	...	1355	...	1535	1635	...	...	1835	...	2035	...
	Les Arcs, Gare SNCF d.	|	...	0645	...	...	|	...	|	...	1235	|	...	|	...	|	|	...	1825	|	...	|	...
23	Ste Maxime, Office du Tourisme d.	0650	...	0720	0750	...	0835	...	1005	...	1310	1320	...	1425	...	1605	1705	...	1900	1905	...	2105	...
27	Grimaud, Saint Pons d.	0700	...	...	0800	...	0845	...	1015	...	...	1330	...	1435	...	1615	1715	...	...	1915	...	2115	...
28	Port Grimaud d.	0702	...	...	0802	...	0847	...	1017	...	...	|	...	1437	...	1617	1717	...	...	|	...	2117	...
29	La Foux a.	0705	...	...	0805	...	0850	...	1020	...	...	1400	...	1440	...	1620	1720	...	...	1945	...	2120	...
35	**St Tropez** Gare Routière a.	0720	...	...	0820	...	0905	...	1035	...	...	1415	...	1455	...	1635	1735	...	...	2000	...	2135	...

St Tropez Gare Routière d.	0600	...	0725	0830	...	0930	...	...	1205	...	1335	...	1615	...	...	1700	...	1845	...	...	2015	...	...
La Foux d.	0610	...	0740	0845	...	0945	...	...	1220	...	1350	...	1630	...	...	1715	...	1900	...	...	2030	...	...
Port Grimaud d.	|	...	0743	0848	...	0948	...	...	1223	...	|	...	1633	...	...	1718	...	1903	...	...	2033	...	...
Grimaud, Saint Pons d.	0630	...	0745	0850	...	0950	...	...	1225	...	1420	...	1635	...	...	1720	...	1905	...	...	2035	...	...
Ste Maxime, Office du Tourisme d.	0640	...	0755	0900	...	1000	1000	...	1235	...	1430	...	1645	1710	...	1730	...	1915	1930	...	2045	...	...
Les Arcs, Gare SNCF a.	|	...	|	...	...	|	1030	...	|	...	|	...	|	1740	...	|	...	|	2000	...	|	...	...
St Aygulf, La Poste d.	0700	...	0825	...	...	1030	...	...	1305	...	1500	...	1715	...	...	1800	...	1945	...	...	2115	...	...
St Raphael Gare Routière a.	0720	...	0845	...	...	1050	...	...	1325	...	1520	...	1735	...	...	1820	...	2005	...	...	2140	...	...

W – Winter only.

Operator: Groupement SUMA, 13340 Rognac
✆ 06 66 44 08 24 www.transports.var.fr

Note: St Raphael Gare Routière (bus station) is situated adjacent to the railway station.

359 NICE - ANNOT - DIGNE - ST AUBAN and VEYNES

2nd class only

km	CP ▲	①	b							
0	**Nice** (Gare CP) d.	...	0625	...	0850	1255	...	1715	1813	...
65	Puget Théniers d.	...	0748	...	1015	1420	...	1839	1937	...
72	Entrevaux d.	...	0756	...	1023	1428	...	1848	1945	...
87	Annot d.	0541	0816	...	1042	1446	...	1908	2001	...
106	Thorame Haute d.	0605	0841	...	1106	1510	...	1932	...	...
118	St André les Alpes d.	0619	0854	...	1119	1524	...	1945	...	...
166	**Digne** a.	0715	0950	...	1216	1620	...	2041	...	...

CP ▲		⚒	†	b					
Digne d.	...	...	...	0729	1055	...	1425	1730	...
St. André les Alpes d.	...	...	...	0826	1153	...	1523	1828	...
Thorame Haute d.	...	...	...	0840	1206	...	1536	1841	...
Annot d.	...	0540	0639	0906	1231	...	1602	1910	...
Entrevaux d.	...	0558	0657	0923	1248	...	1620	1927	...
Puget Théniers d.	...	0606	0705	0931	1256	...	1628	1936	...
Nice (Gare CP) a.	...	0731	0830	1054	1421	...	1752	2057	...

SNCF 🚌 △	🚌 ⚒	🚌	🚌	🚌		🚌	🚌 ⑤f		🚌 ⑧	🚌 ⑥t
Digne (Gare) d.	0525	0825	1140	1155	...	1710	1720	...	1948	2013
Château Arnoux **362** ◧ d.	|	|	|	1225	...	|	1750	...	2020	2038
Sisteron **362** d.	|	|	|	1242	...	|	1807	...	...	2055
Veynes-Dévoluy 362 a.	|	|	|	1340	...	|	1905	...	...	2150
Manosque-Gréoux **362** d.	0610	0910	1225	...	...	1800	...	...	...	...
Aix en Provence TGV a.	0710	1010	1330	...	...	1900	...	...	...	...

SNCF 🚌 △	🚌	🚌 ⚒	🚌	🚌	🚌	🚌 ⑤v	🚌 ⑤f	🚌 ⑦	🚌
Aix en Provence TGV d.	...	0930	1255	...	1520	...	...	...	2055
Manosque-Gréoux **362** d.	...	1028	1353	...	1608	...	...	...	2143
Veynes-Dévoluy 362 d.	0645	|	|	1445	|	1615	2020	2020	|
Sisteron **362** d.	0743	|	|	1543	|	1713	2113	2113	|
Château Arnoux **362** ◧ d.	0800	|	|	1600	|	1730	2130	2130	|
Digne (Gare) a.	0825	1115	1435	1622	1655	1755	2155	2155	2230

b – By 🚌 Thorame Haute - Digne and v.v.
f – Not Dec. 25, Jan. 1.
t – Not May 1, 8.

v – Also Dec. 19 - Jan. 3, Feb. 13 - 28, Apr. 10 - 25.
▲ – Narrow gauge railway, operated by Chemins de Fer de Provence (CP).

△ – No 🚌 service on May 1.
◧ – Château Arnoux - St Auban. Buses serve Town Hall (Mairie), not rail station (however, 1948 from Digne terminates at rail station).

360 MARSEILLE - TOULON - NICE - VENTIMIGLIA

km	All *TGV* trains are [R]	*TGV* 6831 ① g	17471 Ⓐ	4620 4621 [R] B	*TGV* 7989 ⑤–⑦ Y⊗	5771 [R] P	4294 4295 [R] S⊖	4248 4295 [R] L⊖		*EC* 139 [R]§ M	17475	*TGV* 6815 Ⓐ T	17479 Ⓐ T	17479 Ⓐ U	*TGV* 6805 Ⓒ		*TGV* 6171	*TGV* 5102	4652 4653 ★ N		17483 Ⓐ	*TGV* 6173	*TGV* 5148
	Paris Gare de Lyon **350** d.	...	...	...	2220	2225a	...	...	...	...	...	...	...	...	...	...	0746	...	...	...	...	0942	...
	Lille Europe **11** d.	...	...	...	|	|	...	...	...	...	...	...	...	...	...	...	|	0559	...	...	...	|	...
	Metz **379** d.	...	...	...	|	|	...	2040	...	...	...	...	...	...	...	...	|	|	...	...	...	|	0611
	Strasbourg **384** d.	...	...	...	|	|	2058	|	...	...	...	...	...	...	...	...	|	|	...	...	...	|	|
	Dijon **373** d.	...	...	...	|	|	|	|	...	...	...	...	...	...	...	...	|	|	...	...	...	|	0916
	Genève **345** d.	...	...	...	|	|	|	|	...	...	...	...	...	...	...	...	|	|	...	...	...	|	|
	Lyon Part-Dieu **350** d.	0050p	...	...	|	|	|	|	...	...	...	0635	...	...	0737	...	|	0907	...	...	...	|	1107
	Nantes **292** d.	|	...	...	|	|	|	|	...	...	...	|	...	...	|	...	|	|	...	...	...	|	|
	Bordeaux **320** d.	|	...	2157	|	|	|	|	...	...	...	|	...	...	|	...	|	|	0610*	...	...	|	|
	Toulouse **321** d.	|	...	0025	|	|	|	|	...	...	...	|	...	...	|	...	|	|	0817	...	...	|	|
	Montpellier **355** d.	|	...	|	|	|	|	|	...	...	...	|	...	...	|	...	|	|	1016	...	...	|	|
0	**Marseille St Charles** 350 ▶ d.	|	0518	0524	0528	|	0627	0627	...	...	0724	0829	0925	...	0929	...	|	1059	1159	...	1219	|	1259
67	**Toulon** 350 ▶ a.	0541	0601	0610	0619	0637	0712	0712	...	...	0807	0915	1009	...	1013	...	1137	1143	1244	...	1303	|	1343
67	**Toulon** d.	0544	0603	0613	0623	0640	0715	0715	...	...	0810	0918	1012	1012	1016	...	1140	1146	1247	1250	1306	|	1346
100	Carnoules d.	|	0622	|	|	|	|	|	...	...	0829	|	1030	1030	|	...	|	|	|	1321	|	|	|
135	Les Arcs-Draguignan ▷ d.	0622	0642	0651	|	0719	0753	0753	...	...	0850	|	1051	1051	|	...	|	1221	1324	1348	1354	1414	|
158	Fréjus ▷ d.	|	0657	|	|	|	|	|	...	...	0905	|	1106	1106	|	...	|	|	|	...	1408	|	|
162	St Raphaël-Valescure ▷ d.	0640	0702	0710	0724	0742	0810	0810	...	...	0910	1008	1111	1111	1111	...	1230	1239	1341	...	1413	1431	1441
195	**Cannes** ▷ d.	0703	0732	0736	0757	0820	0836	0836	...	...	0934	1035	1135	1135	1136	...	1255	1304	1404	...	1437	1457	1506
206	Antibes ▷ d.	0714	0742	0747	0811	0831	0848	0848	...	...	0944	1046	1144	1144	1147	...	1305	1315	1414	...	1447	1508	1517
229	**Nice Ville** ▷ a.	0739	0803	0807	0829	0854	0909	0909	...	...	1003	1103	1203	1203	1204	...	1324	1332	1434	...	1504	1524	1534
229	**Nice Ville** ▷ d.	...	...	...	...	0859	...	...	...	0949	...	...	...	...	...	...	...	...	...	...	...	...	...
245	Monaco-Monte Carlo ▷ d.	...	...	...	...	0923	...	...	...	1010	...	...	...	...	...	...	...	...	...	...	...	...	...
252	Menton ▷ d.	...	...	...	...	0937	...	...	...	1023	...	...	...	...	...	...	...	...	...	...	...	...	...
262	**Ventimiglia** ▷ a.	...	...	...	...	0951	...	...	...	1035	...	...	...	...	...	...	...	...	...	...	...	...	...

	17487	*TGV* 6175		*EC* 147 [R]§ M	*TGV* 9826 C	4656 4657 ★	Ⓐ	17491 Ⓐ	*TGV* 6177		*TGV* 6818	17495		*TGV* 6179 G	Ⓑ	*TGV* 6829	4658 4659 ★ R	*TGV* 6181	17499 ①–④ m	17499 ⑥ y	*TGV* 6187 ⑤ D	17499 ⑤⑦ q	*TGV* 6183 ⑤ D
Paris Gare de Lyon **350** d.	...	1146	...	...	...	...	...	...	1346	...	...	...	...	1546	...	...	...	1742	...	...	1815	...	1842
Lille Europe **11** d.	...	|	...	...	1030	...	...	...	|	...	...	...	...	|	...	...	...	|	...	...	|	...	|
Metz **379** d.	...	|	...	...	|	...	...	...	|	...	...	...	...	|	...	...	...	|	...	...	|	...	|
Strasbourg **384** d.	...	|	...	...	|	...	...	...	|	...	...	...	...	|	...	...	...	|	...	...	|	...	|
Dijon **373** d.	...	|	...	...	|	...	...	...	|	...	...	...	...	|	...	1616	...	|	...	...	|	...	|
Genève **345** d.	...	|	...	...	|	...	...	...	|	...	1344	...	...	|	...	|	...	|	...	...	|	...	|
Lyon Part-Dieu **350** d.	...	|	...	...	|	...	...	...	|	...	1537	...	...	|	...	1803	...	|	...	...	|	...	|
Nantes **292** d.	...	|	...	...	|	...	...	...	|	...	|	...	...	|	...	|	...	|	...	...	|	...	|
Bordeaux **320** d.	...	|	...	...	|	1010	...	...	|	...	|	...	...	|	...	|	...	|	...	...	|	...	|
Toulouse **321** d.	...	|	...	...	|	1217	...	...	|	...	|	...	...	|	...	|	1613	|	...	...	|	...	|
Montpellier **355** d.	...	|	...	...	|	1416	...	...	|	...	|	...	...	|	...	|	1837	|	...	...	|	...	|
Marseille St Charles 350 ▶ d.	1429	|	...	...	1527	1557	...	1625	|	...	1729	1759	...	|	...	1959	2029	|	2059	2059	2133	2129	|
Toulon 350 ▶ a.	1512	1537	...	...	1611	1643	...	1710	1737	...	1816	1842	...	|	...	2043	2114	2137	2142	2142	2216	2212	2241
Toulon d.	1515	1540	1550	...	1614	1646	1650	1712	1740	1750	1819	1844	1850	|	1950	2046	2117	2140	2145	2145	2219	2223	2244
Carnoules d.	|	|	1620	...	|	|	1720	1733	|	1821	|	|	1921	|	2021	|	|	|	|	|	|	|	|
Les Arcs-Draguignan ▷ d.	1554	|	1648	...	1654	1722	1748	1754	1815	1848	|	1920	1948	2021	2048	|	2153	|	2222	2222	|	2259	|
Fréjus ▷ d.	|	|	...	...	|	|	...	|	|	...	|	1935	...	|	...	|	|	|	|	|	|	|	|
St Raphaël-Valescure ▷ d.	1610	1630	...	...	1711	1738	...	1810	1833	...	1909	1940	...	2039	...	2141	2209	2230	2239	2239	2309	2314	2333
Cannes ▷ d.	1634	1654	...	...	1735	1802	...	1834	1858	...	1935	2004	...	2104	...	2206	2233	2255	2300	2303	2333	2339	2358
Antibes ▷ d.	1644	1706	...	...	1746	1813	...	1844	1908	...	1947	2014	...	2115	...	2217	2244	2306	...	2313	2344	2348	0009
Nice Ville ▷ a.	1703	1724	...	...	1803	1833	...	1903	1924	...	2004	2032	...	2131	...	2237	2304	2324	...	2331	0001	0006	0026
Nice Ville ▷ d.	...	1732	...	1749	...	...	...	...	...	...	...	...	...	...	...	...	...	...	...	...	...	...	...
Monaco-Monte Carlo ▷ d.	...	1754	...	1810	...	...	...	...	...	...	...	...	...	...	...	...	...	...	...	...	...	...	...
Menton ▷ d.	...	1807	...	1824	...	...	...	...	...	...	...	...	...	...	...	...	...	...	...	...	...	...	...
Ventimiglia ▷ a.	...	1821	...	1835	...	...	...	...	...	...	...	...	...	...	...	...	...	...	...	...	...	...	...

VENTIMIGLIA - NICE - TOULON - MARSEILLE 360

All *TGV* trains are Ⓡ					*TGV*			*TGV*	4768		*TGV*		*TGV*	4758	*TGV*	*TGV*			*TGV*	4764	*TGV*		*TGV*
			17470		6172	17474		6854	4769	17478	5198		6174	4759	9864	6176		17482	6886	4765	6178	17486	6168
	⚒			Ⓐ		Ⓐ			★					★				Ⓐ		★			⑦
			▽						Q	△				E	b						G		F
Ventimiglia ▷ d.	...	...	...	...	...	...	...	...	...	...	...	...	0838	...	...	...	...	...	...	...	...	...	...
Menton ▷ d.	...	...	...	...	...	...	...	...	...	...	...	...	0852	...	...	...	...	...	...	...	...	...	...
Monaco-Monte Carlo ▷ d.	...	...	...	...	...	...	...	...	...	...	...	...	0906	...	...	...	...	...	...	...	...	...	...
Nice Ville ▷ a.	...	...	...	...	...	...	...	...	...	...	...	...	0921	...	...	...	...	...	...	...	...	...	...
Nice Ville ▷ d.	...	...	0556	...	0635	0656	...	0723	0827	0835	0925	...	0935	0955	1028	1035	...	1228	1323	1329	1335	1428	1435
Antibes ▷ d.	...	...	0615	...	0654	0715	...	0745	0846	0859	0945	...	0955	1015	1047	1054	...	1247	1343	1349	1356	1446	1455
Cannes ▷ d.	...	...	0626	...	0705	0725	...	0800	0857	0909	0957	...	1006	1026	1058	1105	...	1257	1354	1400	1408	1456	1506
St Raphaël-Valescure ▷ d.	...	...	0648	...	0729	0748	...	0826	0921	0932	1020	...	1030	1050	1123	1130	...	1320	1418	1423	1434	1519	1530
Fréjus ▷ d.	...	...	0653	...	|	0752	...	|	|	0938	|	...	|	|	|	|	...	|	|	|	|	|	|
Les Arcs-Draguignan ▷ d.	0608	0642	0707	0710	|	0806	0810	|	0938	0952	|	...	1046	1106	1139	1147	1210	1335	|	1441	1451	1535	|
Carnoules d.	0635	0708	|	0737	|	|	0838	|	|	1011	|	...	|	|	|	|	1238	|	|	|	|	1554	|
Toulon a.	0704	0738	0742	0808	0815	0843	0907	0916	1013	1029	1111	...	|	1142	1213	|	1308	1409	1509	1516	|	1612	1616
Toulon 350 ▶ d.	0706	...	0744	...	0818	0846	...	0919	1016	1031	1113	...	|	1145	1216	|	...	1411	1512	1519	|	1614	1619
Marseille St Charles 350 ▶ a.	0805	...	0831	...	|	0930	...	1001	1100	1114	1159	...	|	1228	1259	|	...	1455	1557	1601	|	1659	|
Montpellier **355** a.	...	...	...	...	|	...	...	|	1251	...	|	...	|	1409	|	|	...	...	|	1741	|	...	|
Toulouse **321** a.	...	...	...	...	|	...	...	|	1517	...	|	...	|	1612	|	|	...	...	|	1944	|	...	|
Bordeaux **320** a.	...	...	...	...	|	...	...	|	...	...	|	...	|	1823	|	|	...	...	|	2150*	|	...	|
Nantes **292** a.	...	...	...	...	|	...	...	|	...	...	|	...	|	...	|	|	...	...	|	...	|	...	|
Lyon Part-Dieu **350** a.	...	...	...	...	|	...	...	1155	...	...	1350	...	|	...	|	|	...	...	1750	...	|	...	|
Genève **345** a.	...	...	...	...	|	...	...	...	...	...	|	...	|	...	|	|	...	...	1942	...	|	...	|
Dijon **373** a.	...	...	...	...	|	...	...	...	...	...	1539	...	|	...	|	|	...	...	...	...	|	...	|
Strasbourg **384** a.	...	...	...	...	|	...	...	...	...	...	|	...	|	...	|	|	...	...	...	...	|	...	|
Metz **379** a.	...	...	...	...	|	...	...	...	...	...	1849	...	|	...	|	|	...	...	...	...	|	...	|
Lille Europe **11** a.	...	...	...	...	|	...	...	...	...	...	...	...	|	...	1735	|	...	...	...	...	|	...	|
Paris Gare de Lyon **350** a.	...	...	...	...	1210	...	...	...	...	...	...	...	1519	...	...	1615	...	...	...	...	1921	...	2011

	TGV	*EC*		*TGV*	*TGV*			*TGV*			*TGV*			4394	4394		*EC*		*TGV*	4720			
	5184	144	17490	6184	6876			6180	17494		6186		17498	4395	4348		160		7988	4721		5770	
		Ⓡ‡	Ⓐ				Ⓐ				⑦	①–⑥	Ⓐ	Ⓡ	Ⓡ		Ⓡ‡		⑤–⑦	Ⓡ		Ⓡ	
		M						⊕			H	△	△	S	L		M		Y	B		P	
Ventimiglia ▷ d.	...	1525	...	...	...	...	...	...	...	...	...	...	...	...	...	...	1932	...	...	...	...	2008	...
Menton ▷ d.	...	1537	...	...	...	...	...	...	...	...	...	...	...	...	...	...	1944	...	...	...	...	2023	...
Monaco-Monte Carlo ▷ d.	...	1551	...	...	...	...	...	...	...	...	...	...	...	...	...	...	1956	...	...	...	...	2035	...
Nice Ville ▷ a.	...	1610	...	...	...	...	...	...	...	...	...	...	...	...	...	...	2010	...	...	...	...	2056	...
Nice Ville ▷ d.	1528	...	1628	1635	1725	...	...	1735	1757	...	1835	1835	1928	2000	2000	...	...	...	2035	2056	...	2101	...
Antibes ▷ d.	1548	...	1647	1654	1745	...	...	1754	1817	...	1854	1856	1950	2020	2020	...	...	...	2100	2115	...	2121	...
Cannes ▷ d.	1559	...	1658	1705	1757	...	...	1805	1828	...	1905	1907	2001	2032	2032	...	...	...	2115	2126	...	2133	...
St Raphaël-Valescure ▷ d.	1623	...	1722	1730	1823	...	...	1830	1850	...	1931	1932	2023	2057	2057	...	...	...	2143	2151	...	2158	...
Fréjus ▷ d.	|	...	|	|	|	...	...	|	|	...	|	1937	2029	|	|	...	...	...	|	|	...	|	...
Les Arcs-Draguignan ▷ d.	1640	...	1739	|	|	...	1810	|	1906	...	|	1951	2043	2115	2115	...	...	...	|	2207	...	2222	...
Carnoules d.	|	...	|	|	|	...	1837	|	1926	...	|	2015	2103	|	|	...	...	...	|	|	...	|	...
Toulon a.	1712	...	1813	1817	1912	...	1908	1916	1944	...	2016	2037	2121	2150	2150	...	...	...	2230	2242	...	2257	...
Toulon 350 ▶ d.	1715	...	1816	1820	1915	...	...	1919	1947	...	2019	...	2123	2153	2153	...	...	...	2234	2245	...	2301	...
Marseille St Charles 350 ▶ a.	1759	...	1859	|	1959	...	...	|	2029	...	|	...	2211	2237	2237	...	...	...	2318	2329	...	|	...
Montpellier **355** a.	|	...	...	|	|	...	...	|	...	...	|	...	...	|	|	...	...	...	|	|	...	|	...
Toulouse **321** a.	|	...	...	|	|	...	...	|	...	...	|	...	...	|	|	...	...	...	|	0515	...	|	...
Bordeaux **320** a.	|	...	...	|	|	...	...	|	...	...	|	...	...	|	|	...	...	...	|	0811	...	|	...
Nantes **292** a.	|	...	...	|	|	...	...	|	...	...	|	...	...	|	|	...	...	...	|	...	...	|	...
Lyon Part-Dieu **350** a.	1950	...	...	|	2150	...	...	|	...	...	|	...	...	|	|	...	...	...	|	...	...	|	...
Genève **345** a.	|	...	...	|	|	...	...	|	...	...	|	...	...	|	|	...	...	...	|	...	...	|	...
Dijon **373** a.	|	...	...	|	2340	...	...	|	...	...	|	...	...	|	|	...	...	...	|	...	...	|	...
Strasbourg **384** a.	|	...	...	|	...	...	...	|	...	...	|	...	...	0831	|	...	...	...	|	...	...	|	...
Metz **379** a.	|	...	...	|	...	...	...	|	...	...	|	...	...	...	0824	...	...	...	|	...	...	|	...
Lille Europe **11** a.	2253	...	...	|	...	...	...	|	...	...	|	...	...	...	...	...	...	...	|	...	...	|	...
Paris Gare de Lyon **350** a.	...	...	...	2211	...	...	...	2311	...	...	0011	...	...	...	...	...	...	...	0720	...	...	0746a	...

LOCAL TRAINS MARSEILLE - TOULON *Certain trains continue to/from Hyères (Table 352)*

km		⚒		⚒		d	Ⓐd		⚒					Ⓐ				Ⓐ			Ⓐ						
0	**Marseille** d.	0603	0633	0703	0733	0833	0933	1103	1133	1223	1337	1433	1503	1533	1604	1629	1703	1733	1803	1833	1903	1938	2003	2033	2103	2137	2303
27	Cassis d.	0630	0700	0730	0800	0900	1000	1134	1200	1254	1403	1500	1531	1559	1631	1700	1730	1800	1830	1858	1936	2005	2034	2100	2130	2204	2330
37	La Ciotat d.	0637	0707	0737	0807	0907	1007	1141	1207	1301	1410	1507	1538	1607	1638	1707	1737	1807	1837	1905	1944	2012	2041	2107	2137	2211	2337
51	Bandol d.	0649	0719	0749	0819	0919	1019	1153	1219	1314	1422	1519	1551	1619	1650	1719	1749	1819	1849	1918	1956	2024	2054	2119	2149	2223	2349
67	**Toulon** a.	0703	0733	0803	0833	0933	1033	1207	1233	1328	1437	1533	1606	1633	1704	1733	1803	1833	1903	1933	2012	2038	2108	2133	2203	2237	0003

	Ⓑ	Ⓐ	⑥			⚒	Ⓐ						Ⓐ						Ⓐ		Ⓐ					
Toulon d.	0453	0523	0538	0553	0623	0638	0653	0723	0753	0825	0923	1053	1153	1224	1253	1323	1529	1549	1623	1653	1723	1753	1853	1923	2023	2127
Bandol d.	0509	0539	0554	0609	0640	0653	0709	0738	0808	0841	0938	1108	1209	1239	1309	1338	1544	1604	1640	1709	1738	1808	1909	1939	2039	2143
La Ciotat d.	0521	0551	0606	0621	0653	0705	0721	0750	0820	0853	0950	1120	1220	1251	1320	1350	1556	1616	1653	1721	1750	1820	1921	1951	2051	2155
Cassis d.	0528	0558	0613	0628	0700	0712	0728	0757	0827	0900	0958	1127	1228	1258	1328	1358	1603	1623	1700	1728	1757	1827	1928	1958	2058	2202
Marseille a.	0555	0625	0640	0700	0728	0736	0755	0826	0855	0926	1025	1155	1255	1331	1355	1425	1630	1655	1728	1755	1825	1855	1955	2025	2125	2229

B – *CORAIL LUNÉA* – 🛏 1,2 cl. and (2) (reclining) Bordeaux - Nice and v.v. Not Dec. 24, 31. From Hendaye/to Irún on dates in Table **305** (numbered **4630/1** and **4730/1**).

C – (12) Lille Europe (**5164**) - Charles de Gaulle (**9826**) - Nice; (12) Brussels (d 1021) - Nice.

D – ⑤ from Apr. 9 (also May 12).

E – Daily to Feb. 28, ⑥⑦ Mar. 6 - 21, daily from Mar. 27.

F – ⑦ from Apr. 4 (also Apr. 5, May 24).

G – Daily from Apr. 5.

H – ⑦ from Apr. 11 (also Apr. 5, May 24).

L – *CORAIL LUNÉA* – 🛏 1,2 cl. and (2) (reclining) Luxembourg - Metz - Nice and v.v. Not Dec. 24, 31, Jan. 9, 16, 23, 30 from Luxembourg or Nice.

M – (12) and 🍷 Nice - Ventimiglia - Genova - Milano and v.v. (Table **90**).

N – Not on ①–⑤ Mar. 1 - 26. Depart Bordeaux 0600 Jan. 4 - Feb. 28 (also Mar. 6, 7, 13).

P – *TRAIN BLEU* – 🛏 1,2 cl. and (2) (reclining) Paris Austerlitz - Nice - Ventimiglia and v.v. Not Dec. 24, 31. On ⑦ train number from Paris is **15771**.

Q – Dec. 18 - 20, 24, 26, 27, 31, Jan. 2, 3, Feb. 12 - 14, 19 - 21, 26 - 28, Mar. 6, 7, Apr. 5, 17, 24, May 2, 12, 16, 24.

R – Dec. 19, 20, 24, 26, 27, Jan. 1 - 3, Feb. 12 - 14, 19 - 21, 26, 28, Mar. 5, 7, Apr. 2, 5, 10, 16 - 18, May 2, 12, 21.

S – *CORAIL LUNÉA* – 🛏 1,2 cl. and (2) (reclining) Strasbourg - Nice and v.v. Not Dec. 24, 31, Jan. 9, 16, 23, 30 from Strasbourg or Dec. 24, 31, Jan. 9, 16, 23, 30, Mar. 13, 20, 27 from Nice.

T – Ⓐ Dec. 21 - Jan. 22, Ⓐ Apr. 12 - May 28.

U – Ⓐ Dec. 14 - 18, Ⓐ Jan. 25 - Apr. 9, Ⓐ from May 31.

Y – ⑤⑥⑦ (also Dec. 24, 31, Apr. 5, May 12, 13, 24; not Feb. 19, 20, 26, 27, Mar. 5, 6).

a – Paris **Austerlitz**.

b – To Brussels, arrive 1820 (Table **11**).

d – Subject to alteration Marseille - Cassis on Dec. 14 - 18, Ⓐ Jan. 25 - Apr. 9 and Ⓐ from May 31.

g – Also Apr. 6, May 25; not Apr. 5, May 24.

m – Not Dec. 24, 31, Apr. 5, May 12, 13, 24.

p – Lyon **Perrache**.

q – Also Dec. 24, 31, Apr. 5, May 1, 8, 12, 13, 24. On Dec. 18 and ⑤ Jan. 8 - Feb. 26 runs Marseille - Cannes only.

y – Also Dec. 21 - 23, 28 - 30.

TGV – Ⓡ, supplement payable, 🍷.

⊕ – Arrive Paris 2316 on ①–⑤ Jan. 4 - Feb. 26 (also Mar. 5).

⊗ – Depart Paris 2209 on ⑤ Jan. 8 - Feb. 12.

⊖ – Runs approx 30 minutes later Marseille - Nice morning of ①.

△ – Also calls at Cagnes sur Mer (10 minutes after Nice).

▽ – Also calls daily at La Ciotat (d. 0802). On ⑥ depart Toulon 0749, arrive Marseille 0838.

▷ – For local trains Les Arcs - Cannes - Nice - Ventimiglia see Table **361**.

▶ – For local trains Marseille - Toulon see separate panel. For complete *TGV* service Paris - Marseille/Toulon see Table **350**.

★ – *CORAIL TÉOZ*, Ⓡ, 🍷.

§ – Calls to pick up only.

‡ – Calls to set down only.

* – Subject to alteration on May 13 - 16.

See Table 361 for local trains on the Riviera

For the Nice - Nantes night train see page 211

For TGV / Téoz / night trains over this route see Table 360

361 LES ARCS - ST RAPHAEL - CANNES - NICE - MONACO - VENTIMIGLIA

Local trains

km		①–⑤	①–⑤		①–⑤	①–⑥	①–⑥		①–⑥	①–⑥			Ⓐ	①–⑤		①–⑥	①–⑤		①–⑤	①–⑤		①–⑤				①–⑥
		b	c	k									◇												◇	
0	**Les Arcs-Draguignan** .. d.	...	...	...	...	...	...	...	0602	...	...	...	0642	...	...	0656	...	0714	...	...	...	...	...	...	0850	...
23	Fréjus d.	...	...	...	...	...	...	...	|	...	...	...	0657	...	...	0710	...	0728	...	...	...	...	...	...	0905	...
27	St Raphaël-Valescure d.	...	...	...	...	...	0600	...	0621	...	...	0645	0702	...	...	0715	...	0732	...	...	...	...	...	0845	0910	...
31	Boulouris sur Mer d.	...	...	...	...	...	0605	...	0626	...	...	0649	|	...	...	0719	...	0737	...	...	...	...	...	0849	|	...
**	Grasse d.	...	...	...	...	...	|	...	|	...	0637	|	|	...	0713	|	...	|	0747	...	...	...	0837	|	|	...
60	**Cannes** a.	...	...	...	...	...	0631	...	0651	...	0708	0724	0729	...	0738	0748	...	0808	0821	...	...	...	0908	0924	0932	...
60	**Cannes** d.	0440	0510	0540	...	0610	0633	0634	0653	...	0710	0726	0732	...	0740	0749	...	0810	0831	...	0841	...	0910	0926	0934	0940
69	Juan les Pins d.	0449	0519	0549	...	0619	0642	0649	0702	...	0719	0734	|	...	0749	0758	...	0819	0839	...	0850	...	0919	0934	|	0949
71	Antibes d.	0452	0522	0552	...	0622	0646	0652	0705	...	0722	0737	0742	...	0752	0802	...	0822	0842	...	0853	...	0922	0937	0944	0952
80	Cagnes sur Mer d.	0505	0535	0605	...	0636	0656	0705	0718	...	0736	0748	|	0802	0806	0812	...	0835	0853	...	0906	0929	0936	0948	|	1005
94	**Nice Ville** a.	0520	0550	0620	...	0650	0710	0720	0735	...	0750	0759	0803	0814	0820	0825	...	0850	0904	...	0921	0941	0950	0959	1003	1020
94	**Nice Ville** d.	0523	0553	0623	0638	0653	0713	0723	...	0743	0753	...	...	0817	0823	...	0843	0853	...	0917	0923	0943	0953	...	...	1023
99	Villefranche sur Mer d.	0530	0600	0630	|	0700	|	0730	...	|	0801	...	...	|	0831	...	|	0901	...	|	0930	|	1001	...	...	1030
101	Beaulieu sur Mer d.	0534	0603	0634	0647	0703	0722	0734	...	0752	0804	...	...	0826	0834	...	0852	0904	...	0926	0934	0952	1004	...	...	1034
104	Eze d.	0537	0607	0637	|	0707	|	0737	...	|	0808	...	...	|	0838	...	|	0908	...	|	0937	|	1008	...	...	1037
110	**Monaco-Monte Carlo** d.	0547	0617	0647	0656	0717	0732	0747	...	0802	0817	...	...	0836	0847	...	0902	0917	...	0935	0947	1002	1017	...	...	1047
114	Cap Martin-Roquebrune d.	0553	0623	0653	|	0724	|	0753	...	|	0823	...	...	|	0854	...	|	0922	...	|	0953	|	1023	...	...	1053
117	Menton d.	0559	0629	0659	0707	0730	0746	0759	...	0816	0830	...	...	0846	0900	...	0916	0929	...	0946	0959	1017	1030	...	...	1059
127	**Ventimiglia** a.	0612	0642	0712	...	0742	...	0812	...	...	0842	...	...	...	0912	...	...	0942	...	...	1012	1027	1043	...	...	1112

		①–⑤				Ⓐ			①–⑤			①–⑥		①–⑤	Ⓐ			①–⑥		①–⑤		①–⑥		①–⑤	①–⑤	
						◇									◇								◇			
Les Arcs-Draguignan d.	...	...	...	...	...	1051	...	...	...	...	1226	...	...	...	1354	...	...	...	...	...	...	1526	1554	...	...	...
Fréjus d.	...	...	...	...	...	1106	...	...	...	...	1240	...	...	...	1408	...	...	...	...	...	...	1540	|	...	...	...
St Raphaël-Valescure d.	...	...	...	...	1045	1111	...	...	...	...	1245	...	...	1345	1413	...	...	...	...	...	...	1545	1610	...	...	...
Boulouris sur Mer d.	...	...	...	...	1049	|	...	...	...	...	1250	...	...	1350	|	...	...	...	...	...	...	1549	|	...	...	...
Grasse d.	0937	...	1031	1056	|	|	...	...	...	1244	|	...	1337	|	|	...	1437	...	...	...	1537	|	|	...	...	...
Cannes a.	1008	...	1053	1120	1124	1132	←	...	...	1308	1324	...	1408	1425	1434	...	1508	...	...	...	1608	1624	1631	...	...	...
Cannes d.	1010	1040	1055	→	1126	1135	1140	...	1241	1310	1326	1340	1410	1427	1437	...	1510	...	1540	...	1610	1626	1634	...	1640	...
Juan les Pins d.	1019	1049	1104	...	1134	|	1149	...	1250	1319	1333	1349	1419	1434	|	...	1519	...	1549	...	1619	1634	|	...	1649	...
Antibes d.	1022	1052	1107	...	1137	1144	1152	...	1252	1322	1337	1352	1422	1437	1447	...	1522	...	1552	...	1622	1637	1644	...	1652	...
Cagnes sur Mer d.	1036	1106	1121	...	1148	|	1206	...	1305	1336	1348	1405	1436	1447	|	...	1536	...	1605	...	1636	1648	|	1658	1705	...
Nice Ville a.	1050	1120	1135	...	1159	1203	1220	...	1320	1350	1359	1420	1450	1459	1504	...	1550	...	1620	...	1650	1659	1703	1710	1720	...
Nice Ville d.	1053	1123	...	...	...	...	1223	1253	1323	1353	...	1423	1453	...	...	1523	1553	1613	1623	1643	1653	1702	...	1713	1723	1723
Villefranche sur Mer d.	1101	1130	...	...	...	...	1231	1300	1330	1400	...	1430	1501	...	...	1530	1601	|	1630	|	1701	|	...	|	1730	1730
Beaulieu sur Mer d.	1104	1134	...	...	...	...	1234	1303	1333	1404	...	1434	1504	...	...	1533	1604	1622	1634	1652	1704	1711	...	1722	1734	1734
Eze d.	1108	1137	...	...	...	...	1238	1307	1337	1407	...	1437	1508	...	...	1537	1608	|	1637	|	1708	|	...	|	1737	1737
Monaco-Monte Carlo d.	1117	1147	...	...	...	...	1247	1317	1347	1417	...	1447	1517	...	...	1547	1617	1632	1647	1702	1717	1720	...	1732	1747	1747
Cap Martin-Roquebrune d.	1123	1153	...	...	...	...	1254	1323	1353	1424	...	1453	1523	...	...	1553	1623	|	1653	|	1723	...	...	|	1753	1753
Menton d.	1130	1159	...	...	...	...	1300	1330	1359	1430	...	1459	1530	...	...	1600	1630	1646	1659	1716	1730	...	...	1746	1759	1759
Ventimiglia a.	1142	1212	...	...	...	...	1312	1342	1412	1442	...	1512	1542	...	...	1612	1642	...	1712	...	1742	...	...	...	1812	1812

	①–⑤			Ⓑ		①–⑤			Ⓐ		①–⑤						①–⑥			①–⑤			Q		Q	
									◇						◇						z	z	◇	d	◇	h
Les Arcs-Draguignan d.	...	...	1626	...	...	...	...	1726	1754	...	...	...	1826	...	1920	...	1926	...	...	...	...	...	2222	...	2259	...
Fréjus d.	...	...	1645	...	...	...	...	1740	|	...	...	...	1840	...	1935	...	1940	...	...	...	...	...	|	...	|	...
St Raphaël-Valescure d.	...	...	1650	...	...	...	...	1745	1810	...	...	...	1845	...	1940	...	1945	...	...	...	...	...	2239	...	2314	...
Boulouris sur Mer d.	...	...	1655	...	...	...	...	1750	|	...	...	...	1850	...	|	...	1950	...	...	...	...	...	|	...	|	...
Grasse d.	...	1637	|	...	...	...	1737	|	|	...	...	1837	|	...	|	1937	|	...	2037	...	2137	...	|	2237	|	...
Cannes a.	...	1708	1724	...	...	...	1808	1824	1832	...	...	1908	1924	...	2001	2008	2024	...	2108	...	2208	...	2300	2308	2336	...
Cannes d.	...	1710	1726	...	1741	...	1810	1826	1834	...	1840	1910	1926	1940	2004	2010	2026	2040	2110	2140	2210	2240	2303	2310	2339	0010
Juan les Pins d.	...	1719	1734	...	1750	...	1819	1834	|	...	1850	1919	1934	1950	|	2019	2034	2049	2119	2149	2219	2249	|	2319	|	0019
Antibes d.	...	1722	1737	...	1753	...	1822	1837	1844	...	1853	1922	1937	1953	2014	2022	2037	2052	2122	2152	2222	2252	2313	2322	2348	0022
Cagnes sur Mer d.	1725	1736	1748	1758	1806	1828	1836	1848	|	1858	1906	1936	1948	2006	|	2036	2048	2105	2136	2205	2236	2305	|	2336	|	0035
Nice Ville a.	1740	1750	1759	1810	1821	1840	1850	1859	1903	1910	1920	1950	1959	2021	2032	2050	2059	2120	2150	2220	2250	2320	2331	2350	0006	0050
Nice Ville d.	1743	1753	...	1813	1824	1843	1853	...	...	1913	1923	1953	...	2023	...	2053	...	2123	2153	2223	2253	2323	...	2353	...	0053
Villefranche sur Mer d.	|	1801	...	|	1831	|	1900	...	...	|	1931	2001	...	2031	...	2101	...	2130	2201	2230	2300	2330	...	0000	...	0100
Beaulieu sur Mer d.	1753	1804	...	1822	1834	1852	1904	...	...	1922	1934	2004	...	2034	...	2104	...	2134	2204	2234	2304	2334	...	0004	...	0104
Eze d.	|	1808	...	|	1838	|	1907	...	...	|	1938	2008	...	2038	...	2108	...	2137	2208	2237	2307	2337	...	0007	...	0107
Monaco-Monte Carlo d.	1802	1817	...	1832	1847	1902	1917	...	...	1932	1947	2017	...	2047	...	2117	...	2147	2217	2247	2317	2347	...	0017	...	0117
Cap Martin-Roquebrune d.	|	1823	...	|	1853	|	1923	...	...	|	1953	2023	...	2053	...	2123	...	2153	2223	2253	2323	2353	...	0023	...	0123
Menton d.	1816	1830	...	1846	1859	1916	1930	...	...	1947	2000	2030	...	2100	...	2130	...	2159	2230	2259	2330	2359	...	0029	...	0129
Ventimiglia a.	...	1842	...	...	1912	...	1942	...	...	1958	2012	2042	...	2112	...	2142	...	2212	2242	2312	2342	0012	...	...	...	...

						Ⓐ				①–⑤		①–⑤			①–⑤			①–⑤	⑥		①–⑤		①–⑤			①–⑤
	k	k	◇			◇										◇										
Ventimiglia d.	...	0447	...	0517	0547	...	...	...	0617	0631	0647	...	...	0717	...	...	0747	...	...	0817	...	0847	...	...	0947	1017
Menton d.	...	0459	...	0529	0559	...	...	...	0629	0642	0659	0718	...	0729	0742	...	0759	0812	0812	0829	0842	0859	0912	...	0959	1029
Cap Martin-Roquebrune d.	...	0506	...	0537	0606	...	...	...	0636	|	0706	|	...	0736	|	...	0806	|	|	0836	|	0906	|	...	1006	1036
Monaco-Monte Carlo d.	...	0513	...	0544	0613	...	...	...	0643	0658	0713	0733	...	0743	0757	...	0813	0828	0828	0843	0858	0913	0928	...	1013	1043
Eze d.	...	0522	...	0554	0622	...	...	...	0652	|	0722	|	...	0752	|	...	0822	|	|	0852	|	0922	|	...	1022	1052
Beaulieu sur Mer d.	...	0526	...	0558	0626	...	...	...	0656	0707	0726	0746	...	0756	0806	...	0826	0837	0837	0856	0907	0926	0936	...	1026	1056
Villefranche sur Mer d.	...	0529	...	0601	0629	...	...	...	0659	|	0729	|	...	0759	|	...	0829	|	|	0859	|	0929	|	...	1029	1059
Nice Ville a.	...	0536	...	0608	0636	...	...	...	0706	0715	0736	0756	...	0806	0815	...	0836	0845	0845	0906	0915	0936	0945	...	1036	1106
Nice Ville d.	0509	0539	0556	0610	0639	0656	...	0704	0709	0717	0739	0801	0801	0809	0817	0835	0839	0848	...	0909	...	0939	...	1001	1039	1109
Cagnes sur Mer d.	0524	0554	|	0626	0654	|	...	0715	0724	0729	0754	0812	0812	0824	0831	0847	0854	0905	...	0924	...	0954	...	1012	1054	1124
Antibes d.	0537	0606	0615	0640	0707	0715	...	0726	0736	...	0807	0823	0823	0837	...	0859	0907	...	...	0937	...	1007	...	1023	1107	1137
Juan les Pins d.	0540	0609	|	0643	0710	|	...	0729	0740	...	0810	0827	0827	0840	...	|	0910	...	...	0940	...	1010	...	1027	1110	1140
Cannes a.	0549	0618	0624	0653	0718	0723	←	0735	0748	...	0819	0834	0834	0849	...	0907	0919	...	...	0948	...	1019	...	1034	1119	1149
Cannes d.	0558	0620	0626	...	→	0725	0734	0739	...	...	0824	0836	0836	...	...	0909	0923	...	...	...	...	1021	...	1036	1123	...
Grasse a.	0622	0652	|	...	...	|	|	0802	...	...	0852	|	|	...	...	|	0952	...	...	...	...	1045	...	|	1145	...
Boulouris sur Mer d.	...	...	|	...	...	|	0803	...	...	...	...	0910	0910	...	...	|	...	...	...	...	...	...	...	1111	...	...
St Raphaël-Valescure d.	...	...	0648	...	...	0748	0807	...	...	...	...	0914	0914	...	...	0932	...	...	...	...	...	...	...	1116	...	...
Fréjus d.	...	...	0653	...	...	0752	...	...	...	...	...	...	...	...	...	0938	...	...	...	...	...	...	...	1120	...	...
Les Arcs-Draguignan a.	...	...	0705	...	...	0804	...	...	...	...	...	...	...	...	...	0950	...	...	...	...	...	...	...	1133	...	...

		①–⑤	①–⑥	Ⓐ				①–⑤								Ⓑ	⑥	①–⑤	Ⓐ		①–⑤	①–⑥		①–⑤		
				◇							◇								◇							
Ventimiglia d.	1047	...	1117	...	1147	...	...	1216	1247	1317	...	...	1347	1447	...	1517	...	1531	...	1547	...	...	1617	...	1647	...
Menton d.	1059	...	1129	...	1159	...	...	1228	1259	1329	...	...	1359	1459	...	1529	...	1542	...	1559	1612	...	1629	1642	1659	1712
Cap Martin-Roquebrune d.	1106	...	1136	...	1206	...	...	1234	1306	1336	...	...	1406	1506	...	1536	...	|	...	1606	|	...	1636	|	1706	|
Monaco-Monte Carlo d.	1113	...	1143	...	1213	...	...	1241	1313	1343	...	...	1413	1513	...	1543	...	1558	...	1613	1628	...	1643	1657	1713	1728
Eze d.	1122	...	1152	...	1222	...	...	1249	1322	1352	...	...	1422	1522	...	1552	...	|	...	1622	|	...	1652	|	1722	|
Beaulieu sur Mer d.	1126	...	1156	...	1226	...	...	1253	1326	1356	...	...	1426	1526	...	1556	...	1606	...	1626	1637	...	1656	1706	1726	1737
Villefranche sur Mer d.	1129	...	1159	...	1229	...	...	1257	1329	1359	...	...	1429	1529	...	1559	...	|	...	1629	|	...	1659	|	1729	|
Nice Ville a.	1136	...	1206	...	1236	...	...	1303	1336	1406	...	...	1436	1536	...	1606	...	1615	...	1636	1645	...	1706	1714	1736	1745
Nice Ville d.	1139	1201	1209	1228	1239	1257	...	1305	1339	1409	1428	...	...	1539	1601	1609	1609	1618	1628	1639	...	1701	1709	1716	1739	1748
Cagnes sur Mer d.	1154	1212	1224	|	1254	1309	...	1320	1354	1424	|	...	...	1554	1612	1624	1624	1630	|	1654	...	1712	1724	1729	1754	1802
Antibes d.	1207	1223	1237	1247	1307	1319	...	1333	1407	1437	1446	...	...	1607	1623	1637	1637	...	1647	1707	...	1723	1737	...	1807	...
Juan les Pins d.	1210	1226	1240	|	1310	1322	...	1336	1410	1440	|	...	...	1610	1626	1640	1640	...	|	1710	...	1726	1740	...	1810	...
Cannes a.	1219	1233	1249	1255	1319	1329	...	1345	1419	1449	1454	←	...	1619	1633	1649	1649	...	1656	1719	...	1733	1749	...	1819	...
Cannes d.	1228	1235	...	1257	1323	1331	...	...	1423	→	1456	1509	...	1623	1635	...	...	...	1658	1723	...	1735	...	...	1823	...
Grasse a.	1259	|	...	|	1352	|	...	...	1452	...	|	1532	...	1652	|	...	...	...	|	1752	...	|	...	...	1852	...
Boulouris sur Mer d.	...	1309	...	|	...	1406	...	...	...	...	|	...	...	...	1710	...	...	...	|	...	...	1809	...	...	...	...
St Raphaël-Valescure d.	...	1313	...	1320	...	1410	1438	...	...	...	1519	...	...	...	1716	...	...	...	1722	...	...	1815	...	...	...	...
Fréjus d.	...	...	...	|	...	...	1442	...	...	...	|	...	...	...	1720	...	...	...	|	...	...	1819	...	...	...	...
Les Arcs-Draguignan a.	...	...	...	1333	...	...	1455	...	...	...	1533	...	...	...	1733	...	...	...	1737	...	...	1832	...	...	...	...

Local trains VENTIMIGLIA - MONACO - NICE - CANNES - ST RAPHAEL - LES ARCS 361

		①-⑥	⑦		①-⑤	①-⑥		①-⑤			Ⓐ		①-⑤				①-⑤				①-⑤			
	◇					△					◇										n	d	d	
Ventimiglia d.	...	...	...	1717	...	...	1747	...	1817	...	...	1847	...	1917	...	1947	2017	2047	2117	...	2137	...	2332	...
Menton d.	...	...	...	1729	1742	...	1759	1812	1829	1842	...	1859	1912	1929	...	1959	2029	2059	2129	...	2149	...	2344	...
Cap Martin-Roquebrune d.	...	...	...	1736	|	...	1806	|	1836	|	...	1906	|	1936	...	2006	2036	2106	2136	...	2156	...	2351	...
Monaco-Monte Carlo d.	...	1733	...	1743	1758	...	1813	1828	1843	1858	...	1913	1928	1943	...	2013	2043	2113	2143	...	2203	2313	2358	...
Eze d.	...	1743	...	1752	|	...	1822	|	1852	|	...	1922	|	1952	...	2022	2052	2122	2152	...	2212	2322	0007	...
Beaulieu sur Mer d.	...	1747	...	1756	1807	...	1826	1837	1856	1907	...	1926	1937	1956	...	2026	2056	2126	2156	...	2216	2326	0011	...
Villefranche sur Mer d.	...	1751	...	1759	|	...	1829	|	1859	|	...	1929	|	1959	...	2029	2059	2129	2159	...	2219	2329	0014	...
Nice Ville a.	...	1758	...	1806	1815	...	1836	1845	1906	1915	...	1936	1945	2006	...	2036	2106	2136	2206	...	2226	2336	0021	...
Nice Ville d.	1757	1801	1801	1809	1818	1835	1839	...	1909	...	1928	1939	...	2009	...	2039	2109	2139	2209	...	2239	2339	0024	...
Cagnes sur Mer d.	|	1812	1812	1824	1832	1845	1854	...	1924	...	1938	1954	...	2024	...	2054	2124	2154	2224	...	2254	2354	0039	...
Antibes d.	1817	1823	1823	1837	...	1856	1907	...	1937	...	1950	2007	...	2037	...	2107	2137	2207	2237	...	2307	0007	0052	...
Juan les Pins d.	|	1826	1826	1840	...	|	1910	...	1940	...	|	2010	...	2040	...	2110	2140	2210	2240	...	2310	0010	0055	...
Cannes a.	1826	1833	1833	1849	...	1904	1919	...	1949	...	1959	2019	...	2048	...	2119	2149	2219	2249	...	2319	0019	0104	...
Cannes d.	1828	1835	1835	...	...	1907	1923	...	...	...	2001	2023	...	2050	...	2122	...	2223	...	...	...	...	...	...
Grasse a.	|	|	|	...	...	|	1952	...	...	...	|	2052	...	|	...	2152	...	2252	...	...	...	...	...	...
Boulouris sur Mer d.	|	1910	1910	...	...	|	...	...	...	...	|	...	...	2123	...	...	...	...	...	...	...	...	...	...
St Raphaël-Valescure d.	1850	1914	1914	...	...	1932	...	...	...	...	2023	...	...	2127	...	...	...	...	...	...	...	...	...	...
Fréjus d.	|	...	...	...	...	1937	...	...	...	...	2029	...	...	...	...	...	...	...	...	...	...	...	...	...
Les Arcs-Draguignan a.	1904	...	...	...	...	1949	...	...	...	...	2041	...	...	...	...	...	...	...	...	...	...	...	...	...

Q – For days of running see Table **360**.
a – ①-⑤ only.
b – Subject to alteration on Dec. 15-18 and ②-⑤ Jan. 5 - Feb. 26.
c – Subject to alteration Cannes - Nice on Dec. 15-18 and ②-⑤ Jan. 5 - Feb. 26.
d – Subject to alteration on Dec. 14-18 and ①-⑤ Jan. 4 - Feb. 26.
h – Subject to alteration on Dec. 15-19 and ①-⑥ Jan. 5 - Feb. 27 (also Feb. 14, 21).
k – Subject to alteration Cannes - Nice and v.v. on Dec. 14-19 and ②-⑥ Jan. 5 - Feb. 27.
n – Not Mar. 15 - Apr. 2.
z – Not Dec. 13-18 Nice - Ventimiglia.
△ – To/from Toulon (Table **360**).
◇ – To/from Marseille (Table **360**).
** – Grasse - Cannes = *17 km*.

BRIANÇON - GRENOBLE, LYON and MARSEILLE 362

km																							5790	
		⚒		Ⓐ	Ⓐ						⑥	⑥				⑦		Ⓐ		Ⓐ	Ⓒ		🅁	
										v	W	W	⊡			L			E				D§	
0	**Briançon** d.	...	...	0455	...	0612	...	0755	...	0913	1120	1153	1250	...	1500	...	...	1646	1646	1745	1745	...	2030	...
13	L'Argentière les Écrins d.	...	...	0507	...	0625	...	0810	...	0929	1135	1206	1305	...	1513	...	...	1701	1701	1800	1800	...	2045	...
28	Montdauphin-Guillestre d.	...	...	0518	...	0636	...	0823	...	0942	1147	1220	1317	...	1525	...	...	1713	1713	1821	1821	...	2100	...
45	Embrun d.	...	...	0532	...	0654	...	0837	...	0959	1204	1237	1333	...	1547	...	...	1728	1728	1837	1837	...	2117	...
82	**Gap** a.	...	...	0604	...	0727	...	0909	...	1037	1240	1312	1408	...	1628	...	...	1802	1802	1912	1910	...	2155	...
82	**Gap** d.	0503	...	0606	...	0730	...	0911	...	1040	1242	1315	1410	...	1632	1705	...	1805	1805	...	1912	...	2200	...
109	Veynes-Dévoluy a.	0524	...	0625	...	0752	...	0933	...	1108	1306	1346	1436	...	1655	1725	...	1834	1834	...	1932	...	2226	...
109	Veynes-Dévoluy d.	0545	...	0627	0633	▽	...	0935	...	1112	1308	▽	1438	...	1659	1727	...	1836	1836	...	1934	...	2228	...
172	Die d.	|	...	0720	|	...	...	|	...	1213	1408	...	|	...	1752	|	...	|	|	...	|	...	2326	...
244	**Valence Ville** a.	|	...	0824	|	...	...	|	...	1318	1510	...	|	...	1855	|	...	|	|	...	|	...	0029	...
254	Valence TGV **350** a.	|	...	0838	|	...	...	|	...	1331	|	...	|	...	1922	|	...	|	|	...	|	...	|	...
261	Romans-Bourg de Peage a.	|	...	0848	|	...	...	|	...	1342	|	...	|	...	1933	|	...	|	|	...	|	...	|	...
	Lyon Part-Dieu 351 a.	|	...	...	|	...	...	|	...	...	1633	...	|	...	...	|	...	|	|	...	|	...	|	...
	Paris Austerlitz **351** a.	|	...	...	|	...	...	|	...	...	...	...	|	...	...	|	...	|	|	...	|	...	0646	...
159	Sisteron d.	0626	...	...	0718	...	...	1028	...	...	...	...	1523	...	...	1809	...	1917	|	...	2016	...	...	...
176	Château Arnoux-St Auban d.	0639	...	...	0736	...	...	1041	...	...	...	...	1537	...	...	1825	...	1930	|	...	2030	...	...	...
209	Manosque-Gréoux d.	0704	...	...	0803	...	...	1106	...	...	...	...	1605	...	...	1856	...	2002	2002	...	2058	...	...	...
278	Aix en Provence ▷ d.	0751	...	...	0851	...	...	1151	...	...	...	...	1651	...	...	1953	...	2051	2049	...	2151	...	...	...
315	**Marseille St Charles** ▷ a.	0822	...	...	0922	...	...	1222	...	...	...	...	1722	...	...	2024	...	2122	2122	...	2222	...	...	...

		5799																						
	Ⓐ	🅁		⚒	⑥	Ⓐ			⑥			Ⓒ		Ⓐ	⑥				Ⓐ	Ⓑ		Ⓑ	⑤	Ⓑ
		D‡	E		t	x	⊕			v	⊗		▽z		W		▽z						f	
Marseille St Charles ▷ d.	...	...	0536	0636	0636	...	0836	...	...	...	1236	1236	...	...	...	...	...	1636	...	1734	...	1835	1835	...
Aix en Provence ▷ d.	...	...	0620	0712	0712	...	0912	...	...	...	1312	1312	...	...	...	...	...	1712	...	1812	...	1912	1912	...
Manosque-Gréoux d.	...	...	0705	0805	0805	...	0952	...	...	...	1358	1358	...	...	...	...	...	1800	...	1855	...	2003	2003	...
Château Arnoux-St Auban d.	...	...	|	0831	0831	...	1015	...	...	...	1427	1427	...	...	...	...	...	1826	...	1931	...	2031	2031	...
Sisteron d.	...	...	|	0845	0845	...	1029	...	...	...	1446	1446	...	...	...	...	...	1842	...	1945	...	2047	2047	...
Paris Austerlitz **351** d.	...	2205	|	|	|	...	|	...	...	...	|	|	...	...	...	...	...	|	...	|	...	|	|	...
Lyon Part-Dieu 351 d.	...	|	|	|	|	...	|	...	...	...	|	|	...	...	...	...	...	|	...	|	...	|	|	...
Romans-Bourg de Peage d.	...	|	|	|	|	...	|	...	1043	1149	|	|	...	...	1424	...	...	|	1737	|	...	|	|	2018
Valence TGV **365** d.	...	|	|	|	|	...	|	...	1052	1200	|	|	...	...	1432	...	...	|	1747	|	...	|	|	2027
Valence Ville 365 d.	...	0414	|	|	|	...	|	...	1104	1224	|	|	...	...	1458	...	...	|	1803	|	...	|	|	2039
Die d.	...	0521	|	|	|	...	|	...	1215	1330	|	|	...	...	1607	...	...	|	1907	|	...	|	|	2139
Veynes-Dévoluy a.	...	0626	0812	0929	0929	...	1109	...	1314	1428	1535	1535	...	...	1705	...	...	1931	1959	2030	...	2132	2132	2231
Veynes-Dévoluy d.	...	0628	0818	0934	0934	...	1111	...	1317	1439	1537	1537	1608	...	1708	...	1810	1933	2023	2038	...	2134	2134	2233
Gap a.	...	0651	0837	0955	0955	...	1130	...	1339	1502	1556	1556	1630	...	1729	...	1830	1956	2042	2058	...	2156	2156	2253
Gap d.	0623	0654	0840	...	1004	1050	1132	...	1341	1504	...	1558	1654	1733	1733	...	1840	2001	...	...	2120	...	2201	2300
Embrun d.	0655	0735	0921	...	1040	1124	1205	...	1415	1542	...	1634	1729	1806	1806	...	1916	2043	...	...	2200	...	2238	2330
Montdauphin-Guillestre d.	0710	0753	0941	...	1054	1140	1221	...	1431	1558	...	1649	1746	1822	1822	...	1931	2059	...	...	2215	...	2253	2344
L'Argentière les Écrins d.	0720	0811	0953	...	1105	1151	1232	...	1444	1611	...	1702	1801	1837	1837	...	1941	2113	...	...	2226	...	2305	2355
Briançon a.	0733	0832	1006	...	1117	1204	1245	...	1457	1624	...	1717	1815	1850	1850	...	1954	2126	...	...	2238	...	2318	0007

GAP - GRENOBLE *Service is by 🚌 May 31 - June 18*

km		⚒			⑥	⑥	Ⓑ			
				Qv	W		v		b	
	Briançon (see above) d.	...	0612	...	1153	...	...	...	...	...
0	**Gap** d.	0530	0730	1131	1315	1315	1330	1730	1930	...
27	Veynes-Dévoluy d.	0554	0754	1154	1354	1354	1354	1754	2000	...
117	St Georges de Commiers d.	0720	0920	1320	1520	1520	1520	1920	|	...
136	**Grenoble** a.	0744	0944	1344	1544	1544	1544	1944	2144	...

	Q		†						
	⊙	v							
Grenoble d.	0813	1013	1213	...	1413	...	1613	1813	...
St Georges de Commiers d.	0834	1034	1234	...	1434	...	1634	1834	...
Veynes-Dévoluy d.	1008	1210	1408	1408	1608	...	1810	2008	...
Gap a.	1030	1230	1430	1430	1630	...	1830	2029	...
Briançon (see above) a.	...	...	...	...	1815	...	1954	...	...

LOCAL TRAINS MARSEILLE - AIX EN PROVENCE Journey time: 35–45 minutes

From Marseille St Charles: 0536 Ⓐ, 0544 ⚒, 0605 Ⓐ, 0644, 0705 Ⓐ, 0736 ⚒, 0744, 0804 Ⓐ, 0844, 1044, 1105 Ⓐ, 1205, 1305, 1336 Ⓐ, 1344, 1405 Ⓐ, 1423, 1505, 1536 Ⓒ, 1605, 1644 Ⓐ, 1744, 1805 Ⓐ, 1844 †, 1905, 1944, 2005 Ⓐ, 2036, 2044 Ⓐ, 2105, 2144 **u**, 2205 Ⓐ, 2244 Ⓐ **c**.

From Aix en Provence: 0511 Ⓐ, 0551 ⚒, 0611, 0631 ⚒, 0650 Ⓐ, 0731, 0831 Ⓐ, 0911, 1044, 1211, 1231, 1251 Ⓐ, 1311, 1411, 1431 Ⓐ, 1451, 1511, 1551 Ⓐ, 1611, 1631 Ⓐ, 1711, 1731, 1811, 1831 Ⓐ, 1851, 1931 Ⓐ, 1951 Ⓐ, 2031, 2111 †, 2131 Ⓐ, 2231 **u**, 2311 **c**.

D – *CORAIL LUNÉA* – 🛏 1, 2 cl., 💺2 (reclining). Not Dec. 24, 31. Relief trains run on peak dates.
E – ⑥⑦ Jan. 9-31, Mar. 13-28.
L – ⑦ (also May 24; not Dec. 20, 27, Feb. 7, Apr. 4, 11, May 23).
Q – ⚒ to Apr. 24; daily Apr. 26 - May 30.
S – July 1 - Aug. 31.
W – ⑥ Dec. 19 - Mar. 27.

b – Subject to alteration Jan. 25 - Feb. 6.
c – Subject to alteration Feb. 15 - Mar. 12.
f – Not Dec. 25, Jan. 1.
t – Not May 1, 8.
u – Subject to alteration Feb. 22-26, Mar. 1-6.
v – Subject to alteration on Ⓐ Mar. 8 - Apr. 16.

x – Subject to alteration Mar. 29 - Apr. 16.
z – Subject to alteration May 31 - June 18.
▷ – For local trains Marseille - Aix en Provence see below table.
▽ – To/from Grenoble (see panel below main table).
⊕ – Subject to alteration Veynes - Briançon on Ⓐ Mar. 29 - Apr. 16.
⊗ – Subject to alteration Marseille - Veynes on Ⓐ Mar. 8-26.
⊡ – Subject to alteration on Ⓐ Mar. 8-26.
⊙ – Subject to alteration Veynes - Gap on Ⓐ Mar. 29 - Apr. 23.
§ – Train number **15790** on certain dates.

‡ – Train number **15799** on certain dates.

🚌 BRIANÇON (station) - OULX (station)

Connects with TGV trains to/from Paris, Table **44**

Operator: Autocars ResAlp www.autocar-resalp.com. *To Dec. 18, 2009*

Subject to alteration

			S					S
Briançon d.	0845	1055	1410	1645	Oulx d.	0950	1305	1515	1925
Oulx a.	0950	1200	1510	1750	Briançon a.	1055	1410	1620	2030

Also from Briançon 0740 🅁, from Oulx 2015 🅁, to reserve ✆ 04 92 20 47 50.

363 BELLEGARDE - ANNEMASSE - ÉVIAN LES BAINS

km		5674 🅁 N ◧	Ⓐ	①-⑥ x	⚒	⊖	TGV 6501 ⑥ E	①-⑥ x	TGV 6503 ⑥ F	TGV 6509 ⑦ G	⊖	⑥ B	①-⑥ x▽	⚒ k	①-⑥ x	🚌 ⑤-⑦ w	①-⑥ x				Ⓐ	Ⓑ q		🚌	⊕
	Paris Gare de Lyon **341** ... d.	2306a	...	...	...	...	0810	...	0910	0910	...	...	...	...	...	...	...	...	...	...	...	...	...	...	...
	Lyon Part-Dieu **345** ... d.	|	...	...	...	...	|	...	|	|	...	1350	...	...	...	...	...	...	1704c	...	...	...	...	...	...
0	**Bellegarde** ... ▷ d.	0642	0653	...	0834	1032	1119	...	1210	1210	1232	1519	...	1632	...	1715	...	...	1835	...	1931	...	2032	2132	2232
	Genève Eaux Vives **366a** .. d.	|	|	0732	|	|	|	1232	|	|	|	|	1632	|	1732	|	1802	1832	|	1932x	|	...	|	|	|
38	Annemasse ... ▷ a.	0723	0732	0743	0912	1107	1153	1243	1242	1243	1311	1559	1643	1712	1743	1800	1813	1843	1912	1943x	2012	...	2112	2210	2315
38	Annemasse ... d.	0736	...	0753	*0925**	1112	1157	1246	1252	1252	1318	1607	1646	1718	1746	1800	1818	1846	1918	1946	2016	2034	2118	2210	2317
68	Thonon les Bains ... d.	0810	...	0827	*1010**	1140	1231	1315	1323	1323	1347	1639	1715	1744	1815	1850	1845	1915	1950	2015	2041	2059	2144	2255	2341
77	**Évian les Bains** ... a.	0818	...	0837	*1025**	1148	1239	1324	1331	1331	1355	1647	1722	1752	1824	1905	1852	1924	1958	2024	2049	2107	2151	2310	2350

	Ⓐ	Ⓐ		①-⑥ x	Ⓐ ⊡	①-⑥ x		⚒	Ⓐ b	⑥ D	🚌 ⚒	⊖	①-⑥ x▽	TGV 6502 ⑥ D	⊖	TGV 6504 ⑥ F	TGV 6506 ⑦ H	Ⓐ	⑦ d⊖		🚌	①-⑥ x	⊕	①-⑥ x	5676 🅁 P ◧
Évian-les-Bains ... d.	0446	0532	0558	0632	0658	0732	0758	0858	*0925**	1027	1055	1158	1334	1444	1558	1625	1628	*1630**	1702	1732	1745	1832	1903	1932	2030
Thonon-les-Bains ... d.	0455	0541	0608	0641	0708	0741	0808	0908	*0940**	1040	1110	1209	1345	1457	1608	1638	1639	*1645**	1714	1744	1800	1844	1914	1946	2041
Annemasse ... a.	0519	0610	0636	0710	0736	0812	0836	0937	*1030**	1100	1200	1236	1413	1518	1636	1703	1700	*1734**	1741	1811	1850	1911	1943	2014	2107
Annemasse ... ▷ d.	0521	0617	0644	0717	0738	0817	0844	...	1040	1109	...	1244	1417	1523	1644	1713	1721	1744	1744	1817	1850	1917	1945	2016	2118
Genève Eaux Vives **366a** ... a.	|	0628	|	0728	|	0828	|	...	|	|	...	|	1428	|	|	|	|	|	|	1828	|	1928	|	2028	|
Bellegarde ... ▷ a.	0555	...	0719	...	0820	...	0919	...	1120	1149	...	1318	...	1559	1719	1747	|	1819	1819	...	1935	...	2019	...	2151
Lyon Part-Dieu **345** ... a.	...	...	...	...	...	...	1107c	...	...	1338	...	1447c	...	|	...	|	|	...	1953	...	...	...	...	...	|
Paris Gare de Lyon **341** ... a.	...	...	...	...	...	...	...	...	...	...	...	...	...	1900	...	2048	2049	...	...	...	...	...	...	...	0556a

B – ⑥ Dec. 19 - May 1 (also ⑦ Dec. 20 - Jan. 3, Feb. 7 - Mar. 7).
D – ⑥ Dec. 19 - Apr. 24.
E – ⑥ Dec. 19 - Apr. 24 (also Dec. 25, Jan. 1).
F – ⑥ Dec. 20 - Apr. 3 (also Dec. 25, Jan. 1).
G – ⑦ Dec. 20 - Apr. 18 (also Apr. 5).
H – ⑦ Dec. 13 - Apr. 18 (also Apr. 5).
N – ⑤ Dec. 18 - Jan. 1, ⑤ Feb. 5 - Mar. 5.
P – ⑥ Dec. 19 - Jan. 2; ⑥ Feb. 6 - Mar. 6.

a – Paris **Austerlitz**.
b – Subject to alteration Apr. 6 - 16.
c – © only.
d – Also Apr. 5, May 24; not Apr. 4, May 23.
k – Subject to alteration Thonon - Évian from May 3.
q – From Annecy (Table **367**).
w – Also Dec. 24, 31, Apr. 5, May 12, 13, 24.
x – ①-⑥ (not Dec. 25, Jan. 1, Apr. 5, May 13, 24).

TGV –🅁, supplement payable, 🍷.
◧ – 🛏 1, 2 cl. and (2) (reclining).
▷ – See also Table **365**.
▽ – Subject to alteration Mar. 29 - Apr. 2.
⊖ – Subject to alteration Évian - Thonon from May 3.
⊕ – Not Jan. 9.
⊡ – Runs on ⚒ Annemasse - Bellegarde.
* – By 🚌.

364 GENÈVE and ANNECY - CHAMBÉRY - GRENOBLE - VALENCE

km		⚒	⚒	Ⓐ	⚒		Ⓐ	⚒	Ⓐ	Ⓐ		Ⓐ	Ⓐ	Ⓐ	⊖	v	⚒s	q	u	⚒v		Ⓐ	Ⓐ	Ⓐ
0	**Genève** ... **341 345** d.	...	...	...	...	...	...	...	...	*0558*	...	...	...	*0658*	...	...	...	...	1017	...	...	...	...	...
33	Bellegarde ... **341 345** d.	...	...	...	...	...	...	...	...	*0628*	...	...	...	*0730*	...	...	...	...	1049	...	...	...	...	...
66	Culoz ... **345** d.	...	...	...	...	...	...	...	...	0658	...	...	...	0756	...	...	...	...	|	...	...	...	...	1255
	Annecy ... **341 344** d.	...	...	...	...	0600	...	...	0638	|	0700	...	*0716*	|	0800	...	0836	0910	|	...	...	...	...	|
88	Aix les Bains ... **341 344** d.	...	...	...	...	0635	...	0702	0716	0721	0734	...	*0754*	0822	0834	0900	0916	0952	1129	1200	...	...	*1300*	1316
102	**Chambéry** ... **341 344** a.	...	...	...	...	0645	...	0713	0728	0733	0744	...	*0806*	0837	0844	0911	0926	1003	1140	1211	...	...	*1311*	1327
102	**Chambéry** ... d.	0504	...	0554	0614	0648	0654	0720	...	...	0747	0754	0814	...	0847	0914	▬	...	1148	1214	1248	1257	1314	...
116	Montmélian ... d.	0516	...	0607	0626	0659	0708	0733	...	...	0757	0808	0825	...	0858	0926	Ⓐ	...	1200	1226	1300	1310	1326	...
165	**Grenoble** ... a.	0553	...	0653	0712	0735	0753	0821	...	...	0835	0853	0912	...	0935	1012	⊖	...	1235	1312	1335	1359	1412	...
165	**Grenoble** ... d.	0556	0638	0656	...	0738	...	...	...	...	0838	...	...	...	0938	...	1038	...	1238	...	1338	...	...	...
242	Romans-Bourg de Péage ... d.	0655	0730	0754	...	0831	...	...	...	...	0930	...	...	...	1030	...	1130	...	1340	...	1454	...	...	...
249	Valence TGV ... ⊙ d.	0705	0739	0804	...	0841	...	...	...	...	0940	...	...	...	1040	...	1138	...	1355	...	1502	...	...	...
259	**Valence Ville** ... ⊙ a.	0713	0747	0813	...	0849	...	...	...	...	0949	...	...	...	1049	...	1148	...	1404	...	1510	...	...	...

	©	Ⓐ	⚒		Ⓐ				⊡	Ⓐ	⚒					Ⓐ		Ⓑ	⚒	⑦e	Ⓐ	Ⓐ	Ⓑ	Ⓑ§
Genève ... **341 345** d.	...	...	...	...	...	1416	...	...	...	...	...	1624	...	...	1658	...	...	...	...	...	1817	...	1944	...
Bellegarde ... **341 345** d.	...	...	...	...	...	1448	...	...	...	...	...	1655	...	...	1730	...	...	...	...	...	1844	...	2012	...
Culoz ... **345** d.	...	...	...	...	...	1513	...	...	...	...	...	|	...	...	1750	1759	...	...	...	1857	1913	...	2040	...
Annecy ... **341 344** d.	1300	1300	...	1355	...	|	1500	...	1600	...	...	|	1700	*1715**	...	|	1800	...	...	|	|	1900	|	2010
Aix les Bains ... **341 344** d.	1334	1334	...	1434	...	1535	1535	...	1634	...	...	1734	1734	*1758*	...	1821	1834	...	...	1919	1934	1934	2100	2055
Chambéry ... **341 344** a.	1347	1348	...	1445	...	1545	1545	...	1644	...	...	1743	1743	*1809*	...	1835	1843	...	...	1932	1945	1945	2111	2106
Chambéry ... d.	1350	1351	1414	1448	...	1548	1548	1614	1647	1654	1714	1746	1746	1814	...	...	1846	1854	1914	1934	1948	1948	...	2120
Montmélian ... d.	1401	1401	1427	1501	...	1601	1601	1627	1658	1708	1726	1757	1757	1826	...	...	1857	1908	1926	1946	2001	2001	...	2131
Grenoble ... a.	1435	1435	1512	1536	...	1635	1635	1712	1735	1753	1812	1835	1835	1912	...	...	1935	1953	2012	2021	2035	2035	...	2205
Grenoble ... d.	1438	1448	...	1539	...	1638	1638	...	1738	1756	...	1838	1838	...	...	...	1938	1956	...	...	2038	2038	...	...
Romans-Bourg de Péage ... d.	1529	1553	...	1629	1655	1729	1729	...	1829	1914	...	1929	1929	...	...	...	2029	2110	...	...	2129	2129	...	...
Valence TGV ... ⊙ d.	1540	1602	...	1640	1706	1738	1738	...	1839	1924	...	1939	1939	...	...	...	2038	2119	...	...	2138	2138	...	...
Valence Ville ... ⊙ a.	1549	1610	...	1648	1715	1748	1748	...	1848	1932	...	1948	1948	...	...	...	2048	2127	...	...	2149	2149	...	...

	Ⓐ	⚒	⚒	Ⓐ	⚒	R	Ⓐ			Ⓐ		Ⓐ		E	d	z	Ⓐb	Ⓑb	⊕	⚒b	⊕	⊗	b	Ⓐ
Valence Ville ... ⊙ d.	...	...	...	...	...	0514	0533	0609	...	0710	0810	...	...	...	1009	...	...	...	1109	...	1209	1209	1309	...
Valence TGV ... ⊙ d.	...	...	...	...	...	0524	0545	0620	...	0720	0821	...	...	...	1021	...	...	...	1120	...	1220	1220	1322	...
Romans-Bourg de Péage ... d.	...	...	...	...	...	0532	0555	0629	...	0729	0830	...	...	...	1031	...	...	...	1130	...	1230	1230	1334	...
Grenoble ... a.	...	...	...	...	...	0638	0659	0720	...	0819	0920	...	...	...	1120	...	...	...	1220	...	1320	1320	1420	...
Grenoble ... d.	...	...	*0535*	0621	...	0641	0702	0723	0743	...	0923	1004	...	1104	1123	...	1145	1204	1223	1304	1323	1323	1423	1443
Montmélian ... d.	...	...	*0622*	0656	...	0731	0749	0801	0830	...	1000	1055	...	1150	1201	...	1225	1249	1305	1350	1401	1401	1502	1532
Chambéry ... a.	...	...	*0634*	0706	...	0742	0801	0810	0842	...	1009	1104	...	1203	1210	...	1235	1300	1315	1400	1411	1411	1512	1542
Chambéry ... **341 344** d.	0605	0609	0645	0709	0727	*0750*	...	0814	0845	...	1013	1109	...	...	1213	...	...	...	1318	...	1414	1414	1515	...
Aix les Bains ... **341 344** d.	0619	0621	0701	0721	0740	*0804*	...	0832	0856	...	1034	1120	...	...	1230	1234	...	...	1334	...	1434	1430	1534	...
Annecy ... **341 344** a.	0713	|	0752	|	0820	...	...	0909	...	...	1107	...	...	...	|	1321	...	...	1415	...	1514	|	1621	...
Culoz ... **345** a.	...	0636	...	0737	...	...	...	...	...	...	...	...	...	...	1247	...	...	...	...	...	...	|	...	...
Bellegarde ... **341 345** a.	...	0705	...	0802	...	...	...	...	...	...	...	...	...	...	1313	...	...	...	...	...	...	1505	...	...
Genève 347 348 ... **341 345** a.	...	0732	...	0829	...	...	...	...	...	...	...	...	...	...	1342	...	...	...	...	...	...	1532	...	...

		Ⓐ	Ⓐ	Ⓐ		Ⓐ	Ⓐ				Ⓐ	Ⓐ	⚒			Ⓐ						☆‡	‡	
Valence Ville ... ⊙ d.	1409	...	...	...	1509	...	...	...	1609	1609	...	1635	...	1710	...	1725	...	1810	...	1908	...	2009	2109	...
Valence TGV ... ⊙ d.	1420	...	...	...	1520	...	...	...	1620	1620	...	1646	...	1721	...	1736	...	1821	...	1918	...	2020	2120	...
Romans-Bourg de Péage ... d.	1429	...	...	...	1529	...	...	...	1630	1630	...	1655	...	1730	...	1746	...	1830	...	1930	...	2029	2130	...
Grenoble ... a.	1520	...	...	...	1620	...	...	...	1720	1720	...	...	...	1820	...	1901	...	1920	...	2020	...	2120	2220	...
Grenoble ... d.	1523	1543	1604	...	1623	1635	...	1704	1723	1723	1735	...	1804	1823	1843	1904	...	1923	1944	2030	...	2130	2223	...
Montmélian ... d.	1603	1633	1649	...	1701	1722	...	1750	1802	1802	1822	...	1852	1903	1930	1949	...	2001	2032	2106	...	2206	2259	...
Chambéry ... a.	1612	1645	1700	...	1710	1733	...	1800	1811	1811	1833	...	1902	1912	1942	2000	...	2010	2042	2117	...	2215	2308	...
Chambéry ... **341 344** d.	1615	...	...	1705	1713	...	1748	...	1814	1814	...	...	...	1915	1945	...	...	2013	...	2120	...	2218	...	...
Aix les Bains ... **341 344** d.	1634	...	...	1720	1732	...	1804	...	1834	1829	...	...	...	1933	1957	...	...	2033	...	2134	...	2234	...	...
Annecy ... **341 344** a.	1714	...	...	|	1814	...	|	...	1920	|	...	...	...	2009	...	...	...	2104	...	2204	...	2304	...	...
Culoz ... **345** a.	...	...	...	1740	...	...	1823	...	...	1844	...	...	...	...	...	...	...	...	...	...	...	...	...	...
Bellegarde ... **341 345** a.	...	...	...	...	...	...	...	...	...	1903	...	...	...	...	...	...	...	...	...	...	...	...	...	...
Genève 347 348 ... **341 345** a.	...	...	...	...	...	...	...	...	...	1932	...	...	...	...	...	...	...	...	...	...	...	...	...	...

E – ⑤⑦ to Apr. 25 (not Dec. 25, Jan. 1, Feb. 5, 12); ⑤-⑦ from Apr. 30.
R – ②-⑥ (not holidays).
b – Subject to alteration on ①-⑤ Feb. 1 - 12.
d – Not on ①-⑤ Feb. 1 - 12, Mar. 8 - 12, Apr. 5 - 16.
e – Also Apr. 12, May 31; not Apr. 11, May 30.
q – Not Jan. 11 - 13 Aix - Chambéry.
s – From St Gervais (Table **367**).

u – Not on ①-⑤ Feb. 15 - 26, Mar. 15 - 19, Apr. 5 - 16, June 7 - 18.
v – Not Jan. 11 - 13, Feb. 15 - 19, 22 - 26.
z – Depart 1229 on Feb. 14, 20, 21, 27, 28.
⊡ – To Avignon Centre (arrive 2027) on ⑤.
☆ – From Avignon Centre on ⑦, depart 1830 (Table **351**).
⊙ – Additional 🚌 runs 2 - 4 times per hour.
⊕ – Subject to alteration ①-⑤ Feb. 1 - 12, Apr. 26 - May 7.

⊗ – Valence - Aix: see note ⊕. Aix - Genève: not ①-⑤ Mar. 8 - 12, Apr. 5 - 16.
⊖ – Not on ①-⑤ Apr. 12 - 23.
§ – Chambéry - Grenoble: not ①-⑤ Mar. 22 - Apr. 2.
‡ – Subject to alteration on ①-⑤ Mar. 22 - Apr. 2.
* – *1705* on Feb. 20, 27, Mar. 6.

(PARIS / LYON) - ANNECY / GENÈVE - ST GERVAIS 365

Subject to alteration on Apr. 19 - 23 Annecy - La Roche and v.v.

km	*TGV* trains convey 🍷							*TGV*		*TGV*		*TGV*	*TGV*				*TGV*				*TGV*				
				5591				**6561**		**6463**		**6467**	**6473**				**6569**				**6573**				
		Ⓐ	Ⓐ	**Y**		①–⑥	⚒			⑦	①–⑥	⑥	⑥	Ⓐ						⑦	Ⓑ	⚒	Ⓐ		⑥
				🅁◇		**n**			⊖	**M**	**n**⊖	**D**	**E**		⊗		**k**		**R**	**P**	**h**	**e**		**S**	**C**
	Paris Gare de Lyon **341**...d.	...	...	2246a	...	...	...	0710	...	0810	...	0910	1006	...	...	...	1110	...	...	...	1310	...	...	...	...
	Lyon Part-Dieu **345**.........d.	...	...	|	...	...	...	|	0904	|	...	|	|	...	...	...	|	1304	...	...	|	*1504*	...	...	...
	Chambéry **341/4 364**.......d.	...	...	0536	...	...	...	|	|	|	...	|	|	...	...	...	|	|	...	...	|	|	...	...	...
	Aix les Bains **364**.............d.	...	...	0600	...	...	...	|	|	|	...	|	|	...	...	...	|	|	...	...	|	|	...	...	...
0	**Annecy** ....▲d.	...	...	0708	...	...	...	|	|	|	...	|	|	...	...	...	|	|	1622	1648	|	|	...	1722	1735
	Bellegarde ....▽d.	...	...	|	...	...	0834	1007	1032	|	...	1210	|	...	1331	...	1407	1432	|	|	1607	1632	...	|	|
•23	**Genève Eaux-Vives** ▷d.	0602	0702	|	0802	0902	|	...	|	|	1202	|	|	1402	|	...	...	|	|	|	...	|	1702	|	|
•17	Annemasse ....▷a.	0613	0713	|	0813	0913	0912	...	1107	|	1213	1242	|	1413	1412	...	...	1512	|	|	...	1712	1713	|	|
•17	Annemasse ....d.	0618	0718	|	0818	...	0918	...	1118	|	1218	1301	|	...	1418	...	...	1518	|	|	...	...	1718	|	|
39	La Roche sur Foron ....▲a.	0636	0734	0804	0836	...	0936	...	1136	|	1236	|	|	...	1436	...	...	1536	1703	1725	...	...	1736	1812	1823
39	La Roche sur Foron ....d.	0640	0740	0831	0840	...	0940	...	1140	|	1240	|	|	...	1440	...	...	1540	1712	1744	...	...	1740	1825	1833
61	Cluses (Haute-Savoie) ....d.	0706	0806	0851	0906	...	1005	...	1206	1237	1306	1350	1437	...	1506	...	...	1606	1736	1806	...	...	1806	1848	1904
80	Sallanches Megève ....d.	0720	0819	0905	0919	...	1019	...	1219	1253	1319	1406	1453	...	1519	...	...	1620	1754	1817	...	...	1819	1903	1918
86	**St Gervais**........................a.	0726	0825	0911	0925	...	1025	...	1225	1259	1325	1412	1459	...	1525	...	...	1625	1800	1823	...	...	1825	1909	1924

			TGV					*TGV*		
			6577					**6477**		
	Ⓑ	Ⓐ				①–⑥	Ⓐ	⑤	①–⑥	
					△	**n**		**B**	**n**	⊡
Paris Gare de Lyon **341** ... d.	...	...	1504	...	...	...	...	1642	...	...
Lyon Part-Dieu **345** .... d.	...	...	|	1704	1738	...	...	|	...	1904
Chambéry **341/4 364**........ d.	...	...	|	|	|	...	...	|	...	|
Aix les Bains **364** .... d.	...	...	|	|	|	...	...	|	...	|
Annecy ....▲d.	1826	...	|	|	1935	...	...	|	...	|
Bellegarde..................▽d.	|	...	1807	1835	|	...	...	|	...	2032
Genève Eaux-Vives. ▷d.	|	1902	...	|	|	1932	...	|	2032	|
Annemasse ....▷a.	|	1913	...	1912	|	1943	...	|	2043	2112
Annemasse ....d.	|	...	...	1918	|	...	1958	|	...	2118
La Roche sur Foron.........▲a.	1902	...	...	1937	2012	...	2014	|	...	2137
La Roche sur Foron.............d.	1918	...	...	1940	...	...	2019	|	...	2140
Cluses (Haute-Savoie).........d.	1940	...	...	2006	...	...	2042	2201	...	2206
Sallanches Megève.............d.	1955	...	...	2019	...	...	2059	2217	...	2219
St Gervais ....a.	2001	...	...	2025	...	...	2105	2223	...	2225

		TGV						*TGV*			*TGV*
		6564						**6964**			**6568**
			Ⓐ			⚒		Ⓒ		①–⑥	
				V						**n**	
St Gervais.......................d.	0530	...	...	0555	0630	0645	...	0730	...	...
Sallanches Megève..........d.	0535	...	...	0602	0635	0651	...	0735	...	...
Cluses (Haute-Savoie).....d.	0551	...	...	0617	0651	0707	...	0750	...	...
La Roche sur Foron..........a.	0615	...	...	0639	0716	0731	...	0816	...	...
La Roche sur Foron.....▲d.	0619	...	...	0653	0719	0739	...	0820	...	...
Annemasse ....a.	0639	...	...	|	0739	|	...	0839	...	...
Annemasse ....▷d.	0644	...	0647	|	0747	|	...	0844	0847	...
Genève Eaux-Vives. ▷a.	|	...	0658	|	0758	|	...	|	0858	...
Bellegarde ....▽a.	0719	0749	...	|	...	|	...	0919	...	0948
Annecy ....▲a.	|	|	...	0733	...	0820	0830	|	...	|
Aix les Bains **364**..........a.	|	|	...	...	...	0914	0857	|	...	|
Chambéry **341/4 364**.... a.	|	|	...	...	...	0926	|	|	...	|
Lyon Part-Dieu **345**...... a.	0847	|	...	...	...	...	|	1102z	...	|
Paris Gare de Lyon **341** a.	...	1051	...	...	...	...	1207	...	...	1249

		TGV			*TGV*				*TGV*					*TGV*	*TGV*	*TGV*	*TGV*		*TGV*			*TGV*	*TGV*			
		6968		**17582**	**6480**				**6572**	**17572**				**6580**	**6482**	**6486**	**6484**		**6984**			**6584**	**6494**			**5596**
			Ⓐ		⑥	Ⓐ				⑥	⚒		Ⓐ	Ⓐ	⑦	⑥	⑦		Ⓑ		Ⓐ		⑥	Ⓑ		**Z**
				A	**F**	⊖				**E**	⊖				**L**	**H**	**M**	‡	**h**	**s**			**G**		**s**	🅁◇
St Gervais ....d.	0745	...	0830	0853	0930	1130	...	...	1130	1330	1530	...	...	1610	1651	1654	1645	...	1730	...	...	1810	1827	...	2050
Sallanches Megève.............d.	0751	...	0835	0904	0941	1135	...	...	1136	1336	1535	...	...	1621	1700	1703	1650	...	1736	...	...	1821	1833	...	2100
Cluses (Haute-Savoie).........d.	0807	...	0850	0923	1004	1150	...	...	1151	1351	1550	...	...	1639	1718	1720	1707	...	1751	...	...	1837	1849	...	2121
La Roche sur Foron.............a.	0830	...	0916	0939	|	1216	...	...	1216	1416	1616	...	...	|	|	|	1730	...	1816	...	...	|	1913	...	2138
La Roche sur Foron.........▲d.	0843	...	0918	0953	|	1219	...	...	1234	1419	1618	...	...	|	|	|	1743	...	1819	...	...	|	1919	...	2158
Annemasse ....a.	|	...	0939	|	|	1239	...	...	|	1439	1633	...	...	1711	|	1755	|	...	1839	...	...	|	1938	...	|
Annemasse ....▷d.	|	...	0947	|	|	1247	1244	...	|	1445	1644	1647	...	1721	|	1804	|	...	1844	1847	...	|	...	1945	|
Genève Eaux-Vives . ▷a.	|	...	0958	|	|	1258	|	...	|	|	|	1658	...	|	|	|	|	...	|	1858	...	|	...	|	|
Bellegarde..................▽a.	|	...	...	|	|	...	1318	1348	|	1518	1719	...	1748	|	|	|	|	...	1919	...	1948	|	...	2019	|
Annecy ....▲a.	0925	0935	...	1030	|	...	|	|	1318	...	|	...	|	|	|	|	1819	1832	|	...	|	|	...	|	2232
Aix les Bains **364** ....a.	...	1001	...	1107	|	...	|	|	|	...	|	...	|	|	|	|	...	1859	|	...	|	|	...	|	2325
Chambéry **341/4 364**........a.	...	1014	...	|	|	...	|	|	|	...	|	...	|	|	|	|	...	|	|	...	|	|	...	|	2340
Lyon Part-Dieu **345** ....a.	...	|	...	1228	|	...	1447	|	1518	...	1847	...	|	|	|	|	...	|	2047	...	|	|	...	2147	|
Paris Gare de Lyon **341** ... a.	...	1320	...	...	1433	...	...	1649	...	...	...	...	2049	2049	2143	2143	...	2207	...	...	2249*	2347	...	...	0636a

ANNECY - ANNEMASSE / GENÈVE Direct services

			🚌			🚌				🚌	🚌
	Ⓐ	Ⓐ	⚒	Ⓐ	⚒	Ⓑ	Ⓐ	T	Ⓐb	Ⓐ	
Annecy .... d.	0603	0659	0733	0739	0903	1003	1103	1303	1703	1733	1833
La Roche sur Foron.... a.	0648	0732	|	0815	0935	1035	1135	1336	1735	|	1905
La Roche sur Foron.... d.	0650	0738	|	*0820*	0941	1035	1141	1341	1741	|	1905
Annemasse.................. a.	0705	0755	|	*0839*	0955	|	1155	1355	1755	|	|
Genève Eaux-Vives ▷a.	...	...	0853	...	...	1113	...	...	...	1848	1943

			🚌			🚌		🚌		🚌
	Ⓐ	⚒	Ⓐ	Ⓐ	⚒	Ⓑ	y	Ⓐ	Ⓐ	
Genève Eaux-Vives ▷ d.	...	...	0843	...	...	1148	...	1813	...	2003
Annemasse ....d.	0602	0802	|	1002	1202	|	1600	|	1855	2020
La Roche sur Foron....a.	0618	0818	0915	1018	1218	1222	1617	1848	1912	2050
La Roche sur Foron....d.	0621	0825	0915	1021	1221	1222	1621	1848	1919	2050
Annecy.......................a.	0652	0855	0952	1052	1252	1259	1652	1925	1959	2124

A – ⑥ Dec. 19 - May 1 (also ⑦ Dec. 20 - Jan. 3, ⑦ Feb. 7 - Mar. 7).
B – ⑤ Dec. 18 - Apr. 23 (also Dec. 24, 31; not Dec. 25, Jan. 1).
C – ⑥ Dec. 19 - Apr. 24 (also Dec. 25, Jan. 1, Feb. 21, 28, Mar. 7). On Feb. 13, 20, 27, Mar. 6 runs up to 25 minutes earlier.
D – ⑥ Dec. 19 - Apr. 17 (also Dec. 25, Jan. 1).
E – ⑥ Dec. 19 - Apr. 17.
F – ⑥ Dec. 19 - Apr. 24 (also Dec. 25, Jan. 1).
G – ⑥ Dec. 25 - Apr. 3 (also Dec. 25, Jan. 1).
H – ⑥ Dec. 25 - Apr. 24 (also Dec. 25, Jan. 1; not Apr. 5).
L – ⑦ Dec. 20 - Apr. 18 (also Apr. 5).
M – ⑦ Dec. 20 - Apr. 25 (also Apr. 5).
P – ⑦ Dec. 20 - Apr. 25 (also Dec. 25, Jan. 1, Apr. 5).
R – Ⓐ to Apr. 23; Ⓑ from Apr. 26 (also Dec. 13).
S – Ⓑ to Apr. 23 (not Dec. 25, Jan. 1, Feb. 21, 28, Mar. 7); daily from Apr. 25.
T – Not Feb. 13, 14, 20, 21, 27, 28, Mar. 6, Apr. 24, May 1. On ⑥ to May 1 runs 7 minutes earlier.
V – Ⓐ to Apr. 30; ①–⑥ from May 3 (not May 8, 13, 24).
Y – Ⓑ to Mar. 28 (not Dec. 24, 31, Mar. 11); ⑤⑦ from Apr. 2 (also Apr. 5, May 13, 24; not Apr. 4, 30, May 2, 7, 23). Train number is **5594** on certain dates (depart Paris 2302).
Z – Daily to Mar. 28 (not Dec. 14 - 16, 24, 31); ⑤–⑦ from Apr. 2 (also May 12, 13, 24). Train number is **5592** on certain dates.

a – Paris **Austerlitz**.
b – Not Feb. 20, 27, Mar. 6. Runs 12 minutes later La Roche - Annecy on ⑥ Dec. 26 - Apr. 24.

e – Not Feb. 13, 20, 27, Mar. 6.
h – Not Dec. 25, Jan. 1, May 13.
k – Not on ①–⑤ Mar. 8 - 12, Apr. 5 - 16, May 3 - 21.
n – Not Dec. 25, Jan. 1, Apr. 5, May 13, 24.
s – Not Jan. 9.
y – Runs 21 minutes earlier on ✝ Dec. 20 - Apr. 25 (also Feb. 13, 20, 27, Mar. 6).
z – 1107 on Ⓒ.

TGV –🅁, supplement payable, 🍷.

▲ – For connections Annecy - La Roche sur Foron and v.v. see panel below main table.
△ – To Évian les Bains (Table **363**).
▷ – For full service Genève Eaux-Vives - Annemasse and v.v. see Table **366a**.
▽ – Bellegarde - Annemasse: see also Table **363**. For connections Bellegarde - Genève see Table **345**.
◇ – *CORAIL LUNÉA* – 🛏 1, 2 cl. and 💺 (reclining).
⊗ – Subject to alteration Bellegarde - Annemasse on Ⓐ Mar. 22 - Apr. 16.
⊖ – Subject to alteration on ①–⑤ Mar. 8 - 19.
⊡ – Runs 10 - 15 mins later Annemasse - St Gervais on ⑤ to Apr. 23 (also Dec. 24, 31; not Dec. 25, Jan. 1).
‡ – On Feb. 21, 28, Mar. 7 runs 15 minutes earlier, and *TGV* in next column starts from St Gervais (1645) calling at Sallanches (1654) and Cluses (1710).
• – Distance from La Roche sur Foron.
* – 2303 on ①–④ Jan. 4 - Feb. 25.

ST GERVAIS - CHAMONIX 365a

No rail service Apr. 19 - May 7 (service by 🚌)

km				P	P			W							
0	**St Gervais**..................d.	0731	0832	0932	1032	1232	1332	1432	1532	1632	1732	1832	1932	2032	...
9	Les Houches................d.	0756	0856	0956	1056	1256	1356	1456	1556	1656	1756	1856	1956	2056	...
20	**Chamonix** ....a.	0812	0912	1012	1112	1312	1412	1512	1612	1712	1812	1912	2012	2112	...

	Ⓒb	Ⓐ						P				Q			
Chamonix.....................d.	0638	0653	0738	0838	0938	1038	1238	1338	1438	1538	1638	1738	1838	1938	...
Les Houches ....d.	0657	0717	0757	0857	0957	1057	1257	1357	1457	1557	1657	1757	1857	1957	...
St Gervais ....a.	0720	0741	0820	0920	1020	1120	1320	1420	1520	1620	1720	1820	1920	2020	...

b – Also daily Dec. 21 - Jan. 1, Feb. 15 - 26.
P – Dec. 13 - Mar. 28, June 12 - Sept. 12.
Q – Dec. 13 - Mar. 28, June 12 - Sept. 5.
W – ⑥ Feb 2 - Mar. 6.

*Many journeys continue to / from Le Châtelard or Martigny (Table **572**).*

*See Table **9** for additional ski trains to/from Bourg St Maurice*

366 CHAMBÉRY - ALBERTVILLE - BOURG ST MAURICE

TGV trains convey 🍷

km		① g	🚌 ②–⑤ u	Ⓐ	🚌 q	Z	© Y	*TGV* 6417 ⑥ B	Ⓐ X §	b	🚌 b	© Y	*TGV* 6419 ⑦ M	*TGV* 6421 ⑥ C	*TGV* 5106 ⑥▽ D	*TGV* 6429 ⑥ D	*TGV* 6433 ①⑤ U	*TGV* 6427 ⑦ M	© y	Z §	*TGV* 5308 ⑥ A ▷	*TGV* 6435 ⑥⑦ R	Ⓐ X	
	Paris Gare de Lyon **341** d.	...	...	...	...	...	...	0637	...	...	...	...	0742	0838	...	0850	0850	0854	...	...	...	0950	...	...
	Lyon Part Dieu **344** d.	...	...	...	...	...	...	|	...	...	...	...	|	|	...	|	|	|	...	...	...	|	...	...
	Aix les Bains **341/4** d.	...	...	...	...	...	...	|	...	...	...	...	|	|	...	|	|	|	...	...	...	|	...	...
0	**Chambéry** **367** d.	0618	0600	0645	0735	0818	0834	|	1011	1011	...	1010	|	|	1151	1200	|	|	1204	1205	1220	|	1405	...
14	Montmélian **367** d.	0629	0618	0657	0758	0828	|	|	|	|	...	|	|	|	|	|	|	|	|	1216	|	|	|	...
26	St Pierre d'Albigny **367** d.	0638	0636	0710	0813	0837	|	|	|	|	...	|	|	|	|	|	|	|	|	1226	|	|	|	...
62	Albertville a.	0702	0712	0733	0847	0900	0911	1002	1045	1045	...	1045	1122	1206	1223	1230	1230	1230	1238	1249	1254	1339	1443	...
62	Albertville d.	0708	0712	...	0847	0913	0927	1013	1058	...	1055	1104	1134	1216	1233	1240	1240	1240	1251	1302	1304	1351	1451	...
104	Moûtiers-Salins d.	0734	0742	...	0915	0939	1000	1037	1126	...	1123	1134	1154	1241	1256	1303	1310	1302	1315	1327	1336	1411	1517	...
126	Aime la Plagne d.	0748	0756	...	...	0953	1017	1056	1140	...	1140	1149	1209	1256	1312	1319	1326	1318	1333	1340	1352	1426	1531	...
137	Landry d.	0756	|	...	...	1001	1026	1106	1148	...	1150	1159	1217	1305	1321	1330	1336	1328	1342	1348	1403	1436	1539	...
146	**Bourg St Maurice** a.	0804	0815	...	...	1008	1034	1113	1156	...	1200	1207	1224	1312	1328	1337	1343	1335	1350	1355	1410	1443	1546	...

	b	🚌 b	© Y	*TGV* 6437 ⑥ F	*TGV* 6439 ⑥⑦ S	*TGV* 6443 ⑥ E	Z	© Y	Ⓐ	🚌 b	Z	© Y	*TGV* 6447 ⑤ K	d	🚌 Ⓑ	⊡ Z	© Y	*TGV* 6451 ⑤ J	🚌 ⑤⑦ w	*TGV* 6453 ⑤ L	*TGV* 6449 ④ W	5707 🄡◇ BB	*TGV* 6455 ⑤ H	5705 🄡◇ AA
Paris Gare de Lyon **341** d.	...	...	...	1158	1210	1250	...	...	...	...	...	...	1610	...	...	...	...	1858	...	1950	2010	2234a	2302	2302a
Lyon Part Dieu **344** d.	...	...	1230	|	|	|	1441	1441	...	...	...	...	|	1741	...	1941	1941	|	...	|	|	|	|	|
Aix les Bains **341/4** d.	...	...	|	|	|	|	|	|	...	...	...	...	|	|	...	|	|	|	...	2248	|	|	|	|
Chambéry **367** d.	1404	...	1406	|	|	|	1605	1625	1720	...	1818	1830	|	1910	2005	2106	2117	|	2205	2307	2313	|	|	0517
Montmélian **367** d.	|	...	|	|	|	|	|	|	1731	...	1830	|	|	1922	2023	2117	|	|	|	|	|	|	|	|
St Pierre d'Albigny **367** d.	|	...	|	|	|	|	|	|	1740	...	1839	|	|	1932	2038	2125	|	|	|	|	|	|	|	|
Albertville a.	1443	...	1443	1536	1543	1616	1638	1715	1803	...	1902	1910	1950	1956	2103	2149	2152	2236	2250	2338	2346	0513	0540	0555
Albertville d.	...	1445	1456	1546	1555	1627	1651	1731	...	1809	1915	1923	2000	2009	2103	2203	2205	2247	2250	2347	2356	0526	0550	0640
Moûtiers-Salins d.	...	1513	1519	1608	1620	1656	1716	1804	...	1837	1941	1946	2022	2029	2135	2232	2241	2310	2315	0010	0017	0600	0632	0708
Aime la Plagne d.	...	1528	1539	1624	1639	1711	1731	1824	...	1852	1955	2002	2038	2043	...	2246	2302	2326	...	0026	0033	0622	0649	0732
Landry d.	...	1537	1551	1634	1651	1726	1739	1833	...	1902	2003	2011	2048	2051	...	2253	2313	2336	...	0036	0042	0631	0703	0743
Bourg St Maurice a.	...	1550	1559	1641	1658	1733	1746	1840	...	1915	2010	2019	2055	2058	...	2300	2322	2343	...	0043	0049	0639	0710	0751

	🚌 ⚒	© Y	EE	🚌 Ⓐ	Ⓐ	© Y	Z		© Y	Z	*TGV* 6420 ⑥⑦ P		Z §	© Y n	🚌 b	b	Ⓐ X §	*TGV* 6422 ⑥⑦ Q	*TGV* 6424 ⑥ D		© Y	🚌 b	b ⊕	Ⓐ X
Bourg St Maurice d.	...	0517	0535	...	...	0646	0702	...	0807	0810	0851	...	1014	1114	1157	...	1210	1225	1249	...	1351	1359	...	1409
Landry d.	...	0525	0543	...	...	0658	0710	...	0816	0818	0901	...	1023	1124	1204	...	1217	1233	1304	...	1401	1406	...	1417
Aime la Plagne d.	...	0534	0552	...	...	0715	0718	...	0826	0826	0911	...	1031	1134	1212	...	1225	1243	1317	...	1411	1415	...	1426
Moûtiers-Salins d.	0503	0551	0607	0642	...	0736	0735	...	0844	0841	0933	...	1046	1201	1232	...	1240	1320	1339	...	1431	1435	...	1442
Albertville a.	0536	0614	0633	0730	...	0757	0800	...	0905	0905	0953	...	1112	1232	1303	...	1301	1341	1409	...	1452	1506	...	1507
Albertville d.	0536	0629	0644	...	0742	0810	0808	...	0918	0916	1008	...	1125	1256	...	1314	1314	1352	1419	...	1502	...	1517	1517
St Pierre d'Albigny **367** d.	0557	|	0710	...	0806	|	0836	...	|	|	|	...	|	|	...	1333	1333	|	|	...	|	...	1536	1536
Montmélian **367** d.	0612	|	0720	...	0814	|	0845	...	|	|	|	...	|	|	...	1341	1341	|	|	...	|	...	1544	1544
Chambéry **367** a.	0635	0705	0729	...	0824	0846	0855	...	0950	0950	|	...	1156	1332	...	1350	1350	|	|	...	1535	...	1553	1553
Aix les Bains **341/4** a.	0655	|	|	...	...	0910	0911	...	...	...	|	...	...	|	...	...	...	|	|	...	1552	...	...	...
Lyon Part Dieu **344** a.	...	0856	0854	...	...	1028	1028	...	...	...	|	...	...	1516	...	...	...	|	|	...	1729	...	...	...
Paris Gare de Lyon **341** a.	...	...	...	...	...	...	...	...	...	...	1407	...	...	...	...	...	...	1720	1807	...	...	...	...	...

	TGV 6432 ⑥ D	*TGV* 6430 ⑦ N	*TGV* 5182 ⑥▽ D	*TGV* 6434 ①⑤ V		© Y	Z	*TGV* 6444 ⑦ M	*TGV* 6436 ⑥ A	*TGV* 5394 ⑥ A ▷	🚌 Ⓐ	Ⓐ	*TGV* 6438 ⑥ G	🚌 Ⓑ m	🚌 Ⓑ b	© Y	Z	*TGV* 6446 ⑦ M	🚌 ⑤⑦ w	*TGV* 6442 ⑥⑦ T		5710 🄡◇ DD	5706 🄡◇ CC	*TGV* 6456 ⑤ FF
Bourg St Maurice d.	1445	1453	1504	1508	...	1602	1606	1619	1623	1644	...	...	1708	...	1712	1755	1802	1823	...	1905	...	2108	2130	2323
Landry d.	1455	1503	1515	1519	...	1611	1614	1628	1632	1654	...	...	1719	...	1719	1813	1810	1833	...	1915	...	2119	2139	2333
Aime la Plagne d.	1506	1513	1526	1530	...	1621	1622	1637	1642	1709	...	...	1730	...	1728	1822	1819	1842	...	1925	...	2131	2150	2343
Moûtiers-Salins d.	1527	1536	1543	1547	...	1642	1636	1655	1700	1731	1717	...	1748	1748	1748	1838	1834	1900	1928	1948	...	2151	2212	2358
Albertville a.	1545	1553	1610	1605	...	1706	1707	1722	1730	1748	1805	...	1806	1819	1819	1900	1857	1919	2000	2006	...	2222	2240	0022
Albertville d.	1600	1603	1619	1615	...	1720	1715	1732	1742	1758	...	1815	1816	1819	1819	1913	1911	1929	2000	2017	...	2237	2259	0032
St Pierre d'Albigny **367** d.	|	|	|	|	...	|	1738	|	|	|	...	1833	|	1847	1847	|	1933	|	|	|	...	|	|	|
Montmélian **367** d.	|	|	|	|	...	|	1746	|	|	|	...	1842	|	1902	1902	|	1941	|	|	|	...	|	|	|
Chambéry **367** a.	|	|	1647	|	...	1752	1755	|	|	1827	...	1853	|	1925	1925	1951	1951	2004	2050	|	...	2315	2335	|
Aix les Bains **341/4** a.	|	|	...	|	...	|	|	|	|	...	...	...	|	...	...	...	...	|	...	|	...	2329	|	|
Lyon Part Dieu **344** a.	|	|	...	|	...	1921	1916	|	|	...	...	...	|	...	...	...	...	|	...	|	...	|	|	|
Paris Gare de Lyon **341** a.	2005	2007	...	2015	...	...	...	2107	2115	...	...	...	2207	...	...	...	...	2307	...	0007	...	0600a	0621a	0702

A – ⑥ Dec. 19 - Apr. 3 (also Dec. 25, Jan. 1).
B – ⑥ Dec. 19 - Apr. 3.
C – ⑥ Dec. 19 - Apr. 24.
D – ⑥ Dec. 19 - Apr. 24 (also Dec. 25, Jan. 1).
E – ⑥ Dec. 19 - Apr. 3 (also Dec. 25).
F – ⑥ Dec. 19 - Apr. 17 (also Dec. 25).
G – ⑥ Dec. 26 - Apr. 3 (also Dec. 25, Jan. 1).
H – ⑤ Dec. 18 - Apr. 2 (not Dec. 25, Jan. 1).
J – ⑤ Jan. 8 - Apr. 2 (also Dec. 18, 24).
K – ⑤ Jan. 8 - Apr. 23 (also Dec. 18, 24, 31).
L – ⑤ Jan. 8 - Mar. 12 (also Dec. 18).
M – ⑦ Dec. 20 - Apr. 4.
N – ⑦ Dec. 20 - Apr. 25 (also Apr. 5).
P – ⑥⑦ Dec. 19 - Apr. 25.
Q – ⑥⑦ Dec. 19 - Apr. 4 (also Jan. 1).
R – ⑥⑦ Dec. 19 - Apr. 4 (also Dec. 25, Jan. 1, Apr. 5, 11, 18, 25).
S – ⑥⑦ Dec. 19 - Apr. 19 (also Dec. 25, Jan. 1, Apr. 5).
T – ⑥⑦ Dec. 20 - Apr. 25 (also Dec. 25, Jan. 1, Apr. 5).
U – Dec. 18, 21 - 24, 28 - 31, ①⑤ Jan. 4 - Mar. 26 (also Feb. 23 - 25, Mar. 2 - 4). Train **6363** on certain dates.
V – Dec. 18 - 30; ①⑤ Jan. 4 - Apr. 2 (also Feb. 23 - 25, Mar. 2 - 4).

W – ④ Jan. 7 - Mar. 11 (also Dec. 17).
X – Ⓐ Dec. 14 - Apr. 30.
Y – © Dec. 13 - May 2.
Z – Ⓐ Dec. 14 - Apr. 30; daily from May 3.
AA – ①②③④⑥⑦ Dec. 13 - Mar. 6 (not Dec. 14 - 16, 24, 31); daily Mar. 12 - 28; ⑤⑥⑦ from Apr. 2 (also Apr. 5, May 12, 13, 24; not May 2, June 6).
BB – ⑤ Dec. 18 - Jan. 1, ⑤ Feb. 5 - Mar. 5 (also Feb. 20).
CC – Daily Dec. 13 - Mar. 28 (not Dec. 14 - 16, 23, 30); ⑤⑥⑦ from Apr. 2 (also Apr. 12, 29, May 6, 19, 20, 31; not May 21).
DD – Dec. 26, Jan. 2, Feb. 13, 27, Mar. 6 only.
EE – Ⓐ to May 12 (not Jan. 12, 13); ⚒ May 14 - June 19.
FF – ⑤ Jan. 8 - Feb. 26 (also Dec. 18, 31).

a – Paris **Austerlitz**.
b – May 3 - June 25.
d – Daily except ⑤ to Apr. 25 (also Dec. 25, Jan. 1; not Dec. 24, 31, Feb. 20, 21, 27, 28, Mar. 6, 7); Ⓑ from Apr. 26 (also May 1).
g – Also Apr. 6, May 25; not Apr. 5, May 14, 24.
m – Ⓑ Dec. 13 - May 2.

n – Not Dec. 25, Jan. 1, Apr. 5.
q – ①–⑥ Dec. 14 - Apr. 30 (not Dec. 25, Jan. 1, Apr. 5).
u – Not Dec. 25, Jan. 1, Apr. 6, May 13, 25.
w – Also Apr. 5, May 24; not Apr. 4, May 23.
y – © Dec. 13 - May 2 (not Feb. 6, 13, 20, 21, 27, Mar. 6, 7).

TGV – 🄡, supplement payable, 🍷.
◇ – 🛏 1, 2 cl., 2 (reclining).
▽ – To/from Lille Europe (Table **9**).
▷ – To/from Nantes/Rennes (Table **335**).
⊡ – From Dijon on Ⓐ (Table **373**).
⊕ – Subject to alteration ①–⑤ May 3 - 27, also June 2 - 4.
§ – Subject to alteration Mar. 29 - Apr. 2.

366a GENÈVE EAUX-VIVES - ANNEMASSE

Certain journeys continue to/from St Gervais (Table **365**). *Subject to alteration on June 5*

km		Ⓐ	Ⓐ	Ⓐ	Ⓐ	①–⑥ △n		①–⑥ n	①–⑥ n	Ⓐ	①–⑥ n	①–⑥ △n	Ⓐ	Ⓐ	Ⓐ	①–⑥ n	①–⑥ △n	Ⓐ	①–⑥ △n	①–⑥ △n	△	Ⓐ	①–⑥ △n	①–⑥ n	
0	Genève Eaux-Vives d.	0532	0602	0632	0702	0732	0802	0832	0902	0932	1202	1232	1302	1332	1402	1432	1632	1702	1732	1802	1832	1902	1932	2032	...
6	Annemasse a.	0543	0613	0643	0713	0743	0813	0843	0913	0943	1213	1243	1313	1343	1413	1443	1643	1713	1743	1813	1843	1913	1943	2043	...

	Ⓐ	Ⓐ	Ⓐ △	Ⓐ	①–⑥ △n		①–⑥ △n	①–⑥ n	Ⓐ	Ⓐ	①–⑥ n	Ⓐ	Ⓐ	Ⓐ	①–⑥ △n	①–⑥ n	Ⓐ	①–⑥ n	①–⑥ n	△	Ⓐ	①–⑥ △n	①–⑥ △n	
Annemasse d.	0517	0547	0617	0647	0717	0747	0817	0847	0917	0947	1217	1247	1317	1347	1417	1617	1647	1717	1747	1817	1847	1917	2016	...
Genève Eaux-Vives a.	0528	0558	0628	0658	0728	0758	0828	0858	0928	0958	1228	1258	1328	1358	1428	1628	1658	1728	1758	1828	1858	1928	2028	...

n – Not Dec. 25, Jan. 1, Apr. 5, May 13, 24.

△ – To/from Évian les Bains (Table **363**).

CHAMBÉRY - MODANE 367

km		5559						TGV 9241	TGV 6401			TGV 6407							TGV 9249					
		[R] ◇	Ⓐ		⑥	⑥	🚌	❖	⑥			⑥⑦		⑥⑦			Ⓐ				Ⓐ	Ⓐ	†	🚌 ⑤⑦
		N		q	B	F		M	A			R		L				b	T					w
	Paris Gare de Lyon **341** ....d.	2306a	...	...	...	...	...	0742	0742	...	...	1042	...	...	...	...	...	...	1524	...	...	...	...	...
	Lyon St Exupéry ✈ **342** ....d.	|	...	...	...	...	...	|	|	...	...	|	...	...	...	...	...	...	1720	...	...	...	...	...
	Lyon Part Dieu **344** ....d.	|	...	0631	0741	...	...	|	|	...	...	|	...	1313	...	1541	...	1637	|	...	...	...	...	...
	Aix les Bains **341/4** ....d.	0526	...	|	|	...	...	|	|	...	...	|	...	|	...	|	...	|	|	...	...	1951	...	...
0	**Chambéry** .... **366** d.	0555	0641	0807	0911	1016	1005	1045	1049	1210	...	|	1409	1507	1610	1704	1725	1759	1826	...	1905	2008	2006	2205
14	Montmélian .... **366** d.	|	0652	0818	|	|	1023	|	|	1221	...	|	1422	|	1620	|	1736	1811	|	...	1917	2017	2017	2223
26	St Pierre d'Albigny .... **366** d.	|	0701	0827	|	|	1038	|	|	1230	...	|	1430	|	1628	|	1754	1819	|	...	1925	2030	2027	2238
71	St Jean de Maurienne ....d.	0645	0744	0905	0956	1102	1134	1129	1140	1311	...	1434	1513	1556	1711	1756	1830	1857	|	...	2005	2107	2107	2329
83	St Michel-Valloire ....d.	0656	0755	0916	1007	1114	1150	|	1151	1322	...	1446	1522	1607	1722	1807	1839	1907	|	...	2014	2116	2116	2343
99	**Modane** ....a.	0714	0810	0932	1020	1128	1209	1150	1205	1337	...	1500	1536	1620	1736	1823	1852	1921	1925	...	2028	2129	2129	2359

							TGV 9240						TGV 6406			TGV 6414						TGV 9248		5558
	⑥	Ⓐ				Ⓒ				⑥	🚌	⑥	⑥		Ⓒ	⑥⑦		Ⓐ	†		⑥	❖	🚌 ⑤⑦	[R] ◇
	t				Z	Y	T			B		F	A	W	Y §	S			t	V	E	M	w	P
Modane ....d.	0524	0525	0620	0705	0833	0843	0950	1027	...	1130	1220	1325	1354	1421	1438	1604	1620	1715	1715	1833	1846	1920	1921	2130
St Michel-Valloire ....d.	0541	0542	0636	0723	0848	0859	|	1043	...	1148	1237	1342	1410	1437	1454	1620	1639	1728	1728	1849	1902	|	1938	2148
St Jean de Maurienne ....d.	0553	0554	0648	0750	0859	0910	1023	1055	...	1201	1253	1354	1423	1448	1506	1632	1649	1738	1738	1859	1912	|	1954	2201
St Pierre d'Albigny .... **366** d.	0630	0631	0726	0832	0937	|	|	1134	...	|	|	|	|	1525	|	|	1725	1818	1818	1938	|	|	2048	|
Montmélian .... **366** d.	0638	0639	0734	0841	0945	|	|	1143	...	|	1408	|	|	1536	|	|	1736	1827	1827	1947	|	|	2108	|
Chambéry .... **366** a.	0647	0648	0746	0850	0953	0954	1103	1152	...	1255	1432	1445	|	1547	1555	|	1747	1837	1837	1956	1956	2022	2130	2250
Aix les Bains **341/4** ....a.	0700	...	|	...	...	|	|	|	...	|	...	|	|	...	|	|	...	1851	...	|	|	|	...	2335
Lyon Part Dieu **344** ....a.	0843	...	0916	...	...	1116	|	1316	...	1416	...	1612	|	...	1716	|	...	...	...	2116	2116	|	...	|
Lyon St Exupéry ✈ **342** ....a.	...	...	...	...	...	...	|	...	...	...	...	...	|	...	...	|	...	...	...	...	...	2124	...	|
Paris Gare de Lyon **341** ....a.	...	...	...	...	...	...	1403r	...	...	...	...	...	1819	...	...	2019	...	...	...	...	...	2321	...	0556a

A – ⑥ Dec. 19 - Apr. 17 (also Dec. 25, Jan. 1).
B – ⑥ Dec. 19 - Apr. 24.
E – ⑥ Dec. 19 - May 1.
F – ⑥ Dec. 26 - Apr. 24.
L – ⑥⑦ Dec. 19 - May 2.
M – [12] and 🍷 Paris - Milano and v.v. (Table **44**). [R], special 'global' fares payable.
N – ⑤⑥ Dec. 18 - Jan. 2; ⑤ Feb. 5 - Mar. 5.
P – ⑥⑦ Dec. 19 - Jan. 3; ⑥ Feb. 6 - Mar. 6.
R – ⑥⑦ Dec. 19 - Apr. 4 (also Dec. 25, Jan. 1; not Dec. 13).
S – ⑥⑦ Dec. 20 - Apr. 4 (also Dec. 25, Jan. 1).
T – [12] and 🍷 Paris - Torino and v.v. (Table **44**). [R], special 'global' fares payable.
V – Ⓑ to Apr. 30; daily from May 2.
W – Ⓐ Dec. 14 - May 12; ⚒ from May 14.
Y – Ⓒ Dec. 13 - May 2.
Z – Ⓐ Dec. 14 - Apr. 30; daily from May 3.
a – Paris **Austerlitz**.
b – Not Apr. 5, 25, May 2.
q – Not Feb. 23, May 9, 13, 16, 23, 24, 30, June 6, 13, 20.
r – 1359 on ①–⑤.
t – Not May 1, 8.
w – Also Apr. 5, May 24; not Apr. 4, May 23.
TGV – [R], supplement payable, 🍷.
◇ – 🛏 1, 2 cl. and [2] (reclining).
❖ – Subject to confirmation.
§ – To Dijon (Table **373**).

Via Mont Blanc road tunnel — 🚌 CHAMONIX - COURMAYEUR - AOSTA 368

June 2009 - April 2010		[R] §	[R] ‡	[R] §	[R] ‡	[R] §	[R] ‡	[R] § S	[R] ‡ S		[R] § ⚒	[R] ‡ ⚒		[R] §	[R] ‡	[R] ‡	[R] §	[R]
St Gervais (rail station) ....d.	→	0815	...	...	...	...	...	...	...	→	...	...	→	...	...	...	...	...
Chamonix (rail station) ....d.	**June 27 -**	0845	1010	1330	1500	1600	1745	1845	0000	**Sept. 14 -**	0845	1600	**Dec. 19 - Apr. 18**	0845	0945	1500	1600	1700
Courmayeur ....a.	**Sept. 13**	0930	1055	1415	1545	1645	1830	1930	0045	**Dec. 18**	0930	1645	(not Dec. 25)	0930	1030	1545	1645	1745
Aosta (see below) ....a.		*1045*	*1200*	*1630*	*1730*	*1830*	*1930*	*2045*	...		*1045*	*1830*		*1045*	*1200*	*1730*	*1830*	*1930*

		[R] ‡	[R] §	[R] ‡	[R] §	[R] ‡	[R] §	[R] § S	[R] ‡ S		[R] § ⚒	[R] ‡ ⚒		[R] ‡	[R] §	[R] ‡	[R] ‡	[R] §
Aosta (see below) ....d.	→	*0745*	*0945*	*1045*	*1335*	*1545*	*1645*	*1845*	*2145*	→	*0745*	*1335*	→	*0745*	...	*1220*	*1445*	*1545*
Courmayeur ....d.	**June 27 -**	0845	1045	1245	1445	1645	1745	1945	2300	**Sept. 14 -**	0940	1445	**Dec. 19 - Apr. 18**	0845	0945	1400	1600	1700
Chamonix (rail station) ....a.	**Sept. 13**	0930	1130	1330	1530	1730	1830	2030	2345	**Dec. 18**	1025	1530	(not Dec. 25)	0930	1030	1445	1645	1745
St Gervais (rail station) ....a.		...	...	...	...	...	1900	...	...		...	...		...	...	...	...	...

S – July 25 - Aug. 23. § – Operated by SAT, Le Fayet. ‡ – Operated by SAVDA, Aosta.
Reservations by day before departure: SAT, Chamonix station, ✆ +33 (0) 450 530 115 (email chamsat@orange.fr) or SAVDA, Aosta bus station, ✆ +39 0165 842 031.

Connecting 🚌 service **Courmayeur - Pré St Didier - Aosta** (journey 60 minutes): Pré St Didier is 10 mins from Courmayeur. See also Table **586**. Operator: SAVDA, Aosta.
From Courmayeur: 0645, 0800, 0900, 0945, 1100, 1230, 1325, 1430 (⚒, schooldays only), 1530, 1630, 1730, 1830, 1945, 2055, 2155.
From Aosta: 0645, 0745, 0945, 1045, 1220, 1305 (⚒, schooldays only), 1335, 1445, 1545, 1645, 1745, 1845, 1945, 2045, 2145.
Service to Dec. 12, 2009 (no service Dec. 25)

Narrow gauge. 2nd class only — CORSICAN RAILWAYS 369

September 21, 2009 - January 3, 2010 *Certain sections are by 🚌 during reconstruction work*

km		⚒	⚒	⚒ ⊡	⚒	⚒ ⊡	⚒	⚒		⚒	⚒ ⊡	⚒	⚒ ⊡	⚒	⚒	⚒		†	†	†		†	†	†
0	**Bastia** ....d.		0646	...	0857	...	1010	...	...	1532	...	1700	...	...	1821	...	...		0902	1010	...	1700	1818	...
22	Casamozza ....d.		0715	0718	0927	0931	1041	1044	...	1603	1606	1730	1733	...	1853	1856	...		0936	1048	...	1735	1853	...
47	Ponte Leccia ....a.		...	0752	...	1005	...	1116	...	...	1639	...	1806	...	...	1931	...		1011	1121	...	1810	1926	...
47	Ponte Leccia ....d.		...	0754	...	1007	...	1118	...	...	1641	...	1810	1812	...	1933	...		1013	1126	...	1812	1928	1932
98	Ile Rousse ....d.		...	|	...	|	...	1226	...	...	|	...	|	1927	...	|	...		|	1241	...	|	|	2046
120	**Calvi** ....a.		...	|	...	|	...	1259	...	...	|	...	|	2000	...	|	...		|	1314	...	|	|	2119
74	Corté ....d.		...	0828	...	1041	...	...	...	...	1714	...	1843	...	...	2000	...		1047	...	...	1845	1955	...
90	Vivario ....d.		...	0856	...	1109	...	...	...	...	1742	...	1912	...	...	...	...		1116	...	...	1914	...	...
158	**Ajaccio Gare** ....a.		...	1020	...	1232	...	...	...	...	1907	...	2033	...	...	...	...		1239	...	...	2037	...	...

		⚒	⚒	⚒ ⊡	⚒	⚒	⚒ 🚌	⚒	⚒ ⊡	⚒		⚒	⚒ ⊡	⚒	⚒ ⊡	⚒			†	†		†	†	
Ajaccio Gare ....d.		...	...	0623	...	...	...	...	0836	...	...	...	1515	...	1635	...	...		...	0848	...	...	1645	...
Vivario ....d.		...	...	0751	...	...	...	...	1005	...	...	...	1643	...	1806	...	...		...	1016	...	...	1813	...
Corté ....d.		0650	...	0825	...	...	...	...	1039	...	...	...	1717	...	1841	...	...		...	1051	...	...	1848	...
Calvi ....d.		|	...	|	...	0802	...	...	|	...	...	1555	|	...	|	...	...		0820	|	...	1615	|	...
Ile Rousse ....d.		|	...	|	...	0839	...	...	|	...	...	1632	|	...	|	...	...		0857	|	...	1652	|	...
Ponte Leccia ....a.		0717	...	0853	...	0950	...	...	1106	...	...	1743	1744	...	1910	...	...		1008	1118	...	1803	1915	...
Ponte Leccia ....d.		0719	...	0855	...	...	0954	...	1109	...	...	...	1748	...	1912	...	...		1012	1122	...	1815	1918	...
Casamozza ....d.		0752	0756	0927	0932	...	1026	1030	1141	1143	...	...	1821	1824	1945	1950	...		1050	1159	...	1854	1955	...
Bastia ....a.		...	0827	...	1002	...	...	1101	...	1212	...	...	...	1853	...	2018	...		1118	1230	...	1925	2026	...

COMPLETE LOCAL SERVICE BASTIA - CASAMOZZA (for service on † see above)

	⚒	⚒	⚒	⚒	⚒	⚒	⚒	⚒	⚒	⚒	⚒	⚒	⚒	⚒	⚒	⚒	⚒	⚒	⚒	⚒				
Bastia ....d.	0625	0646	0715	0755	0857	0929	1010	1105	1141	1217	1307	1350	1437	1532	1630	1700	1712	1742	1821	1917	...	...	...	...
Casamozza ....a.	0655	0715	0746	0825	0927	1000	1041	1136	1210	1247	1337	1421	1507	1603	1700	1730	1741	1811	1853	1947	...	...	...	...

	⚒	⚒	⚒	⚒	⚒	⚒	⚒	⚒	⚒	⚒	⚒	⚒	⚒	⚒	⚒	⚒	⚒	⚒	⚒	⚒				
Casamozza ....d.	0702	0719	0756	0848	0932	1030	1108	1143	1220	1310	1353	1440	1523	1621	1703	1744	1824	1841	1950	2002	...	...	...	...
Bastia ....a.	0739	0750	0827	0918	1002	1101	1138	1212	1249	1340	1423	1510	1553	1651	1733	1813	1853	1910	2018	2030	...	...	...	...

⊡ – By 🚌 Casamozza - Tatone and v.v. (Tatone is 13 km south of Vivario).
Operator: Chemins de fer Corse (CFC) - operation is contracted to SNCF.
For Calvi - Ajaccio journeys change at Ponte Leccia (use both directions of the table).

370 PARIS - DIJON *TGV services*

Many *TGV* trains continue to / from Besançon or Belfort (Table **374**), Lausanne or Bern (Table **375**)

km	*TGV* trains convey 🍸	*TGV* 6751 Ⓐ	*TGV* 9261	*TGV* 6755 Ⓐ ⊗	*TGV* 6757 Ⓒ		*TGV* 6759 △	*TGV* 6711 ①–⑥ u	*TGV* 9269 ▽	*TGV* 9271 ⑦ d	*TGV* 6713 ⑤ f	*TGV* 6765 Ⓐ	*TGV* 6715 ⑥ t	*TGV* 6719 ⑤ f	*TGV* 9273	*TGV* 6789	*TGV* 6769	*TGV* 9277	*TGV* 6731 D	*TGV* 6773		*TGV* 6735 ①–④ m	*TGV* 6775 ⑤ f	*TGV* 6777 ⑤ f	*TGV* 6777 ⑦ e
0	**Paris Gare de Lyon** d.	0658	0758	0828	0824	...	1028	1124	1258	1358	1410	1427	1427	1512	1558	1658	1728	1758	1858	1928	...	2028	2028	2128	2128
212	Montbard d.	0806	|	|	0932	...	|	1232	|	|	|	|	|	1615	|	1805	|	|	2006	|	...	|	2133	|	|
284	**Dijon** a.	0840	0935	1005	1006	...	1205	1306	1437	1536	1547	1605	1605	1650	1735	1840	1905	1935	2040	2107	...	2205	2207	2305	2305

	TGV 6700 Ⓐ	*TGV* 6704 ⑥ t	*TGV* 6784 Ⓐ		*TGV* 6756	*TGV* 9260	*TGV* 6710 ⑥ t		*TGV* 6714 ⊕	*TGV* 9284 ⊕	*TGV* 6762 ⊕		*TGV* 6766 Ⓐ v	*TGV* 6718 Ⓒ	*TGV* 9268 v	*TGV* 6722 Ⓐ	*TGV* 6726		*TGV* 6774	*TGV* 6776 Ⓑ h	*TGV* 6734 ⑦ e		*TGV* 9272	*TGV* 6770 ⑦ e	*TGV* 9274 ⑤⑦ z
Dijon d.	0620	0650	0653	...	0800	0925	0957	...	1052	1126	1152	...	1359	1457	1524	1621	1652	...	1758	1858	1918	...	2020	2121	2132
Montbard d.	|	0730	0730	...	|	|	|	...	1130	|	|	...	|	|	|	|	1731	...	|	|	1954	...	|	|	|
Paris Gare de Lyon a.	0802	0834	0837	...	0937	1103	1137	...	1237	1303	1333	...	1537	1637	1703	1759	1837	...	1936	2036	2103	...	2159	2303	2315

LILLE - DIJON - BESANÇON

	TGV 5330 ♠ s	*TGV* 5130	
Lille Flandres d.	...	1842	...
Charles de Gaulle ✈ d.	1121	1941	...
Marne la Vallée-Chessy § d.	1136	2000	...
Montbard d.	1244	2106	...
Dijon a.	1318	2139	...
Dole a.	...	2207	...
Besançon a.	...	2232	...

	TGV 5152 Ⓐ	*TGV* 5156 Ⓒ	*TGV* 5348 ♠
Besançon d.	0540	0652	...
Dole d.	0605	0717	...
Dijon d.	0632	0744	1709
Montbard d.	0707	0819	1745
Marne la Vallée-Chessy § a.	0806	0918	1843
Charles de Gaulle ✈ a.	0820	0932	1858
Lille Europe a.	0915	1027	...

MELUN - MARSEILLE

	TGV 6809 ①⑥ b
Melun d.	0733
Fontainebleau-Avon d.	0743
Sens d.	0814
Laroche Migennes d.	0836
Lyon Part Dieu a.	1005
Marseille **350** a.	1208

	TGV 6870 ⑦ e	*TGV* 6824 ⑤ f
Marseille **350** d.	1735	...
Lyon Part Dieu d.	1939	2026
Laroche Migennes a.	2101	2149
Sens a.	2125	2211
Fontainebleau-Avon a.	2153	2238
Melun a.	2206	2250

D – ①–④ to Apr. 1 (not Dec. 24, 31); Ⓐ from Apr. 6.
b – Also Dec. 25, Jan. 1, Apr. 6, May 25; not Apr. 5, May 24.
d – Also Feb. 20, 27, Apr. 5, May 24.
e – Also Apr. 5, May 24.
f – Also Dec. 24, 31, May 12; not Dec. 25, Jan. 1.
h – Not Dec. 25, Jan. 1, May 13.
m – Not Dec. 24, 31, Apr. 5, May 12, 13, 24.
s – Not Apr. 26 - 30, May 3 - 7.
t – Also Dec. 25, Jan. 1, May 13.
u – Not Apr. 4, Apr. 26 - May 7.
v – Not Apr. 6 - 9, 12 - 16.
z – Also Dec. 24, 26, 31, Feb. 27, Mar. 6, Apr. 1, 5, May 12, 24; not Dec. 25, Jan. 1.
TGV – Ⓡ, supplement payable, 🍸.
♠ – To / from Caen and Cherbourg (Table **275**).
⊕ – Not on ①–⑤ Apr. 6 - 23.
⊗ – Not Apr. 26 - May 7.
△ – Not on ①–⑤ Mar. 22 - Apr. 2, Apr. 26 - May 7.
▽ – Not on ①–⑤ Mar. 22 - Apr. 2.
§ – Station for Disneyland Paris.

371 PARIS - SENS - AUXERRE and DIJON *For TGV see Table 370*

km		⚒	⚒	⚒	⊗		⚒⊗			Ⓑd	⚒		Ⓑd		Ⓐ	Ⓒ	Ⓑd	Ⓐ	Ⓒ	Ⓐ	Ⓒ	Ⓑ	Ⓐ	Ⓒ		①–⑤
0	**Paris Bercy** d.	...	...	0620*	0720	0820	0920	1020	1220	...	1320	1420	...	1520	1613	1620	...	1713	1720	1813	1820	...	1913	1920	2020	2220
113	Sens d.	...	...	0729	0818	0915	1021	1115	1315	...	1415	1514	...	1615	1715	1714	...	1815	1815	1915	1915	...	2015	2015	2115	2323
147	Joigny d.	...	...	0752	0834	0931	1038	1131	1331	...	1432	1531	...	1632	1731	1731	...	1832	1832	1931	1931	...	2032	2032	2131	2353
	Auxerre ▷ d.		0722	|	|	|	|	|	|	1322	|	|	1522	|	|	|	1722	|	|	|	|	1922	|	|	|	|
156	Laroche Migennes a.		0735	0758	0840	0938	1044	1138	1338	1335	1438	1538	1535	1639	1738	1738	1735	1838	1839	1938	1938	1935	2038	2038	2138	2359
156	Laroche Migennes d.	0543	0743	0800	0844	0940	1046	1140	1340	1343	1443	1540	1543	1643	1740	1739	1743	1843	1844	1941	1940	1943	2043	2043	2140	...
175	**Auxerre** ▷ a.	|	|	0822	|	0953	|	1153	1353	|	|	1553	|	|	1753	1753	|	|	|	1954	1953	|	|	|	2153	...
197	Tonnerre d.	0611	0811	...	0910	...	1110	...	...	1411	1510	...	1611	1710	...	...	1811	1910	1910	...	...	2011	2110	2110	...	...
243	Montbard d.	0637	0837	...	0938	...	1138	...	...	1437	1538	...	1637	1738	...	...	1838	1938	1938	...	...	2038	2138	2138	...	...
315	**Dijon** a.	0718	0918	...	1016	...	1221	...	...	1517	1615	...	1718	1816	...	...	1918	2016	2016	...	...	2117	2216	2216	...	...

	Ⓐ	Ⓐ	⑥v	Ⓐ	⑥v	⚒		⚒	⚒		⊕	Ⓑ		Ⓒ				Ⓑd	Ⓑd			Ⓑd	⚒	†		Ⓑ
Dijon d.	...	...	...	0546	0546	0646	...	0748	0846	...	0946	1046	...	1225	...	1346	...	1546	1646	...	1746	1825	...	...	1946	2046
Montbard d.	...	...	...	0623	0623	0723	...	0826	0923	...	1024	1123	...	1326	...	1423	...	1623	1723	...	1821	1925	...	...	2023	2124
Tonnerre d.	...	...	...	0649	0651	0751	...	0851	0951	...	1051	1151	...	1351	...	1450	...	1651	1750	...	1849	1951	...	...	2051	2152
Auxerre ▷ d.	0450	*0556*	0600	|	|	|	0809	|	|	1009	|	|	1209	|	1409	|	1609	|	|	1809	|	|	1957	2009	|	|
Laroche Migennes a.	0508	*0610*	0613	0712	0723	0818	0823	0917	1018	1022	1117	1218	1222	1418	1422	1514	1622	1718	1818	1822	1916	2018	2010	2022	2118	2218
Laroche Migennes d.	0515	0613	0624	0714	0730	0826	0825	0923	1026	1024	1123	1226	1224	1426	1424	1520	1624	1724	1826	1824	1922	2026	2011	2024	2124	2228
Auxerre ▷ a.	|	|	|	|	|	0840	|	|	1040	|	|	1244	|	1440	|	|	|	|	1840	|	|	2040	|	|	|	2240
Joigny d.	0523	0620	0633	0721	0738	...	0833	0931	...	1033	1131	...	1233	...	1433	1528	1633	1733	...	1833	1931	...	2020	2033	2131	...
Sens d.	0542	0641	0651	0741	0757	...	0851	0951	...	1051	1151	...	1251	...	1451	1546	1651	1751	...	1851	1949	...	2039	2051	2149	...
Paris Bercy a.	0643	0744	0745	0843	0900	...	0945	1053	...	1144	1245	...	1344	...	1546	1644	1746	1846	...	1946	2044	...	2144	2146	2244	...

LOCAL SERVICES PARIS - LAROCHE MIGENNES ❖

km						△	Ⓐ	Ⓐz	Ⓐz		
0	**Paris Gare de Lyon** d.	0635	0835	1035	1235	1435	1633	1735	1835	1935	2035
45	Melun d.	0702	0902	1103	1302	1502	1657	|	|	2002	2101
60	Fontainebleau-Avon d.	0716	0916	1116	1316	1516	|	|	|	2016	2116
79	Montereau d.	0735	0935	1136	1335	1535	1724	1827	1925	2035	2135
113	Sens d.	0822	1019	1221	1423	1619	1752	1855	1953	2119	2219
147	Joigny d.	0853	1048	1249	1450	1649	1821	1922	2021	2148	2249
156	**Laroche Migennes** a.	0900	1056	1256	1457	1656	1828	1928	2028	2156	2256

	Ⓒ	Ⓐ	Ⓐ	Ⓐ						
Laroche Migennes d.	0603	0617	0642	0717	0803	1003	1203	1403	1603	1803
Joigny d.	0610	0624	0650	0724	0810	1010	1210	1410	1610	1810
Sens d.	0641	0653	0719	0753	0841	1041	1241	1441	1641	1841
Montereau d.	0710	0722	0748	0822	0910	1110	1310	1510	1710	1910
Fontainebleau-Avon d.	0731	|	0808	|	0931	1131	1331	1531	1731	1931
Melun d.	0744	|	0820	0845	0944	1144	1344	1544	1744	1944
Paris Gare de Lyon a.	0811	0810	0850	0911	1011	1213	1411	1611	1811	2012

d – Not Dec. 25, Jan. 1.
r – To / from Dijon (see table above).
v – Not Dec. 26, Jan. 2, May 1, 8.
z – Slower trains calling at Melun and Fontainebleau depart at 1743 Ⓐ, 1843 Ⓐ.
⊕ – Not on ①–⑤ Apr. 6 - 23.
⊗ – Not on ①–⑤ Apr. 26 - May 7.
* – Depart 0615 Jan. 11 - Feb. 12.
❖ – Also from Laroche Migennes at 0403, 0503 ⑥, 0542 Ⓐ, 0703 ⑥, 1503 ⑦, 1703 ⑦.
△ – Similar journeys run at 1635 Ⓒ, 1735 Ⓒ **d**, 1835 Ⓒ.
▷ – Additional local trains Laroche Migennes - Auxerre and v.v. (journey 20 minutes): From Laroche Migennes 0723 ⚒, 0853 ⚒, 1053 ⚒, 1653, 1853, 2053. From Auxerre 0650 Ⓐ, 0659 Ⓒ, 0850 ⚒, 1050, 1250 ⚒, 1650, 1850 Ⓑ **d**, 2050.

371a AUXERRE - AVALLON - AUTUN *2nd class only*

km		Ⓐr		r	⚒r	⚒	⚒r	r		r
	Paris Bercy **371** d.	...	0820	...	...	1220	...	...	1813n	...
	Laroche Mig. **371** d.	0607	0940	...	...	1340	...	...	1940	...
0	**Auxerre** d.	0625	1000	...	1210	1411	...	1801	1955	...
17	Cravant-Bazarnes a.	0644	1016	...	1226	1427	...	1818	2013	...
17	Cravant-Bazarnes d.	0645	1021	1024	1232	1432	1434	1823	2018	2022
53	Clamecy a.	|	1057	|	*1309*c	1506	|	*1921*c	2055	|
86	Corbigny a.	|	1134x	|	|	...	|	|	2136	|
41	Sermizelles-Vézelay § d.	0719	...	1057	1305	...	1507	1854	...	2052
55	**Avallon** a.	0735	...	1113	1321	...	1523	1920	...	2108

	⚒r	r		⑦x	r	⚒r	⚒	⚒r		Nr	Ⓑ	Er
Avallon d.	0552	0659	...	...	1036	1246	...	1647	...	1839	...	1931
Sermizelles-Vézelay § d.	0609	0717	...	...	1100	1306	...	1704	...	1856	...	1948
Corbigny d.	|	|	0628	...	|	|	...	|	...	|	1807x	|
Clamecy d.	*0614*c	|	0705	0906	|	|	1312	|	1658	|	1845	|
Cravant-Bazarnes a.	0641	0744	0741	0940	1132	1339	1346	1737	1734	1929	1926	2016
Cravant-Bazarnes d.	0656	...	0751	0941	1144	...	1351	...	1744	...	1936	2017
Auxerre a.	0714	...	0807	0958	1200	...	1408	...	1759	...	1952	2036
Laroche Mig. **371** a.	...	...	0823	...	...	...	1422	...	1822	...	...	...
Paris Bercy **371** a.	...	...	0945	...	...	...	1546	...	1946	...	...	...

km		⚒	⚒		F	
	Auxerre (see above) d.	...	...	...	1801r	...
0	**Avallon** d.	1118	1530	...	1927	...
42	Saulieu d.	1213	1631	...	2022	...
87	**Autun** a.	1309	1727	...	2118	...
	Étang **374** a.	1328	1751	...	2136	...

			Ⓐ	E
Étang **374** d.	0812	...	1430	...
Autun d.	0835	...	1450	1735
Saulieu d.	0930	...	1546	1830
Avallon a.	1024	...	1639	1924
Auxerre (see above) a.	1200r	...	...	2036r

E – ⑤–⑦ (also Apr. 5, May 13, 24; not Dec. 25, Jan. 1, Apr. 4, May 23).
F – ⑤⑦ (also Apr. 5, May 24; not Dec. 25, Jan. 1, Apr. 4, May 23).
N – ①②③④⑦.

c – Change at Cravant-Bazarnes.
n – 1820 on Ⓒ.
r – Subject to alteration Avallon - Cravant-Bazarnes and v.v. Apr. 6 - June 26.
x – ⑦ (also Apr. 5, May 13, 24; not Apr. 4, May 23).
§ – Station is 9 km from Vézelay.

DIJON and LYON - PARAY LE MONIAL - MOULINS SUR ALLIER 372

Subject to alteration Mar. 15 - Apr. 2 (all services Dijon/Montchanin - Moulins sur Allier and v.v.)

km		Ⓐ			⚒		Ⓐ			
0	**Dijon** ▷ d.	...	...	...	...	...	...	1716	...	...
37	Beaune ▷ d.	...	...	...	...	...	...	1738	...	...
	Chalon sur Saône ▷ d.	0538	...	...	...	...	...	|	...	2009
52	Chagny ▷ d.	0549	...	...	...	...	...	1756	...	2027
81	**Montchanin** ▷ d.	0612	0706	1006	1206	1442	1708	1817	1906	2056
96	Montceau les Mines d.	0625	0719	1020	1223	1457	1722	1829	1921	2110
131	Paray le Monial d.	0659	0754	1053	1256	1531	1801	1901	1954	2143
142	Digoin d.	...	0804	1102	1307	1541	1811	1910	...	...
198	**Moulins sur Allier** a.	...	0856	1151	1359	1631	1859	1953	...	...
	Clermont Ferrand **330** a.	...	...	...	...	...	...	2101r	...	...

		Ⓐ	Ⓐ	⑥⑦					
Clermont Ferrand **330** d.	...	...	0616	0834	...	...	...	...	...
Moulins sur Allier d.	...	...	0734	0942	1204	...	...	1651	1757
Digoin d.	...	...	0816	1025	1253	...	...	1740	1848
Paray le Monial d.	0600	0706	0827	1035	1304	1602	...	1800	1900
Montceau les Mines d.	0636	0742	0859	1106	1338	1635	...	1835	1936
Montchanin ▷ d.	0650	0755	0911	1120	1351	1650	1708	1849	1950
Chagny ▷ d.	...	...	0933	1145	...	...	1732	...	...
Chalon sur Saône ▷ a.	...	...	|	|	...	...	1749	...	...
Beaune ▷ d.	...	...	0945	1157	...	...	...	...	...
Dijon ▷ a.	...	...	1010	1221	...	...	...	...	...

LYON - PARAY LE MONIAL - MOULINS SUR ALLIER

km		c		Ⓐ		Ⓐ
0	**Lyon Perrache** d.	1226	...	1654	1751	1849
4	**Lyon Part Dieu** d.	1239	...	|	1804	|
64	Lamure sur Azergues d.	1329	...	1758	1903	1959
128	Paray le Monial d.	1425	...	1854	2002	2051
139	Digoin d.	1435	...	...	2011	...
195	**Moulins sur Allier** a.	1519	...	...	2053	...
	Orléans **290** a.	|	...	...	2249	...
	Tours **290** a.	1755	...	...	...	...

	⚒	Ⓐz	z	x	⑦e
Tours **290** d.	...	...	...	1213	...
Orléans **290** d.	...	⊡	0707	|	...
Moulins sur Allier d.	...	0613	0901	1444	...
Digoin d.	...	0701	0942	1526	...
Paray le Monial d.	0612	0714	0954	1537	2024
Lamure sur Azergues d.	0706	0808	1049	1631	2118
Lyon Part Dieu a.	|	|	1143	|	2205
Lyon Perrache a.	0810	0910	1158	1727	2217

c – Subject to alteration Feb. 1-5, 8-12.
e – Also Apr. 5, May 13, 24; not Apr. 4, May 23.
r – Change at Moulins sur Allier on † (a. 2110).
x – Subject to alteration Feb. 15-26, Apr. 19-30.
z – Subject to alteration Apr. 6-23.
⊡ – From Nevers (d. 0539).
▷ – For connections Dijon and Chalon sur Saône - Montchanin see Table **374**.

DIJON - CHALON SUR SAÔNE - LYON 373

For *TGV* trains Paris - Mâcon Loché TGV and v.v. see Tables **340/1**

km					*TGV* **6801**	*TGV* **6813**					*TGV* **6811**					*TGV* **6781**	*TGV* **5148/9**						*TGV* **5462**	
		Ⓐ	⚒ ◇	Ⓐ	Ⓐ ♠	①⑥ z♥	Ⓐ	⑥ c	Ⓐ	Ⓒ	Ⓒ ♠	Ⓐ		Ⓐ C		Ⓐ	M	Ⓐ			◇	Ⓐ	P	△
0	*Paris Gare de Lyon* **370** d.	...	...	...	...	...	...	...	...	...	...	...	...	...	...	0658	...	...	...	...	...	...	...	...
315	**Dijon** **372 374** d.	...	...	0533	0549	0616	...	...	0633	0633	0645	...	0718	0733	0833	0846	0916	0933	1008v	1033	...	1120	1124	1223v
352	Beaune **372 374** d.	...	...	0553	|	|	...	...	0653	0653	|	...	0747	0752	0853	0907	|	0953	1046	1053	...	1153	|	1253
367	Chagny **372** d.	...	...	0603	|	|	...	...	0704	0704	|	...	0758	0802	0904	|	|	1003	1058	1103	...	1203	|	1303
382	**Chalon sur Saône** d.	...	...	0616	0624	0652	...	...	0716	0716	0721	...	0808	0815	0915	0924	0954	1016	1108	1116	...	1216	1158	1316
440	Mâcon Ville d.	0553	0632	0646	0653	0722	0712	0725	0746	0746	0752	0816	...	0846	0946	...	1024	1046	...	1146	1232	1246	1227	1346
478	Villefranche sur Saône ⊖ d.	0627	0703	0709	|	|	0735	0759	0809	0814	|	0841	...	0909	1009	...	|	1109	...	1210	1304	1309	|	1409
512	**Lyon Part Dieu** a.	0652	|	0735	0727	0800	0805	|	0835	0839	0831	0905	...	0935	1035	...	1057	1135	...	1235	|	1335	1255	1435
	Grenoble **343** a.	...	|	0911	...	...	|	|	1011	...	...	|	...	...	1211	...	...	1311	...	1411	|	1511	...	1611
512	**Lyon Perrache** a.	...	0733	...	...	...	0817	0827	...	...	...	0917	...	...	...	...	...	...	...	...	1333	...	...	...

			TGV **5117/6**		*TGV* **6829**								*TGV* **6789**		**4264 4265**					**4266 4267**				
	Ⓐ △	△	B ⊗		N	Ⓐ ◇		Ⓐ	◇	Ⓐ	Ⓐ C			Ⓐ	⑤ d		Ⓐ C			A	⚒	⑦ y		⑤⑦ u
Paris Gare de Lyon **370** d.	...	...	...	...	...	...	...	...	...	...	...	...	1658	...	...	...	...	...	...	...	...	...	...	...
Dijon **372 374** d.	1323	1423v	1516	1533	1616	...	1633	1650	...	1721	1733	1833	1843	1850	1908	1918	1933	...	2033	2048	2118	2133	2218	2318
Beaune **372 374** d.	1353	1453	|	1553	|	...	1653	1715	...	1749	1753	1853	1905	1916	|	1947	1953	...	2053	|	2147	2154	2246	2347
Chagny **372** d.	1403	1503	|	1603	|	...	1703	1724	...	1801	1804	1903	|	1925	|	1958	2003	...	2103	|	2158	2205	2258	2358
Chalon sur Saône d.	1416	1516	1551	1616	1651	...	1716	1735	...	1811	1816	1916	1921	1935	1953	2008	2015	...	2116	2124	2208	2217	2309	0008
Mâcon Ville d.	1447	1546	1623	1646	1722	1734	1746	...	1834	...	1846	1946	...	...	2021	...	2046	...	2146	2153	...	2250	...	...
Villefranche sur Saône ⊖ d.	1514	1608	|	1709	|	1804	1809	...	1904	...	1909	2010	...	...	|	...	2109	...	2214	|	...	2313	...	...
Lyon Part Dieu a.	1546	1637	1701	1735	1757	|	1835	...	|	..	1935	2038	...	...	2059	...	2135	...	2237	2229	...	2337	...	...
Grenoble **343** a.	1731	1811	...	1911	...	|	2011	...	|	...	...	2211	...	...	|	...	...	...	|	|	...	|	...	...
Lyon Perrache a.	...	...	...	...	...	1833	...	...	1934	...	...	...	...	...	2114	...	...	...	2251	2242	...	2351	...	...

		TGV **6784**			*TGV* **6786**		**4336 4337**								*TGV* **6850**			*TGV* **6792**	*TGV* **5170**					*TGV* **5198/9**
	Ⓐ	Ⓐ	① g	⚒	⑥ t	Ⓐ	A		§	Ⓐ ◇	Ⓐ	◇		△	Ⓒ ♠	Ⓐ △	△	Ⓐ ⊕	B ▽		Ⓐ		Ⓐ	M
Lyon Perrache d.	...	...	0508	...	...	0608	0635	...	...	0723	...	0823	...	...	...	...	...	...	...	...	...	...	1323	...
Grenoble **343** d.	...	...	|	...	...	|	|	...	0544	|	0644	|	...	0744	...	0844	0944	...	...	...	1044	1144	|	...
Lyon Part Dieu d.	...	...	0522	...	...	0622	0648	...	0722	|	0822	|	...	0922	1000	1022	1122	...	1200	...	1222	1322	|	1400
Villefranche sur Saône ⊖ d.	...	...	0549	...	...	0649	|	...	0749	0754	0849	0856	...	0949	|	1049	1149	...	|	...	1249	1349	1355	|
Mâcon Ville d.	...	...	0611	0611	...	0713	0725	...	0812	0824	0913	0924	...	1013	1038	1112	1213	...	1238	...	1313	1413	1426	1437
Chalon sur Saône d.	0534	0604	0644	0644	0708	0744	0754	0759	0845	...	0945	...	...	1045	1108	1145	1245	1305	1310	...	1349	1445	...	1506
Chagny **372** d.	0545	|	0654	0654	|	0755	|	0809	0855	...	0955	...	...	1055	|	1155	1255	|	|	...	1400	1455	...	|
Beaune **372 374** d.	0555	0622	0705	0705	0727	0804	|	0821	0905	...	1005	...	...	1105	|	1205	1305	1322	|	...	1411	1505	...	|
Dijon **372 374** a.	0620	0640	0724	0724	0747	0823	0827	0849	0924	...	1024	...	...	1124	1143	1234	1334	1344	1354	...	1434	1534x	...	1539
Paris Gare de Lyon **370** a.	...	0837	...	...	0937	...	...	...	...	...	...	...	...	...	...	...	...	1537	...	...	...	...	...	...

															TGV **5464**				*TGV* **6880**		*TGV* **6876**			
	Ⓐ				Ⓑ		Ⓐ	Ⓐ	C		⚒ ◇	Ⓐ	C	Ⓑ ◇	P			Ⓐ	⑤⑦ b♥		N	Ⓐ		
Lyon Perrache d.	...	...	...	...	...	...	1623	1639	...	...	1723	1739	...	1823	...	...	...	...	...	...	...	2203	...	...
Grenoble **343** d.	1244	...	1344	...	1444	...	|	|	...	...	|	|	...	|	...	1744	...	1844	...	1944	...	|	...	...
Lyon Part Dieu d.	1422	...	1522	...	1622	...	|	1652	1722	...	|	1752	1822	|	1900	1922	...	2022	2126	2122	2156	2217	...	...
Villefranche sur Saône ⊖ d.	1449	...	1549	...	1650	...	1656	1719	1749	...	1754	1820	1849	1854	|	1949	...	2048	|	2152	|	2244	...	...
Mâcon Ville d.	1513	...	1613	...	1712	...	1725	1744	1813	...	1824	1845	1913	1924	1937	2013	...	2113	2202	2217	2235	2308	...	...
Chalon sur Saône d.	1545	1625	1645	1725	1745	1749	...	...	1844	...	...	...	1945	...	2006	2045	...	2145	2232	2250	2304	...	...	...
Chagny **372** d.	1555	1639	1655	1739	1755	1803	...	...	1854	...	...	...	1955	...	|	2055	...	2155	|	2259	|	...	...	...
Beaune **372 374** d.	1605	1649	1705	1749	1805	1815	...	...	1905	...	...	...	2005	...	|	2105	...	2205	|	2309	|	...	...	...
Dijon **372 374** a.	1624	1714	1724	1814	1824	1844	...	...	1924	...	...	...	2024	...	2044	2124	...	2224	2305	2328	2340	...	...	...
Paris Gare de Lyon **370** a.	...	...	...	...	...	...	...	...	...	...	...	...	...	...	...	...	...	...	...	...	...	...	...	...

A – 🚃12 Metz - Dijon - Lyon and v.v.
B – 🚃12 and 🍷 Dijon - Montpellier - Toulouse - Bordeaux and v.v.
C – To/from Chambéry (Table **344**).
M – 🚃12 and 🍷 Metz - Lyon - Marseille - Nice and v.v. (Table **350**).
N – 🚃12 and 🍷 Dijon - Lyon - Marseille - Nice and v.v. (Table **350**).
P – 🚃12 and 🍷 Metz - Dijon - Lyon - Montpellier and v.v. (Table **350**).

b – Also Dec. 24, 31, Apr. 5, May 12, 24; not Dec. 25, Jan. 1.
c – Not May 1, 8.
d – Also Dec. 18, 23, 30, Apr. 29, May 6, 19; not Dec. 25, Jan. 1, Apr. 30, May 7, 21.
g – Also Apr. 6, May 25; not Apr. 5, May 24.
t – Also Dec. 25, Jan. 1, May 13.
u – Also Dec. 24, 31, Apr. 5, May 12, 24; not Dec. 25, Jan. 1, Apr. 4, May 23.
v – 10 minutes later on Ⓒ.
x – 1524 on Ⓒ.

y – Also Apr. 5, May 24; not Apr. 4, May 23.
z – Also Dec. 25, Jan. 1, Apr. 6, May 13, 25; not Apr. 5, May 24.

TGV – Ⓡ, supplement payable, 🍷.

♠ – To/from Marseille (Table **350**).
♥ – To/from Montpellier (Table **350**).
◇ – To/from Valence Ville (Table **351**).
⊖ – Villefranche is also served by 🚌 service to Mâcon Loché TGV station, connecting with *TGV* trains to/from Paris (Tables **340/1**).
⊕ – Subject to alteration on Ⓐ Feb. 1-26.
⊗ – On Dec. 14-18 and ①–⑤ Feb. 15 - Mar. 12 depart Dijon 1436 and runs non-stop to Lyon.
△ – Subject to alteration on Dec. 14-18 and ①–⑤ Jan. 25 - Mar. 12.
▽ – On ①–⑤ Feb. 1-26 runs non-stop Lyon - Dijon, arrive 1436.

374 DIJON - MONTCHANIN - ÉTANG - AUTUN and NEVERS

km			⚒k	b	d	⚒c	Ⓑh	Ⓑx		⑤	N
0	**Dijon** **372 373** d.	0603	0702	0903	1053	1329	1603	1703	1803	1900	1903
37	Beaune **372 373** d.	0627	0726	0928	1127	1359	1628	1724	1831	1921	1927
81	Montchanin d.	0659	0754	1002	1155	1426	1705	1753	1902	1949	1954
89	Le Creusot d.	0706	0802	1008	1203	1435	1712	1800	1911	1957	2002
111	**Étang** d.	0720	0816	1022	1217	1449	1726	1813	1926	2010	2016
179	Decize d.	0803	0855	1103	1300	1533	1808	1851	2008	2052	2100
216	**Nevers** a.	0829	0918	1127	1326	1600	1833	1913	2032	2117	2126
	Bourges **290** a.	...	0958	...	...	...	...	2008	...	...	...
	Vierzon **290** a.	...	1017	...	...	...	...	2027	...	...	...
	Tours **290** a.	...	1136	...	...	...	...	2151	...	...	...

	Ⓐ	Ⓐ		⚒z	†			Ⓑ		Ⓑx
Tours **290** d.	...	...	...	0703	...	...	...	...	...	1817
Vierzon **290** d.	...	...	...	0824	...	...	...	...	...	1938
Bourges **290** d.	...	...	...	0842	...	...	...	...	...	1958
Nevers d.	0525	0622	0728	0930	0930	1219	1528	1723	1826	2044
Decize d.	0550	0648	0756	0952	0952	1245	1555	1753	1850	2108
Étang d.	0635	0731	0839	1029	1029	1333	1639	1839	1937	2147
Le Creusot d.	0652	0746	0855	1042	1042	1348	1653	1853	1952	2201
Montchanin d.	0700	0800	0903	1100	1100	1400	1700	1902	2000	|
Beaune **372 373** d.	0730	0829	0930	1130	1130	1429	1732	1931	2030	2233
Dijon **372 373** a.	0751	0854	0949	1150	1150	1504r	1754	1953	2051	2255

km		⚒	Ⓐ	u			Ⓐ	Ⓑ	⑥		
0	**Chalon sur Saône** d.	0608	0701	0909	...	1608	1719	1806	1806	2009	...
15	Chagny d.	0621	0714	0921	...	1625	1738	1823	1823	2027	...
44	Montchanin d.	0650	0743	1015	...	1714	1812	1919	1919	2055	...
52	Le Creusot d.	...	...	1024	...	1729	1821	1931	1931	...	...
74	Étang a.	...	...	1047	...	1751	1845	1955	1955	...	...
89	**Autun** a.	...	...	...	...	...	...	2017	...	...	...

	Ⓐ	Ⓐ	⚒	⚒	⚒n		⑤⑦v	Ⓐ		
Autun d.	...	...	...	...	...	...	1640	...	...	...
Étang d.	...	0603	0655	0750	1300	...	1704	1811	...	...
Le Creusot d.	...	0628	0721	0814	1326	...	1720	1828	...	...
Montchanin d.	0623	0634	0729	0821	1333	1708	1728	1837	1909	2009
Chagny d.	0707	...	0809*	0847	...	1732	1754	...	1936	2035
Chalon sur Saône a.	0723	...	0825	0904	...	1749	1807	...	1948	2048

CONNECTIONS ÉTANG - AUTUN

km		Ⓐ 🚌	⚒	a	🚌		Ⓐ a	⚒ 🚌		Ⓐ 🚌		Ⓑ 🚌	Ⓑ
0	Étang d.	0639	0727	0812	1053	1250	1430	1457	1712	1731	1829	1852	2000
15	Autun a.	0700	0745	0830	1114	1308	1447	1518	1730	1752	1847	1911	2017

	⚒	⚒	⚒ 🚌	⚒ a	🚌	⑤⑦ w	⚒ a	E 🚌	Ⓐ		⑤⑦ w
Autun d.	0609	0749	1217	1310	1607	1640	1733	1807	1808	1852	2119
Étang a.	0627	0806	1238	1328	1628	1657	1751	1828	1827	1910	2136

E – ⑤⑦ (also Apr. 5, May 1, 8, 13, 24).
N – ①②③④⑦ only.
a – To/from Avallon (Table **371a**).
b – Subject to alteration on ①–⑤ Jan. 25 - Feb. 5, Apr. 19-30.
c – Not Dec. 26, Jan. 2. Depart Dijon 1339 on ⑥. On Dec. 14-18 and ①–⑤ Feb. 15 - Mar. 12 depart Dijon 1411, not calling at Beaune or Chagny.
d – Depart Dijon 1103 on ©.
h – Not Dec. 25, Jan. 1.
k – On ①–⑤ Feb. 8-26 runs only to Nevers.
n – Not Jan. 11-15, 18-22.
r – 1451 on ©.
u – Not Jan. 25-29, Feb. 1-5.
v – Also Apr. 5, May 24; not Dec. 25, Jan. 1, Apr. 4, May 23.
w – Also Apr. 5, May 23; not Dec. 25, Jan. 1, Apr. 4, May 23.
x – Not Apr. 4, May 23.
z – Not on ①–⑤ Feb. 1-26.
* – Arrive 0754.

Additional 🚌 Étang - Autun: 2021 ⑤⑦ **E**.

375 DIJON - LAUSANNE and BERN

Special global fares are payable for international journeys. Certain trains continue beyond Lausanne to Aigle or Brig in Winter - see Table **42**

km		⚒	⚒	*TGV* **9261**		Ⓐ	©		*TGV* **9269** b	⚒	*TGV* **9271** ⑦ e	Ⓐ			*TGV* **9273**	*TGV* **9285** ⑤ f		*TGV* **9287** L		*TGV* **9277**		⑤	†
0	*Paris Gare de Lyon* **370** d.	...	...	0758	...	...	...	...	1258	...	1358	...	...	...	1558	1558	...	1658	...	1758	...	...	...
315	**Dijon** **376 377** d.	...	...	0938	...	...	...	...	1440	...	1540	...	...	1654	1738	1738	...	1846	...	1938	...	...	...
361	Dole **376 377** d.	0614	...	|	...	...	1221	...	1505	...	|	...	...	1731	1804	1804	...	|	...	|	...	2141	2141
393	Mouchard **376** d.	0633	...	1018	...	...	1244	...	|	...	|	...	...	1755	|	|	...	1935	...	2018	...	2201	2201
417	Andelot **376** d.	0653	...	|	...	...	1302	...	|	...	|	...	...	1812	|	|	...	|	...	|	...	2218	2218
438	Frasne d.	0710	0816	1050	...	1315	1315	...	1549	1554	1649	1715	...	1827	1848	1857	...	2005	...	2049	...	2233	2233
454	Pontarlier 🏛 a.	0728	0831	|	...	1331	1331	...	|	1609	|	1730	...	1842	|	1904	...	2019	...	|	...	2249	2249
462	Vallorbe 🏛 a.	...	...	1102	...	...	...	...	1602	...	1702	...	...	...	1902	|	...	|	...	2102	...	...	...
508	**Lausanne** a.	...	...	1137	...	...	...	...	1637	...	1737	...	...	...	1940	|	...	|	...	2137	...	...	...
518	Neuchâtel **511** a.	...	...	...	...	...	...	...	...	...	...	...	...	...	...	1947	...	2107	...	...	...	...	...
561	**Bern 511** a.	...	...	...	...	...	...	...	...	...	...	...	...	...	...	2036	...	2140	...	...	...	...	...

	⚒		⚒	*TGV* **9260**		*TGV* **9284** n	*TGV* **9264** n		⑥⑦				*TGV* **9268** d		©	Ⓐ			*TGV* **9272**		*TGV* **9274** ⑤⑦ z		
Bern 511 d.	...	...	...	...	...	0831	...	...	...	...	...	...	...	...	...	...	...	...	...	...	...	...	...
Neuchâtel **511** d.	...	...	...	...	...	0910	...	...	...	...	...	...	...	...	...	...	...	...	...	...	...	...	...
Lausanne d.	...	...	...	0722	...	|	0922	...	...	...	...	...	1322	...	...	...	...	...	1803	...	1922	...	...
Vallorbe 🏛 d.	...	...	...	0757	...	|	0957	...	...	...	...	...	1357	...	...	...	...	...	1840	...	1957	...	...
Pontarlier 🏛 d.	0541	...	0748	|	...	0954	|	...	1151	1151	...	1348	|	...	1610	1645	1803	...	|	...	|	...	...
Frasne d.	0558	...	0804	0814	...	1019	1019	...	1206	1204	...	1403	1414	...	1627	1701	1819	...	1906	...	2014	...	...
Andelot **376** d.	0611	...	...	|	...	|	|	...	1221	...	...	...	|	...	1641	...	1832	...	|	...	|	...	...
Mouchard **376** d.	0628	...	...	0842	...	|	|	...	1238	...	...	...	|	...	1658	...	1850	...	1936	...	2049	...	...
Dole **376 377** d.	0653	...	...	|	...	|	|	...	1300	...	...	...	|	...	1720	...	1906	...	|	...	2106	...	...
Dijon **376 377** a.	...	...	...	0922	...	1123	1123	...	...	...	...	...	1521	...	...	...	...	...	2013	...	2129	...	...
Paris Gare de Lyon **370** a.	...	...	...	1103	...	1303	1303	...	...	...	...	...	1703	...	...	...	...	...	2159	...	2315	...	...

L – Daily except ⑤ (runs Dec. 25, Jan. 1; not Dec. 24, 31, May 12).
b – Not on ①–⑤ Mar. 21 - Apr. 2.
d – Not Apr. 5-9, 12-16.
e – Also Feb. 20, 27, Apr. 5, May 24.
f – Also Dec. 24, 31, May 12; not Dec. 25, Jan. 1.
n – Not on ①–⑤ Apr. 6-23.
z – Also Dec. 24, 26, 31, Feb. 27, Mar. 6, Apr. 1, 5, May 12, 24; not Dec. 25, Jan. 1.
TGV –Ⓡ, supplement payable, 🍷.

376 DOLE / BESANÇON - ST CLAUDE - OYONNAX

km		🚌	⚒					🚌	⑤	⑤⑦ w
0	**Dole** **375 377** d.	...	...	0920	...	...	...	...	...	1834
	Besançon Viotte d.	...	...	|	1110	...	1645	...	1813	|
32	Mouchard **375** d.	...	...	0943	1140	...	1720	...	1845	1858
56	Andelot **375** a.	...	...	1000	1158	...	1741	...	...	1917
56	Andelot d.	...	0712	1005	1203	...	1746	...	...	1922
70	Champagnole d.	...	0732	1016	1215	...	1800	...	...	1935
105	Morez a.	...	0817	1058	1259	...	1846	...	...	2017
105	Morez d.	...	0822	1103	1304	...	1851	...	...	2022
128	**St Claude** a.	0750	0847	1129	1329	...	1916	1925	...	2047
161	Oyonnax (*see below*) a.	0835	...	1207c	...	...	...	2010	...	...

	⚒	🚌		⚒						⑦ e
Oyonnax (*see below*) d.	...	0655	...	...	...	1414c	...	...	...	...
St Claude d.	0613	0740	...	1030	...	1452	...	1644	...	1818
Morez a.	0639	...	...	1056	...	1519	...	1709	...	1845
Morez d.	0644	...	...	1101	...	1524	...	1714	...	1851
Champagnole d.	0729	...	...	1143	...	1606	...	1759	...	1936
Andelot a.	0741	...	...	1155	...	1622	...	1810	...	1946
Andelot **375** d.	0746	...	...	1200	...	1630	...	1814	...	1949
Mouchard **375** d.	0804	...	...	1220	...	1647	...	1838	...	2010
Besançon Viotte a.	|	...	...	1247	...	|	...	1907	...	2031
Dole **375 377** a.	0828	...	...	...	...	1707r	...	...	...	...

🚌 ST CLAUDE - OYONNAX - BOURG EN BRESSE — Bus service

🚌	⚒		⚒				Ⓐ	†	Ⓑ	
St Claude d.	0630	...	...	1140	1240	1425	...	1650	1745	1840
Oyonnax d.	0715	0915	1115	1225	1325	1510	1600	1735	1830	1925
Brion Montréal la Cluse. d.	0735	0935	1135	1250	1345	1530	1625	1755	1855	1950
Bourg en Bresse a.	0825	1025	1225	1350	1435	1620	1715	1845	1955	2040

🚌	Ⓐ	⚒	⚒			⚒			⚒	Ⓑ	
Bourg en Bresse d.	0620	0745	0915	1010	1215	1335	1530	1715	1910	2005	2125
Brion Montréal la Cluse d.	0715	0830	1000	1055	1300	1420	1615	1800	1955	2050	2210
Oyonnax a.	0740	0850	1020	1115	1325	1440	1635	1820	2015	2120	2235
St Claude a.	0825	...	1105	...	1410	...	1720	1905	...	...	2320

🚌 BELLEGARDE - BRION MONTRÉAL LA CLUSE: From Bellegarde 0550 Ⓐ, 1200 ⚒, 1720. From Brion Montréal la Cluse 1310 ⚒, 1830. Journey 50 minutes

c – ③⑥⑦ (also holidays).
e – Also Dec. 25, Jan. 1, Apr. 5, May 13, 24.
r – 1716 on ⑦.
w – Also Dec. 24, 31, Apr. 5, May 12, 13, 24; not Apr. 4, May 23.

DIJON - BESANÇON - BELFORT 377

km												TGV 6751			TGV 6755	TGV 6757				TGV 6759				
		Ⓐ	⑥	Ⓐ	Ⓐ	⚒	⚒	⚒	⚒	Ⓐ	Ⓒ	Ⓐ	Ⓐ	Ⓒ	Ⓐ	Ⓐ ⊗	Ⓒ		⊖	⚒ ⊖		⊖	⚒ ▽	▽	⚒ ⊖
	Paris Gare de Lyon 370 d.	...	...	...	...	...	...	...	...	...	...	...	0658	...	...	0828	0824	...	...	...	1028	...	...	...	...
0	**Dijon** 375 376 d.	...	...	0512	...	...	0607	0641	0705	0734	0734	0800	0843	0945	0948	1008	1009	1039	...	1136	1208	1215	...	1328	...
46	Dole 375 376 d.	...	...	0543	...	...	0645	0714	0739	0806	0806	0832	0909	1016	1021	1035	1035	1109	...	1216	|	1252	...	1358	...
91	**Besançon Viotte** a.	...	...	0617	...	...	0724	0742	0818	0834	0835	0900	0936	1047	1053	1101	1100	1138	...	1253	1257	1328	...	1424	...
91	**Besançon Viotte** 384 d.	0541	0610	0619	0647	0703	...	0744	...	0836	...	...	...	1048	...	...	...	...	1210	...	1303	...	1338	...	1520
170	Montbéliard 384 d.	0642	0713	0723	0744	0810	...	0844	...	0934	...	...	...	1146	...	...	...	...	1310	...	1354	...	1437	...	1621
188	**Belfort** 384 a.	0656	0727	0738	0759	0825	...	0858	...	0949	...	...	...	1200	...	...	...	...	1324	...	1408	...	1453	...	1635

				TGV 6765										TGV 6769			TGV 6773	TGV 6773			TGV 5130/1	TGV 6775		TGV 6777	
	Ⓐ		⑤ f	Ⓐ		Ⓑ			P	Ⓐ q	Ⓐ Q	⑦ Q	⑥		Ⓑ			⑤⑦ w		⑤-⑦ d	L	⑤ f	①-④ m	⑤⑦ w	⑤-⑦ n
Paris Gare de Lyon 370 d.	...	...	...	1427	...	...	...	...	...	...	...	...	...	1728	...	...	1928	1928	...	...	...	2028	...	2128	...
Dijon 375 376 d.	1454	...	1550	1608	1615	1642	1716	...	1750	1814	1833	1834	1851	1908	1916	2003	2111	2111	2117	2117	2142	2210	2219	2308	2315
Dole 375 376 d.	1527	...	1624	|	1647	1727	1750	...	1828	1846	1909	1909	1923	1934	1950	2036	2137	2137	2148	2148	2209	2235	2251	2334	2353
Besançon Viotte a.	1558	...	1656	1703	1724	1803	1818	...	1902	1915	1944	1943	1951	1959	2018	2106	2205	2205	2216	2216	2232	2301	2319	0001	0020
Besançon Viotte 384 d.	...	1630	...	...	1726	...	1820	1835	1906	...	...	...	...	2006	2020	...	...	2208	...	2218	...	...	...	...	...
Montbéliard 384 d.	...	1731	...	...	1830	...	1922	1945	2019	...	...	...	...	2057	2118	...	...	2259	...	2321	...	...	...	...	...
Belfort 384 a.	...	1746	...	...	1848	...	1937	2000	2034	...	...	...	...	2111	2133	...	...	2313	...	2338	...	...	...	...	...

		TGV 6700	TGV 5152/3		TGV 6754				TGV 5156/7	TGV 6756	TGV 6756											TGV 6762	TGV 6762		
	Ⓐ	① g	Ⓐ L	Ⓐ	Ⓐ		P	Ⓐ	Ⓒ L		Ⓐ	⚒ Q	⚒ b	Ⓐ y		Ⓐ						⑥ t	⊕		⚒ ▷
Belfort 384 d.	...	...	...	...	...	0501	...	...	...	...	0552	...	0556	0625	0645	0729	...	0812	0900	0917	...	0944	...	...	...
Montbéliard 384 d.	...	...	...	...	...	0516	...	...	...	...	0606	...	0611	0640	0700	0744	...	0827	0920	0931	...	0958	...	...	...
Besançon Viotte 384 a.	...	...	...	...	...	0620	...	...	...	...	0656	...	0723	0739	0815	0844	...	0930	1018	1033	...	1048	...	...	...
Besançon Viotte d.	0508	0524	0540	0545	0556	...	0626	...	0652	0706	0706	0709	0728	0741	0816	...	0909	...	...	...	1039	1055	1055	...	1227
Dole 375 376 d.	0535	0549	0605	0614	0623	...	0658	0713	0717	0731	0731	0752	0756	0818	0900	...	0938	...	...	...	1110	1122	1122	...	1305
Dijon 375 376 a.	0605	0613	0629	0643	0647	...	0738	0749	0741	0757	0757	0823	0833	0847	0932	...	1011	...	...	...	1141	1145	1145	...	1343
Paris Gare de Lyon 370 a.	...	0800	...	...	0837	...	...	...	...	0937	0937	...	...	...	...	...	...	...	...	...	...	1333	1333	...	...

		TGV 6766								TGV 6774				TGV 6776									TGV 6770		
	▷	Ⓐ v	⑦ s	⚒ ▷	▷			Ⓐ					Ⓐ	Ⓑ h		Ⓐ	Ⓒ	⚒	⚒	Ⓑ	Ⓑ	⑦ u	⑦ e	Ⓐ	
Belfort 384 d.	1138	...	...	1217	1326	...	...	...	1535	1553	...	...	1623	...	...	1710	...	1738	...	1815	...	1910	...	1934	2020
Montbéliard 384 d.	1153	...	...	1231	1340	...	...	...	1550	1607	...	...	1637	...	...	1725	...	1753	...	1830	...	1925	...	1949	2035
Besançon Viotte 384 a.	1256	...	...	1342	1444	...	...	...	1652	1657	...	...	1749	...	...	1824	...	1907	...	1935	...	2025	...	2050	2134
Besançon Viotte d.	...	1301	1310	1345	1446	...	1531	1638	...	1704	1711	1727	1751	1803	...	1826	1835	...	1914	...	2006	...	2032	...	2136
Dole 375 376 d.	...	1327	1341	1416	1525	...	1605	1713	...	1729	1747	1803	1830	1826	...	1911	1911	...	1956	...	2037	...	|	...	2212
Dijon 375 376 a.	...	1352	1411	1450	1559	...	1638	1748	...	1754	1819	1840	1906	1851	...	1940	1940	...	2027	...	2107	...	2118	...	2246
Paris Gare de Lyon 370 a.	...	1537	...	...	...	...	...	...	...	1936	...	...	...	2036	...	...	...	...	...	...	...	...	2303	...	...

L – [12] Lille - Charles de Gaulle ✈ - Besançon and v.v. (Table **370**).
P – Daily to Apr. 13; ⑤ Apr. 16 - June 4; daily from June 6.
Q – To Apr. 13 / from June 6.
b – Not on ①-④ Apr. 14 - May 3.
d – Also Dec. 24, 31, Apr. 5, May 12, 13, 24.
e – Also Apr. 5, May 24.
f – Also Dec. 24, 31, May 12; not Dec. 25, Jan. 1.
g – Also Apr. 6, May 25; not Apr. 5, May 24.
h – Not Dec. 25, Jan. 1, May 13.
m – Not Apr. 5, May 13, 24.
n – Also Dec. 24, 31, Apr. 5, May 13, 24.
q – Not on ①-④ Apr. 14 - June 4.
s – Also Dec. 25, Jan. 1, May 13, 24.
t – Also Dec. 25, Jan. 1, May 13.
u – Also Dec. 25, Jan. 1, Apr. 5, May 13, 24.
v – Not Apr. 6 - 9, 12 - 16.
w – Also Dec. 24, 31, Apr. 5, May 12, 24; not Dec. 25, Jan. 1.
y – Will not run Besançon - Dijon on ⑤ Apr. 16 - June 4 or May 13, 24.

TGV – Ⓡ, supplement payable, 🍷.
⊕ – Not on ①-⑤ Apr. 6 - 23.
⊗ – Not Apr. 26 - May 7.
⊖ – Subject to alteration on ①-⑤ Mar. 22 - Apr. 2.
△ – Not on ①-⑤ Mar. 22 - Apr. 2, Apr. 26 - May 7.
▽ – Not on ①-⑤ Mar. 22 - Apr. 2.
▷ – Not on ①-⑤ Apr. 6 - 16.

BESANÇON - LE LOCLE - LA CHAUX DE FONDS 378

km		A		Ⓐ		⑥t	†	Ⓐb	Ⓐ		†
0	**Besançon Viotte** d.	...	...	0713	1003	1225	1346	1356	1721	1824	2009
67	Morteau d.	0623	0725	0840	1122	1350	1502	1520	1855	1950	2131
80	Le Locle **512** a.	0640	0741	...	1140	...	...	1538	...	2007	...
88	**La Chaux de F 512** a.	0650	0751c	...	1149	...	...	1550	...	2017	...

	⚒	A		Ⓐ	⑥		A	⑥	†	
La Chaux de F 512 d.	...	0658	0810r	...	...	1610	1710	...	...	2041
Le Locle **512** d.	...	0704	0820	...	...	1620	1720	...	...	2051
Morteau d.	0650	0721	0842	1129	1227	1638	1738	1825	2010	2109
Besançon Viotte a.	0812	...	1001	1251	1348	1753	1858	1947	2126	...

A – ①-⑤ (not holidays or Apr. 2).
b – Not May 3 - 7, 10 - 12.
c – *0758* on ©.
r – *0802* on ©.
t – Not May 1, 8.

METZ - NANCY - DIJON 379

km		TGV 5148		TGV 5462		4264 4265	4266 4267		4248 4295	4248 4249
				⊕		⑤ f			N Ⓡ	P Ⓡ
0	**Luxembourg** 388 d.	...	...	...	...	...	...	...	1930	1930
34	Thionville 388 d.	...	...	...	...	...	...	...	2010	2010
64	**Metz** 388 d.	0611	...	0811	...	1530	1713	...	2040	2040
121	**Nancy** 388 d.	0651	...	0856	...	1631	1806	...	2159	2159
154	Toul d.	|	...	|	...	1652	1828	...	2220	2220
198	Neufchâteau d.	|	...	0941	...	1717	1853	...	2247	2247
272	Culmont Chalindrey a.	|	...	|	...	|	1939	...	2332	2332
272	Culmont Chalindrey d.	|	...	|	...	|	1951	...	2355	2355
349	**Dijon** a.	0906	...	1115	...	1848	2036	...	|	|
	Lyon Part-Dieu **373** a.	1057	...	1255	...	2059	2229	...	|	|
	Lyon Perrache **373** a.	|	...	|	...	2114	2242	...	|	|
	Avignon TGV **350** a.	1212	...	|	...	...	...	...	|	|
	Avignon Centre **351** a.	|	...	|	...	...	...	...	0449	|
	Arles **351** a.	|	...	|	...	...	...	...	0511	|
	Montpellier **355** a.	|	...	1455	...	...	...	...	|	0627
	Perpignan **355** d.	|	...	...	...	...	...	...	|	0824
	Portbou **355** a.	|	...	...	...	...	...	...	|	0923
	Marseille **350** a.	1247	...	...	...	...	...	...	0600x	...
	Nice **360** a.	1534	...	...	...	...	...	...	0909x	...

	4394 4348	4348 4349		4336 4337		TGV 5198		TGV 5464	TGV 5464
	N Ⓡ	P Ⓡ				n		①-⑥	⑦
Nice **360** d.	2000	...	...	...	...	0925	...	...	...
Marseille **350** d.	2252	...	...	...	...	1210	...	...	...
Cerbère **355** d.	|	2043	...	...	...	|	...	...	...
Perpignan **355** d.	|	2134	...	...	...	|	...	...	...
Montpellier **355** d.	|	2321	...	...	...	|	...	1648	1648
Arles **351** d.	2335	|	...	...	...	|	...	|	|
Avignon Centre **351** d.	2356	|	...	...	...	|	...	|	|
Avignon TGV **350** d.	|	|	...	...	...	1245	...	|	|
Lyon Perrache **373** d.	|	|	...	0635	...	|	...	|	|
Lyon Part-Dieu **373** d.	|	|	...	0648	...	1400	...	1900	1900
Dijon d.	|	|	...	0839	...	1546	...	2054	2054
Culmont Chalindrey a.	0533	0533	...	0923	...	|	...	|	|
Culmont Chalindrey d.	0553	0553	...	0937	...	|	...	|	|
Neufchâteau d.	0642	0642	...	1025	...	|	...	2228	2228
Toul d.	0708	0708	...	1050	...	|	...	|	|
Nancy 388 a.	0729	0729	...	1109	...	1759	...	2312	2310
Metz 388 a.	0824	0824	...	1206	...	1849	...	2354r	...
Thionville 388 a.	0852	0852	...	...	...	...	...	...	...
Luxembourg 388 a.	0924	0924	...	...	...	...	...	...	...

N – *CORAIL LUNÉA* – 🛏 1,2 cl. and [2] (reclining) Luxembourg - Metz - Nice and v.v. Not Dec. 24, 31, Jan. 9, 16, 23, 30 from Luxembourg or Nice.
P – *CORAIL LUNÉA* – Dec. 13, 18 - 23, 25 - 30, Jan. 1 - 3; ⑤⑦ Jan. 8 - 31; ⑤⑥⑦ Feb. 5 - Mar. 7; ⑤⑦ Mar. 12 - 28; ⑤⑥⑦ from Apr. 2 (also Apr. 5, May 12, 13, 24). 🛏 1, 2 cl. and [2] (reclining) Luxembourg - Metz - Portbou and Cerbère - Metz - Luxembourg.
f – Also Dec. 23, 30, Apr. 29, May 6, 19; not Dec. 25, Jan. 1.
n – Not Mar. 28.
r – Arrive 0035 on nights of Feb. 1 - 4, Mar. 29 - Apr. 1.
x – On ① arrive Marseille 0628, Nice 0937.
TGV – Ⓡ, supplement payable, 🍷.
⊕ – On Feb. 8 - 12, 15 - 19 depart Metz 0820, not calling at Nancy.

380 PARIS - TROYES - BELFORT - MULHOUSE

Timings may vary due to engineering work

km	For TGV see Table 390	1539 Ⓐ	⚒	Ⓐ u	1541 ①-⑥ n	©	1039 ①-⑥ n	Ⓐ	1041 ⑦ e	1841 ⚒	Ⓑ c	1545	1043 ⑦ e	1043 ①-⑥ n	1547	Ⓐ	1045 Ⓑ h	1641 Ⓐ	1047	11641 Ⓐ	1741	1049 ⊕	1643 Ⓐ	1549 E	1645 F
0	**Paris Est** d.	...	...	...	0641	...	0711	...	0812	0942	...	1213z	1243	1313z	1411z	...	1511	1611	1641	1711	1811	1841	1911	2011	2211
110	Nogent sur Seine d.	...	...	0650	0736	...	|	...	0909	1039	...	1308	|	|	1507	...	|	1710	|	1817	1910	|	2010	2108	2308
129	Romilly sur Seine d.	...	...	0702	0750	...	|	...	0924	1052	...	1319	|	|	1519	...	|	1726	|	1838	1930	|	2023	2120	2322
166	**Troyes** d.	0608	...	0722	0811	...	0835	...	0946	1114	...	1340	1408	1437	1540	...	1638	1755	1806	1901	1953	2011	2052	2142	2351
221	Bar sur Aube d.	0636	...	0752	0844	...	|	...	1020	|	...	1412	|	|	1612	...	|	...	1842	...	2027	|	...	2214	...
262	Chaumont 382 d.	0657	...	0813	0906	...	0925	...	1046	1204	...	1433	1500	1527	1634	...	1727	...	1907	...	2052	2059	...	2236	...
296	Langres 382 d.	0717	...	▬	0926	...	|	...	1107	|	...	1453	|	|	1654	...	|	...	1929	...	2113	|	...	2256	...
307	Culmont Chalindrey 382 d.	0726	...	...	0937	...	|	...	1116	|	...	1501	|	|	1707	...	|	...	1939	...	2121	|	...	2308	...
	Dijon 379 a.	0819	...	...	...	...	|	...	|	|	...	...	|	|	▬	...	|	...	|	...	...	|	...	...	...
380	Vesoul d.	...	...	...	...	...	1028	...	1156	1311	...	...	1605	1629	...	...	1828	...	2017	...	...	2202	...	...	...
410	Lure d.	...	...	Ⓐ	...	...	1048	...	1217	...	...	...	1625	1649	†	...	1849	...	2038	...	...	2221	...	...	...
442	**Belfort** ▷ 384 d.	...	0659	0804	...	1057	1110	1155	1243	...	1355	...	1646	1712	1737	1804	1912	...	2102	...	...	2244	...	...	...
491	**Mulhouse** ▷ 384 a.	...	0736	0836	...	1134	...	1232	...	...	1434	...	...	1743a	1815	1849	1947	...	2135	...	...	2312	...	...	...

	1640 ①-⑥ n	11640 Ⓐ	1740 Ⓐ	1940 ⑥ t	1942 Ⓐ	⚒	1742 ⑦ e	1540 ①-⑥ n	1040	1542 Ⓐ ⊗	Ⓐ	†	⑥ v	1042	1840 Ⓑ h	1544 △	Ⓐ	1044 p	1548 q	©	1048 ⑦ d	1046 Ⓐ	1046 ⑥	Ⓑ	⑥ v
Mulhouse ▷ 384 d.	...	...	...	0348	0444	0618	...	...	0743	...	0855	0936	0955	1239	...	...	1555	...	...	1659	...	1819	...	1955	1955
Belfort ▷ 384 d.	...	...	...	0418	0513	0650	...	...	0818	...	0927	1019	1031	1313	...	...	1628	1650	...	1750	1816	1848	1847	2031	2046
Lure d.	...	...	...	0439	0533	▬	...	...	0840	...	▬	...	▬	1333	...	...	...	1710	...	...	1836	1908	1907	...	...
Vesoul d.	...	...	...	0459	0554	...	...	...	0900	...	...	...	...	1353	1516	...	...	1730	...	...	1857	1928	1928	...	...
Dijon 379 d.	...	...	...	|	|	...	...	...	|	0953	©	...	...	|	|	...	...	|	...	...	|	|	|	...	...
Culmont Chalindrey 382 d.	...	...	0522	0537	|	...	0708	0844	|	1047	1047	...	...	|	|	1648	...	|	1817	...	1935	2007	2006	...	...
Langres 382 d.	...	...	0533	0547	|	**1738**	0719	0854	|	1056	1056	...	**1642**	|	|	1658	...	|	1827	...	1946	|	|	...	...
Chaumont 382 d.	...	...	0555	0609	0656	Ⓐ	0741	0914	1002	1116	1116	...	⚒	1454	1618	1718	...	1833	1847	...	2008	2034	2034	...	...
Bar sur Aube d.	...	...	0617	0632	|		0802	0934	|	1137	1137	...		|	|	1739	...	|	1909	...	2030	|	|	...	...
Troyes d.	0506	0556	0651	0705	0746	0805	0835	1010	1047	1210	1210	...	1438	1543	1705	1811	...	1918	1941	...	2106	2120	2120	...	...
Romilly sur Seine d.	0527	0618	0712	0726	|	0827	0856	1030	|	1229	1229	...	1458	|	1726	1831	...	|	2001	...	2127	|	|	...	...
Nogent sur Seine d.	0540	0632	0725	0740	|	0840	0909	1042	|	1241	1241	...	1510	|	1740	1844	...	|	2013	...	2140	|	|	...	...
Paris Est a.	0645	0745	0830	0845	0915	0945	1015	1145	1215	1345	1345	...	1615	1715	1845	1945	...	2045	2115	...	2245	2245r	2245	...	...

E – ⑤⑥⑦ to Mar. 28 (also Dec. 24, 31), daily from Apr. 3.
F – ⑦ to Mar. 28 (also Dec. 24, 31, Apr. 11); Ⓑ from Apr. 25 (not May 13, 23).
a – Ⓐ only.
c – By 🚌 on Ⓐ Feb. 8 - Mar. 5, Mar. 29 - Apr. 16, Apr. 26 - June 4.
d – Also May 24.
e – Also Apr. 5, May 24.
h – Not Dec. 25, Jan. 1, May 13.
n – Not Apr. 5, May 24.
p – Subject to alteration Troyes - Paris Ⓐ Dec. 14 - Feb. 5, Mar. 1 - 12.
q – Subject to alteration Troyes - Paris Dec. 14 - 18, 21 - 23 and ①-⑤ Jan. 4 - Apr. 2.
r – 2323 on Ⓐ to Apr. 23.
t – Also Dec. 25, Jan. 1, May 13.
u – Not Jan. 12 - 22.
v – Not May 1, 8.
z – 4 - 6 minutes earlier on Mar. 15 - 19.
⊕ – Not on ①-⑤ Mar. 1 - 12.
⊗ – Runs up to 30 mins earlier on Ⓐ Mar. 15 - Apr. 2, June 7 - 11.
△ – Subject to alteration Troyes - Paris on Ⓐ Jan. 4 - 22.
▷ – Additional local trains run Belfort - Mulhouse.

381 PARIS - CHÂLONS EN CHAMPAGNE - BAR LE DUC

km		Ⓐ	Ⓐ	Ⓐ	⑥⑦	⑥	Ⓐ △	⑦ d	⊕	2777 ♥		Ⓐ ⊗		Ⓐ	Ⓐ		2785 Ⓑ ♥x		Ⓐ	⑤ k	© z	Ⓐ	⑤ f	† z
0	**Paris Est** d.	0635	0735	0835	0835	1035	1035	1035	1235	1357	...	1435	1635	1735	...	1835	1927	...	1935	1935	2035	2135	2135	2235
95	Château Thierry d.	0723	0823	0922	0923	1123	1123	1123	1323	|	...	1523	1722	1830	...	1930	|	...	2030	2030	2121	2223	2223	2323
142	Épernay d.	0751	0851	0946	0951	1151	1151	1151	1351	|	...	1551	1750	1858	...	1958	|	...	2058	2058	2151	2251	2251	2351
	Champagne-Ardenne TGV d.	|	|	|	|	|	|	|	|	1440	...	|	|	|	...	|	2009	...	|	|	|	|	|	|
*172	**Châlons en Champagne** ▷ d.	0809	0909	1003	1009	1209	1209	1207	1409	1503	...	1609	1808	1913	1920	2015	2033	2038	2113	2115	2207	2307	2309	0007
205	Vitry le François ▷ d.	0827	0927	...	1027	1227	1227	...	1427	1521	1530	1627	1826	...	1939	2033	2052	2058	...	2133	...	...	2327	...
234	**St Dizier** ▷ a.	0845	*0955*	...	*1107*	1245	*1250*	...	1445	|	1550	1645	*1901*e	...	1957	2051	|	2116	...	2151	...	...	|	...
255	**Bar le Duc** ▷ a.	...	0951	...	1051	...	1251	...	...	1545	...	...	1851	...	...	...	2114	...	...	...	...	...	2351	...

	Ⓐ	⚒	⚒	2778 ①-⑥ ♥n	Ⓐ	G		†	⑦ b	⑥ v	⑥	Ⓐ	⑥ s	Ⓐ			Ⓐ	u	Ⓑ		2784 ♥	Ⓐ	†	
Bar le Duc ▷ d.	...	...	...	0614	...	...	...	...	...	...	0936	...	...	...	1132	...	1332	...	...	...	1713	...	...	1936
St Dizier ▷ d.	...	...	0610	|	0637	0737	...	0930	...	0933	|	0941	1102	1122	|	...	|	1537	...	1703	|	1737	1825	|
Vitry le François ▷ d.	...	...	0629	0639	0658	0757	...	0950	...	0952	1001	1001	1122	1141	1157	...	1357	1557	...	1724	1738	1758	1845	2002
Châlons en Champagne ▷ d.	0515	0615	0648	0658	0715	0815	0815	1007	1016	...	1019	1019	1140	...	1215	...	1415	1615	1715	1742	1757	1816	1903	2020
Champagne-Ardenne TGV d.	|	|	...	0720	|	|	|	...	|	...	|	|	...	...	|	...	|	|	|	...	1819	|	|	|
Épernay d.	0534	0632	...	|	0731	0831	0832	...	1035	...	1035	1035	...	...	1231	...	1431	1631	1731	...	|	1832	1919	2036
Château Thierry d.	0600	0700	...	|	0800	0900	0900	...	1100	...	1100	1100	...	...	1300	...	1500	1700	1800	...	|	1900	1948	2100
Paris Est a.	0653	0753	...	0800	0853	0953	0953	...	1153	...	1153	1153	...	...	1353	...	1553	1753	1853	...	1900	1953	2038	2153

G – ①⑥⑦ (also Dec. 25, Jan. 1, Apr. 6, May 13, 25).
b – Also Dec. 25, Jan. 1, Apr. 5, May 24.
d – Also Dec. 25, Jan. 1, May 13, 24.
e – *1855* on ©.
f – Also Dec. 24, 31, May 12; not Dec. 25, Jan. 1.
k – Also Dec. 24, 31, Apr. 5, May 12; not Apr. 4.
n – Not Apr. 5, May 24. From Commercy, depart 0551.
s – Not Dec. 26, Jan. 2.
u – Not on ①-⑤ Apr. 26 - May 12.
v – Not May 1, 8.
x – Not Dec. 25, Jan. 1, May 13. To Commercy, arrive 2137.
z – Not May 23.
▷ – For other trains see Table **382**.
△ – Not Apr. 6 - 23.
⊕ – Depart Paris 1227 on Mar. 1 - 5.
⊗ – Depart Paris 1427 on Mar. 1 - 5.
♥ – *TGV* train, R, supplement payable, 🍸.
* – *188 km* via high-speed line.

382 REIMS - CHÂLONS EN CHAMPAGNE - METZ / NANCY / DIJON

km		②-⑤	⑥ t	Ⓐ	⑥ u	Ⓐ	⊗		⚒		†
0	**Reims** ⊖ d.	...	...	0619	0751	...	...	...	...	1649	...
31	Épernay d.	...	0612	0646	0816	...	...	...	1619	1716	1822
61	**Châlons en Champ. 381** d.	...	0629	0704	0834	...	...	...	1637	1735	1841
94	Vitry le François 381 d.	...	0646	0723	0851	...	...	...	1655	1752	1857
143	Bar le Duc 381 d.	0704	0713	0753	0916	1010	1225	1610	1719	1820	1922
243	**Metz** (*see below*) a.	|	|	|	|	|	|	|	1810	|	2014
183	Commercy d.	0732	0733	0814	0936	1034	1246	1633	...	1841	...
209	Toul d.	0752	0749	0830	0952	1055	1302	1654	...	1857	...
242	**Nancy** a.	0818	0810	0851	1009	1117	1320	1715	...	1915	...

			⊕			Ⓑ	⑥	†	H	⑤ z
Nancy d.	0701	1011	1332	1600	1703	1802	1802	2034	2032	2041
Toul d.	0719	1033	1351	1620	1726	1823	1823	2053	2052	2100
Commercy d.	0733	1053	1411	1637	1747	1837	1837	2107	2107	2114
Metz (*see below*) d.	|	|	|	|	|	|	|	|	|	|
Bar le Duc 381 d.	0755	1116	1436	1658	1813	1859	1857	2128	2127	2136
Vitry le François 381 d.	0822	...	1502	...	...	1925	...	2152	...	2159
Châlons en Champ. 381 d.	0840	...	1519	...	...	1944	...	2209	...	2218
Épernay d.	0901	...	1535	...	...	2012	...	...	...	2234
Reims ⊖ a.	0920	...	...	...	...	2031	...	...	...	...

km		Ⓑ	⑥ v			Ⓑ	©	Ⓐ	N	⑤⑦ b	
0	**Reims** ⊖ d.	0610	0858	1240	...	1640	1732	1748	2001	2000	...
58	**Châlons en Champ. 381** d.	0649	0937	1321	...	1721	1817	1825	2038	2038	...
91	Vitry le François 381 d.	0708	0958	1341	...	1741	1837	1843	2059	2058	...
120	St Dizier 381 d.	0728	1019	1401	...	1802	1855	1901	2119	2118	...
193	Chaumont 380 d.	0818	1104	1446	...	1846	...	...	2203	2202	...
227	Langres 380 d.	0838	1124	1506	...	1906	...	...	2224	2223	...
238	Culmont Chalindrey 380 a.	0846	1133	1514	...	1923	...	...	2232	2231	...
238	Culmont Chalindrey 379 d.	0848	1135	1515	...	*1951*	...	...	...	2233	...
315	**Dijon** 379 a.	0948	1226	1606	...	*2036*	...	...	...	2325	...

	⚒	Ⓐ	① g	⑥⑦				⑤⑦ e	Ⓑ	⑥ d
Dijon 379 d.	...	...	...	*0839*	...	...	1554	1704	1858	1941
Culmont Chalindrey 379 a.	...	...	...	*0923*	...	...	1638	1749	1943	2028
Culmont Chalindrey 380 d.	0539	0658	0928	0945	...	...	1640	1754	1945	2030
Langres 380 d.	0548	0708	0936	0954	...	...	1649	1804	1954	2039
Chaumont 380 d.	0609	0728	0956	1013	...	...	1710	1824	2015	2100
St Dizier 381 d.	0655	0816	1040	1056	...	1703	1758	1911	2058	2144
Vitry le François 381 d.	0716	0835	1102	1116	...	1723	1819	1931	2120	2205
Châlons en Champ. 381 d.	0739	0856	1123	1136	...	1744	1840	1952	2141	2226
Reims ⊖ a.	0823	0934	1158	1210	...	1822	1918	2030	2220	2304

		E	⑤ z
Bar le Duc d.	0723	1230	1921
Metz a.	0815	1323	2014

		E	†	⚒
Metz d.	0829	1332	1830	1830
Bar le Duc a.	0923	1424	1920	1923

E – ①⑤ (also Dec. 24, 31, May 12; not Dec. 25, Jan. 1, Feb. 22 - Mar. 5, Apr. 5, May 24).
H – ①-④ (not holidays).
N – ①②③④⑥ (not Apr. 5, May 1, 8, 12, 13, 24).
b – Also Apr. 5, May 12, 13, 24.
d – Also Dec. 25, Jan. 1; not Dec. 26, Jan. 2.
e – Also Dec. 24, 31, Apr. 5, May 12, 13, 24.
g – Also Apr. 6, May 25; not Apr. 26, May 3.
t – Not May 1, 8.
u – Not May 1, 8. Also runs † from Bar le Duc.
v – Also Dec. 26, Jan. 2.
z – Not Dec. 25, Jan. 1.
⊕ – Not on ①-⑤ Mar. 15 - 19, Apr. 26 - May 14, from May 31.
⊗ – Not on ①-⑤ Feb. 22 - Mar. 19, Apr. 6 - 23, from May 31.

Additional trains: Bar le Duc - Nancy 0605 Ⓐ, 0819 †, 1911; Nancy - Bar le Duc 1937 ⑥.

METZ and NANCY - STRASBOURG 383

km		Ⓐ	⑥ v	Ⓐ	299 ①–⑥	⚒ u	Ⓐ	Ⓐ		Ⓑ h	⑥ v	⑥ v	† s	91 C	Ⓐ	⚒ u⊡	⑥ v	Ⓐ ⊙	† s	Ⓑ h△	Ⓐ ⊕	† s	97 R	⚒ u	Ⓐ	⚒ u
	Luxembourg **388** d.	...	...	...	0543	...	...	...	...	...	...	...	...	1046	...	...	...	...	...	...	...	...	1610	...	...	...
0	**Metz** d.	...	...	...	0630	...	0748	...	0859	...	...	...	...	1131	...	1225	...	1334	1334	...	...	...	1653	...	1711	1742
	Nancy d.	...	...	0614	|	0715	|	0815	|	0915	0915	1115	1115	|	1215	|	1315	|	|	1415	1615	1615	|	1715	|	|
	Lunéville d.	...	...	0632	|	0733	|	0836	|	0932	0934	1132	1135	|	1234	|	1332	|	|	1434	1634	1633	|	1732	|	|
88	Sarrebourg d.	0620	0623	0656	|	0759	0845	0859	0955	1000	1000	1201	1201	|	1259	1328	1402	|	1431	1459	1658	1655	|	1758	1811	|
91	Réding d.	0625	0629	0700	0717	|	|	|	|	|	|	|	|	|	|	1333	|	1422	|	|	|	|	|	1802	1816	1829
114	Saverne d.	0642	0646	0715	0734	0815	0902	0915	1012	1017	1016	1217	1217	|	1315	1349	1417	1438	1448	1516	1714	1712	|	1815	1831	1845
159	**Strasbourg** a.	0718	0720	0739	0800	0839	0931	0937	1040	1039	1039	1239	1239	1248	1344	1415	1439	1505	1514	1539	1739	1735	1812	1840	1859	1908
	Mulhouse **385** a.	0813	...	0843	...	0942	...	...	...	...	1143	...	...	1352	1454	...	...	...	...	...	1844	...	1920	...	...	...
	Basel **385** a.	0838	...	0907	...	1007	...	...	...	...	1207	...	...	1420	1519	...	...	...	...	...	1909	...	1947	...	...	...

	Ⓑ h	⚒ u	⑥ v	Ⓐ	† s	Ⓐ	† s	⑥ v	⑥ v	2583 Ⓑ ♥z	† s	295 Ⓑ B
Luxembourg **388** d.	...	...	...	...	...	...	...	...	...	...	...	2027
Metz d.	...	1824	...	...	...	1928	1932	1932	...	...	2051	2115
Nancy d.	1815	|	1915	1918	1920	|	|	|	2006	2045	|	|
Lunéville d.	1833	|	1933	1936	1937	|	|	|	2024	|	|	|
Sarrebourg d.	1858	1926	1956	1959	2000	2027	|	2027	2046	2124	|	|
Réding d.	|	...	2000	|	|	|	2019	|	|	|	|	|
Saverne d.	1916	...	2014	2015	2015	2045	2036	2045	2103	2142	2151	2211
Strasbourg a.	1941	...	2036	2037	2039	2108	2059	2108	2125	2204	2213	2235
Mulhouse **385** a.	2043	...	...	2146	...	...	...	...	...	...	...	2343
Basel **385** a.	2107	...	...	2211	...	...	...	...	...	...	...	0013

km		2584 ①–⑥ ♥n	Ⓐ	⚒ u	⚒ u	† s	Ⓐ	⑥ v	296 Ⓑ B⊖	
	Basel **385** d.	...	...	...	0537	...	...	...	0646	...
	Mulhouse **385** d.	...	...	...	0559	...	0617	...	0710	...
	Strasbourg d.	0545	0558	0629	0706	0706	0740	0740	0806	...
	Saverne d.	0609	0622	0650	0728	0729	0802	0802	|	...
	Réding d.	|	0638	|	|	|	0817	0817	|	...
0	Sarrebourg d.	0627	0650	0706	0755	0753	0821	0821	|	...
47	Lunéville d.	0650	|	0732	|	|	0845	0844	|	...
80	**Nancy** a.	0709	|	0752	|	|	0904	0902	|	...
	Metz a.	...	0740	...	0846	0842	...	...	0926	...
	Luxembourg **388** a.	...	...	...	...	...	...	...	1014	...

	Ⓐ u	† s	⊙		Ⓐ ⊙	Ⓐ	⑥ v	⑥ v		90 B	⊕	Ⓐ	Ⓐ u	† ◇		96 R	⑥ v	Ⓐ		Ⓐ	† s		Ⓑ h	⑥ v	298 Ⓑ	
Basel **385** d.	0717	...	...	...	...	...	...	...	...	1304	...	...	1517	...	...	1608	...	...	...	1717	...	...	1817	...	...	...
Mulhouse **385** d.	0742	...	...	...	...	...	...	...	...	1334	...	...	1541	...	...	1634	...	...	...	1741	...	...	1841	...	...	...
Strasbourg d.	0841	0840	1002	1026	1143	1217	1220	1237	...	1436	1437	1535	1636	1636	1651	1737	1741	1741	...	1837	1837	1904	1937	1937	2000	...
Saverne d.	0903	0906	1027	1049	1205	1245	1251	1302	...	|	1503	1559	1701	1659	1713	|	1804	1807	...	1903	1900	1929	2003	2003	2023	...
Réding d.	|	|	|	|	1222	|	|	1320	...	|	|	1615	|	|	1730	|	|	|	...	1917	1914	|	|	|	2038	...
Sarrebourg d.	0920	0922	1051	1106	1230	1301	1307	1330	...	|	1519	1631	1719	1717	1741	|	1819	1824	...	1921	1918	1956	2019	2018	|	...
Lunéville d.	0941	0946	|	1133	|	1332	1333	|	...	|	1541	|	|	|	|	|	1847	1849	...	1944	1944	|	2048	2048	|	...
Nancy a.	1001	1004	|	1152	|	1352	1350	|	...	|	1602	|	1757	1757	|	|	1905	1907	...	2002	2003	|	2107	2107	|	...
Metz a.	...	...	1141	...	1327	...	...	1426	...	1554	...	1730	...	...	1830	1854	...	...	...	...	...	2043	...	...	2124	...
Luxembourg **388** a.	...	...	...	...	...	...	...	...	...	1645	...	...	...	...	...	1936	...	...	...	...	...	...	...	...	2214	...

B – [12] Brussels - Basel and v.v. (Table **40**).
C – [12] Brussels - Zürich - Chur (Table **40**).
R – [12] Brussels - Basel - Zürich and v.v. (Table **40**).
e – Also Apr. 2, 5, May 24.
h – Also Dec. 26, May 1, 8.
n – Not Apr. 4, May 25.
s – Also Dec. 26, Apr. 2.
u – Not Dec. 26, Apr. 2.

v – Not Dec. 26, May 1, 8.
z – Not Dec. 25, Jan. 1, May 13.

△ – Subject to alteration on Ⓐ Mar. 8 - 19.
◇ – On Dec. 25, 26, Jan. 1, May 1, 8, 13 will not call at Saverne.
⊕ – Subject to alteration on Ⓐ Mar. 15 - 26.
⊡ – Not on ①–⑤ Dec. 14 - 18, Jan. 25 - Feb. 5.

⊙ – Subject to alteration on Ⓐ Jan. 18 - 29.
⊖ – Not on ①–⑤ Mar. 29 - Apr. 9.

♥ – *TGV* train, Ⓡ, 🍷. To/from Paris (Table **390**).

A Sunday service operates on Apr. 2

STRASBOURG - BELFORT - BESANÇON - LYON 384

🍷 on principal trains

km		①⑥ g	⚒		⚒	⑦ c	4211 4210 ①–⑥ u⊖	*TGV* 5405/4 ⊗	⊖	4213 4212 ⊖	⊖	4215 4214 ⊖		Ⓑ	⑥	Ⓑ	4217 4216 ⑤⑦ d	⊙	4219 4218 R	4221 4220 ⑤ s	4221 4220 ⑦ e		4295 4248 P Ⓡ	4294 4295 N Ⓡ
0	**Strasbourg** 385 d.	...	...	...	...	...	0610	0838	...	1004	...	1147	...	...	...	...	1531	...	1716	1755	1804	...	2058	2058
43	Sélestat 385 d.	...	...	...	...	...	|	|	...	1025	...	|	...	...	...	...	|	...	|	|	|	...	2122	2122
65	Colmar 385 d.	...	...	...	...	...	0638	0904	...	1038	...	|	...	...	...	...	1558	...	1744	|	|	...	2137	2137
106	Mulhouse 385 d.	...	...	...	...	...	0707	0931	...	1109	...	1241	...	...	...	...	1630	...	1814	1902	1901	...	2210	2210
155	**Belfort** a.	...	...	...	...	...	0735	|	...	1137	...	|	...	...	...	...	|	...	1840	1929	1929	...	2237	2237
155	**Belfort** 377 d.	...	...	...	...	...	0755	|	...	1157	...	|	...	...	...	...	|	...	1850	1948	1948	...	2256	2256
173	Montbéliard 377 d.	...	...	...	...	...	|	1007	...	1211	...	1323	...	...	...	...	1710	...	1904	2002	2002	...	2311	2311
252	**Besançon Viotte** 377 a.	...	...	...	...	...	0858	1056	...	1303	...	1418	...	...	...	...	1803	...	1956	2054	2054	...	0004	0004
252	**Besançon Viotte** d.	0453	0606	0639	0722	0850	0900	1058	1235	1305	1337	1420	...	1658	1707	1734	1806	1830	1958	2057	2057	...	0007	0007
292	Mouchard d.	0520	0638	0713	0751	0920	|	|	1315	|	1421	|	...	1744	1743	1807	|	1910	|	|	|	...	|	|
341	Lons-le-Saunier d.	0606	0723	0754	0836	0958	1000	1156	1355	1408	1502	1520	...	1829	1827	1853	1913	1952	2058	2156	2156	...	|	|
405	Bourg-en-Bresse 353 d.	0653	...	0837	...	1039	1041	1236	...	1445	...	|	...	1908	1908	...	|	...	2135	2233	2233	...	|	|
465	**Lyon Part-Dieu** 353 a.	0747	...	0920	...	1123	1123	1316	...	1527	...	1639	...	...	...	...	2028	...	2216	2315	2315	...	|	|
470	**Lyon Perrache** 353 a.	0759	...	0932	...	1135	1137	|	...	1544	...	...	...	...	...	...	2042	...	2230	2329	2329	...	|	|
	Marseille **350** a.	...	...	...	...	...	...	1513	...	...	...	...	...	...	...	...	...	...	...	...	...	...	|	0600r
	Nice **360** a.	...	...	...	...	...	...	...	...	...	...	...	...	...	...	...	...	...	...	...	...	...	|	0909r
	Montpellier **355** a.	...	...	...	...	...	...	...	...	...	...	...	...	...	...	...	...	...	...	...	...	...	0627	...
	Portbou **355** a.	...	...	...	...	...	...	...	...	...	...	...	...	...	...	...	...	...	...	...	...	...	0923	...

	⚒	⚒	⑦	Ⓐ	⑥	4310 4311 ①–⑥ x		4312 4313	⑥	Ⓑ △	4314 4315 ▽	⑥	*TGV* 5430/1 ⊕		4316 4317 ⑤⑦ z	4318 4319 ①–④ m	4318 4319 ⑥	4320 4321 ⑤⑦ z	⑥ t	⑤ f	⑦ b		4394 4395 N Ⓡ	4348 4394 P Ⓡ
Cerbère **355** d.	...	...	...	...	...	...	...	...	...	...	...	...	...	...	...	...	...	...	...	...	...	...	...	2043
Montpellier **355** d.	...	...	...	...	...	...	...	...	...	...	...	...	...	...	...	...	...	...	...	...	...	...	...	2321
Nice **360** d.	...	...	...	...	...	...	...	...	...	...	...	...	...	...	...	...	...	...	...	...	...	...	2000	|
Marseille **350** d.	...	...	...	...	...	...	...	...	...	...	...	...	1246	...	...	...	...	...	...	...	...	...	2252	|
Lyon Perrache 353 d.	...	...	...	...	...	0656	...	0917	...	...	1235	...	|	1538	1654	1654	1732	1824	1919	2108	2108	...	|	|
Lyon Part-Dieu 353 d.	...	...	...	...	...	0712	...	0931	...	...	1249	...	1437	1550	1708	1708	1746	1838	1933	2122	2122	...	|	|
Bourg-en-Bresse 353 d.	0533	...	...	0655	...	0803	...	|	...	...	|	...	1525	1637	1753	1753	1833	|	2017	2218	2218	...	|	|
Lons-le-Saunier d.	0629	0727	0805	0812	0812	0841	1019	1048	1220	1334	|	1416	1600	1719	1830	1830	1912	1955	2059	2300	2300	...	|	|
Mouchard d.	0713	0811	0847	0856	0858	|	1056	|	1323	1422	|	1502	|	1803	|	|	|	|	2133	2337	2338	...	|	|
Besançon Viotte a.	0739	0840	0915	0925	0926	0939	1124	1145	1401	1450	1505	1532	1659	1836	1931	1931	2009	2051	2200	0009	0006	...	0512	0512
Besançon Viotte 377 d.	...	...	...	...	...	0941	...	1147	...	...	1506	...	1701	...	1934	1933	2012	2054	...	...	...	...	0515	0515
Montbéliard 377 d.	...	...	...	...	...	1033	...	|	...	...	1559	...	1749	...	2027	2026	2105	2147	...	...	...	...	0609	0609
Belfort 377 a.	...	...	...	...	...	|	...	1248	...	...	|	...	|	...	|	2038	2117	2200	...	...	...	...	0622	0622
Belfort d.	...	...	...	...	...	|	...	1308	...	...	|	...	|	...	|	2058	2137	2220	...	...	...	...	0642	0642
Mulhouse 385 a.	...	...	...	...	...	1110	...	1332	...	...	1636	...	1823	...	2104	2122	2202	2245	...	...	...	...	0720	0720
Colmar 385 a.	...	...	...	...	...	1137	...	1400	...	...	|	...	1849	...	2132	2150	2229	2320	...	...	...	...	0751	0751
Sélestat 385 a.	...	...	...	...	...	|	...	|	...	...	|	...	|	...	2145	2204	2242	|	...	...	...	...	0806	0806
Strasbourg 385 a.	...	...	...	...	...	1206	...	1436	...	...	1736	...	1918	...	2207	2226	2304	0004	...	...	...	...	0831	0831

N – *CORAIL LUNÉA* – 🛏 1,2 cl. and [2] (reclining) Strasbourg - Nice and v.v. Not Dec. 24, 31, Jan. 9, 16, 23, 30 from Strasbourg or Dec. 24, 31, Jan. 9, 16, 23, 30, Mar. 13, 20, 27 from Nice.
P – *CORAIL LUNÉA* – Dec. 13, 18 - 23, 25 - 30, Jan. 1 - 3; ⑤⑦ Jan. 8 - 31; ⑤⑥⑦ Feb. 5 - Mar. 7; ⑤⑦ Mar. 12 - 28; ⑤⑥⑦ from Apr. 2 (also Apr. 5, May 12, 13, 24). 🛏 1,2 cl., [2] (reclining) Strasbourg - Portbou and Cerbère - Strasbourg.
R – ①②③④⑥ (also Dec. 25, Jan. 1; not Dec. 24, 31, Apr. 5, May 12, 24).
b – Also Dec. 25, Jan. 1, Apr. 5, May 13, 24.

c – Also Dec. 25, Jan. 1, Apr. 5, May 24.
d – Also Dec. 24, 31, Apr. 5, May 12, 24.
e – Also Apr. 5, May 24.
f – Also Dec. 24, 31, May 12; not Dec. 25, Jan. 1.
g – Also Apr. 6, May 25; not Jan. 9, Apr. 5, May 1, 8, 24.
m – Also Dec. 25, Jan. 1; not Dec. 24, 31, Apr. 5, May 12, 24.
r – On ① arrive Marseille 0628, Nice 0937.
s – Also Dec. 24, 31, May 12; not Dec. 25, Jan. 1.
t – Not May 1, 8.
u – Not Dec. 25, Jan. 1, May 24.
x – Not Dec. 25, Jan. 1, Apr. 5, May 24.

z – Also Dec. 24, 31, Apr. 5, May 12, 24; not Dec. 25, Jan. 1.

TGV – Ⓡ, supplement payable, 🍷.

⊖ – Not on ①–⑤ Apr. 5 - 16.
⊕ – Not on ①–⑤ Apr. 12 - 30.
⊗ – Not on ①–⑤ Apr. 6 - 16, May 3 - 21.
△ – Not on ①–⑤ Mar. 22 - Apr. 2.
▽ – Not on ①–⑤ Mar. 22 - Apr. 2, Apr. 12 - 30.
⊙ – 14 - 23 minutes later on ⑤⑦.

385 STRASBOURG - MULHOUSE - BASEL

See also Tables 390 and 384

For faster *TGV* trains Paris - Strasbourg - Mulhouse - Basel see Table **390**. For trains Strasbourg - Mulhouse - Belfort - Lyon see Table **384**.

km	*For TGV see Table* **390**	Ⓐ	Ⓐ	Ⓐ	Ⓐ	⑥ t	Ⓐ	⑥	Ⓐ	⚒ ◇	†	Ⓐ	◇		⚒	†	⚒ ◧	†			91 V ⊕	Ⓒ	Ⓐ ◇	Ⓑ	⑥ t
	Luxembourg 388 d.	...	...	...	...	...	...	...	...	...	...	...	...	...	...	...	...	...	...	...	1046	...	...	...	...
	Metz 383 d.	...	...	...	...	...	...	...	...	...	...	...	...	...	...	...	...	...	...	...	1131	...	...	...	...
0	**Strasbourg** d.	...	...	0521	0621	...	0651	0651	0721	0751	0751	0821	0851	...	0951	0951	1051	1051	1151	...	1251	1351	1351	1451	1451
43	Sélestat d.	...	...	0540	0641	...	0711	0718	0741	0811	0818	0841	0911	...	1011	1011	1112	1118	1212	...	1315	1410	1417	1511	1518
65	Colmar d.	...	...	0552	0653	...	0724	0730	0754	0823	0831	0854	0924	...	1024	1024	1123	1134	1225	...	1330	1422	1429	1524	1530
106	**Mulhouse** ▷ d.	0440	0530	0618	0715	0730	0745	0802	0815	0845	0856	0915	0944	...	1045	1049	1145	1203	1246	...	1355	1445	1454	1545	1550
140	**Basel** ▷ a.	0514	0555	0640	0737	0755	0807	0831	0838	0907	0918	0937	1007	...	1107	1111	1207	1225	1308	...	1420	1507	1518	1610	1612

	⚒	†	Ⓐ		Ⓒ	Ⓐ	⚒ ◇	†		97 R	Ⓐ	⑥ t	†	Ⓐ	†	◇	Ⓐ	†		⑥ t	Ⓐ	†	Ⓒ	295 Ⓑ M	⑥ t
Luxembourg 388 d.	...	...	...	...	...	...	...	...	...	1610	...	...	...	...	...	...	...	...	...	...	...	...	...	2027	...
Metz 383 d.	...	...	...	...	...	...	...	...	...	1653	...	...	...	...	...	...	...	...	...	...	...	...	...	2115	...
Strasbourg d.	1553	1551	1621	1651	...	1721	1751	1751	...	1821	1851	1851	1851	1921	1921	1951	2053	2121	...	2151	2151	2151	...	2251	2251
Sélestat d.	1611	1609	1642	1711	...	1741	1811	1810	...	1845	1911	1910	1919	1944	1942	2012	2112	2150	...	2218	2211	2215	...	2311	2311
Colmar d.	1624	1622	1654	1724	...	1754	1824	1823	...	1859	1924	1923	1935	1957	1956	2024	2125	2204	...	2231	2224	2230	...	2324	2324
Mulhouse ▷ d.	1645	1651	1715	1745	1803	1815	1846	1848	...	1923	1945	1952	2006	2017	2017	2045	2148	2226	...	2252	2243	2254	2305	2348	2343
Basel ▷ a.	1707	1714	1737	1808	1838	1838	1909	1910	...	1947	2008	2014	...	...	...	2107	2211	...	...	2314	...	...	2339	0013	...

For TGV see Table **390**	⚒	Ⓐ	⚒	†	Ⓐ ◇	Ⓐ	⑥ u		296 Ⓑ M⊗	⚒ ◇	Ⓐ		⚒		†	⚒	†	Ⓐ			⚒	†	90 W	Ⓑ	⑥
Basel ▷ d.	...	0517	0537	0537	...	0617	0617	...	0646	0717	0747	0817	0847	...	0917	0947	1006	1047	1117	...	1217	...	1304	1417	1417
Mulhouse ▷ d.	0454	0541	0601	0601	0617	0641	0641	...	0710	0742	0812	0841	0911	...	0941	1012	1030	1111	1140	...	1240	1238	1334	1441	1441
Colmar d.	0518	0601	0627	0627	0646	0703	0709	...	0731	0801	0832	0901	0933	...	1005	1032	1058	1131	1201	...	1301	1306	1356	1501	1501
Sélestat d.	0532	0614	0638	0638	0657	0716	0720	...	0743	0814	0845	0914	0945	...	1017	1044	1109	1144	1214	...	1314	1322	1410	1514	1513
Strasbourg a.	0555	0633	0703	0703	0727	0736	0747	...	0803	0835	0904	0933	1005	...	1036	1104*	1136	1203	1233	...	1333	1354	1433	1533	1540
Metz 383 a.	...	...	0846	...	...	...	...	...	0926	...	...	...	...	...	...	...	...	...	...	...	...	...	1554	...	...
Luxembourg 388 a.	...	...	...	...	...	...	...	...	1014	...	...	...	...	...	...	...	...	...	...	...	...	...	1645	...	...

	⚒ ◇	†	Ⓐ	96 R		Ⓐ	Ⓐ ◇	Ⓒ	†	†	Ⓐ	◇		†	Ⓐ	†	⑥ t			†		Ⓐ	Ⓑ	Ⓑ	
Basel ▷ d.	1518	1517	1547	1606	...	1647	1717	1717	1732	←	1747	1817	...	...	1917	1917	1917	2016	...	2125	2143	2226	2243	...	...
Mulhouse ▷ d.	1541	1541	1611	1634	...	1711	1741	1741	1757	1811	1811	1841	...	1911	1940	1941	1941	2041	...	2149	2218	2252	2317	2323	...
Colmar d.	1600	1601	1633	1657	...	1732	1800	1809	→	1831	1831	1900	...	1931	2001	2008	2010	2101	...	2213	...	...	...	2347	...
Sélestat d.	1615	1613	1646	1710	...	1745	1813	1821	...	1843	1844	1913	...	1945	2014	2023	2025	2114	...	2226	...	...	...	0000	...
Strasbourg a.	1633	1640	1704	1732	...	1804	1833	1840	...	1903	1903	1933	...	2004	2035	2051	2052	2134	...	2249	...	...	...	0026	...
Metz 383 a.	...	...	...	1854	...	...	...	...	...	...	...	...	...	...	...	...	...	...	...	...	...	...	...	...	...
Luxembourg 388 a.	...	...	...	1936	...	...	...	...	...	...	...	...	...	...	...	...	...	...	...	...	...	...	...	...	...

M – JEAN MONNET – [12] Brussels - Basel and v.v.
R – IRIS – [12] Brussels - Basel - Zürich and v.v. (Table **40**).
V – VAUBAN – [12] Brussels - Basel - Zürich - Chur (Table **40**).
W – VAUBAN – [12] Basel - Brussels (Table **40**).
t – Not May 1, 8.

v – Not Dec. 26, May 1, 8.
◧ – Runs 6 minutes earlier on ①.
◇ – To/from Nancy on days in Table **383**.
▷ – Other local trains run.
⊗ – Subject to alteration Mar. 29 - Apr. 3, Apr. 5 - 10.

⊕ – Not Dec. 14 - 18, Jan. 25 - 29, Feb. 1 - 5, ①–⑤ Mar. 29 - Apr. 16.
* – 1113 on ①.

Dec. 26 and Apr. 2 : A Sunday service (†) will operate.

386 NANCY - ÉPINAL - REMIREMONT

km		Ⓐ	⚒	† L	B	⑥ E	⚒	⊕	⑦ u	⚒ ⊗		⚒	2571 ♥		Ⓐ		Ⓐ		⚒		2573 Ⓒ ♥	2573 Ⓐ ♥⊖	Ⓐ	⊖	H	⑤† v
	Paris Est 390 d.	...	...	...	...	...	...	...	...	...	...	...	1212	...	...	...	...	...	...	...	1812	1812	...	...	...	...
0	**Nancy** d.	0605	0705	0707	0720	0725	0820	0905	1006	1119	1205	1303	1346	1405	1506	1605	1703	1720	1805	1904	1945	1950	2006	2105	2204	2254
74	Épinal a.	0705	0759	0800	0821	0832	0914	1000	1100	1215	1301	1400	1427	1458	1600	1701	1800	1820	1901	2000	2026	2030	2112	2157	2300	2354
74	Épinal d.	0720	0801	0802	...	0839	0916	1002	1102	1227	1303	...	1430	1500	1616	1703	1802	...	1903	2002	2029	2033	...	2159	...	...
100	**Remiremont** a.	0750	0825	0828	...	0903	0942	1028	1128	1252	1332	...	1451	1524	1645	1728	1830	...	1929	2028	2052	2054	...	2223	...	...

	⚒ ⊖	2574 Ⓐ ♥⊖		⚒	⚒		2576 Ⓒ ♥	Ⓐ ⊖	⑥⑦	⚒ ⊖	⊖	Ⓐ		⚒	2578 ①–⑥ ♥n	⚒	†	Ⓒ	Ⓐ	Ⓒ L	2580 ⑦ ♥e	Ⓐ	⚒	† L	⚒	Ⓑ ◇
Remiremont d.	0530	0600	0626	0701	...	0833	0907	...	1038	...	1214	1418	...	1536	1603	...	1625	...	1729	1730	1805	...	1835	1839	1934	...
Épinal a.	0555	0622	0654	0729	...	0858	0928	...	1103	...	1245	1443	...	1600	1623	...	1654	...	1757	1758	1826	...	1900	1902	1958	...
Épinal d.	0600	0624	0659	0731	0800	0900	0931	1000	1104	1200	1247	...	1500	1602	1626	1656	1656	1726	1759	1800	1829	1830	1902	1904	2000	2110
Nancy a.	0659	0705	0758	0835	0854	0952	1011	1057	1159	1257	1342	...	1557	1658	1708	1752	1752	1825	1853	1856	1909	1930	1957	1957	2057	2204
Paris Est 390 a.	...	0845	...	...	...	...	1145	...	...	...	...	...	...	...	1845	...	...	...	...	...	2045	...	...	...	...	...

km		⚒	Ⓐ	⑥t	⚒c	Ⓐ	Ⓒ
0	**Nancy** d.	0605r	...	...	...	1750	...
74	Épinal d.	0710	1021	1308	1440	1850	1850
132	Luxeuil les Bains d.	0759	1106	1352	1527	1936	1936
150	Lure 380 d.	0814	1120	1405	1541	1949	1949
182	**Belfort** 380 a.	0834	1140	1423	1601	2010	2010
200	Montbéliard 377 a.	...	...	...	1618	...	...

	⚒	⚒s	†	⚒	⑤	⑦z
Montbéliard 377 d.	0548	...	...	1645	...	...
Belfort 380 d.	0603	1120	1631	1659	1940	1940
Lure 380 d.	0622	1140	1650	1724	2000	2000
Luxeuil les Bains d.	0635	1153	1704	1737	2013	2013
Épinal a.	0720	1240	1753	1825	2059	2059
Nancy a.	...	...	...	...	2158	2158

z – Also Dec. 24, 31, Apr. 5, May 12, 13, 24.
♥ – *TGV* train, Ⓡ, 🍷, supplement payable.
◇ – Depart 2100 on ⑤⑦**z** (see lower panel).
⊖ – Not May 17 - 21.
⊝ – Subject to alteration May 3 - 7, 10 - 12, 17 - 21.
⊕ – Subject to alteration May 3 - 7, 10 - 12.
⊗ – Not Apr. 5 - May 12.

B – Ⓐ to Mar. 12, ⚒ from Mar. 15.
E – ⑥ to Mar. 13.
H – Not ⑤†.
L – To/from Luxembourg (Table **388**).

c – Subject to alteration on Apr. 6 - 9.
e – Also Apr. 5, May 24.
n – Not Apr. 5, May 24.
r – Change at Épinal on ②–⑤.

s – Subject to alteration Mar. 15 - Apr. 16.
t – Not May 1, 8.
u – Also Dec. 25, Jan. 1.
v – Subject to alteration on Jan. 31, Feb. 7.

Additional trains:
Nancy - Épinal 0605 ⚒, 0620 ⚒, 1222 ⚒, 1620 Ⓐ, 1820 Ⓐ. Épinal - Nancy 0500 Ⓐ, 0624 ⑥**t**, 0630 Ⓐ, 1233 ⚒, 1640 Ⓐ.

387 NANCY - ST DIÉ and STRASBOURG - ÉPINAL

km	*Also see below*	⚒	Ⓐ			Ⓐ		2591 ⑦ ♥e			2593 Ⓐ ♥u	2595 ⑦ ♥e
	Paris Est 390 d.	...	...	...	...	...	...	1412	...	...	1812	2012
0	**Nancy** d.	0628	0758	0901	1230	1259	1400	1546	1600	1756	1946	2145
33	Lunéville d.	0655	0825	0923	1249	1324	1422	1606	1620	1821	2007	2205
84	**St Dié** a.	0804	0916	1006	1345	1404	1509	1636	1714	1914	2036	2235

Also see below	2596 ①–⑥ ♥n	Ⓒ	Ⓐ	⑥⑦		Ⓐ	⚒			2598 ⑦ ♥e	
St Dié d.	0720	0853	0855	1059	1214	1449	1558	1640	1755	1923	1944
Lunéville d.	|	0942	0945	1142	1309	1545	1640	1742	1842	1954	2039
Nancy a.	0810	1000	1006	1203	1332	1610	1702	1801	1902	2012	2102
Paris Est 390 a.	0945	...	...	...	...	...	...	...	...	2145	...

Additional trains: **Nancy - St Dié**: 0550 ⚒, 1201 Ⓐ, 1659 Ⓐ, 1726 Ⓐ, 1729 Ⓒ, 1853 †, 1857 ⚒, 1958 Ⓐ, 2000 Ⓒ, 2101 Ⓐ **u**.
St Dié - Nancy: 0521 Ⓐ **v**, 0612 ⚒, 0637 ⚒, 0641 †, 0729 ⚒, 1202 Ⓐ, 1545 †, 1852 Ⓐ.

Strasbourg - St Dié : on Dec. 26 and Apr. 4 a Sunday service will operate.

km		⚒	Ⓐ	Ⓐ	⑦	⑥ t	⑥ t	†	Ⓐ c	Ⓐ ▽	Ⓐ c	⑦	⑥ t	†	Ⓐ	Ⓐ c	Ⓐ	⑥ t	⚒ c	†	Ⓐ	†	†
0	**Strasbourg** d.	...	...	0655	0815	0855	...	0955	0955	...	1205	...	1255	...	...	1555	...	...	1755	1755	...	...	1915
87	St Dié d.	0559	0733	0840	0943	1032	1037	1122	1132	1242	1350	1352	1436	1642	1650	1736	1826	1902	1927	1929	1942	1948	2048
147	**Épinal** a.	0705	0843	...	...	...	1144	...	...	1352	...	1500	...	1748	1808	...	1937	2010	...	...	2049	2053	...

	Ⓐ	Ⓐ	†	⚒	Ⓐ c	⑥ t	†	Ⓐ c	⑥ t	⚒ ▷	Ⓐ c	⑥ t	†	†	Ⓐ	Ⓐ c	†	⑥ t	⑥ t	Ⓐ	†	†	⚒
Épinal d.	0559	...	...	0735	...	...	1025	...	...	1246	...	...	1514	...	1652	...	...	1710	...	1830	1833	...	2042
St Dié d.	0708	0736	0813	0844	0850	0909	1130	1214	1216	1351	1538	1610	1619	1626	1757	1804	1801	1815	1832	1935	1940	2000	2151
Strasbourg a.	...	0901	0935	...	1026	1040	...	1351	1350	...	1717	1740	...	1756	...	1931	1941	...	2015	...	...	2123	...

c – Subject to alteration on Ⓐ Mar. 15 - Apr. 2.
e – Also Apr. 5, May 24.
n – Not Apr. 5, May 24.
t – Not May 1, 8.
u – Not May 17 - 21.
v – Not Apr. 20 - 30.
♥ – *TGV* train, Ⓡ, 🍷, supplement payable.
▽ – Not Apr. 26 - 30.
▷ – Not Apr. 26 - May 12.

LUXEMBOURG - METZ - NANCY 388

For *TGV* trains Luxembourg - Metz - Paris see Table **390**. For long distance trains to the south of France see Table **379**. *A modified service operates on Dec. 26, May 1, 8.*

km				299																	91					
		⚒	⚒	⚒s	⚒	†	⚒	⚒	⚒	Ⓐ	⚒	†	Ⓐ	§	Ⓐu	Ⓒ	Ⓐ§	Ⓐ§	Ⓒ	⑥⑦	S	Ⓐ⊖	§	Ⓐ		Ⓐ
0	**Luxembourg** d.	...	0502	0543	...	...	0614a	...	0655	0715	0730	...	0755	0835	0854	0935	...	1034	...	...	1046	...	1135	...	1235	1255
34	Thionville d.	...	0531	0604	...	...	0642	...	0725	0737	0756	0806	0824	0900	0923	1000	1010	1101	...	1104	1111	...	1200	...	1300	1319
46	Hagondange d.	...	0542	|	...	...	0652	...	0733	0746	0806	0818	0833	0909	0934	1009	1019	1109	...	1113	|	...	1210	...	1309	1331
64	**Metz** a.	...	0600	0627	...	...	0706	...	0745	0757	0818	0836	0845	0921	0953	1022	1031	1120	...	1125	1129	...	1222	...	1321	1343
64	**Metz** d.	0556	...	...	0636	0656	0710	0729	...	0759	0824	0838	*0900*	0924	...	1024	1035	1124	1124	...	...	1157	1224	1259	1324	...
93	Pont-à-Mousson d.	0616	...	...	0658	0726	0727	0749	...	0819	0845	0907	*0918*	0944	...	1044	1056	1144	1144	...	...	1218	1244	1320	1344	...
121	**Nancy** a.	0633	...	...	0717	0759	0743	0807	...	0835	0902	0936	*0935*	1000	...	1100	1113	1200	1201	...	...	1235	1300	1337	1400	...

						97												295								
	①–⑤	⑥⑦			Ⓐ	R	Ⓐ	Ⓐ		Ⓐ		Ⓐ	Ⓐ			Ⓐ	Ⓒ	ⒷM	⑥⑦	⚒	†	†	Ⓐ	⚒	†	△
Luxembourg d.	1330	1330	1430	1535	...	1610	1555	1615	1640	1655	1730	...	1755	1830	1934	2016	...	2027	...	...	2115	...	2145	2215	2235	...
Thionville d.	1351	1351	1453	1559	...	1631	1620	1642	1705	1724	1759	...	1824	1900	1959	2040	...	2051	2104	2142	2142	...	2212	2245	2258	...
Hagondange d.	1401	1401	1503	1608	...	|	1629	1653	1715	1733	1809	...	1835	1909	2008	2050	...	|	2113	2153	2153	...	2223	2253	2306	...
Metz a.	1416	1416	1518	1621	...	1649	1640	1711	1727	1745	1822	...	1850	1921	2019	2108	...	2112	2125	2211	2211	...	2236	2304	2317	...
Metz d.	...	1421	1524	1624	1633	...	*1700*	...	1730	*1800*	1826	1834	1900	1924	2021	2116	2116	...	...	2214	...	2224	...	...	...	2324
Pont-à-Mousson d.	...	1444	1543	1644	|	...	*1719*	...	1752	*1818*	1848	1853	1921	1944	2040	2146	2145	...	...	2234	...	2245	...	...	...	2353
Nancy a.	...	1501	1601	1701	1709	...	*1738*	...	1810	*1835*	1906	1910	1938	2000	2057	2216	2215	...	...	2251	...	2301	...	...	...	0023

															296											
	Ⓐ	Ⓐ	⚒	Ⓐ	⚒	⚒	⚒	Ⓐr	⑦	⚒	†	Ⓐ	Ⓐ	▽	ⒷM	Ⓐ	Ⓒ		Ⓐ⊖	Ⓒ	Ⓐv	▷	▽	Ⓐ‡	‡	Ⓐ‡
Nancy d.	...	...	...	0540	0619	0639	0657	0705	...	0719	0719	0754	...	0819	...	0852	0916	...	0953	1020	...	1122	...	1149	1220	1253
Pont-à-Mousson d.	...	...	...	0603	0636	0702	0715	|	...	0738	0749	0811	...	0836	...	0912	0933	...	1010	1036	...	1139	...	1208	1238	1310
Metz a.	...	...	...	0632	0655	0729	0734	0739	...	0758	0819	0828	...	0855	...	0932	0953	...	1032	1057	...	1158	...	1225	1257	1328
Metz d.	0534	0558	0622	0635	0658	0741	...	0746	0749	0802	...	...	0840	0900	0930	...	...	1019	...	1058	1100	1200	1219	...	1300	...
Hagondange d.	0546	0610	0641	0649	0710	0753	...	0800	0801	0815	...	...	0852	0912	|	...	...	1041	...	1113	1119	1213	1234	...	1314	...
Thionville d.	0557	0619	0653	0702	0727	0804	...	0810	0810	0828	...	...	0902	0923	0952	...	...	1054	...	1124	1129	1224	1247	...	1324	...
Luxembourg a.	0623	0646	0719	0731	0750	0831	...	...	...	0849	...	...	...	0945	1014	...	...	...	...	1150	1156	1247	1315	...	1345	...

				90										96								298				
			Ⓒ	T		Ⓐ	Ⓐ		Ⓐ	Ⓐ		Ⓑ	Ⓐ	R	⚒	†	Ⓐ	Ⓐ		⚒	Ⓐ	Ⓑs	Ⓐ	Ⓐ		
Nancy d.	1319	1418	1418	...	1520	...	*1552*	1619	...	*1651*	1720	1749	...	...	1820	1820	*1853*	1920	...	1924	2020	...	2053	2155	...	2250
Pont-à-Mousson d.	1336	1436	1436	...	1538	...	*1610*	1636	...	*1708*	1736	1807	...	...	1838	1837	*1913*	1938	...	1955	2037	...	2127	2213	...	2321
Metz a.	1355	1457	1457	...	1557	...	*1626*	1657	...	*1728*	1757	1825	...	...	1857	1857	*1932*	1957	...	2024	2057	...	2158	2233	...	2350
Metz d.	1400	1500	1500	1556	1600	1619	1639	1700	1718	1740	1800	...	1839	1856	1900	1900	1939	2000	2020	...	2100	2130	...	...	2321	...
Hagondange d.	1413	1512	1512	|	1613	1634	1653	1715	1732	1751	1813	...	1850	|	1913	1914	1950	2013	2039	...	2113	|	...	...	2338	...
Thionville d.	1424	1521	1523	1620	1624	1647	1703	1727	1742	1803	1824	...	1905	1917	1925	1929	2002	2029	2049	...	2130	2153	...	...	2350	...
Luxembourg a.	1445	...	1544	1645	1650	1715	1730	1752	...	1830	1850	...	1930	1936	1949	1951	2032	2050	...	...	2149	2214	...	...	0017	...

M – JEAN MONNET – (12) Brussels - Basel and v.v. (Table **40**).
R – IRIS – (12) Brussels - Basel - Zürich and v.v. (Table **40**).
S – VAUBAN – (12) Brussels - Basel - Zürich - Chur (Table **40**). Not Dec. 14 - 18, Jan. 25 - 29, Feb. 1 - 5, ①–⑤ Mar. 29 - Apr. 16.
T – VAUBAN – (12) Basel - Brussels (Table **40**).
a – Ⓐ only.
r – To / from Remiremont (Table **386**).
s – To / from Strasbourg (Table **383**).
u – Subject to alteration on Ⓐ Apr. 1 - 16.
v – Subject to alteration on Ⓐ Apr. 12 - 30.
⊖ – Subject to alteration May 3 - 6, 10, 11.
⊖ – Subject to alteration Apr. 26 - 30.
△ – Not Jan. 31 - Feb. 4, Mar. 28 - Apr. 1. On ⑤ Metz 2331, Pont-à-Mousson 0003, Nancy 0034.
▽ – Subject to alteration on Ⓐ Mar. 29 - Apr. 9.
▷ – Subject to alteration on Ⓐ Mar. 29 - Apr. 9, Apr. 26 - 30.
§ – Subject to alteration on Ⓐ Mar. 29 - Apr. 16, Apr. 26 - 30.
‡ – Subject to alteration on Ⓐ Feb. 22 - Mar. 5, Apr. 26 - 30.

PARIS - REIMS - CHARLEVILLE MÉZIÈRES - SEDAN 389

km				*TGV* 2707	*TGV* 2709		*TGV* 2713	*TGV* 2713		*TGV* 2723		*TGV* 2733		*TGV* 2777				*TGV* 2743					*TGV* 2747		
		⊡ ⚒ x	Ⓐ	① g	①–⑥ n	Ⓐ		⑦ e	‡s		‡		△	B	Ⓐ	Ⓒ	⚒			⚒	†	Ⓐ	Ⓑ h	†	Ⓐ
0	**Paris Est** d.	...	...	0657	0757	...	0857	0857	...	1127	...	1257	...	1357	...	...	...	1557	...	...	...	...	1727	...	...
136	Champagne-Ardenne TGV ▷ d.	...	...	|	|	...	|	|	1001	|	...	|	...	1437	1447	1447	...	|	...	...	...	...	|	...	...
147	**Reims** ▷ a.	...	...	0742	0842	...	0942	0942	1008	1212	...	1342	...	...	1455	1455	...	1642	...	...	...	...	1812	...	...
147	**Reims** d.	0705	0741	...	0848	0858	...	0945	1011	...	1228	1345	1407	...	1500	...	1622	...	1648	1719	1729	1756	...	1824	1827
186	Rethel d.	0729	0806	...	|	0923	...	|	1034	...	1253	|	1431	...	1524	...	1646	...	1710	1743	1751	1822	...	1849	1854
235	**Charleville-Mézières** a.	0758	0836	...	0937	0950	...	1031	1101	...	1320	1432	1458	...	1551	...	1714	...	1737	1812	1817	1850	...	1915	1923
255	**Sedan** a.	0821	0857	...	...	1016	...	...	1125	...	1340c	...	1518	...	1611	...	1737	...	1807	1845	1836	...	...	1939	1947

		TGV 2751	*TGV* 2753		*TGV* 2785		*TGV* 2757			*TGV* 2759		*TGV* 2765
		N	⑤⑦ w		Ⓑ Bh	Ⓐ	⑤⑦ w	⑤⑦ w	⑤⑦ w	N	N	⑤⑦ w
Paris Est d.	...	1827	1827	...	1927	...	2004	...	...	2057	...	2127
Champagne-Ardenne TGV ▷ d.	1853	|	|	...	2007	2017	|	...	2107	|	...	|
Reims ▷ a.	1901	1913	1913	...	...	2024	2049	...	2115	2142	...	2213
Reims d.	1904	1916	1916	1938	...	2026	...	2104	2119	...	2152	2216
Rethel d.	1927	1939	1939	2004	...	2048	...	2126	2142	...	2215	|
Charleville-Mézières a.	1954	2006	2006	2031	...	2114	...	2152	2208	...	2242	2303
Sedan a.	2015	2029	...	2058	...	2134	...	2214	...	...	2311	2326

		TGV 2706		*TGV* 2778			*TGV* 2712	
	Ⓐ	Ⓐ	⚒	①–⑥ Bn	Ⓐ	⑥	①–⑥ n	Ⓐ
Sedan d.	...	...	0532	...	0600	0607	...	...
Charleville-Mézières d.	0545	...	0559	...	0628	0631	...	0659
Rethel d.	0614	...	0628	...	0657	0702	...	0729
Reims a.	0635	...	0653	...	0721	0728	...	0754
Reims ▷ d.	...	0645	0658	...	...	...	0745	0805
Champ.-Ardenne TGV ▷ d.	...	|	0706	0720	...	...	|	0815
Paris Est a.	...	0730	...	0800	...	...	0830	...

	TGV 2714			*TGV* 2720		*TGV* 2722		*TGV* 2732				*TGV* 2738	*TGV* 2746		*TGV* 2752		*TGV* 2784		*TGV* 2756			*TGV* 2762		*TGV* 2766	
	Ⓐ	Ⓐ		Ⓒ	⚒ s	①–⑥ n	⚒ ◇		⚒ ◇	⑥ u	Ⓑ z	Ⓑ h	⑥ v	Ⓑ	Ⓑ h	⚒	B	Ⓑ	⑤⑦ w	Ⓑ b			†	⑦ e	
Sedan d.	0700	0708	0737	0756	0853	...	1116	...	1210	1450	1450	...	...	1545	...	1630	...	1704	...	1743	1851	...	2100	...	...
Charleville-Mézières d.	0721	0740	0803	0817	0915	0954	1138	...	1230	1511	1517	...	1526	1605	1621	1706	...	1724	...	1813	1910	...	2115	2126	...
Rethel d.	0750	0812	0832	0846	0942	|	1205	...	1305	1541	1547	...	|	1635	|	1736	...	1758	...	1843	1937	...	...	|	...
Reims a.	0811	0836	0854	0909	1003	1040	1226	...	1333	1602	1608	...	1611	1701	1709	1759	...	1824	...	1907	2000	...	...	2211	...
Reims ▷ d.	0815	...	0900	0915	...	1045	...	1245	...	...	...	1615	1615	...	1715	1801	...	...	1845	1924	...	2015	...	2215	...
Champagne-Ardenne TGV ▷ d.	|	...	0908	|	...	|	...	|	...	...	...	|	|	...	|	1813	1819	...	|	1934	...	|	...	|	...
Paris Est a.	0900	...	...	1000	...	1130	...	1330	...	...	...	1700	1700	...	1800	...	1900	...	1930	...	...	2100	...	2300	...

B – To / from Bar le Duc (Table **381**).
N – ①②③④⑥ (also Dec. 25, Jan. 1; not Dec. 24, 31, Apr. 5, May 12, 24).
b – Also May 1, 8.
c – Ⓒ only.
e – Also Apr. 5, May 24.
g – Also Apr. 6, May 25; not Apr. 5, May 24.
h – Not Dec. 25, Jan. 1, May 13.
m – (2) Longwy - Metz and v.v. (see both directions of table).
n – Not Apr. 5, May 24.
s – Subject to alteration on Ⓐ Apr. 6 - 23.
u – Also holidays.
v – Also Dec. 25, Jan. 1, May 13.
w – Also Dec. 24, 31, Apr. 5, May 12, 24; not Dec. 25, Jan. 1.
x – Subject to alteration on Ⓐ Mar. 29 - Apr. 16.
z – Not holidays. Subject to alteration on Ⓐ Mar. 15 - Apr. 2.
TGV – [R], supplement payable, 🍷.
▷ – For full service see Table **391**.
△ – Subject to alteration on Ⓐ Feb. 22 - Mar. 12, Apr. 6 - 23.
◇ – Subject to alteration on Ⓐ Feb. 15 - 26, Mar. 15 - Apr. 2.
⊡ – An additional journey runs at 0632 on Ⓐ.
‡ – Subject to alteration on Ⓐ Feb. 1 - 12.

CHARLEVILLE MÉZIÈRES - LONGWY and METZ 389a

km		⚒ m	Ⓐ	Ⓐ x	⑥	⚒ △	†	⚒ m	⚒	†	
	Reims 389 d.	...	0632	0705	0706	1407	1407	...	1622	1729	1938
0	**Charleville-Mézières 389** d.	...	0735	0807	0807	1503	1502	...	1719	1822	2039
20	Sedan **389** a.	...	0753	0821	0821	1518	1517	...	1738	1836	2058
20	Sedan d.	...	0755	0822	0822	1519	1518	...	1739	1837	2059
69	Montmédy d.	...	0826	0853	0853	1554	1552	...	1810	1909	2130
91	Longuyon **393** d.	0633	0847	0906	0907	1614	1612	1810	1823	1923	2149
107	**Longwy 393** a.	|	0859	|	|	1627	1624	1822	|	|	2201
	Hayange d.	0705	...	0935	0935	...	...	...	1851	1951	...
170	**Metz** a.	0731	...	0958	0956	...	...	...	1912	2015	...

	Ⓐ	⚒ m	Ⓒ	⚒ s	Ⓑ ◇			⚒ m	
Metz d.	...	...	...	0704	...	...	...	1714	1835
Hayange d.	...	...	...	0728	...	...	...	1739	1857
Longwy 393 d.	0548	0619	0645	|	1013	...	1748	|	|
Longuyon **393** d.	0606	0632	0702	0802	1031	...	1806	1809	1926
Montmédy d.	0620	...	0717	0818	1045	...	1819	...	1940
Sedan a.	0652	...	0748	0852	1114	...	1850	...	2012
Sedan **389** d.	0708	...	0804	0853	1116	...	1851	...	2013
Charleville-Mézières 389 a.	0734	...	0819	0909	1133	...	1905	...	2028
Reims 389 a.	0836	...	...	1003	1228	...	2000	...	2125

FOR NOTES SEE TABLE 389 ABOVE

390 TGV EST EUROPÉEN

PARIS - STRASBOURG - BASEL

For additional connections Strasbourg - Basel see Table **385**

km		TGV 9205 Ⓐ	TGV 9207 Ⓒ	TGV 2405 Ⓐ	TGV 9571	⚒	†	TGV 9211 ②–⑤ w	TGV 9213 ⑥⑦ v		TGV 9215	EC 91 ⊕	TGV 9573	Ⓒ	Ⓐ		TGV 2369 ②–⑥	TGV 2371 ⑦		TGV 2431 ⑤ f	⚒	TGV 9217	TGV 9575 ⊙	
0	**Paris Est** d.	0624	0624	0654	0724	...	...	0824	0824	...	1024	...	1124	...	...	...	1224	1224	...	1324	...	1424	1524	...
405	Saverne a.	|	|	|	|	...	...	|	|	...	|	...	|	...	...	...	|	|	...	1521	...	|	|	...
450	**Strasbourg** a.	0843	0843	0913	0941	...	...	1043	1043	...	1243	...	1341	...	...	...	1443	1443	...	1546	...	1644	1741	...
450	**Strasbourg** 385 d.	0847	0847	...	0945	0951	0951	1047	1047	...	1247	1251	1345	1351	1351	...	1447	1447	1451	...	1553	1648	1745	1751
	Stuttgart Hbf 931 a.	|	|	...	1104	|	|	|	|	...	|	|	1504	|	|	...	|	|	|	...	|	|	1904	|
515	Colmar 385 d.	0914	|	...	...	1024	1024	|	1115	...	|	1330	...	1422	1429	...	1515	1515	1524	...	1624	|	...	1824
556	Mulhouse 385 d.	0937	0937	...	...	1045	1049	1138	1138	...	1332	1355	...	1445	1454	...	1532	1533	1545	...	1645	1730	...	1846
590	**Basel** 385 a.	0956	0956	...	...	1107	1111	1156	1156	...	1351	1420	...	1507	1518	...	...	...	1612	...	1707	1756	...	1910
	Zürich HB 510 a.	1100	1100	...	...	...	...	1300	1300	...	1500	1552	...	...	...	...	...	...	...	...	...	1914	...	...

	TGV 2443 N	TGV 2373 ⑤⑦ u	Ⓐ	⑥ t		TGV 2445 ⑤ f	TGV 2447 ⑦ e		TGV 9577 Ⓑ h	TGV 2449 ⑥ y		TGV 2457		TGV 9219	TGV 2375		TGV 2583 Ⓑ h◇	TGV 2467 Ⓑ h	295 Ⓑ		TGV 2473 ⑤ k	TGV 2469 ⑦ e	TGV 2471 ⑦ e	
Paris Est d.	1624	1624	...	...	...	1654	1654	...	1724	1724	...	1754	...	1824	1924	...	1912	2024	...	...	2124	2124	2154	...
Saverne a.	1820	|	...	...	...	|	1852	...	|	|	...	|	...	|	|	...	2140	|	...	...	|	|	|	...
Strasbourg a.	1846	1843	...	...	...	1913	1916	...	1941	1942	...	2011	...	2043	2143	...	2204	2243	...	...	2345	2345	0013	...
Strasbourg 385 d.	...	1847	1851	1851	...	...	...	...	1946	...	1951	...	...	2047	2147	...	...	...	2251	...	...	...	...	...
Stuttgart Hbf 931 a.	...	|	|	|	...	...	...	...	2105	...	|	...	...	|	|	...	...	...	|	...	...	...	...	...
Colmar 385 d.	...	|	1924	1923	...	...	...	...	...	...	2024	...	...	|	2214	...	...	...	2324	...	...	...	...	...
Mulhouse 385 d.	...	1927	1945	1952	...	...	...	...	...	...	2045	...	...	2132	2232	...	...	...	2348	...	...	...	...	...
Basel 385 a.	...	...	2008	2014	...	...	...	...	...	...	2107	...	...	2151	...	...	...	...	0013	...	...	...	...	...
Zürich HB 510 a.	...	...	...	...	...	...	...	...	...	...	...	...	...	2300	...	...	...	...	...	...	...	...	...	...

	TGV 2402 ① g	TGV 2584 ①–⑥ n◇	Ⓐ	TGV 2404 Ⓐ	Ⓐ	TGV 2350 Ⓐ	TGV 2406 ⑥ v			TGV 2410 Ⓑ h	TGV 2352 ⑥ v	296 Ⓑ ⊗	TGV 9578 ①–⑥ p	TGV 2412 ⑦ d		TGV 9210 ①–⑥ n	TGV 9212 ⑦ e		TGV 9576 ⊙	TGV 9214		Ⓐ	TGV 2424 ①–⑥ n	TGV 2426 ⑦ e
Zürich HB 510 d.	...	...	...	...	...	...	...	...	...	...	...	...	...	...	...	0702	0702	...	...	...	...	...	...	...
Basel 385 d.	...	...	...	...	0517	...	...	...	0537	...	...	0646	...	...	...	0802	0802	...	...	1002	...	1047	...	...
Mulhouse 385 d.	...	...	0454	...	0541	0553	...	...	0601	...	0622	0710	...	...	...	0829	0827	...	...	1024	...	1111	...	...
Colmar 385 d.	...	...	0518	...	0601	0613	...	...	0627	...	0643	0731	...	...	...	|	0846	...	...	1044	...	1131	...	...
Stuttgart Hbf 931 d.	...	...	|	...	|	|	...	...	|	...	|	|	0655	...	...	|	|	...	0855	|	...	|	...	...
Strasbourg 385 a.	...	...	0555	...	0633	0639	...	...	0703	...	0709	0803	0813	...	...	0910	0911	...	1013	1110	...	1203	...	...
Strasbourg d.	0515	0545	...	0615	...	0645	0645	...	...	0715	0715	...	0817	0816	...	0915	0916	...	1017	1115	...	...	1213	1215
Saverne d.	|	0609	...	|	...	|	|	...	...	|	|	...	|	|	...	|	|	...	|	|	...	...	1238	|
Paris Est a.	0734	0845	...	0834	...	0904	0904	...	...	0934	0934	...	1034	1034	...	1134	1134	...	1234	1334	...	...	1434	1434

	⚒	†	TGV 9574 ①–④ m	TGV 9574 ⑤–⑦ s	TGV 2356 ⑤–⑦ s	TGV 9216		TGV 2440	TGV 2448 ⑦ e	⚒	TGV 2446 ⑤ f	TGV 9218	Ⓐ	TGV 2452 ①–⑤ b	TGV 9572 ⑥⑦ c	TGV 9220 Ⓐ	TGV 9222 Ⓒ	TGV 9570 ①–⑤ b	TGV 2360 Ⓐ	TGV 2360 Ⓒ	TGV 2470 ⑤ k	TGV 2472 ⑦ e		TGV 2474 ⑦
Zürich HB 510 d.	...	...	...	...	...	1302	...	...	...	...	...	1502	...	...	...	1627	1627	...	...	...	...	...	...	...
Basel 385 d.	1217	...	...	...	...	1402	...	...	...	1518	...	1602	1647	...	...	1802	1802	...	...	...	...	...	2016	...
Mulhouse 385 d.	1240	1238	...	...	1327	1428	...	...	...	1541	...	1630	1711	...	...	1824	1825	...	1924	1924	...	...	2041	...
Colmar 385 d.	1301	1306	...	...	|	|	...	...	...	1600	...	|	1732	...	...	1844	|	...	|	1943	...	...	2101	...
Stuttgart Hbf 931 d.	|	|	1255	1255	|	|	...	...	...	|	...	|	|	...	1655	|	|	1855	|	|	...	...	|	...
Strasbourg 385 a.	1333	1354	1413	1415	1407	1510	...	...	...	1633	...	1711	1804	...	1813	1910	1910	2015	2010	2010	...	...	2134	...
Strasbourg d.	...	...	1417	1420	1420	1515	...	1615	1641	...	1644	1715	...	1816	1817	1915	1915	2020	2020	2017	2115	2115	...	2215
Saverne d.	...	...	|	|	|	|	...	|	1705	...	|	|	...	|	|	|	|	|	|	|	|	|	...	|
Paris Est a.	...	...	1634	1637	1637	1734	...	1834	1904	...	1904	1934	...	2034	2034	2134	2134	2237	2237	2234	2334	2334	...	0034

PARIS - METZ - LUXEMBOURG

For additional connections Metz - Luxembourg see Table **388**

km		TGV 2601 ① g	TGV 2803 ①–⑥ n	TGV 2503 ☆	TGV 2809 ▽		TGV 2615 △	⊖	TGV 2621	TGV 2827	TGV 2509 Ⓐ ☆	TGV 2629 ⑦ e	TGV 2831	TGV 2833 ⑦ e	TGV 2633 Ⓐ	TGV 2835 Ⓐ	TGV 2837 Ⓒ	TGV 2839 Ⓐ	TGV 2639 Ⓒ	298 Ⓑ	TGV 2643 Ⓐ	TGV 2843 ⑦ e	TGV 2647 ⑤⑦ u	
0	**Paris Est** d.	0639	0709	0812	0839	...	1039	...	1239	1409	1412	1539	1609	1739	1739	1839	1839	1939	1939	...	2039	2039	2139	...
136	Champagne-Ardenne TGV d.	|	|	|	0921	...	|	...	|	|	|	|	|	|	|	|	|	|	|	...	|	|	|	...
236	Meuse TGV a.	|	|	0912	|	...	|	...	|	|	1512	|	|	|	1838	|	1938	|	|	...	|	|	|	...
315	**Metz** a.	0802	0832	...	1008	...	1202	...	1402	1533	...	1702	1732	1902	1908	2002	2008	2102	2102	...	2202	2202	2302	...
315	**Metz** 388 d.	...	0835	...	1012	...	...	1219	...	1537	...	...	1736	1905	...	2005	2012	2106	...	2130	...	2205	...	2321
345	Thionville 388 a.	...	0855	...	1028	...	...	1247	...	1554	...	...	1753	1922	...	2023	2028	2123	...	2151	...	2222	...	2350
379	**Luxembourg** 388 a.	...	0918	...	1052	...	...	1315	...	1617	...	...	1815	1945	...	2045	2051	2145	...	2214	...	2245	...	0017

	TGV 2650 Ⓐ	TGV 2853 Ⓐ	TGV 2857 ⑥ v	TGV 2855 Ⓐ	TGV 2861 ① g	Ⓐ	TGV 2660 ②–⑤ x	TGV 2863 ⑦ e	TGV 2662 ⑥ v	TGV 2865 ①–⑥ ⦵	TGV 2664 ⑦ e	TGV 2537 ☆	TGV 2869		TGV 2672	TGV 2676 Ⓑ h	TGV 2881 ①–⑥ n	TGV 2881 ⑦ e	TGV 2545 Ⓑ h☆	TGV 2684 ⑤⑦ u		TGV 2891 ⑤⑦ u	TGV 2889 N	TGV 2893 ⑦ e
Luxembourg 388 d.	...	0603	0640	0643	0810	0755	...	0807	...	1000	...	...	1308	1430	...	...	1712	1710	...	...	...	1902	1906	2013
Thionville 388 d.	...	0625	0701	0704	0831	0824	...	0828	...	1021	...	...	1329	1453	...	...	1735	1731	...	...	...	1923	1928	2034
Metz 388 a.	...	0645	0719	0721	0849	0845	...	0845	...	1038	...	...	1347	1518	...	...	1752	1749	...	...	...	1943	1945	2051
Metz d.	0625	0650	0725	0725	0855	...	0855	0849	0919	1042	1042	...	1353	...	1555	1655	1755	1755	...	1855	...	1948	1948	2055
Meuse TGV d.	|	0719	|	|	|	...	|	0919	0949	|	|	1245	|	...	|	|	|	|	1847	|	...	|	|	|
Champagne-Ardenne TGV a.	|	|	|	|	|	...	|	|	|	|	|	|	|	...	|	|	|	|	|	|	...	2035	2035	|
Paris Est a.	0749	0819	0849	0849	1019	...	1019	1019	1049	1205	1205	1345	1519	...	1720	1820	1920	1920	1946	2019	...	2119	2119	2219

N – ①②③④⑥ (also Dec. 25, Jan. 1; not Dec. 24, 31, Apr. 5, May 12, 24).

b – Not Dec. 24, 25, 31, Jan. 1, Apr. 5, May 24.
c – Also Dec. 24, 25, 31, Jan. 1, Apr. 5, May 24.
d – Also Dec. 25, Jan. 1, Apr. 5, May 24.
e – Also Apr. 5, May 24.
f – Also Dec. 24, 31, May 12; not Dec. 25, Jan. 1.
g – Also Apr. 6, May 25; not Apr. 5, May 24.
h – Not Dec. 25, Jan. 1, May 13.
k – Also Dec. 24, 31, May 12.
m – Not Dec. 24, 31, Apr. 5, May 12, 13, 24.
n – Not Apr. 5, May 24.
p – Not Dec. 25, Jan. 1, Apr. 5, May 24.
q – Not Dec. 24, 31, Apr. 4, May 23.
s – Also Dec. 24, 31, Apr. 5, May 12, 13, 24.
t – Not May 1, 8.
u – Also Dec. 24, 31, Apr. 5, May 12, 24; not Dec. 25, Jan. 1.
v – Also Dec. 25, Jan. 1, May 13.
w – Not Dec. 25, Jan. 1, May 13.

x – Not Dec. 25, Jan. 1, Apr. 6, May 13, 25.
y – Also Dec. 24, 31, Apr. 4.
z – Also Dec. 24, 31, May 12, 13.

ICE – 🅁 (Paris - Saarbrücken and v.v.); supplement payable.
TGV – 🅁, supplement payable, 🍸.

⊙ – To/from München (Table **32**).
◇ – Via Nancy, calling also at Sarrebourg (Table **383**).
⊡ – Calls at Meuse TGV (see Paris - Metz section).
⊕ – Not Dec. 14 - 18, Jan. 25 - 29, Feb. 1 - 5, ①–⑤ Mar. 29 - Apr. 16.
⊗ – Subject to alteration Mar. 29 - Apr. 3, Apr. 5 - 10.
⊖ – Subject to alteration on Ⓐ Mar. 29 - Apr. 9.
△ – Not Apr. 26 - 30.
▽ – Not Mar. 29 - 31, Apr. 1 - 2, 5 - 9, 26 - 30.
▷ – Not May 17 - 21.
☆ – To/from Nancy (next page).
⦵ – Not Mar. 29 - 31, Apr. 1, 2, 5 - 9, 12 - 16, 26 - 30.

TGV EST EUROPÉEN 390

PARIS - NANCY

Certain trains continue beyond Nancy to Épinal and Remiremont (Table **386**) or to Lunéville and St Dié (Table **387**). Train **2583/4** continues to / from Strasbourg.

km		TGV 2501 ①–⑥ n		TGV 2503 ⊡	TGV 2505 Ⓐ		TGV 2507 Ⓒ	TGV 2571		TGV 2509 Ⓐ ⊡	TGV 2591 ⑦ e		TGV 2513 ⑥ v	TGV 2515 Ⓑ h	TGV 2517 Ⓐ		TGV 2573 ▷	TGV 2583 Ⓑ h		TGV 2519 ①–⑥ n	TGV 2595 ⑦ e		TGV 2521 ⑦ e	
0	**Paris Est** d.	0712	...	0812	0905	...	1042	1212	...	1412	1412	...	1512	1612	1712	...	1812	1912	...	2012	2012	...	2112	...
330	**Nancy** a.	0842	...	0948	1035	...	1212	1342	...	1550	1543	...	1642	1742	1842	...	1942	2042	...	2142	2141	...	2242	...

	TGV 2531 Ⓐ	TGV 2584 ①–⑥ n	TGV 2596 ①–⑥ n	TGV 2533 ⑦ e		TGV 2576 Ⓒ	TGV 2535 Ⓐ		TGV 2537 ⊡	TGV 2539 ①–④ m		TGV 2541 ⑤–⑦ s	TGV 2543 Ⓑ h		TGV 2578 ①–⑥ n	TGV 2545 Ⓑ h⊡		TGV 2547 ⑤⑥ z	TGV 2580 ⑦ e		TGV 2549 Ⓐ	TGV 2598 ⑦ e	TGV 2551 ⑦ e	
Nancy d.	0615	0715	0815	0815	...	1016	1028	...	1210	1345	...	1515	1615	...	1715	1811	...	1915	1915	...	2015	2015	2115	...
Paris Est a.	0745	0845	0945	0945	...	1145	1200	...	1345	1515	...	1645	1745	...	1845	1946	...	2045	2045	...	2145	2145	2245	...

PARIS - SAARBRÜCKEN

🅁 on cross-border journeys and journeys within France

km	*ICE trains with* ✕	ICE 9551 ①–⑥ p	TGV 9553 ①–⑥ n	TGV 9553 ⑦ e		ICE 9555		ICE 9557 Ⓑ q	ICE 9559	
0	**Paris Est** d.	0704	0909	0909	...	1309	...	1709	1905	...
304	Lorraine TGV d.	|	|	|	...	|	...	|	|	...
372	Forbach 🏛 d.	0849	|	1050	...	|	...	|	2049	...
383	**Saarbrücken** Hbf a.	0857	1056	1056	...	1457	...	1857	2057	...
	Frankfurt (Main) Hbf **919** a.	1058	1258	1258	...	1658	...	2058	2258	...

ICE trains with ✕	ICE 9558 ①–⑥ p	ICE 9556 ①–⑥ n	ICE 9556 ⑦ e		ICE 9554		TGV 9552	ICE 9550 Ⓑ q	
Frankfurt (Main) Hbf **919** d.	0600	0901	0901	...	1301	...	1658	1901	...
Saarbrücken Hbf d.	0800	1101	1101	...	1501	...	1903	2101	...
Forbach 🏛 d.	0810	|	1111	...	|	...	1913	2112	...
Lorraine TGV d.	|	|	|	...	|	...	|	|	...
Paris Est a.	0949	1249	1253	...	1650	...	2053	2253	...

← FOR NOTES SEE FOOT OF PREVIOUS PAGE

STRASBOURG - NORTHERN and WESTERN FRANCE 391

	TGV 5420 ①–⑥ n	TGV 5420 ⑦ e	TGV 5486	TGV 5450 ⑦ e△	TGV 5450 ①–⑥ n△	TGV 5476 Ⓒ	TGV 5452 ⑤–⑦ w	TGV 5422	TGV 5452 ①–④ m	TGV 5454	TGV 5438	TGV 5488	TGV 5426 Ⓑ h
Strasbourg d.	0611	0620	0625	0741	0745	0852	1153	1206v	1420	1636r	1648	1756	1900
Lorraine TGV d.	0725	0732	0740	0852	0858	1003	1307	1326	1539	1745	1759	1909	2011
Meuse TGV d.	|	|	|	0911	0923	|	|	|	|	|	1823	|	|
Champagne-Ardenne TGV d.	0812	0812	0828	0944	0949	1045	1347	1407	1624	1832	1858	1949	2057
Marne la Vallée - Chessy a.	|	|	0856	1013	1018	1117	1416	|	1652	1908	|	2020	|
Massy TGV a.	|	|	0930	1058	1058	1157	1458	|	1728	1946	|	2058	|
Paris Charles de Gaulle ✈ a.	0843	0843	|	|	|	|	|	1437	|	|	1934	|	2128
Mantes la Jolie a.	|	|	|	|	|	|	|	|	|	|	2106	|	|
Rouen a.	|	|	|	|	|	|	|	|	|	|	2155c	|	|
Le Havre a.	|	|	|	|	|	|	|	|	|	|	2240c	|	|
TGV Haute Picardie a.	0914	0914	|	|	|	|	|	|	|	|	...	|	|
Arras a.	|	|	|	|	|	|	|	1520	|	|	...	|	|
Douai a.	|	|	|	|	|	|	|	1538	|	|	...	|	|
Lille Europe a.	0946	0946	|	|	|	|	|	1559	|	|	...	|	2223z
Le Mans a.	...	...	1020	|	|	1249	|	...	|	|	...	2151	...
Angers a.	...	...	1059	|	|	|	|	...	|	|	...	2236	...
Nantes a.	...	...	1140	|	|	|	|	...	|	|	...	2314	...
Laval a.	...	...	...	|	|	1332	|	...	|	|	...	...	...
Rennes a.	...	...	...	|	|	1410	|	...	|	|	...	...	...
St Pierre des Corps a.	...	...	...	1153	1153	...	1552	...	1821	2042	...	...	...
Futuroscope a.	...	...	...	1230	1230	...	|	...	|	|	...	...	...
Poitiers a.	...	...	...	1240	1240	...	1633	...	1902	2127	...	...	...
Angoulême a.	...	...	...	1326	1326	...	1719	...	1948	2216	...	...	...
Bordeaux St Jean a.	...	...	...	1430	1430	...	1824	...	2052	2318	...	...	...

	TGV 5400 ①–⑥ n	TGV 5440 ⊖	TGV 5436	TGV 5478	TGV 5402	TGV 5442 Ⓒ ⊖	TGV 5442 Ⓐ	TGV 5480	TGV 5416	TGV 5466 Ⓒ	TGV 5444 ⑦ e	TGV 5446 ①–⑥ u△	
Bordeaux St Jean d.	...	0633	...	...	...	1022	1030	...	...	...	1613	1708	...
Angoulême d.	...	0733	...	...	...	1121	1135	...	...	...	1714	1812	...
Poitiers d.	...	0819	...	...	...	1209	1226	...	...	...	1805	1904	...
Futuroscope d.	...	|	...	...	...	|	|	...	...	...	1815	1915	...
St Pierre des Corps d.	...	0902	...	...	...	1251	1307	...	...	...	1854	1951	...
Rennes d.	...	|	...	...	...	|	|	...	...	1710	|	|	...
Laval d.	...	|	...	...	...	|	|	...	...	1748	|	|	...
Nantes d.	...	|	...	0834	...	|	|	1520	...	|	|	|	...
Angers d.	...	|	...	0913	...	|	|	1556	...	|	|	|	...
Le Mans d.	...	|	...	0956	...	|	|	1640	...	1835	|	|	...
Lille Europe d.	0652	|	...	|	1121	|	|	|	1805	|	|	|	...
Douai d.	|	|	...	|	1142	|	|	|	|	|	|	|	...
Arras d.	|	|	...	|	1201	|	|	|	|	|	|	|	...
TGV Haute Picardie d.	|	|	...	|	1219	|	|	|	|	|	|	|	...
Le Havre d.	|	|	0743	|	|	|	|	|	|	|	|	|	...
Rouen d.	|	|	0833	|	|	|	|	|	|	|	|	|	...
Mantes la Jolie d.	|	|	0917	|	|	|	|	|	|	|	|	|	...
Paris Charles de Gaulle ✈ d.	0746	|	1041	|	1252	|	|	|	1905	|	|	|	...
Massy TGV d.	|	0958	|	1050	|	1349	1402	1730	|	1926	1947	2045	...
Marne la Vallée - Chessy d.	|	1039	|	1128	|	1429	1446	1808	|	2009	2029	2125	...
Champagne-Ardenne TGV a.	0816	1107	1113	1157	1324	1458	1513	1838	1934	2036	2057	2152	...
Meuse TGV a.	|	|	1147	|	|	|	|	|	|	|	2127	2219	...
Lorraine TGV a.	0857	1148	1208	1246	1405	1542	1554	1919	2015	2117	2148	2239*	...
Strasbourg a.	1010	1304	1333	1359	1517	1655	1717	2032	2131	2229	2302	2352*	...

b – Also Dec. 24, 31, Apr. 5, May 12, 13, 24; not Apr. 9, 16, 23.
c – On ⑥ arrive Le Havre 2245. On ⑦ arrive Rouen 2149, Le Havre 2234.
e – Also Apr. 5, May 24.
h – Not Dec. 25, Jan. 1, May 13.
m – Not Dec. 24, 31, Apr. 5, May 12, 13, 24.
n – Not Apr. 5, May 24.
r – 1633 on ⑤⑦ and holidays.
u – Not Dec. 24, 31, Apr. 5, May 24.
v – 1210 on Ⓒ.
w – Also Dec. 24, 31, Apr. 5, May 12, 13, 24.
z – 2227 on ⑦.

TGV – 🅁, supplement payable, 🍸.
⊖ – Subject to alteration Bordeaux - Angoulême on May 13.
⊡ – Subject to alteration on Ⓐ Apr. 6 - 23.
△ – Subject to alteration Bordeaux - Angoulême and v.v. on May 13 - 16.
▽ – Subject to alteration on Ⓐ Jan. 11 - 29, Apr. 6 - 23.
▷ – Subject to alteration on Ⓐ Feb. 1 - 12, Apr. 6 - 23.
* – 4 - 5 minutes later on ⑤.

CONNECTING SERVICE

REIMS - CHAMPAGNE ARNENNE TGV:

Journey 8 - 10 minutes

From Reims:

0658⚒, 0741Ⓒ, 0749Ⓐ, 0805, 0900, 1023Ⓐ⊡, 1024Ⓒ, 1052, 1150⊡, 1306⊡, 1324⑤–⑦b, 1342Ⓐ▽, 1343Ⓒ, 1449Ⓒ, 1458Ⓐ, 1600①–④m, 1801⚒, 1813†, 1820⚒, 1924, 2007, 2034, 2048†, 2136⚒.

From Champagne-Ardenne TGV:

0818⚒, 0824†, 0839Ⓑ, 0843⑥, 1001▷, 1110⊡, 1117⊡, 1209⊡, 1339, 1359⑤–⑦w, 1419, 1447, 1525, 1631①–④m, 1848, 1853, 1957, 2017Ⓑ, 2046Ⓒ, 2050Ⓐ, 2106Ⓐ, 2107†, 2112†, 2202Ⓐ.

CONNECTING 🚌 SERVICES

Bus services connect with the trains in Table **391** on the following routes:

Nancy - Lorraine TGV (journey 35 minutes)

Metz - Lorraine TGV (journey 25 minutes)

Verdun - Meuse TGV (journey 25 minutes)

For further details ✆ 03 87 78 67 09.

CHÂLONS EN CHAMPAGNE - VERDUN 392

2nd class

km		Ⓐd	⑥⑦	Ⓐd	Ⓐ	⑥t	H	†	⑤f	
0	**Châlons en Champagne** d.	0819	1022	1222	1828	2027	2042	2042	2055	...
62	Ste Menehould d.	0905	1109	1311	1928	2114	2130	2129	2142	...
107	**Verdun** a.	0944	1148	1350	2008	2153	2210	2207	2222	...

	①g	⚒	†		Ⓐu	Ⓐ			
Verdun d.	0503	0609	0641	...	1044	1539	...	1845	...
Ste Menehould d.	0541	0647	0720	...	1122	1618	...	1923	...
Châlons en Champagne a.	0631	0735	0807	...	1210	1706	...	2009	...

H – ①–④ (not Dec. 24, 31, Apr. 5, May 12, 13, 19, 20, 24).
d – Subject to alteration Feb. 8 - 19.
f – Also Dec. 24, 31, May 12; not Dec. 25, Jan. 1. To Metz, arrive 2340.
g – Also Apr. 6, May 25; not Apr. 5, May 24.
t – Not May 1, 8.
u – Subject to alteration on Ⓐ Feb. 1 - 19.

392a VERDUN - METZ

km		Ⓐ	⚒	r	🚌 Ⓐ	Ⓒ	Ⓐu	Ⓐ	🚌 Ⓐ	Ⓐ	⑥t	†	⑤f
0	**Verdun** d.	0638	...	1050	1203	...	1238	...	1700	1814	...	1927	2225
40	Conflans-Jarny d.	0718	0736	1128	1256	1318	1318	1636	1752	1852	1852	2006	2307
66	Hagondange **388** d.	|	0813	1204	|	1357	1356	1709	|	1925	1925	|	|
84	**Metz** **388** a.	0752	0825	1217	1335	1411	*1416*	1723	1840	1938	1938	2039	2340

	🚌 Ⓐv	⚒	⚒u	†	🚌 Ⓐ	Ⓐr	†	Ⓐ	⑥t	🚌 Ⓐ
Metz **388** d.	0715	0727	1233	1233	1420	1628	1656	1821	1828	1855
Hagondange **388** d.	|	0739	1247	1247	|	|	1714	|	1844	|
Conflans-Jarny d.	0759	0810	1325	1324	1504	1709	1757	1855	1923	1939
Verdun a.	0845	...	1400	...	1550	1744	1832	1929	1957	2025

f – Also Dec. 24, 31, May 12; not Dec. 25, Jan. 1.
r – Subject to alteration on Ⓐ Feb. 22 - Mar. 5.
t – Not May 1, 8.
u – Subject to alteration Ⓐ Feb. 22 - Mar. 5, Mar. 29 - Apr. 30.
v – Runs one hour earlier on ①.

393 LONGWY - NANCY / LUXEMBOURG

km		Ⓐ	⚒	Ⓐ	⑥t	Ⓐu	†	⑥t	†	Ⓐ	†
0	**Longwy** **389a** d.	0539	0640	0838	1051	1218	1241	1658	1743	1826	1940
16	Longuyon **389a** d.	0552	0654	0851	1104	1232	1254	1711	1757	1839	1953
57	Conflans-Jarny d.	0621	0724	0921	1135	1302	1326	1740	1827	1908	2023
100	Pont-à-Mousson d.	0653	0754	0949	1203	1332	1354	1809	1855	1938	2052
128	**Nancy** a.	0710	0814	1007	1221	1348	1410	1826	1912	1954	2109

	Ⓐ	Ⓐr	⑥t	⑦	⑥t	Ⓐ	†	Ⓐ	Ⓐ	⑥t	†	†
Nancy d.	0605	0848	0906	1006	1254	1402	1707	1734	1836	1856	1937	2246
Pont-à-Mousson d.	0623	0907	0923	1023	1311	1422	1724	1753	1854	1915	1955	2304
Conflans-Jarny d.	0652	0937	0952	1052	1340	1455	1754	1826	1924	1945	2025	2333
Longuyon **389a** d.	0723	1007	1021	1120	1410	1525	1825	1855	1953	2014	2054	0002
Longwy **389a** a.	0735	1020	1033	1132	1422	1537	1836	1908	2005	2027	2106	0016

km		Ⓐb	⚒z	Ⓐ	⚒v	Ⓐ	Ⓐr	⚒v	Ⓐ	
0	**Longwy** d.	0622	0642	0725	0741	*0819*	1316	1843	1910	...
8	Rodange 🛃 d.	0630	0650	0737	0749	0833	1324	1904	1918	...
27	**Luxembourg** a.	0703	0720	0802	0819	0859	1354	1934	2010	...

	⑥v	Ⓐh	Ⓐr	Ⓐ	Ⓐn	Ⓐ	Ⓐ	Ⓐ	⚒v	Ⓐn	Ⓐ
Luxembourg d.	0601	*0735*	1201	1601	1626	1701	1726	1743	1801	1826	1901
Rodange 🛃 d.	0628	0831	1228	1628	1657	1729	1757	1810	1828	1857	1928
Longwy a.	0635	0837	1235	1635	1704	1736	1804	1817	1835	1904	1935

b – Change at Pétange.
h – To Nancy (upper table).
n – To Longuyon (arrive 16 minutes later).
r – Subject to alteration on Apr. 6 - 9.
t – Not May 1, 8.
u – Subject to alteration Mar. 29 - Apr. 9.
v – Not Dec. 26, May 1.
z – From Longuyon on Ⓐ (depart 0621).

LONGWY - METZ Rail service: from Longwy 0619 ⚒, from Metz 1714 ⚒, journey 72 mins.
🚌 service (journey 55 mins):
From Longwy: 0505 Ⓐ, 0735, 0930 ⚒, 1240 ⚒, 1515 ⑤, 1645 Ⓐ, 1838 †, 1920 ⑥**t**, 1930 Ⓐ.
From Metz: 0620 Ⓐ, 0842 ⚒, 0850 †, 1220 ⚒, 1417 ⑤, 1615 Ⓐ, 1805 ⚒, 2020 Ⓒ, 2115 Ⓐ.

394 METZ - FORBACH - SAARBRÜCKEN

km		Ⓐ	Ⓐ	⑥ t	⚒	⚒	†	Ⓐ ◇c	⑥ t	⑦ u	⚒ c	⚒ c	▽c	⊙		Ⓐ	Ⓐ		Ⓐ	Ⓐ	†	⑥ t	Ⓐ		①–④ m	⑤ f	†
0	**Metz** d.	0554	0642	0643	0741	0842	0842	0933	1042	1044	1216	1242	1345	1549	1641	1716	1747	1816	1834	1842	1919	1924	2019	2216	2339	2339
50	St Avold d.	0635	0718	0721	0812	0915	0914	1005	1113	1122	1252	1313	1418	1621	1713	1752	1818	1853	1911	1926	2006	2003	2050	2247	0011	0012
70	Forbach a.	0650	0734	0738	0826	0929	0927	1020	1127	1139	1308	1326	1432	1635	1727	1808	1832	1910	1924	1941	2022	2019	2104	2300	0024	0026
70	Forbach d.	0655	*0743*	0744	*0844*	0937	*0937*	1025	*1140*	1144	*1321*v	*1340*a	1437	1645	*1740*	...	*1844*	1917	*1938*	*1953*	2031	2024	*2117*r	*2314*	*0029*	0031
81	**Saarbrücken** a.	0705	*0752*	0752	*0853*	0945	*0945*	1033	*1149*	1152	*1330*v	*1349*a	1445	1654	*1749*	...	*1853*	1927	*1947*	*2002*	2040	2034	*2126*r	*2323*	*0038*	0039

	⚒ △	⚒	⚒	Ⓐ	Ⓐ	Ⓒ	Ⓐ	†	⚒	Ⓐ d	⑥ t	⚒ d		d	Ⓐ	Ⓒ	Ⓐ	†	Ⓐ	⑥ t	⚒	Ⓑ	†	⚒ ▽	Ⓐ
Saarbrücken d.	0503	*0553*a	*0631*	0651	*0731*	0731	*0831*	*0917*	*0925*	*1131*	1153	...	1233	*1431*	*1631*	1631	...	...	1731	1753	...	*1831*	*1911*	1931	2240
Forbach a.	0511	*0602*a	*0640*	0700	*0740*	0740	*0840*	*0926*	*0934*	*1140*	1202	...	1242	*1440*	*1640*	1642	...	...	1739	1802	...	*1840*	*1920*	1940	2249
Forbach d.	0516	0607	0645	0707	0750	0745	0845	0931	0939	1145	...	1207	1244	1445	1645	1645	1707	1707	1744	...	1807	1847	1925	1945	...
St Avold d.	0533	0623	0659	0723	0805	0800	0900	0947	0952	1200	...	1223	1301	1459	1701	1700	1724	1724	1801	...	1823	1902	1940	2000	...
Metz a.	0610	0705	0734	0801	0837	0830	0932	1023	1023	1233	...	1301	1339	1530	1734	1731	1804	1810	1838	...	1858	1936	2014	2032	...

a – Ⓐ only.
c – Subject to alteration Jan. 25 - Feb. 5.
d – Subject to alteration on Ⓐ Jan. 11 - Feb. 5.
f – Not Dec. 25, Jan. 1, Apr. 2.
m – Not Apr. 5, May 13, 24.
r – ⚒ only.
t – Not May 1, 8.
u – Also May 1, 8.
v – Not ⑤.
◇ – Change at Forbach on ①.
△ – Change at Forbach on Ⓐ.
▽ – Change at Forbach on ⑤.
⊙ – Change at Forbach on ⑤–⑦.

Note: a modified Sunday service operates on Dec. 26, Apr. 2.

METZ - SARREGUEMINES Journey 62 - 73 minutes:
From Metz: 1212 ⚒**c**, 1707 Ⓐ, 1818 ⑥**t**, 1919 Ⓑ.
From Sarreguemines: 0619 ⚒, 0727 Ⓐ, 1210 ⚒**d**, 1714 †.

395 STRASBOURG - SAARBRÜCKEN

km		Ⓐ	Ⓐ		⑥ t	Ⓐ	†		⊕	Ⓐ ⊕	⑥ t		†	Ⓐ ⊕	Ⓐ	⑥ t	Ⓐ	⚒	Ⓐ	†	⑥ t	Ⓐ	†	
0	**Strasbourg** d.	0554	0637	...	0752	0757	0845	...	1100	1230	1300	...	1430	1431	1530	1600	1625	1729	1830	1910	1930	1951	2010	...
71	Diemeringen d.	0645	0732	...	0847	0849	0943	...	1154	1326	1355	...	1522	1522	1622	1655	1729	1832	1929	2003	2023	2045	2112	...
97	Sarreguemines a.	0710	0752	...	0911	0911	1006	...	1217	1349	1418	...	1544	1544	1644	1720	1753	1856	1953	2023	2044	2105	2136	...
97	Sarreguemines 🛃 ▲ d.	0711	...	...	0912	0912	1023	...	1223	1355	1424	...	1555	...	1655	...	...	...	...	2026	2055	2126	...	...
115	**Saarbrücken** Hbf ▲ a.	0727	...	...	0927	0927	1042	...	1244	1415	1441	...	1615	...	1715	...	...	...	...	2043	2115	2143	...	...

	Ⓐ	Ⓐ	⚒	⚒		Ⓒ	Ⓐ ⊕	⑥ t	⚒ ⊕	†	Ⓐ ⊕	⑤ v	①–④ m	†	Ⓒ	Ⓐ	†	Ⓐ
Saarbrücken Hbf ▲ d.	0443	...	...	...	0745	1024	1124	1124	...	1224	1324	1511	1524	...	1714	...	...	1814
Sarreguemines 🛃 ▲ a.	0459	...	...	...	0802	1044	1144	1144	...	1244	1343	1529	1544	...	1732	...	...	1832
Sarreguemines d.	0501	0535	0605	0701	0805	1045	1145	1145	1245	1245	1344	1536	1551	1641	1742	1742	1824	1835
Diemeringen d.	0519	0554	0628	0727	0829	1106	1205	1206	1308	1308	1405	1557	1612	1704	1805	1806	1850	1858
Strasbourg a.	0625	0700	0735	0831	0927	1200	1258	1300	1404	1404	1505	1654	1710	1801	1900	1901	1952	2002

m – Not Apr. 5, May 13, 24.
t – Not May 1, 8.
v – Not Dec. 25, Jan. 1.
⊕ – Subject to alteration Ⓐ Mar. 22 - Apr. 2.

Dec. 26, Apr. 2: a Sunday service operates.

▲ – Additional light rail service operates **Sarreguemines Bahnhof - Saarbrücken Hbf** (line **S1** continuing to / starting from Ludwigstrasse and Riegelsberg Süd). Journey time: 30 minutes.
From Sarreguemines: ⚒ hourly 0516 - 0016, † hourly 0716 - 0016. Runs every 30 minutes 0516 - 0916 and 1216 - 2116 on Ⓐ, 0816 - 1816 on ⑥, 1216 - 1816 on †.
From Saarbrücken: ⚒ hourly 0440 - 2340, † hourly 0740 - 2340. Runs every 30 minutes 0440 - 0840 and 1140 - 2040 on Ⓐ, 0740 - 1740 on ⑥, 1140 - 1740 on †.

396 STRASBOURG - WISSEMBOURG

66 km

	Ⓐ	Ⓐr	Ⓒ	r	⑥t	Ⓐ	r	Ⓒ	Ⓐ		Ⓐ		
Strasbourg d.	0728	0809	0910	1055	1210	1224	1353	1555	1640	1719	1750	1825	1926
Haguenau d.	0803	0843	0942	1125	1242	1251	1429	1649	1706	1743	1822	1857	1953
Wissembourg § a.	0831	0919	1017	1158	1318	1325	1458	1724	1738	1824	1851	1941	2026

	⑥t	Ⓐ	Ⓐr	Ⓒ	Ⓐr	⑥t		r		⚒	†
Wissembourg § d.	0830	0844	0930	1036	1214	1238	1336	1540	1744	1859	2036
Haguenau d.	0901	0918	1003	1110	1303	1318	1402	1609	1822	1940	2103
Strasbourg a.	0935	0950	1035	1142	1326	1350	1425	1634	1855	2017	2137

r – Subject to alteration Ⓐ Mar. 1 - 19.
t – Not May 1, 8.
§ – For connections see Table **918**.
Dec. 26, Apr. 2: a Sunday service operates.

Additional trains from Strasbourg: 0615 ⑥**t**, 0618 Ⓐ; from Wissembourg 0608 Ⓐ, 0640 ⚒, 0727 Ⓐ, 0744 ⑥**t**. Additional trains run Strasbourg - Haguenau (1 - 2 trains per hour).

397 PRIVATE TOURIST RAILWAYS

CHEMIN DE FER DE LA MURE. Scenic electric railway

St Georges de Commiers - La Mure, *30 km*. **Days of running**: daily Apr. 1 - Oct. 31.

	D	B	C	B
St Georges de C. d.	0945	1200	1430	1700
La Mure a.	1135	1345	1620	1835

	B	B	D	C
La Mure d.	0945	1200	1430	1700
St Georges de C. a.	1115	1330	1605	1835

B – July 1 - Aug. 31. **C** – May 1 - Sept. 30. **D** – Apr. 1 - Oct. 31.
For SNCF connections see Table **362**. ✆ 04 76 735 734 www.trainlamure.com

TRAMWAY DU MONT BLANC - Summer season June 13 - Sept. 20

Runs from St Gervais Le Fayet (opposite SNCF station) to Nid d'Aigle (altitude 2380 metres). Journey 70 - 75 mins. The highest rack railway in France. For contact details see next column.

June 13 - July 7 and **Aug. 27 - Sept. 20**:
From St Gervais Le Fayet: 0745, 0910, 1015, 1140, 1340, 1440. *2009 timings*
From Nid d'Aigle: 0900, 1025, 1150, 1325, 1535, 1635.

July 8 - Aug. 26:
From St Gervais Le Fayet: 0715, 0910, 1015, 1045, 1140, 1310, 1340, 1410, 1540, 1640, 1710.
From Nid d'Aigle: 0900, 1025, 1150, 1225, 1250, 1430, 1525, 1550, 1650, 1750, 1840.

TRAMWAY DU MONT BLANC - Winter season Dec. 19 - Apr. 11

Runs from St Gervais Le Fayet (opposite SNCF station) to Bellevue (altitude 1800 metres). Journey 60 minutes.
✆ 04.50.47.51.83, fax 04.50.78.32.75. www.compagniedumontblanc.fr
Depart St Gervais: 0900, 1000 Ⓒ, 1100, 1300, 1430.
Depart Bellevue: 1000, 1100 Ⓒ, 1200, 1430, 1630 (1650 Feb. 6 - Apr. 11).

MER DE GLACE - TRAIN DE MONTENVERS

From Chamonix (200 metres from SNCF station) to Montenvers 'Mer de Glace' (altitude 1913 metres). Journey 20 minutes. A cable car takes visitors to the ice grotto inside the glacier (open Dec. 19 to early October, conditions permitting, but closed for a period in the Spring).
✆ 04.50.53.12.54, fax 04.50.53.83.93. www.compagniedumontblanc.fr

Nov. 9 - Dec. 18: from Chamonix 1000, 1200, 1400, 1500, 1600, returning at 1130, 1330, 1430, 1530, 1630.

Dec. 19 - Apr. 30: from Chamonix hourly 0900 - 1600, returning 1000 and hourly 1030 - 1630.

May 1 - 15: from Chamonix every 30 minutes 0830 - 1700, returning 0900 - 1730.

from May 15: in Summer trains run every 20 - 30 minutes from 0830 (0800 in July / August).

See page 30 for plan of central Paris

PARIS - PARIS AÉROPORTS ✈ 398

CHARLES DE GAULLE ✈ - PARIS

VAL shuttle train: air terminals - RER/TGV station.

Roissyrail (RER line B): Aéroport Charles de Gaulle 2 TGV - Paris Châtelet les Halles. Frequent service 0450-2400.

Journey time from Charles de Gaulle ✈:

Gare du Nord	35 minutes
Châtelet les Halles ★	38 minutes
St Michel Notre Dame	40 minutes
Antony (for Orly ✈, see middle panel)	58 minutes

★ Cross-platform interchange with *RER* for Gare de Lyon.

ORLY ✈ - PARIS (*VAL + RER B*)

VAL light rail: Orly Sud - Orly Ouest - Antony (7 minutes). Frequent service ① - ⑤: 0600 - 2230; ⑦: 0700 - 2300. Cross platform interchange with RER line B (below).

RER line B: Antony - Paris. Frequent service 0510-0010.

Journey time from Antony:

St Michel Notre Dame	20 minutes
Châtelet les Halles ☆	25 minutes
Gare du Nord	29 minutes

☆ Interchange with *RER* for Gare de Lyon.

ORLY ✈ - PARIS (*Orlyrail*)

🚌: Orly ✈ (Ouest and Sud) - Pont de Rungis Aéroport d'Orly station. Frequent shuttle service.

RER line C: Pont de Rungis Aéroport d'Orly - Paris. Every 15 minutes approx. 0500 - 2330 (0530 - 2400 from Paris).

Journey time from Pont de Rungis Aéroport d'Orly:

Paris Austerlitz	24 minutes
St Michel Notre Dame	27 minutes
Musée d'Orsay	31 minutes
Champ de Mars Tour Eiffel	39 minutes

SAVOIE SKI BUSES 399

Winter 2009/2010

🚌 GENÈVE AÉROPORT ✈ - ST GERVAIS - CHAMONIX

Aeroski-Bus

€ ★	Dec. 17, 2009 - Apr. 25, 2010 ⊡		▽	△	▽ b	△	△		
–	**Genève** ✈ Secteur International	d.	0800	1145	1400	1630	1930	...	...
–	**Genève** Gare Routière (bus station)	d.	0830	1115	1430	1600	1910	...	...
31	St Gervais-Le Fayet (Gare SNCF)	a.	0930	1245	1530	1730	2030	...	...
38	Les Contamines ◐	a.	◐	◐	◐	◐	◐	...	...
33	Les Houches, Office de Tourisme	a.	0950	1300	1545	1745	2045	...	...
33	**Chamonix** Gare SNCF	a.	1005	1315	1600	1800	2100	...	...

Dec. 17, 2009 - Apr. 25, 2010 ⊡		△	△	▽ b	△	▽		
Chamonix Gare SNCF	d.	0700	1030	1145	1415	1645	...	...
Les Houches, Office de Tourisme	d.	0710	1040	1155	1425	1700	...	...
Les Contamines ◐	d.	◐	◐	◐	◐	◐	...	...
St Gervais-Le Fayet (Gare SNCF)	d.	0735	1105	1225	1445	1720	...	...
Genève ✈ Secteur International	a.	0845	1205	1325	1545	1835	...	...
Genève Gare Routière (bus station)	a.	0915	1230	1430	1615	1820	...	...

b – Dec. 17 - Apr. 18.
△ – Operated by Société Alpes Transports (SAT), Le Fayet. ▽ – Operated by Veolia.
⊡ – On Dec. 25 only the 1030 Chamonix - Genève and 1600 Genève - Chamonix run.
★ – One-way fare in euros. Return = single x 1.7. Discount for groups (4+).

◐ – Transfer by bus or taxi. Ⓡ (times given on reservation).

Reservations: recommended (book on-line at www.sat-montblanc.com or ✆ +33 (0)450 530 115). Reservation compulsory for return to airport at least 24 hours in advance.

🚌 GENÈVE AÉROPORT ✈ - ST GERVAIS - MEGÈVE

Aeroski-Bus — No service Dec. 25

€ ★	Dec. 19, 2009 - Apr. 3, 2010		Ⓡ	Ⓡ	Ⓡ
–	**Genève** Gare Routière	d.	1100	1410	1840
–	**Genève** ✈ Secteur International	d.	1120	1430	1910
44	**St Gervais** Jardin Public	a.	1220	1530	2015
44	Combloux, Office du Tourisme	a.	1235	1545	2030
44	**Megève** Gare Routière	a.	1245	1555	2040

Dec. 19, 2009 - Apr. 3, 2010		Ⓡ	Ⓡ	Ⓡ
Megève Gare Routière	d.	0930	1400	1700
Combloux, Office du Tourisme	d.	0940	1410	1710
St Gervais Jardin Public	d.	0955	1425	1725
Genève ✈ Secteur International	a.	1050	1535	1855
Genève Gare Routière	a.	1115	1520	1840

Geneve - Grand Bornand - St Jean de Sixt - **La Clusaz**: Service on ⑤⑥⑦ Dec. 19 - Mar. 28. Journey: up to 2 hours. From **Genève** ✈ Secteur International at 0815, 1400 (not ⑤), 1900. From **La Clusaz** at 0645, 1130 (not ⑤), 1715. www.aravis.com. Journeys to airport must be reserved in resort at least 24 hours in advance. Fare €34 to La Clusaz.

★ – One-way fare in euros (return fare is €75). Discount for groups.
Operators: Autocars Borini, Megève and Veolia Transport, Collonges-sous-Salève.

Reservations: compulsory for Megève service (both directions) at least 24 hours in advance. Book on-line at www.borini.com or ✆ +41 22 798 2000 (Accueil France at airport).

🚌 GENÈVE AÉROPORT ✈ - AVORIAZ/CHÂTEL/FLAINE

Aeroski-Bus — No service Dec. 25, Apr. 4

€ ★	Dec. 19, 2009 - Apr. 10, 2010		⑥		⑥	⑥	b ⑥⑦		⑥	
–	**Genève** ✈ Sect. International	d.	...	1120	1300	1330	1345	1430	1705	1830
–	**Genève** Gare Routière	d.	0830	1100	1240	1350	1330	1355	1725	1815
–	Annemasse, Gare Routière	d.	0900	1150	|	|	|	|	|	1900
–	Thonon les Bains ☆	a.	|	|	|	1440	|	|	1825	|
31	La Chapelle-d'Abondance ▷	a.	|	|	|	*1540*	|	|	*1920*	|
35	Châtel ▷	a.	|	|	|	*1545*	|	|	*1925*	|
31	St Jean d'Aulps	a.	|	|	|	1520	|	|	1910	|
24	Taninges, Café Central	a.	0935	1225	1350	|	|	1525	|	1935
42	Sixt-Fer á Cheval ▲	a.	*1000*	*1250*	*1410*	|	|	*1550*	|	*2000*
**47*	Les Carroz § ▲	a.	*1000*	*1250*	*1410*	|	1445	*1550*	|	*2000*
**47*	Flaine § ▲	a.	*1030*	*1320*	*1440*	|	1515	*1620*	|	*2030*
33	Les Gets, Gare Routière	a.	0955	*1245*	1410	|	...	1545	|	1950
36	**Morzine**, Gare Routière	a.	1005	*1255*	1420	1535	...	1555	1925	2005
36	Avoriaz-Prodains ⊡	a.	1015	*1310*	1430	|	...	1610	|	2015
39	**Avoriaz 1800**, Accueil 1800	a.	...	...	...	1610	...	...	1955	...

Dec. 19, 2009 - Apr. 10, 2010			b ⑥⑦	h ⑥	⑥		h ⑥	⑥	b ⑥⑦	
Avoriaz 1800, Accueil 1800	d.	...	...	0930	...	...	1330	...	...	...
Avoriaz-Prodains ⊡	d.	0830	...	|	1130	1415	|	1550	...	1710
Morzine, Gare Routière	d.	0840	...	1010	1140	1425	1400	1600	...	1720
Les Gets, Gare Routière	d.	0850	...	|	1150	1435	|	1610	...	1730
Flaine § ▲	d.	*0755*	1015	|	*1100*	*1345*	|	*1525*	1700	*1640*
Les Carroz § ▲	d.	*0825*	1045	|	*1130*	*1415*	|	*1555*	1730	*1710*
Sixt-Fer á Cheval ▲	d.	*0840*	|	|	*1145*	*1430*	|	*1605*	|	*1725*
Taninges, Café Central	d.	0905	|	|	1210	1455	|	1630	|	1750
St Jean d'Aulps	d.	|	|	1025	|	|	1420	|	|	|
Châtel ▷	d.	|	|	*0950*	|	|	*1345*	|	|	|
La Chapelle-d'Abondance ▷	d.	|	|	*0955*	|	|	*1350*	|	|	|
Thonon les Bains ☆	d.	|	|	1100	|	|	1500	|	|	|
Annemasse, Gare Routière	a.	|	|	|	1245	|	|	1705	|	1825
Genève Gare Routière	a.	1030	1150	1150	1340	1600	1550	1750	1830	1910
Genève ✈ Sect. International	a.	1010	1140	1215	1315	1540	1610	1735	1845	1855

b – ⑥⑦ Dec. 19 - Apr. 18.
h – ⑥ Dec. 26 - Apr. 17.
⊡ – For cable car to Avoriaz village.
★ – One-way fare in euros. Return = single x 1.7. Discounts for groups (4+).
☆ – Calls for connecting services only.

▷ – Change at Thonon les Bains.
▲ – Ⓡ. *Italics* = connection by taxi from/to Taninges.
§ – Office du Tourisme.
* – Direct journeys: €37/39.

Operators: SAT Léman, Annemasse/Veolia.

Reservations: recommended; book on-line at www.altibus.com or ✆ +41 22 594 3599 (Gare-Routière Genève). Reservation compulsory for return to airport at least 24 hours in advance.

Additional direct journey on ⑥⑦ Dec. 19 - Apr. 18: Genève Gare Routière d. 0815 - Flaine a. 0945.

🚌 GENÈVE AÉROPORT ✈ - TARENTAISE SKI RESORTS

Aeroski-Bus — Not Dec. 25 (except **D**)

€ ★	Dec. 5, 2009 - Apr. 18, 2010		⑤–⑦	C ⑥		⑥	⑥	D	C ⑥	
–	**Genève** Gare Routière	d.	...	...	...	...	...	...	...	...
–	**Genève** ✈, Secteur International	d.	1000	1100	1215	1330	1430	1530	1645	1915
57	**Moûtiers-Salins** Gare SNCF	a.	1200	1300	1415	1540	1630	1730	1845	2115
76	Courchevel-Valmorel/Pralognan ♥	a.	*1300*	*1400*	*1515*	*1645*	*1730*	*1830*	*1945*	*2215*
76	Méribel/St Martin de Belleville ♥	a.	*1300*	*1400*	*1515*	*1645*	*1730*	*1830*	*1945*	*2215*
76	Les Menuires/Brides les Bains ♥	a.	*1300*	*1400*	*1515*	*1645*	*1730*	*1830*	*1945*	*2215*
76	Val Thorens ♥	a.	*1330*	*1430*	*1540*	*1710*	*1800*	*1900*	*2015*	*2245*
58	**Aime** Gare SNCF	a.	1220	1320	1435	1600	1650	1750	1905	2135
76	La Plagne ♥	a.	*1330*	*1430*	*1530*	*1700*	*1800*	*1900*	*2000*	*2230*
58	**Bourg St Maurice** Gare SNCF	a.	1240	1340	1500	1620	1710	1810	1925	2155
76	Les Arcs/La Rosière ♥	a.	*1330*	*1430*	*1600*	*1720*	*1810*	*1910*	*2025*	*2245*
61	Tignes le Lac, Cars Martin ♥	a.	*1355*	*1455*	*1535*	*1655*	*1825*	*1925*	*2040*	*2305*
61	Tignes Val Claret, Gare Routière ♥	a.	*1400*	*1500*	*1545*	*1705*	*1830*	*1930*	*2045*	*2310*
61	**Val d'Isère** Cars Martin	a.	1330	1430	1620	1740	1800	1900	2010	2240

Dec. 5, 2009 - Apr. 18, 2010		D	⑥	⑧		⑤–⑦
Val d'Isère Cars Martin	d.	0600	0745	1030	1310	1555
Tignes Val Claret, Gare Routière ♥	d.	0625	0730	1000	1230	1515
Tignes le Lac, Cars Martin ♥	d.	0640	0745	1010	1240	1525
Les Arcs/La Rosière ♥	d.	⊙	⊙	⊙	⊙	⊙
Bourg St Maurice Gare SNCF	d.	0740	0845	1115	1355	1645
La Plagne ♥	d.	⊙	⊙	⊙	⊙	⊙
Aime Gare SNCF	d.	0800	0915	1135	1415	1705
Val Thorens ♥	d.	⊙	⊙	⊙	⊙	⊙
Les Menuires/Brides les Bains ♥	d.	⊙	⊙	⊙	⊙	⊙
Méribel/St Martin de Belleville ♥	d.	⊙	⊙	⊙	⊙	⊙
Courchevel-Valmorel/Pralognan ♥	d.	⊙	⊙	⊙	⊙	⊙
Moûtiers-Salins Gare SNCF	d.	0845	1000	1215	1500	1750
Genève ✈, Secteur International	a.	1040	1210	1415	1700	1950
Genève Gare Routière	a.	...	...	...	...	...

C – Dec. 12 - Mar. 27.
D – Nov. 28 - Apr. 25 (runs Dec. 25).
♥ – Connecting service.
★ – One-way fare in euros. Return = single x 1.7. Discounts for groups (4+).

⊙ – Connection by bus or taxi. Reservation compulsory at local bus or tourist office 48 hours in advance. Departure times given when reservations made.

Operators: Transdev Martin, Bourg St Maurice; Transdev Savoie, Moûtiers; Veolia, Collonges sous Salève.

Reservations: recommended – book on-line at www.alpski-bus.com or contact Accueil France at Aéroport de Genève, ✆ +41 22 798 2000. Reservations for the journey returning to the airport are compulsory at the local bus or tourist office 48 hours in advance, when departure times will be confirmed.

🚌 LYON ✈ - SAVOIE SKI RESORTS

Ski Buses

Coach services operate from Lyon St Exupéry airport to most Savoie ski resorts from late December to mid April. Book on-line at www.altibus.com or ✆ +33 (0)4 79 68 32 96 (or within France ✆ 0 820 320 368). e-mail: admin@altibus.com. Reservations are compulsory, at least seven days in advance.

BOURG ST MAURICE - LES ARCS

During the winter sports period, a funicular railway links Bourg St Maurice with Les Arcs 1600 every 20 minutes. A free bus service connects with each journey, running to Les Arcs 1800 and 2000.

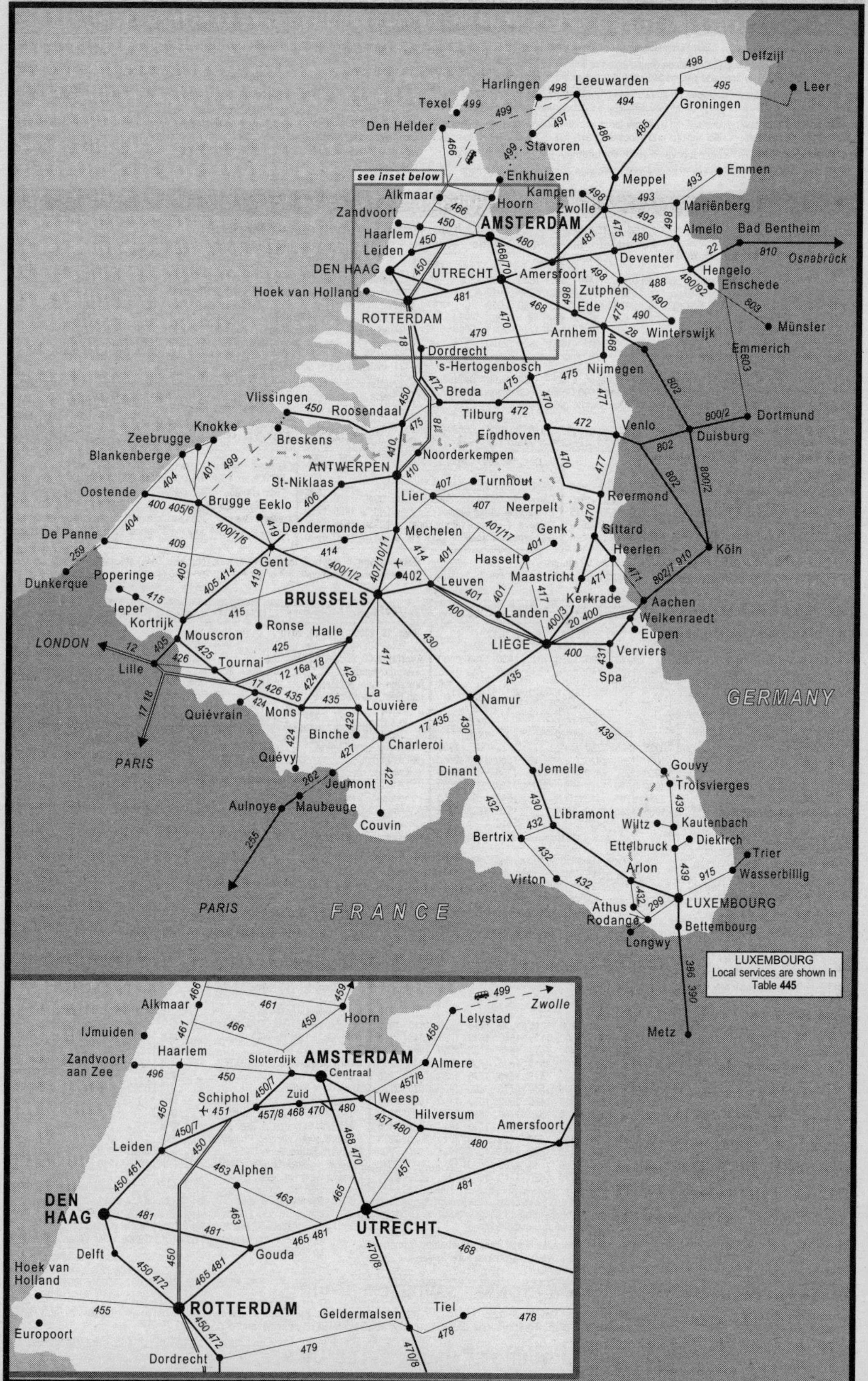
Delfzijl
Leer
Harlingen
Leeuwarden
Groningen
Texel
Den Helder
Stavoren
see inset below
Enkhuizen
Emmen
Alkmaar
Hoorn
Kampen
Meppel
Zandvoort
Zwolle
Mariënberg
AMSTERDAM
Haarlem
Almelo
Bad Bentheim
Leiden
Deventer
Osnabrück
DEN HAAG
UTRECHT
Amersfoort
Hengelo
Enschede
Hoek van Holland
Zutphen
Ede
ROTTERDAM
Münster
Arnhem
Winterswijk
Dordrecht
Emmerich
's-Hertogenbosch
Nijmegen
Vlissingen
Breda
Roosendaal
Tilburg
Dortmund
Knokke
Venlo
Zeebrugge
Breskens
Eindhoven
Duisburg
Blankenberge
Noorderkempen
ANTWERPEN
Oostende
St-Niklaas
Turnhout
Brugge
Eeklo
Lier
Roermond
Neerpelt
De Panne
Dendermonde
Mechelen
Genk
Sittard
Gent
Heerlen
Köln
Dunkerque
Poperinge
Hasselt
Maastricht
BRUSSELS
Leuven
Kerkrade
Ieper
Aachen
Kortrijk
Landen
Welkenraedt
Ronse
Eupen
LONDON
Mouscron
Halle
LIÈGE
Verviers
Lille
Tournai
Spa
GERMANY
Namur
Quiévrain
Mons
La Louvière
Binche
PARIS
Charleroi
Quévy
Dinant
Jemelle
Gouvy
Jeumont
Troisvierges
Aulnoye
Maubeuge
Couvin
Libramont
Wiltz
Kautenbach
Bertrix
Diekirch
Ettelbruck
Trier
Arlon
Wasserbillig
Virton
PARIS
FRANCE
Athus
LUXEMBOURG
Rodange
Bettembourg
Longwy
LUXEMBOURG
Local services are shown in Table 445
Metz
Alkmaar
Hoorn
Zwolle
IJmuiden
Lelystad
Haarlem
Zandvoort aan Zee
Sloterdijk
AMSTERDAM
Centraal
Almere
Schiphol
Zuid
Weesp
Hilversum
Amersfoort
Leiden
Alphen
DEN HAAG
UTRECHT
Delft
Gouda
Hoek van Holland
ROTTERDAM
Geldermalsen
Tiel
Europoort
Dordrecht

BELGIUM and LUXEMBOURG

Operator: Nationale Maatschappij der Belgische Spoorwegen/Société Nationale des Chemins de fer Belges (NMBS/SNCB), Société Nationale des Chemins de fer Luxembourgeois (CFL).

Services: All trains convey first and second classes of seating accommodation unless otherwise indicated. Trains for two or more different destinations are often linked together for part of their journeys, and passengers should be careful to join the correct portion of the train upon boarding.

Timings: Valid from **December 13, 2009** unless otherwise stated in the table, but minor alterations are possible. Local train services may be amended on and around the dates of public holidays (see page 2), and passengers are advised to confirm their train times locally if planning to travel during these periods.

Reservations: Seat reservations are not available for journeys wholly within Belgium or Luxembourg. Reservations for some journeys *between* Belgium and Luxembourg can, however, be made at principal stations and appointed travel agents. *ICE* services to and from Germany require compulsory reservation.

Supplements: Supplements are not payable except for **International** journeys on *EC* trains.

For Dutch-language forms of French-language Belgian names see page 239.

OOSTENDE - BRUSSELS - LIÈGE - AACHEN 400

For *Thalys* trains Paris - Brussels - Köln / Oostende and v.v. – see Tables 16 / 21
For additional services Brugge - Brussels - Liège and v.v. – see Table 401

km				503		1504	504			505	*ICE* 11 [R]		506			507		508			509		510		*ICE* 15 [R]
		†	⚒		Ⓐ	H Ⓐ		Ⓐ			F	Ⓐ		Ⓐ			Ⓐ		Ⓐ			Ⓐ		Ⓐ	F
0	**Oostende 406** d.	...	...	...	...	0356	0435	...	...	0543	...	0546	0643	...	...	0743	...	0843	...	...	0943	...	1043	...	...
22	Brugge ♣ **406** d.	...	...	...	...	0410	0451	...	...	0558	...	0601	0658	...	...	0758	...	0858	...	...	0958	...	1058	...	...
62	Gent Sint-Pieters **406** d.	...	...	...	...	0452	0524	...	...	0624	...	0645	0724	...	...	0824	...	0924	...	...	1024	...	1124	...	...
114	**Brussels Midi / Zuid** a.	...	...	...	...	0528	0555	...	...	0655	...	0722	0755	...	...	0855	...	0955	...	...	1055	...	1155	...	...
114	**Brussels Midi / Zuid** d.	...	...	...	...	0530	0557	0624	...	0657	0725	0724	0757	0824	...	0857	0924	0957	1005	...	1057	1124	1157	1224	1225
116	Brussels Central d.	...	...	...	...	0534	0601	0628	...	0701	|	0728	0801	0828	...	0901	0928	1001	1009	...	1101	1128	1201	1228	|
118	Brussels Nord d.	...	...	...	...	0539	0606	0633	...	0706	0733	0733	0806	0833	...	0906	0933	1006	1014	...	1106	1131	1206	1233	1233
148	Leuven d.	...	...	...	...	0600	0625	|	...	0726	|	|	0826	|	...	0926	|	1026	1032	...	1126	|	1226	|	|
218	**Liège Guillemins** a.	...	...	...	...	...	0703	0719	...	0800	0812	0819	0900	0919	...	1000	1019	1100	1119	...	1200	1219	1300	1319	1312
218	**Liège Guillemins 403** d.	...	...	...	0556	...	0705	0721	0733	0805	0814	0821	0905	0921	0933	1005	1021	1105	1121	1133	1205	1221	1305	1321	1314
	Maastricht **403** a.	...	...	...	|	...	|	0750	|	|	|	0850	|	0950	|	|	1050	|	1150	|	|	1250	|	1350	|
242	Verviers Central d.	...	...	...	0627	...	0727	...	0757	0827	|	...	0927	...	0957	1027	...	1127	...	1157	1227	...	1327	...	|
255	Welkenraedt d.	0554	0559	0640	0639	...	0740	...	0813	0840	|	...	0940	...	1010	1040	...	1140	...	1210	1240	...	1340	...	|
261	**Eupen** a.	|	|	0647	|	...	0747	...	|	0847	|	...	0947	...	|	1047	...	1147	...	|	1247	...	1347	...	|
274	**Aachen Hbf** a.	0611	0616	...	0654	...	...	...	0829	...	0836	...	...	...	1026	...	...	...	...	1226	...	...	...	...	1336
	Köln Hbf **802 910** a.	...	...	...	...	...	...	...	...	...	0915	...	...	...	...	...	...	...	...	...	...	...	...	...	1415

km (via hsl)			511		512			513			514			515	516	*ICE* 17 [R]			517	518		519	520	521	522
				Ⓐ		Ⓐ			Ⓐ	Ⓐ		Ⓐ				F	Ⓐ								
	Oostende 406 d.	...	1143	...	1243	...	...	1343	...	...	1443	...	...	1543	1643	...	...	...	1743	1843	...	1943	2043	2143	2243
	Brugge ♣ **406** d.	...	1158	...	1258	...	...	1358	...	...	1458	...	...	1558	1658	...	...	...	1758	1858	...	1958	2058	2158	2258
	Gent Sint-Pieters **406** d.	...	1224	...	1324	...	...	1424	...	...	1524	...	...	1624	1724	...	...	...	1824	1924	...	2024	2124	2224	2323
	Brussels Midi / Zuid a.	...	1255	...	1355	...	...	1455	...	...	1555	...	...	1655	1755	...	...	...	1855	1955	...	2055	2155	2255	2359
0	**Brussels Midi / Zuid** d.	...	1257	1305	1357	1424	...	1457	1524	...	1557	1624	...	1700	1757	1825	1824	...	1857	1957	...	2057	2157	2257	0001
	Brussels Central d.	...	1301	1309	1401	1428	...	1501	1528	...	1601	1628	...	1704	1801	|	1828	...	1901	2001	...	2101	2201	2301	0005
4	Brussels Nord d.	...	1306	1312	1406	1431	...	1506	1533	...	1606	1633	...	1709	1806	1833	1833	...	1906	2006	...	2106	2206	2306	0010
	Leuven d.	...	1326	1332	1426	|	...	1526	|	...	1626	|	...	1730	1827	|	|	...	1926	2026	...	2126	2226	2326	0030
107	**Liège Guillemins** a.	...	1400	1419	1500	1519	...	1600	1619	...	1700	1719	...	1803	1900	1912	1919	...	2000	2100	...	2200	2300	0019	0123
107	**Liège Guillemins 403** d.	1333	1405	1421	1505	1521	1533	1605	1621	1641	1705	1721	1733	1805	1905	1914	1921	1933	2005	2105	2131	2205	2305	0021	0125
	Maastricht **403** a.	|	|	1450	|	1550	|	|	1650	|	|	1750	|	|	|	|	1950	|	|	|	|	|	|	|	|
	Verviers Central d.	1357	1427	...	1527	...	1557	1627	...	1711	1727	...	1757	1827	1927	|	...	1957	2027	2127	2157	2227	2327	0046	0150
	Welkenraedt d.	1410	1440	...	1540	...	1610	1640	...	1727	1740	...	1810	1840	1940	|	...	2010	2040	2140	2210	2239	2339	0058	0202
	Eupen a.	|	1447	...	1547	...	|	1647	...	|	1747	...	|	1847	1947	|	...	|	2047	2147	|	...	...	...	...
163	**Aachen Hbf** a.	1426	...	...	...	...	1626	...	...	1742	...	...	1826	...	...	1936	...	2024	...	...	2226	...	...	...	...
	Köln Hbf **802 910** a.	...	...	...	...	...	...	...	...	...	...	...	...	...	...	2015	...	...	...	...	...	...	...	...	...

	527	528		529					530			531			*ICE* 16 [R]	532		533			534		535		
			Ⓐ		Ⓐ	Ⓐ	Ⓒ	Ⓐ		Ⓐ	Ⓐ			Ⓐ	F		Ⓐ			Ⓐ		Ⓐ			Ⓐ
Köln Hbf **802 910** d.	...	...	...	...	...	...	...	...	...	...	...	...	...	...	0843	...	...	...	...	...	...	...	...	...	...
Aachen Hbf d.	...	...	...	...	0622	...	0634	...	...	0658	...	...	0834	...	0921	...	...	...	1034	...	...	...	...	1234	...
Eupen d.	...	...	...	0612	|	...	|	...	0712	|	...	0812	|	...	|	0912	...	1012	|	...	1112	...	1212	|	...
Welkenraedt d.	0404	0519	...	0620	0638	0643	0651	...	0720	0723	...	0820	0851	...	|	0920	...	1020	1051	...	1120	...	1220	1251	...
Verviers Central d.	0417	0532	...	0634	...	0657	0704	...	0734	0736	...	0834	0904	...	|	0934	...	1034	1104	...	1134	...	1234	1304	...
Maastricht **403** d.	|	|	...	|	...	|	|	0707	|	|	0809	|	|	0909	|	|	1009	|	|	1109	|	1209	|	|	1309
Liège Guillemins 403 a.	0440	0552	...	0654	...	0721	0727	0737	0754	0807	0839	0854	0927	0939	0943	0954	1039	1054	1127	1139	1154	1239	1254	1327	1339
Liège Guillemins d.	0443	0556	0639	0700	...	0725	...	0742	0800	...	0842	0900	...	0941	0946	1000	1042	1100	...	1142	1200	1242	1300	...	1342
Leuven d.	0537	0637	|	0735	...	0818	...	|	0837	...	|	0937	...	|	|	1037	1130	1137	...	|	1237	1330	1337	...	|
Brussels Nord d.	0556	0656	0729	0756	...	...	...	0829	0856	...	0929	0956	...	1029	1027	1056	1148	1156	...	1229	1256	1348	1356	...	1429
Brussels Central d.	0600	0700	0733	0800	...	...	...	0833	0900	...	0933	1000	...	1033	|	1100	1152	1200	...	1233	1300	1352	1400	...	1433
Brussels Midi / Zuid a.	0603	0703	0736	0803	...	...	...	0836	0903	...	0936	1003	...	1036	1035	1103	1155	1203	...	1236	1303	1355	1403	...	1436
Brussels Midi / Zuid d.	0605	0705	...	0805	...	...	...	...	0905	...	...	1005	...	...	...	1105	...	1205	...	...	1305	...	1405	...	...
Gent Sint-Pieters **406** d.	0639	0739	...	0839	...	...	...	...	0939	...	...	1039	...	...	...	1139	...	1239	...	...	1339	...	1439	...	...
Brugge ♣ **406** d.	0704	0804	...	0904	...	...	...	...	1004	...	...	1104	...	...	...	1204	...	1304	...	...	1404	...	1504	...	...
Oostende 406 a.	0717	0817	...	0917	...	...	...	...	1017	...	...	1117	...	...	...	1217	...	1317	...	...	1417	...	1517	...	...

	536		537			*ICE* 14 [R]	538		539			540			541		542	*ICE* 10 [R]	543		544	1544	1544	545	
		Ⓐ			Ⓐ	F		Ⓐ			Ⓐ		Ⓐ	Ⓐ				F				H Ⓐ	Ⓒ		
Köln Hbf **802 910** d.	...	...	...	...	...	1443	...	...	...	...	...	...	...	...	...	...	...	1943	...	...	...	...	...	...	...
Aachen Hbf d.	...	...	...	1434	...	1521	...	...	...	1634	...	...	...	1756	...	1834	...	2021	...	2034	...	...	...	...	2234
Eupen d.	1312	...	1412	|	...	|	1512	...	1612	|	...	1712	...	|	1812	|	1912	|	2012	|	2112	...	...	2210	|
Welkenraedt d.	1320	...	1420	1451	...	|	1520	...	1620	1651	...	1720	...	1812	1820	1851	1920	|	2020	2051	2120	...	...	2218	2251
Verviers Central d.	1334	...	1434	1504	...	|	1534	...	1634	1704	...	1734	...	...	1834	1904	1934	|	2034	2104	2134	...	...	2232	2304
Maastricht **403** d.	|	1409	|	|	1509	|	|	1609	|	|	1709	|	1809	...	|	|	|	|	|	|	|	...	...	|	|
Liège Guillemins 403 a.	1354	1439	1454	1527	1539	1543	1554	1639	1654	1727	1739	1754	1839	...	1854	1927	1954	2043	2054	2127	2154	...	...	2255	2327
Liège Guillemins d.	1400	1442	1500	...	1541	1546	1600	1642	1700	...	1742	1800	1841	...	1900	...	2000	2046	2100	...	2200	...	2206	2309	...
Leuven d.	1437	|	1537	...	|	|	1637	|	1737	...	|	1837	|	...	1937	...	2037	|	2135	...	2237	2300	2302	0004	...
Brussels Nord d.	1456	1529	1556	...	1629	1627	1656	1729	1756	...	1829	1856	1929	...	1956	...	2056	2127	2156	...	2256	2323	2323	0023	...
Brussels Central d.	1500	1533	1600	...	1633	|	1700	1733	1800	...	1833	1900	1933	...	2000	...	2100	|	2200	...	2300	2327	2327	0027	...
Brussels Midi / Zuid a.	1503	1536	1603	...	1636	1635	1703	1736	1803	...	1836	1903	1936	...	2003	...	2103	2135	2203	...	2303	2330	2330	0030	...
Brussels Midi / Zuid d.	1505	...	1605	...	...	...	1705	...	1805	...	1838	1905	...	...	2005	...	2105	...	2205	...	2305	2336	2336	0032	...
Gent Sint-Pieters **406** d.	1539	...	1639	...	...	...	1739	...	1839	...	1918	1939	...	...	2039	...	2139	...	2239	...	2339	0015	0015	0118	...
Brugge ♣ **406** d.	1604	...	1704	...	...	...	1804	...	1904	...	2000	2004	...	...	2104	...	2204	...	2304	...	0002	0100	0100	0144	...
Oostende 406 a.	1617	...	1717	...	...	...	1817	...	1917	...	2013	2017	...	...	2117	...	2217	...	2317	...	0015	0113	0113	0157	...

F – (12) and 🍷 Brussels - Köln Hbf - Frankfurt ✈ - Frankfurt Hbf and v.v.
H – From / to Hasselt – see Table **401**.

ICE – German high-speed train: special fares payable.
♣ – For Brugge - Zeebrugge and v.v. local service, see note ♣ on next page.

401 KNOKKE / BLANKENBERGE - BRUSSELS - HASSELT, GENK and LIÈGE

For express services (Oostende -) Brugge - Brussels - Liège and v.v. – see Table 400

km				Ⓐ	ⒶG	ⒶO	Ⓐ	ⒶG	Ⓐ	Ⓐ	ⒶG	ⒶB	Ⓐ		Ⓐ	ⒶG	ⒶB	Ⓐ	Ⓐ	ⒶG	Ⓐ	Ⓐ	Ⓐ
	Knokke d.	Ⓐ	...	...	...	...	...	...	...	...	...	...	0605		...	...	...	2005	...	...	...	2105	...
0	Blankenberge d.		...	...	...	...	...	...	...	...	...	0610	|		...	...	2010	|	...	...	2110	|	...
15	**Brugge** ♣ a.		...	...	...	...	...	...	...	...	...	0621	0624		...	...	2021	2024	...	...	2121	2124	...
15	**Brugge 406** ♣ d.		...	...	...	0410	...	...	0531	...	...	0631	0631		...	...	2031	2031	...	...	2131	2131	...
55	Gent Sint-Pieters **406** d.		...	...	...	0452	0503	...	0557	0608	...	0657	0657		2008	...	2057	2057	2108	...	2157	2157	2208
	Denderleeuw d.		...	...	...	0510	0543	...	|	0643	...	|	|	▲	2043	...	|	|	2143	...	|	|	2243
107	**Brussels Midi / Zuid** a.		...	...	...	0528	0606	...	0628	0706	...	0728	0728		2106	...	2128	2128	2206	...	2228	2228	2306
107	**Brussels Midi / Zuid 400** d.		...	0508	0531	0530	0608	0631	0630	0709	0731	0730	0730	and	2108	2131	2130	2130	2213	2231	2230	2230	2308
109	Brussels Central d.		...	0512	0535	0534	0612	0635	0634	0713	0735	0734	0734	at the	2112	2135	2134	2134	2217	2235	2234	2234	2312
111	Brussels Nord d.		...	0518	0540	0540	0618	0640	0640	0718	0740	0740	0740	same	2118	2140	2140	2140	2222	2240	2240	2240	2315
141	Leuven a.		...	0536	0557	0600	0636	0657	0700	0736	0757	0800	0800	minutes	2136	2157	2200	2200	2240	2257	2300	2300	...
141	Leuven d.		...	0538	0559	0610	0638	0659	0710	0738	0759	0810	0810	past	2138	2159	2210	2210	2242	2259	2310	2310	...
	Tienen d.		...	0551	0611	|	0651	0711	|	0751	0811	|	|	each	2151	2211	|	|	2255	2311	|	|	...
	Landen a.		...	0602	0620	|	0702	0721	|	0802	0821	|	|	hour	2202	2221	|	|	2306	2321	|	|	...
	Landen d.		...	0604	0621	|	0704	0721	|	0804	0822	|	|	until	2204	2222	|	|	2308	2322	|	|	...
157	Aarschot **417** d.		...	|	|	0624	|	|	0726	|	|	0824	0824		|	|	2224	2224	|	|	2322	2324	...
175	Diest **417** d.		...	|	|	0635	|	|	0745	|	|	0835	0835		|	|	2235	2235	|	|	2342	2342	...
	Sint-Truiden d.		...	0614	|	|	0714	|	|	0814	|	|	|		2214	|	|	|	2318	|	|	|	...
196	Hasselt **417** d.		...	0631	|	0649	0731	|	0802	0831	|	0849	0849		2231	|	2249	2249	2335	|	2358	2358	...
	Genk a.		...	0648	|	...	0748	|	...	0848	|	...	...		2248	|	...	...	2352	|	...	...	...
	Liège Guillemins 400 a.		...	...	0654	...	...	0754	...	...	0851	...	...		...	2251	...	...	...	2351	...	...	...

km		ⒶB	Ⓐ	Ⓐ	Ⓐ		Ⓒ	Ⓒ	Ⓒ	Ⓒ	Ⓒ	Ⓒ	ⒸB	Ⓒ	Ⓒ		ⒸB	Ⓒ	Ⓒ	ⒸB	Ⓒ	Ⓒ	Ⓒ
0	**Knokke** d.	...	2205	...	2305	Ⓒ	...	...	...	...	...	...	...	0705	...		...	2105	...	...	2205	...	2305
	Blankenberge d.	2210	|	2310	|		...	...	...	...	...	...	0710	|	...		2110	|	...	2210	|	2310	|
22	**Brugge** ♣ a.	2221	2224	2321	2324		...	...	...	...	...	...	0721	0724	...		2121	2124	...	2221	2224	2321	2324
22	**Brugge 406** ♣ d.	2231	2231	...	...		0524	0524	...	0631	0631	...	0731	0731	...		2131	2131	...	2231	2231	...	...
62	Gent Sint-Pieters **406** d.	2257	2257	...	...		0557	0557	0611	0657	0657	0711	0757	0757	0811		2157	2157	2211	2257	2257	...	...
96	Denderleeuw d.	|	|	...	...		|	|	0644	|	|	0744	|	|	0844	▲	|	|	2244	|	|	...	...
119	**Brussels Midi / Zuid** a.	2328	2328	...	...		0628	0628	0704	0728	0728	0804	0828	0828	0904		2228	2228	2304	2328	2328	...	...
119	**Brussels Midi / Zuid 400** d.	...	...	...	...		0630	0630	0706	0730	0730	0806	0830	0830	0906	and	2230	2230	2308	...	...	...	...
121	Brussels Central d.	...	...	...	...		0634	0634	0710	0734	0734	0810	0834	0834	0910	at the	2234	2234	2312	...	...	...	...
123	Brussels Nord d.	...	...	...	...		0639	0639	0713	0739	0739	0813	0839	0839	0913	same	2239	2239	2313	...	...	...	...
152	Leuven a.	...	...	...	...		0658	0658	...	0758	0758	...	0858	0858	...	minutes	2258	2258	...	...	...	...	...
152	Leuven d.	...	...	...	...		0700	0700	...	0800	0800	...	0900	0900	...	past	2300	2300	...	...	...	...	...
170	Tienen d.	...	...	...	...		0711	0711	...	0811	0811	...	0911	0911	...	each	2311	2311	...	...	...	...	...
183	Landen a.	...	...	...	...		0721	0721	...	0821	0821	...	0921	0921	...	hour	2321	2321	...	...	...	...	...
183	Landen d.	...	...	...	...		0729	0732	...	0829	0832	...	0929	0932	...	until	2329	2332	...	...	...	...	...
	Aarschot **417** d.	...	...	...	...		|	|	...	|	|	...	|	|	...		|	|	...	...	...	...	...
	Diest **417** d.	...	...	...	...		|	|	...	|	|	...	|	|	...		|	|	...	...	...	...	...
194	Sint-Truiden d.	...	...	...	...		|	0741	...	|	0841	...	|	0941	...		|	2341	...	...	...	...	...
211	Hasselt **417** d.	...	...	...	...		|	0801	...	|	0901	...	|	1001	...		|	2357	...	...	...	...	...
227	**Genk** a.	...	...	...	...		|	0817	...	|	0917	...	|	1017	...		|	0013	...	...	...	...	...
	Liège Guillemins 400 a.	...	...	...	...		0756	...	...	0856	...	...	0956	...	...		2356	...	...	...	...	...	...

		Ⓐ	Ⓐ	Ⓐ	Ⓐ	Ⓐ	Ⓐ	ⒶB	ⒶG		Ⓐ	Ⓐ	ⒶB	ⒶG	Ⓐ	Ⓐ	ⒶG	Ⓐ	ⒶO	ⒶG		Ⓐ	ⒶO
Liège Guillemins 400 d.	Ⓐ	...	...	...	...	...	...	...	0508		...	...	...	2008	...	...	2108	...	...	2208	...	...	2309
Genk d.		...	...	...	...	⊠	...	...	|		1912	...	...	|	2012	...	|	2112	...	|	...	...	|
Hasselt **417** d.		...	...	...	...	0431	⊡	⊡	|		1931	2011	2011	|	2031	2111	|	2131	2211	|	...	2238	|
Sint-Truiden d.		...	...	...	...	0447	|	|	|		1947	|	|	|	2047	|	|	2147	|	|	...	|	|
Diest **417** d.		...	...	...	...	|	⊡	⊡	|		|	2026	2026	|	|	2126	|	|	2226	|	...	2254	|
Aarschot **417** d.		...	...	...	...	|	0537	0537	|	▲	|	2039	2039	|	|	2139	|	|	2239	|	...	2312	|
Landen a.		...	...	...	...	0456	|	|	0538		1956	|	|	2038	2056	|	2138	2156	|	2238	...	|	2338
Landen d.		...	...	...	...	0458	|	|	0539	and	1958	|	|	2039	2058	|	2139	2158	|	2239	...	|	2340
Tienen d.		...	...	...	...	0510	|	|	0550	at the	2010	|	|	2050	2110	|	2150	2210	|	2250	...	|	2351
Leuven a.		...	...	...	...	0522	0550	0550	0601	same	2022	2050	2050	2101	2122	2150	2201	2222	2250	2301	...	2326	0001
Leuven d.		...	...	...	...	0524	0600	0600	0603	minutes	2024	2100	2100	2103	2124	2200	2203	2224	2300	2303	...	...	0004
Brussels Nord d.		...	...	...	...	0546	0623	0623	0622	past	2046	2123	2123	2122	2146	2223	2222	2246	2323	2322	...	...	0023
Brussels Central d.		...	...	...	...	0550	0627	0627	0626	each	2050	2127	2127	2126	2150	2227	2226	2250	2327	2326	...	...	0027
Brussels Midi / Zuid 400 a.		...	...	...	...	0553	0630	0630	0629	hour	2053	2130	2130	2129	2153	2230	2229	2253	2330	2329	...	...	0030
Brussels Midi / Zuid d.		...	...	...	...	0555	0632	0632	...	until	2055	2132	2132	...	2155	2232	...	2255	2336	...	...	...	0032
Denderleeuw d.		...	...	...	...	0618	|	|	...		2118	|	|	...	2218	|	...	2318	2355	...	...	...	0056
Gent Sint-Pieters **406** d.		...	...	...	...	0652	0703	0703	...		2152	2205	2205	...	2252	2305	...	2352	0015	...	...	...	0118
Brugge 406 ♣ a.		...	...	...	...	...	0727	0727	...		...	2229	2229	...	...	2329	...	...	0055	...	...	...	0143
Brugge ♣ d.		0534	0537	0631	0634	...	0735	0738	...		...	2235	2238	...	...	...	...	...	...	...	...	...	...
Blankenberge a.		|	0548	|	0645	...	|	0749	...		...	|	2249	...	...	...	...	...	...	...	...	...	...
Knokke a.		0553	...	0650	...	...	0754	...	...		...	2254	...	...	...	...	...	...	...	...	...	...	...

		Ⓒ	Ⓒ	Ⓒ	Ⓒ	ⒸB	Ⓒ	Ⓒ	ⒸB	Ⓒ		Ⓒ	ⒸB	Ⓒ		Ⓒ	Ⓒ	Ⓒ		ⒸO	ⒸO		ⒸO
Liège Guillemins 400 d.	Ⓒ	...	...	...	...	...	...	...	0606	...		...	2006	...	...	...	2106	...	...	...	2206	...	2309
Genk d.		...	...	...	...	...	...	0543	|	...		1943	|	...	...	2049	|	...	...	2149	|	...	|
Hasselt **417** d.		...	...	...	...	...	...	0607	|	...		2007	|	...	...	2107	|	...	...	2207	|	...	|
Sint-Truiden d.		...	...	...	...	...	...	0622	|	...		2022	|	...	...	2122	|	...	...	2222	|	...	|
Diest **417** d.		...	...	...	...	...	...	|	|	...		|	|	...	...	|	|	...	...	|	|	...	|
Aarschot **417** d.		...	...	...	...	...	...	|	|	...	▲	|	|	...	...	|	|	...	...	|	|	...	|
Landen a.		...	...	...	...	...	...	0630	0633	...		2030	2033	...	...	2130	2133	...	...	2230	2233	...	2338
Landen d.		...	...	...	...	...	...	0639	0639	...	and	2039	2039	...	...	2139	2139	...	...	2239	2239	...	2340
Tienen d.		...	...	...	...	...	...	0650	0650	...	at the	2050	2050	...	...	2150	2150	...	...	2250	2250	...	2351
Leuven a.		...	...	...	...	...	...	0700	0700	...	same	2100	2100	...	...	2200	2200	...	...	2300	2300	...	0001
Leuven d.		...	...	...	...	...	...	0702	0702	...	minutes	2102	2102	...	...	2202	2202	...	...	2302	2302	...	0004
Brussels Nord d.		...	...	0547	...	...	0647	0723	0723	0747	past	2123	2123	2147	...	2223	2223	2247	...	2323	2323	...	0023
Brussels Central d.		...	...	0551	...	...	0651	0727	0727	0751	each	2127	2127	2151	...	2227	2227	2251	...	2327	2327	...	0027
Brussels Midi / Zuid 400 a.		...	...	0554	...	...	0654	0730	0730	0754	hour	2130	2130	2154	...	2230	2230	2254	...	2330	2330	...	0030
Brussels Midi / Zuid d.		...	...	0556	0632	0632	0656	0732	0732	0756	until	2132	2132	2156	...	2232	2232	2256	...	2336	2336	...	0037
Denderleeuw d.		...	...	0616	|	|	0716	|	|	0816		|	|	2216	...	|	|	2316	...	2355	2355	...	0056
Gent Sint-Pieters **406** d.		...	...	0649	0705	0705	0749	0805	0808	0849		2205	2205	2249	...	2305	2305	2349	...	0015	0015	...	0118
Brugge 406 ♣ a.		...	...	...	0729	0729	...	0829	0829	...		2229	2229	...	...	2329	2329	...	...	0100	0100	...	0142
Brugge ♣ d.		0631	0634	...	0739	0738	...	0838	0838	...		2235	2238	...	...	...	...	...	...	...	...	...	...
Blankenberge a.		|	0645	...	|	0749	...	|	0849	...		|	2249	...	...	...	...	...	...	...	...	...	...
Knokke a.		0650	...	...	0754	...	...	0854	...	...		2254	...	...	...	...	...	...	...	...	...	...	...

B – Passengers may be required to change trains at Brugge on some journeys.
G – From / to St Ghislain / Quiévrain and Mons – see Table **424**.
O – From / to Oostende – see Table **400**.

⊠ – Services from Genk depart at 0512, 0610, 0710, then 0812 and hourly to 1912 (then as shown).

⊡ – Services from Hasselt depart at 0502, 0601, 0701, 0811 and hourly until 1911 (then as shown); Diest depart 0518, 0617, 0717, 0826 and hourly until 1926 (then as shown).

▲ – Times may vary by up to 3 minutes on some journeys.

♣ – **Local service BRUGGE - ZEEBRUGGE and v.v.** Journey 16 minutes. *Subject to alteration.*

From **Brugge**:
to Zeebrugge Dorp station on Ⓐ (not June 26 - Aug. 29): 0609, 0709 and hourly until 2209.
to Zeebrugge Strand station on Ⓐ June 26 - Aug. 29: 0609, 0709 and hourly until 2209.
to Zeebrugge Strand station on Ⓒ May 22 - Sept. 26: 0709 and hourly until 2009.
to Zeebrugge Strand station on Ⓒ until May 21 and from Sept. 27: 0709, 0909, 1109, 1309, 1509, 1709, 1909.

From **Zeebrugge**:
from Dorp station on Ⓐ (not June 26 - Aug. 29): 0634, 0734 and hourly until 1234 then 1333, 1433, 1534 and hourly until 2034, 2133.
from Strand station on Ⓐ June 26 - Aug. 29: 0634, 0734 and hourly until 1234 then 1333, 1433, 1534 and hourly until 2034, 2133.
from Strand station on Ⓒ May 22 - Sept. 26: 0734 and hourly until 1234 then 1333, 1433, 1534 and hourly until 2034.
from Strand station on Ⓒ until May 21 and from Sept. 27: 0734, 0934, 1134, 1333, 1534, 1734, 1934.

BRUSSELS - BRUSSELS NATIONAAL AIRPORT ✈ - LEUVEN 402

km			Ⓐ	Ⓐ	Ⓐ	Ⓐ	Ⓐ	ⒶQ	Ⓐ	Ⓐ	Ⓐ	ⒶQ	Ⓐ	Ⓐ	Ⓐ	ⒶQ	Ⓐ	Ⓐ	▲	Ⓐ	Ⓐ	ⒶQ	Ⓐ
	Gent Sint-Pieters **400/1** d.	Ⓐ	...	...	...	0430	0515	...	...	0530	0615	...	...	0630	0715	...	...	0730	and	1420	1515	...	...
0	**Brussels Midi / Zuid 400/1** d.		0448	0500	0512	0536	0548	0600	0612	0636	0648	0658	0712	0736	0748	0758	0810	0836	at the	1527	1548	1558	1613
2	Brussels Central d.		0452	0504	0516	0540	0552	0604	0616	0640	0652	0702	0716	0740	0752	0802	0814	0840	same	1531	1552	1602	1617
4	Brussels Nord d.		0457	0509	0521	0545	0557	0609	0621	0645	0657	0709	0721	0745	0757	0809	0820	0845	minutes	1636	1557	1609	1622
6	Schaarbeek / Schaerbeek d.		|	|	|	|	|	|	|	|	|	|	|	|	|	|	|	|	past each	|	|	|	|
16	**Brussels Nationaal ✈** a.		0508	0524	0533	0556	0608	0624	0633	0656	0708	0724	0733	0756	0808	0824	0834	0856	hour	1550	1608	1626	1634
16	**Brussels Nationaal ✈** d.		0517	...	0539	...	0617	...	0639	...	0717	...	0739	...	0817	...	0839	...	until	...	1613	...	1639
36	Leuven **400/1** a.		0533	...	0552	...	0633	...	0652	...	0733	...	0752	...	0833	...	0852	...		...	1627	...	1652

	Ⓐ	Ⓐ	ⒶQ	Ⓐ	Ⓐ	Ⓐ	ⒶQ	Ⓐ	Ⓐ	Ⓐ	ⒶQ	Ⓐ	Ⓐ		Ⓐ	ⒶQ	Ⓐ	Ⓐ		Ⓐ	ⒶQ	Ⓐ	
Gent Sint-Pieters **400/1** d.	1520	1615	...	...	1630	1715	...	...	1730	1815	...	...	1830	and	2115	...	...	2130	...	2215	...	...	...
Brussels Midi / Zuid 400/1 d.	1627	1648	1658	1712	1736	1748	1758	1812	1836	1848	1900	1912	1936	at the	2148	2200	2212	2236	...	2248	2300	2312	...
Brussels Central d.	1631	1652	1702	1716	1740	1752	1802	1816	1840	1852	1904	1916	1940	same	2152	2204	2216	2240	...	2252	2304	2316	...
Brussels Nord d.	1636	1657	1711	1721	1745	1757	1809	1821	1845	1857	1909	1921	1945	minutes	2157	2209	2221	2245	...	2257	2309	2321	...
Schaarbeek / Schaerbeek d.	|	|	|	|	|	|	|	|	|	|	|	|	|	past each	|	|	|	|	...	|	|	|	...
Brussels Nationaal ✈ a.	1650	1708	1724	1733	1756	1810	1824	1833	1856	1908	1924	1933	1956	hour	2208	2224	2233	2256	...	2308	2324	2333	...
Brussels Nationaal ✈ d.	...	1713	...	1739	...	1817	...	1839	...	1917	...	1939	...	until	2217	...	2239	...	...	2317	...	2339	...
Leuven **400/1** a.	...	1728	...	1752	...	1833	...	1852	...	1933	...	1952	...		2233	...	2252	...	...	2333	...	2352	...

		Ⓒ		Ⓒ	Ⓒ	Ⓒ	Ⓒ		ⒸQ		Ⓒ	Ⓒ	Ⓒ	ⒸQ		Ⓒ	Ⓒ	Ⓒ	ⒸQ		Ⓒ		
Gent Sint-Pieters **400/1** d.	Ⓒ	...	...	...	...	...	...	...	...	...	...	0530	...	...	and	...	2130	...	...	...	...	...	...
Brussels Midi / Zuid 400/1 d.		0450	...	0506	0523	0536	0550	...	0606	...	0623	0636	0650	0706	at the	2223	2236	2250	2306	...	2323	...	...
Brussels Central d.		0454	...	0510	0527	0540	0554	...	0610	...	0627	0640	0654	0710	same	2227	2240	2254	2310	...	2327	...	...
Brussels Nord d.		0459	...	0515	0532	0545	0559	...	0615	...	0632	0645	0659	0718	minutes	2232	2245	2259	2315	...	2332	...	...
Schaarbeek / Schaerbeek d.		|	...	0518	|	|	|	...	0619	...	|	|	|	0719	past each	|	|	|	2319	...	|	...	...
Brussels Nationaal ✈ a.		0510	...	0529	0543	0556	0610	...	0629	...	0643	0656	0710	0729	hour	2243	2256	2310	2329	...	2343	...	...
Brussels Nationaal ✈ d.		...	...	0538	...	...	...	...	0638	...	...	...	...	0739	until	...	...	...	2338	...	...	...	...
Leuven **400/1** a.		...	...	0551	...	...	...	...	0651	...	...	...	...	0751		...	...	...	2351	...	...	...	...

		Ⓐ	ⒶQ		Ⓐ	Ⓐ	Ⓐ	ⒶQ	Ⓐ	Ⓐ	Ⓐ	ⒶQ		Ⓐ	Ⓐ	Ⓐ		ⒶQ	Ⓐ	Ⓐ					
Leuven **400/1** d.	Ⓐ	...	...	...	0527	...	0608	...	0627	...	0708	...	...	0727	...	0808	...	...	0827	...	...	...	...	...	...
Brussels Nationaal ✈ a.		...	...	...	0543	...	0621	...	0643	...	0721	...	...	0743	...	0821	...	...	0843	...	...	...	...	...	...
Brussels Nationaal ✈ d.		0527	0536	...	0552	0604	0627	0636	0652	0702	0727	0736	...	0752	0810	0827	...	0836	0852	0910	...	...	...	...	...
Schaarbeek / Schaerbeek a.		|	|	...	|	|	|	|	|	|	|	|	...	|	|	|	...	|	|	|	...	...	...	...	...
Brussels Nord a.		0539	0551	...	0603	0615	0639	0651	0703	0715	0739	0752	...	0803	0826	0839	...	0852	0903	0926	...	...	...	...	...
Brussels Central a.		0544	0556	...	0608	0620	0644	0658	0708	0720	0744	0759	...	0808	0829	0844	...	0859	0908	0929	...	...	...	...	...
Brussels Midi / Zuid 400/1 a.		0548	0600	...	0612	0624	0648	0702	0712	0724	0748	0803	...	0812	0833	0848	...	0903	0912	0933	...	...	...	...	...
Gent Sint-Pieters **400/1** a.		...	...	...	0645	0728	...	...	0745	0828	...	...	...	0845	0940	...	...	...	0945	1040	...	...	...	...	...

	Ⓐ	ⒶQ	Ⓐ	Ⓐ	▲	Ⓐ	ⒶQ	Ⓐ	Ⓐ		Ⓐ	Ⓐ	Ⓐ	Ⓐ	Ⓐ	Ⓐ	Ⓐ	Ⓐ	Ⓐ	Ⓐ	Ⓐ		
Leuven **400/1** d.	0908	...	0927	...	and	2008	...	2027	...	...	2108	...	2127	...	2208	...	2227	...	2308	...	2331	...	...
Brussels Nationaal ✈ a.	0921	...	0943	...	at the	2021	...	2043	...	...	2121	...	2143	...	2221	...	2243	...	2321	...	2347	...	...
Brussels Nationaal ✈ d.	0927	0936	0952	1004	same	2027	2036	2052	2104	...	2127	2136	2152	2204	2227	2236	2252	2304	2327	2336	2352	...	...
Schaarbeek / Schaerbeek a.	|	|	|	|	minutes	|	|	|	|	...	|	|	|	|	|	|	|	|	|	|	|	...	...
Brussels Nord a.	0939	0952	1003	1015	past each	2039	2051	2103	2215	...	2139	2151	2203	2215	2239	2251	2303	2315	2339	2351	0003	...	...
Brussels Central a.	0944	0959	1008	1020	hour	2044	2056	2108	2220	...	2144	2156	2208	2220	2244	2256	2308	2320	2344	2356	0008	...	...
Brussels Midi / Zuid 400/1 a.	0948	1002	1012	1024	until	2048	2000	2112	2224	...	2148	2200	2212	2224	2248	2300	2312	2324	2348	2400	0012	...	...
Gent Sint-Pieters **400/1** a.	...	...	1045	1028		...	...	2145	2328	...	...	...	2245	2328	...	...	...	0028	...	...	...	...	...

		Ⓒ	ⒸQ	Ⓒ	Ⓒ	Ⓒ	ⒸQ	▲	Ⓒ	Ⓒ	Ⓒ	ⒸQ		Ⓒ	Ⓒ	Ⓒ	Ⓒ	Ⓒ					
Leuven **400/1** d.	Ⓒ	...	0509	...	...	...	0609	and	...	...	...	2209	...	...	...	...	2309	...	...	...	...	...	...
Brussels Nationaal ✈ a.		...	0524	...	...	...	0624	at the	...	...	...	2224	...	...	...	...	2324	...	...	...	...	...	...
Brussels Nationaal ✈ d.		0517	0532	0550	0604	0617	0631	same	2150	2204	2217	2231	...	2250	2304	2317	2331	2350	...	...	...	...	...
Schaarbeek / Schaerbeek a.		|	0542	|	|	|	0642	minutes	|	|	|	2241	...	|	|	|	2342	|	...	...	...	...	...
Brussels Nord a.		0528	0545	0601	0615	0628	0645	past each	2201	2215	2228	2244	...	2301	2315	2328	2345	0001	...	...	...	...	...
Brussels Central a.		0533	0549	0606	0620	0633	0650	hour	2206	2220	2233	2249	...	2306	2320	2333	2350	0006	...	...	...	...	...
Brussels Midi / Zuid 400/1 a.		0537	0553	0610	0624	0637	0654	until	2210	2224	2237	2253	...	2310	2324	2337	2354	0010	...	...	...	...	...
Gent Sint-Pieters **400/1** a.		...	...	...	0728	...	...		...	2328	...	...	...	...	...	...	...	...	...	...	...	...	...

Q – From / to Mons / Quévy / Quiévrain / St Ghislain – see Table **424**.

▲ – Timings may vary by up to 2 minutes on some journeys.

LIÈGE - MAASTRICHT 403

km		⚒	Ⓐ			⚒						Ⓒ	Ⓐ						Ⓒ	Ⓐ			
0	**Liège Guillemins** d.	0521	0521	...	0621	0621	...	0721	and	1721	...	1821	1832	...	1921	...	2021	...	2121	2123	...	2221	2321
19	Visé a.	0538	0539	...	0638	0639	...	0739	hourly	1739	...	1839	1850	...	1939	...	2039	...	2139	2140	...	2239	2339
32	**Maastricht** a.	...	0550	...	...	0650	...	0750	until	1750	...	1850	1900	...	1950	...	2050	...	2150	2150	...	2250	2350

	Ⓐ	⑥	Ⓐ	Ⓐ	Ⓐ	⑥	†																
Maastricht d.	0558	...	...	...	0707	0709	...	...	0809	and	1909	...	2009	...	2109	...	2209	...	2309	...	0009	...	...
Visé d.	0608	0622	0630	0658	0720	0722	0722	...	0822	hourly	1922	...	2021	...	2122	...	2222	...	2322	...	0022	...	...
Liège Guillemins a.	0624	0639	0649	0718	0737	0739	0739	...	0839	until	1939	...	2039	...	2139	...	2239	...	2339	...	0039	...	...

KNOKKE - OOSTENDE - DE PANNE 404

De Lijn ✆ 059 56 53 53

Belgian Coastal Tramway

From **Knokke** (railway station):
In principle services operate daily 0630 – 2030, with enhanced frequency as follows:
November - Easter: every 20 minutes 1008 – 1748.
Easter - June: every 15 minutes 0858 – 1728.
July and August: every 10 minutes 0803 – 1833.
September and October: every 15 minutes 0858 – 1728.
Exact times are subject to minor variation.

From **De Panne** (railway station):
In principle services operate daily 0600 – 2000, with enhanced frequency as follows:
November - Easter: every 20 minutes 0849 – 1729.
Easter - June: every 15 minutes 0854 – 1739.
July and August: every 10 minutes 0829 – 1929.
September and October: every 15 minutes 0854 – 1739.
Exact times are subject to minor variation.

Knokke → Heist + *0h06* → Zeebrugge + *0h11* → Blankenberge + *0h23* → **Oostende** + *1h00* → Middelkerke + *1h25* → Nieuwpoort + *1h49* → Koksijde + *2h02* → **De Panne** + *2h21*
De Panne → Koksijde + *0h19* → Nieuwpoort + *0h32* → Middelkerke + *0h56* → **Oostende** + *1h19* → Blankenberge + *1h57* → Zeebrugge + *2h05* → Heist + *2h14* → **Knokke** + *2h21*

Connections into NMBS / SNCB rail services are available at Knokke (Table **401**), Zeebrugge (Table **401**), Blankenberge (Table **401**), Oostende (Tables **400/1**) and De Panne (Table **407**). De Panne railway station is situated in Adinkerke.

Dutch-language forms of some **French-language** Belgian names

Aarlen = **Arlon**
Aat = **Ath**
Bergen = **Mons**
Doornik = **Tournai**
Duinkerke = **Dunkerque** (France)
Hoei = **Huy**
Luik = **Liège**
Moeskroen = **Mouscron**
Namen = **Namur**
Nijvel = **Nivelles**
Rijsel = **Lille** (France)
's Gravenbrakel = **Braine le Comte**
Wezet = **Visé**

French-language forms of some **Dutch-language** Belgian names

Anvers = **Antwerpen**
Audenarde = **Oudenaarde**
Bruges = **Brugge**
Courtrai = **Kortrijk**
Dixmude = **Diksmuide**
Furnes = **Veurne**
Gand = **Gent**
Hal = **Halle**
La Panne = **De Panne**
Lierre = **Lier**
Louvain = **Leuven**
Malines = **Mechelen**
Menin = **Menen**
Ostende = **Oostende**
Renaix = **Ronse**
Roulers = **Roeselare**
Saint Nicolas = **Sint Niklaas**
Saint Trond = **Sint Truiden**
Termonde = **Dendermonde**
Tirlemont = **Tienen**
Tongres = **Tongeren**
Ypres = **Ieper**

Some other places outside Belgium

Aken / Aix la Chapelle = **Aachen**
Keulen / Cologne = **Köln**
Londen / Londres = **London**

405 LILLE - KORTRIJK - OOSTENDE and GENT

Lille - Mouscron and v.v. subject to alteration on French and Belgian public holidays

km		Ⓐ		Ⓐ	Ⓒ		Ⓐ	⚒	†		⚒	†						⚒≠	†					
0	**Lille Flandres** § d.	...	...	...	...	...	...	0646	...	...	0805	0810	...	0906	...	1008	...	1108	1108	...	1208	...	1305	...
10	Roubaix § d.	...	...	...	...	...	...	0658	...	...	0816	|	...	|	...	1019	...	1119	|	...	1219	...	|	...
12	Tourcoing § d.	...	...	...	...	...	...	0718	...	...	0820	|	...	|	...	1023	...	1123	|	...	1223	...	|	...
18	Mouscron d.	...	...	...	...	0623	...	0724	0730	...	0827	0830	...	0927	...	1029	...	1129	1130	...	1229	...	1326	...
30	**Kortrijk 415** a.	...	...	...	...	0632	...	0732	0738	...	0838	0838	...	0935	...	1037	...	1138	1138	...	1237	...	1334	...
30	**Kortrijk 414** d.	0443	0535	0548	0608	0634	0648	0740	0743	0748	0840	0843	0848	0948	0940	1040	1048	1140	1143	1148	1240	1248	1348	1340
	Brugge ◇ a.	0527	|	0627	0651	|	0727	|	|	0827	|	|	0927	1027	|	|	1127	|	|	1227	|	1327	1427	|
	Oostende ◇ a.	0547	|	0647	0747	|	0747	|	|	0847	|	|	0947	1047	|	|	1147	|	|	1247	|	1347	1447	|
72	**Gent Sint-Pieters 406 414** a.	...	0603	...	...	0705	...	0805	0803	...	0903	0903	...	...	1003	1103	...	1203	1203	...	1303	...	...	1403
	Antwerpen Centraal **406** a.	...	0654	...	...	0754	...	0854	0854	...	0954	0954	...	...	1054	1154	...	1254	1254	...	1354	...	...	1454

			Ⓐ	Ⓒ				Ⓒ	Ⓐ		Ⓐ	Ⓒ				Ⓒ	Ⓐ		⚒	†		Ⓐ	†	⑥
Lille Flandres § d.	1408	...	...	1508	...	1608	...	1706	1706	...	1806	1806	...	1905	...	2008	2012	...	2105	2109	...	2209	2204	2214
Roubaix § d.	1420	...	...	|	...	1620	...	1718	1718	...	1816	1820	...	|	...	2020	|	...	|	2120	...	2220	|	|
Tourcoing § d.	1424	...	...	|	...	1624	...	1722	1722	...	1820	1824	...	|	...	2024	|	...	|	2124	...	2224	|	|
Mouscron d.	1430	...	1527	1530	...	1630	...	1728	1728	...	1826	1830	...	1925	...	2030	2029	...	2125	2130	...	2230	2230	2230
Kortrijk 415 a.	1438	...	1535	1538	...	1638	...	1736	1736	...	1834	1838	...	1933	...	2038	2037	...	2133	2138	...	2238	2238	2238
Kortrijk 414 d.	1440	1448	1540	1543	1548	1642	1648	1748	1751	1740	1840	1843	1848	1940	1948	2043	2040	2048	2148	2148	2143	2240	2242	2242
Brugge ◇ a.	|	1527	|	|	1627	|	1727	1827	1830	|	|	|	1927	|	2027	|	|	2127	2227	2227	|	|	|	|
Oostende ◇ a.	|	1547	|	|	1647	|	1747	1847	1847	|	|	|	1947	|	2047	|	|	2147	2247	2247	|	|	|	|
Gent Sint-Pieters 406 414 a.	1503	...	1603	1603	...	1703	...	...	...	1803	1903	1903	...	2003	...	2103	2103	...	...	...	2203	2303	2313	2313
Antwerpen Centraal **406** a.	1554	...	1654	1654	...	1754	...	...	...	1854	1954	1954	...	2054	...	2154	2154	...	...	...	2254	2354	0019	0019

km		Ⓐ	⑥t	Ⓐ	Ⓐ	Ⓐ	⚒	†	Ⓒ	⚒			Q	ⒸP		Ⓐ	Ⓒ				†	⚒		
	Antwerpen Centraal **406** d.	...	...	0454	...	...	0606	0606	...	...	0706	...	0806	0806	...	0906	0906	...	1006	1106	...	...	...	1206
	Gent Sint-Pieters 406 414 d.	...	0540	0545	...	...	0657	0657	...	...	0757	...	0857	0857	...	0957	0957	...	1057	1157	...	...	...	1257
0	**Oostende** ◇ d.	...	|	|	0514	0608	|	|	...	0714	|	0814	|	|	0914	|	|	1014	|	|	1114	1114	1214	|
22	Brugge ◇ d.	0507	|	|	0532	0625	|	|	0709	0734	|	0834	|	|	0934	|	|	1034	|	|	1134	1134	1234	|
75	**Kortrijk 414** a.	0554	0611	0609	0610	0705	0717	0717	0758	0812	0821	0912	0921	0917	1012	1022	1017	1112	1121	1221	1212	1212	1312	1321
	Kortrijk 415 d.	...	0612	0612	...	...	0724	0722	...	0822	...	...	0922	0926	...	1025	1022	...	1122	...	1222	1222	...	1323
	Mouscron a.	...	0620	0620	...	...	0732	0730	...	0830	...	...	0930	0934	...	1033	1030	...	1130	...	1230	1233	...	1331
	Tourcoing § a.	...	|	|	...	...	0738	|	...	0837	...	...	0935	0939	...	...	|	...	|	...	|	1238	...	1337
	Roubaix § a.	...	|	|	...	...	0741	|	...	0841	...	...	0939	0943	...	...	|	...	|	...	|	1243	...	1340
	Lille Flandres § a.	...	0636	0636	...	...	0754	0758	...	0854	...	...	0951	0954	...	...	1055	...	1154	...	1252	1256	...	1354

								⊕		⊕									Ⓐ		Ⓒ	Ⓐ		
Antwerpen Centraal **406** d.	...	1306	...	1406	1506	...	...	1606	...	1705	...	1805	1906	...	...	2006	...	2106	2106	...	2206	2206	2306	...
Gent Sint-Pieters 406 414 d.	...	1357	...	1457	1557	...	...	1657	...	1757	...	1857	1957	...	...	2057	...	2157	2157	...	2257	2257	2357	...
Oostende ◇ d.	1314	|	1414	|	|	1514	1614	|	1714	|	1813	|	|	1914	2014	|	2114	|	|	2214	|	|	|	...
Brugge ◇ d.	1334	|	1434	|	|	1534	1634	|	1734	|	1834	|	|	1934	2034	|	2134	|	|	2234	|	|	|	...
Kortrijk 414 a.	1412	1421	1512	1521	1621	1612	1712	1721	1812	1817	1912	1921	2021	2012	2112	2121	2212	2217	2222	2317	2317	2321	0029	...
Kortrijk 415 d.	...	1427	...	1525	...	1623	...	1723	...	1826	...	1927	...	2027	...	2126	...	...	2225	...	...	...	...	...
Mouscron a.	...	1435	...	1533	...	1631	...	1736	...	1834	...	1935	...	2035	...	2134	...	...	2233	...	...	...	...	...
Tourcoing § a.	...	|	...	1538	...	1642	...	1741	...	1839	...	1941	...	|	...	|	...	...	...	...	...	...	...	...
Roubaix § a.	...	|	...	1541	...	1641	...	1746	...	1843	...	1945	...	|	...	|	...	...	...	...	...	...	...	...
Lille Flandres § a.	...	1456	...	1552	...	1656	...	1756	...	1855	...	1955	...	2056	...	2154	...	...	...	...	...	...	...	...

P – May 22 until Sept. 27.
Q – Ⓐ (daily until May 16 and from Sept. 27).
t – Not May. 1 and 8.

⊕ – Change trains at Kortrijk on Ⓒ. ≠ – Change trains at Kortrijk on Ⓐ.
§ – Frequent services Lille Flandres - Lille Europe - Roubaix and Tourcoing are operated by the Lille *VAL* métro (Line 2) or by tram. For *TGV* trains see Table **250**.
◇ – For additional services between Oostende and Brugge see Tables **400/406**.

406 OOSTENDE - GENT - ANTWERPEN

km			Ⓐ	Ⓐ	Ⓐ	Ⓐ	Ⓐ	ⒶL	Ⓐ	▲	ⒶL	Ⓐ	Ⓐ	Ⓐ	ⒶL		Ⓒ	Ⓒ	ⒸL	Ⓒ		ⒸL	Ⓒ	ⒸL
0	**Oostende** § d.	Ⓐ	...	...	0604	...	0703	...	0804	and	...	2104	...	2204	...	Ⓒ	...	0539	...	0639	and	...	2139	...
22	Brugge § d.		...	...	0619	...	0718	...	0819	at the	...	2119	...	2219	...		...	0554	...	0654	at the	...	2154	...
	Kortrijk **405 414** d.		...	0535	|	0634	|	0740	|	same	2040	|	2140	|	2240		0536	|	0637r	|	same	2143	|	2242
62	**Gent Sint-Pieters** § d.		0505	0605	0647	0705	0747	0805	0847	minutes	2105	2147	2205	2247	2305		0605	0620	0705	0720	minutes	2205	2220	2327
89	Lokeren d.		0525	0625	0708	0725	0808	0825	0908	past	2125	2208	2225	2308	2325		0625	0640	0725	0740	past	2225	2240	2346
102	Sint-Niklaas d.		0535	0635	0718	0735	0818	0835	0918	each	2135	2218	2235	2218	2335		0635	0650	0735	0750	each	2235	2250	2355
125	Antwerpen Berchem a.		0549	0649	0734	0749	0834	0849	0934	hour	2149	2236	2249	2336	2349		0649	0707	0749	0807	hour	2249	2307	0014
127	**Antwerpen Centraal** a.		0554	0654	0739	0754	0839	0854	0939	until	2154	2241	2254	2341	2354		0654	0713	0754	0813	until	2254	2313	0019

		ⒶL	Ⓐ	ⒶL	Ⓐ	ⒶL	Ⓐ	▲	ⒶL	Ⓐ	Ⓐ	Ⓐ	Ⓐ		Ⓒ	ⒸL	Ⓒ	ⒸL	Ⓒ		ⒸL	Ⓒ	Ⓒ	Ⓒ
Antwerpen Centraal d.	Ⓐ	0454	0510	0606	0621	0706	0721	and	2106	2119	2206	2232	2306	Ⓒ	0547	0606	0647	0706	0747	and	2106	2147	2206	2306
Antwerpen Berchem d.		0459	0514	0611	0626	0711	0726	at the	2111	2124	2211	2238	2311		0553	0611	0653	0711	0753	at the	2111	2153	2210	2310
Sint-Niklaas d.		0516	0535	0627	0644	0727	0744	same	2127	2144	2227	2304	2327		0612	0627	0712	0727	0812	same	2127	2212	2227	2327
Lokeren d.		0525	0544	0636	0653	0736	0753	minutes	2136	2153	2236	2321	2336		0621	0636	0721	0736	0821	minutes	2136	2221	2236	2336
Gent Sint-Pieters § a.		0541	0603	0655	0713	0755	0813	past	2155	2213	2255	2344	2355		0640	0655	0740	0755	0840	past	2155	2240	2255	2355
Kortrijk **405 414** a.		0609	|	0721	|	0821	|	each	2222	|	2321	...	0029		|	0717	|	0817	|	each	2217	|	2317	0029
Brugge § a.		...	0639	...	0741	...	0841	hour	...	2241	...	...	...		0712	...	0806	...	0906	hour	...	2306	...	...
Oostende § a.		...	0652	...	0756	...	0856	until	...	2256	...	...	...		0728	...	0821	...	0921	until	...	2321	...	...

L – For journeys from/to Lille – see Table **405**.
r – From Kortrijk at 0637, 0743, 0843 and hourly until 2143.

▲ – Timings may vary by up to 2 minutes on some journeys.

§ – For additional services Oostende - Gent see Table **400**; for additional services Brugge - Gent see Tables **400/401**.

407 ANTWERPEN and BRUSSELS - LIER - TURNHOUT and NEERPELT

km			Ⓐ	Ⓐ	Ⓐ	▲	Ⓐ	Ⓐ	Ⓐ	Ⓐ	Ⓐ	Ⓐ	Ⓐ	Ⓐ		Ⓒ	Ⓒ	Ⓒ		Ⓒ	Ⓒ	Ⓒ	Ⓒ
0	**Antwerpen Centraal** d.	Ⓐ	0535	...	0613		2035	...	2113	2151	...	2242	...	2334	Ⓒ	0615	0715	0720		2215	2220	2315	2323
2	Antwerpen Berchem d.		0540	...	0619	and	2040	...	2119	2157	...	2248	...	2340		0621	0721	0726	and	2221	2226	2324	2329
	Brussels Midi/Zuid d.		|	0538	|	at	|	2038	|	|	2138	|	2238	|		|	|	|	at	|	|	|	|
	Mechelen d.		|	0605	|	the	|	2105	|	|	2205	|	2305	|		|	|	|	the	|	|	|	|
14	Lier d.		0550	0622	0629	same	2050	2122	2129	2210	2222	2302	2322	2354		0631	0731	0736	same	2231	2236	2334	2339
34	Herentals d.		0604	0640	0645	minutes	2104	2140	2145	...	2240	2326	2340	0018		0646	0746	0801	minutes	2246	2301	2356	0001
	Turnhout a.		0620	0656	|	past	2120	2156	|	...	2255	|	2355	|		|	|	0815	past	|	2315	|	0015
39	Olen d.		...	...	0650	each	...	...	2150	...	...	2331	...	0023		0651	0751	...	each	2251	...	0002	...
46	Geel d.		...	...	0656	hour	...	...	2156	...	...	2337	...	0029		0657	0757	...	hour	2257	...	0008	...
55	Mol d.		...	...	0708	until	...	...	2208	...	...	2345	...	0036		0708	0808	...	until	2308	...	0014	...
79	**Neerpelt** a.		...	...	0726		...	...	2226	...	...	0003	...	...		0726	0826	...		2326	...	...	...

km			Ⓐ	Ⓐ	Ⓐ	Ⓐ	Ⓐ	▲	Ⓐ	Ⓐ	Ⓐ	Ⓐ	Ⓐ	Ⓐ			Ⓒ	Ⓒ	Ⓒ	Ⓒ	▲	Ⓒ	Ⓒ
	Neerpelt d.	Ⓐ	0434	...	0534	...	...		2034	...	...	2134	...	...	...	Ⓒ	...	0534	...	0634		...	2134
	Mol d.		0457	...	0557	...	...	and	2057	...	...	2157	...	...	...		0456	0557	...	0657	and	...	2157
	Geel d.		0504	...	0604	...	...	at	2104	...	...	2204	...	...	...		0504	0604	...	0704	at	...	2204
	Olen d.		0510	...	0610	...	...	the	2110	...	...	2210	...	...	...		0509	0609	...	0709	the	...	2209
0	Turnhout d.		|	0458	|	0604	0640	same	|	2104	2140	|	2204	←	...		|	|	0645	|	same	2144	|
18	Herentals d.		0517	0521	0617	0621	0657	minutes	2117	2121	2157	2215	2221	2224	...		0515	0615	0704	0715	minutes	2204	2215
38	Lier d.		0532	0539	0632	0639	0711	past	2132	2139	2211	→	2239	2247	...		0530	0630	0725	0730	past	2225	2230
55	Mechelen a.		|	0555	|	0655	|	each	|	2155	|	...	2255	|	...		|	|	|	|	each	|	|
79	**Brussels Midi/Zuid** a.		|	0622	|	0723	|	hour	|	2222	|	...	2322	|	...		|	|	|	|	hour	|	|
	Antwerpen Berchem a.		0541	...	0641	...	0720	until	2141	...	2220	...	...	2302	...		0539	0639	0734	0739	until	2234	2239
	Antwerpen Centraal a.		0547	...	0647	...	0725		2147	...	2225	...	...	2307	...		0545	0645	0740	0745		2240	2245

▲ – Timings may vary by up to 3 minutes on some journeys.

GENT - DE PANNE 409

km			Ⓐ	Ⓐ		Ⓐ		Ⓒ		Ⓒ
	Brussels Nationaal ✈ 402 d.	Ⓐ	...	0552		2052	Ⓒ	...		...
	Brussels Midi/Zuid 401/2 . d.		...	0614		2114		0556r		1956r
0	**Gent Sint-Pieters** d.		0552	0652		2152		0652		2052
30	Tielt d.		0617	0716	and	2216		0716	and	2116
47	Lichtervelde d.		0630	0730	hourly	2230		0730	hourly	2130
66	Diksmuide d.		0644	0744	until	2244		0744	until	2144
81	Veurne d.		0655	0755		2255		0755		2155
86	**De Panne** § a.		0701	0801		2301		0801		2201

		Ⓐ	Ⓐp	▲	Ⓐ		Ⓒ	▲	Ⓒ
De Panne § d.	Ⓐ	0454	0554		2059	Ⓒ	0658		2059
Veurne d.		0502	0602		2106		0706		2106
Diksmuide d.		0513	0613		2117		0717		2117
Lichtervelde d.		0533	0630	and	2133		0732	and	2132
Tielt d.		0545	0641	hourly	2145		0744	hourly	2144
Gent Sint-Pieters a.		0609	0705	until	2209		0809	until	2209
Brussels Midi/Zuid 401/2 a.		0646	0746		2246		0904r		2304r
Brussels Nationaal ✈ 402 a.		0708	0808		2308		...		...

r – Via Denderleeuw (Table **401**).

p – From De Panne at 0554, 0659, 0759 and hourly until 2059.

▲ – Timings may vary by up to 3 minutes on some journeys.

§ – Connection available into the **Belgian Coastal Tramway**. See Table **404** for details. De Panne railway station is situated in Adinkerke.

BRUSSELS - ANTWERPEN - ROOSENDAAL (- AMSTERDAM) 410

FYRA **services.** Most services convey 🍷. **For** *Thalys* **trains Paris - Brussels - Amsterdam and v.v. – see Table 18**

km		A	B	C	B	C												x	x	x		⑥	⑧x
0	**Brussels Midi/Zuid** d.	0618	0715	0718	0813	0818	0918	1018	1118	...	1218	1318	1418	1518	1618	1718	1818	1918	2018	2118	...	2218	2218
2	Brussels Central d.	0622	0719	0722	0817	0822	0922	1022	1122	...	1222	1322	1422	1522	1622	1722	1822	1922	2022	2122	...	2222	2222
24	Mechelen **414** d.	0641	0741	0741	0841	0841	0941	1041	1141	...	1241	1341	1441	1541	1641	1741	1841	1941	2041	2141	...	2241	2241
48	**Antwerpen Centraal** a.	0657	0757	0757	0857	0857	0957	1057	1157	...	1257	1357	1457	1557	1657	1757	1857	1957	2057	2157	...	2257	2257
48	**Antwerpen Centraal** ◧ d.	0700	0800	0800	0900	0900	1000	1100	1200	...	1300	1400	1500	1600	1700	1800	1900	2000	2100	2200	...	2300	2300
89	**Roosendaal** 🏛 ◧ a.	0728	0828	0828	0928	0928	1028	1128	1228	...	1328	1428	1528	1628	1728	1828	1928	2028	2128	2228	...	2328	2328
	Rotterdam CS 450 a.	0806	0906	0906	1006	1006	1106	1206	1306	...	1406	1506	1606	1706	1806	1906	2006	2106	2206	2306	...	0006	0006
	Amsterdam CS 450 a.	0906z	1006z	1006	1106z	1106	1206z	1306z	1406z	...	1506z	1606z	1706z	1806z	1906z	2006z	2106y	2206z	2306z	0006z	...	0106v	...

	A	D								C	B							x	x	x		⑥t
Amsterdam CS 450 d.	...	0554p	0654q	0754z	0854z	0954z	...	1054z	1154z	1254z	1354	1354z	...	1454z	1554z	1654z	1754z	...	1854z	1954z	2054z	...	2154
Rotterdam CS 450 d.	0555	0655	0755	0855	0955	1055	...	1155	1255	1355	1455	1455	...	1555	1655	1755	1855	...	1955	2055	2155	...	2255
Roosendaal 🏛 ◧ d.	0634	0734	0834	0934	1034	1134	...	1234	1334	1434	1534	1534	...	1634	1734	1834	1934	...	2034	2134	2234	...	2334
Antwerpen Centraal ◧ a.	0700	0800	0900	1000	1100	1200	...	1300	1400	1500	1600	1600	...	1700	1800	1900	2000	...	2100	2200	2300	...	2400
Antwerpen Centraal d.	0703	0803	0903	1003	1103	1203	...	1303	1403	1503	1603	1603	...	1703	1803	1903	2003	...	2103	2203	2303	...	0003
Mechelen **414** d.	0721	0821	0921	1021	1121	1221	...	1321	1421	1521	1621	1621	...	1721	1821	1921	2021	...	2121	2221	2321	...	0021
Brussels Central a.	0738	0838	0938	1038	1138	1238	...	1338	1438	1538	1638	1639	...	1738	1838	1938	2038	...	2138	2238	2338	...	0038
Brussels Midi/Zuid a.	0742	0842	0942	1042	1142	1242	...	1342	1442	1542	1642	1643	...	1742	1842	1942	2042	...	2142	2242	2342	...	0042

A – ①–⑥ (also May 1, July 21, Nov. 1, 11; not Dec. 25, 26, Jan. 1, Apr. 5, May 13, 24).
B – ①–⑤ (also July 21, Nov. 1, 11).
C – ⑥⑦ (not July 21, Nov. 1, 11).
D – ①–⑥ (also May 1, July 21, Nov. 1, 10).

p – Not Dec. 25-27, Apr. 5, 30, May 13, 24.
q – Not Jan. 1, Apr. 30.
t – Not Dec. 26, Apr. 30.
v – Not Dec. 26.
x – Not Dec. 31.
y – Not Dec. 31, Apr. 30.
z – Not Apr. 30.

◧ – **Additional local services ANTWERPEN - ROOSENDAAL and v.v.:** Journey 50 minutes.
From **Antwerpen Centraal**: 0635⚒, 0735 and hourly until 2135.
From **Roosendaal**: 0737⚒, 0837 and hourly until 2237.

ANTWERPEN - NOORDERKEMPEN and v.v. *via high-speed line:*
Operates Ⓐ only, journey 15 minutes. *24 km.*
From Antwerpen Centraal: 0637Ⓐ, 0737Ⓐ, 0837, then hourly until 2137.
From Noorderkempen: 0608Ⓐ, 0708Ⓐ, 0808, then hourly until 2108.

CHARLEROI - BRUSSELS - ANTWERPEN 411

		Ⓐ	Ⓐ	Ⓐ	Ⓐ	Ⓐ	Ⓐ	Ⓐ	Ⓐ	Ⓐ	Ⓐ	Ⓐ	Ⓐ	Ⓐ	Ⓐ	Ⓐ	Ⓐ		Ⓐ	Ⓐ	Ⓐ	Ⓐ	Ⓐ	Ⓐ
Charleroi Sud d.	Ⓐ	...	...	...	0433	...	0537	...	0607	...	0635	0705	...	0737	...	0807	...		1737	...	1807	...	1837	1907
Marchienne-au-Pont d.		...	...	...	0438	...	0542	...	|	...	0640	|	...	0742	...	|	...	▲	1742	...	|	...	1842	|
Nivelles d.		...	...	...	0504	...	0552	...	0628	...	0659	0726	...	0801	...	0828	...	and at	1801	...	1828	...	1901	1928
Brussels Midi/Zuid a.		...	...	...	0548	...	0625	...	0653	...	0723	0751	...	0825	...	0853	...	the same	1825	...	1853	...	1925	1953
Brussels Midi/Zuid d.		0421	0453	0533	0555	0605	0628	0632	0655	0704	0728	0755	0804	0828	0832	0855	0905	minutes	1828	1832	1855	1905	1927	1955
Brussels Central d.		0425	0457	0537	0559	0609	0632	0636	0659	0708	0732	0759	0808	0832	0836	0859	0909	past each	1832	1836	1859	1909	1931	1959
Brussels Nord d.		0430	0502	0542	0604	0614	0637	0642	0704	0713	0737	0804	0813	0837	0842	0904	0914	hour	1837	1842	1904	1914	1936	2004
Mechelen **414** d.		0457	0522	0600	0622	0631	0654	0700	0722	0731	0754	0822	0831	0854	0900	0922	0931	until	1854	1900	1922	1931	1954	2022
Antwerpen Berchem a.		0530	0537	0619	0637	0649	0709	0719	0737	0749	0809	0837	0849	0909	0919	0937	0949		1909	1919	1937	1949	2009	2037
Antwerpen Centraal a.		0535	0543	0625	0643	0654	0715	0725	0743	0754	0815	0843	0854	0915	0925	0943	0954		1915	1925	1943	1954	2015	2043

	Ⓐ	Ⓐ	Ⓐ	Ⓐ	Ⓐ	Ⓐ	Ⓐ	Ⓐ	Ⓐ	Ⓐ	Ⓐ	Ⓐ		Ⓒ	Ⓒ	Ⓒ	Ⓒ		Ⓒ	Ⓒ	Ⓒ	Ⓒ	Ⓒ	Ⓒ
Charleroi Sud d.	...	1937	2007	...	2037	2107	...	2137	2207	...	2237	...	Ⓒ	...	0540	...	0640		...	2040	...	2140	...	2240
Marchienne-au-Pont d.	...	1942	|	...	2042	|	...	2142	|	...	2242	...		...	0845	...	0645	▲	...	2045	...	2145	...	2245
Nivelles d.	...	2001	2028	...	2101	2128	...	2201	2228	...	2304	...		...	0603	...	0703	and at	...	2103	...	2203	...	2303
Brussels Midi/Zuid a.	...	2025	2053	...	2125	2153	...	2225	2253	...	2325	...		...	0630	...	0730	the same	...	2130	...	2230	...	2330
Brussels Midi/Zuid d.	2005	2027	2055	2105	2127	2155	2205	2227	2255	2305	2327	2331		0559	0633	0659	0733	minutes	2059	2133	2159	2233	2259	2333
Brussels Central d.	2009	2031	2059	2109	2131	2159	2209	2231	2259	2309	2331	2335		0603	0637	0703	0737	past each	2103	2137	2203	2237	2303	2337
Brussels Nord d.	2014	2036	2104	2114	2136	2204	2214	2236	2304	2314	2334	2340		0908	0642	0708	0742	hour	2108	2142	2208	2242	2308	2342
Mechelen **414** d.	2031	2054	2122	2131	2154	2222	2231	2254	2322	2331	...	0004		0627	0700	0727	0800	until	2127	2200	2227	2300	2327	0000
Antwerpen Berchem a.	2049	2109	2137	2149	2209	2237	2249	2309	2337	2349	...	0033		0648	0716	0748	0816		2148	2216	2248	2316	2348	0016
Antwerpen Centraal a.	2054	2115	2143	2154	2215	2243	2254	2315	2343	2354	...	0038		0653	0722	0753	0822		2153	2222	2253	2322	2353	0022

		Ⓐ	Ⓐ	Ⓐ	Ⓐ	Ⓐ	Ⓐ	Ⓐ	Ⓐ	Ⓐ	Ⓐ	Ⓐ	Ⓐ	Ⓐ	Ⓐ	Ⓐ	Ⓐ		Ⓐ	Ⓐ	Ⓐ	Ⓐ	Ⓐ	Ⓐ
Antwerpen Centraal d.	Ⓐ	0418	0517	0535	0545	0606	0617	0635	0645	0706	0717	0735	0745	0806	0817	0835	0845		1806	1817	1835	1845	1917	1906
Antwerpen Berchem d.		0424	0523	0541	0551	0611	0623	0641	0651	0711	0723	0741	0751	0811	0823	0841	0851	▲	1811	1823	1841	1851	1923	1911
Mechelen **414** d.		0455	0540	0602	0608	0630	0640	0702	0708	0730	0740	0802	0808	0830	0840	0902	0908	and at	1830	1840	1902	1908	1940	1930
Brussels Nord a.		0518	0556	0618	0624	0646	0656	0718	0723	0747	0757	0818	0823	0846	0856	0918	0923	the same	1846	1856	1918	1923	1956	1946
Brussels Central a.		0523	0601	0624	0629	0651	0701	0724	0729	0752	0802	0824	0829	0851	0901	0924	0929	minutes	1851	1901	1923	1929	2001	1951
Brussels Midi/Zuid a.		0527	0605	0628	0633	0655	0705	0728	0733	0756	0806	0828	0833	0855	0905	0928	0933	past each	1855	1905	1927	1933	2005	1955
Brussels Midi/Zuid d.		...	0607	...	0635	...	0707	...	0735	...	0809	...	0835	...	0907	...	0935	hour	...	1907	...	1935	2007	...
Nivelles d.		...	0633	...	0700	...	0733	...	0800	...	0835	...	0900	...	0933	...	1000	until	...	1933	...	2000	2033	...
Marchienne-au-Pont a.		...	|	...	0718	...	|	...	0818	...	|	...	0918	...	|	...	1018		...	|	...	2018	|	...
Charleroi Sud a.		...	0653	...	0723	...	0753	...	0823	...	0855	...	0923	...	0953	...	1023		...	1953	...	2023	2053	...

	Ⓐ	Ⓐ	Ⓐ	Ⓐ	Ⓐ	Ⓐ	Ⓐ	Ⓐ	Ⓐ	Ⓐ	Ⓐ	Ⓐ	Ⓐ			Ⓒ	Ⓒ	Ⓒ	Ⓒ	Ⓒ		Ⓒ	Ⓒ	Ⓒ
Antwerpen Centraal d.	1945	2006	2017	2045	2106	2117	2145	2206	2217	2225	2306	2317	2325	...	Ⓒ	0538	0607	0638	0707	0738		2207	2238	2307
Antwerpen Berchem d.	1951	2011	2023	2051	2111	2123	2151	2211	2223	2230	2311	2323	2330	...		0544	0612	0644	0712	0744	▲	2212	2244	2312
Mechelen **414** d.	2008	2030	2040	2108	2130	2140	2208	2230	2240	2303	2330	2340	0003	...		0602	0635	0702	0735	0802	and at	2235	2302	2235
Brussels Nord a.	2024	2046	2056	2124	2146	2156	2224	2246	2256	2319	2346	2356	0024	...		0618	0652	0718	0752	0818	the same	2252	2318	2252
Brussels Central a.	2029	2051	2101	2129	2151	2201	2229	2251	2301	2338	2351	0001	0029	...		0623	0657	0723	0757	0823	minutes	2257	2323	2257
Brussels Midi/Zuid a.	2033	2055	2105	2133	2155	2205	2233	2255	2305	2342	2355	0005	0033	...		0627	0701	0727	0801	0827	past each	2301	2327	0001
Brussels Midi/Zuid d.	2035	...	2107	2135	...	2207	2235	...	2307	...	...	0007	...	...		0630	...	0730	...	0830	hour	...	2330	...
Nivelles d.	2100	...	2133	2200	...	2233	2300	...	2333	...	...	0047	...	...		0658	...	0758	...	0858	until	...	2358	...
Marchienne-au-Pont a.	2118	...	|	2218	...	|	2318	...	|	...	...	|	...	...		0715	...	0815	...	0915		...	0015	...
Charleroi Sud a.	2123	...	2153	2223	...	2253	2323	...	2353	...	...	0115	...	...		0720	...	0820	...	0920		...	0020	...

▲ – Timings may vary by up to 2 minutes on some journeys.

414 LEUVEN - MECHELEN and MECHELEN - GENT - KORTRIJK

km		Ⓐ	Ⓐ	Ⓒ	Ⓐ		Ⓒ	Ⓐ		Ⓒ	Ⓐ
0	**Mechelen 410** d.	...	...	...	0623	...	0705	0723		2205	2223
27	Dendermonde d.	0435	0542	0631	0643	...	0731	0743	and	2231	2243
57	**Gent Sint-P** a.	0459	0606	0657	0707	...	0757	0807	hourly	2257	2307
57	**Gent Sint-P 405** d.	0500	0608	0709	0709	...	0809	0809	until	2309	2309
99	**Kortrijk 405 415** a.	0533	0641	0742	0742	...	0842	0842		2342	2342

	Ⓐ	Ⓐ	Ⓒ		Ⓐ▲	Ⓒ	▲	Ⓐ	Ⓒ		Ⓐ	Ⓒ
Kortrijk 405 415 d.	0415	0512	0518	...	0618	0618		2118	2118	...	2218	2218
Gent Sint-P 405 a.	0447	0546	0551	...	0651	0651	and	2151	2151	...	2252	2251
Gent Sint-P d.	0452	0548	0603	...	0653	0703	hourly	2153	2203	...	2258	2303
Dendermonde d.	0517	0617	0631	...	0718	0731	until	2218	2231	...	2323	2329
Mechelen 410 a.	0537	0637	0655	...	0737	0755		2237	2255	...	...	...

km		Ⓐ	Ⓐ		Ⓐ	Ⓐp	Ⓒ	and	Ⓐ	Ⓒ	Ⓐ
0	Leuven d.	0515	0548	...	0615	0643	0644	hourly	2215	2244	2248
24	Mechelen a.	0537	0617	...	0637	0713	0710	until	2237	2310	2317

	Ⓐ	Ⓐ	Ⓐ	Ⓒ	Ⓐ	Ⓐ	and	Ⓒ	Ⓐ	Ⓐ		Ⓐ
Mechelen d.	0543	0623	0643	0650	0723	0743	hourly	2214	2223	2243	...	2323
Leuven a.	0613	0645	0713	0716	0745	0813	until	2246	2245	2313	...	2345

p – From Leuven at 0643, 0743, 0848, 0948 and hourly until 2248.

▲ – On Ⓐ Kortrijk d. 0713 (not 0718), Gent a. 0747, d. 0750, Dendermonde d. 0814, Mechelen a. 0837.

415 BRUSSELS - ZOTTEGEM - KORTRIJK - POPERINGE

km		Ⓐ	Ⓒ	Ⓐ	Ⓒ	Ⓐy	▲	Ⓒ	Ⓐ	Ⓒ	Ⓐ
0	**Brussels Nord** d.	0528	...	0632	0722	0732		2122	2132	2222	2232
2	Brussels Central d.	0532	...	0636	0726	0736		2129	2136	2229	2236
4	**Brussels Midi / Zuid** d.	0536	0635	0641	0735	0741		2135	2141	2235	2241
26	Denderleeuw d.	0552	0655	0701	0755	0801	and	2155	2201	2255	2301
46	**Zottegem** d.	0609	0715	0716	0815	0816		2215	2216	2315	2320
63	Oudenaarde **419** d.	0625	0729	0728	0829	0828	hourly	2229	2228	2329	2334
89	**Kortrijk 405 414** a.	0643	0745	0745	0845	0845		2245	2245	2345	2349
89	**Kortrijk** ‡ d.	0644	0751	0750	0851	0850	until	2251	2250	...	...
101	Menen ‡ d.	0658	0804	0803	0904	0903		2304	2303	...	...
123	**Ieper** ‡ d.	0716	0822	0821	0922	0921		2322	2321	...	...
133	**Poperinge** ‡ a.	0723	0829	0828	0929	0928		2329	2328	...	...

	Ⓐ	Ⓒ	Ⓐ	Ⓒ	Ⓐ	Ⓒ	Ⓐx	Ⓒ	▲	Ⓐ	Ⓒ	Ⓐ
Poperinge ‡ d.	0431	...	0524	0531	0625	0631	0731	0731		2031	2031	2131
Ieper ‡ d.	0439	...	0532	0539	0634	0639	0739	0739		2039	2039	2139
Menen ‡ d.	0457	...	0552	0557	0654	0657	0757	0757		2057	2057	2157
Kortrijk ‡ a.	0509	...	0604	0609	0710	0709	0806	0809	and	2109	2109	2209
Kortrijk 405 414 d.	0515	0515	0615	0615	0715	0715	0815	0815		2115	2115	2215
Oudenaarde **419** d.	0533	0532	0633	0632	0733	0732	0833	0832	hourly	2133	2132	2233
Zottegem d.	0545	0547	0646	0647	0746	0747	0846	0847		2146	2147	2246
Denderleeuw d.	0601	0607	0701	0707	0801	0807	0901	0907	until	2201	2207	2305
Brussels Midi/Zuid a.	0619	0625	0719	0725	0819	0825	0919	0925		2219	2225	2323
Brussels Central a.	0624	...	0724	0734	0824	0834	0924	0934		2224	2234	2328
Brussels Nord a.	0628	...	0728	0738	0828	0838	0928	0938		2228	2238	2332

x – A change of train is necessary at Kortrijk on the 1130 and 1431 departures from Poperinge.
y – A change of train is necessary at Kortrijk on the 0732 and 1132 departures from Brussels.

‡ – Additional trains Kortrijk - Poperinge and v.v.: From Kortrijk at 0536 Ⓐ and 0651 Ⓒ. From Poperinge at 2131 Ⓒ.
▲ – Timings may vary by up to 2 minutes on some journeys.

417 ANTWERPEN - HASSELT - LIÈGE

km			Ⓐ	Ⓐ	Ⓐ		Ⓐ	Ⓐ	Ⓐ	Ⓐ				Ⓒ	Ⓒ	Ⓒ		Ⓒ		Ⓒ	Ⓒ	Ⓒ
0	**Antwerpen Centraal** d.	Ⓐ	...	0531	0631		1931	2031	2131	2231	...	...	Ⓒ	...	...	0643		1943	...	2043	2143	2243
2	Antwerpen Berchem d.		...	0536	0636		1936	2036	2136	2236	...	...		...	...	0648		1948	...	2048	2148	2248
14	Lier d.		...	0547	0647	and	1947	2047	2147	2247	...	...		...	...	0658	and	1958	...	2058	2158	2258
41	Aarschot **401** d.		...	0613	0713		2013	2113	2213	2313	...	...		...	...	0724		2024	...	2124	2224	2324
59	Diest **401** d.		...	0625	0725	hourly	2025	2125	2225	2325	...	...		...	...	0737	hourly	2037	...	2137	2241	2337
80	**Hasselt 401** a.		...	0638	0738		2038	2138	2238	2338	...	...		...	...	0750		2050	...	2150	2257	2350
80	**Hasselt** d.		0544	0646	0744	until	2044	2144	...	...	...	...		0558	0658	0756	until	2056	...	2156	2259	...
107	Tongeren d.		0607	0708	0807		2107	2207	...	...	...	...		0618	0718	0818		2118	...	2218	2324	...
135	**Liège Guillemins** a.		0644	0744	0844		2144	...	...	...	...	...		0652	0752	0852		2152	...	...	...	...

		Ⓐ	Ⓐ	Ⓐ	Ⓐ	Ⓐ	Ⓐ		Ⓐ	Ⓐ			Ⓒ	Ⓒ	Ⓒ		Ⓒ		Ⓒ		
Liège Guillemins d.	Ⓐ	...	...	...	0618	0718	0818		2118	2218	...	Ⓒ	...	0608	0708		2008	...	2108	...	...
Tongeren d.		...	...	0559	0654	0754	0854		2154	2254	...		...	0644	0744		2044	...	2144	...	...
Hasselt a.		...	...	0620	0716	0816	0916	and	2216	2316	...		...	0706	0806	and	2106	...	2206	...	...
Hasselt 401 d.		0400	0522	0622	0722	0822	0922		2222	...	...		0610	0710	0810		2110	...	2210	...	...
Diest **401** d.		0416	0536	0636	0736	0836	0936	hourly	2236	...	...		0624	0724	0824	hourly	2124	...	2224	...	...
Aarschot **401** d.		0438	0552	0652	0752	0852	0952		2252	...	...		0641	0741	0841		2141	...	2241	...	...
Lier d.		0509	0614	0714	0815	0914	1014	until	2314	...	...		0703	0803	0903	until	2203	...	2303	...	...
Antwerpen Berchem a.		0522	0624	0724	0824	0924	1024		2324	...	...		0712	0812	0912		2212	...	2312	...	...
Antwerpen Centraal a.		0527	0629	0729	0829	0929	1029		2329	...	...		0717	0817	0917		2217	...	2317	...	...

419 GENT - RONSE and GENT - EEKLO

km		Ⓐ	Ⓐ	Ⓐ	Ⓐ		Ⓐ		Ⓐ			Ⓐ		Ⓐ		Ⓐ	Ⓐ	Ⓐ		Ⓐ		Ⓐ	Ⓒ	Ⓐ
0	**Gent St-Pieters 400/1** d.	...	0555	0701	0727	0801	0901	1001	1101	...	1201	1301	1401	1501	1601	1623	1701	1723	1801	1901	2001	2101	2212	...
7	De Pinte d.	...	0603	0708	0734	0808	0908	1008	1108	...	1208	1308	1408	1508	1608	1630	1708	1730	1808	1908	2008	2108	2220	2220
25	**Oudenaarde 415** a.	...	0625	0729	0757	0829	0929	1029	1129	...	1229	1329	1429	1529	1629	1650	1729	1754	1829	1929	2029	2129	2240	2240
25	**Oudenaarde** d.	0540	0629	0738	0759	0838	0938	1038	1138	...	1238	1338	1438	1538	1638	1659	1738	1757	1838	1938	2038	2138	...	...
39	**Ronse** a.	0550	0639	0748	0809	0848	0948	1048	1148	...	1248	1348	1448	1548	1648	1709	1748	1807	1848	1948	2048	2148	...	...

	Ⓐ	Ⓐ	Ⓐ	Ⓐ	Ⓒ	Ⓐ	Ⓐ		Ⓐ		Ⓐ		Ⓐ		Ⓐ	Ⓐ			Ⓐ		Ⓐ		Ⓐ
Ronse d.	0508	0618	0647	0711	0712	0748	0813	0912	1012	1112	1212	1312	1412	1512	1612	1648	...	1712	1812	1912	2012	2112	2202
Oudenaarde a.	0518	0628	0657	0721	0722	0758	0823	0922	1022	1122	1222	1322	1422	1522	1622	1658	...	1722	1822	1922	2022	2122	2212
Oudenaarde 415 d.	0523	0629	0706	0731	0732	0804	0831	0931	1031	1131	1231	1331	1431	1531	1631	1710	...	1731	1831	1931	2031	2131	2220
De Pinte d.	0543	0650	0727	0752	0753	0826	0852	0952	1052	1152	1252	1352	1452	1552	1652	1732	...	1752	1852	1952	2052	2152	2241
Gent St-Pieters 400/1 a.	0549	0656	0734	0759	0759	0833	0858	0959	1058	1159	1258	1359	1458	1559	1658	1739	...	1759	1858	1959	2058	2159	2247

km			Ⓐ	Ⓐ	Ⓐ	Ⓐ	Ⓐ	Ⓐ		Ⓐ	Ⓐ	Ⓐ	Ⓐ	Ⓐ	Ⓐ		Ⓒ	Ⓒ	Ⓒ	Ⓒ	Ⓒ	Ⓒ	Ⓒ	Ⓒ
0	**Gent St-Pieters 400/1** d.	Ⓐ	0636	0711	0801	0842	0942	1042	and	1742	1759	1842	1942	2042	2142	Ⓒ	0626	0826	1026	1226	1426	1626	1826	2026
7	Gent Dampoort d.		0646	0721	0809	0852	0952	1052	hourly	1752	1809	1852	1952	2052	2152		0636	0836	1036	1236	1436	1636	1836	2036
27	**Eeklo** a.		0711	0747	0834	0919	1016	1117	until	1817	1834	1917	2017	2117	2217		0701	0901	1101	1301	1501	1701	1901	2101

		Ⓐ	Ⓐ	Ⓐ	Ⓐ	Ⓐ		Ⓐ	Ⓐ	Ⓐ	Ⓐ	Ⓐ	Ⓐ	Ⓐ			Ⓒ	Ⓒ	Ⓒ	Ⓒ	Ⓒ	Ⓒ	Ⓒ	Ⓒ
Eeklo d.	Ⓐ	0541	0626	0712	0750	0842	and	1542	1625	1741	1842	1942	2042	2142	...	Ⓒ	0717	0917	1117	1317	1517	1717	1917	2117
Gent Dampoort d.		0609	0652	0739	0818	0910	hourly	1610	1652	1810	1910	2010	2110	2210	...		0743	0943	1143	1343	1543	1743	1943	2143
Gent St-Pieters 400/1 a.		0618	0701	0747	0827	0919	until	1620	1701	1819	1919	2020	2119	2219	...		0752	0952	1152	1352	1552	1752	1952	2152

422 CHARLEROI - COUVIN

km		Ⓐ	Ⓐ	Ⓒ	Ⓐ	Ⓐ	Ⓒ	Ⓐt	Ⓐ	Ⓒ	Ⓐ	Ⓐ	Ⓐ	Ⓒ	Ⓐ	Ⓒ	Ⓐ	Ⓐ	Ⓒ	Ⓐ	Ⓐ	Ⓐ	Ⓐ	Ⓒ	Ⓐ	
0	**Charleroi Sud 435** d.	0618	0714	0754	0804	0909	0954	1010	1105	1154	1207	1311	1405	1402	1541	1554	1613	1717	1754	1819	1851	1918	1952	1954	2107	2230
18	Berzée d.	0634	0730	0815	0820	0924	1015	1032	1121	1215	1223	1328	1421	1423	1557	1615	1629	1732	1815	1835	1907	1934	2008	2015	2123	2251
22	Walcourt d.	0639	0736	0822	0825	0929	1022	1038	1126	1222	1229	1333	1426	1430	1603	1622	1635	1738	1822	1840	1912	1945	2013	2022	2128	2258
35	Philippeville d.	0652	0751	0837	0837	0941	1037	1052	1138	1237	1246	1346	1438	1445	1615	1637	1650	1750	1837	1852	1927	1957	2025	2037	2141	2313
48	Mariembourg ▲ d.	0708	0802	0847	0848	0952	1047	1103	1148	1247	1256	1400	1449	1455	1625	1647	1700	1800	1847	1902	1937	2007	2035	2047	2151	2323
53	**Couvin** a.	0714	0808	0853	0854	0958	1053	1109	1155	1253	1302	1406	1455	1501	1631	1653	1706	1806	1853	1908	1943	2013	2041	2053	2157	2330

	Ⓐ	Ⓒ	Ⓐ	Ⓐ	Ⓒw	Ⓐ	Ⓐ	Ⓒ	Ⓐv	Ⓐ	Ⓒ	Ⓐ	Ⓐ	Ⓒ	Ⓐ	Ⓐ	Ⓒ	Ⓐ	Ⓐ	Ⓒ	Ⓐ	Ⓐ	Ⓒ	Ⓐ	Ⓐ	Ⓒ	Ⓐ
Couvin d.	0448	0507	0546	0635	0707	0733	0840	0907	0923	1034	1107	1156	1249	1259	1353	1504	1507	1532	1653	1707	1808	1909	1907	2000	2056	2059	2123
Mariembourg ▲ d.	0455	0514	0553	0642	0714	0740	0847	0914	0930	1041	1114	1203	1306	1306	1401	1511	1514	1539	1708	1714	1815	1916	1914	2014	2103	2106	2130
Philippeville d.	0506	0525	0605	0653	0725	0752	0858	0925	0942	1053	1125	1214	1319	1317	1412	1522	1525	1551	1723	1725	1827	1928	1925	2026	2114	2117	2142
Walcourt d.	0518	0539	0619	0705	0739	0808	0910	0939	0956	1105	1139	1227	1332	1331	1425	1534	1539	1603	1736	1739	1839	1940	1939	2038	2128	2131	2156
Berzée d.	0525	0546	0623	0709	0746	0812	0914	0946	1001	1111	1146	1233	1336	1338	1431	1540	1546	1610	1743	1746	1845	1944	1946	2042	2133	2138	2203
Charleroi Sud 435 a.	0540	0606	0639	0725	0806	0828	0929	1006	1022	1126	1206	1248	1352	1358	1446	1555	1606	1625	1758	1806	1900	1959	2006	2057	2154	2158	2224

t – Additional journeys on Ⓐ: 0513, 1234, 1507, 1637, 1750, 2010.
v – Additional journeys on Ⓐ: 0419, 05113, 0701, 0755, 1227, 1420, 1553, 1632.
w – Runs 9 minutes earlier June 26 - Aug. 29.

▲ – Service available on certain dates Mariembourg - Treignes and v.v. Some trains operated by steam locomotive. Operator: Chemin de Fer à Vapeur des 3 Vallées (CFV3V), Chaussée de Givet 49-51, 5660 Mariembourg. ✆ / fax +32 60 312 440. Fuller details are shown in our *Tourist Railways* feature annually each July.

BRUSSELS - MONS - QUÉVY and QUIÉVRAIN 424

km	ICD		Ⓐ	Ⓐ	Ⓐ	Ⓐ	Ⓐ	AⒶ	LⒶ	AⒶ		LⒶ	AⒶ	LⒶ	AⒶ	LⒶ	LⒶ		EⒸ	EⒸ		EⒸ	EⒸ	EⒸ	EⒸ
0	**Brussels Nord** d.	Ⓐ	...	...	...	0453	0525	0553	0622	0653		2022	2053	2122	2153	2222	2322	Ⓒ	0546	0647		1947	2047	2147	2246
2	Brussels Central d.		...	...	...	0457	0529	0557	0626	0659	▲♣	2026	2057	2126	2157	2226	2326		0550	0651	▲	1951	2051	2151	2250
4	**Brussels Midi/Zuid** d.		...	...	...	0504	0534	0604	0633	0704	and at	2033	2104	2133	2204	2233	2333		0554	0657	and at	1957	2057	2157	2254
33	Braine-le-Comte d.		...	...	...	0529	0554	0629	0655	0729	the same	2055	2129	2155	2229	2255	2358		0618	0718	the same	2018	2118	2218	2318
39	Soignies d.		...	...	...	0535	0600	0635	0701	0735	minutes	2101	2135	2201	2235	2301	0004		0624	0724	minutes	2024	2124	2224	2324
64	**Mons** a.		...	...	...	0551	0614	0651	0715	0751	past each	2115	2151	2215	2251	2315	0021		0641	0741	past each	2041	2141	2241	2341
64	**Mons 426 435** d.		0453	...	...	0553	0616	0653	0717	0753	hour	2117	2153	2217	...	2317	0022		0649	0749	hour	2049	2149	2249	2349
	Quévy a.		0508	...	...	0608	|	0708	|	0808	until	|	2208	|	...	|	|		|	|	until	|	|	|	|
74	Saint-Ghislain **426** a.		...	0431	0531	...	0627	...	0729	...		2129	...	2229	...	2329	0034		0700	0800		2100	2200	2300	2400
84	**Quiévrain** a.		...	0447	0547	...	0643	...	0747	...		2147	...	...	...	...	...		0726	0826		2126	...	...	...

km			LⒶ	AⒶ	LⒶ	AⒶ	LⒶ	AⒶ	LⒶ	AⒶ	LⒶ	AⒶ		LⒶ	AⒶ	Ⓐ			EⒸ	EⒸ	EⒸ	EⒸ		EⒸ	
	Quiévrain d.	Ⓐ	...	...	0513	...	0613	...	0713	...	0813	...		2113	...	2213	...	Ⓒ	...	...	...	0734		2134	...
	St Ghislain **426** d.		0426	...	0530	...	0630	...	0730	...	0830	...	▲	2130	...	2230	...		0500	0600	0700	0800		2200	...
0	Quévy d.		|	0452	|	0552	|	0650	|	0747	|	0852	and at	|	2152	|	...		|	|	|	|	and at	|	...
15	**Mons 426 435** a.		0437	0507	0543	0607	0643	0707	0743	0802	0843	0907	the same	2143	2207	2243	...		0511	0611	0711	0811	the same	2211	...
	Mons d.		0438	0509	0545	0609	0645	0709	0745	0809	0845	0909	minutes	2145	2209	2245	...		0519	0619	0719	0819	minutes	2219	...
	Soignies d.		0500	0526	0600	0626	0700	0726	0800	0826	0900	0926	past each	2200	2226	2300	...		0537	0637	0737	0837	past each	2237	...
	Braine-le-Comte d.		0507	0533	0607	0633	0707	0733	0807	0833	0907	0933	hour	2207	2233	2307	...		0543	0643	0743	0843	hour	2243	...
	Brussels Midi/Zuid a.		0527	0556	0627	0656	0727	0755	0827	0856	0927	0956	until	2227	2256	2329	...		0604	0703	0803	0903	until	2303	...
	Brussels Central a.		0534	0603	0634	0701	0734	0801	0834	0901	0934	1001		2234	2303	2334	...		0609	0709	0809	0909		2309	...
	Brussels Nord a.		0538	0607	0638	0707	0738	0807	0838	0907	0938	1007		2238	2307	2338	...		0613	0713	0813	0913		2313	...

A – From/to Brussels Nationaal ✈ – see Table **402**.
E – From/to Leuven via Brussels Nationaal ✈ – see Table **402**.
L – From/to Liège – see Table **401**.

▲ – Timings may vary by up to 4 minutes on some journeys.
♣ – Other variations: Brussels Nord d. 1622, Quiévrain a. 1753; Brussels Nord d. 1453, Mons d. 1612, Quévy a. 1627; Brussels Nord d. 1753, Mons d. 1858, Quévy a. 1913.

BRUSSELS - TOURNAI - MOUSCRON 425

km		Ⓐ	Ⓐ	Ⓒr	▲	Ⓐ	Ⓒr	Ⓐ	Ⓒ	Ⓐ	Ⓒ
0	**Brussels Nord** d.	0452	0559	0612		2059	2112	2205	2212	2259	2326
2	Brussels Central d.	0456	0603	0616	and	2103	2116	2209	2216	2303	2330
4	**Brussels Midi/Zuid** d.	0501	0608	0621		2108	2121	2214	2221	2308	2334
55	Ath d.	0543	0644	0659	hourly	2144	2159	2249	2259	2344	0012
67	Leuze d.	0552	0653	0708		2153	2208	2258	2308	2353	0021
85	**Tournai** a.	0603	0704	0719	until	2204	2219	2309	2319	0004	0032
85	**Tournai 435** d.	0607	0706	0736r		2206	2236r	2311	2323	...	...
105	**Mouscron 435** a.	0622	0721	0751r		2221	2251r	2326	2338	...	...

	Ⓐ	Ⓐ	Ⓒ	Ⓐ	Ⓒt	Ⓐ	▲	Ⓒt	Ⓒ	Ⓐ
Mouscron 435 d.	...	0437	0524	0537	0609t	0639		2109t	2216	2239
Tournai 435 a.	...	0452	0539	0552	0624t	0654	and	2124t	2231	2254
Tournai d.	0425	0454	0541	0554	0641	0656		2141	2241	2256
Leuze d.	0437	0506	0553	0606	0653	0708	hourly	2153	2253	2308
Ath d.	0449	0516	0603	0616	0703	0718		2203	2303	2318
Brussels Midi/Zuid a.	0530	0552	0639	0652	0739	0752	until	2239	2339	2352
Brussels Central a.	0536	0557	0644	0657	0744	0757		2344	2344	2357
Brussels Nord a.	0540	0601	0648	0701	0748	0801		2348	2348	0001

r – On † Brussels departures 1312–2012 depart Tournai at xx21▲, arrive Mouscron xx38▲.
t – On † Brussels arrivals 1648–2248 depart Mouscron at xx24▲, arrive Tournai xx39▲.

▲ – Timings may vary by up to 4 minutes on some journeys.

MONS - TOURNAI - LILLE 426

Subject to alteration on Belgian and French holidays

km			Ⓐ	Ⓐ	Ⓐ	Ⓐ	Ⓐ		Ⓐ	Ⓐ	Ⓐ	Ⓐ		Ⓐ	Ⓐ	Ⓐ	Ⓐ		Ⓐ	Ⓐ	Ⓐ		Ⓐ	Ⓐ	Ⓐ	
	Liège G **435** d.	Ⓐ	...	...	0547	0647	0747	...	0847	0947	1047	1147	...	1247	1347	1447	1547	...	1647	1747	1847	...	1947	2047	2247	...
	Namur **435** d.		...	...	0629	0729	0829	...	0929	1029	1129	1229	...	1329	1429	1529	1629	...	1729	1829	1929	...	2029	2129	2229	...
	Charleroi Sud **435** d.		...	0558	0702	0802	0902	...	1002	1102	1202	1302	...	1402	1502	1602	1702	...	1802	1902	2002	...	2102	2202	2302	...
0	**Mons 435** d.		0539	0629	0734	0834	0934	...	1034	1134	1234	1334	...	1434	1534	1634	1734	...	1834	1934	2034	...	2134	2234	2232	...
48	Tournai **435** a.		0602	0652	0757	0857	0957	...	1057	1157	1257	1357	...	1457	1557	1657	1757	...	1857	1957	2057	...	2157	2315	....	...
48	Tournai 🛃 § d.		0615	0654	...	0902	1002	...	1102	1220	1259	...	...	1459	1559	1700	1803	...	1903	2004	2104	...	...	...	...	...
73	**Lille Flandres** a.		0646	0722	...	0920	1022	...	1120	1248	1328	...	...	1524	1621	1726	1829	...	1927	2027	2126	...	...	...	...	...

		†	⑥	Ⓒ	Ⓒ	⑥	†	Ⓒ	†	⑥	⑥	†	Ⓒ		†	⑥	†	⑥	Ⓒ	Ⓒ	Ⓒ	Ⓒ	Ⓒ		Ⓒ	Ⓒ
Liège G **435** d.	Ⓒ	...	...	...	0650	0750	0750	0850	0950	0950	1050	1050	1150	...	1250	1250	1350	1350	1450	1550	1650	1750	1850	...	1950	2050
Namur **435** d.		...	...	0640	0740	0840	0840	0940	1040	1040	1140	1140	1240	...	1340	1340	1440	1440	1540	1640	1740	1840	1940	...	2040	2140
Charleroi Sud **435** d.		0621	0621	0721	0821	0921	0921	1021	1121	1121	1221	1221	1321	...	1421	1421	1521	1521	1621	1721	1821	1921	2021	...	2121	2221
Mons 424 435 d.		0654	0654	0754	0854	0954	0954	1054	1154	1154	1254	1254	1354	...	1454	1454	1554	1554	1654	1754	1854	1954	2054	...	2154	2254
Saint-Ghislain **424** d.		0705	0705	0805	0905	1005	1005	1105	1205	1205	1305	1305	1405	...	1505	1505	1605	1605	1705	1805	1905	2005	2105	...	2205	2305
Tournai **435** a.		0731	0731	0831	0931	1031	1031	1131	1231	1231	1331	1331	1431	...	1531	1531	1631	1631	1731	1831	1931	2031	2131	...	2231	2331
Tournai 🛃 § d.		0732	0732	0839	0932	1032	1032	1133	1232	1232	1334	1336	1432	...	1532	1532	1632	1632	1732	1832	1934	2032	2134	...	...	...
Lille Flandres a.		0750	0757	0900	0950	1050	1056	1151	1250	1256	1355	1354	1450	...	1550	1555	1654	1656	1756	1850	1957	2053	2152	...	...	...

		Ⓐ	Ⓐ	Ⓐ		Ⓐ	Ⓐ	Ⓐ		Ⓐ	Ⓐ	Ⓐ	Ⓐ	Ⓐ		Ⓐ	Ⓐ	Ⓐ		Ⓐ	Ⓐ	Ⓐ		Ⓐ		
Lille Flandres d.	Ⓐ	...	0618	0732	...	...	0930	1031	...	...	1212	1341	1440	1534	...	1630	1737	1839	...	1937	2044	2139	...	...	...	...
Tournai 🛃 § a.		...	0643	0758	...	...	0956	1058	...	...	1241	1359	1458	1558	...	1658	1801	1857	...	1958	2101	2158	...	...	...	...
Tournai **435** d.		0600	0703	0803	...	0903	1003	1103	...	1203	1303	1403	1503	1603	...	1703	1803	1903	...	2003	2103	2203	...	2303	...	...
Mons 435 a.		0626	0726	0826	...	0926	1026	1126	...	1226	1326	1426	1526	1626	...	1726	1826	1926	...	2026	2126	2226	...	2326	...	...
Charleroi Sud **435** a.		0658	0758	0858	...	0958	1058	1158	...	1258	1358	1458	1558	1658	...	1758	1858	1958	...	2058	2158	2258	...	2358	...	...
Namur **435** a.		0731	0831	0931	...	1031	1131	1231	...	1331	1431	1531	1631	1731	...	1831	1931	2031	...	2131	2231	2338	...	...	...	...
Liège G **435** a.		0813	0913	1013	...	1113	1213	1313	...	1413	1513	1613	1713	1813	...	1913	2013	2113	...	2213	2313	0025	...	...	...	...

		Ⓒ	Ⓒ	†	⑥	Ⓒ	Ⓒ	Ⓒ	⑥	†	Ⓒ	⑥	†	Ⓒ	†	⑥	†	⑥	⑥	†	†	⑥	Ⓒ	†	⑥	Ⓒ
Lille Flandres d.	Ⓒ	...		0806	0807	0909	1007	1106	1205	1206	1309	1405	1408	1505	1606	1606	1703	1705	1805	1806	1901	1905	2012	2105	2109	2209
Tournai 🛃 § a.		...		0827	0829	0927	1028	1124	1228	1224	1327	1428	1426	1523	1624	1627	1725	1728	1828	1824	1924	1928	2028	2128	2127	2227
Tournai **435** d.		0629	0729	0829	0829	0929	1029	1129	1229	1229	1329	1429	1429	1529	1629	1629	1729	1729	1829	1829	1929	1929	2029	2129	2129	2235
Saint-Ghislain **424** d.		0656	0756	0856	0856	0956	1056	1156	1256	1256	1356	1456	1456	1556	1656	1656	1756	1756	1856	1856	1956	1956	2056	2156	2156	2302
Mons 424 435 a.		0706	0806	0906	0906	1006	1106	1206	1306	1306	1406	1506	1506	1606	1706	1706	1806	1806	1906	1906	2006	2006	2106	2206	2206	2312
Charleroi Sud **435** a.		0739	0839	0939	0939	1039	1139	1239	1339	1339	1439	1539	1539	1639	1739	1739	1839	1839	1939	1939	2039	2039	2139	2239	2239	...
Namur **435** a.		0820	0920	1020	1020	1120	1220	1320	1420	1420	1520	1620	1620	1720	1820	1820	1920	1920	2020	2020	2120	2120	2220	2320	2320	...
Liège **435** a.		0910	1010	1110	1110	1210	1310	1410	1510	1510	1610	1710	1710	1810	1910	1910	2010	2010	2110	2110	2210	2210	2310	...	...	...

§ – Ticket point is Blandain.

CHARLEROI - JEUMONT 427

km		Ⓐ	Ⓐ	Ⓐ	Ⓐ	Ⓐ	Ⓐ	Ⓐ	Ⓐ	
0	**Charleroi Sud 411 435** d.	0518	0710	0912	1012	1220	1613	1714	1812	...
31	**Jeumont** 🛃 a.	0559	0755	0953	1053	1301	1654	1756	1853	...

	Ⓐ	Ⓐ	Ⓐ	Ⓐ	Ⓐ	Ⓐ	Ⓐ	Ⓐ	
Jeumont 🛃 d.	0629	0809	1006	1106	1307	1706	1806	1906	...
Charleroi Sud 411 435 a.	0716	0855	1048	1148	1348	1747	1848	1948	...

Local services also operate within Belgium: Charleroi - Thuin (*15 km*) - Erquelinnes (*29 km*) and v.v.; approximately hourly on Ⓐ, every 2 hours on Ⓒ.

BRUSSELS - LA LOUVIÈRE - BINCHE 429

km			Ⓐ	Ⓒ	▲	Ⓐ	Ⓒ		Ⓐ	
0	**Brussels Nord** d.	...	0532	0606		2132	2206	...	2232	...
2	Brussels Central d.	...	0536	0610		2136	2210	...	2236	...
4	**Brussels Midi/Zuid** d.	...	0541	0615	and at	2141	2215	...	2241	...
17	Halle d.	...	0552	|	the same	2152	|	...	2252	...
33	Braine-le-Comte a.	...	0604	0637	minutes	2204	2237	...	2304	...
33	Braine-le-Comte d.	...	0605	0639	past each	2205	2239	...	2305	...
52	**La Louvière Centre** d.	...	0623	0656	hour	2223	2256	...	2335	...
55	La Louvière Sud a.	...	0626	0702	until	2226	2302	...	2338	...
64	**Binche** a.	...	0640	0713		2240	2313	...	2350	...

	Ⓐ		Ⓒ	Ⓐ	▲	Ⓒ	Ⓐ	
Binche d.	0520	...	0547	0620		2147	2220	...
La Louvière Sud d.	0534	...	0558	0634		2158	2234	...
La Louvière Centre d.	0538	...	0604	0638	and at	2204	2238	...
Braine-le-Comte a.	0555	...	0621	0655	the same	2221	2255	...
Braine-le-Comte d.	0556	...	0623	0656	minutes	2223	2256	...
Halle d.	0609	...	|	0709	past each	|	2309	...
Brussels Midi/Zuid a.	0619	...	0645	0719	hour	2245	2319	...
Brussels Central a.	0624	...	0650	0724	until	2250	2324	...
Brussels Nord a.	0628	...	0654	0728		2254	2328	...

▲ – Timings may vary by up to 4 minutes on some journeys.

430 BRUSSELS - NAMUR - DINANT and LUXEMBOURG

km		Ⓐ			Ⓐ	Ⓐ	L			L	EC 91 ♦		L	Ⓐ		L		L		L		L		L	EC 97 ♦	
0	**Brussels Midi / Zuid** d.	...	...	...	0533	0600	0603	...	0633	0703	0733	...	0803	...	0833	0903	0933	1003	1033	1103	1133	1203	1233	1303	1309	...
2	Brussels Central d.	...	...	...	0537	0604	0607	...	0637	0707	0737	...	0807	...	0837	0907	0937	1007	1037	1107	1137	1207	1237	1307	1313	...
4	**Brussels Nord** d.	...	...	...	0542	0609	0612	...	0642	0712	0742	...	0812	...	0842	0912	0942	1012	1042	1112	1142	1212	1242	1312	1318	...
10	Brussels Luxembourg d.	...	...	...	0555	0622	0625	...	0655	0725	0755	...	0825	...	0855	0925	0955	1025	1055	1125	1155	1225	1255	1325	1330	...
33	Ottignies d.	...	...	...	0615	|	0645	...	0715	0745	0815	...	0845	...	0915	0945	1015	1045	1115	1145	1215	1245	1315	1345	|	...
48	Gembloux d.	...	...	...	0627	|	0657	...	0727	0757	0827	...	0857	...	0927	0957	1027	1057	1127	1157	1227	1257	1327	1357	|	...
65	**Namur 435** a.	...	...	...	0639	0701	0709	...	0739	0809	0839	...	0909	...	0939	1009	1039	1109	1139	1209	1239	1309	1339	1409	1412	...
65	**Namur** d.	0541	0611	...	0641	0703	0711v	...	0741	0811v	0841	...	0911v	0918	0941	1011v	1041	1111v	1141	1211v	1241	1311v	1341	1411v	1414	...
	Dinant 432 a.	|	0639	...	|	|	0739v	...	|	0839v	|	...	0939v	0946	|	1039v	|	1139v	|	1239v	|	1339v	|	1439v	|	...
94	Ciney d.	0601	...	...	0701	|	...	...	0801	...	0901	...	...	...	1001	...	1101	...	1201	...	1301	...	1401	...	|	...
117	Marloie d.	0616	...	...	0716	|	...	...	0816	...	0916	...	...	...	1016	...	1116	...	1216	...	1316	...	1416	...	|	...
123	Jemelle d.	0623	...	...	0723	|	...	...	0823	...	0923	...	...	...	1023	...	1123	...	1223	...	1323	...	1423	...	|	...
155	Libramont 432 d.	0649	...	...	0748	0806	...	...	0848	...	0948	...	...	...	1048	...	1148	...	1248	...	1348	...	1448	...	1515	...
201	Arlon d.	0722	...	...	0822	0834	...	...	0922	...	1018	...	...	...	1122	...	1222	...	1322	...	1422	...	1522	...	1542	...
229	**Luxembourg** a.	0740	...	...	0840	0852	...	...	0940	...	1036	...	...	...	1140	...	1240	...	1340	...	1445	...	1540	...	1600	...

km			Ⓐ	L			L	Ⓒ	Ⓐ	L	Ⓒ	Ⓐ	L	EC 295 A	EC 295 B	Ⓒ	Ⓐ	Ⓐ	L			L		L	Ⓐ	Ⓒ
	Brussels Midi / Zuid d.	1333	1400	1403	...	1433	1503	1533	1533	1603	1633	1633	1703	1715	1727	1733	1733	1800	1803	...	1833	1903	1933	2003	2033	2033
	Brussels Central d.	1337	1404	1407	...	1437	1507	1537	1537	1607	1637	1637	1707	1719	1731	1737	1737	1804	1807	...	1837	1907	1937	2007	2037	2037
	Brussels Nord d.	1342	1409	1412	...	1442	1512	1542	1542	1612	1642	1642	1712	1724	1736	1742	1742	1809	1812	...	1842	1912	1942	2012	2042	2042
	Brussels Luxembourg d.	1355	1421	1425	...	1455	1525	1555	1554	1625	1655	1654	1725	1751	1751	1755	1754	1822	1825	...	1855	1925	1955	2025	2055	2054
	Ottignies d.	1415	|	1445	...	1515	1545	1615	1615	1645	1715	1715	1745	|	|	1815	1815	|	1845	...	1915	1945	2015	2045	2115	2115
	Gembloux d.	1427	|	1457	...	1527	1557	1627	1628	1657	1727	1728	1757	|	|	1827	1828	|	1857	...	1927	1957	2027	2057	2127	2128
	Namur 435 a.	1439	1459	1509	...	1539	1609	1639	1640	1710	1739	1740	1810	1832	1832	1839	1840	1901	1909	...	1939	2009	2039	2109	2139	2140
0	**Namur** d.	1441	1501	1511v	...	1541	1611v	1641	1642	1711v	1741	1742	1811v	1834	1834	1841	1842	1903	1911v	...	1941	2011v	2041	2111v	2141	2142
27	**Dinant 432** a.	|	|	1539v	...	|	1639v	|	|	1739v	|	|	1839v	|	|	|	|	|	1939v	...	|	2039v	|	2139v	|	|
	Ciney d.	1501	|	...	...	1601	...	1701	1702	...	1801	1802	...	|	|	1901	1902	|	...	...	2001	...	2101	...	2201	2202
	Marloie d.	1516	|	...	...	1616	...	1716	1717	...	1816	1817	...	|	|	1916	1917	|	...	...	2016	...	2116	...	2216	2217
	Jemelle d.	1523	|	...	...	1623	...	1723	1725	...	1823	1825	...	|	|	1923	1925	1940	...	...	2023	...	2123	...	2223	2225
	Libramont 432 d.	1548	1606	...	...	1648	...	1748	1751	...	1848	1851	...	|	|	1948	1951	2006	...	...	2048	...	2148	...	2248	2251
	Arlon d.	1622	1634	...	...	1722	...	1822	1822	...	1922	1922	...	1959	1959	2022	2022	2034	...	...	2122	...	2222	...	2322	2322
	Luxembourg a.	1640	1652	...	...	1740	...	1840	1840	...	1940	1940	...	2017	2017	2040	2040	2052	...	...	2140	...	2240	...	2340	2340

	L	Ⓐ	Ⓒ	Ⓐ L	Ⓒ	Ⓐ	Ⓒ		Ⓒ
Brussels Midi / Zuid d.	2103	2133	2133	2203	2203	2233	2233	...	2333
Brussels Central d.	2107	2137	2137	2207	2207	2237	2237	...	2337
Brussels Nord d.	2112	2142	2142	2212	2212	2242	2242	...	2342
Brussels Luxembourg d.	2125	2155	2154	2225	2225	2255	2255	...	2355
Ottignies d.	2145	2215	2215	2245	2245	2315	2315	...	0022
Gembloux d.	2157	2227	2228	2257	2257	2327	2327	...	0034
Namur 435 a.	2209	2239	2240	2309	2309	2339	2339	...	0046
Namur d.	2211v	2241	2242	2318	...	2341	...	...	...
Dinant 432 a.	2239v	|	|	2346	...	|	...	...	...
Ciney d.	...	2301	2302	...	...	0001	...	...	...
Marloie d.	...	2316	2317	...	...	0016	...	...	...
Jemelle d.	...	2323	2325	...	...	0022	...	...	...
Libramont 432 d.	...	2348	2351	...	...	...	...	...	...
Arlon d.	...	0022	0022	...	...	...	...	...	...
Luxembourg a.	...	0040	0040	...	...	...	...	...	...

	Ⓐ	Ⓒ	Ⓐ		Ⓐ L	Ⓒ	Ⓐ	Ⓒ	L	Ⓐ	Ⓒ	L
Luxembourg d.	...	...	...	...	...	...	...	...	...	0520	...	...
Arlon d.	...	...	...	...	...	...	0440	...	...	0540	0543	...
Libramont 432 d.	...	...	...	...	...	...	0511	...	...	0611	0613	...
Jemelle d.	...	...	0436	...	...	...	0535	...	...	0635	0636	...
Marloie d.	...	...	0445	...	...	...	0544	...	...	0644	0645	...
Ciney d.	...	...	0501	...	...	...	0600	...	...	0700	0701	...
Dinant 432 d.	...	...	|	...	0514	...	|	...	0612x	|	|	0712x
Namur 435 a.	...	...	0519	...	0542	...	0618	...	0641x	0718	0719	0741x
Namur d.	0411	0436	0521	...	0551	0551	0620	0621	0651	0720	0721	0751
Gembloux d.	0432	0449	0535	...	0605	0605	0634	0635	0705	0734	0735	0805
Ottignies d.	0452	0500	0547	...	0617	0617	0647	0648	0718	0747	0747	0818
Brussels Luxembourg a.	0525	0526	0605	...	0635	0635	0705	0705	0735	0805	0805	0835
Brussels Nord a.	0537	0537	0618	...	0648	0648	0718	0718	0748	0818	0818	0848
Brussels Central a.	0541	0542	0623	...	0653	0653	0723	0723	0753	0823	0823	0853
Brussels Midi / Zuid a.	0545	0546	0627	...	0657	0657	0727	0727	0757	0827	0827	0857

	Ⓐ	Ⓒ		Ⓐ	L		L			Ⓐ	L		L	EC 296 ♦	⑥	L		L		L			L			L
Luxembourg d.	0620	0620	...	0658	...	0720	...	0820	...	0900	...	0920	...	1024	1024	...	1120	...	1220	...	1324	...	...	...	1420	...
Arlon d.	0640	0643	...	0718	...	0743	...	0843	...	0920	...	0943	...	1044	1044	...	1146	...	1243	...	1344	...	...	...	1443	...
Libramont 432 d.	0711	0712	...	0746	...	0812	...	0912	...	0946	...	1012	...	1112	1112	...	1212	...	1312	...	1412	...	...	...	1513	...
Jemelle d.	0735	0736	...	0810	...	0836	...	0936	...	|	...	1036	...	1136	1136	...	1236	...	1336	...	1436	...	...	...	1536	...
Marloie d.	0744	0745	...	|	...	0845	...	0945	...	|	...	1045	...	1145	1145	...	1245	...	1345	...	1445	...	...	...	1545	...
Ciney d.	0800	0801	...	|	...	0901	...	1001	...	|	...	1101	...	1201	1201	...	1301	...	1401	...	1501	...	...	...	1601	...
Dinant 432 d.	|	|	...	|	0814x	|	0914x	|	...	|	1014x	|	1114x	|	|	1214x	|	1314x	|	1414x	|	...	1513x	...	|	1614x
Namur 435 a.	0818	0819	...	0846	0842x	0919	0942x	1019	...	1046	1042x	1119	1142x	1219	1219	1242x	1319	1342x	1419	1442x	1519	...	1542x	...	1619	1642x
Namur d.	0820	0821	...	0848	0851	0921	0951	1021	...	1048	1051	1121	1151	1221	1221	1251	1321	1351	1421	1451	1521	...	1551	...	1621	1651
Gembloux d.	0834	0835	...	|	0905	0935	1005	1035	...	|	1105	1135	1205	1235	1235	1305	1335	1405	1435	1505	1535	...	1605	...	1635	1705
Ottignies d.	0847	0847	...	|	0917	0947	1017	1047	...	|	1117	1147	1217	1247	1247	1317	1347	1417	1447	1517	1547	...	1617	...	1647	1717
Brussels Luxembourg a.	0905	0905	...	0929	0935	1005	1035	1105	...	1129	1135	1205	1235	1305	1305	1335	1405	1435	1505	1535	1605	...	1635	...	1705	1735
Brussels Nord a.	0918	0918	...	0941	0948	1018	1048	1118	...	1141	1148	1218	1248	1318	1318	1348	1418	1448	1518	1548	1618	...	1648	...	1718	1748
Brussels Central a.	0923	0923	...	0946	0953	1023	1053	1123	...	1146	1153	1223	1253	1323	1323	1353	1423	1453	1523	1553	1623	...	1653	...	1723	1753
Brussels Midi / Zuid a.	0927	0927	...	0950	0957	1027	1057	1127	...	1150	1157	1227	1257	1327	1327	1357	1427	1457	1527	1557	1627	...	1657	...	1727	1757

		L	Ⓒ	Ⓐ		EC 90 ♦	L	Ⓒ	Ⓐ		L	Ⓐ		L		EC 96 ♦	L		Ⓐ	Ⓒ	Ⓐ	Ⓒ				
Luxembourg d.	1520	...	1620	1620	...	1700	...	1720	1720	...	...	1806	1820	...	1920	2000	...	2020	...	...	2120	2124	2158	2258	2347	...
Arlon d.	1543	...	1640	1643	...	1720	...	1740	1743	...	...	1826	1843	...	1943	2023	...	2043	...	...	2143	2143	2216	2316	0013	...
Libramont 432 d.	1612	...	1711	1712	...	1749	...	1811	1812	...	...	1852	1913	...	2012	|	...	2112	...	...	2212	2212	...	...	...	...
Jemelle d.	1636	...	1735	1736	...	|	...	1835	1836	...	...	|	1937	...	2036	|	...	2136	...	...	2236	2235	...	...	...	...
Marloie d.	1645	...	1744	1745	...	|	...	1844	1845	...	...	|	1945	...	2045	|	...	2145	...	...	2245	...	...	...	...	...
Ciney d.	1701	|	1800	1801	...	|	...	1900	1901	...	...	|	2001	...	2101	|	...	2201	...	...	2301	...	...	...	...	...
Dinant 432 d.	|	1714x	|	|	...	|	1814x	|	|	...	1914x	|	|	2014x	|	|	2114x	|	2214	2221	|	...	...	...	...	...
Namur 435 a.	1719	1742x	1818	1819	...	1846	1842x	1918	1919	...	1942x	1952	2019	2042x	2119	2146	2142x	2219	2242	2249	2319	...	...	...	...	...
Namur d.	1721	1751	1820	1821	...	1848	1851	1920	1921	...	1951	1954	2021	2051	2121	2148	2151	2221	...	...	...	...	...	...	...	...
Gembloux d.	1735	1805	1834	1835	...	|	1905	1934	1935	...	2005	|	2035	2105	2135	|	2205	2235	...	...	...	...	...	...	...	...
Ottignies d.	1747	1817	1847	1847	...	|	1917	1947	1947	...	2017	|	2047	2117	2147	|	2217	2247	...	...	...	...	...	...	...	...
Brussels Luxembourg a.	1805	1835	1905	1905	...	1927	1935	2005	2005	...	2035	2038	2105	2135	2205	2229	2235	2305	...	...	...	...	...	...	...	...
Brussels Nord a.	1818	1848	1918	1918	...	1941	1948	2018	2018	...	2048	2051	2118	2148	2218	2241	2248	2318	...	...	...	...	...	...	...	...
Brussels Central a.	1823	1853	1923	1923	...	1946	1953	2023	2023	...	2053	2056	2123	2153	2223	2246	2253	2323	...	...	...	...	...	...	...	...
Brussels Midi / Zuid a.	1827	1857	1927	1927	...	1950	1957	2027	2027	...	2057	2100	2127	2157	2227	2250	2257	2327	...	...	...	...	...	...	...	...

♦ – NOTES (LISTED BY TRAIN NUMBERS)

90 – VAUBAN – 🚃12: Zürich - Basel - Luxembourg - Brussels.
91 – VAUBAN – 🚃12: Brussels - Luxembourg - Basel - Zürich - Chur.
96/7 – IRIS – 🚃12: Zürich - Basel - Luxembourg - Brussels and v.v. Conveys on ①–⑥: 🍷 Zürich - Basel and v.v.
296 – JEAN MONNET – ⑧: 🚃12 Basel - Strasbourg - Luxembourg - Brussels.

A – JEAN MONNET – ①–⑤: 🚃12 Brussels - Luxembourg - Strasbourg - Basel.
B – JEAN MONNET – ⑦: 🚃12 Brussels - Luxembourg - Strasbourg - Basel.
L – Also conveys on Ⓐ: 🚃12 Brussels - Namur - Liège and v.v. – see Table **435**.

c – Ⓒ only.
v – 7 minutes later on Ⓐ.
x – 7-9 minutes later on Ⓒ.

431 VERVIERS - SPA

16 km Journey time: 23 minutes

From **Verviers Central**:
Ⓐ: 0546, 0647, 0746, 0846 and hourly until 2146.
Ⓒ: 0646, 0746 and hourly until 2146.

From **Spa**:
Ⓐ: 0550, 0652, 0750, 0850 and hourly until 2150.
Ⓒ: 0650, 0750 and hourly until 2150.

All trains continue beyond Spa to Spa-Géronstère (*1 km* from Spa).

ARDENNES LOCAL SERVICES — 432

Additional services operate on Ⓐ at peak times

km																										
			Ⓐ	Ⓐ											Ⓐ		Ⓐ	Ⓒ	Ⓐ	Ⓐ	Ⓐ		Ⓐ			Ⓐ
0	**Libramont 430**	d.	...	...	...	0654	0751	0854	0951	1054	1151	1254	1351	1454	1551	...	1654	1651	1751	1754	1820	1854	1951	...	2054	2151	2323
12	Bertrix	d.	0502	0531	0602	0705	0801	0905	1001	1105	1201	1305	1401	1505	1601	1605	1705	1701	1801	1803	1828	1905	2004	2002	2102	2201	2331
	Dinant 430	a.	0608	0635	0708	0809	|	1009	|	1209	|	1409	|	1609	|	1709	1809	|	|	|	...	2009	|	2106	...	|	...
57	Virton	d.	...	...	...	...	0833	...	1033	...	1233	...	1433	...	1633	...	...	1732	1831	1835	...	...	2036	...	...	2231	...
82	Rodange **445**	d.	...	...	...	...	0905a	...	1103a	...	1259a	...	1503a	...	1703a	...	...	1805	...	1901	...	...	2103a	...	...	...	...
85	Athus **445**	d.	...	...	...	...	0912a	...	1108a	...	1308a	...	1508a	...	1708a	...	...	1813	...	1906	...	...	2108a	...	...	...	...
100	**Arlon 430**	a.	...	...	...	...	0926a	...	1122a	...	1322a	...	1522a	...	1722a	...	...	1828	...	1920	...	...	2122a	...	...	...	...

km																										
				Ⓐ	Ⓒ	Ⓐ	Ⓐ									Ⓐ		Ⓐ		Ⓐ					Ⓐ	Ⓐ
	Arlon 430	d.	...	...	...	0627	...	0737a	...	0938a	...	1138a	...	1338a	...	1538a	1619	...	...	1738a	...	...	...	1938a	...	2038	...
	Athus **445**	d.	...	...	...	0642	...	0752a	...	0953a	...	1153a	...	1353a	...	1553a	1634	...	...	1753a	...	...	...	1953a	...	2053	...
	Rodange **445**	d.	...	...	...	0650	...	0801a	...	1007a	...	1207a	...	1407a	...	1607a	1645	...	...	1802a	...	...	...	2007a	...	2107	...
	Virton	d.	0625	...	...	0724	...	0829	...	1029	...	1229	...	1429	...	1629	1706	...	...	1824	...	...	...	2029	...	2129	...
0	**Dinant 430**	d.	|	0644	0651	|	0751	|	0851	|	1051	|	1251	|	1451	|	...	1651	1723	|	1825	1851	...	|	2051	|	2151
72	Bertrix	d.	0656	0752	0759	0756	0856	0900	0959	1100	1159	1300	1359	1500	1559	1700	...	1759	1830	1856	1936	1959	...	2100	2156	2200	2256
	Libramont 430	a.	0705	0801	0808	0805	...	0909	1008	1109	1208	1309	1408	1509	1608	1709	...	1808	...	1905	1945	2008	...	2109	...	2209	...

a – Ⓐ only.

LIÈGE - NAMUR - CHARLEROI - TOURNAI — 435

For *Thalys* trains Liège - Paris and v.v. – see Table 17

km																								
				Ⓐ	LⒶ	Ⓐ	LⒶ	BⒶ	Ⓐ	LⒶ	BⒶ	Ⓐ	LⒶ	▲	BⒶ	Ⓐ	LⒶ	BⒶ	Ⓐ	Ⓐ	BⒶ	Ⓐ	Ⓐ	Ⓐ	Ⓐ
0	**Liège Guillemins**	d.	Ⓐ	...	...	...	...	0501	...	0547	0559	...	0647		1901	...	1947	2001	...	2047	2101	...	2147	2201	2247
29	Huy	d.		...	...	...	...	0523	...	0608	0621	...	0708		1923	...	2008	2023	...	2108	2123	...	2208	2223	2307
40	Andenne	d.		...	...	...	...	0533	...	|	0632	...	|	and at	1933	...	|	2033	...	|	2133	...	|	2233	2317
59	**Namur 430**	d.		...	...	0449	...	0546	0549	0629	0645	0649p	0729	the same	1946	1949p	2029	2046	2049	2129	2146	2149	2229	2246	2332
76	Jemeppe-sur-Sambre	d.		...	...	0504	...	...	0604	|	...	0704	|	minutes	...	2004	|	...	2104	|	...	2204	|	...	2347
81	Tamines	d.		...	...	0512	...	...	0612	0648	...	0712	0748	past each	...	2012	2048	...	2112	2148	...	2212	2248	...	2355
96	**Charleroi Sud 422**	d.		0419	...	0528	0558	...	0628	0702	...	0728	0802	hour until	...	2028	2102	...	2128	2202	...	2228	2302	...	0010
117	La Louvière Sud	d.		0438	...	0547	0615	...	0647	0719	...	0747	0819		...	2047	2119	...	2147	2219	...	2247	2319	...	...
137	**Mons 426**	a.		0500	0539	0600	0628	...	0700	0732	...	0800	0832		...	2100	2132	...	2200	2232	...	2300	2332	...	...
185	**Tournai 425 426**	a.		0545	0602	0645	0652	...	0745	0757	...	0845	0857		...	2145	2157	...	2245	2315	...	...	...	...	...

			LⒸ	LⒸ	LⒸ		LⒸ	Ⓒ	Ⓒ	Ⓒ
Liège Guillemins	d.	Ⓒ	...	...	0650		1950	2050	2150	2250
Huy	d.		...	...	0713		2013	2113	2213	2313
Andenne	d.		...	...	0723	and at	2023	2123	2223	2323
Namur 430	d.		...	0640	0740	the same	2040	2140	2240	2336
Jemeppe-sur-Sambre	d.		...	0655	0755	minutes	2055	2155	2255	...
Tamines	d.		...	0704	0804	past each	2104	2204	2304	...
Charleroi Sud 422	d.		0621	0721	0821	hour until	2121	2221	2319	...
La Louvière Sud	d.		0639	0739	0839		2139	2239	...	...
Mons 426	a.		0652	0752	0852		2152	2252	...	...
Tournai 425 426	a.		0731	0831	0931		2231	2331	...	...

			Ⓐ	Ⓐ	Ⓐ	BⒶ	Ⓐ	Ⓐ	BⒶ	Ⓐ	LⒶ
Tournai 425 426	d.	Ⓐ	...	...	...	...	0508	0600	...	0607	0703
Mons 426	d.		0500	...	...	...	0600	0628	...	0700	0728
La Louvière Sud	d.		0515	...	...	...	0615	0643	...	0715	0743
Charleroi Sud 422	d.		0534	...	0600	...	0640	0700	...	0734	0800
Tamines	d.		0549	...	0613	...	0655	0713	...	0749	0813
Jemeppe-sur-Sambre	d.		0557	...	|	...	0703	|	...	0757	|
Namur 430	d.		0611	0614	0633	0714	0717	0733	0814	0811	0833
Andenne	d.		...	0628	|	0728	...	|	0828	...	|
Huy	d.		...	0639	0654	0739	...	0754	0839	...	0854
Liège Guillemins	a.		...	0659	0713	0759	...	0813	0859	...	0913

		BⒶ	Ⓐ	LⒶ	▲	BⒶ	Ⓐ	LⒶ	BⒶ	Ⓐ	LⒶ	Ⓐ	Ⓐ	
Tournai 425 426	d.	...	0715	0803		...	2015	2103	...	2115	2203	2215	2303	...
Mons 426	d.	...	0800	0828		...	2059	2128	...	2200	2228	2259	2328	...
La Louvière Sud	d.	...	0815	0843	and at	...	2113	2143	...	2215	2243	...	2343	...
Charleroi Sud 422	d.	...	0834	0900	the same	...	2138	2200	...	2234	2300	...	2358	...
Tamines	d.	...	0849	0913	minutes	...	2153	2213	...	2249	2316	...	...	...
Jemeppe-sur-Sambre	d.	...	0857	|	past each	...	2201	|	...	2257	2324	...	...	...
Namur 430	d.	0913	0918q	0933	hour until	2214	2215q	2233	2314	2311	2340	...	...	...
Andenne	d.	0927	...	|		2228	...	|	2328	...	2354	...	...	...
Huy	d.	0939	...	0954		2239	...	2254	2339	...	0005	...	...	...
Liège Guillemins	a.	0959	...	1013		2259	...	2313	2359	...	0025	...	...	...

			Ⓒ	Ⓒ	Ⓒ	LⒸ	LⒸ		LⒸ	LⒸ	LⒸ
Tournai 425 426	d.	Ⓒ	...	...	0629	0729	0829		2029	2129	2235
Mons 426	d.		...	0608	0708	0808	0908		2108	2208	2312
La Louvière Sud	d.		...	0622	0722	0822	0922	and at	2122	2222	...
Charleroi Sud 422	d.		...	0641	0741	0841	0941	the same	2141	2241	...
Tamines	d.		...	0657	0757	0857	0957	minutes	2157	2257	...
Jemeppe-sur-Sambre	d.		...	0706	0806	0906	1006	past each	2206	2306	...
Namur 430	d.		0624	0724	0824	0924	1024	hour until	2224	2320	...
Andenne	d.		0638	0738	0838	0938	1038		2238	...	...
Huy	d.		0648	0748	0848	0948	1048		2248	...	...
Liège Guillemins	a.		0710	0810	0910	1010	1110		2310	...	...

B – From / to Brussels – see Table **430**.
L – Most journeys run from / to Lille – see Table **426**.
p – Variations: Namur depart 0842, 0942, 1042, 1142, 1242, 1342, 1442.
q – Variations: Namur arrive 1611, 1711, 1811, 1911, 2011, 2111.
▲ – Timings may vary by up to 4 minutes on some journeys.

LIÈGE - LUXEMBOURG — 439

km													
										Ⓐ			
0	**Liège Guillemins**	d.	0718	0918	1118	1318	1518	1618	1718	1750	1918	2118	2318
23	Rivage	d.	0740	0940	1140	1340	1540	1641	1740	1819	1940	2140	2343
31	Aywaille	d.	0749	0949	1149	1349	1549	1650	1749	1828	1949	2149	2353
58	Trois-Ponts	d.	0812	1012	1212	1412	1612	1719	1812	1851	2012	2212	0016
70	Vielsalm	d.	0824	1024	1224	1424	1624	1730	1824	1902	2024	2224	0028
81	**Gouvy**	d.	0835	1035	1235	1435	1635	1740	1835	1912	2035	2235	0037
91	Troisvierges **445**	d.	0845	1045	1245	1445	1645	...	1845	...	2045	2245	...
99	Clervaux **445**	d.	0853	1053	1253	1453	1653	...	1853	...	2053	2253	...
114	Kautenbach **445**	d.	0908	1108	1308	1508	1708	...	1908	...	2108	2310	...
129	Ettelbruck **445**	d.	0921	1121	1321	1521	1721	...	1921	...	2121	2322	...
141	Mersch **445**	d.	0931	1132	1332	1532	1732	...	1932	...	2132	2332	...
160	**Luxembourg 445**	a.	0945	1145	1345	1545	1745	...	1945	...	2145	2345	...

		Ⓐ	Ⓒ	Ⓐ							
Luxembourg 445	d.	...	...	...	0715	0915	1115	1315	1515	1715	1915	2115
Mersch **445**	d.	...	...	...	0729	0929	1129	1329	1529	1729	1929	2129
Ettelbruck **445**	d.	...	...	...	0741	0941	1141	1341	1541	1741	1941	2141
Kautenbach **445**	d.	...	...	...	0753	0953	1153	1353	1553	1753	1953	2153
Clervaux **445**	d.	...	...	...	0808	1008	1208	1408	1608	1808	2008	2208
Troisvierges **445**	d.	...	...	...	0817	1017	1217	1417	1617	1817	2017	2217
Gouvy	d.	0621	0626	0702	0826	1026	1226	1426	1626	1826	2026	2226
Vielsalm	d.	0632	0637	0713	0837	1037	1237	1437	1637	1837	2037	2237
Trois-Ponts	d.	0645	0649	0725	0849	1049	1249	1449	1649	1849	2049	2249
Aywaille	d.	0708	0712	0749	0912	1112	1312	1512	1712	1912	2112	2312
Rivage	d.	0716	0720	0757	0920	1120	1320	1520	1720	1920	2120	2320
Liège Guillemins	a.	0735	0742	0820	0942	1142	1342	1542	1742	1942	2142	2342

Additional journeys on Ⓐ: **Gouvy - Liège and v.v.**: 0507 from Gouvy, 1750 from Liège;
Gouvy - Luxembourg and v.v.: 0542, 0642 from Gouvy, 1615, 1815 from Luxembourg.

LUXEMBOURG – summary of services — 445

In principle, services shown below operate at the same minutes past each hour between 0800 and 2000, but variations are possible.
Only principal stations are listed, and additional services are available at peak times.

Luxembourg (xx15) → Mersch (xx29) → Ettelbruck (xx41) → Kautenbach (xx53) → Clervaux (xx08) → Troisvierges (xx16).

Luxembourg (xx20, also xx50⚒) → Bettembourg (xx31, also xx01⚒) → Noertzange (xx36, also xx06⚒) → Esch-sur-Alzette (xx44, also xx14⚒) → Pétange (xx06, also xx36⚒) → Rodange (xx13, also xx42⚒) → Athus (xx17).

Luxembourg (xx50, also xx20⚒) → Mersch (xx11, also xx41⚒) → Ettelbruck (xx28, also xx55⚒) → Kautenbach (xx42) → Wiltz (xx57).

Luxembourg (xx26) → Pétange (xx51) → Rodange (xx56).

Luxembourg (xx52) → Wasserbillig (xx32).

Luxembourg (xx47) → Kleinbettingen (xx06).

Luxembourg (xx45⚒) → Ettelbruck (xx10⚒, also xx35⚒, xx43†) → Diekirch (xx15⚒, also xx40⚒, xx48†).

Bettembourg (xx34, also xx04⚒) → Dudelange-Centre (xx42, also xx12⚒) → Volmerange-les-Mines (xx48⚒, xx18⚒).

Troisvierges (xx44) → Clervaux (xx53) → Kautenbach (xx08) → Ettelbruck (xx21) → Mersch (xx32) → **Luxembourg** (xx45).

Athus (xx43) → Rodange (xx48, also xx18⚒) → Pétange (xx54, also xx24⚒) → Esch-sur-Alzette (xx18, also xx48⚒) → Noertzange (xx25, also xx55⚒) → Bettembourg (xx30, also xx00⚒) → **Luxembourg** (xx40, also xx10⚒).

Wiltz (xx05) → Kautenbach (xx18) → Ettelbruck (xx35, also xx05⚒) → Mersch (xx49, also xx19⚒) → **Luxembourg** (xx10, also xx40⚒).

Rodange (xx04) → Pétange (xx10) → **Luxembourg** (xx34).

Wasserbillig (xx27) → **Luxembourg** (xx08).

Kleinbettingen (xx15) → **Luxembourg** (xx33).

Diekirch (xx45⚒, also xx12†, xx20⚒) → Ettelbruck (xx51⚒, also xx17†, xx25⚒) → **Luxembourg** (xx15⚒).

Volmerange-les-Mines (xx12⚒, xx42⚒) → Dudelange-Centre (xx18, also xx48⚒) → Bettembourg (xx26, also xx56⚒).

NETHERLANDS

SEE MAP PAGE 236

Operator: **NS** – Nederlandse Spoorwegen (www.ns.nl) – unless otherwise indicated.

Services: Trains convey first- and second-class seated accommodation, unless otherwise indicated in the tables. Some trains consist of portions for two or more destinations, and passengers should be careful to join the correct part of the train. The destination of each train portion is normally indicated beside the entrance doors. Train numbers of internal services are not announced or displayed on stations and are therefore not indicated in these tables. Sleeping cars (🛏) and couchettes (▬) are conveyed on international night trains only.

Validity: **December 13, 2009 - December 11, 2010.**

Holidays: Unless otherwise indicated, services marked ⚒ do not run on ⑦ or on Dec. 25, 26, Jan. 1;
those marked Ⓐ do not run on ⑥⑦ or on Dec. 25, Jan. 1, Apr. 5, 30, May 5, 13, 24;
those marked † run on ⑦ and on Dec. 25, 26, Jan. 1;
those marked Ⓒ run on ⑥⑦ and on Dec. 25, Jan. 1, Apr. 5, 30, May 5, 13, 24.
No trains, other than international services, will run between ± 2000 hours on Dec. 31 and ± 0100 on Jan. 1.

Tickets: There are ticket offices at all main stations. In addition, tickets to all destinations within the Netherlands are available from the ticket machines situated on every station. Tickets not bearing a pre-printed date must be date-stamped in the validating machines at platform entrances. Access to station platforms is strictly limited to persons in possession of a valid travel ticket, and high penalty fares are therefore charged for tickets bought from the conductor on board trains.

Reservations: Seat reservations are available only on international trains to, from, or via France and Germany.

450 AMSTERDAM - DEN HAAG - ROTTERDAM - VLISSINGEN

For INTERNATIONAL TRAINS **Amsterdam – Brussels – Paris**, see Table **18** For NIGHT NETWORK **Utrecht – Amsterdam – Rotterdam**, see Table **454**

km	km*			⑥⑦h	①g	G	H	G	⊡	Ⓐ	⚒	K B	Ⓐ	Ⓐ	⚒	Ⓐ	Ⓐ	K B	⚒v	Ⓐ	L⚡	⚒		Ⓐ	
0	0	**Amsterdam** Centraal ... **458** d.	0011	0010	0010	0010	0041	0040	0127	...	...	...	...	...	0529	0539	0541	0554	...	0559	0626	0610	...	0611	0629
5		Amsterdam Sloterdijk ... **458** d.	0017	0016	0016	0016	0047	0046	0133	...	...	...	...	...	|	0545	0547	|	...	|	|	0616	...	0617	|
17	17	**Schiphol** ✈ .... **457 458** d.	0028	|	|	|	|	|	|	...	...	...	...	...	0543	|	0558	0609	...	0613	0640	|	...	0628	0643
		Haarlem .... d.	|	0028	0028	0029	0059	0106	0144	...	...	...	...	...	|	0557	|	|	...	|	|	0628	...	|	|
44		Leiden Centraal .... **457** d.	0050	0052	0053	0103	0125	0136	...	...	...	...	...	...	0604	0618	0620	|	...	0634	|	0648	...	0650	0704
59		Den Haag Centraal .... a.	0102	|	|	|	0143	0156	...	...	...	...	...	...	|	|	0632	|	...	|	|	|	...	0702	|
		Den Haag Centraal ... **472** d.	...	|	|	|	...	...	...	...	...	...	...	0528	|	|	...	*0628*	...	|	|	|	...	...	|
60		**Den Haag** HS .... **472** d.	...	0111	0116	0122	...	...	...	...	...	...	...	0533	0616	0631	...	0635	...	0646	|	0701	...	...	0716
68		Delft .... **472** d.	...	0122	0127	0133	...	...	...	...	...	...	...	0545	|	0638	...	|	...	|	|	0708	...	...	|
82	70	**Rotterdam** Centraal ..... **472** a.	...	0137	0142	0148	...	...	...	...	...	...	...	0559	0632	0650	...	0654	...	0702	0707	0720	...	...	0732
82		**Rotterdam** Centraal ..... **472** d.	...	...	...	...	...	...	...	...	0517	0555	...	0602	0633	0654	...	0655	...	0703	...	0724	0724	...	0733
89		Rotterdam Lombardijen .... d.	...	...	...	...	...	...	...	...	0528	|	...	0611	|	0701	...	|	...	|	...	0731	0731	...	|
102		Dordrecht .... **472** d.	...	...	...	...	...	...	...	...	0543	0609	...	0626	0649	0715	...	0709	...	0716	...	0743	0743	...	0749
132		**Breda** .... **472** a.	...	...	...	...	...	...	...	...	0608	|	...	|	|	0740	...	|	...	...	...	0808	0808	...	|
140		**Roosendaal** .... a.	...	...	...	...	...	...	...	...	...	0632	...	0656	0712	...	...	0732	...	...	...	...	...	...	0812
140		**Roosendaal** .... d.	...	...	...	...	...	...	...	0616	...	...	0646	0700	0716	...	...	...	0738	...	...	...	...	...	0816
153		Bergen op Zoom .... a.	...	...	...	...	...	...	...	0625	...	...	0655	0710	0725	...	...	...	0747	...	...	...	...	...	0825
190		Goes .... a.	...	...	...	...	...	...	...	0655	...	...	0722	...	0747	...	...	...	0814	...	...	...	...	...	0847
209		Middelburg .... a.	...	...	...	...	...	...	...	0709	...	...	0735	...	0758	...	...	...	0827	...	...	...	...	...	0858
215		**Vlissingen** .... a.	...	...	...	...	...	...	...	0718	...	...	0745	...	0808	...	...	...	0837	...	...	...	...	...	0908

		⚒	m B			⚡		⚒		△		B			⚡			❖				r B		
Amsterdam Centraal .... **458** d.	0640	0641	0654	...	0659	0726	0710	0711	0729	0740	0741	0754	...	0759	0826	0810	0811		2029	2040	2041	2054	...	2059
Amsterdam Sloterdijk .... **458** d.	0646	0647	|	...	|	|	0716	0717	|	0746	0747	|	...	|	|	0816	0817		|	2046	2047	|	...	|
Schiphol ✈ .... **457 458** d.	|	0658	0709	...	0713	0740	|	0728	0743	|	0758	0809	...	0813	0840	|	0828		2043	|	2058	2109	...	2113
Haarlem .... d.	0658	|	|	...	|	|	0728	|	|	0758	|	|	...	|	|	0828	|	and at	|	2058	|	|	...	|
Leiden Centraal .... **457** d.	0718	0720	|	...	0734	|	0748	0750	0804	0818	0820	|	...	0834	|	0848	0850	the	2104	2118	2120	|	...	2134
Den Haag Centraal .... a.	|	0732	|	...	|	|	|	0802	|	|	0832	|	...	|	|	|	0902		|	|	2132	|	...	|
Den Haag Centraal .... **472** d.	|	...	*0728*	...	|	|	|	...	|	|	...	*0828*	...	|	|	|	...	same	|	|	...	*2128*	...	|
Den Haag HS .... **472** d.	0731	...	0735	...	0746	|	0801	...	0816	0831	...	0835	...	0846	|	0901	...	minutes	2116	2131	...	2135	...	2146
Delft .... **472** d.	0738	...	|	...	|	|	0808	...	|	0838	...	|	...	|	|	0908	...		|	2138	...	|	...	|
Rotterdam Centraal ..... **472** a.	0750	...	0754	...	0802	0807	0820	...	0832	0850	...	0854	...	0902	0907	0920	...	past	2132	2150	...	2154	...	2202
Rotterdam Centraal ..... **472** d.	0754	...	0755	...	0803	...	0824	...	0833	0854	...	0855	...	0903	...	0924	...	each	2133	2154	...	2155	...	2203
Rotterdam Lombardijen .... d.	0801	...	|	...	|	...	0831	...	|	0901	...	|	...	|	...	0931	...	hour	|	2201	...	|	...	|
Dordrecht .... **472** d.	0815	...	0809	...	0816	...	0843	...	0849	0912	...	0909	...	0916	...	0943	...	until	2149	2212	...	2209	...	2216
Breda .... **472** a.	0840a	...	|	...	...	...	0908	...	|	...	...	|	...	...	...	1008	...		|	...	...	|	...	...
Roosendaal .... a.	...	...	0832	...	...	...	...	...	0912	...	...	0932	...	...	...	...	...		2212	...	...	2232	...	...
Roosendaal .... d.	...	...	...	0846	...	...	...	...	0916	...	...	...	0946	...	...	...	...		2216	...	...	...	2246	...
Bergen op Zoom .... a.	...	...	...	0855	...	...	...	...	0925	...	...	...	0955	...	...	...	...		2225	...	...	...	2255	...
Goes .... a.	...	...	...	0922	...	...	...	...	0947	...	...	...	1022	...	...	...	...		2247	...	...	...	2322	...
Middelburg .... a.	...	...	...	0935	...	...	...	...	0958	...	...	...	1035	...	...	...	...		2258	...	...	...	2335	...
Vlissingen .... a.	...	...	...	0945	...	...	...	...	1008	...	...	...	1045	...	...	...	...		2308	...	...	...	2345	...

	⚡				†			⑥tB			⚡									E	D	E	⑤⑦f	D	
Amsterdam Centraal .... **458** d.	2126	2110	2111	2129	2129	2140	2141	2154	...	2159	2226	2210	2211	2229	2240	2241	2259	2310	2311	2329	2329	2340	2340	2339	2341
Amsterdam Sloterdijk .... **458** d.	|	2116	2117	|	|	2146	2147	|	...	|	|	2216	2217	|	2246	2247	|	2316	2317	|	|	2346	2346	2345	2347
Schiphol ✈ .... **457 458** d.	2140	|	2128	2143	2143	|	2158	2209	...	2213	2240	|	2228	2243	|	2258	2313	|	2328	2343	2343	|	|	|	2358
Haarlem .... d.	|	2128	|	|	|	2158	|	|	...	|	|	2228	|	|	2258	|	|	2328	|	|	|	2358	2358	2355	|
Leiden Centraal .... **457** d.	|	2148	2150	2204	2204	2218	2220	|	...	2234	|	2248	2250	2304	2318	2320	2334	2348	2350	0004	0004	0018	0018	0024z	0021
Den Haag Centraal .... a.	|	|	2202	|	|	|	2232	|	...	|	|	|	2302	|	|	2332	|	|	0002	|	|	|	|	|	0033
Den Haag Centraal .... **472** d.	|	|	...	|	|	|	...	*2228*	...	|	|	|	...	|	|	...	|	|	...	|	|	|	|	|	...
Den Haag HS .... **472** d.	|	2201	...	2216	2216	2231	...	2235	...	2246	|	2301	...	2316	2331	...	2346	0001	...	0016	0016	0031	0031	0044	...
Delft .... **472** d.	|	2208	...	|	|	2238	...	|	...	|	|	2308	...	|	2338	...	|	0008	...	|	|	0038	0038	0058	...
Rotterdam Centraal ..... **472** a.	2207	2220	...	2232	2232	2250	...	2254	...	2302	2307	2320	...	2332	2350	...	0002	0023	...	0032	0044	0052	0052	0111	...
Rotterdam Centraal ..... **472** d.	...	2224	...	2233	2233	2254	...	2255	...	2303	...	2324	...	2333	2354	...	0003	0024	...	0033	0045	...	0054	0113	...
Rotterdam Lombardijen .... d.	...	2231	...	|	|	2301	...	|	...	|	...	2331	...	|	0001	...	|	0031	...	0044	0057	...	0104	0123	...
Dordrecht .... **472** d.	...	2243	...	2249	2249	2312	...	2309	...	2316	...	2343	...	2349	0012	...	0017	0043	...	0101	0113	...	0118	0137	...
Breda .... **472** a.	...	2308	...	|	|	...	...	|	...	...	...	0008	...	|	...	...	0033e	0112	...	|	|	...	...	...	...
Roosendaal .... a.	...	...	...	2312	2312	...	...	2332	...	...	...	...	...	0014	...	...	...	...	...	0130	0147	...	...	...	...
Roosendaal .... d.	...	...	...	2316	2316	...	...	...	2346	...	...	...	...	0016	...	...	...	...	...	...	...	...	...	...	...
Bergen op Zoom .... a.	...	...	...	2325	2325	...	...	...	2355	...	...	...	...	0025	...	...	...	...	...	...	...	...	...	...	...
Goes .... a.	...	...	...	...	2347	...	...	...	0022	...	...	...	...	0047	...	...	...	...	...	...	...	...	...	...	...
Middelburg .... a.	...	...	...	...	2358	...	...	...	0035	...	...	...	...	0058	...	...	...	...	...	...	...	...	...	...	...
Vlissingen .... a.	...	...	...	...	0008	...	...	...	0045	...	...	...	...	0108	...	...	...	...	...	...	...	...	...	...	...

B – To Brussels (Table **410**).
D – ①–④ (not Apr. 5, May 5, 13, 24).
E – ⑤–⑦ (also Apr. 5, May 5, 13, 24).
G – ②–⑤ (not Apr. 6, May 6, 14, 25).
H – ①⑥⑦ (also Apr. 6, May 6, 14, 25).
K – ①–⑥ (not Dec. 25, 26, Jan. 1, Apr. 5, May 24).
L – ①–⑥ (not Dec. 25, 26, Jan. 1, Apr. 5, May 13, 24).

a – Ⓐ only.

e – ⑤–⑦ (also Apr. 6, May 6, 25; not Dec. 26, 27, Jan. 2).
f – Also Dec. 26; not Apr. 30.
g – Also Dec. 26, 27, Jan. 2.
h – Also Apr. 6, May 6, 14, 25; not Dec. 26, 27, Jan. 2.
m – Not Jan. 1.
r – Not Dec. 31.
t – Also Apr. 5, 30, May 5, 13, 24; not Dec. 26.
v – 8 minutes later on ⑥ (also Apr. 5, 30, May 5, 13, 24).
z – Arrives 0014.

△ – On Ⓐ the services from Amsterdam at 1340, 1440, 1540 and 1640 continue to Breda (arriving 1540, 1640, 1740 and 1840 respectively).
❖ – The 1854 and 1954 from Amsterdam do not run on Dec. 31.
⊡ – 5–10 minutes later on ②③ (not Apr. 6, May 25).
⚡ – *FYRA*. Via high-speed line. Supplement payable. On Dec. 31 the last departure from Amsterdam is at 1826.
* – Via the high-speed line.

451 AMSTERDAM - SCHIPHOL ✈ all trains

From Amsterdam Centraal *17 km*

0002, 0011, 0045, 0145, 0245, 0345, 0445, 0502 ⚒, 0529 ⚒, 0541 Ⓐ, 0544 †, 0559 Ⓐ, 0602, 0611 Ⓐ, 0629, 0632, 0641 ⚒, 0659, 0702, 0711 ⚒, 0729, 0732, 0741, 0759; then 0802–2329 at 02, 11, 29, 32, 41 and 59 minutes past each hour; 2341.

From Schiphol ✈ Journey time: 13–22 minutes

0000, 0008, 0016, 0030, 0100, 0200, 0300, 0400, 0500, 0538 Ⓒ, 0600, 0608, 0616 Ⓐ, 0630 Ⓐ, 0638, 0646, 0700 Ⓐ, 0708, 0716, 0730 ⚒, 0738, 0746, 0800 ⚒, 0808, 0816, 0830, 0838, 0846; then 0900–2330 at 00, 08, 16, 30, 38 and 46 minutes past each hour; 2346.

VLISSINGEN - ROTTERDAM - DEN HAAG - AMSTERDAM 450

For INTERNATIONAL TRAINS **Paris – Brussels – Amsterdam**, see Table **18** For NIGHT NETWORK **Rotterdam – Amsterdam – Utrecht**, see Table **454**

km		Ⓐ	Ⓐ		⚒		Ⓐ	⚒	⚒	†	Ⓐ	⚒	L✗	⚒	⚒		⚒		Ⓐ		✗			Ⓐ	
	Vlissingen d.	...	...	...	...	...	...	...	...	...	...	...	...	...	...	...	...	...	0545	...	...	...	...	0612	...
	Middelburg d.	...	...	...	...	...	...	...	...	...	...	...	...	...	...	...	...	...	0552	...	...	...	...	0619	...
	Goes d.	...	...	...	...	...	...	...	...	...	...	...	...	...	...	...	...	...	0605	...	...	...	...	0632	...
	Bergen op Zoom d.	...	...	...	...	...	...	...	...	...	0533	...	...	...	...	0604a	...	...	0632	...	...	...	...	0704	...
	Roosendaal a.	...	...	...	...	...	...	...	...	...	0544	...	...	...	...	0614a	...	...	0644	...	...	...	...	0715	...
	Roosendaal d.	...	...	...	...	...	...	...	...	...	0547	...	...	...	...	0617a	...	...	0647	...	...	...	...	0718	...
0	**Breda** 472 d.	...	...	...	...	...	...	...	...	...	|	...	...	...	0550a	|	...	0620v	|	...	...	...	0650a	|	...
29	Dordrecht 472 d.	*0437*	...	...	0533	...	...	...	...	...	0612	...	...	...	0622a	0642	...	0652v	0712	0712	...	...	0722a	0742	0742
42	Rotterdam Lombardijen d.	*0450*	...	...	0546	...	...	...	...	...	|	...	...	...	0630a	|	...	0700v	|	|	...	...	0730a	|	|
49	**Rotterdam** Centraal 472 a.	*0500*	...	...	0556	...	...	←	...	...	0626	...	...	...	0639a	0656	...	0709v	0726	0726	...	...	0739a	0756	0756
49	**Rotterdam** Centraal 472 d.	0527	...	0531	→	0559	...	0602	0611	0624	0628	0628	0630	...	0641	0658	...	0711	0728	0728	0730	...	0741	0758	0758
64	Delft 472 d.	|	...	0545	...	|	...	0617	0624	|	|	|	|	...	0654	|	...	0724	|	|	|	...	0754	|	|
72	**Den Haag** HS 472 d.	0547	...	0600	...	0617	...	0630	0632	0647	0647	0647	|	...	0702	0717	...	0732	0747	0747	|	...	0802	0817	0817
	Den Haag Centraal 472 a.	|	...	0603	...	|	...	0633	|	|	|	|	|	...	|	|	...	|	|	|	|	...	|	|	|
	Den Haag Centraal d.	|	0558	...	...	|	0628	...	|	|	|	|	|	0658	|	|	0728	|	|	|	|	0758	|	|	|
88	Leiden Centraal 457 d.	0600	0613	...	...	0630	0643	...	0645	0700	0700	0700	|	0713	0715	0730	0743	0745	0800	0800	|	0813	0815	0830	0830
116	Haarlem d.	|	|	...	...	|	|	...	0706	|	|	|	|	|	0736	|	|	0806	|	|	|	|	0836	|	|
	Schiphol ✈ 457 458 d.	0616	0630	...	...	0646	0700	...	|	0716	0716	0716	0657	0730	|	0746	0800	|	0816	0816	0757	0830	|	0846	0846
130	Amsterdam Sloterdijk 458 a.	|	0643	...	...	|	0713	...	0715	|	|	|	|	0743	0745	|	0813	0815	|	|	|	0843	0845	|	|
135	**Amsterdam** Centraal 458 a.	0633	0650	...	...	0703	0720	...	0722	0733	0733	0733	0711	0750	0752	0803	0820	0822	0833	0833	0811	0850	0852	0903	0903

	⑥t	K B			Ⓐ		✗		▽			B				✗	❖					r B		
Vlissingen d.	0615	...	...	...	0652	...	...	...	...	...	0715	...	...	...	0752	...	and at the same minutes past each hour until	...	...	...	2015	...	...	...
Middelburg d.	0622	...	...	...	0659	...	...	...	...	...	0722	...	...	...	0759	...		...	...	...	2022	...	...	...
Goes d.	0635	...	...	...	0710	...	...	...	...	...	0735	...	...	...	0811	...		...	...	...	2035	...	...	...
Bergen op Zoom d.	0702	...	...	...	0733	...	...	...	...	...	0802	...	...	...	0833	...		...	...	...	2102	...	...	...
Roosendaal a.	0714	...	...	...	0744	...	...	...	...	...	0814	...	...	...	0844	...		...	...	...	2114	...	...	...
Roosendaal d.	...	0730	...	...	0747	...	...	...	...	...	...	0830	...	...	0847	...		...	...	...	...	2130	...	...
Breda 472 d.	...	|	...	0720v	|	...	...	...	0750a	...	...	|	...	0820	|	...		...	...	...	...	|	...	2120
Dordrecht 472 d.	...	0754	...	0752	0812	0812	...	...	0822	0842	...	0854	...	0852	0912	...		...	2122	2142	...	2154	...	2152
Rotterdam Lombardijen d.	...	|	...	0800	|	|	...	...	0830	|	...	|	...	0900	|	...		...	2130	|	...	|	...	2200
Rotterdam Centraal 472 a.	...	0806	...	0809	0826	0826	...	...	0839	0856	...	0906	...	0909	0926	...		...	2139	2156	...	2206	...	2209
Rotterdam Centraal 472 d.	...	0808	...	0811	0828	0828	0830	...	0841	0858	...	0908	...	0911	0928	0930		...	2141	2158	...	2208	...	2211
Delft 472 d.	...	|	...	0824	|	|	|	...	0854	|	...	|	...	0924	|	|		...	2154	|	...	|	...	2224
Den Haag HS 472 d.	...	0826	...	0832	0847	0847	|	...	0902	0917	...	0926	...	0932	0947	|		...	2202	2217	...	2226	...	2232
Den Haag Centraal 472 a.	...	*0833*	...	|	|	|	|	...	|	|	...	*0933*	...	|	|	|		...	|	|	...	*2233*	...	|
Den Haag Centraal d.	...	|	0828	|	|	|	|	0858	|	|	...	|	0928	|	|	|		2158	|	|	...	|	2228	|
Leiden Centraal 457 d.	...	|	0843	0845	0900	0900	|	0913	0915	0930	...	|	0943	0945	1000	|		2213	2215	2230	...	|	2243	2245
Haarlem d.	...	|	|	0906	|	|	|	|	0936	|	...	|	|	1006	|	|		|	2236	|	...	|	|	2306
Schiphol ✈ 457 458 d.	...	0852	0900	|	0916	0916	0857	0930	|	0946	...	0952	1000	|	1016	0957		2230	|	2246	...	2252	2300	|
Amsterdam Sloterdijk 458 a.	...	|	0913	0915	|	|	|	0943	0945	|	...	|	1013	1015	|	|		2243	2245	|	...	|	2313	2315
Amsterdam Centraal 458 a.	...	0906	0920	0922	0933	0933	0911	0950	0952	1003	...	1006	1020	1022	1033	1011		2250	2252	2303	...	2306	2320	2322

		✗					r B					E	D			r B	⑥tB	E	D	†	E	E	D	D	
Vlissingen d.	2052	...	...	...	...	2115	...	...	...	2152	...	...	...	...	2215	...	...	...	...	2252	...	...	...	...	2315
Middelburg d.	2059	...	...	...	...	2122	...	...	...	2159	...	...	...	...	2222	...	...	...	...	2259	...	...	...	...	2322
Goes d.	2111	...	...	...	...	2135	...	...	...	2211	...	...	...	...	2235	...	...	...	...	2311	...	...	...	...	2335
Bergen op Zoom d.	2133	...	...	...	...	2202	...	...	...	2233	...	...	...	...	2302	...	...	...	...	2333	2333	...	2333	...	0002
Roosendaal a.	2144	...	...	...	...	2214	...	...	...	2244	...	...	...	...	2314	...	...	...	...	2344	2344	...	2344	...	0014
Roosendaal d.	2147	...	...	...	...	...	2230	...	...	2247	...	...	...	...	...	2330	2330	...	...	2347	2347	2335	2347	2335	...
Breda 472 d.	|	...	...	...	...	...	|	...	2220	|	...	...	...	...	...	|	|	2320	2320	|	|	|	|	|	...
Dordrecht 472 d.	2212	...	...	2222	2242	...	2254	...	2252	2312	...	2322	2322	*2342*	...	2354	2354	2352	2352	0012	0012	0007	0014	0007	...
Rotterdam Lombardijen d.	|	...	...	2230	|	...	|	...	2300	|	...	2330	2330	|	...	|	|	0000	0000	|	|	0020	|	0020	...
Rotterdam Centraal 472 a.	2226	...	...	2239	2256	...	2306	...	2309	2326	...	2339	2339	*2356*	...	0006	0006	0009	0009	0026	0026	0030	0035	0030	...
Rotterdam Centraal 472 d.	2228	2230	...	2241	2258	...	2308	...	2311	2328	...	2341	2341	0002	...	...	0008	0011	0011	...	...	0032	...	0039	...
Delft 472 d.	|	|	...	2254	|	...	|	...	2324	|	...	2354	2354	0014	...	...	|	0025	0024	...	...	0047	...	0054	...
Den Haag HS 472 d.	2247	|	...	2302	2317	...	2326	...	2332	2347	...	0002	0002	0023	...	...	0026	0032	0044	...	...	0100	...	0107	...
Den Haag Centraal 472 a.	|	|	...	|	|	...	*2333*	...	|	|	...	|	|	|	...	...	|	|	|	...	...	0103	...	0110	...
Den Haag Centraal d.	|	|	2258	|	|	...	|	2328	|	|	2358	|	|	|	...	...	|	|	|	...	...	...	...	...	...
Leiden Centraal 457 d.	2300	|	2313	2315	2330	...	|	2343	2345	0000	0013	0015	0016	0038f	...	...	|	0052	0107	...	...	...	...	...	...
Haarlem d.	|	|	|	2336	|	...	|	|	0006	|	|	0036	0043	|	...	...	|	0113	0137	...	...	...	...	...	...
Schiphol ✈ 457 458 d.	2316	2257	2330	|	2346	...	2352	0000	|	0016	0030	|	|	0100	...	...	0052	|	|	...	...	...	...	...	...
Amsterdam Sloterdijk 458 a.	|	|	2343	2345	|	...	|	0013	0015	|	0043	0045	0057	|	...	...	|	0124	0152	...	...	...	...	...	...
Amsterdam Centraal 458 a.	2333	2311	2350	2352	0003	...	0006	0020	0022	0036	0050	0052	0104	0114	...	...	0106	0131	0158	...	...	...	...	...	...

B – From Brussels (Table **410**).
D – ①–④ (not Apr. 5, May 5, 13, 24).
E – ⑤–⑦ (also Apr. 5, May 5, 13, 24).
K – ①–⑥ (not Dec. 25, 26, Jan. 1, Apr. 5, May 24).
L – ①–⑥ (not Dec. 25, 26, Jan. 1, Apr. 5, May 13, 24).

a – Ⓐ only.
f – 0044 on ②–⑤ (not Apr. 6, May 6, 14, 25).
r – Not Dec. 31.
t – Also Apr. 5, 30, May 5, 13, 24; not Dec. 26.
v – ⚒ only.

▽ – From Breda at 0750 Ⓐ, 0850 Ⓐ, 1550 Ⓐ, 1650 Ⓐ and 1750 Ⓐ. Other services in this pattern start from Dordrecht.
❖ – The 1930 and 2030 from Roosendaal do not run on Dec. 31.
✗ – *FYRA*. Via high-speed line. Supplement payable. On Dec. 31 the last departure from Rotterdam is at 1930.

EINDHOVEN - UTRECHT - AMSTERDAM - ROTTERDAM - EINDHOVEN Night Network 454

Timings may be amended when track maintenance work is taking place. Please check locally.

	y						e	†		A
Eindhoven d.	...	...	0000y	0101y	0201e	0301e	0400	0400	...	...
's-Hertogenbosch d.	...	...	0025y	0125y	0225e	0325e	0425	0425	...	...
Utrecht Centraal d.	...	...	0107	0207	0307	0407	0500	0507	...	...
Amsterdam Centraal d.	...	0045	0145	0245	0345	0445	...	0544	...	2259
Schiphol ✈ d.	...	0102	0203	0303	0403	0503	...	0600	...	2313
Leiden Centraal d.	...	0123	0223	0323	0423	0523	...	0617	...	2334
Den Haag HS d.	...	0138	0238	0338	0438	0538	...	0627	...	2346
Delft d.	...	0146	0246	0346	0446	0546	...	0634	...	|
Rotterdam Centraal a.	0102	0159	0259	0359	0459	0604	...	0651	...	0002
Dordrecht a.	0115	0215z	0315z	0415e	...	...	...	...	...	0016
Breda a.	0136	0236z	0336z	0436e	...	...	...	...	...	0033
Tilburg a.	0153	0253z	0353z	0453e	...	...	...	...	...	0052
Eindhoven a.	0218	0318z	0419z	0518e	...	...	...	...	...	0118

	y							
Eindhoven d.	...	...	...	...	0030y	0130y	0230e	0330e
Tilburg d.	...	...	...	...	0102y	0202y	0302e	0402e
Breda d.	...	...	...	...	0119y	0219y	0319e	0419e
Dordrecht d.	...	...	...	...	0141y	0241y	0341e	0441e
Rotterdam Centraal d.	...	...	0002	0102	0202	0302	0402	0459
Delft d.	...	...	0014	0114h	0214	0314	0414	0510
Den Haag HS d.	...	...	0023	0123	0223j	0323	0423	0523
Leiden Centraal d.	...	...	0038*	0138	0238	0338	0438	0538
Schiphol ✈ d.	...	...	0100	0200	0300	0400	0500	0600
Amsterdam Centraal d.	...	...	0117	0217	0317	0417	0517	0617
Utrecht Centraal a.	0055	...	0151	0252	0352	0452	0551	0651c
's-Hertogenbosch a.	0125	...	0226y	0325z	0425e	...	...	...
Eindhoven a.	0149	...	0247y	0347z	0447e	...	...	...

A – ④–⑥ (also Apr. 5, May 5, 24; not Dec. 25, 26, Jan. 1).
c – Ⓒ only.
e – ⑤–⑦ (also Apr. 5, May 5, 13, 24).
h – Not ③.
j – ①②③④⑥⑦ (also Dec. 25, Jan. 1, Apr. 30).
y – ⑤–⑦ (also Apr. 6, May 6, 25; not Dec. 26, 27, Jan. 2).
z – ⑤–⑦ (not Dec. 26, 27, Jan. 2).
***** – 6–7 minutes later on ②–⑤ (not Apr. 6, May 6, 14, 25).
MAP/INDEX

ROTTERDAM - HOEK VAN HOLLAND 455

For connections to shipping services, see Table **15a**

km		H	Gv	H	Gv			Av	①m	Ⓐ	⚒	Ⓐ	⚒	Ⓐ		Ⓐ		Ⓐ					
0	**Rotterdam** Centraal d.	0013	0013	0043	0056	...	...	0505	0513	0543	0613	0628	0643	0658	0713	0728	0743	0758	0813	0843	and every 30 minutes until	2313	2343
27	**Hoek van Holland** Haven a.	0042	0045	0112	0129	...	...	0537	0542	0612	0642	0658	0712	0728	0742	0758	0812	0828	0842	0912		2342	0012

	H	Gv	H	Gv	H	G		①m	A	Ⓐ	Ⓐ	Ⓐ	⚒	Ⓐ	⚒	Ⓐ		Ⓐ					
Hoek van Holland Haven d.	0007	0007	0037	0050	0107	0135	...	0537	0542	0607	0637	0652	0707	0722	0737	0752	0807	0822	0837	0907	and every 30 minutes until	2307	2337
Rotterdam Centraal a.	0038	0047	0108	0127	0138	0206	...	0608	0613	0638	0708	0723	0738	0753	0808	0823	0838	0853	0908	0938		2338	0008

A – ②–⑤ (not Dec. 25, Jan. 1, Apr. 30, May 5, 13).
G – ②–⑤ (not Apr. 6, May 6, 14, 25).
H – ①⑥⑦ (also Apr. 6, May 6, 14, 25).
m – Not Apr. 5, May 24.
v – Change trains at Vlaardingen Centrum.

457 LEIDEN - AMSTERDAM ZUID - HILVERSUM - UTRECHT and ALMERE - UTRECHT

Stopping trains LEIDEN - AMSTERDAM ZUID - UTRECHT

For fast trains **Schiphol ✈ - Utrecht**, see Table **470**. For direct trains **Leiden - Utrecht** (via Alphen), see Table **463**.

km		Ⓐ	Ⓐ	⚒	⚒					
0	**Leiden** Centraal .. **450** d.	0520	...	...	0618	0648	0718	and at the same minutes past each hour until	2248	2318
27	Schiphol ✈ ... **450 458** d.	0541	0611	...	0641	0711	0741		2311	2341
36	Amsterdam Zuid .. **458** d.	0549	0619	...	0649	0719	0749		2319	2349
41	Duivendrecht .... **458** d.	0556	0626	...	0656	0726	0756		2326	2356
49	Weesp .... **458** a.	0605	0635	...	0705	0735	0805		2335	0005
49	Weesp .... **480** d.	0612	0642	...	0712	0742	0812		2342	0012
58	Naarden-Bussum . **480** d.	0620	0650	0650	0720	0750	0820		2350	0020
64	Hilversum .... **480** d.	0631	0701	0701	0731	0801	0831		0001	0031
81	**Utrecht** Centraal ....a.	0651	0721	0721	0751	0821	0851		0021	0051

Utrecht Centraal .... d.	0538j	0608	0638	and at the same minutes past each hour until	2208	2238	2308	2338
Hilversum .... d.	0559j	0629	0659		2229	2259	2329	2359
Naarden-Bussum .... d.	0609j	0639	0709		2239	2309	2339	0009
Weesp .... a.	0616j	0646	0716		2246	2316	2346	0016
Weesp .... **458** d.	0624	0654	0724		2254	2324	2354	0024
Duivendrecht .... **458** d.	0634	0704	0734		2304	2334	0004	0034
Amsterdam Zuid .... **458** d.	0641	0711	0741		2311	2341	0011	0041
Schiphol ✈ .... **450 458** a.	0650	0718	0748		2318	2348	0019	0048
Leiden Centraal .... **450** a.	0713	0742	0813		2342	0010	...	...

ALMERE - UTRECHT

	Ⓐ	Ⓐ	Ⓐ	Ⓐ	⚒	Ⓑk		⚒			⚒												
Almere Centrum .... d.	0550	0620	0650	0720	0750	0820	...	0850	0920	and at the same minutes past each hour until	1950	2020	...	2120	...	2220	...	2320	...	...	...	...
Naarden-Bussum .... d.	0606	0636	0706	0736	0806	0836	...	0906	0936		2006	2036	...	2136	...	2236	...	2336	...	...	...	...
Hilversum .... d.	0614	0644	0714	0744	0814	0844	...	0914	0944		2014	2044	...	2144	...	2244	...	2344	...	...	...	...
Utrecht Centraal .... a.	0632	0702	0732	0802	0832	0902	...	0932	1002		2032	2102	...	2202	...	2302	...	0002	...	...	...	...

	Ⓐ	⚒	Ⓐ		⚒			⚒												G	H		
Utrecht Centraal .... d.	0628	0658	0728	...	0758	0828	and at the same minutes past each hour until	1858	1928	...	2028	...	2128	...	2228	...	2328	...	0028	0028	...	...
Hilversum .... d.	0646	0716	0746	...	0816	0846		1916	1946	...	2046	...	2146	...	2246	...	2346	...	0046	0046	...	...
Naarden-Bussum .... d.	0652	0722	0752	...	0822	0852		1922	1952	...	2052	...	2152	...	2252	...	2352	...	0052	0058	...	...
Almere Centrum .... a.	0707	0737	0807	...	0837	0907		1937	2007	...	2107	...	2207	...	2307	...	0007	...	0108	0113	...	...

G – ②–⑤ (not Apr. 6, May 6, 14, 25).
H – ①⑥⑦ (also Apr. 6, May 6, 14, 25).
j – 5–6 minutes later on ④⑤⑦ (also Dec. 26; not Apr. 30, May 13).
k – Also Dec. 26; not Apr. 5, 30, May 5, 13, 24.

458 SCHIPHOL ✈ and AMSTERDAM - LELYSTAD

km		Ⓐ	Ⓐ	Ⓐ	ⒶL	⚒	⚒	Ⓐ	ⒶL	⚒	⚒	Ⓐ	ⒶL			⚒	ⒶL			⚒	ⒶL			⚒	ⒶL
0	**Schiphol** ✈ .... **450 457** d.	...	0555	0625	0638	...	0655	0707	0708	...	0725	0737	0738	...	0755	0807	0808	...	0825	0837	0838	...	0855	0907	0908
9	Amsterdam Zuid .... **457** d.	...	0604	0634	|	...	0704	0715	|	...	0734	0745	|	...	0804	0815	|	...	0834	0845	|	...	0904	0915	|
14	Duivendrecht .... **457** d.	...	0611	0641	|	...	0711	0721	|	...	0741	0751	|	...	0811	0821	|	...	0841	0851	|	...	0911	0921	|
	Amsterdam Sloterdijk **450** d.	...	|	|	0652	...	|	|	0722	...	|	|	0752	...	|	|	0822	...	|	|	0852	...	|	|	0922
	Amsterdam Centraal **450** a.	...	|	|	0700	...	|	|	0730	...	|	|	0800	...	|	|	0830	...	|	|	0900	...	|	|	0930
	Amsterdam Centraal **480** d.	0605	|	|	0703	0705	|	|	0733	0735	|	|	0803	0805	|	|	0833	0835	|	|	0903	0905	|	|	0933
22	Weesp .... **457 480** d.	0620	0622	0652	|	0720	0722	|	|	0750	0752	|	|	0820	0822	|	|	0850	0852	|	|	0920	0922	|	|
38	**Almere** Centrum ....d.	...	0634	0704	0725	...	0734	0741	0755	...	0804	0811	0825	...	0834	0841	0855	...	0904	0911	0925	...	0934	0941	0955
44	Almere Buiten ....d.	...	0640	0710	0730	...	0740	0745	0800	...	0810	0815	0830	...	0840	0845	0900	...	0910	0915	0930	...	0940	0945	1000
62	**Lelystad** Centrum ....a.	...	0655	0725	0741	...	0755t	0756	0811	...	0825t	0826	0841	...	0855r	0856	0911	...	0925r	0926	0941	...	0955r	0956	1011

		⚒			⚒				⚒			⚒												
Schiphol ✈ .... **450 457** d.	0925	0937	0938	0955	1007	1008	and at the same minutes past each hour until	1855	1907	1908	1925	1937	1938	1955	...	2025	...	and at the same minutes past each hour until	2255	...	2325	...	2355
Amsterdam Zuid .... **457** d.	0934	0945	|	1004	1015	|		1904	1915	|	1934	1945	|	2004	...	2034	...		2304	...	2334	...	0004
Duivendrecht .... **457** d.	0941	0951	|	1011	1021	|		1911	1921	|	1941	1951	|	2011	...	2041	...		2311	...	2341	...	0011
Amsterdam Sloterdijk **450** d.	|	|	0952	|	|	1022		|	|	1922	|	|	1952	|	...	|	...		|	...	|	...	|
Amsterdam Centraal **450** a.	|	|	1000	|	|	1030		|	|	1930	|	|	2000	|	...	|	...		|	...	|	...	|
Amsterdam Centraal **480** d.	|	|	1003	|	|	1033		|	|	1933	|	|	2003	|	2018	|	2048		|	2318	|	2348	|
Weesp .... **457 480** d.	0952	|	|	1022	|	|		1922	|	|	1952	|	|	2022	2037	2052	2107		2322	2337	2352	0007	0024
Almere Centrum .... d.	1004	1011	1025	1034	1041	1055		1934	1941	1955	2004	2011	2025	2034	2050	2104	2120		2334	2350	0004	0021	0037
Almere Buiten .... d.	1010	1015	1030	1040	1045	1100		1940	1945	2000	2010	2015	2030	2040	2056	2110	2126		2340	2356	0010	0027	0044
Lelystad Centrum .... a.	1025r	1026	1041	1055r	1056	1111		1955r	1956	2011	2025r	2026	2041	2055	2111	2125	2141		2355	0011	0025	0042	0059

			Ⓐ	ⒶL		Ⓐ	ⒶL		Ⓐ		ⒶL		Ⓐ		ⒶL		Ⓐ		ⒶL		Ⓐ			⚒	
Lelystad Centrum .... d.	0433j	0518j	0533	0546	0547c	0603	0616	0618c	0630	0633c	0646	0648c	0700	0703c	0716	0718c	0730	0733c	0746	0748c	0800	0803c	0816	0830	0833r
Almere Buiten .... d.	0448j	0533j	0548	0557	0603	0618	0627	0633	0641	0648	0657	0703	0711	0718	0727	0733	0741	0748	0757	0803	0811	0818	0827	0841	0848
Almere Centrum .... d.	0455j	0540j	0555	0603	0609	0625	0633	0640	0648	0655	0703	0710	0718	0725	0733	0740	0748	0755	0803	0810	0818	0825	0833	0848	0855
Weesp .... **457 480** d.	0509	0554	0609	|	0624	0639	|	0654	|	0709	|	0724	|	0739	|	0754	|	0809	|	0824	|	0839	|	|	0909
Amsterdam Centraal **480** a.	|	0612	|	0626	0642	|	0656	0711	|	|	0726	0741	|	|	0756	0811	|	|	0826	0841	|	|	0856	|	|
Amsterdam Centraal **450** d.	|	...	|	0632	...	|	0702	...	|	|	0732	...	|	|	0802	...	|	|	0832	...	|	|	0902	|	|
Amsterdam Sloterdijk **450** a.	|	...	|	0639	...	|	0709	...	|	|	0739	...	|	|	0809	...	|	|	0839	...	|	|	0909	|	|
Duivendrecht .... **457** d.	0519	...	0619	|	...	0650	|	...	0708	0719	|	...	0738	0750	|	...	0808	0819	|	...	0838	0850	|	0908	0919
Amsterdam Zuid .... **457** a.	0527	...	0627	|	...	0657	|	...	0714	0727	|	...	0744	0757	|	...	0814	0827	|	...	0844	0857	|	0914	0927
Schiphol ✈ .... **450 457** a.	0534	...	0634	0651	...	0704	0721	...	0720	0734	0751	...	0750	0804	0821	...	0820	0834	0851	...	0850	0904	0921	0920	0934

		⚒				⚒			⚒													E		
Lelystad Centrum .... d.	0846	0900	0903r	and at the same minutes past each hour until	1846	1900	1903r	1916	1930	1933r	1946	2003	2018	2033	2048	and at the same minutes past each hour until	2233	2248	2303	2318	2333	2348	0003
Almere Buiten .... d.	0857	0911	0918		1857	1911	1918	1927	1941	1948	1957	2018	2033	2048	2103		2248	2303	2318	2333	2348	0003	0018
Almere Centrum .... d.	0903	0918	0925		1903	1918	1925	1933	1948	1955	2003	2025	2040	2055	2110		2255	2310	2325	2340	2355	0010	0024
Weesp .... **457 480** d.	|	|	0939		|	|	1939	|	|	2009	|	2039	2054	2109	2124		2309	2324	2339	2354	0009	0023	0038
Amsterdam Centraal **480** a.	0926	|	|		1926	|	|	1956	|	|	2026	|	2111	|	2141		|	2341	|	0011	|	0040	|
Amsterdam Centraal **450** d.	0932	|	|		1932	|	|	2002	|	|	2032	|	...	|	...		|	...	|	...	|	...	|
Amsterdam Sloterdijk **450** a.	0939	|	|		1939	|	|	2009	|	|	2039	|	...	|	...		|	...	|	...	|	...	|
Duivendrecht .... **457** d.	|	0938	0950		|	1938	1950	|	2008	2019	|	2050	...	2119	...		2319	...	2350	...	0019	...	0047
Amsterdam Zuid .... **457** a.	|	0944	0957		|	1944	1957	|	2014	2027	|	2057	...	2127	...		2327	...	2357	...	0027	...	0057
Schiphol ✈ .... **450 457** a.	0951	0950	1004		1951	1950	2004	2021	2020	2034	2051	2104	...	2134	...		2334	...	0004	...	0034	...	0105

E – ⑤–⑦ (also Apr. 5, May 5, 13, 24).
L – Runs daily Schiphol - Amsterdam Centraal and v.v.
c – Ⓒ only.
j – 2–3 minutes earlier on †.
r – † only.
t – ⑥ (also Apr. 5, 30, May 5, 13, 24; not Dec. 26).

459 SCHIPHOL ✈ and AMSTERDAM - ENKHUIZEN

km		Ⓐ	Ⓐ		Ⓐ	Ⓒ	Ⓐ	Ⓐ	⑥t	Ⓐ														
	Amersfoort **480** .... d.	...	...	...	...	...	0629	...	...	0659	...	0729v	...	0759v	...	0829	...	0859	and at the same minutes past each hour until	...	2259	...	2329	2359
0	**Amsterdam** Centraal ... **466** d.	0600	0630	...	...	0700	0709	...	0730	0739	...	0809	...	0839	...	0909	...	0939		...	2339	...	0009	0039
	Schiphol ✈ .... d.	|	|	0638	0643	|	|	0713	|	|	0743	|	0813	|	0843	|	0913	|		2313	|	2343	|	|
5	Amsterdam Sloterdijk ... **466** d.	0606	0636	0651	0657	0706	0714	0727	0736	0744	0757	0814	0827	0844	0857	0914	0927	0944		2327	2344	2355	0014	0044
12	Zaandam .... **466** d.	0613	0643	...	0704	0713	|	0734	0743	|	0804	|	0834	|	0904	|	0934	|		2334	|	0004	|	0052
44	Hoorn .... d.	0645	0715	...	0732	0745	0745	0802	0815	0815	0832	0845	0902	0915	0932	0945	1002	1015		0002	0015	0036	0045	0122
62	**Enkhuizen** .... a.	0706	0736	...	...	0806	0806	...	0836	0836	...	0906	...	0936	...	1006	...	1036		...	0036	...	0107	0144

	⚒	⚒	Ⓐ	Ⓐ	Ⓐ	⚒	⚒	⚒	⚒	⚒	⚒													
Enkhuizen .... d.	0439a	...	...	0524	...	0554	...	0624a	...	0654	...	0724	...	0754	...	and at the same minutes past each hour until	2154	...	2224	...	2254	...	2324	2354
Hoorn .... d.	0505	...	0529	0550	0559	0620	0629	0650	0659	0720	0729	0750	0759	0820	0829		2220	2229	2250	2259	2320	2329	2350	0020
Zaandam .... **466** d.	0534	0537	0556	|	0626	|	0656	|	0726	|	0756	|	0826	|	0856		|	2256	|	2326	|	2356	|	0048
Amsterdam Sloterdijk .... **466** a.	0540	0543	0603	0615	0633	0645	0703	0715	0733	0745	0803	0815	0833	0845	0903		2245	2303	2315	2333	2345	0003	0021	0058
Schiphol ✈ .... a.	0552	|	0616	|	0646	|	0716	|	0746	|	0816	|	0846	|	0916		|	2316	|	2346	|	0016	|	|
Amsterdam Centraal .... **466** a.	...	0548	...	0622	...	0651	...	0721	...	0751	...	0821	...	0851	...		2251	...	2321	...	2351	...	0028	0106
Amersfoort **480** .... a.	...	...	...	0701	...	0731	...	0801	...	0831	...	0901	...	0931	...		2332	...	0002	...	...	...	...	...

a – Ⓐ only.
t – Also Apr. 5, 30, May 5, 13, 24; not Dec. 26.
v – ⚒ only.

DEN HAAG - HAARLEM - ALKMAAR - HOORN 461

km				Ⓐ	Ⓐ	Ⓐ	⚒	Ⓐ	⚒	⚒		⚒											
0	**Den Haag** Centraal 450 d.	...	...	...	...	0603	...	0633	...	0703a	...	0733a	0803a	0833a	and at	1833a	1903a	1933a	...	...	...	...
15	Leiden Centraal 450 d.	...	...	...	...	0618	...	0648	...	0718a	...	0748a	0818a	0848a	the same	1848a	1918a	1948a	...	...	...	...
43	**Haarlem** 450 d.	0045	...	...	...	0642	...	0712	...	0742	...	0812	0842	0912	minutes	1912	1942	2012	2042	2142	2242	2342
54	Beverwijk d.	0102	...	...	...	0653	...	0723	...	0753	...	0823	0853	0923	past each	1923	1953	2023	2053	2153	2253	2353
65	Castricum 466 d.	0117	...	...	*0620*	0704	...	0734	...	0804	...	0834	0904	0934	hour until	1934	2004	2034	2104	2204	2304	0004
77	**Alkmaar** 466 d.	0127	...	0616	0646	0716	0716	0746	0746	0816	0816	0846	0916	0946		1946	2016	2045	2116	2216	2316	0016
83	Heerhugowaard 466 a.	...	...	0624	0654	0724	0724	0754	0754	0824	0854	0854	0924	0954		1954	2024	*2058*	2124	2224	2324	0024
100	**Hoorn** a.	...	...	0640	0710	0740	0740	0810	0810	0840	0910	0910	0940	1010		2010	2040	...	2140	2240	2340	0040

	Ⓐ	Ⓐ	⚒	⚒		⚒			⚒														
Hoorn d.	0550	0620	0650	0720	0750	0820	...	0850	0920	...	0950	1020	and at	1820	1850	...	1920	1950	2050	2150	2250	2350
Heerhugowaard 466 d.	0606	0636	0706	0736	0806	0836	...	0906	0936	...	1006	1036	the same	1836	1906	...	1936	2006	2106	2206	2306	0006
Alkmaar 466 d.	0615	0645	0715	0745	0815	0845	0845	0915	0945	0945	1015	1045	minutes	1845	1915	...	1945	2015	2115	2215	2315	0014
Castricum 466 d.	0626	0656	0726	0756	0826	0856	0856	0926	0956	0956	1026	1056	past each	1856	1926	...	1956	2026	2126	2226	2326	...
Beverwijk d.	0638	0708	0738	0808	0838	0908	0908	0938	1008	1008	1038	1108	hour until	1908	1938	...	2008	2038	2138	2238	2338	...
Haarlem 450 a.	0648	0718	0748	0818	0848	0918	0918	0948	1018	1018	1048	1118		1918	1948	...	2018	2048	2148	2248	2348	...
Leiden Centraal 450 a.	0712	0742	0812a	0842a	0912a	0942a	...	1012a	1042a	...	1112a	1142a		1942a	2012a	...	...	...	...	...	...	...
Den Haag Centraal 450 a.	0727	0757	0827a	0857a	0927a	0957a	...	1027a	1057a	...	1127a	1157a		1957a	2027a	...	...	...	...	...	...	...

a – Ⓐ only.

LEIDEN - ALPHEN - UTRECHT and ALPHEN - GOUDA 463

km		Ⓐ	⚒	⚒							
0	**Leiden** Centraal d.	0552	0622	0652	0722	0752	and every	2252	2322	2352	0022
15	Alphen aan den Rijn △ d.	0607	0637	0707	0737	0807	30 minutes	2307	2337	0007	0037
34	Woerden d.	0623	0653	0723	0753	0823	until	2323	2353	0029*	0053
50	**Utrecht** Centraal a.	0635	0705	0735	0805	0835		2335	0005	0040*	0108

	Ⓐ	⚒	⚒					
Utrecht Centraal d.	0555	0625	0655	0725	0755	and every	2355	0025
Woerden d.	0606	0636	0706	0736	0806	30 minutes	0006	0036
Alphen aan den Rijn △ d.	0623	0653	0723	0753	0823	until	0023	0053
Leiden Centraal a.	0637	0707	0737	0807	0837		0037	0107

* – On the mornings of ⑥⑦ (also Apr. 6, May 6, 14, 25; not Dec. 26, 27, Jan. 2) departs Woerden 0023, arrives Utrecht 0035.

△ – Connecting lightrail services run **Alphen** - **Gouda** and v.v. *17 km.* Journey: 20–21 minutes. **From Alphen** at 0019, 0552 Ⓐ, 0619 Ⓐ, 0649 ⚒, 0719 ⚒, 0749 ⚒, 0819, 0849 ⚒ and then at 19 and 49 ⚒ minutes past each hour until 1919, 1949 ⚒; then 2019, 2119, 2219 and 2319. **From Gouda** at 0051, 0621 Ⓐ, 0651 Ⓐ, 0721 ⚒, 0751 ⚒, 0821 ⚒, 0851 and then at 21 ⚒ and 51 minutes past each hour until 2021 ⚒, 2051; then 2151, 2251 and 2351.

AMSTERDAM - GOUDA - ROTTERDAM 465

For fast trains **Amsterdam** – **Rotterdam**, see Table **450**

km		⚒	⚒	⚒						
0	**Amsterdam** Centraal d.	0617	0647	0717	0747	0817		2217	2247	2317
9	Duivendrecht d.	0628	0658	0728	0758	0828	and every	2228	2258	2328
27	Breukelen d.	0649	0719	0749	0819	0849	30 minutes	2249	2319	2349
40	Woerden d.	0658	0728	0758	0828	0858		2258	2328	2358
56	**Gouda** ‡ d.	0712	0742	0812	0842	0912	until	2312	2342	0012
70	Rotterdam Alexander ‡ d.	0724	0754	0824	0854	0924		2324	2354	0024
80	**Rotterdam** Centraal ‡ a.	0735	0805	0835	0905	0935		2335	0005	0045

	Ⓐ	Ⓐ	⚒	⚒					
Rotterdam Centraal ‡ d.	0525	0555	0625	0655	0725	0755		2255	2325
Rotterdam Alexander ‡ d.	0534	0604	0634	0704	0734	0804	and every	2304	2334
Gouda ‡ d.	0549	0619	0649	0719	0749	0819		2319	2349
Woerden d.	0602	0632	0702	0732	0802	0832	30 minutes	2332	0002
Breukelen d.	0611	0641	0711	0741	0811	0841	until	2341	0011
Duivendrecht d.	0630	0700	0730	0800	0830	0900		0000	0030
Amsterdam Centraal a.	0643	0713	0743	0813	0843	0913		0013	0043

‡ – See also Table **483**.

AMSTERDAM - ALKMAAR - DEN HELDER 466

km			②③h	J		①m	G	Ⓐ	Ⓐ	⚒	⑥t	Ⓐ	Ⓐ									E	D
	Arnhem 468 d.	...	...	...	...	...	...	...	...	...	...	...	...	0600a	0630v	0700v	0730	0800		2130	2200	2300	2300
	Utrecht Centraal 468 d.	...	0024	0024	...	...	...	...	...	...	...	...	...	0640v	0710	0740	0810	0840	and every	2210	2240	2340	2340
0	**Amsterdam** Centraal 459 d.	0027	0114	0116	...	0517	0518	...	0547	...	0617	0627	0642	0712	0742	0812	0842	0912	30 minutes	2242	2312	0012	0012
5	Amsterdam Sloterdijk 459 d.	0033	0120	0121	...	0522	0523	...	0552	...	0622	0632	0648	0718	0748	0818	0848	0918	until	2248	2318	0018	0019
12	Zaandam 459 d.	|	0126	0128	...	0529	0532	...	0559	...	0629	0639	0655	0725	0755	0825	0855	0925		2255	2325	0025	0026
29	Castricum 461 d.	0117	0146	0150	...	0550	0600	...	0620	...	0650	0651	0708	0738	0808	0838	0908	0938		2308	2338	0038	0042
41	**Alkmaar** 461 d.	0127	0157	0202	...	0601	0611	0620	0631	0650	0701	0704	0720	0750	0820	0850	0920	0950		2320	2350	0050	0054
48	Heerhugowaard 461 d.	...	0204	0209	...	...	...	0628	...	0658	...	...	0728	0758	0828	0858	0928	0958		2328	2358	0058	0103
83	**Den Helder** a.	...	...	...	...	...	...	0655	...	0725	...	...	0756	0826	0856	0926	0956	1026		2356	0026	0126	0131

	⚒	Ⓐ		Ⓐ	Ⓐ	Ⓒ	⚒	Ⓐ	Ⓒ	⚒	Ⓐ	⚒									E	①②d	③④e
Den Helder d.	...	0504	...	0534	0604	...	0634	0646	...	0704	0716	...	0734	0804		2134	2204	...	2234	...	2334	2334	2334
Heerhugowaard 461 d.	...	0530	...	0600	0630	...	0700	0712	...	0730	0742	...	0800	0830		2200	2230	...	2300	...	0000	0000	0000
Alkmaar 461 d.	0456	0542	0556	0612	0642	0656	0712	0726	0726	0742	0756	0756	0812	0842	and every	2212	2242	...	2312	2326	0012	0010	0016
Castricum 461 d.	0507	0551	0607	0621	0651	0707	0721	0737	0737	0751	0807	0807	0821	0851	30 minutes	2221	2251	...	2321	2337	0029	0021	0029
Zaandam 459 a.	0537	0604	0630	0634	0704	0730	0734	0750	0800	0804	0820	0820	0834	0904	until	2234	2304	...	2334	0000	0052	0105	0105
Amsterdam Sloterdijk 459 a.	0543	0612	0636	0641	0711	0736	0741	0757	0806	0811	0827	0827	0841	0911		2241	2311	...	2341	0005	0059	0111	0111
Amsterdam Centraal 459 a.	0548	0619	0643	0648	0718	0743	0748	0804	0813	0818	0834	0834	0848	0918		2248	2318	...	2348	0013	0104	0117	0117
Utrecht Centraal 468 a.	...	0650	...	0720	0750	...	0820	0835	...	0850	0905	0905	0920	0950		2320	2350	...	0020	...	...	...	...
Arnhem 468 a.	...	0730	...	0800	0830	...	0900	...	...	0930	...	...	1000	1030		2400	0030	...	...	...	...	...	...

D – ①–④ (not Apr. 5, May 5, 13, 24).
E – ⑤–⑦ (also Apr. 5, May 5, 13, 24).
G – ②–⑤ (not Apr. 6, May 6, 14, 25).
J – ①④⑤⑥⑦ (also Apr. 6, May 25).
a – Ⓐ only.
d – Not Apr. 5, May 24.
e – Not May 5, 13.
h – Not Apr. 6, May 25.
m – Not Apr. 5, May 24.
t – Also Apr. 5, 30, May 5, 13, 24; not Dec. 26.
v – ⚒ only.

AMSTERDAM and SCHIPHOL ✈ - ARNHEM - NIJMEGEN 468

For INTERNATIONAL TRAINS **Amsterdam** – **Arnhem** – **Köln**, see Table **28**

For NIGHT NETWORK **Rotterdam** – **Amsterdam** – **Utrecht**, see Table **454**

km		N	⑦w	②③z		Ⓐ	Ⓐ	L	①m	Ⓐ	Ⓐ	Ⓐ	⚒	⚒	⚒	Ⓐ	⚒	†	⚒		⚒		⚒	
	Den Helder 466 d.	...	...	...	...	...	...	...	...	...	...	0504	...	...	0534a	...	0604a	...	...	0634v	...	0704v	...	0734
	Alkmaar 466 d.	...	...	...	...	...	...	...	...	...	...	0542	...	...	0612a	...	0642a	...	...	0712v	...	0742v	...	0812
0	**Amsterdam** Centraal 470 d.	0023	0023	0026	...	...	...	0521	0529	...	...	0623	...	...	0653	...	0723	...	...	0753	...	0823	...	0853
5	Amsterdam Amstel 470 d.	0030	0030	0035	...	...	...	|	|	...	...	0630	...	...	0700	...	0730	...	...	0800	...	0830	...	0900
	Schiphol ✈ 470 d.	|	|	|	...	...	...	|	|	...	...	|	...	...	|	0659	|	...	0729	|	0759	|	0829	|
	Amsterdam Zuid 470 d.	|	|	|	...	...	...	|	|	...	...	|	...	...	|	0708	|	...	0738	|	0808	|	0838	|
39	**Utrecht** Centraal 470 a.	0049	0050	0054	...	...	...	0611	0613	...	...	0650	...	...	0720	0732	0750	...	0802	0820	0832	0850	0902	0920
39	**Utrecht** Centraal d.	0053	0053	0057	...	0553	0607	...	...	0623	0637	0653	0653	0707	0723	0737	0753	0753	0807	0823	0837	0853	0907	0923
79	Ede-Wageningen d.	0120	0123	0127	...	0619	0632	...	...	0648	0702	0718	0718	0732	0748	0802	0818	0820	0832	0848	0902	0918	0932	0948
96	**Arnhem** a.	0130	0136	0139	...	0630	0644	...	...	0700	0714	0730	0730	0744	0800	0814	0830	0830	0844	0900	0914	0930	0944	1000
96	**Arnhem** 475 d.	0136	0141	0144	...	0636	0650	...	...	0706	0720	0736	0736	0750a	0806	0820	0836	0836	0850a	0906	0920a	0936	0950	1006
114	**Nijmegen** 475 a.	0150	0155	0158	...	0650	0703	...	...	0719	0733	0750	0750	0803a	0819	0833	0850	0850	0903a	0919	0933a	0950	1003	1019

	⚒		⚒		⚒		⚒		⚒														
Den Helder 466 d.	...	0804	...	0834	...	0904	...	0934	...	1004	...	1034	...		1904	...	1934	...	2004	2034	2104	2134	2204
Alkmaar 466 d.	...	0842	...	0912	...	0942	...	1012	...	1042	...	1112	...		1942	...	2012	...	2042	2112	2142	2212	2242
Amsterdam Centraal 470 d.	...	0923	...	0953	...	1023	...	1053	...	1123	...	1153	...	and at	2023	...	2053	...	2123	2153	2223	2253	2323
Amsterdam Amstel 470 d.	...	0930	...	1000	...	1030	...	1100	...	1130	...	1200	...	the same	2030	...	2100	...	2130	2200	2230	2300	2330
Schiphol ✈ 470 d.	0859	|	0929	|	0959	|	1029	|	1059	|	1129	|	1159	minutes	|	2029	|	2059	|	|	|	|	|
Amsterdam Zuid 470 d.	0908	|	0938	|	1008	|	1038	|	1108	|	1138	|	1208	past each	|	2038	|	2108	|	|	|	|	|
Utrecht Centraal 470 a.	0932	0950	1002	1020	1032	1050	1102	1120	1132	1150	1202	1220	1232	hour until	2050	2102	2120	2132	2150	2220	2250	2320	2350
Utrecht Centraal d.	0937	0953	1007	1023	1037	1053	1107	1123	1137	1153	1207	1223	1237		2053	2107	2123	2137	2153	2223	2253	2323	2353
Ede-Wageningen d.	1002	1018	1032	1048	1102	1118	1132	1148	1202	1218	1232	1248	1302		2118	2132	2148	2202	2220	2250	2320	2350	0020
Arnhem a.	1014	1030	1044	1100	1114	1130	1144	1200	1214	1230	1244	1300	1314		2130	2144	2200	2214	2230	2300	2330	2400	0030
Arnhem 475 d.	1020	1036	1050	1106	1120	1136	1150	1206	1220	1236	1250	1306	1320		2136	2150	2206	2220	2236	2306	2336	0006	0036
Nijmegen 475 a.	1033	1050	1103	1119	1133	1150	1203	1219	1233	1250	1303	1319	1333		2150	2203	2219	2233	2250	2319	2350	0020	0050

L – ②–⑤ (not Dec. 25, Jan. 1, Apr. 30, May 5, 13).
N – ①④⑤⑥ (also Dec. 27; not May 1, 6, 14).
a – Ⓐ only.
m – Not Apr. 5, May 24.
v – ⚒ only.
w – Also Apr. 6, May 1, 6, 14, 25; not Dec. 27.
z – Not Apr. 6, May 25.

468 NIJMEGEN - ARNHEM - SCHIPHOL ✈ and AMSTERDAM

For INTERNATIONAL TRAINS **Köln – Arnhem – Amsterdam**, see Table **28** For NIGHT NETWORK **Utrecht – Amsterdam – Rotterdam**, see Table **454**

km		Ⓐ	Ⓐ	⚒	Ⓐ	⚒		⚒	⚒		⚒		⚒	†	⚒	⚒		⚒		⚒		⚒		⚒
	Nijmegen 475 d.	...	0534	...	...	0609	...	0627a	0639	...	0656a	0709	0727a	0734	0739	0756a	0809	0827a	0839	0856a	0909	0927	0939	0956
	Arnhem 475 a.	...	0554	...	...	0624	...	0640a	0654	...	0710a	0724	0740a	0754	0754	0810a	0824	0840a	0854	0910a	0924	0940	0954	1010
	Arnhem d.	0546	0600	...	0616	0630	...	0646	0700	...	0716	0730	0746	0800	0800	0816	0830	0846	0900	0916	0930	0946	1000	1016
	Ede-Wageningen d.	0557	0611	...	0627	0641	...	0657	0711	...	0727	0741	0757	0811	0811	0827	0841	0857	0911	0927	0941	0957	1011	1027
	Utrecht Centraal a.	0624	0637	...	0653	0707	...	0723	0737	...	0753	0808	0823	0838	0837	0853	0908	0923	0938	0953	1008	1023	1038	1053
0	**Utrecht** Centraal 470 d.	0628	0640	0640	0658	0710	0710	0728	0740	0740	0758	0810	0828	0840	0840	0858	0910	0928	0940	0958	1010	1028	1040	1058
36	Amsterdam Zuid 470 a.	0651	|	|	0721	|	|	0751	|	|	0821	|	0851	|	|	0921	|	0951	|	1021	|	1051	|	1121
45	**Schiphol** ✈ 470 a.	0659	|	|	0729	|	|	0759	|	|	0829	|	0859	|	|	0929	|	0959	|	1029	|	1059	|	1129
	Amsterdam Amstel 470 a.	...	0658	0658	...	0728	0728	...	0758	0758	...	0828	...	0858	0858	...	0928	...	0958	...	1028	...	1058	...
	Amsterdam Centraal 470 a.	...	0707	0707	...	0737	0737	...	0807	0807	...	0837	...	0907	0907	...	0937	...	1007	...	1037	...	1107	...
	Alkmaar 466 a.	...	0748	0748	...	0818	0818	...	0848	0848	...	0918	...	0948	0948	...	1018	...	1048	...	1118	...	1148	...
	Den Helder 466 a.	...	0826	0826	...	0856	0856	...	0926	0926	...	0956	...	1026	1026	...	1056	...	1126	...	1156	...	1226	...

		⚒																			H	G
Nijmegen 475 d.	1009	1027	1039	1056	1109	1127	1139	and at	1856	1909	1927	1939	1956	2009	2027	2039	2109	2139	2209	2239	2309	...	...
Arnhem 475 a.	1024	1040	1054	1110	1124	1140	1154	the same	1910	1924	1940	1954	2010	2024	2040	2054	2124	2154	2224	2254	2324	...	...
Arnhem d.	1030	1046	1100	1116	1130	1146	1200	minutes	1916	1930	1946	2000	2016	2030	2046	2100	2130	2200	2230	2300	2330	...	...
Ede-Wageningen d.	1041	1057	1111	1127	1141	1157	1211	past each	1927	1941	1957	2011	2027	2041	2057	2111	2141	2211	2241	2311	2341	...	...
Utrecht Centraal a.	1108	1123	1138	1153	1207	1223	1237	hour until	1953	2007	2023	2037	2053	2107	2123	2138	2208	2238	2308	2338	0008	...	...
Utrecht Centraal 470 d.	1110	1128	1140	1158	1210	1228	1240		1958	2010	2028	2040	...	2110	...	2140	2210	2240	2310	2340	...	0025	0026
Amsterdam Zuid 470 a.	|	1151	|	1221	|	1251	|		2021	|	2051	|	...	|	...	|	|	|	|	|	...	|	|
Schiphol ✈ 470 a.	|	1159	|	1229	|	1259	|		2029	|	2059	|	...	|	...	|	|	|	|	|	...	|	|
Amsterdam Amstel 470 a.	1128	...	1158	...	1228	...	1258		...	2028	...	2058	...	2128	...	2158	2228	2258	2328	2358	...	0043	0051
Amsterdam Centraal 470 a.	1137	...	1207	...	1237	...	1307		...	2037	...	2107	...	2137	...	2207	2237	2307	2337	0007	...	0052	0101
Alkmaar 466 a.	1218	...	1248	...	1318	...	1348		...	2118	...	2148	...	2218	...	2248	2318	2348	...	0048j	...	...	...
Den Helder 466 a.	1256	...	1326	...	1356	...	1426		...	2156	...	2226	...	2256	...	2326	2356	0026	...	0126j	...	...	...

G – ②–⑤ (not Apr. 6, May 6, 14, 25). H – ①⑥⑦ (also Apr. 6, May 6, 14, 25). a – Ⓐ only. j – 4–5 minutes later on the mornings of ②–⑤ (not Apr. 6, May 6, 14, 25).

470 AMSTERDAM and SCHIPHOL ✈ - EINDHOVEN - MAASTRICHT and HEERLEN

For NIGHT NETWORK **Amsterdam – Utrecht – Eindhoven**, see Table **454**

km		Ⓐ	Ⓐ	Ⓐ	Ⓐ	Ⓐ	Ⓐ	⚒	Ⓐ		⚒		⚒							❖	L	①m		
0	**Amsterdam** Centraal 468 d.	...	...	...	*0417*	...	0608	...	0638	...	0708	...	0738	...	0808	0838		2108	2138	2208	2238	2238	2307	2338
6	Amsterdam Amstel 468 d.	...	...	...	|	...	0615	...	0645	...	0715	...	0745	...	0815	0845		2115	2145	2215	2245	2245	2315	2345
40	**Utrecht** Centraal 468 a.	...	...	...	*0452*	...	0635	...	0705	...	0735	...	0805	...	0835	0905		2135	2205	2235	2305	2305	2335	0005
40	**Utrecht** Centraal d.	...	...	...	0513	...	0638	...	0708	...	0738	...	0808	0808	0838	0908		2138	2208	2238	2308	2308	2338	...
88	's-Hertogenbosch d.	...	...	*0546*	0557	*0613*	0708	...	0738	...	0808	...	0838	0838	0908	0938		2208	2238	2308	2338	2338	0008	...
120	**Eindhoven** a.	...	...	*0614*	...	*0641*	0728	...	0758	...	0828	...	0858	0858	0928	0958		2228	2258	2328	2358	2358	0027	...
120	**Eindhoven** d.	...	...	0632	...	0702	0732	0732	0802	0802	0832	0832	0902	0902	0932	1002	and every	2232	2302	2332	0002	0002	...	...
149	Weert d.	...	...	0647	...	0717	0747	0747	0817	0817	0847	0847	0917	0917	0947	1017	30 minutes	2247	2317	2347	0017	0020	...	...
173	Roermond d.	...	0639	0703	...	0733	0803	0803	0833	0833	0903	0903	0933	0933	1003	1033	until	2303	2333	0002	0033	0040	...	...
197	Sittard a.	...	0658	0718	...	0748	0818	0818	0848	0848	0918	0918	0948	0948	1018	1048		2318	2348	0018	0048	0058	...	...
197	Sittard d.	0630	0700	0720	...	0750	0820	0820	0850	0850	0920	0920	0950	0950	1020	1050		2320	2350	0019	0050	0100	...	...
219	**Maastricht** a.	0650	0720	0734	...	0804	0834	0834	0904	0904	0934	0934	1004	1004	1035	1104		2334	0005	0034	0106	0115	...	...
			Ⓐ	Ⓐ		Ⓐ	Ⓐ	⚒	Ⓐ		⚒		⚒											
				△		△	△	△	△	△	△	△	△	△	△	△		△	△	△	△	△		
197	Sittard d.	...	0704	0722	...	0752	0822	0822	0852	0852	0922	0922	0952	0952	1022	1052		2322	2352	0022	0052z	0101	...	...
216	**Heerlen** a.	...	0726	0737	...	0807	0837	0837	0907	0907	0937	0937	1007	1007	1037	1107		2337	0007	0037	0109z	0116	...	...

	Ⓐ	Ⓐ	Ⓐ	Ⓐ	⚒	⚒		⚒									E	D						
Heerlen d.	...	...	0523	0553	...	0623	...	0653	...	...	0723	0753		2053	2123	2153	2223	2223	2253	2303	2353	...	...	...
Sittard a.	...	...	0538	0608	...	0638	...	0708	...	...	0738	0808		2108	2138	2208	2238	2238	2308	2326	0008	...	...	...
			▽	▽		▽		▽		...	▽	▽		●	●	●	●	●	●	●				
			Ⓐ	Ⓐ		⚒		⚒		...							E	D				N⊖	†	①m
Maastricht d.	...	...	0523	0553	...	0626	...	0656	...	...	0726	0756		2056	2126	2156	2226	2226	2256	2310	...	2356	2356	2356
Sittard a.	...	...	0540	0610	...	0640	...	0710	...	...	0740	0810		2110	2140	2210	2240	2240	2310	2330	...	0010	0010	0010
Sittard d.	...	...	0543	0613	...	0643	...	0713	...	...	0743	0813	and every	2113	2143	2213	2243	2243	2313	2332	...	0013	0018	0013
Roermond d.	...	...	0559	0629	...	0659	...	0729	...	...	0759	0829	30 minutes	2129	2159	2229	2259	2259	2329	2351	...	0029	0034	0039
Weert d.	...	...	0612	0642	...	0712	...	0742	...	...	0812	0842	until	2142	2212	2242	2312	2312	2342	...	...	0042	0047	0052
Eindhoven a.	...	...	0629	0659	...	0729	...	0759	...	...	0829	0859		2159	2229	2259	2329	2329	2359	...	...	0059	0104	0108
Eindhoven d.	0532	0602	0632	0702	0702	0732	0732	0802	0802	...	0832	0902		2202	2232	2302	2332	2332	*0019*	...	...	...	...	...
's-Hertogenbosch d.	0553	0623	0653	0723	0723	0753	0753	0823	0823	...	0853	0923		2223	2253	2323	2353	2353	*0047*	...	...	...	...	...
Utrecht Centraal a.	0623	0652	0722	0752	0752	0822	0822	0852	0852	...	0922	0952		2252	2322	2352	0022	0022	...	...	...	...	...	...
Utrecht Centraal 468 d.	0625	0655	0725	0755	0755	0825	0825	0855	0855	...	0925	0955		2255	2325	2355	0025	0025	...	...	...	...	...	...
Amsterdam Amstel 468 a.	0643	0713	0743	0813	0813	0843	0843	0913	0913	...	0943	1013		2313	2343	0013	0043	0051	...	...	...	...	...	...
Amsterdam Centraal 468 a.	0652	0722	0752	0822	0822	0852	0852	0922	0922	...	0952	1022		2322	2352	0022	0052	0101	...	...	...	...	...	...

SCHIPHOL ✈ - EINDHOVEN

	Ⓐ	Ⓐ	⚒						
Schiphol ✈ 468 ‡ d.	0614	0644	0644	0714	0744	and every	1914	1944	...
Amsterdam Zuid 468 ‡ d.	0623	0653	0653	0723	0753	30 minutes	1923	1953	...
Utrecht Centraal 468 ‡ a.	0647	0717	0717	0747	0817	until	1947	2017	...
Utrecht Centraal d.	0652	0722	...	0752	0822		1952	2022	...
's-Hertogenbosch a.	0721	0751	...	0821	0851		2021	2051	...
Eindhoven a.	0746	0816	...	0846	0916		2046	2116	...

	Ⓐ	Ⓐ	Ⓐ	⚒					
Eindhoven d.	0614	0644	0714	...	0744	0814	and every	1914	1944
's-Hertogenbosch d.	0638	0708	0738	...	0808	0838	30 minutes	1938	2008
Utrecht Centraal a.	0707	0737	0807	...	0837	0907	until	2007	2037
Utrecht Centraal 468 § d.	0713	0743	0813	0813	0843	0913		2013	2043
Amsterdam Zuid 468 § a.	0736	0806	0836	0836	0906	0936		2036	2106
Schiphol ✈ 468 § a.	0744	0814	0844	0844	0914	0944		2044	2114

D – ①–④ (not Apr. 5, May 5, 13, 24).
E – ⑤–⑦ (also Apr. 5, May 5, 13, 24).
L – ②–⑦ (also Apr. 5, May 24).
N – ②–⑥ (also Apr. 5, May 24; not Dec. 25, 26, Jan. 1).
m – Not Apr. 5, May 24.

z – On ⑥⑦ (also Apr. 6, May 6, 14, 25; not Dec. 26, 27, Jan. 2) Sittard 0101, Heerlen 0116.
‡ – Additional trains Schiphol ✈ - Utrecht at 2014 and every 30 minutes until 2344.
§ – Additional trains Utrecht - Schiphol ✈ at 2113 and every 30 minutes until 2343.

❖ – Timings at Sittard, Maastricht and Heerlen are up to 11 minutes later on certain dates.
⊖ – Timings at Roermond, Weert and Eindhoven are up to 8 minutes later on certain dates.
△ – Heerlen portion detached from train above at Sittard (Heerlen arrivals at 2207 on ©, 2237 on © and 2307 on † require a change of trains at Sittard).
▽ – Heerlen portion attached to train below at Sittard (Heerlen departures at 1923 on ⚒, 1953 on Ⓐ and 2023 on ⚒ require a change of trains at Sittard).
● – Change trains at Sittard.

471 MAASTRICHT - HEERLEN - KERKRADE and AACHEN

km	See note ⊠	Ⓐ	Ⓐ	⚒	⚒								Ⓐ		Ⓐ	⚒		⚒			
0	**Maastricht** d.	0515	0545	0615	0645	0715	0745	and at the	2245	2315	...	A	0700	and every	0930	1000	and every	1230	1300	and every	2230
11	Valkenburg d.	0527	0557	0627	0657	0727	0757	same minutes	2257	2327	...	L	0711	30 minutes	0941	1011	30 minutes	1241	1311	30 minutes	2241
24	**Heerlen** d.	0544	0614	0644	0714	0744	0814	past each	2314	2344	...	S	0722	until	0952	1022	until	1252	1322	until	2252
33	**Kerkrade** Centrum a.	0557	0627	0657	0727	0757	0827	hour until	2327	2357	...	O	...		...	...		...	...		...

See note ⊠	Ⓐ	Ⓐ	⚒	⚒								Ⓐ		Ⓐ	⚒		⚒			
Kerkrade Centrum d.	...	...	0600a	0630	0700v	0730	0800	and at the	2230	2300	...	A	...	and every	...	...	and every	...	...	and every	...
Heerlen d.	0515	0545	0615	0645	0715	0745	0815	same minutes	2245	2315	...	L	0630	30 minutes	0900	0930	30 minutes	1200	1230	30 minutes	2200
Valkenburg d.	0530	0600	0630	0700	0730	0800	0830	past each	2300	2330	...	S	0641	until	0911	0941	until	1211	1241	until	2211
Maastricht a.	0544	0614	0644	0714	0744	0814	0844	hour until	2314	2344	...	O	0652		0922	0954		1222	1252		2222

HEERLEN - AACHEN

km		A	E			⊡				
0	**Heerlen** d.	0528	0628	...	0728	and	2228	...	...	...
10	Herzogenrath 🏛 802 a.	0543	0643	...	0743	hourly	2243	...	...	...
24	**Aachen** Hbf 802 a.	0601	0701	...	0801	until	2301	...	...	...

	A	E			⊡			
Aachen Hbf 802 d.	0632	0732	...	0832	and	2332	...	...
Herzogenrath 🏛 802 d.	0650	0750	...	0850	hourly	2350	...	...
Heerlen a.	0706	0806	...	0906	until	0006	...	...

A – ①–⑤ (not Dec. 24, 25, 31, Jan. 1, Apr. 2, 5, May 13, 24, June 3).
E – ①–⑥ (not Dec. 25, 26, Jan. 1, Apr. 2, 5, May 1, 13, 24, June 3).
a – Ⓐ only.
v – ⚒ only.
⊡ – Last trains on Dec. 31: From Heerlen at 1928, from Aachen at 1832.
⊠ – Operated by **Veolia** (NS tickets valid).

DEN HAAG - EINDHOVEN - VENLO 472

For NIGHT NETWORK **Amsterdam** – **Den Haag** – **Rotterdam** – **Eindhoven**, see Table **454**

km		Ⓐ	Ⓐ	Ⓐ		①m	A	Ⓐ	Ⓐ	⚒	⚒	⚒											
0	**Den Haag** Centraal .... **450** d.	...	...	...	...	0458	0458	...	0551	...	0621	0651	...	...	0721	0751		2121	2151	...	2221	...	2251
2	**Den Haag** HS .... **450** d.	...	...	...	...	0503	0502	...	0556	...	0626	0656	...	...	0726	0756		2126	2156	...	2226	...	2256
10	Delft .... **450** d.	...	...	...	...	0515	0517	...	0603	...	0633	0703	...	...	0733	0803		2133	2203	...	2233	...	2303
24	**Rotterdam** Centraal ...... **450** a.	...	...	...	...	0530	0532	...	0615	...	0645	0715	...	...	0745	0815	and every	2145	2215	...	2245	...	2315
24	**Rotterdam** Centraal ...... **450** d.	...	...	...	...	0532	0533	0547	0617	0617	0647	0717	...	...	0747	0817	30 minutes	2147	2217	...	2247	...	2317
44	Dordrecht .... **450** d.	...	...	...	...	0555	0557	0601	0631	0631	0701	0731	...	...	0801	0831	until	2201	2231	...	2301	...	2331
74	Breda .... **450 475** d.	0540	...	...	...	...	...	0621	0651	0651	0721	0751	...	...	0821	0851		2221	2251	...	2321	...	2351
95	Tilburg .... **475** d.	0553	0558	...	...	...	...	0636	0706	0706	0736	0806	...	...	0836	0906		2236	2306	...	2336	...	0006
132	**Eindhoven** .... a.	...	0627	...	...	...	...	0700	0730	0730	0800	0830	...	...	0900	0930		2300	2330	...	2400	...	0030
132	**Eindhoven** .... d.	...	...	0633	...	...	...	0702	0732	0732	0802	0832	0832	...	0902	0932		2302	2332	...	...	0018	0032
145	Helmond .... d.	...	...	0642	...	...	...	0711	0741	0741	0811	0841	0841	...	0911	0941		2311	2341	...	...	0031	0041
183	**Venlo** .... a.	...	...	0713	...	...	...	0743	0813	0813	0843	0913	0913	...	0943	1013		2343	0013	...	...	...	0113

	Ⓐ	Ⓐ	Ⓐ	Ⓐ	⚒	⚒									E	D							
Venlo .... d.	...	...	0549	0619	...	0649	...	...	0719	0749		2119	2149	...	2219	2219	2249	...	2319	...	...	...	...
Helmond .... d.	...	...	0620	0650	...	0720	...	...	0750	0820		2150	2220	...	2250	2250	2320	...	2350	...	...	...	...
Eindhoven .... a.	...	...	0630	0700	...	0730	...	...	0800	0830		2200	2230	...	2300	2300	2330	...	2400	...	...	...	...
Eindhoven .... d.	0529	0602	0632	0702	0702	0732	0732	...	0802	0832		2202	2232	...	2302	2302	2332	...	...	...	...	...	...
Tilburg .... **475** d.	0555	0625	0655	0725	0725	0755	0755	...	0825	0855	and every	2225	2255	...	2325	2325	2355	...	...	...	...	...	...
Breda .... **450 475** d.	0609	0639	0709	0739	0739	0809	0809	...	0839	0909	30 minutes	2239	2309	...	2339	2339	0009	...	...	...	...	...	...
Dordrecht .... **450** d.	0629	0659	0729	0759	0759	0829	0829	...	0859	0929	until	2259	2329	...	2359	2359	0029	...	...	...	...	...	...
Rotterdam Centraal ...... **450** a.	0642	0712	0742	0812	0812	0842	0842	...	0912	0942		2312	2342	...	0012	0012	0042	...	...	...	...	...	...
Rotterdam Centraal ...... **450** d.	0646	0716	0746	0816	0816	0846	0846	...	0916	0946		2316	2346	...	0016	*0039*	...	0102	...	...	...	...	...
Delft .... **450** a.	0658	0728	0758	0828	0828	0858	0858	...	0928	0958		2328	2358	...	0028	*0054*	...	0114n	...	...	...	...	...
Den Haag HS .... **450** a.	0705	0735	0805	0835	0835	0905	0905	...	0935	1005		2335	0005	...	0035	*0105*	...	0122	...	...	...	...	...
Den Haag Centraal .... **450** a.	0710	0740	0810	0840	0840	0910	0910	...	0940	1010		2340	0010	...	0040	*0110*	...	...	...	...	...	...	...

A – ②–⑤ (not Dec. 25, Jan. 1, Apr. 30, May 5, 13).
D – ①–④ (not Apr. 5, May 5, 13, 24).
E – ⑤–⑦ (also Apr. 5, May 5, 13, 24).
m – Not Apr. 5, May 24.
n – Not ③.

ROOSENDAAL - 's-HERTOGENBOSCH - NIJMEGEN - ARNHEM - ZWOLLE 475

km		Ⓐ	Ⓐ	Ⓐ	⚒	Ⓐ	⚒	Ⓒ	Ⓐ	†	⚒	†	⚒									H		G	
0	**Roosendaal** .... d.	...	...	...	...	0521	...	...	0551	...	0621	0645	0651	...	0721	0751		2121	2151	...	2221	...	2251	...	2321
23	Breda .... **472** d.	...	...	...	...	0540	...	...	0610	...	0640	0704	0710	...	0740	0810		2140	2210	...	2240	...	2310	...	2340
44	Tilburg .... **472** d.	...	...	...	...	0554	...	...	0624	...	0654	0724	0724	...	0754	0824		2154	2224	...	2254	...	2324	...	2354
67	**'s-Hertogenbosch** .... d.	...	...	...	...	0614	...	...	0644	...	0714	0744	0744	...	0814	0844		2214	2244	...	2314	...	2344	...	0010
86	Oss .... d.	...	...	...	...	0626	...	...	0656	...	0726	0756	0756	...	0826	0856	and every	2226	2256	...	2326	...	2356	...	...
110	**Nijmegen** .... **468** d.	...	*0534*	0615	...	0645	0645	*0709*	0715	*0734*	0745	0815	0815	...	0845	0915	30 minutes	2245	2315	...	2345	0003	0015	...	...
129	**Arnhem** .... **468** a.	...	*0554*	0636	...	0706	0706	*0724*	0736	*0754*	0806	0836	0836	...	0906	0936	until	2306	2336	...	0006	0021	0036	...	...
129	**Arnhem** .... d.	...	0600	0640	...	0710	0710	0740	0740	0810	0810	0840	0840	...	0910	0940		2310	2340	...	...	0023	...	0053	...
145	Dieren .... d.	...	0619	0652	...	0722	0722	0752	0752	0822	0822	0852	0852	...	0922	0952		2322	2352	...	...	0042	...	0111	...
159	Zutphen .... d.	0604	0634	0704	0704	0734	0734	0804	0804	0834	0834	0904	0904	...	0934	1004		2334	0004	...	...	0054	...	0124	...
174	Deventer .... d.	0619	0649	0719	0719	0749	0749	0819	0819	0849	0849	0919	0919	...	0949	1019		2349	0019	...	...	...	...	...	...
204	**Zwolle** .... a.	0643	0713	0743	0743	0813	0813	0843	0843	0913	0913	0943	0943	...	1013	1043		0013	0043	...	...	...	...	...	...

	Ⓐ	Ⓐ	Ⓐ	Ⓐ		⚒		⚒		⚒									P	④q		W	P	④q	
Zwolle .... d.	...	...	...	...	...	...	...	0618a	...	0648a	...	0718v	...	0748	0818		2118	2148	2218	2218	2248	...	2318	2318	2348
Deventer .... d.	...	...	...	...	...	...	...	0644a	...	0714a	...	0744v	...	0814	0844		2144	2214	2244	2244	2314	...	2344	2344	0014
Zutphen .... d.	...	...	...	0552	...	*0606*a	...	0657	...	0727	...	0757	...	0827	0857		2157	2227	2257	2257	2327	...	2357	2357	0027
Dieren .... d.	...	...	...	0602	...	*0616*a	...	0707	...	0737	...	0807	...	0837	0907		2207	2237	2307	2307	2337	...	0007	|	0037
Arnhem .... a.	...	...	...	0622	...	*0637*a	...	0720	...	0750	...	0820	...	0850	0920	and every	2220	2250	2320	2320	2350	...	0019	0020	0050
Arnhem .... **468** d.	...	...	0554	0624	...	0654	...	0724	...	0754	0754	0824	...	0854	0924	30 minutes	2224	2254	2324	2324	2354	...	*0036*	*0036*	*0136*
Nijmegen .... **468** d.	...	...	0618	0648	...	0718	...	0748	...	0818	0818	0848	...	0918	0948	until	2248	2318	2348	2348	0014	0023	*0050*	*0050*	*0155*
Oss .... d.	...	...	0633	0703	...	0733	...	0803	...	0833	0833	0903	...	0933	1003		2303	2333	0003	0003	...	0044	...	...	...
's-Hertogenbosch .... d.	...	0619	0649	0719	0719v	0749	0749	0819	0819	0849	0849	0919	...	0949	1019		2319	2349	0019	0025t	...	0102	...	...	...
Tilburg .... **472** d.	*0555*	0637	0707	0737	0737v	0807	0807	0837	0837	0907	0907	0937	...	1007	1037		2337	0007	0037	0047t	...	...	...	...	...
Breda .... **472** d.	0622	0652	0722	0752	0752	0822	0822	0852	0852	0922	0922	0952	...	1022	1052		2352	0022	0057	0108	...	...	...	...	...
Roosendaal .... a.	0641	0711	0741	0811	0811	0841	0841	0911	0911	0941	0941	1011	...	1041	1111		0011	0041	0119	0125	...	...	...	...	...

G – ②–⑤ (not Apr. 6, May 6, 14, 25).
H – ①⑥⑦ (also Apr. 6, May 6, 14, 25).
P – ①②③⑤⑥⑦ (also May 13).
W – Runs 14 minutes later on ②–⑤ (not Apr. 6, May 6, 14, 25).
a – Ⓐ only.
q – Not May 13.
t – Arrives 7 minutes earlier.
v – ⚒ only.

NIJMEGEN - VENLO - ROERMOND 477

Operated by **Veolia** (NS tickets valid)

km					Ⓐ	Ⓐ		Ⓐ	⚒	Ⓐ	⚒	⚒		⚒											
0	**Nijmegen** .... d.	0008	...	...	...	...	...	0538	...	0608	...	0638	...	0708	...	...	0738	0808	and every	2238	2308	...	2338	...	...
24	Boxmeer .... d.	0030	...	...	...	...	...	0600	...	0630	...	0700	...	0730	...	...	0800	0830	30 minutes	2300	2330	...	0000	...	...
39	Venray .... d.	0045	...	...	...	...	...	0615	...	0645	...	0715	...	0745	...	...	0815	0845	until	2315	2345	...	0015	...	...
61	**Venlo** .... d.	0101	...	...	0534	0604	...	0634	0634	0704	0704	0734	0734	0804	0804	...	0834	0904		2334	0004	...	0031	...	...
84	**Roermond** .... a.	...	...	...	0557	0627	...	0657	0657	0727	0727	0757	0757	0827	0827	...	0857	0927		2357	0027	...	...	...	...

					Ⓐ	Ⓐ	⚒	Ⓐ	⚒	Ⓐ		⚒		⚒											
Roermond .... d.	0006	0036	...	...	...	...	...	0606	...	0636	...	0706	...	0736	...	...	0806	0836	and every	2236	2306	...	2336	...	...
Venlo .... d.	0028	0058	...	...	0500	0530	0600	0630	0630	0700	0700	0730	0730	0800	0800	...	0830	0900	30 minutes	2300	2330	...	2358	...	...
Venray .... d.	...	...	...	...	0517	0547	0617	0647	0647	0717	0717	0747	0747	0817	0817	...	0847	0917	until	2317	2347	...	...	...	...
Boxmeer .... d.	...	...	...	...	0530	0600	0630	0700	0700	0730	0730	0800	0800	0830	0830	...	0900	0930		2330	0000	...	...	...	...
Nijmegen .... a.	...	...	...	...	0551	0621	0651	0721	0721	0751	0751	0821	0821	0851	0851	...	0921	0951		2351	0021	...	...	...	...

ARNHEM - TIEL - GELDERMALSEN - UTRECHT and 's-HERTOGENBOSCH 478

km		Ⓐ	Ⓐ	⚒	⚒													
0	**Tiel** .... d.	0552	0622	0652	0722	0752	0822	and every	1952	2022	...	2052	2105	2135	2205	2235	2305	2335
12	Geldermalsen .... a.	0604	0634	0704	0734	0804	0834	30 minutes	2004	2034	...	2104	2116	2146	2216	2247	2316	2347
38	**Utrecht** Centraal .... a.	0632	0702	0732	0802	0832	0902	until	2032	2102	...	2132	2147	2217	2247	2319	2347	0019

	Ⓐ	Ⓐ	Ⓐ	⚒														
Utrecht Centraal .... d.	0528	0558	0628	0658	0728	0758	and every	1928	1958	...	2013	2043	2113	2144	2213	2244	2313	2344
Geldermalsen .... d.	0552	0622	0652	0722	0752	0822	30 minutes	1952	2022	...	2038	2108	2138	2208	2238	2308	2338	0008
Tiel .... a.	0605	0635	0705	0735	0805	0835	until	2005	2035	...	2049	2120	2149	2220	2249	2320	2349	0020

s – Not Dec. 26, Jan. 2, May 1.
t – Also Apr. 5, 30, May 5, 13, 24; not Dec. 26.

ARNHEM - TIEL and v.v. Operated by ***Syntus*** (NS tickets valid). 2nd class only. *44 km*. Journey time: 37 – 39 minutes.
From Arnhem at 0031⑥**s**, 0631Ⓐ, 0701Ⓐ, 0731Ⓐ, 0801Ⓐ, 0831⚒, 0931, 1031 and hourly until 1531; then 1601Ⓐ, 1631, 1701Ⓐ, 1731, 1801Ⓐ, 1831, 1931, 2031, 2131, 2231 and 2331.
From Tiel at 0618Ⓐ, 0648Ⓐ, 0718Ⓐ, 0748⚒, 0818Ⓐ, 0848, 0948 and hourly until 1548; then 1618Ⓐ, 1648, 1718Ⓐ, 1748, 1818Ⓐ, 1848, 1948, 2048, 2151, 2251 and 2351⑥**t**.

GELDERMALSEN - 's-HERTOGENBOSCH and v.v. *22 km*. Journey time: 16 – 17 minutes.
From Geldermalsen at 0540Ⓐ, 0609Ⓐ, 0639Ⓐ, 0709⚒, 0739, 0809, 0839 and every 30 minutes until 2139; then 2239 and 2339.
From 's-Hertogenbosch at 0532Ⓐ, 0602Ⓐ, 0632Ⓐ, 0702⚒, 0732⚒, 0802, 0832 and every 30 minutes until 2202; then 2302.

DORDRECHT - GELDERMALSEN 479

Operated by **Arriva** (NS tickets valid); 2nd class only

km		Ⓐ	⚒	⚒						
0	**Dordrecht** .... d.	0437	0507	0537	0607	0637	and every	2337	0007	0037
10	Sliedrecht .... d.	0447	0517	0547	0617	0647	30 minutes	2347	0017	0047
24	Gorinchem .... d.	0502	0532	0602	0632	0702	until	0002	0032	0058
49	**Geldermalsen** .... a.	0533	0603	0633	0703	0733		0033	0103	...

	Ⓐ	⚒	⚒	⚒						
Geldermalsen .... d.	0539	...	0609	0639	...	0709	0739	and every	0039	0109
Gorinchem .... d.	0604	0604	0634	0704	0704	0734	0804	30 minutes	0104	0134
Sliedrecht .... d.	0616	0616	0646	0716	0716	0746	0816	until	0116	0146
Dordrecht .... a.	0626	0626	0656	0726	0726	0756	0826		0126	0156

480 AMSTERDAM and SCHIPHOL ✈ - AMERSFOORT - DEVENTER - ENSCHEDE

AMSTERDAM CENTRAAL - AMERSFOORT (all trains)

km			⑥⑦d	A	⑥⑦d	Ⓐ	Ⓐ	⚒	Ⓐ	⚒	⚒		⚒											
	Enkhuizen 459 d.	...	...	...	...	...	...	0524a	...	0554	...	0624a	...	0654v	...	0724	...	0754	and at the same minutes past each hour until	...	2154	...	2224	...
0	**Amsterdam** Centraal **458** d.	0005	0035	0043	0135	0557	0605	0627	0635	0657	0705	0727	0735	0757	0805	0827	0835	0857		2235	2257	2305	2327	2335
14	Weesp 457 458 d.	0022	0052	0100	0152	|	0622	|	0652	|	0722	|	0752	|	0822	|	0852	|		2252	|	2322	|	2352
23	Naarden-Bussum 457 d.	0029	0059	0108	0159	|	0629	|	0659	|	0729	|	0759	|	0829	|	0859	|		2259	|	2329	|	2359
29	Hilversum 457 d.	0039	0109	0118	0209	0618	0639	0648	0709	0718	0739	0748	0809	0818	0839	0848	0909	0918		2309	2318	2339	2348	0009
36	Baarn d.	0045	0115	0125	0215	|	0645	|	0715	|	0745	|	0815	|	0845	|	0915	|		2315	|	2345	|	0015
45	**Amersfoort** a.	0055	0123	0133	0223	0631	0653	0701	0723	0731	0753	0801	0823	0831	0853	0901	0923	0931		2323	2332	2353	0002	0024

		†	⚒	Ⓐ	Ⓐ	Ⓐ	Ⓐ		Ⓐ		⚒		⚒										E	
Amersfoort d.	0007	0435	0437	0507	0537	0607	0629	0637	0659	0707	0729	0737	0759	0807	0829	0837	0859	and at the same minutes past each hour until	2237	2259	2307	2329	2337	2359
Baarn d.	0014	0442	0444	0514	0544	0614	|	0644	|	0714	|	0744	|	0814	|	0844	|		2244	|	2314	|	2344	|
Hilversum 457 d.	0021	0452	0451	0521	0551	0621	0641	0651	0711	0721	0741	0751	0811	0821	0841	0851	0911		2251	2311	2321	2341	2351	0011
Naarden-Bussum 457 d.	0029	0500	0500	0530	0600	0630	|	0700	|	0730	|	0800	|	0830	|	0900	|		2300	|	2330	|	0000	|
Weesp 457 458 a.	0037	0507	0508	0537	0607	0637	|	0707	|	0737	|	0807	|	0837	|	0907	|		2307	|	2337	|	0007	|
Amsterdam Centraal **458** a.	0055	0525	0524	0554	0624	0654	0702	0724	0732	0754	0802	0824	0832	0854	0902	0924	0932		2324	2332	2354	0002	0024	0032
Enkhuizen 459 a.	...	...	...	...	...	...	0806	...	0836	...	0906	...	0936	...	1006	...	1036		...	0036	...	0107	...	0144

SCHIPHOL ✈ - AMERSFOORT - DEVENTER - ENSCHEDE

See table **481** for through journeys **Schiphol ✈ - Amersfoort - Groningen / Leeuwarden** and v.v., also **Rotterdam / Den Haag - Amersfoort - Deventer - Enschede** and v.v.

km		Ⓐ	Ⓐ	Ⓐ	w★	⚒				★				★		⊡	⊡					H	G	
0	**Schiphol** ✈ 457 d.	...	0549	0619	0649	0719	...	0749	0819	0849	0919	0949	1019	1049	1119	1149	and at the same minutes past each hour until	2119	2149	2219	2249	2319	...	2349
9	Amsterdam Zuid 457 d.	...	0558	0628	0658	0728	...	0758	0828	0858	0928	0958	1028	1058	1128	1158		2128	2158	2228	2258	2328	...	2358
14	Duivendrecht 457 d.	...	0604	0634	0704	0734	...	0804	0834	0904	0934	1004	1034	1104	1134	1204		2134	2204	2234	2304	2334	...	0004
37	Hilversum 457 d.	...	0621	0651	0721	0751	...	0821	0851	0921	0951	1021	1051	1121	1151	1221		2151	2221	2251	2321	2351	...	0021
53	**Amersfoort** a.	...	0635	0704	0735	0804	...	0835	0904	0935	1004	1035	1104	1135	1204	1235		2204	2235	2304	2335	0004	...	0035
			|	⚒	|			|	|	|	|	|	|	|	|	|		|	|	|	|	H	G	
53	**Amersfoort** d.	...	0637	0707	0737	...	0807	0837	0907	0937	1007	1037	1107	1137	1207	1237		2207	2237	2307	2337	0007	0007	...
96	Apeldoorn d.	0609	0706	0736	0806	...	0836	0906	0936	1006	1036	1106	1136	1206	1236	1306		2236	2306	2336	0006	0036	0036	...
111	**Deventer** d.	0625	0719	0749	0819	...	0849	0919	0949	1019	1049	1119	1149	1219	1249	1319		2249	2319	2349	0019	0049	0059	...
149	Almelo 492 d.	0659	0743	0813	0843	...	0913	0943	1013	1043	1113	1143	1213	1243	1313	1343		2313	2343	0013	0043	0113	0122	...
164	Hengelo 492 a.	0713	0754	0824	0854	...	0924	0954	1024	1054	1124	1154	1224	1254	1324	1354		2324	2354	0024	0054	0124	0134	...
172	**Enschede** 492 a.	0726	0802	0832	*0912*	...	0932	1002	1032	*1112*	1132	1202	1232	*1312*	1332	1402		2332	0003	0035	0103	0132	0143	...

	Ⓐ	⚒	Ⓐ	Ⓐ	⚒	⚒		⚒					z★		♥	♥				n★				
Enschede 492 d.	0455	...	0527	0557	...	0627	...	0657	...	0727	0757	0827	*0856*	0927	0957	and at the same minutes past each hour until	1927	1957	2027	*2056*	2127	2157	2227	*2247*
Hengelo 492 d.	0506	...	0536	0606	...	0636	...	0706	...	0736	0806	0836	0906	0936	1006		1936	2006	2036	2106	2136	2206	2236	*2257*
Almelo 492 d.	0518	...	0548	0618	...	0648	...	0718	...	0748	0818	0848	0918	0948	1018		1948	2018	2048	2118	2148	2218	2248	2333
Deventer d.	0544	...	0614	0644	0644	0714	...	0744	0744	0814	0844	0914	0944	1014	1044		2014	2044	2114	2144	2214	2244	2314	0006
Apeldoorn d.	0557	...	0627	0657	0657	0727	...	0757	0757	0827	0857	0927	0957	1027	1057		2027	2057	2127	2157	2227	2257	2327	0021
Amersfoort a.	0622	...	0652	0722	0722	0752	...	0822	0822	0852	0922	0952	1022	1052	1122		2052	2122	2152	2222	2252	2322	2352	...
	|		Ⓐ	|	|			|	|	|	|	|	|	|	|		|	|	|	|	|	|	|	
Amersfoort d.	0624	0624	0654	0724	0724	...	0754	0824	0824	0854	0924	0954	1024	1054	1124		2054	2124	2154	2224	2254	2324	2354	...
Hilversum 457 d.	0637	0637	0707	0737	0737	...	0807	0837	0837	0907	0937	1007	1037	1107	1137		2107	2137	2207	2237	2307	2337	0007	...
Duivendrecht 457 a.	0655	0655	0725	0755	0755	...	0825	0855	0855	0925	0955	1025	1055	1125	1155		2125	2155	2225	2255	2325	2355	0029	...
Amsterdam Zuid 457 a.	0702	0702	0730	0802	0802	...	0830	0902	0902	0930	1002	1030	1102	1130	1202		2130	2202	2230	2302	2330	0002	0033	...
Schiphol ✈ 457 a.	0709	0709	0738	0809	0809	...	0838	0909	0909	0938	1009	1038	1109	1138	1209		2138	2209	2238	2309	2338	0009	0042	...

A – ①–⑤ (also Dec. 26, 27, Jan. 2; not Apr. 6, May 6, 14, 25).
E – ⑤–⑦ (also Apr. 5, May 5, 13, 24).
G – ②–⑤ (not Apr. 6, May 6, 14, 25).
H – ①⑥⑦ (also Apr. 6, May 6, 14, 25).

a – Ⓐ only.
d – Also Apr. 6, May 6, 14, 25; not Dec. 26, 27, Jan. 2.

n – Not Dec. 24, 31.
v – ⚒ only.
w – Not Dec. 25, Jan. 1.
z – Not Jan. 1.

★ – *IC* train to / from Germany via Bad Bentheim (Table **22**).

⊡ – The services from Schiphol at 1249, 1449, 1649 and 1849 are *IC* trains to Germany via Bad Bentheim (see Table **22**; passengers for Enschede should change trains at Hengelo). The 1849 from Schiphol does not run on Dec. 31.

♥ – The services from Hengelo at 1106, 1306, 1506, 1706 and 1906 are *IC* trains from Germany via Bad Bentheim (see Table **22**; passengers from Enschede depart *1056* / *1256* / *1456* / *1656* / *1856* and change trains at Hengelo). The 1906 from Hengelo terminates at Amersfoort on Dec. 31.

481 ROTTERDAM and DEN HAAG - UTRECHT - AMERSFOORT - ZWOLLE

km		Ⓐ	Ⓐ	Ⓒ	Ⓐ	Ⓐ	⚒	Ⓐ	⑥t	⚒	⚒	†	⚒	⚒		Ⓑr	⑥t		Ⓐ	Ⓒ	⑥t		Ⓐ	Ⓒ	
0	**Rotterdam** Centraal ⊙ d.	...	...	0605	0605	...	...	...	...	0635	...	0705	0705	...	...	...	...	...	0735	0735	0735	...	0805	0805	...
10	Rotterdam Alexander ⊙ d.	...	...	|	0613	...	...	...	...	0643	...	|	0713	...	...	...	...	...	0743	0743	0743	...	0813	0813	...
	Den Haag Centraal ⊙ d.	...	...	|	|	0608	...	...	...	|	0638	|	|	0708	...	...	...	...	|	|	|	0738	|	|	0808
24	Gouda ⊙ d.	...	...	0621	0624	0627	...	...	...	0654	0657	0721	0724	0727	...	...	...	...	0754	0754	0754	0757	0824	0824	0827
56	**Utrecht** Centraal ⊙ a.	...	...	0642	0643	0646	...	...	...	0713	0716	0742	0743	0746	...	...	...	...	0813	0813	0813	0816	0843	0843	0846
56	**Utrecht** Centraal ⊙ d.	0621	0621	...	0651	0651	0651	...	...	0721	0721	...	0751	0751	0751	...	...	...	0817	0821	0821	0821	0847	0851	0851
	Schiphol ✈ 480 d.	|	|	...	|	|	|	0619	...	|	|	...	|	|	|	0719a	0719	0719v	|	|	|	|	|	|	|
77	**Amersfoort** ⊙ a.	0635	0635	...	0705	0705	0705	0704	...	0735	0735	...	0805	0805	0805	0804a	0804	0804v	0831	0835	0835	0835	0901	0905	0905
77	**Amersfoort** d.	0638	0638	...	0707	0707	0707	0708	0708	0738	0738	...	0807	0807	0807	0808	0808	0808	0833	0838	0838	0838	0903	0907	0907
	Deventer 480 a.	|	|	...	0747	0747	0747	|	|	|	|	...	0847	0847	0847	|	|	|	|	|	|	|	|	0947	0947
	Enschede 480 a.	|	|	...	0832	0832	0832	|	|	|	|	...	0932	0932	0932	|	|	|	|	|	|	|	|	...	1032
144	**Zwolle** a.	0714	0714	...	...	...	...	0744	0744	0814	0814	...	...	...	...	0844	0844	0844	0911	0914	0914	0914	0941	...	...
	Leeuwarden 486 a.	|	0814	...	...	...	...	|	|	0914	|	...	...	...	...	|	|	0953	1014	1014	|	|	1053	...	...
	Groningen 485 a.	0814	...	...	...	...	...	0844	0852	...	0914	...	...	...	...	0944	0952	...	...	...	1014	1014	...	...	...

		Ⓒ		⑥t							†		D						⑤f		D				
Rotterdam Centraal ⊙ d.	...	...	0835	0835	...	0905	...	...	...	0935	0935	...	...	1005	...	...	...	1035	1035	...	...	1105	...	...
Rotterdam Alexander ⊙ d.	...	...	0843	0843	...	0913	...	...	...	0943	0943	...	...	1013	...	...	...	1043	1043	...	...	1113	...	...
Den Haag Centraal ⊙ d.	...	...	|	|	0838	|	0908	...	...	|	|	0938	0938	|	1008	...	...	|	|	1038	1038	|	1108	...	...
Gouda ⊙ d.	...	...	0854	0854	0857	0924	0927	...	...	0954	0954	0957	0957	1024	1027	...	...	1054	1054	1057	1057	1124	1127	...	...
Utrecht Centraal ⊙ a.	...	...	0913	0913	0916	0943	0946	...	...	1013	1013	1016	1016	1043	1046	...	...	1113	1113	1116	1116	1143	1146	...	...
Utrecht Centraal ⊙ d.	...	...	0921	0921	0921	0951	0951	...	...	1021	1021	1021	1021	1051	1051	...	...	1121	1121	1121	1121	1151	1151	...	...
Schiphol ✈ 480 d.	0819	0819	|	|	|	|	|	0919	0919	|	|	|	|	|	|	1019	1019	|	|	|	|	|	|	1119	1119
Amersfoort ⊙ a.	0904	0904	0935	0935	0935	1005	1005	1004	1004	1035	1035	1035	1035	1105	1105	1104	1104	1135	1135	1135	1135	1205	1205	1204	1204
Amersfoort d.	0908	0908	0938	0938	0938	1007	1007	1008	1008	1038	1038	1038	1038	1107	1107	1108	1108	1138	1138	1138	1138	1207	1207	1208	1208
Deventer 480 a.	|	|	|	|	|	1047	1047	|	|	|	|	|	|	1147	1147	|	|	|	|	|	|	1247	1247	|	|
Enschede 480 a.	|	|	|	|	|	1132v	1132	|	|	|	|	|	|	1232e	1232	|	|	|	|	|	|	1332h	1332	|	|
Zwolle a.	0944	0944	1014	1014	1014	...	...	1044	1044	1114	1114	1114	1114	...	...	1144	1144	1214	1214	1214	1214	...	...	1244	1244
Leeuwarden 486 a.	|	1053	1114	|	|	...	...	|	1153	1214	|	|	1214	...	...	|	1253	1314	|	|	1314	...	...	|	1353
Groningen 485 a.	1052k	...	...	1114	1114	...	...	1152k	...	...	1214	1214	...	...	...	1252k	...	...	1314	1314	...	...	...	1352k	...

D – ①–④ (not Apr. 5, May 5, 13, 24).
L – ①②③⑤⑥⑦ (also May 13).

a – Ⓐ only.
b – 0506 on ④⑤.
e – ⑤⑥ (also Apr. 5, May 5, 13, 24; not Dec. 25, 26, Jan. 1).
f – ⑤ (not Dec. 25, Jan. 1, Apr. 30).

g – ⑤⑥⑦ (also Apr. 5, May 5, 13, 24).
h – † only.
j – 10 minutes later on Ⓐ.
k – 8 minutes earlier on Ⓐ.
n – ①②③④⑥ (also Apr. 30; not Dec. 26).
p – Later arrivals on dates in Tables **485/6**.
q – 0745 on ⑥t.

r – Also Dec. 26; not Apr. 5, 30 May 5, 13, 24.
t – ⑥ (also Apr. 5, 30, May 5, 13, 24; not Dec. 26).
v – ⚒ only.
w – 0516 on ①.
x – 0053 on ②–⑤ (not Apr. 6, May 6, 14, 25).
y – 0132 on ①⑥⑦ (also Apr. 6, May 6, 14, 25).
z – ①②③④⑥⑦ (also Dec. 25, Jan. 1, Apr. 30).

⊙ – See panel below for other fast trains.
◇ – Runs 6 – 7 minutes later on †.
¶ – Trains start running daily (every 30 minutes) from Rotterdam at 1120 and from Den Haag at 1123.
‡ – Trains start running daily (every 30 minutes) Utrecht - Den Haag at 1129 and Amersfoort - Rotterdam at 1111.

Other fast trains **Rotterdam / Den Haag - Utrecht - Amersfoort** and v.v.

	⚒¶	⚒¶	⚒¶	⚒¶	¶				
Rotterdam Centraal d.	0650	...	0720	...	and every 30 minutes until	2020	...	2050	...
Rotterdam Alexander d.	0658	...	0728	...		2028	...	2058	...
Den Haag Centraal d.	|	0653	|	0723		|	2023	|	2053
Gouda d.	0709	0712	0739	0742		2039	2042	2109	2112
Utrecht Centraal a.	0728	0731	0758	0801		2058	2101	2128	2131
Utrecht Centraal d.	0732	...	0802	...		2102	...	2132	...
Amersfoort a.	0747	...	0817	...		2117	...	2147	...

	⚒‡	⚒‡	⚒‡	⚒‡	‡				
Amersfoort d.	...	0711	...	0741	and every 30 minutes until	...	2041	...	2111
Utrecht Centraal a.	...	0728	...	0758		...	2058	...	2128
Utrecht Centraal d.	0729	0732	0759	0802		2059	2102	2129	2132
Gouda d.	0749	0752	0819	0822		2119	2122	2149	2152
Den Haag Centraal a.	0807	|	0837	|		2137	|	2207	|
Rotterdam Alexander a.	...	0800	...	0830		...	2130	...	2200
Rotterdam Centraal a.	...	0810	...	0840		...	2140	...	2210

ROTTERDAM and DEN HAAG - UTRECHT - AMERSFOORT - ZWOLLE 481

		©		D						⑤f							†					L		g	
Rotterdam Centraal ⊙ d.	1135	1135	...	...	1205	...	...	...	1235	1235	...	1305	...	...	...	1335	1335	...	1405	...	...	...	1435	1435	...
Rotterdam Alexander ⊙ d.	1143	1143	...	...	1213	...	...	...	1243	1243	...	1313	...	...	...	1343	1343	...	1413	...	...	...	1443	1443	...
Den Haag Centraal ⊙ d.			1138	1138		1208	...	...			1238		1308	...	...			1338		1408	...	...			1438
Gouda ⊙ d.	1154	1154	1157	1157	1224	1227	...	...	1254	1254	1257	1324	1327	...	...	1354	1354	1357	1424	1427	...	...	1454	1454	1457
Utrecht Centraal ⊙ a.	1213	1213	1216	1216	1243	1246	...	...	1313	1313	1316	1343	1346	...	...	1413	1413	1416	1443	1446	...	...	1513	1513	1516
Utrecht Centraal ⊙ d.	1221	1221	1221	1221	1251	1251	...	...	1321	1321	1321	1351	1351	...	...	1421	1421	1421	1451	1451	...	...	1521	1521	1521
Schiphol ✈ **480** d.							1219	1219						1319	1319						1419	1419			
Amersfoort ⊙ a.	1235	1235	1235	1235	1305	1305	1304	1304	1335	1335	1335	1405	1405	1404	1404	1435	1435	1435	1505	1505	1504	1504	1535	1535	1535
Amersfoort d.	1238	1238	1238	1238	1307	1307	1308	1308	1338	1338	1338	1407	1407	1408	1408	1438	1438	1438	1507	1507	1508	1508	1538	1538	1538
Deventer **480** a.					1347	1347						1447	1447						1547	1547					
Enschede **480** a.					1432t	1432						1532v	1532						1632z	1632					
Zwolle a.	1314	1314	1314	1314	...	...	1344	1344	1414	1414	1414	...	...	1444	1444	1514	1514	1514	...	...	1544	1544	1614	1614	1614
Leeuwarden **486** a.	1414			1414	...	...		1453	1514			...	...		1553	1614			...	...		1653	1714		
Groningen **485** a.	...	1414	1414	...	...	...	1452k	...	...	1514	1514	...	...	1552k	...	...	1614	1614	...	...	1652k	...	...	1714	1714

	Ⓐ	©			©	Ⓑr	⑥t	⑥t		Ⓐ	©			©	Ⓐ	©		Ⓐ	©			©	Ⓐ	©	
Rotterdam Centraal ⊙ d.	1505	1505	...	...	...	1535	1535	1535	...	1605	1605	...	...	...	1635	1635	...	1705	1705	...	...	...	1735	1735	...
Rotterdam Alexander ⊙ d.	1513	1513	...	...	...	1543	1543	1543	...	1613	1613	...	...	...	1643	1643	...	1713	1713	...	...	...	1743	1743	...
Den Haag Centraal ⊙ d.			1506	...	...				1538			1608	...	...			1638			1708	...	...			1738
Gouda ⊙ d.	1524	1524	1527	...	...	1554	1554	1554	1557	1624	1624	1627	...	...	1654	1654	1657	1724	1724	1727	...	...	1754	1754	1757
Utrecht Centraal ⊙ a.	1543	1543	1546	...	...	1613	1613	1613	1616	1643	1643	1646	...	...	1713	1713	1716	1743	1743	1746	...	...	1813	1813	1816
Utrecht Centraal ⊙ d.	1547	1551	1551	...	...	1617	1621	1621	1621	1647	1651	1651	...	...	1717	1721	1721	1747	1751	1751	...	...	1817	1821	1821
Schiphol ✈ **480** d.				1519	1519								1619	1619							1719	1719			
Amersfoort ⊙ a.	1601	1605	1605	1604	1604	1631	1635	1635	1635	1701	1705	1705	1704	1704	1731	1735	1735	1801	1805	1805	1804	1804	1831	1835	1835
Amersfoort d.	1603	1607	1607	1608	1608	1633	1638	1638	1638	1703	1707	1707	1708	1708	1733	1738	1738	1803	1807	1807	1808	1808	1833	1838	1838
Deventer **480** a.		1647	1647								1747	1747							1847	1847					
Enschede **480** a.		1732	1732								1832h	1832							1932	1932					
Zwolle a.	1641	...	...	1644	1644	1711	1714	1714	1714	1741	...	...	1744	1744	1811	1814	1814	1841	...	...	1844	1844	1911	1914	1914
Leeuwarden **486** a.	1753	...	...		1753	1814	1814			1853	...	...		1853	1914	1914		1953	...	...		1953	2014	2014	
Groningen **485** a.	...	...	...	1752k	...	...	...	1814	1814	...	...	...	1852k	...	...	...	1914	...	...	...	1952k	...	...	...	2014

	Ⓐ	©			©	†	⚒	⑤f			⚒			⚒	†	⚒	n			⚒			⚒		†
Rotterdam Centraal ⊙ d.	1805	1805	...	...	...	1835	1835	1835	...	1905	1905	...	...	...	1935	1935	1935	...	2005	2005	...	...	...	2035	2035
Rotterdam Alexander ⊙ d.	1813	1813	...	...	...	1843	1843	1843	...	1913	1913	...	...	...	1943	1943	1943	...	2013	2013	...	...	...	2043	2043
Den Haag Centraal ⊙ d.			1808	...	...				1838			1908	...	...				1938			2008	...	...		
Gouda ⊙ d.	1824	1824	1827	...	...	1854	1854	1854	1857	1924	1924	1927	...	...	1954	1954	1954	1957	2024	2024	2027	...	...	2054	2054
Utrecht Centraal ⊙ a.	1843	1843	1846	...	...	1913	1913	1913	1916	1943	1943	1946	...	...	2013	2013	2013	2016	2043	2043	2046	...	...	2113	2113
Utrecht Centraal ⊙ d.	1847	1851	1851	...	...	1917	1921	1921	1921	...	1951	1951	...	...	2017	2021	2021	2021	...	2051	2051	...	...	2121	2121
Schiphol ✈ **480** d.				1819	1819					...			1919	1919					...			2019	2019		
Amersfoort ⊙ a.	1901	1905	1905	1904	1904	1931	1935	1935	1935	...	2005	2005	2004	2004	2031	2035	2035	2035	...	2105	2105	2104	2104	2135	2135
Amersfoort d.	1903	1907	1907	1908	1908	1933	1938	1938	1938	...	2007	2007	2008	2008	2033	2038	2038	2038	...	2107	2107	2108	2108	2138	2138
Deventer **480** a.		1947	1947							...	2047	2047							...	2147	2147				
Enschede **480** a.		...	2032							...	2132e	2132							...	2232f	2232				
Zwolle a.	1941	...	...	1944	1944	2011	2014	2014	2014	...	...	...	2044	2044	2111	2114	2114	2114	...	...	...	2144	2144	2214	2214
Leeuwarden **486** a.	2053	...	...		2053	2114	2114			...	...	...		2153	2214	2214			...	...	...		2253	2314	
Groningen **485** a.	...	...	...	2052k	...	...	...	2114	2114	...	...	...	2152k	...	...	...	2214	2214	...	...	...	2252	...	...	2314

		⑥t			⚒	†													⚒	⑤⑥e		z			
Rotterdam Centraal ⊙ d.	...	...	2105	...	...	...	...	2135	...	2205	...	...	...	2235	...	2305	...	...	...	...	2335	2335	...	0005	...
Rotterdam Alexander ⊙ d.	...	...	2113	...	...	...	...	2143	...	2213	...	...	...	2243	...	2313	...	...	...	...	2343	2343	...	0013	...
Den Haag Centraal ⊙ d.	2038	2038		2108	...	...	...		2138		2208	...	...		2238		2308	...	...	...			2338		0008
Gouda ⊙ d.	2057	2057	2124	2127	...	...	...	2154	2157	2224	2227	...	...	2254	2257	2324	2327	...	...	...	2354	2354	2357	0024	0027
Utrecht Centraal ⊙ a.	2116	2116	2143	2146	...	...	...	2213	2216	2243	2246	...	...	2313	2316	2343	2346	...	...	...	0013	0013	0016	0043	0046
Utrecht Centraal ⊙ d.	2121	2121	2151	2151	...	...	...	2221	2221	2251	2251	...	...	2321	2321	2351	2351	...	...	...	...	0021	0021	0051	0051
Schiphol ✈ **480** d.					2119	2119	2119					2219	2219					2319	2319	2319	...				
Amersfoort ⊙ a.	2135	2135	2205	2205	2204	2204	2204	2235	2235	2305	2305	2304	2304	2335	2335	0005	0005	0004	0004	0004	...	0042	0042	0105	0105
Amersfoort d.	2138	2138	2207	2207	2208	2208	2208	2238	2238	2307	2307	2308	2308	2338	2338	0007	0007	0008	0008	0008	...	...	...	...	...
Deventer **480** a.			2247	2247						2347	2347					0047	0047				...	...	...	...	...
Enschede **480** a.			...	2332						...	0032					...	0143y				...	...	...	...	...
Zwolle a.	2214	2214	...	...	2244	2244	2244	2314	2314	...	...	2344	2344	0014	0014	...	...	0049x	0049x	0049	...	...	...	...	...
Leeuwarden **486** a.		2314	...	...			2353	0017		...	...		0053p	...	...	...	...	...		0201	...	...	...	...	...
Groningen **485** a.	2314	...	...	...	2352	0008	...	...	0014	...	...	0052p	...	...	...	...	...	...	0200p	...	...	...	...	...	...

km																									
		Ⓐ	Ⓐ	©◇	Ⓐ	Ⓐ	Ⓐ	Ⓐ	⚒	⚒	†	Ⓐ	Ⓐ	Ⓐ	⚒	⚒	⚒	⚒	⚒	⚒	⚒		Ⓐ	⑥t	©
	Groningen **485** d.	...	...	...	...	...	...	...	...	...	...	...	0510w	...	...	...	...	0546a	...	0616a	...	...	...	...	...
	Leeuwarden **486** d.	...	...	...	...	...	...	...	...	...	...	0500b		...	...	...	0545a		...		...	...	0605	...	...
0	**Zwolle** d.	...	...	...	...	...	0546	...	...	...	...	0616	0616	...	...	...	0646	0646	...	0716	...	...	0711	...	...
	Enschede **480** d.	...	...	...	...	...		...	...	...	...			0527	...	...			...		0627	...		...	...
	Deventer **480** d.	...	...	...	...	...		...	...	...	...			0614	...	...			...		0714	...		0714	...
67	**Amersfoort** a.	...	...	...	...	...	0622	...	...	...	...	0652	0652	0652	...	...	0722	0722	...	0752	0752	...	0747	0752	...
67	**Amersfoort** ⊙ d.	...	...	...	...	0611	0624	...	...	0641a	...	0654	0654	0654	...	0651a	0724	0724	0721a	0754	0754	...	0751	0754	...
	Schiphol ✈ **480** a.	...	...	...	...			...	...		...	0738	0738		...					0838		...			...
88	**Utrecht** Centraal ⊙ a.	...	...	...	...	0628	0640	...	...	0658a	...	...	...	0709	...	0706a	0739	0739	0736a	...	0809	...	0806	0809	...
88	**Utrecht** Centraal ⊙ d.	0559	0602	0609	0629	0632	0644	0647	0659	0702	0710	...	...	0714	0714	0717	0744	0744	0747	...	0814	0814	0817	0817	0817
120	Gouda ⊙ d.	0619	0622	0634	0649	0652	0704	0707	0719	0722	0734	...	...	0734	0734	0737	0804	0804	0807	...	0834	0834	0837	0837	0837
148	**Den Haag** Centraal ⊙ a.	0637			0707		0722		0737			...	...	0752	0752		0822	0822		...	0852	0852			
	Rotterdam Alexander ⊙ d.	...	0630		...	0700	...	0716	...	0730		...	...	...	...	0746	...	...	0816	...	...	...	0846	0846	0846
	Rotterdam Centraal ⊙ a.	...	0640	0650	...	0710	...	0725	...	0740	0750	...	...	...	...	0755	...	...	0825	...	...	...	0855	0855	0855

		Ⓐ	©	©	Ⓐ	⑥t			©		Ⓐ	©	Ⓐ	©			©		†	⑥t	Ⓑr	⚒	†		
Groningen **485** d.	0646v	...	...	0646t	...	...	0706j	...	...	0746	...	...	...	...	0806j	...	...	0846	...	...	...	...	...	0906j	...
Leeuwarden **486** d.		0643	0633t		0705	0705		...	...		0745	0734q	0805	0805		...	...		0845	0845	0845	0905	0905		...
Zwolle d.	0746	0741	0746	0746	0811	0816	0816	...	...	0846	0841	0846	0911	0916	0916	...	...	0946	0946	0941	0946	1011	1016	1016	...
Enschede **480** d.								0727	0727t							0827	...								0927
Deventer **480** d.								0814	0814							0914	0914								1014
Amersfoort a.	0822	0817	0822	0822	0847	0852	0852	0852	0852	0922	0917	0922	0947	0952	0952	0952	0952	1022	1022	1017	1022	1047	1052	1052	1052
Amersfoort ⊙ d.	0824	0821	0824	0824	0851	0854	0854	0854	0854	0924	0921	0924	0951	0954	0954	0954	0954	1024	1024	1021	1024	1051	1054	1054	1054
Schiphol ✈ **480** a.						0938	0938							1038	1038								1138	1138	
Utrecht Centraal ⊙ a.	0839	0836	0839	0839	0906	...	...	0909	0909	0939	0936	0939	1006	...	...	1009	1009	1039	1039	1036	1039	1106	...	...	1109
Utrecht Centraal ⊙ d.	0844	0847	0847	0847	0917	...	...	0914	0917	0944	0947	0947	1017	...	...	1014	1017	1044	1044	1047	1047	1117	...	...	1114
Gouda ⊙ d.	0904	0907	0907	0907	0937	...	...	0934	0937	1004	1007	1007	1037	...	...	1034	1037	1104	1104	1107	1107	1137	...	...	1134
Den Haag Centraal ⊙ a.	0922					...	...	0952		1022				...	...	1052		1122	1122				...	...	1152
Rotterdam Alexander ⊙ d.	...	0916	0916	0916	0946	...	...	...	0946	...	1016	1016	1046	...	...	...	1046	...	...	1116	1116	1146	...	...	...
Rotterdam Centraal ⊙ a.	...	0925	0925	0925	0955	...	...	...	0955	...	1025	1025	1055	...	...	...	1055	...	...	1125	1125	1155	...	...	...

	†			©							D							⑥t							⑤f
Groningen **485** d.	...	0946	...	0946	...	1006j	...	...	1046	...	1046	...	1106j	...	...	1146	...	1146	...	1206j	...	...	1246	...	1246
Leeuwarden **486** d.	...		0945		1005		...	...		1045		1105		...	...		1145		1205		...	...		1245	
Zwolle d.	...	1046	1046	1046	1116	1116	...	...	1146	1146	1146	1216	1216	...	...	1246	1246	1246	1316	1316	...	...	1346	1346	1346
Enschede **480** d.	0927						1027	1027t						1127	1127n						1227	1227e			
Deventer **480** d.	1014						1114	1114						1214	1214						1314	1314			
Amersfoort a.	1052	1122	1122	1122	1152	1152	1152	1152	1222	1222	1222	1252	1252	1252	1252	1322	1322	1322	1352	1352	1352	1352	1422	1422	1422
Amersfoort ⊙ d.	1054	1124	1124	1124	1154	1154	1154	1154	1224	1224	1224	1254	1254	1254	1254	1324	1324	1324	1354	1354	1354	1354	1424	1424	1424
Schiphol ✈ **480** a.					1238	1238						1338	1338						1438	1438					
Utrecht Centraal ⊙ a.	1109	1139	1139	1139	...	...	1209	1209	1239	1239	1239	...	...	1310	1310	1339	1339	1339	...	...	1409	1409	1439	1439	1439
Utrecht Centraal ⊙ d.	1117	1144	1147	1147	...	...	1214	1217	1244	1247	1247	...	...	1314	1317	1344	1347	1347	...	...	1414	1417	1444	1447	1447
Gouda ⊙ d.	1137	1204	1207	1207	...	...	1234	1237	1304	1307	1307	...	...	1334	1337	1404	1407	1407	...	...	1434	1437	1504	1507	1507
Den Haag Centraal ⊙ a.		1222			...	...	1252		1322			...	...	1352		1422			...	...	1452		1522		
Rotterdam Alexander ⊙ d.	1146	...	1216	1216	...	...	...	1246	...	1316	1316	...	...	...	1346	...	1416	1416	...	...	...	1446	...	1516	1516
Rotterdam Centraal ⊙ a.	1155	...	1225	1225	...	...	...	1255	...	1325	1325	...	...	...	1355	...	1425	1425	...	...	...	1455	...	1525	1525

← FOR NOTES SEE PREVIOUS PAGE

481 ZWOLLE - AMERSFOORT - UTRECHT - DEN HAAG and ROTTERDAM

							⚒						Ⓐ	Ⓒ	†	Ⓐ	Ⓒ			Ⓒ			Ⓐ	Ⓒ	Ⓒ
Groningen **485** d.	...	1306j	...	...	1346	...	1346	...	1406j	...	...	1446	...	...	1446	...	...	1506j	...	...	...	1546	...	...	1546
Leeuwarden **486** d.	1305	|	...	...	|	1345	|	1405	|	...	...	|	1445	1445	|	1505	1505	|	...	...	...	|	1545	1545	|
Zwolle d.	1416	1416	...	...	1446	1446	1446	1516	1516	...	...	1546	1541	1546	1546	1611	1616	1616	...	...	...	1646	1641	1646	1646
Enschede **480** d.	|	|	1327	1327g	|	|	|	|	|	1427	1427t	|	|	|	|	|	|	|	1527	1527h	...	|	|	|	|
Deventer **480** d.	|	|	1414	1414	|	|	|	|	|	1514	1514	|	|	|	|	|	|	|	1614	1614	...	|	|	|	|
Amersfoort a.	1452	1452	1452	1452	1522	1522	1522	1552	1552	1552	1552	1622	1617	1622	1622	1647	1652	1652	1652	1652	...	1722	1717	1722	1722
Amersfoort ⊙ d.	1454	1454	1454	1454	1524	1524	1524	1554	1554	1554	1554	1624	1621	1624	1624	1651	1654	1654	1654	1654	...	1724	1721	1724	1724
Schiphol ✈ **480** a.	1538	1538	|	|	|	|	|	1638	1638	|	|	|	|	|	|	|	1738	1738	|	|	...	|	|	|	|
Utrecht Centraal ⊙ a.	...	...	1509	1509	1539	1539	1539	...	...	1609	1609	1639	1636	1639	1639	1706	...	...	1709	1709	...	1739	1736	1739	1739
Utrecht Centraal ⊙ d.	...	...	1514	1517	1544	1547	1547	...	...	1614	1617	1644	1647	1647	1647	1717	...	...	1714	1717	...	1744	1747	1747	1747
Gouda ⊙ d.	...	...	1534	1537	1604	1607	1607	...	...	1634	1637	1704	1707	1707	1707	1737	...	...	1734	1737	...	1804	1807	1807	1807
Den Haag Centraal ⊙ a.	...	...	1552	|	1622	|	|	...	...	1652	|	1722	|	|	|	|	...	...	1752	|	...	1822	|	|	|
Rotterdam Alexander ⊙ d.	...	...	...	1546	...	1616	1616	...	...	...	1646	...	1716	1716	1716	1746	...	...	...	1746	...	...	1816	1816	1816
Rotterdam Centraal ⊙ a.	...	...	...	1555	...	1625	1625	...	...	...	1655	...	1725	1725	1725	1755	...	...	...	1755	...	...	1825	1825	1825

	Ⓐ	Ⓒ			Ⓒ			⑤f	Ⓐ	Ⓒ			Ⓒ			⚒							D		
Groningen **485** d.	...	...	1606j	...	...	1646	...	1646	...	...	1706j	...	...	1746	...	1746	...	1806j	...	...	1846	...	1846	...	1906j
Leeuwarden **486** d.	1605	1605	|	...	...	|	1645	|	1705	1705	|	...	...	|	1745	|	1805	|	...	...	|	1845	|	1905	|
Zwolle d.	1711	1716	1716	...	...	1746	1746	1746	1811	1816	1816	...	...	1846	1846	1846	1916	1916	...	...	1946	1946	1946	2016	2016
Enschede **480** d.	|	|	|	1627	1627	|	|	|	|	|	|	1727	1727	|	|	|	|	|	1827	1827y	|	|	|	|	|
Deventer **480** d.	|	|	|	1714	1714	|	|	|	|	|	|	1814	1814	|	|	|	|	|	1914	1914	|	|	|	|	|
Amersfoort a.	1747	1752	1752	1752	1752	1822	1822	1822	1847	1852	1852	1852	1852	1922	1922	1922	1952	1952	1952	1952	2022	2022	2022	2052	2052
Amersfoort ⊙ d.	1751	1754	1754	1754	1754	1824	1824	1824	1851	1854	1854	1854	1854	1924	1924	1924	1954	1954	1954	1954	2024	2024	2024	2054	2054
Schiphol ✈ **480** a.	|	1838	1838	|	|	|	|	|	|	1938	1938	|	|	|	|	|	2038	2038	|	|	|	|	|	2138	2138
Utrecht Centraal ⊙ a.	1806	...	...	1809	1809	1839	1839	1839	1906	...	...	1909	1909	1939	1939	1939	...	...	2009	2009	2039	2039	2039	...	...
Utrecht Centraal ⊙ d.	1817	...	...	1814	1817	1844	1847	1847	1917	...	...	1914	1917	1944	1947	1947	...	...	2014	2017	2044	2047	2047	...	...
Gouda ⊙ d.	1837	...	...	1834	1837	1904	1907	1907	1937	...	...	1934	1937	2004	2007	2007	...	...	2034	2037	2104	2107	2107	...	...
Den Haag Centraal ⊙ a.	|	...	...	1852	|	1922	|	|	|	...	...	1952	|	2022	|	|	...	...	2052	|	2122	|	|	...	...
Rotterdam Alexander ⊙ d.	1846	...	...	...	1846	...	1916	1916	1946	...	...	...	1946	...	2016	2016	...	...	...	2046	...	2116	2116	...	...
Rotterdam Centraal ⊙ a.	1855	...	...	...	1855	...	1925	1925	1955	...	...	...	1955	...	2025	2025	...	...	...	2055	...	2125	2125	...	...

					⑤⑥e												⑤f					⑤⑥e	K		
Groningen **485** d.	...	...	1946	...	1946	...	2006j	...	...	2046	...	...	2106j	...	...	2146	...	...	...	2206	...	...	...	...	2234
Leeuwarden **486** d.	...	...	|	1945	|	2005	|	...	...	|	2045	2105	|	...	...	|	2145	2145	2205	|	...	...	...	2234	|
Zwolle d.	...	...	2046	2046	2046	2116	2116	...	...	2146	2146	2216	2216	...	...	2246	2246	2246	2316	2316	...	...	...	2346	2346
Enschede **480** d.	1927	1927h	|	|	|	|	|	2027	...	|	|	|	|	2127	...	|	|	|	|	|	2227	2227	...	|	|
Deventer **480** d.	2014	2014	|	|	|	|	|	2114	2114	|	|	|	|	2214	2214	|	|	|	|	|	2314	2314	2314	|	|
Amersfoort a.	2052	2052	2122	2122	2122	2152	2152	2152	2152	2222	2222	2252	2252	2252	2252	2322	2322	2322	2352	2352	2352	2352	2352	0022	0022
Amersfoort ⊙ d.	2054	2054	2124	2124	2124	2154	2154	2154	2154	2224	2224	2254	2254	2254	2254	2324	2324	2324	2354	2354	2354	2354	2354	0024z	0024z
Schiphol ✈ **480** a.	|	|	|	|	|	2238	2238	|	|	|	|	2338	2338	|	|	|	|	|	0042	0042	|	|	|	|	|
Utrecht Centraal ⊙ a.	2109	2109	2139	2139	2139	...	...	2209	2209	2239	2239	...	...	2309	2309	2339	2339	2339	...	...	0009	0009	0009	0039z	0039z
Utrecht Centraal ⊙ d.	2114	2117	2144	2147	2147	...	...	2214	2217	2244	2247	...	...	2314	2317	2344	2344	2347	...	...	...	0014	0017	...	...
Gouda ⊙ d.	2134	2137	2204	2207	2207	...	...	2234	2237	2304	2307	...	...	2334	2337	0004	0004	0007	...	...	...	0034	0037	...	...
Den Haag Centraal ⊙ a.	2152	|	2222	|	|	...	...	2252	|	2322	|	...	...	2352	|	0022	0022	|	...	...	...	0052	|	...	...
Rotterdam Alexander ⊙ d.	...	2146	...	2216	2216	...	...	...	2246	...	2316	...	...	...	2346	...	...	0016	...	...	...	...	0046	...	...
Rotterdam Centraal ⊙ a.	...	2155	...	2225	2225	...	...	...	2255	...	2325	...	...	...	2355	...	...	0025	...	...	...	...	0100	...	...

D – ①–④ (not Apr. 5, May 5, 13, 24).
K – ④–⑥ (also Apr. 5, May 5, 24; not Dec. 25, 26, Jan. 1).
e – Also Apr. 5, May 5, 13, 24; not Dec. 25, 26, Jan. 1.
f – Not Dec. 25, Jan. 1, Apr. 30.
g – ⑤⑥⑦ (also Apr. 5, May 5, 13, 24).
h – † only.
j – 10 minutes later on Ⓐ.
t – ⑥ (also Apr. 5, 30, May 5, 13, 24; not Dec. 26).
y – ⑤⑦ (also Dec. 26; not Apr. 30).
z – On ④⑤ (not May 6, 14) Amersfoort d. 0030, Utrecht a. 0046.
⊙ – See panel at foot of page 252 for other fast trains.

485 ZWOLLE - GRONINGEN

For through journeys from / to **Rotterdam**, see table **481**

km																							
		Ⓐ	Ⓐ	Ⓐ	⑥t	Ⓐ	⚒U	⚒	Ⓐ	Ⓒ	Ⓐ		⚒	Ⓑr	⑥t	Ⓐ		⚒	Ⓐ	Ⓒ	Ⓐ	✣	Ⓐ	Ⓒ
	Den Haag Centraal **481** d.	...	...	...	...	...	...	...	...	...	...	0638v	...	...	...	...	0738	...	...	...	...		...	...
	Schiphol ✈ **480/1** d.	...	...	...	...	...	...	...	0619	...	...	|	...	0719a	0719	...	|	...	0819	0819	...	and at	1919	1919
	Amersfoort **481** d.	...	...	...	...	...	0638a	...	0708	0708t	...	0738v	...	0808	0808	...	0838	...	0908	0908	...	the same	2008	2008
0	**Zwolle** **486** d.	0547	0623	0647	0646	0653	0717	0723	0747	0746	0753	0817	0823	0847	0846	0853	0917	0923	0947	0946	0953	minutes	2047	2046
27	Meppel **486** d.	|	0639	|	0701	0709	|	0739	|	0801	0809	|	0839	|	0901	0909	|	0939	|	1001	1009	past each	|	2101
47	Hoogeveen d.	|	0650	|	0714	0720	|	0750	|	0814	0820	|	0850	|	0914	0920	|	0950	|	1014	1020	hour until	|	2114
77	Assen d.	0626	0709	0726	0733	0739	0756	0809	0826	0833	0839	0856	0909	0926	0933	0939	0956	1009	1026	1033	1039		2126	2133
104	**Groningen** a.	0644	0729	0744	0752	0759	0814	0829	0844	0852	0859	0914	0929	0944	0952	0959	1014	1029	1044	1052	1059		2144	2152

	Ⓐ					†	⚒	†		⑤⑥e	N	⑤⑥e	D
Den Haag Centraal **481** d.	...	1938	...	...	2038	...	...	...	2138	...	...	...	...
Schiphol ✈ **480/1** d.	...	|	...	2019	|	...	2119	2119	|	2219	2219	2319	2319
Amersfoort **481** d.	...	2038	...	2108	2138	...	2208	2208	2238	2308	2308	0008	0008
Zwolle **486** d.	2053	2117	2123	2146	2217	2223	2246	2246	2317	2346	2346	0052	0056
Meppel **486** d.	2109	|	2139	2201	|	2239	2301	2301	|	0001	0001	0110	0111
Hoogeveen d.	2120	|	2150	2214	|	2250	2314	2314	|	0014	0014	0122	0126
Assen d.	2139	2156	2209	2233	2256	2309	2333	2349	2356	0033	0053	0141	0144
Groningen a.	2159	2214	2229	2252	2314	2329	2352	0008	0014	0052	0117	0200	0206

	G	①d	Ⓐ	Ⓐ	Ⓐ	Ⓐ	⚒
Groningen d.	0510	0516	0530	0546	0600	0616	0630
Assen d.	0529	0536	0549	0602	0619	0632	0649
Hoogeveen d.	|	|	0607	|	0637	|	0707
Meppel **486** d.	|	|	0618	|	0648	|	0718
Zwolle **486** a.	0613	0615	0637	0643	0707	0713	0737
Amersfoort **481** a.	0652	0652	...	0722	...	0752	...
Schiphol ✈ **480/1** a.	0738	0738	...	|	...	0838	...
Den Haag Centraal **481** a.	...	...	...	0822	...	...	...

	⚒		Ⓐ	Ⓒ	Ⓐ	⚒		⊠	Ⓐ	Ⓒ	Ⓐ				Ⓐ	Ⓒ	Ⓐ					U		
Groningen d.	0646	...	0700	0706	0716	0730	0746		2000	2006	2016	2030	2046	...	2100	2106	2116	2130	2146	2206	...	2234	...	2330
Assen d.	0702	...	0719	0724	0732	0749	0802	and at	2019	2024	2032	2049	2102	...	2119	2124	2132	2149	2202	2224	...	2255	...	2349
Hoogeveen d.	|	...	0737	0742	|	0807	|	the same	2037	2042	|	2107	|	...	2137	2142	|	2207	|	2242	...	2315	...	0007
Meppel **486** d.	|	...	0748	0756	|	0818	|	minutes	2048	2056	|	2118	|	...	2148	2156	|	2218	|	2256	...	2326	...	0018
Zwolle **486** a.	0743	...	0807	0813	0813	0837	0843	past each	2107	2113	2113	2137	2143	...	2207	2213	2213	2237	2243	2313	...	2343	...	0037
Amersfoort **481** a.	0822	...	...	0852	0852	...	0922	hour until	...	2152	2152	...	2222	...	...	2252	2252	...	2322	2352	...	0022	...	...
Schiphol ✈ **480/1** a.	|	...	...	0938	0938	...	|		...	2238	2238	...	|	...	...	2338	2338	...	|	0042	...	...	...	...
Den Haag Centraal **481** a.	0922	...	...	...	...	...	1022		...	...	...	...	2322	...	...	...	...	...	0022	...	...	...	...	...

D – ①–④ (not Apr. 5, May 5, 13, 24).
G – ②–⑤ (not Dec. 25, Jan. 1, Apr. 30, May 5, 13).
N – ①②③④⑦ (also Dec. 25, 26, Jan. 1; not Apr. 5, May 5, 13, 24).
U – From / to Utrecht (Table **481**).
a – Ⓐ only.
d – Not Apr. 5, May 24.
e – Also Apr. 5, May 5, 13, 24; not Dec. 25, 26, Jan. 1.
r – Also Dec. 26; not Apr. 5, 30, May 5, 13, 24.
t – ⑥ (also Apr. 5, 30, May 5, 13, 24; not Dec. 26).
v – ⚒ only.
✣ – The services from Zwolle at 1623, 1723, 1823, 1923 and 2023 run daily.
⊠ – The services from Groningen at 1530, 1630, 1730, 1830 and 1930 run daily.

486 ZWOLLE - LEEUWARDEN

For through journeys from / to **Rotterdam**, **Den Haag** and **Schiphol** ✈ via **Amersfoort**, see table **481**

km																			
		⑥⑦j	②③g	④⑤h		Ⓐ	Ⓐ	⚒	⚒									B	③④c
0	**Zwolle** **485** d.	0056	0100	0059	...	0550	0620	0650	0720	0750	0820	0850	and at	2220	2250	...	2320	2350	2350
27	Meppel **485** d.	0114	0117	0116	...	0605	|	0705	|	0805	|	0905	the same	|	2305	...	2336	0005	0005
41	Steenwijk d.	0122	0125	0127	...	0614	0644	0714	0744	0814	0844	0914	minutes	2244	2314	...	2345	0014	0020
65	Heerenveen d.	0138	0141	0145	...	0630	0657	0730	0757	0830	0857	0930	past each	2257	2330	...	2358	0030	0038
94	**Leeuwarden** a.	0201	0202	0210	...	0653	0714	0753	0814	0853	0914	0953	hour until	2314	2353	...	0017	0053	0101

	A	④⑤b		Ⓐ	Ⓐ	⑥t	Ⓐ	⚒	†	⚒								
Leeuwarden d.	0500	0506	...	0545	0605	0633	0643	0705	0734	0745	0805	0845	and at	2105	2145	...	2205	2234	2345
Heerenveen d.	0523	0528	...	0601	0627	0655	0659	0727	0755	0801	0827	0901	the same	2127	2201	...	2227	2255	0005
Steenwijk d.	0542	0543	...	0615	0643	0711	0712	0743	0811	0815	0843	0915	minutes	2143	2215	...	2243	2311	0020
Meppel **485** d.	0552	0552	...	0623	0652	0722	0722	0752	0822	|	0852	|	past each	2152	|	...	2252	2322	0030
Zwolle **485** a.	0610	0608	...	0640	0710	0740	0740	0810	0840	0840	0910	0940	hour until	2210	2240	...	2310	2340	0046

A – ①–③ (not Apr. 5, May 5, 24).
B – ①②⑤⑥⑦ (also May 5, 13).
b – Not Dec. 25, Jan. 1, Apr. 30, May 13.
c – Not May 5, 13.
g – Not Apr. 6, May 25.
h – Not May 6, 14.
j – Also Apr. 6, May 6, 14, 25; not Dec. 26, 27, Jan. 2.
t – Also Apr. 5, 30, May 5, 13, 24; not Dec. 26.

OLDENZAAL - HENGELO - ZUTPHEN 488

Operated by **Syntus** (NS tickets valid) 2nd class only

km					Ⓐ	Ⓐ	⚒	⚒					⚒				⚒								
0	**Oldenzaal** d.	0004	0034	...	0604	0634	0704	0734	...	...	0804	0834	0834	and at	2004	2034	2034	...	2104	2134	2204	2234	2304	2334	...
11	Hengelo d.	0016	0046	...	0616	0646	0716	0746	...	...	0816	0844	0846	the same	2016	2044	2046	...	2116	2144	2216	2244	2316	2344	...
26	Goor d.	0031	0100	...	0631	0701	0731	0801	0801	...	0831	...	0901	minutes	2031	...	2101	...	2131	...	2231	...	2331	...	...
39	Lochem d.	0039	...	...	0639	0709	0739	0809	0809	...	0839	...	0909	past each	2039	...	2109	...	2139	...	2239	...	2339	...	...
56	**Zutphen** a.	0053	...	...	0653	0723	0753	0823	0823	...	0853	...	0923	hour until	2053	...	2123	...	2153	...	2253	...	2353	...	...

			Ⓐ	Ⓐ	Ⓐ	Ⓐ	⚒	⚒				⚒				⚒									
Zutphen d.	0006	...	...	...	0606	0636	...	0706	...	...	0736	0806	...	and at	1936	2006	...	...	2036	2106	2136	2206	2236	2306	2336
Lochem d.	0021	...	...	...	0621	0651	...	0721	...	...	0751	0821	...	the same	1951	2021	...	...	2051	2121	2151	2221	2251	2321	2351
Goor d.	0030	...	0531	0601	0631	0701	0701	0731	0731	...	0801	0831	...	minutes	2001	2031	...	...	2101	2131	2201	2231	2301	2331	0001
Hengelo d.	...	...	0546	0616	0646	0716	0716	0746	0746	...	0816	0846	0846	past each	2016	2046	2046	...	2116	2146	2216	2246	2316	2346	0016
Oldenzaal a.	...	...	0556	0626	0656	0726	0726	0756	0756	...	0826	0856	0856	hour until	2026	2056	2056	...	2126	2156	2226	2256	2326	2356	0026

ARNHEM and ZUTPHEN - WINTERSWIJK 490

Operated by **Syntus** (NS tickets valid) 2nd class only

km		Ⓐ	Ⓐ	⚒	Ⓐ		❖			©	
0	**Arnhem** d.	0634	0704	0734	0804	0834	and	2234	2334	2334	...
14	Zevenaar d.	0647	0717	0747	0817	0847	hourly	2247	2347	2347	...
30	Doetinchem d.	0708	0738	0808	0838	0908	until	2308	0007	0008	...
64	**Winterswijk** a.	0741	0811	0841	0911	0941		2341	...	0041	...

	⚒	Ⓐ	⚒		Ⓐ					
Winterswijk d.	0550	0620	0650	...	0720	...	0750	and	2250	...
Doetinchem d.	0623	0653	0723	0723	0753	...	0823	hourly	2323	...
Zevenaar d.	0643	0713	0743	0743	0813	...	0843	until	2343	...
Arnhem a.	0657	0727	0757	0757	0827	...	0857		2357	...

☛ Additional journeys **Arnhem - Winterswijk**: 0904 Ⓐ, 1004 Ⓐ, 1104 Ⓐ, 1204 ⚒, 1304 ⚒, 1404 ⚒, 1504 ⚒, 1604 ⚒, 1704 ⚒, 1804 Ⓐ and 1904 Ⓐ.
Additional journeys **Winterswijk - Arnhem**: 0820 Ⓐ, 0920 Ⓐ, 1020 Ⓐ, 1120 Ⓐ, 1220 ⚒, 1320 ⚒, 1420 ⚒, 1520 ⚒, 1620 ⚒, 1720 ⚒ and 1820 Ⓐ.

km		⑤⑥n		Ⓐ	Ⓐ	⑥t	Ⓐ	©			
0	**Zutphen** d.	0007	...	0701	0801	0807	0901	0907	1007	and	2307
22	Ruurlo d.	0023	...	0717	0817	0823	0917	0923	1023	hourly	2323
43	**Winterswijk** a.	0042	...	0736	0836	0842	0936	0942	1042	until	2342

	Ⓐ	Ⓐ	⑥t	⊙	⊙	Ⓐ	©			
Winterswijk d.	0615	0645	0651	0745	0845	0945	0951	1051	and	2251
Ruurlo d.	0633	0703	0709	0803	0903	1003	1009	1109	hourly	2309
Zutphen a.	0649	0719	0724	0819	0919	1024	1024	1124	until	2324

☛ Additional journeys **Zutphen - Winterswijk**: 0731 Ⓐ, 0831 Ⓐ, 0931 Ⓐ, 1037 Ⓐ, 1137 Ⓐ, 1237 ⚒, 1337 ⚒, 1437 ⚒, 1537 ⚒, 1637 ⚒, 1737 ⚒ and 1837 ⚒.
Additional journeys **Winterswijk - Zutphen**: 0715 Ⓐ, 0815 Ⓐ, 0915 Ⓐ, 1021 Ⓐ, 1121 Ⓐ, 1221 ⚒, 1321 ⚒, 1421 ⚒, 1521 ⚒, 1621 ⚒, 1721 ⚒ and 1821 Ⓐ.

n – Not Dec. 26, Jan. 2, May 1, 14.
t – Also Apr. 5, 30, May 5, 13, 24; not Dec. 26.
❖ – The following trains depart Arnhem at 32 minutes past the hour: 1132 Ⓐ, 1332, 1532, 1732 and 1932.
⊙ – Runs 5–6 minutes later on ©.

ZWOLLE - ENSCHEDE 492

All services are operated by 🚌 between Nijverdal West and Nijverdal (shaded timings). Alternative train services are available via Deventer (tables **475/480**).

km		Ⓐ	⚒	⚒◐	⚒¶	⚒◐					
0	**Zwolle** d.	0634	0704	0734	0804	0834	0904	0934		2304	2334
18	Raalte d.	0650	0720	0750	0820	0850	0920	0950	and	2320	2350
	Nijverdal West a.	0658	0728	0758	0828	0858	0928	0958		2328	2358
	Nijverdal West d.	0706	0736	0806	0836	0906	0936	1006	every 30	2336	0006
32	Nijverdal a.	0721	0751	0821	0851	0921	0951	1021	minutes	2351	0021
32	Nijverdal d.	0733	0803	0833	0903	0933	1003	1033		0003	0033
44	Almelo 480 a.	0747	0817	0847	0917	0947	1017	1047	until	0017	0047
59	Hengelo 480 a.	0802	0832	0902	0932	1002	1032	1102		0032	0102
67	**Enschede** 480 a.	0812	0842	0912	0942	1012	1042	1112		0042	0112

	Ⓐ	⚒	Ⓐ	⚒◐	⚒¶					
Enschede 480 d.	0617	0647	0717	0747	0817	0847	0917		2217	2247
Hengelo 480 d.	0627	0657	0727	0757	0827	0857	0927	and	2227	2257
Almelo 480 d.	0643	0713	0743	0813	0843	0913	0943		2243	2313
Nijverdal a.	0656	0726	0756	0826	0856	0926	0956	every 30	2256	2326
Nijverdal d.	0712	0742	0800	0842	0912	0942	1012	minutes	2312	2342
Nijverdal West a.	0724	0754	|	0854	0924	0954	1024		2324	2354
Nijverdal West d.	0732	0802	◇	0902	0932	1002	1032	until	2332	0002
Raalte d.	0740	0810	0840	0910	0940	1010	1040		2340	0010
Zwolle a.	0757	0727	0857	0927	0957	1027	1057		2357	0027

◐ – Runs daily Nijverdal - Enschede and v.v.
¶ – Runs daily Zwolle - Nijverdal and v.v.
◇ – By 🚌 Nijverdal - Raalte (a. 0825).
☛ Additional Train / 🚌 journeys: Zwolle - Enschede at 0504 Ⓐ, 0534 Ⓐ and 0604 Ⓐ; Enschede - Zwolle at 0517 Ⓐ and 0547 Ⓐ.

ZWOLLE - EMMEN 493

km		D		Ⓐ	Ⓐ	Ⓐ	⚒		⚒			⚒									A			B
0	**Zwolle** d.	0026	...	0556	0626	0656	0726	...	0756	0826	and at	1456	1526	...	1556	1626	and at	2056	2126	...	2156	2226	...	2326
23	Ommen d.	0044	...	0615	0644	0715	0744	...	0815	0844	the same	1515	1544	...	1615	1644	the same	2115	2144	...	2215	2244	...	2344
34	Mariënberg d.	0051	...	|	0651	|	0751	...	|	0851	minutes	|	1551	...	|	1651	minutes	|	2151	...	|	2251	...	2351
55	Coevorden d.	0107	...	0636	0707	0736	0807	...	0836	0907	past each	1536	1607	...	1636	1707	past each	2136	2207	...	2236	2307	...	0007
75	**Emmen** a.	0128	...	0651	0728	0751	0828	...	0851	0928	hour until	1551	1628	...	1651	1728	hour until	2151	2228	...	2251	2328	...	0028

	Ⓐ	Ⓐ	Ⓐ	⚒		⚒			⚒															B	
Emmen d.	0503	0533	0608	0633	...	0708	0733	and at	1508	1533	...	1608	1633	1708	1733	1808	1833	1908	1933	...	2033	2133	2233	2333	...
Coevorden d.	0522	0552	0624	0652	...	0724	0752	the same	1524	1552	...	1624	1652	1724	1752	1824	1852	1924	1952	...	2052	2152	2252	2352	...
Mariënberg d.	0538	0608	|	0708	...	|	0808	minutes	|	1608	...	|	1708	|	1808	|	1908	|	2008	...	2108	2208	2308	0008	...
Ommen d.	0546	0616	0645	0716	...	0745	0816	past each	1545	1616	...	1645	1716	1745	1816	1845	1916	1945	2016	...	2116	2216	2316	0016	...
Zwolle a.	0605	0635	0704	0735	...	0804	0835	hour until	1604	1635	...	1704	1735	1804	1835	1904	1935	2004	2035	...	2135	2235	2335	0035	...

A – ④⑤⑥ (also Apr. 5, May 5, 24; not Dec. 25, 26, Jan. 1).
B – ②–⑥ (also Apr. 5, May 24; not Dec. 25, 26, Jan. 1).
D – ③–⑦ (also Apr. 6, May 25; not Dec. 26, 27, Jan. 2).

LEEUWARDEN - GRONINGEN 494

Operated by **Arriva** (NS tickets valid)

km			Ⓐ	Ⓐ	Ⓐ	Ⓐ		Ⓐ	Ⓐ	Ⓐ	Ⓐ			⑥t	⑥t	⑥t	©	⑥t		⑥t	⑥t	©	©
0	**Leeuwarden** d.		0549	0619	0644	0649	and at the same	1819	1844	1849	1918	...		0636	0706	0801	0806	0836	and at the same	1736	1801	1806	1836
25	Buitenpost d.	Ⓐ	0613	0643	0700	0713	minutes past	1843	1900	1913	1942	...	©	0700	0730	0817	0830	0900	minutes past	1800	1817	1830	1900
54	**Groningen** a.		0638	0709	0719	0738	each hour until	1909	1919	1938	2005	...		0724	0755	0836	0855	0924	each hour until	1824	1836	1855	1924

	⑥t	©	†	†	†					
Leeuwarden d.	1901	1906	1936	2036	2136	...		2006	and	0006
Buitenpost d.	1917	1930	2000	2100	2200	...	DAILY	2030	hourly	0030
Groningen a.	1936	1955	2024	2124	2224	...		2055	until	0055

		Ⓐ	Ⓐ	Ⓐ	Ⓐ		Ⓐ	Ⓐ	Ⓐ	Ⓐ
Groningen d.		0549	0619	0639	0649	and at the same	1819	1839	1849	1919
Buitenpost d.	Ⓐ	0614	0643	0658	0714	minutes past	1843	1858	1914	1941
Leeuwarden a.		0639	0709	0715	0740	each hour until	1909	1915	1939	2006

		⑥t	⑥t	©	⑥t	⑥t		⑥t	⑥t	©	©	⑥t	©	©	⑥t	©	†	†	†					
Groningen d.		0636	0706	0806	0836	0856	and at the same	1636	1656	1706	1736	1756	1806	1836	1856	1906	1936	2036	2136	...		2006	and	0006
Buitenpost d.	©	0701	0730	0830	0901	0915	minutes past	1701	1715	1730	1801	1815	1830	1901	1915	1930	2001	2101	2201	...	DAILY	2030	hourly	0030
Leeuwarden a.		0725	0755	0855	0925	0932	each hour until	1725	1732	1755	1825	1832	1855	1925	1932	1955	2025	2125	2225	...		2055	until	0055

t – Also Apr. 5, 30, May 5, 13, 24; not Dec. 26.

GRONINGEN - NIEUWESCHANS - LEER 495

Operated by **Arriva** ★

km			A	A	A	A		A	A	A	A	A			⑥t	C	⑦k	C	C		C
0	**Groningen** d.		0554	0624	0724	0824	and in the	1924	2024	2124	2224	2324	...		0620	0720	0720	0820	0920	and in the	1620
34	Winschoten d.	Ⓐ	0628	0655	0758	0858	same pattern	1958	2058	2158	2258	2358	...	©	0655	0755	0755	0855	0955	same pattern	1655
46	Nieuweschans 🏛 a.		0639	0706	0809	0909	**every two**	2009	2106	2209	2309	0009	...		0706	0806	0806	0906	1006	**every two**	1706
72	**Leer** (Ostfriesl) a.		0705	...	...	0935	**hours** until	...	2135	...	...	...	...		0735	...	0835	0935	...	**hours** until	1735

	C	C	⑥t	C	C	⑦k	C	C	C
Groningen d.	1720	1820	1820	1920	2020	2020	2120	2220	2320
Winschoten d.	1755	1855	1855	1955	2055	2055	2155	2255	2355
Nieuweschans 🏛 a.	1806	1906	1906	2006	2106	2106	2206	2306	0006
Leer (Ostfriesl) a.	...	...	1935	...	...	2135	...	...	...

		A	A	A	A	A	A	A	A	
Leer (Ostfriesl) d.		...	...	0720	...	...	...	...	1020	and in the
Nieuweschans 🏛 d.	Ⓐ	0644	0718	0748	0818	0848	0918	1018	1048	same pattern
Winschoten d.		0655	0728	0758	0828	0858	0928	1028	1058	**every two**
Groningen a.		0734	0804	0834	0904	0934	1004	1104	1134	**hours** until

	A	A	A			⑥t	C	⑥t	C	⑦k	C	C	⑥t	C		C	⑥t	C	C	⑥t	C	C	C
Leer (Ostfriesl) d.	...	...	2220	...		...	...	0748	...	0848	...	...	1020	1048k	and in the	...	1820	1848k	...	2020	...	2148k	...
Nieuweschans 🏛 d.	2118	2218	2248	...	©	0714	...	0814	0814	0914	0914	1014	1044	1114	same pattern	1814	1844	1914	2014	2044	2114	2214	2314
Winschoten d.	2128	2228	2258	...		0724	0724	0824	0824	0924	0924	1024	1054	1123	**every two**	1824	1854	1924	2024	2054	2124	2223	2324
Groningen a.	2204	2304	2334	...		0800	0800	0900	0900	1000	1000	1100	1130	1200	**hours** until	1900	1930	2000	2100	2130	2200	2300	2400

A – ①–⑤ (not Dec. 25, Jan. 1, Apr. 5, 30, May 5, 13, 24).
C – ⑥⑦ (also Dec. 25, Jan. 1, Apr. 5, 30, May 5, 13, 24).
k – ⑦ (also Dec. 25, 26, Jan. 1).
t – Also Apr. 5, 30, May 5, 13, 24; not Dec. 26.
★ – NS tickets are valid Groningen - Nieuweschans and v.v.

496 AMSTERDAM - ZANDVOORT AAN ZEE

km					Ⓐ	⚒	Ⓒ	Ⓐ	⚒	Ⓒ	Ⓐ	†	⚒	†	⚒								
0	**Amsterdam** Centraal ..... 450 d.	0014	...	...	...	*0610*	0640	0641	...	*0710*	0714	*0740*	0744	*0810*	0814	0844	...	0914	0944	and every	2314	2344	...
5	Amsterdam Sloterdijk ..... 450 d.	0020	...	...	...	*0616*	0646	0647	...	*0716*	0720	*0746*	0750	*0816*	0820	0850	...	0920	0950	30 minutes	2320	2350	...
19	Haarlem ..... 450 d.	0042	...	...	0600	0630	0656	0657	0700	0730	0730	0800	0800	0830	0830	0900	...	0930	1000		2330	0000	...
27	**Zandvoort** aan Zee ..... a.	0053	...	...	0611	0641	...	...	0711	0741	0741	0811	0811	0841	0841	0911	...	0941	1011	until	2341	0011	...

		H	G		H	G			Ⓐ	⚒	⚒												
Zandvoort aan Zee ..... d.	0017	...	...	0058	...	...	...	...	0614	0647	0717	0747	0817	0847	...	0917	0947	and every	2217	2247	...	2317	2347
Haarlem ..... 450 a.	0028	0036	0043	0109	0113	0137	...	...	0625	0658	0728	0759	0828	0859	...	0928	0958	30 minutes	2228	2258	...	2328	2358
Amsterdam Sloterdijk ..... 450 a.	...	0045	0056	...	0124	0152	...	...	0642	0712	0742	0812	0842	0912	...	0942	1012		2242	2312	...	2342	*0015*
Amsterdam Centraal ..... 450 a.	...	0052	0103	...	0131	0158	...	...	0648	0718	0748	0818	0848	0918	...	0948	1018	until	2248	2318	...	2348	*0022*

G – ②–⑤ (not Apr. 6, May 6, 14, 25).

H – ①⑥⑦ (also Apr. 6, May 6, 14, 25).

497 LEEUWARDEN - STAVOREN

Operated by **Arriva** (NS tickets valid); 2nd class only

km		Ⓐ	Ⓐ	⑥t	Ⓐ	Ⓐ	⑥t	Ⓐ	⑥t	†	Ⓐ	⑥t	Ⓐ	Ⓒ		Ⓐ	⑥t	Ⓐ	Ⓒ				⑤⑥h	
0	**Leeuwarden** ..... d.	0523	0550	0603	0621	0650	0703	0750	0803	0803	0821	0835	0850	0903	and at the same	1821	1835	1850	1903	2003	2103	2203	2203	2320
22	Sneek ..... d.	0544	0615	0625	0644	0713	0725	0813	0825	0827	0842	0856	0913	0925	minutes past	1842	1856	1913	1925	2025	2125	2224	2225	2341
51	Stavoren ..... a.	0611	0641	0652	0712	0741	0752	0840	0852	0853	...	...	0940	0952	each hour until	...	...	1940	1952	2052	2152	...	2252	...

	Ⓐ	Ⓐ	⑥t	Ⓐ	⑥t	Ⓒ	Ⓐ	Ⓐ	⑥t	Ⓒ	Ⓐ	⑥t	Ⓐ	Ⓒ		Ⓐ	⑥t	Ⓐ	Ⓒ				⑤⑥h	
Stavoren ..... d.	...	0616	...	0647	0659	...	0716	0747	0759	...	...	...	0847	0859	and at the same	...	...	1847	1859	1959	2059	2159	2315	...
Sneek ..... d.	0617	0647	0701	0717	0729	0729	0747	0817	0829	0829	0847	0901	0917	0929	minutes past	1847	1901	1917	1929	2029	2129	2229	2345	2345
Leeuwarden ..... a.	0638	0709	0722	0738	0752	0752	0809	0838	0852	0852	0909	0923	0938	0952	each hour until	1908	1922	1938	1952	2052	2152	2252	0007	0007

h – Also Apr. 5, May 5, 13, 24; not Dec. 25, 26, Jan. 1.

t – Also Apr. 5, 30, May 5, 13, 24; not Dec. 26.

498 OTHER BRANCH LINES

ALMELO – MARIËNBERG Operated by **Connexxion** (NS tickets valid)

From Almelo:

0622 Ⓐ, 0644 Ⓐ, 0722 ⚒, 0744 ⚒, 0822 ⚒, 0844 ⚒, 0922 ⚒, 0944 ⚒, 1022 ⚒, 1044 ⚒, 1122, 1144 ⚒, 1222, 1244 ⚒, 1322, 1344 ⚒, 1422, 1444 ⚒, 1522, 1544 ⚒, 1622, 1644 ⚒, 1722, 1744 ⚒, 1822 ⚒, 1844 †, 1922 ⚒, 1944 ⑥ **q**, 2022 ⚒, 2044 †, 2122 ⚒ and 2144 †.

19 km Journey time: 22–23 minutes

From Mariënberg:

0649 Ⓐ, 0714 Ⓐ, 0749 ⚒, 0814 ⚒, 0849 ⚒, 0914 ⚒, 0949 ⚒, 1014 ⚒, 1049 ⚒, 1114 ⚒, 1149, 1214 ⚒, 1249, 1314 ⚒, 1349, 1414 ⚒, 1449, 1514 ⚒, 1549, 1614 ⚒, 1649, 1714 ⚒, 1749, 1814 ⚒, 1849 ⚒, 1914 †, 1949 ⚒, 2014 †, 2049 ⚒, 2114 †, 2149 ⚒ and 2214 †.

AMERSFOORT – EDE-WAGENINGEN Operated by **Connexxion** (NS tickets valid)

From Amersfoort:

0011 **L**, 0041 ⑦ **r**, 0111 ⑦ **r**, 0511 Ⓐ, 0541 ⚒, 0611 ⚒, 0641 ⚒, 0711, 0741 and every 30 minutes until until 2341.

34 km Journey time: 35 minutes Amersfoort - Ede, 38 minutes Ede - Amersfoort.

From Ede-Wageningen:

0025, 0055 **L**, 0125 ⑦ **r**, 0155 ⑦ **r**, 0555 Ⓐ, 0625 ⚒, 0655 ⚒, 0725 ⚒, 0755, 0825, 0855 and every 30 minutes until 2355.

APELDOORN – ZUTPHEN

From Apeldoorn:

0004, 0634 Ⓐ, 0704 Ⓐ, 0734 Ⓐ, 0804 ⚒, 0834, 0904, 0934 and every 30 minutes until 2334.

18 km Journey time: 19–20 minutes

From Zutphen:

0604 Ⓐ, 0634 Ⓐ, 0704 Ⓐ, 0734 ⚒, 0804, 0834 and every 30 minutes until 2334.

GRONINGEN – DELFZIJL Operated by **Arriva** (NS tickets valid)

From Groningen:

On Ⓐ at 0521, 0551 and every 30 minutes until 1851; then 1924, 2033, 2133, 2233 and 2333. On ⑥ **t** at 0604, 0633 and at 04 and 33 minutes past each hour until 1804, 1833; then 1933, 2033, 2133, 2233 and 2333. On † at 0633, 0704, 0733, 0833 and hourly until 2333.

38 km Journey time: 37–39 minutes

From Delfzijl:

On Ⓐ at 0603, 0633 and every 30 minutes until 1933, then 2016, 2116, 2216 and 2316. On ⑥ **t** at 0646, 0716 and every 30 minutes until 1916; then 2016, 2116, 2216 and 2316. On † at 0716, 0746, 0816, 0916 and hourly until 2316.

LEEUWARDEN – HARLINGEN ¶ Operated by **Arriva** (NS tickets valid)

From Leeuwarden:

On Ⓐ at 0519, 0619, 0644 and at 19 and 44 minutes past each hour until 1919, 1944; then 2019, 2059, 2159 and 2323. On ⑥ **t** at 0559, 0659, 0733, 0759 and at 33 and 59 minute past each hour until 1933, 1959; then 2059, 2159, 2323. On † at 0759, 0833, 0859, 0959 and hourly until 2159 (also 1233, 1333, 1433, 1733, 1833, 1933 and 2323).

26 km Journey time: 22–24 minutes 2nd class only

From Harlingen:

On Ⓐ at 0551, 0651, 0716, 0751 and at 16 and 51 minutes past each hour until 1916, 1951; then 2016, 2055, 2131, 2231 and 2355. On ⑥ **t** at 0631, 0731, 0806, 0831 and at 06 and 31 minutes past each hour until 2006, 2031; then 2131, 2231 and 2355. On † at 0831, 0906, 0931, 1031 and hourly until 2231 (also 1306, 1406, 1506, 1806, 1906, 2006 and 2355).

ZWOLLE – KAMPEN

From Zwolle:

0103 ⑥⑦ **e**, 0549 Ⓐ, 0619 Ⓐ, 0649 ⚒, 0719 ⚒, 0749 and at 19 ⚒ and 49 minutes past each hour until 1319 ⚒, 1349; then 1419, 1449 and every 30 minutes until 2349.

13 km Journey time: 10 minutes

From Kampen:

0003, 0117 ⑥⑦ **e**, 0603 Ⓐ, 0633 Ⓐ, 0703 ⚒, 0733 ⚒, 0803, 0833 ⚒ and at 03 and 33 ⚒ minutes past each hour until 1303, 1333 ⚒; then 1403, 1433 and every 30 minutes until 2333.

L – ②–⑦ (not Dec. 26, 27, Jan. 2).

e – Also Apr. 6, May 6, 14, 25; not Dec. 26, 27, Jan. 2.

q – Also Dec. 26; not Apr. 5, 30, May 5, 13, 24.

r – Also Apr. 6, May 1, 6, 14, 25; not Dec. 27.

t – Also Apr. 5, 30, May 5, 13, 24; not Dec. 26.

¶ – For ⛴ to/from Terschelling and Vlieland.

499 OTHER 🚌 and ⛴ LINES

ALKMAAR – HARLINGEN ¶ 🚌 *Connexxion Qliner* route **350/351** ★

From Alkmaar rail station:

0524 Ⓐ, 0624 Ⓐ, 0724 ⚒, 0824, 0924 and hourly until 2124.

Journey time: ± 1 hour 40 minutes

From Harlingen Veerbootterminal ¶:

0630 Ⓐ, 0730 Ⓐ, 0830 ⚒, 0930, 1030, 1130, 1230, 1330, 1429 Ⓐ, 1430 Ⓒ, 1529 Ⓐ, 1530 Ⓒ, 1629 Ⓐ, 1630 Ⓒ, 1730, 1830, 1930, 2030, 2130, 2230.

ALKMAAR – LEEUWARDEN 🚌 *Connexxion Qliner* route **350**

From Alkmaar rail station:

0524 Ⓐ, 0624 ⚒, 0724 ⚒, 0824, 0924 and hourly until 2124; also 2224 ⑦.

Journey time: ± 2 hours

From Leeuwarden rail station:

0601 Ⓐ, 0701 ⚒, 0800 ⑦, 0801 ⚒, 0900 ⑦, 0901 ⚒ and hourly until 2200 ⑦, 2201 ⚒.

DEN HELDER – TEXEL ⛴ *TESO*: ✆ +31 (0) 222 36 96 00

🚌 route **33**: Den Helder rail station (departs 20 minutes before ships sail) to Havenhoofd.

From Den Helder Havenhoofd: 0630 ⚒, 0730 ⚒ §, 0830 and hourly until 2030, 2130 **n**.

Journey time: 20 minutes

From Texel ('t Horntje ferryport): 0600 ⚒, 0700 ⚒ §, 0800 and hourly until 2000, 2100 **n**.

🚌 route **33**: Den Helder Havenhoofd (departs 5 minutes after ships arrive) to rail station.

ENKHUIZEN – STAVOREN ⛴ *Rederij V&O* ▲: ✆ +31 (0) 228 32 66 67

From Enkuizen Spoorhaven: 0830 **A**, 1230 **B**, 1630 **A**.

Journey time: 80 minutes Enkhuizen - Stavoren, 85–95 minutes Stavoren - Enkhuizen.

From Stavoren: 1005 **A**, 1405 **B**, 1805 **A**.

LELYSTAD – ZWOLLE 🚌 *Connexxion* route **330**

From Lelystad rail station:

Ⓐ: 0607, 0637 and every 30 minutes until 1907; then 1935, 2035, 2135.
⑥: 0805, 0835 and every 30 minutes until 1935; then 2035, 2135.
⑦: 1235, 1335 and hourly until 2135.

Journey time: 64–68 minutes

From Zwolle rail station:

Ⓐ: 0556, 0626 and every 30 minutes until 1726; then 1759, 1831, 1901, 1931, 2001, 2101.
⑥: 0731, 0801 and every 30 minutes until 1901; then 2001, 2101.
⑦: 1201, 1301 and hourly until 2101.

VLISSINGEN – BRESKENS ⛴ *Veolia Transport Fast Ferries* ▲ Journey time: 20 minutes

0755, 0855 and hourly until 2055; ***also*** 0545 Ⓐ, 0655 Ⓐ, 0720 Ⓐ, 0820 Ⓐ, 1620 Ⓐ, 1720 Ⓐ and 2155 Ⓐ. Additional sailings operate May - September.

BRESKENS ferryport – **BRUGGE** rail station 🚌 *Veolia* route **42** Journey time: 81 minutes

0627 Ⓐ, 0727 ⚒, 0827 ⚒, 0927, 1027 and hourly until 2027.

BRUGGE rail station – **BRESKENS** ferryport 🚌 *Veolia* route **42** Journey time: 76 minutes

0659 ⚒, 0759 ⚒, 0859, 0959 and hourly until 1959; then 2059 ⚒.

BRESKENS – VLISSINGEN ⛴ *Veolia Transport Fast Ferries* ▲ Journey time: 20 minutes

0825, 0925 and hourly until 2125; ***also*** 0615 Ⓐ, 0725 Ⓐ, 0745 Ⓐ, 0850 Ⓐ, 1650 Ⓐ, 1750 Ⓐ and 2225 Ⓐ. Additional sailings operate May - September.

A – Daily Apr. 17 - Sept. 26 (not Apr. 30); ⑥⑦ Oct. 2–17; daily Oct. 23–31.

B – Daily May 1 - Sept. 26.

d – Runs daily Mar. 29 - Oct. 2.

n – Not Dec. 31.

▲ – Conveys foot passengers, cycles and mopeds only.

¶ – For ⛴ to/from Terschelling and Vlieland.

★ – Change at Kop Afsluitdijk on all services.

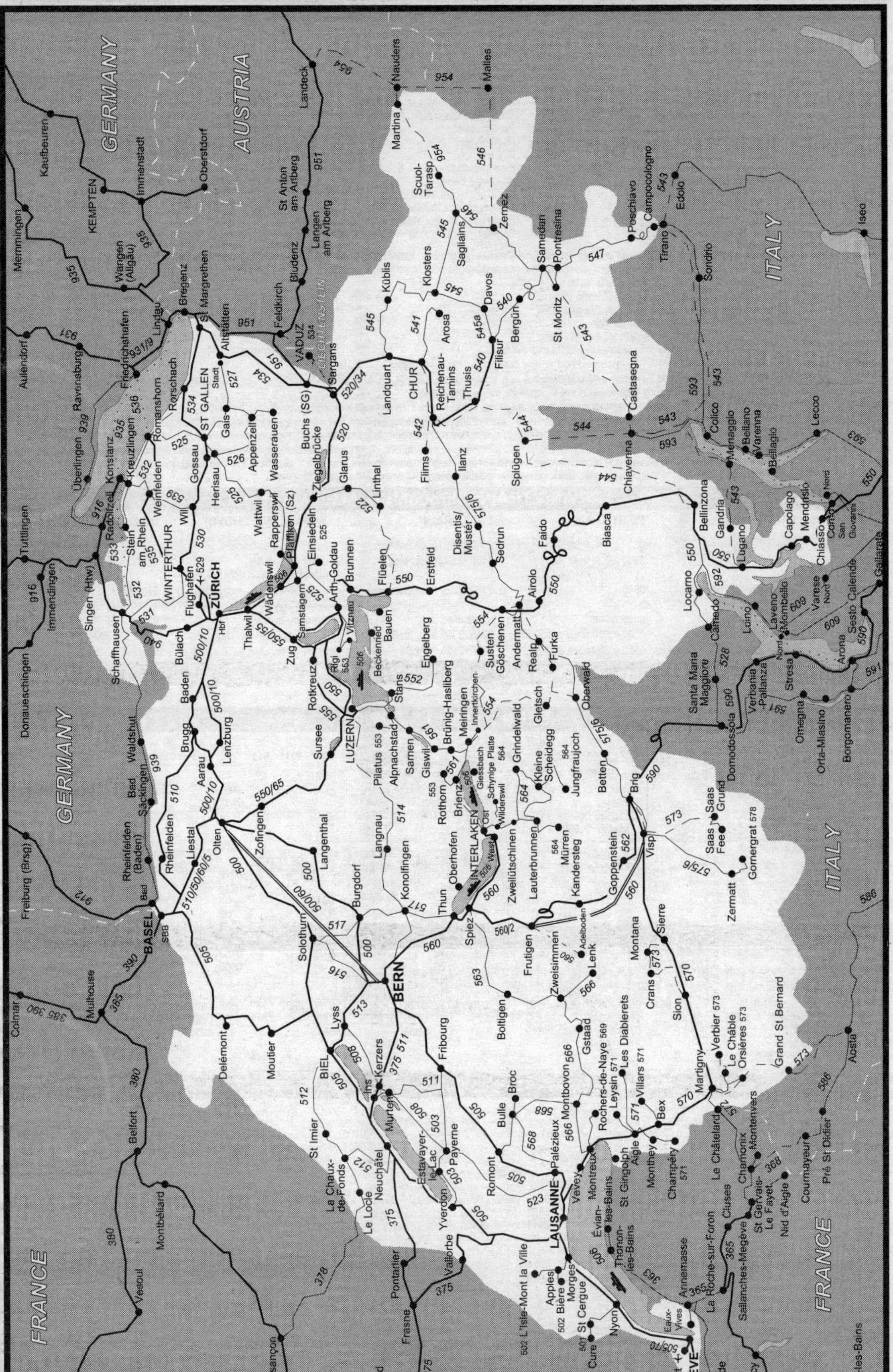
GERMANY
AUSTRIA
FRANCE
ITALY
LIECHTENSTEIN
BASEL
ZÜRICH
BERN
LUZERN
LAUSANNE
GENÈVE
INTERLAKEN
CHUR
ST GALLEN
WINTERTHUR
BIEL
VADUZ
Olten
Brig
Zermatt
Davos
St Moritz
Locarno
Lugano
Bellinzona
Neuchâtel
Fribourg
Montreux
Sion
Martigny
Tirano
Domodossola

SWITZERLAND

Operators: There are numerous operators of which Schweizerische Bundesbahnen (SBB)/Chemins de fer Fédéraux (CFF)/Ferrovie Federali Svizzere (FFS) is the principal. Bus services are provided by PostAuto/Autopostale (PA). Table headings show the operators' initials; abbreviations used in the European Timetable are:

AB	Appenzeller Bahnen	MOB	Montreux - Oberland Bernois	SMC	Sierre - Montana - Crans
BAM	Bière - Apples - Morges	MThB	Mittelthurgau Bahn	SNCF	Société Nationale des Chemins de Fer Français
BLM	Bergbahn Lauterbrunnen - Mürren	MVR	Montreux - Vevey Riviera	SOB	Schweizerische Südostbahn
BLS	BLS Lötschbergbahn	NStCM	Nyon-St Cergue-Morez	SPB	Schynige Platte Bahn
BOB	Berner Oberland Bahnen	PA	PostAuto / Autopostale / AutoDaPosta	THURBO	an alliance of MThB and SBB
BRB	Brienz - Rothorn Bahn	PB	Pilatus Bahn	TMR	Transports de Martigny et Régions
CGN	Compagnie Générale de Navigation	RA	RegionAlps	TPC	Transports Publics du Chablais
CP	CarPostal Suisse	RB	Rigi Bahnen	TPF	Transports Publics Fribourgeois
FART	Ferrovie Autolinee Regionali Ticinesi	RBS	Regionalverkehr Bern - Solothurn	URh	Untersee und Rhein
FS	Ferrovie dello Stato	RhB	Rhätische Bahn	WAB	Wengernalpbahn
GGB	Gornergrat Bahn	RM	Regionalverkehr Mittelland	ZB	Zentralbahn
JB	Jungfraubahn	SBB	Schweizerische Bundesbahnen	ZSG	Zürich Schifffahrtsgesellschaft
MIB	Meiringen - Innertkirchen Bahn	SBS	Schweizerische Bodensee-Schifffahrtsgesellschaft		
MGB	Matterhorn Gotthard Bahn	SGV	Schifffahrtsgesellschaft des Vierwaldstättersees		

Services: All trains convey first and second class seating, **except** where shown otherwise in footnotes or by a '1' or '2' in the train column, or where the footnote shows sleeping and/or couchette cars only. For most local services you **must** be in possession of a valid ticket before boarding your train. Some international trains convey sleeping cars (🛏) and/or couchette cars (▬), descriptions of which appear on page 8.

Train Categories:

TGV	French high-speed **Train à Grande Vitesse**;	*CNL*	**City Night Line** quality international overnight hotel train;
ICE	German high-speed **InterCity Express** train;	*IC*	**InterCity** quality internal express train;
RJ	Austrian high-speed **Railjet** train;	*ICN*	**InterCity Neigezug** high-speed tilting train;
EC	**EuroCity** quality international express train;	*IR*	**InterRegio** fast inter-regional trains;
EN	**EuroNight** quality international overnight express train;	*RE*	**RegioExpress** semi-fast regional trains.

Catering: ✕ – Restaurant; (✕) – Bistro; (🍸) – Bar coach; 🍸 – Minibar.
Details of catering is shown in the tables where known, but as a general guide *ICE*, *RJ*, *EC* and *ICN* trains convey ✕ or (✕), *IC* services convey ✕ or (🍸), and *TGV* and *IR* trains convey (🍸) or 🍸. Catering facilities may not be open for the whole journey.

Timings: Valid from **December 13, 2009** unless otherwise stated in the table. Local services are subject to alteration on **public holidays**.

Supplements: *TGV*, *ICE* and *RJ* high-speed trains may be used for internal Swiss journeys without supplement. For international journeys *TGV* services are priced as 'global' fare, and *EC* trains serving Italy are subject to the payment of a supplement; both types require compulsory reservation for international travel.

Reservations: Seat reservations may be made on all *TGV*, *ICE*, *RJ*, *EC*, *IC* and *ICN* trains. In *EN* and *CNL* night services seat reservations (where seats are conveyed) are compulsory (with a supplement also payable). Reservation is recommended for travel in first class observation cars. Fares in Switzerland are calculated according to distance and many Swiss railways use artificially inflated tariff-kilometres. Distances shown in tables below, however, are actual kilometres.

CAR-CARRYING TRAINS through the ALPINE TUNNELS

BLS, MGB, RhB, SBB

TUNNEL	CAR TERMINALS	FIRST TRAIN*	LAST TRAIN*	NORMAL FREQUENCY	INFORMATION ✆
ALBULA:	Thusis - Samedan	0810 (0750 from Samedan)	2010 (1750 from Samedan)	7 – 11 services per day	081 288 47 16, 081 288 55 11
FURKA:	Oberwald - Realp	0600 (0630 from Realp)	2100 (2130 from Realp)	every 60 minutes, more frequent on ①⑤⑥⑦.	027 927 76 66, 027 927 76 76
LÖTSCHBERG:	Kandersteg - Goppenstein	0550	2350 (2320 from Goppenstein)	every 30 minutes, more frequent 0730 – 1900 on ⑤⑥⑦ and mid-June – mid-Oct.	0900 55 33 33
OBERALP:	Andermatt - Sedrun	unspecified	unspecified	every 60 minutes	027 927 77 07, 027 927 77 40
SIMPLON:	Brig - Iselle (Italy)	0550 (0630 from Iselle)	2215 (2305 from Iselle)	11 – 12 services per day	0900 300 300
VEREINA:	Selfranga (Klosters) - Sagliains	0520 (0550 from Sagliains)	2050 (2120 from Sagliains) Dec. 13 - Apr. 30 and Dec. 1 - 11, services continue for a further 2 hours	every 30 minutes 0850 – 1820	081 288 37 37

* – Not necessarily daily.

500 BERN and BIEL - ZÜRICH

SBB

km		*IR* 1903	*IR* 2005	*IC* 707	*IR* 9051	*IR* 1909	*ICN* 509 ✕	*IR* 2009 Ⓐ	*IC* 809 ✕		*IC* 709 ✕ F	*IR* 9053	*IR* 1911	*ICN* 1511 ✕	*IR* 2011	*IC* 811 ✕		*IC* 711 ✕	*IR* 9055		*IR* 1915	*ICN* 515 ✕	*IR* 2015	*IC* 815 ✕
	Genève Aéroport ✈ **505** d.	...	...	...	...	...	...	...	...	...	...	...	...	...	...	...	...	...	...	...	...	...	...	...
	Genève **505** d.	...	...	...	...	...	...	...	...	...	...	...	...	...	...	...	...	0536	...	...	...	0614	...	...
	Lausanne **505** d.	...	...	...	...	...	...	...	...	...	...	...	...	0539	...	...	...	0620	...	...	...	|	...	...
	Brig **560** d.	...	...	...	...	...	...	...	...	...	...	...	...	|	...	0547	...	|	...	...	...	|	...	0649
	Interlaken Ost **560** d.	...	...	...	...	...	...	...	...	...	...	...	...	|	...	|	...	|	...	...	...	|	...	|
0	**Bern** d.	0421	0440	0530	...	...	...	0539	0602	0607	0632	...	0636	|	0639	0702	0707	0732	...	...	0736	|	0739	0802
23	Burgdorf d.	|	0454	|	...	...	...	0552	|	0620	|	...	|	|	0652	|	0720	|	...	...	|	|	0752	|
47	Langenthal d.	|	0513	|	...	...	...	0611	|	0641	|	...	|	|	0711	|	0741	|	...	...	|	|	0811	|
	Biel/Bienne d.	|	|	|	0515	...	0543	|	|	|	|	0613	|	0644	|	|	|	|	0715	...	|	0746	|	|
	Solothurn d.	|	|	|	0533	...	0601	|	|	|	|	0632	|	0702	|	|	|	|	0733	...	|	0801	|	|
67	**Olten** a.	0446	0525	0555	0557	...	0618	0623	0628	0654	|	0657	0702	0718	0724	|	0754	|	0757	...	0802	0818	0824	|
67	**Olten** d.	0448	0535	0557	0559	0603	0620	...	0631	▬	|	0659	0703	0720	0729	|	▬	|	0759	...	0803	0820	0829	|
80	Aarau d.	0458	0545	|	|	0614	0630	...	|	0653	|	|	0714	0730	|	|	0753	|	|	...	0814	0830	|	|
90	Lenzburg d.	0506	0554	|	|	|	|	...	|	0700	|	|	|	|	|	|	0800	|	|	...	|	|	|	|
	Brugg d.	|	|	|	|	0630	|	...	|	|	|	|	0730	|	|	|	|	|	|	...	0830	|	|	|
	Baden a.	|	|	|	|	0638	|	...	|	|	|	|	0738	|	|	|	|	|	|	...	0838	|	|	|
122	**Zürich HB** a.	|	0619	0628	0630	0654	0656	...	0702	0722	0728	0730	0754	0756	0802	0758	0822	0828	0830	...	0854	0856	0902	0858
	Zürich Flughafen ✈ **530/5** a.	0530	...	0650	0646	...	0720	...	0716	...	0750	0746	...	0820	...	0816	...	0850	0846	...	...	0920	...	0916
	St Gallen **530** a.	...	...	0753	|	...	0815	...	|	...	0853	|	...	0915	...	|	...	0953	|	...	...	1015	...	|
	Konstanz **535** a.	...	...	...	0754	...	...	...	|	...	...	0854	...	...	...	|	...	...	0954	...	...	...	...	|
	Romanshorn **535** a.	...	...	...	...	...	...	...	0818	...	...	...	...	...	...	0918	...	...	...	...	...	...	...	1018

km			*IC* 715 ✕	*IR* 9057	*IR* 1917	*ICN* 1517 ✕	*IR* 2017	*IC* 817 (✕)		*IC* 717 ✕	*IR* 9059	*IR* 1919	*ICN* 519 ✕	*IR* 2019	*IC* 819 ✕		*IC* 719 ✕	*IR* 9061	*IR* 1921	*ICN* 1521 ✕	*IR* 2021	*IC* 821 (✕)		*IC* 721 ✕
	Genève Aéroport ✈ **505** d.	...	0636	...	...	...	...	...	...	0736	...	...	0805	...	...	...	0836	...	...	...	...	...	...	0936
	Genève **505** d.	...	0645	...	...	...	...	...	...	0745	...	...	0814	...	...	...	0845	...	...	...	...	...	...	0945
	Lausanne **505** d.	...	0720	...	...	0745	...	...	...	0820	...	...	|	...	...	...	0920	...	...	0945	...	...	...	1020
	Brig **560** d.	...	|	...	...	|	...	0749	...	|	...	...	|	...	0849	...	|	...	...	|	...	0949	...	|
	Interlaken Ost **560** d.	...	|	...	...	|	...	|	...	|	...	...	|	...	|	...	|	...	...	|	...	|	...	|
	Bern d.	0807	0832	...	0836	|	0839	0902	0907	0932	...	0936	|	0939	1002	1007	1032	...	1036	|	1039	1102	1107	1132
	Burgdorf d.	0820	|	...	|	|	0852	|	0920	|	...	|	|	0952	|	1020	|	...	|	|	1052	|	1120	|
	Langenthal d.	0841	|	...	|	|	0911	|	0941	|	...	|	|	1011	|	1041	|	...	|	|	1111	|	1141	|
0	**Biel/Bienne** d.	|	|	0815	|	0846	|	|	|	|	0915	|	0946	|	|	|	|	1015	|	1046	|	|	|	|
25	Solothurn d.	|	|	0833	|	0901	|	|	|	|	0933	|	1001	|	|	|	|	1033	|	1101	|	|	|	|
60	**Olten** a.	0854	|	0857	0902	0918	0924	|	0954	|	0957	1002	1018	1024	|	1054	|	1057	1102	1118	1124	|	1154	|
60	**Olten** d.	▬	|	0859	0903	0920	0929	|	▬	|	0959	1003	1020	1029	|	▬	|	1059	1103	1120	1129	|	▬	|
73	Aarau d.	0853	|	|	0914	0930	|	|	0953	|	|	1014	1030	|	|	1053	|	|	1114	1130	|	|	1153	|
	Lenzburg d.	0900	|	|	|	|	|	|	1000	|	|	|	|	|	|	1100	|	|	|	|	|	|	1200	|
91	Brugg d.	|	|	|	0930	|	|	|	|	|	|	1030	|	|	|	|	|	|	1130	|	|	|	|	|
100	Baden a.	|	|	|	0938	|	|	|	|	|	|	1038	|	|	|	|	|	|	1138	|	|	|	|	|
122	**Zürich HB** a.	0922	0928	0930	0954	0956	1002	0958	1022	1028	1030	1054	1056	1102	1058	1122	1128	1130	1154	1156	1202	1158	1222	1228
	Zürich Flughafen ✈ **530/5** a.	...	0950	0946	...	1020	...	1016	...	1050	1046	...	1120	...	1116	...	1150	1146	...	1220	...	1216	...	1250
	St Gallen **530** a.	...	1053	|	...	1115	...	|	...	1153	|	...	1215	...	|	...	1253	|	...	1315	...	|	...	1353
	Konstanz **535** a.	...	...	1054	...	...	...	|	...	...	1154	...	...	...	|	...	...	1254	...	...	...	|	...	...
	Romanshorn **535** a.	...	...	...	...	...	...	1118	...	...	...	...	...	...	1218	...	...	...	...	...	...	1318	...	...

F – From Fribourg.

s – Stops to set down only.

SBB BERN and BIEL - ZÜRICH 500

	IR 9063	IR 1923	ICN 523	IR 2023		IC 823		IC 723	IR 9065	IR 1925	ICN 1525	IR 2025		IC 825		IC 725	IR 9067	IR 1927	ICN 527	IR 2027		IC 827		IC 727
			X			X		X			X			(X)		X			X			X		X
Genève Aéroport ✈ **505** d.	...	...	1005	...	...	...	...	1036	...	...	...	...	...	...	...	1136	...	...	1205	...	...	...	...	1236
Genève **505** d.	...	...	1014	...	...	...	...	1045	...	...	...	...	...	...	...	1145	...	...	1214	...	...	...	...	1245
Lausanne **505** d.	...	...	|	...	...	...	...	1120	...	...	1145	...	...	...	...	1220	...	...	|	...	...	...	...	1320
Brig **560** d.	...	...	|	...	...	1049	...	|	...	...	|	...	...	1149	...	|	...	...	|	...	...	1249	...	|
Interlaken Ost **560** d.	...	...	|	...	...	|	...	|	...	...	|	...	...	|	...	|	...	...	|	...	...	|	...	|
Bern d.	...	1136	|	1139	...	1202	1207	1232	...	1236	|	1239	...	1302	1307	1332	...	1336	|	1339	...	1402	1407	1432
Burgdorf d.	...	|	|	1152	...	|	1220	|	...	|	|	1252	...	|	1320	|	...	|	|	1352	...	|	1420	|
Langenthal d.	...	|	|	1211	...	|	1241	|	...	|	|	1311	...	|	1341	|	...	|	|	1411	...	|	1441	|
Biel/Bienne d.	1115	|	1146	|	...	|	|	|	1215	|	1246	|	...	|	|	|	1315	|	1346	|	...	|	|	|
Solothurn d.	1133	|	1201	|	...	|	|	|	1233	|	1301	|	...	|	|	|	1333	|	1401	|	...	|	|	|
Olten a.	1157	1202	1218	1224	...	|	1254	|	1257	1302	1318	1324	...	|	1354	|	1357	1402	1418	1424	...	|	1454	|
Olten d.	1159	1203	1220	1229	...	|	—	|	1259	1303	1320	1329	...	|	—	|	1359	1403	1420	1429	...	|	—	|
Aarau d.	|	1214	1230	|	...	|	1253	|	|	1314	1330	|	...	|	1353	|	|	1414	1430	|	...	|	1453	|
Lenzburg d.	|	|	|	|	...	|	1300	|	|	|	|	|	...	|	1400	|	|	|	|	|	...	|	1500	|
Brugg d.	|	1230	|	|	...	|	|	|	|	1330	|	|	...	|	|	|	|	1430	|	|	...	|	|	|
Baden a.	|	1238	|	|	...	|	|	|	|	1338	|	|	...	|	|	|	|	1438	|	|	...	|	|	|
Zürich HB a.	1230	1254	1256	1302	...	1258	1322	1328	1330	1354	1356	1402	...	1358	1422	1428	1430	1454	1456	1502	...	1458	1522	1528
Zürich Flughafen ✈ **530/5** a.	1246	...	1320	...	...	1316	...	1350	1346	...	1420	...	...	1416	...	1450	1446	...	1520	...	...	1516	...	1550
St Gallen **530** a.	|	...	1415	...	...	|	...	1453	|	...	1515	...	...	|	...	1553	|	...	1615	...	...	|	...	1653
Konstanz **535** a.	1354	...	...	...	...	|	...	...	1454	...	...	...	...	|	...	...	1554	...	...	...	...	|	...	...
Romanshorn **535** a.	...	...	...	...	...	1418	...	...	...	...	...	...	...	1518	...	...	...	...	...	...	...	1618	...	...

	IR 9069	IR 1929	ICN 1529	IR 2029	IC 829		IC 729	IR 9071	IR 1931	ICN 531	IR 2031		IC 831		IC 731	IR 9073	IR 1935	ICN 1535	IR 2035		IC 835		IC 735	IR 9075
			X		X		X			X			X		X			X			(X)		X	
Genève Aéroport ✈ **505** d.	...	...	...	...	...	...	1336	...	...	1405	...	...	...	...	1436	...	...	...	...	...	...	...	1536	...
Genève **505** d.	...	...	...	...	...	...	1345	...	...	1414	...	...	...	...	1445	...	...	...	...	...	...	...	1545	...
Lausanne **505** d.	...	...	1345	...	...	...	1420	...	...	|	...	...	...	...	1520	...	...	1545	...	...	...	...	1620	...
Brig **560** d.	...	...	|	...	1349	...	|	...	...	|	...	...	1449	...	|	...	...	|	...	...	1549	...	|	...
Interlaken Ost **560** d.	...	...	|	...	|	...	|	...	...	|	...	...	|	...	|	...	...	|	...	...	|	...	|	...
Bern d.	...	1436	|	1439	1502	1507	1532	...	1536	|	1539	...	1602	1607	1632	...	1636	|	1639	...	1702	1707	1732	...
Burgdorf d.	...	|	|	1452	|	1520	|	...	|	|	1552	...	|	1620	|	...	|	|	1652	...	|	1720	|	...
Langenthal d.	...	|	|	1511	|	1541	|	...	|	|	1611	...	|	1641	|	...	|	|	1711	...	|	1741	|	...
Biel/Bienne d.	1415	|	1446	|	|	|	|	1515	|	1546	|	...	|	|	|	1615	|	1646	|	...	|	|	|	1715
Solothurn d.	1433	|	1501	|	|	|	|	1533	|	1601	|	...	|	|	|	1633	|	1701	|	...	|	|	|	1733
Olten a.	1457	1502	1518	1524	|	1554	|	1557	1602	1618	1624	...	|	1654	|	1657	1702	1718	1724	...	|	1754	|	1757
Olten d.	1459	1503	1520	1529	|	—	|	1559	1603	1620	1629	...	|	—	|	1659	1703	1720	1729	...	|	—	|	1759
Aarau d.	|	1514	1530	|	|	1553	|	|	1614	1630	|	...	|	1653	|	|	1714	1730	|	...	|	1753	|	|
Lenzburg d.	|	|	|	|	|	1600	|	|	|	|	|	...	|	1700	|	|	|	|	|	...	|	1800	|	|
Brugg d.	|	1530	|	|	|	|	|	|	1630	|	|	...	|	|	|	|	1730	|	|	...	|	|	|	|
Baden a.	|	1538	|	|	|	|	|	|	1638	|	|	...	|	|	|	|	1738	|	|	...	|	|	|	|
Zürich HB a.	1530	1554	1556	1602	1558	1622	1628	1630	1654	1656	1702	...	1658	1722	1728	1730	1754	1756	1802	...	1758	1822	1828	1830
Zürich Flughafen ✈ **530/5** a.	1546	...	1620	...	1616	...	1650	1646	...	1720	...	...	1716	...	1750	1746	...	1820	...	...	1816	...	1850	1846
St Gallen **530** a.	|	...	1715	...	|	...	1753	|	...	1815	...	...	|	...	1853	|	...	1915	...	...	|	...	1953	|
Konstanz **535** a.	1654	...	...	...	|	...	...	1754	...	...	...	...	|	...	...	1854	...	...	...	...	|	...	...	1954
Romanshorn **535** a.	...	...	...	...	1718	...	...	...	...	...	...	...	1818	...	...	...	...	...	...	...	1918	...	...	...

	IR 1937	ICN 537	IR 2037	IC 837			IC 737	IR 9077	IR 1939	ICN 1539	IR 2039	IC 839		IC 739	IR 9079	IR 1941	ICN 541		IR 2041	IC 841		IC 741	IR 2141	IR 1943
		X		X			X			X		(X)		X			X			X		X		
Genève Aéroport ✈ **505** d.	...	1605	...	...	...	...	1636	...	...	...	...	...	...	1736	...	...	1805	...	...	...	...	1836	...	...
Genève **505** d.	...	1614	...	...	...	...	1645	...	...	...	...	...	...	1745	...	...	1814	...	...	...	...	1845	...	...
Lausanne **505** d.	...	|	...	...	...	...	1720	...	...	1745	...	...	...	1820	...	...	|	...	...	...	...	1920	...	...
Brig **560** d.	1541r	|	...	1649	...	...	|	...	1641r	|	...	1749	...	|	...	...	|	...	...	1849	...	|	...	...
Interlaken Ost **560** d.	|	|	...	|	...	...	|	...	|	|	...	|	...	|	...	...	|	...	...	|	...	|	...	...
Bern d.	1736	|	1739	1802	1807	...	1832	...	1836	|	1839	1902	1907	1932	...	1936	|	...	1939	2002	2007	2032	...	2036
Burgdorf d.	|	|	1752	|	1820	...	|	...	|	|	1852	|	1920	|	...	|	|	...	1952	|	2020	|	...	|
Langenthal d.	|	|	1811	|	1841	...	|	...	|	|	1911	|	1941	|	...	|	|	...	2011	|	2041	|	...	|
Biel/Bienne d.	|	1746	|	|	|	...	|	1815	|	1846	|	|	|	|	1915	|	1946	...	|	|	|	|	2015	|
Solothurn d.	|	1801	|	|	|	...	|	1833	|	1901	|	|	|	|	1933	|	2001	...	|	|	|	|	2033	|
Olten a.	1802	1818	1824	|	1854	...	|	1857	1902	1918	1924	|	1954	|	1957	2002	2018	...	2024	|	2054	|	2057	2102
Olten d.	1803	1820	1829	|	—	...	|	1859	1903	1920	1929	|	—	|	1959	2003	2020	...	2029	|	—	|	2059	2103
Aarau d.	1814	1830	|	|	1853	...	|	|	1914	1930	|	|	1953	|	|	2014	2030	...	|	|	2053	|	|	2114
Lenzburg d.	|	|	|	|	1900	...	|	|	|	|	|	|	2000	|	|	|	|	...	|	|	2100	|	|	|
Brugg d.	1830	|	|	|	|	...	|	|	1930	|	|	|	|	|	|	2030	|	...	|	|	|	|	|	2130
Baden a.	1838	|	|	|	|	...	|	|	1938	|	|	|	|	|	|	2038	|	...	|	|	|	|	|	2138
Zürich HB a.	1854	1856	1902	1858	1922	...	1928	1930	1954	1956	2002	1958	2022	2028	2030	2054	2056	...	2102	2058	2122	2128	2130	2154
Zürich Flughafen ✈ **530/5** a.	...	1920	...	1916	...	...	1950	1946	...	2020	...	2016	...	2050	2046	...	2120	...	...	2116	...	2150	...	...
St Gallen **530** a.	...	2015	...	|	...	...	2053	|	...	2115	...	|	...	2153	|	...	2215	...	...	|	...	2253	...	...
Konstanz **535** a.	...	...	...	|	...	...	...	2054	...	...	...	|	...	...	2154	...	...	...	...	|	...	...	...	...
Romanshorn **535** a.	...	...	...	2018	...	...	...	...	...	...	...	2118	...	...	...	...	...	...	...	2218	...	...	...	...

	ICN 1543	IR 2043	IC 843		IR 2143	IC 743	IR 1945		ICN 545	IR 2045	IC 845		IC 745	IR 1947		IC 847	ICN 1547	RE 3647		IC 747	IC 849	ICN 1549		IC 803
	X		(X)			X			X															⑥⑦y
Genève Aéroport ✈ **505** d.	...	...	...	...	...	1936	...	...	2005	...	...	...	2036	...	...	...	...	...	...	2136	...	...	...	...
Genève **505** d.	...	...	...	...	...	1945	...	...	2014	...	...	...	2045	...	...	...	...	...	...	2145	...	...	...	...
Lausanne **505** d.	1945	...	...	...	...	2020	...	...	|	...	...	...	2120	...	...	...	2145	...	...	2220	...	...	...	...
Brig **560** d.	|	...	1949	...	...	|	...	...	|	...	...	...	|	...	...	...	|	...	...	|	...	...	...	...
Interlaken Ost **560** d.	|	...	|	...	...	|	...	...	|	...	...	...	|	...	...	...	|	...	...	|	...	...	...	...
Bern d.	|	2039	2102	2107	...	2132	...	...	|	2137	2202	2207	2232	...	...	2302	|	...	2307	2332	0002	...	0007	0102
Burgdorf d.	|	2052	|	2120	...	|	...	...	|	2152	|	2222	|	...	...	|	|	...	2322	|	|	...	0022	|
Langenthal d.	|	2111	|	2141	...	|	...	...	|	2211	|	2242	|	...	...	|	|	...	2342	|	|	...	0043	|
Biel/Bienne d.	2046	|	|	|	2115	|	...	...	2146	|	|	|	|	...	...	|	2246	...	|	|	|	2346	|	|
Solothurn d.	2101	|	|	|	2133	|	...	...	2203	|	|	|	|	...	...	|	2305	...	|	|	|	0005	|	|
Olten a.	2118	2124	|	2154	2157	2158	...	...	2219	2224	2228	2254	2258	...	...	|	2330	...	2354	2358	0028	0030	0054	0128
Olten d.	2120	...	|	—	...	2200	2203	...	2220	...	2230	—	2300	2303	...	|	2335	2340	—	0000	0033	0035	...	0133
Aarau d.	2130	...	|	2153	...	|	2214	...	2230	...	|	2253	|	2314	...	|	2345	2349	2353	0009	|	0045	...	0143
Lenzburg d.	|	...	|	2200	...	|	|	...	|	...	|	2300	|	|	...	|	|	|	0000	0018	|	0052	...	|
Brugg d.	|	...	|	|	...	|	2230	...	|	...	|	|	|	2330	...	|	|	0003	|	|	|	|	...	|
Baden a.	|	...	|	|	...	|	2238	...	|	...	|	|	|	2338	...	|	|	0013	|	|	|	|	...	|
Zürich HB a.	2156	...	2158	2222	...	2231	2254	...	2256	...	2301	2322	2331	2354	...	2358	0010	0042	0022	0033	0104	0112	...	0207j
Zürich Flughafen ✈ **530/5** a.	2220	...	2216	...	...	...	...	...	2320	...	2316	...	...	...	...	...	0027	...	...	...	...	...	...	...
St Gallen **530** a.	2317	...	|	...	...	...	...	...	0018	...	|	...	...	...	...	...	0125	...	...	...	...	...	...	...
Konstanz **535** a.	...	...	|	...	...	...	...	...	...	...	|	...	...	...	...	...	...	...	...	...	...	...	...	...
Romanshorn **535** a.	...	...	2318	...	...	...	...	...	...	...	0018	...	...	...	...	...	...	...	...	...	...	...	...	...

j – Arrive 0215 on ⑦.

r – ⑥⑦ June 19 - Oct. 24.

y – Also Jan. 1.

500 ZÜRICH - BIEL and BERN

SBB

	IR 3206 Ⓐ	IR 2006	IC 706	IR 2106	IR 3208	IR 2008	IC 808 ✕	ICN 508 ✕	IR 1908	IR 2108	IC 708 ✕		IC 1008 🍷 Ⓐ		IR 2010	IC 810 (✕)	ICN 1510 ✕	IR 1910	IR 9050	IC 710 ✕		IC 1012 🍷 Ⓐ	IR 2012	IC 812 ✕
Romanshorn **535** d.	...	...	...	...	...	...	...	...	...	...	...	...	...	...	...	0538	...	...	...	...	...	...	...	0638
Konstanz **535** d.	...	...	...	...	...	...	...	...	...	...	...	...	...	...	...	|	...	...	0603	...	...	...	...	|
St Gallen **530** d.	...	...	...	...	...	...	...	...	...	...	0511	...	...	...	...	|	0544	...	|	0611	...	...	...	|
Zürich Flughafen ✈ **530/5** d.	...	...	...	...	...	...	...	...	...	...	0613	...	...	...	...	0640	0643	...	0710	0713	...	...	...	0743
Zürich HB d.	...	...	0521	...	...	0558	0600	0604	0606	0630	0632	0638	0647	...	0658	0700	0704	0706	0730	0732	0738	0747	0758	0800
Baden d.	...	...	|	...	...	|	|	|	0622	|	|	|	|	...	|	|	|	0722	|	|	|	|	|	|
Brugg d.	...	...	|	...	...	|	|	|	0632	|	|	|	|	...	|	|	|	0732	|	|	|	|	|	|
Lenzburg d.	...	...	0542	...	...	|	|	|	|	|	|	0659	|	...	|	|	|	|	|	|	0759	|	|	|
Aarau d.	...	...	0549	...	...	|	|	0630	0647	|	|	0705	|	...	|	|	0730	0747	|	|	0805	|	|	|
Olten a.	...	...	0558	...	...	0629	|	0639	0656	0701	|	▬	|	...	0729	|	0739	0756	0801	|	▬	|	0829	|
Olten d.	0506	0536	0603	0603	0606	0636	|	0641	0658	0703	|	0706	|	...	0736	|	0741	0758	0803	|	0806	|	0836	|
Solothurn d.	|	|	|	0628	|	|	|	0659	|	0728	|	|	|	...	|	|	0759	|	0828	|	|	|	|	|
Biel/Bienne a.	|	|	|	0645	|	|	|	0713	|	0745	|	|	|	...	|	|	0813	|	0845	|	|	|	|	|
Langenthal d.	0518	0549	|	...	0618	0649	|	|	|	...	|	0718	|	...	0749	|	|	|	...	|	0818	|	0849	|
Burgdorf d.	0538	0607	|	...	0638	0707	|	|	|	...	|	0738	|	...	0807	|	|	|	...	|	0838	|	0907	|
Bern a.	0553	0621	0629	...	0653	0721	0657	|	0725	...	0729	0753	0745	...	0821	0757	|	0825	...	0829	0853	0845	0921	0857
Interlaken Ost **560** a.	...	...	|	...	...	...	|	|	...	...	|	...	...	...	...	|	|	...	...	|	...	...	...	|
Brig **560** a.	...	...	|	...	...	...	0811	|	...	...	|	...	...	...	...	0911	|	...	...	|	...	...	...	1011
Lausanne **505** a.	...	...	0740	...	...	...	...	|	...	...	0840	...	...	...	...	...	0915	...	...	0940	...	...	...	...
Genève **505** a.	...	...	0815	...	...	...	...	0846	...	...	0915	...	...	...	...	...	...	...	...	1015	...	...	...	...
Genève Aéroport ✈ **505** a.	...	...	0824	...	...	...	...	0855	...	...	0924	...	...	...	...	...	...	...	...	1024	...	...	...	...

	ICN 512 ✕	IR 1912	IR 9052	IC 712 ✕		IR 2016	IC 816 (✕)	ICN 1516 ✕	IR 1916		IR 9054	IC 716 ✕		IR 2018	IC 818 ✕	ICN 518 ✕	IR 1918		IR 9056	IC 718 ✕		IR 2020	IC 820 ✕	ICN 1520 ✕
Romanshorn **535** d.	...	...	...	...	...	...	0741	...	...	...	...	...	...	...	0841	...	...	...	...	...	...	...	0941	...
Konstanz **535** d.	...	...	0703	...	...	...	|	...	...	...	0803	...	...	...	|	...	...	...	0903	...	...	...	|	...
St Gallen **530** d.	0642	...	|	0711	...	...	|	0748	...	...	|	0811	...	...	|	0848	...	...	|	0911	...	...	|	0948
Zürich Flughafen ✈ **530/5** d.	0739	...	0810	0813	...	...	0840	0843	...	...	0910	0913	...	...	0940	0943	...	...	1010	1013	...	...	1040	1043
Zürich HB d.	0804	0806	0830	0832	0838	0858	0900	0904	0906	...	0930	0932	0938	0958	1000	1004	1006	...	1030	1032	1038	1058	1100	1104
Baden d.	|	0822	|	|	|	|	|	|	0922	...	|	|	|	|	|	|	1022	...	|	|	|	|	|	|
Brugg d.	|	0832	|	|	|	|	|	|	0932	...	|	|	|	|	|	|	1032	...	|	|	|	|	|	|
Lenzburg d.	|	|	|	|	0859	|	|	|	|	...	|	|	0959	|	|	|	|	...	|	|	1059	|	|	|
Aarau d.	0830	0847	|	|	0905	|	|	0930	0947	...	|	|	1005	|	|	1030	1047	...	|	|	1105	|	|	1130
Olten a.	0839	0856	0901	|	▬	0929	|	0939	0956	...	1001	|	▬	1029	|	1039	1056	...	1101	|	▬	1129	|	1139
Olten d.	0841	0858	0903	|	0906	0936	|	0941	0958	...	1003	|	1006	1036	|	1041	1058	...	1103	|	1106	1136	|	1141
Solothurn d.	0859	|	0928	|	|	|	|	0959	|	...	1028	|	|	|	|	1059	|	...	1128	|	|	|	|	1159
Biel/Bienne a.	0913	|	0945	|	|	|	|	1013	|	...	1045	|	|	|	|	1113	|	...	1145	|	|	|	|	1213
Langenthal d.	|	|	...	|	0918	0949	|	|	|	...	...	|	1018	1049	|	|	|	...	...	|	1118	1149	|	|
Burgdorf d.	|	|	...	|	0938	1007	|	|	|	...	...	|	1038	1107	|	|	|	...	...	|	1138	1207	|	|
Bern a.	|	0925	...	0929	0953	1021	0957	|	1025	...	...	1029	1053	1121	1057	|	1125	...	...	1129	1153	1221	1157	|
Interlaken Ost **560** a.	|	...	...	|	...	...	|	|	...	...	...	|	...	...	|	|	...	...	...	|	...	...	|	|
Brig **560** a.	|	...	...	|	...	...	1111	|	...	...	...	|	...	...	1211	|	...	...	...	|	...	...	1311	|
Lausanne **505** a.	|	...	...	1040	...	...	...	1115	...	...	...	1140	...	...	...	|	...	...	...	1240	...	...	...	1315
Genève **505** a.	1046	...	...	1115	...	...	...	...	...	...	...	1215	...	...	...	1246	...	...	...	1315	...	...	...	...
Genève Aéroport ✈ **505** a.	1055	...	...	1124	...	...	...	...	...	...	...	1224	...	...	...	1255	...	...	...	1324	...	...	...	...

	IR 1920	IR 9058	IC 720 ✕		IR 2022	IC 822 ✕	ICN 522 ✕	IR 1922		IR 9060	IC 722 ✕		IR 2024	IC 824 (✕)	ICN 1524 ✕	IR 1924	IR 9062	IC 724 ✕		IR 2026	IC 826 ✕	ICN 526 ✕	IR 1926	IR 9064
Romanshorn **535** d.	...	...	...	...	...	1041	...	...	...	...	...	...	...	1141	...	...	...	...	...	...	1241	...	...	...
Konstanz **535** d.	...	1003	...	...	...	|	...	...	...	1103	...	...	...	|	...	...	1203	...	...	...	|	...	...	1303
St Gallen **530** d.	...	|	1011	...	...	|	1048	...	...	|	1111	...	...	|	1148	...	|	1211	...	...	|	1248	...	|
Zürich Flughafen ✈ **530/5** d.	...	1110	1113	...	...	1140	1143	...	...	1210	1213	...	...	1240	1243	...	1310	1313	...	...	1340	1343	...	1410
Zürich HB d.	1106	1130	1132	1138	1158	1200	1204	1206	...	1230	1232	1238	1258	1300	1304	1306	1330	1332	1338	1358	1400	1404	1406	1430
Baden d.	1122	|	|	|	|	|	|	1222	...	|	|	|	|	|	|	1322	|	|	|	|	|	|	1422	|
Brugg d.	1132	|	|	|	|	|	|	1232	...	|	|	|	|	|	|	1332	|	|	|	|	|	|	1432	|
Lenzburg d.	|	|	|	1159	|	|	|	|	...	|	|	1259	|	|	|	|	|	|	1359	|	|	|	|	|
Aarau d.	1147	|	|	1205	|	|	1230	1247	...	|	|	1305	|	|	1330	1347	|	|	1405	|	|	1430	1447	|
Olten a.	1156	1201	|	▬	1229	|	1239	1256	...	1301	|	▬	1329	|	1339	1356	1401	|	▬	1429	|	1439	1456	1501
Olten d.	1158	1203	|	1206	1236	|	1241	1258	...	1303	|	1306	1336	|	1341	1358	1403	|	1406	1436	|	1441	1458	1503
Solothurn d.	|	1228	|	|	|	|	1259	|	...	1328	|	|	|	|	1359	|	1428	|	|	|	|	1459	|	1528
Biel/Bienne a.	|	1245	|	|	|	|	1313	|	...	1345	|	|	|	|	1413	|	1445	|	|	|	|	1513	|	1545
Langenthal d.	|	...	|	1218	1249	|	|	|	...	...	|	1318	1349	|	|	|	...	|	1418	1449	|	|	|	...
Burgdorf d.	|	...	|	1238	1307	|	|	|	...	...	|	1338	1407	|	|	|	...	|	1438	1507	|	|	|	...
Bern a.	1225	...	1229	1253	1321	1257	|	1325	...	...	1329	1353	1421	1357	|	1425	...	1429	1453	1521	1457	|	1525	...
Interlaken Ost **560** a.	...	...	|	...	...	|	|	...	...	...	|	...	...	|	|	...	...	|	...	...	|	|	...	...
Brig **560** a.	...	...	|	...	...	1411	|	...	...	...	|	...	...	1511	|	...	...	|	...	...	1611	|	...	...
Lausanne **505** a.	...	...	1340	...	...	...	|	...	...	...	1440	...	...	...	1515	...	...	1540	...	...	...	|	...	...
Genève **505** a.	...	...	1415	...	...	...	1446	...	...	...	1515	...	...	...	...	...	...	1615	...	...	...	1646	...	...
Genève Aéroport ✈ **505** a.	...	...	1424	...	...	...	1455	...	...	...	1524	...	...	...	...	...	...	1624	...	...	...	1655	...	...

	IC 726 ✕		IR 2028	IC 828 (✕)	ICN 1528 ✕	IR 1928	IR 9066	IC 728 ✕		IR 2030	IC 830 ✕	ICN 530 ✕	IR 1930		IR 9068	IC 730 ✕		IR 2032	IC 832 (✕)	ICN 1532 ✕	IR 1932	IR 9070	IC 732 ✕	
Romanshorn **535** d.	...	...	...	1341	...	...	...	...	...	...	1441	...	...	...	...	...	...	...	1541	...	...	...	...	...
Konstanz **535** d.	...	...	...	|	...	...	1403	...	...	...	|	...	...	...	1503	...	...	...	|	...	...	1603	...	...
St Gallen **530** d.	1311	...	...	|	1348	...	|	1411	...	...	|	1448	...	...	|	1511	...	...	|	1548	...	|	1611	...
Zürich Flughafen ✈ **530/5** d.	1413	...	...	1440	1443	...	1510	1513	...	...	1540	1543	...	...	1610	1613	...	...	1640	1643	...	1710	1713	...
Zürich HB d.	1432	1438	1458	1500	1504	1506	1530	1532	1538	1558	1600	1604	1606	...	1630	1632	1638	1658	1700	1704	1706	1730	1732	1738
Baden d.	|	|	|	|	|	1522	|	|	|	|	|	|	1622	...	|	|	|	|	|	|	1722	|	|	|
Brugg d.	|	|	|	|	|	1532	|	|	|	|	|	|	1632	...	|	|	|	|	|	|	1732	|	|	|
Lenzburg d.	|	1459	|	|	|	|	|	|	1559	|	|	|	|	...	|	|	1659	|	|	|	|	|	|	1759
Aarau d.	|	1505	|	|	1530	1547	|	|	1605	|	|	1630	1647	...	|	|	1705	|	|	1730	1747	|	|	1805
Olten a.	|	▬	1529	|	1539	1556	1601	|	▬	1629	|	1639	1656	...	1701	|	▬	1729	|	1739	1756	1801	|	▬
Olten d.	|	1506	1536	|	1541	1558	1603	|	1606	1636	|	1641	1658	...	1703	|	1706	1736	|	1741	1758	1803	|	1806
Solothurn d.	|	|	|	|	1559	|	1628	|	|	|	|	1659	|	...	1728	|	|	|	|	1759	|	1828	|	|
Biel/Bienne a.	|	|	|	|	1613	|	1645	|	|	|	|	1713	|	...	1745	|	|	|	|	1813	|	1845	|	|
Langenthal d.	|	1518	1549	|	|	|	...	|	1618	1649	|	|	|	...	...	|	1718	1749	|	|	|	...	|	1818
Burgdorf d.	|	1538	1607	|	|	|	...	|	1638	1707	|	|	|	...	...	|	1738	1807	|	|	|	...	|	1838
Bern a.	1529	1553	1621	1557	|	1625	...	1629	1653	1721	1657	|	1725	...	...	1729	1753	1821	1757	|	1825	...	1829	1853
Interlaken Ost **560** a.	|	...	...	|	|	...	...	|	...	...	|	|	...	...	...	|	...	...	|	|	...	...	|	...
Brig **560** a.	|	...	...	1711	|	...	...	|	...	...	1811	|	...	...	...	|	...	...	1911	|	...	...	|	...
Lausanne **505** a.	1640	...	...	...	1715	...	...	1740	...	...	...	|	...	...	...	1840	...	...	...	1915	...	...	1940	...
Genève **505** a.	1715	...	...	...	...	...	...	1815	...	...	...	1846	...	...	...	1915	...	...	...	...	...	...	2015	...
Genève Aéroport ✈ **505** a.	1724	...	...	...	...	...	...	1824	...	...	...	1855	...	...	...	1924	...	...	...	...	...	...	2024	...

SBB ZÜRICH - BIEL and BERN 500

km (via hsl)		IR	IC	ICN	IR	IR	IC		IR	IC	ICN	IR		IR	IC		IR	IC	ICN	ICN	IR	IR	IC	
		2036	836	536	1936	9072	736		2038	838	1538	1938		9074	738		2040	840	1540	540	1940	9076	740	
			✕	✕			✕			✕	✕				✕			✕	✕ ⚒	✕ †			✕	
	Romanshorn **535** d.	...	1641	...	...	...	...	...	...	1741	...	...	...	...	...	...	...	1841	...	...	...	...	...	...
	Konstanz **535** d.	...	|	...	...	1703	...	...	...	|	...	...	...	1803	...	...	...	|	...	...	...	1903	...	...
	St Gallen **530** d.	...	|	1648	...	|	1711	...	...	|	1748	...	...	|	1811	...	...	|	1848	1848	...	|	1911	...
	Zürich Flughafen ✈ **530/5** d.	...	1740	1743	...	1810	1813	...	...	1840	1843	...	...	1910	1913	...	...	1940	1943	1943	...	2010	2013	...
	Zürich HB d.	1758	1800	1804	1806	1830	1832	1838	1858	1900	1904	1906	...	1930	1932	1938	1958	2000	2004	2004	2006	2030	2032	2038
	Baden d.	|	|	|	1822	|	|	|	|	|	|	1922	...	|	|	|	|	|	|	|	2022	|	|	|
	Brugg d.	|	|	|	1832	|	|	|	|	|	|	1932	...	|	|	|	|	|	|	|	2032	|	|	|
	Lenzburg d.	|	|	|	|	|	|	1859	|	|	|	|	...	|	|	1959	|	|	|	|	|	|	|	2059
	Aarau d.	|	|	1830	1847	|	|	1905	|	|	1930	1947	...	|	|	2005	|	|	2030	2030	2047	|	|	2105
	Olten a.	1829	|	1839	1856	1901	|	▬	1929	|	1939	1956	...	2001	|	▬	2029	|	2039	2039	2056	2101	|	▬
0	**Olten** d.	1836	|	1841	1858	1903	|	1906	1936	|	1941	1958	...	2003	|	2006	2036	|	2041	2041	2058	2103	|	2106
	Solothurn d.	|	|	1859	|	1928	|	|	|	|	1959	|	...	2028	|	|	|	|	2059	2059	|	2128	|	|
	Biel/Bienne a.	|	|	1913	|	1945	|	|	|	|	2013	|	...	2045	|	|	|	|	2113	2113	|	2145	|	|
	Langenthal d.	1849	|	|	|	...	|	1918	1949	|	|	|	...	...	|	2018	2049	|	...	|	|	...	|	2118
	Burgdorf d.	1907	|	|	|	...	|	1938	2007	|	|	|	...	...	|	2038	2107	|	...	|	|	...	|	2138
62	**Bern** a.	1921	1857	|	1925	...	1929	1953	2021	1957	|	2025	...	...	2029	2053	2121	2057	...	|	2125	...	2129	2153
	Interlaken Ost **560** a.	...	|	|	...	...	|	...	...	|	|	...	...	...	|	...	...	...	...	|	...	...	|	...
	Brig **560** a.	...	2011	|	...	...	|	...	...	2111	|	...	...	...	|	...	...	...	...	|	...	...	|	...
	Lausanne **505** a.	...	...	|	...	...	2040	...	...	...	2115	...	...	...	2140	...	...	...	...	|	...	...	2240	...
	Genève **505** a.	...	...	2046	...	...	2115	...	...	...	...	...	...	...	2215	...	...	...	...	2246	...	...	2324	...
	Genève Aéroport ✈ **505** a.	...	...	2055	...	...	2124	...	...	...	...	...	...	...	2224	...	...	...	...	2255	...	...	2333	...

km (via hsl)		IR	IC	ICN	IR		IR	IC		IC	IR	ICN	IR	IC		IC	IR	ICN	IR	IC		IC	IR	IC
		2042	842	1542	1942		9078	742		844	2044	1544	1944	744		846	2046	1546	1946	746		800	2002	802
			(✕)					✕ F		✕													⑥⑦q	⑥⑦q
	Romanshorn **535** d.	...	1941	...	...	...	...	...	...	2041	...	...	...	...	...	2141	...	...	...	...	...	...	...	...
	Konstanz **535** d.	...	|	...	...	...	2003	...	...	|	...	...	...	...	...	|	...	...	...	...	...	...	...	...
	St Gallen **530** d.	...	|	1948	...	...	|	2011	...	|	...	2048	...	2111	...	|	...	2144	...	...	...	...	...	...
	Zürich Flughafen ✈ **530/5** d.	...	2040	2043	...	...	2110	2113	...	2140	...	2143	...	2213	...	2240	...	2243	...	...	...	...	...	...
	Zürich HB d.	2058	2100	2104	2106	...	2130	2132	2138	2200	...	2204	2206	2232	2238	2300	...	2304	2306	2332	2338	0000	...	0100
	Baden d.	|	|	|	2122	...	|	|	|	|	...	|	2222	|	|	|	...	|	2322	|	|	|	...	|
	Brugg d.	|	|	|	2132	...	|	|	|	|	...	|	2232	|	|	|	...	|	2332	|	|	|	...	|
	Lenzburg d.	|	|	|	|	...	|	|	2159	|	...	|	|	|	2259	|	...	|	|	|	2359	|	...	|
	Aarau d.	|	|	2130	2147	...	|	|	2205	|	...	2230	2247	|	2305	|	...	2330	2347	|	0005	|	...	|
	Olten a.	2129	|	2139	2156	...	2201	|	...	2232	...	2239	2256	2301	...	2332	...	2339	2356	0001	...	0032	...	0131
0	**Olten** d.	2137	|	2141	...	...	2203	|	...	2235	2237	2241	...	2304	...	2335	2337	2341	...	0004	...	0033	0037	0135
	Solothurn d.	|	|	2159	...	...	2228	|	...	|	|	2258	...	|	...	|	|	0005	...	|	...	|	|	|
58	**Biel/Bienne** a.	|	|	2213	...	...	2245	|	...	|	|	2314	...	|	...	|	|	0022	...	|	...	|	|	|
	Langenthal d.	2149	|	|	...	...	...	|	...	|	2249	|	...	|	...	|	2349	|	...	|	...	|	0049	|
	Burgdorf d.	2209	|	|	...	...	...	|	...	|	2309	|	...	|	...	|	0009	|	...	|	...	|	0109	|
	Bern a.	2223	2157	|	...	...	...	2229	...	2302	2323	|	...	2331	...	0002	0023	|	...	0031	...	0100	0123	0202
	Interlaken Ost **560** a.	...	...	|	...	...	...	...	...	...	...	|	...	...	...	...	...	|	...	...	...	...	...	...
	Brig **560** a.	...	...	|	...	...	...	...	...	...	...	|	...	...	...	...	...	|	...	...	...	...	...	...
	Lausanne **505** a.	...	...	2315	...	...	...	...	...	...	...	0015	...	...	...	...	...	0124p	...	...	...	...	...	...
	Genève **505** a.	...	...	...	...	...	...	...	...	...	...	...	...	...	...	...	...	...	...	...	...	...	...	...
	Genève Aéroport ✈ **505** a.	...	...	...	...	...	...	...	...	...	...	...	...	...	...	...	...	...	...	...	...	...	...	...

F – To Fribourg.
p – ⑥⑦ (also Jan. 1, Apr. 2, 5, May 13, 14, 24; not Dec. 13, 26, 27).
q – Also Jan. 1.
u – Stops to pick up only.

NStCM. Narrow gauge. 2nd class only — NYON - ST CERGUE - LA CURE 501

km		j	k	j	j			j					j			j		j		j		j		j		j					m
0	**Nyon** d.	0525	0556	...	0625	0701	0756	0825	0856	0956	1056	1156	1230	1256	1356	1430	1456	1530	1556	1630	1656	1730	1756	1830	1856	1930	1956	2056	2215	2325	0040
19	St Cergue a.	0600	0628	0631	0700	0734	0828	0900	0928	1028	1128	1228	1304	1328	1428	1504	1528	1604	1628	1704	1728	1804	1828	1904	1928	2004	2028	2128	2246	2356	0111
27	La Cure a.	0616	0644	0644	0716	0748	0844	...	0944	1044	1144	1244	...	1344	1444	...	1544	...	1644	...	1744	...	1844	...	1944	...	...	...	...	...	...

	j		j	⚒	j	j	n	j							j				j			j		j					
La Cure d.	...	...	0618	0649	0718	...	0756	...	...	0856	0956	1056	1156	1256	...	1356	1456	1556	...	...	1656	...	1756	...	1856	1956	...	...	...	...
St Cergue d.	0544	0612	0644	0706	0744	0812	0812	0844	...	0912	1012	1112	1212	1312	1347	1412	1512	1612	1647	...	1712	1747	1812	1847	1912	2012	...	2132	2247	0000
Nyon a.	0616	0644	0716	0741	0816	0844	0844	0916	...	0944	1044	1144	1244	1344	1420	1444	1544	1644	1720	...	1744	1820	1844	1920	1944	2044	...	2204	2320	0032

j – Ⓐ (not Sept. 20).
k – ⑥ (also Sept. 20; not Dec. 26, Jan. 2).
m – ⑥⑦ (not Dec. 26, 27, Jan. 2, 3, Apr. 3, Aug. 1).
n – Ⓒ (also Sept. 20).

BAM. Narrow gauge. 2nd class only — MORGES - BIÈRE and L'ISLE MONT LA VILLE 502

km		⚒		⚒		⚒		⚒			⚒		⚒		⚒			⚒		⚒					F✓
0	**Morges** d.	0616	0702	0738	0846	0946	1046	1138	...	1220	1303	1403	1503	1558	1646	1736	...	1809	1858	1946	2036	2209	2336	...	0103
12	Apples a.	0631	0717	0753	0901	1001	1101	1153	...	1235	1318	1418	1518	1613	1701	1751	...	1824	1913	2001	2051	2224	2351	...	0120
19	**Bière** a.	0644	0730	0806	0914	1014	1114	1206	...	1248	1331	1431	1531	1626	1714	1804	...	1837	1926	2014	2104	2237	0004	...	0131

	⚒		⚒	Ⓐ		⚒		⚒			⚒		⚒		⚒		⚒			⚒					F
Bière d.	0543	0623	0652	0709	0745	0853	0953	1053	1145	...	1227	1310	1353	1453	1605	1653	1726	...	1816	1853	1953	2126	2253	...	0026
Apples d.	0553	0633	0702	0719	0755	0903	1003	1103	1155	...	1237	1320	1403	1503	1615	1703	1736	...	1826	1903	2003	2136	2303	...	0036
Morges a.	0613	0653	0722	0738	0815	0923	1023	1123	1215	...	1257	1340	1423	1523	1635	1723	1756	...	1846	1923	2023	2156	2323	...	0056

km			⚒		Ⓐ🚌	Ⓒ				Ⓐ🚌	Ⓒ		Ⓐ		⚒	A🚌	B	A🚌	C	A🚌	B	D	D		F✓
0	Apples d.	0601	0633	0721	0904	0904	...	1104	1238	1420	1420	1616	1703	1753	1828	1916	1916	2004	2004	2054	2054	2226	2353	...	0121
11	L'Isle Mont la Ville d.	0614	0646	0735	0918	0918	...	1118	1252	1434	1434	1630	1717	1807	1842	1930	1930	2018	2018	2108	2108	2240	0007	...	0135

		⚒			Ⓐ🚌	Ⓒ				Ⓐ🚌	Ⓒ			Ⓐ		⚒	A🚌	B	A🚌	C	A🚌	B	D		F
L'Isle Mont la Ville d.	0616	0647	0739	...	0946	0946	1138	...	1304	1446	1446	1646	...	1720	1810	1846	1946	1946	2036	2036	2120	2120	2246	...	0019
Apples a.	0631	0701	0754	...	1001	1001	1153	...	1319	1501	1501	1701	...	1735	1825	1901	2001	2001	2051	2051	2135	2135	2301	...	0034

A – ①②③④ (not Apr. 5, May 13, 24).
B – ⑤⑥⑦ (also Apr. 5, May 13, 24).
C – ⑤⑥ (also Apr. 5, May 13, 24).
D – ⑤⑥ (not Dec. 25, 26, Jan. 1, 2, Apr. 2).
F – ⑥⑦ (not Dec. 26, 27, Jan. 2, 3, Apr. 3).
✓ – Supplement payable.

SBB YVERDON - FRIBOURG 503

km		Ⓐ		Ⓐ						
0	**Yverdon** d.	0520	0601	0620	...	0701	and	2101	2201	2301
18	Estavayer-le-Lac d.	0538	0619	0638	...	0719	hourly	2119	2219	2319
28	Payerne d.	0553	0630	0653	...	0730	until	2130	2230	2329
50	**Fribourg** a.	0621	0658	0721	...	0758		2158	2259	...

			Ⓐ	Ⓒ				G	⑤⑥
Fribourg d.	...	0601a	0701	0703	0803	and	2203	2303	2342
Payerne d.	0530	0630	0730	0730	0830	hourly	2230	2330	0009
Estavayer-le-Lac d.	0540	0640	0740	0740	0840	until	2240	2340	0019
Yverdon a.	0557	0657	0757	0757	0857		2257	2357	0036

G – ①②③④⑦ only.
a – Ⓐ only.

505 GENÈVE - LAUSANNE - BIEL, BASEL and BERN

SBB

km		ICN 509	IR 2509	ICN 1609	ICN 1511	IR 2511	ICN 611	IR 1711	IC 711	IR 2515	ICN 515	ICN 1615	RE 2615	IC 715	RE 2917	IR 2517	ICN 617	ICN 1517	RE 2617	IC 717	RE 2919	IR 2519	ICN 519	ICN 1619	RE 2619	IC 719
					✕		✕		✕		✕	✕		✕			✕	✕		✕		🍷	✕	✕		✕
			m					B							Ⓐ						Ⓐ					
0	Genève A ✈ 570 d.	...	...	...	...	...	...	0511	...	...	...	...	0612	0636	...	0701	0705	...	...	0736	...	0801	0805	...	...	0836
6	**Genève 570** d.	...	...	...	...	0456	...	0521	0536	0610	0614	...	0621	0645	0649	0710	0714	...	0720	0745	0749	0810	0814	...	0821	0845
27	Nyon **570** d.	...	...	...	...	0510	...	0537	0550	|	0627	...	0637	|	0705	|	0727	...	0736	|	0805	|	0827	...	0837	|
53	Morges **570** d.	...	...	...	...	0528	...	0600	0605	|	0641	...	0700	|	0724	|	0741	...	0800	|	0824	|	0841	...	0900	|
66	**Lausanne 570** a.	...	...	...	...	0540	...	0612	0615	0643	|	...	0712	0718	0737	0743	|	...	0812	0818	0837	0843	|	...	0912	0918
	Lausanne 508 d.	...	0445	...	0539	0545	...	...	0620	0645	|	0645	...	0720	...	0745	|	0745	...	0820	...	0845	|	0845	...	0920
	Yverdon d.	...	|	...	0604	|	...	...	|	|	0704	0707	...	|	...	|	0804	0807	...	|	...	|	0904	0907	...	|
	Neuchâtel d.	...	|	...	0624	|	...	...	|	|	0724	0727	...	|	...	|	0824	0827	...	|	...	|	0924	0927	...	|
	Biel/Bienne a.	...	|	...	0641	|	...	...	|	|	0741	0743k	...	|	...	|	0841	0843k	...	|	...	|	0941	0943k	...	|
	Biel/Bienne d.	0543	|	0549	0644	|	0649	...	|	|	0746	0749	...	|	...	|	0849	0846	...	|	...	|	0946	0949	...	|
	Moutier d.	|	|	0608	|	|	0708	...	|	|	|	0808	...	|	...	|	0908	|	...	|	...	|	|	1008	...	|
	Delémont d.	|	|	0623	|	|	0723	...	|	|	|	0823	...	|	...	|	0923	|	...	|	...	|	|	1023	...	|
	Basel a.	|	|	0653	|	|	0753	...	|	|	|	0853	...	|	...	|	0953	|	...	|	...	|	|	1053	...	|
87	Palézieux **508** d.	|	0501	...	|	0601	...	...	|	0701	|	...	...	|	...	0801	...	|	...	|	...	0901	|	...	...	|
106	Romont d.	|	0516	...	|	0616	...	...	|	0716	|	...	...	|	...	0816	...	|	...	|	...	0916	|	...	...	|
132	Fribourg d.	|	0534	...	|	0634	...	...	0704	0734	|	...	...	0804	...	0834	...	|	...	0904	...	0934	|	...	...	1004
163	**Bern** a.	|	0556	...	|	0656	...	...	0726	0756	|	...	...	0826	...	0856	...	|	...	0926	...	0956	|	...	...	1026
	Olten **500** a.	0618	|	...	0718	|	...	...	|	|	0818	...	...	|	...	|	...	0918	...	|	...	|	1018	...	...	|
	Luzern **565** a.	|	0659	...	|	0800	...	...	|	0900	|	...	...	|	...	1000	...	|	...	|	...	1100	|	...	...	|
	Zürich HB **500** a.	0656	...	...	0756	...	...	...	0828	...	0856	...	...	0928	...	...	...	0956	...	1028	...	...	1056	...	...	1128
	Zürich Flug ✈ **530** a.	0720	...	...	0820	...	...	...	0850	...	0920	...	...	0950	...	...	...	1020	...	1050	...	...	1120	...	...	1150
	St Gallen **530** a.	0815	...	...	0915	...	...	...	0953	...	1015	...	...	1053	...	...	...	1115	...	1153	...	...	1215	...	...	1253

km		IR 2521	ICN 621	ICN 1521	RE 2621	IC 721	IR 2523	ICN 523	ICN 1623	RE 2623	IC 723	IR 2525	ICN 625	ICN 1525	RE 2625	IC 725	IR 2527	ICN 527	ICN 1627	RE 2627	IC 727	IR 2529	ICN 629	ICN 1529	RE 2629	IC 729
		🍷	✕	✕		✕	🍷	✕	✕		✕	🍷	✕	✕		✕	🍷	✕	✕		✕	🍷	✕	✕		✕
	Genève A ✈ 570 d.	0901	0905	...	...	0936	1001	1005	...	...	1036	1101	1105	...	...	1136	1201	1205	...	...	1236	1301	1305	...	...	1336
	Genève 570 d.	0910	0914	...	0921	0945	1010	1014	...	1021	1045	1110	1114	...	1121	1145	1210	1214	...	1221	1245	1310	1314	...	1321	1345
	Nyon **570** d.	|	0927	...	0937	|	|	1027	...	1037	|	|	1127	...	1137	|	|	1227	...	1237	|	|	1327	...	1337	|
	Morges **570** d.	|	0941	...	1000	|	|	1041	...	1100	|	|	1141	...	1200	|	|	1241	...	1300	|	|	1341	...	1400	|
	Lausanne 570 a.	0943	|	...	1012	1018	1043	|	...	1112	1118	1143	|	...	1212	1218	1243	|	...	1312	1318	1343	|	...	1412	1418
0	**Lausanne 508** d.	0945	|	0945	...	1020	1045	|	1045	...	1120	1145	|	1145	...	1220	1245	|	1245	...	1320	1345	|	1345	...	1420
39	Yverdon d.	|	1004	1007	...	|	|	1104	1107	...	|	|	1204	1207	...	|	|	1304	1307	...	|	|	1404	1407	...	|
75	Neuchâtel d.	|	1024	1027	...	|	|	1124	1127	...	|	|	1224	1227	...	|	|	1324	1327	...	|	|	1424	1427	...	|
105	**Biel/Bienne** a.	|	1041	1043k	...	|	|	1141	1143k	...	|	|	1241	1243k	...	|	|	1341	1343k	...	|	|	1441	1443k	...	|
105	**Biel/Bienne** d.	|	1049	1046	...	|	|	1146	1149	...	|	|	1249	1246	...	|	|	1346	1349	...	|	|	1449	1446	...	|
129	Moutier d.	|	1108	|	...	|	|	|	1208	...	|	|	1308	|	...	|	|	|	1408	...	|	|	1508	|	...	|
140	Delémont d.	|	1123	|	...	|	|	|	1223	...	|	|	1323	|	...	|	|	|	1423	...	|	|	1523	|	...	|
179	**Basel** a.	|	1153	|	...	|	|	|	1253	...	|	|	1353	|	...	|	|	|	1453	...	|	|	1553	|	...	|
	Palézieux **508** d.	1001	...	|	...	|	1101	|	...	...	|	1201	...	|	...	|	1301	|	...	...	|	1401	...	|	...	|
	Romont d.	1016	...	|	...	|	1116	|	...	...	|	1216	...	|	...	|	1316	|	...	...	|	1416	...	|	...	|
	Fribourg d.	1034	...	|	...	1104	1134	|	...	...	1204	1234	...	|	...	1304	1334	|	...	...	1404	1434	...	|	...	1504
	Bern a.	1056	...	|	...	1126	1156	|	...	...	1226	1256	...	|	...	1326	1356	|	...	...	1426	1456	...	|	...	1526
	Olten **500** a.	|	...	1118	...	|	|	1218	...	...	|	|	...	1318	...	|	|	1418	...	...	|	|	...	1518	...	|
	Luzern **565** a.	1200	...	|	...	|	1300	|	...	...	|	1400	...	|	...	|	1500	|	...	...	|	1600	...	|	...	|
	Zürich HB **500** a.	...	...	1156	...	1228	...	1256	...	...	1328	...	...	1356	...	1428	...	1456	...	...	1528	...	...	1556	...	1628
	Zürich Flug ✈ **530** a.	...	...	1220	...	1250	...	1320	...	...	1350	...	...	1420	...	1450	...	1520	...	...	1550	...	...	1620	...	1650
	St Gallen **530** a.	...	...	1315	...	1353	...	1415	...	...	1453	...	...	1515	...	1553	...	1615	...	...	1653	...	...	1715	...	1753

km		IR 2531	ICN 531	ICN 1631	RE 2631	IC 731	IC 2535	ICN 635	ICN 1535	RE 2635	IC 735	IR 2537	ICN 537	ICN 1637	RE 2637	IC 737	IR 2539	ICN 639	ICN 1539	RE 2639	IC 739	RE 2941	IR 2541	ICN 541	ICN 1641	RE 2641
		🍷	✕	✕		✕	🍷	✕	✕		✕	🍷	✕	✕		✕	🍷	✕	✕		✕			✕	✕	
																						Ⓐ				
	Genève A ✈ 570 d.	1401	1405	...	...	1436	1501	1505	...	...	1536	1601	1605	...	...	1636	1701	1705	...	...	1736	...	1801	1805	...	...
	Genève 570 d.	1410	1414	...	1421	1445	1510	1514	...	1521	1545	1610	1614	...	1621	1645	1710	1714	...	1721	1745	1749	1810	1814	...	1821
	Nyon **570** d.	|	1427	...	1437	|	|	1527	...	1537	|	|	1627	...	1637	|	|	1727	...	1737	|	1805	|	1827	...	1837
0	Morges **570** d.	|	1441	...	1500	|	|	1541	...	1600	|	|	1641	...	1700	|	|	1741	...	1800	|	1824	|	1841	...	1900
	Lausanne 570 a.	1443	|	...	1512	1518	1543	|	...	1612	1618	1643	|	...	1712	1718	1743	|	...	1812	1818	1837	1843	|	...	1912
	Lausanne 508 d.	1445	|	1445	...	1520	1545	|	1545	...	1620	1645	|	1645	...	1720	1745	|	1745	...	1820	...	1845	|	1845	...
39	Yverdon d.	|	1504	1507	...	|	|	1604	1607	...	|	|	1704	1707	...	|	|	1804	1807	...	|	...	|	1904	1907	...
	Neuchâtel d.	|	1524	1527	...	|	|	1624	1627	...	|	|	1724	1727	...	|	|	1824	1827	...	|	...	|	1924	1927	...
	Biel/Bienne a.	|	1541	1543k	...	|	|	1641	1643k	...	|	|	1741	1743k	...	|	|	1841	1843k	...	|	...	|	1941	1943k	...
	Biel/Bienne d.	|	1546	1549	...	|	|	1649	1646	...	|	|	1746	1749	...	|	|	1849	1846	...	|	...	|	1946	1949	...
	Moutier d.	|	|	1608	...	|	|	1708	|	...	|	|	|	1808	...	|	|	1908	|	...	|	...	|	|	2008	...
	Delémont d.	|	|	1623	...	|	|	1723	|	...	|	|	|	1823	...	|	|	1923	|	...	|	...	|	|	2023	...
	Basel a.	|	|	1653	...	|	|	1753	|	...	|	|	|	1853	...	|	|	1953	|	...	|	...	|	|	2053	...
	Palézieux **508** d.	1501	|	...	...	|	1601	...	|	...	|	1701	|	...	...	|	1801	...	|	...	|	...	1901	|	...	...
	Romont d.	1516	|	...	...	|	1616	...	|	...	|	1716	|	...	...	|	1816	...	|	...	|	...	1916	|	...	...
	Fribourg d.	1534	|	...	...	1604	1634	...	|	...	1704	1734	|	...	...	1804	1834	...	|	...	1904	...	1934	|	...	...
	Bern a.	1556	|	...	...	1626	1656	...	|	...	1726	1756	|	...	...	1826	1856	...	|	...	1926	...	1956	|	...	...
	Olten **500** a.	|	1618	...	...	|	|	...	1718	...	|	|	1818	...	...	|	|	...	1918	...	|	...	|	2018	...	...
	Luzern **565** a.	1700	|	...	...	|	1800	...	|	...	|	1900	|	...	...	|	2000	...	|	...	|	...	2100	|	...	...
	Zürich HB **500** a.	...	1656	...	...	1728	...	...	1756	...	1828	...	1856	...	...	1928	...	...	1956	...	2028	...	...	2056	...	...
	Zürich Flug ✈ **530** a.	...	1720	...	...	1750	...	...	1820	...	1850	...	1920	...	...	1950	...	...	2020	...	2050	...	...	2120	...	...
	St Gallen **530** a.	...	1815	...	...	1853	...	...	1915	...	1953	...	2015	...	...	2053	...	...	2115	...	2153	...	...	2215	...	...

	IC 741	IR 2543	ICN 643	ICN 1543	RE 2643	IC 743	IR 2545	ICN 545	ICN 1645	RE 2645	IC 745	IR 2547	ICN 647	ICN 1547	RE 2647	IC 747	IR 2689	ICN 1647	RE 2649	IR 2691	ICN 1649	RE 2999	IR 2699	RE 2601	IR 2501	RE 2603
	✕		✕	✕		✕		✕	✕		✕					✕										
												⑦w										⑥⑦			x	x
Genève A ✈ 570 d.	1836	1901	1905	...	...	1936	2001	2005	...	...	2036	2047	2105	...	...	2136	2147	...	...	2247	...	...	2347	0012	...	...
Genève 570 d.	1845	1910	1914	...	1921	1945	2010	2014	...	2021	2045	2056	2114	...	2121	2145	2156	...	2221	2256	...	...	2356	0021	...	0118
Nyon **570** d.	|	|	1927	...	1937	|	|	2027	...	2037	|	2110	2127	...	2137	|	2210	...	2237	2310	...	...	0010	0037	...	0137
Morges **570** d.	|	|	1941	...	2000	|	|	2041	...	2100	|	2128	2141	...	2200	|	2228	...	2300	2328	...	...	0028	0100	...	0200
Lausanne 570 a.	1918	1943	|	...	2012	2018	2043	|	...	2112	2118	2140	|	...	2212	2218	2240	...	2312	2340	...	...	0040	0112	...	0212
Lausanne 508 d.	1920	1945	|	1945	...	2020	2045	|	2045	...	2120	2145	|	2145	...	2220	2245	2245	...	2345	2345	...	...	...	0134	...
Yverdon d.	|	|	2004	2007	...	|	|	2104	2107	...	|	|	2204	2207	...	|	|	2307	...	|	0007	...	...	...	|	...
Neuchâtel d.	|	|	2024	2027	...	|	|	2124	2127	...	|	|	2224	2227	...	|	|	2327	...	|	0027	...	...	...	|	...
Biel/Bienne a.	|	|	2041	2043k	...	|	|	2141	2143k	...	|	|	2241	2243k	...	|	|	2343	...	|	0043	...	...	...	|	...
Biel/Bienne d.	|	|	2049	2046	...	|	|	2146	2149	...	|	|	2249	2246	...	|	|	2349	...	|	...	0049	...	...	|	...
Moutier d.	|	|	2108	|	...	|	|	|	2208	...	|	|	2308	|	...	|	|	0008	...	|	...	0108	...	...	|	...
Delémont d.	|	|	2123	|	...	|	|	|	2223	...	|	|	2323	|	...	|	|	0018	...	|	...	0118	...	...	|	...
Basel a.	|	|	2153	|	...	|	|	|	2253	...	|	|	2353	|	...	|	|	...	...	|	...	...	...	...	|	...
Palézieux **508** d.	|	2001	...	|	...	|	2101	|	...	...	|	2201	...	|	...	|	2301	...	...	0001	...	...	...	...	0150	...
Romont d.	|	2016	...	|	...	|	2116	|	...	...	|	2216	...	|	...	|	2316	...	...	0016	...	...	...	...	0205	...
Fribourg d.	2004	2034	...	|	...	2104	2134	|	...	...	2204	2234	...	|	...	2304	2334	...	...	0034	...	...	...	...	0222	...
Bern a.	2026	2056	...	|	...	2126	2156	|	...	...	2226	2256	...	|	...	2326	2356	...	...	0056	...	...	...	...	...	...
Olten **500** a.	|	|	...	2118	...	2158	|	2219	...	...	2258	|	...	2330	...	2358	...	...	...	...	...	...	...	...	...	...
Luzern **565** a.	|	2200	...	|	...	|	2300	|	...	...	|	2400	...	|	...	|	...	...	...	...	...	...	...	...	...	...
Zürich HB **500** a.	2128	...	...	2156	...	2231	...	2256	...	...	2331	...	...	0010	...	0033	...	...	...	...	...	...	...	...	...	...
Zürich Flug ✈ **530** a.	2150	...	...	2220	...	...	...	2320	...	...	...	...	...	0027	...	...	...	...	...	...	...	...	...	...	...	...
St Gallen **530** a.	2253	...	...	2317	...	...	...	0018	...	...	...	...	...	0125	...	...	...	...	...	...	...	...	...	...	...	...

B – To Brig.

k – Connects with train in previous column(s).

m – ① (also Apr. 6, May 25; not Apr. 5, May 24).

w – Also Dec. 25, 26, Jan. 1, 2, Apr. 2, 5, May 13, 24.

x – ⑥⑦ (also Jan. 1, Apr. 2, 5, May 13, 14, 24; not Dec. 26, 27).

SBB BERN, BASEL and BIEL - LAUSANNE - GENÈVE 505

	RE 2602	RE 2604	ICN 1604	ICN 504 Ⓐ	IR 2504	IC 704 ✕	RE 2606	ICN 1506	ICN 606 ✕	IR 2506	IC 706 ✕	RE 2608	ICN 1608 ✕	ICN 508 ✕	IR 2508 🍸	IC 708 ✕	RE 2610	ICN 1510 ✕	ICN 610 ✕	IR 2510 🍸	IC 710 ✕	RE 2612	ICN 1612 ✕	ICN 512 ✕	IR 2512 🍸
St Gallen **530** d.	...	...	...	...	...	...	...	...	...	...	...	...	...	...	...	0511	...	0544	...	...	0611	...	...	0642	...
Zürich Flughafen + **530** d.	...	...	...	...	...	...	...	...	...	...	...	...	...	...	...	0613	...	0643	...	...	0713	...	...	0739	...
Zürich HB **500** d.	...	...	...	...	...	...	...	...	...	...	0521	...	...	0604	...	0632	...	0704	...	...	0732	...	...	0804	...
Luzern **565** d.	...	...	...	...	...	...	...	...	...	...	...	...	...	|	0600	|	...	|	...	0700	|	...	...	|	0800
Olten **500** d.	...	...	...	...	...	...	...	...	...	...	...	...	...	0641	|	|	...	0741	...	|	|	...	...	0841	|
Bern d.	...	...	...	...	0504	0534	...	...	...	0604	0634	...	...	|	0704	0734	...	|	...	0804	0834	...	...	|	0904
Fribourg d.	...	...	...	...	0526	0555	...	...	...	0626	0655	...	...	|	0726	0755	...	|	...	0826	0855	...	...	|	0926
Romont d.	...	...	...	...	0544	|	...	...	...	0644	|	...	...	|	0744	|	...	|	...	0844	|	...	...	|	0944
Palézieux **508** d.	...	...	...	...	0559	|	...	...	...	0659	|	...	...	|	0759	|	...	|	...	0859	|	...	...	|	0959
Basel d.	...	...	...	...	|	|	...	...	...	|	|	...	0603	|	|	|	...	|	0703	|	|	...	0803	|	|
Delémont d.	...	...	...	...	|	|	...	...	0542	|	|	...	0642	|	|	|	...	|	0742	|	|	...	0842	|	|
Moutier d.	...	...	...	...	|	|	...	...	0552	|	|	...	0652	|	|	|	...	|	0752	|	|	...	0852	|	|
Biel/Bienne a.	...	...	...	...	|	|	...	...	0610k	|	|	...	0710	0713k	|	|	...	0813	0810k	|	|	...	0910	0913k	|
Biel/Bienne d.	...	...	0513	0519	|	|	...	0613	0619	|	|	...	0716	0719	|	|	...	0816	0819	|	|	...	0916	0919	|
Neuchâtel d.	...	...	0531	0537	|	|	...	0631	0637	|	|	...	0734	0737	|	|	...	0834	0837	|	|	...	0934	0937	|
Yverdon d.	...	...	0551	0557	|	|	...	0650	0657	|	|	...	0754	0757	|	|	...	0854	0857	|	|	...	0954	0957	|
Lausanne 508 a.	...	...	0612f	|	0615	0640	...	0715	|	0715	0740	...	0815	|	0815	0840	...	0915	|	0915	0940	...	1015	|	1015
Lausanne 570 d.	0448	0548	...	|	0617	0642	0648	...	|	0717	0742	0748	...	|	0817	0842	0848	...	|	0917	0942	0948	...	|	1017
Morges **570** d.	0500	0600	...	0619	|	|	0700	...	0719	|	|	0800	...	0819	|	|	0900	...	0919	|	|	1000	...	1019	|
Nyon **570** d.	0523	0623	...	0633	|	|	0723	...	0733	|	|	0823	...	0833	|	|	0923	...	0933	|	|	1023	...	1033	|
Genève 570 a.	0539	0639	...	0646	0650	0715	0739	...	0746	0750	0815	0839	...	0846	0850	0915	0939	...	0946	0950	1015	1039	...	1046	1050
Genève Aéroport + **570** d.	0548	...	...	0655	0659	0724	...	...	0755	0759	0824	...	...	0855	0859	0924	...	...	0955	0959	1024	...	...	1055	1059

	IC 712 ✕	RE 2614	ICN 1516 ✕	ICN 614 ✕	IR 2516 🍸	IC 716 ✕	RE 2618	ICN 1618 ✕	ICN 518 ✕	IR 2518 🍸	IC 718 ✕	RE 2620	ICN 1520 ✕	ICN 620 ✕	IR 2520 🍸	IC 720 ✕	RE 2622	ICN 1622 ✕	ICN 522 ✕	IR 2522 🍸	IC 722 ✕	RE 2624	ICN 1524 ✕	ICN 624 ✕	IR 2524 🍸
St Gallen **530** d.	0711	...	0748	...	...	0811	...	...	0848	...	0911	...	0948	...	...	1011	...	...	1048	...	1111	...	1148	...	...
Zürich Flughafen + **530** d.	0813	...	0843	...	...	0913	...	...	0943	...	1013	...	1043	...	...	1113	...	...	1143	...	1213	...	1243	...	...
Zürich HB **500** d.	0832	...	0904	...	...	0932	...	...	1004	...	1032	...	1104	...	...	1132	...	...	1204	...	1232	...	1304	...	...
Luzern **565** d.	|	...	|	...	0900	|	...	...	|	1000	|	...	|	...	1100	|	...	...	|	1200	|	...	|	...	1300
Olten **500** d.	|	...	0941	...	|	|	...	...	1041	|	|	...	1141	...	|	|	...	...	1241	|	|	...	1341	...	|
Bern d.	0934	...	|	...	1004	1034	...	...	|	1104	1134	...	|	...	1204	1234	...	...	|	1304	1334	...	|	...	1404
Fribourg d.	0955	...	|	...	1026	1055	...	...	|	1126	1155	...	|	...	1226	1255	...	...	|	1326	1355	...	|	...	1426
Romont d.	|	...	|	...	1044	|	...	...	|	1144	|	...	|	...	1244	|	...	...	|	1344	|	...	|	...	1444
Palézieux **508** d.	|	...	|	...	1059	|	...	...	|	1159	|	...	|	...	1259	|	...	...	|	1359	|	...	|	...	1459
Basel d.	|	...	|	0903	|	|	...	1003	|	|	|	...	|	1103	|	|	...	1203	|	|	|	...	|	1303	|
Delémont d.	|	...	|	0942	|	|	...	1042	|	|	|	...	|	1142	|	|	...	1242	|	|	|	...	|	1342	|
Moutier d.	|	...	|	0952	|	|	...	1052	|	|	|	...	|	1152	|	|	...	1252	|	|	|	...	|	1352	|
Biel/Bienne a.	|	...	1013	1010k	|	|	...	1110	1113k	|	|	...	1213	1210k	|	|	...	1310	1313k	|	|	...	1413	1410k	|
Biel/Bienne d.	|	...	1016	1019	|	|	...	1116	1119	|	|	...	1216	1219	|	|	...	1316	1319	|	|	...	1416	1419	|
Neuchâtel d.	|	...	1034	1037	|	|	...	1134	1137	|	|	...	1234	1237	|	|	...	1334	1337	|	|	...	1434	1437	|
Yverdon d.	|	...	1054	1057	|	|	...	1154	1157	|	|	...	1254	1257	|	|	...	1354	1357	|	|	...	1454	1457	|
Lausanne 508 a.	1040	...	1115	|	1115	1140	...	1215	|	1215	1240	...	1315	|	1315	1340	...	1415	|	1415	1440	...	1515	|	1515
Lausanne 570 d.	1042	1048	...	|	1117	1142	1148	...	|	1217	1242	1248	...	|	1317	1342	1348	...	|	1417	1442	1448	...	|	1517
Morges **570** d.	|	1100	...	1119	|	|	1200	...	1219	|	|	1300	...	1319	|	|	1400	...	1419	|	|	1500	...	1519	|
Nyon **570** d.	|	1123	...	1133	|	|	1223	...	1233	|	|	1323	...	1333	|	|	1423	...	1433	|	|	1523	...	1533	|
Genève 570 a.	1115	1139	...	1146	1150	1215	1239	...	1246	1250	1315	1339	...	1346	1350	1415	1439	...	1446	1450	1515	1539	...	1546	1550
Genève Aéroport + **570** d.	1124	...	...	1155	1159	1224	...	...	1255	1259	1324	...	...	1355	1359	1424	...	...	1455	1459	1524	...	...	1555	1559

	IC 724 ✕	RE 2626	ICN 1626 ✕	ICN 526 ✕	IR 2526 🍸	IC 726 ✕	RE 2628	ICN 1528 ✕	ICN 628 ✕	IR 2528 🍸	IC 728 ✕	RE 2630	ICN 1630 ✕	ICN 530 ✕	IR 2530	IC 730 ✕	RE 2632	ICN 1532 ✕	ICN 632 ✕	IR 2532 🍸	IC 732 ✕	RE 2636	ICN 1636 ✕	ICN 536 ✕	IR 2536
St Gallen **530** d.	1211	...	...	1248	...	1311	...	1348	...	...	1411	...	...	1448	...	1511	...	1548	...	...	1611	...	...	1648	...
Zürich Flughafen + **530** d.	1313	...	...	1343	...	1413	...	1443	...	...	1513	...	...	1543	...	1613	...	1643	...	...	1713	...	...	1743	...
Zürich HB **500** d.	1332	...	...	1404	...	1432	...	1504	...	...	1532	...	...	1604	...	1632	...	1704	...	...	1732	...	...	1804	...
Luzern **565** d.	|	...	...	|	1400	|	...	|	...	1500	|	...	...	|	1600	|	...	|	...	1700	|	...	...	|	1800
Olten **500** d.	|	...	...	1441	|	|	...	1541	...	|	|	...	...	1641	|	|	...	1741	...	|	|	...	...	1841	|
Bern d.	1434	...	...	|	1504	1534	...	|	...	1604	1634	...	...	|	1704	1734	...	|	...	1804	1834	...	...	|	1904
Fribourg d.	1455	...	...	|	1526	1555	...	|	...	1626	1655	...	...	|	1726	1755	...	|	...	1826	1855	...	...	|	1926
Romont d.	|	...	...	|	1544	|	...	|	...	1644	|	...	...	|	1744	|	...	|	...	1844	|	...	...	|	1944
Palézieux **508** d.	|	...	...	|	1559	|	...	|	...	1659	|	...	...	|	1759	|	...	|	...	1859	|	...	...	|	1959
Basel d.	|	...	1403	|	|	|	...	|	1503	|	|	...	1603	|	|	|	...	|	1703	|	|	...	1803	|	|
Delémont d.	|	...	1442	|	|	|	...	|	1542	|	|	...	1642	|	|	|	...	|	1742	|	|	...	1842	|	|
Moutier d.	|	...	1452	|	|	|	...	|	1552	|	|	...	1652	|	|	|	...	|	1752	|	|	...	1852	|	|
Biel/Bienne a.	|	...	1510	1513k	|	|	...	1613	1610k	|	|	...	1710	1713k	|	|	...	1813	1810k	|	|	...	1910	1913k	|
Biel/Bienne d.	|	...	1516	1519	|	|	...	1616	1619	|	|	...	1716	1719	|	|	...	1816	1819	|	|	...	1916	1919	|
Neuchâtel d.	|	...	1534	1537	|	|	...	1634	1637	|	|	...	1734	1737	|	|	...	1834	1837	|	|	...	1934	1937	|
Yverdon d.	|	...	1554	1557	|	|	...	1654	1657	|	|	...	1754	1757	|	|	...	1854	1857	|	|	...	1954	1957	|
Lausanne 508 a.	1540	...	1615	|	1615	1640	...	1715	|	1715	1740	...	1815	|	1815	1840	...	1915	|	1915	1940	...	2015	|	2015
Lausanne 570 d.	1542	1548	...	|	1617	1642	1648	...	|	1717	1742	1748	...	|	1817	1842	1848	...	|	1917	1942	1948	...	|	2020
Morges **570** d.	|	1600	...	1619	|	|	1700	...	1719	|	|	1800	...	1819	|	|	1900	...	1919	|	|	2000	...	2019	2032
Nyon **570** d.	|	1623	...	1633	|	|	1723	...	1733	|	|	1823	...	1833	|	|	1923	...	1933	|	|	2023	...	2033	2050
Genève 570 a.	1615	1639	...	1646	1650	1715	1739	...	1746	1750	1815	1839	...	1846	1850	1915	1939	...	1946	1950	2015	2039	...	2046	2104
Genève Aéroport + **570** d.	1624	...	...	1655	1659	1724	...	...	1755	1759	1824	...	...	1855	1859	1924	...	...	1955	1959	2024	...	...	2055	2113

	IC 736 ✕	RE 2638	ICN 1538 ✕	ICN 638 ✕	IR 2538	IC 738 ✕	RE 2640	ICN 1640 ✕	ICN 1540 ✕ ⚒	ICN 540 ✕ †	IR 2540	IC 740	RE 2642	ICN 642	ICN 1542	IR 2542	IC 742	RE 2644	ICN 1644	ICN 1544	IR 2648	ICN 646	IR 2546	ICN 1546	RE 2600 x
St Gallen **530** d.	1711	...	1748	...	...	1811	...	...	1848	1848	...	1911	...	...	1948	...	2011	...	...	2048	...	...	...	2144	...
Zürich Flughafen + **530** d.	1813	...	1843	...	...	1913	...	...	1943	1943	...	2013	...	...	2043	...	2113	...	...	2143	...	...	...	2243	...
Zürich HB **500** d.	1832	...	1904	...	...	1932	...	...	2004	2004	...	2032	...	...	2104	...	2132	...	...	2204	...	...	...	2304	...
Luzern **565** d.	|	...	|	...	1900	|	...	...	|	|	2000	|	...	...	|	2100	|	...	...	|	...	...	2300	|	...
Olten **500** d.	|	...	1941	...	|	|	...	...	2041	2041	|	|	...	...	2141	|	|	...	...	2241	...	...	|	2341	...
Bern d.	1934	...	|	...	2004	2034	...	...	|	|	2104	2134	...	...	|	2204	2234	...	...	|	2308	...	0008	|	...
Fribourg d.	1955	...	|	...	2026	2055	...	...	|	|	2126	2155	...	...	|	2226	2254	...	...	|	2330	...	0034	|	...
Romont d.	|	...	|	...	2044	|	...	...	|	|	2144	|	...	...	|	2244	...	...	...	|	2348	...	0052j	|	...
Palézieux **508** d.	|	...	|	...	2059	|	...	...	|	|	2159	|	...	...	|	2259	...	...	...	|	0003	...	0107j	|	...
Basel d.	|	...	|	1903	|	|	...	2003	|	|	|	|	...	2103	|	|	...	...	2203	|	|	2303	|	|	...
Delémont d.	|	...	|	1942	|	|	...	2042	|	|	|	|	...	2142	|	|	...	...	2242	|	|	2337	|	|	...
Moutier d.	|	...	|	1952	|	|	...	2052	|	|	|	|	...	2152	|	|	...	...	2252	|	|	...	|	|	...
Biel/Bienne a.	|	...	2013	2010k	|	|	...	2110	2113k	2113k	|	|	...	2210	2213k	|	...	...	2310	2314	|	...	|	0022	...
Biel/Bienne d.	|	...	2016	2019	|	|	...	2116	...	2119	|	|	...	2219e	2216	|	...	...	...	2316	|	...	|	0025x	...
Neuchâtel d.	|	...	2034	2037	|	|	...	2134	...	2137	|	|	...	2237e	2234	|	...	...	...	2334	|	...	|	0043x	...
Yverdon d.	|	...	2054	2057	|	|	...	2154	...	2157	|	|	...	2257e	2254	|	...	...	...	2354	|	...	|	0103x	...
Lausanne 508 a.	2040	...	2115	|	2115	2140	...	2215	...	|	2215	2240	...	|	2315	2315	...	...	...	0015	0019	...	0123j	0124x	...
Lausanne 570 d.	2042	2048	...	|	2120	2142	2148	...	...	|	2220	2245	2248	|	...	2320	...	2348	...	...	0021	...	...	...	0130
Morges **570** d.	|	2100	...	2119	2132	|	2200	...	...	2219	2232	2254	2300	2319e	...	2332	...	0000	...	...	0033	...	...	...	0142
Nyon **570** d.	|	2123	...	2133	2150	|	2223	...	...	2233	2250	2310	2323	2333e	...	2350	...	0023	...	...	0051	...	...	...	0205
Genève 570 a.	2115	2139	...	2146	2204	2215	2239	...	...	2246	2304	2324	2339	2346e	...	0004	...	0039	...	...	0105	...	...	...	0224
Genève Aéroport + **570** d.	2124	...	...	2155	2213	2224	2252	...	...	2255	2313	2333	2352	2355e	...	...	...	...	...	...	...	...	...	...	...

e – † only.
f – Arrive 0615 on Ⓐ.
j – ⑤⑥⑦ (also Jan. 1, Apr. 2, 6, May 13, 14, 25; not Dec. 26, 27).
k – Connects with train in previous column(s).
x – ⑥⑦ (also Jan. 1, Apr. 2, 5, May 13, 14, 24; not Dec. 26, 27).

506 SWISS LAKES

LAC LÉMAN
December 13 - April 17 — Operator: CGN

⚒x	⚒x	⚒x			†y						⚒x			⚒x	⚒x	⚒x				†y					⚒x
...	...	...	...	...	1220	...	...	...	...	...	...	d. Genève ⊗	a.	...	...	...	...	...	...	1500	...	...	...	...	...
...	...	...	...	...	1315	...	...	...	...	...	...	d. Coppet	d.	...	...	...	...	...	...	1410	...	...	...	...	...
...	...	...	...	...	1340	...	...	...	...	...	...	d. Nyon	d.	...	...	...	...	...	...	1345	...	...	...	...	...
...	...	...	...	...	...	...	...	...	...	...	...	d. Yvoire	d.	...	...	...	...	...	...	...	...	...	...	...	...
...	...	...	...	...	...	...	...	...	...	...	...	d. Thonon-les-Bains	d.	...	...	...	...	...	...	...	...	...	...	...	...
0540	0700	0820	1005	1145	...	1315	1445	1615	1800	1920	2045	d. Evian-les-Bains	d.	0530	0654	0815	1000	1135	1305	...	1435	1605	1750	1915	2035
|	|	|	|	|	...	|	|	|	|	|	|	d. Morges	d.	|	|	|	|	|	|	...	|	|	|	|	|
0615	0735	0855	1040	1220	...	1351	1520	1650	1835	1955	2120	a. Lausanne-Ouchy	d.	0455	0622	0740	0925	1100	1230	...	1400	1530	1715	1840	2000

	†y		†y		†y		†y					†y		†y		†y		†y	
...	...	...	1230	...	...	...	...	...	d. Lausanne-Ouchy	a.	...	...	...	...	...	1615	...	...	...
...	1205	...	1335	...	1405	...	1605	...	d. Vevey-Marché	d.	...	1159	...	1359	...	1515	...	1559	...
...	1210	...	1340	...	1410	...	1610	...	d. Vevey-La Tour	d.	...	|	...	|	...	1507	...	|	...
...	1240	...	1405	...	1440	...	1640	...	d. Montreux	d.	...	|	...	|	...	1445	...	|	...
...	1247	...	1412	...	1447	...	1647	...	d. Territet	d.	...	|	...	|	...	1432	...	|	...
...	1255	...	1420	...	1455	...	1655	...	d. Château-de-Chillon	d.	...	|	...	|	...	1425	...	|	...
...	1303	...	...	...	1503	...	1703	...	d. Villeneuve	d.	...	|	...	|	...	...	...	|	...
...	|	...	...	...	|	...	|	...	d. St Gingolph	d.	...	1138	...	1338	...	...	...	1538	...
...	1325	...	...	...	1525	...	1725	...	d. Bouveret	d.	...	1125	...	1325	...	...	...	1525	...
...	1338	...	...	...	1538	...	...	...	a. St Gingolph	d.	...	...	...	...	...	...	...	...	...

VIERWALDSTÄTTERSEE
December 13 - April 1 — Operator: SGV

Ⓐ		⚒	†			†		†		Ⓐ			Ⓐ				†		⚒		†	⚒	⚒	†	Ⓐ
0555	0912	...	...	1012	1200	1312	1412	1512	1612	1718	d. Luzern (Bahnhofquai)	a.	0739	...	1141	1347	1447	1547	...	1647	1747	...	1841	1841	1856
|	0922	...	...	1022	1210	1322	1422	1522	1622	|	d. Verkehrshaus Lido	d.	|	...	|	|	1435	1535	...	1635	1735	...	|	|	|
0622s	0943	...	...	1043	1230	1343	1443	1543	1643	1743	d. Hertenstein	d.	0712	...	1114	1321	1414	1514	...	1614	1714	...	1814	1814	|
0702v	0953	...	...	1053	1240	1353	1453	1553	1653	1753	d. Weggis	d.	0703	...	1105	1312	1405	1505	...	1605	1705	...	1805	1805	|
0643	1009	...	...	1109	1254	1409	1509	1609	1709	1809	d. Vitznau	d.	0646	...	1049	1256	1349	1449	...	1549	1649	...	1749	1749	1811
...	1026	1027	1027	1127	...	1427	1526	1626	1727	...	d. Beckenried	d.	...	1030	1032	...	1332	1432	1530	1532	1632	1730	1732	1732	...
...	...	1045	1045	1145	...	1445	...	...	1745j	...	d. Gersau	d.	...	1014	...	...	1314	1414	1514	...	...	1714	...	1714	...
...	...	1102	1102	1202	...	1502	...	...	1802j	...	d. Treib	d.	...	0957	...	...	1257	1357	1457	...	...	1657	...	1657	...
...	...	1109	1114	1214	...	1514	...	...	1809j	...	d. Brunnen	d.	...	0949	...	...	1249	1349	1449	...	...	1649	...	1649	...
...	...	...	|	1224	...	1524	...	...	...	...	d. Rütli	d.	...	...	...	...	1237	1337	...	...	...	...	...	1637	...
...	...	...	1136	|	...	1536	...	...	...	...	d. Sisikon	d.	...	...	...	...	|	|	...	...	...	...	...	|	...
...	...	...	1143	|	...	1543	...	...	...	...	d. Tellsplatte	d.	...	...	...	...	|	1314	...	...	...	...	...	|	...
...	...	...	1223f	1238	...	1621f	...	...	...	...	d. Bauen	d.	...	...	...	...	1221	1324r	...	...	...	...	...	1621	...
...	...	...	1216f	1245	...	1613f	...	...	...	...	d. Isleten-Isenthal	d.	...	...	...	...	1213	|	...	...	...	...	...	1613	...
...	...	...	1158	1258	...	1558	...	...	...	...	a. Flüelen	d.	...	...	...	...	1200	1300	...	...	...	...	...	1600	...

BRIENZERSEE
Operator: BLS — December 13 - April 1

NO SERVICE	d. Interlaken Ost	a.	NO SERVICE
	d. Bönigen	d.	
	d. Iseltwald	d.	
	d. Giessbach	d.	
	a. Brienz	d.	

THUNERSEE
Operator: BLS — December 13 - April 1

NO SERVICE	d. Thun	a.	NO SERVICE
	d. Hünibach	d.	
	d. Oberhofen	d.	
	d. Gunten	d.	
	d. Spiez	d.	
	d. Faulensee	d.	
	d. Merligen	d.	
	d. Beatenbucht	d.	
	a. Interlaken West	d.	

ZÜRICHSEE
Operator: ZSG — December 13 - April 1

1300	1330	1430	1548	d. Zürich (Bürkliplatz)	a.	1255	1425	1547	1715
1346t	|	1510	1616	d. Erlenbach	d.	1210t	1347	1510t	1645
1338	1356	1518	1622	d. Thalwill	d.	1220	1340	1520	|
...	1403	...	...	d. Oberrieden	d.	...	...	...	|
...	|	...	...	d. Wädenswil	d.	...	...	...	1606
...	1513	...	...	a. Rapperswil	d.	...	...	...	1525

f – Via Flüelen.
j – Connection on ⚒.
r – Via Tellsplatte.
s – Stops to set down only.
t – Via Thalwill.
v – Via Vitznau.
x – Also Dec. 26.
y – Not Dec. 26.

⊗ – Genève has landing stages at: Mont-Blanc, Jardin-Anglais, Pâquis and Eaux-Vives. Services do not call at all landing stages.

Operators:
BLS – Schifffahrt Berner Oberland: ✆ +41 (0)33 334 52 11. (www.bls.ch)
CGN – Compagnie Générale de Navigation: ✆ +41 (0)848 811 848. (www.cgn.ch)
SGV – Schifffahrtsgesellschaft Vierwaldstättersee: ✆ +41 (0)41 367 67 67. (www.lakelucerne.ch)
ZSG – Zürichsee Schifffahrtsgesellschaft: ✆ +41 (0)44 487 13 33. (www.zsg.ch)

508 PAYERNE - MURTEN - KERZERS (- LYSS)
BLS

km			⚒		⚒								Ⓐ	⚒	†	⚒				
0	Payerne 523 ⊡	d.	0556	0633	0701	0734	and at the same minutes past each hour until	2134	2236	0006	Murten ⊡	d.	0514	0602	0603	0643	0702	and at the same minutes past each hour until	2202	2342
11	Avenches ⊡	d.	0609	0648	0710	0748		2148	2248	0017	Avenches ⊡	d.	0522	0611	0611	0649	0711		2211	2350
18	Murten ⊡	a.	0616	0656	0716	0756		2156	2256	0024	Payerne 523 ⊡	a.	0534	0624	0624	0657	0724		2224	0001

km			Ⓐ		Ⓐ		Ⓐ		Ⓐ					Ⓐ		Ⓐ		Ⓐ							
0	Murten	d.	0547	0617	0647	0717	0747	0817	0847	0917	and hourly until	1617	...	1647	1717	1747	1817	1847	1917	...	2017	2117	2217	2317	0025
8	Kerzers ▲	a.	0556	0626	0656	0726	0756	0826	0856	0926		1626	...	1656	1726	1756	1826	1856	1926	...	2026	2126	2226	2326	0034

		Ⓐ	Ⓐ	Ⓐ		Ⓐ		Ⓐ					Ⓐ		Ⓐ		Ⓐ							
Kerzers ▲	d.	0504	0534	0604	0634	0704	0734	0804	0834	and hourly until	1634	...	1704	1734	1804	1834	1904	1934	...	2034	2138	2234	2334	0040
Murten	a.	0513	0543	0613	0643	0713	0743	0813	0843		1643	...	1713	1743	1813	1843	1913	1943	...	2043	2147	2243	2342	0049

⊡ – Additional services operate at peak times.

▲ – **Rail service KERZERS - LYSS and v.v.**: *17 km*, journey 20 minutes.
From **Kerzers**: 0606 and hourly until 2306. From **Lyss**: 0532, 0632 and hourly until 2332, then 0009.

Table 510 notes

◆ – **NOTES** (LISTED BY TRAIN NUMBER)

5 – 🛏12 and ✕ Hamburg - Basel - Zürich.
6 – 🛏12 and ✕ Chur - Basel - Köln - Dortmund (- Hamburg ⑧ **m**).
7 – 🛏12 and ✕ (①-⑥ **n**, Hamburg -) Dortmund - Basel - Chur.
90 – VAUBAN – 🛏12 Zürich - Basel - Luxembourg - Brussels.
91 – VAUBAN – 🛏12 Brussels - Luxembourg - Basel - Zürich - Chur.
96/7 – IRIS – 🛏12 Zürich - Basel - Luxembourg - Brussels and v.v.
100 – ①-⑥ (also Apr. 4, May 23; not Apr. 5, May 24): 🛏12 and ✕ Chur - Zürich - Basel - Hamburg.
101 – 🛏12 and ✕ Hamburg - Basel - Zürich - Chur.
102 – ⑦ (also Apr. 5, May 24; not Apr. 4, May 23): 🛏12 and ✕ Chur - Zürich - Basel - Hamburg - Kiel.
270/1 – 🛏12 and ✕ Zürich - Basel - Frankfurt (Main) and v.v.
272 – ①-⑥ (also Apr. 4, May 23; not Apr. 5, May 24): 🛏12 and ✕ Zürich - Basel - Hamburg. Runs as train **292** on some dates.
372 – ⑦ (also Apr. 5, May 24; not Apr. 4, May 23): 🛏12 and ✕ Zürich - Basel - Berlin Ost.
458/9 – *City Night Line* – For days of running and composition – see Table **73**.
478/9 – *City Night Line* KOMET – For days of running and composition – see Table **73**.

9205 – 🛏12 and (🍷) Paris Est - Basel - Zürich. Runs as train **9207** on some dates.
9210 – 🛏12 and (🍷) Zürich - Basel - Paris Est. Runs as train **9212** on some dates.
9211 – 🛏12 and (🍷) Paris Est - Basel - Zürich. Runs as train **9213** on some dates.
9215 – 🛏12 and (🍷) Paris Est - Basel - Zürich.
9216 – 🛏12 and (🍷) Zürich - Basel - Paris Est.
9217 – 🛏12 and (🍷) Paris Est - Basel - Zürich.
9218 – 🛏12 and (🍷) Zürich - Basel - Paris Est.
9220 – 🛏12 and (🍷) Zürich - Basel (- Paris Est). Runs as train **9222** on some dates.

H – 🛏12 and ✕ Zürich - Basel - Hamburg and v.v.
K – 🛏12 and ✕ Zürich - Basel - Hamburg - Kiel and v.v.

d – ⚒ only.
e – † only.
m – Not Dec. 24, 25, 31, Apr. 2, 4, May 23.
n – Not Dec. 25, 26, Jan. 1, Apr. 3, 5, May 24.
q – ⑥⑦ (also Jan. 1).
s – Stops to set down only.
u – Stops to pick up only.
z – Runs as *IC* train on ©.

SBB — BASEL - ZÜRICH — 510

km		IR 2057	IR 1953	IC 553	IR 2059	IR 1759	ICE 759	IR 1955	IR 1957	IC 559	IR 2061	IR 1761	IC 761	CNL 479	IR 1961	ICN 561	IR 2065	IR 1765	IC 763	CNL 458	IR 1963	IC 565	IR 2067	IR 1767	ICE 5	IR 1967	IC 567	IR 2069	IR 1769
				(✕)		✕	✕						✕		🍷	🍷		✕	✕			(✕)			✕		(✕)		
									Ⓐ					◆		z				◆					◆				
0	**Basel SBB** d.	0440	0513	0533	0540	0547	0607	0613	0630	0633	0640	0647	0707	0710s	0713	0733	0740	0747	0807	0810s	0813	0833	0840	0847	0907	0913	0933	0940	0947
17	Rheinfelden d.	0451	0525	|	0551	|	|	0625	0642	|	0651	|	|	|	0725	|	0751	|	|	|	0825	|	0851	|	|	0925	|	0951	|
	Liestal d.	|	|	|	|	0557	|	|	|	|	|	0657	|	|	|	|	|	0757	|	|	|	|	|	0857	|	|	|	|	0957
	Aarau d.	|	|	|	|	0623	|	|	|	|	|	0723	|	|	|	|	|	0823	|	|	|	|	|	0923	|	|	|	|	1023
	Lenzburg d.	|	|	|	|	0630	|	|	|	|	|	0730	|	|	|	|	|	0830	|	|	|	|	|	0930	|	|	|	|	1030
57	Brugg d.	0520	0600	|	0620	|	|	0700	0715	|	0720	|	|	|	0800	|	0820	|	|	|	0900	|	0920	|	|	1000	|	1020	|
66	Baden d.	0529	0608	|	0629	|	|	0708	0724	|	0729	|	|	0759s	0808	|	0829	|	|	0858s	0908	|	0929	|	|	1008	|	1029	|
88	**Zürich HB** a.	|	0624	0626	|	0652	0700	0724	0740	0726	|	0752	0800	0834j	0824	0826	|	0852	0900	0917	0924	0926	|	0952	1000	1024	1026	|	1052
	Zürich Flug ✈ **530/5** a.	0556	|	...	0656	|	...	...	...	|	0756	|	...	...	...	|	0856	|	...	...	...	|	0956	|	...	...	|	1056	...
	Chur **520** a.	...	0752	...	...	0843	...	...	...	0852	...	0943	...	...	...	0952	...	1043	...	...	...	1052	...	1143	...	...	1152	...	...

	TGV 9205	IR 1969	IC 569	IR 2071	IR 1771	IC 771	IR 1971	IC 571	IR 2073	IR 1773	TGV 9211	IR 1973	ICN 573	IR 2075	IR 1775	IC 775	IR 1975	IC 575	IR 2077	EC 7	TGV 9215	IR 1977	IC 577	IR 2079	IR 91	ICE 73	IR 1979	IC 579
	✕		(✕)					🍷			(🍷)	🍷	🍷				🍷	(✕)			(🍷)		(✕)			✕		🍷
	◆										◆		z							◆	◆				◆	K		
Basel SBB d.	1007	1013	1033	1040	1047	1107	1113	1133	1140	1147	1207	1213	1233	1240	1247	1307	1313	1333	1340	1347	1407	1413	1433	1440	1447	1507	1513	1533
Rheinfelden d.	|	1025	|	1051	|	|	1125	|	1151	|	|	1225	|	1251	|	|	1325	|	1351	|	|	1425	|	1451	|	|	1525	|
Liestal d.	|	|	|	|	1057	|	|	|	|	1157	|	|	|	|	1257	|	|	|	|	1357	|	|	|	|	1457	|	|	|
Aarau d.	|	|	|	|	1123	|	|	|	|	1223	|	|	|	|	1323	|	|	|	|	1423	|	|	|	|	1523	|	|	|
Lenzburg d.	|	|	|	|	1130	|	|	|	|	1230	|	|	|	|	1330	|	|	|	|	1431	|	|	|	|	1530	|	|	|
Brugg d.	|	1100	|	1120	|	|	1200	|	1220	|	|	1300	|	1320	|	|	1400	|	1420	|	|	1500	|	1520	|	|	1600	|
Baden d.	|	1108	|	1129	|	|	1208	|	1229	|	|	1308	|	1329	|	|	1408	|	1429	|	|	1508	|	1529	|	|	1608	|
Zürich HB a.	1100	1124	1126	|	1152	1200	1224	1226	|	1252	1300	1324	1326	|	1352	1400	1424	1426	|	1452	1500	1524	1526	|	1552	1600	1624	1626
Zürich Flug ✈ **530/5** a.	...	...	|	1156	|	...	...	|	1256	|	...	...	|	1356	|	...	...	|	1456	|	...	...	|	1556	|	...	...	|
Chur **520** a.	...	...	1252	...	1343	...	...	1352	...	1443	...	...	1452	...	1543	...	...	1552	...	1643	...	...	1652	...	1743	...	...	1752

	IR 2081	EC 101	IC 781	IR 1981	IC 581	IR 2085	IR 1785	ICE 75	IR 1985	ICN 585	IR 2087	IR 1787	IC 787		TGV 9217	IR 1987	IC 587	IR 2089	IR 1789	ICE 77	IR 1989	IC 589	IR 2091	IR 1791	IC 791	IR 97	IC 591	IR 1793
		✕			🍷			✕		🍷			✕		(🍷)		(✕)			✕		(✕)			✕			(✕)
		◆						H		z					◆					H						◆		
Basel SBB d.	1540	1547	1607	1613	1633	1640	1647	1707	1713	1733	1740	1747	1807	...	1809	1813	1833	1840	1847	1907	1913	1933	1940	1947	2007	2013	2033	2047
Rheinfelden d.	1551	|	|	1625	|	1651	|	|	1725	|	1751	|	|	...	|	1825	|	1851	|	|	1925	|	1951	|	|	2025	|	|
Liestal d.	|	1557	|	|	|	|	1657	|	|	|	|	1757	|	...	|	|	|	|	1857	|	|	|	|	1957	|	|	|	2057
Aarau d.	|	1623	|	|	|	|	1723	|	|	|	|	1823	|	...	|	|	|	|	1923	|	|	|	|	2023	|	|	|	2123
Lenzburg d.	|	1630	|	|	|	|	1730	|	|	|	|	1830	|	...	|	|	|	|	1930	|	|	|	|	2030	|	|	|	2130
Brugg d.	1620	|	|	1700	|	1720	|	|	1800	|	1820	|	|	...	|	1900	|	1920	|	|	2000	|	2020	|	|	2100	|	|
Baden d.	1629	|	|	1708	|	1729	|	|	1808	|	1829	|	|	...	|	1908	|	1929	|	|	2008	|	2029	|	|	2108	|	|
Zürich HB a.	|	1652	1700	1724	1726	|	1752	1800	1824	1826	|	1852	1900	...	1914	1924	1926	|	1952	2000	2024	2026	|	2052	2100	2124	2126	2152
Zürich Flug ✈ **530/5** a.	1656	|	...	...	|	1756	|	...	...	|	1856	|	...	...	...	...	|	1956	|	...	...	|	2056	|	...	...	...	|
Chur **520** a.	...	1843	...	...	1852	...	1943	...	...	1952	...	2045	...	...	...	...	2052	...	2145	...	...	2152	...	2245	...	...	...	2345

	ICE 79	IR 1993	IC 593	IR 1795	TGV 9219	IR 1995	IR 1799	IC 797	IR 1997	IR 1999	IR 1951	
	✕											
	H										q	
Basel SBB d.	2107	2113	2133	2147	2207	2213	2247	2307	2313	0013	0113	...
Rheinfelden d.	|	2125	|	|	|	2225	|	|	2325	0025	0125	...
Liestal d.	|	|	|	2157	|	|	2257	|	|	|	|	...
Aarau d.	|	|	|	2223	|	|	2323	|	|	|	|	...
Lenzburg d.	|	|	|	2230	|	|	2330	|	|	|	|	...
Brugg d.	|	2200	|	|	|	2300	|	|	0000	0100	0200	...
Baden d.	|	2208	|	|	|	2308	|	|	0008	0108	0208	...
Zürich HB a.	2200	2224	2226	2252	2300	2324	2352	2400	0024	0124	0224	...
Zürich Flug ✈ **530/5** a.	...	...	...	...	...	...	...	...	...	...	...	...
Chur **520** a.	...	...	...	...	...	...	...	...	...	...	...	...

	IR 1756	IR 1956	ICE 78	IR 1758	IC 558	IR 2058	IR 1958	TGV 9210	IR 1760	IR 2060	IC 560	IR 1960
			✕	✕				(🍷)			(✕)	
			H					◆				
Chur **520** d.	...	...	...	...	0506d	...	...	...	0513	...	0606	...
Zürich Flug ✈ **530/5** d.	...	...	...	...	|	0604	...	...	|	0704	|	...
Zürich HB d.	0508	0536	0602	0608	0634	|	0636	0702	0708	|	0734	0736
Baden d.	|	0552	|	|	|	0633	0652	|	|	0733	|	0752
Brugg d.	|	0601	|	|	|	0642	0702	|	|	0742	|	0802
Lenzburg d.	0529	|	|	0629	|	|	|	|	0729	|	|	|
Aarau d.	0537	|	|	0637	|	|	|	|	0737	|	|	|
Liestal d.	0601	|	|	0701	|	|	|	|	0801	|	|	|
Rheinfelden d.	|	0635	|	|	|	0717	0734	|	|	0810	|	0834
Basel SBB a.	0612	0651	0657	0712	0727	0734	0747	0757	0812	0823	0827	0847

km		ICE 76	IR 1764	IR 2062	IC 562	IR 1962	IC 768	IR 1766	IR 2066	IC 566	IR 1966	ICE 74	IR 1768	IR 2068	IC 568	IR 1968	EC 102	EC 100	IR 1770	IR 2070	ICN 570	IR 90	ICE 72	IR 1772	IR 2072	IC 572	IR 1972	TGV 9216
		✕	✕		(✕)	🍷				(✕)		✕			🍷	🍷	✕	✕			🍷		✕			(✕)		(🍷)
		K										K					◆	◆			z	◆	H					◆
	Chur **520** d.	...	...	...	0709	...	0713	...	...	0809	...	...	0816	...	0909	...	0916	0916	...	...	1009	...	...	1016	...	1109	...	...
	Zürich Flug ✈ **530/5** d.	...	...	0804	|	...	|	...	0904	|	...	...	|	1004	|	...	|	|	...	1104	|	...	...	|	1204	|	...	...
0	**Zürich HB** d.	0802	0808	|	0834	0836	0902	0908	|	0934	0936	1002	1008	|	1034	1036	1102	1102	1108	|	1134	1136	1202	1208	|	1234	1236	1302
	Baden d.	|	|	0833	|	0852	|	|	0933	|	0952	|	|	1033	|	1052	|	|	|	1133	|	1152	|	|	1233	|	1252	|
	Brugg d.	|	|	0842	|	0902	|	|	0942	|	1002	|	|	1042	|	1102	|	|	|	1142	|	1202	|	|	1242	|	1302	|
32	Lenzburg d.	|	0829	|	|	|	|	0929	|	|	|	|	1029	|	|	|	|	|	1129	|	|	|	|	1229	|	|	|	|
41	Aarau d.	|	0837	|	|	|	|	0937	|	|	|	|	1037	|	|	|	|	|	1137	|	|	|	|	1237	|	|	|	|
77	Liestal d.	|	0901	|	|	|	|	1001	|	|	|	|	1101	|	|	|	|	|	1201	|	|	|	|	1301	|	|	|	|
	Rheinfelden d.	|	|	0910	|	0934	|	|	1010	|	1034	|	|	1110	|	1134	|	|	|	1210	|	1234	|	|	1310	|	1334	|
91	**Basel SBB** a.	0857	0912	0923	0927	0947	0957	1012	1023	1027	1047	1057	1112	1123	1127	1147	1157	1157	1212	1223	1227	1247	1257	1312	1323	1327	1347	1357

	EC 6	IR 2074	IC 574	IR 1974	IC 774	IR 1776	IR 2076	IC 576	IR 96	TGV 9218	IR 1778	IR 2078	IC 578	IR 1978	IC 780	IR 1780	IR 2080	TGV 9220	ICN 580	IR 1980	ICE 372	ICE 272	IR 1782	IR 2082	IC 582	IR 1982	IC 784	IR 1784
	✕		(✕)					(✕)		(🍷)			🍷					(🍷)	✕		✕	✕			(✕)			
	◆								◆	◆								◆	z		◆	◆						
Chur **520** d.	1116	...	1209	...	...	1216	...	1309	...	...	1316	...	1409	...	...	1416	...	...	1509	...	...	...	...	...	1609	...	1616	...
Zürich Flug ✈ **530/5** d.	|	1304	|	...	...	|	1404	|	...	...	|	1504	|	...	...	|	1604	...	|	...	...	...	...	1704	|	...	|	...
Zürich HB d.	1308	|	1334	1336	1402	1408	|	1434	1436	1502	1508	|	1534	1536	1602	1608	|	1627	1634	1636	1702	1702	1708	|	1734	1736	1802	1808
Baden d.	|	1333	|	1352	|	|	1433	|	1452	|	|	1533	|	1552	|	|	1633	|	|	1652	|	|	|	1733	|	1752	|	|
Brugg d.	|	1342	|	1402	|	|	1442	|	1502	|	|	1542	|	1602	|	|	1642	|	|	1702	|	|	|	1742	|	1802	|	|
Lenzburg d.	1329	|	|	|	|	1429	|	|	|	|	1529	|	|	|	|	1629	|	|	|	|	|	|	1729	|	|	|	|	1829
Aarau d.	1337	|	|	|	|	1437	|	|	|	|	1537	|	|	|	|	1637	|	|	|	|	|	|	1737	|	|	|	|	1837
Liestal d.	1401	|	|	|	|	1501	|	|	|	|	1601	|	|	|	|	1701	|	|	|	|	|	|	1801	|	|	|	|	1901
Rheinfelden d.	|	1410	|	1434	|	|	1510	|	1534	|	|	1610	|	1634	|	|	1710	|	|	1734	|	|	|	1810	|	1834	|	|
Basel SBB a.	1412	1423	1427	1447	1457	1512	1523	1527	1547	1557	1612	1623	1627	1647	1657	1712	1723	1736	1727	1747	1757	1757	1812	1823	1827	1847	1857	1912

	IR 2086	IC 586	IR 1984	ICE 270	IR 1786	IR 2088	IC 588	IR 1988	CNL 459	IC 788	IR 1788	IR 2090	IC 590	IR 1990	CNL 478	IC 790	IR 1790	IR 2092	IC 594	IR 1992	ICN 794	IR 1792	IR 1994	IC 798	IR 1794	IR 1996	IR 1798	IR 1752
		(✕)		✕			(✕)			✕							✕											
				◆					◆						◆						z							q
Chur **520** d.	...	1709	...	...	1716	...	1809	...	...	...	1816	...	1909	...	...	...	1916	...	2009e	...	2013	...	...	2113	...	...	...	...
Zürich Flug ✈ **530/5** d.	1804	|	...	...	|	1904	|	...	...	...	|	2004	|	...	...	...	|	2104	|	...	|	...	...	|	...	...	...	...
Zürich HB d.	|	1834	1836	1902	1908	|	1934	1936	1944	2002	2008	|	2034	2036	2042	2102	2108	|	2134	2136	2202	2208	2236	2302	2308	2336	0008	0108
Baden d.	1833	|	1852	|	|	1933	|	1952	1958u	|	|	2033	|	2052	2058u	|	|	2133	|	2152	|	|	2252	|	|	2352	|	|
Brugg d.	1842	|	1902	|	|	1942	|	2002	|	|	|	2042	|	2102	|	|	|	2142	|	2202	|	|	2302	|	|	0002	|	|
Lenzburg d.	|	|	|	|	1929	|	|	|	|	|	2029	|	|	|	|	|	2129	|	|	|	|	2229	|	|	2329	|	0029	0129
Aarau d.	|	|	|	|	1937	|	|	|	|	|	2037	|	|	|	|	|	2137	|	|	|	|	2237	|	|	2337	|	0037	0137
Liestal d.	|	|	|	|	2001	|	|	|	|	|	2101	|	|	|	|	|	2201	|	|	|	|	2301	|	|	0001	|	0101	0202
Rheinfelden d.	1910	|	1934	|	|	2010	|	2034	|	|	|	2110	|	2134	|	|	|	2210	|	2234	|	|	2334	|	|	0034	|	|
Basel SBB a.	1923	1927	1947	1957	2012	2023	2027	2047	2051u	2057	2112	2123	2127	2147	2151u	2157	2212	2223	2227	2247	2257	2312	2347	2357	0012	0047	0112	0212

← FOR NOTES SEE OPPOSITE PAGE

511 BERN and FRIBOURG - NEUCHÂTEL

Valid December 13 - July 11 BLS, TPF*

km																													
		⚒													▲										p			q		
0	Bern ... d.	...	0608	...	0654	0708	...	0754	0808	...	0854	0908	...	0954	and at	1908	...	1954	2008	...	2108	...	2208	...	2234	2308	...	2334	0010
22	Kerzers ... d.	...	0631	...	0711	0731	...	0811	0831	...	0911	0931	...	1011	the same	1931	...	2011	2031	...	2135	...	2231	...	2301	2331	...	0001	0037
	Fribourg ... d.	0532	|	0632	|	|	0732	|	|	0832	|	|	0932	|	minutes	|	1932	|	|	2032	|	2132	|	2232	|	|	2332	|	|
	Murten ... d.	0600	|	0700	|	|	0800	|	|	0900	|	|	1000	|	past each	|	2000	|	|	2100	|	2200	|	2300	|	|	0000	|	|
30	Ins ... d.	0611	0638	0711	0717	0738	0811	0817	0838	0911	0917	0938	1011	1017	hour	1938	2011	2017	2038	2111	2142	2211	2238	2310	2313	2338	0010	0013	0044
43	**Neuchâtel** ... a.	0624	0657	0724	0727	0757	0824	0827	0857	0924	0930	0957	1024	1027	until	1957	2024	2027	2057	2127	2158	2224	2257	...	2326	2357	...	0026	0059

km																														
				⚒													▲													
	Neuchâtel ... d.	0536	0633	0636	0701	0733	0736	0801	0833	0836	0905	0933	0936	1001	1033	1036	and at	1901	1933	1936	2001	2036	2101	2136	2201	2236	2301	2336	0009
0	Ins ... d.	0552	0643	0650	0717	0743	0750	0817	0843	0850	0921	0943	0950	1017	1043	1050	the same	1917	1943	1950	2017	2050	2121	2150	2217	2250	2317	2352	0025
10	Murten ... d.	|	|	0701	|	|	0801	|	|	0901	|	|	1001	|	|	1101	minutes	|	|	2001	|	2101	|	2201	|	2301	|	|	|
32	**Fribourg** ... a.	|	|	0728	|	|	0828	|	|	0928	|	|	1028	|	|	1128	past each	|	|	2028	|	2128	|	2228	|	2328	|	|	|
	Kerzers ... d.	0600	0649	...	0730	0749	...	0830	0849	...	0933	0949	...	1030	1049	...	hour	1930	1949	...	2030	...	2134	...	2230	...	2330	0000	0038
	Bern ... a.	0626	0706	...	0752	0806	...	0852	0907	...	0956	1006	...	1052	1106	...	until	1952	2006	...	2052	...	2156	...	2252	...	2352	0026	0103

p – ①②③④⑦ (also Dec. 25, 26, Jan. 1, 2, Apr. 2).
q – ⑤⑥ (not Dec. 25, 26, Jan. 1, 2, Apr. 2).
▲ – Variations: 1032, 1132 from Fribourg; 0936, 1036 from Neuchâtel, run only Murten - Ins - Neuchâtel and v.v. on Oct. 3.
* – Operators: BLS, Bern - Ins - Neuchâtel; TPF, Fribourg - Ins.

512 BIEL and NEUCHÂTEL - LA CHAUX DE FONDS - LE LOCLE

SBB

km																												
		Ⓐ	Ⓐ																									
0	**Biel/Bienne** ... d.	0508	...	0614	...	0650	0717	...	...	0750	and at	1917	...	...	1950	...	...	2017	...	2117	...	2217	...	2319	...	2350	...	...
28	St Imier ... d.	0543	...	0641	...	0731	0744	...	...	0831	the same	1944	...	...	2031	...	...	2052	...	2152	...	2252	...	2352	...	0028	...	...
	Neuchâtel ... d.	|	0528	|	0631	|	|	0731	0737	|	minutes	|	1931	1937	|	...	2031	|	2037	|	2137	|	2237	|	2337	|	...	...
44	La Chaux de Fonds . d.	0559	0602	0655	0702	0747	0758	0802	0818	0847	past each	1958	2002	2018	2047	...	2059	2110	2115	2210	2215	2310	2315	0010	0015	0044	...	...
52	**Le Locle** ... a.	...	0614	...	0713	...	...	0810	0827	...	hour until	...	2010	2027	...	...	...	...	2123	...	2223	...	2323	...	0023	...	...	...

km																															
0	**Le Locle** ... d.	0546	...	0650	...	0752	...	...	0832	0850	...	...	0932	and at	1850	...	...	1932	1950	...	2032	...	2132	...	2232	...	2332	...
8	La Chaux de Fonds . d.	0557	0559	0701	0702	0801	0802	0813	0842	0901	0902	0913	0942	the same	1901	1902	1913	1942	2001	2002	2042	2051	2142	2151	2242	2251	2342	2351
37	**Neuchâtel** ... a.	0626	|	0729	|	0829	|	|	0919	0929	|	|	1019	minutes	1929	|	|	2019	2030	|	2119	|	2219	|	2319	|	0019	|
	St Imier ... d.	...	0613	...	0716	...	0816	0830	...	...	0916	0930	...	past each	...	1916	1930	...	...	2016	...	2109	...	2209	...	2309	...	0009
	Biel/Bienne ... a.	...	0640	...	0741	...	0841	0909	...	...	0941	1009	...	hour until	...	1941	2009	...	...	2041	...	2141	...	2241	...	2344	...	0041

513 BERN - BIEL

SBB

km																								
		Ⓐ						and at the																⑥⑦j
0	**Bern** ... d.	0500	0530	0600	0612	0630	0642	same minutes	2000	2012	2030	2042	...	2100	2112	2130	2200	2212	2230	2300	2312	2330	0012	0015	0112
23	Lyss ... d.	0523	0553	0623	0630	0653	0700	past each	2023	2030	2053	2100	...	2123	2130	2153	2223	2230	2253	2323	2330	2353	0030	0038	0134
34	**Biel/Bienne** ... a.	0536	0606	0636	0638	0706	0708	hour until	2036	2038	2106	2108	...	2136	2138	2206	2236	2238	2306	2336	2338	0006	0038	0051	0142

							and at the																⑥⑦j
Biel/Bienne ... d.	0518	...	0551	0554	0621	0624	same minutes	1951	1954	2021	2024	...	2051	2054	2121	2124	2154	2221	2224	2254	2321	2324	2354	0026
Lyss ... d.	0530	...	0600	0607	0630	0637	past each	2000	2007	2030	2037	...	2100	2107	2130	2137	2207	2230	2237	2307	2330	2337	0007	0035
Bern ... a.	0554	...	0618	0630	0648	0700	hour until	2018	2030	2048	2100	...	2118	2130	2148	2200	2230	2248	2300	2330	2348	2400	0030	0053

j – Also Jan. 1.

514 BERN - LUZERN via Langnau

BLS

For faster services Bern - (Olten -) Luzern see Tables 505 / 565

km												
0	**Bern** ... § d.	0537a	0612	0637	0712	and at	2137	2212	2237	2312	2342	0012
21	Konolfingen . § d.	0553a	0634	0653	0734	the same	2153	2234	2253	2334	2356	0034
38	Langnau ... § d.	0606	0652	0706	0752	minutes	2206	2252	2306	2352	0008	0052
75	Wolhusen ... d.	0645	...	0745	...	past each	2245	...	2345	...	...	...
96	**Luzern** ... a.	0703	...	0803	...	hour until	2303	...	0010	...	...	...

Luzern ... d.	0557	0657	...	and at	2057	...	2157	...	...	2316	0016
Wolhusen ... d.	0615	0715	...	the same	2115	...	2215	...	...	2344	0040
Langnau ... § d.	0654	0754	0807	minutes	2154	2207	2254	2307	0008	0022	0118
Konolfingen ... § d.	0708	0808	0826	past each	2208	2226	2308	2326	0026	...	...
Bern ... § a.	0726	0826	0848	hour until	2226	2248	2326	2348	0048	...	...

a – Ⓐ only.

Additional services operate Bern - Langnau and v.v.

516 BERN - SOLOTHURN

Valid December 13 - April 18 Narrow gauge. RBS

km						and at the same																	
		⚒																					
0	**Bern RBS** ... d.	0537	...	0605	0635	minutes past	1905	1935	...	2005	...	2041	2111	2141	...	2211	2241	2311	...	2341	...	0011	...
34	Solothurn ... a.	0626	...	0642	0712	each hour until	1942	2012	...	2042	...	2124	2154	2224	...	2254	2324	2354	...	0024	...	0054	...

						and at the same																	
	⚒																						
Solothurn ... d.	0509	0548	...	0618	0648	minutes past	1918	1948	...	2005	...	2035	2107	...	2137	2207	...	2237	2307	...	2337	...	...
Bern RBS ... a.	0552	0625	...	0655	0725	each hour until	1955	2025	...	2050	...	2120	2150	...	2220	2250	...	2320	2350	...	0020	...	...

517 SOLOTHURN - BURGDORF - THUN

BLS

km																											
0	**Solothurn** ... d.	0601	0701	...	0801	0901	...	1001	1101	...	1201	1301	...	1401	1501	...	1601	1701	...	1801	...	1901	...	...	...	...	...
5	Biberist ... d.	0606	0706	...	0806	0906	...	1006	1106	...	1206	1306	...	1406	1506	...	1606	1706	...	1806	...	1906	...	...	...	...	...
21	**Burgdorf** ... a.	0627	0727	...	0827	0927	...	1027	1127	...	1227	1327	...	1427	1527	...	1627	1727	...	1827	...	1927	...	...	...	...	...
21	**Burgdorf** ... d.	0630	0730	*0747*	0830	0930	*0947*	1030	1130	*1147*	1230	1330	*1347*	1430	1530	*1547*	1630	1730	*1747*	1830	*1847*	1930	*1947*	*2047*	*2147*	*2247*	*2347*
28	Hasle-Rüegsau d.	0639	0739	0801	0839	0939	1001	1039	1139	1201	1239	1339	1401	1439	1539	1601	1639	1739	1801	1839	1901	1939	2001	2101	2201	2301	0001
46	Konolfingen ... a.	0700	0800	0822	0900	1000	1022	1100	1200	1222	1300	1400	1422	1500	1600	1622	1700	1800	1822	1900	1922	2000	2022	2122	2222	2322	0022
46	Konolfingen ... d.	0701	0801	0835	0901	1001	1035	1101	1201	1235	1301	1401	1435	1501	1601	1635	1701	1801	1835	1901	1935	2001	2035	2135	2235	2335	0035
61	**Thun** ... a.	0718	0818	0856	0918	1018	1056	1118	1218	1256	1318	1418	1456	1518	1618	1656	1718	1818	1856	1918	1956	2018	2056	2156	2255	2355	0055

	Ⓐ																										
Thun ... d.	0532	0639	0739	0839	0903	0939	1039	1103	1139	1239	1303	1339	1439	1503	1539	1639	1703	1739	1803	1839	1903	1939	2009	2109	2209	2309	0009
Konolfingen ... a.	0553	0658	0758	0858	0924	0958	1058	1124	1158	1258	1324	1358	1458	1524	1558	1658	1724	1758	1824	1858	1924	1958	2031	2130	2230	2330	0030
Konolfingen ... d.	0600	0700	0800	0900	0935	1000	1100	1135	1200	1300	1335	1400	1500	1535	1600	1700	1735	1800	1835	1900	1935	2000	2035	2135	2235	2335	0035
Hasle-Rüegsau. d.	0620	0720	0820	0920	0957	1020	1120	1157	1220	1320	1357	1420	1520	1557	1620	1720	1757	1820	1857	1920	1957	2020	2057	2157	2257	2357	0057
Burgdorf ... a.	0629	0729	0829	0929	*1012*	1029	1129	*1212*	1229	1329	*1412*	1429	1529	*1612*	1629	1729	*1812*	1829	*1912*	1929	*2012*	2029	*2112*	*2212*	*2312*	*0012*	0106
Burgdorf ... d.	0632	0732	0832	0932	...	1032	1132	...	1232	1332	...	1432	1532	...	1632	1732	...	1832	...	1932	...	...	...	...	...	...	...
Biberist ... a.	0650	0750	0850	0950	...	1050	1150	...	1250	1350	...	1450	1550	...	1650	1750	...	1850	...	1950	...	...	...	...	...	...	...
Solothurn ... a.	0657	0757	0857	0957	...	1057	1157	...	1257	1357	...	1457	1557	...	1657	1757	...	1857	...	1957	...	...	...	...	...	...	...

X – ⑦ (also Dec. 25, 26, Jan. 1, 2, Apr. 2, 5, May 13, 24).
h – Change at Hasle-Rüegsau.

Additional services operate:
Solothurn - Burgdorf: 0436Ⓐ, 0518⚒, 0636⚒, 0736⚒, 1236⚒, 1336⚒, 1636, 1736, 1836, 2015, 2115, 2215, 2315, 0015**X**.
Burgdorf - Thun: 0451⚒, 0517Ⓐ, 0547Ⓐ**h**, 0551†, 0647**h**, 0847**h**, 1047**h**, 1247**h**, 1447**h**, 1647**h**.
Thun - Burgdorf: 0503⚒**h**, 0603**h**, 0703**h**, 0803**h**, 1003**h**, 1203**h**, 1403**h**, 1603**h**.
Burgdorf - Solothurn: 0532Ⓐ, 0555⚒, 0632Ⓒ, 0655⚒, 1155⚒, 1255⚒, 1555, 1655, 1755, 1855, 2015, 2115, 2215, 2315.

SBB ZÜRICH - SARGANS - CHUR 520

km																												
		IR	IR		IR	IR	IC		IR	IR	ICN	EC	IR	IC		IR	IR	IC		IR	IC		IR	IC		IR	ICN	
		1755	1953		10759	1759	559		10761	1761	561	163	1765	565		165	1767	567		1777	569		1771	571		1773	573	
			(✕)			✕	🍷				🍷	✕	✕	(✕)				(✕)			(✕)			🍷			🍷	
					x				©		z	♦y															z	
	Basel SBB **510** d.	...	0513	...	...	0547	0633	...	...	0647	0733	...	0747	0833	...	...	0847	0933	...	...	1033	...	1047	1133	...	1147	1233	...
0	**Zürich HB** d.	0612	0637	...	0706	0712	0737	...	0806	0812	0837	0840	0912	0937	...	1006	1012	1037	...	1112	1137	...	1212	1237	...	1312	1337	...
12	Thalwil d.	0622	|	...	|	0722	|	...	|	0822	|	|	0922	|	...	|	1022	|	...	1122	|	...	1222	|	...	1322	|	...
24	Wädenswil d.	0632	|	...	|	0732	|	...	|	0832	|	|	0932	|	...	|	1032	|	...	1132	|	...	1232	|	...	1332	|	...
33	Pfäffikon d.	0641	|	...	0731	0741	|	...	|	0841	|	|	0941	|	...	|	1041	|	...	1141	|	...	1241	|	...	1341	|	...
57	Ziegelbrücke d.	0659	|	...	|	0759	|	...	|	0859	|	|	0959	|	...	|	1059	|	...	1159	|	...	1259	|	...	1359	|	...
90	**Sargans 534** d.	0721	0733	0748	|	0821	0833	0848	0904	0921	0933	0936	1021	1033	1048	|	1121	1133	1148	1221	1233	1248	1321	1333	1348	1421	1433	1448
106	Buchs **534** a.	|	|	0759	|	|	|	0859	|	|	|	0946	|	|	1059	1114	|	|	1159	|	|	1259	|	|	1359	|	|	1459
103	Landquart d.	0736	0743	...	0814	0834	0843	...	0914	0934	0943	...	1034	1043	...	...	1134	1143	...	1234	1243	...	1334	1343	...	1434	1443	...
116	**Chur** a.	0745	0752	...	0823	0843	0852	...	0923	0943	0952	...	1043	1052	...	...	1143	1152	...	1243	1252	...	1343	1352	...	1443	1452	...
	St Moritz **540** a.	...	*0958*	...	...	...	*1058*	...	...	...	*1158*	...	...	*1258*	...	...	...	*1358*	...	...	*1458*	...	...	*1558*	...	...	*1658*	...

	IR	IC	RJ	EC	IC		IR	IC	RJ	EC	IC		IR	ICN		IR	IC		IR	IC	EN		IR	IC		IR	EN	IR
	1775	575	169	7	577		91	579	363	101	581		1785	585		1787	587		1789	589	465		1791	595		1793	467	1797
		(✕)	🍷	✕	(✕)			🍷	🍷	✕	🍷			🍷			(✕)			(✕)								
			W	♦			♦		S	♦											♦						♦	
Basel SBB **510** d.	1247	1333	...	1347	1433	...	1447	1533	...	1547	1633	...	1647	1733	...	1747	1833	...	1847	1933	...	...	1947	...	...	2047	*2133*	...
Zürich HB d.	1412	1437	1440	1512	1537	...	1612	1637	1640	1712	1737	...	1812	1837	...	1912	1937	...	2012	2037	2040	...	2112	2137	...	2212	2240	2312
Thalwil d.	1422	|	|	1522	|	...	1622	|	|	1722	|	...	1822	|	...	1922	|	...	2022	|	|	...	2122	|	...	2222	|	2322
Wädenswil d.	1432	|	|	1532	|	...	1632	|	|	1732	|	...	1832	|	...	1932	|	...	2032	|	|	...	2132	|	...	2232	|	2332
Pfäffikon d.	1441	|	|	1541	|	...	1641	|	|	1741	|	...	1841	|	...	1941	|	...	2041	|	|	...	2141	|	...	2241	|	2341
Ziegelbrücke d.	1459	|	|	1559	|	...	1659	|	|	1759	|	...	1859	|	...	1959	|	...	2059	|	|	...	2159	|	...	2259	|	2359
Sargans 534 d.	1521	1533	1537	1621	1633	1648	1721	1733	1737	1821	1833	1848	1921	1933	1948	2021	2033	2048	2121	2133	2137u	2144	2221	2233	2244	2321	2337	0025
Buchs **534** a.	|	|	1548	|	|	1659	|	|	1748	|	|	1859	|	|	1959	|	|	2059	|	|	2148	2154	|	|	2254	|	2348	|
Landquart d.	1534	1543	...	1634	1643	...	1734	1743	...	1834	1843	...	1934	1943	...	2034	2043	...	2134	2143	...	...	2234	2243	...	2334	...	0040
Chur a.	1543	1552	...	1643	1652	...	1743	1752	...	1843	1852	...	1943	1952	...	2043	2052	...	2143	2152	...	...	2243	2252	...	2343	...	0049
St Moritz **540** a.	...	*1758*	...	...	*1858*	...	...	*1958*	...	...	*2058*	...	...	*2159*	...	...	*2303*	...	...	...	...	...	...	...	...	...	...	...

	IC	IR		EN	IC	IR		IC	IR	EN		IC	IR		IC	EC	RJ	ICN	IR		IC	EC		IC	IR		IC	IR
	558	1760		466	560	1762		562	766	464		566	1768		568	100	362	570	1772		572	6		574	1776		576	1778
					(✕)			(✕)				(✕)			🍷	✕	🍷	🍷			(✕)	✕		(✕)			(✕)	
	⚒			♦						♦						♦	S	z				♦						
St Moritz **540** d.	...	...	...	...	...	...	...	...	...	...	...	...	...	...	*0702*	...	...	*0802*	...	...	*0902*	...	...	*1002*	...	...	*1102*	...
Chur d.	0506	0513	...	...	0606	0613	...	0709	0713	...	...	0809	0816	...	0909	0916	...	1009	1016	...	1109	1116	...	1209	1216	...	1309	1316
Landquart d.	0515	0523	...	...	0615	0623	...	0719	0723	...	...	0819	0826	...	0919	0926	...	1019	1026	...	1119	1126	...	1219	1226	...	1319	1326
Buchs **534** d.	|	|	0603	0610	|	|	0701	|	|	0812	0801	|	|	0901	|	|	1012	|	|	1100	|	|	1201	|	|	1301	|	|
Sargans 534 d.	0525	0539	0618	0620s	0625	0639	0712	0728	0739	0823s	0812	0828	0839	0912	0928	0939	1025	1028	1039	1112	1128	1139	1212	1228	1239	1312	1328	1339
Ziegelbrücke d.	0547	0601	...	|	0647	0701	...	|	0801	|	...	|	0901	...	|	1001	|	|	1101	...	|	1201	...	|	1301	...	|	1401
Pfäffikon d.	|	0619	...	|	|	0719	...	|	0819	|	...	|	0919	...	|	1019	|	|	1119	...	|	1219	...	|	1319	...	|	1419
Wädenswil d.	|	0628	...	|	|	0728	...	|	0828	|	...	|	0928	...	|	1028	|	|	1128	...	|	1228	...	|	1328	...	|	1428
Thalwil d.	|	0638	...	|	|	0738	...	|	0838	|	...	|	0938	...	|	1038	|	|	1138	...	|	1238	...	|	1338	...	|	1438
Zürich HB a.	0623	0648	...	0720	0723	0748	...	0823	0848	0920	...	0923	0948	...	1023	1048	1120	1123	1148	...	1223	1248	...	1323	1348	...	1423	1448
Basel SBB **510** a.	0727	0812	...	...	0827	...	...	0927	0957	...	...	1027	1112	...	1127	1157	...	1227	1312	...	1327	1412	...	1427	1512	...	1527	1612

	RJ	IC	IR		ICN	IR	EC	IC	IC		IC	IR		IC	IR	IR		IC	IR	IR		IC	ICN	IR	IR		IR	
	160	578	1780		580	782	162	582	784		586	1786		588	1788	10790		590	1790	10792		592	794	166	796		1796	
	🍷	🍷			✕		✕	(✕)			(✕)	✕		(✕)				🍷	✕			🍷						
	W				z		♦y									q				v		†	w					
St Moritz **540** d.	...	*1202*	...	...	*1302*	...	...	*1402*	...	...	*1502*	...	...	*1602*	...	...	...	*1702*	...	...	...	*1802*	*1802*	...	...	...	*2002*	...
Chur d.	...	1409	1416	...	1509	1516	...	1609	1616	...	1709	1716	...	1809	1816	1837	...	1909	1916	1937	...	2009	2016	...	2116	...	2216	...
Landquart d.	...	1419	1426	...	1519	1526	...	1619	1626	...	1719	1726	...	1819	1826	1847	...	1919	1926	1947	...	2019	2026	...	2126	...	2226	...
Buchs **534** d.	1412	|	|	1501	|	|	1612	|	|	1701	|	|	1801	|	|	|	1901	|	|	|	2001	|	|	2050	|	2201	|	...
Sargans 534 d.	1425	1428	1439	1512	1528	1539	1625	1628	1639	1712	1728	1739	1812	1828	1839	|	1912	1928	1939	1958	2012	2028	2039	2107	2139	2212	2239	...
Ziegelbrücke d.	|	|	1501	...	|	1601	|	|	1701	...	|	1801	...	|	1901	|	...	|	2001	|	...	|	2101	|	2201	...	2301	...
Pfäffikon d.	|	|	1519	...	|	1619	|	|	1719	...	|	1819	...	|	1919	1930	...	|	2019	|	...	|	2119	|	2219	...	2319	...
Wädenswil d.	|	|	1528	...	|	1628	|	|	1728	...	|	1828	...	|	1928	|	...	|	2028	|	...	|	2128	|	2228	...	2328	...
Thalwil d.	|	|	1538	...	|	1638	|	|	1738	...	|	1838	...	|	1938	|	...	|	2038	|	...	|	2138	|	2238	...	2338	...
Zürich HB a.	1520	1523	1548	...	1623	1648	1720	1723	1748	...	1823	1848	...	1923	1948	1953	...	2023	2048	2053	...	2123	2148	2224	2248	...	2348	...
Basel SBB **510** a.	...	1627	1712	...	1727	...	...	1827	1857	...	1927	2012	...	2027	2112	...	...	2127	2212	...	...	...	2257	...	2357	...	*0112*	...

♦ – **NOTES** (LISTED BY TRAIN NUMBER)

6 – [12] and ✕ Chur - Basel - Köln - Dortmund (- Hamburg ⑧ **m**).
7 – [12] and ✕ (①–⑥ **n**, Hamburg -) Dortmund - Basel - Chur.
91 – VAUBAN – [12] Brussels - Luxembourg - Basel - Zürich - Chur.
100 – [12] and ✕ Chur - Zürich - Basel - Hamburg (- Kiel, ⑦, also Apr. 5, May 24; not Apr. 4, May 23, train number **102**).
101 – [12] and ✕ Hamburg - Basel - Zürich - Chur.
162/3 – TRANSALPIN – [12] and ✕ Wien - Innsbruck - Zürich and v.v.
464/5 – ZÜRICHSEE – 🛏 1, 2 cl., ▬ 2 cl. and [2] Graz - Innsbruck - Feldkirch - Zürich and v.v.; 🛏 1, 2 cl. and ▬ 2 cl. Zagreb (**414/5**) - Villach - Zürich and v.v.; [2] Beograd (**414/5**) - Zagreb - Zürich and v.v.; [12] Buchs - Zürich and v.v.
466/7 – WIENER WALZER – 🛏 1, 2 cl., ▬ 2 cl. and [2] [reclining] Wien - Zürich and v.v.; ▬ 2 cl. and [2] Budapest - Wien - Zürich and v.v.; 🛏 1, 2 cl. and ▬ 2 cl. Praha - Linz - Zürich and v.v.; [12] Buchs - Zürich and v.v.

S – [12] and 🍷 Salzburg - Zürich and v.v.
W – [12] and 🍷 Wien - Zürich and v.v.

m – Not Dec. 24, 25, 31, Apr. 2, 4, May 23.
n – Not Dec. 25, 26, Jan. 1, Apr. 3, 5, May 24.
q – © (daily May 13 - Oct. 24).
s – Stops to set down only.
u – Stops to pick up only.
v – © May 15 - Oct. 24 (also May 13).
w – Runs as *IR* train on ©.
x – May 13 - Oct. 24.
y – Runs as *RJ* train from June 13.
z – Runs as *IC* train on ©.

SBB ZIEGELBRÜCKE - LINTHAL 522

km											©	©
0	Ziegelbrücke d.	0605	and	1905	2005	2105	2205	2305	EXTRA	0823	1023
11	Glarus d.	0621	hourly	1921	2021	2121	2221	2321	SERVICES	0840	1040
16	Schwanden d.	0629	until	1929	2027	2127	2227	2327	▶▶▶	0847	1047
27	Linthal ▲ a.	0647		1947	*2052*y	*2152*y	*2252*y	*2352*j		0900	1100

										©	©
Linthal ▲ d.	0515d	0612	and	2012	*2104*y	*2204*y	*2304*y	EXTRA	1658	1758
Schwanden d.	0534	0630	hourly	2030	2131	2231	2331	SERVICES	1710	1810
Glarus d.	0543	0641	until	2041	2141	2241	2341	▶▶▶	1719	1819
Ziegelbrücke a.	0557	0655		2055	2155	2255	2355		1735	1835

d – ⚒ only.
j – ⑤⑥⑦ (also Apr. 5, May 13, 24). Connection by 🚌.
y – Connection by 🚌.

▲ – 🚌 service **Linthal** - **Flüelen** Bahnhof (Table **550**) and v.v. operates **June 26 - September 26, 2010** over the Klausenpass. 🅁. Journey time: 2 hours 20 minutes. **NO WINTER SERVICE**.

From **Linthal**: 0805©, 0910, 1010, 1505, 1705©. From **Flüelen**: 0550©, 0730, 0930, 1500©, 1530.

Operator: PostAuto Zentralschweiz, Luzern. ✆ (Luzern) 058 448 06 22, fax: 058 667 34 33.

SBB LAUSANNE - PALÉZIEUX - PAYERNE 523

km															Ⓐ										Z
0	**Lausanne 505** d.	0524	0624	0724	0824	0924	1024	1124	...	1224	1324	1424	1524	1624	1700	...	1724	1824	1924	2024	2124	...	2320	...	0247
21	Palézieux **505** d.	0541	0641	0741	0841	0941	1041	1141	...	1241	1341	1441	1541	1641	1718	...	1741	1841	1941	2041	2141	...	2344	...	0310
38	Moudon d.	0600	0700	0800	0900	1000	1100	1200	...	1300	1400	1500	1600	1700	1733	...	1800	1900	2000	2100	2200	...	0003	...	...
58	Payerne **508** a.	0619	0722	0821	0919	1019	1119	1219	...	1321	1419	1519	1619	1721	1752	...	1819	1921	2019	2119	2219	...	0022	...	...

			Ⓐ																					
Payerne **508** d.	0539	0639	0708	0738	0839	...	0939	1039	1139	1238	...	1339	1439	1539	1639	1736	...	1839	1939	...	2039	2139	2239	...
Moudon d.	0559	0659	0725	0759	0859	...	0959	1059	1159	1259	...	1359	1459	1559	1659	1759	...	1859	1959	...	2059	2159	2259	...
Palézieux **505** d.	0618	0718	0742	0818	0918	...	1018	1118	1218	1318	...	1418	1518	1618	1718	1818	...	1918	2018	...	2118	2218	2318	...
Lausanne 505 a.	0636	0736	0800	0836	0936	...	1036	1136	1236	1336	...	1436	1536	1636	1736	1836	...	1936	2036	...	2136	2236	2336	...

Z – ⑥⑦ (also Jan. 1).

525 ARTH GOLDAU - ST GALLEN - ROMANSHORN

SBB, SOB*

km			Ⓐ	IR 2403 V		IR 2405 V					IR 2407	IR 2409 V	IR 2411 V	IR 2413 V	IR 2415 V	IR 2417 V	IR 2419 V	IR 2421 V	IR 2423 V	IR 2425 V	IR 2427 V	IR 2429 V	IR 2431 V	IR 2433 V		
	Luzern **550** d.	...	...	...	...	...	...	...	...	...	...	0740	0840	0940	1040	1140	1240	1340	1440	1540	1640	1740	1840	1940	...	...
0	**Arth Goldau** d.	...	0523	...	...	...	...	0653	...	...	...	0813	0913	1013	1113	1213	1313	1413	1513	1613	1713	1813	1913	2013	2114	2214
20	Biberbrugg ◐ d.	...	0547	...	0550	...	0650	0720	0722	0750	...	0835	0935	1035	1135	1235	1335	1435	1535	1635	1735	1835	1935	2035	2136	2236
26	Samstagern ◐ d.	...	▬	...	0557	...	0657	...	0729	0757	...	|	|	|	|	|	|	|	|	|	|	|	|	|	2144	2244
34	Pfäffikon d.	...	...	...	0615	...	0715	...	0744	0815	...	0854	0954	1054	1154	1254	1354	1454	1554	1654	1754	1854	1954	2054	2158	2258
38	Rapperswil a.	...	...	...	0622	...	0722	...	0750	0822	...	0859	0959	1059	1159	1259	1359	1459	1559	1659	1759	1859	1959	2059	2202	2302
38	Rapperswil d.	...	...	0602**d**	...	0703	...	...	...	...	0803	0903	1003	1103	1203	1303	1403	1503	1603	1703	1803	1903	2003	2103	2203	2303
66	Wattwil d.	...	⚒	0630**d**	...	0730	...	...	...	...	0830	0930	1030	1130	1230	1330	1430	1530	1630	1730	1830	1930	2030	2130	2230	2330
89	Herisau d.	0544	*0608*	0651	...	0751	...	...	...	...	0851	0951	1051	1151	1251	1351	1451	1551	1651	1751	1851	1951	2051	2151	2253	2353
97	**St Gallen** a.	0554	*0617*	0658	...	0758	...	...	...	...	0858	0958	1058	1158	1258	1358	1458	1558	1658	1758	1858	1958	2058	2158	2301	0001
97	**St Gallen 532** d.	0601	0631	0701	...	0801	...	...	...	...	0901	1001	1101	1201	1301	1401	1501	1601	1701	1801	1901	2001	2101	2201	2302	0002
119	**Romanshorn 532** a.	0627	0657	0727	...	0827	...	...	...	...	0927	1027	1127	1227	1327	1427	1527	1627	1727	1827	1927	2027	2127	2227	2329	0029

					IR 2408 V	IR 2410 V	IR 2412 V	IR 2414 V	IR 2416 V	IR 2418 V	IR 2420 V	IR 2422 V	IR 2424 V	IR 2426 V	IR 2428 V	IR 2430 V	IR 2432 V	IR 2434 V		IR 2436						
Romanshorn 532 d.	...	...	0534**d**	...	0634	0734	0834	0934	1034	1134	1234	1334	1434	1534	1634	1734	1834	1934	...	*2034*	...	*2134*	...	*2234*	...	2334
St Gallen 532 a.	...	...	0558**d**	...	0659	0759	0859	0959	1059	1159	1259	1359	1459	1559	1659	1759	1859	1959	...	*2059*	...	*2159*	...	*2259*	...	2359
St Gallen d.	...	...	0600	...	0702	0802	0902	1002	1102	1202	1302	1402	1502	1602	1702	1802	1902	2002	...	2102	...	2202	...	2302	...	0002
Herisau d.	...	...	0608	...	0710	0810	0910	1010	1110	1210	1310	1410	1510	1610	1710	1810	1910	2010	...	2110	...	2211	...	2311	...	0011
Wattwil d.	...	...	0630	...	0732	0832	0932	1032	1132	1232	1332	1432	1532	1632	1732	1832	1932	2032	...	2132	...	2232	...	2332	...	0032
Rapperswil a.	...	...	0657	...	0757	0857	0957	1057	1157	1257	1357	1457	1557	1657	1757	1857	1957	2057	...	2157	...	2257	...	2357	...	...
Rapperswil d.	0548	0636	0700	...	0800	0900	1000	1100	1200	1300	1400	1500	1600	1700	1800	1900	2000	...	2103	...	2203	...	2303	...	0003	...
Pfäffikon d.	0556	0647	0706	...	0806	0906	1006	1106	1206	1306	1406	1506	1606	1706	1806	1906	2006	...	2107	...	2207	...	2307	...	0007	...
Samstagern ◐ d.	0608	0658	0715	...	|	|	|	|	|	|	|	|	|	|	|	|	|	...	2118	...	2218	...	2319	...	0019	...
Biberbrugg ◐ d.	0616	0706	0724	...	0824	0924	1024	1124	1224	1324	1424	1524	1624	1724	1824	1924	2024	...	2125	...	2225	...	...	...	...	...
Arth Goldau a.	0641	0730	0745	...	0846	0946	1046	1146	1246	1346	1446	1546	1646	1746	1846	1946	2046	...	2150	...	2250	...	...	...	...	...
Luzern **550** a.	...	...	...	...	0920	1020	1120	1220	1320	1420	1520	1620	1720	1820	1920	2020	2120	...	...	...	...	...	...	...	...	...

d – ⚒ only.

V – VORALPEN EXPRESS – [12] Luzern - Rapperswil - St Gallen - Romanshorn and v.v. Also conveys (🍷) or 🍷 on most services.

◐ – For service to Einsiedeln see panel below.

* – Operated by SOB, except Rapperswil - Wattwil (SBB).

km												
0	**Wädenswil** d.	0559	0629j	0659j	0734	0804	and every 30 minutes until	2204	2234	2304	2334	0004
6	Samstagern d.	0611	0637j	0707j	0741	0811		2211	2241	2320	2341	0020
11	Biberbrugg ● d.	0620	0650	0720	0750	0820		2220	2250	2327	2350	0027
17	**Einsiedeln** ● a.	0627	0657	0727	0757	0827		2227	2257	2333	2357	0033

Einsiedeln ● d.	0518	0600	0630	0659	0730	0800	and every 30 minutes until	2230	2300	2330	...
Biberbrugg ● d.	0524	0607	0637	0707	0737	0807		2237	2307	2337	...
Samstagern d.	0534	0615	0645	0715	0745	0815		2245	2315	2345	...
Wädenswil a.	0543	0624	0654	0724	0754	0824		2254	2324	2354	...

● – Additional services run Biberbrugg - Einsiedeln and v.v.

j – 4–5 minutes later on Ⓒ.

526 GOSSAU - APPENZELL - WASSERAUEN

Narrow gauge. AB

km		⚒																							2	2	2
0	**Gossau** d.	0548	0647	0717	0747	0817	0847	0917	0947	1017	1047	1117	1147	1247	1347	1447	1517	1547	1617	1647	1717	1747	1847	1947	2047	2147	2312
5	Herisau a.	0553	0653	0723	0753	0823	0853	0923	0953	1023	1053	1123	1153	1253	1353	1453	1523	1553	1623	1653	1723	1753	1853	1953	2053	2153	2318
5	Herisau d.	0554**a**	0654	0724	0754	0824	0854	0924	0954	1024**j**	1054	1124	1154	1254	1354	1454	1524	1554	1624	1654	1724	1754	1854	1954	2054	2154	2319
15	Urnäsch d.	0608**a**	0708	0738	0808	0838	0908	0938	1008	1038**j**	1108	1138	1208	1308	1408	1508	1538	1608	1638	1708	1738	1808	1908	2008	2108	2208	2332
26	**Appenzell** d.	0630**a**	0730	0800	0830	0900	0930	1000	1030	1100**j**	1130	1200	1230	1330	1430	1530	1600	1630	1700	1730	1803	1830	1927	2027	2127	2227	2347
32	**Wasserauen** a.	0641**a**	0741	0811	0841**j**	0911	0941	1011	1041	1111**j**	1141	1211**a**	1241	1341	1441	1541	1611**q**	1641	1711**q**	1741	1814**a**	1841	*1941*y	*2041*y	*2141*y	...	...

																									🚌 j	
Wasserauen d.	...	...	0645**a**	0749	0819	0849**j**	0919	0949	1019	1049**j**	1119	1149**a**	1219	1310	1419	1519	1549**q**	1619	1649**q**	1719	1749**a**	1819	1849	*1942*y	*2042*y	2142	...
Appenzell d.	0603**a**	0633	0703**a**	0803	0833	0903	0933	1003	1033	1103**j**	1133	1203	1233	1333	1433	1533	1603	1633	1703	1733	1803	1833	1903	2003	2103	2153	2203
Urnäsch d.	0620**a**	0650	0720**a**	0820	0850	0920	0950	1020	1050	1120**j**	1150	1220	1250	1350	1450	1550	1620	1650	1720	1750	1820	1850	1920	2020	2120	...	2220
Herisau a.	0636**a**	0706	0736**a**	0836	0906	0936	1006	1036	1106	1136**j**	1206	1236	1306	1406	1506	1606	1636	1706	1736	1806	1836	1906	1936	2036	2136	...	2236
Herisau d.	0637	0707	0737	0837	0907	0937	1007	1037	1107	1137	1207	1237	1307	1407	1507	1607	1637	1707	1737	1807	1837	1907	1937	2037	2137	...	2237
Gossau a.	0643	0713	0743	0843	0913	0943	1013	1043	1113	1143	1213	1243	1313	1413	1513	1613	1643	1713	1743	1813	1843	1913	1943	2043	2143	...	2243

a – Ⓐ only. **j** – May 16 - Oct. 24. **q** – Apr. 2 - Nov. 7. **y** – Connection by 🚌.

527 ST GALLEN - APPENZELL

Narrow gauge rack railway. AB

km		⚒	⚒	Ⓐ			⚒							q								Ⓐ		🚌	🚌	🚌 z
0	**St Gallen** d.	0607	0637**a**	0707	0737**d**	0807	0837	0907	0937	and every 30 minutes until	1607	1637	1707	1722	1737	1807	1837	1907	1937	2007	2037	2107	2137	2230	2330	0030
7	Teufen d.	0624	0654**a**	0724	0754**d**	0824	0854	0924	0954		1624	1654	1724	1738	1754	1824	1854	1924	1954	2024	2054	2124	2154	2242	2342	0042
14	Gais ▲ d.	0640	0710	0740	0810	0849	0910	0940	1010		1640	1710	1740	1750	1810	1840	1910	1940	2010	2039	2109	2139	2210	2252	2352	0052
20	**Appenzell** a.	0651	0721	0751	0821	0859	0921	0951	1021		1651	1721	1751**j**	1801	1821	1851	1921	1951	2021	*2057*y	*2121*y	...	2221	2302	0002	0102

	⚒	Ⓐ	⚒	Ⓐ		⚒									Ⓒ	Ⓐ								🚌	🚌	🚌
Appenzell d.	0508	0608	0638	0701	0708	0738	0808**a**	0838	0908**d**	0938	1008	and every 30 minutes until	1608	1638	1708	1708	1738	1808	1838	1908	1938	2008	2038	2108	2155	2249
Gais ▲ d.	0520	0620	0650	0711	0720	0750	0820	0850	0920	0950	1020		1620	1650	1720	1725	1750	1820	1850	1920	1950	2020	2050	2117	2204	2258
Teufen d.	0533	0633	0703	0724	0733	0803	0833	0903	0933	1003	1033		1633	1703	1733	1738	1803	1833	1903	1933	2003	2033**a**	2103	2127	2215	2308
St Gallen a.	0550	0650	0720	0739	0750	0820	0850	0920	0950	1020	1050		1650	1720	1750	1755	1820	1850	1920	1950	2020	2050**a**	2120	2140	2228	2321

a – Ⓐ only.
d – ⚒ only.
j – Ⓒ (daily Dec. 24 - Jan. 3, July 3 - Aug. 8; also May 12, 14).
q – Ⓐ Dec. 14-23, Jan. 4 - July 2, Aug. 9 - Dec. 10 (not May 12, 14).
y – Connection by 🚌.
z – ⑥⑦ (also Jan. 1, Apr. 2, 5, May 13, 14, 24).

▲ – Rail service **Gais - Altstätten Stadt** and v.v. *8 km*. Journey time: 22 minutes. **Operator**: AB.
From **Gais**: 0551Ⓐ, 0651Ⓐ, 0700Ⓒ, 0800, 0851 and hourly until 1751, then 1911🚌, 2011🚌.
From **Altstätten Stadt**: 0617Ⓐ, 0717Ⓐ, 0725Ⓒ, 0828 and hourly until 1828, then 1928🚌, 2028🚌.
A bus connects Altstätten Stadt with Altstätten SBB station (Table **534**). Journey time: 6 minutes.

528 LOCARNO - DOMODOSSOLA

Subject to alteration FART

km				h	🍷	P 🍷	C 🍷	h	P 🍷	j		
0	**Locarno** d.	0650	0813	0915	1042	1213	1412	1455	1542	1556	1746	1850
20	Camedo 🏛 d.	0726	0849	0949	1117	1249	1446**u**	1530	1618	1635	1826	1929
26	Re ⊗ d.	0743	0905	1005	1135	1304	1504	1545	1633	1650	1844	1944
34	S M Maggiore §⊗ d.	0755	0917	1017	1148	1316	1516	1557	1645	1701	1856	1956
53	**Domodossola** a.	0837	0956	1056	1230	1356	1556	1636	1725	1741	1936	2036

		j	P 🍷	j 🍷	C 🍷	P 🍷	h	🍷	🍷		
Domodossola d.	0535**a**	0825	0925	0945	1025	1125	1158	1405	1525	1805	2025
S. M. Maggiore §⊗ d.	0614**a**	0905	1005	1025	1105	1204	1238	1445	1605	1845	2104
Re ⊗ d.	0624	0917	1017	1037	1117	1216	1250	1457	1617	1857	2116
Camedo 🏛 d.	0640	0933	1034	1056	1136	1232	1306	1514	1637	1913	2132
Locarno a.	0718	1010	1110	1146	1210	1308	1348	1552	1715	1948	2208

C – Conveys observation cars (supplement payable).
P – Conveys observation cars Mar. 22 - Oct. 18 (supplement payable).
a – ①–⑤ only.
h – Mar. 22 - Oct. 18.
j – † Mar. 22 - June 7; daily June 14 - Sept. 6; ⑦ Sept. 13 - Oct. 18 (also Apr. 25, June 2).
u – Stops to pick up only.
⊗ – Request stop.
§ – Full name is Santa Maria Maggiore.

529 ZÜRICH - ZÜRICH FLUGHAFEN ✈

Journey time: 9-13 minutes

Additional services are available at peak times

From **Zürich HB**:
0502, 0520, 0539, 0547, 0601, 0607, 0609, 0617, 0627, 0637, 0639, 0647, 0655, 0707, 0709, 0717, 0727, 0737, 0739, 0747, 0755, 0801, 0807, 0809, 0817, 0827, 0837, 0839, 0847, 0855, and at xx01, xx07, xx09, xx17, xx27, xx37, xx39, xx47, xx55 minutes past each hour until 2001, 2007, 2009, 2017, 2027, 2037, 2039, 2047, 2055, then 2107, 2109, 2117, 2127, 2139, 2147, 2207, 2209, 2217, 2227, 2239, 2247, 2307, 2309, 2327, 0017.

From **Zürich Flughafen**:
0502, 0549, 0602, 0613, 0620, 0632, 0640, 0643, 0651, 0702, 0710, 0713, 0720, 0732, 0739, 0743, 0751, 0802, 0810, 0813, 0820, 0832, 0840, 0843, 0847, 0851, 0902, 0910, 0913, 0920, 0932, 0940, 0943, 0947, 0951, and at xx02, xx10, xx13, xx20, xx32, xx40, xx43, xx47, xx51 minutes past each hour until 2002, 2010, 2013, 2020, 2032, 2040, 2043, 2047, 2051, then 2102, 2110, 2113, 2120, 2132, 2140, 2143, 2202, 2213, 2220, 2232, 2240, 2243, 2302, 2320, 2340, 2343, 0010, 0041.

SBB — ZÜRICH - ST GALLEN — 530

km		IC 705	ICN 507	IC 707		ICN 509	EC 191	IC 709	ICN 1511	IC 711		ICN 515	EC 193	IC 715	ICN 1517	IC 717	ICN 519	IC 719		ICN 1521	IC 721	ICN 523	EC 195	IC 723
			✕	✕		✕	✕	✕	✕	✕		✕	✕	✕	✕	✕	✕	✕		✕	✕	✕	✕	✕
							M	F					M										M	
	Genève Aéroport ✈ **505** d.	...	...	...	...	...	...	...	...	...	...	...	...	0636	...	0736	0805	0836	...	...	0936	1005	...	1036
	Genève **505** d.	...	...	...	...	...	...	...	...	0536	...	0614	...	0645	...	0745	0814	0845	...	...	0945	1014	...	1045
	Lausanne **505** d.	...	...	...	...	...	...	...	0539	0620	...	|	...	0720	0745	0820	|	0920	...	0945	1020	|	...	1120
	Biel **500** d.	...	...	...	...	0543	...	...	0644	|	...	0746	...	|	0846	|	0946	|	...	1046	|	1146	...	|
	Bern **500** d.	...	...	0530	...	|	...	0632	|	0732	...	|	...	0832	|	0932	|	1032	...	|	1132	|	...	1232
0	**Zürich HB 535** d.	0539	0609	0639	...	0709	0716	0739	0809	0839	...	0909	0916	0939	1009	1039	1109	1139	...	1209	1239	1309	1316	1339
10	**Zürich Flughafen ✈ 535** d.	0552	0622	0652	...	0722	0728	0752	0822	0852	...	0922	0928	0952	1022	1052	1122	1152	...	1222	1252	1322	1328	1352
30	Winterthur **535** d.	0607	0637	0707	...	0737	0742	0807	0837	0907	...	0937	0942	1007	1037	1107	1137	1207	...	1237	1307	1337	1342	1407
57	Wil **539** d.	0625	0654	0725	...	0754	|	0825	0854	0925	...	0954	|	1025	1054	1125	1154	1225	...	1254	1325	1354	|	1425
78	Gossau d.	0645	0710	0745	...	0807	|	0845	0907	0945	...	1007	|	1045	1107	1145	1207	1245	...	1307	1345	1407	|	1445
87	**St Gallen** a.	0653	0717	0753	...	0815	0818	0853	0915	0953	...	1015	1018	1053	1115	1153	1215	1253	...	1315	1353	1415	1418	1453

	ICN 1525	IC 725	ICN 527		IC 727	ICN 1529	IC 729	ICN 531	IC 3831	IC 731	ICN 1535	EC 197	IC 735	ICN 537	IC 737	ICN 1539	IC 739		ICN 541	IC 741	ICN 1543	IR 3841	ICN 545	ICN 1547
	✕	✕	✕		✕	✕	✕	✕		✕	✕	✕	✕	✕	✕	✕	✕		✕				✕	
									Ⓐ			M												
Genève Aéroport ✈ **505** d.	...	1136	1205	...	1236	...	1336	1405	...	1436	...	...	1536	1605	1636	...	1736	...	1805	1836	...	...	2005	...
Genève **505** d.	...	1145	1214	...	1245	...	1345	1414	...	1445	...	...	1545	1614	1645	...	1745	...	1814	1845	...	...	2014	...
Lausanne **505** d.	1145	1220	|	...	1320	1345	1420	|	...	1520	1545	...	1620	|	1720	1745	1820	...	|	1920	1945	...	|	2145
Biel **500** d.	1246	|	1346	...	|	1446	|	1546	...	|	1646	...	|	1746	|	1846	|	...	1946	|	2046	...	2146	2246
Bern **500** d.	|	1332	|	...	1432	|	1532	|	...	1632	|	...	1732	|	1832	|	1932	...	|	2032	|	...	|	|
Zürich HB 535 d.	1409	1439	1509	...	1539	1609	1639	1709	1733	1739	1809	1816	1839	1909	1939	2009	2039	...	2109	2139	2209	2239	2309	0017
Zürich Flughafen ✈ 535 d.	1422	1452	1522	...	1552	1622	1652	1722	1745	1752	1822	1828**u**	1852	1922	1952	2022	2052	...	2122	2152	2222	2252	2322	0029
Winterthur **535** d.	1437	1507	1537	...	1607	1637	1707	1737	1800	1807	1837	1842**u**	1907	1937	2007	2037	2107	...	2137	2207	2237	2307	2337	0044
Wil **539** d.	1454	1525	1554	...	1625	1654	1725	1754	|	1825	1854	|	1925	1954	2025	2054	2125	...	2154	2225	2254	2325	2354	0100
Gossau d.	1507	1545	1607	...	1645	1707	1745	1807	|	1845	1907	|	1945	2007	2045	2107	2145	...	2207	2245	2310	2345	0011	0118
St Gallen a.	1515	1553	1615	...	1653	1715	1753	1815	1839	1853	1915	1919**u**	1953	2015	2053	2115	2153	...	2215	2253	2317	2353	0018	0125

		IC 708	ICN 1510	IC 710	ICN 512	IR 3810	IC 712	ICN 1516	IC 716	ICN 518		IC 718	ICN 1520	IC 720	EC 196	ICN 522	IC 722	ICN 1524		IC 724	ICN 526	IC 726	ICN 1528	IC 728
		🍸	✕	✕	✕		✕	✕	✕	✕		✕	✕	✕	✕	✕	✕	✕		✕	✕	✕	✕	✕
						R									M									
St Gallen d.	0432	0511	0544	0611	0642	0644	0711	0748	0811	0848	...	0911	0948	1011	1042	1048	1111	1148	...	1211	1248	1311	1348	1411
Gossau d.	0439	0519	0551	0619	0650	0652	0719	0756	0819	0856	...	0919	0956	1019	|	1056	1119	1156	...	1219	1256	1319	1356	1419
Wil **539** d.	0456	0539	0609	0639	0706	0711	0739	0810	0839	0910	...	0939	1010	1039	|	1110	1139	1210	...	1239	1310	1339	1410	1439
Winterthur **535** d.	0515	0558	0627	0658	0725	0733	0758	0828	0858	0928	...	0958	1028	1058	1119	1128	1158	1228	...	1258	1328	1358	1428	1458
Zürich Flughafen ✈ 535 a.	0529	0611	0641	0711	0737	|	0811	0841	0911	0941	...	1011	1041	1111	1132	1141	1211	1241	...	1311	1341	1411	1441	1511
Zürich HB 535 a.	...	0623	0653	0723	0751	0759	0823	0853	0923	0953	...	1023	1053	1123	1144	1153	1223	1253	...	1323	1353	1423	1453	1523
Bern **500** a.	...	0729	|	0829	|	...	0929	|	1029	|	...	1129	|	1229	...	|	1329	|	...	1429	|	1529	|	1629
Biel **500** a.	...	|	0813	|	0913	...	|	1013	|	1113	...	|	1213	|	...	1313	|	1413	...	|	1513	|	1613	|
Lausanne **505** a.	...	0840	0915	0940	|	...	1040	1115	1140	|	...	1240	1315	1340	...	|	1440	1515	...	1540	|	1640	1715	1740
Genève **505** a.	...	0915	...	1015	1046	...	1115	...	1215	1246	...	1315	...	1415	...	1446	1515	...	...	1615	1646	1715	...	1815
Genève Aéroport ✈ **505** a.	...	0924	...	1024	1055	...	1124	...	1224	1255	...	1324	...	1424	...	1455	1524	...	...	1624	1655	1724	...	1824

	ICN 530	IC 730	EC 194	ICN 1532	IC 732	ICN 536	IC 736		ICN 1538	IC 738	ICN 1540	ICN 540	IC 740	EC 192	ICN 1542	IC 742	ICN 1544	IC 744		EC 190	ICN 1546	ICN 548	ICN 500	
	✕	✕	✕	✕	✕	✕	✕		✕	✕	✕	✕	✕	✕		✕	✕	✕		✕				
			M								⚒	†		M		F				M				
St Gallen d.	1448	1511	1542	1548	1611	1648	1711	...	1748	1811	1848	1848	1911	1942	1948	2011	2048	2111	...	2142	2144	2244	2344	...
Gossau d.	1456	1519	|	1556	1619	1656	1719	...	1756	1819	1856	1856	1919	|	1956	2019	2056	2119	...	|	2151	2251	2351	...
Wil **539** d.	1510	1539	|	1610	1639	1710	1739	...	1810	1839	1910	1910	1939	|	2010	2039	2110	2139	...	|	2210	2310	0010	...
Winterthur **535** d.	1528	1558	1619	1628	1658	1728	1758	...	1828	1858	1928	1928	1958	2019	2028	2058	2128	2158	...	2219	2228	2328	0028	...
Zürich Flughafen ✈ 535 a.	1541	1611	1632	1641	1711	1741	1811	...	1841	1911	1941	1941	2011	2032	2041	2111	2141	2211	...	2232	2241	2341	0041	...
Zürich HB 535 a.	1553	1623	1644	1653	1723	1753	1823	...	1853	1923	1953	1953	2023	2044	2053	2123	2153	2223	...	2244	2253	2353	0053	...
Bern **500** a.	|	1729	...	|	1829	|	1929	...	|	2029	|	|	2129	...	|	2229	|	2331	...	...	|	...	...	...
Biel **500** a.	1713	|	...	1813	|	1913	|	...	2013	|	2113	2113	|	...	2213	...	2314	...	...	...	0022	...	...	...
Lausanne **505** a.	|	1840	...	1915	1940	|	2040	...	2115	2140	...	|	2240	...	2315	...	0015	...	...	...	0124**p**	...	...	...
Genève **505** a.	1846	1915	...	...	2015	2046	2115	...	...	2215	...	2246	2324	...	...	...	...	...	...	...	...	...	...	...
Genève Aéroport ✈ **505** a.	1855	1924	...	...	2024	2055	2124	...	...	2224	...	2255	2333	...	...	...	...	...	...	...	...	...	...	...

F – From/to Fribourg.
M – 🚃12 Zürich - München and v.v.
R – Ⓐ: 🚃12 Rorschach - Zürich.
p – ⑥⑦ (also Jan. 1, Apr. 2, 5, May 13, 14, 24; not Dec. 13, 26, 27).
u – Stops to pick up only.

SBB — WINTERTHUR - SCHAFFHAUSEN — 531

km																							
0	Winterthur d.	0542	0606	0619	0642	and at the same minutes past each hour until	1806	1819	1842	1906	1919	1942	2006	2019	2042	...	2106	2119	2142	2208	2242	2308	2342	...	0012
30	Schaffhausen a.	0614	0638	0644	0714		1838	1844	1914	1938	1944	2014	2038	2044	2114	...	2138	2144	2214	2238	2314	2338	0014	...	0041

					Ⓐ		Ⓐ			Ⓐ													
Schaffhausen d.	0521	0544	0614	0621	0631	0643	0701	0714	0721	0731	0744	0814	0821	0846	and at the same minutes past each hour until	2014	2021	2046	2121	2146	2221	2246	2321	2346
Winterthur a.	0554	0619	0642	0654	0659	0719	0729	0742	0754	0759	0819	0842	0854	0919		2042	2054	2119	2154	2219	2254	2319	2354	0023

SBB, THURBO* — SCHAFFHAUSEN - ROMANSHORN - RORSCHACH — 532

km		⚒																							
0	**Schaffhausen 939/40** d.	...	...	...	0531	...	0601	0631		1701	1731	1801	1831	1901	1931	2001	2031	2101	2131	2201	...	2231	2301	...	0006
20	Stein am Rhein d.	...	...	0527	0557	...	0627	0657		1727	1757	1827	1857	1927	1957	2027	2057	2127	2157	2225	...	2257	2327	...	0034
46	**Kreuzlingen** a.	...	...	0556	0626	...	0656	0726	and at	1756	1826	1856	1926	1956	2026	2056	2126	2156	2226	...	...	2326	2356	...	0100
46	**Kreuzlingen** d.	0500	0530	0600	0630	...	0700	0730	the same	1800	1830	1900	1930	2000	2030	2100	2130	2200	2230	...	2300	2330	...	...	...
47	Kreuzlingen Hafen d.	0502	0532	0602	0632	...	0702	0732	minutes	1802	1832	1902	1932	2002	2032	2102	2132	2202	2232	...	2302	2332	...	...	...
65	**Romanshorn** a.	0525	0555	0625	0655	...	0725	0755	past each	1825	1855	1925	1955	2025	2055	2125	2155	2225	2255	...	2325	2355	...	...	...
65	**Romanshorn** d.	0528	0604**d**	0628	0704**d**	...	0732	0804	hour	1832	1904	1932	2004	2032	2104	2132	...	2232	...	...	2332	...	...	...	...
	St Gallen **525** a.	|	0629**d**	|	0729**d**	...	|	0829	until	|	1929	|	2029	|	2129	|	...	|	...	...	|	...	...	...	...
73	Arbon a.	0536	...	0636	...	...	0741	...		1841	...	1941	...	2041	...	2141	...	2241	...	...	2341	...	...	...	...
79	Rorschach Hafen a.	0543	...	0643	...	...	0748	...		1848	...	1948	...	2048	...	2148	...	2248	...	...	2348	...	...	...	...
80	**Rorschach** a.	0547	...	0647	...	...	0752	...		1852	...	1952	...	2052	...	2152	...	2252	...	...	2352	...	...	...	...

Rorschach d.	...	...	0507	...	0607	...	0707	...	...	0807	...		1807	...	1907	...	2007	...	2107	...	...	2207	...	2307	...
Rorschach Hafen d.	...	...	0508	...	0608	...	0708	...	...	0808	...		1808	...	1908	...	2008	...	2108	...	...	2208	...	2308	...
Arbon d.	...	...	0517	...	0617	...	0717	...	...	0817	...	and at	1817	...	1917	...	2017	...	2117	...	...	2217	...	2317	...
St Gallen **525** d.	...	...	|	...	|	0631**d**	|	0731**d**	...	|	0831	the same	|	1831	|	1931	|	2031	|	...	2131	|	...	|	...
Romanshorn a.	...	...	0527	...	0627	0657**d**	0727	0757**d**	...	0827	0857	minutes	1827	1857	1927	1957	2027	2057	2127	...	2157	2227	...	2327	...
Romanshorn d.	...	...	0532	0602	0632	0702	0732	0802	...	0832	0902	past each	1832	1902	1932	2002	2032	2102	2132	...	2202	2232	...	2332	0032
Kreuzlingen Hafen d.	...	...	0554	0624	0654	0724	0754	0824	...	0854	0924	hour	1854	1924	1954	2024	2054	2124	2154	...	2224	2254	...	2354	0054
Kreuzlingen a.	...	...	0556	0626	0656	0726	0756	0826	...	0856	0926	until	1856	1926	1956	2026	2056	2126	2156	...	2226	2256	...	2356	0056
Kreuzlingen d.	0501	0531	0601	0631	0701	0731	0801	0831	...	0901	0931		1901	1931	2001	2031	2101	2131	...	...	2231	...	2331	...	...
Stein am Rhein d.	0530	0600	0630	0700	0730	0800	0830	0900	...	0930	1000		1930	2000	2030	2100	2130	2200	...	2230	2300	...	2357	...	...
Schaffhausen 939/40 a.	0556	0626	0656	0726	0756	0826	0856	0926	...	0956	1026		1956	2026	2056	2126	2156	2226	...	2256	2326	...	...	...	...

d – ⚒ only.
* – SBB operate Romanshorn - Rorschach; THURBO operate Schaffhausen - Romanshorn.

533 ⛴ SCHAFFHAUSEN - KREUZLINGEN

Valid April 5 - October 18 (no winter service) URh

		✕A		✕B		✕A		✕A	
Schaffhausen d.	...	0910	...	1110	...	1310	...	1510	...
Stein am Rhein d.	...	1115	...	1315	...	1515	...	1715	...
Kreuzlingen Hafen a.	...	1350	...	1550	...	1750	...	1950y	...

		✕A		✕A		✕A		✕C	
Kreuzlingen Hafen d.	...	0900	...	1100	...	1400	...	1600	...
Stein am Rhein d.	...	1130	...	1330	...	1630	...	1830	...
Schaffhausen a.	...	1245	...	1445	...	1745	...	1945y	...

A – © Apr. 5-19; daily Apr. 25 - Oct. 4.

B – † Apr. 26 - June 28; daily July 4 - Sept. 13, Oct. 3-18 (also May 1, June 11, Sept. 20, 27).

C – † Apr. 26 - June 28; daily July 4 - Sept. 13, Sept. 20 - Oct. 4 (also May 1, June 11, Oct. 3).

y – Not Aug. 8.

534 ST GALLEN - BUCHS - CHUR

SBB

km		RE 3803	RE 3805	RE 3807	EC 191	RE 3809	RE 3811	EC 193	RE 3815	RE 3817	RE 3819	RE 3821	EC 195	RE 3823	RE 3825	RE 3827	RE 3829	RE 3833	IR 1787	EC 197	RE 3835	RE 3837	IR 1791		
					M			M					M							M					
0	**St Gallen** d.	0600	0703	0803	0819	0903	1003	1019	1103	1203	1303	1403	1419	1503	1603	1703	1803	1903	...	1919	2003	2103	...	2204	2305
16	Rorschach d.	0621	0721	0821	|	0921	1021	|	1121	1221	1321	1421	|	1521	1621	1721	1821	1921	...	|	2021	2121	...	2222	2322
27	**St Margrethen** d.	0631	0731	0831	0840	0931	1031	1040	1131	1231	1331	1431	1440	1531	1631	1731	1831	1931	...	1940	2031	2131	...	2232	2332
39	Altstätten **527** d.	0642	0742	0842	...	0942	1042	...	1142	1242	1342	1442	...	1542	1642	1742	1842	1942	...	...	2042	2142	...	2243	2343
65	**Buchs 520** ⊖ d.	0701	0801	0901	...	1001	1100	...	1201	1301	1401	1501	...	1601	1701	1801	1901	2001	...	...	2101	2201	...	2306	0006
81	Sargans **520** ⊖ d.	0713	0813	0913	...	1013	1113	...	1213	1313	1413	1513	...	1613	1713	1813	1913	2012	2021	...	2113	2212	2221	2318	0022
93	Landquart **520** d.	0728	0828	0928	...	1028	1128	...	1228	1328	1428	1528	...	1628	1728	1828	1928	...	2036	...	2128	...	2236	...	...
107	**Chur 520** a.	0738	0838	0938	...	1038	1138	...	1238	1338	1438	1538	...	1638	1738	1838	1938	...	2045	...	2138	...	2245	...	...

	IR 1760	RE 3812	RE 3816	RE 3818	RE 3820	EC 196	RE 3822	RE 3824	RE 3826	RE 3828	RE 3830	EC 194	RE 3832	RE 3834	RE 3836	RE 3838	EC 192	RE 3840	RE 3842	EC 190	ICN 792	RE 3844	IR 796		IR 1796
						M						M					M			M	w				
Chur 520 d.	0513	...	0622	0722	0822	...	0922	1022	1122	1222	1322	...	1422	1522	1622	1722	...	1822	1922	...	2013	...	2113	...	2213
Landquart **520** d.	0523	...	0633	0733	0833	...	0933	1033	1133	1233	1333	...	1433	1533	1633	1733	...	1833	1933	...	2023	...	2123	...	2223
Sargans **520** ⊖ d.	0537	0541	0648	0748	0848	...	0948	1048	1148	1248	1348	...	1448	1548	1648	1748	...	1848	1948	...	2037	2048	2137	2144	2237
Buchs 520 ⊖ d.	▬	0600	0701	0801	0901	...	1001	1101	1201	1301	1401	...	1501	1601	1701	1801	...	1901	2001	...	...	2101	...	2157	*2255*
Altstätten **527** d.	0551	0615	0717	0817	0917	...	1017	1117	1217	1317	1417	...	1517	1617	1717	1817	...	1917	2017	...	...	2117	...	2214	*2314*
St Margrethen d.	0605	0626	0729	0829	0929	1020	1029	1129	1229	1329	1429	1520	1529	1629	1729	1829	1920	1929	2029	2120	...	2129	...	2227	*2327*
Rorschach d.	0619	0637	0740	0840	0940	|	1040	1140	1240	1340	1440	|	1540	1640	1740	1840	|	1940	2040	|	...	2140	...	2239	*2339*
St Gallen a.	0638	0656	0756	0856	0956	1041	1056	1156	1256	1356	1456	1541	1556	1656	1756	1856	1941	1956	2056	2141	...	2156	...	2258	*2358*

⊖ – 🚌 services to **VADUZ (LIECHTENSTEIN)**

[line 12]	⚒	⚒	†																		⚒	†	⚒
Buchs (Bahnhof) d.	0533	0603	...	0633	...	0703	0733	...	0803	0833	and at the	2003	2033	...	2103	...	2133	...	2203	...	2233	2233	2303
Vaduz Post d.	0550	0620	0620	0650	...	0720	0750	...	0820	0850	same minutes past each	2020	2050	...	2120	...	2150	...	2220	...	2250	2248	2318
Sargans (Bahnhof) a.	0621	0651	0651	0721	...	0751	0821	...	0851	0921	hour until	2051	2121	...	...	...	2218	...	...	...	2318	...	...

[line 12]	⚒																					⚒	
Sargans (Bahnhof) d.	0606	0636	...	0706	0736	...	0806	0836	...	0906	0936	and at the	1906	1936	...	2006	2040	2106	2140	...	2240	2340	...
Vaduz Post d.	0638	0708	...	0738	0808	...	0838	0908	...	0938	1008	same minutes past each	1938	2008	...	2038	2108	2138	2208	...	2308	0007	...
Buchs (Bahnhof) a.	0655	0725	...	0755	0825	...	0855	0925	...	0955	1025	hour until	1955	2025	...	2055	2125	2155	2225	...	2325	...	...

🚌 [line 14] **Feldkirch** (Bahnhof) - **Vaduz** (Post) and v.v. Journey time: 36 minutes. Service shown operates on Ⓐ; a reduced service operates on ©.
Operator: Liechtenstein Bus Anstalt LBA, Städtle 38, 9490 Vaduz. ✆ +423 236 63 10, fax +423 236 63 11.

From **Feldkirch**: 0625, 0655, 0725, 0755, 0825, 0855 and hourly until 1555, then 1625, 1655, 1725, 1755, 1825, 1855.

From **Vaduz**: 0633, 0703, 0733, 0803, 0833 and hourly until 1133, then 1203, 1233, 1333, 1433, 1533, 1603, 1633, 1703, 1733, 1803, 1833, 1903.

M – (12) and ✕ Zürich - München and v.v.

w – Runs as *IR* train on ©.

535 ZÜRICH - KONSTANZ and ROMANSHORN

SBB

km		IC 807	IR 9051	IC 809	IR 9053	IC 811	IR 9055	IC 815	IR 9057	IC 817	IR 9059	IC 819	IR 9061	IC 821	IR 9063	IC 823	IR 9065	IC 825	IR 9067	IC 827	IR 9069	IC 829	IR 9071	IC 831	IR 9073
		(✕)		✕		✕		✕		(✕)		✕		(✕)		✕		(✕)		✕		✕		✕	
	Brig **560** d.	...	...	...	...	0547	...	0649	...	0749	...	0849	...	0949	...	1049	...	1149	...	1249	...	1349	...	1449	...
	Interlaken Ost **560** d.	...	...	...	...	|	...	|	...	|	...	|	...	|	...	|	...	|	...	|	...	|	...	|	...
	Bern **500** d.	...	...	0602	...	0702	...	0802	...	0902	...	1002	...	1102	...	1202	...	1302	...	1402	...	1502	...	1602	...
	Biel **500** d.	...	0515	|	0613	|	0715	|	0815	|	0915	|	1015	|	1115	|	1215	|	1315	|	1415	|	1515	|	1615
0	**Zürich HB 530** d.	0607	0637	0707	0737	0807	0837	0907	0937	1007	1037	1107	1137	1207	1237	1307	1337	1407	1437	1507	1537	1607	1637	1707	1737
10	**Zürich Flug ✈ 530** d.	0618	0648	0718	0748	0818	0848	0918	0948	1018	1048	1118	1148	1218	1248	1318	1348	1418	1448	1518	1548	1618	1648	1718	1748
30	Winterthur **530** d.	0635	0705	0735	0805	0835	0905	0935	1005	1035	1105	1135	1205	1235	1305	1335	1405	1435	1505	1535	1605	1635	1705	1735	1805
46	Frauenfeld d.	0647	0717	0747	0817	0847	0917	0947	1017	1047	1117	1147	1217	1247	1317	1347	1417	1447	1517	1547	1617	1647	1717	1747	1817
64	Weinfelden **539** ▲ d.	0700	0730	0800	0830	0900	0930	1000	1030	1100	1130	1200	1230	1300	1330	1400	1430	1500	1530	1600	1630	1700	1730	1800	1830
	Kreuzlingen ▲ a.	|	0750	|	0850	|	0950	|	1050	|	1150	|	1250	|	1350	|	1450	|	1550	|	1650	|	1750	|	1850
	Konstanz ▲ a.	|	0754	|	0854	|	0954	|	1054	|	1154	|	1254	|	1354	|	1454	|	1554	|	1654	|	1754	|	1854
86	**Romanshorn** a.	0718	...	0818	...	0918	...	1018	...	1118	...	1218	...	1318	...	1418	...	1518	...	1618	...	1718	...	1818	...

	IC 835	IR 9075	IC 837	IR 9077	IC 839	IR 9079	IC 841	IC 843	IC 845	
	(✕)		✕		(✕)		✕			
Brig **560** d.	1549	...	1649	...	1749	...	1849	1949	...	...
Interlaken Ost **560** d.	|	...	|	...	|	...	|	|	...	...
Bern **500** d.	1702	...	1802	...	1902	...	2002	2102	2202	...
Biel **500** d.	|	1715	|	1815	|	1915	|	|	|	...
Zürich HB 530 d.	1807	1837	1907	1937	2007	2037	2107	2207	2307	...
Zürich Flug ✈ 530 d.	1818	1848	1918	1948	2018	2048	2118	2218	2318	...
Winterthur **530** d.	1835	1905	1935	2005	2035	2105	2135	2235	2335	0045
Frauenfeld d.	1847	1917	1947	2017	2047	2117	2147	2247	2347	0101
Weinfelden **539** ▲ d.	1900	1930	2000	2030	2100	2130	2200	2300	0000	0120
Kreuzlingen ▲ a.	|	1950	|	2050	|	2150	|	|	|	|
Konstanz ▲ a.	|	1954	|	2054	|	2154	|	|	|	|
Romanshorn a.	1918	...	2018	...	2118	...	2218	2318	0018	0140

	IC 810	IR 9050	IC 812	IR 9052	IC 816	IR 9054	IC 818	IR 9056	IC 820	IR 9058
	(✕)		✕		(✕)		✕		✕	
Romanshorn d.	0538	...	0638	...	0741	...	0841	...	0941	...
Konstanz ▲ d.	|	0603	|	0703	|	0803	|	0903	|	1003
Kreuzlingen ▲ d.	|	0607	|	0707	|	0807	|	0907	|	1007
Weinfelden **539** ▲ d.	0559	0629	0659	0729	0759	0829	0859	0929	0959	1029
Frauenfeld d.	0612	0642	0713	0742	0812	0842	0912	0942	1012	1042
Winterthur **530** d.	0625	0655	0728	0755	0825	0855	0925	0955	1025	1055
Zürich Flughafen ✈ 530 a.	0638	0708	0741	0808	0838	0908	0938	1008	1038	1108
Zürich HB 530 a.	0651	0721	0753	0821	0851	0921	0951	1021	1051	1121
Biel **500** d.	|	0845	|	0945	|	1045	|	1145	|	1245
Bern **500** a.	0757	...	0857	...	0957	...	1057	...	1157	...
Interlaken Ost **560** a.	|	...	|	...	|	...	|	...	|	...
Brig **560** a.	0911	...	1011	...	1111	...	1211	...	1311	...

km		IC 822	IR 9060	IC 824	IR 9062	IC 826	IR 9064	IC 828	IR 9066	IC 830	IR 9068	IC 832	IR 9070	IC 836	IR 9072	IC 838	IR 9074	IC 840	IR 9076	IC 842	IR 9078	IC 844	IC 846	IC 848	
		✕		(✕)		✕		(✕)		✕		(✕)		✕		✕		✕		(✕)		✕			
	Romanshorn d.	1041	...	1141	...	1241	...	1341	...	1441	...	1541	...	1641	...	1741	...	1841	...	1941	...	2041	2141	2238	2333
0	**Konstanz** ▲ d.	|	1103	|	1203	|	1303	|	1403	|	1503	|	1603	|	1703	|	1803	|	1903	|	2003	|	|	|	|
1	Kreuzlingen ▲ d.	|	1107	|	1207	|	1307	|	1407	|	1507	|	1607	|	1707	|	1807	|	1907	|	2007	|	|	|	|
24	Weinfelden **539** ▲ d.	1059	1129	1159	1229	1259	1329	1359	1429	1459	1529	1559	1629	1659	1729	1759	1829	1859	1929	1959	2029	2059	2159	2259	2356
	Frauenfeld d.	1112	1142	1212	1242	1312	1342	1412	1442	1512	1542	1612	1642	1712	1742	1812	1842	1912	1942	2012	2042	2112	2212	2312	0011
	Winterthur **530** d.	1125	1155	1225	1255	1325	1355	1425	1455	1525	1555	1625	1655	1725	1755	1825	1855	1925	1955	2025	2055	2125	2225	2325	0027
	Zürich Flug ✈ 530 a.	1138	1208	1238	1308	1338	1408	1438	1508	1538	1608	1638	1708	1738	1808	1838	1908	1938	2008	2038	2108	2138	2238	2338	...
	Zürich HB 530 a.	1151	1221	1251	1321	1351	1421	1451	1521	1551	1621	1651	1721	1751	1821	1851	1921	1951	2021	2051	2121	2151	2251	2351	...
	Biel **500** d.	|	1345	|	1445	|	1545	|	1645	|	1745	|	1845	|	1945	|	2045	|	2145	|	2245	|	|	...	...
	Bern **500** a.	1257	...	1357	...	1457	...	1557	...	1657	...	1757	...	1857	...	1957	...	2057	...	2157	...	2302	0002	...	...
	Interlaken Ost **560** a.	|	...	|	...	|	...	|	...	|	...	|	...	|	...	|	...	...	...	...	...	...	...	...	...
	Brig **560** a.	1411	...	1511	...	1611	...	1711	...	1811	...	1911	...	2011	...	2111	...	...	...	...	...	...	...	...	...

▲ – Additional services operate **Weinfelden - Konstanz and v.v.** journey time: 30–36 minutes.
From **Weinfelden**: 0530Ⓐ, 0602, 0630Ⓐ, 0702, 0735Ⓐ, 0802, 0902, 1002, 1102, 1202, 1302, 1402, 1502, 1602, 1635Ⓐ, 1702, 1735Ⓐ, 1802, 1835Ⓐ, 1902, 2002, 2102, 2202, 2302, 0002.

From **Konstanz**: 0524, 0541Ⓐ, 0621, 0642Ⓐ, 0721, 0748Ⓐ, 0821, 0918, 1018, 1218, 1318, 1418, 1521, 1618, 1648Ⓐ, 1718, 1748Ⓐ, 1818, 1848Ⓐ, 1918, 2021, 2121, 2221, 2321.

SBS — ⛴ ROMANSHORN - FRIEDRICHSHAFEN car ferry service — 536

Journey time: 41 minutes. ✕ available 0836 - 2136 from Romanshorn; 0841 - 2241 from Friedrichshafen. 🍸 on other sailings. Operator: SBS ✆ 071 466 78 88

From **Romanshorn**: 0936 and hourly until 1636.
From **Friedrichshafen**: 0941 and hourly until 1641.

Services shown operate daily. Additional hourly service available on certain dates from 0536 - 0836 and 1736 - 2136 from Romanshorn; 0541 - 0841 and 1741 - 2041, 2241 from Friedrichshafen.

THURBO — WEINFELDEN - WIL — 539

km		Ⓐ		Ⓐ		Ⓐ		and		y
0	Weinfelden **535** d.	0457	0532	0557	0632	0657	0732	hourly	2232	2332
19	Wil **530** a.	0520	0555	0622	0655	0722	0755	until	2255	2355

	Ⓐ		Ⓐ		Ⓐ		and		z
Wil **530** d.	0525	0601	0625	0701	0732	0801	hourly	2301	0011
Weinfelden **535** a.	0550	0624	0650	0724	0757	0824	until	2324	0034

y – ⑤⑥ (also Dec. 31, Apr. 1, 4, May 12, 13, 23).
z – ⑥⑦ (also Jan. 1, Apr. 2, 5, May 13, 14, 24).

Additional services operate Ⓐ: Weinfelden depart 1602, 1702, 1802, 1902; Wil depart 1632, 1732, 1832, 1932.

RhB. Narrow gauge — CHUR - ST MORITZ — 540

For *Glacier Express* services see Table **575**

km		⊗ 2⚒	⚒		◐⊡‡	961 ◆🅁⚡	1325 ◆	951 ◆🅁⚡	953 ◆🅁⚡	◐🍸‡	955 ◆🅁⚡	◐🍸	◐⊡‡	◐🍸‡	◐⊡‡	◐⊡	◐⊡‡	◐⊡	◐	◐‡	◐‡	◐‡	◐	Sy	
0	**Chur 575** d.	0458	...	0644	0758	...	...	0832	0858	0858	0931	0958	1058	1158	1258	1358	1458	1558	1658	1758	1858	1956	2056	...	...
10	Reichenau-Tamins **575** d.	|	...	0657	0808	...	...	|	0908u	0908	|	1008	1108	1208	1308	1408	1508	1608	1708	1808	1908	2007	2107	...	...
27	Thusis d.	0538	...	0730	0830	...	...	|	0930u	0930	|	1030	1130	1230	1330	1430	1530	1630	1730	1830	1930	2033	2133	...	...
41	Tiefencastel d.	0556	...	0747	0847	...	...	0916u	0947u	0947	1016u	1047	1147	1247	1347	1447	1547	1647	1747	1847	1947	2050	2150	...	...
51	**Filisur 545a** d.	0612	...	0802	0902	...	...	0933u	1002u	1002	1033u	1102	1202	1302	1402	1502	1602	1702	1802	1902	2002	2105	2205	...	...
59	Bergün/Bravuogn d.	0630	...	0814	0914	...	...	0947u	1014u	1014	|	1114	1214	1314	1414	1514	1614	1714	1814	1914	2014	2117	2217	...	...
72	Preda d.	0645x	...	0830	0930	...	...	...	|	1030	|	1130	1230	1330	1430	1530	1630	1730	1830	1930	2030	2134	2234	...	...
84	**Samedan** a.	0701	...	0847	0946	...	...	...	|	1046	|	1146	1246	1346	1446	1546	1646	1746	1847	1947	2047	2149	2249	...	...
84	**Samedan 546** d.	...	0712	0850	0950	0923u	1011	...	1049u	1050	|	1150	1250	1350	1450	1550	1650	1750	1850	1950	2050	2151	2251y	2341	...
89	Pontresina **546/7** a.	...	|	|	|	|	|	...	1056	|	1119	|	|	|	|	|	|	|	|	|	|	|	|	|	...
87	Celerina **546/7** d.	...	0715	0853	0953	|	|	...	...	1053	...	1153	1253	1353	1453	1553	1653	1753	1853	1953	2053	2154	2254y	2344	...
89	**St Moritz 546/7** a.	...	0719	0858	0958	0934u	1018	...	...	1058	...	1158	1258	1358	1458	1558	1658	1758	1858	1958	2058	2159	2259y	2348	...

	Ⓐ	Sz	⚒	†	◐	◐‡	◐⊡	◐⊡	◐⊡	◐🍸‡	◐⊡	◐🍸	◐⊡‡	◐⊡‡	950 ◆🅁⚡	952 ◆🅁⚡	1360 ◆	960 ◆🅁⚡	954 ◆🅁⚡	◐⊡‡	◐⊡‡	◐	‡		q
St Moritz 546/7 d.	...	0457	0540z	0557	0702	0802	0902	1002	1102	1202	1302	1402	1502	1602	...	...	1635	◇	...	1702	1802	1902	2002	2102	2120
Celerina **546/7** d.	...	0500	0543z	0600	0705	0805	0905	1005	1105	1205	1305	1405	1505	1605	...	...	|	...	...	1705	1805	1905	2005	2105	|
Pontresina **546/7** d.	...	|	|	|	|	|	|	|	|	|	|	|	|	|	...	1621	|	1638	1702	|	|	|	|	|	|
Samedan 546 a.	...	0504	0548z	0605	0709	0809	0909	1009	1109	1209	1309	1409	1509	1609	...	|	1642	1644	1708s	1709	1809	1909	2009	2109	2127
Samedan d.	0500	...	0550	0605	0717	0817	0917	1017	1117	1217	1317	1417	1517	1617	1627s	|	...	1648	|	1717	1817	1917	2017	...	2130
Preda d.	|	...	0604	0620	0730	0830	0930	1030	1130	1230	1330	1430	1530	1630	|	|	...	|		1730	1830	1931	2031	...	|
Bergün/Bravuogn d.	0529	...	0621	0637	0747	0847	0947	1047	1147	1247	1347	1447	1547	1647	1658s	|	...	1732s	1747s	1747	1847	1948	2048	...	2205
Filisur 545a d.	0542	...	0634	0650	0801	0901	1001	1101	1201	1301	1401	1501	1601	1701	1717s	1717s	...	1744	1800s	1801	1901	2001	2101	...	2221s
Tiefencastel d.	0556	...	0651	0704	0815	0915	1015	1115	1215	1315	1415	1515	1615	1715	1732s	1732s	...	...	1815s	1815	1915	2015	2115	...	2235s
Thusis d.	0612	...	0711	0721	0833	0933	1033	1133	1233	1333	1433	1533	1633	1733	1750s	1750s	...	...	1831s	1833	1933	2033	2133	...	2251s
Reichenau-Tamins **575** d.	0632	...	|	0747	0853	0953	1053	1153	1253	1353	1453	1553	1653	1753	|	|	...	...	1852s	1853	1953	2055	2155	...	|
Chur 575 a.	0645	...	0744	0759	0903	1003	1103	1203	1303	1403	1503	1603	1703	1803	1827	1827	...	...	1903	1903	2003	2109	2209	...	2325

◆ – **NOTES** (LISTED BY TRAIN NUMBER)

950/1 – BERNINA EXPRESS – May 13 - Oct. 24: [12] [observation cars] and 🍸 Tirano - Chur and v.v.
953/4 – BERNINA EXPRESS – Ⓐ Dec. 14 - May 12, Oct. 25 - Dec. 10 (not Dec. 28 - 31): [12] [observation cars] and 🍸 Chur - Pontresina - Tirano and v.v.
952/5 – BERNINA EXPRESS – Ⓒ Dec. 13 - May 9, Oct. 30 - Dec. 11 (also Dec. 28 - 31): [12] [observation cars] and 🍸 Chur - Pontresina - Tirano and v.v.
960/1 – BERNINA EXPRESS – May 13 - Oct. 24: [12] [observation cars] and 🍸 Tirano - St Moritz - Davos and v.v.
1325 – ENGADIN STAR - May 13 - Oct. 24: [12] Landquart - Klosters - St Moritz.
1360 – ENGADIN STAR – Ⓒ (daily May 13 - Oct. 24): [12] St Moritz - Klosters - Landquart.

S – [12] St Moritz - Klosters and v.v.
j – Not ①–⑤ Apr. 12 - Oct. 29.
q – ⑤ Jan. 8 - Mar. 12.
s – Stops to set down only.
u – Stops to pick up only.
w – ①–⑤ Apr. 12 - Oct. 29.
x – Stops on request only.
y – Daily Dec. 13 - Apr. 11; ⑥⑦ Apr. 17 - Oct. 31; daily Nov. 1 - Dec. 11. Bus service on other dates.
z – ⚒ Dec. 14 - Apr. 12; ① Apr. 19 - Nov. 1; ⚒ Nov. 2 - Dec. 11 (not May 24). Bus service on other dates.

⊗ – Mixed train. Times subject to variation.
‡ – Conveys ✕ on some dates.
⊡ – Conveys 🍸 on some dates.
◐ – Conveys [12] [observation cars] Dec. 19 - Mar. 14, 🅁, ⚡.
⚡ – Supplement payable.
◇ – Subject to confirmation.

RhB. Narrow gauge — CHUR - AROSA — 541

km		⚒			w		w		and				z
0	**Chur** d.	0519	0625	0808	0852	0908	0952	1008	and	1908	2004	2104	2300
18	Langwies d.	0600	0709	0849	0931	0949	1031	1049	hourly	1949	2043	2144	2340x
26	Arosa a.	0618	0727	0909	0948	1009	1048	1109	until	2009	2103	2205	2358

	⚒	Ⓐ	Ⓒ								y	
Arosa d.	0556	0628	0651	0748	0848	0948	1048	and	1948	2108	0003	...
Langwies d.	0613	0644	0709	0804	0904	1004	1104	hourly	2004	2123	0018x	...
Chur a.	0656	0726	0752	0852	0952	1052	1152	until	2052	2207	0059	...

w – Ⓒ Jan. 2 - Feb. 28.
x – Stops on request only.
y – Daily Dec. 14 - Apr. 6; ⑥⑦ Apr. 10 - July 18; daily July 19 - Aug. 30; ⑥⑦ Sept. 4 - Nov. 14; daily Nov. 15 - Dec. 11. Bus service on other dates.
z – Daily Dec. 13 - Apr. 5; ⑤⑥ Apr. 9 - July 17; daily July 18 - Aug. 29; ⑤⑥ Sept. 3 - Nov. 13; daily Nov. 14 - Dec. 11. Bus service on other dates.

PA — 🚌 CHUR - FLIMS — 542

🚌 **Chur** (Bahnhof) - **Flims Dorf** (Post), ± 35 minutes, and **Flims Waldhaus** (Post), ± 40 minutes.

From **Chur**:
Ⓐ: 0603, 0640, 0658, 0758, 0858, 0958, 1058, 1120, 1158, 1245, 1258, 1358, 1458, 1558, 1620, 1658, 1720, 1740, 1758, 1820, 1858, 2000, 2100, 2200, 2300.
Ⓒ: 0603⑥, 0658, 0758 and hourly until 1658, 1720⑥, 1758, 1858, 2000, 2100, 2200, 2300.

From **Flims Waldhaus** (± 5 minutes from Flims Dorf):
Ⓐ: 0516, 0613, 0700, 0714 and hourly until 1114, 1149, 1214, 1259, 1314 and hourly until 1814, 1843, 1914, 2013, 2113, 2213, 2313.
Ⓒ: 0516⑥, 0613, 0714 and hourly until 1814, 1914, 2013, 2113, 2213, 2313.

AP, FNM, PA, RhB* — BERNINA and POSCHIAVO 🚌 services — 543

TIRANO - APRICA and EDOLO

	⚒		⚒		Z		⚒		⚒	
Tirano Stazione d.	0840	...	1040	...	1245	...	1435	...	1700	...
Aprica S Pietro a.	0915	...	1115	...	1320	...	1510	...	1740	...
Edolo a.	0945	...	1145	...	...	...	1540	...	1810	...

	Z		⚒		⚒		⚒		⚒	
Edolo d.	...	...	0910	...	1110	...	1510	...	1710	...
Aprica d.	0650	...	0940	...	1140	...	1540	...	1740	...
Tirano Stazione a.	0730	...	1020	...	1220	...	1620	...	1820	...

ST MORITZ and TIRANO - LUGANO

	P🅁		B🅁
St Moritz Bahnhof ◧ d.	1220	...	...
Tirano d.	|	...	1425
Chiavenna Stazione d.	1410	...	|
Menaggio ◐ d.	1505x	...	◐
Lugano Stazione a.	1610s	...	1730
Lugano Via S. Balestra a.	1620	...	1740

	B🅁		Q🅁
Lugano Via S. Balestra d.	0945	...	1120
Lugano Stazione ◐ d.	1000	...	1140u
Menaggio d.	◐	...	1230x
Chiavenna Stazione d.	|	...	1400
Tirano a.	1300	...	|
St Moritz Bahnhof ◧ a.	...	...	1525

B – Bernina Express service. Runs Apr. 1 - Oct. 24.
P – Palm Express service. Runs daily Dec. 18 - Jan. 3; ⑤⑥⑦ Jan. 8 - June 6; daily June 11 - Oct. 24; ⑤⑥⑦ Oct. 29 - Dec. 11 (also Dec. 13).
Q – Palm Express service. Runs daily Dec. 19 - Jan. 4; ①⑥⑦ Jan. 9 - June 7; daily June 12 - Oct. 25; ①⑥⑦ Oct. 30 - Dec. 11 (also Dec. 13, 14).
Z – Schooldays only.
s – Stops to set down only.
u – Stops to pick up only.
x – Calls only if advance reservation is made.

◧ – 🏛 is at Castasegna.
◐ – 🏛 is at Gandria.

* – Operators:
Tirano - Edolo: Automobilistica Perego (AP): ✆ (0342) 701 200; fax (0342) 704 400;
Tirano - Lugano: RhB, Reservation: ✆ Poschiavo (081) 288 54 54; fax (081) 288 54 47;
St Moritz - Lugano: PA, Reservation: ✆ St Moritz (058) 448 35 35; fax (058) 667 49 81.

544 🚌 CHUR - BELLINZONA and CHIAVENNA PA

km																									
			Yh	VRj	VRh	VR		Yh	VR	VRh		VR	VRh		VR	VR		VR	Yh	VRh		VR		R✗g	R✗g
0	Chur Bahnhof 540 d.	...	...	0808	0813	0913	...	...	1008	1113	...	1208	1313	...	1408	1513	...	1608	...	1713	...	1808	...	...	...
40	Thusis Bahnhof 540 d.	0735	...	0835u	0840u	0940u	0935	...	1035u	1140u	1135	1235u	1340u	1335	1435u	1540u	1535	1635u	...	1740u	1735	1835u	1935	2246	2346
64	Splügen Post d.	0809	0820	0904	0904	1004	1009	1020	1104	1204	1209	1304	1404	1409	1504	1604	1609	1704	1715	1804	1809	1904	2007	2326	0026
	San Bernardino Posta a.	0829	|	0923	0923	1023	1029	|	1123	1223	1229	1323	1423	1429	1523	1623	1629	1723	|	1823	1829	1923	2029	...	...
	Chiavenna Stazione ◐ a.	|	1015	|	|	|	|	1215	|	|	|	|	|	|	|	|	|	|	1910	|	|	|	|	...	...
179	Bellinzona Stazione a.	0950	...	1020	1013	1113	1150	...	1220	1313	1350	1420	1513	1550	1620	1713	1750	1820	...	1913	1950	2020	2150	...	...

			Yh		VR	VR		VRh	VR		VRh	VR		VR	Yh	VR		VRh	Yh	VR		VR	R✗g	R✗e
Bellinzona Stazione d.	...	0707	...	0807	0845	0940	1007	1045	1140	1207	1245	1340	1407	1445	...	1540	1607	1645	...	1740	1807	1840r	...	...
Chiavenna Stazione ◐ d.	...	|	0750	|	|	|	|	|	|	|	|	|	|	|	1440	|	|	|	1640	|	|	|	...	...
San Bernardino Posta d.	...	0823	|	0923	0935	1031	1123	1135	1231	1323	1335	1431	1523	1535	|	1631	1723	1735	|	1831	1923	1935	...	...
Splügen Post d.	0745	0845	0940	0945	0953	1051	1145	1153	1251	1345	1353	1451	1545	1553	1630	1651	1745	1753	1830	1851	1945	1953	2342	0042
Thusis Bahnhof 540 d.	0825	0925	...	1025	1020s	1125s	1225	1220s	1325s	1425	1420s	1525s	1625	1620s	...	1725s	1825	1820s	...	1925s	2025	2020s	0009	0109
Chur Bahnhof 540 a.	...	...	...	...	1045	1150	...	1245	1350	...	1445	1550	...	1645	...	1750	...	1845	...	1950	...	2045	...	...

V – San Bernardino Route Express.
Y – Splügen Pass service.

e – ⑥⑦ (also Dec. 25, Jan. 1, Apr. 2, 5, May 13, 24; not Dec. 26, 27, Jan. 2, 3, Apr. 3).
g – ⑤⑥ (not Dec. 25, 26, Jan. 1, 2, Apr. 2).
h – June 12 - Oct. 17.

j – Dec. 13 - June 11, Oct. 18 - Dec. 11.
r – Depart 1845 on ⚒.
s – Stops to set down only.
u – Stops to pick up only.

◐ – 🏦 is at Splügen Pass.
✗ – Supplement payable.
Reservations: ✆ Chur (058) 386 31 66; fax (058) 667 38 51.

545 LANDQUART - KLOSTERS - DAVOS / SCUOL TARASP Narrow gauge. RhB

km																								
		⊗ Ⓐ	⚒	Ⓐ				w		1325 ♦		w			©L		A							
	Chur d.	...	...	0550	...	...	0720	...	0752	...	...	...	0820	0852	...	...	0920	...	1020			1720	...	1820
0	Landquart d.	0451	0525	0615	0647	0747	0749k	0752	0809	0820	0847	0852	0849k	0909	0920	0947	0949k	1047	1049k	and at	1747	1749k	1847	1849k
21	Küblis d.	0511x	0555	0644	0713	0811	0815	0822	...	0847	0911	0922	0915	...	0947	1011	1015	1111	1115	the same	1811	1815	1911	1915
30	Klosters Dorf d.	0524x	0609	0700	0726	|	0828	0844	...	|	|	0944	0928	...	|	|	1028	|	1128	minutes	|	1828	|	1928
32	Klosters 🚗 d.	0529	0617	0706	0734	0828	0834	0851	...	0903	0928	0951	0934	...	1003	1028	1034	1128	1134	past each	1828	1834	1928	1934
	Sagliains 546 🚗 § a.	|	|	|	0754	|	0853	|	...	...	|	|	0953	...	...	|	1053	|	1153	hour	|	1853	|	1953
	Ardez a.	|	|	|	0808	|	0905	|	...	...	|	|	1005	...	...	|	1104	|	1204	until	|	1904	|	2004
	Scuol-Tarasp 546 a.	|	|	|	0819	|	0916	|	...	...	|	|	1016	...	...	|	1116	|	1216		|	1916	|	2016
47	Davos Dorf d.	0550	0640	0728	...	0850	...	0914	...	...	0950	1014	...	...	...	1050	...	1150	...		1850	...	1950	...
50	Davos Platz 545a a.	0556	0647	0734	...	0855	...	0925	...	...	0955	1025	...	...	...	1055	...	1155	...		1855	...	1955	...

									🚌 y
Chur d.	1920	...	1952	...	2052	...	2152	...	...
Landquart d.	1947	...	2047	...	2147	...	2247	...	0043
Küblis d.	2013	...	2113	...	2213	...	2313	...	0112
Klosters Dorf d.	2025	...	2125	...	2225	...	2325	...	0127
Klosters 🚗 d.	2030r	2033	2130r	2133	2230r	2232	2330r	...	0132
Sagliains 546 🚗 § a.	|	2054	|	2154	|	2251	|	...	|
Ardez a.	|	2108	|	2208	|	...	|	...	|
Scuol-Tarasp 546 a.	|	2119	|	2219	|	...	|	...	|
Davos Dorf d.	2053r	...	2153r	...	2253r	...	2353r	...	0147
Davos Platz 545a a.	2057r	...	2157r	...	2257r	...	2357r	...	0153

	⚒		Ⓐ						
Davos Platz 545a d.	0454v	0550t	0627	0655	...	0802	...	0902	...
Davos Dorf d.	0457v	0553t	0630	0658	...	0805	...	0905	...
Scuol-Tarasp 546 d.	|	|	|	|	0738	|	0840	|	0940
Ardez d.	|	|	|	|	0745	|	0848	|	0948
Sagliains 546 🚗 § d.	|	|	|	|	0803	|	0903	|	1003
Klosters 🚗 d.	0520	0617	0654	0724	0825	0832	0925	0932	1025
Klosters Dorf d.	0523	0620	0657	0729	0828	|	0928	|	1028
Küblis d.	0538	0634	0712	0743	0843	0848	0943	0948	1043
Landquart a.	0607	0706	0738	0813	0910	0913k	1010	1013k	1110
Chur a.	0639	0730z	0806	0838	0938	...	1038	...	1138

km																								
										1360 ♦			Lm							p	🚌 q		🚌	
	Davos Platz 545a d.	1002	...	1102	...	1202		...	1702	...	...	1802	...	...	1902	...	2002	...	2102r	2202	2202	...	...	...
	Davos Dorf d.	1005	...	1105	...	1205	and at	...	1705	...	...	1805	...	...	1905	...	2005	...	2105r	2205	2205	...	...	...
0	Scuol-Tarasp 546 d.	|	1040	|	1140	|	the same	1640	|	...	1740	|	...	1840	|	1940	|	2038	|	|	|	2138	...	...
	Ardez d.	|	1048	|	1148	|	minutes	1648	|	...	1748	|	...	1848	|	1948	|	2046	|	|	|	2145	...	...
17	Sagliains 546 🚗 § d.	|	1103	|	1203	|	past each	1703	|	...	1803	|	...	1903	|	2003	|	2103	|	|	|	2203	...	...
39	Klosters 🚗 d.	1032	1125	1132	1225	1232	hour	1725	1732	1754	1825	1832	1854	1925	1932	2024	2029	2124	2129	2227	2227	2229	...	...
	Klosters Dorf d.	|	1128	|	1228	|	until	1728	|	|	1828	|	|	1928	|	▬	2032	▬	2132	▬	...	2232	...	...
	Küblis d.	1048	1143	1148	1243	1248		1743	1748	1813	1843	1848	1913	1943	1948	🚌	2046	🚌	2146	🚌	...	2246	...	...
	Landquart a.	1113k	1210	1213k	1310	1313k		1810	1813k	1836	1910	1913k	1936	2010	2013k	2045	2113	2145	2213	2245	...	2313	2342	...
	Chur a.	...	1238	...	1338	...		1838	...	...	1938	...	...	2038j	...	2109	...	2209	...	2309	...	...	0014	...

♦ – **NOTES** (LISTED BY TRAIN NUMBER)

1325 – ENGADIN STAR – May 13 - Oct. 24: [12] Landquart - St Moritz.
1360 – ENGADIN STAR – © (daily May 13 - Oct. 24): [12] St Moritz - Landquart.

A – RE AQUALINO – [12] Disentis/Mustér - Scuol-Tarasp.
L – [12] Landquart - St Moritz and v.v.

j – Connection on Ⓐ.
k – Connects with train in previous column.
m – © May 13 - Oct. 24.
p – Not ①–⑤ May 10 - Nov. 26.
q – ①–⑤ May 10 - Nov. 26.
r – By connecting 🚌 ①–⑤ May 10 - Nov. 26.
t – By connecting 🚌 ②–⑥ May 11 - Nov. 27.
v – By connecting 🚌 ②–⑥ May 11 - Nov. 27 (not May 13).

w – Dec. 19 - Mar. 7.
x – Stops on request only.
y – ⑥⑦ (also Apr. 2, May 13; not Apr. 3).
z – Connection on ©.

§ – Sagliains station can only be used for changing trains.
⊗ – Mixed train. Times subject to variation.
🚗 – Car-carrying shuttle available (see page 258).

545a DAVOS - FILISUR Narrow gauge. RhB

For *Glacier Express* services see Table **575**

km									
		⚒							
0	Davos Platz 545 d.	0605	0731	0831	0931	and hourly until	1931	2031	...
16	Filisur 540 a.	0630	0756	0856	0956		1956	2056	...

	⚒							
Filisur 540 d.	0635	0804	and hourly until	1904	2004	2107	...	...
Davos Platz 545 a.	0700	0829		1929	2029	2132	...	...

546 PONTRESINA / ST MORITZ - SCUOL TARASP Narrow gauge. RhB

km																									
		⚒ S	⚒ z	⚒	†	⚒	† P			⚒													1360 ♦		
0	St Moritz 540/7 d.	0457z	0536	...	0557	0604	...	...	0702	0724	...	0802	...	0902	...	1002	...	...	1102		...	1602	1635	...	1702
	Pontresina 540/7 d.	|	|	...	|	|	0557	0702	|	|	0802	|	0902	|	1002	|	...	1102	|	and at	1602	|	|	1702	|
5	Samedan 540 a.	0504z	0548	...	0605	0610	0603	0708	0709k	0730	0808	0809k	0908	0909k	1008	1009k	...	1108	1109k	the same	1608	1609k	1642	1708	1709k
5	Samedan d.	0505	...	0600	...	0611	0615	0714	...	0731	0814	...	0914	...	1014	...	...	1114	...	minutes	1614	...	1646	1714	...
15	Zuoz d.	0518	...	0613	...	0624	0628	0727	...	0745	0827	...	0927	...	1027	...	...	1127	...	past each	1627	...	1659	1727	...
32	Zernez ⊖ d.	0538	...	0638	...	...	0647	0747	...	...	0849	...	0949	...	1049	...	...	1149	...	hour	1649	...	1720	1749	...
38	Susch d.	0544	...	0644	...	...	0653	0753	...	...	0855	...	0955	...	1055	...	...	1155	...	until	1655	...	...	1755	...
40	Sagliains 545 § a.	0547	...	0647	...	...	0658	0757	...	...	0900	...	1000	...	1100	...	...	1200	...		1700	...	...	1800	...
57	Scuol-Tarasp 545 a.	...	...	0709	...	...	...	...	...	...	0923	...	1023	...	1123	...	...	1223	...		1723	...	...	1823	...

♦ – **NOTES** (LISTED BY TRAIN NUMBER)

1360 – ENGADIN STAR – © (daily May 13 - Oct. 24): [12] St Moritz - Landquart.

P – [12] Pontresina - Klosters (a. 0722).
S – [12] St Moritz - Klosters (a. 0611).

k – Connects with train in previous column.
z – ⚒ Dec. 14 - Apr. 12; ① Apr. 19 - Nov. 1; ⚒ Nov. 2 - Dec. 11 (not May 24). Bus service on other dates.

§ – Sagliains station can only be used for changing trains.
⊖ – For 🚌 service **Zernez - Malles and v.v.** see next page.

PONTRESINA / ST MORITZ - SCUOL TARASP — 546

Narrow gauge. RhB

	M									
St Moritz 540/7 d.	1735	...	1802	...	1902	...	2002	...	2102	...
Pontresina 540/7 d.	|	1802	|	1902	|	2002	|	2102	|	2202j
Samedan **540** a.	1742	1808	1809k	1908	1909k	2008	2009k	2108	2109k	2208j
Samedan d.	1746	1814	...	1914	...	2014	▬	2114	▬	2214
Zuoz d.	1759	1827	...	1927	...	2027	...	2127	...	2227
Zernez ⊖ d.	1820	1849	...	1949	...	2047	...	2147	...	2247
Susch d.	...	1855	...	1955	...	2053	...	2153	...	2253
Sagliains **545** § a.	...	1900	...	2000	...	2057	2059	2157	2159	2257
Scuol-Tarasp 545 a.	...	1923	...	2023	...	...	2119	...	2219	2317

	⚒	⚒								1325 ♦
Scuol-Tarasp 545 d.	...	0607	...	0649	0738	...	...	0834	...	...
Sagliains **545** § d.	...	|	...	0702	0758	0803	...	0856	...	...
Susch d.	...	0631	...	0705	...	0805	...	0858	...	...
Zernez ⊖ d.	...	0638	...	0713	...	0813	...	0908	...	0933
Zuoz d.	0634	0657	...	0734	...	0834	...	0927	...	0956
Samedan a.	0649	0711	...	0749	...	0849	...	0942	...	1006
Samedan **540** d.	0650	0712	...	0751	...	0851	...	0949	0950	1011
Pontresina 540/7 a.	0656	|	...	0757	...	0857	...	0956	|	|
St Moritz 540/7 a.	...	0719	...	...	...	...	...	...	0958	1018

	L								
Scuol-Tarasp 545 d.	...	0934	...	...	1034	...		1834	...
Sagliains **545** § d.	...	0956	...	...	1056	...	and at	1856	...
Susch d.	...	0958	...	...	1058	...	the same	1858	...
Zernez ⊖ d.	1033	1008	...	...	1108	...	minutes	1908	...
Zuoz d.	1056	1027	...	...	1127	...	past each	1927	...
Samedan a.	1109	1042	...	...	1142	...	hour	1942	...
Samedan **540** d.	1111	1049y	1050	...	1149	1150	until	1949	1950
Pontresina 540/7 a.	|	1056y	|	...	1156	|		1956	|
St Moritz 540/7 a.	1118	...	1058	...	...	1158		...	1958

											r		K		
Scuol-Tarasp 545 d.	...	1934	...	...	...	2038	...	...	2138	...	...	...	...	...	...
Sagliains **545** § d.	...	1956	...	...	...	2058	2103	...	2158	2203	...	...	2257	...	...
Susch d.	...	1958	...	...	...	...	2105	...	...	2205	...	...	2259	...	...
Zernez ⊖ d.	...	2008	...	...	...	...	2113	...	...	2213	...	...	2307	...	...
Zuoz d.	...	2027	...	...	...	...	2134	...	...	2234	...	...	2327	...	...
Samedan a.	...	2042	...	...	...	...	2149	...	...	2249	...	...	2340	...	...
Samedan **540** d.	...	...	2050	2051	...	...	2151	2151	...	2251	2251	...	2341r	...	...
Pontresina 540/7 a.	...	...	|	2057	...	...	2157	|	...	2257	|	...	|	...	...
St Moritz 540/7 a.	...	...	2058	...	...	...	...	2159	...	...	2259	...	2348r	...	...

♦ – **NOTES** (LISTED BY TRAIN NUMBER)

1325 – ENGADIN STAR – May 13 - Oct. 24: (12) Landquart - St Moritz.

K – (12) Klosters (d. 2232) - St Moritz.

L – ©: (12) Landquart - St Moritz.

M – © May 13 - Oct. 24: (12) St Moritz - Landquart.

h – May 13 - Oct. 24.

j – ⑥ (also Dec. 26, Jan. 2).

k – Connects with train in previous column.

r – By connecting 🚌 ①–⑤ Apr. 12 - Oct. 29.

y – By connecting train on Ⓐ Dec. 14 - May 12, Oct. 25 - Dec. 10 (not Dec. 28-31).

§ – Sagliains station can only be used for changing trains.

⊖ – 🚌 service **Zernez - Malles and v.v.** (journey 1 h 35 minutes):
From **Zernez posta**: 0715, 0815 **h**, 0915, 1015 **h**, 1115, 1215 **h**, 1315, 1415 **h**, 1515, 1615 **h**, 1715, 1815 **h**.
From **Malles / Mals bahnhof**: 0703 **h**, 0803 **h**, 0903, 1003 **h**, 1103, 1203 **h**, 1303, 1403 **h**, 1503, 1603 **h**, 1703, 1803 **h**, 1903.

Operator: AutoDaPosta (PA), Agentura Scuol, CH-7550 Scuol. ✆ +41 (0)58 453 28 28, fax +41 (0)58 667 63 94.

ST MORITZ - TIRANO — 547

Narrow gauge. RhB

km		🚌	⊗	⊗	⊗ Ⓐ	©	©		961 ♦ R ⁄	🚌 w		951 ♦ R ⁄		953 ♦ R ⁄	955 ♦ R ⁄	973 ♦ R ⁄	🚌 w					971 ♦ R ⁄	975 ♦ R ⁄		
0	**St Moritz** d.	...	...	...	...	...	0745	0845	0934	...	0945	...	1045	...	...	1122	...	1145	1245	1345	1445	1445	1522	1545	1645
2	Celerina Staz ⊡ d.	...	...	...	...	...	0748	0848	|	...	0948	...	1048	...	...	|	...	1148	1248	1348	1448	|	|	1548	1648
6	**Pontresina** a.	...	...	...	...	...	0755	0855	|	...	0955	...	1055	...	...	|	...	1155	1255	1355	1455	|	|	1555	1655
6	**Pontresina 540** d.	...	...	...	0704	0704j	0809	0904	0952u	...	1009	...	1104	1104	1131	1131u	...	1209	1304	1409	1504	1504u	1531u	1609	1704
12	Morteratsch ⊡ d.	...	...	...	0713	0713j	0818	0913	|	...	1018	...	1113	|	|	|	...	1218	1313	1418	1513	1513u	1542u	1618	1713
17	Bernina Diavolezza ⊡ d.	...	...	...	0723	0723j	0828	0923	1019s	...	1028	...	1123	|	|	|	...	1228	1323	1428	1523	1523u	|	1628	1723
18	Bernina Lagalb ⊡ d.	...	...	...	0725	0725j	0830	0925	|	...	1030	...	1125	|	|	|	...	1230	1325	1430	1525	1525u	|	1630	1725
22	Ospizio Bernina d.	...	...	...	0734	0734j	0839	0934	|	...	1039	...	1134	1134s	1158s	|	...	1239	1334	1439	1534	1534	1603	1639	1734
27	Alp Grüm d.	...	...	...	0746	0746j	0853	0946	1033s	...	1053	1122s	1146	1145s	1210s	1208s	...	1253	1346	1453	1546	1546	1615	1653	1746
44	**Poschiavo** a.	...	...	...	0827	0827j	0935	1027	1113s	...	1135	1200s	1227	1227s	1250s	1250s	...	1335	1427	1535	1627	1627s	1650s	1735	1827
44	**Poschiavo** d.	0610	0626	0736	0829	0829	0938	1029	|	1137	1138v	|	1229	|	|	|	1337	1338v	1429	1538r	1629	|	|	1738	1829
48	Le Prese d.	0616	0634x	0744x	0837	0837	0946	1037	1127s	1142	1146v	1209s	1237	1237s	1258s	1258s	1342	1346v	1437	1546r	1637	1637s	1658s	1746	1837
51	Miralago ⊡ d.	0620	0639	0749	0843	0843	0952	1043	|	1145	1152v	|	1243	|	|	|	1345	1352v	1443	1552r	1643	|	|	1752	1843
54	Brusio ⊡ d.	0624	0647	0757	0851	0851	1000	1051	|	1149	1200v	|	1251	|	|	|	1349	1400v	1451	1600r	1651	|	|	1800	1851
58	Campocologno 🏛 d.	0629	0657	0807	0903	0903	1012	1103	|	1154	1212v	|	1303	|	|	|	1354	1412v	1503	1612r	1703	|	|	1812	1903
61	**Tirano** a.	0638	0712	0823	0912	0912	1021	1112	1203	1200	1221v	1238	1312	1312	1327	1327	1400	1421v	1512	1621r	1712	1712	1727	1821	1912

		⊗ Ⓐ		⊗		⊗		🚌 ⑤h	🚌	
St Moritz d.	1745	...	1845	...	1945	...	2020	...	...	...
Celerina Staz ⊡ d.	1748	...	1848	...	1948	...	2023	...	...	...
Pontresina a.	1755	...	1855	...	1955	...	2030	m	...	...
Pontresina 540 d.	...	1809	▬	1904	▬	2009	...	2057	...	...
Morteratsch ⊡ d.	...	1818	...	1913	...	2018	...	|	...	...
Bernina Diavolezza ⊡ d.	...	1828	...	1921	...	2026	...	|	...	...
Bernina Lagalb ⊡ d.	...	1830	...	1924	...	2029	...	|	...	...
Ospizio Bernina d.	...	1839x	...	1933x	...	2038x	...	|	...	...
Alp Grüm d.	...	1849x	🚌	1942x	...	2047x	...	|	...	...
Poschiavo a.	...	1935	Ⓐ	2029	🚌	2134	...	2135	...	...
Poschiavo d.	...	...	1937	...	2032	...	...	...	2137	...
Le Prese d.	...	...	1943s	...	2038s	...	...	...	2143s	...
Miralago ⊡ d.	...	...	1947s	...	2042s	...	...	...	2147s	...
Brusio ⊡ d.	...	...	1951s	...	2046s	...	...	...	2151s	...
Campocologno 🏛 d.	...	...	1955s	...	2050s	...	...	...	2155s	...
Tirano a.	...	...	2005	...	2100	...	...	...	2205	...

		⊗ ⚒		🚌			970 ♦ R ⁄			972 ♦ R ⁄
Tirano d.	...	...	...	0655	...	0740	0834	...	0850	0850
Campocologno 🏛 d.	...	...	...	0702	...	0752	|	...	0901	|
Brusio ⊡ d.	...	...	...	0706	...	0759	|	...	0909	|
Miralago ⊡ d.	...	...	...	0711	...	0805	|	...	0916	|
Le Prese d.	...	...	...	0714	...	0810	0902u	...	0922	0922u
Poschiavo a.	...	...	...	0730	...	0822	|	...	0931	|
Poschiavo d.	...	0628	...	...	0733	0824	0910u	...	0933	0933u
Alp Grüm d.	...	0705x	...	...	0815	0904	0943s	...	1015	1015
Ospizio Bernina d.	...	0714x	...	...	0824	0912	|	...	1024	1024
Bernina Lagalb ⊡ d.	...	0722	...	...	0832	0920	|	...	1032	1032s
Bernina Diavolezza ⊡ d.	...	0724	...	...	0834	0922	|	...	1034	1034s
Morteratsch ⊡ d.	...	0734	...	...	0844	0931	1013s	...	1044	1044s
Pontresina 540 a.	...	0750	...	...	0858	0950	1027s	...	1058	1058s
Pontresina d.	0720	...	0756	...	0901	0956	|	...	1101	|
Celerina Staz ⊡ d.	0725	...	0802	...	0906	1002	|	...	1106	|
St Moritz a.	0731	...	0808	...	0912	1008	1038	...	1112	1112

		976 ♦ R ⁄			🚌 w			🚌 w		952 ♦ R ⁄	950 ♦ R ⁄	960 ♦ R ⁄		954 ♦ R ⁄	p	q		⊗		⊗		🚌 ⑤h	⊗	⊗	
Tirano d.	0940	1003	1050	1127v	1200	1250	1340v	1400	...	1404	1404	1431	...	1433	1433	1450	1540	1650r	...	1740	...	...	1850	1940	...
Campocologno 🏛 d.	0952	|	1101	1136v	1206	1301	1352v	1406	...	|	|	|	...	|	1442	1501	1552	1701r	...	1752	...	...	1901	1952	...
Brusio ⊡ d.	0959	|	1109	1143v	1210	1309	1359v	1410	...	|	|	|	...	|	1449	1509	1559	1709r	...	1800	...	...	1909	2000	...
Miralago ⊡ d.	1005	|	1116	1149v	1214	1316	1405v	1414	...	|	|	|	...	|	1455	1516	1605	1716r	...	1807	...	...	1916	2007	...
Le Prese d.	1010	1030u	1122	1154v	1217	1322	1410v	1417	...	1432u	1432u	1449u	...	1500u	1500	1522	1610	1721r	...	1812x	...	...	1921x	2012x	...
Poschiavo a.	1022	|	1131	1215v	1223k	1331	1422v	1423k	...	|	|	|	...	|	1512	1531	1622	1732r	...	1823	...	...	1932	2023	...
Poschiavo d.	1024	1044u	1133	1224	...	1333	1424	...	...	1444u	1444u	1507u	...	1513u	1513	1533	1624	1734	...	1825	...	1915	...	...	...
Alp Grüm d.	1104	1122s	1215	1304	...	1415	1504	...	...	1522u	1522u	1545u	...	1558u	1558	1615	1704	1811x	...	1902x	...	|	...	...	...
Ospizio Bernina d.	1112	1132s	1224	1312	...	1424	1512	...	....	|	...	1600u	...	1607u	1607	1624	1712	1820x	...	1911x	...	|	...	...	...
Bernina Lagalb ⊡ d.	1120	|	1232	1320	...	1432	1520	...	...	|	...	|	...	|	1615	1632	1720	1828	...	1919	...	|	...	...	...
Bernina Diavolezza ⊡ d.	1122	|	1234	1322	...	1434	1522	...	...	|	...	|	...	|	1617	1634	1722	1830	...	1921	...	|	...	...	...
Morteratsch ⊡ d.	1131	|	1244	1331	...	1444	1531	...	...	|	...	|	...	|	1626	1644	1731	1840	...	1931	...	|	...	...	...
Pontresina 540 a.	1150	1205s	1258	1350	...	1458	1550	...	...	1604	...	1626s	...	1644	1644	1658	1750	1857	...	1950	...	2000	...	...	...
Pontresina d.	1156	|	1301	1356	...	1501	1556	...	...	...	...	|	...	...	1656	1701	1756	...	1901	...	1956	n	...	...	...
Celerina Staz ⊡ d.	1202	|	1306	1402	...	1506	1602	...	...	...	...	|	...	...	1702	1706	1802	...	1906	...	2002	...	...	...	...
St Moritz a.	1208	1217	1312	1408	...	1512	1608	...	...	...	...	1639	...	...	1708	1712	1808	...	1912	...	2008	...	...	...	...

♦ – **NOTES** (LISTED BY TRAIN NUMBER)

950/1 – BERNINA EXPRESS – May 13- Oct. 24: (12) [observation cars] and 🍸 Chur - Tirano and v.v.

952/5 – BERNINA EXPRESS – © Dec. 13 - May 9, Oct. 30 - Dec. 11 (also Dec. 28-31): (12) [observation cars] and 🍸 Chur - Pontresina - Tirano and v.v.

953/4 – BERNINA EXPRESS – Ⓐ Dec. 14 - May 12, Oct. 25 - Dec. 10 (not Dec. 28-31): (12) [observation cars] and 🍸 Chur - Pontresina - Tirano and v.v.

960/1 – BERNINA EXPRESS – May 13 - Oct. 24: (12) [observation cars] and 🍸 Davos - St Moritz - Tirano and v.v.

970/5 – BERNINA EXPRESS – May 13 - Oct. 24: (12) [observation cars] and 🍸 St Moritz - Tirano and v.v.

971/2 – BERNINA EXPRESS – ②-⑦ Dec. 13 - May 12, Oct. 26 - Dec. 11: (12) [observation cars] St Moritz - Tirano and v.v.

973/6 – BERNINA EXPRESS – May 13 - Oct. 24: (12) [observation cars] and 🍸 Tirano - St Moritz and v.v.

h – Also Dec. 23, Apr. 1, May 12; not Dec. 25, Jan. 1, Apr. 2, May 14.

j – ⑥ only (not Dec. 26, Jan. 2).

k – Connects with train in previous column.

m – From Samedan (d. 2050).

n – To Samedan (a. 2008).

p – Ⓐ Dec. 14 - May 12, Oct. 25 - Dec. 10 (not Dec. 28-31).

q – © (daily May 13 - Oct. 24; also Dec. 28-31).

r – Ⓐ (daily May 10 - Oct. 24).

s – Stops to set down only.

u – Stops to pick up only.

v – May 13 - Oct. 24.

w – Dec. 13 - May 12, Oct. 25 - Dec. 11.

x – Stops on request only.

⊗ – Mixed train. Times subject to variation.

⊡ – Request stop.

⁄ – Supplement payable.

550 LUZERN and ZÜRICH - LOCARNO, CHIASSO and MILANO

SBB, FS

	RE 14063	RE 14065		ICN 663		IR 2257		ICN 10013	EC 13	IR 2159	IR 2409	IR 2259	ICN 667	IR 2163	IR 2411	IR 2263	ICN 10015	EC 15	IR 2165	IR 2413	ICN 671	IR 2267	IR 2415	ICN 10017	EC 17	IR 2169
				🍴				🍴	🍴		(🍷)		🍴		(🍷)		🍴	🍴	🍷	(🍷)	🍴		(🍷)	🍴	🍴	
									◧		R	z			R	x		◧		R			R	q	◧	W
Basel SBB **565** d.	...	...	...	0503	...	...	...	...	...	0603	...	...	...	0703	...	...	...	...	0803	...	0903	...	...	...	...	1003
Olten **565** d.	...	...	...	0530	...	...	...	...	...	0630	...	...	...	0730	...	...	...	...	0830	...	0930	...	...	...	...	1030
Luzern 565 d.	...	...	...	0618	...	...	...	...	...	0718	0740	...	...	0818	0840	...	...	...	0918	0940	1018	...	1040	...	...	1118
Küssnacht am Rigi d.	...	...	...	|	...	...	...	...	...	|	0758	...	...	|	0858	...	...	...	|	0958	|	...	1058	...	...	|
Zürich HB d.	...	...	...	|	...	0609	...	0701	0709	|	|	0731	0809	|	|	0831	0901	0909	|	|	|	1009	|	1101	1109	|
Zug d.	...	...	...	|	...	0631	...	0727	0731	|	|	0757	0831	|	|	0857	0927	0931	|	|	|	1031	|	1127	1131	|
Arth-Goldau a.	...	...	...	0644	...	0646k	...	0744	0748	0744k	0811	0813	0846	0844	0911	0913	0944	0948	0944k	1011	1044	1046k	1111	1144	1148	1144k
Arth-Goldau d.	...	...	...	0650	...	0652	...	0748	0750	0752	▬	0815	0850	0852	▬	0915	0948	0950	0952	▬	1050	1052	▬	1148	1150	1152
Schwyz d.	...	...	...	|	...	0700	...	|	|	0800	...	|	|	0900	...	|	|	|	1000	...	|	1100	...	|	|	1200
Brunnen d.	...	...	...	|	...	0704	...	|	|	0804	...	|	|	0904	...	|	|	|	1004	...	|	1104	...	|	|	1204
Flüelen d.	...	...	...	|	...	0715	...	|	|	0815	...	|	|	0915	...	|	|	|	1015	...	|	1115	...	|	|	1215
Erstfeld d.	...	...	...	|	...	0724	...	|	|	0824	...	|	|	0924	...	|	|	|	1024	...	|	1124	...	|	|	1224
Göschenen d.	...	...	...	|	...	0750	...	|	|	0850	...	0902	|	0950	...	1002	|	|	1050	...	|	1150	...	|	|	1250
Airolo d.	...	...	0657	|	...	0801	...	|	|	0901	...	0913	|	1001	...	1013	|	|	1101	...	|	1201	...	|	|	1301
Faido d.	...	...	0715	|	...	0819	...	|	|	0919	...	|	|	1019	...	|	|	|	1119	...	|	1219	...	|	|	1319
Biasca d.	0552j	0652	0738	|	0805	0840	...	|	|	0940	...	|	|	1040	...	1052	|	|	1140	...	|	1240	...	|	|	1340
Bellinzona a.	0605j	0705	0751	0823	0819k	0853	...	0921	0923	0953	...	1005	1023	1053	...	1105	1121	1123	1153	...	1223	1253	...	1321	1323	1353
Bellinzona ▲ d.	0607	0707	0757	0825	0827	0854	0857	0923	0925	0954	0957	1009	1025	1054	1057	1109	1123	1125	1154	1157	1225	1254	1257	1323	1325	1354
Locarno ▲ a.	|	|	|	|	|	0913	|	|	|	1013	|	|	|	1113	|	|	|	|	1213	|	|	1313	|	|	|	1413
Lugano a.	0637	0737	0827	0846	0857	...	0927	0945	0946	...	1027	1037	1046	...	1127	1137	1145	1146	...	1227	1246	...	1327	1345	1346	...
Lugano d.	0639	0739	0828	...	0858	...	0928	...	0948	...	1028	1039	...	...	1128	1139	...	1148	...	1228	...	...	1328	...	1348	...
Capolago-Riva San Vitale d.	|	|	0842	...	0912	...	0942	...	|	...	1042	|	...	...	1142	|	...	|	...	1242	...	...	1342	...	|	...
Mendrisio d.	0654	0754	0848	...	0918	...	0948	...	|	...	1048	1055	...	...	1148	1155	...	|	...	1248	...	...	1348	...	|	...
Chiasso a.	0701	0801	0856	...	0926	...	0956	...	1008	...	1056	1102	...	...	1156	1202	...	1208	...	1256	...	...	1356	...	1408	...
Chiasso 🏛 d.	...	...	0859	...	...	...	0959	...	1010	...	1059	...	...	...	1159	...	...	1210	...	1259	...	...	1359	...	1410	...
Como San Giovanni § a.	...	...	0903	...	...	...	1003	...	1014	...	1103	...	...	...	1203	...	...	1214	...	1303	...	...	1403	...	1414	...
Milano Centrale § a.	...	...	...	...	...	...	...	...	1050	...	...	...	...	...	...	...	...	1250	...	...	...	...	...	...	1450	...

	IR 2417	ICN 675	IR 2271	IR 2419	EC 19	IR 2173	IR 2421	ICN 679	IR 2275	IR 2423	ICN 10021	EC 21		IR 2177	IR 2425	ICN 683	RE 10683	IR 2279	IR 2427	ICN 10023	EC 23	IR 2181	IR 2429	ICN 687	IR 2283	IR 2431
	(🍷)	🍴		(🍷)	🍴		(🍷)	🍴		(🍷)	🍴	🍴			(🍷)	🍴			(🍷)	🍴	🍴		(🍷)	🍴		(🍷)
	R		T	R	◧	W	R			R	n	◧			R				R	y	◧		R			R
Basel SBB **565** d.	...	1103	...	...	...	1203	...	1303	...	...	...	...	...	1403	...	1503	...	...	...	...	...	1603	...	1703	...	...
Olten **565** d.	...	1130	...	...	...	1230	...	1330	...	...	...	...	...	1430	...	1530	...	...	...	...	...	1630	...	1730	...	...
Luzern 565 d.	1140	1218	...	1240	...	1318	1340	1418	...	1440	...	...	...	1518	1540	1618	...	...	1640	...	...	1718	1740	1818	...	1840
Küssnacht am Rigi d.	1158	|	...	1258	...	|	1358	|	...	1458	...	...	...	|	1558	|	...	...	1658	...	...	|	1758	|	...	1858
Zürich HB d.	|	|	1209	|	1309	|	|	|	1409	|	1501	1509	...	|	|	|	...	1609	|	1701	1709	|	|	|	1809	|
Zug d.	|	|	1231	|	1331	|	|	|	1431	|	1527	1531	...	|	|	|	...	1631	|	1727	1731	|	|	|	1831	|
Arth-Goldau a.	1211	1244	1246k	1311	1348	1344k	1411	1444	1446k	1511	1544	1548	...	1544k	1611	1644	...	1646k	1711	1744	1748	1744k	1811	1844	1846k	1911
Arth-Goldau d.	▬	1250	1252	▬	1350	1352	▬	1450	1452	▬	1548	1550	...	1552	▬	1650	...	1652	▬	1748	1750	1752	▬	1850	1852	...
Schwyz d.	...	|	1300	...	|	1400	...	|	1500	...	|	|	...	1600	...	|	...	1700	...	|	|	1800	...	|	1900	...
Brunnen d.	...	|	1304	...	|	1404	...	|	1504	...	|	|	...	1604	...	|	...	1704	...	|	|	1804	...	|	1904	...
Flüelen d.	...	|	1315	...	|	1415	...	|	1515	...	|	|	...	1615	...	|	...	1715	...	|	|	1815	...	|	1915	...
Erstfeld d.	...	|	1324	...	|	1424	...	|	1524	...	|	|	...	1624	...	|	...	1724	...	|	|	1824	...	|	1924	...
Göschenen d.	...	|	1350	...	|	1450	...	|	1550	...	|	|	...	1650	...	|	...	1750	...	|	|	1850	...	|	1950	...
Airolo d.	...	|	1401	...	|	1501	...	|	1601	...	|	|	...	1701	...	|	...	1801	...	|	|	1901	...	|	2001	...
Faido d.	...	|	1419	...	|	1519	...	|	1619	...	|	|	...	1719	...	|	...	1819	...	|	|	1919	...	|	2019	...
Biasca d.	...	|	1440	...	|	1540	...	|	1640	...	|	|	...	1740	...	|	...	1840	...	|	|	1940	...	|	2040	...
Bellinzona a.	...	1423	1453	...	1523	1553	...	1623	1653	...	1721	1723	...	1753	...	1823	...	1853	...	1921	1923	1953	...	2023	2053	...
Bellinzona ▲ d.	1357	1425	1454	1457	1525	1554	1557	1625	1654	1657	1723	1725	...	1754	1757	1825	...	1854	1857	1923	1925	1954	1957	2025	2054	...
Locarno ▲ a.	|	|	1513	|	|	1613	|	|	1713	|	|	|	...	1813	|	|	...	1913	|	|	|	2013	|	|	|	...
Lugano a.	1427	1446	...	1527	1546	...	1627	1646	...	1727	1745	1746	...	...	1827	1846	...	...	1927	1945	1946	...	2027	2046	2126	...
Lugano d.	1428	...	...	1528	1548	...	1628	...	...	1728	...	1748	...	...	1828	...	1851	...	1928	...	1948	...	2028	2048	2127	...
Capolago-Riva San Vitale d.	1442	...	...	1542	|	...	1642	...	...	1742	...	|	...	...	1842	...	|	...	1942	...	|	...	2042	|	2142	...
Mendrisio d.	1448	...	...	1548	|	...	1648	...	...	1748	...	|	...	...	1848	...	1906	...	1948	...	|	...	2048	|	2149	...
Chiasso a.	1456	...	...	1556	1608	...	1656	...	...	1756	...	1808	...	...	1856	...	1913	...	1956	...	2008	...	2056	2110	2158	...
Chiasso 🏛 d.	1459	...	...	1559	1610	...	1659	...	...	1759	...	1810	...	...	1859	...	...	...	1959	...	2010	...	...	...	...	...
Como San Giovanni § a.	1503	...	...	1603	1614	...	1703	...	...	1803	...	1814	...	...	1903	...	...	...	2003	...	2014	...	...	...	...	...
Milano Centrale § a.	...	...	...	...	1650	...	...	...	...	...	...	1850	...	...	...	...	...	...	...	...	2050	...	...	...	...	...

	ICN 10025	EC 25	IR 2187	IR 2433	ICN 691	IR 2289	ICN 693	IR 2191	IR 2197	IR 2293	IR 2295
	🍴	🍴		(🍷)	🍴						
	w	◧		R							
Basel SBB **565** d.	...	...	1803	...	1903	...	...	2003	...	...	...
Olten **565** d.	...	...	1830	...	1930	...	...	2030	...	...	...
Luzern 565 d.	...	...	1918	1940	2018	...	...	2118	2218	...	...
Küssnacht am Rigi d.	...	...	|	1958	|	...	...	|	|	...	...
Zürich HB d.	1901	1909	|	|	|	2009	2109	|	|	2209	2309
Zug d.	1927	1931	|	|	|	2031	2131	|	|	2231	2331
Arth-Goldau a.	1944	1948	1944k	2011	2044	2046k	2146	2144k	2244	2246	2346
Arth-Goldau d.	1948	1950	1952	...	2050	2052	2150	2154	...	2254	*2355*
Schwyz d.	|	|	2000	...	|	2100	|	2202	...	|	*0003*
Brunnen d.	|	|	2004	...	|	2104	|	2206	...	|	*0006*
Flüelen d.	|	|	2015	...	|	2115	|	2216	...	|	*0016*
Erstfeld d.	|	|	2024	...	|	2124	|	2226	...	2316	*0025*
Göschenen d.	|	|	2050	...	|	2150	|	...	...	2340	...
Airolo d.	|	|	2101	...	|	2201	|	...	...	2351	...
Faido d.	|	|	2119	...	|	2219	|	...	...	0009	...
Biasca d.	|	|	2140	...	|	2240	|	...	...	0030	...
Bellinzona a.	2121	2123	2153	...	2223	2253	2323	...	...	0042	...
Bellinzona ▲ d.	2123	2125	2154	...	2225	...	2325	...	...	0043	...
Locarno ▲ a.	|		|	...	|	...	|	...	...	|	...
Lugano a.	2145	2146	2226	...	2246	...	2346	...	...	0114	...
Lugano d.	...	2148	2227	...	2248	...	2348	...	...	0116	...
Capolago-Riva San Vitale d.	...	|	2242	...	|	...	|	...	...	0130	...
Mendrisio d.	...	|	2249	...	2304	...	0004	...	...	0138	...
Chiasso a.	...	2208	2258	...	2312	...	0012	...	...	0146	...
Chiasso 🏛 d.	...	2210	...	...	...	...	...	...	...	...	...
Como San Giovanni § a.	...	2214	...	...	...	...	...	...	...	...	...
Milano Centrale § a.	...	2250	...	...	...	...	...	...	...	...	...

	ICN 650	IR 2164	IR 2166	ICN 654	IR 2408	IR 2272	ICN 658	IR 2410	IR 2170		EC 12
	🍴			🍴	(🍷)		🍴	(🍷)			🍴
					R			R			◧
Milano Centrale § d.	...	...	...	...	...	...	...	...	...	...	0710
Como San Giovanni § d.	...	...	...	...	...	...	...	...	...	0725h	0745
Chiasso 🏛 a.	...	...	...	...	...	...	...	...	...	0731h	0750
Chiasso d.	0446	...	...	0546	...	0611	0641	...	0711	0733	0752
Mendrisio d.	0454	...	...	0554	...	0620	0650	...	0720	0742	|
Capolago-Riva San Vitale d.	|	...	...	|	...	|	|	...	|	0745	|
Lugano a.	0510	...	...	0610	...	0635	0705	...	0735	0800	0810
Lugano d.	0512	...	...	0612	...	0637	0712	...	0737	0800	0812
Locarno ▲ d.	|	...	...	|	...	|	|	...	|	|	|
Bellinzona ▲ a.	0534	...	...	0634	...	0705	0734	...	0805	0830	0834
Bellinzona d.	0536	...	0606	0636	...	0706	0736	...	0806	0839	0836
Biasca d.	|	...	0618	|	...	0718	|	...	0818	0855	|
Faido d.	|	...	0640	|	...	0740	|	...	0840	...	|
Airolo d.	|	...	0658	|	...	0758	|	...	0858	...	|
Göschenen d.	|	...	0708	|	...	0808	|	...	0908	...	|
Erstfeld d.	|	0626	0733	|	...	0833	|	...	0933	...	|
Flüelen d.	|	0636	0742	|	...	0842	|	...	0942	...	|
Brunnen d.	|	0651	0754	|	...	0854	|	...	0954	...	|
Schwyz d.	|	0656	0758	|	...	0858	|	...	0958	...	|
Arth-Goldau a.	0709	0706k	0806	0809k	...	0906	0909k	...	1006	...	1009k
Arth-Goldau d.	0713	0714	0814	0813	0848	0913	0914	0948	1014	...	1013
Zug d.	0729	|	|	0829	|	0929	|	|	|	...	1029
Zürich HB a.	0751	|	|	0851	|	0951	|	|	|	...	1051
Küssnacht am Rigi d.	...	|	|	...	0859	...	|	0959	|	...	...
Luzern 565 a.	...	0741	0841	...	0920	...	0941	1020	1041	...	...
Olten **565** a.	...	0827	0927	...	...	...	1027	...	1127	...	...
Basel SBB **565** a.	...	0853	0953	...	...	...	1053	...	1153	...	...

R – VORALPEN EXPRESS – [12] Luzern - St Gallen - Romanshorn and v.v.
T – [12] Zürich - Locarno. Oct. 18 - Dec. 11 runs as WILHELM TELL EXPRESS Flüelen - Locarno. [R]
W – [12] Basel - Locarno and v.v. May 1 - Oct. 17 runs as WILHELM TELL EXPRESS Flüelen - Locarno and v.v. [R]

h – ①-⑤ (not Dec. 25, Jan. 1, 6, Apr. 5, June 2, Nov. 1, Dec. 8).
j – Ⓐ (also Apr. 2, Dec. 9, 10; not Jan. 6, Mar. 19, June 3, 29, Nov. 1).
k – Connects with train in previous column(s).
n – ⑤⑦ Mar. 7 - Oct. 31.
q – ⑥ Mar. 6 - Oct. 30 (also Apr. 2, May 13).

w – ⑤ (not Dec. 25, Jan. 1, Apr. 2).
x – Mar. 6 - Oct. 31.
y – Ⓐ (daily Mar. 6 - Nov. 5; not Apr. 2, 5, May 13, 24).
z – ⑥ (also ⑦ July 4 - Nov. 7).

◧ – Supplement payable in Italy and for international journeys.

△ – Also conveys [car] [observation car].

▲ – For additional services Locarno - Bellinzona and v.v. – see panel on page 275.
§ – For additional services Como San Giovanni - Milano Porta Garibaldi and v.v. – see panel on page 275.

FS, SBB — MILANO, CHIASSO and LOCARNO - ZÜRICH and LUZERN — 550

km			IR 2276	RE 10662	ICN 662		IR 2174	EC 14		IR 2280	ICN 666		IR 2178		ICN 10016	EC 16		IR 2282	ICN 670		IR 2182	ICN 10018	EC 18		IR 2286	ICN 674
					✕			✕			✕				✕	✕			✕			✕	✕			✕
							W	◧		T			W		n	◧							◧			
0	**Milano Centrale** .....§ d.	...	...	...	...	...	...	0910	...	...	...	...	...	...	...	1110	...	...	...	...	...	...	1310	...	...	...
47	Como San Giovanni..§ d.	0755	...	...	...	0855	...	0945	0955	...	...	1055	...	...	...	1145	1155	...	...	1255	...	...	1345	1355	...	...
51	**Chiasso** 🏛 .... a.	0801	...	...	...	0901	...	0950	1001	...	...	1101	...	...	...	1150	1201	...	...	1301	...	...	1350	1401	...	...
51	**Chiasso** .... d.	0803	...	0847	...	0903	...	0952	1003	...	...	1103	...	...	...	1152	1203	...	...	1303	...	...	1352	1403	...	...
58	Mendrisio .... d.	0812	...	|	...	0912	...	|	1012	...	...	1112	...	...	...	|	1212	...	...	1312	...	...	|	1412	...	...
63	Capolago-Riva San Vitale d.	0815	...	|	...	0915	...	|	1015	...	...	1115	...	...	...	|	1215	...	...	1315	...	...	|	1415	...	...
77	**Lugano** .... a.	0830	...	0908	...	0930	...	1010	1030	...	...	1130	...	...	...	1210	1230	...	...	1330	...	...	1410	1430	...	...
77	**Lugano** .... d.	0830	...	...	0912	0930	...	1012	1030	...	1112	1130	...	...	1210	1212	1230	...	1312	1330	...	1410	1412	1430	...	1512
	Locarno .... ▲ d.	|	0845	...	|	|	0945	|	|	1045	|	|	1145	...	|	|	|	1245	|	|	1345	|	|	|	1445	|
106	Bellinzona .... ▲ a.	0900	0904	...	0934	1000	1004	1034	1100	1104	1134	1200	1204	...	1232	1234	1300	1304	1334	1400	1404	1432	1434	1500	1504	1534
106	Bellinzona .... d.	▬	0906	...	0936	▬	1006	1036	▬	1106	1136	▬	1206	...	1235	1236	▬	1306	1336	▬	1406	1435	1436	▬	1506	1536
125	Biasca .... d.	...	0918	...	|	...	1018	|	...	1118	|	...	1218	...	|	|	...	1318	|	...	1418	|	|	...	1518	|
151	Faido .... d.	...	0940	...	|	...	1040	|	...	1140	|	...	1240	...	|	|	...	1340	|	...	1440	|	|	...	1540	|
171	Airolo .... d.	...	0958	...	|	...	1058	|	...	1158	|	...	1258	...	|	|	...	1358	|	...	1458	|	|	...	1558	|
187	Göschenen .... d.	...	1008	...	|	...	1108	|	...	1208	|	...	1308	...	|	|	...	1408	|	...	1508	|	|	...	1608	|
216	Erstfeld .... d.	...	1033	...	|	...	1133	|	...	1233	|	...	1333	...	|	|	...	1433	|	...	1533	|	|	...	1633	|
225	Flüelen .... d.	*IR*	1042	...	|	*IR*	1142	|	*IR*	1242	|	*IR*	1342	...	|	|	*IR*	1442	|	*IR*	1542	|	|	*IR*	1642	|
237	Brunnen .... d.	**2412**	1054	...	|	**2414**	1154	|	**2416**	1254	|	**2418**	1354	...	|	|	**2420**	1454	|	**2422**	1554	|	|	**2424**	1654	|
240	Schwyz .... d.	(🍷)	1058	...	|	(🍷)	1158	|	(🍷)	1258	|	(🍷)	1358	...	|	|	(🍷)	1458	|	(🍷)	1558	|	|	(🍷)	1658	|
248	**Arth-Goldau** .... a.	**R**	1106	...	1109**k**	**R**	1206	1209**k**	**R**	1306	1309**k**	**R**	1406	...	1408**k**	1409**k**	**R**	1506	1509**k**	**R**	1606	1608**k**	1609**k**	**R**	1706	1709**k**
248	**Arth-Goldau** .... d.	1048	1113	...	1114	1148	1214	1213	1248	1313	1314	1348	1414	...	1410	1413	1448	1513	1514	1548	1614	1610	1613	1648	1713	1714
264	Zug .... d.	|	1129	...	|	|	|	1229	|	1329	|	|	|	...	1426	1429	|	1529	|	|	|	1626	1629	|	1729	|
293	**Zürich HB** .... a.	|	1151	...	|	|	|	1251	|	1351	|	|	|	...	1449	1451	|	1551	|	|	|	1649	1651	|	1751	|
*	Küssnacht am Rigi .... d.	1059	...	...	|	1159	|	...	1259	...	|	1359	|	...	...	...	1459	...	|	1559	|	...	...	1659	...	|
*	**Luzern 565** .... a.	1120	...	...	1141	1220	1241	...	1320	...	1341	1420	1441	...	...	...	1520	...	1541	1620	1641	...	...	1720	...	1741
	Olten **565** .... a.	...	...	...	1227	...	1327	...	...	...	1427	...	1527	...	...	...	...	...	1627	...	1727	...	...	...	...	1827
	Basel SBB **565** ...... a.	...	...	...	1253	...	1353	...	...	...	1453	...	1553	...	...	...	...	...	1653	...	1753	...	...	...	...	1853

		IR 2188	ICN 10020	EC 20		IR 2288		IR 2290	ICN 678		IR 2192	ICN 10022	EC 22	RE 14082		IR 2294	ICN 682		IR 2196	ICN 10024	EC 24		IR 2298	ICN 686		
			✕	✕					✕			✕	✕				✕			✕	✕			✕		
				◧		m							◧	j						p	◧					
Milano Centrale .....§ d.	...	...	...	1510	...	...	...	...	...	...	...	...	1710	...	...	...	...	...	...	...	1910	...	...	...	...	...
Como San Giovanni ..§ d.	1455	...	...	1545	...	...	1555	...	...	1655	...	...	1745	...	1755	...	...	1855	...	...	1945	1955	...	...	2055	...
Chiasso 🏛 .... a.	1501	...	...	1550	...	...	1601	...	...	1701	...	...	1750	...	1801	...	...	1901	...	...	1950	2001	...	...	2101	...
Chiasso .... d.	1503	...	...	1552	...	1556	1603	...	...	1703	...	...	1752	1757	1803	...	...	1903	...	...	1952	2003	...	...	2103	...
Mendrisio .... d.	1512	...	...	|	...	1604	1612	...	...	1712	...	...	|	1804	1812	...	...	1912	...	...	|	2012	...	...	2112	...
Capolago-Riva San Vitale. d.	1515	...	...	|	...	|	1615	...	...	1715	...	...	|	|	1815	...	...	1915	...	...	|	2015	...	...	2115	...
Lugano .... a.	1530	...	...	1610	...	1619	1630	...	...	1730	...	...	1810	1819	1830	...	...	1930	...	...	2010	2030	...	...	2130	...
Lugano .... d.	1530	...	1610	1612	...	1621	1630	...	1712	1730	...	1810	1812	1821	1830	...	1912	1930	...	2010	2012	2030	...	2112	2130	...
Locarno .... ▲ d.	|	1545	|	|	...	|	|	1645	|	|	1745	|	|	|	|	1845	|	|	1945	|	|	|	2045	|	|	...
Bellinzona .... ▲ a.	1600	1604	1632	1634	...	1647	1700	1704	1734	1802	1804	1832	1834	1847	1900	1904	1934	2000	2004	2032	2034	2100	2104	2134	2200	...
Bellinzona .... d.	▬	1606	1635	1636	...	1654	▬	1706	1736	▬	1806	1835	1836	...	▬	1906	1936	...	2006	2035	2036	...	2106	2136	...	...
Biasca .... d.	...	1618	|	|	...	1707	...	1718	|	...	1818	|	|	...		1918	|	...	2018	|	|	...	2118	|	...	...
Faido .... d.	...	1640	|	|	...	|	...	1740	|	...	1840	|	|	...	...	1940	|	...	2040	|	|	...	2140	|	...	...
Airolo .... d.	...	1658	|	|	...	1745	...	1758	|	...	1858	|	|	...	...	1958	|	...	2058	|	|	...	2158	|	...	...
Göschenen .... d.	...	1708	|	|	...	1757	...	1808	|	...	1908	|	|	...	...	2008	|	...	2108	|	|	...	2208	|	...	...
Erstfeld .... d.	...	1733	|	|	...	|	...	1833	|	...	1933	|	|	...	...	2033	|	...	2133	|	|	...	2233	|	...	...
Flüelen .... d.	*IR*	1742	|	|	...	|	*IR*	1842	|	*IR*	1942	|	|	...	*IR*	2042	|	...	2142	|	|	...	2242	|	...	...
Brunnen .... d.	**2426**	1754	|	|	...	|	**2428**	1854	|	**2430**	1954	|	|	...	**2432**	2054	|	...	2154	|	|	...	2254	|	...	...
Schwyz .... d.	(🍷)	1758	|	|	...	|	(🍷)	1858	|	(🍷)	1958	|	|	...	(🍷)	2058	|	...	2158	|	|	...	2258	|	...	...
Arth-Goldau .... a.	**R**	1806	1808**k**	1809**k**	...	1844	**R**	1906	1909**k**	**R**	2006	2008**k**	2009**k**	...	**R**	2106	2109**k**	...	2206	2208**k**	2209**k**	...	2306	2309**k**	...	...
Arth-Goldau .... d.	1748	1814	1810	1813	...	1846	1848	1913	1914	1948	2014	2010	2013	...	2048	2113	2115	...	2214	2210	2213	...	2313	2314	...	...
Zug .... d.	|	|	1826	1829	...	1903	|	1929	|	|	|	2026	2029	...	|	2129	|	...	|	2226	2229	...	2329	|	...	...
Zürich HB .... a.	|	|	1849	1851	...	1928	|	1951	|	|	|	2049	2051	...	|	2151	|	...	|	2249	2251	...	2351	|	...	...
Küssnacht am Rigi .... d.	1759	|	...	...	...	...	1859	...	|	1959	|	...	...	...	2059	...	|	...	|	...	...	...	...	|	...	...
Luzern 565 .... a.	1820	1841	...	...	...	...	1920	...	1941	2020	2041	...	...	...	2120	...	2141	...	2241	...	...	...	...	2341	...	...
Olten **565** .... a.	...	1927	...	...	...	...	...	...	2027	...	2127	...	...	...	...	...	2227	...	2327	...	...	...	...	0027	...	...
Basel SBB **565** ...... a.	...	1953	...	...	...	...	...	...	2053	...	2153	...	...	...	...	...	2253	...	2353	...	...	...	...	0053	...	...

▲ – Additional services **BELLINZONA - LOCARNO and v.v.**:

km				and at the same minutes past each hour until					j			j					and at the same minutes past each hour until							
0	Bellinzona ..... d.	0500	0530		1600	1630	...	1700	1716	1730	1800	1816	1830	...	1900	1930		2300	2330	...	0000	0046	...	...
21	Locarno .... a.	0527	0557		1627	1657	...	1727	1742	1757	1827	1842	1857	...	1927	1957		2327	2357	...	0024	0110	...	...

					and at the same minutes past each hour until					j			j					and at the same minutes past each hour until					
Locarno .... d.	0533	...	0603	0633		1603	1633	...	1703	1717	1733	1803	1817	1833	...	1903	1933		2303	2333	...	0014	0044	0114
Bellinzona ..... a.	0557	...	0627	0657		1627	1657	...	1727	1742	1757	1827	1842	1857	...	1927	1957		2327	2357	...	0036	0106	0136

§ – Additional services **MILANO PORTA GARIBALDI - COMO SAN GIOVANNI and v.v.** (2nd class only):

	⚒				and at the same minutes past each hour until			
Milano Porta Garibaldi. d.	0608	0638	0738	0838		2038	2138	2238
Monza .... d.	0625	0655	0755	0855		2055	2155	2255
Como San Giovanni .... a.	0708	0738	0838	0938		2138	2238	2338

				and at the same minutes past each hour until				
Como San Giovanni .... d.	0723	0823	0923		1923	2023	2123	2223
Monza .... d.	0805	0905	1005		2005	2105	2205	2305
Milano Porta Garibaldi .... a.	0826	0922	1022		2022	2122	2222	2322

♦ – **NOTES** (LISTED BY TRAIN NUMBER)

24 – 🚃12 and ✕ Venezia - Milano - Zürich.

R – VORALPEN EXPRESS – 🚃12 Romanshorn - St Gallen - Luzern.

T – 🚃12 Locarno - Zürich. Oct. 18 - Dec. 11 runs as WILHELM TELL EXPRESS Locarno - Flüelen. 🅁

W – 🚃12 Locarno - Basel. May 1 - Oct. 17 runs as WILHELM TELL EXPRESS Locarno - Flüelen. 🅁

j – Ⓐ (also Apr. 2, Dec. 9, 10; not Jan. 6, Mar. 19, June 3, 29, Nov. 1).

k – Connects with train in previous column(s).

m – ⑦ July 4 - Oct. 31.

n – ⑤⑦ Mar. 7 - Oct. 31.

p – ⑦ Mar. 7 - Oct. 31.

◧ – Supplement payable in Italy and for international journeys.

△ – Also conveys 🚃1 [observation car].

▲ – For additional services Locarno - Bellinzona and v.v. see panel.

* – Other distances: Arth-Goldau *0*, Küssnacht am Rigi *12 km*, Luzern *28 km*.

552 LUZERN - STANS - ENGELBERG

Narrow gauge rack railway. ZB

km		⚒						T			T								🚌			🚌			🚌		🚌
0	**Luzern 561** d.	0609	0623	0641	0711	0741	0811	0834	0841	0911	0934	0941	1011		1941	2011	...	2041	...	2111	2141	...	2211	2241	...	2341	...
9	Hergiswil **561** d.	0625	0635	0655	0725	0755	0825	|	0855	0925	|	0955	1025	and	1955	2025	...	2055	...	2125	2155	...	2225	2255	...	2355	...
11	Stansstad d.	0629	0639	0659	0730	0759	0830	|	0859	0930	|	0959	1030	hourly	1959	2030	...	2059	...	2130	2159	...	2230	2259	...	2359	...
15	Stans d.	0633	0643	0704	0735	0803	0835	0852	0903	0935	0952	1003	1035	until	2003	2035	...	2104	...	2133	2204	...	2233	2304	...	0004	...
19	Dallenwil d.	0640	...	0708a	0740	...	0840	|	...	0940	|	...	1040		...	2040	...	2108	2111	...	2208	2211	...	2308	2311	0008	0011
34	**Engelberg** a.	0712	...	...	0812	...	0912	0923	...	1012	1023	...	1112		...	2112	...	...	2132	...	...	2232	...	...	2332	...	0032

				Ⓐ									T			T						🚌		🚌		🚌	
Engelberg d.	...	...	...	...	0645	...	0745	...		1545	...	...	1628	1645	...	1728	1745	...		2045	...	2145	...	2245	...	2345	...
Dallenwil d.	0550	0607	...	0709	0718	0749a	0818	...	and	1618	...	...	|	1718	1749	|	1818	...	and	2118	...	2206	2212	2306	2312	0006	0012
Stans d.	0555	0613	0655	0717	0725	0755	0825	0855	hourly	1625	1655	...	1707	1725	1755	1807	1825	1855	hourly	2125	2155	...	2225	...	2317	...	0018
Stansstad d.	0600	0617	0700	0721	0730	0800	0830	0900	until	1630	1700	...	|	1730	1800	|	1830	1900	until	2130	2200	...	2230	...	2321	...	0022
Hergiswil **561** d.	0604	0624	0705	0725	0734	0805	0834	0905		1634	1705	...	|	1734	1805	|	1834	1905		2134	2205	...	2234	...	2324	...	0025
Luzern 561 a.	0615	0636	0719	0734	0749	0819	0849	0919		1649	1719	...	1726	1749	1819	1826	1849	1919		2149	2219	...	2249	...	...	...	...

T – TITLIS EXPRESS – Ⓒ Dec. 13 - Apr. 5; ⑥⑦ July 3 - Oct. 10.

a – Ⓐ only.

553 MOUNTAIN RAILWAYS IN CENTRAL SWITZERLAND

2nd class only. RB

km			p		S							p	q
0	Arth-Goldau d.	0800	0910	1010	1015	1110	1210	1310	1410	1510	1610	1710	1810
9	Rigi Kulm a.	0845	0947	1047	1205	1147	1247	1347	1447	1547	1647	1747	1847

		p					S				p	q
Rigi Kulm d.	0900	1004	1104	1204	1304	1404	1405	1504	1604	1704	1804	1904
Arth-Goldau a.	0948	1048	1148	1248	1348	1448	1535	1548	1648	1748	1848	1948

km		Dec. 13	m		and		m	m	m	m	May 23			r	w				r		and			
0	Rigi Kulm d.	to	0910	1000	hourly	1700	1800	1900	2000	2240	to	0910	1000	1050	1100	1200	1300	1400	1430	1500	hourly	2000	2240	...
7	Vitznau a.	May 22	0949	1040	until	1740	1840	1940	2040	2320	Sept. 12	0949	1040	1140	1140	1240	1340	1440	1515	1540	until	2040	2320	...

	Dec. 13	m		and		m	m	m	m	May 23				r			and						
Vitznau d.	to	0835	0915	hourly	1615	1715	1815	1915	2205	to	0835	0915	1015	1050	...	1115	hourly	1915	...	2205	...	...	...
Rigi Kulm a.	May 22	0905	0945	until	1645	1745	1845	1945	2235	Sept. 12	0905	0945	1045	1120	...	1145	until	1945	...	2235	...	...	...

ALPNACHSTAD - PILATUS KULM. Narrow gauge rack railway. *5 km*. Journey time: 30 minutes uphill, 40 minutes downhill. **Operator**: PB, ✆ 041 329 11 11.
Services run daily **early May - November 21** (weather permitting). **No winter service** (December - April).

From **Alpnachstad**: 0815 **j**, 0855, 0935, 1015, 1055, 1135, 1215, 1300, 1340, 1420, 1500, 1550, 1630 **j**, 1710 **j**, 1750 **k**, 1830 **n**.

From **Pilatus Kulm**: 0850 **j**, 0930, 1010, 1050, 1130, 1210, 1255, 1335, 1415, 1455, 1545, 1625, 1705 **j**, 1745 **j**, 1825 **k**, 1910 **n**.

BRIENZ - BRIENZER ROTHORN. Narrow gauge rack railway. *8 km*. Most services operated by steam train. Journey time: 55–60 minutes uphill, 60–70 minutes downhill.
Operator: BRB, ✆ 033 952 22 22. Service valid **June 5 - October 24**, and is subject to weather conditions on the mountain and demand. Extra trains may run at busy times. **No winter service**.

From **Brienz**: 0730 **y**, 0830, 0940, 1045, 1145, 1258, 1358, 1458, 1558.

From **Brienzer Rothorn**: 0830 **y**, 0935, 1115, 1220, 1328, 1428, 1528, 1628, 1710.

S – 🚂 Steam train. Runs ⑥⑦ July 3 - Sept. 26. Supplement payable (from Arth-Goldau only, CHF 10).
j – Until Oct. 30.
k – May 23 - Aug. 28.
m – May 1 - 22.
n – June 27 - Aug. 28.
p – ⑥⑦ Dec. 13 - 20; daily Dec. 21 - Mar. 21; Ⓒ Mar. 27 - Apr. 25; daily May 1 - Oct. 31; ⑥⑦ Nov. 6 - Dec. 11 (also Nov. 1, Dec. 8).
q – Daily Dec. 19 - Jan. 3; ⑤⑥⑦ Apr. 30 - June 20; daily June 26 - Aug. 29; ⑤⑥⑦ Sept. 3 - Oct. 31 (also May 13, 24, June 3).
r – † May 23 - July 4; daily July 10 - Aug. 22 (also Aug. 29, Sept. 5, 12).
w – ①-⑥ May 25 - July 3, Aug. 23 - Sept. 11.
y – ⑦ Aug. 1 - Sept. 19.

554 🚌 MEIRINGEN - ANDERMATT

Service June 19 - October 3, 2010 (no winter service) PA

	R	R		R	R	R	R		R	R
Meiringen Bahnhof d.	0920	...	...	1100	...	1330	1330	...	1520	...
Susten Passhöhe d.	|	1010	...	|	...	|	1440	...	|	...
Göschenen Bahnhof d.	|	1049	...	|	...	|	1519	...	|	...
Grimsel Passhöhe d.	1055	|	...	1220	...	1444	|	...	1630	...
Gletsch Post d.	1105	|	...	1230	...	1455	|	...	1640	...
Oberwald Bahnhof a.	1119	|	...	1244	...	1508	|	...	1654	...
Oberwald Bahnhof d.	...	|	...	...	1340	...	|	...	...	1715
Gletsch Post d.	...	|	...	...	1350	...	|	...	...	1725
Furka Passhöhe d.	...	|	...	...	1425	...	|	...	...	1751
Realp Post d.	...	|	...	...	1451	...	|	...	...	1817
Andermatt Bahnhof a.	...	1104	...	...	1510	...	1534	...	...	1835

	R	R	R	R		R	R	R	R	R
Andermatt Bahnhof d.	...	0830	0915	...	...	1140	...	...	1545	1545
Realp Post d.	...	0842	|	...	...	|	...	...	1557	|
Furka Passhöhe d.	...	0906	|	...	...	|	...	...	1621	|
Gletsch Post d.	...	1005	|	...	...	|	...	...	1651	|
Oberwald Bahnhof a.	...	1020	1210	...	...	1510	...	...	1706	|
Oberwald Bahnhof d.	...	1030	...	1330	...	...	1530	1700	...	|
Gletsch Post d.	...	1046	...	1345	...	...	1545	1716	...	|
Grimsel Passhöhe d.	...	1130	...	1410	...	...	1610	1732	...	|
Göschenen Bahnhof d.	0900	|	...	|	...	...	|	|	...	1601
Susten Passhöhe d.	0940	|	...	|	...	...	|	|	...	1641
Meiringen Bahnhof a.	...	1230	...	1514	...	...	1714	1836	...	1805

555 ZÜRICH FLUGHAFEN ✈ - ZÜRICH - LUZERN

SBB

km															Ⓐ			Ⓐ				Ⓐ			
0	**Zürich Flughafen ✈ 530/5** d.	...	...	...	...	...	...	...	0847	...	and at	1547	...	...	...	1647	...	...	1747	...	...	...	1847	...	1947
10	**Zürich HB 530/5** d.	0535	0604	0635	0704	0735	0804	0835	0904	0935	the same	1604	1635	...	1641	1704	1735	1741	1804	1835	...	1841	1904	1935	2004
22	Thalwil d.	0545	0614	0645	0714	0745	0814	0845	0914	0945	minutes	1614	1645	...	1654	1714	1745	1754	1814	1845	...	1854	1914	1945	2014
39	Zug d.	0602	0629	0702	0729	0802	0829	0902	0929	1002	past each	1629	1702	...	1712	1729	1802	1812	1829	1902	...	1912	1929	2002	2029
49	Rotkreuz d.	0610	|	0710	|	0810	|	0910	|	1010	hour	|	1710	...	1721	|	1810	1821	|	1910	...	1921	|	2010	|
67	**Luzern** a.	0625	0649	0725	0749	0825	0849	0925	0949	1025	until	1649	1725	...	1739	1749	1825	1839	1849	1925	...	1939	1949	2025	2049

									w⚡	w⚡	w⚡
Zürich Flughafen ✈ 530/5 d.	...	2047	...	...	...	...	...	...	...	...	...
Zürich HB 530/5 d.	2035	2104	2135	2204	2235	2304	2335	0007	0135	0235	0335
Thalwil d.	2045	2114	2145	2214	2245	2314	2345	0017	|	|	|
Zug d.	2102	2129	2202	2229	2302	2329	0002	0035	0155	0255	0355
Rotkreuz d.	2110	|	2210	|	2310	|	0010	0046	0202	0302	0402
Luzern a.	2125	2149	2225	2249	2325	2349	0025	0107	0225	0325	0425

				Ⓐ				Ⓐ	
Luzern d.	0455	0528	0610	0620	0635	...	0710	0720	0735
Rotkreuz d.	0513	0548	|	0636	0648	...	|	0736	0748
Zug d.	0526	0558	0631	0648	0658	...	0731	0748	0758
Thalwil d.	0542	0616	0646	0705	0716	...	0746	0805	0816
Zürich HB 530/5 a.	0555	0625	0656	0719	0725	...	0756	0819	0825
Zürich Flughafen ✈ 530/5 a.	0613	...	...	...	...	...	0813	...	...

																						w	w⚡	w⚡
Luzern d.	0810	0835	and at	1510	1535	...	1610	1635	1710	1735	1810	1835	1910	1935	2010	2035	2110	2135	2210	2235	2310	2335	0035	0135	0235
Rotkreuz d.	|	0848	the same	|	1548	...	|	1648	|	1748	|	1848	|	1948	|	2048	|	2148	|	2248	|	2348	0048	0146	0246
Zug d.	0831	0858	minutes	1531	1558	...	1631	1658	1731	1758	1831	1858	1931	1958	2031	2058	2131	2158	2231	2258	2331	2358	0058	0153	0253
Thalwil d.	0846	0916	past each	1546	1616	...	1646	1716	1746	1816	1846	1916	1946	2016	2046	2116	2146	2216	2246	2316	2346	0016	0116	|	|
Zürich HB 530/5 a.	0856	0925	hour	1556	1625	...	1656	1725	1756	1825	1856	1925	1956	2025	2056	2125	2156	2225	2256	2325	2356	0025	0125	0225	0325
Zürich Flughafen ✈ 530/5 a.	0913	...	until	1613	...	...	1713	...	1813	...	1913	...	2013	...	...	...	...	...	...	...	...	...	...	...	

w – ⑥⑦ (also Jan. 1, Apr. 2, 5, May 13, 14, 24).

⚡ – Supplement payable.

SBB — BASEL - BERN - INTERLAKEN and BRIG — 560

km		IC	IC	ICE	IC	IC	EC	IC	IC	ICE	ICE	IC	IC	IC	IC	IC	ICE	IR	IC	IC	IC	IC	IC	ICE	IC	EC	IC	IC	IC
		953	806	1055	955	808	51	959	810	1061	371	812	1063	965	816	1067	271	1467	818	1069	969	820	1071	373	822	57	973	824	1075
			(✕)		✕	✕	◧	(✕)	(✕)		✕	✕	✕		(✕)	(✕)	✕		✕	✕	✕	✕	✕	✕	✕	◧	(✕)	(✕)	✕
											♦						♦							B					
	Romanshorn **535** d.	...	...	...	...	...	...	...	0538	...	...	0638	...	...	0741	...	...	...	0841	...	...	0941	...	...	1041	...	...	1141	...
	Zürich Flug ✈ **535** d.	...	...	...	...	...	...	...	0640	...	...	0743	...	...	0840	...	...	...	0940	...	...	1040	...	...	1140	...	...	1240	...
	Zürich HB **500** d.	...	...	...	...	0600	...	...	0700	...	...	0800	...	...	0900	...	...	...	1000	...	...	1100	...	...	1200	...	...	1300	...
0	**Basel SBB** d.	...	...	0524	0601	|	0628	0701	|	0728	0801	|	0828	0901	|	0928	1001	...	|	1028	1101	|	1128	1201	|	1228	1301	|	1328
14	Liestal d.	...	...	0534	|	|	0638	|	|	0738	|	|	0838	|	|	0938	|	...	|	1038	|	|	1138	|	|	1238	|	|	1338
39	Olten d.	...	...	0559	0629	|	0700	0729	|	0800	0829	|	0900	0929	|	1000	1029	...	|	1100	1129	|	1200	1229	|	1300	1329	|	1400
101	**Bern** a.	...	...	0627	0656	0657k	0727	0756	0757k	0827	0856	0857k	0927	0956	0957k	1027	1056	...	1057k	1127	1156	1157k	1227	1256	1257k	1327	1356	1357k	1427
101	**Bern** d.	0604	0607	0635	0704	0707	0735	0804	0807	0835	0904	0907	0935	1004	1007	1035	...	1104	1107	1135	1204	1207	1235	1304	1307	1335	1404	1407	1435
132	Thun d.	0622	0625	0654	0722	0725	0754	0822	0825	0854	0922	0925	0954	1022	1025	1054	...	1123	1125	1154	1222	1225	1254	1322	1325	1354	1422	1425	1454
142	**Spiez** a.	0631	0634	0702	0731	0734	0802	0831	0834	0902	0931	0934	1002	1031	1034	1102	...	1131	1134	1202	1231	1234	1302	1331	1334	1402	1431	1434	1502
142	**Spiez** d.	0633	0636	0703	0733	0736	0805	0833	0836	0903	0933	0936	1005	1033	1036	1103	...	1133	1136	1205	1233	1236	1303	1333	1336	1405	1433	1436	1503
	Interlaken West d.	0652	|	0723	0752	|	|	0852	|	0923	0952	|	|	1052	|	1123	...	1153	|	|	1252	|	1323	1352	|	|	1452	|	1523
	Interlaken Ost a.	0657	|	0728	0757	|	|	0857	|	0928	0957	|	|	1057	|	1128	...	1157	|	|	1257	|	1328	1357	|	|	1457	|	1528
197	Visp d.	...	0703	...	...	0803	0832	...	0903	...	...	1003	1032	...	1103	...	...	...	1203	1232	...	1303	...	...	1403	1432	...	1503	...
206	**Brig** a.	...	0711	...	...	0811	0840	...	0911	...	...	1011	1040	...	1111	...	...	...	1211	1240	...	1311	...	...	1411	1440	...	1511	...
	Milano C **590** a.	...	...	...	...	...	1035	...	...	...	...	...	...	...	...	...	...	...	...	...	...	...	...	...	...	1640	...	...	...

	ICE	IC	IC	IC	IC	IC	IC	IC	IC	IC	IC	EC	ICE	IC	IC	ICE	IC	IC	ICE	IC	IC	IC	IC	IC	IC		IC	ICE	IC
	375	826	1077	977	828	1079	979	830	1081	981	832	59	277	836	1085	987	838	1087	279	1089	1091	991	1093	1095	1097		993	947	949
	✕	✕	✕	✕	(✕)	(✕)	(✕)	✕	✕	✕	(✕)	◧	✕	✕	(✕)		✕	✕	✕	✕			🍷				✕		
	B n												B						B	①–⑥	⑦			①–⑥	⑦				L
Romanshorn **535** d.	...	1241	...	...	1341	...	...	1441	...	...	1541	...	...	1641	...	...	1741	...	...	...	...	...	...	...	...	...	...	...	...
Zürich Flug ✈ **535** d.	...	1340	...	...	1440	...	...	1540	...	...	1640	...	...	1740	...	...	1840	...	...	...	...	...	...	...	...	...	...	...	...
Zürich HB **500** d.	...	1400	...	...	1500	...	...	1600	...	...	1700	...	...	1800	...	...	1900	...	...	...	...	...	...	...	...	...	...	...	...
Basel SBB d.	1401	|	1428	1501	|	1528	1601	|	1628	1701	|	1728	1801	|	1828	1901	|	1928	2001	2028	2028	2101	2128	...	...	...	2201	*2301*	...
Liestal d.	|	|	1438	|	|	1538	|	|	1638	|	|	1738	|	|	1838	|	|	1938	|	2038	2038	|	2138	...	...	...	|	|	...
Olten d.	1429	|	1500	1529	|	1600	1629	|	1700	1729	|	1800	1829	|	1900	1929	|	2000	2029	2100	2100	2129	2200	...	...	...	2229	*2330*	...
Bern a.	1456	1457k	1527	1556	1557k	1627	1656	1657k	1727	1756	1757k	1827	1856	1857k	1927	1956	1957k	2027	2056	2127	2127	2156	2227	...	...	...	2256	*2357*	...
Bern d.	1504	1507	1535	1604	1607	1635	1704	1707	1735	1804	1807	1835	1904	1907	1935	2004	2007	2035	2107	2135	2135	2207	...	2235	2235	...	2308	0008	0108
Thun d.	1522	1525	1554	1622	1625	1654	1722	1725	1754	1822	1825	1854	1922	1925	1954	2022	2025	2054	2125	2154	2154	2225	...	2254	2254	...	2326	0028	0133
Spiez a.	1531	1534	1602	1631	1634	1702	1731	1734	1802	1831	1834	1902	1931	1934	2002	2031	2034	2102	2134	2202	2202	2234	...	2302	2302	...	2335	0038	0143
Spiez d.	1533	1536	1605	1633	1636	1703	1733	1736	1805	1833	1836	1905	1933	1936	2003	2033	2036	2105	2135	2205	2205	2235	...	2305	2305	...	2336	0038	0143
Interlaken West d.	1552	|	|	1652	|	1723	1752	|	|	1852	|	|	1952	|	2023	2049	|	|	2152	|	|	2252	...	|	|	...	2354	0052	0200
Interlaken Ost a.	1557	|	|	1657	|	1728	1757	|	|	1857	|	|	1956	|	2028	2054	|	|	2156	|	|	2257	...	f	|	...	2359	0059	0206
Visp d.	...	1603	1632	...	1703	...	...	1803	1832	...	1903	1932	...	2003	...	...	2103	2132	...	2232	|	...	...	2335	f	...	...	...	...
Brig a.	...	1611	1640	...	1711	...	...	1811	1840	...	1911	1940	...	2011	...	...	2111	2140	...	2240	2301	...	...	2343	0009	...	...	...	...
Milano C **590** a.	...	...	...	...	...	...	...	...	...	...	...	2135	...	...	...	...	...	...	...	...	...	...	...	...	...	...	...	...	...

km		IC		IC	ICE	IC	IC	IC	IC	IC	ICE	IC	IC	IC	IC	EC	IR	IC	ICE	IC	IC	IC	IC	ICE	IC	IC	IC	IC	EC
		952		1058	278	811	1060	956	815	1064	276	817	1066	962	819	50	1464	821	374	1070	968	823	1072	370	825	1074	974	827	52
		✕		✕	✕	✕	(✕)	(✕)	✕	✕	✕	(✕)	(✕)	✕	✕	◧		(✕)	✕	(✕)	✕	✕	✕	✕	(✕)	✕	(✕)	✕	◧
					B						B								♦					B p					
	Milano C **590** d.	...	...	...	...	...	...	...	...	...	...	...	...	...	...	0725	...	...	...	...	...	...	...	...	...	...	...	...	1120
	Brig d.	...	...	...	...	0547	...	...	0649	0720	...	0749	...	...	0849	0920	...	0949	...	...	...	1049	1120	...	1149	...	...	1249	1320
	Visp d.	...	...	...	...	0554	...	...	0657	0728	...	0757	...	...	0857	0928	...	0957	...	...	...	1057	1128	...	1157	...	...	1257	1328
0	**Interlaken Ost** d.	...	...	0521	0601	f	0627	0701	|	|	0801	|	0831	0901	|	|	1001	|	...	1031	1101	|	|	1201	|	1231	1301	|	|
2	Interlaken West d.	...	...	0526	0606	|	0632	0706	|	|	0806	|	0836	0906	|	|	1006	|	...	1036	1106	|	|	1206	|	1236	1306	|	|
18	**Spiez** a.	...	...	0548	0622	0624	0652	0722	0724	0753	0822	0824	0852	0922	0924	0953	1022	1024	...	1052	1122	1124	1153	1222	1224	1252	1322	1324	1353
	Spiez d.	0520	...	0550	0623	0625	0654	0723	0725	0754	0823	0825	0854	0923	0925	0954	1023	1025	...	1054	1123	1125	1154	1223	1225	1254	1323	1325	1354
	Thun d.	0530	...	0601	0633	0636	0704	0733	0736	0804	0833	0836	0904	0933	0936	1004	1033	1036	...	1104	1133	1136	1204	1233	1236	1304	1333	1336	1404
	Bern a.	0552	...	0623	0652	0654k	0723	0752	0754k	0823	0852	0854k	0923	0952	0954k	1023	1052	1054k	...	1123	1152	1154k	1223	1252	1254k	1323	1352	1354k	1423
	Bern d.	0604	...	0634	0704	0702	0734	0804	0802	0834	0904	0902	0934	1004	1002	1034	...	1102	1104	1134	1204	1202	1234	1304	1302	1334	1404	1402	1434
	Olten d.	0632	...	0705	0732	|	0805	0832	|	0905	0932	|	1005	1032	|	1105	...	|	1132	1205	1232	|	1305	1332	|	1405	1432	|	1505
	Liestal d.	|	...	0721	|	|	0821	|	|	0921	|	|	1021	|	|	1121	...	|	|	1221	|	|	1321	|	|	1421	|	|	1521
	Basel SBB a.	0655	...	0732	0755	|	0832	0855	|	0932	0955	|	1032	1055	|	1132	...	|	1155	1232	1255	|	1332	1355	|	1432	1455	|	1532
	Zürich HB **500** a.	...	...	...	...	0758	...	...	0858	...	...	0958	...	...	1058	...	...	1158	...	...	...	1258	...	...	1358	...	...	1458	...
	Zürich Flug ✈ **535** a.	...	...	...	...	0816	...	...	0916	...	...	1016	...	...	1116	...	...	1216	...	...	...	1316	...	...	1416	...	...	1516	...
	Romanshorn **535** a.	...	...	...	...	0918	...	...	1018	...	...	1118	...	...	1218	...	...	1318	...	...	...	1418	...	...	1518	...	...	1618	...

	IC	IC	IC	ICE	IC	IC	IC	IC	ICE	IC	IC	IC	IC	IC	IC	IC	IC	IC	IC	IC	EC	IC	ICE	IC	ICE	IC	ICE	IC	IC
	978	829	1078	376	831	1080	982	835	1082	986	837	1086	988	839	1088	990	841	1092	992	843	56	845	994	1096	996	851	998	853	1098
	✕	✕	✕	✕	✕	✕	(✕)	(✕)		-✕	✕	✕	✕	(✕)	(✕)	(✕)	✕	✕	✕	(✕)	◧								
				♦																						①–⑥		⑦	⑤⑥
Milano C **590** d.	...	...	...	...	...	...	...	...	...	...	...	...	...	...	...	...	...	...	...	...	1825	...	...	...	...	...	...	...	...
Brig d.	...	1349	...	...	1449	1520	...	1549	...	...	1649	1720	...	1749	...	...	1849	1920	...	1949	2020	...	...	2120	...	2220	...	2226	...
Visp d.	...	1357	...	...	1457	1528	...	1557	...	...	1657	1728	...	1757	...	...	1857	1928	...	1957	2028	...	...	2128	...	2228	...	|	...
Interlaken Ost d.	1401	|	1431	1501	|	|	1601	|	1631	1701	|	|	1801	|	1831	1901	|	|	2001	|	|	...	2101	|	2201	|	2301	|	2333
Interlaken West d.	1406	|	1436	1506	|	|	1606	|	1636	1706	|	|	1806	|	1836	1906	|	|	2006	|	|	...	2106	|	2206	|	2306	|	2338
Spiez a.	1422	1424	1452	1522	1524	1553	1622	1624	1652	1722	1724	1753	1822	1824	1852	1922	1924	1953	2022	2024	2053	...	2122	2153	2222	2253	2322	2322	2354
Spiez d.	1423	1425	1454	1523	1525	1554	1623	1625	1654	1723	1725	1754	1823	1825	1854	1923	1925	1954	2023	2025	2054	...	2123	2154	2223	2254	2323	2325	2355
Thun d.	1433	1436	1504	1533	1536	1604	1633	1636	1704	1733	1736	1804	1833	1836	1904	1933	1936	2004	2033	2036	2104	...	2133	2204	2233	2304	2333	2336	0005
Bern a.	1452	1454k	1523	1552	1554k	1623	1652	1654k	1723	1752	1754k	1823	1852	1854k	1923	1952	1954k	2023	2052	2054k	2123	...	2152k	2223	2252	2323	2352	2354	0024
Bern d.	1504	1502	1534	1604	1602	1634	1704	1702	1734	1804	1802	1834	1904	1902	1934	2004	2002	2034	2104	2102	2134	2202	2204	...	2304	...	...	...	...
Olten a.	1532	|	1605	1632	|	1705	1732	|	1805	1832	|	1905	1932	|	2005	2032	|	2105	2132	|	2205	2228	2232	...	2332	...	...	...	...
Liestal a.	|	|	1621	|	|	1721	|	|	1821	|	|	1921	|	|	2021	|	|	2121	|	|	2221	|	|	...	|	...	...	...	...
Basel SBB a.	1555	|	1632	1655	|	1732	1755	|	1832	1855	|	1932	1955	|	2032	2055	|	2132	2155	|	2232	|	2255	...	2355	...	...	...	...
Zürich HB **500** a.	...	1558	...	...	1658	...	...	1758	...	...	1858	...	...	1958	...	...	2058	...	...	2158	...	2301	...	...	...	...	...	...	...
Zürich Flug ✈ **535** a.	...	1616	...	...	1716	...	...	1816	...	...	1916	...	...	2016	...	...	2116	...	...	2216	...	2316	...	...	...	...	...	...	...
Romanshorn **535** a.	...	1718	...	...	1818	...	...	1918	...	...	2018	...	...	2118	...	...	2218	...	...	2318	...	0018	...	...	...	...	...	...	...

♦ – **NOTES** (LISTED BY TRAIN NUMBER)

271 – 12 and ✕ Frankfurt - Basel - Bern.
371 – 12 and ✕ (Karlsruhe, ①–⑤, not Dec. 24, 25, 31, Jan. 1, Apr. 2, 5, May 24 -) Basel - Interlaken.
374 – 12 and ✕ Bern - Basel - Berlin Ost.
376 – 12 and ✕ Interlaken - Basel - Frankfurt (- Hamburg ⑤⑦, also Dec. 23, 30, Apr. 1, 5, May 12, 24; not Dec. 25, Jan. 1, Apr. 2, 4, May 14, 23).

B – 12 and ✕ Interlaken - Basel - Berlin Ost and v.v.
L – MOONLINER – ⑥⑦ (also Jan. 1).

f – Via Frutigen.
k – Connects with train in previous column.
n – Runs as train **291** on † (also Apr. 3; not Jan. 2, Apr. 2, May 13).
p – Runs as train **290** on some dates.
s – Stops to set down only.
u – Stops to pick up only.
✓ – Supplement payable.
◧ – Supplement payable for journeys from / to Italy.

SWITZERLAND

561 LUZERN - INTERLAKEN

ZB. Narrow gauge rack railway

km		Ⓐ	P				⚒				P						P									P	
0	**Luzern 552** d.	...	...	...	0537	0606	0637	0655	0708	0737	0755	0808	0837	0855	0908	0937	0955	1008	1037	1055	1108	1137	1155	1208	1237	1255	1308
9	Hergiswil **552** d.	...	...	...	0553	0623	0653	0706	0723	0753	0806	0823	0853	0906	0923	0953	1006	1023	1053	1106	1123	1153	1206	1223	1253	1306	1323
13	Alpnachstad d.	...	...	...	0558	0628	0658	|	0728	0758	|	0828	0858	|	0928	0958	|	1028	1058	|	1128	1158	|	1228	1258	|	1328
15	Alpnach Dorf d.	...	...	...	0601	0631	0701	0711	0731	0801	0811	0831	0901	0911	0931	1001	1011	1031	1101	1111	1131	1201	1211	1231	1301	1311	1331
21	Sarnen d.	...	...	...	0609	0639	0709	0720	0739	0809	0820	0839	0909	0920	0939	1009	1020	1039	1109	1120	1139	1209	1220	1239	1309	1320	1339
23	Sachseln d.	...	...	...	0614	0644	0714	|	0744	0814	|	0844	0914	|	0944	1014	|	1044	1114	|	1144	1214	|	1244	1314	|	1344
29	Giswil d.	...	...	...	0626	0651	0721	0730	0751	0821	0830	0851	0921	0930	0951	1021	1030	1051	1121	1130	1151	1221	1230	1251	1321	1330	1351
36	Lungern d.	...	...	...	0639	...	▬	0744	...	▬	0844	...	▬	0944	▬	▬	1044	...	▬	1144	...	▬	1244	...	▬	1344	...
40	Brünig Hasliberg d.	...	...	...	0656	...	...	0756	...	...	0856	...	...	0956	...	...	1056	...	...	1156	...	...	1256	...	...	1356	...
45	**Meiringen ●** a.	...	...	...	0711	...	...	0812	...	...	0912	...	...	1012	...	...	1112	...	...	1212	...	...	1312	...	...	1412	...
45	**Meiringen ●** d.	0547	0614	0647	0720	...	0744	0821	...	0844	0921	...	0944	1021	...	1044	1121	...	1144	1221	...	1244	1321	...	1344	1421	...
58	**Brienz** d.	0559	0626	0701	0734	...	0800	0838	...	0900	0938	...	1000	1038	...	1100	1138	...	1200	1238	...	1300	1338	...	1400	1438	...
65	Oberried d.	0609	0638	0713	0744	...	0812	|	...	0912	|	...	1012	|	...	1112	|	...	1212	|	...	1312	|	...	1412	|	...
74	**Interlaken Ost** a.	0622	0651	0724	0755	...	0824	0855	...	0924	0955	...	1024	1055	...	1124	1155	...	1224	1255	...	1324	1355	...	1424	1455	...

					P									P						P							
Luzern 552 d.	1337	1355	1408	1437	1455	1508	1537	1555	1608	1637	1655	1708	1737	1755	1808	1837	1855	1908	1937	1955	2008	2037	2108	2137	2208	2311	0030
Hergiswil **552** d.	1353	1406	1423	1453	1506	1523	1553	1606	1623	1653	1706	1723	1753	1806	1823	1853	1906	1923	1953	2006	2023	2053	2123	2153	2223	2326	0043
Alpnachstad d.	1358	|	1428	1458	|	1528	1558	|	1628	1658	|	1728	1758	|	1828	1858	|	1928	1958	|	2028	2058	2128	2158	2228	2330	0048
Alpnach Dorf d.	1401	1411	1431	1501	1511	1531	1601	1611	1631	1701	1711	1731	1801	1811	1831	1901	1911	1931	2001	2011	2031	2101	2131	2201	2231	2332	0050
Sarnen d.	1409	1420	1439	1509	1520	1539	1609	1620	1639	1709	1720	1739	1809	1820	1839	1909	1920	1939	2009	2020	2039	2109	2139	2209	2239	2340	0057
Sachseln d.	1414	|	1444	1514	|	1544	1614	|	1644	1714	|	1744	1814	|	1844	1914	|	1944	2014	|	2044	2114	2144	2214	2244	2344	0100
Giswil d.	1421	1430	1451	1521	1530	1551	1621	1630	1651	1721	1730	1751	1821	1830	1851	1921	1930	1951	2021	2030	2051	2121	2152	2221	2251	2351	0108
Lungern d.	▬	1444	...	▬	1544	...	▬	1644	...	▬	1744	...	▬	1844	...	...	1944	...	▬	2044	▬	...	2206	▬	...	▬	...
Brünig Hasliberg d.	...	1456	...	...	1556	...	...	1656	...	...	1756	...	...	1856	...	...	1956	...	...	2101	...	...	2217	...	...	...	...
Meiringen ● a.	...	1512	...	...	1612	...	...	1712	...	...	1812	...	...	1912	...	...	2012	...	...	2116	...	...	2232	...	...	⑤⑥j	...
Meiringen ● d.	1444	1521	...	1544	1621	...	1644	1721	...	1744	1821	...	1844	1921	...	...	...	...	2018	...	2118	...	...	2239	...	2325	...
Brienz d.	1500	1538	...	1600	1638	...	1700	1738	...	1800	1838	...	1900	1935	...	...	...	...	2032	...	2132	...	...	2251	...	2338	...
Oberried d.	1512	|	...	1612	|	...	1712	|	...	1812	|	...	1912	1944	...	...	...	...	2042	...	2142	...	...	2301	...	2348	...
Interlaken Ost a.	1524	1555	...	1624	1655	...	1724	1755	...	1824	1855	...	1924	1956	...	...	...	...	2055	...	2155	...	...	2313	...	2359	...

		⚒		P		Ⓐ		Ⓐ		P										P						P	
Interlaken Ost d.	...	...	...	...	...	0555	...	0627	...	0704	0733	...	0804	...	0833	...	0904	...	0933	1004	...	1033	1104	1133	...	1204	1233
Oberried d.	...	...	...	...	...	0608	...	0639	...	0714	0746	...	|	...	0846	...	|	...	0946	|	...	1046	|	1146	...	|	1246
Brienz d.	...	...	...	...	...	0625	...	0650	...	0724	0757	...	0824	...	0857	...	0924	...	0957	1024	...	1057	1124	1157	...	1224	1257
Meiringen ● a.	...	...	...	...	...	0637	...	0703	...	0735	0809	...	0835	...	0909	...	0935	...	1009	1035	...	1109	1135	1209	...	1235	1309
Meiringen ● d.	...	...	...	0546	...	▬	0646	▬	...	0746	▬	...	0846	...	▬	...	0946	...	▬	1046	...	▬	1146	▬	...	1246	▬
Brünig Hasliberg d.	...	...	...	0557	...	...	0657	...	...	0757	...	...	0857	...	...	...	0957	...	...	1057	...	...	1157	...	...	1257	...
Lungern d.	...	...	...	0610	...	...	0710	...	...	0810	...	...	0910	...	...	...	1010	...	...	1110	...	...	1210	...	...	1310	...
Giswil d.	0506	0536	0606	0627	0636	0706	0729	0736	0806	0829	0836	0906	0929	0936	1006	...	1029	1036	1106	1129	1136	1206	1229	1236	1306	1329	1336
Sachseln d.	0515	0545	0615	0634	0645	0715	|	0745	0815	|	0845	0915	|	0945	1015	...	|	1045	1115	|	1145	1215	|	1245	1315	|	1345
Sarnen d.	0520	0550	0620	0640	0650	0720	0740	0750	0820	0840	0850	0920	0940	0950	1020	...	1040	1050	1120	1140	1150	1220	1240	1250	1320	1340	1350
Alpnach Dorf d.	0525	0555	0625	0645	0655	0725	0745	0755	0825	0845	0855	0925	0945	0955	1025	...	1045	1055	1125	1145	1155	1225	1245	1255	1325	1345	1355
Alpnachstad d.	0530	0600	0630	|	0700	0730	|	0800	0830	|	0900	0930	|	1000	1030	...	|	1100	1130	|	1200	1230	|	1300	1330	|	1400
Hergiswil **552** d.	0538	0608	0638	0654	0708	0738	0754	0808	0838	0854	0908	0938	0954	1008	1038	...	1054	1108	1138	1154	1208	1238	1254	1308	1338	1354	1408
Luzern 552 a.	0552	0622	0652	0704	0722	0752	0804	0822	0852	0904	0922	0952	1004	1022	1052	...	1104	1122	1152	1204	1222	1252	1304	1322	1352	1404	1422

								P						P								P					⑥⑦
Interlaken Ost d.	...	1304	...	1333	1404	1433	...	1504	1533	...	1604	1633	...	1704	1733	...	1804	1833	...	1904	1933	2008	...	2105	2202	2317	0005
Oberried d.	...	1314	...	1346	|	1446	...	|	1546	...	|	1646	...	|	1746	...	|	1846	...	|	1946	2020	...	2117	2213	2328	0016
Brienz d.	...	1324	...	1357	1424	1457	...	1524	1557	...	1624	1657	...	1724	1757	...	1824	1857	...	1924	1957	2031	...	2129	2223	2338	0026
Meiringen ● a.	...	1335	...	1409	1435	1509	...	1535	1609	...	1635	1709	...	1735	1809	...	1835	1909	...	1935	2009	2043	...	2141	2235	2350	0038
Meiringen ● d.	...	1346	...	▬	1446	▬	...	1546	▬	...	1646	▬	...	1746	▬	...	1846	▬	...	1946	▬	...	2051	▬	▬	...	...
Brünig Hasliberg d.	...	1357	...	...	1457	...	...	1557	...	...	1657	...	...	1757	...	...	1857	...	...	1957	...	...	2102	...	...	...	...
Lungern d.	...	1410	...	...	1510	...	...	1610	...	...	1710	...	...	1810	...	...	1910	...	...	2010	...	...	2115	...	...	...	...
Giswil d.	1406	1429	1436	1506	1529	1536	1606	1629	1636	1706	1729	1736	1806	1829	1836	1906	1929	1936	2006	2029	2106	...	2136	2206	2306	...	...
Sachseln d.	1415	|	1445	1515	|	1545	1615	|	1645	1715	|	1745	1815	|	1845	1915	|	1945	2015	|	2115	...	2145	2215	2315	...	...
Sarnen d.	1420	1440	1450	1520	1540	1550	1620	1640	1650	1720	1740	1750	1820	1840	1850	1920	1940	1950	2020	2040	2120	...	2150	2220	2320	...	...
Alpnach Dorf d.	1425	1445	1455	1525	1545	1555	1625	1645	1655	1725	1745	1755	1825	1845	1855	1925	1945	1955	2025	2045	2125	...	2155	2225	2325	...	...
Alpnachstad d.	1430	|	1500	1530	|	1600	1630	|	1700	1730	|	1800	1830	|	1900	1930	|	2000	2030	|	2130	...	2200	2230	2330	...	...
Hergiswil **552** d.	1438	1454	1508	1538	1554	1608	1638	1654	1708	1738	1754	1808	1838	1854	1908	1938	1954	2008	2038	2054	2138	...	2208	2238	2338	...	...
Luzern 552 a.	1452	1504	1522	1552	1604	1622	1652	1704	1722	1752	1804	1822	1852	1904	1922	1952	2004	2022	2052	2104	2152	...	2222	2252	2352	...	...

P – GOLDENPASS PANORAMIC – Conveys (1) [observation car] and (12). Also conveys ✕ on most services (Reservation recommended for observation car).

j – Not Dec. 25, 26, Jan. 1, 2, Apr. 2.

n – ⚒ Dec. 14 - May 12; daily May 13 - Aug. 22; ①–⑥ Aug. 23 - Dec. 11.

q – © May 13 - Aug. 22.

● – Rail service **Meiringen - Innertkirchen** and v.v. Narrow gauge. 2nd class only. *5 km*. Journey time: 11 minutes. **Operator**: MIB. Trains run from **Meiringen MIB** (300 metres from ZB station).

From **Meiringen MIB**: 0617Ⓐ, 0642Ⓐ, 0717, 0742, 0817⚒, 0842, 0942, 1042, 1117Ⓐ, 1142, 1217⚒, 1242, 1317**n**, 1342, 1417**q**, 1442, 1517**q**, 1542, 1617**n**, 1642, 1717Ⓐ, 1742, 1817Ⓐ, 1842, 1917, 1942, 2049, 2149, 2300⑤⑥.

From **Innertkirchen**: 0557Ⓐ, 0628Ⓐ, 0700, 0728, 0800, 0828⚒, 0900, 1000, 1100, 1128Ⓐ, 1200, 1228⚒, 1300, 1328**n**, 1400, 1428**q**, 1500, 1528**q**, 1600, 1628**n**, 1700, 1728Ⓐ, 1800, 1828Ⓐ, 1900, 1928, 2000, 2100, 2220⑤⑥.

562 SPIEZ - BRIG (via Lötschberg pass)

BLS

km		*RE* 3253	*RE* 3255 T	*RE* 3257	*RE* 3259	*RE* 3261		*CNL* 1179 ♦		*RE* 3263	*RE* 3265	*RE* 3267	*RE* 3269	*RE* 3271	*RE* 3273		*RE* 3275	*RE* 3277	*RE* 3279	*RE* 3281	*RE* 3283	*RE* 3285		*IC* 1097 ⑦	*RE* 3251
	Bern d.	...	...	0740	0840	0940	...	...	...	1040c	1140e	1240e	1340e	1440e	1540e	...	1640	1740	1840	1940	...	...	...	2235	...
0	**Spiez** d.	0612	0712	0812	0912	1012	...	1047s	...	1112	1212	1312	1412	1512	1612	...	1712	1812	1912	2012	2112	2212	...	2305	0012
14	Frutigen ● d.	0625	0725	0825	0925	1025	...	1059s	...	1125	1225	1325	1425	1525	1625	...	1725	1825	1925	2025	2125	2225	...	2317	0025
31	Kandersteg 🚗 d.	0642	0742	0842	0942	1042	...	1116s	...	1142	1242	1342	1442	1542	1642	...	1742	1842	1942	2042	2142	2242	...	2333	0042
48	Goppenstein 🚗 d.	0657	0757	0857	0957	1057	...	1130s	...	1157	1257	1357	1457	1557	1657	...	1757	1857	1957	2057	2157	2257	...	2345	0053
74	**Brig** a.	0724	0824	0924	1024	1124	...	1156	...	1224	1324	1424	1524	1624	1724	...	1824	1924	2024	2124	2224	2324	...	0009	0120

	RE 3256	*IC* 811 R	*RE* 3256	*RE* 3258	*RE* 3260	*RE* 3262	*RE* 3264	*RE* 3266	*RE* 3268		*RE* 3270	*RE* 3272	*RE* 3274	*RE* 3276	*RE* 3278		*CNL* 1178 ♦		*RE* 3280	*RE* 3282	*RE* 3284	*RE* 3286	*RE* 3288	
Brig d.	0516	0547	...	0636	0736	0836	0936	1036	1136	...	1236	1336	1436	1536	1636	...	1700	...	1736	1836	1936	2040	2207	...
Goppenstein 🚗 d.	0542	|	...	0701	0801	0901	1001	1101	1201	...	1301	1401	1501	1601	1701	...	1723u	...	1801	1901	2001	2105	2232	...
Kandersteg 🚗 d.	0553	|	←	0712	0812	0912	1012	1112	1212	...	1312	1412	1512	1612	1712	...	1738u	...	1812	1912	2012	2116	2243	...
Frutigen ● d.	0609	0613	0632	0732	0832	0932	1032	1132	1232	...	1332	1432	1532	1632	1732	...	1757u	...	1832	1932	2032	2132	2301	...
Spiez a.	→	0624	0647	0747	0847	0947	1047	1147	1247	...	1347	1447	1547	1647	1747	...	1813u	...	1847	1947	2047	2147	2314	...
Bern a.	...	0654	0720	0820	0920	1020c	1120e	1220e	1320e	...	1420e	1520e	1620	1720	1820	...	...	...	1920	...	...	...	...	...

♦ – **NOTES** (LISTED BY TRAIN NUMBER)

1178/9 – *City Night Line* KOMET – For days of running and composition – see Table **73**.

R – (12) and ✕ Brig - Romanshorn.
T – From Thun.
c – © only.
e – † only.
s – Stops to set down only.
u – Stops to pick up only.

🚗 – Car-carrying shuttle available (see page 258).

● – 🚌 **SERVICE FRUTIGEN - ADELBODEN and v.v.**: 20 km, journey 30 minutes.
Operator: AFA, 3715 Adelboden. ✆ +41 (0)33 673 74 74, fax +41 (0)33 673 74 70.
From **Frutigen**: 0615Ⓐ, 0631, 0700Ⓐ, 0731, 0800, 0831, 0900©, 0931, 1000©, 1031 and hourly until 1631, then 1700, 1731, 1800, 1831, 1900, 1931, 2031, 2134, 2231, 2331.
From **Adelboden**: 0535Ⓐ, 0550, 0622Ⓐ, 0650, 0730, 0750, 0830©, 0850, 0930©, 0950, 1050 and hourly until 1550, then 1630, 1650, 1730, 1750, 1830, 1850, 1950, 2050, 2150, 2228.

BLS — SPIEZ - ZWEISIMMEN — 563

km		⚒	†	⚒	†	†	⚒		©q	†	⚒	G		⚒	†			⚒	†	⚒	†	G	⚒	†	⚒	†	†	⚒
	Interlaken Ost **560** d.	...		...			...	...	...		...	0908	...	...		...	...	...		...		1308	...		...		1508	1508
0	**Spiez 560** d.	0605	0608	0707	0712	0735	0740	0812	0845	0912	0914	0935	1012	1107	1112	1135	...	1209	1212	1309	1312	1335	1409	1412	1508	1512	1535	1541
11	Erlenbach im Simmental d.	0624	0627	0723	0728	0750	0756	0828	|	0928	0929	0949	1028	1122	1128	1150	...	1227	1228	1326	1328	1349	1426	1428	1525	1528	1550	1555
26	Boltigen d.	0642	0645	0741	0746	0810	0811	0846	0909	0946	0947	1009	1046	1146	1146	1209	...	1245	1246	1345	1346	1408	1444	1446	1544	1546	1610	1610
35	**Zweisimmen** a.	0652	0655	0751	0756	0819	0820	0856	0919	0956	0957	1019	1056	1156	1156	1219	...	1256	1256	1356	1356	1419	1454	1456	1554	1556	1619	1619

	⚒	†	Ⓐ		G		Ⓐ					
Interlaken Ost **560** d.	...	...	...	...	1708	...	...	...	...	...	...	...
Spiez 560 d.	1607	1612	1642	1712	1742	1814	1843	1912	2012	2107	2207	2339
Erlenbach im Simmental d.	1627	1628	1655	1728	1755	1828	1856	1930	2030	2122	2222	2354
Boltigen d.	1645	1646	1710	1746	1811	1846	1912	1947	2047	2140	2240	0012
Zweisimmen a.	1656	1656	1720	1756	1820	1856	1921	1957	2057	2150	2250	0022

	Ⓐ	⚒	†	Ⓐ	⚒	†	Ⓐ					
Zweisimmen d.	0540	0556	0559	0634	0657	0701	0732	...	0801	0900	0937	1001
Boltigen d.	0547	0606	0609	0645	0706	0710	0741	...	0810	0909	0947	1010
Erlenbach im Simmental d.	0605	0625	0628	0701	0725	0729	0757	...	0829	0929	1003	1029
Spiez 560 a.	0619	0640	0643	0718	0740	0744	0812	...	0843	0946	1021	1045
Interlaken Ost **560** a.	...	...	...	...	...	...	...	...	...	...	...	...

	†	⚒	G			⚒	†			⚒	†	⚒	†	G			©q										
Zweisimmen d.	1101	1107	1138	...	1200	1259	1301	1337	...	1359	1401	1458	1501	1536	...	1600	1636	1701	1738	...	1801	1903	2003	2108	2208	2307	...
Boltigen d.	1110	1116	1147	...	1210	1308	1310	1346	...	1409	1410	1507	1510	1545	...	1610	1645	1710	1746	...	1810	1912	2012	2117	2217	2316	...
Erlenbach im Simmental d.	1129	1134	1203	...	1228	1327	1329	1402	...	1427	1429	1526	1529	1606	...	1628	|	1729	1806	...	1829	1931	2031	2135	2235	2334	...
Spiez 560 a.	1144	1150	1221	...	1244	1346	1344	1421	...	1443	1443	1541	1544	1621	...	1643	1711	1742	1821	...	1843	1946	2046	2150	2250	2351	...
Interlaken Ost **560** a.	...	...	1250	...	...	...	...	1450	...	...	...	...	...	1650	...	...	...	...	1850	...	...	...	...	...	...	...	...

G – GOLDEN PASS PANORAMIC – Ⓡ for groups.

q – Also Apr. 5; not Dec. 26, Jan. 2.

Narrow gauge rack railway. BOB, WAB, JB — INTERLAKEN - KLEINE SCHEIDEGG - JUNGFRAUJOCH — 564

km						j	v			j	j			j	j			j	v			j	j			j	
0	**Interlaken Ost** d.	0635	0635	0705	0705	0735	0735	0805	0805	0835	0835	0905	0905	0935	0935	1005	1005	1035	1035	1105	1105	1135	1135	1205	1205	1235	1305
3	Wilderswil ▲ d.	0640	0640	0710	0710	0740	0740	0810	0810	0840	0840	0910	0910	0940	0940	1010	1010	1040	1040	1110	1110	1140	1140	1210	1210	1240	1310
8	Zweilütschinen d.	0646	0647	0716	0717	0746	0747	0816	0817	0846	0847	0916	0917	0946	0947	1016	1017	1046	1047	1116	1117	1146	1147	1216	1217	1246	1316
12	**Lauterbrunnen** ● a.	0655	|	0725	|	0755	|	0825	|	0855	|	0925	|	0955	|	1025	|	1055	|	1125	|	1155	|	1225	|	1255	1325
	change trains		|		|		|		|	j	|		|		|		|	j	|		|		|		|	j	
12	**Lauterbrunnen** d.	0659	|	0739	|	0804	|	0830	|	0913	|	0939	|	1004	|	1030	|	1113	|	1139	|	1204	|	1230	|	1313	1339
16	Wengen a.	0712	|	0753	|	0818	|	0844	|	0927	|	0953	|	1018	|	1044	|	1127	|	1153	|	1218	|	1244	|	1327	1353
16	Wengen d.	0715	|	0759	|	0824j	|	0849	|	0934	|	0959	|	1024j	|	1049	|	1134	|	1159	|	1224j	|	1249	|	1334	1359
19	Grindelwald a.	|	0709	|	0739	|	0809	|	0839	|	0909	|	0939	|	1009	|	1039	|	1109	|	1139	|	1209	|	1239	|	|
	change trains	|	|	|	|	|	j	|	|	|	j	|	|	|	j	|	|	|	j	|	|	|	j	|	|	|	|
19	Grindelwald d.	|	0717	|	0747	|	0817	|	0847	|	0917	|	0947	|	1017	|	1047	|	1117	|	1147	|	1217	|	1247	|	|
20	Grindelwald Grund d.	|	0725	|	0755	|	0825	|	0855	|	0925	|	0955	|	1025	|	1055	|	1125	|	1155	|	1225	|	1255	|	|
23	**Kleine Scheidegg** a.	0739	0750	0824	0820	0849j	0850	0914	0920	1004	0950	1024	1020	1049j	1050	1114	1120	1204	1150	1224	1220	1249j	1250	1314	1320	1402	1424

				j			j	j			j	j			v			⚒	⚒								
Interlaken Ost d.	1305	1405	1405	1435	1505	1505	1535	1535	1605	1605	1635	1635	1705	1705	1735	1805	1805	1835	1835	1905	1905	2001	2005	2101	2105	2201	2205
Wilderswil ▲ d.	1310	1410	1410	1440	1510	1510	1540	1540	1610	1610	1640	1640	1710	1710	1740	1810	1810	1840	1840	1910	1910	2006	2010	2106	2110	2206	2210
Zweilütschinen d.	1317	1416	1417	1447	1516	1517	1546	1547	1616	1617	1646	1647	1716	1717	1746	1816	1817	1846	1847	1916	1917	2012	2016	2112	2116	2212	2216
Lauterbrunnen ● a.	|	1425	|	|	1525	|	1555	|	1625	|	1655	|	1725	|	1755	1825	|	1855	|	1925	|	2021	|	2121	|	2221	|
change trains	|		|	|		|		|		|		|		|			|		|		|		|		|		|
Lauterbrunnen d.	|	1430	|	|	1539	|	1604	|	1630	|	1713	|	1739	|	1804	1830	|	1904	|	1930	|	2030	|	2130	|	2230	|
Wengen a.	|	1444	|	|	1553	|	1618	|	1644	|	1727	|	1753	|	1818	1844	|	1918	|	1944	|	2044	|	2144	|	2244	|
Wengen d.	|	1449	|	|	1559	|	1624k	|	1649	|	...	|	1759j	|	...	...	|	...	|	...	|	...	|	...	|	...	|
Grindelwald a.	1339	|	1439	1509	|	1539	|	1609	|	1639	...	1709	|	1739	...	...	1839	...	1909	...	1939	...	2035	...	2135	...	2235
change trains		|		j	|		|	j	|			j	|	j					j								
Grindelwald d.	1347	|	1447	1517	|	1547	|	1617	|	1647	...	1717	|	1747	...	...	1847	...	1917	...	...	...	...	...	...	...	...
Grindelwald Grund d.	1355	|	1455	1525	|	1555	|	1625	|	1655	...	1722	|	1755	...	...	1852	...	1922	...	...	...	...	...	...	...	...
Kleine Scheidegg a.	1420	1514	1520	1550	1624	1620	1649k	1650k	1714	1720	...	...	1824j	1820	...	...	...	...	...	...	...	...	...	...	...	...	...

												j		t				j				j				j	
Kleine Scheidegg d.	...	...		...	...	...	...	...	...	...	...	...	0744t	0803	0831	0833	0856j	0903	0925	0933	0944j	1003	1031	1033	1056j	1103	1125
Grindelwald Grund d.	...	...		...	...	...	...	0708	...	0738	...	0808	|	0838	|	0908	|	0938	|	1008	|	1038	|	1108	|	1138	|
Grindelwald a.	...	...		...	...	...	...	0712	...	0742	...	0812	|	0842	|	0912	|	0942	|	1012	|	1042	|	1112	|	1142	|
change trains			⚒							v			|	j	|		|	j	|		|	j	|		|	j	|
Grindelwald d.	0519	...	0546	...	0619	...	...	0719	...	0749	...	0819	|	0849	|	0919	|	0949	|	1019	|	1049	|	1119	|	1149	|
Wengen a.	|	...	|	...	|	...		|	...	|	...	|	0815t	|	0904	|	0929j	|	0953	|	1015j	|	1104	|	1129j	|	1153
Wengen d.	|	0512	|	0606	|	0641	0713	|	0737	|	0802	|	0828	|	0911	|	0937	|	1002	|	1028	|	1111	|	1137	|	1202
Lauterbrunnen a.	|	0528	|	0623	|	0657	0729	|	0754	|	0819	|	0845	|	0928	|	0954	|	1019	|	1045	|	1128	|	1154	|	1219
change trains	|		|		|	v		|	j	|		|	j	|		|	j	|		|	j	|		|	j	|	
Lauterbrunnen ● d.	|	0534	|	0633	|	0703	0733	|	0803	|	0833	|	0903	|	0933	|	1003	|	1033	|	1103	|	1133	|	1203	|	1233
Zweilütschinen d.	0540	0544	0611	0643	0643	0713	0743	0743	0813	0813	0843	0843	0913	0913	0943	0943	1013	1013	1043	1043	1113	1113	1143	1143	1213	1213	1243
Wilderswil ▲ d.	0546	0549	0617	0649	0649	0719	0749	0749	0819	0819	0849	0849	0919	0919	0949	0949	1019	1019	1049	1049	1119	1119	1149	1149	1219	1219	1249
Interlaken Ost a.	0550	0554	0622	0654	0654	0724	0754	0754	0824	0824	0854	0854	0924	0924	0954	0954	1024	1024	1054	1054	1124	1124	1154	1154	1224	1224	1254

							j				j				j				j			j					
Kleine Scheidegg d.	1133	1231	1233	1325	1333	1344j	1403	1431	1433	1456j	1503	1525	1533	1544j	1603	1631	1633	1656j	1703	1725	1733	1833	1830j	...	...	...	...
Grindelwald Grund d.	1208	|	1308	|	1408	|	1438	|	1508	|	1538	|	1608	|	1638	|	1708	|	1738	|	1808	1908	|	...	...	...	...
Grindelwald a.	1212	|	1312	|	1412	|	1442	|	1512	|	1542	|	1612	|	1642	|	1712	|	1742	|	1812	1912	|	...	...	...	...
change trains		|		|		|	j	|		|	j	|		|	j	|		|	v	|			|				
Grindelwald d.	1219	|	1319	|	1419	|	1449	|	1519	|	1549	|	1619	|	1649	|	1719	|	1749	|	1819	1919	|	2019	...	2119	...
Wengen a.	|	1304	|	1353	|	1415j	|	1504	|	1529j	|	1553	|	1615j	|	1704	|	1726j	|	1753	|	|	1858j	|	...	|	...
Wengen d.	|	1311	|	1402	|	1428	|	1511	|	1537	|	1602	|	1628	|	1711	|	1737	|	1802	|	|	1902	|	2002	|	2108
Lauterbrunnen a.	|	1328	|	1419	|	1445	|	1528	|	1554	|	1619	|	1645	|	1728	|	1754	|	1819	|	|	1919	|	2019	|	2125
change trains	|		|		|	j	|		|	j	|		|	j	|		|	v	|		|	|		|		|	
Lauterbrunnen ● d.	|	1333	|	1433	|	1503	|	1533	|	1603	|	1633	|	1703	|	1733	|	1803	|	1833	|	|	1933	|	2033	|	2133
Zweilütschinen d.	1243	1343	1343	1543	1443	1513	1513	1543	1543	1613	1613	1643	1643	1713	1713	1743	1743	1813	1813	1843	1843	1940	1944	2040	2044	2140	2144
Wilderswil ▲ d.	1249	1349	1349	1449	1449	1519	1519	1549	1549	1619	1619	1649	1649	1719	1719v	1749	1749	1819	1819	1849	1849	1946	1950	2046	2050	2146	2150
Interlaken Ost a.	1254	1354	1354	1454	1454	1524	1524	1554	1554	1624	1624	1654	1654	1724	1724v	1754	1754	1824	1824	1854	1854	1950	1954	2050	2054	2150	2154

At times of heavy snowfall (November 1 - April 30) the Eigergletscher - Jungfraujoch service is subject to cancellation

km				t		t		t			t		t		t			t		t			t	
0	**Kleine Scheidegg** d.	0800	0830	0900	0930	1000	1030	1100	1130	...	1200	1230	1300	1330	1400	1430	...	1500	1530	1630	...	1730	1840	...
2	Eigergletscher d.	0810	0840	0910	0940	1010	1040	1110	1140	...	1210	1240	1310	1340	1410	1440	...	1510	1540	1640	...	1740	1850	...
9	**Jungfraujoch** a.	0852	0922	0952	1022	1052	1122	1152	1222	...	1252	1322	1352	1422	1452	1522	...	1552	1622	1716	...	...	...	...

	t		t			t			t		t			t		t			t			t	
Jungfraujoch d.	0900	0930	1000	...	1030	1100	1130	...	1200	1230	1300	1330	...	1400	1430	1500	1530	...	1600	1640	...	1745	...
Eigergletscher d.	0940	1010	1040	...	1110	1140	1210	...	1240	1310	1340	1410	...	1440	1510	1540	1610	...	1640	1710	...	1810	...
Kleine Scheidegg a.	0950	1020	1050	...	1120	1150	1220	...	1250	1320	1350	1420	...	1450	1520	1550	1620	...	1650	1720	...	1820	...

h – June 19 - Sept. 26.
j – Dec. 13 - Apr. 11, May 1 - Oct. 24.
k – Jan. 23 - Apr. 11, May 1 - Oct. 24.
m – Dec. 19 - Apr. 11, May 22 - Oct. 17.
t – May 1 - Oct. 24.
v – ①–⑥ (also ⑦ Dec. 13 - Apr. 17, May 2 - Oct. 30).

Additional trains run between Lauterbrunnen, Wengen and Jungfraujoch and between Grindelwald and Jungfraujoch.

● – Cableway operates **Lauterbrunnen - Grütschalp**, and narrow gauge railway **Grütschalp - Mürren**, *total: 5 km.* **Operator**: BLM. Journey time: 20 minutes allowing for the connection.
From **Lauterbrunnen**: 0610, 0631, 0701, 0731, 0801 and every 30 minutes◆ until 1831, then 1931, 2031 **m**.
From **Mürren**: 0606, 0636, 0706 and every 30 minutes◆ until 1906, then 2006 **m**.
◆ – Additional services available Dec. 19 - Apr. 11, May 22 - Oct. 17.

▲ – Narrow gauge rack railway operates **May 22 - Oct. 17 Wilderswil - Schynige Platte.** *7 km.* Journey time: 52 minutes. **Operator**: SPB, ✆ 033 828 73 51. Service may be reduced In bad weather.
From **Wilderswil**: 0725, 0805 **h**, 0845, 0925, 1005, 1045, 1125, 1205 **h**, 1245, 1325, 1405, 1445, 1525, 1605 **h**, 1645.
From **Schynige Platte**: 0821, 0901 **h**, 0941, 1021, 1101, 1141, 1221 **h**, 1301, 1341, 1421, 1501, 1541, 1621, 1701 **h**, 1753.

565 BASEL, OLTEN and BERN - LUZERN SBB

km		IR 2451	ICN 663	RE 3557	IR 2509	IR 2159	IR 2453	RE 3559	IR 2511	IR 2163		IR 2455	RE 3561	IR 2515	IR 2165	IR 2457	RE 3565	IR 2517	ICN 671	IR 2459	RE 3567	IR 2519	IR 2169	IR 2461	RE 3569	IR 2521	ICN 675
									🍷					🍷				🍷	✕			🍷				🍷	✕
		Ⓐ	G		m	L				L					L				G				L				G
	Genève Aéroport + 505 d.	...	...	...	...	...	...	...	...	...	...	...	...	...	...	...	...	0701	...	...	...	0801	...	...	...	0901	...
	Genève 505 d.	...	...	...	...	...	...	...	0456	...	...	...	...	0610	...	...	...	0710	...	...	...	0810	...	...	...	0910	...
	Lausanne 505 d.	...	...	...	0445	...	...	...	0545	...	...	...	...	0645	...	...	...	0745	...	...	...	0845	...	...	...	0945	...
0	**Basel SBB** d.	...	0503	...	|	0603	0615	...	|	0703	...	0715	...	|	0803	0815	...	|	0903	0915	...	|	1003	1015	...	|	1103
14	Liestal d.	...	|	...	|	|	0627	...	|	|	...	0727	...	|	|	0827	...	|	|	0927	...	|	|	1027	...	|	|
21	Sissach d.	...	|	...	|	|	0633	...	|	|	...	0733	...	|	|	0833	...	|	|	0933	...	|	|	1033	...	|	|
39	**Olten** a.	...	0528	...	|	0628	0647	...	|	0728	...	0747	...	|	0828	0847	...	|	0928	0947	...	|	1028	1047	...	|	1128
39	**Olten** d.	0549	0530	0606	|	0630	0649	0706	|	0730	...	0749	0806	|	0830	0849	0906	|	0930	0949	1006	|	1030	1049	1106	|	1130
	Bern d.	|	|	|	0600	|	|	|	0700	|	...	|	|	0800	|	|	|	0900	|	|	|	1000	|	|	|	1100	|
47	Zofingen d.	0558	|	0612	0628	|	0658	0712	0728	|	...	0758	0812	0828	|	0858	0912	0928	|	0958	1012	1028	|	1058	1112	1128	|
69	Sursee d.	0611	|	0632	0641	|	0711	0732	0741	|	...	0811	0832	0841	|	0911	0932	0941	|	1011	1032	1041	|	1111	1132	1141	|
95	**Luzern** a.	0630	0605	0656	0700	0705	0730	0756	0800	0805	...	0830	0856	0900	0905	0930	0956	1000	1005	1030	1056	1100	1105	1130	1156	1200	1205

	IR 2463	RE 3571	IR 2523	IR 2173	IR 2465	RE 3573	IR 2525	ICN 679	IR 2467	RE 3575	IR 2527	IR 2177	IR 2469	RE 3577	IR 2529	ICN 683	IR 2471	RE 3579	IR 2531	IR 2181	IR 2473	RE 3581	IR 2535	ICN 687	IR 2475	RE 3585	IR 2537
			🍷				🍷	✕			🍷				🍷	✕			🍷				🍷	✕			🍷
				L				G				L				G				L				C			
Genève Aéroport + 505 d.	...	...	1001	...	...	...	1101	...	...	...	1201	...	...	...	1301	...	...	...	1401	...	...	...	1501	...	...	...	1601
Genève 505 d.	...	...	1010	...	...	...	1110	...	...	...	1210	...	...	...	1310	...	...	...	1410	...	...	...	1510	...	...	...	1610
Lausanne 505 d.	...	...	1045	...	...	...	1145	...	...	...	1245	...	...	...	1345	...	...	...	1445	...	...	...	1545	...	...	...	1645
Basel SBB d.	1115	...	|	1203	1215	...	|	1303	1315	...	|	1403	1415	...	|	1503	1515	...	|	1603	1615	...	|	1703	1715	...	|
Liestal d.	1127	...	|	|	1227	...	|	|	1327	...	|	|	1427	...	|	|	1527	...	|	|	1627	...	|	|	1727	...	|
Sissach d.	1133	...	|	|	1233	...	|	|	1333	...	|	|	1433	...	|	|	1533	...	|	|	1633	...	|	|	1733	...	|
Olten a.	1147	...	|	1228	1247	...	|	1328	1347	...	|	1428	1447	...	|	1528	1547	...	|	1628	1647	...	|	1728	1747	...	|
Olten d.	1149	1206	|	1230	1249	1306	|	1330	1349	1406	|	1430	1449	1506	|	1530	1549	1606	|	1630	1649	1706	|	1730	1749	1806	|
Bern d.	|	|	1200	|	|	|	1300	|	|	|	1400	|	|	|	1500	|	|	|	1600	|	|	|	1700	|	|	|	1800
Zofingen d.	1158	1212	1228	|	1258	1312	1328	|	1358	1412	1428	|	1458	1512	1528	|	1558	1612	1628	|	1658	1712	1728	|	1758	1812	1828
Sursee d.	1211	1232	1241	|	1311	1332	1341	|	1411	1432	1441	|	1511	1532	1541	|	1611	1632	1641	|	1711	1732	1741	|	1811	1832	1841
Luzern a.	1230	1256	1300	1305	1330	1356	1400	1405	1430	1456	1500	1505	1530	1556	1600	1605	1630	1656	1700	1705	1730	1756	1800	1805	1830	1856	1900

	IR 2187	IR 2477	RE 3587	IR 2539	ICN 691	IR 2479	RE 3589	IR 2541	IR 2191	IR 2481	RE 3591	IR 2543	IR 2193	IR 2483	RE 3593	IR 2545	IR 2195	IR 2485	RE 3595	IR 2547	IR 2199	IR 2487	RE 3597	IR 2151	IR 2489	IR 2153	
					✕																						
	C				C				E											⑦w						⑥⑦q	
Genève Aéroport + 505 d.	...	...	...	1701	...	...	...	1801	...	...	...	1901	...	...	...	2001	...	...	...	2047	...	...	...	...	...	...	...
Genève 505 d.	...	...	...	1710	...	...	...	1810	...	...	...	1910	...	...	...	2010	...	...	...	2056	...	...	...	...	...	...	...
Lausanne 505 d.	...	...	...	1745	...	...	...	1845	...	...	...	1945	...	...	...	2045	...	...	...	2145	...	...	...	...	...	...	...
Basel SBB d.	1803	1815	...	|	1903	1915	...	|	2003	2015	...	|	2103	2115	...	|	2203	2215	...	|	2303	2315	...	0003	0015	0101	...
Liestal d.	|	1827	...	|	|	1927	...	|	|	2027	...	|	|	2127	...	|	|	2227	...	|	|	2327	...	|	0027	0110	...
Sissach d.	|	1833	...	|	|	1933	...	|	|	2033	...	|	|	2133	...	|	|	2233	...	|	|	2333	...	|	0033	0116	...
Olten a.	1828	1847	...	|	1928	1947	...	|	2028	2047	...	|	2128	2147	...	|	2228	2247	...	|	2328	2347	...	0028	0047	0128	...
Olten d.	1830	1849	1906	|	1930	1949	2006	|	2030	2049	2106	|	2130	2149	2206	|	2230	2249	2306	|	2330	2349	0006	0033	...	0136	...
Bern d.	|	|	|	1900	|	|	|	2000	|	|	|	2100	|	|	|	2200	|	|	|	2300	|	|	|	|	...	|	...
Zofingen d.	|	1858	1912	1928	|	1958	2012	2028	|	2058	2112	2128	|	2158	2212	2228	|	2256	2312	2328	|	2356	0012	|	...	0143	...
Sursee d.	|	1911	1932	1941	|	2011	2032	2041	|	2111	2132	2141	|	2211	2232	2241	|	...	2332	2341	|	...	0034	0051	...	0157	...
Luzern a.	1905	1930	1956	2000	2005	2030	2056	2100	2105	2130	2156	2200	2205	2230	2256	2300	2305	...	2356	2400	0005	...	0056	0110	...	0215	...

km (via hsl)		RE 3554	IR 2452	IR 2160	IR 2508	RE 3558	IR 2454	IR 2162	IR 2510	RE 3560	IR 2456	IR 2164	IR 2512	RE 3562	IR 2458	IR 2166	IR 2516	RE 3566	IR 2460	ICN 658		IR 2518	RE 3568	IR 2462	IR 2170	IR 2520	RE 3570
									🍷				🍷				🍷			✕		🍷				🍷	
			Ⓐ									E				B				C					C		
	Luzern d.	0456	0530	0554	0600	0604	0630	0654	0700	0704	0730	0754	0800	0804	0830	0854	0900	0904	0930	0954	...	1000	1004	1030	1054	1100	1104
	Sursee d.	0521	0548	|	0618	0626	0648	|	0718	0726	0748	|	0818	0826	0848	|	0918	0926	0948	|	...	1018	1026	1048	|	1118	1126
0	Zofingen d.	0543	0602	|	0632	0645	0702	|	0732	0745	0802	|	0832	0845	0902	|	0932	0945	1002	|	...	1032	1045	1102	|	1132	1145
63	**Bern** a.	|	|	|	0700	|	|	|	0800	|	|	|	0900	|	|	|	1000	|	|	|	...	1100	|	|	|	1200	|
	Olten a.	0552	0610	0627	|	0652	0710	0727	|	0752	0810	0827	|	0852	0910	0927	|	0952	1010	1027	...	|	1052	1110	1127	|	1152
	Olten d.	...	0612	0629	|	...	0712	0729	|	...	0812	0829	|	...	0912	0929	|	...	1012	1029	...	|	...	1112	1129	|	...
	Sissach d.	...	0627	|	|	...	0727	|	|	...	0827	|	|	...	0927	|	|	...	1027	|	...	|	...	1127	|	|	...
	Liestal d.	...	0633	|	|	...	0733	|	|	...	0833	|	|	...	0933	|	|	...	1034	|	...	|	...	1133	|	|	...
	Basel SBB a.	...	0644	0653	|	...	0744	0753	|	...	0844	0853	|	...	0944	0953	|	...	1044	1053	...	|	...	1144	1153	|	...
	Lausanne 505 a.	...	...	...	0815	...	...	...	0915	...	...	...	1015	...	...	...	1115	...	...	...	...	1215	...	...	...	1315	...
	Genève 505 a.	...	...	...	0850	...	...	...	0950	...	...	...	1050	...	...	...	1150	...	...	...	...	1250	...	...	...	1350	...
	Genève Aéroport + 505 a.	...	...	...	0859	...	...	...	0959	...	...	...	1059	...	...	...	1159	...	...	...	...	1259	...	...	...	1359	...

	IR 2464	ICN 662	IR 2522	RE 3572	IR 2466	IR 2174	IR 2524	RE 3574	IR 2468	ICN 666	IR 2526	RE 3576	IR 2470	IR 2178		IR 2528	RE 3578	IR 2472	ICN 670	IR 2530	RE 3580	IR 2474	IR 2182	IR 2532	RE 3582	IR 2476	ICN 674
		✕	🍷				🍷			✕	🍷			🍷		🍷			✕	🍷				🍷			✕
		C				L				G				L					G				L				G
Luzern d.	1130	1154	1200	1204	1230	1254	1300	1304	1330	1354	1400	1404	1430	1454	...	1500	1504	1530	1554	1600	1604	1630	1654	1700	1704	1730	1754
Sursee d.	1148	|	1218	1226	1248	|	1318	1326	1348	|	1418	1426	1448	|	...	1518	1526	1548	|	1618	1626	1648	|	1718	1726	1748	|
Zofingen d.	1202	|	1232	1245	1302	|	1332	1345	1402	|	1432	1445	1502	|	...	1532	1545	1602	|	1632	1645	1702	|	1732	1745	1802	|
Bern a.	|	|	1300	|	|	|	1400	|	|	|	1500	|	|	|	...	1600	|	|	|	1700	|	|	|	1800	|	|	|
Olten a.	1210	1227	|	1252	1310	1327	|	1352	1410	1427	|	1452	1510	1527	...	|	1552	1610	1627	|	1652	1710	1727	|	1752	1810	1827
Olten d.	1212	1229	|	...	1312	1329	|	...	1412	1429	|	...	1512	1529	...	|	...	1612	1629	|	...	1712	1729	|	...	1812	1829
Sissach d.	1227	|	|	...	1327	|	|	...	1427	|	|	...	1527	|	...	|	...	1627	|	|	...	1727	|	|	...	1827	|
Liestal d.	1233	|	|	...	1333	|	|	...	1433	|	|	...	1533	|	...	|	...	1633	|	|	...	1733	|	|	...	1833	|
Basel SBB a.	1244	1253	|	...	1344	1353	|	...	1444	1453	|	...	1544	1553	...	|	...	1644	1653	|	...	1744	1753	|	...	1844	1853
Lausanne 505 a.	...	...	1415	...	...	...	1515	...	...	...	1615	...	...	...	...	1715	...	...	...	1815	...	...	...	1915	...	...	...
Genève 505 a.	...	...	1450	...	...	...	1550	...	...	...	1650	...	...	...	...	1750	...	...	...	1850	...	...	...	1950	...	...	...
Genève Aéroport + 505 a.	...	...	1459	...	...	...	1559	...	...	...	1659	...	...	...	...	1759	...	...	...	1859	...	...	...	1959	...	...	...

	IR 2536	RE 3586	IR 2478	IR 2188	IR 2538	RE 3588	IR 2480		ICN 678	IR 2540	RE 3590	IR 2482	IR 2192	IR 2542	RE 3592	IR 2484	ICN 682	IR 2544	RE 3594	IR 2486	IR 2196	IR 2546	RE 3596	IR 2488	ICN 686	RE 3598	IR 2150
	🍷			🍷					✕																		
				L					G				L				G				L				G		⑥⑦q
Luzern d.	1800	1804	1830	1854	1900	1904	1930	...	1954	2000	2004	2030	2054	2100	2104	2130	2154	2200	2204	...	2254	2300	2304	...	2354	0004	0049
Sursee d.	1818	1826	1848	|	1918	1926	1948	...	|	2018	2026	2048	|	2118	2126	2148	|	2218	2226	...	|	2318	2326	...	|	0026	0108
Zofingen d.	1832	1845	1902	|	1932	1945	2002	...	|	2032	2045	2102	|	2132	2145	2202	|	2232	2245	2302	|	2332	2345	0005	|	0045	0121
Bern a.	1900	|	|	|	2000	|	|	...	|	2100	|	|	|	2200	|	|	|	2300	|	|	|	2400	|	|	|	|	|
Olten a.	|	1852	1910	1927	|	1952	2010	...	2027	|	2052	2110	2127	|	2152	2210	2227	...	2252	2310	2327	|	2352	0012	0027	0052	0128
Olten d.	|	...	1912	1929	|	...	2012	...	2029	|	...	2112	2129	|	...	2212	2229	...	...	2312	2329	|	...	0013	0029	...	0136
Sissach d.	|	...	1927	|	|	...	2027	...	|	|	...	2127	|	|	...	2227	|	...	...	2327	|	|	...	0027	|	...	|
Liestal d.	|	...	1933	|	|	...	2033	...	|	|	...	2133	|	|	...	2233	|	...	...	2333	|	|	...	0033	|	...	0153
Basel SBB a.	|	...	1944	1953	|	...	2044	...	2053	|	...	2144	2153	|	...	2244	2253	...	...	2344	2353	|	...	0044	0053	...	0202
Lausanne 505 a.	2015	...	...	...	2115	...	...	...	...	2215	...	...	...	2315	...	...	...	...	...	...	...	0123j	...	...	...	...	...
Genève 505 a.	2104	...	...	...	2204	...	...	...	...	2304	...	...	...	0004	...	...	...	...	...	...	...	...	...	...	...	...	...
Genève Aéroport + 505 a.	2113	...	...	...	2213	...	...	...	...	2313	...	...	...	...	...	...	...	...	...	...	...	...	...	...	...	...	...

B – ⑫ Bellinzona - Basel.
C – ⑫ Basel - Chiasso and v.v.
E – ⑫ Basel - Erstfeld and v.v.
G – ⑫ Basel - Lugano and v.v.
L – ⑫ Basel - Locarno and v.v.

j – ⑤⑥⑦ (also Jan. 1, Apr. 2, 6, May 13, 14, 25; not Dec. 26, 27).
q – Also Jan. 1.
m – ① (also Apr. 6, May 25; not Apr. 5, May 24).
w – Also Dec. 25, 26, Jan. 1, 2, Apr. 2, 5, May 13, 24.

LENK - ZWEISIMMEN - MONTREUX — 566

Narrow gauge. MOB

km		Ⓐ		Ⓐ				Ⓒ												Ⓐ		Ⓐ					⑤⑥
0	**Lenk** d.	0611	0634	0703	0737	0837	0937	1003	1037	1103	1137	1237	1303	1337	1437	1537	1603	1637	1737	1803	1842	1903	1937	2037	2132	2232	2326
13	**Zweisimmen** a.	0629	0652	0721	0755	0855	0955	1021	1055	1121	1155	1255	1321	1355	1455	1555	1621	1655	1755	1821	1900	1921	1955	2055	2150	2250	2344

km						2111 🍷 G		Ⓒz	y	3115 🍷 G		2119 (🍴) C			3123 🍷 G★			2129 (🍷) [R]T	2127 🍷 G	2229 🍷 G	Ⓐ	2131 (🍷) C	Ⓒ	Ⓐ			
0	**Zweisimmen** d.	0411	0518	0605	0700	0826	0905	0923	1005	1026	1105	1226	...	1305	1426	1505	1515	...	1626	1705	1724	1826	1905	1926	2005	2105	2155
9	Saanenmöser d.	0426	0532	0619	0714	0841	0919	0938	1020	1041	1119	1241	...	1319	1441	1519	1530	...	1641	1719	1738	1841	1919	1941	2019	2119	2208
11	Schönried d.	0431	0537	0624	0719	0846	0924	0943	1024	1046	1124	1246	...	1324	1446	1524	1535	...	1646	1724	1743	1846	1924	1946	2024	2124	2212
16	**Gstaad** d.	0440	0547	0634	0730	0856	0937	0952	1033	1056	1137	1256	...	1337	1456	1537	1544	...	1656	1737	1752	1856	1937	1956	2037	2135	2222
19	Saanen d.	0444	0551	0639	0735	0901	0942	0956	1037	1101	1142	1301	...	1342	1501	1542	1548	...	1701	1742	1756	1901	1942	2000	2042	2140	2226s
23	Rougemont d.	0450	0556	0645	0741	0906	0948	...	...	1106	1148	1306	...	1348	1506	1548	...	...	1706	1748	...	1906	1948	2006	2048	2146	2231s
29	Château d'Oex d.	0503	0610	0706	0806	0916	1006	...	...	1116	1206	1316	...	1406	1516	1606	...	...	1716	1806	...	1916	2006	2015	2106	2206	2240
40	**Montbovon** d.	0522	0631	0723	0826	0931	1026	...	...	1131	1226	1331	...	1426	1531	1626	...	1711	1731	1826	...	1931	2026	2030	2130	2233	...
51	Les Avants § d.	0544	0652	0743	0847	0952	1047	...	...	1152	1247	1352	...	1447	1552	1647	...	|	1752	1847	...	1952	2047	2051	2150	2253	...
55	Chamby ⊙ § d.	0555	0659	0750	0854	1000	1054	...	...	1200	1254	1400	...	1454	1600	1654	...	|	1800	1854	...	2000	2054	2103	2156	2300	...
58	Chernex § d.	0601	0704	0756	0900	1005	1100	...	...	1205	1300	1405	...	1500	1605	1700	...	|	1805	1900	...	2005	2100	2109	2201	2305	...
62	**Montreux** § a.	0610	0713	0805	0910	1013	1110	...	...	1213	1310	1413	...	1510	1613	1710	...	1810	1813	1910	...	2013	2110	2118	2210	2315	...

	Ⓐ	Ⓐ	Ⓒ	Ⓐ	Ⓒ		2112 🍷 G	Ⓒz	2216 🍷 C	2118 (🍷) [R]T	y	3118 🍷 G★		2124 🍷 G			3126 🍷 G			2128 🍷 C		Ⓐ	2134 🍷 G★	2234 🍷 G			
Montreux § d.	...	...	...	0540	0550	0635	0745	...	0847	0925	...	0945	1045	1145	...	1245	1345	...	1445	1545	1645	...	1745	1845	1945	2045	2145
Chernex § d.	...	...	...	0550	0600	0645	0755	...	0855	|	...	0955	1054	1155	...	1254	1355	...	1454	1555	1654	...	1755	1854	1954	2059	2201
Chamby ⊙ § d.	...	...	...	0556	0605	0650	0800	...	0900	|	...	1000	1100	1200	...	1300	1400	...	1500	1600	1700	...	1800	1900	2000	2104	2206
Les Avants § d.	...	...	...	0604	0613	0658	0807	...	0912	|	...	1007	1112	1207	...	1312	1407	...	1512	1607	1712	...	1807	1912	2008	2112	2214
Montbovon d.	...	...	...	0622	0632	0722	0828	...	0932	1012	...	1028	1132	1228	...	1332	1428	...	1532	1628	1732	...	1828	1932	2032	2132	2234
Château d'Oex d.	...	0541	0550	0639	0652	0737	0843	...	0949	...	...	1043	1149	1243	...	1349	1443	...	1549	1643	1749	...	1843	1949	2049	2149	2249
Rougemont d.	...	0555	0603	0651	0709	0750	0853	...	1003	...	...	1053	1203	1253	...	1403	1453	...	1603	1653	1803	...	1853	2003	2103	2203	2303
Saanen d.	0514	0601	0620	0657	0715	0756	0859	1000	1009	...	1048	1059	1209	1259	...	1409	1459	1552	1609	1659	1809	1821	1859	2009	2109	2209	2309
Gstaad d.	0519	0606	0625	0703	0721	0803	0905	1005	1014	...	1054	1105	1214	1305	...	1414	1505	1557	1614	1705	1814	1827	1905	2014	2114	2214	2314
Schönried d.	0528	0614	0634	0711	0730	0812	0914	1014	1023	...	1103	1114	1223	1314	...	1423	1514	1606	1623	1714	1823	1836	1914	2023	2123	2223	2323
Saanenmöser d.	0533	0618	0639	0715	0735	0817	0918	1019	1028	...	1107	1118	1228	1318	...	1428	1518	1611	1628	1718	1828	1841	1918	2028	2128	2228	2328
Zweisimmen a.	0547	0631	0653	0729	0750	0834	0932	1034	1043	...	1123	1132	1243	1332	...	1443	1532	1625	1643	1732	1843	1854	1932	2043	2143	2243	2343

	Ⓐ		Ⓐ				Ⓒ													Ⓐ		Ⓐ					⑤⑥
Zweisimmen d.	0550	0611	0634	0703	0803	0903	0937	1003	1037	1103	1137	...	1203	1303	1403	1503	1537	1603	1703	1737	1803	1824	1903	2003	2103	2155	2255
Lenk a.	0608	0629	0652	0721	0821	0921	0956	1021	1056	1121	1156	...	1221	1321	1421	1521	1556	1621	1721	1756	1821	1842	1921	2021	2121	2213	2313

§ – ADDITIONAL SERVICES LES AVANTS - MONTREUX and v.v. (2nd class only):

	Ⓐ	Ⓐ		q		q		Ⓐ			
Les Avants d.	0710	0815	...	1323	...	1720	...	1800	...	2320	...
Chamby ⊙ d.	0717	0822	...	1330	...	1728	...	1807	...	2327	...
Chernex d.	0723	0834	...	1335	...	1734	...	1812	...	2332	...
Montreux a.	0736	0844	...	1345	...	1744	...	1824	...	2342	...

	Ⓐ	Ⓐ		q		q		Ⓐ			
Montreux d.	0643	0740	...	1216	...	1606	...	1714	...	2251	2345
Chernex d.	0653	0757	...	1226	...	1617	...	1724	...	2304	2355s
Chamby ⊙ d.	0658	0804	...	1231	...	1622	...	1729	...	2309	0000s
Les Avants a.	0706	0811	...	1238	...	1629	...	1736	...	2316	0007

C – GOLDEN PASS CLASSIC – [12] and (🍴).
G – GOLDEN PASS PANORAMIC – conveys [12] [observation cars].
T – TRAIN DU CHOCOLAT – ①③④ May 3 - June 30; daily July 1 - Aug. 31; ①③④ Sept. 1 - 28: conveys [1] only.

q – Ⓐ Dec. 14 - 18, Jan. 4 - Feb. 5, Feb. 15 - Mar. 26, Apr. 12 - July 2, Aug. 23 - Oct. 15, Nov. 1 - Dec. 10 (not May 14, Sept. 20).
s – Stops to set down only.
y – May 1 - Oct. 31.
z – Dec. 13 - Apr. 25.

★ – Also conveys VIP accommodation. [R]
⊙ – Chamby is a request stop.

MONTBOVON - BULLE - PALÉZIEUX — 568

Narrow gauge. 2nd class only. TPF

Châtel-St Denis - Palézieux and v.v. subject to 🚌 replacement July 12 - August 20

km		Ⓐ	Ⓐ		⚒																			611 [R] F w		🚌
0	**Montbovon** d.	...	0540	...	0640	0723	0840	0940	1040	1140	...	1240	1340	1440	...	1540	1640	1740	...	1840	1940	2040	...	2130	...	2140
13	Gruyères d.	...	0558	...	0658	0745	0858	0958	1058	1158	...	1258	1358	1458	...	1558	1658	1758	...	1858	1958	2058	...	|	...	2158
17	**Bulle** ▲ a.	...	0608	...	0708	0753	0908	1008	1108	1208	...	1308	1408	1508	...	1608	1708	1808	...	1908	2008	2108	...	2204	...	2208
17	**Bulle** d.	0513	...	0613	0713	0813	0913	1013	1113	1213	...	1313	1413	1513	...	1613	1713	1813	...	1913	2013	2113	...	...	...	...
37	Châtel-St Denis a.	0539	...	0639	0739	0839	0939	1039	1139	1239	...	1339	1439	1539	...	1639	1739	1839	...	1939	2039	2139	...	...	...	...
37	Châtel-St Denis d.	0542	...	0642	0742	0842	0942	1042	1142	1242	...	1342	1442	1542	...	1642	1742	1842	...	1942	2042	2142	...	...	...	...
44	**Palézieux** a.	0555	...	0655	0755	0855	0955	1055	1155	1255	...	1355	1455	1555	...	1655	1755	1855	...	1955	2055	2155	...	...	...	...

	Ⓐ	⚒																610 [R] F w					🚌		
Palézieux d.	...	...	0605a	0705	0805d	0905	1005	...	1105	1205	1305	1405	...	1505	1605	1705	...	...	1805	1905	...	2005	...	2105	2205
Châtel-St Denis a.	...	...	0616a	0716	0816d	0916	1016	...	1116	1216	1316	1416	...	1516	1616	1716	...	...	1816	1916	...	2016	...	2116	2216
Châtel-St Denis d.	...	...	0619a	0719	0819d	0919	1019	...	1119	1219	1319	1419	...	1519	1619	1719	...	...	1819	1919	...	2019	...	2119	2219
Bulle a.	...	...	0647a	0747	0847d	0947	1047	...	1147	1247	1347	1447	...	1547	1647	1747	...	...	1847	1947	...	2047	...	2147	2247
Bulle ▲ d.	0452	0552	0652	0756	0852	0952	1052	...	1152	1252	1352	1452	...	1552	1652	1752	...	1830	1852	...	1952	...	2052	...	...
Gruyères d.	0459	0559	0659	0803	0859	0959	1059	...	1159	1259	1359	1459	...	1559	1659	1759	...	|	1859	...	1959	...	2059	...	...
Montbovon a.	0520	0620	0720	0824	0920	1020	1120	...	1220	1320	1420	1520	...	1620	1720	1820	...	1904	1920	...	2020	...	2120	...	...

F – TRAIN FONDUE – [1] [observation car], [12] and 🍴 Montbovon - Bulle and v.v. [R].
a – Ⓐ only.
d – ⚒ only.
q – Not June 3, Nov. 1, Dec. 8.
w – Jan. 9, 16, 30, Feb. 6, 13, 20, Mar. 6, 20, Apr. 10, 24, Nov. 6, 20, 27.
x – Not Dec. 26, Jan. 2.

▲ – Local TPF rail services **Bulle** - **Broc** (*5 km*, journey time 11 minutes), **Bulle** - **Romont** (*18 km*, journey time 22 minutes); TPF 🚌 service **Bulle** - **Fribourg** (*28 km*, journey time 32 minutes, line **346**). Other services available (some via Sorens) journey time 45 – 60 minutes, line **336**.

From **Bulle**: 0619Ⓐ, 0713⚒, 0813, 0913⚒, 1013, 1113Ⓐ, 1154Ⓐ, 1213Ⓒ, 1313, 1413Ⓐ, 1513, 1554Ⓐ, 1613⑥**x**, 1713, 1813, 1913.
From **Broc**: 0632Ⓐ, 0732⚒, 0832, 0932⚒, 1032, 1132Ⓐ, 1232Ⓒ, 1249Ⓐ, 1332, 1432Ⓐ, 1532, 1632⚒, 1732, 1832, 1932.

From **Bulle**: 0546Ⓐ, 0646, 0746⚒, 0846, 1046, 1204, 1318Ⓐ, 1418, 1518Ⓐ, 1618, 1718, 1818, 1918.
From **Romont**: 0619Ⓐ, 0719, 0819⚒, 0919, 1119, 1247, 1347Ⓐ, 1447, 1547Ⓐ, 1647, 1747, 1847, 1947.

From **Bulle** (Gare) 🚌 service: 0556Ⓐ**q**, 0626, 0656Ⓐ**q**, 0726, 0756Ⓐ**q** and in the same pattern until 1926, 1956Ⓐ**q**, then 2026, 2056, 2145, 2245, 2345⑤⑥.

From **Fribourg** (Gare) 🚌 service: 0602Ⓐ**q**, 0632Ⓐ**q**, 0702, 0732Ⓐ**q** and in the same pattern until 1902, 1932Ⓐ**q**, then 2002, 2102, 2202, 2302, 0040⑥⑦.

MONTREUX - CAUX - ROCHERS DE NAYE — 569

Narrow gauge rack railway. 2nd class only. MVR

Caux - Rochers de Naye and v.v.: no service during bad weather; special service Nov. 25 - Dec. 11

km									B						B											
0	**Montreux** d.	0545	0645	0745	...	0847	0946	1047	1048	...	1146	1247	1346	...	...	1446	1546	1647	1746	...	1847	1947	2047	2147	2247
3	Glion ▲ d.	0558	0658	0758	...	0900	1000	1100	1102	...	1200	1300	1400	...	...	1500	1600	1700	1800	...	1900	2000	2100	2200	2300
5	Caux a.	0609	0709	0809	...	0911	1011	1111	1116	...	1211	1311	1411	1420	...	1511	1611	1711	1811	...	1911	2011	2111	2211	2311
10	**Rochers de Naye** a.	...	...	...	...	0941	1041	1141	1208	...	1241	1341	1441	1508	...	1541	1641	1741r	1841t	...	...	...	...	...	...

											B				B										
Rochers de Naye d.	...	...	...	...	...	0946	1046	...	1146	1246	1320	...	1346	1446	1520	...	1546	1646	1746r	1846t	...	...	...	...	...
Caux d.	0612	0712	...	0812	0916	1016	1116	...	1216	1316	1355	...	1416	1516	1555	...	1616	1716	1816	1916	...	2016	2116	2216	...
Glion ▲ d.	0625	0725	...	0825	0929	1029	1129	...	1229	1329	...	...	1429	1529	1616	...	1629	1729	1829	1929	...	2029	2129	2229	...
Montreux a.	0637	0737	...	0837	0941	1041	1141	...	1241	1341	...	...	1441	1541	1630	...	1641	1741	1841	1941	...	2041	2141	2241	...

B – BELLE EPOQUE – ⑥⑦ July 3 - Aug. 29. Runs only in good weather.
r – May 29 - Sept. 26.
t – June 26 - Aug. 29.

▲ – Funicular railway operates **Glion** - **Territet** and v.v. (no service Oct. 25 - 29): 0525, 0545, 0600 and every 15 minutes until 2100, then 2115, 2145, 2215, 2245, 2315, 2350, 0020, 0050, 0130⑥⑦. **Operator**: MVR, ✆ 0900 245 245.

570 GENÈVE - LAUSANNE - SION - BRIG SBB

km		IR 1709	IR 1411	EC 35		IR 1711	IR 1415	IR 1715	IR 1417	EC 37		IR 1717	IR 1419	IR 1719	IR 1421	IR 1721	IR 1423	IR 1723		IR 1425	TGV 9261	IR 1725	IR 1427	IR 1727	IR 1429	EC 39	IR 1729
				◧						◧ V											(🍷) ♦					◧	
0	Genève A ✈ 505 ..d.	...	...	...	...	0512	0547	0627	0647	...	...	0724	0747	0827	0847	0927	0947	1027	...	1047	...	1127	1147	1227	1247	...	1327
6	**Genève 505** .....d.	...	...	0545	...	0521	0556	0636	0656	0742	...	0733	0756	0836	0856	0936	0956	1036	...	1056	...	1136	1156	1236	1256	1342	1336
27	Nyon **505** .....d.	...	...	|	...	0537	0610	0650	0710	|	...	0747	0810	0850	0910	0950	1010	1050	...	1110	...	1150	1210	1250	1310	|	1350
53	Morges **505** .....d.	...	...	|	...	0600	0628	0705	0728	|	...	0802	0828	0905	0928	1005	1028	1105	...	1128	...	1205	1228	1305	1328	|	1405
66	**Lausanne 505** .....a.	...	...	0617	...	0612k	0640	0715	0740	0815	...	0812k	0840	0915	0940	1015	1040	1115	...	1140k	...	1215	1240	1315	1340	1415	1415
66	**Lausanne** ..... ▲ d.	...	0545	0620	...	0624	0645	0720	0745	0820	...	0824	0845	0920	0945	1020	1045	1120	...	1150	1157	1220	1245	1320	1345	1420	1420
84	Vevey ..... ▲ d.	...	0559	|	...	0638	0659	0734	0759	|	...	0838	0859	0934	0959	1034	1059	1134	...	1204	|	1234	1259	1334	1359	|	1434
92	**Montreux** ..... ▲ d.	...	0605	0639	...	0644	0705	0740	0805	0839	...	0844	0905	0940	1005	1040	1105	1140	...	1210	1217	1240	1305	1340	1405	1439	1440
105	Aigle ..... ▲ d.	...	0616	|	...	0655	0716	0751	0816	|	...	0855	0916	0951	1016	1051	1116	1151	...	1221	1230	1251	1316	1351	1416	|	1451
114	Bex .....d.	...	0623	|	...	|	0723	|	0823	|	...	|	0923	|	1023	|	1123	|	...	1227	|	|	1323	|	1423	|	|
118	St Maurice .....d.	...	0628	|	...	|	0728	|	0828	|	...	|	0928	|	1028	|	1128	|	...	1232	|	|	1328	|	1428	|	|
133	Martigny .....d.	...	0638	|	...	0712	0738	0808	0838	|	...	0912	0938	1008	1038	1108	1138	1208	...	1243	1249	1308	1338	1408	1438	|	1508
158	**Sion** .....d.	0624	0654	0714	...	0728	0754	0824	0854	0914	...	0928	0954	1024	1054	1124	1154	1224	...	1258	1306	1324	1354	1424	1454	1514	1524
174	Sierre .....d.	0634	0704	|	...	0738	0804	0834	0904	|	...	0938	1004	1034	1104	1134	1204	1234	...	1308	1317	1334	1404	1434	1504	|	1534
184	Leuk .....d.	0642	0712	|	...	|	0812	0842	0912	|	...	|	1012	1042	1112	1142	1212	1242	...	|	1326	1342	1412	1442	1512	|	1542
203	Visp .....d.	0655	0722	|	...	0755	0824	0855	0924	|	...	0955	1024	1055	1124	1155	1224	1255	...	1324	1338	1355	1424	1455	1524	|	1555
212	**Brig** .....a.	0702	0730	0740	...	0802	0830	0902	0930	0940	...	1002	1030	1102	1130	1202	1230	1302	...	1330	1345	1402	1430	1502	1530	1540	1602
	Milano C **590** .....a.	...	...	0935	...	...	...	...	...	1135	...	...	...	...	...	...	...	...	...	...	...	...	...	...	...	1735	...

	IR 1431	IR 1731		IR 1435	IR 1735	IR 1437	TGV 9267	IR 1737		IR 1439	IR 1739	IR 1441	IR 1741	EC 41	IR 1443	TGV 9273	IR 1743	IR 1445		IR 1745	IR 1447	IR 1747	RE 2747	IR 1749	IR 1449	RE 2701	
							(🍷) ♦							◧		(🍷) ♦										q	
Genève A ✈ 505 ..d.	1347	1427	...	1447	1527	1547	...	1627	...	1647	1727	1747	1827	...	1847	...	1927	1947	...	2027	...	2127	...	2227	2312	...	...
Genève 505 .....d.	1356	1436	...	1456	1536	1556	...	1636	...	1656	1736	1756	1836	1842	1856	...	1936	1956	...	2036	...	2136	...	2236	2321	...	...
Nyon **505** .....d.	1410	1450	...	1510	1550	1610	...	1650	...	1710	1750	1810	1850	|	1910	...	1950	2010	...	2050	...	2150	...	2250	2337	...	...
Morges **505** .....d.	1428	1505	...	1528	1605	1628	...	1705	...	1728	1805	1828	1905	|	1928	...	2005	2028	...	2105	...	2205	...	2305	0000	...	...
Lausanne 505 .....a.	1440	1515	...	1540k	1615	1640	...	1715	...	1740	1815	1840k	1915	1915	1940	...	2015	2040	...	2115	...	2215	...	2315	0012	...	...
Lausanne ..... ▲ d.	1445	1520	...	1550	1620	1645	1657	1720	...	1745	1820	1850	1920	1917	1945	1957	2020	2045	...	2120	2145	2220	2245	2320	0024	0132	...
Vevey ..... ▲ d.	1459	1534	...	1604	1634	1659	|	1734	...	1759	1834	1904	1934	|	1959	|	2034	2059	...	2134	2159	2234	2259	2334	0038	0146	...
Montreux ..... ▲ d.	1505	1540	...	1610	1640	1705	1717	1740	...	1805	1840	1910	1940	1939	2005	2017	2040	2105	...	2140	2205	2240	2305	2340	0044	0152	...
Aigle ..... ▲ d.	1516	1551	...	1621	1651	1716	1727	1751	...	1816	1851	1921	1951	|	2016	2028	2051	2116	...	2151	2216	2251	2316	2351	0055	0203	...
Bex .....d.	1523	|	...	1627	|	1723	...	|	...	1823	|	1927	|	|	2023	|	2057	2123	...	|	2223	2258	2323	2358	0102	0210	...
St Maurice .....d.	1528	|	...	1632	|	1728	...	|	...	1828	|	1932	|	|	2028	|	2103	2128	...	|	2228	2303	2327	0003	0107	0214	...
Martigny .....d.	1538	1608	...	1643	1708	1738	...	1808	...	1838	1908	1943	2008	|	2038	2045	2113	2138	...	2208	2238	2313	...	0013	0117	...	...
Sion .....d.	1554	1624	...	1658	1724	1754	...	1824	...	1854	1924	1958	2024	2014	2054	2103	2127	2154	...	2224	...	2329	...	0029	0131	...	...
Sierre .....d.	1604	1634	...	1708	1734	1804	...	1834	...	1904	1934	2008	2034	|	2104	2116	...	2204	...	2234	...	2339	...	0039	...	...	...
Leuk .....d.	1612	1642	...	|	1742	1812	...	1842	...	1912	1942	|	2042	|	2112	2125	...	2212	...	2242	...	2347	...	0047	...	...	...
Visp .....d.	1624	1655	...	1724	1755	1824	...	1855	...	1924	1955	2024	2055	|	2124	2140	...	2224	...	2255	...	2359	...	0059	...	...	...
Brig .....a.	1630	1702	...	1730	1802	1830	...	1902	...	1930	2002	2030	2102	2040	2130	2147	...	2230	...	2302	...	0005	...	0105	...	...	...
Milano C **590** .....a.	...	...	...	...	...	...	...	...	...	...	...	...	...	2235	...	...	...	...	...	...	...	...	...	...	...	...	...

	IR 1402	IR 1702	IR 1404	IR 1706	IR 1400	IR 1406	IR 1708	IR 1408	IR 1710	IR 1410	IR 1712	IR 1412	IR 1714	IR 1414	IR 1718		EC 32	IR 1418	IR 1720	TGV 9268	IR 1420	IR 1722	IR 1422	IR 1724	IR 1424	IR 1726	EC 34
					Ⓐ				♦								◧			(🍷) ♦							◧
Milano C **590** .....d.	...	...	...	...	...	...	...	...	...	...	...	...	...	...	...	...	0825	...	...	...	...	...	...	...	...	...	1225
Brig .....d.	...	...	0428	...	...	0528	0600	0628	0657	0728	0757	0828	0857	0928	0957	...	1023	1028	1057	1101	1128	1157	1228	1257	1328	1357	1423
Visp .....d.	...	...	0436	...	...	0536	0607	0636	0707	0736	0807	0836	0907	0936	1007	...	|	1036	1107	1110	1136	1207	1236	1307	1336	1407	|
Leuk .....d.	...	...	0447	...	...	0547	0618	0647	0718	0747	0818	0847	0918	0947	1018	...	|	|	1118	1123	1147	1218	1247	1318	1347	1418	|
Sierre .....d.	...	...	0455	...	...	0555	0626	0655	0726	0755	0826	0855	0926	0955	1026	...	|	1051	1126	1132	1155	1226	1255	1326	1355	1426	|
Sion .....d.	...	0426	0506	0537	...	0606	0637	0706	0737	0806	0837	0906	0937	1006	1037	...	1051	1102	1137	1143	1206	1237	1306	1337	1406	1437	1451
Martigny .....d.	...	0440	0520	0551	0610	0620	0651	0720	0751	0820	0851	0920	0951	1020	1051	...	|	1116	1151	1205	1220	1251	1320	1351	1420	1451	|
St Maurice .....d.	...	0451	0531	|	0625	0631	|	0731	|	0831	|	0931	|	1031	|	...	|	1126	|	|	1231	|	1331	|	1431	|	|
Bex .....d.	...	0456	0536	|	0631	0636	|	0736	|	0836	|	0936	|	1036	|	...	|	1131	|	|	1236	|	1336	|	1436	|	|
Aigle ..... ▲ d.	...	0503	0543	0608	0638	0643	0708	0743	0808	0843	0908	0943	1008	1043	1108	...	|	1138	1208	1229	1243	1308	1343	1408	1443	1508	|
Montreux ..... ▲ d.	...	0514	0554	0619	0649	0654	0719	0754	0819	0854	0919	0954	1019	1054	1119	...	1124	1149	1219	1248	1254	1319	1354	1419	1454	1519	1524
Vevey ..... ▲ d.	...	0521	0601	0626	0655	0701	0726	0801	0826	0901	0926	1001	1026	1101	1126	...	|	1156	1226	|	1301	1326	1401	1426	1501	1526	|
Lausanne ..... ▲ a.	...	0535	0615	0640	0709	0715	0740	0815	0840	0915	0940	1015	1040	1115	1140	...	1140	1210	1240	1308	1315	1340	1415	1440	1515	1540	1540
Lausanne 505 .....d.	0520	0540	0620	0645	0711	0720	0745	0820	0845	0920	0945	1020	1045	1120	1145	...	1145	1220	1245	...	1320	1345	1420	1445	1520	1545	1545
Morges **505** .....d.	0532	0549	0632	0654	0727	0732	0754	0832	0854	0932	0954	1032	1054	1132	1154	...	|	1232	1254	...	1332	1355	1432	1454	1532	1554	|
Nyon **505** .....d.	0550	0605	0650	0710	0743	0750	0810	0850	0910	0950	1010	1050	1110	1150	1210	...	|	1250	1310	...	1350	1410	1450	1510	1550	1610	|
Genève 505 .....a.	0604	0619	0704	0724	0758	0804	0824	0904	0924	1004	1024	1104	1124	1204	1224	...	1218	1304	1324	...	1404	1424	1504	1524	1604	1624	1618
Genève A ✈ 505 ..a.	0613	0628	0713	0733	...	0813	0833	0913	0933	1013	1033	1113	1133	1213	1233	...	...	1313	1333	...	1413	1433	1513	1533	1613	1633	...

	IR 1426	IR 1728	IR 1428	TGV 9272	IR 1730	IR 1430	IR 1732	TGV 9274	IR 1432	IR 1736	IR 1436		IR 2536	EC 36	IR 1738	IR 1438	IR 2538	IR 1740	IR 1440	IR 2540	EC 42	IR 1442	IR 2542		IR 1444	IR 2648	RE 2700
				(🍷) ♦				(🍷) ♦						◧							◧ V						q
Milano C **590** .....d.	...	...	...	...	...	...	...	...	...	...	...	...	...	1720	...	...	...	...	...	...	1920	...	...	...	...	...	...
Brig .....d.	1428	1457	1528	1541	1557	1628	1657	...	1728	1757	1828	...	...	1923	1857	1928	...	1957	2028	...	2123	2128	...	...	2228	...	...
Visp .....d.	1436	1507	1536	1549	1607	1636	1707	...	1736	1807	1836	...	...	|	1907	1936	...	2007	2036	...	|	2136	...	...	2236	...	...
Leuk .....d.	|	1518	1547	1602	1618	1647	1718	...	1747	1818	|	...	...	|	1918	1947	...	2018	2047	...	|	2147	...	...	2247	...	...
Sierre .....d.	1451	1526	1555	1611	1626	1655	1726	...	1755	1826	1851	...	...	|	1926	1955	...	2026	2055	...	|	2155	...	...	2255	...	...
Sion .....d.	1502	1537	1606	1626	1637	1706	1737	...	1806	1837	1902	...	...	1951	1937	2006	...	2035	2106	...	2151	2206	...	...	2306	...	...
Martigny .....d.	1516	1551	1620	1642	1651	1720	1751	...	1820	1851	1916	...	...	|	1951	2020	...	...	2120	...	|	2220	...	...	2320	...	...
St Maurice .....d.	1526	|	1631	|	|	1731	|	...	1831	|	1926	...	...	|	|	2031	...	...	2131	...	|	2231	...	...	2331	...	0041
Bex .....d.	1531	|	1636	|	|	1736	|	...	1836	|	1931	...	...	|	|	2036	...	...	2136	...	|	2236	...	...	2336	...	0046
Aigle ..... ▲ d.	1538	1608	1643	1714	1708	1743	1808	1835	1843	1908	1938	...	...	|	2008	2043	...	...	2143	...	|	2243	...	...	2343	...	0053
Montreux ..... ▲ d.	1549	1619	1654	1727	1719	1754	1819	1849	1854	1919	1949	...	...	2024	2019	2054	...	...	2154	...	2224	2254	...	...	2354	...	0104
Vevey ..... ▲ d.	1556	1626	1701	|	1726	1801	1826	|	1901	1926	1956	...	...	|	2026	2101	...	...	2201	...	|	2301	...	...	0001	...	0110
Lausanne ..... ▲ a.	1610	1640	1715	1745	1740	1815	1840	1908	1915	1940	2010	...	...	2040	2040	2115	...	...	2215	...	2240	2315	...	...	0015	...	0124
Lausanne 505 .....d.	1620	1645	1720	...	1745	1820	1845	...	1920	1945	...	...	2020	2045	2045	...	2120	...	...	2220	2242	...	2320	...	...	0021	...
Morges **505** .....d.	1632	1654	1732	...	1754	1832	1854	...	1932	1954	...	...	2032	|	2054	...	2132	...	...	2232	|	...	2332	...	...	0033	...
Nyon **505** .....d.	1650	1710	1750	...	1810	1850	1910	...	1950	2010	...	...	2050	|	2110	...	2150	...	...	2250	|	...	2350	...	...	0051	...
Genève 505 .....a.	1704	1724	1804	...	1824	1904	1924	...	2004	2024	...	...	2104	2118	2124	...	2204	...	...	2304	2315	...	0004	...	...	0105	...
Genève A ✈ 505 ..a.	1713	1733	1813	...	1833	1913	1933	...	2013	2037	...	...	2113	...	2133	...	2213	...	...	2313	...	...	...	...	...	...	...

♦ – **NOTES** (LISTED BY TRAIN NUMBER)

9261 – ⑥ Dec. 19 - Apr. 3, July 10 - Aug. 28: [12] and (🍷) Paris - Brig.
9267 – ⑦ Dec. 20 - Mar. 28, July 4 - Aug. 29 (also Apr. 5): [12] and (🍷) Paris - Aigle.
9268 – ⑥ Dec. 19 - Apr. 3, July 10 - Aug. 28 (also Dec. 25, Jan. 1): [12] and (🍷) Brig - Paris.
9272 – ⑥ Dec. 19 - Apr. 3, July 10 - Aug. 28: [12] and (🍷) Brig - Paris.
9273 – ④⑤ Dec. 18 - Jan. 1; ⑤ Jan. 8 - Apr. 2, July 9 - Aug. 27: [12] and (🍷) Paris - Brig.
9274 – ⑦ Dec. 20 - Mar. 28, July 4 - Aug. 29 (also Apr. 5): [12] and (🍷) Aigle - Paris.

V – [12] and ✕ Genève - Milano - Venezia and v.v.

k – Connects with train in previous column.
q – ⑥⑦ (also Jan. 1, Apr. 2, 5, May 13, 14, 24; not Dec. 26, 27).
s – Stops to set down only.
u – Stops to pick up only.
◧ – Supplement payable for journeys from / to Italy.

2nd class only — Local services from VEVEY, AIGLE and BEX — 571

VEVEY - BLONAY: Narrow gauge. *6 km*. Journey time: 14–16 minutes. **Operator**: MVR.

From **Vevey**: 0603⚒, 0622, 0655⚒, 0714Ⓐ, 0739, 0803⚒, 0825Ⓐ, 0839, 0903⚒, 0939, 1003⚒, 1039, 1103⚒, 1139, 1211⚒, 1239, 1303⚒, 1339, 1403⚒, 1439Ⓒ, 1503⚒, 1539, 1603⚒, 1625Ⓐ, 1639, 1703⚒, 1725Ⓐ, 1739, 1803⚒, 1825Ⓐ, 1839, 1911Ⓐ, 1925Ⓐ, 1939, 2003Ⓐ, 2043, 2143, 2243, 2343, 0043⑥⑦ (also Jan. 1).

From **Blonay**: 0541⚒, 0605, 0638⚒, 0657, 0716Ⓐ, 0733⚒, 0805, 0819Ⓐ, 0841⚒, 0905, 0941⚒, 1005, 1041⚒, 1105, 1133⚒, 1205, 1241⚒, 1305, 1341⚒, 1405, 1441⚒, 1505, 1533⚒, 1605, 1619Ⓐ, 1641⚒, 1705, 1719Ⓐ, 1741⚒, 1805, 1819Ⓐ, 1841Ⓐ, 1905, 1919Ⓐ, 1933Ⓐ, 2005, 2116, 2216, 2316, 0019⑥⑦ (also Jan. 1).

AIGLE - LEYSIN: Narrow gauge rack railway. *6 km*. Journey time: 29–39 minutes. **Operator**: TPC.

From **Aigle**: 0550⚒, 0620Ⓒ, 0720Ⓐ, 0756, 0900, 0956 and hourly until 2056, then 2256.

From **Leysin** Grand Hotel: 0525, 0624Ⓐ, 0653Ⓒ, 0753, 0857, 0953 and hourly until 2153, then 2327.

AIGLE - LES DIABLERETS: Narrow gauge. *23 km*. Journey time: 45–55 minutes. **Operator**: TPC.

From **Aigle**: 0618, 0720, 0820, 0955, 1059, 1140Ⓐ, 1155Ⓒ, 1240Ⓐ, 1255Ⓒ, 1355, 1455, 1603, 1659, 1803, 1855, 2055, 2155.

From **Les Diablerets**: 0611Ⓒ, 0622Ⓐ, 0713, 0811, 0948, 1045, 1150, 1250, 1332Ⓐ, 1348Ⓒ, 1506, 1548, 1708, 1748, 1904, 2048, 2148.

AIGLE - CHAMPÉRY: Narrow gauge rack railway. 2nd class only. **Operator**: TPC.

km		⚒			⚒				⚒		⚒		⚒					⚒								⑥y	
0	**Aigle** d.	0518	0619	0720	0807	0822	0922	1022	1105	1120	1155	1224	1255	1320	1422	1520	1624	1655	1722	1824	1855	1955	2055	2153	2255	...	2355
11	Monthey Ville d.	0547	0645	0748	0826	0848	0948	1048	1124	1148	1214	1248	1314	1348	1448	1548	1648	1714	1748	1848	1921	2021	2114	2213	2314	2330	0014
23	**Champéry** a.	0620	0720	0821	...	0921	1021	1130	...	1221	...	1321	...	1421	1521	1628	1721	...	1821	1921	1954	2054	...	2245	...	0003	...

		⚒		⚒					⚒		⚒		⚒						⚒						z		⑦w
Champéry d.	...	...	0600	0631a	0700d	0734	0834	0934	...	1034	...	1134	...	1301	1334	1434	1534	1632	...	1734	1834	1934	2034	2134	2246	...	0004
Monthey Ville d.	0540	0611	0641	0712	0742	0814	0914	1014	1042	1112	1127	1216	1231	1342	1414	1512	1616	1714	1729	1816	1914	2016	2116	2216	2321	2317	0039
Aigle a.	0600	0631	0703	0732	0802	0834	0934	1034	1102	1132	1147	1236	1251	1402	1434	1532	1636	1735	1749	1836	1934	2036	2136	2236	...	2337	...

BEX - VILLARS: *12 km*. Journey time: 40–46 minutes. All trains call at Bex (Place du Marché), and Bévieux (*3 km* and 10 minutes from Bex). **Operator**: TPC.

From **Bex**: 0633, 0739, 0839, 0939, 1039, 1149, 1239, 1339, 1457, 1549, 1639, 1742, 1842, 1934, 2105.

From **Villars**: 0541, 0644, 0733, 0833, 0933, 1033, 1143, 1233, 1333, 1433, 1543, 1633, 1737, 1837, 1947, 2042.

a – Ⓐ only.
d – ⚒ only.
w – Also Aug. 2.
y – Also Aug. 1.
z – Change at Monthey En Place for connection to Aigle.

2nd class only. SNCF, TMR — MARTIGNY - CHAMONIX — 572

Narrow gauge rack railway. Through journeys operate as MONT BLANC EXPRESS. Passengers may be required to change trains at Vallorcine

km					N	H	K			y	N	H	K			y			y						
0	**Martigny** d.	0538	0640	0801	0843	0901	0901	...	1001	...	1043	1101	1101	1201	1301	1401	1501	1601	...	...	1801	1901	2001	2122	2222
7	Salvan d.	0554	0657	0817	0859	|	0917	...	1017	...	1059	|	1117	1217	1317	1417	1517	1617	...	...	1817	1917	2017	2138	2238
9	Les Marécottes d.	0558	0701	0821	0903	0921	0921	...	1021	...	1103	1121	1121	1221	1321	1421	1521	1621	...	...	1821	1921	2021	2142	2242
14	Finhaut d.	0610	0713	0833	0917	0933	0933	...	1033	...	1117	1133	1133	1233	1333	1433	1533	1633	...	...	1833	1933	2033	2154	2255
18	Le Châtelard Frontière 🏛 d.	0621	0731	0845	0927	0944	0944	0945	1044	1045	1126	1144	1144	1245	1345	1445	1544	1644	1645	1745	1845	1945	2044	2205	2305
21	**Vallorcine** a.	...	0737x	0851	...	...	...	0951	...	1051	...	...	...	1251y	1351	1451	...	...	1651	1751	1851	1951	...	...	...
		▬	|	|				|	▬ y	|			▬	|	|	|		▬	|	|	|	|			
21	**Vallorcine** d.	0700	0800x	0900	...	...	...	1000	1030	1100	...	...	1200	1300y	1400	1500	...	1600	1656	1800	1900	2000	...	...	...
28	Argentière Haute Savoie d.	0716	0816	0916	...	...	...	1016	1049	1116	...	...	1216	1316y	1416	1516	...	1616	1715	1816	1916	2016	...	...	...
32	Les Tines d.	0726	0826	0926	...	...	...	1026	1059	1126	...	...	1226	1326y	1426	1526	...	1626	1726	1826	1926	2026	...	...	...
36	**Chamonix** a.	0733	0833	0933	...	...	...	1033	1107	1133	...	...	1233	1333y	1433	1533	...	1633	1733	1833	1933	2033	...	...	...
	St Gervais **365a** a.	0820	0920	*1020*y	...	...	...	1120	...	...	...	...	1320	1420y	1520	*1620*	...	1720	*1820*	1920	2020	...	...	...	...

	x	L		N		H	y	y		N		H	K	y				y		J	y				
St Gervais **365a** d.	0632	0652	0731	...	0832	...	...	0932	...	...	*1032*y	...	...	...	...	1232	1332	...	1532	...	1632	1732	1832	1932	...
Chamonix d.	0716	0737	0816	...	0916	...	0945	1016	...	...	1116	...	...	1216	...	1316	1416	1516	1616	1643	1716	1816	1916	2016	...
Les Tines d.	0727	0747	0827	...	0927	...	0954	1027	...	...	1127	...	...	1227	...	1327	1427	1527	1627	1652	1727	1827	1927	2027	...
Argentière Haute Savoie d.	0736	0756	0836	...	0936	...	1004	1036	...	...	1136	...	...	1236	...	1336	1436	1536	1636	1702	1736	1836	1936	2036	...
Vallorcine a.	0752	...	0852	...	0952	...	1022	1052	...	...	1152	...	...	1252	...	1352	1452	1552	1652	1718	1752	1852	1952	2052	...
	▬	▬	|		|		▬ K	|			|			|		|	|	▬ y	▬		▬	|	|	▬	
Vallorcine d.	...	0759x	0859	...	0959	...	...	1059	...	...	1159	...	...	1259	...	1359	1459	...	*1659*y	...	1759	1859	1959	...	...
Le Châtelard Frontière 🏛 d.	0633	0808	0908	0952	1005	1008	1008	1105	1108	1152	1205	1208	1208	1305	1308	1408	1505	1508	1708	...	1808	1908	2008	2113	2213
Finhaut d.	0642	0817	0917	1001	...	1017	1017	...	1117	1201	...	1217	1217	...	1317	1417	...	1517	1717	...	1817	1917	2017	2122	2222
Les Marécottes d.	0654	0829	0929	1013	...	1029	1029	...	1129	1213	...	1229	1229	...	1329	1429	...	1529	1729	...	1829	1929	2029	2134	2234
Salvan d.	0658	0833	0933	1017	...	|	1033	...	1133	1217	...	|	1233	...	1333	1433	...	1533	1733	...	1833	1933	2033	2138	2238
Martigny a.	0720	0855	0955	1038	...	1055	1055	...	1155	1238	...	1255	1255	...	1355	1455	...	1555	1755	...	1855	1955	2055	2159	2259

H – June 12 - Sept. 12.
J – Daily Dec. 13 - Apr. 5; Ⓐ Apr. 6 - June 11; daily June 12 - Sept. 12; Ⓐ Sept. 13 - Dec. 11.
K – Dec. 13 - June 11, Sept. 13 - Dec. 11.
L – Dec. 13 - June 30, Sept. 1 - Dec. 11.
N – June 5 - Sept. 12.
x – July 1 - Aug. 31.
y – Dec. 13 - Apr. 5, June 12 - Sept. 12.
* – Runs if passengers are present at Les Marécottes.

In the event of deep snow or very bad weather, certain trains may be suspended between Vallorcine and Argentière.

SION VALLEY RESORTS — 573

MARTIGNY - ORSIÈRES▲ and LE CHÂBLE: *19 km*, 26 minutes to both resorts. ▲ – A change of train is necessary at Sembrancher. **Operator**: RA.

From **Martigny**: 0616Ⓐ, 0813, 0923, 1013, 1130, 1213, 1313, 1413, 1523, 1613Ⓒ, 1647, 1723, 1813, 1913, 2013, 2123⑤⑥.

From **Orsières and Le Châble**: 0544Ⓐ, 0648, 0809, 0919, 1009, 1057, 1209, 1309, 1409, 1519, 1609, 1643Ⓒ, 1719, 1809, 1909, 2048⑤⑥.

LE CHÂBLE - VERBIER: 🚌 service. Journey time: ± 25 minutes. **Operator**: PA.

From **Le Châble Gare**: 0650⚒, 0715†, 0805⚒, 0850, 0955, 1050 **r**, 1135 **t**, 1255, 1355, 1455 **p**, 1610, 1715, 1806, 1900, 1955 **q**, 2050 **q**, 2155⑤⑥ **n**.
From **Verbier Post**: 0615⚒, 0720⚒, 0740†, 0845⚒, 0925, 1025, 1225, 1330, 1430 **p**, 1525, 1640, 1740, 1835, 1930, 2020 **q**, 2115 **q**, 2220⑤⑥ **n**.

MARTIGNY - AOSTA: 🚌 service via Grand St Bernard tunnel. Service runs daily throughout the year. Journey time: ± 2 hours. **Operator**: TMR / SAVDA.

From **Martigny Gare**: 0825, 1655. From **Aosta Stazione**: 0802, 1620 (🚌 to Orsières arrive 1805, then train forward depart 1809, Martigny arrive 1835).

SION - CRANS-SUR-SIERRE: 🚌 service. Journey time: ± 45 minutes. **Operator**: PA.

From **Sion Gare**: 0645⚒, 0745, 0845⚒, 1000, 1045⚒, 1150, 1230⚒ 1345, 1545, 1650, 1800, 1910.

From **Crans-sur-Sierre Post**: 0645, 0745⚒, 0835, 0935⚒, 1050, 1135⚒, 1245, 1345⚒, 1545, 1645, 1805, 1905.

SIERRE - CRANS-sur-SIERRE - MONTANA: 🚌 service. Principal stop in **Crans-sur-Sierre** is Hotel Scandia (± 40 minutes from Sierre, ± 8 minutes from Montana. **Operator**: SMC.

From **Sierre Gare**: 0745, 0845, 0945⚒**z**, 1045⚒**z**, 1130, 1201⚒**z**, 1230⚒**z**, 1340, 1440⚒**z**, 1540, 1658, 1745, 1940, 2030, 2207.

From **Montana Gare**: 0607⚒**z**, 0642, 0743†**y**, 0839⚒**z**, 1003, 1043⚒**z**, 1133⚒**z**, 1230, 1334⚒**z**, 1438, 1603, 1638, 1733⚒**z**, 1818, 1907, 2048.

BRIG - SAAS-FEE: 🚌 service. Journey time: 50–70 minutes. All services call at **Visp** (Bahnhof Süd) ± 20 minutes from Brig, and **Saas Grund** (Post) ± 12 minutes from Saas Fee.

From **Brig (Bahnhof)**: 0420, 0545, 0615, 0645, 0715 and every 30 minutes until 1115, then 1140, 1215, 1251, 1315, 1345 and every 30 minutes until 1845, then 1945, 2045, 2215⑤⑥ **x**.

From **Saas-Fee**: 0531, 0602, 0631, 0702, 0731, 0802, 0826, and at xx02 and xx26 minutes past each hour until 1926, then 2026, 2330⑤⑥ **x**.

Operator: PA. Seat reservation **compulsory** from Saas Fee to Brig on journeys 0802 - 1802. Reserve seats at least two hours before departure: ✆ 058 454 26 16.

n – Dec. 18 - Apr. 10.
p – ⚒ (also † Dec. 20 - Apr. 11).
q – Dec. 19 - Apr. 11.
r – Not ③ schooldays.
t – ③ schooldays only.
x – Not Dec. 25, 26, Jan. 1, 2, Apr. 2.
y – Also Mar. 19, June 3, Nov. 1, Dec. 8; not Apr. 2.
z – Also Apr. 2; not Mar. 19, June 3, Nov. 1, Dec. 8.

575 GLACIER EXPRESS — MGB, RhB*

Glacier Express through services (compulsory reservation). **No service Nov. 1 - Dec. 11.** For local services see Table **576**. Narrow gauge rack railway

km			900	910		902	904	906	908
		WINTER SERVICE ▶▶▶	⊡ W 🍴	⊡ 🍴	SUMMER SERVICE ▶▶▶	★ S 🍴🍷	★ T 🍴	★ 🍴	★ 🍴
0	**Zermatt** d.		...	1000		0900	0913	1000	1013
21	St Niklaus △ d.		...	1037		0936	|	|	|
36	Visp △ d.		1005	1107		1007	1025	1107	1125
45	**Brig** △ d.		1017	1117		1018	1040	1118	1140
62	Fiesch △ d.		1043	1143		1043	|	|	|
86	Oberwald △ d.	**Dec. 13**	1111	1212	**May 13**	1111	|	|	|
113	**Andermatt** a.	**to**	1136	1236	**to**	1136	1200	1236	1300
113	**Andermatt** d.	**May 12**	1155	1255	**Oct. 31**	1155	1224	1243	1304
132	Sedrun △ d.		|	|		|	|	|	|
142	**Disentis/Mustér** ▽ a.		1258	1356		|	|	|	|
	Chur ▽ a.		1438	1537		1447	1447	1514	1514
	Thusis ▽ a.		...	1628		|	1528	1602	1602
	Tiefencastel ▽ a.		...	1647		1550	1547	1626	1626
	Filisur 545a ▽ a.		...	1701		1611	1601	|	|
	Davos Platz **545a** a.		...	|		1648	|	|	|
	Bergün/Bravuogn ▽ a.		...	1714		...	1614	1655	1655
	Samedan 546 ▽ a.		...	1746		...	1646	1731	1731
	Celerina **546/7** ▽ a.		...	1753		...	1653	1736	1736
	St Moritz 546/7 a.		...	1758		...	1658	1742	1742

		901	903		905	907	909	911
	WINTER SERVICE ▶▶▶	⊡ W 🍴	⊡ 🍴	SUMMER SERVICE ▶▶▶	★ 🍴	★ 🍴	★ T 🍴	★ S 🍴🍷
St Moritz 546/7 d.		...	0902		0917	0917	1002	...
Celerina **546/7** △ d.		...	0905		|	|	1005	...
Samedan 546 △ d.		...	0917		0927	0927	1017	...
Bergün/Bravuogn △ d.		...	0947		|	|	1047	...
Davos Platz **545a** d.		...	|		|	|	|	1041
Filisur 545a △ d.	**Dec. 13**	...	1001	**May 13**	|	|	1101	|
Tiefencastel △ d.	**to**	...	1015	**to**	1032	1032	|	1131
Thusis △ d.	**May 12**	...	1033	**Oct. 31**	1050	1050	|	|
Chur △ d.		1015	1115		1127	1127	1227	1227
Disentis/Mustér △ d.		1139	1239		|	|	|	|
Sedrun ▽ a.		|	|		|	|	|	|
Andermatt a.		1249	1349		1349	1410	1449	1510
Andermatt d.		1254	1354		1356	1420	1456	1520
Oberwald ▽ a.		1325	1420		|	|	|	1543
Fiesch ▽ a.		1355	1451		|	|	|	1612
Brig ▽ a.		1423	1523		1523	1541	1623	1643
Visp ▽ a.		1437	1537		1537	1603	1637	1707
St Niklaus ▽ a.		...	|		|	|	|	1753
Zermatt a.		...	1652		1652	1711	1752	1831

All Glacier Express trains convey (12) [observation cars]. Reservations for 🍴 are obligatory in advance through Railgourmino swissAlps AG, ✆ Chur (081) 300 15 15 (meals are served between 1100 and 1330 at your seat). Further information: www.glacierexpress.ch

S – May 13 - Oct. 17.
T – June 5 - Oct. 17.
W – Dec. 25 - Jan. 3, Jan. 30 - May 12.
⊡ – Ⓡ (reservation fee including supplement: 13 CHF).
★ – Ⓡ (reservation fee including supplement: 33 CHF).

△ – Calls to pick up only.
▽ – Calls to set down only.
* – For operators see foot of page.

576 *Local Services* ZERMATT - BRIG - ANDERMATT (- GÖSCHENEN) - DISENTIS - CHUR — MGB, RhB*

Narrow gauge rack railway. For *Glacier Express* through services see Table **575**

ZERMATT - BRIG

km										
0	**Zermatt** d.	0539	0613	0739		1839	1913	2013	2113	2213
8	Täsch d.	0551	0625	0751	and	1851	1925	2025	2125	2225
21	St Niklaus d.	0617	0653	0817	every	1917	1953	2053	2153	2249
29	Stalden-Saas d.	0638	0712	0838	hour	1938	2012	2112	2212	2310
36	Visp a.	0647	0722	0847	until	1947	2022	2122	2222	2320
36	Visp d.	0652	0722	0852	△	1952	2025	2125	2225	2321
45	**Brig** a.	0703	0736	0903		2003	2035	2135	2235	2329

										①–⑥	⑦
Brig d.	0510	0553		1453	1608	1653		2053	2225	2308
Visp a.	0520	0604	and	1504	1620	1704	and	2104	2236	2318
Visp d.	0529	0610	every	1510	1625	1710	every	2110	2240	2323
Stalden-Saas d.	0539	0620	hour	1520	1636	1720	hour	2120	2251	2333
St Niklaus d.	0556	0638	until	1538	1655	1738	until	2138	2309	2351
Täsch d.	0622	0702	▽	1602	1721	1802	▽	2202	2333	0015
Zermatt a.	0633	0714		1614	1734	1814		2214	2344	0025

VISP - BRIG - ANDERMATT

km									①–⑥	⑦
	Visp d.	...	0708	0808		1908	2008	2108	2236	2255
0	**Brig** d.	0623	0723	0823	and	1923	2023	2123	2250	2310
7	Mörel d.	0633	0733	0833	every	1933	2033	2133	2259	2319
10	Betten d.	0639	0739	0839	hour	1939	2039	2139	2305	2325
17	Fiesch d.	0658	0758	0858	until	1958	2058	2157	2323	2343
41	Oberwald 🚗 d.	0744	0844	0944		2044	2144	*2237z*	...	...
59	Realp ▲ 🚗 § d.	0805	0905	1005		2105	2205t	...	...	...
68	**Andermatt** a.	0820	0920	1020		2120	2220t	...	...	...

							t				y
Andermatt d.	...	...	0737	0837		1837	1909	1937	2037	...	...
Realp ▲ 🚗 § d.	...	...	0750	0850	and	1850	1922	1950	2050	...	...
Oberwald 🚗 d.	*0612z*	0713	0813	0913	every	1913	1942	2013	2113	...	*2250z*
Fiesch d.	0657	0757	0857	0957	hour	1957	2027	2057	2157	...	2326
Betten d.	0716	0816	0916	1016	until	2016	2048	2116	2216	...	2344
Mörel d.	0724	0824	0924	1024		2024	2055	2124	2224	...	2351
Brig a.	0733	0833	0933	1033		2033	2103	2133	2233	...	0001
Visp a.	0750	0850	0950	1050		2050	...	2150	...	...	...

ANDERMATT - DISENTIS

km		🚌		w◇		w◇		w◇			w◇		n		w◇								🚌	🚌 v	🚌 v	
0	**Andermatt** 🚗 d.	...	0727	0755	0827	0855	0927	0955	...	1027	1055	1127	1227	1327	1355	...	1427	1527	1627	1727	1827	...	...	...	...	...
10	Oberalppass d.	...	0750	0815	0850	0915	0950	1015	...	1050	1115	1150	1250	1350	1415	...	1450	1550	1650	1750	1850	...	...	...	...	...
19	Sedrun 🚗 d.	0705	0817	...	0917	...	1017	...	...	1117	...	1217	1317	1417	...	...	1517	1617	1717	1817	1917	...	2001	2101	2201	...
29	**Disentis/Mustér** a.	0728	0836	...	0936	...	1036	...	...	1136	...	1236	1336	1436	...	...	1536	1636	1736	1836	1936	...	2021	2121	2221	...

	🚌	n	r						r	n		n	r			w					🚌	🚌	🚌 v	🚌 v	
Disentis/Mustér d.	0640	0708	0714	0814	0914	...	1014	1114	1220	1214	...	1314	...	1414	1514	...	1614	1714	1814	...	1919	2022	2122	2222	...
Sedrun 🚗 d.	0652	0731	0731	0831	0931	...	1031	1131	1240	1231	...	1331	...	1431	1531	...	1631	1731	1831	...	1936	2038	2138	2238	...
Oberalppass d.	...	0753	0753	0853	0953	...	1053	1153	1301	1253	...	1353	1353	1453	1553	1626	1653	1753	1853	...	...	...	...	...	...
Andermatt 🚗 a.	...	0822	0822	0922	1022	...	1122	1222	...	1322	...	1422	1422	1522	1622	1652	1722	1822	1922	...	...	...	...	...	...

DISENTIS - CHUR

km			⚒								
0	**Disentis/Mustér** d.	0545	0615	0645	0745	and	1745	1845	1945	2045	...
12	Trun d.	0601	0630	0701	0801	every	1801	1901	2001	2101	...
30	Ilanz d.	0624	0653	0724	0824	hour	1824	1924	2024	2124	...
49	Reichenau-Tamins d.	0650	0720	0750	0850	until	1850	1950	2050	2150	...
59	**Chur** a.	0704	0734	0804	0902		1902	2002	2104	2204	...

	⚒									
Chur d.	0611	0656	0756	0856	and	1756	1856	1959	2059	2259
Reichenau-Tamins d.	0625	0705	0805	0905	every	1805	1905	2013	2113	2310
Ilanz d.	0653	0733	0833	0933	hour	1833	1933	2042	2142	2336
Trun d.	0714	0753	0853	0953	until	1853	1953	2101	2201	2355
Disentis/Mustér a.	0731	0811	0911	1011		1911	2011	2119	2219	0012

GÖSCHENEN - ANDERMATT

km												
0	**Göschenen** d.	0753	0812	0853	and hourly	1812	1853	1912	2012	2112	2153
4	**Andermatt** a.	0803	0822	0903	until	1822	1903	1922	2022	2122	2203

Andermatt d.	0725	0748	0828	0848	and hourly	1828	1848	1948	2048	2128
Göschenen a.	0739	0803	0842	0903	until	1842	1903	2003	2103	2142

n – Dec. 13 - May 12, Nov. 1 - Dec. 11.
r – May 13 - Oct. 31.
t – ⑤ Dec. 18 - Mar. 19, May 14 - Oct. 29 (not Dec. 25, Jan. 1).
v – Dec. 13 - Apr. 11.

w – Dec. 19 - Mar. 21.
y – On ⑦ runs 20 minutes later Fiesch - Brig.
z – Connection by 🚌.
◇ – Subject to favourable weather conditions.
§ – Realp is a request stop.

△ – Additional services Zermatt - Visp: 1113, 1213, 1613, 1713, 1813.
▽ – Additional services Visp - Zermatt: 0843, 0943, 1043, 1243, 1843.
▲ – 🚂 service (summer only, not daily) runs Realp - Furka - Gletsch and v.v. Operator: Dampfbahn Furka-Bergstrecke ✆ 0848 000 144.
🚗 – Car-carrying shuttle available (see page 258).
* – For operators see foot of page.

578 ZERMATT - GORNERGRAT — Narrow gauge rack railway. GGB

Journey 33 minutes, *9 km*. Additional winter-sports journeys run Dec. 21 - Apr. 17 between Riffelalp and Gornergrat. *Services are liable to be suspended in bad weather*

Dec. 13 - Apr. 25, June 3 - Oct. 17, Nov. 27 - Dec. 11

From Zermatt: 0710, 0800, 0824, 0848, 0912*, 0936*, 1000*, 1024*, 1048*, 1112*, 1136, 1200, 1224, 1248, 1312, 1336, 1400, 1424, 1448, 1512, 1536, 1600, 1624, 1712, 1800, 1924 **p**.
From Gornergrat: 0755, 0843, 0907, 0931, 0955, 1019, 1043, 1107, 1131, 1155, 1219, 1243, 1307, 1331, 1355, 1419, 1443, 1507, 1531, 1555, 1619, 1643, 1707, 1755, 1857, 2007 **p**.

Apr. 26 - June 2, Oct. 18 - Nov. 26

From Zermatt: 0710 **r**, 0824, 0936 **q**, 1024, 1136, 1224, 1336, 1424, 1536 **q**, 1624, 1712 **q**, 1800 **q**.
From Gornergrat: 0755 **r**, 0931, 1019 **q**, 1131, 1219, 1331, 1419, 1531, 1619 **q**, 1707, 1755 **q**, 1857 **q**.

p – Dec. 13 - Apr. 18, June 19 - Sept. 26.
q – Apr. 26 - June 2, Oct. 18 - Nov. 1.
r – Daily Apr. 26 - June 2, Oct. 18 - Nov. 1; ①–⑤ Nov. 2 - 26.
* – Duplicated by non-stop journeys Dec. 13 - Apr. 18 (journey 29 minutes).

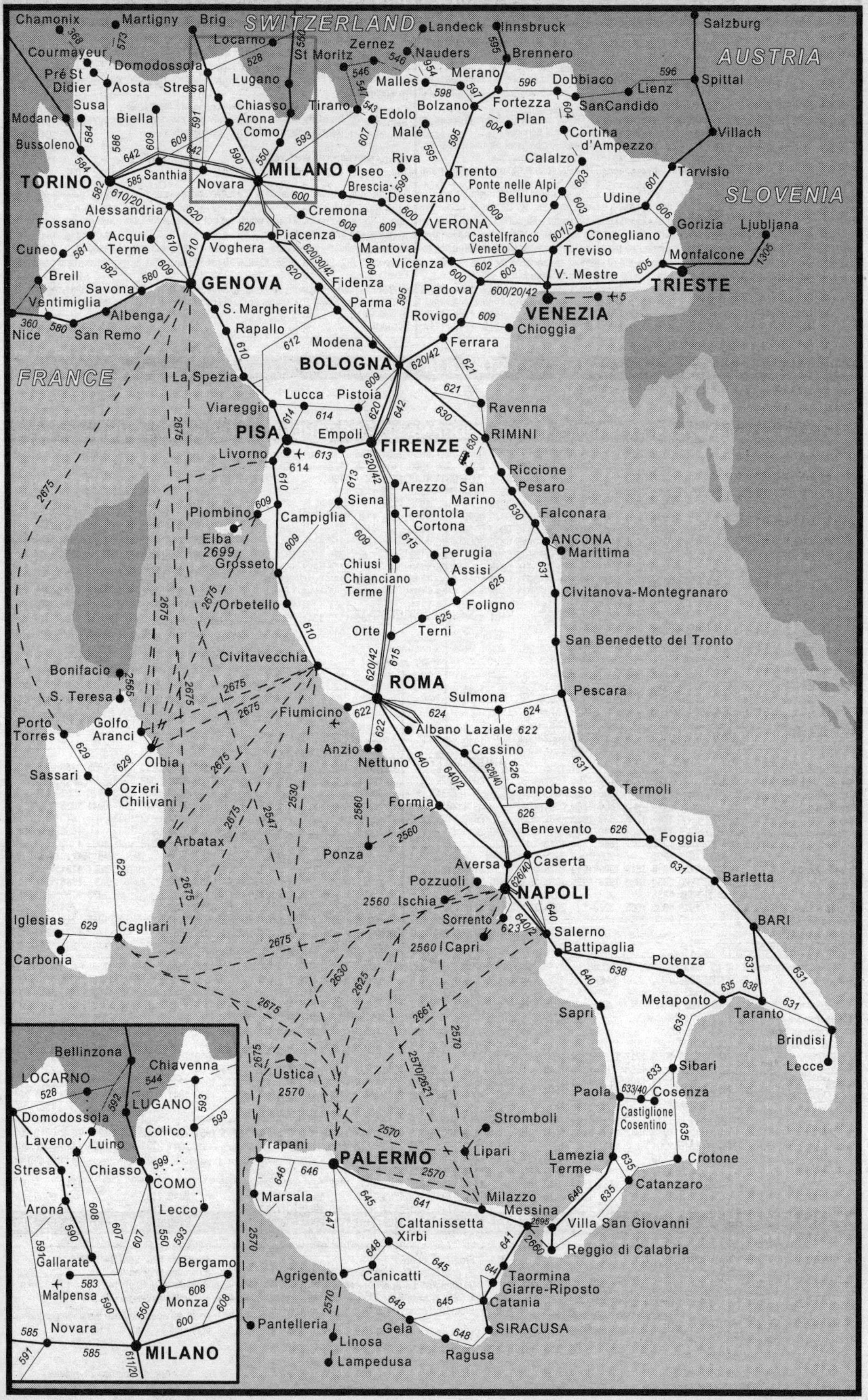

A list of Scenic Rail Routes appears elsewhere in the timetable – see Contents page

ITALY

Operator: Trenitalia, a division of Ferrovie dello Stato SpA (FS), unless otherwise noted.

Services: All trains convey First and Second classes of travel unless otherwise shown by a figure "2" at the top of the column, or in a note in the Table heading. Overnight sleeping car (🛏) or couchette (▬) trains do not necessarily convey seating accommodation or may convey only second class seats - refer to individual footnotes. Excelsior sleeping cars offer en-suite facilities. Descriptions of sleeping and couchette cars appear on page 8. Refreshment services (✕ or 🍷) where known, may only be available for part of the journey, and may be added to or taken away from trains during the currency of the timetable.

Train Categories: There are 8 categories of express train:

AV	**Alta Velocità**	premium fare ETR 500 services using high-speed lines.	*ESc*	**Eurostar City**	fast services at premium fare.
E	**Espresso**	semi-fast or international services.	*IC*	**InterCity**	internal day express; supplement payable.
EC	**EuroCity**	international express; supplement payable.	*ICN*	**InterCityNight**	internal night express.
EN	**EuroNight**	higher standard of overnight express.		Other services are classified:	
ES	**Eurostar Italia**	high speed (ETR 450 / 460 / 500) services at premium fare.	*R*	**Regionale**	Local train.

Timings: Valid from **December 13, 2009** unless otherwise stated. Readers should note, however, that only partial information was available at press date and further changes are likely – only *AV*, *ES*, *ESc*, *EC* and *EN* trains have been updated. Details of local services and accommodation conveyed, particularly on domestic night trains, may change.

Trains may be cancelled or altered at holiday times – for public holiday dates see page 2. Some international trains which are not available for local travel are not shown in this section; these include some *City Night Line* services running between Germany and Italy – see International pages.

Tickets: Tickets must be date-stamped by the holder before boarding the train using the self-service validating machines – this applies to all tickets except passes.

Reservations: Reservations are **compulsory** for all journeys by services for which a **train category** (*AV*, *EC*, *EN*, *ES*, *ESc*, *IC*, *ICN*, *E*) is shown in the timing column and passengers boarding without a prior reservation may be surcharged.

Supplements Supplements are calculated according to class of travel and total distance travelled (minimum 10km, maximum 3000km), and are payable on all *EC* and *IC* trains, regardless of the number of changes of train. A higher fare (including supplement) is payable for travel by *AV*, *ES* and *ESc* trains. Some trains are only available to passengers holding long distance tickets and the restrictions applying to these are noted in the tables.

580 VENTIMIGLIA - GENOVA

km		*IC* 651				*IC* 515				*IC* 657				*EC* 139										*IC* 693			
		✕		✕		🍷	2	Ⓒ 2	Ⓐ 2		C2	2	✕ T	🍷 ♦	† T	Ⓐ	2	† C2	✕ T2	† 2		2	†	♦	Ⓒ	Ⓐ 2	✕
0	**Ventimiglia** 🏛 **581** d.	0445	0507	0517	...	0633	0646	0750	0750	0858	0908	0948	1048	1058	1107	...	1150	1206	1206	1220	...	1354r	1420	1458	...	...	1526
5	Bordighera d.	0452	0514	0524	...	0640	0655	0757	0757	0905	0917	0956	1055	1105	1115	...	1157	1216	1216	1229	...	1401r	1427	1505	...	...	1533
16	**San Remo 581** d.	0502	0522	0533	...	0650	0704	0806	0806	0915	0928	1006	1104	1115	1128	...	1205	1226	1226	1237	...	1409r	1435	1515	...	...	1542
24	Taggia-Arma d.	0508	0528	0539	...	|	0710	0812	0812	|	0937	1015	1110	|	1136	...	1212	1233	1233	1243	...	1414	1441	|	...	...	1548
39	Imperia Porto Maurizio d.	0521	0541	0551	...	0707	0722	0824	0824	0932	—	1032	1123	1132	1154	...	1229	...	...	1255	...	1432	1453	1532	...	...	1600
41	Imperia Oneglia d.	|	0545	0555	...	|	0732	0828	0828	|	...	1036	1129	|	1159	...	1236	...	...	1259	...	1437	1458	|	...	...	1605
46	Diano Marina d.	|	0551	0601	...	0715	0738	0835	0835	0940	...	1042	...	1140	—	...	1242	...	...	1305	...	1443	1504	1540	...	...	1612
61	Alassio d.	0541	0604	0626	...	0730	0756	0849	0849	0956	✕	1056	...	1156	Ⓒ	...	1302	...	...	1329	...	1502	1523	1556	1609	1609	1639
67	**Albenga** d.	0549	0611	0636	0657	0738	0803	0855	0855	1004	1015	1104	...	1204	1214	1214	1312	...	...	1336	1413	1512	1531	1604	1616	1616	1649
76	Loano d.	|	0622	0651	0711	|	0817	0905	0905	|	1024	1122	...	|	1223	1223	1321	...	...	1350	1422	1521	1546	|	1624	1624	1704
79	Pietra Ligure d.	|	0626	0655	0716	|	0822	0915	0915	|	1028	1130	...	|	1228	1228	1330	...	...	1354	1426	1531	1551	|	1628	1628	1708
85	Finale Ligure Marina d.	0603	0634	0704	0725	0752	0831	0923	0923	1018	1035	1138	...	1218	1235	1235	1338	...	...	1403	1433	1538	1602	1618	1635	1635	1716
108	**Savona** d.	0619	0655	0726	0747	0807	0900k	0941	0958	1033	1110	1157j	...	1233	1253	1255	1408	...	...	1433	1452	1601	1618	1633	1655	1655	1732
120	Varazze d.	|	0704	0735	0759	|	0913k	0956	1013	|	1124	1211j	...	|	1301	1304	1423	...	...	1447	1501	1615	...	|	1704	1704	*1754*
151	**Genova** Piazza Principe § a.	0702	0744	0815	0844	0849	1002	1052	1101	1106	1209	1301	...	1306	1332	1344	1509	...	...	1541	1532	1701	...	1706	1732	1747	*1839*
	Milano Centrale **610** a.	0855	0945	...	...	|	...	...	...	1255	...	...	...	1450	1535	...	...	...	...	...	1737	...	...	1850	1938	...	...
	Pisa Centrale **610** a.	...	...	...	...	1057	...	...	...	...	...	...	...	...	...	...	...	...	...	...	...	...	...	...	...	...	...
	Roma Termini **610** a.	...	...	...	...	1414	...	...	...	...	...	...	...	...	...	...	...	...	...	...	...	...	...	...	...	...	...

			IC 1537	*IC* 669				*EC* 147		*IC* 1539		
	P	†	Ⓒ	Ⓐ	† T	✕ T	✕ 2	🍷 ♦		🍷 †	2	
Ventimiglia 🏛 **581** d.	1554	...	1645	1658	1723	1723	1754	1858	...	1935	1951	...
Bordighera d.	1601	...	1652	1705	1730	1730	1801	1905	...	1942	1958	...
San Remo 581 d.	1610	...	1702	1715	1739	1739	1809	1915	...	1952	2006	...
Taggia-Arma d.	1616	...	1708	1721	1744	1744	1815	|	...	1958	2012	...
Imperia Porto Maurizio d.	1629	...	1722	1734	1756	1756	1832	1932	...	2011	2029	...
Imperia Oneglia d.	1634	...	|	|	1800	1800	1837	|	...	|	2034	...
Diano Marina d.	1641	...	|	|	1806	1806	1843	1940	...	|	2040	...
Alassio d.	1702	...	1741	1756	1832	1838	1902	1956	...	2039	2102	2224
Albenga d.	1710	1725	1749	1804	1840	1846	1910	2004	2010	2048	2113	2232
Loano d.	1721	1736	1757	|	1856	1859	1918	|	2020	|	2121	2240
Pietra Ligure d.	1730	1747	1807	|	1900	1909	1922	|	2024	|	2130	2244
Finale Ligure Marina d.	1738	1755	1815	1818	1909	1919	1929	2018	2031	2105	2138	2251
Savona d.	1758j	1820	1830	1833	1928	1935	1955	2033	2049	2123	2201	2312
Varazze d.	1812j	1831	1838	|	...	...	2010	|	2058	|	2215	2325
Genova P P § a.	1901	1918	1906	1906	...	...	2056	2106	2136	2214	2301	0009
Milano Centrale **610** a.	...	2130	2050	2050	...	...	...	2250	2335	2359	...	...
Pisa Centrale **610** a.	...	...	...	...	...	...	...	...	...	...	...	...
Roma Termini **610** a.	...	...	...	...	...	...	...	...	...	...	...	...

							IC 692			
	✕ 2	2	2	T	✕	†	♦	r 2	T	
Roma Termini **610** d.	...	...	...	...	...	...	...	...	...	...
Pisa Centrale **610** d.	...	...	...	...	...	...	...	...	...	...
Milano Centrale **610** d.	...	...	...	...	...	0625	0700	...	...	0820
Genova P P § d.	0523	0608	0644	*0715*	0753	0842	0855	0859	...	1026
Varazze d.	0606	0653	0729	*0808*	0839	0926	|	0946	...	1057
Savona d.	0621	0710	0745	0848	0907	0938	0928	1007	1029	1110
Finale Ligure Marina d.	0637	0729	0801	0905	0926	0957	0941	1038	1054	1123
Pietra Ligure d.	0643	0737	0807	0914	0932	1003	|	1045	1100	1131
Loano d.	0648	0742	0812	0919	0937	1009	|	1050	1105	1136
Albenga d.	0655	0804	0821	0929	0948	1024	1003	1103	1114	1144
Alassio d.	0702	0812	0829	0936	...	...	1011	1110	1132	...
Diano Marina d.	0725	0834	0851	0959	...	...	1024	1141	1156	...
Imperia Oneglia d.	0731	0841	0857	1007	...	...	|	1148	1203	...
Imperia Porto Maurizio d.	0735	0845	0904	1011	...	...	1033	1153	1207	...
Taggia-Arma d.	0746	0856	0916	1023	...	...	|	1204	1218	...
San Remo 581 d.	0752	0905	0926	1030	...	...	1050	1211	1224	...
Bordighera d.	0801	0917	0939	1042	...	...	1100	1221	1234	...
Ventimiglia 🏛 **581** a.	0808	0926	0948	1050	...	...	1107	1231	1241	...

	IC 650	*IC* 1536			*EC* 144										*EC* 160						*IC* 660				*IC* 538		*IC* 668
	Ⓐ	🍷 Ⓒ	2		🍷 ♦	✕ 2	†	T		Ⓐ 2	Q 2	Ⓐ 2	Ⓒ 2	T2	🍷 ♦	✕	† 2	✕ 2	Ⓐ	Ⓒ		2	Ⓐ	Ⓒ	🍷		
Roma Termini **610** d.	...	...	...	...	...	...	...	...	...	...	...	...	...	...	...	...	...	...	...	...	...	...	...	...	1546	...	...
Pisa Centrale **610** d.	...	...	...	...	...	...	...	...	...	...	...	...	...	...	...	...	...	...	...	...	...	...	...	...	1900	...	...
Milano Centrale **610** d.	0905	0905	...	...	1110	...	...	...	...	...	...	...	...	...	1510	...	...	...	...	1625	1700	...	...	1825	|	2025	2105
Genova Piazza Principe § d.	1055	1055	1059	1217	1255	1259	1259	...	1417	...	...	1459	1459	...	1655	1717	1738	1746	1817	1830	1855	1859	2017	2038	2112	2231	2255
Varazze d.	|	1121	1144	1258	|	1345	1345	...	1458	...	...	1544	1544	...	|	1758	1819	1828	1858	1904	|	1944	2058	2112	|	2310	|
Savona d.	1129	1132	1213	1308	1329	1411	1411	...	1508	1540	1538	1613	1613	1631t	1729	1813	1829	1841	1912	1914	1929	2008	2108	2122	2146	2333	2329
Finale Ligure Marina d.	1141	1144	1235	1324	1341	1433	1433	...	1524	1600	1602	1635	1635	1647t	1741	1836	1844	1900	1932	1932	1941	2031	2124	2142	2158	2351	2341
Pietra Ligure d.	|	1150	1241	1331	|	1439	1439	...	1530	1613	1613	1641	1641	1653t	|	1842	1850	1908	1938	1938	|	2038	2131	2148	|	2357	|
Loano d.	|	1156	1246	1336	|	1444	1444	...	1535	1619	1619	1646	1646	1658t	|	1847	1855	1913	1943	1943	|	2044	2136	2153	|	0002	|
Albenga d.	1203	1207	1254	1347	1403	1453	1453	...	1544	1631	1631	1653	1653	1709	1803	1854	1905	1925	1951	1951	2003	2052	2147	2201	2212	0012	0003
Alassio d.	1211	1215	1301	...	1411	1501	1501	...	1555	1638	1638	1703	1703	1722	1811	1901	1917	1934	...	...	2011	2101	2155	2209	2220	0020	0011
Diano Marina d.	|	|	1316	...	1424	1516	1525	...	...	1708	1708	1719	1729	1750	1824	1917	1941	2000	...	...	|	2116	...	...	2233	0035	0024
Imperia Oneglia d.	|	|	1322	...	|	1522	1536	1604	...	1714	1714	1725	1736	1801	|	1923	1952	2006	...	...	|	2122	...	...	|	0041	|
Imperia Porto Maurizio d.	1230	1241	1328	...	1433	1531	1542	1609	...	1718	1721	1733	1741	1806	1833	1931	1957	2010	...	...	2030	2127	...	...	2242	|	0033
Taggia-Arma d.	1242	1253	1343	...	|	1543	1553	1621	...	1729	1734	1745	1753	1817	|	1943	2010	2021	...	...	2042	2138	...	...	|	0055	|
San Remo 581 d.	1250	1302	1350r	...	1450	1550	1600	1628	...	1735	1741	1751	1759	1823	1850	1950	2017	2027	...	...	2050	2144	...	...	2258	0101	0050
Bordighera d.	1300	1312	1400r	...	1500	1600	1610	1638	...	1744	1750	1800	1809	1833	1900	2000	2027	2037	...	...	2100	2154	...	...	2308	0110	0100
Ventimiglia 🏛 **581** a.	1307	1320	1409r	...	1507	1607	1617	1646	...	1752	1757	1811	1820	1840	1907	2007	2035	2047	...	...	2107	2204	...	...	2315	0117	0107

♦ – **NOTES** (LISTED BY TRAIN NUMBER)

139 – RIVIERA DEI FIORI – [12] and 🍷 Nice - Genova (**140**) - Milano.
147 – SANREMO – [12] and 🍷 Nice - Genova (**148**) - Milano.
144 – SANREMO – [12] and 🍷 Milano (**143**) - Genova - Nice.
160 – RIVIERA DEI FIORI – [12] and 🍷 Milano (**159**) - Genova - Nice.
692 – ANDREA DORIA – [12] Milano (**691**) - Genova - Ventimiglia.
693 – ANDREA DORIA – [12] Ventimiglia - Genova (**694**) - Milano.

C – From / to Cuneo.
P – Ⓐ until Sept. 11; daily from Sept. 14: [12] Ventimiglia - La Spezia - Parma.
Q – † (also ⑥ from Sept. 5).
T – From / to Torino.

j – 4 minutes later from Sept. 14.
k – 8 minutes later on Ⓐ.
r – Ⓐ (daily from Sept. 14).
t – 4 – 5 minutes later on Ⓒ.
§ – Local services may use the underground platforms.

CUNEO - NICE, VENTIMIGLIA and SAN REMO 581

2nd class only

km																											
		f	d	d	c		T	d			Ld	Lc	T	d		c		d	c	b			y				🚌
	Torino P.N. **582** d.	...	...	...	...	...	...	...	...	...	0730	0730	0835	...	...	...	...	...	...	...	...	...	...	...	...	...	...
0	**Cuneo** d.	...	...	0602	0604	...	0655	0726	0833	...	0904	0904	1012	1033	...	1204	1304	1400	1504	...	1604	1704	...	1807	1905	2008	2205
29	Limone 🏛 d.	...	...	0639	0641	...	0742	0802	0910	...	0939	0939	1049	1110	...	1242	1347	1435	1550	...	1644	1747	...	1849	1943	2049	2249
47	Tende d.	0610	...	0658	0700	...	0802	...	0928	...	0957	0957	1107	...	1210	1306	1405	...	1608	...	1722	1809	1835	1916	2006	...	...
75	Breil sur Roya a.	0647	...	0732	0734	...	0834	...	0957	...	1025	1025	1137	...	1249	1346	1441	...	1643	...	1802	1844	1911	1945	2034	...	...
75	Breil sur Roya d.	0651	0649	0734	0736	0738	0841	...	...	1008	1026	1026	1139	...	1250	1348	1443	...	1645	1716	1813	1846	1936	1947	2036	...	...
*	**Nice Ville** a.	0755	|	|	|	0841	|	...	...	1106	|	|	|	...	1355	|	|	...	|	1825	1917	|	2038	|	|	...	...
96	**Ventimiglia** a.	...	0716	0759	0801	...	0905	...	...	...	1045	1045	1203	...	...	1420	1510	...	1718	...	...	1910	...	2020	2101	...	...
96	**Ventimiglia 580** d.	...	...	...	...	...	0908	...	...	...	1048	1107	1206	...	...	...	...	...	...	...	...	...	...	...	...	...	...
112	**San Remo 580** a.	...	...	...	...	...	0927	...	...	...	1103	1127	1225	...	...	...	...	...	...	...	...	...	...	...	...	...	...

	🚌 z	d	d	d	c						c		T				d	c	T	d	L					
San Remo 580 d.	...	...	...	...	...	...	...	...	...	...	...	...	1143	...	...	...	...	...	1535	...	1628	...	...	...	...	...	...
Ventimiglia 580 a.	...	...	...	...	...	...	...	...	...	...	...	...	1200	...	...	...	...	...	1553	...	1646	...	...	...	...	...	...
Ventimiglia d.	...	...	0540	...	0645	...	0816	0907	...	...	1050	...	1204	...	1348	...	...	...	1556	...	1649	...	1756	...	1947	...	...
Nice Ville d.	...	...	|	...	|	0721	|	|	0905	...	|	...	|	1236	|	...	...	...	|	...	|	1704	|	1755	|	1920	...
Breil sur Roya a.	...	...	0602	...	0711	0828	0840	0934	1003	...	1115	...	1229	1340	1417	...	...	...	1620	...	1713	1808	1822	1905	2017	2025	...
Breil sur Roya d.	...	...	0604	...	0713	...	0842	0936	1005	...	1117	...	1231	1347	1419	...	...	...	1622	...	1715	...	1824	1923	2035	...	...
Tende d.	...	...	0637	...	0803	...	0910	1020	1049	...	1156	...	1305	1428	1455	...	...	...	1700	...	1750	...	1859	2007	2108	...	...
Limone 🏛 d.	0600	0642	0703	0815	0826	...	0938	1048	...	1120	1217	...	1325	1452	1515	1600	1616	1724	1748	1812	...	1918	2028	2127	...	...
Cuneo a.	0644	0720	0745	0855	0903	...	1011	1126	...	1155	1257	...	1357	1526	1550	1640	1656	1754	1827	1846	...	1957	2100	2200	...	...
Torino P.N. **582** a.	...	...	...	...	...	...	...	...	...	...	...	...	...	...	...	...	...	1925	...	2030	...	...	...	...	...	...

L – (2) Torino - Imperia Oneglia and v.v.
T – From / to Taggia-Arma.
b – ⑦ (also French public holidays).
c – ⑦ (also Italian public holidays).
d – ①–⑥ (not Italian public holidays).
f – ①–⑥ (not French public holidays).
y – ⑦ until Sept. 6 (also July 14, Aug. 15).
z – Not Aug. 2 - 30.
* – Nice - Breil sur Roya: *44 km*.

TORINO - CUNEO and SAVONA 582

Most trains 2nd class only

km																													
		⚒	†z	†	⚒	⚒	V	†	⚒	⚒	†z	⑥y	L	†V	⚒V	†z	⚒		⚒	†	†	⚒	†	⚒		†	⚒	†	⚒
0	**Torino P N** d.	...	0545	...	0555	...	0620	0655	0700	...	0725	0725	0730	0800	0800	0835	0835	...	0900	0940	...	1030	1035	1100	1135	...	1200	1235	1235
52	Savigliano d.	...	|	...	0642	...	0717	0744	0750	...	0810	0810	0825	0849	0853	0923	0923	...	0953	1028	...	1123	1121	1150	1222	...	1253	1323	1322
64	Fossano d.	0602	0625	0636	0652	0707	0727	0755	0801	0808	0822	0822	0836	0857	0903	0932	0935	...	1002	1037	1040	1134	1130	1200	1232	1240	1303	1332	1332
90	**Cuneo** a.	|	|	|	0721	|	|	0829	0829	|	|	|	0902	|	|	|	1000	...	|	1058	|	1157	|	|	1255	|	|	|	1355
83	Mondovi d.	0621	0639	0654	...	0726	0741	...	...	0826	0840	0840	...	0911	0919	0945	...	...	1018	...	1059	...	1144	1216	...	1259	1325	1345	...
103	Ceva d.	0644	0654	0712	...	0742	0756	...	...	0846	0900	0900	...	0926	0933	1000	...	...	1033	...	1118	...	1200	1232	...	1318	1339	1400	...
153	**Savona** a.	0744	0742	0809	...	0843	0845	...	...	0940	0949	0949	...	1019	1026	1046	...	...	1122	...	1215	...	1248	1320	...	1415	1425	1447	...

	⚒	†	†	⚒	⚒V	†V	⚒	⚒		†	⚒	†		⚒	⚒		†	⚒	⚒	†	⚒		†	⚒	⚒				
Torino P N d.	1300	1325	...	1330	1400	1400	1435	1500	1535	...	1600	...	1635	1700	1725	1735	...	1800	1835	1835	1900	1935	2000	2000	2100	2135	2235	2340	...
Savigliano d.	1353	1415	...	1421	1453	1453	1522	1552	1623	...	1650	...	1723	1747	1802	1823	...	1846	1922	1922	1953	2023	2046	2049	2150	2223	2328	0028	...
Fossano d.	1403	1425	1430	1432	1503	1503	1533	1602	1632	1640	1659	1728	1732	1756	1812	1833	1845	1855	1932	1931	2003	2032	2055	2058	2159	2232	2338	0038	...
Cuneo a.	|	1449	|	1455	|	|	1555	|	1654	|	|	|	1755	|	1835	1855	|	|	1955	|	|	2055	|	|	|	2255	2400	0100	...
Mondovi d.	1419	...	1449	...	1518	1518	...	1619	...	1658	1715	1741	...	1815	...	...	1906	1909	...	1943	2019	...	2113	2116	2217	...	...	...	...
Ceva d.	1434	...	1508	...	1533	1532	...	1633	...	1718	1731	1758	...	1832	...	...	1928	1932	...	1958	2033	...	2133	2136	2235	...	...	...	...
Savona a.	1522	...	1606	...	1627	1628	...	1734	...	1821	1823	1852	...	1920	...	...	2023	2022	...	2046	2122	...	2226	2230	...	...	...	...	...

	⚒		⚒	⚒	⚒	⚒	⚒	†	⚒	⚒	†		⚒	⚒	†	⚒	⑥	Ⓐ	†	†	⚒	†	†	†z	⚒	†		⚒	⚒
Savona d.	...	...	...	...	0515	...	0548	...	...	0626	0628	...	0724	...	0725	0748	...	...	...	0911	0942	0942	...	1111	...	1140	...	1240	...
Ceva d.	...	...	0535	...	0613	...	0652	...	...	0729	0729	...	0831	...	0835	0847	...	...	...	0958	1030	1036	...	1158	...	1237	...	1327	...
Mondovi d.	...	...	0551	...	0626	...	0705	...	...	0746	0746	...	0845	...	0851	0905	...	...	...	1012	1044	1055	...	1211	...	1257	...	1346	...
Cuneo d.	0435	0500	|	0555	|	0645	|	0705	0725	|	|	0813	|	0836	|	|	0905	0905	0908	|	|	|	1103	|	1203	|	1303	|	1403
Fossano d.	0458	0524	0607	0623	0640	0708	0718	0728	0749	0802	0802	0836	0857	0902	0905	0922	0928	0928	0931	1027	1059	1112	1127	1227	1227	1315	1331	1403	1427
Savigliano d.	0508	0534	0617	0633	0648	0718	0727	0737	0758	0811	0811	0846	...	0911	...	...	0937	0937	0941	1037	1110	...	1137	1237	1237	...	1340	1412	1437
Torino P N a.	0600	0625	0710	0730	0735	0755	0815	0825	0835	0900	0900	0935	...	1000	...	...	1025	1035	1030	1125	1205t	...	1225	1325	1325	...	1425	1500	1525

	†	⚒	†		⚒	⚒	†	⚒	†		†	⚒	†		†z	⚒	†	L		©z		Ⓐ	⑥	†	⚒	⚒	⚒	†	†z
Savona d.	1311	1340	1341	...	1442	...	1500	1538	1540	...	1621	1638	1703	...	1713	1735	1745	...	1838	1854	...	...	...	...	2036	...	2116	2117	2136
Ceva d.	1358	1432	1437	...	1530	...	1549	1627	1634	...	1709	1725	1754	...	1812	1830	1838	...	1928	1946	...	...	...	...	2129	...	2215	2207	2224
Mondovi d.	1412	1446	1456	...	1547	...	1605	1642	1653	...	1723	1740	1809	...	1826	1844	1857	...	1943	2001	...	...	...	...	2146	...	2228	2221	2238
Cuneo d.	|	|	|	1503	|	1603	|	|	|	1703	|	|	|	1756	|	|	|	1902	|	|	2003	2105	2105	2105	|	2205	|	|	|
Fossano d.	1429	1501	1514	1527	1602	1627	1627	1659	1710	1727	1738	1758	1826	1826	1839	1859	1915	1927	1959	2015	2027	2129	2129	2141	2201	2229	2240	2236	2251
Savigliano d.	1438	1510	...	1537	1611	1636	1636	1708	...	1737	1747	1807	...	1836	1848	1908	...	1938	2008	2024	2037	2138	2138	2150	2210	2239	2248	2245	2259
Torino P N a.	1525	1600	...	1625	1700	1725	1725	1800	...	1830	1835	1900	...	1925	1930	2000	...	2030	2100	2110	2125	2239t	2230	2235	2300	2335	2345	2335	2345

ADDITIONAL SERVICES FOSSANO - CUNEO and v.v. (2nd class only):

	⚒	†	⚒		⚒	†		†	⚒	⚒	†	⚒		⚒	†		⚒	⚒	⚒	⚒	†		⚒		
Fossano d.	0622	0735	0749	...	0907	0917	...	1134	1207	1307	1336	1407	...	1507	1535	...	1606	1707	1800	1900	1935	...	2007	2107	...
Cuneo a.	0644	0758	0811	...	0930	0947	...	1157	1229	1330	1359	1429	...	1529	1558	...	1630	1730	1830	1930	1959	...	2029	2130	...

	⚒		†	⚒		†	⚒	⚒		†	⚒	⚒		†	⚒	†	⚒		⚒	⚒		⚒	†		
Cuneo d.	0403	...	1000	1132	...	1200	1231	1331	...	1401	1431	1531	...	1600	1631	1657	1731	...	1810	1914	...	2031	2205	...	...
Fossano a.	0425	...	1022	1155	...	1222	1253	1353	...	1424	1453	1555	...	1622	1653	1718	1753	...	1832	1944	...	2053	2227	...	...

L – (2) Torino - Ventimiglia - Imperia Oneglia and v.v.
V – From / to Ventimiglia.
t – Torino **Porta Susa**.
y – Until Sept. 5 (not holidays).
z – Until Sept. 6.

MILANO MALPENSA AEROPORTO ✈ 583

FNM *Malpensa Express*

45 km, journey 40 minutes (50 minutes by 🚌). All rail services call at Milano Nord Bovisa (7 minutes from Cadorna, 33 minutes from Malpensa). Special fare payable.

From **Milano Cadorna**: 0410 🚌, 0457, 0527 and every 30 minutes until 2257, then 2327 🚌.

Operator: Ferrovie Nord Milano, Piazzale Cadorna 14, 20123 Milano. ✆ + 39 02 85 111, fax: + 39 02 85 11 708.

From **Malpensa Aeroporto**: 0553, 0623, 0653 and every 30 minutes until 2353, then 0023 🚌, 0130 🚌.

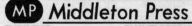

584 MODANE - OULX - TORINO

2nd class only except where shown

Additional connections operate Susa - Bussolena by 🚌 (all journeys on † are by 🚌). Timings in *italics*: change at Bussoleno.

km															EC 9241									
			†	⚒	⚒	⚒	⚒	†	⚒	⚒	†	⚒	†	⚒	⚒	P⊗	⚒	†	⚒	Ⓐ	©	⚒	Ⓐ	Ⓐ	©
0	**Modane**	d.	...	...	...	...	...	...	...	...	...	...	...	...	...	1155	...	...	...	...	...	...	...	...	...
20	Bardonecchia	d.	0513	0555	...	0650	...	0713	0810	...	0913	1005	1108	...	*1152*	1220	*1302*	1313	1405	*1502*	1513	...	1632	...	1713
31	Oulx ▲	d.	0526	0606	...	0701	...	0727	0823	...	0926	1017	1121	...	*1205*	1230	*1315*	1326	1417	*1514*	1527	...	1644	...	1726
⊖	Susa	d.	|	|	0618	|	0737	|	|	0944	|	|	|	1155	1232	|	1342	|	|	1543	|	1643	|	1738	|
61	Bussoleno	d.	0556	0637	0643	0733	0749	0757	0854	0954	0955	1053	1152	1205	1242	|	1352	1355	1452	1553	1557	1653	1715	1748	1755
106	**Torino Porta Nuova**	a.	0645	0715	0742	0810	0840	0845	0945	1045	1045	1145	1240	1255	1340	|	1445	1445	1545	1645	1645	1745	1805	1840	1845
107	**Torino Porta Susa**	a.	...	...	...	...	...	...	...	...	...	...	...	...	...	1317	...	...	...	...	...	...	...	...	...
	Milano Centrale **585**	a.	...	...	...	...	...	...	...	...	...	...	...	...	...	...	...	...	...	...	...	...	...	...	...

					EC 9247			EC 9249			
		Ⓐ	†	⚒	P⊗	Ⓐ	©	P	⚒	Ⓐ	©
Modane	d.	...	...	...	1820	...	...	1930	...	...	...
Bardonecchia	d.	1740	1805	...	1847	*1900*	1923	1957	2019	*2058*	2113
Oulx ▲	d.	1750	1816	...	1857	*1913*	1937	2007	2031	*2111*	2126
Susa	d.	|	|	1843	|	1943	|	|	|	2143	|
Bussoleno	d.	1818	1844	1853	|	1953	2006	|	2100	2153	2155
Torino Porta Nuova	a.	1915	1915	1945	|	2045	2055	|	2150	2245	2245
Torino Porta Susa	a.	...	...	...	1945	...	...	2100	...	...	...
Milano Centrale **585**	a.	...	...	...	...	...	...	...	...	...	...

					EC 9240					EC 9242
		⚒	⚒		P	⚒	†	⚒	†	P⊗
Milano Centrale **585**	d.	...	...	...	...	...	...	...	...	...
Torino Porta Susa	d.	...	...	...	0805	...	...	...	...	0940
Torino Porta Nuova	d.	0610	0655	0720	|	0815	0835	0910	0915	|
Bussoleno	d.	0701	0749	0810	|	0911	0906	0957	1004	|
Susa	a.	|	0758	|	|	0920	|	|	|	|
Oulx ▲	d.	0732	...	0838	0900	...	0930	1024	1035	1030
Bardonecchia	d.	0742	...	0852	0912	...	0940	1034	1050	1040
Modane	a.	...	...	...	0938	...	...	...	...	1105

															EC 9248										
		⚒	⚒		⚒	†	⚒	⚒	©	Ⓐ	⚒	Ⓐ	©	Ⓐ	P⊗	Ⓐ	Ⓐ	©	Ⓐ	Ⓐ	©	Ⓐ	⚒	©	Ⓐ
Milano Centrale **585**	d.	...	...	...	...	...	...	...	...	...	...	...	...	...	...	...	...	...	...	...	...	...	...	...	...
Torino Porta Susa	d.	1020	...	...	...	...	...	...	...	...	...	...	...	...	1735	...	...	...	...	...	...	...	...	...	...
Torino Porta Nuova	d.	|	1100	1130	1215	1315	1315	1420	1520	1520	1615	1700	1715	1715	|	1755	1815	1815	1845	1915	1915	1940	2020	2130	2130
Bussoleno	d.	1111	1154r	1220	1310	1405	1415	1519	1610	1616	1711	1738	1816	1816	|	1834	1907	1906	1936	2006	2006	2030	2111	2223	2226
Susa	a.	1120	1203r	|	1320	|	|	1528	|	1625	1720	|	|	1825	|	|	1916	|	|	2015	|	|	2120	|	2235
Oulx ▲	§ d.	*1148*	...	1248	*1346*	1433	1445	...	1640	*1653*	...	1807	1849	...	1825	1905	...	1934	2009	...	2034	2058	...	2250	*2322**
Bardonecchia	§ d.	*1200*	...	1300	*1400*	1445	1457	...	1652	*1705*	...	1817	1902	...	1840	1916	...	1947	2022	...	2047	2110	...	2302	*2341**
Modane	a.	...	...	...	...	...	...	...	...	...	...	...	...	...	1905	...	...	...	...	...	...	...	...	...	...

P – [12] and ✕ Paris - Torino and v.v. (Table **44**). Special 'global' fares payable.
r – 12 minutes later on ⑥.

* – By 🚌.
⊗ – Subject to confirmation.
▲ – Station for the resorts of Cesana, Claviere and Sestriere.
⊖ – Bussoleno - Susa: *8 km*.

585 TORINO - MILANO

km											y														
0	**Torino Porta Nuova 586**	d.	0450	0550	...	0650	...	0750	0850	...	1050	...	1150	1250	...	1350	...	1450	1550	...	1650	1750	1850	...	...
6	**Torino Porta Susa 586**	d.	0459	0559	...	0659	...	0759	0859	...	1103	...	1159	1259	...	1359	...	1459	1559	...	1659	1759	1859	...	...
29	Chivasso **586**	d.	0516	0616	...	0714	...	0816	0916	...	1120	...	1216	1316	...	1416	...	1516	1616	...	1716	1816	1916	...	...
60	Santhià	d.	0533	0633	...	0734	...	0833	0933	...	1143	...	1233	1333	...	1433	...	1533	1633	...	1733	1833	1933	...	...
79	Vercelli	d.	0546	0646	...	0746	...	0846	0946	...	1200	...	1246	1346	...	1446	...	1546	1646	...	1746	1846	1946	...	...
101	Novara	d.	0603	0703	...	0801	...	0903	1003	...	1214	...	1303	1403	...	1503	...	1603	1703	...	1803	1903	2003	...	...
153	**Milano Centrale**	a.	0645	0745	...	0842	...	0945	1045	...	1250	...	1345	1445	...	1545	...	1645	1745	...	1845	1945	2045	...	...
	Verona Porta Nuova **600**	a.	...	...	...	...	...	...	...	...	...	...	...	...	...	...	...	...	...	...	...	...	...	...	...
	Venezia Santa Lucia **600**	a.	...	...	...	...	...	...	...	...	...	...	...	...	...	...	...	...	...	...	...	...	...	...	...

Torino Porta Nuova 586	d.	...	1950	2055	...	2150	2250	...	...	...
Torino Porta Susa 586	d.	...	1959	2104	...	2159	2259	...	...	...
Chivasso **586**	d.	...	2016	2121	...	2216	2316	...	...	...
Santhià	d.	...	2033	2138	...	2233	2333	...	...	...
Vercelli	d.	...	2046	2151	...	2246	2346	...	...	...
Novara	d.	...	2103	2207	...	2303	0003	...	...	...
Milano Centrale	a.	...	2145	2248	...	2345	0045	...	...	...
Verona Porta Nuova **600**	a.	...	...	...	...	...	...	...	...	...
Venezia Santa Lucia **600**	a.	...	...	...	...	...	...	...	...	...

									y	
Venezia Santa Lucia **600**	d.	...	...	...	...	...	...	...	...	...
Verona Porta Nuova **600**	d.	...	...	...	...	...	...	...	...	...
Milano Centrale	d.	0015	0515	...	0600	0715	...	0815	0915	...
Novara	d.	0059	0559	...	0645	0759	...	0859	0959	...
Vercelli	d.	0116	0614	...	0700	0814	...	0914	1014	...
Santhià	d.	0127	0625	...	0713	0825	...	0925	1025	...
Chivasso **586**	d.	0148	0644	...	0730	0844	...	0944	1044	...
Torino Porta Susa 586	a.	0206	0700	...	0748	0900	...	1000	1100	...
Torino Porta Nuova 586	a.	...	0710	...	0800	0910	...	1010	1115	...

															Ⓐz										
Venezia Santa Lucia **600**	d.	...	...	...	...	...	...	...	...	...	...	...	...	...	...	...	...	...	...	...	...	...	...	...	...
Verona Porta Nuova **600**	d.	...	...	...	...	...	...	...	...	...	...	...	...	...	...	...	...	...	...	...	...	...	...	...	...
Milano Centrale	d.	1115	1215	...	1315	...	1415	1515	...	1615	...	1715	1815	...	1848	1915	...	2015	2115	...	2215	2301	...	...	...
Novara	d.	1159	1259	...	1359	...	1459	1559	...	1659	...	1759	1859	...	1929	1959	...	2059	2159	...	2259	0012	...	...	...
Vercelli	d.	1214	1314	...	1414	...	1514	1614	...	1714	...	1814	1914	...	1943	2014	...	2114	2214	...	2314	...	...	...	...
Santhià	d.	1225	1325	...	1425	...	1525	1625	...	1725	...	1825	1925	...	1955	2025	...	2125	2225	...	2325	...	...	...	...
Chivasso **586**	d.	1244	1344	...	1444	...	1544	1644	...	1744	...	1844	1944	...	2013	2044	...	2144	2244	...	2344	...	...	...	...
Torino Porta Susa 586	a.	1300	1400	...	1500	...	1600	1700	...	1800	...	1900	2000	...	2034	2100	...	2200	2300	...	2400	...	...	...	...
Torino Porta Nuova 586	a.	1310	1410	...	1510	...	1610	1710	...	1810	...	1910	2010	...	...	2110	...	2210	2310	...	0010	...	...	...	...

p – Milano **Porta Garibaldi**.
s – Calls to set down only.
u – Calls to pick up only.

y – Not Aug. 3-30.
z – Not Aug. 1-30.

586 TORINO - AOSTA - PRÉ ST DIDIER

Most trains 2nd class only

km																												
					⚒	⚒			†		⚒	†	⚒				Ⓐ	Ⓐ		⚒	⚒	†		⚒	†	†	
0	**Torino Porta Nuova 585**	d.	...	...	...	0625	0735	0825	0930	...	1125	*1150*	*1150*	*1225*	1325	1425	...	*1450*	...	1625	*1650*	1725	1725	1825	1920	1920	2025	2225
6	Torino Porta Susa **585**	d.	...	...	...	0634	0744	0835	0941	...	1136	*1159*	*1159*	*1235*	1334	1433	...	*1459*	...	1636	*1659*	1734	1734	1834	1928	1928	2034	2234
29	Chivasso **585**	d.	...	...	...	0706	0806	0900	1011	...	1200	1219	1253	*1303*	1400	1500	...	1520	...	1703	1720	1758	1803	1902	2000	2006	2101	2300
62	Ivrea	d.	...	0624	0650	0747	0836	0925	1037	...	1225	1304	1338	1338	1425	1529	...	1610	1637	1728	1805	1834	1834	1928	2025	2037	2126	2326
79	Pont Saint Martin	d.	...	0642	0712	0801	0853	0944	1051	...	1239	1323	1352	1354	1439	1544	...	▬	1652	1742	1833	1850	1848	1942	2046	2054	2147	2340
91	Verrès	d.	...	0701	0728	0812	0910	0955	1108	...	1251	1333	1409	1409	1450	1556	...	...	1707	1753	1850	1901	1859	1953	2057	2112	2158	2351
104	Chatillon-Saint Vincent	d.	...	0714	0741	0826	0922	1008	1122	...	1311	1344	1421	1421	1509	1615	...	...	1718	1811	1902	1914	1912	2013	2115	2125	2211	0004
129	**Aosta**	a.	...	0735	0811	0853	0940	1032	1142	...	1332	1408	1444	1452	1532	1635	...	...	1750	1832	1924	1935	1933	2034	2136	2144	2232	0025
	change trains					d			†	⚒		d				©	Ⓐ	©				Ⓐ	©					
129	**Aosta**	d.	0642	0744	...	0903	...	1041	1147	1240	1337	1439	...	...	1541	1642	1711	1744	...	1846	...	1946	1948	...	...	...	...	...
161	**Pré St Didier** ▲	a.	0733	0835	...	0954	...	1132	1238	1327	1428	1530	...	...	1632	1733	1758	1835	...	1937	...	2037	2039	...	...	...	...	...

CONTINUED ON NEXT PAGE

PRÉ ST DIDIER - AOSTA - TORINO 586

			⚒					⚒	†									Ⓒ	Ⓐ		Ⓒ	Ⓐ	Ⓒ	Ⓐ	Ⓒ	
Pré St Didier ▲ d.	...	...	0639	...	0741	0900	1038	1140	1144	...	...	...	1334	1436	1538	...	...	1639	1702		1741	1837	1843	1943	1945	2047
Aosta a.	...	...	0726	...	0828	0947	1125	1227	1231	...	...	...	1421	1523	1625	...	...	1726	1753		1828	1928	1930	2030	2032	2134
change trains								▬	d	⚒		⚒			†	⚒		d	⚒	Ⓐ	†	⚒	d		d	⚒
Aosta d.	0510	0625	...	0737	0836	1034	1148	...	1236	1336	...	1415	1429	1536	1637	1637	...	1735	1759	...	1833	1846	1937	...	2037	2141
Chatillon-Saint Vincent d.	0530	0646	...	0759	0858	1055	1210	...	1255	1358	...	1435	1451	1557	1657	1657	...	1756	1823	...	1853	1914	1957	...	2059	2200
Verrès d.	0542	0701	...	0812	0910	1108	1222	...	1309	1409	...	1450	1505	1611	1709	1707	...	1809	1833	...	1912	1927	2010	...	2112	2210
Pont Saint Martin d.	0552	0712	...	0822	0921	1118	1239	...	1322	1425	...	1503	1515	1621	1720	1721	...	1820	1850	...	1922	1942	2020	...	2123	2223
Ivrea d.	0606	0724	...	0835	0936	1131	1257	...	1337	1447	...	1517	1528	1636	1740	1742	...	1833	1909	...	1941	2004	2036	...	2137	2236
Chivasso **585** d.	0647	0808	...	0906	1007	1206	1335	1344	1407	1534	1544	...	1602	1710	1811	1833	1844	1905	1953	2027	2015	2048	2106	...	2208	2318
Torino Porta Susa **585** a.	0709	0825	...	0923	1030	1233	...	1400	1425	...	1600	...	1621	1725	1830	...	1900	1922	...	2051	2034	...	2124	...	2225	2339
Torino Porta Nuova 585 a.	0720	0835	...	0935	1040	1245	...	1410	1435	...	1610	...	1635	1740	1840	...	1910	1935	...	2100	2045	...	2135	...	2235	2350

d – Daily.

▲ – A connecting 🚌 service is available Pré St Didier - Courmayeur and v.v. (see Table **368**).

BRIG - STRESA - MILANO 590

For night trains from Genève / Basel to Roma and Venezia see Table **82**

km								*EC* **35**		*EC* **51**		*EC* **37**					*EC* **57**			*EC* **39**					*EC* **59**	*EC* **41**	
		2	2	2	2	2	2	◧	2	◧	2	◧	2		2	2	◧		2	◧	2	2		2	◧	◧	2
						⚒	†					V	⑥⑦						⚒								
	Genève Aéroport **570** d.	...	...	...	...	...	...	...	...	...	...	...	...	...	...	...	...	...	...	...	...	...	...	...	...	...	...
	Genève **570** d.	...	...	...	...	...	...	0545	...	...	...	0742	...	...	...	...	...	...	...	1342	...	...	...	...	...	1842	...
	Lausanne **570** d.	...	...	...	...	...	...	0620	...	...	...	0820	...	...	...	...	...	...	...	1420	...	...	...	...	...	1917	...
	Basel **560** d.	...	...	...	...	...	...	|	...	0628	...	|	...	...	...	...	1228	...	...	|	...	...	...	...	1728	|	...
	Bern **560** d.	...	...	...	...	...	...	|	...	0735	...	|	...	...	...	...	1335	...	...	|	...	...	...	...	1835	|	...
0	**Brig** 🏛 d.	...	...	...	...	...	...	0744	...	0844	...	0944	1107	...	...	...	1444	...	...	1544	...	...	...	...	1944	2044	...
42	**Domodossola** 🏛 § a.	...	...	...	...	...	...	0812	...	0912	...	1012	1145	...	...	...	1512	...	...	1612	...	...	...	...	2012	2112	...
42	**Domodossola** d.	0455	0555	0605	0655	0728	0750	0817	0825	0917	0948	1017	...	...	1255	1357	1517	1525	1605	1617	1655	1810	1855	1955	2017	2117	2155
72	Verbania-Pallanza d.	0516	0616	0627	0716	0747	0817	|	0846	|	1014	|	...	...	1316	1433	|	1546	1633	|	1716	1836	1915	2024	|	|	2223
77	Baveno d.	|	|	0632	|	|	0822	|	|	|	1019	|	...	...	|	1438	|	|	1638	|	|	1841	|	2029	|	|	2228
81	Stresa d.	0523	0623	0638	0723	0755	0827	0839	0853	0939	1024	|	...	...	1323	1443	1539	1553	1642	1639	1723	1845	1923	2039	|	2139	2232
98	Arona d.	0536	0635	0657	0736	0808	0851	|	0906	|	1049	|	...	...	1336	1502	|	1606	1700	|	1736	1903	1936	2059	|	|	2251
124	Gallarate d.	0558	0655	0731	0758	0832	0922	|	0928	|	1128	1104	...	...	1358	1532	|	1628	1731	|	1758	1932	1958	2128	2104	|	2321
150	Rho d.	|	|	0800	|	0900	0944	|	|	|	1149	|	...	...	|	1559	|	|	1800	|	|	1959	|	2150	|	|	2345
165	**Milano Porta Garibaldi** a.	|	0733	0815	0835	0915	0957	|	|	|	1207	|	...	...	|	1613	|	|	1813	|	|	2013	|	2203	|	|	2357
167	**Milano Centrale** a.	0635	...	...	...	...	...	0935	1004	1035	...	1135	...	...	1435	...	1640	1705	...	1735	1835	...	2035	...	2135	2235	...

			EC **50**		*EC* **32**				*EC* **52**		*EC* **34**						*EC* **36**			*EC* **56**			*EC* **42**				
		2	◧	2	◧		2		◧		◧		2	2	2		◧	2		◧			◧	2	2		
						⚒	⑥	†															V				
Milano Centrale d.	...	...	0725	0755	0825	...	...	...	1120	...	1225	...	1325	...	1525	...	1720	...	1725	1825	...	...	1920	1925	...	2125	...
Milano Porta Garibaldi d.	0455	0617	|	|	|	0900	...	0900	|	...	|	1246	|	1447	|	1600	|	1647	|	|	1755	1835	|	|	2047	|	...
Rho d.	0514	0630	|	|	|	0912	...	0912	|	...	|	1300	|	1500	|	|	|	1701	|	|	|	|	|	|	2100	|	...
Gallarate d.	0543	0654	0756	0832	|	0931	...	0931	|	...	|	1327	1401	1527	1600	1636	|	1727	1802	|	1831	1915	1956	2002	2128	2200	...
Arona d.	0611	0724	|	0853	|	0959	...	1007	|	...	|	1348	1421	1555	1621	1711	|	1754	1824	|	1911	1936	|	2021	2157	2221	...
Stresa d.	0631	0743	|	0906	0921	1018	...	1027	1221	...	1321	1408	1434	1613	1634	1732	1821	1812	1837	1921	1930	1956	|	2034	2216	2234	...
Baveno d.	0635	0747	|	|	|	1023	...	1031	|	...	|	1412	|	1617	|	1736	|	1816	|	|	1935	2000	|	|	2220	|	...
Verbania-Pallanza d.	0640	0752	|	0914	|	1028	...	1037	|	...	|	1417	1442	1622	1642	1741	|	1821	1845	|	1940	2005	|	2042	2225	2242	...
Domodossola a.	0708	0818	0843	0935	0943	1105	...	1108	1243	...	1343	1437	1505	1643	1705	1810	1843	1850	1905	1943	2000	2027	2043	2105	2253	2305	...
Domodossola 🏛 § d.	...	...	0848	...	0948	...	1215	...	1248	...	1348	...	...	...	...	...	1848	...	...	1948	...	...	2048	...	...	...	...
Brig 🏛 a.	...	...	0916	...	1016	...	1253	...	1316	...	1416	...	...	...	...	...	1916	...	...	2016	...	...	2116	...	...	...	...
Bern **560** a.	...	...	1023	...	|	...	...	...	1423	...	|	...	...	...	...	...	|	...	...	2123	...	...	|	...	...	...	...
Basel **560** a.	...	...	1132	...	|	...	...	...	1532	...	|	...	...	...	...	...	|	...	...	2232	...	...	|	...	...	...	...
Lausanne **570** a.	...	...	...	...	1140	...	...	...	...	...	1540	...	...	...	...	...	2040	...	...	...	...	...	2240	...	...	...	...
Genève **570** a.	...	...	...	...	1218	...	...	...	...	...	1618	...	...	...	...	...	2118	...	...	...	...	...	2315	...	...	...	...
Genève Aéroport **570** a.	...	...	...	...	...	...	...	...	...	...	...	...	...	...	...	...	...	...	...	...	...	...	...	...	...	...	...

Local service BRIG - DOMODOSSOLA and v.v. (2nd class only):

km		Ⓐ		🚌	⑥z		🚌 Ⓐ		🚌	⑥z		Ⓒ		🚌	🚌	⑥z	🚌	🚌	Ⓐ			🚌		🚌		🚌	
0	**Brig** d.	0610	0715*	...	0820	0850*	...	1015*	...	1015	1044	1107	1150*	...	*1325*r	1419	*1450*r	*1615*r	1707	1807	1915*	...	2050*	...	2215*	...	0019
23	Iselle di Trasquera § d.	0630	0736	0750	|	0911	0920	1036	1050	|	|	1127	1211	1220	1350	|	1520	1650	1727	1827	1936	1950	2111	2120	2236	2250	0039
42	**Domodossola** a.	0648	...	0820	0848	...	0948	...	1120	1043	1112	1145	...	1248	1420	1447	1548	1720	1745	1845	...	2020	...	2148	...	2320	0057

		Ⓐ		⚒	🚌		🚌 Ⓐ		🚌		🚌		⑥x	🚌		🚌		🚌		🚌		🚌		🚌		🚌	
Domodossola d.	0354	0515	0615	0705	0720	...	0850	...	1020	...	1150	...	1215	1320	...	1450	...	1620	...	1750	...	1920	...	2050	...	2220	...
Iselle di Trasquera § d.	0417	0539	0639	0727	0748	0805	0918	0930	1048	1105	1218	1230	1239	1348	1405	1518	1530	1648	1705	1818	1830	1948	2005	2118	2130	2248	2305
Brig a.	0432	0553	0653	0742	...	0825*	...	0949*	...	1125*	...	1249*	1253	...	1425*	...	1549*	...	1725*	...	1849*	...	2025*	...	2149*	...	2325*

V – 🚃12 and 🍷 Genève - Milano - Venezia Santa Lucia and v.v.
r – Connection by train from Brig Autoquai (see note *).
x – Not Dec. 26, Jan. 2.
z – *IR* train (1, 2 class). Not Dec. 26, Jan. 2.

§ – Ticket point is **Iselle**.
* – Brig Autoquai (allow 8 minutes walk from Brig station).

DOMODOSSOLA and ARONA - NOVARA 591

2nd class only except where shown

km		⚒p		S	Ⓐx		⚒p		q	y	⚒p	Ⓒ	Ⓒ	🚌 Ⓐ	⚒			q	⚒p	⚒	⚒		q	†		q	Ⓐw	Ⓒ
0	**Domodossola** d.	0523	...	0618	0618	...	0615	...	0653	...	0755	...	...	1100	...	...	...	1236	1340	...	...	...	1557	...	...	1747	1902	1902
38	Omegna d.	0618	...	|	|	...	0657	...	0751	...	0850	...	...	1201	...	...	...	1337	1431	...	...	...	1645	...	...	1842	1945	1943
44	Pettenasco d.	0625	...	|	|	...	0704	...	0759	...	0857	...	...	1208	...	...	...	1344	|	...	...	...	1651	...	...	1850	1951	1950
47	Orta-Miasino d.	0629	...	|	|	...	0708	...	0804	...	0901	...	...	1212	...	...	...	1354	1442	...	...	...	1655	...	...	1855	1959	1959
60	Borgomanero d.	0642	...	|	|	...	0721	...	0819	...	0916	...	...	1232	1253	...	...	1409	1458	...	...	...	1714	...	...	1908	2017	2017
	Arona d.	|	0637	0704	0704	...	|	0756	|	...	|	1002	1205	▬	|	...	1400	|	|	...	...	1636	|	...	1845	|	|	|
	Oleggio d.	|	0700	0721	0721	...	|	0818	|	...	|	1022	1228	...	|	...	1424	|	|	...	...	1658	|	...	1911	|	|	|
90	**Novara** a.	0713	0719	0733	0734	0735	0752	0836	0854	0907	0951	1040	1246	1313	1328	1423	1441	1450	1533	1605	1706	1717	1753	1909	1931	1942	2046	2046
157	Alessandria a.	...	...	0822	...	0822	...	...	...	1021	...	...	...	1429	...	1534	...	...	...	1718	1820	...	...	2018	...	...	...	...

km		⚒p	⚒	q			🚌	b	d	t		⚒p			⚒	q	Ⓐw	z	q			Ⓐw		Ⓒ	Ⓐw		n	S
	Alessandria d.	...	...	...	...	...	...	...	...	...	...	...	...	1240	1355	...	...	1535	...	...	1643	...	1741	...	...	...	2040	2119
0	**Novara** d.	0538	0553	0634	0653	0805	...	0912	1002	1223	1254	1350	1412	1414	1506	1519	1632	1648	1732	1739	1753	1822	1853	1920	1920	1926	2152	2203
17	Oleggio d.	|	0610	|	0722	|	...	0928	1023	|	1311	|	1441	...	...	|	|	...	|	1759	...	|	...	|	|	1942	...	2218
37	**Arona** a.	|	0635	|	0742	|	...	0952	1047	|	1334	|	1504	...	...	|	|	...	|	1823	...	|	...	|	|	2004	...	2231
	Borgomanero d.	0608	...	0722	...	0838	0845	...	...	1252	...	1425	...	...	...	1556	1700	...	1809	...	...	1912	...	2003	2003	...	...	|
	Orta-Miasino d.	0630	...	0736	...	...	0907	...	...	1306	...	1443	...	...	...	1612	1713	...	1825	...	...	1932	...	2017	2017	...	...	|
	Pettenasco d.	0635	...	0741	...	...	0913	...	...	1311	...	1448	...	...	...	1617	1718	...	1830	...	...	1937	...	2021	2021	...	...	|
	Omegna d.	0658	...	0800	...	...	0920	...	...	1323	...	1458	...	...	...	1624	1725	...	1843	...	...	1944	...	2027	2027	...	...	|
93	**Domodossola** a.	0744	...	0850	...	...	1011	...	...	1413	...	1548	...	...	...	1716	1805	...	1936	...	...	2018	...	2113	2113	...	...	2314

S – Ⓒ until Aug. 2; daily Aug. 3-30.
b – By 🚌 on Ⓐ (depart Novara 0910, arrive Arona 1007).
d – By 🚌 on Ⓐ (depart Novara 1010, arrive Arona 1107).

n – On † until Sept. 6 depart Alessandria 2047, arrive Novara 2135.
p – Not Aug. 15-21.

q – Not Aug. 17-21.
t – Not ⚒ Aug. 15-21.
w – Not Aug. 15-23.

x – Not Aug. 1-30.
y – Not Aug. 10-23.
z – Not ⚒ Aug. 9-23.

Selected details only received by press date – see page 286

592 BELLINZONA - LUINO

2nd class only

km											
0	**Bellinzona 550** d.	0554	0754	...	0950	*1154*	...	*1354*	*1554*	*1754*	...
9	Cadenazzo d.	0606	0806	...	1006j	1206	...	1406	1606	1806	...
27	Pino-Tronzano 🏛 d.	0627	0827	...	1027j	1227	...	1427	1627	1827	...
40	**Luino 608** a.	0644	0844	...	1044j	1244	...	1444	1644	1844	...

Luino 608 d.	0705	...	1115	1315	...	1515	...	1715	1915	...
Pino-Tronzano 🏛 d.	0722	...	1131	1331	...	1531	...	1731	1931	...
Cadenazzo a.	0744	...	1152	1352	...	1552	...	1752	1952	...
Bellinzona 550 a.	0754	...	*1204*	*1404*	...	*1604*	...	1800	2008	...

Operator: FS – Ferrovie dello Stato / FFS – Ferrovie Federali Svizzere.

j – Runs 6 minutes later on some dates.

593 MILANO - COLICO - TIRANO

km		2 ⚒v		2 †	2 ▷	2 ⚒	2 †			⚒			2 Ⓐ		⚒	2 ⚒				2	🚌	▷	2	2
0	**Milano Centrale** ▷ d.	...	0620	0625p	0649p	0720	0720	0820	1020	1125	1220	1420	1520p	1620	1720	1750	1820	1920	2020	2125	...	2149p	2250	2350
12	Monza ▷ d.	...	0634	0643	0709	0734	0734	0834	1034	1138	1234	1434	1534	1634	1734	1804	1834	1934	2034	2139	...	2209	2308	0008
50	Lecco ▷ d.	...	0702	0718	0751	0801	0802	0902	1102	1208	1302	1502	1602	1702	1802	1836	1902	2001	2102	2209	...	2251	2350	0052
72	Varenna-Esino d.	...	0724	0753	...	...	0824	0924	1124	...	1324	1524	...	1724	1824	...	|	2024	2124	2240	...	...	...	...
75	Bellano-Tartavalle Terme d.	...	0733	0802	...	...	0833	0933	1133	...	1333	1533	...	1733	1833	...	1933	2033	2133	2245	...	...	...	...
89	**Colico** a.	...	0747	0823	...	...	0847	0947	1147	...	1347	1547	...	1747	1847	...	1947	2047	2147	2300	2305	...	...	...
116	Chiavenna ▲ a.	...	|	0848	...	...	|	|	|	...	|	|	...	|	|	...	|	|	|	...	|	...	...	...
130	Sondrio a.	0652	0821	...	...	...	0921	1021	1221	...	1422	1622	...	1821	1921	...	2021	2121	2221	...	2347	...	...	...
156	**Tirano** a.	0734	0850	...	...	...	1007	1050	1250	...	1450	1650	...	1850	...	...	2050	2151	...	...	...	...	...	...

	2 ▽			2 ⚒		⚒						2 ⚒	2 Ⓐ		2 †		2 †	2 ⚒		2 †r	2 ⚒	2 ▽	2	2
Tirano d.	...	...	0610	...	0710	...	0910	1110	...	1310	1510	...	...	1710	...	...	1810	...	1910	1952	...	...		2123
Sondrio d.	...	0528	0638	...	0738	...	0938	1138	...	1338	1538	...	...	1738	...	...	1838	...	1938	2038	...	...	2123	2200
Chiavenna ▲ d.	...	|	|	...	|	...	|	|	...	|	|	...	...	|	1802	...	|	...	|	|	...	...	|	...
Colico d.	...	0601	0716	...	0816	...	1016	1216	...	1416	1616	...	...	1816	1837	...	1916	...	2016	2116	2116	...	2203	...
Bellano-Tartavalle Terme d.	...	0616	0732	...	0832	...	1032	1232	...	1432	1632	...	...	1832	1901	...	1932	...	2032	2132	2132	...	2219	...
Varenna-Esino d.	...	0621	0737	...	0837	...	1037	1237	...	1437	1637	...	...	1837	1906	...	1937	...	2037	2137	2137	...	2224	...
Lecco ▽ d.	0609	0653	0759	0826	0859	0957	1059	1259	...	1459	1659	1729	1757	1859	1946	...	1959	1959	2059	2159	2159	2209	2248	...
Monza ▽ d.	0652	0727	0827	0857	0927	1027	1127	1327	...	1527	1727	1757	1827	1927	2014	...	2027	2027	2127	2227	2227	2252	2322	...
Milano Centrale ▽ a.	0711p	0740	0840	0910	0940	1040	1140	1340	...	1540	1740	1810	1840p	1940	2030p	...	2040	2040	2140	2240	2240	2311p	2335	...

p – Milano **Porta Garibaldi**.
r – † (daily Aug. 3-30).
v – Not Aug. 2-30.
▷ – Local trains run Milano Porta Garibaldi - Lecco hourly 0649 - 2149.
▽ – Local trains run Lecco - Milano Porta Garibaldi hourly 0609 - 2209.

▲ – **Local service COLICO - CHIAVENNA**: Journey 28–35 minutes, 2nd class only. *Services operated by 🚌 Aug. 2-30 – timings may vary).*

From **Colico**: 0550, 0707, 0810 ⚒, 0846 ⚒, 1002, 1046 ⚒, 1202, 1246 ⚒, 1402, 1446 ⚒, 1602, 1646 ⚒, 1802, 1852 ⚒, 2002.

From **Chiavenna**: 0626, 0745 ⚒, 0843 ⚒, 0928 ⚒, 1043, 1128 ⚒, 1243, 1328 ⚒, 1443, 1528 ⚒, 1643, 1728 ⚒, 1845, 1930 ⚒, 2040.

595 INNSBRUCK - BOLZANO / BOZEN - VERONA - BOLOGNA

km			2 ⚒	2	2	2 ⚒	2	2 Ⓐ	1871 2 L	2	*IC* 717 🍷 ♦	2 ©	2 ©	2	2		*EC* 81 ✕	2	2	2	2	2 ⚒	*EC* 85 ✕	2	2
	München Hbf **951** d.	...	...	...	...	...	...	...	...	...	...	...	...	...	...	...	0731	...	...	...	...	...	0931	...	...
0	**Innsbruck Hbf** ▷ d.	...	...	0516	...	0546	0616	...	0700	0716	...	...	...	0816	...	...	0927	...	0916	...	1016	...	1127	1116	1216
18	Matrei ▷ d.	...	...	0534	...	0604	0634	...	0718	0734	...	...	...	0834	...	...	|	...	0934	...	1034	...	|	1134	1234
23	Steinach in Tirol ▷ d.	...	...	0539	...	0609	0639	...	0723	0739	...	...	...	0839	...	...	|	...	0939	...	1039	...	|	1139	1239
37	**Brennero** 🏛 ▷ a.	...	...	0555	...	0624	0655	...	0737	0755	...	...	...	0855	...	...	|	...	0955	...	1055	...	|	1155	1255
						2d	▬		|	2⚒				©			|		2		2		|	2	2
37	**Brennero** 🏛 d.	...	...	0605	...	0638		...	0739	0804	...	...	0838	0908g	0938	...	|	...	1038	...	1138	...	|	1238	1308
60	Vipiteno / Sterzing d.	...	...	0626	...	0657	...	...	0758	0823	...	...	0857	0927g	0957	...	|	...	1057	...	1157	...	|	1257	1327
78	Fortezza / Franzensfeste d.	...	0542	0646	...	0715	...	...	0814	0841	...	...	0915	0945g	1015	...	1052	...	1115	...	1215	...	1252	1315	1345
89	Bressanone / Brixen d.	...	0554	0656	...	0725	...	...	...	0851	...	...	0925	0955g	1025	...	1102	...	1125	...	1225	...	1302	1325	1355
99	Chiusa / Klausen d.	...	0602	0704	...	0733	2	...	...	0859	...	...	0933	1003g	1033	...	|	...	1133	...	1233	...	|	1333	1403
127	**Bolzano / Bozen** a.	...	0626	0728	...	0759	⚒	...	...	0925	...	...	0959	1029g	1059	...	1134	...	1159	...	1259	...	1334	1359	1429
127	**Bolzano / Bozen** d.	0500	0630	0731	0737	▬	0831	0907	...	▬	0931	0937	...	1031	▬	...	...	1137	▬	1231	...	1304	1336	...	1431
143	Ora / Auer d.	0512	0642	0743	0755	...	0843	0925	...	...	0943	0955	...	1043	...	...	...	1155	...	1243	...	1322	|	...	1443
165	Mezzocorona d.	0526	0655	0756	0816	...	0856	0942	...	...	0958	1016	...	1056	...	...	...	1216	...	1256	...	1343	|	...	1456
182	**Trento** ▲ d.	0540	0712	0810	0832	...	0910	0957	...	...	1012	1032	...	1110	...	...	...	1232	...	1310	...	1355	1410	...	1510
206	Rovereto d.	0554	0726	0825	0846	...	0925	1012	...	...	1028	1046	...	1125	...	...	...	1246	2	1325	...	...	1426	...	1525
274	**Verona Porta Nuova** a.	0647	0818	0917	0952	©	1017	...	...	...	1111	1159	...	1217	...	...	...	1352	⚒	1417	...	...	1507	...	1617
274	**Verona Porta Nuova** d.	0659	...	...	...	0959	...	...	...	1147	1131	...	...	...	1259	...	...	...	1415	1457	...	...	1521	...	1659
388	**Bologna Centrale** a.	0832	...	...	...	1132	...	...	...	1332	1315	...	...	...	1432	...	...	...	1604	1634	...	...	1636	...	1832
	Milano Centrale **600** a.	...	...	...	...	...	...	...	...	...	...	...	...	...	...	...	...	...	...	...	...	...	...	...	...
	Venezia Santa Lucia **600** a.	...	...	...	...	...	...	...	...	...	...	...	...	...	...	...	...	...	...	...	...	...	...	...	...
	Firenze SMN **620** a.	...	...	...	...	...	...	...	...	...	...	...	...	...	...	...	...	...	...	...	...	...	...	...	...
	Roma Termini **620** a.	...	...	...	...	...	...	...	...	...	...	...	...	...	...	...	...	...	...	...	...	...	...	...	...

	2	*EC* 87 ✕	2	2	2	2	1875 2 L⑤	*EC* 89 *EC* 92 🍷	2	2	*E* 1595 ♦	2	2	1873 2 L	*EC* 83 🍷	2	2	2	*E* 925 *E* 837 Q	2	2	*E* 1601 ♦		*EN* 485 ♦	*EN* 363 B
München Hbf **951** d.	...	1131	...	...	...	...	...	1331	...	...	...	...	...	...	1531	...	...	...	...	...	...	...	...	2103	2103
Innsbruck Hbf ▷ d.	...	1327	...	1316	1416	...	1503	1527	...	1516	...	1616	...	1701	1727	...	1715	1816	...	1916	2016	...	...	2305	2305
Matrei ▷ d.	...	|	...	1334	1434	...	1521	|	...	1534	...	1634	...	1719	|	...	1734	1834	...	1934	2034	...	...	|	|
Steinach in Tirol ▷ d.	...	|	...	1339	1439	...	1526	|	...	1539	...	1639	...	1724	|	...	1739	1839	...	1939	2039	...	...	|	|
Brennero 🏛 ▷ a.	...	|	...	1355	1455	...	1540	|	...	1555	...	1655	...	1740	|	...	1755	1855	...	1955	2055	...	...	|	|
		|		2	2		|	|		2		2		|	|		2	2		2	2			|	|
Brennero 🏛 d.	1338	|	...	1438	1508	1538	1543	|	...	1638	...	1708	1738	1743	|	...	1838	1908	...	2008	2108	...	...	|	|
Vipiteno / Sterzing d.	1357	|	...	1457	1527	1557	1603	|	...	1657	...	1727	1757	1804	|	...	1857	1927	...	2027	2127	...	...	|	|
Fortezza / Franzensfeste d.	1415	1452	...	1515	1545	1615	1620	1652	...	1715	...	1745	1815	1820	1852	...	1915	1945	...	2045	2145	2154	...	0029	0029
Bressanone / Brixen d.	1425	1502	...	1525	1555	1625	...	1702	...	1725	...	1755	1825	...	1902	...	1925	1955	...	2055	2155	2205	...	0038	0038
Chiusa / Klausen d.	1433	|	...	1533	1603	1633	...	|	...	1733	...	1803	1833	...	|	...	1933	2003	...	2103	2203	|	...	|	|
Bolzano / Bozen a.	1500	1534	...	1559	1629	1659	...	1734	...	1759	...	1829	1859	...	1934	...	1959	2029	...	2129	2229	2236	...	0107	0107
Bolzano / Bozen d.	...	1536	1537	...	1631	...	...	1736	1737	...	1837	1831	...	...	1936	1937	...	2031	2050	...	2231r	2301	...	0109	0109
Ora / Auer d.	...	|	1555	...	1643	...	...	|	1755	...	1854	1843	...	...	|	1955	...	2043	2103	...	2248r	2314	...	|	|
Mezzocorona d.	...	|	1616	...	1656	...	...	|	1816	...	1915	1856	...	...	|	2016	...	2056	2124	...	2310r	2330	...	|	|
Trento ▲ d.	...	1610	1632	...	1710	...	...	1810	1832	...	1929	1910	...	...	2010	2032	...	2110	2139	...	2323r	2348	...	0142	0142
Rovereto d.	...	1626	1646	...	1725	...	...	1826	1846	...	1945	1925	...	...	2026	2046	...	2125	2155	...	...	0006	...	|	|
Verona Porta Nuova a.	...	1707	1759	...	1817	...	...	1907	1952	...	2032	2017	...	...	2107	2152	...	2217	2237	...	...	|	...	0237	0237
Verona Porta Nuova d.	...	...	...	...	1848	...	...	1922	...	...	2052	2106	...	...	...	...	...	...	2240	...	...	|	...	0305	0440
Bologna Centrale a.	...	...	...	...	2032	...	...	|	...	...	2228	2234	...	...	...	...	...	...	0058	...	...	|	...	0420	|
Milano Centrale **600** a.	...	...	...	...	...	...	...	2135p	...	...	|	...	...	...	...	...	...	...	|	...	...	|	...	|	|
Venezia S.L. **600** a.	...	...	...	...	...	...	...	...	...	...	|	...	...	...	...	...	...	...	|	...	...	|	...	|	0638
Firenze SMN **620** a.	...	...	...	...	...	...	...	...	...	...	2344c	...	...	...	...	...	...	...	|	...	...	|	...	0618	...
Roma Termini **620** a.	...	...	...	...	...	...	...	...	...	...	...	...	...	...	...	...	...	...	0609t	...	...	0837t	...	0905	...

FOR NOTES SEE NEXT PAGE

ADDITIONAL TRAINS INNSBRUCK - BRENNERO

2nd class

	⚒	⚒	⚒	⚒	⚒	⚒	⚒			
Innsbruck Hbf d.	0846	1045	1246	1446	1646	1846	1946	2116	2216	2316
Matrei d.	0904	1104	1304	1504	1704	1904	2004	2134	2234	2334
Steinach in Tirol d.	0908	1108	1308	1508	1708	1908	2009	2138	2239	2339
Brennero 🏛 a.	...	...	...	...	...	...	2023	...	2255	2355

			⚒		⚒	⚒	⚒	⚒	⚒	⚒
Brennero 🏛 d.	0535	0605	0635	0705	...	...	...	...	...	...
Steinach in Tirol d.	0552	0622	0652	0722	0852	1052	1252	1452	1652	1852
Matrei d.	0557	0627	0657	0727	0857	1057	1257	1457	1657	1857
Innsbruck Hbf a.	0613	0643	0713	0743	0914	1113	1313	1513	1713	1913

BOLOGNA - VERONA - BOLZANO / BOZEN - INNSBRUCK 595

	2 ⚒	1870 2 L	2	2 ⑥	2	*E* 1602 ♦	2 ⚒	*E* 824 *E* 924 R	2 ⚒h	*EC* 82 🍷	2	2	2	*E* 1594 ♦	2	*EC* 93 *EC* 88 🍷	2	2 †	2	*EC* 80 ✕	2		2	2 ⚒	2 ⚒w
Roma Termini **620** d.	...	...	...	...	...	2157t	...	2205t	...	...	...	...	...	...	...	...	...	...	...	...	...	...	...	...	...
Firenze SMN **620** d.	...	...	...	...	...	|	...	|	...	...	...	...	...	...	...	...	...	...	...	...	...	...	...	...	...
Venezia Santa Lucia **600** d.	...	...	...	...	...	|	...	|	...	...	...	...	...	...	...	...	...	...	...	...	...	...	...	...	...
Milano Centrale **600** d.	...	...	...	...	...	|	...	|	...	...	...	...	...	...	...	0640p	...	...	...	...	...	...	...	...	...
Bologna Centrale d.	...	...	...	...	...	|	...	0400	0503	...	...	...	0604	0535	0643	|	0748	...	...	...	...	0948x	...	...	1048
Verona Porta Nuova a.	...	...	...	...	...	|	...	0610	0655	...	...	...	0744	0802	0823	0837	0926	...	...	...	...	1122x	...	...	1226
Verona Porta Nuova d.	...	...	...	*0525*	...	|	0609	0620	...	0705	...	0747	▬	0805	...	0905	▬	0947	...	...	...	1147	...	1209	...
Rovereto d.	...	...	...	*0612*	...	0626s	0715	0721	...	0747	*0751*z	0837	...	0857	...	0947	...	1037	...	...	*1150*a	1237	...	1315	...
Trento ▲ d.	...	...	*0558*z	*0628*	...	0644s	0731	0739	...	0804	*0807*z	0853	...	0913	...	1004	...	1053	...	...	*1207*a	1253	...	1331	...
Mezzocorona d.	...	...	*0613*z	*0641*	...	0657s	0744	0752	...	|	*0818*z	0905	...	0926	...	|	...	1105	...	...	*1218*a	1305	...	1344	...
Ora / Auer d.	...	...	*0634*z	*0704*	...	0713s	0805	0810	...	|	*0839*z	0919	...	0945	...	|	2	1119	...	...	*1235*a	1319	...	1405	...
Bolzano / Bozen a.	...	...	*0652*z	*0722*	...	0732s	0822	0843	...	0842	*0856*z	0930	2	1006	...	1042	©	1131	...	...	*1252*a	1330	...	1422	...
Bolzano / Bozen d.	0605	...	0700	0729	0800	0809s	...	...	...	0843	0901	0932	1000	...	...	1043	1100	...	1200	1241	1300	1332	1400	...	...
Chiusa / Klausen d.	0630	...	0725	0754	0825	|	...	...	...	|	0925	0955	1025	...	...	|	1125	...	1225	|	1325	1355	1425	...	...
Bressanone / Brixen d.	0638	...	0734	0802	0834	0843s	...	...	...	0910	0934	1004	1034	...	...	1110	1134	...	1234	1310	1334	1404	1434	...	...
Fortezza / Franzensfeste d.	0650	0720	0745	0812	0845	0856s	...	...	...	0923	0945	1015	1045	...	...	1123	1145	...	1245	1323	1345	1415	1445	...	...
Vipiteno / Sterzing d.	0709	0739	0803	0833	0903	...	...	...	...	|	1003	1033	1103	...	...	|	1203	...	1303	|	1403	1433	1503	...	...
Brennero 🏛 a.	0729	0758	0822	0852	0922	...	...	...	...	|	1022	1052	1122	...	...	1148	1222	...	1322	|	1422	1452	1522	...	...
	2d	|		2	2					|		2	2			|	2d		2	|		2	2		
Brennero 🏛 ▷ d.	0735	0805	...	0905	1005	...	...	...	...	|	...	1105	1205	...	...	1200	1305	...	1405	|	...	1505	1605	...	...
Steinach in Tirol ▷ d.	0752	0822	...	0922	1022	...	...	...	...	|	...	1122	1222	...	...	|	1322	...	1422	|	...	1522	1622	...	...
Matrei ▷ d.	0757	0827	...	0927	1027	...	...	...	...	|	...	1127	1227	...	...	|	1327	...	1427	|	...	1527	1627	...	...
Innsbruck Hbf ▷ a.	0814	0843	...	0943	1043	...	...	...	...	1032	...	1143	1243	...	...	1232	1343	...	1443	1432	...	1543	1643	...	...
München Hbf **951** a.	...	...	...	...	...	...	...	...	...	1225	...	...	...	...	...	1425	...	...	...	1625	...	...	...	...	...

	EC 84 ✕	2		2	2 Ⓐ	*EC* 86 ✕	2		1874 2 L⑦k	2		2	1872 2 L		2	2 Ⓐ		2 Ⓐb	2 ⚒		*IC* 718 🍷 ♦			*EN* 358 B	*EN* 484 ♦
Roma Termini **620** d.	...	...	...	...	...	...	...	...	...	...	...	...	...	...	...	...	...	...	...	...	...	...	...	...	1905
Firenze SMN **620** d.	...	...	...	...	...	...	...	...	...	...	...	...	...	...	...	...	...	...	...	...	...	...	...	...	2138
Venezia Santa Lucia **600** d.	...	...	...	...	...	...	...	...	...	...	...	...	...	...	...	...	...	...	...	...	...	...	...	2251	|
Milano Centrale **600** d.	...	...	...	...	...	...	...	...	...	...	...	...	...	...	...	...	...	...	...	...	...	...	...	|	|
Bologna Centrale d.	1155	...	1148	...	...	...	...	1348	...	...	...	...	...	1548	...	...	1748	...	*1848*r	1948	1956	2118	...	|	2305
Verona Porta Nuova a.	1253	...	1324	...	...	...	...	1522	...	...	...	...	...	1722	...	...	1922	...	*2035*r	2122	2146	2248	...	0025	0020
Verona Porta Nuova d.	1305	...	1343	...	1409	1505	...	1547	...	...	...	*1609*a	...	1747	...	1809	1947	2009	2109	2147	2207	...	...	0101	0101
Rovereto d.	1347	...	1437	...	1515	1547	*1550*a	1637	...	*1651*a	...	*1715*a	...	1837	...	1915	2037	2115	2215	2237	2251	...	...	|	|
Trento ▲ d.	1404	*1411*a	1453	...	1531	1604	*1607*a	1653	...	*1707*a	...	*1731*a	...	1853	...	1931	2053	2131	2231	2253	2308	...	...	|	|
Mezzocorona d.	|	*1423*a	1505	...	1544	|	*1618*a	1705	...	*1718*a	...	*1744*a	...	1905	...	1944	2105	2144	2244	2305	2320	...	...	|	|
Ora / Auer d.	|	*1439*a	1519	...	1605	|	*1635*a	1719	...	*1735*a	...	*1805*a	...	1919	...	2005	2119	2205	2305	2319	2334	...	...	|	|
Bolzano / Bozen a.	1442	*1455*a	1530	...	1622	1642	*1652*a	1730	...	*1752*a	...	*1822*a	...	1930	...	2022	2130	2222	2322	2331	2350	...	...	|	|
Bolzano / Bozen d.	1443	1500	1532	1600	...	1643	1700	1732	...	1800	...	1832	...	1932	2000	*2030*	2132	*2258*	...	...	...	...	...	|	|
Chiusa / Klausen d.	|	1525	1555	1625	...	|	1722	1755	...	1825	...	1855	...	1955	2025	*2055*	2155	*2322*	...	...	...	...	...	|	|
Bressanone / Brixen d.	1510	1534	1604	1634	...	1710	1730	1804	...	1834	...	1904	...	2004	2034	*2104*	2204	*2331*	...	...	...	...	...	|	|
Fortezza / Franzensfeste d.	1523	1545	1615	1645	...	1723	1741	1815	1841	1845	...	1915	1945	2015	2045	*2121*	2215	*2340*	...	...	...	...	...	|	|
Vipiteno / Sterzing d.	|	1603	1633	1703	...	|	1801	1833	1856	1903	...	1933	2003	2033	2103	...	2233	...	...	...	...	...	...	|	|
Brennero 🏛 a.	|	1622	1652	1722	...	|	1822	1852	1913	1922	...	1952	2021	2052	2122	...	2252	...	...	...	...	...	...	|	|
	|		2	2		|		2	|			2	|	2			2							|	|
Brennero 🏛 ▷ d.	|	...	1705	1805	...	|	...	1905	1918	...	...	2005	2023	2105	...	...	2305	...	...	...	...	...	...	|	|
Steinach in Tirol ▷ d.	|	...	1722	1822	...	|	...	1922	1933	...	...	2022	|	2122	...	...	2322	...	...	...	...	...	...	|	|
Matrei ▷ d.	|	...	1727	1827	...	|	...	1927	1938	...	...	2027	|	2127	...	...	2327	...	...	...	...	...	...	|	|
Innsbruck Hbf ▷ a.	1632	...	1743	1843	...	1832	...	1943	1954	...	...	2043	2056	2143	...	...	2343	...	...	...	...	...	...	0431	0431
München Hbf **951** a.	1825	...	...	...	...	2025	...	...	...	...	...	...	...	...	...	...	...	...	...	...	...	...	...	0630	0630

♦ – **NOTES** (LISTED BY TRAIN NUMBER)

484/5 – LUPUS – 🛏 1, 2 cl. (Excelsior), 🛏 1, 2 cl., ▬ 2 cl. and [2] Roma (**234/5**) - Bologna - München and v.v. Supplement payable. Train numbers **35484/5** Aug. 3 - 22.

717 – ADIGE – [12] and 🍷 Bolzano - Verona - Mantova (d. 1205) - Modena (d. 1253) - Bologna - Lecce. Train number **35417** Aug. 3 - 23.

718 – ADIGE – [12] and 🍷 Lecce - Bologna - Modena (d. 2023) - Mantova (d. 2115) - Verona - Bolzano. Train number **35418** Aug. 3 - 23.

1594 – ⑤ June 19 - Sept. 11 (from Reggio): 🛏 1,2 cl. (T2), ▬ 2 cl. and [2] Reggio di Calabria - Bolzano.

1595 – ⑥ June 20 - Sept. 12: 🛏 1,2 cl. (T2), ▬ 2 cl. and [2] Bolzano - Reggio di Calabria.

1601 – July 25 - Sept. 6: 🛏 1,2 cl. (Excelsior), 🛏 1,2 cl. (T2), 🛏 1,2 cl., ▬ 2 cl. (4 berth) San Candido (**1600**) - Fortezza - Bolzano - Roma Tiburtina. Train number **35401** Aug. 3 - 22.

1602 – July 24 - Sept. 5 (from Roma): 🛏 1,2 cl. (Excelsior), 🛏 1,2 cl. (T2), 🛏 1,2 cl. and ▬ 2 cl. (4 berth) Roma Tiburtina - Bolzano - Fortezza (**1603**) - San Candido. Train number **35402** Aug. 3 - 22 (from Roma).

B – 🛏 1, 2 cl. (Excelsior), 🛏 1, 2 cl., ▬ 2 cl. and [2] Venezia - Verona (**484/5**) - München Hbf and v.v.

L – [2] Innsbruck - San Candido - Lienz and v.v. (Table **596**).

Q – ①②④⑤⑥⑦ (also Dec. 9; not Dec. 10). 🛏 1, 2 cl. (Excelsior), 🛏 1, 2 cl., ▬ 2 cl. (4 / 6 berth) and [2] Bolzano - Bologna - Lecce; 🛏 1, 2 cl. (Excelsior), 🛏 1, 2 cl., ▬ 2 cl. (4 berth) and [2] Bolzano - Bologna (**837**) - Napoli.

R – ①③④⑤⑥⑦ (also Dec. 8; not Dec. 9): 🛏 1, 2 cl. (Excelsior), 🛏 1, 2 cl. ▬ 2 cl. (4 / 6 berth) and [2] Lecce - Bologna - Bolzano; 🛏 1, 2 cl. (Excelsior), 🛏 1, 2 cl., ▬ 2 cl. (4 berth) and [2] Napoli (**824**) - Bologna (**924**) - Bolzano.

OTHER TRAIN NAMES: **81/188** VAL GARDENA / GRODNERTAL, **82/83** PAGANINI, **86/87** TIEPOLO, **88/89** LEONARDO DA VINCI.

a – Ⓐ only.
b – Runs on Ⓑ Trento - Bolzano; daily Bolzano - Fortezza.
c – Firenze **Campo di Marte**.
d – Daily.
g – ⑥ only.
h – Change at Poggio Rusco (0557 / 0603).
k – Not Oct. 25.
p – Milano **Porta Garibaldi**.
r – Ⓑ (not Aug. 15, and days before holidays).
s – Stops to set down only.
t – Roma **Tiburtina**.
w – Not Aug. 2 - 30.
x – © only.
z – ⚒ only.

▷ – For additional trains Innsbruck - Brennero and v.v. see foot of page 290. Austrian holiday dates apply Innsbruck - Brennero and v.v.

▲ – **TRENTO - MALÉ - MARILLEVA**

To Malé *56 km* 70–90 mins, to Marilleva *65 km*, 90–100 mins

⚒: 19 departures to Malé, 14 to Marilleva.
†: 15 departures to Malé, 10 to Marilleva.

Operator: Trentino transporti S.p.A, Via Innsbruck 65, 38100 Trento. ✆ +39 0 461 821000, fax +39 0 461 031407.

2nd class except where shown — FORTEZZA / FRANZENSFESTE - SAN CANDIDO / INNICHEN - LIENZ 596

km		⚒	⚒		1871	1603 A				⚒			⚒				⚒			1875 ⑤		①–⑥		1873	◇	
	Innsbruck Hbf **595** d.	...	...	...	0700	...	...	...	...	...	...	...	...	...	...	...	...	...	...	1503	...	...	...	1701	...	...
	Brennero 🏛 **595** d.	...	...	...	0739	...	...	...	...	...	...	...	...	...	...	...	...	...	...	1543	...	...	...	1743	...	...
0	**Fortezza / Franzensfeste** d.	...	0650	...	0815	0919	0950	...	1050	...	1150	1250	...	1350	...	1450	...	1550	...	1621	1650	...	1751	1821	1850	...
33	Brunico / Bruneck d.	...	0730	...	0852	1007	1030	...	1130	...	1230	1330	...	1430	...	1530	...	1630	...	1704	1730	...	1830	1905	1930	...
61	Dobbiaco / Toblach d.	...	0801	...	0925	1042	1101	...	1201	...	1301	1401	...	1501	...	1601	...	1701	...	1740	1801	...	1901	1941	2001	...
65	**San Candido / Innichen** a.	...	0806	...	0931	1048	1106	...	1206	...	1306	1406	...	1506	...	1606	...	1706	...	1747	1806	...	1906	1947	2006	...
65	**San Candido / Innichen** 🏛 d.	0640	...	0909	0933	...	...	1109	...	1209	...	...	1409	...	1509	...	1609	...	1709	1753	...	1822	...	1949	...	2009
78	Sillian 🏛 d.	0653	...	0922	0946	...	...	1122	...	1222	...	...	1422	...	1522	...	1622	...	1722	1806	...	1835	...	2003	...	2022
108	**Lienz** a.	0725	...	0953	1017	...	...	1153	...	1253	...	...	1453	...	1553	...	1653	...	1753	1836	...	1906	...	2033	...	2052

A – July 24 - Sept. 5 (from Roma): 🛏 1,2 cl. (Excelsior), 🛏 1,2 cl. (T2), 🛏 1,2 cl., ▬ 2 cl. (4 berth) Roma Tiburtina - Bolzano - Fortezza - San Candido. Train number **35403** Aug. 3 - 22 (from Roma). Calls to set down only.

◇ – Additional journeys Fortezza - San Candido: 1950, 2020.

Certain journeys are operated by SAD

596 LIENZ - SAN CANDIDO / INNICHEN - FORTEZZA / FRANZENSFESTE

2nd class except where shown

	1870																	1874			1872			1600	
					Ⓐ			⚒			⚒				⚒			⑦k	①–⑥					A	
Lienz d.	0515	...	*0706*	...	...	...	*0957*	1106	...	...	1306	...	1406	...	1506	...	*1606*	1624	1706	...	1735	...	*1845*	...	...
Sillian d.	0545	...	*0737*	...	...	...	*1038*	1139	...	...	1339	...	1439	...	1539	...	*1639*	1655	1739	...	1807	...	*1918*	...	...
San Candido / Innichen 🏛 a.	0558	...	*0750*	...	...	...	*1051*	1152	...	...	1352	...	1452	...	1552	...	*1652*	1708	1752	...	1820	...	*1931*	...	...
San Candido / Innichen 🏛 d.	0600	0655	0755	0849	0933	0955	1055	...	1155	1255	...	1355	...	1455	...	1555	1655	1711	...	1755	1825	1855	1955	2008	2055
Dobbiaco / Toblach d.	0606	0701	0801	0858	0939	1001	1101	...	1201	1301	...	1401	...	1501	...	1601	1701	1717	...	1801	1831	1901	2001	2013	2101
Brunico / Bruneck d.	0637	0732	0831	0932	1007	1032	1132	...	1232	1332	...	1432	...	1532	...	1632	1732	1802	...	1832	1905	1932	2032	2103	2133
Fortezza / Franzensfeste a.	0719	0810	0910	1010	1040	1110	1210	...	1310	1410	...	1510	...	1610	...	1710	1810	1840	...	1910	1944	2010	2110	2140	2210
Brennero 🏛 **595** a.	0758	...	...	...	...	...	...	...	...	...	...	...	...	...	...	...	...	1913	...	...	2021	...	...	...	...
Innsbruck Hbf **595** a.	0843	...	...	...	...	...	...	...	...	...	...	...	...	...	...	...	...	1954	...	...	2056	...	...	...	...

A – July 25 - Sept. 6: 🛏 1, 2 cl. (Excelsior), 🛏 1,2 cl. (T2), 🛏 1,2 cl., 🛏 2 cl. (4 berth) San Candido - Fortezza - Bolzano - Roma Tiburtina. Train number **35400** Aug. 3 - 22. Calls to pick up only.

k – Not Oct. 25.

Certain journeys are operated by SAD

597 BOLZANO / BOZEN - MERANO / MERAN

2nd class only

km		⚒				⚒§	©	Ⓐ§	⚒§		⚒§		⚒§		⚒§		⚒§		⚒§		⚒§		⚒§		⚒§		
	Brennero **595** d.	...	0538	0638	...	...	0838	...	...	0938	...	1038	...	1138	...	1238	...	1338	...	1438	...	1538	...	1638	...	1738	1838
0	**Bolzano / Bozen** d.	0630	0701	0802	0903	0935	1002	1003	1035	1102	1135	1202	1235	1302	1335	1402	1435	1502	1535	1602	1635	1702	1735	1802	1835	1902	2002
32	Merano / Meran a.	0712	0744	0844	0944	1014	1044	1044	1114	1144	1214	1244	1314	1344	1414	1444	1514	1544	1614	1644	1714	1744	1814	1844	1914	1944	2044

	⚒		⚒		⚒§		⚒§	©	⚒§		⚒§		⚒§		⚒§		⚒§		⚒§		⚒§		⚒§		⚒§		
Merano / Meran d.	0609	0716	0746	0816	0846	0916	0946	1016	1046	1116	1146	1216	1246	1316	1346	1416	1446	1516	1546	1616	1646	1716	1746	1816	1846	1916	2016
Bolzano / Bozen a.	0658	0758	0826	0859	0926	0958	1026	1058	1126	1158	1226	1258	1326	1358	1426	1459	1526	1558	1626	1658	1726	1757	1826	1857	1926	1958	2058
Brennero **595** a.	0822	0922	...	1022	...	1122	...	1222	...	1322	...	1422	...	1522	...	1622	...	1722	...	1822	...	1922	...	...	...	...	...

§ – Operated by SAD (for contact details see Table **598**).

Additional journeys: from Bolzano / Bozen 0547 ⚒, 0736 ⚒§, 0835 ⚒§, 1935 ⚒§, 2035, 2202 ⚒§; from Merano / Meran 0701 Ⓐ, 1946 Ⓐ§, 2046 ⚒§, 2146.

598 MERANO / MERAN - MALLES / MALS

2nd class only SAD

km																									
0	Merano / Meran d.	0542	0635	0718	0746	0816	0916	0946	1016	1116	1146	1216	1316	1346	1416	1516	1546	1616	1716	1746	1816	1916	1946	2046	2246
60	Malles / Mals **546 / 954** a.	0700	0754	0838	0855	0938	1038	1055	1138	1238	1255	1338	1438	1455	1538	1638	1655	1738	1838	1855	1938	2038	2055	2155	2355

Malles / Mals **546 / 954** d.	0547	0611	0703	0720	0820	0903	0920	1020	1103	1120	1220	1303	1320	1420	1503	1520	1620	1703	1720	1820	1903	1920	2020	2120	...
Merano / Meran a.	0702	0732	0813	0843	0943	1013	1043	1143	1213	1243	1343	1413	1443	1543	1613	1643	1743	1813	1843	1943	2013	2043	2143	2234	...

Trains call at Silandro / Schlanders 46–54 minutes after leaving Merano, 24–28 minutes after leaving Malles.

Ferrovia della Val Venosta Operator: Servizi Autobus Dolomiti (SAD), Via Conciapelli 60, I - 39100 Bolzano. ✆ +39 0471 97 12 59, fax +39 0471 97 00 42.

599 ITALIAN LAKES (LAGO MAGGIORE, GARDA, COMO)

Lago Maggiore: ⛴ services link Arona, Stresa, Baveno, Laveno, Luino and Locarno throughout the year on an irregular schedule. For details contact the operator below:
Operator: Navigazione sul Lago Maggiore, Viale F. Baracca 1, 28041 Arona, Italy. ✆ + 39 0322 233 200. Fax: + 39 0322 249 530.

Lago di Garda: ⛴ services link Desenzano, Peschiera, Garda, Salo, Gardone and Riva, (April to September only), on an irregular schedule. For details contact the operator below:
Operator: Navigazione sul Lago di Garda, Piazza Matteotti, 25015 Desenzano del Garda, Italy. ✆ + 39 30 91 41 321, 2, 3. Fax: + 39 30 91 44 640.

Lago di Como: ⛴ services link Como, Bellagio, Menaggio, Varenna, Bellano and Colico (April to September only) on an irregular schedule. For details contact the operator below:

Hydrofoil service **November 2, 2009 - March 28, 2010**:

	⚒	†		⚒	⚒x	†z	⚒w		⚒	Ⓐw	x	Ⓑv	⑥
Como d.	0733	1110	...	1225	1330	1400	1420	...	1615	1710	1810	1910	1910
Tremezzo d.	0819r	1153	...	1302	1419	1443	1507	...	1651	1757	1857	1947	1957
Bellagio d.	0813r	1200	...	1309	1439r	1450	1514	...	1658	1804	1905	1953	2004
Menaggio d.	0808	1208	...	1316	1430	1457	1521	...	1704	1812	1913	1959	2012
Bellano d.	...	1218	...	1328	1455	...	...	...	1713	1821	1929	2011	2028
Colico a.	...	1251	...	1355	1528	...	...	...	1740	...	1959	2034	2058

	⚒	⚒y	†q	⚒		⚒	†z	⚒w	x		⚒	Ⓐw	⑥t
Colico d.	0604	0622	0722	...	...	1356	...	...	1610	...	1741	...	1959
Bellano d.	0628	0653	0753	...	...	1424	...	...	1644	...	1806	1822	|
Menaggio d.	0641	0703	0803	0808	...	1435	1518	1522	1655	...	1814	1843	2030
Bellagio d.	0647	0712	0812	0814	...	1442	1527	1531	1704	...	1820	1852	2039
Tremezzo d.	0653	0718	0818	0820	...	1448	1533	1537	1710	...	1826	1858	|
Como a.	0730	0805	0905	0857	...	1525	1617	1624	1754	...	1857	1940	2117

q – Not Dec. 26.
r – Via Menaggio.
t – Not Jan. 2.
v – Not Dec. 24, 26, 27, 31, Jan. 3.
w – Not Dec. 21 - Jan. 5.
x – Not Jan. 2, 4, 5.
y – Not Dec. 28, Jan. 2, 4, 5.
z – Not Dec. 26, 27, Jan. 3.

Operator: Navigazione Lago di Como, Via Per Cernobbio 18, 22100 Como, Italy. ✆ +39 (0) 31 579 211, fax: +39 (0) 31 570 080.

600 MILANO - VERONA - VENEZIA

km			*EN*			*ESc*		*EC*	*ESc*			*ESc*		*ESc*		*ESc*	*ESc*		*ESc*	*ESc*		*EC*	*ESc*
			363			**9701**		**93**	**9703**			**9707**		**9709**		**9711**	**9713**		**9791**	**9715**		**37**	**9719**
				2	2	🍷		🍷	🍷			🍷		🍷		🍷	🍷	2	🍷	🍷		🍷	🍷
			♦		⚒			♦										†	©			♦	Ⓐ
0	**Milano Centrale** d.	0015	...	...	...	0635	0625	0640p	0735	0725	...	0805	0825	0835	...	0905	0935	0920p	1035	1135	...	1205	1235
4	Milano Lambrate d.	0022	...	...	...	|	0633	|	|	0733	...	|	0833	|	...	|	|	0932	|	|	1130	|	|
34	Treviglio d.	0049	...	...	...	|	0655	|	|	0755	...	|	0855	|	...	|	|	0955	|	|	1155	|	|
83	Brescia d.	0136	...	...	0601	0723	0735	0743	0823	0835	...	0853	0935	0923	...	0953	1023	1030	1123	1223	1235	1253	1323
111	Desenzano-Sirmione d.	0152	...	...	0626	0737	0751	0808	|	0851	...	0907	0951	0937	...	|	1037	1046	|	|	1251	|	1337
125	Peschiera del Garda § d.	0202	...	...	0635	|	0801	0818	0843	0901	...	|	1001	|	...	1013	|	1055	1143	1243	1301	1313	|
148	**Verona Porta Nuova** a.	0223	...	...	0654	0757	0820	0837	0857	0915	...	0927	1020	0957	...	1027	1057	1110	1157	1257	1316	1327	1357
148	**Verona Porta Nuova** d.	...	0440	0634	0702	0759	...	...	0859	0918	...	0929	...	0959	...	1029	1059	1113	1159	1259	1318	1329	1359
200	Vicenza d.	...	0520	0725	0747	0826	...	...	0926	0959	...	0956	...	1026	...	1056	1126	1147	1226	1326	1359	1356	1426
230	Padova **620** d.	...	0554	0752	0815	0843	...	...	0943	1020	...	1013	...	1043	...	1113	1143	1208	1243	1343	1420	1412	1443
258	**Venezia Mestre 620** a.	...	0625	0826	0838	0858	...	...	0958	1038	...	1028	...	1058	...	1128	1158	1236	1258	1358	1443	1428	1458
258	**Venezia Mestre 620** d.	...	0628	0828	0840	0900	...	...	1022	1040	...	1030	...	1100	...	1130	1200	1238	1300	1400	1445	1430	1500
267	**Venezia Santa Lucia 620** a.	...	0638	0840	0852	0910	...	...	|	1049	...	1040	...	1110	...	1140	1210	1249	1310	1410	1455	1440	1510
	Trieste Centrale **605** a.	...	...	...	...	...	...	...	1208	...	...	...	...	...	...	...	...	...	...	...	...	...	...

			ESc			*ESc*		*ESc*		*ESc*		*ESc*		*ESc*		*ESc*		*ESc*			*ESc*		
			9723			**9727**		**9729**		**9733**		**9735**		**9737**		**9739**		**9741**			**9743**		
			🍷			🍷		🍷		🍷		🍷		🍷		🍷		🍷			🍷		
	Ⓐ	†																	⚒				
Milano Centrale d.	1225	1305p	1335	1325	...	1435	1425	1505	1525	1605	...	1635	1625	1705	...	1735	1725	1805	1800	...	1835	1825	...
Milano Lambrate d.	1233	1325	|	1333	...	|	1433	|	1533	|	...	|	1633	|	...	|	1733	|	1808	...	|	1833	...
Treviglio d.	1255	1344	|	1355	...	|	1455	|	1553	|	...	|	1655	|	...	|	1755	|	1827	...	|	1855	...
Brescia d.	1335	1429	1423	1435	...	1523	1535	1553	1635	1653	...	1723	1735	1753	...	1823	1835	1853	1902	...	1923	1935	...
Desenzano-Sirmione d.	1351	1445	|	1451	...	1537	1551	|	1651	1707	...	|	1751	1807	...	|	1851	1907	...	...	|	1951	...
Peschiera del Garda § d.	1401	1454	1443	1501	...	|	1601	1613	1701	|	...	|	1801	|	...	|	1901	|	...	...	1943	2001	...
Verona Porta Nuova a.	1420	1511	1457	1520	...	1557	1620	1627	1720	1727	...	1755	1820	1827	...	1855	1915	1927	...	...	1957	2020	...
Verona Porta Nuova d.	...	1514	1459	...	...	1559	...	1629	...	1729	...	1757	...	1829	...	1857	1918	1929	...	...	1959	...	...
Vicenza d.	...	1557	1526	...	...	1626	...	1656	...	1756	...	|	...	1856	...	|	1952	1956	...	...	2024	...	...
Padova **620** d.	...	1616	1543	...	...	1643	...	1713	...	1813	...	1836	...	1913	...	1936	2012	2013	...	...	...	...	...
Venezia Mestre 620 a.	...	1642	1558	...	...	1658	...	1728	...	1828	...	1850	...	1928	...	1950	2038	2028	...	...	...	...	...
Venezia Mestre 620 d.	...	1644	1600	...	...	1700	...	1730	...	1830	...	1852	...	1945	...	1952	2040	2045	...	...	...	...	...
Venezia Santa Lucia 620 a.	...	1656	1610	...	...	1710	...	1740	...	1840	...	1902	...	|	...	2002	2051	|	...	...	...	...	...
Trieste Centrale **605** a.	...	...	...	...	...	...	...	...	...	...	...	...	...	2122	...	...	...	2222	...	...	...	...	...

FOR NOTES SEE NEXT PAGE

MILANO - VERONA - VENEZIA — 600

	ESc 9745 🍷		*ESc* 9749 🍷			*ESc* 9753 🍷 ◆			
Milano Centrale d.	1905	1925	2005	2025	...	2105	2125	2230	...
Milano Lambrate d.	|	1933	|	2033	...	|	2133	2238	...
Treviglio d.	|	1955	|	2053	...	|	2153	2258	...
Brescia d.	1953	2035	2053	2135	...	2157	2235	2335	...
Desenzano-Sirmione d.	2007	2051	|	2151	...	2213	2251	2351	...
Peschiera del Garda § d.	|	2101	2103	2201	...	2223	2301	0001	...
Verona Porta Nuova a.	2027	2120	2127	2215	...	2244	2320	0020	...
Verona Porta Nuova d.	2029	...	2129	2218	...	2247	...	...	...
Vicenza d.	2056	...	2156	2252	...	2320	...	...	...
Padova **620** d.	2113	...	2213	2310	...	2338	...	...	...
Venezia Mestre 620 a.	2128	...	2228	2339	...	2356	...	...	...
Venezia Mestre 620 d.	2130	...	2230	2341	...	...	...	...	...
Venezia Santa Lucia 620 a.	2140	...	2240	2352	...	...	...	...	...
Trieste Centrale **605** a.	...	...	...	...	...	...	...	...	...

		2 Ⓒ	Ⓐ		*ESc* 9700 🍷 ◆		*ESc* 9702 🍷		*ESc* 9704 🍷
Trieste Centrale **605** d.	...	...	...	...	...	...	...	...	...
Venezia Santa Lucia 620 d.	...	0514	0514	...	...	...	0620	...	0658
Venezia Mestre 620 a.	...	0524	0524	...	...	...	0630	...	0708
Venezia Mestre 620 d.	...	0526	0526	...	0532	...	0632	...	0710
Padova **620** d.	...	0545	0545	...	0554	...	0648	...	0726
Vicenza d.	...	0605	0605	...	0615	...	0705	...	|
Verona Porta Nuova a.	...	0637	0651	...	0643	...	0730	...	0803
Verona Porta Nuova d.	0540	0640	0654	...	0646	...	0732	0740	0805
Peschiera del Garda § d.	0557	0654	0709	...	0701	...	0747	0757	|
Desenzano-Sirmione d.	0607	0705	0720	...	0712	...	|	0807	|
Brescia d.	0627	0727	0739	...	0733	...	0809	0827	0839
Treviglio d.	0705	0803	0816	...	|	...	|	0903	|
Milano Lambrate d.	0728	0815	0837	...	|	...	|	0929	|
Milano Centrale a.	0735	0835	0845	...	0825	...	0855	0935	0925

	ESc 9706 🍷 ◆		*ESc* 9708 🍷 Ⓐ		*ESc* 9710 🍷	*ESc* 9712 🍷		*ESc* 9792 🍷 Ⓒ	*ESc* 9714 🍷		*ESc* 9716 🍷			*ESc* 9718 🍷		*ESc* 9722 🍷			*ESc* 9726 🍷		*ESc* 9730 🍷	*ESc* 9732 🍷	
Trieste Centrale **605** d.	...	...	...	...	0635	...	...	...	...	...	0938	...	...	...	...	...	...	...	...	...	...	...	...
Venezia Santa Lucia 620 d.	...	...	0750	...	|	0858	...	0950	1050	...	|	...	1109	1150	...	1250	...	...	1350	...	1450	1520	1504
Venezia Mestre 620 a.	...	...	0800	...	0815	0908	...	1000	1100	...	1116	...	1120	1200	...	1300	...	...	1400	...	1500	1530	1513
Venezia Mestre 620 d.	...	...	0802	...	0832	0910	...	1002	1102	...	1132	...	1122	1202	...	1302	...	...	1402	...	1502	1532	1515
Padova **620** d.	...	...	0818	...	0848	0926	...	1018	1118	...	1148	...	1145	1218	...	1318	...	...	1418	...	1518	1548	1541
Vicenza d.	0805	...	0835	...	0905	|	...	1035	1135	...	1205	...	1205	1235	...	1335	...	...	1435	...	1535	1605	1608
Verona Porta Nuova a.	0830	...	0900	...	0930	1003	...	1100	1200	...	1230	...	1239	1300	...	1400	...	...	1500	...	1600	1630	1642
Verona Porta Nuova d.	0832	0840	0902	...	0932	1005	...	1102	1202	1206	1232	...	1240	1302	1340	1402	1440	...	1502	1540	1602	1632	1645
Peschiera del Garda § d.	0847	0857	|	...	|	1017	...	1117	|	1222	|	...	1257	1317	1357	|	1457	...	1517	1557	|	1647	1658
Desenzano-Sirmione d.	|	0907	0922	...	0952	|	...	|	1222	|	1252	...	1307	|	1407	1422	1507	...	|	1607	1622	|	1707
Brescia d.	0909	0927	0939	...	1009	1039	...	1139	1239	1249	1309	...	1327	1339	1427	1439	1527	...	1539	1627	1639	1709	1727
Treviglio d.	|	1003	|	...	|	|	...	|	|	1325	|	...	1403	|	1503	|	1603	...	|	1703	|	|	1803
Milano Lambrate d.	|	1031	|	...	|	|	...	|	|	1349	|	...	1435	|	1529	|	1629	...	|	1731	|	|	1829
Milano Centrale a.	0955	...	1025	...	1055	1125	...	1225	1325	1355	1355	...	1445	1425	1535	1525	1635	...	1625	1740	1725	1755	1835

	EC 42 🍷 ◆		*ESc* 9738 🍷			*ESc* 9740 🍷	2 †	*ESc* 9742 🍷	*EC* 92 🍷 ◆		2 †	*ESc* 9746 🍷	*ESc* 9748 🍷		2 ⚒	2 †	*ESc* 9750 🍷				†	*EN* 358 ◆	
Trieste Centrale **605** d.	...	...	...	...	...	...	...	...	...	...	...	...	1702	...	...	...	...	...	...	...	...	...	...
Venezia Santa Lucia 620 d.	1620	...	1650	1705	...	1720	1742	1750	...	...	1809	1820	|	...	1853	1904	1950	...	...	2034	2109	2251	...
Venezia Mestre 620 a.	1630	...	1700	1716	...	1730	1752	1800	...	...	1821	1830	1848	...	1905	1916	2000	...	...	2046	2120	2301	...
Venezia Mestre 620 d.	1632	...	1702	1718	...	1732	1754	1802	...	...	1823	1832	1902	...	1907	1918	2002	...	...	2048	2122	2304	...
Padova **620** d.	1648	...	1718	1741	...	1748	1816	1818	...	...	1856	1848	1918	...	1939	1954	2018	...	...	2124	2142	2328	...
Vicenza d.	1705	...	1735	1808	...	1805	1834	1835	...	...	1917	1905	1935	...	2006	2021	2035	...	...	2151	2202	2347	...
Verona Porta Nuova a.	1730	...	1800	1842	...	1830	1919	1900	...	...	1956	1930	2000	...	2054	2116	2100	...	...	2240j	2240	0025	...
Verona Porta Nuova d.	1732	1740	1802	1845	...	1832	1922	1902	1922	1940	2007	1932	2002	2040	...	...	2102	2140	...	...	2243	...	...
Peschiera del Garda § d.	1747	1757	|	1858	...	1847	1946	|	1946	1957	2030	|	2017	2057	...	...	|	2157	...	...	2300	...	...
Desenzano-Sirmione d.	|	1807	1822	1907	...	|	1959	1922	1958	2007	2039	1952	|	2107	...	...	2122	2207	...	...	2310	...	...
Brescia d.	1809	1827	1839	1927	...	1909	2014	1939	2017	2027	2057	2009	2039	2127	...	...	2139	2227	...	...	2332	...	...
Treviglio d.	|	1903	|	2003	...	|	...	|	|	2103	2134	|	|	2203	...	...	|	2303	...	...	0001	...	...
Milano Lambrate d.	|	1932	|	2032	...	|	...	|	|	2129	2153	|	|	2229	...	...	|	2329	...	...	0022	...	...
Milano Centrale a.	1855	1940	1925	2040	...	1955	...	2025	2135p	2135	2210p	2055	2125	2235	...	...	2225	2335	...	...	0030	...	...

◆ – **NOTES** (LISTED BY TRAIN NUMBER)

37 – (12) and ✕ Genève - Milano - Venezia.
42 – (12) and 🍷 Venezia - Milano - Genève.
92 – LEONARDO DA VINCI – (12) and 🍷 München (**89**) - Verona - Milano.
93 – LEONARDO DA VINCI – (12) and 🍷 Milano - Verona (**88**) - München.
358 – 🛏 1, 2 cl. (Excelsior), 🛏 1, 2 cl., ▬ 2 cl. and (2) Venezia - Verona (**484**) - München.
363 – 🛏 1, 2 cl. (Excelsior), 🛏 1, 2 cl., ▬ 2 cl. and (2) München (**485**) - Verona - Venezia.
9702 – (12) and 🍷 Venezia Mestre - Milano. Conveys (subject to confirmation): 🛏 1, 2 cl. and ▬ 2 cl. (4 berth) Wien (**235**) - Venezia Mestre - Milano.
9706 – (12) and 🍷 Udine (**9705**) - Treviso - Vicenza - Milano.
9753 – (12) and 🍷 Milano - Venezia Mestre. Conveys (subject to confirmation): 🛏 1, 2 cl. and ▬ 2 cl. (4 berth) Milano - Venezia Mestre (**234**) - Wien.

j – Arrive 2248 on †.
p – Milano **Porta Garibaldi**.
s – Calls to set down only.
u – Stops to pick up only.
§ – Station for Gardaland Park. Free shuttle bus available.

VENEZIA - UDINE - VILLACH — 601

km		*E* 1236 ⚡ ◆	*E* 1238 ⚡ ◆	*EN* 234 ⚡ ◆		Ⓐp	q		*ICN* 774 ◆		⚒	⚒	†				2 ⚒		Ⓐ		⚒y			2	
0	**Venezia** Santa Lucia **603** d.	...	...	...	...	0526	0526	0547	0604	0704	0718	0904	0904	1004	...	1204	1304	1404	1504	...	1604	1704	1804	1904	...
9	**Venezia** Mestre a.	...	...	...	...	0536	0536	0558	0614	0714	0729	0914	0914	1014	...	1214	1314	1414	1514	...	1614	1714	1814	1914	...
9	**Venezia** Mestre **603** d.	0036	0036	0130	...	0538	0538	0600	0616	0716	0731	0916	0916	1016	...	1216	1316	1416	1516	...	1616	1716	1816	1916	...
30	Treviso Centrale d.	|	|	|	...	0558	0558	0622	0636	0735	0753	0935	0937	1035	...	1235	1338	1435	1538	...	1635	1737	1835	1938	...
57	Conegliano **603** d.	|	|	|	...	0618	0617	0644	0656	0754	0819	0954	1003	1054	...	1254	1356	1454	1557	...	1654	1757	1854	1956	...
74	Sacile d.	|	|	|	...	0642	0630	0657	0712	0807	0837	1007	1020	1107	...	1307	1414	1507	1610	...	1707	1810	1907	2009	...
87	Pordenone d.	|	|	|	...	0653	0641	0710	0724	0817	0849	1017	1031	1117	...	1317	1423	1517	1620	...	1717	1820	1917	2019	...
136	**Udine** a.	|	|	|	...	0730	0722	0751	0805	0853	0931	1053	1112	1153	...	1353	1502	1553	1656	...	1753	1856	1953	2055	...
136	**Udine** d.	|	|	|	...	0734	0734	...	...	0856	0934	...	...	1156r	...	1356	...	1556	1659	...	1756	1859v	1956	...	...
	Trieste Centrale **606** a.	|	|	|	...	0846	0856	...	...	1004	1050	...	...	1304r	...	1504	...	1704	1807	...	1904	2007v	2104	...	...
230	Tarvisio Boscoverde 🏛 a.	0304	0304	0339	...	...	...	...	...	...	...	...	...	...	...	...	...	...	...	...	...	...	...	...	...
258	**Villach Hbf** a.	0341	0341	0415	...	...	...	...	...	...	...	...	...	...	...	...	...	...	...	...	...	...	...	...	...

◆ – **NOTES** (LISTED BY TRAIN NUMBER)

234 – ALLEGRO TOSCA – 🛏 1, 2 cl. (Excelsior), 🛏 1,2 cl., ▬ 2 cl. and (2) Roma - Venezia Mestre - Villach - Wien.
774 – MARCO POLO – 🛏 1, 2 cl., ▬ 2 cl. (4 berth) and (2) Napoli - Roma Tiburtina - Venezia Santa Lucia - Udine.
1236 – ALLEGRO ROSSINI – ⑥ Mar. 27 - Sept. 25: 🛏 1, 2 cl. (T2), ▬ 2 cl. and (2) Firenze - Venezia Mestre - Villach - Wien.
1238 – ALLEGRO ROSSINI – Dec. 29, 30, Jan. 1 - 6, Apr. 5, May 13, 24, June 3: 🛏 1, 2 cl. (T2), ▬ 2 cl. and (2) Firenze - Venezia Mestre - Villach - Wien.

p – From Sept. 7.
q – ⚒ until Sept. 5; ⑥ Sept. 12 - Dec. 12 (not holidays).
r – ①⑥† (also Dec. 9).
v – Ⓐ (⚒ until Sept. 5).
y – Also Aug. 15.
⚡ – Supplement payable.

601 VENEZIA - UDINE - VILLACH

		ESc 9743 🍷 ♦	*AV* 9420 🍷 ♦	2	*EN* 236 ⟋ ♦				
Venezia Santa Lucia **603**	d.	2004	...	...	2056	2105	...	2204	2304	2356
Venezia Mestre	a.	2014	...	...	2106	|	...	2214	2315	0006
Venezia Mestre **603**	d.	2016	...	2040	2108	2118u	...	2216	2317	0008
Treviso Centrale	d.	2035	2120	2056	2129	2142	...	2235	2338	0027
Conegliano **603**	d.	2054	2140	2115	2149	2205	...	2254	0000	0046
Sacile	d.	2107	2154	|	2202	|	...	2307	0013	0059
Pordenone	d.	2117	2202	2136	2214	2228	...	2317	0023	0109
Udine	a.	2153	2232	2208	2256	2307	...	2353	0058	0145
Udine	d.	2156	...	...	...	2309	...	0003	...	...
Trieste Centrale **606**	a.	2304	...	...	...	|	...	0131	...	...
Tarvisio Boscoverde 🏛	a.	...	...	...	...	0005	...	...	...	...
Villach Hbf	a.	...	...	...	...	0042	...	...	...	...

		EN 235 ⟋ ♦	*E* 1237 ⟋ ♦	*E* 1239 ⟋ ♦		2	*ESc* 9705 🍷 ♦	*AV* 9403 🍷 ♦			*EN* 237 ⟋ ♦
Villach Hbf	d.	0006	0045	0045	...	...	...	...	...	...	0445
Tarvisio Boscoverde 🏛	d.	0041	0123	0123	...	...	...	...	...	...	0533
Trieste Centrale **606**	d.	|	|	|	...	...	...	...	...	0502	|
Udine	a.	|	|	|	...	...	...	...	...	0623	0633
Udine	d.	|	|	|	...	0510	0540	0550	...	0628	0636
Pordenone	d.	|	|	|	...	0547	0609	0619	...	0705	0713
Sacile	d.	|	|	|	...	0559	0620	|	...	0715	|
Conegliano **603**	d.	|	|	|	...	0615	0631	0640	...	0727	0738
Treviso Centrale	d.	|	|	|	...	0642	0650	0701	...	0746	0801
Venezia Mestre **603**	a.	0252	0332	0332	...	0713	...	0722	...	0805	0821s
Venezia Mestre	d.	...	...	...	...	0714	...	...	...	0807	|
Venezia Santa Lucia **603**	a.	...	...	...	...	0726	...	...	...	0817	0834

					2 †			†	⚒			⚒	2 ⚒		2			⚒		Ⓐ			*ICN* 771 ♦		
Villach Hbf	d.	...	...	...	...	...	...	...	...	...	...	...	...	...	...	...	...	...	...	...	...	...	...	...	...
Tarvisio Boscoverde 🏛	d.	...	...	...	...	...	...	...	...	...	...	...	...	...	...	...	...	...	...	...	...	...	...	...	...
Trieste Centrale **606**	d.	...	0558x	0656	...	0856	...	...	...	1056	...	1126	...	1256	...	1456	...	...	1656	1755	1856	...	...	2042	...
Udine	a.	...	0728	0804	...	1004	...	...	...	1204	...	1253	...	1404	...	1604	...	...	1804	1903	2004	...	...	2204	...
Udine	d.	...	0742	0807	0911	1007	...	1043	1102	1207	...	1258	1329	1407	1502	1607	...	1702	1807	1906	2007	...	2122	2207	...
Pordenone	d.	...	0819	0844	0948	1044	...	1123	1139	1244	...	1335	1409	1444	1539	1644	...	1739	1844	1944	2044	...	2158	2244	...
Sacile	d.	...	0830	0854	0959	1054	...	1137	1149	1254	...	1345	1423	1454	1549	1654	...	1749	1854	1954	2054	...	2210	2254	...
Conegliano **603**	d.	...	0849	0906	1011	1106	...	1155	1201	1306	...	1403	1441	1506	1601	1706	...	1801	1906	2005	2106	...	2223	2306	...
Treviso Centrale	d.	...	0915	0925	1030	1125	...	1222	1222	1325	...	1422	1508	1525	1622	1725	...	1822	1925	2023	2125	...	2242	2325	...
Venezia Mestre **603**	a.	...	0937	0944	1052	1144	...	1244	1244	1344	...	1444	1530	1544	1644	1744	...	1844	1944	2044	2144	...	2302	2344	...
Venezia Mestre	d.	...	0939	0946	1054	1146	...	1246	1246	1346	...	1446	1532	1546	1646	1746	...	1846	1946	2046	2146	...	2304	2346	...
Venezia Santa Lucia **603**	a.	...	0949	0956	1105	1156	...	1256	1256	1356	...	1456	1542	1556	1656	1756	...	1856	1956	2056	2156	...	2313	2356	...

♦ – **NOTES** (LISTED BY TRAIN NUMBER)

235 – ALLEGRO TOSCA – 🛏 1, 2 cl. (Excelsior), 🛏 1,2 cl., ▬ 2 cl. and (2) Wien - Villach - Venezia Mestre - Roma.
236 – ALLEGRO DON GIOVANNI – 🛏 1,2 cl., ▬ 2 cl. and (2) Venezia - Villach - Salzburg - Wien.
237 – ALLEGRO DON GIOVANNI – 🛏 1,2 cl., ▬ 2 cl. and (2) Wien - Salzburg - Villach - Venezia.
771 – MARCO POLO – 🛏 1, 2 cl., ▬ 2 cl. (4 berth) and (2) Udine - Venezia Santa Lucia - Napoli.
1237 – ALLEGRO ROSSINI – ⑤ Mar. 26 - Sept. 24 (from Wien): 🛏 1, 2 cl. (T2), ▬ 2 cl. and (2) Wien - Villach - Venezia Mestre - Firenze.
1239 – ALLEGRO ROSSINI – Dec. 28 - 30, Jan. 1 - 5, Apr. 4, May 12, 23, June 2 (from Wien): 🛏 1, 2 cl. (T2), ▬ 2 cl. and (2) Firenze - Villach - Venezia Mestre - Roma.

9403/20 – (12) and 🍷 Udine - Venezia Mestre - Roma Termini and v.v.
9705 – (12) and 🍷 Udine - Treviso - Milano.
9743 – (12) and 🍷 Milano - Treviso - Udine.

s – Calls to set down only.
u – Calls to pick up only.
x – Depart 0604 on †.
⟋ – Supplement payable.

602 VICENZA - TREVISO

2nd class only except where shown

km			⚒	⚒		⚒	⚒	⚒z	†			†	⚒	⚒	⚒		⚒		†	⚒	⚒z			⚒	*ESc* 9743 U	
0	**Vicenza**	d.	0546	0615	0654	0810	0839	0918	0918	...	1120	1330	1404	1507	1550	1630	1700	...	1730	1800	1900	1928	...	2007	2026	...
24	Cittadella	d.	0611	0640	0718	0835	0904	0943	0943	...	1145	1355	1429	1532	1615	1655	1721	...	1756	1824	1924	1952	...	2031	2047	...
36	Castelfranco Veneto	d.	0634	0702	0743	0850	0929	1004	1004	...	1207	1410	1452	1548	1635	1711	1737	...	1811	1840	1945	2008	...	2047	2100	...
60	**Treviso Centrale**	a.	0656	0727	0808	...	0951	1027	1027	...	1230	1433	1516	1610	1658	1732	1756	...	1835	1905	2007	2030	...	2110	2118	...

		⚒	⚒	⚒		*ESc* 9706 U	⚒		⚒	†	⚒	†		⚒y		⚒		⚒z	⚒			⚒		Ⓐx	†	
Treviso Centrale	d.	0528	0547	0613	...	0653	0702	0731	...	0938	1009	1138	...	1240	1332	1432	1538	1640	1711	1750	...	1838	...	2012	2046	...
Castelfranco Veneto	d.	0547	0614	0637	...	0714	0726	0756	0942	1004	1038	1207	...	1304	1400	1456	1601	1705	1741	1812	...	1902	...	2037	2116	...
Cittadella	d.	0600	0629	0652	...	0729	0746	0811	0959	1020	1052	1222	...	1317	1415	1510	1617	1719	1757	1827	...	1917	...	2053	2132	...
Vicenza	a.	0626	0656	0719	...	0803	0814	0837	1025	1046	1120	1249	...	...	1440	1537	1645	1745	1822	1855	...	1944	...	2123	2200	...

U – (12) Milano - Vicenza - Treviso - Udine and v.v.
x – Not July 25 - Aug. 30.
y – From Sept. 7.
z – Not Aug. 2 - 30.

603 VENEZIA and PADOVA - BELLUNO and CALALZO

2nd class only except where shown

km			*E* 1606 H	qz	⚒	†z		⚒z	⚒				⚒y	z	z			z		z		z	z		Ⓐ	z		
0	**Venezia** Santa Lucia **601**	d.	...	...	...	0643	...	0804	...	...	...	...	...	1226	1326	...	...	1529	...	...	...	1726	...	...	1826	1943	...	...
9	Venezia Mestre **601**	d.	...	...	...	0656	...	0816	...	...	...	...	...	1239	1339	...	...	1542	...	...	...	1739	...	...	|	1955	...	...
57	Conegliano **601**	d.	...	0627	...	0746	...	0903	...	...	...	...	1240	1337	1435	...	...	1647	...	1747	...	1837	...	...	|	2038	...	...
71	Vittorio Veneto	d.	...	0643	...	0811	...	0917	...	...	...	...	1257	1353	1456	...	...	1703	...	1807	...	1853	...	...	|	2051	...	...
	Padova	d.	...	|	0600	|	0649	|	...	0933	...	1134	|	|	|	1250	1345	|	1534	|	1705	|	...	1812	|	|	1916	2120
	Castelfranco Veneto	d.	...	|	0629	|	0725	|	...	1002	...	1203	|	|	|	1322	1425	|	1614	|	1733	|	...	1846	|	|	1950	2155
	Montebelluna	d.	...	|	0643	|	0747	|	...	1020	...	1217	|	|	|	1336	1443	|	1627	|	1751	|	...	1908	1932	|	2008	2207
	Feltre	d.	...	|	0733	|	0834	|	...	1054	...	1250	|	|	|	1425	1531	|	1711	|	1827	|	...	1943	2017	|	2041	2241
	Belluno	d.	0619	|	0816	|	0908	|	...	1125	1156	1325	|	|	|	1513	1601	|	1753r	|	1909	|	...	2018	2048	|	2114	2312
98	Ponte nelle Alpi	a.	|	0718	0824	0846	0917	0948	...	...	1204	1333	1328	1427	1526	1523	...	1734	1802	1843	*1926*	1924	...	...	...	2122	2121	...
98	Ponte nelle Alpi	§ d.	|	0726	0826	0856	0920e	0957	0953	...	1205	1334	1335	...	1527	1531	...	1742	1808	1845	...	1932	1952	...	...	2124	2127j	...
	Belluno	§ a.	|	|	|	|	|	|	1001	...	|	|	1343	...	1534	|	...	|	|	1853	...	|	2000	...	...	2132	|	...
135	**Calalzo** ▲	a.	0730	0805	0915	0936	1003e	1046	...	...	1254	1422	...	...	...	1614	...	1825	1850	...	...	2018	...	...	...	...	2212j	...

km			⚒		z		z				⚒z	†z	z								z				z		z	*E* 1607 L
0	**Calalzo** ▲	d.	...	...	...	0638	...	0813	...	...	0941	1007	...	1229	1313	...	...	1506	...	1622	...	1723	...	1852	...	1930	2036	2056
	Belluno	§ d.	...	...	0604	|	0732	|	...	1015	|	|	1126	|	|	...	1542	|	...	|	1725	|	1917	|	1941	|	|	|
37	Ponte nelle Alpi	§ a.	...	...	0612	0721	0739	0854	...	1023	1024	1048	1134	1313	1401	...	1550	1552	...	1703	1733	1806	1926	1930	1949	2019	2115	|
37	Ponte nelle Alpi	d.	...	...	0613	0723	0741	0854	...	...	1033	1056	1135	1315	...	1429	...	1559z	1557	1704	1735	1807	...	1931	1951	2020	2127	|
44	**Belluno**	d.	0528	0608	|	0735	|	0909	1018	...	|	|	|	1326	...	1437	...	|	1605	1713	|	1816	...	1939	|	2027	|	2144
75	Feltre	d.	0601	0643	|	0809	|	0945	1055	...	|	|	|	1400	...	1507	...	|	1638	1750	|	1848	...	2016	|	...	|	...
110	Montebelluna	d.	0644	0728	|	0848	|	1019	1129	...	|	|	|	1444	...	1542	...	|	1714	1828	|	1926	...	2057	|	...	|	...
127	Castelfranco Veneto	d.	0703	0744	|	0902	|	1034	1143	...	|	|	|	1504	...	1604	...	|	1733	1846	|	1943	...	2113	|	...	|	...
158	**Padova**	a.	0741	0818	|	0936	|	1110	1217	...	|	|	|	1538	...	1643	...	|	1808	1917	|	2017	...	2148	|	...	|	...
	Vittorio Veneto	d.	...	...	0644	...	0810	...	...	...	1101	1124	1204	...	...	...	...	1628z	...	...	1806	...	...	...	2018	...	2153	...
	Conegliano **601**	a.	...	...	0659	...	0822	...	...	...	1115	1138	1218	...	...	...	...	1646z	...	...	1818	...	...	...	2033	...	2206	...
	Venezia Mestre **601**	a.	...	...	0752	...	0914	...	...	...	1202	1230	1304	...	...	...	...	...	...	...	1915	...	...	...	2130	...	2254	...
	Venezia Santa Lucia **601**	a.	...	...	0805	...	0928	...	...	...	1216	1243	1317	...	...	...	...	...	...	...	1928	...	...	...	2143	...	2307	...

H – ⑤ June 19 - July 17; daily July 24 - Sept. 4 (from Roma): 🛏 1, 2 cl. (Excelsior), 🛏 1,2 cl. and ▬ 2 cl. (4 berth) Roma Tiburtina - Belluno - Calalzo-Cortina.
L – ⑥ June 20 - July 18; daily July 25 - Sept. 5: 🛏 1, 2 cl. (Excelsior), 🛏 1,2 cl. and ▬ 2 cl. (4 berth) Calalzo-Cortina - Belluno - Roma Tiburtina.
e – † only.
j – 11 minutes later July 25 - Sept. 5.
q – From Treviso, depart 0605.
r – Arrive 1740.
y – Not July 26 - Sept. 13.
z – Not Aug. 31 - Sept. 13.
§ – See other direction of table for further connections.
▲ – Full name of station is Calalzo-Pieve di Cadore-Cortina.

Note - connections at Ponte nelle Alpi may be shown in previous column.

VAL GARDENA / GRÖDNERTAL and CORTINA 🚌 services 604

Service 445/446	⚒										
San Candido / Innichen .. d.	...	0843	...	1043	...	1343	...	1543	...	1743	...
Dobbiaco / Toblach ♣ .... d.	0700	0855	0905	1055	1105	1355	1405	1555	1605	1755	1805
Cortina .... a.	0750	...	0955	...	1155	...	1455	...	1655	...	1855

Service 445/446	⚒										
Cortina .... d.	0810	...	1010	...	1315	...	1510	...	1710	...	1910
Dobbiaco / Toblach ♣ .... d.	0855	0905	1055	1105	1400	1405	1555	1605	1755	1805	1955
San Candido / Innichen .... a.	...	0915	...	1115	...	1415	...	1615	...	1815	...

♣ – Dobbiaco town. Services also call at Dobbiaco railway station en route between Dobbiaco town and Cortina (5 minutes from town stop).

Service 350	⚒									
Bolzano / Bozen ♦ ..... d.	0642	0826	...	1054	1226	...	...	1726	...	1926
Ponte Gardena / Waidbruck . d.	0715	0857	1057	1125	1257	1357	1657	1757	1857	1957
Ortisei / St Ulrich ▲ ...... d.	0745	0927	1127	1157	1327	1427	1727	1827	1927	2027
Santa/St Cristina ▲ ..... d.	0755	0937	1137	1207	1337	1437	1737	1837	1937	2037
Selva / Wolkenstein ▲ d.	0804	0946	1146	1216	1346	1446	1746	1846	1946	2046
Plan ▲ .... a.	0807	0949	1149	1219	1349	1449	1749	1849	1949	2049

Service 350	⚒									
Plan ▲ .... d.	0607	0707	0837	0907	1037	1307	1337	1507	1707	1737
Selva / Wolkenstein ▲ ...... d.	0610	0710	0840	0910	1040	1310	1340	1510	1710	1740
Santa/St Cristina ▲ .... d.	0619	0719	0849	0919	1049	1319	1349	1519	1719	1749
Ortisei / St Ulrich ▲ .... d.	0631	0731	0901	0931	1101	1331	1401	1531	1731	1801
Ponte Gardena / Waidbruck .. d.	0659	0759	0931	0959	1131	1359	1431	1559	1759	1831
Bolzano / Bozen ♦ .... a.	...	0830	1002	...	1202	1430	...	1630	...	1902

♦ – Bolzano / Bozen town. Services also call at railway station (2 minutes from town stop). ▲ – Extra buses run Ortisei/St Ulrich - Plan and v.v. in summer.

Timings are valid **September 14, 2009 - June 12, 2010** (San Candido / Innichen - Dobbiaco / Toblach and v.v. (route 446) valid until December 12 only).
Operator: Servizi Autobus Dolomiti, Via Conciapelli 60, 39100, Bolzano / Bozen. ✆ : + 39 0471 450111 Fax: + 39 0471 970042.

🚌 service **30 Cortina - Calalzo**. 35 km. Journey time: 55 minutes. Timings are valid **September 14, 2009 - June 9, 2010**.

From **Cortina Autostazione** (Bus Station): 0535⚒, 0625⚒, 0650⚒, 0700†, 0725 **S**, 0800† **y**, 0832⚒, 0850†, 0930⚒, 1115, 1220⚒, 1240⚒, 1315⚒, 1345⚒, 1345† **z**, 1402, 1505, 1605⚒, 1705, 1725†, 1755⚒, 1920⚒, 1940, 2010⚒ **w**.

From **Calalzo Stazione** (FS rail station): 0625⚒, 0647 **S**, 0658, 0740⚒, 0830, 0935⚒, 1010†, 1100⚒, 1215⚒, 1305, 1400⚒, 1455, 1620, 1755⚒, 1835†, 1900⚒, 2025⚒, 2035†.

Operator: Dolomitibus, via Col Da Ren 14, 32100, Belluno, Italy. ✆ +39 00 437 217 111, fax +39 00 437 940 522.

S – Schooldays only. **w** – Dec. 19 - Apr. 3. **y** – Not Dec. 20 - Mar. 21. **z** – Dec. 20 - Mar. 21.

VENEZIA - TRIESTE 605

km			ICN 773	ICN 777				ESc 9703										ESc 9737		IC 707	ESc 9741	EN 241			
		y	♦	♦	2 ⚒			🍷 V			†	⚒						🍷 V		M	🍷 V	♦⊖		x	
	Roma Termini **620** .... d.	...	2236t	...	...	...	...	...	...	...	...	...	...	...	...	...	...	...	...	1444	...	...	...	...	...
0	**Venezia Santa Lucia** .... d.	0018	|	...	0732	0911	0948	...	...	1211	1311	1311	1411	1511	1611	1711	1811	...	1936	|	...	2120	...	2257	...
9	**Venezia Mestre 600** .... d.	0030	0532	0703	0745	0923	1000	1022	...	1223	1323	1323	1423	1523	1623	1723	1823	1945	1949	2111	2045	2132	...	2312	...
42	Santa Dona di Piave-Jesolo d.	0054	0558	0732	0809	0947	1024	1044	...	1247	1347	1347	1447	1547	1647	1747	1847	|	2016	2134	|	2156	...	2346	...
69	Portogruaro-Caorle .... d.	0115	0616	0801	0831	1008	1045	1101	...	1308	1408	1408	1508	1608	1708	1808	1908	2021	2037	2150	2121	2214	...	0010	...
83	Latisana-Lignano .... d.	0126	0628	0817	0844	1019	1056	1114	...	1319	1419	1419	1519	1619	1719	1819	1919	|	2050	2202	|	2226	...	0022	...
101	San Giorgio di Nogaro .... d.	0139	0640	0833	0857	1032	1109	|	...	1332	1432	1438	1532	1632	1732	1832	1932	|	2104	|	|	|	...	0037	...
112	Cervignano-Aquileia-Grado .. d.	0147	0650	0845	0905	1040	1117	1131	...	1340	1440	1446	1540	1640	1740	1840	1940	|	2112	2219	|	2243	...	0044	...
129	Monfalcone **606** .... d.	0200	0704	0901	0919	1053	1130	1145	...	1353	1453	1459	1553	1653	1753	1853	1953	2058	2125	2234	2158	2258	...	0057	...
157	**Trieste Centrale 606** .... a.	0223	0728	0928	0942	1116	1153	1208	...	1418	1516	1522	1616	1719	1816	1916	2016	2122	2148	2258	2222	...	...	0120	...

			EN 240			ESc 9710		IC 702				ESc 9716							ESc 9748				ICN 778		ICN 772
	2		♦⊖			🍷 V		M				🍷 V							V		Ⓑv	w	♦	2 Ⓐ	♦
Trieste Centrale 606 .... d.	...	0430	...	0532	...	0635	0641	0704	...	0818	0918	0938	1144	1244	1344	1444	1544	1644	1702	1744	1844	1918	1946	2021	2154
Monfalcone **606** .... d.	...	0453	0544	0555	...	0658	0704	0729	...	0841	0941	1001	1207	1307	1407	1507	1607	1707	1727	1807	1907	1941	2012	2048	2220
Cervignano-Aquileia-Grado .. d.	...	0505	0556	0607	...	|	0717	0742	...	0853	0953	|	1219	1319	1419	1519	1619	1719	1740	1819	1919	1954	2026	2101	2233
San Giorgio di Nogaro .... d.	...	0514	|	0616	...	|	0724	|	...	0902	1002	|	1228	1328	1428	1528	1628	1728	|	1828	1928	2003	2035	2110	2242
Latisana-Lignano .... d.	...	0526	0614	0629	...	|	0743	0802	...	0915	1015	|	1241	1341	1441	1541	1641	1741	1800	1841	1941	2021	2050	2129	2256
Portogruaro-Caorle .... d.	0512	0537	0625	0640	...	0737	0753	0813	...	0926	1026	1040	1252	1352	1452	1552	1652	1752	1810	1852	1952	2032	2103	2141	2308
Santa Dona di Piave-Jesolo . d.	0536	0557	0642	0703	...	|	0815	0830	...	0946	1046	|	1312	1412	1512	1612	1712	1812	1826	1912	2012	2059	2121		2325
Venezia Mestre 600 .... a.	0611	0622	0704	0728	...	0815	0849	0854	...	1011	1111	1116	1337	1437	1537	1637	1737	1837	1848	1937	2037	2136	2149	...	2349
Venezia Santa Lucia .... a.	0624	0634	0716	0740	...	...	0902	|	...	1024	1124	...	1349	1449	1549	1649	1749	1849	...	1949	2049	2149	...	...	|
Roma Termini **620** .... a.	...	...	...	...	...	...	...	1516	...	...	...	...	...	...	...	...	...	...	...	...	...	...	...	...	0656t

♦ – **NOTES** (LISTED BY TRAIN NUMBER)

240 – VENEZIA – 🛏 1,2 cl., ▬ 2 cl. and [2] Budapest - Zagreb - Ljubljana - Venezia; ▬ 2 cl. Beograd (**412**) - Zagreb - Venezia. Conveys 🛏 1,2 cl. Bucureşti (**1821**) - Arad (**354**) - Budapest - Venezia.

241 – VENEZIA – 🛏 1,2 cl., ▬ 2 cl. and [2] Venezia - Ljubljana - Zagreb - Budapest; ▬ 2 cl. Venezia - Zagreb (**413**) - Beograd. Conveys 🛏 1,2 cl. Venezia - Budapest (**355**) - Arad (**1822**) - Bucureşti.

772 – MARCO POLO – 🛏 1,2 cl. (T2), 🛏 1,2 cl., ▬ 2 cl. (4 berth) and [2] Trieste - Venezia Mestre (**771**) - Napoli.

773 – MARCO POLO – 🛏 1,2 cl. (T2), 🛏 1,2 cl., ▬ 2 cl. (4 berth) and [2] Napoli (**774**) - Venezia Mestre - Trieste.

777 – TERGESTE – ▬ 2 cl. (4 berth) and [12] Lecce (**776**) - Venezia Mestre - Trieste. Train number **35477** Aug. 31 - Sept. 19 (from Lecce).

778 – TERGESTE – ▬ 2 cl. (4 berth) and [12] Trieste - Venezia Mestre (**779**) - Lecce. Train number **35478** Aug. 31 - Sept. 19.

M – MIRAMARE – [12] Trieste - Venezia Mestre (**703/6**) - Roma and v.v.
V – [12] and 🍷 Milano - Trieste and v.v.
r – ⑥⑦ until Sept. 13.
t – Roma **Tiburtina**.
v – Not Aug. 14, Dec. 7.
w – Not Aug. 8, 22.
x – Not Aug. 8, 15, 22.
y – Not Aug. 9, 16, 23.
⊖ – Ⓡ and special fares payable for journeys to / from Slovenia.

UDINE - TRIESTE 606

Most services 2nd class only

km		⚒		⚒		⚒	Ⓐz	y			⚒	†	q	r		w		p	⚒m			Ⓐ	†		x	v	
	Venezia SL **601** .... d.	...	...	...	...	...	0526	0526	...	0704	0718	...	1004	...	...	...	1204	...	...	...	1404	...	...	...	1504	1504	...
0	**Udine 601** .... d.	0552	...	0630	0655	0730	0734	0734	...	0856	0934	1000	1156	1207	...	1245	1356	1420	1420	...	1556	1627	1629	...	1659	1704	...
33	Gorizia Centrale .... d.	0628	...	0654	0733	|	0801	0805	...	0920	1003	1036	1220	1234	...	1318	1420	1452	1458	...	1620	1700	1705	...	1723	1736	...
55	Monfalcone **605** .... d.	0655	...	0717	0759	0813	0823	0828	...	0941	1025	1101	1241	1305	...	1343	1441	1516	1523	...	1641	1722	1730	...	1744	1800	...
83	**Trieste Centrale 605** a.	0721	...	0740	0828	0836	0846	0856	...	1004	1050	1130	1304	1329	...	1409	1504	1540	1552	...	1704	1750	1802	...	1807	1829	...

		†	⑥m	Ⓐ			Ⓒ	Ⓐz	Ⓐm			
Venezia SL **601** .... d.	1604	...	1704	1704	...	1804	...	...	...	2004	2204	...
Udine 601 .... d.	1756	1814	1859	1859	...	1956	2021	2036	2036	2156	0003	...
Gorizia Centrale .... d.	1820	1839	1923	1923	...	2020	2054	2109	2109	2220	0038	...
Monfalcone **605** .... d.	1841	1900	1944	1944	...	2041	2116	2131	2131	2241	0103	...
Trieste Centrale 605 a.	1904	1923	2007	2007	...	2104	2142	2157	2157	2304	0131	...

	⚒	⚒	†			⚒	†		†	
Trieste Centrale 605 ..... d.	0502	0558	0604	...	0656	0735	0735	0856	0956	...
Monfalcone **605** .... d.	0527	0623	0629	...	0719	0803	0758	0919	1024	...
Gorizia Centrale .... d.	0551	0648	0653	...	0740	0826	0818	0940	1048	...
Udine 601 .... a.	0623	0728	0728	...	0804	0857	0843	1004	1123	...
Venezia SL **601** .... a.	0817	0949	0949	...	0956	...	...	1156	...	...

		⚒	†			⚒	x			⑦n	⑥	Ⓐm	Ⓐz	Ⓐ			Ⓐ	⑥h	Ⓐj		Ⓐ			⚒		⑥h	Ⓑk
Trieste Centrale 605 d.	1056	1126	1208	...	1256	1330	1411	...	1456	1551	1559	1602	1603	1631	...	1656	1722	1722	1734	...	1755	1856	...	1935	2042	2216	2221
Monfalcone **605** .... d.	1119	1154	1237	...	1319	1400	1434	...	1519	1618	1622	1630	1628	1659	...	1719	1750	1750	1757	...	1818	1919	...	2003	2108	2239	2244
Gorizia Centrale .... d.	1140	1219	1301	...	1340	1425	|	...	1540	1641	1643	1653	1651	1722	...	1740	1814	1814	|	...	1839	1940	...	2027	2131	2300	2305
Udine 601 .... a.	1204	1253	1338	...	1404	1504	1517	...	1604	1710	1709	1723	1724	1755	...	1804	1849	1849	1837	...	1903	2004	...	2058	2204	2324	2329
Venezia SL **601** .... a.	1356	1456	...	...	1556	...	...	...	1756	...	...	...	...	...	...	1956	...	2056	...	...	2056	2156	...	...	2356	...	...

h – Not holidays.
j – Not Aug. 14.
k – Also Aug. 15.
m – Until Sept. 5.
n – Also Dec. 8.
p – † until Aug. 30; daily Sept. 6 - Dec. 12.
q – ①⑥† (also Dec. 9).
r – ②③④⑤ (also Dec. 9; not holidays).
v – ⑥ until Sept. 5 (also Aug. 14; not holidays).
w – ⚒ until Sept. 5; daily Sept. 6 - Dec. 12.
x – Ⓐ until Sept. 4; ⚒ from Sept. 7 (not Aug. 14).
y – ⚒ until Sept. 5; ⑥ Sept. 12 - Dec. 12 (not holidays).
z – From Sept. 7.

607 FERROVIE NORD MILANO services

BRESCIA - EDOLO : *103 km* Journey: approximately 120 – 150 minutes 2nd class only

From **Brescia**: 0556⚒**r**, 0703†, 0703**s**, 0903, 1103, 1303, 1503, 1703, 1754Ⓐ**r**, 1903.
From **Edolo**: 0550⚒**r**, 0643⚒**r**, 0750, 0950, 1150, 1350, 1550, 1750, 1950†, 1950**s**.

MILANO - COMO LAGO : *46 km* Journey: 52 – 65 minutes 2nd class only

From **Milano Cadorna**: Hourly 0740 – 2040 (also 0900, 1000⑦**n**, 1400†, 1810, 2110).
On Ⓐ (not Aug. 3-21) runs every 30 minutes 0610-0740, 1140-2110.

From **Como Lago**: Hourly 0617 – 2117 (also 0547⚒, 0647⚒, 0747⚒, 1836†, 1856⑦**n**).
On Ⓐ (not Aug. 3-21) runs every 30 minutes 0547-0817, 1217-2017.

n – ⑦ Mar. 29 - Sept. 27. **r** – Not Aug. 1-23. **s** – Aug. 1-23.

MILANO - VARESE - LAVENO : *72 km* Journey: 87 – 107 mins 2nd class only

From **Milano Cadorna**: 0605⚒**r**, 0635, 0705Ⓐ**r**, 0750, 0850, 0920⑦**n**, 0935, 1035, 1135, 1205⚒**r**, 1235**s**, 1250**r**, 1350, 1435Ⓒ, 1435**s**, 1450Ⓐ**r**, 1535, 1605Ⓐ**r**, 1650, 1720Ⓐ**r**, 1750, 1820Ⓐ, 1850, 1920Ⓐ**r**, 1935Ⓒ, 1935**s**, 2020Ⓐ**r**, 2035Ⓒ, 2035**s**.
From **Laveno Mombello**: 0537Ⓐ**r**, 0607⚒, 0637, 0707Ⓐ**r**, 0737, 0807Ⓐ**r**, 0837, 0937, 1037, 1137, 1237, 1307⚒**r**, 1337, 1437, 1537, 1637, 1737, 1807Ⓐ**r**, 1837, 1937, 2037.
Additional journeys run Milano Cadorna - Varese (journey 64 minutes).

Operator: Ferrovie Nord Milano, Piazzale Cadorna 14, 20123 Milano.
✆ + 39 02 20 222 www.lenord.it For 🚌 Edolo - Tirano see Table **543**.

608 MILANO local services

MILANO - BERGAMO : Some services 2nd class only

km		Ⓐz		Ⓐ	Ⓒ	Ⓐ	Ⓒ			Ⓐ					Ⓐ	Ⓒ	Ⓐ	Ⓒ	Ⓐ	Ⓒ					
0	**Milano Centrale** ◇ d.	0525p	0610	0710	0710	0810	0810	0910	1110	1210p	1310	1410	1510	1610	1710	1710	1810	1810	1910	1910	2010	2110	2210	2345	...
34	Treviglio Ovest d.	0608	|	|	0750	|	0850	0950	1150	1306	1350	1450	1550	1650	|	1750	|	1850	|	1950	2050	2150	2250	0026	...
56	**Bergamo** a.	0630	0658	0758	0813	0858	0913	1013	1213	1328	1413	1513	1613	1713	1758	1813	1858	1913	1958	2013	2113	2213	2313	0045	...

	Ⓒ	Ⓐ	⑥	Ⓐy				Ⓐz								Ⓒ	Ⓐ								
Bergamo d.	0547	0602	0647	0720	0732	0802	...	0832	0947	1147	...	1247	1347	1447	1602	1647	1702	1747	1847	...	1947	2047	2147	2247	...
Treviglio Ovest d.	0605	|	0705	|	0747	|	...	0847	1005	1205	...	1305	1405	1505	|	1705	|	1805	1905	...	2005	2105	2205	2305	...
Milano Centrale ◇ a.	0650	0650	0750	0820p	0830	0850	...	0950p	1050	1250	...	1350	1450	1550	1650	1750	1750	1850	1950	...	2050	2150	2250	2350	...

Additional trains run approximately hourly Milano Porta Garibaldi - Bergamo via Monza, journey 64 minutes, *43 km*.

MILANO - LUINO : *91 km* 2nd class only

	⚒	⚒	⑥x	⚒				Ⓐ		⚒	
Milano P G d.	0515	0656	*0830*	*1230*	*1330*	*1530*	*1730*	1745	*1830*	1856	*2202*v
Gallarate **590** d.	0601	0735	0913	1313	1413	1613	1813	1826	1913	1937	2256
Laveno Mombello d.	0650	0820	0952	1349	1449	1649	1849	1904	1951	2014	2328
Luino 592 a.	0707	0835	1008	1408	1508	1708	1908	1919	2008	2032	2347

	⚒	⚒		Ⓒ	⚒		⚒			⚒	
Luino 592 d.	0632	0723	0852	1252	1352	1452	1552	1652	1752	1952	2052
Laveno Mombello d.	0649	0738	0912	1312	1412	1512	1612	1712	1812	2016	2112
Gallarate **590** a.	0725	0804	0947	1347	1447	1547	1647	1747	1847	2047	2147
Milano P G a.	0804	0846	*1030*	*1430*	*1530*	*1630*	*1730*	*1830*	*1930*	*2130*	*2255*v

Additional journeys (change at Gallarate): from **Milano P G** 0530†, 0730†, 0930†, 1130†, 1430⚒, 1630⚒, 1930; from **Luino** 0552Ⓐ, 0752†, 1052†, 1852†, 2152Ⓒ.

MILANO - CREMONA - MANTOVA :

km				w			⚒		Ⓐ	Ⓒ		
0	**Milano C** d.	0620	0815	1022n	1215	1415	1620	1720	1850	1848n	2020	...
60	Codogno d.	0704	0904	1104	1304	1504	1708	1804	1930	1930	2104	...
88	Cremona d.	0735	0926	1126	1326	1524	1729	1823	1949	1949	2124	...
151	**Mantova** a.	0832	1017	1217	1413	1617	1815	1917	2045	2045	2217	...

			⚒				w			2†	
Mantova d.	0520	0612	0647	0943	1143	1437	1543	1737	1943	1953	...
Cremona d.	0618	0658	0734	1030	1230	1525	1630	1835	2030	2056	...
Codogno a.	0641	0720	0754	1051	1254	1546	1653	1853	2053	2136	2151
Milano C a.	0745	0801n	0840	1145	1345	1640	1749n	1950	2145	...	2245

NOTES – SEE FOOT OF PAGE

609 Local services in NORTHERN and CENTRAL ITALY

2nd class only

ALESSANDRIA - ACQUI TERME : *34 km* Journey 28 – 38 minutes

From **Alessandria**: 0619⚒, 0700⚒, 0752†**m**🅁, 0911, 1136, 1243, 1337⚒, 1609†, 1641Ⓐ, 1741, 1937.
From **Acqui Terme**: 0615⚒, 0700⚒, 0706†, 0740⚒, 0946, 1320, 1510, 1546⚒, 1727†**r**, 1820⚒, 2021†**m**🅁.

BOLOGNA - PORRETTA TERME : *59 km* Journey 60 – 72 minutes

From **Bologna Centrale**: 0552⚒, 0630⚒, 0704, 0804⚒, 0904, 1004⚒, 1104, 1204, 1304, 1404, 1504, 1604, 1704, 1734⚒**w**, 1804, 1834Ⓐ**z**, 1904, 1934Ⓐ**z**, 2004, 2104.
From **Porretta Terme**: 0500⚒, 0550, 0608⚒, 0640**w**, 0718, 0750⚒, 0822, 0922⚒, 1022, 1122⚒, 1222, 1322, 1422, 1522, 1622, 1722, 1821, 1921, 2021, 2050Ⓐ**z**, 2122Ⓐ**z**.

CAMPIGLIA - PIOMBINO : *16 km* Journey 22 – 30 minutes

From **Campiglia Marittima**: 0603⚒, 0710⚒, 1016Ⓒ**k**, 1330Ⓐ, 1339⑥**h**, 1533, 1647, 1737Ⓐ, 1804, 1839Ⓒ**t**, 1930†**t**, 2100†**t**.
From **Piombino Marittima**: 0638⚒, 0746⚒, 0916, 1053Ⓒ**k**, 1132Ⓒ**t**, 1520⚒, 1609, 1725, 1812Ⓐ, 1841, 2010†**t**.

GENOVA - ACQUI TERME : *58 km* Journey 65 – 81 minutes

From **Genova Piazza Principe**:
⚒: 0612, 0714, 0902, 1021Ⓐ, 1222, 1322, 1422, 1548, 1712Ⓐ, 1747, 1822Ⓐ, 1922, 2043.
†: 0612, 0736, 0907, 1039, 1206, 1342, 1437, 1607, 1747, 1922, 2043.
From **Acqui Terme**:
⚒: 0520, 0610, 0703, 0740, 0851Ⓐ, 1025, 1215, 1316, 1414, 1554, 1716, 1817, 2049.
†: 0602, 0736, 0900, 1034, 1203, 1334, 1601, 1748, 1916, 2049.

Subject to alteration August 8 – 31

PORRETTA TERME - PISTOIA : *40 km* Journey 48 – 55 minutes

From **Porretta Terme**: 0540⚒, 0647⚒, 0719†, 0720⚒, 0817, 0926⚒, 1021, 1324, 1428, 1521, 1727, 1921.
From **Pistoia**: 0515⚒, 0614, 0705†, 0712⚒, 0825⚒, 0921, 1224, 1316, 1422, 1621, 1721, 1926.

Subject to alteration August 15 – 31

ROVIGO - CHIOGGIA : *57 km* *Subject to alteration Aug. 15 – Sept. 13*

	⚒	†m	⚒	†q	⚒	†	⚒	⚒q	†	⚒	⚒	†q	⚒
Rovigo d.	0622	0748	0810	0917	1017	1217	1249	1421	1455	1617	1817	1817	1943
Adria d.	0657	0821	0835	0945	1045	1246	1322	1450	1523	1648	1843	1844	2016
Chioggia a.	0739	0855	0911	1021	1120	1321	1356	1532	1558	1724	1920	1920	2050

	⚒	†	⚒	⚒	†q	⚒	†	⚒	⚒	†	⚒		⚒
Chioggia d.	0651	0744	0756	0938	1030	1244	1337	1444	1609	1615	1739	1937	2100
Adria d.	0724	0820	0836	1014	1107	1321	1413	1517	1647	1652	1814	2013	2129
Rovigo a.	0751	0847	0902	1045	1134	1347	1440	1545	1713	1718	1845	2043	2148

SANTHIÀ - ARONA : *65 km* Journey 60 – 73 minutes

From **Santhià**: 0640⚒, 0840, 0908†, 1240⚒, 1352, 1443Ⓐ, 1640Ⓐ, 1744, 1845.
From **Arona**: 0655, 1120†, 1155⚒, 1347⚒, 1511, 1730, 1810Ⓐ, 1845†, 1908†, 1955.
Trains call at Borgomanero approximately 45 mins from Santhia and 15 mins from Arona.

SANTHIÀ - BIELLA SAN PAOLO : *27 km* Journey 20 – 35 minutes

From **Santhià**: 0637⚒, 0737⚒, 0755†, 0837⚒, 0900†, 0940†, 0951⚒, 1152⚒, 1237⚒, 1240†, 1355⚒, 1437, 1552⚒, 1637⚒, 1640†, 1737⚒, 1837†, 1846⚒, 1925Ⓐ, 1959, 2048, 2142.
From **Biella**: 0548, 0624⚒, 0711Ⓐ, 0723⚒, 0750†, 0802⚒, 0851†, 0902⚒, 0944⚒, 1145, 1301⚒, 1350⚒, 1353†, 1500⚒, 1545, 1702⚒, 1748†, 1801⚒, 1832⚒, 1952, 2042.

Subject to alteration August 1 – 31

SIENA - CHIUSI-CHIANCIANO TERME : *89 km* Journey 71 – 94 minutes

From **Siena**: 0557⚒, 0601†, 0801†, 0806⚒, 1004†, 1216⚒, 1328⚒, 1357⚒, 1404†, 1448, 1601†, 1604⚒, 1659⚒, 1743⚒, 1804†, 1815⚒, 1927⚒, 2004†, 2019⚒.
From **Chiusi**: 0430⚒, 0605⚒, 0627†, 0707⚒, 0832†, 0914⚒, 1031†, 1038⚒, 1232†, 1350⚒, 1510⚒, 1632†, 1707⚒, 1832†, 1843⚒, 1928⚒, 2031†, 2038⚒, 2132.

SIENA - GROSSETO : *102 km* Journey 77 – 107 minutes

From **Siena**: 0602⚒, 0753, 1218, 1329, 1543, 1744, 1839, 1943.
From **Grosseto**: 0500, 0620⚒, 0722, 0934, 1334, 1547⚒, 1645, 1758, 1953.

TRENTO - CASTELFRANCO VENETO - VENEZIA : *Subject to alteration Aug. 1 – 30*

km				⚒	⚒		⚒				
0	**Trento** d.	*0705*	0805	*0905*	*1005*	*1105*	*1205*	*1305*	*1505*	*1605*	*1705*
31	Levico Terme d.	*0755*	0855	*0955*	*1055*	*1155*	*1255*	*1355*	*1555*	*1655*	*1755*
44	Borgo Valsugana Centro d.	*0809*	0909	*1009*	*1109*	*1209*	*1309*	*1409*	*1609*	*1709*	*1809*
97	Bassano del Grappa a.	*0903*	1006	*1106*	*1206*	*1306*	*1406*	*1506*	*1706*	*1806*	*1906*
97	Bassano del Grappa d.	0908	1008	1121	1223	1342	1431	1533	1740	1812	1922
116	Castelfranco Veneto d.	0926	1028	1147	1242	1405	1455	1604	1805	1834	1941
148	Venezia Mestre a.	1001	1108	1232	1332	1459	1532	1659	1901	1932	2032
157	**Venezia Santa Lucia** a.	1014	1122	1246	1346	1513	1546	1713	1914	1946	2046

			†	⚒		⚒				
Venezia Santa Lucia d.	0546	0727	0827	0857	1127	1327	1523	1627	1727	1927
Venezia Mestre d.	0600	0741	0841	0911	1141	1341	1537	1642	1741	1941
Castelfranco Veneto d.	0651	0836	0926	1011	1227	1433	1631	1744	1832	2032
Bassano del Grappa a.	0712	0859	0951	1035	1250	1457	1650	1807	1855	2053
Bassano del Grappa d.	*0717*	0915	1015	*1115*	*1315*	*1515*	*1715*	1815	*1915*	2108
Borgo Valsugana Centro d.	*0825*	1025	1126	*1225*	*1425*	*1626*	*1825*	1925	*2025*	2205
Levico Terme d.	*0844*	1044	1144	*1244*	*1444*	*1644*	*1844*	1944	*2044*	2218
Trento a.	*0927*	1127	1227	*1327*	*1527*	*1727*	*1927*	2027	*2127*	2257

VERONA PORTA NUOVA - MANTOVA - MODENA :

km		⚒	⚒		⚒	A	⚒w		⚒				
0	**Verona P N** d.	0631	0758	0856	0931	1131	1230	1357	1545	1658	1743	1900	1959
37	Mantova d.	0725	0843	0934	1020	1205	1330	1445	1635	1745	1834	1949	2050
56	Suzzara d.	0748	0906	0953	1041	|	1354	1509	1656	1810	1900	2009	2114
98	**Modena** a.	0835	0952	1027r	1126r	1251	1445	1552	1738	1901	1948	2102	2156

	⚒		⚒w	⚒				⚒			⚒	†	A
Modena d.	0605	0658r	0813	0906	...	1329	1422	1522	1630	1741	1837	...	2023
Suzzara d.	0656	0747	0905	0954	...	1421	1508	1608	1720	1834	1922	...	|
Mantova d.	0724	0825	0933	1010	1221	1446	1530	1642	1739	1901	1948	1948	2115
Verona P N a.	0813	0920	1020	...	1306	1533	1603	1734	*1836*	1949	2042	2042	2146

NOTES FOR TABLES 608 / 9

A – ADIGE – Not Aug. 3-23: 12 and 🍷 Bolzano - Verona - Bologna - Lecce and v.v. (*IC* **717 / 8**).
h – Not holidays.
k – From Aug. 29.
m – Until Sept. 6.
n – Milano **Lambrate**.
p – Milano **Porta Garibaldi**.
q – From Sept. 20.
r – Not Aug. 3-23.
t – Until Aug. 23.
v – Milano Porta Garibaldi **Passante**.
w – Not Aug. 2-30.
x – Not Aug. 15.
y – Not Aug. 3-28.
z – Nof Aug. 1-30.
◇ – Services from Centrale also call at Lambrate (8 mins from Centrale).

TORINO and MILANO - GENOVA - PISA - ROMA 610

km			IC 501 🍷 ⚒	ES 9305 🍷		ESc 9761 🍷	⚒	2 †	IC 645 🍷		†A	IC 517 Ⓐ	⚒	IC 691 🍷 ◆	IC 515 🍷 ◆			F	2 ⚒	2 †	2	IC 1533 🍷 ©	IC 647 🍷 Ⓐ	A	2	Ⓐ
0	**Torino Porta Nuova 620** .. d.	...	...	...	...	...	...	...	...	0520	...	0635	...	...	...	...	...	...	...	...	0720	...	...	...	0820	...
56	Asti **620** d.	...	...	...	...	...	...	...	...	0606	...	0713	...	...	...	...	...	...	...	...	0806	...	...	...	0906	...
91	Alessandria **620** d.	...	...	...	...	...	...	...	...	0628	...	0732	...	...	...	...	...	...	...	...	0833	...	...	...	0930	...
112	Novi Ligure d.	...	...	...	...	...	...	...	...	0650	...	0745	...	...	...	...	...	...	...	...	0850	...	...	...	0943	...
	Milano Centrale d.	...	...	...	...	...	...	...	0605	|	0625	|	0625	0700	...	...	...	...	0720	0720	|	0805	0805	0820	|	0850
	Pavia d.	...	...	...	...	...	...	...	0635	|	0700	|	0700	0735	...	...	...	...	0753	0753	|	0835	0835	0855	|	0915
	Voghera **620** d.	...	...	...	...	...	...	...	|	|	0716	|	0716	0751	...	...	...	...	0811	0811	|	0851	0851	0911	|	0933
	Tortona **620** d.	...	...	...	...	...	...	...	0700	|	0729	|	0729	|	...	...	...	...	0824	0824	|	|	|	0923	|	...
166	**Genova Piazza Principe** .. a.	...	...	...	...	...	...	...	0744	0749	0822	0830	0836	0842	...	...	...	...	0908	0910	0943	0942	0942	1014	1032	...
166	**Genova Piazza Principe** .. d.	...	...	...	0606	0652	0711	0711	0747	0752	—	...	|	...	0852	...	...	...	0911	0913	...	0947	0947	...	1035	...
169	Genova Brignole d.	...	...	0600	0615	0700	0720	0720	0758	0803	...	...	0847	...	0900	...	...	...	0920	0922	...	0958	0958	...	1041	...
194	Santa Margherita-Portofino d.	...	...	|	0647	|	0757	0757	0822	0834	...	...	...	...	|	...	...	...	0957	1000	...	1022	1030	...	...	...
196	Rapallo d.	...	...	|	0652	0723	0801	0801	0827	0838	...	...	...	...	0923	...	...	...	1002	1005	...	1027	1036	...	...	...
205	Chiavari d.	...	...	|	0701	0732	0809	0809	0836	0846	...	...	...	...	0932	...	...	...	1011	1014	...	1036	1045	...	...	...
212	Sestri-Levante d.	...	0515	|	0710	|	0816	0816	0844	0856	...	...	...	...	|	...	...	...	1025	1027	...	1044	1053	...	...	...
235	Levanto d.	...	|	|	0730	|	0836	0836	0858	0924	...	...	...	...	|	...	...	...	1054	1053	...	1058	1111	...	...	...
249	Riomaggiore d.	...	|	|	|	|	0856	0858	|	0949	2	...	...	...	|	...	...	...	1121	1123	...	|	|	...	...	...
256	**La Spezia Centrale** d.	...	0546	0651	0749	0806	0912	0907	0919	1000	1012	...	...	...	1006	...	...	...	1132	1132	...	1119	1138	...	...	...
272	Sarzana d.	...	0559	|	—	|	0928	*0928*	|	...	1028	...	...	...	|	...	1041	1058	...	...	...	|	|	...	...	...
282	Carrara-Avenza d.	...	0608	|	...	|	0936	*0936*	|	...	1035	...	...	...	|	...	1050	1106	...	...	...	1137	|	...	...	...
289	Massa Centro d.	...	0616	|	...	0827	0942	*0942*	0947	...	1041	...	...	...	|	...	1058	1113	...	...	...	1145	1205	...	...	...
310	Viareggio d.	...	0630	0717	...	0840	1004	*1004*	1002	...	1102	...	...	...	1038	...	1127	1137	...	...	...	1206	1223	...	...	...
331	**Pisa Centrale** d.	0545	0649	0732	0745	0900	1038	*1038*	1021	...	1135	...	...	...	1100	1145	1147	1205	...	...	...	1224	1248	...	...	...
	Firenze SMN **614** a.	|	|	|	|	|	...	...	|	...	...	...	...	...	|	|	|	...	...	...	...	|	|	...	...	...
351	**Livorno Centrale** d.	0604	0706	0746	0804	0916	...	...	1038	...	...	...	...	...	1116	1204	1207	...	...	...	...	1242	1305	...	...	...
374	Rosignano d.	0621	|	|	0821	|	...	...	...	...	...	...	...	...	|	1221	...	...	...	...	...	|	|	...	...	...
385	Cecina d.	0630	0729	|	0830	0937	...	...	...	...	...	...	...	...	1138	1230	...	...	...	...	...	1306	1339	...	...	...
420	Campiglia Marittima d.	0653	0748	|	0853	|	...	...	...	...	...	...	...	...	|	1253	...	...	...	...	...	1325	1400	...	...	...
437	Follonica d.	0704	0758	|	0904	|	...	...	...	...	...	...	...	...	|	1304	...	...	...	...	...	1336	1411	...	...	...
479	Grosseto d.	0732	0819	|	0932	1016	...	...	...	...	...	...	...	...	1228	1332	...	...	...	...	...	1400	1433	...	...	...
517	Orbetello d.	0754	0837	|	0954	|	...	...	...	...	...	...	...	...	|	1354	...	...	...	...	...	...	...	...	...	...
556	Tarquinia d.	0827	|	|	1027	|	...	...	...	...	...	...	...	...	|	1427	...	...	...	...	...	...	...	...	...	...
586	**Civitavecchia** d.	0841	0917	|	1041	1105	...	...	...	...	...	...	...	...	1322	1441	...	...	...	...	...	...	...	...	...	...
595	Santa Marinella d.	0848	|	|	1048	|	...	...	...	...	...	...	...	...	|	1448	...	...	...	...	...	...	...	...	...	...
617	Ladispoli-Cerveteri d.	0904	|	|	1104	|	...	...	...	...	...	...	...	...	|	1504	...	...	...	...	...	...	...	...	...	...
660	**Roma Ostiense** a.	0937	1000	|	1137	|	...	...	...	...	...	...	...	...	1400	1537	...	...	...	...	...	...	...	...	...	...
667	**Roma Termini** a.	0950	1014	0959	1150	1150	...	...	...	...	...	...	...	...	1414	1550	...	...	...	...	...	...	...	...	...	...
	Napoli Centrale **640** a.	...	1236	...	...	...	...	...	...	...	...	...	...	...	...	...	...	...	...	...	...	...	...	...	...	...

km		IC 649 🍷 ◆	ESc 9765 🍷		EC 143 🍷 ◆	IC 523 🍷 ◆	2	IC 653 🍷			†	⚒	ESc 9769 🍷	IC 655 🍷	2	IC 529 ⚒	2 A	EC 159 🍷 ◆	ESc 9771 🍷	2	2	G	IC 605 🍷	IC 537		©A
	Torino Porta Nuova 620 .. d.	...	...	...	...	1105	1120	...	...	...	...	...		...	1320	1405	...	...	...	...	1520	...	...	1605	...	...
	Asti **620** d.	...	...	...	...	1143	1206	...	...	...	...	...	...	...	1406	1443	...	...	...	...	1606	...	...	1643	...	...
	Alessandria **620** d.	...	...	...	...	1202	1233	...	...	...	...	...	...	...	1433	1502	...	...	...	...	1633	...	...	1702	...	...
	Novi Ligure d.	...	...	...	...	|	1249	...	...	...	...	...	...	...	1450	1515	...	...	...	...	1648	...	...	1715	...	...
0	**Milano Centrale** d.	0905	...	...	1110	|	|	1205	...	...	1225	1225	1310	1400	|	|	1420	1510	...	...	|	...	1600	|	...	1625
39	Pavia d.	0935	...	...	1135	|	|	1235	...	...	1300	1300	1335	1435	|	|	1455	1535	...	...	|	...	1635	|	...	1659
65	Voghera **620** d.	|	...	...	1151	|	|	|	...	...	1316	1316	|	1451	|	|	1512	1551	...	...	|	...	1651	|	...	1715
82	Tortona **620** d.	1000	...	...	|	|	|	1300	...	...	1328	1328	|	|	|	|	1523	|	...	...	|	...	|	|	...	1726
154	**Genova Piazza Principe** .. a.	1042	...	...	1242	1249	1334	1342	...	...	1418	1434	1442	1542	1536	1553	1613	1642	...	...	1734	...	1742	1753	...	1816
	Genova Piazza Principe .. d.	...	1052	...	...	1252	1336	1347	...	1411	|	|	1452	1547	1539	1556	...	...	1652	...	1736	...	1748	1802	1811	...
	Genova Brignole d.	...	1100	...	...	1300	1342	1358	...	1420	1427	1442	1500	1558	1548	1602	...	...	1700	...	1742	...	1758	1808	1820	...
	Santa Margherita-Portofino .. d.	...	|	...	...	|	...	1422	...	1456	...	...	|	|	1626	...	...	...	|	...	—	...	1822	...	1849	...
	Rapallo d.	...	1123	...	...	|	...	1427	...	1500	...	...	1523	1627	1630	...	...	...	1723	...	...	...	1827	...	1853	...
	Chiavari d.	...	1132	...	...	|	...	1436	...	1508	...	...	1532	1636	1638	...	...	...	1732	...	...	...	1836	...	1901	...
	Sestri-Levante d.	...	|	...	...	1334	...	1444	...	1518	...	...	|	1644	1648	...	...	...	|	...	...	...	1844	...	1911	...
	Levanto d.	...	|	...	...	|	...	1458	...	1538	...	...	|	1658	1724	...	...	...	|	...	...	...	1858	...	1931	...
	Riomaggiore d.	...	|	...	...	|	...	|	...	1552	...	...	|	|	1751	...	...	...	|	...	...	...	|	...	1953	...
	La Spezia Centrale d.	...	1206	...	...	1406	...	1518	...	1600	...	...	1606	1718	1800	...	...	...	1806	1812	...	...	1919	...	2000	...
	Sarzana d.	...	|	...	...	|	...	...	...	...	...	...	|	—	...	...	...	...	|	1828	...	...	|	...	...	...
	Carrara-Avenza d.	...	|	...	...	1423	...	...	...	...	...	...	|	...	...	...	...	...	|	1835	...	...	1940	...	...	...
	Massa Centro d.	...	1227	...	...	|	...	...	...	...	...	...	1627	...	...	...	...	...	1827	1841	...	...	|	...	...	...
	Viareggio d.	...	1240	...	...	1441	...	...	...	...	...	...	1640	...	...	...	...	...	1840	1902	⑤⑥	...	1957	...	...	...
	Pisa Centrale d.	...	1300	1345	...	1500	...	...	1545	...	...	...	1700	1745	...	...	...	...	1900	1924	1956	1956	2015	...	...	...
	Firenze SMN **614** a.	...	|	|	...	|	...	...	|	...	...	...	|	|	...	...	...	...	|	...	|	|	|	...	...	...
	Livorno Centrale d.	...	1316	1404	...	1516	...	...	1604	...	...	...	1716	1804	...	...	...	...	1916	...	2014	2014	2030	...	...	...
	Rosignano d.	...	|	1421	...	|	...	...	1621	...	...	...	|	1821	...	...	...	...	|	...	2031	2031	...	...	...	...
	Cecina d.	...	|	1430	...	|	...	...	1630	...	...	...	|	1830	...	...	...	...	|	...	2040	2040	...	...	...	...
	Campiglia Marittima d.	...	|	1453	...	1553	...	...	1653	...	...	...	1750	1853	...	...	...	...	|	...	2103	2103	...	...	...	...
	Follonica d.	...	1357	1504	...	|	...	...	1704	...	...	...	|	1904	...	...	...	...	|	...	2114	2114	...	...	...	...
	Grosseto d.	...	1416	1532	...	1628	...	...	1732	...	...	...	1816	1932	...	...	...	...	2015	...	2142	2142	...	...	...	...
	Orbetello d.	...	|	1554	...	|	...	...	1754	...	...	...	|	1954	...	...	...	...	2032	...	2204	2204	...	...	...	...
	Tarquinia d.	...	|	1627	...	|	...	...	1827	...	...	...	|	2027	...	...	...	...	|	...	2236	2236	...	...	...	...
	Civitavecchia d.	...	1505	1641	...	1722	...	...	1841	...	...	...	1905	2041	...	...	...	...	2108	...	2250	2250	...	...	...	...
	Santa Marinella d.	...	|	1648	...	|	...	...	1848	...	...	...	|	2048	...	...	...	...	|	...	2257	2257	...	...	...	...
	Ladispoli-Cerveteri d.	...	|	1704	...	|	...	...	1904	...	...	...	|	2104	...	...	...	...	|	...	2312	2312	...	...	...	...
	Roma Ostiense a.	...	|	1737	...	1800	...	...	1937	...	...	...	|	2137	...	...	...	...	|	...	2339	2339	...	...	...	...
	Roma Termini a.	...	1550	1750	...	1814	...	...	1950	...	...	...	1950	2150	...	...	...	...	2150	...	2354	2357t	...	...	...	...
	Napoli Centrale **640** a.	...	...	...	...	2036	...	...	...	...	...	...	...	...	...	...	...	...	...	...	...	...	...	...	...	...

◆ – **NOTES** (LISTED BY TRAIN NUMBER)

143 – SANREMO – 12 and 🍷 Milano - Genova (**144**) - Nice.
159 – RIVIERA DEI FIORI – 12 and 🍷 Milano - Genova (**160**) - Nice.
515 – TIRRENO – 12 and 🍷 Ventimiglia - Genova - Roma.
523 – CAPODIMONTE – 12 and 🍷 Torino - Salerno.
649 – MAMELI – 12 Milano - Genova (**650**) - Ventimiglia. Train numbers **1535/6** on ©.
691 – ANDREA DORIA – 12 and 🍷 Milano - Genova (**692**) - Ventimiglia.

A – To Albenga.
F – FRECCIA DELLA VERSILIA – 12 Bergamo - Fidenza - Aulla - Pisa.
G – ①②③④⑦ only.
t – Roma Tiburtina.

610 TORINO and MILANO - GENOVA - PISA - ROMA

			E 1941	IC 659	ESc 9773				IC 661	IC 541				IC 663	IC 543		IC 665		ICN 761	IC 667		ICN 799			IC 1571
		2		🍷	🍷		2		🍷				2		🍷	2	🍷			🍷	2			2	🍷
	Ⓐ	⚒	♦	♦				Ⓐ			©A	Ⓐ	⑤q		Ⓑp			V	♦	♦		♦			†
Torino Porta Nuova 620 d.	...	...	1655	...	...	...	1720	...	...	1805	...	...	...	...	1905	1920	...	...	2050	...	2120	2155	...	2225	...
Asti **620** d.	...	...	1730	...	...	...	1806	...	...	1843	...	...	...	...	1943	2006	...	...	2126	...	2206	2237	...	2317	...
Alessandria **620** d.	...	...	1750	...	...	...	1831	...	...	1902	...	...	...	...	2002	2033	...	...	2146	...	2230	2300	...	2339	...
Novi Ligure d.	...	...	|	...	...	...	1847	...	...	1915	...	...	...	...	|	2049	...	...	2159	...	2247	|	...	2355	...
Milano Centrale d.	1625	1635	|	1700	...	1705	|	1742	1800	|	1825	1825	1853g	1905	|	|	2010	2025	|	2105	|	|	2225	|	...
Pavia d.	1700	1712	|	1736	...	|	|	1819	1835	|	1902	1904	|	1935	|	|	2035	2059	|	2135	|	|	2300	|	...
Voghera **620** d.	1716	1733	|	1751	...	|	|	1844	1851	|	1918	1922	|	1951	|	|	2055	2115	|	2151	|	|	2316	|	...
Tortona **620** d.	1729	1745	|	|	...	|	|	1856	1903	|	1930	1936	|	|	|	|	|	2127	|	|	|	|	2329	|	...
Genova Piazza Principe a.	1818	...	1837	1842	...	|	1934	...	1945	1953	2025	2028	|	2042	2049	2135	2148	2217	2237	2242	2333	2350	0030	0052	...
Genova Piazza Principe d.	|	...	1840	...	1852	|	1937	...	1948	1957	...	|	|	|	2052	2137	2151	...	2240	...	2334	2353	|	0054	...
Genova Brignole d.	1829	...	1849	...	1900	|	1948	...	1958	2003	...	2037	|	2051	2100	2143	2200	...	2249	...	2340	0002	0038	0100	...
Santa Margherita-Portofino d.	...	...	|	...	|	|	2031	...	2022	...	...	...	|	...	|	...	2221	...	|	...	...	|	...	...	...
Rapallo d.	...	...	|	...	1923	w	2035	...	2027	...	...	...	w	...	2123	...	2226	...	|	...	...	0028	...	...	...
Chiavari d.	...	...	|	...	1932	|	2045	...	2036	...	...	...	|	...	2133	...	2235	...	|	...	...	0038	...	...	...
Sestri-Levante d.	...	...	|	...	|	|	2054	...	2044	...	...	...	|	...	2141	...	2246	...	|	...	...	|	...	...	...
Levanto d.	...	...	|	...	|	|	2126	...	2058	...	...	...	|	...	|	...	2300	...	|	...	...	|	...	...	...
Riomaggiore d.	...	...	|	...	|	|	2152	...	|	...	...	...	|	...	|	...	|	...	|	...	...	|	...	...	...
La Spezia Centrale d.	...	...	1955	...	2006	|	2200	...	2119	...	...	...	|	...	2212	...	2319	...	2358	...	...	0127	...	...	...
Sarzana d.	...	...	|	...	|	2044	...	...	|	...	...	...	2241	...	2225	...	...	...	|	...	...	|	...	...	...
Carrara-Avenza d.	...	...	|	...	|	2052	...	...	|	...	...	...	2249	...	2234	...	...	...	|	...	...	|	...	...	...
Massa Centro d.	...	...	|	...	2027	2058	...	...	2141	...	...	...	2257	...	2241	...	...	...	|	...	...	|	...	...	...
Viareggio d.	...	...	|	...	2040	2117	...	...	2156	...	...	...	2318	...	2254	...	...	...	0030	...	...	|	...	...	...
Pisa Centrale d.	...	...	2047	...	2100	2138	...	...	2215	...	...	...	2337	...	2313	...	...	...	0050	...	...	0219	...	...	...
Firenze SMN **614** a.	...	...	|	...	|	|	...	...	|	...	...	...	|	...	|	...	...	...	|	...	...	|	...	...	...
Livorno Centrale d.	...	...	2104	...	2116	2153	...	...	2230	...	...	...	2353	...	2329	...	...	...	0107	...	...	0240	...	...	0527
Rosignano d.	...	...	|	...	|	...	...	...	...	...	...	...	...	...	...	...	...	...	|	...	...	|	...	...	|
Cecina d.	...	...	|	...	|	...	...	...	...	...	...	...	...	...	...	...	...	...	|	...	...	|	...	...	0550
Campiglia Marittima d.	...	...	|	...	|	...	...	...	...	...	...	...	...	...	...	...	...	...	|	...	...	|	...	...	0612
Follonica d.	...	...	|	...	2157	...	...	...	...	...	...	...	...	...	...	...	...	...	|	...	...	|	...	...	0628
Grosseto d.	...	...	2209	...	2216	...	...	...	...	...	...	...	...	...	...	...	...	...	0217	...	...	0358	...	...	0655
Orbetello d.	...	...	...	...	|	...	...	...	...	...	...	...	...	...	...	...	...	...	|	...	...	|	...	...	0713
Tarquinia d.	...	...	...	...	|	...	...	...	...	...	...	...	...	...	...	...	...	...	|	...	...	|	...	...	|
Civitavecchia d.	...	...	...	...	2305	...	...	...	...	...	...	...	...	...	...	...	...	...	|	...	...	0455	...	...	0752
Santa Marinella d.	...	...	...	...	|	...	...	...	...	...	...	...	...	...	...	...	...	...	|	...	...	|	...	...	|
Ladispoli-Cerveteri d.	...	...	...	...	|	...	...	...	...	...	...	...	...	...	...	...	...	...	|	...	...	|	...	...	|
Roma Ostiense a.	...	...	...	...	|	...	...	...	...	...	...	...	...	...	...	...	...	...	|	...	...	|	...	...	0831
Roma Termini a.	...	...	...	...	2350	...	...	...	...	...	...	...	...	...	...	...	...	...	|	...	...	0551	...	...	0844
Napoli Centrale **640** a.	...	...	...	...	...	...	...	...	...	...	...	...	...	...	...	...	...	...	0558f	...	...	0911	...	...	1114

			ICN 796		IC 648	IC 500	IC 652	E 1940		IC 502		IC 654	ICN 768			IC 504	IC 656		ESc 9762	IC 658					IC 662
	2			2	🍷		🍷					🍷				🍷		2	🍷	🍷		2	2		🍷
			♦				♦	♦	V		⚒		♦			⚒				♦	P		†		
Napoli Centrale **640** d.	...	...	2108	...	...	...	...	...	...	...	...	...	...	...	...	...	...	...	...	...	...	...	...	...	...
Roma Termini d.	...	...	2350	...	...	...	...	...	...	...	...	...	...	...	...	...	...	...	0610	...	...	...	...	0609	...
Roma Ostiense d.	...	...	|	...	...	...	...	...	...	...	...	...	...	...	...	...	...	...	|	...	...	...	...	0619	...
Ladispoli-Cerveteri d.	...	...	|	...	...	...	...	...	...	...	...	...	...	...	...	...	...	...	|	...	...	...	...	0649	...
Santa Marinella d.	...	...	|	...	...	...	...	...	...	...	...	...	...	...	...	...	...	...	|	...	...	...	...	0705	...
Civitavecchia d.	...	...	0052	...	...	...	...	...	...	...	...	...	...	...	...	...	...	...	0653	...	...	...	...	0715	...
Tarquinia d.	...	...	|	...	...	...	...	...	...	...	...	...	...	...	...	...	...	...	|	...	...	...	...	0729	...
Orbetello d.	...	...	|	...	...	...	...	...	...	...	...	...	...	...	...	...	...	0559a	|	...	...	...	...	0802	...
Grosseto d.	...	...	0154	...	...	...	...	...	...	...	...	...	...	...	...	...	...	0628	0743	...	...	0755	...	0828	...
Follonica d.	...	...	|	...	...	...	...	...	...	...	...	...	...	...	...	...	...	0654	|	...	...	0826	...	0854	...
Campiglia Marittima d.	...	...	|	...	...	...	...	...	...	...	...	...	...	...	...	...	...	0707	0809	...	...	0840	...	0905	...
Cecina d.	...	...	|	...	...	...	...	...	...	...	...	...	...	...	...	...	...	0732	|	...	...	0908	...	0928	...
Rosignano d.	...	...	|	...	...	...	...	...	...	...	...	...	...	...	...	...	...	0740	|	...	...	0916	...	0936	...
Livorno Centrale d.	...	...	0311	...	...	...	...	0441	...	...	...	0526	0542	...	0550	0632	...	0811	0843	...	...	0937	...	1000	...
Firenze SMN **614** d.	...	...	|	...	...	...	...	|	...	...	...	|	|	...	|	|	...	|	|	...	...	|	...	|	...
Pisa Centrale d.	...	...	0328	...	...	...	...	0502	...	...	...	0544	0600	...	0608	0649	...	0826	0900	...	...	0957	...	1015	...
Viareggio d.	...	...	|	...	...	...	...	|	...	...	...	0601	0618	...	0627	0706	...	...	0917	...	...	▬	...	...	...
Massa Centro d.	...	...	|	...	...	...	...	|	...	...	...	0616	|	...	0644	0719	...	...	0931	...	...	...	...	...	...
Carrara-Avenza d.	...	...	|	...	...	...	...	|	...	...	...	|	|	...	0650	0726	...	...	|	...	...	...	...	...	...
Sarzana d.	...	...	|	...	...	...	...	|	...	...	0606	|	0642	...	0700	0735	...	...	|	...	...	...	...	...	...
La Spezia Centrale d.	...	...	0416	...	0502	...	...	0550	...	...	0627	0640	0701	...	|	0750	...	...	0953	...	1000	...	...	...	1040
Riomaggiore d.	...	...	|	...	|	...	...	|	...	...	|	|	|	...	|	|	...	...	|	...	1009	...	...	...	|
Levanto d.	...	...	|	...	0525	...	...	|	...	...	0644	0701	|	...	|	|	...	...	|	...	1023	...	...	...	1101
Sestri-Levante d.	...	0434	|	...	0541	...	...	|	...	...	0701	0716	|	...	|	0818	...	...	|	...	1043	...	...	...	1116
Chiavari d.	...	0445	0510	...	0552	...	...	|	...	...	0711	0724	|	...	|	0827	...	...	1027	...	1053	...	...	...	1124
Rapallo d.	...	0453	0520	...	0601	...	...	|	...	...	0721	0733	|	...	w	0836	...	...	1036	...	1101	...	...	...	1133
Santa Margherita-Portofino d.	...	0457	|	...	0607	...	...	|	...	...	0726	0739	|	...	|	|	...	...	|	...	1105	...	...	...	|
Genova Brignole d.	0535	0536	0555	0617	0635	0657	...	0730	...	0750	0804	0810	0835	...	|	0902	0910	...	1102	...	1142	...	...	...	1210
Genova Piazza Principe a.	|	0542	0601	|	0641	|	...	0736	...	|	0810a	0816	0841	...	|	0908	|	...	1108	...	...	⚒	...	...	1216
Genova Piazza Principe d.	0543	0545	0604	0625	0644	0708	0719	0739	0758	0808	...	0819	0844	...	|	0912	0919	...	...	1119	...	1125	1145	...	1219
Tortona **620** d.	|	0634	|	|	|	|	|	|	0844	|	...	0859	|	...	|	|	|	...	...	|	...	1233	1233	...	|
Voghera **620** d.	|	0646	|	|	0734	|	0808	|	0856	|	...	0912	|	...	|	|	1008	...	...	1208	...	1246	1246	...	1308
Pavia d.	|	0707	|	|	0751	|	0825	|	0912	|	...	0928	|	...	|	|	1025	...	...	1225	...	1302	1302	...	1325
Milano Centrale a.	|	0740	|	|	0820	|	0855	|	0945	|	...	0955	|	...	1025	|	1055	...	...	1255	...	1335	1335	...	1355
Novi Ligure d.	0635	...	|	0707	...	0741	...	|	...	0841	...	...	0925	...	...	|	...	...	...	...	...	...	...	...	...
Alessandria **620** d.	0657	...	0705	0726	...	0757	...	0827	...	0857	...	...	0941	...	...	0957	...	...	...	...	...	...	...	...	...
Asti **620** d.	0720	...	0739	0751	...	0816	...	0847	...	0916	...	...	1002	...	...	1016	...	...	...	...	...	...	...	...	...
Torino Porta Nuova 620 a.	0810	...	0820	0840	...	0855	...	0940	...	0955	...	...	1045	...	...	1055	...	...	...	...	...	...	...	...	...

♦ – **NOTES** (LISTED BY TRAIN NUMBER)

652 – MAZZINI – ⚒: [12] and 🍷 Ventimiglia (**651**) - Genova - Milano.
658 – CRISTOFORO COLOMBO – [12] and 🍷 Ventimiglia (**657**) - Genova - Milano.
659 – CRISTOFORO COLOMBO – [12] and 🍷 Milano - Genova (**660**) - Ventimiglia.
667 – MAZZINI – [12] and 🍷 Milano - Genova (**668**) - Ventimiglia.
761 – SCILLA – 🛏 1, 2 cl., ▬ 2 cl. and [12] Torino - Reggio; ▬ 2 cl. (4 berth) and [2] Torino - Lamezia (**763**) - Reggio.
768 – SCILLA – 🛏 1, 2 cl., ▬ 2 cl. and [12] Reggio - Torino; ▬ 2 cl. (4 berth) and [2] Reggio (**766**) - Lamezia - Torino.
796 – 🛏 1, 2 cl., ▬ 2 cl. (4 berth) and [2] Napoli - Torino; 🛏 1, 2 cl. (T2), 🛏 1, 2 cl., ▬ 2 cl. (4 berth) and [2] Roma - Torino.
799 – 🛏 1, 2 cl., ▬ 2 cl. (4 berth) and [2] Torino - Napoli; 🛏 1, 2 cl. (T2), 🛏 1, 2 cl., ▬ 2 cl. (4 berth) and [2] Torino - Roma.
1940 – TRENO DEL SOLE – 🛏 1, 2 cl. and ▬ 2 cl. (4 berth) Palermo - Torino; 🛏 1, 2 cl. and ▬ 2 cl. (4 berth) Siracusa (**1942**) - Messina - Torino.
1941 – TRENO DEL SOLE – 🛏 1, 2 cl. and ▬ 2 cl. (4 berth) Torino - Palermo; 🛏 1, 2 cl. and ▬ 2 cl. (4 berth) Torino - Messina (**1945**) - Siracusa.

A – To Albenga.
P – [12] Parma - Aulla - La Spezia - Genova. Runs up to 7 minutes later Sestri-Levante - Genova on ②③.
V – From / to Ventimiglia.
a – Ⓐ only.
f – Napoli **Campi Flegrei**.
g – Milano **Porta Garibaldi**.
p – Not Aug. 15, and days before holidays.
q – Also Dec. 7; not Dec. 4.
w – Via Fidenza and Aulla.

ROMA - PISA - GENOVA - MILANO and TORINO 610

		ESc 9764	EC 140						IC 606			IC 516			IC 518	IC 664			ESc 9768	IC 694		IC 524	IC 666			
	2	🍷	🍷 ◆	2	Ⓐ	© A			🍷	2		🍷 ◆	A		Ⓐ	🍷		2	🍷	🍷 ◆		⚒	🍷		2	⚒
Napoli Centrale **640** d.	...	...	...	...	...	...	...	...	...	...	...	0730	...	...	...	...	...	...	...	...	...	...	...	...	...	...
Roma Termini d.	...	0810	...	...	...	...	...	...	...	...	...	0946	...	...	...	...	1009	...	1210	...	...	...	...	1209	...	...
Roma Ostiense d.	...	|	...	...	...	...	...	...	...	...	...	0957	...	...	...	...	1019	...	|	...	...	...	...	1219	...	...
Ladispoli-Cerveteri d.	...	|	...	...	...	...	...	...	...	...	...	|	...	...	...	...	1049	...	|	...	...	...	...	1249	...	...
Santa Marinella d.	...	|	...	...	...	...	...	...	...	...	...	|	...	...	...	...	1105	...	|	...	...	...	...	1305	...	...
Civitavecchia d.	...	0853	...	...	...	...	...	...	...	...	...	1037	...	...	...	...	1115	...	1253	...	...	...	...	1315	...	...
Tarquinia d.	...	|	...	...	...	...	...	...	...	...	...	|	...	...	...	...	1129	...	|	...	...	...	...	1329	...	...
Orbetello d.	...	0928	...	...	...	...	...	...	...	...	...	|	...	...	...	...	1202	...	|	...	...	...	...	1402	...	...
Grosseto d.	...	0946	...	...	...	...	...	...	...	...	...	1130	...	...	...	...	1228	...	1343	...	...	...	...	1428	...	...
Follonica d.	...	|	...	...	...	...	...	...	...	...	...	1151	...	...	...	...	1254	...	1401	...	...	...	...	1454	...	...
Campiglia Marittima d.	...	|	...	...	...	...	...	...	...	...	...	|	...	...	...	...	1305	...	|	...	...	...	...	1505	...	...
Cecina d.	...	|	...	...	...	...	...	...	...	...	...	|	...	...	...	...	1328	...	|	...	...	...	...	1528	...	...
Rosignano d.	...	|	...	...	...	...	...	...	...	...	...	|	...	...	...	...	1336	...	|	...	...	...	...	1536	...	...
Livorno Centrale d.	...	1043	...	...	...	...	...	...	1126	...	...	1242	...	...	...	1326	1400	1418	1443	...	...	...	...	1600	...	...
Firenze SMN **614** d.	...	|	...	...	...	...	...	...	|	...	...	|	...	...	...	|	|	|	|	...	...	...	...	|	...	...
Pisa Centrale d.	...	1100	...	...	...	...	1109	...	1144	1236	...	1300	...	...	...	1344	1415	1436	1500	...	...	...	...	1615	1636	...
Viareggio d.	...	1117	...	...	...	...	1127	...	1202	1257	...	|	...	...	...	1402	...	1457	1517	...	...	...	...	▬	1657	...
Massa Centro d.	...	1131	...	...	...	...	1144	...	|	1317	...	1327	...	...	...	1416	...	1517	|	...	...	...	...	...	1717	...
Carrara-Avenza d.	...	|	...	...	...	...	1150	...	1219	1323	...	|	...	...	...	|	...	1523	1533	...	...	...	...	...	1723	...
Sarzana d.	...	|	...	...	...	...	1201	...	|	1331	...	|	...	...	...	|	...	1531	|	...	...	...	...	...	1731	...
La Spezia Centrale d.	...	1153	...	...	...	...	1219	1222	1240	1346	...	1353	...	1400	...	1440	...	1546	1553	...	...	...	1640	...	1746	...
Riomaggiore d.	...	|	...	...	...	...	...	1231	|	▬	...	|	...	1409	...	|	...	▬	|	...	...	...	|	...	▬	...
Levanto d.	...	|	...	...	...	...	...	1245	1301	...	...	|	...	1423	...	1501	...	...	|	...	...	...	1701	...	...	...
Sestri-Levante d.	...	|	...	...	...	...	...	1305	1316	...	...	|	...	1444	...	1516	...	...	|	...	...	...	1716	...	...	...
Chiavari d.	...	1227	...	...	...	...	...	1315	1324	...	...	1427	...	1454	...	1524	...	...	1627	...	...	...	1724	...	...	...
Rapallo d.	...	1236	...	...	...	...	...	1323	1333	...	...	1436	...	1502	...	1533	...	...	1636	...	...	...	1733	...	...	...
Santa Margherita-Portofino d.	...	|	...	...	...	...	...	1327	1339	←	...	|	...	1506	...	1539	...	2	|	...	...	...	1739	...	...	...
Genova Brignole d.	1217	1302	...	1325	1336	...	...	1413	1410	1416	...	1502	...	1545	1557	1610	...	1617	1702	...	...	1757	1810	1816	†	1917
Genova Piazza Principe a.	|	1308	...	|	|	...	...	→	1416	1422	...	1508	...	1551	|	1616	...	|	1708	...	...	|	1816	|	A	|
Genova Piazza Principe d.	1225	...	1319	1333	1345	1345	...	...	1419	1425	...	1512	1546	...	1608	1619	...	1625	...	1719	1745	1808	1819	1825	1935	1925
Tortona **620** d.	|	...	|	|	1433	1433	...	...	|	|	...	|	1634	...	|	1700	...	|	...	|	1833	|	1859	|	2026	2026
Voghera **620** d.	|	...	1408	|	1446	1446	...	...	1508	|	...	|	1647	...	|	|	...	|	...	1808	1846	|	|	|	2038	2038
Pavia d.	|	...	1425	|	1502	1502	...	...	1525	|	...	|	1703	...	|	1725	...	|	...	1825	1902	|	1925	|	2055	2055
Milano Centrale a.	|	...	1450	|	1535	1535	...	...	1555	|	...	|	1737	...	|	1755	...	|	...	1850	1938	|	1955	|	2130	2130
Novi Ligure d.	1309	...	...	1414	...	...	...	...	...	1509	...	|	...	...	1641	...	...	1709	...	...	...	1841	...	1909	...	...
Alessandria **620** d.	1329	...	...	1429	...	...	...	...	...	1529	...	1557	...	...	1657	...	...	1729	...	...	...	1857	...	1929	...	...
Asti **620** d.	1351	...	...	1451	...	...	...	...	...	1551	...	1616	...	...	1716	...	...	1751	...	...	...	1916	...	1951	...	...
Torino Porta Nuova 620 a.	1440	...	...	1540	...	...	...	...	...	1640	...	1655	...	...	1755	...	...	1840	...	...	...	1955	...	2040	...	...

	ESc 9770	IC 670				IC 1534	IC 672				IC 538	EC 148					ES 9308			ESc 9774		IC 1572	IC 546			
	🍷	🍷 ◆	2		2 ⑦t	🍷 ©	🍷 Ⓐ		F	2	🍷 ◆	🍷 ◆	A				🍷	2		🍷		🍷 ⑥q	🍷 ⑧p		2	2
Napoli Centrale **640** d.	...	...	...	...	...	...	...	...	...	...	1324	...	...	...	...	...	...	...	...	...	...	1724	1724	...	...	...
Roma Termini d.	1410	...	...	...	...	...	...	1409	...	...	1546	...	...	1609	...	...	1800	...	...	1810	1809	1946	1946	2009	2109	2209
Roma Ostiense d.	|	...	...	...	...	...	...	1419	...	...	1557	...	...	1619	...	...	|	...	...	|	1820	1957	1957	2019	2120	2220
Ladispoli-Cerveteri d.	|	...	...	...	...	...	...	1449	...	...	|	...	...	1649	...	...	|	...	...	|	1849	|	|	2049	2151	2257
Santa Marinella d.	|	...	...	...	...	...	...	1505	...	...	|	...	...	1705	...	...	|	...	...	|	1905	|	|	2105	2207	2312
Civitavecchia d.	1453	...	...	...	...	...	...	1515	...	...	1637	...	...	1715	...	...	|	...	...	1853	1915	2037	2038	2115	2216	2321
Tarquinia d.	|	...	...	...	...	...	...	1529	...	...	|	...	...	1729	...	...	|	...	...	|	1929	|	|	2129	2229	2333e
Orbetello d.	|	...	...	...	...	...	...	1602	...	...	|	...	...	1802	...	...	|	...	...	|	2002	2113	2113	2202	2302	0006e
Grosseto d.	1543	...	...	...	...	1604	1610	1628	...	...	1729	...	...	1828	...	...	|	...	...	1943	2028	2131	2131	2228	2329	0033e
Follonica d.	|	...	...	...	...	1625	1632	1654	...	...	|	...	...	1854	...	...	|	...	...	2001	2054	2153	2153	2254	...	...
Campiglia Marittima d.	|	...	...	...	...	1636	1643	1705	...	...	|	...	...	1905	...	←	|	...	...	|	2105	2205	2205	2305	...	...
Cecina d.	1622	...	...	...	...	1655	1702	1728	...	...	1816	...	...	1927	...	1927	|	...	...	|	2128	2222	2222	2328	...	...
Rosignano d.	|	...	...	...	...	|	|	1736	...	...	|	...	...	→	...	1936	|	...	...	|	2136	|	|	2336	...	...
Livorno Centrale d.	1643	...	...	...	1703	1718	1726	1800	...	...	1842	...	...	▬	1850	2000	2013	...	...	2043	2200	2245	2247	0001	...	...
Firenze SMN **614** d.	|	...	...	...	|	|	|	|	...	...	|	...	...	...	|	|	|	...	...	|	|	...	|	|	...	...
Pisa Centrale d.	1700	...	...	...	1720	1736	1744	1815	1822	1836	1900	...	...	...	1909	2015	2027	...	...	2100	2220	...	2304	0015	...	...
Viareggio d.	1717	...	...	...	1736	1753	1802	...	1840	1857	1917	...	...	...	1927	▬	2039	...	...	2117	▬	...	2321	...	...	...
Massa Centro d.	1731	...	...	...	1753	1813	1816	...	1858	1917	|	...	...	...	1944	...	|	...	...	2131	...	...	2334	...	...	...
Carrara-Avenza d.	|	...	...	...	1759	1820	|	...	1904	1923	|	...	...	...	1951	...	|	...	...	|	...	...	2340	...	...	...
Sarzana d.	|	...	...	...	1807	|	|	...	1911	1931	|	...	...	...	2000	...	|	...	...	|	2	...	2349	...	...	...
La Spezia Centrale d.	1753	...	1713	1800	|	1840	1840	...	▬	1946	1953	...	...	2000	|	...	2107	...	2116	2153	2222	...	0006	...	...	...
Riomaggiore d.	|	...	1722	1809	|	|	|	...	...	...	|	...	...	2009	|	...	|	...	2124	|	2231	...	|	...	...	...
Levanto d.	|	...	1746	1823	|	1901	1901	...	...	...	|	...	...	2022	|	...	|	...	2137	|	2248	...	|	...	...	...
Sestri-Levante d.	|	...	1817	1844	|	1916	1916	...	...	...	|	...	...	2042	|	...	|	...	2157	|	2308	...	0040	...	...	...
Chiavari d.	1826	...	1828	1854	|	1924	1924	...	...	...	2027	...	...	2052	|	...	|	...	2207	2227	2315	...	...	...	...	...
Rapallo d.	1835	...	1840	1902	w	1933	1933	...	...	...	2036	...	...	2103	w	...	|	...	2214	2236	2323	...	...	...	...	...
Santa Margherita-Portofino d.	|	...	1845	1906	|	1939	1939	...	2	...	|	...	...	2107	|	*IC*	|	...	2218	|	2327	...	...	...	...	...
Genova Brignole d.	1902	...	1935	1945	|	2010	2010	...	2024	...	2102	...	...	2154	|	**1540**	2159	2224	2255	2303	0016	...	...	...	...	...
Genova Piazza Principe a.	1908	...	1941	1951	|	2016	2016	...	|	...	2108	...	...	2200	|	†	...	|	...	2309	...	...	...	...	...	...
Genova Piazza Principe d.	...	1919	1944	...	|	2019	2019	...	2032	...	...	2119	2149	...	|	2227	...	2232	...	2312	...	...	...	...	...	...
Tortona **620** d.	...	2000	2032	...	|	|	|	...	|	...	...	|	2236	...	|	|	...	|	...	|	...	...	...	...	...	...
Voghera **620** d.	...	|	2045	...	|	2108	2108	...	|	...	...	2208	2247	...	|	2316	...	|	...	|	...	...	...	...	...	...
Pavia d.	...	2025	2102	...	|	2125	2125	...	|	...	...	2225	2303	...	|	2333	...	|	...	0012	...	...	...	...	...	...
Milano Centrale a.	...	2050	2140	...	2202g	2155	2155	...	|	...	...	2250	2335	...	2320	2359	...	|	...	0040	...	...	...	...	...	...
Novi Ligure d.	...	...	...	...	...	...	...	...	2114	...	...	...	...	...	...	...	...	2313	...	...	...	...	...	...	...	...
Alessandria **620** d.	...	...	...	...	...	...	...	...	2134	...	...	...	...	...	...	...	...	2331	...	...	...	...	...	...	...	...
Asti **620** d.	...	...	...	...	...	...	...	...	2155	...	...	...	...	...	...	...	...	2351	...	...	...	...	...	...	...	...
Torino Porta Nuova 620 a.	...	...	...	...	...	...	...	...	2240	...	...	...	...	...	...	...	...	0040	...	...	...	...	...	...	...	...

◆ – **NOTES** (LISTED BY TRAIN NUMBER)

140 – RIVIERA DEI FIORI – 12 and 🍷 Nice (**139**) - Genova - Milano.
148 – SANREMO – 12 and 🍷 Nice (**147**) - Genova - Milano.
516 – CAPODIMONTE – 12 and 🍷 Salerno - Torino.
538 – TIRRENO – 12 and 🍷 Napoli - Ventimiglia.
670 – MAMELI – 12 Ventimiglia (**669**) - Genova - Milano. Train number **1537/8** on ©.
694 – ANDREA DORIA – 12 and 🍷 Ventimiglia (**693**) - Genova - Milano.

A – From Albenga.
F – FRECCIA DELLA VERSILIA – 12 Pisa - Aulla - Fidenza - Bergamo.

e – † only.
g – Milano **Porta Garibaldi**.
p – Not Aug. 15, and days before holidays.
q – Also Aug. 15, and days before holidays.
t – Also Dec. 8; not Dec. 6.
w – Via Aulla, Fidenza.

612 PARMA and FIDENZA - SARZANA and LA SPEZIA

Most services 2nd class only

km																											
		⚒				⚒y	H		B			⚒y		⚒	⚒y						F	⚒	⑤j		⚒	⚒	†
	Milano Centrale d.	...	...	...	...	...	...	0650	...	...	...	...	...	...	...	...	...	...	...	1705	...	...	1853g	...	...	...	...
0	**Parma** d.	...	...	0515	0611	...	0748	|	...	...	1248	...	1346	...	...	1448	1548	1648	1740	|	1901	1948	|	2048	2148	2238	2238
*	**Fidenza** ▲ d.	...	...	|	|	0736	|	0834	0913	...	|	1342	|	...	1447	|	|	|	|	1843	|	|	2031	|	|	|	|
23	Fornovo ▲ d.	...	...	0533	0646	0753	0813	0900	0930	...	1317	1409	1414	...	1514	1517	1614	1717	1806	1901	1920	2014	2057	2115	2214	2308	2308
61	Borgo Val di Taro d.	...	0547	0605	0730	...	0846	0936	1001	...	1353	...	1446	...	...	1553	1646	1753	1846	1945	1957	2046	2142	2153	2246	2343	2343
79	Pontremoli d.	0545	0603	0628	0745	...	0902	0953	1019	1318	1409	...	1502	1542	...	1609	1702	1809	1902	2001	2019	2102	2158	2210	2301	2359	0001
100	Aulla Lunigiana d.	0609	0623	0658	0809	...	0920	1021	1039	1344	...	...	1520	1609	...	...	1720	...	1920	2022	2045	2120	2218	2229	...	...	0021
108	San Stefano di Magra d.	0615	0631	0704	0815	...	0927	1028	1047	1351	...	...	1526	1615	...	...	1726	...	1926	2032	2052	2126	2225	2236	...	...	0028
116	**Sarzana** a.	|	0640	|	|	...	|	1040	1057	|	...	...	|	|	...	...	|	...	|	2043	|	|	2240	|	...	...	|
	Pisa C **610** a.	|	0737	|	|	...	|	1147	1205	|	...	...	|	|	...	...	|	...	|	2135	|	|	2334	|	...	...	|
	Livorno **610** a.	|	...	|	|	...	|	1207	...	|	...	...	|	|	...	...	|	...	|	2153	|	|	2353	|	...	...	|
120	**La Spezia Centrale** a.	0633	...	0722	0833	...	0942	...	...	1409	...	...	1540	1633	...	...	1740	...	1940	...	2113	2140	...	2254	...	...	0046

	⚒	⚒	q			H	⚒	Ⓐv	Ⓒw		⚒y	⚒		⚒y		⚒	⚒	⑦k	x	†z	⚒	B			G	J	
La Spezia Centrale d.	...	...	0540	0620	...	0752	0820	1020	1020	1228	...	1420	...	...	1620	...	1727	...	1818	1824	1901	...	...	2020	2102	2108	...
Livorno **610** d.	...	...	|	|	0550	|	|	|	|	|	...	|	...	...	|	...	|	1703	|	|	|	...	1850	|	|	|	...
Pisa C **610** a.	...	...	|	|	0608	|	|	|	|	|	...	|	...	...	|	...	|	1720	|	|	|	1822	1909	|	|	|	...
Sarzana d.	...	...	|	|	0700	|	|	|	|	|	...	|	...	...	|	...	|	1807	|	|	|	1912	2000	|	|	|	2100
San Stefano di Magra d.	...	...	0553	0634	0709	0810	0834	1034	1034	1242	...	1434	...	...	1634	...	1744	1816	1834	1835	1919	1923	2009	2034	2113	2119	2126
Aulla Lunigiana d.	...	...	0600	0640	0716	0818	0840	1040	1040	1249	...	1440	...	...	1640	...	1751	1823	1840	1841	...	1930	2016	2040	2120	2126	2133
Pontremoli d.	0510	0551	0627	0659	0740	0838	0859	1059	1059	1314	...	1459	1551	...	1659	1751	1814	1848	1859	1859	...	1951	2036	2059	2142	2145	2155
Borgo Val di Taro d.	0526	0608	0648	0715	0803	0854	0916	1114	1115	1332	...	1515	1608	...	1715	1808	...	1903	1915	1915	...	2008	2052	2115	2202	2202	...
Fornovo ▲ d.	0606	0645	0725	0747	0844	0926	0957	...	1147	1413	1414	1547	1645	1706	1746	1846	...	1937	1947	1947	...	2043	2136	2147	2244	2244	...
Fidenza ▲ a.	|	|	|	|	0904	|	|	...	|	|	1442	|	|	1734	|	|	...	2003	|	|	...	2103	2154	|	|	|	...
Parma a.	0630	0708	0745	0808	|	0940	1016	...	1208	1436	...	1608	1708	...	1808	1916	...	|	2008	2008	...	...	|	2208	2308	2308	...
Milano Centrale a.	...	...	...	...	1025	...	...	...	...	...	...	...	...	...	...	...	...	2202g	...	...	...	...	2320	...	...	...	...

B – FRECCIA DELLA VERSILIA – [12] Bergamo - Pisa and v.v.
F – [12] Bologna - Parma - La Spezia - Genova.
G – Sept. 14 - Dec. 12: [12] Ventimiglia - La Spezia - Parma.
H – [12] Parma - La Spezia - Genova and v.v.
J – June 14 - Sept. 13: [12] (Ⓐ Ventimiglia -) Savona - La Spezia - Parma.

g – Milano **Porta Garibaldi**.
j – Also Dec. 7; not Dec. 4.
k – Also Dec. 8; not Dec. 6.
q – Daily June 14 - Aug. 2; † Aug. 9 - 23; daily Aug. 30 - Dec. 12.
v – Until Nov. 27.
w – Daily from Nov. 28.
x – ⚒ June 14 - Sept. 13; daily Sept. 14 - Dec. 12.

y – Not Aug. 2 - 30.
z – Until Sept. 13.

▲ – **Fidenza - Fornovo and v.v. additional services**:
From Fidenza: 1242⚒y, 1631⚒y, 1742⚒y.
From Fornovo: 0703⚒y, 1209⚒y, 1553⚒y.

* – Fidenza - Fornovo is *25 km*.

613 FIRENZE - SIENA, PISA, PISA AEROPORTO ✈ and LIVORNO

Most services 2nd class only

km																												
		⚒		⚒						⚒	D					†	⚒	⚒		⚒	⚒		⚒				⚒	
0	**Firenze SMN 614** d.	0430	0535	...	0610	0628	0637	0727	...	0732	0755	0757	0810	0805	0827	0850	0857	0910	0927	0957	1010	1027	1037	1057	1110	1127	1157	1210
34	Empoli d.	0506	0602	0627	0647	0655	0714	0759	0806	0808	0822	0830	0840	0845	0859	0927	0930	0940	0959	1030	1040	1059	1114	1130	1140	1159	1230	1240
	Poggibonsi d.	|	|	0705	|	0729	|	|	0848	|	|	|	0915	|	|	|	|	1015	|	|	1115	|	|	|	1215	|	|	1315
	Siena a.	|	|	0731	|	0752	|	|	0914	|	|	|	0938	|	|	|	|	1038	|	|	1138	|	|	|	1238	|	|	1338
81	**Pisa Centrale 614** ¶ d.	0555	0643	...	0732	...	0802	0834	...	0851	0856	0906	...	0925	0934	1007	1010	...	1034	1106	...	1134	1202	1206	...	1234	1306	...
	Pisa Aeroporto ✈ ¶ a.	|	|	...	...	...	0807	|	...	...	...	...	...	0930	|	...	...	...	|	...	...	|	1207	...	...	|	...	...
101	**Livorno** a.	0612	0656	...	...	...	...	0849	...	...	...	...	...	...	0949	...	...	...	1049	...	...	1149	...	...	...	1249	...	...

km																												
					⚒	⚒						⚒		⚒					⚒	⚒					Ⓐ			
	Firenze SMN 614 d.	1227	...	1257	1310	1327	...	1337	1357	1410	1427	...	1457	1510	1527	...	1537	1557	1610	1627	1657	1710	1727	1737	1757	1810	1827	1857
0	Empoli d.	1259	1308	1330	1340	1359	1408	1414	1430	1440	1459	1508	1530	1540	1559	1608	1614	1630	1640	1659	1730	1740	1759	1814	1830	1840	1859	1930
38	Poggibonsi d.	|	1349	|	1415	|	1449	|	|	1515	|	1549	|	1615	|	1649	|	|	1715	|	|	1815	|	|	|	1915	|	|
63	**Siena** a.	|	1414	|	1438	|	1514	|	|	1538	|	1614	|	1638	|	1714	|	|	1738	|	|	1838	|	|	|	1938	|	|
	Pisa Centrale 614 ¶ d.	1334	...	1406	...	1434	...	1504	1506	...	1534	...	1606	...	1634	...	1659	1706	...	1734	1806	...	1834	1904	1906	...	1934	2006
	Pisa Aeroporto ✈ ¶ a.	|	...	...	...	|	...	...	...	...	|	...	...	...	|	...	...	...	...	|	...	...	|	|	...	...	|	...
	Livorno a.	1349	...	...	...	1449	...	1520	...	...	1549	...	...	...	1649	...	...	...	...	1749	...	...	1849	1922	...	...	1949	...

			⚒			⚒							
Firenze SMN 614 d.	1910	1927	...	1957	2010	2027	2037	2057	2127	...	2157	2307	0037
Empoli d.	1940	1959	2008	2030	2040	2059	2114	2130	2159	2208	2233	2343	0114
Poggibonsi d.	2015	|	2049	|	2115	|	|	|	|	2249	|	|	|
Siena a.	2038	|	2114	|	2138	|	|	|	|	2314	|	|	|
Pisa Centrale 614 ¶ d.	...	2034	...	2109	...	2131	2202	2209	2234	...	2322	0032	0159
Pisa Aeroporto ✈ ¶ a.	...	|	...	|	...	...	2207	|	|	...	|	|	...
Livorno a.	...	2049	...	2124	...	...	...	2224	2249	...	2337	0047	...

			⚒					⚒	†	⚒	
Livorno d.	...	0521	...	0620	...	...	...	0711	...	...	0730
Pisa Aeroporto ✈ ¶ d.	...	|	...	|	...	0641	...	|	...	...	|
Pisa Centrale 614 ¶ d.	0415	0539	...	0638	...	0654	...	0729	0729	...	0754
Siena d.	|	|	0550	|	0627	|	0639	|	|	0702	|
Poggibonsi d.	|	|	0615	|	0649	|	0703	|	|	0728	|
Empoli d.	0452	0618	0653	0709	0723	0731	0752	0802	0802	0820	0831
Firenze SMN 614 a.	0527	0652	0728	0737	0750	0803	0828	0833	0833	0855	0903

km																												
		⚒				⚒	†	⚒	⚒	⚒				⚒	⚒				⚒						⚒	⚒	⚒	
	Livorno d.	...	0811	...	...	0911	0911	...	...	1011	...	...	1111	...	...	...	1211	...	...	1311	...	...	1343	1411	...	...	1511	...
0	Pisa Aeroporto ✈ ¶ d.	...	|	...	...	|	|	...	...	|	...	...	|	...	1143	...	|	...	1243	|	...	...	|	|	...	...	|	...
2	**Pisa Centrale 614** ¶ d.	...	0829	...	...	0929	0929	...	0954	1029	1054	1101	1129	...	1154	...	1229	...	1254	1329	...	1354	1401	1429	...	1454	1529	1554
	Siena d.	0732	|	0818	0847	|	|	0918	|	|	|	|	|	1118	|	1141	|	1218	|	|	1318	|	|	|	1418	|	|	|
	Poggibonsi d.	0809	|	0846	0909	|	|	0946	|	|	|	|	|	1146	|	1212	|	1246	|	|	1346	|	|	|	1446	|	|	|
	Empoli d.	0852	0902	0921	0940	1002	1017	1021	1031	1102	1131	1147	1202	1221	1231	1252	1302	1321	1331	1402	1421	1431	1447	1502	1521	1531	1602	1631
	Firenze SMN 614 a.	...	0933	0950	1010	1033	1046	1050	1103	1133	1203	1223	1233	1250	1303	...	1333	1350	1403	1433	1450	1503	1523	1533	1550	1603	1633	1703

				⚒									⚒	†	z	⚒				⚒	D	Ⓒy					†y
Livorno d.	...	1543	1611	...	...	1711	...	...	...	1811	...	...	...	...	1911	...	...	2006	...	...	...	2035	...	2111	...	...	2258
Pisa Aeroporto ✈ ¶ d.	...	|	|	...	...	|	...	...	1753	|	...	...	...	...	|	...	...	|	...	...	...	|	...	|	...	2220	|
Pisa Centrale 614 ¶ d.	...	1601	1629	...	1654	1729	...	1754	1801	1829	...	1854	1901	1913	1929	...	1954	2029	...	2038	2058	2051	2101	2129	...	2230	2316
Siena d.	1518	|	|	1618	|	|	1718	|	|	|	1818	|	|	|	|	1918	|	|	2018	|	|	|	|	|	2118	|	|
Poggibonsi d.	1546	|	|	1646	|	|	1746	|	|	|	1846	|	|	|	|	1946	|	|	2046	|	|	|	|	|	2146	|	|
Empoli d.	1621	1647	1702	1721	1731	1802	1821	1831	1847	1902	1921	1931	1947	1953	2002	2021	2031	2102	2121	2111	2128	2135	2147	2202	2221	2315	2347
Firenze SMN 614 a.	1650	1723	1733	1750	1803	1833	1850	1903	1923	1933	1950	2003	2023	2024	2033	2050	2103	2133	2150	2142	2155	2209	2223	2233	2250	2350	0020

D – *ESc* – [12] Firenze - Pisa - Torino and v.v. Ⓡ.

y – Until Aug. 23.
z – ⚒ June 14 - Aug. 23; daily Aug. 24 - Dec. 12.

¶ – For complete service Pisa - Pisa Aeroporto see Table **614** (page 301).

614 FIRENZE - LUCCA - VIAREGGIO and PISA

Most services 2nd class only

km																								
		⚒	⚒	⚒									†	Ⓐ									⚒	
0	**Firenze SMN 613** d.	0510	...	...	...	0605	0708	...	0808	...	0908	...	1008	...	...	1208	...	and at	1908	...	2008	...	2115	2208
17	Prato Centrale d.	0533	...	...	...	0627	0729	...	0829	...	0929	...	1029	...	...	1229	...	the same	1929	...	2029	...	2138	2229
34	Pistoia d.	0551	...	...	...	0644	0745	...	0845	...	0945	...	1045	...	...	1245	...	minutes	1945	...	2045	...	2153	2245
47	Montecatini Centro d.	0604	...	...	...	0703	0805	...	0905	...	1005	...	1105	...	...	1305	...	past each	2005	...	2105	...	2205	2305
78	Lucca ⊡ d.	0650	0653	0708	0742	0755	0831	0842	0931	0942	1031	1042	1131	1242	1312	1331	1342	hour	2031	2042	2131	2142	2231	2331
101	**Viareggio** a.	0711	|	|	|	|	0849	|	0949	|	1049	|	1149	|	|	1349	|	until	2049	|	2149	|	2249	2349
	Pisa Centrale 613 ⊡ a.	...	0716	0740	0812	0825	...	0912	...	1012	...	1107	...	1312	1342	...	1412		...	2112	...	2212	...	...

⊡ – Additional services operate Lucca - Pisa Centrale on ⚒.

PISA and VIAREGGIO - LUCCA - FIRENZE 614

Most services 2nd class only

km		⚒																				q	⚒		
0	**Pisa Centrale 613** . ⊡ d.	0620	...	...	0704	0750	...	0850	...	0950	...	...	1250	...	1343	...	1450	...	and at	1950	...	2050	...	2150	...
	Viareggio .... d.	|	0630	0714	|	|	0811	|	0911	|	1011	1211	|	1311	|	1411	|	1511	the same	|	2011	|	2111	|	2211
24	Lucca .... ⊡ d.	0645	0650	0731	0736	0822	0832	0917	0932	1017	1032	1232	1317	1332	1408	1432	1517	1532	minutes	2017	2032	2117	2132	2217	2232
	Montecatini Centro ..... d.	...	0716	0758	...	...	0857	...	0957	...	1057	1257	...	1357	...	1457	...	1557	past each	...	2057	...	2158	...	2257
	Pistoia .... d.	...	0732	0812	...	...	0912	...	1012	...	1112	1312	...	1412	...	1512	...	1612	hour	...	2112	...	2214	...	2312
	Prato Centrale .... d.	...	0747	0828	...	...	0928	...	1028	...	1130	1328	...	1428	...	1528	...	1628	until	...	2128	...	2230	...	2328
	Firenze SMN 613 ...... a.	...	0806	0852	...	...	0952	...	1100	...	1159	1352	...	1452	...	1552	...	1652		...	2152	...	2252	...	2350

⊡ – Additional services operate Pisa Centrale - Lucca on ⚒.

q – Daily June 14 - July 26; † July 27 - Aug. 23; daily Aug. 24.

¶ – **Full service PISA Centrale - PISA Aeroporto ✈ and v.v.**: *2 km*, journey 5 minutes. Most services 2nd class only.

From **Pisa Centrale**: 0620, 0720, 0750, 0802, 0822⚒, 0850, 0925, 0950, 1020⚒, 1050, 1120, 1202⚒, 1220, 1250, 1320, 1350, 1420, 1450, 1520, 1550, 1620, 1650, 1720, 1742, 1820, 1850, 1920, 1950, 2020, 2050, 2120, 2202.

From **Pisa Aeroporto**: 0641, 0735, 0810, 0835, 0905, 0935⚒, 1005, 1035, 1105, 1135, 1143⚒, 1235, 1243⚒, 1305, 1335, 1405, 1435, 1505, 1535, 1605, 1635, 1705, 1735, 1753, 1835, 1905, 1935, 2005, 2035, 2105, 2135, 2220.

FIRENZE - PERUGIA - FOLIGNO and ROMA 615

Faster express trains Firenze - Arezzo - Chiusi - Roma are shown in Table 620

km		*ICN* 771 ♦	*ES* 9321 🍷 ⚒	⚒	†	2 ⚒	*IC* 579 ⚒	2 ⚒	*EN* 235 ♦	⚒	*AV* 9501 🍷 ♦	†	2 ⚒			*IC* 585 🍷 ♦		⚒			*IC* 703 🍷 ♦	2	2 ⚒		*IC* 591 🍷 ♦	2
0	**Firenze SMN** .... d.	...	...	...	...	...	0550	...	0630	0645	0700	0709	...	0802	0913	1027r	...	1102	1113	1213	1227r	1313	...	1413	1427r	1513
88	Arezzo .... d.	0458	...	...	...	...	0630	...	|	0746	0736	0814	...	0914	1014	1106	...	1147	1214	1314	1306	1414	...	1514	1506	1614
106	Castiglion Fiorentino ... d.	|	...	...	...	...	|	...	|	0759	|	0827	...	0927	1027	|	...	1203	1227	1327	|	1427	...	1527	|	1627
122	Terontola .... d.	0520	...	...	...	0625	0650	0709	|	0812	|	0840	0840	0940	1040	|	...	1221	1240	1340	|	1440	1445	1540	|	1640
134	Passignano ▲ .... d.	|	...	...	...	0638	|	0720	|	|	|	|	0853	0951	|	|	...	1234	|	1351	|	|	1458	1551	|	|
165	**Perugia** .... a.	|	...	...	...	0718	|	0750	|	|	|	|	0936	1023	|	|	...	1301	|	1419	|	|	1533	1619	|	|
165	**Perugia 625** .... d.	|	0643	0700	0723	0723	|	0751	|	|	|	|	0938	1025	|	|	1118	1303	|	1421	|	|	1540	1621	|	|
176	Ponte San Giovanni d.	|	0653	0710	0733	0734	|	0805	|	|	|	|	0952	1034	|	|	1131	1312	|	1430	|	|	1549	1630	|	|
189	Assisi **625** .... d.	|	0705	0721	0745	0752	|	0823	|	|	|	|	1012	1046	|	|	1144	1329	|	1441	|	|	1600	1642	|	|
200	Spello .... d.	|	|	0730	0754	0801	|	0832	|	|	|	|	1021	1055	|	|	1153	1339	|	1457	|	|	1609	1650	|	|
205	**Foligno 625** .... a.	|	0716	0735	0800	0807	|	0837	|	|	|	|	1028	1101	|	|	1200	1345	|	1502	|	|	1615	1656	|	|
133	Castiglion del Lago ..... d.	|	|	...	|	...	|	...	|	0820	|	0848	...	...	1048	|	|	...	1248	...	|	1448	...	...	|	1648
151	Chiusi ▼ .... d.	0541	|	...	|	...	0710	...	0732	0838	|	0903	...	...	1101	1145	|	...	1301	...	1345	1515	...	...	1545	1715
191	Orvieto .... d.	|	|	...	|	...	0731	...	0757	0905	|	0930	...	...	1127	1209	|	...	1327	...	1409	1542	...	...	1609	1742
233	Orte **625** .... d.	|	0816	...	0936	...	|	...	|	0943	|	1005	...	...	1202	1238	1317	...	1402	...	1438	1617	...	...	1638	1817
311	Roma Tiburtina **625** .... a.	0656	0847s	...	1011	...	|	...	|	1050	|	1040	...	...	1244	|	1352	...	1437	...	|	1652	...	...	|	1852
316	**Roma Termini 625** .... a.	...	0858	...	1019	...	0824	...	0905	1100	0845	1051	...	...	1254	1316	1403	...	1448	...	1516	1703	...	...	1716	1903

		ES 9333 🍷		*IC* 705 🍷 ♦		2 ⚒		*IC* 595 🍷 ♦				*IC* 597 🍷 ♦
Firenze SMN .... d.	...	...	1613	1627r	1713	...	1813	1827r	1913	2013	2113	2138
Arezzo .... d.	...	...	1714	1706	1814	...	1914	1906	2014	2114	2214	2223
Castiglion Fiorentino .. d.	...	...	1727	|	1827	...	1927	|	2027	2127	2227	|
Terontola .... d.	...	...	1740	|	1840	1853	1940	1927	2040	2140	2240	2249
Passignano ▲ .... d.	...	...	1751	|	|	1907	1951	|	|	2151	|	|
Perugia .... a.	...	...	1819	|	|	1935	2019	|	|	2222	|	2316
Perugia 625 .... d.	1718	1804	1821	|	|	1941	2021	|	|	2227	|	2318
Ponte San Giovanni d.	1732	1814	1831	|	|	1952	2031	|	|	2236	|	2327
Assisi **625** .... d.	1745	1825	1843	|	|	...	2043	|	|	2247	|	2336
Spello .... d.	1754	|	1853	|	|	...	2053	|	|	2256	|	|
Foligno 625 .... a.	1759	1839	1900	|	|	...	2101	|	|	2302	|	2350
Castiglion del Lago .... d.	|	|	...	|	1848	...	...	|	2048	...	2248	...
Chiusi ▼ .... d.	|	|	...	1745	1915	...	...	1945	2115	...	2301	...
Orvieto .... d.	|	|	...	1809	1942	...	...	2009	2142	...	2327	...
Orte **625** .... d.	1917	1946	...	1838	2017	...	...	2038	2217	...	0002	...
Roma Tiburtina **625** ... a.	1952	2020s	...	|	2052	...	...	|	2252	...	0037	...
Roma Termini 625 .... a.	2003	2030	...	1916	2103	...	...	2116	2303	...	0048	...

	2 ⚒	*IC* 580 🍷 ♦	2 ⚒		*IC* 578 ✕	2 ⚒				*IC* 582 🍷 ♦		
Roma Termini 625 . d.	...	...	...	0557	0635	...	0657	...	0755	0841	0905	0905
Roma Tiburtina **625** . d.	...	...	...	0605	|	...	0705	...	0803	|	0913	0913
Orte **625** .... d.	...	...	...	0642	0713	...	0742	...	0840	0922	0950	0950
Orvieto .... d.	...	...	...	0716	0745	...	0816	...	|	0950	1024	1024
Chiusi ▼ .... d.	...	...	...	0750	0809	...	0855	...	|	1013	1055	1055
Castiglion del Lago . d.	...	...	...	0804	|	...	0912	...	|	|	1111	1111
Foligno 625 .... d.	0526	0600	0640	|	|	0736	|	0924	0956	|	|	|
Spello .... d.	0532	|	0645	|	|	0742	|	0930	1002	|	|	|
Assisi **625** .... d.	0541	0612	0653	|	|	0751	|	0939	1011	|	|	|
Ponte S. Giovanni . d.	0553	0629	0711	|	|	0804	|	0951	1035	|	|	|
Perugia 625 .... a.	0601	0638	0720	|	|	0812	|	0959	1045	|	|	|
Perugia .... d.	0603	0640	0722	|	|	0814	|	1001	...	|	|	|
Passignano ▲ .... d.	0639	|	0754	|	|	0854	|	1028	...	|	|	|
Terontola .... d.	0656	0710	0807	0814	0832	0909	0921	1040	...	|	1120	1120
Castiglion Fiorentino . d.	0709	|	...	0828	|	...	0942	|	...	|	1133	1133
Arezzo .... d.	0727	0735	...	0840	0857	...	0957	1101	...	1053	1145	1145
Firenze SMN .... a.	0837	0817	...	0947	0938	...	1047	1149	...	1133r	1247	1247

		IC 704 🍷 ♦	2		⚒	*IC* 586 🍷 ♦			*ES* 9328 🍷	*IC* 706 🍷 ♦		2 ⚒	*IC* 1554 🍷 ♦		*IC* 592 🍷 ♦	*IC* 1590 ♦		*IC* 594 Ⓑp	2 ⚒	*EN* 234 ♦		2 ⚒	2	*ES* 9336 🍷 Ⓑh	*AV* 9536 🍷 ♦	*ICN* 774 ♦
Roma Termini 625 .... d.	...	1044	1105	...	1157	1244	1257	...	1332	1444	1500	...	...	...	1644	...	1657	1755	...	1905	...	...	1857	2000	2015	...
Roma Tiburtina **625** ... d.	...	|	1113	...	1205	|	1305	...	1340u	|	1508	...	1532	...	|	1658	1705	|	...	|	...	...	1905	2008u	|	2236
Orte **625** .... d.	...	1122	1150	...	1242	1322	1342	...	1412	1522	1546	...	|	...	1722	|	1742	|	...	|	...	...	1942	2043	|	|
Orvieto .... d.	...	1150	1224	...	|	1350	1416	...	|	1550	1620	...	1657	...	1750	1801	1816	1848	...	1955	...	...	2016	|	2102	|
Chiusi ▼ .... d.	...	1213	1255	...	|	1413	1455	...	|	1613	1655	...	1720	...	1813	1827	1855	1912	...	2019	...	...	2055	|	2122	0007
Castiglion del Lago .... d.	...	|	1311	...	|	|	1511	...	|	|	1711	...	|	...	|	|	1911	|	...	|	...	...	2111	|	|	|
Foligno 625 .... d.	1103	|	|	1303	1351	|	|	1503	1515	|	|	1625	|	1703	|	|	|	|	1820	|	1903	1934	|	2154	|	|
Spello .... d.	1109	|	|	1309	1402	|	|	1509	|	|	|	1630	|	1709	|	|	|	|	1830	|	1909	1940	|	|	|	|
Assisi **625** .... d.	1118	|	|	1318	1412	|	|	1518	1531	|	|	1643	|	1718	|	|	|	|	1843	|	1918	1949	|	2206	|	|
Ponte San Giovanni d.	1130	|	|	1331	1431	|	|	1530	1550	|	|	1656	|	1731	|	|	|	|	1856	|	1931	2001	|	2217	|	|
Perugia 625 .... a.	1139	|	|	1339	1440	|	|	1538	1558	|	|	1705	|	1739	|	|	|	|	1905	|	1940	2011	|	2226	|	|
Perugia .... d.	1141	|	|	1341	...	|	|	1539	...	|	|	1707	|	1741	|	|	|	|	...	|	1942	2020	|	...	|	|
Passignano ▲ .... d.	1208	|	|	1409	...	|	|	1609	...	|	|	1752	|	1809	|	|	|	|	...	|	2009	2049	|	...	|	|
Terontola .... d.	1220	|	1320	1420	...	|	1520	1620	...	|	1720	1804	|	1820	|	1844	1920	1931	...	|	2020	2100	2120	...	|	0025
Castiglion Fiorentino .. d.	1233	|	1333	1433	...	|	1533	1633	...	|	1733	...	|	1833	|	|	1933	|	...	|	2033	...	2133	...	|	|
Arezzo .... d.	1245	1253	1345	1445	...	1453	1545	1645	...	1653	1745	...	1755	1845	1853	1912	1945	1957	...	|	2045	...	2145	...	2151	0047
Firenze SMN .... a.	1347	1333r	1447	1547	...	1533r	1647	1747	...	1733r	1847	...	1854r	1949	1933r	2015r	2047	2038	...	2124	2147	...	2247	...	2225	0145c

♦ – **NOTES** (LISTED BY TRAIN NUMBER)

234/5 – ALLEGRO TOSCA – 🛏 1,2 cl. (Excelsior), 🛏 1,2 cl., ▬ 2 cl. and [2] Roma - Wien and v.v.; 🛏 1,2 cl. (Excelsior), 🛏 1,2 cl., ▬ 2 cl. and [2] Roma - Bologna (**484/5**) - München and v.v. Supplement payable.

580/97 – TACITO – [12] and 🍷 Terni - Milano and v.v.

582/95 – VESUVIO – [12] and 🍷 Napoli - Milano and v.v.

585/92 – BRERA – [12] and 🍷 Milano - Napoli and v.v.

586/91 – PARTENOPE – [12] and 🍷 Napoli - Milano and v.v.

703 – MIRAMARE – [12] and 🍷 Trieste (**702**) - Venezia Mestre - Napoli.

704/5 – MATILDE SERAO – [12] and 🍷 Napoli - Venezia and v.v.

706 – MIRAMARE – [12] and 🍷 Roma (**707**) - Venezia Mestre - Trieste.

771/4 – MARCO POLO – 🛏 1,2 cl., ▬ 2 cl. (4 berth) and [2] Napoli - Udine and v.v.; 🛏 1,2 cl. (T2), 🛏 1,2 cl., ▬ 2 cl. (4 berth) and [2] Napoli - Venezia Mestre (**772/3**) - Trieste and v.v.

1554 – CARACCIOLO – ⑦ (also Dec. 8; not Dec. 6): [12] and 🍷 Salerno - Milano.

1590 – ASPROMONTE – ⑦ (also Dec. 8; not Dec. 6): [12] Reggio - Milano. Train number **1588** from Sept. 13.

9501/36 – [12] and 🍷 Bologna - Napoli and v.v.

c – Firenze **Campo di Marte**.
h – Not Dec. 25, 26, Apr. 4, May 1, Oct. 31, and days before holidays.
p – Not Aug. 15, and days before holidays.
r – Firenze **Rifredi**.
s – Stops to set down only.
u – Stops to pick up only.

▲ – Passignano sul Trasimeno.
▼ – Chiusi - Chianciano Terme.

Additional local services are available on ⚒ Firenze - Chiusi and v.v. serving Arezzo, Castiglion Fiorentino, Terontola-Cortona and Castiglion del Lago.

620 MILANO, TORINO and VENEZIA - BOLOGNA - FIRENZE - ROMA

km		IC 579	ICN 771	E 907		EN 235		EN 1239	EN 1237				AV 9551	ESc 9859			ESc 9801		IC 585	IC 713			ESc 9803	
		⚒	◆	◆		⊡ ◆		⊡ ◆	⊡ ◆				🍷	🍷 ◆			🍷 A	⚒	🍷	🍷 ◆	R		🍷 C	L
0	**Milano** Centrale d.	...	...	...	...	...	...	...	...	...	...	...	0545	0600	...	...	0635	...	0705	...	...	...	0735	0650
	Venezia Santa Lucia **600** d.	...	2330	...	...	...	...	...	...	...	...	...	|	|	0557	...	|	0657	|	0715	...	0720	|	|
	Venezia Mestre **600** d.	...	0021	...	...	0311	...	0357	0357	...	...	...	|	|	0609	...	|	0709	|	0728	...	0734	|	|
	Padova **600** d.	...	0045	...	...	|	...	|	|	...	0535	...	|	|	0633	...	|	0733	|	0750	...	0807	|	|
	Rovigo d.	...	0119	...	...	|	...	|	|	...	0607	...	|	|	0707	...	|	0810	|	0821	...	0843	|	|
	Ferrara **621** d.	...	0141	...	...	0419	...	|	|	...	0631	...	|	|	0731	...	|	0831	|	0842	...	0902	|	|
	Torino P N **610** d.	...	|	2250	...	|	...	|	|	...	|	...	|	|	|	...	|	|	|	|	...	|	|	|
	Asti **610** d.	...	|	2332	...	|	...	|	|	...	|	...	|	|	|	...	|	|	|	|	...	|	|	|
	Alessandria **610** d.	...	|	2356	...	|	...	|	|	...	|	...	|	|	|	...	|	|	|	|	...	|	|	|
	Tortona **610** d.	...	|	0014	...	|	...	|	|	...	|	...	|	|	|	...	|	|	|	|	0649	|	|	|
	Voghera **610** d.	...	|	0027	...	|	...	|	|	...	|	...	|	|	|	...	|	|	|	|	0703	|	|	|
72	Piacenza d.	...	|	0105	...	|	...	|	|	...	|	...	0627	0648	|	...	0722	|	0750	|	0754	|	0822	0810
107	Fidenza d.	...	|	|	...	|	...	|	|	...	|	...	|	|	|	...	|	|	|	|	0816	|	|	0832
129	Parma d.	...	|	|	...	|	...	|	|	...	|	...	0656	0716	|	...	0750	|	0814	|	0830	|	0850	...
157	Reggio Emilia d.	...	|	|	...	|	...	|	|	...	|	...	0712	0733	|	...	0805	|	0829	|	0847	|	0905	...
182	Modena d.	...	|	|	...	|	...	|	|	...	|	...	0726	0747	|	...	0819	|	0842	|	0901	|	0919	...
219	**Bologna** Centrale **630** a.	...	0217	0234	...	0448	...	|	|	...	0704	...	0750	...	0804	...	0842	0904	0904	0912	0928	0938	0942	...
219	**Bologna** Centrale d.	...	0222	...	...	0515	...	|	|	...	...	...	0753	...	...	...	...	...	0908	...	...	...	...	...
300	Prato d.	...	|	...	...	|	...	|	|	...	...	...	|	...	...	...	...	...	1016	...	...	...	...	...
314	Firenze Campo di Marte d.	...	|	...	...	|	...	|	|	...	...	...	|	...	...	...	...	...	1027r	...	...	...	...	...
316	**Firenze** SMN a.	...	|	...	...	0618	...	0705	0705	...	...	...	0830	...	...	...	...	...	|	...	...	...	...	...
316	**Firenze** SMN d.	0550	|	...	...	0630	...	...	...	...	...	...	0840	...	...	...	...	...	|	...	...	...	...	...
404	Arezzo d.	0630	0458	...	...	|	...	...	...	...	...	...	|	...	...	...	...	...	1106	...	...	...	...	...
467	Chiusi-Chianciano Terme d.	0710	0541	...	...	0732	...	...	...	...	...	...	|	...	...	...	...	...	1145	...	...	...	...	...
627	Roma Tiburtina a.	|	0656	...	...	|	...	...	...	...	...	...	|	...	...	...	...	...	|	...	...	...	...	...
632	**Roma** Termini **640** a.	0824	|	...	...	0905	...	...	...	...	...	...	1015	...	...	...	...	...	1316	...	...	...	...	...
	Napoli C **640** a.	...	1000	...	...	...	...	...	...	...	...	...	...	...	...	...	...	...	1550	...	...	...	...	...

km				IC 1591			IC 703	IC 553	ESc 9807		IC 1545			IC 591		ESc 9811		E 823			ESc 9813	IC 705		IC 593
			P	◆			◆	🍷 ◆	🍷 C		🍷 ◆	A		🍷	†	🍷 C		◆		A	🍷 A	🍷		✗
	Milano Centrale d.	...	0730	0735	...	...	...	0915	0935	...	0950	...	...	1100	...	1135	...	1145	...	...	1235	...	...	...
0	**Venezia** Santa Lucia **600** d.	0757	|	|	...	...	...	|	|	...	|	...	1057	|	...	|	...	|	1157	...	|	1309	1257	...
9	**Venezia** Mestre **600** d.	0809	|	|	...	...	0920	|	|	...	|	...	1109	|	...	|	...	|	1209	...	|	1322	1309	...
37	Padova **600** d.	0833	|	|	...	...	0941	|	|	...	|	...	1133	|	...	|	...	|	1233	...	|	1341	1333	...
81	Rovigo d.	0907	|	|	...	...	1008	|	|	...	|	...	1207	|	...	|	...	|	1307	...	|	1410	1405	...
113	Ferrara **621** d.	0931	|	|	...	...	1028	|	|	...	|	...	1231	|	...	|	...	|	1331	...	|	1428	1433	...
	Torino P N **610** d.	|	|	|	...	0605	|	|	|	...	|	...	|	|	...	|	...	|	|	...	|	|	|	...
	Asti **610** d.	|	|	|	...	0651	|	|	|	...	|	...	|	|	...	|	...	|	|	...	|	|	|	...
	Alessandria **610** d.	|	|	|	...	0716	|	|	|	...	|	...	|	|	...	|	...	|	|	...	|	|	|	...
	Tortona **610** d.	|	|	|	...	0750	|	|	|	...	|	...	|	|	...	|	...	|	|	...	|	|	|	...
	Voghera **610** d.	|	|	|	...	0803	|	|	|	...	|	...	|	|	...	|	...	|	|	...	|	|	|	...
	Piacenza d.	|	0835	0842	...	0843	|	0956	1022	...	|	1052	|	1151	1208	1222	...	1231	|	1252	1322	|	|	...
	Fidenza d.	|	0858	0907	...	...	|	|	|	...	|	1115	|	|	1232	|	...	|	|	1315	|	|	|	...
	Parma d.	|	0911	0921	...	...	|	1023	1050	...	1100	1130	|	1217	1245	1250	...	|	|	1330	1350	|	|	...
	Reggio Emilia d.	|	0927	0938	...	...	|	1038	1105	...	|	1146	|	1235	1303	1305	...	|	|	1347	1405	|	|	...
	Modena d.	|	0941	0953	...	...	|	1053	1119	...	1130	1200	|	1248	1319	1319	...	|	|	1401	1419	|	|	...
160	**Bologna** Centrale **630** a.	1004	1012	1022	...	...	1054	1114	1142	...	1150	1228	1304	1309	1346	1342	...	1354	1404	1428	1442	1454	1504	...
	Bologna Centrale d.	...	...	1032	...	...	1102	...	...	...	...	...	...	1313	...	...	...	1359	...	...	...	1508	...	...
	Prato d.	...	...	1131	...	...	1216	...	...	...	...	...	...	1416	...	...	...	1504	...	...	...	1616	...	...
	Firenze Campo di Marte d.	...	...	1203	...	...	1227r	...	...	...	...	...	...	1427r	...	...	...	1525	...	...	...	1627r	...	...
	Firenze SMN a.	...	...	|	...	...	|	...	...	...	...	...	...	|	...	...	...	|	...	...	...	|	...	...
	Firenze SMN d.	...	...	|	...	...	|	...	...	...	...	...	...	|	...	...	...	|	...	...	...	|	...	1755
	Arezzo d.	...	...	|	...	...	1306	...	...	...	...	...	...	1506	...	...	...	|	...	...	...	1706	...	1835
	Chiusi-Chianciano Terme d.	...	...	1306	...	...	1345	...	...	...	...	...	...	1545	...	...	...	|	...	...	...	1745	...	1912
	Roma Tiburtina a.	...	...	1441	...	...	|	...	...	...	...	...	...	|	...	...	...	1837	...	...	...	|	...	|
	Roma Termini **640** a.	...	...	|	...	...	1516	...	...	...	...	...	...	1716	...	...	...	...	...	...	...	1916	...	2040
	Napoli C **640** a.	...	...	1722	...	...	1750	...	...	...	...	...	...	1938	...	...	...	...	...	...	...	2138	...	...

km		ESc 9815	IC 1557		ESc 9817			IC 595		ESc 9819		IC 715		ESc 9821				E 1921	ESc 9823		IC 597	ESc 9829		
		🍷 T	🍷 ◆		🍷 B	A		🍷		🍷 B		◆		🍷 E	A			◆	🍷 E	L	🍷 ◆	🍷 p		
	Milano Centrale d.	1335	1350	...	1435	...	...	1500	...	1535	...	...	...	1635	...	...	...	1620	1735	1705	1745	2035	...	...
	Venezia Santa Lucia **600** d.	|	|	1357	|	...	1457	|	...	|	...	1527	1557	|	...	1657	...	|	|	|	|	|	...	1757
	Venezia Mestre **600** d.	|	|	1409	|	...	1509	|	...	|	...	1541	1609	|	...	1709	...	|	|	|	|	|	...	1809
	Padova **600** d.	|	|	1433	|	...	1533	|	...	|	...	1602	1633	|	...	1733	...	|	|	|	|	|	...	1833
	Rovigo d.	|	|	1507	|	...	1607	|	...	|	...	1625	1707	|	...	1807	...	|	|	|	|	|	...	1907
	Ferrara **621** d.	|	|	1531	|	...	1631	|	...	|	...	1643	1731	|	...	1831	...	|	|	|	|	|	...	1931
0	**Torino** P N **610** d.	|	|	|	|	...	|	|	1420	|	...	|	|	|	...	|	...	|	|	|	|	|	1620	|
56	Asti **610** d.	|	|	|	|	...	|	|	1506	|	...	|	|	|	...	|	...	|	|	|	|	|	1706	|
91	Alessandria **610** d.	|	|	|	|	...	|	|	1533	|	...	|	|	|	...	|	...	|	|	|	|	|	1733	|
113	Tortona **610** d.	|	|	|	|	...	|	|	1550	|	...	|	|	|	...	|	...	|	|	|	|	|	1750	|
130	Voghera **610** d.	|	|	|	|	...	|	|	1603	|	...	|	|	|	...	|	...	|	|	|	|	|	1803	|
188	Piacenza d.	1422	1442	|	1522	1452	|	1548	1643	1622	...	|	|	1722	1652	|	...	1705	1822	1812	1843	2122	1843	|
	Fidenza d.	|	1459	|	|	1515	|	1605	...	|	...	|	|	|	1715	|	...	|	|	1835	|	|	...	|
	Parma d.	1450	1511	|	1550	1529	|	1617	...	1650	...	|	|	1750	1729	|	...	1736	1850	...	1915	2150	...	|
	Reggio Emilia d.	1505	1526	|	1605	1545	|	1631	...	1705	...	|	|	1805	1745	|	...	1753	1905	...	1926	2205	...	|
	Modena d.	1519	1540	|	1619	1600	|	1644	...	1719	...	|	|	1819	1759	|	...	1808	1919	...	1941	2219	...	|
	Bologna Centrale **630** a.	1542	1600	1604	1642	1628	1704	1704	...	1742	...	1712	1804	1842	1828	1904	...	|	1942	...	2004	2242	...	2004
	Bologna Centrale d.	...	1604	...	...	...	...	1708	...	...	...	...	...	...	...	...	...	|	...	...	2008	...	...	...
	Prato d.	...	1704	...	...	...	...	1816	...	...	...	...	...	...	...	...	...	|	...	...	2059	...	...	...
	Firenze Campo di Marte d.	...	1730	...	...	...	...	1827r	...	...	...	...	...	...	...	...	...	2035	...	...	|	...	...	...
	Firenze SMN a.	...	|	...	...	...	...	|	...	...	...	...	...	...	...	...	...	|	...	...	2116	...	...	...
	Firenze SMN d.	...	|	...	...	...	...	|	...	...	...	...	...	...	...	...	...	|	...	...	2138	...	...	...
	Arezzo d.	...	|	...	...	...	...	1906	...	...	...	...	...	...	...	...	...	|	...	...	2221	...	...	...
	Chiusi-Chianciano Terme d.	...	|	...	...	...	...	1945	...	...	...	...	...	...	...	...	...	|	...	...	...	...	...	...
	Roma Tiburtina a.	...	1958	...	...	...	...	|	...	...	...	...	...	...	...	...	...	2315	...	...	...	...	...	...
	Roma Termini **640** a.	...	|	...	...	...	...	2116	...	...	...	...	...	...	...	...	...	...	...	...	...	...	...	...
	Napoli C **640** a.	...	2223	...	...	...	...	2342	...	...	...	...	...	...	...	...	...	...	...	...	...	...	...	...

◆ – **NOTES** (LISTED BY TRAIN NUMBER)

234 – ALLEGRO TOSCA – 🛏 1,2 cl. (Excelsior), 🛏 1,2 cl., ▬ 2 cl. and [2] Roma - Venezia Mestre - Villach - Wien; 🛏 1,2 cl. (Excelsior), 🛏 1,2 cl., ▬ 2 cl. and [2] Roma - Bologna (**484**) - München.

235 – ALLEGRO TOSCA – 🛏 1,2 cl. (Excelsior), 🛏 1,2 cl., ▬ 2 cl. and [2] Wien - Villach - Venezia Mestre - Roma; 🛏 1,2 cl. (Excelsior), 🛏 1,2 cl., ▬ 2 cl. and [2] München (**485**) - Bologna - Roma.

553 – MURGE – [12] and 🍷 Milano - Taranto (**554**) - Metaponto (**555**) - Crotone.

568 – MURGE – [12] and 🍷 Crotone (**566**) - Metaponto (**567**) - Taranto - Milano.

580 – TACITO – [12] and 🍷 Terni - Milano.

597 – TACITO – [12] Milano - Terni.

703 – MIRAMARE – [12] Trieste (**702**) - Venezia Mestre - Napoli.

706 – MIRAMARE – [12] and 🍷 Roma - Venezia Mestre (**707**) - Trieste.

713 – ADRIATICO – [12] and 🍷 Venezia - Bari.

714 – ADRIATICO – [12] and 🍷 Bari - Venezia.

715 – MANIN – [12] Venezia - Pescara.

716 – MANIN – [12] Pescara - Venezia.

751 – TOMMASO CAMPANELLA – 🛏 1,2 cl., ▬ 2 cl. and [12] Milano - Reggio; ▬ 2 cl. (4 berth) and [2] Milano - Lamezia (**753**) - Reggio.

752 – TOMMASO CAMPANELLA – 🛏 1,2 cl., ▬ 2 cl. and [12] Reggio - Milano; ▬ 2 cl. (4 berth) and [2] Reggio (**750**) - Lamezia - Milano.

771 – MARCO POLO – 🛏 1,2 cl., ▬ 2 cl. (4 berth) and [2] Udine - Napoli; 🛏 1,2 cl. (T2), 🛏 1,2 cl., ▬ 2 cl. (4 berth) and [2] Trieste (**772**) - Venezia - Napoli.

774 – MARCO POLO – 🛏 1,2 cl., ▬ 2 cl. (4 berth) and [2] Napoli - Udine; 🛏 1,2 cl. (T2), 🛏 1,2 cl., ▬ 2 cl. (4 berth) and [2] Napoli - Venezia Mestre (**773**) - Trieste.

CONTINUED ON NEXT PAGE →

MILANO, TORINO and VENEZIA - BOLOGNA - FIRENZE - ROMA 620

			ESc	E				E	E		ICN	IC		E		ICN	E	E	E	ICN	ICN	ICN	ICN	
			9825	1931				1595	1991		751	549		923		781	833	901	837	785	1911	779	35479	
			🍸 A	♦	R		2 ⑤x	♦	♦		♦	R		♦		♦	♦	♦	♦	♦	♦	♦	♦	
Milano Centrale d.	1820	...	1835	...	...	...	1853g	...	1943g	...	2000	2005	...	2040	...	2100	2200	...	...	2300	2320	...	...	...
Venezia Santa Lucia **600** d.	|	1857	|	1909	...	1957	|	...	|	...	|	|	...	|	...	|	|	...	...	|	|	...	...	...
Venezia Mestre **600** d.	|	1909	|	1925	...	2009	|	...	|	...	|	|	...	|	...	|	|	...	...	|	|	2211	2211	...
Padova **600** d.	|	1933	|	1949	...	2033	|	...	|	...	|	|	...	|	...	|	|	...	...	|	|	2236	2236	...
Rovigo d.	|	2007	|	2022	...	2107	|	...	|	...	|	|	...	|	...	|	|	...	...	|	|	2316	2316	...
Ferrara **621** d.	|	2031	|	2047	...	2131	|	...	|	...	|	|	...	|	...	|	|	...	...	|	|	2336	2336	...
Torino P N **610** d.	|	|	|	|	...	|	|	...	|	...	|	|	1820	|	...	|	|	2105	...	|	|	...	...	...
Asti **610** d.	|	|	|	|	...	|	|	...	|	...	|	|	1906	|	...	|	|	2139	...	|	|	...	...	...
Alessandria **610** d.	|	|	|	|	...	|	|	...	|	...	|	|	1933	|	...	|	|	2206	...	|	|	...	...	...
Tortona **610** d.	|	|	|	|	1850	|	|	...	|	...	|	|	1950	|	...	|	|	2222	...	|	|	...	...	...
Voghera **610** d.	|	|	|	|	1903	|	|	...	|	...	|	|	2003	|	...	|	|	2235	...	|	|	...	...	...
Piacenza d.	1912	|	1922	|	1952	|	2004	...	|	...	2044	2051	2043	2139	2152	2204	2254	2314	...	2346	0011	...	...	...
Fidenza d.	1937	|	|	|	2015	|	2028	...	|	...	|	2112	...	2158	2215	|	2319	|	...	|	|	...	...	...
Parma d.	1951	|	1950	|	2030	|	...	...	|	...	|	2124	...	2217	2230	2243	2333	2351	...	0018	0101	...	...	...
Reggio Emilia d.	2008	|	2005	|	2046	|	...	...	|	...	|	2139	...	2234	2247	2303	2351	0010	...	0038	|	...	...	...
Modena d.	2022	|	2019	|	2100	|	...	...	2207	...	|	2152	...	2250	2304	2318	0008	0027	...	0055	|	...	...	...
Bologna Centrale **630** a.	2052	2104	2042	2120	2128	2204	...	...	2228	...	2200	2218	...	2314	2337	2352	0039	0054	...	0124	|	...	...	...
Bologna Centrale d.	...	...	...	2148	...	...	...	2233	2233	...	2208	...	...	...	...	...	0044	...	0115	...	|	...	...	...
Prato d.	...	...	...	|	...	...	...	|	|	...	|	...	...	...	...	...	|	...	|	...	|	...	...	...
Firenze Campo di Marte d.	...	...	...	2247	...	...	...	2344	2355	...	2325	...	...	...	...	...	|	...	|	...	|	...	...	...
Firenze SMN a.	...	...	...	...	...	...	...	...	...	...	...	...	...	...	...	...	|	...	|	...	|	...	...	...
Firenze SMN d.	...	...	...	...	...	...	...	...	...	...	...	...	...	...	...	...	|	...	|	...	|	...	...	...
Arezzo d.	...	...	...	...	...	...	...	...	...	...	...	...	...	...	...	...	|	...	|	...	|	...	...	...
Chiusi-Chianciano Terme d.	...	...	...	...	...	...	...	...	...	...	...	...	...	...	...	...	|	...	|	...	|	...	...	...
Roma Tiburtina a.	...	...	...	...	...	...	...	...	...	...	...	...	...	...	...	...	0452	...	0609	...	0730	...	...	...
Roma Termini **640** a.	...	...	...	...	...	...	...	...	...	...	...	...	...	...	...	...	|	...	|	...	|	...	...	...
Napoli C **640** a.	...	...	...	...	...	...	...	...	...	...	...	...	...	...	...	...	0734	...	0926	...	1012	...	...	...

	E	ICN	E	ICN	ICN	ICN	ICN		E	E		ICN	E		E		E	ESc	IC		ICN			E
	824	774	900	776	35476	780	1910		1992	1594		784	830		906		926	9802	550		752			1920
	♦	♦	♦	♦	♦	♦	♦		♦	♦		♦	♦	⚒	♦		♦	k	R	L	♦		A	♦
Napoli C **640** d.	1845	1957	...	...	...	...	2030	...	...	2259	...	...	2150	...	...	...	...	...	...	...	...	...	...	...
Roma Termini **640** d.	|	|	...	...	...	...	2306	...	...	|	...	...	|	...	...	...	...	...	...	...	...	...	...	...
Roma Tiburtina d.	2205	2236	...	...	...	...	|	...	...	|	...	...	0047u	...	...	...	...	...	...	...	0428	...	...	...
Chiusi-Chianciano Terme d.	2350	0007	...	...	...	...	|	...	...	|	...	...	|	...	...	...	...	...	...	...	|	...	...	...
Arezzo d.	0032	0047	...	...	...	...	|	...	...	|	...	...	|	...	...	...	...	...	...	...	|	...	...	...
Firenze SMN a.	|	|	...	...	...	...	|	...	...	|	...	...	|	...	...	...	...	...	...	...	|	...	...	...
Firenze SMN d.	|	|	...	...	...	...	|	...	...	|	...	...	|	...	...	...	...	...	...	...	|	...	...	...
Firenze Campo di Marte d.	|	0148	...	...	...	...	|	...	0416	|	...	...	|	...	...	...	...	...	...	...	0638	...	...	0653
Prato d.	|	|	...	...	...	...	|	...	|	|	...	...	|	...	...	...	...	...	...	...	|	...	...	|
Bologna Centrale **630** a.	0300	0313	...	...	...	...	|	...	0518	0528	...	...	0552	...	...	...	...	...	...	...	0752	...	...	|
Bologna Centrale d.	...	0318	0325	...	...	0412	|	0452	0523	...	0530	0548	0557	0602	0618	0627	0702	0722	0741	...	0756	0756	0830	|
Modena d.	...	|	|	...	...	0435	|	0521	|	...	0556	0612	0623	|	0639	0653	0730	0741	0801	...	|	|	0856	0842
Reggio Emilia d.	...	|	|	...	...	0453	|	0536	|	...	0611	0629	0641	|	0654	0708	0747	0755	0816	...	|	|	0910	0857
Parma d.	...	|	|	...	...	0512	0521	0553	|	...	0628	0648	0702	|	0713	0724	|	0810	0833	...	|	|	0929	0914
Fidenza d.	...	|	|	...	...	|	|	0607	|	...	0642	|	|	|	|	0739	|	|	0845	0907	|	|	0945	|
Piacenza d.	...	|	0446	...	...	0554	0602	0638	|	...	0708	0730	0814	|	0752	0817	0832	0841	0908	0932	0919	|	1006	1020
Voghera **610** d.	...	|	0524	...	...	|	|	0721	|	...	|	|	|	|	0833	0859	|	|	|	|	|	|	...	|
Tortona **610** d.	...	|	0537	...	...	|	|	0736	|	...	|	|	|	|	0847	0912	|	|	|	|	|	|	...	|
Alessandria **610** d.	...	|	0554	...	...	|	|	0800	|	...	|	|	|	|	0905	...	|	|	|	|	|	|	...	|
Asti **610** d.	...	|	0625	...	...	|	|	0822	|	...	|	|	|	|	0927	...	|	|	|	|	|	|	...	|
Torino P N **610** a.	...	|	0705	...	...	|	|	0910	|	...	|	|	|	|	1010	...	|	|	|	|	|	|	...	|
Ferrara **621** d.	...	0349	...	0516	0516	|	|	...	|	...	|	|	|	0637	...	...	|	|	|	|	|	0830	...	|
Rovigo d.	...	0411	...	0538	0538	|	|	...	|	...	|	|	|	0659	...	...	|	|	|	|	|	0854	...	|
Padova **600** d.	...	0450	...	0621	0621	|	|	...	|	...	|	|	|	0738	...	...	|	|	|	|	|	0929	...	|
Venezia Mestre **600** a.	...	0508	...	0643	0643	|	|	...	|	...	|	|	|	0801	...	...	|	|	|	|	|	0951	...	|
Venezia Santa Lucia **600** a.	...	0526	...	...	...	|	|	...	|	...	|	|	|	0813	...	...	|	|	|	|	|	1003	...	|
Milano Centrale a.	...	...	...	...	...	0705	0725	...	0925g	...	0800	0820	0920	...	...	...	0920	0930	1000	1025	1005	...	...	1130

	ESc			E		IC	IC				ESc	E				IC	IC		ESc					
	9806			1930		580	578				9810	834				582	714		9814					
	🍸 A			♦	A	🍸 ♦	✕				🍸 E	♦	A			🍸	🍸 ♦		🍸 T	A			A	
Napoli C **640** d.	...	...	...	...	...	...	...	...	...	...	...	...	...	...	...	0614	...	...	...	...	...	...	...	...
Roma Termini **640** d.	...	...	...	...	...	...	0635	...	...	...	...	...	...	...	...	0841	...	...	...	...	...	...	...	...
Roma Tiburtina d.	...	...	...	...	...	...	|	...	...	...	...	0613	...	...	...	|	...	...	...	...	...	...	...	...
Chiusi-Chianciano Terme d.	...	...	...	...	...	...	0809	...	...	...	...	|	...	...	...	1013	...	...	...	...	...	...	...	...
Arezzo d.	...	...	...	...	...	0735	0857	...	...	...	...	|	...	...	...	1053	...	...	...	...	...	...	...	...
Firenze SMN a.	...	...	...	...	...	0817	0938	...	...	...	...	|	...	...	...	|	...	...	...	...	...	...	...	...
Firenze SMN d.	...	...	...	...	...	0829	...	...	...	...	...	|	...	...	...	|	...	...	...	...	...	...	...	...
Firenze Campo di Marte d.	...	...	...	0723	...	|	...	...	...	...	...	0918	...	...	...	1136r	...	...	...	...	...	...	...	...
Prato d.	...	...	...	|	...	0844	...	...	...	...	...	0942	...	...	...	1145	...	...	...	...	...	...	...	...
Bologna Centrale **630** a.	...	...	...	0928	...	0952	...	...	...	...	...	1100	...	...	...	1243	...	...	...	...	...	...	...	...
Bologna Centrale d.	0918	0900	...	|	0930	0956	...	...	...	1000	1118	1108	1130	...	1156	1247	1256	...	1318	1330	...	1356	1430	...
Modena d.	0940	|	...	|	0956	1015	...	...	...	|	1140	|	1156	...	|	1308	|	...	1340	1356	...	|	1456	...
Reggio Emilia d.	0954	|	...	|	1010	1029	...	...	...	|	1154	|	1210	...	|	1322	|	...	1354	1410	...	|	1510	...
Parma d.	1009	|	...	|	1027	1044	...	...	...	|	1209	|	1227	...	|	1337	|	...	1409	1427	...	|	1527	...
Fidenza d.	|	|	...	|	1040	|	...	...	...	|	|	|	1240	...	|	1355	|	...	|	1440	...	|	1540	...
Piacenza d.	1041	|	...	|	1110	1117	...	...	1117	|	1241	1228	1306	...	|	1418	|	...	1441	1506	...	|	1606	...
Voghera **610** d.	|	|	...	|	...	|	...	...	1159	|	|	|	...	...	|	|	|	...	|	...	...	|	...	...
Tortona **610** d.	|	|	...	|	...	|	...	...	1212	|	|	|	...	...	|	|	|	...	|	...	...	|	...	...
Alessandria **610** d.	|	|	...	|	...	|	...	...	1229	|	|	|	...	...	|	|	|	...	|	...	...	|	...	...
Asti **610** d.	|	|	...	|	...	|	...	...	1251	|	|	|	...	...	|	|	|	...	|	...	...	|	...	...
Torino P N **610** a.	|	|	...	|	...	|	...	...	1340	|	|	|	...	...	|	|	|	...	|	...	...	|	...	...
Ferrara **621** d.	|	0930	...	1021	...	|	...	...	...	1031	|	|	...	...	1230	|	1323	...	|	...	...	1430	...	...
Rovigo d.	|	0954	...	1044	...	|	...	...	...	1054	|	|	...	...	1254	|	1341	...	|	...	...	1454	...	...
Padova **600** d.	|	1029	...	1120	...	|	...	...	...	1129	|	|	...	...	1329	|	1410	...	|	...	...	1529	...	...
Venezia Mestre **600** a.	|	1051	...	1137	...	|	...	...	...	1151	|	|	...	...	1351	|	1436	...	|	...	...	1551	...	...
Venezia Santa Lucia **600** a.	|	1103	...	1150	...	|	...	...	...	1203	|	|	...	...	1403	|	1449	...	|	...	...	1603	...	...
Milano Centrale a.	1125	...	...	...	...	1200	...	...	...	...	1325	1320	...	...	...	1500	...	...	1530	...	...	...	...	...

♦ – **NOTES** (CONTINUED FROM PREVIOUS PAGE)

776 – TERGESTE – Not Aug. 31 - Sept. 19 (from Lecce): ▬ 2 cl. (4 berth) and [12] Lecce - Venezia Mestre (**777**) - Trieste; 🛏 1,2 cl. (Excelsior), 🛏 1,2 cl. (T2), 🛏 1,2 cl. and [12] Lecce - Venezia Mestre (**1598**) - Venezia Santa Lucia.

779 – TERGESTE – Not Aug. 31 - Sept. 19: ▬ 2 cl. (4 berth) and [12] Trieste (**778**) - Venezia Mestre - Lecce; 🛏 1,2 cl. (Excelsior), 🛏 1,2 cl. (T2), 🛏 1,2 cl. and [12] Venezia Santa Lucia (**1599**) - Mestre - Lecce.

780 – FRECCIA SALENTINA – 🛏 1,2 cl. (Excelsior), 🛏 1,2 cl. (T2), 🛏 1,2 cl., ▬ 2 cl. (4 berth) and [12] Lecce - Milano.

781 – FRECCIA SALENTINA – 🛏 1,2 cl. (Excelsior), 🛏 1,2 cl. (T2), 🛏 1,2 cl., ▬ 2 cl. (4 berth) and [12] Milano - Lecce.

784 – FRECCIA DEL LEVANTE – ▬ 2 cl. and [12] Crotone - Metaponto (**783**) - Taranto (**784**) - Milano; 🛏 1,2 cl. (Excelsior), 🛏 1,2 cl. (T2), 🛏 1,2 cl., ▬ 2 cl. and [12] Taranto - Milano.

785 – FRECCIA DEL LEVANTE – ▬ 2 cl. and [12] Milano - Taranto (**786**) - Metaponto (**787**) - Crotone; 🛏 1,2 cl. (Excelsior), 🛏 1,2 cl. (T2), 🛏 1,2 cl., ▬ 2 cl. and [12] Milano - Taranto.

823 – FRECCIA DEL SUD – ①③⑤⑦: [2] Milano - Catania - Agrigento; [2] Milano - Catania (**827**) - Siracusa.

824 – ①③④⑤⑥⑦ (also Dec. 8; not Dec. 9): 🛏 1,2 cl. (Excelsior), 🛏 1,2 cl., ▬ 2 cl. (4 berth) and [2] Napoli - Bologna (**924**) - Bolzano.

830 – ②④⑦: ▬ 2 cl. and [2] Salerno - Milano.

833 – ①③⑤: ▬ 2 cl. and [2] Milano - Salerno.

834 – FRECCIA DEL SUD – ②④⑥⑦ (from Agrigento and Siracusa): [2] Agrigento - Catania - Milano; [2] Siracusa (**836**) - Catania - Milano.

CONTINUED ON NEXT PAGE →

620 ROMA - FIRENZE - BOLOGNA - VENEZIA, TORINO and MILANO

		ESc 9816 🍷 C	IC 704 🍷	A	ESc 9818 🍷 A				IC 1550 ♦	ESc 9820 🍷 A		IC 586 🍷	ESc 9822 🍷 B		A			ESc 9824 🍷 E	R	IC 706 🍷 ♦		IC 568 🍷 ♦	ESc 9826 🍷 C	A
Napoli C **640**	d.	...	0824	...	...	...	...	...	...	...	...	1024	...	...	...	...	...	...	...	...	...	...	...	...
Roma Termini **640**	d.	...	1044	...	...	...	...	...	...	...	...	1244	...	...	...	...	...	...	...	1444	...	...	...	...
Roma Tiburtina	d.	...	|	...	...	...	...	...	...	...	...	|	...	...	...	...	...	...	...	|	...	...	...	...
Chiusi-Chianciano Terme	d.	...	1213	...	...	...	...	...	...	...	...	1413	...	...	...	...	...	...	...	1613	...	...	...	...
Arezzo	d.	...	1253	...	...	...	...	...	...	...	...	1453	...	...	...	...	...	...	...	1653	...	...	...	...
Firenze SMN	a.	...	|	...	...	...	...	...	...	...	...	|	...	...	...	...	...	...	...	|	...	...	...	...
Firenze SMN	d.	...	|	...	...	...	...	...	...	...	...	|	...	...	...	...	...	...	...	|	...	...	...	...
Firenze Campo di Marte	d.	...	1336r	...	...	...	...	...	...	...	...	1536r	...	...	...	...	...	...	...	1736r	...	...	...	...
Prato	d.	...	1345	...	...	...	...	...	...	...	...	1545	...	...	...	...	...	...	...	|	...	...	...	...
Bologna Centrale **630**	a.	...	1453	...	...	...	...	...	...	...	...	1659	...	...	...	...	...	...	...	1828	...	...	...	...
Bologna Centrale	d.	1418	1504	1530	1518	...	1556	...	1606	1618	1656	1703	1722	...	1730	1756	...	1818	1830	1832	1856	1856	1918	1930
Modena	d.	1440	|	1556	1540	...	|	...	1628	1640	|	1725	1741	...	1756	|	...	1840	1856	|	|	1915	1940	1956
Reggio Emilia	d.	1454	|	1610	1554	...	|	...	1643	1654	|	1745	1754	...	1810	|	...	1854	1910	|	|	1929	1954	2010
Parma	d.	1509	|	1627	1609	...	|	...	1659	1709	|	1800	1809	...	1827	|	...	1909	1927	|	|	1945	2009	2027
Fidenza	d.	|	|	1640	|	...	|	...	|	|	|	|	|	...	1840	|	...	|	1940	|	|	|	|	2040
Piacenza	d.	1541	|	1706	1641	...	|	1717	1727	1741	|	1823	1841	...	1910	|	1917	1941	2027t	|	|	2020	2041	2106
Voghera **610**	d.	|	|	...	|	...	|	1759	|	|	|	|	|	...	...	|	1957	|	2108	|	|	|	|	...
Tortona **610**	d.	|	|	...	|	...	|	1812	|	|	|	|	|	...	...	|	2009	|	2120	|	|	|	|	...
Alessandria **610**	d.	|	|	...	|	...	|	1829	|	|	|	|	|	...	...	|	2029	|	...	|	|	|	|	...
Asti **610**	d.	|	|	...	|	...	|	1851	|	|	|	|	|	...	...	|	2049	|	...	|	|	|	|	...
Torino P N **610**	a.	|	|	...	|	...	|	1940	|	|	|	|	|	...	...	|	2140	|	...	|	|	|	|	...
Ferrara **621**	d.	|	1533	...	|	...	1630	...	|	|	1730	|	|	...	...	1830	...	|	...	1914	1930	|	|	...
Rovigo	d.	|	1551	...	|	...	1654	...	|	|	1754	|	|	...	...	1854	...	|	...	1935	1954	|	|	...
Padova **600**	d.	|	1619	...	|	...	1729	...	|	|	1829	|	|	...	...	1929	...	|	...	2016	2029	|	|	...
Venezia Mestre **600**	a.	|	1637	...	|	...	1751	...	|	|	1851	|	|	...	...	1951	...	|	...	2045	2051	|	|	...
Venezia Santa Lucia **600**	a.	|	1649	...	|	...	1803	...	|	|	1903	|	|	...	...	2003	...	|	...	...	2103	|	|	...
Milano Centrale	a.	1625	...	...	1730	...	...	...	1815	1825	...	1905	1925	...	...	...	...	2030	...	...	...	2105	2125	...

		2 L⑦j		P	ESc 9828 🍷 B	IC 1546 ♦	IC 1554 🍷 ♦		A	IC 592 🍷	IC 716 ♦	L	ESc 9830 🍷 C		ESc 9858 🍷 ♦	IC 1590 ♦		EN 1236 ⊡ ♦	EN 1238 ⊡ ♦	IC 594 Ⓑq		EN 234 ⊡ ♦	AV 9558 🍷	
Napoli C **640**	d.	...	...	...	...	...	1307	...	...	1424	...	...	...	...	...	1442	...	...	...	...	...	...	...	...
Roma Termini **640**	d.	...	...	...	...	...	|	...	...	1644	...	...	...	...	...	|	...	...	...	1755	...	1905	1930	...
Roma Tiburtina	d.	...	...	...	...	...	1532	...	...	|	...	...	...	...	...	1658	...	...	...	|	...	|	|	...
Chiusi-Chianciano Terme	d.	...	...	...	...	...	1720	...	...	1813	...	...	...	...	...	1827	...	...	...	1912	...	2019	|	...
Arezzo	d.	...	...	...	...	...	1755	...	...	1853	...	...	...	...	...	1912	...	...	...	1957	...	|	|	...
Firenze SMN	a.	...	...	...	...	...	|	...	...	|	...	...	...	...	...	|	...	...	...	2038	...	2124	2104	...
Firenze SMN	d.	...	...	...	...	...	|	...	...	|	...	...	...	...	...	|	...	2055	2055	...	...	2138	2114	...
Firenze Campo di Marte	d.	...	...	...	...	...	1857r	...	...	1936r	...	...	...	...	...	2008	...	|	|	...	...	|	|	...
Prato	d.	...	...	...	...	...	1912	...	...	1945	...	...	...	...	...	2029	...	|	|	...	...	|	|	...
Bologna Centrale **630**	a.	...	...	...	...	...	2013	...	...	2052	...	...	...	...	...	2127	...	|	|	...	...	2255	2154	...
Bologna Centrale	d.	...	1956	2003	2006	...	2017	...	2030	2056	2106	...	2118	...	...	2137	...	|	|	...	2235	2320	2157	...
Modena	d.	...	|	2030	2030	1935	2041	...	2056	2115	|	...	2140	...	2229	2205	...	|	|	...	|	|	2219	...
Reggio Emilia	d.	...	|	2057	2048	|	2054	...	2110	2130	|	...	2154	...	2243	2219	...	|	|	...	|	|	2233	...
Parma	d.	...	|	2117	2109	2000	2109	...	2127	2145	|	...	2209	...	2258	2235	...	|	|	...	|	|	2249	...
Fidenza	d.	2016	|	2132	|	|	2124	...	2140	|	|	2204	|	...	|	2246	...	|	|	...	|	|	|	...
Piacenza	d.	2040	|	2158	2141	|	2150	...	2206	2220	|	2227	2241	...	2330	2304	...	|	|	...	|	|	2323	...
Voghera **610**	d.	|	|	|	|	|	|	...	...	|	|	|	|	...	|	|	...	|	|	...	|	|	|	...
Tortona **610**	d.	|	|	|	|	|	|	...	...	|	|	|	|	...	|	|	...	|	|	...	|	|	|	...
Alessandria **610**	d.	|	|	|	|	|	|	...	...	|	|	|	|	...	|	|	...	|	|	...	|	|	|	...
Asti **610**	d.	|	|	|	|	|	|	...	...	|	|	|	|	...	|	|	...	|	|	...	|	|	|	...
Torino P N **610**	a.	|	|	|	|	|	|	...	...	|	|	|	|	...	|	|	...	|	|	...	|	|	|	...
Ferrara **621**	d.	|	2030	|	|	|	|	...	...	|	2133	|	|	...	|	|	...	|	|	...	2307	2350	|	...
Rovigo	d.	|	2056	|	|	|	|	...	...	|	2150	|	|	...	|	|	...	|	|	...	2328	|	|	...
Padova **600**	d.	|	2129	|	|	|	|	...	...	|	2219	|	|	...	|	|	...	|	|	...	2400	0041	|	...
Venezia Mestre **600**	a.	|	2151	|	|	|	|	...	...	|	2237	|	|	...	|	|	...	0011	0011	...	...	0102	|	...
Venezia Santa Lucia **600**	a.	|	2203	|	|	|	|	...	...	|	2250	|	|	...	|	|	...	...	...	...	...	...	|	...
Milano Centrale	a.	2202g	...	2310	2230	2135	2240	...	...	2300	...	2320	2325	...	0025	2350	...	...	...	...	...	...	0005	...

♦ – **NOTES** (CONTINUED FROM PREVIOUS PAGE)

837 – ①②④⑤⑥⑦; also Dec. 9, not Dec. 10 (from Bolzano): 🛏 1, 2 cl. (Excelsior), 🛏 1, 2 cl., ▬ 2 cl. (4 berth) and [2] Bolzano (**925**) - Bologna - Napoli.

900 – Daily June 14 - Sept. 13; ⑦ Sept. 20 - Nov. 29; also Dec. 8 (from Bari): ▬ 2 cl. and [2] Bari - Torino.

901 – FRECCIA ADRIATICA – 🛏 1,2 cl. (T2), 🛏 1, 2 cl., ▬ 2 cl. and [2] Torino - Lecce; ▬ 2 cl. and [2] Torino - Bari (**903**) - Taranto (**904**) - Metaponto (**905**) - Catanzaro Lido.

906 – FRECCIA ADRIATICA – 🛏 1,2 cl. (T2), 🛏 1, 2 cl., ▬ 2 cl. and [2] Lecce - Torino; ▬ 2 cl. and [2] Catanzaro Lido (**908**) - Metaponto (**909**) - Taranto (**910**) - Bari - Torino.

907 – Daily June 14 - Sept. 12; ⑤ Sept. 18 - Dec. 11 (from Torino): ▬ 2 cl. and [2] Torino - Bari.

923 – 🛏 1, 2 cl. (T2), ▬ 2 cl. (4/6 berth) and [2] Milano - Lecce.

926 – 🛏 1, 2 cl. (T2), ▬ 2 cl. (4/6 berth) and [2] Lecce - Milano.

1236 – ALLEGRO ROSSINI – ⑥ Mar. 27 - Sept. 25: 🛏 1, 2 cl. (T2), ▬ 2 cl. and [2] Firenze - Venezia Mestre - Villach - Wien.

1237 – ALLEGRO ROSSINI – ⑤ Mar. 26 - Sept. 24 (from Wien): 🛏 1, 2 cl. (T2), ▬ 2 cl. and [2] Wien - Villach - Venezia Mestre - Firenze.

1238 – ALLEGRO ROSSINI – Dec. 29, 30, Jan. 1-6, Apr. 5, May 13, 24, June 3: 🛏 1, 2 cl. (T2), ▬ 2 cl.and [2] Firenze - Venezia Mestre - Villach - Wien.

1239 – ALLEGRO ROSSINI – Dec. 28-30, Jan. 1-5, Apr. 4, May 12, 23, June 2 (from Wien): 🛏 1, 2 cl. (T2), ▬ 2 cl. and [2] Wien - Villach - Venezia Mestre - Firenze.

1545 – GARGANO – ⑥ (not Aug. 15): [12] and 🍷 Milano - Lecce.

1546 – GARGANO – ⑦ (also Dec. 8; not Dec. 6): [12] and 🍷 Lecce - Milano.

1549 – APULIA – ⑤: [12] and 🍷 Milano - Bari.

1550 – APULIA – ⑦ (also Dec. 8; not Dec. 6): [12] Bari - Milano.

1554 – CARACCIOLO – ⑦ (also Dec. 8; not Dec. 6): [12] and 🍷 Salerno - Milano.

1557 – CARACCIOLO – ⑤: [12] and 🍷 Milano - Salerno.

1590 – ASPROMONTE – ⑦ (also Dec. 8; not Dec. 6): [12] Reggio - Milano. Train number **1588** from Sept. 13.

1591 – ASPROMONTE – ⑥ (also Aug. 14; not Aug. 15): [12] Milano - Reggio. Train number **1589** from Sept. 12.

1594 – ⑤ June 19 - Sept. 11: 🛏 1,2 cl. (T2), ▬ 2 cl. and [2] Reggio - Bolzano.

1595 – ⑥ June 20 - Sept. 12 (from Bolzano): 🛏 1,2 cl. (T2), ▬ 2 cl. and [2] Bolzano - Reggio.

1910 – 🛏 1,2 cl. (Excelsior), 🛏 1,2 cl. (T2), 🛏 1,2 cl., ▬ 2 cl. (4 berth) and [2] Napoli - Milano.

1911 – 🛏 1,2 cl. (Excelsior), 🛏 1,2 cl. (T2), 🛏 1,2 cl., ▬ 2 cl. (4 berth) and [2] Milano - Napoli.

1920 – TRINACRIA – 🛏 1, 2 cl. (T2), 🛏 1,2 cl. and ▬ 2 cl. (4/6 berth) Palermo - Milano; 🛏 1, 2 cl. (T2), 🛏 1,2 cl. and ▬ 2 cl. (4/6 berth) Siracusa (**1922**) - Messina - Milano.

1921 – TRINACRIA – 🛏 1, 2 cl. (T2), 🛏 1,2 cl. and ▬ 2 cl. (4/6 berth) Milano - Palermo and v.v.; 🛏 1, 2 cl. (T2), 🛏 1,2 cl. and ▬ 2 cl. (4/6 berth) Milano - Messina (**1923**) - Siracusa.

1930 – FRECCIA DELLA LAGUNA – 🛏 1, 2 cl. and ▬ 2 cl. (4 berth) Siracusa - Venezia; 🛏 1, 2 cl. and ▬ 2 cl. (4 berth) Palermo (**1932**) - Messina - Venezia; 🛏 1, 2 cl. and ▬ 2 cl. (4 berth) Reggio (**1934**) - Villa SG - Venezia.

1931 – FRECCIA DELLA LAGUNA – 🛏 1,2 cl. and ▬ 2 cl. (4 berth) Venezia - Siracusa; 🛏 1, 2 cl. and ▬ 2 cl. (4 berth) Venezia - Messina (**1933**) - Palermo; 🛏 1, 2 cl. and ▬ 2 cl. (4 berth) Venezia - Villa SG (**1935**) - Reggio.

1991 – MONGIBELLO – ①⑤ June 15 - Sept. 28 (also Dec. 4, 9): 🛏 1, 2 cl. (T2), ▬ 2 cl. and [2] Milano - Siracusa; ▬ 2 cl. (4 berth) and [2] Milano - Messina (**1993**) - Palermo.

1992 – MONGIBELLO – ④⑦ until Sept. 27 (also Dec. 3, 8): 🛏 1, 2 cl. (T2), ▬ 2 cl. and [2] Siracusa - Milano; ▬ 2 cl. (4 berth) and [2] Palermo (**1990**) - Messina - Milano.

9858/9 – ⑥⑦ June 13 - Sept. 12: [12] and 🍷 Milano - Ravenna - Ancona and v.v.

35476 – TERGESTE – Aug. 31 - Sept. 19 (from Lecce): ▬ 2 cl. (4 berth) and [12] Lecce - Venezia Mestre (**35477**) - Trieste; 🛏 1, 2 cl. (Excelsior), 🛏 1, 2 cl. (T2), 🛏 1, 2 cl. and [12] Lecce - Venezia Mestre (**1598**) - Venezia Santa Lucia.

35479 – TERGESTE – Aug. 31 - Sept. 19: ▬ 2 cl. (4 berth) and [12] Trieste (**35478**) - Venezia Mestre - Lecce; 🛏 1, 2 cl. (Excelsior), 🛏 1, 2 cl. (T2), 🛏 1, 2 cl. and [12] Venezia Santa Lucia (**1599**) - Mestre - Lecce.

A – From/to Ancona.
B – From/to Bari.
C – From/to Lecce.
E – From/to Pescara.
L – [12] Milano - Aulla - Livorno and v.v.
M – [12] and 🍷 Milano - Pescara and v.v.
P – ⑥⑦: [2] Milano - Pescara and v.v.
R – From/to Rimini.
T – From/to Taranto.

g – Milano **Porta Garibaldi**.
j – Also Dec. 8; not Dec. 6.
k – Not ⑥⑦ June 13 - Sept. 12.
p – Not ⑤⑥ June 12 - Sept. 11.
q – Not Aug. 15, and days before holidays.
r – Firenze **Rifredi**.

s – Stops to set down only.
t – Arrive 2006.
u – Stops to pick up only.
v – ①②③④⑦ (not Aug. 15, and days before holidays).
w – Not Aug. 8-22.
x – Also Dec. 7; not Dec. 4.
y – Not Aug. 9-23.

⊡ – Supplement payable.

FERRARA and BOLOGNA - RAVENNA - RIMINI 621

2nd class only except where shown

For express services Bologna - Faenza - Rimini see Table 630

km		ES 9325 ♦	⚒y	y		⚒	⚒x	⚒		†n	⚒p	z	q		ESc 9859 ♦	⚒x		†n	†r	m		j	y			⚒x
0	**Ferrara 620** d.	...	...	0557	...	...	0717	...	...	0816	0817	0817	0850	...	...	0913	...	1010	....	1030	...	...	1215	...	...	1309
	Bologna C 630 d.	...	...	|	...	0650	|	...	0758	|	|	|	|	...	...	|	0906	|	1008	|	1106	...	|	...	1306	|
	Imola d.	...	...	|	...	0712	|	...	0823	|	|	|	|	...	...	|	0935	|	1036	|	1136	...	|	...	1336	|
	Castelbolognese d.	...	...	|	...	0719	|	...	0832	|	|	|	|	...	...	|	0942	|	1042	|	1142	...	|	...	1342	|
	Lugo d.	...	...	|	...	0734	|	...	0846	|	|	|	|	...	...	|	1000	|	1056	|	1200	...	|	...	1400	|
74	**Ravenna** a.	...	...	0715	...	0803	0830	...	0913	0921	0928	0928	0953	...	1009	1025	1025	1118	1116	1129	1225	...	1324	...	1425	1432
74	**Ravenna** d.	0607	0635	...	0733	...	...	0832	0922	...	0933	0935	0954	...	1019	...	...	1121	1121	1131	...	1239	...	1336	...	...
95	Cervia d.	|	0656	...	0756	...	...	0900	0943	...	1002	1002	1015	...	1052	...	...	1138	1138	1148	...	1304	...	1400	...	...
103	Cesenatico d.	|	0702	...	0802	...	...	0906	0956	...	1009	1009	1022	...	1103	...	...	1145	1144	1155	...	1310	...	1406	...	...
124	**Rimini 630** a.	0645	0732	...	0836	...	...	0936	1017	...	1036	1037	1100	...	1120	...	...	1214	1218	1228	...	1337	...	1437	...	...

	j		y		⚒	ES 9335 ♦	⚒k			†	⚒		⚒x	†	⚒	Ⓐ	y			y					ICN 779 ♦	ICN 35479 ♦
Ferrara 620 d.	...	...	1414	...	...	...	...	...	1615	...	...	...	1701	...	...	...	1814	...	...	2014	...	...	...	...	2338	2338
Bologna C 630 d.	...	1406	|	...	1506	...	...	1606	|	...	...	1706	|	...	...	1755	|	1806	1906	|	2006	...	2206	...	|	|
Imola d.	...	1436	|	...	1536	...	...	1635	|	...	...	1734	|	...	...	|	|	1835	1935	|	2034	...	2236	...	|	|
Castelbolognese d.	...	1442	|	...	1542	...	...	1642	|	...	...	1742	|	...	...	1821	|	1842	1942	|	2042	...	2242	...	|	|
Lugo d.	...	1501	|	...	1600	...	...	1700	|	...	...	1800	|	...	...	1834	|	1900	2000	|	2100	...	2256	...	|	|
Ravenna a.	...	1525	1529	...	1625	...	...	1725	1725	...	...	1825	1814	...	...	1855	1926	1925	2025	2124	2125	...	2320	...	0029	|
Ravenna d.	1435	1535	...	1535	...	1630	1647	...	...	1730	1735	...	...	1835	1835	...	...	1935	...	...	...	2135	...	...	0031	|
Cervia d.	1502	1557	...	1557	...	1654	1710	...	...	1758	1758	...	...	1856	1900	...	...	1959	...	...	...	2157	...	...	|	|
Cesenatico d.	1508	1603	...	1603	...	1702	1717	...	...	1805	1805	...	...	1908	1907	...	...	2005	...	...	...	2204	...	...	|	|
Rimini 630 a.	1535	1631	...	1631	...	1734	1751	...	...	1836	1836	...	...	1933	1933	...	...	2035	...	...	...	2233	...	...	0111	0111

km		ICN 776 ♦	ICN 35476 ♦			j	⚒			⚒x	†t		⚒	⚒	⚒x	†t			⚒x	f	†		⚒x		ES 9322 ♦	
	Rimini 630 d.	0333	0333	...	...	0518	...	...	0620	...	...	0651	0736	...	...	...	0820	0921	...	1020	...	...	...	...	1157	1230
	Cesenatico d.	|	|	...	...	0550	...	...	0646	...	...	0722	0803	...	...	...	0852	0955	...	1054	...	...	...	...	1222	1257
	Cervia d.	|	|	...	...	0557	...	...	0657	...	...	0728	0809	...	...	...	0859	1001	...	1100	...	...	...	...	1229	1303
	Ravenna a.	0411	|	...	...	0615	...	...	0719	...	...	0748	0829	...	...	...	0920	1020	...	1118	...	...	...	...	1243	1324
0	**Ravenna** d.	0413	|	...	0503	...	0620	0630	...	0726	0735	0754	...	0835	0840	0931	0935	...	1031	...	1134	1135	1226	1235	...	...
28	Lugo d.	|	|	...	0528	...	|	0659	...	|	|	0812	...	0901	|	|	1000	...	|	...	|	1200	|	1300	...	...
42	Castelbolognese d.	|	|	...	0544	...	|	0716	...	|	|	|	...	0916	|	|	1016	...	|	...	|	1216	|	1316	...	...
50	Imola d.	|	|	...	0551	...	|	0724	...	|	|	|	...	0923	|	|	1023	...	|	...	|	1223	|	1323	...	...
84	**Bologna C 630** a.	|	|	...	0620	...	|	0748	...	|	|	0852	...	0954	|	|	1053	...	|	...	|	1254	|	1354	...	...
	Ferrara 620 a.	0514	0514	...	...	...	0739	...	...	0846	0848	...	...	...	0950	1049	...	...	1142	...	1248	...	1347	...	...	...

	y		j	⚒x		h	⚒k	m	Ⓐ	y		g		w	q		ESc 9858 ♦	⚒	†	y	⚒	†v			y	
Rimini 630 d.	...	...	1320	...	1420	...	1520	1551	...	1615	...	1720	...	...	1731	...	2001	1820	1838	...	1920	1920	...	2020	...	...
Cesenatico d.	...	...	1353	...	1454	...	1549	1624	...	1702	...	1750	...	...	1806	...	2036	1852	1907	...	1952	1952	...	2052	...	...
Cervia d.	...	...	1359	...	1501	...	1558	1633	...	1709	...	1757	...	...	1813	...	2044	1859	1914	...	1958	1958	...	2059	...	...
Ravenna a.	...	...	1421	...	1521	...	1622	1652	...	1729	...	1820	...	...	1833	...	2058	1920	1932	...	2020	2020	...	2120	...	...
Ravenna d.	1350	1335	...	1444	1531	1540	...	1702	1635	1736	1735	...	1835	1824	1845	...	...	...	1935	1950	...	...	2035	...	2134	...
Lugo d.	|	1400	...	|	1600	|	...	|	1700	|	1800	...	1900	|	|	...	...	...	2000	|	...	...	2100	...	|	...
Castelbolognese d.	|	1416	...	|	1616	|	...	|	1716	|	1816	...	1917	|	|	...	...	...	2016	|	...	...	2116	...	|	...
Imola d.	|	1423	...	|	1623	|	...	|	1723	|	1822	...	1923	|	|	...	...	...	2023	|	...	...	2123	...	|	...
Bologna C 630 a.	|	1454	...	|	1654	|	...	|	1752	|	1854	...	1952	|	|	...	...	...	2054	|	...	...	2154	...	|	...
Ferrara 620 a.	1505	...	...	1608	...	1658	...	1812	...	1849	...	...	...	1936	1952	...	...	...	...	2103	...	...	...	...	2241	...

♦ – **NOTES** (LISTED BY TRAIN NUMBER)

776 – TERGESTE – Not Aug. 31 - Sept. 19 (from Lecce): ▬ 2 cl. (4 berth) and (12) Lecce - Venezia Mestre (**777**) - Trieste; 🛏 1,2 cl. (Excelsior), 🛏 1,2 cl. (T2), 🛏 1,2 cl. and (12) Lecce - Mestre (**1598**) - Venezia Santa Lucia.

779 – TERGESTE – Not Aug. 31 - Sept. 19: ▬ 2 cl. (4 berth) and (12) Trieste (**778**) - Venezia Mestre - Lecce; 🛏 1,2 cl. (Excelsior), 🛏 1,2 cl. (T2), 🛏 1,2 cl. and (12) Venezia Santa Lucia (**1599**) - Mestre - Lecce.

9322 – June 13 - Sept. 4: (12) and 🍷 Roma - Ancona - Ravenna.

9325 – (12) and 🍷 Ravenna - Rimini - Roma.

9335 – June 13 - Sept. 4: (12) and 🍷 Ravenna - Ancona - Roma.

9858 – ⑥⑦ June 13 - Sept. 12: (12) and 🍷 Ancona - Modena - Milano.

9859 – ⑥⑦ June 13 - Sept. 12: (12) and 🍷 Milano - Modena - Ancona.

35476 – TERGESTE – Aug. 31 - Sept. 19 (from Lecce): ▬ 2 cl. (4 berth) and (12) Lecce - Venezia Mestre (**35477**) - Trieste; 🛏 1,2 cl. (Excelsior), 🛏 1,2 cl. (T2), 🛏 1,2 cl. and (12) Lecce - Mestre (**1598**) - Venezia Santa Lucia.

35479 – TERGESTE – Aug. 31 - Sept. 19: ▬ 2 cl. (4 berth) and (12) Trieste (**35478**) - Venezia Mestre - Lecce; 🛏 1,2 cl. (Excelsior), 🛏 1,2 cl. (T2), 🛏 1,2 cl. and (12) Venezia Santa Lucia (**1599**) - Mestre - Lecce.

f – † (daily June 29 - Aug. 29).
g – Daily June 14 - Sept. 13; ⚒ Sept. 14 - Dec. 12.
h – ⚒ June 15 - Aug. 29; daily Sept. 21 - Dec. 12.
j – Daily June 14 - Sept. 19; ⚒ Sept. 21 - Dec. 12.
k – From Aug. 31.
m – Until Aug. 30.
n – From Sept. 27.
p – Not June 21 - Sept. 20.
q – July 26 - Aug. 30.
r – Until Sept. 6.
t – Not Aug. 31 - Sept. 26.
v – Until Sept. 13.
w – Daily June 14 - Aug. 30; ⚒ Sept. 21 - Dec. 12.
x – Not Aug. 30 - Sept. 20.
y – Not Aug. 31 - Sept. 20.
z – June 21 - Aug. 30.

ROMA AIRPORTS ✈ and other local services 622

ROMA FIUMICINO AIRPORT ✈

Leonardo Express rail service Roma Termini - Roma Fiumicino ✈. *26 km* Journey time: 31 minutes. Special fare payable.

From **Roma Termini**: 0552, 0622, 0652, and every 30 minutes until 2252.

From **Roma Fiumicino**: 0636, 0706, 0736, and every 30 minutes until 2336.

Additional rail service (2nd class only) operates from Roma Tiburtina **and** Roma Ostiense - Roma Fiumicino ✈. *26 km* Journey times: Tiburtina - ✈ 41 – 42 minutes; Ostiense - ✈ 27 minutes.

From **Roma Tiburtina** (Ostiense 15 minutes later): 0505, 0533, 0548⚒, 0603, 0618⚒, 0633, 0648⚒, and every 15 minutes (30 †) until 2033, then 2103, 2133, 2203, 2233.

From **Roma Fiumicino** ✈: 0557, 0627, 0642⚒, 0657, 0712⚒, 0727, 0742⚒, 0757, and every 15 minutes (30 †) until 2127, then 2157, 2227, 2257, 2327.

A reduced service operates in July and August

ROMA CIAMPINO AIRPORT ✈

Frequent services operate Roma Termini - Ciampino and v.v., journey approximately 15 minutes. There is a 🚌 service between Ciampino station and airport.

ROMA - ANZIO and v.v. *57 km* Journey time: 56 – 68 minutes. 2nd class only. All services continue to Nettuno (*3 km* and 4 – 6 minutes from Anzio).

From **Roma Termini**:
⚒: 0505, 0607, 0710, 0807, 0907 and hourly until 1407, then 1428, 1507, 1607, 1709, 1807, 1907, 1930, 2007, 2107, 2148.
†: 0710, 0807, 0907, 1107, 1307, 1407, 1607, 1807, 2007, 2148.

From **Anzio**:
⚒: 0452, 0558, 0632, 0658, 0733, 0754, 0836, 0937 and hourly until 1837, then 1935, 2037, 2150.
†: 0632, 0733, 0836, 0937, 1237, 1437, 1637, 1837, 1935, 2150.

ROMA - CIAMPINO - ALBANO LAZIALE and v.v. *29 km* Journey time: 40 – 58 minutes. 2nd class only.

From **Roma Termini**: 0534⚒, 0720, 0837, 1000⚒, 1210, 1306⚒, 1406, 1506⚒, 1606, 1706⚒, 1806, 1906⚒, 2006, 2106⚒.

From **Albano Laziale**: 0632⚒, 0702⚒, 0739⚒, 0820, 1019⚒, 1023†, 1119⚒, 1335, 1420⚒, 1520⚒, 1524†, 1620⚒, 1720⚒, 1724†, 1820⚒, 1920⚒, 1924†, 2020⚒, 2120⚒, 2124†, 2213⚒.

All trains call at Ciampino, Marino Laziale and Castel Gandolfo approximately 15, 30 and 35 minutes from Roma, 6, 11 and 30 minutes from Albano Laziale respectively.

623 NAPOLI - SORRENTO, BAIANO and SARNO

2nd class only | Circumvesuviana Ferrovia

Services depart from Napoli Porta Nolana station and call at Napoli Piazza Garibaldi ▲ 2 minutes later. *Subject to alteration July 1 - August 31.*

NAPOLI (Porta Nolana) - SORRENTO and v.v. Journey: 55-68 minutes. *45 km.* All services call at Ercolano, Pompei Villa di Misteri, Castellammare di Stabia, Vico Equense and Meta.

From **Napoli:** 0509⚒, 0539, 0609⚒, 0640, 0644⚒, 0709, 0739⚒, 0811, 0822, 0839, 0909, 0939 and every 30 minutes until 1309, 1341, 1409, 1439, 1511, 1522⚒, 1539, 1609, 1639, 1709, 1741, 1809, 1839, 1911, 1939, 2009, 2039, 2109, 2139, 2209, 2242.

From **Sorrento:** 0501, 0537, 0607⚒, 0625, 0655, 0722, 0738⚒, 0755, 0826, 0852⚒, 0907, 0937 and every 30 minutes until 1307, 1325, 1356, 1422, 1455, 1526, 1552⚒, 1607, 1637, 1707, 1725, 1756, 1822, 1855, 1926, 2007, 2037, 2107, 2137, 2225.

NAPOLI (Porta Nolana) - BAIANO and v.v. Journey 60 minutes.

From **Napoli:** 0517⚒, 0548, 0618⚒, 0648, 0718, 0748, 0818, 0848⚒, 0918, 0948⚒, 1018, 1048⚒, 1118, 1148⚒, 1218, 1248, 1318, 1348⚒, 1418†, 1430⚒, 1448⚒, 1518, 1548Ⓐ, 1618, 1648Ⓐ, 1718†, 1730⚒, 1748Ⓐ, 1818, 1848Ⓐ, 1918, 1948, 2018, 2048.

From **Baiano:** 0502, 0532⚒, 0602, 0632⚒, 0700, 0730, 0802, 0832, 0902, 0932, 1002, 1032⚒, 1102, 1132⚒, 1202, 1232⚒, 1302, 1332⚒, 1402, 1430, 1502, 1532⚒, 1602, 1632⚒, 1702, 1730Ⓐ, 1802, 1832Ⓐ, 1902, 1932Ⓐ, 2002, 2032Ⓐ, 2102.

NAPOLI (Porta Nolana) - SARNO and v.v. Journey 65 minutes. All services call at Poggiomarino (49 minutes from Napoli, 12 minutes from Sarno).

From **Napoli:** 0502⚒, 0532, 0602⚒, 0632, 0722, 0802, 0832⚒, 0902, 0932⚒, 1002, 1032⚒, 1102, 1132⚒, 1202, 1232, 1302, 1332⚒, 1402, 1432⚒, 1502, 1532Ⓐ, 1602, 1632Ⓐ, 1702, 1732Ⓐ, 1802, 1832Ⓐ, 1902, 1932, 2002, 2042, 2102**p**.

From **Sarno:** 0453, 0519⚒, 0549, 0619⚒, 0649, 0719, 0741, 0759, 0819, 0849, 0919, 0949, 1019⚒, 1049, 1119⚒, 1149, 1219⚒, 1249, 1349, 1419, 1449, 1519⚒, 1549, 1619⚒, 1649, 1719Ⓐ, 1749, 1819Ⓐ, 1849, 1919Ⓐ, 1949, 2019Ⓐ, 2049.

p – To Poggiomarino only.

▲ – Adjacent to **Napoli Centrale** main line station - connection is by moving walkway. Operator: Circumvesuviana Ferrovia ✆ +39 081 77 22 444, fax +39 081 77 22 450.

Frequent 🚌 services operate along the Amalfi Coast between Sorrento and Salerno. Up to 20 services on ⚒, less frequent on †. Change of buses at Amalfi is necessary. Operator: SITA, Via Campegna 23, 80124 Napoli. ✆ +39 081 610 67 11, fax +39 081 239 50 10.

624 ROMA - PESCARA

2nd class only

km					⚒	Ⓐ				⚒	
0	**Roma Tiburtina** ▲ d.	...	0751	1046	1157	1250	1426	1626	1832j	1943	2048
40	Tivoli ▲ d.	...	0844	1147	1236	|	1508	|	1910	2045	2132
108	Avezzano d.	0606	0951	1256	1349	1433	1618	1816	2025	2209	2242
172	Sulmona **626** d.	0729	1050	1410	...	1537	1716	1912	2135	...	...
226	Chieti a.	0831	1130	1515	...	1631	1805	2003	2215	...	...
240	**Pescara C** a.	0849	1149	1533	...	1655	1825	2021	2233	...	...

				Ⓐ		⚒					
Pescara C d.	...	...	0620	0645	0920	1242	1409	1600	...	1758	1904
Chieti d.	...	...	0637	0709	0939	1300	1427	1617	...	1823	1921
Sulmona **626** d.	...	0550	0728	0824	1025	1402	1514	1712	1736	1925	2010
Avezzano d.	0457	0651	0820	0924	1129	*1521*	1615	...	1901	...	2110
Tivoli ▲ d.	0610	0759	|	|	1235	...	1717	...	2029	...	2221
Roma Tiburtina ▲ a.	0658	0844t	1000	1100	1312	...	1750r	...	2125	...	2300

j – Depart 1838 on †.
r – Arrive 1800 on ⚒.
t – Roma **Termini**.
▲ – Additional services operate Roma Tiburtina - Tivoli and v.v., journey 55–60 minutes.

625 ROMA - FOLIGNO - ANCONA

km		2 ⚒	2 ⚒	2 ⚒	*IC* **580** T	2 †	2 ⚒		*ES* **9320** 🍷 S		*ES* **9324** 🍷	2 Ⓐ	2 ⚒z	⚒	⚒		*ES* **9328** 🍷		*ES* **9330** 🍷		*ES* **9332** 🍷 V		Ⓑ		*ES* **9334** 🍷	*ES* **9336** 🍷 Ⓑh		
0	**Roma Termini 615** d.	...	...	...	...	...	...	0550	0732	0755	0922	...	...	1130	1157	1304	1332	1357	1530	1557	1730	...	1757	1830	1932	2000	2030	2236
5	**Roma Tiburtina 615** d.	...	...	...	...	...	...	0558	0740u	0803	|	...	...	1139	1205	1312	1340u	1405	|	1605	|	...	1805	1838	1940u	2008u	2039	2244
83	Orte **615** d.	...	...	...	...	...	...	0635	|	0840	|	...	...	1215	1242	1350	1412	1442	|	1642	|	...	1842	1917	|	2043	2115	2321
112	Terni d.	...	...	...	0502	...	...	0656	0833	0901	1016	...	...	1236	1303	1409	1430	1506	1622	1707	1821	...	1917	1954	2027	2103	2146	2342
141	Spoleto d.	...	...	...	0529	...	...	0718	0852	0930	|	...	...	1306	1332	1434	1457	1530	|	1743	|	...	1941	2021	2054	2130	2208	0011
167	**Foligno** a.	...	...	...	0552	...	...	0738	0905	0951	1050	...	...	1326	1349	1449	1512	1547	1659	1803	1854	...	1958	2038	2109	2152	2225	0030
167	**Foligno 615** d.	...	...	0550	0600	0620	0645	0740	0907	0956	1052	1158	...	1328	1351	1450	1515	1549	1701	1806	1856	1903	2000	2042	2111	2154	2228	...
	Assisi **615** a.	...	...	|	0611	|	|	|	|	1010	|	|	...	|	1411	1504	1529	|	|	|	|	1918	2014	|	|	2204	|	...
	Perugia **615** a.	...	...	|	0638	|	|	|	|	1045	|	|	...	|	1440	1528	1558	|	|	|	|	1940	2045	|	|	2226	|	...
224	**Fabriano** d.	0500	0600	0643	...	0715	0743	0845	0953	...	1134	1300	...	1419	...	...	...	1659	1745	1910	1934	...	...	2140	2156	...	2332	...
268	Jesi d.	0542	0642	0733	...	0756	0830	0922	1022	...	1213	1348	1426	1512	...	...	...	1736	1813	1949	2003	...	...	2212	2227	...	0009	...
286	Falconara Marittima **630** d.	0557	0706	0747	...	0811	0851	0938	1034	...	1227	1406	1443	1529	...	...	...	1752	1827	2006	2015	...	...	2224	2240	...	0023	...
295	**Ancona 630** a.	0608	0718	0800	...	0825	0905	0955	1043	...	1236	1417	1455	1540	...	...	...	1803	1836	2019	...	...	...	2238	2250	...	0035	...
	Ancona Marittima a.	0618	0729a	0809	...	...	0914	...	...	...	...	...	1505	...	...	...	...	...	...	...	...	...	...	...	...	...	...	...

		ES **9321** 🍷 ⚒	*ES* **9323** 🍷	†	2 ⚒	*ES* **9325** 🍷 V	2 ⚒			*ES* **9327** 🍷	2 ⚒		2 Ⓐy	2	*ES* **9331** 🍷		2 ⚒z	*ES* **9333** 🍷	2 Ⓐ		2 ⚒y	*ES* **9337** 🍷 S	2	2		2 ⚒	2	*IC* **597** T
Ancona Marittima d.	...	...	...	...	...	...	0645	...	...	...	1226a	...	1404	...	...	...	1535	...	1617	...	1721a	...	1821a	...	...	1940	...	...
Ancona 630 d.	0336	...	0618	...	...	*0717**	0655	0808	...	1110	1235	1408	1414	...	1518	...	1544	...	1626	1650	1730	1853	1830	...	1908	1949	2128	...
Falconara Marittima **630** d.	0347	...	0628	...	...	0743	0706	0818	...	1119	1247	1418	1426	...	1531	...	1556	...	1638	1703	1741	1903	1841	...	1919	2001	2139	...
Jesi d.	0359	...	0643	...	...	0756	0725	0832	...	1131	1304	1432	1443	...	1542	...	1614	...	1657	1718	1759	1915	1902	...	1933	2020	2155	...
Fabriano d.	0435	...	0715	...	...	0825	0813	0914	...	1205	1352	1514	1534	...	1614	...	1658	...	1741	1811	1852	2002	2002	...	2017	2100	2249	...
Perugia **615** d.	|	0643	|	0723	0751	|	...	|	1118	|	|	|	...	1621	|	1718	|	1804	...	|	...	|	...	2021	|	...	|	2318
Assisi **615** d.	|	0705	|	0745	0823	|	...	|	1144	|	|	|	...	1642	|	1745	|	1825	...	|	...	|	...	2043	|	...	|	2336
Foligno 615 a.	0519	0716	0757	0800	0837	0900	...	1001	1200	1250	1459	1610	...	1656	1656	1759	1804	1839	...	1908	...	2036	...	2101	2105	...	2340	2350
Foligno d.	0531	0718	0759	0803	...	0902	...	1003	1203	1252	1507	1611	...	...	1658	1801	...	1841	...	1909	...	2038	...	...	2106	...	...	2354
Spoleto d.	0557	0735	|	0824	...	|	...	1019	1221	1307	1531	1628	...	...	|	1822	...	1857	...	1925	...	2053	...	...	2123	...	...	0010
Terni d.	0623	0758	0834	0909	...	0936	...	1049	1255	1329	1558	1658	...	...	1733	1855	...	1919	...	1953	...	2123	...	...	2145	...	...	0035
Orte **615** d.	0649	0816	|	0936	...	|	...	1117	1317	|	...	1718	...	...	|	1917	...	1948	...	2016	...	|	...	...	2208	...	...	...
Roma Tiburtina 615 a.	0724	0847s	|	1011	...	|	...	1152	1352	1419s	...	1752	...	...	|	1952	...	2020s	...	2108	...	2204s	...	...	2245	...	...	...
Roma Termini 615 a.	0738	0858	0924	1019	...	1024	...	1203	1403	1428	...	1803	...	...	1824	2003	...	2030	...	2118	...	2219	...	...	2256	...	...	...

R – [12] and 🍷 Roma - Rimini and v.v.
S – June 13 - Sept. 4: [12] and 🍷 Roma - Ancona - Ravenna and v.v.
T – TACITO – [12] Terni - Perugia - Milano and v.v.
V – [12] and 🍷 Ravenna - Rimini - Roma and v.v.
a – Ⓐ only.
h – Not Dec. 25, 26, Apr. 4, May 1, Oct. 31, and days before holidays.
s – Stops to set down only.
u – Stops to pick up only.
y – Not July 25 - Aug. 23.
z – Not July 26 - Aug. 23.
* – By 🚌 from/to Falconara Marittima.

626 ROMA - CASERTA - NAPOLI and FOGGIA

km		⚒	C q	*E* **833** Z	2 ⚒w	2 ⚒		C	*E* **837** Z	2 †	*ES* **9351** 🍷	2 ⚒w	2		C r	*IC* **677** 🍷	C	*ES* **9353** 🍷	2 x	⚒r	*ES* **9355** 🍷	⚒	2 y	C	2 ⚒
0	**Roma Termini** d.	...	...	0501t	...	...	...	0615	0617t	...	0845	...	0725	...	...	0820	0915	1115	...	...	1445	...	1315	...	1401
138	Cassino d.	...	...	|	0657	...	...	0738	0759	...	|	...	0930	...	...	0950	1036	|	1317	...	|	...	1449	...	|
	Sulmona 624 d.	...	...	|	|	...	...	|	|	...	|	0632	|	...	...	|	|	|	|	...	|	...	|	...	|
	Castel di Sangro d.	...	...	|	|	...	...	|	|	...	|	0748	|	...	...	|	|	|	|	...	|	...	|	...	|
	Pescolanciano-Chiauci d.	...	...	|	|	...	...	|	|	...	|	|	|	...	...	|	|	|	|	...	|	...	|	...	|
	Campobasso d.	0518r	0545	|	|	0624r	...	|	|	0710q	|	|	|	...	0828	|	|	|	|	1219	|	1311r	|	1415r	|
	Carpinone d.	0559r	0631	|	|	0718r	...	|	|	0754q	|	0839	|	...	0922	|	|	|	|	1307	|	1400r	|	1500	|
	Isernia d.	0609	0641	|	|	0736	...	0822	|	0805	|	0849	|	...	0932	|	1118	|	|	1319	|	1412	|	1510	|
170	Vairano-Caianello d.	0648	...	|	0727	0814	...	...	|	0851	|	0931	1011	...	...	1008	...	|	1347	1404	|	1457	1510	...	|
216	Caserta d.	0714	...	|	0816	0842	...	...	0853	0920	1002	1005	1056	...	...	1039	...	1227	1431	...	1557	1530	1542	...	1617
	Napoli Centrale a.	0748	...	0734	0858	0916	...	...	0926	0952	|	1047	...	...	...	|	...	|	1512	...	|	1603	...	...	|
279	Benevento d.	...	...	...	...	...	...	...	...	...	1040	...	...	...	...	1127	...	1316	...	...	|	...	...	...	1724
380	**Foggia 631** a.	...	...	...	...	...	...	...	...	...	1153	...	...	...	...	1248	...	1418	...	...	1733	...	...	...	...
	Bari Centrale **631** a.	...	...	...	...	...	...	...	...	...	1302	...	...	...	...	1420	...	1530	...	...	1844	...	...	...	...
	Lecce **631** a.	...	...	...	...	...	...	...	...	...	1410	...	...	...	...	...	...	...	...	...	2006	...	...	...	...

FOR NOTES SEE OPPOSITE PAGE

ROMA - CASERTA - NAPOLI and FOGGIA 626

km				*ES*	*ES*															*ES*			*E*	*E*	*E*	*ICN*
				9357	**9385**															**9359**			**891**	**951**	**35451**	**789**
		⚒C	†C	🍷	🍷T		†Cr	⚒Cr	2v	2†	2⚒	⚒		m	†C	2y	C	⚒C	†C	🍷	2Ⓐ	2⑥	Z	Z	Z	Y
	Roma Termini d.	1415	1420	1645	1638	...	...	...	...	1647	1647	1715	...	...	1728	1815	...	1940	1942	1945	*1915*	...	2225	2330	2330	2358
	Cassino d.	1543	1545	|	|	...	...	...	...	1844	1854	1847	...	...	1855	1950	...	|	|	|	2130	2130	|	0108	0108	0140
0	**Sulmona 624** d.	|	|	|	|	...	...	...	1544	|	|	|	...	...	|	|	...	|	|	|	|	|	|	|	|	|
77	Castel di Sangro d.	|	|	|	|	...	...	...	1700	|	|	|	...	...	|	|	...	|	|	|	|	|	|	|	|	|
106	Pescolanciano-Chiauci d.	|	|	|	|	...	...	...	1731	|	|	|	...	...	|	|	...	|	|	|	|	|	|	|	|	|
	Campobasso d.	|	|	|	|	...	1628r	1630r	|	|	|	|	...	1803r	|	|	1943r	|	|	|	|	|	|	|	|	|
119	Carpinone d.	|	|	|	|	...	1715	1714	1744	|	|	|	...	1853r	|	|	2030	|	|	|	|	|	|	|	|	|
130	Isernia d.	1627	1627	|	|	...	1725	1723	1757	|	|	|	...	1904	1942	|	2040	2145	2147	|	|	|	|	|	|	|
176	Vairano-Caianello d.	...	...	|	|	...	...	...	1838	1913	1926	1910	...	1958	...	2013	...	...	...	|	2200	2200	|	|	|	|
222	Caserta d.	...	...	1756	1825	...	...	...	1921	1957	2010	1942	...	2028	...	2044	...	...	...	2057	2258	2258	0036	0155	0155	0236
256	**Napoli Centrale** a.	...	...	|	|	...	...	...	2002	...	...	...	...	2100	...	2126	...	...	...	|	2339	2339	...	|	|	|
	Benevento d.	...	...	1835	1910	...	...	...	...	...	...	...	...	...	...	...	...	...	...	|	...	...	...	|	|	0330
	Foggia 631 a.	...	...	1948	2040	...	...	...	...	...	...	...	...	...	...	...	...	...	...	2233	...	...	...	n	n	0453
	Bari Centrale **631** a.	...	...	2110	2157	...	...	...	...	...	...	...	...	...	...	...	...	...	...	2344	...	...	...	|	|	0635
	Lecce **631** a.	...	...	2233	...	...	...	...	...	...	...	...	...	...	...	...	...	...	...	...	...	...	...	0845	1007	0820

km		*ICN*															*ES*			*ES*						
		788															**9350**			**9352**						
		Y	2†	2⚒	2⚒	2y	C		2⚒p	2⚒	C	2		C	⚒r	C	🍷		⚒	🍷	2	2	C	k	C	w
	Lecce **631** d.	2228	...	...	...	...	...	...	...	...	...	...	...	...	...	...	0550	...	...	...	...	...	...	...	...	...
	Bari Centrale **631** d.	0015	...	...	...	...	...	...	...	...	...	...	...	...	...	...	0716	...	...	0950	...	...	...	...	...	...
	Foggia 631 d.	0159	...	...	...	...	...	...	...	...	...	...	...	...	...	...	0827	...	...	1123	...	...	...	...	...	...
	Benevento d.	0327	...	...	0515	...	...	...	...	...	...	...	...	...	...	...	|	...	...	1227	...	...	...	...	...	...
	Napoli Centrale d.	|	...	...	|	...	...	...	0551	...	...	0750	...	...	...	...	|	...	1214	|	...	...	...	1415	...	1527
	Caserta d.	0418	0510	0510	0605	0612	...	...	0622	0714	...	0827	...	...	...	...	1003	...	1244	1305	1313	1340	...	1445	...	1602
	Vairano-Caianello d.	|	0556	0557	|	0647	...	...	0655	0748	...	0911	...	...	...	...	|	...	1317	|	1359	1411	...	1521	...	1647
	Isernia d.	|	|	|	|	|	0642	...	0735	|	0823	|	...	0933	1050	1119	|	...	1413	|	|	|	1511	1603	1628	1801
0	Carpinone d.	|	|	|	|	|	|	...	0750	|	0834	|	...	|	1101	1130	|	...	1424r	|	|	|	|	1615r	1640	1815
48	**Campobasso** d.	|	|	|	|	|	|	...	|	|	0918r	|	...	|	1153	1215r	|	...	1522r	|	|	|	|	1709r	1730r	|
	Pescolanciano-Chiauci d.	|	|	|	|	|	|	...	0805	|	...	|	...	|	...	...	|	...	...	|	|	|	|	...	...	1828
	Castel di Sangro d.	|	|	|	|	|	|	...	0844	|	...	|	...	|	...	...	|	...	...	|	|	|	|	...	...	1901
	Sulmona 624 d.	|	|	|	|	|	|	...	1003	|	...	|	...	|	...	...	|	...	...	|	|	|	|	...	...	2018
	Cassino a.	|	0624	0630	|	0710	0729	...	...	0811	...	0950	...	1013	...	...	|	...	...	|	1431	1435	1553	...	...	...
	Roma Termini a.	0629	0838	0835	0812	0848	0853	...	...	0945	...	...	...	1140	...	...	1115	...	...	1415	1646	1625	1716	...	...	...

km					*ES*						*E*		*ES*		*IC*		*ES*			*ES*	*E*	*ICN*	*E*	*E*	*E*	*E*
					9354						**824**		**9356**		**678**		**9394**			**9358**	**830**	**752**	**892**	**956**	**35456**	**898**
		2⚒	2†		🍷	⚒C	†C		2⚒	†C	Z		🍷		🍷	C	🍷R	⚒Cr	†Cr	🍷	Z	Z	Z	Z	Z	Z
	Lecce **631** d.	...	...	...	1250	...	...	...	...	...	...	...	...	...	...	...	...	...	...	1728	...	...	...	2048	1935	...
	Bari Centrale **631** d.	...	...	...	1412	...	...	...	...	...	...	...	1716	...	1625	...	1709	...	...	1900	...	...	...	|	|	...
	Foggia 631 d.	...	...	...	1523	...	...	...	...	...	...	...	1827	...	1810	...	1833	...	...	2011	...	...	...	n	n	...
	Benevento d.	...	...	...	1627	...	...	...	...	...	...	...	|	...	1938	...	2001	...	...	2127	...	...	...	|	|	...
	Napoli Centrale d.	1535	1547	...	|	...	...	1730	1749	...	1845	1943	|	...	|	...	|	...	...	|	2150	...	...	|	|	...
	Caserta d.	1614	1624	...	1705	...	...	1800	1832	...	1917	2014	2003	...	2030	...	2050	...	...	2205	2224u	0158	0347	0426	0426	0448
	Vairano-Caianello d.	1658	1709	...	|	...	...	1841	1917	...	|	2042	|	...	2056	...	|	...	...	|	|	|	|	|	|	|
0	Isernia d.	|	|	...	|	1724	1726	1922	|	1943	|	2124	|	...	|	2041	|	2146	2148	|	|	|	|	|	|	|
	Carpinone d.	|	|	...	|	|	|	1933r	|	1954	|	2135r	|	...	|	|	|	|	|	|	|	|	|	|	|	|
	Campobasso d.	|	|	...	|	|	|	2028r	|	2046r	|	2220r	|	...	|	|	|	2240	2245	|	|	|	|	|	|	|
	Pescolanciano-Chiauci d.	|	|	...	|	|	|	...	|	...	|	...	|	...	|	|	|	...	...	|	|	|	|	|	|	|
	Castel di Sangro d.	|	|	...	|	|	|	...	|	...	|	...	|	...	|	|	|	...	...	|	|	|	|	|	|	|
	Sulmona 624 d.	|	|	...	|	|	|	...	|	...	|	...	|	...	|	|	|	...	...	|	|	|	|	|	|	|
60	Cassino a.	1734	1743	...	|	1805	1804	...	1950	...	2013	...	|	...	2118	2125	|	...	...	|	|	|	|	|	|	|
198	**Roma Termini** a.	...	...	...	1815	1925	1928	...	...	...	2152t	...	2115	...	2244	2250	2258	...	...	2315	0038t	0417t	0617	0635	0635	0708

C – (12) Roma - Isernia - Campobasso and v.v.
R – ⑦ (also Apr. 5, Nov. 1; not Apr. 4, Oct. 31): (12) and 🍷 Taranto - Roma.
T – ⑤ (also Dec. 24, 31; not Dec. 25, Jan. 1: (12) and 🍷 Roma - Taranto.
Y – For days of running and composition – see Table **631**.
Z – For days of running and composition – see Table **640**.

k – Not Sept. 13.
m – Not Sept. 12.
n – Via Taranto.
p – Not Aug. 1 - 31.

q – From Sept. 14.
r – From Sept. 13.
t – Roma **Tiburtina**.
u – Stops to pick up only.

v – Not July 31 - Aug. 30.
w – Not Aug. 1 - 30.
x – † Aug. 1 - 30; daily Aug. 31 - Dec. 12.
y – Not † June 28 - Aug. 30.

SARDINIA 629

Some trains 2nd class only

km		†S	⚒S	⚒	†	⚒	†	†		⚒		⚒	⚒	†P	⚒P	⚒		†S	⚒S		†	⚒	⚒C	†		⚒	⚒		Ⓐ		
0	Cagliari d.	0630	0640	0700	0901	1000	1010	1140	...	1200	...	1330	1400	1444	1453	1530	...	1636	1640	...	1654	1700	1740	1754	...	1830	1900	1930	2020	2037	...
17	Decimomannu d.	0641	0651	0711	0915	1010	1027	1153	...	1215	...	1350	1417	1456	1507	1544	...	|	|	...	1711	1713	1754	1806	...	1844	1914	1949	|	2049	...
95	Oristano d.	0740	0754	0819	1040	1115	1139	1306	...	1314	1320	1514	1535	1607	1607	1642	...	1736	1736	...	1824	1825	1854	1916	...	2000	2030	2103	2120	2201	...
154	Macomer d.	0826	0845	...	1146	1209z	...	...	...	...	1417	...	...	1705	1705	...	...	1823	1820	...	1917	1926	1946	...	...	...	...	...	...	...	...
214	Ozieri-Chilivani a.	0919	0926	...	...	...	...	...	...	...	1507	...	...	1753	1753	...	...	1906	...	...	...	...	2035	...	...	...	...	...	...	...	...

km			⚒	†	†	y	†S	⚒S	†	⚒		P	†S	⚒
0	Ozieri-Chilivani d.	...	0711	...	0738	0853	0925	0934	1029	1043	1521	1758	1915	2040
47	Sassari d.	0700	0759	0801	0827	0935	1006	1013	1111	1125	1605	1843	2003	2123
66	Porto Torres d.	0718	0814	0819	...	...	...	...	...	...	1623d	1900	...	...
67	Porto Torres M a.	0720	0816	0821	...	...	...	...	...	...	1625d	1904	...	...

	†S		†	⚒	†P	⚒P	⚒	S	⚒	⚒P	†S		†y
Porto Torres M d.	...	0730	...	...	0920	0926	...	...	1647d	1820	...	1915	...
Porto Torres d.	...	0733	...	...	0923	0929	...	...	1650d	1823	...	1919	...
Sassari d.	0654	0748	0800	0803	0940	0947	1330	1430	1708	1844	1847	1935	1940
Ozieri-Chilivani a.	0734	...	0841	0844	1027	1034	1411	1512	1749	1931	1935	...	2027

km		⚒	⚒	†	⚒	†	⚒		⚒	⚒				C
0	Ozieri-Chilivani d.	...	0640	0745	0851	0924	0937	...	...	1413	1518	1800	1913	2037
71	Olbia d.	0648	0747	0853	0951	1030	1043	1310	1415	1521	1617	1909	2011	2141
92	Golfo Aranci a.	0711	...	...	...	...	...	1334	1440	...	*1648*	...	2037	...

	†	†C	⚒C	⚒	†	⚒		⚒					
Golfo Aranci d.	...	...	0724	...	...	...	1340	1525	...	1747	...	2044	...
Olbia d.	0635	0744	0749	0822	0920	0928	1403	1550	1647	1811	1925	2104	...
Ozieri-Chilivani a.	0736	0845	0848	0929	1022	1036	*1510*	...	1751	*1936*	2032	...	...

km		⚒	⚒	†	⚒	⚒	⚒	†	⚒S		†S	†C	⚒C		†P	⚒P		⚒z	†	⚒	†	⚒	S		⚒	⚒	†	⚒		⚒P	†S
0	Ozieri-Chilivani d.	...	...	...	...	...	...	...	...	...	0741	0847	0850	...	1034	1041	...	...	...	...	...	...	1517	...	...	...	...	...	...	1941	1942
60	Macomer d.	...	...	...	...	...	0655	...	0808	...	0827	0933	0946	...	1120	1127	...	...	...	...	1427	...	1607	...	1724	...	...	...	...	2027	2028
120	Oristano d.	0450	0530	0542	0600	0642	0753	0753	0852	...	0913	1022	1035	...	1208	1212	...	1413	1445	1449	1522	1610	1657	...	1826	1914	1948	2032	...	2123	2118
197	Decimomannu d.	0549	0643	0648	0714	|	0850	0854	|	...	1003	1117	1131	...	1312	1308	...	1509	1550	1555	1636	1725	1757	...	1948	2018	2055	2153	...	2214	2222
214	Cagliari a.	0607	0704	0705	0728	0746	0906	0910	0946	...	1018	1132	1145	...	1329	1323	...	1524	1611	1609	1658	1738	1812	...	2001	2033	2116	2206	...	2230	2237

km		⚒								x					x		x					†							
0	Cagliari d.	0520	0543	...	0620	0644	...	0748	0848	0920	1120	1220	1340	1420	...	1520	...	1720	1820	1920	2047	0728	1128	1435	1640	1723	1838	1952	2047
17	Decimomannu d.	0534	0557	...	0634	0704	...	0808	0906	0935	1133	1234	1355	1440	...	1533	...	1740	1840	1940	2105	0747	1147	1452	1658	1741	1856	2011	2105
46	Villamassargia ⊡ a.	|	0631	0641	0705	0735	0741	0835	0933	0959	1156	1259	1421	1505	1510	1558	1604	1805	1905	2005	2128	0809	1209	1516	1720	1810	1919	2034	2128
	Carbonia Stato a.	0605	|	0655	|	|	0755	|	|	1015	|	|	|	1524	|	1614	|	1824	|	|	|	|	|	|	|	|	|	|	|
55	Iglesias a.	...	0649	...	0719	0749	...	0845	0941	...	1205	1315	1435	...	1517	...	1613	...	1917	2017	2138	0819	1219	1526	1730	1820	1929	2044	2138

km		⚒										z					x		x			†							
	Iglesias d.	...	0630	0700	...	0730	0800	...	0900	...	1030	...	1254	1347	1454	...	1654	...	1854	...	1954	0620	0830	1339	1545	1740	1845	1941	2054
0	Carbonia Stato d.	0620	|	|	0718	|	|	0828	|	1021	|	1243	|	|	|	1540	|	1648	|	1848	|	|	|	|	|	|	|	|	|
22	Villamassargia ⊡ d.	0634	0639	0709	0733	0739	0809	0842	0909	1035	1040	1257	1302	1356	1507	1601	1702	1707	1902	1907	2007	0628	0838	1347	1553	1748	1853	1948	2103
	Decimomannu d.	...	0703	0736	...	0803	0837	0901	0936	...	1107	...	1325	1428	1534	1625	...	1729	...	1927	2032	0652	0900	1410	1616	1811	1922	2012	2132
	Cagliari a.	...	0724	0754	...	0824	0857	0916	0956	...	1126	...	1338	1443	1547	1646	...	1747	...	1943	2045	0709	0919	1428	1634	1829	1940	2032	2152

C – Cagliari - Olbia / Golfo Aranci and v.v.
P – Cagliari - Porto Torres and v.v.
S – Cagliari - Sassari and v.v.
d – ⚒ only.
x – From Sept. 1.
y – From Sept. 7.

z – From Sept. 14.
⊡ – Full name is Villamassargia-Domusnovas.

Narrow gauge services on Sardinia are operated by Ferrovie della Sardegna (FdS), Via Cugia 1, 09129 Cagliari. ✆ +39 070 342341. Cagliari - Sorgono (166km), Macomer - Bosa Marina (45km), Mandas - Arbatax (160km), Macomer - Nuoro (63km), Sassari - Alghero San Agostino (35km), Sassari - Palau Marina (150km), Sassari - Sorso (11km). Services operate to differing frequencies; some lines have an occasional tourist service only. Fuller details are shown in our *Tourist Railways* feature annually each July.

630 MILANO - BOLOGNA - RIMINI - ANCONA

km		E 901 ♦	ICN 785 ♦	E 925 ♦	E 907 ♦	2 ⚒	2 †	2 ⚒		ES 9325 🍷 ♦	2 ⚒				ESc 9801 🍷		ESc 9803 🍷	IC 713 🍷	ESc 9859 🍷 z	2 ⑥⑦	Ⓒ	Ⓐ	IC 553 🍷		ESc 9807 🍷	
	Torino Porta Nuova **620** d.	2105	...	...	2250	...	...	...	...	...	...	...	...	...	...	...	...	...	...	...	...	...	...	...	...	...
	Venezia S L **620** d.	|	...	...	|	...	...	...	...	...	...	...	...	...	...	...	...	0715	...	...	...	...	...	...	...	...
0	**Milano Centrale 620** d.	|	2300	...	|	...	...	...	...	...	...	...	...	...	0635	...	0735	|	0600	0730	...	...	0915	...	0935	...
219	**Bologna Centrale 620** a.	0054	0124	...	0234	...	...	...	...	...	...	...	...	...	0842	...	0942	0912	|	1012	...	...	1114	...	1142	...
219	**Bologna Centrale** d.	0059	0130	0139	0239	...	...	...	0444	...	...	0638	0738	...	0850	0838	0950	0920	r	1017	1038	1038	1120	1138	1150	1238
254	Imola d.	|	|	|	|	...	...	...	0512	...	...	0701	0805	...	|	0902	|	|	|	1042	1101	1104	|	1200	|	1301
261	Castelbolognese d.	|	|	|	|	...	...	...	0519	...	...	0708	0812	...	|	0909	|	|	|	|	1108	1121	|	1207	|	1308
269	Faenza d.	|	|	|	|	...	...	...	0526	...	...	0717	0819	...	|	0917	|	0951	|	1052	1115	1136	1151	1215	|	1317
284	Forlì d.	|	|	|	|	...	...	...	0536	...	...	0728	0830	...	0923	0932	|	1001	|	1103	1125	1157	1201	1227	|	1332
302	Cesena d.	|	|	|	|	...	...	...	0551	...	...	0741	0843	...	0935	0945	|	1013	|	1114	1142	1214	1213	1243	|	1345
331	**Rimini ●** d.	0202	0237	0245	|	0550	0600	0620	0620	0647	0717	0807	0909	...	0958	1007	1047	1036	1123	1134	1207	1247	1236	1316	1247	1407
340	Riccione d.	|	|	|	|	0600	0608	0631	...	|	0727	0817	0917	...	|	1017	|	1047	1132	1144	1217	1256	|	1326	|	1417
349	Cattolica d.	|	|	|	|	0610	0615	0641	...	|	0737	0826	0924	...	|	1026	|	1056	1138	1151	1226	1306	|	1336	|	1427
364	Pesaro d.	|	|	|	|	0621	0626	0651	...	0707	0749	0838	0935	...	1020	1038	1107	1110	1150	1203	1238	1319	1302	1347	1307	1438
376	Fano d.	|	|	|	|	0629	0634	0659	...	|	0757	0846	0943	...	|	1046	|	|	1158	|	1246	1327	|	1355	|	1446
398	Senigallia d.	|	|	|	|	0643	0648	0714	...	|	0811	0901	0958	...	|	1101	|	1128	1210	1223	1301	1341	|	1408	|	1501
415	Falconara Marittima **625** d.	|	|	|	|	0659	0702	0732	...	0732	0830	0911	1008	...	|	1111	|	|	1221	|	1311	1357	|	1422	|	1511
423	**Ancona 625** a.	0257	0333	0341	0440	0712	0717	0749	...	...	0843	0924	1024	...	1055	1124	1138	1147	1231	1243	1324	1410	1334	1436	1338	1524
	Ancona Marittima **625** a.	|	|	|	|	0721	...	0758	...	...	0852	...	...	...	...	...	|	|	...	|	...	...	|	...	|	...
	Pescara Centrale **631** a.	0422	0459	0523	0624	...	...	...	...	...	...	...	...	...	...	...	1249	1325	...	1436	...	...	1509	...	1449	...
	Bari Centrale **631** a.	0749	0826	0915	1040	...	...	...	...	...	...	...	...	...	...	...	1535	1640	...	...	...	...	1841	...	1735	...
	Lecce **631** a.	0955	...	1118	...	...	...	...	...	...	...	...	...	...	...	...	1704	...	...	...	...	...	...	...	1904	...

	IC 717 🍷 ♦	2 ⚒	ESc 9811 🍷			ESc 9813 🍷	ES 9335 🍷 ♦		ESc 9815 🍷 T			ESc 9817 🍷	IC 715 🍷		ESc 9819 🍷		ESc 9821 🍷		ESc 9823 🍷		ESc 9825 🍷		IC 549	E 923 ♦	ICN 781 ♦	ICN 779 ♦
Torino Porta Nuova **620** d.	...	...	...	...	...	...	...	...	...	...	...	...	...	...	...	...	...	...	...	...	...	...	...	...	...	...
Venezia S L **620** d.	...	...	...	...	...	...	...	...	...	...	...	...	1527	...	...	...	...	...	...	...	...	...	...	...	...	2211v
Milano Centrale 620 d.	...	...	1135	...	...	1235	...	...	1335	...	...	1435	|	...	1535	...	1635	...	1735	...	1835	...	2005	2040	2100	|
Bologna Centrale 620 a.	...	...	1342	...	...	1442	...	...	1542	...	...	1642	1712	...	1742	...	1842	...	1942	...	2042	...	2218	2314	2352	|
Bologna Centrale d.	1320	...	1350	1338	1438	1450	...	1538	1550	...	1638	1650	1720	1738	1750	1838	1850	...	1950	2038	2050	2138	2222	2319	2357	r
Imola d.	|	...	|	1401	1501	|	...	1603	|	...	1659	|	|	1805	|	1903	|	...	|	2101	|	2202	|	|	|	|
Castelbolognese d.	|	...	|	1408	1508	|	...	1610	|	...	1706	|	|	1812	|	1910	|	...	|	2108	|	2209	|	|	|	|
Faenza d.	1351	...	|	1417	1517	|	...	1619	|	...	1717	|	1751	1820	|	1917	|	...	|	2117	|	2217	2251	|	|	|
Forlì d.	1401	...	|	1428	1532	1523	...	1630	|	...	1732	|	1801	1831	|	1928	1923	...	2023	2128	2123	2229	2301	|	0034	|
Cesena d.	1413	...	|	1441	1545	1535	...	1642	|	...	1745	|	1813	1845	|	1941	1935	...	2035	2141	2135	2246	2313	|	|	|
Rimini ● d.	1436	1443	1447	1507	1607	1558	1736	1713	1647	...	1807	1747	1836	1911	1847	2007	1958	...	2058	2207	2158	2319	2336	0030	0104	0113
Riccione d.	1447	1455	|	1516	1617	|	1744	1724	|	...	1816	|	|	1920	|	2017	|	...	|	2217	|	...	...	0041	|	|
Cattolica d.	1456	1504	|	1523	1626	1608	1752	1734	|	...	1826	|	1850	1930	|	2026	|	...	|	2226	|	...	...	|	|	|
Pesaro d.	1510	1516	1507	1534	1638	1620	1802	1746	1707	...	1838	1807	1903	1942	1907	2038	2020	...	2120	2238	2220	...	...	0101	|	|
Fano d.	|	1524	|	1542	1646	|	1810	...	|	...	1846	|	1912	1950	|	2046	|	...	|	2246	|	...	...	|	|	|
Senigallia d.	1528	1539	|	1557	1701	|	1822	...	|	...	1901	|	|	2005	|	2101	|	...	|	2301	|	...	...	|	|	|
Falconara Marittima **625** d.	|	1551	|	1607	1711	|	|	...	|	...	1914	|	1935	2023	|	2111	|	...	|	2311	|	...	...	|	|	|
Ancona 625 a.	1547	1605	1538	1619	1724	1655	1843	...	1738	...	1924	1839	1947	2037	1938	2124	2055	...	2155	2324	2255	...	...	0135	0202	0209
Ancona Marittima **625** a.	|	1614a	|	...	...	...	...	...	|	...	...	|	|	...	|	...	|	...	|	...	...	...	...	|	|	|
Pescara Centrale **631** a.	1725	...	1649	...	...	...		...	1849	...	...	1949	2125	...	2049	...	2220	...	2330	...	...	...	...	0256	0329	0338
Bari Centrale **631** a.	2047	...	1935	...		...	...	...	2135	...	...	2235	...	...	2335	...	...		...	...	...	...	...	0618	0645	0705
Lecce **631** a.	2225	...	2104	...	...	...	...	...	...	...	...	...	...	...	...	...	...	...	...	...	...	...	...	0810	0830	0902

	E 900 ♦	E 924 ♦	ICN 780 ♦	ICN 776 ♦	ICN 784 ♦	E 906 ♦	E 926 ♦	IC 550			ESc 9806 🍷			Ⓐ	Ⓒ	ESc 9810 🍷		IC 714 🍷		ES 9322 🍷 ♦	ESc 9814 🍷 T		ESc 9816 🍷		ESc 9818 🍷	
Lecce **631** d.	...	1805	1907	1927	...	2125	2205	...	...	...	...	...	...	...	...	...	...	...	...	...	...	...	0700	...	...	...
Bari Centrale **631** d.	1955	2022	2100	2124	2259	2338	2359	...	...	...	...	...	...	...	...	...	...	0510	...	...	0729	...	0829	...	...	...
Pescara Centrale **631** d.	2350	0001	0029	0100	0204	0241	0321	...	...	...	...	...	...	...	...	0740	...	0820	...	...	1014	...	1114	...	...	...
Ancona Marittima **625** d.	|	|	|	|	|	|	|	...	...	...	...	...	...	...	...	|	...	|	...	...	|	...	|	...	...	...
Ancona 625 d.	0124	0133	0158	0233	0330	0406	0445	...	0545	0635	0710	0740	...	0800	0835	0910	...	1015	1035	1053	1127	1135	1227	1246	1310	...
Falconara Marittima **625** d.	|	|	|	|	|	|	|	...	0555	0646	|	0751	...	0811	0845	|	...	|	1043	|	|	1145	|	1257	|	...
Senigallia d.	|	|	|	|	|	|	|	...	0607	0700	|	0805	...	0821	0855	|	...	|	1053	1108	|	1159	|	1307	|	...
Fano d.	|	|	|	|	|	|	|	...	0621	0714	|	0819	...	0835	0909	|	...	1042	1107	1120	|	1213	|	1321	|	...
Pesaro d.	|	|	|	|	|	|	|	...	0631	0724	0741	0828	...	0843	0918	0941	...	1052	1116	1129	|	1223	1256	1330	1341	...
Cattolica d.	|	|	|	|	|	|	|	...	0642	0735	|	0839	...	0854	0929	|	...	1105	1127	1139	|	1234	|	1341	|	...
Riccione d.	|	|	|	|	|	|	|	...	0650	0745	|	0845	...	0904	0939	|	...	|	1136	1147	|	1244	|	1351	|	...
Rimini ● d.	|	0230	0256	0333	0427	0502	0541	0613	0703	0800	0808	0900	...	0930	0953	1008	...	1126	1155	1155	1219	1300	1319	1403	1408	...
Cesena d.	|	|	|	|	0448	|	|	0637	0721	0818	0827	0918	...	0953	1011	1027	...	1145	1213	...	|	1318	|	1421	1427	...
Forlì d.	|	|	|	|	0501	|	|	0649	0734	0831	0839	0931	...	1007	1023	1039	...	1157	1226	...	|	1331	|	1434	1439	...
Faenza d.	|	|	|	|	|	|	|	0700	0744	0842	|	0942	...	1020	1034	|	...	1207	1238	...	|	1342	|	1444	|	...
Castelbolognese d.	|	|	|	|	|	|	|	|	0750	0850	|	0950	...	1032	1041	|	...	|	1250	...	|	1349	|	1450	|	...
Imola d.	|	|	|	|	|	|	|	|	0756	0857	|	0957	...	1051	1055	|	...	|	1257	...	|	1356	|	1456	|	...
Bologna Centrale a.	0320	0330	0408	r	0543	0612	0652	0736	0822	0922	0914	1022	...	1122	1122	1114	...	1246	1322	...	1314	1422	1414	1522	1514	...
Bologna Centrale 620 d.	0325	...	0412	|	0548	0618	0702	0741	...	...	0918	...	...	...	...	1118	...	1256	...	...	1318	...	1418	...	1518	...
Milano Centrale 620 a.	|	...	0705	|	0820	|	0920	1000	...	...	1125	...	...	...	...	1325	...	|	...	...	1530	...	1625	...	1730	...
Venezia S L **620** a.	|	...	...	0643v	...	|	...	...	...	...	...	...	...	...	...	...	...	1449	...	...	...	...	...	...	...	...
Torino Porta Nuova **620** a.	0705	...	...	...	...	1010	...	...	...	...	...	...	...	...	...	...	...	...	...	...	...	...	...	...	...	...

	2 ⚒m	2 ⚒	ESc 9820 🍷	2 Ⓐ		ESc 9822 🍷	2 ⚒	ESc 9824 🍷	IC 568 🍷 ♦	IC 1546 🍷 ⑦n		2 ⑥⑦	IC 718 🍷 ♦	ESc 9826 🍷	2 ⚒	2 Ⓐ	ESc 9828 🍷	IC 716 🍷		ESc 9830 🍷	2 Ⓐm	ESc 9858 🍷 z	2 ⚒	ES 9332 🍷 R		
Lecce **631** d.	...	...	...	...	...	...	...	...	...	0940	...	...	1020	1200	...	...	...	...	...	1400	...	...	...	...	...	...
Bari Centrale **631** d.	...	...	...	...	...	1129	...	...	1113	1120	...	...	1203	1329	...	...	1405	...	...	1529	...	...	...	...	...	...
Pescara Centrale **631** d.	...	...	...	...	...	1414	...	1445	1435	1444	...	1505	1530	1614	...	...	1700	1630	...	1814	...	...	...	...	...	...
Ancona Marittima **625** d.	1314	1334	...	1412	...	|	1545a	|	|	|	...	|	|	|	1713a	1735	|	|	...	|	1917	...	1948	...	...	...
Ancona 625 d.	1323	1343	1410	1421	1435	1527	1554	1610	1620	1627	1635	1658	1708	1727	1722	1744	1813	1810	1835	1927	1926	1847	1957	...	2035	...
Falconara Marittima **625** d.	1334	1355	|	1433	1447	|	1606	|	|	|	1644	1708	|	|	1734	1756	|	1822	1845	|	1938	1857	2006	2025	2046	...
Senigallia d.	1348	1412	|	1450	1457	|	1620	|	|	|	1656	1719	1724	|	1752	1812	|	1833	1859	|	1952	1907	2019	|	2100	...
Fano d.	1403	1427	|	1505	1511	|	1634	|	|	|	1710	1733	|	|	1806	1828	|	|	1913	|	2007	1919	2034	|	2115	...
Pesaro d.	1413	1435	1441	1513	1520	1556	1642	1641	1652	1703	1718	1744	1743	1756	1815	1836	1844	1852	1923	1956	2017	1928	2044	2047	2125	...
Cattolica d.	...	1446	|	1524	1531	|	1653	1651	|	1715	1729	1756	1756	|	...	1848	|	|	1934	|	...	1940	2055	|	2136	...
Riccione d.	...	1456	|	1534	1541	|	1702	1708	|	1724	1740	1806	1807	|	...	1858	|	1910	1943	|	...	1948	2105	|	2145	...
Rimini ● d.	...	1510	1508	1548	1555	1619	1715	|	1726	1734	1755	1832	1826	1819	...	1912	1905	1926	1955	2019	...	2001	2120	2107	2200	...
Cesena d.	...	...	1527	...	1613	|	...	1727	1745	1752	1813	1850	1845	|	...	...	|	1945	2013	|	...	|	...	...	2220	...
Forlì d.	...	...	1539	...	1626	|	...	1739	1757	1805	1826	1904	1857	|	...	...	|	1957	2026	|	...	|	...	...	2233	...
Faenza d.	...	...	|	...	1638	|	...	|	1807	|	1838	1915	1907	|	...	...	|	2007	2043	|	...	|	...	...	2244	...
Castelbolognese d.	...	...	|	...	1650	|	...	|	|	|	1850	|	|	|	...	...	|	|	2051	|	...	r	...	...	2250	...
Imola d.	...	...	|	...	1657	|	...	|	|	|	1856	1928	|	|	...	...	|	|	2057	|	...	|	...	...	2256	...
Bologna Centrale a.	...	...	1614	...	1722	1714	...	1814	1846	|	1922	1958	1946	1914	...	...	2000	2048	2122	2114	...	|	...	...	2322	...
Bologna Centrale 620 d.	...	...	1618	...	...	1722	...	1818	1856	|	...	2003	...	1918	...	...	2006	2106	...	2118	...	|	...	...	...	...
Milano Centrale 620 a.	...	...	1825	...	...	1925	...	2030	2105	2135	...	2310	...	2125	...	...	2230	|	...	2325	...	0025	...	...	...	...
Venezia S L **620** a.	...	...	...	...	...	...	...	...	...	...	...	...	...	...	...	...	...	2250	...	...	...	...	...	...	...	...
Torino Porta Nuova **620** a.	...	...	...	...	...	...	...	...	...	...	...	...	...	...	...	...	...	...	...	...	...	...	...	...	...	...

FOR NOTES SEE OPPOSITE PAGE

ANCONA - BARI - LECCE 631

km				*E*	*ICN*	*ICN*	*E*	*ICN*	*E*		*E*	*E*	*ICN*	*E*		*E*		*ES*				*IC*	*ES*	*ESc*		
				923	**789**	**781**	**951**	**779**	**35451**		**903**	**901**	**785**	**925**		**907**		**9351**				**677**	**9353**	**9803**		
		2	2							2					2		2	🍷	2	2	2	🍷	🍷	🍷	2	2
		⚒		♦	♦	♦	♦	♦	♦	⚒	A	♦	♦	♦	⚒	♦	⚒m		⚒	⚒					⚒	⚒
	Torino Porta Nuova **620** . d.	...	...	...	...	...	...	...	...	...	2105	2105	...	...	...	2250	...	...	...	...	...	...	...	...	...	...
	Venezia S L **620** d.	...	...	...	...	...	...	2211v	...	...	|	|	...	...	...	|	...	...	...	...	...	...	...	...	...	...
	Milano C **620/30** d.	...	...	2040	...	2100	...	|	...	...	|	|	2300	...	...	|	...	...	...	...	...	...	...	0735	...	...
	Bologna C **620/30** d.	...	...	2319	...	2357	...	r	...	...	0059	0059	0130	0139	...	0239	...	...	...	...	...	...	...	0950	...	...
0	**Ancona 625/30** d.	...	...	0137	...	0205	...	0212	...	...	0259	0259	0336	0343	...	0443	...	...	...	0625	0730	...	...	1141	...	...
43	Civitanova-Montegranaro d.	...	...	|	...	|	...	|	...	...	|	|	|	|	...	0512	...	...	...	0704	0805	...	...	|	...	...
85	San Benedetto del Tronto d.	...	...	|	...	|	...	|	...	...	|	|	|	0437	...	0538	...	...	...	0738	0839	...	...	|	...	...
146	**Pescara Centrale** a.	...	...	0256	...	0329	...	0338	...	...	0422	0422	0459	0523	...	0624	...	...	...	0835	0931	...	...	1249	...	...
146	**Pescara Centrale** d.	...	...	0300	...	0332	...	0341	...	...	0425	0425	0502	0526	...	0627	...	...	...	▬	▬	...	...	1252	...	...
236	Termoli d.	...	...	0403	...	|	...	0445	...	...	0530	0530	0608	0636	...	0744	...	...	...	...	...	...	...	1343	...	...
	Roma Termini **626** d.	...	...	|	2358	|	...	|	...	...	|	|	|	|	...	|	...	0845	...	...	...	0820	1115	|	...	...
323	**Foggia 626** a.	...	...	0450	0453	0524	...	0540	...	...	0625	0625	0700	0743	...	0837	...	1153	...	...	...	1248	1418	1429	...	...
323	**Foggia** d.	...	...	0453	0508	0530	...	0544	...	...	0633	0633	0704	0747	...	0843	...	1202	...	...	...	1303	1427	1432	...	...
391	Barletta d.	...	...	0533	0544	0606	...	0621	...	...	0707	0707	0745	0821	...	0938	...	1231	...	2	2	1335	1458	1504	...	...
446	**Bari Centrale** a.	...	...	0618	0635	0645	...	0705	...	...	0749	0749	0826	0915	...	1040	...	1302	...	⚒	⚒	1420	1530	1535	...	...
446	**Bari Centrale** ▲ d.	0505	0537	0623	0639	0649	...	0709	...	0714	0804	0805	0849	0930	1015	...	1148	1306	1249	1317	1405	...	...	1539	1543	1606
	Gioia del Colle d.	|	|	|	|	|	...	|	...	0803	0835	|	0933	|	1058	...	|	|	|	1403	|	...	...	|	|	1647
	Taranto 638 ▲ a.	|	|	|	|	|	0657	|	0819	0845	0914	|	1009	|	1141	...	|	|	|	1454	|	...	...	|	|	1731
	Crotone **635** a.	|	|	|	|	|	|	|	|	...	1245	|	1400	|	...	...	|	|	|	...	|	...	...	|	|	...
487	Monopoli d.	0537	0609	0652	0702	0715	|	0743	|	...	...	0837	...	0959	...	...	1221	1330	1323	...	1430	...	...	|	1608	...
501	Fasano d.	0545	0617	0702	0713	0725	|	0754	|	...	...	0848	...	1010	...	...	1231	1339	1331	...	1440	...	...	|	1616	...
521	Ostuni d.	0559	0631	0715	0728	0738	|	0808	|	...	...	0902	...	1023	...	...	1247	1351	1342	...	1451	...	...	|	1630	...
557	**Brindisi** ▲ d.	0626	0658	0740	0753	0804	0814	0832	0936	...	...	0926	...	1047	...	...	1333	1410	1407	...	1516	...	...	1637	1656	...
596	**Lecce** a.	0658	0730	0810	0820	0830	0845	0902	1007	...	...	0955	...	1118	...	...	1403	1434	1440	...	1547	...	...	1704	1727	...

	IC				*ESc*		*IC*	*ES*			*IC*		*ESc*	*ES*		*ESc*	*ES*	*ESc*	*E*	*ESc*		*IC*	*ES*	*ESc*	*ESc*	
	713				**9807**		**553**	**9355**			**717**		**9811**	**9357**		**9815**	**9395**	**9817**	**981**	**9819**		**715**	**9359**	**9821**	**9823**	
	🍷	2	2	2	🍷	2	🍷	🍷	2	2	🍷	2	🍷	🍷		🍷	🍷	🍷		🍷	2		🍷	🍷	🍷	
		⑥⑦	⚒								♦	⚒					⑤q		♦							
Torino Porta Nuova **620** d.	...	...	...	...	...	...	...	...	...	...	...	...	...	...	...	...	...	...	...	...	...	...	...	...	...	...
Venezia S L **620** d.	0715	...	...	...	...	...	...	...	...	...	...	...	...	...	...	...	...	...	...	...	...	1527	...	...	...	...
Milano C **620/30** d.	|	0730	...	...	0935	...	0915	...	...	...	...	...	1135	...	...	1335	...	1435	...	1535	...	|	...	1635	1735	...
Bologna C **620/30** d.	0920	1017	...	...	1150	...	1120	...	...	...	1320	...	1350	...	...	1550	...	1650	...	1750	...	1720	...	1850	1950	...
Ancona 625/30 d.	1150	1246	...	...	1341	...	1337	...	...	...	1550	...	1541	...	...	1741	...	1841	...	1941	...	1950	...	2058	2158	...
Civitanova-Montegranaro d.	1216	1320	...	...	|	...	1406	...	...	...	1616	...	|	...	...	|	...	|	...	|	...	2020	...	|	|	...
San Benedetto del Tronto d.	1248	1352	...	...	|	...	1429	...	...	...	1648	...	|	...	...	|	...	|	...	|	...	2046	...	2139	2239	...
Pescara Centrale a.	1325	1436	...	...	1449	...	1509	...	...	...	1725	...	1649	...	...	1849	...	1949	...	2049	...	2125	...	2220	2330	...
Pescara Centrale d.	1328	...	...	...	1452	...	1512	...	...	...	1728	...	1652	...	...	1852	...	1952	...	2052	...	▬	...	...	...	...
Termoli d.	1428	...	...	...	1543	...	1620	...	...	...	1828	...	1743	...	...	1943	...	2043	...	2143	...	...	...	...	...	...
Roma Termini **626** d.	|	...	...	...	|	...	|	1445	...	...	|	...	|	1645	...	|	1638	|	...	|	...	...	1945	...	...	...
Foggia 626 a.	1528	...	...	...	1628	...	1723	1733	...	...	1921	...	1828	1948	...	2028	2040	2128	...	2228	...	...	2233	...	...	...
Foggia d.	1531	...	...	...	1631	...	1727	1742	...	...	1924	...	1831	1957	...	2031	2052	2131	...	2231	...	...	2242	...	...	...
Barletta d.	1603	...	...	...	1702	...	1801	|	...	...	1959	...	1903	2027	...	2102	2123	2203	...	2302	...	...	|	...	...	...
Bari Centrale a.	1640	...	...	...	1735	...	1841	1844	...	...	2047	...	1935	2110	...	2135	2157	2235	...	2335	...	2	2344	...	...	...
Bari Centrale ▲ d.	...	...	1718	1738	1739	1824	1907	1848	1935	1944	2051	2058	1939	2114	...	2149	2211	...	2256	...	2310	2320	...	...	...	...
Gioia del Colle d.	...	...	1754	|	|	1906	1939	|	|	2026	|	|	|	|	...	2222	2245	...	2345	...	|	0008	...	...	...	...
Taranto 638 ▲ a.	...	...	1834	|	|	1953	2014	|	|	2112	|	|	|	|	...	2257	2320	...	0029	...	|	0051	...	...	...	...
Crotone **635** a.	...	...	...	|	|	...	2359	|	|	...	|	|	|	|	...	...	...	...	...	...	|	...	...	...	...	...
Monopoli d.	...	...	...	1812	|	...	...	|	2011	...	2114	2132	|	|	...	...	...	...	...	...	2342	...	...	...	...	...
Fasano d.	...	...	...	1822	|	...	...	|	2019	...	2124	2141	|	|	...	...	...	...	...	...	2350	...	...	...	...	...
Ostuni d.	...	...	...	1835	|	...	...	|	2033	...	2137	2155	|	|	...	...	...	...	...	...	0004	...	...	...	...	...
Brindisi ▲ d.	...	...	...	1924k	1840	...	...	1944	2100	...	2200	2219	2037	2208	...	...	...	...	...	...	0028	...	...	...	...	...
Lecce a.	...	...	...	1955	1904	...	...	2006	...	...	2225	2251	2104	2233	...	...	...	...	...	...	0100	...	...	...	...	...

♦ – **NOTES FOR TABLES 630/1** (LISTED BY TRAIN NUMBER)

568 – MURGE – [12] and 🍷 Crotone (**566**) - Metaponto (**567**) - Taranto - Milano.
717/8 – ADIGE – [12] Bolzano - Verona - Bologna - Lecce and v.v. Train numbers **35417/8** Aug. 3-23.
776 – TERGESTE – ▬ 2 cl. (4 berth) and [12] Lecce - Venezia Mestre (**777**) - Trieste; 🛏 1,2 cl. (Excelsior), 🛏 1,2 cl. (T2), 🛏 1,2 cl. and [12] Lecce - Venezia Mestre (**1598**) - Venezia Santa Lucia. Train number **35476** Aug. 31 - Sept. 19.
779 – TERGESTE – ▬ 2 cl. (4 berth) and [12] Trieste (**778**) - Venezia Mestre - Lecce; 🛏 1,2 cl. (Excelsior), 🛏 1,2 cl. (T2), 🛏 1,2 cl. and [12] Venezia Santa Lucia (**1599**) - Venezia Mestre - Lecce. Train number **35479** Aug. 31 - Sept. 19.
780/1 – FRECCIA SALENTINA – 🛏 1,2 cl. (Excelsior), 🛏 1,2 cl. (T2), 🛏 1,2 cl., ▬ 2 cl. (4 berth) and [12] Lecce - Milano and v.v.
784 – FRECCIA DEL LEVANTE – ▬ 2 cl. and [12] Crotone (**782**) - Metaponto (**783**) - Taranto - Milano; 🛏 1,2 cl. (Excelsior), 🛏 1,2 cl. (T2), 🛏 1,2 cl., ▬ 2 cl. and [12] Taranto - Milano.
785 – FRECCIA DEL LEVANTE – ▬ 2 cl. and [12] Milano - Taranto (**786**) - Metaponto (**787**) - Crotone; 🛏 1,2 cl. (Excelsior), 🛏 1,2 cl. (T2), 🛏 1,2 cl., ▬ 2 cl. and [12] Milano - Taranto.
789 – TAVOLIERE – 🛏 1,2 cl., ▬ 2 cl. (4 berth) and [12] Roma - Lecce.
900 – Daily June 14 - Sept. 13; ⑦ Sept. 20 - Nov. 29; also Dec. 8 (from Bari): ▬ 2 cl. and [2] Bari - Torino.
901 – FRECCIA ADRIATICA – 🛏 1,2 cl. (T2), 🛏 1,2 cl., ▬ 2 cl. and [2] Torino - Lecce; ▬ 2 cl. and [2] Torino (**901**) - Bari (**903**) - Taranto (**904**) - Metaponto (**905**) - Catanzaro Lido.
906 – FRECCIA ADRIATICA – 🛏 1,2 cl. (T2), 🛏 1,2 cl., ▬ 2 cl. and [2] Lecce - Torino; ▬ 2 cl. and [2] Catanzaro Lido (**908**) - Metaponto (**909**) - Taranto (**910**) - Bari (**906**) - Torino.
907 – Daily June 14 - Sept. 12; ⑤ Sept. 18 - Dec. 11 (from Torino): ▬ 2 cl. and [2] Torino - Bari.
923 – 🛏 1,2 cl. (T2), ▬ 2 cl. (4/6 berth) and [2] Milano - Lecce.
924 – ①③④⑤⑥⑦ (also Dec. 8; not Dec. 9): 🛏 1,2 cl. (Excelsior), 🛏 1,2 cl., ▬ 2 cl. (4/6 berth) and [2] Lecce - Bologna - Bolzano.
925 – ①②④⑤⑥⑦; also Dec. 9, not Dec. 10 (from Bolzano): 🛏 1,2 cl. (Excelsior), 🛏 1,2 cl., ▬ 2 cl. (4/6 berth) and [2] Bolzano - Bologna - Lecce.
926 – 🛏 1,2 cl. (T2), ▬ 2 cl. (4/6 berth) and [2] Lecce - Milano.
951 – Not July 1 - Aug. 30 (from Roma): [2] Roma - Lecce; [2] Roma - Metaponto (**953**) - Catanzaro Lido.
981 – Ⓐ: [2] Bari - Taranto (**982**) - Metaponto (**983**) - Villa S G - Reggio di Calabria.
9322/35 – June 13 - Sept. 4: [12] and 🍷 Roma - Ancona - Ravenna and v.v.
9325 – [12] and 🍷 Ravenna - Rimini - Roma.
35451 – July 1 - Aug. 30 (from Roma): [2] Roma - Lecce; [2] Roma - Sibari (**35455**) - Catanzaro Lido.

A – FRECCIA ADRIATICA – ▬ 2 cl. and [2] Torino (**901**) - Bari - Taranto (**904**) - Metaponto (**905**) - Catanzaro Lido.
R – [12] and 🍷 Roma - Rimini and v.v.
T – From/to Taranto.

a – Ⓐ only.
f – Until Sept. 13.
k – Arrive 1903.
m – Not July 26 - Aug. 23.
n – Also Dec. 8; not Dec. 6.
p – Not Aug. 15.
q – Also Dec. 24, 31; not Dec. 25, Jan. 1.
r – Via Ravenna.
v – Venezia **Mestre**.
z – ⑥⑦ June 13 - Sept. 12.

▲ – For additional services Taranto - Brindisi/Bari and v.v. – see below.
● – For 🚌 service Rimini - San Marino and v.v. – see below.

▲ – **LOCAL SERVICES TARANTO - BRINDISI/BARI and v.v.** 2nd class only

TARANTO - BRINDISI and v.v.: 70 km, journey 61–84 minutes.

From **Taranto**: 0516⚒, 0536⚒, 0624, 0851⚒**m**, 1205⚒, 1247⚒**m**, 1355⚒**m**, 1437⚒, 1616⚒**m**, 1817, 1906.

From **Brindisi**: 0541⚒, 0704⚒**m**, 0813⚒, 1154⚒**m**, 1324, 1409⚒**m**, 1434⚒, 1630, 1728⚒**m**, 1803⚒, 2025.

TARANTO - BARI and v.v. (additional services): 115 km, journey 83–110 minutes.

From **Taranto**: 0440⚒, 0500†, 0547⚒, 0634, 0708⚒**m**, 0815⚒**m**, 1023†, 1220⚒, 1531⚒, 1907†, 1923⚒.

From **Bari**: 0350, 0556⚒**m**, 0647⚒**m**, 0811†, 1420, 1605†, 1742⚒**m**.

● – 🚌 service available **Rimini - San Marino and v.v.**, 27 km, journey 40–50 minutes. Departures from Rimini (FS railway station). Operator: F.lli Benedettini s.a. ✆ +378 90 67 48.

631 LECCE - BARI - ANCONA

km		ESc	IC	ESc			ES		E		ESc		ES	ESc	ESc	IC	IC		IC			ESc		ES		ESc
		9810	714	9814			9350		990		9816		9352	9824	9822	568	1546		718			9826		9354		9828
		🍷		🍷	2		🍷	2		2	🍷	2	🍷	🍷	🍷	🍷	🍷	2	🍷	2	2	🍷	2	🍷	2	🍷
								⚒	♦	⚒		⚒m					⑦n	⑥⑦	♦	⚒			⚒m		⚒	
	Lecce d.	...	...	...	0456	...	0550	0546	...	0605	0700	0800	...	...	...	...	0940	...	1020	1041	1055	1200	1230	1250	...	...
	Brindisi ▲ d.	...	...	...	0527	...	0615	0623	...	0635	0725	0824	...	...	...	...	1005	...	1047	1110	1129	1224	1302	1313	...	...
	Ostuni d.	...	...	...	0550	...	|	0647	...	0657	|	|	...	...	...	...	1025	...	1107	1132	1156	|	1328	|	...	...
	Fasano d.	...	...	...	0604	...	|	0700	...	0711	|	|	...	...	...	...	1038	...	1120	1145	1229	|	1343	|	...	...
	Monopoli d.	...	...	...	0613	...	|	0709	...	0720	|	0900	...	...	...	...	1048	...	1130	1155	1238	|	1352	|	...	...
	Crotone **635** d.	...	...	...	|	...	|	|	...	|	|	|	...	...	...	...	|	...	|	|	|	|	|	|	...	...
0	**Taranto 638 ▲** d.	...	...	0600	|	...	|	|	0608	|	|	|	...	...	...	0941	|	...	|	|	|	|	|	|	1336	...
62	Gioia del Colle d.	...	...	0634	|	...	|	|	0657	|	|	|	...	...	...	1013	|	...	|	|	|	|	|	|	1419	...
115	**Bari Centrale ▲** a.	...	...	0715	0651	...	0712	0745	0746	0758	0825	0930	...	...	...	1048	1116	...	1159	1227	1313	1325	1430	1408	1502	...
	Bari Centrale d.	...	0510	0729	...	...	0716	...	...	...	0829	...	0950	...	1129	1113	1120	...	1203	...	...	1329	▬	1412	...	1405
	Barletta d.	...	0547	0802	...	...	|	...	...	...	0902	...	1030	...	1202	1149	1200	...	1248	...	...	1402	...	1442	...	1436
	Foggia a.	...	0623	0832	...	...	0818	...	...	...	0932	...	1114	...	1232	1224	1234	...	1328	...	...	1432	...	1514	...	1508
	Foggia 626 d.	...	0627	0835	...	...	0827	...	...	...	0935	...	1123	...	1235	1227	1239	...	1331	...	...	1435	...	1523	...	1511
	Roma Termini **626** a.	...	|	|	...	...	1115	...	...	...	|	...	1415	...	|	|	|	...	|	...	...	|	*IC*	1815	...	|
	Termoli d.	...	0719	0923	...	...	...	...	...	...	1023	...	...	...	1323	1334	1344	...	1426	...	...	1523	**716**	...	...	1609
	Pescara Centrale a.	...	0817	1011	...	...	...	...	...	...	1111	...	...	...	1411	1432	1441	...	1527	...	...	1611		...	...	1657
	Pescara Centrale d.	0740	0820	1014	...	...	...	...	...	...	1114	...	...	1445	1414	1435	1444	1505	1530	...	...	1614	1630	...	...	1700
	San Benedetto del Tronto d.	0818	0900	|	...	...	...	...	...	...	|	...	...	1523	|	1521	1527	1545	1611	...	...	|	1711	...	...	|
	Civitanova-Montegranaro d.	|	0927	|	...	...	...	...	...	...	|	...	...	|	|	1545	1556	1616	1638	...	...	|	1738	...	...	|
	Ancona 625/30 a.	0907	1012	1124	...	...	...	...	...	...	1224	...	...	1607	1524	1617	1624	1655	1705	...	...	1724	1807	...	...	1810
	Bologna C **620/30** a.	1114	1246	1314	...	...	...	...	...	...	1414	...	...	1814	1714	1846	|	1958	1946	...	...	1914	2048	...	...	2000
	Milano C **620/30** a.	1325	|	1530	...	...	...	...	...	...	1625	...	...	2030	1925	2105	2135	2310	...	...	...	2125	|	...	...	2230
	Venezia S L **620** a.	...	1449	...	...	...	...	...	...	...	...	...	...	...	...	...	...	...	...	...	...	...	2250	...	...	...
	Torino Porta Nuova **620** a.	...	...	...	...	...	...	...	...	...	...	...	...	...	...	...	...	...	...	...	...	...	...	...	...	...

	ESc			IC			ES	ES				ES			E	E		ICN	ICN	E	E		ICN	E	E	E
	9830			678			9394	9356				9358			900	924		780	776	35456	956		784	906	908	926
	🍷	2	2	🍷	2	2	🍷	🍷	2	2	2	🍷	2	2			2					2				
			⚒m		⚒m	†	⑦n			⚒m			⚒		♦	♦	⚒	♦	♦	♦	♦		♦	♦	A	♦
Lecce d.	1400	1345	...	...	1430	...	...	...	1530	1645	...	1728	1745	...	...	1805	...	1907	1927	1935	2048	1950	...	2125	...	2205
Brindisi ▲ d.	1425	1418	...	...	1506	...	...	...	1603	1710	...	1751	1815	...	...	1834	...	1932	1956	2009	2123	2033	...	2154	...	2236
Ostuni d.	|	1441	...	...	1528	...	...	...	1627	|	...	1811	1839	...	...	1856	...	1955	2019	|	|	2057	...	2215	...	2258
Fasano d.	|	1455	...	...	1541	...	...	...	1640	|	...	1823	1853	...	...	1910	...	2009	2033	|	|	2111	...	2228	...	2311
Monopoli d.	|	1504	...	...	1551	...	...	...	1649	1746	...	1832	1902	...	...	1922	...	2020	2045	|	|	2125	...	2240	...	2321
Crotone **635** d.	|	|	...	...	|	...	...	...	|	|	...	|	|	...	...	|	...	|	|	|	|	|	1730	|	1802	|
Taranto 638 ▲ d.	|	|	1426	...	|	1522	1550	...	|	|	1648	|	|	1805	...	|	1905	|	|	2113	2236	|	2120	|	2156	|
Gioia del Colle d.	|	|	1510	...	|	1602	1622	...	|	|	1729	|	|	1850	...	|	1948	|	|	...	...	|	2204	|	2237	|
Bari Centrale ▲ a.	1525	1543	1556	...	1630	1647	1700	...	1727	1815	1816	1856	1940	1937	...	1958	2031	2053	2119	...	...	2200	2241	2315	2314	2352
Bari Centrale d.	1529	...	...	1625	...	...	1709	1716	...	...	...	1900	...	...	1955	2022	...	2100	2124	...	...	...	2259	2338	2338	2359
Barletta d.	1602	...	...	1712	...	...	1751	|	...	...	...	1931	...	...	2043	2116	...	2138	2211	...	...	...	2332	0011	0011	0044
Foggia a.	1632	...	...	1752	...	...	1824	1818	...	...	...	2002	...	...	2130	2155	...	2221	2256	...	...	...	0010	0046	0046	0125
Foggia 626 d.	1635	...	...	1810	...	...	1833	1827	...	...	...	2011	...	...	2136	2159	...	2225	2300	...	...	...	0013	0050	0050	0130
Roma Termini **626** a.	|	...	...	2244	...	...	2258	2115	...	...	...	2315	...	...	|	|	...	|	|	...	...	...	|	|	|	|
Termoli d.	1723	...	...	...	...	...	...	...	...	...	...	...	...	...	2238	2255	...	2320	2357	...	...	...	|	|	|	0220
Pescara Centrale a.	1811	...	...	...	...	...	...	...	...	...	...	...	...	...	2347	2359	...	0026	0057	...	...	...	0201	0238	0238	0319
Pescara Centrale d.	1814	...	...	...	...	...	...	...	...	...	...	...	...	...	2350	0001	...	0029	0100	...	...	...	0204	0241	0241	0321
San Benedetto del Tronto d.	|	...	...	...	...	...	...	...	...	...	...	...	...	...	0030	0040	...	|	|	...	...	...	|	|	|	|
Civitanova-Montegranaro d.	|	...	...	...	...	...	...	...	...	...	...	...	...	...	0054	|	...	|	|	...	...	...	|	|	|	|
Ancona a.	1924	...	...	...	...	...	...	...	...	...	...	...	...	...	0122	0130	...	0155	0229	...	...	...	0327	0403	0403	0443
Bologna C **620/30** a.	2114	...	...	...	...	...	...	...	...	...	...	...	...	...	0320	0330	...	0408	r	...	...	...	0543	0612	0612	0652
Milano C **620/30** a.	2325	...	...	...	...	...	...	...	...	...	...	...	...	...	|	...	...	0705	|	...	...	...	0820	|	|	0920
Venezia S L **620** a.	...	...	...	...	...	...	...	...	...	...	...	...	...	...	|	...	...	...	0643v	...	...	...	...	|	|	...
Torino Porta Nuova **620** a.	...	...	...	...	...	...	...	...	...	...	...	...	...	...	0705	...	...	...	...	...	...	...	...	1010	1010	...

♦ – **NOTES** (LISTED BY TRAIN NUMBER)

718 – ADIGE – [12] Lecce - Bologna - Verona - Bolzano. Train number **35418** Aug. 3-23.

776 – TERGESTE – ▬ 2 cl. (4 berth) and [12] Lecce - Venezia Mestre (**777**) - Trieste; 🛏 1,2 cl. (Excelsior), 🛏 1,2 cl. (T2), 🛏 1,2 cl. and [12] Lecce - Venezia Mestre (**1598**) - Venezia Santa Lucia. Train number **35476** Aug. 31 - Sept. 19.

780 – FRECCIA SALENTINA – 🛏 1,2 cl. (Excelsior), 🛏 1,2 cl. (T2), 🛏 1,2 cl., ▬ 2 cl. (4 berth) and [12] Lecce - Milano.

784 – FRECCIA DEL LEVANTE – ▬ 2 cl. and [12] Crotone (**782**) - Metaponto (**783**) - Taranto - Milano; 🛏 1,2 cl. (Excelsior), 🛏 1,2 cl. (T2), 🛏 1,2 cl., ▬ 2 cl. and [12] Taranto - Milano.

788 – TAVOLIERE – 🛏 1,2 cl., ▬ 2 cl. (4 berth) and [12] Lecce - Roma.

900 – Daily June 14 - Sept. 13; ⑦ Sept. 20 - Nov. 29; also Dec. 8 (from Bari): ▬ 2 cl. and [2] Bari - Torino.

906 – FRECCIA ADRIATICA – 🛏 1,2 cl. (T2), 🛏 1,2 cl., ▬ 2 cl. and [2] Lecce - Torino; ▬ 2 cl. and [2] Catanzaro Lido (**908**) - Metaponto (**909**) - Taranto (**910**) - Bari (**906**) - Torino.

924 – ①③④⑤⑥⑦ (also Dec. 8; not Dec. 9): 🛏 1,2 cl. (Excelsior), 🛏 1,2 cl., ▬ 2 cl. (4/6 berth) and [2] Lecce - Bologna - Bolzano.

926 – 🛏 1,2 cl. (T2), ▬ 2 cl. (4/6 berth) and [2] Lecce - Milano.

956 – Not July 1 - Aug. 30: [2] Lecce - Roma; [2] Catanzaro Lido (**954**) - Metaponto - Roma.

990 – Ⓐ (from Reggio): [2] Reggio di Calabria (**986**) - Villa S G - Metaponto (**989**) - Taranto - Bari.

35456 – July 1 - Aug. 30: [2] Lecce - Roma; [2] Catanzaro Lido (**954**) - Sibari - Roma.

A – FRECCIA ADRIATICA – ▬ 2 cl. and [2] Catanzaro Lido - Metaponto (**909**) - Taranto (**910**) - Bari (**906**) - Torino.

m – Not July 26 - Aug. 23.

n – Also Apr. 5, Nov. 1; not Apr. 4, Oct. 31.

r – Via Ravenna.

v – Venezia **Mestre**.

▲ – For additional services Taranto - Brindisi / Bari and v.v. – see page 309.

633 ROMA and LAMEZIA - PAOLA - COSENZA - SIBARI ○

km		2	2	2	2	2	2	2	IC 511/2	2	2
		⚒	©	†v		⚒		⚒	S	Ⓑy	
	Roma Termini **640** d.	...	...	...	...	...	...	...	1420	...	...
	Napoli Centrale **640** d.	...	0648	...	0854	...	1250	...	1648	...	1842
	Lamezia Terme **640** d.	...	|	...	|	...	|	...	|	...	|
0	**Paola 640** ▲ d.	...	1100	...	1300	...	1700	...	2025	...	2251
21	Castiglione-Cosentino ▲ a.	...	1116	...	1318	...	1723	...	2048	...	2308
26	**Cosenza** ▲ a.	...	1125	...	1325	...	1730	...	2054	...	2315
—	**Cosenza** d.	1045	...	1243	...	1417	...	1817	2107	2117	...
0	Castiglione-Cosentino d.	1051	...	1249	...	1423	...	1823	|	2123	...
60	**Sibari** a.	1145	...	1353	...	1522	...	1915	2155	2219	...

	2	2	IC 535/6	2	2	2	2	2	2	2
		⚒	S	©	⚒		Ⓐ	⚒	⚒	
Sibari d.	...	0715	1000	...	1310	...	1505	...	1655	...
Castiglione-Cosentino a.	...	0812	|	...	1401	...	1601	...	1750	...
Cosenza a.	...	0818	1055	...	1407	...	1607	...	1802	...
Cosenza ▲ d.	0530	...	1110	1225	...	1425	...	1622	...	1825
Castiglione-Cosentino ▲ d.	0537	...	1117	1232	...	1434	...	1629	...	1832
Paola 640 ▲ a.	0550	...	1135	1250	...	1450	...	1643	...	1850
Lamezia Terme **640** a.	|	...	|	|	...	|	...	...	...	|
Napoli Centrale **640** a.	1013	...	1512	1715	...	1915	...	...	...	2301
Roma Termini **640** a.	...	...	1733	...	...	...	...	...	...	...

S – SILA – [2] Roma (**507/30**) - Sibari (**513/34**) - Crotone and v.v.

v – Until Sept. 6.

x – Until Sept. 12.

y – Also Aug. 15.

▲ – Additional services PAOLA - COSENZA and v.v. 2nd class only.

From **Paola**: 0535⚒, 0630⚒, 0700⚒, 0727⚒, 0730†, 0752⚒, 0830⚒, 0900⚒, 0935⚒, 0945†, 1136†, 1202⚒, 1230⚒, 1230†x, 1330⚒, 1400⚒, 1430, 1530⚒, 1600⚒, 1730⚒, 1830, 1930⚒, 2050†, 2110⚒, 2200⚒, 2230.

From **Cosenza**: 0555⚒, 0625⚒, 0650, 0725⚒, 0750⚒, 0805†v, 0825⚒, 0855, 1030†, 1125⚒, 1155⚒, 1250, 1325⚒, 1350⚒, 1450⚒, 1525⚒, 1605†, 1622⚒, 1700⚒, 1750, 1850⚒, 1950, 2025, 2125, 2220⚒.

REGGIO DI CALABRIA - SIBARI - TARANTO 635

Most services 2nd class only

km		E 986 ♦	E 951 ♦	⚒	E 35452 ♦	IC 566 ♦	⚒	IC 534 ♦	†	⚒q	⚒	⚒	†	⚒	⚒	⚒	⚒	†	⚒	†	⚒	⚒	⚒	⚒	†	ICN 782 ♦
0	**Reggio di Calabria 640** d.	2340	...	...	...	...	...	...	0630	0637	...	...	0825	0837	...	...	...	1025	1037	...	...	1237	...	...	...	...
30	Melito di Porto Salvo d.	|	...	...	...	...	...	...	0706	0702	...	...	0902	0902	...	...	...	1102	1102	...	...	1302	...	...	...	...
96	Locri d.	|	...	...	...	...	...	...	0812	0810	...	...	1007	1007	...	...	...	1210	1210	...	...	1409	...	...	...	...
101	Siderno d.	|	...	...	...	...	...	...	0818	0818	...	...	1012	1013	...	...	...	1215	1219	...	...	1420	...	...	...	...
112	Roccella Jonica d.	|	...	...	...	...	...	...	0831	0833	...	...	1024	1027	...	...	...	1231	1234	...	...	1434	...	...	...	...
160	Soverato d.	|	...	...	...	...	...	...	0923	0910	...	...	1113	1114	...	...	...	1317	1310	...	...	1506	...	...	...	...
178	Catanzaro Lido a.	|	...	...	...	...	...	...	0940	0925	...	...	1130	1130	...	...	...	1335	1325	...	...	1525	...	...	...	...
	Catanzaro Lido ▲ d.	|	...	...	...	...	0540	...	0950	0930a	...	...	1140	1140	1135	...	1230	1345	1340	1346	1346	▬	1530	...	...	...
	Catanzaro ▲ d.	|	...	...	...	...	|	...	0959	|	...	...	1153	1153	|	...	|	1353	1353	|	|	...	|	...	...	...
	Lamezia Terme ▲ a.	0117	...	...	...	...	|	...	1037	|	...	...	1237	1237	|	...	|	1430	1437	|	|	...	|	...	...	...
238	**Crotone** d.	|	...	...	...	0605	0627	0800	▬	1022a	...	...	...	...	1221	...	1320	...	...	1436	1442	...	1617	...	1650	1730
325	Rossano d.	|	...	...	...	0710	0734	0912	...	1117a	...	...	...	...	1337	...	1438	...	...	1546	1557	...	1733	...	1806	1849
336	Corigliano Calabro d.	|	...	...	...	0721	0744	0927	...	1127a	...	...	...	...	1346	...	1447	...	...	1555	1608	...	1743	...	1815	1901
351	**Sibari** a.	0313	...	...	...	0731	0757	0944	⚒	1139a	...	...	...	...	1356	...	1458	...	...	1605	1620	Ⓐ	1755	...	1825	1915
351	**Sibari** d.	0333	...	0510	0630	0734	...	...	1003	...	1155	1245	...	...	...	1400	...	...	...	...	...	1645	1758	1830	...	1918
366	Trebisacce d.	|	...	0525	0639	0749	...	...	1019	...	1216	1258	...	...	...	1415	...	...	...	...	...	1701	1810	1846	...	1933
430	Metaponto **638** d.	0455	0609	0630	0739	0847	...	...	1130	...	1321	1359	...	...	...	1520	...	...	...	...	...	1804	1918	1945	...	2023
473	**Taranto 631/8** a.	0550	0650	0716	0812	0924	...	...	*1226*	...	1402	1446	...	...	...	1600	...	...	...	...	...	1843	2006	2024	...	2100
	Bari Centrale **631** a.	0746	...	...	...	1048	...	...	...	...	...	...	...	...	...	...	...	...	...	...	...	...	...	...	...	2241

	E 908 ♦	⚒	E 954 ♦	ICN 766 ♦	†	⚒	⚒	E 35454 ♦	ICN 750 ♦	⚒	E 890 ♦
Reggio di Calabria 640 d.	...	1437	...	1610	1625	1637	...	...	1710	1837	1910
Melito di Porto Salvo d.	...	1502	...	1633	1700	1702	...	...	1733	1902	1938
Locri d.	...	1609	...	1740	1806	1809	...	...	1840	2006	2104
Siderno d.	...	1614	...	1747	1810	1819	...	...	1847	2012	2113
Roccella Jonica d.	...	1633	...	1803	1824	1832	...	...	1903	2033	2131
Soverato d.	...	1710	...	1847	1913	1911	...	...	1944	2115	2214
Catanzaro Lido a.	...	1725	...	1902	1930	1925	...	...	2000	2130	2230
Catanzaro Lido ▲ d.	1710	...	1815	1917	1940	...	1935	2005	2015	...	2245
Catanzaro ▲ d.	|	...	|	1928	1953	...	|	|	2025	...	2256
Lamezia Terme ▲ a.	|	...	|	2003	2030	...	|	|	2100	...	2335
Crotone d.	1802	...	1916	...	...	...	2026	2109	...	...	...
Rossano d.	1916	...	2033	...	...	...	2138	2230	...	...	...
Corigliano Calabro d.	1928	...	2045	...	...	...	2147	2245	...	...	...
Sibari a.	1939	...	2055	...	...	...	2158	2302	...	...	...
Sibari d.	1942	...	2058	...	...	...	...	...	...	...	...
Trebisacce d.	2002	...	2115	...	...	...	...	...	...	...	...
Metaponto **638** d.	2054	...	2220	...	...	...	...	...	...	...	...
Taranto 631/8 a.	2138	...	...	...	...	...	...	...	...	...	...
Bari Centrale **631** a.	2314	...	...	...	...	...	...	...	...	...	...

	⚒	E 893 ♦	⚒	†	⚒	E 35455 ♦	⚒	⚒	E 953 ♦	ICN 753 ♦
Bari Centrale **631** d.	...	...	...	...	...	...	...	...	...	...
Taranto 631/8 d.	...	...	...	...	...	...	0508	...	...	...
Metaponto **638** d.	...	...	...	...	...	...	0553	...	0615	...
Trebisacce d.	...	...	...	...	...	...	0654	...	0709	...
Sibari a.	...	...	...	...	...	...	0703	...	0727	...
Sibari d.	...	...	...	...	0602	0635	0705	...	0739	...
Corigliano Calabro d.	...	...	...	...	0612	0652	0722	...	0800	...
Rossano d.	...	...	...	...	0620	0711	0735	...	0812	...
Crotone d.	...	...	...	...	0735	0844	0859	...	0931	...
Lamezia Terme ▲ d.	...	0545	0713	...	|	|	|	0913	|	0940
Catanzaro ▲ d.	...	0627	0752	...	|	|	|	0952	|	1022
Catanzaro Lido ▲ a.	...	0635	0800	...	0825	0948	0957	1000	1025	1030
Catanzaro Lido d.	0610	0650	0810	0808	...	...	...	1010	...	1045
Soverato d.	0624	0710	0824	0825	...	...	...	1023	...	1058
Roccella Jonica d.	0705	0810	0904	0914	...	...	...	1102	...	1138
Siderno d.	0717	0832	0916	0927	...	...	...	1116	...	1150
Locri d.	0722	0839	0925	0933	...	...	...	1122	...	1156
Melito di Porto Salvo d.	0828	1008	1028	1044	...	...	...	1228	...	1252
Reggio di Calabria 640 a.	0853	1040	1053	1120	...	...	...	1253	...	1315

km		⚒	ICN 763 ♦	⚒	E 904 ♦	ICN 786 ♦	⚒	†	⚒	⚒	⚒	⚒	⚒	†	⚒	⚒		⚒	⚒	⚒	Ⓐ	IC 513 ♦	IC 554 ♦	E 35456 ♦	E 956 ♦	E 982 ♦
	Bari Centrale **631** d.	...	...	...	0804	0849	...	...	...	...	...	...	...	...	...	...	...	...	...	...	...	...	1907	...	...	2256
	Taranto 631/8 d.	0645	...	...	0931	1031	...	...	...	...	1147	...	...	...	...	1438	...	1709	...	1816	1931	...	2032	2128	2244	0048
	Metaponto **638** d.	0737	...	...	1011	1111	...	...	...	...	1238	...	...	...	...	1519	...	1802	...	1920	2024	...	2118	2202	2330	0215
	Trebisacce d.	0845	...	...	1057	1215	...	...	...	...	1339	...	...	...	...	1616	...	1913	...	2031	2134	...	2210	2248	...	|
	Sibari a.	0900	...	...	1110	1226	...	...	...	...	1353	...	...	...	...	1631	...	1930	...	2050	2148	...	2224	2300	...	0308
	Sibari d.	...	...	...	1113	1229	...	...	...	...	▬	1400	1532	...	...	▬	1710	...	1955	...	...	2208	2227	...	...	0328
	Corigliano Calabro d.	...	...	...	1128	1245	...	...	...	...	...	1410	1545	...	...	...	1721	...	2005	...	...	2219	2244	...	...	|
	Rossano d.	...	...	...	1139	1257	...	...	...	...	...	1418	1554	...	...	...	1734	...	2013	...	...	2229	2256	...	...	|
	Crotone d.	...	...	...	1248	1400	...	...	...	...	†	1534	1713	...	...	...	1845	...	2135	...	...	2330	2359	...	...	|
0	Lamezia Terme ▲ d.	...	1040	...	|	...	1313	1313	...	1513	1513	|	|	1708	1713	...	|	...	...	...	...	...	...	...	...	0512
38	Catanzaro ▲ d.	...	1117	...	|	...	1352	1352	...	1552	1552	|	|	1747	1752	...	|	...	...	...	...	...	...	...	...	|
47	Catanzaro Lido ▲ a.	...	1125	...	1345	...	1400	1400	...	1600	1600	1625	1805	1755	1800	†	1930	...	...	...	...	...	...	...	...	|
	Catanzaro Lido d.	...	1140	1210	...	...	1410	1410	1512	1610	1610	...	...	1805	1810	1845	...	...	...	...	...	...	...	...	...	|
	Soverato d.	...	1155	1224	...	...	1424	1427	1529	1629	1632	...	...	1822	1824	1914	...	...	...	...	...	...	...	...	...	|
	Roccella Jonica d.	...	1233	1304	...	...	1505	1515	1617	1705	1720	...	...	1916	1905	2015	...	...	...	...	...	...	...	...	...	|
	Siderno d.	...	1246	1316	...	...	1520	1527	1629	1717	1732	...	...	1928	1917	2027	...	...	...	...	...	...	...	...	...	|
	Locri d.	...	1254	1321	...	...	1525	1532	1634	1723	1741	...	...	1934	1923	2033	...	...	...	...	...	...	...	...	...	|
	Melito di Porto Salvo d.	...	1350	1429	...	...	1628	1635	1755	1828	1847	...	...	2052	2028	2144	...	...	...	...	...	...	...	...	...	|
	Reggio di Calabria 640 a.	...	1415	1453	...	...	1653	1712	1833	1853	1923	...	...	2128	2053	2210	...	...	...	...	...	...	...	...	...	0655

♦ – **NOTES** (LISTED BY TRAIN NUMBER)

513 – SILA – [2] Roma (**507**) - Paola (**511**) - Cosenza (**512**) - Sibari - Crotone.
534 – SILA – [2] Crotone - Sibari (**535**) - Cosenza (**536**) - Paola (**530**) - Roma.
554 – MURGE – [12] Milano (**553**) - Taranto - Metaponto (**555**) - Crotone.
566 – MURGE – [12] Crotone - Metaponto (**567**) - Taranto (**568**) - Milano.
750/3 – TOMMASO CAMPANELLA – ▬ 2 cl. (4 berth) and [2] Reggio di Calabria - Lamezia (**751/2**) - Milano and v.v.
763/6 – SCILLA – ▬ 2 cl. (4 berth) and [2] Torino (**761/8**) - Lamezia - Reggio di Calabria and v.v.
782/6 – FRECCIA DEL LEVANTE – ▬ 2 cl. and [12] Crotone - Metaponto (**783/7**) - Taranto (**784/5**) - Milano and v.v.
890/3 – 🛏 1, 2 cl., ▬ 2 cl. and [2] Reggio di Calabria - Lamezia (**894/5/8**) - Roma and v.v.
904 – FRECCIA ADRIATICA – ▬ 2 cl. and [2] Torino (**901**) - Bari (**903**) - Taranto - Metaponto (**905**) Catanzaro Lido.
908 – FRECCIA ADRIATICA – ▬ 2 cl. and [2] Catanzaro Lido - Metaponto (**909**) - Taranto (**910**) - Bari (**906**) - Torino.
951/6 – Not July 1 - Aug. 30 (from Roma and Lecce): [2] Roma - Lecce and v.v.
953 – Not July 1 - Aug. 30 (from Roma): [2] Roma (**951**) - Sibari - Catanzaro Lido.
954 – Not July 1 - Aug. 30: [2] Catanzaro Lido - Metaponto (**956**) - Roma.
982 – Ⓐ: [2] Bari (**981**) - Taranto - Metaponto (**983**) - Reggio di Calabria.
986 – Ⓐ: [2] Reggio di Calabria - Metaponto (**989**) - Taranto (**990**) - Bari.
35452 – July 1 - Aug. 30 (from Roma): [2] Roma (**35451**) - Sibari - Metaponto (**35453**) - Lecce.
35454 – July 1 - Aug. 30: [2] Catanzaro Lido - Sibari (**35457**) - Paola (**35458**) - Roma.
35455 – July 1 - Aug. 30 (from Roma): [2] Roma (**35451**) - Sibari - Catanzaro Lido.
35456 – July 1 - Aug. 30: [2] Lecce - Metaponto (**35457**) - Paola (**35458**) - Roma.
a – Ⓐ only.
q – Not Aug. 15.

▲ – **LAMEZIA TERME - CATANZARO LIDO and v.v. (additional services)**:
Journey 50–75 minutes. All trains call at Catanzaro; 33–56 minutes from Lamezia Terme, 10–15 minutes from Catanzaro Lido. 2nd class only.
From **Lamezia Terme**: 0613, 0813⚒, 1113⚒, 1213, 1413⚒, 1613⚒, 1813⚒, 1913, 2113⚒.
From **Catanzaro Lido**: 0640⚒, 0740, 0840, 0940⚒, 1240⚒, 1440⚒, 1540⚒, 1640, 1740⚒, 1840⚒, 1940⚒.

NAPOLI - POTENZA - TARANTO 638

km		E 951 ♦	E 35453 ♦	IC 675 🍷	2 ⚒q	2 †q	2 ⚒	2 ⚒	x	2 ⚒	2 x	ES 9363 🍷	x
	Roma T **640** d.	2330	2330	0627	...	...	...	...	...	...	...	1545	...
0	**Napoli C 640** d.	|	|	0848	...	...	0916	...	1355p	...	1624	1742	1820
26	Pompei d.	|	|	|	...	...	|	...	1436	...	1654	|	1853
54	Salerno d.	0243	0243	0926	0930	0930	0957	...	1459	...	1719	1819	1936
74	Battipaglia d.	0307	0315	0943	1000	0959	1016	...	1521	...	1735	1837	1956
166	**Potenza** Centrale d.	0440	|	1057r	1134	1142	...	1415	1707	1735	1922	1954	2140
273	Metaponto **635** d.	0609	0739	1218r	...	...	...	1554	...	1912	2042	2119	...
317	**Taranto 635** a.	0650	0812	1252r	...	...	...	1636	...	*2006*	2125	2153	...

	2 ⚒	2 †	2 ⚒	ES 9360 🍷 ⚒	ES 9380 🍷 †	2	IC 676 🍷	2 ⚒	⚒q	E 35456 ♦	E 956 ♦
Taranto 635 d.	...	...	0520	0616	0730	1005	1400r	1408	...	2128	2244
Metaponto **635** d.	...	...	0605	0650	0805	1043	1436r	1501	...	2202	0005
Potenza Centrale d.	0520	0617	0739	0811	0926	1217	1559r	1640	1843	|	0133
Battipaglia d.	0651	0751	...	0925	1100	1344	1717	...	2034	0304	0304
Salerno d.	0712	0808	...	0942	1121	1405	1735	...	2053	0322	0322
Pompei a.	0733	0829	...	|	1138	1435	|	...	...	|	|
Napoli C 640 a.	0815	0938f	...	1018	1202	1509	1812	...	...	|	|
Roma T **640** a.	...	...	...	1215	1402	...	2033	...	...	0635	0635

♦ – **NOTES** (LISTED BY TRAIN NUMBER)

951/6 – Not July 1 - Aug. 30: [2] Roma - Lecce and v.v.; [2] Roma - Metaponto (**953/4**) - Catanzaro Lido and v.v.
35453/6 – July 1 - Aug. 30: [2] Roma (**35451/8**) - Sibari (**35452/7**) - Metaponto - Lecce and v.v.; [2] Roma - Sibari (**35454/5**) - Catanzaro Lido and v.v.

f – Napoli **Campi Flegrei**.
p – Napoli **Piazza Garibaldi**.
q – Not July 1 - Aug. 30.
r – Not July 1 - Aug. 31.
x – From Sept. 7.

640 ROMA - NAPOLI - COSENZA and REGGIO DI CALABRIA

km		E 1991	E 1595		ICN 751		ICN 761			E 833			ES 9371		ICN 799	IC 675	E 837	ES 9387	IC 723	ICN 771	ICN 1911		IC 1571	IC 589
						2			2		2		🍷	2		🍷		🍷	🍷					
		♦	♦		♦		♦			♦			n		♦	♦	♦	p	♦	♦	♦		♦	①-⑥
	Torino P N **610** d.	...	...	...	...	...	2050	...	...	...	...	...	...	...	2155	...	...	...	...	...	...	...	...	...
	Milano C **620** d.	1943g	...	...	2000	...	|	...	...	2200	...	...	...	...	|	...	...	...	...	...	2320	...	...	...
	Venezia S L **620** d.	|	...	...	|	...	|	...	...	|	...	...	...	...	|	...	...	...	...	2330	|	...	...	...
	Bologna C **620** d.	2233	2233	...	2208	...	|	...	...	0044	...	...	...	...	|	...	0115	...	...	0222	|	...	...	...
0	**Roma Termini 620** d.	|	|	...	|	...	|	...	...	0501t	0541	...	0645	...	0612	0627	0617t	0645	0737	0713t	0735t	...	0900	0927
62	Latina d.	|	|	...	|	...	|	...	...	0540	0618	...	|	...	0650	0658	|	|	|	|	|	...	0934	0958
129	Formia d.	|	|	...	|	...	|	...	...	0626	0709	...	|	...	0753	0737	|	|	0840	0855	|	...	1009	1035
195	Aversa d.	|	|	...	|	...	|	...	...	0712	0755	...	|	...	0846	0812	|	|	0912	|	|	...	1048	1113
	Caserta **626** d.	|	|	...	0446	...	|	...	...	|	|	...	|	...	|	|	0853	|	|	|	|	...	|	|
214	**Napoli Centrale 620/6** a.	|	|	...	|	...	0558f	...	...	0734	0823	...	0830	...	0911	0836	0926	0830	0930	1000	1012	...	1114	1136
214	**Napoli Centrale** d.	|	|	...	|	0550	0602f	...	0648	0754	...	...	0842	0854	...	0848	...	0842	0942	...	...	...	...	1148
240	Pompei d.	|	|	...	|	0618	|	...	0718	0825	...	...	|	0923	...	|	...	|	|	...	...	...	...	|
268	Salerno d.	0531	0520	...	0540	0643	0657	...	0742	0854	...	...	0919	0944	...	0926	...	0919	1019	...	...	...	...	1231
288	Battipaglia d.	|	|	...	0558	0701	0715	...	0801	...	...	...	|	1001	...	0941	...	|	|	...	...	...	...	1247
318	Agropoli d.	|	0559	...	0618	0724	0733	...	0824	...	...	...	|	1024	...	...	...	0948	|	...	...	...	...	|
349	Ascea d.	|	0623	...	0647	0750	0756	...	0848	...	...	...	|	1050	...	...	...	|	|	...	...	...	...	|
395	Sapri d.	|	0659	...	0717	0840	0831	...	0928	...	...	...	1029	1126	...	...	...	1036	1133	...	...	...	...	1353
407	Maratea d.	|	|	...	0728	0856	0842	...	0938	...	...	...	|	1138	...	...	...	|	|	...	...	...	...	1403
455	Belvedere Marittimo d.	|	|	...	|	0947	|	...	1009	...	...	...	|	1221	...	...	...	|	|	...	...	...	...	|
489	Paola d.	0747	0801	...	0820	1015	0933	...	1100	...	...	...	1118	1300	...	...	...	1130	1225	...	...	...	...	1453
	Cosenza a.	|	|	...	|	...	|	...	1125c	...	...	...	|	1325	...	...	...	|	|	...	...	...	...	|
546	**Lamezia Terme C** a.	0827	0838	...	0900	...	1015	...	...	...	...	...	1152	...	...	...	...	1208	1300	...	...	...	...	1529
546	**Lamezia Terme C** d.	0830	0903	...	0908	...	1025	...	...	...	...	...	1155	...	...	...	...	1211	1303	...	...	...	...	1532
638	Gioia Tauro d.	|	0949	...	0956	...	1107	...	...	...	...	...	1235	...	...	...	...	1253	|	...	...	...	...	1615
675	Villa San Giovanni **641** a.	0945	1020	...	1027	...	1138	...	...	...	...	...	1304	...	...	...	...	1321	1410	...	...	...	...	1644
675	Villa San Giovanni d.	...	1042	...	1030	...	1141	...	...	...	...	...	1307	...	...	...	...	1324	...	...	...	...	...	1647
690	**Reggio di Calabria 635** a.	...	1100	...	1050	...	1203	...	...	...	...	...	1320	...	...	...	...	1340	...	...	...	...	...	1700

	IC 501	ES 9373				IC 727	IC 1573				IC 585	ES 9375		IC 507		IC 1589	IC 1591		IC 703		ES 9363	IC 521		
		🍷	2	2		🍷		2		2	🍷	🍴				🍷	🍷	2			🍷	🍷	2	2
	♦	⚒				♦	⑦	⚒q						♦		♦	♦		♦		♦			
Torino P N **610** d.	...	...	...	...	...	...	...	...	...	...	...	...	...	...	...	...	...	...	...	...	...	...	...	...
Milano C **620** d.	...	...	...	...	...	...	...	...	...	...	0705	...	...	...	...	0735	0735	...	...	...	...	...	...	...
Venezia S L **620** d.	...	...	...	...	...	...	...	...	...	...	|	...	...	...	...	|	|	...	0920z	...	...	...	...	...
Bologna C **620** d.	...	...	...	...	...	...	...	...	...	...	0908	...	...	...	...	1032	1032	...	1102	...	...	...	...	...
Roma Termini 620 d.	1027	1045	...	1049	...	1128	1145	...	...	1249	1337	1345	...	1420	...	1445t	1445t	1449	1537	...	1545	1627	...	1649
Latina d.	1058	|	...	1127	...	1158	1216	...	...	1327	1414	|	...	1458	...	1517	1517	1527	1614	...	|	1658	...	1727
Formia d.	1135	|	...	1213	...	1235	1253	...	...	1413	1451	|	...	1535	...	1556	1556	1613	1651	...	|	1733	...	1813
Aversa d.	1212	|	...	1259	...	1312	1326	...	...	1459	1525	|	...	1613	...	1653	1653	1701	1725	...	|	1813	...	1901
Caserta **626** d.	|	|	...	|	...	|	|	...	...	|	|	|	...	|	...	|	|	|	|	...	|	|	...	|
Napoli Centrale 620/6 a.	1236	1230	...	1323	...	1330	1346	...	...	1522	1550	1530	...	1636	...	1722	1722	1736	1750	...	1730	1836	...	1928
Napoli Centrale d.	...	1242	1250	...	...	1342	1358	1350	...	...	...	1542	...	1648	...	1734	1734	...	...	...	1742	1848	1842	...
Pompei d.	...	|	1320	...	...	|	|	1418	...	...	...	|	...	|	...	|	|	...	...	...	|	|	1920	...
Salerno d.	...	1315	1342	...	...	1419	1435	1442	...	...	...	1615	...	1731	...	1811	1811	...	...	...	1819	1931	1942	...
Battipaglia d.	...	|	1401	...	...	|	1453	1501	...	...	...	|	...	1747	...	|	|	...	...	...	1835	1947	2001	...
Agropoli d.	...	|	1425	...	...	|	|	1523	...	...	...	|	...	1803	...	|	|	...	...	...	...	|	2021	...
Ascea d.	...	|	1453	...	...	|	|	1549	...	...	...	|	...	1828	...	1901	1901	...	...	...	...	|	2048	...
Sapri d.	...	1423	1541	...	...	1527	1559	1630	...	...	...	1723	...	1901	...	1936	1936	...	...	...	...	2051	2122	...
Maratea d.	...	|	1551	...	...	|	1609	...	...	...	...	|	...	|	...	|	|	...	...	...	...	2102	2132	...
Belvedere Marittimo d.	...	|	1627	...	...	|	|	...	...	...	...	|	...	|	...	|	|	...	...	...	...	|	2210	...
Paola d.	...	1510	1700	...	...	1618	1705	...	...	...	...	1809	...	2006	...	2043	2043	...	...	...	...	2151	2251	...
Cosenza a.	...	|	1730	...	...	|	|	...	...	...	...	|	...	|	...	|	|	...	...	...	...	|	2315	...
Lamezia Terme C a.	...	1540	...	...	...	1650	1744	...	...	...	...	1840	...	2040	...	2123	2123	...	...	...	...	2227	...	...
Lamezia Terme C d.	...	1543	...	...	...	1653	1747	...	...	...	...	1843	...	2043	...	2126	2126	...	...	...	...	2230	...	...
Gioia Tauro d.	...	1624	...	...	...	|	1830	...	...	...	...	1924	...	2123	...	2207	2300	...	...	...	...	2313	...	...
Villa San Giovanni **641** a.	...	1651	...	...	...	1755	1901	...	...	...	...	1951	...	2151	...	2235	2329	...	...	...	...	2340	...	...
Villa San Giovanni d.	...	1654	...	...	...	...	1904	...	...	...	...	1954	...	2154	...	2238	2332	...	...	...	...	2343	...	...
Reggio di Calabria 635 a.	...	1705	...	...	...	...	1920	...	...	...	...	2005	...	2208	...	2250	2345	...	...	...	...	2355	...	...

km		ES 9377	IC 591		IC 523		ES 9381	IC 705	E 853	E 823	IC 1557	ICN 1925	IC 595	ICN 1939	E 891		E 1921	E 985	E 895	E 1941	E 951	E 35451	E 1935	E 1931	
		🍷		2	🍷	2	🍷	🍷					🍷												
						⑧	m		♦	♦	⑤	♦		♦	♦		♦	♦	♦	♦	♦	♦	K	♦	
	Torino P N **610** d.	...	...	...	1105	...	...	...	...	...	...	...	...	...	...	...	...	...	...	1655	...	...	...	...	...
	Milano C **620** d.	...	...	...	|	...	...	...	...	1145	1350	...	1500	...	...	...	1620	...	...	|	...	...	...	...	...
	Venezia S L **620** d.	...	...	...	|	...	...	1309	...	|	|	...	|	...	...	...	|	...	...	|	...	...	1909	1909	...
	Bologna C **620** d.	...	...	...	|	...	...	1508	...	1359	1604	...	1708	...	...	...	|	...	...	|	...	...	2148	2148	...
0	**Roma Termini 620** d.	1730	1738	...	1827	1850	1915	1939	1838	1842t	2011t	2030	2137	2126	2225	...	2320t	...	2300	|	2330	2330	|	|	...
	Latina d.	|	1808	...	1858	1928	|	2008	|	|	2052	2101	2208	2158	2301	...	|	...	|	|	|	|	|	|	...
	Formia d.	|	1843	...	1935	2018	|	2043	|	|	2130	2139	2243	2234	2346	...	|	...	|	|	|	|	|	|	...
	Aversa d.	|	1917	...	2009	2101	|	2116	|	|	|	|	2318	|	|	...	|	...	|	|	|	|	|	|	...
216	Caserta **626** d.	|	|	...	|	|	|	|	2051	2051	|	|	|	|	0039	...	|	...	|	|	0155	0155	|	|	...
	Napoli Centrale 620/6 a.	1845	1938	...	2036	2128	2030	2138	|	|	2223	2236	2342	2326	|	...	|	...	|	|	|	|	|	|	...
	Napoli Centrale d.	1857	...	1950	2048	...	2042	...	|	|	2235	2248	...	2338	|	...	|	...	|	|	|	|	|	|	...
	Pompei d.	|	...	2019	|	...	|	...	|	|	|	|	...	|	|	...	|	...	|	|	|	|	|	|	...
287	Salerno d.	1929	...	2041	2123	...	2114	...	|	|	2312	2326	...	|	|	...	|	...	0204	|	0243	0243	0440	0440	...
——	Battipaglia d.	|	...	2101	...	...	|	...	|	|	...	|	...	|	|	...	|	...	|	|	0305	0315	|	|	...
	Agropoli d.	|	...	2125	...	...	|	...	|	|	...	|	...	|	|	...	|	...	|	|	...	|	|	|	...
	Ascea d.	|	...	2153	...	...	|	...	|	|	...	|	...	|	|	...	|	...	|	|	...	|	|	|	...
	Sapri d.	|	...	2230	...	...	|	...	|	|	...	|	...	|	0248	...	|	...	0342	|	...	|	0557	0557	...
	Maratea d.	|	...	...	...	...	|	...	|	|	...	|	...	|	|	...	|	...	|	|	...	|	|	|	...
	Belvedere Marittimo d.	|	...	...	...	...	|	...	|	|	...	|	...	|	|	...	|	...	|	|	...	|	|	|	...
0	Paola d.	2102	...	...	...	...	2247	...	2355	2355	...	|	...	|	0350	...	|	...	0444	|	...	0515	0652	0652	...
26	Cosenza a.	|	...	...	...	...	|	...	|	|	...	|	...	|	|	...	|	...	|	|	...	...	|	|	...
	Lamezia Terme C a.	2129	...	...	...	...	2314	...	0032	0032	...	|	...	|	0427	...	|	...	0526	0542	...	...	0726	0726	...
	Lamezia Terme C d.	2132	...	...	...	...	...	...	0035	0035	...	|	...	|	0430	...	|	0515	0538	0545	...	...	0729	0729	...
	Gioia Tauro d.	|	...	...	...	...	...	...	|	|	...	|	...	|	0521	...	|	0604	0722	0631	...	...	0814	0814	...
	Villa San Giovanni **641** a.	2226	...	...	...	...	...	...	0145	0145	...	0335	...	0435	0605	...	0610	0639	0758	0705	...	...	0845	0845	...
	Villa San Giovanni d.	2229	...	...	...	...	...	...	...	...	...	...	...	...	0608	...	...	0642	0813	...	...	...	0900	...	...
	Reggio di Calabria 635 a.	2242	...	...	...	...	...	...	...	...	...	...	...	...	0630	...	...	0655	0830	...	...	...	0924	...	...

♦ – **NOTES FOR TABLES 640/1** (LISTED BY TRAIN NUMBER)

501 – CARDUCCI – ⚒: [12] and 🍷 Sestri Levante - Napoli.
507 – SILA – [12] Roma - Reggio; [2] Roma - Paola (**511**) - Cosenza (**512**) - Sibari (**513**) - Crotone.
530 – SILA – [12] Reggio - Roma; [2] Crotone (**534**) - Sibari (**535**) - Cosenza (**536**) - Paola - Roma.
538 – TIRRENO – [12] Napoli - Ventimiglia.
546 – CARDUCCI – ⑧ (not Aug. 15, and days before holidays): [12] and 🍷 Napoli - Sestri Levante.
675 – JONIO – [12] and 🍷 Roma - Taranto.
676 – JONIO – [12] and 🍷 Taranto - Roma.
703 – MIRAMARE – [12] Trieste (**702**) - Venezia Mestre - Napoli.
723 – PELORITANO – [12] and 🍷 Roma - Palermo; [12] Roma - Messina (**721**) - Siracusa.
724 – ARCHIMEDE – [12] and 🍷 Siracusa - Roma; [12] Palermo (**730**) - Messina - Roma.
727 – ARCHIMEDE – [12] and 🍷 Roma - Siracusa; [12] Roma - Messina (**729**) - Palermo.
728 – PELORITANO – [12] and 🍷 Palermo - Roma; [12] Siracusa (**722**) - Messina - Roma.
751 – TOMMASO CAMPANELLA – 🛏 1, 2 cl., ▬ 2 cl. and [12] Milano - Reggio; ▬ 2 cl. (4 berth) and [2] Milano - Lamezia (**753**) - Reggio.
752 – TOMMASO CAMPANELLA – 🛏 1, 2 cl., ▬ 2 cl. and [12] Reggio - Milano; ▬ 2 cl. (4 berth) and [2] Reggio (**750**) - Lamezia - Milano.
761 – SCILLA – 🛏 1, 2 cl., ▬ 2 cl. and [12] Torino - Reggio; ▬ 2 cl. (4 berth) and [2] Torino - Lamezia (**763**) - Reggio.
768 – SCILLA – 🛏 1, 2 cl., ▬ 2 cl. and [12] Reggio - Torino; ▬ 2 cl. (4 berth) and [2] Reggio (**766**) - Lamezia - Torino.
771 – MARCO POLO – 🛏 1, 2 cl., ▬ 2 cl. (4 berth) and [2] Udine - Napoli; 🛏 1, 2 cl. (T2), 🛏 1, 2 cl., ▬ 2 cl. (4 berth) and [2] Trieste (**772**) - Venezia - Napoli.

CONTINUED ON NEXT PAGE →

REGGIO DI CALABRIA and COSENZA - NAPOLI - ROMA 640

	E 898	E 894	E 892	E 1920		E 854	E 834	E 956	E 35458	ICN 1924	E 986		IC 582	ICN 1938		IC 516	IC 704	ES 9368			ES 9360	IC 586	ES 9372	ES 9380
												2	🍷		2	🍷		🍷	2	2	🍷		🍷	🍷
	♦	♦	♦	♦		X	Y	♦	♦	♦	♦	①–⑥		♦				q			♦			♦
Reggio di Calabria 635 d.	2030	2040	2140	...	...	...	...	...	...	...	2340	...	...	...	...	...	...	...	...	...	...	...	0718	...
Villa San Giovanni **641** a.	2046	2056	2154	...	...	...	...	...	...	...	2355	...	...	...	...	...	...	...	...	...	...	...	0731	...
Villa San Giovanni d.	2115	2125	2157	2120	...	2310	2310	...	...	2350	2358	...	...	0145	...	...	...	...	...	...	...	...	0734	...
Gioia Tauro d.	2205	2205	2242	|	...	|	|	...	...	|	0030	...	...	|	...	...	...	...	...	...	...	...	|	...
Lamezia Terme C a.	2330	2330	2340	|	...	0014	0014	...	...	|	0114	...	...	|	...	...	...	...	...	...	...	...	0828	...
Lamezia Terme C d.	0022	0022	2343	|	...	0017	0017	...	...	|	...	...	...	|	...	...	...	0631	...	...	...	...	0831	...
Cosenza d.	|	|	|	|	...	|	|	...	...	|	...	...	...	|	...	...	...	|	...	0530	...	...	|	...
Paola d.	0111	0111	0033	|	...	0100	0100	...	0037	|	...	...	...	|	...	...	...	0701	...	0553	...	...	0901	...
Belvedere Marittimo d.	|	|	|	|	...	|	|	...	|	|	...	...	...	|	...	...	...	|	...	0622	...	...	|	...
Maratea d.	|	|	|	|	...	|	|	...	|	|	...	...	...	|	...	...	...	|	...	0706	...	...	|	...
Sapri d.	0211	0211	0130	|	...	|	|	...	|	|	...	...	...	|	...	...	...	|	0615	0720	...	...	|	...
Ascea d.	|	|	|	|	...	|	|	...	|	|	...	...	...	|	...	...	...	|	0649	0813	...	...	|	...
Agropoli d.	|	|	|	|	...	|	|	...	|	|	...	...	...	|	...	...	...	|	0717	0840	...	...	|	...
Battipaglia d.	|	|	|	|	...	|	|	0304	0304	|	...	...	...	|	...	...	...	|	0742	0902	0925	...	|	1100
Salerno d.	0346	0346	0255	|	...	|	|	0322	0322	|	...	...	...	|	...	0643	...	0834	0801	0922	0942	...	1034	1121
Pompei d.	|	|	|	|	...	|	|	|	|	|	...	...	...	|	...	|	...	|	0822	0940	|	...	|	1138
Napoli Centrale a.	|	0440	|	|	...	|	|	|	|	0449	...	...	...	0619	...	0718	...	0903	0905	1013	1018	...	1103	1202
Napoli Centrale 620/6 d.	|	0452	|	|	...	|	|	|	|	0501	...	0530	0614	0631	0637	0730	0824	0915	...	...	1030	1024	1115	1214
Caserta **626** d.	0448	|	0347	|	...	|	|	0426	0426	|	...	|	|	|	|	|	|	|	...	...	|	|	|	|
Aversa d.	0510	0510	|	|	...	|	|	|	|	|	...	0547	0636	|	0657	0748	0842	|	...	...	|	1046	|	|
Formia d.	0547	0547	0440	|	...	|	|	0523	0523	0554	...	0633	0715	0734	0746	0825	0915	|	...	...	|	1121	|	|
Latina d.	0632	0632	0530	|	...	|	|	0558	0558	0640	...	0709	0750	0817	0834	0859	0950	|	...	...	|	|	|	|
Roma Termini 620 a.	0708	0708	0617	|	...	0605	0608t	0635	0635	0723	...	0753	0823	0856	0918	0933	1023	1030	...	...	1215	1223	1230	1402
Bologna C **620** a.	...	...	...	|	...	...	1100	...	...	...	...	...	1243	...	...	|	1453	...	...	...	...	1659	...	...
Venezia S L **620** a.	...	...	...	|	...	...	|	...	...	...	...	...	|	...	...	|	1649	...	...	...	...	|	...	...
Milano C **620** a.	...	...	...	1130	...	...	1320	...	...	...	...	...	1500	...	...	|	...	...	...	...	...	1905	...	...
Torino P N **610** a.	...	...	...	...	...	...	...	...	...	...	...	...	...	...	...	1655	...	...	...	...	...	...	...	...

	IC 522		IC 1554	ES 9376	IC 538	IC 592		IC 1590	IC 1588					IC 530		IC 728		IC 546	IC 1572		IC 676		ES 9378	E 824
	🍷	2	🍷	✖		🍷		🍷	🍷		2	2	2	🍷	2	🍷	2	🍷		2	🍷	2	🍷	
		①–⑥	♦		♦			♦	♦		⚒	†		♦		♦		♦	♦		♦		⑧v	♦
Reggio di Calabria 635 d.	0652	...	...	0855	...	...	...	0840	0925	...	...	...	...	0930	...	...	...	...	...	...	...	...	1355	...
Villa San Giovanni **641** a.	0707	...	...	0906	...	...	...	0856	0939	...	...	...	...	0945	...	...	...	...	...	...	...	...	1406	...
Villa San Giovanni d.	0710	...	...	0909	...	...	...	0859	0942	...	...	...	...	0948	...	1210	...	...	...	...	...	...	1409	...
Gioia Tauro d.	0740	...	...	0935	...	...	...	0928	1010	...	...	...	...	1019	...	|	...	...	...	...	...	...	1435	...
Lamezia Terme C a.	0820	...	...	1012	...	...	...	1053	1053	...	...	...	...	1100	...	1306	...	...	...	...	...	...	1512	...
Lamezia Terme C d.	0823	...	...	1015	...	...	...	1056	1056	...	...	...	...	1103	...	1309	...	...	...	...	...	...	1515	...
Cosenza d.	|	...	...	|	...	...	...	|	|	...	...	...	...	|	...	|	...	...	...	1225c	...	1425	|	...
Paola d.	0900	...	...	1047	...	...	...	1133	1133	...	...	...	...	1205	1157	1344	...	...	...	1253	...	1453	1547	...
Belvedere Marittimo d.	|	...	...	|	...	...	...	|	|	...	...	...	...	|	1228	|	...	...	...	1322	...	1527	|	...
Maratea d.	0950	...	...	|	...	...	...	|	|	...	...	...	...	|	1312	|	...	...	...	1404	...	1610	|	...
Sapri d.	1001	...	...	1135	...	...	...	1226	1226	...	...	...	1245	1301	1325	1433	...	...	...	1421	...	1622	1635	...
Ascea d.	|	...	...	|	...	...	...	1255	1255	...	...	...	1325	1337	1403	|	...	...	...	1459	...	1703	|	...
Agropoli d.	|	...	...	|	...	...	...	|	|	...	...	...	1356	1359	1437	|	...	...	...	1532	...	1731	|	...
Battipaglia d.	1106	...	...	|	...	...	...	|	|	...	...	...	1425	1420	1501	|	...	...	...	1602	1717	1757	|	...
Salerno d.	1128	...	1207	1242	...	...	...	1356	1356	...	...	...	1444	1436	1521	1544	...	...	...	1622	1735	1820	1742	...
Pompei d.	|	...	1230	|	...	...	...	|	|	...	...	...	1502	|	1541	|	...	...	...	1643	|	1841	|	...
Napoli Centrale a.	1212	...	1255	1318	...	...	...	1430	1430	...	...	...	1537	1512	1615	1618	...	...	...	1715	1812	1915	1818	...
Napoli Centrale 620/6 d.	1224	1230	1307	1330	1324	1424	...	1442	1442	...	1430	1430	...	1524	...	1630	1638	1724	1724	...	1824	...	1830	1845
Caserta **626** d.	|	|	|	|	|	|	...	|	|	...	|	|	...	|	...	|	|	|	|	...	|	...	|	1917
Aversa d.	1246	1252	|	|	1346	1442	...	1459	1459	...	1452	1502	...	1546	...	1646	1653	1746	1746	...	1846	...	|	|
Formia d.	1323	1344	1401	|	1423	1515	...	1542	1542	...	1544	1551	...	1623	...	1726	1744	1823	1823	...	1923	...	|	|
Latina d.	1359	1430	1438	|	1459	1550	...	1618	1618	...	1630	1637	...	1659	...	1759	1830	1859	1859	...	1959	...	|	|
Roma Termini 620 a.	1433	1511	1527t	1515	1533	1623	...	1653t	1653t	...	1713	1720	...	1733	...	1833	1913	1933	1933	...	2033	...	2015	2152t
Bologna C **620** a.	...	...	2013	...	...	2052	...	2127	2127	...	...	...	...	...	...	...	...	...	...	...	...	...	...	0300
Venezia S L **620** a.	...	...	|	...	...	|	...	|	|	...	...	...	...	...	...	...	...	...	...	...	...	...	...	...
Milano C **620** a.	...	...	2240	...	...	2300	...	2350	2350	...	...	...	...	...	...	...	...	...	...	...	...	...	...	...
Torino P N **610** a.	...	...	...	...	...	...	...	...	...	...	...	...	...	...	...	...	...	...	...	...	...	...	...	...

		IC 724	ICN 774	IC 590	ICN 1910		ICN 796			ES 9386	ES 9380	E 830		E 1992		E 1594		E 1940	ICN 768		ICN 752	E 1934	E 1930	
	2	🍷		🍷		2		2		🍷	🍷		2											
		♦	♦		♦		♦	⑦		p	n	♦		♦		♦		♦	♦		♦	L	♦	
Reggio di Calabria 635 d.	...	...	...	1455	...	...	...	...	...	1625	1645	...	...	...	...	1615	...	...	1820	...	1935	1925	...	...
Villa San Giovanni **641** a.	...	...	...	1509	...	...	...	...	...	1639	1657	...	...	...	...	1630	...	...	1837	...	1948	1943	...	...
Villa San Giovanni d.	...	1450	...	1512	...	...	...	...	...	1642	1700	...	...	1745	...	1653	...	1835	1840	...	1951	2025	2025	...
Gioia Tauro d.	...	|	...	1540	...	...	...	...	...	1711	1728	...	...	|	...	1732	...	|	1913	...	2021	2057	2057	...
Lamezia Terme C a.	...	1555	...	1623	...	...	...	...	...	1749	1807	...	...	1848	...	1820	...	1944	2000	...	2107	2143	2143	...
Lamezia Terme C d.	...	1558	...	1626	...	...	...	...	...	1752	1810	...	...	1851	...	1855	...	1947	2025	...	2130	2146	2146	...
Cosenza d.	...	|	...	|	...	...	...	...	...	|	|	...	1825	|	...	|	...	|	|	...	|	|	|	...
Paola d.	...	1633	...	1704	...	...	...	1653	...	1831	1845	...	1853	1926	...	1937	...	2023	2104	...	2215	2223	2223	...
Belvedere Marittimo d.	...	|	...	|	...	...	...	1726	...	|	|	...	1925	|	...	|	...	|	|	...	|	|	|	...
Maratea d.	...	|	...	1754	...	...	...	1811	...	|	|	...	2010	|	...	|	...	|	2150	...	2305	|	|	...
Sapri d.	...	1722	...	1805	...	...	...	1821	...	1928	1934	...	2020	|	...	2034	...	2116	2205	...	2322	2316	2316	...
Ascea d.	...	|	...	|	...	...	...	1903	...	|	|	...	2101	|	...	2108	...	|	2236	...	2353	|	|	...
Agropoli d.	...	|	...	|	...	...	...	1937	...	2011	|	...	2138	|	...	2130	...	|	2303	...	0022	|	|	...
Battipaglia d.	...	|	...	1916	...	...	...	2002	...	|	|	...	2202	|	...	|	...	|	2328	...	0047	|	|	...
Salerno d.	...	1832	...	1933	...	...	...	2022	...	2042	2042	2035	2221	2134	...	2208	...	2233	2344	...	0104	0037	0037	...
Pompei d.	...	|	...	|	...	...	...	2041	...	|	|	2102	|	|	...	|	...	|	|	...	|	|	|	...
Napoli Centrale a.	...	1909	...	2012	...	...	...	2113	...	2118	2118	2138	2301	|	...	2247	...	|	|	...	|	|	|	...
Napoli Centrale 620/6 d.	1836	1921	1957	2024	2030	2048	2108	...	...	2130	2130	2150	...	|	...	2259	...	|	|	...	|	|	|	...
Caserta **626** d.	|	|	|	|	|	|	|	...	...	|	|	2224u	...	|	...	|	...	|	0037	...	0158	|	|	...
Aversa d.	1853	1937	|	2044	|	2106	2129	...	...	|	|	|	...	|	...	|	...	|	|	...	|	|	|	...
Formia d.	1944	2012	2113	2123	|	2154	2211	...	...	|	|	2318u	...	|	...	|	...	|	|	...	|	|	|	...
Latina d.	2030	2048	2151	2159	|	2245	2257	...	...	|	|	2356u	...	|	...	|	...	|	|	...	|	|	|	...
Roma Termini 620 a.	2112	2122	2231t	2233	2245	2330	2336	...	...	2315	2315	0047t	...	|	...	|	...	|	|	...	0417t	|	|	...
Bologna C **620** a.	...	...	0313	...	|	...	|	...	...	...	...	0552	...	0518	...	0528	...	|	|	...	0752	0928	0928	...
Venezia S L **620** a.	...	...	0526	...	|	...	|	...	...	...	...	|	...	|	...	...	...	|	|	...	|	1150	1150	...
Milano C **620** a.	...	...	...	...	0725	...	|	...	...	...	...	0920	...	0925g	...	...	...	|	|	...	1005	...	...	...
Torino P N **610** a.	...	...	...	...	...	...	0820	...	...	...	...	...	...	...	...	...	...	0940	1045	...	...	...	...	...

♦ – **NOTES FOR TABLES 640 / 1** (CONTINUED FROM PREVIOUS PAGE)

774 – MARCO POLO – 🛏 1, 2 cl., ▬ 2 cl. (4 berth) and (2) Napoli - Udine; 🛏 1,2 cl. (T2), 🛏 1, 2 cl., ▬ 2 cl. (4 berth) and (2) Napoli - Venezia Mestre (**773**) - Trieste.

796 – 🛏 1, 2 cl., ▬ 2 cl. (4 berth) and (2) Napoli - Torino.

799 – 🛏 1, 2 cl., ▬ 2 cl. (4 berth) and (2) Torino - Napoli.

823 – FRECCIA DEL SUD – ①③⑤⑦: (2) Milano - Catania - Agrigento; (2) Milano - Catania (**827**) - Siracusa.

824 – ①③④⑤⑥⑦ (also Dec. 8; not Dec. 9): 🛏 1,2 cl. (Excelsior), 🛏 1, 2 cl., ▬ 2 cl. (4 berth) and (2) Napoli - Bologna (**924**) - Bolzano.

830 – ②④⑦: ▬ 2 cl. and (2) Salerno - Milano.

833 – ①③⑤: ▬ 2 cl. and (2) Milano - Salerno.

837 – ①②④⑤⑥⑦; also Dec. 9, not Dec. 10 (from Bolzano): 🛏 1,2 cl. (Excelsior), 🛏 1, 2 cl., ▬ 2 cl. (4 berth) and (2) Bolzano (**925**) - Bologna - Napoli.

853 – FRECCIA DEL SUD – ②④⑥: (2) Roma - Catania - Agrigento; (2) Roma - Catania (**857**) - Siracusa.

891 – ⑤: ▬ 2 cl. and (2) Roma - Reggio.

892 – ⑦ (also Dec. 8; not Dec. 6): ▬ 2 cl. and (2) Reggio - Roma.

894 – Not ⑥ June 20 - Sept. 12: 🛏 1, 2 cl., ▬ 2 cl. and (2) Reggio - Roma; 🛏 1, 2 cl., ▬ 2 cl. and (2) Reggio (**890**) - Lamezia - Roma.

895 – 🛏 1, 2 cl., ▬ 2 cl. and (2) Roma - Reggio; 🛏 1, 2 cl., ▬ 2 cl. and (2) Roma - Lamezia (**893**) - Reggio.

898 – ⑥ June 20 - Sept. 12: 🛏 1, 2 cl., ▬ 2 cl. and (2) Reggio - Roma; 🛏 1, 2 cl., ▬ 2 cl. and (2) Reggio (**890**) - Lamezia - Roma.

951 – Not July 1 - Aug. 30: (2) Roma - Lecce; (2) Roma - Metaponto (**953**) - Catanzaro Lido.

CONTINUED ON NEXT PAGE →

Selected details only received by press date – see page 286

641 VILLA SAN GIOVANNI - MESSINA - SIRACUSA and PALERMO

km		*E* 853 ♦	*E* 823 ♦	2 ⚒	2 ⚒	2 ⚒	*ICN* 1925 ♦	2 ⚒	*ICN* 1939 ♦	2	*E* 1921 ♦	*E* 1923 A	*E* 1945 B	*E* 1941 ♦	*E* 1931 ♦	*E* 1933 C	*E* 1993 D	*E* 1991 ♦	2 ⚒	2 ⚒	2 ⚒	2 †	2 ⚒	2 ⚒	2 ⑥	2 Ⓐ
0	**Villa San Giovanni 640** d.	0205	0205	...	...	...	0350	...	0450	...	0625	0625	0725	0725	0900	0900	1000	1000	...	...	...	...	...	...	...	...
9	**Messina** Centrale a.	0335	0335	...	...	...	0515	...	0615	...	0755	0755	0855	0855	1035	1035	1135	1135	...	...	...	...	...	...	...	...
9	**Messina** Centrale d.	0400	0400	0445	0525	0525	0539	0550	0638	0705	0825	0830	0916	0923	1057	1105	1200	1205	1215	1232	1310	1350	1410	1420	1530	1530
	Taormina-Giardini d.	0439	0439	|	0604	|	|	|	0741	|	|	0916	1004	|	1133	|	|	1256	1323	|	1403	1453	1512	|	|	|
	Giarre-Riposto **644** d.	0455	0455	|	0623	|	|	|	0804	|	|	0931	1020	|	1150	|	|	1310	1340	|	1420	1516	1527	|	|	|
	Catania Centrale a.	0520	0520	|	0643	|	|	|	0831	|	|	0957	1044	|	1218	|	|	1338	1403	|	1444	1545	1550	|	|	|
	Catania Centrale d.	0609	0609	|	0647	|	|	|	0844	|	|	1004	1048	|	1232	|	|	1343	1410	|	...	...	...	|	|	|
	Augusta d.	0659	0659	|	0746	|	|	|	0940	|	|	1053	1146	|	1325	|	|	1451	1511	|	...	...	...	|	|	|
	Siracusa 648 a.	0729	0729	|	0810	|	|	|	1000	|	|	1120	1215	|	1355	|	|	1515	1545	|	...	...	...	|	|	|
45	Milazzo d.	...	...	0508	...	0546	0603	0621	...	0729	0853	...	...	0947	...	1130	1223	...	...	1306	...	...	...	1444	1603	1603
174	Cefalù d.	...	...	0702	...	0740	0800	0854	...	0914	1054	...	...	1141	...	1323	1439	...	...	1522	...	...	...	1650	1837	1840
204	Termini Imerese **645/7** d.	...	...	0729	...	0808	0826	0921	...	0937	1116	...	...	1208	...	1343	1511	...	...	1554	...	...	...	1710	1906	1906
241	**Palermo C 645/7** a.	...	...	0755	...	0840	0850	0947	...	1000	1140	...	...	1234	...	1415	1535	...	...	1625	...	...	...	1736	1930	1930

	2 †	*IC* 723 🍷 ♦	*IC* 721 🍷 E	2 ⚒	2 Ⓐ	2 †	2	2 ⚒	*IC* 729 🍷 F	*IC* 727 ♦	2 ⚒
Villa San Giovanni 640 d.	...	1425	1425	...	...	...	...	...	1807	1807	...
Messina Centrale a.	...	1543	1553	...	...	...	...	...	1923	1933	...
Messina Centrale d.	1530	1556	1606	1620	1715	1725	1830	1835	1936	1950	2145
Taormina-Giardini d.	|	|	1645	1711	|	1811	|	1930	|	2027	2227
Giarre-Riposto **644** d.	|	|	1701	1729	|	1827	|	1945	|	2042	2243
Catania Centrale a.	|	|	1725	1757	|	1852	|	2008	|	2107	2305
Catania Centrale d.	|	|	1730	1801	|	1854	|	2010	|	2110	...
Augusta d.	|	|	1815	1848	|	1941	|	2101	|	2204	...
Siracusa 648 a.	|	|	1838	1910	|	2010	|	2130	|	2230	...
Milazzo d.	1603	1619	...	...	1738	...	1853	...	2000	...	...
Cefalù d.	1839	1758	...	...	1931	...	2056	...	2139	...	...
Termini Imerese **645/7** d.	1902	1823	...	...	1956	...	2125	...	2203	...	...
Palermo C 645/7 a.	1937	1850	...	...	2020	...	2155	...	2228	...	...

	2 ⚒	2 ⚒	2 ⚒	2 ⚒		*IC* 728 🍷 ♦	*IC* 722 N	2	2	2 †
Palermo C 645/7 d.	...	0405	0605	...	...	0730	...	0805	...	0845
Termini Imerese **645/7** d.	...	0431	0632	...	...	0756	...	0830	...	0926
Cefalù d.	...	0455	0701	...	...	0824	...	0853	...	0951
Milazzo d.	...	0718	0855	...	...	0955	...	1056	...	1215
Siracusa 648 d.	0505	|	|	0630	...	|	0800	|	0845	|
Augusta d.	0526	|	|	0658	...	|	0822	|	0909	|
Catania Centrale a.	0607	|	|	0744	...	|	0905	|	1000	|
Catania Centrale d.	0612	|	|	0747	...	|	0908	|	1003	|
Giarre-Riposto **644** d.	0636	|	|	0808	...	|	0934	|	1026	|
Taormina-Giardini d.	0700	|	|	0825	...	|	0950	|	1044	|
Messina Centrale a.	0750	0752	0920	0921	...	1025	1030	1120	1135	1250
Messina Centrale d.	...	...	...	...	...	1040	1040	...	...	...
Villa San Giovanni 640 a.	...	...	...	...	...	1150	1150	...	...	...

km		*IC* 730 P	*IC* 724 🍷 ♦	2 ⚒	2 ⚒y	2 †	2 ⚒	*E* 1990 Q	*E* 1992 ♦	2 ⚒	2 ⚒	*E* 1942 R	*E* 1940 ♦	*E* 1930 ♦	*E* 1932 S	2 Ⓐ	*E* 1922 T	*E* 1920 ♦	2 ⚒	*E* 854 X	*E* 834 Y	2	*ICN* 1924 ♦	2	*ICN* 1938 ♦	
	Palermo C 645/7 d.	1005	...	1135	...	...	1135	1130	...	...	1305	...	1330	...	1458	1525	...	1600	...	...	...	1805	1840	2030	...	...
	Termini Imerese **645/7** d.	1031	...	1201	...	...	1201	1204	...	...	1333	...	1356	...	1527	1556	...	1628	...	...	...	1834	1907	2057	...	...
	Cefalù d.	1055	...	1224	...	...	1224	1233	...	...	1358	...	1422	...	1553	1616	...	1651	...	...	...	1903	1932	2119	...	...
	Milazzo d.	1234	...	1437	...	...	1437	1446	...	...	1553	...	1609	...	1746	1810	...	1846	...	...	...	2102	2122	2256	...	...
0	**Siracusa 648** d.	|	1030	|	...	...	|	|	1220	...	|	1350	|	1510	|	|	1615	|	1700	1730	1730	|	|	|	2025	...
31	Augusta d.	|	1054	|	...	...	|	|	1241	...	|	1413	|	1538	|	|	1640	|	1725	1755	1755	|	|	|	2045	...
87	**Catania Centrale** a.	|	1141	|	...	...	|	|	1334	...	|	1457	|	1625	|	|	1723	|	1817	1850	1850	|	|	|	2142	...
87	**Catania Centrale** d.	|	1146	|	1350	1350	|	|	1339	1422	|	1500	|	1643	|	|	1727	|	1820	1912	1912	|	|	|	2202	...
117	Giarre-Riposto **644** d.	|	1210	|	1418	1418	|	|	1406	1448	|	1526	|	1712	|	|	1758	|	1851	1938	1938	|	|	|	2230	...
135	Taormina-Giardini d.	|	1228	|	1448	1441	|	|	1424	1511	|	1542	|	1733	|	|	1821	|	1913	1957	1957	|	|	|	2248	...
182	**Messina** Centrale a.	1305	1310	1503	1547	1545	1503	1520	1530	1605	1625	1625	1630	1815	1820	1835	1905	1910	2006	2050	2050	2130	2150	2320	2330	...
182	**Messina** Centrale d.	1320	1320	...	...	...	...	1550	1550	...	...	1650	1650	1835	1835	...	1930	1930	...	2110	2110	...	2210	...	2350	...
191	**Villa San Giovanni 640** a.	1425	1425	...	...	...	...	1715	1715	...	...	1810	1810	2000	2000	...	2055	2055	...	2235	2235	...	2335	...	0115	...

♦ – **NOTES FOR TABLES 640/1** (CONTINUED FROM PREVIOUS PAGE)

956 – Not July 1 - Aug. 30 (from Lecce): [2] Lecce - Roma; [2] Catanzaro Lido (**954**) - Metaponto - Roma.
985 – ①–⑥, not days after holidays (from Bari): [2] Bari (**981**) - Taranto (**982**) - Metaponto (**983**) - Reggio.
986 – Ⓐ: [2] Reggio - Metaponto (**989**) - Taranto (**990**) - Bari.
1554 – CARACCIOLO – ⑦ (also Dec. 8; not Dec. 6): [12] and 🍷 Salerno - Milano.
1571 – CARDUCCI – †: [12] Livorno - Napoli.
1572 – CARDUCCI – ⑥ (also Aug. 15, and days before holidays): [12] Napoli - Livorno.
1588 – ASPROMONTE – ⑦ Sept. 13 - Nov 29 (also Dec. 8): [12] Reggio - Milano.
1589 – ASPROMONTE – ⑥ Sept. 12 - Dec. 12: [12] Milano - Reggio.
1590 – ASPROMONTE – ⑦ until Sept. 6: [12] Reggio - Milano.
1591 – ASPROMONTE – ⑥ June 20 - Sept. 5 (also Aug. 14; not Aug. 15): [12] Milano - Reggio.
1594 – ⑤ June 19 - Sept. 11: 🛏 1,2 cl. (T2), ▬ 2 cl. and [2] Reggio - Bolzano.
1595 – ⑥ June 20 - Sept. 12 (from Bolzano): 🛏 1,2 cl. (T2), ▬ 2 cl. and [2] Bolzano - Reggio.
1910 – 🛏 1,2 cl. (Excelsior), 🛏 1,2 cl. (T2), 🛏 1,2 cl., ▬ 2 cl. (4 berth) and [2] Napoli - Milano.
1911 – 🛏 1,2 cl. (Excelsior), 🛏 1,2 cl. (T2), 🛏 1,2 cl., ▬ 2 cl. (4 berth) and [2] Milano - Napoli.
1920 – TRINACRIA – 🛏 1,2 cl. (T2), 🛏 1,2 cl. and ▬ 2 cl. (4/6 berth) Palermo - Milano; [2] Palermo - Messina; 🛏 1,2 cl. (T2), 🛏 1,2 cl. and ▬ 2 cl. (4/6 berth) Siracusa (**1922**) - Messina - Milano.
1921 – TRINACRIA – 🛏 1,2 cl. (T2), 🛏 1,2 cl. and ▬ 2 cl. (4/6 berth) Milano - Palermo; [2] Messina - Palermo; 🛏 1,2 cl. (T2), 🛏 1,2 cl. and ▬ 2 cl. (4/6 berth) Milano - Messina (**1923**) - Siracusa.
1924 – IL GATTOPARDO – 🛏 1,2 cl. (Excelsior), 🛏 1,2 cl. (T2), 🛏 1,2 cl., ▬ 2 cl. (4 berth) and [2] Palermo - Roma.
1925 – IL GATTOPARDO – 🛏 1,2 cl. (Excelsior), 🛏 1,2 cl. (T2), 🛏 1,2 cl., ▬ 2 cl. (4 berth) and [2] Roma - Palermo.
1930 – FRECCIA DELLA LAGUNA – 🛏 1,2 cl. and ▬ 2 cl. (4 berth) Siracusa - Venezia; 🛏 1,2 cl. and ▬ 2 cl. (4 berth) Palermo (**1932**) - Messina - Venezia; 🛏 1,2 cl. and ▬ 2 cl. (4 berth) Reggio (**1934**) - Villa SG - Venezia.
1931 – FRECCIA DELLA LAGUNA – 🛏 1,2 cl. and ▬ 2 cl. (4 berth) Venezia - Siracusa; 🛏 1,2 cl. and ▬ 2 cl. (4 berth) Venezia - Messina (**1933**) - Palermo; 🛏 1,2 cl. and ▬ 2 cl. (4 berth) Venezia - Villa SG (**1935**) - Reggio.
1938 – BELLINI – 🛏 1,2 cl. (Excelsior), 🛏 1,2 cl. (T2), 🛏 1,2 cl., ▬ 2 cl. (4 berth) and [2] Siracusa - Roma.
1939 – BELLINI – 🛏 1,2 cl. (Excelsior), 🛏 1,2 cl. (T2), 🛏 1,2 cl., ▬ 2 cl. (4 berth) and [2] Roma - Siracusa.
1940 – TRENO DEL SOLE – 🛏 1,2 cl. and ▬ 2 cl. (4 berth) Palermo - Torino; [2] Palermo - Messina; 🛏 1,2 cl. and ▬ 2 cl. (4 berth) Siracusa (**1942**) - Messina - Torino.
1941 – TRENO DEL SOLE – 🛏 1,2 cl. and ▬ 2 cl. (4 berth) Torino - Palermo; [2] Messina - Palermo; 🛏 1,2 cl. and ▬ 2 cl. (4 berth) Torino - Messina (**1945**) - Siracusa.
1991 – MONGIBELLO – ①⑤ June 15 - Sept. 28 (also Dec. 4, 9): 🛏 1,2 cl. (T2), ▬ 2 cl. and [2] Milano - Siracusa; ▬ 2 cl. (4 berth) and [2] Milano - Messina (**1993**) - Palermo.
1992 – MONGIBELLO – ④⑦ until Sept. 27 (also Dec. 3, 8): 🛏 1,2 cl. (T2), ▬ 2 cl. and [2] Siracusa - Milano; ▬ 2 cl. (4 berth) and [2] Palermo (**1990**) - Messina - Milano.

9360 – ⚒: [12] and 🍷 Taranto - Roma.
9363 – [12] and 🍷 Roma - Taranto.
9380 – †: [12] and 🍷 Taranto - Roma.
35451 – July 1 - Aug. 30: [2] Roma - Taranto - Lecce; [2] Roma - Sibari (**35455**) - Catanzaro Lido.
35458 – July 1 - Aug. 30 (from Lecce): [2] Lecce - Roma; [2] Catanzaro Lido (**35454**) - Paola - Roma.

A – TRINACRIA – 🛏 1,2 cl. (T2), 🛏 1,2 cl. and ▬ 2 cl. (4/6 berth) Milano (**1921**) - Messina - Siracusa.
B – TRENO DEL SOLE – 🛏 1,2 cl. and ▬ 2 cl. (4 berth) Torino (**1941**) - Messina - Siracusa.
C – FRECCIA DELLA LAGUNA – 🛏 1,2 cl. and ▬ 2 cl. (4 berth) Venezia (**1931**) - Messina - Palermo.
D – MONGIBELLO – ▬ 2 cl. (4 berth) and [2] Milano (**1991**) - Messina - Palermo.
E – PELORITANO – [12] Roma (**723**) - Messina - Siracusa.
F – ARCHIMEDE – [12] Roma (**727**) - Messina - Palermo.
K – FRECCIA DELLA LAGUNA – 🛏 1,2 cl. and ▬ 2 cl. (4 berth) Venezia (**1931**) - Villa SG - Reggio.
L – FRECCIA DELLA LAGUNA – 🛏 1,2 cl. and ▬ 2 cl. (4 berth) Reggio - Villa SG (**1930**) - Venezia.
N – PELORITANO – [12] Siracusa - Messina (**728**) - Roma.
P – ARCHIMEDE – [12] Palermo - Messina (**724**) - Roma.
Q – MONGIBELLO – ▬ 2 cl. (4 berth) and [2] Palermo - Messina (**1992**) - Milano.
R – TRENO DEL SOLE – 🛏 1,2 cl. and ▬ 2 cl. (4 berth) Siracusa - Messina (**1940**) - Torino.
S – FRECCIA DELLA LAGUNA – 🛏 1,2 cl. and ▬ 2 cl. (4 berth) Palermo - Messina (**1930**) - Venezia.
T – TRINACRIA – 🛏 1,2 cl. (T2), 🛏 1,2 cl. and ▬ 2 cl. (4/6 berth) Siracusa - Messina (**1920**) - Milano.
X – FRECCIA DEL SUD – ①③⑤: [2] Agrigento - Catania - Roma; [2] Siracusa (**856**) - Catania - Roma.
Y – FRECCIA DEL SUD – ②④⑥⑦: [2] Agrigento - Catania - Milano; [2] Siracusa (**836**) - Catania - Milano.

c – © only.
e – ⑥ only.
f – Napoli **Campi Flegrei**.
g – Milano **Porta Garibaldi**.
m – Ⓑ from Apr. 25.
n – Not June 13 - Sept. 4.
p – June 13 - Sept. 4.
q – ①–⑥ from Apr. 26.
t – Roma **Tiburtina**.
u – Stops to pick up only.
v – Not Dec. 25, 26, Apr. 4, May 1, Oct. 31, and days before holidays.
y – Not ⑥ July 11 - Aug. 30.
z – Venezia **Mestre**.

ALTA VELOCITÀ (*AV*) – high-speed services 642

km		*AV* 9501 A	*AV* 9551 M	*AV* 9503 Ⓑj	*AV* 9601 Ⓐ	*AV* 9401 ⚒j	*AV* 9603 Ⓐj	*AV* 9505	*AV* 9451 R	*AV* 9605 Ⓐj	*AV* 9607 Ⓐj	*AV* 9403 U	*AV* 9507	*AV* 9609 Ⓐj	*AV* 9553 z	*AV* 9593 y	*AV* 9611 Ⓐj	*AV* 9405	*AV* 9509	*AV* 9613 Ⓐj	*AV* 9555 Ⓐx	*AV* 9595 Ⓐw	*AV* 9407	*AV* 9453	*AV* 9511
	Venezia Santa Lucia ♣ d.	...	...	...	...	0627	...	...	...	...	...	...	...	...	...	...	...	0827	...	...	...	...	0927	...	...
	Venezia Mestre ♣ d.	...	...	...	...	0639	...	...	...	...	...	0739	...	...	...	...	...	0839	...	...	...	...	0939	...	...
	Padova d.	...	...	...	...	0655	...	...	...	...	...	0755	...	...	...	...	...	0855	...	...	...	...	0955	...	...
	Torino Porta Nuova d.	...	...	...	...	|	...	...	...	...	0640	|	...	...	0740	0740	...	|	...	...	0840	0840	|	...	...
	Verona Porta Nuova d.	...	...	...	...	|	...	...	0755	...	|	|	...	...	|	|	...	|	...	...	|	|	|	1007	...
	Milano Centrale a.	...	...	...	...	|	...	...	|	...	0740	|	...	...	0832g	|	...	|	...	...	0932g	|	|	|	...
0	**Milano** Centrale d.	...	0545	0615	0630	|	0700	0715	|	0730	0800	|	0815	0830	0835g	|	0900	|	0915	0930	0935g	|	|	|	1015
	Milano Rogoredo d.	...	|	|	|	|	|	|	|	0742	|	|	|	|	|	0852	|	|	|	|	|	0952	|	|	|
214	**Bologna** Centrale a.	...	0750	0720	|	|	|	0820	0844	|	|	0850	0920	|	0944	0944	|	0950	1020	|	1044	1044	1050	1057	1120
—	**Bologna** Centrale d.	0610	0753	0723	|	|	|	0823	0847	|	|	0853	0923	|	0947	0947	|	0953	1023	|	1047	1047	1053	1100	1123
	Firenze SMN a.	0650	0830	0800	|	|	|	0900	0924c	|	|	0930	1000	|	1025c	1025c	|	1030	1100	|	1125c	1125c	1130	1136c	1200
0	**Firenze** SMN d.	0700	0840	0810	|	|	|	0910	0927c	|	|	0940	1010	|	1027c	1027c	|	1040	1110	|	1127c	1127c	1140	1139c	1210
	Roma Tiburtina a.	|	|	|	|	|	|	|	|	1027	|	|	|	|	|	|	|	|	|	|	|	|	|	|	|
261	**Roma** Termini a.	0845	1015	0945	0929	0955	0959	1045	1055	|	1059	1113	1145	1129	1150	1150	1159	1213	1245	1229	1250	1250	1313	1305	1345
261	**Roma** Termini d.	0900	...	1000	0945	...	1018	1100	...	|	...	...	1200	...	...	...	...	...	1300	...	...	...	...	...	1400
479	**Napoli** Centrale a.	1010	...	1110	1055	...	1125	1210	...	1140	...	...	1310	...	...	...	...	...	1410	...	...	...	...	...	1510
	Salerno a.	...	...	...	...	...	...	...	...	...	...	...	...	...	...	...	...	...	...	...	...	...	...	...	...

	AV 9409	*AV* 9513	*AV* 9411	*AV* 9515	*AV* 9517	*AV* 9415	*AV* 9619 Ⓑj	*AV* 9519 9521	*AV* 9623 Ⓑj	*AV* 9417	*AV* 9523 9525	*AV* 9557 Ⓑz	*AV* 9597 Ⓑy	*AV* 9627 Ⓑj	*AV* 9419	*AV* 9527	*AV* 9629	*AV* 9421	*AV* 9631 Ⓑ	*AV* 9529	*AV* 9559 z	*AV* 9599 y	*AV* 9635 Ⓑj	*AV* 9423	*AV* 9531
Venezia Santa Lucia ♣ d.	1027	...	1127	...	...	1327	...	...	...	1427	...	...	...	...	1527	...	...	1627	...	...	...	...	...	1727	...
Venezia Mestre ♣ d.	1039	...	1139	...	...	1339	...	...	...	1439	...	...	...	...	1539	...	...	1639	...	...	...	...	...	1739	...
Padova d.	1055	...	1155	...	...	1355	...	...	...	1455	...	...	...	...	1555	...	...	1655	...	...	...	...	...	1755	...
Torino Porta Nuova d.	|	...	|	...	...	|	...	...	...	|	...	1440	1440	...	|	...	...	|	...	...	1640	1640	...	|	...
Verona Porta Nuova d.	|	...	|	...	...	|	...	...	...	|	...	|	|	...	|	...	...	|	...	...	|	|	...	|	...
Milano Centrale a.	|	...	|	...	...	|	...	...	...	|	...	1532g	|	...	|	...	...	|	...	...	1732g	|	...	|	...
Milano Centrale d.	|	1115	|	1215	1315	|	1400	1415	1500	|	1515	1535g	|	1600	|	1615	1630	|	1700	1715	1735g	|	1800	|	1815
Milano Rogoredo d.	|	|	|	|	|	|	|	|	|	|	|	|	1552	|	|	|	1642	|	|	|	|	1752	|	|	|
Bologna Centrale a.	1150	1220	1250	1320	1420	1450	|	1520	|	1550	1620	1644	1644	|	1650	1720	|	1750	|	1820	1844	1844	|	1850	1920
Bologna Centrale d.	1153	1223	1253	1323	1423	1453	|	1523	|	1553	1623	1647	1647	|	1653	1723	|	1753	|	1823	1847	1847	|	1853	1923
Firenze SMN a.	1230	1300	1330	1400	1500	1530	|	1600	|	1630	1700	1723c	1723c	|	1730	1800	|	1830	|	1900	1925c	1925c	|	1930	2000
Firenze SMN d.	1240	1310	1340	1410	1510	1540	|	1610	|	1640	1710	1725c	1725c	|	1740	1810	|	1840	|	1910	1927c	1927c	|	1940	2010
Roma Tiburtina a.	|	|	|	|	|	|	|	|	|	|	|	|	|	|	|	|	1927	|	|	|	|	|	|	|	|
Roma Termini a.	1413	1445	1513	1545	1645	1713	1659	1745	1759	1813	1845	1850	1850	1859	1913	1945	|	2013	1959	2045	2050	2050	2059	2113	2145
Roma Termini d.	...	1500	...	1600	1700	...	...	1800	...	...	1900	...	...	...	...	2000	|	...	...	2100	...	...	2115	...	...
Napoli Centrale a.	...	1610	...	1710	1810	...	...	1910	...	...	2010	...	...	...	...	2110	2040	...	...	2210	...	...	2225	...	...
Salerno a.	...	...	...	...	...	...	...	1959	...	...	2059	...	...	...	...	...	...	...	...	...	...	...	...	...	...

	AV 9637 Ⓑj	*AV* 9457	*AV* 9639 Ⓑj	*AV* 9425	*AV* 9533	*AV* 9427 Ⓑh	*AV* 9643 Ⓑj	*AV* 9535 Ⓑ	*AV* 9647 Ⓑj	*AV* 9537 Ⓑj
Venezia Santa Lucia ♣ d.	...	...	...	1827	...	1927	...	...	...	...
Venezia Mestre ♣ d.	...	...	...	1839	...	1939	...	...	...	...
Padova d.	...	...	...	1855	...	1955	...	...	...	...
Torino Porta Nuova d.	...	...	...	|	1800	|	...	...	...	2030
Verona Porta Nuova d.	...	1855	...	|	|	|	...	...	...	|
Milano Centrale a.	...	|	...	|	1900	|	...	...	...	2130
Milano Centrale d.	1830	|	1900	|	1915	|	2000	2015	2100	2145
Milano Rogoredo d.	1842	|	|	|	|	|	|	|	|	|
Bologna Centrale a.	|	1944	|	1950	2020	|	|	2120	|	2250
Bologna Centrale d.	|	1947	|	1953	2023	|	|	2123	|	...
Firenze SMN a.	|	2024c	|	2030	2100	|	|	2200	|	...
Firenze SMN d.	|	2027c	|	2040	2110	|	|	...	|	...
Roma Tiburtina a.	2127	|	|	|	|	|	|	...	|	...
Roma Termini a.	|	2155	2159	2213	2245	2255	2259	...	2359	...
Roma Termini d.	|	...	...	...	...	...	...	...	...	...
Napoli Centrale a.	2240	...	...	...	...	...	...	...	...	...
Salerno a.	...	...	...	...	...	...	...	...	...	...

	AV 9500 ①–⑥j	*AV* 9502 ⚒	*AV* 9504 ①–⑥j	*AV* 9600 Ⓐ	*AV* 9400 ⚒j	*AV* 9602 Ⓐj	*AV* 9604 Ⓐj	*AV* 9506	*AV* 9402	*AV* 9606 Ⓐj
Salerno d.	...	...	...	...	...	...	...	...	...	...
Napoli Centrale d.	...	...	...	...	...	...	0620	...	...	...
Roma Termini a.	...	...	...	...	...	...	|	...	...	...
Roma Termini d.	...	...	0615	0630	0645	0700	|	0715	0745	0800
Roma Tiburtina d.	...	...	|	|	|	|	0733	|	|	|
Firenze SMN a.	...	...	0750	|	|	|	|	0850	0920	|
Firenze SMN d.	...	0700	0800	|	|	|	|	0900	0930	|
Bologna Centrale a.	...	0737	0837	|	|	|	|	0937	1007	|
Bologna Centrale d.	0640	0740	0840	|	|	|	|	0940	1010	|
Milano Rogoredo d.	|	|	|	|	|	|	1020	|	|	|
Milano Centrale a.	0745	0845	0945	0929	|	0959	1030	1045	|	1059
Milano Centrale d.	0800	...	1000	...	|	...	...	...	|	...
Verona Porta Nuova a.	|	...	|	...	|	...	...	...	|	...
Torino Porta Nuova a.	0900	...	1100	...	|	...	...	...	|	...
Padova d.	...	...	...	...	0951	...	...	...	1107	...
Venezia Mestre ♣ a.	...	...	...	...	1005	...	...	...	1121	...
Venezia Santa Lucia ♣ a.	...	...	...	...	1017	...	...	...	1133	...

	AV 9452	*AV* 9508 9510	*AV* 9608 Ⓐj	*AV* 9550 z	*AV* 9590 y	*AV* 9404	*AV* 9610 Ⓐj	*AV* 9512	*AV* 9612 Ⓐj	*AV* 9552 Ⓐz	*AV* 9592 Ⓐy	*AV* 9406	*AV* 9514	*AV* 9408	*AV* 9516 9518	*AV* 9410	*AV* 9520	*AV* 9412	*AV* 9522	*AV* 9414	*AV* 9618 Ⓑj	*AV* 9524	*AV* 9416	*AV* 9622 Ⓑj	*AV* 9454
Salerno d.	...	0602	...	...	...	...	...	...	...	...	...	...	...	...	0902	...	...	...	...	...	...	...	...	...	...
Napoli Centrale d.	...	0650	0705	...	...	...	...	0750	...	...	...	...	0850	...	0950	...	1050	...	1150	...	...	1250	...	...	...
Roma Termini a.	...	0800	0815	...	...	...	...	0900	...	...	...	...	1000	...	1100	...	1200	...	1300	...	...	1400	...	...	...
Roma Termini d.	0805	0815	0830	0840	0840	0845	0900	0915	0930	0940	0940	0945	1015	1045	1115	1145	1215	1245	1315	1345	1400	1415	1445	1500	1505
Roma Tiburtina d.	|	|	|	|	|	|	|	|	|	|	|	|	|	|	|	|	|	|	|	|	|	|	|	|	|
Firenze SMN a.	0928c	0950	|	1005c	1005c	1020	|	1050	|	1105c	1105c	1120	1150	1220	1250	1320	1350	1420	1450	1520	|	1550	1620	|	1630c
Firenze SMN d.	0930c	1000	|	1007c	1007c	1030	|	1100	|	1107c	1107c	1130	1200	1230	1300	1330	1400	1430	1500	1530	|	1600	1630	|	1633c
Bologna Centrale a.	1013	1037	|	1045	1045	1107	|	1137	|	1145	1145	1207	1237	1307	1337	1407	1437	1507	1537	1607	|	1637	1707	|	1713
Bologna Centrale d.	1016	1040	|	1048	1048	1110	|	1140	|	1148	1148	1210	1240	1310	1340	1410	1440	1510	1540	1610	|	1640	1710	|	1716
Milano Rogoredo d.	|	|	|	|	1142	|	|	|	|	|	1242	|	|	|	|	|	|	|	|	|	|	|	|	|	|
Milano Centrale a.	|	1145	1129	1155g	|	|	1159	1245	1229	1255g	|	|	1345	|	1445	|	1545	|	1645	|	1659	1745	|	1759	|
Milano Centrale d.	|	...	...	1158g	|	|	...	...	...	1258g	|	|	...	|	...	|	...	|	...	|	1715	...	|	...	|
Verona Porta Nuova a.	1105	...	...	|	|	|	...	...	...	|	|	|	...	|	...	|	...	|	...	|	|	...	|	...	1805
Torino Porta Nuova a.	...	...	...	1250	1250	|	...	...	...	1350	1350	|	...	|	...	|	...	|	...	|	1815	...	|	...	...
Padova d.	...	...	...	...	...	1207	...	...	...	...	...	1307	...	1407	...	1507	...	1607	...	1707	...	...	1807	...	...
Venezia Mestre ♣ a.	...	...	...	...	...	1221	...	...	...	...	...	1321	...	1421	...	1521	...	1621	...	1721	...	...	1821	...	...
Venezia Santa Lucia ♣ a.	...	...	...	...	...	1233	...	...	...	...	...	1333	...	1433	...	1533	...	1633	...	1733	...	...	1833	...	...

	AV 9526	*AV* 9554 Ⓑz	*AV* 9594 Ⓑy	*AV* 9418	*AV* 9626 Ⓑj	*AV* 9528	*AV* 9628	*AV* 9420 U	*AV* 9630 Ⓑ	*AV* 9530	*AV* 9556 z	*AV* 9596 y	*AV* 9422 Ⓑh	*AV* 9634 Ⓑj	*AV* 9456 B	*AV* 9532	*AV* 9636 Ⓑj	*AV* 9424	*AV* 9638 Ⓑj	*AV* 9534	*AV* 9558 M	*AV* 9642 Ⓑj	*AV* 9536 A	*AV* 9646 Ⓑj	
Salerno d.	...	...	...	...	...	...	...	...	...	...	...	...	...	...	...	...	...	...	...	...	...	...	...	...	...
Napoli Centrale d.	1350	...	...	...	1435	1450	1520	...	1535	1550	...	...	...	...	...	1650	1720	...	...	1750	...	...	1850	...	...
Roma Termini a.	1500	...	...	...	1542	1600	|	...	1642	1700	...	...	...	...	...	1800	|	...	...	1900	...	...	2000	...	...
Roma Termini d.	1515	1540	1540	1545	1600	1615	|	1645	1700	1715	1737	1737	1745	1800	1805	1815	|	1845	1900	1915	1930	2000	2015	2100	...
Roma Tiburtina d.	|	|	|	|	|	|	1633	|	|	|	|	|	|	|	|	|	1833	|	|	|	|	|	|	|	...
Firenze SMN a.	1650	1703c	1703c	1720	|	1750	|	1820	|	1850	1900c	1900c	|	|	1930c	1950	|	2020	|	2050	2104	|	2225	|	...
Firenze SMN d.	1700	1705c	1705c	1730	|	1800	|	1830	|	1900	1902c	1902c	|	|	1933c	2000	|	2030	|	2100	2114	|	2235	|	...
Bologna Centrale a.	1737	1745	1745	1807	|	1837	|	1907	|	1937	1945	1945	|	|	2013	2037	|	2107	|	2137	2154	|	2316	|	...
Bologna Centrale d.	1740	1748	1748	1810	|	1840	|	1910	|	1940	1948	1948	|	|	2016	2040	|	2110	|	2140	2157	|	...	|	...
Milano Rogoredo d.	|	|	1842	|	|	|	1920	|	|	|	|	2042	|	|	|	|	2120	|	|	|	|	|	...	|	...
Milano Centrale a.	1845	1855g	|	|	1859	1945	1930	|	1959	2045	2055g	|	|	2059	|	2145	2130	|	2159	2245	0005	2259	...	2359	...
Milano Centrale d.	...	1858g	|	|	...	...	...	|	...	...	2058g	|	|	...	|	...	...	|	...	...	...	...	...	...	...
Verona Porta Nuova a.	...	|	|	|	...	...	...	|	...	...	|	|	|	...	2105	...	...	|	...	...	...	...	...	...	...
Torino Porta Nuova a.	...	1950	1950	|	...	...	...	|	...	...	2150	2150	|	...	...	...	...	|	...	...	...	...	...	...	...
Padova d.	...	...	...	1907	...	...	...	2007	...	...	...	...	2051	...	...	...	...	2207	...	...	...	...	...	...	...
Venezia Mestre ♣ a.	...	...	...	1921	...	...	...	2021	...	...	...	...	2105	...	...	...	...	2221	...	...	...	...	...	...	...
Venezia Santa Lucia ♣ a.	...	...	...	1933	...	...	...	...	...	...	...	...	2117	...	...	...	...	2233	...	...	...	...	...	...	...

A – Via Arezzo – see Table **615**.
B – To Brescia (a. 2155).
M – Via Modena – see Table **620**.
R – From Brescia (d. 0705).
U – From / to Udine – see Table **601**.

c – Firenze **Campo di Marte**.
g – Milano **Porta Garibaldi**.
h – Not Dec. 25, 26, Apr. 4, May 1, Aug. 1 - 22, Oct. 31, and days before holidays.

j – Not Aug. 1 - 22.
r – Milano **Rogoredo**.
w – Dec. 28 - June 12.
x – Not Dec. 28 - June 12.

y – Dec. 28 - Jan. 10.
z – Not Dec. 28 - Jan. 10.
♣ – Local journeys are not permitted Venezia Santa Lucia - Mestre and v.v.

644 CATANIA - RANDAZZO - RIPOSTO
Ferrovia Circumetnea

Winter service valid from September 21, 2009. No service on †

km		⚒	⚒	⚒	⚒	⚒	⚒	⚒	⚒	⚒	⚒	⚒	⚒	⚒	⚒
0	**Catania ▲** d.	0541	0636	0744	...	0924	...	1104	1204	1325	1445	1640	1822	1918	2012
20	Paternò d.	0616	0714	0820	...	1001	...	1140	1239	1401	1520	1716	1858	1955	2046
36	Adrano d.	0646	0748	0850	...	1031	...	1211	1313	1433	1553	1746	1929	2025	...
52	Bronte d.	0718	0821	0920	...	1101	...	1241	1345	1503	1623	1816	1959	2057	...
71	Randazzo d.	0750	0852	0951	1010	1132	1145	1318	1416	1533	1654	1847	2030	2127	...
109	Giarre **640** a.	0857	...	...	1116	...	1255	1433	...	...	1801	...	...	...	...
111	**Riposto** a.	0901	...	...	1120	...	1259	1437	...	...	1805	...	...	...	...

	⚒	⚒	⚒	⚒	⚒	⚒	⚒	⚒	⚒	⚒	⚒	⚒	⚒	⚒
Riposto d.	...	...	0627	0831	...	1002	...	...	1229	...	1343	1455	...	1810
Giarre **640** d.	...	...	0632	0836	...	1007	...	...	1234	...	1348	1500	...	1815
Randazzo d.	0507	0645	0751	0946	0954	1116	1209	1314	1347	1432	1459	1612	1710	1926
Bronte d.	0538	0717	0821	...	1024	...	1242	1345	...	1504	...	...	1741	1958
Adrano d.	0610	0750	0850	...	1053	...	1314	1411	...	1532	...	...	1810	2025
Paternò d.	0642	0821	0920	...	1123	...	1344	1442	...	1602	...	...	1840	2057
Catania ▲ a.	0716	0855	0953	...	1157	...	1418	1515	...	1636	...	...	1914	2130

▲ – Catania Borgo station. The Metropolitana di Catania operates a metro service Borgo - Porto and v.v. (3.8 km) via Catania Centrale station. Weekdays only, every 15 minutes 0700 – 2045.

645 PALERMO and AGRIGENTO - CATANIA
2nd class only except where shown

km		⚒	⚒	⚒	m	⚒	y		x	⚒	⚒	⚒v	n	⚒		†	⚒	A	⚒	G	†w	z	🚌 ⚒	
0	**Palermo C 647** d.	...	...	0555	0635	...	...	...	...	1205	...	...	...	...	1435	...	...	...	...	1722	...	...	...	...
37	Termini Imerese **647** d.	...	...	0622	0704	...	...	...	...	1231	...	...	...	...	1502	...	...	...	...	1752	1830	...	...	...
70	Roccapalumba Alia **647** d.	...	...	0649	0745	...	...	...	...	1301	...	...	1437	...	1531	1535	1535	...	1740	1823	1856	...	1945	...
	Agrigento C 647 d.	...	...	|	|	0813	1046	...	1225	|	1314	1345	|	...	1647	|	|	1500	|	|	|	1850	|	...
	Aragona-Caldare **647** d.	...	...	|	|	0832	1103	...	1247	|	1331	1404	|	1440	...	|	|	1517	|	|	|	1907	|	...
	Canicattì **648** d.	...	...	|	|	0916	1145	...	1323	|	1409	1442	|	1518	...	|	|	1606	|	|	|	1941	|	...
	Caltanissetta Xirbi **648** a.	...	...	0739	0852	|	|	...	|	1352	|	|	1530	|	...	1620	1625	|	1836	1912	1942	|	2135	...
	Caltanissetta C **648** d.	0542	0627	0754	0908	0948	1223	...	1353	1410	1445	1510	1546	1551	...	|	1641	1643	1855	1925	2000	2006	...	...
127	Caltanissetta Xirbi **648** d.	0551	0637	...	...	...	1233	...	1403	...	...	...	...	1558	...	1621	...	1654	...	...	...	2014	...	...
154	Enna d.	0613	0715	...	...	...	1256	...	1426	...	...	...	...	...	...	1643	...	1725	...	...	...	2038	...	...
243	**Catania Centrale** a.	0733	0835	...	...	...	1425	...	1540	...	...	...	...	...	...	1800	...	1842	...	...	...	2150	...	...

km		⚒	⚒	⚒	B		G ⚒	⚒	†	G †	†	⚒	⚒	⚒	†	⚒	†q			⚒	⚒	†v	G	
	Catania Centrale d.	...	...	...	0550	...	...	...	0715	...	...	1040	...	...	1335	1415	...	...	...	1605	...	1605	...	1830
	Enna d.	...	...	...	0714	...	...	...	0833	...	...	1204	...	...	1451	1539	...	...	...	1727	...	1727	...	1946
0	Caltanissetta Xirbi **648** a.	...	...	...	0752	...	...	...	0855	...	...	1228	...	...	1517	1601	...	...	...	1748	...	1748	1918	2010
6	Caltanissetta C **648** d.	0453	0600	0620	0806	...	0805	0835	0909	0910	1050	1245	1420	1513	1527	|	1620	...	...	|	1735	1806	1926	2023
	Caltanissetta Xirbi **648** d.	0508	0615	|	|	...	0820	|	|	0922	1107	...	1435	1531	|	1604	1632	...	...	1750	|	...	|	...
35	Canicattì **648** d.	|	|	0653	0847	...	|	0912	0945	|	|	...	|	|	1613	|	|	...	...	|	1812	...	2000	...
65	Aragona-Caldare **647** d.	|	|	0724	0925	...	|	0946	1014	|	|	...	|	|	1644	|	|	...	...	|	1844	...	...	...
78	**Agrigento C 647** a.	|	|	0741	0940	...	|	1004	1030	|	|	...	|	|	1700	|	|	...	...	|	1905	...	...	...
	Roccapalumba Alia **647** d.	0601	0711	...	...	...	0912	...	...	1015	1157	...	1525	1625	...	1703	1727	1736	...	1845	...	...	...	...
	Termini Imerese **647** d.	...	0736	...	...	...	0943	...	...	1041	...	...	...	...	...	1731	1756	1803	...	1912	...	...	...	...
	Palermo C 647 a.	...	0800	...	...	...	1017	...	...	1109	...	...	...	...	...	1800	1824	1830	...	1940	...	...	...	...

A – FRECCIA DEL SUD – On ②④⑥⑦ (train number **834**) (2) Agrigento - Milano. On ①③⑤ (train number **854**) (2) Agrigento - Roma.
B – FRECCIA DEL SUD – On ①②④⑥ (train number **823**) (2) Milano - Agrigento. On ③⑤⑦ (train number **853**) (2) Roma - Agrigento.
G – (2) Palermo - Gela and v.v.
m – Ⓐ until Aug. 28; ⚒ Aug. 31 - Dec. 12.
n – Daily July 27 - Aug. 1; ⚒ Aug. 2 - Dec. 12.
q – Not July 12 - Aug. 29.
v – From Sept. 13.
w – Aug. 2 - 30.
x – From Aug. 31.
y – July 27 - Aug. 30.
z – From July 27.

CATANIA - GELA and v.v. 2nd class only, *137 km*, journey 2½ hours (approximately).
From **Catania**: 0558⚒, 1223⚒, 1316⚒, 1437⚒, 1748⚒.
From **Gela**: 0545⚒, 0655⚒, 1240⚒, 1325⚒, 1428⚒, 1730⚒.

646 PALERMO - TRAPANI
2nd class only.

km		⚒	⚒	⚒🚌	†	m	⚒	†	⚒	⚒	⚒	†	†	⚒	⚒	⚒	⚒	⚒	⚒	†	†	⚒	⚒		⚒			⚒
0	**Palermo Centrale ▲** d.	...	...	...	...	...	0638	0740	0839	...	0929	0938	...	...	1129	...	1329	...	1429	1429	...	...	...	1709	1739	...	1829	1929
32	Piraineto ▲ d.	...	...	...	...	...	0747	0841	0941	0950	1019	1035	...	...	1219	...	1419	...	1519	1519	...	...	...	1809	1839	1845	1919	2020
73	Castellammare del Golfo d.	...	0644	...	...	...	0836	0920	...	1037	1110	1118	...	...	1259	...	1514	...	1558	1558	...	...	...	...	...	1926	2004	2107
79	Alcamo Diramazione d.	...	0652	0656	...	...	0844	0927	...	1044	1117	1125	1134	...	1311	1313	1522	1528	1607	1607	1610	...	...	...	...	1935	2012	2114
121	Castelvetrano d.	0624	0730	|	0828	0828	0920	1003	...	1124	|	|	1212	1316	|	1404	|	1604	1647	1648	|	1715	1815	...	...	2015	|	2150
144	Mazara del Vallo d.	0642	0754	|	0847	0851	0939	1027	...	1146	|	|	1239	1339	|	1428	|	1623	...	1711	|	1734	1838	...	...	2033	|	...
165	Marsala d.	0703	0813	|	0911	0913	0958	1044	...	1205	|	|	1255	1401	|	1451	|	1647	...	1730	|	1759	1903	...	...	2055	|	...
196	**Trapani** a.	0735	0840	0736	0937	0940	1022	1115	...	1234	1158	1205	1326	1435	1350	1520	1604	1713	...	1757	1651	1833	1928	...	...	2125	2048	...

km		⚒	⚒	⚒	†	⚒		⚒	⚒	†	⚒	†	†	⚒	⚒	⚒	†	⚒	⚒			†		🚌		⚒		
0	**Trapani** d.	0500	0523	0618	0706	0605	...	0838	...	0843	0843	1012	1125	1215	1155	1240	1246	1330	1423	1426	...	1701	1600	1920	1820	1938	2028	...
	Marsala d.	|	|	|	|	0635	...	|	...	0910	0912	|	1152	|	1228	1313	1319	1402	1450	|	...	|	1626	|	1845	2005	2054	...
	Mazara del Vallo d.	|	|	|	|	0705	...	|	...	0932	0940	|	1210	|	1244	1338	1338	1427	1509	|	...	|	1644	|	1903	2034	2109	...
	Castelvetrano d.	|	|	|	|	0731	...	|	...	1004	1001	|	1235	|	1304	1403	1403	1447	1529	|	...	|	1707	|	1922	2054	2130	...
47	Alcamo Diramazione d.	0537	0601	0655	0747	0809	...	0918	...	1040	1045	1052	...	1255	1343	1440	1440	...	...	1506	...	1740	1745	2000	2013	...	...	...
53	Castellammare del Golfo d.	0544	...	0702	0754	0816	...	0926	...	...	1052	1059	...	...	1350	...	...	...	...	1513	...	...	1753	...	2022	...	...	...
94	Piraineto ▲ d.	0625	...	0746	|	0855	0907	1010	1027	...	1137	1144	...	...	1434	...	...	...	...	1555	1607	...	1834	...	2111	...	...	...
126	**Palermo Centrale ▲** a.	0727	...	0837	0936	...	0957	...	1127	...	1237	1237	...	...	1537	...	...	...	...	...	1657	...	2006	...	2200	...	...	...

m – Ⓐ until Aug. 28; ⚒ Aug. 31 - Dec. 12.
▲ – Additional services operate Palermo Centrale - Piraineto and v.v.

647 PALERMO - AGRIGENTO
2nd class only

km		⚒m				⚒		⚒	†k	⚒		⚒	
0	**Palermo C 645** d.	0735	0835	1035	1235	1335	1435	1535	1635	1635	1735	1835	2015
37	Termini-Imerese **645** d.	0803	0901	1101	1301	1402	1502	1601	1702	1702	1801	1901	2046
70	Roccapalumba-Alia **645** d.	0836	0936	1129	1329	1434	1533	1635	1732	1736	1835	1938	2116
125	Aragona-Caldare **645** d.	0928	1028	1224	1429	1521	1628	1725	1828	1828	1933	2038	2203
139	**Agrigento C 645** a.	0947	1045	1245	1447	1547	1647	1745	1845	1845	1950	2055	2221

	⚒	⚒	⚒			m	⚒	q			
Agrigento C 645 d.	0450	0538	0653	0825	1057	1325	1410	1525	1607	1808	2005
Aragona-Caldare **645** d.	0508	0556	0710	0843	1114	1343	1430	1545	1629	1829	2023
Roccapalumba-Alia **645** d.	0605	0650	0806	0936	1209	1436	1533	1634	1736	1920	2117
Termini-Imerese **645** d.	0635	0721	0832	1004	1235	1504	1604	1703	1803	1946	2145
Palermo C 645 a.	0700	0750	0900	1030	1300	1530	1630	1730	1830	2011	2213

k – From Sept. 13.
m – Not ⑥ July 11 - Aug. 29.
q – ⚒ until Sept. 12; daily Sept. 13 - Dec. 12.

648 SIRACUSA - CALTANISSETTA
2nd class only

km		⚒G	†G	⚒		†	⚒	†	⚒j	⚒	⚒		
0	**Siracusa 640** d.	...	...	0520	1010	...	...	1255	...	1400	1745	...	2028
62	Pozzallo d.	...	...	0629	1112	...	...	1357	...	1514	1850	...	2129
92	Modica d.	...	...	0715	1154	...	...	1442	1352	1546	1928	2000	2210
112	Ragusa d.	...	...	0742	1221	...	...	1507	1418	...	...	2023	...
153	Vittoria d.	...	...	0824	1303	...	...	...	1505	...	...	2106	...
183	Gela d.	0620	0708	0850	1330	1420	1420	...	1533	...	...	2135	...
218	Licata d.	0654	0738	...	...	1453	1453	...	1612	...	...	...	...
264	Canicattì **645** d.	0735	0834	...	...	1540	1540	...	1659	...	...	...	...
293	**Caltanissetta C 645** d.	0805	0910	...	...	1612	1617	...	1733	...	...	...	...
299	Caltanissetta Xirbi **645** a.	0812	0917	...	...	1619	...	...	1742	...	...	...	...

	⚒	⚒	⚒	†	⚒	⚒	†	⚒		G
Caltanissetta Xirbi **645** d.	...	...	...	...	...	...	...	...	...	1918
Caltanissetta C 645 d.	...	...	...	...	0545	...	...	...	...	1926
Canicattì **645** d.	...	...	...	...	0615	...	...	...	...	2001
Licata d.	...	...	...	...	0653	...	...	...	...	2041
Gela d.	...	...	...	0640	0731	1250	1415	1415	1721	2113
Vittoria d.	...	...	...	0711	0803	1324	1446	1446	1752	...
Ragusa d.	...	...	0800	0801	0900	1420	1539	1540	1843	...
Modica d.	0540	0622	0823	0823	0920	1441	1608	1602	1904	...
Pozzallo d.	0611	0653	0855	0855	...	1513	1640	...	1937	...
Siracusa 640 a.	0720	0755	0958	0958	...	1620	1740	...	2045	...

G – (2) Palermo - Gela and v.v.
j – Until Sept. 12.

MALTA

Bus services are operated by ATP (www.atp.com.mt) on behalf of the Government's Transport Department ADT (www.maltatransport.com) and operate frequently throughout Malta.

649 PRINCIPAL BUS SERVICES
Approx frequency (in minutes) shown in *italics*

Routes from Valletta: 1/2/4/6 Vittoriosa (*15*), 3 Senglea (*20-30*), 8 Airport (*30*), 10-13 Birzebugia (*10-15*), 17-21 Zabbar / Marsascala (*20-30*), 27/127 Marsaxlokk (*30*), 32/34 Zurrieq (*15-20*), 45/145 Cirkewwa for Gozo ferry (*20*), 49/58-59 Mosta / Bugibba (*10*), 55-56 Naxxar (*15-20*), 62/64/66/67/68 Sliema / St Julians (*5*), 80/81/84 Rabat / Dingli (*15*), 88 Zebbug (*15*), 89 Siggiewi (*20-30*).
Routes from Sliema: 65 Mosta / Rabat (*30*), 645 Bugibba / Cirkewwa for Gozo ferry (*30*), 652 Bugibba / Golden Bay (*30*). **Gozo**: service 25 Victoria - Mgarr connects with ferries.

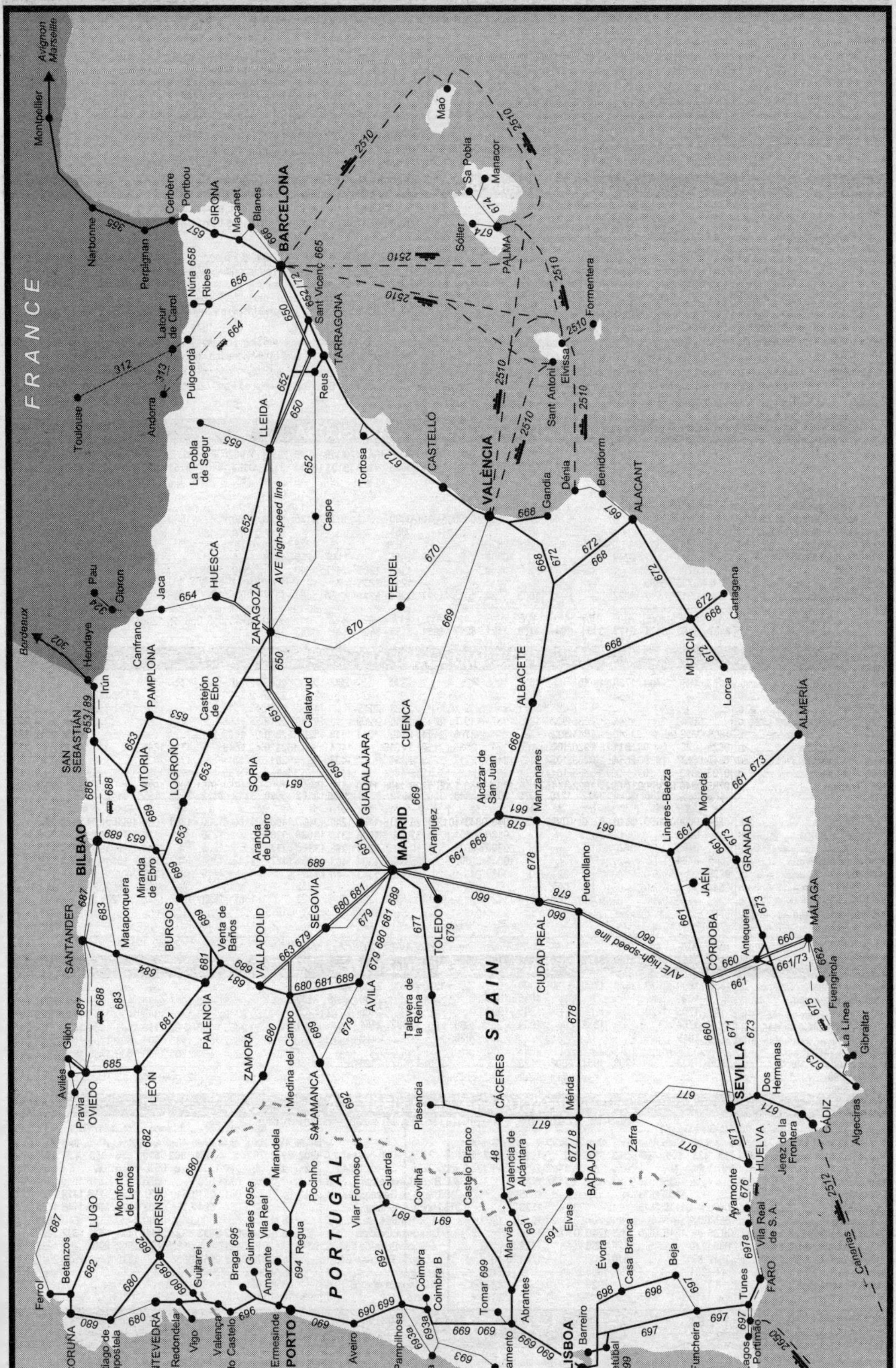
FRANCE
SPAIN
PORTUGAL
Montpellier
Avignon Marseille
Narbonne
Perpignan
Cerbère
Portbou
Toulouse
Andorra
Latour de Carol
Puigcerdà
Núria 658
Ribes
GIRONA
Maçanet
Blanes
BARCELONA
Sant Vicenç 665
TARRAGONA
Reus
LLEIDA
La Pobla de Segur
Tortosa
CASTELLÓ
VALÈNCIA
Gandia
Dénia
Benidorm
ALACANT
Caspe
AVE high-speed line
Maó
Sa Pobla
Manacor
Sóller
PALMA
Eivissa
Sant Antoni
Formentera
Bordeaux
Pau
Oloron
Hendaye
Irún
Canfranc
Jaca
HUESCA
ZARAGOZA
TERUEL
SAN SEBASTIÁN
PAMPLONA
Castejón de Ebro
VITORIA
LOGROÑO
Calatayud
CUENCA
SORIA
GUADALAJARA
BILBAO
Miranda de Ebro
Aranda de Duero
MADRID
Aranjuez
Alcázar de San Juan
Manzanares
ALBACETE
MURCIA
Cartagena
Lorca
ALMERÍA
SANTANDER
Mataporquera
BURGOS
Venta de Baños
VALLADOLID
SEGOVIA
TOLEDO 679
Puertollano
CIUDAD REAL
Linares-Baeza
Moreda
JAÉN
GRANADA
Gijón
Avilés
Pravia
OVIEDO
LEÓN
PALENCIA
ZAMORA
Medina del Campo
ÁVILA
Talavera de la Reina
SALAMANCA
Plasencia
CÁCERES
Mérida
Zafra
BADAJOZ
CÓRDOBA
Antequera
MÁLAGA
Fuengirola
SEVILLA
Dos Hermanas
La Línea
Gibraltar
Algeciras
CÁDIZ
Jerez de la Frontera
HUELVA
Ayamonte
Vila Real de S.A.
FARO
Tunes
Lagos
Portimão
Funcheira
Beja
Évora
Casa Branca
Barreiro
Setúbal 699
LISBOA
Cascais
Sintra 699
Entroncamento
Caldas da Rainha
Tomar 699
Abrantes
Marvão
Valencia de Alcántara
Elvas
Castelo Branco
Covilhã
Guarda
Vilar Formoso
Coimbra
Coimbra B
Figueira da Foz
Pampilhosa
Aveiro
PORTO
Ermesinde
Amarante
Regua
Pocinho
Vila Real
Mirandela
Guimarães 695a
Braga 695
Viana do Castelo
Valença
Guillarei
Vigo
Redondela
PONTEVEDRA
Santiago de Compostela
A CORUÑA
Ferrol
Betanzos
LUGO
Monforte de Lemos
OURENSE
Canarias
Madeira
AVE high-speed line

SPAIN

Operator: **Renfe Operadora** – unless otherwise indicated.

Services: On long-distance trains first class is known as *Preferente* and second class as *Turista*; a 'super-first class' – *Club* – is additionally available on *AVE* and some *Avant* trains. Unless otherwise indicated (by '2' in the train column or [2] in the notes), all trains convey both first- and second-class seating accommodation.

🍷 indicates a buffet car (*cafetería*) or a mobile trolley service. 🍴 indicates a full restaurant car service or the availability of hot meals served from the buffet car. Meals are served free of extra charge to holders of *Club* and *Preferente* tickets on all *AVE* trains and to holders of *Preferente* tickets on *Alaris*, *Altaria*, *Alvia*, *Euromed*, and *Trenhotel* services. Note that catering services may not be available throughout a train's journey, particularly in the case of trains with multiple origins / destinations.

Train categories:

Alaris: Fast tilting trains.

Altaria (*Alta*): Talgo trains which can change gauge and run on the high-speed lines as well as the broad-gauge system.

Alta Velocidad Española (*AVE*): High-speed trains running on the standard-gauge lines.

AVE-Lanzadera (*AL*): New regional high-speed gauge-changing trains.

Alvia: New high-speed gauge-changing trains.

Arco: Quality day express trains.

Avant (*Av*): Medium-distance high-speed trains on the standard-gauge lines.

Diurno (*D*): Ordinary long-distance day trains.

Estrella (*Estr*): Night trains, conveying 🛏, ▬, [1] and [2] as indicated.

Euromed (*Em*): Trains similar of similar construction to *AVE* but running on the broad-gauge Barcelona - València - Alacant route.

Talgo: Quality express trains using light, articulated stock.

Trenhotel (*Hotel*): Quality night express trains (see Services, above)

▬ indicates coaches equipped with couchettes: for occupancy of these a standard supplement is payable in addition to the normal *Turista* fare. 🛏 indicates sleeping-cars with single, double, and 3- or 4-berth compartments. The *Turista* fare is payable plus a sleeping-car supplement corresponding to the type and standard of accommodation. ***Trenhotel*** services additionally convey *Gran Clase* accommodation: *de luxe* single- and double-occupancy compartments with *en suite* shower and toilet. *Preferente* fare is payable for travel in *Gran Clase* plus a sleeping-car supplement corresponding to the type and standard of accommodation.

Local (*Media Distancia*) and suburban (*Cercanías*) trains are shown without an indication of category except for some fast ***Tren Regional Diesel*** (*TRD*), ***R-598*** services and ***Media Distancia*** (*MD*).

Reservations: Reservations are **compulsory** for all journeys by services for which a **train category** (e.g. *D*, *TRD*) is shown in the timing column. A reservation fee paid to the conductor on board the train costs more than one bought in advance. Advance purchase of tickets is also available for travel by services for which a train number is shown.

Supplements: Higher fares, incorporating a supplement, are payable for travel by *Alaris*, *Altaria*, *Alvia*, *Arco*, *AVE*, *Euromed*, *InterCity*, *Talgo*, and *Trenhotel* services. 'Global' fares – i.e. inclusive of meals and accommodation – are payable for travel by the international hotel trains from Barcelona to Milano / Paris / Zürich and v.v., and Madrid - Paris and v.v.

Timings: Timings have been compiled from the latest information supplied by operators.

650 MADRID - ZARAGOZA - BARCELONA — High-speed services

km		Av	Av	AVE	Av	AVE	AVE	AVE	AVE	AVE	AVE	Av	AVE	AVE	AVE	AVE	Av	AVE	Av	Alvia	AVE	AVE	
		8077	**8087**	**3063**	**8477**	**3071**	**3271**	**3073**	**3081**	**3083**	**3093**	**8127**	**3103**	**3113**	**3123**	**3133**	**8167**	**3151**	**8567**	**609**	**3153**	**3161**	
		M		D		C	B	b	R			y				b		E				⑧f	
	Sevilla **660** d.	...	...	...	...	...	...	...	...	...	...	...	...	...	...	...	...	...	...	...	...	...	...
	Málaga **660** d.	...	...	...	...	...	...	...	...	...	...	...	...	...	...	...	...	...	...	...	...	...	...
0	**Madrid** Puerta de Atocha d.	...	...	0630	...	0700	0720	0730	0800	0830	0930	...	1030	1130	1230	1330	...	1500	...	1505	1530	1600	...
64	Guadalajara - Yebes d.	...	...	|	...	|	|	|	|	|	0954	...	|	|	|	1354	...	|	...	1531	|	|	...
221	Calatayud d.	...	...	|	0735	|	|	0828	|	|	|	...	|	1228	|	|	...	|	1600	1618	1628	|	...
307	**Zaragoza** Delicias d.	...	...	0749	0805	|	|	0855	|	0949	1055	...	1149	1255	1349	1455	...	|	1630	...	1655	|	...
447	Lleida d.	0705	0805	|	...	|	|	0940	|	|	1140	1205	|	1340	|	1540	1605	|	...	...	1740	|	...
526	Camp de Tarragona d.	0735	0835	|	...	|	|	1011	|	|	1211	1235	|	1411	|	1611	1635	|	...	...	1811	|	...
621	**Barcelona** Sants a.	0817	0917	0927	...	0943	1003	1054	1043	1127	1254	1317	1327	1454	1527	1654	1717	1738	....	...	1854	1838	...

	Av	AVE	AVE	AVE	AVE	AVE	AVE	AVE	Av	AVE	AVE	Av	AVE	AVE	AVE	AVE							
	8187	**3163**	**3171**	**3173**	**3181**	**3941**	**3183**	**3191**	**8217**	**3991**	**3193**	**8607**	**3201**	**3203**	**3403**	**3211**							
			⑧		⑧q			⑧f	y				S	y	⑧j	P							
Sevilla **660** d.	...	...	...	...	...	1600	...	...	...	...	...	...	...	...	...	...	...	...	...	...	...	...	...
Málaga **660** d.	...	...	...	...	...	|	...	...	...	1650	...	...	...	...	...	...	...	...	...	...	...	...	...
Madrid Puerta de Atocha d.	...	1630	1700	1730	1800	|	1830	1900	...	|	1930	...	2000	2030	2045	2100	...	...	...	...	...	...	...
Guadalajara - Yebes d.	...	|	|	1754	|	|	|	|	...	|	|	...	|	|	2109	|	...	...	...	...	...	...	...
Calatayud d.	...	|	|	|	|	|	|	|	...	|	2028	2045	|	|	2149	|	...	...	...	...	...	...	...
Zaragoza Delicias d.	...	1749	|	1855	|	1934	1949	|	...	2040	2055	2115	|	2149	2215	|	...	...	...	...	...	...	...
Lleida d.	1805	|	|	1940	|	2022	|	|	2105	2124	2140	...	|	|	2300	|	...	...	...	...	...	...	...
Camp de Tarragona d.	1835	|	|	2011	|	2056	|	|	2135	2150	2211	...	|	|	2329	|	...	...	...	...	...	...	...
Barcelona Sants a.	1917	1927	1938	2054	2043	2139	2127	2143	2217	2233	2254	...	2238	2327	0012	2338	...	...	...	...	...	...	...

	Av	AVE	AVE	Av	AVE	AVE	AVE	AVE	AVE	AVE	AVE	Av	AVE	AVE	AVE	AVE	AVE	AVE	Av	AVE	Av	AVE	
	8476	**3062**	**3260**	**8066**	**3072**	**3270**	**3070**	**3082**	**3940**	**3080**	**3092**	**8096**	**3090**	**3102**	**3990**	**3112**	**3122**	**3132**	**8556**	**3142**	**8146**	**3152**	
		T	C	V	b	B	H			K			⑧h					⑧		b	e		
Barcelona Sants d.	...	0600	0630	0610	0700	0720	0730	0800	0815	0830	0900	0910	0930	1000	1030	1100	1200	1300	...	1400	1410	1500	...
Camp de Tarragona d.	...	0636	|	0649	|	|	|	0836	0851	|	|	0949	|	1036	1106	|	1236	|	...	1436	1449	|	...
Lleida d.	...	0705	|	0720	|	|	|	0905	0920	|	|	1020	|	1105	1135	|	1305	|	...	1505	1520	|	...
Zaragoza Delicias d.	0645	0754	|	...	0832	|	|	0954	1009	|	1032	...	|	1154	1227	1232	1354	1432	1500	1554	...	1632	...
Calatayud d.	0715	|	|	...	|	|	|	1019	|	|	|	...	|	|	|	|	1419	|	1530	|	...	|	...
Guadalajara - Yebes d.	...	0853	|	...	|	|	|	|	|	|	|	...	|	1253	|	|	|	|	...	1653	...	|	...
Madrid Puerta de Atocha a.	...	0923	0908	...	0957	1003	1013	1123	|	1113	1157	...	1213	1323	|	1357	1523	1557	...	1723	...	1757	...
Málaga **660** a.	...	...	...	...	...	...	...	...	|	...	...	...	...	...	1615	...	...	...	...	...	...	...	...
Sevilla **660** a.	...	...	...	...	...	...	...	...	1352	...	...	...	...	...	...	...	...	...	...	...	...	...	...

	AVE	AVE	Av	AVE	AVE	AVE	AVE	Av	Av	AVE	AVE	AVE	Av	AVE									
	3150	**3162**	**8166**	**3160**	**3172**	**3170**	**3182**	**8186**	**8606**	**3180**	**3192**	**3202**	**8206**	**3212**									
	E			⑧p		⑧				Q		k		d									
Barcelona Sants d.	1530	1600	1610	1630	1700	1730	1800	1810	...	1830	1900	2000	2010	2100	...	...	...	...	...	...	...	...	...
Camp de Tarragona d.	|	1636	1649	|	|	|	1836	1849	...	|	|	2036	2049	2136	...	...	...	...	...	...	...	...	...
Lleida d.	|	1705	1720	|	|	|	1905	1920	...	|	|	2105	2120	2205	...	...	...	...	...	...	...	...	...
Zaragoza Delicias d.	|	1754	...	|	1832	|	1954	...	2005	|	2032	2154	...	2254	...	...	...	...	...	...	...	...	...
Calatayud d.	|	1819	...	|	|	|	|	...	2035	|	|	2219	...	|	...	...	...	...	...	...	...	...	...
Guadalajara - Yebes d.	|	|	...	|	|	|	2053	...	...	|	|	|	...	|	...	...	...	...	...	...	...	...	...
Madrid Puerta de Atocha a.	1808	1923	...	1908	1957	2008	2123	...	...	2108	2157	2323	...	0017	...	...	...	...	...	...	...	...	...
Málaga **660** a.	...	...	...	...	...	...	...	...	...	...	...	...	...	...	...	...	...	...	...	...	...	...	...
Sevilla **660** a.	...	...	...	...	...	...	...	...	...	...	...	...	...	...	...	...	...	...	...	...	...	...	...

Madrid – Logroño, Pamplona / Iruña, Huesca – Barcelona

	Alvia	Alvia	Alvia	Alvia	Alvia	AVE	Alvia	Alvia	Alvia	AVE	Alvia	Alvia
	601	**533**	**433**	**605**	**609**	**3363**	**621**	**537**	**701**	**3393**	**437**	**801**
	h	W	F	N		⑤⑦v	J	W	A	k	F	G
Madrid PA ¶ d.	0735	...	...	1035	1505	1605	...	...	1835	1905	...	1935
Guadalajara - Yebes d.	|	...	...	1101	1531	|	...	...	1901	1929	...	|
Calatayud d.	|	...	...	1146	1618	|	...	...	1948	2009	...	|
Logroño **653** a.	|	...	1014	|	|	|	...	...	2158	|	1909	|
Pamplona / Iruña **653** a.	1035	1003	|	1340	1825	|	1710	1757	...	|	|	2240
Zaragoza Delicias d.	...	1156	1210	...	...	1727	1906	1951	...	2036	2103	...
Huesca **654** a.	...	|	|	...	...	1810	|	|	...	2120	|	...
Lleida d.	...	1247	1301	...	...	...	1958	2046	...	...	2159	...
Camp de Tarragona d.	...	1318	1335	...	...	...	2028	2117	...	...	2229	...
Barcelona Sants a.	...	1359	1415	...	...	...	2110	2158	...	...	2310	...

	Alvia	AVE	Alvia	Alvia	Alvia	Alvia	Alvia	Alvia	Alvia	Alvia	AVE	Alvia
	802	**3272**	**702**	**534**	**434**	**602**	**622**	**606**	**530**	**430**	**3592**	**610**
	Z	b	L	W	F	c	J	⑧g	W	F	⑤⑦v	t
Barcelona Sants d.	...	...	...	0735	0735	...	0920	...	1645	1645	...	...
Camp de Tarragona d.	...	...	...	0813	0813	...	0957	...	1724	1724	...	...
Lleida d.	...	...	...	0844	0844	...	1026	...	1756	1756	...	...
Huesca **654** d.	...	0810	...	|	|	...	|	...	|	|	1935	...
Zaragoza Delicias d.	...	0855	...	0934	0934	...	1115	...	1847	1847	2020	...
Pamplona / Iruña **653** d.	0645	|	...	1117	|	1126	1308	1435	2032	|	|	1954
Logroño **653** d.	|	|	0752	...	1122	|	...	|	...	2038	|	|
Calatayud d.	|	0920	0952	...	...	1317	...	|	...	...	|	2153
Guadalajara - Yebes d.	|	0958	1038	...	...	1403	...	|	...	...	|	2241
Madrid PA ¶ a.	0950	1029	1106	...	...	1433	...	1738	...	...	2141	2310

A – ⑧ (not Dec. 24).
B – ①–④ (not Dec. 21 - Jan. 7).
C – ①–⑤ (not Dec. 24 - Jan. 8).
D – ①–⑥ (not Dec. 25, 26, Jan. 1, 2, 6).
E – ①–⑤ (not Dec. 24 - Jan. 8).
F – [12] Barcelona - Bilbao and v.v. (Table **653**).
G – ⑧ (not Dec. 24, 25, 26, 31, Jan. 2).
H – ①–⑤ (not Dec. 25, Jan. 1, 6).
J – [12] and 🍷 Vigo - Barcelona and v.v.
K – ①–⑥ (not Dec. 24 - Jan. 8).
L – ①–⑥ (not Dec. 25).
M – ①–⑤ (not Dec. 8, 25, Jan. 1, 6).
N – ①–⑥ (also Dec. 27, Jan. 3).
P – ⑧ (not Dec. 21 - Jan. 8).
Q – ⑧ (not Dec. 24 - Jan. 8).
R – ①–⑥ (not Dec. 25, Jan. 1, 6).
S – ④⑤⑦ from Jan. 14.
T – ①–⑥ (not Dec. 25, 26, Jan. 1, 2, 6).
V – ①–⑤ (not Dec. 25, 31, Jan. 1, 6).
W – [12] Barcelona - Irún and v.v.
Z – ①–⑥ (not Dec. 25, 26, Jan. 1).
b – Not Dec. 25, Jan. 1.
c – Not Jan. 1.
e – Not Dec. 25, 26, Jan. 1, 6.
d – Not Dec. 24, 26, 31.
f – Not Dec. 24 - Jan. 8.
g – Also Dec. 19, 26.

NOTES continued on next page →

MADRID - SORIA and ZARAGOZA 651

km	*For high-speed trains see Table 650*	2 ①–⑤	2 ⑥⑦		2 ①–⑤ T	17308 2		2 ⑥⑦ U	17012 2	2 ①–⑥		2	17302 2 ⑤		2	2 ⑦	17406 2 ⑤		2 ⑦	17304 2	2	*Estr* 370 C	*Hotel* 995 🍷 F	*Hotel* 945 🍷 B	
0	**Madrid** Chamartín d.	...	...	...	0700	0815	...	0915	1030	...	...	...	1548	...	...	...	1715	...	...	1915	2025	2250	2332t	2348t	...
55	Guadalajara d.	...	...	...	0739	0853	...	0952	1105	...	...	1528	1626	...	...	1751	1751	...	...	1955	2105	2328	|	|	...
138	Sigüenza d.	...	...	...	0842	0945	...	1055	1158	...	...	1631	1720	...	...	1854	1854	...	...	2052	2207	0020	|	|	...
248	**Soria** a.	...	...	...	|	1112	...	|	|	...	...	...	1850	...	...	|	...	...	...	2215	|	|	|	|	...
178	Arcos de Jalón d.	0650	0855	...	0910	...	...	1124	1223	1255	...	...	...	...	1735j	1922	...	...	...	...	2236	0047	|	|	...
241	Calatayud d.	0736	0939	...	...	...	...	...	1259	1341	...	...	...	...	1825	...	...	...	2100	...	...	0126	|	|	...
339	**Zaragoza** Delicias a.	0855	1102	...	...	...	...	...	1400	1452	...	...	...	...	1945	...	...	...	2220	...	...	0249	0455	0515	...

For high-speed trains see Table 650		*Estr* 373 C	2 ①–⑤ T		17305 2 ①–⑤ T	2 ⑥⑦ U	17303 2 ⑥⑦ U		2 ①–⑤		2 ⑥⑦	2		2 b	2 ⑤	2		17309 2	17011 2	17311 2 ⑦	2	2	*Hotel* 996 🍷 F	*Hotel* 946 🍷 B	
Zaragoza Delicias d.	...	0312	...	...	...	...	...	...	0745	...	0915	...	...	...	...	1510	...	...	1725	...	...	2020	2350	0020	...
Calatayud d.	...	0427	...	...	...	...	...	...	0909	...	1035	...	...	...	...	1626	...	...	1823	...	...	2139	|	|	...
Arcos de Jalón d.	...	0508	0611	...	...	0840	...	...	0957	...	1125	1230	...	...	...	1715f	...	...	1900	...	1935o	2228	|	|	...
Soria d.	...	|	|	...	0740	|	0845	...	...	...	...	|	...	...	...	...	...	1740	|	1825	|	...	|	|	...
Sigüenza d.	...	0536	0642	...	0900	0911	1006	...	...	...	...	1301	...	1645	1700	...	...	1903	1925	1947	2005	...	|	|	...
Guadalajara a.	...	0628	0743	...	0949	1012	1054	...	...	...	...	1402	...	1746	1801	...	...	1954	2015	2039	2103	...	|	|	...
Madrid Chamartín a.	...	0721	0823	...	1028	1052	1135	...	...	...	...	...	...	...	1840	...	...	2035	2055	2123	2143	...	0445t	0505t	...

B – ANTONIO MACHADO – (not Dec. 24, 26, 31): 🛏 and [1] Barcelona - Zaragoza - Sevilla - Cádiz and v.v.
C – COSTA BRAVA – (not Dec. 24, 26, 31): 🛏 1, 2 cl., ▬ 2 cl. and [2] Madrid - Barcelona - Portbou / Cerbère and v.v.
F – GIBRALFARO – (Not Dec. 24, 26, 31): 🛏 and [1] Barcelona - Zaragoza - Córdoba - Málaga and v.v.
T – ①–⑤ (not Dec. 8, 25, 31, Jan. 1).
U – ⑥⑦ (also Dec. 8, 25, 31, Jan. 1).

b – Not ⑤.
f – ⑤ only.
j – ⑤⑦ only.
o – ⑦ only.
t – Madrid **Puerta de Atocha**.

ZARAGOZA - BARCELONA 652

km	*For high-speed trains see Table 650*	*Hotel* 995 F🍷 ¶	*Hotel* 945 B🍷 ¶	2	*Hotel* 931 A🍷 ¶	2	*Hotel* 921 G🍷 ¶	2	15650 2 ①–⑤	2	2	2 ⑥⑦	2	2	2	2	2 ①–⑤	2 ①–⑥	2 ⑦	2	2	2	2	*Estr* 370 C	
	Madrid Chamartín **651** d.	2332f	2348f	...	...	...	...	...	...	...	...	...	...	...	...	...	...	...	...	...	...	...	...	2250	...
0	**Zaragoza** Delicias d.	0500	0520	...	0543	...	0632	...	0627	...	...	0905	...	1218	...	...	1508	...	...	1635	...	2029	2101	0254	...
114	Caspe d.	|	|	...	|	...	|	0720	|	...	...	|	...	1345	...	...	|	...	...	1808	...	2200	|	0346	...
★	Lleida d.	|	|	...	0645	0715	0730	|	0836	...	...	1121	1310	|	1545	...	1720	1748	1748	|	...	...	2322	|	...
239	Reus d.	|	|	0643	|	|	|	0911	...	1110	1210	...	1437	1540	1714	1841	...	|	|	2013	2118	...	...	0552	...
257	Tarragona **672** d.	0624t	0644t	0700	0722t	|	0804t	0925	...	1125	1225	...	1454	1557	1729	1857	...	|	|	2030	2134	...	...	0609	...
282	Sant Vicenç de Calders **672** d.	|	|	0719	|	0845	|	0945	...	1145	1245	...	1515	1618	1747	1917	...	1913	1923	2049	2200	...	...	0628	...
342	**Barcelona** Sants **672** a.	0725	0745	0809	0808	0935	0845	1035	...	1235	1335	...	1605	1705	1835	2009	...	2005	2017	2136	2302	...	...	0736	...
345	Barcelona Pass. de Gràcia a.	...	...	0815	...	0944	...	1045	...	1244	1344	...	1614	1714	1844	2015	...	2012	2023	2143	2307	...	...	|	...
	Cerbère **657** a.	...	...	|	...	|	...	|	...	|	|	...	|	|	|	|	...	|	|	|	|	...	...	1035	...
350	**Barcelona** França a.	...	...	0823	...	0952	...	1055	...	1252	1353	...	1623	1722	1852	2024	...	2020	2032	2152	2316	...	...	...	...

For high-speed trains see Table 650	2 ①–⑥	2 ①–⑤	2 ⑦	2	2 ⑥	4 2	2	2	2	2	15657 2	2	2 ⑧z	2	2	2	2	2	*Hotel* 922 G🍷 ¶	*Hotel* 932 A🍷 ¶	2	*Hotel* 996 F🍷 ¶	*Hotel* 946 B🍷 ¶	*Estr* 373 C	
Barcelona França d.	...	...	...	0617	...	0650	0717	0847	0946	1147	...	1347	...	1546	1648	1717	1847	2018	...	...	2118	...	...	...	...
Portbou **657** d.	...	...	...	|	...	|	|	|	|	|	...	|	...	|	|	|	|	|	...	...	|	...	...	1940	...
Barcelona Pass. de Gràcia d.	...	...	...	0626	...	0659	0726	0856	0956	1156	...	1355	...	1556	1656	1726	1855	2026	...	...	2126	...	...	|	...
Barcelona Sants **672** d.	...	...	...	0633	...	0706	0733	0903	1003	1203	...	1403	...	1603	1703	1733	1903	2033	2020	2045	2133	2145	2205	2220	...
Sant Vicenç de Calders **672** d.	...	...	...	0718	...	0807	0818	0948	1047	1248	...	1447	...	1648	1747	1818	1947	2118	|	|	2222	|	|	2317	...
Tarragona **672** d.	...	...	...	0739	...	|	0839	1009	1108	1308	...	1509	...	1708	1809	1837	|	2139	2103t	2133t	2243	2226t	2246t	2341	...
Reus d.	...	...	...	0754	...	|	0855	1028	1123	1326	...	1529	...	1724	1827	1852	|	2154	|	|	2258	|	|	2356	...
Lleida d.	...	0620	...	...	0925	0955	...	|	...	1455	1500	1646	1820	|	1953	|	2111	...	2142	2219	...	|	|	|	...
Caspe d.	0655	|	0828	...	|	...	...	1237	...	...	|	...	|	1920	...	2052	...	...	|	|	...	|	|	0135	...
Zaragoza Delicias a.	0823	0851	0956	...	1153	...	...	1411	...	...	1720	...	2025	2100	...	...	...	...	2238	2319	...	2345	0005	0307	...
Madrid Chamartín **651** a.	...	...	...	...	...	...	...	...	...	...	...	...	...	...	...	...	...	...	...	...	...	0445f	0505f	0721	...

A – PÍO BAROJA – (not Dec. 24, 26, 31): 🛏 and [1] (reclining) Barcelona - Gijón and v.v.
B – ANTONIO MACHADO – (not Dec. 24, 26, 31): 🛏 and [1] Barcelona - Zaragoza - Sevilla - Cádiz and v.v.
C – COSTA BRAVA – (not Dec. 24, 26, 31): 🛏 1, 2 cl., ▬ 2 cl. and [2] Madrid - Barcelona - Portbou / Cerbère and v.v.
F – GIBRALFARO – (Not Dec. 24, 26, 31): 🛏 and [1] Barcelona - Zaragoza - Córdoba - Málaga and v.v.
G – GALICIA – (not Dec. 24, 26, 31): 🛏 and [1] (reclining) Barcelona - A Coruña and Vigo and v.v.

f – Madrid **Puerta de Atocha**.

t – Camp de Tarragona.
z – On ⑦ depart Lleida 1815, arrive Zaragoza 2028.
¶ – Via high speed line.
★ – Leida - Reus: *90 km.*
Lleida - Sant Vicenç: *106 km.*
Zaragoza - Lleida: *189 km.*

Notes continued from previous page, Table 650.

h – Not Dec. 25, 26, 27, Jan. 1, 3.
j – Not Dec. 21, 24, 28, 31, Jan. 4.
k – Not Dec. 24, 31.
p – Not Dec. 23, 24, 25, 27 - 31, Jan. 1, 3 - 7.
q – Not Dec. 24, 25, 27 - 31, Jan. 1, 2, 4 - 8.
t – Not Dec. 24, 25, 26, Jan. 2.
v – Also Dec. 24, 31; not Dec. 25, 27, Jan. 1, 3, 8.
y – Not Dec. 24, 25, 31.

☛ *AVE* trains convey ✕ and 🍷.
Alvia trains convey 🍷.
Avant trains (*Av*) are *Turista* class only.

653 ZARAGOZA - IRÚN and BILBAO

km		18069	18071	16023	16023	Alvia 601	Alvia 534	Alvia 434	Alvia 622	18021	Talgo 633	18073	16025	18023	16017	18075	16027	Alvia 530	Alvia 430	18077	Alvia 701	Alvia 801	18079	Hotel 922	Hotel 932	
		2 P	2	2	2	h	M	Q	J	2	p	2	2	2	2	2	2	M	Q	2	🍸	🍸	2	G 🍸	A 🍸	
		①	①–⑥	①–⑥	①–⑥	🍸	j	j	🍸					⑤			⑦				⑧ r	⑧ q	⑧	¶	¶	
	Barcelona Sants **652** d.	...	...	...	...	...	0735	0735	0920	...	...	...	...	...	...	...	...	1645	1645	...	...	...	...	2020	2045	...
	Madrid Pta de Atocha **650** d.	...	...	...	...	0735	|	|	|	...	...	...	...	...	...	...	...	|	|	...	1835	1935	...	|	|	...
0	**Zaragoza** Delicias d.	...	0638	...	...	|	0934	0934	1115	1140	1420	1425	...	1651	...	1748	...	1847	1847	1918	|	|	2117	2250	2322	...
94	Castejón de Ebro ★ d.	...	0732	0737	...	0943	|	|	1211	1245	1512	1533	1540	1748	...	1849	1904	1942	1946	2025	|	|	2224	0014	0056	...
182	**Pamplona / Iruña** d.	...	|	0837	0857	1035	1119	|	1310	1356	|	|	1637	1856	1940	|	2012	2034	|	|	|	2240	...	|	|	...
234	Altsasu **689** d.	...	|	...	0928y	...	|	|	|	...	|	|	1716y	...	2015y	|	...	2105	|	|	|	...	...	|	|	...
275	Vitoria / Gasteiz **689** d.	...	|	...	1000	...	|	|	1403	...	|	|	1752	...	2045	|	...	|	|	|	|	...	...	|	|	...
321	San Sebastián / Donostia d.	...	|	...	...	...	1302s	|	|	...	|	|	...	...	...	|	...	2222	|	|	|	...	...	|	|	...
337	**Irún** **689** a.	...	|	...	...	...	1325	|	|	...	|	|	...	...	...	|	...	2242	|	|	|	...	...	|	|	...
339	Hendaye **689** a.	...	|	...	...	...	...	|	|	...	|	|	...	...	...	|	...	...	|	|	|	...	...	|	|	...
171	**Logroño** d.	0736	0838a	...	...	...	...	1124	|	...	1604	1629	...	...	...	1954	...	...	2040	2128c	2158	...	...	0102	0149	...
242	Miranda de Ebro **689** d.	0832	...	...	...	...	...	1217	1424	...	...	...	...	...	...	...	...	...	2133	...	...	...	...	...	...	...
347	**Bilbao** Abando **689** a.	...	...	...	...	...	...	1348	...	...	...	...	...	...	...	...	...	...	2303	...	...	...	...	...	...	...

	18070	Alvia 802	18072	Alvia 702	16007	18074	Alvia 533	Alvia 433	Talgo 630	16022	18076	16021		18020	Alvia 621	Alvia 537	Alvia 437	18022	Alvia 610	16011	18078	18017	Hotel 931	Hotel 921		
		S	2	R	2	2	M	Q	p	2	2	2	2	2	J	M	Q	2	k	2	2	2 P	A 🍸	G 🍸		
	①–⑤	🍸		🍸	①–⑥		j	j		①–⑥			c		🍸	🍸	🍸	⑦	🍸			⑦	¶	¶		
Bilbao Abando **689** d.	...	...	...	...	...	...	...	0746	...	...	...	...	...	...	...	...	1645	...	...	...	...	...	...	...	...	...
Miranda de Ebro **689** d.	...	...	...	...	...	...	...	0918	...	...	...	...	...	...	1556	...	1814	...	...	...	...	2130	...	...	...	...
Logroño d.	...	...	0730a	0752	...	...	...	1014	1045	...	1415	...	1645	...	|	...	1909	...	...	...	2012	2230	0305	0403	...	...
Irún **689** d.	...	...	|	|	...	...	0800	|	|	...	|	...	|	...	|	1600	|	...	...	...	|	...	|	|	...	...
San Sebastián / Donostia d.	...	...	|	|	...	...	0818	|	|	...	|	...	|	...	|	1618	|	...	...	...	|	...	|	|	...	...
Vitoria / Gasteiz **689** d.	...	...	|	|	0750	...	|	|	|	...	|	1530	|	...	1617	|	|	...	...	1905	|	...	|	|	...	...
Altsasu **689** d.	...	...	|	|	0820y	...	0932	|	|	...	|	1601y	|	...	|	|	|	...	...	1936y	|	...	|	|	...	...
Pamplona / Iruña d.	...	0645	|	|	0852	0920e	1003	|	|	1400	|	1635	|	1645	1710	1757	|	1905	1954	2013	|	...	|	|	...	...
Castejón de Ebro d.	0625	0735	0830	|	...	1030	1059	1109	1136	1503	1511	...	1739	1747	1808	|	|	2011	|	2113	2121	...	0359	0456	...	...
Zaragoza Delicias a.	0733	|	0940	|	...	1138	1153	1206	1229	...	1613	...	...	1850	1904	1946	2058	2105	|	...	2230	...	0538	0629	...	...
Madrid Pta de Atocha **650** a.	...	0950	...	1106	...	...	|	|	...	...	...	...	...	...	|	|	|	...	2310	...	...	...	|	|	...	...
Barcelona Sants **652** a.	...	...	...	...	...	...	1359	1415	...	...	...	...	...	...	2110	2158	2310	...	...	...	...	...	0808	0845	...	...

A – PÍO BAROJA – (not Dec. 24, 26, 31): 🛏 and (1) (reclining) Barcelona - Gijón and v.v.
G – GALICIA – (not Dec. 24, 26, 31): 🛏 and (1) (reclining) Barcelona - A Coruña and Vigo and v.v.
J – (12) and 🍸 Barcelona - Vigo and v.v.
M – (12) Barcelona - Irún and v.v.
P – To / from Valladolid.
Q – (12) Barcelona - Bilbao and v.v.
R – ①–⑥ (not Dec. 25).
S – ①–⑥ (not Dec. 7, 8, 25, 26, Jan. 1).

a – ①–⑤ (not Dec. 25, Jan. 1).
c – ⑤⑥⑦.
e – ① only.

h – Not Dec. 25, 26, 27, Jan. 1, 3.
k – Not Dec. 24, 25, 26, Jan. 2.
j – Not Dec. 25, 26, 27, Jan. 1, 2, 3.
p – To / from Salamanca (Table **689**).
q – Not Dec. 6, 7, 24, 25, 31.
r – Not Dec. 24.
s – Stops to set down only.
y – Altsasu Pueblo (*230 km*).

¶ – Via high speed line.
★ – Calatayud - Castejón: *140 km.*

654 ZARAGOZA - HUESCA - CANFRANC

2nd class (except *AVE* trains)

km			MD 15660		TRD 15646			AVE 3363	MD 15662	MD 18504	AVE 3393	MD 15664
			E					C		B	p	
	Madrid ◇ **650** d.	...	...	...	...	...	...	1605	...	...	1905	...
0	**Zaragoza** Delicias d.	0659	0841	...	1147	...	1513	1727	1800	1943	2036	2044
58	Tardienta d.	0750	0919	...	1230	...	1603	|	1838	|	2107	2121
80	**Huesca** d.	0813	0933	...	1249	...	1621	1810	1851	2042	2120	2135
115	Ayerbe d.	0856	...	...	1322	...	1659	...	...	...	...	...
174	Sabiñánigo d.	0959	...	...	1424	...	1810	...	...	...	...	...
190	Jaca d.	1022	...	...	1441	...	1831	...	...	...	...	...
215	**Canfranc 324** a.	1054	...	...	...	...	1903	...	...	...	...	...

	MD 18511	MD 15661	AVE 3272			MD 15663		TRD 15647	MD 15665	AVE 3592	
	B	E	q							C	
Canfranc 324 d.	...	...	...	0915	...	...	...	✣	...	...	1725
Jaca d.	...	...	...	0945	...	...	...	1538	...	...	1756
Sabiñánigo d.	...	...	...	1002	...	...	...	1555	...	...	1813
Ayerbe d.	...	...	...	1104	...	...	...	1657	...	...	1916
Huesca d.	0702	0735	0810	1157	...	1536	...	1738	1908	1935	2001
Tardienta d.	|	0751	0822	1215	...	1550	...	1754	1923	|	2016
Zaragoza Delicias a.	0802	0832	0850	1310	...	1631	...	1840	2002	2015	2114
Madrid ◇ **650** a.	...	...	1029	...	...	...	...	...	...	2141	...

B – From / to València.
C – ⑤⑦ (also Dec. 8, 24, 31; not Dec. 6, 25, 27, Jan. 1, 3, 8).
E – ①–⑤ (not Dec. 6, 25, Jan. 1, 6).

p – Not Dec. 24, 31.
q – Not Dec. 25, Jan. 1.

✣ – 🚌 Canfranc - Jaca bus station (± *2 km* from rail station): daily at 1300 from Canfranc; journey 30 minutes; operated by *Mancobús.*
◇ – Madrid Puerta de Atocha.

655 LLEIDA - LA POBLA DE SEGUR

FGC 2nd class

km											
0	**Lleida** d.	0600	0715	0905	...	1145	1345	1515	1750	...	2030
27	Balaguer d.	0623	0744	0934	...	1214	1419	1544	1819	...	2059
77	Tremp d.	...	...	1039	...	...	1524	...	...	...	2204
90	**La Pobla de Segur** a.	...	...	1055	...	...	1540	...	...	...	2220

La Pobla de Segur d.	...	0640	...	...	...	1256	...	...	...	1805
Tremp d.	...	0655	...	...	...	1311	...	...	...	1820
Balaguer d.	0630	0800	0945	...	1225	1416	...	1600	1830	1925
Lleida a.	0659	0830	1014	...	1254	1446	...	1629	1859	1955

656 BARCELONA - PUIGCERDÀ - LATOUR DE CAROL

2nd class

km												
0	**Barcelona** Sants d.	...	0700	0757	0917	1106	1206	1406	1516	1706	1857	2015
33	Granollers - Canovelles d.	...	0741	0836	0952	1148	1241	1447	1553	1747	1933	2051
74	Vic d.	...	0819	0922	1034	1234	1319	1522	1626	1822	2010	2129
90	Torelló d.	...	0834	0939	1051	1249	1335	1535	1644	1838	2029	2144
110	Ripoll d.	...	0855	1005	1112	1311	1357	1555	1706	1902	2053	2205
124	Ribes de Freser **658** a.	...	0914	1023	1134	...	1416	...	1727	1923	2114	...
145	La Molina a.	...	0951	...	1211	...	1454	...	1804	2004	2148	...
159	Puigcerdà a.	0801	1010	...	1231	...	1515	...	1824	2024	2209	...
163	**Latour de Carol** 🚌**312** a.	0807	1017	...	1238	...	1522	...	1831	...	...	...

	Ⓐ										
Latour de Carol 🚌**312** d.	...	...	0815	1031	...	1315	...	1628	...	1842	...
Puigcerdà d.	...	0631	0822	1042	...	1326	...	1636	...	1853	...
La Molina d.	...	0653	0844	1105	...	1348	...	1658	...	1916	...
Ribes de Freser **658** d.	...	0724	0916	1137	...	1420	...	1729	...	1948	...
Ripoll d.	0634	0745	0938	1157	1329	1440	1639	1751	1832	2007	...
Torelló d.	0654	0806	0958	1217	1356	1505	1706	1819	1858	2031	...
Vic d.	0708	0821	1013	1233	1413	1520	1724	1838	1912	2046	...
Granollers - Canovelles d.	0742	0857	1051	1308	1506	1600	1808	1912	1953	2118	...
Barcelona Sants a.	0819	0937	1128	1346	1549	1637	1858	1949	2036	2158	...

BARCELONA - GIRONA - PORTBOU 657

For hotel trains Barcelona - Paris and v.v., see Table **13**; Barcelona - Zürich and v.v., see Table **49**; Barcelona - Milano and v.v., see Table **90**

km		MD		MD			MD	Estr	Talgo	MD			MD	MD			MD		MD			MD	
		15901		15834			30557	370	73	10577			15909	15095			15079		15005			30911	
		[R] 2	2	[R] 2	2	2	[R] 2		🍷	[R] 2	2	2	[R] 2	[R] 2	2	2	[R] 2	2	[R] 2	2	2	[R] 2	
		①-⑤	①-⑤	①-⑤	⑥	①-⑤	⑥⑦	B	T	①-⑤	⑥⑦	①-⑤	⑥⑦	①-⑤	⑥⑦	①-⑤	⑥⑦	①-⑤	①-⑤	⑥⑦	①-⑤	⑦	
		p	p	p		p	q				q	p	q	p	q	p	q	p		q	p	q	
0	**Barcelona** Sants .... **666** d.	0556	0616	0646	0646	0716	0746	0753	0845f	0816	0846	0916	0946	1016	1046	1116	1146	1146	1246	1246	1316	1346	...
3	Barcelona Passeig de Gràcia .... d.	0601	0620	0651	0650	0720	0751	|	|	0821	0850	0920	0951	1021	1050	1120	1151	1151	1251	1250	1320	1351	...
31	Granollers Centre .... d.	|	0649	|	0719	0755	|	0829	|	|	0919	0949	|	|	1119	1149	|	|	|	1319	1349	|	...
72	Maçanet - Massanes .... **666** d.	0655	0726	0748	0756	0836	0848	|	|	0918	0959	1026	1048	1118	1156	1226	1248	1248	1348	1356	1426	1448	...
86	Caldes de Malavella .... d.	0706	0737	0759	0807	0847	0859	0906	|	0929	1010	1037	1059	1129	1207	1237	1259	1259	1359	1407	1437	1459	...
102	**Girona** .... d.	0718	0752	0811	0822	0902	0911	0925	0955	0941	1025	1052	1111	1141	1222	1252	1311	1311	1411	1422	1452	1511	...
118	Flaçà .... d.	0730	0807	0823	0837	0917	0923	0938	|	0953	1040	1107	1123	1153	1237	1307	1323	1323	1423	1437	1507	1523	...
143	Figueres .... d.	0746	0830	0839	0900	0940	0940	0958	1025	1010	1103	1130	1140	1210	1300	1330	1340	1339	1439	1500	1530	1540	...
162	Llançà .... d.	...	0845	...	0915	0955	0953	1016	|	1023	1118	1145	1153	1223	1315	1345	1353	...	...	1515	1545	1553	...
169	**Portbou** 🏛 .... a.	...	0855	...	0925	1005	1000	1025	1048	1030	1128	1155	1200	1230	1325	1355	1400	...	...	1525	1555	1600	...
171	**Cerbère** 🏛 .... **355** a.	...	0900	...	0930	1010	...	1035	1111	...	1133	1200	...	...	1330	1400	...	...	...	1530	1600	...	...

	MD		MD			MD		Talgo		MD	MD	MD				MD	MD						
	30597		15915			30599		460		15081	30583	30583				15087	30589						
	[R] 2	2	[R] 2	2	2	[R] 2	2	🍷	2	[R] 2	[R] 2	[R] 2	2	2	2	[R] 2	[R] 2	2	2	2	2		
	①-⑤	⑥	⑦		Ⓑ	Ⓑ	⑦	M		①-⑤	①-⑤	⑥	⑦	①-⑤		①-⑤	⑥⑦	①-⑤	⑦	①-⑤	⑥⑦		
	p		q							p				p		p							
Barcelona Sants .... **666** d.	1416	1416	1446	1516	1546	1616	1616	1642	1716	1746	1816	1816	1816	1846	1916	1946	2016	2016	2046	2116	2146	...	...
Barcelona Passeig de Gràcia .... d.	1421	1421	1451	1520	1551	1621	1621	|	1720	1751	1821	1821	1821	1851	1920	1951	2021	2021	2051	2121	2151	...	...
Granollers Centre .... d.	|	|	|	1549	|	|	|	|	1749	|	|	|	|	|	1949	|	|	|	|	|	|	...	...
Maçanet-Massanes .... **666** d.	1518	1518	1548	1626	1648	1718	1718	|	1826	1848	1918	1918	1918	1948	2026	2051	2118	2118	2152	2221	2253	...	...
Caldes de Malavella .... d.	1529	1529	1559	1637	1659	1729	1729	|	1837	1859	1929	1929	1929	1959	2037	2102	2129	2129	2203	2232	2304	...	...
Girona .... d.	1541	1541	1611	1652	1709	1741	1741	1748	1852	1911	1941	1941	1941	2011	2059	2114	2141	2141	2214	2242	2314	...	...
Flaçà .... d.	1553	1553	1623	1707	...	1753	1753	|	1907	1923	1953	1953	1953	2023	2114	2126	2153	2153	2226	...	...	...	...
Figueres .... d.	1609	1610	1640	1730	...	1809	1809	1815	1930	1939	2010	2009	2009	2039	2137	2142	2209	2209	2242	...	...	...	...
Llançà .... d.	...	1623	1653	1745	...	...	...	|	1945	...	2023	...	...	...	2152	...	...	...	...	...	...	...	...
Portbou 🏛 .... a.	...	1630	1700	1755	...	...	...	1837	1955	...	2030	...	...	...	2202	...	...	...	...	...	...	...	...
Cerbère 🏛 .... **355** a.	...	...	...	1800	...	...	...	1902	2000	...	...	...	...	...	...	...	...	...	...	...	...	...	...

				MD					MD	MD		MD		Talgo		MD		MD			MD	MD	
				30560					15064	30566		30568		463		30570		15090			15072	15072	
	2	2	2	[R] 2	2	2	2	2	[R] 2	[R] 2	2	[R] 2	2	🍷	2	[R] 2	2	[R] 2	2	2	[R] 2	[R] 2	
	①-⑤	⑥	①-⑤	①-⑤	⑥	⑦	①-⑤	①-⑥	⑦	①-⑥		Ⓑ	⑥	N					①-⑤		⑥⑦	①-⑤	
			p	p	p	q	p	p	q	p									p		q	p	
Portbou 🏛 .... **355** d.	...	...	...	...	...	...	...	0659	...	...	0829	...	...	0952	1029	1126	1229	1326	...	1429	1526	...	...
Llançà .... d.	...	...	...	...	...	...	...	0708	...	...	0838	...	...	|	1038	1133	1238	1333	...	1438	1533	...	...
Figueres .... d.	...	...	0556	0640	0640	...	0710	0724	0740	0817	0854	0947	0947	1013	1054	1147	1254	1347	1417	1454	1547	1547	...
Flaçà .... d.	...	...	0612	0656	0656	...	0727	0746	0756	0833	0916	1003	1003	|	1116	1203	1316	1403	1433	1516	1603	1603	...
Girona .... d.	0611	0626	0626	0710	0710	0710	0741	0802	0810	0847	0932	1017	1017	1042	1132	1217	1332	1417	1447	1532	1617	1617	...
Caldes de Malavella .... d.	0621	0637	0637	0721	0721	0721	0752	0816	0821	0857	0946	1027	1027	|	1146	1227	1346	1427	1457	1546	1627	1627	...
Maçanet - Massanes .... **666** d.	0632	0648	0648	0732	0732	0732	0803	0827	0832	0908	0957	1038	1038	|	1157	1238	1357	1438	1508	1557	1638	1638	...
Granollers Centre .... d.	|	|	|	|	|	|	|	0902	|	|	1032	|	|	|	1232	|	1432	|	|	1632	|	|	...
Barcelona Passeig de Gràcia .... a.	0734	0748	0748	0834	0834	0834	0905	0934	0934	1004	1104	1134	1134	|	1304	1334	1504	1534	1605	1704	1734	1734	...
Barcelona Sants .... **666** a.	0739	0753	0753	0839	0839	0839	0909	0939	0939	1009	1109	1139	1139	1146	1309	1339	1509	1539	1609	1709	1739	1739	...

			MD		MD			Talgo	MD	MD					Estr	MD		MD					
			30518		30592			70	15918	15074					373	15000		15904					
	2	2	[R] 2	2	[R] 2	2	2	🍷	[R] 2	[R] 2	2	2	2	2		[R] 2	2	[R] 2					
	Ⓑ	⑥	①-⑤	⑦	⑥⑦	①-⑤	①-⑤	T	⑦	Ⓑ	⑦	⑥	①-⑤	⑥⑦	C	①-⑤	⑥⑦	①-⑤					
			p		q	p	p		q		q		p	q		p	q	p					
Portbou 🏛 .... **355** d.	1559	1629	...	...	1726	...	1727	1753	1756	...	1829	...	1859	1931	1940	...	2030	2036	...	...	...	...	...
Llançà .... d.	1608	1638	...	...	1733	...	1736	|	1803	...	1838	...	1908	1940	1950	...	2038	2044	...	...	...	...	...
Figueres .... d.	1624	1654	1717	...	1747	...	1752	1812	1817	1847	1854	1854	1924	1956	2005	2017	2051	2058	...	...	...	...	...
Flaçà .... d.	1646	1716	1733	...	1803	...	1814	|	1833	1903	1916	1916	1946	2018	2023	2033	2108	2114	...	...	...	...	...
Girona .... d.	1702	1732	1747	1747	1817	1817	1830	1838	1847	1917	1932	1932	2002	2034	2042	2047	2122	2128	...	...	...	...	...
Caldes de Malavella .... d.	1716	1746	1757	1757	1827	1827	1844	|	1857	1927	1946	1946	2016	2048	2055	2058	2134	2139	...	...	...	...	...
Maçanet-Massanes .... **666** d.	1727	1757	1808	1808	1838	1838	1901	|	1908	1938	1957	1957	2027	2059	|	2109	2145	2150	...	...	...	...	...
Granollers Centre .... d.	1802	1832	|	|	|	|	1934	|	|	|	2032	2032	2102	2138	2131	|	2218	2222	...	...	...	...	...
Barcelona Passeig de Gràcia .... a.	1834	1904	1904	1904	1934	1934	2004	|	2004	2034	2104	2104	2134	2208	|	2205	2247	2252	...	...	...	...	...
Barcelona Sants .... **666** a.	1839	1909	1909	1909	1939	1939	2009	1959f	2009	2039	2109	2109	2139	2213	2206	2209	2252	2256	...	...	...	...	...

B – COSTA BRAVA – (not Dec. 24, 26, 31): 🛏 1, 2 cl., 🛏 2 cl. and (2) Madrid - Barcelona - Cerbère.

– COSTA BRAVA – (not Dec. 24, 26, 31): 🛏 1, 2 cl., 🛏 2 cl. and (2) Portbou - Barcelona - Madrid.

M – MARE NOSTRUM – (12) Lorca - Montpellier.

N – MARE NOSTRUM – (12) Montpellier - Cartagena.

T – CATALÁN TALGO – (12) Barcelona - Montpellier and v.v.

f – Barcelona França.

p – Not Dec. 8, 25, 31, Jan. 1.

q – Also Dec. 8, 25, 31, Jan. 1.

2nd class VALL DE NÚRIA 658

Ribes Enllaç - **Queralbs** - **Núria** rack railway *No service Nov. 1 - 26, 2009*

High Season ⑥⑦ (daily Dec. 23 - Jan. 6, June 20 - Sept. 13; not Nov. 1 - 22). See Note ⊖.
From Ribes: 0920, 1010, 1100, 1150, 1240, 1330, 1420, 1510, 1600, 1650, 1740.
From Núria: 0830, 1010, 1100, 1150, 1240, 1330, 1420, 1510, 1600, 1650, 1740, 1830.

Low Season ①-⑤ (except dates above). No service Nov. 1 - 26.
From Ribes: 0930, 1110, 1250, 1455, 1640, 1730, 1830⑤, 2030⑤.
From Núria: 0830, 1020, 1200, 1400, 1545, 1730, 1820, 1920⑤.

Journey times **Ribes** – **Queralbs** (*6 km*) 20 minutes, **Ribes** – **Núria** (*12 km*) 40 minutes.

Operator: Ferrocarrils de la Generalitat de Catalunya (FGC) ✆ +34 972 73 20 30.

⊖ – Reduced service Dec. 25. Extra evening services run on ⑤.

2nd class AEROPORT ✈ BARCELONA 659

Local rail service *Cercanías* (suburban) line **C2**.

Aeroport ✈ - Barcelona Sants – Barcelona Passeig de Gràcia

Journey time: 22 minutes Sants, 27 minutes Passeig de Gràcia

From Aeroport:

0608, 0638, 0708, 0738 and every 30 minutes until 2308, 2338.

From Barcelona Sants:

0535, 0609, 0639, 0709 and every 30 minutes until 2239, 2309.

660 MADRID - CÓRDOBA - SEVILLA and MÁLAGA — High-speed services

km		AVE	AVE	AVE	AVE	AVE	AVE	AVE	AVE	Alta	Alta	AVE	AVE	Alvia	AVE	AVE	AVE	AVE	AVE	AVE	AVE	AVE	AVE	AVE	
		2260	2062	2070	2270	2072	2080	2280	2090	9218	9366	2092	2100	9320	2102	2110	3940	2112	2120	2122	2130	3990	2140	2142	
		①–⑤	①–⑤	①–⑤			①–⑥	①–⑥			★		①–⑥		①–⑥										
		b	e	f	k	k	k	k		k	k		k	k				g			k				
	Barcelona Sants **650** d.	...	...	...	...	...	...	...	...	...	...	...	...	...	...	...	0815	...	...	...	...	1030	...	...	...
0	**Madrid** Puerta de Atocha d.	0630	0635	0700	0730	0735	0800	0830	0900	0905	0905	0935	1000	1005	1035	1100	|	1130	1200	1235	1300	|	1400	1435	...
171	Ciudad Real d.	0719	|	|	|	|	|	|	0951	1007	1007	1026	|	1057	|	|	1205	|	|	1326	1351	|	|	|	...
210	Puertollano d.	0734	|	|	|	|	|	|	1007	1023	1023	1044	|	1114	|	|	1221	|	|	1342	1407	|	|	|	...
345	**Córdoba** d.	0820	0825	0844	|	|	0944	1014	1052	1110	1110	1127	1144	1157	1219	1244	1306	1314	1344	1427	1452	1513	1544	1619	...
470	**Sevilla** a.	0905	|	0930	0950	|	1030	1100	1135	|	|	|	1230	1247	|	1330	1352	|	1430	|	1535	|	1630	|	...
	Cádiz **671** a.	...	|	...	...	|	...	...	...	|	|	|	...	1428	|	...	...	|	...	|	...	|	...	|	...
	Huelva **671** a.	...	|	...	...	|	...	...	...	|	|	|	...	...	|	...	...	|	...	|	...	|	...	|	...
419	Puente Genil - Herrera ¶ a.	...	0848	...	...	|	...	...	...	|	|	|	...	...	|	...	...	|	...	1448	...	1534	...	|	...
455	Antequera - Santa Ana § a.	...	0901	...	...	|	...	...	...	1148	1148	|	...	...	|	...	...	|	...	1501	...	1547	...	|	...
	Algeciras **673** a.	...	|	...	...	|	...	...	...	|	*1445*	|	...	...	|	...	...	|	...	|	...	|	...	|	...
	Granada **673** a.	...	|	...	...	|	...	...	...	1342	...	|	...	...	|	...	...	|	...	|	...	|	...	|	...
513	**Málaga** María Zambrano a.	...	0930	...	...	1014	...	...	...	...	...	1223	...	...	1315	...	...	1410	...	1530	...	1615	...	1715	...

	AVE	AVE	AVE	Alvia	AVE	AVE	AVE	Alta	Alta	AVE	AVE	AVE	AVE	Alvia	AVE	AVE	AVE	AVE	AVE	AVE	Hotel	Hotel	AVE		
	2150	2152	2160	9332	2360	2162	2170	9234	9330	2172	2180	2182	2190	9386	2390	2192	2200	2202	2210	2212	996	946	2220		
	⑧	⑤⑦			⑤⑦				★				⑧		⑧	⑤⑦					A	B			
	p	g	q	q	m	k		q	q						q	g	b	g	q	y	✕	✕	y		
Barcelona Sants **650** d.	...	...	...	...	...	...	...	...	...	...	...	...	...	...	...	...	...	...	...	...	2145	2205	...	...	...
Madrid Puerta de Atocha d.	1500	1535	1600	1610	1630	1635	1700	1705	1705	1735	1800	1835	1900	1905	1930	1935	2000	2035	2100	2135	0447	0507	2200	...	...
Ciudad Real d.	|	|	|	1702	|	|	1751	|	|	1826	|	|	1951	|	|	|	|	|	|	2226	|	|	2251	...	...
Puertollano d.	|	|	|	1718	|	|	1807	|	|	1844	|	|	2007	|	|	|	|	|	|	2242	|	|	2307	...	...
Córdoba d.	|	|	1744	1803	1814	1819	1852	1909	1909	1927	1944	|	2052	2055	2114	2119	2144	|	2244	2327	0708	0728	2352	...	...
Sevilla a.	1720	|	1830	1855	1900	|	1935	|	|	|	2030	|	2135	|	2200	|	2230	|	2330	|	|	0839	0035	...	...
Cádiz **671** a.	...	|	...	2044	...	|	...	|	|	|	...	|	...	|	...	|	...	|	...	|	|	1031	...	...	...
Huelva **671** a.	...	|	...	...	...	|	...	|	|	|	...	|	...	2245	...	|	...	|	...	|	|	...	...	...	...
Puente Genil - Herrera ¶ a.	...	|	...	...	...	|	...	|	|	1948	...	|	...	...	...	|	...	|	...	2348	0737	...	...	...	...
Antequera - Santa Ana § a.	...	|	...	...	...	|	...	|	|	2001	...	|	...	...	...	|	...	|	...	0001	0754	...	...	...	...
Algeciras **673** a.	...	|	...	...	...	|	...	|	2315	|	...	|	...	...	...	|	...	|	...	|	|	...	...	...	...
Granada **673** a.	...	|	...	...	...	|	...	2141	...	|	...	|	...	...	...	|	...	|	...	|	|	...	...	...	...
Málaga María Zambrano a.	...	1810	...	...	...	1915	...	...	...	2030	...	2110	...	...	...	2215	...	2305	...	0030	0825	...	...	...	...

	AVE	AVE	AVE	AVE	AVE	AVE	AVE	AVE	AVE	AVE	Alvia	AVE	Alvia	AVE	AVE	Alta	Alta	AVE	AVE	AVE	AVE	AVE	AVE	AVE	
	2261	2061	2263	2073	2271	2071	2083	2281	2081	2093	9365	2091	9317	2101	2113	9367	9219	2111	2123	2121	2131	2143	2141	2153	
	①–⑤	①–⑤	①–⑤			①–⑥	①–⑤	①–⑥			①–⑥	①–⑥				★							⑧		
	p	k	e	k	k	k	k	k			j	k	k			k	k		g		k		p		
Málaga María Zambrano d.	...	...	0635	0710	...	...	0800	...	...	0900	...	...	...	...	1100	...	...	...	1200	...	...	1400	...	1500	...
Granada **673** d.	...	...	|	|	...	...	|	...	...	|	...	...	...	...	|	...	0945	...	|	...	...	|	...	|	...
Algeciras **673** d.	...	...	|	|	...	...	|	...	...	|	...	...	...	...	|	0805	|	...	|	...	...	|	...	|	...
Antequera - Santa Ana § d.	...	...	0701	|	...	...	|	...	...	0926	...	...	...	...	|	|	|	...	|	...	...	1426	...	|	...
Puente Genil - Herrera ¶ d.	...	...	0714	|	...	...	|	...	...	|	...	...	...	...	|	|	|	...	|	...	...	1439	...	|	...
Huelva **671** d.	...	...	|	|	...	...	|	...	...	|	0800	...	...	...	|	|	|	...	|	...	...	|	...	|	...
Cádiz **671** d.	...	...	|	|	...	...	|	...	...	|	|	...	0805	...	|	|	|	...	|	...	...	|	...	|	...
Sevilla d.	0615	0645	|	|	0715	0745	|	0815	0845	|	|	0945	0953	1045	|	|	|	1145	|	1245	1345	|	1445	|	...
Córdoba d.	0658	0729	0739	|	0803	|	0856	0858	0929	0959	0954	1028	1047	1129	1156	1213	1213	1229	1256	1328	|	1504	1529	1556	...
Puertollano d.	0740	|	0821	|	0845	|	|	|	|	1041	|	1110	1130	|	|	|	|	|	|	1413	|	1546	|	|	...
Ciudad Real d.	0755	|	0837	|	0859	|	|	|	|	1057	|	1124	1145	|	|	|	|	|	|	1427	|	1602	|	|	...
Madrid Puerta de Atocha a.	0850	0915	0932	0940	0955	1005	1040	1045	1115	1150	1145	1220	1238	1315	1340	1429	1429	1415	1440	1520	1605	1655	1715	1740	...
Barcelona Sants **650** a.	...	...	...	...	...	...	...	...	...	...	...	...	...	...	...	...	...	...	...	...	...	...	...	...	...

	AVE	AVE	AVE	AVE	AVE	AVE	AVE	Alvia	AVE	AVE	Alvia	AVE	AVE	AVE	AVE	AVE	Alta	Alta	AVE	Hotel	Hotel	AVE	AVE		
	2151	2163	3941	2361	2161	3991	2173	9383	2171	2183	9333	2181	2391	2193	2191	2203	9331	9237	2201	995	945	2213	2211		
		⑤⑦			⑤⑦			⑦				⑧	⑧	⑤⑦			★			A	B				
		g		q	k			h					q	g	q	g	q	q	w	✕	✕	k	d		
Málaga María Zambrano d.	...	1600	...	...	...	1650	1700	...	...	1805	...	...	...	1900	...	2000	...	...	...	2005	...	2100	...	...	...
Granada **673** d.	...	|	...	...	...	|	|	...	...	|	...	...	...	|	...	|	...	1800	...	|	...	|	...	...	...
Algeciras **673** d.	...	|	...	...	...	|	|	...	...	|	...	...	...	|	...	|	1650	|	...	|	...	|	...	...	...
Antequera - Santa Ana § d.	...	|	...	...	...	1715	1726	...	...	|	...	...	...	|	...	|	1950	1950	...	2031	...	2126	...	...	...
Puente Genil - Herrera ¶ d.	...	|	...	...	...	1728	1739	...	...	|	...	...	...	|	...	|	|	|	...	2046	...	2139	...	...	...
Huelva **671** d.	...	|	...	...	...	|	|	1623	...	|	...	...	...	|	...	|	|	|	...	|	...	|	...	...	...
Cádiz **671** d.	...	|	...	...	...	|	|	|	...	|	1626	...	...	|	...	|	|	|	...	|	1824	|	...	...	...
Sevilla d.	1545	|	1600	1615	1645	|	|	|	1745	|	1811	1845	1915	|	1945	|	|	|	2045	|	2011	|	2145	...	...
Córdoba d.	1629	|	1645	1700	1729	1753	1804	1816	1829	|	1903	1929	|	2002	2029	|	2031	2031	2129	2118	2124	2204	2228	...	...
Puertollano d.	|	|	1727	1742	|	|	|	|	|	|	1946	|	|	|	|	|	2120	2120	|	|	|	2247	2312	...	...
Ciudad Real d.	|	|	1741	1756	|	|	|	|	|	|	2001	|	|	|	|	|	2138	2138	|	|	|	2303	2326	...	...
Madrid Puerta de Atocha a.	1815	1840	|	1850	1915	|	1948	2008	2015	2040	2056	2115	2135	2145	2215	2235	2250	2250	2315	2330	2345	2355	0020	...	...
Barcelona Sants **650** a.	...	...	2139	...	...	2233	...	...	...	...	...	...	...	...	...	...	...	...	...	0725	0745	...	...	...	...

A – GIBRALFARO – (Not Dec. 24, 26, 31): 🛏 and 1 Barcelona - Zaragoza - Córdoba - Málaga and v.v.
B – ANTONIO MACHADO – (not Dec. 24, 26, 31): 🛏 and 1 Barcelona - Zaragoza - Sevilla - Cádiz and v.v.
b – Not Dec. 24, 25, 26, 31, Jan. 1, 5, 6.
d – Not Dec. 24, 26, 31.
e – Not Dec. 21 - Jan. 8.
f – Not Dec. 25, 26, Jan. 1.
g – Not Dec. 20 - Jan. 9.
h – Also Dec. 7, 8, 25, 26, 27, Jan. 1, 2, 4, 5, 6.
j – Not Dec. 7, 8, 25, 26, 27, Jan. 1, 2, 4, 5, 6.
k – Not Dec. 25, Jan. 1.
m – Not Jan. 1, 3.
p – Not Dec. 24, 25, 31, Jan. 1, 6.
q – Not Dec. 24, 31.
w – Not Dec. 24, 25, 26, 31, Jan. 1.
y – Not Dec. 24, 26, 31.
§ – ± *17 km* from Antequera.
★ – Oct. 26 - Mar. 25: 🚌 Antequera - Ronda - Algeciras and v.v.
¶ – ± *8 km* from Puente Genil.
☛ All trains convey 🍷. *AVE* trains also convey ✕.

Madrid – Puertollano *Avant* high-speed shuttle services

Turista class; 🍷

		8260		8080		8100			8130	8140		8150		8170	8180	8190	8200	8210	8220					
		A								C		B			D		⑧	E	⑧p					
Madrid Puerta de Atocha d.	...	0640	...	0815	...	1015	...	...	1315	1415	...	1545	...	1715	1815	1915	2015	2115	2215	...	...	...	...	...
Ciudad Real d.	...	0736	...	0911	...	1111	...	...	1411	1511	...	1641	...	1811	1911	2011	2111	2211	2311	...	...	...	...	...
Puertollano a.	...	0753	...	0928	...	1128	...	...	1428	1528	...	1658	...	1828	1928	2028	2128	2228	2328	...	...	...	...	...

		8261		8271	8471	8081		8101		8121			8151	8161	8171	8181	8191	8201	8211					
		A		E	C								B	C		⑦q		D	p					
Puertollano d.	...	0625	...	0700	0745	0815	...	1015	...	1215	...	...	1515	1615	1715	1815	1915	2015	2115	...	...	...	...	...
Ciudad Real d.	...	0642	...	0717	0802	0832	...	1032	...	1232	...	...	1532	1632	1732	1832	1932	2032	2132	...	...	...	...	...
Madrid Puerta de Atocha a.	...	0738	...	0813	0858	0928	...	1128	...	1328	...	...	1628	1728	1828	1928	2028	2128	2228	...	...	...	...	...

A – ①–⑤ (not Dec. 7, 8, 24, 25, 31, Jan. 1, 6).
B – ①–⑥ (not Dec. 8, 25, Jan. 1, 6).
C – ①–⑤ (not Dec. 24 - Jan. 6).
D – ⑧ (not Dec. 24 - Jan. 6).
E – ①–⑥ (not Dec. 8, 24, 25, 31, Jan. 1, 6).
p – Not Dec. 24, 31.
q – Also Jan. 6.

Málaga – Córdoba – Sevilla *Avant* high-speed shuttle services

Turista class; 🍷

	8654	8664	8664	8694	8664	8744	8764	8784	8804
	A	A			A		A		
Málaga María Zambrano d.	...	0645	...	0910	...	1430	1615	1810	2015
Antequera - Santa Ana § d.	...	0711	...	0936	...	1456	1641	1836	2041
Puente Genil - Herrera ¶ d.	...	0726	...	0950	...	1510	1655	1850	2055
Córdoba a.	...	0750	...	1015	...	1535	1720	1915	2120
Córdoba d.	0650	0755	0755	1020	1255	1540	1725	1920	2125
Sevilla a.	0735	0840	0840	1105	1340	1625	1810	2005	2210

	8075	8085	8095	8095	8125	8155	8175	8195	8215	
	A	A	⑥⑦				A			
Sevilla d.	0650	0800	0920	0920	1230	1540	1755	1935	2135	...
Córdoba a.	0735	0845	1005	1005	1315	1625	1840	2020	2220	...
Córdoba d.	0740	0850	1010	...	1320	1630	1845	2025	...	...
Puente Genil - Herrera ¶ d.	0803	0913	1033	...	1343	1653	1908	2048	...	...
Antequera - Santa Ana § d.	0817	0927	1047	...	1357	1707	1922	2102	...	...
Málaga María Zambrano a.	0845	0955	1115	...	1425	1735	1950	2130	...	...

A – ①–⑤ (not Dec. 7, 8, 25, Jan. 1, 6).
§ – ± *17 km* from Antequera.
¶ – ± *8 km* from Puente Genil.

MADRID - GRANADA, ALMERÍA and MÁLAGA — 661

For other trains Madrid – Córdoba – Granada / Málaga and v.v. via the AVE high-speed line, see Table **660**

km		17008	AL 9070	13097	13068	Talgo 276	MD 18030	13058	Arco 697	Arco 697	Arco 697	13035	17804		13073	Talgo 278	MD 18032	MD 18034	MD 18036	17000	Hotel 897	Hotel 996	Estr 940	
		2	Ⓡ🍷	2	2	🍷	Ⓡ2	2	2🍷	2🍷	2🍷	2	2	2	2	🍷	Ⓡ2	Ⓡ2	Ⓡ2	2	✕	✕	🍷	
		①–⑤																						
		V	J		A	g		⑤⑥	N	G	H	D	B		D	h	E	Ⓑf			R	S	P	
0	**Madrid** Chamartín § d.	0754	...	...	...	0800	0916	...	...	...	...	...	...	...	...	1514	1535	1720	1913	2040	...	...	...	...
8	**Madrid** Atocha Cercanías § d.	0813	...	...	...	0818	0930	...	...	...	...	...	1328	...	...	1532	1548	1738	1932	2055	...	...	...	...
57	Aranjuez § d.	0856	...	...	...	|	1008	...	...	...	...	...	1409	...	...	|	1623	|	2007	2129	...	...	...	...
	Barcelona Sants **672** d.	|	...	...	...	|	|	...	0800	0800	0800	...	|	...	...	|	|	|	|	|	2130	2145	...	...
	València Nord **668** d.	|	...	...	...	|	|	...	1128	1128	1128	...	|	...	...	|	|	|	|	|	0051	|	...	...
157	Alcázar de San Juan **678** d.	0948	...	...	...	0937	1058	...	1455	1455	1455	...	1501	...	...	1653	1710	1853	2055	2228	0401	|	...	...
	Bilbao Abando **689** d.	...	...	...	...	|	|	...	|	|	|	...	|	...	...	|	|	|	|	...	|	|	2125	...
206	Manzanares **678** d.	...	...	...	...	|	1122	...	1518	1518	1518	...	1527	...	...	1719	1734	1916	2120	...	|	|	0535	...
323	Linares - Baeza a.	...	...	...	...	1117	1237	...	1636	1636	1636	...	...	...	...	1837	1853	2033	2235	...	0538	|	0650	...
323	Linares - Baeza d.	...	...	...	...	1119	1238	...	1646	1655	1655	...	...	1730	...	1838	1854	2033	2236	...	0548	|	0651	...
441	Moreda d.	...	...	...	...	|	|	...	|	1836	1836	...	...	1917	...	|	|	|	|	...	|	|	|	...
499	**Granada** **673** a.	...	...	...	...	|	|	...	|	|	1930	...	...	2006	...	|	|	|	|	...	0835	|	|	...
466	Guadix **673** d.	...	...	...	...	1301	|	...	|	1858	...	...	...	...	...	2025	|	|	|	...	...	|	|	...
565	**Almería** **673** a.	...	...	...	...	1412	|	...	|	2018	...	...	...	...	...	2136	|	|	|	...	...	|	|	...
¶	**Jaén** d.	...	0730	1000	...	...	1320	...	|	...	...	1650	...	...	1840	...	1938	2116	2318	...	...	|	|	...
371	Andújar d.	...	0810	1040	...	...	...	...	1721	...	...	1738	...	...	1922	...	...	...	...	...	...	|	|	...
450	**Córdoba** a.	...	0902	1136	...	...	...	...	1815	...	...	1830	...	...	2011	...	...	...	...	...	...	0705	0824	...
450	**Córdoba** d.	...	...	...	1215	...	...	1645	1825	...	...	...	...	...	...	...	...	...	...	...	...	0708	0824	...
501	Montilla d.	...	...	...	1252	...	...	1729	1900	...	...	...	...	...	...	...	...	...	...	...	...	|	|	...
527	Puente Genil d.	...	...	...	1314	...	...	1751	1919	...	...	...	...	...	...	...	...	...	...	...	...	0739**p**	0938	...
574	Bobadilla **673** d.	...	...	...	1352	...	...	1827	1954	...	...	...	...	...	...	...	...	...	...	...	...	|	1013	...
643	**Málaga** María Zambrano **673** a.	...	...	...	...	...	...	...	2116	...	...	...	...	...	...	...	...	...	...	...	...	0825	1115	...

	18047	MD 18031		MD 18033	Talgo 277	13093	Arco 694	Arco 694	Arco 694	17041		MD 18035	17801	13047	MD 18037	13071	13067	13069	Talgo 279	AL 9181	Hotel 894	Hotel 995	Estr 941	
	2	Ⓡ2		Ⓡ2	🍷	2	2🍷	2🍷	2🍷	2	2	Ⓡ2	2	2	Ⓡ2	2	2	2	🍷	Ⓡ🍷	✕	✕	🍷	
	①–⑤	E			g		H	G	N	C			B	D		D	A	⑤⑥	h	J	R	T	Q	
Málaga María Zambrano **673** d.	...	...	...	...	...	...	...	...	0710	...	...	...	...	...	...	...	...	...	...	...	...	2005	2235	...
Bobadilla **673** d.	...	...	...	...	...	...	...	...	0802	...	...	...	...	...	...	...	1600	1915	...	...	...	|	2328	...
Puente Genil d.	...	...	...	...	...	...	...	...	0832	...	...	...	...	...	...	...	1635	1954	...	...	...	2046**p**	2359	...
Montilla d.	...	...	...	...	...	...	...	...	0853	...	...	...	...	...	...	...	1657	2015	...	...	...	|	|	...
Córdoba a.	...	...	...	...	...	...	...	...	0934	...	...	...	...	...	...	...	1736	2054	...	...	...	2115	0057	...
Córdoba d.	...	...	...	...	...	0800	...	...	1000	...	...	...	...	1447	...	1623	...	...	...	2042	...	2118	0058	...
Andújar d.	...	...	...	...	...	0858	...	...	1051	...	...	...	...	1543	...	1718	...	...	...	2134	...	|	|	...
Jaén d.	...	0620	...	0838	...	0945	...	...	|	...	...	1538	...	1634	1718	1812	...	...	...	2218	...	|	|	...
Almería **673** d.	...	|	...	|	0705	...	0740	...	|	...	...	|	...	...	|	...	...	...	1605	...	...	|	|	...
Guadix **673** d.	...	|	...	|	0816	...	0907	...	|	...	...	|	...	...	|	...	...	...	1718	...	...	|	|	...
Granada **673** d.	...	|	...	|	|	...	|	0845	|	...	1335	|	...	...	|	...	...	...	|	...	2155	|	|	...
Moreda d.	...	|	...	|	|	...	0931	0937	|	...	1425	|	...	...	|	...	...	...	|	...	|	|	|	...
Linares - Baeza a.	...	0702	...	0920	0958	...	1105	1110	1123	...	1558	1617	...	...	1757	...	...	...	1910	...	0028	|	0215	...
Linares - Baeza d.	...	0703	...	0921	0959	...	1147	1147	1147	...	...	1618	...	...	1758	...	...	...	1911	...	0040	|	0216	...
Manzanares **678** d.	...	0821	...	1041	|	...	1308	1308	1308	1520	...	1741	1809	...	1925	...	...	...	2034	...	|	|	0333	...
Bilbao Abando **689** a.	...	|	...	|	|	...	|	|	|	|	...	|	|	...	|	...	...	...	|	...	|	|	1229	...
Alcázar de San Juan **678** d.	0551	0849	...	1107	1141	...	1353	1353	1353	1550	...	1807	1836	...	1949	...	...	...	2101	...	0230	|	...	...
València Nord **668** a.	|	|	...	|	|	...	1650	1650	1650	|	...	|	|	...	|	...	...	...	|	...	0505	|	...	...
Barcelona Sants **672** a.	|	|	...	|	|	...	2050	2050	2050	|	...	|	|	...	|	...	...	...	|	...	0929	0725	...	...
Aranjuez § d.	0644	0934	...	1152	|	...	...	...	...	1652	...	1850	1927	...	2032	...	...	...	|	...	...	...	...	...
Madrid Atocha Cercanías § a.	0722	1008	...	1226	1305	...	...	...	...	1728	...	1926	2006	...	2107	...	...	...	2218	...	...	...	...	...
Madrid Chamartín § a.	0737	1022	...	1240	1320	...	...	...	...	1742	...	1940	...	...	2120	...	...	...	2236	...	...	...	...	...

A – ①②③④⑦.
B – To / from Badajoz (Table **678**).
C – From Ciudad Real.
D – To / from Sevilla.
E – ①–⑤ (not Dec. 25, 31, Jan. 1).
G – GARCÍA LORCA – ①④⑥.
H – GARCÍA LORCA – ③⑤⑦.
J – To / from Cádiz (Table **671**).

N – GARCÍA LORCA – [2] Barcelona - Málaga and v.v.; [12] Barcelona - Córdoba - Sevilla and v.v. (Table **671**).
P – PICASSO – Dec. 4: 🛏, ━ and [12] Bilbao - Málaga (Table **689**).
Q – PICASSO – Dec. 8: 🛏, ━ and [12] Málaga - Bilbao (Table **689**).
R – ALHAMBRA – (not Dec. 24, 26, 31): 🛏 and [1] (reclining) Barcelona - Granada and v.v.
S – GIBRALFARO – (Not Dec. 24, 26, 31): 🛏 and [1] Barcelona - Málaga. Calls at Antequera - Santa Ana 0754.
T – GIBRALFARO – (Not Dec. 24, 26, 31): 🛏 and [1] Málaga - Barcelona. Calls at Antequera - Santa Ana 2031.
V – ①–⑤ (not Nov. 9, Dec. 7, 8).
f – Not Dec. 24, 31, Jan. 1.
g – Not Dec. 25, Jan. 1.
h – Not Dec. 24, 31.

p – Puente Genil - **Herrera**.
¶ – Linares - Jaen: *59 km*. Jaen - Andújar: *54 km*.
§ – Madrid - Alcázar and v.v. (see also Table **667**).

MÁLAGA - TORREMOLINOS - FUENGIROLA — 662

2nd class

km				⚒		⚒			
0	**Málaga** María Zambrano d.	0519	0549	0619	0649	0719	0749	and	2219
8	Aeropuerto ✈ d.	0534	0604	0634	0704	0734	0804	every	2234
16	**Torremolinos** d.	0546	0616	0646	0716	0746	0816	30	2246
20	Benalmádena d.	0553	0623	0653	0723	0753	0823	minutes	2253
31	**Fuengirola** a.	0609	0639	0709	0739	0809	0839	until	2309

		⚒		⚒						
Fuengirola d.	0617	0647	0717	0747	0817	and	2217	2247	2317	...
Benalmádena d.	0630	0700	0730	0800	0830	every	2230	2300	2330	...
Torremolinos d.	0637	0707	0737	0807	0837	30	2237	2307	2337	...
Aeropuerto ✈ d.	0649	0719	0749	0819	0849	minutes	2249	2319	2349	...
Málaga María Zambrano a.	0703	0743	0813	0843	0913	until	2303	2333	0003	...

MADRID - VALLADOLID — 663

High-speed services

km		AVE 4069	Alvia 4071	Alvia 4073	Alvia 4087	Alvia 4087	AL 8089	AL 8109	Alvia 4111		Alvia 4133	AVE 4149	Talgo 151	Talgo 151	Alvia 4141	AL 8159	Alvia 4167	Alvia 4167	AL 8179	Alvia 4183	Alvia 4181	AL 8199	Alvia 4201	AL 8219
		①–⑤	①–⑥	①–⑥	①–⑥		①–⑤	⑥⑦					①–⑥	①–⑥				Ⓑ	⑤		Ⓑ			
		f	A	f	w		2 f	2 t								2		C	2	b	h		h	2 b
	Alacant Terminal **668** d.	...	...	...	...	...	...	...	...	...	...	...	...	...	1035n	...	...	...	...	1400	...	...	...	...
0	**Madrid** Chamartín d.	0635	0650	0740	0800	0800	0835	1030	1100	...	1330	1400	1420	1420	1440	1530	1610	1610	1730	1805	1830	1915	2015	2100
68	Segovia Guiomar ¶ d.	|	|	|	0833	0833	0906	1101	|	...	|	|	1453	1453	1516	1601	1643	1643	1801	1841	|	1946	|	2131
	A Coruña **680** a.	|	|	|	|	|	|	|	|	...	|	|	2208	|	|	|	|	|	|	|	|	|	|	|
	Pontevedra **680** a.	|	|	|	|	|	|	|	|	...	|	|	...	2226	|	|	|	|	|	|	|	|	|	|
180	**Valladolid** Campo Grande a.	0737	0801	0851	0917	0917	0945	1140	1211	...	1441	1456	...	...	1559	1640	1732	1732	1840	1924	1945	2025	2125	2210
	Gijón Cercanías **681** a.	...	1155	|	|	|	...	...	1605	...	|	...	...	...	2002	...	|	|	...	|	2339	...	...	...
	Santander **681** a.	...	...	1207	|	|	...	...	...	...	1755	...	...	...	...	...	|	|	...	2242	...	...	...	...
	Bilbao Abando **689** a.	...	...	...	1252	|	...	...	...	...	...	...	...	...	...	...	|	2111	...	...	...	...	...	...
	Hendaye **689** a.	...	...	...	...	1354	...	...	...	...	...	...	...	...	...	...	2203	...	...	...	...	...	...	...

	AL 8278	Alvia 4060	AVE 4088	AL 8108	Alvia 4072	Alvia 4070	Alvia 4086	Alvia 4086	Alvia 4100	AL 8168	AVE 4178	Alvia 4142	Alvia 4140		AL 8198	Talgo 152	Talgo 152	AL 8218	Alvia 4166	Alvia 4166		Alvia 4180	Alvia 4182	
	①–⑤	①–⑥	①–⑤			①–⑥		①–⑥								Ⓑ	Ⓑ	⑤⑥⑦		Ⓑ		Ⓑ	Ⓑ	
	2 f	y	f	2	y	f		D		2								2 t		q		B	b	
Irún **689** d.	...	...	...	...	...	...	0825	...	...	...	...	...	...	...	...	...	...	...	1620	...	...	...	...	...
Bilbao Abando **689** d.	...	...	...	...	...	...	|	0855	...	...	...	...	...	...	...	...	...	...	|	1710	...	...	...	...
Santander **681** d.	...	...	...	...	0705	...	|	|	...	...	...	1405	...	...	...	...	...	...	|	|	...	...	1920	...
Gijón Cercanías **681** d.	...	...	...	...	|	0715	|	|	1025	...	...	|	1400	...	...	...	...	...	|	|	...	1815	|	...
Valladolid Campo Grande d.	0645	0804	0830	0920	1021	1114	1240	1240	1420	1530	1700	1718	1801	...	1935	...	...	2030	2048	2048	...	2210	2237	...
Pontevedra **680** d.	|	|	|	|	|	|	|	|	|	|	|	|	|	...	|	1250	...	|	|	|	...	|	|	...
A Coruña **680** d.	|	|	|	|	|	|	|	|	|	|	|	|	|	...	|	|	1310	|	|	|	...	|	|	...
Segovia Guiomar ¶ d.	0723	|	|	0958	1106	|	1325	1325	|	1608	|	|	1846	...	2013	2033	2033	2108	2133	2133	...	|	|	...
Madrid Chamartín a.	0755	0920	0932	1030	1143	1229	1400	1400	1540	1640	1756	1833	1923	...	2045	2108	2108	2140	2208	2208	...	2325	2352	...
Alacant Terminal **668** a.	...	...	...	...	1558	...	...	...	...	...	...	...	2338p	...	...	...	...	...	...	...	...	...	...	...

A – ①–⑥ (not Dec. 7, 25, Jan. 1, 6).
B – Ⓑ (not Dec. 7, 24, 31).
C – Ⓑ (not Dec. 7, 24, 31, Apr. 4).
D – ①–⑥ (not Dec. 8, 25, 31, Jan. 6).

b – Not Dec. 24, 31.
f – Not Dec. 25, Jan. 1, 6.
h – Not Dec. 7, 24, 31.
j – Also Dec. 31, Jan. 6; not Dec. 25, 1, 2.

n – Not ⑦.
p – Not ⑥.
q – Not Dec. 8, 24, 31.
t – Also Dec. 25, Jan. 1, 6.

w – Not Dec. 8, 25, Jan. 1, 6.
y – Not Dec. 25, Jan. 1.
☛ All trains convey 🍷. *AVE* trains also convey ✕.
¶ – *4 km* from city centre.

664 BARCELONA - ANDORRA

From **Barcelona** Nord bus station: 0615, 1030, 1300Ⓑ, 1500, 1900.
From **Andorra la Vella** bus station: 0600, 1030, 1500, 1700Ⓑ, 1915.

Journey 3 hrs 15 mins. Operator: Alsina Graells, Barcelona (ALSA) ✆ +34 902 42 22 42.
Additional slower services also operate.

From **Barcelona** Sants railway station: 0615, 0815, 1145, 1345, 1545, 1815, 2045, 2345.
From **Andorra la Vella** bus station: 0615, 0815, 1115, 1315, 1515, 1815, 2015, 2215.
Journey 3 hours (continues to / from Barcelona ✈). Operator: Autocars Nadal ✆ +376 805 151.

665 SITGES — 2nd class

Local rail service **Barcelona - Sitges - Sant Vicenç de Calders**.
From Barcelona Sants: 0606, 0636 and every 30 minutes until 2206; then 2306.
From Sant Vicenç: 0600, 0615, 0632Ⓐ, 0643Ⓐ, 0658, 0732, 0751, 0816, 0831, 0903, 0933 and every 30 minutes until 2103; then 2200.

Additional trains operate **Barcelona - Sitges** and v.v.

Journey times: **Barcelona** – **Sitges** (*34 km*) 30 minutes,
Barcelona – **Sant Vicenç** (*60 km*) 57 minutes.

666 BARCELONA - MATARÓ, BLANES and MAÇANET — 2nd class

Cercanías (suburban) line **C1**. For faster services Barcelona - Maçanet via Granollers, see Table **657**.
Approximate journey times (in mins) to / from **Barcelona** Sants: Mataró (43), Arenys de Mar (55), Calella (71), Pineda de Mar (74), Malgrat de Mar (80), Blanes (85), Maçanet-Massanes (98).

Barcelona Sants – **Mataró** and v.v. *35 km*
Ⓐ: 4–6 trains per hour.
From Barcelona 0555–2311; from Mataró 0526–2234.
Ⓒ: 2–4 trains per hour.
From Barcelona 0612–2300; from Mataró 0559–2220.

Barcelona Sants – **Blanes** *67 km*
0612, 0642 and every 30 mins. until 2042, then 2124, 2158, 2233.
Blanes - **Barcelona** Sants
0603, 0633, 0653, 0703, 0733 and every 30 mins. until 2103, 2144.

Barcelona Sants – Blanes – **Maçanet-Massanes** *82 km*
0612, 0712 and hourly until 1912, then 2042, 2158.
Maçanet-Massanes – Blanes – **Barcelona** Sants
0620, 0650, 0720, 0820 and hourly until 2020, then 2130.

667 ALACANT - BENIDORM - DÉNIA — 2nd class

By tram (route L1)									N
Alacant Mercado ⊙ d.	0544	0614	every	1944	2014	2044	2114	2144	2325z
El Campello d.	0609	0639	30	2009	2039	2109	2139	2209	2350
La Vila Joiosa d.	0638	0708	minutes	2038	2108	2138	2208	2238	0017
Benidorm a.	0653	0723	until	2053	2123	2153	2223	2253	0034
By train (route L9)									
Benidorm d.	0659	...		2059	...	2159	...	...	...
Altea d.	0714	...	every	2114	...	2211	...	...	...
Calpe d.	0730	...	hour	2130	...	...	...	...	...
Teulada d.	0745	...	until	2145	...	...	...	...	...
Gata d.	0754	...		2154	...	...	...	...	...
Dénia a.	0808	...		2208	...	...	...	...	...

By train (route L9)									
Dénia d.	...	...	...	0620	...		2020	...	...
Gata d.	...	...	...	0635	...		2035	...	...
Teulada d.	...	...	...	0644	...	every	2044	...	...
Calpe d.	...	...	...	0659	...	hour	2059	...	...
Altea d.	...	0616	...	0716	...	until	2116	...	2216
Benidorm a.	...	0629	...	0729	...		2129	...	2229
By tram (route L1)	P								
Benidorm d.	0053	0635	0705	0735	0805	every	2135	2205	...
La Vila Joiosa d.	0109	0653	0723	0753	0823	30	2153	2223	...
El Campello d.	0142	0723	0753	0823	0853	minutes	2223	2253	...
Alacant Mercado ⊙ a.	0208z	0748	0818	0848	0918	until	2248	2318	...

N – ④⑤⑥ July 2 - Sept. 12 (also departure at 0055 next day).
P – ⑤⑥⑦ July 3 - Sept. 13 (also departure at 0223).
z – **Alacant** Puerta del Mar.
⊙ – ± 900 m from Alacant Renfe station.
Operator: Tram Metropolitano / FGV ✆ 900 72 04 72 www.fgvalicante.com

668 MADRID - CARTAGENA, ALACANT and VALÈNCIA

km		*Hotel* 894 ✕ C	18024 2 ①–⑤	*Alaris* 1074 ✕ G	2 ⑥⑦	*Alvia* 1076 🍸 D	*Alta* 220 🍸 E	*Alaris* 1084 ✕ K	*Alaris* 1094 ✕ ①–⑥	*Alvia* 1096 🍸 p	18081 2	*Alta* 222 🍸	*Alaris* 1414 ✕	*Alvia* 4072 🍸 S	*Arco* 694 🍸 A	*Alta* 228 🍸 Ⓑh	*Alaris* 1144 ✕ Ⓑp	*Alvia* 1146 🍸	18040 33040 2	*Alaris* 1454 ✕	2 ⑤⑦	*Alvia* 1166 🍸	*Alta* 224 🍸	*Alaris* 1174 ✕ w	18044 2 ⑤
0	**Madrid** Chamartín ‡ d.	...	...	0640	...	0654	0713	0740	0842	0900	...	0940	1100	1203	...	1234	1340	1400	1419	1500	...	1600	1629	1640	1639
8	**Madrid** Atocha Cercanías ‡ d.	...	...	0700	...	0712	0731	0800	0900	0918	...	1000	1120	1220	...	1253	1400	1418	1433	1518	...	1618	1647	1700	1653
57	Aranjuez ‡ d.	...	...	|	...	|	|	|	|	|	...	|	|	1251	...	|	|	|	1509	|	...	|	|	|	1724
	Badajoz **678** d.	...	...	|	...	|	|	|	|	|	...	|	|	|	0715	|	|	|	|	|	...	|	|	|	|
	Ciudad Real **678** d.	...	0551y	|	...	|	|	|	|	|	0918	|	|	|	1157	|	|	|	|	|	...	|	|	|	|
157	Alcázar de San Juan ‡ a.	...	0657y	|	...	0824	0848	|	|	|	1029	|	|	1334	1315	|	|	|	1608	1629	...	|	|	|	1824
157	Alcázar de San Juan d.	0230	0700	|	0800	0828	0849	|	|	|	1032	|	|	1336	1353	|	|	|	1609	1630	...	|	|	|	1828
288	**Albacete** d.	0327	0820	0903	0922	0926	0947	1003	1103	1124	1145	1210	1323	1431	1453	1505	1602	1626	1728	1724	1733	1828	1856	1902	1941
354	Hellín d.	|	|	|	|	|	1022	|	|	|	|	|	|	|	|	|	|	|	...	|	|	|	|	|	...
458	Alcantarilla d.	|	|	|	|	|	1133	|	|	|	|	|	|	|	|	|	|	|	...	|	|	|	|	|	...
466	Murcia **672** d.	|	|	|	|	|	1143	|	|	|	|	1351	|	|	|	1644	|	|	...	|	|	|	2047	|	...
531	**Cartagena** **672** a.	|	|	|	|	|	...	|	|	|	|	1442	|	|	|	1726	|	|	...	|	|	|	2132	|	...
424	Elda-Petrer d.	|	|	|	|	1030	...	|	|	1222	1259	...	|	1530	|	...	|	1726	...	|	|	1930	...	|	...
464	**Alacant** Terminal a.	|	|	|	|	1102	...	|	|	1250	1328	...	|	1558	|	...	|	1753	...	|	|	1959	...	|	...
435	Xátiva **672** d.	|	0935	|	1047	...	...	1054	|	...	...	...	1414	...	1553	...	|	...	...	1817	1915	...	...	|	...
491	**València** Nord △ **672** a.	0505	1016	1027	1125	...	...	1128	1225	...	...	...	1447	...	1650	...	1725	...	...	1849	2000	...	...	2025	...
	Barcelona Sants **672** a.	0929	...	...	...	...	...	...	|	...	...	...	...	...	2050	...	...	...	...	...	...	...	...	|	...
553	Gandia △ a.	...	...	...	...	...	...	...	1323g	...	...	...	...	...	...	...	...	...	...	...	...	...	...	2121v	...

	Alaris 1184 ✕ t	*Alvia* 1186 🍸 Ⓑd	*Talgo* 74 🍸 Q	*Alaris* 1194 ✕	18032 2	*Alta* 226 🍸 Ⓑq	*Alvia* 4140 🍸 N	*Alaris* 1504 ✕ Ⓑj	17000 2	*Alaris* 11504 ✕ ⑦c
Madrid Chamartín ‡ d.	1740	1800	1813	1840	1818	1900	1943	2000	2040	2056
Madrid Atocha Cercanías ‡ d.	1800	1818	1828	1900	1832	1918	2000	2018	2055	2115
Aranjuez ‡ d.	|	|	|	|	1907	|	|	|	2129	|
Alcázar de San Juan ‡ a.	|	|	1939	|	1957	2033	2114	|	2228	|
Alcázar de San Juan d.	|	|	1940	|	2010b	2034	2116	|	...	|
Albacete d.	2002	2026	2039	2103	2124b	2135	2211	2223	...	2324
Hellín d.	|	|	|	|	...	2210	|	|	...	|
Alcantarilla d.	|	|	|	|	...	|	|	|	...	|
Murcia **672** d.	|	|	|	|	...	2327	|	|	...	|
Cartagena **672** a.	|	|	|	|	...	0013	|	|	...	|
Elda-Petrer d.	|	2125	2147	|	...	...	2313	|	...	|
Alacant Terminal a.	|	2150	2215	|	...	...	2338	|	...	|
Xátiva **672** d.	|	...	...	2154	...	...	...	|	...	|
València Nord △ **672** a.	2125	...	...	2227	...	...	...	2345	...	0048
Barcelona Sants **672** a.	...	...	...	...	...	...	...	...	...	...
Gandia △ a.	...	...	...	...	...	...	...	...	...	...

	Hotel 897 ✕ C	18047 2 ①–⑤		18041 2 ①–⑤	*Alta* 221 🍸 L	18049 2 ⑥⑦	*Alaris* 1065 ✕ U	*Alvia* 1077 🍸 H	*Alaris* 1075 ✕ Tp	*Alaris* 1085 ✕ ①–⑥
Gandia △ d.	...	...	...	...	...	...	...	...	...	...
Barcelona Sants **672** d.	2130	...	...	...	...	...	...	...	...	...
València Nord △ **662** d.	0051	...	...	...	...	...	0650	...	0750	0850
Xátiva **672** d.	|	...	...	...	...	...	0721	...	|	|
Alacant Terminal d.	|	...	...	...	...	...	|	0700	|	|
Elda-Petrer d.	|	...	...	...	...	...	|	0727	|	|
Cartagena **672** d.	|	...	...	...	0530	...	|	|	|	|
Murcia **672** d.	|	...	...	...	0611	...	|	|	|	|
Alcantarilla d.	|	...	...	...	|	...	|	|	|	|
Hellín d.	|	...	...	...	|	...	|	|	|	|
Albacete d.	0243	0427e	...	0627	0750	0724z	0813	0826	0913	1013
Alcázar de San Juan a.	0346	0550e	...	0735	|	0834z	|	|	|	|
Alcázar de San Juan ‡ d.	...	0551	...	0736	|	0835	|	|	|	|
Aranjuez ‡ d.	...	0644	...	0832	|	0934	|	|	|	|
Madrid Atocha Cercanías ‡ a.	...	0722	...	0912	1004	1014	1023	1034	1123	1223
Madrid Chamartín ‡ a.	...	0737	...	0928	1021	1028	1037	1048	1138	1237

A – GARCÍA LORCA – [2] Badajoz - Alcázar - Barcelona and v.v.
C – ALHAMBRA – (not Dec. 24, 26, 31): 🛏 and [1] (reclining) Granada - Alcázar - Barcelona and v.v.
D – ①–⑤ (not Dec. 8, 25, Jan. 1, 6).
E – ①–⑤ (not Dec. 25, Jan. 1, 6).
G – ①–⑥ (not Dec. 7, 8, 25, Jan. 1, 6).
H – ①–⑥ (not Dec. 8, 25, Jan. 1, 6).
K – [12] Madrid - València - Castelló de la Plana (- Benicàssim June 16 - Oct. 12) and v.v. (Table **672**).
L – ①–⑥ (not Dec. 25, 26, Jan. 1, 2, 6).
N – Ⓑ. [12] Gijón - Alacant.
P – ①–⑥. [12] Alacant - Gijón.
Q – ⑥. [12] A Coruña and Pontevedra - Alacant.
R – ⑦. [12] Alacant - A Coruña and Pontevedra.

S – From / to Santander.
T – [12] Madrid - València - Castelló de la Plana and v.v. (Table **672**).
U – ①–⑥ (not Dec. 7, 8, 25, Jan. 1, 6).

b – Not ⑥.
c – Not Dec. 27.
d – Not Dec. 24, 25, 31, Jan. 1.
e – ① only.
f – Not Dec. 6, 7, 24, 25, 28, 31, Jan. 1.
g – Also Dec. 8.
h – Not Dec. 7, 25, Jan. 1.
j – Not Dec. 6, 7.
k – Also Nov. 29, Dec. 8.
p – Not Dec. 25, Jan. 1.

q – Also Jan. 2; not Dec. 24, 25, 27, 28, 31, Jan. 1, 4.
r – Dec. 25, Jan. 5 only.
t – Not Dec. 24, 31.
v – ⑤ only.
w – Not Dec. 26, Jan. 2.
x – ⑦ (also Jan. 6).
y – ① only.
z – ⑥ only.

‡ – See also Table **661**.
△ – See next page.

VALÈNCIA, ALACANT and CARTAGENA - MADRID 668

	Talgo 85 🍷 R	Alta 223 🍷	Alvia 4141 🍷 P	Alaris 1415 ✕	Alvia 1127 🍷	Arco 697 🍷 A	Alta 229 🍷 ⑧p	Alvia 4183 🍷 S	Alaris 1445 ✕ ⑧p	2 ⑤⑦	Alaris 1155 ✕ K	Alta 1167 🍷 ⑧	18043 33043 2	Alaris 1165 ✕ J	Alta 225 🍷	18083 2	Alaris 1175 ✕ p	18045 2 ⑦	Alvia 1187 🍷	18027 2	Alaris 1185 ✕	Alta 227 🍷 ⑧d	Alvia 1207 🍷 ⑧h	Alaris 1505 ✕ f	Alaris 11505 ✕ r
Gandia △ d.	...	...	...	...	...	...	...	...	...	...	...	...	...	1540k	...	...	...	...	...	...	...	...	...	...	...
Barcelona Sants **672** d.	...	...	...	...	...	0800	...	...	...	...	...	...	...	|	...	...	...	...	...	...	...	...	...	...	...
València Nord △ **672** d.	...	...	...	1125	...	1128	...	...	1420	1433	1550	...	...	1650	...	...	1750	...	...	1805	1850	...	...	2020	2120
Xátiva **672** d.	...	...	...	1156	...	1224	...	...	|	1515	|	...	...	|	...	...	1821	...	...	1841	|	...	...	2052	|
Alacant Terminal d.	0935	...	1035	|	1205	|	...	1400	|	|	|	1605	...	|	...	1700	|	...	1805	|	|	...	2000	|	|
Elda - Petrer d.	1002	...	1057	|	1232	|	...	1426	|	|	|	1631	...	|	...	1728	|	...	1832	|	|	...	2023	|	|
Cartagena **672** d.	|	0850	|	|	|	|	1215x	|	|	|	|	|	...	|	1555	|	|	...	|	|	|	1820	|	|	|
Murcia **672** d.	|	0936	|	|	|	|	1258	|	|	|	|	|	...	|	1643	|	|	...	|	|	|	1905	|	|	|
Alcantarilla d.	|	0945	|	|	|	|	|	|	|	|	|	|	...	|	|	|	|	...	|	|	|	|	|	|	|
Hellín d.	|	1049	|	|	|	|	|	|	|	|	|	|	...	|	|	|	|	...	|	|	|	2024	|	|	|
Albacete d.	1109	1127	1156	1249	1329	1337	1446	1523	1541	1702	1712	1730	1740	1813	1833	1844	1913	1916	1931	1958	2012	2103	2118	2145	2242
Alcázar de San Juan a.	1204	1232	|	|	|	1437	|	1615	|	...	|	|	1853	|	|	1957	2006	2022	|	2125	|	2200	2210	|	|
Alcázar de San Juan ‡ d.	1205	1233	|	|	|	1510	|	1616	|	...	|	|	1854	|	|	2007	2007	2023	|	2128x	|	2201	2211	|	|
Ciudad Real **678** a.	|	|	|	|	|	1621	|	|	|	...	|	|	|	|	|	2115	|	|	|	2240x	|	|	|	|	|
Badajoz **678** a.	|	|	|	|	|	2145	|	|	|	...	|	|	|	|	|	...	|	|	|	...	|	|	|	|	|
Aranjuez ‡ d.	|	|	|	|	|	...	|	1700	|	...	|	|	1953	|	|	...	|	2123	|	...	|	|	|	|	|
Madrid Atocha Cercanías ‡ a.	1320	1359	1404	1500	1542	...	1704	1733	1751	...	1920	1940	2034	2021	2045	...	2126	2156	2142	...	2222	2317	2325	2353	0051
Madrid Chamartín ‡ a.	1335	1415	1419	1514	1556	...	1718	1748	1805	...	1934	1955	2048	2035	2100	...	2140	2210	2156	...	2236	2332	2339	0007	0105

FOR NOTES SEE PREVIOUS PAGE

△ – *Cercanías* (suburban) line **C1**: **Valencia** - **Gandia** and v.v. 2nd class. Journey time: 54–60 minutes.

From **València** Nord
Ⓐ: 0611, 0641 and every 30 minutes until 1941; then 1956, 2033, 2041, 2111, 2141, 2211, 2241.
Ⓒ: 0641, 0741 and hourly until 2241.

From **Gandia**
Ⓐ: 0605, 0640, 0655, 0710, 0725, 0740, 0755, 0825, 0840, 0855, 0915, 0925, 0955 and every 30 minutes until 2225.
Ⓒ: 0655, 0755 and hourly until 2055; then 2225.

MADRID - CUENCA - VALÈNCIA 669

2nd class

km		14160	18760 A	18160		18162		18164		18766
0	**Madrid** Atocha Cercanías d.	...	...	*0820*	...	*1155*	...	*1530*	...	*1910*
8	Villaverde Bajo d.	...	...	0858	...	1230	...	1607	...	1947
49	Aranjuez **661 668** d.	...	0610	0925	...	1257	...	1635	...	2017
201	**Cuenca** d.	0740	0837	1140r	...	1450	...	1852	...	2225
327	Requena d.	0927	...	1322	...	1631	...	2037	...	...
399	**València** Sant Isidre ◧ a.	1049	...	1445	...	1752	...	2150	...	...

	18761 ①–⑤	18161	18763 A	14501	18765	14161	18771 B	18769 C	14163
València Sant Isidre ◧ d.	...	0814	...	1232	...	1514	...	...	1814
Requena d.	...	0947	...	1344	...	1651	...	...	1940
Cuenca d.	0705	1138	1320	1552	1620	1841	1848	1855	2135
Aranjuez **661 668** d.	0908	1327	1536	...	1819	...	2052	2052	...
Villaverde Bajo a.	0939	1358	1611	...	1852	...	2121	2121	...
Madrid Atocha Cercanías a.	*1005*	*1425*	*1635*	...	*1915*	...	*2145*	*2145*	...

A – ①–⑤ (not Dec. 8, 25, Jan. 1).
B – ⑦ (also Dec. 8, 25, Jan. 1).
C – ①–⑥ (not Dec. 8, 25, Jan. 1).
r – Arrives 1119.
◧ – *Renfe* rail tickets to / from València are valid on *MetroValencia* services between Sant Isidre and either Plaça d'Espanya (on Line 1) or Bailén (on Line 5) – both are adjacent to València Nord main railway station. Allow at least 15 minutes for the transfer.

VALÈNCIA - TERUEL - ZARAGOZA 670

2nd class

km				*TRD** 18502		*MD* 18504 H		*TRD* 18518		
0	**València** Nord d.	...	...	0942	...	1527	...	1647	...	1844
34	Sagunt d.	...	...	1010	...	|	...	1717	...	1914
65	Segorbe d.	...	...	1037	...	|	...	1747	...	1943
171	**Teruel** d.	0653	...	1211	...	1745	...	1922	...	2132
242	Calamocha d.	0748	...	1255	...	|	...	2006	...	...
305	Cariñena d.	0858	...	1337	...	|	...	2057	...	...
359	**Zaragoza** Delicias a.	0948	...	1414	...	1942	...	2135	...	...
361	**Zaragoza** El Portillo a.	0952	...	1419	...	1947	...	2140	...	...

			MD 18511 H		*TRD* 18517		*TRD** 18513		
Zaragoza El Portillo d.	...	...	0754	...	0900	...	1550	...	1923
Zaragoza Delicias d.	...	...	0802	...	0905	...	1555	...	1928
Cariñena d.	...	...	|	...	0946	...	1632	...	2013
Calamocha d.	...	...	|	...	1036	...	1724	...	2119
Teruel d.	0800	...	1002	...	1122	...	1811	...	2212
Segorbe d.	0938	...	|	...	1256	...	1945	...	...
Sagunt d.	1012	...	|	...	1327	...	2014	...	...
València Nord a.	1042	...	1220	...	1352	...	2042	...	...

H – To / from Huesca (Table **654**).
* – Reservation on these trains is not compulsory, but is recommended on ⑤⑦.

CÓRDOBA - SEVILLA - HUELVA and CÁDIZ 671

km		*MD* 13000 ①–⑤ Ⓡ2f	*MD* 13002 ①–⑥ Ⓡ2f	13030 2 ①–⑤ f	*Hotel* 946 ✕ A	*MD* 13004 Ⓡ2	13037 2	*AL* 9070 Ⓡ🍷 J	13021 2	*MD* 13020 Ⓡ2	*MD* 13008 ①–⑤ Ⓡ2f	*Alvia* 9320 k	*MD* 13010 Ⓡ2	13032 2	*MD* 13012 ①–⑤ Ⓡ2f	13039 2	*MD* 13014 Ⓡ2	13028 2	*MD* 13016 Ⓡ2	*Alvia* 9332 j	13035 2 J	*Arco* 697 G	*MD* 13018 2	*Alvia* 9386	13095 2	*MD* 13044 Ⓡ2
	Madrid Pta de Atocha **660** d.	...	...	...	...	...	...	...	...	...	...	1005	...	...	...	...	...	...	...	1610	...	...	...	1905	...	...
0	**Córdoba** **660** d.	...	...	0715	0728	...	...	0904	0938	...	...	1157	...	1335	...	...	...	1610	...	1803	1832	1840	...	2055	...	...
51	Palma del Río d.	...	...	0744	|	...	...	|	1009	...	...	|	...	1404	...	...	...	1640	...	|	1901	|	...	|	...	...
129	**Sevilla** **660** a.	...	...	0831	0839	...	...	0953	1058	...	...	1247	...	1456	...	...	...	1730	...	1855	1949	1955	...	|	...	...
129	**Sevilla** **673** § d.	0638	0755	...	0845	0905	0910	0957	...	1100	1205	1250	1405	...	1535	1630	1700	...	1808	1858	...	...	2005	|	2050	2138
204	La Palma del Condado d.	|	|	...	|	|	1010	|	...	|	|	|	|	...	|	1731	|	...	|	|	...	...	|	2217s	2150	|
244	**Huelva** a.	|	|	...	|	|	1045	|	...	|	|	|	|	...	|	1807	|	...	|	|	...	...	|	2245	2223	|
145	Dos Hermanas **673** § d.	0652	0808	...	|	0918	...	1009	...	1113	1218	|	1420	...	1550	...	1713	...	1821	|	...	...	2018	...	...	2151
162	Utrera § d.	0704	|	...	|	0929	...	|	...	|	1231	|	|	...	1601	...	|	...	1832	|	...	...	|	...	...	2202
236	Jerez de la Frontera d.	0745	0903	...	0951	1016	...	1056	...	1206	1316	1344	1515	...	1646	...	1812	...	1919	2002	...	...	2115	...	...	2244
250	Puerto de Santa María d.	0755	0913	...	1001	1026	...	1106	...	1216	1326	1355	1525	...	1656	...	1822	...	1929	2013	...	...	2125	...	...	2254
271	San Fernando - Bahía Sur. d.	0819	0937	...	1018	1047	...	1122	...	1235	1351	1412	1549	...	1720	...	1839	...	1951	2030	...	...	2150	...	...	2313
284	**Cádiz** a.	0834	0952	...	1031	1100	...	1138	...	1248	1404	1428	1604	...	1734	...	1853	...	2004	2044	...	...	2203	...	...	2328

	MD 13001 ①–⑤ Ⓡ2f	13023 2 ①–⑤ f	*Arco* 694 G	13041 2	MD 13003 ①–⑥ Ⓡ2f	*Alvia* 9365 ①–⑥ p	13025 2	*Alvia* 9317 k	*MD* 13005 Ⓡ2	*MD* 13007 ①–⑤ Ⓡ2f	*MD* 13009 Ⓡ2	13047 2 J	*MD* 13011 ①–⑤ Ⓡ2f	13071 2 J	*MD* 13013 ①–⑤ Ⓡ2f	13043 2	*MD* 13015 Ⓡ2	*Alvia* 9383 ⑦ q	*Alvia* 9333 j	*MD* 13045 Ⓡ2	*AL* 9181 Ⓡ🍷 J	13031 2	13049 2	*Hotel* 945 ✕ A	*MD* 13019 Ⓡ2	*MD* 13033 Ⓡ2
Cádiz d.	0540	...	...	...	0645	...	...	0805	0855	1005	1110	...	1300	...	1355	...	1500	...	1626	1705	1805	...	...	1824	1913	2015
San Fernando - Bahía Sur d.	0554	...	...	...	0700	...	...	0816	0906	1017	1121	...	1311	...	1410	...	1515	...	1642	1718	1815	...	...	1835	1924	2029
Puerto de Santa María d.	0614	...	...	...	0724	...	...	0837	0926	1039	1140	...	1331	...	1434	...	1540	...	1700	1738	1831	...	...	1855	1944	2048
Jerez de la Frontera d.	0624	...	...	...	0735	...	...	0850	0936	1050	1150	...	1341	...	1444	...	1551	...	1713	1748	1841	...	...	1905	1955	2058
Utrera § d.	0705	...	...	...	0819	...	...	|	|	|	|	...	1422	...	|	...	1632	...	|	|	|	...	...	|	2044	2141
Dos Hermanas **673** § d.	0718	...	...	...	0831	...	...	|	1029	1149	1241	...	1434	...	1535	...	1644	...	|	1836	1935	...	...	|	2056	2153
Huelva d.	|	...	...	0710	|	0800	...	|	|	|	|	...	|	...	|	1425	|	1623	|	|	|	...	1855	|	|	|
La Palma del Condado d.	|	...	...	0739	|	0826	...	|	|	|	|	...	|	...	|	1458	|	1649	|	|	|	...	1927	|	|	|
Sevilla **673** § a.	0734	...	...	0844	0844	|	...	0950	1045	1204	1257	...	1448	...	1548	1557	1657	|	1806	1850	1948	...	2027	2006	2111	2209
Sevilla **660** d.	...	0750	0820	...	...	|	0900	0953	...	...	...	1325	...	1500	...	...	...	|	1811	...	1952	2015	...	2011	...	...
Palma del Río d.	...	0840	|	...	...	|	0949	|	...	...	...	1414	...	1548	...	...	...	|	|	...	|	2107	...	|	...	...
Córdoba **660** a.	...	0911	0937	...	...	0952	1027	1045	...	...	...	1445	...	1621	...	...	...	1814	1901	...	2042	2138	...	2121	...	...
Madrid Pta de Atocha **660** a.	...	...	...	...	...	1145	...	1238	...	...	...	...	...	...	...	...	...	2008	2046	...	...	...	...	2345	...	...

A – ANTONIO MACHADO – (not Dec. 24, 26, 31): 🛏 and (1) Barcelona - Córdoba - Cádiz and v.v.
G – GARCÍA LORCA – (12) Barcelona - València - Sevilla and v.v.
J – From / to Jaén (Table **661**).
f – Not Dec. 7, 8, 25, Jan. 1.
j – Not Dec. 24, 31.
k – Not Dec. 25, Jan. 1.
p – Not Dec. 7, 8, 25, 26, 27, Jan. 1, 2, 4, 5, 6.
q – Also Dec. 7, 8, 25, 26, 27, Jan. 1, 2, 4, 5, 6.
s – Stops to set down only.
§ – Frequent suburban services operate Sevilla - Utrera and v.v.

672 BARCELONA - VALÈNCIA - ALACANT - CARTAGENA

km			Alaris			Em		Arco		Em		Em		Alaris			Talgo	Alaris			Em	Talgo		Em	
			1075	2	2	1071		697		1091	18093	1101	18093	1111			463	1155			1341	165		1161	
		2	🍷	①–⑤	①–⑥	🍷	2	🍷	2	🍷	2	🍷	2	🍷	2	2	🍷	🍷	2	2	🍷	🍷	2	🍷	2
			f			P	⑥	F						g		⑤⑦	J				⑧f				
	Portbou **657** d.	...	...	...	...	...	...	...	...	...	...	...	...	...	...	...	0952	...	...	...	...	...	...	...	...
0	**Barcelona** França d.	...	...	...	0548	...	...	...	0746	...	0919	...	...	...	1047	...	|	...	...	1318	...	...	1446	...	1618
5	Barcelona Passeig de Gràcia d.	...	...	...	0556	...	...	...	0755	...	0927	...	...	...	1055	...	|	...	...	1326	...	...	1456	...	1626
8	**Barcelona** Sants **652** d.	...	...	...	0603	0700	...	0800	0803	0900	0933	1000	...	1100	1103	...	1200	...	...	1333	1430	1500	1503	1600	1633
68	Sant Vicenç de Calders **652** d.	...	...	...	0648	|	...	|	0848	|	1017	|	...	|	1147	...	|	...	...	1416	|	|	1547	|	1716
82	Altafulla - Tamarit d.	...	...	...	0658	|	...	|	|	|	1028	|	...	|	1158	...	|	...	...	1426	|	|	1558	|	1727
93	**Tarragona** **652** d.	...	...	...	0707	0754	...	0856	0909	0955	1039	1055	...	1155	1207	...	1254	...	...	1435	1524	1555	1608	1657	1738
103	Port Aventura d.	...	...	...	0720	|	...	|	0917	|	1047	|	...	|	1216	...	|	...	...	1443	|	|	1616	|	1747
105	Salou d.	...	...	...	0724	|	...	0907	0922	|	1051	|	...	1204	1219	...	1307	...	...	1447	|	1606	1620	|	1751
163	L'Aldea - Amposta d.	...	...	...	0807	|	...	0940	1006	|	1138	|	←	1237	1302	...	1335	...	...	1532	|	1633	1710	|	1836
176	Tortosa d.	...	...	0645	0817	|	0751	|	1015	|	1149	|	1151	|	1312	...	|	...	1330	1542	|	|	1720	|	1847
202	Vinaròs d.	...	...	0720	...	|	0828	0956	...	|	→	|	1227	1253	▬	...	1350	...	1404	▬	|	1648	▬	|	▬
208	Benicarló - Peñíscola d.	...	...	0726	...	|	0833	1002	...	|	...	|	1233	1259	...	...	1355	...	1410	...	|	1654	...	|	...
268	Benicàssim d.	...	...	0804	...	|	0914	|	...	|	...	|	1310	1329	...	...	1419	1442c	1448	...	|	1719	...	|	...
280	Castelló de la Plana d.	...	0650	0815	...	0915	0922	1036	...	1117	...	1215	1319	1338	2	...	1427	1455	1457	...	1643	1727	...	1812	2
353	**València** Nord a.	...	0740	0907	...	0959	1019	1121	...	1159	...	1300	1412	1430	①–④	...	1515	1540	1553	2	1730	1821	...	1859	⑤
353	**València** Nord **668** d.	0704	0750	...	...	1005	...	1128	...	...	...	1306	...	1435	1433	1515	1520	1550	...	1620	...	1827	...	1905	1935
409	Xátiva **668** d.	0738	|	...	...	|	...	1224	...	...	...	|	...	|	1513	1551	1607	|	...	1657	...	1906	...	|	2017
	Madrid Chamartín **668** a.	|	1138	...	...	|	...	|	...	...	...	|	...	|	|	|	|	1934	...	|	...	|	...	|	|
	Badajoz **678** a.	|	▬	...	...	|	...	2145	...	...	...	|	...	|	|	|	|	...	...	|	...	|	...	|	|
	Granada **661** a.	|	...	...	...	|	...	1930	...	...	...	|	...	|	|	|	|	...	...	|	...	|	...	|	|
	Almería **661** a.	|	...	...	...	|	...	2028	...	...	...	|	...	|	|	|	|	...	...	|	...	|	...	|	|
	Málaga **661** a.	|	...	...	...	|	...	2116	...	...	...	|	...	|	|	|	|	...	...	|	...	|	...	|	|
	Sevilla **671** a.	|	...	...	...	|	...	1955	...	...	...	|	...	|	|	|	|	...	...	|	...	|	...	|	|
495	Elda - Petrer d.	0837	...	...	...	|	...	...	...	...	...	|	...	|	1616	1648	1701	...	...	1753	...	1946	...	|	2107
536	**Alacant** a.	0903	...	...	...	1140	...	...	...	...	...	1500	...	1645	1651	1717	1724	...	...	1819	...	2019	...	2040	2132
536	**Alacant** § d.	0908	...	...	...	...	...	...	...	...	...	...	...	...	...	...	1734	...	...	1824	...	2039	...	...	...
614	Murcia § a.	1028	2	...	...	...	...	...	...	...	...	...	...	...	...	...	1849	...	...	1935	...	2147	2	...	...
614	Murcia **668** § d.	...	1208	...	...	...	...	...	...	...	...	...	...	...	...	...	1905	...	...	1944	...	2151	2155	...	...
677	**Lorca** Sutullena § a.	...	|	...	...	...	...	...	...	...	...	...	...	...	...	...	|	...	...	|	...	2252	|	...	...
679	**Cartagena** **668** § a.	...	1258	...	...	...	...	...	...	...	...	...	...	...	...	...	1952	...	...	2033	...	...	2245	...	...

	Talgo		Em		Alaris		Em		Hotel	
	1171		1181		1391		1401		897	
	🍷	2	🍷	2	🍷	2	🍷	2	✕	
		⑦					⑧p		B	
Barcelona França d.	...	...	...	1748	...	1917	...	2046	...	...
Barcelona Passeig de Gràcia d.	...	...	...	1756	...	1925	...	2056	...	...
Barcelona Sants **652** d.	1700	...	1800	1803	1930	1933	2030	2103	2130	...
Sant Vicenç de Calders **652** d.	|	...	|	1848	|	2017	|	2147	|	...
Altafulla - Tamarit d.	|	...	|	1900	|	2029	|	2159	|	...
Tarragona **652** d.	1755	...	1854	1909	2025	2040	2123	2208	2224	...
Port Aventura d.	|	...	|	1923	|	2050	|	2219	|	...
Salou d.	1807	...	|	1928	2038	2055	|	2223	2238	...
L'Aldea - Amposta d.	1841	...	|	2017	2112	2142	|	2306	|	...
Tortosa d.	|	...	|	2028	|	2153	|	2316	|	...
Vinaròs d.	1858	1903	|	...	2129	2228	|	...	|	...
Benicarló - Peñíscola d.	1904	1908	|	...	2135	...	|	...	|	...
Benicàssim d.	1933	1948	|	...	2203	...	|	...	|	...
Castelló de la Plana d.	1941	1957	2013	...	2212	...	2241	...	2359	...
València Nord a.	2025	2052	2059	...	2303	...	2325	...	0049	...
València Nord **668** d.	2031	...	2105	...	...	...	...	...	0051	...
Xátiva **668** d.	2125	...	|	...	...	...	...	...	|	...
Granada **661** a.	|	...	|	...	...	...	...	...	0835	...
Elda - Petrer d.	2203	...	|	...	...	...	...	...	...	...
Alacant a.	2223	...	2240	...	...	...	...	...	...	...
Alacant § d.	2238	...	...	...	...	...	...	...	...	...
Murcia § a.	2343	...	...	...	...	...	...	...	...	...
Murcia **668** § d.	...	...	...	...	...	...	...	...	...	...
Lorca Sutullena § a.	...	...	...	...	...	...	...	...	...	...
Cartagena **668** § a.	...	...	...	...	...	...	...	...	...	...

		Hotel	Em			Em			
		894	1362			1282			
	2	✕	🍷	2	2	🍷	2	2	
	①–⑥	B	Z				①–⑥		
Cartagena **668** § d.	...	...	...	...	...	...	...	...	...
Lorca Sutullena § d.	...	...	...	...	...	...	...	...	...
Murcia **668** § a.	...	...	...	...	...	...	...	...	...
Murcia § d.	...	...	...	...	...	...	0555	...	...
Alacant § a.	...	...	...	...	...	...	0718	...	...
Alacant d.	...	...	...	...	...	0655	0721	...	...
Elda - Petrer d.	...	...	...	...	...	|	0753	...	...
Granada **661** d.	...	2155	...	...	...	|	|	...	...
Xátiva **668** d.	...	|	...	...	...	|	0847	...	...
València Nord **668** a.	...	0505	...	...	...	0827	0933	...	...
València Nord d.	...	0511	0640	...	...	0835	...	...	...
Castelló de la Plana d.	...	0606	0717	...	...	0918	...	...	...
Benicàssim d.	...	|	|	...	...	|	...	...	...
Benicarló - Peñíscola d.	...	|	|	...	...	|	...	...	...
Vinaròs d.	...	|	|	0710	...	|	...	...	...
Tortosa d.	0615	|	|	0748	0918	|	...	1045	...
L'Aldea - Amposta d.	0626	|	|	0800	0930	|	...	1055	...
Salou d.	0707	0740	|	0843	1013	|	...	1142	...
Port Aventura d.	0710	|	|	0845	1023	|	...	1145	...
Tarragona **652** d.	0721	0755	0836	0856	1032	1040	...	1156	...
Altafulla - Tamarit d.	|	|	|	0904	1038	|	...	|	...
Sant Vicenç de Calders **652** d.	0743	|	|	0917	1057	|	...	1216	...
Barcelona Sants **652** a.	0835	0929	0947	1005	1146	1142	...	1305	...
Barcelona Passeig de Gràcia a.	0844	...	...	1014	1151	...	...	1315	...
Barcelona França a.	0853	...	...	1023	1200	...	...	1325	...

	Talgo		Em	Alaris		Talgo	Alaris		Em	Em		Arco		Talgo		Em			Em	Alaris		Talgo		Alaris	
	1102		1112	1084		460	1142		1152	1162		694	18096	264		1182	18096		1392	1202		1212	14202	1184	
	🍷	2	🍷	🍷	2	🍷	🍷	2	🍷	🍷	2	🍷	2	🍷	2	🍷	2	2	🍷	🍷	2	🍷	2	🍷	2
	L					K			⑧f	⑧		G						⑧	Q		⑧	⑦y		h	⑦
Cartagena **668** § d.	...	...	...	...	...	...	...	...	...	...	...	...	...	1255	...	...	...	...	...	...	...	...	1650	...	...
Lorca Sutullena § d.	...	...	...	...	...	0820	...	...	...	...	...	...	...	|	...	...	...	...	...	...	...	...	|	...	...
Murcia **668** § a.	...	...	...	...	...	0920	...	...	...	...	...	...	...	1339	...	...	...	...	...	...	...	...	1741	...	...
Murcia § d.	0635	...	...	...	...	0945	...	...	...	...	...	...	...	1353	...	...	...	...	...	...	...	1647	1747	...	...
Alacant § a.	0746	...	...	...	...	1054	...	...	...	...	...	...	...	1453	...	...	...	...	...	...	...	1758	1858	...	...
Alacant d.	0806	...	0925	...	...	1109	...	...	...	1420	...	...	...	1523	...	1616	...	1728	...	1820v	...	1818	1902	...	1933
Elda - Petrer d.	0831	...	|	...	...	1135	...	...	...	|	...	...	...	1547	...	|	...	1803	...	|	...	1846	1930	...	2010
Sevilla **671** d.	|	...	|	...	...	|	...	...	...	|	...	0820	...	|	...	|	...	|	...	|	...	|	|	...	|
Málaga **661** d.	|	...	|	...	...	|	...	...	...	|	...	0710	...	|	...	|	...	|	...	|	...	|	|	...	|
Almería **661** d.	|	...	|	...	...	|	...	...	...	|	...	0740	...	|	...	|	...	|	...	|	...	|	|	...	|
Granada **661** d.	|	...	|	...	...	|	...	...	...	|	...	0845	...	|	...	|	...	|	...	|	...	|	|	...	|
Badajoz **678** d.	|	...	|	...	...	|	...	...	...	|	...	0715	...	|	...	|	...	|	...	|	...	|	|	...	|
Madrid Chamartín **668** d.	|	...	|	0740	...	|	...	...	...	|	...	|	...	|	...	|	...	|	...	|	...	|	|	1740	|
Xátiva **668** d.	0916	...	|	1054	...	1213	...	...	...	|	...	1553	...	1626	...	|	...	1852	...	|	...	1933	2024	|	2102
València Nord **668** a.	0953	...	1055	1128	...	1257	...	...	...	1555	...	1650	...	1708	...	1800	...	1932	...	1950v	...	2019	2106	2125	2138
València Nord d.	1000	1035	1105	1133	...	1308	1405	...	1505	1605	...	1655	1700	1715	...	1805	...	...	1935	2005	2010	2035	...	2130	...
Castelló de la Plana d.	1043	1134	1144	1222	...	1352	1451	...	1546	1647	...	1744	1759	1803	...	1845	...	...	2016	2048	2104	2120	...	2215	...
Benicàssim d.	1050	1142	|	1229c	...	1401	1500	...	|	|	...	|	1807	1811	...	|	←	...	|	2056	2112	2129	...	...	...
Benicarló - Peñíscola d.	1119	1226	|	...	...	1426	1533	...	|	|	...	1815	1847	1833	...	|	1848	...	|	2123	2149	2157	...	...	...
Vinaròs d.	1125	1232	|	...	...	1431	1539	...	|	|	...	1820	→	1838	...	|	1855	...	|	2129	2155	2203	...	...	...
Tortosa d.	|	1307	|	...	1324	|	|	1554	|	|	1725	|	...	|	1850	|	1936	...	|	|	2230	|	...	...	...
L'Aldea - Amposta d.	1140	...	|	...	1336	1447	1555	1605	|	|	1735	1836	...	1853	1903	|	1950	...	|	2144	2241	2219	...	...	...
Salou d.	1215	...	|	...	1413	1520	1630	1645	|	|	1818	1914	...	1927	1943	|	2039	...	|	2213	...	2255	...	...	...
Port Aventura d.	|	...	|	...	1416	|	|	1647	|	|	1821	|	...	|	|	|	2041	...	|	|	...	|	...	...	...
Tarragona **652** d.	1234	...	1309	...	1428	1539	1641	1658	1710	1811	1830	1928	...	1940	1957	2010	2100	...	2137	2242	...	2306	...	...	...
Altafulla - Tamarit d.	|	...	|	...	1435	|	|	1706	|	|	1838	|	...	|	2005	|	2108	...	|	|	...	|	...	...	...
Sant Vicenç de Calders **652** d.	|	...	|	...	1447	|	|	1718	|	|	1849	1947	...	|	2017	|	2118	...	|	|	...	|	...	...	...
Barcelona Sants **652** a.	1339	...	1409	...	1535	1637	1739	1805	1809	1910	1935	2050	...	2039	2105	2109	2205	...	2237	2346	...	2358	...	...	...
Barcelona Passeig de Gràcia a.	...	...	...	...	1544	|	...	1814	...	...	1944	...	...	...	2111	...	2214	...	...	...	...	...	...	...	...
Barcelona França a.	...	...	...	...	1552	|	...	1822	...	...	1953	...	...	...	2120	...	2222	...	...	...	...	...	...	...	...
Cerbère **657** a.	...	...	...	...	...	1902	...	...	...	...	...	...	...	...	...	...	...	...	...	...	...	...	...	...	...

B – ALHAMBRA – (not Dec. 24, 26, 31): 🛏 and [1] (reclining) Barcelona - Granada and v.v.
F – GARCÍA LORCA – Daily: [12] Barcelona - Sevilla. Daily: [2] Barcelona - Badajoz and Malaga. ①④⑥: [2] Barcelona - Almería. ③⑤⑦: [2] Barcelona - Granada.
G – GARCÍA LORCA – Daily: [12] Sevilla - Barcelona. Daily: [2] Badajoz and Málaga - Barcelona. ③⑤⑦: [2] Almería - Barcelona. ①④⑥: [2] Granada - Barcelona.
J – MARE NOSTRUM – [12] Montpellier - Cartagena.
K – MARE NOSTRUM – [12] Lorca - Montpellier.
L – Murcia - València ①–⑥. València - Barcelona daily.
Q – ⑧ (not Dec. 7, 24, 25, 31, Jan. 1).

P – ①–⑥ (not Dec. 25, 26, Jan. 1, 6).
Z – ①–⑥ (not Dec. 7, 25, Jan. 1).

c – June 16 - Oct. 12.
f – Not Dec. 25, Jan. 1.
g – Not Dec. 27, Jan. 3.
h – Not Dec. 24, 31.
p – Not Dec. 6, 7, 24, 25, 31, Jan. 1.
v – ①–⑥.

y – Also Dec. 8; not Dec. 6.

§ – Additional local trains operate between these stations.

2nd class — SEVILLA and ALGECIRAS - MÁLAGA, GRANADA and ALMERÍA — 673

For trains **Sevilla** – **Málaga** and v.v. via **Córdoba**, see Table **660**

km		*R-598* 13920	13061 C	*R-598* 13900	13063 ✤	*Alta* 9218 p	*Alta* 9367 p★	*R-598* 13902	*R-598* 13926		*R-598* 13904	13077 ✤		*R-598* 13910 E	*R-598* 13922	13065 ✤	*R-598* 13906	*R-598* 13924	*Alta* 9234 q	*Alta* 9331 q★	13079 D	*R-598* 13908		
0	**Sevilla** ¶ d.	0700	...	0735	...	...	...	1105	1150	...	1300	...	...	1510	1605	...	1705	1740	...	...	...	2010	...	...
15	Dos Hermanas ¶ d.	0713u	...	0749u	...	...	...	1119u	1203u	...	1314u	...	...	1524u	1618u	...	1719u	1753u	...	...	...	2024u	...	...
	Algeciras d.	|	...	|	0705	...	0805	|	|	...	|	1215	...	|	|	1550	|	|	...	1650	1850	|	...	...
	San Roque - La Línea d.	|	...	|	0719	...	|	|	|	...	|	1229	...	|	|	1603	|	|	...	|	1903	|	...	...
	Ronda d.	|	0712	|	0857	...	0935	|	|	...	|	1411	...	|	|	1735	|	|	...	1815	2047	|	...	...
	Madrid Pta de Atocha **660** d.	|	|	|	|	0905	1429	|	|	...	|	|	...	|	|	|	|	|	1705	2250	...	|	...	...
167	Bobadilla **661** d.	|	0800	0913	0948	|	...	1247	|	...	1439	1508	...	1646	|	1835	1844	|	|	...	...	2149	...	...
236	**Málaga** M. Zambrano ... **661** a.	|	0909	1014	|	|	...	1341	|	...	1539	|	...	1740	|	|	1939	|	|	...	...	2246	...	...
183	Antequera d.	0843	...	...	1004	1149	...	...	1337	...	...	1524	...	...	1747	1848	...	1943	2014	...	...	...	...	...
290	**Granada** a.	1000	...	...	1133	1342	...	...	1459	...	...	1649	...	...	1909	2017	...	2102	2141	...	...	...	...	...
290	**Granada** **661** d.	1004	...	...	...	...	...	...	1503	...	...	...	...	...	1913	...	...	2106	...	...	...	...	...	...
372	Guadix **661** d.	1107	...	...	...	...	...	...	1600	...	...	...	...	...	2016	...	...	2203	...	...	...	...	...	...
471	**Almería** **661** a.	1221	...	...	...	...	...	...	1717	...	...	...	...	...	2124	...	...	2311	...	...	...	...	...	...

km		13074 D	*R-598* 13901	13064 ✤	*R-598* 13941	*Alta* 9366 p★		*Alta* 9219 p	*R-598* 13903	*R-598* 13943		*R-598* 13905	13076 ✤		*R-598* 13907	*R-598* 13945	13062 ✤	13057 C	*Alta* 9330 q★	*Alta* 9237 q	*R-598* 13909 ⑤⑦	*R-598* 13911	*R-598* 13947	
0	**Almería** **661** d.	...	...	...	0600	...	...	...	...	0925	...	...	...	...	...	1420	...	...	...	...	...	...	1805	...
99	Guadix **661** d.	...	...	...	0717	...	...	...	...	1037	...	...	...	...	...	1530	...	...	...	...	...	...	1923	...
181	**Granada** **661** a.	...	...	...	0814	...	...	...	...	1129	...	...	...	...	...	1627	...	...	...	...	...	...	2019	...
181	**Granada** d.	...	...	0715	0818	...	...	0945	...	1133	...	...	1355	...	...	1632	1720	...	...	1800	...	...	2023	...
288	Antequera d.	...	...	0841	0942	...	...	1108	...	1247	...	...	1520	...	...	1752	1850	...	...	1950	...	...	2145	...
	Málaga M. Zambrano ... **661** d.	...	0740	|	|	...	...	|	1040	|	...	1405	|	...	1635	|	|	1843	...	|	1905	2013	|	...
304	Bobadilla **661** d.	...	0834	0857	|	...	...	|	1132	|	...	1455	1538	...	1725	|	1902	1948	...	|	1956	2106	|	...
	Madrid Pta de Atocha **660** d.	...	|	|	|	0905	...	1429	|	|	...	|	|	...	|	|	|	|	1705	2250	|	|	|	...
376	Ronda d.	0750	|	0958	|	1319	...	...	|	|	...	|	1636	...	|	|	1959	2042	2144	...	|	|	|	...
468	San Roque - La Línea d.	0924	|	1130	|	|	...	...	|	|	...	|	1820	...	|	|	2128	...	|	...	|	|	|	...
480	**Algeciras** a.	0939	|	1146	|	1445	...	...	|	|	...	|	1836	...	|	|	2141	...	2315	...	|	|	|	...
456	Dos Hermanas ¶ a.	...	0956s	...	1109s	...	...	...	1255s	1413s	...	1621s	...	...	1851s	1930s	...	...	...	...	2120s	2231s	2316s	...
471	**Sevilla** ¶ a.	...	1010	...	1127	...	...	...	1310	1430	...	1639	...	...	1907	1945	...	...	...	...	2137	2245	2332	...

C – ①–⑥ (not Dec. 7, 8, 25, Jan. 1).
D – ①–⑤ (not Dec. 7, 8, 24, Jan. 1).
E – ①⑤⑦ (also Dec. 8; not Dec. 7, 25, 27, Jan. 1).
p – Not Dec. 25, Jan. 1.
q – Not Dec. 24, 31.
s – Stops to set down only.
u – Stops to pick up only.
★ – Oct. 26 - Mar. 25: 🚌 Algeciras - Ronda - Antequera and v.v.
✤ – Oct. 26 - Mar. 25: 🚌 Algeciras - Ronda and v.v.
¶ – Frequent suburban services run Sevilla - Dos Hermanas and v.v.

SFM 2nd class — PALMA DE MALLORCA - INCA - SA POBLA and MANACOR — 674

km			Ⓐ	Ⓐ	Ⓐ	Ⓐ	Ⓐ	Ⓐ	and at the same	Ⓐ	Ⓐ	Ⓐ	Ⓐ	Ⓐ			Ⓒ	Ⓒ	Ⓒ	Ⓒ	and at the same	Ⓒ	Ⓒ	Ⓒ	Ⓒ
0	**Palma** d.	Ⓐ	0544	0609	0624	0644	0709	0724	minutes	2024	2044	2109	2124	2209	...	Ⓒ	0604	0634	0704	0734	minutes	2034	2104	2134	2204
7	Marratxi d.		0559	0619	0639	0659	0719	0739	past	2039	2059	2119	2139	2219	...		0619	0649	0719	0749	past	2049	2119	2149	2219
29	**Inca** d.		0624	0644	0703	0724	0744	0803	each	2103	2124	2144	2204	2244	...		0644	0714	0744	0814	each	2114	2144	2214	2244
***	sa Pobla a.		0641	|	...	0741	|	...	hour	...	2141	|	2221	|	...		|	0731	|	0831	hour	2131	|	2231	|
64	**Manacor** a.		...	0715	...	...	0815	...	until	...	...	2215	...	2315	...		0715	...	0815	...	until	...	2215	...	2315

		Ⓐ	Ⓐ	Ⓐ	and at the same	Ⓐ	Ⓐ	Ⓐ	Ⓐ	Ⓐ			Ⓒ	Ⓒ	Ⓒ	Ⓒ	Ⓒ	and at the same	Ⓒ	Ⓒ	Ⓒ	Ⓒ	Ⓒ		
Manacor d.	Ⓐ	...	0622	...	minutes	...	...	2122	...	2222	...	Ⓒ	0622	0722	...	0822	...	minutes	2022	...	2122	...	2222	...	...
sa Pobla d.		...	|	0656	past	2056	...	|	2156	|	...		|	|	0806	|	0906	past	|	2106	|	2206	|	...	...
Inca d.		0634	0654	0714	each	2114	2134	2154	2214	2254	...		0654	0754	0824	0854	0924	each	2054	2124	2154	2224	2254	...	...
Marratxi d.		0658	0718	0738	hour	2138	2158	2218	2238	2318	...		0718	0818	0848	0918	0948	hour	2118	2148	2218	2248	2318	...	...
Palma a.		0713	0728	0753	until	2153	2213	2228	2253	2328	...		0733	0833	0903	0933	1003	until	2133	2203	2233	2303	2333	...	...

Operator: Serveis Ferroviaris de Mallorca (SFM) ✆ +34 971 752 245.

*** – *19 km* Inca - sa Pobla.

PALMA DE MALLORCA - SÓLLER
0800, 1050, 1305, 1515, 1900.
28 km Journey time: 55 minutes.

SÓLLER - PALMA DE MALLORCA
0700, 0910, 1155, 1410, 1800.
Operator: Ferrocarril de Sóller (FS) ✆ +34 971 752 051.

A connecting tram service operates **Sóller** - **Port de Sóller**.
5 km. Journey time: 15–20 minutes. Not all services shown.

From Sóller: 0700, 0800, 0900, 1000, 1100, 1200, 1300, 1405, 1500, 1600, 1700, 1800, 1900, 2030.
From Port de Sóller: 0730, 0830, 0930, 1030, 1125, 1230, 1330, 1430, 1530, 1630, 1725, 1830, 1930, 2025.

🚌 MÁLAGA and ALGECIRAS - LA LÍNEA (for Gibraltar) — 675

There are no cross-border 🚌 services: passengers to / from Gibraltar must cross the frontier on foot (walking-time about 5 minutes) and transfer to / from Gibraltar local 🚌 services

🚌 **MÁLAGA** bus stn – **LA LÍNEA** bus station (for **Gibraltar**)
From Málaga: 0700, 1130▽, 1400, 1630, 1915⑦.
From La Línea: 0850, 1030, 1630▽, 1745, 2045⑦.
Journey time: 3 hours. Operator: Automóviles Portillo, Málaga ✆ +34 902 143 144.
▽ – Journey operated by Alsina Graells (see Table **664** for contact details).

🚌 **ALGECIRAS** bus station - **LA LÍNEA** bus station (for **Gibraltar**)
From Algeciras: Ⓐ: 0700 and every 30 minutes until 2130, also 2230.
⑥: every 45 mins 0700 – 2115, also 2230. †: every 45 mins 0800 – 2130, also 2230.
From La Línea: Ⓐ: 0700, 0745 and every 30 minutes until 2215, also 2315.
⑥: every 45 mins 0700 – 2200, also 2315. †: 0700, 0845 then every 45 mins until 2215, also 2315.
Journey time: 45 mins. Operator: Transportes Generales Comes SA, Algeciras ✆ +34 956 653 456.

DAMAS ☆ — 🚌 SEVILLA - AYAMONTE - FARO - LAGOS — 676

	→		⚒		Ⓐ	Ⓒ		Ⓑ	†	⑥	Ⓐ	→		⚒	Ⓒ	Ⓐ	Ⓐ			Ⓐ		†	⚒
Sevilla Plaza de Armas ... d.	**Summer**	*0730*	0930	1130	1230	*1330*	1530	*1800*	1900	1930	2000	**Winter**	*0730*	0930	1100	1130	1230	*1330*	1530	*1630*	*1730*x	1900	1930
Huelva d.	July 4 -	0900	1100	1300	1400	1500	1700	1930	2030	2100	2130	from	0900	1100	1230	1300	1400	1515r	1700	1800	1930	2030	2100
Ayamonte a.	Sept. 6	1000	1200	1400	1500	1600	1800	2030	2130	2200	2230	Sept. 7	1000	1200	1330	1400	1500	1615r	1800	1900	2030	2130	2200

	→	Ⓐ			Ⓐ	Ⓑ	⚒	†	Ⓐ			→	Ⓐ				⚒	⑥	Ⓐ	†	Ⓐ		
Ayamonte d.	**Summer**	0715	*0845*	0930z	*1145*	*1400*	1530	1615	1630	*1730*	1900	**Winter**	0645	*0845*	0930z	*1145*	*1400*	1500	1530	1615	1630	*1730*	1930
Huelva d.	July 4 -	0830	1000	1100	1300	1500	1700	1730	1800	1900x	2000	from	0800	1000	1100	1300	1500	1630	1700	1730	1800	1900	2030
Sevilla Plaza de Armas ... a.	Sept. 6	1000	1130	1230	1430	1630	1830	1900	1930	2030x	2130	Sept. 7	0930	1130	1230	1430	1630	1800	1830	1900	1930	2030	2200

⛴ **Ayamonte - Vila Real de Santo António Guadiana** Journey time: 10 minutes Operator: Empresa de Transportes do Rio Guadiana, Vila Real ✆ +351 281 543 152.
July - Sept every 30 minutes (from Ayamonte (ES) 0930 - 2100, from Vila Real (PT) 0830 - 2000). October - June sails every 40 minutes ⚒, every 60 minutes † (limited evening service).

INTERNATIONAL 🚌 SERVICE Joint EVA △ / DAMAS ☆ service *for international journeys only* No service Dec. 25, Jan. 1.

Sevilla, Plaza de Armas d.		0730	0800	1330	1615		0730	1615
Huelva d.	→	0845	0915	1445	1730	→	0845	1730
Ayamonte 🏛 ES d.	**Summer**	|	1000	|	1815	**Winter**	0930	1815
Vila Real de Santo António 🏛 PT a.		|	0925	|	1740		0855	1740
Faro, Av. da República a.	July 4 -	0920	1040	1520	1855	from	1010	1855
Albufeira, Alto dos Caliços a.	Sept. 6	1000	1125	1600	1940	Sept. 7	1055	1940
Portimão, Largo do Dique a.		|	1200	|	2015		1130	2015
Lagos, Rossio de S. João a.		1045	1230	1645	2045		1200	2045

Lagos, Rossio de S. João d.		0615	0730	1230	1445		0630	1345
Portimão, Largo do Dique d.	→	|	0800	|	1515	→	0700	1415
Albufeira, Alto dos Caliços d.	**Summer**	0700	0835	1315	1550	**Winter**	0735	1450
Faro, Av. da República d.		0740	0920	1355	1635		0820	1535
Vila Real de Santo António 🏛 PT d.	July 4 -	|	1035	|	1750	from	0935	1650
Ayamonte 🏛 ES a.	Sept. 6	|	1200	|	1915	Sept. 7	1100	1815
Huelva a.		1015	1245	1630	2000		1145	1905
Sevilla, Plaza de Armas a.		1130	1400	1745	2115		1300	2015

r – 15 minutes later on Ⓑ.
x – 30 minutes later on ⑦.
z – 15 minutes later on Ⓒ.
✤ – Subject to confirmation.

☆ – DAMAS, Huelva ✆ +34 959 256 900. www.damas-sa.es
△ – EVA, Faro ✆ +351 289 899 700. www.eva-bus.com
ES – Spain (Central European Time).
PT – Portugal (West European Time).

Sevilla Plaza de Armas bus station is ± 2 km from Sevilla (Santa Justa) rail station.
Huelva bus station is ± 1 km from the rail station.
Ayamonte bus station is ± 1.5 km from the ferry terminal.

677 MADRID - CÁCERES - BADAJOZ

km																									
			R-598			*R-598*			*R-598*	*R-598*							*TRD*		*Talgo*		*TRD*			*Hotel*	
			17904	**18772**		**17902**	**18774**		**17014**	**17900**				**17804**		**17702**	**17016**	**17824**	**194**	**17704**	**17018**	**17706**	**17708**	**332**	
		2	2	2	2	2	2	2	2	2	2	2	2	2	2	2	2	2	🍷	2	2	2	2	🅁✕	
		①⑥	**J**	**J**	**J**	**K**	**K**	**K**			**P**	⑦					**B**	⑤⑦		①–⑤	⑧**j**	**G**	**H**	**A**	
0	**Madrid** Chamartín ... d.	...	...	...	...	...	...	...	...	...	...	...	...	...	...	...	...	...	1625	...	...	...	...	2225	...
8	**Madrid** Atocha Cercanías ... d.	...	...	...	...	...	...	...	0741	0953	...	...	...	1328	...	1400	1527	1527	1640	1730	1909	1940	2020	|	...
146	Talavera de la Reina ... d.	...	...	...	...	...	...	...	0902	1121	...	...	...	|	...	1605	1653	1706	1803	1925	2034	2135	2222	0008	...
278	Plasencia ... a.	...	...	...	...	...	...	...	1022	1242	...	...	...	◧	...	...	1820	1838	|	...	2148	...	...	|	...
278	Plasencia ... d.	...	0538	...	...	0720	...	...	1025	1245	...	...	...	|	...	...	...	...	|	...	2151	...	...	|	...
343	**Cáceres** ... d.	...	0644	...	...	0830	...	...	1141	1350	...	...	1900	|	...	...	...	...	2004	...	2301	...	...	0151	...
409	Mérida ... a.	...	0751	...	...	0938	...	...	1245	1458	...	...	2006	2012	...	...	...	...	2101	...	0006	...	...	...	...
409	Mérida ... **678** d.	...	0755	0800	0900	0945	0945	1100	...	1503	1510	...	...	2024	2042	...	...	...	2113	...	...	...	...	...	...
469	**Badajoz** ... **678** a.	...	0840	|	0946	1025	|	1146	...	1540	|	...	...	2115	|	...	...	...	2153	...	...	...	...	...	...
475	Zafra ... d.	0550	...	0858	...	...	1043	...	...	...	1604	...	...	...	2137	...	...	...	...	...	...	...	...	...	...
649	Sevilla ... a.	|	...	1218	...	...	1401	...	...	...	...	...	...	...	...	...	...	...	...	...	...	...	...	...	...
521	Fregenal de la Sierra ... d.	0641	...	...	...	...	...	...	...	...	...	1545	...	...	...	...	...	...	...	...	...	...	...	...	...
660	Huelva ... a.	0935	...	...	...	...	...	...	...	...	...	1840	...	...	...	...	...	...	...	...	...	...	...	...	...

	Hotel		*TRD*	*TRD*			*Talgo*								*R-598*			*R-598*		*TRD*			*R-598*		
	335	**17705**	**17021**	**17023**			**197**						**17707**	**17801**	**17027**	**17801**		**17907**		**17025**	**17817**	**18779**	**17909**		
	🅁✕	2	2	2	2	2	🍷	2	2	2	2	2	2	2	2	2	2	2		2	2	2	2	2	
	A		**C**	⑥**q**	**J**	**J**		**J**	**K**	**K**	⑥⑦	⑦					**P**			**D**	**E**			⑤⑦	
Huelva ... d.	...	...	...	...	...	...	...	...	...	...	...	0950	...	...	...	...	...	...	...	...	...	...	...	1905	...
Fregenal de la Sierra ... d.	...	...	...	...	...	...	...	...	...	...	...	1245	...	...	...	...	...	...	...	...	...	...	...	2200	...
Sevilla ... d.	...	...	...	...	...	...	...	...	...	...	...	...	...	...	...	...	...	...	...	...	...	1550	...	|	...
Zafra ... d.	...	...	...	...	0655	...	...	...	0845	...	...	...	...	...	...	...	1402	...	...	...	...	1911	...	2249	...
Badajoz ... **678** d.	...	...	...	...	|	0700	0735	...	|	0855	...	...	...	1240	...	...	|	1420	...	...	...	|	1958	...	...
Mérida ... **678** a.	...	...	...	...	0745	0748	0808	...	0935	0943	...	...	...	1326	...	←	1452	1456	...	...	...	2005	2037	...	...
Mérida ... d.	...	...	0545	0620	...	...	0820	0905	...	...	0950	...	...	1328	1335	1328	...	1500	...	...	...	...	2045	...	...
Cáceres ... d.	0508	...	0646	0721	...	...	0925	1010	...	...	1055	...	...	→	1436	|	...	1602	...	...	...	...	2155	...	...
Plasencia ... a.	|	...	0757	0835	...	...	|	...	...	...	...	...	...	...	1543	|	...	1702	...	...	...	...	2315	...	...
Plasencia ... d.	|	...	0800	0850	...	...	|	...	...	...	...	...	...	...	1545	◧	...	1705	...	1911	1944	...	...	...	...
Talavera de la Reina ... d.	0714	0905	0922	1019	...	...	1125	...	...	...	...	...	1430	...	1710	|	...	1820	...	2031	2115	...	...	...	...
Madrid Atocha Cercanías ... a.	|	1050	1054	1157	...	...	1253	...	...	...	...	...	1615	...	1844	2006	...	1956	...	2212	2300	...	...	...	...
Madrid Chamartín ... a.	0903	...	...	...	...	...	1311	...	...	...	...	...	...	...	...	...	...	...	...	...	...	...	...	...	...

A – LUSITANIA *Hotel Train* – 🛏 *Gran Clase* (1, 2 berths), 🛏 *Preferente* (1, 2 berths), 🛏 1, 2 cl. (T4), (12) and ✕ Madrid - Cáceres - Lisboa and v.v. Special fares apply (Table **45**). Not Dec. 24, 31.
B – ①②③④⑥.
C – ①–⑤ (not Dec. 8, 25, Jan. 1).
D – ①②③④⑥ (also Dec. 6; not Dec. 8, 24, 31).
E – ⑤⑦ (also Dec. 8; not Dec. 6, 25, 27).
G – ①–⑥ (not Dec. 8, 24, 31).
H – ⑦ (also Dec. 8).
J – ①–⑤ (not Dec. 7, 8, 25, Jan. 1).
K – ⑥⑦ (also Dec. 7, 8).
P – From / to Puertollano (Table **678**).
j – Not Dec. 24, 31.
q – Also Dec. 8.
◧ – Via Ciudad Real (Table **678**).

678 ALCÁZAR DE SAN JUAN - BADAJOZ

km										
								Arco		**18027**
							17804	**697**	**18083**	**V**
		2	2	2	2	2	2	2	2	2
		A		⑥	**B**	**Z**		**G**	**C**	⑦**p**
	Madrid Atocha Cercanías. **661 / 8** d.	...	...	...	...	...	1328	...	...	...
	Albacete **661** ... d.	...	...	...	...	...	|	1337	1844	1958
0	**Alcázar de San Juan** ... **661** d.	...	0750	...	1240	...	1501	1510	2007	2128
50	Manzanares ... **661** d.	...	0819	...	1309	...	1528	1540	2037	2157
114	Ciudad Real ... **660** d.	...	0857	...	1347	...	1612	1637	2115	2240
153	Puertollano ... **660** d.	...	...	...	...	1132	1647	1718	...	...
265	Cabeza del Buey ... d.	0610	...	0740	...	1316	1831	1911	...	...
392	Mérida ... **677** a.	0750	...	0924	...	1457	2012	2046	...	...
451	**Badajoz** ... **677** a.	*0840*	...	*1025*	...	*1540*	2115	2145	...	...

	18024		*Arco*					
	V	**18081**	**694**	**17041**	**17801**			
	2	2	2	2	2	2	2	2
	①**q**	**C**	**G**			**Z**	⑧**k**	⑧**j**
Badajoz ... **677** d.	...	...	0715	...	1240	*1420*	...	...
Mérida ... **677** d.	...	...	0756	...	1328	1506	...	2050
Cabeza del Buey ... d.	...	...	0927	...	1503	1645	...	2233
Puertollano ... **660** d.	...	...	1106	...	1643	1841	...	...
Ciudad Real ... **660** d.	0551	0918	1157	1441	1726	...	2150	...
Manzanares ... **661** d.	0629	0958	1244	1520	1809	...	2227	...
Alcázar de San Juan ... **661** a.	0657	1029	1315	1549	1835	...	2257	...
Albacete **661** ... a.	0819	1144	1452	|	|	...	...	...
Madrid Atocha Cercanías. **661 / 8.** a.	...	...	...	1728	2006	...	...	...

A – ①–⑤ (not Dec. 7, 8, 25, Jan. 1).
B – ①–⑥ (not Dec. 7, 8).
C – COSTA DE LA MANCHA – (2) Alacant - Ciudad Real and v.v.
G – GARCÍA LORCA – (2) Barcelona - Badajoz and v.v.
V – (2) València - Ciudad Real and v.v.
Z – To / from Zafra (Table **677**).
j – Not Dec. 6, 7, 24, 25, 31.
k – Not Dec. 7, 8, 24, 31.
p – Also Dec. 8.
q – Also Dec. 9.

679 MADRID - TOLEDO, SEGOVIA and SALAMANCA

2nd class

km		*AV*	*AV*	*AV*	*AV*	*AV*	*AV*	*AV*	*AV*	*AV*	*AV*	*AV*	*AV*
		8062	**8072**	**8292**	**8302**	**8102**	**8322**	**8132**	**8152**	**8172**	**8182**	**8192**	**8212**
		A	**F**			**D**					**B**		
0	**Madrid** △ ... d.	0650	0750	0920	1020	1050	1220	1350	1550	1750	1850	1950	2150
75	**Toledo** ... a.	0720	0820	0950	1050	1120	1250	1420	1620	1820	1920	2020	2220

	AV	*AV*	*AV*	*AV*	*AV*	*AV*		*AV*	*AV*	*AV*	*AV*	*AV*
	8273	**8073**	**8283**	**8093**	**8103**	**8123**		**8153**	**8173**	**8183**	**8193**	**8213**
	A	**B**	**F**							**D**		**F**
Toledo ... d.	0650	0730	0800	0930	1030	1230	...	1530	1730	1830	1930	2130
Madrid △ ... a.	0720	0800	0832	1000	1100	1300	...	1600	1800	1900	2000	2200

km		*AL*	*AL*	*AL*	*AL*		*AL*	*AL*	*AL*	*AL*	*AL*	
		8089	**8109**	**8119**	**8129**		**8159**	**8179**	**8199**	**8209**	**8219**	
		F	**C**	**F**	**C**					**B**		
0	**Madrid** Chamartín ... d.	0835	1030	1115	1200	...	1530	1730	1915	2000	2100	...
68	**Segovia** Guiomar ¶ a.	0905	1100	1146	1231	...	1600	1800	1946	2031	2130	...

	AL	*AL*	*AL*	*AL*	*AL*		*AL*		*AL*	*AL*	*AL*
	8078	**8278**	**8088**	**8098**	**8108**		**8168**		**8188**	**8198**	**8218**
	G	**F**	**F**	**C**							**H**
Segovia Guiomar ¶ d.	0700	0723	0800	0905	0958	...	1608	...	1820	2013	2108
Madrid Chamartín ... a.	0732	0755	0832	0937	1030	...	1640	...	1852	2045	2140

km		**E**							**E**		
0	**Madrid** Atocha C. ... d.	0733	...	1001	1202	1401	1602	1802	2002	...	...
8	Madrid Chamartín ... d.	0747	...	1016	1216	1415	1616	1816	2016	...	...
108	**Segovia** ... a.	0935	...	1204	1402	1603	1757	2003	2213	...	...

	E							**E**		
Segovia ... d.	0755	...	1055	1255	1455	1650	1855	2055	...	...
Madrid Chamartín ... a.	0938	...	1237	1437	1637	1837	2037	2236	...	...
Madrid Atocha C. ... a.	0951	...	1250	1450	1650	1850	2050	2249	...	...

km		*MD*	*MD*	*MD*	*MD*	*MD*	*MD*	*MD*	*MD*	*MD*	
		18201	**18901**	**18903**	**18905**	**18907**	**18913**	**18919**	**18909**	**18911**	
							①–⑥	⑤⑥⑦			
0	**Madrid** Chamartín ... ◧ d.	...	0845	1105	1340	1545	1707	1843	2000	2113	...
122	Ávila ... ◧ d.	0712	1015	1238	1514	1715	1840	2014	2132	2245	...
233	**Salamanca** ... a.	0838	1122	1349	1625	1825	1951	2129	2237	2350	...

	MD	*MD*	*MD*	*MD*	*MD*	*MD*	*MD*	*MD*	*MD*	*MD*
	18910	**18900**	**18912**	**18902**	**18918**	**18904**	**18202**	**18906**	**18908**	**18202**
	①–⑥				⑤⑥⑦		①–⑥			⑦
Salamanca ... d.	0545	0747	0958	1225	1455	1542	1643	1800	2002	2059
Ávila ... ◧ d.	0652	0855	1112	1335	1612	1650	1811	1910	2113	2228
Madrid Chamartín ... ◧ a.	0830	1028	1244	1509	1751	1822	...	2045	2245	...

A – ①–⑤ (not Dec. 7, 8, 24, 25, 31, Jan. 1, 6).
B – ①–⑤ (not Dec. 8, Dec. 24 - Jan. 6).
C – ⑥⑦ (also Dec. 8, 25, Jan. 1, 6).
D – ⑥⑦ (also Dec. 7, 8, 25).
E – ①–⑤ (not Dec. 8, 25, Jan. 1).
F – ①–⑤ (not Dec. 25, Jan. 1, 6).
G – ①–⑤ (not Dec. 24, 25, 31, Jan. 1, 6).
H – ⑤⑥⑦ (also Dec. 8, 24, 31, Jan. 6; not Jan. 1, 3).
f – Not Dec. 24, 31.
◧ – See also Tables **680**, **681**, **689**.
△ – Madrid Puerta de Atocha.
MD – Medium Distance Plus 🅁.
AV – ***Avant*** high-speed services. Single class. 🍷.
AL – ***AVE-Lanzadera*** regional high-speed gauge-changing trains.
¶ – 4 km from city centre. For long-distance high-speed services calling at Segovia Guiomar, see Table **663**.

MADRID - ZAMORA - VIGO, PONTEVEDRA and A CORUÑA 680

For services to / from A Coruña via León, see Table **682**

km			R-598 12412	Hotel 851	R-598 12414	Hotel 851	R-598 12022	MD		R-598 12418				Hotel 922			R-598 12422	R-598 12424	MD	R-598 12428			R-598 12430	
		2	2	✕	2	✕	2	2	2	2	2	2	2	🍷	2	2	2	2	2	2	2	2	2	
		①–⑥	P	C		D			①–⑤			①–⑤	①–⑤	G	⑥	⑥⑦	P				①–⑤		P	
0	**Madrid** Chamartín ... **681 689** d.	...	...	2230	...	2230	...	...	...	...	...	...	...	...	...	...	...	...	...	...	...	...	...	...
121	Ávila ... **681 689** d.	...	...	0003	...	0003	...	...	...	...	...	...	...	...	...	...	...	...	...	...	...	...	...	...
	Irún **689** ... d.	...	...	|	...	|	...	...	...	...	...	...	...	...	...	...	...	...	...	...	...	...	...	...
	Barcelona Sants **652** ... d.	...	...	|	...	|	...	...	...	...	...	...	...	2020	...	...	...	...	...	...	...	...	...	...
	Miranda de Ebro **681 689** ... d.	...	...	|	...	|	...	...	...	...	...	...	...	|	...	...	...	...	...	...	...	...	...	...
207*	Medina del Campo... **681 689** d.	...	...	0053	...	0053	...	...	...	...	...	...	...	|	...	...	...	...	...	...	...	...	...	...
297	**Zamora** ... d.	...	...	0149	...	0149	...	...	...	...	...	...	...	|	...	...	...	...	...	...	...	...	...	...
404	Puebla de Sanabria ... d.	...	...	0314	...	0314	...	...	...	...	...	0635	...	|	0745	...	...	...	...	...	...	...	...	...
547	**Ourense** ... d.	...	...	0520	...	0540	0657	...	...	...	...	0827	0841	0906	0933	0947	...	...	...	...	...	1430	...	...
641	Guillarei ... d.	...	...	|	...	0655	|	...	...	...	...	...	1015	1030	...	1120	...	...	...	...	...	|	...	...
	Vigo ... d.	...	0535	|	0630	|	|	0705	0803	0855	0940	...	|	|	...	|	1040	1215	1305	1400	1420	|	1520	...
666	Redondela ... d.	...	0545	|	|	0720	|	0720	0816	|	0953	...	1035	1051	...	1140	|	1225	1319	|	1431	|	|	...
678	**Vigo** ... a.	...	|	|	|	0733s	|	|	|	|	|	...	1051	1102	...	1151	|	|	|	|	|	|	|	...
684	**Pontevedra** ... d.	...	0606	|	0656	0825	|	0744	0832	0927	1017	...	...	...	...	...	1108	1245	1343	1427	1450	|	1550	...
717	Vilagarcía de Arousa ... d.	...	0626	|	0718	...	|	0811	...	0948	1041	...	...	...	...	...	1128	1306	1406	1447	...	|	1610	...
677	Santiago de Compostela ... d.	0635	0705	0723	0756	...	0830	0901	...	1021	1124	...	...	...	...	...	1204	1340	1448	1520	...	1618	1643	...
751	**A Coruña** ... a.	0731	0749	0819	0845	...	0915	1007	...	1106	1218	...	...	...	...	...	1246	1428	1547	1603	...	...	1728	...

	MD		R-598 12434	R-598 12436	Arco 283	Arco 283				R-598 12440	Talgo 85	Talgo 151	R-598 12442	Talgo 85	Talgo 151	MD 12609		Alvia 622						
	2	2	2	2	2	2	2	2	2	2	🍷	🍷	2	🍷	🍷	2	2	🍷	2	2	2	2		
					B	A		⑦	①–⑤		K⑦	①–⑥		H⑦	①–⑥	h		E	①–⑤	⑦		J		
Madrid Chamartín ... **681 689** d.	...	...	...	...	...	...	...	...	...	...	1355	1420	...	1355	1420	...	...	...	...	...	1430	...	...	...
Ávila ... **681 689** d.	...	...	...	...	...	...	...	...	...	...	1526	|	...	1526	|	...	...	...	...	...	1602	...	...	...
Irún **689** ... d.	...	...	...	...	...	0845	...	...	...	...	|	◧	...	|	◧	...	...	...	...	...	|	...	...	...
Barcelona Sants **652** ... d.	...	...	...	...	...	|	...	...	...	...	|	|	...	|	|	...	...	0920	...	...	|	...	...	...
Miranda de Ebro **681 689** ... d.	...	...	...	...	1116	1116	...	...	...	...	|	|	...	|	|	...	...	1425	...	...	|	...	...	...
Medina del Campo... **681 689** d.	...	...	...	...	|	|	...	...	...	...	1619	1600	...	1619	1600	...	...	|	...	...	1646	1806	...	...
Zamora ... d.	...	...	...	...	|	|	...	...	...	...	1707	1649	...	1707	1649	...	...	|	...	...	...	1907	...	...
Puebla de Sanabria ... d.	...	...	...	...	|	|	...	1750	...	...	1820	1800	...	1820	1800	...	...	|	...	...	...	2029	...	...
Ourense ... d.	...	1527	...	...	1805	1830	...	1945	...	...	2003	1945	...	2009	2000	2022	2039	2057	...	...	...	...	...	...
Guillarei ... d.	...	1650	...	...	1929	|	...	...	...	...	|	|	...	2120	2112	2145	|	|	...	...	...	...	...	...
Vigo ... d.	1545	|	1705	1815	|	|	1845	...	1930	1955	|	|	2100	|	|	|	|	|	2213	2230	...	...	...	...
Redondela ... d.	1558	1711	|	|	1950	|	1901	...	1942	|	|	|	|	2140s	2131s	2205	|	2232	2226	2245	...	...	...	...
Vigo ... a.	|	1724	|	|	2006	|	|	...	|	|	|	|	|	2154	2144	2215	|	2250	|	|	...	...	...	...
Pontevedra ... d.	1619	...	1732	1846	...	|	1923	...	1959	2023	|	|	2126	2247	2226	...	|	...	2247	2307	...	...	...	...
Vilagarcía de Arousa ... d.	1645	...	1752	1906	...	|	1946	...	...	2043	|	|	2147	...	...	...	|	...	2311	2328	...	...	...	...
Santiago de Compostela ... d.	1730	...	1826	1938	...	2010	2030	...	...	2117	2132	2123	2227	...	...	...	2231	...	2352	0007	...	...	...	...
A Coruña ... a.	1829	...	1909	2022	...	2108	2129	...	...	2205	2226	2208	2310	...	...	...	...	...	...	...	...	...	...	...

km			18010		R-598 12411		MD 12604	Alvia 621	R-598 12413			R-598 12417	Arco 280	Arco 280	Talgo 74	R-598 12419	Talgo 74	MD	R-598 12423		Talgo 152	R-598 12425	MD	Talgo 152
		2	2	2	2	2	2	🍷	2	2	2	2	2	2	🍷	2	🍷	2	2	2	🍷	2	2	🍷
		J	①–⑥	①–⑥	P	①–⑤	h	E		①–⑤	⑥		A	B	H⑥	P	K⑥		P	⑥⑦	Ⓑ			Ⓑ
0	**A Coruña** ... d.	...	...	...	0540	...	...	...	0655	...	...	0750	0826	...	...	0822	0900	0927	1030	...	...	1150	1225	1310
74	Santiago de Compostela ... d.	...	...	0545	0626	0645	...	...	0738	...	0807	0837	0917	...	...	0908	0954	1021	1114	...	...	1234	1318	1357
116	Vilagarcía de Arousa ... d.	...	...	0637	0702	|	...	...	0812	...	|	0907	|	...	...	0937	|	1103	1144	...	...	1303	1400	|
149	**Pontevedra** ... d.	...	...	0655	0722	|	...	...	0832	0845	|	0927	|	...	0845	0956	|	1131	1203	...	1250	1323	1426	|
	Vigo ... d.	...	...	|	|	|	0652	0755	|	|	|	|	|	0925	0930	|	|	|	|	...	1337	|	|	|
167	Redondela ... d.	...	...	0720	0741	|	0704	0806	0853	0907	|	|	|	0936	0941	|	|	1155	|	...	1349	|	1452	|
179	**Vigo** ... a.	...	...	0737	0752	|	|	|	0905	0921	|	0958	|	|	|	1029	|	1210	1231	...	|	1354	1505	|
192	Guillarei ... d.	...	...	...	...	|	0724	|	...	...	|	...	|	0954	0959	...	|	...	...	...	1408	...	...	|
	Ourense ... d.	...	...	...	...	0836	0844	0927	...	...	0957	...	1115	1115	1138	...	1138	...	...	1510	1546	...	...	1546
	Puebla de Sanabria ... d.	0715	...	...	...	...	...	|	...	...	...	...	|	|	1320	...	1320	...	...	1718	1728	...	...	1728
	Zamora ... d.	0832	...	...	...	...	...	|	...	...	...	...	|	|	1430	...	1430	...	...	...	1847	...	...	1847
	Medina del Campo... **681 689** d.	0927	1032	...	...	...	...	|	...	...	...	...	|	|	1533	...	1533	...	...	...	1938	...	...	1938
	Miranda de Ebro **681 689** ... a.	...	|	...	...	...	...	1555	...	...	...	...	1755	1755	|	...	|	...	...	...	|	...	...	|
	Barcelona Sants **652** ... a.	...	|	...	...	...	...	2110	...	...	...	...	|	...	|	...	|	...	...	...	|	...	...	|
	Hendaye **689** ... a.	...	|	...	...	...	...	...	...	...	...	...	2040	...	|	...	|	...	...	...	◧	...	...	◧
	Ávila ... **681 689** d.	...	1121	...	...	...	...	...	...	...	...	...	...	...	1620	...	1620	...	...	...	|	...	...	|
	Madrid Chamartín ... **681 689** a.	...	1309	...	...	...	...	...	...	...	...	...	...	...	1752	...	1752	...	...	...	2108	...	...	2108

		R-598 12429				R-598 12431		Hotel 921		R-598 12435		R-598 12437			R-598 12023		Hotel 852	MD	R-598 12441	Hotel 852				
	2	2	2	2	2	2	2	🍷	2	2	2	2	2	2	2		✕	2	2	✕	2	2		
	①–⑤				①–④			G	⑤				①–⑤				D			C	①–⑤	⑦		
A Coruña ... d.	...	1355	...	...	...	1445	1523	...	...	1655	...	1750	...	1850	1945	...	...	2000	2050	2145	2210	2230	...	...
Santiago de Compostela ... d.	...	1439	...	1455	...	1528	1621	...	...	1738	...	1833	...	1944	2032	...	...	2057	2133	2235	2302	2327	...	...
Vilagarcía de Arousa ... d.	...	1513	...	|	...	1559	1707	...	...	1808	...	1902	...	2030	|	...	...	2141	2205	|	...	...	...	...
Pontevedra ... d.	1510	1532	...	|	...	1619	1731	...	...	1828	...	1923	2025	2100	|	...	2130	2205	2226	|	...	...	...	...
Vigo ... d.	|	|	1447	|	...	|	|	1810	...	|	2012	|	|	|	|	...	2220u	|	|	|	...	...	...	...
Redondela ... d.	1527	|	1459	|	...	|	1753	1820	...	|	2024	|	2043	2127	|	...	2236	2227	|	|	...	...	...	...
Vigo ... a.	1540	1603	|	|	...	1648	1805	|	...	1859	|	1954	2056	2140	|	...	|	2242	2259	|	...	...	...	...
Guillarei ... d.	...	...	1521	|	...	...	...	1841	...	...	2046	...	...	...	|	...	2258	...	...	|	...	...	...	...
Ourense ... d.	...	...	1646	1640	1725	...	...	1948	2010	...	2221	...	...	...	2201	...	0035	...	...	0035	...	...	...	...
Puebla de Sanabria ... d.	...	...	...	...	1939	...	...	|	2215	...	...	...	...	...	...	...	0233	...	...	0233	...	...	...	...
Zamora ... d.	...	...	...	...	...	...	...	|	...	...	...	...	...	...	...	...	0400	...	...	0400	...	...	...	...
Medina del Campo... **681 689** d.	...	...	...	...	...	...	...	|	...	...	...	...	...	...	...	...	0540	...	...	0540	...	...	...	...
Miranda de Ebro **681 689** ... a.	...	...	...	...	...	...	...	|	...	...	...	...	...	...	...	...	|	...	...	|	...	...	...	...
Barcelona Sants **652** ... a.	...	...	...	...	...	...	...	0845	...	...	...	...	...	...	...	...	|	...	...	|	...	...	...	...
Hendaye **689** ... a.	...	...	...	...	...	...	...	...	...	...	...	...	...	...	...	...	|	...	...	|	...	...	...	...
Ávila ... **681 689** d.	...	...	...	...	...	...	...	...	...	...	...	...	...	...	...	...	0625	...	...	0625	...	...	...	...
Madrid Chamartín ... **681 689** a.	...	...	...	...	...	...	...	...	...	...	...	...	...	...	...	...	0805	...	...	0805	...	...	...	...

A – CAMINO DE SANTIAGO – [12] and 🍷 Irún / Hendaye - Miranda de Ebro - Ourense - A Coruña and v.v.
B – CAMINO DE SANTIAGO – [2] Bilbao - Miranda de Ebro - Ourense - Vigo and v.v.
C – RÍAS GALLEGAS *Hotel Train* – (not Dec. 24, 26, 31): 🛏 and [2] Madrid - A Coruña and v.v.
D – RÍAS GALLEGAS *Hotel Train* – (not Dec. 24, 26, 31): 🛏 and [2] Madrid - Pontevedra and v.v.
E – [12] and 🍷 Barcelona - Vigo and v.v.
G – GALICIA – (not Dec. 24, 26, 31): 🛏 and [1] (reclining) Barcelona - Vigo and v.v.
H – [12] Alacant - Pontevedra and v.v.
J – [2] Valladolid - Puebla de Sanabria and v.v.
K – [12] Alacant - A Coruña and v.v.

P – ①–⑤ (not Dec. 7, 8, 25, Jan. 1).

h – To/from Ponferrada. (Table **682**).
s – Stops to set down only.
u – Stops to pick up only.

◧ – Via high-speed line.
* – *153 km* Madrid - Medina del Campo via high-speed line.

681 MADRID - LEÓN

km		18009	4071	4073	18101	283	4111	18215	18001	4133	622	4141	18003	18217	18105	4183	4181	18791	18791	18005	4201	751	922	932	
			Alvia	Alvia		Arco	Alvia			Alvia	Alvia	Alvia				Alvia	Alvia				Alvia	Hotel	Hotel	Hotel	
		2	①–⑥	①–⑥	2		♀	2	2	♀	2622	2622	2	2	2	♀	♀	2	2	2	♀		♀		
		①–⑥	K	f		B					E	X			T	Rg	Ⓑh	⑤	⑤		h	A	G	D	
0	**Madrid** Chamartín . **680 689** d.	...	0650	0740	...	...	1100	...	1130	1330	...	1440	1430	...	...	1805	1830	1645	...	1814	2015	2230	...	...	...
121	Ávila .... **680 689** d.	...	◧	◧	...	...	◧	...	1309	◧	...	◧	1602	...	...	◧	◧	1823	...	1950	◧	0002	...	...	...
207	Medina del Campo. **680 689** d.	0655	│	│	...	...	│	...	1354	│	...	│	1647	...	...	│	│	1913	...	2035	│	0051	...	...	...
249	**Valladolid** C. Grande.... **689** d.	0737	0803	0853	0935	...	1213	1235	1421	1443	...	1601	1714	1755	1810	1926	1947	1940	...	2100	2127	0122	...	...	...
286	Venta de Baños .... **689** d.	0804	│	│	1008	...	│	1308	1445	│	...	│	1738	1825	1843	│	│	2002	...	2124	│	0147	...	...	...
	Barcelona Sants **652**.....d.	│	│	│	│	...	│	│	│	│	0920	│	│	│	│	│	│	│	...	│	│	│	2020	2045	...
	Irún **689** ....d.	│	│	│	│	0845	│	│	│	│	│	│	│	│	│	│	│	│	...	│	│	│	│	│	...
	Bilbao Abando **689**........d.	│	│	│	│	0915	│	│	│	│	│	│	│	│	│	│	│	│	...	│	│	│	│	│	...
	Miranda de Ebro......... **689** d.	│	│	│	│	1116	│	│	│	│	1425	│	│	│	│	│	│	│	...	│	│	│	│	│	...
	Burgos Rosa de Lima **689** d.	│	│	│	│	1211	│	│	│	│	1521	│	│	│	│	│	│	│	...	│	│	│	0249	0355	...
297	Palencia...................... **689** d.	0815	0836	0926	1020	1258	1245	1320	1455	1516	1608	1634	1748	1836	1855	1959	2016	2014	2020	2134	2201	0157	0341	0449	...
	Santander **684**..................a.	│	│	1207	1334	│	│	│	│	1755	│	│	│	│	2216	2242	│	│	2330	│	│	│	│	│	...
420	**León**.................................a.	0927	0936	...	...	1401	1344	1440	1604	...	1709	1737	1856	2000	...	...	2118	2127	...	2244	2305	0258	0445	0557	...
	Gijón Cercanías **685**.........a.	...	1155	...	...	│	1605	...	...	...	│	2002	...	...	...	...	2339	│	...	...	...	│	│	0830	...
	Ponferrada **682**.................a.	...	...	...	...	1533	...	...	...	...	1838	...	...	...	...	...	...	2328	...	...	...	0428	0622	...	...
	Vigo **682**...........................a.	...	...	...	...	2006	...	...	...	...	2250	...	...	...	...	...	...	...	...	...	...	│	1102	...	...
	A Coruña **682**...................a.	...	...	...	...	2108	...	...	...	...	...	...	...	...	...	...	...	...	...	...	...	│	1055	...	...
	Ferrol **682**.........................a.	...	...	...	...	...	...	...	...	...	...	...	...	...	...	...	...	...	...	...	...	0913	...	...	...

	4060	18002	4072	4070		4100	621	18004	280	18214	4142	4140	18102	18006	18216	18104	18790	18790	4180	4192	18008	931	921	752	
	Alvia		Alvia	Alvia		Alvia	Alvia		Arco		Alvia	Alvia							Alvia	Alvia		Hotel	Hotel	Hotel	
	①–⑥	2	♀	①–⑥	2	2621	2621	2		2	♀	♀	2	2	2	2	2	2	Ⓑ	Ⓑ	2	♀	♀	Ⓑ	
	p		Rq	f	⑥⑦		E		C			Y			⑦	①–⑥	⑦	⑦	L	g		D	G	A	
Ferrol **682** .... d.	...	...	...	...	...	...	...	...	...	...	...	...	...	...	...	...	...	...	...	...	...	...	...	2100	...
A Coruña **682**.................. d.	...	...	...	...	...	...	...	...	0826	...	...	...	...	...	...	...	...	...	...	...	...	...	1800	│	...
Vigo **682** .... d.	...	...	...	...	...	...	0755	...	0925	...	...	...	...	...	...	...	...	...	...	...	...	...	1810	│	...
Ponferrada **682** .... d.	...	...	...	...	...	...	1142	...	1334	...	...	...	...	...	...	...	...	1700	...	...	...	...	2237	0145	...
Gijón Cercanías **685**......... d.	...	...	...	0715	...	1025	│	...	│	...	...	1400	...	...	...	...	...	│	1815	...	...	2048	│	│	...
León .... d.	0630	0713	...	0937	...	1247	1312	1320	1507	1500	...	1624	...	1652	1737	...	...	1908	2035	...	2050	2328	0014	0324	...
Santander **684**................. d.	│	│	0705	│	0820	│	│	│	│	│	1405	│	1415	│	│	1655	1720	│	│	1920	│	│	│	│	...
Palencia .... **689** d.	0730	0818	0947	1040	1141	1348	1416	1426	1611	1622	1644	1727	1732	1757	1849	2017	2019	2025	2136	2203	2208	0031	0122	0426	...
Burgos Rosa de Lima **689** d.	│	│	│	│	│	│	1501	│	1659	│	│	│	│	│	│	│	│	│	│	│	│	0120	0215	│	...
Miranda de Ebro........ **689** a.	│	│	│	│	│	│	1555	│	1755	│	│	│	│	│	│	│	│	│	│	│	│	│	│	│	...
Bilbao Abando **689**........ a.	│	│	│	│	│	│	│	│	2000	│	│	│	│	│	│	│	│	│	│	│	│	│	│	│	...
Hendaye **689** .... a.	│	│	│	│	│	│	│	│	2040	│	│	│	│	│	│	│	│	│	│	│	│	│	│	│	...
Barcelona Sants **652**..... a.	│	│	│	│	│	│	2110	│	...	│	│	│	│	│	│	│	│	│	│	│	│	0808	0845	│	...
Venta de Baños........... **689** d.	│	0825	│	│	1152	│	...	1436	...	1633	│	│	1741	1807	1858	2028	2029	2035	│	│	2218	...	...	│	...
Valladolid C. Grande ... **689** d.	0804	0849	1021	1114	1220	1420	...	1458	...	1705	1718	1801	1809	1828	1922	2100	2052	2100	2210	2237	2246	...	...	0500	...
Medina del Campo..**680 689** a.	│	0917	│	│	...	│	...	1523	...	...	│	│	...	1853	1951	...	...	2132	│	│	2323	...	...	0526	...
Ávila ....**680 689** a.	◧	1001	◧	◧	...	◧	...	1608	...	...	◧	◧	...	1938	2037	...	...	2216	◧	◧	...	...	...	0623	...
Madrid Chamartín ..**680 689** a.	0920	1139	1143	1229	...	1540	...	1742	...	...	1833	1923	...	2121	2214	...	...	2352	2325	2352	...	...	...	0805	...

☛ **FOR NOTES**, SEE TABLE **682** BELOW.

682 LEÓN - VIGO, FERROL and A CORUÑA

km			12021				922	922							283	283			12609	622	723			18791	751
			R-598				Hotel	Hotel							Arco	Arco			MD	Alvia	Arco				Hotel
		2	2	2	2	2	♀		2	2	2	2	2	2	2	♀	2	2	2	1623	1623	2	2	2	
		①–⑤	①–⑤	①–⑤	①–⑤	⑥⑦	G	G	⑥⑦	⑥⑦	①–⑤	⑦			B	B				E		T	⑤	⑤	A
	Madrid Chamartín ‡ d.	...	...	...	...	...	...	...	...	...	...	...	...	...	...	...	...	...	...	...	...	...	...	1645	2230
	Barcelona Sants... ‡ d.	...	...	...	...	...	2020	2020	...	...	...	...	...	...	...	...	...	...	...	0920	...	...	...	│	│
	Irún ....‡ d.	...	...	...	...	...	│	│	...	...	...	...	...	...	...	0845	...	...	...	│	...	...	...	│	│
	Bilbao Abando......‡ d.	...	...	...	...	...	│	│	...	...	...	...	...	...	0915	│	...	...	...	│	...	...	...	│	│
0	**León** ....d.	...	...	...	...	...	0450	0450	...	...	0710	...	...	...	1403	1403	...	...	...	1711	...	2005	...	2128	0300
52	Astorga..........................d.	...	...	...	...	...	0522	0522	...	...	0749	...	...	...	1431	1431	...	...	...	1740	...	2045	...	2209	0331
128	**Ponferrada** ....d.	...	...	0600	...	...	0624	0624	0700	...	0901	...	...	...	1534	1534	...	...	1757	1839	...	2155	...	2325	0429
238	Monforte de Lemos.....a.	...	...	0743	...	...	0755	0755	0841	...	...	...	...	...	1704	1704	...	...	1931	2011	...	...	...	...	0556
238	Monforte de Lemos.....d.	...	...	0748	0752	...	0820	0815	0844	0857	...	1121	...	...	1719	1719	1825	...	1936	2014	2055	...	2138	...	0611
285	Ourense........... **680** d.	...	...	0841	│	...	│	0906	0947	│	...	1224	...	...	1805	1830	│	...	2022	2057	│	...	2220	...	│
416	**Vigo**................. **680** a.	...	...	1051	│	...	│	1102	1151	│	...	...	...	...	2006	│	│	...	2215	2250	│	...	...	...	│
309	Lugo...............................d.	...	...	...	0852	...	0913	...	...	0957	...	...	...	...	...	│	1924	...	...	...	2157	...	...	...	0706
	Ferrol ....d.	0700	0915	...	│	0921	│	...	...	│	...	...	1430	1705	...	▲	│	2020	...	...	│	...	...	...	│
402	Betanzos - Infesta........d.	0753	1000	...	1012	1015	1030	...	...	1127	...	...	1530	1753	...	│	2057	2119	...	...	2324	...	...	...	0825
445	**Ferrol** ....a.	│	│	...	│	│	│	...	...	│	...	...	│	│	...	│	│	│	...	...	│	...	...	...	0913
428	**A Coruña**............ **680** a.	0820	1022	...	1039	1040	1055	...	...	1153	...	...	1556	1821	...	2108	2124	2147	...	...	2354	...	...	...	...

				12604	720	621	12020		280	280			18790					921	921				752		
				MD	Arco	Alvia	R-598		Arco	Arco								Hotel	Hotel				Hotel		
	2	2	2	2	1621	1621	2	2	♀	2	2	2	2	2	2	2			♀	2	2	2			
	①–⑤	⑥	①–⑤			E	①–⑤		C	C	⑥⑦	①–⑥	⑦			⑦		G	G				A		
A Coruña............ **680** d.	...	...	0625	...	0650	...	0725	0827	0826	...	1056	...	...	1440	...	...	...	...	1800	1840	1858	2029	...	...	...
Ferrol ....d.	...	...	│	...	│	...	│	│	│	...	│	...	...	│	...	...	...	...	│	│	│	│	2100	...	...
Betanzos - Infesta........d.	...	...	0655	...	0714	...	0752	0857	│	...	1125	...	...	1510	...	...	...	...	1822	1909	1927	2059	2155	...	...
Ferrol ....a.	...	...	0748	...	│	...	0832	│	▲	...	1215	...	...	1559	...	...	...	...	│	│	2012	2147	│	...	...
Lugo...............................d.	...	...	...	...	0829		...	1022	│	...	...	...	...	...	...	...	...	...	1927	2036	...	...	2308	...	...
Vigo................. **680** d.	...	...	...	0652	│	0755	...	│	│	0925	...	...	...	...	1447	...	...	1810	│	│	...	...	│	...	...
Ourense........... **680** d.	...	0805	...	0846	│	0927	...	│	1115	1115	...	...	...	...	1648	1740	...	1948	│	│	...	...	│	...	...
Monforte de Lemos......a.	...	0850	...	0928	0941	1005	...	1121	1155	1155	...	...	...	...	1734	1824	...	2028	2023	2137	...	...	0000	...	...
Monforte de Lemos......d.	...	...	...	0933	...	1010	...	...	1205	1205	...	...	...	...	1739	...	...	2056	2056	...	...	...	0015	...	...
Ponferrada.................d.	0712	...	...	1107	...	1142	...	...	1334	1334	...	1700	1700	...	1945	...	...	2237	2237	...	...	...	0145	...	...
Astorga..........................d.	0823	...	...	...	...	1242	...	...	1433	1433	...	1825	1825	...	2105	...	...	2339	2339	...	...	...	0243	...	...
León ....a.	0900	...	...	...	...	1310	...	...	1505	1505	...	1903	1903	...	2144	...	...	0009	0009	...	...	...	0322	...	...
Bilbao Abando.......‡ a.	...	...	...	...	...	│	...	...	│	2000	...	...	│	...	...	...	...	│	│	...	...	...	│	...	...
Hendaye ....‡ a.	...	...	...	...	...	│	...	...	2040	...	...	...	│	...	...	...	...	│	│	...	...	...	│	...	...
Barcelona Sants....‡ a.	...	...	...	...	...	2110	...	...	...	...	...	...	│	...	...	...	...	0845	0845	...	...	...	│	...	...
Madrid Chamartín..‡ a.	...	...	...	...	...	...	...	...	...	...	...	...	2352	...	...	...	...	...	...	...	...	...	0805	...	...

A – ATLÁNTICO – ②③④⑤⑥⑦ (not Dec. 24, 26, 31): 🛏, ▬ and (1) Madrid - Ferrol and v.v.
B – CAMINO DE SANTIAGO – (12) and ♀ Irún - A Coruña. (2) Bilbao - Vigo.
C – CAMINO DE SANTIAGO – (12) and ♀ A Coruña - Hendaye. (2) Vigo - Bilbao.
D – PÍO BAROJA – (not Dec. 24, 26, 31): 🛏 and (1) (reclining) Barcelona - Gijón and v.v.
E – (12) and ♀ Barcelona - Vigo and v.v.
G – GALICIA – (not Dec. 24, 26, 31): 🛏 and (1) (reclining) Barcelona - A Coruña and Vigo and v.v. ♀ Barcelona - A Coruña and v.v.
K – ①–⑥ (not Dec. 7, 25, Jan. 1, 6).

L – Ⓑ (not Dec. 7, 24, 31).
R – (12) Alacant - Madrid - Santander and v.v.
T – ①②③④⑥⑦.
X – From Alacant on ①–⑥.
Y – To Alacant on Ⓑ.
f – Not Dec. 25, Jan. 1, 6.

g – Not Dec. 24, 31.
h – Not Dec. 7, 24, 31.
p – Not Dec. 8, 25, Jan. 1.
q – Not Dec. 25, Jan. 1.
▲ – Via Santiago (Table 680).
‡ – See Table 681 (above).
◧ – Via high-speed line (Table 663).

683 LEÓN - BILBAO

FEVE narrow-gauge

1400 →	1445 →	1535 →	1636 →	1717 →	1801 →	1935 →	2042 →	2130
León	La Vecilla	Cistierna	Guardo	Vado Cervera	Mataporquera	Espinosa	Balmaseda	**Bilbao** Concordia
2148	← 2059	← 2018	← 1921	← 1841	← 1800	← 1623	← 1519	← 1430

PALENCIA - SANTANDER 684

km		Alvia 4073 🍷 A	2		Alvia 4133	2	2 C	Alvia 4183 🍷 Ep	2 ⑤
	Madrid Chamartín **681 689** d.	0740	...	...	1330	...	...	1805	...
	Valladolid C. Grande **681 689** d.	0853	0935	...	1443	1455	1810	1926	...
0	**Palencia** d.	0926	1020	...	1516	1537	1855	1959	2020
98	Aguilar de Campoo d.	1027	1136	...	|	1701	2007	2101	2131
110	Mataporquera **683** ‡ d.	|	1146	...	|	1712	2016	|	2141
129	Reinosa § d.	1052	1202	...	|	1730	2036	2127	2156
188	Torrelavega § d.	1141	1300	...	1730	1826	2140	2217	2257
218	**Santander** § a.	1207	1334	...	1755	1900	2216	2242	2330

	2 ①–⑤	Alvia 4072 🍷 Eq	2 ⑥⑦	Alvia 4142 🍷	2	2 ①–⑥	2 ⑦	Alvia 4182 🍷 B	
Santander § d.	...	0705	0820	1405	1415	1655	1720	1920	...
Torrelavega § d.	...	0730	0854	1430	1450	1730	1747	1945	...
Reinosa § d.	0715	0819	0957	|	1551	1833	1842	2034	...
Mataporquera **683** ‡ d.	0734	|	1013	|	1607	1849	1857	|	...
Aguilar de Campoo d.	0744	0843	1028	|	1619	1859	1904	2058	...
Palencia a.	0859	0945	1140	1642	1731	2016	2018	2201	...
Valladolid C. Grande **681 689** a.	0943	1019	1220	1716	1809	2100	2052	2235	...
Madrid Chamartín **681 689** a.	...	1143	...	1833	...	...	...	2352	...

A – ①–⑥ (not Dec. 25, Jan. 1, 6).
B – ⑧ (not Dec. 24, 31).
C – ①②③④⑥⑦.
E – From / to Alacant.
p – Not Dec. 24, 31.
q – Not Dec. 25, Jan. 1.
§ – Additional local services operate between these stations.
‡ – Walking distance to the narrow gauge station is 600 metres.

LEÓN - OVIEDO - GIJÓN 685

km		Hotel 932 A	Alvia 4071 ①–⑥ D		2	Alvia 4111 🍷	Alvia 4141 🍷 C	2 ⑧	Alvia 4181 🍷 ⑧h	
	Barcelona Sants **681** d.	2045	...	...	...	...	...	...	...	...
	Madrid Chamartín **681** d.	|	0650	...	...	1100	1440	...	1830	...
0	**León** d.	0601	0938	...	1315	1344	1739	1939	2120	...
109	Pola de Lena § a.	|	|	...	1449	|	1857	2122	|	...
140	**Oviedo** ▽ § a.	0757	1126	...	1523	1532	1930	2203	2310	...
172	**Gijón** Cercanias § a.	0830	1155	...	1553	1605	2002	2243	2339	...

	2 ①–⑤	Alvia 4070 ①–⑥ f	Alvia 4100 🍷	2	Alvia 4140 🍷 B		Alvia 4180 ⑧ E	Hotel 931 A	
Gijón Cercanias § d.	0650	0715	1025	1300	1400	...	1815	2048	...
Oviedo ▽ § d.	0729	0743	1054	1336	1428	...	1843	2126	...
Pola de Lena § d.	0807	|	1125	1418	1500	...	|	|	...
León a.	1008	0935	1245	1601	1622	...	2033	2325	...
Madrid Chamartín **681** a.	...	1229	1540	...	1923	...	2325	|	...
Barcelona Sants **681** a.	...	...	...	...	...	...	...	0808	...

A – PÍO BAROJA (not Dec. 24, 26, 31): 🛏 and 💺 (reclining) Barcelona - Gijón and v.v.
B – To Alacant on ⑧.
C – From Alacant on ①–⑥.
D – ①–⑥ (not Dec. 7, 25, Jan. 1, 6).
E – ⑧ (not Dec. 7, 24, 31).
f – Not Dec. 25, Jan. 1, 6.
h – Not Dec. 7, 24, 31.

▽ – **OVIEDO – AVILÉS** and v.v. ***Renfe Cercanías*** (suburban) service. *31 km.* Journey time: ± 38 minutes.
From Oviedo: Approximately 1 train each hour 0550 Ⓐ, 0616 Ⓐ, then 0716 until 2216. **From Avilés**: Approximately 1 train each hour 0641 Ⓐ, 0741 Ⓐ, then 0841 until 2311.
Additional services on Ⓐ.

§ – **GIJÓN – OVIEDO – POLA de LENA** and v.v. ***Renfe Cercanías*** (suburban) service. *63 km.* Journey time: ± 78 minutes.
From Pola de Lena: Approximately 1–2 trains each hour from 0630 until 2200. **From Gijón**: Approximately 1–2 trains each hour from 0600 until 2230.

EuskoTren (narrow gauge) SAN SEBASTIÁN - BILBAO 686

					Ⓐ	Ⓐd				
Hendaye **689** d.		0847c	1947c		...	...	...		...	...
San Sebastián ⊡ Amara d.	F	0918	2018	S	0547	0647	0747		1947	2047
Zarautz d.	A	0945	2045	L	0620	0720	0820	and	2020	2120
Zumaia d.	S	0953	2053	O	0629	0729	0829	hourly	2029	2129
Eibar d.	T	1036	2136	W	0713	0813	0913		2113	2215
Durango d.	→	1101	2201	→	0742	0842	0942	until	2142	2246
Bilbao Bolueta ⊖ a.		1134	2234		0818	0918	1018		2218	...
Bilbao Atxuri § a.		1138	2238		0822	0922	1022		2222	...

					Ⓐ	Ⓐ				
Bilbao Atxuri § d.		0934	2034		...	0600	0700		2000	2100
Bilbao Bolueta ⊖ d.	F	0939	2039	S	...	0603	0703	and	2003	2103
Durango d.	A	1012	2112	L	0539	0641	0741	hourly	2041	2141
Eibar d.	S	1035	2135	O	0613	0713	0813		2113	2213
Zumaia d.	T	|	|	W	0700	0800	0900	until	2200	...
Zarautz d.	→	1122	2222	→	0708	0808	0908		2208	...
San Sebastián ⊡ Amara a.		1147	2247		0739	0839	0939		2239	...
Hendaye **689** a.		1215c	2315c		...	...	...		...	...

c – © only.
d – Daily Eibar - Bilbao.
⊡ – San Sebastián / Donostia.
§ – Bilbao Atxuri ⇆ Bilbao Concordia: ± *1000 m.* Linked by tram approx every 10 minutes, journey 6 minutes. Bilbao Concordia is adjacent to Bilbao Abando (*Renfe*).
⊖ – Metro interchange.
Operator: EuskoTren. 2nd class, narrow gauge.
Distance: San Sebastian - Bilbao *108* km.

FEVE (narrow gauge) BILBAO - SANTANDER - OVIEDO - FERROL 687

		Ⓐ			S	ⒶW	S		S	
Bilbao Concordia § d.	...	...	...	0802	...	...	...	1302	...	1930
Marrón d.	...	0720	...	0940	...	...	...	1434	...	2106
Treto d.	...	0731	...	0950	...	...	...	1444	...	2116
Santander a.	...	0828	...	1100	...	...	...	1558	...	2215
Santander ▽ d.	...	...	0910	...	...	...	...	1610	...	...
Torrelavega ▽ d.	...	...	0937	...	...	...	...	1638	...	...
Cabezón de la Sal ▽ d.	...	...	1007	...	...	...	...	1707	...	...
Unquera d.	...	...	1044	...	...	...	...	1743	...	...
Llanes d.	0755	...	1113	...	1400	1430	1725	1813	2020	...
Ribadesella d.	0832	...	1153	...	1436	1507	1804	1852	2055	...
Oviedo a.	1029	...	1340	...	1629	1707	...	2040	2254	...

		Ⓐ		ⒶW	S		S		S	
Oviedo d.	...	...	0905	1035	1035	...	1435	1535	...	1855
Ribadesella d.	...	0710	1100	1241	1241	...	1635	1735	1853	2054
Llanes d.	...	0745	1139	1317	1317	...	1710	1814	1928	2130
Unquera d.	...	...	1208	...	...	...	...	1843	▬	...
Cabezón de la Sal ▽ d.	...	...	1249	...	...	...	...	1924		...
Torrelavega ▽ d.	...	...	1316	...	...	...	...	1949		...
Santander ▽ a.	...	...	1346	...	...	...	...	2017	Ⓐ	...
Santander d.	0800	...	1400	...	...	1900	...	...	2035	...
Treto d.	0900	...	1503	...	...	2000	...	...	2133	...
Marrón d.	0911	...	1514	...	...	2011	...	...	2143	...
Bilbao Concordia § a.	1046	...	1646	...	...	2146	...	...	...	...

					Ⓐ					
Oviedo △ d.	...	...	0747	...	...	...	...	...	1447	...
Gijón Cercanías △ d.	...	0732	|	0932	...	...	1132	1432	|	1832
Avilés △ d.	...	0814	|	1018	...	...	1218	1518	|	1918
Pravia △ d.	...	0844	0847	1048	...	...	1248	1548	1552	1948
Luarca d.	...	...	0956	...	...	...	...	...	1703	...
Navia d.	...	...	1021	...	...	...	...	...	1728	...
Ribadeo d.	0650	...	1112	...	...	1445	...	...	1817	...
Viveiro d.	0756	...	1220	...	...	1553	...	...	1923	...
Ortigueira d.	0833	...	1257	...	1500	1630	...	...	2000	...
Ferrol a.	0949	...	1409	...	1611	1740	...	...	2111	...

							Ⓐ			
Ferrol d.	...	...	0810	...	1030	...	1345	1518	...	1845
Ortigueira d.	...	...	0923	...	1143	...	1456	1631	...	1959
Viveiro d.	...	...	0959	...	1219	...	...	1707	...	2035
Ribadeo d.	...	...	1110	...	1325	...	...	1818	...	2148
Navia d.	...	...	1158	...	...	...	...	1907	...	...
Luarca d.	...	...	1223	...	...	...	...	1932	...	...
Pravia △ d.	0848	1148	1331	1348	...	1648	...	2049	2048	...
Avilés △ a.	0926	1226	|	1428	...	1728	...	|	2128	...
Gijón Cercanías △ a.	1008	1308	|	1508	...	1808	...	|	2208	...
Oviedo △ a.	...	...	1428	...	...	...	...	2148	...	...

S – July 1 - Aug. 31.
W – Sept. 1 - June 30.
▽ – Additional trains run Santander - Cabezón de al Sal and v.v.
△ – Additional trains run Oviedo / Gijón - Pravia and v.v.
§ – Bilbao Concordia is adjacent to Bilbao Abando (*Renfe*).
Operator: FEVE. 2nd class, narrow gauge.

ALSA ★ 🚌 IRÚN - BILBAO - SANTANDER - GIJÓN 688

🚌	▽ ①–⑥			▼ ⑧	▼ ⑥	①–⑥	⑦	⑤S				▼ ⑧	⑥		W	▽ ⑧		▼				▽ ⑤⑦		⑦	
Irún RENFE rail station d.	...	...	...	0645	...	0745	...	...	...	0845	...	...	...	1100	1215	...	1345	1445	...	1645	1830	...	2045	2115	2355
San Sebastián / Donostia d.	...	...	...	0710	...	0810	...	...	...	0910	...	...	...	1125	1240	...	1410	1510	...	1710	1855	...	2110	2140	0020
Bilbao TermiBus § d.	0600	...	0700	0830	0830	0930	0930	1000	1015	1030	1130	1230	1230	1330	1400	1430	1530	1630	1730	1830	2030	2100	2230	2300	0145
Santander § d.	0715	0830	0830	0950	0950	1100	1115	1130	1145	1215	1300	1350	1400	1530	...	1545	1700	1750	1900	2000	2200	2215	2350	0020	0330
Oviedo a.	1000*	1145	...	1205	1205	...	...	1530*	...	1530	...	1605	...	1845	...	1800	...	2005	2145	2300	...	0030	...	...	0600
Gijón a.	0930	1215	...	1235	1235	...	...	1445	...	1600	...	1635	...	1915	...	1830	...	2035	2215	2330	...	0100	...	...	0700

🚌		①–⑥			⊖ ①–⑥	▼	▽ ①–⑥	W	⑦	①–⑥	▽ ①–⑥		⑤⑦	▼ ⑧	▼ ⑥			▼ ①–④	▼ ⑤⑦			▽ ⑧		▽ ⑤	▽ ⑦
Gijón d.	0014	...	...	...	...	0715	...	...	0815	0815	0915	1115	...	1315	1315	...	1515	1615	1615	...	1715	1915	2015	2115	2115
Oviedo d.	0100	...	...	...	...	0745	...	...	0845	0845	0945	1145	...	1345	1345	...	1545	1645	1645	...	1745	1945	2045	2145	2145
Santander § d.	0345	0545	0700	0800	0930	1005	1200	...	1200	1230	1200	1500	1530	1605	1605	1700	1900	1905	1905	...	2030	2200	2340	2359	2359
Bilbao TermiBus § d.	0515	0730	0840	0930	1130	1120	1315	1400	1400	1415	1315	1630	1730	1720	1720	1830	2045	2020	2020	2045	2200	2315	...	0115	0115
San Sebastián / Donostia a.	0640	0840	1000	...	1240	1230	...	1510	1600	1615	...	...	1840	...	1830	1940	2155	2130	...	2155	2310	...	...	...	0225
Irún RENFE rail station a.	0700	0910	1030	...	1310	1305	...	1545	1630	1645	...	...	1910	...	1905	2010	2225	2205	...	2225	2340	...	...	...	0300

S – ⑤ June 1 - Aug. 31.
W – ①–⑤ Oct. 1 - May 31.
⊖ – Runs daily Santander - Bilbao.
▼ – *Clase Supra* luxury coach.
▽ – *Eurobús* luxury coach.
§ – Additional services operate Bilbao - Santander and v.v.
★ – ALSA: ✆ +34 913 270 540 www.alsa.es
* – Calls after Gijon.

689 MADRID and SALAMANCA - BILBAO and IRÚN

km							Talgo	Estr		TRD	Alvia	Alvia	TRD				D	D					Alvia	
△		16007		16001	16203	18401	630	941	17201	18302	4087	4087	18314		18061	16003	410	410	17203		16021	16021	620	
		①–⑥	2	2	2	2		♀	2	2	♀	♀f	2	2	2	2	2	2	2	2	2	2	♀	2
		N 2	①–⑤			①–⑥	q	P		①–⑤		①–⑥	⑥	Y			♀					N	B	①–⑤
0	**Madrid** Chamartín ...... 680 681 d.	...	...	...	...	...	...	...	...	...	0800	0800	...	...	0830	...	...	...	...	...	...	...	...	...
**	Aranda de Duero .... d.	...	...	...	...	...	...	...	...	...	|	|	...	...	|	...	...	...	...	...	...	...	...	...
121	Ávila .... 680 681 d.	...	...	...	...	...	...	0704	0715	...	|	|	...	...	0959	...	...	...	1048	...	...	...	...	...
	Salamanca .... d.	...	...	...	...	...	0640	|	|	0715	|	|	0813	...	|	...	1030	1030	|	...	...	...	...	...
207	Medina del Campo...... 680 681 d.	...	...	...	...	...	0721	0747	0803	0806	|	|	0908	0928	1044	...	1120	1120	1137	...	...	...	...	...
250	**Valladolid** Campo Grande. 681 d.	...	...	...	...	0700	0749	0817	0831	0841	0919	0919	0942	1014	1111	...	1151	1151	1208	1235	...	...	...	...
286	Venta de Baños .... 681 d.	...	...	...	...	0726	|	|	...	...	|	|	...	...	1134	...	1215	1215	...	1308	...	...	...	...
298	Palencia .... 681 d.	...	...	...	...	0739	|	|	...	...	|	|	...	...	1147	...	|	|	...	1318	...	...	1416	...
371	**Burgos** Rosa de Lima .... 681 d.	...	...	...	...	0830	0856	0923	...	...	1022	1022	...	...	1235	...	1304	1304	...	...	...	...	1501	...
460	Miranda de Ebro .... 653 d.	...	0720	...	0900	...	...	1013	...	...	1117	1120	...	...	1340	...	1425	1440	...	...	1501	...	1556	1715
565	**Bilbao** Abando .... 653 a.	...	|	...	|	...	...	1229	...	...	|	1252	...	...	|	...	|	1632	...	...	|	...	|	|
494	Vitoria / Gasteiz .... 653 d.	0750	0746	0928	0927	...	...	...	...	...	1140	...	...	...	1412	1417	1503	...	...	...	1528	1530	1617	1742
	Barcelona Sants 653 .... a.	|	...	|	...	...	...	...	...	...	|	...	...	...	...	|	|	...	...	...	...	|	2110	...
537	Altsasu .... 653 d.	0820n	...	0954	...	...	...	...	...	...	|	...	...	...	...	1445	1528	...	...	...	...	1601n	...	...
624	**San Sebastián / Donostia** ▲ 653 d.	...	...	1110	...	...	...	...	...	...	1324	...	...	...	...	1600	1644	...	...	...	...	...	...	...
641	**Irún** .... ▲ 653 a.	...	...	1135	...	...	...	...	...	...	1348s	...	...	...	...	1623	1704s	...	...	...	...	...	...	...
643	Hendaye .... ▲ 653 a.	...	...	...	...	...	...	...	...	...	1354	...	...	...	...	...	1713	...	...	...	...	...	...	...

	TRD	Arco	Arco					Talgo	Alvia	Alvia	TRD				TRD		TRD				Hotel	Hotel	Estr	
	18306	280	280	17221	18063	16005	16011	201	4167	4167	18316	17225	18017	18065	18312	18719	18324		17111	18007	931	921	310	
	2		2	2	2	2	2		♀	⑧	2	2	2	2	①–⑥	2	2	2	2	2	♀	♀	♀	
		D	E				N	⑧j		R	⑦k	⑧	K	⑧	2h	①–⑥	⑦	⑦	⑤	⑧	A	G	S	
Madrid Chamartín .... 680 681 d.	...	...	...	...	1313	...	...	1430	1610	1610	...	...	...	1730	...	...	...	...	1932	2030	...	...	...	...
Aranda de Duero .... d.	...	...	...	...	|	...	...	1643	|	|	...	...	...	|	...	...	...	...	|	|	...	...	...	...
Ávila .... 680 681 d.	...	...	...	1410	1445	...	...	|	|	|	...	1720	...	1910	...	...	...	...	2128	2159	...	...	...	...
Salamanca .... d.	1350	...	...	|	|	...	...	|	|	|	1705	|	...	|	2010	...	2102	...	|	|	...	...	0005	...
Medina del Campo....... 680 681 d.	1448	...	...	1458	1530	...	...	|	|	|	1758	1808	...	1955	2105	...	2201	...	2222	2244	...	...	0057	...
Valladolid Campo Grande.. 681 d.	1515	...	...	1538	1557	...	...	|	1734	1734	1837	1847	1900	2022	2139	2200	2236	2245	2252	2311	...	...	0130	...
Venta de Baños .... 681 d.	1537	...	...	...	1618	...	...	|	|	|	...	...	1921	2046	...	2233	...	2317	...	2338	...	...	|	...
Palencia .... 681 d.	1543	1611	1611	...	1629	...	...	|	|	|	...	...	1935	2059	...	2243	...	2328	...	2348	0031	0122	|	...
Burgos Rosa de Lima........ 681 d.	...	1659	1659	...	1717	...	...	1800	1837	1837	...	...	2023	2146	...	...	...	...	...	...	0120	0215	0254	...
Miranda de Ebro .... 653 d.	...	1805	1832	...	1818	...	...	...	1935	1939	...	...	2125	2248	...	...	...	...	...	...	|	|	0355	...
Bilbao Abando .... 653 a.	...	|	2000	...	|	...	...	...	|	2111	...	...	...	|	...	...	...	...	...	...	|	|	|	...
Vitoria / Gasteiz .... 653 d.	...	1828	...	...	1845	1900	1905	...	1956	...	...	...	...	2315	...	...	...	...	...	...	|	|	0424	...
Barcelona Sants 653 .... a.	...	|	...	...	...	|	|	...	|	...	...	...	...	...	...	...	...	...	...	...	0808	0845	|	...
Altsasu .... 653 d.	...	1854	...	...	...	1929	1936n	...	|	...	...	...	...	...	...	...	...	...	...	...	...	...	|	...
San Sebastián / Donostia ▲ 653 d.	...	2010	...	...	...	2050	...	...	2135	...	...	...	...	...	...	...	...	...	...	...	...	...	0634	...
Irún .... ▲ 653 a.	...	2032s	...	...	...	2108	...	...	2157s	...	...	...	...	...	...	...	...	...	...	...	...	...	0658s	...
Hendaye .... ▲ 653 a.	...	2040	...	...	...	...	...	...	2203	...	...	...	...	...	...	...	...	...	...	...	...	...	0710	...

km		Hotel	Hotel		TRD			TRD						Alvia	Alvia		Arco	Arco	TRD			Alvia		
		922	932	18000	18300		18702	18304	18010	18069	17218	16000	16023	4086	4086	17202	283	283	18308	17220	18012	623		
		G	A	2	2	2	2r	2	2	2	2	2	①–⑥	♀	①–⑥	2	2		2	2	2	♀	2	2
		♀	♀	①–⑥	①–⑤	①–⑤	①–⑤	⑥	①–⑥	L		①–⑥	N 2		U		E	D				B	⑦	Y
0	**Irún** .... ▲ 653 d.	...	...	...	...	...	...	...	...	...	...	0640	...	0825	...	...	...	0845	...	...	...	...	...	...
17	**San Sebastián / Donostia** ▲ 653 d.	...	...	...	...	...	...	...	...	...	...	0657	...	0842	...	...	...	0902	...	...	...	...	...	...
104	Altsasu .... 653 d.	...	...	...	...	...	...	...	...	...	...	0814	0928n	|	...	...	...	1015	...	...	...	...	...	...
	Barcelona Sants 653 .... d.	2020	2045	...	...	...	...	...	...	...	...	|	|	|	...	...	...	|	...	...	...	0920	...	...
147	Vitoria / Gasteiz .... 653 d.	|	|	...	...	...	...	...	0716	...	...	0845	1000	1014	...	...	...	1038	...	...	1340	1403	...	...
	Bilbao Abando .... 653 d.	|	|	...	...	...	...	...	|	...	...	...	...	|	0855	...	0915	|	...	...	|	|	...	...
180	Miranda de Ebro .... 681 d.	|	|	...	...	...	...	...	0739	0837	...	...	...	1039	1034	...	1116	1116	...	...	1403	1425	...	...
270	**Burgos** Rosa de Lima .... 681 d.	0249	0355	...	...	...	...	...	0839	0942	...	...	...	1130	1127	...	1211	1211	...	...	1501	1521	...	...
353	Palencia .... 681 d.	0338	0439	0630	...	0733	0900	...	0932	1037	...	...	...	|	|	...	1256	1256	1315	...	1552	1606	...	...
355	Venta de Baños .... 681 d.	...	...	0640	...	0744	0910	...	0942	1056	...	...	...	|	|	...	...	...	1324	...	1602	...	...	...
391	**Valladolid** Campo Grande. 681 d.	...	...	0701	0726	0815	0943	0945	1006	1120	1125	...	...	1240	1237	1315	...	...	1348	1415	1623	...	1725	1735
434	Medina del Campo...... 680 681 d.	...	...	0729	0803	...	...	1018	1032	...	1204	...	...	|	|	1348	...	...	1417	1454	1654	...	1750	1805
504	**Salamanca** .... a.	...	...	|	0859	...	...	1118	|	...	|	...	...	|	|	|	...	...	1515	|	|	...	|	...
	Ávila .... 680 681 d.	...	...	0814	...	...	...	...	1121	...	1255	...	...	|	|	1437	...	...	...	1545	1739	...	1837	...
	Aranda de Duero .... d.	...	...	|	...	...	...	...	|	...	...	...	...	|	|	...	...	...	...	...	|	...	|	...
	Madrid Chamartín ...... 680 681 a.	...	...	0943	...	...	...	...	1309	...	...	...	...	1400	1357	...	...	...	...	...	1924	...	2026a	...

		D	D	Talgo	TRD			Alvia	Alvia			TRD	Talgo					Estr			Estr			
		413	413	633	18318	16002	17200	4166	4166	16025	18014	18310	200		18408	16017	16208	940	16004	16004	313			
	2	2	2		2	2	2	♀	♀	2	2	2		2	2	2	2	♀	2	2	♀			
	①–⑤		♀	q	⑦k			⑧		N			⑧j	⑧	⑧	N		Q			T			
Irún .... ▲ 653 d.	...	...	1320	...	...	1517	...	...	1620	...	...	...	...	...	...	...	...	...	1937	...	2200	...	...	...
San Sebastián / Donostia ▲ 653 d.	...	...	1337	...	...	1535	...	...	1639	...	...	...	...	...	...	...	...	...	1956	...	2220	...	...	...
Altsasu .... 653 d.	...	...	1448	...	...	1652	...	...	|	1716n	...	...	...	...	...	2015n	...	...	2114	...	|	...	...	...
Barcelona Sants 653 .... d.	...	...	|	...	...	|	...	...	|	|	...	...	...	...	...	|	...	...	|	...	|	...	...	...
Vitoria / Gasteiz .... 653 d.	1430	...	1515	...	...	1721	...	...	1817	1752	1755	...	...	1850	...	2045	2055	...	2142	2150	0015	...	...	...
Bilbao Abando .... 653 d.	|	1400	|	...	...	...	...	1710	|	...	|	...	...	|	...	...	|	2125	...	|	|	...	...	...
Miranda de Ebro .... 681 d.	1457	1602	1602	...	...	...	...	1844	1844	...	1816	...	...	1917	1920	...	2122	2257	...	2214	0040	...	...	...
Burgos Rosa de Lima .... 681 d.	...	1704	1704	1752	...	...	...	1940	1940	...	1917	...	1955	...	2024	...	...	2353	...	...	0159	...	...	...
Palencia .... 681 d.	...	|	|	|	...	...	...	|	|	...	2013	...	|	...	2120	...	...	|	...	...	|	...	...	...
Venta de Baños .... 681 d.	...	1748	1748	|	...	...	...	|	|	...	2023	...	|	...	2130	...	...	|	...	...	|	...	...	...
Valladolid Campo Grande.. 681 d.	...	1813	1813	1900	1905	...	1946	2048	2048	...	2050	2055	|	...	2200	...	...	0058	...	...	0320	...	...	...
Medina del Campo....... 680 681 d.	...	1844	1844	1924	1939	...	2024	|	|	...	2114	2130	|	...	...	...	...	0126	...	...	0353	...	...	...
Salamanca .... a.	...	1937	1937	2006	2036	...	|	|	|	...	|	2225	|	...	...	...	...	|	...	...	0448	...	...	...
Ávila .... 680 681 d.	...	...	...	...	...	...	2114	|	|	...	2202	...	|	...	...	...	...	0210	...	...	...	...	...	...
Aranda de Duero .... d.	...	...	...	...	...	...	...	|	|	...	|	...	2104	...	...	...	...	...	...	...	...	...	...	...
Madrid Chamartín .... 680 681 a.	...	...	...	...	...	...	...	2208	2208	...	2342	...	2325	...	...	...	...	...	...	...	...	...	...	...

A – PÍO BAROJA – (not Dec. 24, 26, 31): [sleeper] and [1] (reclining) Barcelona - Gijón and v.v.
B – [1,2] and ♀ Vigo - Palencia - Barcelona and v.v.
D – CAMINO DE SANTIAGO – [1,2] and ♀ A Coruña - Ourense - Miranda de Ebro - Irún / Hendaye and v.v.
E – CAMINO DE SANTIAGO – [2] Vigo - Ourense - Miranda de Ebro - Bilbao and v.v.
G – GALICIA – (not Dec. 24, 26, 31): [sleeper] and [1] (reclining) Barcelona - A Coruña and Vigo and v.v.
K – To Logroño on ⑥.
L – From Logroño on ①.
N – To / from Pamplona (Table **653**).
P – PICASSO – Dec. 4 (one day later from Ávila): [sleeper], [couchette] and [1,2] Málaga - Bilbao (Table **661**).
Q – PICASSO – Dec. 8: [sleeper], [couchette] and [1,2] Bilbao - Málaga (Table **661**).

R – ⑧ (not Dec. 7, 24, 31).
S – SUREX – [sleeper], [couchette] and [1,2] Lisboa - Hendaye. Not Dec. 24, 31.
T – SUREX – [sleeper], [couchette] and [1,2] Irún - Lisboa. Not Dec. 24, 31.
U – ①–⑥ (not Dec. 8, 25, 31).
Y – [2] Puebla de Sanabria - Valladolid and v.v.

a – Continues to Madrid Atocha (arrive 2042).
f – Not Dec. 8, 25, Jan. 1, 6.
h – Not Dec. 8, 25, Jan. 1.
j – Not Dec. 7.
k – Also Dec. 8.

n – Altsasu Pueblo.
p – Not Dec. 8, 24, 31.
q – To / from Zaragoza (Table **653**).
r – From Reinosa (Table **684**).
s – Stops to set down only.

* – Train number from Vitoria.
** – Madrid - Aranda: *168 km.* Aranda - Burgos: *115 km.*
§ – Train number to Vitoria.
△ – Via Ávila.

▲ – **SAN SEBASTIÁN** - **IRÚN** and v.v. ***Renfe Cercanías*** (suburban) service. *17 km.* Journey time: ± 23 minutes.

From San Sebastián: Approximately 2–3 trains each hour from 0630 until 2300.

From Irún: Approximately 2–3 trains each hour from 0522 until 2222.

▲ – **SAN SEBASTIÁN** (Amara) - **IRÚN** (Colón, near Renfe station) - **HENDAYE** (SNCF station) and v.v. ***EuskoTren*** (narrow-gauge) service. *22 km.* Journey time: ± 37 minutes.

From San Sebastián: 0555 Ⓐ, 0615 Ⓑ, 0645 Ⓐ, 0715, 0745 and every 30 minutes until 2145 then 2315 ⑥ **s**; also at 1148 Ⓒ **n**, 2248 Ⓒ **n**. On ⑦ also hourly 0015–0615 (2-hourly winter).
From Hendaye (A): 0647 Ⓐ, 0703 Ⓑ, 0733 Ⓐ, 0803, 0833 and every 30 minutes until 2233 then 0003 ⑦ **s**; also at 0847 Ⓒ **n**, 1947 Ⓒ **n**. On ⑦ also hourly 0103–0703 (2-hourly winter).

A – 4 minutes later from Irún. n – Non-stop journey, not calling at Irún (journey 27–29 minutes). From / to Bilbao (Table **686**). s – Summer only (late-June to mid-Sept).

PORTUGAL

SEE MAP PAGE 317

Operator: CP – Comboios de Portugal (www.cp.pt).

Train categories: ***Alfa Pendular*** – *AP* – high-quality tilting express trains. ***Intercidades*** – *IC* – high-quality express trains linking the main cities of Portugal to Lisboa and Porto. ***Interregional*** – *IR* – 'semi-fast' links usually calling at principal stations only. ***Regional*** and ***Suburbano*** – local stopping trains (shown without train numbers).

Higher fares are payable for travel by *AP* and *IC* trains, also the international **Sud Expresso** service (Lisboa - Hendaye / Irún - Lisboa), and there is an additional supplement for travel by *AP* trains. The **Lusitânia** *Hotel Train* service (Lisboa - Madrid and v.v.) is shown in Table **45**, special fares apply. The Porto - Vigo trains are classified *IN*.

Services: All services shown with a train number convey first and second class accommodation (on *Alfa Pendular* trains termed, respectively, *Conforto* and *Turística*) unless otherwise indicated. *Regional* and *Suburbano* trains convey second-class seating only.

AP, *IC*, *IR* and international trains convey a buffet car (*carruagem-bar*) and there is an at-seat service of meals to passengers in 1st class on *AP* and certain *IC* trains. Sleeping- (🛏) and couchette (🛏) cars are of the normal European types described on page 8.

Reservations: Reservations are compulsory for travel by *AP* and *IC* trains, also the *Sud Expresso* and *Lusitania*. Seat reservation is not normally available on other services.

Timings: Timings do not usually change on set dates in Portugal, and amendments may come into effect at short notice.

LISBOA - COIMBRA - PORTO 690

Reservations compulsory on all *AP* and *IC* trains. For local trains Entroncamento - Coimbra / Coimbra - Aveiro / Aveiro - Porto see Table **699**

km		*AP* 121 Ⓐ	*AP* 131 △	*IC* 521 ①–⑥	*AP* 123 ①–⑥ n	*IC* 511 ◇	*IC* 523	*AP* 182	*IC* 525	*AP* 125 ⚒	*IR* 821 ⑤ f	*IC* 513 ◇	*AP* 133 △	*IC* 527	*AP* 135 Ⓑ h△	310 311 S 🅁	*AP* 127	*IC* 621 ☆	*AP* 184	*IC* 515 ◇	*AP* 137 △	*IC* 529	*AP* 129	*IC* 531
	Faro **697** d.	...	...	...	...	...	...	0655	...	...	...	...	...	...	...	...	...	...	1455	...	...	...	...	...
0	**Lisboa** Sta Apolónia ▷ d.	0600	0700	0730	0800	0830	0930	|	1130	1200	...	1330	1400	1530	1600	1606	1700	1730	|	1828	1900	1930	2000	2130
7	**Lisboa** Oriente ▷ d.	0609	0709	0739	0809	0839	0939	1009	1139	1209	...	1339	1409	1539	1609	1614	1709	1739	1809	1837	1909	1939	2009	2139
31	Vila Franca de Xira ▷ d.	|	|	0752	|	0852	0952	|	1152	|	...	1352	|	1552	|	|	|	1752	|	1850	|	1952	|	2152
75	Santarém ▷ d.	|	|	0813	0840	0915	1013	|	1213	|	...	1415	|	1613	|	|	|	1813	|	1913	|	2013	2040	2213
107	**Entroncamento** ▷ d.	|	|	0833	0900	0936	1033	|	1233	|	1358	1435	|	1633	|	1719	|	1833	|	1934	|	2033	2100	2233
131	Fátima ⊙ d.	|	|	|	|	0949	|	|	|	|	1414	1449	|	|	|	1733	|	|	|	1947	|	|	|	|
171	Pombal d.	|	|	0906	0929	1013	1109	|	1306	|	1438	1512	|	1706	|	1757	|	1909	|	2011	|	2106	2129	2309
199	Alfarelos d.	|	|	|	|	1027	|	|	1320	|	1456	1526	|	1720	|	|	|	|	|	2025	|	|	|	|
218	**Coimbra** B ▶ d.	0746	0846	0931	0952	1041	1134	1146	1333	1346	1510	1540	1546	1733	1746	1826	1846	1933	1946	2039	2046	2131	2152	2334
232	Pampilhosa d.	|	|	|	|	1053	|	|	1343	|	1521	1551	|	1743	|	1841	|	|	|	2051	|	|	|	|
273	Aveiro d.	0811	0911	1000	1016	...	1200	1211	1401	1411	1552	...	1611	1801	1811	...	1911	2000	2011	...	2111	2200	2216	0000
318	Espinho d.	|	|	1024	1037	...	1224	|	1423	|	1623	...	|	1823	|	...	|	2024	|	...	|	2224	2237	0024
334	Vila Nova de Gaia d.	0838	0939	1033	1046	...	1233	1238	1433	1438	1633	...	1639	1833	1838	...	1938	2034	2038	...	2139	2233	2246	0033
337	**Porto** Campanhã ▽ a.	0844	0944	1039	1052	...	1239	1244	1439	1444	1639	...	1644	1839	1844	...	1944	2039	2044	...	2144	2239	2252	0039

	①–⑥	*AP* 180	*AP* 130 △	*IC* 520 ①–⑥ n	*AP* 120 ①–⑥ n	312 313 S 🅁	*IC* 510 ◇	*IC* 620 ☆	*AP* 122 ⚒	*IC* 522	*AP* 124 Ⓑ b	*IC* 524	*AP* 132 △	*IC* 512 ◇	*IC* 526	*AP* 186	*AP* 126	*IC* 528	*AP* 128 Ⓑ	*AP* 134 △	*IC* 514 ◇	*IC* 530	*IR* 820 ⑦	*AP* 136 Ⓑ h△
Porto Campanhã ▽ d.	0123	0547	0647	0652	0745	...	...	0852	0947	1052	1147	1252	1347	...	1452	1547	1647	1652	1745	1847	...	1952	1956	2047
Vila Nova de Gaia d.	0128	0552	0652	0657	0750	...	...	0857	0952	1057	1152	1257	1352	...	1457	1552	1652	1657	1750	1852	...	1957	2002	2052
Espinho d.	0141	|	|	0708	0800	...	...	0908	|	1108	|	1308	|	...	1508	|	|	1708	1800	|	...	2008	2012	|
Aveiro d.	0216	0621	0721	0732	0821	...	...	0931	1021	1131	1221	1331	1421	...	1529	1621	1721	1731	1821	1921	...	2031	2042	2121
Pampilhosa d.	0247	|	|	|	|	0838	0907	|	|	1148	|	|	|	1507	1546	|	|	|	|	|	2007	|	2106	|
Coimbra B ▶ d.	0300	0645	0745	0800	0845	0851	0919	0957	1045	1158	1245	1357	1445	1519	1557	1645	1745	1757	1845	1945	2019	2057	2117	2145
Alfarelos d.	0315	|	|	|	|	|	0933	|	|	1211	|	|	|	1533	1610	|	|	|	|	|	2033	|	2131	|
Pombal d.	0334	|	|	0825	0908	0919	0948	1022	|	1225	|	1423	|	1548	1625	|	|	1823	1908	|	2048	2123	2147	|
Fátima ⊙ d.	0403	|	|	|	|	0942	1012	|	|	|	|	|	|	1612	|	|	|	|	|	|	2112	|	|	|
Entroncamento ▷ d.	0421	|	|	0858	0938	0956	1025	1058	|	1258	|	1458	|	1625	1658	|	|	1858	1938	|	2125	2158	2225	|
Santarém ▷ d.	0446	|	|	0917	0958	|	1045	1117	|	1317	|	1517	|	1645	1717	|	|	1917	1958	|	2145	2217	2245	|
Vila Franca de Xira ▷ d.	0524	|	|	0940	|	|	1109	1140	|	1340	|	1540	|	1709	1740	|	|	1940	|	|	2209	2240	2322	|
Lisboa Oriente ▷ a.	0542	0822	0922	0952	1029	1054	1121	1152	1222	1352	1422	1552	1622	1721	1752	1822	1922	1952	2029	2122	2221	2252	2341	2322
Lisboa Sta Apolónia ▷ a.	0553	|	0930	1000	1038	1103	1130	1200	1230	1400	1430	1600	1630	1730	1800	|	1930	2000	2038	2130	2230	2300	2349	2330
Faro **697** a.	...	1155	...	...	...	...	...	...	...	...	...	...	...	...	...	2155	...	...	...	...	...	...	...	...

S – SUD EXPRESSO – see Table **692**.
b – Not public holidays.
f – If ⑤ is a public holiday runs previous day.
h – Not Oct. 5, Dec. 25.
n – Not Oct. 5.
⊙ – Fátima station is *20* km from Fátima.
◇ – Lisboa - Guarda and v.v. (Table **692**).
☆ – Lisboa - Porto - Guimarães and v.v. (Table **695a**).
△ – Lisboa - Porto - Braga and v.v. (Table **695**).
▷ – For other fast trains see Table **691**, for local trains see Table **699**.
▽ – Local services run Porto Campanhã - Porto São Bento.
▶ – Local trains run Coimbra B - Coimbra and v.v. (journey 4 mins).

LISBOA - ABRANTES - ELVAS and COVILHÃ 691

km		⚒		*IC* 541			*IC* 543				*IC* 545
0	**Lisboa** Sta Apolónia ▷ d.	...	...	0818	...	...	1318	1618	...	...	1918
7	**Lisboa** Oriente ▷ d.	...	...	0826	...	...	1327	1628	...	...	1926
31	Vila Franca de Xira ▷ d.	...	...	0843	...	...	1340	1644	...	...	1943
75	Santarém ▷ d.	...	...	0909	...	...	1404	1713	...	...	2009
107	**Entroncamento** ▷ d.	...	0746	0931	0949	1150	1424	1753	1845	1943	2035
135	Abrantes d.	...	0821	0958	1029	1224	1445	1826	1920	2015	2056
175	Torre das Vargens d.	...	|	|	1110	|	|	|	2002	|	|
240	Marvão Beirã 🏛 a.	...	|	|	*1221*v	|	|	|	*2112*v	|	|
217	Portalegre ⊖ d.	...	|	|	1203	|	|	|	2056	|	|
266	**Elvas** ⊙ a.	...	|	|	1318	|	|	|	2211	|	|
199	Ródão d.	...	0930	1049	...	1322	1536	1939	...	2119	2147
229	Castelo Branco a.	...	1001	1114	...	1352	1601	2008	...	2150	2212
229	Castelo Branco d.	0619	*1009*	1130	...	*1438*	1618	*2013*	...	...	2228
283	Fundaõ d.	0724	*1112*	1211	...	*1546*	1657	*2116*	...	...	2309
301	**Covilhã** a.	0748	*1136*	1230	...	*1610*	1717	*2140*	...	...	2328

	①–⑥		*IC* 540				*IC* 542	*IC* 544	
Covilhã d.	*0430*r	...	0709	*0843*	*1250*	...	1456	1758	1825
Fundaõ d.	*0449*r	...	0725	*0903*	*1310*	...	1512	1814	1845
Castelo Branco a.	*0550*r	...	0808	*1005*	*1412*	...	1555	1857	1947
Castelo Branco d.	0555	...	0824	1015	1424	...	1611	1913	...
Ródão d.	0625	...	0850	1049	1454	...	1637	1939	...
Elvas ⊙ d.	|	0453	|	|	|	1400	|	|	...
Portalegre ⊖ d.	|	0609	|	|	|	1516	|	|	...
Marvão Beirã 🏛 d.	|	*0554*v	|	|	|	*1459*v	|	|	...
Torre das Vargens d.	|	0710	|	|	|	1615	|	|	...
Abrantes d.	0723	0746	0941	1153	1559	1651	1728	2030	...
Entroncamento ▷ d.	0804	0820	1002	1221	1629	1725	1751	2056	...
Santarém ▷ d.	0830	...	1022	...	...	...	1810	2116	...
Vila Franca de Xira ▷ d.	0915	...	1049	...	...	...	1838	2140	...
Lisboa Oriente ▷ a.	0932	...	1101	...	...	...	1851	2151	...
Lisboa Sta Apolónia ▷ a.	0941	...	1111	...	...	...	1900	2200	...

r – ⚒ only.
v – Change at Torre das Vargens.
▷ – For other fast trains see Table **690**, for local trains see Table **699**.
△ – 🚌 dep. Covilhã 0535, 1140, 1618; dep. Guarda 0710, 1322, 1820.
⊙ – *16 km* from Badajoz (no rail service across the border).
⊖ – Station is *10 km* from Portalegre.

For the LUSITANIA Lisboa - Madrid night train via Marvão Beirã see Table **45**.

COVILHÃ - GUARDA *Currently replaced by* 🚌 △

km								
0	Covilhã d.	0553	1140	1618	Guarda d.	0725	1337	1830
46	Guarda a.	0708	1255	1733	Covilhã a.	0838	1450	1942

(LISBOA -) COIMBRA - GUARDA - VILAR FORMOSO 692

km		⚒	*IC* 511		*IC* 513	Ⓑ	310/1 S		*IC* 515	⑤r
	Lisboa Sta Apolónia **690** d.	...	0830	...	1330	...	1606	...	1828	...
	Lisboa Oriente **690** d.	...	0839	...	1339	...	1614	...	1837	...
0	**Coimbra** d.	0704	*1030*	1200	*1529*	1602	*1750*	1828	*1951*	...
2	**Coimbra** B d.	0708	1041	1206	1540	1606	1826	1835	2039	...
16	Pampilhosa d.	0721	1054	1218	1552	1619	1842	1853	2052	...
51	Santa Comba Dão d.	0803	1120	1251	1620	1654	1909	1938	2118	...
83	Nelas d.	0835	1140	1319	1641	1726	1936	2010	2138	...
95	Mangualde d.	0845	1148	1330	1650	1736	1945	2020	2146	...
171	**Guarda** a.	0945	1240	1438	1745	1845	2040	2125	2239	2250
218	Vilar Formoso 🏛 PT a.	...	*1345*	...	*1838*	*1933*	2109	...	...	2324
220	Fuentes d'Oñoro 🏛 ES d.	...	...	...	...	...	2232	...	...	...
346	**Salamanca** a.	...	...	...	...	...	0002	...	...	...

	①v	⚒	313 S	⚒	*IC* 510		*IC* 512	①–⑥	⑦n	*IC* 514
Salamanca d.	...	...	0455	...	...	...	...	...	...	...
Fuentes d'Oñoro 🏛 ES d.	...	...	0640	...	...	...	...	...	...	...
Vilar Formoso 🏛 PT d.	...	...	0610	0632	...	...	*1207*	...	...	*1707*
Guarda d.	0029	0500	0639	0715	0722	1040	1322	1622	1622	1813
Mangualde d.	0126	0557	0734	...	0814	1148	1414	1739	1739	1908
Nelas d.	0134	0607	0743	...	0822	1157	1422	1751	1751	1916
Santa Comba Dão d.	0201	0638	0805	...	0841	1226	1441	1820	1820	1938
Pampilhosa d.	0230	0714	0838	...	0907	1305	1507	1853	1853	2007
Coimbra B a.	0242	0728	0849	...	0917	1319	1517	1905	1905	2017
Coimbra a.	...	0734	*0859*	...	*0945*	1324	*1545*	1910	*1923*	*2028*
Lisboa Oriente **690** a.	...	...	1054	...	1121	...	1721	...	2131	2221
Lisboa Sta Apolónia **690** a.	...	...	1103	...	1130	...	1730	...	2141	2230

S – SUD EXPRESSO – 🛏 1, 2 cl., 🛏 2 cl. and (2) Lisboa - Hendaye / Irún - Lisboa (Table **46**); ✕ Lisboa - Vilar Formosa and v.v. 🅁. Not Dec. 24, 31. Only for passengers making international journeys (unless space is available).
n – Also Oct. 5; not Oct. 4.
r – If ⑤ is a public holiday will run instead on ④.
v – Also Oct. 6; not Oct. 5, Nov. 30, Dec. 7.
ES – Spain (Central European Time).
PT – Portugal (West European Time).

693 LISBOA - CALDAS DA RAINHA - FIGUEIRA DA FOZ / COIMBRA *Linha do Oeste*

km										*IR* 805					*IR* 807	*IR* 809				*IR* 901			
		①-⑥	Ⓐ	Ⓐ	Ⓒ	Ⓐ	Ⓐ	Ⓒn			Ⓐ	Ⓐ	Ⓒn				Ⓐ	Ⓐ	Ⓒn		Ⓐ	Ⓐ	⑦n
0	**Lisboa** Oriente ▷ d.	0507s	0538	...	0555s	...	...	...	...	...	...	...	...	...	...	...	1717	...	...	...	1947	...	...
7	Entrecampos ▷ d.	0518	0547	...	0606	0707	...	...	...	1034*	1037	...	...	...	1434*	1634*	1727	...	...	1844*	1957	...	...
9	Sete Rios ▷ d.	0523	0551	...	0611	0711	...	...	...	1037	1041	...	...	...	1437	1637	1731	...	...	1847	2001	...	...
22	Agualva - Cacém ⊙ ▷ d.	0540	0613	...	0629	0733	...	0739	...	1054	1103	...	1116	...	1454	1654	1753	...	1810	1909	2023	...	2102
26	Mira Sintra - Meleças ▷ d.	0545	0618	0635	0635	0738	0747	0747	...	1100	1108	1122	1122	...	1500	1700	1758	1818	1818	1915	2028	2109	2109
72	Torres Vedras d.	0645	...	0735	0735	...	0851	0851	...	1146	...	1223	1223	...	1546	1743	...	1916	1916	2005	...	2207	2207
95	Bombarral d.	0710	...	0800	0800	...	0917	0917	...	1206	...	1247	1247	...	1606	1806	...	1941	1941	2026	...	2232	2232
114	**Caldas da Rainha** a.	0732	...	0822	0822	...	0939	0939	...	1218	...	1309	1309	...	1618	1818	...	2003	2003	2038	...	2254	2254

				IR 804				*IR* 806		*IR* 808				*IR* 900									
	⑥r	Ⓐ	Ⓐ		Ⓒr	Ⓐ	Ⓐ				Ⓒr	Ⓐ	Ⓐ		Ⓒr	Ⓐ	Ⓐ		⑥	⑦r	Ⓐ	Ⓐ	Ⓑ
Caldas da Rainha d.	0517	0517	...	0658	0737	0737	...	0828	...	1109	1339	1339	...	1509	1741	1741	...	...	1900	1900	1900	...	2132
Bombarral d.	0538	0538	...	0711	0759	0759	...	0841	...	1121	1400	1400	...	1521	1805	1805	...	...	1921	1921	1921	...	2153
Torres Vedras d.	0603	0603	...	0736	0824	0824	...	0906	...	1145	1426	1426	...	1545	1831	1831	...	...	1946	1946	1946	...	2222
Mira Sintra - Meleças ▷ d.	0710	0708	0729	0822	0931	0931	0949	0952	...	1232	1532	1531	1549	1632	1935	1934	1939	...	2050	2050	2047	2109	2322
Agualva - Cacém ⊙ ▷ a.	0715	...	0733	0827	0936	...	0953	0957	...	1237	1537	...	1553	1637	1939	...	1943	...	2055	2055	...	2113	2327
Sete Rios ▷ a.	...	...	0756	0850	...	...	1016	1020	...	1300	...	...	1616	1700	...	...	2006	...	2113	...	...	2136	2347
Entrecampos ▷ a.	...	...	0759	0853*	...	...	1020	1023*	...	1303*	...	...	1620	1703*	...	...	2009	...	2117	...	...	2140	2352
Lisboa Oriente ▷ a.	...	...	0810	...	...	...	...	...	...	...	...	...	...	...	...	...	2020	...	2127s	...	...	...	0002s

km		*IR* 801			*IR* 803	
		①-⑥				
0	**Caldas da Rainha** d.	0620	0850	1322	1620	1858
13	São Martinho do Porto d.	0628	0904	1335	1628	1911
47	Marinha Grande d.	0659	0943	1414	1659	1950
57	Leiria d.	0710	0951	1423	1708	1959
104	Bifurcação de Lares ▽ a.	|	1047	1512	|	2050
111	**Figueira da Foz** a.	*0847*z	1055	1526	*1856*x	2100
118	Alfarelos ▽ d.	0800	...	...	1800	...
138	**Coimba** B ▽ a.	0816	...	...	1817	...
140	**Coimbra** ▽ a.	*0826*	...	...	1827	...

		IR 800			*IR* 802
	①-⑥				Ⓑ
Coimbra ▽ d.	...	*0845*	...	...	1900
Comiba B ▽ d.	...	0904	...	...	1910
Alfarelos ▽ d.	...	0921	...	...	1928
Figueira da Foz d.	0618	*0908*z	1106	1604	*1915*z
Bifurcação de Lares ▽ d.	0632	|	1116	1612	|
Leiria d.	0711	1015	1206	1707	2022
Marinha Grande d.	0722	1026	1217	1718	2032
São Martinho do Porto d.	0758	1054	1252	1754	2101
Caldas da Rainha a.	0812	1105	1306	1808	2111

n – From Monte Abraão (depart 8 minutes earlier).
r – To Monte Abraão (arrive 9 minutes later).
s – Lisboa **Santa Apolónia**.
x – Not ⑥. Change at Verride.
z – Change at Verride.

▷ – For suburban services see Table **699**.
▽ – See Table **693a** for connections to / from Coimbra.
⊙ – Connections to / from Lisboa Rossio every 20 minutes (see Table **699**).
* – Terminal platforms (Entrecampos - Poente).

693a FIGUEIRA DA FOZ - COIMBRA

km		⚒	⚒	Ⓐ						Ⓐ							
0	**Figueira da Foz** d.	0632	0710	0741	0811	0908	1025	1118	1315	1410	1515	1615	1710	1815	1915	2010	2228
8	Bifurcação de Lares d.	0644	0721	0753	0822	0919	1036	1129	1326	|	1527	1626	1721	1826	1929	2021	2239
22	Alfarelos d.	0702	0740	0810	0842	0942	1055	1147	1346	1431	1546	1646	1741	1846	1949	2041	2258
42	**Coimbra** B a.	0730	0807	0828	0911	1010	1122	1215	1414	1459	1614	1714	1808	1914	2016	2110	2325
44	**Coimbra** a.	0739	0816	0837	0925	1019	1131	1224	1423	1508	1623	1723	1817	1923	2028	2121	2334

	▽	▽	▽
Figueira da Foz d.	0637	1242	1925
Pampilhosa d.	0806	1409	2056
Coimbra B a.	0820	1424	2110
Coimbra B d.	0821	1425	*2133*
Comibra a.	0826	1429	*2137*

	⚒	⚒								Ⓐ		Ⓑ	Ⓐ			
Coimbra d.	0535	0642	0753	0912	0953	...	1251	1353	1451	1654	1706	1750	1835	1951	2222	0019
Coimbra B d.	0544	0652	0802	0923	1002	...	1259	1402	1500	1703	1715	1759	1846	2000	2231	0027
Alfarelos d.	0611	0719	0821	0949	1030	...	1326	1431	1526	1721	1742	1826	1907	2017	2258	0055
Bifurcação de Lares d.	0631	0738	0837	1007	1053	...	1344	1449	1545	|	1801	1845	|	2036	2316	0113
Figueira da Foz a.	0645	0750	0847	1018	1105	...	1355	1500	1556	1743	1812	1856	1928	2048	2327	0124

	▽	▽	▽
Coimbra d.	*0627*	1246	1928
Coimbra B a.	*0631*	1250	1932
Coimbra B d.	0655	1252	1934
Pampilhosa d.	0711	1309	1951
Figueira da Foz a.	0837	1436	2119

For main line trains calling at Alfarelos see Table **690**. Other trains: Coimbra - Alfarelos Table **699**, Figuerira da Foz - Bif. de Lares Table **693**.

▽ – Rail service currently suspended.

694 PORTO - RÉGUA - POCINHO

km	*Numbered trains: IR*			861	863	867	869	873	877	961	
		Ⓐ									
0	**Porto** São Bento d.	0630	...		0915	...	1319		...	1920	...
3	**Porto** Campanhã d.	0635	...	0725	0920	1115	1324	1520	1715	1925	2156
12	Ermesinde d.	0647	...	0736	0929	1124	1333	1529	1726	1938	2206
50	Caíde d.	0723	0727	0810	1003	1203	1407	1603	1804	2012	2240
59	Livração ▷ d.	...	0740	0820	1012	1212	1416	1612	1812	2021	2254
64	Marco de Canaveses d.	...	0747	0827	1019	1219	1423	1619	1819	2028	2301
107	**Régua** ▷ a.	...	0844	0915	1106	1305	1510	1707	1908	2119	2358
	Pocinho (below) a.	...	...	1039	...	...	...	...	2033	...	...

		862	864	866	870	874	878	962		
Pocinho (below) d.	...	...	...	...	...	...	...	...	...	...
Régua ▷ d.	0605	0730	0858	1045	1243	1449	1659	1901	2032	...
Marco de Canaveses d.	0703	0815	0944	1132	1331	1536	1745	1946	2132	...
Livração ▷ d.	0709	0821	0950	1138	1337	1542	1751	1952	2138	...
Caíde d.	0727	0833	1002	1150	1349	1554	1803	2004	2155	2213
Ermesinde d.	0803	0905	1035	1222	1421	1626	1838	2039	...	2259
Porto Campanhã a.	0814	0915	1045	1230	1430	1635	1850	2049	...	2310
Porto São Bento a.	...	...	...	1236	...	...	1855	2055	...	2315

km	*Numbered trains: IR*	861	△	865	871	871	875	875	△	877	
					N	S	S	N			
	Porto Campanhã d.	0725	...	...	...	...	...	...	...	1715	...
0	**Régua** d.	0916	...	1116	1531	1557	1718	1729	...	1909	...
23	Pinhão d.	0943	...	1142	1557	1627	1754	1755	...	1935	...
36	Tua a.	0957	1026	1156	1612	1641	1808	1810	1815	1949	...
90	Mirandela a.	|	1213	|	|	|	|	|	2010	|	...
68	**Pocinho** a.	1039	...	1240	1658	1724	1854	1854	...	2033	...

	860	△	868		872	876		▽	960	
					⚒	†				
Pocinho d.	0654	...	1113	...	1318	1528	...	...	1731	1905
Mirandela d.	|	0937	|	...	|	|	...	1614	|	|
Tua d.	0736	1126	1157	...	1400	1612	...	1802	1815	1950
Pinhaõ d.	0751	...	1213	...	1416	1628	...	...	1831	2005
Régua a.	0816	...	1238	...	1441	1654	...	...	1856	2030
Porto Campanhã a.	...	...	...	...	...	...	...	...	...	...

▷ NARROW-GAUGE BRANCHES. *Both branches are currently operated by* 🚌 *in the following timings:*

23 km	Ⓐ					Ⓐ		
Livração d.	0610	0715	0830	1215	1620	1820	2050	...
Amarante a.	0650	0755	0910	1250	1700	1900	2130	...
	Ⓐ						Ⓐ	
Amarante d.	0520	0620	0735	1050	1250	1700	1900	2050
Livração a.	0600	0700	0815	1130	1325	1740	1940	2130

26 km		①-⑤			
Régua d.	0706	0846	1120	1520	1920
Vila Real a.	0800	0939	1213	1613	2015
		①-⑤			
Vila Real d.	0700	0944	1351	1755	1915
Régua a.	0755	1038	1445	1850	2010

N – Not when train **S** runs. S – ⑥ May 30 - Oct. 3.
△ – By taxi Tua - Cachão and v.v. ▽ – By taxi.

🚂 steam-hauled tourist train: ⑥ May 30 - Oct. 3, 2009
Régua d. 1446 → Pinhão d. 1543 → Tua a. 1605.
Tua d. 1706 → Pinhão d. 1746 → Régua 1822.

695 PORTO - BRAGA

km						*AP* 131								*AP* 133				*AP* 135					*AP* 137			
		△	△	Ⓐ						△					△	△	Ⓐ	Ⓑh						Ⓐ		
	Lisboa Sta Ap. **690**. d.	...	...	...	...	0700	...	...	...	...	...	...	...	1400	...	...	...	1600	...	...	...	...	1900	...	...	...
0	**Porto** São Bento ▷ d.	0645	0745	0825	0845	|	0945	1045	1145	1245	1345	1445	1545	|	1645	1745	1825	|	1845	1925	1945	2045	|	2145	2245	0025
3	**Porto** Campanhã ▷ d.	0650	0750	0830	0850	0946	0950	1050	1150	1250	1350	1450	1550	1646	1650	1750	1830	1846	1850	1930	1950	2050	2146	2150	2250	0030
12	Ermesinde ▷ d.	0702	0802	0842	0902	|	1002	1102	1202	1302	1402	1502	1602	|	1702	1802	1841	|	1902	1942	2002	2102	|	2202	2302	0042
26	Trofa ▷ d.	0718	0818	0859	0918	|	1018	1118	1218	1318	1418	1518	1618	|	1718	1818	1854	|	1918	1959	2018	2118	|	2218	2318	0055
35	Famalicão ▷ d.	0729	0829	0908	0929	1018	1029	1129	1229	1329	1429	1529	1629	1718	1729	1829	1901	1918	1929	2008	2029	2129	2218	2229	2329	0104
42	Nine ▷ d.	0737	0837	0913	0937	|	1037	1137	1237	1337	1437	1537	1637	|	1737	1837	1906	|	1937	2013	2037	2137	|	2237	2337	0109
57	**Braga** a.	0758	0858	0925	0958	1031	1058	1158	1258	1358	1458	1558	1658	1731	1758	1858	1916	1931	1958	2025	2058	2158	2231	2258	2358	0129

		AP 130												*AP* 132							*AP* 134				*AP* 136	
			Ⓐ		Ⓐ	Ⓒ	Ⓐ								▽				Ⓐ			Ⓐ			Ⓑh	d
Braga d.	0530	0604	0608	0630	0705	0730	0744	0805	0830	0930	1030	1130	1230	1304	1330	1430	1530	1630	1713	1730	1804	1815	1830	1930	2004	2030
Nine ▷ d.	0550	|	0620	0650	0717	0750	0754	0817	0850	0950	1050	1150	1250	|	1350	1450	1550	1650	1723	1750	|	1827	1850	1950	|	2050
Famalicão ▷ d.	0558	0619	0626	0658	0723	0758	0759	0823	0858	0958	1058	1158	1258	1319	1358	1458	1558	1658	1728	1758	1819	1833	1858	1958	2019	2058
Trofa ▷ d.	0610	|	0635	0710	0735	0810	0807	0835	0910	1010	1110	1210	1310	|	1410	1510	1610	1710	1736	1810	|	1842	1910	2010	|	2110
Ermesinde ▷ d.	0629	|	0649	0729	0749	0829	0819	0849	0929	1029	1129	1229	1329	|	1429	1529	1629	1729	1748	1829	|	1857	1929	2029	|	2129
Porto Campanhã ▷ a.	0641	0645	0701	0741	0801	0841	0831	0901	0941	1041	1141	1241	1341	1345	1441	1541	1641	1741	1756	1841	1845	1910	1941	2041	2045	2141
Porto São Bento ▷ a.	0645	|	0705	0745	0805	0845	0835	0905	0945	1045	1145	1245	1345	|	1445	1545	1645	1745	1800	1845	|	1915	1945	2045	|	2145
Lisboa Sta Ap. **690**. a.	...	0930	...	...	...	...	...	...	...	...	...	...	...	1630	...	...	...	...	...	...	2130	...	...	...	2330	...

d – Additional journeys run at 2130 Ⓒ, 2230 Ⓐ, 2326.
h – Not Apr. 10, May 1, Oct. 5, Dec. 25.
▷ – For other trains see Table **696**.
▽ – Additional journey: 1308 Ⓐ (journey time 1 hour).
△ – Additional journeys: 0625 Ⓐ, 0725 Ⓐ, 1225 Ⓐ, 1625 Ⓐ, 1725 Ⓐ (journey time 1 hour).

PORTO - GUIMARÃES 695a

60 km

												IC **621**
				Ⓐ				Ⓐ		Ⓐ		
Lisboa Sta Ap. **690**	d.	...	...	...	...	...	...	...	...	...	...	1730
Porto São Bento	▷ d.	0715	0815	1015	1115	1215	1415	1615	1715	1815	1915	2015	|
Porto Campanhã	▷ d.	0720	0820	1020	1120	1220	1420	1620	1720	1820	1920	2020	2041
Ermesinde	▷ d.	0732	0832	1032	1132	1232	1432	1632	1732	1832	1932	2032	|
Trofa	▷ d.	0748	0850	1050	1150	1250	1450	1650	1750	1848	1950	2050	2101
Guimarães	a.	0833	0933	1133	1233	1333	1533	1733	1833	1933	2033	2133	2140

			IC **620**										
										Ⓐ			
Guimarães	d.	0654	0743	0754	0854	0954	1154	1354	1554	1709	1809	1954	2054
Trofa	▷ d.	0740	0825	0840	0940	1040	1240	1440	1640	1759	1900	2040	2140
Ermesinde	▷ d.	0758	|	0858	0958	1058	1258	1458	1658	1819	1919	2058	2158
Porto Campanhã	▷ a.	0810	0845	0910	1010	1110	1310	1510	1710	1831	1931	2110	2210
Porto São Bento	▷ a.	0815	|	0915	1015	1115	1315	1515	1715	1835	1935	2115	2215
Lisboa Sta Ap. **690**	a.	...	1200	...	...	...	...	...	...	...	...	...	...

▷ – See also Tables **695** and **696**.

Additional trains: **Porto - Guimarães** 0615, 2115 Ⓒ, 2215 Ⓐ, 2315; **Guimarães - Porto** 0554 Ⓐ, 1909 Ⓐ, 2254.

PORTO - VIANA DO CASTELO - VALENÇA - VIGO 696

km											
			IR **851** Ⓐ	*IN* **421**		*IR* **853**	*IR* **855**	*IN* **423**		*IR* **857** Ⓐ	
0	**Porto** Campanhã	▷ d.	0555	0755	...	1245	1555	1755	...	2005	...
12	Ermesinde	▷ d.	0605	0807	...	1255	1607	1807	...	2016	...
23	Trofa	▷ d.	0618	0826	...	1310	1624	1827	...	2033	...
32	Famalicão	▷ d.	0629	0836	...	1321	1635	1837	...	2044	...
39	**Nine**	▷ d.	0636	0843	...	1328	1642	1844	...	2051	...
51	Barcelos	d.	0646	0858	...	1338	1653	1854	...	2105	...
82	**Viana do Castelo**	d.	0734	0930	...	1414	1728	1931	...	2139	...
116	Vila Nova de Cerveira	d.	0808	1003	...	1445	1758	2001	...	2209	...
130	**Valença**	▦ PT d.	0820	1017	...	1457	1811	2015	...	2222	...
134	Tui	▦ ES d.	...	1135	...	...	...	2130	...	...	...
162	Redondela **681**	d.	...	1159	...	...	...	2156	...	...	...
174	**Vigo 681**	a.	...	1214	...	...	...	2212	...	...	...

		Ⓐ		*IN* **420**	*IR* **850**		*IR* **852**	*IR* **854**	*IN* **422**	
Vigo 681	d.	...	...	0740	...	...	...	...	1942	...
Redondela **681**	d.	...	...	0754	...	...	...	...	1957	...
Tui	▦ ES d.	...	...	0829	...	...	...	...	2037	...
Valença	▦ PT d.	0548	...	0737	0951	...	1414	1742	1945	...
Vila Nova de Cerveira	d.	0602	...	0750	1004	...	1427	1757	2000	...
Viana do Castelo	d.	0643	...	0825	1037	...	1459	1832	2032	...
Barcelos	d.	0730	...	0859	1113	...	1534	1913	2104	...
Nine	▷ d.	0745	...	0913	1124	...	1546	1925	2115	...
Famalicão	▷ d.	0752	...	0921	1132	...	1554	1933	2123	...
Trofa	▷ d.	0801	...	0930	1141	...	1603	1942	2132	...
Ermesinde	▷ d.	0824	...	0946	1157	...	1619	1957	2146	...
Porto Campanhã	▷ a.	0835	...	0955	1210	...	1630	2010	2155	...

ADDITIONAL LOCAL TRAINS

		Ⓐ	Ⓒ	Ⓐ		Ⓐ			Ⓐ	Ⓒ	Ⓑ
Porto São Bento **695**	d.	*0625*	*0645*	*0825*	*0945*	*1245*	*1345*	*1625***a**	*1825*	*1845*	*2045*
Nine	d.	0717	0742	0918	1059	1355	1455	1729	1924	2006	2142
Barcelos	d.	0731	0756	0932	1114	1410	1509	1743	1937	2023	2156
Viana do Castelo	a.	0817	0842	1018	1158	1454	1556	1829	2021	2108	2240
Viana do Castelo	d.	*0824*	*0846*	*1036*	...	...	*1606*	*1831*	...	...	...
Vila Nova de Cerveira	d.	*0909*	*0931*	*1121*	...	...	*1651*	*1915*	...	...	...
Valença	▦ d.	*0925*	*0947*	*1137*	...	...	*1707*	*1931*	...	...	...

			Ⓐ		Ⓐ	Ⓒ	Ⓐ			
Valença	▦ d.	...	*0623*	...	*1102*	*1123*	...	*1503*	...	*1826*
Vila Nova de Cerveira	d.	...	*0639*	...	*1120*	*1139*	...	*1519*	...	*1842*
Viana do Castelo	a.	...	*0724*	...	*1205*	*1224*	...	*1604*	...	*1929*
Viana do Castelo	d.	0536	0733	0934	1211	1229	1313	1610	1729	1937
Barcelos	d.	0619	0818	1019	1255	1313	1409	1654	1813	2024
Nine	a.	0634	0833	1034	1310	1328	1424	1709	1828	2039
Porto São Bento **695**	a.	*0745*	*0945*	*1145*	*1405*	*1445*	*1545*	*1800***a**	*1945*	*2145*

a – Ⓐ only. ▷ – See also Table **695**. ES – Spain (Central European Time). PT – Portugal (West European Time).

LISBOA - PINHAL NOVO - TUNES - FARO 697

km Δ					*AP* **180**	*IC* **570**		*IC* **572**	*IC* **574**		*AP* **186**	*IC* **576** E
	Porto Campanhã **690**	d.	...	...	0547	...	...	...	...	...	1547	...
	Coimbra B **690**	d.	...	...	0645	...	...	...	...	...	1645	...
0	**Lisboa** Oriente	⊙ d.	...	...	0840	1020	...	1320	1720	...	1840	1920
7	Entrecampos	⊙ d.	...	...	0851	1030	...	1330	1730	...	1851	1930
18	Pragal	⊙ d.	...	...	|	1044	...	1344	1744	...	|	1944
	Barreiro	d.	...	0643	|	|	...	|	|	1807	|	|
47	Pinhal Novo	⊙ d.	...	0655	0930	1106	...	1406	1806	1821	1931	2006
60	Setúbal	d.	...	0707	|	1114	...	1414	1818	1830	|	2021
110	Alcácer do Sal	d.	...	0753	|	1154	...	1447	1851	1920	|	2054
134	Grândola	d.	...	0809	|	1208	...	1502	1907	1935	|	2108
**	**Beja**	d.	0755	|	|	|	1417	|	|	|	|	|
196	Funcheira	d.	0851	0857	|	1241	1513	1538	1940	2047r	|	2141
280	**Tunes**	▷ d.	...	1014	1127	1344	...	1649	2043	2155	2128	2245
285	Albufeira	▷ d.	...	1020	1133	1349	...	1654	2048	2201	2134	2251
302	Loulé	▷ d.	...	1034	1146	1401	...	1711	2100	2215	2147	2303
318	**Faro**	▷ a.	...	1048	1155	1411	...	1721	2110	2228	2155	2313

			AP **182**	*IC* **670**		*IC* **672**		*AP* **184**		*IC* **674**	*IC* **676** F
Faro	▷ d.	0548	0655	0920	...	1320	...	1455	1553	1700	1858
Loulé	▷ d.	0603	0706	0931	...	1332	...	1506	1607	1711	1909
Albufeira	▷ d.	0617	0719	0944	...	1349	...	1518	1621	1723	1921
Tunes	▷ d.	0622	0725	0952	...	1356	...	1524	1626	1729	1928
Funcheira	d.	0730	|	1107	1110	1458	1518	|	1742	1831	2047
Beja	a.	|	|	|	1210	|	1616	|	|	|	|
Grândola	d.	0824	|	1140	...	1531	...	|	1831	1906	2123
Alcácer do Sal	d.	0840	|	1153	...	1545	...	|	1851	1920	2137
Setúbal	d.	0934	|	1225	...	1617	...	|	1943	1952	2212
Pinhal Novo	⊙ d.	0945	0923	1233	...	1625	...	1723	1956	2005	2224
Barreiro	a.	0957	|	|	...	|	...	|	2008	|	|
Pragal	⊙ a.	...	|	1250	...	1643	...	|	...	2023	2243
Entrecampos	⊙ a.	...	0957	1303	...	1656	...	1757	...	2036	2256
Lisboa Oriente	⊙ a.	...	1004	1312	...	1705	...	1804	...	2045	2305
Coimbra B **690**	a.	...	1145	...	...	...	...	1945	...	...	...
Porto Campanhã **690**	a.	...	1244	...	...	...	...	2044	...	...	...

LOCAL TRAINS LAGOS - TUNES - FARO

				⚒		⚒						
0	**Lagos**	d.	0611	0655	0826	1037	1253	1410	1624	1810	1915	2016
18	Portimão	d.	0629	0713	0849	1055	1311	1428	1642	1828	1933	2034
29	Silves	d.	0644	0728	0904	1111	1326	1443	1657	1848	1949	2048
42	Algoz	d.	0700	0744	0921	1127	1342	1459	1717	1904	2009	2110
46	**Tunes**	a.	0706	0750	0927	1133	1348	1504	1723	1909	2014	2115
46	**Tunes**	▷ d.	0707	0755	0933	1138	1355	1505	1728	1910	2015	*2155*
52	Albufeira	▷ d.	0718	0802	0944	1146	1402	1517	1735	1921	2022	*2201*
69	Loulé	▷ d.	0733	0819	1003	1204	1417	1533	1751	1942	2042	*2215*
85	**Faro**	▷ a.	0751	0837	1018	1219	1432	1548	1806	1957	2057	*2228*

			⚒				⚒					⑤v
Faro	▷ d.	0712	0927	1055	1300	1617	1730	1827	1910	2010	...	...
Loulé	▷ d.	0733	0944	1112	1317	1634	1751	1844	1927	2027	...	...
Albufeira	▷ d.	0749	1003	1132	1332	1654	1807	1900	1943	2048	...	...
Tunes	▷ a.	0754	1008	1137	1337	1659	1812	1905	1949	2053	...	...
Tunes	d.	0755	1013	1139	1349	1701	1813	1910	1950	2054	2200	2250
Algoz	d.	0801	1019	1145	1354	1707	1818	1916	1957	2100	2205	2255
Silves	d.	0817	1035	1201	1410	1723	1834	1931	2015	2115	2221	2311
Portimão	d.	0832	1055	1216	1428	1738	1849	1950	2034	2130	2236	2326
Lagos	a.	0850	1113	1234	1446	1756	1907	2008	2052	2148	2255	2345

E – ⑤ (daily June 1 - Aug. 31).
F – ⑦ (daily June 1 - Aug. 31), also Oct. 5; not Oct. 4.
r – Arrive 2027.
v – If ⑤ is a public holiday runs instead on ④.
⊙ – See Table **698** for other fast trains, Table **699** for local services. Trains also call at Sete Rios.
▷ – Also see other section of table above or below.
** – Beja - Funcheira: *62 km*
Δ – Via Setúbal (subtract *9* km for direct trains).

FARO - VILA REAL DE SANTO ANTÓNIO 697a

									Ⓐ				Ⓐ
0	**Faro**	d.	0734	0925	1225	1434	1625	1730	1825	1925	2125	2235	2325
10	Olhão	d.	0745	0941	1240	1445	1641	1741	1841	1941	2141	2246	2336
32	Tavira	d.	0816	1010	1308	1511	1710	1810	1910	2010	2210	2314	0004
56	**Vila Real** §	a.	0845	1039	1339	1540	1739	1839	1939	2039	2239	2343	0033

			Ⓐ								
Vila Real §	d.	0547	0617	0716	0941	1141	1310	1543	1741	1841	2041
Tavira	d.	0613	0648	0746	1013	1213	1340	1613	1813	1913	2113
Olhão	d.	0637	0714	0813	1040	1241	1407	1640	1840	1940	2140
Faro	a.	0648	0724	0824	1051	1252	1418	1651	1851	1951	2151

§ – Vila Real de Santo António. (± *1 500 m* from bus station / ferry terminal).

Additional journeys on Ⓐ:
Faro - Tavira 0758, 1025, 1130, 1323, 1525; Tavira - Faro 0913, 1119, 1312, 1513, 1711.

LISBOA - PINHAL NOVO - ÉVORA and BEJA 698

km				b	*IC* **690**	*IC* **592**		*IC* **694**			*IC* **696**	*IC* **594**
0	**Lisboa** Oriente	⊙ d.	...	...	0810	0910	...	1410	...	...	1810	1910
7	Entrecampos	⊙ d.	...	...	0821	0921	...	1421	...	...	1821	1921
18	Pragal	⊙ d.	...	...	0835	0935	...	1435	...	...	1835	1935
47	**Pinhal Novo**	⊙ d.	...	0706	0858	0958	...	1458	...	...	1901	2001
88	Vendas Novas	d.	...	0748	0924	1024	...	1524	...	...	1934	2036
	Évora	d.	0616	|	|	|	1200	|	1524	1745	|	|
122	Casa Branca	a.	0636	0819	0949	1049	1220	1549	1544	1805	1959	2101
122	Casa Branca	d.	0641	0819	0950	1050	1225	1550	1553	1812	2000	2102
148	Évora	a.	|	|	1008	|	|	1608	|	|	2018	|
185	**Beja**	a.	0735	0915	...	1131	1323	...	1650	1905	...	2143

		IC **598**	*IC* **590**			*IC* **692**		d	*IC* **698**	*IC* **596**	
Beja	d.	...	0814	0930	1256	...	1618	1720	...	1914	1946
Évora	d.	0638	|	|	|	1338	|	|	1838	|	|
Casa Branca	a.	0656	0856	1023	1351	1356	1714	1810	1855	1958	2038
Casa Branca	d.	0657	0857	1028	1358	1357	1718	1811	1856	1959	2043
Évora	a.	|	|	1049	1419	|	1739	|	|	|	2104
Vendas Novas	d.	0721	0923	...	...	1421	...	1839	1920	2023	...
Pinhal Novo	⊙ d.	0751	0951	...	...	1451	...	1920	1951	2051	...
Pragal	⊙ a.	0813	1013	...	...	1513	...	...	2013	2113	...
Entrecampos	⊙ a.	0826	1026	...	...	1526	...	...	2026	2126	...
Lisboa Oriente	⊙ a.	0835	1036	...	...	1535	...	...	2036	2135	...

b – From Barreiro, depart 0651. **d** – To Barreiro, arrive 1935. ⊙ – See Table **697** for other fast trains and Table **699** for local services. *IC* trains also call at Sete Rios.

699 OTHER LOCAL SERVICES

LISBOA - ESTORIL - CASCAIS

26 km (Estoril *24 km*)

Ⓐ													
Lisboa Cais do Sodre .d.	0530	every	0700	every	1000	every	1700	every	2030	every	2200	every	0130
Estoril .d.	0606	30	0728	15	1029	20	1729	15	2059	20	2236	30	0206
Cascais .a.	0610	mins	0732	mins	1033	mins	1733	mins	2103	mins	2240	mins	0210

Ⓒ						*	*			
Lisboa Cais do Sodre .d.	0530	every	0730	0800	every	1920	1940	2000	every	0130
Estoril .d.	0606	30	0806	0829	20	1949	2016	2036	30	0206
Cascais .a.	0610	mins	0810	0833	mins	1953	2020	2040	mins	0210

Ⓐ											
Cascais .d.	0530	0600	0630	0648	every	2048	2108	2130	every	0130
Estoril .d.	0534	0604	0634	0652	15-20 ◧	2052	2112	2134	30	0134
Lisboa Cais do Sodre .a.	0610	0640	0703	0720	mins	2121	2141	2210	mins	0210

Ⓒ								*	*			
Cascais .d.	0530	every	0700	every	0803	every	1903	1923	1943	2000	every	0130
Estoril .d.	0534	30	0707	20	0807	20	1907	1927	1947	2004	30	0134
Lisboa Cais do Sodre .a.	0610	mins	0743	mins	0836	mins	1936	1956	2023	2040	mins	0210

◧ – Every 15 minutes 0648 - 0948, every 20 minutes 1008 - 1648, every 15 minutes 1703 - 1948, every 20 minutes 2008 - 2108.

* – Every 30 mins 1900 - 2000 October - early May.

LISBOA ROSSIO - SINTRA

27 km

	Ⓐ					Ⓒ		
Lisboa Rossio .. d.	0621	every	2201	every	0131	0601	every	0121
Monte Abraão .... d.	0639	20	2219	30	0149	0619	20	0139
Agualva - Cacém d.	0646	mins	2226	mins	0156	0626	mins	0146
Sintra .... a.	0700	△	2240		0210	0640	⊖	0200

	Ⓐ					Ⓒ				
Sintra .... d.	0556	every	2156	every	0056	0516	every	2116	every	0046
Agualva - Cacém . d.	0610	20	2210	30	0110	0530	20	2130	30	0100
Monte Abraão .... d.	0618	mins	2218	mins	0118	0538	mins	2138	mins	0108
Lisboa Rossio .. a.	0636	▽	2236		0136	0556		2156		0126

△ – Every 10 minutes 0611 - 0941, 1641 - 2021.

▽ – Every 10 minutes 0546 - 0916, 1616 - 1936 (also at 0506, 0526).

⊖ – Every 30 minutes 2121 - 0121.

LISBOA ORIENTE - MIRA SINTRA-MELEÇAS

See also Table 693

	Ⓐ				Ⓒ		
Lisboa Oriente .... d.	0538	▲		▲	0638		0008
Roma Areeiro .... d.	0545	0605		2255	0645	every	0015
Entrecampos .... d.	0547	0607	every	2257	0647	30	0017
Sete Rios .... d.	0551	0611	10-20	2301	0651	mins	0021
Monte Abraão .... d.	0605	0625	mins	2315	0705		0035
Agualva - Cacém .... d.	0613	0633	△	2323	...		...
Mira Sintra - Meleças ...a.	0618	0638		2328	...		...

	Ⓐ						Ⓒ		
Mira Sintra - Meleças ... d.	0639	0649		2209	2239	2309	...		...
Agualva - Cacém .... d.	0643	0653	every	2213	2243	2313	...		...
Monte Abraão .... d.	0651	0701	10-20	2221	2251	2321	0551		2321
Sete Rios .... d.	0706	0716	mins	2236	2306	2336	0606	every	2336
Entrecampos .... d.	0709	0719		2240	2310	2339	0609	30	2339
Roma Areeiro .... d.	0711	0722		2242	2312	2341	0611	mins	2341
Lisboa Oriente .... a.	0720	▼		▼	...	2350	0620		2350

△ – Every 30 minutes 2155 - 2255 (also to Cacém 2325, 2355, 0025).

▲ – From Oriente every 30 mins 0538 - 0938, 1638 - 1938 (also every 30 mins 0717 - 0847, 1647 - 1947). Connections Oriente to Roma Areeiro also run every 30 mins 0657 - 2327.

▼ – Through journeys Mira Sintra Meleças to Oriente: every 30 mins 0639 - 0839, 1609 - 1939 (also every 30 mins 0629 - 0859, 1629 - 1929). Connections Roma Areeiro to Oriente also run every 30 mins 0619 - 2219. Additional journeys Cacém - Oriente run 0513 - 0624.

LISBOA - PINHAL NOVO - SETÚBAL

Operator: Fertagus. CP tickets not valid.

	Ⓐ					Ⓒ		
Roma Areeiro .... d.	0542		2242	2357	0042	0642		2342
Entrecampos .... d.	0544	and	2244	2359	0044	0644	and	2344
Sete Rios .... d.	0548	every	2248	0003	0048	0648	every	2348
Pragal .... d.	0559	hour	2259	0014	0059	0659	hour	2359
Pinhal Novo .... d.	0627	until	2327	0042	0127	0727	until	0027
Setúbal .... a.	0640		2340	0055	0140	0740		0040

	Ⓐ								Ⓒ		
Setúbal .... d.	0547	0657		1857	1927	2017		0017	0557		2257
Pinhal Novo .... d.	0601	0711	and	1911	1941	2031	and	0031	0611	and	2311
Pragal .... d.	0629	0739	every	1939	2009	2059	every	0059	0639	every	2339
Sete Rios .... d.	0640	0750	hour	1950	2020	2110	hour	0110	0650	hour	2350
Entrecampos .... d.	0643	0753	until	1953	2023	2113	until	0113	0653	until	2353
Roma Areeiro .... a.	0645	0755		1955	2025	2115		0115	0655		2355

Additional journeys on Ⓐ: from Roma Areeiro 1812, 1912, 2012, from Setúbal 0627, 0727, 0827. *Fertagus* trains operate every 10 - 20 mins (30 evenings and Ⓒ) Roma Areeiro - Pragal - Coina.

Catamaran LISBOA - BARREIRO

Soflusa / Transtejo

From Lisboa Terreiro do Paço: By ⛴ journey time 20 minutes. *10* km

Ⓐ: 0545, 0610, 0640; every 5–10 minutes 0655–0920; 0940, 1005; every 30 minutes 1020–1550; 1615, 1630; every 10–15 minutes 1650–2040; 2105, 2130, 2200, 2230, 2300, 2330, 0000, 0030, 0100, 0130, 0230.

Ⓒ: 0545, 0610, 0640, 0710, 0740, 0805, 0830, 0855, 0920 and every 30 minutes until 2120, 2200, 2230, 2300, 2330, 0000, 0030, 0100, 0130, 0230.

From Barreiro Barcos: By ⛴ journey time 20 minutes. *10* km

Ⓐ: 0515, 0545, 0615; every 5–10 minutes 0630–0925; 0940, every 30 minutes 0955–1455; 1525, 1545, 1600; every 10–15 minutes 1620–2000; 2015, 2040, 2100, 2130, 2200, 2230, 2300, 2330, 0000, 0030, 0100, 0200.

Ⓒ: 0515, 0545, 0615, 0645, 0715, 0740, 0805, 0830, 0855 and every 30 minutes until 2055, 2130, 2200, 2230, 2300, 2330, 0000, 0030, 0100, 0200.

BARREIRO - SETÚBAL

See also Tables **697** and **698**

km					
0	**Barreiro** .... d.	0625	and	2325	0029
15	Pinhal Novo .... d.	0644	hourly	2344	0048
28	**Setúbal** .... a.	0655	until	2355	0059

	Ⓒ			
Setúbal .... d.	0548	0648	and	2348
Pinhal Novo .... d.	0600	0700	hourly	0000
Barreiro .... a.	0618	0718	until	0018

Additional journeys on Ⓐ:
From Barreiro: 0555, 0655, 0756, 0855, 1655, 1755, 1855, 1955.
From Setúbal: 0510, 0618, 0718, 0818, 0918, 1718, 1818, 1918, 2021.
All journeys continue beyond Setúbal to Praias do Sado A (8 minutes).

LISBOA - ENTRONCAMENTO - TOMAR

km			Ⓐ	⚒		⑥	Ⓐ		Ⓐ	Ⓐ		Ⓐ		Ⓐ			Ⓐ§		Ⓐ§				Ⓐ	
0	**Lisboa** Santa Apolónia .... ▷ d.	0015	0548	0648	0748	0806	0848	0948	1048	1148	1248	1348	1448	1548	1618	1648	1718	1748	1818	1848	1948	2048	2148	2248
7	**Lisboa** Oriente .... ▷ d.	0024	0556	0656	0756	0814	0856	0956	1056	1156	1256	1356	1456	1556	1628	1656	1726	1756	1826	1856	1956	2056	2156	2256
31	Vila Franca de Xira .... d.	0042	0615	0715	0815	0835	0913	1015	1113	1215	1313	1415	1515	1615	1644	1715	1742	1815	1842	1915	2015	2115	2213	2313
75	Santarém .... d.	0119	0658	0758	0858	0920	0950	1058	1152	1258	1350	1458	1552	1706	1713	1758	1819	1858	1918	1958	2058	2152	2250	2350
107	Entroncamento .... d.	0145	0724	0824	0923	0941	1016	1124	1218	1324	1416	1524	1617	1731	1737	1824	1841	1923	1940	2024	2128	2218	2316	0016
130	**Tomar** .... a.	...	0755	0855	0950	...	...	1155	1245	...	1443	1555	1651	1758	...	1855	1902	1954	2001	2055	2155	2251	2343	0043

	⚒	Ⓐ	Ⓐ§		Ⓐ§		⚒		Ⓐ			Ⓐ		Ⓐ					Ⓐ	Ⓑ	⑥	Ⓐ	
Tomar .... d.	...	0515	0557	0614v	0657	0710v	...	0802	...	1009	1109v	...	1315	...	1509	1609	1702	1802	1913	2002	*2002*	...	2210
Entroncamento .... d.	0421	0543	0618	0641	0719	0741	0804	0836	0924	1036	1141	1236	1343	1436	1542	1637	1736	1836	1942	2036	2035	2143	2242
Santarém .... d.	0446	0608	0639	0706	0740	0806	0830	0901	0949	1101	1207	1302	1408	1502	1607	1702	1801	1901	2007	2101	2101	2205	2307
Vila Franca de Xira .... d.	0524	0646	0707	0744	0816	0844	0915	0946	1031	1146	1245	1346	1446	1546	1645	1746	1845	1946	2045	2146	2146	2246	2345
Lisboa Oriente .... ▽ a.	0542	0703	0723	0803	0831	0903	0932	1002	1048	1202	1302	1402	1503	1602	1702	1802	1902	2002	2102	2202	2202	2302	0002
Lisboa Santa Apolónia .... ▽ a.	0553	0711	0731	0811	0841	0911	0941	1011	1057	1211	1311	1411	1511	1611	1711	1811	1911	2011	2111	2211	2211	2311	0010

▷ – Additional local trains Santa Apolónia - Oriente: hourly 0536 - 0136 (on Ⓐ also runs every 30 minutes 0536 - 0936, 1636 - 2036).

▽ – Additional local trains Oriente - Santa Apolónia: hourly 0615 - 0115 (on Ⓐ also runs every 30 minutes 0615 - 1015, 1715 - 2115).

v – ⚒ only.

§ – *IR* train.

ENTRONCAMENTO - COIMBRA

km		Ⓐ			⚒						Ⓐ		Ⓑ
0	**Entroncamento** ... d.	0442	0542	0659	0742	0842	1142	1242	1542	1742	1845	1959	2132
24	Fátima ⊙ .... d.	0503	0603	0720	0809	0903	1203	1309	1603	1809	1913	2020	2153
64	Pombal .... d.	0535	0635	0751	0842	0941	1234	1342	1635	1842	1945	2052	2225
91	Alfarelos .... d.	0558	0658	0815	0905	1004	1257	1405	1658	1905	2009	2120	2248
111	Coimbra B .... a.	0624	0718	0841	0925	1030	1317	1424	1718	1924	2032	2139	2314
111	Coimbra B .... d.	0631	0723	0849	0932	1035	1325	1430	*1742*	1935	*2041*	2147	...
113	**Coimbra** .... a.	0635	0729	0853	0936	1039	1329	1434	*1746*	1939	*2046*	2151	...

	①–⑥	Ⓐ					Ⓐ			Ⓑ
Coimbra .... d.	*0635*	0716	0837	1039	1329	1623	1723	1817	1914	2013
Coimbra B .... a.	*0639*	0720	0841	1043	1333	1627	1727	1821	1918	2017
Coimbra B .... d.	0650	0725	0853	1049	1338	1632	1735	1826	1925	2022
Alfarelos .... d.	0707	0747	0910	1116	1411	1658	1758	1858	1958	2049
Pombal .... d.	0731	0827	0934	1140	1435	1722	1831	1922	2022	2112
Fátima ‡ .... d.	0802	0900	1005	1212	1507	1754	1905	1954	2054	2152
Entroncamento .. a.	0824	0920	1032	1232	1527	1814	1928	2014	2114	2213

⊙ – Station is *20 km* from Fátima.

AVEIRO - COIMBRA

km					Ⓐ			Ⓐ					
0	**Aveiro** .... d.	0649	0749	0949	1049	1133	1223	1349	1449	1533	1749	1949	2149
41	Pampilhosa .... d.	0725	0825	1025	1126	1210	1300	1425	1525	1610	1825	2025	2226
55	Coimbra B .... a.	0740	0840	1040	1140	1224	1314	1440	1540	1624	1840	2040	2240
57	**Coimbra** .... a.	0745	0845	1047	1146	1230	1318	1446	1545	1632	1846	2046	2246

		⚒								
Coimbra .... d.	0635	0745	0845	1056	1338	1446	1638	1846	1946	2210
Coimbra B .... d.	0640	0750	0850	1101	1348	1451	1646	1850	1951	2215
Pampilhosa .... d.	0655	0805	0905	1116	1404	1505	1702	1905	2006	2231
Aveiro .... a.	0732	0843	0943	1153	1441	1543	1739	1943	2043	2308

Additional trains: **Aveiro - Coimbra**: 0549 ⚒, 0849 Ⓐ, 1633 Ⓐ, 1849 Ⓐ, 2049 Ⓐ. **Coimbra - Aveiro**: 0545 Ⓐ, 1004 Ⓐ, 1146 Ⓐ, 1240 Ⓐ, 1545 Ⓐ, 1738 Ⓐ, 2046 Ⓐ.

Suburban trains run **Porto - Espinho - Aveiro** approx. hourly.

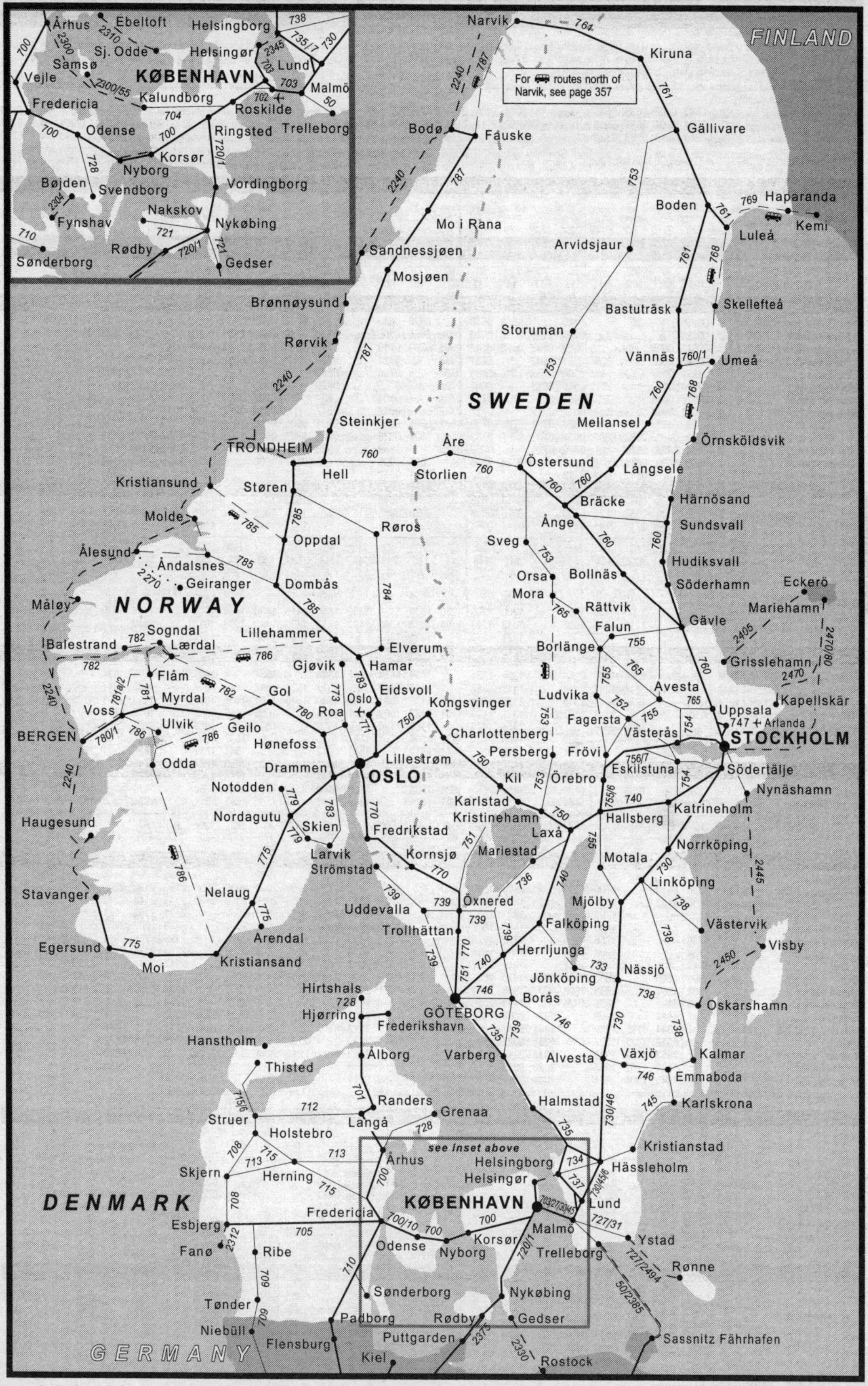
FINLAND
SWEDEN
NORWAY
DENMARK
GERMANY
KØBENHAVN
For routes north of Narvik, see page 357
see inset above
Narvik
Kiruna
Gällivare
Boden
Haparanda
Kemi
Luleå
Arvidsjaur
Skellefteå
Bastuträsk
Storuman
Vännäs
Umeå
Mellansel
Örnsköldsvik
Östersund
Långsele
Bräcke
Ånge
Härnösand
Sundsvall
Sveg
Hudiksvall
Söderhamn
Orsa
Mora
Bollnäs
Rättvik
Falun
Gävle
Eckerö
Mariehamn
Borlänge
Avesta
Grisslehamn
Kapellskär
Ludvika
Fagersta
Uppsala
Arlanda
Västerås
STOCKHOLM
Södertälje
Nynäshamn
Charlottenberg
Persberg
Frövi
Eskilstuna
Kil
Karlstad
Kristinehamn
Örebro
Laxå
Hallsberg
Katrineholm
Norrköping
Mariestad
Motala
Linköping
Mjölby
Västervik
Visby
Öxnered
Falköping
Herrljunga
Jönköping
Nässjö
Oskarshamn
Uddevalla
Trollhättan
GÖTEBORG
Borås
Alvesta
Växjö
Kalmar
Emmaboda
Karlskrona
Varberg
Halmstad
Kristianstad
Hässleholm
Helsingborg
Helsingør
Lund
Malmö
Trelleborg
Ystad
Rønne
Sassnitz Fährhafen
Rostock
Bodø
Fauske
Mo i Rana
Sandnessjøen
Mosjøen
Brønnøysund
Rørvik
Steinkjer
TRONDHEIM
Hell
Åre
Storlien
Kristiansund
Støren
Molde
Oppdal
Røros
Ålesund
Åndalsnes
Geiranger
Dombås
Måløy
Sogndal
Lærdal
Balestrand
Lillehammer
Elverum
Hamar
Gjøvik
Eidsvoll
Kongsvinger
Flåm
Myrdal
Voss
Gol
Geilo
Roa
Oslo
Ulvik
BERGEN
Hønefoss
Odda
Lillestrøm
Drammen
OSLO
Notodden
Nordagutu
Haugesund
Skien
Larvik
Strömstad
Fredrikstad
Kornsjø
Stavanger
Nelaug
Arendal
Egersund
Moi
Kristiansand
Hirtshals
Hjørring
Frederikshavn
Hanstholm
Ålborg
Thisted
Randers
Struer
Langå
Grenaa
Holstebro
Århus
Skjern
Herning
Fredericia
Esbjerg
Odense
Nyborg
Korsør
Fanø
Ribe
Sønderborg
Nykøbing
Tønder
Padborg
Rødby
Gedser
Niebüll
Flensburg
Puttgarden
Kiel
Ebeltoft
Sj. Odde
Samsø
Vejle
Kalundborg
Roskilde
Ringsted
Bøjden
Svendborg
Vordingborg
Nakskov
Fynshav

DENMARK

Operators: The principal operator is Danske Statsbaner (DSB). Arriva Tog (AT) operate many local services in Jutland.

Services: InterCity (*IC*) and InterCityLyn (*Lyn*) trains offer *Business* (1st class), *Standard* (2nd class), and on some services *Hvilepladser* ('quiet' seats) and *Familiepladser* ('family' seats). These services often consist of two or more portions for different destinations and care should be taken to join the correct portion. Other trains convey 1st and 2nd (standard) classes of accommodation unless otherwise shown.

Timings: Valid from **December 13, 2009** unless otherwise stated. Alterations may be made on and around the dates of public holidays (see **Holiday periods** below for known changes to schedules).

Reservations: Seat reservations (currently 20 DKK) are recommended for travel on *IC* and *Lyn* trains (especially at peak times) and may be purchased a maximum of two months and a minimum of 15 minutes before departure of the train from its *originating* station. Passengers may board the train without a reservation but are not guaranteed a seat. Reservations are also available on EuroCity (*EC*) trains. It is not possible to reserve seats on other types of train. Special reservation rules may apply during holiday periods.

Supplements: Supplements are payable for travel to and from Germany by InterCityExpress (*ICE*) and EuroCity (*EC*) trains; also for journeys København – Høje Taastrup – Nykøbing Falster and v.v. by *ICE* and *EC* train. On DSB trains, a higher fare is payable for journeys in the Greater København area between 0100 and 0500 hours.

Holiday periods: Danske Statsbaner services will be amended as follows: a ⑤ service will operate on Dec. 23, Mar. 31, Apr. 29, May 12; a ⑥ service will operate on Dec. 24, 31, Apr. 3; a ⑦ service will operate on Dec. 25, 26, Jan. 1, Apr. 1, 2, 4, 5, 30, May 13, 23, 24.

Arriva services will be amended as follows: a ⑥ service will operate on Dec. 24, 31, Apr. 3, May 22, June 5; a ⑦ service will operate on Dec. 25, 26, Jan. 1, Apr. 1, 2, 5, 6, 30, May 13, 23, 24.

700 KØBENHAVN - ODENSE - FREDERICIA - ÅRHUS

km		*IC* 191 A	*IC* 805	*IC* 109 A ①–⑤	*Lyn* 11 F ①–⑥	*IC* 113 A ①–⑥	*IC* 917 S	*Lyn* 15 F ①–⑥	*IC* 117 A	*IC* 821 E	*Lyn* 19 F ①–⑥	*IC* 121 A		*IC* 925 S	*Lyn* 23 F	*IC* 125 A	*IC* 829 E	*Lyn* 27 F	*IC* 129 A	*IC* 933 S	*IR* 1643 ⑥z	*Lyn* 29 F	*IC* 133 A	*IR* 1665 A ⑤y
0	**København Lufthavn** ... d.	0020	0140	...	...	0440	...	0528	0540	...	0620	0640	...	...	0728	0740	...	...	0840	...	...	...	0940	...
11	**København H 721** .... § d.	0038	0207	...	...	0500	0530	0550	0600	0630	0650	0700	...	0730	0750	0800	0830	0850	0900	0930	0941	0950	1000	0956
31	Høje Taastrup **721** ..... § d.	0051	0221	...	...	0513	0543	0603	0613	0643	0703	0713	...	0743	0803	0813	0843	0903	0913	0943	|	1003	1013	|
42	Roskilde **721** .... § d.	0059	0233	...	...	0521	0552	|	0621	0652	|	0721	...	0752	|	0821	0852	|	0921	0952	|	|	1021	1016
75	Ringsted **721** .... d.	0122	0256	...	...	0536	0607	|	0636	0707	|	0736	...	0807	|	0836	0907	|	0936	1007	1015	|	1036	1033
104	Slagelse .... d.	0141	0316	...	...	0555	0625	|	0655	0725	|	0755	...	0825	|	0855	0925	|	0955	1025	1038	|	1055	1049
119	Korsør .... d.	0151	0326	...	...	0604	0634	|	0704	0734	|	0804	...	0834	|	0904	0934	|	1004	1034	|	|	1104	|
143	Nyborg .... d.	0206	0342	0514	...	0617	0647	|	0717	0747	|	0817	...	0847	|	0917	0947	|	1017	1047	1100	|	1117	1110
171	**Odense** .... a.	0228	0359	0530	...	0630	0701	0705	0730	0801	0805	0830	...	0901	0905	0930	1001	1005	1030	1101	1118	1105	1130	1125
171	**Odense 729** .... d.	0230	0401	0533	0607	0636	0703	0707	0733	0803	0807	0833	...	0903	0907	0933	1003	1007	1033	1103	1120	1107	1133	1136
221	Middelfart **710** .... d.	0258	0428	0559	|	0700	0726	|	0758	0826	|	0858	...	0926	|	0958	1026	|	1058	1126	|	|	1158	|
231	**Fredericia** .... a.	0305	0436	0606	0637	0709	...	0737	0806	...	0837	0906	...	...	0937	1006	...	1037	1106	...	1158	1137	1206	1210
231	**Fredericia 705/10/5** ..... d.	0307	...	0612	0641	0712	...	0741	0812	...	0841	0912	...	...	0941	1012	...	1041	1112	...	1200	1141	1212	1220
257	Vejle **715** .... d.	0323	...	0627	0656	0727	...	0756	0827	...	0856	0927	...	...	0956	1027	...	1056	1127	...	1218	1156	1227	1238
288	Horsens .... d.	0340	...	0643	0713	0743	...	0813	0843	...	0913	0943	...	...	1013	1043	...	1113	1143	...	1236	1213	1243	1258
317	Skanderborg **713** .... d.	0356	...	0658	0729	0758	...	0828	0858	...	0928	0958	...	...	1028	1058	...	1128	1158	...	1252	1228	1258	1316
340	**Århus 713** .... a.	0410	...	0711	0741	0811	...	0841	0911	...	0941	1011	...	...	1041	1111	...	1141	1211	...	1305	1241	1311	1331

	IC 837 E	*Lyn* 41 F	*ICE* 386 ♦	*IC* 137 A	*IC* 941 S	*Lyn* 43 F		*IC* 141 A	*IC* 845 E	*Lyn* 45 F	*IC* 145 A	*IC* 949 S	*Lyn* 47 F	*IC* 149 A	*IR* 1639 E ⑤x	*IC* 853 E	*Lyn* 51 F	*IC* 153 A		*IR* 1653 ⑤w	*IC* 957 S	*Lyn* 55 F	*IC* 157 A	*IR* 1655 ⑤x
København Lufthavn .... d.	...	...	...	1040	...	...	...	1140	...	...	1240	...	...	1340	...	...	...	1440	...	...	...	...	1540	...
København H 721 ...... § d.	1030	1050	...	1100	1130	1150	...	1200	1230	1250	1300	1330	1350	1400	1416	1430	1450	1500	...	1516	1530	1550	1600	1616
Høje Taastrup **721** ...... § d.	1043	1103	...	1113	1143	1203	...	1213	1243	1303	1313	1343	1403	1413	1430	1443	1503	1513	...	1530	1543	1603	1613	1629
Roskilde **721** .... § d.	1052	|	...	1121	1152	|	...	1221	1252	|	1321	1352	|	1421	1440	1452	|	1521	...	1540	1552	|	1621	1639
Ringsted **721** .... d.	1107	|	...	1136	1207	|	...	1236	1307	|	1336	1407	|	1436	|	1507	|	1536	...	|	1607	|	1636	1657
Slagelse .... d.	1125	|	...	1155	1225	|	...	1255	1325	|	1355	1425	|	1455	1512	1525	|	1555	...	1612	1625	|	1655	1715
Korsør .... d.	1134	|	...	1204	1234	|	...	1304	1334	|	1404	1434	|	1504	|	1534	|	1604	...	|	1634	|	1704	|
Nyborg .... d.	1147	|	...	1217	1247	|	...	1317	1347	|	1417	1447	|	1517	1533	1547	|	1617	...	1633	1647	|	1717	1736
Odense .... a.	1201	1205	...	1230	1301	1305	...	1330	1401	1405	1430	1501	1505	1530	1549	1601	1605	1630	...	1649	1701	1705	1730	1751
Odense 729 .... d.	1203	1207	...	1233	1303	1307	...	1333	1403	1407	1433	1503	1507	1533	...	1603	1607	1633	...	1657	1703	1707	1733	1757
Middelfart **710** .... d.	1226	|	...	1258	1326	|	...	1358	1426	|	1458	1526	|	1558	...	1626	|	1658	...	|	1726	|	1758	|
Fredericia .... a.	...	1237	...	1306	...	1337	...	1406	...	1437	1506	...	1537	1606	...	...	1637	1706	...	1727	...	1737	1806	1827
Fredericia 705/10/5 ...... d.	...	1241	1304	1312	...	1341	...	1412	...	1441	1512	...	1541	1612	...	...	1641	1712	...	1729	...	1741	1812	1829
Vejle **715** .... d.	...	1256	1320	1327	...	1356	...	1427	...	1456	1527	...	1556	1627	...	...	1656	1727	...	1745	...	1756	1827	1845
Horsens .... d.	...	1313	1336	1343	...	1413	...	1443	...	1513	1543	...	1613	1643	...	...	1713	1743	...	1803	...	1813	1843	1903
Skanderborg **713** .... d.	...	1328	|	1358	...	1428	...	1458	...	1528	1558	...	1628	1658	...	...	1728	1758	...	1820	...	1828	1858	1920
Århus 713 .... a.	...	1341	1402	1411	...	1441	...	1511	...	1541	1611	...	1641	1711	...	...	1741	1811	...	1834	...	1841	1911	1934

	Lyn 53 ①–④	*IC* 861 E	*Lyn* 59 F	*ICE* 380 ♦	*IC* 161 A	*IC* 965 S	*Lyn* 63 F	*IC* 165 A	*IC* 869 E	*Lyn* 65 F		*EN* 483 [R] ♦⊡	*IC* 169 A	*IC* 973 S	*Lyn* 69	*IC* 173 A	*IC* 877	*Lyn* 73 ⑤–⑦	*IC* 177	*IC* 981	*IC* 179	*IC* 885	*IC* 189	
København Lufthavn .... d.	...	...	...	...	1640	...	...	1740	...	...	...	...	1840	...	...	1940	...	...	2040	...	2140	...	2308	...
København H 721 ...... § d.	1627	1630	1650	...	1700	1730	1750	1800	1830	1850	...	1842	1900	1930	1950	2000	2030	2050	2100	2130	2200	2230	2330	...
Høje Taastrup **721** ...... § d.	|	1643	1703	...	1713	1743	1803	1813	1843	1903	...	1904	1913	1943	2003	2013	2043	2103	2113	2143	2213	2243	2344	...
Roskilde **721** .... § d.	|	1652	|	...	1721	1752	|	1821	1852	|	...	|	1921	1952	|	2021	2052	|	2121	2152	2221	2252	2353	...
Ringsted **721** .... d.	|	1707	|	...	1736	1807	|	1836	1907	|	...	1931	1936	2007	|	2036	2107	|	2136	2207	2236	2307	0013	...
Slagelse .... d.	1713	1725	|	...	1755	1825	|	1855	1925	|	...	|	1955	2025	|	2055	2125	|	2155	2225	2255	2327	0033	...
Korsør .... d.	|	1734	|	...	1804	1834	|	1904	1934	|	...	|	2004	2034	|	2104	2134	|	2204	2234	2304	2338	0044	...
Nyborg .... d.	1732	1747	|	...	1817	1847	|	1917	1947	|	...	|	2017	2047	|	2117	2147	|	2217	2247	2317	2353	0059	...
Odense .... a.	1745	1801	1805	...	1830	1901	1905	1930	2001	2005	...	2025	2030	2101	2105	2130	2201	2205	2230	2301	2334	0011	0117	...
Odense 729 .... d.	...	1803	1807	...	1833	1903	1907	1933	2003	2007	...	...	2033	2103	2107	2133	2203	2207	2233	2303	2336	0013	0119	...
Middelfart **710** .... d.	...	1826	|	...	1858	1926	|	1958	2026	|	...	...	2058	2126	|	2158	2226	|	2258	2326	0005	0039	0145	...
Fredericia .... a.	...	...	1837	...	1906	...	1937	2006	...	2037	...	...	2106	...	2137	2205	...	2237	2305	...	0014	0048	0154	...
Fredericia 705/10/5 ...... d.	...	...	1841	1706	1912	...	1941	2012	...	2041	...	...	2112	...	2141	2211	...	2241	2311	...	0016	...	0156	...
Vejle **715** .... d.	...	...	1856	1721	1927	...	1956	2027	...	2056	...	...	2127	...	2156	2226	...	2256	2326	...	0032	...	0212	...
Horsens .... d.	...	...	1913	1737	1943	...	2013	2043	...	2113	...	...	2143	...	2213	2244	...	2313	2345	...	0049	...	0230	...
Skanderborg **713** .... d.	...	...	1928	1752	1958	...	2028	2058	...	2128	...	...	2158	...	2228	2300	...	2328	0000	...	0106	...	0247	...
Århus 713 .... a.	...	...	1941	1804	2011	...	2041	2111	...	2141	...	...	2211	...	2241	2314	...	2341	0014	...	0120	...	0301	...

	IC 190 F	*IC* 100	*IC* 800 ①–⑤	*IC* 802 ①–⑥	*Lyn* 2 ①–⑤	*IC* 804 ①–⑤	*Lyn* 4 ①–⑤	*IC* 808 ①–⑥	*IC* 810 ⑦	*Lyn* 8 ①–⑤	*IC* 904/6 ①–⑤	*Lyn* 6 ①–⑤	*IC* 108	*Lyn* 10 A ①–⑤	*IC* 910 S p	*IC* 908 S q	*EN* 482 [R] ♦⊡	*IC* 112 A	*Lyn* 14 F ①–⑥	*IC* 812 E	*ICE* 381 ♦	*IC* 116 A	*Lyn* 18 F	*IC* 916 S
Århus 713 729 .... d.	0151	...	...	...	0420	...	...	...	...	...	...	0545	0559g	0628	...	...	...	0702	0728	...	0754	0759	0828	...
Skanderborg **713** .... d.	0206	...	...	...	0435	...	...	...	...	...	...	0558	0613g	0641	...	...	...	0714	0741	...	0808	0814	0841	...
Horsens .... d.	0223	...	...	...	0451	...	...	...	...	...	...	0613	0628g	0656	...	...	...	0729	0756	...	0824	0829	0856	...
Vejle **715** .... d.	0243	...	...	...	0509	...	...	...	...	...	...	0630	0646g	0713	...	...	...	0748	0813	...	0841	0848	0913	...
Fredericia 715 .... a.	0259	...	...	...	0523	...	...	...	...	...	...	0645	0701g	0728	...	...	...	0804	0828	...	0856	0904	0928	...
Fredericia 705 710 .... d.	0303	0402d	...	0506	0528	0536	...	0601	0606	...	...	0649	0706	0733	...	...	...	0809	0833	...	...	0909	0933	...
Middelfart **710** .... d.	0311	0410d	...	0514	|	0544	...	0609	0614	...	0645	|	0714	|	0746	0746	...	0817	|	0845	...	0917	|	0945
Odense .... a.	0340	0436d	...	0541	0600	0611	...	0639	0644	...	0711	0720	0743	0803	0807	0811	...	0845	0903	0909	...	0945	1003	1011
Odense 729 .... d.	0342	0440	0515	0545	0602	0615	0629	0642	0646	0656	0715	0729	0745	0807	0812	0815	0829	0848	0907	0915	...	0948	1007	1015
Nyborg .... d.	0402	0500	0528	0600	0616	0628	0643	0658	0700	0712	0728	0743	0800	|	0825	0828	|	0903	|	0928	...	1003	|	1028
Korsør .... d.	0415	0513	0541	0613	|	0641	|	0712	0713	|	0741	|	0813	|	0838	0841	|	0916	|	0941	...	1016	|	1041
Slagelse .... d.	0426	0523	0552	0623	0635	0652	0701	0722	0723	0732	0752j	|	0823	|	0847	0852	|	0926	|	0952	...	1026	|	1052
Ringsted **721** .... d.	0445	0540	0610	0640	|	0710	|	0740	0740	|	0810j	|	0840	|	0909	0910	0916	0940	|	1010	...	1040	|	1110
Roskilde **721** .... § a.	0508	0556	0628	0656	|	0724	|	0756	0756	|	0824j	|	0856	|	0927	0924	|	0956	|	1027	...	1056	|	1124
Høje Taastrup **721** ...... § a.	0519	0606	0637	0706	0710	0734	|	0806	0806	|	0834	0839	0906	0910	0935	0934	0945	1006	1010	1035	...	1105	1110	1134
København H 721 ...... § a.	0536	0619	0653	0719	0723	0749	0753	0819	0819	0827	0849	0852	0919	0923	0949	0949	1006	1019	1023	1049	...	1119	1123	1149
København Lufthavn ...... a.	0559	0639	...	...	0741	...	...	...	...	0851	...	...	0939	...	...	...	...	1039	...	...	...	1139	...	...

FOR NOTES SEE FACING PAGE

ÅRHUS - FREDERICIA - ODENSE - KØBENHAVN 700

	IR	*IC*	*Lyn*	*IC*	*IC*	*Lyn*	*IC*	*IC*	*Lyn*	*IC*	*IC*	*Lyn*	*IC*	*IC*	*Lyn*	*IC*	*IC*	*ICE*	*Lyn*	*IC*	*IR*	*IC*	*Lyn*	*IC*	*IC*
	1658	**120**	**24**	**820**	**124**	**26**	**924**	**128**	**28**	**828**	**132**	**40**	**932**	**136**	**42**	**836**	**140**	**387**	**44**	**940**	**1646**	**144**	**46**	**844/6**	**148/50**
		A	**F**	**E**	**A**	**F**	**S**	**A**	**F**	**E**	**A**	**F**	**S**	**A**	**F**	**E**	**A**		**F**	**S**		**A**	**F**	**E**	**A**
	⑥**k**																	♦			⑦**v**				
Århus 713 729 ....d.	0836	0900	0928	...	1000	1028	...	1100	1128	...	1200	1228	...	1300	1328	...	1400	1424	1428	...	1437	1500	1528	...	1600
Skanderborg **713** ....d.	|	0914	0941	...	1014	1041	...	1114	1141	...	1214	1241	...	1314	1341	...	1414	|	1441	...	|	1514	1541	...	1614
Horsens.......................d.	0905	0929	0956	...	1029	1056	...	1129	1156	...	1229	1256	...	1329	1356	...	1429	1451	1456	...	1505	1529	1556	...	1629
Vejle **715** ....d.	0923	0948	1013	...	1048	1113	...	1148	1213	...	1248	1313	...	1348	1413	...	1448	1508	1513	...	1523	1548	1613	...	1648
Fredericia 715 ....a.	0938	1004	1028	...	1104	1128	...	1204	1228	...	1304	1328	...	1404	1428	...	1504	1521	1528	...	1538	1604	1628	...	1704
Fredericia 705 710......d.	0943	1009	1033	...	1109	1133	...	1209	1233	...	1309	1333	...	1409	1433	...	1509	...	1533	...	1543	1609	1633	...	1709
Middelfart **710**.............d.	|	1017	|	1045	1117	|	1145	1217	|	1245	1317	|	1345	1417	|	1445	1517	...	|	1546	|	1617	|	1645	1717
Odense ....a.	1015	1045	1103	1111	1145	1203	1211	1245	1303	1311	1345	1403	1411	1445	1503	1511	1545	...	1603	1611	1615	1645	1703	1711	1745
Odense 729 ....d.	1019	1048	1107	1115	1148	1207	1215	1248	1307	1315	1348	1407	1415	1448	1507	1515	1548	...	1607	1615	1620	1648	1707	1715	1748
Nyborg..........................d.	1034	1103	|	1128	1203	|	1228	1303	|	1328	1403	|	1428	1503	|	1528	1603	...	|	1628	1636	1703	|	1728	1803
Korsør ....d.	|	1116	|	1141	1216	|	1241	1316	|	1341	1416	|	1441	1516	|	1541	1616	...	|	1641	|	1716	|	1741	1816
Slagelse ....d.	1058	1126	|	1152	1226	|	1252	1326	|	1352	1426	|	1452	1526	|	1552	1626	...	|	1652	1658	1726	|	1752**r**	1826
Ringsted **721** ....d.	1115	1140	|	1210	1240	|	1310	1340	|	1410	1440	|	1510	1540	|	1610	1640	...	|	1710	1715	1740	|	1810**r**	1840
Roskilde **721**............ § a.	1131	1156	|	1224	1256	|	1324	1356	|	1424	1456	|	1524	1556	|	1624	1656	...	|	1724	1731	1756	|	1824**r**	1856
Høje Taastrup **721** .... § a.	1140	1205	1210	1234	1306	1308	1334	1405	1410	1434	1505	1510	1534	1605	1610	1634	1705	...	1710	1734	1740	1805	1810	1835	1905
København H 721.... § a.	1154	1219	1223	1249	1319	1323	1349	1419	1423	1449	1519	1523	1549	1619	1623	1649	1719	...	1723	1749	1754	1819	1823	1849	1919
København Lufthavn.....a.	...	1239	...	...	1339	...	...	1439	...	...	1539	...	...	1639	...	...	1739	...	...	...	...	1839	...	...	1939

	Lyn	*IC*	*IR*	*IC*	*IC*	*IR*	*Lyn*	*IC*	*IC*	*Lyn*	*IC*	*IC*	*IR*	*Lyn*	*IC*	*IC*	*Lyn*	*IC*	*IC*	*Lyn*	*IC*	*IC*	*IC*	*IC*	
	50	**948/50**	**1654**	**158**	**152**	**1640**	**54**	**852**	**156**	**56**	**956**	**160**	**1666**	**60**	**860**	**164**	**64**	**964**	**168**	**68**	**868**	**172**	**176**	**180**	
	F	**S**		**A**	**A**	**E**	**F**	**E**	**A**	**A**	**S**	**A**	**A**	**F**	**E**	**A**	**A**	**S**	**A**		**E**	**A**	**A**	**A**	
			⑦**v**	⑤	⑥–④	⑤**x**							⑤**y**							⑦					
Århus 713 729 ....d.	1628	...	1637	1700	1700	...	1728	...	1800	1828	...	1859	1914	1928	...	1959	2028	...	2100	2128	...	2200	2259	2359	...
Skanderborg **713** ....d.	1641	...	|	1713	1713	...	1741	...	1814	1841	...	1913	1931	1941	...	2013	2041	...	2114	2141	...	2214	2313	0014	...
Horsens.......................d.	1656	...	1705	1728	1729	...	1756	...	1829	1856	...	1928	1946	1956	...	2028	2056	...	2129	2156	...	2230	2329	0030	...
Vejle **715** ....d.	1713	...	1723	1748	1748	...	1813	...	1848	1913	...	1946	2004	2013	...	2046	2113	...	2148	2213	...	2248	2350	0051	...
Fredericia 715 ....a.	1728	...	1738	1804	1804	...	1828	...	1904	1928	...	2001	2018	2028	...	2101	2128	...	2204	2230	...	2304	0006	0107	...
Fredericia 705 710......d.	1733	...	1742	1806	1809	...	1833	...	1909	1933	...	2006	2020	2033	...	2106	2133	...	2206	2235	...	2306	0011	0110	...
Middelfart **710**.............d.	|	1745	|	1815	1818	...	|	1845	1917	|	1945	2014	|	|	2045	2114	|	2145	2214	|	2245	2313	0018	0117	...
Odense ....a.	1803	1811	1815	1842	1845	...	1903	1911	1945	2003	2011	2042	2051	2103	2111	2142	2203	2211	2245	2307	2314	2346	0048	0147	...
Odense 729 ....d.	1807	1815	1820	1845	1848	1852	1907	1915	1948	2007	2015	2045	2052	2107	2115	2145	2207	2215	2247	2309	2318	2348	0050	...	...
Nyborg..........................d.	|	1828	1836	1900	1903	1907	|	1928	2003	|	2028	2100	2108	|	2128	2200	|	2228	2306	|	2332	0006	0109	...	...
Korsør ....d.	|	1841	|	1913	1916	|	|	1941	2016	|	2041	2113	|	|	2141	2213	|	2241	2319	|	2345	0019	0122	...	...
Slagelse ....d.	|	1852**j**	1858	1923	1926	1928	|	1952	2026	|	2052	2123	2139	|	2152	2223	|	2252	2330	|	2356	0030	0133	...	...
Ringsted **721** ....d.	|	1910**j**	1915	1940	1940	1944	|	2010	2040	|	2110	2140	2155	|	2210	2240	|	2311	2346	|	0017	0049	0153	...	...
Roskilde **721**............ § a.	|	1924**j**	1931	1956	1956	2011	|	2024	2056	|	2124	2156	2216	|	2224	2256	|	2330	0005	|	0033	0108	0212	...	...
Høje Taastrup **721** .... § a.	1910	1935	1940	2005	2005	2020	2010	2034	2105	2110	2134	2205	2225	2210	2234	2305	2310	2338	0013	0029	0040	0115	0220	...	...
København H 721.... § a.	1923	1949	1954	2019	2019	2036	2023	2049	2119	2123	2149	2219	2239	2223	2249	2319	2323	2355	0026	0045	0055	0131	0236	...	...
København Lufthavn.....a.	1943	...	...	2039	2039	...	...	...	2139	2143	...	2239	...	2247	...	2339	2343	...	0108	...	...	0208	0308	...	...

A – From / to Aalborg on some days (see Table **701**).
E – From / to Esbjerg (Table **705**).
F – From / to Frederikshavn on some days. A change of train may be necessary at Aalborg (see Table **701**).
S – From / to Sønderborg (Table **710**).

d – ①–⑥ only.
g – ⑥ only.
j – Runs up to 3 minutes later on ①–④ from Aug. 9.
k – Dec. 19 - June 19, Aug. 21 - Dec. 11 (not Dec. 24, 31, Jan. 2, Apr. 3).

p – ①–④ Dec. 14 - June 24, Aug. 9 - Dec. 9.
q – ⑤–⑦ Dec. 13 - June 26; daily June 27 - Aug. 7; ⑤–⑦ Aug. 8 - Dec. 11.
r – Runs up to 3 minutes later on ①–④ until June 24 and from Aug. 9.
v – Dec. 13 - June 20, Aug. 22 - Dec. 5 (not Dec. 25 - 27, Jan. 1, 3, Apr. 1, 2, 4, 5, 30, May 13, 23).
w – Dec. 18 - June 18, Aug. 20 - Dec. 10 (not Mar. 31, May 14).
x – Dec. 18 - June 18, Aug. 20 - Dec. 10 (not Dec. 23, Mar. 31, May 14).
y – Apr. 16 - June 18, Aug. 27 - Oct. 15 (not Apr. 29, May 12, 14, 28).
z – Dec. 19 - June 19, Aug. 21 - Dec. 11 (not Dec. 24, 31, Jan. 2, Apr. 3).

§ – *IC* and *Lyn* trains are not available for local journeys. Frequent local trains run between Roskilde and København.
⊡ – For passengers making international journeys only.
♦ – For days of running and composition see Table **710**.

ÅRHUS - AALBORG - FREDERIKSHAVN 701

2nd class only (*IC* & *Lyn* 1st & 2nd class)

km		*IC*			*Lyn*			*IC*	*IC*		*IC*	*Lyn*	*IC*	*Lyn*		*IC*		*Lyn*	*IC*	*Lyn*	*IC*	*Lyn*	*IC*	*Lyn*		*IC*	
		191			**7**			**105**	**107**		**109/11**	**11**	**113**	**15**		**117**		**19**	**121**	**23**	**125**	**27**	**129**	**29**		**133**	
			①–⑤	①–⑤	①–⑤	①–⑥	⑥⑦	①–⑤	①–⑤	⑥⑦		①–⑥		①–⑥	⑦		⑦	①–⑥							⑤	**z**	①–⑤
0	**Århus 712 729** d.	0416	...	0453	0530	...	0543	0552	0625	0649**g**	0717	0748	0817	0848	...	0917	...	0948	1017	1048	1117	1148	1217	1248	1310	1317	...
46	Langå **712**....... d.	0444	...	0523	|	...	0613	0619	0652	0713**g**	0744	|	0844	|	...	0944	...	|	1044	|	1144	|	1244	|	1340	1344	...
59	Randers.......... d.	0454	...	0534	0602	...	0624	0628	0701	0723**g**	0755	0820	0855	0920	...	0955	...	1020	1055	1120	1155	1220	1255	1320	1350	1355	...
91	Hobro.............. d.	0513	...	0553	0620	...	0643	0644	0717	0739**g**	0812	0838	0912	0938	...	1012	...	1038	1112	1138	1212	1238	1312	1338	1410	1412	...
140	**Aalborg**.......... a.	0551	...	0634	0651	...	0724	0724	0756	0817**g**	0852	0909	0952	1009	...	1052	...	1109	1155	1209	1252	1309	1352	1409	1452	1452	...
140	**Aalborg**.......... d.	0554	0621	...	*0656*	0721	...	...	0759	0821	...	0921	...	1021	1021	...	1121	1121**h**	...	1221**h**	...	1321**h**	...	1421**t**	...	...	1500
188	Hjørring **729**.... d.	0639	0700	...	*0742*	0803	...	...	0842	0903	...	1003	...	1103	1103	...	1203	1203**h**	...	1303**h**	...	1403**h**	...	1503**t**	...	...	1540
225	**Frederikshavn** a.	0708	0729	...	*0812*	0831	...	...	0912	0927	...	1030	...	1128	1128	...	1231	1231**h**	...	1328**h**	...	1431**h**	...	1528**t**	...	...	1605

	IR	*Lyn*		*IC*	*Lyn*		*IC*		*Lyn*		*IC*	*Lyn*	*IC*	*Lyn*	*IC*	*Lyn*	*IC*	*Lyn*	*IC*		*Lyn*	*IC*	*Lyn*		*IC*		*IC*
	1665	**41**		**137**	**43**		**141**		**45**		**145**	**47**	**149**	**51**	**153**	**55**	**157**	**59**	**161**		**63**	**165**	**65/7**		**169**		**173/5**
	⑤**w**		①–⑤	⑥⑦		①–⑤	⑤–⑦	①–④		①–⑤										⑥	⑧		⑧	⑥		⑥⑦**x**	
Århus 712 729.d.	1338	1348	1410	1417	1448	...	1517	1510	1548	...	1617	1648	1717	1748	1817	1848	1917	1948	2017	...	2048	2117	2148	...	2217	...	2320
Langå **712** ....d.	1419	|	1440	1444	|	...	1544	1540	|	...	1644	|	1744	|	1844	|	1944	|	2044	...	|	2144	|	...	2244	...	2350
Randers...............d.	1431	1420	1450	1455	1520	...	1555	1550	1620	...	1655	1720	1755	1820	1855	1920	1955	2020	2055	...	2120	2155	2220	...	2255	...	0000
Hobro ....d.	1454	1438	1510	1512	1538	...	1612	1610	1638	...	1712	1738	1812	1838	1912	1938	2012	2038	2112	...	2138	2212	2238	...	2312	...	0018
Aalborg..............a.	1535	1509	1552	1552	1609	...	1652	1652	1709	...	1752	1809	1852	1909	1952	2009	2052	2109	2152	...	2209	2252	2309	...	2355	...	0055
Aalborg..............d.	...	1521**t**	...	...	1621**v**	1649	...	...	1721	1750	...	1821	...	1921	...	2021	...	2121	...	2221	2221	...	2319	2319	...	0021	...
Hjørring **729**.......d.	...	1603**t**	...	...	1705**v**	1741	...	...	1803	1841	...	1903	...	2003	...	2103	...	2203	...	2303	2303	...	0000	0000	...	0103	...
Frederikshavn .a.	...	1631**t**	...	...	1733**v**	1813	...	...	1828	1913	...	1931	...	2031	...	2128	...	2232	...	2328	2328	...	0028	0028	...	0131	...

	Lyn	*IC*	*Lyn*	*IC*	*Lyn*		*IC*		*Lyn*	*IC*			*Lyn*	*IC*	*Lyn*	*IC*	*Lyn*	*IC*	*Lyn*	*IC*	*Lyn*	*IC*	*Lyn*	*IC*	*Lyn*	*IC*	*Lyn*
	10	**112/4**	**14**	**116**	**18**		**120**		**24**	**124**			**26**	**128**	**28**	**132**	**40**	**136**	**42**	**140**	**44**	**144**	**46**	**148/50**	**50**	**152/4/8**	**54**
	①–⑤	①–⑥	①–⑥		①–⑥	⑦		⑧	①–⑥	⑥⑦	①–⑤	①–⑤															
Frederikshavn .d.	...	...	0435**a**	...	0537	0537	...	0630	0633**g**	...	...	0733	0737**c**	...	0836**j**	...	0933	...	1037	...	1133**h**	...	1237	...	1333**h**	...	1433**v**
Hjørring **729**.......d.	...	...	0506**a**	...	0605	0605	...	0705	0705**g**	...	...	0804	0806**c**	...	0906**j**	...	1006	...	1106	...	1206**h**	...	1306	...	1406**h**	...	1506**v**
Aalborg..............a.	...	...	0550**a**	...	0650	0650	...	0752	0750**g**	...	...	0843	0850**c**	...	0950**j**	...	1050	...	1150	...	1250**h**	...	1350	...	1450**h**	...	1550**v**
Aalborg..............d.	0502	0517	0602	0617	0702	...	0717	...	0802	0817	0817	...	0902	0917	1002	1017	1102	1117	1202	1217	1302	1317	1402	1417	1502	1517	1602
Hobro ....d.	0532	0557	0632	0657	0732	...	0757	...	0832	0857	0858	...	0932	0957	1032	1057	1132	1157	1232	1257	1332	1357	1432	1457	1532	1557	1632
Randers...............d.	0548	0614	0648	0714	0748	...	0814	...	0848	0914	0918	...	0948	1014	1048	1114	1148	1214	1248	1314	1348	1414	1448	1514	1548	1614	1648
Langå **712** ....d.	|	0624	|	0724	|	...	0824	...	|	0924	0929	...	|	1024	|	1124	|	1224	|	1324	|	1424	|	1524	|	1624	|
Århus 712..........a.	0621	0653	0721	0753	0821	...	0853	...	0921	0953	1000	...	1021	1053	1121	1153	1221	1253	1321	1353	1421	1453	1521	1553	1621	1653	1721

	IC			*Lyn*	*IC*	*IR*			*Lyn*	*IC*			*Lyn*	*IC*	*Lyn*		*IC*		*Lyn*	*IC*		*IC*		*IC*		*IC*	
	156			**56**	**160**	**1666**			**60**	**164**			**64**	**166/8**	**68**		**172**		**72**	**176**		**180**		**184**		**190**	
	z	⑤	①–⑤		**z**	⑤**w**	⑤**r**	①–⑤			①–⑤		⑧		⑧	①–⑥		⑥⑦	①–⑤					**y**	⑤⑥		
Frederikshavn .d.	...	...	1450	1529**h**	...	...	...	1547	1633**h**	...	1651	1737	...	...	1833**v**	1833	...	1937	1937	...	2033	...	2137	...	...	2251	...
Hjørring **729**.......d.	...	...	1540	1606**h**	...	...	...	1640	1706**h**	...	1741	1806	...	...	1906**v**	1906	...	2006	2006	...	2106	...	2206	...	...	2323	...
Aalborg..............a.	...	...	1623	1650**h**	...	...	...	1723	1750**h**	...	1823	1850	...	...	1950**v**	1950	...	2050	2050	...	2150	...	2250	...	...	2400	...
Aalborg..............d.	1617	1617	...	1702	1717	1717	1717	...	1802	1817	...	...	1902	1917	2002	...	2017	...	2102	2117	...	2217	...	2317	2317	0005	...
Hobro ....d.	1657	1658	...	1732	1757	1758	1758	...	1832	1857	...	...	1932	1957	2032	...	2057	...	2132	2157	...	2257	...	2357	0058	0045	...
Randers...............d.	1714	1718	...	1748	1814	1818	1818	...	1848	1914	...	...	1948	2014	2048	...	2114	...	2148	2214	...	2314	...	0014	0018	0104	...
Langå **712** ....d.	1724	1729	...	|	1824	1829	1829	...	|	1924	...	...	|	2024	|	...	2124	...	|	2224	...	2324	...	0024	0029	0115	...
Århus 712..........a.	1753	1801	...	1821	1853	1903	1903	...	1921	1953	...	...	2021	2053	2121	...	2153	...	2221	2253	...	2353	...	0056	0101	0145	...

a – ①–⑤ only.
c – ⑥⑦ only.
g – ⑥ only.
h – Connection on ⑤.
j – Connection on ①–④.

r – Dec. 18 - May 28, June 25 - Aug. 20, Oct. 22 - Dec. 10 (not Apr. 16, 23, May 7, 21).
t – Connection on ⑧.
v – Connection on ①–⑤.

w – Apr. 16 - June 18, Aug. 27 - Oct. 15 (not Apr. 29, May 12, 14, 28).
x – Also Dec. 26, 27, 31, Jan. 2, Apr. 2, 3, 5, May 1, 24.
y – ①②③④⑦ only.
z – ①②③④⑥⑦ only.

703 HELSINGØR - KØBENHAVN - KØBENHAVN LUFTHAVN (KASTRUP) ✈ - MALMÖ

km																						
0	**Helsingør** § d.	0012j	0112j	0212j	0312j	...	...	...	0435	0455	0515	and	1855	1915	1935	1952	and	2252	...	2312	2332	2352
43	Østerport ⊡ § d.	0055	0155	0255	0355	0425	0445	0505	0515	0535	0555	every	1935	1955	2015	2035	every	2335	...	2355	0015	0035
46	**København H 700/20/1** ⊡ § d.	0103	0203	0303	0403	0435	0455	0515	0523	0543	0603	20	1943	2003	2023	2043	20	2343	...	0003	0021	0041
58	Køb Lufthavn (Kastrup) ✈ ⊡ a.	0116	0216	0316	0416	0447	0507	0527	0536	0556	0616	minutes	1956	2016	2036	2056	minutes	2356	...	0016	...	...
	Malmö Syd / Svågertorp a.	0128	0228	0328	0428	...	...	...	0548	0608	0628	until	2008	2028	2048	2108	until	0008	...	0028	...	...
94	**Malmö C** a.	0138	0238	0338	0438	...	...	...	0558	0618	0638		2018	2038	2058	2118		0018	...	0038	...	...

Malmö C d.	0022	0122	0222	0322	0422	...	0502	0522	0542	and	1822	1842	1902	1922	and	2322	...	...	...	...	...
Malmö Syd / Svågertorp d.	0031	0131	0231	0331	0431	...	0511	0531	0551	every	1831	1851	1911	1931	every	2331	...	...	...	...	...
Køb Lufthavn (Kastrup) ✈ ⊡ d.	0044	0144	0244	0344	0444	0504	0524	0544	0604	20	1844	1904	1924	1944	20	2344	...	...	0024	...	...
København H 700/20/1 ⊡ § d.	0059	0159	0259	0359	0459	0519	0539	0559	0619	minutes	1859	1919	1939	1959	minutes	2359	...	0019	0039	...	...
Østerport ⊡ § a.	0106	0206	0306	0406	0506	0526	0546	0606	0626	until	1906	1926	1946	2006	until	0006	...	0026	0046	...	...
Helsingør § a.	0148j	0248j	0348j	0448j	0544	0604	0624	0644	0704		1944	2004	2024	2048		0048	...	0108	0128	...	...

j – ⑥⑦ only. ⊡ – Additional services operate Østerport - Kastrup and v.v. § – Additional services operate ①–⑤ København H - Helsingør and v.v.

704 KØBENHAVN - KALUNDBORG

Roskilde - Holbæk and v.v. subject to alteration March 13 - June 13 owing to engineering work

km		①–⑤	⑥	①–⑤	⑥⑦	①–⑤		①–⑤	⑥⑦		①–⑤	⑥⑦		①–⑤		①–⑤	①–⑤			①–⑤	①–⑤		①–⑤		①–⑤	
0	**København H** d.	0507	0537	0537	0637	0637	...	0734	0737		1334	1337	...	1434	1437	1507	1534	1537	...	1607	1634	1637	1707	...	1734	1737
20	Høje Taastrup d.	0521	0551	0551	0651	0651	...	0747	0751	and	1347	1351	...	1447	1451	1521	1547	1551	...	1621	1647	1651	1721	...	1747	1751
31	Roskilde d.	0533	0601	0601	0701	0701	...	0756	0801	hourly	1356	1401	...	1456	1501	1533	1556	1601	...	1633	1656	1701	1733	...	1756	1801
67	Holbæk a.	0605	0635	0635	0735	0735	...	0823	0835	until	1423	1435	...	1523	1535	1605	1623	1635	...	1705	1723	1735	1805	...	1823	1835
67	Holbæk d.	0609	0636	0652	0736	0736	...	0825	0836		1425	1436	...	1525	1536c	1608	1625	1636c	...	1708	1725	1736c	1808	...	1825	1836c
111	Kalundborg a.	0650	0712	0734	0812	0821	...	0906	0912		1506	1512	...	1603	1612c	1647	1703	1712c	...	1739	1803	1812c	1839	...	1903	1912c

	①–⑤									
København H d.	1807	1837	...	1937		2337	...	0034	...	...
Høje Taastrup d.	1821	1851	...	1951	and	2351	...	0048	...	...
Roskilde d.	1833	1901	...	2001r	hourly	0001r	...	0101	...	...
Holbæk a.	1905	1935	...	2035	until	0035	...	0132	...	...
Holbæk d.	1908	1936	...	2036		0036	...	0133	...	...
Kalundborg a.	1939	2012	...	2112		0112	...	0209	...	...

	①–⑤	①–⑤	⑥	①–⑤	⑥⑦	①–⑤	①–⑤	①–⑤	⑥⑦	①–⑤	①–⑤
Kalundborg d.	0426	0450	0450	0520	0550	0557	0605	0627	0648	0650	0735
Holbæk a.	0458	0527	0528	0558	0628	0627	0644	0709	0728	0727	0808
Holbæk d.	0459	0528	0529	0559	0629	0628	0659	0711	0729	0728	0810
Roskilde a.	0533	0601	0603	0633	0703	0701	0733	0739	0803	0801	0839
Høje Taastrup a.	0543	0613	0613	0643	0713	0713	0743	0748	0813	0813	0848
København H a.	0558	0628	0628	0658	0728	0738	0758	0801	0828	0831	0901

	①–⑤		⑥⑦	①–⑤		⑥⑦	①–⑤		⑥⑦	①–⑤	⑥⑦	①–⑤	⑥⑦	①–⑤	⑥⑦	①–⑤	⑥⑦					⑦	①–⑥	⑦	①–⑥
Kalundborg d.	0745	...	0748	0833		1348	1433	...	1448	1540	1548	1632	1648	1740	1748	1840	1848	...	1948	2048	2148	2248	2248	2348	2348
Holbæk a.	0824	...	0828	0910	and	1428	1510	...	1528	1623	1628	1723	1728	1823	1828	1923	1928	...	2028	2128	2228	2328	2328	0028	0028
Holbæk d.	0828	...	0829	0911	hourly	1429	1511	...	1529	1628	1629	1728	1729	1828	1829	1928	1929	...	2029	2129	2229	2329	2329	0029	0029
Roskilde a.	0901	...	0903	0939	until	1503	1539	...	1603	1701	1703	1801	1803	1901	1903	2001	2003	...	2103	2203	2303	0003	0003	0103	0103
Høje Taastrup a.	0913	...	0913	0948		1513	1548	...	1613	1713	1713	1813	1813	1913	1913	2013	2013	...	2113t	2213t	2313t	0012	0016	0112	0116
København H a.	0928	...	0928	1001		1528	1601	...	1628	1728	1728	1828	1828	1928	1928	2028	2028	...	2128t	2228t	2328t	0032	0034	0128	0134

c – ⑥⑦ only. r – 3 minutes later on ①–⑥. t – 3–4 minutes later on ①–⑥. Additional services operate København - Holbæk and v.v.

705 FREDERICIA - ESBJERG

2nd class only (*IC* & *Lyn* 1st & 2nd class)

km		*IC* 191									*IC* 821			*IC* 829		*IC* 861			*IC* 869			*IC* 877			E	*IR* 1639
				①–⑤	①–⑥	①–⑤	①–⑤																	m	X	⑤x
	København 700 d.	0038	...	...	...	...	...	...	...	...	0630	...	...	0830		1630	...	...	1830	...	...	2030	...	...	T	1416
	Odense 700 d.	0230	...	...	...	...	...	...	...	...	0803	...	...	1003		1803	...	...	2003	...	...	2203	...	...	R	1557
	Middelfart 700 d.	0258	...	...	...	...	...	...	...	...	0827	...	...	1027	and in	1827	...	...	2027	...	...	2227	...	...	A	|
	Århus 700 d.	|	...	...	...	...	...	...	0607	...	|	...	...	|	the same	|	...	...	|	...	...	|	...	...		|
0	**Fredericia 700/10** d.	0305	0314	0414	0531	0545	0614	0645	0713	0745	|	0845	0945	|	pattern	|	1845	1945	|	2043	2145	|	2319	0024	T	|
20	Kolding **710** d.	...	0331	0429	0546	0602	0630	0702	0726	0802	0843	0902	1002	1043	until	1843	1902	2002	2043	2059	2200	2243	2336	0040	R	1635
33	Lunderskov **710** d.	...	0342	0439	0555	0613	0639	0713	0734	0813	|	0913	1013	|		|	1913	2013	|	2110	2211	|	2346	0050	A	|
44	Vejen d.	...	0351	0448	0605	0623	0648	0723	0742	0823	0857	0923	1023	1057		1857	1923	2023	2057	2120	2221	2257	2355	0059	I	|
72	Bramming **709** a.	...	0415	0512	0628	0648	0713	0748	0805	0848	0912	0948	1048	1112		1912	1948	2048	2112	2145	2245	2312	0018	0123	N	|
88	**Esbjerg** a.	...	0427	0525	0641	0700	0726	0803	0822	0903	0924	1003	1103	1124		1924	2003	2103	2124	2203	2258	2324	0031	0136		1714

		IC 190			*Lyn* 806				*IC* 812			*IC* 820			*IC* 828		*IC* 860			*IC* 868		*IC* 176		E	*IR* 1640
			①–⑤	①–⑥	①–⑤		①–⑤			①–⑤														X	⑤x
Esbjerg d.	0150	...	0448	0530	0557	0615	0649	0715	0741	0751	0815	0941	1015	1115	1141		1941	2015	2115	2141	2245	...	2350	T	1732
Bramming **709** d.	0201	...	0500	0541	0608	0627	0659	0727	0753	0803	0827	0953	1027	1127	1153		1953	2027	2127	2153	2257	...	0002	R	|
Vejen d.	0223	...	0525	0602	0623	0652	0721	0752	0809	0829	0852	1009	1052	1152	1209	and in	2009	2052	2152	2209	2322	...	0027	A	|
Lunderskov **710** d.	0231	...	0534	0609	|	0700	0729	0800	|	0838	0900	|	1100	1200	|	the same	|	2100	2200	|	2330	...	0035		|
Kolding **710** d.	0240	...	0544	0618	0639	0710	0738	0810	0828	0849	0910	1028	1110	1210	1228	pattern	2028	2110	2210	2228	2340	...	0045	T	1814
Fredericia 700/10 a.	0257	0303	0559	0632	|	0726	0752	0826	|	0904	0926	|	1126	1226	|	until	|	2126	2226	|	2356	0011	0101	R	|
Århus 700 a.	...	|	...	...	|	...	0857	...	|	...	...	|	...	...	|		|	...	...	|	...	|	...	A	|
Middelfart 700 a.	...	0311	...	...	|	...	...	...	0845	...	...	1045	...	...	1245		2045	...	...	2245	...	0018	...	I	|
Odense 700 a.	...	0340	...	...	0715	...	...	...	0909	...	...	1111	...	...	1311		2111	...	...	2314	...	0048	...	N	1850
København 700 a.	...	0536	...	...	0852	...	...	...	1049	...	...	1249	...	...	1449		2249	...	...	0055	...	0236	...		2036

m – Runs 4 minutes later on ⑥ (also Dec. 25, 26, Mar. 31, Apr. 1, 4, 29, May 12, 23). Additional services operate Fredericia - Esbjerg and v.v. on ①–⑤.
x – Dec. 18 - June 18, Aug. 20 - Dec. 10 (not Dec. 23, 31, May 14).

708 ESBJERG - SKJERN and SKJERN - STRUER

2nd class only. Operator: *AT*

km																			⑥	†	⑥					
0	**Esbjerg 705** ⊗ d.	Ⓐ	0431	0529	0617	0709	0834	0931	1023	1130	1223	1314	and	1614	1739	1835	2035	2235	Ⓒ	0512	0656	0730	0930	and every	1930	2135
17	Varde ⊗ d.		0451	0549	0641	0736	0854	0953	1043	1153	1243	1340	hourly	1640	1803	1855	2055	2255		0532	0716	0750	0950	two hours	1950	2201
60	**Skjern 713** a.		0528	0626	0722	0813	0931	1030	1123	1230	1323	1423	until	1723	1844	1933	2132	2332		0609	0753	0827	1027	until	2027	2238

km																	⑥	†	⑥	†	⑥						
0	**Skjern 713** d.	Ⓐ	0436	0530	0630	0723	0832	0932	1032		1732	1936	2136	...	Ⓒ	0441	0615	0615	0802	0831	1031		2031	...	2324	...
23	Ringkøbing a.		0454	0549	0650	0743	0855	0955	1055	and	1755	1955	2155	...		0459	0634	0634	0821	0850	1050	and every	2050	...	2343	...
23	Ringkøbing d.		0455	0550	0651	0744	0856	0956	1056	hourly	1756	1956	2200	...		0501	0635	0635	0822	0851	1051	two hours	2051	...	2344	...
71	Holstebro a.		0540	0631	0731	0831	0934	1034	1134	until	1834	2034	2238	...		0549	0713	0713	0900	0929	1129	until	2129	...	0022	...
71	Holstebro **715** d.		0546	0639	...	0849	0935	1035	1135		1835	2035	2242	...		0557	0718	...	0921	0930	1130		2130	...	0023	...
86	**Struer 715** a.		0605	0656	...	0904	0949	1049	1149		1849	2049	2256	...		0610	0735	...	0935	0944	1144		2144	...	0036	...

															⑥		†	⑥							
Struer 715 d.	Ⓐ	0445	0525	0620	...	0832	0933		1633	1820	2020	2228	...	Ⓒ	0501	...	0626	0703	...	0903		1903	...	2203	...
Holstebro **715** a.		0501	0537	0638	...	0847	0948	and	1648	1834	2034	2242	...		0515	...	0640	0717	...	0921	and every	1921	...	2221	...
Holstebro d.		0507	0542	0656	0746	0849	0949	hourly	1649	1835	2035	2243	...		0516	...	0641	0730	...	0930	two hours	1930	...	2222	...
Ringkøbing a.		0547	0625	0741	0827	0931	1031	until	1731	1914	2114	2322	...		0555	...	0724	0809	...	1009	until	2009	...	2302	...
Ringkøbing d.		0551	0625	0745	0832	0932	1032		1732	1914	2114	2322	...		0555	...	0730	0809	...	1009		2009	...	2303	...
Skjern 713 a.		0611	0649	0805	0852	0952	1052		1752	1935	2134	2342	...		0615	...	0750	0829	...	1029		2029	...	2323	...

																		⑥	†	⑥					
Skjern 713 d.	Ⓐ	0534	0628	0653	0814	0900	0959	1054	1159	1254	and	1654	1754	1938	2138	2346	Ⓒ	0625	0806	0833	1033	and every	2033	...	2325
Varde ⊗ d.		0616	0709	0739	0857	0950	1042	1133	1242	1339	hourly	1739	1834	2015	2215	0023		0710	0843	0910	1110	two hours	2110	...	0002
Esbjerg 705 ⊗ a.		0639	0732	0802	0917	1010	1102	1153	1302	1402	until	1802	1857	2035	2235	0043		0730	0903	0930	1130	until	2130	...	0022

⊗ – Additional services operate Esbjerg - Varde and v.v.

ESBJERG - TØNDER - NIEBÜLL 709

Operator: *AT*. 2nd class only

Esbjerg - Niebüll and v.v. direct services operate on Ⓒ March 27 - October 24 only (not Apr. 1, 30); on other dates a change of train is necessary at Tønder

km																												
		⑥	Ⓐ	Ⓐ	Ⓒ	Ⓐ	⑥	Ⓐ	Ⓒ	Ⓐ	Ⓐ	Ⓒ	Ⓐ	Ⓐ	Ⓒ	Ⓐ	Ⓐ	Ⓒ	Ⓐ	Ⓐ	Ⓒ	Ⓐ	Ⓒ	Ⓐ		Ⓒ		
0	**Esbjerg 705** ⊗ d.	0507	0506	0622	0707	0722	0807	0807	0907	0907	1007	1107	1107	1207	1307	1307	1407	1507	1507	1607	1707	1707	1907	1907	2000	2107	2200	2303
16	Bramming **705** ⊗ d.	0521	0521	0637	0721	0737	0821	0822	0921	0921	1021	1121	1121	1221	1321	1321	1421	1521	1521	1621	1721	1721	1921	1921	2014	2121	2214	2317
33	Ribe ⊗ d.	0544	0544	0657	0744	0800	0839	0841	0944	0943	1044	1144	1144	1244	1344	1344	1444	1544	1544	1644	1744	1744	1944	1944	2032	2143	2233	2335
80	**Tønder** a.	0631	0637	0746	0831	...	...	0929	1031	1031	1131	1231	1231	1331	1431	1431	1531	1631	1631	1731	1831	1831	2031	2031	...	...	2320	...
		│	—	—	│				│	—		│	—	—	│	—	—	│		—	│	—	│	—				
		│	Ⓐq	Ⓐ	│				│	Ⓐ		│	Ⓐ	Ⓐz	│	Ⓐ	Ⓐz	│		Ⓐz	│	Ⓐ	│	Ⓐt				
80	**Tønder** ▲ ⊡ d.	0634v	0722	0834	0834y	...	...	...	1034	1034	...	1234	1234	1334	1434	1434	1534	1634j	...	1734	1834	1834	2034x	2034	...	...	...	...
97	Niebüll **821** ▲ ⊡ a.	0653v	0741	0853	0853y	...	...	...	1053	1053	...	1253	1253	1353	1453	1453	1553	1653j	...	1753	1853	1853	2053x	2053	...	...	...	...

					Ⓐz	Ⓐ	Ⓒ		Ⓐ	Ⓒ	Ⓐ	Ⓒ	Ⓐz	Ⓐ	Ⓒ	Ⓐz		Ⓒ	Ⓐz		Ⓒ	Ⓐ	⑦m	Ⓐt	Ⓒ			
Niebüll **821** ▲ ⊡ d.	...	...	...	...	0701	0806	0806r	...	1006	1006	1206	1206	1306	1406	1406	1506	...	1606j	1706	...	1806	1806	1906	2006	2006x	...	...	...
Tønder ▲ ⊡ a.	...	...	...	...	0720	0824	0825r	...	1025	1025	1225	1225	1325	1425	1425	1525	...	1625j	1725	...	1825	1825	1925	2025	2025x	...	...	...
					—	—	│		—	│	—	│	—	—	│	—		│	—		│	—	—	—	│			
	Ⓐ	Ⓐ	Ⓒ	Ⓐ	Ⓐ	Ⓐ	│	Ⓐ	Ⓐ	│	Ⓐ	│	Ⓐ	Ⓐ	│	Ⓐ	Ⓐ	│	Ⓐ	Ⓒ	│	Ⓐ		Ⓐ	│			
Tønder d.	...	0604	0637g	0646	...	0830	0837	0933	1035	1037	1235	1237	1335	1435	1437	1535	1635	1637	1735	...	1837	1835	...	2035	2037	...	...	2324
Ribe ⊗ d.	0601	0658	0725	0740	0819	0924	0925	1025	1125	1125	1325	1325	1425	1525	1525	1625	1725	1725	1825	1843	1925	1925	2043	2125	2125	2235	2339	0012
Bramming **705** ⊗ a.	0619	0716	0742	0758	0840	0942	0942	1043	1142	1142	1342	1342	1442	1542	1542	1642	1742	1742	1842	1900	1942	1942	2100	2142	2142	2252	2356	0029
Esbjerg 705 ⊗ a.	0634	0735	0756	0815	0855	0956	0956	1057	1156	1156	1356	1356	1456	1556	1556	1656	1756	1756	1856	1914	1956	1956	2114	2156	2156	2310	0010	0043

g – ⑥ only.
j – Not Apr. 1, 30.
m – Not Apr. 4, May 23.
q – Also Dec. 24, 31.
r – ⑥ (also Apr. 1, 30; not May 1).

t – Mar. 27 - Oct. 24.
v – Mar. 27 - Oct. 24 (not Apr. 3, May 1).
x – Mar. 27 - Oct. 24 (also Apr. 2, 4, May 24).
y – ⑥ (also Apr. 1, 2, 30, May 13).
z – Also Dec. 24, 31, Apr. 1, 30.

⊗ – Additional services operate Esbjerg - Ribe and v.v.
▲ – Bus service operates Niebüll - Tønder and v.v. up to 4 times daily on ⚒. Operator: Autokraft Niebüll. ✆ +49 0 46 61 87 75, fax +49 0 46 61 80 89.
⊡ – Niebüll - Tønder nominally operated by Nord-Ostsee-Bahn GmbH, Kiel. ✆ +49 (0) 180 10 180 11. Niebüll - Tønder - Esbjerg direct services operated by *AT*.

FREDERICIA - SØNDERBORG and FLENSBURG (- HAMBURG) 710

km		*IC* 191	*IC* 190	*Lyn* 2				*IC* 917	*Lyn* 15		*IC* 821	*ICE* 381		*IC* 925	*Lyn* 23		*IC* 829		*IC* 933	*Lyn* 29		*IC* 837		*IC* 941	*Lyn* 43		*IC* 845
				①–⑤					①–⑥			♦															
	København **700** d.	0038	...	...	...	...	...	0530	0550	...	0630	...	...	0730	0750	...	0830	...	0930	0950	...	1030	...	1130	1150	...	1230
	Odense **700** d.	0230	...	...	...	...	...	0703	0707	...	0803	...	...	0903	0907	...	1003	...	1103	1107	...	1203	...	1303	1307	...	1403
	Århus **700** d.	│	0151	0420	...	0428a	0607	│	│	...	│	0754	0807	│	│	...	│	1007	│	│	...	│	1207	│	│	...	│
0	**Fredericia 700** d.	0305	0259	0523	0541	0557	0713	│	0737	0801	│	0858	0913	│	0937	1001	│	1113	│	1137	1201	│	1313	│	1337	1401	│
*	Middelfart **700** d.	...	...	—	│	│	│	0727	...	│	0827	│	│	0927	...	│	1027	│	1127	...	│	1227	│	1327	...	│	1427
20	Kolding **705** d.	...	...	...	0555	0614	0725	0743	...	0814	0843	0911	0925	0943	...	1014	1043	1125	1143	...	1214	1243	1325	1343	...	1414	1443
33	Lunderskov **705** d.	...	...	...	0603	0625	0733	0751	...	0824	—	│	...	0951	...	1024	...	—	1151	...	1224	...	—	1351	...	1424	—
60	Vojens d.	...	...	①–⑤	0628	0649	—	0808	...	0849	...	│	...	1009	...	1049	...	...	1208	...	1249	...	...	1411	...	1449	...
95	Tinglev d.	...	...	0657	0648k	0716	...	0835	...	0914	...	│	...	1035	...	1114	...	...	1235	...	1314	...	...	1435	...	1514	...
136	**Sønderborg** a.	...	...	│	0728	│	...	0912	...	│	...	│	...	1112	...	│	...	...	1312	...	│	...	...	1512	...	│	...
110	Padborg 🛃 **823** a.	...	...	0712	...	0726	0733	...	...	0926	0933	1002	...	...	...	1126	...	1133	...	...	1326	...	1333	...	...	1526	1533
122	**Flensburg** 🛃 **823** a.	...	...	...	...	...	0746	...	...	...	0946	1022	...	...	...	...	...	1146	...	...	...	...	1346	...	...	...	1546
302	*Hamburg Hbf* **823** a.	...	...	...	...	...	1014	...	...	...	1214	1232	...	...	...	...	...	1414	...	...	...	...	1614	...	...	...	1814

	IC 145		*ICE* 387	*IC* 949	*Lyn* 47		*IC* 853		*IC* 957	*Lyn* 55		*IC* 861		*IC* 965	*Lyn* 63		*IC* 869	*EN* 483		*IC* 973	*Lyn* 69		*IC* 877	*IC* 981	*IC* 180	*IC* 189	
			♦															♦ ⊡									
København **700** d.	1300	...	...	1330	1350	...	1430	...	1530	1550	...	1630	...	1730	1750	...	1830	1842	...	1930	1950	...	2030	2130	...	2330	...
Odense **700** d.	1433	...	...	1503	1507	...	1603	...	1703	1707	...	1803	...	1903	1907	...	2003	2027	...	2103	2107	...	2203	2303	...	0119	...
Århus **700** d.	│	1407	1424	│	│	...	│	1607	│	│	...	│	1807	│	│	...	│	│	2007	│	│	...	│	│	2359	│	...
Fredericia 700 d.	1506	1513	1524	│	1537	1601	│	1713	│	1737	1801	│	1913	│	1937	2001	│	│	2113	│	2137	2201	│	│	0107	0154	0201
Middelfart **700** d.	...	│	│	1527	...	│	1627	│	1727	...	│	1827	│	1927	...	│	2027	│	│	2127	—	│	2227	2327	...	...	│
Kolding **705** d.	...	1525	1537	1546	...	1614	1643	1725	1747	...	1814	1843	1925	1943	...	2014	2043	2107	2125	2143	...	2214	2243	2343	...	...	0214
Lunderskov **705** d.	...	...	│	1554	...	1624	...	—	1755	...	1824	...	—	1951	...	2024	—	│	...	2151	...	2224	...	2351	...	...	0222
Vojens d.	...	...	│	1611	...	1649	...	...	1812	...	1849	...	...	2008	...	2049	...	│	...	2208	...	2249	...	0008	...	...	0239
Tinglev d.	...	...	│	1635	...	1714	...	...	1835	...	1914	...	...	2035	...	2114	...	│	...	2235	2240	2314	...	0031	...	...	0300
Sønderborg a.	...	...	│	1712	...	│	...	...	1912	...	│	...	...	2112	...	│	...	│	...	2312	│	│	...	0109	...	...	0338
Padborg 🛃 **823** a.	...	...	1630	...	...	1726	...	1733	...	...	1926	...	1933	...	...	2126	2133	2158	...	...	2254	2326	...	...	...	...	...
Flensburg 🛃 **823** a.	...	...	1652	...	...	...	...	1746	...	...	...	...	1946	...	...	...	2146	2231	...	...	...	...	...	...	...	...	...
Hamburg Hbf **823** a.	...	...	1853	...	...	...	...	2014	...	...	...	...	2237z	...	...	...	...	0028	...	...	...	...	...	...	...	...	...

	IC 904/6			*IC* 108	*IC* 908/10	*EN* 482		*IC* 812		*IC* 116	*IC* 916		*IC* 820		*IC* 124	*IC* 924		*IC* 828		*ICE* 386	*IC* 132	*IC* 932		*IC* 836		*IC* 140	*IC* 940
	①–⑤		①–⑤			♦ ⊡	①–⑥					p								♦							
Hamburg Hbf **823** d.	...	...	...	...	...	0358	...	...	...	...	...	*0620z*	...	...	...	...	0843	...	...	0930	...	...	1043	...	...	...	...
Flensburg 🛃 **823** d.	...	...	...	...	...	0551	0707	...	...	...	...	0907	...	...	...	...	1107	...	...	1132	...	...	1307	...	...	...	...
Padborg 🛃 **823** d.	...	...	0528	...	...	0623	0718	...	0734	...	...	0918	...	0934	...	...	1118	...	1134	1150	...	...	1318	...	1334	...	...
Sønderborg d.	0500	...	│	...	0557	│	—	...	│	...	0757	—	...	│	...	0957	—	...	│	│	...	1157	—	...	│	...	1357
Tinglev d.	0543	...	0548v	...	0637	│	...	...	0745	...	0837	...	...	0945	...	1037	...	...	1145	│	...	1237	...	...	1345	...	1437
Vojens d.	0603	...	0614	...	0659	│	...	...	0811	...	0859	...	...	1011	...	1059	...	...	1211	│	...	1259	...	...	1411	...	1459
Lunderskov **705** d.	0621	...	0637	...	0719	│	0729a	...	0835	...	0917	...	...	1035	...	1115	...	...	1235	│	...	1315	...	...	1435	...	1515
Kolding **705** d.	0630	0634	0646	...	0728	0734	0738	0828	0845	...	0928	0940	1028	1045	...	1128	1140	1228	1245	1249	...	1328	1340	1428	1445	...	1532
Middelfart **700** a.	0645	│	│	...	0746	│	│	0845	│	...	0945	│	1045	│	...	1145	│	1245	│	│	...	1345	│	1445	│	...	1546
Fredericia 700 a.	│	0648	0702	0706	│	│	0752	│	0858	0909	│	0952	│	1058	1109	│	1152	│	1258	1302	1309	│	1352	│	1458	1509	│
Århus **700** a.	│	0759	...	│	│	│	0859	│	...	│	│	1059	│	...	│	│	1259	│	...	1402	│	│	1457	│	...	│	│
Odense **700** a.	0711	...	...	0743	0811	0816	...	0909	...	0945	1011	...	1111	...	1145	1211	...	1311	...	...	1345	1411	...	1511	...	1545	1611
København **700** a.	0849	...	...	0919	0949	1006	...	1049	...	1119	1149	...	1249	...	1319	1349	...	1449	...	...	1519	1549	...	1649	...	1719	1749

		IC 844/6		*ICE* 380	*IC* 148/50	*IC* 948/50		*IC* 852		*IC* 156	*IC* 956		*IC* 860		*IC* 164	*IC* 964		*IC* 868		*IC* 172		*IC* 976	*IC* 176	*IC* 179		*IC* 189	*IC* 190
				♦																							
Hamburg Hbf **823** d.	1243	...	...	1330	...	...	1443	...	...	...	...	1643	...	...	...	...	1843	...	...	...	...	...	...	...	...	...	...
Flensburg 🛃 **823** d.	1507	...	...	1532	...	...	1707	...	...	...	...	1907	...	...	...	...	2107	...	...	...	...	...	...	...	...	...	...
Padborg 🛃 **823** d.	1518	...	1534	1550	...	...	1718	...	1734	...	...	1918	...	1934	...	...	2118	...	2134	...	2222	...	...	...	...	...	...
Sønderborg d.	—	...	│	│	...	1557	—	...	│	...	1757	—	...	│	...	1957	—	...	│	...	│	2157	...	...	2352	...	...
Tinglev d.	...	...	1545	│	...	1637	...	...	1745	...	1837	...	...	1945	...	2037	...	...	2145	...	2232	2237	...	...	0030	...	...
Vojens d.	...	...	1611	│	...	1659	...	...	1811	...	1859	...	...	2011	...	2059	...	...	2211	...	—	2259	...	...	0051	...	...
Lunderskov **705** d.	...	...	1635	│	...	1715	...	...	1835	...	1915	...	...	2034	...	2115	...	...	2235	...	...	2315	...	...	0111	...	...
Kolding **705** d.	1540	1628	1645	1650	...	1728	1740	1828	1845	...	1928	1940	2028	2044	...	2128	2140	2228	2245	...	*IC*	2325	...	...	0119	...	...
Middelfart **700** a.	│	1645	│	│	...	1745	│	1845	│	...	1945	│	2045	│	...	2145	│	2245	│	...	**177**	│	...	...	│	...	...
Fredericia 700 a.	1552	│	1658	1703	1709	│	1752	│	1858	1909	│	1952	│	2057	2106	│	2152	│	2258	2306	2311	2338	0011	0016	0133	0156	0303
Århus **700** a.	1657	│	...	1804	│	│	1857	│	...	│	│	2057	│	2211	│	│	2257	│	...	│	0028	...	│	0120	...	0301	│
Odense **700** a.	...	1711	...	...	1745	1811	...	1911	...	1945	2011	...	2111	...	2142	2211	...	2314	...	2346	...	...	0048	...	...	...	0340
København **700** a.	...	1849	...	...	1919	1949	...	2049	...	2119	2149	...	2249	...	2319	2355	...	0055	...	0131	...	...	0236	...	...	...	0536

♦ – **NOTES** (LISTED BY TRAIN NUMBER)

380/1 – [12] and 🍷 Berlin - Hamburg - Århus and v.v.
386/7 – [12] and 🍷 Århus - Fredericia - Hamburg and v.v.
482 – *City Night Line* HANS CHRISTIAN ANDERSEN – 🛏 1, 2 cl., ▬ 2 cl., [2] [reclining] and 🍴 (⑥ Dec. 26 - Apr. 10, Innsbruck -) München - København; 🛏 1, 2 cl., ▬ 2 cl. (4 / 6 berth), [2] [reclining] and 🍴 Basel - Frankfurt - København; 🛏 1, 2 cl., ▬ 2 cl., [2] [reclining] and 🍷 Amsterdam - Köln - København. Ⓡ.
483 – *City Night Line* HANS CHRISTIAN ANDERSEN – 🛏 1, 2 cl., ▬ 2 cl., [2] [reclining] and 🍴 København - München (- Innsbruck, ⑤ Dec. 25 - Apr. 9 from København); 🛏 1, 2 cl., ▬ 2 cl. (4 / 6 berth), [2] [reclining] and 🍴 København - Frankfurt - Basel; 🛏 1, 2 cl., ▬ 2 cl., [2] [reclining] and 🍷 København - Köln - Amsterdam. Ⓡ.

a – ①–⑤ only.
k – Connects with train in previous column.
p – Daily to Apr. 17; ①–⑥ from Apr. 19.
v – Arrive 0539.
z – Change at Neumünster (see Table **823**).
⊡ – For passengers making international journeys only.
* – Middelfart - Kolding: *23 km*.

712 ÅRHUS - VIBORG - STRUER

2nd class only (IC & Lyn 1st & 2nd class). Operator: *AT*

km		Ⓐ											z			Ⓒ	⑥		⑥				†			
	København 700 d.		...	...	...	...	...	...	...		...	...	...	...	...		...	...	...	...	...	...	...	...		...
0	**Århus 700** ⊗ d.		0517	0617	0724	0824	0924	1024	1224		1824	2024	2124	2224	2324		0449	0617	0724	0824	0924	1024	1124	1224		1824
46	Langå **700** ⊗ a.		0548	0648	0756	0856	0956	1056	1256	and	1856	2056	2156	2256	2356		0531	0648	0756	0856	0956	1056	1156	1256	and	1856
46	Langå ⊗ d.		0553	0653	0800	0900	1000	1100	1300	hourly	1900	2100	2200	2300	0000		0535	0653	0800	0900	1000	1100	1200	1300	hourly	1900
86	Viborg ⊗ d.		0633	0733	0835	0935	1035	1135	1335	until	1935	2136	2236	2336	0036		0609	0733	0836	0936	1036	1136	1236	1336	until	1936
116	Skive d.		0702	0800	0900	1000	1100	1200	1400		2000	2159	2300	0000	0100		0633	0800	0900	1000	1100	1200	1300	1400		2000
148	**Struer** a.		0727	0827	0925	1025	1125	1225	1425		2025	...	2325	0025	0125		0658	0825	0925	1025	1125	1225	1325	1425		2025

		⑥					725 ①–⑤	1625 ⑥	757	765 ⑤†y
København 700 d.	...	...	...	...	...	DSB	0800	0800	1600	1800
Århus 700 ⊗ d.	2024	2124	2224	2324	...	*IC*	1124	1124	1924	2124
Langå **700** ⊗ a.	2056	2156	2256	2356	...	services	1156	1156	1956	2156
Langå ⊗ d.	2100	2200	2300	0000	...	▶▶▶▶	1200	1200	2000	2200
Viborg ⊗ d.	2136	2236	2336	0036	...		1235	1236	2036	2236
Skive d.	2159	2300	0000	0100	...		1300	1300	2100	2300
Struer a.	...	2325	0025	0125	...		1325	1325	2125	2325

	Ⓐ									▲	
Struer d.		0440	0510	0540	0610	0637	0700	0803	0859		1659
Skive d.		0506	0536	0606	0636	0706	0729	0831	0928	and	1729
Viborg ⊗ d.		0532	0602	0632	0702	0738	0758	0858	0958	hourly	1758
Langå ⊗ a.		0606	0637	0706	0737	0812	0832	0932	1032	until	1832
Langå **700** ⊗ d.		0611	0641	0711	0741	0817	0837	0937	1037		1837
Århus 700 ⊗ a.		0643	0713	0743	0813	0849	0909	1009	1109		1909
København 700 a.		...	...	...	...	...	...	...	...		...

						Ⓒ	⑥	⑥												728 ①–⑤	1628 ⑥⑦	1652 ⑤y	752 ⑦	768 ①–⑤	1668 ⑦	
Struer d.	1742	1942	2042	...	2242		...	0539	0631	0742	...	0942		2042	...	2242	...	DSB		0834	0842	1434	1442	1842	1842	...
Skive d.	1812	2012	2112	2212	2312		...	0606	0706	0812	...	1012	and	2112	2212	2312	...	*IC*		0901	0912	1501	1512	1912	1912	...
Viborg ⊗ d.	1838	2038	2138	2238	2338		0529	0633	0738	0838	...	1038	hourly	2138	2238	2338	...	services		0938	0938	1538	1538	1938	1938	...
Langå ⊗ a.	1912	2112	2212	2312	0012		0603	0707	0812	0912	...	1112	until	2212	2312	0012	...	▶▶▶▶		1012	1012	1612	1612	2012	2012	...
Langå **700** ⊗ d.	1917	2117	2217	2317	0017		0608	0712	0817	0917	...	1117		2217	2317	0017	...			1017	1017	1617	1617	2017	2017	...
Århus 700 ⊗ a.	1949	2149	2249	2349	0049		0640	0744	0849	0949	...	1149		2249	2349	0049	...			1049	1049	1649	1649	2049	2049	...
København 700 a.	...	...	...	...	...		...	...	...	...	...	...		...	...	...	...			1419	1419	2019	2019	0026	0026	...

y – Also Dec. 23, Mar. 31, Apr. 29, May 12.
z – ①②③④ (not Dec. 23, Mar. 31, Apr. 29, May 12).

▲ – Timings may vary by up to 3 minutes on some journeys.
⊗ – Additional services operate Århus - Viborg and v.v.

See **Table 715** below for direct services Struer - Herning - København and v.v.

713 ÅRHUS - HERNING - STRUER

2nd class only. Operator: *AT*

km		Ⓐ																Ⓒ	⑥									
0	**Århus 700** ⊗ d.		0457	0557	0714	0846	0914	and at	1646	1714	1746	1846	1946	2046	2146	2246	2346		0546	0745	and	1746	1846	1946	2046	2146	2246	2346
23	Skanderborg **700** ⊗ d.		0517	0620	0734	0906	0934	the same	1706	1734	1806	1906	2006	2106	2206	2306	0008		0606	0806	every	1806	1906	2006	2106	2206	2306	0008
53	Silkeborg ⊗ d.		0546	0655	0807	0937	1007	minutes	1737	1807	1837	1937	2037	2137	2237	2337	0037		0635	0837	two	1837	1937	2037	2137	2237	2337	0037
94	**Herning** ⊗ a.		0632	0735	0847	1017	1047	past	1817	1847	1917	2017	2117	2217	2317	0015	0115		0712	0917	hours	1917	2017	2117	2217	2317	0022	0115
94	**Herning 715** d.		0656	0748	0850	...	1050	each hour	...	1850	...	2044	...	2244	...	...	...		0744	0944	until	1944	...	...	2244	...	...	...
136	**Skjern** a.		0737	0828	0927	...	1127	until	...	1927	...	2121	...	2321	...	...	...		0821	1021		2021	...	...	2321	...	...	...

	Ⓐ																Ⓒ	⑥	Ⓒ	†	†	⑥				Ⓒ		
Skjern d.		0559	0650	0741	0838	0938	1138	...	and at	1738	...	...	1943	...	2143	...		...	0617j	...	0809	0843	1043	and	2043	...	2328	...
Herning 715 a.		0638	0727	0818	0918	1018	1218	...	the same	1818	...	...	2021	...	2221	...		...	0655j	...	0847	0921	1121	every	2121	...	0006	...
Herning ⊗ d.		0652	0752	0821	0921	1021	1221	1251	minutes	1821	1851	1951	2051	2151	2251	...		0551	0656	0751	0851	0951	1151	two	2151	2251	0007	...
Silkeborg ⊗ d.		0735	0836	0902	1002	1102	1302	1336	past	1902	1936	2036	2136	2236	2336	...		0636	0736	0836	0936	1036	1236	hours	2236	2336	0050	...
Skanderborg **700** ⊗ a.		0805	0905	0930	1030	1130	1330	1405	each hour	1930	2005	2105	2205	2305	0005	...		0705	0805	0905	1005	1105	1305	until	2305	0005	0117	...
Århus 700 ⊗ a.		0825	0924	0951	1051	1151	1351	1424	until	1951	2024	2124	2224	2324	0025	...		0724	0824	0924	1024	1124	1324		2324	0025	0137	...

j – ⑥ only.

⊗ – Additional services operate Århus - Herning and v.v.

715 FREDERICIA - STRUER - THISTED

2nd class only (IC & Lyn 1st & 2nd class)

km		*IC* 791	①–⑤	①–⑥	①–⑤	①–⑤	①–⑤	*IC* 113 ①–⑥		*IC* 117		*IC* 721	*IC* 125		*IC* 729	*IC* 133		*IC* 737 ①–⑤	*IC* 1637 ⑥⑦	*IC* 141		①–④	*IC* 745	①–⑤	*IC* 149	
	København 700 d.	0038	...	...	...	...	...	0500	...	0600	...	0700	0800	...	0900	1000	...	1100	1100	1200	...	...	1300	...	1400	...
	Odense 700 d.	0230	...	...	...	...	...	0636	...	0733	...	0833	0933	...	1033	1133	...	1233	1233	1333	...	...	1433	...	1533	...
0	**Fredericia 700** d.	0307	...	0502	...	0600	...	0712	0701	0812	0759	0912	1012	1016	1112	1212	1215	1312	1312	1412	1415	...	1512	...	1612	1615
26	Vejle **700** d.	0324	...	0524	...	0625	...	0726	0731	0826	0833	0934	1026	1033	1134	1226	1233	1334	1334	1426	1434	...	1534	...	1626	1634
99	Herning a.	0416	...	0631	...	0733	...	...	0834	...	0934	1034	...	1134	1234	...	1334	1434	1434	...	1534	...	1634	...	...	1734
99	Herning **713** d.	0417	0537	0642	0656	...	0753	...	0835	...	0935d	1035	...	1135	1235	...	1335	1435	1435	...	1535	1609	1635	1709	...	1735
140	Holstebro **708** d.	0449	0626	0718	0738	...	0834	...	0906	...	1006d	1106	...	1206	1306	...	1406	1506	1506	...	1606	1649	1706	1749	...	1806
155	**Struer 708** a.	0501	0639	0735	0756	...	0847	...	0919	...	1019d	1119	...	1219	1319	...	1419	1519	1519	...	1619	1706	1719	1806	...	1819
229	*Thisted 716* a.	...	...	...	...	...	...	...	...	...	...	...	...	...	...	...	...	1651	1657	...	...	...	...	...	...	...

	IC 753	*IC* 755 ①–④	*IC* 157	⑤–⑦	*IC* 761	*IC* 165	Ⓑ	*IC* 769	*IC* 173	Ⓑ	*IC* 777
København 700 d.	1500	1600	1600	...	1700	1800	...	1900	2000	...	2100
Odense 700 d.	1633	1733	1733	...	1833	1933	...	2033	2133	...	2233
Fredericia 700 d.	1712	1812	1812	1815	1912	2012	2015	2112	2211	2214	2311
Vejle **700** d.	1734	1834	1826	1834	1934	2026	2034	2134	2225	2235	2334
Herning a.	1834	1934	...	1934	2034	...	2134	2234	...	2334	0034
Herning **713** d.	1835	1935	...	1935	2035	...	2135	2235	...	2335	0035
Holstebro **708** d.	1906	2006	...	2006	2106	...	2206	2306	...	0006	0106
Struer 708 a.	1919	2019	...	2019	2119	...	2219	2319	...	0019	0119
Thisted 716 a.	...	...	...	...	2248	...	...	...	...	...	...

	Lyn 706 ①–⑤	①–⑤	*Lyn* 710 ①–⑤	①–⑤	⑥	①–⑤	*Lyn* 14 ①–⑥	①–⑤	*IC* 716	①–⑤	①–⑤
Thisted 716 d.	...	...	...	...	...	...	...	...	...	...	...
Struer 708 d.	0434	0509	0533	...	0543	0551	...	0609	0644	0704	0720
Holstebro **708** d.	0454	0524	0547	...	0557	0606	...	0630	0701	0717	0739
Herning **713** a.	0524	0555	0613	←	0628	0642	...	0710	0733	0748	0810
Herning d.	0528	→	0617	0632	0631	0652	...	...	0738	...	...
Vejle **700** d.	0625	...	0709	0731	0735	0804	0813	...	0834	...	...
Fredericia 700 a.	0641	...	0725	0749	0753	0825	0828	...	0850	...	...
Odense 700 a.	0720	...	0803	...	...	...	0903	...	0945	...	...
København 700 a.	0852	...	0923	...	...	...	1023	...	1119	...	...

	①–⑤	⑥	*IC* 120	*IC* 1624 ⑥⑦	*IC* 724 ①–⑤		*IC* 128	*IC* 732		*IC* 136	*IC* 740		*IC* 144	*IC* 748/50	①–④		*IC* 152/8	*IC* 756		*IC* 160	*IC* 1664 ⑥⑦	*IC* 764 ①–⑤	Ⓑ	*IC* 168		*IC* 776
Thisted 716 d.	...	...	...	0713	0728	...	...	...	...	...	...	...	...	...	...	...	...	...	...	...	1713	1718	...	...	...	...
Struer 708 d.	0741	0751	...	0851	0851	0951	...	1051	1151	...	1251	1351	...	1451	1502	1551	...	1651	1751	...	1851	1851	1951	...	2051	2151
Holstebro **708** d.	0800	0805	...	0905	0905	1005	...	1105	1205	...	1305	1405	...	1505	1522	1605	...	1705	1805	...	1905	1905	2005	...	2105	2205
Herning **713** a.	0834	0835	...	0935	0935	1035	...	1135	1235	...	1335	1435	...	1535	1558	1635	...	1735	1835	...	1935	1935	2035	...	2135	2235
Herning d.	0836	0836	...	0936	0936	1036	...	1136	1236	...	1336	1436	...	1536	...	1636	...	1736	1836	...	1936	1936	2036	...	2136	2236
Vejle **700** d.	0935	0935	0948	1035	1035	1135	1148	1235	1335	1348	1435	1535	1548	1634	...	1734	1748	1835	1935	1946	2035	2035	2135	2148	2235	2335
Fredericia 700 a.	0953	0953	1004	1053	1053	1153	1204	1253	1353	1404	1453	1553	1604	1653	...	1753	1804	1853	1953	2001	2053	2053	2153	2204	2253	2353
Odense 700 a.	...	...	1045	1145	1145	...	1245	1345	...	1445	1545	...	1645	1745	...	...	1845	1945	...	2042	2142	2142	...	2245	...	0048
København 700 a.	...	...	1219	1319	1319	...	1419	1519	...	1619	1719	...	1819	1919	...	...	2019	2119	...	2219	2319	2319	...	0026	...	0236

d – ①–⑥ only.

716 STRUER - THISTED

2nd class only (IC 1st & 2nd class). Operator: *AT* (IC trains: *DSB*)

km		Ⓐ								*IC* 737 K			*IC* 761 K			Ⓒ	⑥					*IC* 1637 K			*IC* 761 K	
0	Struer d.		0448	0545	0800	1032	1232	1333	1432	1532	1651	1853	2129	2337	...		0541	0746	0946	1146	1346	1535	1746	1946	2129	2337
74	Thisted a.		0609	0727	0921	1151	1351	1454	1555	1651	1816	2016	2248	0055	...		0659	0904	1104	1304	1504	1657	1904	2104	2248	0055

	Ⓐ			*IC* 724 K							*IC* 764 K				Ⓒ	⑥	*IC* 1624 K					*IC* 1664 K				
Thisted d.		0512	0615	0728	0824	0958	1158	1357	1458	1618	1718	1918	2215	...		0508	0713	0913	1113	1313	1508	1713	1913	...	2215	...
Struer a.		0633	0733	0847	0942	1120	1320	1520	1620	1741	1837	2037	2336	...		0629	0834	1034	1234	1434	1626	1834	2034	...	2336	...

K – From / to København (Table **715**).

KØBENHAVN - RØDBY - PUTTGARDEN (- HAMBURG) 720

EC services only. For local trains see Table 721

km		*ICE* 38 B	*ICE* 238		*ICE* 36		*EC* 34 q	*ICE* 32		*EC* 30 y
0	**København H** ....d.	0745	0945	...	1145	...	1345	1545	...	1745
20	Høje Taastrup ....● d.	0758	0958	...	1158	...	1358	1558	...	1758
91	Næstved ....● d.	0833	1033	...	1233	...	1433	1633	...	1833
	Vordingborg ....d.	0847	1047	...	1247	...	1447	1647	...	1847
147	Nykøbing (Falster) ....● d.	0912	1112	...	1312	...	1512	1712	...	1912
183	Rødby .... ⛴ ▲ a.	0934	1134	...	1334	...	1534	1734	...	1934
202	**Puttgarden** .... ⛴ ▲ d.	1042	1242	...	1442	...	1642	1842	...	2042
291	*Lübeck* **825** ....a.	1136	1336	...	1536	...	1736	1936	...	2136
353	*Hamburg Hbf* **825** ....a.	1216	1416	...	1616	...	1816	2016	...	2216

	EC 31 z		*ICE* 33		*ICE* 35		*ICE* 237	*ICE* 37 B	*EC* 39 q
Hamburg Hbf **825** ....d.	0725	...	0928	...	1328	...	1525	1728	1928
Lübeck **825** ....d.	0806	...	1006	...	1406	...	1606	1806	2006
Puttgarden .... ⛴ ▲ a.	0905	...	1105	...	1505	...	1705	1905	2105
Rødby .... ⛴ ▲ d.	1005	...	1205	...	1605	...	1805	2005	2205
Nykøbing (Falster) ....● a.	1029	...	1229	...	1629	...	1829	2029	2229
Vordingborg ....a.	1103		1303		1703		1903	2103	2303
Næstved ....● a.	1119	...	1319	...	1719	...	1919	2119	2319
Høje Taastrup ....● a.	1158	...	1358	...	1758	...	1958	2158	2358
København H ....a.	1211	...	1411	...	1811	...	2011	2211	0011

B – (12) and 🍷 København - Berlin and v.v.

q – June 18 - Aug. 22.
y – Dec. 13 - Jan. 10, Mar. 12 - Oct. 24 (not Dec. 24, 31).
z – Dec. 14 - Jan. 11, Mar. 13 - Oct. 25 (not Dec. 25, Jan. 1).

▲ – Through trains are conveyed by ⛴ Rødby - Puttgarden and v.v. ✕ on board ship. Passengers to/from Rødby or Puttgarden may be required to leave or join the train on board the train-ferry. See **Table 2375** for other available sailings.
● – From København stops to pick up only; to København stops to set down only.

KØBENHAVN - NYKØBING - RØDBY 721

km		4201 ①-⑤	4203 ①-⑤		①-⑤		①-⑤			①-⑥			①-⑥				①-⑥	4229		W		①-⑥		①-⑤	⑥⑦
0	**København H 700** .....d.	...	...	0511	...	0611	0641	0711	0811	0845	0911	1011	1045	1111	...	1211	1245	...	1311	1345	1411	1445	1511	1541	1611
20	Høje Taastrup **700** .....d.	...	...	0525	...	0625	0654	0725	0825	0858	0925	1025	1058	1125	...	1225	1258	...	1325	1358	1425	1458	1525	1555	1625
31	Roskilde **700** ....d.	...	...	0535	...	0635	0702	0735	0835	|	0935	1035	|	1135	...	1235	|	...	1335	|	1435	|	1535	1612	1635
64	Ringsted **700** ....d.	...	...	0553	...	0653	0720	0753	0853	|	0953	1053	|	1153	...	1253	|	...	1353	|	1453	|	1553	1629	1653
91	Næstved ....d.	...	...	0611	0655	0711	0737	0811	0911	0933	1011	1111	1133	1211	...	1311	1333	...	1411	1433	1511	1533	1611	1647	1711
118	Vordingborg ....d.	...	...	0629	0715	0729	0751	0829	0929	0947	1029	1129	1147	1229	...	1329	1347	...	1429	1447	1529	1547	1629	1714	1729
147	Nykøbing (Falster) .... ⊙ d.	0512	0650	0658	0738	0758	0811	0858	0958	1007	1058	1158	1207	1258	...	1358	1407	1412	1458	1507	1558	1607	1658	1738	1758
183	**Rødby** ....a.	0539	0712	...	...	...	...	...	...	...	...	...	...	...	...	...	...	1434	...	...	...	...	...	...	...

	2245 ①-⑤	①-⑤	⑧		①-⑤	1249 X		⑧		⑦		2261 ⑦	4261 ①-⑥	⑦	⑦	①-⑥	⑦	⑦	①-⑥	⑦	①-⑥			⑥⑦	Y
København H § **700** ....d.	1611	1641	1645	1711	1741	1745	1811	1845	1911	1945	...	2011	2011	2045	2111	2111	2145	2211	2211	2311	2311	...	0011	0107	...
Høje Taastrup § **700** ....d.	1625	1655	1658	1725	1755	1758	1825	1858	1925	1958	...	2025	2025	2058	2125	2125	2158	2225	2225	2325	2325	...	0025	0123	...
Roskilde § **700** ....d.	1635	1712	|	1735	1812	|	1835	|	1935	|	...	2035	2035	|	2135	2135	|	2235	2235	2335	2335	...	0035	0137	...
Ringsted § **700** ....d.	1653	1729	|	1753	1829	|	1853	|	1953	|	...	2053	2058	|	2153	2158	|	2253	2258	2353	2358	...	0058	0158	0207
Næstved § ....d.	1711	1747	1733	1811	1847	1833	1911	1933	2011	2033	...	2111	2115	2133	2211	2215	2233	2311	2315	0011	0015	...	0115	...	0227
Vordingborg ....d.	1729	1814	1747	1829	1914	1847	1929	1947	2029	2047	...	2129	2133	2147	2229	2233	2247	2329	2333	0029	0033	...	0134	...	...
Nykøbing (Falster) .... ⊙ d.	1803	1838	1807	1858	1938	1912	1958	2007	2058	2107	...	2159	2159	2207	2254	2255	2317	2354	2355	0054	0054	...	0155	...	...
Rødby ....a.	1829	...	...	...	...	1934	...	...	...	...	...	2228	2228	...	...	...	...	...	...	...	...	...	...	...	...

	①-⑤	2202 ①-⑤	⑥⑦	①-⑤	①-⑤		①-⑤	1210 ①-⑤			①-⑤	①-⑤	2214 ①-⑤		①-⑥		①-⑥			Z		①-⑥			①-⑥
Rødby ....d.	...	0426	...	...	...	...	...	0606	...	...	...	...	0722	...	...	...	...	...	...	...	...	...	...	...	...
Nykøbing (Falster) .... ⊙ d.	0444	0451	0451	0519	0544	0551	0615	0638	...	0649	0713	0738	0749	...	0838	0849	0938	0949	...	1038	1049	1138	1149	1249	1338
Vordingborg ....d.	0503	0515	0515	0544	0604	0615	0644	0704	...	0715	0744	0806	0815	...	0904	0915	1004	1015	...	1104	1115	1204	1215	1315	1404
Næstved ....d.	0520	0533	0533	0602	0620	0633	0702	0720	...	0733	0802	0821	0833	...	0920	0933	1020	1033	...	1120	1133	1220	1233	1333	1420
Ringsted **700** ....d.	|	0551	0551	0621	|	0651	0721	|	...	0751	0821	|	0851	...	|	0951	|	1051	...	|	1151	|	1251	1351	|
Roskilde **700** ....a.	|	0608	0608	0638	|	0708	0738	|	...	0813	0838	|	0908	...	|	1008	|	1108	...	|	1208	|	1308	1408	|
Høje Taastrup **700** ....a.	0558	0616	0616	0650	0658	0717	0750	0758	...	0822	0850	0858	0917	...	0958	1017	1058	1117	...	1158	1217	1258	1317	1417	1458
København H 700 ....a.	0611	0631	0631	0706	0711	0732	0806	0811	...	0838	0906	0912	0932	...	1011	1032	1111	1132	...	1211	1232	1311	1332	1432	1511

		①-⑥			4246	⑥⑦	①-⑥			⑧				⑦	⑦	①-⑥		⑦	①-⑥	⑦	①-⑥	4274 ①-⑥	2274 ⑦	Y	
Rødby ....d.	...	...	...	...	1446	...	...	...	...	...	...	...	...	...	...	...	...	...	...	...	...	2238	2238	...	...
Nykøbing (Falster) .... ⊙ d.	1349	1438	1449	...	1510	1538	1538	1549	1649	1738	...	1749	1849	1938	1948	1948	...	2049	2049	2149	2149	2302	2302	...	...
Vordingborg ....d.	1415	1504	1515	...	...	1604	1604	1615	1715	1804	...	1815	1915	2004	2015	2015	...	2115	2115	2215	2215	2324	2325	...	...
Næstved ....d.	1433	1520	1533	...	...	1620	1620	1633	1733	1820	...	1833	1933	2020	2033	2033	...	2133	2133	2233	2233	2340	2342	0124	...
Ringsted **700** ....d.	1451	|	1551	...	...	|	1634	1651	1751	|	...	1851	1951	|	2051	2051	...	2151	2151	2251	2251	2357	0000	0144	...
Roskilde **700** ....a.	1508	|	1608	...	...	|	|	1708	1808	|	...	1908	2008	|	2108	2112	...	2208	2212	2308	2312	0016	0017	...	...
Høje Taastrup **700** ....a.	1517	1558	1617	...	...	1658	1658	1717	1817	1858	...	1917	2017	2058	2117	2121	...	2217	2221	2317	2321	0024	0026	...	...
København H 700 ....a.	1532	1611	1632	...	...	1711	1711	1732	1832	1911	...	1932	2032	2111	2132	2136	...	2232	2236	2332	2336	0039	0042	...	...

W – ①-⑥ Dec. 14 - June 17, Aug. 23 - Dec. 11.
X – ⑧ Jan. 11 - Mar. 11, Oct. 25 - Dec. 10.
Y – ⑦ Apr. 17 - Sept. 18 (not May 23).
Z – ①-⑥ Jan. 12 - Mar. 12, Oct. 26 - Dec. 11.

⊙ – Trains run approximately hourly (more frequent on ①-⑤) Nykøbing (Falster) - Nakskov and v.v., journey 45 minutes (A/S Lollandbanen).

KØBENHAVN - YSTAD - RØNNE 727

km			z	y	⑦x	w	v			A				B	C		D			🚌	🚌	
0	**København H** ....d.	Dec. 13	0639	1007	1339	1659	2039	Jan. 4	0639	1339	1659	Mar. 1	0639	1007	1339	1659	2039	...	Jan. 19, 20	0745	1730	...
11	Kastrup ✈ ....d.	to	0652	1020	1352	1712	2052	to	0652	1352	1712	to	0652	1020	1352	1712	2052	...	and	0815	1800	...
76	**Ystad** ....a.	Jan. 3	0757	1133	1457	1827	2152	Feb. 28	0757	1458	1827	Apr. 28	0757	1132	1458	1827	2152	...	Apr. 20, 21	0930	1915	...
	Ystad ⛴ ....d.	▶▶▶▶	*0830*	*1200*	*1530*	*1900*	*2230*	▶▶▶▶	*0830*	*1530*	*1900*	▶▶▶▶	*0830*	*1200*	*1530*	*1900*	*2230*	...	▶▶▶▶	*1000*	*1945*	...
	Rønne ⛴ ....a.		*0945*	*1315*	*1645*	*2015*	*2345*		*0945*	*1645*	*2015*		*0945*	*1315*	*1645*	*2015*	*2345*	...		*1230*	*2215*	...

		z	y	⑦x	w	v			A				B	C		D			🚌	🚌	
Rønne ⛴ ....d.	Dec. 13	*0645*	*1015*	*1345*	*1715*	*2045*	Jan. 4	*0645*	*1345*	*1715*	Mar. 1	*0645*	*1015*	*1345*	*1715*	*2045*	...	Jan. 19, 20	*0645*	*1630*	...
Ystad ⛴ ....a.	to	*0800*	*1130*	*1500*	*1830*	*2200*	to	*0800*	*1500*	*1830*	to	*0800*	*1130*	*1500*	*1830*	*2200*	...	and	*0915*	*1900*	...
Ystad ....d.	Jan. 3	0817	1147	1518	1847	2220	Feb. 28	0817	1518	1847	Apr. 28	0817	1147	1518	1847	2220	...	Apr. 20, 21	0950	1935	...
Kastrup ✈ ....a.	▶▶▶▶	0917	1254	1619	1947	2319	▶▶▶▶	0917	1619	1947	▶▶▶▶	0917	1254	1619	1947	2319	...	▶▶▶▶	1105	2050	...
København H ....a.		0931	1309	1633	2001	2333		0931	1633	2001		0931	1309	1633	2001	2333	...		1135	2120	...

A – ⑤ Feb. 5 - 26.
B – ⑥ Mar. 27 - Apr. 28 (also Mar. 28, 31, Apr. 1 - 3, 5, 6).
C – ⑤⑥⑦ (also Mar. 27, 31, Apr. 1, 5, 19, 26; not Apr. 2, 4).
D – ⑦ Mar. 27 - Apr. 28 (also Mar. 27, 31, Apr. 5).

v – Dec. 18, 23, 27.
w – Not Dec. 24, 31.
x – Also Dec. 18, 19, 23, Jan. 1; not Dec. 20.
y – Dec. 19, 20, 23 - 31.
z – Not Jan. 1.

728 BRANCH LINES in Denmark

2nd class only

ÅRHUS - GRENAA: 69 km

	①–⑥	①–⑥			and							
Århus d.	0514	0614	...	0714	hourly	2214	...	2324	...	...	...	...
Grenaa a.	0626	0726	...	0828	until	2328	...	0037	...	...	...	...

	①–⑤	①–⑤	①–⑥	①–⑥		and						
Grenaa d.	0502	0532	0632	0732	0832	hourly	1832	1933	2033	2133	2233	2339
Århus a.	0614	0644	0744	0844	0945	until	1945	2045	2145	2245	2347	0053

ODENSE - SVENDBORG: 48 km

	①–⑥			①–⑥	and		①–⑥		and				
Odense d.	0531	0631	0731	0801	hourly	1631	1701	1731	hourly	2231	2341	...	...
Svendborg a.	0612	0712	0812	0843	until	1712	1743	1812	until	2312	0022	...	...

	①–⑤	①–⑥			①–⑥	and		①–⑥		and			
Svendborg d.	0520	0620	0720	0820	0850	hourly	1720	1750	1820	hourly	2220	2330	0030
Odense a.	0602	0702	0802	0902	0931	until	1802	1831	1902	until	2302	0012	0121

HJØRRING - HIRTSHALS: Valid December 13 - June 25

Nordjyske Jernbaner A/S *18 km* Journey 22 minutes

From **Hjørring**: *On Dec. 24, 28-31 a ⑥ service operates.*

①–⑤: 0454, 0546, 0611, 0640, 0708, 0741, 0810, 0906, 1006, 1106, 1206, 1306, 1411, 1511, 1611, 1641, 1711, 1741, 1811, 1906, 2106, 2306.

⑥: 0706, 0806, and hourly until 1406, then 1606, 1706, 1806 **x**, 1906 **x**, 2106 **x**, 2306 **x**.

⑦: 0806, 0906, 1106, 1206, 1306, 1406, 1606, 1706, 1806, 1906, 2106, 2306.

From **Hirtshals / Color Line**: *On Dec. 24, 28-31 a ⑥ service operates.*

①–⑤: 0520, 0612, 0641, 0706, 0740, 0811, 0837, 0937, 1037, 1137, 1237, 1342, 1442, 1542, 1642, 1712, 1742, 1812, 1837, 2010, 2137, 2332.

⑥: 0737, 0837, and hourly until 1437, 1637, 1737, 1837 **x**, 2014 **x**, 2137 **x**, 2332 **x**.

⑦: 0837, 0937, 1137, 1237, 1337, 1437, 1637, 1737, 1837, 2014, 2137, 2332.

x – Not Dec. 24, 31.

ICELAND

There are no railways in Iceland but bus services serve all major settlements (some are only served in summer, particularly in the eastern part of the country). Principal bus services enabling a circuit around the country are shown below - see the right hand column for operating dates of each journey. See www.bsi.is and www.austurleid.is for further information.

729 PRINCIPAL BUS SERVICES

Winter 2009–2010

Clockwise direction	*depart / arrive*	*Anti-clockwise direction*	*depart / arrive*	*Days of operation (applies to both directions)*
Reykjavik - Akureyri △:	d. 0830 a. 1430*	Akureyri - Reykjavik △:	d. 0830 a. 1430*	Daily May 1 - Sept. 30; ①–⑥ Oct. 1 - May 31.
	d. 1500 a. 2100		d. 1500 a. 2100	⑦ Oct. 1 - Apr. 30.
	d. 1700 a. 2300		d. 1700 a. 2300	⑤ Oct. 1 - Apr. 30; ⑤⑦ May 1 - June 14; daily June 15 - Aug. 31; ⑤⑦ Sept. 1 - 30.
Akureyri - Egilsstadir:	d. 0800 a. 1155	Egilsstadir - Akureyri:	d. 1300 a. 1645	Daily June 1 - Aug. 31. Limited winter service.
Egilsstadir - Hofn:	d. 0745 a. 1100	Hofn - Egilsstadir:	d. 1700 a. 2015	Daily June 1 - Aug. 31. No winter service.
Hofn - Reykjavik:	d. 1100 a. 1855	Reykjavik - Hofn:	d. 0830 a. 1615	Daily June 1 - Sept. 14.
	d. 1200 a. 1900		d. 1400 a. 2025	⑤⑦ Sept. 18 - May 30.
	d. 1200 a. 1900		d. 1500 a. 2125	② Sept. 15 - May 25.

Blue Lagoon: departures several times per day from Reykjavik, also infrequent departures from Kevlavik Airport to Blue Lagoon.

Egilsstadir - Seydisfjördur (for Smyril ferry, Table **2285**) June 1 - Aug. 31: depart Egilsstadir 0950 Ⓐ, 1300 ③⑥⑦ **b**, 1345 ④, 1705 Ⓐ; depart Seydisfjördur 0820 Ⓐ, 1220 ③⑥⑦ **b**, 1250 ④, 1610 Ⓐ. A limited service operates in winter.

Reykjavik - Thingvellir - Geysir - Gulfoss: depart Reykjavik 1100 July 1 - Aug. 31, arriving back at 1930 (also 0830 to Geysir, arriving back 1600).

b – June 28 - Aug. 10. * – 1415 June 1 - Aug. 31.

△ – Additional journey runs via interior *Kjolur* route via Geysir and Gulfoss daily June 18 - Sept. 4: Reykjavik 0800 → Akureyri 1700; Akureyri 0800 → Reykjavik 1700. Reservation compulsory.

SWEDEN

SEE MAP PAGE 337

Operators: Most services are operated by **Statens Järnvägar** - Swedish State Railways (*SJ*). There is, however, a number of other operators which run services shown within the European Timetable; these are indicated by their initials in the relevant table heading, or at the top of each train column where more than one operator runs services on the same route.
AEX – Arlanda Express (A-Train AB). *MER* – MerResor. *Øtåg* – Øresundståg. *ST* – Svenska Tågkompaniet AB. *VEO* – Veolia Transport.
The Regional Public Transport Authority is responsible for many local services, known collectively as Länstrafik (*LT*). Those shown within these pages are abbreviated as follows:
LTAC – Länstrafiken Västerbotten. *Skåne* – Skånetrafiken. *V* – Västtrafik. *VTAB* – Värmlandstrafik.

Services: Trains convey first and second classes of accommodation, unless otherwise shown. The fastest trains are classified *X2000* (high-speed trains). Sleeping cars (🛏) are of two basic types with a range of supplements: older cars (those without showers) have one berth in first class, two or three berths in second class. Newer cars either have compartments with shower and WC (one or two berth, first class only) or have shower and WC available in the car (one or two berths in first class, two berths in second class). Couchette cars (▬) have six berths and are second class only. Refreshment services (✕, 🍸, Bistro or Shop) may be available for part of the journey only.

Timings: Valid from **December 13, 2009** except where indicated otherwise. Alterations may be made on and around the dates of public holidays.

Tickets: Through journeys between Länstrafik and Statens Järnvägar, Veolia Transport or Svenska Tågkompaniet are possible with a combined ticket known as 'Tågplus'. Similarly, Arlanda Express may be combined with Statens Järnvägar journeys. However, Veolia Transport and Svenska Tågkompaniet have their own fare structures and tickets cannot be combined with those of Statens Järnvägar.

Reservations: Seat reservation is compulsory on all *X2000* and night trains, and for through journeys to København (excluding local and *Skåne* services). Reserved seats are not labelled and, if occupied, must be claimed by presenting the seat ticket on the train.

Supplements: Special supplements are payable for travel on *X2000* high-speed trains.

730 STOCKHOLM - MALMÖ - KØBENHAVN

km				*X2000*	*X2000*			*X2000*			*X2000*			*X2000*	*X2000*		*X2000*		*X2000*		*X2000*	*VEO*	*X2000*	235	
		67	69	519	521	273	221	523	223	225	525	201	277	527	529	229	531		533	233	535	7153	537	237	289
		🅁	🅁	🅁✕	🅁✕			🅁✕			🅁✕			🅁✕	🅁✕		🅁✕		🅁✕		🅁✕	2	🅁✕		
		♦	♦	Ⓐz	⚒	Ⓐn	Ⓐ	Ⓐ	⑥	Ⓐ		⚒n	Ⓐn	⑤y							⑤†x	⑥n			Ⓐn
0	**Stockholm** Central ‡ d.	...	...	0521	0621	0651	0706	0721	0800	0814	0821	0825	0855	0921	1021	1040	1121	...	1221	1240	1321	1408	1421	1440	1451
15	Flemingsberg ‡ d.	...	...	|	|	|	0717	|	0811	0825	|	|	|	|	1032	1051	|	...	|	1251	1332	|	1432	1451	|
36	Södertälje Syd ‡ d.	...	...	0539	0639	|	0728	|	0821	0835	0839	0845	|	0940	|	1102	1139	...	1239	1302	|	|	|	1502	|
	Katrineholm **740 754** d.	...	...	|	|	|	|	0814	|	|	|	|	|	|	|	|	|	...	|	|	|	|	|	|	|
103	Nyköping d.	...	...	|	|	|	0810	|	0901	0925	|	|	|	|	|	1142	|	...	|	1342	|	1515	|	1542	|
162	**Norrköping** d.	0500s	0529s	0635	0735	0813	0850	0837	0941	1006	0935	0953	1015	1037	1135	1227	1235	...	1335	1427	1435	1553	1535	1627	1611
209	Linköping d.	0534s	0559s	0700	0800	0841	0916	0902	1007	1032	1000	1022	1043	1102	1200	1253	1300	...	1400	1453	1500	1622	1600	1653	1640
241	**Mjölby 755** d.	|	|	|	0815	...	...	|	...	...	1015	|	...	|	1215	...	|	...	1415	...	|	|	1615	...	...
277	Tranås d.	|	|	0729	|	...	...	|	...	...	|	|	...	|	|	...	|	...	|	...	|	|	|	...	...
329	**Nässjö 733** d.	0640s	0703s	0753	0853	...	...	0953	...	...	1053	1122	...	1153	1253	...	1353	...	1453	...	1553	1731	1653	...	...
416	Alvesta d.	0728s	0750s	0827	0927	...	...	1027	...	...	1127	1206	...	1227	1327	...	1427	...	1527	...	1627	1814	1727	...	...
514	Hässleholm **745/6** a.	0814s	0835s	0902	1002	...	...	1105	...	...	1202	1248	...	1302	1402	...	1502	...	1602	...	1702	1902	1802	...	...
581	Lund **745/6** § a.	0920s	0920s	0931	1031	...	...	1134	...	...	1231	1324	...	1331	1431	...	1531	...	1631	...	1731	1940	1831	...	...
597	**Malmö C 745/6** a.	|	|	0946	1046	...	...	1149	...	...	1246	|	...	1346	1446	...	1546	...	1646	...	1746	|	1846	...	...
597	**Malmö C 703** d.	|	|	...	1059	...	...	...	...	...	1259	|	...	...	1459	...	...	...	1659	...	...	|	1859	...	...
	Malmö Syd / Svågertorp a.	0946	0946	...	|	...	...	...	...	...	|	1346	...	...	|	...	...	...	|	...	...	2002	|	...	...
633	København (Kastrup) ✈ **703** a.	...	...	...	1119s	...	...	...	...	...	1319s	...	...	...	1519s	...	...	...	1719s	...	...	...	1919s	...	...
645	**København H 703** a.	...	...	...	1133	...	...	...	...	...	1333	...	...	...	1533	...	...	...	1733	...	...	...	1933	...	...

♦ – **NOTES** (LISTED BY TRAIN NUMBER)

67 – † Dec. 14 - Mar. 7; ④† Mar. 8 - Apr. 11 (from Duved): 🛏, ▬ and 2 Duved - Stockholm - Malmö; ✕ and Bistro Duved - Sundsvall; ✕ Norrköping - Malmö.

69 – ④⑤⑥ Dec. 13 - Mar. 6; ⑤⑥ Mar. 7 - Apr. 10: 🛏, ▬ and 2 Storlien (**77**) - Stockholm - Malmö; 🍸 Norrköping - Malmö.

n – Jan. 11 - June 19.
s – Stops to set down only.
x – Not Dec. 21 - Jan. 9.
y – Not Dec. 28 - Jan. 10.
z – Not Dec. 21 - Jan. 10.

‡ – Most trains on this table do not convey passengers for local journeys between Stockholm and Södertälje Syd and v.v. Local trains run every 30 minutes Stockholm Central - Södertälje Hamn - Södertälje Centrum and v.v. (journey 42 mins). 🚌 Södertälje Syd - Södertälje Centrum runs every 30 minutes.

§ – From Malmö stops to pick up only, to Malmö stops to set down only. Frequent local trains run between Lund and Malmö.

STOCKHOLM - MALMÖ - KØBENHAVN 730

	539	7143	291	203	541	241	293	503	513	543	505	263	263	545	245	7155	7123	299	249	247	251		1	7149	7121
	X2000	VEO			X2000			X2000	X2000	X2000	X2000			X2000		VEO	VEO							VEO	VEO
	R ✕	2			R ✕			R ✕	R ✕	R ✕	R ✕	q		R ✕		2	2		t				R	2	2
	Ⓑ	H	Ⓐ n	Ⓑ		Ⓑ	Ⓐ t	Ⓑ x	◆	Ⓑ m	Ⓑ w	①–④	J			⑤ t	◆	G q	①–④	† q			◆	◆	◆
Stockholm Central ‡ d.	1521	1538	1551	1615	1621	1640	1644	1706	1721	1721	1740	1745	1745	1821	1840	1900	1900	1930	2040	2040	2145	...	2306	2315	2358
Flemingsberg ‡ d.	1532	|	|	|	|	1651	1655	|	1732	1732	|	1756	1756	|	1851	|	|	|	2051	2051	2156	...	|	|	|
Södertälje Syd ‡ d.	|	|	|	|	1639	1702	|	|	|	|	1758	1808	1808	1839	1902	|	|	1949	2102	2102	2208	...	2331u	|	|
Katrineholm **740 754** d.	|	|	|	|	|	|	|	|	|	|	|	|	|	|	|	|	|	|	|	|	|	...	|	|	|
Nyköping d.	|	1637	|	|	|	1742	|	|	|	|	|	1850	1850	|	1942	1954	|	|	2142	2142	2249	...	|	|	|
Norrköping d.	1635	1728	1709	1754	1735	1827	1808	|	1835	1835	|	1928	1938	1935	2027	2040	2040	2055	2222	2224	2329	...	0048	0053	0136
Linköping d.	1700	1803	1737	1825	1800	1853	1835	1840	1900	1900	|	...	2003	2000	2053	2108	2115	2122	2248	2252	2355	...	0123	0128	0203
Mjölby 755 d.	|	|	...	|	1815	...	...	|	|	|	|	...	...	2015	...	|	|	...	...	...	...	...	|	|	|
Tranås d.	|	|	...	|	|	...	...	|	1929	1929	|	...	...	|	...	|	|	...	...	...	...	...	|	|	|
Nässjö 733 d.	1753	1908	...	1939	1853	...	...	|	1953	1955	|	...	...	2053	...	2213	2217	...	...	...	...	...	|	|	0312
Alvesta d.	1827	1959	...	2037	1927	...	...	|	...	2029	2033	...	...	2127	...	2256	2303	...	...	...	...	...	|	0355	0358
Hässleholm **745/6** a.	1902	2046	...	2121	2002	...	...	2034	...	2104	2108	...	...	2202	...	2344	2354	...	...	...	...	...	0445s	0509	0449
Lund **745/6** § a.	1931	2122	...	2159	2031	...	...	2102	...	2133	2137	...	...	2231	...	0019	0033	...	...	...	...	...	0604s	0613s	0526s
Malmö C 745/6 a.	1946	|	...	|	2046	...	...	2116	...	2148	2155	...	...	2246	...	|	|	...	...	...	...	...	0627	|	|
Malmö C 703 d.	...	|	...	|	...	...	...	...	...	2159	2205	...	...	...	...	|	|	...	...	...	...	...	...	|	|
Malmö Syd / Svågertorp a.	...	2147	...	2220	...	...	...	...	...	|	|	...	...	...	...	0042	0056	...	...	...	...	...	...	0647	0547
København (Kastrup) ✈ **703** a.	...	...	...	...	...	...	...	...	...	2219s	2227s	...	...	...	...	...	...	...	...	...	...	...	...	...	...
København H 703 a.	...	...	...	...	...	...	...	...	...	2233	2241	...	...	...	...	...	...	...	...	...	...	...	...	...	...

	218	260	270	220	520	222	272	512	224	522	524	516	226	526	526	7140	528	230	202	530	7152	532	234	534	236
					X2000			X2000		X2000	X2000	X2000		X2000	X2000	VEO	X2000			X2000	VEO	X2000		X2000	
					R ✕			R ✕		R ✕	R ✕	R ✕		R ✕	R ✕	2	R ✕			R ✕	2	R ✕		R ✕	
	Ⓐ	Ⓐ t	Ⓐ t	Ⓐ	Ⓐ z	Ⓐ	Ⓐ n	◆	⑥	Ⓐ	Ⓐ z	◆		†	⚒	⑥	⚒		⚒ n		L	⑤⑥ v	Ⓑ		⑥
København H 703 d.	...	...	...	...	...	...	...	...	...	...	...	...	...	...	0619	...	...	...	...	...	...	...	...	1019	...
København Kastrup ✈ **703** d.	...	...	...	...	...	...	...	...	...	...	...	...	...	...	0631u	...	...	...	...	...	...	...	...	1032u	...
Malmö Syd / Svågertorp d.	...	...	...	...	...	...	...	...	...	...	...	...	...	...	|	0712	...	...	...	...	0913	...	...	|	...
Malmö C 703 a.	...	...	...	...	...	...	...	...	...	...	...	...	...	...	0701	|	...	...	...	...	|	...	...	1052	...
Malmö C 745/6 d.	...	...	...	...	...	...	...	...	...	0511	0614	...	...	0714	0714	|	0814	...	0817	0915	|	1013	...	1114	...
Lund **745/6** § d.	...	...	...	...	...	...	...	...	...	0525	0628	...	...	0728	0728	0731	0828	...	0831	0928	0930	1028	...	1128	...
Hässleholm **745/6** d.	...	...	...	...	...	...	...	...	...	0554	0657	...	...	0757	0757	0806	0857	...	0905	0957	1005	1057	...	1157	...
Alvesta **746** d.	...	...	...	...	...	...	...	...	...	0631	0734	...	...	0834	0834	|	0934	...	0949	1034	1053	1134	...	1234	...
Nässjö 733 d.	...	...	...	...	...	...	...	0642	...	0705	0808	0808	...	0908	0908	|	1008	...	1032	1108	1137	1208	...	1308	...
Tranås d.	...	...	...	...	...	...	...	0703	...	|	|	|	...	|	|	|	|	...	|	|	|	|	...	|	...
Mjölby 755 d.	...	...	...	...	...	...	...	|	...	0740	|	|	...	0943	0943	|	|	...	|	1143	|	|	...	1343	...
Linköping d.	0506	0528e	0600	0615	0638	0700	0724	0740	0750	0800	0900	0900	0905	1000	1000	1031	1100	1105	1135	1200	1234	1257	1305	1400	1410
Norrköping 754 d.	0534	0556	0627	0643	0702	0728	0751	0804	0818	0824	0924	0924	0933	1024	1024	1100	1124	1133	1204	1224	1302	1322	1333	1424	1438
Nyköping d.	0617	0645	|	0724	|	0808	|	|	0859	|	|	|	1013	|	|	|	|	1213	|	|	1343	|	1413	|	1518
Katrineholm **740 754** a.	|	|	|	|	|	|	|	|	|	|	|	|	|	|	|	|	|	|	|	|	|	|	|	|	|
Södertälje Syd ‡ a.	0656	0725	0730	0805	0757	0847	|	0900	0938	0919	|	|	1052	1118	1118	|	|	1252	1310	1319	|	|	1452	1518	1557
Flemingsberg ‡ a.	0706	0736	0741	0816	0807	0856	|	0911	0948	|	1026	1026	1102	|	|	|	1226	1302	|	|	|	1424	1502	|	1607
Stockholm Central ‡ a.	0720	0750	0754	0831	0820	0909	0920	0923	1001	0939	1039	1039	1115	1139	1139	1235	1239	1315	1335	1339	1458	1437	1515	1539	1620

	536	238	7154	538	290	540	244	242	292	542	544	246	204	206	546	7120	7122	66	68	548	550	7148	8	2	208
	X2000		VEO	X2000		X2000				X2000	X2000				X2000	VEO	VEO			X2000	X2000	VEO			
	R ✕		2	R ✕		R ✕				R ✕	R ✕				R ✕	2	2	R	R	R ✕	R ✕	2	R	R	R
		Ⓑ	⑤ t		Ⓐ n	Ⓑ	⑥	Ⓑ	Ⓐ n		Ⓑ	Ⓑ	⑤†	K		◆	◆	◆	◆	† x	Ⓑ	④	◆	◆	◆
København H 703 d.	...	...	...	1219	...	...	...	...	...	1419	...	...	...	...	1619	...	...	...	...	...	1819	...	...	...	...
København Kastrup ✈ **703** d.	...	...	...	1232u	...	...	...	...	...	1432u	...	...	...	...	1632u	...	...	...	...	...	1832u	...	...	...	...
Malmö Syd / Svågertorp d.	...	...	1205	|	...	...	...	...	...	|	...	...	1600	1600	|	1638	1638	1742	1742	...	|	2157	...	...	2257
Malmö C 703 a.	...	...	|	1252	...	...	...	...	...	1452	...	...	|	|	1652	|	|	|	|	...	1852	|	...	...	|
Malmö C 745/6 d.	1214	...	|	1314	...	1414	...	...	...	1514	1611	...	|	|	1714	|	|	|	|	1812	1914	|	2248	2248	|
Lund **745/6** § d.	1228	...	1225	1328	...	1428	...	...	...	1528	1626	...	1632	1632	1728	1656	1654	1759u	1759u	1828	1928	2216u	2303u	2303u	2315u
Hässleholm **745/6** d.	1257	...	1303	1357	...	1457	...	...	...	1557	1654	...	1706	1706	1757	1731	1743	1831u	1831u	1857	1957	2302	0013u	2359u	0013u
Alvesta **746** d.	1334	...	1354	1434	...	1534	...	...	...	1634	1734	...	1758	1758	1834	1819	1838	1917u	1917u	1934	2034	0009	|	|	|
Nässjö 733 d.	1408	...	1441	1508	...	1608	...	...	...	1708	1808	...	1840	1840	1908	1912	1929	2014u	2014u	2008	2108	|	|	|	|
Tranås d.	|	...	|	|	...	|	...	...	...	|	|	...	|	|	|	|	|	|	|	|	2129	|	|	|	|
Mjölby 755 d.	|	...	|	1543	...	|	...	...	...	1743	|	...	|	|	1943	|	|	|	|	|	|	|	|	|	|
Linköping d.	1458	1505	1550	1600	1615	1658	1705	1705	1715	1800	1858	1905	1939	1945	2000	2015	2040	2117u	2117u	2057	2200	0237	0315s	0315s	0315s
Norrköping 754 d.	1522	1533	1635	1624	1643	1722	1733	1733	1743	1824	1922	1933	2009	2013	2024	2046	2111	2145u	2145u	2122	2224	0355	0349s	0349s	0349s
Nyköping d.	|	1613	|	|	|	|	1814	1814	|	|	|	2013	|	|	|	|	|	...	...	|	|	|	|	|	|
Katrineholm **740 754** a.	|	|	|	|	|	|	|	|	|	|	|	|	|	|	|	|	|	...	...	|	|	|	|	|	|
Södertälje Syd ‡ a.	|	1652	|	1718	|	|	1853	1857	|	1918	|	2052	|	|	2119	|	|	...	...	|	2318	|	0528s	0528s	0528s
Flemingsberg ‡ a.	1624	1702	|	|	|	1827	1903	1907	|	|	2027	2102	|	|	|	|	|	...	...	|	|	|	|	|	|
Stockholm Central ‡ a.	1639	1715	1813	1739	1805	1839	1916	1920	1905	1939	2039	2115	2135	2145	2139	2221	2252	...	...	2235	2339	0600	0556	0556	0556

◆ – **NOTES** (LISTED BY TRAIN NUMBER)

1 – Ⓑ (not Dec. 23 - Jan. 9): 🛏 and ▬ (also [2] until Dec. 22, and from June 14) Stockholm - Malmö.
2 – Ⓑ Dec. 13 - 22; Ⓐ Jan. 10 - June 13; Ⓐ June 14 - 19: 🛏 and ▬ (also [2] until Dec. 22, and from June 14) Malmö - Stockholm.
8 – † Jan. 10 - June 19: 🛏 and ▬ Malmö - Stockholm.
66 – ⑥ Dec. 13 - Mar. 7; ③⑥ Mar. 8 - Apr. 11: 🛏, ▬ and [2] Malmö - Stockholm - Duved; ✕ and [Bio] Malmö - Stockholm; ✕ Sundsvall - Duved.
68 – ③④⑤ Dec. 13 - Mar. 7; ④⑤ Mar. 8 - Apr. 11: 🛏, ▬ and [2] Malmö - Stockholm (**76**) - Storlien; ✕ Malmö - Stockholm.
208 – † Jan. 10 - June 19: ▬ Malmö - Stockholm.
512 – Ⓐ (not Dec. 21 - Jan. 10): [12] and ✕ Jönköping - Nässjö - Stockholm.
513 – Ⓑ (not Dec. 20 - Jan. 9): [12] and ✕ Stockholm - Nässjö - Jönköping.
516 – ⑥ (not Dec. 21 - Jan. 10): [12] and ✕ Jönköping - Nässjö - Stockholm.
7120 – ⑥ Dec. 19 - Apr. 10: ▬, [2] and ✕ Malmö - Storlien.
7121 – † Dec. 20 - Apr. 11: ▬, [2] and ✕ Storlien - Malmö.
7122 – ③ Dec. 29 - Apr. 7: ▬, [2] and ✕ Malmö - Duved.
7123 – ④ Dec. 30 - Apr. 10 (from Duved): ▬, [2] and ✕ Duved - Malmö.
7149 – † Apr. 12 - June 19: ▬ and [2] Stockholm - Malmö.

G – ①②③④† only.
H – ⑤† (also ①②③④⑥ Dec. 26 - Jan. 10).
J – ⑤ (Ⓐ Dec. 24 - Jan. 5).
K – ④ (also ①②③ from Jan. 11).
L – † Dec. 13 - 20; daily Dec. 26 - Jan. 10; † Jan. 11 - June 19.
e – ① only.
m – Dec. 20 - Jan. 9.
n – Jan. 11 - June 19.
q – Not Dec. 24 - Jan. 5.
s – Stops to set down only.
u – Stops to pick up only.
t – Not Dec. 24 - Jan. 6.
v – Not Dec. 24 - Jan. 10.
w – Not Dec. 20 - Jan. 9.
x – Not Dec. 21 - Jan. 9.
z – Not Dec. 21 - Jan. 10.
‡ – see page 344.
§ – see page 344.

MALMÖ - YSTAD 731

Operator: *Skåne* 65 km Journey time: 45 minutes 2nd class only

From **Malmö**: 0019②③④⑤⑥†, 0119Ⓒ, 0545⚒, 0619Ⓐ, 0645Ⓐ, 0719, 0745Ⓐ, 0819, 0919, 1019, 1119, 1219, 1319, 1419, 1445Ⓐ, 1519, 1545Ⓐ, 1619, 1645Ⓐ, 1719, 1745Ⓐ, 1819, 1845Ⓐ, 1919, 2019, 2119, 2219, 2319.

From **Ystad**: 0510Ⓐ, 0540Ⓐ, 0610⚒, 0640Ⓐ, 0710⚒, 0740Ⓐ, 0810, 0840Ⓐ, 0910, 1010, 1110, 1210, 1310, 1410, 1440Ⓐ, 1510, 1540Ⓐ, 1610, 1640Ⓐ, 1710, 1740Ⓐ, 1810, 1840Ⓐ, 1910, 1940Ⓐ, 2010, 2110, 2210, 2310, 0010Ⓒ.

SKÖVDE - JONKÖPING - NÄSSJÖ 733

2nd class only except where shown

km																													
		Ⓐ	Ⓐ S q	Ⓐ	⑥ S q	Ⓐ	⑥	Ⓐ	Ⓐ	Ⓐ		⑥	⑥		Ⓐ	Ⓐ		Ⓐ	⚒		†	Ⓐ	Ⓑ		Ⓑ	Ⓑ		Ⓑ	⑥
0	**Skövde 740** d.	*0450*	...	*0557*	...	0627	0656	0658	0725	...	0854	0925	...	1054	1124	...	1254	1355	...	1454	1532	1552	...	1702	1800	...	1849j	2057	*2237*
	Göteborg d.	|	...	|	...	|	|	|	|	0657	|	|	0902	|	|	1102	|	|	1302	|	|	|	1502	|	|	1707	|	|	|
30	Falköping **740** d.	0511	...	0621	...	0650	0716	0718	0747	0820	0916	0943	1020	1114	1142	1220	1316	1413	1420	1514	1548	1610	1616	1725	1818	1828	1916	2120	2258
100	Jönköping a.	0551	...	0707	...	0739	0756	0758	0829	0902	1001	...	1100	1159	...	1301	1401	...	1500	1601	...	...	1702	1810	...	1911	2001	2208	2343
100	Jönköping d.	0553	0610	0710	0735	0742	0800	0802	...	0904	1010	...	1102	1201	...	1310	1407	...	1509	1607	...	...	1708	1812	...	1914	2003	2210	2345
143	**Nässjö 730** a.	0624	0637	0741	0802	0816	0838	0838	...	0942	1041	...	1140	1238	...	1341	1441	...	1548r	1642	...	...	1741	1843	...	1945	2041	2241	0016

	Ⓐ	Ⓐ	Ⓐ	⑥	⚒	Ⓐ	⑥		Ⓐ	Ⓐ			⑥		Ⓐ	Ⓐ		Ⓐ	Ⓑ	Ⓐ	†		Ⓑ	Ⓑ		Ⓑ S p			
Nässjö 730 d.	0449	0545	0702	0725	0824	...	...	0921	1017	...	1120	...	1225	1317	1420	...	1523	1552	1617	...	...	1721	1819	...	1921	2002	...	2120	...
Jönköping a.	0521	0622	0737	0759	0900	...	...	0953	1050	...	1150	...	1300	1350	1454	...	1559	1623	1658	...	...	1752	1851	...	1954	2032	...	2152	...
Jönköping d.	0523	0625	0740	0801	0902	...	...	1001	1102	...	1201	...	1304	1401	1501	...	1601	1632	1702	...	...	1754	1853	...	2003	...	...	2154	...
Falköping **740** a.	0606	0706	0833	0842	0945	0950	1019	1045	1143	1152	1245	...	1344	1445	1543	1550	1646	1718	1742	1754	1756	1842	1942	1950	2044	...	...	2235	2243
Göteborg a.	|	|	|	|	1057	|	|	|	1257	|	|	...	1457	|	1657	|	|	|	1857	|	|	|	2057	|	|	...	...	...	|
Skövde 740 a.	0629	0735	0854	0902	...	1008	1037	1106	...	1210	1306	...	...	1506	...	1608	1707	1738	...	1815	1814	1902	...	2008	2106	...	...	...	2301

S – *X2000*: [12] and ✕ Stockholm - Nässjö - Jönköping and v.v. R and special supplement payable. Train numbers **512/3/6**.
j – Depart 1856 on Ⓒ.
p – Not Dec. 20 - Jan. 9.
q – Not Dec. 21 - Jan. 10.
r – Arrive 1543 on ⑤⑥.

734 HÄSSLEHOLM - HELSINGBORG

Operator: *Skåne* Journey 55–65 minutes *77 km*

From **Hässleholm**: 0525Ⓐ, 0622⚒, 0722, 0822, and hourly until 2222, then 2322⚒.

From **Helsingborg**: 0536Ⓐ, 0636, 0736, and hourly until 1636, then 1736⑥, 1740Ⓑ, 1836Ⓒ, 1840Ⓐ, 1936, 2036, 2136, 2236, 2336⚒.

735 GÖTEBORG - MALMÖ - KØBENHAVN

km			Øtåg	Øtåg		Øtåg	Øtåg	X2000	Øtåg	Øtåg		Øtåg	Øtåg		Øtåg	Øtåg	X2000	Øtåg	Øtåg		Øtåg	Øtåg			Øtåg	Øtåg	Øtåg
					10881			481			601			609			485			603			661	605			
					[R]			[R]✗									[R]✗										
			Ⓐ	Ⓐ	♦	⚒	Ⓐ	⚒	Ⓐ	Ⓐ	Ⓐ		Ⓐ	⑥		Ⓐ			Ⓐ			Ⓐ	⑤			Ⓐ	Ⓐ
	Oslo Sentral **770**	d.	...	...	...	...	...	...	...	...	...	...	...	...	...	...	...	...	...	...	...	...	...	...	...	...	...
0	**Göteborg**	d.	...	...	...	0542a	0612	0627	0642	0712	0727	0742d	0842	0927	0942	1042	1132	1142	1242	1327	1342	1442	1457	1527	1542	1612	1642
28	Kungsbacka	d.	...	...	...	0600a	0630	|	0700	0730	|	0800d	0900	|	1000	1100	|	1200	1300	|	1400	1500	1515u	|	1600	1630	1700
76	Varberg	d.	...	...	0551s	0621a	0651	0701	0721	0751	0803	0821d	0921	1003	1021	1121	1202	1221	1321	1403	1421	1521	1538	1603	1621	1651	1721
106	Falkenberg	d.	...	...	|	0636a	0706	0717	0736	0806	0818	0836d	0936	1017	1036	1136	1218	1236	1336	1418	1436	1536	1555	1618	1636	1706	1736
150	**Halmstad**	d.	0504	0604	0625s	0704	0725	0739	0804	0825	0839	0904	1004	1035	1104	1204	1240	1304	1404	1437	1504	1604	1617	1639	1704	1725	1804
*	Hässleholm	a.	|	|	|	|	...	0830	|	...	|	|	|	|	|	|	1332	|	|	|	|	|	1718	|	|	...	|
173	Laholm	d.	0515	0615	|	0715	...	|	0815	...	|	0915	1015	|	1115	1215	|	1315	1415	|	1515	1615	|	|	1715	...	1815
185	Båstad	d.	0523	0623	|	0723	...	|	0823	...	|	0923	1023	|	1123	1223	|	1323	1423	|	1523	1623	|	|	1723	...	1823
210	Ängelholm	d.	0545	0645	|	0745	...	|	0845	...	|	0945	1045	|	1145	1245	|	1345	1445	|	1545	1645	|	|	1745	...	1845
237	**Helsingborg**	a.	0604	0704	0733s	0804	...	|	0904	...	0928	1004	1104	1134	1204	1304	|	1404	1504	1528	1604	1704	|	1728	1804	...	1904
237	**Helsingborg 737**	d.	0610	0710	|	0810	...	|	0910	...	0930	1010	1110	1137	1210	1310	|	1410	1510	1530	1610	1710	|	1730	1810	...	1910
259	Landskrona **737**	d.	0622	0722	|	0822	...	|	0922	...	|	1022	1122	|	1222	1322	|	1422	1522	|	1622	1722	|	|	1822	...	1922
290	Lund **737**	a.	0637	0737	0813s	0837	...	0900	0937	...	1002s	1037	1137	1202s	1237	1337	1400	1437	1537	1600s	1637	1737	1800s	1800s	1837	...	1937
306	**Malmö 737**	a.	0652	0752	|	0852	...	0915	0952	...	1017s	1052	1152	1217s	1252	1352	1415	1452	1552	1615s	1652	1752	|	1815s	1852	...	1952
306	**Malmö 703**	d.	0702	0802	|	0902	...	0929	1002	...	|	1102	1202	|	1302	1402	1425	1502	1602	|	1702	1802	|	|	1902	...	2002
	Malmö Syd / Svågertorp	a.	0710	0810	0835	0910	...	|	1010	...	|	1110	1210	|	1310	1410	|	1510	1610	|	1710	1810	1823	|	1910	...	2010
342	København (Kastrup) ✈ **703**	a.	0723	0823	...	0923	...	0947s	1023	...	1047s	1123	1223	1247s	1323	1423	1447s	1523	1623	1647s	1723	1823	...	1847s	1923	...	2023
354	**København H 703**	a.	0737	0837	...	0937	...	1001	1037	...	1100	1137	1237	1301	1337	1437	1500	1537	1637	1701	1737	1837	...	1901	1937	...	2037

		Øtåg	X2000	Øtåg	Øtåg	Øtåg		Øtåg	Øtåg	X2000	Øtåg	Øtåg
			495				607			445		
			[R]✗							[R]✗		
		Ⓐ	Ⓑ		Ⓐ	Ⓐ			Ⓐ	S Ⓑ	⚒	
Oslo Sentral **770**	d.	...	...	...	...	...	...	...	...	...	...	...
Göteborg	d.	1712	1727	1742	1812	1842	1927	1942	2042	2132	2142	2242
Kungsbacka	d.	1730	|	1800	1830	1900	|	2000	2100	2150	2200	2300
Varberg	d.	1751	1801	1821	1851	1921	2003	2021	2119	2209	2221	2321
Falkenberg	d.	1806	1817	1836	1906	1936	2018	2036	2136	2225	2236	2336
Halmstad	d.	1825	1839	1904	1925	2004	2039	2104	2204	2244	2255	2355
Hässleholm	a.	...	1931	|	...	|	|	|	|	...	...	...
Laholm	d.	...	|	1915	...	2015	|	2115	2215	...	...	...
Båstad	d.	...	|	1923	...	2023	|	2123	2223	...	...	...
Ängelholm	d.	...	|	1945	...	2045	|	2145	2245	...	...	...
Helsingborg	a.	...	|	2004	...	2104	2128	2204	2304	...	...	...
Helsingborg 737	d.	...	|	2010	...	2110	2130	2210	2310	...	...	...
Landskrona **737**	d.	...	|	2022	...	2122	|	2222	2322	...	...	...
Lund **737**	a.	...	2000	2037	...	2137	2202s	2237	2337	...	...	...
Malmö 737	a.	...	2015	2052	...	2152	2217s	2252	2352	...	...	...
Malmö 703	d.	...	2029	2102	...	2202	|	2302	...	...	...	...
Malmö Syd / Svågertorp	a.	...	|	2110	...	2210	|	2310	...	...	...	...
København (Kastrup) ✈ **703**	a.	...	2047s	2123	...	2223	2247s	2323	...	...	...	...
København H 703	a.	...	2101	2137	...	2237	2301	2337	...	...	...	...

		X2000	Øtåg	Øtåg	Øtåg	Øtåg	X2000	Øtåg	Øtåg	X2000	Øtåg
		422					426			484	
		[R]✗					[R]✗			[R]✗	
		S Ⓐ§	Ⓐ	Ⓐ	Ⓐ	⚒	S ⑥	Ⓐ	Ⓐ	Ⓐ	
København H 703	d.	...	...	...	...	...	...	...	0523	0530	0623
København (Kastrup) ✈ **703**	d.	...	...	...	...	...	...	...	0536	0540u	0636
Malmö Syd / Svågertorp	d.	...	...	...	...	...	...	...	0548	|	0648
Malmö 703	a.	...	...	...	...	...	...	...	0558	0601	0658
Malmö 737	d.	...	...	...	...	0508a	...	...	0608	0617	0708
Lund **737**	d.	...	...	...	...	0522a	...	...	0622	0629	0722
Landskrona **737**	d.	...	...	...	...	0538a	...	...	0638	|	0738
Helsingborg 737	a.	...	...	...	...	0550a	...	...	0650	|	0750
Helsingborg	d.	...	...	...	...	0553a	...	...	0653	|	0753
Ängelholm	d.	...	...	...	...	0613a	...	...	0713	|	0813
Båstad	d.	...	...	...	...	0637a	...	...	0737	|	0837
Laholm	d.	...	...	...	...	0644a	...	...	0744	|	0844
Hässleholm	d.	...	...	...	...	|	...	...	|	0700	|
Halmstad	d.	0520	0532	0602	0632	0702	0720	0732	0802	0750	0902
Falkenberg	d.	0538	0549	0619	0649	0719	0739	0749	0819	0808	0919
Varberg	d.	0554	0604	0634	0704	0734	0754	0804	0834	0822	0934
Kungsbacka	d.	0613	0627	0657	0727	0757	0813	0827	0857	|	0957
Göteborg	a.	0631	0647	0717	0747	0817	0832	0847	0917	0905	1017
Oslo Sentral **770**	a.	...	...	...	...	...	...	...	...	...	...

		X2000		Øtåg	Øtåg		Øtåg	Øtåg		Øtåg	Øtåg	X2000	Øtåg		Øtåg	Øtåg		Øtåg	Øtåg	X2000	Øtåg	Øtåg	Øtåg			Øtåg	Øtåg
		486	600			608			602			492		660			604			496				10880	610		
		[R]✗										[R]✗								[R]✗				[R]			
		⑥	Ⓐ	Ⓐ		⑥	Ⓐy			Ⓐ			Ⓐ	†	Ⓐ			Ⓐ	Ⓐ	Ⓑ		Ⓐ		♦			⚒
København H 703	d.	0657	0659	0723	0823	0859	0923	1023	1100	1123	1223	1259	1323	...	...	1423	1459	...	1523	1559	1623	1723	1823	...	1859	2023	2223
København (Kastrup) ✈ **703**	d.	0712u	0712u	0736	0836	0912u	0936	1036	1111u	1136	1236	1312u	1336	...	...	1436	1511u	...	1536	1612u	1636	1736	1836	...	1911u	2036	2236
Malmö Syd / Svågertorp	d.	|	|	0748	0848	|	0948	1048	|	1148	1248	|	1348	1437	...	1448	|	...	1548	|	1648	1748	1848	1855	|	2048	2248
Malmö 703	a.	0735	|	0758	0858	|	0958	1058	|	1158	1258	1335	1358	|	...	1458	|	...	1558	1635	1658	1758	1858	|	|	2058	2258
Malmö 737	d.	0742	0742u	0808	0908	0942u	1008	1108	1142u	1208	1308	1345	1408	|	...	1508	1542u	...	1608	1645	1708	1808	1908	|	1942u	2108	2308
Lund **737**	d.	0754	0756u	0822	0922	0954u	1022	1122	1154u	1222	1322	1357	1422	1455u	...	1522	1554u	...	1622	1659	1722	1822	1922	1915u	1953u	2122	2322
Landskrona **737**	d.	|	|	0838	0938	|	1038	1138	|	1238	1338	|	1438	|	...	1538	|	...	1638	|	1738	1838	1938	|	|	2138	2340
Helsingborg 737	a.	|	|	0850	0950	1021	1050	1150	1221	1250	1350	|	1450	|	...	1550	1621	...	1650	|	1750	1850	1950	|	2029	2150	2352
Helsingborg	d.	|	|	0853	0953	1025	1053	1153	1225	1253	1353	|	1453	|	...	1553	1625	...	1653	|	1753	1853	1953	1944u	2030	2153	2353
Ängelholm	d.	|	|	0913	1013	|	1113	1213	|	1313	1413	|	1513	|	...	1613	|	...	1713	|	1813	1913	2013	|	|	2213	0013
Båstad	d.	|	|	0937	1037	|	1137	1237	|	1337	1437	|	1537	|	...	1637	|	...	1737	|	1837	1937	2037	|	|	2237	0037
Laholm	d.	|	|	0944	1044	|	1144	1244	|	1344	1444	|	1544	|	...	1644	|	...	1744	|	1844	1944	2044	|	|	2244	0044
Hässleholm	d.	0830	0830	|	|	|	|	|	|	|	|	1428	|	1532	...	|	|	...	|	1728	|	|	|	|	|	|	|
Halmstad	d.	0920	0923	1002	1102	1123	1202	1302	1319	1402	1502	1521	1602	1628	1632	1702	1723	1732	1802	1818	1902	2002	2102	2043u	2122	2302	0056
Falkenberg	d.	0937	0940	1019	1119	1140	1219	1319	1337	1419	1519	1538	1619	1657	1649	1719	1740	1749	1819	1837	1919	2019	2119	|	2139	2319	...
Varberg	d.	0952	0955	1034	1134	1155	1234	1334	1354	1434	1534	1554	1634	1711	1704	1734	1755	1804	1834	1851	1934	2034	2134	2119u	2154	2334	...
Kungsbacka	d.	|	|	1057	1157	|	1257	1357	|	1457	1557	|	1657	1735s	1727	1757	|	1827	1857	|	1957	2057	2157	...	|	2356	...
Göteborg	a.	1030	1030	1117	1217	1230	1317	1417	1432	1517	1617	1632	1717	1752	1747	1817	1830	1847	1917	1932	2017	2117	2217	...	2229	0017	...
Oslo Sentral **770**	a.	...	...	...	...	...	...	...	...	...	...	...	...	...	...	...	...	...	...	...	...	...	...	...	...	...	...

♦ – **NOTES** (LISTED BY TRAIN NUMBER)

10880 – ⑥ Dec. 13 - Apr. 11: couchette, sleeper and ✗ Malmö - Göteborg - Duved.

10881 – † Dec. 19 - Apr. 11 (from Duved): couchette, sleeper and ✗ Duved - Göteborg - Malmö.

S – [12] and ✗ Stockholm - Göteborg - Halmstad and v.v.

a – Ⓐ only.

d – ⚒ only.

s – Stops to set down only.

u – Stops to pick up only.

y – Jan. 4 - June 19.

§ – Train number **412** Dec. 21 - Jan. 10.

X2000 - High speed train. Special supplement payable.

* – Halmstad - Hässleholm: *91 km*.

736 HALLSBERG - MARIESTAD - LIDKÖPING - HERRLJUNGA

Operator: *V* 2nd class only

km			Ⓐ	Ⓐ	Ⓐ	Ⓐ	⑥	Ⓐ	Ⓒ	Ⓐ	Ⓐ	†	⑥	⑥	Ⓐ	Ⓐ	†	†	Ⓐ	⑥	Ⓐ	†	Ⓐ	⑥	Ⓐ	†	Ⓐ	†	Ⓐ
0	**Hallsberg 740**	d.	...	...	...	...	...	...	...	0852	...	...	1025	...	1045	...	1140	...	...	...	1443	...	...	1626	1639	...	...	1851	1950
30	Laxå **740**	d.	...	...	...	...	...	...	...	0909	...	...	1042	...	1102	...	1157	...	...	...	1500	...	...	1643	1656	...	...	1908	2007
92	Mariestad	d.	...	0540	0650	...	...	0756	0835	1001	...	...	1142	...	1151	...	1246	1405	1435	1440	1554	1629	1705	1736	1746	1815	...	1959	2058
146	Lidköping	a.	...	0620	0741	...	...	0852	0915	1049	...	...	1230	...	...	...	...	1453	1515	1520	1642	1709	1756	1824	*1846*	1903	...	2047	2146
146	Lidköping	d.	0537	0622	...	0756	0800	0853	0917	...	1105	1205	...	1312	...	1315	...	1500	1518	1520	1714	1720	...	...	...	1905	2006	...	...
201	**Herrljunga 740**	a.	0622	0702	...	0844	0847	0953	0957	...	1154	1251	...	1401	...	1402	...	1550	1600	1600	1804	1759	...	...	...	1956	2052	...	...
	Göteborg **740**	a.	...	0757	...	...	...	...	1047	...	...	...	...	...	...	...	...	...	1647	1647	...	1847	...	...	...	...	...	...	...

		Ⓐ	Ⓐ	⑥	Ⓐ	Ⓐ	Ⓐ	†	⑥	Ⓐ	Ⓐ	Ⓐ	⑥	Ⓐ	†	Ⓐ	†	Ⓐ	†	Ⓐ	Ⓒ	Ⓐ	Ⓐ	†	⚒	Ⓐ	†	†	Ⓐ
Göteborg **740**	d.	...	...	...	...	...	...	...	...	0932	...	...	1102	...	1132	...	...	...	...	...	...	...	...	...	1712	...	1912	...	...
Herrljunga 740	d.	...	...	...	0705	...	0912	...	1000	1019	...	...	1146	1200	1216	...	1308	1412	...	...	1602	1602	...	...	1807	1858	2001	2100	2110
Lidköping	a.	...	...	...	0754	...	1001	...	1047	1058	...	...	1224	1247	1301	...	1355	1500	...	...	1649	1649	...	...	1849	1945	2038	2147	2157
Lidköping	d.	0458	0528	0717	...	0757	...	0920	1049	1100	...	...	1232	...	1302	1327	...	...	1517	1542	...	1703	...	1712	1851	...	2050	...	...
Mariestad	d.	0550	0623	0807	...	0847	...	1009	1137	1138	1155	1213	1310	...	1342	1417	...	...	1607	1637	...	1752	1759	1800	1929	...	2128	...	...
Laxå **740**	d.	0638	...	0855	...	0937	...	1057	...	...	1243	1301	...	...	...	1505	...	...	1655	...	...	...	1846	...	...	...	...	...	...
Hallsberg 740	a.	0655	...	0913	...	0955	...	1115	...	...	1301	1319	...	...	...	1523	...	...	1713	...	...	...	1904	...	...	...	...	...	...

KØBENHAVN - LUFTHAVN (KASTRUP) ✈ - MALMÖ - HELSINGBORG 737

Operator: *Skåne* (Ø – *Øtåg*)

km																									
		Ⓐ2	ØⒶ	Ⓐ2	Ⓐ2	Ø	ØⒶ		2	Ⓐ2	Ø	Ⓐ	2	Ø		2	Ø	2	Ø	2	Ø		2	Ø	2
	København H 703 d.	...	...	...	...	0523	...	...	...	...	0623	...	...	0723	...	...	0823	...	0923	...	1023	...	...	1123	...
	Lufthavn (Kastrup) 703 d.	...	...	...	...	0536	...	...	...	...	0636	...	...	0736	...	...	0836	...	0936	...	1036	...	...	1136	...
0	**Malmö 703 735** d.	0438	0508	0538	...	0608	...	...	0638	...	0708	...	0738	0808	...	0838	0908	0938	1008	1038	1108	...	1138	1208	1238
16	Lund 735 d.	0451	0522	0551	0617	0622	0646	...	0651	0717	0722	0748	0751	0822	...	0851	0922	0951	1022	1051	1122	...	1151	1222	1251
48	Landskrona 735 d.	0515	0538	0615	0645	0638	0702	...	0715	0745	0738	0804	0815	0838	...	0915	0938	1015	1038	1115	1138	...	1215	1238	1315
69	**Helsingborg 735** a.	0532	0550	0632	0702	0650	0716	...	0732	0802	0750	0818	0832	0850	...	0932	0950	1032	1050	1132	1150	...	1232	1250	1332

	Ø	2	Ø		Ⓐ2		Ø	ØⒶ	2	Ⓐ2		Ø	ØⒶ	2	Ⓐ2		Ø	ØⒶ	2	Ⓐ2		Ø	2	Ø	2
København H 703 d.	1223	...	1323	...	...	...	1423	...	...	...	...	1523	...	...	...	...	1623	...	...	...	...	1723	...	1823	...
Lufthavn (Kastrup) 703 d.	1236	...	1336	...	...	...	1436	...	...	...	...	1536	...	...	...	...	1636	...	...	...	...	1736	...	1836	...
Malmö 703 735 d.	1308	1338	1408	1438	...	...	1508	...	1538	...	...	1608	...	1638	...	...	1708	...	1738	...	...	1808	1838	1908	1938
Lund 735 d.	1322	1351	1422	1451	1517	...	1522	1548	1551	1617	...	1622	1648	1651	1717	...	1722	1748	1751	1817	...	1822	1851	1922	1951
Landskrona 735 d.	1338	1415	1438	1515	1545	...	1538	1604	1615	1645	...	1638	1704	1715	1745	...	1738	1804	1815	1845	...	1838	1915	1938	2015
Helsingborg 735 a.	1350	1432	1450	1532	1602	...	1550	1618	1632	1702	...	1650	1718	1732	1802	...	1750	1818	1832	1902	...	1850	1932	1950	2032

	Ø	2	Ø	2	Ø	2	Ø	⚒2	2H	
København H 703 d.	1923	...	2023	...	2123	...	2223	...	...	...
Lufthavn (Kastrup) 703 d.	1936	...	2036	...	2136	...	2236	...	...	...
Malmö 703 735 d.	2008	2038	2108	2138	2208	2238	2308	2338	0100	...
Lund 735 d.	2022	2051	2122	2151	2222	2251	2322	2351	0114	...
Landskrona 735 d.	2040	2115	2138	2215	2240	2315	2340	0015	0138	...
Helsingborg 735 a.	2052	2132	2150	2232	2252	2332	2352	0032	0155	...

	ØⒶ	2	Ⓐ2	Ø		2	ØⒶ	Ⓐ2	Ø	2
Helsingborg 735 d.	0506	0527	0553	0610	...	0627	0642	0653	0710	0727
Landskrona 735 d.	0520	0545	0611	0622	...	0645	0655	0711	0722	0745
Lund 735 d.	0539	0610	0634	0639	...	0710	0711	0734	0739	0810
Malmö 703 735 a.	0552	0624	...	0652	...	0723	...	...	0752	0823
Lufthavn (Kastrup) 703 a.	0623	...	...	0723	...	...	...	...	0823	...
København H 703 a.	0637	...	...	0737	...	...	...	...	0837	...

	ØⒶ	Ⓐ2	Ø	2	Ⓐ2	Ø	2		Ø	2	Ø	2	Ø	2		Ø	2	Ø	2	Ⓐ2	Ø		2	Ⓐ2	Ø
Helsingborg 735 d.	0742	0753	0810	0827	0853	0910	0927	...	1010	1027	1110	1127	1210	1227	...	1310	1327	1410	1427	1453	1510	...	1526	1553	1610
Landskrona 735 d.	0755	0811	0822	0845	0911	0922	0945	...	1022	1045	1122	1145	1222	1245	...	1322	1345	1422	1445	1511	1522	...	1548	1611	1622
Lund 735 d.	0811	0834	0839	0910	0934	0939	1010	...	1039	1110	1139	1210	1239	1310	...	1339	1410	1439	1510	1534	1539	...	1612	1634	1639
Malmö 703 735 a.	...	...	0852	0923	...	0952	1023	...	1052	1123	1152	1223	1252	1323	...	1352	1423	1452	1523	...	1552	...	1623	...	1652
Lufthavn (Kastrup) 703 a.	...	...	0923	...	...	1023	...	...	1123	...	1223	...	1323	...	...	1423	...	1523	...	...	1623	...	...	...	1723
København H 703 a.	...	...	0937	...	...	1037	...	...	1137	...	1237	...	1337	...	...	1437	...	1537	...	...	1637	...	...	...	1737

		ØⒶ	Ⓐ2		Ø	2	ØⒶ		Ⓐ2	Ø	2	Ø	2		Ø	2	Ø	2		Ø	2	Ø	⚒2		2H
Helsingborg 735 d.	1627	1642	1653	...	1710	1726	1742	...	1753	1810	1827	1910	1927	...	2010	2027	2110	2127	...	2210	2227	2310	2327	...	0027
Landskrona 735 d.	1645	1655	1711	...	1722	1744	1755	...	1811	1822	1845	1922	1945	...	2022	2045	2122	2145	...	2222	2245	2322	2345	...	0045
Lund 735 d.	1710	1711	1734	...	1739	1809	1811	...	1834	1839	1910	1939	2010	...	2039	2110	2139	2210	...	2239	2310	2339	0010	...	0108
Malmö 703 735 a.	1724	...		...	1752	1820	...	...	...	1852	1923	1952	2023	...	2052	2124	2152	2224	...	2252	2323	2355	0023	...	*0130*
Lufthavn (Kastrup) 703 a.	...	...	...	...	1823	...	...	...	...	1923	...	2023	...	...	2123	...	2223	...	...	2323	...	...	...	...	...
København H 703 a.	...	...	...	...	1837	...	...	...	...	1937	...	2037	...	...	2137	...	2237	...	...	2337	...	...	...	...	...

H – ②③④⑤⑥† only.

Ø – Operated by *Øtåg*.

SECONDARY LINES in South - East Sweden 738

2nd class only except where shown

km	Operator: *KLT*	Ⓐ		⚒											Ⓑ
0	Västervik d.	0541	...	0623	0747	...	1107	1405	...	1606	...	1802	...	1922
116	Linköping a.	0731	...	0813	0932	...	1245	1545	...	1755	...	1943	...	2104

Operator: *KLT*	Ⓐ								Ⓑ				Ⓑ
Linköping d.	0545	0912	...	1112	...	1412	1612	...	1717	...	1918	...	2114
Västervik a.	0727	1052	...	1251	...	1548	1757j	...	1904	...	2104	...	2257

km	Operator: *KLT*	Ⓐ‡	Ⓐ‡	⑥‡		‡	‡	‡		‡	‡	Ⓑ‡		Ⓑ‡
0	Linköping d.	...	0534	...	...	0823	1023	1223	...	1423	1623	1822	...	2023
123	Hultsfred d.	0620	0713	0713	...	1008	1206	1405	...	1606	1805	2003	...	2201
159	Berga a.	0644	0737	0737	...	1032	1230	1429	...	1630	1829	2027	...	...
159	Berga d.	0649	0742	0742	...	1037	1235	1434	...	1635	1834	2032	...	...
235	Kalmar 746 a.	0748	0845	0845	...	1137	1335	1534	...	1734	1932	2128	...	...

Operator: *KLT*	Ⓐ‡	Ⓐ‡	⑥‡		‡	‡		‡	‡	‡		Ⓑ‡	Ⓑ‡
Kalmar 746 d.	...	0544	...	...	0839	1035	...	1234	1434	1634	...	1831	2120
Berga a.	...	0641	...	...	0935	1133	...	1333	1532	1732	...	1931	2222
Berga d.	...	0646	...	...	0940	1138	...	1338	1537	1737	...	1936	2226
Hultsfred d.	0540	0712	0712	...	1006	1205	...	1404	1603	1803	...	2003	2249
Linköping a.	0723	0845	0845	...	1145	1341	...	1540	1740	1939	...	2139	...

km	*KLT* 🚌 service	⚒			†		⚒					Ⓐ	Ⓑ	Ⓑ
0	Berga d.	0740	0940	1035	1135	1235	1340	1435	1535	1735	1835	1935	2035	2225
29	Oskarshamn a.	0812	1012	1107	1207	1307	1412	1507	1615	1807	1907	2007	2107	2257

KLT 🚌 service	⚒						⚒		†		⚒	†	Ⓑ
Oskarshamn d.	0705	0900	1000	1100	1200	1300	1400	1500	1600	1700	1800	1955	2150
Berga a.	0735	0930	1030	1130	1230	1330	1430	1530	1630	1730	1830	2025	2220

km	Operator: *MER*		Ⓐ				Ⓒ		Ⓐ				⑤†	
0	Nässjö d.	...	0702	...	0918	...	1316	...	1525	...	1721	...	1916	...
83	Hultsfred a.	...	0818	...	1037	...	1433	...	1639	...	1839	...	2031	...

Operator: *MER*		Ⓐ								⑤†	
Hultsfred d.	...	0628	...	0929	...	1327	...	1729	...	1922	...
Nässjö a.	...	0743	...	1043	...	1440	...	1846	...	2040	...

j – Arrive 1753 on ⑤⑥†.

‡ – Also conveys 1st class.

VARBERG and GÖTEBORG - UDDEVALLA - STRÖMSTAD 739

2nd class only except where shown

Currently operated by 🚌 Strömstad - Skee and v.v.

km																											
			V																				V				
																				X2000 479	*X2000* 473						
		Ⓐ	⚒	Ⓐ	⚒	⑥		⑥	Ⓐ		†		⑥	Ⓐ	Ⓐ	†	Ⓐ	Ⓒ	Ⓐ	Ⓒ	†Sj	ⒶSr	Ⓑ	†	Ⓐ	⑥	Ⓐ	†
0	**Varberg 735** d.	...	...	0613	0709a	0741	...	0950	0954	...	1142	...	1340	1348	1444	...	1544	1549	1641	...	...	...	...	1815	1842	1952	1955	2144
84	Borås 746 a.	...	...	0727	0831a	0852	...	1104	1105	...	1252	...	1451	1458	1600	...	1702	1703	1804	...	...	...	...	1931	1958	2105	2111	2258
	Borås d.	0600	...	▬	0833	▬	1005	▬	...	1202	▬	1403	▬	1503	1603	1603	1704	▬	1806	1806	...	...	...	2002	2010	▬	...	...
127	Herrljunga 740 a.	0638	...	...	0910	...	1042	...	...	1239	...	1440	...	1540	1640	1640	1742	...	1843	1843	...	...	...	2039	2047	...	...	...
	Herrljunga d.	0644	...	...	0921	...	1118c	...	...	1318a	...	1518	...	▬	1713	1718	1746	...	...	1919g	1924	1933	...	2116	2055	...	...	...
191	Vänersborg d.	0734	...	...	1007	...	1204c	...	...	1406a	...	1604	V	...	1800	1808	1834	...	...	2007g	2004	2013	...	2202	2141	...	...	...
195	Öxnered 750 d.	0740	...	V	1013	V	1210c	V	...	1411a	V	1610	⚒	V	1806	1815	1840	V	...	2013g	|	|	...	2208	2147	V	...	...
	Göteborg ▲ d.	|	0647	0847	|	1047	|	1247	...	|	1447	|	1547	1647	|	1830	|	1847	...	|	|	|	1947	|	|	2047	...	...
217	Uddevalla C ▲ a.	0756	0758	0958	1029	1158	1226c	1358	...	1428a	1558	1626	1702	1758	1822	...	1856	1957	...	2029g	2027	2035	2058	2223	2202	2158	...	...
	Uddevalla C d.	...	0803	...	...	1203	...	1408b	...	...	1608	...	...	...	...	...	...	2004g	...	...	...	...	2103	...	...	...	...	...
302	Skee 🚌 a.	...	0913	...	...	1313	...	1524b	...	...	1724	...	...	...	...	...	...	2114g	...	...	...	...	2213	...	...	...	...	...
309	**Strömstad** 🚌 a.	...	*0933*	...	...	*1333*	...	*1544b*	...	...	*1744*	...	...	...	...	...	...	*2134*	...	...	...	...	*2233*	...	...	...	...	...

km																											
					X2000 472	V	V		V		V	V		V			V		V	V				V	V			V
		Ⓐ	⑥	Ⓐ	ⒶSr	⚒	Ⓐ	⚒	⑥	†		⚒				Ⓒ		Ⓑ	Ⓐ	Ⓒ	Ⓐ	Ⓒ	Ⓐ	Ⓐ	†	Ⓐ	†	
0	**Strömstad** 🚌 d.	...	...	...	...	...	*0626*	...	*0626*	...	...	...	...	*1029*	...	...	...	...	*1422*	*1422*	...	...	...	*1622*	*1622*	...	...	*1829*
	Skee 🚌 d.	...	...	...	...	...	0646	...	0646	...	...	...	...	1049	...	...	...	...	1442	1442	...	...	...	1642	1642	...	...	1849
92	Uddevalla C a.	...	...	...	...	...	0757	...	0757	...	...	...	...	1201	...	...	...	...	1556	1555	...	...	...	1755	1755	...	...	2001
	Uddevalla C ▲ d.	...	...	0524	0540	0709	0806	0801	0809	0933	1009	1109	1133d	1206	1328	...	1409	1533	1606	1609	1632	1736	...	1806	1809	1915	1933	2009
180	**Göteborg** ▲ a.	...	...	|	|	0822	0922	|	0922	|	1122	1222	|	1322	|	...	1522	|	1722	1722	|	|	...	1922	1922	|	|	2122
	Öxnered 750 d.	...	...	0540	|	▬	...	0817	▬	0949	▬	▬	1149d	▬	1347	...	▬	1549	...	▬	1648	1751	...	...	...	1931	1949	...
	Vänersborg d.	...	...	0546	0559	...	...	0823	...	0955	...	...	1155d	...	1355	...	...	1555	...	...	1654	1759	...	...	...	1937	1955	...
	Herrljunga 746 a.	...	...	0633	0641	...	...	0909	...	1040	⚒	...	1240d	...	1445	...	Ⓐ	1643	...	...	1744	1846	...	...	...	2029	2041	...
	Herrljunga d.	0548	...	0647	...	...	...	0916	...	1116	1116	...	1316	...	1518	...	1618	1721	...	...	1750	1924	1933	...	...	2053	2116	...
	Borås 746 a.	0627	...	0724	...	†	...	0953	⑥	1153	1153	Ⓒ	1353	Ⓐ	1559	...	1700	1803	...	†	1833	1959	2008	...	...	2128	2151	...
	Borås d.	0628	0658	0729	...	0900	...	1001a	1043	...	1200a	1257	...	1500	1604a	1642	1702	1808a	...	1831	...	...	2010	...	...	...	2158	...
	Varberg 735 a.	0741	0814	0840	...	1010	...	1116a	1154	...	1310a	1414	...	1617	1717a	1753	1815	1918a	...	1942	...	...	2121	...	...	...	2311	...

S – (12) and ✕ Stockholm - Herrljunga - Uddevalla and v.v.

a – Ⓐ only.
b – Ⓑ only.
c – Ⓒ only.

d – ⚒ only.
g – ⑥ only.
j – Not Dec. 14 - Jan. 9.
r – Not Dec. 21 - Jan. 10.

▲ – Additional services Göteborg - Uddevalla and v.v. Operator: Västtrafik:
From Göteborg: 0747Ⓐ, 0947⚒, 1147⚒, 1347⚒, 1717Ⓐ, 1747Ⓑ.
From Uddevalla: 0611Ⓐ, 0641Ⓐ, 0809†, 0909⚒, 1309⚒, 1509⚒, 1709Ⓑ, 1809⑥, 1909Ⓑ.

740 STOCKHOLM - HALLSBERG - GÖTEBORG

For Stockholm - Hallsberg - Karlstad / Oslo and v.v. services see Table 750

km		Ⓐ	2 Ⓐ	2 Ⓐ	77 R ♦	73 R ♦	2 Ⓐ	X2000 401 R✕ ①–④j	2 ⑥	X2000 421 R✕ Ⓐ	159 ⚒y	621 🍷 Ⓐq	X2000 423 R✕ Ⓐj	97 R ♦	X2000 425 R✕ ⚒	X2000 415 R✕ †	163 x	X2000 427 R✕ ⚒	101 Ⓐp	2 ⑥	X2000 429 R✕	167	103 Ⓒn	2 Ⓐ	X2000 433 R✕	171
0	**Stockholm** C **730** d.	...	...	...	...	...	...	0600	...	0610	...	0636	0714	...	0810	0810	0707d	0914	0902	...	1010	0907	1051	...	1210	1107
15	Flemingsberg ‡ d.	...	...	...	...	...	...	|	...	|	...	0647	0725	...	|	|	|	0925	|	...	|	|	|	...	|	|
36	Södertälje Syd ‡ d.	...	...	...	...	...	...	|	...	0628	...	0657	|	...	0828	0828	|	0936	0922	...	1028	|	1111	...	1228	|
108	Flen **730** d.	...	...	...	...	...	...	|	...	|	...	0732	|	...	|	|	V	|	|	...	|	V	|	...	|	V
131	Katrineholm **730** d.	...	...	...	...	...	...	|	...	0706	...	0745	|	...	0906	|	|	|	|	...	1106	|	|	...	1306	|
197	**Hallsberg 755/6** a.	...	...	...	...	...	...	|	...	|	...	0816	0830	0838	|	0926	|	|	|	...	|	|	|	...	|	|
	Örebro C **755/6** d.	...	...	...	0548c	0548	...	|	...	|	0710	▬	|	|	|	|	0910	|	|	...	|	1110	|	...	|	1310
197	**Hallsberg** d.	...	...	...	0608s	0608s	...	|	...	|	0733	...	0832	|	|	0928	0933	|	|	...	|	1133	|	...	|	1333
227	Laxå **736** d.	...	...	...	|	|	...	|	...	|	0748	2	|	|	|	|	0948	|	|	...	|	1148	|	...	|	1348
272	Töreboda d.	...	...	...	|	|	...	|	...	|	0809	†	|	|	|	|	1009	|	|	...	|	1209	|	...	|	1409
311	**Skövde** d.	0450	0557	0635	0708s	0708s	0732	|	0732	0811	0832	0832	0915	0930	1011	1011	1032	1115	1130	1132	1211	1232	1308	1332	1411	1432
341	Falköping d.	0508	0615	0650	|	|	0748	|	0750	|	0850	0850	|	|	|	|	1050	|	|	1150	|	1250	|	1350	|	1450
375	Herrljunga **736/9** a.	0528	0635	0708	0742s	0742s	|	|	0808	0835	0906	0908	|	1003s	|	|	1106	|	|	1208	|	1306	|	1408	1435	1506
	Borås a.	|	|	|	|	|	|	|	|	|	|	|	|	|	|	|	|	|	|	|	|	|	|	|	|	|
410	Alingsås a.	0549	0656	0727	|	|	|	|	0828	|	0927	0928	|	|	1046s	1046s	1127	|	|	1228	1246s	1327	|	1428	|	1527
455	**Göteborg** a.	0617	0732	0802	0837	0837	0847	0852	0857	0917	0957	0957	1017	1052	1117	1117	1157	1217	1247	1257	1317	1357	1422	1457	1517	1557
	Oslo S **770** a.	...	...	...	...	...	...	...	...	...	...	...	...	...	...	...	...	...	...	...	...	...	...	...	...	...

	633 Ⓐ	X2000 435 R✕ Ⓐ	2	X2000 437 R✕	175	637	X2000 439 R✕ Ⓑ	2	105 Y	639 Ⓑ	X2000 441 R✕ Ⓑk	X2000 411 R✕ Z	179	107 †n	641 Ⓐr		X2000 479 R✕ ♦	X2000 473 R✕ ♦	X2000 443 R✕ Ⓑ	643 Ⓐv	X2000 405 R✕ Ⓑm	X2000 445 R✕	183	X2000 447 R✕ m	X2000 449 R✕ Ⓑ	651 Ⓑ
Stockholm C **730** d.	1225	1315	...	1410	1307	1425	1515	...	1525	1530	1610	1610	1507	1625	1625	...	1645	1651	1710	1730	1736	1810	1707	1910	2010	2205
Flemingsberg ‡ d.	1236	1326	...	|	|	1436	|	...	|	1541	|	|	|	|	1636	...	|	|	|	1749	|	|	|	1921	|	2216
Södertälje Syd ‡ d.	1248	|	...	1428	|	1448	|	...	1547	1553	1628	1628	|	1645	1647	...	1705	1710	1728	1803	|	1828	|	|	2028	2228
Flen **730** d.	1324	|	...	|	V	1525	|	...	|	1629	|	|	V	|	1725	...	|	|	|	1839	|	|	V	|	|	2311
Katrineholm **730** d.	1338	|	...	1506	|	1538	|	...	1632	1643	1706	1706	|	|	1738	...	|	|	|	1853	|	1906	|	2006	2106	2325
Hallsberg 755/6 a.	1412	1431	...	|	|	1612	1630	...	1702	1717	|	|	|	|	1814	...	|	|	1826	1938	|	|	|	|	2130	2400
Örebro C **755/6** d.	...	|	...	|	1510	...	|	...	|	...	|	|	1710	|	...	...	|	|	|	...	|	|	1910	|	|	▬
Hallsberg d.	...	1433	...	|	1533	...	1630	...	1704	...	|	|	1733	|	...	...	|	|	1828	...	|	|	1933	|	2132	...
Laxå **736** d.	...	|	...	|	1548	...	|	...	|	...	|	|	1748	|	...	...	|	|	|	...	|	|	1948	|	|	**147**
Töreboda d.	...	|	...	|	1609	...	|	...	|	...	|	|	1809	|	...	...	1829	1838	|	...	|	|	2009	|	|	⑤⑥
Skövde d.	...	1516	1532c	1611	1632	...	1713	1732g	1755	...	1811	1811	1832	1840	...	...	1846	1855	1911	...	|	2011	2032	2111	2215	2237
Falköping d.	...	|	1550	|	1650	...	|	1750	1811	...	|	|	1850	|	...	...	1901	1910	|	...	|	|	2050	|	|	2255
Herrljunga **736/9** a.	...	|	1608	|	1706	...	1737	1808	|	...	|	1835	1906	|	...	...	1917	1926	|	...	|	2035	2106	|	|	2313
Borås a.	...	|	|	|	|	...	|	|	|	...	|	|	|	|	...	...	...	...	|	...	|	|	|	|	|	|
Alingsås a.	...	|	1628	1646s	1727	...	|	1828	1844s	...	|	|	1927	|	...	...	...	...	1947s	...	|	|	2127	2147s	|	2333
Göteborg a.	...	1617	1657	1717	1757	...	1817	1857	1922	...	1917	1917	1957	2002	...	...	...	...	2017	...	2022	2117	2157	2217	2317	0002
Oslo S **770** a.	...	...	...	...	...	...	...	...	...	...	...	...	...	...	...	...	...	...	...	...	...	...	...	...	...	...

	620 Ⓐ	X2000 420 R✕ Ⓐm	X2000 402 R✕ ①–④j	X2000 400 R✕ Ⓐj	X2000 472 R✕ ♦	164 ⚒	X2000 422 R✕ ⚒j	X2000 412 R✕ Ⓐw	2 Ⓐ	X2000 424 R✕ Ⓐ	168	X2000 426 R✕ ⚒	X2000 416 R✕ †	100 Ⓐp	2 ⚒	X2000 428 R✕ ⚒	172	X2000 430 R✕	102 ⑥p	104 †n	X2000 432 R✕ ⑤†m	176	636 10636 Ⓑv	X2000 434 R✕	2 ⚒	X2000 404 R✕ †m
Oslo S **770** d.	...	...	...	...	...	...	...	...	...	...	...	...	...	...	...	...	...	...	...	...	...	...	...	...	...	...
Göteborg d.	...	0507	0554	0600	...	0602	0642	0642	0657	0742	0802	0842	0842	0832	0902	0942	1002	1042	1032	1102	1142	1202	...	1242	1302	1312
Alingsås d.	...	0534u	|	|	...	0629	0707u	|	0730	0807u	0830	|	0907	|	0930	1007u	1030	1107u	|	|	|	1230	...	|	1330	|
Borås d.	...	|	|	|	...	|	|	|	|	|	|	|	|	|	|	|	|	|	|	|	|	|	...	|	|	|
Herrljunga **736/9** d.	...	0548	|	|	0646	0652	|	0720	0750	|	0852	0920	|	0915	0950	|	1052	|	|	|	|	1252	...	1320	1350	|
Falköping d.	...	0604	|	|	0702	0711	|	|	0809	|	0911	|	|	|	1011	|	1111	|	1129	|	|	1311	...	|	1409	|
Skövde d.	...	0622	|	|	0721	0729	0747	0747	▬	0847	0929	0947	0947	0955	1029a	1047	1129	1147	1155	1213	1242	1329	...	1347	...	1412
Töreboda d.	...	|	|	|	0736	0746	|	|	...	|	0946	|	|	|	...	|	1146	|	|	|	|	1346	...	|	...	|
Laxå **736** d.	...	|	|	|	|	0808	|	|	...	|	1008	|	|	|	...	|	1208	|	|	|	|	1408	...	|	...	|
Hallsberg a.	...	0703	|	|	0808	0825	|	|	**624**	|	1025	|	|	|	...	|	1225	|	|	|	1324	1425	...	|	...	1454
Örebro C **755/6** a.	...	|	|	|	|	0848	|	|	⑥	|	1048	|	|	|	...	|	1248	|	|	|	|	1448	...	|	...	|
Hallsberg 755/6 d.	0627	0707	|	|	0810	|	|	|	0835	|	|	|	|	|	...	|	|	|	|	|	1326	|	1341	|	...	1456
Katrineholm **730** a.	0700	0731	|	|	|	|	0851	0851	0908	|	|	1051	1051	|	...	|	|	1251	|	|	|	|	1414	1451	...	|
Flen **730** a.	0715	|	|	|	|	V	|	|	0922	|	V	|	|	|	...	|	V	|	|	|	|	V	1428	|	...	|
Södertälje Syd ‡ a.	0751	|	|	|	0909	|	0929	0929	0958	|	|	1129	1129	1150	...	1224	|	1329	1349	1407	1424	|	1504	1529	...	|
Flemingsberg ‡ a.	0802	0821	|	|	|	|	|	|	1010	1031	|	|	|	|	...	|	|	|	|	|	|	|	1516	|	...	|
Stockholm C **730** a.	0816	0835	0839	0846	0930	1053	0950	0950	1024	1045	1253	1150	1150	1214	...	1245	1453	1350	1414	1431	1445	1653	1530	1550	...	1614

	X2000 436 R✕ Ⓑ	640 †	180	X2000 438 R✕	2 Ⓑ	106 Ⓐp	X2000 440 R✕ Ⓑ	194 Q	184 j ①–④	X2000 406 R✕ ①–④j	2 Ⓐ	X2000 442 R✕	108 †	98 R ♦	2 Ⓑ	X2000 444 R✕ Ⓑ	648 Ⓑ	188	X2000 446 R✕	76 R ♦	70 R ♦	Ⓑ	152 2	X2000 450 R✕ Ⓑj	2	2 P
Oslo S **770** d.	...	...	...	...	...	...	...	...	...	...	...	...	...	...	...	...	...	...	...	...	...	...	...	...	...	...
Göteborg d.	1342	...	1402	1442	1502	1512	1542	1602	1602	1612	1627	1642	1632	1700	1707	1742	...	1802	1842	1900	1900	1907	2002	2042	2132	2302
Alingsås d.	1407u	...	1430	|	1530	|	1607u	1630	1630	|	1700	|	|	|	1737	1810u	...	1830	|	|	|	1933	2030	|	2200	2330
Borås d.	|	...	|	|	|	|	|	|	|	|	|	|	|	|	|	|	...	|	|	|	|	|	|	|	|	|
Herrljunga **736/9** d.	|	...	1452	|	1550	|	|	1652	1655	|	1732	|	1715	1744u	1757	|	...	1852	1920	1946u	1946u	1955	2050	|	2220	2349
Falköping d.	|	...	1511	|	1609	|	|	1711	1714	|	1754	|	|	|	1820	|	...	1911	|	|	|	2016	2111	|	2243	0009
Skövde d.	1447	...	1529	1542	...	1629	1647	1729	1732	|	1815	1745	1755	1820	▬	1847	...	1929	1947	2017u	2017u	2037	2131	2145	2301	0029
Töreboda d.	|	...	1546	|	...	|	|	1746	1749	|	...	|	|	|	...	|	...	1946	|	|	|	...	2149	|	...	...
Laxå **736** d.	|	...	1608	|	...	|	|	1808	1812	|	...	|	|	|	...	|	...	2008	|	|	|	...	...	|	...	...
Hallsberg a.	|	...	1630	|	...	|	|	1825	1834	|	...	|	|	1915	**646**	1930	...	2025	|	2110u	2110u	...	...	2226	...	...
Örebro C **755/6** a.	|	...	1652	|	...	|	|	1848	1857	|	...	|	|	1935	Ⓐv	|	...	2048	|	2130g	...	...	...	|	...	...
Hallsberg 755/6 d.	|	1541	|	|	...	|	|	|	|	|	...	|	|	...	1849	1932	2008	|	|	...	...	...	...	2228	...	...
Katrineholm **730** d.	|	1614	|	1646	...	1745	|	|	|	|	...	1851	|	...	1919	|	2041	|	2051	...	...	...	...	|	...	...
Flen **730** d.	|	1628	V	|	...	|	|	V	V	|	...	|	|	...	1932	|	2100	V	|	...	...	...	...	|	...	...
Södertälje Syd ‡ a.	1624	1704	|	1724	...	1836	|	|	|	|	...	1929	1949	...	2007	|	2140	|	2129	...	...	...	...	2326	...	...
Flemingsberg ‡ a.	|	1716	|	|	...	|	1832	|	|	|	...	|	|	...	2018	2037	2152	|	|	...	...	...	...	|	...	...
Stockholm C **730** a.	1645	1731	1853	1745	...	1900	1845	2053	2105	1909	...	1950	2014	...	2031	2050	2206	2253	2150	...	...	...	...	2346	...	...

♦ – **NOTES** (LISTED BY TRAIN NUMBER)

70 – ①②† Dec. 13 - May 2; Ⓑ May 3 - June 19: 🛏, ▬ and (2) Göteborg - Stockholm (**86**) - Storlien; ✕ and (Bio) Göteborg - Stockholm.

73 – ①②③ Dec. 13 - May 2; Ⓑ May 3 - June 19 (from Storlien, one day later from Örebro): 🛏, ▬ and (2) Storlien (**87**) - Stockholm - Göteborg; ✕ and (Bio) Örebro - Göteborg.

76 – ③④⑤⑥ Dec. 13 - May 2: 🛏, ▬ and (2) Göteborg - Stockholm - Storlien; ✕ and (Bio) Göteborg - Stockholm; ✕ Sundsvall - Storlien.

77 – ④⑤⑥† Dec. 13 - May 2 (from Storlien, one day later from Örebro): 🛏, ▬ and (2) Storlien - Göteborg; ✕ and (Bio) Storlien - Sundsvall; ✕ Örebro - Göteborg.

97/8 – 🛏, ▬ and (2) Luleå (**91/2**) - Gävle - Göteborg and v.v.; 🍷 Gävle - Göteborg and v.v.

472/3 – Ⓐ (not Dec. 21 - Jan. 10): (12) and ✕ Stockholm - Herrljunga - Uddevalla and v.v.

479 – † (not Dec. 14 - Jan. 9): (12) and ✕ Stockholm - Herrljunga - Uddevalla.

P – ①②③④† only.
Q – ⑤⑥† (daily Dec. 21 - Jan. 10).
V – Via Västerås – see Table **756**.
Y – ⑤ (also ①–④ from Jan. 11).
Z – ⑥ (daily Dec. 19 - Jan. 9).

a – Ⓐ only.
c – Ⓒ only.
d – ⚒ only.
g – ⑥ only.
j – Not Dec. 21 - Jan. 10.
k – Not Dec. 19 - Jan. 9.
m – Not Dec. 21 - Jan. 9.
n – Jan. 10 - June 19.
p – Jan. 11 - June 19.

q – Not Dec. 24 - Jan. 6.
r – Not Dec. 24 - 27.
s – Stops to set down only.
u – Stops to pick up only.
v – Not Dec. 24 - Jan. 5.
w – Dec. 21 - Jan. 10.
x – Runs as train **193** on †.
y – Runs as train **157** on ⑥.

X2000 – High speed train. Special supplement payable.
(Bio) – Cinema / bistro car.
‡ – Most trains on this table do not convey passengers for local journeys between Stockholm and Södertälje Syd or v.v. Local trains run every 30 minutes Stockholm Central - Södertälje Hamn - Södertälje Centrum and v.v. (journey 42 mins). 🚌 Södertälje Syd - Södertälje Centrum runs every 30 minutes.

Operator: *Øtåg* KØBENHAVN - MALMÖ - KRISTIANSTAD - KARLSKRONA 745

km																									
		Ⓐ	Ⓐ																						
0	**København H 703/30** d.	...	...	0543	0643	0743	0803	0843	0903	0943	1003	1043	1103	1143	1203	1243	1303	1343	1403	1443	1503	1543	1603	1643	1703
12	Kastrup ✈ **703/30** d.	...	...	0556	0656	0756	0816	0856	0916	0956	1016	1056	1116	1156	1216	1256	1316	1356	1416	1456	1516	1556	1616	1656	1716
36	**Malmö** Syd / Svågertorp d.	...	...	0608	0708	0808	0828	0908	0928	1008	1028	1108	1128	1208	1228	1308	1328	1408	1428	1508	1528	1608	1628	1708	1728
47	**Malmö C 703** a.	...	...	0618	0718	0818	0838	0918	0938	1018	1038	1118	1138	1218	1238	1318	1338	1418	1438	1518	1538	1618	1638	1718	1738
47	**Malmö C 730/46** d.	...	0528	0628	0728	0828	0848	0928	0948	1028	1048	1128	1148	1228	1248	1328	1348	1428	1448	1528	1548	1628	1648	1728	1748
63	Lund **730/46** d.	...	0542	0642	0742	0842	0902	0942	1002	1042	1102	1142	1202	1242	1302	1342	1402	1442	1502	1542	1602	1642	1702	1742	1802
81	Eslöv **746** d.	...	0552	0652	0752	0852	0912	0952	1012	1052	1112	1152	1212	1252	1312	1352	1412	1452	1512	1552	1612	1652	1712	1752	1812
130	Hässleholm **730/46** a.	...	0616	0716	0816	0916	0936	1016	1036	1116	1136	1216	1236	1316	1336	1416	1436	1516	1536	1616	1636	1716	1736	1816	1836
130	Hässleholm d.	0516	0618	0718	0818	0918	...	1018	...	1118	...	1218	...	1318	...	1418	...	1518	...	1618	...	1718	...	1818	...
160	**Kristianstad** a.	0537	0637	0737	0837	0937	...	1037	...	1137	...	1237	...	1337	...	1437	...	1537	...	1637	...	1737	...	1837	...
160	**Kristianstad** d.	0546	0646	0746**d**	0846	0946**a**	...	1046	...	1146**d**	...	1246	...	1346**d**	...	1446	...	1546	...	1646	...	1746**b**	...	1846	...
191	Sölvesborg d.	0607	0707	0807**d**	0907	1007**a**	...	1107	...	1207**d**	...	1307	...	1407**d**	...	1507	...	1607	...	1707	...	1807**b**	...	1907	...
222	Karlshamn d.	0632	0732	0832**d**	0932	1032**a**	...	1132	...	1232**d**	...	1332	...	1432**d**	...	1532	...	1632	...	1732	...	1832**b**	...	1932	...
260	Ronneby d.	0700	0800	0900**d**	1000	1100**a**	...	1200	...	1300**d**	...	1400	...	1500**d**	...	1600	...	1700	...	1800	...	1900**b**	...	2000	...
290	**Karlskrona** a.	0722	0822	0922**d**	1022	1122**a**	...	1222	...	1322**d**	...	1422	...	1522**d**	...	1622	...	1722	...	1822	...	1922**b**	...	2022	...

										Ⓒ
København H 703/30 d.	1743	1803	1843	1903	1943	2003	2043	2143	2243	0003
Kastrup ✈ **703/30** d.	1756	1816	1856	1916	1956	2016	2056	2156	2256	0016
Malmö Syd / Svågertorp d.	1808	1828	1908	1928	2008	2028	2108	2208	2308	0028
Malmö C 703 a.	1818	1838	1918	1938	2018	2038	2118	2218	2318	0038
Malmö C 730/46 d.	1828	1848	1928	1948	2028	2048	2128	2228	2328	0053
Lund **730/46** d.	1842	1902	1942	2002	2042	2102	2142	2242	2342	0113
Eslöv **746** d.	1852	1912	1952	2012	2052	2112	2152	2252	2352	0126
Hässleholm **730/46** a.	1916	1936	2016	2036	2116	2136	2216	2316	0016	0155
Hässleholm d.	1918	...	2018	...	2118	...	2218	2318	0018	0157
Kristianstad a.	1937	...	2037	...	2137	...	2237	2337	0037	0215
Kristianstad d.	1946**b**	...	2046	...	2146**b**	...	2246	...	...	...
Sölvesborg d.	2007**b**	...	2107	...	2207**b**	...	2307	...	...	...
Karlshamn d.	2032**b**	...	2132	...	2232**b**	...	2332	...	...	...
Ronneby d.	2100**b**	...	2200	...	2300**b**	...	0000	...	...	...
Karlskrona a.	2122**b**	...	2222	...	2322**b**	...	0022	...	...	...

Karlskrona d.	...	0438**a**	...	0538**d**	...	0638**a**	...	0738	...	0838**a**
Ronneby d.	...	0502**a**	...	0602**d**	...	0702**a**	...	0802	...	0902**a**
Karlshamn d.	...	0530**a**	...	0630**d**	...	0730**a**	...	0830	...	0930**a**
Sölvesborg d.	...	0552**a**	...	0652**d**	...	0752**a**	...	0852	...	0952**a**
Kristianstad a.	...	0614**a**	...	0714**d**	...	0814**a**	...	0914	...	1014**a**
Kristianstad d.	0520	0623	...	0723	...	0823	...	0923	...	1023
Hässleholm a.	0540	0640	...	0740	...	0840	...	0940	...	1040
Hässleholm **730/46** d.	0542	0642	0724	0742	0824	0842	0924	0942	1024	1042
Eslöv **746** d.	0606	0706	0747	0806	0847	0906	0947	1006	1047	1106
Lund **730/46** d.	0617	0717	0757	0817	0857	0917	0957	1017	1057	1117
Malmö C 730/46 a.	0632	0732	0812	0832	0912	0932	1012	1032	1112	1132
Malmö C 703 d.	0642	0742	0822	0842	0922	0942	1022	1042	1122	1142
Malmö Syd / Svågertorp a.	0650	0750	0830	0850	0930	0950	1030	1050	1130	1150
Kastrup ✈ **703/30** a.	0703	0803	0843	0903	0943	1003	1043	1103	1143	1203
København H 703/30 a.	0717	0817	0857	0917	0957	1017	1057	1117	1157	1217

Karlskrona d.	...	0938	...	1038**d**	...	1138	...	1238**d**	...	1338	...	1438	...	1538	...	1638**b**	...	1738	...	1838**b**	...	1938	...	2038**b**	2138
Ronneby d.	...	1002	...	1102**d**	...	1202	...	1302**d**	...	1402	...	1502	...	1602	...	1702**b**	...	1802	...	1902**b**	...	2002	...	2102**b**	2202
Karlshamn d.	...	1030	...	1130**d**	...	1230	...	1330**d**	...	1430	...	1530	...	1630	...	1730**b**	...	1830	...	1930**b**	...	2030	...	2130**b**	2230
Sölvesborg d.	...	1052	...	1152**d**	...	1252	...	1352**d**	...	1452	...	1552	...	1652	...	1752**b**	...	1852	...	1952**b**	...	2052	...	2152**b**	2252
Kristianstad a.	...	1114	...	1214**d**	...	1314	...	1414**d**	...	1514	...	1614	...	1714	...	1814**b**	...	1914	...	2014**b**	...	2114	...	2214**b**	2314
Kristianstad d.	...	1123	...	1223	...	1323	...	1423	...	1523	...	1623	...	1723	...	1823	...	1923	...	2023	...	2123	...	2223	2323
Hässleholm a.	...	1140	...	1240	...	1340	...	1440	...	1540	...	1640	...	1740	...	1840	...	1940	...	2040	...	2140	...	2240	2340
Hässleholm **730/46** d.	1124	1142	1224	1242	1324	1342	1424	1442	1524	1542	1624	1642	1724	1742	1824	1842	1924	1942	2024	2042	2124	2142	2224	2242	2342
Eslöv **746** d.	1147	1206	1247	1306	1347	1406	1447	1506	1547	1606	1647	1706	1747	1806	1847	1906	1947	2006	2047	2106	2147	2206	2247	2306	0006
Lund **730/46** d.	1157	1217	1257	1317	1357	1417	1457	1517	1557	1617	1657	1717	1757	1817	1857	1917	1957	2017	2057	2117	2157	2217	2257	2317	0017
Malmö C 730/46 a.	1212	1232	1312	1332	1412	1432	1512	1532	1611	1632	1712	1732	1811	1832	1912	1932	2012	2032	2112	2132	2212	2232	2312	2332	0032
Malmö C 703 d.	1222	1242	1322	1342	1422	1442	1522	1542	1622	1642	1722	1742	1822	1842	1922	1942	2022	2042	2122	2142	2222	2242	2322	...	...
Malmö Syd / Svågertorp a.	1230	1250	1330	1350	1430	1450	1530	1550	1630	1650	1730	1750	1830	1850	1930	1950	2030	2050	2130	2150	2230	2250	2330	...	...
Kastrup ✈ **703/30** a.	1243	1303	1343	1403	1443	1503	1543	1603	1643	1703	1743	1803	1843	1903	1943	2003	2043	2103	2143	2203	2243	2303	2343	...	...
København H 703/30 a.	1257	1317	1357	1417	1457	1517	1557	1617	1657	1717	1757	1817	1857	1917	1957	2017	2057	2117	2157	2217	2257	2317	2357	...	...

a – Ⓐ only. **b** – Ⓑ only. **d** – ⚒ only.

KØBENHAVN - MALMÖ and GÖTEBORG - KALMAR and KARLSKRONA 746

km																											
		Øtåg Ⓐ	*Øtåg* Ⓐ	*Øtåg* Ⓐ	Ⓐ	*Øtåg*	*Øtåg* Ⓐ	*Øtåg* †	*Øtåg* ⚒	⚒	*Øtåg* Ⓐ	*Øtåg*	*Øtåg*	Ⓒ	Ⓐ	*Øtåg* Ⓐ	*Øtåg* Ⓒ	*Øtåg* Ⓐ	*Øtåg*		*Øtåg* Ⓐ		*Øtåg*	Ⓑ	*Øtåg*	*Øtåg* Ⓑ	*Øtåg*
0	**København 703** d.	...	...	0603	...	0703	0803	0903	0903	...	1003	1103	1203	...	...	1303	1303	1403	1503	...	1603	...	1703	...	1903	2003	2103
12	Kastrup ✈ **703** d.	...	...	0616	...	0716	0816	0916	0916	...	1016	1116	1216	...	...	1316	1316	1416	1516	...	1616	...	1716	...	1916	2016	2116
47	**Malmö 703** a.	...	...	0638	...	0738	0838	0938	0938	...	1038	1138	1238	...	...	1338	1338	1438	1538	...	1638	...	1738	...	1938	2038	2138
47	**Malmö 730/45** d.	...	0548	0648	...	0748	0848	0948	0948	...	1048	1148	1248	...	...	1348	1348	1448	1548	...	1648	...	1748	...	1948	2048	2148
63	Lund **730/45** d.	...	0602	0702	...	0802	0902	1002	1002	...	1102	1202	1302	...	...	1402	1402	1502	1602	...	1702	...	1802	...	2002	2102	2202
80	Eslöv **745** d.	...	0612	0712	...	0812	0912	1012	1012	...	1112	1212	1312	...	...	1412	1412	1512	1612	...	1712	...	1812	...	2012	2112	2212
130	Hässleholm **730/45** d.	...	0639	0739	...	0839	0939	1039	1039	...	1139	1239	1339	...	...	1439	1439	1539	1639	...	1739	...	1839	...	2039	2139	2239
181	Älmhult d.	...	0702	0802	...	0902	1002	1102	1102	...	1202	1302	1402	...	...	1502	1502	1602	1702	...	1802	...	1902	...	2102	2202	2302
	Göteborg ▲ d.	...	|	|	0607	|	|	|	|	0907	|	|	|	1212	1212	|	|	|	|	...	|	1607	|	1807	|	|	|
	Borås ▲ d.	...	|	|	0706	|	|	|	|	1004	|	|	|	1307	1307	|	|	|	|	...	|	1704	|	1902	|	|	|
	Limmared d.	...	|	|	0734	|	|	|	|	1032	|	|	|	1335	1335	|	|	|	|	...	|	1734	|	1930	|	|	|
	Värnamo d.	...	|	|	0814	|	|	|	|	1111	|	|	|	1417	1427	|	|	|	|	...	|	1818	|	2014	|	|	|
228	Alvesta **730** a.	...	0721	0821	0840	0921	1021	1121	1121	1137	1221	1321	1421	1443	1453	1521	1521	1621	1721	...	1821	1843	1921	2038	2121	2221	2321
228	Alvesta ▲ d.	0606	0723	0826	0844	0934	1027	1134	1151	1144	1241	1334	1431	1445	1455	1534	1534	1641	1734	...	1827	1845	1934	2044	2134	2225	2323
245	**Växjö** ▲ d.	0628	0734	0836	0906	0946	1037	1146	1201	1158	1300	1346	1441	1458	1508	1546	1546	1657	1746	...	1837	1859	1946	2102	2146	2236	2335
302	Emmaboda a.	0703	0805	...	0937	1020	...	1220	...	1229	1333	1421	...	1529	1539	1621	1621	1729	1820	...	...	1930	2020**b**	2133	2220	...	0008
302	Emmaboda ● d.	0706	0806	...	0939	1022	...	1230	...	1231	1340	1422	...	1531	1552	1624	1629	1731	1827	...	...	1932	2028**b**	2135	2222	...	0010
330	Nybro d.	0722	0821	...	0954	1036	...	1244	...	1246	1354	1436	...	1546	1609	1638	1643	1745	1841	...	...	1947	2042**b**	2150	2236	...	0024
359	**Kalmar** a.	0737	0836	...	1010	1051	...	1300	...	1302	1414	1452	...	1603	1625	1653	1658	1801	1856	...	...	2003	2057**b**	2206	2251	...	0039

km																											
		Øtåg Ⓐ	Ⓐ	*Øtåg* Ⓐ	*Øtåg* ⚒	*Øtåg*	⚒	*Øtåg* ⚒	*Øtåg*	*Øtåg* Ⓐ	*Øtåg* ⚒	*Øtåg* †			*Øtåg* Ⓐ	*Øtåg*	*Øtåg* Ⓑ	*Øtåg*	Ⓐ	Ⓒ	*Øtåg* Ⓐ	*Øtåg*	Ⓑ	*Øtåg* Ⓐ	*Øtåg*	*Øtåg* Ⓑ	*Øtåg* Ⓐ
	Kalmar d.	...	0500	...	0555**a**	0707	0804	...	0909	...	1055	1109	1157	...	...	1309	1345**a**	1500	1553	1556	...	1701	1753	...	1903	1956	2106
	Nybro d.	...	0516	...	0610**a**	0723	0820	...	0925	...	1111	1125	1213	...	...	1325	1402**a**	1516	1609	1614	...	1717	1813	...	1919	2014	2122
	Emmaboda ● a.	...	0530	...	0624**a**	0737	0834	...	0938	...	1124	1138	1228	...	...	1338	1416**a**	1529	1624	1629	...	1730	1827	...	1932	2028	2135
	Emmaboda d.	...	0532	...	0626**a**	0739	0835	...	0940	...	1126	1140	1230	...	...	1340	1422**a**	1540	1626	1631	...	1740	1829	...	1940	2030	2140
	Växjö ▲ d.	0518	0606	0620	0658	0811	0906	0900	1012	1120	1206	1212	1300	...	1320	1412	1513	1612	1704	1702	1720	1812	1904	1920	2012	2102	2212
	Alvesta ▲ a.	0531	0619	0631	0710	0824	0919	0911	1025	1131	1219	1225	1313	...	1331	1425	1524	1625	1715	1715	1731	1825	1915	1931	2025	2115	2225
0	Alvesta **730** d.	0533	0622	0633	0712	0833	0925	0933	1033	1133	1233	1233	1315	...	1333	1433	1533	1633	1717	1717	1733	1833	1917	1933	2035	...	...
49	Värnamo d.	|	0655	|	|	|	0952	|	|	|	|	|	1342	...	|	|	|	|	1748	1748	|	|	1945	|	|	...	...
110	Limmared d.	|	0735	|	|	|	1032	|	|	|	|	|	1421	...	|	|	|	|	1830	1830	|	|	2027	|	|	...	...
149	Borås ▲ a.	|	0804	|	|	|	1100	|	|	|	|	|	1449	...	|	|	|	|	1859	1859	|	|	2055	|	|	...	...
222	**Göteborg** ▲ a.	|	0901	|	|	|	1157	|	|	|	|	|	1552	...	|	|	|	|	1957	1957	|	|	2152	|	|	...	...
	Älmhult d.	0553	...	0653	0732	0853	...	0953	1053	1153	1253	1253	...	...	1353	1453	1553	1653	...	...	1753	1853	...	1953	2055	...	...
	Hässleholm **730/45** a.	0616	...	0716	0755	0916	...	1016	1116	1216	1316	1316	...	...	1416	1516	1616	1716	...	...	1816	1916	...	2016	2118	...	...
	Eslöv **745** a.	0646	...	0746	0820	0946	...	1046	1146	1246	1346	1346	...	...	1446	1546	1646	1746	...	...	1846	1946	...	2046	2146	...	...
	Lund **730/45** a.	0657	...	0757	0831	0957	...	1057	1157	1257	1357	1357	...	...	1457	1557	1657	1757	...	...	1857	1957	...	2057	2157	...	...
	Malmö 730/45 a.	0712	...	0812	0846	1012	...	1112	1212	1312	1412	1412	...	...	1512	1611	1712	1811	...	...	1912	2012	...	2112	2212	...	...
	Malmö 703 d.	0722	...	0822	0902**a**	1022	...	1122	1222	1322	1422	1422	...	...	1522	1622	1722	1822	...	...	1922	2022	...	2122	2222	...	...
	Kastrup ✈ **703** a.	0743	...	0843	0923**a**	1043	...	1143	1243	1343	1443	1443	...	...	1543	1643	1743	1843	...	...	1943	2043	...	2143	2243	...	...
	København 703 a.	0757	...	0857	0937**a**	1057	...	1157	1257	1357	1457	1457	...	...	1557	1657	1757	1857	...	...	1957	2057	...	2157	2257	...	...

● – CONNECTING SERVICES **Emmaboda - Karlskrona and v.v.:**

km													
		Ⓐ	⑥	Ⓐ	†	⚒	†			Ⓑ	⑥	Ⓑ	
0	Emmaboda d.	0708	0841	0943	1025	1129	1234	1426	1632	1832	1937	2140	...
57	Karlskrona a.	0751	0925	1026	1108	1212	1317	1509	1715	1915	2025	2225	...

	Ⓐ	⑥	Ⓑ	⚒	†	⚒	†		Ⓑ	⑥	†	Ⓐ
Karlskrona a.	0444	0747	0851	1034	1142	1252	1333	1533	1733	1844	1933	2047
Emmaboda d.	0527	0830	0934	1118	1225	1335	1416	1617	1816	1927	2016	2130

a – Ⓐ only. **b** – Ⓑ only. ▲ – Additional trains run Göteborg - Borås and v.v., and Alvesta - Växjö and v.v.

747 STOCKHOLM - STOCKHOLM ARLANDA ✈ — Arlanda Express. Operator: A-Train AB (*AEX*)

Journey time: 20 minutes. All services stop at Arlanda Södra (17 minutes from Stockholm, 2 minutes from Arlanda Norra). Södra serves terminals 2, 3 and 4; Norra serves terminal 5.

From **Stockholm Central:** 0435, 0505, 0520, 0535, 0550, 0605, 0620, 0635, 0650 and at the same minutes past each hour until 2205, 2220, 2235, 2305, 2335, 0005, 0035.

From **Arlanda Norra:** 0505, 0535, 0550, 0605, 0620, 0635, 0650 and at the same minutes past each hour until 2205, 2220, 2235, 2250, 2305, 2335, 0005, 0035, 0105.

Minor alterations to schedules are possible at peak times

750 STOCKHOLM - HALLSBERG - KARLSTAD - OSLO

km		*VTAB*	*X2000*	*VTAB*		*VTAB*			*VTAB*	*VTAB*	*X2000*	*VTAB*		*X2000*	*VTAB*	*VTAB*			*VTAB*		*VTAB*	*X2000*	*VTAB*		*VTAB*
			451		**625**		**629**	**627**			**453**		**633**	**455**			**637**	**637**		**639**		**459**		**647**	
		2	R ✕	2	✕	2			2	2	R ✕	2	🍷	R ✕	2	2			2		2	R ✕	2	🍷	2
		Ⓐ	Ⓐ	Ⓐ		Ⓐ	Ⓐ	⑥	Ⓒ	Ⓐ	†	Ⓐ	Ⓐ	Ⓐ	Ⓐ	Ⓐ	⑥	Ⓑ	⑥	Ⓑ	Ⓐ	Ⓑ	†		Ⓑ
0	**Stockholm** C **730/40** .. d.	...	0615	...	0829	...	1025	1025	...	...	1215	...	1225	1415	...	...	1425	1425	...	1530	...	1715	...	1915	...
15	Flemingsberg **730/40** .. d.	...	|	...	0840	...	1036	1036	...	...	|	...	1236	|	...	...	1436	1436	...	1541	...	|	...	1926	...
36	Södertälje Syd **730/40** .. d.	...	0633**u**	...	0852	...	1048	1048	...	...	1233**u**	...	1248	1433**u**	...	...	1448	1448	...	1553	...	1733**u**	...	1938	...
108	Flen **730/40** .... d.	...	|	...	0928	...	1124	1124	...			...	1324	|	...	...	1525	1525	...	1629	...	|	...	2014	...
131	Katrineholm **730/40** .... d.	...	0712	...	0942	...	1138	1138	...	...	1311	...	1338	1511	...	...	1539	1538	...	1643	...	1811	...	2028	...
197	**Hallsberg 740** .... a.	...	0736	...	1016	...	1212	1212	...	...	1335	...	1412	1535	...	...	1612	1612	...	1717	...	|	...	2102	...
197	**Hallsberg** .... d.	...	0738	...	1020	...	1215	1215	...	...	1337	...	1415	1537	...	...	1615	1615	...	1722	...	1837**u**	...	2105	...
263	Degerfors .... d.	...	0805	...	1052	...	1245	1245	...	...	1405	...	1446	1605	...	...	1645	1645	...	1804	...	1902	...	2135	...
289	Kristinehamn .... d.	0608	0822	...	1109	...	1303	1308	...	...	1421	1446	1503	1621	...	1630	1707	1707	...	1819	1842	1918	...	2151	...
329	**Karlstad 751** .... a.	0639	0845	...	1130	...	1329	1328	...	...	1441	1512	1526**k**	1639	...	1659	1729	1729	...	1848	1920	1940	...	2215	...
329	**Karlstad** .... d.	0642	...	0855	1134	1246	1348	...	1345	1427	...	1534	1559	...	1647	1710	...	1731	1750	...	1928	1945	1957	...	2225
349	Kil .... d.	0658	...	0909	1148	1259	1401	...	1359	1441	...	1549	1612	...	1702	1727	...	1753	1804	...	1946	2001	2011	...	2241
397	Arvika .... d.	0746	...	0942	1216	1335	...	...	1435	1530	...	1622	...	...	1737	1806	...	1826	1841	...	2018	2027	2048	...	2318
432	Charlottenberg 🏛 ...... a.	0812	...	1004	1236	1359	...	...	1459	1556	...	1645	...	...	1805	1832	...	1847	1907	...	...	...	2114	...	2350
474	Kongsvinger .... a.	...	...	1032	1306	...	...	...	...	...	...	1712	...	...	...	...	...	1916	...	...	...	...	...	...	...
574	**Oslo** Sentral .... a.	...	...	1149	1436	...	...	...	...	...	...	1831	...	...	...	...	...	2040	...	...	...	...	...	...	...

		X2000	*X2000*	*VTAB*		*VTAB*	*VTAB*	*VTAB*			*VTAB*		*X2000*			*VTAB*		*VTAB*		*VTAB*	*X2000*	*VTAB*		*VTAB*	*VTAB*
	622	**452**	**454**		**626**				**630**	**630**		**634**	**456**	**638**	**640**		**642**		**644**		**458**		**648**		
		R ✕	R ✕	2		2	2	2			2	✕	R ✕	🍷		2		2	🍷	2	R ✕	2		2	2
	Ⓐ	Ⓐ	⑥	Ⓐ	Ⓐ	Ⓐ	Ⓒ	Ⓐ	Ⓑ	⑥	⑥	⑥	Ⓐ	Ⓐ	†	Ⓐ	Ⓐ	⚒	Ⓒ	†	Ⓑ	Ⓐ	Ⓑ	Ⓐ	Ⓐ
Oslo Sentral .... d.	...	...	...	...	...	...	...	...	0725	...	...	0924	...	...	...	...	...	1329**a**	...	...	...	...	1549	...	1929
Kongsvinger .... d.	...	...	...	...	...	...	...	...	0850	...	...	1046	...	...	...	...	...	1439**a**	...	...	...	...	1717	...	2047
Charlottenberg 🏛 .... d.	...	...	...	0621	...	0720	0814	0832	0917	...	1000	1115	...	...	...	1407	...	1507	...	1547	...	1623	1745	2033	2117
Arvika .... d.	...	0553	0634	0649	...	0756	0839	0856	0941	...	1028	1136	...	...	...	1433	...	1532	...	1614	...	1651	1807	2058	2148
Kil .... d.	...	0618	0700	0727	...	0832	0917	0932	1010	...	1105	1210	...	1341	...	1510	...	1612	1540**g**	1649	...	1730	1835	2131	2224
Karlstad 751 .... a.	...	0633	0712	0740	...	0845	0930	0946	1023	...	1118	1224	...	1400	...	1522	...	1625	1552**g**	1702	...	1743	1855	2144	2237
Karlstad .... d.	0600	0639	0715	0745	0822	...	...	...	1026	1026	...	1226	1315	1420	1424	...	1622	...	1632	...	1712	1754	1855	...	...
Kristinehamn .... d.	0623	0657	0734	0810	0852	...	...	...	1048	1048	...	1251	1334	1444	1451	...	1654	...	1654	...	1737	1820	1920	...	...
Degerfors .... d.	0638	0710	0747	...	0906	...	...	...	1110	1110	...	1305	1347	1503	1505	...	1708	...	1708	...	1749	...	1936	...	...
Hallsberg .... a.	0710	|	0815	...	0938	...	...	...	1140	1140	...	1338	1416	1538	1538	...	1740	...	1740	...	1819	...	2006	...	...
Hallsberg 740 .... d.	0712	|	0817	...	0941	...	...	...	1142	1142	...	1341	1418	1541	1541	...	1742	...	1742	...	1821	...	2008	...	...
Katrineholm **730/40** ...... a.	0745	|	0841	...	1014	...	...	...	1215	1215	...	1414	1442	1614	1614	...	1815	...	1815	...	1845	...	2041	...	...
Flen **730/40** .... a.	0814	|	|	...	1028	...	...	...	1229	1229	...	1428	|	1628	1628	...	1832	...	1832	...	|	...	2100	...	...
Södertälje Syd **730/40** ... a.	0850	|	0918**s**	...	1104	...	...	...	1305	1305	...	1504	1524**s**	1704	1704	...	1908	...	1908	...	1924**s**	...	2140	...	...
Flemingsberg **730/40** ... a.	0902	|	|	...	1116	...	...	...	1317	1317	...	1516	|	1716	1716	...	1920	...	1920	...	|	...	2152	...	...
Stockholm C **730/40** ... a.	0915	0850	0939	...	1130	...	...	...	1330	1330	...	1530	1545	1731	1731	...	1935	...	1935	...	1945	...	2206	...	...

a – Ⓐ only.
g – ⑥ only.
k – Connects into train in previous column.
s – Stops to set down only.
u – Stops to pick up only.
X2000 – High speed train. Special supplement payable.

751 KARLSTAD - GÖTEBORG

km		2Ⓐ	Ⓐ	⑥		⑥	†	Ⓐ	⚒	†	†	Ⓐ	
0	**Karlstad 750** .... d.	...	0601	0700	0904	1231	1310	1348	1559	1559	1757	1856	...
19	Kil .... d.	...	0621	0717	0919	1246	1329	1402	1615	1615	1815	1914	...
70	Säffle .... d.	...	0654	0748	0956	1318	1402	1434	1647	1656	1846	1945	...
87	Åmål .... d.	*0532*	0707	0758	1007	1329	1413	1445	1657	1706	1856	1956	...
128	Mellerud .... d.	*0556*	0734	0824	1033	1356	1438	1511	1723	1731	1924	2021	...
169	Öxnered .... a.	0628	0801	0848	1056	1418	1502	1534	1756	1754	1955	2044	...
179	Trollhättan .... a.	0634	0808	0855	1103	1425	1509	1541	1804	1804	2002	2051	...
251	**Göteborg** .... a.	0729	0855	0944	1150	1513	1553	1632	1852	1852	2049	2138	...

	Ⓐ	⑥	Ⓒ	Ⓐ	⑥	†	Ⓐ	Ⓐ	Ⓒ	†	†	Ⓐ
Göteborg .... d.	0707	0817	1012	1107	1307	1407	1507	1707	1712	1812	1912	1912
Trollhättan .... d.	0756	0903	1058	1155	1352	1454	1553	1751	1757	1902	1958	1958
Öxnered .... d.	0805	0911	1106	1204	1400	1503	1606	1800	1805	1916	2006	2007
Mellerud .... d.	0826	0933	1127	1226	1427	1524	1627	1822	1826	1938	2026	2032
Åmål .... d.	0851	1003	1152	1251	1452	1549	1653	1847	1850	2009	2051	2101
Säffle .... d.	0904	1019	1204	1304	1505	1601	1708	1900	1908	...	2103	2113
Kil .... a.	0936	1052	1238	1339	1538	1634	1748	1941	1941	...	2137	2148
Karlstad 750 ...... a.	0951	1107	1258	1400	1552	1649	1804	1956	1956	...	2151	2203

752 VÄSTERÅS - LUDVIKA — Operator: *ST* 2nd class only

km		⚒	Ⓐ	⑥	⚒	†				Ⓐ	Ⓑ
0	**Västerås 756** .... d.	0615	0815	0815	1015	1015	1215	1415	1615	1815	2015
80	Fagersta C .... d.	0713	0916	0912	1113	1112	1312	1514	1713	1914	2114
129	**Ludvika** .... a.	0755	0957	...	1155	...	...	1556	1755	1956	2157

	⚒	⚒	Ⓑ	⑥	⚒	†			Ⓑ	Ⓐ
Ludvika .... d.	0605	0804	1005	...	1205	...	...	1605	1805	2005
Fagersta C .... d.	0648	0848	1048	1048	1248	1248	1448	1648	1848	2048
Västerås 756 .... a.	0745	0945	1145	1145	1345	1345	1545	1745	1945	2145

Additional services operate on Ⓐ only **Västerås - Fagersta and v.v.:**
From **Västerås**: 0715, 0915, 1115, 1315, 1515, 1715, 1915, 2115.
From **Fagersta**: 0548, 0748, 0948, 1148, 1348, 1548, 1748, 1948.

753 KRISTINEHAMN - MORA - ÖSTERSUND - GÄLLIVARE — INLANDSBANAN — 2010 service (subject to alteration) Summer only

km		🚂B		C	
0	**Kristinehamn 750** ... d.	0810	...	...	...
40	Nykroppa .... d.	|	...	...	...
66	**Persberg** .... d.	0915	...	...	...
—	Vansbro .... d.	1125	...	...	...
0	**Mora 765** .... d.	1220	...	1440	...
14	Orsa .... d.	...	...	1455	...
137	Sveg .... d.	...	...	1718	...
321	**Östersund 760** .... a.	...	...	2044	...

	C		🚂B	
Östersund 760 ..... d.	0722	...	...	...
Sveg .... d.	1052	...	...	...
Orsa .... d.	1303	...	...	...
Mora 765 .... d.	1317	...	1350	...
Vansbro .... d.	...	...	1438	...
Persberg .... d.	...	...	1640	...
Nykroppa .... d.	...	...	|	...
Kristinehamn 750 a.	...	...	1745	...

km		D	
0	**Östersund 760** .... d.	0715	...
115	Ulriksfors .... d.	0909	...
244	Vilhelmina .... d.	1145	...
312	Storuman .... d.	1303	...
384	Sorsele .... d.	1427	...
473	Arvidsjaur .... d.	1602	...
646	Jokkmokk .... d.	1938	...
746	**Gällivare 761** .... a.	2149	...

	E	
Gällivare 761 .... d.	0650	...
Jokkmokk .... d.	0843	...
Arvidsjaur .... d.	1241	...
Sorsele .... d.	1425	...
Storuman .... d.	1528	...
Vilhelmina .... d.	1701	...
Ulriksfors .... d.	1857	...
Östersund 760 ...... a.	2037	...

All rail services operated by Railbus.
B – June 28 - Aug. 1.
C – June 7 - Aug. 29 (not June 25, 26).
D – June 7 - Aug. 28 (not June 25, 26).
E – June 8 - Aug. 29 (not June 25, 26).
🚂 – Steam trains operate ⑤⑥ July 10 - Aug. 8, 2009 Arvidsjaur - Slagnäs and v.v. (*53 km*); depart 1745, arrive back 2200. ✆ +46 (0)70 356 72 47.

Operator: Inlandsbanan AB, Box 561, 831 27, Östersund.
✆ +46 (0)63 19 44 00, fax +46 (0)63 19 44 06.

754 NORRKÖPING - VÄSTERÅS - SALA — 2nd class only

km		Ⓐ	Ⓐ	⚒	⚒			Ⓐx	Ⓑ		Ⓑ
0	**Norrköping 730** .... d.	...	0632	0832	1033	1232	1432	1529	1632	1833	2032
48	Katrineholm **730** .... d.	...	0658	0900	1100	1300	1500	1555	1700	1859	2100
71	Flen **730** .... d.	...	0711	0913	1113	1313	1513	1614	1713	1912	2113
112	Eskilstuna .... d.	0552	0752	0952	1152	1352	1552	1652	1752	1952	2152
160	**Västerås** .... a.	0625	0825	1025	1225	1425	1625	1725	1825	2025	2225
160	**Västerås** .... d.	0627	0827	1027	1227	1427	1627**b**	1727	1827	2027**b**	...
199	Sala **765** .... a.	0650	0850	1050	1250	1450	1650**b**	1750	1850	2050**b**	...

	Ⓐ	⚒			⚒	Ⓑ	Ⓐx		Ⓑ	Ⓐ
Sala **765** .... d.	...	0710**a**	0910**d**	1110	1310	1510	1610	1710**b**	1910	2110
Västerås .... a.	...	0733**a**	0933**d**	1133	1333	1533	1633	1733**b**	1933	2133
Västerås .... d.	0535	0735	0935	1135	1335	1535	1635	1735	1935	2135
Eskilstuna .... d.	0609	0809	1009	1209	1409	1609	1722	1809	2009	2207
Flen **730** .... d.	0644	0844	1044	1244	1444	1644	1805	1844	2044	...
Katrineholm **730** .... d.	0658	0900	1100	1300	1500	1658	1820	1900	2100	...
Norrköping 730 .... a.	0724	0926	1126	1326	1526	1723	1847	1926	2126	...

a – Ⓐ only.
b – Ⓑ only.
d – ⚒ only.
x – Not Dec. 24 - Jan. 5.

Operator: *ST*

MJÖLBY - HALLSBERG - ÖREBRO - GÄVLE 755

Valid December 13 - May 14

km																								98			
		Ⓐ	Ⓐ	Ⓐ	⚒	Ⓐ	Ⓐ	Ⓐ	⑥	⚒	†	⚒	†	⚒		Ⓐ		Ⓐ	Ⓐx		Ⓑ			ⓇG	Ⓑ	Ⓑ	Ⓑ
0	**Mjölby 730** d.	...	...	...	...	...	0600	...	...	0812	...	1012	1012	...	...	...	1212	...	...	1412	...	1612	...	...	1812	...	2012
27	Motala d.	...	...	...	...	...	0617	...	...	0829	...	1029	1029	...	...	...	1229	...	...	1429	...	1629	...	...	1829	...	2029
96	**Hallsberg** a.	...	...	...	...	...	0657	...	...	0906	...	1106	1106	...	...	...	1306	...	...	1506	...	1710	...	...	1906	...	2106
	Hallsberg 756 d.	...	...	...	0516	0650	0718	0819	...	0924	...	1114	1125	...	...	...	1314	1344	...	1514	...	1720	...	1915	1941	1948	2120
121	**Örebro C 756** a.	...	...	...	0535	0709	0737	0838	...	0943	...	1133	1144	...	...	...	1333	1403	...	1533	...	1739	...	1935	2000	2007	2139
	Örebro C d.	...	...	...	0537	0710	0748	0900	0900	0947	...	1146	1146	1300	...	...	1342	1430	...	1547	1707	1747b	...	1937	2001	2017	...
146	Frövi d.	...	...	...	0552	0725	0803	0915	0915	1002	...	1201	1201	1315	...	...	1357	1447	...	1602	1722	1802b	...	|	2016	2032	...
204	Kopparberg d.	...	...	...	0636	|	0847	|	|	1046	...	1245	1245	|	...	...	1442	1536	...	1654	|	1846b	...	|	2101	|	...
232	Grängesberg d.	...	...	...	0702	|	0914	|	|	1107	...	1312	1312	|	...	...	1502	...	...	1718	|	1921b	...	|	2126	|	...
247	Ludvika d.	...	...	0625	0712	|	0925	|	|	1119	...	1323	1323	|	...	...	1513	...	1612	1729	|	1932b	...	|	2137	|	...
295	**Borlänge** a.	...	...	0702	0753	|	0953	|	|	1150	...	1354	1354	|	...	...	1553	...	1645	1757	|	2000b	...	|	2206	|	...
	Borlänge 765 d.	0557	...	0709	0810	|	1013	|	|	1218	1218	1416	1416	|	...	1508	1616	...	1656	1818	|	2017b	...	|	2215	|	...
317	Falun **761** d.	0630	...	0730	0826	|	1032	|	|	1236	1236	1435	1435	|	...	1528	1634	...	1714	1836	|	2036b	...	|	2232	|	...
	Fagersta d.	|	0600	|	|	0814	|	1006	1006	|	|	|	|	1358	...	|	|	...	|	|	1806	|	...	|	...	2120	...
	Avesta Krylbo d.	|	0637	|	|	0840	|	1030	1031	|	|	|	|	1423	...	|	|	...	|	|	1830	|	...	2128	...	2142	...
371	Storvik d.	0710	0715	0813	0906	0922	1110	1114	1108	1312	1312	1511	1511	1505	...	1611	1711	...	1751	1914	1909	2113b	...	|	...	2216	...
385	Sandviken d.	0721	0726	0826	0917	0933	1121	1125	1119	1323	1323	1521	1521	1516	...	1622	1722	...	1801	1925	1920	2124b	...	|	...	2231	...
408	**Gävle 760** a.	0736	0746	0847	0933	0947	1136	1140	1134	1338	1338	1544	1544	1531	...	1647	1737	...	1816	1940	1935	2139b	...	2227	...	2245	...

km							97																				
		Ⓐ	Ⓐ	Ⓐ	⚒	Ⓐ	ⓇG	Ⓐx	⑥		Ⓐ	⚒		†		Ⓐ	Ⓐ	Ⓒ	Ⓐ		Ⓑ	Ⓑ	Ⓐ	†	Ⓑ	Ⓑ	Z
0	**Gävle 760** d.	...	0425	...	...	...	0510	0520	...	0621d	0720	0812	0818d	1014	1022	1212	1222	1222	1414	1420	1618	1625	1720	1818	1824	2022	2027
23	Sandviken d.	...	0441	...	...	...	|	0537	...	0638d	0741	0829	0834d	1031	1038	1229	1238	1238	1431	1437	1635	1642	1741	1835	1841	2039	2044
37	Storvik d.	...	0456	...	...	...	|	0547	...	0648d	0751	0839	0844d	1041	1048	1239	1248	1248	1442	1447	1647	1652	1751	1844	1851	2049	2054
95	Avesta Krylbo d.	...	0536	...	...	...	0609	|	...	|	|	0923	|	1123	|	1320	|	|	1523	|	|	1734	|	1928	|	|	2135
130	Fagersta d.	...	0600	...	...	...	|	|	0745	|	|	0948	|	1148	|	1347	|	|	1557	|	|	1803	|	1958	|	|	2205
	Falun **761** d.	...	|	0508e	...	0605	|	0656	|	0725d	0832	|	0921d	|	1127	|	1326	1326	|	1526	1726	|	1834	...	1928	2128	...
	Borlänge 765 a.	...	|	0528e	...	0622	|	0722	|	0742d	0849	|	0938d	|	1143	|	1343	1343	|	1543	1743	|	1855	...	1944	2145	...
	Borlänge d.	...	|	0534	0534g	0649	|	0726	|	0800d	...	|	1000	|	1200	|	1400	1400	|	1600b	1800	|	...	...	2000	...	...
	Ludvika d.	...	|	0613	0611g	0718	|	0757	|	0831d	...	|	1029	|	1229	|	1429	1429	|	1629b	1831	|	...	...	2029	...	...
	Grängesberg d.	...	|	0622	0620g	0727	|	...	|	0840d	...	|	1038	|	1238	|	1438	1438	|	1638b	1846	|	...	...	2038	...	...
	Kopparberg d.	...	|	0642	0640g	0747	|	...	|	0903d	...	|	1107	|	1303	|	1503	1503	|	1658b	1907	|	...	...	2101	...	...
202	Frövi d.	0553	0643	0727	0725g	0834	|	...	0829	0951d	...	1032	1152	1231	1353	1439	1550	1550	1640	1746b	1957	1846	...	...	2153	...	...
228	**Örebro C** a.	0608	0658	0742	0740g	0849	0804	...	0844	1006d	...	1047	1207	1246	1408	1454	1605	1605	1655	1801b	2012	1900	...	...	2209	...	...
	Örebro C 756 d.	0613	0705	0744	0815	0852	0814	...	...	1017	...	...	1214	...	1416	1456	1606	1622	1735	1812b	2016	1902	...	...	2212	...	...
252	**Hallsberg 756** a.	0632	0723	0803	0834	0912	0838	...	...	1036	...	...	1233	...	1436	1514	1625	1641	1753	1831b	2035	1921	...	...	2232	...	...
	Hallsberg a.	0648	...	...	0845	...	...	...	...	1045	...	...	1245	...	1445	...	...	1651	...	1845b	2045	...	...	...	...	...	...
	Motala d.	0727	...	...	0927	...	...	...	...	1127	...	...	1327	...	1527	...	...	1731	...	1927b	2127	...	...	...	...	...	...
	Mjölby 730 a.	0743	...	...	0943	...	...	...	...	1143	...	...	1343	...	1543	...	...	1747	...	1945b	2143	...	...	...	...	...	...

G – sleeper, couchette and 2nd class Luleå (**91/2**) - Gävle - Göteborg and v.v.; 🍷 Gävle - Göteborg and v.v.
Z – ①②③④† only.
b – Ⓑ only.
d – ⚒ only.
e – ① only.
g – ⑥ only.
x – Not Dec. 24 - Jan. 10.

STOCKHOLM - VÄSTERÅS - ÖREBRO - HALLSBERG 756

km		159		97	163		167	171		175		179		991		183		756			187	764		772		
		Ⓐ	Ⓐ	Ⓡ◆	⚒	⚒x			⚒x		Ⓐ			Ⓐ	Ⓐ		Ⓐ	Ⓐx	†	Ⓐx		Ⓑ	Ⓐx		①-④x	⑤⑥x
0	**Stockholm C** ⊡ d.	...	0607	...	0707	0807	0907	1107	1207	1307	1407	1507	1607	1630	1637	1707	1737	1753	1807	1837	1907	2007	2107	2207	2307	2337
72	Enköping ⊡ d.	...	0645	...	0748	0845	0948	1148	1245	1348	1445	1548	1645	|	1718	1748	1818	1840	1848	1915	1948	2048	2145	2245	2348	0015
107	**Västerås 752** ⊡ d.	0609	0702	0704	0809	0902	1009	1209	1302	1409	1502	1609	1702	|	1739	1809	1837	1902	1907	1930	2009	2109	2200	2302	0007	0030
141	Köping d.	0627	0718x	|	0827	0918	1027	1227	1318	1427	1518x	1627	1718x	|	1757	1827	...	1918	...	...	2027	2127	...	2318b	...	...
159	Arboga **757** d.	0641	0731x	|	0841	0931	1041	1241	1331	1441	1531x	1641	1731x	1814	...	1841	...	1931	...	...	2041	2141	...	2331b	...	...
205	**Örebro** a.	0704	0751x	0804	0904	0951	1104	1304	1351	1504	1551x	1704	1751x	1838	...	1904	...	1952	...	...	2104	2205	...	2352b	...	...
205	**Örebro 755** ▲ d.	0710	...	0804	0910	...	1110	1310	...	1510	...	1710	...	1840	...	1910	...	1955	...	...	2107	2208	...	2355b	...	...
230	**Hallsberg 755** ▲ a.	0730	...	0838	0930	...	1130	1330	...	1530	...	1730	...	1900	...	1930	...	2015	...	...	2127	2228	...	0015b	...	...
	Göteborg a.	0957	...	1052	1157	...	1357	1557	...	1757	...	1957	...	...	...	2157	...	...	...	...	...	...	...	...	...	...

	982		711	781		715		719		164	723		168	172		176		180		194	184	98		188	76	70
	Ⓐ	Ⓐ	Ⓐ	Ⓐx	Ⓐx	⚒	Ⓐx	⚒x	y	⚒	†	⚒x			x		Ⓑx		Ⓐx	Y	Z	Ⓡ◆	Ⓑx		Ⓡ◆	Ⓡ◆
Göteborg d.	...	...	...	...	...	...	...	...	...	0602	...	...	0802	1002	...	1202	...	1402	...	1602	1602	1700	...	1802	1900	1900
Hallsberg 755 ▲ d.	0430	...	0530	0600	...	0633a	...	0745g	...	0828	0845	...	1028	1228	...	1428	...	1632	...	1828	1837	1915	...	2028	2110u	2110u
Örebro 755 ▲ a.	0450	...	0550	0620	...	0653a	...	0805g	...	0848	0905	...	1048	1248	...	1448	...	1652	...	1848	1857	1935	...	2048	|	|
Örebro d.	0452	...	0553	0622	...	0656a	...	0808	...	0856	0908	1008	1056	1256	1408d	1456	1608a	1656	1808	1856	1900	1937	...	2056	2130u	2130u
Arboga **757** d.	0515	...	0616	|	...	0721a	...	0831	...	0921	0931	1031	1121	1321	1431d	1521	1631a	1721	1831	1921	1926	|	...	2121	|	|
Köping d.	|	...	0627	|	0706	0731a	...	0840	...	0931	0940	1040	1131	1331	1440d	1531	1640a	1731	1840	1931	1936	|	...	2131	|	|
Västerås 752 ⊡ d.	|	0630	0653	0714	0730	0800	0823	0900	0900	0953	1000	1100	1153	1353	1500	1553	1700	1753	1900	1953	2004	2036	2053	2153	2220	2220
Enköping ⊡ d.	|	0643	0710	|	0743	0813	0840	0913	0913	1010	1013	1113	1210	1410	1513	1610	1713	1810	1912b	2010	2021	...	2110	2210	...	...
Stockholm C ⊡ a.	0650	0723	0753	0804	0823	0853	0923	0953	0953	1053	1053	1153	1253	1453	1553	1653	1753	1853	1953b	2053	2105	...	2153	2253	...	...

Y – ⑤⑥† (also ①–④ Dec. 21 - Jan. 10).
Z – ①–④ (not Dec. 21 - Jan. 10).
a – Ⓐ only.
b – Ⓑ only.
d – ⚒ only.
g – ⑥ only.
u – Stops to pick up only.
x – Not Dec. 24 - Jan. 5.
y – Dec. 24 - Jan. 5.
◆ – For days of running and composition see Tables **740/60**.
▲ – Additional services operate Hallsberg - Örebro and v.v.
⊡ – Additional services operate Stockholm - Västerås and v.v.

STOCKHOLM - ESKILSTUNA - ARBOGA 757

km		Ⓐ	2Ⓐ	Ⓐ	2⚒	Ⓐ	⑥				Ⓐr	Ⓐ	Ⓒ	2	Ⓑ	2Ⓐ	2Ⓐ		Ⓐr	Ⓐ	†r		Ⓐ	Ⓒ	r ①–④	⑤⑥r
0	**Stockholm C** d.	...	...	0625	...	0725	0751	0851	1055	1251	1351	1447	1451	...	1544	...	1630	1655	1725	1751	1751	1851	2051	2151	2251	2325
36	Södertälje Syd d.	...	...	0646	...	0746	0812	0912	1116	1312	1412	1508	1512	...	1605	...	1653	1716	1748	1812	1812	1912	2112	2212	2312	2346
67	Läggesta ● d.	...	...	0703	...	0804	0829	0929	1133	1329	1429	1526	1529	...	1626	...	1711	1733	1806	1829	1829	1929	2129	2229	2329	0003
83	Strängnäs d.	...	0625r	0723	...	0822	0840	0940	1144	1340	1440	1537	1540	...	1637	...	1727	1744	1817	1840	1840	1940	2140	2240	2340	0014
115	Eskilstuna a.	...	0641r	0741	...	0836	0854	0954	1158	1354	1454	1551	1554	...	1651	...	1743	1758	1835	1854	1854	1954	2154	2254	2354	0028
115	Eskilstuna d.	0549	0649	...	0807	...	...	*1007*	*1207*	*1407*	...	...	...	1607	...	1709	1745	1807	...	1859	...	2000	2200	...	...	...
141	Kungsör d.	0604	0707	...	0820	...	...	*1020*	*1220*	*1420*	...	...	...	1620	...	1722	1803	1820	...	1912	...	2013	2213	...	...	...
159	**Arboga 756** a.	0616	0717	...	0831	...	...	*1031*	*1231*	*1431*	...	...	...	1631	...	1733	1813	1829	...	1924	...	2025	2225	...	...	...
	Örebro **756** a.	...	...	...	...	...	...	...	...	...	...	...	...	...	...	...	1838	...	...	...	...	...	2248r	...	...	...

	Ⓐr	2Ⓐ	Ⓐr	Ⓐ	⑥	Ⓐ	2Ⓐ	⚒	⚒	2⚒		2		2		Ⓑr	2		2Ⓐ	Ⓑ	2Ⓒ	Ⓒ	2Ⓐ	Ⓐ		
Örebro **756** d.	...	0452	...	...	...	...	...	...	...	...	...	...	...	...	...	...	...	...	...	...	...	...	...	...	...	...
Arboga 756 d.	...	0515	...	0632	...	...	0729	...	...	0929	...	1129	...	1329	...	...	1529	...	1636	...	1729	...	1738	...	1935	2135
Kungsör d.	...	0524	...	0641	...	...	0738	...	...	0938	...	1138	...	1338	...	...	1538	...	1645	...	1738	...	1747	...	1944	2144
Eskilstuna a.	...	0540	...	0658	...	...	0754	...	...	0953	...	1153	...	1353	...	...	1553	...	1700	...	1753	...	1802	...	2000	2200
Eskilstuna d.	0506	0542	0642	0700	0702	0720	...	0802	0906	...	1006	...	1206	...	1406	1506	...	1606	...	1706	...	1806	...	1813	2006	2206
Strängnäs d.	0520	0558	0658	0716	0716	0734	...	0816	0920	...	1020	...	1220	...	1420	1520	...	1620	...	1720	...	1820	...	1829	2020	2220
Läggesta ● d.	0528	0607	|	0726	0724	0743	...	0824	0928	...	1028	...	1228	...	1428	1528	...	1628	...	1728	...	1828	...	1843	2028	2228
Södertälje Syd d.	0547	0627	|	0745	0743	0802	...	0843	0947	...	1047	...	1247	...	1447	1547	...	1647	...	1747	...	1847	...	1902	2047	2247
Stockholm C a.	0609	0650	0735	0809	0805	0824	...	0905	1009	...	1109	...	1309	...	1509	1609	...	1709	...	1809	...	1909	...	1924	2109	2309

r – Not Dec. 24 - Jan. 5.
● – Summer only narrow gauge service operates Läggesta nedre - Mariefred. Operator: Östra Södermanlands Järnväg ✆ +46 (0)159 210 00, fax +46 (0)159 210 06.

760 STOCKHOLM - GÄVLE - STORLIEN and UMEÅ

km		X2000		X2000	X2000	X2000		X2000	X2000	X2000	X2000	X2000		X2000	X2000				VEO	VEO						
		560	80	564	568	572	84	576	578	580	10582	582	94	584	442	92	98	10880	7120	7122		66	68	76	86	70
		R✕		R✕	R✕	R✕	✕	R✕	R✕	R✕	R✕	R✕	R	R✕	R✕	R	R					R	R	R	R	R
		Ⓐ	A	⚒	Ⓑ		B		Ⓑ	Ⓑ	C	Ⓐm	♦		Ⓑw	♦	♦	♦	♦	♦		♦	♦	♦	♦	♦
	Malmö Syd **730** .. d.	...	...	...	...	...	...	...	...	...	...	...	...	...	...	...	...	1855	1638	1638	...	1742	1742	...	...	...
	Göteborg **740** .... d.	...	...	...	...	...	...	...	...	...	...	...	...	...	1642	...	1700	2232	|	|	...	|	|	1900	...	1900
0	**Stockholm C 765** . ⊗ d.	0630	0758	0828	1030	1230	1314	1430	1600	1630	1716	1721	1812	1830	2000	2042	|	2155	2246	2320	...	2325u	2345u	2345u	2350	2350u
39	Arlanda C ✈ **765**◧ ⊗ d.	0648	0819	0848	1048	1248	1334	1448	1618	1648	1737	1740	|	1848	2018	|	|	|	2309	2344	...	|	|	|	0019	0019
69	Uppsala **765** .... ⊗ d.	0707u	0838u	0907u	1107u	1307u	1357u	1507u	1637u	1707u	1758u	1758u	1858u	1907u	2037	2124u	|	2235	2328	0005	...	|	|	|	0043u	0043u
182	**Gävle** .... ⊗ a.	0754	0939	0954	1154	1354	1452	1554	1724	1754	1847	1847	1950	1954	2124	2223	2227	|	0027	0107	...	|	|	|	0140	0140
182	**Gävle 755** .... d.	0757	0941	0957	1157	1357	1453	1557	1727	1757	1850	1850	1953	1957	...	2250	2250	2342u	0027	0107	...	|	|	|	0143	0143
260	Söderhamn .... d.	0834	|	1034	1234	1434	|	1634	|	1835	1927	1927	|	2034	...	|	|	|	|	|	...	|	|	|	0235	0235
314	Hudiksvall .... d.	0900	|	1100	1300	1500	|	1700	|	1900	1952	1952	|	2100	...	|	|	|	|	|	...	|	|	|	|	|
402	**Sundsvall** .... a.	0952y	|	1152y	1352y	1556	|	1752	|	1952	2052	2052	|	2155	...	|	|	|	|	|	...	0318	0340	0340	0409	0409
——	**Sundsvall 768** ...... ⊖ d.	...	|	1154q	...	...	|	1802g	|	1955d	...	...	|	...	...	|	|	|	|	|	...	0328	0400	0400	0425	0425
*	Härnösand **768** ..... a.	...	|	|	...	...	|	|	|	2040d	...	...	|	...	...	|	|	|	|	|	...	|	|	|	|	|
	Bollnäs .... d.	...	|	|	...	...	|	|	|	...	...	...	2050	...	...	2355	2355	|	|	|	...	|	|	|	|	|
	Ånge .... ⊖ d.	...	1226	1311q	...	...	|	1907g	2005	...	...	...	2228	...	...	0139	0139	|	0500r	0435t	...	0440s	0513s	0513s	0540	0540
0	Bräcke .... ⊖ d.	...	1245	1329q	...	...	1826	1924g	2023	...	...	...	2252	...	...	|	|	|	|	|	...	0503s	0536s	0536s	0602	0602
	Östersund 753 . ⊖ a.	...	1328	1416q	...	...	1908	2003g	2115	...	...	...	|	...	...	|	|	0540s	0612	0612	...	0552	0637	0637	0654	0654
	Östersund .... ▲ d.	...	1334z	...	...	...	1913v	...	2120j	...	...	...	|	...	...	|	|	|	0630	0630	...	0600	0640	0640	0658	0658
	Åre .... ▲ d.	...	1454z	...	...	...	2029v	...	2227j	...	...	...	|	...	...	|	|	0700s	0756	0756	...	0729s	0808s	0808s	0827	0827
	Duved .... ▲ d.	...	...	...	...	...	2041v	...	2235j	...	...	...	|	...	...	|	|	0723	0810	0810	...	0754	0827s	0827s	0841	0841
	Storlien 🏛 .... ▲ a.	...	...	...	...	...	...	...	...	...	...	...	|	...	...	|	|	...	0859	...	...	...	0917	0917	1000	1000
131	Långsele .... d.	...	...	...	...	...	...	...	...	...	...	...	0027	...	...	0329	0329	...	...	...	...	...	...	...	...	...
341	Vännäs .... a.	...	...	...	...	...	...	...	...	...	...	...	0305	...	...	0606	0606	...	...	...	...	...	...	...	...	...
372	**Umeå 761/8** .... a.	...	...	...	...	...	...	...	...	...	...	...	...	...	...	0631	0631	...	...	...	...	...	...	...	...	...

km		VEO		VEO							X2000		X2000		X2000	X2000	X2000	X2000		X2000	X2000	X2000				X2000
		7123	83	7121	10881	67	87	73	77	69	561	93	563	281	565	567	571	575	81	579	583	587	85	97	91	423
						R	R	R	R	R	R✕	R	R✕		R✕	R✕	R✕	R✕		R✕	R✕	R✕	✕	R	R	R✕
		♦	E	♦	♦	♦	♦	♦	♦	♦	Ⓐ	♦	Ⓐ	j	Ⓐ				D		Ⓑ		F	♦	♦	Ⓐm
	Umeå 761/8 .... d.	...	...	...	...	...	...	...	...	...	...	...	...	...	...	...	...	...	...	...	...	...	...	2050	2050	...
	Vännäs .... d.	...	...	...	...	...	...	...	...	...	...	2344	...	...	...	...	...	...	...	...	...	...	...	2125	2125	...
	Långsele .... d.	...	...	...	...	...	...	...	...	...	...	0215	...	...	...	...	...	...	...	...	...	...	...	0002	0002	...
0	**Storlien** 🏛 .... ▲ d.	...	...	1455	...	...	1700	1700	1805	1805	...	|	...	...	...	...	...	...	...	...	...	...	...	|	|	...
48	Duved .... ▲ d.	1025	1345	1536	1628	1719	1757	1757	1858u	1858u	...	|	...	2245	...	...	...	...	0902	...	...	...	...	|	|	...
57	Åre .... ▲ d.	1035	1409	1604	1711u	1803u	1843	1843	1939u	1939u	...	|	...	2253	...	...	...	...	0927	...	...	...	1532z	|	|	...
162	**Östersund** .... ▲ a.	1153	1519	1728	|	1952	2020	2020	2100	2100	...	|	...	2359	...	...	...	...		...	...	...	1707z	|	|	...
162	**Östersund 753** . ⊖ d.	1153	1523	1728	1851u	2003	2052	2052	2121	2121	...	|	...	...	0600	...	0800c	...	1040	...	...	1547n	1710	|	|	...
233	Bräcke .... ⊖ d.	|	|	|	|	2111u	2145	2145	2207u	2207u	...	0351	...	...	0640	...	0840c	...	1122	...	...	1628n	1754	|	|	...
263	Ånge .... ⊖ d.	1317	|	1832	|	2132u	2208	2208	2229u	2229u	...	0410	...	...	0700	...	0900c	...	|	...	...	1648n	1813	0147	0147	...
432	Bollnäs .... d.	|	|	|	|	|	|	|	|	|	...	0600	...	...	|	...	|	...	|	...	...	|	|	0343	0343	...
	Härnösand **768** ..... d.	|	|	|	|	|	|	|	|	|	...	|	0511e	...	|	...	|	...	|	...	...	|	|	|	|	...
*	**Sundsvall 768** ...... ⊖ a.	|	|	|	|	2241	2318	2318	2338	2338	...	|	0603e	...	|	...	1005c	...	|	...	...	1758n	|	|	|	...
	Sundsvall .... d.	|	|	|	|	2249	2325	2325	2345	2345	0508	|	0608	...	|	0808	1008y	1208y	|	1408y	1608	1808	|	|	|	...
	Hudiksvall .... d.	|	|	|	|	|	0033	0033	|	|	0558	|	0658	...	|	0858	1058	1258	|	1458	1658	1858	|	|	|	...
	Söderhamn .... d.	|	|	|	|	|	|	|	|	|	0626	|	0726	...	|	0926	1126	1326	|	1526	1726	1926	|	|	|	...
531	**Gävle 755** .... a.	1639	1906s	2144	|	|	0152s	0152s	|	|	0703	0710	0803	...	0928	1003	1203	1403	1359	1603	1806	2003	2049s	0458	0458	...
	Gävle .... ⊗ d.	1639	|	2144	|	|	|	|	|	|	0706	0715	0806	...	0931	1006	1206	1406	1402	1606	1806	2006	|	0510	0510	0526
	Uppsala **765** .... ⊗ a.	1759	2000s	2245	|	|	0249s	0249s	|	|	0751s	0831s	0851s	...	1021s	1051s	1251s	1451s	1501s	1651s	1851s	2051s	2155s	|	0602s	0621
	Arlanda C ✈ **765**◧ ⊗ a.	|	|	2309	|	|	0312	0312	|	|	0809	|	0909	...	1039	1109	1309	1509	1523	1709	1911	2109	2214	|	|	0639
	Stockholm C 765 . ⊗ a.	1841	2037	2333	|	|	0337	|	|	|	0830	0915	0930	...	1100	1130	1330	1530	1546	1730	1932	2130	2237	|	0645	0700
	Göteborg **740** .... a.	|	...	|	0422	|	...	0837	0837	|	...	...	...	...	...	...	...	...	...	...	...	...	...	1052	...	1017
	Malmö Syd **730** .. a.	0035	...	0547	0835	0946	...	...	...	0946	...	...	...	...	...	...	...	...	...	...	...	...	...	...	...	...

STOCKHOLM - GÄVLE and v.v. (additional services) :

	Ⓐx	Ⓐ			Ⓑ	K	Ⓐm	⑥	Ⓑx	Ⓑ
Stockholm C. ....d.	0728	0930	1130	1330	1528	1616	1621	1630	1728	1930
Arlanda C ✈ .... ◧ d.	0748	0948	1148	1348	1548	1637	1640	1648	1748	1948
Uppsala **765** ....d.	0807	1007	1207	1407	1607	1658	1658	1707	1807	2007
Gävle 755 ....a.	0858	1054	1258	1458	1658	1800	1800	1758	1858	2058

	Ⓐ	Ⓐx	⚒	⚒x					Ⓑx	
Gävle 755 ....d.	0626	0726	0906	1102	...	1306	1502	1702	1902	...
Uppsala **765** ....a.	0721	0821	0951	1151	...	1351	1551	1751	1951	...
Arlanda C ✈ .... ◧ a.	0739	0840	1009	1209	...	1409	1609	1809	2009	...
Stockholm C.........................a.	0800	0901	1030	1230	...	1430	1630	1830	2030	...

SUNDSVALL - ÖSTERSUND and v.v. local services (2nd class only) : Operator: *VEO*

		Ⓐ	Ⓐ		†		Ⓐ	†		
Sundsvall ....d.	0455	0747	1025	...	...	1410	1635	1800	...	2340
Ånge...............................d.	0608	0903	1137	...	1220	1526	1749	1917	...	0052
Bräcke.............................d.	0623	0920	1154	...	1236	1542	1806	1932	...	...
Östersund ....a.	0714	1006	1244	...	1321	1624	1852	2018	...	...

	Ⓐ	Ⓐ			Ⓑ	Ⓐ	†			
Östersund.........................d.	...	0738	1144	...	1340	1642	1655	...	2049	...
Bräcke ....d.	...	0825	1224	...	1425	1729	1742	...	2136	...
Ånge...................................d.	0613	0843	1244	...	1444	1749	1806	...	2154	...
Sundsvall.........................a.	0727	0957	1358	...	1558	1903	1927	...	2309	...

♦ – NOTES FOR TABLES 760/761 (LISTED BY TRAIN NUMBER)

66 – ⑥ Dec. 13 - Mar. 7; ③⑥ Mar. 8 - Apr. 11 (from Malmö): 🛏, ▬ and [2] Malmö - Stockholm - Duved; ✕ and [Bio] Malmö - Stockholm; ✕ Sundsvall - Duved.

67 – † Dec. 14 - Mar. 7; ④† Mar. 8 - Apr. 11: 🛏, ▬ and [2] Duved - Stockholm - Malmö; ✕ and [Bio] Duved - Sundsvall; ✕ Norrköping - Malmö.

68 – ③④⑤ Dec. 13 - Mar. 7; ④⑤ Mar. 8 - Apr. 11 (from Malmö): 🛏, ▬ and [2] Malmö - Stockholm (**76**) - Storlien; ✕ Malmö - Stockholm.

69 – ④⑤⑥ Dec. 13 - Mar. 6; ⑤⑥ Mar. 7 - Apr. 10: 🛏, ▬ and [2] Storlien (**77**) - Stockholm - Malmö; 🍷 Norrköping - Malmö.

70 – ①②† Dec. 13 - May 2; Ⓑ May 3 - June 19 (from Göteborg): 🛏, ▬ and [2] Göteborg - Stockholm (**86**) - Storlien; ✕ and [Bio] Göteborg - Stockholm.

73 – ①②③ Dec. 13 - May 2; Ⓑ May 3 - June 19: 🛏, ▬ and [2] Storlien (**87**) - Stockholm - Göteborg; ✕ and [Bio] Örebro - Göteborg.

76 – ③④⑤⑥ Dec. 13 - May 2 (from Göteborg): 🛏, ▬ and [2] Göteborg - Stockholm - Storlien; ✕ and [Bio] Göteborg - Stockholm; ✕ Sundsvall - Storlien. Conveys ③④⑤ Dec. 13 - Mar. 7; ④⑤ Mar. 8 - Apr. 11: 🛏, ▬ and [2] Malmö (**68**) - Stockholm - Storlien.

77 – ④⑤⑥† Dec. 13 - May 2: 🛏, ▬ and [2] Storlien - Göteborg; ✕ and [Bio] Storlien - Sundsvall; ✕ Örebro - Göteborg. Conveys ④⑤⑥ Dec. 13 - Mar. 6; ⑤⑥ Mar. 7 - Apr. 10: 🛏, ▬ and [2] Storlien - Stockholm (**69**) - Malmö.

86 – Daily Dec. 13 - May 2; Ⓑ May 3 - June 19: 🛏, ▬ and [2] Stockholm - Storlien; ✕ Östersund - Duved. Conveys ①②† Dec. 13 - May 2; Ⓑ May 3 - June 19: 🛏, ▬ and [2] Göteborg (**70**) - Stockholm - Storlien.

87 – Daily Dec. 13 - May 2; Ⓑ May 3 - June 19: 🛏, ▬ and [2] Storlien - Stockholm; ✕ Duved - Östersund. Conveys ①②③ Dec. 13 - May 2; Ⓑ May 3 - June 19: 🛏, ▬ and [2] Storlien - Stockholm (**73**) - Göteborg.

91 – 🛏, ▬ and [2] Luleå - Stockholm; 🛏, ▬, [2] and ✕ Luleå - Gävle (**97**) - Göteborg.

92 – 🛏, ▬ and [2] Stockholm - Luleå; 🛏, ▬, [2] and ✕ Göteborg (**98**) - Gävle - Luleå.

93 – 🛏, ▬, [2] and ✕ Narvik - Stockholm; 🛏, ▬ and [2] Luleå (**7006**) - Boden - Stockholm; [2] Narvik - Boden (**7007**) - Luleå.

94 – 🛏, ▬, [2] and ✕ Stockholm - Narvik; 🛏, ▬ and [2] Stockholm - Boden (**7005**) - Luleå; [2] Luleå (**7004**) - Boden - Narvik.

97/8 – 🛏, ▬ and [2] Luleå (**91/2**) - Gävle - Göteborg and v.v.; 🍷 Gävle - Göteborg and v.v.

7004/7 – [2] Narvik (**93/94**) - Boden - Luleå and v.v.

7005/6 – 🛏, ▬ and [2] Stockholm (**93/94**) - Boden - Luleå and v.v.

7120 – ⑥ Dec. 19 - Apr. 10: ▬, [2] and ✕ Malmö - Storlien.

7121 – † Dec. 20 - Apr. 11: ▬, [2] and ✕ Storlien - Malmö.

7122 – ③ Dec. 29 - Apr. 7: ▬, [2] and ✕ Malmö - Duved.

7123 – ④ Dec. 30 - Apr. 10 (from Duved): ▬, [2] and ✕ Duved - Malmö.

10880 – ⑥ Dec. 13 - Apr. 11 (from Malmö): 🛏, ▬ and ✕ Malmö - Göteborg - Duved.

10881 – † Dec. 19 - Apr. 11: 🛏, ▬ and ✕ Duved - Göteborg - Malmö.

ÖSTERSUND - TRONDHEIM and v.v. : Operator: *VEO*

km		2	2
0	**Östersund** ... d.	0718	1627
105	Åre .... d.	0842	1745
114	Duved .... d.	0850	1753
162	Storlien 🏛 .... a.	0928	1830
268	**Trondheim**... a.	1110	2012

	2	2
Trondheim .... d.	0750	1650
Storlien 🏛 ...... d.	0935	1835
Duved .... d.	1011	1911
Åre .... d.	1024	1927
Östersund ..... a.	1136	2039

A – Daily Dec. 13 - May 2; Ⓐ May 3 - June 19.
B – ④⑤⑥† Dec. 13 - May 2; ⑤† May 3 - June 19.
C – † (also Ⓐ Dec. 21 - Jan. 10).
D – ①⑥† Dec. 14 - May 3.
E – † Dec. 27 - May 2.
F – Daily Dec. 13 - May 2; Ⓑ May 3 - June 19.
G – Ⓐ Dec. 13 - June 13.
H – June 6 - 19. Riksgränsen stop is at hotel.
J – June 7 - 19. Riksgränsen stop is at hotel.
K – † Dec. 13 - 20; Ⓐ Dec. 21 - 23; Ⓑ Jan. 6 - 10; † Jan. 11 - June 19.

c – Ⓒ only.
d – ①②③④† until May 27.
e – Until May 30.
f – Feb. 1 - June 6.
g – ⑥ only.
j – ④⑤ Dec. 13 - May 2.
k – May 3 - June 19.
m – Not Dec. 21 - Jan. 10.
n – ⑥ May 3 - June 19.
p – Jan. 31 - June 5.
q – ⑥ May 8 - June 19.
r – Arrive 0359.
s – Stops to set down only.
t – Arrive 0400
u – Stops to pick up only.
v – ④⑤⑥† Dec. 13 - May 2.
w – Not Dec. 20 - Jan. 9.
x – Not Dec. 24 - Jan. 5.
y – ①–⑤ May 10 - June 19 connection by 🚌.
z – Dec. 13 - May 2.

◇ – Ticket point.
▲ – For Östersund - Storlien - Trondheim services see panel.
⊖ – For Sundsvall - Östersund local services see panel.
⊗ – For additional services Stockholm - Gävle and v.v. see panel.
◧ – From Stockholm stops to pick up only; to Stockholm stops to set down only.
* – Ånge - Sundsvall: *94 km*; Boden - Luleå: *36 km*; Härnösand - Sundsvall: *68 km*.

UMEÅ - LULEÅ - KIRUNA - NARVIK 761

km		🚌 J	90 2f🍷	7004 ♦	94 ♦	7005 ♦	96 2🍷	92 ♦		7000 ⚒	7002 †	7022 2G
0	**Umeå 760/8** d.	...	...	...	...	...	...	0641	...	...	...	1630
31	Vännäs d.	...	...	...	0305	...	...	|	...	...	...	|
142	Bastuträsk d.	...	...	...	0411	...	...	0831	...	...	...	1749
270	Älvsbyn d.	...	...	...	0525	...	...	0953	...	...	...	1904
316	**Boden** a.	...	...	...	0605	0629	...	1030	...	...	...	1930
*	**Luleå 768/9** d.	...	...	0541	|	0653	1001	1110	...	1632	1840	2008
316	**Boden** d.	...	...	0605	0622	...	1041	...	...	1712	1907	...
484	Gällivare **753** d.	...	...	...	0818	...	1244	...	...	1913	2105	...
584	**Kiruna** d.	0709	0709	...	0931	...	1404	...	...	2019	2210	...
677	Abisko Östra d.	0822	0822	...	1029	...	1505	...	...	...	...	...
686	Björkliden d.	0836	0836	...	1046	...	1520	...	...	...	...	...
706	Vassijaure ◇ d.	0856	0856	...	|	...	1549	...	...	...	...	...
713	Riksgränsen 🏛 d.	0906	0909	...	1139	...	1602	...	...	...	...	...
753	**Narvik** a.	1001	1001	...	1240	...	1651	...	...	...	...	...

	7021 2G	7001 ⚒z	7011 ⚒k	7003 †	91 ♦	95 2🍷	7006 ♦	93 ♦	7007 ♦	99 2p🍷	🚌 H
Narvik d.	...	...	...	...	...	1026	...	1450	...	1742	1742
Riksgränsen 🏛 d.	...	...	...	...	...	1119	...	1538	...	1838	1838
Vassijaure ◇ d.	...	...	...	...	...	1138	...	|	...	1845	1847
Björkliden d.	...	...	...	...	...	1159	...	1612	...	1911	1914
Abisko Östra d.	...	...	...	...	...	1215	...	1631	...	1926	1928
Kiruna d.	...	0538	0538	0750	...	1332	...	1736	...	2046	2046
Gällivare **753** d.	...	0643	0643	0902	...	1445	...	1842	...	...	...
Boden a.	...	0835	0837	1055	...	1648	...	2035	2040	...	...
Luleå 768/9 a.	0541	0858	0903	1120	1632	1724	1957	|	2104	...	...
Boden d.	0610	...	...	...	1725	...	2027	2055	...	...	...
Älvsbyn d.	0635	...	...	...	1751	...	...	2121	...	...	...
Bastuträsk d.	0744	...	...	...	1908	...	...	2237	...	...	...
Vännäs d.	|	...	...	...	|	- ...	...	2344	...	...	...
Umeå 760/8 a.	0913	...	...	...	2040	...	...	...	...	...	...

FOR NOTES SEE PREVIOUS PAGE

STOCKHOLM - BORLÄNGE - MORA 765

km		ST Ⓐ	10010 Ⓐx	ST	40 ⊖ Ⓐ	ST ⑥	16 x ①–④	18 D	ST	22 Ⓑx	44 ⑥	ST Ⓑ	54 Ⓑw	10024 Ⓐx	26 E	46 †	ST ⚒	58 ⑤x	X2000 596 †v	30 ⊖ Ⓐ	ST	X2000 590 Ⓐy	48 ⊖	38 F	ST Ⓑ	50 B	52 ⑤
0	**Stockholm** C. **760** d.	...	0614	...	0745	...	0845	0945	...	1145	1145	...	1145	1245	1345	1345	...	1445	1545	1545	...	1650	1745	1945	...	2211	2216
37	Arlanda C ✈ **760** ◧ d.	...	0634	...	0807	...	0907	1007	...	1207	1207	...	1207	1307	1407	1407	...	1507	1607	1607	...	1709	1808	2007	...	2231	2237
66	Uppsala **760** d.	...	0656	...	0826	...	0926	1026	...	1226	1226	...	1226	1326	1426	1426	...	1526	1626u	1626	...	1732u	1826	2026	...	2256	2256
128	Sala **754** d.	...	0745	...	0901	...	1001	1101	...	1301	1301	...	1301	1401	1501	1501	...	1601	1700	1701	...	|	1901	2101	...	2331	2331
161	Avesta Krylbo d.	...	0804	...	0920	...	1020	1120	...	1320	1320	...	1320	1420	1520	1520	...	1633	1718	1720	...	1820	1920	2120	...	2350	2350
226	**Borlänge** a.	...	0851	...	1007	...	1100	1207	...	1407	1407	...	1407	1505	1607	1607	...	1746	1753	1808	...	1900	2007	2207	...	0033	0033
	Borlänge 755 ● d.	0639	0853	0902	1010	1020	1102	1209	1220	1409	1410	1418	1424	...	1609	1610	1619	1750	1753	1808	1820	1900	2010	2209	2228	0035	0035
250	Falun **755** ● a.	|	0910	|	|	|	1119	1226	|	1426	|	|	|	...	1626	|	|	|	1811	1827	|	1919	|	2226	|	0052	0052
269	Leksand d.	0710	...	0933	1051	1051	...	...	1251	...	1449	1449	1509	...	...	1652	1650	1830	...	...	1851	...	2049	...	2259	...	...
289	Rättvik d.	0726	...	0949	1112	1111	...	...	1311	...	1510	1509	1528	...	...	1712	1711	1849	...	...	1911	...	2110	...	2315	...	...
329	**Mora 753** ♣ a.	0749	...	1012	1137	1134	...	...	1334	...	1535	1535	1553	...	...	1737	1734	1919	...	...	1934	...	2136	...	2338	...	...
330	Mora Strand ♣ a.	0755	...	1017	...	1139	...	...	1339	...	...	1540	...	...	...	...	1739	...	...	...	1939	...	...	...	2343	...	...

	51 ⚒	10011 Ⓐx	ST Ⓐ	X2000 591 Ⓐy	41 Ⓐ	ST ⑥	X2000 595 ⑥y	ST Ⓑ	19 Ⓑm	43 ⑥	ST	23 ⚒	25 x ①–④	45 Ⓑ	ST ⑥	27 ⑥	ST	31 Ⓑ	59 †z	55 Ⓑw	47 ⑥	ST Ⓑ	35 Ⓑx	49 †	ST ⚒	39 Ⓐx	ST Ⓑ
Mora Strand ♣ d.	...	...	0512	...	...	0627	...	0823	...	...	1027	...	...	...	1227	...	1425	...	...	...	...	1627	...	...	1827	...	2025
Mora 753 ♣ d.	...	...	0517	...	0622	0632	...	0828	...	0820	1032	...	...	1228	1232	...	1430	...	1442	1609	1622	1632	...	1822	1832	...	2030
Rättvik d.	...	...	0540	...	0647	0655	...	0851	...	0845	1055	...	...	1253	1255	...	1453	...	1509	1634	1647	1655	...	1847	1855	...	2053
Leksand d.	...	...	0555	...	0710	0710	...	0906	...	0904	1110	...	...	1313	1310	...	1509	...	1531	1653	1709	1710	...	1909	1910	...	2108
Falun **755** ● d.	0334	0532	|	0614	|	|	0734	|	0934e	|	|	1134	1234	|	|	1334	|	1533	|	|	|	|	1734	|	|	1934	|
Borlänge 755 ● a.	0351	0549	0627	0635	0749	0742	0751	0941	0951e	0944	1143	1151	1251	1351	1342	1351	1541	1550	1606	1734	1748	1742	1751	1948	1942	1951	2140
Borlänge d.	0353	0551	...	0637	0752	...	0753	...	0953	0953	...	1153	1253	1353	...	1353	...	1553	1608	1753	1753	...	1753	1953	...	1953	...
Avesta Krylbo d.	0440	0636	...	0714	0840	...	0840	...	1040	1040	...	1240	1337	1440	...	1440	...	1640	1659	1840	1840	...	1840	2040	...	2040	...
Sala **754** a.	0459	0656	...	|	0859	...	0859	...	1059	1059	...	1259	1356	1459	...	1459	...	1659	1727	1859	1859	...	1859	2059	...	2059	...
Uppsala **760** a.	0534	0733	...	0801s	0933	...	0933s	...	1133s	1133	...	1333	1433	1533	...	1533	...	1733	1816	1933	1933	...	1933	2133	...	2133	...
Arlanda C ✈ **760** ◧ a.	0557	0753	...	0822	0953	...	0953	...	1153	1153	...	1353	1453	1553	...	1553	...	1753	1836	1953	1953	...	1953	2153	...	2153	...
Stockholm C. **760** a.	0619	0816	...	0840	1016	...	1016	...	1216	1216	...	1416	1516	1616	...	1616	...	1816	1900	2018	2018	...	2018	2216	...	2216	...

B – ①②③④† only.
D – Ⓒ (daily Dec. 24 - Jan. 5).
E – ⚒ Dec. 13 - 23; ⑥ Dec. 24 - Jan. 5; ⚒ Jan. 6 - June 19.
F – Ⓑ Dec. 13 - 23; † Dec. 24 - Jan. 5; Ⓑ Jan. 6 - June 19.

e – † only.
m – Not Ⓐ Dec. 24 - Jan. 5.
s – Stops to set down only.
u – Stops to pick up only.

v – Not Dec. 14 - Jan. 9.
w – Dec. 24 - Jan. 5.
x – Not Dec. 24 - Jan. 5.
y – Not Dec. 21 - Jan. 10.
z – Not Dec. 28 - Jan. 5.

⊖ – Train number **100xx** or **200xx** on some dates.
♣ – Local journeys are not permitted Mora - Mora Strand and v.v.
● – Additional services operate Borlänge - Falun and v.v.
◧ – From Stockholm calls to pick up only; to Stockholm calls to set down only.

Operator: *LTAC* 🚌 SUNDSVALL - UMEÅ - LULEÅ - HAPARANDA 768

			Ⓑ				Ⓐ				
Sundsvall 760 ‡ d.	...	...	...	0800	1000	1200	...	1400	1600	1800	...
Härnösand § d.	...	...	...	0900	1100	1300	...	1500	1700	1900	...
Örnsköldsvik § d.	...	...	...	1030	1230	1430	...	1630	1830	2030	...
Umeå 761 § a.	...	...	...	1205	1405	1605	...	1805	2005	2210	...
Umeå § d.	0545	0800	1000	1215	1415	1615	1725	1815	2015	...	...
Skelleftea § d.	0810	1030	1225	1420	1620	1820	2000	2020	2220	...	...
Piteå § d.	0930	1150	1350	1535	1735	1935	2125	2135	2335	...	...
Luleå 769 § a.	1025	1240	1440	1625	1825	2025	2220	2225	0025	...	...
Haparanda 769 § a.	1310	1535	1740	1850	2050	2250	0100	...	...	...	...

								Ⓐ		†	Ⓐ
Haparanda 769 § d.	...	...	0520	0720	...	1120	1200	1335	1610	1810	1810
Luleå 769 § d.	...	0545	0750	0950	1150	1350	1500	1620	1900	2045	2055
Piteå § d.	...	0640	0845	1045	1245	1445	1605	1725	2000	2140	2155
Skelleftea § d.	...	0755	1000	1200	1400	1600	1740	1850	2125	2300	2310
Umeå 761 § a.	...	0950	1155	1355	1555	1755	1950	2100	2335	0120	0130
Umeå § d.	0805	1005	1205	1405	1605	1805	...	...	...	...	...
Örnsköldsvik § d.	0940	1140	1340	1540	1740	1940	...	...	...	...	...
Härnösand § d.	1105	1305	1505	1705	1905	2105	...	...	...	...	...
Sundsvall 760 ‡ a.	1200	1400	1600	1800	2000	2200	...	...	...	...	...

§ – Bus station.

‡ – All buses originate / terminate at Sundsvall bus station (journey 5–10 minutes).

🚌 LULEÅ - HAPARANDA and HAPARANDA - TORNIO - KEMI 769

Luleå - Haparanda valid June 14 - December 12, 2009; Haparanda - Tornio - Kemi valid August 13, 2009 - June 6, 2010

	Ⓐ	Ⓒ			Ⓑ			Ⓐ		⑥	Ⓐ
Luleå Bus Station **768** § d.	0810	0830	1050	1310	1510	1635	1835	1930	2035	2240	2240
Haparanda Bus Station 🏛 § a.	1035	1050	1310	1535	1740	1850	2050	2150	2250	0055	0100

	Ⓐ			Ⓐ			Ⓐ	Ⓒ		
Haparanda Bus Station 🏛 § d.	0440	0520	0720	0910	1120	1200	1335	1400	1610	1810
Luleå Bus Station **768** § a.	0700	0740	0940	1140	1340	1425	1600	1625	1835	2035

	①–⑤	①–⑥	①–⑤	①–⑤	①–⑥	⑥⑦	①–⑤	①–⑤	⑥x	①–⑥		①–⑤	x	①–⑥	①–⑤	x	①–⑤	①–⑥		①–⑤	x	x	①–⑤	①–⑤
Haparanda Bus Station 🏛 § d.	0515	0615	...	0715	0815	...	0915	1115	...	1215	...	1315	...	1415	1515	...	...	1615	...	...	...	...	1815	2015
Tornio Bus Station 🏛 ‡ d.	0625	0725	0740	0825	0925	1005	1025	1225	1235	1325	...	1425	1500	1525	1625	1655	1700	1725	...	1855	1855	1920	1925	2125
Kemi Railway Station **790** ‡ d.	|	|	0812	|	|	|	|	|	|	|	...	|	|	|	|	1718	1723	|	...	1918	|	|	|	|
Kemi Bus Station ‡ a.	0700	0800	0810	0900	1000	1035	1100	1300	1310	1400	...	1500	1525	1600	1700	1720	1725	1800	...	1920	1920	1952	2000	2200

	①–⑤	①–⑤	①–⑤	①–⑥	①–⑤	①–⑥	①–⑤	①–⑥		①–⑤	①–⑤	①–⑥	①–⑤	①–⑤	①–⑤	①–⑤	①–⑥	①–⑤	x	①–⑥	x	⑥⑦	①–⑤	①–⑤
Kemi Bus Station ‡ d.	0605	0645	0705	0805	0905	0910	0925	1005	...	1205	1305	1405	1430	1505	1510	1530	1605	1705	1715	1805	1830	1850	2005	2205
Kemi Railway Station **790** ‡ d.	|	0646	|	|	|	0915	0920	|	...	|	|	|	1432	|	1511	1525	|	|	|	|	1835	1851	|	|
Tornio Bus Station 🏛 ‡ d.	0638	0715	0738	0838	0938	0950	0955	1038	...	1238	1338	1438	1500	1538	1550	1605	1638	1738	1750	1838	1910	1925	2038	2238
Haparanda Bus Station 🏛 § a.	0550	...	0650	0750	0850	...	...	0950	...	1150	1250	1350	...	1450	...	...	1550	1650	...	1750	...	...	1950	2150

r – Haparanda railway station (currently no rail service).
x – Runs †. However, runs on the last day only when there are two consecutive holidays (not June 20, Oct. 31, Dec. 25, 26, Jan. 1, 6, Apr. 2, 4, May 1, 13).

‡ – Finnish time.
§ – Swedish time.

Additional local services operate Tornio - Kemi and v.v.

Operators:
Luleå - Haparanda; Länstrafiken Norrbotten; www.ltnbd.se
Tornio - Kemi; Veljekset Salmela; www.veljeksetsalmela.fi
Haparanda - Tornio - Kemi direct services; www.netmatkat.palvelee.fi

Veljekset Salmela also operate Haparanda - Tornio - Kemi direct services (international rail tickets valid):
From Haparanda: 0850⑥⑦, 0945⑥, 1030①–⑤, 1120⑥**x**, 1155①–⑤, 1210⑥, 1300①–⑤, 1325⑥, 1450①–⑤, 1805①–⑤, 1805⑥**x**.
From Kemi: 0745①–⑤, 0910①–⑥, 0955①–⑤, 1125①–⑤, 1125⑥, 1315①–⑤, 1415⑥, 1500①–⑤, 1620①–⑤, 1625⑥, 1715⑥**x**, 1850⑥⑦, 1900①–⑤, 2050①–⑤, 2155①–⑤, 2245⑥.

Approximate walking distances:
Haparanda bus station - Tornio bus station 800 metres; Kemi railway station - Kemi bus station 200 metres.

NORWAY

SEE MAP PAGE 337

Operator: Norges Statsbaner (NSB).

Services: All trains convey second class seating accommodation. Many services, as identified in the notes, also convey *NSB Komfort* accommodation (see below). Sleeping-cars (🛏) have one-, two-, and three-berth compartments; passengers may reserve a berth in any category with either a first or second-class ticket. Most long distance express trains convey a bistro car (✕) serving hot and cold meals, drinks and snacks. 🍷 indicates that drinks and light refreshments are available from automatic vending machines.

Timings: NSB services are valid **December 13, 2009 - June 12, 2010**. Dec. 25, 26, Jan. 1, Apr. 1, 2, 5, May 1, 13, 17, 24 are public holidays. **All services are subject to alteration Dec. 24 - Jan. 1** (alterations to domestic services during this period are **not** shown in the tables below; ✆ +47 815 00 888 to confirm travel arrangements).

Reservations: Seat reservation is highly recommended on long-distance routes Oslo - Kristiansand - Stavanger (Table **775**), Oslo - Bergen (Table **780**), Oslo - Trondheim / Åndalsnes (Table **785**) and Trondheim - Bodø (Table **787**).

Supplements: A supplement is payable (90 NOK) to use *NSB Komfort* accommodation, a dedicated area provided on many trains with complimentary tea / coffee and newspapers.

770 OSLO - HALDEN - GÖTEBORG

Most trains convey NSB Komfort and 🍷

km	Norwegian train number	103	105	107	109	109	111	113	115	117	117	119	121	141	123	143	125	125	127	129	131	133	135	137	139
	Swedish train number		391			393	▲	▲			395							397	399						
		Ⓐ	A	⚒z		⑥k	⚒z		⚒z		Ⓑm	⚒z		Ⓐw	p	Ⓐw		⑥t	Ⓑr		Ⓑq		Ⓑq	Ⓑn	
0	**Oslo** Sentral ....d.	0600	0700	0800	0900	0900	1000	1100	1200	1300	1300	1400	1500	1530	1600	1632	1700	1700	1800	1900	2000	2100	2200	2300	2359
60	Moss ....d.	0643	0744	0843	0943	0943	1043	1143	1243	1343	1343	1443	1543	|	1644	|	1743	1743	1843	1943	2043	2143	2243	2343	0050
94	Fredrikstad ....d.	0709	0810	0910	1009	1009	1109	1209	1309	1409	1409	1509	1609	1637	1711	1739	1810	1810	1909	2010	2109	2209	2309	0009	0117
109	Sarpsborg ....d.	0729	0825	0925	1024	1024	1124	1224	1324	1424	1424	1523	1623	1653	1725	1753	1825	1825	1924	2025	2125	2225	2323	0023	0130
137	**Halden** ....a.	0749	0845	0945	1044	1044	1144	1244	1344	1444	1444	1543	1643	1719	1746	1818	1845	1845	1944	2045	2145	2245	2343	0043	0150
137	**Halden** ★ ....d.	...	0851	...	...	1050	...	...	...	...	1450	...	...	...	...	...	...	1848	1953	...	...	...	...	...	...
268	Öxnered **751** ....a.	...	1004	...	...	1204	...	...	...	...	1604	...	...	...	...	...	...	2001	2107	...	...	...	...	...	...
278	Trollhättan **751** ....a.	...	1011	...	...	1211	...	...	...	...	1611	...	...	...	...	...	...	2009	2114	...	...	...	...	...	...
350	**Göteborg 751** ....a.	...	1055	...	...	1254e	...	...	...	...	1659f	...	...	...	...	...	...	2054e	2155f	...	...	...	...	...	...

Swedish train number								390		▲	392	▲				394					396		398		
Norwegian train number	102	104	142	106	144	108	110	112	112	114	116	116	118	120	122	124	124	126	128	130	132	132	134	136	138
	Ⓐ	Ⓐ	Ⓐw	⚒z	Ⓐw		⚒z	A		⚒z	⑥k		⚒z		p	Ⓑm		Ⓑq		Ⓑq	⑥t		Ⓑr	Ⓑn	
Göteborg 751 ....d.	...	...	...	...	...	...	...	0645	...	...	0845g	...	...	...	...	1245h	...	...	...	...	1639g	...	1745h	...	...
Trollhättan **751** ....d.	...	...	...	...	...	...	...	0729	...	...	0929	...	...	...	...	1328	...	...	...	...	1725	...	1831	...	...
Öxnered **751** ....d.	...	...	...	...	...	...	...	0735	...	...	0936	...	...	...	...	1335	...	...	...	...	1731	...	1838	...	...
Halden ★ ....a.	...	...	...	...	...	...	...	0848	...	...	1049	...	...	...	...	1448	...	...	...	...	1843	...	1951	...	...
Halden ....d.	0400	0500	0532	0558	0632	0658	0800	0900	0900	1000	1100	1100	1200	1300	1400	1500	1500	1600	1700	1800	1900	1900	2000	2100	2200
Sarpsborg ....d.	0422	0522	0553	0620	0653	0720	0822	0923	0923	1022	1122	1122	1222	1322	1422	1521	1521	1621	1723	1823	1922	1922	2023	2123	2223
Fredrikstad ....d.	0437	0537	0607	0634	0707	0734	0837	0937	0937	1037	1137	1137	1237	1337	1437	1535	1535	1635	1737	1837	1937	1937	2037	2137	2237
Moss ....d.	0503	0603	0633	0701	0733	0801	0903	1003	1003	1103	1203	1203	1303	1403	1503	1601	1601	1701	1803	1903	2003	2003	2103	2203	2303
Oslo Sentral ....a.	0545	0645	0715	0745	0815	0845	0945	1045	1045	1145	1245	1245	1345	1445	1545	1645	1645	1745	1845	1945	2045	2045	2145	2245	2345

A – ①–⑤ (not Dec. 24, 25, 31, Jan. 1, Apr. 1, 2, 5, May 13, 17, 24).
e – 11 minutes later on Feb. 20. 31 minutes later on June 5 (by 🚌 from Trollhättan).
f – 26–30 minutes later on June 6 (by 🚌 from Trollhättan).
g – 29–35 minutes **earlier** on June 5 (by 🚌 to Trollhättan).
h – 35 minutes **earlier** on June 6 (by 🚌 to Trollhättan).
k – Also Dec. 24, 31; not Dec. 26, Apr. 3, May 1.
m – Also Dec. 26, Apr. 3, May 1; not Dec. 24, 31.
n – Not Apr. 1, 2, May 23.
p – Not Apr. 1–4, May 1, 23.
q – Not Apr. 1–4, May 23.
r – Also Dec. 26, Apr. 3, May 1; not Dec. 24, 25, 31.
t – Not Dec. 26, Apr. 3, May 1.
w – Not Mar. 29, 30, 31, May 14.
z – Not Apr. 3.
▲ – On ①–⑤ from Apr. 6 by 🚌 Oslo - Fredrikstad and v.v.
★ – 🛃 at Kornsjø (*km169*).

771 OSLO - OSLO ✈ GARDERMOEN

See also Table 783

Operated by NSB Gardermobanen AS.
Special fares apply.
✆ +47 23 15 90 00
fax +47 23 15 90 01.

Daily services (journey time: 22 minutes)
Trains call at Lillestrøm 10 minutes from Oslo
From Oslo Sentral every 20 minutes 0445 - 0005.
From Gardermoen every 20 minutes 0536 - 0056.

Additional services on Ⓑ (journey time: 19 minutes)
Non-stop services
From Oslo Sentral every 20 minutes: 0615 - 2235 on Ⓐ, 1215 - 2315 on ⑦.
From Gardermoen every 20 minutes: 0646 - 2306 on Ⓐ, 1246 - 2346 on ⑦.

773 OSLO - GJØVIK

All trains convey NSB Komfort and 🍷

km				h					Ⓐ				Ⓐ
0	**Oslo** S.... ‡ d.	0007	...	0707	0907	1107	1307	1507	1613	1707	1907	2107	2307
56	Roa.... ‡ d.	0107	...	0805	1004	1203	1403	1605	1711	1809	2004	2205	0008
70	Jaren.... ‡ d.	0123	...	0821	1020	1219	1419	1621	1728	1824	2020	2220	0024
99	Eina ....d.	0146	...	0845	1044	1243	1442	1644	1755	1847	2044	2243	0047
110	Raufoss ....d.	0156	...	0855	1054	1253	1452	1654	1806	1857	2054	2253	0057
122	**Gjøvik** ....a.	0206	...	0905	1104	1303	1502	1704	1816	1907	2104	2303	0107

	Ⓐ	⑥⑦c	Ⓐ	Ⓐ	d							
Gjøvik ....d.	0433	0533	0549	0635	0738	0937	1136	1332	1535	1734	1937	2134
Raufoss ....d.	0444	0544	0600	0645	0749	0948	1147	1343	1546	1745	1948	2145
Eina ....d.	0454	0554	0610	0654	0759	0958	1157	1353	1556	1756	1958	2155
Jaren .... ‡ d.	0517	0617	0633j	0717	0822	1021	1220	1417	1620	1823	2021	2219
Roa.... ‡ d.	0533	0633	0650j	0734	0838	1037	1236	1434	1637	1839	2037	2236
Oslo S.. ‡ a.	0629	0731	0750j	0834	0935	1133	1334	1532	1734	1935	2134	2333

c – Also May 13, 17; not Apr. 3, 4.
d – Not Apr. 1–4, May 24.
h – Not Apr. 1–5, May 24.
j – 7–11 minutes later Mar. 29–31, May 14.
‡ – Additional trains operate Oslo - Jaren and v.v.

775 OSLO - KRISTIANSAND - STAVANGER

km				73			77	79	81	81	
		769	771	773	773	775	777	779		781	705
		Ⓐ	⚒z	⚒z		Ⓑq	e		p	⑤⑦v	Ⓑr
		✕□	✕□	✕□	✕□	✕□	✕□	✕□	✕□	✕□	♣✕
0	**Oslo** Sentral .... § d.	...	...	0711	...	...	1111	1507	1709	1709	2247
41	Drammen .... § d.	...	...	0748u	...	...	1148u	1544u	1745u	1745u	2337u
87	Kongsberg .... § d.	...	...	0821	...	...	1222	1621	1817	1817	0017
134	Nordagutu ....d.	...	...	0856	...	...	1256	1657	1851	1851	0055x
151	Bø ....d.	...	...	0910	...	...	1311	1711	1905	1905	0111
209	Neslandsvatn ....d.	...	...	0954	...	...	1357	1755	1950	1950	0158x
225	Gjerstad ....d.	...	...	1007	...	...	1412	1809	2003	2003	0211x
270	Nelaug ....d.	...	...	1040	...	...	1449	1845	2036	2036	0246x
353	**Kristiansand** ....a.	...	...	1138	...	...	1555	1943	2134	2134	0352
353	**Kristiansand** ....d.	0520	0805	1146	1146	1415	1610	1950	...	2200	0407
465	Moi ....d.	0643	0929	1312	1312	1543	1741	2117	...	2330	0540x
514	Egersund .... ◇ d.	0725	1006	1350	1350	1620	1818	2155	...	0017	0620
573	Sandnes Sentrum ... ◇ d.	0807	1051	1450	1450	1706	1906	2237	...	0058	0709s
587	**Stavanger** .... ◇ a.	0821	1104	1504	1504	1719	1919	2250	...	0110	0721

			776	778	780	782	784	784	786	
	70	72	76		80	82		84		706
	Ⓐ	⑥k	e	Ⓐ	e	Ⓑm	e	⑤f	Ⓑh	Ⓑr
	✕□	✕□	✕□	✕□	✕□	✕□	✕□	✕□	✕□	♣✕
Stavanger .... ◐ d.	...	...	0603	0903	1033	1403	1603	1603	1933	2220
Sandnes Sentrum ◐ d.	...	...	0616	0917	1047	1417	1617	1617	1947	2234
Egersund .... ◐ d.	...	...	0704	1005	1130	1504	1704	1704	2029	2331
Moi ....d.	...	...	0739	1040	1208	1542	1742	1742	2105	0011
Kristiansand ....a.	...	...	0902	1205	1342	1709	1905	1905	2228	0143
Kristiansand ....d.	0530	0740	0910	...	1405	1717	...	1913	...	0215
Nelaug ....d.	0626	0839	1009	...	1508	1815	...	|	...	0328x
Gjerstad ....d.	0656	0912	1044	...	1543	1849	...	|	...	0404x
Neslandsvatn ....d.	0709	0925	1056	...	1556	1902	...	|	...	0416x
Bø ....d.	0752	1013	1140	...	1642	1952	...	2131	...	0504
Nordagutu ....d.	0806	1027	1156	...	1659	2006	...	|	...	0519x
Kongsberg .... ¶ d.	0844	1104	1237	...	1737	2040	...	2217	...	0600
Drammen .... ¶ a.	0921s	1146s	1317s	...	1820s	2120s	...	2255s	...	0642s
Oslo Sentral .... ¶ a.	0956	1232	1356	...	1856	2156	...	2332	...	0726

Nelaug - Arendal

km		Ⓐ	⑥k	†b	⚒z		e	d		Ⓑn	
0	Nelaug ....d.	0630	0845	1015	1045	...	1510	1845	...	2040	...
36	Arendal ....a.	0705	0920	1050	1120	...	1545	1920	...	2115	...

	Ⓐ	⑥k	e		e	Ⓑm	⑥w		Ⓑn	
Arendal ....d.	0545	0800	0930	...	1410	1735	1800	...	1955	...
Nelaug ....a.	0620	0835	1005	...	1445	1810	1835	...	2030	...

b – Also Apr. 3; not May 17.
d – Not May 16.
e – Not May 17.
f – Also May 12; not Apr. 2, May 14.
h – Not Apr. 1–4, May 16, 23.
k – Not Apr. 3, May 1.
m – Not Apr. 1, 2, May 13, 16, 23.
n – Not Apr. 1–4, May 13, 16, 17, 23.
p – Not Apr. 1–4, May 1, 13, 16, 17, 22, 23.
q – Not Apr. 1–4, May 13, 17, 23.
r – Not Apr. 1–4, May 13, 16, 23.
s – Stops to set down only.
t – Also May 1.
u – Stops to pick up only.
v – Also Apr. 5, May 12, 24; not Apr. 2, 4, May 14, 16, 23.
w – Also Apr. 1, 2, May 13, 23.
x – Stops on request.
z – Not Apr. 3.
♣ – Conveys 🛏 and ▭2. Reservation recommended.
□ – Reservation recommended. Conveys *NSB Komfort*.
§ – Additional local trains **Oslo** S - **Drammen** (39 minutes) - **Kongsberg** (80–82 minutes): 0017, 0617 ⚒**z**, 0717 ⚒**z**, 0817, 0917 and hourly until 2317.
¶ – Additional local trains **Kongsberg** - **Drammen** (44–51 minutes) - **Oslo** S (85–90 minutes): 0453 Ⓐ, 0553 ⚒**z**, 0653, 0750, 0853, 0953, 1053, 1150, 1253, 1353, 1453, 1550, 1650, 1751, 1853, 1953, 2053, 2148 and 2253.
◇ – Additional local trains **Egersund** - **Sandnes** Sentrum (52 minutes) - **Stavanger** (68 minutes): 0506 Ⓐ, 0536 Ⓐ, 0606 Ⓐ, 0636 ⚒, 0706 Ⓐ, 0736 ⚒, 0836 ⚒, 0936, 1036, 1136, 1236, 1336, 1436, 1536, 1606 Ⓐ, 1636, 1706 Ⓐ, 1736, 1836, 1936, 2036, 2136, 2236 and 2336.
◐ – Additional local trains **Stavanger** - **Sandnes** Sentrum (17 minutes) - **Egersund** (67 minutes): 0510 Ⓐ, 0540 Ⓐ, 0610 ⚒, 0710 ⚒, 0810 ⚒, 0910, 1010, 1110, 1210, 1310, 1410, 1440 Ⓐ, 1510, 1540 Ⓐ, 1610, 1640 Ⓐ, 1710, 1810, 1910, 2010, 2110, 2210, 2310 Ⓑt and 2340.

PORSGRUNN - NORDAGUTU - NOTODDEN 779

No service on ©

km		Ⓐ	Ⓐ	Ⓐ	Ⓐ	Ⓐ	Ⓐ	Ⓐ	Ⓐ
0	**Porsgrunn** ..... 783 d.	...	0636	0751	0926	1211	1425	1551	1706
9	Skien .... 783 d.	0544	0645	0800	0935	1220	1434	1600	1715
43	Nordagutu ....d.	0613	0722	0832	1009	1258e	1508	1634	1749
62	**Notodden** ....a.	0633	0742	0852	1029	1320	1528	1654	1809

	Ⓐ	Ⓐ	Ⓐ	Ⓐ	Ⓐ	Ⓐ	Ⓐ	Ⓐ
Notodden ....d.	0642	0812	0929	1124	1428	1554	1709	1847
Nordagutu ....d.	0703	0833	0950	1145	1449	1615	1730	1908
Skien ....783 a.	0733	0903	1019	1214	1519	1645	1759	1939
Porsgrunn ...783 a.	0742	0912	*1043**	*1239*	1528	1700	*1843**	*2043**

e – Arrives 1250.

* – By 🚌 from Skien.

OSLO - BERGEN 780

km		609 M R	61 ✕□		601 ✕□	1405 ⑦W	607 ⑦E R	603 ⑤F R	63 z ✕□		605 ⑧n NR
0	**Oslo Sentral** .... 783 d.	0631	0811	...	1031	...	1227	1433	1607	...	2309
41	Drammen .... △ 783 d.	0712	0848	...	1112	...	1305	1512	1644	...	2354
112	Hønefoss ....d.	0816	0938	...	1222	...	1414	1619	1737	...	0056
208	Nesbyen ....d.	|	1046	...	1341	...	1532	1744	1845	...	0223
225	Gol ....d.	0935	1101	...	1354	...	1545	1800	1900	...	0239
250	Ål ....d.	0955	1124	...	1419	1519	1608	1832	1921	...	0305
275	Geilo ....d.	1015	1145	...	1442	1540	1630	1855	1942	...	0328
286	Ustaoset ....d.	|	1156	...	1454	1552	1643	1905	1953	...	0341
324	Finse ....d.	1110	1225	...	1526	1624	1717	1937	2021	...	0417
354	**Myrdal** .... 781 a.	1141	1253	...	1551	1649	1746	2006	2045	...	0445
403	**Voss** .... 781 a.	1311	1341	...	1637	1736	1834	2048	2128	...	0532
443	Dale .... ▽ 781 a.	|	|	...	1709x	|	1903x	|	2156x	...	0608
480	Arna .... ▽ 781 a.	1410	1441	...	1740	1840	1935	2155	2228x	...	0644
489	**Bergen** .... 781 a.	1422	1452	...	1752	1850	1945	2204	2235	...	0656

	62 ✕□		602 ✕□		604 ⑤⑦ GR	64 z ✕□	610 M R	1404 ⑤T		606 ⑧n NR
Bergen .... 781 d.	0758	...	1028	...	1458	1558	1610	1628	...	2258
Arna .... △ 781 d.	0806	...	1037	...	1506	1606	1618	1637	...	2307
Dale .... △ 781 d.	0836x	...	1107x	...	|	|	|	|	...	2344x
Voss .... 781 d.	0907	...	1139	...	1608	1710	1736	1710	...	0015
Myrdal .... 781 d.	0950	...	1225	...	1657	1752	1828	1825	...	0105
Finse ....d.	1017	...	1254	...	1730	1818	1900	1854	...	0138
Ustaoset ....d.	1046	...	1326	...	1800	1845	|	1927	...	0209
Geilo ....d.	1058	...	1339	...	1812	1857	1946	1939	...	0224
Ål ....d.	1121	...	1400	...	1833	1919	2007	1957	...	0246
Gol ....d.	1141	...	1423	...	1858	1938	2028	...	...	0308
Nesbyen ....d.	1152	...	1436	...	1909	1949	2041	...	...	0321
Hønefoss ....d.	1304	...	1554	...	2023	2059	2201	...	...	0442
Drammen ..... ▽ 783 a.	1353	...	1655	...	2125	2155	2303	...	...	0539
Oslo Sentral ..... 783 a.	1432	...	1732	...	2212	2232	2346	...	...	0626

E – ⑦ to May 9 (also Apr. 5).
F – ⑤ to May 7 (also Mar. 31, May 12; not Apr. 2).
G – ⑤⑦ to Mar. 9 (also Mar. 31, Apr. 5, May 12; not Apr. 2).
M – From May 18.

N – Conveys 🛏, 2, and ✕.
R – Reservation recommended.
T – Jan. 8 - Mar. 19.
W – Jan. 10 - Mar. 21.

n – Not Apr. 1, 2, May 13, 16, 23.
x – Stops on request only.
z – Not Apr. 3.

□ – Reservation recommended. Conveys *NSB Komfort*.
△ – Trains stop to pick up ony.
▽ – Trains call to set down only.

MYRDAL - VOSS - BERGEN and MYRDAL - FLÅM 781

Service to May 1 (subject to alteration Dec. 24 - Jan. 1)

km		⑦	Ⓐ	605 A ✕◇	Ⓐ	Ⓐ	Ⓐ	⚒z			Ⓐ	61 ✕◇	b	Ⓐ		601 Ⓑ ✕◇	601 ⑥ ✕◇	⑥⑦	Ⓐ	607 ⑦e ◇	⑦c		603 ⑤f ◇	⑤f	63 z ✕◇
	Oslo Sentral **780** .....d.	...	...	2309p	...	...	...	...	...	...	...	0811	...	...	...	1031	1031	...	...	1227	...	...	1433	...	1607
0	**Myrdal** ....d.	...	...	0445	...	...	...	...	...	1110	...	1258	...	...	...	1556	1556	...	...	1751	1825	...	2006	2015	2047
18	Mjølfjell ....d.	...	...	|	...	...	0745	...	...	1128x	...	|	...	1515	...	|	1610x	...	...	|	1841x	...	|	2030x	|
49	**Voss** ....a.	...	...	0532	...	...	0816	...	...	1206	...	1341	...	1547	...	1637	1637	...	...	1834	1915	...	2048	2100	2128
49	**Voss** ....d.	...	0515	0537	0617	0720	0835	0835	1050	...	1250	1343	1435	1552	1552	1640	1640	1655	1753	1836	1920	1920	2048	...	2130
89	Dale ....d.	0128	0543	0608	0646	0749	0907	0907	1122	...	1318	|	1503	1623	1623	1709r	1709r	1728	1824	1903r	1950	1950	|	...	2156r
104	Vaksdal ....d.	0143	0559	0626	0705	0805	0924	0924	1140	...	1336	|	1522	1639	1639	|	|	1742	1840	|	2009	2009	|	...	|
126	Arna ....‡ d.	0200	0617	0644s	0727	0826	0946	0946	1157	...	1356	1441s	1543	1657	1657	1740s	1740s	1758	1857	1935s	2026	2026	2155s	...	2228r
135	**Bergen** ....‡ a.	0208	0625	0656	0735	0835	0954	0954	1205	...	1405	1452	1552	1705	1705	1752	1752	1805	1905	1945	2034	2034	2204	...	2235

	⑦		Ⓐ	Ⓐ	62 ✕◇		602 ①–⑥ ✕◇	602 ⑦ ✕◇	Ⓐ			Ⓐ	⑦c	604 ⑤⑦ v◇	Ⓐ	64 z ✕◇	Ⓐ	d	⑤f	Ⓐ			Ⓑn	⑥k	606 Ⓑn ✕◇
Bergen ....‡ d.	0035	...	...	0657	0758	0840	1028	1028	1110	...	1310	1310	1310	1458	1510	1558	1610	1710	1710	1810	1928	...	2128	2258	2258
Arna ....‡ d.	0044	...	...	0707	0806u	0848	1037u	1037u	1118	...	1318	1318	1318	1506u	1518	1606u	1618	1718	1718	1818	1936	...	2136	2306	2307u
Vaksdal ....d.	0101	...	...	0726	|	0905	|	|	1140	...	1336	1336	1336	|	1539	|	1639	1742	1742	1840	1953	...	2153	2324	2326x
Dale..............................d.	0118	...	...	0748	0836x	0924	1107y	1107y	1156	...	1355	1355	1355	|	1554	|	1655	1756	1756	1857	2008	...	2212	2340	2344x
Voss ....a.	...	...	...	0820	0905	0953	1135	1135	1226	...	1425	1425	1425	1605	1625	1708	1727	1825	1825	1932	2039	...	2240	0010	0013
Voss ....d.	...	...	0700	...	0907	0958	1139	1139	...	...	...	1432	1432	1608	...	1710	...	...	1840	...	...	...	...	...	0015
Mjølfjell ....d.	...	...	0732	...	|	1029x	|	1206x	...	...	...	1504	1506	|	...	|	...	...	1911x	...	...	...	...	...	|
Myrdal ....a.	...	...	...	...	0947	1046	1220	1220	...	...	...	...	1523	1652	...	1750	...	...	1928	...	...	...	...	...	0101
Oslo Sentral **780** ......a.	...	...	...	...	1432	...	1732	1732	...	...	...	...	...	2212	...	2232	...	...	...	...	...	...	...	...	0626

Myrdal - Flåm ⊠

km								z				
0	Myrdal ....d.	0955	...	1300	...	1600	...	1755	...	...	...	...
20	Flåm ....a.	1040	...	1350	...	1645	...	1840	...	...	...	...

							z				
Flåm ....d.	0900	...	1130	...	1450	...	1700	...	...	...	...
Myrdal ....a.	0940	...	1210	...	1540	...	1740	...	...	...	...

A – ①–⑥ (not Jan. 2, Apr. 2, 3).
b – Not Apr. 1, 2, 3.
c – Also Apr. 5, May 1.
d – Not Apr. 1 – 5.
e – Also Apr. 5.

f – Also Mar. 31; not Apr. 2.
k – Not Apr. 3, May 1.
n – Not Apr. 1, 2.
p – Previous day.
r – Stops on request to set down only.
s – Stops to set down only.

u – Stops to pick up only.
v – Also Mar. 31, Apr. 5; not Apr. 2
x – Stops on request.
y – Stops on request to pick up only.
z – Not Apr. 3.

‡ – Additional local services operate.
◇ – Reservation recommended. See also Table **780**.
⊠ – **Operator**: Flåm Utvikling AS. ✆ +47 57 63 21 00. 30% discount available for rail pass holders.

Oct. 1, 2009 - Apr. 30, 2010 ⛴ FLÅM - GUDVANGEN and 🚌 GUDVANGEN - VOSS 781a

	⛴	🚌 Ⓑ
Flåm .... d.	1510	...
Gudvangen .... a.	1720	...
Gudvangen .... d.	...	1803e
Voss .... a.	...	1905

	🚌	⛴
Voss .... d.	1000	...
Gudvangen .... a.	1100	...
Gudvangen .... d.	...	1130
Flåm .... a.	...	1340

e – Bus stop on E16 main road.

🚌 operators : Sogn Billag ✆ +47 57 67 66 00. Skyss ✆ +47 5523 9550.
⛴ operator : Fylkesbaatane i Sogn og Fjordane ✆ +47 57 75 70 00.

Oct. 1, 2009 - Apr. 30, 2010 ⛴ / 🚌 GOL and FLÅM - BALESTRAND - BERGEN 782

	⛴ Ⓐ	⛴ ⑥	🚌	🚌	⛴ ⑦	🚌	🚌	🚌	🚌 s	🚌 ⑤⑦	🚌 s
Gol skysstasjon .... d.	...	...	...	...	...	...	...	...	1325	...	1900
Sogndal ⊕ .... d.	...	...	...	0750	...	...	1430	...	|	...	|
Kaupangersenteret . d.	...	...	...	0805	...	...	1445	...	|	...	|
Øvre Årdal ◇ ...... d.	*0530*e	...	0745	|	...	1430	|	1430	|	2030	|
Lærdal .... d.	*0605*e	...	0845	0845	...	1525	1525	|	1525	|	2105
Kaupangersenteret..... d.	*0640*e	...	|	|	...	|	|	1540k	1600	2140	2140
Sogndal ⊕ .... d.	0705	0705	|	|	1540	|	|	1555k	1620	2155	2205
Flåm .... d.	|	|	0930	0930	|	1620	1620	...	|	...	|
Leikanger .... d.	0730	0730	|	|	1605	|	|	...	1645	...	2230
Balestrand .... d.	0750	0750	|	|	1625	|	|	...	1735	...	2310
Voss .... a.	|	|	1035	1035	|	1730	1730	...	...	...	...
Bergen □ .... a.	1140	1150z	1230	1230	2010	1915	1915	...	...	...	...

	🚌 s	🚌	🚌	🚌 s	🚌	⛴ ⑥	🚌	🚌	⛴ Ⓑ	🚌 s	🚌 ⑤⑦
Bergen □ .... d.	...	0855	0855	...	...	1415v	1535	1535	1630	...	...
Voss .... d.	...	1045	1045	...	...	|	1725	1725	|	...	...
Balestrand .... d.	1005	|	|	1310	...	1820	|	|	2020	2120b	...
Leikanger.................. d.	1045	|	|	1350	...	1835	|	|	2045	2200b	...
Flåm .... a.	|	1155	1155	|	...	|	1835	1835	|	|	...
Sogndal ⊕................ d.	1130	|	|	1430	1430	1900	|	|	2120	2230	2230
Kaupangersenteret. d.	1145	|	|	1445	1445	...	|	|	...	2245	2245
Lærdal .... d.	1225	1250	1255	1525	|	...	1920	1920	...	2325	|
Øvre Årdal ◇.... a.	|	|	1345	|	1605	...	|	2040	...	|	0010
Kaupangersenteret a.	|	1320	...	|	...	...	2000	...	...	|	...
Sogndal ⊕ .... a.	|	1335	...	|	...	...	2015	...	...	|	...
Gol skysstasjon ..... a.	1415	...	...	1715	...	...	...	...	...	0120	...

b – Ⓑ only.
e – By 🚌 to Sogndal.
k – 20 minutes later on ⑥⑦.
s – Change 🚌 at Sogndal.
v – Change boats at Sollibotn (d. 1555).

z – Change boats at Sollibotn (d. 1005).

◇ – Øvre Årdal Farnes.
⊕ – 🚌: Sogndal skysstasjon. ⛴: Sogndal kai.
□ – 🚌: Bus station. ⛴: Strandkaiterminal.

🚌 operator : Sogn Billag ✆ +47 57 67 66 00.
⛴ operator : Fylkesbaatane i Sogn og Fjordane ✆ +47 57 75 70 00.

783 LILLEHAMMER - OSLO - SKIEN

All trains convey *NSB Komfort* and 🍷

km		Ⓐ	Ⓐ	Ⓐ	Ⓒ	⚒z	Ⓑt	⑥k	⚒◇	Ⓑt	⑥k	⚒z		Ⓐ	⑥k	†w	⚒z	⑦b	Ⓐ		Ⓑq		Ⓑq		Ⓑq	
0	**Lillehammer** 785 d.	...	0402	0523	0523	0618	0717	0717	0818	0913	0913	1018	1110	1211	1211	1315	1315	1414	1414	1509	1620	1714	1811	1920	2012	2117
58	**Hamar** 785 d.	...	0450	0612	0612	0706	0806	0806	0907	1007	1007	1107	1203	1307r	1307r	1407	1407	1503	1503	1604	1708	1807	1908r	2008	2107	2205
117	Eidsvoll d.	...	0535	0656	0656	0756	0856	0856	0956	1056	1056	1156	1256	1356	1356	1456	1456	1556	1556	1656	1756	1856	1956	2056	2156	2256
133	Oslo ✈ ● 771 785 d.	...	0546	0708	0708	0808	0908	0908	1008	1108	1108	1208	1308	1408	1408	1508	1508	1608	1608	1708	1808	1908	2008	2108	2208	2308
164	Lillestrøm 771 785 d.	...	0601	0723	0723	0823	0923	0923	1023	1123	1123	1223	1323	1423	1423	1523	1523	1623	1623	1723	1823	1923	2023	2123	2223	2323
185	**Oslo** Sentral 771 785 a.	...	0612	0734	0734	0834	0934	0934	1034	1134	1134	1234	1334	1434	1434	1534	1534	1634	1634	1734	1834	1934	2034	2134	2234	2334
185	**Oslo** Sentral d.	0537	0643	0743	0743	0843	0943	0943	1043	1143	1143	1243	1343	1443	1443	1543	1543	1643	1643	1743	1843	1943	2043	2143	2243	2343
225	Drammen d.	0616	0722	0822	0822	0922	1022	1022	1122	1222	1222	1322	1422	1522	1522	1622	1622	1722	1722	1822	1922	2022	2122	2222	2322	0022
259	Holmestrand d.	0640	0746	0846	0846	0946	1046	1046	1146	1246	1246	1346	1446	1546	1546	1646	1646	1746	1746	1846	1946	2046	2146	2246	2346	0046
273	Skoppum d.	0651	0757	0857	0857	0957	1057	1057	1157	1257	1257	1357	1457	1557	1557	1657	1657	1757	1757	1857	1957	2057	2157	2257	2357	0057
289	Tønsberg d.	0716	0816	0916	0916	1016	1116	1116	1216	1316	1316	1416	1516	1616	1616	1716	1716	1816	1816	1916	2016	2116	2216	2311	0011	0111
308	Torp ✈ d.	0729	0829	0929	0929	1029	1129	1129	1229	1329	1329	1429	1529	1629	1629	1729	1729	1829	1829	1929	2029	2129	2229	2324	0024	0124
313	**Sandefjord** d.	0738	0838	0938	0938	1038	1138	1138	1238	1338	1338	1438	1538	1638	1638	1738	1738	1838	1838	1938	2038	2138	2237	2332	0032	0132
332	Larvik a.	0751	0851	0951	0951	1051	1151	1151	1251	1351	1351	1451	1551	1651	1651	1751	1751	1851	1851	1951	2051	2151	2250	2345	0045	0145
332	Larvik d.	*0752**	*0852**	0956	*0952**	*1052**	*1152**	1153	*1252**	*1352**	1353	*1452**	*1552**	*1652**	1653	*1752**	1756	*1852**	1856	1956	*2052**	2153	2252	2347	0047	0147
366	Porsgrunn 779 d.	*0815**	*0915**	1033	*1015**	*1115**	*1215**	1229	*1315**	*1415**	1429	*1515**	*1615**	*1715**	1729	*1815**	1833	*1915**	1932	2034	*2115**	2229	2327	0022	0122	0222
375	**Skien** 779 a.	*0833**	*0933**	1041	*1033**	*1133**	*1233**	1237	*1333**	*1433**	1437	*1533**	*1633**	*1733**	1737	*1833**	1841	*1933**	1940	2042	*2133**	2237	2335	0030	0130	0230

	Ⓐd	Ⓐ		Ⓐd	⚒z	Ⓐd		⚒z	Ⓐ	Ⓒ	⚒z	Ⓐ	Ⓒ	n	⑥z	Ⓑw	Ⓑq	⚒z	†w	Ⓑq	⚒z	†w	Ⓑq		Ⓑq	
Skien 779 d.	...	0338	0436	0501	0536	0555	0631	0737	*0825**	0835	*0925**	*1025**	1030	*1125**	*1225**	1229	*1325**	*1425**	1436	*1520**	*1620**	1636	*1725**	*1825**	*1925**	*2025**
Porsgrunn 779 d.	...	0347	0445	0511	0545	0605	0645	0747	*0843**	0845	*0943**	*1043**	1040	*1143**	*1243**	1239	*1343**	*1443**	1446	*1543**	*1643**	1646	*1743**	*1843**	*1943**	*2043**
Larvik a.	...	0421	0519	0545	0620	0639	0720	0820	*0910**	0920	*1010**	*1110**	1114	*1210**	*1310**	1314	*1410**	*1510**	1520	*1610**	*1710**	1720	*1810**	*1910**	*2010**	*2110**
Larvik d.	...	0423	0521	0547	0622	0641	0722	0822	0922	0922	1022	1122	1122	1222	1322	1322	1422	1522	1522	1622	1722	1722	1822	1922	2022	2122
Sandefjord d.	...	0438	0536	0602	0637	0656	0737	0837	0937	0937	1037	1137	1137	1237	1337	1337	1437	1537	1537	1637	1737	1737	1837	1937	2037	2137
Torp ✈ d.	...	0441	0539	0605	0640	0659	0740	0840	0940	0940	1040	1140	1140	1240	1340	1340	1440	1540	1540	1640	1740	1740	1840	1940	2040	2140
Tønsberg d.	...	0500	0558	0624	0659	0719	0759	0859	0959	0959	1059	1159	1159	1259	1359	1359	1459	1559	1559	1659	1759	1759	1859	1959	2059	2159
Skoppum d.	...	0513	0611	0637	0713	0732	0813	0913	1013	1013	1113	1213	1213	1313	1413	1413	1513	1613	1613	1713	1813	1813	1913	2013	2113	2213
Holmestrand d.	...	0524	0622	0653	0724	0746	0824	0924	1024	1024	1124	1224	1224	1324	1424	1424	1524	1624	1624	1724	1824	1824	1924	2024	2124	2224
Drammen d.	...	0553	0653	0720	0751	0814	0851	0951	1051	1051	1151	1251	1251	1351	1451	1451	1551	1651	1651	1751	1851	1851	1951	2051	2151	2251
Oslo Sentral a.	...	0630	0732	0758	0828	0852	0928	1028	1128	1128	1228	1328	1328	1428	1528	1528	1628	1728	1728	1828	1928	1928	2028	2128	2228	2328
Oslo Sentral 771 785 d.	...	0637	0737	...	0837	...	0937	1037	1137	1137	1237	1337	1337	1437	1537	1537	1637	1737	1737	1837	1937	1937	2037	2137	...	2337
Lillestrøm 771 785 d.	...	0649	0749	...	0849	...	0949	1049	1149	1149	1249	1349	1349	1449	1549	1549	1649	1749	1749	1849	1949	1949	2049	2149	...	2349
Oslo ✈ ● 771 785 d.	...	0705	0805	...	0905	...	1005	1105	1205	1205	1305	1405	1405	1505	1605	1605	1705	1805	1805	1905	2005	2005	2105	2205	...	0005
Eidsvoll d.	...	0716	0816	...	0916	...	1016	1116	1216	1216	1316	1416	1416	1516	1616	1616	1716	1816	1816	1916	2016	2016	2116	2216	...	0016
Hamar 785 d.	0704	0805	0905	...	1004	...	1106	1202	1303	1303	1408	1505	1505	1606	1709	1709	1805	1902	1902	2009	2105	2105	2203	2307	...	0104
Lillehammer 785 a.	0752	0853	0950	...	1053	...	1154	1248	1350	1350	1458	1556	1556	1655	1758	1758	1902	1955	1955	2101	2152	2152	2248	2352	...	0149

b – Also Apr. 5, May 13, 17, 24; not Apr. 4, May 23.
d – Not Mar. 29, 30, 31, May 14.
k – Not Apr. 3, May 1.
n – Not Apr. 1–4, May 1, 23.
q – Not Apr. 1, 2, 4, May 23.
r – Arrives 9–11 minutes earlier.
t – Also Apr. 3, May 1.
w – Also Apr. 3.
z – Not Apr. 3.
* – By 🚌.
◇ – Not Apr. 3. Change trains at Oslo on Ⓐ.
● – Oslo Lufthavn Gardermoen.

784 HAMAR - RØROS - TRONDHEIM

km		Ⓐ	⑥k	Ⓐ	⚒	Ⓑm	Ⓐ	Ⓒ	m	Ⓑ	Ⓑe	
0	**Hamar** d.	...	...	0810	1009	1209	...	...	1608	1811	2014	...
32	Elverum d.	...	...	0833	1034	1234	...	...	1633	1834	2039	...
64	Rena d.	...	...	0855	1059	1256	...	...	1655	1859	2101	...
120	Koppang d.	...	...	0937	1141	1338	...	...	1737	1941	2143	...
273	**Røros** a.	...	...	1130	1335	1529	...	...	1930	2131	2334	...
273	**Røros** d.	0505	0705	...	...	...	1535	1630	1937	...	...	...
384	Støren 785 d.	0640	0835	...	...	...	1709	1802	2108	...	...	...
435	**Trondheim** S. 785 a.	0735	0930	...	...	...	1800	1855	2200	...	...	...

	Ⓐ	⚒	Ⓐ	m	Ⓑm	†v		Ⓐ		⑦c
Trondheim S. 785 d.	...	...	0540	0950	...	1345	...	1615	...	2040
Støren 785 d.	...	...	0640	1041	...	1440	...	1709	...	2134
Røros a.	...	...	0815	1212	...	1611	...	1845	...	2305
Røros d.	0427	0619	0824	1218	1411	1622	1622	...	...	...
Koppang d.	0617	0809	1017	1417	1606	1817	1817	...	...	...
Rena d.	0659	0854	1059	1459	1654	1859	1859	...	...	...
Elverum d.	0721	0916	1121	1521	1716	1921	1921	...	...	...
Hamar a.	0746	0941	1146	1546	1741	1946	1946	...	...	...

c – Also Apr. 5, May 13, 17, 24; not Apr. 4, May 16, 23.
e – Not Apr. 1, 2, 4, May 16, 23.
k – Not Apr. 3, May 1.
m – Not May 17.
v – Also Apr. 3; not May 1.

785 OSLO - LILLEHAMMER - ÅNDALSNES and TRONDHEIM

km		407	41	2341	313	2343	45	2345	47	2347	329	405
		Ⓐd			⚒z	ⒶM			Ⓑh	Ⓑh	Ⓑq	Ⓑr
		R	R	▲R		R	R	▲R	R	▲R		R
		✕⊡	✕⊡	🍷	🍷⊡	🍷	✕⊡	🍷	✕⊡	🍷	🍷⊡	✕N
0	**Oslo** Sentral 783 d.	...	0807	...	1037	...	1417	...	1607	...	1837	2305
21	Lillestrøm 783 d.	...	0819u	...	1049	...	1430u	...	1619u	...	1849	2327u
52	Oslo ✈ ⊖ 783 d.	...	0833u	...	1105	...	1445u	...	1633u	...	1905	2346u
127	**Hamar** 783 d.	...	0929	...	1202	...	1537	...	1730	...	2009	0045
185	**Lillehammer** 783 d.	...	1015	...	1248	1301	1623	...	1813	...	2109	0139
243	Ringebu d.	...	1058	...	...	1344	1705	...	1855	...	2152	0233
267	Vinstra d.	...	1113	...	...	1402	1722	...	1912	...	2209	0251
298	Otta d.	...	1138	...	...	1426	1747	...	1934	...	2233	0320
344	Dombås d.	...	1210	1215	...	1500	1824	1828	2006	2008	2306	0402
458	**Åndalsnes** ▲ a.	...	|	1332	...	1619	|	1944	|	2124	...	|
430	Oppdal d.	0645	1308	...	...	...	1923	...	2105	...	...	0512
502	Støren 784 d.	0735	1357	...	...	...	2017	...	2155	...	...	0608
553	**Trondheim** S. 784 a.	0830	1445	...	...	...	2100	...	2243	...	...	0700

	308	2340	316	2342	42	2344	44	2346	46	406
	⚒y	ⒶM				Ⓑh	Ⓑh			Ⓑr
		R		▲R	R	▲R	R	▲R	R	R
	🍷⊡	🍷	🍷⊡	🍷	✕⊡	🍷	✕⊡	🍷	✕⊡	✕N
Trondheim S. 784 d.	...	...	...	...	0825	...	1408	...	1525	2305
Støren 784 d.	...	...	...	...	0909	...	1452	...	1609	2355
Oppdal d.	...	...	...	...	1005	...	1545	...	1700	0058
Åndalsnes ▲ d.	...	0742	...	0933	|	1445	|	1635	|	|
Dombås d.	0513	0904	...	1055	1103	1613	1644	1756	1802	0210
Otta d.	0545	0934	...	...	1137	...	1714	...	1834	0249
Vinstra d.	0609	0957	...	...	1158	...	1741	...	1856	0313
Ringebu d.	0625	1013	...	...	1216	...	1757	...	1919	0332
Lillehammer 783 d.	0717	1059	1110	...	1300	...	1846	...	2005	0419
Hamar 783 d.	0806	...	1203	...	1350	...	1930	...	2049	0512
Oslo ✈ ⊖ 783 d.	0908	...	1308	...	1443s	...	2015s	...	2143s	0606s
Lillestrøm 783 d.	0923	...	1323	...	1501s	...	2031s	...	2201s	0626s
Oslo Sentral 783 a.	0934	...	1334	...	1513	...	2042	...	2212	0643

🚌 ⊠	⚒					Ⓐ	Ⓐ			Ⓑ¶	Ⓑ¶
Åndalsnes d.	0730	0950	1345	1345	...	1630	1655	1955	2015	2130	2130
Molde a.	0900	1120	1510	|	...	|	1820	|	2135	2250	|
Ålesund a.	...	...	...	1555	...	1840	...	2200	...	...	2345

🚌 ⊠	Ⓐ			Ⓑ	Ⓑ					
Ålesund d.	...	0705	...	...	1200	...	1405	...	...	2100
Molde d.	0620	|	0800	1300	|	1450	|	2015	2200	|
Åndalsnes a.	0740	0920	0920	1425	1435	1610	1620	2130	2315	2320

🚌 ⊠			Ⓐ				⑤⑦		Ⓑ		
Oppdal skysstasjon d.	0530	...	1050	...	1315	...	1810	...	2130	...	...
Kristiansund a.	0905	...	1430	...	1635	...	2130	...	0040	...	...

🚌 ⊠	⚒		Ⓐ					⑤⑦		
Kristiansund d.	0630	...	1040	...	...	1315	...	1635	...	2040
Oppdal skysstasjon a.	0940	...	1420	...	...	1640	...	2010	...	0005

M – Until May 28.
N – Conveys 🛏 and 🛏2.
R – Reservation recommended.
d – Not Mar. 29, 30, 31.
h – Not Apr. 1, 2, May 13, 16, 17, 23.
q – Not Apr. 1, 2, 4, May 23.
r – Not Apr. 1, 2, May 13, 16, 23.
s – Stops to set down only.
u – Stops to pick up only.
y – Not Jan. 2, Apr. 3.
z – Not Apr. 3.
▲ – Services to / from Åndalsnes are subject to alteration from May 29.
⊡ – Conveys *NSB Komfort.*
⊖ – Oslo Lufthavn Gardermoen (see also Table **771**).
⊠ – Subject to confirmation.
¶ – By Taxi (only available for passengers from train **2347**). Runs on request only – please inform the on train staff.

786 SOUTHWEST NORWAY 🚌 LINKS

BERGEN - TRONDHEIM (Operator: NOR-WAY Bussekspress ✆ +47 815 44 444)
Bergen ⊡ d. 1630 → Oppdal a. 0435 → Trondheim a. 0645.
Trondheim d. 2000 → Oppdal d. 2210 → Bergen ⊡ a. 0945.

BERGEN - ÅLESUND (Operator: NOR-WAY Bussekspress ✆ +47 815 44 444)
Bergen ⊡ d. 0800 → Ålesund a. 1735 (1720 on ⑥).
Ålesund d. 1100 → Bergen ⊡ a. 2020.

BERGEN - LILLEHAMMER (Operator: NOR-WAY Bussekspress ✆ +47 815 44 444)
Bergen ⊡ d. 0855 → Voss d. 1045 → Flåm d. 1155 → Lillehammer skysstasjon a. 1745.
Lillehammer skysstasjon d. 1035 → Flåm d. 1620 → Voss a. 1730 → Bergen ⊡ a. 1915.

BERGEN - KRISTIANSAND (Operator: NOR-WAY Bussekspress ✆ +47 815 44 444)
Bergen ⊡ d. 0730 → Odda d. 1115 → Haukeli a. 1250, d. 1445 → Kristiansand a. 1855.
Kristiansand d. 0845 → Haukeli a. 1250, d. 1445 → Odda a. 1630 → Bergen ⊡ a. 1955.

BERGEN - ODDA ★ 🚌/⛴ *Journey time: 3 hrs 15 m – 3 hrs 40 m.*
From Bergen ⊡ at 0730, 1130, 1430 Ⓑ, 1730 ⑦ and 2030 Ⓑ.
From Odda ⊡ at 0535 ⚒, 1230, 1635 and 2035 Ⓑ.

GEILO - ODDA ★ *Journey time: 3 hrs 25 m. Summer services only: May 1 - Sept. 30, 2009.*
From Geilo railway station at 1150. From Odda ⊡ at 0720, 1230 Ⓑ **S**.

VOSS - ULVIK ★ *Journey time: 50–65 minutes.*
From Voss at 0845 Ⓐ, 1005 ⚒ **V**, 1140 Ⓐ, 1530 Ⓐ **z**, 1645 ⑥ **R**, 1735 Ⓑ and 2135 Ⓑ.
From Ulvik ⊡ at 0725 Ⓐ, 0855 ⚒ **V**, 1410 Ⓐ **z**, 1525 Ⓑ **V** and 1810 Ⓑ.

R – Until Sept. 26.
S – June 22 - Aug. 16 only. Journey time: 3 hrs 50 m.
V – Daily until Oct. 2.
z – Also ⑥ from Oct. 3.
⊡ – Bus station.
★ – Operator: Skyss ✆ +47 5523 9550.

TRONDHEIM - BODØ and NARVIK — 787

Subject to alteration Dec. 24 - Jan. 1

km		1781 Ⓐn 🍷	1783 Ⓐ 🍷	475 b 🍴N	🚌 ◇	473 ⚒v 🍷	473 Ⓐ 🍷R	1785 Ⓐn 🍷	471 m 🍴R	1791 Ⓐ 🍷	🚌 ◇	479 Ⓑd 🍷R	477 Ⓑr 🍷R
0	**Trondheim** S § d.	...	...	2335	...	...	...	...	0740	...	...	...	1558
33	Værnes ✈ ‡... § d.	...	...	0005	...	...	...	...	0815	...	...	...	1631u
34	Stjørdal......... § d.	...	...	0010	...	...	...	...	0820	...	...	...	1637u
126	Steinkjer .... § d.	...	...	0129	...	...	...	...	0946	...	...	...	1801u
220	Grong .... d.	...	...	0240	...	...	...	...	1053	...	...	...	1907
406	Mosjøen .... d.	...	...	0457	...	0650	0650	...	1309	...	...	1645	2120
498	Mo i Rana......... d.	...	...	0608	...	0754	0800	...	1420	...	...	1747	2225
648	Rognan.............. d.	0542	0642	0802	...	...	0954	1145	1615	1740	...	1936	...
	Bodø ⊖........ d.	|	|	|	0700	...	|	|	|	|	1615	|	...
674	Fauske .... a.	0603	0703	0825	0815	...	1014	1206	1637	1800	1730	1956	...
674	Fauske .... d.	0603	0703	0830	0855	...	1016	1206	1646	1809	1810	2001	...
	Narvik ⊡ ...... a.	|	|	|	1330	...	|	|	|	|	2300	|	...
729	**Bodø**............... a.	0642	0742	0910	...	...	1055	1253	1726	1848	...	2040	...

	478 c 🍷R	470 Ⓐ 🍷	1784 Ⓐn 🍷	🚌 ◇	472 m 🍴R	1786 Ⓐn 🍷	1790 Ⓐ 🍷	474 Ⓑd 🍷R	🚌 ◇	476 b 🍴N
Bodø............. d.	...	0748	1015	...	1215	1340	1605	1728	...	2110
Narvik ⊡ ... d.	...	|	|	0700	|	|	|	|	1610	|
Fauske .... a.	...	0828	1100	1200	1255	1419	1644	1807	2110	2149
Fauske .... d.	...	0828	1100	1215	1258	...	1646	1808	2130	2153
Bodø ⊖..... a.	...	|	|	1325	|	...	|	|	2240	|
Rognan.......... d.	...	0848	1120	...	1320	...	1705	1832	...	2214
Mo i Rana...... d.	0820	1032n	...	...	1531	...	...	2017	...	0015
Mosjøen......... d.	0928	1136n	...	...	1641	...	...	2118	...	0140
Grong .... d.	1146	...	...	...	1905	...	...	...	...	0426
Steinkjer ..... § d.	1250	...	...	...	2016	...	...	...	...	0540
Stjørdal....... § d.	1404	...	...	...	2134	...	...	...	...	0704
Værnes ✈ ‡ § d.	1406	...	...	...	2136	...	...	...	...	0706
Trondheim . § a.	1439	...	...	...	2210	...	...	...	...	0740

Local services Trondheim - Steinkjer and v.v.

km	▶	Ⓐ	⚒z					Ⓐn		Ⓐn			Ⓑe
0	**Trondheim** S ... d.	0610	0710	0910	1110	1310	1510	1539	1710	1810	1910	2110	2310
31	Hell ● .... d.	0643	0743	0943	1143	1343	1543	1613	1743	1843	1943	2143	2343
33	Værnes ✈ ‡ ● .. d.	0645	0745	0945	1145	1345	1545	1615	1745	1845	1945	2145	2345
34	Stjørdal............. d.	0652	0752	0952	1152	1352	1552	1620	1752	1852	1952	2152	2349
126	**Steinkjer**......... a.	0816	0916	1116	1319	1516	1716	1744	1916	2016	2116	2313	0107

▶	Ⓐ	t							Ⓐn	
Steinkjer .... d.	0528	0728	0928	1128	1328	1528	1728	1925	2028	2128
Stjørdal.......... d.	0652	0852	1052	1252	1452	1652	1852	2052	2152	2252
Værnes ✈ ‡ ● d.	0654	0854	1054	1254	1454	1654	1854	2054	2154	2254
Hell ● .... d.	0657	0857	1057	1257	1457	1657	1857	2057	2157	2257
Trondheim S. a.	0732	0932	1132	1332	1532	1732	1932	2132	2229	2332

N – Conveys 🛏 and 🛋. Reservation recommended.
R – Reservation recommended.
b – Not Apr. 1, 2, 3, May 1, 13, 16, 22.
c – Not Apr. 1, 2, 3, May 1, 16, 17, 22, 23.
d – Not Apr. 1, 2, 4, May 13, 16, 23.
e – Not Apr. 1, 2, 4, May 16, 23.
m – Not May 17.
n – Not Mar. 29, 30, 31.

r – Not Apr. 1, 2, May 16, 23.
t – Not Apr. 1 – 5, May 23, 24.
u – Stops to pick up only.
v – Not Apr. 3, May 22.
z – Not Apr. 3.
● – Trains stop on request.
⊡ – Bus station.
⊖ – Bodø Busstorget.

‡ – Station for Trondheim Airport.
§ – See also panel below main table.
◇ – Operator: Cominor. ✆ +47 7692 3500.
▶ – **Additional services** Trondheim - Stjørdal - Steinkjer and v.v.: **From Trondheim** at 0510 Ⓐ **n**, 0810 Ⓐ, 1010 Ⓐ **n**, 1210 Ⓐ, 1410 Ⓐ, 1439 Ⓐ **n** and 1610 Ⓐ. **From Steinkjer** at 0600 Ⓐ **n**, 0628 Ⓐ, 0657 Ⓐ **n**, 0828 Ⓐ, 1028 Ⓐ, 1228 Ⓐ **n**, 1428 Ⓐ, 1628 Ⓐ **n** and 1828 Ⓐ.

LAPLAND 🚌 LINKS — 789

Narvik – Tromsø – Alta

Operator: Cominor

km		①–⑤	①–⑥			Ⓑ	Ⓑ			⑦	
0	**Narvik** bus station ...... d.	0520	...	...	...	1250	1250	1530	...	1840	...
	Narvik rail station .... d.	|	...	...	...	1257	1257	|	...	1847	...
181	Nordkjosbotn .... d.	0820	0820	...	...	1615	1615	1845	...	2150	...
252	**Tromsø** Prostneset . d.	0925	0925	...	1600	|	1725	1945	...	2250	...
241	Lyngseidet.................. d.	...	...	...	1745	1745	...	...	...	...	...
465	**Alta** .... a.	...	...	...	2230	2230	...	...	...	...	...

km		①–⑤			①–⑥	①–⑤	⑥	⑦	⑦	⑦
0	**Alta** .... d.	...	...	...	1045	1045	1045	...	1400	1400
224	Lyngseidet.................. d.	...	...	...	1545	1545	1545	...	1910	1910
293	**Tromsø** Prostneset . d.	0615	1000	1600	|	1725	1800	1900	|	2050
	Nordkjosbotn .... d.	0730	1105	1705	1705	...	...	2010	2010	...
	Narvik rail station .... a.	1025	1410	|	|	...	...	|	|	...
	Narvik bus station ...... a.	1030	1415	2010	2010	...	...	2310	2310	...

Alta – Hammerfest – Karasjok – Kirkenes

Operator: FFR Veolia Transport

km		①–⑤	⑦	①–⑤	①–⑤ ◇	①③	⑤⑦	①–④	①–④ ◇	⑤⑦	⑤⑦ ◇
0	**Alta** .... d.	...	...	0635	...	...	...	1430	...	1500	...
	Hammerfest .... d.	...	...	|	0710	...	...	|	1500	|	1540
87	Skaidi .... a.	...	...	0800	0805	...	...	1605	1600	1635	1635
87	Skaidi .... d.	...	...	0810	0810	...	...	1615	1615	1645	1645
	Hammerfest .... a.	...	...	0900	|	...	...	1705	|	1745	|
112	Olderfjord .... d.	...	...	...	0845	...	...	...	1650	...	1720
212	Honningsvåg ★....... a.	...	...	...	1025	...	...	...	1830	...	1900
174	Lakselv .... d.	...	...	...	1010	...	...	...	1755	...	1835
248	Karasjok .... d.	...	...	...	1125	1200	1410	...	1910	...	1950
429	Tanabru..................... d.	0830	1130	...	...	1500	1715	...	...	...	...
571	**Kirkenes** .... a.	1050	1350	...	...	1720	1950	...	...	...	...

km		①–⑤ ◇	①–⑤	⑥**S**	**Q**	①–④ ◇	①–④	⑤⑦ ◇	⑤⑦	Ⓑ
	Kirkenes .... d.	...	...	...	0805	...	...	...	...	1510
	Tanabru..................... d.	...	...	...	1035	...	...	...	...	1800
	Karasjok .... d.	0515	...	...	1310	1350	...	1430	...	...
	Lakselv .... d.	0725	...	...	...	1520	...	1605	...	...
	Honningsvåg ★....... d.	0640	...	1400	...	1440	...	1510	...	...
	Olderfjord .... d.	0845	...	1650	...	1650	...	1720	...	...
0	Hammerfest .... d.	|	0810	|	...	|	1615	|	1635	...
57	Skaidi .... a.	0905	0905	1710	...	1710	1710	1740	1735	...
57	Skaidi .... d.	0915	0915	1720	...	1720	1720	1750	1750	...
	Hammerfest .... a.	1010	|	1815	...	1815	|	1845	|	...
144	**Alta** .... a.	...	1035	...	...	...	1840	...	1915	...

Rovaniemi – Muonio – Tromsø

Operator: Eskelisen Lapin Linjat

km		◐		C
0	**Rovaniemi** bus station d.	0800	1130	1130
157	Kittilä .... d.	1040	1335	1335
238	Muonio .... d.	1300z	1450	1505
327	Karesuvanto .... d.	1435	...	1625
440	Kilpisjärvi ⊡ .... FI d.	1625	...	1810
535	Nordkjosbotn .... NO d.	...	...	1830
608	**Tromsø** Prostneset .... a.	...	...	1930

		D	◐
Tromsø Prostneset .. d.	...	0730	...
Nordkjosbotn ...... NO d.	...	0830	...
Kilpisjärvi ⊡ .... FI d.	...	1110	1315
Karesuvanto .... d.	...	1240	1515
Muonio .... d.	1410	1410	1700
Kittilä........................ d.	1535	1535	1835
Rovaniemi bus station a.	1740	1740	2040

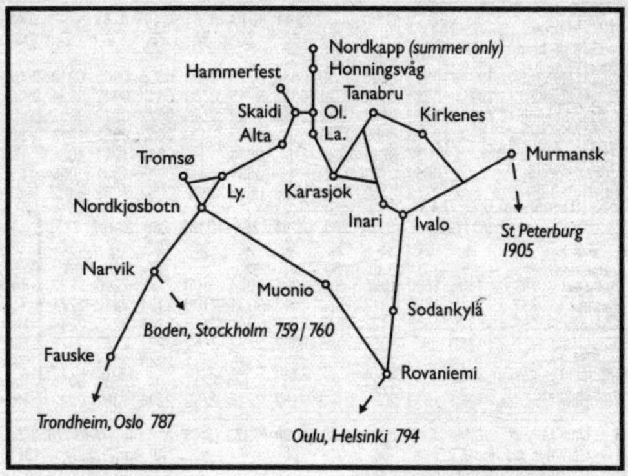

Rovaniemi – Karasjok, Nordkapp, Tanabru, Kirkenes and Murmansk

km	Operator:	G	G ⊖	S	G/M ①③⑤	E	E **H**	P ①–⑥	E	G/L Ⓑ	G **A**
0	**Rovaniemi** bus station d.	0800	...	...	...	1145	1145	1520	1720	2000	2255
	Rovaniemi rail station d.	0820	...	...	...	1100	1100	1525	1645	2010	2300
130	Sodankylä................... d.	1020	...	...	...	1345	1345	1730	1915	2200	0105
305	Ivalo .... FI d.	1250	1300	...	1530	1625	1625	1935	2130	0015	0310
345	Inari...................... FI d.	...	1340	...	|	1700	1700	...	2205	...	...
461	Karasjok............ NO a.	...	...	...	|	1755	1755	...	|	...	...
536	Lakselv, Statoil........ a.	...	...	...	|	...	1855	...	|	...	...
735	**Nordkapp** .... a.	...	...	...	|	...	2220	...	|	...	...
	Tanabru......... NO a.	...	...	...	|	...	...	...	2355r	...	...
	Kirkenes, Europris NO d.	...	...	1500	|	...	...	...	...	...	...
	Murmansk .... RU a.	...	...	2100v	2300	...	...	...	...	...	...

Operator:	P ⑥	G **A**	E	G ①–⑤	G/L ①–⑥	E **J**	E	S	G/M ①③⑤	G	G
Murmansk .... RU d.	...	...	...	...	...	...	...	0700v	0830	...	...
Kirkenes .... NO a.	...	...	...	...	...	...	...	1100	|	...	...
Tanabru .... NO d.	...	...	0330t	...	...	...	...	...	|	...	...
Nordkapp .... d.	...	...	|	...	...	0100	...	...	|	...	...
Lakselv, Statoil .... d.	...	...	|	...	...	0810	...	...	|	...	...
Karasjok............ NO d.	...	...	|	...	...	0915	0915	...	|	...	...
Inari....................... FI d.	...	...	0715	1105	...	1210	1210	...	|	1415	...
Ivalo .... FI d.	0530	0615	0820	1140	1215	1320	1320	...	1400	1450	1615
Sodankylä.................. d.	0755	0900	1045	...	1500	1550	1550	...	...	...	1845
Rovaniemi rail station . a.	0945	1045	1225	...	1715	1730	1730	...	...	...	2030
Rovaniemi bus station a.	0950	1050	1230	...	1710	1735	1735	...	...	...	2035

Operator codes:
E – Eskelisen Lapin Linjat.
G – Gold Line.
L – Liikenne O. Niemelä.
M – Murmanskavtotrans.
P – Pikakuljetus Rovaniemi.
S – Pasvikturist AS.

A – ①–⑤ until June 4.
C – June 1 - Sept. 19.
D – June 2 - Sept. 20.
H – June 1 - Aug. 22.
J – June 2 - Aug. 23.
N – June 8 - Aug. 23.
P – June 9 - Aug. 24.
Q – ①③⑤⑦.
S – June 13 - Aug. 22.

r – ③④⑤⑦ (daily May 31 - Sept. 20).
t – ①④⑤⑥ (daily June 1 - Sept. 19).
v – Murmansk Vorovskogo gate.
z – Arrives 1200.

⊖ – Runs one hour later on ⑥⑦.
⊡ – Trekking centre (Retkeilykeskus).
◇ – Two routes: Hammerfest - Olderfjord - Karasjok and v.v.; Hammerfest - Olderfjord - Honningsvåg and v.v.
◐ – Operator: Gold Line.

★ – **Honningsvåg - Nordkapp** and v.v. *34 km.* Journey 45 minutes. Summer service May 4 - Sept. 6, 2009. **From Honningsvåg** (Nordkapphuset) at 1045 and 2130 **N**. **From Nordkapp** at 0015 **P** and 1315.

FI – Finland (East European Time).
NO – Norway (Central European Time).
RU – Russia (Moskva Time).

FINLAND

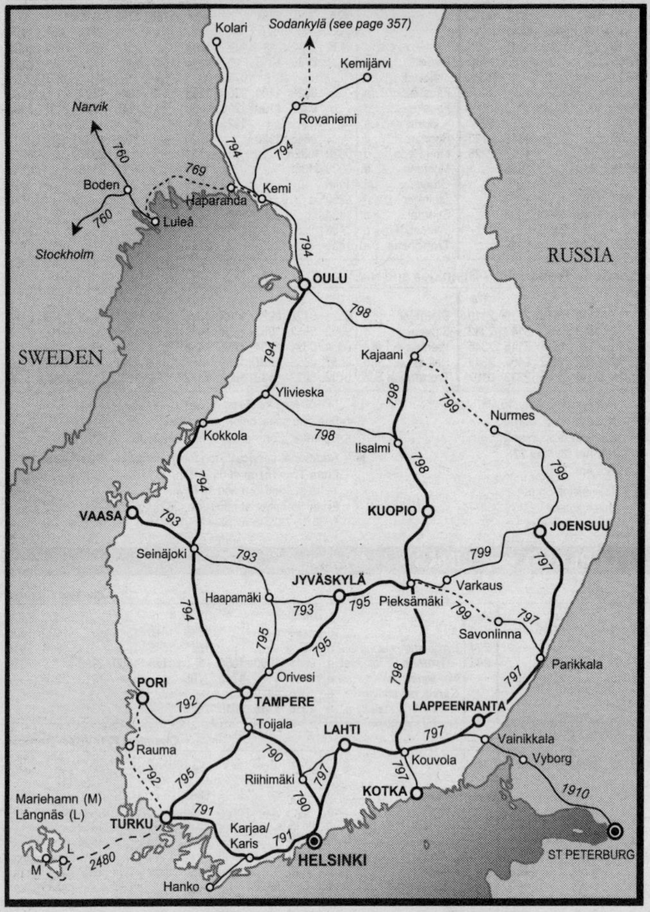

Operator: **VR** – VR-Yhtymä Oy (www.vr.fi).

Tickets and train types: For all except purely local journeys, tickets are always sold for travel by a specific train or combination of trains. There are four different pricing-scales, corresponding to each of the following train types (in descending order of cost):

- ▶ **S 220 Pendolino** (e.g. *S* **123**) – high-speed tilting trains (220 km/h), with 1st (*Business*) and 2nd class seats. Reservation compulsory.
- ▶ **InterCity** (e.g. *IC* **124**) – quality fast trains between major centres, with 1st and 2nd class seats, all reservable.
- ▶ **Express**, *pikajunat* (train number only shown, e.g. **128**) – other fast trains, with 2nd class seats, all reservable. Night expresses convey sleeping-cars and 2nd class seats only (marked ★ in the tables).
- ▶ **Regional**, *taajamajunat* (no train number shown) – stopping-trains, normally with 2nd class seats only.

S 220, InterCity and Express tickets include a seat reservation when purchased in advance.

Rail tickets are **not** valid on 🚌 services (except Kemi - Tornio). However, special combined train / bus fares are available on certain routes.

Services: ✕ indicates a train with a restaurant car.

Trains marked 🍷 convey a buffet car or a *MiniBistro* trolley service.

Complimentary light meals are served to holders of Plus and Business Plus tickets.

A supplement is payable for travel in sleeping-cars (🛏) in addition to the appropriate **Regional** fare – 2nd class for a berth in a 2- or 3-person cabin, 1st class for occupancy of a single-berth cabin. Sleeper supplements cost up to 50% more on peak nights in mid-winter. Seated passengers on night express trains pay the 2nd class **Express** fare.

Timings: Timings are valid, unless otherwise indicated, **Dec. 13, 2009 - June 6, 2010**.

In these tables Ⓐ = ①-⑤, ⚒ = ①-⑥.

Changes to the normal service pattern are likely to occur on and around the dates of public holidays: Dec. 25, 26, Jan. 1, 6, Apr. 2, 5, May 1, 13, 23. On Dec. 23, 31 services run as on ⑤. A special service operates on Dec. 24 (with a very limited service in the afternoon and no overnight departures). A special service also operates on Dec. 25 (no long-distance services operate in the morning). A modified sunday service operates on Dec. 26.

790 HELSINKI - TAMPERE

For through journeys to / from **Oulu** and **Rovaniemi**, see table **794**. For through journeys to / from **Jyväskylä** and **Pieksämäki**, see table **795**.

km			*IC* 161		*S* 41	*IC* 83	*IC* 43	*IC* 165	*IC* 85		*S* 45	*IC* 47	*IC* 169	*IC* 171		*S* 87	*IC* 49	*IC* 173	*S* 89	*IC* 175		*S* 53	*IC* 55	*S* 91	*IC* 177		*IC* 57
		2 Ⓐ	Ⓐ	2 ⚒	✕ ⚒	✕	✕	🍷 ⚒	🍷	2	✕	✕	🍷	🍷	2	✕	✕	🍷	✕ Ⓑ	✕	2	✕	✕	✕	🍷	2	✕ Ⓑ
0	**Helsinki** .... **797** d.	0519	0606	0619	0630	0706	0730	0806	0906	0919	0930	1006	1106	1206	1219	1230	1306	1406	1430	1506	1519	1530	1606	1630	1706	1719	1730
3	Pasila .... **797** d.	0524	0612	0624	0636	0712	0736	0812	0912	0924	0936	1012	1112	1212	1224	1236	1312	1412	1436	1512	1524	1536	1612	1636	1712	1724	1736
16	Tikkurila ⊙ **797** d.	0532	0622	0632	0646	0722	0746	0822	0922	0932	0946	1022	1122	1222	1232	1246	1322	1422	1446	1522	1532	1546	1622	1646	1722	1732	1746
71	Riihimäki .... d.	0613	0652	0713	|	0752	|	0852	0952	1013	|	1052	1152	1252	1313	|	1352	1452	|	1552	1613	|	1652	|	1752	1813	|
108	Hämeenlinna ... d.	0636	0711	0736	|	0811	|	0911	1011	1036	|	1111	1211	1311	1336	|	1411	1511	|	1611	1636	|	1711	|	1811	1836	|
147	Toijala .... d.	0659	0731	0759	|	0831	|	0931	1031	1059	|	1131	1231	1331	1359	|	1431	1531	|	1631	1659	|	1731	|	1831	1859	|
187	**Tampere** .... a.	0722	0752	0822	0756	0852	0902	0952	1052	1122	1056	1152	1252	1352	1422	1356	1452	1552	1556	1652	1722	1656	1752	1756	1852	1922	1902

	IC 179	*S* 59	*IC* 181	**265**	*IC* 93	**267**	*IC* 185	**269**	*IC* 187	**273**
	🍷	✕	🍷	✕ ★	✕	✕ ★	✕ ⊖	✕ ★	🍷 Ⓑ	✕ ★
Helsinki .... **797** d.	1806	1830	1906	1926	2006	2023	2100	2123	2206	2223
Pasila .... **797** d.	1812	1836	1912	1934	2012	2031	2106	2131	2212	2231
Tikkurila ⊙ **797** d.	1822	1846	1922	1948	2022	2044	2116	2144	2222	2244
Riihimäki .... d.	1852	|	1952	2026	2052	2122	2152	2222	2252	2322
Hämeenlinna..... d.	1911	|	2011	2052	2111	2148	2211	2248	2311	2348
Toijala............... d.	1931	|	2031	|	2131	|	2231	|	2331	0015
Tampere .... a.	1952	1956	2052	2142	2152	2238	2252	2336	2352	0042

	264	**266**	*IC* 160	**270**	*IC* 162	**274**	**272**	*S* 80	*S* 40	*IC* 164		*S* 82	*S* 42
	✕ ★	✕ ★	Ⓐ	✕ ★	✕ Ⓐ	✕ ★	✕ ★	✕ Ⓐ	✕ Ⓐ	🍷 ⚒	2	✕ ⚒	✕ ⚒
Tampere .... d.	0405	0440	0533	0548	0604	0611	0636	0657	0702	0707	0732	0757	0802
Toijala .... d.	0434	0507	0554	0615	0626	0638	0737	|	|	0728	0755	|	|
Hämeenlinna .... d.	0502	0534	0615	0642	0647	0705	0804	|	|	0749	0818	|	|
Riihimäki .... d.	0531	0600	0635	0708	0707	0732	0832	|	|	0809	0852	|	|
Tikkurila ⊙ ...... **797** a.	0610	0635	0702	0746	0737	|	0942	0810	0815	0837	0928	0910	0915
Pasila .... **797** a.	0622	0647	0711	0758	0746	0828	0953	0819	0824	0846	0936	0919	0924
Helsinki .... **797** a.	0630	0654	0717	0806	0752	0836	1000	0825	0830	0852	0941	0925	0930

	IC 166	*S* 84	*IC* 44	*S* 46	*IC* 86	*IC* 170	*IC* 48		*IC* 174	*IC* 176	*IC* 50		*S* 52	*IC* 88	*S* 62	*IC* 180		*IC* 54	*S* 90	*IC* 182		*S* 56	*IC* 184	*IC* 58	*IC* 92	*S* 60	*S* 94
	🍷 ⚒	✕ ⚒	✕ ◧	✕	✕	🍷	✕	2	🍷	🍷	✕	2	✕	🍷	✕	✕	2	✕	✕	🍷	2	✕	🍷	✕	🍷	✕ Ⓑ	✕
Tampere .... d.	0807	0902	0907	1002	1007	1107	1207	1237	1307	1407	1507	1537	1602	1607	1702	1707	1737	1807	1902	1907	1937	2002	2007	2102	2107	2202	2302
Toijala............... d.	0828	|	0928	|	1028	1128	1228	1300	1328	1428	1528	1600	|	1628	|	1728	1800	1828	|	1928	2000	|	2028	|	2128	2221	2321
Hämeenlinna..... d.	0849	|	0949	|	1049	1149	1249	1323	1349	1449	1549	1623	|	1649	|	1749	1823	1849	|	1949	2023	|	2049	|	2149	2239	2339
Riihimäki .... d.	0909	|	1009	|	1109	1209	1309	1352	1409	1509	1609	1652	|	1709	|	1809	1852	1909	|	2009	2052	|	2109	|	2209	2256	2356
Tikkurila ⊙ **797** a.	0937	1015	1037	1115	1137	1237	1337	1428	1437	1537	1637	1728	1715	1737	1815	1837	1928	1937	2015	2037	2128	2115	2137	2221	2237	2321	0021
Pasila .... **797** a.	0946	1024	1046	1124	1146	1246	1346	1436	1446	1546	1646	1736	1724	1746	1824	1846	1936	1946	2024	2046	2136	2124	2146	2230	2246	2330	0030
Helsinki .... **797** a.	0952	1030	1052	1130	1152	1252	1352	1441	1452	1552	1652	1741	1730	1752	1830	1852	1941	1952	2030	2052	2141	2130	2152	2236	2252	2336	0036

Additional regional trains Helsinki - Riihimäki and v.v. ⊠

				Ⓐ							
Helsinki ....d.	0036	0136	...	0548	...	0648	and	2248	...	2336	...
Pasila ....d.	0041	0141	...	0553	...	0653	hourly	2253	...	2341	...
Tikkurila ⊙ .....d.	0058	0158	...	0602	...	0702	until	2302	...	2358	...
Riihimäki ....a.	0150	0250	...	0646	...	0746		2346	...	0050	...

			Ⓐ	Ⓒ							
Riihimäki ....d.	0414	...	0514	0514	...	0614	and	2214	...	2314	...
Tikkurila ⊙ .....d.	0505	...	0558	0605	...	0658	hourly	2258	...	0005	...
Pasila ....a.	0520	...	0607	0620	...	0707	until	2307	...	0020	...
Helsinki.........a.	0525	...	0612	0625	...	0712		2312	...	0025	...

⊖ – ①②③④⑦.
◧ – Train number **188** on ⑦.
⊙ – For Helsinki ✈ Vantaa.
⊠ – 2nd class only.
★ – Overnight train to / from northern Finland. Conveys 🛏 and 2. For through cars and days of running see Table **794**.

HELSINKI - TURKU and HANKO 791

km		IC 121	IC 159	S 123		IC 125	S 127	IC 129		IC 131	IC 133	IC 135		IC 137		IC 139		IC 141		143	S 145		IC 147	IC 149		IC 153
		🍷	🍷 Ⓐ	🍴 ⚒		🍷	🍴 ⚒	🍷	2 ⚒	🍷	🍷	🍷	2	🍷	2 Ⓐ	🍷	2 Ⓐ	🍷	2	2🍴	🍴	2 Ⓑ	🍷 Ⓑ	🍷		
0	**Helsinki** d.	0546	0634	0738	...	0903	1003	1103	1133	1203	1303	1403	1433	1503	1533	1603	1633	1703	1733	1803	1903	1933	2003	2103	...	2303
3	Pasila d.	0552	0640	0745	...	0909	1009	1109	1138	1209	1309	1409	1438	1509	1538	1609	1638	1709	1738	1809	1909	1938	2009	2109	...	2309
20	Espoo d.	0605	0653	0758	...	0922	1022	1122	|	1222	1322	1422	|	1522	|	1622	|	1722	|	1822	1922	|	2022	2122	...	2322
87	Karjaa / Karis ★ d.	0645	0736	0834	...	1003	1103	1203	1239	1303	1403	1503	1539	1603	1639	1703	1739	1803	1839	1903	2003	2039	2103	2203	...	0006
138	Salo d.	0712	0803	0857	...	1030	1130	1230	...	1330	1430	1530	...	1630	...	1730	...	1830	...	1930	2030	...	2130	2230	...	0033
194	**Turku** a.	0744	0833	0925	...	1100	1200	1300	...	1400	1500	1600	...	1700	...	1800	...	1900	...	2000	2100	...	2200	2300	...	0103
197	Turku satama a.	0753	...	...	...	...	...	...	...	...	...	...	...	...	...	*1819*	...	1912	...	2012	...	...	...	...	...	...

			IC 122		IC 124			S 126	IC 128	IC 130		S 132	IC 134	IC 136		S 138	IC 140	IC 142		IC 144	IC 146	IC 148		IC 150	IC 152	154
		2 Ⓐ	🍷 Ⓐ	2 Ⓐ	🍷	2 ⚒	2 ⑦	🍴 ⚒	🍷 Ⓐ	🍷		🍴 ⚒	🍷	🍷	2 ⚒	🍴	🍷	🍷	2	🍷	🍷	🍷	2	🍷	🍷	2🍴
	Turku satama d.	...	...	...	...	...	...	...	0738	0815	...	...	...	...	...	...	...	...	...	...	...	...	...	...	1945	2045
	Turku d.	...	0544	...	0638	...	...	0735	0755	0855	...	1000	1100	1200	...	1300	1400	1500	...	1600	1700	1800	...	1900	2000	2100
	Salo d.	...	0616	...	0710	...	...	0805	0830	0932	...	1032	1132	1232	...	1332	1432	1532	...	1632	1732	1832	...	1932	2032	2132
	Karjaa / Karis ★ d.	0600	0643	0650	0737	0752	0800	0828	0900	1000	...	1100	1200	1300	1304	1400	1500	1600	1615	1700	1800	1900	1918	2000	2100	2200
	Espoo a.	|	0722	|	0813	|	0852	0900	0938	1038	...	1138	1238	1338	|	1438	1538	1638	|	1738	1838	1938	|	2038	2138	2238
	Pasila a.	0707	0736	0753	0826	0853	0916	0913	0951	1051	...	1151	1251	1351	1407	1451	1551	1651	1722	1751	1851	1951	2022	2051	2151	2251
	Helsinki a.	0712	0742	0759	0832	0858	0921	0919	0957	1057	...	1157	1257	1357	1412	1457	1557	1657	1727	1757	1857	1957	2027	2057	2157	2257

★ – **KARJAA / KARIS - HANKO** and v.v. *50 km.* Journey time: 40 minutes (55–60 minutes by 🚌). 2nd class only.
Karjaa - Hanko at 0743, 0835 Ⓐ 🚌, 1010, 1220 🚌, 1310, 1410 Ⓐ 🚌, 1510, 1610 Ⓐ 🚌, 1710, 1910 and 2210.
Hanko - Karjaa at 0540 Ⓐ 🚌, 0640, 0720 Ⓐ 🚌, 0910, 1050 Ⓐ 🚌, 1210, 1410, 1435 🚌, 1610, 1810, 1900 Ⓐ 🚌 and 2110.

TAMPERE and TURKU - PORI 792

2nd class only

km		⚒									
0	**Tampere** d.	0807	...	1215	1415	1615	1815	2205	...	...	...
135	**Pori** a.	0937	...	1345	1556	1748	1948	2335	...	...	...

	⚒									
Pori d.	0520	0715	...	1015	...	1415	1615	1815	...	...
Tampere a.	0650	0850	...	1145	...	1545	1747	1945	...	...

km		🚌	🚌	🚌	🚌	🚌	🚌	🚌	🚌	🚌	🚌
0	**Turku** bus station d.	0600	0815	1100	...	1500	1500	1730	1800	...	2030
93	Rauma bus station d.	|	0945	1230	1615	|	1640	1855	|	1945	2155
144	**Pori** bus station a.	0820	1035	1320	1720	1720	...	...	2020	2050	2240

	🚌	🚌	🚌	🚌	🚌	🚌	🚌	🚌	🚌	🚌
Pori bus station d.	0600	0830	...	1030	1230	...	1720	1930	1945	...
Rauma bus station d.	0645	|	1040	1135	1320	1535	1810	|	2050	2210
Turku bus station a.	0820	1050	1220	...	1450	1700	1940	2150	...	2345

JYVÄSKYLÄ - SEINÄJOKI - VAASA 793

km										IC 57	
		⚒2	⚒2	2		2	2	2	2	Ⓑ🍴	2
0	**Jyväskylä** d.	...	0733	...	...	1033	...	...	1633	...	...
78	Haapamäki d.	...	0844	...	...	1144	...	...	1744	...	...
151	Alavus d.	...	0953	...	...	1253	...	...	1853	...	...
	Helsinki **794** d.	...	|	...	...	|	...	...	|	1730	...
196	Seinäjoki a.	...	1025	...	...	1325	...	...	1925	2030	...
196	Seinäjoki d.	0930	1038	1038	...	1338	1638	1816	1943	2045	2115
270	**Vaasa** a.	1032	1136	1136	...	1436	1736	1918	2045	2137	2213

		IC 44									
	⚒2	⚒🍴	⑦2	2		2	2	2	Ⓑ2	2	Ⓑ2
Vaasa d.	0553	0622	0742	0922	...	1222	1453	1522	1808	1808	1935
Seinäjoki a.	0642	0720	0840	1020	...	1320	1439	1620	1906	1906	2033
Seinäjoki d.	...	0738	...	1034	...	...	...	1634	1934	...	...
Helsinki **794** a.	...	1052	...	|	...	...	...	|	|	...	...
Alavus d.	...	...	...	1107	...	...	...	1707	2007	...	...
Haapamäki d.	...	...	...	1215	...	...	...	1815	2114	...	...
Jyväskylä a.	...	...	...	1327	...	...	...	1927	2225	...	...

TAMPERE - OULU, KOLARI and ROVANIEMI 794

km		273					S 41				IC 43	701		S 45	IC 47	703	S 61	IC 49	IC 49	IC 173	S 53	IC 55	IC 57	S 59	265	267	269
		★ T	🚌 Ⓐ	🚌 Ⓐ		2	🍴 ⚒	2	🚌 ⚒	🚌 Ⓐ	🍴	2🍴 K	🚌	🍴	🍴	2🍴 J	‡🍴 Ⓑ	🍴 Ⓑ	🍴	🍷 Ⓑ	🍴	🍴	🍴 Ⓑ V	🍴	★	★ B	★ A
	Helsinki **790** d.	2223	...	...	...	...	0630	...	...	...	0730	...	...	0930	1006	...	1230	1306	1306	1406	1530	1606	1730	1830	1926	2023	2123
0	**Tampere** d.	0115	...	...	...	...	0800	...	...	...	0905	...	...	1100	1200	...	1400	1500	1500	1600	1700	1802	1905	2000	2211	2308	2359
75	Parkano d.	0211	...	...	...	...	|	...	...	...	0943	...	...	|	1238	...	|	1538	1538	1638	1736	1842	1948	|	2309	|	|
159	Seinäjoki a.	0307	...	...	...	...	0904	...	...	...	1020	...	...	1204	1315	...	1514	1619	1619	1720	1808	1929	2030	2104	0018	0104	0205
159	Seinäjoki d.	0310	...	...	...	...	0907	...	...	...	1032	...	...	1207	1330	...	...	1631	1631	...	1811	1933	...	2109	0021	0200	0208
292	Kokkola d.	0450	...	...	...	0641	1025	...	...	...	1156	...	...	1320	1504	...	...	1804	1804	...	1940	2104	...	2226	0230	0412	0345
371	Ylivieska d.	0548	...	...	...	0736	1109	...	...	...	1245	...	...	1410	1555	...	...	1854	1854	...	2028	2155	...	2310	0341	0509	0443
493	**Oulu** a.	0726	...	...	...	0850	1222	...	...	...	1359	...	...	1515	1712	...	...	2007	2007	...	2133	2309	...	0012	0503	0638	0615
493	**Oulu** d.	0755	...	...	...	...	...	1237	...	...	...	1407	...	...	...	1727	...	2023	...	...	...	...	...	...	0522	0643	0632
599	Kemi a.	0909	...	0920	...	...	...	1338	...	1432	...	1507	...	...	...	1826	...	2123	...	...	...	...	...	...	0630	0752	0737
808	**Kolari** ● a.	|	...	1305	...	...	...	|	...	1805	...	|	...	...	...	|	...	|	...	...	...	...	...	...	|	|	1040
713	**Rovaniemi** a.	1041	1135	...	...	...	...	1507	1520	...	...	1629	1640	...	...	1948	...	2246	...	...	...	...	...	...	0753	0932	...
796	Kemijärvi ⊡ a.	...	1250	...	...	...	...	...	1645	...	...	...	1815	...	...	...	...	...	...	...	...	...	...	...	0945	...	...

	S 40	S 42	IC 44	S 46	S 46	IC 48			IC 50	IC 50	S 52	S 62		708	IC 54		710	S 56	IC 58	S 60		264		266	270	272	274
	🍴 Ⓐ	🍴 ⚒	🍴 ⚒V	🍴 ⑦	🍴 ⚒	🍴	🚌 Ⓐ	🚌 Ⓐ	🍴 ⚒	🍴	🍴	🍴	🚌 ⚒	2🍴 J	🍴	🚌	🍴 P	🍴	🍴	🍴 Ⓑ	2	★ C	🚌 Ⓐ	★U	★ D	★ E	★
Kemijärvi ⊡ d.	...	...	...	...	...	...	...	0525	...	...	...	...	0840	...	...	1115	...	...	...	...	...	...	...	...	...	...	1900
Rovaniemi d.	...	...	...	...	...	...	...	0645	0715	...	...	...	0950	1007	...	1230	1250	...	...	...	1630	1717	...	1800	...	...	2110
Kolari ● d.	...	...	...	...	...	...	0415	...	|	...	...	...	...	|	...	▬	|	...	...	...	|	|	1605	|	1845	1845	|
Kemi d.	...	...	...	...	...	...	0725	...	0837	...	...	...	...	1125	...	...	1410	...	...	...	1753	1855	1918	1939	2153	2153	2234
Oulu a.	...	...	...	...	...	...	...	...	0937	...	...	...	...	1225	...	...	1519	...	...	...	1857	2023	...	2058	2259	2259	2343
Oulu d.	...	...	...	...	0545	0650	...	...	0950	0950	1140	...	...	...	1250	...	...	1540	1550	1745	1902	2030	...	2134	2324	2324	2352
Ylivieska d.	...	...	...	...	0650	0812	...	...	1107	1107	1247	...	...	...	1412	IC 182	...	1647	1711	1852	2026	2214	...	2314	0047	0047	0109
Kokkola d.	...	0526	*0549*	*0717*	0735	0902	...	...	1156	1156	1337	...	...	...	1502	🍷	...	1731	1802	1937	2120	2320	...	0018	0203	0203	0226
Seinäjoki a.	...	0647	*0715*	*0843*	0847	1028	...	...	1328	1328	1444	...	...	...	1628	Ⓑ	...	1849	1928	2048	...	0113	...	0203	0348	0348	0408
Seinäjoki d.	0550	0650	0738	0850	0850	1038	...	...	1338	1338	1447	1545	...	...	1638	1738	...	1852	1938	2050	...	0116	...	0205	0351	0351	0410
Parkano d.	0623	0723	0816	|	|	1116	...	...	1416	1416	|	|	...	...	1716	1821	...	|	2017	|	...	|	...	0315	|	|	|
Tampere a.	0656	0756	0858	0959	0959	1158	...	...	1457	1457	1557	1656	...	...	1758	1903	...	1956	2059	2156	...	0400	...	0405	0537	0537	0548
Helsinki **790** a.	0830	0930	1052	1130	1130	1352	...	...	1652	1652	1730	1830	...	...	1952	2052	...	2130	2236	2336	...	0630	...	0654	0806	1000	0836

A – ③⑤⑥ Dec. 16 - Jan. 24; daily Jan. 27 - May 1.
B – ⑤ (also ⑥ Feb. 20 - Apr. 17).
C – ⑦ (also ⑥ Feb. 20 - Apr. 17).
D – ⑥ Dec. 19 - Jan. 23; ⑤⑥ Jan. 29 - May 1.
E – ④⑦ Dec. 13 - Jan. 28; ①②③④⑦ Jan. 31 - May 2.
J – From / to Kajaani (Table **798**).

K – From Kouvola (on ⚒) and Kuopio (Table **798**).
P – To Pieksämäki (Table **798**).
T – Also conveys 🛏 Turku (**933**) - Tampere - Rovaniemi.
U – Also conveys 🛏 Rovaniemi - Tampere (**904**) - Turku.
V – From / to Vaasa (Table **793**).

‡ – Train number **87** Helsinki - Tampere.
★ – Conveys 🛏, ▭2 and 🍴.
● – 🚌 services operate to / from Kolari keskusta in the town centre (approximately 3 km from the rail station).
⊡ – 🚌 services operate to / from the bus station.

TURKU - TAMPERE - PIEKSÄMÄKI 795

km		S 81 §	IC 905	IC 83	IC 165		909	IC 85	IC 47	911	S 87	IC 49	IC 917	IC 173	S 89		S 53	921	923	S 91	S 59	IC 927	IC 927	931	IC 93	933
		K🍴 Ⓐ	🍷	🍴	🍷 ⚒	2	2	🍷	🍴	2🍴	🍴	🍴	🍷	🍷	🍴 Ⓑ	2	🍴	2🍴	2	🍴	🍴	🍴	K🍴 Ⓑ	2🍴	🍴 Ⓑ	2 R
0	Turku satama d.	...	...	...	...	...	0836	...	...	...	...	...	...	...	...	...	...	...	...	...	...	...	...	1950	...	2050
3	**Turku** d.	...	0700	...	...	...	0905	...	...	1005	...	...	1305	...	...	...	...	1505	1605	...	...	1805	1805	2005	...	2105
69	Loimaa d.	...	0741	...	...	...	0944	...	...	1044	...	...	1344	...	...	...	...	1544	1644	...	...	1844	1844	2044	...	2147
	Helsinki **790** d.	0630	|	0706	0806	...	|	0906	1006	|	1230	1306	|	1406	1430	...	1530	|	|	1630	1830	|	|	|	2006	|
131	Toijala d.	|	0825	0831	0931	...	1025	1031	1131	1125	|	1431	1425	1531	|	...	|	1625	1725	|	|	1925	1925	2125	2131	2234
171	**Tampere** a.	0756	0847	0852	0952	...	1047	1052	1152	1147	1356	1452	1447	1552	1556	...	1656	1647	1747	1756	1956	1947	1947	2147	2152	2300
171	**Tampere** d.	0805	...	0905	...	1005	...	1105	...	1205	1405	...	1505	...	1605	1615	...	1705	...	1805	...	2005	2005	...	2205	...
213	Orivesi d.	|	...	0930	...	1031	...	|	...	1230	|	...	1530	...	|	1641	...	1730	...	1832	...	2030	2030	...	2232	...
285	Haapamäki a.	|	...	|	...	1124	...	|	...	|	|	...	|	...	|	1734	...	|	...	|	...	|	|	...	|	...
269	Jämsä d.	0858	...	1006	...	...	...	1205	...	1306	1500	...	1606	...	1656	...	...	1806	...	1906	...	2106	2106	...	2307	...
326	Jyväskylä d.	0927	...	1045	...	...	...	1235	...	1345	1527	...	1645	...	1730	...	...	1840	...	1946	...	2136	2140	...	2337	...
406	**Pieksämäki** a.	1009	...	1134	...	...	...	...	...	1434	...	...	1734	...	1812	...	...	1934	...	2028	...	...	2231	...	...	...

K – To Kuopio (Table **798**).
R – ▭2 Turku - Tampere; 🛏 Turku - Tampere (**273**) - Rovaniemi.
§ – Train number **41** Helsinki - Tampere.

795 PIEKSÄMÄKI - TAMPERE - TURKU

	904 2 T	S80 ✕ Ⓐ	906 2 A	2 ⚒	S82 ✕ ⚒	S84 K✕ ⚒	IC86 ✕	IC912 🍷		916 2✕	IC48 ✕	2	IC176 🍷	IC922 ✕	IC50 ✕	IC88 🍷	924 2✕	928 2✕	IC54 ✕	S90 ✕	2	S56 ✕	IC92 🍷	IC934 🍷	936 2 ⑦	S94 ✕
Pieksämäki d.	...	...	...	...	0530	0643	...	...	...	0924	...	...	...	1224	...	...	...	1524	...	...	...	...	1828	...	...	2051
Jyväskylä d.	...	0530	...	...	0630	0730	0822	...	...	1022	...	...	...	1322	...	1425	...	1622	...	1735	...	...	1922	...	...	2137
Jämsä d.	...	0557	...	...	0657	0757	0856	...	...	1054	...	...	...	1354	...	1458	...	1654	...	1804	...	...	1954	...	...	2204
Haapamäki d.	...	|	...	...	|	|	|	...	...	|	...	1221	...	|	...	|	...	|	...	|	1821	...	|	...	...	|
Orivesi d.	...	|	...	0717	|	0827	0931	...	...	1129	...	1317	...	1429	...	|	...	1729	...	|	1917	...	2029	...	...	|
Tampere a.	...	0650	...	0742	0750	0850	0955	...	...	1153	...	1342	...	1453	...	1553	...	1753	...	1853	1942	...	2053	...	...	2253
Tampere d.	0556	0657	0711	...	0757	0902	1007	1011	...	1211	1207	...	1407	1511	1507	1607	1611	1811	1807	1902	...	2002	2107	2111	2211	2302
Toijala d.	0623	|	0735	...	|	|	1028	1035	...	1235	1228	...	1428	1535	1528	1628	1635	1835	1828	|	...	|	2128	2135	2235	2321
Helsinki **790** a.	|	0825	|	...	0925	1030	1152	|	...	|	1352	...	1552	|	1652	1752	|	|	1952	2030	...	2130	2252	|	|	0036
Loimaa d.	0706	...	0813	...	...	...	...	1113	...	1313	...	...	...	1613	...	...	1713	1916	...	...	...	...	...	2215	2313	...
Turku a.	0750	...	0850	...	...	...	...	1150	...	1355	...	...	...	1655	...	...	1750	1955	...	...	...	...	...	2252	2350	...
Turku satama a.	0802	...	...	...	...	...	...	...	...	...	...	...	...	...	...	...	1819	*2012*	...	...	...	...	...	...	...	...

A – ①–⑤ (also ⑦ Feb. 21 - Apr. 25). K – From Kuopio (Table **798**). T – [2] Tampere - Turku; 🛏 Rovaniemi (**866**) - Tampere (**904**) - Turku.

797 HELSINKI - KOUVOLA - JOENSUU

km		2 Ⓐm	S1 ✕	IC71 J✕	IC3 ✕	2	IC73 K✕	IC107 🍷 Ⓐ	IC5 ✕	2	IC109 🍷	S7 ¶✕	IC77 J✕	IC77 §✕ Ⓑ	2 Ⓐ	IC111 🍷 Ⓑ	2	IC11 ✕	S79 C✕	IC113 ✕	2 Ⓑ		2		2
0	**Helsinki** 790 d.	0519	0712	0812	1012	*1041*	1112	1212	1300	*1341*	1412	1512	1612	1612	1641	1712	*1741*	1812	1912	2012	2241	Other	0641		2241
3	Pasila 790 d.	0524	0718	0818	1018	*1046*	1118	1218	1306	*1346*	1418	1518	1618	1618	1646	1718	*1746*	1818	1918	2018	2246	local	0646	and	2246
16	Tikkurila ⊙ 790 d.	0532	0728	0828	1028	*1055*	1128	1228	1316	*1355*	1428	1528	1628	1628	1655	1728	*1755*	1828	1928	2028	2255	trains	0655	hourly	2255
104	**Lahti** d.	0650	0802	0908	1108	1155	1208	1308	1402	1450	1508	1602	1708	1708	1743	1808	1850	1908	2002	2108	2342	→	0741	until	2341
166	**Kouvola** a.	0730	0835	0940	1140	1235	1240	1340	1435	1530	1540	1635	1740	1740	1823	1843	1930	1940	2035	2140	0022		...		...
166	**Kouvola** d.	...	0837	...	1142	...	...	1342	1437	...	...	1641	...	1748	...	...	...	1942	...	2142	...		...		...
252	Lappeenranta d.	...	0922	...	1227	...	...	1425	1522	...	...	1732	...	1834	...	...	...	2027	...	2227	...		...		...
288	Imatra d.	...	0948	...	1253	...	...	...	1548	...	...	1755	...	1900	...	...	...	2058	...	2251	...		...		...
352	Parikkala d.	...	1029	...	1334	...	...	...	1629	...	...	|	...	1941	...	...	...	2139	...	...	...		...		...
482	**Joensuu** a.	...	1139	...	1444	...	...	...	1739	...	...	1933	...	2051	...	...	...	2249	...	...	...		...		...

	2 ⚒	IC102 🍷 Ⓐ	2 Ⓐ	IC104 ✕ ⚒	S2 ✕ ⚒	S70 J✕ ⚒	2	IC4 ✕	IC74 J✕	2	IC6 ✕	IC68 K✕	S8 ✕	S76 K✕	IC118 🍷 Ⓐ	2	IC114 🍷	IC10 ✕	IC66 K✕ Ⓑ	IC78 J✕	IC12 ✕		2		2
Joensuu d.	...	...	...	...	0519	...	...	0614r	...	...	0914	...	1219	...	...	...	...	1514	...	...	1819		...		...
Parikkala d.	...	...	...	...	0627	...	...	0727r	...	...	1027	...	1332	...	...	...	...	1627	...	...	1939		...		...
Imatra d.	...	...	...	0600	0704	...	...	0808	...	...	1108	...	1413	...	...	...	...	1708	...	...	2020		...		...
Lappeenranta d.	...	...	...	0628	0727	...	...	0834	...	...	1134	...	1439	...	1540	...	...	1734	...	...	2046		...		...
Kouvola a.	...	...	...	0711	0810	...	...	0917	...	...	1217	...	1522	...	1623	...	...	1817	...	...	2128		...		...
Kouvola d.	0500	0620	0635	0715	0812	0825	0830	0920	1120	1125	1220	1420	1525	1622	1626	1630	1720	1820	1920	2025	2130		...		...
Lahti d.	0540	0654	0717	0754	0848	0900	0910	0954	1154	1205	1254	1454	1600	1658	1705	1710	1754	1854	1954	2100	2203	Other	0617		2317
Tikkurila ⊙ 790 a.	0627	0732	0806	0832	0922	0932	*1005*	1032	1232	*1305*	1332	1532	1632	1732	1744	*1805*	1832	1932	2032	2142	2247	local	0706	and	0005
Pasila 790 a.	0635	0741	0815	0841	0931	0941	*1014*	1041	1241	*1314*	1341	1541	1641	1741	1754	*1814*	1841	1941	2041	2151	2257	trains	0715	hourly	0014
Helsinki 790 a.	0640	0748	0821	0848	0937	0948	*1019*	1048	1248	*1319*	1348	1548	1648	1748	1800	*1819*	1848	1948	2048	2157	2304	→	0721	until	0019

Branch lines **KOUVOLA - KOTKA** and **PARIKKALA - SAVONLINNA** (2nd class only)

km		⚒					Ⓑ		⚒					Ⓑ
0	**Kouvola** d.	0637	0842	1247	1535	1752	2147	Kotka satama d.	0732	1027	1432	1625	1916	2240
51	**Kotka** a.	0719	0924	1329	1617	1834	2229	**Kotka** d.	0735	1030	1435	1628	1919	2243
52	Kotka satama a.	0722	0927	1332	1619	1837	2232	**Kouvola** a.	0818	1113	1518	1711	2002	2326

km		⚒				Ⓑ			⚒					
0	**Parikkala** d.	0732	1032	1337	1632	1944	2142	**Savonlinna** d.	0529	...	0927	1232	1527	1839
33	Retretti d.	0800	1100	1405	1700	2012	2210	Retretti d.	0552	...	0950	1255	1550	1902
59	**Savonlinna** a.	0826	1126	1431	1726	2038	2236	**Parikkala** a.	0622	...	1020	1325	1620	1932

Local connecting trains **RIIHIMÄKI - LAHTI**
59 km. Journey time: 35–41 minutes. 2nd class only.

From Riihimäki at 0013, 0613 ⚒, 0713, 0813 and hourly until 2213.

From Lahti at 0452 Ⓐ, 0544 Ⓐ, 0628 ⑥, 0706 ⚒, 0806, 0911, 1006, 1106 and hourly until 1606; then 1711, 1806, 1906, 2006, 2106 and 2206.

C – [12] Helsinki - Kuopio (- Kajaani Ⓑ).
J – To / from Kajaani (Table **798**).
K – To / from Kuopio (Table **798**).
m – Change trains at Riihimäki (a. 0608, d. 0613).
r – ⚒ only.
§ – Train number **9** Kouvola - Joensuu.
¶ – Conveys [12] Helsinki - Kouvola (**75**) - Kuopio on Ⓑ (Table **798**).
⊙ – For Helsinki ✈ Vantaa.

798 KOUVOLA - KUOPIO - OULU

km		2 ⚒	2 ⚒		701 2✕ ⚒R	701 2✕ R	S81* ✕ Ⓐ	IC71 ✕	703 2✕ R	IC73 ✕	705 2✕	2	707 2✕	707 2✕ Ⓑ	S75‡ ✕ Ⓑ	IC77 ✕	709 2✕ Ⓑ	S79 ✕	S79 ✕ Ⓑ	IC927 T✕ Ⓑ
	Helsinki **797** d.	...	...	...	...	...	0630	0812	...	1112	...	...	*1412*	*1412*	1512	1612	*1712*	1912	1912	...
0	**Kouvola** d.	...	...	...	0632	...	◇	0953	...	1253	...	...	1548	1548	1644	1755	1848	2042	2042	...
113	Mikkeli d.	...	...	...	0752e	...	|	1058	...	1358	...	...	1700	1700	1744	1905	1957	2139	2139	...
184	Pieksämäki d.	...	...	...	0846k	...	1011	1146	...	1446	...	...	1746	1746	1826	1953	2044	2219	2219	2233
273	**Kuopio** d.	...	...	...	0947	0947	1058	1247	...	1542	1547	...	1841	1847	1913	2049	2136	2309	2312	2323
358	Iisalmi d.	...	0545	...	1048	1048	...	1348	...	...	1648	1654	...	1948	...	2147	...	...	0009	...
512	Ylivieska a.	...	0727	...	|	|	...	|	...	...	|	1829	...	|	...	|	...	...	|	...
441	Kajaani d.	0620	|	...	1144	1144	...	1440	1512	...	1746e	...	...	2056v	...	2234	...	...	0054	...
484	Paltamo d.	0652	|	...	1215	1215	...	...	1543	...	1818	...	...	2129	...	...	...	...	...	...
633	**Oulu** a.	0834	*0850*	...	1355	1355	...	...	1724	...	1956	...	...	2314	...	...	...	...	...	...

	700 2✕ ⚒	S70 ✕ ⚒	S84 ✕ ⚒		IC74 ✕		704 2✕ ⚒	IC68 ✕	S76 ✕	706 2✕	IC66 ✕ Ⓑ	708 2✕ R	IC54 ✕	2	IC78 ✕	710 2✕ R	S94 ✕	714 2✕ Ⓑ	2 Ⓑ	2 Ⓑ
Oulu d.	...	...	...	...	...	...	0712	...	...	1005	...	1237	1250	...	...	1529	...	...	*1902*	2019
Paltamo d.	...	...	...	...	...	...	0849	...	...	1146	...	1415	|	...	...	1705	...	...	|	2200
Kajaani d.	...	0400	...	...	0620	...	0920	...	...	1220	...	1446	|	...	1520	1747	...	...	|	2229
Ylivieska d.	...	|	...	...	|	...	|	...	...	|	...	...	1410	1428	|	|	...	...	2030	...
Iisalmi d.	...	0448	...	...	0715	...	1015	...	...	1315	...	...	...	1605	1615	1843	...	...	2213	...
Kuopio d.	0408	0545	0555	...	0820e	...	1112	1120	1350	1420e	1605	...	...	...	1720e	1951	...	...	...	...
Pieksämäki d.	0513	0638	0643	...	0916	...	...	1216	1441	1518	1700	...	...	...	1822e	2044	2051	2108	...	...
Mikkeli d.	0600	0721	|	...	1003	...	...	1303	1522	1605	1747	...	...	...	1907	...	|	2204	...	...
Kouvola a.	0709	0815	◇	...	1107	...	...	1407	1615	1711	1905	...	...	...	2009	...	◇	2313	...	...
Helsinki **797** a.	*0848*	0948	1030	...	1248	...	...	1548	1748	*1848*	2048	...	...	...	2157	...	0036	...	...	...

R – To / from Rovaniemi (Table **794**).
T – From Turku (Table **795**).

e – Arrives 8–9 minutes earlier.
k – Arrives 0835.
v – Arrives 2041.

* – Train number **41** Helsinki - Tampere.
‡ – Train number **7** Helsinki - Kouvola.
◇ – Via Tampere (Table **795**).

799 PIEKSÄMÄKI - JOENSUU - NURMES - KAJAANI

2nd class only

km		🚌 Ⓐ			🚌 Ⓐ		🚌	🚌 ⚒		Ⓑ	🚌 Ⓑ	
0	**Pieksämäki** d.	0655	...	1148	1235	1448	1640	1800	1829	2055	2240	...
49	Varkaus d.	0750	...	1223	1310	1522	1725	1835	1903	2130	2315	...
183	**Joensuu** ⊙ a.	1000	...	1353	...	1653	1920	...	2035	2303	...	...

	🚌 ⚒		🚌 ⚒		🚌 Ⓐ	🚌 ⑥	🚌 Ⓐ	🚌 ⑦		Ⓑ
Joensuu ⊙ d.	...	0700	0910	1218	...	...	1500	1515	1605	1828
Varkaus d.	0545	0836	1120	1357	1605	1715	1720	1725	1743	2007
Pieksämäki a.	0620	0909	1155	1430	1650	1750	1755	1800	1815	2039

km		🚌 ⚒		🚌 ⑦	🚌 ⚒	🚌 ⚒	🚌		🚌 Ⓑ¶	🚌 Ⓐ	🚌 Ⓑ	🚌 ⑦
0	**Joensuu** ⊙ d.	0900	1147	1210	1405	1520	1630	1755	2100	2115	2315	2315
104	Lieksa ⊙ a.	|	1308	|	|	1705	|	1916	|	2245	0045	|
160	Nurmes ⊙ a.	1055	1353	1400	1610	...	1830	2001	2320	...	...	0135
274	**Kajaani** bus station a.	1255	...	1600	1805	...	2030	...	...	...	...	...

	🚌 ⚒		🚌 ⚒	🚌 ⑦	🚌 Ⓑ	🚌	🚌	🚌 Ⓐ		🚌
Kajaani bus station d.	...	...	0540	...	...	1040	...	...	...	1710
Nurmes ⊙ d.	...	0640	0750	0915	...	1235	...	...	1540	1905
Lieksa ⊙ d.	0510	0726	|	1005	1005	|	1250	1410	1626	1950
Joensuu ⊙ a.	0645	0845	1010	1150	1150	1430	1435	1600	1745	2130

🚌 (◇) **PIEKSÄMÄKI – SAVONLINNA** (bus station) at 1020 ⚒, 1520, 1830 ⑤⑦ and 2100 ⑦.
🚌 (◇) **SAVONLINNA** (bus station) – **PIEKSÄMÄKI** at 0655 ⚒, 1230, 1530 ⑤⑦ and 1800 ⑦.

⊙ – 🚌 timings are at the bus station.
¶ – 15 minutes later until Dec. 31.
◇ – *123 km.* Journey time: 1 hr 50 m - 2 hrs 5 m.

GERMANY

Operator: Principal operator is Deutsche Bahn Aktiengesellschaft (DB). Many regional services are run by independent operators – these are specified in the table heading (or by footnotes for individual trains).

Services: Trains convey first- and second-class seating accommodation unless otherwise shown (by '2' in the column heading, a footnote or a general note in the table heading). Overnight sleeping car (🛏) and couchette (▬) trains do not necessarily convey seating accommodation - refer to individual footnotes for details. Descriptions of sleeping and couchette cars appear on page 8.

There are various categories of trains in Germany. The type of train is indicated by the following letter codes above each column (or by a general note in the table heading):

ICE	**InterCity Express**	German high-speed (230–320 km/h) train. Higher fares payable.
EC	**EuroCity**	International express train.
IC	**InterCity**	Internal express train.
THA	**Thalys**	International high-speed train. Special fares.
TGV	**Train à Grande Vitesse**	French high-speed (320 km/h) train.
RJ	**Railjet**	Austrian high-speed train.
IRE	**InterRegio Express**	Regional express train.
RE	**Regional Express**	Semi-fast train.
RB	**Regional Bahn**	Stopping train.
CNL	**City Night Line**	Quality overnight express train. Most services convey *Deluxe* sleeping cars (1/2 berth) with en-suite shower and WC, *Economy* sleeping cars (1/2/4 berth), couchettes (4/6 berth) and reclining seats. Reservation compulsory. See also page 8.
EN	**Euro Night**	International overnight express train. See also page 8.
D	**Durchgangszug**	Or **Schnellzug** – other express train (day or night).
S-Bahn		Suburban stopping train.

Other operators:

ALX	**Arriva-Länderbahn-Express**	Operated by Arriva / Regentalbahn AG - Die Länderbahn. Runs trains on the route Hof - Regensburg - München - Oberstdorf / Lindau.
X	**InterConnex**	Long-distance routes operated by Veolia Verkehr GmbH. **DB tickets are not valid.**

Timings: Valid **December 13**, 2009 - **June 12**, 2010 (except where shown otherwise in the table heading).

Many long distance trains operate on selected days only for part of the journey. These are often indicated in the train composition footnote by showing the dated journey segment within brackets. For example '(12) Leipzig - Hannover (- Dortmund ⑦)' means that the train runs daily (or as shown in the column heading) between Leipzig and Hannover, but only continues to Dortmund on Sundays. Additional footnotes / symbols are often used to show more complex running dates, e.g. '(12) (München ⊡ -) Nürnberg - Hamburg' means that the train runs only on dates in note ⊡ between München and Nürnberg, but runs daily (or as shown in the column heading) between Nürnberg and Hamburg.

International overnight trains that are not intended for internal German journeys are not usually shown in the German section. Please refer to the International section for details of these services. A number of other international overnight trains (which may be used for certain internal journeys) run over long distances without a public stop making it difficult to show them clearly in the relevant German tables. For ease of reference a summary of these trains can be found in international table **54**. A summary of domestic overnight trains München - Hamburg / Berlin and v.v. can be found in the special table at the foot of this page.

Engineering work may occasionally disrupt services at short notice (especially at weekends and during holiday periods), so it is advisable to check timings locally before travelling. The locations of known service alterations are summarised in the shaded panel below.

Supplements: A 'Sprinter' supplement (€16 in first class, €11 in second class) is payable for travel by limited stop *ICE* ***SPRINTER*** trains **1090–1097**. Special 'global' fares are payable for international journeys on *Thalys* trains. A variable supplement (*Aufpreis*) is payable for travel by overnight *CNL* and *EN* trains, the cost of which depends on the type of accommodation required (sleeper, couchette or reclining seat).

Catering: Two types of catering are indicated in the tables: 🍷 Bordbistro – hot and cold drinks, snacks and light meals; ✕ Bordrestaurant – full restaurant car service (bordbistro also available). First class passengers on *ICE* and *IC* trains benefit from an at-seat service. On overnight trains 🍷 indicates that drinks and light snacks are available, usually from the sleeping or couchette car attendant (the refreshment service may only be available to sleeping and couchette car passengers).

Reservations: Reservation is compulsory for travel by *CNL*, *Thalys* and other trains marked Ⓡ. Seat reservations are also available on *ICE*, *EC* and *IC* trains (€5 first class, €4 second class).

Holidays: Dec. 25, 26, Jan. 1, Apr. 2, 5, May 1, 13, 24 are German national public holidays (trains marked ⚒ or Ⓐ do not run). In addition there are other regional holidays as follows: Jan. 6 – Heilige Drei Könige (Epiphany) and June 3 – Fronleichnam (Corpus Christi). On these days the regional service provided is usually that applicable on ⑦ (please refer to individual footnotes for details).

ENGINEERING WORK SUMMARY

- **Hannover - Hamburg**: Dec. 14–21. Certain northbound *ICE* services are diverted with Hamburg arrivals up to 25 minutes later. Southbound services may be delayed by up to 7 minutes.
- **Rostock - Bützow**: Dec. 14–22 (also until 0800 on Dec. 23). All services from / to Rostock via Bützow or Güstrow are subject to alteration. Journey times on the Stralsund - Rostock - Hamburg route are extended by up to 30 minutes (earlier departures / later arrivals possible).
- **Wolfsburg - Braunschweig - Hildesheim - Göttingen**: Dec. 24–27. *ICE* services are diverted, not calling at Braunschweig or Hildesheim.
- **Hannover - Magdeburg**: Dec. 24–27. *IC* services are diverted, not calling at Braunschweig or Helmstedt. Earlier departures / later arrivals at Hannover Hbf.
- **Koblenz - Wiesbaden**: Dec. 28 - Jan. 18. All rail services via St Goarshausen are suspended. A replacement 🚌 service operates during this period.
- **Hamburg - Bremen - Osnabrück**: Jan. 5–21. Certain southbound *EC* / *IC* trains depart Hamburg and Bremen up to 11 minutes earlier.
- **Weimar - Erfurt - Gotha**: Jan. 16 (also until 0730 on Jan. 17). *ICE* trains are replaced by 🚌 Weimar - Erfurt - Gotha and v.v. *IC* trains are diverted between Halle (Saale) and Kassel (via Nordhausen and Leinefelde). Journey times extended (please confirm timings locally).
- **Basel - Freiburg**: Jan. 23, 24 (also Jan. 22 from 1530). Trains **104/5**, **2100/2/3/5** do not operate Basel - Freiburg and v.v. Other services may be delayed by up to 24 minutes.
- **Hildesheim - Berlin**: Jan. 23, 24, 25 (also Jan. 22 from 1600): *ICE* trains from Hildesheim to Berlin may be delayed by up to 28 minutes.
- **Koblenz - Mainz**: Jan. 30, 31, Feb. 6, 7. Most long-distance services are diverted with delays of up to 15 minutes possible (trains will not call at Bingen).
- **Ulm - Augsburg**: Feb. 27 - May 16. Certain *IC* trains do not operate Ulm - München and v.v. Certain *ICE* trains are diverted between Stuttgart and Augsburg and do not call at Ulm. Full details can be found in Table **930**.
- **Strasbourg - Offenburg / Karlsruhe**: Mar. 6, 7. All services are subject to alteration.
- **Nürnberg - Regensburg**: May 22 - June 6. Services diverted via Ingolstadt. During this period eastbound timings Regensburg - Passau - Wien and westbound timings Nürnberg - Würzburg - Frankfurt and beyond are up to 60 minutes later.
- **Hannover - Magdeburg**: From May 1. Many long-distance services are diverted via Stendal and do not call at Braunschweig or Helmstedt. Earlier departures / later arrivals possible at Hannover and Magdeburg (up to 20 minutes).
- **Stuttgart**. June 10 - July 28. Regional services via Bietigheim-Bissingen (to/from Heilbronn and Vaihingen) are subject to alteration.

German Domestic Overnight Trains Summary

See international Table 54 for a summary of international overnight trains from / to / via Germany.

		CNL 1286 ⊙	*CNL* 1246 A ◇	*CNL* 1244 B ◇	
München Hbf	d.	2051	2051	2051	...
München Ost	d.	2152	2152	2152	...
Augsburg Hbf	d.	|	|	|	...
Potsdam Hbf	a.	|	0734	0813	...
Berlin Wannsee	a.	|	0747	0825	...
Berlin Zoo	a.	|	0820	0850	...
Berlin Hbf	a.	|	0828	0856	...
Berlin Ostbahnhof	a.	|	0840	0904	...
Berlin Lichtenberg	a.	|	0858	0943	...
Hannover Hbf	a.	0525	...	...	...
Bremen Hbf	a.	0642	...	...	...
Hamburg Hbf	a.	0753	...	...	...
Hamburg Altona	a.	0808	...	...	...

		RE 4435	*CNL* 1287 ⊙	*CNL* 1245 C ◇	*CNL* 1247 E ◇	
Hamburg Altona	d.	...	2113	...	...	...
Hamburg Hbf	d.	...	2127	...	...	...
Bremen Hbf	d.	2118	|	...	...	...
Hannover Hbf	d.	2238	2323	...	...	...
Berlin Lichtenberg	d.	...	|	1940	2038	...
Berlin Ostbahnhof	d.	...	|	1955	2053	...
Berlin Hbf	d.	...	|	2006	2103	...
Berlin Zoo	d.	...	|	2013	2114	...
Berlin Wannsee	d.	...	|	2054	2154	...
Potsdam Hbf	d.	...	|	2102	2202	...
Augsburg Hbf	a.	...	0622	0622	0622	...
München Hbf	a.	...	0705	0705	0705	...
München Ost	a.	...	0726	0726	0726	...

A – Until Apr. 30.
B – From May 1.
C – From Apr. 30.
E – Until Apr. 29.

⊙ – PYXIS. Conveys 🛏 1, 2 cl., ▬ 2 cl., (2) (reclining) and 🍷.
◇ – CAPELLA. Conveys 🛏 1, 2 cl., ▬ 2 cl., (2) (reclining) and 🍷.

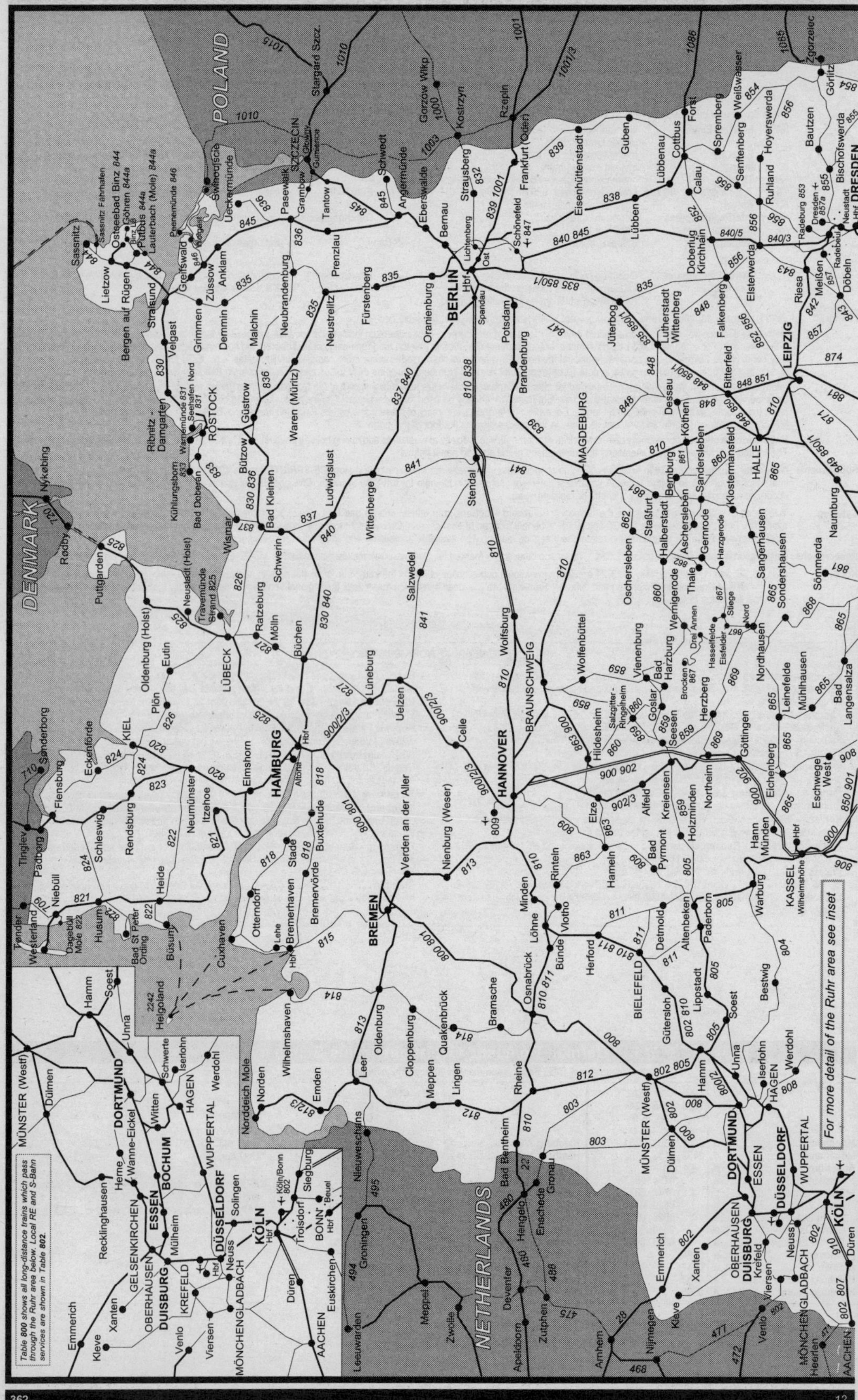
DENMARK
POLAND
NETHERLANDS
Table 800 shows all long-distance trains which pass through the Ruhr area below. Local RE and S-Bahn services are shown in Table 802.
For more detail of the Ruhr area see inset
HAMBURG
BERLIN
HANNOVER
BREMEN
LEIPZIG
DRESDEN
MAGDEBURG
BRAUNSCHWEIG
KIEL
LÜBECK
ROSTOCK
SZCZECIN
HALLE
BIELEFELD
KASSEL
DORTMUND
ESSEN
DÜSSELDORF
DUISBURG
KÖLN
BOCHUM
WUPPERTAL
HAGEN
BONN
AACHEN
MÖNCHENGLADBACH
MÜNSTER (Westf)
OBERHAUSEN
GELSENKIRCHEN
KREFELD
Sassnitz
Stralsund
Greifswald
Schwerin
Wismar
Flensburg
Westerland
Husum
Cuxhaven
Wilhelmshaven
Oldenburg
Osnabrück
Emden
Norden
Leer
Rheine
Hamm
Paderborn
Göttingen
Wolfsburg
Stendal
Potsdam
Frankfurt (Oder)
Cottbus
Görlitz
Helgoland

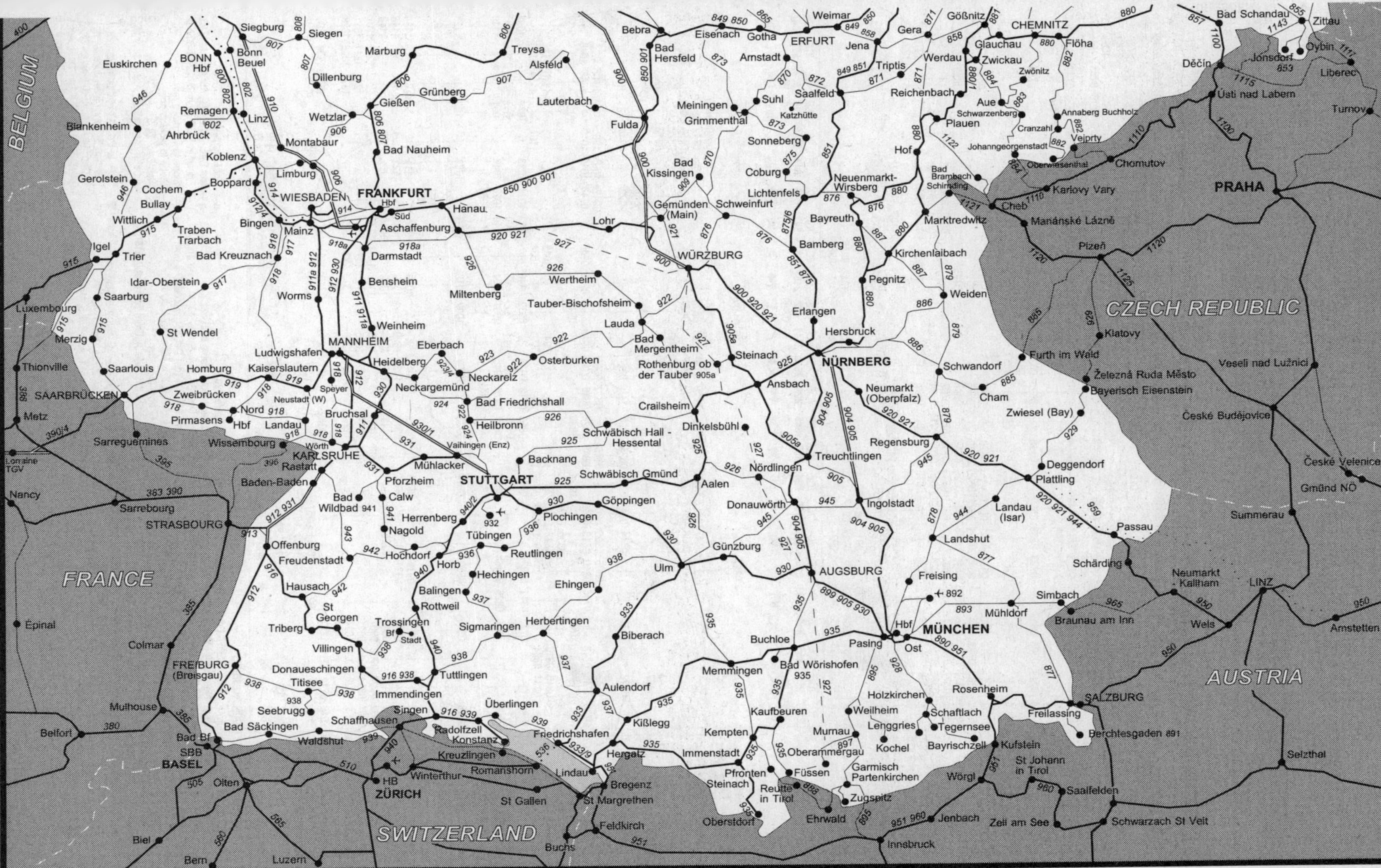
12
BELGIUM
FRANCE
SWITZERLAND
AUSTRIA
CZECH REPUBLIC
PRAHA
FRANKFURT
WIESBADEN
MANNHEIM
KARLSRUHE
STUTTGART
WÜRZBURG
NÜRNBERG
AUGSBURG
MÜNCHEN
CHEMNITZ
ERFURT
SALZBURG
LINZ
ZÜRICH
BASEL
STRASBOURG
SAARBRÜCKEN
Bonn Hbf
Bonn Beuel
Siegburg
Siegen
Euskirchen
Blankenheim
Remagen
Ahrbrück
Linz
Koblenz
Gerolstein
Cochem
Bullay
Wittlich
Traben-Trarbach
Boppard
Bingen
Mainz
Trier
Igel
Luxembourg
Merzig
Saarburg
Idar-Oberstein
Bad Kreuznach
St Wendel
Saarlouis
Thionville
Metz
Homburg
Kaiserslautern
Zweibrücken
Pirmasens
Nord
Hbf
Neustadt (W)
Landau
Wissembourg
Wörth
Sarreguemines
Lorraine TGV
Nancy
Sarrebourg
Rastatt
Baden-Baden
Offenburg
Freudenstadt
Hausach
Triberg
St Georgen
Villingen
Donaueschingen
Titisee
Seebrugg
Freiburg (Breisgau)
Colmar
Mulhouse
Belfort
Épinal
Bad Säckingen
Waldshut
Schaffhausen
Singen
Bad Bf
SBB
Olten
Biel
Bern
Luzern
Winterthur
HB
Kreuzlingen
Romanshorn
St Gallen
Buchs
Feldkirch
St Margrethen
Bregenz
Lindau
Hergatz
Friedrichshafen
Konstanz
Radolfzell
Überlingen
Immendingen
Tuttlingen
Trossingen
Bf
Stadt
Rottweil
Balingen
Hechingen
Tübingen
Reutlingen
Horb
Hochdorf
Nagold
Herrenberg
Calw
Bad Wildbad
Pforzheim
Mühlacker
Vaihingen (Enz)
Bruchsal
Speyer
Ludwigshafen
Worms
Heidelberg
Neckargemünd
Eberbach
Neckarelz
Osterburken
Bad Friedrichshall
Heilbronn
Backnang
Plochingen
Göppingen
Schwäbisch Gmünd
Aalen
Schwäbisch Hall - Hessental
Crailsheim
Dinkelsbühl
Nördlingen
Donauwörth
Günzburg
Ulm
Ehingen
Herbertingen
Sigmaringen
Biberach
Aulendorf
Kißlegg
Memmingen
Kempten
Immenstadt
Oberstdorf
Pfronten Steinach
Reutte in Tirol
Füssen
Ehrwald
Oberammergau
Murnau
Garmisch Partenkirchen
Zugspitz
Kochel
Lenggries
Tegernsee
Schaftlach
Holzkirchen
Weilheim
Kaufbeuren
Buchloe
Bad Wörishofen
Pasing
Ost
Freising
Landshut
Mühldorf
Simbach
Braunau am Inn
Rosenheim
Freilassing
Berchtesgaden
Kufstein
Wörgl
Jenbach
Innsbruck
St Johann in Tirol
Saalfelden
Zell am See
Schwarzach St Veit
Selzthal
Wels
Neumarkt - Kallham
Amstetten
Schärding
Passau
Plattling
Deggendorf
Landau (Isar)
Regensburg
Ingolstadt
Treuchtlingen
Neumarkt (Oberpfalz)
Schwandorf
Cham
Zwiesel (Bay)
Bayerisch Eisenstein
Železná Ruda Město
Furth im Wald
Klatovy
Plzeň
Veselí nad Lužnicí
České Budějovice
České Velenice
Gmünd NÖ
Summerau
Mariánské Lázně
Cheb
Karlovy Vary
Chomutov
Ústí nad Labem
Děčín
Bad Schandau
Zittau
Oybin
Jonsdorf
Liberec
Turnov
Annaberg Buchholz
Vejprty
Oberwiesenthal
Cranzahl
Johanngeorgenstadt
Schwarzenberg
Aue
Zwönitz
Zwickau
Glauchau
Flöha
Gößnitz
Werdau
Plauen
Reichenbach
Bad Brambach
Schirnding
Marktredwitz
Hof
Gera
Triptis
Jena
Weimar
Gotha
Eisenach
Arnstadt
Saalfeld
Katzhütte
Suhl
Meiningen
Grimmenthal
Sonneberg
Coburg
Lichtenfels
Neuenmarkt-Wirsberg
Bayreuth
Kirchenlaibach
Pegnitz
Weiden
Hersbruck
Erlangen
Bamberg
Schweinfurt
Bad Kissingen
Gemünden (Main)
Lohr
Steinach
Ansbach
Rothenburg ob der Tauber
Bad Mergentheim
Lauda
Tauber-Bischofsheim
Wertheim
Miltenberg
Aschaffenburg
Hanau
Süd
Darmstadt
Bensheim
Weinheim
Bad Nauheim
Gießen
Wetzlar
Limburg
Montabaur
Dillenburg
Marburg
Grünberg
Alsfeld
Treysa
Lauterbach
Fulda
Bebra
Bad Hersfeld
363

800 KOBLENZ - KÖLN - DORTMUND - HAMBURG

km		ICE	IC	IC	IC	ICE	IC	IC	IC	IC	ICE	ICE	IC	CNL	CNL	ICE	ICE	ICE	ICE	ICE	ICE	ICE	IC	IC	ICE
		949	2020	2128	2128	541	2214	2314	2145	2355	853	843	2331	40478	418	608	1095	553	543	918	328	328	2212	2143	826
		①m		①g	Ⓐn	①–⑥	V		①–⑥	①g	①–⑥		⊡	R [R]	R [R]		♥ [R]	①–⑥		⑤f	P	Q		①–⑥	
						d✕	✕	✕♦	e🍷	🍷♦	e✕	✕	N🍷	🍷♦	🍷♦	K✕	⚡✕	e✕	✕	🍷	A🍷	A🍷	✕♦	e🍷	🍷
	Basel SBB 🚌 **912** d.	...	...	...	...	...	...	...	...	...	...	...	...	2207	...	2326	...	...	...	...	...	...	...	...	...
	Karlsruhe Hbf **912** d.	...	...	...	...	...	...	...	...	...	...	...	...	0018	...	0129	...	...	...	...	...	...	...	...	...
	München Hbf **904 930** d.	...	...	...	...	...	...	...	...	...	...	...	...	|	2243	|	...	...	...	...	...	...	...	...	0032g
	Stuttgart Hbf **930** d.	...	...	...	...	...	...	...	...	...	...	...	...	|	0125	|	...	...	...	...	...	...	...	...	0305
	Nürnberg Hbf **920** d.	...	...	...	...	...	...	...	...	...	...	...	...	|	|	|	...	...	...	...	...	...	...	...	|
	Frankfurt (Main) Hbf **910/2** d.	...	2324	...	...	...	...	...	...	...	...	...	...	|	|	0315	...	...	...	0510	0510	...	...	...	0544
	Frankfurt Flughafen ✈ § d.	...	2338	...	...	...	...	...	...	...	...	...	...	|	|	0346r	...	...	...	0524	0524	...	...	...	0601
	Mainz Hbf **912** d.	...	0001	...	...	...	...	...	...	...	...	...	...	|	|	0408	...	...	...	|	|	...	...	...	|
0	**Koblenz** Hbf d.	...	0057	...	...	...	...	...	...	...	...	...	...	0446s	0446s	0503	...	0547	...	|	|	...	0606	...	|
18	Andernach d.	...	0109	...	...	...	...	...	...	...	...	...	...	|	|	|	...	|	...	|	|	...	0618	...	|
39	Remagen d.	...	0121	...	...	...	...	...	...	...	...	...	...	|	|	|	...	|	...	|	|	...	0631	...	|
59	**Bonn** Hbf d.	...	0135	...	...	...	...	...	...	...	...	...	...	0519s	0519s	0544	...	0622	...	|	|	...	0644	...	|
	Köln/Bonn Flughafen ✈ d.	...	|	...	...	...	...	...	...	...	...	...	...	|	|	|	...	|	...	0628	0628	...	|	...	|
93	**Köln** Hbf a.	...	0155	...	...	...	...	...	...	...	...	...	...	0542s	0542s	0605	...	0642	...	0639	0639	...	0705	...	|
93	**Köln** Hbf d.	0149	0210	0410	...	0429	0510	0510	0510	...	0545	0529	0541	|	|	0609	0616	0648	0626	0646	0646	0646	0710	0710	|
94	**Köln** Messe/Deutz d.	|	|	|	...	|	|	|	|	...	|	|	|	|	|	|	|	|	|	|	|	|	|	|	0708
	Solingen Hbf d.	|	|	|	...	|	|	|	0530	...	0604	|	|	|	|	|	|	|	|	|	|	|	|	0730	|
	Wuppertal Hbf d.	|	|	|	...	|	|	|	0543	...	0617	|	|	|	|	|	|	0716	|	|	|	|	|	0743	|
	Hagen Hbf d.	|	|	|	...	|	|	|	0601	...	0634	|	|	|	|	|	|	0734	|	|	|	|	|	0801	|
133	**Düsseldorf** Hbf d.	0213	0234	0433	...	0453	0533	0533	|	0546	|	0553	0604	0608s	0608s	0633	0639u	|	0653	0713	0713	0713	0733	|	0729
140	Düsseldorf Flughafen ✈ d.	0221	0241	|	...	0501	|	|	|	0553	|	0600	0611	|	|	|	|	|	0700	|	|	|	|	|	|
157	**Duisburg** Hbf d.	0231	0252	0446	...	0511	0546	0546	|	0604	|	0610	0621	0628s	0628s	0646	0651u	|	0710	0726	0726	0726	0746	|	0751
165	Oberhausen Hbf d.	|	|	|	...	|	|	|	|	|	|	|	|	0637	0637	|	|	|	|	|	0732	0732	|	|	|
167	Mülheim (Ruhr) Hbf d.	0239	0300	|	...	|	|	|	|	|	|	|	|	...	...	|	|	|	|	|	...	...	|	|	|
176	**Essen** Hbf d.	0247	0308	0459	...	0523	0559	0559	|	0618	|	0623	0637	...	...	0659	0703u	|	0723	0736	...	...	0759	|	0804
	Gelsenkirchen Hbf d.	|	|	|	...	|	|	|	|	|	|	|	0647	...	...	|	|	|	|	...	...	...	|	|	|
	Wanne-Eickel Hbf d.	|	|	|	...	|	|	|	|	|	|	|	0653	...	...	|	|	|	|	...	...	...	|	|	|
	Recklinghausen Hbf d.	|	|	|	...	|	|	|	|	|	|	|	0701	...	...	|	|	|	|	...	...	...	|	|	|
192	Bochum Hbf d.	0257	0318	0511	...	0534	0611	0611	|	0629	|	0635	|	...	...	0711	|	|	0735	...	...	...	0811	|	0816c
210	**Dortmund** Hbf a.	0308	0329	0521	...	0545	0621	0621	0620	0639	|	0646	|	...	...	0721	|	|	0746	...	...	...	0821	0820	0827c
210	**Dortmund** Hbf **805** d.	0311	0332	0525	0525	0547	0625	0625	0628	0642	|	0648	|	...	...	0725	|	|	0748	...	...	...	0825	0828	...
	Hamm (Westf) **805** a.	0327	0352	|	|	0602	|	|	0643	0702	0702	0707	|	...	...	|	|	0802	0807	...	...	...	|	0843	...
	Hamm (Westf) d.	0330	0354	|	|	0604	|	|	0645	0707	0711	0711	|	...	...	|	|	0811	0811	...	...	...	|	0845	...
	Hannover Hbf **810** a.	0458	|	|	|	0728	|	|	0818	|	0828	0828	|	...	...	|	|	0928	0928	...	...	...	|	1018	...
	Leipzig Hbf **810** a.	|	|	|	|	|	|	|	1120	|	|	|	|	...	...	|	|	|	|	...	...	...	|	1320	...
	Berlin Hbf **810** a.	0655	|	|	|	0908	|	|	...	1316	1011	1011	|	...	...	|	|	1108	1108	...	...	...	|	...	...
266	Münster (Westf) Hbf **801** d.	...	0417	0557	0557	...	0657	0657	...	...	...	...	0728	...	...	0757	|	...	...	...	...	...	0857	...	...
316	Osnabrück Hbf **801** d.	...	0450	0623	0623	...	0723	0723	...	...	...	...	...	...	...	0823	|	...	...	...	...	...	0923	...	...
438	**Bremen** Hbf **801** d.	...	0555	0725	0725	...	0817	0817	...	...	...	...	...	...	...	0917	|	...	...	...	...	...	1017	...	...
553	**Hamburg** Hbf **801** a.	...	0651	0833	0833	...	0912	0912	...	...	...	...	...	...	...	1012	0945	...	...	...	...	...	1112	...	...
560	**Hamburg** Altona a.	...	0705	0853	0853	...	0927	...	...	...	...	...	...	...	...	...	0959	...	...	...	...	...	...	...	...

	IC	ICE	ICE	ICE	IC	ICE	IC	IC	ICE	ICE	ICE	ICE	IC	IC	ICE	IC	ICE	ICE	IC	ICE	IC	ICE	ICE	ICE	ICE
	2357	855	855	845	2333	616	2320	2120	824	555	545	226	2310	2141	822	2157	857	847	331	614	2028	820	557	557	547
	①–⑥	Ⓐ			⊖		V		①–⑤						①–⑥							①–⑤	⑥z		
	e🍷	T✕	✕	✕	N🍷	🍷	✕	✕♦	a D 🍷	✕	E✕	A🍷	✕♦	🍷	e🍷	🍷♦	✕	✕	🍷♦	🍷	🍷	a🍷	T✕	✕	✕
Basel SBB 🚌 **912** d.	...	...	...	...	...	...	...	...	...	...	...	...	...	...	...	...	...	...	...	...	...	...	...	...	...
Karlsruhe Hbf **912** d.	...	...	...	...	...	...	...	...	...	...	...	...	...	...	...	...	...	...	...	...	...	...	...	...	...
München Hbf **904 930** d.	...	...	...	...	...	0317	...	...	...	...	...	...	...	...	0448g	...	...	...	...	0523	...	0551	...	...	...
Stuttgart Hbf **930** d.	...	...	...	...	...	0551	...	...	...	...	...	...	...	...	|	...	...	...	...	0751	...	|	...	...	...
Nürnberg Hbf **920** d.	...	...	...	...	...	|	...	...	...	...	...	...	...	...	0600	...	...	...	...	|	0530	0700	...	...	...
Frankfurt (Main) Hbf **910/2** d.	...	...	...	...	...	|	0542	0542	0702	...	...	0729	0638	...	0810	...	...	...	...	|	0742	0910	...	...	...
Frankfurt Flughafen ✈ § d.	...	...	...	...	...	0709	0558	0558	0715	...	...	0743	0657	...	0824	...	...	...	...	0909	0758	0924	...	...	...
Mainz Hbf **912** d.	...	...	...	...	...	|	0617	0617	|	...	...	|	0717	...	|	...	...	...	...	|	0820	|	...	...	...
Koblenz Hbf d.	...	0643	...	...	...	|	0712	0712	|	...	...	|	0812	...	|	...	...	...	0843e	|	0912	|	0943	...	...
Andernach d.	...	0657	...	...	...	|	|	|	|	...	...	|	|	...	|	...	...	...	0856e	|	|	|	0957	...	...
Remagen d.	...	|	...	...	...	|	|	|	|	...	...	|	|	...	|	...	...	...	0908e	|	|	|	|	...	...
Bonn Hbf d.	...	0722	...	...	...	|	0744	0744	|	0825e	...	|	0844	...	|	...	...	...	0922e	|	0944	|	1022	...	...
Köln/Bonn Flughafen ✈ d.	...	|	...	0712	...	|	|	|	|	|	...	|	|	...	|	...	...	...	|	|	|	|	|	...	1012j
Köln Hbf a.	...	0742	...	|	...	0805	0805	0805	|	0845e	...	0832	0905	...	|	...	...	...	0942e	1005	1005	|	1042	...	|
Köln Hbf d.	0715	0748	0748	|	0746	0810	0810	0810	|	0848	0826	0846	0910	0913	|	0905	0948	...	0946	1010	1010	|	1048	1048	|
Köln Messe/Deutz d.	|	|	|	0730	|	|	|	|	0824	|	0830	|	|	|	0917	|	|	...	|	|	|	1017	|	|	1030j
Solingen Hbf d.	|	|	|	|	|	|	0830	0830	|	|	|	|	|	0931	|	|	|	...	|	|	1030	|	|	|	|
Wuppertal Hbf d.	|	0816	0816	|	|	|	0843	0843	|	0916	|	|	|	0943	|	|	1016	...	|	|	1043	|	1116	1116	|
Hagen Hbf d.	|	0834	0834	|	|	|	0901	0901	|	0934	|	|	|	1001	|	|	1034	...	|	|	1101	|	1134	1134	|
Düsseldorf Hbf d.	0746	|	|	0753	0811	0833	|	|	0845	|	0853	0913	0933	|	0939	0946	|	0953	1011	1033	|	1039	|	|	1053
Düsseldorf Flughafen ✈ d.	0753	|	|	0800	|	|	|	|	|	|	0900	|	|	|	|	0953	|	1000	|	|	|	|	|	|	1100
Duisburg Hbf d.	0804	|	|	0810	0826	0846	|	|	0857	|	0910	0926	0946	|	0951	1004	|	1010	1026	1046	|	1051	|	|	1110
Oberhausen Hbf d.	|	|	|	|	0833	|	|	|	|	|	|	0933	|	|	|	|	|	|	1033	|	|	|	|	|	|
Mülheim (Ruhr) Hbf d.	|	|	|	|	|	|	|	|	|	|	|	...	|	|	|	|	|	|	|	|	|	|	|	|	|
Essen Hbf d.	0818	|	|	0823	|	0859	|	|	0914	|	0923	...	0959	|	1002	1018	|	1023	|	1059	|	1102	|	|	1123
Gelsenkirchen Hbf d.	|	|	|	|	0845	|	|	|	|	|	|	...	|	|	...	|	|	|	1045	|	|	...	|	|	|
Wanne-Eickel Hbf d.	|	|	|	|	0851	|	|	|	|	|	|	...	|	|	...	|	|	|	1051	|	|	...	|	|	|
Recklinghausen Hbf d.	|	|	|	|	0859	|	|	|	|	|	|	...	|	|	...	|	|	|	1059	|	|	...	|	|	|
Bochum Hbf d.	0829	|	|	0835	|	0911	|	|	0926	|	0935	...	1011	|	...	1029	|	1035	|	1111	|	...	|	|	1135
Dortmund Hbf a.	0839	|	|	0846	|	0921	0921	0921	0936	|	0946	...	1021	1020	...	1039	|	1046	|	1121	1121	...	|	|	1146
Dortmund Hbf **805** d.	0842	|	|	0848	|	...	0925	0925	...	|	0948	...	1025	1028	...	1042	|	1048	|	...	1125	...	|	|	1148
Hamm (Westf) **805** a.	0902	0902	0902	0907	|	...	|	|	...	1002	1007	...	|	1043	...	1102	1102	1107	|	...	|	...	1202	1202	1207
Hamm (Westf) d.	0907	0911	0911	0911	|	...	|	|	...	1011	1011	...	|	1045	...	1107	1111	1111	|	...	|	...	1211	1211	1211
Hannover Hbf **810** a.	|	1028	1028	1028	|	...	|	|	...	1128	1128	...	|	1218	...	|	1228	1228	|	...	|	...	1328	1328	1328
Leipzig Hbf **810** a.	|	|	|	|	|	...	|	|	...	|	|	...	|	1520	...	|	|	|	|	...	|	...	|	|	|
Berlin Hbf **810** a.	1518	1211	1211	1211	|	...	|	|	...	1308	1308	...	|	...	...	1719	1411	1411	|	...	|	...	1508	1508	1508
Münster (Westf) Hbf **801** d.	...	...	...	...	0927	...	0957	0957	...	...	...	...	1057	...	...	...	...	...	1127	...	1157	...	...	...	...
Osnabrück Hbf **801** d.	...	...	...	...	...	...	1023	1023	...	...	...	...	1123	...	...	...	...	...	...	...	1223	...	...	...	...
Bremen Hbf **801** d.	...	...	...	...	...	...	1117	1117	...	...	...	...	1217	...							1317	...	...	...	...
Hamburg Hbf **801** a.	...	...	...	...	...	...	1212	1212	...	...	...	...	1312	...							1412	...	...	...	...
Hamburg Altona a.	...	...	...	...	...	...	1226	...	...	...	...	...	...	...							1427	...	...	...	...

*See Table **802** for Rhein-Ruhr local RE and S-Bahn services*

♦ – **NOTES** (LISTED BY TRAIN NUMBER)

331 – [12] and 🍷 (Luxembourg ①–⑥**e** -) Köln - Emden. Runs with train number **231** and continues to Norddeich Mole on ①②③④⑥ to Mar. 25.

418 – POLLUX – 🛏 1, 2 cl., 🛌 2 cl., [2] and 🍷 München - Amsterdam. Starts from Innsbruck on ⑥ Dec. 26 - Apr. 10 (Table **21**).

2120 – From Mar. 27. FEHMARN – [12] and ✕ Frankfurt - Lübeck - Puttgarden.

2157 – [12] and 🍷 Köln - Kassel - Erfurt - Halle - Berlin (- Stralsund ⑥**q**). Train number **2257** on ⑥ (also Dec. 24, 25, 31, Apr. 2, 4, May 23)

2212 – RÜGEN – [12] and ✕ Koblenz - Rostock - Stralsund - Ostseebad Binz.

2310 – NORDFRIESLAND – [12] and ✕ Frankfurt - Köln - Westerland.

2314 – From Mar. 27. DEICHGRAF – [12] and ✕ Köln - Westerland.

2355 – STRELASUND – [12] Düsseldorf - Kassel - Erfurt - Halle - Berlin - Stralsund - Ostseebad Binz.

40478 – PEGASUS – 🛏 1, 2 cl., 🛌 2 cl., [2] (reclining) and 🍷 Zürich - Amsterdam. Starts from Brig on ⑥ Dec. 26 - Apr. 10.

A – To Amsterdam (Table **28**).
D – From Darmstadt Hbf (d. 0637).
E – From Aachen Hbf (d. 0740) and Düren (d. 0758) on ①–⑥**e**.

K – To Kiel (Table **820**).
N – To Norddeich Mole (Table **812**).
P – ①–④ (not Dec. 24, Apr. 5, May 13, 24, June 3).
Q – ①–④ until Mar. 25 (not Dec. 24); ①②③④⑥ from Mar. 27 (not Apr. 3, 5, May 13, 24, June 3).
R – ④–⑦ (daily from Mar. 25).
T – Ⓐ (not Dec. 24, 31, June 3). From Trier (Table **915**).
V – Until Mar. 26.

a – Not Dec. 24, 25, 31, Jan. 1, Apr. 2, 5, May 24.
c – ⑥⑦ (also Dec. 24, 25, 31, Jan. 1, Apr. 2).
d – Not Dec. 25, 26, Jan. 1, Apr. 2, 3, 5, May 24.
e – ①–⑥ (not Dec. 25, 26, Jan. 1, Apr. 3, 5, May 24).
f – Not Dec. 25, Jan. 1, Apr. 2.
g – ① (also Apr. 6, May 25; not Apr. 5, May 24).
j – ①–⑤ (not Dec. 25, Jan. 1, Apr. 2, 5, May 24).
m – Also Apr. 6, May 25; not Dec. 21, 28, Apr. 5, May 24.

n – Not Dec. 24, 31.
q – Not Dec. 24, 25, 31, Apr. 2, 4, May 23.
r – Frankfurt Flughafen Regionalbahnhof.
s – Stops to set down only.
u – Stops to pick up only.
z – Also Dec. 24, 31, Apr. 2, May 13, June 3; not Dec. 26, Apr. 3, May 15, June 5.
♥ – ①–④ to Dec. 17 and from Mar. 29 (not Apr. 5, May 13, 24, June 3).
⊡ – ① Dec. 14 - Jan. 4; ① Mar. 8–22; ①④⑤⑥⑦ Mar. 27 - Apr. 12; ① Apr. 19 - May 3; ①④⑤⑥⑦ from May 8.
⊖ – ⚒ (daily from Mar. 22).
⚡ – *ICE **SPRINTER***. Supplement payable.
§ – Frankfurt Flughafen Fernbahnhof. See also Tables **910** and **912**.

KOBLENZ - KÖLN - DORTMUND - HAMBURG 800

	IC	*IC*	*ICE*	*IC*	*ICE*	*IC*	*IC*	*ICE*	*ICE*	*IC*	*ICE*	*ICE*	*ICE*	*ICE*	*ICE*	*ICE*	*ICE*	*ICE*	*IC*	*ICE*	*ICE*	*IC*	*IC*	*ICE*	*ICE*
	2010	**2010**	**128**	**2116**	**602**	**2049**	**2359**	**859**	**849**	**333**	**612**	**1126**	**1026**	**726**	**559**	**1049**	**549**	**126**	**2114**	**1018**	**600**	**2047**	**2151**	**951**	**941**
	①–⑤	⑤**f**			①–④	⑤–⑦	⑤⑦					①⑦	②–⑥	①–⑥		⑦**m**	①–⑥	**E**		⑤**f**	⑥**k**	Ⓑ**q**			
	d 🍷	🍷	**A** 🍷	🍴♦	**h** 🍷	**z** 🍷	🍷♦	🍴	🍴	🍷♦	🍷	🍴♦	🍴♦	**e** 🍷	🍴	🍴	**e** 🍴	**A** 🍷	🍴	🍷	🍷	🍷	🍷♦	🍴	🍴
Basel SBB ▦ **912**......... d.	...	...	...	...	0712	...	...	...	...	...	...	...	...	...	...	...	...	...	...	...	...	...	...	...	...
Karlsruhe Hbf **912**......... d.	...	...	...	...	0901	...	...	...	...	...	...	...	...	...	...	...	...	...	...	1109	1109	...	...	...	...
München Hbf **904 930**...... d.	...	...	...	...	|	...	...	...	...	...	0723	0545**g**	...	0755	...	...	...	...	...	|	|	...	...	...	...
Stuttgart Hbf **930**............ d.	0714	0714	...	0737	|	...	...	...	...	...	0951	|	...	|	...	...	...	...	0937	|	|	...	...	...	...
Nürnberg Hbf **920**......... d.	|	|	...	|	|	...	...	...	...	...	|	0729**g**	0729	0900	...	...	...	...	|	|	|	...	...	...	...
Frankfurt (Main) Hbf **910/2**. d.	|	|	0929	|	|	...	...	...	...	...	|	0942	0942	1110	...	...	...	1129	|	|	|	...	...	...	...
Frankfurt Flughafen ✈ §... d.	|	|	0943	|	1009	...	...	...	...	...	1109	0958	0958	1124	...	...	...	1143	|	1209	1209	...	...	...	...
Mainz Hbf **912**............... d.	0848	0848	|	0920	|	...	...	...	...	...	|	1020	1020	|	...	...	...	|	1120	|	|	...	...	...	...
Koblenz Hbf..................... d.	0943	0943	|	1012	|	...	...	...	...	1043	|	1112	1112	|	...	...	...	|	1212	|	|	...	...	...	...
Andernach.......................... d.	0956	0956	|	|	|	...	...	...	...	1056	|	|	|	|	...	...	...	|	|	|	|	...	...	...	...
Remagen............................. d.	1008	1008	|	|	|	...	...	...	...	1108	|	|	|	|	...	...	...	|	|	|	|	...	...	...	...
Bonn Hbf.......................... d.	1022	1022	|	1044	|	...	...	...	...	1122	|	1144	1144	|	1223**e**	...	...	|	1244	|	|	...	...	...	...
Köln/Bonn Flughafen ✈.... d.	|	|	|	|	|	...	...	...	...	|	|	|	|	|	|	...	1212	|	|	|	|	...	...	...	1312**w**
Köln Hbf.......................... a.	1042	1042	1032	1105	1105	...	...	...	...	1142	1205	1205	1205	|	1242**e**	...	|	1232	1305	1305	1305	...	...	...	|
Köln Hbf.......................... d.	1045	1045	1046	1110	1110	1113	1120	1148	...	1146	1210	1210	1210	|	1248	...	|	1246	1310	1314	1310	1313	...	1348	|
Köln Messe/Deutz.............. d.	|	|	|	|	|	|	|	|	...	|	|	|	|	1217	|	...	1230	|	|	|	|	|	...	|	1330**w**
Solingen Hbf....................... d.	|	|	|	|	1130	1131	|	|	...	|	|	|	|	|	|	...	|	|	|	|	1330	1331	...	|	|
Wuppertal Hbf.................... d.	|	|	|	|	1143	1143	|	1216	...	|	|	1243	1243	|	1316	...	|	|	|	|	1343	1343	...	1416	|
Hagen Hbf......................... d.	|	|	|	|	1201	1201	|	1234	...	|	|	1301	1301	|	1334	...	|	|	|	|	1401	1401	...	1434	|
Düsseldorf Hbf.................. d.	1107	1117	1113	1133	|	|	1146	|	1153	1212	1233	|	|	1239	|	1230	1253	1314	1333	1342	|	|	1346	|	1353
Düsseldorf Flughafen ✈....... d.	...	|	|	|	|	|	1153	|	1200	|	|	|	|	|	|	1240	1300	|	|	|	|	|	1353	|	1400
Duisburg Hbf.................... d.	...	1130	1126	1146	|	|	1204	|	1210	1226	1246	|	|	1251	|	1310	1310	1328	1346	1355	|	|	1404	|	1410
Oberhausen Hbf.................. d.	...	|	1133	|	|	|	|	|	|	1233	|	|	|	|	|	|	|	1333	|	|	|	|	|	|	|
Mülheim (Ruhr) Hbf.............. d.	...	1137	...	|	|	|	|	|	|	|	|	|	|	|	|	|	|	...	|	|	|	|	|	|	|
Essen Hbf........................ d.	...	1145	...	1159	|	|	1218	|	1223	|	1259	|	|	1304	|	1323	1323	...	1359	1406	|	|	1418	|	1423
Gelsenkirchen Hbf.............. d.	...	|	...	|	|	|	|	|	|	1245	|	|	|	|	|	|	|	...	|	...	|	|	|	|	|
Wanne-Eickel Hbf............... d.	...	|	...	|	|	|	|	|	|	1251	|	|	|	|	|	|	|	...	|	...	|	|	|	|	|
Recklinghausen Hbf........... d.	...	|	...	|	|	|	|	|	|	1259	|	|	|	|	|	|	|	...	|	...	|	|	|	|	|
Bochum Hbf........................ d.	...	1156	...	1211	|	|	1229	|	1235	|	1311	|	|	1316**r**	|	1335	1335	...	1411	...	|	|	1429	|	1435
Dortmund Hbf.................... a.	...	1208	...	1221	1220	1220	1239	|	1246	|	1321	1321	1321	1330**r**	|	1346	1346	...	1421	...	1420	1420	1439	|	1446
Dortmund Hbf............ **805** d.	...	1211	...	1225	...	1228	1242	|	1248	|	...	1325	1325	...	|	1348	1348	...	1425	...	...	1428	1442	|	1448
Hamm (Westf)........... **805** a.	...	1233	...	|	...	1243	1302	1302	1307	|	...	|	|	...	1402	1407	1407	...	|	...	...	1443	1502	1502	1507
Hamm (Westf).................. d.	...	1235	...	|	...	1245	1307	1311	1311	|	...	|	|	...	1411	1411	1411	...	|	...	...	1445	1507	1511	1511
Hannover Hbf **810**......... a.	...	1400	...	|	...	1418	|	1428	1428	|	...	|	|	...	1528	1528	1528	...	|	...	...	1618	|	1628	1628
Leipzig Hbf **810**......... a.	...	|	...	|	...	1720	|	|	|	|	...	|	|	...	|	|	|	...	|	...	...	1920	|	|	|
Berlin Hbf **810**.............. a.	...	1550	...	|	...	...	1918	1611	1611	|	...	|	|	...	1708	1708	1708	...	|	...	...	...	2118**c**	1811	1811
Münster (Westf) Hbf....... **801** d.	...	...	...	1257	...	...	...	...	...	1327	...	1357	1357	...	...	...	...	...	1457	...	...	...	...	...	...
Osnabrück Hbf............. **801** d.	...	...	...	1323	...	...	...	...	...	...	...	1423	1423	...	...	...	...	...	1523	...	...	...	...	...	...
Bremen Hbf................ **801** d.	...	...	...	1417	...	...	...	...	...	...	...	1517	1517	...	...	...	...	...	1617	...	...	...	...	...	...
Hamburg Hbf............. **801** a.	...	...	...	1511	...	...	...	...	...	...	...	1612	1612	...	...	...	...	...	1712	...	...	...	...	...	...
Hamburg Altona................ a.	...	...	...	...	...	...	...	...	...	...	...	...	...	...	...	...	...	...	1727	...	...	...	...	...	...

	IC	*ICE*	*IC*	*ICE*	*ICE*	*ICE*	*ICE*	*IC*	*IC*	*IC*	*ICE*	*IC*	*IC*	*ICE*	*ICE*	*ICE*	*IC*	*IC*	*IC*	*IC*	*ICE*	*IC*	*ICE*	*ICE*	*ICE*
	335	**610**	**2024**	**722**	**651**	**641**	**124**	**1920**	**1916**	**2112**	**508**	**2045**	**2153**	**953**	**943**	**928**	**2014**	**2004**	**2006**	**1808**	**518**	**2026**	**628**	**653**	**643**
								⑦**w**	⑤**f**		⑥**k**	Ⓑ**p**	Ⓑ**q**	Ⓑ**q**		⑥**k**	①–⑤	⑦	⑥	⑦**w**					
	🍷♦	🍷	🍴♦	🍷	🍴	🍴	**A** 🍷		**S** 🍷	🍴	🍷	🍷	🍷♦	🍴	🍴	🍷	🍷♦	🍷♦	🍷♦	♦	🍷		🍷	🍴	🍴
Basel SBB ▦ **912**......... d.	...	...	...	...	...	...	...	...	...	...	1112	...	...	...	...	...	...	...	...	...	...	...	...	...	...
Karlsruhe Hbf **912**......... d.	...	...	...	...	...	...	...	...	...	...	1300	...	...	...	...	...	...	1221	1221	...	...	...	...	...	...
München Hbf **904 930**...... d.	...	0923	...	0955	...	...	...	...	0841**x**	...	|	...	...	...	...	1055	...	|	|	...	1123	...	1155	...	...
Stuttgart Hbf **930**............ d.	...	1151	...	|	...	...	...	...	1114	1137	|	...	...	...	...	|	1209	|	|	...	1351	...	|	...	...
Nürnberg Hbf **920**......... d.	...	|	0928	1100	...	...	...	...	|	|	|	...	...	...	...	1200	|	|	|	...	|	...	1300	...	...
Frankfurt (Main) Hbf **910/2**. d.	...	|	1142	1310	...	...	1329	1215	|	|	|	...	...	...	...	1410	|	|	|	...	|	1344	1510	...	...
Frankfurt Flughafen ✈ §... d.	...	1309	1158	1324	...	...	1343	1228	|	|	1409	...	...	...	...	1424	|	|	|	...	1509	1358	1524	...	...
Mainz Hbf **912**............... d.	...	|	1220	|	...	...	|	1248	1248	1320	|	...	...	...	...	|	1342	1342	1342	...	|	1420	|	...	...
Koblenz Hbf..................... d.	1243	|	1312	|	...	...	|	1343	1343	1412	|	...	...	...	...	|	1443	1443	1443	...	|	1512	|	...	...
Andernach.......................... d.	1256	|	|	|	...	...	|	1356	1356	|	|	...	...	...	...	|	1456	1456	1456	...	|	|	|	...	...
Remagen............................. d.	1308	|	|	|	...	...	|	1408	1408	|	|	...	...	...	...	|	1508	1508	1508	...	|	|	|	...	...
Bonn Hbf.......................... d.	1322	|	1344	|	1425	...	|	1422	1422	1444	|	...	...	...	...	|	1522	1522	1522	...	|	1544	|	...	...
Köln/Bonn Flughafen ✈.... d.	|	|	|	|	|	...	|	|	|	|	|	...	...	...	...	|	|	|	|	...	|	|	|	...	1612
Köln Hbf.......................... a.	1342	1405	1405	|	1445	...	1432	1442	1442	1505	1505	...	...	...	...	|	1542	1542	1542	...	1605	1605	|	...	|
Köln Hbf.......................... d.	1346	1410	1410	|	1448	...	1446	1445	1445	1510	1510	1513	...	1548	...	|	1546	1546	1546	1539	1610	1610	|	1648	|
Köln Messe/Deutz.............. d.	|	|	|	1417	|	...	|	|	|	|	|	|	...	|	...	1548	|	|	|	|	|	|	1617	|	1630
Solingen Hbf....................... d.	|	|	1430	|	|	...	|	|	|	|	1530	1531	...	|	...	|	|	|	|	|	|	1630	|	|	|
Wuppertal Hbf.................... d.	|	|	1443	|	1516	...	|	|	|	|	1543	1543	...	1616	...	1616	|	|	|	|	|	1643	|	1716	|
Hagen Hbf......................... d.	|	|	1501	|	1534	...	|	|	|	|	1601	1601	...	1634	...	1635	|	|	|	|	|	1701	|	1734	|
Düsseldorf Hbf.................. d.	1412	1433	|	1439	|	1453	1514	1518	1518	1533	|	|	1546	|	1553	|	1612	1612	1612	1617	1633	|	1639	|	1653
Düsseldorf Flughafen ✈....... d.	|	|	|	|	|	1500	|	|	|	|	|	|	1553	|	1600	|	|	|	|	|	|	|	|	|	1700
Duisburg Hbf.................... d.	1426	1446	|	1451	|	1510	1528	1532	1532	1546	|	|	1604	|	1610	|	1626	1626	1626	1630	1646	|	1651	|	1710
Oberhausen Hbf.................. d.	1433	|	|	|	|	|	1533	|	|	|	|	|	|	|	|	|	1633	1633	|	|	|	|	|	|	|
Mülheim (Ruhr) Hbf.............. d.	|	|	|	|	|	|	...	|	|	|	|	|	|	|	|	|	|	|	1633	|	|	|	|	|	|
Essen Hbf........................ d.	|	1459	|	1502	|	1523	...	1545	1545	1559	|	|	1618	|	1623	|	|	|	1641	1643	1659	|	1702	|	1723
Gelsenkirchen Hbf.............. d.	1445	|	|	...	|	|	...	|	|	|	|	|	|	|	|	|	1645	1645	|	|	|	|	...	|	|
Wanne-Eickel Hbf............... d.	1451	|	|	...	|	|	...	|	|	|	|	|	|	|	|	|	1651	1651	|	|	|	|	...	|	|
Recklinghausen Hbf........... d.	1459	|	|	...	|	|	...	|	|	|	|	|	|	|	|	|	1659	1659	|	|	|	|	...	|	|
Bochum Hbf........................ d.	|	1511	|	...	|	1535	...	1556	1556	1611	|	|	1629	|	1635	|	|	|	1652	|	1711	|	...	|	1735
Dortmund Hbf.................... a.	|	1521	1521	...	|	1546	...	1608	1608	1621	1620	1620	1639	|	1646	1655	|	|	1703	1700	1721	1721	...	|	1746
Dortmund Hbf............ **805** d.	|	...	1525	...	|	1548	...	1611	1611	1625	...	1628	1642	|	1648	...	|	|	...	1702	...	1725	...	|	1748
Hamm (Westf)........... **805** a.	|	...	|	...	1602	1607	...	1633	1633	|	...	1643	1702	1702	1707	...	|	|	...	|	...	|	...	1802	1807
Hamm (Westf).................. d.	|	...	|	...	1611	1611	...	1635	1635	|	...	1645	...	1711	1711	...	|	|	...	|	...	|	...	1811	1811
Hannover Hbf **810**......... a.	|	...	|	...	1728	1728	...	1759	1800	|	...	1818	...	1828	1828	...	|	|	...	|	...	|	...	1928	1928
Leipzig Hbf **810**......... a.	|	...	|	...	|	|	...	|	|	|	...	2120	...	|	|	...	|	|	...	|	...	|	...	|	|
Berlin Hbf **810**.............. a.	|	...	|	...	1908	1908	...	1951	1951	|	...	...	...	2011	2011	...	|	|	...	|	...	|	...	2108	2108
Münster (Westf) Hbf....... **801** d.	1527	...	1557	...	...	...	...	...	...	1657	...	...	...	...	...	...	1727	1727	...	1738	...	1757	...	...	...
Osnabrück Hbf............. **801** d.	...	...	1623	...	...	...	...	...	...	1723	...	...	...	...	...	...	...	...	...	1813	...	1823	...	...	...
Bremen Hbf................ **801** d.	...	...	1717	...	...	...	...	...	...	1817	...	...							...	1907**b**	...	1917	...	...	...
Hamburg Hbf............. **801** a.	...	...	1812	...	...	...	...	...	...	1912	...	...							...	2006	...	2012	...	...	...
Hamburg Altona................ a.	...	...	1827	...	...	...	...	...	...	1926	...	...							...	...	...	2026	...	...	...

*See Table **802** for Rhein - Ruhr local RE and S-Bahn services*

♦ – **NOTES** (LISTED BY TRAIN NUMBER)

333/5 – [12] and 🍷 Luxembourg - Koblenz - Emden - Norddeich Mole.
1026 – ②–⑥ to May 21 and from June 8 (not Dec. 25, 26, Jan. 1, Apr. 3, 6, May 13). [12] and 🍴 Regensburg - Frankfurt - Köln - Kiel.
1126 – ①⑦ (also Dec. 25, 26, Jan. 1, Apr. 3, 6, May 13); daily May 22 - June 7. [12] and 🍴 (München ① **g** -) Frankfurt - Köln - Kiel.
1808 – [12] Köln - Hamburg - Westerland.
2004 – ⑦ (also Jan. 1, Apr. 5, May 13, 24, June 3; not Apr. 4, May 23). BODENSEE – [12] and 🍷 Konstanz - Mannheim - Emden.
2006 – ⑥ (also Dec. 24, 25, 31, Apr. 2, 4, May 23). BODENSEE – [12] and 🍷 Konstanz - Mannheim - Dortmund.
2014 – ①–⑤ (not Dec. 24, 25, 31, Jan. 1, Apr. 2, 5, May 13, 24, June 3). [12] and 🍷 Stuttgart - Mannheim - Emden.
2024 – [12] and 🍴 Passau - Regensburg - Frankfurt - Köln - Hamburg.
2116 – [12] and 🍴 Stuttgart - Heidelberg - Köln - Hamburg - Stralsund (- Greifswald ①–⑤ **a**).
2151 – [12] and 🍷 Düsseldorf - Kassel - Erfurt - Halle (- Berlin ⑥⑦ **c**).
2153 – [12] and 🍷 Düsseldorf - Kassel - Erfurt (- Halle ⑦ **w**).
2359 – ⑤⑦ (also Dec. 23, 30, Apr. 1, 5, May 12, 24; not Dec. 25, Jan. 1, Apr. 2, 4, May 14, 23). [12] and 🍷 Köln - Kassel - Erfurt - Halle - Berlin - Stralsund.

A – To Amsterdam (Table **28**).
E – From Mar. 26.
S – From Salzburg (Table **890**).

a – Not Dec. 24, 25, 31, Jan. 1, Apr. 2, 5, May 24.
b – Not Jan. 3 - Mar. 28.
c – ⑥⑦ (also Dec. 24, 25, 31, Jan. 1, Apr. 2, 5, May 24).
d – Not Dec. 24, 25, 31, Jan. 1, Apr. 2, 5, May 13, 14, 24, June 3, 4.
e – ①–⑥ (not Dec. 25, 26, Jan. 1, Apr. 3, 5, May 24).
f – Also Dec. 23, 30, Apr. 1, May 12, June 2; not Dec. 25, Jan. 1, Apr. 2, May 14, June 4.
g – ① (also Apr. 6, May 13, 22, 25–29, June 1–5; not Apr. 5, May 24). Departs München 0614 on May 13, 22, 26–29, June 1–5.
h – Not Dec. 23, 24, 30, 31, Apr. 1, 5, May 24.
k – Also Dec. 24, 25, 31, Apr. 2, 4, May 23.
m – ⑦ (also Dec. 25, 26, Jan. 1, Apr. 3, 5, May 24). From Mönchengladbach Hbf (d. 1205) and Neuss (d. 1217).
p – Not Dec. 24, 25, 31, Apr. 2, 4, May 13, 23.
q – Not Dec. 24, 25, 31, Apr. 2, 4, May 23.
r – ⑥ (also Dec. 24, 31, Apr. 2, 4, May 23).
w – ⑦ (also Apr. 5, May 24; not Apr. 4, May 23).
x – Not Mar. 5 - May 12.
z – Also Dec. 23, 24, 30, 31, Apr. 1, 5, May 24.

§ – Frankfurt Flughafen Fernbahnhof. See also Tables **910** and **912**.

800 KOBLENZ - KÖLN - DORTMUND - HAMBURG

	IC	EC	EC	ICE	ICE	IC	ICE	ICE	ICE	ICE	IC	ICE	IC	ICE	ICE	ICE	IC	ICE	EC	IC	ICE	ICE	ICE	ICE	ICE
	2012	**100**	**102**	**506**	**806**	**2155**	**1226**	**122**	**955**	**945**	**337**	**516**	**2022**	**624**	**655**	**645**	**118**	**914**	**6**	**2041**	**606**	**104**	**622**	**957**	**947**
		①–⑥	⑦		①–⑤	⑦**w**	⑥**k**			⑧**q**								①–⑤		⑦**w**	①–⑥	**n**		⑧**q**	
	🍷♦	✕♦	✕♦	🍷	**a**🍷	🍷♦	🍷	**A**🍷	✕	✕	🍷♦	🍷	🍷	🍷	✕	✕	🍷♦	**a**🍷	✕♦	🍷	**e**🍷	🍷♦	🍷	✕	✕
Basel SBB 🏛 **912** d.	...	1218	1218	...	...	...	...	...	...	...	...	...	...	...	...	...	...	...	1420	...	...	1512	...	...	...
Karlsruhe Hbf **912** d.	...	1412	1412	1509	1509	...	...	...	...	...	...	...	...	...	...	...	...	...	1612	...	...	1700	...	...	...
München Hbf **904 930** d.	...	|	|	|	|	...	1255	...	...	...	...	1323	...	1355	...	...	...	...	|	...	...	|	1455	...	...
Stuttgart Hbf **930** d.	1314	|	|	|	|	...	|	...	...	...	...	1551	...	|	...	...	1512	...	|	...	...	|	|	...	...
Nürnberg Hbf **920** d.	|	|	|	|	|	...	1400	...	...	...	...	|	...	1500	...	...	|	...	|	...	...	|	1600	...	...
Frankfurt (Main) Hbf **910/2** d.	|	|	|	|	|	...	1610	1629	...	...	...	|	1542	1710	...	...	|	1717	|	...	...	|	1810	...	...
Frankfurt Flughafen ✈ § d.	|	|	|	1609	1609	...	1624	1643	...	...	...	1709	1558	1724	...	...	|	1732	|	...	...	1809	1824	...	...
Mainz Hbf **912** d.	1448	1520	1520	|	|	...	|	|	...	...	...	|	1620	|	...	...	1648	|	1720	...	...	|	|	...	...
Koblenz Hbf d.	1543	1612	1612	|	|	...	|	|	...	...	1643	|	1712	|	...	...	1743	|	1812	...	...	|	|	...	...
Andernach d.	1556	|	|	|	|	...	|	|	...	...	1656	|	|	|	...	...	1756	|	|	...	...	|	|	...	...
Remagen d.	1608	|	|	|	|	...	|	|	...	...	1708	|	|	|	...	...	1808	|	|	...	...	|	|	...	...
Bonn Hbf d.	1622	1644	1644	|	|	...	|	|	...	...	1722	|	1744	|	...	...	1822	|	1844	...	...	|	|	...	...
Köln/Bonn Flughafen ✈ d.	|	|	|	|	|	...	|	|	...	...	|	|	|	|	...	1812**q**	|	|	|	...	...	|	|	...	...
Köln Hbf a.	1642	1705	1705	1705	1705	...	|	1739	...	...	1742	1805	1805	|	...	|	1842	|	1905	...	...	1905	|	...	...
Köln Hbf d.	1646	1710	1710	1710	1714	...	|	1746	1748	...	1745	1810	1810	|	1848	|	1845	|	1910	1913	1913	1917	|	1948	1926
Köln Messe/Deutz d.	|	|	|	|	|	...	1730	|	|	...	|	|	|	1817	|	1830**q**	|	1851	|	|	|	|	1922	|	|
Solingen Hbf d.	|	|	|	1730	|	...	|	|	|	...	|	1830	|	|	|	|	|	|	|	1931	1931	|	|	|	|
Wuppertal Hbf d.	|	|	|	1743	|	...	|	|	1816	...	|	1843	|	|	1916	|	|	|	|	1943	1944	|	|	2016	|
Hagen Hbf d.	|	|	|	1801	|	...	|	|	1834	...	|	1901	|	|	1934	|	|	|	|	2001	2002	|	|	2034	|
Düsseldorf Hbf d.	1714	1733	1733	|	1738	1746	1753	1813	|	1753	1817**c**	|	1833	1839	|	1853	1911	1917	1933	|	|	1940	1944	|	1953
Düsseldorf Flughafen ✈ d.	|	|	|	|	|	1753	1800	|	|	1800	|	|	|	|	|	1900	|	|	|	|	|	|	|	|	2000
Duisburg Hbf d.	1727	1746	1746	|	1750	1804	1810	1826	|	1810	1830	|	1846	1851	|	1910	1924	1930	1946	|	|	1953	1956	|	2010
Oberhausen Hbf d.	|	|	|	|	1756	|	|	1833	|	|	1837	|	|	|	|	|	|	|	|	|	|	1958	|	|	|
Mülheim (Ruhr) Hbf d.	1734**h**	|	|	|	...	|	|	...	|	|	|	|	|	|	|	|	|	|	|	|	|	...	|	|	|
Essen Hbf d.	1740	1759	1759	|	...	1818	1823	...	|	1823	|	|	1859	1904	|	1923	1936	1942	1959	|	|	...	2011	|	2023
Gelsenkirchen Hbf d.	|	|	|	|	...	|	|	...	|	|	1849	|	|	|	|	|	1946	|	|	|	|	...	|	|	|
Wanne-Eickel Hbf d.	|	|	|	|	...	|	|	...	|	|	|	|	|	|	|	|	1952	|	|	|	|	...	|	|	|
Recklinghausen Hbf d.	|	|	|	|	...	|	|	...	|	|	1900	|	|	|	|	|	2000	|	|	|	|	...	|	|	|
Bochum Hbf d.	1753	1811	1811	|	...	1829	1835	...	|	1835	|	|	1911	1916	|	1935	|	1953	2011	|	|	...	2026	|	2035
Dortmund Hbf a.	1805	1821	1821	1820	...	1839	1846	...	|	1846	|	1920	1921	1929	|	1946	|	2003	2021	2020	2021	...	2038	|	2046
Dortmund Hbf **805** d.	1828	1825	1825	...	...	1842	1848	...	|	1848	|	...	1925	...	|	1948	|	...	2025**q**	2028	...	...	...	|	2048
Hamm (Westf) **805** a.	1843	|	|	...	...	1902	1906	...	1902	1907	|	...	|	...	2002	2007	|	...	|	2043	...	...	...	2102	2107
Hamm (Westf) d.	1845	|	|	...	...	...	...	...	1911	1911	|	...	|	...	2011	2011	|	...	|	2045	...	...	...	2111	2111
Hannover Hbf **810** a.	2018	|	|	...	...	...	...	...	2028	2028	|	...	|	...	2128	2128	|	...	|	2218	...	...	...	2228	2228
Leipzig Hbf **810** a.	2323**w**	|	|	...	...	...	...	...	|	|	|	...	|	...	|	|	|	...	|	...	...	...	...	|	|
Berlin Hbf **810** a.	...	|	|	...	...	...	...	...	2221	2221	|	...	|	...	2308	2308	|	...	|	...	...	...	...	0016	0016
Münster (Westf) Hbf **801** d.	...	1857	1857	...	...	...	...	...	...	...	1928	...	1957	...	...	...	2029	...	2057**q**	...	...	...	...	...	...
Osnabrück Hbf **801** d.	...	1923	1923	...	...	...	...	...	...	...	...	...	2023	...	...	...	...	...	2123**q**	...	...	...	...	...	...
Bremen Hbf **801** d.	...	2017	2017	...	...	...	...	...	...	...	...	...	2117	...	...	...	...	...	2221**q**	...	...	...	...	...	...
Hamburg Hbf **801** a.	...	2112	2112	...	...	...	...	...	...	...	...	...	2212	...	...	...	...	...	2315**q**	...	...	...	...	...	...
Hamburg Altona a.	...	2127	...	...	...	...	...	...	...	...	...	...	2226	...	...	...	...	...	2330**q**	...	...	...	...	...	...

	EC	ICE	ICE	ICE	ICE	ICE	ICE	ICE	IC	IC	IC	ICE	ICE	ICE	ICE	ICE	ICE	ICE	CNL	IC	IC	ICE	ICE	ICE	ICE
	114	**26**	**514**	**1220**	**926**	**912**	**120**	**657**	**2339**	**2318**	**2318**	**1002**	**502**	**528**	**810**	**24**	**512**	**526**	**457**	**1910**	**2110**	**500**	**524**	**22**	**522**
				⑦**z**	⑥**t**	①–③	**Y**	⑦**w**	⑧**q**		⑧**q**	⑥**k**	⑧**q**		⑧**q**			⑧**q**	🅁	⑦**w**	⑧**q**				
	✕♦	**B**✕	🍷	🍷	🍷	**m**🍷	**A**🍷	✕	🍷			🍷	🍷	**G**🍷	🍷	**B**✕	🍷	🍷	🍷♦		✕	🍷	🍷	**B**✕	🍷
Basel SBB 🏛 **912** d.	...	...	...	...	...	...	...	...	...	...	...	...	...	...	...	...	...	...	...	...	...	1912	...	...	...
Karlsruhe Hbf **912** d.	...	...	...	...	...	...	...	...	...	...	...	1909	1909	...	...	...	...	...	...	...	...	2101	...	...	...
München Hbf **904 930** d.	1340	...	1523	1555	1555	...	...	...	...	...	...	|	|	1650	...	...	1723	1755	...	1612**r**	...	|	1855	...	1951
Stuttgart Hbf **930** d.	1610	...	1751	|	|	...	...	...	...	1741	1741	|	|	|	...	...	1951	|	...	1914	1914**j**	|	|	...	|
Nürnberg Hbf **920** d.	|	1528	|	1700	1700	...	...	...	...	|	|	|	|	1800	...	1727	|	1900	...	|	|	|	2000	1927	2100
Frankfurt (Main) Hbf **910/2** d.	|	1742	|	1910	1910	1929	1929	...	...	|	|	|	|	2010	2016	1942	|	2110	...	|	|	|	2210	2146	2310
Frankfurt Flughafen ✈ § d.	|	1758	1909	1924	1924	1943	1943	...	...	|	|	2009	2009	2024	2032	1958	2109	2124	...	|	|	2209	2224	2159	2329
Mainz Hbf **912** d.	1742	1820	|	|	|	|	|	...	...	1920	1920	|	|	|	|	2020	|	|	...	2048	2120	|	|	2220	|
Koblenz Hbf d.	1843	1912	|	|	|	|	|	...	1943	2012	2012	|	|	|	|	2112	|	|	...	2143	2212	|	|	2312	|
Andernach d.	1856	|	|	|	|	|	|	...	1956	|	|	|	|	|	|	|	|	|	...	2156	|	|	|	|	|
Remagen d.	1908	|	|	|	|	|	|	...	2008	|	|	|	|	|	|	|	|	|	...	2208	|	|	|	|	|
Bonn Hbf d.	1922	1944	|	|	|	|	|	2025	2022	2044	2044	|	|	|	|	2144	|	|	...	2222	2244	|	|	2344	|
Köln/Bonn Flughafen ✈ d.	|	|	|	|	2028	|	|	|	|	|	|	|	|	|	2139	|	|	|	...	|	|	|	2330	|	|
Köln Hbf a.	1942	2005	2005	|	2039	2039	2039	2045	2042	2105	2105	2105	2105	|	|	2205	2205	2219	...	2242	2305	2309	|	0005	0039
Köln Hbf d.	1946	2010	2010	|	2046	2046	2046	2048	2045	...	2110	2110	2110	|	|	2210	2210	2232	2228	2245	...	2314	|	0010**v**	0044
Köln Messe/Deutz d.	|	|	|	2017	|	|	|	|	|	...	|	|	|	2117	2150	|	|	|	|	|	...	|	2345	|	|
Solingen Hbf d.	|	2030	|	|	|	|	|	|	|	...	|	|	2130	|	|	2230	|	|	|	|	...	|	|	|	|
Wuppertal Hbf d.	|	2043	|	|	|	|	|	2116	|	...	|	|	2143	|	|	2243	|	|	2314	|	...	|	|	|	|
Hagen Hbf d.	|	2101	|	|	|	|	|	2134	|	...	|	|	2201	|	|	2301	|	|	|	|	...	|	|	|	|
Düsseldorf Hbf d.	2012	|	2033	2039	2113	2113	2113	|	2117**c**	...	2133	2133	|	2139	2212	|	2233	2258	2202*	2309	...	2337	0007	0034**v**	0106
Düsseldorf Flughafen ✈ d.	|	|	|	|	|	|	|	|	|	...	|	|	|	|	|	|	|	|	|	|	...	2345	|	|	0113
Duisburg Hbf d.	2025	|	2046	2052	2126	2126	2126	|	2130	...	2146	2146	|	2151	2225	|	2246	2312	2147*	2322	...	2354	0020	0047**v**	0124
Oberhausen Hbf d.	|	|	|	|	|	|	2133	|	|	...	|	|	|	|	|	|	|	|	2139*	|	...	|	|	|	|
Mülheim (Ruhr) Hbf d.	2033	|	|	|	|	|	...	|	2137	...	|	|	|	|	|	|	|	|	|	2330	...	|	|	|	|
Essen Hbf d.	2041	|	2059	2104	2138	2138	...	|	2145	...	2159	2159	|	2204	2237	|	2259	2325	|	2338	...	0007	0032	0059**v**	0136
Gelsenkirchen Hbf d.	|	|	|	|	|	|	...	|	|	...	|	|	|	|	|	|	|	|	|	|	...	|	|	|	|
Wanne-Eickel Hbf d.	|	|	|	|	|	|	...	|	|	...	|	|	|	|	|	|	|	|	|	|	...	|	|	|	|
Recklinghausen Hbf d.	|	|	|	|	|	|	...	|	|	...	|	|	|	|	|	|	|	|	|	|	...	|	|	|	|
Bochum Hbf d.	2051	|	2111	2116	2149	2149	...	|	2156	...	2211	2211	|	2216	2248	|	2311	2335	|	2349	...	0018	0043	0111**v**	0146
Dortmund Hbf a.	2102	2120	2121	2129	2159	2159	...	|	2207	...	2221	2221	2220	2228	2300	2320	2321	2345	|	2359	...	0028	0054	0121**v**	0157
Dortmund Hbf **805** d.	...	...	2125	2132**x**	...	...	...	|	...	...	2225**w**	2228	2228	...	...	...	2325	...	2356	...	...	...	...	...	...
Hamm (Westf) **805** a.	...	...	|	2147**x**	...	...	...	2202	...	...	|	2248	2248	...	...	...	|	...	|	...	...	...	...	...	...
Hamm (Westf) d.	...	...	|	2149**x**	...	...	...	2211	...	...	|	2250	2250	...	...	...	|	...	0014	...	...	...	...	...	...
Hannover Hbf **810** a.	...	...	|	2317**x**	...	...	...	2328	...	...	|	0018	0018	...	...	...	|	...	|	...	...	...	...	...	...
Leipzig Hbf **810** a.	...	...	|	...	...	...	...	|	...	...	|	...	...	...	...	...	|	...	|	...	...	...	...	...	...
Berlin Hbf **810** a.	...	...	|	...	...	...	...	0112	...	...	|	...	...	...	...	...	|	...	0421	...	...	...	...	...	...
Münster (Westf) Hbf **801** d.	...	...	2200	...	...	...	...	...	...	...	2254**w**	...	...	...	...	...	2357	...	...	...	...	...	...	...	...
Osnabrück Hbf **801** d.	...	...	2227	...	...	...	...	...	...	...	...	...	...	...	...	...	...	...	...	...	...	...	...	...	...
Bremen Hbf **801** d.	...	...	2323	...	...	...	...	...	...	...	...	...	...	...	...	...	...	...	...						
Hamburg Hbf **801** a.	...	...	0019	...	...	...	...	...	...	...	...	...	...	...	...	...	...	...	...						
Hamburg Altona a.	...	...	0033	...	...	...	...	...	...	...	...	...	...	...	...	...	...	...	...						

*See Table **802** for Rhein-Ruhr local RE and S-Bahn services*

♦ – **NOTES** (LISTED BY TRAIN NUMBER)

6 – [12] and ✕ Chur - Zürich - Basel - Karlsruhe - Dortmund (- Hamburg ⑧**q**).
100 – ①–⑥ (also Apr. 4, May 23; not Apr. 5, May 24). [12] and ✕ Chur - Zürich - Basel - Hamburg.
102 – ⑦ (also Apr. 5, May 24; not Apr. 4, May 23). [12] and ✕ Chur - Zürich - Basel - Köln - Kiel.
104 – ICE INTERNATIONAL – [12] and 🍷 Basel - Köln - Arnhem - Utrecht - Amsterdam.
114 – WÖRTHERSEE – [12] and ✕ Klagenfurt - Villach - Salzburg - Dortmund.
118 – [12] and 🍷 Salzburg - Innsbruck - Bregenz - Lindau - Ulm - Stuttgart - Münster.
337 – [12] and 🍷 Luxembourg - Trier - Koblenz - Münster (- Emden ♥).
457 – PHOENIX – 🛏 1, 2 cl., ▬ 2 cl. and [2] Amsterdam - Dresden - Praha (Table **28**); 🛏 1, 2 cl., ▬ 2 cl. and [2] (*CNL* **40447** – BOREALIS) Amsterdam - København (Table **50**); 🛏 1, 2 cl., ▬ 2 cl. and [2] (*EN* **447** – JAN KIEPURA) Amsterdam - Warszawa (Table **24**); conveys 🛏 1, 2 cl. Amsterdam - Warszawa - Moskva (Table **24**). For overnight journeys only.
2012 – ALLGÄU – [12] and 🍷 Oberstdorf - Köln - Hannover (- Magdeburg ⑤⑦**b**) (- Leipzig ⑦**w**).
2155 – [12] and 🍷 Düsseldorf - Kassel - Erfurt.

A – To Amsterdam (Table **28**).
B – [12] and ✕ Wien - Passau - Regensburg - Dortmund. Runs up to 60 minutes later May 22 - June 6.
G – On ⑥ runs with train number **924** and starts from Garmisch (d. 1515).
Y – ④⑤⑦ (also Dec. 23, Apr. 5, May 12, 24, June 2; not Dec. 24, 25, 31, Apr. 2, 4, May 23).

a – Not Dec. 24, 25, 31, Jan. 1, Apr. 2, 5, May 24.
b – Also Dec. 23, 30, Apr. 1, 5, May 12, 24; not Dec. 25, Jan. 1, Apr. 2, 4, May 23.
c – Arrives 10–11 minutes earlier.
e – Not Dec. 25, 26, Jan. 1, Apr. 3, 5, May 24.
h – ①②③④⑥⑦ (also Dec. 25, Jan. 1, Apr. 2, May 14; not Dec. 23, 30, Apr. 1, May 12).
j – 1937 on ⑤⑦ (also Apr. 5, May 24).
k – Also Dec. 24, 25, 31, Apr. 2, 4, May 23.
m – Not Dec. 23, Apr. 5, May 12, 24, June 2.
n – Not Dec. 24, 31.
q – ⑧ (not Dec. 24, 25, 31, Apr. 2, 4, May 23).
r – Not Feb. 28 - May 16.
t – Also Dec. 24, 25, 31, Apr. 2.
v – Not Dec. 25, Jan. 1.
w – ⑦ (also Apr. 5, May 24; not Apr. 4, May 23).
x – Not Apr. 4, May 23.
z – Also Apr. 5, May 24.
♥ – ⑧ to Mar. 19 (not Dec. 24, 25, 31); daily from Mar. 21.
* – Calls before Köln.
§ – Frankfurt Flughafen Fernbahnhof ✈. See also Tables **910** and **912**.

HAMBURG - DORTMUND - KÖLN - KOBLENZ 800

km		ICE 523	ICE 1123	ICE 948	ICE 511	ICE 23	CNL 456	ICE 711	ICE 925	ICE 525	ICE 501	IC 2319	IC 2338	ICE 813	ICE 527	ICE 25	ICE 513	ICE 815	EC 115	ICE 529	ICE 503	EC 7	IC 119	ICE 646	ICE 656
		①-⑤	⑥ b	① m	① g		R	①-⑤	⑥⑦	①-⑤		①-⑥	①-⑥	①-⑤	①-⑥			①-⑥						①-⑤	①-⑤
		a 🍷	🍷		🍷	✕♦	🍷♦	a	c 🍷	a 🍷	🍷	e	e 🍷	a 🍷	G 🍷	✕♦	🍷	e 🍷	✕♦	🍷	🍷	✕♦	🍷♦	a ✕	a ✕
	Hamburg Altona d.	...	...	...	...	...	...	...	...	...	...	...	...	...	...	...	...	...	...	...	...	0428e	...	...	...
	Hamburg Hbf 801 d.	...	...	...	...	...	...	...	...	...	...	...	...	...	...	...	...	...	...	...	...	0442e	...	...	...
	Bremen Hbf 801 d.	...	...	...	...	...	...	...	...	...	...	...	...	...	...	...	...	...	...	...	...	0540e	...	...	...
	Osnabrück Hbf 801 d.	...	...	...	...	...	...	...	...	...	...	...	...	...	...	...	...	...	...	...	...	0637e	...	...	...
	Münster (Westf) Hbf 801 d.	...	...	...	...	...	...	...	...	...	...	0503g	...	...	...	...	0601	...	0631	...	...	0703e	0727	...	...
	Berlin Hbf 810 d.	...	...	0036	...	...	0032	...	...	...	...	│	...	...	...	...	│	...	│	...	...	│	│	0427	0427
	Leipzig Hbf 810 d.	...	...	│	...	...	│	...	...	...	...	│	...	...	...	...	│	...	│	...	...	│	│	│	│
	Hannover Hbf 810 d.	...	...	0231	...	...	│	...	...	...	...	│	...	...	0410g	...	│	...	│	...	0540	│	│	0621	0621
	Hamm (Westf) a.	...	...	0359	...	...	0429	...	...	...	...	│	...	...	0548g	...	│	...	│	...	0713	│	│	0748	0748
0	Hamm (Westf) 805 d.	...	...	0401	...	...	│	...	...	...	...	│	...	...	0552g	...	│	...	│	...	0715	│	│	0752	0754
	Dortmund Hbf 805 a.	...	...	0418	...	...	0450	...	...	...	...	0533g	...	...	0614g	...	0633	...	│	...	0732	0733e	│	0809	│
	Dortmund Hbf d.	0406	0423	0421	0437	0437v	│	0502	0502	0523	0537	0537	0552	0600	0623	0636	0637	0652	│	0723c	0737	0737	│	0812	│
	Bochum Hbf d.	0417	0434	0433	│	0448v	│	0513	0513	0535	│	0548	0603	│	0635	│	0648	0704	│	0735c	│	0748	│	0825	│
	Recklinghausen Hbf d.	│	│	│	│	│	│	│	│	│	│	│	│	│	│	│	│	│	0700	│	│	│	0757	│	│
	Wanne-Eickel Hbf d.	│	│	│	│	│	│	│	│	│	│	│	│	│	│	│	│	│	0709	│	│	│	0806	│	│
	Gelsenkirchen Hbf d.	│	│	│	│	│	│	│	│	│	│	│	│	│	│	│	│	│	0715	│	│	│	0812	│	│
	Essen Hbf d.	0428	0445	0444	│	0459v	│	0524	0524	0553	│	0559	0615	│	0653	│	0659	0715	│	0753	│	0759	0823	0836	│
	Mülheim (Ruhr) Hbf d.	│	│	│	│	│	│	│	│	│	│	│	0624	│	│	│	│	│	│	│	│	│	0831	│	│
	Oberhausen Hbf d.	│	│	│	│	│	0737*	│	│	│	│	│	│	│	│	│	│	│	0727	│	│	│	│	│	│
	Duisburg Hbf d.	0440	0459	0457	│	0512v	0715*	0536	0536	0608	│	0612	0632	│	0708	│	0712	0729	0735	0808	│	0812	0838	0849	│
	Düsseldorf Flughafen ✈ d.	│	│	0507	│	│	│	│	│	│	│	│	│	│	│	│	│	│	│	│	│	│	│	0859	│
	Düsseldorf Hbf d.	0455	0513	0518	│	0527v	0654*	0551	0551	0621	│	0627	0652	│	0721	│	0727	0748	0752	0821	│	0827	0852	0908	│
48	**Hagen** Hbf d.	│	│	│	0457	│	│	│	│	│	0557	│	│	0622	│	0657	│	│	│	│	0757	│	│	│	0824
75	Wuppertal Hbf d.	│	│	│	0514	│	0538	│	│	│	0614	│	│	0638	│	0714	│	│	│	│	0814	│	│	│	0841
93	Solingen Hbf d.	│	│	│	0527	│	│	│	│	│	0627	│	│	0651	│	0727	│	│	│	│	0827	│	│	│	│
120	**Köln** Messe/Deutz a.	0515	0533	│	│	│	│	0613	0613	0642	│	│	│	│	0742	│	│	0808	│	0842	│	│	│	0928	│
121	**Köln** Hbf a.	│	│	0540	0545	0550v	0614	│	│	│	0646	0650	0715	0709	│	0746	0749	│	0815	│	0846	0850	0915	│	0909
	Köln Hbf d.	│	│	0543	0555	0553	...	│	│	│	0655	0653	0718	0720	│	0753	0755	│	0818	│	0855	0853	0918	│	...
	Köln/Bonn Flughafen ✈ a.	0529	0545	0604	│	│	...	│	0629	│	│	│	│	│	│	│	│	0819	│	│	│	│	│	0943	...
	Bonn Hbf d.	│	│	...	│	0614	...	│	│	│	│	0714	0737	│	│	0814	│	│	0837	│	│	0914	0937	...	...
	Remagen d.	│	│	...	│	│	...	│	│	│	│	│	0751	│	│	│	│	│	0851	│	│	│	0951	...	...
	Andernach d.	│	│	...	│	│	...	│	│	│	│	│	0803	│	│	│	│	│	0903	│	│	│	1003	...	...
	Koblenz Hbf a.	│	│	...	│	0646	...	│	│	│	│	0746	0816	│	│	0846	│	│	0915	│	│	0946	1015	...	...
	Mainz Hbf 912 a.	│	│	...	│	0738	...	0744	│	│	│	0837	...	│	│	0938	│	│	1013	│	│	1037	1111	...	...
	Frankfurt Flughafen ✈ § a.	0634	0634	...	0651	0759	...	│	0734	0734	0751	│	...	0826	0834	0959	0851	0926	│	0934	0951	│	│	...	...
	Frankfurt (Main) Hbf 910/2 a.	0648	0648	...	│	0813	...	│	0748	0748	│	│	...	0841	0848	1013	│	0941	│	0948	│	│	│	...	...
	Nürnberg Hbf 920 a.	0859	0859	...	│	1028	...	│	0959	0959	│	│	...	...	1059	1228	│	...	│	1159	│	│	│	...	...
	Stuttgart Hbf 930 a.	│	│	...	0808	...	...	0923	│	│	│	1018	...	...	│	...	1008	...	1153	│	│	│	1246	...	...
	München Hbf 904 930 a.	1005	1005	...	1033	...	...	...	1106	1106	│	...	...	...	1205	...	1233	...	1417	1305	│	│	...	...	...
	Karlsruhe Hbf 912 a.	...	...	...	...	...	...	...	...	...	0858	...	...	...	...	...	...	...	...	...	1050	1147	...	...	...
	Basel SBB 🏛 912 a.	...	...	...	...	...	...	...	...	...	1047	...	...	...	...	...	...	...	...	...	...	1337	...	...	...

	ICE 621	ICE 1121	ICE 1094	ICE 121	ICE 515	ICE 27	ICE 923	IC 2007	IC 2005	IC 2015	ICE 946	ICE 956	ICE 105	EC 101	IC 2013	ICE 644	ICE 654	ICE 625	IC 2023	ICE 517	IC 336	ICE 927	ICE 944	ICE 954	IC 2156
	⊡	⑦ h	♥ R	⊡			⑦ w		⑤⑥	①-④	①-⑥	①-⑥	v			①-⑥						⑦ t		①-⑥	①-⑥
	🍷	🍷	⚡ ✕	A 🍷	🍷	✕♦	🍷	🍷♦	🍷♦	🍷♦	e ✕	e ✕	A 🍷	✕♦	🍷♦	e ✕	✕	🍷	🍷	🍷	🍷♦	🍷	✕	d ✕	e ♦
Hamburg Altona d.	...	...	0558	...	0523	...	...	...	...	...	...	...	...	0632	...	...	...	...	0732	...	...	...	...	...	...
Hamburg Hbf 801 d.	...	...	0612	...	0538	...	...	...	...	...	...	...	...	0646	...	...	...	...	0746	...	...	...	...	...	...
Bremen Hbf 801 d.	...	...	│	...	0637	...	...	...	...	...	...	...	...	0744	...	...	...	...	0844	...	...	...	...	...	...
Osnabrück Hbf 801 d.	...	...	│	...	0732	...	...	...	...	...	...	...	...	0837	...	...	...	...	0937	...	...	...	...	...	...
Münster (Westf) Hbf 801 d.	...	...	│	...	0801	...	...	...	0832	0832	...	...	...	0903	...	...	...	...	1003	...	1032	...	...	...	...
Berlin Hbf 810 d.	...	...	│	...	│	...	...	...	│	│	0536	0536	...	│	...	0650	0650	...	│	...	│	...	0748	0748	...
Leipzig Hbf 810 d.	...	...	│	...	│	...	...	...	│	│	│	│	...	│	0437g	│	│	...	│	...	│	...	│	│	...
Hannover Hbf 810 d.	...	...	│	...	│	...	...	...	│	│	0731	0731	...	│	0740	0831	0831	...	│	...	│	...	0931	0931	...
Hamm (Westf) a.	...	...	│	...	│	...	...	...	│	│	0848	0848	...	│	0912	0948	0948	...	│	...	│	...	1048	1048	...
Hamm (Westf) 805 d.	...	...	│	...	│	...	...	...	│	│	0852	0854	...	│	0914	0952	0954	1000w	│	...	│	...	1052	1054	1056
Dortmund Hbf 805 a.	...	...	│	...	0833	...	...	...	│	│	0909	│	...	0933	0932	1009	│	1020w	1033	...	│	...	1109	│	1115
Dortmund Hbf d.	0816k	0821	│	...	0837	0837	0853	0852	│	│	0912	│	...	0937	0952	1012	│	1023w	1036	1037	│	1100	1112	│	1117
Bochum Hbf d.	0829k	0833	│	...	│	0848	0904	│	│	│	0925	│	...	0948	1003	1025	│	1035w	│	1048	│	│	1125	│	1129
Recklinghausen Hbf d.	│	│	│	...	│	│	│	│	0901	0901	│	│	...	│	│	│	│	│	│	│	1101	│	│	│	│
Wanne-Eickel Hbf d.	│	│	│	...	│	│	│	0910	0910	0910	│	│	...	│	│	│	│	│	│	│	1110	│	│	│	│
Gelsenkirchen Hbf d.	│	│	│	...	│	│	│	0916	0916	0916	│	│	...	│	│	│	│	│	│	│	1116	│	│	│	│
Essen Hbf d.	0840	0853	0853s	...	│	0859	0917	│	│	│	0936	│	...	0959	1015	1036	│	1053	│	1059	│	│	1136	│	1141
Mülheim (Ruhr) Hbf d.	│	│	│	...	│	│	│	│	│	│	│	│	...	│	1023	│	│	│	│	│	│	│	│	│	│
Oberhausen Hbf d.	│	│	│	0900	│	│	│	0928	0928	0928	│	│	1000	│	│	│	│	│	│	│	1128	│	│	│	│
Duisburg Hbf d.	0855	0908	│	0908	│	0912	0930	0935	0935	0935	0949	│	1008	1012	1031	1049	│	1108	│	1112	1135	│	1149	│	1155
Düsseldorf Flughafen ✈ d.	│	│	│	│	│	│	│	│	│	│	0959	│	│	│	│	1059	│	│	│	│	│	│	1159	│	1206
Düsseldorf Hbf d.	0913	0923	0916s	0923	│	0927	0948	0953	0949	0949	1005	│	1022	1027	1051	1108	│	1121	│	1127	1149	│	1208	│	1212
Hagen Hbf d.	│	│	│	│	0857	│	│	│	│	│	...	0924	│	│	│	│	1024	│	1057	│	│	1121	│	1124	...
Wuppertal Hbf d.	│	│	│	│	0914	│	│	│	│	│	...	0941	│	│	│	│	1041	│	1114	│	│	1137	│	1141	...
Solingen Hbf d.	│	│	│	│	0927	│	│	│	│	│	...	│	│	│	│	│	│	│	1127	│	│	│	│	│	...
Köln Messe/Deutz a.	0934	0943	│	0943	│	│	│	│	│	│	...	│	│	│	│	1128	│	1142	│	│	│	│	1228w	│	...
Köln Hbf a.	│	│	0941	│	0946	0950	1012	1015	1012	1012	...	1009	1045	1050	1115	│	1109	│	1146	1149	1212	1209	│	1209	...
Köln Hbf d.	│	│	...	│	0955	0953	1019	1018	1018	1018	...	...	1055	1053	1118	│	1112e	│	1153	1155	1218	1219	│	...	...
Köln/Bonn Flughafen ✈ a.	│	│	...	│	│	│	│	│	│	│	...	...	│	│	│	1142	│	│	│	│	│	│	1242w	...	...
Bonn Hbf d.	│	│	...	│	│	1014	│	1037	1037	1037	...	...	│	1114	1137	...	1132e	│	1214	│	1237	│	...	...	...
Remagen d.	│	│	...	│	│	│	│	1051	1051	1051	...	...	│	│	1151	...	...	│	│	│	1251	│	...	...	...
Andernach d.	│	│	...	│	│	│	│	1103	1103	1103	...	...	│	│	1203	...	...	│	│	│	1303	│	...	...	...
Koblenz Hbf a.	│	│	...	│	│	1046	│	1115	1115	1115	...	...	│	1146	1215	...	...	│	1246	│	1316	│	...	...	...
Mainz Hbf 912 a.	│	│	...	│	│	1138	│	1212	1212	1212	...	...	│	1237	1311	...	...	│	1338	│	...	│	...	...	...
Frankfurt Flughafen ✈ § a.	1026	1034	...	1034	1051	1159	1126	│	│	│	...	...	1151	│	│	...	...	1234	1359	1251	...	1326	...	...	...
Frankfurt (Main) Hbf 910/2 a.	1041	1048	...	1050	│	1213	1141	│	│	│	...	...	│	│	│	...	...	1248	1412	│	...	1344	...	...	...
Nürnberg Hbf 920 a.	1259	1259	...	...	│	1428	1359	│	│	│	...	...	│	│	│	...	...	1459	...	│	...	1559	...	...	...
Stuttgart Hbf 930 a.	│	│	...	...	1208	...	│	│	│	1358	...	...	│	│	1446	...	...	│	...	1408	...	│	...	...	...
München Hbf 904 930 a.	1405	1405	...	...	1433	...	1505	│	│	...	...	...	│	│	...	...	...	1605	...	1633	...	1705	...	...	...
Karlsruhe Hbf 912 a.	...	...	...	...	...	...	...	1334	1334	...	...	...	1258	1347	...	...	...	...	...	...	...	...	...	...	...
Basel SBB 🏛 912 a.	...	...	...	...	...	...	...	...	...	...	...	...	1447	1537	...	...	...	...	...	...	...	...	...	...	...

♦ – **NOTES** (LISTED BY TRAIN NUMBER)

7 – [12] and ✕ (Hamburg ①-⑥ **e** -) Dortmund - Basel - Zürich - Chur.

23/5/7 – [12] and ✕ Dortmund - Regensburg - Passau - Wien.

101 – [12] and ✕ Hamburg - Köln - Karlsruhe - Basel - Zürich - Chur.

115 – WÖRTHERSEE – [12] and ✕ Münster - Salzburg - Villach - Klagenfurt.

119 – [12] and 🍷 Münster - Ulm - Lindau - Bregenz - Innsbruck.

336 – [12] and 🍷 (Emden ● -) Münster - Koblenz - Trier - Luxembourg.

456 – PHOENIX – 🛏 1, 2 cl., ▬ 2 cl. and [2] Praha - Dresden - Amsterdam (Table **28**); 🛏 1, 2 cl., ▬ 2 cl. and [2] (*CNL* **40483** – BOREALIS) København - Amsterdam (Table **50**); 🛏 1, 2 cl., ▬ 2 cl. and [2] (*EN* **446** – JAN KIEPURA) Warszawa - Amsterdam (Table **24**); 🛏 1, 2 cl. Moskva - Warszawa - Amsterdam (Table **24**). For overnight journeys only.

2005 – ⑤⑥ (also Dec. 23, 24, 30, 31, Apr. 1, May 12, June 2; not Dec. 25, 26, Jan. 1, Apr. 3). BODENSEE – [12] and 🍷 Emden - Mannheim - Konstanz.

2007 – Runs on Dec. 25, 26, Jan. 1, Apr. 3, 4, May 23 only. BODENSEE – [12] and 🍷 Dortmund - Mannheim - Konstanz.

2013 – ALLGÄU – [12] (Leipzig ① **g** -) (Magdeburg ①-⑥ **e** -) Hannover - Köln - Ulm - Oberstdorf.

2015 – ①-④ (not Dec. 23, 24, 30, 31, Apr. 1, 5, May 12, 24, June 2). [12] and 🍷 Emden - Stuttgart.

2156 – [12] and 🍷 Erfurt - Kassel - Düsseldorf.

A – From Amsterdam (Table **28**).

G – ①-⑥ (not Dec. 25, Jan. 1, Apr. 5, May 24). To Garmisch on ⑥ (a. 1335).

a – Not Dec. 24, 25, 31, Jan. 1, Apr. 2, 5, May 24.

b – Also Dec. 24, 31, Apr. 2; not Dec. 26, Apr. 3.

c – ⑥⑦ (also Dec. 24, 25, 31, Jan. 1, Apr. 2, 5, May 24).

d – Not Dec. 25, 26, Jan. 1, Apr. 3.

e – ①-⑥ (not Dec. 25, 26, Jan. 1, Apr. 3, 5, May 24).

g – ① (also Apr. 6, May 25; not Apr. 5, May 24).

h – Also Dec. 25, 26, Jan. 1, Apr. 5, May 24.

k – Also Dec. 24, 31, Apr. 2; not Dec. 26.

m – Also Apr. 6, May 25; not Dec. 21, 28, Apr. 5, May 24.

s – Stops to set down only.

t – Also Dec. 25, 26, Jan. 1, Apr. 3, 5, May 24.

v – Not Dec. 25, Jan. 1.

w – ⑦ (also Apr. 5, May 24; not Apr. 4, May 23).

⊡ – ①-⑥ (not Dec. 25, 26, Jan. 1, Apr. 5, May 24).

● – ①-⑥ to Mar. 20 (not Dec. 25, 26, Jan. 1); daily from Mar. 22.

♥ – ①-④ to Dec. 17 and from Mar. 29 (not Apr. 5, May 13, 24, June 3).

* – Arrival times. Calls after Köln.

⚡ – *ICE* ***SPRINTER***. Supplement payable.

§ – Frankfurt Flughafen Fernbahnhof. See also Tables **910** and **912**.

800 HAMBURG - DORTMUND - KÖLN - KOBLENZ

	IC 2044	ICE 507	IC 2113	ICE 123	IC 1911	ICE 642	ICE 652	ICE 629	IC 2025	ICE 519	IC 334	ICE 942	ICE 952	IC 2154	ICE 921	IC 2046	ICE 509	IC 2115	ICE 125	IC 2011	IC 2246	IC 2011	ICE 640	ICE 650	ICE 723
	①–⑥	⑦d			⑤⑦			⑧q						①–⑥	⑤–⑦	⑥⑦	①–⑤			H	⑤f	⑦w			⑧q
	e🍷	🍷	✕	A🍷	r	✕	✕	🍷		🍷	🍷◆	✕	✕	e🍷	b🍷	h🍷	a🍷	✕◆	A🍷	🍷	🍷	🍷	✕	✕	🍷
Hamburg Altona ... d.	...	...	0832	...	...	...	...	...	0932	...	...	...	...	...	...	...	...	...	...	...	...	...	...	...	...
Hamburg Hbf ... **801** d.	...	...	0846	...	...	...	...	...	0946	...	...	...	...	...	...	...	...	1046	...	...	...	...	...	...	...
Bremen Hbf ... **801** d.	...	...	0944	...	...	...	...	...	1044	...	...	...	...	...	...	...	...	1144	...	...	...	...	...	...	...
Osnabrück Hbf ... **801** d.	...	...	1037	...	...	...	...	...	1137	...	...	...	...	...	...	...	...	1237	...	...	...	...	...	...	...
Münster (Westf) Hbf ... **801** d.	...	...	1103	...	...	...	...	...	1203	...	1232	...	...	...	...	...	...	1303	...	...	...	...	...	...	...
Berlin Hbf **810** ... d.	...	...	|	...	...	0850	0850	...	|	...	|	0948	0948	0639	...	...	...	|	...	...	...	1008	1050	1050	...
Leipzig Hbf **810** ... d.	0639	...	|	...	...	|	|	...	|	...	|	|	|	|	...	0839k	...	|	...	...	0839	|	|	|	...
Hannover Hbf **810** ... d.	0940	...	|	...	...	1031	1031	...	|	...	|	1131	1131	|	...	1140	...	|	...	...	1140	1157	1231	1231	...
Hamm (Westf) ... a.	1112	...	|	...	...	1148	1148	...	|	...	|	1248	1248	1252	...	1312	...	|	...	...	1312	1324	1348	1348	...
Hamm (Westf) ... **805** d.	1114	...	|	...	...	1152	1154	...	|	...	|	1252	1254	1256	...	1314	...	|	...	...	1325	1326	1352	1354	...
Dortmund Hbf ... **805** a.	1132	...	1133	...	...	1209	|	...	1233	...	|	1309	|	1315	...	1332	...	1333	...	...	1346	1346	1409	|	...
Dortmund Hbf ... d.	1137	1137	1137	...	1152	1212	|	1223w	1236	1237	|	1312	|	1317	1323c	1337	1337	1337	...	...	1352	1352	1412	|	...
Bochum Hbf ... d.	|	|	1148	...	1204	1225	|	1235w	|	1248	|	1325	|	1329	1335c	|	|	1348	...	...	1403	1403	1425	|	...
Recklinghausen Hbf ... d.	|	|	|	...	|	|	|	|	|	|	1301	|	|	|	|	|	|	|	...	...	|	|	|	|	...
Wanne-Eickel Hbf ... d.	|	|	|	...	|	|	|	|	|	|	1310	|	|	|	|	|	|	|	...	...	|	|	|	|	...
Gelsenkirchen Hbf ... d.	|	|	|	...	|	|	|	|	|	|	1316	|	|	|	|	|	|	|	...	...	|	|	|	|	...
Essen Hbf ... d.	|	|	1159	...	1214	1236	|	1253	|	1259	|	1336	|	1341	1353	|	|	1359	...	...	1414	1414	1436	|	1453
Mülheim (Ruhr) Hbf ... d.	|	|	|	...	1222	|	|	|	|	|	|	|	|	|	|	|	|	|	...	...	1422	1422	|	|	|
Oberhausen Hbf ... d.	|	|	|	1226	|	|	|	|	|	|	1328	|	|	|	|	|	|	|	1426	...	|	|	|	|	|
Duisburg Hbf ... d.	|	|	1212	1234	1230	1249	|	1308	|	1312	1335	1349	|	1355	1408	|	|	1412	1434	...	1430	1430	1449	|	1508
Düsseldorf Flughafen ✈ ... d.	|	|	|	|	|	1259	|	|	|	|	|	1359	|	1406	|	|	|	|	|	...	|	|	1500	|	|
Düsseldorf Hbf ... d.	|	|	1227	1248	1252	1305	|	1321	|	1327	1349	1408	|	1412	1421	|	|	1427	1448	1451	1451	1451	1506	|	1521
Hagen Hbf ... d.	1157	1157	|	|	|	...	1224	|	1257	|	|	|	1324	...	|	1357	1357	|	|	|	|	|	...	1424	|
Wuppertal Hbf ... d.	1214	1214	|	|	|	...	1241	|	1314	|	|	|	1341	...	|	1414	1414	|	|	|	|	|	...	1441	|
Solingen Hbf ... d.	1226	1227	|	|	|	...	|	|	1327	|	|	|	|	...	|	1426	1427	|	|	|	|	|	...	|	|
Köln Messe/Deutz ... a.	|	|	|	|	|	...	|	1342	|	|	|	1428	|	...	1442	|	|	|	|	|	|	|	...	|	1542
Köln Hbf ... a.	1245	1246	1250	1312	1315	...	1309	|	1346	1349	1412	|	1409	...	|	1445	1446	1450	1512	1515	1515	1515	...	1509	|
Köln Hbf ... d.	...	1255	1253	1328	1318	...	1312	|	1353	1355	1418	|	...	...	|	...	1455	1453	1528	1518	1518	1518	...	...	|
Köln/Bonn Flughafen ✈ ... a.	...	|	|	|	|	...	|	|	|	|	|	1443	...	...	|	...	|	|	|	|	|	|	...	...	|
Bonn Hbf ... d.	...	|	1314	|	1337	...	1332	|	1414	|	1437	...	...	...	|	...	|	1514	|	1537	1537	1537	...	...	|
Remagen ... d.	...	|	|	|	1351	...	...	|	|	|	1451	...	...	...	|	...	|	|	|	1551	1551	1551	...	...	|
Andernach ... d.	...	|	|	|	1403	...	...	|	|	|	1503	...	...	...	|	...	|	|	|	1603	1603	1603	...	...	|
Koblenz Hbf ... a.	...	|	1346	|	1415	...	...	|	1446	|	1516	...	...	...	|	...	|	1546	|	1615	1615	1615	...	...	|
Mainz Hbf **912** ... a.	...	|	1437	|	1511	...	...	|	1538	|	...	...	...	...	|	...	|	1637	|	1711	1711	1711	...	...	|
Frankfurt Flughafen ✈ § ... a.	...	1351	|	1416	|	...	...	1434	1559	1451	...	...	...	...	1534	...	1551	|	1616	|	|	|	...	...	1634
Frankfurt (Main) Hbf **910/2** a.	...	|	|	1430	|	...	...	1448	1613	|	...	...	...	...	1548	...	|	|	1630	|	|	|	...	...	1648
Nürnberg Hbf **920** ... a.	...	|	|	...	|	...	...	1659	...	|	...	...	...	...	1759	...	|	|	...	|	|	|	...	...	1859
Stuttgart Hbf **930** ... a.	...	|	1622	...	1646	...	...	|	...	1608	...	...	...	...	|	...	|	1825	...	1846	1846	1846	...	...	|
München Hbf **904 930** ... a.	...	|	...	...	...	...	...	1805	...	1832	...	...	...	...	1905	...	|	...	...	...	2123	...	...	...	2005
Karlsruhe Hbf **912** ... a.	...	1450	...	...	...	...	...	...	...	...	...	...	...	...	...	...	1658	...	...	...	...	...	...	...	...
Basel SBB 🏛 **912** ... a.	...	...	...	...	...	...	...	...	...	...	...	...	...	...	...	...	1847	...	...	...	...	...	...	...	...

	IC 2027	IC 2327	ICE 611	IC 332	IC 332	ICE 940	ICE 950	IC 2152	ICE 725	IC 2048	IC 2311	ICE 127	ICE 327	IC 1915	ICE 548	ICE 558	ICE 727	ICE 1025	ICE 1125	ICE 613	IC 330	ICE 848	ICE 858	IC 2150	ICE 729
		⑤			⑧q			⑤⑦				⑧G	⑥G	⑤⑦			⑧q		⑤						
	✕◆	✕◆	🍷	🍷◆	🍷◆	✕	✕	🍷◆	🍷	🍷	✕◆	A🍷	A🍷	z	✕	✕	🍷	✕◆	✕◆	🍷	🍷◆	✕	✕	🍷◆	🍷
Hamburg Altona ... d.	1132	...	...	...	...	...	...	...	...	...	...	...	...	...	...	...	...	...	...	...	...	...	...	...	...
Hamburg Hbf ... **801** d.	1146	1146	...	...	...	...	...	...	...	...	1246	...	...	...	...	...	...	1346	1346	...	...	...	...	...	...
Bremen Hbf ... **801** d.	1244	1244	...	...	...	...	...	...	...	...	1344	...	...	...	...	...	...	1444	1444	...	...	...	...	...	...
Osnabrück Hbf ... **801** d.	1337	1337	...	...	...	...	...	...	...	...	1437	...	...	...	...	...	...	1537	1537	...	...	...	...	...	...
Münster (Westf) Hbf ... **801** d.	1403	1403	...	1431	1431	...	...	...	...	...	1503	...	...	...	...	...	...	1602	1602	...	1631	...	...	...	...
Berlin Hbf **810** ... d.	|	|	...	|	|	1148	1148	0839f	...	...	|	...	...	1208	1249	1249	...	|	|	...	|	1348	1348	1039	...
Leipzig Hbf **810** ... d.	|	|	...	|	|	|	|	|	...	1039	|	...	...	|	|	|	...	|	|	...	|	|	|	|	...
Hannover Hbf **810** ... d.	|	|	...	|	|	1331	1331	|	...	1340	|	...	...	1357	1431	1431	...	|	|	...	|	1531	1531	|	...
Hamm (Westf) ... a.	|	|	...	|	|	1448	1448	1452	...	1512	|	...	...	1524	1548	1548	...	|	|	...	|	1648	1648	1652	...
Hamm (Westf) ... **805** d.	|	|	...	|	|	1452	1454	1456	...	1514	|	...	...	1526	1552	1554	...	|	|	...	|	1652	1654	1656	...
Dortmund Hbf ... **805** a.	1433	1433	...	|	|	1509	|	1515	...	1532	1533	...	...	1546	1609	|	...	1633	1633	...	|	1709	|	1715	...
Dortmund Hbf ... d.	1436	1436	1437	|	|	1512	|	1517	1523w	1537	1537	...	...	1552	1612	|	...	1636	1636	1637	|	1712	|	1717	...
Bochum Hbf ... d.	|	|	1448	|	|	1525	|	1529	1535w	|	1548	...	...	1603	1625	|	...	|	|	1648	|	1725	|	1729	...
Recklinghausen Hbf ... d.	|	|	|	1500	1500	|	|	|	|	|	|	...	...	|	|	|	...	|	|	|	1700	|	|	|	...
Wanne-Eickel Hbf ... d.	|	|	|	1509	1509	|	|	|	|	|	|	...	...	|	|	|	...	|	|	|	1709	|	|	|	...
Gelsenkirchen Hbf ... d.	|	|	|	1516	1516	|	|	|	|	|	|	...	...	|	|	|	...	|	|	|	1716	|	|	|	...
Essen Hbf ... d.	|	|	1459	|	|	1536	|	1541	1553	|	1559	...	...	1614	1636	|	1653	|	|	1659	|	1736	|	1741	1753
Mülheim (Ruhr) Hbf ... d.	|	|	|	|	|	|	|	|	|	|	|	...	...	1622	|	|	|	|	|	|	|	|	|	|	|
Oberhausen Hbf ... d.	|	|	|	1528	1528	|	|	|	|	|	|	1626	1626	|	|	|	|	|	|	|	1728	|	|	|	|
Duisburg Hbf ... d.	|	|	1512	1535	1535	1549	|	1555	1608	|	1612	1634	1634	1630	1649	|	1708	|	|	1712	1735	1749	|	1755	1808
Düsseldorf Flughafen ✈ ... d.	|	|	|	|	|	1559	|	1606	|	|	|	|	|	|	1659	|	|	|	|	|	|	1759	|	1807	|
Düsseldorf Hbf ... d.	|	|	1527	1549	1549	1605	|	1612	1621	|	1627	1648	1648	1651	1709	|	1721	|	|	1727	1749	1805	|	1814	1821
Hagen Hbf ... d.	1457	1457	|	|	|	...	1524	...	|	1557	|	|	|	|	|	1624	|	1657	1657	|	|	...	1724	...	|
Wuppertal Hbf ... d.	1514	1514	|	|	|	...	1541	...	|	1614	|	|	|	|	|	1641	|	1714	1714	|	|	...	1741	...	|
Solingen Hbf ... d.	1527	1527	|	|	|	...	|	...	|	1626	|	|	|	|	|	|	|	|	|	|	|	...	|	...	|
Köln Messe/Deutz ... a.	|	|	|	|	|	...	|	...	1642	|	|	|	|	|	1729	|	1742	|	|	|	|	...	|	...	1842
Köln Hbf ... a.	1546	1546	1549	1612	1612	...	1609	...	|	1645	1650	1712	1712	1715	|	1709	|	1746	1746	1749	1812	...	1809	...	|
Köln Hbf ... d.	1553	1553	1555	...	1618	...	...	...	|	...	1653	1720	1728	1718	|	...	|	1753	1753	1755	1818	...	...	...	|
Köln/Bonn Flughafen ✈ ... a.	|	|	|	...	|	...	...	...	|	...	|	|	|	|	1743	...	|	|	|	|	|	...	...	...	|
Bonn Hbf ... d.	1614	1614	|	...	1637	...	...	...	|	...	1714	|	|	1737	...	...	|	1814	1814	|	1837	...	...	...	|
Remagen ... d.	|	|	|	...	1651	...	...	...	|	...	|	|	|	1751	...	...	|	|	|	|	1851	...	...	...	|
Andernach ... d.	|	|	|	...	1703	...	...	...	|	...	|	|	|	1803	...	...	|	|	|	|	1903	...	...	...	|
Koblenz Hbf ... a.	1646	1646	|	...	1716	...	...	...	|	...	1746	|	|	1815	...	...	|	1846	1846	|	1916	...	...	...	|
Mainz Hbf **912** ... a.	1738	1738	|	...	...	...	...	...	|	...	1837	|	|	1911	...	...	|	1938	1938	|	...	...	...	...	|
Frankfurt Flughafen ✈ § ... a.	1759	1759	1651	...	...	...	...	...	1734	...	|	1814	1816	|	...	...	1834	1959	1959	1851	...	...	...	...	1934
Frankfurt (Main) Hbf **910/2** a.	1813	1813	|	...	...	...	...	...	1748	...	|	1830	1830	|	...	...	1848	2013	2013	|	...	...	...	...	1948
Nürnberg Hbf **920** ... a.	2028	2028	|	...	...	...	...	...	1959	...	|	...	...	|	...	...	2058	2224	2224	|	...	...	...	...	2159
Stuttgart Hbf **930** ... a.	...	...	1808	...	...	...	...	...	|	...	2023	...	...	2046	...	...	|	|	...	2008	...	...	...	...	|
München Hbf **904 930** ... a.	...	...	2033	...	...	...	...	...	2105	...							2205	2350	...	2233	...	...	...	...	2308
Karlsruhe Hbf **912** ... a.	...	...	...	...	...	...	...	...	...	...							...	...	...	...	...	...	...	...	...
Basel SBB 🏛 **912** ... a.	...	...	...	...	...	...	...	...	...	...							...	...	...	...	...	...	...	...	...

*See Table **802** for Rhein-Ruhr local RE and S-Bahn services*

◆ – **NOTES** (LISTED BY TRAIN NUMBER)

330 – NORDERNEY – ⟨12⟩ and 🍷 Norddeich Mole - Emden - Koblenz - Luxembourg.
332 – ⟨12⟩ and 🍷 Norddeich Mole - Emden - Köln (- Luxembourg ⑧**q**).
334 – ⟨12⟩ and 🍷 Norddeich Mole - Emden - Koblenz - Luxembourg.
1025 – ①②③④⑥⑦ (also Dec. 25, Apr. 2, May 28, June 4; not Dec. 23, 30, Apr. 1). ⟨12⟩ and ✕ Kiel - Köln - Frankfurt - München.
1125 – ⑤ (also Dec. 23, 30, Apr. 1; not Dec. 25, Apr. 2, May 28, June 4). ⟨12⟩ and ✕ Kiel - Köln - Frankfurt - Regensburg.
2027 – ①②③④⑥⑦ (also Dec. 25, Jan. 1, Apr. 2, May 14; not Dec. 23, 30, Apr. 1, May 12, June 12). ⟨12⟩ and ✕ Hamburg - Köln - Regensburg - Passau.
2115 – ⟨12⟩ and ✕ (Greifswald ①–⑤**a** -) Stralsund - Hamburg - Köln - Stuttgart.
2150 – ⟨12⟩ and 🍷 (Stralsund ①–⑥**e** -) Berlin - Halle - Erfurt - Kassel - Düsseldorf. Train number **2250** on ⑦ (also Dec. 25, 26, Jan. 1, Apr. 3, 5, May 24).
2152 – ⑤⑦ (also Dec. 23, 30, Apr. 1, 5, May 12, 24; not Dec. 25, Jan. 1, Apr. 2, 4, May 14, 23). ⟨12⟩ and 🍷 (Berlin ⑤**f** -) Halle - Erfurt - Kassel - Düsseldorf.
2311 – NORDFRIESLAND – ⟨12⟩ and ✕ Westerland - Köln - Heidelberg - Stuttgart.
2327 – ⑤ (also Dec. 23, 30, Apr. 1, May 12, June 12; not Dec. 25, Jan. 1, Apr. 2, May 14). LÜBECKER BUCHT – ⟨12⟩ and ✕ Puttgarden - Lübeck - Köln - Regensburg - Passau.

A – From Amsterdam (Table **28**).
G – From Mar. 26.
H – ①②③④⑦ (not Dec. 23, 24, 30, 31, Apr. 1, 4, May 12, 13, 23, June 2, 3).

a – Not Dec. 24, 25, 31, Jan. 1, Apr. 2, 5, May 24.
b – Also Dec. 23, 24, 30, 31, Apr. 1, 5, May 12, 24, June 2; not May 14, June 4.
c – ⑥⑦ (also Dec. 24, 25, 31, Jan. 1, Apr. 2, 5, May 24).
d – Also Dec. 25, 26, Jan. 1, Apr. 3, 5, May 24.
e – Not Dec. 25, 26, Jan. 1, Apr. 3, 5, May 24.
f – Also Dec. 23, 30, Apr. 1, May 12; not Dec. 25, Jan. 1, Apr. 2, May 14.
h – Also Dec. 24, 31, Apr. 2, 5, May 24; not Dec. 26, Apr. 3, 4, May 23.
k – ⑥ (also Dec. 24, 31, Apr. 2).
q – Not Dec. 24, 25, 31, Apr. 2, 4, May 23.
r – Also Dec. 23, 30, Apr. 1, 5, May 12, 24, June 2; not Dec. 25, Jan. 1, Apr. 2, 4, May 14, 23, June 4.
w – ⑦ (also Apr. 5, May 24; not Apr. 4, May 23).
z – also Dec. 23, 30, Apr. 1, 5, May 24; not Dec. 25, Jan. 1, Apr. 2, 4, May 14, 23.

§ – Frankfurt Flughafen ✈ Fernbahnhof See also Tables **910** and **912**.

HAMBURG - DORTMUND - KÖLN - KOBLENZ 800

	IC	IC	IC	IC	ICE	ICE	ICE	ICE	ICE	ICE	IC	ICE	IC	IC	ICE	ICE	ICE	ICE	IC	ICE	IC	IC	IC	ICE	ICE
	2140	2213	1917	1917	129	929	821	546	556	556	2029	615	2332	2334	846	1046	856	856	2356	605	2142	2215	2315	227	544
			⑤⑦t	⑦w		⑥⑦	①–⑤			①–⑤			Y	X	Q	⑤v		Ⓑ			Ⓑq	C			
	🍷	✕♦	🍷	🍷	A🍷	🍷♦	a🍷	✕	✕	a✕	🍷	🍷	E🍷	N🍷	✕	J✕	✕	T✕	🍷♦	🍷	🍷	✕	✕♦	A🍷	D✕
Hamburg Altona ... d.	...	...	...	...	...	...	...	...	...	...	1532	...	...	...	...	...	...	...	...	...	...	1632	...	...	...
Hamburg Hbf ... **801** d.	...	1446	...	...	...	...	...	...	...	...	1546	...	...	...	...	...	...	...	...	...	...	1646	1646	...	...
Bremen Hbf ... **801** d.	...	1544	...	...	...	...	...	...	...	...	1644	...	...	...	...	...	...	...	...	...	...	1744	1744	...	...
Osnabrück Hbf ... **801** d.	...	1637	...	...	...	...	...	...	...	...	1737	...	...	...	...	...	...	...	...	...	...	1837	1837	...	...
Münster (Westf) Hbf ... **801** d.	...	1703	...	...	...	...	...	...	...	...	1803	...	1832	1832	...	...	...	...	...	...	...	1903	1903	...	...
Berlin Hbf **810** ... d.	...	|	1358	1358	...	...	...	1450	1450	1450	|	...	|	|	1548	1548	1548	1548	1239	...	...	|	|	...	1650
Leipzig Hbf **810** ... d.	1239	|	|	|	...	...	...	|	|	|	|	...	|	|	|	|	|	|	|	...	1439	|	|	...	|
Hannover Hbf **810** ... d.	1540	|	1558	1558	...	...	...	1631	1631	1631	|	...	|	|	1731	1731	1731	1731	|	...	1740	|	|	...	1831
Hamm (Westf) ... a.	1712	|	1723	1723	...	...	...	1748	1748	1748	|	...	|	|	1848	1848	1848	1848	1852	...	1912	|	|	...	1948
Hamm (Westf) ... **805** d.	1714	|	1725	1725	...	...	...	1752	1754	1754	|	...	|	|	1852	1852	1854	1854	1856	...	1914	|	|	...	1952
Dortmund Hbf ... **805** a.	1732	1733	1746	1746	...	...	...	1809	|	|	1833	...	|	|	1909	1909	|	|	1915	...	1932	1933	1933	...	2009
Dortmund Hbf ... d.	1737	1737	1752	1752	...	...	...	1812	|	|	1836	1837	|	|	1912	1912	|	|	1917	1923	1937	1937	1937	...	2012
Bochum Hbf ... d.	|	1748	1803	1803	...	...	...	1825	|	|	|	1848	|	|	1925	1925	|	|	1929	1937	|	1948	1948	...	2025
Recklinghausen Hbf ... d.	|	|	|	|	...	...	...	|	|	|	|	|	1901	1901	|	|	|	|	|	|	|	|	|	...	|
Wanne-Eickel Hbf ... d.	|	|	|	|	...	...	...	|	|	|	|	|	1910	1910	|	|	|	|	|	|	|	|	|	...	|
Gelsenkirchen Hbf ... d.	|	|	|	|	...	...	...	|	|	|	|	|	1916	1916	|	|	|	|	|	|	|	|	|	...	|
Essen Hbf ... d.	|	1759	1814	1814	...	1840	...	1836	|	|	|	1859	|	|	1936	1936	|	|	1941	1949	|	1959	1959	...	2036
Mülheim (Ruhr) Hbf ... d.	|	|	1822	1822	...	|	...	|	|	|	|	|	|	|	|	|	|	|	|	|	|	|	|	...	|
Oberhausen Hbf ... d.	|	|	|	|	1826	|	1847	|	|	|	|	|	1928	1928	|	|	|	|	|	|	|	|	|	2026	|
Duisburg Hbf ... d.	|	1812	1830	1830	1834	1855	1855	1849	|	|	|	1912	1935	1935	1949	1949	|	|	1955	2004	|	2012	2012	2034	2049
Düsseldorf Flughafen ✈ ... d.	|	|	|	|	|	|	|	1904	|	|	|	|	|	|	1959	|	|	|	2006	2014	|	|	|	|	2059
Düsseldorf Hbf ... d.	|	1827	1851	1851	1848	1908	1908	1912	|	|	|	1927	1949	1949	2008	2014	|	|	2017	2022	|	2027	2027	2048	2108
Hagen Hbf ... d.	1757	|	|	|	|	|	|	|	1824	1824	1857	|	|	|	|	...	1924	1924	|	|	1957	|	|	|	|
Wuppertal Hbf ... d.	1814	|	|	|	|	|	|	|	1841	1841	1914	|	|	|	|	...	1941	1941	|	|	2014	|	|	|	|
Solingen Hbf ... d.	1826	|	|	|	|	|	|	|	|	|	1927	|	|	|	|	...	|	|	|	|	2026	|	|	|	|
Köln Messe/Deutz ... a.	|	|	|	|	|	1928	1928	1933	|	|	|	|	|	|	|	...	|	|	|	2042	|	|	|	|	|
Köln Hbf ... a.	1845	1850	1915	1915	1912	|	|	|	1909	1909	1946	1949	2012	2012	2033	...	2009	2009	2042v	|	2045	2050	2050	2112	2133
Köln Hbf ... d.	...	1853	...	1918	1920	|	|	|	1912b	1912	1953	1957	...	...	...	...	...	2018	...	|	...	2053	2053	2120	...
Köln/Bonn Flughafen ✈ ... a.	...	|	...	|	|	|	|	1945	|	|	|	|	...	...	...	...	...	|	...	|	...	|	|	|	...
Bonn Hbf ... d.	...	1914	...	1937	|	|	|	...	1932b	1937	2014	|	...	...	...	...	...	2041	...	|	...	2114	2114	|	...
Remagen ... d.	...	|	...	1951	|	|	|	...	...	|	|	|	...	...	...	...	...	|	...	|	...	|	|	|	...
Andernach ... d.	...	|	...	2003	|	|	|	...	...	|	|	|	...	...	...	...	...	2104	...	|	...	|	|	|	...
Koblenz Hbf ... a.	...	1946	...	2015	|	|	|	...	...	2010	2046	|	...	...	...	...	...	2116	...	|	...	2146	2146	|	...
Mainz Hbf **912** ... a.	...	2037	...	2111	|	|	|	...	...	...	2141	|	...	...	...	...	...	...	...	|	...	2238	2238	|	...
Frankfurt Flughafen ✈ § ... a.	...	|	...	|	2014	2034	2034	...	...	...	2159	2054	...	...	...	...	...	...	...	2151	...	2258	2258	2214	...
Frankfurt (Main) Hbf **910/2** a.	...	|	...	|	2030	2048	2048	...	...	...	2213	|	...	...	...	...	...	...	...	|	...	2310	2310	2230	...
Nürnberg Hbf **920** ... a.	...	|	...	|	...	2259	2259f	...	...	...	0038	|	...	...	...	...	...	...	...	|	...	...	...	...	...
Stuttgart Hbf **930** ... a.	...	2222	...	|	...	|	|	...	...	...	...	2208	...	...	...	...	...	...	...	|	...	...	...	...	...
München Hbf **904 930** ... a.	...	...	...	|	...	0008	0008f	...	...	...	...	0034	...	...	...	...	...	...	...	|	...	...	...	...	...
Karlsruhe Hbf **912** ... a.	...	...	...	2224	...	...	...	...	...	...	...	...	...	...	...	...	...	...	...	2300	...	...	...	...	...
Basel SBB 🏛 **912** ... a.	...	...	...	...	...	...	...	...	...	...	...	...	...	...	...	...	...	...	...	0058y	...	...	...	...	...

	ICE	IC	IC	ICE	IC	ICE	ICE	IC	IC	IC	ICE	ICE	ICE	CNL	CNL	ICE	ICE	ICE	ICE	IC	IC	IC	IC	ICE	IC
	554	2321	2121	617	2330	844	854	2354	2307	2144	913	542	552	419	40419	329	609	842	852	2352	2146	2309	2309	540	2021
		C			R		Ⓑq	⑦w		Ⓑq	⑥h			B 🅁	B 🅁	P			⑦w	⑦w	⑦w		⑤–⑦		
	✕	✕	✕♦	🍷	N🍷	✕	✕		✕		🍷	✕	✕	🍷♦	🍷♦	A🍷	K✕	✕	✕	♦		n	m		
Hamburg Altona ... d.	...	1732	...	...	...	...	...	...	1832	...	...	...	...	...	...	...	...	...	...	...	...	2032	2032	...	...
Hamburg Hbf ... **801** d.	...	1746	1746	...	...	...	...	...	1846	...	...	...	...	...	...	...	1946	...	...	...	...	2046	2046	...	2246
Bremen Hbf ... **801** d.	...	1844	1844	...	...	...	...	...	1944	...	...	...	...	...	...	...	2044	...	...	...	...	2143	2143	...	2347
Osnabrück Hbf ... **801** d.	...	1937	1937	...	...	...	...	...	2037	...	...	...	...	...	...	...	2137	...	...	...	...	2238	2238	...	0045
Münster (Westf) Hbf ... **801** d.	...	2003	2003	...	2032	...	...	...	2103	...	...	...	...	...	...	...	2202	...	...	...	...	2304	2304	...	0113
Berlin Hbf **810** ... d.	1650	|	|	...	|	1749	1749	1439	|	...	...	1850	1850	...	...	...	|	1948	1948	1639	...	|	|	2106	|
Leipzig Hbf **810** ... d.	|	|	|	...	|	|	|	|	|	1639	...	|	|	...	...	...	|	|	|	|	1839	|	|	|	|
Hannover Hbf **810** ... d.	1831	|	|	...	|	1931	1931	|	|	1940	...	2031	2031	...	...	...	|	2131	2131	|	2140	|	|	2300	|
Hamm (Westf) ... a.	1948	|	|	...	|	2048	2048	2052	|	2110	...	2148	2148	...	...	...	|	2248	2248	2252	2310	|	|	0029	0131
Hamm (Westf) ... **805** d.	1954	|	|	...	|	2052	2054	2056	|	2112	...	2152	2152	...	...	...	|	2252	2254	2256	2312	|	|	0031	0133
Dortmund Hbf ... **805** a.	|	2033	2033	...	|	2109	|	2115	2133	2132	...	2209	|	...	...	...	2233	2309	|	2315	2332	2333	2333	0049	0149
Dortmund Hbf ... d.	|	2036	2036	2037	|	2112	|	2117	2137	2137	2137	2212	|	...	...	...	2237	2312	|	2317	2337	...	2337	0051	0152
Bochum Hbf ... d.	|	|	|	2048	|	2125	|	2129	2148	|	|	2225	|	...	...	...	2249	2325	|	2329	|	...	2348	0103	0203
Recklinghausen Hbf ... d.	|	|	|	|	2101	|	|	|	|	|	|	|	|	...	...	...	|	|	|	|	|	...	|	|	|
Wanne-Eickel Hbf ... d.	|	|	|	|	2110	|	|	|	|	|	|	|	|	...	...	...	|	|	|	|	|	...	|	|	|
Gelsenkirchen Hbf ... d.	|	|	|	|	2116	|	|	|	|	|	|	|	|	...	...	...	|	|	|	|	|	...	|	|	|
Essen Hbf ... d.	|	|	|	2059	|	2136	|	2141	2159	|	|	2236	|	...	...	...	2259	2336	|	2341	|	...	2359	0114	0214
Mülheim (Ruhr) Hbf ... d.	|	|	|	|	|	|	|	|	|	|	|	|	|	...	...	...	|	|	|	|	|	...	|	|	|
Oberhausen Hbf ... d.	|	|	|	|	2128	|	|	|	|	|	|	|	|	2248	2248	2258	|	|	|	|	|	...	|	|	|
Duisburg Hbf ... d.	|	|	|	2112	2135	2151	|	2156	2212	|	|	2249	|	2256u	2256u	2306	2312	2349	|	2355	|	...	0012	0129	0229
Düsseldorf Flughafen ✈ ... d.	|	|	|	|	|	2201	|	2208	|	|	|	2259	|	|	|	|	|	2359	|	0006	|	...	|	0139	0239
Düsseldorf Hbf ... d.	|	|	|	2127	2149	2209	|	2216	2227	|	|	2308	|	2312u	2312u	2320	2327	0007	|	0014	|	...	0027	0147	0247
Hagen Hbf ... d.	2024	2057	2057	|	|	|	2124	|	|	2157	2157	|	2224	|	|	|	|	|	2324	|	2357	...	|	|	|
Wuppertal Hbf ... d.	2041	2114	2114	|	|	|	2141	|	|	2214	2214	|	2241	|	|	|	|	|	2341	|	0014	...	|	|	|
Solingen Hbf ... d.	|	2127	2127	|	|	|	|	|	|	2226	2227	|	2253	|	|	|	|	|	|	|	0026	...	|	|	|
Köln Messe/Deutz ... a.	|	|	|	|	|	|	|	|	|	|	|	|	|	|	|	|	|	|	|	|	|	...	|	|	0307
Köln Hbf ... a.	2109	2146	2146	2149	2212	2231	2209	2240	2250	2245	2246	2330	2312	|	|	2343	2350	0029	0009	0035	0045	...	0050	0209	0345
Köln Hbf ... d.	...	2153	2153	2155	...	...	2218w	...	2253	...	2255	...	2318q	2346u	2346u	...	2353	...	...	...	...	...	...	0214z	0353
Köln/Bonn Flughafen ✈ ... a.	...	|	|	|	...	...	|	...	|	...	2306	...	|	|	|	...	|	...	...	...	...	...	...	0225z	0328*
Bonn Hbf ... d.	...	2214	2214	|	...	...	2237w	...	2314	...	|	...	2339q	0007u	0007u	...	0014	...	...	...	...	...	...	...	0416
Remagen ... d.	...	|	|	|	...	...	|	...	2328	...	|	...	...	|	|	...	|	...	...	...	...	...	...	...	0431
Andernach ... d.	...	|	|	|	...	...	|	...	2341	...	|	...	...	|	|	...	|	...	...	...	...	...	...	...	0447
Koblenz Hbf ... a.	...	2246	2246	|	...	...	2311w	...	2354	...	|	...	...	0043u	0043u	...	0046	...	...	...	...	...	...	...	0500
Mainz Hbf **912** ... a.	...	2338	2338	|	...	...	...	...	...	...	|	...	...	|	|	...	0141	...	...	...	...	...	...	...	0626
Frankfurt Flughafen ✈ § ... a.	...	2359	2359	2255	...	...	...	...	...	...	0010	...	...	|	|	...	0202r	...	...	...	...	...	...	...	0645
Frankfurt (Main) Hbf **910/2** a.	...	0013	0013	|	...	...	...	...	...	...	0023	...	...	|	|	...	0217	...	...	...	...	...	...	...	0702
Nürnberg Hbf **920** ... a.	...	...	...	|	...	...	...	...	...	...	...	...	...	|	|	...	|	...	...	...	...	...	...	...	...
Stuttgart Hbf **930** ... a.	...	...	...	0053j	...	...	...	...	...	...	...	...	...	0417	|	...	|	...	...	...	...	...	...	...	...
München Hbf **904 930** ... a.	...	...	...	...	...	...	...	...	...	...	...	...	...	0716	|	...	|	...	...						
Karlsruhe Hbf **912** ... a.	...	...	...	...	...	...	...	...	...	...	...	...	...	...	0437	...	0345	...	...						
Basel SBB 🏛 **912** ... a.	...	...	...	...	...	...	...	...	...	...	...	...	...	...	0654	...	0547	...	...						

*See Table **802** for Rhein - Ruhr local RE and S-Bahn services*

♦ – **NOTES** (LISTED BY TRAIN NUMBER)

419 – POLLUX – 🛏 1, 2 cl., ▬ 2 cl., [2] (reclining) and 🍷 Amsterdam - München (Amsterdam - München - Innsbruck on ⑤ Dec. 25 - Apr. 9).

929 – ⑥⑦ (also Dec. 24, 25, 31, Apr. 2, 5, May 24; not Apr. 4, May 23). [12] and 🍷 Essen - Frankfurt (- Nürnberg - München ⑦**w**).

2121 – From Mar. 27. FEHMARN – [12] Puttgarden - Lübeck - Frankfurt.

2213 – RÜGEN – [12] and ✕ Ostseebad Binz - Stralsund - Köln - Stuttgart.

2315 – From Mar. 27. DEICHGRAF – [12] and ✕ Westerland - Stuttgart.

2352 – [12] Stralsund - Berlin - Halle - Erfurt - Kassel - Köln.

2356 – [12] and 🍷 (Ostseebad Binz ①–⑥ -) Stralsund - Berlin - Halle - Erfurt - Kassel - Düsseldorf (- Köln ⑤**v**). Train number **2254** on ⑤**v**.

40419 – PEGASUS – 🛏 1, 2 cl., ▬ 2 cl., [2] (reclining) and 🍷 Amsterdam - Zürich (Amsterdam - Zürich - Brig on ⑤ Dec. 25 - Apr. 9).

A – From Amsterdam (Table **28**).

B – ①⑤⑥⑦ (daily fom Mar. 26).

C – Until Mar. 26.

D – To Düren (a. 2154) and Aachen Hbf (a. 2216) on ⑦**w**.

E – From Emden (Table **812**).

J – To Neuss Hbf (a. 2026) and Mönchengladbach Hbf (a. 2040).

K – From Kiel (Table **820**).

N – From Norddeich Mole (Table **812**).

P – ⑦ Dec. 13 - Mar. 21; ⑤⑦ from Mar. 26 (also Apr. 5, May 24, June 1; not Apr. 2, 4, May 23).

Q – ①②③④⑥⑦ (also Dec. 25, Jan. 1, Apr. 2, May 14, June 4; not Dec. 23, 30, Apr. 1, May 12, June 2).

R – ⑦ Dec. 13 - Jan. 3; ⑦ Mar. 7 – 21; ③–⑦ Mar. 26 - Apr. 11; ⑦ Apr. 18 - May 2; ③–⑦ from May 7.

T – Ⓑ (not Dec. 24, 25, 31, Apr. 2, 4, May 14, 23). To Trier (Table **915**). ✕ Berlin - Köln.

X – ①–④ Dec. 14 - Mar. 25 (not Dec. 24, 31).

Y – ⑤⑦ to Mar. 21 (not Dec. 25); daily from Mar. 26.

a – Not Dec. 24, 25, 31, Jan. 1, Apr. 2, 5, May 24.

b – Ⓑ (not Dec. 24, 25, 31, Jan. 1, Apr. 2, 4, May 23).

f – Frankfurt - München on ⑤ (also Dec. 23, 30, Apr. 1, May 12, June 2; not Dec. 25, Jan. 1, Apr. 2).

h – Also Dec. 24, 25, 31, Apr. 2, 4, May 23.

j – 0040 on the mornings of ①⑦.

m – Also Dec. 23, 30, Apr. 1, 5, May 12, 24.

n – Not Dec. 24.

q – Ⓑ (not Dec. 24, 25, 31, Apr. 2, 4, May 23).

r – Frankfurt Flughafen ✈ Regionalbahnhof.

t – Also Dec. 23, 30, Apr. 1, 5, May 12, 24; not Dec. 25, Jan. 1, Apr. 2, 4, May 14, 23.

u – Stops to pick up only.

v – ⑤ (also Dec. 23, 30, Apr. 1, May 12, June 2; not Dec. 25, Jan. 1, Apr. 2, May 14, June 4).

w – ⑦ (also Apr. 5, May 24; not Apr. 4, May 23).

y – Karlsruhe - Basel on ①②③④⑦ (not Dec. 23, 24, 30, 31, Apr. 1, 4, May 23). Basel **Badischer Bahnhof** (not SBB).

z – ①–⑤ only.

***** – Calls at Köln/Bonn Flughafen before Köln Hbf.

§ – Frankfurt Flughafen Fernbahnhof. See also Tables **910** and **912**.

801 Local services MÜNSTER - OSNABRÜCK - BREMEN - HAMBURG

See Table **800** for fast trains

Münster (Westf) Hbf - **Osnabrück** Hbf and v.v. Operated by WestfalenBahn. Journey time: 36 minutes.
From Münster (Westf) Hbf at 0504 Ⓐ **n**, 0604 ⚒, 0634 Ⓐ, 0704, 0734 Ⓐ, 0804, 0904 and hourly until 1604, then 1634 Ⓐ **n**, 1704, 1734 Ⓐ **n**, 1804, 1904, 2004, 2104, 2204 and 2304.
From Osnabrück Hbf at 0519 Ⓐ **n**, 0549 Ⓐ **n**, 0619 ⚒, 0719, 0749 Ⓐ **n**, 0819, 0919 and hourly until 1619, then 1649 Ⓐ **n**, 1719, 1749 Ⓐ **n**, 1819, 1919, 2019, 2119, 2219 and 2319.

Osnabrück Hbf - **Bremen** Hbf and v.v. *RE* services. Journey time: 72–74 minutes. Certain trains continue to / start from Bremerhaven (see Table **815**).
From Osnabrück Hbf at 0538 ⚒, 0638 ⚒, 0738, 0838 **w**, 0938, 1038 **w**, 1138, 1238 ⚒ **w**, 1338, 1438 **w**, 1538, 1638 **w**, 1738, 1838 **w**, 1938 Ⓑ **D**, 2038 and 2138.
From Bremen Hbf 0506 ⚒, 0606 ⚒ **y**, 0706 **E**, 0806 **w**, 0906, 1006 **w**, 1106, 1209 **w**, 1306, 1406 **w**, 1506, 1606 ⚒ **w**, 1706, 1806, 1906, 2006 Ⓑ **B**, 2106 and 2253.

Bremen Hbf - **Hamburg** Hbf and v.v. *metronom* (operated by metronom Eisenbahngesellschaft). Journey time: 73–80 minutes.
From Bremen Hbf at 0513 **r**, 0618 Ⓐ, 0628 Ⓒ, 0645 ⚒, 0728, 0828, 0928, 1028, 1128, 1228, 1328, 1428, 1528, 1628 **m**, 1728, 1828 **m**, 1928, 2028 **n**, 2128 and 2228 **n**.
From Hamburg Hbf at 0015 ⑦, 0515 ⚒, 0615, 0715 **r**, 0815, 0915, 1015, 1115, 1215, 1315 **r**, 1415, 1515, 1615 **m**, 1652 Ⓐ **m**, 1715, 1815 **m**, 1915, 2015 **n**, 2115, 2215 † and 2315 **t**.

B – Ⓑ to Jan. 1 and from Mar. 29 (not Dec. 24, 31).
D – Ⓑ (also Dec. 26, May 1; not Dec. 24, 31); daily Jan. 1 - Apr. 2.
E – ⚒ (daily Jan. 2 - Apr. 1).
m – Not Dec. 24.
n – Not Dec. 24, 31.
r – Not Jan. 1.
t – Not Dec. 31.
w – Not Jan. 2 - Mar. 28.
y – Not Jan. 2 - Mar. 29.

802 RHEIN – RUHR LOCAL SERVICES

RE / RB services

Services in this table (pages 372–374) are shown route by route. Sub-headings indicate the route number and principal stations served.

RE1 Aachen - Köln - Düsseldorf - Duisburg - Dortmund - Hamm ⊡ *RE6* Düsseldorf - Duisburg - Dortmund - Bielefeld - Minden ⊡

km																								
																		n				⑤⑥f	
0	**Aachen** Hbf.. 807 910 d.	...	...	...	...	0451e	...	0551	...	0651	...		...	1751	...	1851	...	1951	...	2051	2151	2251	2351	2351
31	Düren .... 807 d.	...	...	...	...	0517e	...	0617	...	0717	...		...	1817	...	1917	...	2017	...	2117	2217	2317	0017	0017
70	**Köln** Hbf ...... 807 910 a.	...	...	...	...	0544e	...	0644	...	0744	...		...	1844	...	1944	...	2044	...	2144	2244	2344	0044	0044
70	**Köln** Hbf ....d.	...	...	...	...	0549	...	0649	...	0749	...		...	1849	...	1949	...	2049	...	2149	2249	2349	0049	...
71	**Köln** Messe/Deutz ......d.	...	...	...	...	0552	...	0652	...	0752	...	and at	...	1852	...	1952	...	2052	...	2152	2252	2352	0052	...
83	Leverkusen Mitte ....d.	...	...	...	...	0604	...	0704	...	0804	...		...	1904	...	2004	...	2104	...	2204	2304	0004	0104	...
110	**Düsseldorf** Hbf ....d.	0422c	...	0522	...	0622	0654e	0722	0754r	0822	0854	the same	1854	1922	...	2022	...	2122	...	2222	2322	0022	0122	...
117	Düsseldorf Flughafen ✈ d.	0428c	...	0528	...	0628	0702e	0728	0802r	0828	0902		1902	1928	...	2028	...	2128	...	2228	2328	0028	0128	...
134	**Duisburg** Hbf ....d.	0438	...	0538	...	0638	0715e	0738	0815r	0838	0915	minutes	1915	1938	...	2038	...	2138	...	2238	2338	0038	0138	...
144	Mülheim (Ruhr) Hbf......d.	0444	...	0544	...	0644	0721e	0744	0821r	0844	0921		1921	1944	...	2044	...	2144	...	2244	2344	0044	0144	...
153	**Essen** Hbf ....d.	0453	...	0553	...	0653	0729e	0753	0829r	0853	0929	past each	1929	1953	...	2053	...	2153	...	2253	2353	0053	0153	...
169	Bochum Hbf............d.	0505	...	0605	...	0705	0741e	0805	0841r	0905	0941		1941	2005	...	2105	...	2205	...	2305	0005	0105	0205	...
187	**Dortmund** Hbf...........d.	0517	0555	0617	0655	0717	0755	0817	0855	0917	0955	hour until	1955	2017	2055	2117	2155	2217	*2255*	2317	0017	0117	0217	...
218	**Hamm** (Westf) ..... 810 d.	0545	0615	0640	0715	0745	0815	0840	0915	0945	1015		2015	2040	2115	2145	2215	2245	2322	2345	0045	0145	0245	...
268	Gütersloh Hbf .... 810 d.	...	0649	...	0749	...	0849	...	0949	...	1049		2049	...	2149	...	2249	...	2355	...	...	...	...	...
285	**Bielefeld** Hbf....... 810 a.	...	0658	...	0758	...	0858	...	0958	...	1058		2058	...	2158	...	2258	...	0008	...	...	...	...	...
299	Herford .... 810 a.	...	0707r	...	0807	...	0907	...	1007	...	1107		2107	...	2207r	...	2307b	...	...	...	...	...	...	...
309	Löhne .... 810 a.	...	0713r	...	0813	...	0913	...	1013	...	1113		2113	...	2213r	...	2313b	...	...	...	...	...	...	...
315	Bad Oeynhausen . 810 a.	...	0718r	...	0818	...	0918	...	1018	...	1118		2118	...	2218r	...	2318b	...	...	...	...	...	...	...
330	**Minden** (Westf) ... 810 a.	...	0730r	...	0830	...	0930	...	1030	...	1130		2130	...	2230r	...	2330b	...	...	...	...	...	...	...

				⚒r																		⑤⑥f	
Minden (Westf) ..... 810 d.	...	...	...	0528e	...	0628r	...	0728r	...	0828	...		1728	...	1828	...	1928	...	2028	...	2128	...	...	2228r
Bad Oeynhausen ... 810 d.	...	...	...	0539e	...	0639r	...	0739r	...	0839	...		1739	...	1839	...	1939	...	2039	...	2139	...	...	2239r
Löhne .... 810 d.	...	...	...	0544e	...	0644r	...	0744r	...	0844	...		1744	...	1844	...	1944	...	2044	...	2144	...	...	2244r
Herford .... 810 d.	...	...	...	0550e	...	0650r	...	0750r	...	0850	...		1750	...	1850	...	1950	...	2050	...	2150	...	...	2250r
Bielefeld Hbf .... 810 d.	...	...	...	0559	...	0659	...	0759	...	0859	...	and at	1759	...	1859	...	1959	...	2059	...	2159	...	...	2259
Gütersloh Hbf .... 810 d.	...	...	...	0608	...	0708	...	0808	...	0908	...		1808	...	1908	...	2008	...	2108	...	2208	...	...	2308
Hamm (Westf)....... 810 d.	0415	0515	0615	0644	0720	0744	0815	0844	0920	0944	1015	the same	1844	1920	1944	2015	2044	2115	2144	2215	2244	2315	2315	2344
Dortmund Hbf............d.	0444	0544	0644	0706	0744	0806	0844	0906	0944	1006	1044		1906	1944	2004	2044	2104	2144	2204	2244	2304	2344	2344	0004
Bochum Hbf..............d.	0455	0555	0655	0719	0755	0819	0855	0919	0955	1019	1055	minutes	1919	1955	...	2055	...	2155	...	2255	...	2355	2355	...
Essen Hbf.................d.	0508	0608	0708	0732	0808	0832	0908	0932	1008	1032	1108		1932	2008	...	2108	...	2208	...	2308	...	0008	0008	...
Mülheim (Ruhr) Hbf.......d.	0514	0614	0714	0738	0814	0838	0914	0938	1014	1038	1114	past each	1938	2014	...	2114	...	2214	...	2314	...	0014	0014	...
Duisburg Hbf..............d.	0523	0623	0723	0748	0823	0848	0923	0948	1023	1048	1123		1948	2023	...	2123	...	2223	...	2323	...	0021	0023	...
Düsseldorf Flughafen ✈ d.	0531	0631	0731	0757	0831	0857	0931	0957	1031	1057	1131	hour until	1957	2031	...	2131	...	2231	...	2331	...	...	0031	...
Düsseldorf Hbf ....d.	0540	0640	0740	0805	0840	0905	0940	1005	1040	1105	1140		2005	2040	...	2140	...	2240	...	2340	...	...	0040	...
Leverkusen Mitte ....d.	0555	0655	0755	...	0855	...	0955	...	1055	...	1155		...	2055	...	2155	...	2255	...	2355	...	...	0055	...
Köln Messe/Deutz ....d.	0609	0709	0809	...	0909	...	1009	...	1109	...	1209		...	2109	...	2209	...	2309	...	0009	...	...	0109	...
Köln Hbf ....a.	0612	0712	0812	...	0912	...	1012	...	1112	...	1212		...	2112	...	2212	...	2312	...	0012	...	...	0112	...
Köln Hbf .... 807 910 d.	0615	0715	0815	...	0915	...	1015	...	1115	...	1215		...	2115	...	2215	...	2315	...	0015	...	...	0115	...
Düren .... 807 d.	0639	0739	0839	...	0939	...	1039	...	1139	...	1239		...	2139	...	2239	...	2339	...	0039	...	...	0139	...
Aachen Hbf... 807 910 a.	0707	0807	0907	...	1007	...	1107	...	1207	...	1307		...	2207	...	2307	...	0007	...	0107	...	...	0207	...

RE2 Mönchengladbach - Duisburg - Essen - Gelsenkirchen - Münster ⊡ *RB33* Aachen - Mönchengladbach - Duisburg ⊡ *RB42* Essen - Münster

km																								
		Ⓐe	⚒r			⚒r																⊖		
0	**Aachen** Hbf................d.	...	*0413*	...	*0513*	*0513*	...	0538r	*0613*	...	0638		*1813*	...	1838	*1913*	...	1938	*2013*	...	2038	*2113*	...	2238
62	**Mönchengladbach** Hbf d.	...	0521	...	0621	0621	...	0637	0721	...	0737		1921	...	1937	2021	...	2037	2121	...	2137	2221	...	2337
71	Viersen.......................d.	...	0531	...	0631	0631	...	0645	0731	...	0745	and at	1931	...	1945	2031	...	2045	2131	...	2145	2231	...	2345
86	Krefeld Hbf ....d.	...	0542	...	0642	0642	...	0659	0742	...	0759		1942	...	1959	2042	...	2059	2142	...	2159	2242	...	2359
107	**Duisburg** Hbf ....d.	...	0601	...	0701	0701	...	0724	0801	...	0824	the same	2001	...	2024	2101	...	2124	2201	...	2224	2301	...	0024
117	Mülheim (Ruhr) Hbf......d.	...	0607	...	0707	0707	...	...	0807	...	...		2007	...	...	2107	...	...	2207	...	...	2307	...	...
126	**Essen** Hbf..................d.	0515	0615	0648	0713	0715	0748	...	0815	0848	...	minutes	2015	2048	...	2115	2148	...	2215	2248	...	2317	2348	...
134	Gelsenkirchen Hbf ....d.	0524	0624	0656	...	0724	0756	...	0824	0856	...		2024	2056	...	2124	2156	...	2224	2256	...	2325	2356	...
139	Wanne-Eickel Hbf ....d.	0529	0629	0701	...	0729	0801	...	0829	0901	...	past each	2029	2101	...	2129	2201	...	2229	2301	...	2330	0001	...
149	Recklinghausen Hbf....d.	0537	0637	0709	...	0737	0809	...	0837	0909	...		2037	2109	...	2137	2209	...	2237	2309	...	2338	0009	...
164	Haltern am See ....d.	0549	0649	0719	...	0749	0819	...	0849	0919	...	hour until	2049	2119	...	2148	2219	...	2248	2319	...	2349	0019	...
177	Dülmen........................d.	0559	0659	0728	...	0759	0828	...	0859	0928	...		2059	2128	...	...	2228	...	...	2328	...	...	0028	...
206	**Münster** (Westf) Hbf....a.	0621	0721	0749	...	0821	0849	...	0921	0949	...		2121	2149	...	...	2249	...	...	2349	...	...	0049	...

	⚒r	⚒r		⚒r																				
Münster (Westf) Hbf.....d.	0411	...	...	0511	0537e	...	0611	0637r	...	0711	0737r	...	0811	0837	...	0911		2037	...	2111	...	...	2211	2311
Dülmen.........................d.	0432	...	...	0532	0558e	...	0632	0658r	...	0732	0758r	...	0832	0858	...	0932		2058	...	2132	...	...	2232	2332
Haltern am See ....d.	0441	0508	...	0541	0608r	...	0641	0708	...	0741	0808	...	0841	0908	...	0941	and at	2108	...	2141	2208	...	2241	2341
Recklinghausen Hbf.....d.	0451	0521	...	0551	0621r	...	0651	0721	...	0751	0821	...	0851	0921	...	0951		2121	...	2151	2221	...	2251	2351
Wanne-Eickel Hbf ....d.	0500	0529	...	0600	0629r	...	0700	0729	...	0800	0829	...	0900	0929	...	1000	the same	2129	...	2200	2229	...	2300	0000
Gelsenkirchen Hbf ....d.	0504	0534	...	0604	0634r	...	0704	0734	...	0804	0834	...	0904	0934	...	1004		2134	...	2204	2234	...	2304	0004
Essen Hbf......................d.	0515	0545	...	0615	0645	...	0714	0745	...	0814	0845	...	0914	0945	...	1014	minutes	2145	...	2214	2245	...	2314	0014
Mülheim (Ruhr) Hbf.......d.	...	0551	...	...	0651	...	...	0751	...	...	0851	...	...	0951	...	...		2151	...	...	2251	...	...	...
Duisburg Hbf...............d.	...	0559	0636	...	0659	0736	...	0759	0836	...	0859	0936	...	0959	1036	...	past each	2159	2236	...	2259	2336	...	...
Krefeld Hbf ....d.	...	0619	0700	...	0719	0800	...	0819	0900	...	0919	1000	...	1019	1100	...		2219	2300	...	2319	0000	...	...
Viersen ....d.	...	0633	0713	...	0733	0813	...	0833	0913	...	0933	1013	...	1033	1113	...	hour until	2233	2313	...	2333	0013	...	...
Mönchengladbach Hbf a.	...	0642	0720	...	0742	0820	...	0842	0920	...	0942	1020	...	1042	1120	...		2242	2320	...	2342	0020	...	...
Aachen Hbf..................a.	...	*0745*	0820	...	*0845*	0920	...	*0945*	1020	...	*1045*	1120	...	*1145*	1220	...		*2345*	0020	...	*0045*	...	...	...

RE3 Düsseldorf - Duisburg - Gelsenkirchen - Dortmund - Hamm ⊡ ◇

km											
0	**Düsseldorf** Hbf ....d.	0545	0645	0745	0845		1845	1945	2045		2345
7	Düsseldorf Flughafen ✈ d.	0553	0653	0753	0853		1853	1953	2053		2353
24	**Duisburg** Hbf ....a.	0603	0703	0803	0903	and	1903	2003	2103	and	0003
24	**Duisburg** Hbf .... d.	0610	0710	0810	0910		1910	2010	2110		0010
32	Oberhausen Hbf ....d.	0616	0716	0816	0916	hourly	1916	2016	2116	hourly	0016
48	Gelsenkirchen Hbf ......d.	0629	0729	0829	0929		1929	2029	2129		0029
53	Wanne-Eickel Hbf ....d.	0634	0734	0834	0934	until	1934	2034	2134	until	0034
57	Herne ....d.	0638	0738	0838	0938		1938	2038	2138		0038
78	**Dortmund** Hbf............a.	0657	0757	0857	0957		1957	2057	2157		0057
109	**Hamm** (Westf) Hbf.......a.	0729e	0829e	0929e	1029r		2029e	2129e	...		...

Hamm (Westf) Hbf....d.	0529e	0629e	0729e	0829r		1729r	1829e	...		...
Dortmund Hbf..........d.	0603	0703	0803	0903		1803	1903	2003		2303
Herne ....d.	0620	0720	0820	0920	and	1820	1920	2020	and	2320
Wanne-Eickel Hbf .....d.	0624	0724	0824	0924		1824	1924	2024		2324
Gelsenkirchen Hbf ....d.	0629	0729	0829	0929	hourly	1829	1929	2029	hourly	2329
Oberhausen Hbf........d.	0643	0743	0843	0943		1843	1943	2043		2343
Duisburg Hbf ....a.	0648	0748	0848	0948	until	1848	1948	2048	until	2348
Duisburg Hbf ....d.	0652	0752	0852	0952		1852	1952	2052		2352
Düsseldorf Flughafen.d.	0702	0802	0902	1002		1902	2002	2102		0002
Düsseldorf Hbf ....a.	0710	0810	0910	1010		1910	2010	2110		0010

b – Ⓑ (also Dec. 24, 31; not Dec. 26, May 1).
c – Ⓒ (also Dec. 24, 31, June 3).
e – Ⓐ (not Dec. 24, 31, June 3).
f – Also Dec. 23, 24, 30, 31, Apr. 1, 4, May 12, 23, June 2.
n – Not Dec. 24, 31.
r – ⚒ (not June 3).
⊖ – Change trains at Essen on ①②③④⑥⑦ (through train on ⑤).
⊡ – See note and shaded panel on page 371.
◇ – Operated by **eurobahn** Keolis Deutschland GmbH & Co. KG.

RE4 Aachen - Mönchengladbach - Düsseldorf - Wuppertal - Dortmund ⊡ *RE13* Venlo - Mönchengladbach - Düsseldorf - Wuppertal - Hamm ⊡ ◇

km			⚒r	⚒r	Ⓐe		⚒r																	
0	**Aachen** Hbf .... **471** d.	0253	0413	...	...	0513	...	0613	...	0713	...		...	1713	...	1813	...	1913	...	2013	...	2113	...	2238
14	Herzogenrath .... **471** d.	0307	0427	...	...	0527	...	0627	...	0727	...		...	1727	...	1827	...	1927	...	2027	...	2127	...	2253
58	Rheydt Hbf ....d.	0341	0503	...	...	0603	...	0703	...	0803	...		...	1803	...	1903	...	2003	...	2103	...	2203	...	2330
	Venlo 🏛 ....d.	|	|	0505	0505	|	0605	|	0705	|	0805	and at	1705	|	1805	|	1905	|	2005	|	2105	|	2205	|
	Kaldenkirchen ....d.	|	|	0510	0510	|	0610	|	0710	|	0810		1710	|	1810	|	1910	|	2010	|	2110	|	2210	|
	Viersen ....d.	|	|	0527	0527	|	0627	|	0727	|	0827	the same	1727	|	1827	|	1927	|	2027	|	2127	|	2227	|
62	**Mönchengladbach** Hbf d.	0349	0510	0545j	0545j	0610	0645j	0710	0745j	0810	0845j		1745j	1810	1845j	1910	1945j	2010	2045j	2110	2145j	2210	2235	2336
79	Neuss Hbf ....d.	0403	0524	0557	0557	0624	0657	0724	0757	0824	0857	minutes	1757	1824	1857	1924	1957	2024	2057	2124	2157	2224	...	...
90	**Düsseldorf** Hbf ....a.	0413	0534	0608	0608	0634	0708	0734	0808	0834	0908		1808	1834	1908	1934	2008	2034	2108	2134	2208	2234	...	...
90	**Düsseldorf** Hbf ....d.	f	0540e	...	0612	0640r	0712	0740	0812	0840	0912	past each	1812	1840	1912	1940	2012	2040	...	2140	...	2240	...	...
117	**Wuppertal** Hbf ....d.	...	0602e	...	0632	0702r	0732	0802	0832	0902	0932		1832	1902	1932	2002	2032	2102	...	2202	...	2302	...	...
144	**Hagen** Hbf..................d.	...	0630e	...	0658	0730r	0758	0830	0858	0930	0958	hour until	1858	1930	1955	2030	2055	2130	...	2230	...	2330	...	...
159	Witten.........................d.	...	0641e	...	|	0741r	|	0841	|	0941	|		|	1941	|	2041	|	2141	...	2241	...	2341	...	...
175	**Dortmund** Hbf............d.	...	0651e	...	|	0751r	|	0851	|	0951	|		|	1951	|	2051	|	2151	...	2251	...	2351	...	...
	Schwerte (Ruhr).......d.	...	...	...	0708	...	0808e	...	0908r	...	1008		1908	...	*2031*	...	*2131*	...	...	...	...	...	...	...
	Unna ....d.	...	...	...	0720	...	0820e	...	0920r	...	1020		1920	...	*2043*	...	*2143*	...	...	...	...	...	...	...
	Hamm (Westf) ....d.	...	...	...	0734	...	0834e	...	0934r	...	1034		1934	...	*2057*	...	*2157*	...	...	...	...	...	...	...

km			⚒r																					
0	**Hamm** (Westf) ....d.	...	...	...	...	0622e	...	0722e	...	0822e	...	0922r	...	1022		1722	...	1822	...	1922	...	...	...	...
19	Unna ....d.	...	...	...	...	0635e	...	0735e	...	0835e	...	0935r	...	1035		1735	...	1835	...	1935	...	...	...	...
35	Schwerte (Ruhr).......d.	...	...	...	...	0647e	...	0747e	...	0847e	...	0947r	...	1047		1747	...	1847	...	1947	...	...	...	...
	Dortmund Hbf............d.	...	...	...	0609e	|	0709r	|	0809	|	0909	|	1009	|	and at	|	1809	|	1909	|	2009	...	2109	2209
	Witten.........................d.	...	...	...	0619e	|	0719r	|	0819	|	0919	|	1019	|		|	1819	|	1919	|	2019	...	2119	2219
48	**Hagen** Hbf..................d.	...	...	0602e	0632e	0702r	0732r	0802	0832	0902	0932	1002	1032	1102	the same	1802	1832	1902	1932	2002	2032	...	2132	2232
75	**Wuppertal** Hbf ....d.	...	...	0625e	0658e	0725r	0758r	0825	0858	0925	0958	1025	1058	1125		1825	1858	1925	1958	2025	2058	...	2158	2258
102	**Düsseldorf** Hbf ....a.	...	...	0645e	0719e	0745r	0819r	0845	0919	0945	1019	1045	1119	1145	minutes	1845	1919	1945	2019	2045	2119	...	2219	2319
102	**Düsseldorf** Hbf ....d.	0548r	0622	0648r	0722	0748	0822	0848	0922	0948	1022	1048	1122	1148		1848	1922	1948	2022	2048	2122	2148	2222	2322
113	Neuss Hbf ....d.	0601r	0636	0701r	0736	0801	0836	0901	0936	1001	1036	1101	1136	1201	past each	1901	1936	2001	2036	2101	2136	2201	2236	2336
130	**Mönchengladbach** Hbf d.	0625j	0649	0725j	0749	0825j	0849	0925j	0949	1025j	1049	1125j	1149	1225j		1925j	1949	2025j	2049	2125j	2149	2225j	2249	2349
139	Viersen ....d.	0633	|	0733	|	0833	|	0933	|	1033	|	1133	|	1233	hour until	1933	|	2033	|	2133	|	2233	|	|
157	Kaldenkirchen ....d.	0652	|	0752	|	0852	|	0952	|	1052	|	1152	|	1252		1952	|	2052	|	2152	|	2252	|	|
167	**Venlo** 🏛 ....a.	0656	|	0756	|	0856	|	0956	|	1056	|	1156	|	1256		1956	|	2056	|	2156	|	2256	|	|
	Rheydt Hbf ....d.	...	0654	...	0754	...	0854	...	0954	...	1054	...	1154	...		...	1954	...	2054	...	2154	...	2254	2354
	Herzogenrath .... **471** d.	...	0729	...	0829	...	0929	...	1029	...	1129	...	1229	...		...	2029	...	2129	...	2229	...	2329	0029
	Aachen Hbf .... **471** a.	...	0745	...	0845	...	0945	...	1045	...	1145	...	1245	...		...	2045	...	2145	...	2245	...	2345	0045

RE5 Koblenz - Bonn - Köln - Düsseldorf - Duisburg - Emmerich ⊡

km				Ⓐe	v◐	⚒r															n◐	n◐		n◐	n◐
0	**Koblenz** Hbf...............d.	...	...	0516	0526	0616	0716	0816	0916	1016	1116	1216	1316	1416	1516	1616	1716	1816	1916	2016	2026	2126	...	2226	2326
18	Andernach ....d.	...	...	0527	0544	0627	0727	0827	0927	1027	1127	1227	1327	1427	1527	1627	1727	1827	1927	2027	2044	2144	...	2244	2344
29	Bad Breisig ....d.	...	...	0534	0554	0634	0734	0834	0934	1034	1134	1234	1334	1434	1534	1634	1734	1834	1934	2034	2054	2154	...	2254	2354
39	Remagen.....................d.	...	...	0542	0611j	0642	0742	0842	0942	1042	1142	1242	1342	1442	1542	1642	1742	1842	1942	2042	2111j	2211j	...	2311j	0011j
59	**Bonn** Hbf ....d.	...	...	0601	0632	0701	0801	0901	1001	1101	1201	1301	1401	1501	1601	1701	1801	1901	2001	2101	2132	2232	...	2332	0032
93	**Köln** Hbf ....a.	...	...	0628	0701	0728	0828	0928	1028	1128	1228	1328	1428	1528	1628	1728	1828	1928	2028	2128	2201	2301	...	0001	0101
93	**Köln** Hbf .... ♥ d.	...	0631r	0631	▬	0731	0831	0931	1031	1131	1231	1331	1431	1531	1631	1731	1831	1931	2031	2131	...	...	*2349*	...	...
106	Leverkusen Mitte ....d.	...	0645r	0645	...	0745	0845	0945	1045	1145	1245	1345	1445	1545	1645	1745	1845	1945	2045	2145	...	...	*0004*	...	...
133	**Düsseldorf** Hbf ....d.	...	0703r	0703	...	0803	0903	1003	1103	1203	1303	1403	1503	1603	1703	1803	1903	2003	2103	2203	...	...	*0022*	...	...
140	Düsseldorf Flughafen ✈ d.	...	0710r	0710	...	0810	0910	1010	1110	1210	1310	1410	1510	1610	1710	1810	1910	2010	2110	2210	...	...	*0028*	...	...
157	**Duisburg** Hbf ....d.	0620	0720	0720	0820	0820	0920	1020	1120	1220	1320	1420	1520	1620	1720	1820	1920	2020	2120	2220	...	...	0044	...	...
165	Oberhausen Hbf ....d.	0628	0728	0728	0828	0828	0928	1028	1128	1228	1328	1428	1528	1628	1728	1828	1928	2028	2128	2228	...	...	0051	...	...
192	Wesel ....d.	0659	0755	0755	0855	0855	0955	1055	1155	1255	1355	1455	1555	1655	1755	1855	1955	2055	2155	2255	...	...	0119	...	...
226	**Emmerich** ....a.	0725	0821	0821	0925	0925	1021	1125	1221	1325	1421	1525	1621	1725	1821	1925	2021	2125	2227	2327	...	...	0152	...	...

	Ⓐe	v◐	⚒r		⚒r														n◐		n◐	n◐			
Emmerich ....d.	...	...	0433e	0533	0533	0636	0740	0836	0940	1036	1140	1236	1340	1436	1540	1636	1740	1836	...	1940	...	...	2036	2140	2236
Wesel ....d.	...	...	0506e	0606	0606	0706	0806	0906	1006	1106	1212	1306	1412	1506	1612	1706	1812	1906	...	2012	...	...	2106	2206	2309
Oberhausen Hbf ....d.	...	...	0534e	0634	0634	0734	0834	0934	1034	1134	1234	1334	1434	1534	1634	1734	1834	1934	...	2034	...	...	2134	2234	2337
Duisburg Hbf..............d.	...	...	0542	0640	0642	0742	0842	0942	1042	1142	1242	1342	1442	1542	1642	1742	1842	1942	...	2042	...	...	2140	2240	2343
Düsseldorf Flughafen ✈ .d.	...	...	0550	▬	0650	0750	0850	0950	1050	1150	1250	1350	1450	1550	1650	1750	1850	1950	...	2050	...	...	*2202*	*2302*	▬
Düsseldorf Hbf ....d.	...	...	0558	...	0658	0758	0858	0958	1058	1158	1258	1358	1458	1558	1658	1758	1858	1958	...	2058	...	...	*2210*	*2310*	...
Leverkusen Mitte ....d.	...	...	0614	...	0714	0814	0914	1014	1114	1214	1314	1414	1514	1614	1714	1814	1914	2014	...	2114	...	...	...	...	⑤⑥
Köln Hbf .... ★ a.	...	...	0629	...	0729	0829	0929	1029	1129	1229	1329	1429	1529	1629	1729	1829	1929	2029	...	2129	...	...	...	...	d◐
Köln Hbf ....d.	0532	0556	0632	0732	0732	0832	0932	1032	1132	1232	1332	1432	1532	1632	1732	1832	1932	2032	2056	*2138*	2156	2256	...	...	2356
Bonn Hbf ....d.	0558	0627	0658	0758	0758	0858	0958	1058	1158	1258	1358	1458	1558	1658	1758	1858	1958	2058	2127	*2208*	2227	2327	...	...	0027
Remagen.......................d.	0615	0654j	0715	0815	0815	0915	1015	1115	1215	1315	1415	1515	1615	1715	1815	1915	2015	2115	2154j	*2233*	2254j	2354j	...	...	0054j
Bad Breisig ....d.	0623	0703	0723	0823	0823	0923	1023	1123	1223	1323	1423	1523	1623	1723	1823	1923	2023	2123	2203	...	2303	0003	...	...	0103
Andernach ....d.	0630	0714	0730	0830	0830	0930	1030	1130	1230	1330	1430	1530	1630	1730	1830	1930	2030	2130	2214	...	2314	0014	...	...	0114
Koblenz Hbf.................a.	0642	0731	0742	0842	0842	0942	1042	1142	1242	1342	1442	1542	1642	1742	1842	1942	2042	2142	2231	...	2331	0031	...	...	0131

RE7 Krefeld - Köln - Wuppertal - Hagen - Hamm - Münster (- Rheine: Table 812) ⊡

km		Ⓐe									
0	**Krefeld** Hbf ....d.	...	...	0535r	0635		1935	2035	2135	2235	2335
19	Neuss Hbf ....d.	...	...	0553r	0653		1953	2053	2153	2253	2353
57	**Köln** Hbf ....a.	...	...	0618r	0718	and	2018	2118	2218	2318	0018
57	**Köln** Hbf .... ♥ d.	...	0521e	0621r	0721		2021	2121	2221	*2352*	*0052*
85	Solingen Hbf..................d.	...	0543e	0643r	0743	hourly	2043	2143	2243	*0020*	*0120*
103	**Wuppertal** Hbf ....d.	...	0556e	0656r	0756		2056	2156	2256	*0037*	*0137*
130	**Hagen** Hbf.....................d.	0521	0621	0721	0821	until	2121	2221	2321	...	...
143	Schwerte (Ruhr) ....d.	0531	0631	0731	0831		2131	2231	2331	...	...
159	Unna ....d.	0543	0643	0743	0843		2143	2243	2343	...	...
178	**Hamm** (Westf) ....d.	0559	0659	0759	0859		2159	2259	0010z	...	...
214	**Münster** (Westf) Hbf.....d.	0622	0722	0822	0922		2229	2329	0040	...	...

	⚒r	⚒k								
Münster (Westf) Hbf . d.	...	...	0529e	0634		2034	...	...	2134	2234
Hamm (Westf)..........d.	...	0501	0601	0701		2101	...	...	2201	2301
Unna..........................d.	...	0514	0614	0714		2114	...	...	2214	2314
Schwerte (Ruhr) ....d.	...	0527	0627	0727	and	2127	...	...	2227	2327
Hagen Hbf.................d.	0439e	0539	0639	0739		2139	...	...	2237	2337
Wuppertal Hbf..........d.	0504e	0604	0704	0804	hourly	2204	*2221*	2321	...	...
Solingen Hbf ....d.	0515e	0615	0715	0815		2215	*2238*	2338	...	...
Köln Hbf............. ★ a.	0538e	0638	0738	0838	until	2238	*2305*	0005	...	...
Köln Hbf....................d.	0542	0642	0742	0842		2242	2342	...	...	...
Neuss Hbf...................d.	0607	0707	0807	0907		2307	0007	...	...	...
Krefeld Hbf ....a.	0625	0725	0825	0925		2325	0025	...	...	...

RE10 Düsseldorf - Krefeld - Kleve ⊠

km		⚒r	Ⓐe			Ⓐe				
0	**Düsseldorf** Hbf ....d.	0609	0639	0709		1939	2009	2109	2209	2309
27	**Krefeld** Hbf ....d.	0637	0707	0737	and at	2007	2037	2137	2237	2337
57	Geldern ....d.	0702	0732	0802	the same	2032	2102	2202	2302	0002
66	Kevelaer........................d.	0709	0739	0809	minutes	2039	2109	2209	2309	0009
72	Weeze............................d.	0715	0745	0815	past each	2045	2115	2215	2315	0015
79	Goch ....d.	0721	0751	0821	hour until	2051	2121	2221	2321	0021
92	**Kleve** ....a.	0734	0804	0834		2104	2134	2234	2334	0034

	⚒r		Ⓐe		Ⓐe				
Kleve.........................d.	0525	0619	0649		1749	1819	1919		2219
Goch............................d.	0538	0636	0706	and at	1806	1836	1936		2236
Weeze ....d.	0545	0645	0715	the same	1815	1845	1945	and	2245
Kevelaer ....d.	0551	0651	0721	minutes	1821	1851	1951	hourly	2251
Geldern.......................d.	0558	0658	0728	past each	1828	1858	1958	until	2258
Krefeld Hbf ....d.	0626	0726	0756	hour until	1856	1926	2026		2326
Düsseldorf Hbf ....a.	0652	0752	0822		1922	1952	2052		2352

d – ⑤⑥ (also Apr. 1, 4, May 12, 23, June 2); runs daily Köln - Remagen.
e – Ⓐ (not Dec. 24, 31, June 3).
f – To Düsseldorf Flughafen Terminal ✈ (a. 0425).
j – Arrives 8 – 10 minutes earlier.
k – ⚒ (also June 3); runs daily Köln - Krefeld.
n – Not Dec. 24, 31.
r – ⚒ (not June 3).
v – Not Dec. 25, Jan. 1.
z – Arrives 2357.

⊡ – See shaded panel for a summary of the principal Rhein – Ruhr *RE* routes.
♥ – Trains also call at Köln Messe/Deutz (3 minutes after Köln Hbf).
★ – Trains also call at Köln Messe/Deutz (4 minutes before Köln Hbf).
◐ – Operated by TransRegio Deutsche Regionalbahn GmbH.
◇ – *RE13* operated by **eurobahn** Keolis Deutschland GmbH & Co. KG.
⊠ – Operated by Nord West Bahn GmbH.

	RE1	*RE2*	*RE3*	*RE4*	*RE5*	*RE6*	*RE7*	*RE13*	*RB33*
Aachen Hbf	●	...	...	●	...	...	...	...	●
Köln Hbf	●	...	...	|	●	...	●	...	|
Mönchengladbach Hbf	|	●	...	●	|	...	|	●	●
Düsseldorf Hbf	●	|	●	●	●	●	|	●	|
Duisburg Hbf	●	●	●	|	●	●	|	|	●
Essen Hbf	●	●	|	|	...	●	|	|	...
via Gelsenkirchen	|	●	●	|	...	|	|	|	...
via Wuppertal and Hagen	|	|	|	●	...	|	●	●	...
Dortmund Hbf	●	|	●	●	...	●	|	|	...
Hamm (Westf)	●	|	●	...	...	●	●	●	...
Münster (Westf) Hbf	...	●	...	...	...	...	●	...	...

802 RHEIN – RUHR LOCAL SERVICES

RE / RB services

RB8/27 Mönchengladbach - Köln - Königswinter - Koblenz

km		Ⓐe	⚒r	⚒r		⚒r						▲									Ⓑq			
0	**Mönchengladbach** ⊖ d.	0440	0503e	0540	0603e	0640	0703e	0740	0803e	0840	...		1340	...	1440	1503e		1740	1803e	1840	1903e	1940	2040	2140
3	Rheydt Hbf ⊖ d.	0444	0507e	0544	0607e	0644	0707e	0744	0807e	0844	...		1344	...	1444	1507e		1744	1807e	1844	1907e	1944	2044	2144
22	Grevenbroich ⊖ d.	0502	0528e	0602	0628e	0702	0728e	0802	0828e	0902	...	and at	1402	...	1502	1528e	and at	1802	1828e	1902	1928e	2002	2102	2202
56	**Köln** Hbf ⊖ a.	0535	0600e	0635	0700e	0735	0800e	0835	0900e	0935	...		1435	...	1535	1600e		1835	1900e	1935	2000e	2035	2135	2235
56	**Köln** Hbf 807 d.	0538	0601t	0638	0701t	0738	0801t	0838	0901t	0938	1001t	the same	1438	1501t	1538	1601t	the same	1838	1901t	1938	2001t	2101	2201	2301
57	**Köln** Messe/Deutz d.	0541	0604t	0641	0704t	0741	0804t	0841	0904t	0941	1004t		1441	1504t	1541	1604t		1841	1904t	1941	2004t	2104	2204	2304
71	Köln/Bonn Flughafen ✈ d.	0550	|	0650	|	0750	|	0850	|	0950	|	minutes	1450	|	1550	|	minutes	1850	|	1950	|	|	|	|
83	Troisdorf 807 d.	0601	0623	0701	0723	0801	0823	0901	0923	1001	1023		1501	1523	1601	1623		1901	1923	2001	2023	2123	2223	2323
92	**Bonn** Beuel d.	0611	0633	0711	0733	0811	0833	0911	0933	1011	1033	past each	1511	1533	1611	1633	past each	1911	1933	2011	2033	2133	2233	2333
100	Königswinter d.	0620	0643	0720	0743	0820	0843	0920	0943	1020	1043		1520	1543	1620	1643		1920	1943	2020	2043	2143	2243	2343
105	Bad Honnef d.	0626	0649	0726	0749	0826	0849	0926	0949	1026	1049	hour until	1526	1549	1626	1649	hour until	1926	1949	2026	2049	2149	2249	2349
115	Linz (Rhein) d.	0637	0702	0735t	0802	0835	0902	0935	1002	1035	1102		1535	1602	1635	1702		1935	2002	2035	2102	2202	2302	0001
122	Bad Hönningen d.	0642	0709	0740t	0809	0840	0909	0940	1009	1040	1109		1540	1609	1640	1709		1940	2009	2040j	2109n	2209n	2309n	...
138	Neuwied d.	0655	0724	0752t	0824	0852	0924	0952	1024	1052	1124		1552	1624	1652	1724		1952	2024	2052j	2124n	2224n	2324n	...
◊153	**Koblenz** Hbf a.	0716	0740	0813t	0840	0913	0940	1013	1040	1113	1140		1613	1640	1713	1740		2013	2040	2113j	2140n	2240n	2340n	...

	⚒r			Ⓐe		Ⓐe	⑥k		⚒r													Ⓑq		
Koblenz Hbf d.	...	...	0515r	0536	0618r	0636	0648	0718	0748	0818	0848		1218	1248	1318	1348	1418		1818	1848	1918	1948	2018	2118n
Neuwied d.	...	...	0532r	0558	0632r	0658	0708	0732	0808	0832	0908		1232	1306	1332	1408	1432		1832	1908	1932	2008	2032	2132n
Bad Hönningen d.	...	...	0546r	0612	0646r	0712	0719	0746	0819	0846	0919	and at	1246	1317	1346	1419	1446	and at	1846	1919	1946	2019	2046	2146n
Linz (Rhein) d.	0453	...	0553	0619	0653	0719	0724	0753	0824	0853	0924		1253	1322	1353	1424	1453		1853	1924	1953	2024	2053	2153
Bad Honnef d.	0503	...	0603	0630	0703	0730	0733	0803	0833	0903	0933	the same	1303	1333	1403	1433	1503	the same	1903	1933	2003	2033	2103	2203
Königswinter d.	0509	...	0609	0636	0709	0736	0739	0809	0839	0909	0939		1309	1339	1409	1439	1509		1909	1939	2009	2039	2109	2209
Bonn Beuel d.	0518	...	0618	0646	0718	0746	0749	0818	0849	0918	0949	minutes	1318	1349	1418	1449	1518	minutes	1918	1949	2018	2049	2118	2218
Troisdorf 807 d.	0528	...	0628	0659	0728	0759	0759	0828	0859	0928	0959		1328	1359	1428	1459	1528		1928	1959	2028	2059	2128	2228
Köln/Bonn Flughafen ✈ d.	|	...	|	0708	|	0808	0808	|	0908	|	1008	past each	|	1408	|	1508	|	past each	|	2008	|	2108	|	|
Köln Messe/Deutz d.	0550	0619	0650	0719	0750	0819	0819	0850	0919	0950	1019		1350	1419	1450	1519	1550		1950	2019	2050	2119	2150	2250
Köln Hbf 807 a.	0553	0622	0653	0722	0753	0822	0822	0853	0922	0953	1022	hour until	1353	1422	1453	1522	1553	hour until	1953	2022	2053	2122	2153	2253
Köln Hbf ⊖ d.	0559e	0625	0659e	0725	0759e	0825	0825	...	0925	...	1025		...	1425	1459e	1525	1559e		1959e	2025	...	2125	2225	2325
Grevenbroich ⊖ d.	0630e	0655	0730e	0755	0830e	0855	0855	...	0955	...	1055		...	1455	1530e	1555	1630e		2030e	2055	...	2155	2255	2355
Rheydt Hbf ⊖ d.	0651e	0715	0751e	0815	0851e	0915	0915	...	1015	...	1115		...	1515	1551e	1615	1651e		2051e	2115	...	2215	2315	0015
Mönchengladbach ⊖ a.	0656e	0720	0756e	0820	0856e	0920	0920	...	1020	...	1120		...	1520	1556e	1620	1656e		2056e	2120	...	2220	2320	0020

S-Bahn 13 Köln - Köln/Bonn Flughafen ✈ - Troisdorf

				Ⓒz		Ⓒz	Ⓐe		Ⓐe	Ⓒz	Ⓐe			Ⓐe	Ⓒz	Ⓐe							
Köln Hbf d.	0011	0041	0241	0241	0341	0341	0421	0441	0501	0511	0521	0541	and at the same	2001	2011	2021	2041	2111	2141	2211	2241	2311	2341
Köln Messe/Deutz d.	0013	0043	0243	0243	0343	0343	0423	0443	0503	0513	0523	0543	minutes past	2003	2013	2023	2043	2113	2143	2213	2243	2313	2343
Köln/Bonn Flughafen ✈ d.	0026	0056	0255	0256	0355	0356	0436	0456	0516	0526	0536	0556	each hour until	2016	2026	2036	2056	2126	2156	2226	2256	2326	2356
Troisdorf a.	0036	0108	...	0308	...	0408	0448	0508	0528	0536	0548	0608		2028	2036	2048	2108	2136	2208	2236	2308	2336	0008

					Ⓒz		Ⓒz		Ⓐe	Ⓒz	Ⓐe			Ⓐe	Ⓒz	Ⓐe							
Troisdorf d.	0023	0053	0123	...	0303	...	0403	...	0513	0523	0533	0553	and at the same	2013	2023	2033	2053	2123	2153	2223	2253	2323	2353
Köln/Bonn Flughafen ✈ d.	0034	0104	0134	...	0314	0314	0414	0414	0524	0534	0544	0604	minutes past	2024	2034	2044	2104	2134	2204	2234	2304	2334	0004
Köln Messe/Deutz a.	0046	0116	0146	...	0326	0326	0426	0426	0536	0546	0556	0616	each hour until	2036	2046	2056	2116	2146	2216	2246	2316	2346	0016
Köln Hbf a.	0049	0119	0149	...	0329	0329	0429	0429	0539	0549	0559	0619		2039	2049	2059	2119	2149	2219	2249	2319	2349	0019

Dortmund - Unna - Soest ◇

km			Ⓒz		⚒r		⚒r	Ⓐe			Ⓐe			Ⓐe									
0	**Dortmund** Hbf 805 d.	0007	0107	...	0507	...	0607	0637	...	0707	0737	and at the same	1907	1937	...	2007	...	2107	...	2207	...	2307	...
23	Unna d.	0032	0132	...	0532	...	0632	0702	...	0732	0802	minutes past	1932	2002	...	2032	...	2132	...	2232	...	2332	...
53	**Soest** 805 a.	0055	0155	...	0555	...	0655	0725	...	0755	0825	each hour until	1955	2025	...	2055	...	2155	...	2255	...	2355	...

		Ⓒz		⚒r	Ⓐe	⚒r	Ⓐe			Ⓐe			Ⓐe									
Soest 805 d.	0003	0103	...	0503	0533	0603	0633	...	0703	0733	and at the same	1803	1833	...	1903	...	2003	...	2103	...	2203	...	2303
Unna d.	0027	0127	...	0527	0557	0627	0657	...	0727	0757	minutes past	1827	1857	...	1927	...	2027	...	2127	...	2227	...	2327
Dortmund Hbf 805 a.	0051	0151	...	0551	0621	0651	0721	...	0751	0821	each hour until	1851	1921	...	1951	...	2051	...	2151	...	2251	...	2351

RB 53 Dortmund - Schwerte - Iserlohn

km		Ⓐe	Ⓐe	Ⓐe		Ⓐe		Ⓐe			Ⓐe		Ⓐe		Ⓐe		Ⓐe		Ⓐe		Ⓐe			b
0	**Dortmund** Hbf d.	0523	0553	0623	0653	0723	0753	0823	0853	and at the same	1523	1553	1623	1653	1723	1753	1823	1853	1923	1953	2023	2053	2153	2323
18	Schwerte (Ruhr) d.	0545	0615	0645	0715	0745	0815	0842	0915	minutes past	1542	1615	1645	1715	1745	1815	1842	1915	1942	2015	2042	2115	2215	2344
38	**Iserlohn** a.	0608	0638	0708	0738r	0808	0838	...	0938	each hour until	...	1638	1708	1738	1808	1838	...	1938	...	2038	...	2138	2238	...

	Ⓐe	Ⓐe	Ⓐe		Ⓐe		Ⓐe		Ⓐe			Ⓐe		Ⓐe		Ⓐe		Ⓐe		Ⓐe			
Iserlohn d.	...	0523	...	0617e	0647	0717r	0747	0817	...	0917	and at the same	...	1617	1647	1717	1747	1817	...	1917	...	2017	2117	2217
Schwerte (Ruhr) d.	0520	0550	0620	0650	0720	0750	0820	0850	0920	0950	minutes past	1620	1650	1720	1750	1820	1850	1920	1950	2020	2050	2150	2250
Dortmund Hbf a.	0539	0609	0639	0709	0739	0809	0839	0909	0939	1009	each hour until	1639	1709	1739	1809	1839	1909	1939	2009	2039	2109	2209	2309

RB30 BONN - REMAGEN (*20 km*) - AHRBRÜCK (*48 km*) and v.v.

From Bonn Hbf at 0749 ⚒**r**, 0849 and hourly until 1749, 1849 **n**, 1949 **n**, 2049 **n**.
Trains depart Remagen 22 minutes later. Journey time from Bonn: 67 minutes.

From Ahrbrück at 0704 ⚒**r**, 0804 and hourly until 1904, 2004 **n** (also 2104 **n** and 2204 **n** to Remagen only). Journey time to Remagen 43 minutes, Bonn 64 minutes.

RB31 DUISBURG - MOERS - XANTEN and v.v. (45 km, journey time: 45 minutes) ⊠

From Duisburg Hbf at: 0556 ⚒**r**, 0710 ⚒**r**, 0810, 0910 and hourly until 2310.
From Xanten at: 0500 ⚒**r**, 0600 ⚒**r**, 0700, 0800 and hourly until 2200.
Trains call at Moers 18 minutes from Duisburg, 28 minutes from Xanten.

OTHER USEFUL S-BAHN LINKS

Services operate every 20 minutes (every 30 minutes evenings and weekends)

Service	*Route (journey time in minutes)*
S1	Solingen Hbf - Düsseldorf Hbf (22) - Düsseldorf Flughafen ✈ (35) - Duisburg Hbf (53) - Essen Hbf (72) - Bochum Hbf (90) - Dortmund Hbf (113).
S3	Oberhausen Hbf - Mülheim Hbf (8) - Essen Hbf (17).
S9	Essen Hbf - Wuppertal Hbf (47).
S11	Düsseldorf Flughafen Terminal ✈ - Düsseldorf Hbf (12) - Neuss Hbf (31) - Köln Hbf (82).

b – To Bestwig (Table **804**).
e – Ⓐ (not Dec. 24, 31, June 3).
j – Linz - Koblenz on † (also June 3).
k – Also Dec. 24, 31; not Dec. 26, May 1.
n – Not Dec. 24, 31.
q – Also Dec. 26, May 1; not Dec. 24, 31.
r – ⚒ (not June 3).
t – 2–3 minutes later on Ⓐ**e**.
w – Also June 3.
z – Also Dec. 24, 31, June 3.
⊠ – Operated by Nord West Bahn GmbH.
◊ – Via Koblenz-Lützel (*159 km* via Ehrenbreitstein).
▲ – On Ⓐ**e** the 1040 and 1140 from Mönchengladbach departs Linz 2 mins later, Bad Hönningen 4 mins later, Neuwied 5 mins later, arrives Koblenz 5 mins later.
⊖ – Additional trains Mönchengladbach Hbf - Köln Hbf and v.v.
From Mönchengladbach at 0440 ⑥**k**, 0540 †**w**, 0640 †**w**, 1840 ⑥**k**, 2240, 2340.
From Köln Hbf at 0025, 0525 ⚒**r**, 0725 Ⓒ**z**, 0825 †**w**, 0925 †**w**, 2125 ⑥**k**.
◇ – Operated by **eurobahn** Keolis Deutschland GmbH & Co. KG (2nd class only).

803 DORTMUND and MÜNSTER - ENSCHEDE

2nd class only

km	△	Ⓐe	⚒r						⑦w	
0	**Dortmund** Hbf d.	0552	0652	0752r	0852		1852	1952	1952	2052
44	Dülmen d.	0640	0740	0840r	0940	and	1940	2040	2040	2140
61	Coesfeld (Westf) d.	0705	0801	0901	1001	hourly	2001	2053	2101	2153
96	Gronau (Westf) d.	0739	0839	0939	1039	until	2039	...	2139	...
103	**Enschede** a.	0750	0850	0950	1050		2050	...	2150	...

△	Ⓐe	⚒r	⚒r	⚒r					
Enschede d.	...	...	0556e	0656	...	0756		1956	2056
Gronau (Westf) d.	...	0525e	0621	0708	...	0821	and	2021	2107
Coesfeld (Westf) d.	0506	0603	0703	0803	0803	0903	hourly	2103	...
Dülmen d.	0520	0617	0717	0817	0817	0917	until	2117	...
Dortmund Hbf a.	0607	0707	0807	0907	0907	1007		2207	...

km	♥	Ⓐe	Ⓐe	⚒r						⑤⑥v
0	**Münster** (Westf) Hbf d.	0508	0608	0708	...	0808	and	2108	2208	2308
56	Gronau (Westf) d.	0604	0709	0809	0809	0909	hourly	2209	2309	0009
63	**Enschede** a.	0620	0720	0820	0820	0920	until	2220	2320n	0020

♥	⚒r	Ⓐe	⑥k					⑤⑥v	⑤⑥v
Enschede d.	...	0626	0626	0726t	0826	and	2126	2226	2326
Gronau (Westf) d.	0544	0644	0644	0744	0844	hourly	2144	2244	2344
Münster (Westf) Hbf a.	0644	0744	0744	0844	0944	until	2244	2344	0044

e – Ⓐ (not June 3).
k – Also Dec. 24, 31; not Dec. 26, May 1.
n – Not Dec. 24, 31.
r – ⚒ (not June 3).
t – ①–⑥ (not Dec. 25, 26, Jan. 1, Apr. 5, May 13, 24).
v – Also Feb. 11, Apr. 4, May 12, 23, June 2; not Apr. 2.
w – Also Dec. 25, 26, Jan. 1, Apr. 5, May 13, 24.
△ – Operated by Prignitzer Eisenbahn GmbH. German holiday dates apply.
♥ – Operated by DB (*RB* services). German holiday dates apply.

HAGEN - KASSEL 804

RE services

km		⚒r	Ⓐt	⑥k	⚒r	Ⓐt	⑥k														Ⓒz			D
0	**Hagen** Hbf ... **802** d.	...	0509	...	...	0603	0613	0713	0813	0913	1013	1113	1213	1313	1413	1513	1613	1713	1813	1913	2013	2013	2113	2213	*2321*
14	Schwerte (Ruhr) ... **802** d.	...	0519	...	...	0616	0623	0723	0823	0923	1023	1123	1223	1323	1423	1523	1623	1723	1823	1923	2023	2023	2123	2223	2349
57	Arnsberg (Westf) ... d.	...	0549	...	...	0649	0656	0756	0856	0956	1056	1156	1256	1356	1456	1556	1656	1756	1856	1956	2056	2056	2156	2256	0020
77	Meschede ... d.	...	0607	...	...	0708	0715	0815	0915	1015	1115	1215	1315	1415	1515	1615	1715	1815	1915	2015	2115	2115	2215	2315	0038
86	Bestwig ... d.	...	0614	0623	...	0717	0723	0823	0923	1023	1123	1223	1323	1423	1523	1623	1723	1823	1923	2023	2122	2123	2222	2322	0045
100	Brilon Wald ... d.	...	0628	0638	...	0733	0738	0838	0938	1038	1138	1238	1338	1438	1538	1638	1738	1838	1938	2038	...	2138	...	...	...
152	Warburg (Westf) ... a.	...	0714	0720	...	0820	0820	0920	1020	1120	1220	1320	1420	1520	1620	1720	1820	1920	2020	2120	...	2220	...	...	...
152	Warburg (Westf) ... **805** d.	0601	0720	0721	0801	...	...	0921	...	1121	...	1321	...	1521	...	1721	...	1921	...	*2141*	...	...	...	...	...
205	**Kassel** Hbf ... a.	0656	0759	0759	0857	...	...	0959	...	1159	...	1359	...	1559	...	1759	...	1959	...	*2237*	...	...	...	...	...
209	**Kassel** Wilhelmshöhe .. **805** a.	...	0809	0809	...	...	...	1009	...	1209	...	1409	...	1609	...	1809	...	2009	...	...	...	...	...	...	...

	⚒r	⚒r	⚒r		Ⓐt	⑥k		Ⓐt	⚒r															⚒r	†h
Kassel Wilhelmshöhe ... **805** d.	...	...	...	...	...	...	...	...	...	...	0748	...	0948	...	1148	...	1348	...	1548	...	1748	...	1948	...	...
Kassel Hbf ... d.	...	...	...	...	*0516*	*0516*	...	0618	...	...	0758	...	0958	...	1158	...	1358	...	1558	...	1758	...	1958	2028	2258
Warburg (Westf) ... **805** a.	...	...	...	...	*0610*	*0610*	...	0714	...	...	0835	...	1035	...	1235	...	1435	...	1635	...	1835	...	2035	2122	2353
Warburg (Westf) ... d.	...	...	0532y	...	0632	0638	...	...	0738	...	0838	0938	1038	1138	1238	1338	1438	1538	1638	1738	1838	1938	2038	...	...
Brilon Wald ... d.	...	...	0622	...	0719	0722	...	...	0822	...	0922	1022	1122	1222	1322	1422	1522	1622	1722	1822	1922	2022	2122	...	...
Bestwig ... d.	0436	0536	0636	0636	0736	0736	0736	...	0836	0836	0936	1036	1136	1236	1336	1436	1536	1636	1736	1836	1936	2036	2136	...	...
Meschede ... d.	0443	0543	0643	0643	0743	0743	0743	...	0843	0843	0943	1043	1143	1243	1343	1443	1543	1643	1743	1843	1943	2043	2143	...	...
Arnsberg (Westf) ... d.	0501	0601	0701	0701	0801	0801	0801	...	0901	0901	1001	1101	1201	1301	1401	1501	1601	1701	1801	1901	2001	2101	2201	...	...
Schwerte (Ruhr) ... **802** d.	0535	0635	0735	0735	0835	0835	0835	...	0935	0935	1035	1135	1235	1335	1435	1535	1635	1735	1835	1935	2035	2135	2235	...	...
Hagen Hbf ... **802** a.	0545	0645	0745	0745	0845	0845	0845	...	0945	0945	1045	1145	1245	1345	1445	1545	1645	1745	1845	1945	2045	2145	2245	...	...

D – From Dortmund Hbf (d. 2323).
h – Also June 3.
k – Also Dec. 24, 31; not Dec. 26, May 1.
r – Not June 3.
t – Not Dec. 24, 31, June 3.
y – 0538 on ⑥ (also Dec. 24, 31).
z – Also Dec. 24, 31, June 3.

DORTMUND and MÜNSTER - PADERBORN - KASSEL 805

RE / *RB* services except where shown

km		Ⓐt ◇	⑥k ◇		*IC* 2355 ①–⑥ e ◐	Ⓐt ◇	Ⓒz ◇		*IC* 2357 🍷	Ⓐt ◇	Ⓒz ◇		*IC* 2157 § 🍷	Ⓐt ◇	Ⓒz ◇		*IC* 2359 ⑤⑦ b 🍷	Ⓐt ◇	Ⓒz ◇		*IC* 2151 🍷	Ⓐt ◇	Ⓒz ◇		*IC* 2153 Ⓑq 🍷
	Köln Hbf **800** ... d.	...	...	...	🍷	...	...	...	0715e	...	...	...	0905	...	...	...	1120	...	...	...	...	...	...	...	...
	Düsseldorf Hbf **800** ... d.	...	...	...	0546g	...	...	...	0746e	...	...	...	0946	...	...	...	1146	...	...	...	1346	...	...	...	1546
0	**Dortmund** Hbf ... **802** d.	...	...	...	0642	...	...	...	0842	...	...	...	1042	...	...	...	1242	...	...	...	1442	...	...	...	1642
	Münster (Westf) Hbf .. **802** d.	0510	0510	0634	|	0710	0710	0834	|	0910	0910	1034	|	1110	1110	1234	|	1310	1310	1434	|	1510	1510	1634	|
31	Hamm (Westf) ... **802** a.	0537	0537	0659	0702	0737	0737	0859	0902	0937	0937	1059	1102	1137	1137	1259	1302	1337	1337	1459	1502	1537	1537	1659	1702
31	Hamm (Westf) ... d.	0546	0552	...	0707	0746	0752	...	0907	0946	0952	...	1107	1146	1152	...	1307	1346	1352	...	1507	1546	1552	...	1707
57	Soest ... **802** d.	0602	0608	...	0722	0802	0808	...	0922	1002	1008	...	1122	1202	1208	...	1322	1402	1408	...	1522	1602	1608	...	1722
77	Lippstadt ... d.	0614	0620	...	0733	0814	0820	...	0933	1014	1020	...	1133	1214	1220	...	1333	1414	1420	...	1533	1614	1620	...	1733
109	**Paderborn** Hbf . ⊖ **809 811** d.	0642	0642	...	0749	0842	0842	...	0949	1042	1042	...	1149	1242	1242	...	1349	1442	1442	...	1549	1642	1642	...	1749
126	Altenbeken ... ⊖ **809 811** d.	0654	0654	...	0804	0854	0854	...	1004	1054	1054	...	1204	1254	1254	...	1404	1454	1454	...	1604	1654	1654	...	1804
163	Warburg (Westf) ... **804** d.	0716	0716	...	0826	0916	0916	...	1026	1116	1116	...	1226	1316	1316	...	1426	1516	1516	...	1626	1716	1716	...	1826
220	**Kassel** Wilhelmshöhe .. **804** a.	*0809*	*0809*	...	0857	*1009*	*1009*	...	1057	*1209*	*1209*	...	1257	*1409*	*1409*	...	1457	*1609*	*1609*	...	1657	*1809*	*1809*	...	1857
	Erfurt Hbf **850** ... a.	...	...	...	1029	...	...	...	1229	...	...	...	1429	...	...	...	1629	...	...	...	1829	...	...	...	2029
	Halle (Saale) Hbf **850** ... a.	...	...	...	1158	...	...	...	1358	...	...	...	1558	...	...	...	1758	...	...	...	1958	...	...	...	2200w
	Berlin Hbf **850** ... a.	...	...	...	1316	...	...	...	1518	...	...	...	1719	...	...	...	1918	...	...	...	2118c	...	...	...	...
	Stralsund **845** ... a.	...	...	...	1624	...	...	...	...	...	...	...	2036q	...	...	...	2225	...	...	...	...	...	...	...	...

	Ⓐt ◇	Ⓒz ◇	*IC* 2155 ⑦w 🍷	◇	Ⓐt ◇	Ⓒz ◇	◇	◇	◇	◇
Köln Hbf **800** ... d.	...	...	...	...	...	...	...	...	...	...
Düsseldorf Hbf **800** ... d.	...	...	1746	...	...	...	...	...	...	...
Dortmund Hbf ... **802** d.	...	...	1842	...	...	...	...	...	...	...
Münster (Westf) Hbf .. **802** d.	1710	1710	|	1840v	1910	1910	*2034*	*2134*	*2234*	2310
Hamm (Westf) ... **802** a.	1737	1737	1902	1906v	1937	1937	*2059*	*2159*	*2259*	2337
Hamm (Westf) ... d.	1746	1752	1907	1916	1946	2007	2107	2207	2307	0007
Soest ... **802** d.	1802	1808	1922	1932	2002	2023	2123	2223	2323	0023
Lippstadt ... d.	1814	1820	1933	1944	2014	2035	2135	2235	2335	0035
Paderborn Hbf .. ⊖ **809 811** d.	1842	1842	1949	2009	2058j	2100	2200	2300	2359	0100
Altenbeken ... ⊖ **809 811** d.	1854	1854	2004	...	2110	2111	...	...	...	...
Warburg (Westf) ... **804** d.	1916	1916	2026	...	2133	2134	...	...	...	...
Kassel Wilhelmshöhe ... **804** a.	*2009*	*2009*	2057	...	*2237*h	*2237*h	...	...	...	...
Erfurt Hbf **850** ... a.	...	...	2229	...	...	...	...	...	...	...
Halle (Saale) Hbf **850** ... a.	...	...	...	...	...	...	...	...	...	...
Berlin Hbf **850** ... a.	...	...	...	...	...	...	...	...	...	...
Stralsund **845** ... a.	...	...	...	...	...	...	...	...	...	...

	⚒r ◇	◇	Ⓐt ◇	Ⓒz ◇	Ⓒz ◇	Ⓐt ◇	Ⓒz ◇	Ⓐt ◇	*IC* 2156 ①–⑥ e 🍷	
Stralsund **845** ... d.	...	...	...	...	...	...	...	...	...	...
Berlin Hbf **850** ... d.	...	...	...	...	...	...	...	...	...	...
Halle (Saale) Hbf **850** ... d.	...	...	...	...	...	...	...	...	...	...
Erfurt Hbf **850** ... d.	...	...	...	...	...	...	...	...	0725	...
Kassel Wilhelmshöhe **804** d.	...	...	...	...	...	...	*0748*	*0748*	0900	...
Warburg (Westf) ... **804** d.	...	...	0624	0639	...	...	0839	0839	0934	...
Altenbeken ... ⊖ **809 811** d.	...	...	0647	0702	...	...	0902	0902	0956	...
Paderborn Hbf ⊖ **809 811** d.	0513	0621	0721j	0716	0816	0821	0916	0921	1010	...
Lippstadt ... d.	0536	0644	0744	0736	0836	0844	0936	0944	1026	...
Soest ... **802** d.	0548	0656	0756	0748	0848	0856	0948	0956	1037	...
Hamm (Westf) ... a.	0606	0714	0814	0806	0906	0914	1006	1014	1052	...
Hamm (Westf) ... **802** d.	0620	0720	0820	0820	0920	0920	1020	1020	1056	1059
Münster (Westf) Hbf **802** a.	0647	0747	0847	0847	0947	0947	1047	1047	|	1122
Dortmund Hbf ... **802** a.	...	...	...	...	...	...	...	...	1115	...
Düsseldorf Hbf **800** ... a.	...	...	...	...	...	...	...	...	1212	...
Köln Hbf **800** ... a.	...	...	...	...	...	...	...	...	...	...

	Ⓒz ◇	Ⓐt ◇	*IC* 2154 ①–⑥ e 🍷		Ⓒz ◇	Ⓐt ◇	*IC* 2152 ⑤⑦ b 🍷		Ⓒz ◇	Ⓐt ◇	*IC* 2150 ‡ 🍷		Ⓒz ◇	Ⓐt ◇	*IC* 2356 ¶ ◐ 🍷		Ⓒz ◇	Ⓐt ◇	*IC* 2354 🍷		◇	*IC* 2352 ⑦w 🍷	◇	①–⑥ m ◇	◇
Stralsund **845** ... d.	...	...	...	...	...	...	...	...	...	...	0737e	...	...	...	0937	...	...	...	...	...	...	1337	...	...	...
Berlin Hbf **850** ... d.	...	...	0639	...	...	...	0839f	...	...	...	1039	...	...	...	1239	...	...	...	1439	...	...	1639	...	...	...
Halle (Saale) Hbf **850** ... d.	...	...	0800	...	...	...	1000	...	...	...	1200	...	...	...	1400	...	...	...	1600	...	...	1800	...	...	...
Erfurt Hbf **850** ... d.	...	...	0926	...	...	...	1126	...	...	...	1326	...	...	...	1526	...	...	...	1726	...	...	1926	...	...	...
Kassel Wilhelmshöhe ... **804** d.	*0948*	*0948*	1100	...	*1148*	*1148*	1300	...	*1348*	*1348*	1500	...	*1548*	*1548*	1701	...	*1748*	*1748*	1900	...	*1948*	2100	...	...	...
Warburg (Westf) ... **804** d.	1039	1039	1134	...	1239	1239	1334	...	1439	1439	1534	...	1639	1639	1734	...	1839	1839	1934	...	2039	2134	...	2139	...
Altenbeken ... ⊖ **809 811** d.	1102	1102	1156	...	1302	1302	1356	...	1502	1502	1556	...	1702	1702	1756	...	1902	1902	1956	...	2102	2156	...	2202	...
Paderborn Hbf .. ⊖ **809 811** d.	1116	1121	1210	...	1316	1321	1410	...	1516	1521	1610	...	1716	1721	1810	...	1916	1921	2010	...	2116	2210	2216	2215	2311
Lippstadt ... d.	1136	1144	1226	...	1336	1344	1426	...	1536	1544	1626	...	1736	1744	1826	...	1936	1944	2026	...	2139	2226	2239	...	2334
Soest ... **802** d.	1148	1156	1237	...	1348	1356	1437	...	1548	1556	1637	...	1748	1756	1837	...	1948	1956	2037	...	2151	2237	2251	...	2346
Hamm (Westf) ... a.	1206	1214	1252	...	1406	1414	1452	...	1606	1614	1652	...	1806	1814	1852	...	2006	2014	2052	...	2209	2252	2309	...	0004
Hamm (Westf) ... **802** d.	1220	1220	1256	1259	1420	1420	1456	1459	1620	1620	1656	1659	1820	1820	1856	1859	2020	2020	2056	2059	*2259*	2256	*2315*	...	*0010*x
Münster (Westf) Hbf .. **802** a.	1247	1247	|	1322	1447	1447	|	1522	1647	1647	|	1722	1847	1847	|	1922	2047	2047	|	2122	*2329*	|	|	...	*0040*x
Dortmund Hbf ... **802** a.	...	...	1315	...	...	...	1515	...	...	...	1715	...	...	...	1915	...	...	...	2115	...	...	2315	*2342*	...	...
Düsseldorf Hbf **800** ... a.	...	...	1412	...	...	...	1612	...	...	...	1814	...	...	...	2015	...	...	...	2214w	...	...	0012	...	...	...
Köln Hbf **800** ... a.	...	...	...	...	...	...	...	...	...	...	...	...	...	...	2042p	...	...	...	2240w	...	...	0035	...	...	...

Paderborn - Holzminden ⊡

km		Ⓐt	⚒r	⚒r					Ⓐt	Ⓒz		Ⓒz
0	**Paderborn** Hbf ... d.	0453	0553	0653	0753	and	1953	2053	2106	2206	2315
17	Altenbeken ... d.	0507	0606	0707	0807	hourly	2007	2107	2119	2219	2329
66	**Holzminden** ... a.	0553	0658y	0753	0853	until	2053	2153	2202	2302	0012

	Ⓐt	⚒r	⚒r				Ⓐt	Ⓒz	Ⓒz
Holzminden ... d.	0450	0604	0704	0804	and	2104	2204	2208	2316
Altenbeken ... d.	0537	0652	0752	0852	hourly	2152	2252	2252	0001
Paderborn Hbf ... a.	0551	0705	0805	0905	until	2205	2305	2305	0015

b – Also Dec. 23, 30, Apr. 1, 5, May 12, 24; not Dec. 25, Jan. 1, Apr. 2, 4, May 14, 23.
c – ⑥⑦ (also Dec. 24, 25, 31, Jan. 1, Apr. 2, 5, May 24).
e – ①–⑥ (not Dec. 25, 26, Jan. 1, Apr. 3, 5, May 24).
f – ⑤ (also Dec. 23, 30, Apr. 1, May 12; not Apr. 2, May 14).
g – ① (also Apr. 6, May 25; not Apr. 5, May 24).
h – Kassel **Hbf**.
j – Arrives 20 – 21 minutes earlier.
k – ⑥ (also Dec. 24, 31; not Dec. 26, May 1).
m – Also Apr. 4, May 23; not Jan. 1, Apr. 5, May 13, 24, June 3.
p – ⑤ (also Dec. 23, 30, Apr. 1, May 12, June 2; not Dec. 25, Jan. 1, Apr. 2, May 14, June 4).
q – Ⓑ (not Dec. 24, 25, 31, Apr. 2, 4, May 23).
r – Not June 3.
t – Not Dec. 24, 31, June 3.
v – On Ⓒ (also Dec. 24, 31, June 3) depart Münster *1834*, arrive Hamm *1859*.
w – ⑦ (also Apr. 5, May 24; not Apr. 4, May 23).
x – Not Dec. 25, Jan. 1.
y – 0651 on ⑥ (also Dec. 24, 31).
z – Also Dec. 24, 31, June 3.
◐ – To / from Ostseebad Binz (Table **844**).
§ – Train number **2257** on ⑥ (also Dec. 24, 25, 31, Apr. 2, 4, May 23).
‡ – Train number **2250** on ⑦ (also Dec. 25, 26, Jan. 1, Apr. 3, 5, May 24).
¶ – Train number **2254** on ⑤ (also Dec. 23, 30, Apr. 1, May 12, June 2; not Dec. 25, Jan. 1, Apr. 2, May 14, June 4).
◇ – Operated by **eurobahn** Keolis Deutschland GmbH & Co. KG (2nd class only).
⊖ – See panel below for Holzminden connections.
⊡ – Operated by Nord West Bahn (2nd class only).

806 FRANKFURT - GIESSEN - KASSEL

See Table **900** for faster *ICE* services Frankfurt - Kassel - Hannover - Hamburg and v.v.

km		RE	RE	IC	RE	IC	RE	IC	RE	IC	RE	IC	IC	RE	IC	RE	IC	RE	IC	IC	IC	RE	RE	IC	RE
		4120	**4100**	**2378**	**4102**	**2376**	**4104**	**2374**	**4106**	**2372**	**4108**	**2370**	**2270**	**4110**	**2276**	**4112**	**2274**	**4114**	**2272**	**2172**	**2282**	**4116**	**4118**	**1874**	**4120**
		✝h	⚒y	①–⑥				⊖				♥	⑤⑦r		¶				①–⑤	⑦w	⑥	⑤–⑦	①–④	⑦w	
				e🍷		🍷		🍷		🍷		K🍷	K🍷		🍷		🍷		a🍷	S🍷	A🍷	b	m		
	Karlsruhe Hbf **911** d.	...	...	...	...	0702e	...	0910	...	1110c	...	1310	1310	...	1510	...	1710	...	1910	...	...	...	...	...	...
	Heidelberg Hbf **911** d.	...	...	...	...	0746e	...	0946	...	1146c	...	1346	1346	...	1546	...	1746	...	1946	1946	...	...	...	2124	...
0	**Frankfurt (Main)** Hbf **807** d.	0508	0521	0649	0718	0852	0921	1052	1121	1252	1321	1452	1452	1521	1652	1720	1852	1921	2052	2052	2052	2121	2121	2223	2324
34	Friedberg (Hess) **807** d.	0531	0545	0717	0745	0916	0945	1116	1145	1316	1345	1516	1516	1545	1716	1745	1916	1945	2116	2116	2116	2145	2145	2247	2345
38	Bad Nauheim **807** d.	0535	|	|	|	|	|	|	|	|	|	|	|	|	|	|	|	|	|	|	|	|	|	|	|
66	**Gießen** **807** d.	0604	0604	0735	0804	0935	1004	1135	1204	1335	1404	1535	1535	1604	1735	1804	1935	2004	2135	2135	2135	2204	2204	2306	0008
96	Marburg (Lahn) d.	0621	0621	0751	0821	0951	1021	1151	1221	1351	1421	1551	1551	1621	1751	1821	1951	2021	2151	2151	2151	2221	2221	2322	0028
118	Stadtallendorf d.	0636	0636	|	0836	|	1036	|	1236	|	1436	|	|	1636	|	1836	|	2036	|	|	|	2236	2236	|	0043
138	Treysa d.	0651	0651	0815	0851	1015	1051	1215	1251	1415	1451	1615	1615	1651	1815	1851	2015	2051	2215	2215	2215	2250	2250	2347	0058
166	Wabern d.	0707	0707	0834	0907	1034	1107	1234	1307	1434	1507	1634	1634	1707	1834	1907	2034	2107	2234	2234	2234	2308	...	0006	...
196	**Kassel** Wilhelmshöhe ‡ a.	0727	0727	0853	0927	1053	1127	1253	1327	1453	1527	1653	1653	1727	1855	1927	2053	2127	2253	2253	2253	2328	...	0026	...
200	**Kassel** Hbf ‡ a.	0734	0734	|	0934	|	1134	|	1334	|	1534	|	|	1734	|	1934	|	2135	...	...	...	2335	...	...	...
	Hannover Hbf **902** a.	...	...	0956	...	1156	...	1356	...	1556	...	1756	1756	...	1957	...	2156r	...	...	...	...	...	...	...	...
	Hamburg Hbf **902** a.	...	...	1127	...	1328	...	1529	...	1730	...	1927	1927	...	2128	...	2326w	...	...	...	...	...	...	...	...
	Stralsund **830** a.	...	...	...	...	1630	...	...	...	2032	...	...	2230	...	...	...	...	...	...	...	...	...	...	...	...

	RE	RE	RE	IC	RE	RE	IC	IC	RE	RE	IC	RE	IC	RE	IC	RE	IC	RE	IC	RE	IC	RE	IC	IC	RE
	25051	**4121**	**4101**	**2273**	**4123**	**4103**	**2271**	**2275**	**25007**	**4105**	**2277**	**4107**	**2279**	**4109**	**2371**	**4111**	**2373**	**4113**	**2375**	**4115**	**2377**	**4117**	**2379**	**1899**	**4119**
		Ⓐt	⑥k	①–⑥	Ⓐt	ⓒz	①–④	⑤v															⑤f	⑦w	
				e🍷			d	S			🍷		🍷		K🍷		🍷		🍷		O🍷		🍷	B	
Stralsund **830** d.	...	...	...	...	...	...	...	...	...	...	...	...	0527e	...	...	...	0927	...	...	...	1327	...	1527	...	...
Hamburg Hbf **902** d.	...	...	...	...	...	...	...	...	...	...	0628e	...	0828e	...	1028	...	1228	...	1428	...	1628	...	1828	...	...
Hannover Hbf **902** d.	...	...	...	...	...	...	0600	0600	...	...	0800e	...	1000e	...	1200	...	1400	...	1600	...	1800	...	2000	2100	...
Kassel Hbf ‡ d.	...	0401	0423	...	0611	0615	|	|	...	0823	|	1023	|	1223	|	1423	|	1623	|	1823	|	2023	|	|	2222
Kassel Wilhelmshöhe ‡ d.	...	0406	0429	0502	0617	0621	0703	0703	...	0829	0903	1029	1103	1229	1303	1429	1503	1629	1703	1829	1903	2029	2103	2204	2227
Wabern d.	...	0424	0448	0523	0639	0646	0723	0723	...	0848	0923	1048	1123	1248	1323	1448	1523	1648	1723	1848	1923	2048	2123	2225	2250
Treysa d.	...	0440	0505	0540	0701	0705	0740	0740	0815	0905	0940	1105	1140	1305	1340	1505	1540	1705	1740	1905	1940	2105	2140	2243	2309
Stadtallendorf d.	...	0455	0519	|	0716	0719	|	|	0829	0919	|	1119	|	1319	|	1519	|	1719	|	1919	|	2119	|	2300	2323
Marburg (Lahn) d.	0408	0512	0535	0605	0734	0735	0805	0805	0849	0935	1005	1135	1205	1335	1405	1535	1605	1735	1805	1935	2005	2135	2205	2314	2339
Gießen **807** d.	0439	0536	0553	0623	0753	0753	0823	0823	0922	0953	1023	1153	1223	1353	1423	1553	1623	1753	1823	1953	2023	2153	2223	2332	0008
Bad Nauheim **807** d.	0505	0554	|	|	|	|	|	|	0938	|	|	|	|	|	|	|	|	|	|	|	|	|	|	2351	0031
Friedberg (Hess) **807** d.	0510	0600	0613	0642	0812	0812	0842	0842	0942	1012	1042	1212	1242	1412	1442	1612	1642	1812	1842	2012	2042	2212	2242	2356	0036
Frankfurt (Main) Hbf **807** a.	0536	0625	0634	0704	0837	0837	0904	0904	1007	1034	1104	1234	1304	1434	1504	1636	1704	1837	1904	2034	2104	2234	2304	0021	0059
Heidelberg Hbf **911** a.	...	...	...	0812	...	...	1012	1012	...	...	1212c	...	1412	...	1612	...	1812	...	2012q	...	2246j	...	...	...	...
Karlsruhe Hbf **911** a.	...	...	...	0850	...	...	1050	...	...	...	1250c	...	1450	...	1650	...	1850	...	2050a	...	2325j	...	...	...	...

A – From Saarbrücken (Table **919**).
B – From Berlin (Table **810**).
K – From / to Konstanz (Table **916**).
O – From Ostseebad Binz (Table **844**).
S – From / to Stuttgart (Table **930**).

a – ①–⑤ (not Dec. 24, 25, 31, Jan. 1, Apr. 2, 5, May 24).
b – Also Dec. 24, 31, Apr. 5, May 13, 24, June 3.
c – ⑥⑦ (also Apr. 5, May 24; not Apr. 4, May 23).
d – Not Dec. 23, 24, 30, 31, Apr. 1, 5, May 12, 24.
e – ①–⑥ (not Dec. 25, 26, Jan. 1, Apr. 3, 5, May 24).
f – Also Dec. 23, 30, Apr. 1, May 12; not Dec. 25, Jan. 1, Apr. 2, May 14.
h – Also June 3.
j – ⑤⑦ (also Apr. 5, May 24; not Dec. 25, Apr. 2, 4, May 23). On ⑦ (also Apr. 5, May 24) Heidelberg a. 2212, Karlsruhe a. 2251.
k – Also Dec. 24, 31; not Dec. 26, May 1.
m – Not Dec. 24, 31, Apr. 5, May 13, 24, June 3.
q – ⑧ (not Dec. 24, 25, 31, Apr. 2, 4, May 23).
r – ⑤⑦ (also Dec. 23, 30, Apr. 1, 5, May 12, 24; not Dec. 25, Jan. 1, Apr. 2, 4, May 14, 23).
t – Not Dec. 24, 31, June 3.
v – Also Dec. 23, 30, Apr. 1, May 12; not Dec. 25, Jan. 1, Apr. 2, May 14.
w – ⑦ (also Apr. 5, May 24; not Apr. 4, May 23).
y – Not June 3.
z – Also Dec. 24, 31, June 3.
♥ – ①②③④⑥ (also Dec. 25, Jan. 1, Apr. 2, 4, May 14, 23; not Dec. 23, 30, Apr. 1, 5, May 12, 24).
⊖ – On ⑤**f** runs with train number **2174** and continues to Rostock (Table **830**).
¶ – On ⑦**w** runs with train number **2286** and continues to Rostock (Table **830**).
‡ – See also Tables **804** / **901**.

807 AACHEN - KÖLN - SIEGEN - GIESSEN - FRANKFURT

RE / RB services

km																									
				ⓒz	⑥k		Ⓐt	Ⓐt	Ⓐt		⚒r	⚒r	✝h		⚒r	✝h		⚒r	✝h					Ⓑq	⑥k
0	**Aachen** Hbf **802 910** d.	...	...	...	...	...	...	...	...	...	0513t	0613t	...	0713t	0813	...	0913	1013	1013	1113	1213	...	1313	1413	1413
31	Düren **802** d.	...	...	0303	...	...	...	...	...	...	0545t	0645t	...	0745t	0845	...	0945	1045	1045	1145	1245	...	1345	1445	1445
70	**Köln** Hbf **802 910** a.	...	...	0340	...	...	...	...	...	...	0612t	0712t	...	0812t	0912	...	1012	1112	1112	1212	1312	...	1412	1512	1512
70	**Köln** Hbf **802 910** d.	...	...	0341	...	...	...	0431	...	...	0623	0723	0723	0823	0923	0923	1023	1123	1123	1223	1323	...	1423	1523	1523
71	**Köln** Messe/Deutz **802 910** d.	...	...	0343	...	...	...	0433	...	...	0626	0726	0726	0826	0926	0926	1026	1126	1126	1226	1326	...	1426	1526	1526
91	Troisdorf **802** d.	...	...	0409	...	...	...	0454	...	...	0640	0740	0740	0840	0940	0940	1040	1140	1140	1240	1340	...	1440	1540	1540
95	Siegburg/Bonn **910** d.	...	...	0414	...	...	...	0459	...	...	0645	0745	0745	0845	0945	0945	1045	1145	1145	1245	1345	...	1445	1545	1545
102	Hennef (Sieg) d.	...	...	0420	...	...	...	0506	...	...	0650	0750	0750	0850	0950	0950	1050	1150	1150	1250	1350	...	1450	1550	1550
114	Eitorf d.	...	...	0431	...	...	...	0517	...	...	0659	0759	0759	0859	0959	0959	1059	1159	1159	1259	1359	...	1459	1559	1559
136	Au (Sieg) d.	...	...	0455	0500	...	0515	0539	0545	...	0717	0817	0817	0917	1017	1017	1117	1217	1217	1317	1417	...	1517	1617	1617
142	Wissen (Sieg) d.	...	...	▬	0507	...	0522	▬	0552	...	0722	0822	0822	0922	1022	1022	1122	1222	1222	1322	1422	...	1522	1622	1622
154	Betzdorf (Sieg) d.	...	...	...	0521	...	0536	...	0606	...	0733	0833	0833	0933	1033	1033	1133	1233	1233	1333	1433	...	1533	1633	1633
171	**Siegen** a.	...	...	...	0546	...	0601	...	0631	...	0752	0852	0852	0952	1052	1052	1152	1252	1252	1352	1452	...	1552	1652	1652
												|	▬		|	▬		|	▬		|			|	▬
		Ⓐt	Ⓐt	⚒r	⑥k	Ⓐt	A★	C★	Ⓐt		d	|		◇	|			|			|			|	
171	**Siegen** d.	...	0456	...	0554	0554	0615	0619	0654	...	0802	0854	...	1002	1054	...	1202	1254	...	1402	1454	...	1602	1654	...
203	Dillenburg d.	0424	0523	...	0617	0622	0640	0646	0728	0733r	0826	0917	0933	1026	1117	1133	1226	1317	1333	1426	1517	1533	1626	1717	1733
209	Herborn d.	0432	0528	...	0622	0627	0646	0652	0734	0740r	0831	0922	0940	1031	1122	1140	1231	1322	1340	1431	1522	1540	1631	1722	1740
231	Wetzlar **906** d.	0454	0547	...	0637	0648	0703	0702	0752	0802r	0845	0936	1002	1045	1136	1202	1245	1336	1402	1445	1536	1602	1645	1736	1802
244	**Gießen** **906** a.	0505	|	...	0646	0658	0714	0721	0802	0814r	0855	0946	1014	1055	1146	1214	1255	1346	1414	1455	1546	1614	1655	1746	1814
244	**Gießen** **806** d.	0514	|	0628	0653	0705	0729	0729	0809	0828	0902	*0953*	1028	1102	*1153*	1228	1302	*1353*	1428	1502	*1553*	1628	1702	*1753*	1828
272	Bad Nauheim **806** d.	0538	0609	0653	|	0723	0746	0746	0826	0853	|	|	1053	|	|	1253	|	|	1453	|	|	1653	|	|	1853
276	Friedberg (Hess) **806** d.	0542	|	0658	0712	0728	0752	0752	0830	0858	0922	*1012*	1058	1122	*1212*	1258	1322	*1412*	1458	1522	*1612*	1658	1722	*1812*	1858
310	**Frankfurt** (Main) Hbf **806** a.	0607	0640	0727	0734	0753	0813	0813	0858	0927	0944	*1034*	1127	1144	*1234*	1327	1344	*1434*	1527	1544	*1636*	1727	1744	*1837*	1927

		Ⓑq	⑥k								m
Aachen Hbf **802 910** d.	1513	1613	1613	1713	...	1813	1913	...	...	...	...
Düren **802** d.	1545	1645	1645	1745	...	1845	1945	...	...	...	...
Köln Hbf **802 910** a.	1612	1712	1712	1812	...	1912	2012	...	...	...	...
Köln Hbf **802 910** d.	1623	1723	1723	1823	...	1923	2023	...	2123	2223	2323
Köln Messe/Deutz **802 910** d.	1626	1726	1726	1826	...	1926	2026	...	2126	2226	2326
Troisdorf **802** d.	1640	1740	1740	1840	...	1940	2040	...	2140	2240	2340
Siegburg/Bonn **910** d.	1645	1745	1745	1845	...	1945	2045	...	2145	2245	2345
Hennef (Sieg) d.	1650	1750	1750	1850	...	1950	2050	...	2150	2250	2350
Eitorf d.	1659	1759	1759	1859	...	1959	2059	...	2159	2259	2359
Au (Sieg) d.	1717	1817	1817	1917	...	2017	2117	...	2217	2317	0017
Wissen (Sieg) d.	1722	1822	1822	1922	...	2022	2122	...	2224	2324	0024
Betzdorf (Sieg) d.	1733	1833	1833	1933	...	2033	2133	...	2239	2339	0039
Siegen a.	1752	1852	1852	1952	...	2052	2152	...	2302	0002	0102
		|	▬			|	▬		⊖	▬	
		|		◇		|	Ⓐt		|		
Siegen d.	1802	1854	...	2002	...	2054	...	...	2307	...	...
Dillenburg d.	1826	1917	1933	2026	...	2117	2233	...	2332	...	...
Herborn d.	1831	1922	1940	2031	...	2122	2240	...	2337	...	...
Wetzlar **906** d.	1845	1936	2002	2045	...	2136	2302	...	2351	...	...
Gießen **906** a.	1855	1946	2014	2055	...	2146	2314	...	0001	...	...
Gießen **806** d.	1902	*1953*	2028	2102	2118	*2153*	2322	2322	...	0008	...
Bad Nauheim **806** d.	|	|	2053	|	2140	|	2345	2345	...	0031	...
Friedberg (Hess) **806** d.	1922	*2012*	2058	2122	2143	*2212*	2348	2348	...	0036	...
Frankfurt (Main) Hbf **806** a.	1944	*2034*	2127	2144	2207	*2234*	0010	0010	...	0059	...

			⚒r		Ⓐt	⑥k	Ⓐt	Ⓐt	
Frankfurt (Main) Hbf **806** d.	0032	...	*0521*	...	...	0621	0630	*0718*	0750
Friedberg (Hess) **806** d.	0058	...	*0545*	...	...	0645	0657	*0745*	0815
Bad Nauheim **806** d.	0102	...	|	...	...	|	0701	|	0819
Gießen **806** a.	0126	...	*0602*	...	...	0702	0724	*0802*	0835
Gießen **906** d.	▬	...	0613	...	0652	0709	0740	0809	0840r
Wetzlar **906** d.	...	...	0622	...	0703	0718	0750	0818	0850r
Herborn d.	...	...	0635	...	0728	0732	0812	0833	0912r
Dillenburg d.	...	...	0640	...	0737	0737	0822	0839	0922r
Siegen a.	...	...	0705	...	0801	0801	...	0906	▬
			|					|	
	⚒r		|	✝z		d		|	ⓒz
Siegen d.	0454	0608	0707	0707	...	0808	...	0908	0908
Betzdorf (Sieg) d.	0515	0626	0726	0726	...	0826	...	0926	0926
Wissen (Sieg) d.	0527	0636	0736	0736	...	0836	...	0936	0936
Au (Sieg) d.	0535	0642	0742	0742	...	0842	...	0942	0942
Eitorf d.	0555	0659	0759	0759	...	0859	...	0959	0959
Hennef (Sieg) d.	0608	0709	0809	0809	...	0909	...	1009	1009
Siegburg/Bonn **910** d.	0614	0714	0814	0814	...	0914	...	1014	1014
Troisdorf **802** d.	0619	0719	0819	0819	...	0919	...	1019	1019
Köln Messe/Deutz **802 910** d.	0633	0733	0833	0833	...	0933	...	1033	1033
Köln Hbf **802 910** a.	0636	0736	0836	0836	...	0936	...	1036	1036
Köln Hbf **802 910** d.	0647t	0747t	0847	...	...	0947	...	1047	1047
Düren **802** d.	0715t	0815t	0915	...	...	1015	...	1115	1115
Aachen Hbf **802 910** a.	0745t	0845t	0945	...	...	1045	...	1145	1145

A – ①–⑤ (not Dec. 24, 25, 31, Apr. 2, 5, May 13, 24, June 3).
C – ⑥⑦ (also Dec. 24, 25, 31, Apr. 2, 5, May 13, 24, June 3).
d – Daily from Siegen.
h – Also June 3.
k – Also Dec. 24, 31; not Dec. 26, May 1.
m – Not Dec. 24.
q – Also Dec. 26, May 1; not Dec. 24, 31.
r – ⚒ (not June 3).
t – Ⓐ (not Dec. 24, 31, June 3).
z – Also Dec. 24, 31, June 3.
◇ – Change trains at Gießen on Ⓐt.
⊖ – Change trains at Siegen on Ⓐt.
★ – *EC* **113**. (12) and ✕ Siegen - Stuttgart - München - Salzburg - Klagenfurt.

RE / RB services — FRANKFURT - GIESSEN - SIEGEN - KÖLN - AACHEN — 807

			⚒r			⚒r		⊡							†h	Ⓐt			Ⓑq	★✕					
Frankfurt (Main) Hbf ..... 806 d.	0821	0831	*0921*	1021	1031	*1121*	1221	1231	*1321*	1421	1431	*1521*	1621	1631	*1720*	1730	1821	1831	*1921*	2001	2031	*2121*	2152	2228	*2324*
Friedberg (Hess) .... 806 d.	0845	0859	*0945*	1045	1059	*1145*	1245	1259	*1345*	1445	1459	*1545*	1645	1657	*1745*	|	1845	1859	*1945*	2024	2059	*2145*	2215	2256	*2345*
Bad Nauheim .... 806 d.	|	0903	|	|	1103	|	|	1303	|	|	1503	|	|	1701	|	1757	|	1903	|	2029	2103	|	2219	2300	|
Gießen .... 806 a.	0902	0928	*1002*	1102	1128	*1202*	1302	1328	*1402*	1502	1528	*1602*	1702	1728	*1802*	|	1902	1928	*2002*	2044	2128	*2202*	2236	2324	*0004*
Gießen .... 906 d.	0909	0940	1009	1109	1140	1209	1309	1340	1409	1509	1540	1609	1709	1740	1809	|	1909	1940	2009	2056	2140	2209	2240t	2329	0011
Wetzlar .... 906 d.	0918	0950	1018	1118	1150	1218	1318	1350	1418	1518	1550	1618	1718	1750	1818	1820	1918	1950	2018	2106	2150	2218	2250t	2340	0022
Herborn .... d.	0932	1012	1033	1132	1212	1233	1332	1412	1433	1532	1612	1633	1732	1812	1833	1836	1932	2012	2033	2122	2212	2233	2312t	0002	0047
Dillenburg .... d.	0937	1022	1039	1137	1222	1239	1337	1422	1439	1537	1622	1639	1737	1822	1839	1841	1937	2022	2039	2128	2222	2239	2322t	0010	0102
Siegen .... a.	1001	—	1106	1201	—	1306	1401	...	1506	1601	...	1706	1801	—	1906	1906	2001	—	2106	2157	—	2306	—	—	0137

		†h			†h									⑥k				⑥k		m		Ⓑq	Ⓐt	⑥w	
Siegen .... d.	1008	1108	1108	1208	1308	1308	1408	...	1508	1608	...	1708	1808	1908	1908	1908	2008	2108	2108	2208	...	2313	2313	2359	...
Betzdorf (Sieg) .... d.	1026	1126	1126	1226	1326	1326	1426	...	1526	1626	...	1726	1826	1926	1926	1926	2026	2126	2126	2226	...	2336	2336	0023	...
Wissen (Sieg) .... d.	1036	1136	1136	1236	1336	1336	1436	...	1536	1636	...	1736	1836	1936	1936	1936	2036	2136	2136	2236	...	...	2348	0034	...
Au (Sieg) .... d.	1042	1142	1142	1242	1342	1342	1442	...	1542	1642	...	1742	1842	1942	1942	1942	2042	2142	2142	2242	2320	...	2357	0043	...
Eitorf .... d.	1059	1159	1159	1259	1359	1359	1459	...	1559	1659	...	1759	1859	1959	1959	1959	2059	2159	2159	2259	2339	...	...	...	...
Hennef (Sieg) .... d.	1109	1209	1209	1309	1409	1409	1509	...	1609	1709	...	1809	1909	2009	2009	2009	2109	2209	2209	2309	2353	...	...	...	...
Siegburg/Bonn .... 910 d.	1114	1214	1214	1314	1414	1414	1514	...	1614	1714	...	1814	1914	2014	2014	2014	2114	2214	2214	2314	2359	...	...	...	...
Troisdorf .... 802 d.	1119	1219	1219	1319	1419	1419	1519	...	1619	1719	...	1819	1919	2019	2019	2019	2119	2219	2219	2319	0003	...	...	...	...
Köln Messe/Deutz .. 802 910 d.	1133	1233	1233	1333	1433	1433	1533	...	1633	1733	...	1833	1933	2033	2033	2033	2133	2233	2233	2333	0027	...	...	...	...
Köln Hbf .... 802 910 a.	1136	1236	1236	1336	1436	1436	1536	...	1636	1736	...	1836	1936	2036	2036	2036	2136	2236	2236	2336	0029	...	...	...	...
Köln Hbf .... 802 910 d.	1147	1247	1247	1347	1447	1447	1547	...	1647	1747	...	1847	1947	...	...	*2047*	...	...	...	...	...	...	...	...	...
Düren .... 802 d.	1215	1315	1315	1415	1515	1515	1615	...	1715	1815	...	1915	2015	...	...	*2115*	...	...	...	...	...	...	...	...	...
Aachen Hbf .... 802 910 a.	1245	1345	1345	1445	1545	1545	1645	...	1745	1845	...	1945	2045	...	...	*2145*	...	...	...	...	...	...	...	...	...

h – Also June 3.
k – Also Dec. 24, 31; not Dec. 26, May 1.
m – Not Dec. 24.
q – Also Dec. 26, May 1; not Dec. 24, 31.
r – Not June 3.
t – Ⓐ (not Dec. 24, 31, June 3).
w – Not Dec. 26, May 1.
z – Also Dec. 24, 31, June 3.
⊡ – Change trains at Gießen on ⚒r.
★ – *EC* **112**. (12) and ✕ Klagenfurt - Villach - Salzburg - München - Stuttgart - Siegen.

ABELLIO Rail NRW — ESSEN - HAGEN - SIEGEN — 808

km																									
		Ⓐe	Ⓐe	Ⓐe	Ⓐe	Ⓒz		⚒r		⚒r		⚒r			⚒r		Ⓐe		Ⓐe		Ⓐe				
0	**Essen** Hbf .... ⊡ d.	...	...	...	...	...	0634e	...	0734e	...	0834r	...	0934	and at	...	1634	...	1734	...	1834	...	1934	...	...	...
16	Bochum Hbf .. ⊡ d.	...	...	...	...	...	0647e	...	0747e	...	0847r	...	0947	the same	...	1647	...	1747	...	1847	...	1947	...	...	...
30	Witten Hbf .... ⊡ d.	...	...	...	...	...	0657e	...	0757e	...	0857r	...	0957	minutes	...	1657	...	1757	...	1857	...	1957	...	...	...
45	**Hagen** Hbf .... ⊡ a.	...	...	...	...	...	0709e	...	0809e	...	0909r	...	1009	past each	...	1709	...	1809	...	1909	...	2009	...	...	...
45	**Hagen** Hbf .... d.	...	...	0540	0610	0615	0715	0740	0815	0840	0915	0940	1015	hour until	1640	1715	1740	1815	1840	1915	1940	2015	2115	2215	2315
75	Altena (Westf) ... d.	...	...	0605	0636	0640	0740	0805	0840	0905	0940	1005	1040		1705	1740	1805	1840	1905	1940	2005	2040	2140	2240	2340
84	Werdohl .... d.	...	...	0614	0645	0649	0749	0814	0849	0914	0949	1014	1049		1714	1749	1814	1849	1914	1949	2014	2049	2149	2249	2349
106	Finnentrop .... d.	0502	0558	0631	0703	0707	0807	0831	0907	0931	1007	1031	1107		1731	1807	1831	1907	1931	2007	2031	2107	2207	2307	0007
119	Lennestadt ♥ ... d.	0515	0610	0643	0715	0718	0818	0843	0918	0943	1018	1043	1118		1743	1818	1843	1918	1943	2018	2043	2119	2219	2319	0019
141	Kreuztal .... d.	0537	0633	0706	0738	0739	0837	0906	0937	1006	1037	1106	1137		1806	1837	1906	1937	2006	2037	2106	2142	2242	2342	0042
152	**Siegen** .... a.	0550	0644	0719	0750	0749	0849	0919	0949	1019	1049	1119	1149		1819	1849	1919	1949	2020	2049	2119	2154	2254	2354	0054

	⚒r	Ⓐe		⚒r		Ⓐe		Ⓐe			⚒r			⚒r		Ⓐe		Ⓐe		Ⓐe				n
Siegen .... d.	...	0402	...	0504	...	0543	0612	0635	0712	...	0743	0812	and at	1543	1612	1643	1712	1743	1812	1843	1912	2011	2111	2211	2311
Kreuztal .... d.	...	0413	...	0515	...	0554	0622	0647	0722	...	0754	0822	the same	1554	1622	1654	1722	1754	1822	1854	1922	2022	2122	2222	2323
Lennestadt ♥ ..... d.	...	0436	...	0537	...	0617	0641	0710	0741	...	0817	0841	minutes	1617	1641	1717	1741	1817	1841	1917	1941	2045	2145	2245	2347
Finnentrop .... d.	0453	0453	...	0553	0553	0630	0653	0730	0754	...	0830	0853	past each	1630	1653	1730	1753	1830	1853	1930	1953	2058	2158	2258	2400
Werdohl .... d.	0510	0510	...	0610	0610	0647	0710	0747	0810	...	0847	0910	hour until	1647	1710	1747	1810	1847	1910	1947	2010	2115	2215	2315	...
Altena (Westf) ..... d.	0518	0518	...	0618	0618	0655	0718	0755	0818	...	0855	0918		1655	1718	1755	1818	1855	1918	1955	2018	2123	2223	2323	...
Hagen Hbf .... a.	0546	0546	...	0646	0646	0724	0746	0824	0846	...	0924	0946		1724	1746	1824	1846	1924	1946	2024	2046	2152	2252	2352	...
Hagen Hbf ..... ⊡ d.	...	...	...	0651e	...	...	0751e	...	0851r	...	...	0951		...	1751	...	1851	...	1951	...	...	...	...	...	...
Witten Hbf ...... ⊡ d.	...	...	...	0702e	...	...	0802e	...	0902r	...	...	1002		...	1802	...	1902	...	2002	...	...	...	...	...	...
Bochum Hbf ... ⊡ d.	...	...	...	0714e	...	...	0814e	...	0914r	...	...	1014		...	1814	...	1914	...	2014	...	...	...	...	...	...
Essen Hbf ..... ⊡ a.	...	...	...	0729e	...	...	0829e	...	0929r	...	...	1029		...	1829	...	1929	...	2029	...	...	...	...	...	...

Additional services Essen - Hagen and v.v.

	⚒r									
Essen Hbf .... d.	0508	0608	0708	and	1908	2008	2108	2208	2308	...
Bochum Hbf .... d.	0522	0622	0722	hourly	1922	2022	2122	2222	2322	...
Witten Hbf .... d.	0533	0633	0733	until	1933	2033	2133	2233	2333	...
Hagen Hbf .... a.	0546	0646	0746		1946	2046	2146	2246	2346	...

	⚒r								
Hagen Hbf .... d.	0517	0617	0717	and	1917	2017	2117	2217	2317
Witten Hbf .... d.	0531	0631	0731	hourly	1931	2031	2131	2231	2331
Bochum Hbf .... d.	0541	0641	0741	until	1941	2041	2141	2241	2341
Essen Hbf .... a.	0556	0656	0756		1956	2056	2156	2256	2356

e – Ⓐ (not Dec. 24, 31, June 3).
n – Not Dec. 24, 31.
r – ⚒ (not June 3).
z – Also Dec. 24, 31, June 3.
⊡ – See also panel below main table.
♥ – Lennestadt - Altenhundem.

S-Bahn 5 — PADERBORN - HAMELN - HANNOVER - HANNOVER FLUGHAFEN ✈ — 809

km																									
						Ⓑn	⑥k		⚒	†				⚒	†				⚒	†				⚒	†
0	**Paderborn** Hbf ..... 805 811 d.	...	...	...	...	0512e	...	...	0615	...	...	0715	...	0815	...	...	0915	...	1015	...	...	1115	...	1215	...
17	Altenbeken .... 805 811 d.	...	...	...	...	0524e	...	...	0627	...	...	0727	...	0827	...	...	0927	...	1027	...	...	1127	...	1227	...
56	Bad Pyrmont .... d.	...	...	0505r	...	0602e	0605	0635e	0702	0705	0735e	0802	...	0902	0905	...	1002	...	1102	1105	...	1202	...	1302	1305
75	Hameln .... a.	...	...	0519r	...	0616e	0619	0649e	0716	0719	0749e	0816	...	0916	0919	...	1016	...	1116	1119	...	1216	...	1316	1319
75	Hameln .... d.	0420e	0450e	0520	0550r	0620	0620	0650r	0720	0720	0750r	0820	0850r	0920	0920	0950r	1020	1050r	1120	1120	1150r	1220	1250r	1320	1320
133	**Hannover** Hbf .... a.	0503e	0533e	0603	0633r	0703	0703	0733r	0803	0803	0833r	0903	0933r	1003	1003	1033r	1103	1133r	1203	1203	1233r	1303	1333r	1403	1403
133	**Hannover** Hbf .... d.	0505	0535	0605	0635	0705	0705	0735	0805	0805	0835	0905	0935	1005	1005	1035	1105	1135	1205	1205	1235	1305	1335	1405	1405
148	**Hannover** Flughafen ✈ ...... a.	0523	0553	0623	0653	0723	0723	0753	0823	0823	0853	0923	0953	1023	1023	1053	1123	1153	1223	1223	1253	1323	1353	1423	1423

				⚒	†				⚒	†				Ⓐe	Ⓒz				Ⓐe	Ⓒz					A
Paderborn Hbf ...... 805 811 d.	...	1315	...	1415	...	...	1515	...	1615	...	...	1715	...	1815	...	...	1915	...	2015	...	...	2115	...	...	...
Altenbeken .... 805 811 d.	...	1327	...	1427	...	...	1527	...	1627	...	...	1727	...	1827	...	...	1927	...	2027	...	...	2127	...	...	...
Bad Pyrmont .... d.	1335e	1402	...	1502	1505	...	1602	1635e	1702	1705	...	1802	1835e	1902	1905	...	2002	...	2102	2105	...	2202	...	2305	2305
Hameln .... a.	1349e	1416	...	1516	1519	...	1616	1649e	1716	1719	...	1816	1849e	1916	1919	...	2016	...	2116	2119	...	2216	...	2319	2319
Hameln .... d.	1350r	1420	1450r	1520	1520	1550r	1620	1650r	1720	1720	1750e	1820	1850e	1920	1920	1950e	2020	2050e	2120	2120	...	2220	...	2320	2320
Hannover Hbf .... a.	1433r	1503	1533r	1603	1603	1633r	1703	1733r	1803	1803	1833e	1903	1933e	2003	2003	2033e	2103	2133e	2203	2203	...	2303	...	0003	0003
Hannover Hbf .... d.	1435	1505	1535	1605	1605	1635	1705	1735	1805	1805	1835	1905	1935	2005	2005	2035	2105	2135	2205	2205	2235	2305	2335	...	0005
Hannover Flughafen ✈ .... a.	1453	1523	1553	1623	1623	1653	1723	1753	1823	1823	1853	1923	1953	2023	2023	2053	2123	2153	2223	2223	2253	2323	2353	...	0023

		B	Ⓐe	⚒		⚒					†	⚒				†	⚒				†	⚒			
Hannover Flughafen ✈ .... d.	0006	0036	...	...	0506	0536	0536	0606	0636	0706	0736	0736	0806	0836	0906	0936	0936	1006	1036	1106	1136	1136	1206	1236	1306
Hannover Hbf .... a.	0023	0053	...	...	0523	0553	0553	0623	0653	0723	0753	0753	0823	0853	0923	0953	0953	1023	1053	1123	1153	1153	1223	1253	1323
Hannover Hbf .... d.	...	0100	0455	...	0525e	0555	...	0625r	0655	0725r	0755	0755	0825r	0855	0925r	0955	0955	1025r	1055	1125r	1155	1155	1225r	1255	1325r
Hameln .... a.	...	0144	0540	...	0610e	0640	...	0710r	0740	0810r	0840	0840	0910r	0940	1010r	1040	1040	1110r	1140	1210r	1240	1240	1310r	1340	1410r
Hameln .... d.	...	...	0544g	0544	0611e	0644	...	0711e	0744	...	0841	0844	...	0944	...	1041	1044	...	1144	...	1241	1244	1311e	1344	...
Bad Pyrmont .... d.	...	...	0600g	0600	0625e	0700	...	0725e	0800	...	0855	0900	...	1000	...	1055	1100	...	1200	...	1255	1300	1325e	1400	...
Altenbeken .... 805 811 d.	...	...	0633g	0633	...	0733	...	...	0833	...	...	0933	...	1033	...	...	1133	...	1233	...	...	1333	...	1433	...
Paderborn Hbf .... 805 811 a.	...	...	0646g	0646	...	0746	...	...	0846	...	...	0946	...	1046	...	...	1146	...	1246	...	...	1346	...	1446	...

	†	⚒				†	⚒				Ⓒz	Ⓐe				Ⓒz	Ⓐe								
Hannover Flughafen ✈ .... d.	1336	1336	1406	1436	1506	1536	1536	1606	1636	1706	1736	1736	1806	1836	1906	1936	1936	2006	2036	2106	2136	2206	2236	2306	2336
Hannover Hbf .... a.	1353	1353	1423	1453	1523	1553	1553	1623	1653	1723	1753	1753	1823	1853	1923	1953	1953	2023	2053	2123	2153	2223	2253	2323	2353
Hannover Hbf .... d.	1355	1355	1425r	1455	1525r	1555	1555	1625r	1655	1725r	1755	1755	1825e	1855	1925e	1955	1955	2025e	2055	2125e	2155	...	2255	...	2355
Hameln .... a.	1440	1440	1510r	1540	1610r	1640	1640	1710r	1740	1810r	1840	1840	1910e	1940	2010e	2040	2040	2110e	2140	2210e	2240	...	2340	...	0040
Hameln .... d.	1441	1444	...	1544	1611e	1641	1644e	...	1744	1811e	1841	1844	...	1944	...	2041	2044	...	2144	...	2241	...	2341	...	...
Bad Pyrmont .... d.	1455	1500	...	1600	1625e	1655	1700e	...	1800	1825e	1855	1900	...	2000	...	2055	2100	...	2200	...	2255	...	2355	...	...
Altenbeken .... 805 811 d.	...	1533	...	1633	...	...	1733e	...	1833	...	...	1933	...	2033	...	...	2133	...	2233	...	...	...	...	...	...
Paderborn Hbf .... 805 811 a.	...	1546	...	1646	...	...	1746e	...	1846	...	...	1946	...	2046	...	...	2146	...	2246	...	...	...	...	...	...

A – ⑤–⑦ (also Dec. 24, 31, Apr. 1, 5, May 12, 13, 24).
B – ①⑥⑦ (also Dec. 25, Jan. 1, Apr. 2, 6, May 13, 14, 25).
e – Ⓐ (not Dec. 24, 31).
g – ① (also Apr. 6, May 14, 25; not Apr. 5, May 24).
k – Also Dec. 24, 31.
n – Not Dec. 24, 31.
r – ⚒ only.
z – Also Dec. 24, 31.

810 HAMM and BAD BENTHEIM - HANNOVER - BERLIN and LEIPZIG

km	km	See note △	CNL 457	ICE 1741	ICE 949	ICE 649	IC 2031	RE 14201	ICE 841	ICE 841	IC 2147	RE 14003	IC 2241	ICE 541	ICE 541	ICE 876	IC 2033	RE 14203	EC 341	ICE 1092	IC 2145	ICE 843	ICE 853	ICE 696	IC 2145
			🅁	①–⑤	①m	①–⑤	①–⑥	⚒⊖	①g	①–⑥	①–⑤	⚒⊖	①–⑥	①–⑥		①–⑥			①–⑥	①–⑤	①–⑥		①–⑥	①g	①–⑥
			B 🍷	d R		d	e		🍴	e 🍴	d 🍷		e M 🍷	h 🍴	🍴	e D	🍷		A	d E ⚡🍴	e 🍷	🍴	e 🍴	L 🍴	e 🍷
		Koblenz Hbf **800** d.	...	...	...	...	...	...	...	...	...	...	...	...	...	...	...	...	...	...	...	...	...	...	...
		Bonn Hbf **800** d.	...	...	...	...	...	...	...	...	...	...	...	...	...	...	...	...	...	...	...	...	...	...	...
		Köln/Bonn Flughafen ✈ **800** d.	...	...	...	...	...	...	...	...	...	...	...	...	...	...	...	...	...	...	...	...	...	...	...
		Köln Hbf **800** d.	2228	...	0149	...	...	...	...	...	...	...	...	0429	...	...	...	...	...	...	0510	0529	0545	...	...
		Wuppertal Hbf **800** d.	2314	...	|	...	...	...	...	...	...	...	...	|	...	...	...	...	...	...	0543	|	0617	...	...
		Hagen Hbf **800** d.	|	...	|	...	...	...	...	...	...	...	...	|	...	...	...	...	...	...	0601	|	0634	...	...
		Düsseldorf Hbf **800 802** d.	2202	...	0213	...	...	...	...	...	...	...	...	0453	...	...	...	...	...	...	|	0553	|	...	...
		Dortmund Hbf **800 802** d.	2356	...	0311	...	...	...	...	...	...	...	...	0547	...	...	...	...	...	...	0628	0648	|	...	...
0		**Hamm** (Westf) **802** d.	0014	...	0330	...	...	...	...	...	...	...	...	0604	...	...	...	...	...	...	0645	0711	0711	...	...
50		Gütersloh Hbf **802** d.	|	...	0351	...	...	...	...	...	...	...	...	0629	...	...	...	...	...	...	0705	|	|	...	...
67		**Bielefeld** Hbf **802** d.	0043	...	0403	...	...	0424	0537	...	...	...	...	0640	...	...	...	0624	...	...	0717	0737	0737	...	...
81		Herford **802** d.	|	...	0413	...	...	0433	|	...	...	...	...	|	...	...	...	0633	...	...	0727	|	|	...	...
		Schiphol ✈ **22** ⊡ d.	|	...	|	...	...	|	|	...	...	...	...	|	...	...	...	|	...	...	|	|	|	...	...
		Bad Bentheim 🛃 **811** d.	|	...	|	...	...	|	|	...	...	...	...	|	...	...	...	|	...	...	|	|	|	...	...
		Rheine **811** d.	|	...	|	...	...	|	|	...	...	...	...	|	...	...	...	|	...	...	|	|	|	...	...
		Osnabrück Hbf **811** d.	|	...	|	...	...	|	|	...	...	0515	0604	|	...	...	...	|	...	...	|	|	|	...	...
		Bünde (Westf) **811** d.	|	...	|	...	...	|	|	...	...	0539	0626	|	...	...	...	|	...	...	|	|	|	...	...
91		Löhne (Westf) **802** d.	|	...	|	...	...	0440	|	...	...	0550	|	|	...	...	...	0640	...	...	|	|	|	...	...
97		Bad Oeynhausen **802** d.	|	...	|	...	...	0445	|	...	...	0555	0639	|	...	...	...	0645	...	...	0737	|	|	...	...
112		Minden (Westf) **802** d.	|	...	0430	...	...	0507t	0600	...	...	0607	0649	|	...	...	...	0707t	...	...	0749	|	|	...	...
		Basel SBB **912** d.	|	...	|	...	...	|	|	...	...	|	|	|	...	...	...	|	...	...	|	|	|	...	...
		Stuttgart Hbf **930** d.	|	...	|	...	...	|	|	...	...	|	|	|	...	...	...	|	...	...	|	|	|	...	...
		Frankfurt (Main) Hbf **900** d.	|	...	|	...	...	|	|	...	...	|	|	|	...	0510g	...	|	...	0614	|	|	|	...	...
		Oldenburg (Oldb) **813** d.	|	...	|	...	...	|	|	...	...	|	|	|	...	|	0535e	|	...	|	|	|	|	...	...
		Bremen Hbf **813** d.	|	...	|	...	...	|	|	...	...	|	|	|	...	|	0609	|	...	|	|	|	|	...	...
177		**Hannover** Hbf a.	|	...	0458	...	...	0550	0628	...	...	0650	0718	0728	...	|	0714	0750	...	|	0818	0828	0828	...	←
177		**Hannover** Hbf △ d.	|	...	0501	0527	0536	0555	0631	0631	0636	0655	0721	0731	0731	|	0736	0755	...	|	→	0831	0831	...	0836
212		Peine △ d.	|	...	|	|	|	0624	|	|	|	0724	|	|	|	|	|	0824	...	|	...	|	|	...	|
238	0	**Braunschweig** Hbf △ ‡ d.	|	...	|	0601z	0610	0641	|	|	0711	0741	|	|	|	0800	0810	0841	...	|	...	|	|	0900	0911
274		Helmstedt △ ‡ d.	|	...	|	|	0632	*0720*a	|	|	|	...	|	|	|	|	0832	...	...	|	...	|	|	|	|
322		**Magdeburg** Hbf △ ‡ a.	|	...	|	|	0657	...	|	|	0755	...	|	|	|	|	0857	...	...	|	...	|	|	|	0955
322		**Magdeburg** Hbf ‡ d.	|	0626	|	|	0703	...	|	|	0759	...	|	|	|	|	0903	...	...	|	...	|	|	|	0959
372		Köthen ‡ d.	|	0655	|	|	0732	...	|	|	0830	...	|	|	|	|	0932	...	...	|	...	|	|	|	1030
408		**Halle (Saale)** Hbf ‡ d.	|	0718	|	|	0755	...	|	|	0853	...	|	|	|	|	0955	...	...	|	...	|	|	|	1053
426		Leipzig/Halle Flughafen ✈ ‡ a.	|	0728	|	|	0805	...	|	|	0903	...	|	|	|	|	1005	...	...	|	...	|	|	|	1103
446		**Leipzig** Hbf ‡ a.	|	0743	|	|	0820	...	|	|	0920	...	|	|	|	|	1020	...	...	|	...	|	|	|	1120
	32	Wolfsburg d.	|	...	0534	0620	...	...	0705	0705	...	...	0755	|	|	0818	...	...	...	|	...	0905	0905	0918	...
	107	Stendal **838** d.	|	...	0603	0647	...	...	0733	0733	...	...	0826	|	|	|	...	...	0847	|	...	|	|	|	...
	199	**Berlin** Spandau **838** a.	|	...	0641	0721	...	...	0806	0806	...	...	0903	0854	0854	0911	...	...	0923	0937	...	0956	0956	1009	...
	215	**Berlin** Hbf **838** a.	0421	...	0655	0736	...	...	0820	0820	...	...	0920	0908	0908	0925	...	...	0937	0951	...	1011	1011	1024	...
	220	**Berlin** Ostbahnhof **838** a.	0430	...	0706	0748	...	...	0831	0831	...	...	0930	0919	0919	0936	...	...	0948j	1002	...	1022	1022	1036	...

See note △	RE 14005	IC 2243	ICE 543	ICE 553	ICE 874	IC 2035	RE 14205	IC 2143	ICE 845	ICE 855	ICE 694	IC 2143	RE 14007	IC 141	ICE 545	ICE 555	ICE 872	IC 2037	RE 14207	IC 2141	ICE 847	ICE 857	ICE 692	IC 2141	RE 14009
		¶		①–⑥				①–⑥				①–⑥													
		🍷	🍴	e 🍴	C 🍴	🍷		e 🍷	🍴	T 🍴	🍴	e 🍷		🍷	X 🍴	🍴	🍴	N 🍷		🍷	🍴	🍴	🍴	🍷	
Koblenz Hbf **800** d.	...	...	...	0547	...	...	...	...	...	0643y	...	...	...	...	...	...	...	...	...	...	...	...	...	...	...
Bonn Hbf **800** d.	...	...	...	0622	...	...	...	...	...	0722y	...	...	...	...	...	0825e	...	...	...	...	...	...	...	...	...
Köln/Bonn Flughafen ✈ **800** d.	...	...	...	|	...	...	...	...	0712	|	...	...	...	...	...	|	...	...	...	...	...	...	...	...	...
Köln Hbf **800** d.	...	...	0626	0648	...	...	...	0710	|	0748	...	...	...	...	0826	0848	...	...	...	0913	...	0948	...	...	...
Wuppertal Hbf **800** d.	...	...	|	0716	...	...	...	0743	|	0816	...	...	...	...	|	0916	...	...	...	0943	...	1016	...	...	...
Hagen Hbf **800** d.	...	...	|	0734	...	...	...	0801	|	0834	...	...	...	...	|	0934	...	...	...	1001	...	1034	...	...	...
Düsseldorf Hbf **800 802** d.	...	...	0653	|	...	...	...	|	0753	|	...	...	...	...	0853	|	...	...	...	|	0953	|	...	...	...
Dortmund Hbf **800 802** d.	...	...	0748	|	...	...	...	0828	0848	|	...	...	...	...	0948	|	...	...	...	1028	1048	|	...	...	...
Hamm (Westf) **802** d.	...	...	0811	0811	...	...	...	0845	0911	0911	...	...	...	...	1011	1011	...	...	...	1045	1111	1111	...	...	...
Gütersloh Hbf **802** d.	...	...	|	|	...	...	...	0905	|	|	...	...	...	...	|	|	...	...	...	1105	|	|	...	...	...
Bielefeld Hbf **802** d.	...	...	0838	0838	...	...	0824	0917	0937	0937	...	...	...	...	1038	1038	...	...	1024	1117	1137	1137	...	...	...
Herford **802** d.	...	...	|	|	...	...	0833	0927	|	|	...	...	...	...	|	|	...	...	1033	1127	|	|	...	...	...
Schiphol ✈ **22** ⊡ d.	...	...	|	|	...	...	|	|	|	|	...	...	...	0649v	|	|	...	...	|	|	|	|	...	...	...
Bad Bentheim 🛃 **811** d.	*0557*a	0721e	|	|	...	...	|	|	|	|	...	...	*0757*r	0928v	|	|	...	...	|	|	|	|	...	...	*0957*
Rheine **811** d.	0638	0735e	|	|	...	...	|	|	|	|	...	...	0838	0942v	|	|	...	...	|	|	|	|	...	...	1038
Osnabrück Hbf **811** d.	0716	0804	|	|	...	...	|	|	|	|	...	...	0916	1008v	|	|	...	...	|	|	|	|	...	...	1116
Bünde (Westf) **811** d.	0738	0826	|	|	...	...	|	|	|	|	...	...	0938	|	|	|	...	...	|	|	|	|	...	...	1138
Löhne (Westf) **802** d.	0750	|	|	|	...	...	0840	|	|	|	...	...	0950	|	|	|	...	...	1040	|	|	|	...	...	1150
Bad Oeynhausen **802** d.	0755	0839	|	|	...	...	0845	0937	|	|	...	...	0955	1039v	|	|	...	...	1045	1137	|	|	...	...	1155
Minden (Westf) **802** d.	0807	0849	|	|	...	...	0907t	0949	|	|	...	...	1007	1049v	|	|	...	...	1107t	1149	|	|	...	...	1207
Basel SBB **912** d.	|	|	|	|	...	...	|	|	|	|	...	...	|	|	|	|	0608	...	|	|	|	|	...	...	|
Stuttgart Hbf **930** d.	|	|	|	|	...	...	|	|	|	|	0651	...	|	|	|	|	|	...	|	|	|	|	0851	...	|
Frankfurt (Main) Hbf **900** d.	|	|	|	|	0713	...	|	|	|	|	0813	...	|	|	|	|	0913	...	|	|	|	|	1013	...	|
Oldenburg (Oldb) **813** d.	|	|	|	|	|	0735	|	|	|	|	|	...	|	|	|	|	|	0935	|	|	|	|	|	...	|
Bremen Hbf **813** d.	|	|	|	|	|	0809	|	|	|	|	|	...	|	|	|	|	|	1009	|	|	|	|	|	...	|
Hannover Hbf a.	0850	0918	0928	0928	|	0914	0950	1018	1028	1028	|	←	1050	1118v	1128	1128	|	1114	1150	1218	1228	1228	|	←	1250
Hannover Hbf △ d.	0855	0921	0931	0931	|	0936	0955	→	1031	1031	|	1036	1055	1121	1131	1131	|	1136	1155	→	1231	1231	|	1236	1255
Peine △ d.	0924	|	|	|	|	|	1024	...	|	|	|	|	1124	|	|	|	|	|	1224	...	|	|	|	|	1324
Braunschweig Hbf △ ‡ d.	0941	|	|	|	1000	1010	1041	...	|	|	1100	1111	1141	|	|	|	1200	1210	1241	...	|	|	1300	1311	1341
Helmstedt △ ‡ d.	...	|	|	|	|	1032	...	...	|	|	|	|	...	|	|	|	|	1232	...	...	|	|	|	|	▬
Magdeburg Hbf △ ‡ a.	...	|	|	|	|	1057	...	...	|	|	|	1155	...	|	|	|	|	1257	...	...	|	|	|	1355	...
Magdeburg Hbf ‡ d.	...	|	|	|	|	1103	...	...	|	|	|	1159	...	|	|	|	|	1303	...	...	|	|	|	1359	...
Köthen ‡ d.	...	|	|	|	|	1132	...	...	|	|	|	1230	...	|	|	|	|	1332	...	...	|	|	|	1430	...
Halle (Saale) Hbf ‡ d.	...	|	|	|	|	1155	...	...	|	|	|	1253	...	|	|	|	|	1355	...	...	|	|	|	1453	*IC*
Leipzig/Halle Flughafen ✈ ‡ a.	...	|	|	|	|	1205	...	...	|	|	|	1303	...	|	|	|	|	1405	...	...	|	|	|	1503	**1931**
Leipzig Hbf ‡ a.	...	|	|	|	|	1220	...	...	|	|	|	1320	...	|	|	|	|	1420	...	...	|	|	|	1520	⑤f
Wolfsburg d.	...	0955	|	|	1018	...	...	...	1105	1105	|	...	...	1155	|	|	1218	...	...	...	1305	1305	|	...	U
Stendal **838** d.	...	1026	|	|	|	...	...	...	|	|	|	...	...	1226	|	|	|	...	...	...	|	|	|	...	1406
Berlin Spandau **838** a.	...	1103	1053	1053	1110	...	...	...	1156	1156	1206	...	...	1303	1253	1253	1310	...	...	...	1356	1356	1406	...	1442
Berlin Hbf **838** a.	...	1120	1108	1108	1125	...	...	...	1211	1211	1221	...	...	1320	1308	1308	1325	...	...	...	1411	1411	1421	...	1459
Berlin Ostbahnhof **838** a.	...	1131	1119	1119	1136	...	...	...	1222	1222	1232	...	...	1331	1319	1319	1336	...	...	...	1422	1422	1432	...	...

A – ①–⑥ (Not Dec. 25, 26, 31, Jan. 1, Apr. 3, 5, May 24). WAWEL – (12) Hamburg - Uelzen - Berlin - Cottbus - Forst 🛃 - Wrocław - Kraków. Arrives Berlin Hbf 0933 from May 3.
B – PHOENIX – 🛏 1, 2 cl., ▬ 2 cl. and (2) Amsterdam - Köln - Berlin - Dresden - Praha (Table **28**); 🛏 1, 2 cl., ▬ 2 cl. and (2) (*EN* **447** – JAN KIEPURA) Amsterdam - Köln - Berlin - Warszawa (Table **24**); conveys 🛏 1, 2 cl. Amsterdam - Moskva (Table **24**). For overnight journeys only.
C – (12) and 🍴 (Basel Bad. Bf ①**g** -) Karlsruhe - Mannheim - Frankfurt - Berlin.
D – (12) and 🍴 (Frankfurt ①**g** -) Kassel - Berlin.
E – From Darmstadt Hbf (d. 0543).
L – From Kassel (Table **900**).
M – From Münster (Westf) Hbf (d. 0538).
N – From Norddeich Mole (Table **813**).
R – To Dresden (Table **842**).
T – From Trier (Table **915**) on Ⓐ**y**.
U – From Uelzen (Table **841**).
X – From Aachen Hbf (d. 0740) and Düren (d. 0758) on ①–⑥**e**.

a – Ⓐ (not Dec. 24, 31).
d – Not Dec. 24, 25, 31, Jan. 1, Apr. 2, 5, May 24.
e – ①–⑥ (not Dec. 25, 26, Jan. 1, Apr. 3, 5, May 24).
f – Also Dec. 23, 30, Apr. 1, May 12; not Dec. 25, Jan. 1, Apr. 2, May 14.
g – ① (also Apr. 6, May 25; not Apr. 5, May 24).
h – Not Dec. 25, 26, Jan. 1, Apr. 2, 3, 5, May 24.
j – Until May 1.
m – Also Apr. 6, May 25; not Dec. 21, 28, Apr. 5, May 24.
r – ⚒ only.
t – Arrives 10 minutes earlier.
v – Not Dec. 25, Jan. 1.
y – Ⓐ (not Dec. 24, 31, June 3).
z – Until Apr. 30.

¶ – Train number **2343** on ⑦ (also Dec. 25, 26, Jan. 1, Apr. 3, 5, May 24).
⊖ – Runs daily Hannover - Braunschweig.
⚡ – *ICE SPRINTER*. 🅁 and supplement payable.
⊡ – Schiphol timings are subject to alteration on Apr. 30.
‡ – See panel on page 379 for additional local services.
△ – Services between Hannover and Magdeburg are subject to alteration from May 1. See Engineering Work Summary on page 361.

HAMM and BAD BENTHEIM - HANNOVER - BERLIN and LEIPZIG 810

	IC	ICE	ICE	ICE	IC	RE	IC	IC	ICE	ICE	ICE	IC	RE	IC	IC	ICE	ICE	ICE	ICE	IC	IC	IC	RE	IC	ICE
See note △	143	547	557	278	2039	14209	2010	2049	849	859	690	2049	14011	145	245	1049	549	559	276	2131	2131	2239	14211	2047	941
							⑤f	⑤–⑦						Ⓑq	⑥k	⑦d	①–⑥			H	G	R		Ⓑq	
	🍷	✕	♣✕	A✕	🍷		T🍷	c🍷	✕	✕	✕	🍷		S🍷	🍷	♥✕	e✕	✕	A✕	L🍷	L🍷			🍷	✕
Koblenz Hbf **800** d.	...	...	0943h	...	...	...	0943	...	...	...	...	...	...	...	...	...	...	...	...	...	...	...	...	...	...
Bonn Hbf **800** d.	...	...	1022h	...	...	...	1022	...	...	...	...	...	...	...	...	...	...	1223e	...	...	...	...	...	...	...
Köln/Bonn Flughafen ✈ **800** d.	...	1012a	|	...	...	...	|	...	...	...	...	...	...	...	...	...	1212	|	...	...	...	...	...	...	1312w
Köln Hbf **800** d.	...	|	1048	...	...	...	1045	1113	...	1148	...	...	...	...	...	...	|	1248	...	...	...	...	...	1313	|
Wuppertal Hbf **800** d.	...	|	1116	...	...	...	|	1143	...	1216	...	...	...	...	...	...	|	1316	...	...	...	...	...	1343	|
Hagen Hbf **800** d.	...	|	1134	...	...	...	|	1201	...	1234	...	...	...	...	...	...	|	1334	...	...	...	...	...	1401	|
Düsseldorf Hbf **800 802** d.	...	1053	|	...	...	...	1117	|	1153	|	...	...	...	...	...	1230	1253	|	...	...	...	...	...	|	1353
Dortmund Hbf **800 802** d.	...	1148	|	...	...	...	1211	1228	1248	|	...	...	...	...	...	1348	1348	|	...	...	...	...	...	1428	1448
Hamm (Westf) **802** d.	...	1211	1211	...	...	...	1235	1245	1311	1311	...	...	...	...	...	1411	1411	1411	...	...	...	...	...	1445	1511
Gütersloh Hbf **802** d.	...	|	|	...	...	...	1255	1305	|	|	...	...	...	...	...	|	|	|	...	...	...	...	...	1505	|
Bielefeld Hbf **802** d.	...	1238	1238	...	...	1224	1305	1317	1337	1337	...	...	...	...	...	1438	1438	1438	...	...	...	...	1424	1517	1537
Herford **802** d.	...	|	|	...	...	1233	1315	1327	|	|	...	...	...	...	...	|	|	|	...	...	...	...	1433	1527	|
Schiphol ✈ **22** ⊡ d.	0849	|	|	...	...	|	|	|	|	|	...	...	...	1049	1049	|	|	|	...	...	...	...	|	|	|
Bad Bentheim 🏛 **811** d.	1128	|	|	...	...	|	|	|	|	|	...	...	*1157*	1328	1328	|	|	|	...	...	...	...	|	|	|
Rheine **811** d.	1142	|	|	...	...	|	|	|	|	|	...	...	1238	1342	1342	|	|	|	...	...	...	...	|	|	|
Osnabrück Hbf **811** d.	1208	|	|	...	...	|	|	|	|	|	...	...	1316	1408	1408	|	|	|	...	...	...	...	|	|	|
Bünde (Westf) **811** d.	1229	|	|	...	...	|	|	|	|	|	...	...	1338	|	|	|	|	|	...	...	...	...	|	|	|
Löhne (Westf) **802** d.	|	|	|	...	...	1240	|	|	|	|	...	...	1350	|	|	|	|	|	...	...	...	...	1440	|	|
Bad Oeynhausen **802** d.	|	|	|	...	...	1245	|	1337	|	|	...	...	1355	1439	1439	|	|	|	...	...	...	...	1445	1537	|
Minden (Westf) **802** d.	1249	|	|	...	...	1307t	|	1349	|	|	...	...	1407	1449	1449	|	|	|	...	...	...	...	1507t	1549	|
Basel SBB **912** d.	|	|	|	0812	...	|	|	|	|	|	...	...	|	|	|	|	|	|	1012	...	...	...	|	|	|
Stuttgart Hbf **930** d.	|	|	|	|	...	|	|	|	|	|	1051	...	|	|	|	|	|	|	|	...	...	...	|	|	|
Frankfurt (Main) Hbf **900** d.	|	|	|	1113	...	|	|	|	|	|	1213	...	|	|	|	|	|	|	1313	...	...	...	|	|	|
Oldenburg (Oldb) **813** d.	|	|	|	|	1135	|	|	|	|	|	|	...	|	|	|	|	|	|	|	1335	1335	...	|	|	|
Bremen Hbf **813** d.	|	|	|	|	1209	|	|	|	|	|	|	...	|	|	|	|	|	|	|	1409	1409	...	|	|	|
Hannover Hbf a.	1318	1328	1328	|	1314	1350	1400	1418	1428	1428	|	←	1450	1518	1518	1528	1528	1528	|	1514	1514	...	1550	1618	1628
Hannover Hbf △ d.	1321	1331	1331	|	1336	1355	1403	→	1431	1431	|	1436	1455	1521	1521	1531	1531	1531	|	1517	1536	...	1555	→	1631
Peine △ d.	|	|	|	|	|	1424	|	...	|	|	|	|	1524	|	|	|	|	|	|	|	|	...	1624	...	|
Braunschweig Hbf △ ‡ d.	|	|	|	1400	1410	1441	|	...	|	|	1500	1511	1541	|	|	|	|	|	1600	|	1610	...	1641	...	|
Helmstedt △ ‡ d.	|	|	|	|	1432	...	|	...	|	|	|	|	...	|	|	|	|	|	|	|	1632	...	...	...	|
Magdeburg Hbf △ ‡ a.	|	|	|	|	1457	...	|	...	|	|	|	1555	...	|	|	|	|	|	|	|	1657	...	...	...	|
Magdeburg Hbf ‡ d.	|	|	|	|	1503	...	|	...	|	|	|	1559	...	|	|	|	|	|	|	|	1700	1703	...	...	|
Köthen ‡ d.	|	|	|	|	1532	...	|	...	|	|	|	1630	...	|	|	|	|	|	|	|	|	1732	...	...	|
Halle (Saale) Hbf ‡ d.	|	|	|	|	1555	...	|	...	|	|	|	1653	...	|	|	|	|	|	|	|	|	1755	...	...	|
Leipzig/Halle Flughafen ✈ ‡ a.	|	|	|	|	1605	...	|	...	|	|	|	1703	...	|	|	|	|	|	|	|	|	1805	...	...	|
Leipzig Hbf ‡ a.	|	|	|	|	1620	...	|	...	|	|	|	1720	...	|	|	|	|	|	|	|	|	1820	...	...	|
Wolfsburg d.	1355	|	|	1418	...	...	1438	...	1505	1505	|	...	...	1555	1555	|	|	|	1618	|	|	...	...	...	1705
Stendal **838** d.	1426	|	|	|	...	...	|	...	|	|	|	...	...	1626	1626	|	|	|	|	1642	|	...	...	...	|
Berlin Spandau **838** a.	1503	1453	1453	1511	...	...	1541	...	1556	1556	1606	...	...	1701	1701	1654	1654	1654	1711	1721	|	...	...	...	1756
Berlin Hbf **838** a.	1520	1508	1508	1525	...	...	1550	...	1611	1611	1621	...	...	1712	1720	1708	1708	1708	1725	1738	1827	...	...	...	1811
Berlin Ostbahnhof **838** a.	1531	1519	1519	1536	...	...	...	...	1622	1622	1633	...	...	...	1730	1719	1719	1719	1736	1748	1838	...	...	...	1822

	ICE	ICE	IC	RE	IC	ICE	ICE	ICE	IC	RE	IC	IC	IC	ICE	ICE	ICE	IC	RE	IC	ICE	ICE	ICE	IC	RE	ICE
See note △	951	598	2047	14013	147	641	651	374	2133	14213	1920	1916	2045	943	953	596	2045	14015	149	643	653	370	2135	14215	1090
			Ⓑq								⑦w	⑤f	Ⓑb		Ⓑq		Ⓑb					Ⓑq			Ⓑr
	✕	✕	🍷		🍷	✕	✕	B✕	🍷		F	T🍷	🍷	✕	✕	✕	🍷		🍷	✕	✕	A✕	N🍷		✕⚡
Koblenz Hbf **800** d.	...	...	...	...	...	...	...	...	...	...	1343	1343	...	...	...	...	...	...	...	...	...	...	...	...	...
Bonn Hbf **800** d.	...	...	...	...	...	...	1425	...	...	...	1422	1422	...	...	...	...	...	...	...	...	...	...	...	...	...
Köln/Bonn Flughafen ✈ **800** d.	...	...	...	...	...	...	|	...	...	...	|	|	...	...	...	...	...	...	...	1612	...	...	...	...	...
Köln Hbf **800** d.	1348	...	...	...	...	...	1448	...	...	...	1445	1445	1513	...	1548	...	...	...	...	|	1648	...	...	...	...
Wuppertal Hbf **800** d.	1416	...	...	...	...	...	1516	...	...	...	|	|	1543	...	1616	...	...	...	...	|	1716	...	...	...	...
Hagen Hbf **800** d.	1434	...	...	...	...	...	1534	...	...	...	|	|	1601	...	1634	...	...	...	...	|	1734	...	...	...	...
Düsseldorf Hbf **800 802** d.	|	...	...	...	...	1453	|	...	...	...	1518	1518	|	1553	|	...	...	...	...	1653	|	...	...	...	...
Dortmund Hbf **800 802** d.	|	...	...	...	...	1548	|	...	...	...	1611	1611	1628	1648	|	...	...	...	...	1748	|	...	...	...	...
Hamm (Westf) **802** d.	1511	...	...	...	...	1611	1611	...	...	...	1635	1635	1645	1711	1711	...	...	...	...	1811	1811	...	...	...	...
Gütersloh Hbf **802** d.	|	...	...	...	...	|	|	...	...	...	1655	1655	1705	|	|	...	...	...	...	|	|	...	...	...	...
Bielefeld Hbf **802** d.	1537	...	...	...	...	1638	1638	...	...	1624	1705	1705	1717	1737	1737	...	...	...	...	1838	1838	...	...	1824	...
Herford **802** d.	|	...	...	...	...	|	|	...	...	1633	1715	1715	1727	|	|	...	...	...	...	|	|	...	...	1833	...
Schiphol ✈ **22** ⊡ d.	|	...	...	...	1249	|	|	...	...	|	|	|	|	|	|	...	...	...	1449	|	|	...	...	|	...
Bad Bentheim 🏛 **811** d.	|	...	...	*1357*	1528	|	|	...	...	|	|	|	|	|	|	...	...	*1557*	1728	|	|	...	...	|	...
Rheine **811** d.	|	...	...	1438	1542	|	|	...	...	|	|	|	|	|	|	...	...	1638	1742	|	|	...	...	|	...
Osnabrück Hbf **811** d.	|	...	...	1516	1608	|	|	...	...	|	|	|	|	|	|	...	...	1716	1808	|	|	...	...	|	...
Bünde (Westf) **811** d.	|	...	...	1538	1629	|	|	...	...	|	|	|	|	|	|	...	...	1738	|	|	|	...	...	|	...
Löhne (Westf) **802** d.	|	...	...	1550	|	|	|	...	...	1640	|	|	|	|	|	...	...	1750	|	|	|	...	...	1840	...
Bad Oeynhausen **802** d.	|	...	...	1555	|	|	|	...	...	1645	|	|	1737	|	|	...	...	1755	1839	|	|	...	...	1845	...
Minden (Westf) **802** d.	|	...	...	1607	1649	|	|	...	...	1707t	|	|	1749	|	|	...	...	1807	1849	|	|	...	...	1907t	...
Basel SBB **912** d.	|	...	...	|	|	|	|	1212	...	|	|	|	|	|	|	...	...	|	|	|	|	1412	...	|	...
Stuttgart Hbf **930** d.	|	1251	...	|	|	|	|	|	...	|	|	|	|	|	|	1451	...	|	|	|	|	|	...	|	1651
Frankfurt (Main) Hbf **900** d.	|	1413	...	|	|	|	|	1513	...	|	|	|	|	|	|	1613	...	|	|	|	|	1713	...	|	1813
Oldenburg (Oldb) **813** d.	|	|	...	|	|	|	|	|	1535	|	|	|	|	|	|	|	...	|	|	|	|	|	1735	|	|
Bremen Hbf **813** d.	|	|	...	|	|	|	|	|	1609	|	|	|	|	|	|	|	...	|	|	|	|	|	1809	|	|
Hannover Hbf a.	1628	|	←	1650	1718	1728	1728	|	1714	1750	1759	1800	1818	1828	1828	|	←	1850	1918	1928	1928	|	1914	1950	|
Hannover Hbf △ d.	1631	|	1636	1655	1721	1731	1731	|	1736	1755	1802	1803	→	1831	1831	|	1836	1855	1921	1931	1931	|	1936	1955	|
Peine △ d.	|	|	|	1724	|	|	|	|	|	1824	|	|	...	|	|	|	|	1924	|	|	|	|	|	2024	|
Braunschweig Hbf △ ‡ d.	|	1700	1711	1741	|	|	|	1800	1810	1841	|	|	...	|	|	1900	1911	1941	|	|	|	2000	2010	2041	|
Helmstedt △ ‡ d.	|	|	|	...	|	|	|	|	1832	...	|	|	...	|	|	|	|	...	|	|	|	|	2032	...	|
Magdeburg Hbf △ ‡ a.	|	|	1755	...	|	|	|	|	1857	...	|	|	...	|	|	|	1955	...	|	|	|	|	2057	...	|
Magdeburg Hbf ‡ d.	|	|	1759	...	|	|	|	|	1903	...	|	|	...	|	|	|	1959	...	|	|	|	|	2103	...	|
Köthen ‡ d.	|	|	1830	...	|	|	|	|	1932	...	|	|	...	|	|	|	2030	...	|	|	|	|	2132	...	|
Halle (Saale) Hbf ‡ d.	|	|	1853	...	|	|	|	|	1955	...	|	|	...	|	|	|	2055	...	|	|	|	|	2155	...	|
Leipzig/Halle Flughafen ✈ ‡ a.	|	|	1903	...	|	|	|	|	2005	...	|	|	...	|	|	|	2103	...	|	|	|	|	2205	...	|
Leipzig Hbf ‡ a.	|	|	1920	...	|	|	|	|	2020	...	|	|	...	|	|	|	2120	...	|	|	|	|	2219	...	|
Wolfsburg d.	1705	|	...	...	1755	|	|	1818	...	...	1837	1837	...	1905	1905	|	...	...	1955	|	|	2018	...	...	|
Stendal **838** d.	|	|	...	...	1826	|	|	|	...	...	|	|	...	|	|	|	...	...	2026	|	|	|	...	...	|
Berlin Spandau **838** a.	1756	1806	...	...	1903	1854	1854	1911	...	...	1941	1941	...	1957	1957	2006	...	...	2103	2053	2053	2111	...	...	2137
Berlin Hbf **838** a.	1811	1821	...	...	1920	1908	1908	1925	...	...	1951	1951	...	2011	2011	2021	...	...	2120	2108	2108	2126	...	...	2148
Berlin Ostbahnhof **838** a.	1822	1832	...	...	1931	1919	1919	1936	...	...	...	...	...	2021	2021	2032	...	...	2130	2120	2120	2137	...	...	...

A – From Interlaken via Bern (Table **560**).
B – From Bern (Table **560**).
F – From Frankfurt (Table **912**).
G – Until Apr. 30.
H – From May 1.
L – OSTFRIESLAND – 🚃12 and 🍷 Emden - Berlin (- Cottbus Ⓑq).
N – From Norddeich Mole on dates in Table **813**.
R – Ⓑ (also June 12; daily Dec. 13 - Mar. 26). From Warnemünde (via Rostock and Schwerin) on ⑤⑦ from Mar. 28 (also June 12). See also Tables **830**, **837** and **841**.
S – To Szczecin (Table **845**).
T – From Stuttgart via Mainz (Table **912**).

a – ①–⑤ (not Dec. 25, Jan. 1, Apr. 2, 5, May 24).
b – Not Dec. 24, 25, 31, Apr. 2, 4, May 13, 23.
c – Also Dec. 23, 24, 30, 31, Apr. 1, 5, May 24.
d – Also Dec. 25, 26, Jan. 1, Apr. 3, 5, May 24.
e – ①–⑥ (not Dec. 25, 26, Jan. 1, Apr. 3, 5, May 24).
f – Also Dec. 23, 30, Apr. 1, May 12, June 2; not Dec. 25, Jan. 1, Apr. 2, May 14, June 4.
h – ⑥ (also Dec. 24, 31, Apr. 2, May 13, June 3; not Dec. 26, Apr. 3, May 15, June 5).
j – Not Dec. 24, 31, Jan. 6.
k – Also Dec. 24, 25, 31, Apr. 2, 4, May 23.
n – Not Dec. 24, 31.
q – Not Dec. 24, 25, 31, Apr. 2, 4, May 23.
r – Not Dec. 24, 25, 31, Jan. 1, Apr. 2, 4, May 23.
t – Arrives 10 minutes earlier.
w – ⑦ (also Apr. 5, May 24; not Apr. 4, May 23).
z – Also Dec. 24, 25, 31, Jan. 1, Apr. 2, 5, May 24.

⊡ – Schiphol timings are subject to alteration on Apr. 30.
♥ – From Mönchengladbach Hbf (d. 1205).
♣ – From Trier (Table **915**) on ⑥h.
⚡ – *ICE* ***SPRINTER***. 🄡 and supplement payable.

❖ – The 1617 and 1817 from Braunschweig do not run on Dec. 24, 31.
△ – Services between Hannover and Magdeburg are subject to alteration from May 1. See Engineering Work Summary on page 361.
‡ – See panel below main table for additional *RE* / *RB* services.

	Ⓐ		❖	Ⓐn	n	Ⓐn
Braunschweig Hbf d.	0617	0717	then hourly on Ⓐ,	2017	2117	2217
Helmstedt d.	0645	0745	every **two** hours	2045	2145	2245
Magdeburg Hbf a.	0729	0829	on Ⓒ until	2129	2229	2329

	Ⓐj	Ⓐj	a n	⑥⑦z			
Magdeburg Hbf d.	0407	0504	0555	0607	0707	and	2207
Köthen d.	0447	0545	0635	0647	0747	hourly	2247
Halle (Saale) Hbf a.	0515	0615	0703	0715	0815	until	2315

Halle (Saale) Hbf d.	0511	0523	and at the same	2211	2223	2326
Leipzig/Halle Flughafen ✈ d.	0524	|	minutes past	2224	|	2337
Leipzig Hbf a.	0538	0559	each hour until	2238	2259	2351

810 HAMM and BAD BENTHEIM - HANNOVER - BERLIN and LEIPZIG

See note △	IC 2012	ICE 945	ICE 955	IC 2012	ICE 594	RE 14017	IC 241	IC 241	ICE 645	ICE 655	ICE 870	IC 2137	RE 14217	IC 2041	ICE 947	ICE 957	ICE 592	RE 14019	ICE 1220	RE 14219	ICE 657	ICE 372	ICE 1743	ICE 502	ICE 1002
		⑧q		⑤⑦r	⑥j		⑧q	⑤⑦				⑧q		⑦w		⑧q			⑦w		⑦w	⑦w	⑦w	⑧q	⑥h
	🍷♦	✕	✕	🍷♦	✕		🍷	r🍷	✕	✕	✕	🍷		🍷	✕	✕	✕		🍷♦		✕	Z✕		K🍷	K🍷
Koblenz Hbf **800** d.	1543	...	...	...	...	...	...	...	...	...	...	...	...	...	...	...	...	...	...	...	...	...	...	...	...
Bonn Hbf **800** d.	1622	...	...	...	...	...	...	...	...	...	...	...	...	...	...	...	...	...	...	...	2025	...	...	...	...
Köln/Bonn Flughafen ✈ **800** d.	|	...	...	...	...	...	...	...	1812q	...	...	...	...	...	...	...	...	...	...	...	|	...	...	...	...
Köln Hbf **800** d.	1646	...	1748	...	...	...	...	...	|	1848	...	...	...	1913	1926	1948	...	...	2017d	...	2048	...	...	2110	2110
Wuppertal Hbf **800** d.	|	...	1816	...	...	...	...	...	|	1916	...	...	...	1943	|	2016	...	...	|	...	2116	...	...	2143	|
Hagen Hbf **800** d.	|	...	1834	...	...	...	...	...	|	1934	...	...	...	2001	|	2034	...	...	|	...	2134	...	...	2201	|
Düsseldorf Hbf **800 802** d.	1714	1753	|	...	...	...	...	...	1853	|	...	...	...	|	1953	|	...	...	2039	...	|	...	...	|	2133
Dortmund Hbf **800 802** d.	1828	1848	|	...	...	...	...	...	1948	|	...	...	...	2028	2048	|	...	...	2132	...	|	...	...	2228	2228
Hamm (Westf) **802** d.	1845	1911	1911	...	...	...	...	...	2011	2011	...	...	...	2045	2111	2111	...	...	2149	...	2211	...	...	2250	2250
Gütersloh Hbf **802** d.	1905	|	|	...	...	...	...	...	|	|	...	...	...	2105	|	|	...	...	2209	...	|	...	...	2310	2310
Bielefeld Hbf **802** d.	1917	1937	1937	...	...	...	...	...	2038	2038	...	...	2024	2117	2137	2137	...	...	2219	2224	2238	...	...	2320	2320
Herford **802** d.	1927	|	|	...	...	...	...	...	|	|	...	...	2033	2127	|	|	...	...	|	2233	|	...	...	2330	2330
Schiphol ✈ **22** ⊡ d.	|	|	|	...	...	...	1649	1649	|	|	...	...	|	|	|	|	...	...	|	|	|	...	...	|	|
Bad Bentheim 🏛 **811** d.	|	|	|	...	...	*1757*	1928	1928	|	|	...	...	|	|	|	|	...	*1957*	|	|	|	...	...	|	|
Rheine **811** d.	|	|	|	...	...	1838	1942	1942	|	|	...	...	|	|	|	|	...	2038	|	|	|	...	...	|	|
Osnabrück Hbf **811** d.	|	|	|	...	...	1916	2008	2008	|	|	...	...	|	|	|	|	...	2116	|	|	|	...	...	|	|
Bünde (Westf) **811** d.	|	|	|	...	...	1938	2029	2029	|	|	...	...	|	|	|	|	...	2138	|	|	|	...	...	|	|
Löhne (Westf) **802** d.	|	|	|	...	...	1950	|	|	|	|	...	...	2040	|	|	|	...	2150	|	2240	|	...	...	|	|
Bad Oeynhausen **802** d.	1937	|	|	...	...	1955	|	|	|	|	...	...	2045	2137	|	|	...	2155	|	2245	|	...	...	|	|
Minden (Westf) **802** d.	1949	|	|	...	...	2007	2049	2049	|	|	...	...	2107t	2149	|	|	...	2207	2247	2257	|	...	...	2347	2347
Basel SBB **912** d.	|	|	|	...	...	|	|	|	|	|	1612	...	|	|	|	|	...	|	|	...	|	1812	...	|	|
Stuttgart Hbf **930** d.	|	|	|	...	1651	|	|	|	|	|	|	...	|	|	|	|	1851	|	|	...	|	|	...	|	|
Frankfurt (Main) Hbf **900** d.	|	|	|	...	1813	|	|	|	|	|	1913	...	|	|	|	|	2013	|	|	...	|	2113	...	|	|
Oldenburg (Oldb) **813** d.	|	|	|	...	|	|	|	|	|	|	|	1935	|	|	|	|	|	|	|	...	|	|	...	|	|
Bremen Hbf **813** d.	|	|	|	...	|	|	|	|	|	|	|	2009	|	|	|	|	|	|	|	...	|	|	...	|	|
Hannover Hbf a.	2018	2028	2028	←	|	2050	2118	2118	2128	2128	|	2114	2150	2218	2228	2228	|	2250	2317	...	2328	|	...	0018	0018
Hannover Hbf △ d.	→	2031	2031	2036	|	2055	...	2121	2131	2131	|	2136	2155	...	2231	2231	|	2255	...	...	2331	|	2350	...	...
Peine △ d.	...	|	|	|	|	2124	...	|	|	|	|	2157	2224	...	|	|	|	2324	...	...	|	|	|	...	...
Braunschweig Hbf △ ‡ d.	...	|	|	2111	2100	2141	...	|	|	|	2200	2212	2241	...	|	|	2300	2341	...	...	|	2359	0026	...	...
Helmstedt △ ‡ d.	...	|	|	|	|	...	...	|	|	|	|	2235	▬	...	|	|	|	...	...	...	|	|	|	...	...
Magdeburg Hbf △ ‡ a.	...	|	|	2155	|	...	...	|	|	|	|	2300	n	...	|	|	|	...	...	...	|	|	0113	...	...
Magdeburg Hbf ‡ d.	...	|	|	2203w	|	...	...	|	|	|	|	...	2308v	...	|	|	|	...	...	...	|	|	...	...	...
Köthen ‡ d.	...	|	|	2235w	|	...	...	|	|	|	|	...	2348	...	|	|	|	...	...	...	|	|	...	...	...
Halle (Saale) Hbf ‡ d.	...	|	|	2258w	|	...	...	|	|	|	|	...	0016	...	|	|	|	...	...	...	|	|	...	...	...
Leipzig/Halle Flughafen ✈ ‡ a.	...	|	|	2308w	|	...	...	|	|	|	|	...	*0042*	...	|	|	|	...	...	...	|	|	...	...	...
Leipzig Hbf ‡ a.	...	|	|	2323w	|	...	...	|	|	|	|	...	*0057*	...	|	|	|	...	...	...	|	|	...	...	...
Wolfsburg d.	...	2105	2105	...	2118	...	...	2155	|	|	2218	...	...	...	2305	2305	2318	...	...	...	0005	0018	...	...	...
Stendal **838** d.	...	2133	2133	...	|	...	...	2226	|	|	|	...	...	...	2333	2333	|	...	...	...	|	|	...	...	...
Berlin Spandau **838** a.	...	2206	2206	...	2211	...	...	2303	2253	2253	2311	...	...	...	0006	0006	0012	...	...	...	0057	0111	...	...	...
Berlin Hbf **838** a.	...	2221	2221	...	2226	...	...	2320	2308	2308	2325	...	...	...	0016	0016	0023	...	...	...	0112	0125	...	...	...
Berlin Ostbahnhof **838** a.	...	2232	2232	...	2237	...	...	2330	2320	2320	2336	...	...	...	...	...	...	...	...	...	0122	0136	...	...	...

km	See note △	CNL 456	ICE 948	ICE 527	RE 14002	ICE 503	ICE 656	ICE 646	RE 14202	IC 2136	IC 242	ICE 373	RE 14004	IC 2013	ICE 593	ICE 956	ICE 946	IC 2013	ICE 1091	RE 14204	IC 2134	ICE 375	ICE 654	ICE 644	IC 240
		Ⓡ	①m	①g	⚒		①–⑤	①–⑤	⚒⊖	①–⑤	①–⑥	①–⑤		①–⑥	⑥⑦	①–⑥	①–⑥		①–⑤			①–⑥		①–⑥	①–⑥
		🍷♦		♦		K🍷	a✕	a✕		a	e🍷	aA		e♦	s✕	e✕	e✕	🍷♦	a⚡ ✕		🍷♦	eA	✕	e✕	e🍷
0	**Berlin** Ostbahnhof **838** d.	0022	0026	...	...	...	0417	0417	...	...	...	0421	...	...	0520	0525	0525	...		...	...	0621	0640	0640	0626
5	**Berlin** Hbf **838** d.	0032	0036	...	...	...	0427	0427	...	...	...	0432	...	...	0531	0536	0536	...	0608	...	...	0632	0650	0650	0637
21	**Berlin** Spandau **838** d.	|	0054	...	...	...	0441	0441	...	...	...	0447	...	...	0546	0552	0552	...	0618	...	...	0647	0705	0705	0654
113	Stendal **838** d.	|	0127	...	...	...	0518	0518	...	...	...	|	...	...	|	0626	0626	...	|	...	...	|	|	|	0735
188	Wolfsburg d.	|	0155	...	...	...	0546	0546	...	...	...	0540	...	...	0640	0655	0655	...	|	...	...	0740	|	|	0805
	Leipzig Hbf ‡ d.	|	|	...	...	...	|	|	...	...	...	|	...	0437g	|	|	|	...	|	...	0539a	|	|	|	|
	Leipzig/Halle Flughafen ✈ ‡ d.	|	|	...	...	...	|	|	...	...	...	|	...	0450g	|	|	|	...	|	...	0552a	|	|	|	|
	Halle (Saale) Hbf ‡ d.	|	|	...	...	...	|	|	...	...	...	|	...	0504g	|	|	|	...	|	...	0607a	|	|	|	|
	Köthen ‡ d.	|	|	...	...	...	|	|	...	...	...	|	...	0525g	|	|	|	...	|	...	0628a	|	|	|	|
	Magdeburg Hbf ‡ a.	|	|	...	...	...	|	|	...	...	...	|	...	0556g	|	|	|	...	|	...	0656a	|	|	|	|
	Magdeburg Hbf △ ‡ d.	|	|	...	...	...	|	|	...	0501	...	|	...	0600	|	|	|	...	|	...	0700	|	|	|	|
	Helmstedt △ ‡ d.	|	|	...	...	...	|	|	...	0528	...	|	...	0628	|	|	|	...	|	...	0728	|	|	|	|
	Braunschweig Hbf △ ‡ d.	|	|	...	0420	...	|	|	0520	0551	...	0558	0620	0651	0658	|	|	...	|	0720	0751	0758	|	|	|
	Peine △ d.	|	|	...	0437	...	|	|	0537	0606	...	|	0637	|	|	|	|	...	|	0737	|	|	|	|	|
263	**Hannover** Hbf △ a.	|	0228	...	0505	...	0618	0618	0605	0626	...	|	0705	0723	|	0728	0728	←	|	0805	0823	|	0828	0828	0837
263	**Hannover** Hbf d.	|	0231	0410	0509	0540	0621	0621	0609	0645	0640	|	0709	→	|	0731	0731	0740	|	0809	0845	|	0831	0831	0840
	Bremen Hbf **813** a.	|	|	|	|	|	|	|	|	0751	|	|	|	...	|	|	|	|	|	|	0951	|	|	|	|
	Oldenburg (Oldb) **813** a.	|	|	|	|	|	|	|	|	0822	|	|	|	...	|	|	|	|	|	|	1022	|	|	|	|
	Frankfurt (Main) Hbf **900** a.	|	|	|	|	|	|	|	|	...	|	0844	|	...	0944	|	|	|	0942	|	...	1044	|	|	|
	Stuttgart Hbf **930** a.	|	|	|	|	|	|	|	|	...	|	|	|	...	1108	|	|	|	1108	|	...	|	|	|	|
	Basel SBB **912** a.	|	|	|	|	|	|	|	|	...	|	1147	|	...	...	|	|	|	...	|	...	1347	|	|	|
328	Minden (Westf) **802** d.	|	0302	0447	0555	0612	0651	0651	0702	...	0712	...	0752	...	...	|	|	0812	...	0902t	...	...	|	|	0912
343	Bad Oeynhausen **802** d.	|	|	|	0607	|	|	|	0714	...	0722	...	0804	...	...	|	|	0822	...	0914	...	...	|	|	|
349	Löhne (Westf) **802** d.	|	|	|	0611	|	|	|	0719	...	|	...	0811	...	...	|	|	|	...	0919	...	...	|	|	|
359	Bünde (Westf) **811** d.	|	|	|	0622	|	|	|	|	...	|	...	0821	...	...	|	|	|	...	|	...	...	|	|	0932
396	**Osnabrück** Hbf **811** d.	|	|	|	0647	|	|	|	|	...	0753	...	0847	...	...	|	|	|	...	|	...	...	|	|	0953
444	Rheine **811** d.	|	|	|	0723	|	|	|	|	...	0821	...	0923	...	...	|	|	|	...	|	...	...	|	|	1021
465	Bad Bentheim 🏛 **811** a.	|	|	|	*0803*	|	|	|	|	...	0834	...	*1003*	...	...	|	|	|	...	|	...	...	|	|	1034
655	*Schiphol* ✈ **22** ⊡ a.	|	|	|	...	|	|	|	|	...	1109	...	...	...	...	|	|	|	...	|	...	...	|	|	1309
	Herford **802** d.	|	0320	0504	...	0632	0710	0710	0727	...	...	...	...	...	...	|	|	0833	...	0927	...	...	|	|	...
	Bielefeld Hbf **802** d.	0356	0330	0514	...	0641	0720	0720	0736	...	...	...	...	...	...	0822	0822	0842	...	0936	...	...	0922	0922	...
	Gütersloh Hbf **802** d.	|	0340	0524	...	0651	|	|	...	...	...	...	...	...	...	|	|	0852	...	...	...	...	|	|	...
	Hamm (Westf) **802** a.	0429	0359	0548	...	0713	0748	0748	...	...	...	...	...	...	...	0848	0848	0912	...	...	...	...	0948	0948	...
	Dortmund Hbf **800 802** a.	0450	0418	0614	...	0732	|	0809	...	...	...	...	...	...	...	|	0909	0932	...	...	...	...	|	1009	...
	Düsseldorf Hbf **800 802** a.	0654	0514	0719	...	|	|	0905	...	...	...	...	...	...	...	|	1005	1045	...	...	...	...	|	1105	...
	Hagen Hbf **800** a.	|	|	|	...	0755	0822	|	...	...	...	...	...	...	...	0922	...	|	...	...	...	...	1022	|	...
	Wuppertal Hbf **800** a.	0538	|	|	...	0812	0839	|	...	...	...	...	...	...	...	0939	...	|	...	...	...	...	1039	|	...
	Köln Hbf **800** a.	0614	0540	0742d	...	0846	0909	|	...	...	...	...	...	...	...	1009	...	1115	...	...	...	...	1109	|	...
	Köln/Bonn Flughafen ✈ **800** d.	...	0604	...	...	...	...	0943	...	...	...	...	...	...	...	...	...	|	...	...	...	...	|	1142	...
	Bonn Hbf **800** a.	...	...	...	...	...	...	...	...	...	...	...	...	...	...	...	...	1135	...	...	...	...	1132e	...	...
	Koblenz Hbf **800** a.	...	...	...	...	...	...	...	...	...	...	...	...	...	...	...	...	1215	...	...	...	...	...	...	...

♦ – **NOTES** (LISTED BY TRAIN NUMBER)

456 – PHOENIX – 🛏 1, 2 cl., ━ 2 cl. and (2) Praha - Dresden - Berlin - Köln - Amsterdam (Table **28**); 🛏 1, 2 cl., ━ 2 cl. and (2) (*EN* **446** – JAN KIEPURA) Warszawa - Berlin - Köln - Amsterdam (Table **24**); conveys 🛏 1, 2 cl. Moskva - Amsterdam (Table **24**). For overnight journeys only.

527 – (12) and 🍷 Hannover - Köln Messe/Deutz - Frankfurt - Nürnberg - München.

1220 – (12) and 🍷 München - Köln Messe/Deutz - Hannover.

2012 – ALLGÄU – (12) and 🍷 Oberstdorf - Stuttgart - Köln - Hannover (- Magdeburg ⑤⑦**r**) (- Leipzig ⑦**w**).

2013 – ALLGÄU – (12) and 🍷 (Leipzig ①**g** -) (Magdeburg ①–⑥**e** -) Hannover - Köln - Stuttgart - Oberstdorf.

2134 – BORKUM – (12) and 🍷 (Leipzig ①–⑤**a** -) Magdeburg - Oldenburg - Emden.

A – (12) and ✕ Berlin - Basel - Bern - Interlaken.
K – (12) and 🍷 Karlsruhe - Köln - Hannover and v.v.
Z – From Zürich (Table **510**).

a – ①–⑤ (not Dec. 24, 25, 31, Jan. 1, Apr. 2, 5, May 24).
d – Köln **Messe/Deutz**.
e – ①–⑥ (not Dec. 25, 26, Jan. 1, Apr. 3, 5, May 24).
g – ① (also Apr. 6, May 25; not Apr. 5, May 24).
h – Also Dec. 24, 25, 31, Apr. 2, 4, May 23.
j – Also Dec. 24, 25, 31, Apr. 2, 4, May 23; not Dec. 26, Jan. 2.
m – Also Apr. 6, May 25; not Dec. 21, 28, Apr. 5, May 24.
n – Not Dec. 24, 31.
q – ⑧ (not Dec. 24, 25, 31, Apr. 2, 4, May 23).
r – Also Dec. 23, 30, Apr. 1, 5, May 12, 24; not Dec. 25, Jan. 1, Apr. 2, 4, May 14, 23.
s – Also Dec. 24, 25, 31, Jan. 1, Apr. 2, 5, May 24; not Dec. 26, Jan. 2.
t – Arrives 10 minutes earlier.
v – 2311 on ⑧ from May 2 (not May 23).
w – ⑦ (also Apr. 5, May 24; not Apr. 4, May 23).

⊖ – Runs daily Braunschweig - Hannover.
⚡ – *ICE* ***SPRINTER***. Ⓡ and supplement payable.
△ – Services Hannover - Magdeburg and v.v. are subject to alteration from May 1. See Engineering Work Summary on page 361.
⊡ – Schiphol timings are subject to alteration on Apr. 30.
‡ – See panels on pages 379 and 381 for additional local services.

LEIPZIG and BERLIN - HANNOVER - BAD BENTHEIM and HAMM 810

	RE	IC	ICE	ICE	ICE	IC	RE	IC	IC	ICE	ICE	ICE	IC	IC	RE	IC	IC	ICE	ICE	ICE	IC	IC	IC	RE	IC
See note △	14006	2044	595	954	944	2044	14206	2238	2132	871	652	642	148	248	14008	2046	2246	597	952	942	2046	2246	2011	14208	2130
		①–⑥		①–⑥		①–⑥		R					①–⑥	⑦h		M	⑤f				⑥⑦	⑤f	⑦w		
		e🍷	✕	d✕	✕	e🍷			O🍷	✕	✕	✕	e S	🍷		🍷	L🍷	✕	✕	✕	c🍷	L🍷	T🍷		🍷
Berlin Ostbahnhof 838 d.	...	...	0726	0738	0738	...	...	...	0720	0821	0840	0840	🍷	0826	...	...	...	0926	0938	0938	...	...	...	...	...
Berlin Hbf 838 d.	...	...	0737	0748	0748	...	...	...	0731	0832	0850	0850	0839	0837	...	...	...	0937	0948	0948	...	...	1008	...	...
Berlin Spandau 838 d.	...	...	0751	0803	0803	...	...	...	|	0847	0905	0905	0854	0854	...	...	...	0951	1003	1003	...	...	1018	...	...
Stendal 838 d.	...	...	|	|	|	...	...	...	|	|	|	|	0935	0935	...	...	...	|	|	|	...	...	|	...	...
Wolfsburg d.	...	...	|	0855	0855	...	...	...	|	0940	|	|	1005	1005	...	...	...	|	1055	1055	...	...	1121	...	...
Leipzig Hbf ‡ d.	...	0639	|	|	|	...	...	0739	|	|	|	|	|	|	...	0839	0839	|	|	|	...	...	|	...	0939
Leipzig/Halle Flughafen ✈ ‡ d.	...	0652	|	|	|	...	...	0752	|	|	|	|	|	|	...	0852	0852	|	|	|	...	...	|	...	0952
Halle (Saale) Hbf ‡ d.	...	0707	|	|	|	...	...	0807	|	|	|	|	|	|	...	0907	0907	|	|	|	...	...	|	...	1007
Köthen ‡ d.	...	0728	|	|	|	...	...	0828	|	|	|	|	|	|	...	0928	0928	|	|	|	...	...	|	...	1028
Magdeburg Hbf ‡ a.	...	0756	|	|	|	...	...	0855	0858	|	|	|	|	|	...	0956	0956	|	|	|	...	...	|	...	1056
Magdeburg Hbf △ ‡ d.	...	0802	|	|	|	...	...	...	0901	|	|	|	|	|	...	1002	1002	|	|	|	...	...	|	...	1100
Helmstedt △ ‡ d.	...	|	|	|	|	...	...	...	0928	|	|	|	|	|	...	|	|	|	|	|	...	...	|	...	1128
Braunschweig Hbf △ ‡ d.	0820	0851	0858	|	|	...	0920	...	0951	0958	|	|	|	|	1020	1051	1051	1058	|	|	...	...	|	1120	1151
Peine △ d.	0837	|	|	|	|	...	0937	...	|	|	|	|	|	|	1037	|	|	|	|	|	...	...	|	1137	|
Hannover Hbf △ a.	0905	0923	|	0928	0928	←	1005	...	1023	|	1028	1028	1037	1037	1105	1123	1123	|	1128	1128	←	←	1154	1205	1223
Hannover Hbf d.	0909	→	|	0931	0931	0940	1009	...	1045	|	1031	1031	1040	1040	1109	→	→	|	1131	1131	1140	1140	1157	1209	1245
Bremen Hbf **813** a.	|	...	|	|	|	|	|	...	1151	|	|	|	|	|	|	...	...	|	|	|	|	|	|	|	1351
Oldenburg (Oldb) **813** a.	|	...	|	|	|	|	|	...	1222	|	|	|	|	|	|	...	...	|	|	|	|	|	|	|	1422
Frankfurt (Main) Hbf **900** a.	|	...	1144	|	|	|	|	...	...	1244	|	|	|	|	|	...	...	1344	|	|	|	|	|	|	...
Stuttgart Hbf **930** a.	|	...	1308	|	|	|	|	...	...	|	|	|	|	|	|	...	...	1508	|	|	|	|	|	|	...
Basel SBB **912** a.	|	...	...	|	|	|	|	...	...	1547	|	|	|	|	|	...	...	...	|	|	|	|	|	|	...
Minden (Westf) 802 d.	0952	...	...	|	|	1012	1102t	...	...	...	|	|	1112	1112	1152	...	...	...	|	|	1212	1212	|	1302t	...
Bad Oeynhausen 802 d.	1004	...	...	|	|	1022	1114	...	...	...	|	|	1122	1122	1204	...	...	...	|	|	1222	1222	|	1314	...
Löhne (Westf) 802 d.	1011	...	...	|	|	|	1119	...	...	...	|	|	|	|	1211	...	...	...	|	|	|	|	|	1319	...
Bünde (Westf) 811 d.	1021	...	...	|	|	|	|	...	...	...	|	|	|	|	1221	...	...	...	|	|	|	|	|	|	...
Osnabrück Hbf 811 d.	1047	...	...	|	|	|	|	...	...	...	|	|	1153	1153	1247	...	...	...	|	|	|	|	|	|	...
Rheine 811 d.	1123	...	...	|	|	|	|	...	...	...	|	|	1221	1221	1323	...	...	...	|	|	|	|	|	|	...
Bad Bentheim 🏛 811 a.	*1203*	...	...	|	|	|	|	...	...	...	|	|	1234	1234	*1403*	...	...	...	|	|	|	|	|	|	...
Schiphol ✈ **22** ⊡ a.	...	...	...	|	|	|	|	...	...	...	|	|	1509	1509	...	...	...	...	|	|	|	|	|	|	...
Herford 802 d.	...	...	...	|	|	1033	1127	...	...	...	|	|	...	...	...	...	...	...	|	|	1233	1233	1244	1327	...
Bielefeld Hbf 802 d.	...	...	...	1022	1022	1042	1136	...	...	...	1122	1122	...	...	...	...	...	...	1222	1222	1242	1242	1253	1336	...
Gütersloh Hbf 802 d.	...	...	...	|	|	1052	...	...	...	...	|	|	...	...	...	...	...	...	|	|	1252	1252	1303	...	...
Hamm (Westf) 802 a.	...	...	...	1048	1048	1112	...	...	...	...	1148	1148	...	...	...	...	...	...	1248	1248	1312	1312	1324	...	...
Dortmund Hbf **800 802** a.	...	...	...	|	1109	1132	...	...	...	...	|	1209	...	...	...	...	...	...	|	1309	1332	1346	1346	...	...
Düsseldorf Hbf **800 802** a.	...	...	...	|	1205	|	...	...	...	...	|	1305	...	...	...	...	...	...	|	1405	|	1442	1442	...	...
Hagen Hbf **800** a.	...	...	...	1122	|	1155	...	...	...	...	1222	...	...	...	...	...	...	...	1322	|	1355	|	|	...	...
Wuppertal Hbf **800** a.	...	...	...	1139	|	1212	...	...	...	...	1239	...	...	...	...	...	...	...	1339	|	1412	|	|	...	...
Köln Hbf **800** a.	...	...	...	1209	|	1245	...	...	...	...	1309	...	...	...	...	...	...	...	1409	|	1445	1515	1515	...	...
Köln/Bonn Flughafen ✈ **800** d.	...	...	...	...	1242w	...	...	...	...	...	|	...	...	...	...	...	...	...	...	1443	...	|	|	...	...
Bonn Hbf **800** a.	...	...	...	...	...	...	...	...	...	...	1332	...	...	...	...	...	...	...	...	...	...	1535	1535	...	...
Koblenz Hbf **800** a.	...	...	...	...	...	...	...	...	...	...	...	...	...	...	...	...	...	...	...	...	...	1615	1615	...	...

	ICE	ICE	ICE	IC	RE	IC	ICE	ICE	ICE	IC	IC	RE	IC	ICE	ICE	ICE	IC	RE	IC	ICE	ICE	ICE	IC	IC	RE
See note △	277	650	640	146	14010	2048	599	950	940	2048	1915	14210	2038	279	558	548	144	14012	2140	691	858	848	2140	1917	14212
											⑤⑦													⑤⑦r	
	A✕	✕	✕	🍷		🍷	✕	✕	✕	🍷	zT		🍷	A✕	✕	✕	🍷		🍷	✕	✕	✕	🍷	K🍷	
Berlin Ostbahnhof 838 d.	1021	1040	1040	1026	...	...	1126	1138	1138	...	...	...	...	1221	1238	1238	1226	...	...	1326	1338	1338	...	...	...
Berlin Hbf 838 d.	1032	1050	1050	1037	...	...	1137	1148	1148	...	1208	...	...	1232	1249	1249	1236	...	...	1337	1348	1348	...	1358	...
Berlin Spandau 838 d.	1047	1105	1105	1054	...	...	1151	1203	1203	...	1218	...	...	1247	1304	1304	1254	...	...	1351	1403	1403	...	1408	...
Stendal 838 d.	|	|	|	1135	...	...	|	|	|	...	|	...	...	|	|	|	1335	...	...	|	|	|	...	1449	...
Wolfsburg d.	1140	|	|	1205	...	...	|	1255	1255	...	1321	...	...	1340	|	|	1405	...	...	|	1455	1455	...	1521	...
Leipzig Hbf ‡ d.	|	|	|	|	...	1039	|	|	|	...	|	...	1139	|	|	|	|	...	1239	|	|	|	...	|	...
Leipzig/Halle Flughafen ✈ ‡ d.	|	|	|	|	...	1052	|	|	|	...	|	...	1152	|	|	|	|	...	1252	|	|	|	...	|	...
Halle (Saale) Hbf ‡ d.	|	|	|	|	...	1107	|	|	|	...	|	...	1207	|	|	|	|	...	1307	|	|	|	...	|	...
Köthen ‡ d.	|	|	|	|	...	1128	|	|	|	...	|	...	1228	|	|	|	|	...	1328	|	|	|	...	|	...
Magdeburg Hbf ‡ a.	|	|	|	|	...	1156	|	|	|	...	|	...	1256	|	|	|	|	...	1356	|	|	|	...	|	...
Magdeburg Hbf △ ‡ d.	|	|	|	|	...	1202	|	|	|	...	|	...	1300	|	|	|	|	...	1402	|	|	|	...	|	...
Helmstedt △ ‡ d.	|	|	|	|	...	|	|	|	|	...	|	...	1328	|	|	|	|	...	|	|	|	|	...	|	...
Braunschweig Hbf △ ‡ d.	1158	|	|	|	1220	1251	1258	|	|	...	|	1320	1351	1358	|	|	|	1420	1451	1458	|	|	...	|	1520
Peine △ d.	|	|	|	|	1237	|	|	|	|	...	|	1337	|	|	|	|	|	1437	|	|	|	|	...	|	1537
Hannover Hbf △ a.	|	1228	1228	1237	1305	1323	|	1328	1328	←	1354	1405	1423	|	1428	1428	1437	1505	1523	|	1528	1528	←	1555	1605
Hannover Hbf d.	|	1231	1231	1240	1309	→	|	1331	1331	1340	1357	1409	1445	|	1431	1431	1440	1509	→	|	1531	1531	1540	1558	1609
Bremen Hbf **813** a.	|	|	|	|	|	...	|	|	|	|	|	|	1551	|	|	|	|	|	...	|	|	|	|	|	|
Oldenburg (Oldb) **813** a.	|	|	|	|	|	...	|	|	|	|	|	|	1622	|	|	|	|	|	...	|	|	|	|	|	|
Frankfurt (Main) Hbf **900** a.	1444	|	|	|	|	...	1544	|	|	|	|	|	...	1644	|	|	|	|	...	1744	|	|	|	|	|
Stuttgart Hbf **930** a.	|	|	|	|	|	...	1708	|	|	|	|	|	...	|	|	|	|	|	...	1908	|	|	|	|	|
Basel SBB **912** a.	1747	|	|	|	|	...	...	|	|	|	|	|	...	1947	|	|	|	|	...	...	|	|	|	|	|
Minden (Westf) 802 d.	...	|	|	1312	1352	...	...	|	|	1412	|	1502t	...	...	|	|	1512	1552	...	...	|	|	1612	|	1702t
Bad Oeynhausen 802 d.	...	|	|	|	1404	...	...	|	|	1422	|	1514	...	...	|	|	1522	1604	...	...	|	|	1622	|	1714
Löhne (Westf) 802 d.	...	|	|	|	1411	...	...	|	|	|	|	1519	...	...	|	|	|	1611	...	...	|	|	|	|	1719
Bünde (Westf) 811 d.	...	|	|	1332	1421	...	...	|	|	|	|	|	...	...	|	|	|	1621	...	...	|	|	|	|	|
Osnabrück Hbf 811 d.	...	|	|	1353	1447	...	...	|	|	|	|	|	...	...	|	|	1553	1647	...	...	|	|	|	|	|
Rheine 811 d.	...	|	|	1421	1523	...	...	|	|	|	|	|	...	...	|	|	1621	1723	...	...	|	|	|	|	|
Bad Bentheim 🏛 811 a.	...	|	|	1434	*1603*	...	...	|	|	|	|	|	...	...	|	|	1634	*1803*	...	...	|	|	|	|	|
Schiphol ✈ **22** ⊡ a.	...	|	|	1709	...	...	...	|	|	|	|	|	...	...	|	|	1909	...	...	...	|	|	|	|	|
Herford 802 d.	...	|	|	...	...	...	...	|	|	1433	1444	1527	...	...	|	|	...	...	...	...	|	|	1633	1644	1727
Bielefeld Hbf 802 d.	...	1322	1322	...	...	...	...	1422	1422	1442	1453	1536	...	...	1522	1522	...	...	...	...	1622	1622	1642	1653	1736
Gütersloh Hbf 802 d.	...	|	|	...	...	...	...	|	|	1452	1503	...	...	...	|	|	...	...	...	...	|	|	1652	1703	...
Hamm (Westf) 802 a.	...	1348	1348	...	...	...	...	1448	1448	1512	1524	...	...	...	1548	1548	...	...	...	...	1648	1648	1712	1723	...
Dortmund Hbf **800 802** a.	...	|	1409	...	...	...	...	|	1509	1532	1546	...	...	...	|	1609	...	...	...	...	|	1709	1732	1746	...
Düsseldorf Hbf **800 802** a.	...	|	1506	...	...	...	...	|	1605	|	1642	...	...	...	|	1705	...	...	...	...	|	1805	|	1842	...
Hagen Hbf **800** a.	...	1422	...	...	...	...	...	1522	...	1555	|	...	...	...	1622	|	...	...	...	...	1722	...	1755	|	...
Wuppertal Hbf **800** a.	...	1439	...	...	...	...	...	1539	...	1612	|	...	...	...	1639	|	...	...	...	...	1739	...	1812	|	...
Köln Hbf **800** a.	...	1509	...	...	...	...	...	1609	...	1645	1715	...	...	...	1709	|	...	...	...	...	1809	...	1845	1915	...
Köln/Bonn Flughafen ✈ **800** d.	...	...	...	...	...	...	...	...	...	...	|	...	...	...	...	1743	...	...	...	...	...	...	...	|	...
Bonn Hbf **800** a.	...	...	...	...	...	...	...	...	...	...	1735	...	...	...	...	...	...	...	...	...	...	...	...	1935w	...
Koblenz Hbf **800** a.	...	...	...	...	...	...	...	...	...	...	1815	...	...	...	...	...	...	...	...	...	...	...	...	2015w	...

A – To Interlaken via Bern (Table **560**).
K – To Karlsruhe (Table **912**) on ⑦**w**.
L – To München via Stuttgart (Tables **912**/**930**).
M – ①②③④⑥ (also Apr. 2; not Dec. 23, 26, 30, Apr. 1, 3, 5, May 12, 24).
O – OSTFRIESLAND – 12 (Cottbus ①–⑥**e** -) Berlin - Oldenburg (- Norddeich Mole on dates in Table **813**).
P – ①–⑥ (not Dec. 24, 25, 31, Jan. 1, Apr. 2, 5, May 13, 24).
R – ①–⑥ (daily Dec. 13 - Mar. 27). To Warnemünde (via Schwerin and Rostock) on ⑤⑥ from Mar. 27. See also Tables **841**, **837** and **830**.
S – From Szczecin (Table **845**).
T – To Stuttgart via Mainz (Table **912**).

b – Not Dec. 25.
c – Also Dec. 24, 31, Apr. 2, 5, May 24; not Dec. 26, Apr. 3, 4, May 23.
d – Not Dec. 25, 26, Jan. 1, Apr. 3.
e – Not Dec. 25, 26, Jan. 1, Apr. 3, 5, May 24.
f – Also Dec. 23, 30, Apr. 1, May 12; not Dec. 25, Jan. 1, Apr. 2, May 14.
h – Also Dec. 25, 26, Jan. 1, Apr. 3, 5, May 24.
n – Not Dec. 24, 31.
r – Also Dec. 23, 30, Apr. 1, 5, May 12, 24; not Dec. 25, Jan. 1, Apr. 2, 4, May 14, 23.
t – Arrives 10 minutes earlier.
w – ⑦ (also Apr. 5, May 24; not Apr. 4, May 23).
z – Also Dec. 23, 30, Apr. 1, 5, May 24; not Dec. 25, Jan. 1, Apr. 2, 4, May 14, 23.

◇ – Later service (daily): Leipzig Hbf d. 2337, Leipzig/Halle Flughafen d. 2352, Halle (Saale) Hbf a. 0005.
⊕ – Runs 14 minutes later on ⑦**w**.
⊡ – Schiphol timings are subject to alteration on Apr. 30.

❖ – The 1430, 1630 and 1830 from Magdeburg do not run on Dec. 24, 31.
△ – Services between Magdeburg and Hannover are subject to alteration from May 1. See Engineering Work Summary on page 361.
‡ – See panel below main table for additional *RE*/*RB* services.

						◇
Leipzig Hbf d.	0451	0505	and at the same	2151	2205	2237
Leipzig/Halle Flughafen ✈ d.	0506	|	minutes past	2206	|	2252
Halle (Saale) Hbf a.	0518	0541	each hour until	2218	2241	2305

	b						n
Halle (Saale) Hbf d.	0010	...	0543	and	2143	...	2245
Köthen d.	0039	...	0612	hourly	2212	...	2314
Magdeburg Hbf a.	0123	...	0651	until	2251	...	2353

		Ⓐ	❖	n	P	n⊕
Magdeburg Hbf d.	0530	0630	then hourly on Ⓐ,	1930	2030	2200
Helmstedt d.	0614	0714	every **two** hours	2014	2114	2244
Braunschweig Hbf a.	0642	0742	on © until	2042	2142	2313

810 LEIPZIG and BERLIN - HANNOVER - BAD BENTHEIM and HAMM

See note △	IC 2036	ICE 873	ICE 556	ICE 546	IC 142	RE 14014	IC 2142 ⑧q	ICE 693	ICE 856	ICE 846 E	ICE 1046 ⑤	IC 2142 ⑧q	RE 14214	IC 2034	ICE 875	ICE 554	ICE 544	IC 140	EC 340 ⑧	RE 14016	ICE 695 ⑥h	IC 2144 ⑧q	ICE 854	ICE 844	IC 2144 ⑧q
	N🍷	✕	✕	✕	🍷		🍷	✕	T✕	✕	✕♦	🍷		🍷	✕	✕	A✕	🍷	♦		✕	🍷	✕	✕	
Berlin Ostbahnhof 838 d.	...	1421	1440	1440	1426	...	...	1526	1538	1538	1538	...	...	...	1621	1640	1640	1626	1725r	...	1722	...	1738	1738	...
Berlin Hbf 838 d.	...	1432	1450	1450	1437	...	...	1537	1548	1548	1548	...	...	...	1632	1650	1650	1637	1737	...	1733	...	1749	1749	...
Berlin Spandau 838 d.	...	1449	1505	1505	1454	...	...	1551	1603	1603	1603	...	...	...	1649	1705	1705	1654	1752	...	1747	...	1803	1803	...
Stendal 838 d.	...	|	|	|	1535	...	...	|	|	|	|	...	...	...	|	|	|	1735	1824	...	|	...	|	|	...
Wolfsburg d.	...	1540	|	|	1605	...	...	|	1655	1655	1655	...	...	...	1740	|	|	1805	...	...	|	...	1855	1855	...
Leipzig Hbf ‡d.	1339	|	|	|	|	...	1439	|	|	|	|	...	...	1539	|	|	|	|	...	...	|	1639	|	|	...
Leipzig/Halle Flughafen ✈ ‡d.	1352	|	|	|	|	...	1452	|	|	|	|	...	...	1552	|	|	|	|	...	...	|	1652	|	|	...
Halle (Saale) Hbf ‡d.	1407	|	|	|	|	...	1507	|	|	|	|	...	...	1607	|	|	|	|	...	...	|	1707	|	|	...
Köthen ‡d.	1428	|	|	|	|	...	1528	|	|	|	|	...	...	1628	|	|	|	|	...	...	|	1728	|	|	...
Magdeburg Hbf ‡a.	1456	|	|	|	|	...	1556	|	|	|	|	...	...	1656	|	|	|	|	...	...	|	1756	|	|	...
Magdeburg Hbf △ ‡d.	1500	|	|	|	|	...	1602	|	|	|	|	...	...	1700	|	|	|	|	...	...	|	1802	|	|	...
Helmstedt △ ‡d.	1528	|	|	|	|	...	|	|	|	|	|	...	...	1728	|	|	|	|	...	...	|	|	|	|	...
Braunschweig Hbf △ ‡d.	1551	1558	|	|	|	1620	1651	1658	|	|	|	...	1720	1751	1758	|	|	|	...	1820	1858	1851	|	|	...
Peine △ d.	|	|	|	|	|	1637	|	|	|	|	|	...	1737	|	|	|	|	|	...	1837	|	|	|	|	...
Hannover Hbf △ a.	1623	|	1628	1628	1637	1705	1723	|	1728	1728	1728	←	1805	1823	|	1828	1828	1837	...	1905	|	1923	1928	1928	←
Hannover Hbf d.	1645	|	1631	1631	1640	1709	→	|	1731	1731	1731	1740	1809	1845	|	1831	1831	1840n	...	1909	|	→	1931	1931	1940
Bremen Hbf **813** a.	1751	|	|	|	|	|	...	|	|	|	|	|	|	1951	|	|	|	|	...	|	|	...	|	|	|
Oldenburg (Oldb) **813** a.	1822	|	|	|	|	|	...	|	|	|	|	|	|	2022	|	|	|	|	...	|	|	...	|	|	|
Frankfurt (Main) Hbf **900** a.	...	1844	|	|	|	|	...	1944	|	|	|	|	|	...	2044	|	|	|	...	|	2142	...	|	|	|
Stuttgart Hbf **930** a.	...	|	|	|	|	|	...	2108	|	|	|	|	|	...	|	|	|	|	...	|	2309	...	|	|	|
Basel SBB **912** a.	...	2147	|	|	|	|	...	...	|	|	|	|	|	...	2355	|	|	|	...	|	...	...	|	|	|
Minden (Westf) 802 d.	...	...	|	|	1712	1752	...	...	|	|	|	1812	1902t	...	...	|	|	1912n	...	1952	...	...	|	|	2012
Bad Oeynhausen 802 d.	...	...	|	|	|	1804	...	...	|	|	|	1822	1914	...	...	|	|	1922n	...	2004	...	...	|	|	2022
Löhne (Westf) 802 d.	...	...	|	|	|	1811	...	...	|	|	|	|	1919	...	...	|	|	|	...	2011	...	...	|	|	|
Bünde (Westf) 811 d.	...	...	|	|	1732	1821	...	...	|	|	|	|	...	...	...	|	|	|	...	2021	...	...	|	|	|
Osnabrück Hbf 811 d.	...	...	|	|	1753	1847	...	...	|	|	|	|	...	...	...	|	|	1953n	...	2047	...	...	|	|	|
Rheine 811 d.	...	...	|	|	1821	1923	...	...	|	|	|	|	...	...	...	|	|	2021n	...	2123	...	...	|	|	|
Bad Bentheim 🏛 811 a.	...	...	|	|	1834	*2003*	...	...	|	|	|	|	...	...	...	|	|	2034n	...	*2203*	...	...	|	|	|
Schiphol ✈ 22 ⊡ a.	...	...	|	|	2109j	...	...	...	|	|	|	|	...	...	...	|	|	2309n	...	...	...	...	|	|	|
Herford 802 d.	...	...	|	|	...	...	...	...	|	|	|	1833	1927	...	...	|	|	...	...	...	...	...	|	|	2033
Bielefeld Hbf 802 d.	...	...	1722	1722	...	...	...	...	1822	1822	1822	1842	1936	...	...	1922	1922	...	...	...	...	...	2022	2022	2042
Gütersloh Hbf 802 d.	...	...	|	|	...	...	...	...	|	|	|	1852	...	...	...	|	|	...	...	...	...	...	|	|	2052
Hamm (Westf) 802 a.	...	...	1748	1748	...	...	...	...	1848	1848	1848	1912	...	...	...	1948	1948	...	...	...	...	...	2048	2048	2110
Dortmund Hbf **800 802** a.	...	...	|	1809	...	...	...	...	|	1909	1909	1932	...	...	...	|	2009	...	...	...	...	...	|	2109	2132
Düsseldorf Hbf **800 802** a.	...	...	|	1910	...	...	...	...	|	2005	2014	|	...	...	...	|	2105	...	...	...	...	...	|	2207	|
Hagen Hbf **800** a.	...	...	1822	|	...	...	...	...	1922	|	...	1955	...	...	...	2022	|	...	...	...	...	...	2122	|	2155
Wuppertal Hbf **800** a.	...	...	1839	|	...	...	...	...	1939	|	...	2012	...	...	...	2039	|	...	...	...	...	...	2139	|	2212
Köln Hbf **800** a.	...	...	1909	|	...	...	...	...	2009	2033	...	2045	...	...	...	2109	2133	...	...	...	...	...	2209	2231	2245
Köln/Bonn Flughafen ✈ **800** d.	...	...	|	1945	...	...	...	...	|	...	...	...	...	...	...	...	...	...	...	...	...	...	|	...	...
Bonn Hbf **800** a.	...	...	1932b	...	...	...	...	...	2039p	...	...	...	...	...	...	...	...	...	...	...	...	...	2235w	...	...
Koblenz Hbf **800** a.	...	...	2010a	...	...	...	...	...	2116p	...	...	...	...	...	...	...	...	...	...	...	...	...	2311w	...	...

See note △	ICE 1093 ⑧d	RE 14216	IC 2032	ICE 877	ICE 552	ICE 542	IC 2242	RE 14018	IC 1899 ⑦w	IC 2146 ⑧q	ICE 697 ⑧q	ICE 852 ⑦w	ICE 842	ICE 832 B	ICE 862 ⑤f	IC 2146 ⑦w	IC 1932 ⑦w	IC 1930 ⑦w	IC 2030 ⑧q	ICE 879 ⑦w	IC 2240 ⑦w	ICE 540	IC 1740 C	ICE 850 ⑦w	IC 2340 ⑤v
	✕⟋		🍷	✕♦	✕	✕	L🍷		♦	🍷	✕♦	✕	✕	✕	✕		♦	U🍷		✕♦	M🍷	✕	D	✕	
Berlin Ostbahnhof 838 d.	1754	...	...	1822	1840	1840	1826	...	...	...	1926	1938	1938	1938	1938	...	...	...	...	2021	...	2056	...	2138	2323
Berlin Hbf 838 d.	1805	...	...	1833	1850	1850	1837	...	1908	...	1937	1948	1948	1948	1948	...	...	2026	...	2032	2041	2106	...	2148	2334
Berlin Spandau 838 d.	1819	...	...	1849	1905	1905	1854	...	1919	...	1951	2003	2003	2003	2003	...	1958	2036	...	2047	2053	2121	...	2203	2348
Stendal 838 d.	|	...	...	|	|	|	1935	...	|	...	|	|	|	|	|	...	2035	2111	...	|	2135	2155	...	2235	|
Wolfsburg d.	|	...	...	1940	|	|	2006	...	2021	...	|	2055	2055	2055	2055	...	|	▬	...	2140	2206	2222	...	2303	0051
Leipzig Hbf ‡d.	|	...	1739	|	|	|	|	...	|	1839	|	|	|	|	|	...	|	...	1939	|	|	|	2011	|	|
Leipzig/Halle Flughafen ✈ ‡d.	|	...	1752	|	|	|	|	...	|	1852	|	|	|	|	|	...	|	...	1952	|	|	|	2025	|	|
Halle (Saale) Hbf ‡d.	|	...	1807	|	|	|	|	...	|	1907	|	|	|	|	|	...	|	...	2007	|	|	|	2038	|	|
Köthen ‡d.	|	...	1828	|	|	|	|	...	|	1928	|	|	|	|	|	...	|	*RE*	2028	|	|	|	2058	|	|
Magdeburg Hbf ‡a.	|	...	1856	|	|	|	|	...	|	1956	|	|	|	|	|	...	|	**14218**	2056	|	|	|	2127	|	|
Magdeburg Hbf △ ‡d.	|	...	1900	|	|	|	|	...	|	2002	|	|	|	|	|	...	|		2100	|	|	|	2201w	|	|
Helmstedt △ ‡d.	|	...	1928	|	|	|	|	...	|	|	|	|	|	|	|	...	|		2128	|	|	|	|	|	|
Braunschweig Hbf △ ‡d.	|	1920	1951	1958	|	|	|	2020	|	2051	2058	|	|	|	|	...	|	2120	2151	2158	|	|	2247w	|	|
Peine △ d.	|	1937	|	|	|	|	|	2037	|	|	|	|	|	|	|	...	|	2137	|	|	|	|	|	|	|
Hannover Hbf △ a.	|	2005	2023	|	2028	2028	2037	2105	2055	2123	|	2128	2128	2128	2128	←	2142	2205	2223	|	2237	2256	2320w	2334	0128
Hannover Hbf d.	|	2009	2045	|	2031	2031	2040	2109	2100	→	|	2131	2131	2145	2145	2140	2145	2209	...	|	2240	2300	...	2344	...
Bremen Hbf **813** a.	|	|	2151	|	|	|	|	|	|	...	|	|	|	2244	2244	|	2244	|	...	|	|	|	...	0044	...
Oldenburg (Oldb) **813** a.	|	|	2222q	|	|	|	|	|	|	...	|	|	|	...	2317	|	2315	|	...	|	|	|	...	0123	...
Frankfurt (Main) Hbf **900** a.	2142	|	...	2244	|	|	|	|	0021	...	2344k	|	|	...	...	|	...	|	...	0058	|	|	...	...	...
Stuttgart Hbf **930** a.	2309	|	...	...	|	|	|	|	...	...	...	|	|	...	...	|	...	|	...	...	|	|	...	...	...
Basel SBB **912** a.	...	|	...	...	|	|	|	|	...	...	...	|	|	...	...	|	...	|	...	...	|	|	...	...	...
Minden (Westf) 802 d.	...	2102t	...	...	|	|	2112	2152	...	...	...	|	|	...	...	2212	...	2302t	...	...	2312	|	...	...	...
Bad Oeynhausen 802 d.	...	2114	...	...	|	|	2122	2204	...	...	...	|	|	...	...	2222	...	2314	...	...	2322	|	...	...	...
Löhne (Westf) 802 d.	...	2119	...	...	|	|	|	2211	...	...	...	|	|	...	...	|	...	2319	...	...	|	|	...	...	...
Bünde (Westf) 811 d.	...	|	...	...	|	|	2135	2221	...	...	...	|	|	...	...	|	...	|	...	...	2335	|	...	...	...
Osnabrück Hbf 811 d.	...	|	...	...	|	|	2159	2246	...	...	...	|	|	...	...	|	...	|	...	...	2358	|	...	...	...
Rheine 811 d.	...	|	...	...	|	|	*2246*	*2346*	...	...	...	|	|	...	...	|	...	|	...	...	...	|	...	...	...
Bad Bentheim 🏛 811 a.	...	|	...	...	|	|	...	...	...	...	...	|	|	...	...	|	...	|	...	...	...	|	...	...	...
Schiphol ✈ 22 ⊡ a.	...	|	...	...	|	|	...	...	...	...	...	|	|	...	...	|	...	|	...	...	...	|	...	...	...
Herford 802 d.	...	2127	...	...	|	|	...	...	...	...	...	|	|	...	...	2233	...	2327	...	...	...	2345	...	...	...
Bielefeld Hbf 802 d.	...	2136	...	...	2122	2122	...	...	...	...	...	2222	2222	...	...	2242	...	2336	...	...	...	2356	...	...	...
Gütersloh Hbf 802 d.	...	...	...	...	|	|	...	...	...	...	...	|	|	...	...	2252	...	...	...	...	...	0006	...	...	...
Hamm (Westf) 802 a.	...	...	...	...	2148	2148	...	...	...	...	...	2248	2248	...	...	2310	...	...	...	...	...	0029	...	...	...
Dortmund Hbf **800 802** a.	...	...	...	...	|	2209	...	...	...	...	...	|	2309	...	...	2332	...	...	...	...	...	0049	...	...	...
Düsseldorf Hbf **800 802** a.	...	...	...	...	|	2305	...	...	...	...	...	|	0005	...	...	|	...	...	...	...	...	0145	...	...	...
Hagen Hbf **800** a.	...	...	...	...	2222	|	...	...	...	...	...	2322	|	...	...	2355	...	...	...	...	...	|	...	...	...
Wuppertal Hbf **800** a.	...	...	...	...	2239	|	...	...	...	...	...	2339	|	...	...	0012	...	...	...	...	...	|	...	...	...
Köln Hbf **800** a.	...	...	...	...	2312	2330	...	...	...	...	...	0009	0029	...	...	0045	...	...	...	...	...	0209	...	...	...
Köln/Bonn Flughafen ✈ **800** d.	...	...	...	...	|	...	...	...	...	...	...	...	...	...	...	...	...	...	...	...	...	0225z	...	...	...
Bonn Hbf **800** a.	...	...	...	...	2339q	...	...	...	...	...	...	...	...	...	...	...	...	...	...	...	...	...	...	...	...
Koblenz Hbf **800** a.	...	...	...	...	...	...	...	...	...	...	...	...	...	...	...	...	...	...	...	...	...	...	...	...	...

♦ – NOTES (LISTED BY TRAIN NUMBER)

340 – ⑧ (not Dec. 24, 25, 30, 31, Apr. 2, 4, May 23). WAWEL – [12] Kraków - Forst 🏛 - Cottbus - Berlin - Uelzen - Hamburg. Departs Berlin Hbf 1742 from May 3.

697 – [12] and ✕ Berlin - Kassel (- Frankfurt ⑤⑦ k).

877/9 – [12] and ✕ Berlin - Mannheim - Karlsruhe.

1046 – ⑤ (also Dec. 23, 30, Apr. 1, May 12, June 2; not Dec. 25, Jan. 1, Apr. 2, May 14, June 4). [12] and ✕ Berlin - Düsseldorf - Mönchengladbach Hbf (a. 2040).

1899 – [12] Berlin - Kassel - Gießen - Frankfurt.

1932 – [12] Stralsund - Berlin Spandau - Bremen - Oldenburg.

A – To Düren (a. 2154) and Aachen Hbf (a. 2216) on ⑦w.

B – ①②③④⑥ (also Dec. 25, Apr. 2; not Dec. 23, 30, Apr. 1, 5, May 24).

C – ①②③④⑦ (not Dec. 23, 24, 30, 31, Apr. 1, 4, May 23).

D – From Dresden (Table **842**). Conveys ✕ on ⑦w.

E – ①②③④⑥⑦ (also Dec. 25, Jan. 1, Apr. 2, May 14, June 4; not Dec. 23, 30, Apr. 1, May 12, June 2).

L – To Münster (Westf) Hbf on ⑧q (a. 2225).

M – To Münster (Westf) Hbf (a. 0024).

N – To Norddeich Mole (Table **813**).

T – To Trier (Table **915**) on ⑧p.

U – To Uelzen (Table **841**).

a – ①–⑤ (not Dec. 24, 25, 31, Jan. 1, Apr. 2, 5, May 24).

b – ⑧ (not Dec. 24, 25, 31, Jan. 1, Apr. 2, 4, May 23).

d – Not Dec. 24, 25, 31, Jan. 1, Apr. 2, 4, May 23.

f – Also Dec. 23, 30, Apr. 1; not Dec. 25, Apr. 2.

h – Also Dec. 24, 25, 31, Jan. 1, Apr. 2, 4, May 23.

j – On Dec. 31 terminates at Amersfoort (a. 2022).

k – ⑤⑦ (also Dec. 23, 30, Apr. 1, 5, May 24; not Dec. 25, Apr. 2, 4, May 23).

n – Not Dec. 24, 31.

p – ⑧ (not Dec. 24, 25, 31, Apr. 2, 4, May 14, 23).

q – ⑧ (not Dec. 24, 25, 31, Apr. 2, 4, May 23).

r – Until May 2.

t – Arrives 10 minutes earlier.

v – Also Dec. 23, 30, Apr. 1, May 12; not Dec. 25, Jan. 1, Apr. 2, May 14.

w – ⑦ (also Apr. 5, May 24; not Apr. 4, May 23).

z – ①–⑤ only.

⟋ – *ICE SPRINTER*. 🅁 and supplement payable.

⊡ – Schiphol timings are subject to alteration on Apr. 30.

‡ – See panel on page 381 for additional local services.

△ – Services between Magdeburg and Hannover are subject to alteration from May 1. See Engineering Work Summary on page 361.

BIELEFELD - PADERBORN and BAD BENTHEIM — 811

Nord West Bahn; Westfalenbahn

Bielefeld Hbf - **Paderborn** Hbf via Hövelhof (*44 km*). Operated by Nord West Bahn. On Dec. 24, 31 services run as on ⑥. On June 3 services run as on ⑦. Journey time: 62 – 75 minutes.
From Bielefeld at 0432 Ⓐ, 0528 Ⓐ, 0539 ⑥ **k**, 0616 Ⓐ, 0639 ⑥ **k**, 0739 ⚒, 0839 ⚒, 0939, 1039 ⚒, 1139, 1239 ⚒, 1339, 1439 ⚒, 1539, 1639 ⚒, 1739, 1839 ⚒, 1939, 2039 ⚒, 2139 and 2239 ⚒.
From Paderborn at 0504 Ⓐ, 0513 ⑥ **k**, 0604 Ⓐ, 0613 ⑥ **k**, 0628 Ⓐ, 0713 ⚒, 0813 ⚒, 0913, 1013 ⚒, 1113, 1213 ⚒, 1313, 1413 ⚒, 1513, 1613 ⚒, 1713, 1813 ⚒, 1913, 2013 ⚒, 2113 and 2213 ⚒.

km	⊖	⚒v		⚒v							F
0	**Bielefeld** Hbf d.	0750	0850	0950	1050	1250	1450	1650	1850	2050	2250
11	Oerlinghausen d.	0803	0903	1003	1103	1303	1503	1703	1903	2103	2303
31	Detmold a.	0820	0920	1020	1120	1320	1520	1720	1920	2120	2320
60	Altenbeken a.	...	0946	...	1146	1346h	1546	1746	1946	...	2345

⊖	Ⓐe	⚒v		⚒v							
Altenbeken d.	0610	0713e	0813	...	1013	1213	1413h	1613	1813	2013	...
Detmold d.	0637	0740	0840	0940	1040	1240	1440	1640	1840	2040	2240
Oerlinghausen d.	0655	0801	0901	1001	1101	1301	1501	1701	1901	2101	2301
Bielefeld Hbf a.	0706	0812	0912	1012	1112	1312	1512	1712	1912	2112	2312

km	⊡	Ⓐe	⚒v						F⊖	
	Bielefeld Hbf **810** d.	0509	0609	0709	and	2109	...	2209	2250	...
0	Herford d.	0530	0633	0733	hourly	2133	...	2233	|	...
28	Detmold d.	0559	0702	0802	until	2202	...	2258	2320	...
57	Altenbeken ‡ a.	0624	0727	0827		2227	...	...	2345	...
74	**Paderborn** Hbf ‡ a.	0638	0741	0841		2241	...	...	2358	...

⊡	Ⓐe	⚒v								F⊖
Paderborn Hbf ‡ d.	...	0518	...	0621	and	2021	...	2121	...	2232
Altenbeken ‡ d.	...	0530	...	0633	hourly	2033	...	2133	...	2245
Detmold d.	0458	0558	...	0701	until	2101	...	2201	...	2322
Herford a.	0524	0624	...	0727		2127	...	2227	...	2350
Bielefeld Hbf **810** a.	0548	0648	...	0748		2148	...	2248	...	0007

km	⊡ See also Table **810**	⚒	⚒							
0	**Bielefeld** Hbf d.	0509	0609	...	0709		2109	2209	2309	...
14	Herford a.	0520	0620	...	0720	and	2120	2220	2320	...
14	Herford d.	0533	0633	...	0733		2133	2233	2333	...
28	Bünde (Westf) d.	0546	0646	...	0746	hourly	2146	2246	2346	...
65	**Osnabrück** Hbf d.	0614	0714	...	0814	until	2214	2314	0012	...
113	**Rheine** a.	0646	0746	...	0846		2246	2346	...	...
134	Bad Bentheim a.	0703	0803	...	0903		2303	...	...	...

⊡ See also Table **810**	⚒	⚒								
Bad Bentheim d.	...	...	0557a	0657r	0757r	0857		1957	2057	2157
Rheine d.	...	0514	0614a	0714r	0814	0914	and	2014	2114	2214
Osnabrück Hbf d.	0448	0548	0648	0748	0848	0948		2048	2148	2248
Bünde (Westf) d.	0513	0613	0713	0813	0913	1013	hourly	2113	2213	2313
Herford a.	0527	0627	0727	0827	0927	1027	until	2127	2227	2327
Herford d.	0537	0637	0737	0837	0937	1037		2137	2237	2337
Bielefeld Hbf a.	0548	0648	0748	0848	0948	1048		2148	2248	2348

F – ⑤–⑦ (also Dec. 24, 31, Apr. 5, May 13, 24, June 3).
a – Ⓐ (not Dec. 24, 31).
e – Ⓐ (not Dec. 24, 31, June 3).
h – ⑤† only.
k – Not Dec. 26, May 1.
r – ⚒ only.
v – Not June 3.
‡ – See also Tables **805/9**.
⊖ – 2nd class only. Operated by Nord West Bahn.
⊡ – Operated by WestfalenBahn.

MÜNSTER - EMDEN - NORDDEICH — 812

RE services except where shown

km		Ⓐn	⚒	⚒		*IC* 2331 A 🍷			*IC* 2333 H 🍷			*IC* 231 C L🍷	*IC* 331 E 🍷♦	*IC* 2132 D 🍷	©z	Ⓐn		*IC* 333 L🍷			*IC* 335 L🍷			*IC* 2014 ①–⑤ 🍷♦	*IC* 2004 ⑦b 🍷♦
	Köln Hbf **800** d.	...	...	...	...	0541	...	...	0746	...	...	0946	0946	...	...	...	...	1146	...	...	1346	...	...	1546	1546
0	**Münster** (Westf) Hbf. § d.	0502	...	0602	0702	0731	0805	0905	0931	1005	1105	1131	1131	...	1205	1205	1305	1331	1405	1505	1531	1605	1705	1731	1731
39	Rheine § d.	0534	0534	0634	0734	0756	0834	0934	0956	1034	1134	1156	1156	...	1234	1234	1334	1356	1434	1534	1556	1634	1734	1756	1756
70	Lingen (Ems) d.	0556	0556	0656	0756	0815	0856	0956	1015	1056	1156	1215	1215	...	1256	1256	1356	1415	1456	1556	1615	1656	1756	1815	1815
91	Meppen d.	0611	0611	0711	0811	0829	0911	1011	1029	1111	1211	1229	1229	...	1311	1329t	1411	1429	1511	1611	1629	1711	1811	1829	1829
137	Papenburg (Ems) d.	0643	0643	0743	0843	0856	0943	1043	1056	1143	1243	1256	1256	...	1343	1403	1443	1456	1543	1643	1656	1743	1843	1856	1856
154	Leer (Ostfriesl) **813** d.	0656	0656	0756	0856	0918j	0956	1056	1109	1156	1256	1309	1309	1319	1356	1415	1456	1509	1556	1656	1709	1756	1856	1909	1909
180	**Emden** Hbf **813** a.	0713	0713	0813	0913	0933	1013	1113	1125	1213	1313	1325	1325	1336	1413	1432	1513	1525	1613	1713	1725	1813	1913	1926	1926
180	**Emden** Hbf **813** d.	0735	0735	0843	...	0936	1043	...	1141	1243	...	1328	...	1341	1443	1443	...	1527	1643	...	1728	1843	...	...	...
209	Norden **813** d.	0807	0807	0907	...	1003	1107	...	1205	1307	...	1352	...	1409	1507	1507	...	1550	1707	...	1753	1907	...	...	...
215	**Norddeich** **813** a.	0813	0813	0913	...	1009	1113	...	1211	1313	...	1359	...	1415	1513	1513	...	1557	1713	...	1759	1913	...	...	...
	Norddeich Mole **813** a.	0817	0817	0918	...	1014	1118	...	1217	1318	...	1404	...	1421	1518	1518	...	1604	1718	...	1804	1918	...	...	...

	IC 2036 🍷♦			*IC* 337 N L🍷		n	n	¶	¶ v
Köln Hbf **800** d.	...	...	...	1745	...	...	...	...	...
Münster (Westf) Hbf. § d.	...	1805	1905	1931	2005	2105	2211	2311	0011
Rheine § d.	...	1834	1934	1956	2034	2134	2251	2343	0043
Lingen (Ems) d.	...	1856	1956	2015	2056	2156	2312	...	...
Meppen d.	...	1911	2011	2029	2111	2211	2326	...	...
Papenburg (Ems) d.	...	1943	2043	2056	2143	2243	2358	...	...
Leer (Ostfriesland) **813** d.	1925	1956	2056	2109	2156	2256	0010	...	...
Emden Hbf **813** a.	1942	2013	2113	2125	2213	2313	0027	...	...
Emden Hbf **813** d.	1945	2043	...	...	2243	...	...	...	...
Norden **813** d.	2008	2107	...	...	2307	...	...	...	...
Norddeich **813** a.	2015	2113	...	...	2313	...	...	...	...
Norddeich Mole **813** a.	2021	...	...	...	...	...	...	...	...

	Ⓐn	⚒	⚒	⚒	*IC* 2015 ①–④ 🍷♦	*IC* 2005 ⑤⑥d 🍷♦	Ⓐn	©z		*IC* 2037 🍷♦	*IC* 336 M L🍷
Norddeich Mole **813** d.	...	...	...	...	...	...	...	...	...	0737	...
Norddeich **813** d.	...	...	...	0532	...	...	...	...	0642	0740	...
Norden **813** d.	...	...	...	0538	...	...	...	...	0648	0747	...
Emden Hbf **813** a.	...	...	...	0602	...	...	...	...	0716	0812	...
Emden Hbf **813** d.	...	0450	0550	0604	0634	0634	0642	0650	0750	0814	0834
Leer (Ostfriesland) **813** d.	...	0506	0606	0621	0653	0653	0658	0706	0806	0831	0853
Papenburg (Ems) d.	...	0516	0616	...	0704	0704	0709	0716	0816	...	0904
Meppen d.	...	0550	0650	...	0731	0731	0744	0750	0850	...	0931
Lingen (Ems) d.	...	0604	0704	...	0744	0744	0804	0804	0904	...	0944
Rheine § d.	0528	0628	0729	...	0804	0804	0829	0829	0929	...	1004
Münster (Westf) Hbf § a.	0554	0654	0756	...	0829	0829	0856	0856	0956	...	1029
Köln Hbf **800** a.	...	...	...	...	1012	1012	...	...	...	...	1212

			IC 334 L🍷			Ⓐn	*IC* 332 🍷♦	Ⓐn	©z		*IC* 330 L🍷			*IC* 2135 D 🍷	*IC* 2332 F 🍷	*IC* 2334 K 🍷			*IC* 2330 B 🍷			n	¶		n
Norddeich Mole **813** d.	...	0840	0953	...	1040	...	1136	...	...	1240	1354	...	1440	1539	...	1558	...	1640	1754	...	1840	...	...	2040	...
Norddeich **813** d.	...	0842	0956	...	1042	...	1139	...	...	1242	1402	...	1442	1542	...	1602	...	1642	1802	...	1842	...	...	2042	...
Norden **813** d.	...	0848	1004	...	1048	...	1146	...	...	1248	1409	...	1448	1549	...	1609	...	1648	1809	...	1848	...	...	2048	...
Emden Hbf **813** a.	...	0916	1026	...	1116	...	1213	...	...	1316	1431	...	1516	1611	...	1631	...	1716	1831	...	1916	...	...	2116	...
Emden Hbf **813** d.	0850	0950	1034	1050	1150	1224	1234	...	1250	1350	1434	1450	1550	1619	1634	1634	1650	1750	1834	1850	1950	2050	...	2118	2214
Leer (Ostfriesland) **813** d.	0906	1006	1053	1106	1206	1241	1253	...	1306	1406	1453	1506	1606	1636	1653	1653	1706	1806	1853	1906	2006	2106	...	2135	2229
Papenburg (Ems) d.	0916	1016	1104	1116	1216	1251	1304	←	1316	1416	1504	1516	1616	...	1704	1704	1716	1816	1904	1916	2016	2116	...	▬	2239
Meppen d.	0950	1050	1131	1150	1250	1325	1331	1337	1350	1450	1531	1550	1650	...	1731	1731	1750	1850	1931	1950	2050	2150	...	...	2313
Lingen (Ems) d.	1004	1104	1144	1204	1304	→	1344	1351	1404	1504	1544	1604	1704	...	1744	1744	1804	1904	1944	2004	2104	2204	...	n ¶	2327
Rheine § d.	1029	1129	1204	1229	1327	...	1404	1429j	1429	1529	1604	1629	1729	...	1804	1804	1829	1929	2004	2029	2129	2229	2252	2352	2349
Münster (Westf) Hbf. § a.	1056	1156	1229	1256	1356	...	1429	1456	1456	1556	1629	1656	1756	...	1829	1829	1856	1956	2029	2056	2156	2256	2325	0025	...
Köln Hbf **800** a.	...	...	1412	...	...	...	1612	...	...	...	1812	...	...	...	2012	2012	...	...	2212	...	...	...	...	...	...

Additional trains Münster - Rheine and v.v.

	¶		¶			¶		¶	¶
Köln Hbf **802** d.	...	0621r	...	0821	each train	...	1821	...	...
Münster (Westf) Hbf d.	0735	0824	0935	1024	runs every **two** hours	1935	2024	2135	2235
Rheine a.	0808	0851	1008	1051	until	2008	2051	2208	2308

	¶⚒r	Ⓐe			¶		¶			¶
Rheine d.	0452	0606	0617	0706	0752	0906	0952	each train	1906	1952
Münster (Westf) Hbf a.	0525	0632	0650	0732	0825	0932	1025	runs every **two** hours	1932	2025
Köln Hbf **802** a.	...	0838	...	0938	...	1138	...	until	2138	...

♦ – **NOTES** (LISTED BY TRAIN NUMBER)

331 – BORKUM – [12] and 🍷 (Luxembourg ★ -) Köln - Emden.
332 – [12] and 🍷 Norddeich Mole - Köln (- Luxembourg Ⓑ **q**).
2004/5 – BODENSEE – [12] and 🍷 Konstanz - Karlsruhe - Koblenz - Köln - Emden and v.v.
2014 – ①–⑤ (not Dec. 24, 25, 31, Jan. 1, Apr. 2, 5, May 13, 24, June 3). [12] and 🍷 Stuttgart - Koblenz - Köln - Emden.
2015 – ①–④ (not Dec. 23, 24, 30, 31, Apr. 1, 5, May 12, 24, June 2). [12] and 🍷 Emden - Köln - Koblenz - Stuttgart.
2036/7 – [12] and 🍷 Leipzig - Hannover - Bremen - Norddeich Mole and v.v.

A – ① Dec. 14 - Jan. 4; ① Mar. 8 – 22; ①④⑤⑥⑦ Mar. 27 - Apr. 12; ① Apr. 19 - May 3; ①④⑤⑥⑦ from May 8.
B – ⑦ Dec. 13 - Jan. 3; ⑦ Mar. 7 – 21; ③–⑦ Mar. 26 - Apr. 11; ⑦ Apr. 18 - May 2; ③–⑦ from May 7.
C – ①②③④⑥ to Mar. 25.
D – Daily Dec. 26 - Jan. 3 (also Dec. 13, 18, 20); ⑤⑦ Jan. 8 - Mar. 14; daily from Mar. 19. See also Table **813**.
E – ⑤⑦ to Mar. 21; daily from Mar. 26.
F – ⑤⑦ to Mar. 21 (not Dec. 25); daily from Mar. 26.
H – ⚒ (daily from Mar. 22).
K – ①–④ Dec. 14 - Mar. 25 (not Dec. 24, 31).
L – From / to Luxembourg (Table **915**).
M – ①–⑥ to Mar. 20 (not Dec. 25, 26, Jan. 1); daily from Mar. 22.
N – Ⓑ to Mar. 19 (not Dec. 24, 25, 31); daily from Mar. 21.

b – Also Jan. 1, Apr. 5, May 13, 24, June 3; not Apr. 4, May 23.
d – Also Dec. 23, 24, 30, 31, Apr. 1, May 12, June 2; not Dec. 25, 26, Jan. 1, Apr. 3.
e – Not Dec. 24, 31, June 3.
j – Arrives 11 minutes earlier.
n – Not Dec. 24, 31.
q – Not Dec. 24, 25, 31, Apr. 2, 4, May 23.
r – ⚒ (not June 3).
t – Arrives 1310.
v – Not Dec. 25, Jan. 1.
z – Also Dec. 24, 31.

★ – ⑤ to Mar. 19 (not Dec. 25, Jan. 1); ①–⑥ from Mar. 26 (not Apr. 3, 5, May 24).
¶ – Operated by WestfalenBahn.
§ – See panel below main table for additional trains.

813 NORDDEICH - EMDEN - BREMEN - HANNOVER

km		RE 4401	RB 14801	ICE 531	RE 4403	RE 14531	IC 2033	IC 2033	RE 4407	ICE 533	RE 4407	RE 14533	IC 2035	RE 4411	ICE 1035	ICE 535	RE 4411	IC 2037	RE 4415	ICE 537	RE 4415	RE 14535	IC 2039	RE 4419	ICE 539	RE 4419
			Ⓐ n	①–⑤ a ✕		⚒ n	①–⑥ e 🍷	🍷		①–⑥ e ✕			🍷		⑤t F ✕	A ✕		🍷		✕			🍷		✕	
◧	**Norddeich Mole** 812 d.	...	...	...	...	...	...	...	...	...	...	...	...	...	...	...	...	0737	0840	...	...	...	...	1040	...	...
0	**Norddeich** 812 d.	...	...	...	...	...	...	...	...	...	...	0532r	...	0642	...	...	...	0740	0842	...	...	0922	...	1042	...	...
6	Norden 812 d.	...	...	...	...	...	...	...	...	...	...	0538r	...	0648	...	...	...	0747	0848	...	...	0928	...	1048	...	...
35	**Emden** Hbf 812 d.	...	...	...	...	0418	...	...	0518	...	...	0604	...	0718	...	...	...	0814	0918	...	...	1018	...	1118	...	...
61	Leer (Ostfriesland) **812** a.	...	...	...	...	0435	...	...	0535	...	...	0621	...	0735	...	...	...	0831	0935	...	...	1035	...	1135	...	...
61	Leer (Ostfriesland) d.	...	...	...	...	0442	...	...	0542	...	...	0632	...	0742	...	...	...	0841	0942	...	...	1042	...	1142	...	...
101	Bad Zwischenahn d.	...	...	...	...	0510	...	...	0613	...	...	0707	...	0813	...	...	...	0918	1013	...	...	1112	...	1213	...	...
116	**Oldenburg** (Oldb) a.	...	...	...	...	0521	...	...	0623	...	...	0719	...	0823	...	...	...	0930	1023	...	...	1123	...	1223	...	...
116	**Oldenburg** (Oldb) d.	...	0409	0447g	...	...	0535	...	0635	0642	...	...	0735	0835	...	...	...	0935	1035	...	...	...	1135	1235	...	...
147	Delmenhorst d.	...	0438	|	...	...	0553	...	0654	|	...	...	0753	0854	...	...	...	0953	1054	...	...	...	1153	1254	...	...
161	**Bremen** Hbf a.	...	0451	0512g	...	...	0603	...	0705	0709	←	...	0803	0905	...	...	←	1003	1105	...	←	...	1203	1305	...	←
161	**Bremen** Hbf ◇ d.	0418	...	0514	0518	...	0609	0609	→	0714	0718	...	0809	→	0914	0914	0918	1009	→	1114	1118	...	1209	→	1314	1318
196	Verden (Aller) ◇ d.	0442	...	|	0542	...	0629	0629	...	|	0742	...	0829	...	|	|	0942	1029	...	|	1142	...	1229	...	|	1342
227	Nienburg (Weser) ◇ d.	0504	...	|	0604	...	0647	0647	...	|	0804	...	0847	...	|	|	1004	1047	...	|	1204	...	1247	...	|	1404
283	**Hannover** Hbf ◇ a.	0538	...	0614	0638	...	0714	0714	...	0814	0838	...	0914	...	1013	1014	1038	1114	...	1214	1238	...	1314	...	1414	1438
	Magdeburg Hbf ⊖ a.	...	...	|	...	...	0857	0857	...	|	...	...	1057	...	...	|	...	1257	...	|	...	...	1457	...	|	...
	Berlin Hbf **810** a.	...	...	|	...	...	|	|	...	|	...	...	|	...	...	|	...	|	...	|	...	...	|	...	|	...
	Leipzig Hbf **810** a.	...	...	|	...	...	1020	1020	...	|	...	...	1220	...	...	|	...	1420	...	|	...	...	1620	...	|	...
	Nürnberg Hbf **900** a.	...	...	0930	...	...	...	...	...	|	...	...	...	...	...	1329	...	...	...	|	...	...	...	...	|	...
	München Hbf **900** a.	...	...	1044	...	...	...	...	...	1304	...	...	...	...	...	1444	...	...	...	1707	...	...	...	...	1903	...

	IC 2131	RE 4423	ICE 631	RE 4423	RE 14537	IC 2133	RE 4427	ICE 633	RE 4427	IC 2135	IC 2135	RE 4431	ICE 635	ICE 635	RE 4431	RE 14539	IC 2137	RE 4433	RE 4435	ICE 637	RE 4435	RB 14837	RE 4437	RE 14541 14839	RE 4439	RB 14841
	C 🍷		✕			🍷		✕		★ 🍷	🍷		✕	⑦w ✕			Ⓑq ¶			⑦w ✕						n
Norddeich Mole 812 d.	...	1240	...	...	...	...	1440	...	...	1539	...	1640	...	...	...	...	...	...	1840	...	...	...	...	...	2040	...
Norddeich 812 d.	...	1242	...	...	...	...	1442	...	...	1542	...	1642	...	...	...	...	...	...	1842	...	...	...	...	...	2042	...
Norden 812 d.	...	1248	...	...	...	...	1448	...	...	1549	...	1648	...	...	...	...	...	...	1848	...	...	...	...	...	2048	...
Emden Hbf 812 d.	1219	1318	...	...	1418	...	1518	...	...	1619	...	1718	...	...	...	1818	...	...	1918	...	...	...	...	2018	2118	...
Leer (Ostfriesland) **812** a.	1236	1335	...	...	1435	...	1535	...	...	1636	...	1735	...	...	...	1835	...	...	1935	...	...	...	...	2035	2135	...
Leer (Ostfriesland) d.	1242	1342	...	...	1442	...	1542	...	...	1641	...	1742	...	...	...	1842	...	...	1942	...	...	...	...	2042	2142	...
Bad Zwischenahn d.	1321	1413	...	...	1512	...	1613	...	...	1718	...	1813	...	...	...	1912	...	...	2013	...	...	...	...	2112	2213	...
Oldenburg (Oldb) a.	1331	1423	...	...	1523	...	1623	...	...	1730	...	1823	...	...	...	1923	...	...	2023	...	...	...	...	2123	2223	...
Oldenburg (Oldb) d.	1335	1435	...	...	...	1535	1635	...	...	1735	1735	1835	...	...	...	...	1935	...	2035	...	...	2109	...	2137	2235	2340
Delmenhorst d.	1353	1454	...	...	...	1553	1654	...	...	1753	1753	1854	...	...	...	...	1953	...	2054	...	...	2138	...	2204	2254	0009
Bremen Hbf a.	1403	1505	...	←	...	1603	1705	...	←	1803	1803	1905	...	...	←	...	2003	...	2105	...	←	2151	...	2220	2305	0022
Bremen Hbf ◇ d.	1409	→	1514	1518	...	1609	→	1714	1718	1809	1809	→	1914	1914	1918	...	2009	2018	→	2114	2118	...	2218	...	2311	...
Verden (Aller) ◇ d.	1429	...	|	1542	...	1629	...	|	1742	1829	1829	...	|	|	1942	...	2029	2042	...	|	2142	...	2242	...	2343	...
Nienburg (Weser) ◇ d.	1447	...	|	1604	...	1647	...	|	1804	1847	1847	...	|	|	2004	...	2047	2104	...	|	2204	...	2304	...	0004	...
Hannover Hbf ◇ a.	1514	...	1614	1638	...	1714	...	1814	1838	1914	1914	...	2014	2014	2038	...	2114	2138	...	2213	2238	...	2338	...	0038	...
Magdeburg Hbf ⊖ a.	1657z	...	|	...	...	1857	...	|	...	2057	2057	...	|	|	...	...	2300	...	...	...	...	...	...	...	...	...
Berlin Hbf **810** a.	1827z	...	|	...	...	|	...	|	...	|	|	...	|	|	...	...	...	...	...	...	...	...	...	...	...	...
Leipzig Hbf **810** a.	...	...	|	...	...	2020	...	|	...	2219	2219	...	|	|	...	...	...	...	...	...	...	...	...	...	...	...
Nürnberg Hbf **900** a.	...	...	|	...	...	...	...	|	...	...	...	...	2324	2324	...	...	...	...	...	...	...	...	...	...	...	...
München Hbf **900** a.	...	...	2102	...	...	...	...	2302	...	...	...	...	...	0041	...	...	...	...	...	...	...	...	...	...	...	...

	RE 4400	RB 14800	RB 14802	RE 4402	RE 4404	IC 2136	RE 14534	RE 4406	ICE 636	RE 4406	IC 2134	RE 4410	ICE 634	RE 4410	IC 2132	IC 2132	RE 4414	ICE 632	RE 4414	IC 2130	RE 14536	RE 4418	ICE 630	RE 4418	IC 2038	RE 14538
		⚒ n				①–⑥ e			①–⑤ a ✕		🍷		✕		C 🍷	★ C 🍷		✕		🍷			✕		🍷	
München Hbf **900** d.	...	...	...	...	...	...	...	...	...	...	...	...	0515a	...	...	...	...	0648	...	...	...	...	0915	...	...	...
Nürnberg Hbf **900** d.	...	...	...	...	...	...	...	...	...	...	...	...	0630	...	...	...	...	|	...	...	...	...	1028	...	...	...
Leipzig Hbf **810** d.	...	...	...	...	...	...	...	...	...	...	0539a	...	|	...	...	...	...	|	...	0939	...	...	|	...	1139	...
Berlin Hbf **810** d.	...	...	...	...	...	...	...	...	...	...	|	...	|	...	0731	0731	...	|	...	|	...	...	|	...	|	...
Magdeburg Hbf ⊖ d.	...	...	...	...	...	0501a	...	...	...	...	0700	...	|	...	0901	0901	...	|	...	1100	...	...	|	...	1300	...
Hannover Hbf ◇ d.	0021	...	...	0521	0617	0645	...	0721	0745	...	0845	0921	0945	...	1045	1045	1121	1145	...	1245	...	1321	1345	...	1445	...
Nienburg (Weser) ◇ d.	0055	...	...	0555	0655	0713	...	0755	|	...	0913	0955	|	...	1113	1113	1155	|	...	1313	...	1355	|	...	1513	...
Verden (Aller) ◇ d.	0116	...	...	0616	0716	0730	...	0816	|	...	0930	1016	|	...	1130	1130	1216	|	...	1330	...	1416	|	...	1530	...
Bremen Hbf ◇ a.	0139	...	...	0641	0741	0751	...	0841	0844	←	0951	1039	1044	←	1151	1151	1239	1244	←	1351	...	1441	1444	←	1551	...
Bremen Hbf d.	...	0444	0543	0654	...	0755	...	→	...	0854	0955	→	...	1054	1155	1155	→	...	1254	1355	...	→	...	1454	1555	...
Delmenhorst d.	...	0455	0556	0704	...	0806	...	...	...	0904	1006	...	...	1104	1206	1206	...	...	1304	1406	...	...	...	1504	1606	...
Oldenburg (Oldb) a.	...	0518	0623	0723	...	0822	...	...	...	0923	1022	...	...	1123	1222	1222	...	...	1323	1422	...	...	...	1523	1622	...
Oldenburg (Oldb) d.	...	0533	0626	0733	...	...	0833	...	...	0933	1033	...	...	1133	...	1224	...	...	1333	...	1433	...	...	1533	...	1633
Bad Zwischenahn d.	...	0545	0638	0745	...	...	0845	...	...	0945	1044	...	...	1145	...	1236	...	...	1345	...	1445	...	...	1545	...	1645
Leer (Ostfriesland) a.	...	0615	0707	0815	...	...	0915	...	...	1015	1115	...	...	1215	...	1307	...	...	1415	...	1515	...	...	1615	...	1715
Leer (Ostfriesland) **812** d.	...	0625	0715	0825	...	...	0925	...	...	1025	1120	...	...	1225	...	1319	...	...	1425	...	1522	...	...	1625	...	1722
Emden Hbf 812 d.	...	0643	0735	0843	...	...	0942	...	...	1043	1137	...	...	1243	...	1341	...	...	1443	...	1538	...	...	1643	...	1738
Norden 812 d.	...	0707	0807	0907	...	...	...	...	...	1107	...	...	...	1307	...	1409	...	...	1507	...	...	...	...	1707	...	...
Norddeich 812 a.	...	0713	0813	0913	...	...	...	...	...	1113	...	...	...	1313	...	1415	...	...	1513	...	...	...	...	1713	...	...
Norddeich Mole 812 a.	...	0717	0817	0918	...	...	...	...	...	1118	...	...	...	1318	...	1421	...	...	1518	...	...	...	...	1718	...	...

	RE 4422	ICE 538	RE 4422	IC 2036	RE 4426	ICE 536	RE 4426	IC 2034	RE 14540	RE 4430	ICE 776	RE 4430	IC 2032	IC 2032	RE 14542	RE 4434	ICE 832	ICE 862	IC 1932	RE 4440	RE 4440	RE 4436	ICE 732	ICE 732	RE 4438	ICE 850
		✕		🍷		✕		🍷			Ⓑq F ✕		🍷	Ⓑq 🍷	Ⓑn		⊡ ✕	⑤f ✕	⑦w H		⑥		G ✕	L ✕		⑦w ✕
München Hbf **900** d.	...	1052	...	...	...	1251	...	...	...	...	...	...	...	...	...	...	...	...	...	...	...	...	1820	1820	...	...
Nürnberg Hbf **900** d.	...	|	...	...	...	|	...	...	...	...	...	...	...	...	...	...	...	...	...	...	...	...	1933	1933	...	...
Leipzig Hbf **810** d.	...	|	...	1339	...	|	...	1539	...	...	...	...	1739	1739	...	...	...	...	...	...	...	...	|	|	...	...
Berlin Hbf **810** d.	...	|	...	|	...	|	...	|	...	...	...	...	|	|	...	...	1948	1948	1958s	...	...	...	|	|	...	2148
Magdeburg Hbf ⊖ d.	...	|	...	1500	...	|	...	1700	...	...	...	...	1900	1900	...	...	|	|	|	...	...	...	|	|	...	|
Hannover Hbf ◇ d.	1521	1545	...	1645	1721	1745	...	1845	...	1921	1949	...	2045	2045	...	2121	2145	2145	2145	...	...	2221	2251	2251	2321	2344
Nienburg (Weser) ◇ d.	1555	|	...	1713	1755	|	...	1913	...	1955	|	...	2113	2113	...	2155	|	|	|	...	...	2255	|	|	2355	|
Verden (Aller) ◇ d.	1616	|	...	1730	1816	|	...	1930	...	2016	|	...	2130	2130	...	2216	|	|	|	...	...	2316	|	|	0016	|
Bremen Hbf ◇ a.	1639	1644	←	1751	1839	1844	←	1951	...	2039	2048	←	2151	2151	...	2241	2244	2244	2244	...	...	2339	2349	2349	0039	0044
Bremen Hbf d.	→	...	1654	1755	→	...	1854	1955	...	→	2050a	2055	...	2155	...	...	...	2246	2247	2254	2254	...	...	2352	...	0047
Delmenhorst d.	...	...	1704	1806	...	...	1904	2006	...	...	|	2105	...	2206	...	...	...	2259	2258	2304	2304	...	...	|	...	0101
Oldenburg (Oldb) a.	...	...	1723	1822	...	...	1923	2022	...	...	2115a	2124	...	2222	...	...	...	2317	2315	2323	2323	...	...	0017	...	0123
Oldenburg (Oldb) d.	...	...	1733	1833	...	...	1933	...	2033	...	...	2133	...	...	2233	...	...	...	...	...	2333	...	...	...	...	...
Bad Zwischenahn d.	...	...	1745	1844	...	...	1945	...	2045	...	...	2145	...	...	2245	...	...	...	...	...	2345	...	...	...	...	...
Leer (Ostfriesland) a.	...	...	1815	1915	...	...	2015	...	2115	...	...	2215	...	...	2315	...	...	...	...	...	0015	...	...	...	...	...
Leer (Ostfriesland) **812** d.	...	...	1825	1925	...	...	2025	...	2122	...	...	2225	...	...	2322	...	...	...	...	...	0025	...	...	...	...	...
Emden Hbf 812 d.	...	...	1843	1945	...	...	2043	...	2138	...	...	2243	...	...	2338	...	...	...	...	...	0041	...	...	...	...	...
Norden 812 d.	...	...	1907	2008	...	...	2107	...	...	...	...	2307	...	...	...	...	...	...	...	...	...	...	...	...	...	...
Norddeich 812 a.	...	...	1913	2015	...	...	2113	...	...	...	...	2313	...	...	...	...	...	...	...	...	...	...	...	...	...	...
Norddeich Mole 812 a.	...	...	1918	2021	...	...	...	...	...	...	...	...	...	...	...	...	...	...	...	...	...	...	...	...	...	...

A – ①②③④⑥⑦ (also Dec. 25, Jan. 1, Apr. 2, May 14, June 4; not Dec. 23, 30, Apr. 1, May 12, June 2).
C – To / from Cottbus on dates in Table **838**.
F – From / to Frankfurt (Table **900**).
G – From Garmisch (d. 1624) on ⑥.
H – From Stralsund (Table **845**).
L – ①②③④⑦ (not Dec. 23, 24, 30, 31, Apr. 1, 4, May 23).

a – ①–⑤ (not Dec. 24, 25, 31, Jan. 1, Apr. 2, 5, May 24).
e – ①–⑥ (not Dec. 25, 26, Jan. 1, Apr. 3, 5, May 24).
f – Also Dec. 23, 30, Apr. 1; not Dec. 25, Apr. 2.
g – ① (also Apr. 6, May 25; not Apr. 5, May 24).
n – Not Dec. 24, 31.
q – Not Dec. 24, 25, 31, Apr. 2, 4, May 23.
r – ⚒ only.
s – Berlin **Spandau**.
t – Also Dec. 23, 30, Apr. 1, May 12, June 2; not Dec. 25, Jan. 1, Apr. 2, May 14, June 4.
w – Also Apr. 5, May 24; not Apr. 4, May 23.
z – From May 1 does not call at Magdeburg and arrives Berlin Hbf 1738.

⊡ – ①②③④⑥ (also Dec. 25, Apr. 2; not Dec. 23, 30, Apr. 1, 5, May 24).
★ – Daily Dec. 26 - Jan. 3 (also Dec. 13, 18, 20); ⑤⑦ Jan. 8 - Mar. 14; daily from Mar. 19.
¶ – Conveys 🍷 on ⑤⑦.
◧ – Norddeich Mole is 300 metres from Norddeich.
⊖ – See also Table **810**. Magdeburg timings are subject to alteration from May 1.
◇ – Other *RE* trains Bremen - Verden - Nienburg - Hannover and v.v. From Bremen Hbf at 0618 and every two hours until 1818. From Hannover Hbf at 0821 and every two hours until 2021.

OSNABRÜCK - OLDENBURG - WILHELMSHAVEN — 814

Nord West Bahn

km		⚒	Ⓐ		Ⓐ								Ⓐ			B							⚒		†
0	**Osnabrück** Hbf d.	...	0442	0602	0626	0702	0802	0902	1002	1102	1202	1302	1326	1402	1502	...	1602	1702	1802	1902	2002	2102	...	2253	2253
20	Bramsche d.	...	0500	0617	0641	0717	0817	0917	1017	1117	1217	1317	1348	1417	1517	...	1617	1717	1817	1917	2017	2117	...	2313	2313
50	Quakenbrück d.	...	0540	0640	0710	0740	0840	0940	1040	1140	1240	1340	1410	1440	1540	...	1640	1740	1840	1940	2040	2140	...	2340	2340
72	Cloppenburg d.	...	0556	0656	0740	0756	0856	0956	1056	1156	1256	1356	1442	1456	1556	...	1656	1756	1856	1956	2056	2156	...	2356	2356
113	**Oldenburg** (Oldb) a.	...	0629	0729	0819	0829	0929	1029	1129	1229	1329	1429	1519	1529	1629	...	1729	1829	1929	2029	2129	2229	...	0029	0029
113	**Oldenburg** (Oldb) d.	0536	0636	0736	...	0836	0936	1036	1136	1236	1336	1436	...	1536	1636	1706	1736	1836	1936	2036	2136	2236	2336	...	0039
143	Varel (Oldb) d.	0559	0659	0759	...	0859	0959	1059	1159	1259	1359	1459	...	1559	1659	1729	1759	1859	1959	2059	2159	2259	2359	...	0103
165	**Wilhelmshaven** a.	0619	0719	0819	...	0919	1019	1119	1219	1319	1419	1519	...	1619	1719	1748	1819	1919	2019	2119	2219	2319	0019	...	0122

	Ⓐ	⚒	Ⓐ	⚒	ⒶD	Ⓐ								Ⓑk									Ⓒ		
Wilhelmshaven d.	...	0444	...	0544	0613	...	0644	0744	0844	0944	1044	1144	1244	1344	...	1444	1544	1644	1744	1844	1944	2044	2044	2144	2243
Varel (Oldb) d.	...	0502	...	0602	0631	...	0702	0802	0902	1002	1102	1202	1302	1402	1402	1502	1602	1702	1802	1902	2002	2102	2102	2202	2301
Oldenburg (Oldb) a.	...	0525	...	0625	0653	...	0725	0825	0925	1025	1125	1225	1325	1425	1425	1525	1625	1725	1825	1925	2025	2125	2125	2225	2324
Oldenburg (Oldb) d.	0412	0529	0557	0629	...	0657	0729	0829	0929	1029	1129	1229	1329	1429	1429	1529	1629	1729	1829	1929	2029	...	2129	2229	...
Cloppenburg d.	0444	0606	0632	0706	...	0732	0806	0906	1006	1106	1206	1306	1406	1506	1506	1606	1706	1806	1906	2006	2106	...	2206	2302	...
Quakenbrück d.	0459	0621	0650	0721	...	0750	0821	0921	1021	1121	1221	1321	1421	1522	1522	1621	1721	1821	1921	2021	2122	...	2221	2321	...
Bramsche d.	0521	0642	0710	0742	...	0810	0842	0942	1042	1142	1242	1342	1442	1542	1542	1642	1742	1842	1942	2042	2142	...	2242	2342	...
Osnabrück Hbf a.	0540	0658	0727	0758	...	0827	0858	0958	1058	1158	1258	1358	1458	1558	1558	1658	1758	1858	1958	2058	2158	...	2258	2358	...

B – From Bremen Hbf (d. 1631). D – To Bremen Hbf (a. 0727). k – Also Dec. 26, May 1. **Operator**: Nord West Bahn GmbH. ✆ +49 (0) 1805 60 01 61.

BREMEN - BREMERHAVEN - CUXHAVEN — 815

RE / RB services

km			⚒				Ⓐn	ⒸN		b	Q	⑥D	P			⚒			Ⓐn	†F	⑥C			Ⓐn		
	Osnabrück Hbf **800/1** d.	...	...	0538r	...	...	0638	...	0738	...	...	...	...	0938	...	...	1138	...	...	...	...	1338	...	1438j	1538	
0	**Bremen** Hbf d.	0004	0534	0656	...	0734	0756	0757	0856	0934	0934	...	...	1056	1134	...	1256	1334	...	1357	1357	1456	1534	1556	1656	1734
21	Osterholz-Scharmbeck d.	0022	0552	0710	...	0752	0810	0811	0910	0952	0952	...	...	1110	1152	...	1310	1352	...	1411	1411	1510	1552	1610	1710	1752
63	**Bremerhaven** Hbf d.	0057	0627	0732	0736	0827	0832	0837	0932	1026	1027	1029	1036	1132	1227	1236	1332	1427	1436	1436	1436	1532	1627	1632	1732	1827
66	**Bremerhaven**-Lehe d.	0102	0632	0737	0742	0832	0837	0843	0937	...	1032	1034	1042	1137	1232	1242	1337	1432	1442	1442	1442	1537	1632	1637	1737	1832
106	**Cuxhaven** a.	...	*0727*	...	0827	...	*0927*	0922	*1027*	...	...	1127	1127	*1227*	...	1327	*1427*	...	1527	1520	1527	*1627*	...	*1727*	*1827*	...

	Ⓐn			Ⓐn		Ⓑk			Ⓐ	⚒	†	
Osnabrück Hbf **800/1** d.	1638j	1738	...	...	...	1938	...	...	2038	...	...	
Bremen Hbf d.	1756	1856	1934	...	2034	2056	...	2134	2156	...	2157	2304
Osterholz-Scharmbeck d.	1810	1910	1952	...	2052	2110	...	2152	2210	...	2211	2322
Bremerhaven Hbf d.	1832	1932	2027	2036	2127	2132	2136	2227	2232	2236	2238	2357
Bremerhaven-Lehe d.	1837	1937	2032	2042	2132	2137	2142	2232	2237	2242	2244	0002
Cuxhaven a.	*1927*	*2027*	...	2127	...	...	2227	...	...	2327	2323	...

	⚒	⚒	Ⓐn	⚒		⚒	Ⓐn		
Cuxhaven d.	...	...	*0509*	...	...	0639	...	...	*0739*
Bremerhaven-Lehe d.	0407	0528	0554	0623	0628	0719	0723	0728	0823
Bremerhaven Hbf d.	0412	0533	0559	0628	0633	0724	0728	0733	0828
Osterholz-Scharmbeck d.	0447	0608	0633	0650	0708	...	0750	0808	0850
Bremen Hbf a.	0505	0626	0656	0703	0726	...	0803	0826	0903
Osnabrück Hbf **800/1** a.	0620z	...	...	0820	...	...	0920j	...	1020

	Ⓐn			ⒸN	Ⓐn			⚒			⚒			E	Ⓐn			Ⓐn			Ⓐn		Ⓐ		Ⓐn	⑤⑥
Cuxhaven d.	*0839*	...	*0939*	1033	1039	...	*1139*	1239	...	*1339*	1439	...	*1539*	1633	*1639*	...	*1739*	1839	...	*1939*	2039	...	...	*2139*	2239	...
Bremerhaven-Lehe d.	0923	0928	1023	1112	1119	1128	1223	1319	1328	1423	1519	1528	1623	1712	1723	1728	1823	1919	1928	2023	2119	2128	2128	2228	2319	2328
Bremerhaven Hbf d.	0928	0933	1028	1118	1124	1133	1228	1324	1333	1428	1524	1533	1628	1718	1728	1733	1828	1924	1933	2028	2124	2133	2133	2233	2324	2333
Osterholz-Scharmbeck d.	0950	1008	1050	1143	...	1208	1250	...	1408	1450	...	1608	1650	1743	1750	1808	1850	...	2008	2050	...	2208	2208	2308	...	0008
Bremen Hbf a.	1003	1026	1103	1158	...	1226	1303	...	1426	1503	...	1626	1703	1758	1803	1826	1903	...	2026	2103	...	2226	2226	2326	...	0026
Osnabrück Hbf **800/1** a.	1120j	...	1220	...	...	...	1420	...	...	1620	...	...	1820	...	1920	...	2020	...	...	2220	...	...	0013	...	...	...

C – ⑥ from Mar. 27 (not May 1).
D – ⑥ from Apr. 3 (not May 1).
E – † to Mar. 21; Ⓒ from Mar. 28.
F – From Apr. 2.
N – From Mar. 27.
P – ⚒ to Mar. 26; Ⓐ from Mar. 29.
Q – Daily to Mar. 26; Ⓑ from Mar. 28 (also May 1).
b – Not Mar. 27.
j – Not Jan. 4 - Mar. 26.
k – Also Dec. 26, May 1; not Dec. 24, 31.
n – Not Dec. 24, 31.
r – ⚒ only.
z – Jan. 2 - Mar. 27 only.

HAMBURG - CUXHAVEN and BREMERHAVEN — 818

metronom; EVB

Hamburg - Buxtehude - Cuxhaven ⊖

km		Ⓐn‡	⚒	‡	Ⓐn‡	Ⓐ	⚒	⚒		⚒	t	⚒		⚒		⚒		⚒		p		n	Ⓐn	Ⓒ	‡
0	**Hamburg** Hbf § d.	0448	...	0528	0558	...	...	0707	0807	0907	1007	1107	1207	1307	1407	1506	1607	1707	1807	1907	2007	2107	2207	2310	2328
12	**Hamburg** Harburg § d.	0501	...	0541	0611	0624	...	0724	0824	0924	1024	1124	1224	1324	1424	1524	1624	1724	1824	1924	2024	2124	2224	2327	2341
33	**Buxtehude** § d.	0526	...	0606	0636	0638	...	0738	0838	0938	1038	1138	1238	1338	1438	1538	1638	1738	1838	1938	2038	2138	2238	2341	0006
54	Stade § d.	0547	0551	0627	...	0656	0656	0756	0856	0956	1056	1156	1256	1357	1456	1556	1656	1756	1856	1956	2056	2156	2256	2359	0027
102	Otterndorf d.	...	0633	...	...	0738	0738	0838	0938	1038	1138	1238	1338	1441	1538	1638	1738	1838	1938	2038	2138	2238	2338	0041	...
116	**Cuxhaven** a.	...	0645	...	...	0750	0750	0850	0950	1050	1150	1250	1350	1453	1550	1650	1750	1850	1950	2050	2150	2250	2350	0053	...

	Ⓐ	⚒	Ⓐ	⚒	⑦w	‡	⚒	t	t		⚒		⚒		⚒	m	⚒m		n	Ⓒ	Ⓐ	‡	‡	Ⓒ	Ⓐn
Cuxhaven d.	0434	0510	0551	0610	0636	...	0651	0752	0910	1010	1110	1210	1310	1410	1510	1610	1710	1810	1910	2010	2039	...	...	2210	2239
Otterndorf d.	0446	0521	0603	0621	0648	...	0703	0804	0921	1021	1121	1221	1321	1421	1521	1621	1721	1821	1921	2021	2050	...	...	2221	2250
Stade § d.	0527	0603	0645	0703	0731	0735	0745	0846	1003	1103	1203	1303	1403	1503	1603	1703	1803	1903	2003	2103	2131	2135	2235	2303	2331
Buxtehude § d.	0546	0621	0702	0721	...	0755	0802	0903	1021	1121	1221	1321	1421	1521	1621	1721	1821	1921	2021	2121	...	2155	2255	2321	...
Hamburg Harburg § a.	0600	0636	0717	0736	...	0820	0817	0918	1036	1136	1236	1336	1436	1536	1636	1736	1836	1936	2036	2136	...	2220	2320	2336	...
Hamburg Hbf § a.	*0619*	0656	0736	0758	...	0834	0836	0938	1054	1155	1256	1357	1454	1556	1658	1757	1858	1956	2057	2156	...	2234	2334	2353	...

Buxtehude - Bremervörde - Bremerhaven △

km		Ⓐ	Ⓐn	Ⓐn	Ⓐn	Ⓐn		Ⓐn	Ⓐn		Ⓐn		⑥	⑥k	⑥k	⊡	⑥k	⑥	†	†		†
0	Buxtehude d.		0537	0637	0717	0837	and hourly	1337	1452	and hourly	2152	...		0737	0842	and hourly	1942	2142		0742	and every **two**	2142
39	Bremervörde a.		0619	0721	0819	0919	until	1419	1534	until	2234	...		0819	0924	until	2024	2224		0824	hours until	2224

	Ⓐ	Ⓐn	Ⓐn		Ⓐn	Ⓐn		Ⓐn			⑥	⑥k	⑥k	⑥k	❖	⑥k	⑥		†	†		†
Bremervörde d.		0425	0525	and hourly	1325	1440	and hourly	1940	...	...		0625	0725	0830	and hourly	1830	2030	...		0630	and every **two**	2030
Buxtehude a.		0509	0609	until	1409	1524	until	2024	...	...		0709	0809	0914	until	1914	2114	...		0714	hours until	2114

km		⚒		Ⓐn				Ⓐn	Ⓒd	Ⓐn		Ⓐn		Ⓐn	Ⓒd			
0	Bremervörde d.	0538	0638	0738	0838	1038	1238	1338	1438	1538	1638	1738	1838	1938	2038	...	...	...
39	**Bremerhaven** Hbf a.	0621	0721	0821	0921	1121	1321	1421	1521	1621	1721	1821	1921	2021	2121	...	...	...

	Ⓐn	⚒		Ⓐn	Ⓒd	Ⓐn	Ⓒd	Ⓐn			Ⓐn		Ⓐn		⚒n	†	Ⓒd	Ⓐn
Bremerhaven Hbf d.	0539	0639	0739	0839	0939	1039	1139	1239	1339	1539	1639	1739	1839	1939	2039	2139	2239	2352
Bremervörde a.	0622	0724	0822	0922	1022	1122	1222	1322	1422	1622	1722	1822	1922	2022	2122	2222	2322	0034

⊡ – The 1642 and 1842 departures do not run on Dec. 24, 31.
❖ – The 1530 and 1730 departures do not run on Dec. 24, 31.
‡ – Hamburg S-Bahn (2nd class only).
§ – Additional S-Bahn trains operate.
⊖ – Operated by metronom Eisenbahngesellschaft mbH.
△ – Operated by Eisenbahnen und Verkehrsbetriebe Elbe-Weser GmbH.

d – Also Dec. 24, 31.
k – Also Dec. 24, 31; not Dec. 26, May 1.
m – Not Dec. 24.
n – Not Dec. 24, 31.
p – Not Dec. 24, 31, Jan. 1.
t – Not Jan. 1.
w – Also Dec. 25, Apr. 2, May 13, 24; not Dec. 27.

HAMBURG - KIEL — 820

RE services except where shown

km									ICE 608	ICE 76	ICE 1026 1126	ICE 74	ICE 892 Ⓑq	ICE 974 Ⓑq	EC 102 ⑦w
		v	⚒				n		B	Z	A	Z	R	S	C
0	**Hamburg** Hbf **823** d.	0028	0520	0620	and	2220	2323	also	1015	1538	1615	1738	1859	2040	2115
37	Elmshorn **823** d.	0100	0551	0650	hourly	2250	2353		|	|	|	|	|	|	|
73	Neumünster **823** d.	0133	0617	0716	until	2316	0019		1103	1626	1703	1829	1952	2128	2203
111	**Kiel** Hbf a.	0200	0638	0736		2336	0039		1121	1644	1721	1847	2010	2147	2221

									ICE 973 ①-⑥	ICE 73	ICE 791 ①-⑥	ICE 1025 1125		ICE 673	ICE 609
	Ⓐn		v				n		eS	Z	eR	A		K	B
Kiel Hbf d.	0404	0521	0621	0721	and	2221	2321	also	0612	0712	0753	1238	...	1712	1838
Neumünster **823** d.	0425	0542	0642	0742	hourly	2242	2343		0631	0730	0811	1257	...	1730	1857
Elmshorn **823** d.	0457	0609	0709	0809	until	2309	0010		|	|	|	|	...	|	|
Hamburg Hbf **823** a.	0530	0637	0737	0837		2337	0040		0720	0820	0903	1343	...	1819	1943

A – (12) and ✕ Nürnberg - Frankfurt - Köln - Kiel and v.v.
B – (12) and ✕ Basel - Karlsruhe - Frankfurt - Köln - Kiel and v.v.
C – (12) and ✕ Chur - Zürich - Basel - Karlsruhe - Köln - Kiel.
K – (12) and ✕ Kiel - Hannover - Frankfurt - Karlsruhe (- Basel ⑤⑥ r).
R – (12) and ✕ Berlin - Kiel and v.v.
S – (12) and ✕ Kiel - Hannover - Frankfurt - Stuttgart and v.v.
Z – (12) and ✕ Kiel - Hannover - Frankfurt - Karlsruhe - Basel - Zürich and v.v.

e – Not Dec. 25, 26, Jan. 1, Apr. 3, 5, May 24.
n – Not Dec. 24, 31.
q – Not Dec. 24, 25, 31, Apr. 2, 4, May 23.
r – Also Dec. 23, 24, 30, Apr. 1, 4; not Dec. 25, Jan. 1.
v – Not Dec. 25, Jan. 1.
w – Also Apr. 5, May 24; not Apr. 4, May 23.

821 HAMBURG - WESTERLAND

DB; NOB

km		◇	◇	◇	◇	◇	◇	◇	◇	◇	◇	◇	◇	IC● 2314	◇	◇	IC● 2074	IC● 2072	◇	◇	◇	◇	IC● 2310	◇	IC● 2170
			Ⓐ		Ⓒv		Ⓐ		⑥⑦ W	Q			S	S ✕	W		⑥⑦ D🍷	①–⑤ D🍷			Ⓐ	Ⓒ	F✕		P J🍷
	Köln Hbf **800** d.	...	...	...	...	...	...	...	...	...	...	...	...	0510	...	...	...	...	...	...	...	...	0910	...	...
	Berlin Hbf **840** d.	...	...	...	...	...	...	...	...	...	...	...	...	|	...	...	0823	0823	...	...	...	...	|	...	...
	Hamburg Hbf ... **820** d.	...	...	...	...	...	*0500‡*	...	*0620**	*0620**	*0720**	*0820**	*0843**	0915	*0920**	*1020**	1048	1048	*1120**	*1220**	*1243**	*1250‡*	1315	*1420**	1448
0	**Hamburg** Altona d.	...	...	...	...	...	0524	...	0633	0633	0733	0833	0901	|	0933	1033	|	|	1133	1233	1303	1310	|	1433	|
30	Elmshorn **820** d.	...	...	...	...	...	0545	...	0655	0655	0755	0855	0922	|	0955	1055	|	|	1155	1255	1322	1332	|	1455	|
64	Itzehoe a.	...	...	...	...	...	0611	...	0720	0720	0820	0920	0948	1003	1020	1120	1142	1142	1220	1320	1345	1357	1404	1520	1544
64	Itzehoe d.	...	0456	...	0538	...	0612	...	0721	0721	0821	0921	0950	1016	1021	1121	1144	1144	1221	1321	1346	1358	1416	1521	1546
123	Heide (Holst) a.	...	0540	...	0622	...	0656	...	0756	0756	0856	0956	1027	1052	1056	1156	1218	1218	1256	1356	1420	1432	1453	1556	1619
123	Heide (Holst) d.	...	0549	...	0623	...	0702	...	0802	0802	0902	1002	1028	1054	1102	1202	1220	1220	1302	1402	1421	1433	1455	1602	1621
157	Husum a.	...	0615	...	0649	...	0728	...	0827	0828	0928	1028	1052	1117	1128	1228	1242	1242	1328	1429	1448	1458	1518	1628	1643
157	Husum d.	0558	...	0630	...	0658	0730	0730	...	0830	0930	1030	1100	1119	1130	1230	1244	1244	1330	1430	1500	1500	1520	1630	1645
197	Niebüll a.	0628	...	0658	...	0728	0758	0758	...	0858	0958	1058	1128	1145	1158	1258	1310	1310	1400	1458	1528	1528	1546	1658	1710
197	Niebüll d.	0631	...	0701	...	0731	0801	0801	...	0901	1001	1101	1131	1201	1201	1301	1331	1331	1401	1501	1531	1531	1601	1701	1731
237	**Westerland** (Sylt) a.	0705	...	0735	...	0805	0835	0835	...	0937	1035	1135	1207	1234	1235	1337	1404	1406	1435	1535	1605	1605	1634	1735	1804

	◇	◇	◇	◇	◇	IC 1808	◇	◇	◇	◇	
						⑦z	n		n	n ⊖	n
Köln Hbf **800** d.	...	...	...	...	...	1539	...	...	...	...	...
Berlin Hbf **840** d.	...	...	...	...	...	|	...	...	...	...	...
Hamburg Hbf .... **820** d.	*1520**	*1620**	*1720**	*1820**	*1920**	2009	*2020**	*2120**	...	*2220**	*2240‡*
Hamburg Altona d.	1533	1633	1733	1833	1933	|	2033	2133	...	2233	2302
Elmshorn **820** d.	1555	1655	1755	1855	1955	|	2055	2155	...	2255	2329
Itzehoe a.	1620	1720	1820	1920	2020	2057	2120	2220	...	2320	2359
Itzehoe d.	1621	1721	1821	1921	2021	2109	2121	2221	...	2321	...
Heide (Holst) a.	1656	1756	1856	1956	2056	2143	2203	2303	...	0003	...
Heide (Holst) d.	1702	1802	1902	2002	2102	2145	2204	2304	...	0004	...
Husum a.	1728	1828	1928	2028	2128	2212	2230	2330	...	0030	...
Husum d.	1730r	1830n	1930	2030n	2130	2219	2232	...	2333	...	...
Niebüll a.	1758r	1858n	1958	2058n	2158	2244	2300	...	0001	...	...
Niebüll d.	1801r	1901n	2001	2101n	2201	2247	2301	...	0002	...	...
Westerland (Sylt) a.	1835r	1935n	2035	2135n	2235	2314	2335	...	0034	...	...

	◇	◇	◇	◇	◇	◇	◇	◇	◇	IC 2001
	v	Ⓐ	Ⓐ	v	Ⓒv	Ⓐ	v			①g
Westerland (Sylt) d.	0000	...	0423	...	*0522*	0522	0622	0722	0822	0856
Niebüll a.	0030	...	0453	...	*0559*	0559	0659	0759	0859	0929
Niebüll d.	0031	...	0454	...	*0600*	0601	0701	0801	0901	0931
Husum a.	0101	...	0522	...	*0628*	0629	0729	0830	0929	0955
Husum d.	...	0423	...	0525	0631	0631	0731	0831	0931	0957
Heide (Holst) a.	...	0448	...	0550	0656	0656	0756	0856	0956	1018
Heide (Holst) d.	...	0450	...	0552	0702	0702	0802	0902	1002	1020
Itzehoe a.	...	0536	...	0636	0736	0736	0836	0936	1036	|
Itzehoe d.	...	0537	...	0637	0737	0737	0837	0937	1037	|
Elmshorn **820** d.	...	0603	...	0703	0803	0803	0903	1003	1103	|
Hamburg Altona a.	...	0625	...	0725	0825	0825	0925	1025	1125	1135
Hamburg Hbf **820** a.	...	*0637**	...	*0737**	*0837**	*0837**	*0937**	*1037**	*1137**	...
Berlin Hbf **840** a.	...	...	...	...	...	...	...	...	...	...
Köln Hbf **800** a.	...	...	...	...	...	...	...	...	...	...

	IC● 2311	◇	◇	◇	IC● 2171	IC● 2181	◇	◇	◇	◇	IC● 2315	◇	◇	IC● 2073	IC● 2075	◇	◇	◇	◇	◇	◇	◇	◇	◇	◇
	H✕				⑤–⑦ L🍷	N 🍷		ⒸS	ⒶS	W	S G✕			①–⑤ D🍷	⑥⑦ D🍷					n	Y	⑤⑥ W		n	
Westerland (Sylt) d.	0926	0952	1022	1122	1156	1156	1222	1252	1252	1322	1326	1422	1522	1552	1552	1622	1722	1822	1922	2022	2022	...	2122	...	2255
Niebüll a.	0959	1029	1059	1159	1229	1229	1259	1329	1329	1359	1359	1459	1559	1629	1629	1659	1759	1859	1959	2059	2059	...	2159	...	2326
Niebüll d.	1013	1031	1101	1201	1245	1245	1301	1331	1331	1401	1413	1501	1601	1645	1645	1701	1801	1901	2001	2101	2101	...	2201	...	2329
Husum a.	1039	1059	1130	1230	1310	1310	1330	1357	1359	1429	1439	1529	1629	1710	1710	1730	1829	1929	2029	2129	2129	...	2229	...	2358
Husum d.	1041	1101	1131	1231	1312	1312	1331	1358	1400	1431	1441	1531	1631	1712	1712	1731	1831	1931	2031	...	2131	2132	...	2244	...
Heide (Holst) a.	1102	1129	1156	1256	1333	1333	1356	1420	1422	1456	1502	1556	1656	1733	1733	1756	1856	1956	2056	...	2156	2157	...	2309	...
Heide (Holst) d.	1104	1131	1202	1302	1335	1335	1402	1421	1423	1502	1504	1602	1702	1735	1735	1802	1902	2002	2102	...	2202	2202	...	2310	...
Itzehoe a.	1139	1204	1236	1336	1412	1412	1436	1455	1458	1536	1539	1636	1736	1810	1810	1836	1936	2036	2146	...	2246	2246	...	2354	...
Itzehoe d.	1155	1205	1237	1337	1414	1414	1437	1456	1459	1537	1555	1637	1737	1812	1812	1837	1937	2037	2147	...	2247	2247	...	...	...
Elmshorn **820** d.	|	1228	1303	1403	|	|	1503	|	|	1603	|	1703	1803	|	|	1903	2003	2103	2214	...	2314	2314	...	...	...
Hamburg Altona a.	|	1250	1325	1425	|	|	1525	1540	1543	1625	|	1725	1825	|	|	1925	2025	2125	2235	...	2335	2335	...	...	...
Hamburg Hbf .... **820** a.	1242	*1311‡*	*1337**	*1437**	1511	1511	*1537**	*1601‡*	*1601‡*	*1637**	1642	*1737**	*1837**	1909	1909	*1937**	*2037**	*2137**	*2252n*	...	*0001‡*	*0001‡*	...	...	...
Berlin Hbf **840** a.	|	...	...	...	...	...	...	...	...	...	|	...	...	2123	2123	...	...	...	...	...	...	...	...	...	...
Köln Hbf **800** a.	1650	...	...	...	...	...	...	...	...	...	2050	...	...	...	...	...	...	...	...	...	...	...	...	...	...

D – SYLTER STRAND. From / to Dresden on dates in Table **840**.
F – NORDFRIESLAND – [12] and ✕ Frankfurt - Koblenz - Köln - Westerland.
G – DEICHGRAF – [12] and ✕ Westerland - Köln - Koblenz - Frankfurt.
H – NORDFRIESLAND – [12] and ✕ Westerland - Köln - Heidelberg - Stuttgart.
J – WATTENMEER – [12] and 🍷 (Frankfurt ⑥⑦ -) Hannover - Westerland.
L – ⑤–⑦ (also Dec. 23, 24, 30, 31, Apr. 1, 5, May 12, 24; not Dec. 25, Jan. 1).
WATTENMEER – [12] and 🍷 Westerland - Hannover - Frankfurt.
N – ① to Mar. 22; ①–④ from Mar. 29 (not Apr. 1, 5, May 12, 24).
WATTENMEER – [12] and 🍷 Westerland - Hannover - Göttingen.
P – ④–⑦ to Mar. 21 (also Dec. 22, 23, 29, 30; not Dec. 24, 31); daily from Mar. 25.

Q – Ⓐ (daily from Mar. 22).
S – From Mar. 27.
W – Until Mar. 26.
Y – ①②③④⑦ (not Dec. 24, 31).

g – Also Apr. 6, May 25; not Apr. 5, May 24.
n – Not Dec. 24, 31.
r – Not Dec. 24.
v – Not Dec. 25, Jan. 1.
z – Also Apr. 5, May 24; not Apr. 4, May 23.

* – Change trains at Elmshorn.
‡ – S-Bahn connection Hamburg Hbf - Hamburg Altona and v.v.
⊖ – On ⑦ from Mar. 28 (also Apr. 5, May 13, 24; not Apr. 4, May 23) Itzehoe a. 2318, d. 2319, Heide a. 0005, d. 0006, Husum a. 0033.
● – From Mar. 27 conveys [2] to / from Dagebüll Mole (Table **822**).
◇ – Operated by Nord-Ostsee-Bahn GmbH.
🍷 (trolley service) available on most trains Hamburg - Westerland and v.v.

822 SCHLESWIG-HOLSTEIN BRANCH LINES

Neumünster - Heide - Büsum ⊠

km		⚒		⚒	⑥k		Ⓐn													r	r		n		n
0	Neumünster d.	...	...	...	0537	...	0537	...	0737	...	0937	...	1137	...	1337	...	1537	...	1737	...	1937	...	...	...	2137
63	Heide a.	...	...	...	0646	...	0710	...	0846	...	1046	...	1246	...	1446	...	1646	...	1846	...	2046	...	...	...	2246
63	Heide d.	0451	...	0601	0701	0701	...	0801	0901	1001	1101	1201	1301	1401	1501	1601	1701	1801	1901r	2001	2101	...	2208	...	...
87	Büsum a.	0517	...	0627	0727	0727	...	0827	0927	1027	1127	1227	1327	1427	1527	1627	1727	1827	1927r	2027	2127	...	2234	...	...

	⚒	⚒		⚒	⑥k														r	r	r		n	
Büsum d.	...	0521	...	0631	0631	...	0731	0831	0931	1031	1131	1231	1331	1431	1531	1631	1731	1831	1931	2031	2131	...	2238	...
Heide a.	...	0547	...	0657	0657	...	0757	0857	0957	1057	1157	1257	1357	1457	1557	1657	1757	1857	1957	2057	2157	...	2304	...
Heide d.	0517	...	...	...	0717	0717	...	0917	...	1117	...	1317	...	1517	...	1717	...	1917	...	2117	...	...	2317	...
Neumünster a.	0625	...	...	...	0825	0825	...	1025	...	1228	...	1425	...	1625	...	1825	...	2025	...	2225	...	...	0025	...

Husum - Bad St Peter Ording ◇

km		⚒b	v				n	n	n	n
0	Husum d.	0437	0537	0637	and	1837	1937	2037	2137	2237
21	Tönning d.	0502	0602	0702	hourly	1902	2002	2102	2202	2302
43	Bad St Peter Ording a.	0528	0628	0728	until	1928	2028	2128	2228	2328

	⚒b	v				n	n	n	n
Bad St Peter Ording d.	0534	0634	0734	and	1934	2034	2134	2234	2334
Tönning d.	0605	0705	0805	hourly	2005	2105	2205	2305	0005
Husum a.	0624	0724	0824	until	2024	2124	2224	2324	0024

Niebüll - Dagebüll Mole ⊡

km	*Until Mar. 26*	Ⓐ	🚌 Ⓒ	⚒		🚌 Ⓐn		n d		d	♥z	⑤⑦f
0	Niebüll neg d.	0635	0705	0805	0905	1035	1135	1316	1405	1716	1810	1910
14	Dagebüll Mole a.	0654	0720	0822	0924	1055	1154	1335	1424	1735	1829	1929

Until Mar. 26	Ⓐ	🚌 Ⓒ	⚒e		🚌 Ⓐn		x			♥n	⑤⑦g
Dagebüll Mole d.	0705	0725	0825	0935	1100	1200	1339	1435	1739	1835	1935
Niebüll neg a.	0724	0740	0844	0954	1120	1219	1355	1454	1755	1854	1954

km	*From Mar. 27*					★	★		★	★	♥	A
	Hamburg Hbf a.	...	...	...	...	0915	1048	...	1315	1448	...	...
	Niebüll a.	...	...	...	...	1145	1310	...	1546	1710	...	...
0	Niebüll neg d.	0805	0905	1035	1135	1200	1325	1425	1605	1720	1815	1910
14	Dagebüll Mole a.	0822	0924	1054	1151	1216	1350	1450	1624	1739	1834	1929

From Mar. 27	⚒	★		★	Ⓑ★	⑥★		★			B
Dagebüll Mole d.	0835	0935	1100	1200	1325	1340	1435	1605	1739	1840	1935
Niebüll neg a.	0851	0954	1119	1226	1350	1359	1451	1629	1755	1856	1954
Niebüll d.	...	1013	...	1245	1413	1413	...	1645	...	...	...
Hamburg Hbf a.	...	1242	...	1511	1642	1642	...	1909	...	...	...

A – ⑤–⑦ (also Apr. 1, 12; not Apr. 2–4, Mar. 27).
B – ⑤–⑦ (also Apr. 1, May 12, 24; not Apr. 2–4).
b – Runs 7 minutes earlier on ⑥ from Mar. 27.
d – Runs 4 minutes later Dec. 25 - Jan. 10.
e – Dec. 28 - Jan. 9 Dagebüll d. 0835, Niebüll a. 0851.
f – Also Dec. 26; not Mar. 26.

g – Also Dec. 26.
k – Also Dec. 24, 31; not Dec. 26, May 1.
n – Not Dec. 24, 31.
r – Not Dec. 24.
v – Not Dec. 25, Jan. 1.

x – Not Dec. 24 - Jan. 10.
z – not Dec. 24, 26, 31.
♥ – ①②③④⑥.
★ – Conveys [2] (*IC*) from / to Hamburg and beyond (see Table **821**).

⊠ – **Operator**: Schleswig-Holstein-Bahn GmbH.
◇ – **Operator**: Nord-Ostsee-Bahn GmbH.
⊡ – **Operator**: Norddeutsche Eisenbahngesellschaft Niebüll GmbH. ✆ +49 (0) 4661 98088 90. Niebüll neg station is situated a short distance from the Niebüll DB station forecourt.

HAMBURG - NEUMÜNSTER - FLENSBURG - PADBORG 823

RE / RB services except where shown

km		①–⑥ v	CNL 482 ®S A🍷	⚒	©z	Ⓐn	d			ICE 386 🍷					ICE 380 ◇🍷								IC 1284 ⑦w M🍷		e n	IC 1870 ⑦w ◇
0	**Hamburg** Hbf .... 820 d.	2323p	0358	...	0520k	0520	0620	0720	0843	0930	0920	1043	1120	1243	1330	1320	1443	1520	1643	1720	1843	1920	2032	2050	2120	2233
37	Elmshorn .... 820 d.	2353p	|	...	0551k	0551	0650	0750	0910	|	0950	1110	1150	1310	|	1350	1510	1550	1710	1750	1910	1950	|	2117	2150	|
73	Neumünster .... 820 d.	0033	0445	0533	0635	0656	0733	0835	0933	1022	1035	1133	1235	1333	1422	1435	1533	1635	1733	1835	1933	2033	2121	2143	2233	2321
112	Rendsburg .... 824 d.	0104	|	0604	0708	0727	0804	0908	1004	1049	1108	1204	1308	1404	1449	1508	1604	1708	1804	1908	2004	2104	2149	2217	2304	2349
136	Schleswig .... 824 d.	0121	|	0621	0725	0744	0821	0925	1020	1105	1125	1220	1325	1420	1505	1525	1620	1725	1820	1925	2020	2121	2204	2233	2321	0005
174	**Flensburg** .... a.	0152	0549	0652	0753	0813	0852	0953	1045	1125	1153	1245	1353	1445	1525	1553	1645	1753	1845	1953	2045	2152	2226	2258	2352	0027
174	**Flensburg** .... 710 d.	...	0551	0707	...	...	0907	...	1107	1132	...	1307	...	1507	1532	...	1707	...	1907	...	2107	...	...	...	...	...
186	**Padborg** 🏛 .... 710 a.	...	0602	0718	...	...	0918	...	1118	1143	...	1318	...	1518	1543	...	1718	...	1918	...	2118	...	...	...	...	...
	Århus **700** .... a.	...	...	...	...	...	...	...	...	1402	...	...	...	...	1804	...	...	...	...	...	...	...	...	...	...	...

	⚒	d v	d	d				ICE 381 ◇🍷		IC 1871 ⑤f ◇						ICE 387 🍷			IC 1889 ⑦w N					CNL 483 ®▲ A🍷	Ⓑn
Århus **700** .... d.	...	...	...	...	...	...	...	0754	...	...	...	...	...	...	...	1424	...	...	...	...	...	...	...	...	...
Padborg 🏛 .... 710 d.	...	...	...	...	0733	...	0933	1010	...	...	1133	...	1333	...	1533	1640	...	1733	...	...	1933	...	2133	2218	...
Flensburg .... 710 a.	...	...	...	...	0746	...	0946	1022	...	...	1146	...	1346	...	1546	1652	...	1746	...	...	1946	...	2146	2231	...
Flensburg .... d.	0410	0510	0609	0710	0809	0910	1009	1024	1110	1201	1209	1310	1409	1510	1609	1654	1710	1809	1854	1910	2008	2110	...	2233	2310
Schleswig .... 824 d.	0438	0538	0634	0738	0834	0938	1034	1045	1138	1223	1234	1338	1434	1538	1634	1716	1738	1834	1916	1938	2038	2138	...	|	2338
Rendsburg .... 824 d.	0457	0557*	0650	0757	0850	0957	1050	1101	1157	1241	1250	1357	1450	1557	1650	1733	1757	1850	1934	1957	2057	2157	...	|	2357
Neumünster .... 820 a.	0526	0625*	0721	0826	0921	1026	1121	1130	1226	1308	1321	1428	1521	1626	1721	1758	1826	1921	1959	2026	2126	2226	...	2333	0026
Elmshorn .... 820 a.	0607	0707	0745	0907	0945	1107	1145	|	1307	1337	1345	1507	1545	1707	1745	|	1907	1945	|	2107	2207	2307	...	|	...
Hamburg Hbf .... 820 a.	0637	0737	0814	0937	1014	1137	1214	1232	1337	1408	1414	1537	1614	1737	1814	1853	1937	2014	2050	2137	2237	2337	...	0028	...

A – HANS CHRISTIAN ANDERSEN – 🛏 1, 2 cl., 🛏 2 cl. and (2) München - København and v.v. See also Table **900**. For Basel cars (train number **472/3** – AURORA) and Amsterdam via Köln cars (train number **40447/40483** – BOREALIS) see international table **54**. For overnight journeys only.
M – (12) and 🍷 (Dec. 20 - Apr. 5: Schwarzach -) München - Flensburg.
N – To Nürnberg (Table **900**).
S – On ⑦ from Dec. 27 Neumünster d. 0504, Flensburg a. 0636, d. 0638, Padborg a. 0704.
d – Daily to Apr. 17; ①–⑥ from Apr. 19.
e – Daily to Apr. 16; Ⓑ from Apr. 18.
f – Also Dec. 23, 30, Apr. 1, May 12; not Dec. 25, Jan. 1, Apr. 2, May 14.
k – ⑥ (also Dec. 24, 31; not Dec. 26, May 1).
n – Not Dec. 24, 31.
p – Previous day.
v – Not Dec. 25, Jan. 1.
w – Also Apr. 5, May 24; not Apr. 4, May 23.
z – Also Dec. 24, 31; not ⑦ Apr. 18 - June 3.
* – 6–7 minutes later on ⑦ Mar. 7 - Apr. 11.
◇ – From / to Berlin (Table **840**).
▲ – On ⑥ from Apr. 17 Padborg d. 2120, Flensburg a. 2133, d. 2135, Neumünster a. 2240, Hamburg Hbf a. 2342.

KIEL - HUSUM and FLENSBURG 824

RB services

km	△	⚒							n	n	n
0	**Kiel** Hbf .... d.	0344	0501f	0556d	0701d	0801	and hourly until	2001	2101	2201e	2301e
40	Rendsburg . 823 d.	0431	0534	0634	0734	0834		2034	2134	2234	2334
65	Schleswig .. 823 d.	0449	0552	0652	0752	0852		2052	2152	2252	2352
102	**Husum** .... a.	0521	0624	0724	0824	0924		2124	2224	2324	0024

△	⚒						n	n	Ⓑn
Husum .... d.	0422	0529	0635	0735	and hourly until	2035	2135	2235	2335
Schleswig .... 823 d.	0454	0601	0707	0807		2107	2207	2307	0007
Rendsburg .... 823 d.	0514	0621	0727	0827		2127	2227	2327	0027
Kiel Hbf .... a.	0549	0654d	0759d	0859		2159	2259e	2359e	0059

km		Ⓐn	⚒					n	n	n	
0	**Kiel** Hbf .... d.	0403	0520	0642	0742	and hourly until	2042	2142	2242	2342	...
29	Eckernförde ..... d.	0430	0553	0710	0809		2109	2209	2309	0011	...
50	Süderbrarup ...... d.	0448	0613	0729	0829		2129	2229	2329	0031	...
81	**Flensburg** .... a.	0518	0641	0756	0856		2156	2256	2358	0058	...

	⚒	v					n		n
Flensburg .... d.	0445	0545	...	0703	and hourly until	2103	2203	...	2323
Süderbrarup .... d.	0512	0612	...	0729		2129	2229	...	2350
Eckernförde .... d.	0530	0630	...	0749		2149	2249	...	0011
Kiel Hbf .... a.	0604	0700	...	0816		2216	2316	...	0038

d – Daily to Apr. 17; ①–⑥ from Apr. 19.
e – Daily to Apr. 16 (not Dec. 24, 31); Ⓑ from Apr. 18.
f – Daily to Mar. 6; ①–⑥ from Mar. 8.
n – Not Dec. 24, 31.
v – Not Dec. 25, Jan. 1.
△ – Kiel - Husum operator: Nord-Ostsee-Bahn GmbH. ✆ +49 (0) 180 10 180 11.

HAMBURG - LÜBECK - PUTTGARDEN 825

RB / RE services except where shown

km	SEE NOTE ▲	v	⚒				EC 31 E R				ICE 33 R🍷						IC 2120 G F			ICE 35 BR				ICE 237 R🍷		
0	**Hamburg** Hbf .... d.	0026	0510	0610	...	0710	0725	0810	...	0910	0928	1010	...	1110	1210	...	1233	...	1310	1328	1410	...	1510	1525	1610	...
40	Bad Oldesloe .... d.	0049	0534	0634	...	0734	|	0834	...	0934	|	1034	...	1134	1234	...	|	...	1334	|	1434	...	1534	|	1634	...
63	**Lübeck** Hbf .... a.	0106	0551	0651	...	0751	0804	0851	...	0951	1004	1051	...	1151	1251	...	1310	...	1351	1404	1451	...	1551	1604	1651	...
							|				|				H	H	|	G		|				|		
63	**Lübeck** Hbf .... d.	...	0612	0712	0712	0812	0806	0912	0912	1012	1006	1112	1112	1212	1312	1312	1313	1319	1412	1406	1512	1512	1612	1606	1712	1712
93	Neustadt (Holst)..... a.	...	0656	0752	|	0851	|	0952	|	1051	|	1152	|	1251	1352	|	|	1401	1451	|	1552	|	1651	|	1752	|
115	Oldenburg (Holst)...... d.	...	...	...	0813	...	0838	...	1013	...	1038	...	1213	...	...	1413	1411	...	...	1438	...	1613	...	1638	...	1813
151	**Puttgarden** 🏛 .... a.	...	...	...	0840	...	0905	...	1040	...	1105	...	1240	...	...	1440	1436	...	...	1505	...	1640	...	1705	...	1840
	København H **720** .. a.	...	...	...	...	...	1211	...	...	...	1411	...	...	...	...	...	...	...	...	1811	...	...	...	2011	...	...

SEE NOTE ▲		ICE 37 R🍷						ICE 584 Ⓑq M			
Hamburg Hbf .... d.	1710	1728	1810	...	1910	2010	...	2103	2110	2210	2330
Bad Oldesloe .... d.	1734	|	1834	...	1934	2034	...	|	2134	2234	2353
Lübeck Hbf .... a.	1751	1804	1851	...	1951	2051	...	2139	2151	2251	0010
		|							n	n	
Lübeck Hbf .... d.	1812	1806	1912	1912	2012	2112	2112	...	2212	2312	...
Neustadt (Holst) ..... a.	1851	|	1952	|	2051	2152	|	...	2251	2345	...
Oldenburg (Holst) ...... d.	...	1838	...	2013	...	...	2213	...	...	0017	...
Puttgarden 🏛 .... a.	...	1905	...	2040	...	...	2240	...	...	0044	...
København H **720** .. a.	...	2211	...	...	...	...	...	...	...	...	...

SEE NOTE ▲		Ⓐn	ICE 583 ①–⑥ e M	v	Ⓐn					IC 2327 A	
København H **720** d.	...	...	...	...	...	...	...	...	...	...	...
Puttgarden 🏛 .... d.	...	...	...	0528	0629	...	0725	...	...	0907	0925
Oldenburg (Holst)... d.	...	...	...	0553	0654	...	0750	...	...	0933	0950
Neustadt (Holst) d.	...	0522	...	0622	|	0716j	|	0816	0922	|	|
Lübeck Hbf .... a.	...	0555	...	0655	0755	0755	0855	0855	0955	1032	1055
	⚒	d								|	
Lübeck Hbf .... d.	0510	0610	0617	0710	...	0810	...	0910	1010	1036	...
Bad Oldesloe .... d.	0527	0627	|	0727	...	0827	...	0927	1027	|	...
Hamburg Hbf .... a.	0550	0651	0654	0751	...	0851	...	0951	1051	1117	...

SEE NOTE ▲		ICE 38 BR				ICE 238 R🍷				ICE 36 R🍷		IC 2121 G F	H					ICE 32 R🍷				EC 30 D R				n
København H **720** .. d.	...	0745	...	...	...	0945	...	...	...	1145	...	...	...	...	...	...	...	1545	...	...	...	1745	...	...	...	...
Puttgarden 🏛 .... d.	...	1042	...	1125	...	1242	...	1325	...	1442	...	1507	1525	...	...	1725	...	1842	...	1925	...	2042	...	2125	...	...
Oldenburg (Holst) ...... d.	...	1106	...	1150	...	1306	...	1350	...	1506	...	1533	1550	...	...	1750	...	1906	...	1950	...	2106	...	2150	...	...
Neustadt (Holst) ..... d.	1016	|	1122	|	1216	|	1322	|	1416	|	1522	|	|	1616	1722	|	1816	|	1922	|	2016	|	2122	|	2216	2316
Lübeck Hbf .... a.	1055	1136	1155	1255	1255	1336	1355	1455	1455	1536	1555	1632	1655	1655	1755	1855	1855	1936	1955	2055	2055	2136	2155	2255	2255	2348
		|				|				|		|						|				|				v
Lübeck Hbf .... d.	1110	1138	1210	...	1310	1338	1410	...	1510	1538	1610	1636	...	1710	1810	...	1910	1938	2010	...	2110	2138	2210	...	2310	0018
Bad Oldesloe .... d.	1127	|	1227	...	1327	|	1427	...	1527	|	1627	|	...	1727	1827	...	1927	|	2027	...	2127	|	2227	...	2327	0035
Hamburg Hbf .... a.	1151	1216	1251	...	1351	1416	1451	...	1551	1616	1651	1716	...	1751	1851	...	1951	2016	2051	...	2151	2216	2251	...	2351	0100

Lübeck - Travemünde ⊠

km		H	G		H	G	
0	**Lübeck** Hbf ....d.	0801	0803	and at the same minutes past each hour until	2101	2103	...
18	Travemünde Skandinavienkai ....a.	0817	0819		2117	2119	...
21	**Travemünde** Strand ....a.	0823	0825		2123	2125	...

	H	G		H	G		
Travemünde Strand ....d.	0831	0834	and at the same minutes past each hour until	2131	2134	...	...
Travemünde Skandinavienkai.....d.	0836	0839		2136	2139	...	...
Lübeck Hbf ....a.	0853	0856		2153	2156	...	...

A – ⑤ (also Dec. 23, 30, Apr. 1, May 12, June 12; not Dec. 25, Jan. 1, Apr. 2, May 14). LÜBECKER BUCHT – (12) Puttgarden - Köln - Frankfurt - Passau.
B – (12) and 🍷 Berlin - Hamburg - København and v.v.
D – Daily Dec. 13 - Jan. 10 and from Mar. 12 (not Dec. 24, 31).
E – Daily Dec. 14 - Jan. 11 and from Mar. 13 (not Dec. 25, Jan. 1).
F – FEHMARN – (12) Frankfurt - Köln - Puttgarden and v.v.
G – From Mar. 27.
H – Until Mar. 26.
M – To / from München (Table **900**).
R – Reservation recommended.
d – Daily from Lübeck.
e – not Dec. 25, 26, Jan. 1, Apr. 3, 5, May 24.
j – 0722 on © (also Dec. 24, 31).
n – Not Dec. 24, 31.
q – Not Dec. 24, 25, 31, Apr. 2, 4, May 23.
v – Not Dec. 25, Jan. 1.
▲ – Regional services between Lübeck and Neustadt / Puttgarden are subject to alteration from Mar. 27.
⊠ – On Dec. 14, Jan. 11, 25, Feb. 1, 22, Mar. 22 Apr. 12, 19, 26, May 3, 10 trains are replaced by 🚌 0800 - 1400.

826 KIEL - LÜBECK - BAD KLEINEN

RE/RB services

km			m	Ⓐ S				S				S				P			n N				n H	n	n
0	**Kiel** Hbf .... d.	...	0444	...	...	0544	0644	...	and in	1344	1444	...	...	1544	1644	...	1744	1844	...	1944	2044	2144	...	2244	2344
33	Plön .... d.	...	0516	...	...	0616	0716	...	the same	1416	1516	...	...	1616	1716	...	1816	1916	...	2016	2116	2216	...	2316	0016
47	Eutin .... d.	...	0530	...	...	0630	0730	...	pattern	1430	1530	...	...	1630	1730	...	1830	1930	...	2030	2130	2230	...	2330	0030
80	**Lübeck** Hbf .... a.	...	0558	...	...	0658	0758	...	every **two**	1458	1558	...	...	1658	1758	...	1858	1958	...	2058	2158	2258	...	2400	0058
80	**Lübeck** Hbf .... d.	0504	...	0602	...	*0704*	...	0802	hours until	*1504*	...	1602	...	*1704*	...	1802	*1904*	...	2002	*2104*	...	...	2306	...	...
119	Grevesmühlen .. d.	0538	...	0637	...	*0740*	...	0837		*1540*	...	1637	...	*1740*	...	1837	*1940*	...	2037	*2140*	...	...	2341	...	...
142	**Bad Kleinen** ..... a.	0553	...	0655	...	*0755*	...	0855		*1555*	...	1655	...	*1755*	...	1855	*1955*	...	2055	*2155*	...	...	2359	...	...

	Ⓒ w	Ⓐ n		m	⚒	Ⓐ H		Ⓐ		N			S			S			n S			n S	n		n
Bad Kleinen ...... d.	...	...	...	...	...	0432	...	0518	*0603*	0703	...	*0803*	0903	...	and in	1703	...	*1803*	1903	...	*2003*	2103	...	2203	...
Grevesmühlen ... d.	...	...	...	...	...	0446	...	0540	*0617*	0721	...	*0817*	0921	...	the same	1721	...	*1817*	1921	...	*2017*	2121	...	2221	...
Lübeck Hbf .... a.	...	...	...	...	...	0525	...	0623	*0654*	0756	...	*0854*	0956	...	pattern	1756	...	*1854*	1956	...	*2054*	2156	...	2256	...
Lübeck Hbf .... d.	0020	0020	...	0401	0501	...	0601	...	0703	...	0803	0903	...	1003	every **two**	...	1803	1903	...	2003	2101	...	2201	...	2301
Eutin .... d.	0050	0049	...	0429	0528	...	0628	...	0728	...	0828	0928	...	1028	hours until	...	1828	1928	...	2028	2129	...	2229	...	2329
Plön .... d.	0105	0104	...	0444	0543	...	0643	...	0742	...	0843	0943	...	1043		...	1843	1943	...	2043	2144	...	2244	...	2344
Kiel Hbf .... a.	0136	0143	...	0515	0615	...	0715	...	0815	...	0915	1015	...	1115		...	1915	2015	...	2115	2215	...	2315	...	0015

H – From / to Schwerin (Table **830**).
N – To / from Neubrandenburg (Table **836**).
P – To Pasewalk (Table **836**).
S – To / from Szczecin (Table **836**).
m – Not Dec. 25.
n – Not Dec. 24, 31.
v – Also Dec. 24, 31; not Dec. 25, Jan. 1.

827 LÜBECK - BÜCHEN - LÜNEBURG

RB services

km		Ⓐ n					❖		n	n
0	**Lübeck** Hbf .... d.	0506	0606	0707	0810	0910		2110	2220	2324
9	Lübeck Flughafen ✈ ... d.	0514	0614	0715	0818	0918	and	2118	2228	2332
22	Ratzeburg .... d.	0528	0628	0730	0830	0930		2130	2242	2344
31	Mölln (Lauenburg) .... d.	0535	0634	0737	0837	0937	hourly	2137	2249	2351
50	Büchen .... a.	0546	0646	0749	0849	0949		2149	2301	0004
50	Büchen .... d.	0558	0655	0758	0858	1003	until	2203	2321	...
79	**Lüneburg** .... a.	0620	0717	0820	0920	1025		2225	2343	...

	⚒	Ⓐ n	Ⓒ z				⊠		n
Lüneburg .... d.	0522	0628	0628	0730	0826	0937		2037	2245
Büchen .... a.	0544	0649	0649	0751	0847	0959	and	2059	2307
Büchen .... d.	0558	0658	0710	0810	0910	1010		2110	2324
Mölln (Lauenburg) .... d.	0610	0710	0721	0822	0922	1022	hourly	2122	2336
Ratzeburg .... d.	0617	0717	0731	0831	0931	1031		2131	2345
Lübeck Flughafen ✈ d.	0626	0726	0740	0840	0940	1040	until	2140	2354
Lübeck Hbf .... a.	0634	0734	0748	0848	0948	1048		2148	0003

n – Not Dec. 24, 31.
z – Also Dec. 24, 31.
❖ – The following services from Lübeck run 5–7 minutes later Büchen - Lüneburg: 1610, 1710 Ⓐ **n**, 1810 and 2010.
⊠ – Certain services run 3–7 minutes **earlier** Lüneburg - Büchen (departures from Lüneberg at 1030, 1230, 1430 and 1534).

830 HAMBURG - ROSTOCK - STRALSUND

km		*RB*	*RE*	*RE*	*RE*	*RE*	*RE*	*IC*	*RE*	*RE*	*RE*	*IC*	*RE*	*RE*	*IC*	*IC*	*RE*	*RE*	*IC*	*RE*	*RE*	*IC*	*RE*	*RE*	*IC*
	See note ▲	**33287**	**33203**	**33205**	**33090**	**33001**	**33207**	**2186**	**33023**	**33005**	**33209**	**2184**	**33007**	**33211**	**2182**	**2238**	**33009**	**33213**	**2212**	**33011**	**33215**	**2376**	**33013**	**33217**	**2116**
				Ⓐ	Ⓐ			① g	Ⓐ n			①–⑥				B									
					L							e ◆			◆	◆			✕ ◆			🍷 ◆			✕ ◆
0	**Hamburg** Hbf .... d.	*0004*r	...	...	...	...	...	0541	*0524*	0634	...	0744	0836	...	0944	...	1028	...	1117	1228	...	1344	1428	...	1516
47	Büchen .... d.	0102	...	...	...	0504a	...	|	*0559*t	0704	...	|	0905	...	|	...	1058	...	|	1304	...	|	1458	...	|
123	**Schwerin** Hbf .... a.	0151	...	...	...	0549a	...	0635	*0651*	0749	...	0835	0950	...	1035	...	1149	...	1208	1349	...	1435	1549	...	1612
123	**Schwerin** Hbf **836 837** d.	...	...	...	0412	0551	...	0637	0704	0751	...	0837	0951	...	1037	1055	1151	...	1210	1351	...	1437	1551	...	1614
140	Bad Kleinen ... **836 837** d.	...	...	...	0426	0602	...	|	0718	0802	...	|	1002	...	|	1107	1202	...	|	1402	...	|	1602	...	|
181	Bützow .... **836** d.	...	...	...	...	0629	...	0711	0746	0829	...	0911	1029	...	1111	1132	1229	...	1244	1429	...	1511	1629	...	1648b
211	**Rostock** Hbf .... a.	...	...	...	...	0651	...	0732	0810	0851	...	0932	1051	...	1132	1152	1251	...	1304	1451	...	1532	1651	...	1706
211	**Rostock** Hbf .... d.	...	0453	0553	...	...	0700	0738	...	...	0901	0938	...	1101	1138k	...	...	1301	1317	...	1501	1538	...	1701	1717
240	Ribnitz-D'garten West . d.	...	0516	0617	...	...	0723	0759	...	...	0922	1000	...	1122	1200k	...	...	1322	1339	...	1522	1600	...	1722	1739
265	Velgast .... d.	...	0540	0638	...	...	0740	0816	...	...	0940	1016	...	1140	1216k	...	...	1340	1354	...	1540	1616	...	1740	1754
283	**Stralsund** .... a.	...	0555	0655	...	...	0755	0830	...	...	0955	1030	...	1155	1230k	...	...	1355	1412	...	1555	1630	...	1755	1812
	Ostseebad Binz **844** a.	...	|	|	...	...	|	0932	...	...	|	1132	...	|	...	...	...	|	1516	...	|	1748h	...	|	...
	Sassnitz **844** .... a.	...	0655	0755	...	...	0855	...	...	...	1055	...	...	1255	...	...	...	1455	...	...	1655	...	...	1855	...

	IC	*RE*	*RE*	*IC*	*RE*	*RE*	*IC*	*IC*	*RE*	*IC*	*RE*
See note ▲	**2174**	**33015**	**33219**	**2372**	**33017**	**33221**	**2188**	**2270**	**33019**	**2286**	**33021**
	⑤						①–④	⑤⑦		⑦ w	
	🍷 ◆			A 🍷			z	🍷 ◆		🍷 ◆	
Hamburg Hbf .... d.	1542	1634	...	1743	1835	...	1944	1944	2034	2146	2248
Büchen .... d.	|	1704	...	|	1904	...	|	|	2104	2210	2318
Schwerin Hbf .... a.	1635	1749	...	1835	1949	...	2035	2035	2149	2241	0003
Schwerin Hbf **836 837** d.	1637	1751	...	1837	1951	...	2037	2037	2151	2249	0004
Bad Kleinen ... **836 837** d.	|	1802	...	|	2002	...	|	|	2202	|	0015
Bützow .... **836** d.	1711	1829	...	1911	2029	...	2111	2111	2229	2323	0041
Rostock Hbf .... a.	1732	1851	...	1932	2051	...	2132	2132	2251	2343	0103
Rostock Hbf .... d.	...	...	1901	1938	...	2101	...	2138	...	...	...
Ribnitz-Damgarten West d.	...	...	1922	2000	...	2122	...	2200	...	...	...
Velgast .... d.	...	...	1940	2016	...	2140	...	2216	...	...	...
Stralsund .... a.	...	...	1955	2032	...	2155	...	2230	...	...	...
Ostseebad Binz **844** . a.	...	...	|	...	...	|	...	...	...	...	...
Sassnitz **844** .... a.	...	...	2055	...	...	2255	...	...	...	...	...

	RE	*RE*	*IC*	*RE*	*RE*	*IC*	*RE*	*RE*	*IC*
See note ▲	**33000**	**33030**	**2189**	**33002**	**33204**	**2279**	**33206**	**33004**	**2115**
	Ⓐ n		①–⑥		Ⓐ	①–⑥			
			m 🍷			e A			✕ ◆
Sassnitz **844** .... d.	...	...	...	...	0402	...	0505	...	...
Ostseebad Binz **844** .... d.	...	...	...	...	|	...	|	...	...
Stralsund .... d.	...	...	...	...	0454	0527	0600	...	0727
Velgast .... d.	...	...	...	...	0508	0541	0615	...	0741
Ribnitz-Damgarten West .... d.	...	...	...	...	0525	0555	0632	...	0755
Rostock Hbf .... a.	...	...	...	...	0547	0616	0654	...	0819
Rostock Hbf .... d.	...	...	0458	0505	...	0625	...	0707	0825
Bützow .... **836** d.	...	...	0519	0527	...	0647	...	0729	0847
Bad Kleinen .... **836 837** d.	...	...	0544	0551	...	|	...	0753	|
Schwerin Hbf ...... **836 837** a.	...	...	0555	0601	...	0721	...	0803	0921
Schwerin Hbf .... d.	0355	0457	0604	0615	...	0723	...	0806	0923
Büchen .... d.	0447	0552	0636	0702	...	|	...	0853	|
Hamburg Hbf .... a.	0517	0624	0701	0729	...	0819	...	0924	1019

	RE	*RE*	*IC*	*RE*	*RE*	*IC*	*RE*	*RE*	*IC*	*IC*	*RE*	*RE*	*IC*	*RE*	*RE*	*IC*	*IC*	*RE*	*RE*	*IC*	*RE*	*RE*	*RB*	*RE*	*RE*
See note ▲	**33208**	**33006**	**2373**	**33210**	**33008**	**2213**	**33212**	**33010**	**2239**	**2377**	**33214**	**33012**	**2379**	**33216**	**33014**	**2183**	**2183**	**33218**	**33016**	**2185**	**33220**	**33018**	**33286**	**33222**	**33095**
									C							⑦ w	⑤ f			⑦ w					
			A 🍷			✕ ◆			◆	🍷 ◆			🍷 ◆			H ✕	🍷			H					v L
Sassnitz **844** .... d.	0705	...	...	0905	...	...	1105	...	...	...	1305	...	...	1505	...	...	...	...	...	...	1905	...	...	2103	...
Ostseebad Binz **844** . d.	|	...	...	|	...	1029	|	...	...	1229	|	...	...	|	...	1629	...	1707	...	...	|	...	...	|	...
Stralsund .... d.	0800	...	0927	1000	...	1127	1200	...	...	1327	1400	...	1527	1600	...	1727	1727	1800	...	1927	2000	...	...	2200	...
Velgast .... d.	0816	...	0941	1016	...	1141	1216	...	...	1341	1416	...	1541	1616	...	1741	1741	1816	...	1941	2016	...	...	2216	...
Ribnitz-Damgarten West d.	0833	...	0955	1033	...	1155	1233	...	...	1400	1433	...	1555	1633	...	1800	1800	1833	...	1955	2033	...	...	2233	...
Rostock Hbf .... a.	0855	...	1019	1055	...	1219	1255	...	...	1419	1455	...	1619	1655	...	1820	1820	1855	...	2019	2055	...	...	2255	...
Rostock Hbf .... d.	...	0907	1025	...	1107	1243	...	1307	1404	1425	...	1507	1625	...	1707	1825	1825	...	1907	2025	...	2107	...	*2307*	...
Bützow .... **836** d.	...	0929	1047	...	1129	1305	...	1329	1426	1447	...	1529	1647	...	1729	1847	1847	...	1929	2047	...	2129	...	*2329*	...
Bad Kleinen ... **836 837** d.	...	0953	|	...	1153	|	...	1353	1449	|	...	1553	|	...	1753	|	|	...	1953	|	...	2153	...	*2353*	0006
Schwerin Hbf **836 837** a.	...	1003	1121	...	1203	1337	...	1403	1500	1521	...	1603	1721	...	1803	1921	1921	...	2003	2121	...	2203	...	*0003*	0019
Schwerin Hbf .... d.	...	1012	1123	...	1206	1339	...	1406	...	1523	...	1606	1723	...	1806	1923	1923	...	2006	2123	...	...	2212	...	...
Büchen .... d.	...	1058	|	...	1258	|	...	1453	...	|	...	1658	|	...	1853	|	|	...	2053	|	...	...	2315	...	...
Hamburg Hbf .... a.	...	1127	1215	...	1327	1430	...	1522	...	1615	...	1727	1817	...	1922	2015	2015	...	2122	2216	...	...	*0018*s	...	...

◆ – **NOTES** (LISTED BY TRAIN NUMBER)

2115/6 – [12] and ✕ (Greifswald ①–⑤ **d** -) Stralsund - Köln - Koblenz - Heidelberg - Stuttgart and v.v.
2174 – [12] and 🍷 Karlsruhe - Frankfurt - Hannover - Hamburg - Rostock.
2182 – [12] (Kassel ①–⑤ **d** -) (Hannover ①–⑥ **e** -) Hamburg - Stralsund.
2184 – ARKONA – [12] and 🍷 (Hannover ①–⑤ **d** -) Hamburg - Ostseebad Binz.
2212 – RÜGEN – [12] and ✕ Koblenz - Köln - Hamburg - Ostseebad Binz.
2213 – RÜGEN – [12] and ✕ Ostseebad Binz - Hamburg - Köln - Koblenz - Heidelberg - Stuttgart.
2238/9 – WARNOW – [12] Leipzig - Magdeburg - Stendal - Rostock - Warnemünde and v.v.
2270 – ⑤⑦ (also Dec. 23, 30, Apr. 1, 5, May 12, 24; not Dec. 25, Jan. 1, Apr. 2, 4, May 14, 23). SCHWARZWALD – [12] and 🍷 Konstanz - Karlsruhe - Frankfurt - Hannover - Stralsund.
2286 – [12] and 🍷 Karlsruhe - Frankfurt - Hannover - Hamburg - Rostock.
2376 – [12] and 🍷 (Karlsruhe ①–⑥ **e** -) Frankfurt - Hannover - Hamburg - Stralsund (- Ostseebad Binz ⑥).
2377 – ARKONA – [12] and 🍷 Ostseebad Binz - Hamburg - Hannover - Frankfurt (- Karlsruhe ⑤⑦ **y**).
2379 – [12] and 🍷 Stralsund - Hamburg - Hannover (- Göttingen ⑤⑦ **j**) (- Frankfurt ⑤ **f**).

A – [12] and 🍷 Stralsund - Hamburg - Hannover - Frankfurt - Karlsruhe and v.v.
B – ⑤⑥ from Mar. 27. Continues to Warnemünde (a. 1212).
C – ⑤⑦ from Mar. 28 (also June 12). From Warnemünde (d. 1348).
H – To Hannover (Table **902**).
L – To / from Lübeck (Table **826**).
a – Ⓐ only.
b – Not ⑥.
d – Not Dec. 24, 25, 31, Jan. 1, Apr. 2, 5, May 24.
e – Not Dec. 25, 26, Jan. 1, Apr. 3, 5, May 24.
f – Also Dec. 23, 30, Apr. 1, May 12; not Dec. 25, Jan. 1, Apr. 2, May 14.
g – Also Apr. 6, May 25; not Apr. 5, May 24.
h – ⑥ only.
j – Also Dec. 23, 30, Apr. 1, 5, May 12, 24; not Dec. 25, Jan. 1, Apr. 2, 4, May 14, 23.
k – On ⑥ from May 15 (also Mar. 27) departs Rostock 1149, Ribnitz 1217, Velgast 1237, arrives Stralsund 1249.
m – Not Dec. 25, 26, Jan. 1, 2, Apr. 3, 5, May 14, 15, 24.
n – Not Dec. 24, 31.
r – *S-Bahn* connection. Change trains at Aumühle (a. *0036*, d. 0042).
s – *S-Bahn* connection. Change trains at Aumühle (a. 2335, d. *2346*).
t – *0553* on ① (also Apr. 6, May 25).
v – Not Dec. 25, Jan. 1.
w – Also Apr. 5, May 24; not Apr. 4, May 23.
y – Also Apr. 5, May 24; not Dec. 25, Apr. 2, 4, May 23.
z – Not Dec. 23, 24, 30, 31, Apr. 1, 5, May 12, 24.
▲ – Subject to alteration Dec. 14–23. See page 361.

S-Bahn — ROSTOCK - WARNEMÜNDE and SEEHAFEN NORD — 831

Rostock Hbf - Rostock Seehafen Nord and v.v. *12 km.* Journey time: 18 minutes. **Rostock Überseehafen ferry terminal** is situated just over 1 km from Seehafen Nord station.
From Rostock Hbf at 0434 Ⓐ, 0534 Ⓐ, 0634, 0734 Ⓐ, 0834, 0934, 1034, 1134, 1234, 1334, 1434, 1534, 1634, 1734, 1834, 1934, 2034 and 2134.
From Rostock Seehafen Nord at 0506 Ⓐ, 0603 Ⓐ, 0706, 0806 Ⓐ, 0906, 1006, 1106, 1206, 1306, 1403, 1506, 1603, 1706, 1806, 1906, 2006, 2106 and 2206.

Rostock Hbf - Warnemünde and v.v. *13 km.* Journey time: 20 – 21 minutes. On Dec. 24, 28, 29, 30, 31 services run as on Ⓒ.
From Rostock Hbf on Ⓐ at 0001, 0401, 0431, 0446, 0501, 0516, 0531, 0546, 0556 and every 10 – 15 minutes until 2016; then 2039, 2101, 2141, 2201, 2231 and 2301 (also 2331 on ⑤).
From Rostock Hbf on Ⓒ at 0001, 0431, 0501, 0531, 0601, 0631, 0701, 0716 and every 15 minutes until 2016; then 2039, 2101, 2141, 2201, 2231 and 2301 (also 2331 on ⑥).
From Warnemünde on Ⓐ at 0037, 0407, 0432, 0507, 0522, 0532 and every 10 – 15 minutes until 2037; then 2107, 2137, 2207, 2237 and 2307 (also 2337 on ⑤).
From Warnemünde on Ⓒ at 0037, 0432, 0507, 0532, 0552, 0607, 0637, 0707, 0737, 0752 and every 15 minutes until 2037; then 2107, 2137, 2207, 2237 and 2307 (also 2337 on ⑥).

Niederbarnimer Eisenbahn (2nd class only) — BERLIN - KOSTRZYN — 832

km								
0	**Berlin** Lichtenberg ...... d.	0534	0634	each train	1934	2034	...	...	...
23	Strausberg ...... d.	0552	0652	runs every	1952	2052	...	...	...
80	**Kostrzyn** 🏛 ...... a.	0652	0742	**two** hours until	2052	2142	...	...	...

Kostrzyn 🏛 ...... d.	0503	...	0558	0706	each train	1958	2106	...
Strausberg ...... d.	0611	...	0711	0811	runs every	2111	2211	...
Berlin Lichtenberg ... a.	0628	...	0728	0828	**two** hours until	2128	2228	...

RE services — WISMAR - ROSTOCK — 833

km			Ⓐ								
0	**Wismar** ...... d.	0442	0542	...	0642	and	2042	...	2142	...
22	Neubukow ...... d.	0511	0611	...	0711	hourly	2111	...	2211	...
41	Bad Doberan ▲ ...... d.	0530	0630	...	0730	until	2130	...	2230	...
57	**Rostock** Hbf ...... a.	0551	0651	...	0751		2151	...	2250	...

	Ⓐ								
Rostock Hbf ...... d.	0412	0509	...	0606	and	2106	...	2206	...
Bad Doberan ▲ ...... d.	0432	0532	...	0632	hourly	2132	...	2225	...
Neubukow ...... d.	0451	0551	...	0651	until	2151	...	...	...
Wismar ...... a.	0515	0615	...	0715		2215	...	...	...

▲ – **BAD DOBERAN - OSTSEEBAD KÜHLUNGSBORN WEST**. All services worked by steam locomotive. 2nd class only. Journey time: 40 minutes.
Operator: Mecklenburgische Bäderbahn Molli GmbH, Am Bahnhof, 18209 Bad Doberan. ✆ +49 (0) 38203 4150, Fax +49 (0) 38203 41512. **Service until Mar. 31, 2010**.
From **Bad Doberan** at 0835 Ⓐ, 1035, 1235, 1435 and 1640. From **Kühlungsborn West** at 0643 Ⓐ, 0935, 1135, 1342 and 1535.

ROSTOCK and STRALSUND - NEUSTRELITZ - BERLIN - LUTHERSTADT WITTENBERG — 835

km		*RE*	*RE*	*RE*	*RE*	*RE*	*RE*	*ICE*	*RE*		*RE*	*ICE*	*RE*	*RE*	*RE*	*RE*		*RE*	*ICE*	*RE*	*X*	*RE*	*RE*	*RE*	
		38305	**38329**	**33101**	**38307**	**33043**	**33103**	**1609**	**38309**	⊙	**33105**	**1611**	**38311**	**33045**	**33107**	**38313**	⊙	**33109**	**1615**	**38315**	**80004**	**33047**	**33111**	**38317**	⊙
			Ⓒ	Ⓐ				**A M**				**C M**							**E M**		⊠ **L**				
	Warnemünde **831** ...... d.	...	...	...	...	...	...	0658	...	...	...	0902	...	...	...	...	...	...	1302	...	1415	...	...	...	...
0	**Rostock** Hbf ...... ★ d.	...	...	0438	...	...	0634	0724	...	...	0834	0924	...	...	1034	...	...	1234	1324	...	1432	...	1453	...	...
34	Güstrow ...... ★ d.	...	...	0502	...	...	0657	|	...	...	0857	|	...	...	1057	...	...	1257	|	...	1456	...	|	...	...
85	Waren (Müritz) ...... d.	...	...	0534	...	...	0734	0806	...	...	0934	1006	...	...	1134	...	...	1334	1406	...	1528	...	1536	...	...
	Stralsund ...... d.	...	...	|	0502	0602e	|	|	0702	0802	|	|	0902	1002	|	1102	1202	|	|	1302	|	1402	|	1502	1602
	Grimmen ...... d.	...	...	|	0523	0623e	|	|	0723	0823	|	|	0923	1023	|	1123	1223	|	|	1323	|	1423	|	1523	1623
	Demmin ...... d.	...	...	|	0546	0646e	|	|	0746	0846	|	|	0946	1046	|	1146	1246	|	|	1346	|	1446	|	1546	1646
	Neubrandenburg ...... a.	...	...	|	0627	0728e	|	|	0828	0928	|	|	1028	1128	|	1228	1328	|	|	1428	|	1528	|	1628	1728
	Neubrandenburg ...... d.	0429	...	|	0632	0731	|	|	0832	0931	|	|	1032	1131	|	1232	1331	|	|	1432	|	1531	|	1632	1731
121	**Neustrelitz** Hbf ...... d.	0458	...	0600	0700	0756	0800	0832	0900	0956	1000	1032	1100	1156	1200	1300	1356	1400	1432	1500	1553	1556	1600	1700	1756
141	Fürstenberg (Havel) ...... d.	0510	...	0613	0713	...	0813	|	0913	...	1013	|	1113	...	1213	1313	...	1413	|	1513	|	...	1613	1713	...
162	Gransee ...... d.	0527	...	0628	0727	...	0828	|	0927	...	1028	|	1127	...	1228	1327	...	1428	|	1527	|	...	1628	1727	...
191	Oranienburg ...... d.	0550	...	0650	0750	...	0850	|	0950	...	1050	|	1150	...	1250	1350	...	1450	|	1550	|	...	1650	1750	...
218	**Berlin** Gesundbrunnen ...... d.	0611	...	0711	0811	...	0911	0939	1011	...	1111	1138	1211	...	1311	1411	...	1511	1540	1611	1658	...	1711	1811	...
223	**Berlin** Hbf ...... △ d.	0617	0717	0717	0817	...	0917	0952j	1017	...	1117	1152j	1217	...	1317	1417	...	1517	1552j	1617	1703	...	1717	1817	...
231	**Berlin** Südkreuz ...... △ d.	0624	0724	0724	0824	...	0924	0959	1024	...	1124	1159	1224	...	1324	1424	...	1524	1559	1624	...	...	1724	1824	...
276	Luckenwalde ...... d.	0655	0754	0754	0855	...	0954	|	1055	...	1154	|	1255	...	1354	1455	...	1554	|	1655	...	...	1754	1855	...
289	Jüterbog ...... d.	0703	0802	0802	0903	...	1002	|	1103	...	1202	|	1303	...	1402	1503	...	1602	|	1703	...	...	1802	1903	...
	Falkenberg (Elster) ...... a.	0746	|	|	0946	...	|	|	1146	...	|	|	1346	...	|	1546	...	|	|	1746	...	...	|	1946	...
321	**Lutherstadt Wittenberg** △ a.	...	0829	0829	...	...	1029	1033	...	...	1229	1233	...	...	1429	...	...	1629	1633	...	...	...	1829	...	...

	RE	*RE*	*RE*	*RE*	*RE*	*RE*		*RE*	*RE*	
	33113	**38319**	**38591**	**33049**	**33115**	**38321**	⊙	**33117**	**33051**	⊙
			Ⓒ **k**				Ⓑ			
Warnemünde **831** ...... d.	...	...	1800	...	...	...	...	...	...	...
Rostock Hbf ...... ★ d.	1634	...	1819	...	1834	...	...	2034	...	...
Güstrow ...... ★ d.	1657	...	|	...	1857	...	...	2057	...	...
Waren (Müritz) ...... d.	1734	...	1905	...	1934	...	...	2134	...	...
Stralsund ...... d.	|	1702	|	1802	|	1902	2002	|	2102	...
Grimmen ...... d.	|	1723	|	1823	|	1923	2023	|	2123	...
Demmin ...... d.	|	1746	|	1846	|	1946	2046	|	2146	...
Neubrandenburg ...... a.	|	1828	|	1928	|	2028	2128	|	2229	...
Neubrandenburg ...... d.	|	1832	|	1931	|	2032	2131	|	▬	2253
Neustrelitz Hbf ...... d.	1800	1900	1931	1956	2000	2100	2156	2200	...	2326
Fürstenberg (Havel) ...... d.	1813	1913	1944	...	2013	2113	...	2213	...	▬
Gransee ...... d.	1828	1927	|	...	2028	2127	...	2228	*RE*	*RE*
Oranienburg ...... d.	1850	1950	2022	...	2050	2150	...	2251	**38335**	**38333**
Berlin Gesundbrunnen ...... d.	1911	2011	2044	...	2111	2211	...	2312		Ⓒ **Q**
Berlin Hbf ...... △ d.	1917	2017	2048	...	2117	2217	...	2316	2320	0015
Berlin Südkreuz ...... △ d.	1924	2024	...	...	2124	2223	...	...	2327	0022
Luckenwalde ...... d.	1954	2055	...	...	2154	2302	...	...	0004	0100
Jüterbog ...... d.	2002	2103	...	...	2202	2312	...	...	0011	0108
Falkenberg (Elster) ...... a.	|	2146	...	...	|	2356	...	...	...	|
Lutherstadt Wittenberg .. △ a.	2029	...	...	...	2229	...	...	...	...	0124

km		*RE*		*RE*	*RE*	*RE*	*RE*	*RE*	*RE*	
		33100	⊙	**38306**	**33102**	**33044**	**38308**	**38590**	**33104**	⊙
		Ⓐ			**H**			Ⓒ **k**		
	Lutherstadt Wittenberg △ d.	...	...	...	0526	...	...	...	0728	...
0	**Falkenberg** (Elster) ...... d.	...	...	...	|	...	0609	...	|	...
49	Jüterbog ...... d.	...	...	0453	0554	...	0653	...	0756	...
62	Luckenwalde ...... d.	...	...	0501	0602	...	0701	...	0803	...
107	**Berlin** Südkreuz ...... △ d.	...	...	0534	0634	...	0734	...	0834	...
115	**Berlin** Hbf ...... △ d.	0444	...	0544	0644	...	0744	0814	0844	...
120	**Berlin** Gesundbrunnen ...... d.	0449	...	0549	0649	...	0749	0820	0849	...
147	Oranienburg ...... d.	0509	...	0609	0709	...	0809	0841	0909	...
176	Gransee ...... d.	0533	...	0634	0733	...	0834	|	0933	...
197	Fürstenberg (Havel) ...... d.	0548	...	0648	0748	...	0848	0915	0948	...
218	**Neustrelitz** Hbf ...... d.	0605j	0603	0701	0801	0803	0901	0928	1001	1003
253	**Neubrandenburg** ...... a.	|	0631	0729	|	0828	0929	|	|	1028
253	**Neubrandenburg** ...... d.	|	0633	0733	|	0833	0933	|	|	1033
295	Demmin ...... d.	|	0709	0809	|	0909	1009	|	|	1109
319	Grimmen ...... d.	|	0729	0829	|	0929	1029	|	|	1129
342	**Stralsund** ...... a.	|	0751	0851	|	0951	1051	|	|	1151
	Waren (Müritz) ...... d.	0631	...	...	0831	...	...	0953	1031	...
	Güstrow ...... ★ d.	0702	...	...	0902	...	...	|	1102	...
	Rostock Hbf ...... ★ a.	0723	...	...	0923	...	...	1038v	1123	...
	Warnemünde **831** ...... a.	...	...	...	...	...	...	1058v	...	...

	RE	*ICE*	*RE*	*RE*	*X*	*RE*	*RE*		*RE*	*RE*	*RE*	*RE*	*RE*		*RE*	*ICE*	*RE*	*RE*	*RE*	*RE*	*RE*	*RE*	*RE*	*RE*	*RE*
	38310	**1614**	**33106**	**33046**	**80003**	**38312**	**33108**	⊙	**38314**	**33110**	**33048**	**38316**	**33112**	⊙	**38318**	**1606**	**33114**	**33050**	**38320**	**33116**	**38322**	**38322**	**38328**	**38332**	**38324**
		E N			⊠ **L**									Ⓑ ¶		**B M**		Ⓑ ¶				**P**		⑤⑥ **f**	
Lutherstadt Wittenberg .. △ d.	...	0922	0926	...	...	...	1126	...	...	1326	...	...	1526	...	...	1722	1726	...	...	1930	...	...	2126	...	...
Falkenberg (Elster) ...... d.	0809	|	|	...	...	1009	|	...	1209	|	...	1409	|	...	1609	|	|	...	1809	|	2009	2009	|	...	2209
Jüterbog ...... d.	0853	|	0954	...	...	1053	1154	...	1253	1354	...	1453	1554	...	1653	|	1754	...	1853	1957	2053	2053	2154	...	2253
Luckenwalde ...... d.	0901	|	1002	...	...	1101	1202	...	1301	1402	...	1501	1602	...	1701	|	1802	...	1901	2005	2101	2101	2201	...	2301
Berlin Südkreuz ...... △ d.	0934	0959	1034	...	...	1134	1234	...	1334	1434	...	1534	1634	...	1734	1800	1834	...	1934	2035	2134	2134	2239	...	2338
Berlin Hbf ...... △ d.	0944	1014	1044	...	1059	1144	1244	...	1344	1444	...	1544	1644	...	1744	1812	1844	...	1944	2044	2141	2144	2247	2313	2345
Berlin Gesundbrunnen ...... d.	0949	1020	1049	...	1105	1149	1249	...	1349	1449	...	1549	1649	...	1749	1820	1849	...	1949	2049	▬	2149	2251	2318	...
Oranienburg ...... d.	1009	|	1109	...	|	1209	1309	...	1409	1509	...	1609	1709	...	1809	|	1909	...	2009	2109	...	2209	...	2337	...
Gransee ...... d.	1034	|	1133	...	|	1234	1333	...	1434	1533	...	1634	1733	...	1834	|	1933	...	2034	2133	⊙	2234	...	2358	...
Fürstenberg (Havel) ...... d.	1048	|	1148	...	|	1248	1348	...	1448	1548	...	1648	1748	...	1848	|	1948	...	2048	2148	Ⓑ	2248	...	0013	...
Neustrelitz Hbf ...... d.	1101	1128	1201	1203	1208	1301	1401	1403	1501	1601	1603	1701	1801	1803	1901	1929	2001	2003	2101	2201	2203	2303	...	0027	...
Neubrandenburg ...... a.	1129	|	|	1228	|	1329	|	1429	1529	|	1628	1729	|	1828	1929	|	|	2028	2129	|	2228	2330	...	0054	...
Neubrandenburg ...... d.	1133	|	|	1233	|	1333	|	1433	1533	|	1633	1733	|	1833	1933	|	|	2033	2133	|	...	...	...	...	...
Demmin ...... d.	1209	|	|	1309	|	1409	|	1509	1609	|	1709	1809	|	1909	2009	|	|	2109	2209	|	...	...	...	...	...
Grimmen ...... d.	1229	|	|	1329	|	1429	|	1529	1629	|	1729	1829	|	1929	2029	|	|	2129	2229	|	...	...	...	...	...
Stralsund ...... a.	1251	|	|	1351	|	1451	|	1551	1651	|	1751	1851	|	1951	2051	|	|	2151	2251	|	...	...	...	...	...
Waren (Müritz) ...... d.	...	1153	1225	...	1232	...	1431	...	...	1631	...	...	1831	...	...	1953	2031	...	...	2231	...	...	...	...	...
Güstrow ...... ★ d.	...	|	|	...	1303	...	1502	...	...	1702	...	...	1902	...	...	|	2102	...	...	2302	...	...	...	...	...
Rostock Hbf ...... ★ a.	...	1233	1304	...	1324	...	1523	...	...	1723	...	...	1923	...	...	2033	2123	...	...	2323	...	...	...	...	...
Warnemünde **831** ...... a.	...	1247	...	...	1357	...	...	...	...	...	...	...	...	...	...	2048	...	...	...	...	...	...	...	...	...

A – ①–⑤ (not Dec. 24, 25, 31, Jan. 1, Apr. 2, 5, May 24).
B – Ⓑ (not Dec. 24, 25, 31, Apr. 2, 4, May 23).
C – ⑥ (also Dec. 24, 31, Apr. 2; not Dec. 26, Apr. 3).
E – ⑥ from June 5.
H – From Halle on Ⓒ (not Dec. 25). See Table **848**.
L – From / to Leipzig (Table **851**).
M – 12 and ✕ Warnemünde - Leipzig - Nürnberg - München and v.v.
N – 12 and ✕ Nürnberg - Leipzig - Warnemünde.

P – ①②③④⑦ (not Apr. 4, May 23).
Q – Ⓒ (not Dec. 25). To Halle (Table **848**).

e – ①–⑥ only.
f – Also Apr. 4, May 23.
j – Arrives 5 – 9 minutes earlier.
k – Not Dec. 25, 26, 27, Jan. 1.
v – 28 – 33 minutes later on Dec. 19, 20.

¶ – Runs daily Neustrelitz - Neubrandenburg.
△ – See Tables **850/1** for other *ICE* / *IC* services Berlin - Lutherstadt Wittenberg and v.v.
⊠ – Operated by Veolia Verkehr GmbH. **DB tickets not valid**.
⊙ – Operated by Ostseeland Verkehr GmbH.
★ – Dec. 14 – 22 (also before 0800 on Dec. 23) trains are diverted between Rostock and Waren and do not call at Güstrow. Rostock timings may also vary during this period.

836 LÜBECK and SCHWERIN - PASEWALK - SZCZECIN and UECKERMÜNDE

DB (*RE* services); OLA ‡

km			‡	Ⓐ		‡	Ⓐ	Ⓒ	‡		‡		‡Ⓐ	‡		‡		‡		‡		‡	‡⑤f	n	‡⑦
0	**Lübeck** Hbf 826 d.	...	...	...	...	...	0602	...	...	0802	...	1002	...	...	1202	...	1402	...	1602	...	1802	...	...	2002	...
	Schwerin Hbf 830/7 d.	...	...	0442	...	0551	|	0640	0751	|	0951	|	...	1151	|	1351	|	1551	|	1751	|	1951	1951	|	2151
62	Bad Kleinen 826 830/7 d.	...	...	0504	...	0602	0704	0704	0802	0904	1002	1104j	...	1202	1304	1402	1504	1602	1704	1802	1904	2002	2002	2104	2202
103	Bützow 830 d.	...	...	0534	...	0632	0734	0734	0832	0934	1032	1134	...	1232	1334	1432	1534	1632	1734	1832	1934	2032	2032	2134	2232
117	Güstrow a.	...	...	0543	...	0641	0743	0743	0841	0943	1041	1143	...	1241	1343	1441	1543	1641	1743	1841	1943	2041	2041	2143	2241
117	Güstrow d.	...	...	0558	...	0709	0758	0758	0909	0958	1109	1158	...	1309	1358	1509	1558	1709	1758	1909	1958	2109	2109	2158	2309
146	Teterow d.	...	...	0623	...	0733	0823	0823	0933	1023	1133	1223	...	1333	1423	1533	1623	1733	1823	1933	2023	2133	2133	2223	2333
160	Malchin d.	...	0537a	0634	...	0744	0834	0834	0944	1034	1144	1234	...	1344	1434	1544	1634	1744	1834	1944	2034	2144	2144	2234	2344
204	**Neubrandenburg** a.	...	0611a	0708	...	0824	0908	0908	1024	1108	1224	1308	...	1424	1508	1624	1708	1824	1908	2024	2108	2224	2224	2308	0018
204	**Neubrandenburg** d.	0516a	0612	0712	0712	0832	0912	0912	1032	1112	1232	1312	...	1433	1512	1632	1712	1832	1912	2032	2133	...	2232	...	...
257	**Pasewalk** a.	0600a	0701	0800	0800	0915	1000	1000	1115	1200	1315	1400	...	1515	1600	1715	1800	1915	2003	2115	2218	...	2316	...	...
257	**Pasewalk** ◧ d.	0601	0714	0801	0801	0921	1001	1001	1121	1201	1321	1401	1404	1521	1601	1721	1801	1927	2004	2121n	...	...	2328	...	...
287	Ueckermünde ◧ a.	|	0752	|	|	0952	|	|	1152	|	1352	|	1438	1552	|	1752	|	1958	|	2152n	...	...	|	...	...
284	Grambow d.	0625	...	0825	0825	...	1025	1025	...	1225	...	1425	...	...	1625	...	1825	...	2028	...	...	...	2351	...	...
294	Szczecin Gumience ⊞ d.	0635	...	0834	0834	...	1034	1035	...	1240	...	1440	...	...	1640	...	1840	...	2037	...	...	...	0001	...	...
299	**Szczecin** Główny a.	0640	...	0840	0840	...	1040	1040	...	1245	...	1445	...	...	1645	...	1845	...	2043	...	...	...	0005	...	...

	‡⑥t	‡	Ⓐ	‡	Ⓐ		‡	‡Ⓐ		‡		‡		‡		‡	‡Ⓐ		‡		‡		‡	‡⑦	
Szczecin Główny d.	0013	...	...	...	0453	...	...	...	0656	...	0856	...	1056	...	1256	...	...	1456	...	1656	...	1853	...	...	2056
Szczecin Gumience ⊞ d.	0019	...	...	...	0502	...	...	...	0702	...	0902	...	1102	...	1302	...	...	1502	...	1702	...	1901	...	...	2102
Grambow d.	0029	...	...	...	0512	...	...	...	0712	...	0912	...	1112	...	1312	...	...	1512	...	1712	...	1911	...	...	2112
Ueckermünde ◧ d.	|	...	...	...	|	...	0559r	0659	|	0759	|	0959	|	1159	|	1403	1454	|	1559	|	1759	|	2005	2005	|
Pasewalk ◧ a.	0051	...	...	...	0535	...	0631r	0731	0735	0831	0935	1031	1135	1231	1335	1438	1526	1535	1631	1735	1831	1934	2037	2037	2136
Pasewalk d.	0052	...	...	...	0541	...	0643	...	0741	0843	0941	1043	1141	1243	1341	1443	...	1541	1643	1741	1843	1946	2043	2043	2146
Neubrandenburg a.	0130	...	...	...	0628	...	0728	...	0828	0928	1028	1128	1228	1328	1428	1528	...	1628	1728	1828	1928	2028	2128	2128	2231
Neubrandenburg d.	...	...	0448	0528	0638	0638	0735	...	0838	0935	1038	1135	1238	1335	1438	1535	...	1638	1736	1838	1936	2038	...	2135	...
Malchin d.	...	...	0521	0607	0715	0715	0807	...	0915	1007	1115	1207	1315	1407	1515	1607	...	1715	1808	1915	2008	2115	...	2207	...
Teterow d.	...	...	0532	0624	0730	0730	0819	...	0930	1019	1130	1219	1330	1419	1530	1619	...	1730	1819	1930	2019	2130	...	2219	...
Güstrow a.	...	...	0556	0648	0756	0756	0848	...	0956	1048	1156	1248	1356	1448	1556	1648	...	1756	1848	1956	2048	2156	...	2248	...
Güstrow d.	...	0508	0608	0708	0808	0808	0908	...	1008	1108	1208	1308	1408	1508	1608	1708	...	1808	1908	2008	2108	2208	...	2308	...
Bützow 830 d.	...	0517	0619	0717	0819	0819	0917	...	1019	1117	1219	1317	1419	1517	1619	1717	...	1819	1917	2019	2117	2219	...	2317	...
Bad Kleinen 826 830/7 a.	...	0550	0648	0752	0848	0848	0952	...	1048	1152	1248	1352	1457	1552	1648	1752	...	1848	1952	2048	2152	2248	...	2352	...
Schwerin Hbf 830/7 a.	...	0601	|	0803	|	|	1003	...	|	1203	|	1403	|	1603	|	1803	...	|	2003	|	2203	2302	...	0003	...
Lübeck Hbf 826 a.	...	...	0756	...	0956	0956	...	...	1156	...	1356	...	1556	...	1756	...	...	1956n	...	2156n	...	...	...	...	...

a – Ⓐ only.
f – Also Apr. 1; not Apr. 2.
j – 1056 on ⑤⑥ from Mar. 27.
n – Not Dec. 24, 31.
r – ⚒ only.
t – Also Apr. 2; not Apr. 3.
‡ – Operated by Ostseeland Verkehr (OLA).
◧ – Additional trains Pasewalk - Ueckermünde and v.v. (operated by OLA ‡): **From Pasewalk** at 0521 ⚒ and 0608 Ⓐ. **From Ueckermünde** at 2159 n.

837 WISMAR - SCHWERIN - BERLIN

RE services except where shown

km		Ⓐ		⚒ ◇	Ⓐn ◇			Ⓐn ◇					◇		*IC* 2239 A L			Ⓐn ◇		◇		◇		◇		Ⓐ
0	**Wismar** d.	0427	...	0539	...	0644	0732	...	0844	0933	1044	1133	1244	1333	...	1430	1533	...	1644	1733	...	1846	1933	2044	2140	2244
16	Bad Kleinen a.	0440	...	0554	...	0659	0748	...	0859	0948	1059	1148	1259	1348	...	1445p	1548	...	1700	1748	...	1900	1948	2059	2155	2300
16	Bad Kleinen 830/6 d.	0441	...	0557	...	0701	0758	...	0901	0958	1101	1158	1301	1358	1449	1501	1558	...	1701	1758	...	1901	1958	2101	2158	2302
32	**Schwerin** Hbf 830/6 a.	0454	...	0609	...	0712	0810	...	0912	1010	1112	1210	1312	1410	1500	1512	1610	...	1712	1810	...	1913	2010	2112	2209	2313
32	**Schwerin** Hbf d.	...	0517	0610	0648	0713	0817	0846	0913	1017	1113	1217	1313	1417	1502	1513	1617	1648	1713	1811	...	1914	2017	2113	▬	...
72	Ludwigslust a.	...	0547	0639	0712	0746	0847	0910	0945	1047	1145	1247	1345	1447	1524	1545	1647	1713	1745	1840	...	1946	2047	2146	...	...
72	Ludwigslust 840 d.	...	0548	0648	...	...	0848	...	...	1048	...	1248	...	1448	1526	...	1648	...	...	1850	...	...	...	2148	...	...
116	Wittenberge 840 d.	...	0612	0712	...	...	0912	...	...	1112	...	1312	...	1512	1545	...	1712	...	...	1914	2112	...	...	2212	2302	...
207	Nauen d.	...	0705	0805	...	...	1005	...	...	1205	...	1409	...	1605	...	...	1805	...	...	2006	2205	...	...	...	2355	...
229	**Berlin** Spandau 840 a.	...	0719	0819	...	...	1019	...	...	1219	...	1423	...	1619	...	...	1819	...	...	2022	2219	...	...	...	0010	...
241	**Berlin** Hbf 840 a.	...	0729	0829	...	...	1029	...	...	1229	...	1433	...	1629	...	...	1829	...	...	2031	2229	...	...	...	0025	...

	⚒		⚒ ◇				Ⓐ ◇		*IC* 2238 B L							Ⓐn ◇			Ⓐn ◇			◇				
Berlin Hbf 840 d.	...	0426	0521	...	...	0730	...	...	...	0930	...	1130	...	1330	...	...	1530	...	...	1730	...	...	1930	2030	2130	2230
Berlin Spandau 840 d.	...	0436	0531	...	...	0740	...	...	...	0940	...	1140	...	1340	...	...	1540	...	...	1740	...	...	1940	2040	2140	2240
Nauen d.	...	0452	0545	...	...	0754	...	...	...	0954	...	1154	...	1354	...	...	1554	...	...	1754	...	...	1954	2054	2154	2254
Wittenberge 840 d.	...	0548	0650	...	...	0850	...	...	1012	1050	...	1250	...	1450	...	...	1650	...	...	1850	...	...	2049	2150	2249	2355
Ludwigslust 840 a.	...	0611	0713	...	...	0913	...	...	1029	1113	...	1313	...	1513	...	...	1713	...	...	1913	...	...	...	2213	▬	...
Ludwigslust d.	0514a	0612	0714	...	0812	0914	0938	1012	1031	1114	1212	1314	1412	1514	1612	1638	1714	1812	1845	1914	2012	2054	...	2214	...	...
Schwerin Hbf a.	0544a	0645	0744	...	0845	0944	1004	1045	1053	1144	1245	1344	1445	1544	1645	1704	1744	1845	1909	1944	2045	2125	...	2246	...	...
Schwerin Hbf 830/6 d.	0545	0646	0745	0745	0846	0945	...	1046	1055	1145	1246	1345	1446	1545	1646	...	1745	1846	...	1945	2046	2145	...	...	2253	...
Bad Kleinen 830/6 a.	0558	0658	0758	0758	0858	0958	...	1058	1105p	1158	1258	1358	1458	1558	1658	...	1758	1858	...	1958	2058	2158	...	...	2306	...
Bad Kleinen d.	0605	0701	0805	0805	0901	1005	...	1110	...	1205	1301	1405	1501	1605	1701	...	1805	1901	...	2005	2101	2205	...	...	2307	...
Wismar a.	0620	0717	0820	0820	0916	1020	...	1125	...	1220	1316	1420	1516	1620	1716	...	1820	1916	...	2020	2116	2220	...	...	2322	...

A – ⑤⑦ from Mar. 28 (also June 12).
B – ⑤⑥ from Mar. 27.
L – WARNOW – (12) Leipzig - Magdeburg - Stendal - Rostock - Warnemünde and v.v.
a – Ⓐ only.
n – Not Dec. 24, 31.
p – Connects with train in previous column.
◇ – Connects at Ludwigslust with fast *ICE*, *EC* or *IC* train to / from Berlin (see Table **840**).

838 *Subject to alteration from May 3* STENDAL - BERLIN - LÜBBEN - COTTBUS

RE services except where shown

km				⚒				*EC* 341 t A										*IC* 2131 Ⓑq E 🍷							
0	**Stendal** 810 d.	...	0448	0526	...	0631	...	0847v	0831	...	1031	...	1231	...	1431	...	1631	...	...	1831	...	2031	...	2220n	...
34	Rathenow 810 a.	...	0504	0551	...	0656	...	|	0856	...	1056	...	1256	...	1456	...	1656	...	...	1856	...	2056	...	2245n	...
34	Rathenow 810 d.	0405a	0505	...	0605	0705	0805	|	0910	1005	1110	1205	1310	1405	1510	1605	1710	...	1805	1910	2005	2110	2205	2310	...
92	**Berlin** Spandau 810 d.	0449a	0549	...	0648	0749	0849	0925v	0950	1049	1149	1249	1349	1448	1549	1648	1749	...	1848	1949	2049	2149	2249	2347	...
104	**Berlin** Zoo d.	0458a	0558	...	0658	0758	0858	|	0958	1058	1158	1258	1358	1457	1558	1658	1758	...	1858	1958	2058	2158	2258	2356	...
108	**Berlin** Hbf 810 d.	0503a	0603	...	0703	0803	0903	0941	1004	1103	1203	1303	1403	1503	1603	1703	1803	1831	1903	2003	2103	2203	2303	2400	0040
113	**Berlin** Ostbahnhof 810 d.	0513	0613	...	0713	0813	0913	0951	1013	1113	1213	1313	1413	1513	1613	1713	1813	1841	1913	2013	2113	2213	2313	...	0049
146	Königs Wusterhausen d.	0540	0640	...	0740	0840	0940	|	1040	1140	1240	1340	1440	1540	1640	1740	1840	|	1940	2040	2140	2240	2340	...	0113
192	Lübben (Spreewald) d.	0610	0710	...	0810	0910	1010	1043	1110	1210	1310	1410	1510	1610	1710	1810	1910	1933	2010	2110	2219	2319	0019	...	0149
203	Lübbenau (Spreew) d.	0619	0717	...	0817	0917	1017	1053	1117	1217	1317	1417	1517	1620	1717	1817	1917	1943	2017	2117	2226	2326	0026	...	0156
233	**Cottbus** a.	0645	0745	...	0843	0943	1043	1109	1143	1243	1343	1443	1543	1643	1743	1843	1943	1958	2043	2143	2248	...	0047	...	0213

		Ⓐ	⚒			*IC* 2132 ①–⑥ N 🍷											*EC* 340 n B								
Cottbus d.	...	...	...	0418	0516	0602	0616	0716	0816	0916	1016	1116	1216	1316	1416	1516	1602	1616	1716	1816	1916	2016	2113	...	2310
Lübbenau (Spreew) d.	0039	...	...	0439	0539	0619	0639	0739	0839	0939	1039	1139	1239	1339	1439	1539	1620	1639	1739	1839	1939	2039	2135	...	2331
Lübben (Spreewald) d.	0047	...	...	0447	0547	0628	0647	0747	0847	0947	1047	1147	1247	1347	1447	1547	1629	1647	1747	1847	1947	2047	2142	...	2338
Königs Wusterhausen d.	0119	...	...	0519	0619	|	0719	0819	0919	1019	1119	1219	1319	1419	1519	1619	|	1719	1819	1919	2019	2119	2221	...	0019
Berlin Ostbahnhof 810 d.	0147	...	...	0547	0647	0720	0747	0847	0947	1047	1147	1247	1347	1447	1547	1647	1725	1747	1847	1947	2047	2147	2247	...	0047
Berlin Hbf 810 d.	0158a	...	...	0558	0658	0727	0758	0858	0958	1058	1158	1258	1358	1458	1558	1658	1737	1758	1858	1958	2058	2158	2258	0015	0058
Berlin Zoo d.	0203a	0504	...	0604	0704	...	0804	0904	1004	1104	1204	1304	1404	1504	1604	1704	|	1804	1904	2004	2104	2204	2304	0021	0103
Berlin Spandau 810 d.	...	0513	...	0613	0713	...	0813	0913	1013	1113	1213	1313	1413	1513	1613	1713	1752z	1813	1913	2013	2113	2213	2313	0029	...
Rathenow 810 a.	...	0554	...	0655	0754	...	0849	0955	1049	1154	1249	1354	1449	1554	1651	1754	|	1851	1954	2051	2155	2250	2355	0102	...
Rathenow 810 d.	...	...	0557	0702	...	...	0902	...	1102	...	1302	...	1502	...	1702	...	|	1902	...	2102	...	...	2356	...	...
Stendal 810 a.	...	...	0621	0727	...	...	0927	...	1127	...	1327	...	1527	...	1727	...	1824z	1927	...	2127	...	...	0012	...	...

A – WAWEL – (12) (Hamburg ①–⑥ v -) Berlin - Forst ⊞ - Wrocław - Katowice - Kraków.
B – WAWEL – (12) Kraków - Katowice - Wrocław - Forst ⊞ - Berlin (- Hamburg Ⓑ z).
E – OSTFRIESLAND – (12) Emden - Oldenburg - Bremen - Hannover - Magdeburg - Cottbus. On May 2 Berlin Hbf d. 1742, Berlin Ostbahnhof d. 1754, Cottbus a. 2003 (not calling at Lübben or Lübbenau).
N – ①–⑥ (not Dec. 25, 26, Jan. 1, Apr. 3, 5, May 24). OSTFRIESLAND – (12) Cottbus - Magdeburg - Hannover - Bremen - Oldenburg. Continues to Norddeich Mole on dates in Table **813**.
a – Ⓐ only.
n – Not Dec. 24, 31.
q – not Dec. 24, 25, 31, Apr. 2, 4, May 23.
t – Not Dec. 25, 31.
v – ①–⑥ (not Dec. 25, 26, 31, Jan. 1, Apr. 3, 5, May 24).
z – Ⓑ (not Dec. 24, 25, 30, 31, Apr. 2, 4, May 23).

MAGDEBURG - BERLIN - FRANKFURT (ODER) - COTTBUS — 839

RE services

km																								
				Ⓐ	Ⓒ									P🍷					E♣					
0	**Magdeburg** Hbf ... d.	...	...	0446v	0458z	...	0604	...	0706	...	and at the same minutes past each hour until	1606	...	1700	1706	...	1806	...	1851	1906	2006	2104	2204	2317
79	**Brandenburg** Hbf ... d.	0422	0500	0600	0600	0622*	0700	0722*	0800	0822		1700	1722	1742	1800	1822	1900	1922	|	2000	2100	2156	2256	0022
114	Potsdam Hbf ... d.	0451	0522	0622	0622	0652	0722	0752	0822	0852		1722	1752	1800	1822	1852	1922	1952	2005	2022	2122	2222	2322	0052
123	Berlin Wannsee ... d.	0457	0529	0629	0629	0659	0730	0759	0829	0859		1729	1759	1809	1829	1859	1929	1959	2012	2029	2129	2229	2329	0059
138	**Berlin** Zoo ... d.	0510	0542	0642	0642	0712	0742	0812	0842	0912		1742	1812	|	1842	1912	1942	2012	2032	2042	2142	2242	2342	0112
142	**Berlin** Hbf ... d.	0515	0548	0648	0648	0718	0748	0818	0848	0918		1748	1818	1831	1848	1918	1948	2018	|	2048	2148	2248	2348	0118
147	**Berlin** Ostbahnhof ... 1001 d.	0523	0559	0659	0659	0729	0759	0829	0859	0929		1759	1829	1841	1859	1929	1959	2029	2048	2059	2159	2259	2359	0128
194	Fürstenwalde (Spree) ... d.	0607	0632	0732	0732	0807	0832	0907	0932	1007		1832	1907	|	1932	2007	2032	2107	...	2137	2237	2337	0037	...
228	**Frankfurt (Oder)** ... 1001 a.	0629	0702	0802	0802	0826	0902	0926	1002	1026		1902	1926	⊖	2002	2026	2102	2126	...	2206	2306	0006	0106	...
	Cottbus (see below) ... a.	...	...	...	...	...	...	...	...	...		...	...	1958b	...	2129	...	2249	...	2316	0030	...	...	...

	Ⓒ							N🍷	C♣															⑤⑥j
Cottbus (see below) ... d.	...	...	...	...	0341	...	0441	0602e	...	0511	0543	...	...	and at the same minutes past each hour until	...	...	...	...	...	...	...	...	...	...
Frankfurt (Oder) ... 1001 d.	...	...	0351	...	0451	0533	0554	⊖	...	0633	0654	0733	0754		1833	1854	1933	1954	2029	2126	2224	...	2323	2323
Fürstenwalde (Spree) ... d.	...	...	0419	...	0519	0551	0624	|	...	0651	0724	0751	0824		1851	1924	1951	2024	2051	2153	2251	...	2351	2351
Berlin Ostbahnhof ... 1001 d.	0129	...	0459	0530	0559	0629	0659	0720	0708	0729	0759	0829	0859		1929	1959	2029	2059	2129	2229	2326	2330	0029	0029
Berlin Hbf ... d.	0140	...	0510	0540	0610	0640	0710	0731	|	0740	0810	0840	0910		1940	2010	2040	2110	2140	2240	...	2340	0040	0040
Berlin Zoo ... d.	0147	...	0517	0547	0617	0647	0717	|	0722	0747	0817	0847	0917		1947	2017	2047	2115	2147	2247	...	2347	0047	0047
Berlin Wannsee ... d.	0200	...	0530	0600	0630	0700	0730	0750	0736	0800	0830	0900	0930		2000	2030	2100	...	2200	2300	...	0000	0100	0100
Potsdam Hbf ... d.	0208	...	0538	0608	0638	0708	0738	0758	0744	0808	0838	0908	0938		2008	2038	2108	...	2208	2308	...	0008	0108	0108
Brandenburg Hbf ... d.	0237	...	0600	0637	0700	0737	0800	0817	|	0837	0900	0937	1000		2037	2100	2140	...	2237	2338	...	0037	0137	0138
Magdeburg Hbf ... a.	...	...	0653	...	0753	...	0853	0858	0904	...	0953	...	1053		...	2153	2238	...	...	0031	...	...	...	0223

km		Ⓐ	Ⓐ							
0	**Frankfurt (Oder)** ... d.	0404	0434	0534	and hourly until	1934	2028	2128	2208	2309
23	Eisenhüttenstadt ... d.	0425	0455	0555		1955	2049	2149	2229	2330
48	Guben ... d.	0447	0517	0617		2017	2106	2212	2251	2353
86	**Cottbus** ... a.	0522	0552	0652		2052	2129	2249	2316	0030

					Ⓐ					
Cottbus ... d.	0341	0441	0511	0543	0607	0707	and hourly until	1907	2107	2307
Guben ... d.	0403	0506	0548	0605	0642	0742		1942	2142	2342
Eisenhüttenstadt ... d.	0424	0528	0609	0626	0703	0803		2003	2202	0003
Frankfurt (Oder) ... a.	0448	0551	0631	0650	0724	0824		2024	2222	0024

C – ⑥⑦ (also Dec. 24, Jan. 1, Apr. 2, 5, May 13, 24).
E – ⑤–⑦ (also Dec. 23, 31, Apr. 1, 5, 29, May 12, 13, 24).
N – *IC* **2132**. To Norddeich (Tables **810**/**813**).
P – Until Apr. 30. *IC* **2131**. From Emden (Tables **813**/**810**).
b – Ⓑ (not Dec. 24, 25, 31, Apr. 2, 4).
e – ①–⑥ (not Dec. 25, 26, Jan. 1, Apr. 3, 5, May 24). 0532 from May 3.
j – Also Dec. 31, Apr. 1, 4, May 12, 23
v – Change trains at Genthin (a. *0527*, d. 0537).
z – Not Dec. 25.
⊖ – Via Lübben (Table **838**).
♣ – *HARZ-BERLIN-EXPRESS*. [2] Berlin - Halberstadt - Thale (Table **862**) / Vienenburg (Table **860**) and v.v. Operated by Veolia Verkehr Sachsen-Anhalt GmbH. **DB tickets not valid**.
* – 4 minutes later on Ⓐ.

HAMBURG - BERLIN - DRESDEN — 840

km		*CNL* 457	*EC* 171	*ICE* 1607	*EC* 173	*ICE* 1507	*ICE* 705	*ICE* 1209	*EC* 175	*ICE* 791	*ICE* 709	*EC* 177	*ICE* 793	*ICE* 803	*ICE* 38 381	*EC* 379	*ICE* 795	*IC* 1105	*IC* 1871	*EC* 179	*ICE* 797	*ICE* 901	*IC* 2071	*ICE* 891	*ICE* 905
				①–⑥	¶	①–⑤	①–⑤	⑥⑦		①–⑥									⑤f					Ⓑq	
		A	✕♦	e M	✕♦	a M	a ✕	b M	✕♦	e K	✕	✕♦	✕	✕	B 🍷	✕♦	✕		F	✕♦	✕	✕	✕	✕	✕
0	**Hamburg** Altona ... d.	...	...	0546	0614	0651	0752	0752	0817	✕	0952	...	1036	1152	...	...	1254	1352	...	...	1431	1552	1615	1652	1750
7	**Hamburg** Hbf ... 830 d.	...	...	0600	0628	0708	0806	0806	0831	0908	1006	...	1051	1206	1239	...	1308	1406	1411	...	1454	1606	1629	1708	1804
54	Büchen ... 830 d.	...	...	|	0656	|	|	|	0856	|	|	...	|	|	|	...	|	|	1433	...	|	|	1656	|	|
122	Ludwigslust ... 837 d.	...	...	0645	0722	|	|	|	0922	|	|	...	|	|	|	...	1351	|	1459	...	|	|	1722	|	1846
167	Wittenberge ... 837 d.	...	...	0702	0741	|	|	|	0941	|	|	...	|	|	|	...	1408	|	|	...	|	|	1741	|	|
280	**Berlin** Spandau ... 837 d.	...	...	0739	0825	|	0937	0937	1025	|	1137	...	|	1337	|	...	|	1538	1559	...	|	1737	1825	|	1939
292	**Berlin** Hbf ... 837 a.	...	...	0747	0833	0844	0945	0945	1033	1044	1145	...	1231	1345	1427	...	1452	1546	1610	...	1631	1745	1833	1844	1947
292	**Berlin** Hbf ... 845 d.	...	0636	0752	0836	0858	|	0952	1036	|	|	1236	|	|	|	1436	|	|	|	1636	|	|	1836	|	|
300	**Berlin** Südkreuz .. 845 d.	...	0643	0756	0843	0903	0953	0957	1043	1052	1154	1243	1239	1354	|	1443	1500	1555	1618	1643	1639	1754	1843	1852	1956
	Berlin Ostbahnhof ... a.	0457	|	...	|	...	...	...	|	...	...	|	...	...	1438	|	...	...	...	|	...	...	|	...	...
432	Elsterwerda .. 843 845 d.	|	0756	...	|	...	...	...	|	...	...	1356	...	...	...	|	...	...	...	1756	...	...	1956	...	...
485	**Dresden** Neustadt ... a.	|	|	...	|	...	...	...	|	...	...	|	...	...	...	|	...	...	...	|	...	...	|	...	...
489	**Dresden** Hbf ... 843 a.	0707	0852	...	1052	...	...	...	1252	...	...	1452	...	...	...	1652	...	...	...	1852	...	...	2050	...	...

	ICE 893	*IC* 2075	*IC* 2075	*IC* 2077	*IC* 2073	*IC* 2073	*IC* 1107	*ICE* 897	*ICE* 1005	*IC* 1877	*ICE* 1007
	Ⓑq	⑥⑦	⑦t	③m	P	③	Ⓑq	⑥h		④z	⑤⑦
	L ✕	S 🍷	S 🍷	🍷	S 🍷	S 🍷		✕	✕		r ✕
Hamburg Altona ... d.	1853	...	...	...	...	...	1952	1952	2102	2144	2152
Hamburg Hbf ... 830 d.	1908	1921	1921	...	1921	1921	2006	2006	2121	2159	2206
Büchen ... 830 d.	|	1945	1945	...	1945	1945	|	|	|	|	|
Ludwigslust ... 837 d.	|	2012	2012	...	2012	2012	|	|	2204	|	|
Wittenberge ... 837 d.	|	2031	2031	...	2031	2031	|	|	2222	|	|
Berlin Spandau ... 837 d.	2040	2115	2115	...	2115	2115	|	|	2258	2336	2335
Berlin Hbf ... 837 a.	2048	2123	2123	...	2123	2123	2143	2144	2313	2350	2345
Berlin Hbf ... 845 d.	2055	2127	2127	2127	2127	2132	|	|	|	|	|
Berlin Südkreuz ... 845 d.	2059	2131	2133	2133	2133	2136	2152	2152	|	|	2354
Berlin Ostbahnhof ... a.	...	...	|	|	|	...	...	...	2323	2400	...
Elsterwerda ... 843 845 d.	...	...	|	|	|	...	...	...	...	...	...
Dresden Neustadt ... a.	...	...	|	2332	2332	...	...	...	...	...	...
Dresden Hbf ... 843 a.	...	...	2334	2340	2340	...	...	...	...	...	...

	ICE 1006	*ICE* 1004	*ICE* 790	*ICE* 792	*IC* 2072	*IC* 2072	*IC* 2076	*IC* 2074	*IC* 2074
		①–⑤		①–⑥	①–⑤	N	④j	⑥c	⑥⑦
	✕	d ✕	L ✕	e ✕	S 🍷	S 🍷	🍷	S 🍷	S 🍷
Dresden Hbf ... 843 d.	...	...	...	...	...	0554	0554	0554	...
Dresden Neustadt ... d.	...	...	...	...	...	0602	0602	0602	...
Elsterwerda ... 843 845 d.	...	...	...	...	...	0658	0658	0658	...
Berlin Ostbahnhof ... d.	...	...	...	...	...	|	|	|	...
Berlin Südkreuz ... 845 d.	0509	0547	0655	0808	0814	0814	0812	0814	0814
Berlin Hbf ... 845 a.	|	|	0700	0813	0819	0819	0820	0819	0819
Berlin Hbf ... 837 d.	0517	0555	0713	0817	0823	0823	...	0823	0823
Berlin Spandau ... 837 d.	0527	0605	0723	0827	0832	0832	...	0832	0832
Wittenberge ... 837 d.	0606	0644	|	|	0914	0914	...	0914	0914
Ludwigslust ... 837 d.	0624	0701	|	|	0934	0934	...	0934	0934
Büchen ... 830 d.	|	|	|	|	1001	1001	...	1001	1001
Hamburg Hbf ... 830 a.	0707	0745	0852	0956	1024	1024	...	1024	1024
Hamburg Altona ... a.	...	0759	0915	1014	...	...	...	...	...

	IC 2070	*ICE* 904	*IC* 1106	*ICE* 796	*EC* 178	*ICE* 35 380	*ICE* 808	*ICE* 798	*EC* 176	*ICE* 804	*ICE* 890	*EC* 378	*ICE* 800	*IC* 1100	*ICE* 892	*EC* 174	*ICE* 706	*ICE* 708	*EC* 172	*ICE* 1604	*IC* 1870	*ICE* 1504	*EC* 170	*ICE* 1502	*CNL* 456
								Ⓑq					⑥h	Ⓑq	Ⓑq			⑤⑦	‡	Ⓑq	⑦w			n	
	✕	✕		✕	✕♦	B 🍷	✕	✕	✕♦	✕	✕	✕♦	✕		K ✕	✕♦	✕	r ✕	✕♦	M ✕	F	M ✕	✕♦	M ✕	A
Dresden Hbf ... 843 d.	0654	...	...	...	0904	...	...	...	1104	...	...	1304	...	...	...	1504	...	...	1704	...	...	...	1904	...	2053
Dresden Neustadt ... d.	0702	...	...	...	|	...	...	...	|	...	...	|	...	...	...	|	...	...	|	...	...	...	|	...	2101
Elsterwerda ... 843 845 d.	0756	...	...	...	|	...	...	...	|	...	...	1356	...	...	...	|	...	...	|	...	...	...	1956	...	|
Berlin Ostbahnhof ... d.	|	...	...	...	|	1116	...	...	|	...	...	|	...	...	...	|	...	...	|	...	...	...	|	...	2333
Berlin Südkreuz ... 845 d.	0912	0917	1008	1107	1110	|	1208	1307	1315	1408	1512	1515	1609	1609	1708	1715	1809	1908	1915	2000	...	2055	2113	2251	...
Berlin Hbf ... 845 a.	0919	|	|	|	1117	|	|	|	1320	|	|	1520	|	|	|	1720	|	|	1920	2015	...	2105	2120	2256	...
Berlin Hbf ... 837 d.	...	0925	1017	1116	...	1126	1217	1316	1323	1417	1525	...	1617	1617	1716	1723	1817	1916	1923	2017	2021	2126	...	2300	...
Berlin Spandau ... 837 d.	...	|	1027	|	...	|	1227	|	1333	1427	|	...	1627	1627	|	1733	1827	|	1933	2027	2031	2136	...	|	...
Wittenberge ... 837 d.	...	|	|	|	...	|	|	|	1418	|	1610	...	|	|	|	1818	|	|	2018	|	2118	|	...	|	...
Ludwigslust ... 837 d.	...	|	|	|	...	|	|	|	1438	|	1628	...	|	|	|	1838	|	|	2038	|	2137	|	...	|	...
Büchen ... 830 d.	...	|	|	|	...	|	|	|	1506	|	|	...	|	|	|	1906	|	|	2106	|	|	|	...	|	...
Hamburg Hbf ... 830 a.	...	1101	1157	1252	...	1318	1356	1452	1527	1556	1709	...	1756	1757	1852	1928	1956	2052	2133	2156	2224	2305	...	0033	...
Hamburg Altona ... a.	...	1121	1217	1316	...	...	1412	1506	1540	1622	1721	...	1813	1811	...	1943	2012	2110	2147	2213	...	2321	...	0058	...

♦ – **NOTES** (LISTED BY TRAIN NUMBER)

170/1 – HUNGARIA – [12] and ✕ Budapest - Bratislava - Praha - Děčín - Berlin and v.v.
172/3 – VINDOBONA – [12] and ✕ Villach - Wien - Břeclav - Praha - Děčín - Berlin - Hamburg and v.v.
174/5 – JAN JESENIUS – [12] and ✕ Budapest - Bratislava - Praha - Děčín - Berlin - Hamburg and v.v.
176 – ALOIS NEGRELLI – [12] and ✕ Brno - Praha - Děčín - Berlin - Hamburg.
177 – JOHANNES BRAHMS – [12] and ✕ Berlin - Děčín - Praha - Břeclav - Wien; [2] Berlin - Břeclav (**277**) - Bratislava.
178 – JOHANNES BRAHMS – [12] and ✕ Praha - Děčín - Berlin.
179 – ALOIS NEGRELLI – [12] and ✕ Berlin - Děčín - Praha.
378 – [12] and ✕ Wien - Břeclav - Praha - Děčín - Berlin - Stralsund (- Binz ♥); [2] Bratislava (**278**) - Břeclav (**378**) - Stralsund / Ostseebad Binz.
379 – [12] and ✕ (Binz ♥ -) Stralsund - Berlin - Děčín - Praha - Brno.

A – PHOENIX – 🛏 1, 2 cl., ▬ 2 cl. and [2] (Ⓡ) Praha - Berlin - Köln - Amsterdam and v.v. (see Table **54**). Conveys [2] (*D* **60456/7**) Praha - Berlin and v.v.
B – [12] (**35/8**) and 🍷 Berlin - Hamburg - Puttgarden - København and v.v.; [12] (**380/1**) and 🍷 Berlin - Hamburg - Flensburg - Århus and v.v.

F – To / from Flensburg (Table **823**).
K – From / to Kiel (Table **820**).
L – To / from Leipzig (Table **851**).
M – [12] and ✕ München - Nürnberg - Jena - Leipzig - Hamburg and v.v.
N – ①②③⑤ (also Dec. 31, May 13; not Dec. 25, Jan. 1, Apr. 5, May 24).
P – ①②④⑤. On Dec. 24, 25, 31, Apr. 2 does not run Berlin - Dresden.
S – SYLTER STRAND – To / from Westerland (Table **821**).

a – Not Dec. 24, 25, 31, Jan. 1, Apr. 2, 5, May 24.
b – Also Dec. 24, 25, 31, Jan. 1, Apr. 2, 5, May 24.
c – Not Dec. 26, Apr. 3.
d – Not Dec. 25, Jan. 1, May 24.
e – Not Dec. 25, 26, Jan. 1, Apr. 3, 5, May 24.
f – Also Dec. 23, 30, Apr. 1, May 12; not Dec. 25, Jan. 1, Apr. 2, May 14.
h – Also Dec. 24, 25, 31, Apr. 2, 4, May 23.
j – Not Dec. 31, May 13.
m – Not Dec. 30, May 12.
n – Not Dec. 24, 31.
q – Not Dec. 24, 25, 31, Apr. 2, 4, May 23.
r – Also Dec. 23, 30, Apr. 1, 5, May 12, 24; not Dec. 25, Jan. 1, Apr. 2, 4, May 14, 23.
t – Not Apr. 4, May 23.
w – Also Apr. 5, May 24; not Apr. 4, May 23.
z – Also Dec. 22, 29, Mar. 31, May 11; not Dec. 24, 31, Apr. 1, May 13.
♥ – See Table **844** for running dates.
‡ – Terminates at Berlin on Dec. 24, 31.
¶ – Starts from Berlin on Dec. 25, Jan. 1.

841 MAGDEBURG - STENDAL - UELZEN and WITTENBERGE

RE / RB services except where shown

km		⚒	Ⓐa		Ⓐ	Ⓒ			H		IC 2238 D R															EC 340 L W
0	**Magdeburg** Hbf d.	0357	...	0508	0603	0603	0608	0708	0756r	0808	0857	0903	0908	1008	1103	1108	1208	1303	1308	1408	1503	1508	1608	1703	1708	...
58	Stendal a.	0442	...	0556	0642	0642	0656	0756	0832r	0858	0933	0942	0956	1056	1142	1156	1256	1342	1356	1456	1542	1556	1656	1742	1756	...
58	Stendal d.	0449	0458	0558	0643	0643	0658a	0758	0833	...	0937	0943	0958	...	1143	1158	1258a	1343	1358	1503a	1543	1558	1658a	1743	1758	1826
113	**Wittenberge** a.	|	0537	0637	|	|	0737a	0837	0908	...	1010	|	1037	...	|	1237	1337a	|	1437	1541a	|	1637	1737a	|	1837	|
116	Salzwedel a.	0530	...	...	0713	0719	...	...	...	...	...	1013	...	...	1213	...	...	1413	...	...	1613	...	...	1813	...	1851
116	Salzwedel d.	0536	...	...	0714	0720	...	...	...	...	...	1014	...	...	1214	...	...	1414	...	...	1614	...	...	1814	...	1853
167	**Uelzen** a.	0608	...	...	0746	0751	...	...	...	...	...	1045	...	...	1245	...	...	1445	...	...	1645	...	...	1845	...	1929

		n		⑥			IC 1930 ⑦w		Ⓑz		n
Magdeburg Hbf d.	1808	1903	1908	1908	...	2008	...	2108	...	2213	2318
Stendal a.	1856	1942	1956	1956	...	2056	b	2156	...	2301	0006
Stendal d.	1858	1943	...	2008	2008	2101	2123	2217n	2213	...	...
Wittenberge a.	1937	|	...	|	|	2140	|	2256n	|	...	...
Salzwedel a.	...	2013	...	2048	2048	...	2151	...	2253	...	...
Salzwedel d.	...	2014	...	...	...	...	2153	...	...	...	...
Uelzen a.	...	2045	...	...	...	...	2216	...	...	...	...

	Ⓐa		Ⓐa		H			⚒		EC 341 G W	
Uelzen d.	...	...	...	...	...	...	...	0620	...	0756	...
Salzwedel a.	...	...	...	...	...	...	...	0652	...	0818	...
Salzwedel d.	...	...	0458	...	0531	0600	...	0653	...	0820	...
Wittenberge d.	...	...	|	0517a	|	|	0617a	|	0717	|	0817a
Stendal a.	...	...	0540	0555a	0601	0641	0655a	0724t	0755	0845	0855a
Stendal d.	0353	0457	0542	0557	0606	0645	0657	0725t	0757	...	0857
Magdeburg Hbf a.	0440	0544	0622	0643	0648	0725	0744	0802t	0843	...	0943

			H						IC 1931 ⑤f				IC 2239 E R										n	Ⓐa	n	v
Uelzen d.	0824	...	...	...	...	1102	...	...	1250	1302	...	...	1502	...	...	...	1702	...	...	1902	...	...	2103	...	...	...
Salzwedel a.	0857	...	...	...	...	1133	...	...	1321	1333	...	...	1533	...	...	...	1733	...	...	1933	...	...	2134	...	...	...
Salzwedel d.	0902	...	...	...	...	1134	...	...	1323	1334	...	...	1534	...	...	...	1734	...	...	1934	2016	...	2135	2218	...	...
Wittenberge d.	|	0918	1017	...	1117	|	...	1317	|	|	1422a	1517	|	1547	1617a	1717	|	1822a	1917	|	|	2058	|	|	2227	0002
Stendal a.	0944	0956	1055	...	1155	1208	...	1355	1404	1410	1458a	1555	1608	1619	1655a	1755	1808	1858a	1955	2008	2056	2136	2213	2302	2305	0040
Stendal d.	...	0957	1057	1057	1157	1211	1257	1357	b	1411	1458	1557	1611	1623	1657	1757	1811	1858	1957	2011	2057	2144	2214p	...	2307	...
Magdeburg Hbf a.	...	1043	1143	1143	1243	1251	1343	1443	...	1451	1544	1643	1651	1659	1743	1843	1851	1944	2043	2051	2143	2230	2302p	...	2354	...

D – ⑤⑥ from Mar. 27.
E – ⑤⑦ from Mar. 28 (also June 12).
G – ①–⑥ (not Dec. 25, 26, 31, Jan. 1, Apr. 3, 5, May 24).
H – ①–⑥ (not Dec. 25, 26, Jan. 1, 2, Apr. 3, 5, May 13, 24).
L – Ⓑ (not Dec. 24, 25, 30, 31, Apr. 2, 4, May 23).
R – WARNOW – [12] Leipzig - Halle - Magdeburg - Schwerin - Rostock - Warnemünde and v.v.
W – WAWEL – [12] Kraków - Forst 🏛 - Cottbus - Berlin - Hamburg and v.v.

a – Ⓐ (not Dec. 24, 31, Jan. 6).
b – From / to Berlin (Table **810**).
f – Also Dec. 23, 30, Apr. 1, May 12; not Dec. 25, Jan. 1, Apr. 2, May 14.
n – Not Dec. 24, 31.
p – On Ⓑ from May 2 (not May 23) Stendal d. 2225, Magdeburg a. 2310.
r – From May 1 Magdeburg d. 0750, Stendal a. 0828.
t – From May 3 Stendal a. 0725, d, 0728, Magdeburg a. 0804.
v – Not Dec. 25, Jan. 1.
w – Also Apr. 5, May 24; not Apr. 4, May 23.
z – Not Dec. 24, 25, 31, Jan. 1, Apr. 2, 4, May 23.

842 LEIPZIG - DRESDEN

km		◧	◧ Ⓐ	Ⓒ			RE 17441 v	RE 17443 ⚒	RE 17445	CNL 459 Ⓡ N🍷	D 61459 2F	RE 17447 ⚒	ICE 1741 ①–⑤ aB	RE 17449	ICE 1553 ①–⑤ aG	RE 17451 ⚒	ICE 1543 ⑦m ✕	ICE 1543 ①–⑥ e✕	RE 17453	ICE 1555 ①–⑥ e✕	RE 17455 ⚒	ICE 1545 ①–⑥ e✕	ICE 1745 ⑦d 🍷	RE 17457
	Frankfurt Flughafen § **850** d.	...	...	...	...	...	...	...	...	...	...	...	...	...	...	...	...	...	...	...	...	0811	...	...
	Frankfurt (Main) Hbf **850** d.	...	...	...	...	...	...	...	...	0055z	...	...	...	...	0517g	...	...	0618	...	0721	...	|	0822	...
0	**Leipzig** Hbf d.	0010	0010	0120	...	...	...	0458	0558	|	0651	0658	0751	0758	0851	0858	0951	0951	0958	1051	1058	1151	1151	1158
26	Wurzen d.	0039	0039	0151	...	...	...	0519	0619	|	|	0719	|	0819	|	0919	|	|	1019	|	1119	|	|	1219
53	Oschatz d.	...	0058	0211	...	...	...	0539	0639	|	|	0739	|	0839	|	0939	|	|	1039	|	1139	|	|	1239
66	Riesa d.	...	...	...	...	...	0448	0548	0648	0720	0722	0748	0823	0848	0923	0948	1023	1023	1048	1123	1148	1223	1223	1248
102	Coswig **843 856 857** d.	...	...	...	...	...	0519	0619	0719	|	|	0819	|	0919	|	1019	|	|	1119	|	1219	|	|	1319
110	Radebeul Ost **857** d.	...	...	...	...	...	0528	0628	0728	|	|	0828	|	0928	|	1028	|	|	1128	|	1228	|	|	1328
116	**Dresden** Neustadt **856 857** a.	...	...	...	...	...	0535	0635	0734	0756	0756	0835	0856	0935	1006	1035	1056	1106	1135	1206	1235	1306	1306	1334
120	**Dresden** Hbf **843 856 857** a.	...	...	...	...	...	0542	0642	0742	0804	0804	0842	0904	0942	1014	1042	1104	1114	1142	1214	1242	1314	1314	1342

	ICE 1557 ①–⑥ eS ✕	ICE 1597 ⑦d A🍷	RE 17459 ⚒	ICE 1547 ✕	RE 17461	ICE 1559 A✕	RE 17463	ICE 1549 ✕	RE 17465	ICE 1651 A✕	RE 17467	ICE 1641 ✕	RE 17469	ICE 1653 A✕	RE 17471 Ⓑ	ICE 1643 n ✕	RE 17473	ICE 1602 Ⓑq M✕	RE 17475	ICE 1645 ⑦ ✕	ICE 1645 ①–⑥ n✕	◧	ICE 1657 ⑤⑦f A✕	RE 17477 n
Frankfurt Flughafen § **850** d.		0901	...	1011	...	1102	...	1211	...	1302	...	1411	...	1503	...	1611	...	...	...	1811	1811	...	1902	...
Frankfurt (Main) Hbf **850** d.	0921	0921	...	|	...	1119	...	|	...	1319	...	|	...	1520	...	|	...	...	...	|	|	...	1919	...
Leipzig Hbf d.	1251	1251	1258	1351	1358	1451	1458	1551	1558	1651	1658	1751	1758	1851	1858	1951	1958	2051	2058	2151	2151	2208	2256	2306
Wurzen d.	|	|	1319	|	1419	|	1519	|	1619	|	1719	|	1819	|	1919	|	2019	|	2119	|	|	2237	|	2326
Oschatz d.	|	|	1339	|	1439	|	1539	|	1639	|	1739	|	1839	|	1939	|	2039	|	2139	|	|	...	|	2346
Riesa d.	1323	1323	1348	1423	1448	1523	1548	1623	1648	1723	1748	1823	1848	1923	1948	2023	2048	2123	2148	2223	2223	...	2328	2355
Coswig **843 856 857** d.	|	|	1419	|	1519	|	1619	|	1719	|	1819	|	1919	|	2019	|	2119	|	2219	|	|	...	|	0026
Radebeul Ost **857** d.	|	|	1428	|	1528	|	1628	|	1728	|	1828	|	1928	|	2028	|	2128	|	2228	|	|	...	|	|
Dresden Neustadt **856 857** a.	1406	1406	1435	1506	1535	1606	1635	1706	1734	1806	1835	1906	1935	2006	2035	2106	2135	2206	2235	|	2306	...	|	|
Dresden Hbf **843 856 857** a.	1414	1414	1442	1514	1542	1614	1642	1714	1742	1814	1842	1914	1942	2014	2042	2114	2142	2214	2242	2314	2314	...	0014	0041

	◧ Ⓐ		†	RE 17440 ⚒	ICE 1644 ①–⑤ a✕	RE 17442	ICE 1605 ①–⑥ eM	RE 17444 ⚒	ICE 1642 ①–⑥ e✕	RE 17446	ICE 1652 A✕	RE 17448 ⚒	ICE 1640 ✕	RE 17450	ICE 1650 A✕	RE 17452 ⚒	ICE 1548 ✕	RE 17454	ICE 1558 A✕	RE 17456 ⚒	ICE 1546 ✕	RE 17458	ICE 1556 A✕	RE 17460
Dresden Hbf **843 856 857** d.	...	...	...	0413	0444	0523	0549	0623	0649	0723	0754	0823	0854	0923	0954	1023	1054	1123	1154	1223	1254	1323	1354	1423
Dresden Neustadt **856 857** d.	...	...	...	0420	0452	0530	0557	0630	0657	0730	0802	0830	0902	0930	1002	1030	1102	1130	1202	1230	1302	1330	1402	1430
Radebeul Ost **857** d.	...	...	...	0426	|	0538	|	0638	|	0738	|	0838	|	0938	|	1038	|	1138	|	1238	|	1338	|	1438
Coswig **843 856 857** d.	...	...	...	0433	|	0544	|	0644	|	0744	|	0844	|	0944	|	1044	|	1144	|	1244	|	1344	|	1444
Riesa d.	...	...	...	0503	0525	0613	0635	0713	0735	0813	0835	0913	0935	1013	1035	1113	1135	1213	1235	1313	1335	1413	1435	1513
Oschatz d.	0400	...	0500	0512	|	0622	|	0722	|	0822	|	0922	|	1022	|	1122	|	1222	|	1322	|	1422	|	1522
Wurzen d.	0419	...	0519	0531	|	0641	|	0741	|	0841	|	0941	|	1041	|	1141	|	1241	|	1341	|	1441	|	1541
Leipzig Hbf a.	0447	...	0548	0553	0557	0703	0707	0803	0807	0903	0907	1003	1007	1103	1107	1203	1207	1303	1307	1403	1407	1503	1507	1603
Frankfurt (Main) Hbf **850** a.	...	...	...	...	|	...	...	...	|	...	1241	...	|	...	1441	...	|	...	1641	...	|	...	1841	...
Frankfurt Flughafen § **850** a.	...	...	...	...	0950	...	...	...	1150	...	1257	...	1350	...	1457	...	1550	...	1657	...	1750	...	1857	...

	ICE 1544 ①–⑤ h✕	ICE 1744 ⑦w ✕	RE 17462	ICE 1554 n A✕	ICE 1594 Ⓑq S✕	RE 17464	ICE 1542 Ⓑq ✕	RE 17466	ICE 1552 n ✕	RE 17468	ICE 1740 H	RE 17470 Ⓑ	ICE 1550 ⑦w ✕	RE 17472	D 61458 2E	CNL 458 Ⓡ N🍷		◧		RE 17474 ①–⑥ n	RE 17478 ⑦		RE 17476 ①–⑤ r	RE 17480 ⑥⑦
Dresden Hbf **843 856 857** d.	1454	1454	1523	1554	1554	1623	1654	1723	1754	1823	1854	1923	1954	2023	2104	2104	...	...	...	2223	2226	...	2323	2326
Dresden Neustadt **856 857** d.	1502	1502	1530	1602	1602	1630	1702	1730	1802	1830	1902	1930	2002	2030	|	|	...	...	...	2230	|	...	2330	|
Radebeul Ost **857** d.	|	|	1538	|	|	1638	|	1738	|	1838	|	1938	|	2038	|	|	...	...	...	2238	|	...	2338	|
Coswig **843 856 857** d.	|	|	1544	|	|	1644	|	1744	|	1844	|	1944	|	2044	|	|	...	...	...	2244	2244	...	2344	2344
Riesa d.	1535	1535	1613	1635	1635	1713	1735	1813	1835	1913	1935	2013	2035	2113	2144	2144	...	...	...	2313	2313	...	0012	0012
Oschatz d.	|	|	1622	|	|	1722	|	1822	|	1922	|	2022	|	2122	|	|	...	...	...	2322	2322	...	...	...
Wurzen d.	|	|	1641	|	|	1741	|	1841	|	1941	|	2041	|	2141	|	|	...	2220	...	2341	2341	...	...	...
Leipzig Hbf a.	1607	1607	1703	1707	1707	1803	1807	1903	1907	2003	2005	2103	2107	2203	2215	|	...	2248	...	0003	0003	...	...	...
Frankfurt (Main) Hbf **850** a.	1942	|	...	2041	2041	...	|	...	2254	...	...	...	0056	...	...	0359z	...	...	...	...	...	...	...	...
Frankfurt Flughafen § **850** a.	...	1950	...	2057	...	...	2150	...	...	...	...	...	...	...	...	...	...	...	...	...	...	...	...	...

A – From / to Wiesbaden (Table **912**).
B – From Magdeburg (Table **810**).
E – [2] Praha - Erfurt.
F – [2] Fulda - Praha.
G – [12] and ✕ (Frankfurt ① g -) Eisenach - Dresden.
H – ①②③④⑦ (not Dec. 23, 24, 30, 31, Apr. 1, 4, May 23). [12] Dresden - Leipzig - Magdeburg (- Hannover ⑦ w). Conveys ✕ on ⑦ w.
M – [12] and ✕ München - Nürnberg - Leipzig - Dresden and v.v.
N – CANOPUS – 🛏 1, 2 cl., ━ 2 cl., [2] (reclining) and 🍷 Praha - Karlsruhe - Basel - Zürich and v.v.
S – From / to Saarbrücken (Table **919**).

a – Not Dec. 24, 25, 31, Jan. 1, Apr. 2, 5, May 24.
d – Also Dec. 25, 26, Jan. 1, Apr. 3, 5, May 24.
e – ①–⑥ (not Dec. 25, 26, Jan. 1, Apr. 3, 5, May 24).
f – Also Dec. 23, 30, Apr. 1, 5, May 24; not Dec. 25, Apr. 2, 4, May 23.
g – ① (also Apr. 6, May 25; not Apr. 5, May 24).
h – Not Dec. 24, 25, 31, Apr. 2, 5, May 24.
m – Also Dec. 25, 26, Jan. 1, Apr. 3, 5, May 24.
n – Not Dec. 24, 31.
q – Not Dec. 24, 25, 31, Apr. 2, 4, May 23.
r – Not Dec. 24, 25, 31.
v – Not Dec. 25, 26, Jan. 1.
w – Also Apr. 5, May 24; not Apr. 4, May 23.
z – Frankfurt (Main) **Süd**.

◧ – Operated by Mitteldeutsche Regiobahn.
§ – Frankfurt Flughafen Fernbahnhof ✈.

(BERLIN -) ELSTERWERDA - CHEMNITZ and DRESDEN — 843

RE / RB services except where shown

See Tables **851** / **874** for Berlin - Chemnitz via Leipzig. See Table **840** for direct *EC* and *IC* services Berlin - Dresden and v.v.

km					Ⓐ	Ⓐ	*EC* 171 ✕						*EC* 177 ✕				Ⓐ		*EC* 179 ✕		V	*IC* 2071 ✕	x		x
	Berlin Hbf **845** d.	...	...	...	0423	...	0636	...	0726	...	0926	...	1236	...	1326	...	1426	...	1636	...	1751z	1836	...	1926	...
0	**Elsterwerda** d.	...	0453a	0603a	0612	0703	0754	0803	0926e	1003	1128e	1203	1354	1403	1528e	1603	1620e	1703a	1754	1803	1936	1954	2003	2128	2215
24	Riesa a.	...	0518a	0628a	...	0728	...	0828	...	1028	...	1228	...	1428	...	1628	...	1728a	...	1828	1954	...	2028	...	2240
24	Riesa d.	0441	0541	0641	...	0741	...	0841	...	1041k	...	1241k	...	1441	...	1641	...	1741	...	1841	1955	...	2041	...	2241
50	Döbeln Hbf d.	0504	0604	0709	...	0804	...	0904	...	1104	...	1309	...	1504	...	1704	...	1804	...	1904	2015	...	2104	...	2304
91	**Chemnitz** Hbf a.	0552	0652	0752	...	0852	...	0952	...	1152t	...	1352t	...	1552	...	1752	...	1852	...	1952	2048	...	2152	...	2352

		IC 2072 G✕		*IC* 2070 ✕	H V					Ⓑd	*EC* 378 ✕	⑥w	L V				Ⓐ				*EC* 170 ✕	Ⓑ	x	Ⓐ	x
Chemnitz Hbf d.	0505	...	0605	...	0637	0805	...	1005r	...	1205	...	1105*	1237	1405	...	1505	...	1605	...	1805	...	1905	2005	2105	2212
Döbeln Hbf d.	0547	...	0647	...	0712	0847	...	1047j	...	1247	...	1307	1312	1447	...	1547	...	1647	...	1847	...	1947	2047	2147	2254
Riesa a.	0611	...	0711	...	0730	0911	...	1111j	...	1311	...	1331	1331	1511	...	1611	...	1711	...	1911	...	2011	2111	2211	2318
Riesa d.	0616a	...	0716	...	0742	0932	...	1132	...	1316	...	1332	1345	1516	...	1632a	...	1732	...	1916	...	2032a	2132c	2232	...
Elsterwerda a.	0638a	0658	0738	0756	0804	0954	1032h	1154	1232h	1338	1356	1354	1404	1538	1632h	1654a	1736	1754	1832	1940	1956	2054a	2154c	2254	...
Berlin Hbf **845** a.	...	0820	...	0919	1007z	...	1232	...	1432	...	1520	*1632*	1607z	...	1832	...	1932	...	2032	...	2120	...	...	...	...

km		Ⓐ	Ⓐ	Ⓐ					⑥⑦	
0	Elsterwerda-Biehla d.	0440	0540	0640	0740	0940	and every	2140	...	...
2	**Elsterwerda** d.	0445	0545	0645	0745	0945	two hours	2145	2353	...
41	Coswig **842 856/7** d.	0524	0624	0724	0824	1024	until	2224	0032	...
59	**Dresden** Hbf **842 856/7** a.	0546	0646	0746	0846	1046		2246	0054	...

		Ⓐ					
Dresden Hbf **842 856/7** d.	0510	0610	0710	0910	and every	1910	2110
Coswig **842 856/7** d.	0532	0632	0732	0932	two hours	1932	2132
Elsterwerda a.	0611	0711	0811	1011	until	2011	2211
Esterwerda-Biehla a.	0619	0719	0819	1019		2019	...

G – ①–⑥ (not Dec. 25, 26, Jan. 1, Apr. 3, 5, May 24). Train number **2074** on ⑥, **2076** on ④.
H – ①–⑥ (not Dec. 25, Jan. 1, Apr. 5, May 24).
L – ⑦ (also Dec. 25, Jan. 1, Apr. 5, May 24).
V – Operated by Vogtlandbahn. **DB tickets not valid**.

a – Ⓐ only.
c – Ⓒ only.
d – Runs daily from May 16.
e – 7–10 minutes later from Mar. 21 (see Table **845**).

h – 8 minutes **earlier** from Mar. 21 (see Table **845**).
j – 20 minutes later on ⑥ until May 15.
k – 2 minutes **earlier** on ⑥ until May 15.
r – 0905 on ⑥ until May 15 (by 🚌 Mittweida - Döbeln).
t – 60 minutes later on ⑥ until May 15 (by 🚌 Döbeln - Mittweida).

w – Until May 15.
x – Not Dec. 24, 31.
z – Berlin **Zoo**.
* – By 🚌 Mittweida - Döbeln.

STRALSUND - OSTSEEBAD BINZ / SASSNITZ — 844

RE / RB services except where shown

km		Ⓐ			Ⓐ	Ⓐ					*IC* 2186 ①g		A		A	*IC* 2184 ①–⑥ e H		A		A		A		A	*IC* 2212 ✕♦
	Hamburg Hbf **830** d.	...	...	...	...	...	...	...	...	...	0541	...	...	...	...	0744	...	...	...	...	...	...	...	...	1117
	Rostock Hbf **830** d.	...	...	0453	...	0553	...	...	0700	...	0738	...	...	0901	...	0938	...	...	1101	...	...	...	1301	...	1317
0	**Stralsund** d.	0504	...	0604	...	0704	0704	...	0804	...	0842	0904	...	1004	...	1042	1104	...	1204	...	1304	...	1404	...	1425
29	Bergen auf Rügen d.	0533	...	0633	...	0733	0733	...	0833	...	0907	0933	...	1033	...	1107	1133	...	1233	...	1333	...	1433	...	1450
39	Lietzow (Rügen) d.	0542	...	0642	0644	0742	0742	0744	0842	0844	|	0942	0944	1042	1044	|	1142	1144	1242	1244	1342	1344	1442	1444	|
	Ostseebad Binz a.	|	...	|	0657	|	|	0757	|	0857	0932	0955	|	|	1057	1132	1155	|	|	1257	1355	|	|	1457	1516
51	**Sassnitz** a.	0556	...	0655	...	0755	0755	...	0855	...	...	...	0957	1055	...	...	...	1157	1255	...	...	1357	1455	...	...

		A		A	*IC* 2355 🍷♦	*IC* 2376 ⑥ 🍷♦					*EC* 378 ✕♦										Ⓑ			
Hamburg Hbf **830** d.	...	...	...	...	...	1344	...	...	...	...	...	...	...	...	...	...	...	...	...	...	...	...	...	...
Rostock Hbf **830** d.	...	...	1501	...	...	1538	...	...	1701	...	...	...	...	1901	...	...	...	2101	...	...	...	...	...	...
Stralsund d.	1504	...	1604	...	1642	1656	1704	...	1804	...	1832	1904	...	2004	...	2104	...	2204	...	...	2311	...	...	...
Bergen auf Rügen d.	1533	...	1633	...	1707	1721	1733	...	1833	...	1855	1933	...	2033	...	2133	...	2233	...	...	2340	...	...	...
Lietzow (Rügen) d.	1542	1544	1642	1644	|	|	1742	1744	1842	1844	|	1942	1944	2042	2044	2142	2144	2242	2244	...	...	...	...	...
Ostseebad Binz a.	1555	|	|	1657	1732	1748	1756	|	|	1857	1917	1955	|	|	2057	2155	|	|	2257	...	...	...	...	...
Sassnitz a.	...	1557	1655	...	...	...	...	1757	1855	...	...	...	1957	2055	...	...	2157	2255	...	...	...	...	...	...

km		Ⓐ				Ⓐ	⚒					*IC* 2356 ①–⑥ ♦	A		A		*IC* 2213 ✕♦		*EC* 379 ✕♦	A			A		*IC* 2377 🍷♦
	Sassnitz d.	0402	...	0505	...	...	0605	...	0705	...	0805	...	...	0905	1003	...	...	...	...	...	1105	...	1203	...	...
0	**Ostseebad Binz** d.	|	...	|	...	0603	|	0703	|	0803	|	0843	0903	|	|	1007	1029	...	1042	1103	|	...	|	1207	1229
12	Lietzow (Rügen) d.	0416	...	0520	...	0616	0620	0716	0720	0816	0820	|	0916	0920	1017	1020	|	...	|	1116	1120	...	1217	1220	|
22	Bergen auf Rügen d.	0424	...	0528	...	...	0628	...	0728	...	0828	0908	...	0928	...	1028	1056	...	1108	...	1128	...	...	1228	1255
51	**Stralsund** a.	0453	...	0557	...	...	0657	...	0757	...	0857	0932	...	0957	...	1057	1119	...	1130	...	1157	...	...	1257	1318
	Rostock Hbf **830** a.	0547	...	0654	...	...	...	...	0855	...	...	...	...	1055	...	...	1219	...	...	...	1255	...	...	...	1419
	Hamburg Hbf **830** a.	...	...	...	...	...	...	...	...	...	...	...	...	...	...	...	1430	...	...	...	...	...	...	...	1615

	A		A		A		A		*IC* 2183 ⑦w H✕			*IC* 1852 ⑦w B												
Sassnitz d.	...	1305	1403	...	...	1505	1603	...	...	1703	...	...	1803	...	...	...	1905	2003	...	...	2103	...	2203	...
Ostseebad Binz d.	1303	|	|	1407	1503	|	|	1607	1629	|	1707	1757	|	1807	...	1903	|	|	2007	2103	|	...	|	2207
Lietzow (Rügen) d.	1316	1320	1417	1420	1516	1520	1617	1620	|	1717	1720	|	1817	1820	...	1917	1920	2017	2020	2116	2120	...	2217	2220
Bergen auf Rügen d.	...	1328	...	1428	...	1528	...	1628	1654	...	1728	1818	...	1828	...	...	1928	...	2028	...	2128	...	...	2228
Stralsund a.	...	1357	...	1457	...	1557	...	1657	1718	...	1757	1847	...	1857	...	...	1957	...	2057	...	2157	...	...	2257
Rostock Hbf **830** a.	...	1455	...	...	...	1655	...	...	1820	...	1855	...	...	...	...	...	2055	...	...	...	2255	...	...	...
Hamburg Hbf **830** a.	...	...	...	...	...	...	...	...	2015	...	...	...	...	...	...	...	...	...	...	...	...	...	...	...

♦ – **NOTES** (LISTED BY TRAIN NUMBER)

378 – Daily Dec. 18 - Jan. 2; ⑤⑥ from Mar. 26 (also Apr. 1, 4, May 12, 23). [12] and ✕ Wien - Praha - Berlin - Ostseebad Binz.
379 – Daily Dec. 19 - Jan. 3; ⑥⑦ from Mar. 27 (also Apr. 2, 5, May 13, 24). [12] and ✕ Ostseebad Binz - Berlin - Praha - Brno.
2212 – RÜGEN – [12] and ✕ Koblenz - Köln - Hamburg - Ostseebad Binz.
2213 – RÜGEN – [12] and ✕ Ostseebad Binz - Hamburg - Köln - Stuttgart.
2355 – STRELASUND – [12] and 🍷 (Düsseldorf ① **g** -) (Dortmund ①–⑥ **e** -) Erfurt - Halle - Berlin - Ostseebad Binz.
2356 – [12] and 🍷 Ostseebad Binz - Berlin - Halle - Erfurt - Kassel - Düsseldorf. Train number **2254** on ⑤ (also Dec. 23, 30, Apr. 1, May 12, June 2; not Dec. 25, Jan. 1, Apr. 2, May 14, June 4).
2376 – [12] and 🍷 Karlsruhe - Frankfurt - Hannover - Hamburg - Ostseebad Binz.
2377 – ARKONA – [12] and 🍷 Ostseebad Binz - Hamburg - Hannover - Frankfurt (- Karlsruhe on dates in Table **911**).

A – Ⓐ (daily from May 10).
B – To Berlin (Table **845**).
H – From / to Hannover (Table **902**).

e – Not Dec. 25, 26, Jan. 1, Apr. 3, 5, May 24.
g – Also Apr. 6, May 25; not Apr. 5, May 24.
w – Also Apr. 5, May 24; not Apr. 4, May 23.

BERGEN AUF RÜGEN - PUTBUS - LAUTERBACH and RÜGENSCHE BÄDERBAHN — 844a

Preßnitztalbahn ●

km		Ⓐ	Ⓒ						n	n	
0	**Bergen** auf Rügen d.	0540	0640	0740	0940	1140	1340	1540	1740	1940	...
10	**Putbus** a.	0548	0648	0748	0948	1148	1348	1548	1748	1948	...
12	**Lauterbach** Mole a.	0554	0654	0753	0954	1154	1354	1554	1754	1954	...

	Ⓐ	Ⓒ							n	n
Lauterbach Mole d.	0604	0704	0800	...	1104	1304	1504	1704	1904	2000
Putbus d.	0611	0711	0811	...	1111	1311	1511	1711	1911	2011
Bergen auf Rügen a.	0620	0720	0820	...	1120	1320	1520	1720	1920	2020

RÜGENSCHE BÄDERBAHN **SERVICE UNTIL MAY 12**

km							n				
0	**Lauterbach** Mole d.	...	...	...	...	...	...	...	...	...	...
2	**Putbus** a.	...	...	...	...	...	...	...	...	...	...
2	**Putbus** d.	0808	1008	1208	1408	1608	1808	...	...	...	...
14	Binz Lokalbahn ▲ d.	0840	1040	1240	1440	1640	1840	...	...	...	...
22	Sellin (Rügen) Ost d.	0909	1109	1309	1509	1709	1909	...	...	...	...
27	**Göhren** (Rügen) a.	0924	1124	1324	1524	1724	1924	...	...	...	...

						n				
Göhren (Rügen) d.	0952	1152	1352	1552	1752	1952	...	...	...	...
Sellin (Rügen) Ost d.	1011	1211	1411	1611	1811	2011	...	...	...	...
Binz Lokalbahn ▲ d.	1040	1240	1440	1640	1840	2040	...	...	...	...
Putbus a.	1106	1306	1506	1706	1906	2106	...	...	...	...
Putbus d.	...	...	...	...	...	...	...	...	...	...
Lauterbach Mole a.	...	...	...	...	...	...	...	...	...	...

n – Not Dec. 24, 31.

● – Eisenbahn-Bau- und Betriebsgesellschaft Preßnitztalbahn mbH.

▲ – 2½ km from Ostseebad Binz DB station.

845 ELSTERWERDA - BERLIN - STRALSUND

RE / RB services except where shown

km				*IC* 2115 ①–⑤ J✕	¶		Ⓐn	Ⓒt	Ⓐ		ⒸS	◧		Ⓐ		*IC* 2351 P 🍷	*IC* 2351 H 🍷			*IC* 2353 K🍷			*IC* 2355 G🍷	
		Ⓐ																						
0	**Elsterwerda** 840 d.	...	...	...	...	...	0422	0432	0536	...	...	...	0627	0736	...	...	...	0832	...	...	1032x	...	...	1232x
20	Doberlug-Kirchhain d.	...	...	...	...	...	0451	0451	0551	...	...	...	0646	0751	...	...	...	0851	...	...	1051	...	...	1251
132	**Berlin** Südkreuz 840 d.	...	...	...	...	...	0626	0626	0726	0726	...	...	0826	0926	0926	...	0912	1026	1127	1118	1226	1327	1312	1426
140	**Berlin** Hbf 840 d.	...	...	...	...	0532	0634	0634	0734	0734	0808	0759	0834	0934	0934	0938	0938	1034	1134	1138	1234	1334	1338	1434
145	**Berlin** Gesundbrunnen d.	...	...	...	...	0537	0639	0639	0739	0739	0814	|	0839	0939	0939	0944	0944	1039	1139	1144	1239	1339	1344	1439
166	Bernau (b. Berlin) d.	...	...	...	...	0551	0653	0653	0753	0753	0829	0836	0853	0953	0953	0959	0959	1053	1153	1159	1253	1353	1359	1453
188	Eberswalde Hbf d.	...	...	...	0506	0607	0707	0707	0807	0807	0843	0850	0907	1007	1007	1014	1014	1107	1207	1214	1307	1407	1414	1507
214	Angermünde a.	...	...	...	0526	0625	0726	0726	0825	0825	0859	0905	0926	1025	1025	1030	1030	1126	1225	1230	1326	1425	1430	1526
214	Angermünde d.	...	...	...	0533	0634	0733	0733	0834	0834	0901	...	0933	1034	1034	1032	1032	1133	1234	1232	1333	1434	1432	1533
	Schwedt (Oder) a.	...	...	...	|	0656	|	|	0856	0856	|	...	|	1056	1056	|	|	|	1256	|	|	1456	|	|
251	Prenzlau d.	...	...	...	0600	...	0800	0800	...	...	0924	...	1000	...	...	1056	1056	1200	...	1256	1400	...	1456	1600
276	**Pasewalk** d.	0423	...	...	0618	...	0817	0817	...	...	|	...	1017	...	...	1112	1112	1217	...	1312	1417	...	1512	1617
319	Anklam d.	0457	...	...	0649	...	0849	0849	...	...	|	...	1049	...	...	1140	1140	1249	...	1340	1449	...	1540	1649
335	Züssow 846 d.	0515	...	...	0705	...	0905	0905	...	...	1016	...	1105	...	...	1152	1152	1305	...	1352	1505	...	1552	1705
353	Greifswald 846 d.	0530	...	0701	0721	...	0921	0921	...	...	1030	...	1121	...	...	1205	1205	1321	...	1405	1521	...	1605	1721
384	**Stralsund** 846 a.	0553	...	0722	0744	...	0943	0943	...	...	1051	...	1143	...	...	1224	1224	1347	...	1424	1543	...	1624	1743

		EC 378 B✕		*IC* 145 Ⓑq A	Ⓐ		*IC* 2157 Ⓑq L🍷		Ⓐ		*IC* 2359 ⑤⑦ r L		⑤⑥ v	Ⓐ	Ⓒ	⑦w		Ⓒ	Ⓐ	Ⓐ	①–⑥ h		
Elsterwerda 840 d.	...	1356	1432	...	1536x	...	...	1632x	1736	...	...	1832	1832	1936	...	...	...	2032	2032	...	...	...	...
Doberlug-Kirchhain d.	...	|	1451	...	1551	...	...	1651	1751	...	...	1851	1851	1951	...	...	...	2051	2051	...	...	...	...
Berlin Südkreuz 840 d.	1527	1515	1626	...	1726	1726	1713	1826	1926	1926	1912	2026	2026	2126	2126	...	...	2229	2225	2229	...	...	2325
Berlin Hbf 840 d.	1534	1538	1634	1728	1734	1734	1751	1834	1934	1934	1938	2034	2034	2134	2134	...	...	2236	...	2236	...	...	2334
Berlin Gesundbrunnen d.	1539	1544	1639	1734	1740	1740	1757	1839	1939	1939	1944	2039	2039	2139	2139	...	...	2241	...	2241	...	...	2339
Bernau (b. Berlin) d.	1553	1559	1653	1750	1757	1757	1812	1853	1953	1953	1959	2053	2053	2153	2153	...	...	2255	...	2255	...	...	2353
Eberswalde Hbf d.	1607	1614	1707	1805	1813	1813	1827	1907	2007	2007	2014	2107	2107	2207	2207	...	...	2314	...	2314	...	...	0011
Angermünde a.	1625	1630	1726	1821	1831	1831	1843	1926	2025	2025	2030	2126	2126	2225	2225	...	...	2332	...	2332	...	...	...
Angermünde d.	1634	1632	1733	...	1834	1834	1845	1933	2034	2034	2032	2133	2133	2234	2234	2233	...	2334	...	2334	2336	...	...
Schwedt (Oder) a.	1656	|	|	...	1856	1856	|	|	2056	2056	|	|	|	2256	2256	|	...	2356	...	2356	|	...	...
Prenzlau d.	...	1656	1800	...	...	...	1908	2000	...	...	2056	2200	2200	...	...	2301	...	...	...	...	0004	...	...
Pasewalk d.	...	1712	1817	...	...	...	1923	2024j	...	...	2112	2216	2224	...	...	2318	...	...	...	...	0020	...	...
Anklam d.	...	1740	1849	...	...	...	1952	2055	...	...	2140	...	2255	...	...	2350	...	...	...	...	...	...	...
Züssow 846 d.	...	1752	1905	...	...	...	2004	2109	...	...	2152	...	2309	...	...	0003	...	...	...	...	...	...	...
Greifswald 846 d.	...	1805	1921	...	...	...	2017	2124	...	...	2205	...	2324	...	...	0017	...	...	...	...	...	...	...
Stralsund 846 a.	...	1824	1943	...	...	...	2036	2145	...	...	2225	...	2345	...	...	0039	...	...	...	...	...	...	...

km		Ⓐ		Ⓒ	Ⓐ		①g			Ⓐ		*IC* 148 ①–⑥ e A			*IC* 2150 ①–⑥ e D			*IC* 2356 E🍷			*EC* 379 C✕		Ⓐ	
	Stralsund 846 d.	...	...	...	...	...	0320	...	...	...	0413	...	...	0613	0737	...	0813	0937	...	1013	1138	...	...	1213
	Greifswald 846 d.	...	...	...	...	...	0354	...	...	...	0434	...	...	0634	0758	...	0834	0958	...	1034	1159	...	...	1234
	Züssow 846 d.	...	...	...	...	...	0407	...	...	...	0450	...	...	0650	0810	...	0850	1010	...	1050	1211	...	...	1250
	Anklam d.	...	...	...	...	...	0418	...	...	...	0503	...	...	0703	0822	...	0903	1022	...	1103	1223	...	...	1303
	Pasewalk d.	...	...	...	...	...	0442	0442	...	...	0544j	...	...	0744j	0849	...	0944j	1049	...	1144j	1250	...	...	1344j
	Prenzlau d.	...	...	...	...	...	0458	0458	...	...	0600	...	...	0800	0905	...	1000	1105	...	1200	1306	...	...	1400
0	Schwedt (Oder) d.	...	...	...	...	...	|	|	0507	0507	|	...	0707	|	|	0907	|	|	1107	|	|	1307	1307	|
23	Angermünde a.	...	...	...	...	...	0524	0524	0529	0529	0627	...	0729	0827	0925	0929	1027	1125	1129	1227	1326	1329	1329	1427
	Angermünde d.	...	...	...	0432	...	...	...	0530	0530	0632	0727	0732	0832	0927	0932	1032	1127	1132	1232	1327	1332	1332	1432
	Eberswalde Hbf d.	...	...	0446	0452	...	...	...	0550	0550	0652	0744	0752	0852	0945	0952	1052	1145	1152	1252	1345	1352	1352	1452
	Bernau (b. Berlin) d.	...	...	0507	0507	...	...	...	0607	0607	0707	0801	0807	0907	1001	1007	1107	1201	1207	1307	1401	1407	1407	1507
	Berlin Gesundbrunnen d.	0418	...	0520	0520	...	...	...	0620	0620	0720	0816	0820	0920	1016	1020	1120	1216	1220	1320	1416	1420	1420	1520
	Berlin Hbf 840 d.	0423	...	0526	0526	...	...	...	0626	0626	0726	0820	0826	0926	1021*	1026	1126	1221*	1226	1326	1421*	1426	1426	1526
	Berlin Südkreuz 840 d.	0430	...	0533	0533	...	...	...	0632	0633	0733	...	0832	0933	1044	1032	1133	1244	1232	1333	1441	1432	1433	1533
	Doberlug-Kirchhain d.	0557	...	0712	0712	...	...	...	...	0805	0908	...	...	1110	...	...	1310	...	...	1510	...	...	1605	1710
	Elsterwerda 840 a.	0612	...	0730	0730	...	...	...	...	0820	0926z	...	...	1128z	...	...	1328	...	...	1528z	...	...	1620z	1728

	IC 2352 P N🍷		Ⓐ		*IC* 2350 Ⓑq 🍷	*IC* 2350 ⑦w R🍷		Ⓐ		*IC* 1932 ⑦w M	*IC* 2358 ⑥b		*IC* 2116 ①–⑤ J✕		*IC* 1852 ⑦w O	△	ⒸS				Ⓒd	Ⓐm	n ●2
Stralsund 846 d.	1337	...	...	1415	1537	1537	...	...	1613	1709	1737	...	1814	1825	1859	...	1911	...	2013	...	...	...	2304
Greifswald 846 d.	1358	...	...	1436	1558	1558	...	...	1634	1730	1758	...	1834	1845	1920	...	1931	...	2034	...	...	...	2328
Züssow 846 d.	1410	...	...	1450	1610	1610	...	...	1650	|	1810	...	...	1859	|	...	1952	...	2050	...	...	...	2342
Anklam d.	1422	...	...	1503	1622	1622	...	...	1703	1751	1822	...	...	1912	1941	...	|	...	2103	...	...	...	...
Pasewalk d.	1449	...	...	1544j	1649	1649	...	...	1744j	1818	1849	...	...	1944	2008	...	|	...	2144j	...	...	...	...
Prenzlau d.	1505	...	...	1600	1705	1705	...	...	1800	1834	1905	...	...	2000	2024	...	2041	...	2200	...	...	...	...
Schwedt (Oder) d.	|	1507	1507	|	|	|	1707	1707	|	|	|	1907	...	|	|	...	|	2107	|	...	2307	2307	...
Angermünde a.	1525	1529	1529	1627	1726	1726	1729	1729	1827	1854	1925	1929	...	2027	2044	...	2103	2129	2227	...	2329	2329	...
Angermünde d.	1527	1532	1532	1632	1728	1728	1732	1732	1832	1856	1927	1932	...	2032	2046	2058	2104	2132	2232	...	2334	2334	...
Eberswalde Hbf d.	1545	1552	1552	1652	1745	1745	1752	1752	1852	1914	1945	1952	...	2052	2104	2114	2121	2152	2252	...	2354	2354	...
Bernau (b. Berlin) d.	1601	1607	1607	1707	1801	1801	1807	1807	1907	1930	2001	2007	...	2107	2120	2132	2140	2208	2307	...	0009	0009	...
Berlin Gesundbrunnen d.	1616	1620	1620	1720	1816	1816	1820	1820	1920	1945	2014*	2020	...	2120	2133*	|	2155	2222	2320	...	0022	0025	...
Berlin Hbf 840 d.	1621*	1626	1626	1726	1821	1839	1826	1826	1926	...	2021*	2026	...	2127	2140*	2206	2159	2228	2326	...	0026	...	...
Berlin Südkreuz 840 d.	1644	1632	1633	1733	...	1844	1832	1833	1933	...	2029	2032	...	2136	2148	...	...	2234	2332	...	...	...	...
Doberlug-Kirchhain d.	...	...	1805	1910	...	...	...	2005	2110	...	...	...	...	2310	...	...	...	...	...	...	...	...	...
Elsterwerda 840 a.	...	...	1820	1928	...	...	...	2020	2128	...	...	...	...	2328	...	...	...	...	...	...	...	...	...

ANGERMÜNDE - SZCZECIN

km			◧	⑥⑦	①–⑤				q A		T
0	**Angermünde** d.	0737	0907	1034	1134	1334	1534	1741	1839	1951	2234
40	Tantow (ticket point) d.	0813	0936	1110	1210	1410	1610	1820	|	2030	2310
59	Szczecin Gumience 🚌 d.	0825	0948	1122	1222	1422	1622	1832	1927	2045	2321
64	**Szczecin** Głowny a.	0831	0954	1128	1228	1428	1628	1838	1933	2050	2328

		e A						△	T
Szczecin Głowny d.	0522	0613	0915	1232	1432	1632	1755	2010	2132
Szczecin Gumience 🚌 d.	0528	0620	0921	1238	1438	1638	1801	2016	2138
Tantow (ticket point) d.	0541	0636u	0938	1251	1451	1651	1818	2029	2151
Angermünde a.	0616	0707	1013	1326	1526	1726	1853	2057	2226

A – *IC* **145/8**. [12] Amsterdam - Berlin - Angermünde - Szczecin and v.v.
B – [12] and ✕ Wien - Praha - Dresden - Stralsund (- Ostseebad Binz ⊖).
C – [12] and ✕ (Ostseebad Binz ⊖ -) Stralsund - Dresden - Praha - Brno.
D – [12] and 🍷 Stralsund - Berlin - Halle - Erfurt - Kassel - Düsseldorf.
E – [12] and 🍷 (Ostseebad Binz ①–⑥ -) Stralsund - Berlin - Halle - Erfurt - Kassel - Düsseldorf. Train number **2254** on ⑤**f**.
G – STRELASUND – [12] and 🍷 (Düsseldorf ①**g** -) (Dortmund ①–⑥**e** -) Erfurt - Halle - Berlin - Ostseebad Binz.
H – ①⑤ Dec. 14 - Mar. 26 (also Dec. 23, 29, 30, Jan. 2; not Dec. 25, Jan. 1); ①–⑥ from Mar. 29 (not Apr. 3, 5, May 24). From Halle (Table **850**).
J – ①–⑤ (not Dec. 24, 25, 31, Jan. 1, Apr. 2, 5, May 24). [12] and ✕ Greifswald - Rostock - Hamburg - Köln - Stuttgart and v.v.
K – [12] and 🍷 (Kassel ①**g** -) Erfurt - Halle - Berlin - Stralsund.
L – [12] Köln - Kassel - Erfurt - Halle - Berlin - Stralsund.
M – [12] Stralsund - Berlin Spandau - Hannover - Bremen - Oldenburg.
N – [12] and 🍷 Stralsund - Berlin - Halle - Erfurt (- Kassel - Köln ⑦**w**).
O – From Ostseebad Binz (Table **844**).
P – ①⑤⑦ Dec. 13 - Mar. 26 (also Dec. 23, 29, 30, Jan. 2; not Dec. 25); daily from Mar. 28.

R – To Würzburg via Halle, Erfurt and Fulda (Table **850**).
S – Ⓒ from May 1 (also Apr. 2–5).
T – ⑤–⑦ (also Dec. 24, Apr. 5, May 13, 24, June 3).

b – Also Dec. 24, 31, Apr. 2, 4, May 13.
d – Also Dec. 24, 31, Apr. 1, May 12.
e – ①–⑥ (not Dec. 25, 26, Jan. 1, Apr. 3, 5, May 24).
f – Also Dec. 23, 30, Apr. 1, May 12, June 2; not Dec. 25, Jan. 1, Apr. 2, May 14, June 4.
g – Also Apr. 6, May 25; not Apr. 5, May 24.
h – Also Apr. 4, May 23; not Apr. 5, May 24.
j – Arrives 8–11 minutes earlier.
m – Not Dec. 24, 31, Apr. 1, May 12.
n – Not Dec. 24, 31.
q – Ⓑ (not Dec. 24, 25, 31, Apr. 2, 4, May 23).
r – Also Dec. 23, 30, Apr. 1, 5, May 12, 24; not Dec. 25, Jan. 1, Apr. 2, 4, May 14, 23.
t – Also Dec. 24, 31.

u – Stops to pick up only.
v – Also Dec. 24, 31, Apr. 1, 4, May 12, 23.
w – Also Apr. 5, May 24; not Apr. 4, May 23.
x – 8–12 minutes **earlier** from Mar. 21 (by 🚌 to Hohenleipisch).
z – 7–10 minutes later from Mar. 21 (by 🚌 from Hohenleipisch).

* – Arrival time.
● – Operated by Usedomer Bäderbahn.
¶ – Change at Angermünde on ②–⑥ (not Dec. 25, 26, Jan. 1, 2, Apr. 2, 3, 6, May 13, 14, 25).
◧ – [2] Berlin Zoo (d. 0753) - Berlin Ostbf (d. 0811) - Angermünde - Szczecin.
△ – [2] Szczecin - Angermünde - Berlin Ostbf (a. 2155) - Berlin Zoo (a. 2212).
⊖ – See Table **844** for running dates to / from Ostseebad Binz.

Usedomer Bäderbahn (2nd class only) STRALSUND - ZÜSSOW - ŚWINOUJŚCIE *Service until May 12* 846

km		Ⓐ									n	n	n	n	n	n
0	**Stralsund** 845 d.	...	0521a	...	0721v	...	0921	then	1521	...	1721	...	1921	...	2202	2304
31	Greifswald 845 d.	...	0545a	...	0745v	...	0945	hourly from	1545	...	1745	...	1945	...	2226	2328
49	Züssow 845 d.	...	0604a	0704	0804	0904	1004	Züssow	1604	1704	1804	1904	2008	2110	2241	2343
67	Wolgast d.	0530	0630	0730	0830	0930	1030	and every	1630	1730	1830	1930	2030	2130	2301	0001
77	Zinnowitz ▲ d.	0548	0648	0748	0848	0948	1048	two hours	1648	1748	1848	1948	2048	2151	2319	...
104	Seebad Heringsdorf d.	0630	0730	0830	0930	1030	1130	from	1730	1830	1930	2030	2130	2230	2355	...
106	Seebad Ahlbeck d.	0634	0734	0834	0934	1034	1134	Stralsund	1734	1834	1934	2034	2134	2234	0000	...
110	**Świnoujście** Centrum a.	0639	0739	0839	0939	1039	1139		1739	1839	1939	2039	2139	2239	0005	...

	Ⓐ	v	Ⓐe	©d									n	n	n	n
Świnoujście Centrum d.	0418	0518	0554	0618	0718	0818	0918	1018	then	1518	1618	1718	1818	1918	2018	2218
Seebad Ahlbeck d.	0424	0524	0600	0624	0724	0824	0924	1024	hourly to	1524	1624	1724	1824	1924	2024	2224
Seebad Heringsdorf d.	0433	0533	0609	0633	0733	0833	0933	1033	Züssow	1533	1633	1733	1833	1933	2033	2233
Zinnowitz ▲ d.	0511	0611	0648	0711	0811	0910	1011	1111	and every	1611	1711	1811	1911	2011	2110	2311
Wolgast d.	0529	0629	0729j	0729	0829	0929	1029	1129	two hours	1629	1729	1829	1929	2029	2135	2327
Züssow 845 a.	0547	0647	0747	0747	0847	0947	1047	1147	to	1647	1747	1847n	1947	2047	2153	...
Greifswald 845 a.	0617	...	0817	0817	...	1017	...	1217	Stralsund	...	1817n	...	2003	...	2217	...
Stralsund 845 a.	0641	...	0841	0841	...	1041	...	1241		...	1841n	...	2027	...	2241	...

a – Ⓐ only.
d – © (also May 21); runs daily Dec. 19 - Jan. 3, Feb. 6–21, Mar. 27 - Apr. 7.
e – Not Dec. 21 - Jan. 1, Feb. 8–19, Mar. 29 - Apr. 7, May 21.
j – Arrives 0703.
n – Not Dec. 24, 31.
v – Not Dec. 25, Jan. 1.

▲ – **Zinnowitz - Peenemünde** and v.v. (*12 km*, journey 14 minutes): **From Zinnowitz** at 0431 Ⓐ, 0512 Ⓐ, 0612 **v**, 0659 Ⓐ **e**, 0712 © **d**, 0812 and hourly until 1712, 1812 **n**, 1912 **n**, 2012 **n** and 2112 **n**. **From Peenemünde** at 0452 Ⓐ, 0530 Ⓐ, 0630 **v**, 0717 Ⓐ **e**, 0730 © **d**, 0830, 0930 and hourly until 1730, 1830 **n**, 1930 **n**, 2030 **n** and 2130 **n**.

RE services BERLIN SCHÖNEFELD ✈ - BERLIN - DESSAU 847

km			Ⓐe																	Ⓐ	♣		◇		◇
0	**Berlin** Schönefeld ✈ d.	0425e	0525	0625r	0725	0825	0925	1025	1125	1225	1325	1425	1525	1625	1725	1825	1925	2025	2125	2225	2225		0655		2255
19	**Berlin** Ostbahnhof d.	0443	0543	0643	0743	0843	0943	1043	1143	1243	1343	1443	1543	1643	1743	1843	1943	2043	2143	2243	2243		0713	and	2313
24	**Berlin** Hbf d.	0454	0554	0654	0754	0854	0954	1054	1154	1254	1354	1454	1554	1654	1754	1854	1954	2054	2154	2254	2254	also	0724	hourly	2324
28	**Berlin** Zoo d.	0500	0600	0700	0800	0900	1000	1100	1200	1300	1400	1500	1600	1700	1800	1900	2000	2100	2200	2259	2300		0729	until	2329
43	**Berlin** Wannsee d.	0516	0616	0717	0816	0916	1016	1116	1216	1316	1416	1516	1616	1716	1816	1916	2016	2116	2216	...	2316		...		...
95	Belzig d.	0603	0703	0803	0902	1003	1102	1203	1303	1403	1503	1603	1703	1803	1902	2003	2102	2203	2303	...	0002		...		...
139	Roßlau (Elbe) 848 a.	0636	0736	0836	...	1036	...	1236c	1336a	1436	1536a	1636	1736a	1836	...	2036	...	2236	2336q	...	...		...		...
144	**Dessau** Hbf 848 a.	0649	0749	0849	...	1049	...	1249c	1349a	1449	1549a	1649	1749a	1849	...	2049	...	2243	2343q	...	...		...		...

	Ⓐe																	Ⓐ					⊙		⊙
Dessau Hbf 848 d.	...	...	0520t	0617a	0711	0811e	0911c	1011a	1111c	...	1311	1411a	1511	1611a	1711	1811a	1911c	2011	2111c	2317	...		...		...
Roßlau (Elbe) 848 d.	...	...	0528t	0624a	0724	0824e	0924c	1024a	1124c	...	1324	1424a	1524	1624a	1724	1824a	1924c	2024	2124c	2324	...		...		...
Belzig d.	0400	0500	0600	0700	0800	0900	1000	1100	1200	1300	1400	1500	1600	1700	1800	1900	2000	2100	2200	0000	...		...		...
Berlin Wannsee d.	0443	0543	0643	0743	0843	0943	1043	1143	1243	1343	1443	1543	1643	1743	1843	1943	2043	2143	2243	0043	...		...		...
Berlin Zoo d.	0501	0602	0701	0802	0901	1002	1101	1202	1301	1402	1501	1602	1701	1802	1901	2002	2101	2202	2301	0101	...		0528	and	2129
Berlin Hbf d.	0507	0607	0707	0807	0907	1007	1107	1207	1307	1407	1507	1607	1707	1807	1907	2007	2107	2207	2307	0107	...	also	0534	hourly	2134
Berlin Ostbahnhof d.	0518	0618	0718	0818	0918	1018	1117	1218	1317	1418	1517	1618	1718	1818	1918	2018	2118	2218	2316	0116	...		0545	until	2145
Berlin Schönefeld ✈ a.	0536	0636r	0736	0836	0936	1036	1136	1236	1336	1436	1536	1636	1736	1836	1936	2036	2136	2236	...	...	...		0603		2203

a – Ⓐ only.
e – Ⓐ (not Dec. 24, 31).
c – © only.
e – Ⓐ (not Dec. 24, 31).
q – ⑦ (also Dec. 25, Jan. 1, Apr. 2, 5, May 13, 24).
r – ⚒ only.
t – ①–⑥ only.
♣ – ①–④ (not Apr. 5, May 13, 24).
◇ – To Berlin Spandau (arrives 14 minutes after Berlin Zoo).
⊙ – From Berlin Spandau (departs 11–13 minutes before Berlin Zoo).

RE / RB services MAGDEBURG - DESSAU - LEIPZIG and HALLE 848

km		©z	©¶			v		v																	
0	**Magdeburg** Hbf d.	...	...	...	...	...	...	0512	...	...	0612r	...	...	0712	...	...	0812	...	...	0912	...	...	1012	...	...
	Falkenberg (Elster) d.	B	...	...	...	...	...	|	0524k	...	|	0624e	...	|	0724	...	|	...	...	|	0924	...	|	...	...
	Lutherstadt Wittenberg ♥ d.	0125	...	0406r	0445	0510	0544	|	0610	0645	|	0710	0745	|	0810	0845	|	0910	0945	|	1010	1045	|	1110	1145
56	Roßlau (Elbe) 847 d.	|	...	0438r	|	0542	|	0605	0642	|	0705r	0742	|	0805	0842	|	0859	0942	|	1005	1042	|	1059	1142	|
61	**Dessau** Hbf 847 a.	|	...	0445r	|	0549	|	0613	0649	|	0713r	0749	|	0813	0849	|	0907	0949	|	1013	1049	|	1107	1149	|
61	**Dessau** Hbf d.	|	...	0452	|	0552	|	0614	0652	|	0714	0752	|	...	0852	|	0914	0952	|	...	1052	|	1114	1152	|
87	Bitterfeld ♥ a.	0146	...	0516	0516	0615	0615	0632	0716	0716	0732	0815	0816	...	0916	0916	0931	1015	1016	...	1116	1116	1131	1215	1216
87	Bitterfeld ♥ d.	0147	0152	0520	0520	0620	0620	0632	0720	0720	0732	0820	0820	...	0920	0920	0932	1020	1020	...	1120	1120	1132	1220	1220
	Halle (Saale) Hbf ♥ a.	0207	|	|	0545	0645	|	|	|	0745	|	|	0845	...	0945	|	|	|	1045	...	1145	|	|	|	1245
120	**Leipzig** Hbf ♥ a.	...	0225	0549	...	...	0649	0658	0749	...	0758	0849	...	...	...	0949	0958	1049	...	...	...	1149	1158	1249	...

km																									
	Magdeburg Hbf d.	1112	...	...	1212	...	...	1312	...	...	1412	...	...	1512	...	...	1612	...	...	1712	...	...	1812	...	...
0	**Falkenberg** (Elster) d.	|	...	...	|	1224	...	|	...	...	|	...	...	|	1524	...	|	...	...	|	1724	...	|	1824e	...
54	Lutherstadt Wittenberg ♥ d.	|	1210	1245	|	1310	1345	|	1410	1445	|	1510	1545	|	1610	1645	|	1710	1745	|	1810	1845	|	1910	1945
86	Roßlau (Elbe) 847 d.	1205	1242	|	1259	1342	|	1405	1442	|	1459	1542	|	1605	1642	|	1659	1742	|	1805	1842	|	1859	1942	|
91	**Dessau** Hbf 847 a.	1213	1249	|	1307	1349	|	1413	1449	|	1507	1549	|	1613	1649	|	1707	1749	|	1813	1849	|	1907	1949	|
91	**Dessau** Hbf d.	...	1252	|	1314	1352	|	...	1452	|	1514	1552	|	...	1652	|	1714	1752	|	...	1852	|	1914	1952	|
117	Bitterfeld ♥ a.	...	1316	1316	1331	1415	1416	...	1516	1516	1531	1615	1616	...	1716	1716	1731	1815	1816	...	1916	1916	1931	2015	2016
117	Bitterfeld ♥ d.	...	1320	1320	1332	1420	1420	...	1520	1520	1532	1620	1620	...	1720	1720	1732	1820	1820	...	1920	1920	1932	2020	2020
147	**Halle** (Saale) Hbf ♥ a.	...	1345	|	|	|	1445	...	1545	|	|	|	1645	...	1745	|	|	|	1845	...	1945	|	|	|	2045
	Leipzig Hbf ♥ a.	...	...	1349	1358	1449	...	...	...	1549	1558	1649	...	...	...	1749	1758	1849	...	...	...	1949	1958	2049	...

										n
Magdeburg Hbf d.	1912	...	...	2012	...	...	2112	...	...	2312
Falkenberg (Elster) d.	|	1924	...	|	...	...	|	2124	...	|
Lutherstadt Wittenberg ♥ d.	|	2010	2056	|	...	2145	|	2210	2245	|
Roßlau (Elbe) 847 d.	2005	2042	|	2053	...	|	2205	2242	|	0004
Dessau Hbf 847 a.	2013	2049	|	2101	...	|	2213	2249	|	0019*
Dessau Hbf d.	...	...	|	2104	2152	|	...	2252	|	...
Bitterfeld ♥ a.	...	...	2126	2127	2216	2216	...	2316	2316	...
Bitterfeld ♥ d.	...	...	2131	2130	2220	2220	...	2320	2320	...
Halle (Saale) Hbf ♥ a.	...	...	2155	|	2245	|	...	|	2345	...
Leipzig Hbf ♥ a.	...	...	...	2159	...	2249	...	2355	...	...

	v	Ⓐ	Ⓐe	Ⓐe	©z		©	©	Ⓐe	⚒r
Leipzig Hbf ♥ d.	...	0411	...	...	...	...	...	0511	...	...
Halle (Saale) Hbf ♥ d.	...	|	0415	...	0427	...	0515	|	...	0547e
Bitterfeld ♥ a.	...	0439	0439	...	0452	...	0539	0539	...	0611e
Bitterfeld ♥ d.	...	0443	0443	...	0452	...	0543	0543	...	0613e
Dessau Hbf a.	...	|	0508	...	|	...	|	0608	...	0637e
Dessau Hbf 847 d.	0427*	|	0511	...	|	0542	|	0611	0617	0641
Roßlau (Elbe) 847 d.	0442	|	0518	0529	|	0550	|	0618	0629	0648
Lutherstadt Wittenberg ♥ d.	|	0515	0549	|	0524	|	0615	0649	|	|
Falkenberg (Elster) a.	|	...	0638	|	R	|	...	...	|	|
Magdeburg Hbf a.	0537	...	...	0620	...	0646	...	...	0720	0746

Leipzig Hbf ♥ d.	0611	...	...	...	0711	0757f	0811	...	...	...	0911	0957f	1011	...	...	...	1111	1157f	1211	...	...	...	1311	1357f	1411
Halle (Saale) Hbf ♥ d.	|	0615	...	0715	|	|	|	0815	...	0915	|	|	|	1015	...	1115	|	|	|	1215	...	1315	|	|	|
Bitterfeld ♥ a.	0639	0639	...	0739	0739	0825	0839	0839	...	0939	0939	1025	1039	1039	...	1139	1139	1225	1239	1239	...	1339	1339	1425	1439
Bitterfeld ♥ d.	0643	0643	...	0743	0743	0827	0843	0843	...	0943	0943	1027	1043	1043	...	1143	1143	1227	1243	1243	...	1343	1343	1427	1443
Dessau Hbf a.	|	0708	...	|	0808	0846	|	0908	...	|	1008	1046	|	1108	...	|	1208	1248	|	1308	...	|	1408	1448	|
Dessau Hbf 847 d.	|	0711	0742	|	0811	0850	|	0911	0942	|	1011	1050	|	1111	1142	|	1211	1250	|	1311	1342	|	1411	1450	|
Roßlau (Elbe) 847 d.	|	0718	0750	|	0818	0858	|	0918	0950	|	1018	1058	|	1118	1150	|	1218	1258	|	1318	1350	|	1418	1458	|
Lutherstadt Wittenberg ♥ d.	0715	0751	|	0815	0849	|	0915	0949	|	1015	1051	|	1115	1149	|	1215	1249	|	1315	1351	|	1415	1449	|	1515
Falkenberg (Elster) a.	...	0838	|	...	...	|	...	...	|	...	1138	|	...	...	|	...	...	|	...	1438	|	...	...	|	...
Magdeburg Hbf a.	...	...	0846	...	...	0946	...	...	1046	...	...	1146	...	...	1246	...	...	1346	...	...	1446	...	...	1546	...

																					n	G			
Leipzig Hbf ♥ d.	...	...	...	1511	1557f	1611	...	...	...	1711	1757f	1811	...	...	...	1911	1957f	2011	...	...	2111	2211	...	...	2311
Halle (Saale) Hbf ♥ d.	1415	1446e	1515	|	|	|	1615	1646e	1715	|	|	|	1815	...	1915	|	|	|	2016	2115	|	|	...	2247	|
Bitterfeld ♥ a.	1439	1510e	1539	1539	1625	1639	1639	1710e	1739	1739	1825	1839	1839	...	1939	1939	2025	2039	2039	2139	2139	2237	...	2311	2339
Bitterfeld ♥ d.	1443	1512e	1543	1543	1627	1643	1643	1712e	1743	1743	1827	1843	1843	...	1943	1943	2027	2043	2043	2143	2143	2238	...	2312	2343
Dessau Hbf a.	1508	1536e	|	1608	1648	|	1708	1736e	|	1808	1848	|	1908	...	|	2008	2046	|	2108	|	2208	2256	...	2336	|
Dessau Hbf 847 d.	1511	1542	|	1611	1650	|	1711	1742	|	1811	1850	|	1911	1942	|	2011t	2047	|	2111	|	2211g	2257	2306	...	|
Roßlau (Elbe) 847 d.	1518	1550	|	1618	1658	|	1718	1750	|	1818	1858	|	1918	1950	|	2018t	2055	|	2118	|	2218g	2305	2313	...	|
Lutherstadt Wittenberg ♥ d.	1551	|	1615	1653	|	1715	1751	|	1814	1849	|	1915	1951	|	2014	2049t	|	2115	2151	2214	2249g	|	2344	...	0015
Falkenberg (Elster) a.	1638	|	...	1746e	|	...	1838	|	...	...	|	...	2038	|	...	...	|	...	2238b	...	...	|	...	...	...
Magdeburg Hbf a.	...	1646	...	...	1746	...	...	1846	...	...	1946	...	...	2046	...	...	2146	...	...	...	...	2359	...	...	...

B – From Berlin (Table **835**).
G – ⑤–⑦ (also Jan. 6, Apr. 5, May 13, 24).
R – To Rostock via Berlin (Table **835**).
b – ⑧ (not Dec. 24, 25, 31, Apr. 4, May 23).
e – Ⓐ (not Dec. 24, 31, Jan. 6).
f – 2 minutes later until Mar. 13.
g – ①–④ (not Dec. 24, 31, Jan. 6, Apr. 5, May 13, 24).
k – ①–⑥ (not Dec. 25, 26, Jan. 1, Apr. 5, May 24).
n – Not Dec. 24, 31.
r – ⚒ (not Dec. 24, 31, Jan. 6).
t – ⚒ only.
v – Not Dec. 25, Jan. 1.
z – Not Dec. 25.
* – By 🚌.
¶ – Operated by Mitteldeutsche Regiobahn.
♥ – See Tables **850** and **851** for *ICE* and *IC* services Lutherstadt Wittenberg - Bitterfeld - Halle / Leipzig and v.v.

849 Local services LEIPZIG and HALLE - EISENACH and SAALFELD *RB services*

See Tables **850** and **851** for faster *IC* and *ICE* services

km		Ⓐn	d	Ⓐn				Ⓐn	Ⓒz											n	◧	n	n		H
0	**Halle** (Saale) Hbf .... d.	0420	...	...	0522	...	0622	...	...	0722	...	0822	...		1822	...	1922	...	2022	...	2122	...	2222	...	*2325*
32	Weißenfels................ d.	0453	...	...	0553	...	0653	...	...	0753	...	0853	...		1853	...	1953	...	2053	...	2153	...	2253	...	2358
46	Naumburg (Saale) Hbf d.	0503	0503	...	0603	0613	0703	0707	0713	0803	...	0903	0913	each train	1903	1913	2003	...	2103	...	2203	...	2303	2313	0008
59	Großheringen............ d.	0513	0513	0520	0613	|	0713	|	|	0813	0822	0913	|		1913	|	2013	2022	2113	2122	2213	2222	2320r	|	0018
	Jena Paradies .... d.	|	|	0546	|	0648	|	0740	0748	|	0848	|	0948	runs every	|	1948	|	2048	|	2148	|	2248	|	2346	|
	Göschwitz (Saale) .. d.	|	|	0551	|	0653	|	0753r	0753	|	0853	|	0953		|	1953	|	2053	|	2153	|	2253	|	2351	|
	Rudolstadt (Thür) ... d.	|	|	0618	|	0721	|	0821	0821	|	0921	|	1021	two hours	|	2021	|	2121	|	2221	|	2321	|	...	|
	Saalfeld (Saale)..... a.	|	|	0627	|	0730	|	0830	0830	|	0930	|	1030		|	2030	|	2132	|	2233	|	2330	|	...	|
87	Weimar .... **858** d.	0540	0540	...	0638	...	0740	...	...	0840	...	0940	...	until	1940	...	2040	...	2140	...	2240	...	2353f	...	0043
108	**Erfurt** Hbf.......... **858** d.	0559	0559	...	0700	...	0800	...	...	0900	...	1000	...		2005r	...	2100	...	2205r	...	2313t	...	0013	...	0101
136	Gotha .... d.	0624	0624	...	0724	...	0827	...	...	0924	...	1027	...		2033	...	2124	...	2230	...	2344	...	0037	...	...
165	**Eisenach**................. a.	0647	0647	...	0747	...	0850	...	...	0947	...	1050	...		2056	...	2147	...	2253	...	0008	...	0101	...	...

km			Ⓐn																		L	n		n	n
	Eisenach................. d.	0405a	...	0507v	...	0607	...	0707	...	0811	...	0907		...	1707	...	1811	...	1907	...	2011	...	2107n	*2215*	...
	Gotha .... d.	0429a	...	0532v	...	0632	...	0732	...	0835	...	0932		...	1732	...	1835	...	1932	...	2035	...	2132n	*2241*	...
	Erfurt Hbf.......... **858** d.	0453	...	0600	...	0700	...	0800	...	0900	...	1000	each train	...	1800	...	1900	...	2000	...	2100	...	2200	2312	...
	Weimar .... **858** d.	0511	...	0620	...	0719	...	0819	...	0919	...	1019		...	1819	...	1919	...	2019	...	2119	...	2219	2333	...
0	**Saalfeld** (Saale)..... d.	|	0508	|	0618	|	0724	|	0824	|	0930	|	runs every	1730	|	1824	|	1930	|	2024	|	2132	|	|	2235
10	Rudolstadt (Thür) ... d.	|	0517	|	0628	|	0733	|	0833	|	0939	|		1739	|	1833	|	1939	|	2033	|	2141	|	|	2244
42	Göschwitz (Saale) .. d.	|	0544	|	0658	|	0801	|	0901	|	1005	|	two hours	1805	|	1901	|	2005	|	2101	|	2207	|	|	2312
47	**Jena** Paradies .... d.	|	0549	|	0703	|	0806	|	0906	|	1011	|		1811	|	1906	|	2011	|	2106	|	2213	|	|	2316
75	Großheringen............ d.	0534	|	0644	0728	0744	|	0844	0932	0944	|	1044	until	|	1844	1932	1944	2037	2044	2132	2144	|	2244	2356	...
	Naumburg (Saale) Hbf d.	0545	0625	0654	...	0754	0840	0854	...	0954	1045	1054		1845	1854	...	1954	...	2054	...	2154	2247	2254	0005	...
	Weißenfels................ d.	0556	0635e	0705	...	0805	...	0905	...	1005	...	1105		...	1905	...	2005	...	2105	...	2204	...	2305	0015	...
	Halle (Saale) Hbf .... a.	0629	0707e	0738	...	0838	...	0938	...	1038	...	1138		...	1938	...	2038	...	2138	...	*2240*	...	2341	0047	...

Leipzig - Weißenfels and v.v. ⊠

From Leipzig Hbf at 0418 Ⓐ, 0503 Ⓒ, 0518 Ⓐ, 0618 Ⓐ, 0647 Ⓒ, 0747 Ⓐ, 0847, 0947 Ⓐ, 1047, 1147 Ⓐ, 1247, 1347 Ⓐ, 1447, 1547 Ⓐ, 1647, 1747 Ⓐ, 1847, 1947 Ⓐ, 2047 and 2317.
From Weißenfels at 0426, 0526 Ⓐ, 0626, 0726 Ⓐ, 0826, 0926 Ⓐ, 1026, 1126 Ⓐ, 1226, 1326 Ⓐ, 1426, 1526 Ⓐ, 1626, 1726 Ⓐ, 1826, 1926 Ⓐ, 2026 and 2205.

Eisenach - Bebra and v.v. ✣

From Eisenach at 0452 Ⓐ **n**, 0530 Ⓐ **n**, 0614 ⚒, 0712 ⚒, 0812, 0912 ⚒, 1012, 1112 Ⓐ **n**, 1212, 1312 Ⓐ **n**, 1412, 1512 Ⓐ **n**, 1612, 1712 Ⓐ **n**, 1812, 1912 Ⓐ **n**, 2012, 2112 Ⓐ **n** and 2212 Ⓒ **z**.
From Bebra at 0504 Ⓐ **n**, 0606 ⚒, 0659 Ⓐ **n**, 0706 Ⓒ **z**, 0806 ⑥ **k**, 0906, 1006 Ⓐ **n**, 1106, 1206 Ⓐ **n**, 1306 Ⓒ **z**, 1315 Ⓐ **n**, 1406 Ⓐ **n**, 1506, 1606 Ⓐ **n**, 1706, 1806 Ⓐ **n**, 1906, 2006 Ⓐ **n** and 2106.

H – From Leipzig Hbf (d. 2317).
L – To Leipzig Hbf (a. 2245).
a – Ⓐ (not Dec. 24, 31).
d – Not Dec. 25.
e – Not Jan. 6.
f – Arrives 2342.
k – Also Dec. 24, 31; not Dec. 26, May 1.
n – Not Dec. 24, 31.
r – Arrives 7–9 minutes earlier.
t – Arrives 2257.
v – Not Dec. 25, Jan. 1.
z – Also Dec. 24, 31.
◧ – On Dec. 24, 31 terminates at Erfurt.
⊠ – Journey 40–46 minutes.
✣ – Journey 36–41 minutes. 2nd class only. Operated by CANTUS Verkehrsgesellschaft.

850 BERLIN and LEIPZIG - ERFURT - KASSEL and FRANKFURT

Alternative regional services: Table **835** Berlin - Lutherstadt Wittenberg. Table **848** Lutherstadt Wittenberg - Halle. Table **849** Leipzig / Halle - Erfurt - Eisenach - Bebra.

km		*IC*	*IC*	*ICE*	*ICE*	*ICE*	*ICE*	*ICE*	*IC*	*ICE*	*ICE*	*IC*	*ICE*	*IC*	*ICE*	*ICE*	*IC*	*IC*	*ICE*	*IC*	*ICE*	*ICE*	*IC*	*ICE*	*IC*
		1850	**1850**	**1646**	**1646**	**1656**	**1503**	**1644**	**2156**	**1654**	**291**	**2154**	**1642**	**2154**	**1607**	**1652**	**2152**	**2152**	**1640**	**2152**	**1209**	**1650**	**2150**	**1548**	**2150**
		①**g**	Ⓐ¶	①**g**	①–⑤	①–⑥	①–⑥	①–⑥	①–⑥	①–⑥	⑦**d**	①–⑥		①–⑥	**1727**		①–⑥			⑤⑦	**1609**		◐		◐
					a	**e**	**e** ⊖	**e**	**e**	**e**	**E**	**e**		**e**	⊖		**e**			**r**	⊖				
				✕	✕	✕	✕	✕	🍷	✕	✕	🍷	✕	🍷	✕	✕	🍷	🍷	✕	🍷	✕	✕	🍷	✕	🍷
	Stralsund **845** ....d.	...	...	...	...	...	...	...	...	...	...	...	...	...	...	...	...	...	...	...	...	...	0737e	...	...
	Berlin Hbf.................... **851** d.	0043	...	...	...	...	0441	...	...	0548	0549	0639	...	...	0752	...	0839	...	...	...	0952	...	1039	...	...
	Berlin Südkreuz........... **851** d.	0050	...	...	...	...	0448	...	...	0554	0556	0646	...	...	0759	...	0846	...	...	...	0959	...	1046	...	...
	Lutherstadt Wittenberg . **851** d.	0124	...	...	...	...	0524	...	...	0633	0631	0721	...	...	0835	...	0921	...	...	...	1035	...	1121	...	...
	Bitterfeld .... **851** d.	0141	...	...	...	...	0540	...	...	0649	0648	0738	...	...	|	...	0938	...	...	...	|	...	1138	...	...
	Halle (Saale) Hbf ....d.	0203	...	...	...	...	0602	...	...	|	|	0800	...	...	|	...	1000	1000	...	...	|	...	1200	...	...
	Dresden Hbf **842** ....d.	|	...	...	...	...	|	0444a	...	|	|	|	0649e	...	|	0754	|	|	0854	...	|	0954	|	1054	...
0	**Leipzig** Hbf .... **851** d.	0235	...	0404	...	0458	|	0602	...	0715	0710	|	0811	...	0905	0915	|	|	1011	...	1105	1115	|	1211	...
40	Weißenfels.........................d.	|	...	|	...	|	|	|	...	|	|	0825	|	...	...	|	1025	1025	|	...	...	|	1225	|	...
54	Naumburg (Saale) Hbf... **851** d.	|	...	0438	...	0534	0634	0640	...	|	|	0836	|	..	...	|	1036	1036	|	...	...	|	1236	|	...
95	Weimar .... **858** d.	0336	...	0501	...	0556	...	0704	...	0808	|	0901	0906	←	...	1008	1101	1101	1106	←	...	1208	1301	1306	←
117	**Erfurt** Hbf .... **858** d.	0353	...	0518	0518	0619	...	0719	0725	0824	0823	0917	0922	0926	...	1024	1117	1117	1122	1126	...	1224	1317	1322	1326
144	Gotha ....d.	0411	...	0536	0536	0636	...	0735	0743	0841	|	→	|	0943	...	1041	→	→	|	1143	...	1241	→	|	1343
173	**Eisenach**...........................d.	0426	...	0552	0552	0652	...	0752	0758	0856	0855	...	0952	0958	...	1056	...	...	1152	1158	...	1256	...	1352	1358
	Bebra .... **901** d.	0500	0500	|	|	|	...	|	0823	|	|	...	|	1023	...	|	...	...	|	1223	...	|	...	|	1423
	Kassel Wilhelmshöhe **901** a.	|	|	|	|	|	...	|	0858	|	|	...	|	1058	...	|	...	...	|	1258	...	|	...	|	1458
	Düsseldorf Hbf **800** ......a.	|	|	|	|	|	...	|	1212	|	|	...	|	1412	...	|	...	...	|	1612	...	|	...	|	1814
230	Bad Hersfeld .... **901** d.	0511	0511	0619	0619	0720	...	0819	...	|	|	...	1019	...	...	|	...	...	1219	...	...	|	...	1419	...
272	Fulda .... **900/1** d.	0540	0540	0644	0644	0744	...	0844	...	0944	0947	...	1044	...	...	1144	...	...	1244	...	...	1344	...	1444	...
353	Hanau Hbf .... **900/1** d.	0623	0623	|	|	|	...	|	...	|	1029	...	|	...	...	|	...	...	|	...	...	|	...	|	...
372	**Frankfurt** (Main) Süd ....a.	|	|	0740	0740	|	...	0937	...	|	|	...	1137	...	...	|	...	...	1337	...	...	|	...	1537	...
376	**Frankfurt** (Main) Hbf.. **900/1** a.	0642	0642	|	|	0841	...	|	...	1041	1044	...	|	...	...	1241	...	...	|	...	...	1441	...	|	...
	Frankfurt Flughafen ✈ §..a.	...	...	0750	0750	0857	...	0950	...	1057	...	...	1150	...	...	1257	...	...	1350	...	...	1457	...	1550	...
	Wiesbaden Hbf **912** ....a.	...	...	...	...	0938	...	...	...	1138	...	...	...	...	...	1338	...	...	...	...	...	1538	...	...	...

	ICE	*ICE*	*IC*	*ICE*	*IC*	*ICE*	*ICE*	*IC*	*IC*	*ICE*	*ICE*	*IC*	*ICE*	*ICE*	*ICE*	*IC*	*IC*	*IC*	*ICE*	*IC*	*ICE*	*ICE*	*IC*	*ICE*	*ICE*
	1611	**1558**	**2356**	**1546**	**2356**	**1613**	**1556**	**1858**	**2354**	**1544**	**1744**	**2354**	**1615**	**1554**	**1594**	**1856**	**1854**	**2352**	**1542**	**2352**	**1617**	**1552**	**2350**	**1717**	**1737**
								⑦**w**		①–⑤	⑦**w**		**n**	**n**	Ⓑ**q**	⑦**w**	⑦**w**		Ⓑ**q**	⑦**w**		**n**	⑦**w**	①–⑥	⑦**w**
	⊖		**O**		**O**	⊖		**T**	**B**	**h**		**B**	⊖		**R**						⊖		**L**	**z**	
	✕	✕	🍷	✕	🍷	✕	✕	🍷	🍷	✕	✕	🍷	✕	✕	✕			🍷	✕	🍷	✕	✕	🍷	♣✕	♥✕
Stralsund **845** ....d.	...	...	0937	...	...	...	...	...	...	...	...	...	...	...	...	...	...	1337j	...	...	...	...	1537	...	...
Berlin Hbf .... **851** d.	1152	...	1239	...	...	1352	...	...	1439	...	...	...	1552	...	...	...	...	1639	...	...	1752	...	1839	1850	1858
Berlin Südkreuz .... **851** d.	1159	...	1246	...	...	1359	...	...	1446	...	...	...	1559	...	...	...	...	1646	...	...	1759	...	1846	1856	1905
Lutherstadt Wittenberg.. **851** d.	1235	...	1321	...	...	1435	...	...	1521	...	...	...	1635	...	...	...	...	1721	...	...	1835	...	1921	|	|
Bitterfeld .... **851** d.	|	...	1338	...	...	|	...	...	1538	...	...	...	|	...	...	...	...	1738	...	...	|	...	1938	1954	|
Halle (Saale) Hbf..................d.	|	...	1400	...	...	|	...	...	1600	...	...	...	|	...	...	1700	...	1800	...	...	|	...	2000	2016	|
Dresden Hbf **842** ....d.	|	1154	|	1254	...	|	1354	...	|	1454	1454	...	|	1554	1554	|	...	|	1654	...	|	1754	|	|	|
Leipzig Hbf................ **851** d.	1305	1315	|	1411	...	1505	1515	1543	|	1611	1611	...	1705	1715	1715	|	1743	|	1811	...	1905	1915	|	|	2012
Weißenfels ....d.	...	|	1425	|	...	...	|	|	1625	|	|	...	...	|	|	|	|	1825	|	...	...	|	2025	|	|
Naumburg (Saale) Hbf ... **851** d.	...	|	1436	|	...	...	|	1618	1636	|	|	...	...	|	|	1732	1818	1836	|	...	...	1951	2035	2056	2047
Weimar........................ **858** d.	...	1408	1501	1506	←	...	1608	1645	1701	1706	1706	←	...	1808	1808	1801	1845	1901	1906	←	...	2015	2104	2120	2111
Erfurt Hbf....................... **858** d.	...	1424	1517	1522	1526	...	1624	1704	1717	1722	1722	1726	...	1824	1824	1818	1904	1917	1922	1926	...	2030	2122	2135	2129
Gotha ....d.	...	1441	→	|	1543	...	1641	1730	→	|	|	1743	...	1841	1841	1835	1930	→	|	1943	...	2047	2139	...	|
Eisenach............................d.	...	1456	...	1552	1558	...	1656	1746	...	1752	1752	1758	...	1856	1856	1902	1946	...	1952	1958	...	2103	2153	...	2158
Bebra .... **901** d.	...	|	...	|	1623	...	|	|	...	|	|	1823	...	|	|	|	|	...	|	2023	...	|	→	...	|
Kassel Wilhelmshöhe. **901** a.	...	|	...	|	1658	...	|	|	...	|	|	1858	...	|	|	|	|	...	|	2058	...	|	...	...	|
Düsseldorf Hbf **800** .... a.	...	|	...	|	2015	...	|	|	...	|	|	2214w	...	|	|	|	|	...	|	0012	...	|	...	...	|
Bad Hersfeld.................. **901** d.	...	|	...	1619	...	...	|	|	...	1819	1819	...	...	|	|	|	|	...	2019	...	...	|	...	...	2227
Fulda .... **900/1** d.	...	1544	...	1644	...	...	1744	1838	...	1844	1844	...	...	1944	1944	1954	2038	...	2044	...	...	2159x	...	...	2251
Hanau Hbf .... **900/1** d.	...	|	...	|	...	...	|	|	...	|	|	...	...	|	|	|	|	...	2125	...	...	2240	...	...	2335
Frankfurt (Main) Süd............ a.	...	|	...	1737	...	...	|	|	...	|	1937	...	...	|	|	|	|	...	2138	...	...	|	...	...	|
Frankfurt (Main) Hbf .. **900/1** a.	...	1641	...	|	...	...	1841	1932	...	1942	|	...	...	2041	2041	2052	2142	...	|	...	...	2254	...	...	2351
Frankfurt Flughafen ✈ § .. a.	...	1657	...	1750	...	...	1857	...	...	...	1950	...	...	2057	...	...	...	...	2150	...	...	...	...	...	...
Wiesbaden Hbf **912**......... a.	...	1738	...	...	...	...	1938	...	...	...	...	...	...	2138	...	...	...	...	...	...	...	...	...	...	...

A – CANOPUS – 🛏 1, 2 cl., ▬ 2 cl., (2) (reclining) and 🍷 Praha - Karlsruhe - Basel - Zürich and v.v.
B – (12) and 🍷 Berlin - Kassel - Dortmund (- Köln ⑦**w**).
D – STRELASUND – (12) and 🍷 (Düsseldorf ①**g** -) (Dortmund ①–⑥**e** -) Erfurt - Berlin - Ostseebad Binz.
E – (12) and ✕ Interlaken - Bern - Basel - Karlsruhe - Berlin and v.v.

NOTES CONTINUED ON NEXT PAGE →

FRANKFURT and KASSEL - ERFURT - LEIPZIG and BERLIN 850

Alternative regional services: Table **835** Berlin - Lutherstadt Wittenberg. Table **848** Lutherstadt Wittenberg - Halle. Table **849** Leipzig / Halle - Erfurt - Eisenach - Bebra.

	IC 2350 ⑦w L 🍷	*ICE* 1619 ⑥⑦ m ✕	*ICE* 1550 ⑦w ✕	*ICE* 893 ⑧q ✕	*D* 61458 P 2	*CNL* 458 🅁 A 🍷	*IC* 61258 2	*CNL* 1258 🅁 Z ✕		
Stralsund **845** d.	...	...	...	...	...	...	...	...	...	...
Berlin Hbf **851** d.	...	1952	...	2055	...	...	2222	2222	...	...
Berlin Südkreuz **851** d.	...	2000	...	2101	...	...	2230	2230	...	...
Lutherstadt Wittenberg **851** d.	...	2035	...	2138	...	...	2310	2310u	...	...
Bitterfeld **851** d.	...	|	...	|	...	...	2327	2327u	...	...
Halle (Saale) Hbf d.	...	|	...	|	...	...	2351	2351u	...	...
Dresden Hbf **842** d.	...	|	1954	|	2104	2104	|	|	...	...
Leipzig Hbf **851** d.	...	2105	2112	2209	2229	2229	|	|	...	...
Weißenfels d.	...	...	|	...	|	|	|	|	...	...
Naumburg (Saale) Hbf **851** d.	...	...	2144	...	2308	2308u	0022	0022u	...	...
Weimar **858** d.	...	...	2207	...	2333	2333u	0049	0049u	...	...
Erfurt Hbf **858** d.	...	...	2224	...	2350	0123u	0105	0123u	...	...
Gotha d.	←	...	2241	...	...	|	...	|	...	...
Eisenach d.	2202	...	2258	...	...	|	...	|	...	...
Bebra **901** d.	|	...	|	...	...	|	...	|	...	...
Kassel Wilhelmshöhe **901** a.	|	...	|	...	...	|	...	|	...	...
Düsseldorf Hbf **800** a.	|	...	|	...	...	|	...	|	...	...
Bad Hersfeld **901** d.	2234	...	2326	...	...	|	...	|	...	...
Fulda **900/1** d.	2301	...	2351	...	...	|	...	|	...	...
Hanau Hbf **900/1** d.	...	...	0035	...	...	|	...	|	...	...
Frankfurt (Main) Süd a.	...	...	0049	...	...	0359	...	0359	...	...
Frankfurt (Main) Hbf **900/1** a.	...	...	0056	...	...	...	...	...	...	...
Frankfurt Flughafen ✈ § a.	...	...	...	...	...	...	...	...	...	...
Wiesbaden Hbf **912** a.	...	...	...	...	...	...	...	...	...	...

km		*CNL* 1259 🅁 Z ✕	*IC* 61259 2	*CNL* 459 🅁 A 🍷	*D* 61459 P 2	*ICE* 1616 ①–⑤ a ✕	*ICE* 1516 v ✕	*IC* 2351 ①–⑥ e 🍷	*IC* 2351 N 🍷	*ICE* 1553 ①g ✕
	Wiesbaden Hbf **912** d.	...	...	...	...	...	...	...	...	...
0	**Frankfurt** Flughafen ✈ § d.	...	...	...	...	...	...	...	...	...
	Frankfurt (Main) Hbf **900/1** d.	...	...	...	...	...	...	...	...	0517
11	**Frankfurt** (Main) Süd d.	0055	...	0055	...	...	...	...	...	|
—	Hanau Hbf **900/1** d.	|	...	|	...	...	...	...	...	|
	Fulda **900/1** d.	|	...	|	0341	...	...	...	...	0611
	Bad Hersfeld **901** d.	|	...	|	0410	...	...	...	...	0635
	Düsseldorf Hbf **800** d.	|	...	|	|	...	...	...	...	|
0	**Kassel** Wilhelmshöhe **901** d.	|	...	|	|	...	...	...	...	|
54	Bebra **901** d.	|	...	|	|	...	...	...	...	|
99	**Eisenach** d.	|	...	0440s	0447	...	0602a	...	...	0702
128	Gotha d.	|	...	0500s	0502	...	0617a	...	...	0718
155	**Erfurt** Hbf **858** d.	0413s	0443	0518s	0523	...	0635	...	...	0735
177	Weimar **858** d.	0458s	0500	0538s	0540	...	0653	...	...	0752
218	Naumburg (Saale) Hbf **851** d.	0524s	0526	0603s	0605	...	0715	...	...	0814
232	Weißenfels d.	|	|	|	|	...	|	...	...	|
	Leipzig Hbf **851** a.	|	|	0641	0641	0651	0747	...	...	0846
	Dresden Hbf **842** a.	|	|	0804	0804	|	|	...	...	1014
264	**Halle** (Saale) Hbf d.	0557s	0600	...	...	|	|	0801	0801	...
294	Bitterfeld **851** d.	0618s	0620	...	...	0709	|	0820	0820	...
331	Lutherstadt Wittenberg **851** d.	0634s	0636	...	...	0725	|	0836	0836	...
421	**Berlin** Südkreuz **851** a.	0710	0710	...	...	0800	0853	0909	0909	...
429	**Berlin** Hbf **851** a.	0718	0718	...	...	0807	0900	0918	0918	...
	Stralsund **845** a.	...	...	...	...	...	...	...	1224	...

	ICE 1553 ①–⑤ a ✕	*ICE* 1614 ①–⑥ e⊖ ✕	*IC* 2353 ①g 🍷	*ICE* 1543 ①–⑥ e ✕	*IC* 2353 🍷	*ICE* 1555 ①–⑥ e ✕	*ICE* 1612 ①–⑥ e⊖ ✕	*IC* 2355 ①–⑥ eD 🍷	*ICE* 1545 ①–⑥ e ✕	*ICE* 1745 ⑦d 🍷	*IC* 2355 D 🍷	*ICE* 1557 ①–⑥ eR ✕	*ICE* 1597 ⑦d 🍷	*ICE* 1610 ⊖ ✕	*IC* 2357 G 🍷	*ICE* 1547 ✕	*IC* 2357 G 🍷	*ICE* 1559 ✕	*ICE* 1608 ⊖ ✕	*IC* 2157 ◧ 🍷	*ICE* 1549 ✕	*IC* 2157 ◧ 🍷	*IC* 1853 ⑤ K	*ICE* 1651 ✕	*ICE* 1606 ⊖ ✕
Wiesbaden Hbf **912** d.	...	...	...	...	...	...	...	...	...	...	...	...	0824	...	...	...	...	1024	...	...	...	...	...	1224	...
Frankfurt Flughafen ✈ § d.	...	...	...	...	...	...	...	...	0811	...	...	...	0901	...	...	1011	...	1102	...	...	1211	...	...	1302	...
Frankfurt (Main) Hbf **900/1** d.	...	...	...	0618	...	0721	...	...	|	0822	...	0921	0921	...	...	|	...	1119	...	...	|	...	1302	1319	...
Frankfurt (Main) Süd d.	...	...	...	|	...	|	...	...	0822	|	...	|	|	...	...	1022	...	|	...	...	1222	...	|	|	...
Hanau Hbf **900/1** d.	...	...	...	0634	...	|	...	...	|	|	...	|	|	...	...	|	...	|	...	...	|	...	|	|	...
Fulda **900/1** d.	...	...	...	0714	...	0814	...	...	0914	0914	...	1013	1013	...	...	1114	...	1213	...	...	1314	...	1400	1413	...
Bad Hersfeld **901** d.	...	...	...	0738	...	|	...	...	0938	0938	...	|	|	...	...	1138	...	|	...	...	1338	...	1426	|	...
Düsseldorf Hbf **800** d.	...	...	...	|	...	|	...	0546g	|	|	...	|	|	...	0746e	|	...	|	...	0946	|	...	|	|	...
Kassel Wilhelmshöhe **901** d.	...	...	0659	|	...	|	...	0859	|	|	...	|	|	...	1059	|	...	|	...	1259	|	...	|	|	...
Bebra **901** d.	...	...	0735	|	...	|	...	0935	|	|	...	|	|	...	1135	|	...	|	...	1335	|	...	|	|	...
Eisenach d.	0702	...	0800	0807	...	0902	...	1000	1007	1007	...	1102	1102	...	1200	1207	...	1302	...	1400	1407	...	1457	1502	...
Gotha d.	0718	...	0815	|	←	0917	...	1015	|	|	←	1117	1117	...	1215	|	←	1317	...	1415	|	←	|	1517	...
Erfurt Hbf **858** d.	0735	...	0829	0835	0839	0934	...	1029	1035	1035	1039	1134	1134	...	1229	1235	1239	1334	...	1429	1435	1439	1528	1534	...
Weimar **858** d.	0752	...	→	0853	0859	0950	...	→	1053	1053	1059	1150	1150	...	→	1253	1259	1350	...	→	1453	1459	1554	1550	...
Naumburg (Saale) Hbf **851** d.	0814	...	...	|	0924	|	...	...	|	|	1124	|	|	...	...	|	1324	|	...	...	|	1524	1621	|	...
Weißenfels d.	|	...	...	|	0933	|	...	...	|	|	1133	|	|	...	...	|	1333	|	...	...	|	1533	1631	|	...
Leipzig Hbf **851** a.	0846	0851	...	0945	|	1046	1051	...	1145	1145	|	1246	1246	1251	...	1345	|	1446	1451	...	1545	|	|	1646	1651
Dresden Hbf **842** a.	1014	|	...	1114	|	1214	|	...	1314	1314	|	1414	1414	|	...	1514	|	1614	|	...	1714	|	|	1814	|
Halle (Saale) Hbf d.	...	|	...	...	1000	...	|	...	...	...	1200	...	...	|	...	...	1400	...	|	...	...	1600	1657	...	|
Bitterfeld **851** d.	...	|	...	...	1020	...	|	...	...	...	1220	...	...	|	...	...	1420	...	|	...	...	1620	...	...	|
Lutherstadt Wittenberg **851** d.	...	0922	...	...	1036	...	1122	...	...	...	1236	...	...	1322	...	...	1436	...	1522	...	...	1636	...	...	1722
Berlin Südkreuz **851** a.	...	1006	...	...	1115	...	1206	...	...	...	1310	...	...	1406	...	...	1509	...	1606	...	...	1710	...	...	1800
Berlin Hbf **851** a.	...	1013	...	...	1123	...	1213	...	...	...	1316	...	...	1413	...	...	1518	...	1613	...	...	1719	...	...	1810
Stralsund **845** a.	...	...	...	...	1424	...	...	...	...	...	1624	...	...	...	...	...	...	...	...	...	...	2036q	...	...	...

	IC 2359 ⑤⑦ r 🍷	*ICE* 1641 ✕	*IC* 2359 ⑤⑦ r 🍷	*IC* 2259 ①–④ ⊕ 🍷	*ICE* 1653 ✕	*ICE* 1604 1704 n⊖ ✕	*IC* 2151 🍷	*ICE* 1643 n ✕	*IC* 2151 🍷	*IC* 2151 ⑥⑦ c 🍷	*IC* 1859 ⑤f 🍷	*IC* 2204 ①–④ ⊙ 🍷	*ICE* 290 ⑥k E ✕	*ICE* 1655 ⑧q ✕	*IC* 2153 ⑧q 🍷	*ICE* 1645 n ✕	*ICE* 1502 n ⊖ ✕	*IC* 2153 ⑦w 🍷	*ICE* 1657 ⑧q 🍷	*ICE* 1600 ⑤⑦ b⊖ ✕	*IC* 2155 ⑦w 🍷	*ICE* 1747 ⑦w ✕	*ICE* 1647 ①–⑥ t ✕	*ICE* 1659 ⑧q ✕	*ICE* 1659 ⑤⑦ ‡ ✕
Wiesbaden Hbf **912** d.	...	...	...	...	1424	...	...	...	...	...	...	...	...	1624	...	...	...	...	1824	...	...	...	...	2024	2024
Frankfurt Flughafen ✈ § d.	...	1411	...	...	1503	...	...	1611	...	...	...	...	...	1703	...	1811	...	...	1902	...	...	2011	...	2102	2102
Frankfurt (Main) Hbf **900/1** d.	...	|	...	...	1520	...	...	|	...	...	1615	1617	1713	1720	...	|	...	...	1919	...	...	|	2022	2119	2119
Frankfurt (Main) Süd d.	...	1422	...	...	|	...	...	1622	...	...	|	|	|	|	...	1822	...	...	|	...	...	2022	|	|	|
Hanau Hbf **900/1** d.	...	|	...	...	|	...	...	|	...	...	|	1637	1729	|	...	|	...	...	|	...	...	2037	2037	|	|
Fulda **900/1** d.	...	1514	...	...	1613	...	...	1714	...	...	1721	1719	1811	1813	...	1914	...	...	2013	...	...	2117	2117	2213	2213
Bad Hersfeld **901** d.	...	1538	...	...	|	...	...	1738	...	...	1749	1749	|	|	...	1938	...	...	|	...	...	2142	2142	|	|
Düsseldorf Hbf **800** d.	1146	|	...	...	|	...	1346	|	...	...	|	|	|	|	1546	|	...	...	|	...	1746	|	|	|	|
Kassel Wilhelmshöhe **901** d.	1459	|	...	...	|	...	1659	|	...	...	|	|	|	|	1859	|	...	...	|	...	2059	|	|	|	|
Bebra **901** d.	1535	|	...	...	|	...	1735	|	...	...	|	1801	|	|	1935	|	...	...	|	...	2135	|	|	|	|
Eisenach d.	1600	1607	...	...	1702	...	1800	1807	...	...	|	...	1903	1902	2000	2007	...	...	2101	...	2200	2209	2209	2301	2301
Gotha d.	1615	|	←	...	1717	...	1815	|	←	←	1831	...	|	1917	2015	|	...	←	2116	...	2215	2226	2226	2316	2316
Erfurt Hbf **858** d.	1629	1635	1639	1639	1734	...	1829	1835	1839	1839	1855	...	1934	1936	2029	2035	...	2039	2133	...	2229	2245	2245	2331	2335
Weimar **858** d.	→	1653	1659	1659	1750	...	→	1853	1859	1859	1913	...	|	1952	→	2053	...	2059	2150	...	...	2303	2303	...	2353
Naumburg (Saale) Hbf **851** d.	...	|	1724	1724	|	...	...	|	1924	1924	1938	...	|	|	...	|	...	2128	2213	...	...	2325	2325	...	0016
Weißenfels d.	...	|	1733	1733	|	...	...	|	1933	1933	1948	...	|	|	...	|	...	2138	|	...	...	|	|	...	|
Leipzig Hbf **851** a.	...	1745	|	|	1846	1851	...	1945	|	|	2017	...	2046	2046	...	2145	2149	|	2250	2259	...	0047	0047	...	0058
Dresden Hbf **842** a.	...	1914	|	|	2014	|	...	2114	|	|	...	...	|	|	...	2314	|	|	0014y	|	...	|	|	...	...
Halle (Saale) Hbf d.	...	...	1800	1800	...	|	...	...	1958	2000	...	...	|	|	...	...	|	2200	...	|	...	2353*	2353*	...	...
Bitterfeld **851** d.	...	...	1820	1820	...	|	...	...	...	2020	...	...	|	|	...	...	|	...	...	|	...	...	...	...	...
Lutherstadt Wittenberg **851** d.	...	...	1836	1836	...	1922	...	...	...	2036	...	...	|	2122	...	...	|	...	...	2334	...	...	...	...	...
Berlin Südkreuz **851** a.	...	...	1910	1910	...	2008	...	...	...	2110	...	...	2152	2205	...	...	2249	...	...	0018	...	...	...	...	...
Berlin Hbf **851** a.	...	...	1918	1918	...	2015	...	...	...	2118	...	...	2159	2212	...	...	2256	...	...	0025	...	...	...	...	...
Stralsund **845** a.	...	...	2225	...	...	...	...	...	...	...	...	...	...	...	...	...	...	...	...	...	...	...	...	...	...

NOTES (CONTINUED FROM PREVIOUS PAGE)

G – 🚃12 and 🍷 (Köln - Düsseldorf ①–⑥ **e** -) Dortmund - Kassel - Erfurt - Berlin.
K – ⑤ (also Dec. 23, 30, Apr. 1; not Dec. 25, Jan. 1, Apr. 2). From Karlsruhe (Table **911**).
L – To Gemünden (a. 2332) and Würzburg (a. 2356).
N – ①⑤ Dec. 14 - Mar. 26 (also Dec. 23, 29, 30, Jan. 2; not Dec. 25, Jan. 1); ①–⑥ from Mar. 29 (not Apr. 3, 5, May 24).
O – From Ostseebad Binz on ①–⑥ (Table **844**). Train number **2254** on ⑤ (also Dec. 23, 30, Apr. 1, May 12, June 2; not Dec. 25, Jan. 1, Apr. 2, May 14, June 4).
P – From / to Praha (Table **1100**).
R – To / from Saarbrücken (Table **919**).
T – To Stuttgart (Tables **911**/**930**).
Z – SIRIUS – 🛏 1, 2 cl., 🛏 2 cl., 🚃2 (reclining) and ✕ Berlin - Basel - Zürich and v.v.

a – ①–⑤ (not Dec. 24, 25, 31, Jan. 1, Apr. 2, 5, May 24).
b – Also Dec. 23, 30, Apr. 1, 5, May 12, 24, June 2; not Dec. 25, Jan. 1, Apr. 2, 4, May 14, 23, June 4.
c – Also Dec. 24, 25, 31, Jan. 1, Apr. 2, 5, May 24.
d – Also Dec. 25, 26, Jan. 1, Apr. 3, 5, May 24.
e – ①–⑥ (not Dec. 25, 26, Jan. 1, Apr. 3, 5, May 24).
f – Also Dec. 23, 30, Apr. 1, May 12; not Dec. 25, Jan. 1, Apr. 2, May 14.
g – ① (also Apr. 6, May 25; not Apr. 5, May 24).
h – Not Dec. 24, 25, 31, Apr. 2, 5, May 24.
j – ①⑤⑦ Dec. 13 - Mar. 26 (also Dec. 23, 29, 30, Jan. 2; not Dec. 25); daily from Mar. 28.
k – Also Dec. 24, 25, 31, Apr. 2, 4, May 23.
m – Also Dec. 25, Apr. 2, 5, May 24.
n – Not Dec. 24, 31.
q – ⑧ (not Dec. 24, 25, 31, Apr. 2, 4, May 23).
r – Also Dec. 23, 30, Apr. 1, 5, May 12, 24; not Dec. 25, Jan. 1, Apr. 2, 4, May 14, 23.
s – Stops to set down only.
t – Also Apr. 4, May 23; not Apr. 5, May 24.
u – Stops to pick up only.
v – Not Dec. 25, Jan. 1.
w – ⑦ (also Apr. 5, May 24; not Apr. 4, May 23).
x – Arrives 2151.
y – Leipzig - Dresden on ⑤⑦‡.
z – Also Apr. 4, May 23; not Dec. 24, 31, Apr. 5, May 24.

⊙ – Not Dec. 23, 24, 30, 31, Apr. 1, 5, May 12, 13, 24, June 2, 3.
⊕ – Not Dec. 23, 24, 30, 31, Apr. 1, 5, May 12, 13, 24.
¶ – Not Dec. 24, 31, May 14, June 3, 4.
‡ – Also Dec. 23, 30, Apr. 1, 5, May 24; not Dec. 25, Apr. 2, 4, May 23.
♣ – Conveys 🚃12 (*ICE* **1517**) Berlin - Bitterfeld - Nürnberg - München (Table **851**).
♥ – Conveys 🚃12 (*ICE* **1757**) Berlin - Naumburg - Nürnberg - München (Table **851**).
§ – Frankfurt Flughafen Fernbahnhof.
⊖ – See also Table **851**.
* – Arrival time (calls before Leipzig).
◧ – Train number **2257** on ⑥**k**.
◐ – Train number **2250** on ⑦**d**.

851 BERLIN - LEIPZIG - SAALFELD - NÜRNBERG

Alternative regional services: Table **835** Berlin - Lutherstadt Wittenberg. Table **848** Lutherstadt Wittenberg - Leipzig. Table **849** Leipzig / Halle - Saalfeld. Table **875** Lichtenfels - Nürnberg.

km		RB 16841	ICE 1501	RB 16843	ICE 1603	RB 16847	ICE 1644	ICE 1503	ICE 1654	ICE 291	ICE 1605	IC 2154	ICE 1505	RE 3483	ICE 1607	ICE 1727	X 80002	IC 2152	IC 2152	ICE 1507	ICE 1707	ICE 1707	RE 3485	ICE 1209	ICE 1609
		Ⓐn	Ⓐd		①–⑤		①–⑥	①–⑥	①–⑥	⑦h	①–⑥	①–⑥			①–⑥	⑦h		①–⑥		①–⑤	⑥k	⑥⑦		⑥⑦r	①–⑤
			✕		a✕		e	e✕	e⊖	⊖	e D	e⊖	✕	◧	e✕	✕	△	e⊖	⊖	a✕	✕	r✕	◧	P✕	a R
0	**Berlin** Gesundbrunnen ....d.	...	...	...	...	...	...	0434	0541	0541	✕	0631	0644	...	...	0744	0740	0831	...	...	0850	...	...	...	0939
	Hamburg Hbf **840** ....d.	...	...	...	...	...	...	|	|	|	...	|	|	...	0600	|	|	|	...	0708	|	...	...	0806	|
5	**Berlin** Hbf .... **850** d.	...	...	...	...	...	...	0441	0548	0549	...	0639	0652	...	0752	0752	0756	0839	...	0858	0858	...	...	0952	0952
13	**Berlin** Südkreuz .... **850** d.	...	...	...	...	...	...	0448	0554	0556	...	0646	0659	...	0759	0759	|	0846	...	0905	0905	...	...	0959	0959
103	Lutherstadt Wittenberg . **850** d.	...	...	...	...	...	...	0524	0633	0631	...	0721	0736	...	0835	0835	|	0921	...	|	|	...	...	1035	1035
140	Bitterfeld .... **850** d.	...	...	...	...	...	...	0540	0649	0648	...	0738	|	...	|	|	|	0938	...	|	|	...	...	|	|
173	**Leipzig** Hbf ....a.	...	...	...	...	...	...	|	0705	0705	...	|	0805	...	0905	0905	0915	|	...	1005	1005	...	...	1105	1105
173	**Leipzig** Hbf .... **850** d.	...	...	...	0458	...	0602	|	▬	...	0711	|	0816	...	0911	0911	...	|	...	1016	1016	1016	...	1111	1111
	Halle (Saale) Hbf .... **850** d.	...	...	...	|	...	|	0602	*RE*	...	|	0800	|	...	|	|	...	1000	1000	|	|	|	...	|	|
227	Naumburg (Saale) Hbf ... **850** d.	...	...	...	0541	...	0638	0645	**3481**	...	|	0834	0851	...	|	|	...	1034	1033	1051	1051	1051	...	|	|
266	**Jena** Paradies ....d.	...	...	...	0606	0614j	...	0711	◧	...	0806	...	0917	...	1006	1006	...	...	...	1117	1117	1117	...	1206	1206
313	**Saalfeld** (Saale) ....d.	0433	...	0524	0634	0657	...	0741	0752	...	|	...	0946	0952	|	|	...	...	...	1146	1146	1146	1152	|	|
377	Kronach ....d.	0533	...	0629	|	0803	...	|	0841	...	|	...	|	1041	|	|	...	...	...	|	|	|	1241	|	|
400	Lichtenfels ....d.	0555	0628	0651	0729	0826	...	0832	0853	...	0925	...	|	1053	1125	1125	...	...	...	|	|	|	1253	1325	1325
432	**Bamberg** ....d.	...	0647	...	0745	...	...	0849	...	...	0942	...	|	...	1142	1142	...	...	...	|	|	|	...	1342	1342
470	Erlangen ....d.	...	0707	...	|	...	...	0908	...	...	1002	...	|	...	1202	1202	...	...	...	|	|	|	...	1402	1402
494	**Nürnberg** Hbf ....a.	...	0725	...	0820	...	...	0930	...	...	1020	...	1125	...	1228	1228	...	...	...	1325	1325	1325	...	1420	1420
	München Hbf **904** ....a.	...	0840	...	0948	...	...	1122*	...	...	1149	...	1250	...	1422*	1422*	...	...	...	1450	1450	1450	...	1543	1549

	IC 2150 2250	ICE 1509	RE 3487	ICE 1611	IC 2254 2356	ICE 109	RE 3489	ICE 1613	IC 2354	ICE 1213	RE 3491	ICE 1615	IC 2352	ICE 1515	X 80004	ICE 1617	ICE 1617	IC 2350	ICE 1517	ICE 1757	ICE 1619	ICE 893	CNL 1247	ICE 1621	IC 2016
								⊙				n		n			⑤⑦	⑦w	①–⑥	⑦w	⑥⑦	⑧q	Ⓡ	⑤f	⑦w
	🍷⊖	✕	◧	R✕	🍷⊖	N✕	◧	✕	🍷⊖	P✕	◧	S✕	🍷⊖	✕	●△	✕	y✕	🍷⊖	♣✕	♥✕	‡✕	✕	B🍷	✕	✕
Berlin Gesundbrunnen ....d.	1016§	1051	...	1138	1216	1250	...	1344	1431	1451	...	1540	...	1650	1658	1744	1744	1816	1842	1850	1942	...	...	2148	...
Hamburg Hbf **840** ....d.	|	|	...	|	|	|	...	|	|	|	...	|	...	|	|	|	|	|	|	|	|	1908	...	|	...
Berlin Hbf .... **850** d.	1039	1058	...	1152	1239	1258	...	1352	1439	1458	...	1552	1639	1657	1706	1752	1752	1839	1850	1858	1952	2055	2103	2155	2158
Berlin Südkreuz .... **850** d.	1046	1105	...	1159	1246	1305	...	1359	1446	1505	...	1559	1646	1705	|	1759	1759	1846	1857	1905	2000	2101	|	2201	2204
Lutherstadt Wittenberg .. **850** d.	1121	|	...	1235	1321	|	...	1435	1521	|	...	1635	1721	|	|	1835	1835	1921	|	|	2035	2138	|	2237	2239
Bitterfeld .... **850** d.	1138	|	...	|	1338	|	...	|	1538	|	...	|	1738	|	|	|	|	1938	1948	|	|	|	|	|	|
Leipzig Hbf ....a.	|	1205	...	1305	|	1405	...	1505	|	1605	...	1705	|	1805	1830	1905	1905	|	2005	2005	2105	2209	|	2307	2309
Leipzig Hbf .... **850** d.	|	1216	...	1311	|	1416	...	1511	|	1616	...	1711	|	1816	▬	...	1911	|	2020	2012	▬	...	|	...	...
Halle (Saale) Hbf .... **850** d.	1200	|	...	|	1400	|	...	|	1600	|	...	|	1800	|	*RE*	...	|	2000	|	|	*RE*	...	|	...	...
Naumburg (Saale) Hbf ... **850** d.	1234	1251	...	|	1434	1451	...	|	1634	1651	...	|	1834	1851	**3493**	...	|	2033	2052	2052	**3495**	...	|	...	...
Jena Paradies ....d.	...	1317	...	1406	...	1517	...	1606	...	1717	...	1806	...	1917		...	2006	...	2117	2117		...	|	...	...
Saalfeld (Saale) ....d.	...	1346	1352	|	...	1546	1552	|	...	1746	1752	|	...	1946	1952	...	|	...	2146	2146	2152	...	|	...	...
Kronach ....d.	...	|	1441	|	...	|	1641	|	...	|	1841	|	...	|	2041	...	|	...	|	|	2247	...	|	...	...
Lichtenfels ....d.	...	|	1453	1525	...	|	1653	1725	...	|	1853	1925	...	|	2053	...	2125	...	2236	2236	2310	...	|	...	...
Bamberg ....d.	...	|	...	1542	...	|	...	1742	...	|	...	1942	...	2050	...	...	2142	...	2253	2253	...	...	|	...	...
Erlangen ....d.	...	|	...	1602	...	|	...	1802	...	|	...	2002	...	|	...	...	2202	...	2313	2313	...	...	|	...	...
Nürnberg Hbf ....a.	...	1525	...	1628	...	1725	...	1828	...	1925	...	2028	...	2126	...	...	2220	...	2334	2334	...	...	|	...	...
München Hbf **904** ....a.	...	1650	...	1822*	...	1838	...	2023*	...	2050	...	2225*	...	2251	...	...	2351w	...	0059	0059	...	...	0705	...	...

	ICE 790	ICE 1518	RB 16918	RB 16900	ICE 1616	CNL 1246	RB 16902	ICE 1516	RB 16842	ICE 1614	X 80003	RE 3480	ICE 1514	ICE 1514	ICE 1714	IC 2353	ICE 1612	RE 3482	ICE 1512	IC 2355	ICE 1610	RE 3484	ICE 108	IC 2357	ICE 1608
	①–⑥	①g	©v	Ⓐn	①–⑤	Ⓡ	Ⓐn	v	①–⑥	①–⑥			①–⑤	⑧m	⑥k		①–⑥								
	e✕				a✕	A🍷		✕		e S	●△		a✕	✕	✕	🍷⊖	e✕	◧	✕	🍷⊖	✕	◧	N✕	🍷⊖	✕
München Hbf **904** ....d.	...	0012	...	...	...	2051	...	...	...	✕	...	...	0431*	...	0516	...	0530*	...	0719	...	0743*	...	0920	...	0945*
Nürnberg Hbf ....d.	...	0222	...	...	...	|	...	...	...	0520	...	...	0634	...	0634	...	0737	...	0833	...	0937	...	1033	...	1137
Erlangen ....d.	...	0243	...	...	...	|	...	...	...	0540	...	...	|	...	|	...	0756	...	|	...	0956	...	|	...	1156
Bamberg ....d.	...	0304	...	...	...	|	...	...	...	0601	...	...	|	...	|	...	0816	...	|	...	1016	...	|	...	1216
Lichtenfels ....d.	...	0322	...	...	...	|	...	...	0543	0621	...	0704	|	...	|	...	0833	0904	|	...	1033	1104	|	...	1233
Kronach ....d.	...	|	...	...	...	|	...	...	0607	|	...	0717	|	...	|	...	|	0917	|	...	|	1117	|	...	|
Saalfeld (Saale) ....d.	...	0414	0428	0436	...	|	0508	...	0709	0717	...	0808	0815	...	0815	...	|	1008	1015	...	|	1208	1215	...	|
Jena Paradies ....d.	...	0441	0525	0525	...	|	0549	...	...	0744	...	...	0843	...	0843	...	0954	...	1043	...	1154	...	1243	...	1354
Naumburg (Saale) Hbf ... **850** d.	...	0504	0558	0558	...	|	0625	0715	...	|	...	...	0908	...	0908	0924	|	...	1108	1124	|	...	1308	1324	|
Halle (Saale) Hbf .... **850** a.	...	|	|	|	...	|	0707	|	...	|	...	...	|	...	|	0958	|	...	|	1158	|	...	|	1358	|
Leipzig Hbf .... **850** a.	...	0548	*0641*	*0641*	...	|	...	0747	...	0846	...	...	0946	...	0946	|	1046	...	1146	|	1246	...	1346	|	1446
Leipzig Hbf ....d.	0551t	...	...	...	0651	|	...	0751	...	0851	0925	...	0951	0951	0951	|	1051	...	1151	|	1251	...	1351	|	1451
Bitterfeld .... **850** d.	|	...	...	...	0709	|	...	|	...	|	|	...	|	|	|	1020	|	...	|	1220	|	...	|	1420	|
Lutherstadt Wittenberg .. **850** d.	|	...	...	...	0725	|	...	|	...	0922	|	...	|	|	|	1036	1122	...	|	1236	1322	...	|	1436	1522
Berlin Südkreuz .... **850** a.	0653	...	...	...	0800	|	...	0853	...	1006	|	...	1103	1103	1103	1115	1206	...	1303	1310	1406	...	1503	1509	1606
Berlin Hbf .... **850** a.	0700	...	...	...	0807	0828	...	0900	...	1013	1050	...	1110	1110	1110	1123	1213	...	1310	1316	1413	...	1510	1518	1613
Hamburg Hbf **840** ....a.	0852	...	...	...	|	...	...	|	...	|	|	...	|	|	|	|	|	...	|	|	|	...	|	|	|
Berlin Gesundbrunnen ....a.	...	...	...	...	0815	...	...	0907	...	1022	1103	...	1117	1117	1117	1142	1223	...	1317	1342	1423	...	1517	1525	1623

	RE 3486	ICE 1208	IC 2157 2257	ICE 1606	RE 3488	ICE 1206	IC 2259 2359	ICE 1604	ICE 1704	X 80005	RE 3490	ICE 1504	IC 2151	IC 2151	ICE 1602	ICE 290	ICE 1655	RE 3492	ICE 1502	IC 2153	ICE 1600	RE 3494	ICE 1500	ICE 1500	ICE 1647 1747
								⑧q	⑥x					⑥⑦r	⑧q	⑥u	⑧q		n	⑦w	⑤⑦		n	⑦w	
	◧	P✕	🍷⊖	R✕	◧	P✕	⑧c	✕	✕	△	◧	✕	🍷⊖	🍷⊖	D✕	✕⊖	✕⊖	◧	✕	⊖	b✕		✕	✕	⊖
München Hbf **904** ....d.	...	1119	...	1225	...	1319z	🍷⊖	1341*	1341*	...	...	1519	...	...	1621	...	...	...	1719	...	1745*	...	1919	1919	...
Nürnberg Hbf ....d.	...	1233	...	1337	...	1433	...	1537	1537	...	...	1633	...	...	1737	...	...	...	1833	...	1937	...	2034	2034	...
Erlangen ....d.	...	|	...	1356	...	|	...	1556	1556	...	...	|	...	...	1756	...	...	...	|	...	1956	...	2055	2055	...
Bamberg ....d.	...	|	...	1416	...	|	...	1616	1616	...	...	|	...	...	1816	...	...	...	|	...	2016	...	2115	2115	...
Lichtenfels ....d.	1304	|	...	1433	1504	|	...	1633	1633	...	1704	|	...	...	1833	...	...	1904	|	...	2033	2103	2133	2133	...
Kronach ....d.	1317	|	...	|	1517	|	...	|	|	...	1717	|	...	...	|	...	...	1917	|	...	|	2118	|	|	...
Saalfeld (Saale) ....d.	1408	1415	...	|	1608	1615	...	|	|	...	1808	1815	...	...	|	...	...	2008	2015	...	2127	2208	2225	2225	...
Jena Paradies ....d.	...	1443	...	1555	...	1643	...	1754	1754	...	...	1843	...	...	1954	...	...	...	2043	...	2156	...	2252	2252	...
Naumburg (Saale) Hbf ... **850** d.	...	1508	1524	|	...	1708	1724	|	|	...	...	1908	1924	1924	|	...	...	...	2108	2128	2219	...	2316	2316	2325
Halle (Saale) Hbf .... **850** a.	...	|	1558	|	...	|	1758	|	|	...	...	|	1958	1958	|	...	...	...	|	2200	|	...	|	|	2353
Leipzig Hbf .... **850** a.	...	1546	|	1646	...	1746	|	1846	1846	...	...	1946	...	|	2046	...	...	...	2146	...	2250	...	2355	2355	...
Leipzig Hbf ....d.	...	1551	|	1651	...	1751	|	1851	1851	1855	...	1951	...	|	...	2051	2051	...	2149	...	2259	...	...	2359	...
Bitterfeld .... **850** d.	...	|	1620	|	...	|	1820	|	|	|	...	|	...	2020	...	|	|	...	|	...	|	...	...	|	...
Lutherstadt Wittenberg .. **850** d.	...	|	1636	1722	...	|	1836	1922	1922	|	...	|	...	2036	...	|	2122	...	|	...	2334	...	...	0035	...
Berlin Südkreuz .... **850** a.	...	1703	1710	1800	...	1903	1910	2000	2008	|	...	2053	...	2110	...	2152	2205	...	2249	...	0018	...	...	0120	...
Berlin Hbf .... **850** a.	...	1710	1719	1810	...	1910	1918	2015	2015	2014	...	2105	...	2118	...	2159	2212	...	2256	...	0025	...	...	0127	...
Hamburg Hbf **840** ....a.	...	|	|	|	...	|	|	2156	|	...	...	2305	...	|	...	|	|	...	0033	...	|	...	...	|	...
Berlin Gesundbrunnen ....a.	...	1717	1755	1819	...	1917	1942	...	2022	...	...	...	...	2125	...	2208	2221	...	...	...	0032	...	...	0134	...

A – CAPELLA – 🛏 1, 2 cl., 🛏 2 cl. and 💺 (reclining) München - Berlin. From May 1 runs with train number **1244** and arrives Berlin Hbf 0856. See overnight trains summary on page 361 for other calling points.
B – CAPELLA – 🛏 1, 2 cl., 🛏 2 cl. and 💺 (reclining) Berlin - München. From Apr. 30 runs with train number **1245** and departs Berlin Hbf 2006. See overnight trains summary on page 361 for other calling points.
D – To / from Dresden (Table **842**).
N – From / to Innsbruck via Kufstein (Table **951**).
P – From / to Innsbruck via Garmisch on dates in Table **895**.
R – 💺 and ✕ Warnemünde - Rostock - Berlin - München and v.v. See Table **835** for running dates and timings from / to Warnemünde.
S – To / from Warnemünde via Rostock on ⑥ from June 5 (Table **835**).

a – Not Dec. 24, 25, 31, Jan. 1, Apr. 2, 5, May 24.
b – Also Dec. 23, 30, Apr. 1, 5, May 12, 24, June 2; not Dec. 25, Jan. 1, Apr. 2, 4, May 14, 23, June 4.
c – Not Dec. 24, 25, 31, Jan. 1, Apr. 2, 4, May 13, 14, 23.
d – Not Dec. 24, 31, Jan. 6, June 3.
e – Not Dec. 25, 26, Jan. 1, Apr. 3, 5, May 24.
f – Also Dec. 23, 30, Apr. 1, May 12; not Dec. 25, Jan. 1, Apr. 2, May 14.
g – Also Apr. 6, May 25; not Apr. 5, May 24.
h – Also Dec. 25, 26, Jan. 1, Apr. 3, 5, May 24.
j – 0612 (not Dec. 24, 31).
k – Also Dec. 24, 31, Apr. 2; not Dec. 26, Apr. 3.
m – Also Dec. 26, Apr. 3; not Dec. 24, 31, Apr. 2.
n – Not Dec. 24, 31.
q – Not Dec. 24, 25, 31, Apr. 2, 4, May 23.
r – Also Dec. 24, 25, 31, Jan. 1, Apr. 2, 5, May 24.
t – 0545 on ① (also Apr. 6, May 25).
u – Also Dec. 24, 25, 31, Apr. 2, 4, May 23.
v – Not Dec. 25, Jan. 1.
w – ⑦ (also Apr. 5, May 24; not Apr. 4, May 23).
x – Also Dec. 25, Apr. 2, 4, May 23.
y – Also Dec. 23, 30, Apr. 1, 5, May 12, 24; not Dec. 25, Jan. 1, Apr. 2, 4, May 14, 23.
z – 1315 on ⑦w.

‡ – Also Dec. 25, Apr. 2, 5, May 24.
⊙ – On Dec. 24, 31 runs Berlin - Leipzig only.
⊖ – See also Table **850**.
§ – 1029 on ⑦w.
♣ – ①–⑥ (also Apr. 4, May 23; not Dec. 24, 31, Apr. 5, May 24). Conveys 💺 (*ICE* **1717**) Berlin - Bitterfeld - Halle - Erfurt (Table **850**).
♥ – Conveys 💺 (*ICE* **1737**) Berlin - Naumburg - Erfurt - Frankfurt.
◧ – To / from Bayreuth and Hof (Table **876**).
△ – *InterConnex*. Operated by Veolia Verkehr GmbH. **DB tickets are not valid.**
● – To / from Warnemünde via Rostock (Table **835**).
* – Earlier arrival / later departure possible by changing trains at Nürnberg (Table **904**).

COTTBUS - LEIPZIG — 852

RE / RB services

Service to Mar. 13. See page 542 for service from Mar. 14.

km											
		⚒									
0	**Cottbus** ● d.	0503	0703	0903	1103	1303	1503	1703	1903	2002	2302
24	Calau (Niederl) ● d.	0521	0721	0921	1121	1321	1521	1721	1921	2020	2320
46	Finsterwalde ● d.	0534	0734	0934	1134	1334	1534	1734	1934	2035	2335
56	Doberlug-Kirchhain ● d.	0542	0742	0942	1142	1342	1542	1742	1942	2043	2343
79	Falkenberg (Elster) ● a.	0558	0758	0958	1158	1358	1558	1758	1958	2109	0009
79	Falkenberg (Elster) **856** d.	0558	0758	0958	1158	1358	1558	1758	1958	...	...
97	Torgau **856** d.	0612	0812	1012	1212	1412	1612	1812	2012	...	...
124	Eilenburg **856** d.	0640	0840	1040	1240	1440	1640	1840	2040	...	...
149	**Leipzig** Hbf **856** a.	0700	0900	1100	1300	1500	1700	1900	2100	...	...

			⚒						
Leipzig Hbf **856** d.	...	*0607*	0707	0907	1107	1307	1507	1707	1907	2107
Eilenburg **856** d.	...	*0628*	0728	0928	1128	1328	1528	1728	1928	2128
Torgau **856** d.	...	*0650*	0750	0950	1150	1350	1550	1750	1950	2150
Falkenberg (Elster) **856** a.	...	*0708*	0802	1002	1202	1402	1602	1802	2002	2202
Falkenberg (Elster) ♥ d.	0526	0730	0803	1003	1203	1403	1603	1803	2003	2203
Doberlug-Kirchhain ♥ d.	0549	0749	0816	1016	1216	1416	1616	1816	2016	2216
Finsterwalde ♥ d.	0557	0756	0823	1023	1223	1423	1623	1823	2023	2223
Calau (Niederl) ♥ d.	0611	0810	0836	1036	1236	1436	1636	1836	2036	2236
Cottbus ♥ a.	0631	0830	0856	1056	1256	1456	1656	1856	2056	2256

● – Additional trains Cottbus - Falkenberg at 0602 Ⓐ, 0802, 1202, 1402, 1602 and 1802.

♥ – Additional trains Falkenberg - Cottbus at 0623 Ⓐ, 0855, 1255, 1455, 1655 and 1855.

STEAM TRAINS IN SACHSEN — 853

km										
		Ⓐe							⊡	
	Dresden Hbf (S-Bahn) **857** d.	*0430*	...	*0800*	*1000*	*1230*	*1400*	*1630*	*1800*	...
0	Radebeul Ost d.	0456	...	0826	1026	1256	1426	1656	1826	...
8	Moritzburg d.	0525	...	0853	1055	1323	1455	1723	1853	...
16	Radeburg a.	0546	...	...	1116	...	1516	...	...	...

	Ⓐe								⊡
Radeburg d.	0611	...	...	...	1139	...	1539	...	...
Moritzburg d.	0634	...	0903	...	1203	1333	1603	1733	1903
Radebeul Ost a.	0701	...	0930	...	1230	1400	1630	1800	1930
Dresden Hbf (S-Bahn) **857** a.	*0723*	...	*0955*	...	*1255*	*1423*	*1655*	*1823*	*1955*

km																								
				🍷	©d‡		🍷		©d‡		🍷		©d‡		🍷			©d		🍷	🍷	🍷	🍷	🍷	🍷
0	Zittau d.	High season	0900	0919	0955	...	1119	...	1155	...	1319	...	1355	...	1519	...	...	1722	Low season	0919	...	...	1339	...	...
9	Bertsdorf d.	★	0950	0950	1035	1041	1150	1150	1235	1241	1350	1350	1435	1441	1550	1550	1641	1753	♣	0950	1040	1130	1410	1502	1551
12	Kurort Oybin a.	→	|	1002	|	1053	1202	|	|	1253	1402	|	|	1453	1602	|	|	1805	→	1002	|	1142	1422	|	1603
13	Kurort Jonsdorf a.		1001	...	1046	...	...	1201	1246	...	...	1401	1446	...	...	1601	1652	...		...	1052	...	...	1513	...

			🍷		©d‡		🍷		©d‡		🍷		©d‡		🍷		©d		🍷	🍷	🍷	🍷	🍷	🍷
Kurort Jonsdorf d.	High season	1014	...	...	1106	1214	...	...	1306	1414	...	...	1506	1614	...	1738	...	Low season	...	1103	...	...	1525	...
Kurort Oybin d.	★	|	1014	1105	|	|	1214	1305	|	|	1414	1505	|	|	1614	|	1816	♣	1014	|	1156	1435	|	1614
Bertsdorf d.	→	1026	1026	1116	1118	1226	1226	1316	1318	1426	1426	1516	1518	1626	1626	1753	1829	→	1025	1115	1209	1446	1537	1626
Zittau a.		...	1053	...	1147	...	1253	...	1347	...	1453	...	1547	...	1653	1820	1856		...	...	1238	...	...	1653

Operators: Radebeul service – BVO Bahn GmbH, Betriebsleitung Lößnitzgrundbahn, Am Bahnhof 1, 01468 Moritzburg. ✆ +49 (0) 35207 89290. www.loessnitzgrundbahn.de
Zittau service – SOEG - Sächisch Oberlausitzer Eisenbahngesellschaft mbH, Bahnhofstraße 41, 02763 Zittau. ✆ +49 (0) 3583 540540. www.soeg-zittau.de

d – © from Apr. 24 (also May 14, June 3, 4).
e – Not Dec. 23 - Jan. 1, Feb. 8–19, Apr. 1–9, May 14.
⊡ – From Apr. 2.
‡ – Diesel train.
★ – Dec. 19 - Jan. 3, Jan. 30 - Feb. 21, Mar. 27 - Apr. 11 and from Apr. 24.
♣ – Dec. 13–18, Jan. 4–29, Feb. 22 - Mar. 26, Apr. 12–23.

SEUSSLITZ - DRESDEN - BAD SCHANDAU — 853a

Mar. 27 - Oct. 31, 2010

Special dates: May 1 "Steamship Parade", May 12 "Riverboat - Shuffle", Aug. 14 "Fleet Parade". Contact the operator for service details on these dates.

	A	B			A	A	A	A		A	A	C
Seußlitz d.	...	...	...	...	...	...	...	...	...	...	1315	...
Meißen d.	...	...	...	...	...	...	...	...	...	...	1445	1615
Radebeul d.	...	...	...	...	...	...	...	...	...	...	1630	1800
Dresden ⊡ d.	...	0830	0900	1000	1030	...	1200	1330	1400	1600	1800	1930
Pillnitz d.	...	1020	1050	1130	1200	...	1330	1500	1530	1730	...	...
Pirna d.	0930	1130	1200	...	1300	1430	...	1600	...	...	...	...
Königstein d.	1130	1400	1430	...	1500	1630	...	1800	...	...	...	...
Bad Schandau a.	1215	...	...	...	1600	1715	...	1845	...	...	...	...

	A		A	C	A		A	B		A	A	A
Bad Schandau d.	...	...	0930	...	...	...	1230	...	...	...	1630	1730
Königstein d.	...	...	1000	...	...	...	1300	1430	1500	...	1700	1800
Pirna d.	...	...	1115	...	...	...	1415	1600	1630	...	1815	1915
Pillnitz d.	...	1145	1200	...	1345	1545	...	1645	1715	1745	1900	...
Dresden ⊡ d.	0945	1245	1300	1415	1445	1645	...	1800	1830	1845	2000	...
Radebeul d.	1045	...	...	1515	...	...	...	...	...	...	...	...
Meißen d.	1145	...	...	1615	...	...	...	...	...	...	...	...
Seußlitz a.	1245	...	...	...	...	...	...	...	...	...	...	...

A – Apr. 24 - Oct. 17.
B – ④⑤⑥ Apr. 24 - Oct. 16.
C – May 2 - Oct. 3.
⊡ – Dresden Terrassenufer.

Operator: Sächsische Dampfschiffahrts GmbH & Co. Conti Elbschiffahrts KG.
Hertha-Lindner Straße 10, D-01067 Dresden. ✆ +49 (0) 351 866 090, Fax +49 (0) 351 866 09 88.

COTTBUS - GÖRLITZ - ZITTAU — 854

ODEG ★ 2nd class only

km																										
		Ⓐe	Ⓐe	Ⓐe								Ⓐe											⚒e	Ⓐe		
0	**Cottbus** d.	...	...	0503	...	0603	0703	0803	0903	1003	1103	1103	1203	1303	1403	1503	1603	1703	1803	1903	2003	2103	2103	2203	2303	...
24	Spremberg d.	...	...	0522	...	0622	0722	0822	0922	1022	1121	1122	1222	1322	1422	1522	1622	1722	1822	1921	2022	2122	2122	2222	2322	...
42	Weißwasser d.	...	0433	0535	0535	0635	0735	0835	0935	1035	...	1135	1235	1335	1435	1535	1635	1735	1835	...	2035	2135	2135	2235	2342	...
72	Horka d.	...	0457	0600	0600	0700	0800	0900	1000	1100	...	1200	1300	1400	1500	1600	1700	1800	1900	...	2100	2200	2200	2300	0003	...
93	**Görlitz** a.	...	0512	0615	0615	0715	0815	0915	1015	1115	...	1215	1315	1415	1515	1615	1715	1815	1915	...	2115	2215	2215	2315	0018	...
93	**Görlitz** d.	0417	0520	0620	0620	0719	0820	0920	1021	1119	...	1219	1317	1419	1520	1617	1720	1820	1919	...	2120	...	2220	...	...	...
127	**Zittau** a.	0456	0554	0654	0654	0758	0854	0954	1055	1158	...	1258	1356	1458	1554	1656	1754	1854	1958	...	2154	...	2254	...	...	...

	Ⓐe	Ⓐe							Ⓐe													Ⓐ			
Zittau d.	...	0404	...	0501	0601	0706	0801	0901	1003	...	1106	1206	1304	1406	1501	1604	1701	...	1906	...	2101	2201	...	...	...
Görlitz a.	...	0438	...	0540	0640	0740	0840	0940	1040	...	1140	1240	1338	1440	1540	1638	1740	...	1940	...	2140	2240	...	...	...
Görlitz d.	0346	0441	0441	0544	0644	0744	0844	0944	1045	...	1144	1244	1344	1444	1544	1644	1744	...	1944	...	2144	2244	...	...	...
Horka d.	0401	0456	0456	0558	0658	0758	0858	0958	1058	...	1158	1258	1358	1458	1558	1658	1758	...	1958	...	2158	2258	...	...	...
Weißwasser d.	0425	0520	0520	0620	0720	0820	0920	1020	1120	...	1220	1320	1420	1520	1620	1720	1820	...	2020	...	2220	2319	...	...	...
Spremberg d.	0438	0538	0538	0638	0738	0838	0938	1038	1138	1138	1238	1338	1438	1538	1638	1738	1838	1938	2038	...	2238	...	...	...	...
Cottbus a.	0457	0557	0557	0657	0757	0857	0957	1057	1157	1157	1257	1357	1457	1557	1657	1757	1857	1957	2057	...	2257	...	...	...	...

e – Not Dec. 24, 31.

★ – Ostdeutsche Eisenbahn GmbH ✆ +49 (0) 3581 764 89 10. www.odeg.info

DRESDEN - GÖRLITZ and ZITTAU — 855

RE / RB services

km																										
			⚒			r												m							n	n
0	**Dresden** Hbf d.	0532	0609	0637	0709	0732	0809	0909	1009	1109	1209	1309	1331	1409	1509	1609	1709	1731	1809	1909	2009	2109	2209	2209	2309	2340
4	Dresden Neustadt d.	0540	0616	0645	0716	0737	0816	0916	1016	1116	1216	1316	1337	1416	1516	1616	1716	1737	1816	1916	2016	2116	2215	2215	2316	2346
41	Bischofswerda d.	0621	0645	0720	0745	|	0845	0945	1045	1145	1245	1345	|	1445	1545	1645	1745	|	1845	1945	2045	2145	2255	2258	2345	0022
79	Ebersbach (Sachs) d.	0702	|	|	0814	|	|	1014	|	1214	|	1414	|	|	1614	|	1814	|	|	2014	|	2214	2332	|	0014	|
83	Neugersdorf d.	0706	|	|	0819	|	|	1019	|	1219	|	1419	|	|	1619	|	1819	|	|	2019	|	2219	2336	|	0019	|
105	**Zittau** a.	0729	|	|	0838	|	|	1038	|	1238	|	1438	|	|	1638	|	1838	|	|	2038	|	2238	2358	|	0038	|
	Liberec **1117** a.	...	|	|	0918	|	|	...	|	1318	|	...	|	|	1718	|	...	|	|	2118n	|	...	...	|	...	|
	Bautzen d.	...	0657	0735	**T**	0812	0857	...	1057	...	1257	...	1412	1457	**W**	1657	...	1812	1857	...	2057	...	...	2313	...	0036
	Löbau (Sachs) d.	...	0711	0754	...	|	0911	...	1111	...	1311	...	|	1511	...	1711	...	|	1911	...	2111	...	...	2332	...	0055
	Görlitz a.	...	0726	0815	...	0840	0926	...	1126	...	1326	...	1440	1526	...	1726	...	1840	1926	...	2126	...	...	2352	...	0116
	Wrocław Gł **1085** a.	...	...	...	...	1102	...	...	...	...	...	...	1702	...	...	...	...	2102	...	...	...	...	...	...	...	...

km																										
		⚒n	v		⚒			r														m			n	n
	Wrocław Gł **1085** d.	...	...	...	...	...	...	0705	...	...	...	...	...	...	1305	...	...	...	...	...	...	1805	...	...	...	...
0	**Görlitz** d.	...	...	0545	0645	...	0826	0921	...	1026	...	1226	...	1426	1521	...	1626	...	1826	...	1945	2021	...	2145	2234	...
24	Löbau (Sachs) d.	...	...	0600	0700	...	0841	|	...	1041	...	1241	...	1441	|	...	1641	...	1841	...	2006	|	...	2206	2255	...
46	Bautzen d.	...	...	0613	0715	...	0855	0949	...	1055	...	1255	**T**	1455	1549	...	1655	...	1855	...	2024	2049	**W**	2224	2313	...
	Liberec **1117** d.	...	...	|	|	...	|	|	0838	|	...	|	1238	|	|	...	|	1638	|	...	|	|	2035n	|	|	...
	Zittau d.	0354	0515	|	|	0719	|	|	0919	|	1119	|	1319	|	|	1519	|	1719	|	1919	|	|	2119	|	|	2225
	Neugersdorf d.	0418	0535	|	|	0739	|	|	0939	|	1139	|	1339	|	|	1539	|	1739	|	1939	|	|	2139	|	|	2249
	Ebersbach (Sachs) d.	0423	0539	|	|	0743	|	|	0943	|	1143	|	1343	|	|	1543	|	1743	|	1943	|	|	2143	|	|	2253
65	Bischofswerda d.	0501	0609	0625	0726	0814	0907	|	1014	1107	1214	1307	1414	1507	|	1614	1707	1814	1907	2014	2040	|	2214	2240	2328	2331
102	Dresden Neustadt a.	0534	0639	0653	0753	0842	0934	1025	1042	1134	1242	1334	1442	1534	1625	1642	1734	1842	1934	2042	2114	2125	2242	2314	...	0005
106	**Dresden** Hbf a.	0545	0645	0659	0800	0850	0945	1030	1050	1145	1250	1348	1450	1545	1630	1650	1748	1850	1945	2050	2121	2130	2250	2321	...	0012

T – To / from Tanwald on ⑥⑦ (also Dec. 24, 25, Jan. 1, Apr. 5). See Table **1141**.
W – To / from Tanwald on ⑥⑦ (also Dec. 25, Jan. 1, Apr. 5). See Table **1141**.
m – Not Dec. 24.
n – Not Dec. 24, 31.
r – Not Jan. 1.
v – Not Dec. 25, Jan. 1.

856 DRESDEN and LEIPZIG - RUHLAND - COTTBUS and HOYERSWERDA *RE services*

Service to Mar. 13. See page 542 for service from Mar. 14.

km	km																							
					v								⊠										n	r
	0	**Dresden** Hbf .. 842 843 857 d.	...	...	0541	...	...	0645	0741	...	...	0845		1741	...	...	1845	1941	...	...	2045	...	2141	...
	18	Coswig .... 842 843 857 d.	...	...	0604	...	...	0704	0804	...	...	0904		1804	...	...	1904	2004	...	...	2104	...	2204	...
0		**Leipzig** Hbf .... 852 d.	...	...	|	...	0607	|	|	...	0807	|	each train	|	...	1807	|	|	...	2007	|	...	|	2316
25		Eilenburg .... 852 d.	...	...	|	...	0628	|	|	...	0828	|		|	...	1828	|	|	...	2028	|	...	|	2341
52		Torgau .... 852 d.	...	...	|	...	0650	|	|	...	0850	|	runs every	|	...	1850	|	|	...	2050	|	...	|	0002
70		Falkenberg (Elster) .... 852 d.	0411a	E	|	0611a	0710	|	|	0811a	0910	|		|	1811e	1910	|	|	2011e	2110	|	...	|	0016
94		Elsterwerda-Biehla ◇ .... d.	0431a	0524	|	0631a	0734	|	|	0831a	0934	|	two hours	|	1831e	1934	|	|	2031e	2134	|	...	|	...
120	73	Ruhland .... a.	0452a	0546	0655	0652a	0755	0757	0855	0852a	0955	0957		1855	1852e	1955	1957	2055	2052e	2155	2157	...	2248	...
120	73	Ruhland .... d.	0505	0604	0656	0705	0802	0800	0856	0905	1002	1000	until	1856	1905	2002	2000	2056	2105	2202	2200	...	2256	...
145		Hoyerswerda ★ .... a.	|	|	0719	|	0825	|	0919	|	1025	|		1919	|	2025	|	2119	|	2225	|	...	2319	...
	86	Senftenberg .... d.	0516	0615	...	0716	...	0810	...	0916	...	1010		...	1916	...	2010	...	2116	...	2210	2348	...	...
	120	**Cottbus** .... 852 a.	0548	0648	...	0748	...	0840	...	0948	...	1040		...	1948	...	2040	...	2148	...	2240	0018	...	...

		v									⊡												n	
Cottbus .... 852 d.	0417	...	0514	...	0608	...	0714	...	0808	...		1513	...	1608	...	1714	...	1808	...	1914	...	2008	...	2208
Senftenberg .... d.	0446	...	0544	...	0640	...	0744	...	0840	...		1544	...	1640	...	1744	...	1840	...	1944	...	2040	...	2241
Hoyerswerda ★ .... d.	|	0438	|	0531	|	0638	|	0731	|	0838	each train	|	1531	|	1638	|	1731	|	1838	|	1931	|	2038	|
Ruhland .... a.	0457	0501	0553	0555	0651	0701	0753	0755	0851	0901		1553	1555	1651	1701	1753	1755	1851	1901	1953	1955	2051	2101	2252
Ruhland .... d.	0505a	0502	0600	0601	0705a	0702	0800	0801	0905a	0902	runs every	1600	1601	1705e	1702	1800	1801	1905e	1902	2000	2001	2105e	2102	2253
Elsterwerda-Biehla ◇ .... d.	0530a	|	|	0623	0728a	|	|	0823	0928a	|		|	1623	1728e	|	|	1823	1928e	|	|	2023	2128e	|	2316
Falkenberg (Elster) ..... 852 d.	0552a	|	|	0652	0750a	|	|	0852	0950a	|	two hours	|	1652	1750e	|	|	1852	1950e	|	|	2052	2150e	|	L
Torgau .... 852 d.	...	|	|	0712	...	|	|	0912	...	|		|	1712	...	|	|	1912	...	|	|	2112	...	|	...
Eilenburg .... 852 d.	...	|	|	0740	...	|	|	0940	...	|	until	|	1740	...	|	|	1940	...	|	|	2140	...	|	...
Leipzig Hbf .... 852 a.	...	|	|	0800	...	|	|	1000	...	|		|	1800	...	|	|	2000	...	|	|	2204	...	|	...
Coswig .... 842 843 857 d.	...	0552	0647	...	...	0752	0852	...	...	0952		1652	...	...	1752	1852	...	...	1952	2052	...	...	2152	...
Dresden Hbf ... 842 843 857 a.	...	0614	0703	...	...	0814	0908	...	...	1014		1708	...	...	1814	1908	...	...	2014	2108	...	...	2214	...

E – From Elsterwerda (d. 0521).
L – To Elsterwerda (a. 2319).
a – Ⓐ only.
d – Also Dec. 24, 31.
e – Ⓐ (not Dec. 24, 31).
n – Not Dec. 24, 31.
r – Not Dec. 31.

t – Ⓐ (not Dec. 23 - Jan. 1, Feb. 8 – 19). Journey time is 84 minutes.
v – Not Dec. 25, Jan. 1.
w – Ⓒ (daily Dec. 23 - Jan. 3, Feb. 6 – 21).
⊠ – The 1211 and 1411 from Falkenberg run daily throughout. The 1611 from Falkenberg does not run on Dec. 24, 31 between Falkenberg and Ruhland
⊡ – The 1208 and 1408 from Cottbus run daily throughout.

◇ – See Table **843** for connections from / to Elsterwerda.
★ – **Hoyerswerda - Görlitz** and v.v. *73 km*. Journey time: 60 – 72 minutes. Operated by Ostdeutsche Eisenbahn GmbH (ODEG). 2nd class only.
From Hoyerswerda at 0454 Ⓐ **e**, 0622 Ⓐ **e**, 0649 Ⓒ, 0832 Ⓐ, 1032, 1230, 1430, 1629, 1724 ⑦, 1832, 2032 and 2232.
From Görlitz at 0513 Ⓐ **e**, 0616 Ⓒ **d**, 0635 Ⓐ **e**, 0825, 1025, 1223 Ⓒ **w**, 1235 Ⓐ **t**, 1423 Ⓒ **w**, 1435 Ⓐ **t**, 1622, 1825 and 2025.

857 BAD SCHANDAU - DRESDEN - MEISSEN - LEIPZIG *RB / S-Bahn services*

km	S-Bahn																						
														n		①–⑥	⑦	⑦	⑥⑦	r	A	①⑦	
0	**Bad Schandau** ⊡ .... 1100 d.	0441a	0511f	0541a	0611	0641		1741	1811	1841	1911	1941	2011	...	2111	2211	2211	...	...	2311	2311	...	0011
23	Pirna .... d.	0505v	0535f	0605	0635	0705	and at	1805	1835	1905	1935	2005	2035	2105	2135	2235	2235	...	2305	2335	2335	...	0035
40	**Dresden** Hbf 842/3 856 1100 d.	0530	0600	0630	0700	0730	the same	1830	1900	1930	2000	2030	2100	2130	2200	2300	2300	...	2330	0000	0000	...	0058
44	**Dresden** Neustadt .. 842 856 d.	0537	0607	0637	0707	0737	minutes	1837	1907	1937r	2007	2037n	2107	2137	2207	2307	2306	...	2336	0006	0007	...	...
50	Radebeul Ost .... d.	0547	0617	0647	0717	0750	past each	1850	1917	1950r	2017	2050n	2117	2150	2217	2317	*2334**	...	*0004**	...	0017	...	...
58	Coswig .... 842/3 856 d.	0558	0628	0658	0728	0800	hour until	1900	1928	2000r	2028	2100n	2128	2200	2228	2328	*2351**	2358	*0021**	...	0028	0035	...
68	**Meißen** .... a.	0607	0637	0707	0737	0809		1909	1937	2009r	2037	2109n	2137	2209	2237	2337	...	0007	...	...	0037	0044	...

S-Bahn																						
		f								n		n	⑦	A	⑥	⑥⑦	⑦	①–⑥	①–⑤	r	A	②–⑥	①⑦
Meißen .... d.	...	0519	0546	0619		1846	1919	1946	2019	2046	2119	2149	2210	2219	2219	...	...	2249	2319	2352	2352	...	...
Coswig .... 842/3 856 d.	...	0528	0556	0628	and at	1856	1928	1956	2028	2056	2128	2158	2219	2228	2228	...	*2231**	2258	2328	0001	0001	...	*0007**
Radebeul Ost .... d.	...	0538	0605	0638	the same	1905	1938	2005	2038	2105	2138	2208	...	2238	2238	...	*2248**	2308	2338	...	0011	...	*0024**
Dresden Neustadt ...... 842 856 d.	...	0548	0616	0648	minutes	1916	1948	2016	2048	2116	2148	2218	...	2248	2248	2248	2318	2318	2348	...	0021	...	0054
Dresden Hbf . 842/3 856 1100 d.	0500	0600	0630	0700	past each	1930	2000	2030	2100	2130	2200	2230	...	2300	2300	2300	2330	2330	2355	...	0028	0034	0103
Pirna .... d.	0524	0624	0654	0724	hour until	1954	2024	2053	2124	2153	2224	2253	...	2324	2335	2335	2353	2353	...	...	...	0058	0126
Bad Schandau ⊡ .... 1100 a.	0546	0646	0716	0746		2016	2046	...	2146	...	2246	...	...	2346	2357	2357	...	...	...	...	...	0120	...

km											
0	**Meißen** .... d.	...	...	0725a	0925	1125	1325	1525	1725	1925	2125
21	Nossen .... d.	...	0556a	0756	0956	1156	1356	1556	1756	1956	2156
29	Roßwein .... d.	...	0606a	0806	1006	1206	1406	1606	1806	2006	2206
40	Döbeln Hbf .... d.	0526	0626	0826	1026	1226	1426	1626	1826	2026	2226
53	Leisnig .... d.	0539	0639	0839	1039	1239	1439	1639	1839	2039	2239
68	Großbothen .... d.	0556	0656	0856	1056	1256	1456	1656	1856	2056	2257
75	Grimma ob Bf .... d.	0604	0704	0904	1104	1304	1504	1704	1904	2104	2304
106	**Leipzig** Hbf .... a.	0640	0736	0936	1136	1336	1540	1740	1936	2136	2337

	Ⓐ										
Leipzig Hbf .... d.	...	0615	0815	1015	1215	1415	1615	1815	1915	2115	2317
Grimma ob Bf .... d.	...	0648	0848	1048	1248	1448	1648	1848	1948	2148	2349
Großbothen .... d.	...	0655	0855	1055	1255	1455	1655	1855	1955	2155	2356
Leisnig .... d.	...	0709	0909	1109	1309	1509	1709	1909	2009	2209	0010
Döbeln Hbf .... d.	0524	0724	0924	1124	1324	1524	1724	1924	2024	2224	0024
Roßwein .... d.	0536	0736	0936	1136	1336	1536	1736	1936	2036a	2236	...
Nossen .... d.	0551	0751	0951	1151	1351	1551	1751	1951	2046a	2246	...
Meißen .... a.	0616	0816	1016	1216	1416	1616	1816	2016	...	...	...

A – ①–⑤ (not Dec. 31). a – Ⓐ only. f – Not Jan. 1. n – Not Dec. 24, 31. r – Not Dec. 31. v – Not Dec. 25, Jan. 1. * – By 🚐

⊡ – A frequent ferry services links the railway station with Bad Schandau town centre. **Operator**: Oberelbische Verkehrsgesellschaft Pirna - Sebnitz mbH. ✆ +49 (0) 3501 7920. Depart Bad Schandau, Bahnhof 0700 and every 30 minutes until 2100 (10 minute journey). Depart Bad Schandau, Elbkai 0650 and every 30 minutes until 2050 (5 minute journey).

857a DRESDEN - DRESDEN FLUGHAFEN ✈ *S-Bahn*

km								
0	**Dresden** Hbf .... d.	0418	0448	and at the same	2248	2318	...	...
4	**Dresden** Neustadt ...... d.	0425	0455	minutes past	2255	2325	...	...
15	**Dresden** Flughafen ✈ a.	0440	0510	each hour until	2310	2340	...	...

Dresden Flughafen ✈ .... d.	0446	0516	and at the same	2316	2346	...	...	...
Dresden Neustadt .... a.	0459	0529	minutes past	2329	2359	...	...	...
Dresden Hbf .... a.	0507	0537	each hour until	2337	0007	...	...	...

858 CHEMNITZ / ZWICKAU - GERA - ERFURT *RB / RE services*

km		⑥k	Ⓐn	G	Ⓐn	⚒▶	⚒G	G	▶	G	▶	G	▶	G	▶	G	▶	G	▶	L	Ⓒp	n▶	n	n
0	**Chemnitz** Hbf .... 880 d.	...	...	...	...	0625n	...	...	0825	...	1025	...	1225	...	1425	...	1625	...	1825	...	*1859*	2025	...	...
32	Glauchau (Sachs) .... 880 d.	...	...	...	...	0652n	...	...	0852	...	1052	...	1252	...	1452	...	1652	...	1852	...	1927	2052	...	...
	Zwickau (Sachs) Hbf .. 881 d.	...	...	...	...	|	0658n	...	|	0858	|	1058	|	1258	|	1458	|	1658	|	1858	|	|	2058	...
	Werdau .... 881 d.	...	...	...	...	|	0707n	...	|	0907	|	1107	|	1307	|	1507	|	1707	|	1907	|	|	2107	...
48	Gößnitz .... 881 a.	...	...	...	...	0713n	0722n	...	0913	0922	1113	1122	1313	1322	1513	1522	1713	1722	1913	1922	1947	2113	2122	...
48	Gößnitz .... d.	...	...	...	...	—	0727n	...	—	0927	—	1127	—	1327	—	1527	—	1727	—	1927	1948	—	2127	...
83	**Gera** Hbf .... a.	...	...	...	...	...	0756n	...	...	0956	...	1156	...	1356	...	1556	...	1756	...	1956	2023	n	2156	...
83	**Gera** Hbf .... d.	0437	0443	0601	0624	0702	0802	0802	0902	1002	1102	1202	1302	1402	1502	1602	1702	1802	1902	2002	...	2133	2203	2337
123	Göschwitz (Saale) .... d.	0508	0518	0628	0652	0729	0829	0829	0929	1029	1129	1229	1329	1429	1529	1629	1729	1829	1929	2029	...	2210	2230	0013
128	**Jena** West .... d.	0513	0523	0634	0658	0735	0835	0835	0935	1035	1135	1235	1335	1435	1535	1635	1735	1835	1935	2035	...	2215	2235	0018
151	Weimar .... 849 850 d.	0534	0546	0650	0717	0751	0851	0851	0951	1051	1151	1251	1351	1451	1551	1651	1751	1851	1951	2051	...	2236	2302z	0039
172	**Erfurt** Hbf .... 849 850 a.	*0557*	0602	0706	0730	0807	0907	0907	1007	1107	1207	1307	1407	1507	1607	1707	1807	1907	2007	2107	...	*2257*	2318	*0101*

	w	w	⚒n	⚒n	Ⓐn	⑥	Ⓒp		G	G		G		G		G		G		G		G	n	n
Erfurt Hbf .... 849 850 d.	0020	0437	...	...	*0516e*	...	...	0644	0749	0849	0949	1049	1149	1249	1349	1449	1549	1649	1749	1849	1949	2049	2149	*2312*
Weimar .... 849 850 d.	0050	0456	...	...	0545	0622	...	0701	0806	0906	1006	1106	1206	1306	1406	1506	1606	1706	1806	1906	2006	2106	2206	2334
Jena West .... d.	0110	0517	...	...	0606	0644	...	0723	0823	0923	1023	1123	1223	1323	1423	1523	1623	1723	1823	1923	2023	2123	2223	2354
Göschwitz (Saale) .... d.	0114	0522	...	...	0611	0649	...	0728	0828	0928	1028	1128	1228	1328	1428	1528	1628	1728	1828	1928	2028	2128	2228	0006
Gera Hbf .... a.	...	0554	...	...	0646	0724	...	0754	0854	0954	1054	1154	1254	1354	1454	1554	1654	1754	1854	1954	2054	2154	2254	0042
Gera Hbf .... d.	...	...	0600	...	...	...	0734	0800	—	1000	—	1200	—	1400	—	1600	—	1800	—	2000n	—	...	...	...
Gößnitz .... a.	...	...	0629	◄	...	...	0810	0829	◄	1029	◄	1229	◄	1429	◄	1629	◄	1829	◄	2029n	n◄	...	...	...
Gößnitz .... 881 d.	...	...	0632	0637	...	...	0811	0833	0837	1032	1037	1232	1237	1433	1437	1632	1637	1832	1837	2032n	2037	...	...	...
Werdau .... 881 d.	...	...	0648	|	...	...	|	0849	|	1048	|	1248	|	1449	|	1648	|	1848	|	2048n	|	...	...	...
Zwickau (Sachs) Hbf ... 881 a.	...	...	0656	|	...	...	|	0856	|	1056	|	1256	|	1456	|	1656	|	1856	|	2056n	|	...	...	...
Glauchau (Sachs) .... 880 d.	...	...	...	0702	...	...	0830	...	0902	...	1102	...	1302	...	1502	...	1702	...	1902	...	2102	...	...	...
Chemnitz Hbf .... 880 a.	...	...	...	0730	...	...	*0859*	...	0930	...	1130	...	1330	...	1530	...	1730	...	1930	...	2130	...	...	...

G – To / from Göttingen (Table **865**).
L – To Leinefelde (Table **865**).
e – Not Dec. 24 – 31, May 14.
k – Not Dec. 26, May 1.
n – Not Dec. 24, 31.
p – Also Dec. 24, 31.
w – Not Dec. 25.
z – Arrives 2249.
▶ – Attached to train in the next column at Gößnitz.
◄ – Detached from train in previous column at Gößnitz.

RB services — BRAUNSCHWEIG - BAD HARZBURG, GOSLAR and HERZBERG — 859

km		Ⓐ								Ⓒ	Ⓐ			Ⓐ		Ⓐ		n	n	n	n		Ⓑw			
0	**Braunschweig** Hbf ... d.	0513	0626	0707	0826	0907	1026	1107	1226	1307	1322	1426	1507	1551	1626	1639	1707	1826	1907	2026	2107	...	2220	...	...	...
12	Wolfenbüttel .... d.	0523	0636	0716	0836	0916	1036	1116	1236	1316	1331	1436	1516	1601	1636	1650	1716	1836	1916	2036	2116	...	2229	...	...	...
39	Vienenburg .... **860** d.	0547	0702	0741	0902	0941	1102	1141	1302	1341	1356	1502	1541	1626	1702	1716	1741	1902	1941	2102	2141	...	2254	...	...	...
47	**Bad Harzburg 860** a.	|	0710	|	0910	|	1110	|	1310	|	|	1510	|	1634	1710	|	|	1910	|	2110	|	...	|	...	...	...
58	**Goslar** .... **860** a.	0601	...	0754	...	0954	...	1154	...	1354	1409	...	1554	...	...	1729	1754	...	1954	...	2154	...	2307	...	...	...

km		Ⓐ	Ⓐ	⚒	⚒	⚒							Ⓒ	Ⓐ						n	n		n			
0	**Goslar** .... **860** d.	0452	0526	...	0627	...	0809	...	1009	...	1209	...	1409	1423	...	1609	...	1809	...	2009	...	...	2215	...	...	...
	Bad Harzburg 860 d.	|	0547	0547	|	0651	|	0851	|	1051	|	1251	|	|	1451	|	1651	|	1851	|	2051	...	|	...	...	...
13	Vienenburg .... **860** d.	0505	0556	0556	0639	0701	0822	0901	1022	1101	1222	1301	1422	1436	1501	1621	1701	1822	1901	2022	2101	...	2227	...	...	...
40	Wolfenbüttel .... d.	0529	0620	0620	0703	0725	0846	0925	1046	1125	1246	1325	1446	1500	1525	1646	1725	1846	1925	2046	2125	...	2252	...	...	...
52	**Braunschweig** Hbf ... a.	0538	0629	0629	0712	0734	0855	0934	1055	1134	1255	1334	1455	1509	1534	1655	1734	1855	1934	2055	2134	...	2302	...	...	...

km		Ⓐn	Ⓐ			⚒			⚒			⚒			Ⓐ			Ⓐ			Ⓐ	n	n	Ⓐn		nB
0	**Braunschweig** Hbf ... d.	0503	0603	0703	0803	0803	0903	1003	1003	1103	1203	1203	1303	1403	1403	1503	1603	1603	1703	1803	1803	1903	2003	2003	...	2203
31	Salzgitter-Ringelheim d.	0529	0629	0729	0829	0829	0929	1029	1029	1129	1229	1229	1329	1429	1429	1529	1629	1629	1729	1829	1829	1929	2029	2029	...	2229
52	Seesen .... d.	0545	0645	0745	0844	0845	0945	1044	1045	1145	1244	1245	1345	1444	1445	1545	1644	1645	1745	1844	1845	1945	2044	2045	...	2244
71	Osterode (Harz) Mitte . d.	0607	0707	0807	...	0907	1007	...	1107	1207	...	1309	1407	...	1507	1607	...	1707	1807	...	1907	2007	...	2107	...	...
83	**Herzberg** (Harz) .... a.	0621	0721	0821	...	0921	1021	...	1121	1221	...	1325	1421	...	1521	1621	...	1721	1821	...	1921	2021	...	2121	...	...

	Ⓐn	Ⓐ	Ⓐ	ⒸB	Ⓐ	Ⓒ	⚒			⚒			⚒			Ⓐ			Ⓐ			Ⓐ		n	Ⓐn	n
Herzberg (Harz) .... d.	**B**	0534	0634	...	0730	0734	0834	...	0934	1034	...	1134	1234	...	1334	1434	...	1534	1634	...	1734	1834	...	1934	2034	...
Osterode (Harz) Mitte . d.	...	0547	0647	...	0745	0747	0847	...	0947	1047	...	1147	1247	...	1347	1447	...	1547	1647	...	1747	1847	...	1947	2047	...
Seesen .... d.	0513	0613	0713	0713	0813	0813	0913	0913	1013	1113	1113	1213	1313	1313	1413	1513	1513	1613	1713	1713	1813	1913	1913	2013	2113	2113
Salzgitter-Ringelheim . d.	0529	0629	0729	0729	0829	0829	0929	0929	1029	1129	1129	1229	1329	1329	1429	1529	1529	1629	1729	1729	1829	1929	1929	2029	2129	2129
Braunschweig Hbf.... a.	0551	0651	0751	0751	0851	0851	0951	0951	1051	1151	1151	1251	1351	1351	1451	1551	1551	1651	1751	1751	1851	1951	1951	2051	2151	2151

km		Ⓐn	Ⓐ	⚒											Ⓐ	Ⓒ	Ⓐ			n	n		†		nB	
0	**Bad Harzburg** ... **860** d.	...	0618	...	...	0736	0820	0936	1022	1136	1222	1323	1422	1536	...	1622	1622	1736	1820	1936	2022	...	...	...	...	...
11	Goslar .... **860** d.	0532	0632	...	...	0757	0835	0957	1035	1157	1235	1357	1435	1557	...	1635	1635	1757	1835	1957	2035	...	...	...	...	...
34	Seesen .... d.	0551	0651	...	...	0816	0854	1016	1054	1216	1254	1416	1454	1616	...	1654	1654	1816	1854	2016	2054	...	...	...	2249	...
48	Bad Gandersheim ..... d.	0601	0701	...	...	0827	0904	1027	1104	1227	1304	1427	1504	1627	...	1704	1704	1827	1904	2027	2104	...	...	...	2300	...
54	**Kreiensen** .... a.	0607	0706	...	...	0832	0911	1032	1111	1232	1311	1432	1511	1632	...	1711	1711	1832	1911	2032	2111	...	...	...	2307	...
54	**Kreiensen** .... **903** d.	0627	0708	0754	...	0839t	0923	1039t	1123	1239t	1323	1439t	1523	1639t	1650	1723	1750	1839t	1923n	2039t	2123	...	2238	...	...	...
98	**Holzminden** .... a.	0700	0742	0827	...	|	0956	|	1156	|	1356	|	1556	|	1723	1756	1823	|	1956n	|	2156	...	2311	...	...	...
	Northeim (Han) ... **903** a.	...	...	...	...	0854t	...	1054t	...	1254t	...	1454t	...	1654t	...	...	...	1854t	...	2054t	...	...	...	...	...	...
	Göttingen .... **903** a.	...	...	...	...	0909t	...	1109t	...	1309t	...	1509t	...	1709t	...	...	...	1909t	...	2109t	...	...	...	...	...	...

	Ⓐn	Ⓐ	Ⓐ	ⒸB	⑥k	Ⓐ										t	D	Ⓐ	E	Ⓐ	Ⓒ	Ⓐn	n	n	n	†
Göttingen ....**903** d.	**B**	...	...	...	...	...	...	0848t	...	1048t	...	1248t	...	1448t	...	1648	1648t	...	...	...	...	...	1848t	...	2048t	...
Northeim (Han).....**903** d.	...	...	...	...	...	...	...	0902t	...	1102t	...	1302t	...	1502t	...	1702	1702t	...	...	...	...	...	1902t	...	2102t	...
Holzminden .... d.	...	...	0530n	...	0654	0710	0758	|	0958	|	1158	|	1358	|	1558	|	|	1654	1654	1754	1758	1834	|	1958	|	2034
Kreiensen ....**903** a.	...	...	0604n	...	0728	0744	0832	0917t	1032	1117t	1232	1317t	1432	1517t	1632	1717	1717t	1728	1728	1828	1832	1908	1917t	2032	2117t	2108
Kreiensen .... d.	0457	0535	0641	0657	0746	0746	0842	0923	1042	1123	1242	1323	1442	1523	1642	...	1723	...	1750	1842	1842	...	1923	2042	2123	...
Bad Gandersheim ...... d.	0502	0540	0646	0702	0751	0751	0848	0928	1048	1128	1248	1328	1448	1528	1648	...	1728	...	1755	1848	1848	...	1928	2048	2128	...
Seesen .... d.	0512	0551	0657	0712	0802	0802	0858	0939	1058	1139	1258	1339	1458	1539	1658	...	1739	...	1806	1858	1858	...	1939	2058	2139	...
Goslar ....**860** a.	...	0610	0716	...	0821	0821	0917	0957	1117	1157	1317	1357	1517	1557	1717	...	1757	...	1825	1917	1917	...	1957	2117	2157	...
Bad Harzburg .....**860** a.	...	0633	0729	...	0840	0840	0930	1017	1130	1217	1338	1417	1530	1617	1730	...	1817	...	1840	1930	1930	...	2017	2130	...	...

B – [12] Braunschweig - Seesen - Kreiensen and v.v.
D – ⑤–⑦ (also Apr. 5, May 13, 24).
E – ①–④ (not Apr. 5, May 13, 24).
k – Not Dec. 26, May 1.
n – Not Dec. 24, 31.
t – Not ⑦ Jan. 3 - Mar. 21.
w – Also Dec. 26, May 1; not Dec. 24, 31.

DB (*RE* services); *Harz Elbe Express* ◇ — HANNOVER - BAD HARZBURG - HALLE — 860

km			Ⓐ	Ⓐ			Ⓐ	Ⓐn	Ⓒ	⚒	⚒	⚒														
0	**Hannover** Hbf.......... d.	0019	...	...	...	...	...	...	...	...	0546	...	...	0651	...	0748	0855	...	0948	1055	...	1148	1255	...	1348	1449
36	**Hildesheim** Hbf .... d.	0049	...	...	...	...	...	...	...	...	0614	...	...	0721	...	0814	0921	...	1014	1121	...	1214	1321	...	1414	1521
70	Salzgitter-Ringelheim d.	▬	...	...	...	...	...	...	...	...	0643	...	...	0744	...	0843	0944	...	1043	1144	...	1243	1344	...	1443	1544
89	Goslar **859** .... d.	...	...	...	...	...	0526	0611	...	...	0658	0703	...	0759	...	0858	0959	...	1058	1159	...	1258	1359	...	1458	1559
100	**Bad Harzburg 859** ... a.	...	...	...	...	...	0538	|	...	...	0711	|	...	0809	...	0911	1009	...	1111	1209	...	1311	1409	...	1511	1609
100	**Bad Harzburg 859** ... d.	...	...	...	...	...	0547	|	...	0651	...	|	...	0815	*0851*	...	1015	*1051*	▬	1215	*1251*	▬	1415	*1451*	...	1615
108	Vienenburg **859** .... d.	...	...	...	...	...	0554	0623	...	0658	...	0713	...	0824	0911	...	1024	1111	...	1224	1311	...	1424	1511	...	1624
124	Ilsenburg .... d.	...	...	0449	...	0531	▬	0635	0626	...	...	0726	...	0835	0926	...	1035	1126	...	1235	1326	...	1435	1526	...	1635
133	Wernigerode .... d.	...	...	0501	...	0542	...	0645	0637	...	...	0737	...	0842	0937	...	1042	1137	...	1242	1337	...	1442	1537	...	1642
157	**Halberstadt** .... a.	...	...	0519	...	0601	Ⓐ	0657	0655	...	...	0753	...	0854	0953	...	1054	1153	...	1254	1353	...	1454	1553	...	1654
157	**Halberstadt** .... d.	0344r	0444	0524	0524	...	0606	0659	0659	...	...	0801	0801	0859	1001	...	1059	...	1201	1259	...	1401	1459	1601	...	1659
190	Aschersleben .... d.	0410	0515	0553	0553	...	0639	0719	0724	...	...	0829	0829	0919	1029	...	1119	...	1229	1319	...	1429	1519	1629	...	1719
201	Sandersleben (Anh) .... d.	0424	0528	0606	0606	...	0649	0726	0734	...	...	0846	0846	0926	1046	...	1126	...	1246	1326	...	1446	1526	1646	...	1726
219	Könnern .... ⊡ d.	0438	0544	0621	0621	...	0701	0737	0746	...	...	0900	0900	0937	1100	...	1137	...	1300	1337	...	1500	1537	1700	...	1737
248	**Halle** (Saale) Hbf .... a.	0507	0616	0653	0653	...	0729	0754	0805	...	...	0929	0929	0954	1129	...	1154	...	1329	1354	...	1529	1554	1729	...	1754

								n	n	n	n	
Hannover Hbf .... d.	...	1548	1655	...	1748	1855	...	1948	2045	...	2148	2319
Hildesheim Hbf......... d.	...	1614	1721	...	1814	1921	...	2014	2109	...	2214	2349
Salzgitter-Ringelheim . d.	...	1643	1744	...	1843	1944	...	2043	2131	...	2243	▬
Goslar **859** .... d.	...	1658	1759	...	1858	1959	...	2058	2147	2152	2257	...
Bad Harzburg 859 .... a.	...	1711	1809	...	1911	2009	...	2111	|	2204	...	...
Bad Harzburg 859 .... d.	*1651*	▬	1815	*1851*	...	2015	*2051*n	...	|	...	...	...
Vienenburg **859** .... d.	1711	...	1824	1911	...	2024	2111	...	2157	...	...	...
Ilsenburg .... d.	1726	...	1835	1926	...	2039	2126	...	2208	...	...	2303
Wernigerode .... d.	1737	...	1842	1937	...	2046	2137	...	2216	...	...	2314
Halberstadt .... a.	1753	...	1854	1953	...	2058	2153	...	2228	...	...	2331
Halberstadt .... d.	**A**	1801	1859	2001	...	2105	...	...	2229	...	...	...
Aschersleben .... d.	...	1829	1919	2029	...	2125	...	...	2247	...	...	...
Sandersleben (Anh) ..... d.	...	1846	1926	2046	...	2132	...	...	2254	...	...	...
Könnern .... ⊡ d.	...	1900	1937	2100	...	2143	...	...	2304	...	...	...
Halle (Saale) Hbf .... ⊡ a.	...	1929	1954	2129	...	2200	...	...	2321	...	...	...

	Ⓐn	Ⓐ	Ⓐn	⑥	Ⓒ	Ⓐ		Ⓐ	
Halle (Saale) Hbf .... d.	...	...	...	...	...	0422	...	0517	0602
Könnern .... ⊡ d.	...	...	...	...	...	0439	...	0546	0621
Sandersleben (Anh) .... d.	...	...	...	...	...	0452	...	0606	0631
Aschersleben .... d.	...	...	...	...	...	0502	...	0623	0639
Halberstadt .... a.	...	...	...	...	...	0530	...	0652	0657
Halberstadt .... d.	...	0441	...	0500	...	0543	...	...	0703
Wernigerode .... d.	...	0502	...	0518	...	0559	...	...	0717
Ilsenburg .... d.	...	0518	...	0533	...	0609	...	...	0725
Vienenburg **859** .... d.	...	0531	...	0547	...	0623	...	...	0738
Bad Harzburg 859 .... a.	...	|	...	|	...	|	...	...	0746
Bad Harzburg 859 .... d.	...	|	0540	|	...	|	0642	...	0752
Goslar **859** .... d.	0457	0542	0554	0559	0605	0640	0656	...	0808
Salzgitter-Ringelheim .... d.	0511	...	0608	...	0616	0652	0710	...	0819
Hildesheim Hbf .... d.	0543	...	0639	...	0640	0720	0743	...	0843
Hannover Hbf .... a.	0609	...	0707	...	0706	0747	0810	...	0906

		Ⓒ	Ⓐ														n			n		n			E	
Halle (Saale) Hbf .... d.	...	0623	0623	0809	0832	...	1009	1032	...	1209	...	1232	1409	1432	...	1609	...	1632	1809	...	1832	2009	2032	2256	2256	...
Könnern .... ⊡ d.	...	0651	0702z	0824	0900	...	1024	1100	...	1224	...	1300	1424	1500	...	1624	...	1700	1824	...	1900	2024	2105	2327	2327	...
Sandersleben (Anh) .... d.	...	0705	0714	0834	0914	...	1034	1114	...	1234	...	1314	1434	1514	...	1634	...	1714	1834	...	1914	2034	2119	2340	2340	...
Aschersleben .... d.	...	0718	0730	0841	0930	...	1041	1130	...	1241	...	1330	1441	1530	...	1641	...	1730	1841	...	1930	2042	2136	2358	2358	...
Halberstadt .... a.	...	0746	0757	0900	0957	**B**	1100	1157	...	1300	...	1357	1500	1557	...	1700	...	1757	1900	...	1957	2101	2203	0027	0027	...
Halberstadt .... d.	...	0804	0804	0903	▬	1004	1103	▬	1204	1303	...	1404	1503	▬	1604	1703	...	1804	1903	...	2009	2103	*2230*	▬	0030	0030
Wernigerode .... d.	...	0822	0822	0917	...	1022	1117	...	1222	1317	...	1422	1517	...	1622	1717	...	1822	1917	...	2026	2117	*2247*	...	0048	0048
Ilsenburg .... d.	...	0836	0836	0925	...	1036	1125	...	1236	1325	...	1436	1525	...	1636	1725	...	1836	1925	...	2038	2125	*2258*	...	0058	0058
Vienenburg **859** .... d.	...	0848	0848	0938	...	1048	1138	...	1248	1338	...	1448	1538	...	1648	1738	...	1848	1938	...	2050	2138	...	...	...	...
Bad Harzburg 859 .... a.	...	*0910*	*0910*	0946	...	*1110*	1146	...	*1310*	1346	...	*1510*	1546	...	*1710*	1746	...	*1910*	1946	...	*2110*	2146	...	...	...	...
Bad Harzburg 859 .... d.	0845	...	...	0952	1045	...	1152	1245	...	1352	1445	...	1552	1645	...	1752	1845	...	1952	2045	▬	2206	...	...	...	...
Goslar **859** .... d.	0859	...	...	1008	1059	...	1208	1259	...	1408	1459	...	1608	1659	...	1808	1859	...	2008	2059	...	2218	...	...	...	...
Salzgitter-Ringelheim . d.	0913	...	...	1019	1113	...	1219	1313	...	1419	1513	...	1619	1713	...	1819	1913	...	2019	2113	...	...	...	...	...	...
Hildesheim Hbf .... d.	0943	...	...	1043	1143	...	1243	1343	...	1443	1543	...	1643	1743	...	1843	1943	...	2043	2143	2207	...	...	2307	...	...
Hannover Hbf .... a.	1010	...	...	1106	1210	...	1306	1410	...	1506	1610	...	1706	1810	...	1906	2010	...	2106	2210	2238	...	...	2338	...	...

A – To Berlin via Magdeburg on ⑤–⑦ (also Dec. 23, 31, Apr. 1, 5, 29, May 12, 13, 24). See Tables **862** / **839**.
B – From Berlin via Magdeburg on ⑥⑦ (also Dec. 24, Jan. 1, Apr. 2, 5, May 13, 24). See Tables **839** / **862**.
E – ①–⑥ (not Dec. 26, Jan. 1, 6, Apr. 2, 5, May 1, 13, 24).
n – Not Dec. 24, 31.

r – ⚒ only.
z – Arrives 0650.
◇ – *Harz Elbe Express* (*HEX*). Operated by Veolia Verkehr Sachsen-Anhalt GmbH.

⊡ – **Bernburg - Könnern** and v.v. (*16 km*, journey 23–26 minutes) ◇.
From Bernburg (trains marked ◧ continue to Halle): 0512 Ⓐ, 0628 Ⓐ, 0647 ⑥ ◧, 0734 Ⓐ ◧, 0830 Ⓒ, 0934 ◧, 1133 ◧ and every two hours until 1933 ◧; then 2032.
From Könnern (trains marked ◐ start from Halle, departing 29–31 minutes earlier): 0546 Ⓐ, 0656 Ⓐ, 0743 Ⓒ ◐, 0801 Ⓐ ◐, 0904 Ⓒ, 1001 ◐, 1201 ◐ and every two hours until 2001 ◐; then 2237 ◐.

861 MAGDEBURG - SANGERHAUSEN - ERFURT and DESSAU - ASCHERSLEBEN

RE / RB services

Magdeburg - Erfurt and Aschersleben

km		Ⓐn	Ⓐe	Ⓐe	Ⓐe			⑥								Ⓐe	Ⓑq	Ⓒz	Ⓐe					n		
0	**Magdeburg** Hbf d.	...	0400	...	0512	0612	0712	0712	0826	0912	1026	1112	1226	1312	1426	1457	...	1512	1533	1626	1712	1826	1912	2026	2112	2244
37	Staßfurt d.	...	0432	...	0549	0652	0747	0747	0853	0947	1054	1147	1254	1347	1454	1535	...	1547	1606	1654	1747	1854	1947	2054	2147	2326
44	Güsten d.	...	0440	...	0556	0659	0757	0802	0859	0954	1059	1154	1259	1354	1459	1543	...	1554	1614	1659	1754	1859	1954	2059	2154	2334
	Aschersleben a.	...	0452	0538	0608	|	0808	|	|	1006	|	1206	|	1406	|	|	...	1606	1625	|	1806	|	2006	|	2206	2345
60	Sandersleben d.	...	▬	0549	▬	0711	▬	0815	0911	▬	1111	▬	1311	▬	1511	1554	1554	▬	▬	1711	▬	1911	...	2111	...	...
66	Hettstedt d.	...	...	0556	...	0718	...	0822	0918	...	1118	...	1318	...	1518	1601	1601	...	...	1718	...	1918	...	2118	...	...
75	Klostermansfeld d.	...	v	0605	...	0727	...	0831	0927	...	1127	...	1327	...	1527	1610	1610	Ⓐn	Ⓒt	1727	...	1927	...	2127	...	...
97	**Sangerhausen** d.	0514	0546	0626	0644	0747	0835	0902	0947	1035	1147	1235	1347	1435	1547	1629	1629	1635	1638	1747	1906	1947	...	2147	...	...
142	Sömmerda d.	0553	0631	0703	0730	0832	0921	...	1032	1121	1232	1321	1432	1521	1632	...	...	1723	1721	1832	1954	2032	...	2232	...	...
167	**Erfurt** Hbf a.	0610	0653	0719	0751	0853	0941	...	1053	1141	1253	1341	1453	1541	1653	...	...	1743	1741	1853	2015	2053	...	2253	...	...

	Ⓐe	Ⓐe	Ⓒz	Ⓐe	Ⓐe	Ⓒb	Ⓐn	Ⓐn								Ⓐe				⑥		Ⓐn	Ⓒt			n
Erfurt Hbf d.	...	...	...	...	...	0507	0514	0613	0706	0814	0906	1014	1106	1214	1306	...	1414	1506	1614	...	1706	1747	1814	1906	2016	2236
Sömmerda d.	...	...	...	...	...	0526	0531	0635	0730	0835	0928	1035	1128	1235	1328	...	1435	1528	1635	...	1728	1804	1835	1928	2037	2257
Sangerhausen d.	...	...	...	0510	...	0609	0609	0725	0816	0920	1016	1118	1216	1318	1416	...	1514	1616	1720k	1738	1816	1852	1921	2016	2120	2340
Klostermansfeld d.	...	...	...	0530	...	0629	0629	▬	0836	▬	1036	▬	1236	▬	1436	...	▬	1636	▬	1757	1836	...	...	2036	▬	...
Hettstedt d.	...	...	...	0539	...	0639	0639	...	0846	...	1046	...	1246	...	1446	...	...	1646	...	1807	1846	...	...	2046	...	...
Sandersleben d.	...	...	...	0553	...	0655	0655	...	0855	...	1055	...	1255	...	1455	...	Ⓒz	1655	...	1814	1855	...	...	2055	...	...
Aschersleben d.	0448	0529	0548	|	0623	|	|	0748	|	0948	|	1148	|	1348	|	1545	1548	|	1748	|	|	1948	...	|	2148	...
Güsten d.	0500	0541	0600	0605	0635	0708	0708	0800	0908	1000	1108	1200	1308	1400	1508	1557	1600	1708	1800	1826	1908	2000	...	2108	2200	...
Staßfurt d.	0508	0549	0608	0614	0645	0714	0714	0808	0914	1008	1114	1208	1314	1408	1514	1608	1608	1714	1808	1833	1914	2008	...	2114	2208	...
Magdeburg Hbf a.	0540	0624	0640	0640	0717	0740	0740	0840	0940	1040	1140	1240	1340	1440	1540	1640	1640	1740	1840	1911	1940	2040	...	2140	2249	...

Dessau - Aschersleben

km		Ⓐe	Ⓒw	Ⓐe		Ⓐe		Ⓒz	Ⓐe			Ⓐe						Ⓐe	Ⓒz							n
0	**Dessau** Hbf d.	0419	0457	0526	0602	0650	...	0711	0730	0802	0913	1002	1002	1113	1202	1313	1402	1513	1513	1602	1713	1802	1913	2002	2111	2303
21	Köthen a.	0442	0520	0554	0623	0714	...	0733	0751	0823	0933	1023	1023	1133	1223	1333	1423	1533	1533	1623	1733	1823	1933	2023	2133	2324
21	Köthen d.	0451	0525	0554	0633	0718	...	0735	0755	0833	0935	1033	...	1135	1233	1335	1433	1535	1535	1633	1735	1833	1935	2033	2135	2325
42	Bernburg d.	0512	0546	0615	0653	0738	...	0756	0817	0853	0956	1053	...	1156	1253	1356	1453	1556	1556	1653	1756	1853	1956	2053	2156	2346
54	Güsten d.	0522	0557	0626	0703	0749	0757	0807	0827	0903	1007	1103	...	1207	1303	1407	1503	1606	1607	1703	1807	1903	2007	2103	2207	2357
66	**Aschersleben** a.	0533	0608	0634	0714	...	0808	0819	0836	0914	1019	1114	...	1219	1314	1419	1514	1615	1619	1714	1819	1914	2019	2114	2219	0009

	v	Ⓐe	Ⓒz	Ⓐe		Ⓒz		Ⓐe			Ⓐe						Ⓐe	Ⓒz						n	n	
Aschersleben d.	0431	0517	0559	0559	0650	0738	0748	...	0850	0938	1050	...	1138	1250	1338	1450	1535	1538	1650	1738	1850	1938	...	2046	...	2138
Güsten d.	0443	0529	0610	0610	0702	0750	0759	0805	0902	0950	1103	...	1150	1303	1350	1503	1550	1550	1703	1750	1903	1950	...	2057	2111	2150
Bernburg d.	0456	0541	0620	0620	0714	0802	...	0819	0914	1002	1114	...	1202	1314	1402	1514	1602	1602	1714	1802	1914	2002	...	...	2123	2202
Köthen a.	0517	0602	0639	0639	0735	0823	...	0840	0933	1023	1134	...	1223	1334	1423	1534	1623	1623	1734	1823	1934	2023	...	...	2141	2223
Köthen d.	0522	0603	0640	0640	0735	0825	...	0841	0935	1025	1135	1135	1225	1335	1425	1535	1625	1625	1735	1825	1935	2033	...	...	2142	2224
Dessau Hbf a.	0546	0630	0703	0706	0756	0844	...	0906	0956	1044	1156	1156	1244	1356	1444	1556	1644	1644	1756	1844	1956	2055	...	...	2204	2246

b – Also Dec. 24, 31; not Dec. 25, Jan. 1.
e – Not Dec. 24, 31, Jan. 6.
k – 1714 on Ⓐ (not Dec. 24, 31).
n – Not Dec. 24, 31.
q – Not Dec. 24, 25, 31, Jan. 1, 6, Apr. 2, 4, May 13, 23.
t – Also Dec. 24, 31.
v – Not Dec. 25, Jan. 1.
w – Also Dec. 24, 31, Jan. 6; not Dec. 25, Jan. 1.
z – Also Dec. 24, 31, Jan. 6.

862 MAGDEBURG - HALBERSTADT - THALE

HEX ◇

km		v	Ⓐe						C▲	Ⓐe	Ⓒz		Ⓒz	Ⓐe		Ⓒz	Ⓐe								n	n
	Berlin Ostbf 839 d.	...	...	...	...	...	...	...	0708																	
0	**Magdeburg** Hbf d.	...	0446	...	0555v	0710	0810	0910	0910	0944	1010	*1110*	1144	1210	1310	1344	1410	1510	1610	1710	1810	1907	2015	2127	2217	2318
39	Oschersleben (Bode) d.	...	0520	...	0633v	0741	0841	0941	0941	1024	1041	*1141*	1224	1241	1341	1424	1441	1541	1641	1741	1841	1948	2041	2205	2258	2356
59	**Halberstadt** a.	...	0540	...	0654v	0756	0856	0956	0956	1045	1056	*1156*	1245	1256	1356	1445	1456	1556	1656	1756	1856	2006	2057	2225	2319	0016
59	**Halberstadt** d.	0500	...	0607	0706	0806	0906	1006	1006	1106	1106	1206	1306	1306	1406	1506	1506	1606	1706	1806	1906	2009	2106	2234	...	0026
77	Quedlinburg a.	0515	...	0623	0723	0823	0923	1023	1023	1123	1123	1223	1323	1323	1423	1523	1523	1623	1723	1823	1923	2026	2123	2249	...	0041
77	Quedlinburg d.	0519	...	0630	0730	0830	0930	1030	1030	1130	1130	1230	1330	1330	1430	1530	1530	1630	1730	1830	1930	2030	2130	2251	...	0042
87	**Thale** Hbf a.	0531	...	0642	0742	0842	0942	1042	1042	1142	1142	1242	1342	1342	1442	1542	1542	1642	1742	1842	1942	2042	2142	2303	...	0053

	Ⓐe	v		Ⓐe			Ⓐe	Ⓒz				Ⓐe	Ⓒz				Ⓐe			B▲						n
Thale Hbf d.	...	...	0505v	...	0616v	0716	0816	0816	0916	1016	1116	1216	1216	1316	1416	1516	...	1616	1716	1716	1816	1916	2016	2116	2155	2345
Quedlinburg a.	...	...	0517v	...	0628v	0728	0828	0828	0928	1028	1128	1228	1228	1328	1428	1528	...	1628	1728	1728	1828	1928	2028	2128	2207	2357
Quedlinburg d.	...	...	0517v	...	0629v	0733	0833	0833	0933	1033	1133	1233	1233	1333	1433	1533	...	1633	1733	1733	1833	1933	2033	2133	2208	2358
Halberstadt a.	...	...	0537v	...	0645v	0749	0849	0849	0949	1049	1149	1249	1249	1349	1450	1549	...	1649	1749	1749	1849	1949	2049	2149	2224	0014
Halberstadt d.	0349	0450	0541	0613	0701	0801	0901	0912	1001	1112	*1201*	1301	1312	1401	1501	1601	1615	1701	1801	1801	1905	2015	2105	2208n	...	...
Oschersleben (Bode) d.	0406	0512	0602	0629	0716	0816	0916	0933	1016	1133	*1216*	1316	1333	1416	1516	1616	1635	1716	1816	1816	1921	2037	2121	2230n	...	...
Magdeburg Hbf a.	0440	0549	0645	0658	0742	0842	0942	1014	1042	1214	*1242*	1342	1414	1442	1544	1642	1712	1742	1842	1842	1948	2114	2150	2306n	...	...
Berlin Ostbf 839 a.	...	...	...	...	...	...	...	...	...	...	...	...	...	...	...	...	...	...	...	2048	...	...	...	...	...	...

B – ⑤–⑦ (also Dec. 23, 31, Apr. 1, 5, 29, May 12, 13, 24).
C – ⑥⑦ (also Dec. 24, Jan. 1, Apr. 2, 5, May 13, 24).
e – Not Jan. 6.
n – Not Dec. 24, 31.
v – Not Dec. 25, Jan. 1.
z – Also Jan. 6.
◇ – *Harz Elbe Express*. Operated by Veolia Verkehr Sachsen-Anhalt GmbH.
▲ – *HARZ-BERLIN-EXPRESS*. **DB tickets not valid for journeys from / to Berlin.** Conveys (2.) Berlin - Halberstadt - Vienenburg and v.v. (Table **860**).

863 BÜNDE - HAMELN - HILDESHEIM - BRAUNSCHWEIG

DB (RB services); eurobahn ★

km		⚒	Ⓐe	⚒	⚒		Ⓐe						Ⓐe	Ⓒz	Ⓐe	Ⓐe					Ⓐe					Ⓑr
0	**Bünde** (Westf) 810 d.	...	...	...	0632e	...	0730	...	0832e	...	1032e	...	1232	...	...	1332	...	1432e	...	1632e	1732	...	1832e	...		
10	Löhne (Westf) 810 d.	...	0545	...	0645	...	0745	...	0845	0945e	1045	1145e	1245	1245	...	1345	...	1445	1545e	1645	1745	...	1845	1945e	2045	2045
22	Vlotho d.	...	0559	...	0659	...	0759	...	0859	0959e	1059	1159e	1259	1259	...	1359	...	1459	1559e	1659	1759	...	1859	1959e	2059	2059
39	Rinteln d.	...	0610	...	0710	...	0810	...	0910	1010e	1110	1210e	1310	1310	...	1410	...	1510	1610e	1710	1810	...	1910	2010e	2110	2110
63	**Hameln** d.	0528	0628	0628	0728	0728	0828	0828	0928	1028	1128	1228	1327	1328	1335	1428	1428	1528	1628	1728	1828	1828	1928	2028	2127	2128
92	Elze a.	0553	0653	0653	0753	0753	0852	0852	0953	1052	1153	1252	...	1353	1402	1452	1452	1553	1652	1753	1852	1852	1953	2052	...	2153
92	Elze d.	0602	0702	0702	0802	0802	0907	0907	1002	1107	1202	1307	...	1402	1403	1507	1507	1602	1707	1802	1907	1907	2002	2107	...	2202
110	**Hildesheim** Hbf a.	0620	0720	0720	0820	0820	0925	0925	1020	1125	1220	1325	...	1420	1422	1525	1525	1620	1725	1820	1925	1925	2020	2125	...	2220

	Ⓐe	⚒	⚒	Ⓐe			Ⓐe			Ⓐe			Ⓐe			Ⓐe			Ⓐe			Ⓐe				Ⓑr
Hildesheim Hbf d.	...	0537	0634	0634	0737	0834	0834	0937	1034	1034	1137	1234	1234	1337	1434	1434	1537	1634	1634	1737	1834	1834	1937	2034	...	2137
Elze a.	...	0553	0650	0650	0753	0850	0850	0953	1050	1050	1153	1250	1250	1353	1450	1450	1553	1650	1650	1753	1850	1850	1953	2050	...	2153
Elze d.	...	0602	0702	0702	0802	0902	0902	1002	1102	1102	1202	1302	1302	1402	1502	1502	1602	1702	1702	1802	1902	1902	2002	2102	...	2202
Hameln d.	0529	0629	0727	0729	0829	0927	0929	1029	1127	1129	1229	1327	1329	1429	1527	1529	1629	1727	1729	1829	1927	1929	2029	2127	...	2227
Rinteln d.	0546	0646	...	0746	0846	...	0946	1046	...	1146	1246	...	1346	1446	...	1546	1646	...	1746	1846	...	1946	2046	...	...	...
Vlotho d.	0602	0702	...	0802	0902	...	1002	1102	...	1202	1302	...	1402	1502	...	1602	1702	...	1802	1902	...	2002	2102	...	...	...
Löhne (Westf) 810 a.	0613	0713	...	0813	0913	...	1013	1113	...	1213	1313	...	1413	1513	...	1613	1713	...	1813	1913	...	2013	2113	...	...	...
Bünde (Westf) 810 a.	0626	0725e	...	0825	...	...	1025	...	...	1225	1325e	...	1425	...	...	1625	1725e	...	1825	...	...	...	...	...	...	...

Hildesheim - Braunschweig

km				◇			◇	◇		◇	◇		◇	◇		◇		◇		◇	◇		◇		◇	◇
		Ⓐe		A	⚒												Ⓐe		m			n	Ⓑq	n		
0	**Hildesheim** Hbf d.	0559	0659	0734	0753	0859	0934	1034	1059	1134	1234	1259	1334	1434	1459	1534	1559	1634	1659	1734	1834	1859	1934	2059	2134	2234
43	**Braunschweig** Hbf a.	0645	0745	0758	0845	0945	0958	1058	1145	1158	1258	1345	1358	1458	1545	1558	1645	1658	1745	1758	1858	1945	1958	2145	2158	2258

			◇		◇	◇		◇	◇		◇	◇		◇		◇		◇		◇			◇			
	⚒	Ⓐe	A												Ⓐ				Ⓐe		⚒m	†		n	Ⓑq	Ⓒ
Braunschweig Hbf d.	0615	0658	0758	0815	0857	0958	1015	1057	1158	1215	1257	1358	1415	1457	1515	1558	1615	1657	1715	1758	1815	1817	1958	2015	2057	2215
Hildesheim Hbf a.	0652	0730	0823	0856	0923	1023	1056	1123	1223	1256	1323	1423	1456	1523	1556	1623	1656	1723	1756	1823	1856	1856	2023	2056	2123	2256

A – ①–⑥ (not Dec. 25, 26, Jan. 1, Apr. 3, 5, May 24).
e – Ⓐ (not Dec. 24, 31).
m – Not Dec. 24.
n – Not Dec. 24, 31.
q – Not Dec. 24, 25, 31, Apr. 2, 4, May 23.
r – Also Dec. 26, May 1; not Dec. 24, 31.
z – Also Dec. 24, 31.
◇ – *ICE* train (see Table **900**). Does not operate via Hildesheim Dec. 24 – 27.
★ – Löhne - Hildesheim operated by **eurobahn** Keolis Deutschland GmbH & Co. KG.

CANTUS Verkehrsgesellschaft (2nd class only) — GÖTTINGEN - KASSEL local services — 864

For fast trains Göttingen - Kassel Wilhelmshöhe and v.v. see Tables **900** (*ICE* services) and **902** (*IC* services).

km		Ⓐn	⑥k	⑥k	Ⓐn	©d	Ⓐn	⚒		⚒			©d	Ⓐn			Ⓐn	©d	Ⓑw	Ⓐn	©d	Ⓑw	⚒	Ⓑw	Ⓐn	©◇
0	**Göttingen** .... **908** d.	0443	0444	0543	0600	0702	0714	0814	0914	1018	1114	1218	1314	1332	1418	1514	1614	1618	1714	1814	1818	1914	2014	2118	2214	2335
20	Eichenberg .... **908** a.	0457	0458	0557	0613	0716	0728	0828	0928	1032	1128	1232	1328	1346	1432	1528	1628	1632	1728	1828	1832	1928	2028	2132	2228	2350
20	Eichenberg .... **865** d.	0502	0502	0603	0623	0723	0733	0833	0933	1033	1133	1233	1333	1349	1433	1533	1633	1633	1733	1833	1833	1933	2033	2133	2237	2354
43	Hann Münden .... **865** d.	0523	0523	0623	0643	0743	0753	0853	0953	1053	1153	1253	1353	1409	1453	1553	1653	1653	1753	1853	1853	1953	2053	2153	2258	0015
67	**Kassel** Hbf ⊡ .... **865** a.	0543	0543	0643	0703	0803	0813	0913	1013	1113	1213	1313	1413	1430	1513	1613	1713	1713	1813	1913	1913	2013	2113	2213	2319	0036

	Ⓐn		Ⓐn	⑥k	Ⓐn	©d	⚒	†	⚒	⚒						Ⓑw		Ⓐn	©d		Ⓑw	⚒			Ⓐn	©d
Kassel Hbf ⊡ .... **865** d.	0416	...	0535	0546	0626	0636	0746	0846	0846	0946	1046	1146	1246	1346	1446	1546	1646	1746	1746	1846	1946	2046	2146	...	2314	2346
Hann Münden .... **865** d.	0436	...	0555	0606	0646	0656	0806	0906	0906	1006	1106	1206	1306	1406	1506	1606	1706	1806	1806	1906	2006	2106	2206	...	2334	0006
Eichenberg .... **865** a.	0456	...	0615	0626	0706	0716	0826	0926	0926	1026	1126	1226	1326	1426	1526	1626	1726	1826	1826	1926	2026	2126	2226	...	2356	0026
Eichenberg .... **908** d.	0458	...	0624	0627	0707	0722	0832	0927	0932	1032	1127	1232	1327	1432	1527	1632	1727	1827	1832	1927	2032	2127	2227	...	0002	0027
Göttingen .... **908** a.	0513	...	0637	0640	0721	0735	0845	0940	0945	1045	1140	1245	1340	1445	1540	1645	1740	1840	1845	1940	2045	2140	2240	...	0015	0040

d – Also Dec. 24, 31.
k – Also Dec. 24, 31; not Dec. 26, May 1.
n – Not Dec. 24, 31.
w – Also Dec. 26, May 1; not Dec. 24, 31.
◇ – © (also Dec. 24, 31). Runs 10 – 11 minutes later on ⑥ (also Dec. 24, 31; not Dec. 26, May 1).
⊡ – See Tables **804**, **806** and **901** for connecting trains to / from Kassel Wilhelmshöhe.

DB (*RE* / *RB* services); EIB ◇ — ERFURT and HALLE - LEINEFELDE - KASSEL and GÖTTINGEN — 865

km		⚒r	◇Ⓐ	⚒r		Ⓐt	Ⓐ◇		◇	◇Ⓐ	◇©	G			◇	◇	A		◇	◇	A		◇	◇
0	**Erfurt** Hbf .... **849 850** d.	...	0402	...	0430	...	...	...	...	*0559*	0558	0710	...	...	...	0811	0910	...	...	1011	1110	...	...	1211
27	Gotha .... **849 850** d.	...	|	...	0504	...	0539	...	0636	0636	|	0737	...	...	0839	|	0937	...	1039	|	1137	...	1239	|
48	Bad Langensalza .... d.	...	0452	...	0515	...	0602	...	0653	0654	0702	0749	...	...	0856	0902	0949	...	1056	1102	1149	...	1256	1302
67	Mühlhausen (Thür) .... d.	...	0509	...	0528	...	0617	...	▬	0714	0718	0802	...	...	▬	0918	1002	...	▬	1118	1202	...	▬	1318
	Halle (Saale) Hbf .... ◧ d.	...	|	...	|	...	|	0446	...	|	|	|	0535	0704	...	|	|	0904	...	|	|	1104	...	|
	Lutherstadt Eisleben .... ◧ d.	...	|	...	|	...	|	0520	...	|	|	|	0614	0734	...	|	|	0934	...	|	|	1134	...	|
	Sangerhausen .... ◧ d.	...	|	...	|	...	|	0542	...	|	|	|	0636	0753	...	|	|	0953	...	|	|	1153	...	|
	Nordhausen .... ◧ a.	...	|	...	|	...	|	0617	...	|	|	|	0710	0821	...	|	|	1021	...	|	|	1221	...	|
	Nordhausen .... d.	...	|	0502	|	...	|	0622	0659	|	|	|	*0751*r	0822	0851	|	|	1022	1051	|	|	1222	1251	|
94	**Leinefelde** .... a.	...	0535	0544	0546	...	0641	0655	0737	0741	0741	0818	*0833*r	0855	0933	0941	1018	1055	1133	1141	1218	1255	1333	1341
94	**Leinefelde** .... d.	0426	0536	...	0548	0607	...	0656	...	0742	0742	0820	...	0856	...	0942	1020	1056	...	1142	1220	1256	...	1342
110	Heilbad Heiligenstadt .... d.	0440	0551	...	0559	0621	...	0706	...	0757	0757	0831	...	0906	...	0957	1031	1106	...	1157	1231	1306	...	1357
144	**Göttingen** .... a.	|	|	...	0625	|	...	|	...	|	|	0852	...	|	...	|	1052	|	...	|	1252	|	...	|
125	Eichenberg .... **864** a.	0454	0604	...	...	0635	...	0717	...	0811	0811	...	...	0917	...	1011	...	1117	...	1211	...	1317	...	1411
148	Hann Münden .... **864** a.	*0522*	0626	...	...	*0708*x	...	0736	...	0831	0831	...	...	0936	...	1031q	...	1136	...	1231a	...	1336	...	1431b
172	**Kassel** Hbf .... **864** a.	*0543*	0647	...	...	*0730*x	...	0753c	...	|	|	...	...	0953c	...	|	...	1153c	...	|	...	1353c	...	|
176	**Kassel** Wilhelmshöhe .... **864** a.	...	...	...	...	...	...	0754a	...	0851	0851	...	...	0954a	...	1051q	...	1154a	...	1251a	...	1355a	...	1451b

	A		◇	◇	A		◇	◇	⑦E	A	①–⑥			n◇	n◇	A	n	n◇	n◇	nA	n	n◇	n◇	n
Erfurt Hbf .... **849 850** d.	1310	...	...	1411	1510	...	...	1611	...	1710	h	...	...	...	1811	1910	...	...	2011	2110	...	...	2221	...
Gotha .... **849 850** d.	1337	...	1439	|	1537	...	1639	|	...	1737	...	...	...	1839	|	1937	...	2039	|	2137	...	2249	|	...
Bad Langensalza .... d.	1349	...	1456	1502	1549	...	1656	1702	...	1749	...	...	...	1856	1902	1949	...	2056	2102	2150	...	2306	2311	...
Mühlhausen (Thür) .... d.	1402	...	▬	1518	1602	...	▬	1718	...	1802	...	...	...	▬	1917	2002	...	▬	2118	2204	...	...	2327	...
Halle (Saale) Hbf .... ◧ d.	|	1304	...	|	|	1504	...	|	1604	|	1604	...	1704	...	|	|	1904	...	|	|	2104	...	|	2234
Lutherstadt Eisleben .... ◧ d.	|	1334	...	|	|	1534	...	|	1636	|	1635	...	1734	...	|	|	1934	...	|	|	2135	...	|	2305
Sangerhausen .... ◧ d.	|	1353	...	|	|	1553	...	|	1654	|	1657	...	1753	...	|	|	1953	...	|	|	2155	...	|	2328
Nordhausen .... ◧ a.	|	1421	...	|	|	1621	...	|	1722	|	1731	...	1821	...	|	|	2021	n	|	|	2228	...	|	0001
Nordhausen .... d.	|	1422	1451	|	|	1622	1651	|	1723	|	...	1751	1822	1851	|	|	2022	2101	|	|	*2233*	...	|	...
Leinefelde .... a.	1418	1455	1533	1541	1618	1655	1733	1741	1752	1818	...	1833	1855	1933	1939	2018	2055	2140	2141	2221	*2316*	...	2345	...
Leinefelde .... d.	1420	1456	...	1542	1620	1656	...	1742	1754	1820	...	1834	1856	...	1942	2020	2056	...	2145	▬	...	...	...	...
Heilbad Heiligenstadt .... d.	1431	1506	...	1557	1631	1706	...	1757	1806	1831	...	1847	1906	...	1957	2031	2106	...	2200	...	...	...	...	...
Göttingen .... a.	1452	|	...	|	1652	|	...	|	|	1852	...	...	|	...	|	2052	|	...	|	Ⓐn	...	...	...	...
Eichenberg .... **864** a.	...	1517	...	1611	...	1717	...	1811	|	...	...	...	1917	...	2011	...	2117	...	2214	2237	...	...	...	...
Hann Münden .... **864** a.	...	1536	...	1631	...	1736	...	1831	|	...	...	...	1936	...	2031k	...	2136	...	...	2257	...	...	...	...
Kassel Hbf .... **864** a.	...	1553c	...	|	...	1753c	...	|	|	...	...	...	1953c	...	|	...	2153	...	...	2319	...	...	...	...
Kassel Wilhelmshöhe .... **864** a.	...	1554a	...	1651	...	1754a	...	1851	1851	...	...	...	1954a	...	2050k	...	...	...	...	...	...	...	...	...

km		v	v	Ⓐt	⚒	Ⓐt	◇	◇	ⒶG	Ⓐ	©	Ⓐ◇	A	◇			A	◇			A	◇		
0	**Kassel** Wilhelmshöhe .... **864** d.	...	...	...	...	...	...	...	...	...	...	...	...	...	...	0804a	...	0907	...	1004a	...	1107q	...	1204a
	Kassel Hbf .... **864** d.	...	...	0416	...	...	...	...	...	0602	0605	...	...	0657a	...	0805c	...	|	...	1005c	...	|	...	1205c
23	Hann Münden .... **864** d.	...	...	0436	...	...	...	...	...	0618	0621	...	...	0717a	...	0821	...	0926	...	1021	...	1126q	...	1221
46	Eichenberg .... **864** d.	...	...	0456	0510r	...	...	...	...	0636	0640	...	...	0738a	...	0840	...	0946	...	1040	...	1146	...	1240
	Göttingen .... d.	...	...	...	|	...	...	...	0603	|	|	...	0708	|	...	|	0908	|	...	|	1108	|	...	|
61	Heilbad Heiligenstadt .... d.	...	0446t	...	0524r	0559	...	...	0631	0649	0652	...	0730	0752a	...	0852	0930	1000	...	1052	1130	1200	...	1252
77	**Leinefelde** .... a.	...	0502t	...	0538r	0613	...	...	0641	0659	0702	...	0741	0808a	...	0902	0941	1015	...	1102	1141	1215	...	1302
77	**Leinefelde** .... d.	0443r	0503	...	0539	0613	0608a	...	0642	0700	0703	0708	0743	0821	0823	0903	0943	1021	1023	1103	1143	1221	1223	1303
119	**Nordhausen** .... a.	0525r	|	...	0620	0653	|	...	|	0733	0736	|	|	|	0905	0936	|	|	1106	1136	|	|	1304	1336
119	**Nordhausen** .... ◧ d.	0528	|	...	0622	...	|	...	|	0738	0738	|	|	|	▬	0938	|	|	▬	1138	|	|	▬	1338
157	Sangerhausen .... ◧ d.	0559	|	...	0657	...	|	...	|	0808	0808	|	|	|	...	1008	|	|	...	1206	|	|	...	1408
179	Lutherstadt Eisleben .... ◧ d.	0619	|	...	0719	...	|	...	|	0828	0828	|	|	|	...	1028	|	|	...	1228	|	|	...	1428
217	**Halle** (Saale) Hbf .... ◧ d.	0650	|	...	0749	...	|	...	|	0900	0900	|	|	|	...	1100	|	|	...	1300	|	|	...	1500
—	Mühlhausen (Thür) .... d.	...	0525	...	...	...	0636	...	0659	...	...	0731	0800	0844	◇	...	1000	1044	◇	...	1200	1244	◇	...
0	Bad Langensalza .... a.	...	0536	...	...	...	0652	0658	0708	...	...	0747	0810	0859	0902	...	1010	1059	1102	...	1210	1259	1302	...
	Gotha .... **849 850** a.	...	0551	...	...	...	|	0716	0720	...	...	0810	0822	|	0920	...	1022	|	1120	...	1222	|	1320	...
38	**Erfurt** Hbf .... **849 850** a.	...	0617	...	...	...	0747	...	0746	...	...	...	0847	0958	...	...	1047	1158	...	...	1247	1358	...	...

	A	Ⓐm	◇	H	Ⓐm		A	◇			A	⑤F	◇			G	◇		n	n◇	n	n◇	n	n◇
Kassel Wilhelmshöhe .... **864** d.	...	...	1307a	...	...	1404a	...	1507b	...	1604a	...	1704	1708	...	1804a	...	1907	...	2004a	...	...	2109k	...	...
Kassel Hbf .... **864** d.	...	...	|	...	*1318*x	1405c	...	|	...	1605c	...	|	|	...	1805c	...	|	...	2005c	...	...	|	...	*2146*
Hann Münden .... **864** d.	...	...	1326a	...	*1340*x	1421	...	1526b	...	1621	...	|	1726	...	1821	...	1926	...	2021	...	...	2126k	...	*2206*
Eichenberg .... **864** d.	...	...	1346	...	1412	1440	...	1548	...	1640	...	|	1746	...	1840	...	1947	...	2040	...	...	2147	...	2233
Göttingen .... d.	1308	...	|	...	|	|	1508	|	...	|	1708	|	|	...	|	1908	|	...	|	...	2108	|	...	|
Heilbad Heiligenstadt .... d.	1330	...	1400	...	1426	1452	1530	1602	...	1652	1730	1749	1800	...	1852	1930	2001	...	2052	...	2131	2201	...	2247
Leinefelde .... a.	1341	...	1415	...	1440	1502	1541	1617	...	1702	1741	1759	1815	...	1902	1941	2016	...	2102	...	2142	2215	...	2303
Leinefelde .... d.	1343	1346	1421	1423	1442	1503	1543	1621	1623	1703	1743	1801	1821	1823	1903	1943	2021	2023	2103	2108	2143	2222	*2225*	...
Nordhausen .... a.	|	1427	|	1504	1526	1536	|	|	1704	1737	|	1830	|	1904	1936	|	|	2105	2136	|	|	|	*2306*	...
Nordhausen .... ◧ d.	|	...	|	▬	...	1538	|	|	▬	1738	|	1832	|	▬	1938	|	|	▬	2138	|	|	|	2319	...
Sangerhausen .... ◧ d.	|	...	|	...	...	1608	|	|	...	1808	|	1903	|	...	2008	|	|	...	2208	|	|	|	2353	...
Lutherstadt Eisleben .... ◧ d.	|	...	|	...	...	1628	|	|	...	1828	|	1921	|	...	2028	|	|	...	2228	|	|	|	0011	...
Halle (Saale) Hbf .... ◧ d.	|	...	|	...	...	1700	|	|	...	1900	|	1949	|	...	2100	|	|	...	2301	|	|	|	0051	...
Mühlhausen (Thür) .... d.	1400	...	1444	◇	...	...	1600	1644	◇	...	1800	...	1844	n◇	...	2000	2044	n◇	...	2135	2200	2245	...	...
Bad Langensalza .... a.	1410	...	1459	1502	...	...	1610	1659	1702	...	1810	...	1859	1902	...	2010	2059	2102	...	2149	2210	2300	...	...
Gotha .... **849 850** a.	1422	...	|	1520	...	...	1622	|	1720	...	1822	...	|	1920	...	2022	|	2120	...	|	2222	2333	...	...
Erfurt Hbf .... **849 850** a.	1447	...	1558	...	...	...	1647	1758	...	...	1847	...	1958	...	...	2047	2158	...	...	2244	2250	0003	...	...

A – From / to Chemnitz and Zwickau (Table **858**).
E – ⑦ (also Apr. 5, May 24; not Apr. 4, May 23). *IC* **1848**. From Leipzig Hbf (d. 1525) to Frankfurt (Main) Hbf (a. 2040).
F – ⑤ (Also Dec. 23, 30, Apr. 1, May 12; not Dec. 25, Jan. 1, Apr. 2, May 14). *IC* **1851**. From Frankfurt (Main) Hbf (d. 1517) to Leipzig Hbf (a. 2042). 🍷.
G – From / to Gera (Table **858**).
H – © (daily Dec. 19 - Jan. 3, Jan. 30 - Feb. 7, Mar. 27 - Apr. 11).
L – ①②③④⑥⑦ (also Dec. 25, Jan. 1, Apr. 2, May 14; not Dec. 23, 30, Apr. 1, May 12).

a – Ⓐ only.
b – Ⓑ only.
c – © only.
h – Also Apr. 4, May 23; not Apr. 5, May 24.
k – ⑤–⑦ (also Apr. 1, 5, May 12, 13, 24, June 2, 3).
m – Not Dec. 21 - Jan. 1, Feb. 1 – 5, Mar. 29 - Apr. 9.
n – Not Dec. 24, 31.
q – † only.
r – ⚒ (not Dec. 24, 31).
t – Ⓐ (not Dec. 24, 31).
v – Not Dec. 25, Jan. 1.
x – Not June 3.

◇ – Operated by Erfurter Bahn GmbH (2nd class only).
◧ – See panel below for additional services Halle - Nordhausen and v.v.

				Ⓐ	⚒						
Halle (Saale) Hbf .... d.	0014	...	...	0628	0804	1004	1204	1404	...	1804	2004
Lutherstadt Eisleben .... d.	0055	...	...	0703	0835	1035	1235	1435	...	1835	2035
Sangerhausen .... d.	0117	...	...	0730	0857	1057	1257	1457	...	1857	2057
Nordhausen .... d.	...	...	...	0803	0931	1131	1331	1531	...	1931	2131

	⚒			Ⓐ	©	Ⓐ	©	Ⓑ	⑥	L	
Nordhausen .... d.	0415	0821	1021	1221	1221	1421	1421	1621	1621	1821	2053
Sangerhausen .... d.	0452	0857	1057	1257	1257	1457	1457	1657	1657	1857	2130
Lutherstadt Eisleben .... d.	0513	0919	1119	1314	1319	1514	1519	1714	1719	1919	2151
Halle (Saale) Hbf .... a.	0527	0948	1148	1348	1348	1548	1551	1748	1748	1948	2230

867 HARZER SCHMALSPURBAHNEN

2nd class only

Nordhausen - Wernigerode: *Die Harzquerbahn*; Eisfelder Talmühle - Stiege - Alexisbad - Quedlinburg: *Die Selketalbahn*; Drei Annen Hohne - Brocken: *Die Brockenbahn*

Winter service: November 2, 2009 - April 23, 2010

km		v	🚂🍷	C🚂	🚂	🚂🍷	r🚂	r🚂	r🚂	L🚂	n	
0	**Wernigerode** § d.	0725	0910	1025	1155	...	1255	1455	...	1555	1625	...
15	Drei Annen Hohne a.	0803	0948	1103	1233	...	1342	1533	...	1649	1707	...
15	Drei Annen Hohne d.	0810	1005	1120	1240	1235	1350	1540	1557	1705	1710	...
20	Schierke d.	|	1024	1139	|	1254	1409	|	1616	1728	|	...
34	**Brocken** a.	|	1054	1209	|	1324	1440	|	1646	1758	|	...
19	Elend d.	0822	▬	▬	1252	▬	▬	1552	...	...	1722	...
28	Sorge d.	0841	...	...	1311	...	...	1611	...	...	1741	...
31	Benneckenstein d.	0850	...	🚋	1320	...	...	1620	...	...	1750	...
44	Eisfelder Talmühle a.	0919	©z	Ⓐn	1349	...	🚋	1649	...	...	1819	...
44	Eisfelder Talmühle d.	...	0921	0921	...	1401		1659	...	...	...	1831
50	Ilfeld d.	...	0942	0942	...	1416	1442	1714	...	...	...	1846
61	**Nordhausen** Nord § a.	...	1009*	1009*	...	1438e	1509*	1739	...	...	...	1909*

	v	🚂🍷	🚂🍷	C🚂	🚂🍷	r	r🚂	J🚂	N🚂	L🚂	n
Nordhausen Nord § d.	0831*	...	1016	...	...	1317	...	...	...	...	1746*
Ilfeld d.	0859	...	1043	...	...	1343	...	...	...	...	1813
Eisfelder Talmühle a.	0913	...	1057	...	...	1357	...	...	...	...	1827
Eisfelder Talmühle d.	0937	...	1107	...	...	▬	1407	...	...	...	1837
Benneckenstein d.	1007	...	1137	...	...	...	1437	...	...	...	1909
Sorge d.	1015	...	1145	...	...	🚂	1445	...	...	...	1917
Elend d.	1035	...	1205	...	...	r	1505	...	...	...	1938
Brocken d.	|	1106	|	1221	1338	1451	|	1656	1723	1808	|
Schierke d.	|	1141	|	1258	1411	1526	|	1727	1756	1841	|
Drei Annen Hohne a.	1046	1153	1216	1309	1423	1538	1516	1738	1808	1853	1949
Drei Annen Hohne d.	1108	...	1253	1353	1453	...	1553	1753	1823	1908	1953
Wernigerode § a.	1145	...	1330	1430	1533	...	1633	1830	1900	1945	2030

km		v	v	P🚂				¶	Pn	Pn	n	n
0	**Quedlinburg** § △ d.	0830	...	1030v	1130v	...	...	1430r	1630	...	1730	2030
8	**Gernrode** △ d.	0847	...	1047	1147	...	...	1447r	1647	...	1747	2045
18	Mägdesprung d.	0918	...	1118	1219	...	...	1518r	1718	...	1818	▬
	Harzgerode d.	|	0928	|	|	1325	1525	|	|	1825	|	...
23	Alexisbad a.	0932	0938	1132	1232	1335	1535	1532r	1732	1835	1833	n◐
23	Alexisbad d.	▬	0942	1139	1239	1339	▬	1539	1739	▬	1839	1839‡
26	**Harzgerode** a.	...	|	1149	1249	|	...	|	1749	...	|	1849‡
26	Silberhütte d.	...	0954	...	...	1351	...	1551	▬	...	1851	...
30	Straßberg (Harz) d.	...	1005	...	...	1403	...	1603	...	...	1903	...
35	Güntersberge d.	...	1014	...	...	1412	...	1612	...	...	1912	...
	Hasselfelde d.	1007	|	...	...	|	1500	|	1748	...	|	...
44	Stiege a.	1028	1030	...	...	1428	1521	1628	1809	...	1928	...
44	Stiege d.	...	1031	...	...	1429	1533	1629	1810	...	1931	...
48	**Hasselfelde** a.	...	|	...	...	1450	|	1650	|	...	|	...
53	Eisfelder Talmühle d.	...	1059	...	...	...	1557	...	1831	1857	1958	...
59	Ilfeld d.	...	1114	...	...	...	1612	...	1846	1914	2013	...
70	**Nordhausen** Nord § a.	...	1138	...	...	...	1638	...	1909*	1938	2039*	...

	v	v			P🚂			n	n◐	n	Pn
Nordhausen Nord § d.	0631*	...	0831*	...	...	...	1117	1617	...	...	🚂
Ilfeld d.	0659	...	0859	...	...	...	1143	1643	...	...	...
Eisfelder Talmühle d.	0714	...	0921	...	...	...	1203	1659	...	...	...
Hasselfelde d.	|	0800	|	1007	...	...	|	|	1700	...	...
Stiege a.	0734	0821	0941	1028	...	...	1223	1719	1721	...	...
Stiege d.	0735	0822	0942	1036	...	...	1236	1723	1736	...	...
Hasselfelde a.	0756	|	1003	|	...	...	|	1744	|	...	...
Güntersberge d.	▬	0838	▬	1053	...	...	1252	▬	1752	...	...
Straßberg (Harz) d.	...	0848	...	1102	...	...	1302	...	1802	...	...
Silberhütte d.	...	0859	...	1114	...	...	1313	t	1813	...	...
Harzgerode d.	...	|	...	|	...	1225	|	1525	|	1825k	1925
Alexisbad a.	...	0910	v	1125	...	1235	1324	1535	1824	1835k	1935
Alexisbad d.	...	0914	1001	1139	1201	1301	1339	1601	1839‡	1901	2001
Harzgerode a.	...	0924	|	1149	|	|	1349	|	1849‡	|	|
Mägdesprung d.	v	...	1015	...	1220	1315	...	1615	...	1915	2015
Gernrode △ d.	0759	...	1059f	...	1259	1359f	...	1659f	...	1959f	2045
Quedlinburg § △ a.	0815	...	1115	...	1315r	1415r	...	1715n	...	2015	...

C – ⑥⑦ (daily Dec. 19 - Feb. 21 and from Mar. 27).
J – To Jan. 29 and from Mar. 27 (not Dec. 24).
L – From Mar. 27.
N – Jan. 30 - Mar. 26.
P – Dec. 12 - Apr. 23 (not Mar. 8–19).

e – © (also during school holidays).
f – Arrives 14 minutes earlier.
k – 23 minutes later Nov. 2 - Dec. 11 and Mar. 8–19.

n – Not Dec. 24, 31.
r – Not Dec. 24.
t – Not Dec. 31.
v – Not Jan. 1.
z – Also Dec. 24, 31.

🚂 – Steam train.
🚋 – Nordhausen Stadtbahn.
* – Nordhausen **Bahnhofsplatz**.

§ – Adjacent to DB station.
¶ – Operated by 🚂 between Gernrode and Hasselfelde Dec. 12 - Mar. 7 and Mar. 20 - Apr. 23 (passengers from Quedlinburg change trains at Gernrode).
◐ – Operated by 🚂 Dec. 12 - Mar. 7 and Mar. 20 - Apr. 23.
‡ – Nov. 2 - Dec. 11 and Mar. 8–19 Alexisbad d. 1835, Harzgerode a. 1844.
△ – Additional services Quedlinburg - Gernrode and v.v.
From Quedlinburg at 1330 🚂 **P r**. **From Gernrode** at 0959 🚂 **P v**, 1559 **P n**.

Operator: Harzer Schmalspurbahnen GmbH, Friedrichstrasse 151, 38855 Wernigerode.
✆ + 49 (0) 3943 558 151. Fax + 49 (0) 3943 558 148.

868 ERFURT - NORDHAUSEN

RE / RB services

km		Ⓐn	⚒												Ⓐn	©z				n
0	**Erfurt** Hbf d.	...	0440	0604	0704	0804	0904	1004	1104	1204	1304	1404	1504	1604	1704	1704	1804	1904	2004	2144
27	Straußfurt d.	...	0505	0626	0730	0826	0930	1026	1130	1226	1330	1426	1530	1626	1730	1730	1826	1930	2026	2209
60	Sondershausen d.	0452	0552	0700	0810	0859	1010	1059	1210	1259	1410	1500	1610	1659	1803	1810	1859	2010	2055	2247
80	**Nordhausen** a.	0516	0615	0719	0833	0919	1033	1119	1233	1319	1433	1521	1633	1719	1826	1833	1919	2033	2115	2312

	Ⓐn	⚒		Ⓐn	©z										Ⓐn	©z			n
Nordhausen d.	0424	0527	0637	0723	0728	0837	0928	1037	1128	1237	1328	1439	1528	1637	1720	1728	1837	1928	2138
Sondershausen d.	0454	0553	0659	0753	0753	0859	0953	1059	1153	1259	1353	1501	1553	1659	1746	1753	1859	1953	2159
Straußfurt d.	0527	0627	0731	0827	0827	0931	1027	1131	1227	1331	1427	1531	1627	1731	1827	1827	1931	2027	2229
Erfurt Hbf a.	0552	0652	0752	0852	0852	0952	1052	1152	1252	1352	1452	1552	1652	1752	1852	1852	1952	2052	2251

n – Not Dec. 24, 31.
z – Also Dec. 24, 31.

869 NORDHAUSEN - GÖTTINGEN

RB services

km		①g	⚒	v												m	n	n	Ⓑn
0	**Nordhausen** d.	0438	0538	0638	0738	0838	0938	1038	1138	1238	1338	1438	1538	1638	1738	1838	1938	2038	2142
20	Walkenried d.	0500	0603	0703	0803	0903	1003	1103	1203	1303	1403	1503	1603	1703	1803	1903	2003	2103	2203
23	Bad Sachsa d.	0506	0608	0708	0808	0908	1008	1108	1208	1308	1408	1508	1608	1708	1808	1908	2008	2108	2208
37	Bad Lauterberg ⊡ d.	0516	0619	0719	0819	0919	1019	1119	1219	1319	1419	1519	1619	1719	1819	1919	2019	2119	2219
43	Herzberg (Harz) d.	0523	0626	0726	0826	0926	1026	1126	1226	1329	1426	1526	1626	1726	1826	1926	2026	2126	2226
70	Northeim (Han) 903 a.	0547	0650	0750	0850	0950	1050	1150	1250	1353	1450	1550	1650	1750	1850	1950	2050	2150	2250
90	**Göttingen** 903 a.	0605	0715	0808	0909	1008	1109	1208	1309	1411	1509	1608	1709	1808	1909	2008	2109	2208	2308

	Ⓐn	⚒	v												n	n	n	E
Göttingen 903 d.	0407	0538	0638	0749	0848*	0949	1048*	1149	1248*	1349	1448*	1549	1648*	1749	1848*	1949	2048*	2149
Northeim (Han) 903 d.	0506	0606	0702f	0806	0906	1006	1106	1206	1306	1406	1506	1606	1706	1806	1906	2006	2106	2206
Herzberg (Harz) d.	0530	0630	0730	0830	0930	1030	1130	1230	1330	1430	1530	1630	1730	1830	1930	2030	2130	2230
Bad Lauterberg ⊡ d.	0536	0636	0736	0836	0936	1036	1136	1236	1336	1436	1536	1636	1736	1836	1936	2036	2136	2236
Bad Sachsa d.	0547	0647	0747	0847	0947	1047	1147	1247	1347	1447	1547	1647	1747	1847	1947	2047	2147	2247
Walkenried d.	0552	0652	0752	0852	0952	1052	1152	1252	1352	1452	1552	1652	1752	1852	1952	2052	2205r	2252
Nordhausen a.	0615	0715	0815	0915	1015	1115	1215	1315	1415	1515	1615	1715	1815	1915	2015	2115	2227	2315

E – ⑤–⑦ (also Apr. 5, May 13, 24).
f – 0706 on ©.
g – Also Apr. 6, May 25; not Apr. 5, May 24.
m – Not Dec. 24.
n – Not Dec. 24, 31.
r – Arrives 2152.
v – Not Dec. 25, Jan. 1.
* – 38 minutes earlier on ⑦ Jan. 3 - Mar. 21.
⊡ – Bad Lauterberg im Harz Barbis

870 ERFURT - MEININGEN - SCHWEINFURT - WÜRZBURG

DB (*RE* services); *STB*; *EB*

km				▽ Ⓐn			▽		▽		▽		▽		▽		▽					▽ n	★	⑦w	▽ n
0	**Erfurt** Hbf 872 d.	...	...	0413	0506	...	0647	0732	0847	0932	1047	1132	1247	1332	1447	1532	1647	1732	1830	1932	...	2047	2216	2234	2357
23	Arnstadt Hbf 872 d.	...	...	0434	0523	...	0709	0750	0909	0950	1109	1150	1309	1350	1509	1550	1709	1750	1847	1950	...	2109	2233	2251	0019
31	Plaue (Thür) d.	...	...	0444	0529	...	0719	0758	0919	0958	1119	1158	1319	1358	1519	1558	1719	1758	1854	1958	...	2119	2241	2259	0029
37	Gräfenroda d.	...	...	0449	0534	...	0724	0803	0924	1003	1124	1203	1324	1403	1524	1603	1724	1803	1859	2003	...	2124	2246	2304	0034
53	Oberhof (Thür) d.	...	...	0503	0546	...	0744	0815	0944	1015	1144	1215	1344	1415	1544	1615	1744	1815	1910	2015	...	2144	2257	2316	0049
58	Zella-Mehlis d.	...	...	0509	0551	...	0751	0819	0951	1019	1151	1219	1351	1419	1551	1619	1751	1819	1915	2019	...	2151	2302	2320	0054
64	Suhl d.	...	...	0515	0557	...	0758	0825	0958	1025	1158	1225	1358	1425	1558	1625	1758	1825	1921	2025	...	2158	2308	2326	0100
84	Grimmenthal 873 a.	...	...	0536	0609	...	0814	0835	1014	1035	1214	1235	1414	1435	1614	1635	1814	1835	1938	2035	...	2214	2318	2337	0116
92	**Meiningen** 873 a.	...	...	0544	0633a	...	0821	0848	1021	1048	1221	1248	1421	1448	1621	1648	1821	1848	1949	2048	...	2221	2325	2344	0123
				▬	|		▬	|	▬	|	▬	|	▬	|	▬	|	▬	|	▬	|					
		◇ Ⓐe	Ⓐe	◇	|	◇ Ⓐe	◇	|	◇	|	◇	|	◇	|	◇	|	◇	|	◇	|	◇ Ⓐe				
	Meiningen 873 d.	0424	...	0530	0549a	0646	0741	0822	0945	1022	1145	1222	1345	1422	1545	1622	1745	1822	1945	2022n	2055	...	...	...	...
84	Grimmenthal 873 d.	|	...	|	0610	|	|	0836	|	1036	|	1236	|	1436	|	1636	|	1836	|	2036	|	...	...	...	...
110	Mellrichstadt d.	0447	...	0553	0630	0712	0808	0849	1009	1049	1209	1249	1409	1449	1609	1649	1809	1849	2009	2049	2122	...	...	...	...
124	Bad Neustadt (Saale) d.	0456	...	0605	0638	0721	0818	0857	1018	1057	1218	1257	1418	1457	1618	1657	1818	1857	2018	2057	2141	...	...	...	...
134	Münnerstadt d.	0504	...	0613	0647	0729	0828	0904	1028	1104	1228	1304	1428	1504	1628	1704	1828	1904	2028	2104	2149	...	...	...	...
149	Ebenhausen (Unterfr) d.	0514	0518	0631	0701	0742	0841	0917	1041	1117	1241	1317	1441	1517	1641	1717	1841	1917	2040	2117	2202	...	...	...	...
163	**Schweinfurt** Hbf 876 a.	...	0532	0643	0716	0754	0852	0926	1052	1126	1252	1326	1452	1526	1652	1726	1852	1926	2052	2126	2214	...	...	...	...
206	**Würzburg** Hbf 876 a.	...	0617	0719	0747	0823	0923	0958	1123	1158	1323	1358	1523	1558	1723	1758	1923	1958	2151g	2158	2253	...	...	...	...

a – Ⓐ only.
e – Not Dec. 24, 31, Jan. 6, June 3.
g – *2123* on © (also Dec. 24, 31, Jan. 6, June 3).
n – Not Dec. 24, 31.
w – Also Apr. 5, May 24; not Apr. 4, May 23.
★ – ①–⑥ (also Apr. 4, May 23; not Dec. 24, 31, Apr. 5, May 24).
▽ – Operated by Süd Thüringen Bahn (2nd class only).
◇ – Operated by Erfurter Bahn (2nd class only).

DB (*RE* services); *STB*; *EB*

WÜRZBURG - SCHWEINFURT - MEININGEN - ERFURT 870

							◇	◇	◇		◇		◇		◇		◇		◇		◇			◇	◇
							Ⓐe	Ⓐe	Ⓒd															Ⓐe	
Würzburg Hbf .. 876 ● d.	...	...	...	...	*0501*r	...	...	*0602*	*0602*	0801	*0836*	1001	*1036*	1201	*1236*	1401	*1436*	1601	*1636*	1801	*1836*	2001		*2036*	*2139*z
Schweinfurt Hbf 876 ● d.	...	...	...	...	0539	...	0619	0648	0705	0830	0906	1030	1106	1230	1306	1430	1506	1630	1706	1830	1906	2030	...	2106	2224
Ebenhausen (Unterf) ● d.	...	...	...	...	0549	...	0635	0701	0720	0840	0920	1040	1120	1240	1320	1440	1520	1640	1720	1840	1920	2040	...	2120	2238
Münnerstadt d.	...	...	...	...	0558	...	0648	0712	0731	0849	0931	1049	1131	1249	1331	1449	1531	1649	1731	1849	1931	2049	...	2131	2249
Bad Neustadt (Saale) d.	...	...	...	...	0605	...	0656	0722	0740	0857	0940	1057	1140	1257	1340	1457	1540	1657	1740	1857	1940	2057	...	2140	2258
Mellrichstadt d.	...	...	...	...	0614	...	0710	0731	0749	0906	0949	1106	1149	1306	1349	1506	1549	1706	1749	1906	1949	2106	...	2149	2307
Grimmenthal 873 a.	...	...	...	...	0629	...	|	|	|	0919	|	1119	|	1319	|	1519	|	1719	|	1919	|	2120	...	|	|
Meiningen 873 a.	...	...	...	...	|	...	0732	0756	0816	*0932*	1016	*1132*	1216	*1332*	1416	*1532*	1616	*1732*	1816	*1932*	2016	*2132*n	...	2213	2330
		▽		▽	|		▽			|	▽	|	▽	|	▽	|	▽	|	▽	|	▽	|	▽		
	Ⓐn	Ⓐn	v																		n		n		
Meiningen 873 d.	0340	0409	0510	0527	*0619*	0711	0733	...	...	*0907*	0933	*1107*	1133	*1307*	1333	*1507*	1533	*1707*	1733	*1907*	1933	*2107*	2133	...	...
Grimmenthal 873 d.	0346	0417	0517	0538	0630	0720	0740	...	...	0920	0940	1120	1140	1320	1340	1520	1540	1720	1740	1920	1940	2121	2140	...	...
Suhl d.	0358	0437	0531	0557	0641	0731	0758	...	...	0931	0958	1131	1158	1331	1358	1531	1558	1731	1758	1931	1958	2132	2158	...	...
Zella-Mehlis d.	0404	0449	0538	0603	0647	0737	0805	...	...	0937	1005	1137	1205	1337	1405	1537	1605	1737	1805	1937	2005	2138	2205	...	...
Oberhof (Thür) d.	0409	0455	0543	0608	0652	0743	0811	...	...	0943	1011	1143	1211	1343	1411	1543	1611	1743	1811	1943	2011	2144	2211	...	...
Gräfenroda d.	0419	0511	0556	0627	0703	0753	0827	...	...	0953	1027	1153	1227	1353	1427	1553	1627	1753	1827	1953	2027	2154	2227	...	...
Plaue (Thür) d.	0424	0518	0600	0639	0707	0758	0838	...	...	0958	1038	1158	1238	1358	1438	1558	1638	1758	1838	1958	2038	2159	2240	...	...
Arnstadt Hbf 872 d.	0432	0526	0609	0648	0714	0806	0848	...	...	1006	1048	1206	1248	1406	1448	1606	1648	1806	1848	2006	2048	2206	2248	...	...
Erfurt Hbf 872 a.	0449	0547	0624	0708	0729	0822	0908	...	...	1022	1108	1222	1308	1422	1508	1622	1708	1822	1908	2022	2108	2222	2308	...	...

d – Also Dec. 24, 31, Jan. 6, June 3.
e – Not Dec. 24, 31, Jan. 6, June 3.
n – Not Dec. 24, 31.
r – ⚒ (not Jan. 6, June 3).
v – Not Dec. 25, Jan. 1.
z – *2144* on Ⓒ **d**.
▽ – Operated by Süd Thüringen Bahn (2nd class only).
◇ – Operated by Erfurter Bahn (2nd class only).
● – Trains between Würzburg, Schweinfurt and Ebenhausen are often combined with a service to Bad Kissingen. Passengers should take care to join the correct portion for their destination.

RE / *RB* services

LEIPZIG - GERA - HOF and SAALFELD 871

km																											
		Ⓐe	⚒n	v					⑥H	G	R					R					R					n	n
0	**Leipzig** Hbf d.	...	...	...	0503**e**	*0625*	0719**e**	0719	0826	0826**j**	...	0919	1025	1119	1225	...	1319	1425	1519	1625	...	1719	1825	1919	2025	*2125*	2325
45	Zeitz d.	...	0445**e**	...	0557**e**	*0704*	0805**e**	0805	0904	0904	...	1005	1104	1205	1304	...	1405	1504	1605	1704	...	1805	1904	2005	2104	*2211*	0014
72	**Gera** Hbf a.	...	0516**e**	...	0624**e**	*0726*	0832**e**	0832	0926	0926	...	1032	1126	1232	1326	...	1432	1526	1632	1726	...	1832	1926	2032	2126	*2238*	0041
72	**Gera** Hbf d.	0435	0518	0609	0628	0744	0835	...	0928	0943	1009	1035	1145	1236	1345	1409	1438	1545	1635	1745	1809	1835	1945	2035	*2201*n	2302	...
84	Weida d.	0455	0533	0621	0644	0759	0850	...	|	1003	1021	1050	1203	1252	1403	1421	1452	1603	1653	1803	1821	1850	2003	2050	*2214*n	2321	...
156	**Hof** Hbf a.	|	|	0726	|	|	|	...	|	|	1126	|	|	|	|	1526	|	|	|	|	1926	|	|	|	...	|	...
99	Triptis d.	0508	0547	...	0657	0816	0909	...	|	1016	...	1109	1216	1309	1416	...	1509	1616	1709	1816	...	1909	2016	2109	...	2334	...
108	Neustadt (Orla) d.	0516	0555	...	0704	0824	0916	...	|	1024	...	1116	1224	1316	1424	...	1516	1624	1716	1824	...	1916	2024	2116	...	2342	...
139	**Saalfeld** (Saale) a.	0551	0627	...	0729	0854	0940	...	1018	1054	...	1140	1254	1340	1454	...	1540	1654	1740	1854	...	1940	2054	2140	...	0011	...

	⚒n	Ⓐe	⚒n					R					R				Ⓒz	Ⓐe	R	G	⑥L		◇		n	n	n
Saalfeld (Saale) d.	...	...	0506	...	0622	0723	0819	...	0905	1019	1105	1219	...	1305	1419	1505	1619	1619	...	1705	1735	1819	1905	2019	...	2134	2229
Neustadt (Orla) d.	...	...	0537	...	0648	0752	0848	...	0940	1048	1140	1248	...	1340	1448	1540	1648	1648	...	1740	|	1848	1940	2048	...	2203	2258
Triptis d.	...	...	0548	...	0658	0801	0855	...	0949	1055	1149	1255	...	1349	1455	1549	1655	1655	...	1749	|	1855	1949	2055	...	2211	2306
Hof Hbf d.	...	...	|	...	|	|	|	0834	|	|	|	|	1234	|	|	|	|	|	1634	|	|	|	|	|	2045	|	|
Weida d.	...	*0453*	0601	...	0712	0815	0910	0938	1002	1110	1202	1310	1338	1402	1510	1602	1710	1715	1738	1802	|	1910	2002	2110	2150	2224	2319
Gera Hbf a.	...	*0507*	0614	...	0723	0827	0921	0948	1015	1121	1215	1321	1348	1415	1521	1615	1721	1726	1748	1815	1829	1921	2015	2121	2200	2235	2332
Gera Hbf ◧ d.	0452	0528	0630	0630	...	0830	...	...	1030	...	1230	...	...	1430	...	1630	...	...	...	1830	1830	...	2030	...	...	2238	...
Zeitz ◧ d.	0520	0556	0654	0654	...	0854	...	...	1054	...	1254	...	...	1454	...	1654	...	...	...	1854	1854	...	2054	...	...	2307	...
Leipzig Hbf ◧ a.	0613	0645	0732	0732	...	0932	...	...	1132	...	1332	...	...	1532	...	1732	...	...	...	1932	1932	...	2132	...	...	2354	...

G – Change trains at Gera until May 1 (also on ⑥ from May 8).
H – ⑥ from May 1. To Rottenbach (1053), Obstfelderschmiede (1123), Katzhütte (1141).
L – ⑥ from May 1. From Katzhütte (1617), Obstfelderschmiede (1635), Rottenbach (1702).
R – To / from Regensburg (Table **879**).
e – Ⓐ (not Dec. 24, 31).
j – 0825 until Mar. 13.
n – Not Dec. 24, 31.
v – Not Dec. 25, Jan. 1.
z – Also Dec. 24, 31.
◇ – Change trains at Gera on ⑥.
◧ – Additional journeys Gera - Zeitz - Leipzig: From Gera Hbf at 0712, 0912 and every **two** hours until 1912.

RE / *RB* services

ERFURT - SAALFELD and ROTTENBACH - KATZHÜTTE 872

km		⚒n				C	n		n	n
0	**Erfurt** Hbf 870 d.	0454	0638	*0737*	0840	then each	*1937*	2040	*2142*	2252
23	Arnstadt Hbf 870 d.	0517	0655	0802	0900	train runs	2002	2100	2212	2310
38	Stadtilm d.	0536	0708	0816	0912	every	2016	2112	2226	2324
54	Rottenbach d.	0553	0721	0835	0925	**two** hours	2035	2125	2245	2337
62	Bad Blankenburg d.	0601	0728	0842	0932	until	2042	2132	2252	2344
70	**Saalfeld** (Saale) a.	0610	0736	0850	0940		2050	2140	2300	2352

	⚒n					⊠		n	n
Saalfeld (Saale) d.	0506	0612	0704	0819	0907	then each	2019	2107	2229
Bad Blankenburg d.	0513	0619	0711	0826	0914	train runs	2026	2114	2236
Rottenbach d.	0521	0626	0723	0833	0927	every	2033	2127	2243
Stadtilm d.	0535	0639	0737	0846	0942	**two** hours	2046	2142	2256
Arnstadt Hbf 870 a.	0549	0653	0751	0858	0955	until	2058	2155	2308
Erfurt Hbf 870 a.	0612	0712	*0818*	0916	*1018*		2116	*2218*	2326

km		Ⓐ			A			⑤⑦f	
0	Rottenbach d.	0546	0641	0730	then each train	1841	1930	2041	...
15	Obstfelderschmiede ¶ a.	0610	0705	0754	runs every **two**	1905	1954	2105	...
25	Katzhütte a.	0628	0723	0812	hours until	1923	2012	2123	...

	Ⓐ				B			⑤⑦f
Katzhütte d.	0540	...	0635	0746	then each train	1835	1946	2035
Obstfelderschmiede ¶ d.	0558	...	0653	0804	runs every **two**	1853	2004	2053
Rottenbach a.	0622	...	0717	0828	hours until	1917	2028	2117

A – On ⑥ from May 1 the 1041 and 1641 from Rottenbach run 18 – 19 minutes later.
B – On ⑥ from May 1 the 1035 and 1635 from Katzhütte run 18 – 19 minutes **earlier**.
C – On ⑥ from May 1 Saalfeld a. 1054 (not 1050).
f – Also Apr. 5, May 24; not Apr. 4, May 23.
⊠ – The 1907 from Saalfeld does not run on Dec. 24, 31.
¶ – Station for the *Oberweißbacher Bergbahn* to Lichtenhain and Cursdorf.
n – Not Dec. 24, 31.

Süd Thüringen Bahn (2nd class only)

EISENACH - MEININGEN - SONNEBERG 873

km																									
		Ⓐ	Ⓐ	Ⓐ										Ⓒ	Ⓐ		Ⓒ	Ⓐ				n	n	n	n
0	**Eisenach** d.	...	0400	0452	...	0608**t**	0715	0815	0915	1015	1115	1215	1315	1415	1415	1515	1615	1615	1715	1815	1915	2015	2115	2220	2310
27	Bad Salzungen d.	...	0426	0521	...	0641**t**	0741	0841	0941	1041	1141	1241	1341	1441	1441	1541	1641	1641	1741	1841	1941	2041	2141	2250	2333
41	Wernshausen d.	...	0441	0539	...	0657**t**	0757	0857	0957	1057	1157	1257	1357	1457	1457	1557	1657	1657	1757	1857	1957	2057	2157	2304	...
61	**Meiningen** a.	...	0458	0600	...	0713**t**	0813	0913	1013	1113	1213	1313	1413	1513	1513	1613	1713	1713	1813	1913	2013	2113	2213	2321	...
61	**Meiningen** 870 d.	0417	0549	0619	0619	0719	0822	0919	1022	1119	1222	1319	1422	1519	1519	1622	1719	1719	1822	1919**n**	2022**n**	2119	...	...	...
68	Grimmenthal 870 d.	0423	0556	0631	0631	0731	0831	0931	1031	1131	1231	1331	1431	1531	1541**k**	1631	1731	1741**k**	1831	1931**n**	2031**n**	2131	...	...	...
82	Themar d.	0440	0609	0644	0644	0744	0844	0944	1044	1144	1244	1344	1444	1544	1553	1644	1744	1753	1844	1944**n**	2044**n**	2144	...	...	...
94	Hildburghausen d.	0454	0621	0700	0700	0800	0900	1000	1100	1200	1300	1400	1500	1600	1606	1700	1800	1806	1900	2000**n**	2100**n**	2156	...	...	...
109	**Eisfeld** d.	0514	0643	0716	0716	0814	0916	1014	1116	1214	1316	1414	1516	1614	1621	1716	1814	1821	1916	2014**n**	2114**n**	2211	...	...	...
141	**Sonneberg** (Thür) Hbf a.	0558	0727	0800	0800	...	1000	...	1200	...	1400	...	1600	...	...	1800	...	...	2000	...	...	...	...	...	...

	Ⓐ	Ⓐ	Ⓐ	t	Ⓐ												Ⓒ	Ⓐ		Ⓒ	Ⓐ			n
Sonneberg (Thür) Hbf d.	...	...	...	...	...	...	...	0600	...	0802	...	1002	...	1202	...	1402	...	...	1602	...	1630	1802	...	2002
Eisfeld d.	...	...	0412	...	0540	...	...	0645	0745	0845	0945	1045	1145	1245	1345	1445	1545	1545	1645	1745	1745**f**	1845	1945	2045
Hildburghausen d.	...	...	0427	...	0555	...	...	0659	0759	0859	0959	1059	1159	1259	1359	1459	1559	1606	1659	1759	1806	1859	1959	2059
Themar d.	...	...	0438	...	0611	...	...	0711	0811	0911	1011	1111	1211	1311	1411	1511	1611	1617	1711	1811	1817	1911	2011	2111
Grimmenthal 870 d.	...	...	0455	...	0627	...	...	0726	0829	0926	1029	1126	1229	1326	1429	1526	1629	1629	1726	1829	1829	1926	2029	2126
Meiningen 870 a.	...	...	0501	...	0633	...	...	0732	0835	0932	1035	1132	1235	1332	1435	1532	1635	1635	1732	1835	1835	1932	2035	2132
Meiningen d.	...	0423	0503	0549	0639	0639	...	0739	0839	0939	1039	1139	1239	1339	1439	1539	1639	1639	1739	1839	1839**n**	1939**n**	2039**n**	2139
Wernshausen d.	...	0441	0520	0608	0657	0657	...	0757	0857	0957	1057	1157	1257	1357	1457	1557	1657	1657	1757	1857	1857**n**	1957**n**	2057**n**	2157
Bad Salzungen d.	0410	0453	0533	0621	0711	0711	...	0811	0911	1011	1111	1211	1311	1411	1511	1611	1711	1711	1811	1911	1911**n**	2011**n**	2111**n**	2211
Eisenach a.	0438	0519	0556	0646	0740	0740	...	0840	0940	1040	1140	1240	1340	1440	1540	1640	1740	1740	1840	1940	1940**n**	2040**n**	2140**n**	2236

f – Arrives 1713.
k – Arrives 16 minutes earlier.
n – Not Dec. 24, 31.
t – Not Dec. 25, 26, Jan. 1.

RE services

LEIPZIG - CHEMNITZ 874

km		v	①–⑥					n
0	**Leipzig** Hbf d.	0526	0631	0731	and	2131	...	2339
33	Bad Lausick d.	0550	0650	0750	hourly	2150	...	0002
44	Geithain d.	0558	0658	0758	until	2158	...	0010
66	Burgstädt d.	0612	0712	0812		2212	...	0025
81	**Chemnitz** Hbf a.	0625	0725	0825		2225	...	0038

	v	①–⑥		❖			n
Chemnitz Hbf d.	0424	0532	0632	and	2032	...	2244
Burgstädt d.	0436	0544	0644	hourly	2044	...	2256
Geithain d.	0450	0559	0659	until	2059	...	2311
Bad Lausick d.	0458	0607	0707		2107	...	2321
Leipzig Hbf a.	0520	0625	0725		2125	...	2352

n – Not Dec. 24, 31.
v – Not Dec. 25, Jan. 1.
❖ – On ②④⑥⑦ Chemnitz d. 1330 (not 1332).

875 NÜRNBERG - COBURG - SONNEBERG

RE / RB services

See Table **851** for faster *ICE* services Nürnberg - Erlangen - Bamberg - Lichtenfels and v.v.

km		Ⓐe	Ⓐe	Ⓐe																						2Ⓐe
0	**Nürnberg** Hbf ‡ d.	...	0429	...	0552	...	0651	0744	0839	...	0846	0944	1039	...	1045	1144	1149	1239	...	1245	1344	1439	...	1445	1544	1614
8	Fürth (Bay) Hbf ‡ d.	...	0438	...	0601	...	0659	0752	0846	...	0854	0952	1046	...	1053	1152	1158	1246	...	1253	1352	1446	...	1453	1552	1622
24	Erlangen ‡ d.	...	0456	...	0613	...	0719	0806	0900	...	0913	1006	1100	...	1112	1206	1216	1300	...	1312	1406	1500	...	1512	1606	1634
39	Forchheim (Oberfr) ‡ d.	...	0510	...	0621	...	0733	0816	0908	...	0928	1016	1108	...	1128	1216	1230	1308	...	1328	1416	1508	...	1528	1616	1645
62	**Bamberg** ‡ a.	...	0532	...	0636	...	0753	0831	0924	...	0949	1031	1124	...	1149	1231	1251	1324	...	1349	1431	1524	...	1549	1631	1702
62	**Bamberg** 876 d.	0449	...	0538	0638	0741	0755	0838	0926	0941	0954	1038	1126	1141	1154	1238	1252	1326	1340	1354	1438	1526	1541	1554	1638	1717
	Würzburg Hbf 876 a.	|	...	|	|	|	|	|	1023	|	|	|	1223	|	|	|	|	1423	|	|	|	1623	|	|	|	|
94	Lichtenfels 876 a.	0517	...	0610	0656	0800	0824	0856	...	1000	1023	1056	...	1200	1223	1256	1319	...	1400	1423	1456	...	1600	1623	1656	1746
94	Lichtenfels d.	0524	...	0622	0658	0810	0839	0906	...	1010	1039	1106	...	1210	1239	1306	1336e	...	1410	1439	1506	...	1610	1639	1706	1754
114	**Coburg** a.	0553	...	0642	0718	0833	0906	0930	...	1029	1106	1130	...	1229	1306	1330	1403e	...	1429	1506	1530	...	1629	1706	1730	1814
114	**Coburg** d.	0554	...	0701	0724	0835	...	0932	...	1035	...	1132	...	1235	...	1332	...	...	1435	...	1532	...	1635	1707q	1732	...
135	**Sonneberg** (Thür) Hbf a.	0621	...	0725	0745	0857	...	0954	...	1057	...	1154	...	1257	...	1354	...	...	1457	...	1554	...	1657	1738q	1754	...

Nürnberg Hbf ‡ d.	1639	...	1645	1744	1839	...	1944	2040	...	2145	2253
Fürth (Bay) Hbf ‡ d.	1646	...	1653	1752	1846	...	1952	2049	...	2154	2307
Erlangen ‡ d.	1700	...	1712	1806	1900	...	2006	2103	...	2207f	2325
Forchheim (Oberfr) ‡ d.	1708	...	1728	1816	1908	...	2016	2113	...	2217f	2339
Bamberg ‡ a.	1724	...	1749	1831	1924	...	2031	2129	...	2232f	2358
Bamberg 876 d.	1726	1741	1754	1838	1926	1941	2038	2138c	2141	2236f	0021
Würzburg Hbf 876 a.	1824	|	|	|	2024	|	|	2251c	|	|	|
Lichtenfels 876 a.	...	1800	1823	1856	...	2000	2056	...	2205	2301f	0048
Lichtenfels d.	...	1810	1840	1909	...	2010	2109	...	2212	2316	...
Coburg a.	...	1829	1906	1930	...	2029	2126	...	2238	2336	...
Coburg d.	...	1835	...	1932	...	2035	...	...	2239	...	...
Sonneberg (Thür) Hbf a.	...	1857	...	1954	...	2057	...	...	2301	...	...

	Ⓐe	Ⓐe	Ⓒz	Ⓐe			Ⓐe	Ⓒz		
Sonneberg (Thür) Hbf d.	0433	...	...	0518	0612	...	0648	0656	...	0732e
Coburg a.	0456	...	...	0542	0634	...	0721	0721	...	0800e
Coburg d.	0457	0518	0518	0543	0636	0652e	0724	0732	...	0802e
Lichtenfels a.	0517	0539	0539	0604	0656	0717e	0749	0753	...	0823e
Lichtenfels 876 d.	0518	0542	0542	0605	0658	0736	0800	0800	...	0840
Würzburg Hbf 876 d.	|	|	|	|	|	|	|	|	0728t	|
Bamberg 876 a.	0547	0612	0612	0632	0722	0806	0819	0819	0834	0908
Bamberg ‡ d.	0549	0617	0628	0636	0727	0809	...	...	0836	0910
Forchheim (Oberfr) ‡ d.	0605	0631	0642	0650	0743	0831	...	...	0850	0930
Erlangen ‡ d.	0616	0645	0654	0714v	0755	0846	...	...	0900	0945
Fürth (Bay) Hbf ‡ d.	0628	0700	0708	0727	0808	0903	...	...	0913	1002
Nürnberg Hbf ‡ a.	0637	0708	0716	0734	0817	0912	...	...	0921	1011

																								⊡		2
Sonneberg (Thür) Hbf d.	0807	...	0907	...	1007	...	1107	...	1207	...	1307	...	1407	...	1507	...	1607	...	1707	...	1807	...	1907	...	2007	2140
Coburg a.	0829	...	0929	...	1029	...	1129	...	1229	...	1329	...	1429	...	1529	...	1629	...	1729	...	1829	...	1929	...	2029	2203
Coburg d.	0835	0858	0932	...	1035	1058	1132	...	1235	1258	1332	...	1435	1458	1532	...	1635	1658	1732	...	1835	1858	1932	...	2035	2204
Lichtenfels a.	0852	0920	0951	...	1052	1120	1151	...	1252	1320	1351	...	1452	1520	1551	...	1652	1720	1751	...	1852	1920	1951	...	2052	2225
Lichtenfels 876 d.	0902	0936	1000	...	1102	1136	1200	...	1302	1337	1400	...	1502	1536	1600	...	1702	1736	1800	...	1902	1936	2000	...	2102	2314
Würzburg Hbf 876 d.	|	|	|	0936	|	|	|	1136	|	|	|	1336	|	|	|	1536	|	|	|	1736	|	|	|	1936	|	|
Bamberg 876 a.	0922	1006	1019	1034	1122	1206	1219	1234	1322	1406	1419	1434	1522	1606	1619	1634	1722	1806	1819	1834	1922	2006	2019	2034	2127	2342
Bamberg ‡ d.	0930	1010	...	1036	1130	1210	...	1236	1325	1410	...	1436	1530	1610	...	1636	1730	1810	...	1836	1930	2009	...	2036	2130	2343
Forchheim (Oberfr) ‡ d.	0943	1030	...	1050	1143	1230	...	1250	1345	1430	...	1450	1543	1630	...	1650	1743	1830	...	1850	1943	2030	...	2050	2143	0004
Erlangen ‡ d.	0955	1045	...	1100	1155	1245	...	1300	1355	1445	...	1500	1555	1645	...	1700	1755	1845	...	1900	1955	2045j	...	2100	2155	0018
Fürth (Bay) Hbf ‡ d.	1008	1102	...	1113	1208	1302	...	1313	1408	1502	...	1513	1608	1702	...	1713	1808	1902	...	1913	2008	2102j	...	2113	2209	0036
Nürnberg Hbf ‡ a.	1017	1111	...	1121	1217	1311	...	1321	1417	1511	...	1521	1617	1711	...	1721	1817	1911	...	1921	2017	2111j	...	2121	2217	0045

c – Ⓒ (also Dec. 24, 31, Jan. 6, June 3). On † (also Jan. 6, June 3) Bamberg d. 2148, Würzburg a. 2254.
e – Ⓐ (not Dec. 24, 31, Jan. 6, June 3).
f – Mar. 1 - May 30 Erlangen d. 2213, Forchheim d. 2226, Bamberg a. 2245, d. 2247, Lichtenfels a. 2312. On Ⓒ to Feb. 28 and from June 5 (also Dec. 24, 31, Jan. 6, June 3) Bamberg d. 2244, Lichtenfels a. 2309.
j – Mar. 1 - May 30 Erlangen d. 2053, Fürth d. 2114, Nürnberg a. 2122.
q – ①–④ (not Dec. 24, 31, Jan. 6, Apr. 5, May 13, 24, June 3).
r – Not Jan. 6, June 3.
t – 0732 on Ⓒ (also Dec. 24, 31, Jan. 6, June 3).
v – Arrives 0701.
z – Also Dec. 24, 31, Jan. 6, June 3.
⊡ – To Feb. 28 and from May 31.
‡ – Additional *RB* services Nürnberg - Bamberg and v.v.
From Nürnberg Hbf at 0011, 0106, 0618 ⚒**r**, 0750, 0950, 1350, 1516 Ⓐ**e**, 1550, 1715 Ⓐ**e**, 1750, 1845, 1950 and 2048.
From Bamberg at 0347 Ⓐ**e**, 0444 ⚒**r**, 0505, 0543 Ⓒ**z**, 0604 Ⓒ**z**, 0704, 1110, 1310, 1510, 1652 Ⓐ**e**, 1710, 1910 and 2210.
See Table **921** for other trains Nürnberg - Fürth and v.v.

876 WÜRZBURG - BAMBERG - HOF

RE / RB services

km		Ⓐe		⑥k	Ⓐe						Ⓐe	Ⓒz	S	S					S	S	⊠		S	S	
0	**Würzburg** Hbf 870 d.	...	...	0501	0501	...	...	0602	...	...	0728	0732	...	...	0809	0836	0836	0936	...	...		1736	...	...	1809
43	Schweinfurt Hbf 870 d.	...	...	0538	0543	...	...	0636	...	...	0803	0803	...	...	0842	0903	0903	1003	...	...		1803	...	...	1842
68	Haßfurt d.	...	...	0556	0600	...	...	0653	...	...	0816	0816	...	...	0858	0918	0918	1017	...	...		1817	...	...	1858
100	**Bamberg** a.	...	...	0620	0625	...	...	0719	...	...	0834	0834	...	...	0923	0936	0936	1034	...	...	each train	1834	...	...	1923
100	**Bamberg** 851 875 d.	...	0449e	▬	...	0638	0638	...	0741	0741	0836	0836	0838	0838	...	0941	0941	1036	1038	1038		1836	1838	1838	...
	Nürnberg Hbf 875 a.	...	|	...	...	|	|	...	|	|	0921	0921	|	|	...	|	|	1121	|	|	runs every	1921	|	|	...
132	Lichtenfels 851 875 d.	0442	0550	...	...	0700	0700	...	0802	0802	...	...	0900	0900	...	1002	1002	...	1100	1100		...	1900	1900	...
162	Kulmbach d.	0510	0618	...	...	0718	0718	...	0821	0821	...	...	0918	0918	...	1021	1021	...	1118	1118	two hours	...	1918	1918	...
174	Neuenmarkt-Wirsberg a.	0524	0631	...	...	0727	0727	...	0833	0833	...	...	0927	0927	...	1033	1033	...	1127	1127		...	1927	1927	...
174	Neuenmarkt-Wirsberg d.	0525	0632	0637	...	0729	0733	...	0835	0837	...	...	0929	0933	...	1035	1037	...	1129	1133	until	...	1929	1933	...
196	**Bayreuth** Hbf a.	0548	|	0659	...	|	0755	...	0856	|	...	...	|	0955	...	1056	|	...	|	1155		...	|	1955	...
203	Münchberg 880 d.	...	0657	...	...	0754	...	...	...	0900	...	...	0954	...	...	...	1100	...	1154	...		...	1954	...	...
216	Schwarzenbach d.	...	0709	...	...	0804	...	...	...	0909	...	...	1004	...	...	...	1109	...	1204	...		...	2004	...	...
227	**Hof** Hbf 880 a.	...	0720	...	...	0816	...	...	...	0920	...	...	1014	...	...	...	1120	...	1214	...		...	2015	...	...

								Ⓐe¶	Ⓒz	Ⓐe	
Würzburg Hbf 870 d.	1836	1836	1936	...	2009	2036	2036	...	2139	2139	2300
Schweinfurt Hbf 870 d.	1903	1903	2003	...	2042	2103	2103	...	2205	2217	2334
Haßfurt d.	1918	1918	2017	...	2058	2118	2118	...	2219	2233	2350
Bamberg a.	1936	1936	2034	...	2123	2136	2136	...	2237	2257	0016
Bamberg 851 875 d.	1941	1941	2036b	2038	...	2141	2141	2236	2244*	▬	...
Nürnberg Hbf 875 a.	|	|	2121b	|	...	|	|	|	|	...	...
Lichtenfels 851 875 d.	2002	2002	...	2107	...	2206	2206	2301	2309*	2318	...
Kulmbach d.	2021	2021	...	2134	...	2226	2226	...	...	2342	...
Neuenmarkt-Wirsberg a.	2033	2033	...	2147	...	2238	2238	...	...	2354	...
Neuenmarkt-Wirsberg d.	2035	2037	...	2147	...	2240	2242	...	...	2355	...
Bayreuth Hbf a.	2056	|	...	2214	...	2300	|	...	...	0023	...
Münchberg 880 d.	...	2100	...	...	...	...	2306	...	...	...	...
Schwarzenbach d.	...	2109	...	...	...	...	2315	...	...	...	...
Hof Hbf 880 a.	...	2120	...	...	...	...	2327	...	...	...	...

	Ⓒz	Ⓐe		Ⓐe	Ⓐe			⚒r			
Hof Hbf 880 d.	...	...	...	...	...	0525	...	...	0638	...	...
Schwarzenbach d.	...	...	...	...	...	0533	...	...	0647	...	...
Münchberg 880 d.	...	...	...	...	...	0543	...	...	0656	...	...
Bayreuth Hbf d.	...	...	...	0458	...	|	0550	...	|	0703	...
Neuenmarkt-Wirsberg a.	...	...	...	0519	...	0606	0610	...	0721	0725	...
Neuenmarkt-Wirsberg d.	...	...	...	0520	...	0613	0613	...	0728	0728	...
Kulmbach d.	...	...	...	0532	...	0622	0622	...	0738	0738	...
Lichtenfels 851 875 d.	...	...	...	0601	...	0650f	0650f	...	0800	0800	...
Nürnberg Hbf 875 d.	...	...	...	|	...	|	|	...	|	|	...
Bamberg 851 875 a.	...	...	...	0632	...	0717e	0717e	...	0819	0819	...
Bamberg d.	0446	0455	0617	...	0643	...	...	0726	0824	0824	0838
Haßfurt d.	0508	0516	0634	...	0707	...	...	0742	0841	0841	0900
Schweinfurt Hbf 870 d.	0526	0543	0650	...	0725	...	...	0758	0856	0856	0918
Würzburg Hbf 870 a.	0600	0617	0719	...	0800	...	...	0823	0923	0923	0951

	S	S					♥				S	S						⑥k	Ⓐe	†h					
Hof Hbf 880 d.	...	0744	...	0841	...	...		1640	...	...	...	1744	...	1841	...	1940	...	...	...	...	2041	...	...	...	2237
Schwarzenbach d.	...	0752	...	0849	...	...		1648	...	...	...	1752	...	1849	...	1950	...	...	...	...	2049	...	...	...	2248
Münchberg 880 d.	...	0803	...	0858	...	...		1659	...	...	...	1803	...	1858	...	2002	...	...	...	...	2058	...	...	...	2301
Bayreuth Hbf d.	0801	|	...	|	0903	...	each train	|	1703	...	1801	|	...	|	1903	|	2003	...	...	...	|	2103	...	2203	|
Neuenmarkt-Wirsberg a.	0823	0828	...	0921	0925	...		1721	1725	...	1823	1828	...	1921	1925	2025	2029	...	...	...	2121	2125	...	2231	2328
Neuenmarkt-Wirsberg d.	0830	0830	...	0928	0928	...	runs every	1728	1728	...	1830	1830	...	1928	1928	▬	2030	...	...	...	2128	2128	...	2232	▬
Kulmbach d.	0838	0838	...	0938	0938	...		1738	1738	...	1838	1838	...	1938	1938	...	2038	...	...	...	2138	2138	...	2244	...
Lichtenfels 851 875 d.	0857	0857	...	1000	1000	...	two hours	1800	1800	...	1857	1857	...	2000	2000	...	2057	...	...	...	2200	2200	...	2305	...
Nürnberg Hbf 875 d.	|	|	0839	|	|	...		|	|	...	|	|	1839	|	|	...	|	2040	...	2040	|	|	...	|	...
Bamberg 851 875 a.	0922	0922	0924	1019	1019	...	until	1819	1819	...	1922	1922	1924	2019	2019	Ⓑw	2127	2129	...	2129	2224	2224	...	2342	...
Bamberg d.	...	...	0926	1024	1024	1038		1824	1824	1838	...	...	1926	2024z	2024z	2038	...	2138	2145	2148	...	...	2259	...	0007
Haßfurt d.	...	...	0942	1041	1041	1100		1841	1841	1900	...	...	1942	2041z	2041z	2100	...	2159	2202	2205	...	...	2322	...	0031
Schweinfurt Hbf 870 d.	...	...	0958	1056	1056	1118		1856	1856	1918	...	...	1958	2056z	2056z	2118	...	2218	2219	2222	...	...	2342	...	0051
Würzburg Hbf 870 a.	...	...	1023	1123	1123	1151		1923	1923	1951	...	...	2024	2123z	2123z	2151	...	2251	2253	2254	...	...	0016	...	0124c

S – From / to Saalfeld (Table **851**).
b – To Feb. 28 and from May 31.
c – ⑥⑦ (also Apr. 5, May 24; not Dec. 26).
e – Ⓐ (not Dec. 24, 31, Jan. 6, June 3).
f – Arrives 0642.
h – Also Jan. 6, June 3.
k – Also Dec. 24, 31; not Dec. 26, May 1.
r – Not Jan. 6, June 3.
w – Also May 1; not Dec. 24, 31.
z – Ⓒ (also Dec. 24, 31, Jan. 6, June 3).
* – 3 minutes later Mar. 6 - May 30.
¶ – Runs 11 minutes later Mar. 1 - May 28.
⊠ – Bamberg d. 1340 (not 1341).
The 1209 from Würzburg to Bamberg runs on Ⓒ (daily Dec. 24 - Jan. 6, Feb. 13–21, Mar. 27 - Apr. 11 and May 22 - June 6).

LANDSHUT - MÜHLDORF - SALZBURG — 877

RB services

km		⑥k	Ⓐe	m						w	w
0	**Landshut** (Bay) Hbf d.	...	...	0609r	0836	1036	1236	1436	1636	1836	2036
55	Mühldorf (Oberbay) a.	...	...	0712r	0928	1128	1328	1528	1728	1928	2128
55	Mühldorf (Oberbay) d.	0603	0606	0743	0943	1143	1343	1543	1743	1943	2146
120	Freilassing **890/1** a.	0702	0711	0841	1041	1241	1441	1641	1841	2041	2240
126	**Salzburg** Hbf **890/1** a.	0717	0725	0851	1051	1317	1451	1651	1851	2117	2248

	Ⓐe	⚒r							w	w
Salzburg Hbf **890/1** d.	0459	...	0650y	0908	1108	1242	1508	1708	1907	...
Freilassing **890/1** d.	0529	...	0720	0920	1120	1320	1520	1720	1920	2116f
Mühldorf (Oberbay) a.	0622	...	0814	1014	1214	1414	1614	1814	2014	2215f
Mühldorf (Oberbay) d.	...	0633	0830	1030	1230	1430	1630	1830	2030	2242
Landshut (Bay) Hbf a.	...	0723	0921	1121	1321	1521	1721	1921	2121	2328

e – Not Dec. 24, 31, Jan. 6, June 3.
f – ⑤ only.
k – Also Dec. 24, 31; not Dec. 26, May 1.
m – Change trains at Mühldorf on Ⓐe.
r – ⚒ (not Jan. 6, June 12).
w – Not Dec. 24.
y – 0704 on ⑥⑦ (also Dec. 25, Jan. 1, 6, Apr. 5, May 13, 24, June 3).

MÜNCHEN - REGENSBURG — 878

DB (RE services); ALX

km			ALX		ALX	ALX		ALX		ALX		ALX		ALX		ALX	ALX	ALX		ALX		ALX		ALX	ALX
		N		N		P	N		N		N		N	Ⓐe	Ⓐe	©z	P	Ⓑ	N		N				t
0	**München** Hbf **944** d.	0544	0644	0744	0844	0901	0943	1044	1144	1244	1344	1444	1544	1603	1642	1644	1702	1702	1744	1844	1944	2044	2124	2244	2355
42	Freising **944** d.	0610	0709	0808	0909	|	1008	1109	1208	1309	1408	1509	1608	1629	1708	1708	1728	1728	1808	1909	2008	2110	2148	2311	0019
76	Landshut (Bay) Hbf **944** d.	0635	0732	0832	0931	0946	1032	1132	1233	1332	1432	1532	1632	1650	1732	1732	1749	1749	1832	1932	2032	2132	2218	2335	0041
99	Neufahrn (Niederbay) d.	0652	0748	0849	0948	|	1049	1148	1249	1347	1449	1547	1649	|	1749	1749	|	|	1849	1948	2049	2148	2235	2351	0057
138	**Regensburg** Hbf a.	0716	0811	0914	1011	1022	1114	1211	1314	1411	1514	1611	1714	1726	1816	1816	1826	1826	1915	2011	2122	2211	2303	0019	0123
	Schwandorf **879 885** a.	...	0846	...	...	1058	...	1246	...	1446	...	1646	...	...	...	...	1901	1901	...	2046	...	2252	...	...	...
	Hof Hbf **879** a.	...	1018	...	...	...	...	1418	...	...	...	1818	...	...	...	...	...	2036	...	2220	...	...	...	...	...

	ALX	ALX		ALX	ALX		ALX		ALX		ALX		ALX	ALX		ALX		ALX	ALX		ALX			ALX	
	⚒r		Ⓐe	©z	Ⓐe	Ⓐe		N		N		N	P		N		N			N		N		P	N
Hof Hbf **879** d.	...	...	...	...	...	...	0535h	...	0740	...	0940	...	...	...	...	1340	...	...	...	...	1740	...	...	...	...
Schwandorf **879 885** d.	...	0501h	...	...	...	...	0708	...	0908	...	1108	...	1303	...	...	1511	...	1708	...	...	1908	...	...	2105	...
Regensburg Hbf d.	0443	0546	0622	0647	0647	0659	0746	0844	0946	1044	1146	1244	1341	1346	1444	1546	1644	1746	1834	1844	1947	2044	...	2141	2244
Neufahrn (Niederbay) d.	0508	0611	0648	0712	0712	0727	0811	0910	1010	1110	1210	1310	|	1410	1510	1610	1710	1810	|	1910	2011	2117		|	2316
Landshut (Bay) Hbf **944** d.	0526	0627	0707	0728	0733	0746	0827	0929	1027	1129	1227	1329	1419	1428	1529	1627	1729	1827	1911	1929	2027	2134	2147	2220	2335
Freising **944** d.	0547	0649	0730	0750	|	0809	0848	0951	1048	1151	1248	1349	|	1449	1549	1648	1749	1848	1931	1951	2048	...	2209	2241	2356
München Hbf **944** a.	0615	0717	0758	0819	0819	0835	0915	1017	1115	1217	1315	1417	1502	1515	1617	1715	1817	1915	1958	2017	2115	...	2235	2306	0022

N – To/from Nürnberg (Table **921**).
P – (12) München - Schwandorf - Furth im Wald 🛃 - Praha and v.v. See also Tables **57** and **885**.
e – Not Dec. 24, 31, Jan. 6, June 3.
h – ①–⑥ only.
r – Not Jan. 6, June 3.
t – Not Dec. 31.
z – Also Dec. 24, 31, Jan. 6, June 3.
ALX – *Arriva-Länderbahn-Express*. Operated by Arriva / Regentalbahn AG - Die Länderbahn. Conveys 🍷.

REGENSBURG - HOF — 879

DB (RE services); ALX; Vogtlandbahn

km		2			2	ALX	2		2	ALX		2	ALX		2	ALX		2	ALX	ALX	2	2	ALX	2	ALX
		Ⓐe	G	Ⓐe		🍷		G		🍷	⑤f		🍷	G		🍷			🍷	Ⓑ🍷			🍷		🍷
	München Hbf **878** d.	...	...	...	...	0644	...	...	...	1044	...	...	1244	...	...	1444	...	...	1702	1702	...	...	1844	...	2044
0	**Regensburg** Hbf **885** d.	...	0628	0729	0730z	0821	0931	1037	1130	1221	1322	1331	1421	1430	1530	1621	1737	...	1835	1835	...	1930	2021	2131	2221
42	Schwandorf **885** a.	...	0654	0756	0759z	0846	1000	1103	1159	1246	1348	1400	1446	1457	1559	1646	1758	...	1901	1901	...	1959	2046	2200	2252
42	Schwandorf d.	0502	0655	...	0801	0847	1001	1104	1201	1247	1349	1401	...	1459	1601	1647	1759	1802	...	1907	1914	2002	2047	2209	2345
86	Weiden (Oberpf) a.	0541	0720	...	0841	0913	1041	1128	1241	1313	1418	1441	...	1521	1641	1713	1823	1841	...	1932	1952	2042	2113	2249	0024
86	Weiden (Oberpf) d.	0552	0721	...	0852	0914	1052	1129	1252z	1314	1419	1452	...	1522	1652	1714	1824	1852	...	1933	1953e	2052	2114	2252	...
137	Marktredwitz **880** d.	0634	0755	...	0934	0950	1134	1202	1334z	1350	1455	1534	...	1555	1734	1750	1857	1934	...	2008	2035e	2134	2152	2334	...
179	**Hof** Hbf **880** a.	0710	0819	...	1010	1018	1210	1225	1410z	1418	1524	1610	...	1619	1810	1818	1924	2010	...	2036	2111e	2210	2220	0010	...

	ALX		2	ALX		ALX	2	ALX	2		2	2	ALX	2		ALX	2	ALX	2			2		2	2
	①–⑥	Ⓐe	©z	H🍷		🍷		🍷		G		Ⓐe	🍷		G	🍷		🍷		⑦w	G			Ⓐe	
Hof Hbf **880** d.	🍷	...	...	0535	0642	0740	0748	0940	0948	1140	1148	...	1340	1348	1540	...	1548	1740	1748	1837	1944	1948	...	2048	2248
Marktredwitz **880** d.	...	...	...	0602	0708	0807	0824	1007	1024	1202	1224	...	1407	1424	1602	...	1624	1807	1824	1904	2006	2024	...	2124	2324
Weiden (Oberpf) a.	...	...	...	0639	0741	0840	0904	1041	1104	1233	1304	...	1441	1504	1633	...	1704	1841	1904	1940	2037	2104	...	2204	0004
Weiden (Oberpf) d.	0414e	0522	0522	0640	0742	0841	0914	1042	1114	1234	1314z	1321	1442	1514	1634	...	1714	1842	1914	1941	2038	2109z	...	2217	...
Schwandorf a.	0454e	0547	0602	0707	0808	0907	0954	1107	1154	1256	1354z	1400	1510	1554	1656	...	1754	1907	1952	2008	2100	2150z	...	2255	...
Schwandorf **885** d.	0501	0548	0604	0708	0810	0908	1002	1108	1202	1309	1402z	1402	1511	1602	1702	1708	1804	1908	2006h	2008	2111	...	2206	2303	...
Regensburg Hbf **885** a.	0536	0615	0634	0737	0837	0937	1034	1136	1234	1337	1434z	1434	1536	1634	1730	1736	1836	1936	2037h	2037	2141	...	2237	2332	...
München Hbf **878** a.	0717	...	...	0915	...	1115	...	1315	...	...	...	...	1715	...	...	1915	...	2115	...	...	...	...	...	...	...

G – To/from Gera (Table **871**).
H – ①–⑥ (daily Schwandorf - München).
e – Ⓐ (not Dec. 24, 31, Jan. 6, June 3).
f – Also Dec. 23, 30, Apr. 1, May 12, June 2; not Dec. 25, Jan. 1, Apr. 2, May 14, June 4.
h – On ⑦**w**: Schwandorf d. 1953, Regensburg a. 2027.
w – Also Apr. 5, May 24; not Apr. 4, May 23.
z – © (also Dec. 24, 31, Jan. 6, June 3).
ALX – *Arriva-Länderbahn-Express*. Operated by Regentalbahn AG - Die Länderbahn.

NÜRNBERG - HOF - DRESDEN — 880

IRE / RE / RB services

km				Ⓐn		L	Ⓐn			⚒	H									Ⓐn	E				
0	**Nürnberg** Hbf ● d.	0012	...	...	...	...	...	0545	0545	0642	0648	0648	0748	0748	0842	0848	0848	0948	0948	1042	1048	1048	1148	1148	1242
28	Hersbruck (r Pegnitz) ● d.	0031	...	...	...	...	...	0606	0606	|	0706	0706	0806	0806	|	0906	0906	1006	1006	|	1106	1106	1206	1206	|
67	Pegnitz ● a.	0053	...	...	...	...	...	0627	0627	|	0727	0727	0827	0827	|	0927	0927	1027	1027	|	1127	1127	1227	1227	|
67	Pegnitz d.	0054	...	...	...	...	...	0629	0635	|	0729	0733	0829	0835	|	0929	0933	1029	1035	|	1129	1133	1229	1235	|
	Bayreuth Hbf **876** d.	0114	...	...	...	...	...	|	0654	0732	|	0754	|	0854	0932	|	0954	|	1054	1132	|	1154	|	1254	1332
	Münchberg **876** d.	...	...	...	...	...	...	|	...	0805	|	...	|	...	1005	|	...	|	...	1205	|	...	|	...	1405
94	Kirchenlaibach d.	...	...	...	...	...	...	0643	...	|	0743	...	0843	...	|	0943	...	1043	...	|	1143	...	1243	...	|
125	Marktredwitz **879** d.	...	...	...	...	...	...	0702	...	|	0812	...	0902	...	|	1012	...	1102	...	|	1212	...	1302	...	|
167	**Hof** Hbf **876 879** a.	...	...	...	...	...	...	0724	...	0823	▬	...	0924	...	1023	...	...	1124	...	1222	▬	...	1324	...	1423
167	**Hof** Hbf **881** d.	...	...	0428	0525	0610	0626	0728	...	0828	...	...	0928	...	1028	...	...	1128	...	1228	...	...	1328	...	1428
215	Plauen (Vogtl) ob Bf **881** d.	...	...	0455	0555	0636	0655	0755	...	0855	...	...	0955	...	1055	...	...	1155	...	1255	...	...	1355	...	1455
240	Reichenbach (Vogtl) ob Bf **881** d.	...	...	0509	0609	0651	0709	0809	...	0909	...	...	1009	...	1109	...	...	1209	...	1309	...	...	1409	...	1509
263	**Zwickau** (Sachs) Hbf d.	...	...	0526	0626	0706	0726	0826	...	0926	0933	...	1026	...	1126	...	...	1226	...	1326	1333	...	1426	...	1526
279	Glauchau (Sachs) **858** d.	...	...	0535	0634	...	0735	0834	...	0935	0949	...	1034	...	1135	...	...	1234	...	1335	1349	...	1434	...	1535
311	**Chemnitz** Hbf **858** d.	...	0430	0600	0700	...	0800	0900	...	1000	1030	...	1100	...	1200	...	...	1300	...	1400	1430	...	1500	...	1600
324	Flöha d.	...	0442	0614	0714	...	0814	0914	...	1014	1042	...	1114	...	1214	...	...	1314	...	1414	1442	...	1514	...	1614
350	Freiberg (Sachs) d.	...	0507	0631	0731	...	0831	0931	...	1031	1107	...	1131	...	1231	...	...	1331	...	1431	1507	...	1531	...	1631
390	**Dresden** Hbf a.	...	0551	0702	0802	...	0902	1002	...	1102	1151	...	1202	...	1302	...	...	1402	...	1502	1551	...	1602	...	1702

					Ⓐn						E				n									⚒r	†w
Nürnberg Hbf ● d.	1248	1248	1348	1348	1442	1448	1448	1548	1548	1642	1648	1648	1748	1748	1842	1848	1848	1948	1948	2055	2148	2148	2250	2250	2250
Hersbruck (r Pegnitz) ● d.	1306	1306	1406	1406	|	1506	1506	1606	1606	|	1706	1706	1806	1806	|	1906	1906	2006	2006	2114	2206	2206	2309	2309	2309
Pegnitz ● a.	1327	1327	1427	1427	|	1527	1527	1627	1627	|	1728	1728	1827	1827	|	1927	1927	2027	2027	2136	2227	2227	2331	2331	2331
Pegnitz d.	1329	1333	1429	1435	|	1529	1533	1629	1635	|	1729	1733	1829	1835	|	1929	1933	2029	2035	2137	2234	2240	2332	2332	2337
Bayreuth Hbf **876** d.	|	1354	|	1454	1532	|	1554	|	1654	1732	|	1754	|	1854	1932	|	1954	|	2054	2156	|	2257	2351	2352	|
Münchberg **876** d.	|	...	|	...	1605	|	...	|	...	1805	|	...	|	...	2005	|	▬	|	▬	...	|	...	...	0030	|
Kirchenlaibach d.	1343	...	1443	...	|	1543	...	1643	...	|	1743	...	1843	...	|	1943	...	2043	...	...	2252	...	...	|	2352
Marktredwitz **879** d.	1412	...	1502	...	|	1612	...	1702	...	|	1812	...	1902	...	|	2013	...	2102	...	...	2313	...	...	|	0010
Hof Hbf **876 879** a.	...	...	1524	...	1623	▬	...	1724	...	1823	...	...	1924	...	2023	▬	...	2124	n ◇	...	2341	...	...	0050	0033
Hof Hbf **881** d.	...	...	1528	...	1628	...	...	1728	...	1828	...	...	1928	...	2040	...	...	...	2224	...	...	...	...	...	...
Plauen (Vogtl) ob Bf **881** d.	...	...	1555	...	1655	...	...	1755	...	1855	...	...	1955	...	2107	...	...	...	2312	...	...	...	...	...	...
Reichenbach (Vogtl) ob Bf. **881** d.	...	...	1609	...	1709	...	...	1809	...	1909	...	...	2009	...	2121	...	...	...	2335	...	...	...	...	...	...
Zwickau (Sachs) Hbf d.	...	...	1626	...	1726	1733	...	1826	...	1926	...	...	2026	...	2136	2141	2233	...	...	...	...	...	...	...	...
Glauchau (Sachs) **858** d.	...	...	1634	...	1735	1749	...	1834	...	1935	...	...	2034	...	2145	2156	2249	...	...	...	...	...	...	...	...
Chemnitz Hbf **858** d.	...	...	1700	...	1800	1830	...	1900	...	2000	...	...	2100	...	2208	2230	2330	...	...	...	...	...	...	...	...
Flöha d.	...	...	1714	...	1814	1842	...	1914	...	2014	...	...	2114	...	2219c	2243	2342	...	...	...	...	...	...	...	...
Freiberg (Sachs) d.	...	...	1731	...	1831	1907	...	1931	...	2031	...	...	2131	...	2237c	2308	0006	...	...	...	...	...	...	...	...
Dresden Hbf a.	...	...	1802	...	1902	1951	...	2002	...	2102	...	...	2202	...	2303c	2351	...	...	...	...	...	...	...	...	...

E – To Cheb (Table **1121**).
H – To Cheb on ©**z** (Table **1121**).
L – To Leipzig (Table **881**).
c – Chemnitz - Dresden on © only.
n – Not Dec. 24, 31.
r – Not Jan. 6, June 3.
w – Also Jan. 6, June 3.
z – Also Dec. 24, 31, Jan. 6, June 3.
◇ – Operated by Vogtlandbahn. 2nd class only.
● – Most trains between Nürnberg and Pegnitz convey portions for two separate destinations. Passengers should take care to join the correct portion for their destination.

880 DRESDEN - HOF - NÜRNBERG

IRE / RE services

km		p	Ⓐe	Ⓒz	Ⓒz	Ⓐe	v					①g	⚒			H							Ⓐn		
0	**Dresden** Hbf ..... d.	...	...	...	...	...	...	...	...	...	...	0455	...	0555	...	...	...	0655	0755	...	...	...	0855	0906	0955
40	Freiberg (Sachs) ..... d.	...	...	...	...	...	...	...	...	...	0449	0526	...	0627	...	...	...	0726	0827	...	...	...	0926	0949	1027
66	Flöha ..... d.	...	...	...	...	...	...	...	...	...	0513	0545	...	0643	...	...	...	0745	0843	...	...	...	0945	1013	1043
79	**Chemnitz** Hbf ..... **858** d.	...	...	...	...	...	0415	...	...	...	0530	0559	0559	0659	...	...	...	0759	0859	...	...	...	0959	1030	1059
111	Glauchau (Sachs) ..... **858** d.	...	...	...	...	...	0449	...	...	...	0604	0621	0621	0722	...	...	...	0821	0922	...	...	...	1021	1104	1122
127	**Zwickau** (Sachs) Hbf ..... d.	...	...	...	...	...	0506	0522	...	...	0621	0633	0633	0733	...	...	...	0833	0933	...	...	...	1033	1121	1133
150	Reichenbach (Vogtl) ob Bf **881** d.	...	...	...	...	...	▬	0537	...	...	▬	0650	0650	0750	...	...	...	0850	0950	...	...	...	1050	▬	1150
175	Plauen (Vogtl) ob Bf ..... **881** d.	...	...	...	...	...	...	0552	...	...	...	0706	0706	0806	...	...	...	0906	1006	...	...	...	1106	...	1206
223	**Hof** Hbf ..... **881** a.	...	...	...	...	...	...	0625	...	...	...	0733	0733	0833	...	...	...	0933	1033	...	...	...	1133	...	1233
223	**Hof** Hbf ..... **876 879** d.	...	0420	0517	...	*0447*	...	0628	...	...	...	0737	0737	0837	...	...	...	0937	1037	...	...	...	1137	...	1237
	Marktredwitz ..... **879** d.	...	0442	0539	...	0548	...	0656	...	0744	...	|	|	0900	...	0944	...	|	1059	...	1144	...	|	...	1259
	Kirchenlaibach ..... d.	...	0506	0555	...	0605	...	0711	...	0811	...	|	|	0915	...	1011	...	|	1115	...	1211	...	|	...	1315
247	Münchberg ..... **876** d.	...	|	|	...	|	Ⓐe	|	...	|	...	0753	0753	|	...	|	...	0953	|	...	|	...	1153	...	|
295	**Bayreuth** Hbf ..... **876** d.	0502	|	|	0556	|	0605	|	0713	|	0812	0827	0827	|	0912	|	1012	1027	|	1112	|	1212	1227	1305	|
322	Pegnitz ..... a.	0523	0527	0612	0617	0623	0628	0731	0737	0828	0833	|	|	0931	0936	1028	1033	|	1131	1136	1228	1233	|	1326	1333
322	Pegnitz ..... d.	0529	0529	0619	0619	0630	0630	0739	0739	0836	0836	|	|	0939	0939	1036	1036	|	1139	1139	1236	1236	|	1336	1336
361	Hersbruck (r Pegnitz) ..... d.	0552	0552	0642	0642	0653	0653	0801	0801	0858	0858	|	|	1001	1001	1058	1058	|	1201	1201	1258	1258	|	1358	1358
389	**Nürnberg** Hbf ..... a.	0607	0607	0700	0700	0710	0710	0817	0817	0915	0915	0919	0919	1018	1018	1115	1115	1119	1218	1218	1315	1315	1319	1415	1415

	C							Ⓐn								Ⓑn							⑤f	n	
Dresden Hbf ..... d.	...	...	1055	1155	...	...	...	1255	1355	...	...	...	1455	1555	...	1655	1706	...	1755	...	1855	1955	2055	2106	2306
Freiberg (Sachs) ..... d.	...	...	1126	1227	...	...	...	1326	1427	...	...	...	1526	1627	...	1726	1749	...	1827	...	1926	2027	2126	2149	2349
Flöha ..... d.	...	...	1145	1243	...	...	...	1345	1443	...	...	...	1545	1643	...	1745	1813	...	1843	...	1945	2043	2145	2213	0013
Chemnitz Hbf ..... **858** d.	...	...	1159	1259	...	...	...	1359	1459	...	...	...	1559	1659	...	1759	1830	...	1859	...	1959	2059	2159	2230	0026*
Glauchau (Sachs) ..... **858** d.	...	...	1221	1322	...	...	...	1421	1522	...	...	...	1621	1722	...	1821	1904	...	1922	...	2021	2122	2221	2304	...
Zwickau (Sachs) Hbf ..... d.	...	...	1233	1333	...	...	...	1433	1533	...	...	...	1633	1733	...	1834	1921	...	1933	...	2033	2132	2233	2321	...
Reichenbach (Vogtl) ob Bf. **881** d.	...	...	1250	1350	...	...	...	1450	1550	...	...	...	1650	1750	...	1851	▬	...	1950	...	2050	*2210*	2250	...	...
Plauen (Vogtl) ob Bf ..... **881** d.	...	...	1306	1406	...	...	...	1506	1606	...	...	...	1706	1806	...	1906	...	...	2006	...	2106	*2235*	2309	...	...
Hof Hbf ..... **881** a.	...	...	1333	1432	...	...	...	1533	1633	...	...	...	1733	1833	...	1933	...	...	2033	...	2133	...	2336	...	...
Hof Hbf ..... **876 879** d.	...	...	1337	1437	...	...	...	1537	1637	...	...	...	1737	1837	...	1937	C	...	2037	...	2137	...	...	...	...
Marktredwitz ..... **879** d.	1331t	...	|	1459	...	1544	...	|	1659	...	1744	...	|	1859	...	|	1944	...	2059	...	|	...	...	...	...
Kirchenlaibach ..... d.	1411	...	|	1515	...	1611	...	|	1715	...	1811	...	|	1915	...	|	2011	...	2115	...	|	...	...	...	...
Münchberg ..... **876** d.	|	...	1353	|	...	|	...	1553	|	...	|	...	1753	|	...	1953	|	...	|	...	2153	...	...	...	...
Bayreuth Hbf ..... **876** d.	|	1412	1427	|	1512	|	1612	1627	|	1712	|	1812	1827	|	1912	2027	|	2012	|	2116	2228	...	...	...	...
Pegnitz ..... a.	1428	1433	|	1531	1536	1628	1633	|	1731	1736	1828	1833	|	1931	1936	|	2028	2033	2131	2136	2247	...	...	...	...
Pegnitz ..... d.	1436	1436	|	1539	1539	1636	1636	|	1739	1739	1836	1836	|	1939	1939	|	2036	2036	2139	2139	2248	...	...	...	...
Hersbruck (r Pegnitz) ..... d.	1458	1458	|	1601	1601	1658	1658	|	1801	1801	1858	1858	|	2001	2001	|	2108	2108	2201	2201	2312	...	...	...	...
Nürnberg Hbf ..... a.	1515	1515	1519	1618	1618	1715	1715	1719	1818	1818	1915	1915	1919	2018	2018	2119	2124	2124	2218	2218	2328	...	...	...	...

C – From Cheb (Table **1121**).
H – From Cheb on Ⓒ**z** (Table **1121**).
e – Not Dec. 24, 31, Jan. 6, June 3.
f – Also Apr. 1; not Dec. 25, Apr. 2.
g – Also Apr. 6, May 25; not Apr. 5, May 24.
n – Not Dec. 24, 31.
p – Change trains at Pegnitz on Ⓐ**e**.
t – 1344 on Ⓒ**z**.
v – Not Dec. 25, Jan. 1.
z – Also Dec. 24, 31, Jan. 6, June 3.
***** – Arrives 0048 on the mornings of ②–④ (by 🚌 from Niederwiesa, d. *0023*).

881 HOF and ZWICKAU - LEIPZIG

RE / RB services

km		w	w	①–⑥		①–⑤													Ⓐ	Ⓒ			
	Hof Hbf ..... **880** d.	...	...	...	*0428*a	...	0610	*0626*a	...	*0828*r	...	...	*1028*	...	...	*1228*a	...	...	1428	1433	...	...	*1628*a
	Plauen (Vogtl) ob Bf ..... **880** d.	...	...	...	*0455*a	*0507*a	0636	*0655*a	*0701*	0900	...	*0907*	*1055*	...	...	1300	...	*1307*	1455	1501	...	*1507*	*1655*g
	Reichenbach (Vogtl) ob Bf ..... **880** d.	...	...	...	*0509*a	*0532*a	0651	*0709*a	*0725*	0915	...	*0932*	1114	...	...	1315	...	*1332*	1515	1515	...	*1532*	1714
0	**Zwickau** (Sachs) Hbf ..... **858 880** d.	0342	...	0511	0542	0613	0714	0742	0811	|	0942	1011	|	1142	1211	|	1342	1411	|	|	1542	1611	|
9	Werdau ..... **858** d.	0352	...	0521	0552	0621	0722	0752	0821	0925	0952	1021	1125	1152	1221	1325	1352	1421	1525	1525	1552	1621	1725
29	Gößnitz ..... **858** d.	0410	...	0536	0610	0636	0737	0810	0836	0940	1010	1036	1140	1210	1236	1340	1410	1436	1540	1540	1610	1636	1740
45	Altenburg ..... d.	0425	0525	0550	0625	0650	0750	0825	0850	0954	1025	1050	1154	1225	1250	1354	1425	1450	1554	1554	1625	1650	1754
89	**Leipzig** Hbf ..... a.	0519	0620	0631	0719	0732	0833	0919	0932	1035	1119	1132	1235	1319	1332	1435	1519	1532	1635	1635	1720	1732	1835

	n			n	n	⊡	n	n
Hof Hbf ..... **880** d.	...	...	*1828*	...	...	*2040*	...	...
Plauen (Vogtl) ob Bf ..... **880** d.	...	*1701*a	*1855*	...	*1901*	*2107*	...	...
Reichenbach (Vogtl) ob Bf ..... **880** d.	...	*1725*a	1914	...	*1925*	*2121*	...	...
Zwickau (Sachs) Hbf ..... **858 880** d.	1742	1811	|	1942	2011	2142	...	...
Werdau ..... **858** d.	1752	1821	1925	1952	2021	2152	...	...
Gößnitz ..... **858** d.	1810	1836	1940	2010	2036	2210	...	...
Altenburg ..... d.	1825	1850	1954	2025	2050	2225	2225	2325
Leipzig Hbf ..... a.	1919	1932	2035	2119	2132	2319	2319	0019

km		v		①–⑤	Ⓐ				
0	**Leipzig** Hbf ..... d.	0013	...	0427	0434	0534	0626	0721	0734
44	Altenburg ..... d.	0107	...	0507	0528	0628	0709	0802	0828
60	Gößnitz ..... **858** d.	...	...	0520	0543	0643	0723	0815	0843
80	Werdau ..... **858** d.	...	...	0537	0602	0702	0739	0831	0902
	Zwickau (Sachs) Hbf ..... **858 880** a.	...	...	0545	0614	0713	0748	|	0914
97	Reichenbach (Vogtl) ob Bf ..... **880** a.	...	...	*0628*a	*0649*	*0749*	*0835*	0843	*0949*
122	Plauen (Vogtl) ob Bf ..... **880** a.	...	...	*0700*a	*0705*	*0805*	*0859*	*0905*	*1005*
170	**Hof** Hbf ..... **880** a.	...	...	...	*0733*	*0833*	...	*0933*	*1033*

														Ⓑ				n	n		n		n
Leipzig Hbf ..... d.	0828	0921	0934	1028	1121	1134	1228	1321	1334	1428	1521	1534	1628	1726	1734	1828	1921	1934	2028	2121	2134	...	2228
Altenburg ..... d.	0909	1002	1028	1109	1202	1228	1309	1402	1428	1509	1602	1628	1709	1806	1828	1909	2002	2028	2108	2202	2228	...	2308
Gößnitz ..... **858** d.	0922	1015	1043	1122	1215	1243	1322	1415	1443	1522	1615	1643	1722	1819	1843	1922	2015	2043	2122	2215	2243	...	2322
Werdau ..... **858** d.	0939	1031	1102	1139	1231	1302	1339	1431	1502	1539	1631	1702	1739	1836	1902	1939	2031	2102	2137	2231	2302	...	2337
Zwickau (Sachs) Hbf ..... **858 880** a.	0948	|	1114	1148	|	1314	1349	|	1514	1549	|	1714	1749	1844	1913	1949	|	2113	2148	|	2313	...	2348
Reichenbach (Vogtl) ob Bf ..... **880** a.	*1024*	1043	*1149*	...	1243	*1349*	*1435*a	1443	*1549*	*1635*	1643	*1749*	*1835*	*1933*	*1949*	*2024*	2043	...	*2209*j	2243	...	...	...
Plauen (Vogtl) ob Bf ..... **880** a.	*1050*	1059	*1205*	...	1257	*1405*	*1500*a	*1505*t	*1605*	*1700*	*1705*	*1805*	*1900*	*1959*	*2005*	*2050*	2057	...	*2235*j	2302	...	...	...
Hof Hbf ..... **880** a.	...	*1133*a	*1233*	...	1326	*1432*	...	*1533*a	*1633*	...	*1733*	*1833*	...	...	*2033*	...	2126	...	...	*2336*f	...	...	...

a – Ⓐ (not Dec. 24, 31).
f – ⑤ (also Apr. 1; not Dec. 25, Apr. 2).
g – *1642* on Ⓒ (also Dec. 24, 31).
j – Change trains at Lichtentanne (a. 2142; d. *2152*).
n – Not Dec. 24, 31.
r – ⚒ only.
t – *1522* on Ⓒ (also Dec. 24, 31).
v – Not Dec. 25, Jan. 1.
w – Not Jan. 1.
⊡ – ①②③④⑦ (not Dec. 24, 31).

882 CHEMNITZ - VEJPRTY - CHOMUTOV

DB (RB services); ČD

km								A	⑥⑦z	n	n
0	**Chemnitz** Hbf ..... **880** d.	0736	0836	0936	1136	1336	1436	1536	1636	1836	2036
13	Flöha ..... **880** d.	0747	0847	0947	1147	1347	1447	1547	1647	1847	2047
31	Zschopau ..... d.	0810	0908	1010	1210	1410	1510	1610	1710	1910	2110
57	Annaberg-Buchholz Unt. d.	0846	0940	1046	1246	1446	1546	1646	1746	1946	2146
64	Cranzahl ⊖ ..... d.	0900	1000r	1100	1259	1459	1607	1706	1807	2006	2159
74	Bärenstein (Annab) ..... d.	0912c	1012	1112	...	...	1619a	...	1819	...	...
75	Vejprty 🏛 ..... a.	0914c	1014	1114	...	...	1621a	...	1821	...	...
75	Vejprty 🏛 ..... d.	...	1019z	...	...	...	...	...	*1824*	...	...
133	Chomutov ..... a.	...	1141z	...	...	...	...	...	*1951*	...	...

							⑥⑦z	⑥⑦z	n	n
Chomutov ..... d.	...	*0803*z	...	...	...	...	1620	...	...	...
Vejprty 🏛 ..... a.	...	*0930*z	...	...	...	...	1742	...	...	...
Vejprty 🏛 ..... d.	...	0943c	1143	...	...	1636a	1752	1843	...	...
Bärenstein (Annab) ..... d.	...	0945c	1145	...	...	1638a	1754	1845	...	...
Cranzahl ⊖ ..... d.	0757	0957	1157	1357	1550	1650	1806	1857	1950	2048
Annaberg Buchholz Unt. d.	0810	1010	1210	1410	1610	1710	1816	1910	2010	2110
Zschopau ..... d.	0846	1046	1246	1446	1646	1746	1848	1946	2046	2146
Flöha ..... **880** a.	0908	1108	1308	1508	1708	1808	1908	2008	2108	2208
Chemnitz Hbf ... **880** a.	0919	1119	1319	1519	1719	1819	1919	2019	2119	2219

⊖ – **Cranzahl - Kurort Oberwiesenthal** *Fichtelbergbahn* (17 km, narrow gauge steam). Journey: 60 minutes.
Operator: SDG Sächsische Dampfeisenbahngesellschaft GmbH, Bahnhofstraße 7, 09484 Kurort Oberwiesenthal. ✆ + 49 (0) 37348 151 0.
From **Cranzahl** at 1010, 1110**k**, 1310, 1510**k**, 1710 and 1810**m**. From **Kurort Oberwiesenthal** at 0850, 0940**k**, 1140, 1340**k**, 1540 and 1640**m**.

A – ①–⑤ (not Dec. 25, Jan. 1, Apr. 5).
a – Ⓐ only.
c – Ⓒ only.
k – Not Mar. 1–26.
m – Ⓒ (not Mar. 6–21; runs daily Dec. 25 - Jan. 3).
n – Not Dec. 24, 31.
r – Arrives 0950.
z – ⑥⑦ (also Dec. 25, Jan. 1, Apr. 5).

883 CHEMNITZ - AUE

RB services

km			Ⓐ	Ⓒ							n	n
0	**Chemnitz** Hbf ..... d.	0610	0810	0821	0910	1110	1310	1510	1710	1910	2110	2240
27	Thalheim ..... d.	0658	0853	0857	0958	1158	1358	1558	1758	1958	2200	2320
36	Zwönitz ..... d.	0709	0904	0906	1009	1209	1409	1609	1809	2009	2211	2331
47	Lößnitz unt Bf. ⊗ d.	0720	0915	|	1020	1220	1420	1620	1820	2020	2222	2342
51	**Aue** (Sachs) ..... a.	0725	0920	0920	1025	1225	1425	1625	1825	2025	2227	2347

	v	Ⓐ								n	Ⓒ	n
Aue (Sachs) ..... d.	0403	0531	0629	0820	0929	1129	1329	1529	1729	1929	2031	2129
Lößnitz unt Bf ⊗ d.	0408	0536	0634	0826	0934	1134	1334	1534	1734	1934	2036	2134
Zwönitz ..... d.	0420	0548	0646	0837	0946	1146	1346	1546	1746	1946	2048	2146
Thalheim ..... d.	0436	0558	0658	0858	0958	1158	1358	1558	1758	1958	2058	2156
Chemnitz Hbf .. a.	0515	0640	0740	0940	1040	1240	1440	1640	1840	2040	2140	2234

n – Not Dec. 24, 31.
v – Not Dec. 25, Jan. 1.
⊗ – Trains stop on request only.

DB; ČD (2nd class only) — ZWICKAU - JOHANNGEORGENSTADT - KARLOVY VARY — 884

km		Ⓐ				n	n	n	Ⓒ
0	**Zwickau** (Sachs) Hbf ... d.	0505	...	0605	and	1905	2005	2105	2205	2205
27	Aue (Sachs) ... d.	0539	0539	0639	hourly	1939	2039	2139	2239	2239
37	Schwarzenberg (Erzg) . d.	0556	0556	0656	until	1956	2056	2156	2251	2256
56	**Johanngeorgenstadt** . a.	0621	0621	0721		2021	2121	2221	...	2321

	Ⓐ	v			n	n	n	Ⓒ
Johanngeorgenstadt ... d.	0430	0530	0630	and	1930	2030	2130	2230
Schwarzenberg (Erzg) ... d.	0454	0554	0654	hourly	1954	2054	2154	2254
Aue (Sachs) ... d.	0507	0607	0707	until	2007	2107	2207	2307
Zwickau (Sachs) Hbf ... a.	0539	0639	0739		2039	2139	2239	2339

km	▶	Ⓐ			Ⓐ		Ⓒ	Ⓐ		d	n
0	**Johanngeorgenstadt** . d.	...	0726v	1032	...	*1240c*	1439	*1439*	1542	1734	*2046*
1	Potučky 🏛 ... d.	0600	0729v	1038	1243	*1243c*	1442	*1442*	1545	1737	*2049*
28	Nejdek ... d.	0700	0821	1127	1334	1420	1534	1551	1635	1836	2225
44	**Karlovy Vary** ... a.	0727	0847	1153	1401	1446	1600	1618	1701	1902	2250
47	**Karlovy Vary** dolní ... a.	0734	0854	1159	1407	1454	1606	1626	1707	1908	2256

▶	Ⓒv	v	⊖		Ⓐ	Ⓒ	d⊖	n	n
Karlovy Vary dolní ... d.	0507	0546a	0745	0952	1210	1259	1459	1755	2103
Karlovy Vary ... d.	0513	0552a	0751	0958	1216	1306	1506	1802	2109
Nejdek ... d.	0539	0620	0821	1026	1305f	1334	1534	1831	2135
Potučky 🏛 ... d.	...	0710	0912	1118	1355	1422	1623	1920	*2309r*
Johanngeorgenstadt ... a.	...	0712	0914	1120c	1357	1424	1625	1922	...

a – Ⓐ only.
c – Ⓒ only.
d – Not Dec. 24.
f – Arrives 1242.
n – Not Dec. 24, 31.
r – Not Dec. 24–31.
v – Not Dec. 25, Jan. 1.
⊖ – Change trains at Nejdek on Ⓐ.
▶ – Czech holiday dates apply (see page 2).

DB (*RE* / *RB* services); ČD — REGENSBURG - SCHWANDORF - FURTH IM WALD - PLZEŇ — 885

km		2	2 Ⓐe		351 ‡🍷	2 t			2	2	355 ‡🍷	2 Ⓐe	Ⓐe	2 Ⓒz	2	2	‡🍷	353 ‡🍷			2	357 ‡🍷	2 Ⓐm	2	2	2
	München Hbf **878** .. d.	...	...	...	...	...	...	...	...	...	0901	...	...	...	...	...	1244	...	...	...	...	1702	...	...	...	...
0	**Regensburg** Hbf **879** d.	...	*0521*	0628	...	...	0832	...	*0931*	...	1031	*1130*	...	*1230*	...	*1331*	1421	...	1632	...	*1737*	1835	...	*1930*	*2031*	*2221*
	Nürnberg Hbf **886** .. d.	...	|	|	0600	...	|	0752	|	...	|	|	...	|	...	|	|	1405	|	1553	|	|	...	|	|	|
42	**Schwandorf** ...... **879** d.	...	0553	0654	0704	...	0902	0905	1004	...	1108	1202	...	1305	...	1405	1446	1508	1659	1705	1804	1909	...	2006	2110	2306
90	Cham (Oberpf) ... d.	...	0633	▬	0736	...	▬	0940	1039	...	1136	1243	1247	1339	...	1439	...	1536	▬	1740	1839	1937	...	2046	2145	2342
109	**Furth im Wald** 🏛 ..... a.	...	0650	2	0749	...	...	0956	1056	...	1149	...	1305	1356	...	1456	...	1549	...	1758	1856	1951	...	2102	2202	2359f
109	**Furth im Wald** 🏛 ..... d.	...	...	*0703*	0750	0906	2 ⊕	...	...	*1103t*	1150	...	...	...	*1403c*	*1516*	...	1550	2	*1806*	...	1952	...	...	...	...
131	Domažlice ... d.	0606	...	0731	0810	0929	0934	...	...	1131	1210	...	...	...	1434	*1539*	...	1610	1640	*1835*	...	2012	2231	...	...	...
190	**Plzeň** Hlavni ... a.	0731	...	0851	0857	...	1054	...	...	1251	1257	...	...	...	1555	...	...	1657	1755	*1955*	...	2059	2337	...	...	...
	Praha Hlavní **1120** . a.	...	...	...	1058	...	...	...	...	...	1458	...	...	...	...	...	...	1858	...	...	...	2258	...	...	...	...

	2 Ⓐe	2		‡🍷	2 ⑥k	2	350 ‡🍷	2 t	2		2 t	2	354 ‡🍷	2 ⑥⑦c	2 Ⓒz	2	2	2	352 ‡🍷	2	2	2	2	356 ‡🍷	2	2 t
Praha Hlavní **1120** .. d.	...	...	...	...	...	...	0504	...	...	...	...	...	0904	...	...	...	...	...	1304	...	...	...	...	1704	...	...
Plzeň Hlavni ... d.	...	...	...	...	...	...	0700	*0705*	...	...	*0808*	...	1100	*1105*	...	...	*1208*	...	1500	...	...	...	...	1900	...	2259
Domažlice ... d.	...	0529	...	...	...	...	0746	0829	...	...	1029	...	1146	1229	...	...	1429	...	1546	1638	...	...	...	1946	...	0013
Furth im Wald 🏛 ...... a.	...	0552	...	...	...	...	0810	0852	...	...	1052	...	1210	1252	...	...	1452	...	1610	1701	...	...	...	2012	...	...
Furth im Wald 🏛 ...... d.	0448	...	0612	...	0653	0657e	0812	▬	0901	1002	▬	1101	1212	...	1256	1401	...	1501	1612	▬	1704	1800	1901	2014	2106	...
Cham (Oberpf) ... d.	0503	...	0629	...	0710	0715	0826	‡🍷	0917	1017	...	1117	1226	...	1317	1417	...	1517	1626	‡🍷	1718	1817	1917	2028	2122	...
Schwandorf .... **879** a.	0539	...	0702	0708	...	0754	0853	0908	0955	1054	1100	1155	1256	...	1357	1455	...	1555	1653	1708	1757	1855	1956	2056	2200	...
Nürnberg Hbf **886** ... a.	|	...	0806j	|	...	|	0956	|	|	1222	|	|	|	...	|	|	...	|	1756	|	|	|	|	|	|	...
Regensburg Hbf . **879** a.	*0615*	...	...	0737	...	*0832*	...	0937	*1034*	...	1129	*1234*	1331	...	*1434*	*1529*	...	*1634*	...	1736	*1836*	*1929*	*2037*	2133	*2237*	...
München Hbf **878** ... a.	...	...	...	0915	...	...	...	1115	...	...	...	...	1502	...	...	...	...	...	...	1915	...	...	...	2306	...	...

c – ⑥⑦ (also Jan. 6, June 3).
e – Ⓐ (not Dec. 24, 31, Jan. 6, June 3).
f – ⑤⑥ only.
j – 0823 on Ⓒ z.
k – Also Dec. 24, 31; not Dec. 26, May 1.
m – Not Dec. 31.
t – Not Dec. 24, 25, 31.
z – Also Dec. 24, 31, Jan. 6, June 3.
⊕ – ①–⑥ (not Dec. 25, 26, Jan. 1, 2, Apr. 5).
‡ – *ALX* in Germany (operated by Arriva / Regentalbahn AG - Die Länderbahn).

RE services — NÜRNBERG - SCHWANDORF and WEIDEN — 886

Nürnberg - Schwandorf

km				Ⓐe	P‡									P‡		Ⓐe						‡		A		
0	**Nürnberg** Hbf .... ◧ d.	0012	...	0434	0600	0648	0752	0848	0953	1048	1136	1248	1353	1405	1448	1536	1553	1648	1736	1753	1848	1940	2055	2112	2148	2253
28	Hersbruck (r Pegnitz) ◧ d.	0029	...	0449	|	0712	0812	0912	1012	1112	1151	1312	1412	|	1512	1551	1612	1712	1751	1812	1912	|	2117	|	2212	2312
68	Amberg ... d.	0101	...	0526	0647	0743	0843	0943	1043	1143	1229	1341	1441	1450	1543	1629	1643	1744	1828	1843	1943	2033	2146	2152	2246	2347
94	**Schwandorf** ... a.	...	...	0543	0703	0757	0859	0957	1057	1157	1243	1357	1457	1507	1557	1644	1703	1758	1846	1857	1957	2052	2203v	2205	2301	0001
	Furth im Wald **885** . a.	...	...	...	0749	...	0956	...	...	...	...	...	...	1549	...	...	1758	...	...	...	...	...	...	...	...	...

	‡	⚒r	†w	Ⓐe	⚒r	†w	Ⓐe	Ⓒz		P‡									P‡							
Furth im Wald **885** .. d.	...	...	...	...	...	...	0612	0612	...	0812	...	...	1002	...	...	...	...	...	1612	...	...	...	...	...	...	...
Schwandorf ... d.	0411	0509	0516	0544	0557	0609	0703	0709	0809	0854	0912	1009	1112	1209	1309	1407	1509	1609	1654	1712	1809	1911	2009	2113	2205	2341
Amberg ... d.	0430	0529	0532	0603	0615	0626	0721	0733	0824	0912	0926	1024	1126	1224	1326	1426	1524	1626	1712	1729	1824	1925	2024	2132	2222	0005
Hersbruck (r pegnitz) .. d.	0505	0606	0606	|	0648	0707	0754	0808	0908	|	1007	1108	1207	1308	1406	1508	1607	1708	|	1807	1908	2007	2108	2207	2306	...
Nürnberg Hbf ... a.	0522	0621	0621	0656	0706	0723	0810	0823	0923	0956	1022	1123	1222	1323	1421	1523	1622	1723	1756	1822	1923	2022	2124	2222	2321	...

Nürnberg - Weiden

km		Ⓐe								
0	**Nürnberg** Hbf .... ◧ d.	0434	0533	0625	0737	0836	and	2036	...	2253
28	Hersbruck (r Pegnitz) ◧ d.	0449	0548	0644	0752	0851	hourly	2051	...	2312
97	**Weiden** (Oberpf) .... a.	0542	0645	0745	0845	0945	until	2145	...	0007

	⚒r			✥					
Weiden (Oberpf) ... d.	0506	0612	0710	and	1809	1910	2010	...	2213
Hersbruck (r Pegnitz) ... a.	0605	0706	0807	hourly	1907	2006	2106	...	2305
Nürnberg Hbf ... a.	0621	0723	0823	until	1923	2022	2124	...	2321

A – May 22 - June 6 only.
P – To / from Praha (Table **885**).
e – Not Dec. 24, 31, Jan. 6, June 3.
r – Not Jan. 6, June 3.
v – Not May 22 - June 6.
w – Also Jan. 6, June 3.
z – Also Dec. 24, 31, Jan. 6, June 3.
‡ – Operated by *ALX* (Arriva / Regentalbahn AG - Die Länderbahn). Conveys 🍷.
✥ – Certain trains depart Weiden at 09 minutes past the hour.
◧ – Certain trains from Nürnberg and Hersbruck convey portions for two separate destinations. Passengers should take care to join the correct portion for their destination.

RB services — BAYREUTH - WEIDEN — 887

km		Ⓐe	Ⓐe			Ⓐe					Ⓐe			Ⓐe			Ⓐe		Ⓐe		Ⓐe		Ⓑh			
0	**Bayreuth** Hbf ... d.	0440	0543	0615	0716	0818	0818	0918	1018	1118	1218	1218	1318	1418	1418	1518	1618	1618	1644	1718	1818	1818	1918	1918	2018	2230
19	Kirchenlaibach .. a.	0457	0600	0632	0739	0839	0839	0939	1039	1139	1239	1239	1339	1439	1439	1539	1639	1639	1701	1739	1839	1839	1939	1939	2039	2247
19	Kirchenlaibach .. d.	*0532*	...	0655	0746	0846	...	0946	...	1146	1246	...	1346	1446	...	1546	1646	...	...	1746	1846	...	1953	...	...	...
59	**Weiden** ... a.	*0607*	...	0725	0817	0917	...	1017	...	1217	1317	...	1417	1517	...	1617	1717	...	...	1817	1917	...	2029	...	...	...

	Ⓐe	Ⓐe	⚒r	Ⓐe	Ⓑh		Ⓐe					Ⓐe			Ⓐe			Ⓐe			Ⓐe				Ⓒz	
Weiden ... d.	0428	0524	...	0631	...	0731	0831	...	0931	...	1131	1231	...	1331	1431	...	1531	1631	...	1731	1831	...	1937	...	2131	...
Kirchenlaibach ... a.	0500	0557	...	0707	...	0808	0908	...	1008	...	1208	1308	...	1408	1508	...	1608	1708	...	1808	1908	...	2008	...	2203	...
Kirchenlaibach ... d.	0509	0608	0651	0717	0717	0819	0919	0919	1019	1119	1219	1319	1319	1419	1519	1519	1619	1719	1719	1819	1919	1919	2019	2119	...	2207
Bayreuth Hbf ... a.	0526	0629	0707	0734	0734	0836	0936	0936	1036	1136	1236	1336	1336	1436	1536	1536	1636	1736	1736	1836	1936	1936	2036	2136	...	2224

e – Not Dec. 24, 31, Jan. 6, June 3.
h – Also Dec. 26, May 1; not Dec. 24, 31.
r – Not Jan. 6, June 3.
z – Also Dec. 24, 31, Jan. 6, June 3.

RB services; 2nd class only — KEMPTEN - REUTTE IN TIROL - GARMISCH-PARTENKIRCHEN — 888

km		①–⑥								
0	**Kempten** (Allgäu) Hbf ... d.	k	0719	0917	1017	1117	1317	1517	1717	1917
18	Oy-Mittelberg ... d.	...	0749	0948	1048	1148	1348	1549	1748	1948
24	Nesselwang ... d.	...	0800	0959	1059	1159	1359	1600	1759	1959
31	Pfronten-Ried ... d.	0631	0813	1013	1113	1213	1413	1613	1813	2013
33	**Pfronten-Steinach** 🏛 ... d.	0635	0818	1018	1128	1218	1418	1618	1818	2018
38	Vils in Tirol 🏛 ... d.	0643	0826	1033	1137	1226	1426	1626	1841	2026
48	**Reutte in Tirol** ... a.	0658	0841	1048	1152	1241	1441	1641	1856	2041
	Change trains	d			|					
48	**Reutte in Tirol** ... d.	0700	0903	1103	1154t	1303	1503	1703	1903	...
68	Lermoos ... d.	0726	0929	1129	1221t	1329	1529	1729	1929	...
71	Ehrwald Zugspitzbahn 🏛 ... d.	0731	0934	1134	1226t	1334	1534	1734	1934	...
93	**Garmisch**-Partenkirchen ... a.	0756	0959	1201	...	1359	1559	1759	1959	...

			⑥⑦c							
Garmisch-Partenkirchen .. d.	...	0804	0906	1004	1204	1404	1604	...	1804	2006
Ehrwald Zugspitzbahn 🏛 . d.	...	0829	0935	1029	1229	1429	1629	1757a	1829	2031
Lermoos ... d.	...	0833	0940	1033	1233	1433	1633	1801a	1833	2035
Reutte in Tirol ... a.	...	0859	1005	1059	1259	1459	1659	1825a	1859	2100
Change trains			⑥⑦c					|		
Reutte in Tirol ... d.	0717	0917	1017	1103	1317	1517	1717	1826	1917	2105
Vils in Tirol 🏛 ... d.	0731	0931	1031	1117	1331	1531	1731	1839	1931	2119
Pfronten-Steinach 🏛 ... d.	0741	0941	1041	1128	1341	1541	1743	1850	1943	2139
Pfronten-Ried ... d.	0747	0947	1047	1145	1347	1547	1747	1854	1947	2145
Nesselwang ... d.	0801	1001	1101	1201	1401	1601	1801	1903	2001	2206
Oy-Mittelberg ... d.	0812	1012	1112	1212	1412	1612	1812	1914	2012	2218
Kempten (Allgäu) Hbf ... a.	0843	1042	1143	1243	1443	1643	1843	1943	2042	2251

a – ①–⑤ (not Dec. 25, Jan. 1, 6, Apr. 5, May 13, 24, June 3).
c – Also Dec. 25, Jan. 1, 6, Apr. 5, May 13, 24, June 3.
d – Runs daily from Reutte.
k – Not Dec. 25, 26, Jan. 1, 6, Apr. 5, May 1, 13, 24, June 3.
t – ①–⑤ (not Dec. 24 - Jan. 6, Feb. 8–12, Mar. 29 - Apr. 6, May 13, 24, 25, June 3).

890 MÜNCHEN - SALZBURG

km		RB 30061	RB 30063	RB 30001	RB 30003	RJ 61	RE 30007	EC 111	RE 30009	RJ 63	RE 30011	EC 317	RE 30013	RJ 65	RE 30015	EC 113	RE 30017	RJ 67	RE 30019	IC 2083	EC 115	RE 30021	RJ 69	RE 30023
		Ⓐt	Ⓐt	Ⓐt																				
			2			B🍷		✕♦		B🍷		🍷♦		B🍷		✕♦		B🍷		🍷♦	✕♦		B🍷	
	Frankfurt Hbf 911 d.	...	...	...	...	...	...	...	...	...	...	...	...	...	...	0820	...	...	...	...	...	...	...	...
	Stuttgart Hbf 930 d.	...	...	...	...	...	...	...	...	...	...	0758	...	...	...	0958	...	...	...	...	1158	...	...	...
0	**München** Hbf 951 d.	...	...	0552	0639	0727	0742	0827	0848	0927	0942	1027	1048	1127	1142	1227	1242	1327	1342	...	1427	1446	1527	1542
10	München Ost 951 d.	...	...	0601	0647	|	0750	0836	0856	|	0950	1036	1056	|	1150	1236	1250	|	1350	1414	1436	1455	|	1550
65	Rosenheim 951 d.	0541	...	0641	0731	|	0831	0907	0931	|	1031	1106	1131	|	1231	1307	1331	|	1431	1444	1506	1531	|	1631
82	Bad Endorf d.	0553	...	0653	0742	|	0842	|	0942	|	1042	|	1142	|	1242	|	1342	|	1442	1456	|	1542	|	1642
90	Prien am Chiemsee d.	0600	...	0701	0750	|	0850	0925	0950	|	1050	1124	1150	|	1250	1325	1350	|	1450	1504	1524	1550	|	1650
118	Traunstein d.	0623	0652	0725	0814	|	0914	0943	1014	|	1114	1143	1214	|	1314	1343	1414	|	1514	1525	1543	1614	|	1714
147	Freilassing 891 d.	0643	0716	0746	0834	|	0934	1002	1034	|	1134	1202	1234	|	1334	1402	1434	|	1534	1544	1602	1634	|	1734
153	**Salzburg** Hbf ⊞ 891 a.	*0705*	0725	0756	0842	0856	0942	1009	1042	1058	1142	1209	1242	1258	1342	1409	1442	1456	1542	...	1609	1642	1656	1742
	Wien Westbahnhof 950 a.	...	...	...	...	1140	...	...	...	1340	...	...	...	1540	...	...	...	1740	...	...	...	...	1940	...

	EC 319	RE 30025	RE 30027	RE 30051	ICE 261	RE 30029	RE 30031	EC 117	RE 30033	IC 2265	IC 1865	RE 30035	EC 391	RE 30037	RB 27097	RE 30039		RE 30041		D 499	EN 463	RB 30043 30045	RE 30043	RB 30067
		Ⓐt	Ⓒz	Ⓐt		Ⓒz	Ⓐt	Ⓑq		Ⓑ¶	●				m								⑤⑥	Ⓐt
	🍷♦				✕			🍷♦		🍷♦			🍷♦				2			🍷♦	🍷♦	d	f	
Frankfurt Hbf 911 d.	1220	...	...	...	...	...	...	1420	...	...	...	...	1620	...	...	...	...	...	...	...	...	...	...	...
Stuttgart Hbf 930 d.	1358	...	...	...	...	...	...	1558	...	1653	...	...	1758	...	...	...	...	...	...	...	...	...	...	...
München Hbf 951 d.	1627	1632	1648	1648	1723	1742	1752	1827	1847	1927	1927	1942	2024	2046	...	2142	...	2246	...	2340	2340	2350	2350	...
München Ost 951 d.	1636	1642	1656	1656	|	1750	1800	1836	1855	1936	1936	1950	2034	2054	...	2150	...	2254	...	|	|	2358	2358	...
Rosenheim 951 d.	1706	1714	1731	1731	|	1831	1831	1907	1931	2007	2007	2031	2107	2131	...	2231	...	2331	...	0019	0019	0037	0038	0042
Bad Endorf d.	|	1726	1742	1743	|	1842	1842	|	1942	2020	2020	2042	2120	2142	...	2242	...	2343	...	|	|	...	0050	0055
Prien am Chiemsee d.	1724	1733	1750	1750	|	1850	1850	1925	1950	2028	2028	2050	2128	2150	...	2250	...	2350	...	|	|	...	0057	0102
Traunstein d.	1743	1759	1814	1814	|	1914	1914	1943	2014	2046	2046	2114	2146	2214	...	2314	...	0014	...	|	|	...	0120	0127
Freilassing 891 d.	1802	1822	1834	1836	|	1934	1934	2002	2034	2108	2108	2134	2205	2235	2241	2333	0005	0034	...	|	|	...	0141	0149
Salzburg Hbf ⊞ 891 a.	1809	1829	1842	...	1858	1942	1942	2009	2042	2120	2120	2142	2212	...	2248	...	0017	0042	...	0117	0117	...	0148	...
Wien Westbahnhof 950 a.	...	...	...	...	2140	...	...	...	...	...	...	...	...	...	...	...	...	...	...	...	0545h	...	...	...

	RB 30000	EN 462	D 498	RB 30002		RE 30004	IC 2290	RE 30006	RE 30008	RE 30010	IC 2264	IC 1916	IC 1864	RE 30012		RE 30014	EC 390	RE 30016	ICE 260	RE 30018	IC 2082	EC 318	RE 30020	RJ 262
	Ⓐt			Ⓐt	Ⓐt		①-⑥	Ⓐt	Ⓐt	Ⓒz	⊡	⑤	⊖	Ⓐt	①-⑤		①-⑥							
		🍷♦	🍷♦		2		e🍷				🍷♦	🍷♦			y 2		e♦		✕		🍷♦	🍷♦		
Wien Westbahnhof 950 d.	...	0009h	...	...	...	...	...	...	...	...	...	...	...	...	...	...	...	...	0614	...	...	...	...	0820
Salzburg Hbf ⊞ 891 d.	...	0428	0428	...	0459	...	0545	...	...	...	0639	0639	0639	...	0650	0704c	0751	0812	0902	0912	...	0951	1012	1102
Freilassing 891 d.	0413	|	|	0451	0510	0521	0555	0600	0623	0623	0648	0648	0648	0652	0704	0724	0759	0824	|	0924	0942	0959	1024	|
Traunstein d.	0433	|	|	0511	...	0543	0613	0628	0643	0643	0706	0706	0706	0720	...	0744	0817	0844	|	0944	1000	1017	1044	|
Prien am Chiemsee d.	0457	|	|	0534	...	0607	0631	0652	0707	0707	0724	0724	0724	0744	...	0808	0835	0908	|	1008	1022	1035	1108	|
Bad Endorf d.	0504	|	|	0541	...	0615	0639	0700	0714	0714	0732	0732	0732	0751	...	0815	|	0915	|	1015	1030	|	1115	|
Rosenheim 951 d.	0519	0529	0529	0556	...	0630	0653	0715	0729	0729	0748	0748	0748	0805	...	0830	0855	0930	|	1030	1044	1055	1130	|
München Ost 951 a.	0557	0602	0602	0634	...	0702	0721	0745	0758	0806	0818	0818	0818	0842	...	0901	0923	1007	|	1101	1112	1122	1207	|
München Hbf 951 a.	0606	0615	0615	0644	...	0712	0733	0800	0808	0816	0833	0833	0833	0853	...	0911	0933	1018	1030	1111	...	1133	1218	1230
Stuttgart Hbf 930 a.	...	...	...	...	...	...	1001	...	...	...	1107	1107	...	...	...	...	1201	...	...	...	...	1401	...	...
Frankfurt Hbf 911 a.	...	...	...	...	...	...	1140	...	...	...	...	...	...	...	...	...	1340	...	...	...	...	1540	...	...

	RE 30022	EC 114	RE 30024	RJ 60	RE 30028	EC 112	RE 30030		RE 30032	EC 316	RE 30034	RJ 64	RE 30036		RE 30038	RJ 66	RE 30040	EC 110	RE 30042	RJ 68	RE 30044		RB 30068	RB 30058
																							m	m
		✕♦		B🍷		✕♦				🍷♦		B🍷				B🍷		✕♦		🍷				
Wien Westbahnhof 950 d.	...	...	...	1020	...	...	...	...	...	...	...	1420	...	...	...	1620	...	...	...	1820	...	...	...	...
Salzburg Hbf ⊞ 891 d.	1112	1151	1212	1302	1312	1351	1412	...	1512	1551	1612	1702	1712	...	1812	1902	1912	1951	2012	2102	2112	...	2258	...
Freilassing 891 d.	1124	1159	1224	|	1324	1359	1424	...	1524	1559	1624	|	1724	...	1824	|	1924	1959	2024	|	2124	...	2305	...
Traunstein d.	1144	1217	1244	|	1344	1417	1444	...	1544	1617	1644	|	1744	...	1844	|	1944	2017	2044	|	2144	...	2327	...
Prien am Chiemsee d.	1208	1235	1308	|	1408	1435	1508	...	1608	1635	1708	|	1808	...	1908	|	2008	2035	2108	|	2208	...	2351	2356
Bad Endorf d.	1215	|	1315	|	1415	|	1515	...	1615	|	1715	|	1815	...	1915	|	2015	|	2115	|	2215	...	...	0003
Rosenheim 951 d.	1230	1255	1330	|	1430	1455	1530	...	1630	1657	1730	|	1830	...	1930	|	2030	2055	2130	|	2230	...	...	0015
München Ost 951 a.	1307	1323	1407	|	1501	1522	1607	...	1707	1724	1807	|	1901	...	2008	|	2101	2122	2207	|	2301	...		
München Hbf 951 a.	1318	1333	1417	1430	1512	1533	1617	...	1717	1735	1817	1833	1911	...	2018	2034	2111	2133	2217	2230	2312	...		
Stuttgart Hbf 930 a.	...	1600	...	...	...	1801	...	...	...	2001	...													
Frankfurt Hbf 911 a.	...	...	...	...	...	1940																		

♦ – **NOTES** (LISTED BY TRAIN NUMBER)

110/1 – (12) and ✕ Klagenfurt - Villach - München and v.v.; (12) Beograd (**210/1**) - Vinkovci - Zagreb - Dobova ⊞ - Ljubljana - Jesenice ⊞ - Villach - München and v.v.

112/3 – (12) and ✕ Klagenfurt - Villach - München - Frankfurt - Siegen and v.v.; (12) Zagreb (**212/3**) - Dobova ⊞ - Ljubljana - Jesenice ⊞ - Villach - München - Frankfurt - Siegen and v.v.

114 – WÖRTHERSEE – (12) and ✕ Klagenfurt - Villach - München - Mannheim - Köln - Dortmund.

115 – WÖRTHERSEE – (12) and ✕ Münster - Köln - Mannheim - München - Villach - Klagenfurt.

117 – (12) and 🍷 Frankfurt - Salzburg - Villach - Klagenfurt.

316/7 – (12) and 🍷 Graz - Selzthal - Bischofshofen - Salzburg - Mannheim - Saarbrücken and v.v.

318/9 – (12) and 🍷 Graz - Selzthal - Bischofshofen - Salzburg - Frankfurt and v.v.

390 – (12) and 🍷 Linz - Salzburg - Frankfurt.

391 – (12) and 🍷 Frankfurt - Salzburg (- Linz Ⓑq).

462/3 – KÁLMÁN IMRE – 🛏 1,2 cl., ▬ 2 cl., (2) and 🍷 Budapest - Wien - München and v.v. Conveys Dec. 13 - Jan. 9 (from Bucureşti), Dec. 13 - Jan. 11 (from München) 🛏 1,2 cl., Bucureşti - Timişoara - Budapest - München and v.v.

498 – LISINSKI – 🛏 1,2 cl., ▬ 2 cl. and (2) Zagreb - Dobova ⊞ - Ljubljana - Jesenice ⊞ - Villach - München; (2) Beograd (**414**) - Zagreb (**498**) - München. Mar. 27 - Sept. 18 (from Rijeka) conveys ▬ 2 cl. (also 🛏 1,2 cl. Apr. 29 - Sept. 18) Rijeka (**480**) - Ljubljana (**296**) - München.

499 – LISINSKI – 🛏 1,2 cl., ▬ 2 cl. and (2) München - Villach - Jesenice ⊞ - Ljubljana - Dobova ⊞ - Zagreb; (2) München - Zagreb (**415**) - Beograd. Mar. 28 - Sept. 19 conveys ▬ 2 cl. (also 🛏 1,2 cl. Apr. 30 - Sept. 19) München - Ljubljana (**481**) - Rijeka.

1916 – ⑤ to Feb. 26 and from May 21 (also Dec. 23, 30, June 2; not Dec. 25, Jan. 1, June 4). (12) and 🍷 Salzburg - Köln - Dortmund - Berlin.

2082/3 – KÖNIGSSEE – (12) Berchtesgaden - Augsburg - Hamburg and v.v. See Table **900** for timings to / from Hamburg.

2264/5 – (12) and 🍷 Salzburg - Karlsruhe and v.v.

B – (12) and 🍷 München - Wien - Hegyeshalom ⊞ - Györ - Budapest and v.v.

c – ⑥⑦ (also Dec. 25, Jan. 1, 6, Apr. 5, May 13, 24, June 3).
d – Not Dec. 31.
e – Not Dec. 25, 26, Jan. 1, Apr. 3, 5, May 24.
f – Also Dec. 23, 24, 30, Jan. 5, Apr. 1, 4, May 12, 23, June 2.
h – Wien **Hütteldorf**.
m – Not Dec. 24.
q – Not Dec. 24, 25, 31, Apr. 2, 4, May 23.
t – Not Dec. 24, 31, Jan. 6, June 3.
y – Not Dec. 25, Jan. 1, 6, Apr. 5, May 13, 24, June 3.
z – Also Dec. 24, 31, Jan. 6, June 3.

⊡ – ①②③④⑥ to Feb. 25 and from May 17 (also June 4; not Dec. 23, 26, 30, May 24, June 2).
¶ – Ⓑ to Feb. 26 and from May 17 (not Dec. 24, 25, 31).
⊖ – ①-⑥ Feb. 27 - May 15 (not Apr. 3, 5).
● – Ⓑ Feb. 28 - May 16 (not Apr. 2, 4).

891 SALZBURG - FREILASSING - BERCHTESGADEN

Berchtesgadener Land Bahn *

km		Ⓐt		⚒r									H											E
0	**Salzburg** Hbf 890 d.	*0612*	*0650k*	*0742*	*0812*	0912	...	and at	1412	...	1512	1542	...	1612	...	1712	...	1812	...	1912	...	*2012*	*2112*	*2226*	*2321*
6	Freilassing 890 a.	*0624*	*0704k*	*0754*	*0820*	0924	...	the same	1424	...	1524	1554	...	1624	...	1724	...	1824	...	1924	...	*2020*	*2120*	*2233*	*2330*
6	Freilassing d.	0632	0717	0801	0847	0929	0947	minutes	1429	1447	1529	...	1559	1629	1647	1729	1747	1829	1847	1929	1947	2047	2137	2247	2337
21	Bad Reichenhall d.	0651	0738	0822	0914	0946	1004	past each	1446	1504	1546	...	1618	1646	1704	1746	1804	1846	1904	1946	2004	2104	2154	2305	2354
39	**Berchtesgaden** Hbf. a.	0724	0808	0855	0956	...	1038	hour until	...	1538	...	...	1656	...	1738	...	1838	...	1937	...	2038	2134	2223	2334	0023

	Ⓐt	⚒r	Ⓐt				H																	
Berchtesgaden Hbf d.	...	0620	...	0707	...	0820	0836	0920	...	and at	1420	...	1520	...	1620	...	1720	...	1820	...	1920	2020	2224	...
Bad Reichenhall d.	0534	0655	...	0737	0811	0851	0910	0951	1011	the same	1451	1511	1551	1605	1651	1711	1751	1811	1851	1911	1951	2051	2254	...
Freilassing a.	0550	0712	...	0754	0828	0912	0927	1012	1028	minutes	1512	1528	1615	1626	1712	1728	1812	1828	1912	1928	2012	2112	2313	...
Freilassing 890 d.	0605	...	0716	*0805*	0837	...	0934	*1034*	1037	past each	*1534*	1537	*1634*	1637	*1734*	1737	*1822j*	1837	*1934*	1937	*2034*	*2134*	...	0005
Salzburg Hbf 890 a.	0617	...	0725	*0817*	0847	...	0942	*1042*	1047	hour until	*1542*	1547	*1642*	1647	*1742*	1747	*1829j*	1847	*1942*	1947	*2042*	*2142*	...	0017

E – ⑤-⑦ (also Jan. 6, Apr. 5, May 13, 24, June 3).
H – *IC* **2082/3**: KÖNIGSSEE – (12) and 🍷 Berchtesgaden - Hamburg and v.v. Train category *RE* Berchtesgaden - Freilassing and v.v.
j – On Ⓒ (also Dec. 24, 31, Jan. 6, June 3) Freilassing d. *1834*, Salzburg a. *1842*.
k – On ⑥⑦ (also Dec. 25, Jan. 1, 6, Apr. 5, May 13, 24, June 3) Salzburg d. *0704*, Freilassing a. *0712*.
r – Not Jan. 6, June 3.
t – Not Dec. 24, 31, Jan. 6, June 3.
* – Services to / from Bad Reichenhall or Berchtesgaden (except train H) are operated by Berchtesgadener Land Bahn GmbH (Salzburg AG / Arriva). ✆ +43 (0) 662 4480 6109. 2nd class only. Other trains are operated by either DB or ÖBB.

892 FLUGHAFEN MÜNCHEN ✈ (S-Bahn services S1, S8)

2nd class only

km		S8	S8	S8	S8		S8	S1	S8	S1	S8	S1	S8		S1	S8	S1	S8	S1	S8	S8
0	**München** Pasing d.	0005	0045	0125	0305	and every	0445	...	0505	...	0525	...	0545	and at the	...	2245	...	2305	...	2325	2345
7	**München** Hbf (low level) d.	0015	0055	0135	0315	20 minutes	0455	0503	0515	0523	0535	0543	0555	same minutes	2243	2255	2303	2315	2323	2335	2355
11	**München** Ost d.	0024	0104	0144	0324	until	0504	|	0524	|	0544	|	0604	past each	|	2304	|	2324	|	2344	0004
44	**München Flughafen** Terminal ✈ a.	0055	0135	0215	0355		0535	0546	0555	0606	0615	0626	0635	hour until	2326	2335	2346	2355	0006	0015	0035

km*		S8	S8	S8	S8		S8	S1	S8	S1	S8	S1	S8		S1	S8	S1	S8	S1	S8	S1
0	**München Flughafen** Terminal ✈ d.	0004	0044	0124	0404	and every	0544	0551	0604	0611	0624	0631	0644	and at the	2251	2304	2311	2324	2331	2344	2351
	München Ost a.	0035	0115	0155	0435	20 minutes	0615	|	0635	|	0655	|	0715	same minutes	|	2335	|	2355	|	0015	|
41	**München** Hbf (low level) a.	0045	0125	0205	0445	until	0625	0637	0645	0657	0705	0717	0725	past each	2337	2345	2357	0005	0017	...	0037
	München Pasing a.	0055	0135	0215	0455		0635	...	0655	...	0715	...	0735	hour until	...	2355	...	0015	...	...	...

* – Via Neufahrn (b Freising).

☛ Many **S1** trains from München Hbf are combined with a Freising service - travel in the rear portion for the Airport.

893 MÜNCHEN - MÜHLDORF - SIMBACH

km			Ⓐe	⑥	⑦v	⚒r								Ⓒz	Ⓐe	Ⓒz	Ⓐe	Ⓒz	Ⓐe			Ⓐe				
0	**München** Hbf ● d.	...	0559	0559g	0604	0707	0807z	0906	1008	1107	1207	1307	1407	1507	1522	1607	1619	1707	1727	1748	1807	1823	1907	2028	2129	2228
10	**München** Ost d.	...	0616	0617g	0617	0717	0817	0917	1017	1117	1217	1317	1417	1517	1532	1617	1638	1717	1739	1758	1817	1838	1916	2038	2139	2238
85	**Mühldorf** (Oberbay) a.	...	0722	0722g	0722	0816	0924	1016	1116	1216	1316	1417	1517	1618	1631	1718	1732	1816	1829	1853	1919	1930	2021	2142	2238	2333
		A	d	|	|	d								Ⓒz	|		d	Ⓒz	|	|		|		n	n	
85	**Mühldorf** (Oberbay) d.	0637	0737	0737	0737	0837	0937	1037	1137	1227	1337	1437	1537	1637	1633	..	1737	1831	1832	1857	1938	1938	2032	2146	2246	...
124	**Simbach** (Inn) a.	0714	0813	0813	0813	0924	1013	1113	1213	1258	1413	1513	1613	1713	1707	...	1813	1908	1906	1919	2016	2016	2103	2217	2317	...
	Linz Hbf **962** a.	0850	...	0950	0950	...	...	...	...	...	...	...	...	...	...	...	...	...	...	2057	...	...	...	...	...	...

		Ⓐe	⑥k	Ⓐe	Ⓐe			G										Ⓐe	Ⓒz			Ⓒz		Ⓐe	n	n
Linz Hbf **962** d.	...	...	...	...	...	...	...	0653	...	...	...	...	...	...	...	...	...	...	...	...	...	...	1810	1810	...	...
Simbach (Inn) d.	...	0507	0547	0554	0648	0648	0749	0826	0900	0949	1049	1149	1259	1349	1449	1549	...	1638	1649	...	1749	1844	1952	1952	2108	2222
Mühldorf (Oberbay) a.	...	0540	0619	0628	0724	0724	0822	0850	0932	1021	1124	1221	1332	1421	1521	1621	...	1717	1721	...	1821	1933	2024	2024	2140	2257
	①–⑥	Ⓐe	Ⓒz	|	|	Ⓒz		|								Ⓒz	Ⓐe					Ⓒz	Ⓒz	|		
Mühldorf (Oberbay) d.	0522	0546	0623	0637	0730	0729	0830	0851	0937	1029	1137	1228	1339	1428	1538	1629	1633	...	...	1737	1839	1939	2029	2032	2146	...
München Ost a.	0625	0640	0725	0722	0822	0826	0926	0939	1045	1127	1246	1327	1443	1526	1646	1726	1746	...	...	1846	1943	2043	2126	2142	2247	...
München Hbf ● a.	0636	0655	0737	0737	0837	0836	0938	0948	1055	1137	1256	1337	1454	1537	1656	1738	1803	...	...	1856	1954	2057	2137	2153	2257	...

A – ①–⑤ (not Dec. 25, Jan. 1, 6, Apr. 5, May 13, 24, June 3).
G – [12] (Kleinreifling ⚒ -) Garsten - Linz - München.
d – Daily from Mühldorf.
e – Not Dec. 24, 31, Jan. 6, June 3.
g – Not Dec. 26, May 1
k – Also Dec. 24, 31; not Dec. 26, May 1.
n – Not Dec. 24.
r – Not Jan. 6, June 3.
v – Also Dec. 25, Jan. 1, 6, Apr. 5, May 13, 24, June 3.
z – Ⓒ (also Dec. 24, 31, Jan. 6, June 3).
● – Connecting trains München Hbf - Ost and v.v. are S-Bahn services operating from / to the underground platforms at München Hbf.

895 MÜNCHEN - GARMISCH - INNSBRUCK

DB; ÖBB (2nd class only in Austria)

km		¶	Ⓐe				ICE 987 ⑥N				ICE 527 ⑥D		ICE 583 ⑥L				ICE 1209 ⑥K	X		X			ICE 1213 ⑤K	n	n	n
0	**München** Hbf d.	...	0538	0630	0732	0832	0846	0932	1032	1132	1209	1232	1312	1332	1432	1532	1545	1632	1732	1832	1932	2032	2054	2132	2232	2333
7	München Pasing d.	...	0545	0638	0739	0839	|	0939	1039	1139	|	1239	|	1339	1439	1539	|	1639	1739	1839	1939	2039	|	2139	2240	2340
40	Tutzing d.	...	0609	0701	0801	0901	0921	1001	1101	1201	1242	1301	1342	1401	1501	1601	1622	1701	1801	1901	2001	2101	2141	2201	2301	0001
54	Weilheim (Oberbay) d.	...	0631	0711	0814	0911	|	1011	1111	1211	|	1311	|	1411	1511	1611	|	1711	1811	1911	2011	2111	|	2211	2312	0013
75	Murnau d.	...	0650	0730	0832	0930	|	1030	1130	1230	|	1330	|	1430	1530	1630	|	1730	1830	1930	2030	2130	|	2230	2330	0031
101	**Garmisch**-Partenk. a.	...	0717	0759	0857	0957	1019	1057	1157	1257	1335	1357	1443	1457	1557	1657	1720	1757	1857	1957	2057	2157	2234	2257	2357	0057
101	**Garmisch**-Partenk. d.	0629	0727	0804	0904	1004	...	1100	1204	1300	...	1404	...	1504	1604	1700f	1723	1804	1900	2004	2100	2200	2237	2300	0000	...
118	**Mittenwald** ▦ d.	0656	0754	0826	0926	1026	...	1122	1226	1321	...	1426	...	1525	1626	1722f	|	1826	1922	2026	2122	2222	|	2322	0022	...
125	Scharnitz ⊡ d.	0704	...	0834	...	1034	...	...	1234	...	...	1434	...	...	1634	...	|	1834	...	2034	...	...	|	...	...	...
135	Seefeld in Tirol ⊡ d.	0716	...	0846	...	1046	...	...	1246	...	...	1446	...	...	1646	...	1833	1846	...	2046	...	...	2333	...	...	...
160	**Innsbruck** Hbf ⊡ a.	0753	...	0922	...	1123	...	...	1323	...	...	1523	...	...	1723	...	1906	1923	...	2123	...	...	0004	...	...	...

	⚒r	Ⓐe	Ⓒz	Ⓐe				ICE 1208 ⑥K		ICE 788 ⑥H		ICE 1206 WK					ICE 924 ⑥D		ICE 732 ⑥B					n		n
Innsbruck Hbf ⊡ d.	...	...	...	...	...	0638	...	0739	0838	...	...	0939	1038	...	1238	...	...	1438	...	...	1638	...	1838	...	2038	...
Seefeld in Tirol ⊡ d.	...	...	...	...	...	0715	...	0818	0915	...	...	1018	1115	...	1315	...	...	1515	...	...	1715	...	1915	...	2115	...
Scharnitz ⊡ d.	...	...	...	...	...	0727	...	|	0927	...	...	|	1127	...	1327	...	...	1527	...	...	1727	...	1927	...	2127	...
Mittenwald ▦ d.	...	...	0537	0556	0632t	0737	0837	|	0937	...	1037	|	1136	1237	1337	1437	...	1537	...	1637	1737	1837	1937	2037	2137	2237
Garmisch-Partenk. a.	...	...	0559	0618	0658t	0759	0859	0923	0959	...	1059	1119	1158	1259	1359	1459	...	1559	...	1659	1759	1859	1959	2059	2159	2259
Garmisch-Partenk. d.	0504	0558	0604	0623	0659t	0804	0904	0938	1004	1039	1104	1124	1206	1304j	1404	1504	1515	1604	1624	1704	1804	1904	2004	2104	2204n	2304
Murnau d.	0530	0625	0631	0651	0730	0831	0931	|	1031	|	1130	|	1230	1333	1430	1530	|	1630	|	1731	1831	1931	2030	2130	2232n	2330
Weilheim (Oberbay) d.	0548	0648	0649	0716	0749	0849	0949	|	1049	|	1149	|	1249	1349	1449	1549	|	1649	|	1749	1850	1949	2049	2149	2249n	2348
Tutzing d.	0559	0700	0700	0729	0800	0900	1000	1039	1100	1138	1200	|	1300	1400	1500	1600	1618	1700	|	1800	1900	2000	2100	2200	2300n	0000
München Pasing a.	0621	0721	0721	0753	0819	0919	1020	|	1120	|	1220	|	1320	1420	1520	1620	|	1720	|	1820	1920	2021	2120	2220	2320n	0019
München Hbf a.	0629	0728	0728	0800	0827	0927	1027	1111	1127	1210	1227	1257	1327	1427	1527	1627	1645	1727	1756	1827	1927	2029	2127	2226	2327n	0027

München - Tutzing - Kochel

km			Ⓐe	Ⓐe	Ⓐe	Ⓐe	Ⓐe	Ⓐe	Ⓐe	Ⓐe	Ⓐe	Ⓐe	Ⓐe	Ⓐe	Ⓐe		Ⓐe	Ⓐe			Ⓒz	Ⓒz		Ⓒz	Ⓒb	Ⓒb	Ⓒb
0	**München** Hbf d.	Ⓐ	0640	0758	0832	0932	1032	1132	1232	1332	1446	1546	1646	1746	1832	and	2232	2333	...	Ⓒ	0630	0732	and	2032	2132	2232	2333
7	München Pasing d.		0647	0805	0839	0939	1039	1139	1239	1339	1453	1553	1653	1754	1839	hourly	2240	2340	...		0638	0739	hourly	2039	2139	2240	2340
40	Tutzing d.		0715	0831	0904	1004	1104	1204	1310	1420	1519	1620	1720	1820	1904	until	2305	2400	...		0704	0804	until	2104	2204	2305	2400
75	**Kochel** a.		0748	0904	0935	1035	1135	1235	1348	1453	1553	1653	1753	1853	1935		2336	0036	...		0735	0835		2135	2235	2336	0036

		Ⓐe	Ⓐe	Ⓐe	Ⓐe	Ⓐe		Ⓐe	Ⓐe	Ⓐe	Ⓐe	Ⓐe	Ⓐe	Ⓐe	Ⓐe	Ⓐe	Ⓐe	Ⓐe			Ⓒz	Ⓒz		Ⓒz	Ⓒb	Ⓒb	Ⓒb
Kochel d.	Ⓐ	0517	0602	0638	0726	0813	and	1213	1300	1403	1503	1603	1703	1803	1913	2013	2113	2213	...	Ⓒ	0618	0713	and	2013	2113	2213	2313
Tutzing a.		0550	0636	0710	0809	0852	hourly	1252	1333	1439	1539	1645	1745	1845	1952	2052	2152	2252	...		0652	0752	hourly	2052	2152	2252	2352
München Pasing a.		0614	0701	0741	0832	0919	until	1320	1359	1503	1604	1712	1820	1920	2021	2120	2220	2320	...		0721	0819	until	2120	2220	2320	0019
München Hbf a.		0621	0708	0749	0839	0927		1327	1405	1511	1612	1719	1827	1927	2029	2127	2226	2327	...		0728	0827		2127	2226	2327	0027

B – ZUGSPITZE – [12] and ✕ Garmisch - Nürnberg - Hannover - Bremen.
D – WETTERSTEIN – [12] and 🍷 Dortmund - Köln - Frankfurt - Nürnberg - Garmisch and v.v.
H – WERDENFELSER LAND – [12] and ✕ Garmisch - Nürnberg - Hannover - Hamburg.
K – KARWENDEL – [12] and ✕ Innsbruck - Garmisch - Nürnberg - Leipzig - Berlin and v.v.
L – WERDENFELSER LAND – [12] and ✕ Lübeck - Hamburg - Hannover - Garmisch.
N – ZUGSPITZE – [12] and ✕ Nürnberg - Garmisch.
W – ⑦ (also Apr. 5, May 24; not Apr. 4, May 23).
X – Change trains at Garmisch on Ⓐe.
b – Also Dec. 31, Jan. 6, June 3.
e – Not Dec. 24, 31, Jan. 6, June 3.
f – 4 minutes later on Ⓒz.
j – 1308 on Ⓐe.
n – Not Dec. 24.
r – Not Jan. 6, June 3.
t – On Ⓒz: Mittenwald d. 0633, Garmisch a. 0700, d. 0704.
z – Also Dec. 24, 31, Jan. 6, June 3.
¶ – Change trains at Mittenwald on Dec. 24, 31, Apr. 2.
⊡ – Additional ÖBB trains Scharnitz - Seefeld - Innsbruck and v.v.
From Scharnitz at 0004, 0634, 0734 ⚒, 0904, 1304, 1504, 1704, 1904 and 2134.
From Innsbruck Hbf at 0708 ⚒, 0808, 1208, 1408, 1608, 1808, 2008 and 2308.

A rack railway operates between Garmisch-Partenkirchen and the Zugspitz mountain: departures at 0815 and hourly to 1415, returning from Bf Zugspitzplatt at 0930 and hourly to 1630. All trains call at Eibsee (30 minutes from Garmisch, 49 minutes from Zugspitzplatt). Service may be suspended in bad weather conditions – please check locally before travelling. Cable cars run between Eibsee and Zugspitzgipfel (Eibsee-Seilbahn) and between Zugspitzplatt and Zugspitzgipfel summit (Gletscherbahn). **Operator**: Bayerische Zugspitzbahn AG ✆ + 49 (0) 88 21 7970.

897 MURNAU - OBERAMMERGAU

RB services

km		Ⓐe	Ⓐe						Ⓐe	Ⓒz	Ⓐe	Ⓒz									A	A
0	**Murnau** d.	0600	0647	0742	0842	0942	1042	1142	1235	1242	1324	1342	1442	1542	1642	1742	1842	1942	2042	2142	2335	
12	Bad Kohlgrub d.	0619	0707	0802	0902	1002	1102	1202	1254	1302	1343	1402	1502	1602	1702	1802	1902	2002	2102	2202	2353	
20	Unterammergau d.	0633	0721	0816	0916	1016	1116	1216	1308	1316	1357	1416	1516	1616	1716	1816	1916	2016	2116	2216	0007	
24	**Oberammergau** a.	0638	0726	0821	0921	1021	1121	1221	1313	1321	1402	1421	1521	1621	1721	1821	1921	2021	2121	2221	0012	

	Ⓐe		Ⓐe					Ⓐe	Ⓒz	Ⓐe	Ⓒz								n	A	B
Oberammergau d.	0555	0643	0738	0838	0938	1038	1138	1230	1238	1318	1338	1438	1538	1638	1738	1838	1938	2038	2138	2243	2315
Unterammergau d.	0559	0647	0742	0842	0942	1042	1142	1234	1242	1322	1342	1442	1542	1642	1742	1842	1942	2042	2142	2247	2319
Bad Kohlgrub d.	0618	0706	0801	0901	1001	1101	1201	1253	1301	1342	1401	1501	1601	1701	1801	1901	2001	2101	2201	2303	2335
Murnau a.	0636	0725	0819	0919	1019	1119	1219	1312	1319	1401	1419	1519	1619	1719	1819	1919	2019	2119	2219	2321	2354

A – Daily Dec. 13 - May 14 (not Dec. 24); ①③ from May 17.
B – ②④⑤⑥⑦ from May 15.
e – Not Dec. 24, 31, Jan. 6, June 3.
n – Not Dec. 24.
z – Also Dec. 24, 31, Jan. 6, June 3.

900 NÜRNBERG and FRANKFURT - HAMBURG

See Table **901** for local services Frankfurt - Fulda - Kassel. See Table **902** for other *IC* services Frankfurt - Gießen - Kassel - Göttingen - Alfeld - Hannover - Hamburg.

km		*ICE*	*IC*	*CNL*	*IC*	*EN*	*IC*	*CNL*	*EN*	*ICE*	*ICE*	*ICE*	*ICE*	*ICE*	*ICE*	*ICE*	*ICE*	*ICE*	*ICE*	*ICE*	*ICE*	*ICE*	*ICE*	*RE*
		990	**2178**	**1286**	**2184**	**490**	**2176**	**478**	**490**	**988**	**876**	**672**	**1092**	**888**	**696**	**774**	**684**	**634**	**874**	**670**	**886**	**694**	**772**	**34606**
		①g	①–⑤	R	①–⑤	t	①–⑤	R	⊖	①–⑥	①–⑥		①–⑤	①–⑤	①g	①–⑥				◧				
			a🍷	✕♦	a🍷	♦	a🍷	✕♦	♦	e✕	e✕	✕♦	a D ⁄✕	a✕	✕	e✕	✕	✕	✕	✕	✕	✕	✕	
	Zürich HB **510** d.	...	...	...	...	...	...	2042	...	...	...	...		...	...	...	...	...	...	...	...	...	...	...
	Basel SBB **912** d.	...	...	...	...	...	...	2207	...	...	...	...	...	...	...	...	...	...	0412b	0513c	...	...	...	...
	Karlsruhe Hbf **912** d.	...	...	...	...	...	...	0018	...	...	...	...	...	...	...	...	...	...	0558	0651e	...	...	...	...
	Ulm Hbf **930** d.	2204p	...	...	...	...	...	|	...	...	...	...	...	...	...	...	...	...	|	|	...	...	...	...
	Stuttgart Hbf **930** d.	2305p	...	...	...	...	...	|	...	...	...	...	...	...	...	0509	...	...	|	|	...	0651	0727	...
	Mannheim Hbf **912 930** d.	2351p	...	...	...	...	...	|	...	...	...	...	...	...	...	0605	...	...	0631	0716e	...	0731	0806	...
	Frankfurt Flughafen + § d.	0029	...	...	...	...	...	|	...	...	...	0539	...	...	...	0642	...	...	|	|	...	|	0842	...
	Frankfurt (Main) Hbf **850** d.	0055	...	...	...	...	...	|	...	0504	0510g	0555	0614	...	...	0658	...	...	0713	0758	...	0813	0858	...
	Hanau Hbf **850** d.	0112	...	...	...	...	...	|	...	0520	0526g	0611	|	...	...	|	...	...	0729	|	...	0829	|	...
	München Hbf **904** d.	|	...	2051	...	...	...	|	...	|	|	|	|	...	...	|	0515a	0515a	|	|	0620	|	|	...
	Augsburg Hbf **904** d.	|	...	|	...	...	...	|	...	|	|	|	|	...	...	|	|	|	|	|	|	|	|	...
0	**Nürnberg** Hbf **920 921** d.	|	...	|	...	0132	...	|	0218	|	|	|	|	0534	...	|	0630	0630	|	|	0733	|	|	0804
102	**Würzburg** Hbf **920 921** d.	|	...	|	...	0228	...	|	0313	|	|	|	|	0631	...	|	0730	0730	|	|	0831	|	|	0919
195	Fulda **850** d.	0158	...	|	...	|	...	|	|	0604	0609g	|	|	0707	...	|	0803	0803	0811	|	0904	0911	|	...
285	**Kassel** Wilhelmshöhe d.	|	...	|	...	|	...	|	|	0636	0643	0723	|	0739	0742	0822	0835	0835	0843	0922	0936	0943	1022	...
330	Göttingen d.	0325	...	|	...	0508	0548	0611s	0641	0656	0703	0743	|	0759	0805	0843	0856	0856	0903	0943	0956	1003	1043	...
	Hildesheim Hbf d.	|	...	|	...	|	|	|	|	|	0734	|	|	|	0834	|	|	|	0934	|	|	1034	|	...
	Braunschweig Hbf a.	|	...	|	...	|	|	|	|	|	0758	|	|	|	0858	|	|	|	0958	|	|	1058	|	...
430	**Hannover** Hbf a.	0421	...	0525s	...	0613	0656	0702s	0753	0732	|	0817	|	0832	|	0917	0932	0932	|	1017	1032	|	1117	...
430	**Hannover** Hbf d.	0424	0511	|	0555	0617	0659	|	0804	0736	|	0820	|	0836	|	0920	0936	0945	|	1020	1036	|	1120	...
	Berlin Hbf **810** a.	|	|	|	|	|	|	|	|	|	0925	|	0951	|	1024	|	|	|	1125	|	|	1221	|	...
	Bremen Hbf **813** a.	|	|	0642	|	|	|	|	|	|	...	|	...	|	...	|	|	1044	...	|	|	...	|	...
608	**Hamburg** Hbf a.	0543	0644	0753	0728	0750	0827	0906z	1003	0853	...	0934	...	0953	...	1035	1055	...	...	1134	1155	...	1234	...
615	**Hamburg** Altona a.	...	0659	0808	...	0804	0841	0935z	1021	0909	...	0950	...	1008	...	1049	1109	...	...	...	1209	...	1250	...

	ICE	*ICE*	*ICE*	*ICE*	*ICE*	*ICE*	*IC*	*ICE*	*ICE*	*ICE*	*ICE*	*ICE*	*ICE*	*ICE*	*ICE*	*RE*	*ICE*	*ICE*	*ICE*	*ICE*	*ICE*	*ICE*	*IC*	*IC*
	682	**632**	**872**	**78**	**882**	**692**	**2170**	**770**	**680**	**630**	**278**	**76**	**880**	**690**	**578**	**34614**	**588**	**538**	**276**	**74**	**788**	**598**	**2082**	**1886**
							⑥⑦																	⑥
	✕	✕	✕	✕	✕	✕	🍷♦	✕	✕	✕	R✕	K✕	✕	✕	✕		✕	✕	R✕	K✕	G✕	✕	🍷♦	🍷♦
Zürich HB **510** d.	...	...	...	0602	...	...	...	...	...	...	...	0802	...	...	...	...	...	...	...	1002	...	...	...	...
Basel SBB **912** d.	...	...	0608	0704	...	...	...	...	...	...	0812	0904	...	...	...	...	...	...	1012	1104	...	...	...	...
Karlsruhe Hbf **912** d.	...	...	0800	0851	...	...	...	...	...	...	1000	1051	...	...	...	...	...	...	1200	1251	...	...	...	...
Ulm Hbf **930** d.	...	...	|	|	...	0751a	...	...	...	...	|	|	...	0951	...	...	...	...	|	|	...	1151	...	...
Stuttgart Hbf **930** d.	...	...	|	|	...	0851	...	0927	...	...	|	|	...	1051	1127	...	...	...	|	|	...	1251	...	...
Mannheim Hbf **912 930** d.	...	...	0831	0916	...	0931	...	1006	...	...	1031	1116	...	1131	1206	...	...	...	1231	1316	...	1331	...	...
Frankfurt Flughafen + § d.	...	...	|	|	...	|	...	1042	...	...	|	|	...	|	1242	...	...	...	|	|	...	|	...	...
Frankfurt (Main) Hbf **850** d.	...	...	0913	0958	...	1013	1017	1058	...	...	1113	1158	...	1213	1258	...	...	...	1313	1358	...	1413	...	...
Hanau Hbf **850** d.	...	...	0929	|	...	1029	1038	|	...	...	1129	|	...	1229	|	...	...	...	1329	|	...	1429	...	...
München Hbf **904** d.	0648	0648	|	|	0820	|	|	|	0915	0915	|	|	1020	|	|	...	1052	1052	|	|	1219	|	1114o	...
Augsburg Hbf **904** d.	0732	0732	|	|	|	|	|	|	|	|	|	|	|	|	|	...	1132	1132	|	|	|	|	1229	...
Nürnberg Hbf **920 921** d.	|	|	|	|	0933	|	|	|	1028	1028	|	|	1133	|	|	1204	|	|	|	|	1333	|	|	1323x
Würzburg Hbf **920 921** d.	0930	0930	|	|	1031	|	|	|	1130	1130	|	|	1231	|	|	1319	1330	1330	|	|	1431	|	1440	1423
Fulda **850** d.	1003	1003	1011	|	1104	1111	1122	|	1203	1203	1211	|	1304	1311	|	...	1403	1403	1411	|	1504	1511	1518	1524
Kassel Wilhelmshöhe d.	1035	1035	1043	1122	1136	1143	1159	1222	1235	1235	1243	1322	1336	1343	1422	...	1435	1435	1443	1522	1536	1543	1554	1601
Göttingen d.	1056	1056	1103	1143	1156	1203	1220	1243	1256	1256	1303	1343	1356	1403	1443	...	1456	1456	1503	1543	1556	1603	1614	1621
Hildesheim Hbf d.	|	|	1134	|	|	1234	|	|	|	|	1334	|	|	1434	|	...	|	|	1534	|	|	1634	|	|
Braunschweig Hbf a.	|	|	1158	|	|	1258	|	|	|	|	1358	|	|	1458	|	...	|	|	1558	|	|	1658	|	|
Hannover Hbf a.	1132	1132	|	1217	1232	|	1258	1317	1332	1332	|	1417	1432	|	1517	...	1532	1532	|	1617	1632	|	1654	1659
Hannover Hbf d.	1136	1145	|	1220	1236	|	1301	1320	1336	1345	|	1420	1436	|	1520	...	1536	1545	|	1620	1636	|	1658	1702
Berlin Hbf **810** a.	|	|	1325	|	|	1421	|	|	|	|	1525	|	|	1621	|	...	|	|	1725	|	|	1821	|	|
Bremen Hbf **813** a.	|	1244	...	|	|	...	|	|	|	1444	...	|	|	...	|	...	|	1644	...	|	|	...	|	1811
Hamburg Hbf a.	1253	...	...	1334	1353	...	1428	1435	1454	...	...	1534	1554	...	1634	...	1654	...	...	1734	1754	...	1828	1907
Hamburg Altona a.	1308	...	...	1350	1408	...	...	1449	1512	...	...	...	1608	...	1657	...	1709	...	...	...	1808	...	1842	1921

	ICE	*RE*	*ICE*	*ICE*	*ICE*	*ICE*	*ICE*	*ICE*	*IC*	*ICE*	*ICE*	*ICE*	*ICE*	*ICE*	*ICE*	*ICE*	*ICE*	*ICE*	*ICE*	*IC*	*IC*	*IC*	*ICE*	*ICE*
	576	**34618**	**586**	**536**	**374**	**72**	**786**	**596**	**1284**	**974**	**574**	**584**	**1084**	**370**	**776**	**70**	**784**	**1090**	**594**	**1880**	**1878**	**1878**	**572**	**582**
									⑦w	Ⓑq	⑥h	Ⓑq	⑥h	Ⓑq	Ⓑq			Ⓑv	⑥j	⑦w	⑤⑦	④¶		‡
	✕		✕	✕	B✕	✕	✕	✕	🍷♦	K✕	✕	L✕	✕	R✕	N✕	✕	✕	⁄✕	✕	E🍷	d🍷	🍷	✕	✕
Zürich HB **510** d.	...	...	...	...	...	1202	...	...	...	...	...	...	...	...	...	...	...	...	...	...	...	...	...	...
Basel SBB **912** d.	...	...	...	...	1212	1304	...	...	...	...	...	...	...	1412	...	1504	...	...	...	...	...	...	...	...
Karlsruhe Hbf **912** d.	...	...	...	...	1400	1451	...	...	...	...	...	...	...	1600	...	1651	...	...	...	...	...	...	...	...
Ulm Hbf **930** d.	...	...	...	...	|	|	...	1351r	...	...	...	...	...	|	...	|	...	1551	1551	...	...	...	...	...
Stuttgart Hbf **930** d.	1327	...	...	...	|	|	...	1451	...	1527	1527	...	...	|	...	|	...	1651	1651	...	...	...	1727	...
Mannheim Hbf **912 930** d.	1406	...	...	...	1431	1516	...	1531	...	1606	1606	...	...	1631	...	1716	...	1731	1731	...	...	...	1806	...
Frankfurt Flughafen + § d.	1442	...	...	...	|	|	...	|	...	1642	1642	...	...	|	...	|	...	|	|	...	...	...	1842	...
Frankfurt (Main) Hbf **850** d.	1458	...	...	...	1513	1558	...	1613	...	1658	1658	...	...	1713	1716	1758	...	1813	1813	...	1822	1822	1858	...
Hanau Hbf **850** d.	|	...	...	...	1529	|	...	1629	...	|	|	...	...	1729	1741	|	...	|	1829	...	1838	1838	1914	...
München Hbf **904** d.	|	...	1251	1251	|	|	1420	|	1345	|	|	1514	1514	|	|	|	1616	|	|	1545	|	|	|	1714
Augsburg Hbf **904** d.	|	...	1331	1331	|	|	|	|	1425	|	|	|	|	|	|	|	|	|	|	1624	|	|	|	|
Nürnberg Hbf **920 921** d.	|	1404	|	|	|	|	1533	|	|	|	|	1628	1628	|	|	|	1733	|	|	|	|	|	|	1828
Würzburg Hbf **920 921** d.	|	1519	1530	1530	|	|	1631	|	1635	|	|	1730	1730	|	|	|	1831	|	|	1835	|	|	|	1930
Fulda **850** d.	|	...	1603	1603	1611	|	1704	1711	1717	|	|	1803	1803	1811	|	|	1907	|	1911	1914	1921	1930	|	2003
Kassel Wilhelmshöhe d.	1622	...	1635	1635	1643	1722	1736	1743	1754	1822	1822	1835	1835	1843	1851	1922	1939	|	1943	1950	1959	2007	2025	2035
Göttingen d.	1643	...	1656	1656	1703	1743	1756	1803	1815	1843	1843	1856	1856	1903	1912	1943	1959	|	2005	2012	2021	2028	2045	2056
Hildesheim Hbf d.	|	...	|	|	1734	|	|	1834	|	|	|	|	|	1934	|	|	|	|	2034	|	|	|	|	|
Braunschweig Hbf a.	|	...	|	|	1758	|	|	1858	|	|	|	|	|	1958	|	|	|	|	2058	|	|	|	|	|
Hannover Hbf a.	1717	...	1732	1732	|	1817	1832	|	1856	1917	1917	1932	1932	|	1946	2017	2032	|	|	2051	2100	2109	2118	2132
Hannover Hbf d.	1721	...	1736	1745	|	1820	1836	|	1859	1920	1920	1936	1936	|	1949	2020	2036	|	|	2055	2105	2114	2121	2136
Berlin Hbf **810** a.	|	...	|	|	1925	|	|	2021	|	|	|	|	|	2126	|	|	|	2148	2226	|	2250	2259	|	|
Bremen Hbf **813** a.	|	...	|	1844	...	|	|	...	|	|	|	|	|	...	2048	|	|	...	...	|	...	...	|	|
Hamburg Hbf a.	1834	...	1853	...	...	1934	1953	...	2028	2037	2038	2054	2054	...	...	2137	2154	...	...	2225	...	...	2239	2254
Hamburg Altona a.	1850	...	1907	...	...	1950	2008	...	...	...	2052	...	2109	...	...	2153	2208	...	...	2239	...	...	2253	2308

♦ – **NOTES** (LISTED BY TRAIN NUMBER)

478 – ④–⑦ (daily from Mar. 25). KOMET – [sleeper] 1, 2 cl., [couchette] 2 cl., [2] (reclining) and ✕ Zürich - Hamburg.

490 – HANS ALBERS – [sleeper] 1, 2 cl., [couchette] 2 cl., [2] and 🍷 Wien - Linz - Passau - Regensburg - Hamburg; conveys [2] (*D* **60490**) Nürnberg - Hamburg.

672 – [12] and ✕ Wiesbaden Hbf (d. 0500) - Mainz Hbf (d. 0511) - Frankfurt - Hamburg.

1284 – [12] and 🍷 (Schwarzach ● -) München - Flensburg. Also calls at Ansbach (d. 1540).

1286 – PYXIS – [sleeper] 1, 2 cl., [couchette] 2 cl., [2] (reclining) and 🍷 München - Hamburg.

1886 – ROTTALER LAND – [12] and 🍷 Passau - Hamburg. Also calls at Gemünden (d. 1447).

2082 – KÖNIGSSEE – [12] and 🍷 Berchtesgaden - Hamburg; [12] Oberstdorf (**2084**) - Augsburg (**2082**) - Hamburg. Also calls at Treuchtlingen, Gunzenhausen, Ansbach and Steinach (Table **905a**).

2170 – WATTENMEER – [12] and 🍷 Frankfurt - Westerland. See also Tables **902**/**821**.

B – From Bern (Table **560**).
D – From Darmstadt Hbf (d. 0543).
E – Also calls at Donauwörth (d. 1644), Treuchtlingen (d. 1707) and Ansbach (d. 1740).
G – From Garmisch (d. 1039) on ⑥.
K – To Kiel (Table **820**).
L – To Lübeck (Table **825**).
N – To Oldenburg on ①–⑤ **a** (Table **813**).
R – From Interlaken via Bern (Table **560**).

a – ①–⑤ (not Dec. 24, 25, 31, Jan. 1, Apr. 2, 5, May 24).
b – ① (also Apr. 6, May 25; not Apr. 5, May 24). Basel **Badischer Bahnhof**.
c – ⑥ (also Dec. 24, 31; not Dec. 26, Apr. 3). Basel **Badischer Bahnhof**.
d – Also Apr. 5, May 24; not Dec. 25, 27, Jan. 1, Apr. 2, 4, May 14, 23.
e – ①–⑥ (not Dec. 25, 26, Jan. 1, Apr. 3, 5, May 24).
g – ① (also Apr. 6, May 25; not Apr. 5, May 24).
h – Also Dec. 24, 25, 31, Apr. 2, 4, May 23.

j – Also Dec. 24, 25, 31, Apr. 2, 4, May 23; not Dec. 26, Jan. 2.
o – München **Ost**.
p – Previous day.
q – Not Dec. 24, 25, 31, Apr. 2, 4, May 23.
r – Not Dec. 25, 27, Jan. 1.

s – Stops to set down only.
t – Not May 22 - June 7.
v – Not Dec. 24, 25, 31, Jan. 1, Apr. 2, 4, May 23.
w – Also Apr. 5, May 24; not Apr. 4, May 23.
x – Not May 22, 29, June 5.

z – On ⑥ arrives Hamburg Hbf 0829, Altona 0843. On ⑦ (also Dec. 25, Jan. 1, Apr. 5, May 24) arrives Hamburg Hbf 0836, Altona 0859.

⊖ – May 22 - June 7 only. On ⑥ Göttingen d. 0645, Hannover a. 0744, d. 0747, Hamburg Hbf a. 0947, Altona a. 1004. On ①⑦ Göttingen d. 0611, Hannover a. 0742, d. 0746, Hamburg Hbf a. 0947, Altona 1004.
● – From Schwarzach (via Wörgl) Dec. 20 - Apr. 5 (Tables **960** and **951**).
◧ – Train number **674** on ⑤ (also Dec. 23, 30, Apr. 1, May 12; not Dec. 25, Jan. 1, Apr. 2, May 14).
‡ – Train number **1082** on ⑤ (also Dec. 23, 30, Apr. 1, May 12, June 2; not Dec. 25, Jan. 1, Apr. 2, May 14, June 4.
¶ – Also Dec. 22, 23, 29, 30, Mar. 31, May 11, 12; not Dec. 24, 31, May 13. From May 6 departs Fulda 1921, Kassel 1959, Göttingen 2021.
§ – Frankfurt Flughafen Fernbahnhof.
⁄ – *ICE* ***SPRINTER***. R and supplement payable.

NÜRNBERG and FRANKFURT - HAMBURG 900

See Table **901** for local services Frankfurt - Fulda - Kassel and v.v. See Table **902** for other *IC* services Frankfurt - Gießen - Kassel - Göttingen - Alfeld - Hannover - Hamburg and v.v.

	ICE 870	*ICE* 376	*ICE* 782	*ICE* 732	*ICE* 782	*ICE* 732	*ICE* 592	*ICE* 782	*ICE* 732	*ICE* 570	*ICE* 524	*ICE* 580	*ICE* 580	*ICE* 980	*ICE* 292	*ICE* 272	*ICE* 372	*CNL* 482	*CNL* 482	*ICE* 780	*ICE* 590	*ICE* 992	*ICE* 698	*ICE* 920
		⑤⑦j	⑦	⑦	①–⑥	①–⑥		①–⑥	①–⑥	⑦w		①–④	⑦w	⑤f	⑥s	①–⑤	⑦w	Ⓐ	Ⓒ	⑦w	⑥n	⑦w	⑤f	⑦w
	✕	R✕	✕	⊖✕	✕	Q✕	✕	✕	Q✕	✕	🍷	m✕	✕	✕	✕	a✕	✕	✕♦	✕♦	✕	✕	✕	✕	🍷
Zürich HB **510** d.	...	...	...	...	...	...	...	...	...	...	...	...	...	...	1702	1702	1702	...	...	...	...	...	...	...
Basel SBB **912** d.	1612	1704	...	...	...	...	...	...	...	...	...	...	...	...	1812	1812	1812	...	...	...	...	...	...	...
Karlsruhe Hbf **912** d.	1801	1851	...	...	...	...	...	...	...	...	...	...	...	...	2000	2000	2000	...	...	...	...	...	...	...
Ulm Hbf **930** d.	|	|	...	...	...	...	1751	...	...	...	...	...	...	...	|	|	|	...	...	...	1951	1951	1951	...
Stuttgart Hbf **930** d.	|	|	...	...	...	...	1851	...	...	1927	...	...	...	...	|	|	|	...	...	...	2051	2051	2051	...
Mannheim Hbf **912 930** d.	1831	1916	...	...	...	...	1931	...	...	2006	...	...	...	...	2031	2031	2031	...	...	...	2131	2131	2131	...
Frankfurt Flughafen ✈ § d.	|	|	...	...	...	...	|	...	...	2042	...	...	...	...	|	|	|	...	...	...	|	|	|	...
Frankfurt (Main) Hbf **850** d.	1913	1958	...	...	...	...	2013	...	...	2058	...	...	...	...	2113	2113	2113	...	...	...	2222	2222	2222	...
Hanau Hbf **850** d.	1929	|	...	...	...	...	2029	...	...	|	...	...	...	...	2129	2129	2129	...	...	...	2238	2238	2238	...
München Hbf **904** d.	|	|	1820	1820	1820	1820	|	...	...	|	1855	1849	1849	1849	|	|	|	1900	1915	2020	|	|	|	2255
Augsburg Hbf **904** d.	|	|	|	|	|	|	|	...	...	|	|	1932	1932	1932	|	|	|	|	|	|	|	|	|	|
Nürnberg Hbf **920 921** d.	|	|	1933	1933	1933	1933	|	...	...	|	2000	|	|	|	|	|	|	2135	2135	2140	|	|	|	0006
Würzburg Hbf **920 921** d.	|	|	2031	2031	2031	2031	|	...	...	|	2054	2131	2131	2131	|	|	|	2233	2233	2237	|	|	|	0101
Fulda **850** d.	2011	|	2104	2104	2104	2104	|	...	...	|	...	2204	2204	2204	2211	2211	2211	2343u	2343u	2311	2323	2323	2323	...
Kassel Wilhelmshöhe d.	2043	2122	2136	2136	2136	2136	2140	←	←	2222	...	...	2236	2236	2243	2243	2243	|	|	2342	2353	2356	0034	...
Göttingen d.	2103	2143	2157	2157	2155	2155	2201	2205	2205	2243	...	...	2256	2258	2306	2305	2303	|	|	...	...	0047	...	...
Hildesheim Hbf d.	2134	|	|	|	→	→	2234	|	|	|	...	...	|	|	|	|	2334	|	|	...	...	|	...	...
Braunschweig Hbf a.	2158	|	|	|	...	...	2258	|	|	|	...	...	|	|	|	|	2358	|	|	...	...	|	...	...
Hannover Hbf a.	|	2217	2232	2232	...	...	|	2240	2240	2317	...	...	2332	2357	2341	0003	|	|	|	...	...	0146	...	...
Hannover Hbf d.	|	2220	2236	2251	...	...	|	2244	2251	2320	...	...	2336	...	2344	0006	|	|	|	...	...	...	...	...
Berlin Hbf **810** a.	2325	|	|	|	...	...	0023	|	|	|	...	...	|	...	|	|	0125	|	|	...	...	...	...	...
Bremen Hbf **813** a.	...	|	|	2349	...	...	...	|	2349	|	...	...	|	...	|	|	...	|	|	...	...	...	...	...
Hamburg Hbf a.	...	2342	2358	...	...	...	...	0007	...	0037	...	...	0103	...	0111	0134	...	0356	0356	...	...	...	...	...
Hamburg Altona a.	...	2357	0013	...	...	...	...	0022	...	0052	...	...	0118	...	0125	0148	...	...	...	...	...	...	...	...

km		*ICE* 5	*CNL* 483	*CNL* 483	*CNL* 483	*ICE* 827	*ICE* 591	*ICE* 591	*ICE* 999	*ICE* 781	*ICE* 781	*ICE* 373	*ICE* 531	*ICE* 581	*ICE* 571	*ICE* 1097	*ICE* 593	*ICE* 1091	*ICE* 783	*ICE* 71	*ICE* 375	*ICE* 533	*ICE* 583	*ICE* 1083
		①g	B	⑦p	①g	Ⓐv	①–⑤	①–⑥	⑦w	①⑥	①–⑥	①–⑤	①–⑤	¶	①–⑥	ⒶD	⑥⑦	①–⑤	①–⑥		①–⑥	①–⑥	①–⑥	⑦d
			✕♦	✕♦	✕♦		a✕	y✕	✕	b✕	e✕	aR	aE	✕	e✕	⚡✕	k✕	a⚡	e✕	✕	eR	eN	e♦	✕
	Hamburg Altona d.	...	...	...	...	...	0304	...	...	...	...	✕	✕	0443	0505	0552	...	✕	0541c	0604	✕	✕	✕	0647
	Hamburg Hbf d.	0025	0031	0031r	0031	...	0318	...	...	...	...	...	...	0457	0519	0609	...	...	0600c	0618	...	...	0700	0701
	Bremen Hbf **813** d.	|	|	|	|	...	|	...	...	...	...	...	0514	|	|	|	...	...	|	|	...	0714	|	|
	Berlin Hbf **810** d.	|	|	|	|	...	|	...	...	...	...	0432	|	|	|	|	0531	0608	|	|	0632	|	|	|
	Hannover Hbf a.	0147	|	|	|	...	0459	...	...	...	...	|	0614	0621	0638	0719	|	|	0724	0738	|	0814	0823	0821
	Hannover Hbf d.	0150	|	|	|	...	0518	0518	...	0526	...	|	0626	0626	0641	0722	|	|	0726	0741	|	0826	0826	0826
0	**Braunschweig** Hbf d.	|	|	|	|	...	|	|	...	|	...	0558	|	|	|	|	0657	|	|	|	0758	|	|	|
43	Hildesheim Hbf d.	|	|	|	|	...	|	|	...	|	...	0625	|	|	|	|	0725	|	|	|	0825	|	|	|
121	Göttingen d.	0247	|	|	|	...	0555	0555	...	0602	...	0655	0702	0702	0717	|	0755	|	0802	0817	0855	0902	0902	0902
166	**Kassel** Wilhelmshöhe d.	|	|	|	|	...	0616	0616	0616	0623	...	0716	0723	0723	0738	|	0816	|	0826	0838	0916	0923	0923	0923
256	Fulda **850** d.	0418	0456	0513	0513	...	0647	0647	0647	0656	0656	0747	0755	0755	|	|	0847	|	0858	|	0947	0955	0955	0955
	Würzburg Hbf **920 921** d.	|	0536	0551	0551	0603	|	|	|	0729	0729	|	0831	0831	|	|	|	|	0930	|	|	1031	1031	1031
	Nürnberg Hbf **920 921** a.	|	0644	0646	|	0656	|	|	|	0824	0824	|	0930	0930	|	|	|	|	1024	|	|	|	|	|
	Augsburg Hbf **904** a.	|	|	|	|	|	|	|	|	|	|	|	|	|	|	|	|	|	|	|	|	1223	1223	1223
	München Hbf **904** a.	|	0900	0900	0900	0806	|	|	|	0942	0942	|	1044	1044	|	|	|	|	1143	|	|	1304	1304	1304
337	Hanau Hbf **850** d.	0506	...	...	...	...	0730	0730	0730	...	...	0829	...	...	|	|	0929	|	...	|	1029	...	...	...
360	**Frankfurt** (Main) Hbf **850** a.	0529	...	...	...	...	0745	0745	0745	...	...	0844	...	...	0900	0928	0944	0942	...	1000	1044	...	...	...
	Frankfurt Flughafen ✈ § a.	0550	...	...	...	...	|	|	|	...	...	|	...	...	0916	...	|	|	...	|	|	...	...	...
	Mannheim Hbf **912 930** a.	0625	...	...	...	...	0828	0828	0828	...	...	0928	...	...	0953	...	1028	1028	...	1042	1128	...	...	...
	Stuttgart Hbf **930** a.	|	...	...	...	...	0908	0908	0908	...	...	|	...	...	1034	...	1108	1108	...	|	|	...	...	...
	Ulm Hbf **930** a.	|	...	...	...	...	1006x	1006x	1006x	...	...	|	...	...	...	...	1206x	1206x	...	|	|	...	...	...
	Karlsruhe Hbf **912** a.	0650	...	...	...	...	...	...	...	...	...	0958	...	...	...	...	...	...	...	1106	1158	...	...	...
	Basel SBB **912** a.	0847	...	...	...	...	...	...	...	...	...	1147	...	...	...	...	...	...	...	1255	1347	...	...	...
	Zürich HB **510** a.	1000	...	...	...	...	...	...	...	...	...	...	...	...	...	...	...	...	...	...	...	...	...	...

	RE 34613	*ICE* 973	*ICE* 573	*IC* 1887	*IC* 2083	*ICE* 595	*ICE* 785	*ICE* 73	*ICE* 1035	*ICE* 871	*ICE* 535	*ICE* 585	*ICE* 575	*IC* 1879	*ICE* 597	*ICE* 787	*ICE* 75	*ICE* 277	*ICE* 537	*ICE* 587	*RE* 34621	*ICE* 577	*ICE* 599	*ICE* 789
		①–⑥	⑦d	⑥					⑤f		A	⊙		⑤◇										
		eK	✕	🍷♦	🍷♦	✕	✕	K✕	✕	✕	✕	✕	✕	🍷	✕	✕	✕	R✕	✕	✕		✕	✕	✕
Hamburg Altona d.	...	✕	0709	0620	0714	...	0747	...	...	...	...	0847	0909	0914	...	0947	1009	...	...	1047	...	1109	...	1147
Hamburg Hbf d.	...	0724	0724	0635	0728	...	0803	0824	...	...	...	0901	0924	0928	...	1001	1024	...	...	1101	...	1124	...	1201
Bremen Hbf **813** d.	...	|	|	0736	|	...	|	|	0914	...	0914	|	|	|	...	|	|	...	1114	|	...	|	...	|
Berlin Hbf **810** d.	...	|	|	|	|	0737	|	|	|	0832	|	|	|	|	0937	|	|	1032	|	|	...	|	1137	|
Hannover Hbf a.	...	0838	0838	0846	0857	|	0921	0938	1013	|	1014	1023	1038	1056	|	1121	1138	|	1214	1223	...	1238	|	1321
Hannover Hbf d.	...	0841	0841	0849	0900	|	0926	0941	1016	|	1026	1026	1041	1059	|	1126	1141	|	1226	1226	...	1241	|	1326
Braunschweig Hbf d.	...	|	|	|	|	0857	|	|	|	0958	|	|	|	|	1057	|	|	1158	|	|	...	|	1257	|
Hildesheim Hbf d.	...	|	|	|	|	0925	|	|	|	1025	|	|	|	|	1125	|	|	1225	|	|	...	|	1325	|
Göttingen d.	...	0917	0917	0928	0941	0955	1002	1017	|	1055	1102	1102	1117	1140	1155	1202	1217	1255	1302	1302	...	1317	1355	1402
Kassel Wilhelmshöhe d.	...	0938	0938	0951	1005	1016	1023	1038	1109	1116	1123	1123	1138	1203	1216	1223	1238	1316	1323	1323	...	1338	1416	1423
Fulda **850** d.	...	|	|	1028	1043	1047	1055	|	|	1147	1155	1155	|	1241	1247	1255	|	1347	1355	1355	...	|	1447	1455
Würzburg Hbf **920 921** d.	1040	|	|	1118	1121	|	1129	|	|	|	1231	1231	|	|	|	1329	|	|	1431	1431	1440	|	|	1529
Nürnberg Hbf **920 921** a.	1154	|	|	1232z	|	|	1224	|	|	|	1329	1329	|	|	|	1424	|	|	|	|	1554	|	|	1624
Augsburg Hbf **904** a.	...	|	|	...	1329	|	|	|	|	|	|	|	|	|	|	|	|	|	1626	1626	...	|	|	|
München Hbf **904** a.	...	|	|	...	1412o	|	1339	|	|	|	1444	1444	|	|	|	1543	|	|	1707	1707	...	|	|	1739
Hanau Hbf **850** d.	...	|	|	...	...	1129	...	|	|	1229	...	...	|	|	1329	...	|	1429	...	...	...	|	1529	...
Frankfurt (Main) Hbf **850** a.	...	1100	1100	...	...	1144	...	1200	1240	1244	...	...	1300	1336	1344	...	1400	1444	...	...	...	1500	1544	...
Frankfurt Flughafen ✈ § a.	...	1116	1116	...	...	|	...	|	...	|	...	...	1316	...	|	...	|	|	...	...	...	1516	|	...
Mannheim Hbf **912 930** a.	...	1153	1153	...	...	1228	...	1242	...	1328	...	...	1353	...	1428	...	1442	1528	...	...	...	1553	1628	...
Stuttgart Hbf **930** a.	...	1234	1234	...	...	1308	...	|	...	|	...	...	1434	...	1508	...	|	|	...	...	...	1634	1708	...
Ulm Hbf **930** a.	...	...	...	...	...	1406h	...	|	...	|	...	...	...	...	1606x	...	|	|	...	...	...	...	1806x	...
Karlsruhe Hbf **912** a.	...	...	...	...	...	...	...	1306	...	1358	...	...	...	...	...	...	1506	1558	...	...	...	...	...	...
Basel SBB **912** a.	...	...	...	...	...	...	...	1455	...	1547	...	...	...	...	...	...	1655	1747	...	...	...	...	...	...
Zürich HB **510** a.	...	...	...	...	...	...	...	1600	...	...	...	...	...	...	...	...	1800	...	...	...	...	...	...	...

♦ – **NOTES** (LISTED BY TRAIN NUMBER)

482 – HANS CHRISTIAN ANDERSEN – 🛏 1, 2 cl., 🛌 2 cl. and (2) München - Ingolstadt Hbf (d. 1943 Ⓐ**t** / 2013 Ⓒ**H**) - Flensburg - København. See also Tables **50** / **823**. Starts from Innsbruck on ⑥ Dec. 26 - Apr. 10. 🅁 for overnight journeys. For Warszawa and Moskva cars see Table **24**.

483 – HANS CHRISTIAN ANDERSEN – 🛏 1, 2 cl., 🛌 2 cl. and (2) København - Flensburg - Ingolstadt Hbf (a. 0810) - München. See also Tables **50** / **823**. On ⑤ Dec. 25 - Apr. 10 runs København - München - Innsbruck. 🅁 for overnight journeys. For Warszawa and Moskva cars see Table **24**.

583 – WERDENFELSER LAND – (12) and ✕ Lübeck - München (- Garmisch ⑥).

1887 – ROTTALER LAND – (12) and 🍷 Hamburg - Passau. Also calls at Gemünden (d. 1057).

2083 – KÖNIGSSEE – (12) and 🍷 Hamburg - Berchtesgaden; (12) Hamburg - Augsburg (**2085**) - Oberstdorf. Also calls at Steinach, Ansbach, Gunzenhausen and Treuchtlingen (Table **905a**).

- **A** – ①②③④⑥⑦ (also Dec. 25, Jan. 1, Apr. 2, May 14, June 4; not Dec. 23, 30, Apr. 1, May 12, June 2).
- **B** – ②–⑥ (also May 24; not Dec. 25, Apr. 6, May 25).
- **D** – Ⓐ (not Dec. 24, 31). To Darmstadt Hbf (a. 0950).
- **E** – From Oldenburg on ①**g** (d. 0447).
- **H** – Until Apr. 25.
- **K** – From Kiel (Table **820**).
- **N** – From Oldenburg (d. 0642).
- **Q** – From Garmisch (d. 1624) on ⑥. To Oldenburg on dates in Table **813**.
- **R** – From / to Interlaken via Bern (Table **560**).

- **a** – Not Dec. 24, 25, 31, Jan. 1, Apr. 2, 5, May 24.
- **b** – Also Dec. 24, 31, Apr. 2, 6, May 13, 25; not Dec. 26, Jan. 2, Apr. 3, 5, May 15, 24.
- **c** – On ⑥ (also Apr. 2, May 13) departs Hamburg Altona 0552, Hamburg Hbf 0605.
- **d** – Also Dec. 25, 26, Jan. 1, Apr. 3, 5, May 24.
- **e** – Not Dec. 25, 26, Jan. 1, Apr. 3, 5, May 24.
- **f** – Also Dec. 23, 30, Apr. 1, May 12, June 2; not Dec. 25, Jan. 1, Apr. 2, May 14, June 4.
- **g** – Also Apr. 6, May 25; not Apr. 5, May 24.
- **h** – Not Dec. 25, 27, Jan. 1, Feb. 27 - May 16.

- **j** – Also Dec. 23, 30, Apr. 1, 5, May 12, 24; not Dec. 25, Jan. 1, Apr. 2, 4, May 14, 23.
- **k** – Also Dec. 24, 25, 31, Jan. 1, Apr. 2, 5, May 24; not Dec. 26, Jan. 2.
- **m** – Also Jan. 1, May 14, June 4; not Dec. 23, 24, 30, 31, Apr. 1, 5, May 12, 24, June 2.
- **n** – Also Apr. 2, May 14; not Apr. 3.
- **o** – München **Ost**.
- **p** – Also Dec. 25, Apr. 5.
- **r** – 0011 from Apr. 18.
- **s** – Also Dec. 24, 25, 31, Apr. 2, 4, May 23.
- **t** – Not May 25 - June 4.
- **u** – Stops to pick up only.
- **v** – Not Dec. 24, 31, Jan. 6, June 3.
- **w** – Also Apr. 5, May 24; not Apr. 4, May 23.
- **x** – Not Feb. 27 - May 16.
- **y** – Also Apr. 4, May 23; not Dec. 25, Apr. 5, May 24.
- **z** – Not May 22, 29, June 5.

- ◇ – Also Dec. 23, 30, Apr. 1, May 12; not Dec. 25, Jan. 1, Apr. 2, May 14.
- ¶ – Train number **1081** on ⑥⑦ (also Dec. 24, 25, 31, Jan. 1, Apr. 2, 5, May 24).
- ⊙ – Train number **1085** on ⑤**f**.
- ⊖ – To Oldenburg (not Apr. 4, May 23). See Table **813**.
- ⚡ – *ICE* ***SPRINTER***. 🅁 and supplement payable.
- § – Frankfurt Flughafen Fernbahnhof.

900 HAMBURG - FRANKFURT and NÜRNBERG

See Table **902** for other *IC* services Hamburg - Hannover - Alfeld - Göttingen - Kassel - Gießen - Frankfurt. See Table **901** for local services Kassel - Fulda - Frankfurt.

	ICE	*ICE*	*ICE*	*ICE*	*RE*	*ICE*	*IC*	*ICE*	*ICE*	*ICE*	*ICE*	*ICE*	*ICE*	*RE*	*ICE*	*IC*	*ICE*	*ICE*	*ICE*	*ICE*	*ICE*	*ICE*	*RE*	*ICE*
	77	**279**	**539**	**589**	**34625**	**579**	**1881**	**691**	**881**	**79**	**873**	**631**	**681**	**34629**	**771**	**2171**	**693**	**883**	**671**	**875**	**633**	**683**	**34633**	**773**
							⑤⑦t									⑤–⑦		◐						
	✕	✕♦	✕	✕		✕	E🍷	✕	✕	✕	✕	✕	✕		✕	🍷♦	✕	✕	✕	✕	✕	✕		✕
Hamburg Altona d.	1208	...	...	1247	...	1309	1314	...	1347	1409	...	...	1447	...	1509	...	...	...	1609	...	...	1647	...	1709
Hamburg Hbf d.	1224	...	...	1301	...	1324	1328	...	1401	1424	...	...	1501	...	1524	1528	...	1603	1624	...	...	1701	...	1724
Bremen Hbf **813** d.	|	...	1314	|	...	|	|	...	|	|	...	1514	|	...	|	|	...	|	|	...	1714	|	...	|
Berlin Hbf **810** d.	|	1232	|	|	...	|	|	1337	|	|	1432	|	|	...	|	|	1537	|	|	1632	|	|	...	|
Hannover Hbf a.	1338	|	1414	1423	...	1438	1453	|	1521	1538	|	1614	1623	...	1638	1658	|	1723	1738	|	1814	1823	...	1838
Hannover Hbf d.	1341	|	1426	1426	...	1441	1456	|	1526	1541	|	1626	1626	...	1641	1702	|	1726	1741	|	1826	1826	...	1841
Braunschweig Hbf d.	|	1358	|	|	...	|	|	1457	|	|	1558	|	|	...	|	|	1657	|	|	1758	|	|	...	|
Hildesheim Hbf d.	|	1425	|	|	...	|	|	1525	|	|	1625	|	|	...	|	|	1725	|	|	1825	|	|	...	|
Göttingen d.	1417	1455	1502	1502	...	1517	1535	1555	1602	1617	1655	1702	1702	...	1717	1741	1755	1802	1817	1855	1902	1902	...	1917
Kassel Wilhelmshöhe d.	1438	1516	1523	1523	...	1538	1559	1616	1623	1638	1716	1723	1723	...	1738	1803	1816	1823	1838	1916	1923	1923	...	1938
Fulda **850** d.	|	1547	1555	1555	...	|	1633	1647	1655	|	1747	1755	1755	...	|	1840	1847	1855	|	1947	1955	1955	...	|
Würzburg Hbf **920 921** d.	|	|	1631	1631	1640	|	1716	|	1729	|	|	1831	1831	1840	|	|	|	1929	|	|	2031	2031	2040	|
Nürnberg Hbf **920 921** a.	|	|	|	|	1754	|	|	|	1824	|	|	|	|	1955	|	|	|	2024	|	|	|	|	2154	|
Augsburg Hbf **904** a.	|	|	1822	1822	...	|	1930	|	|	|	|	2022	2022	...	|	|	|	|	|	|	2222	2222	...	|
München Hbf **904** a.	|	|	1903	1903	...	|	2011	|	1939	|	|	2102	2102	...	|	|	|	2139	|	|	2302	2302	...	|
Hanau Hbf **850** d.	|	1629	...	...	...	|	...	1729	...	|	1829	...	...	...	|	1925	1929	...	|	2029	...	...	...	|
Frankfurt (Main) Hbf **850** a.	1600	1644	...	...	...	1700	...	1744	...	1800	1844	...	...	...	1900	1950	1944	...	2000	2044	...	...	...	2100
Frankfurt Flughafen ✈ § a.	|	|	...	...	...	1716	...	|	...	|	|	...	...	...	1916	...	|	...	|	|	...	...	...	2116
Mannheim Hbf **912** a.	1642	1728	...	...	...	1753	...	1828	...	1842	1928	...	...	...	1953	...	2028	...	2042	2128	...	...	...	2153
Stuttgart Hbf **930** a.	|	|	...	...	...	1834	...	1908	...	|	|	...	...	...	2034	...	2108	...	|	|	...	...	...	2249
Ulm Hbf **930** a.	|	|	...	...	...	...	...	2006j	...	|	|	...	...	...	...	...	2206	...	|	|	...	...	...	...
Karlsruhe Hbf **912** a.	1706	1758	...	...	...	...	...	...	...	1906	1958	...	...	...	...	...	...	...	2107	2158	...	...	...	...
Basel SBB **912** a.	1855	1947	...	...	...	...	...	...	...	2055	2147	...	...	...	...	...	...	...	2300w	2355	...	...	...	...
Zürich HB **510** a.	2000	...	...	...	...	...	...	...	...	2200	...	...	...	...	...	...	...	...	...	...	...	...	...	...

	IC	*ICE*	*ICE*	*ICE*	*ICE*	*ICE*	*ICE*	*ICE*	*ICE*	*ICE*	*IC*	*ICE*	*ICE*	*ICE*	*ICE*	*IC*	*ICE*	*IC*	*ICE*	*CNL*	*EN*	*CNL*	*ICE*	*ICE*
	1897	**695**	**1093**	**885**	**673**	**877**	**635**	**685**	**1517**	**775**	**1899**	**697**	**697**	**887**	**1087**	**2350**	**879**	**1889**	**879**	**479**	**491**	**1287**	**889**	**1089**
	⑦w	⑥h	Ⓑp						**1757**	⑦w	⑦w	Ⓑq	⑤⑦	Ⓑq	⑥k	⑦w	⑦w	⑦w	⑦w	[R]		[R]	⑦w	⑤f
	🍷	✕	✕⚡	✕	✕♦	✕	✕	✕	n✕	✕		✕	r✕	A✕	A✕	♦	✕	F	✕	✕♦	🍷♦	✕♦		
Hamburg Altona d.	...	...	...	1745	...	...	...	1847	...	1909	...	...	...	1947	1947	...	...	...	...	1903z	2018	2113	2301	2338
Hamburg Hbf d.	...	...	...	1801	1824	...	...	1901	...	1924	...	...	...	2001	2001	...	...	2101	...	1918z	2033	2127	2314	2352
Bremen Hbf **813** d.	...	...	...	|	|	...	1914	|	...	|	...	...	...	|	|	...	...	|	...	|	|	|	|	|
Berlin Hbf **810** d.	1658c	1733	1805	|	|	1833	|	|	...	|	1909	1937	1937	|	|	1839	2032	|	...	|	|	|	|	|
Hannover Hbf a.	1844c	|	|	1923	1938	|	2014	2023	...	2038	2055	|	|	2121	2121	|	|	2219	...	|	2223	|	0044	0142
Hannover Hbf d.	1901	|	|	1926	1941	|	2026	2026	...	2041	2100	|	|	2126	2137	|	|	2222	...	2216u	2226	2323u	...	...
Braunschweig Hbf d.	|	1857	|	|	|	1958	|	|	...	|	|	2057	2057	|	|	|	2158	|	...	|	|	|	...	...
Hildesheim Hbf d.	|	1925	|	|	|	2025	|	|	...	|	|	2125	2125	|	|	|	2225	|	...	|	|	|	...	...
Göttingen d.	1942	1955	|	2002	2017	2055	2102	2102	...	2117	2142	2155	2155	2202	2212	|	2255	2300	...	2332u	2325	|	...	...
Kassel Wilhelmshöhe d.	2004	2016	|	2026	2038	2116	2123	2123	...	2138	2204	2213	2215	2223	2233	|	2316	2322	←	|	|	|	...	...
Fulda **850** d.	2047	2047	|	2058	|	2147	2155	2155	...	|	|	...	2247	2255	2304	2307	2346	2357	2358	|	|	|	...	...
Würzburg Hbf **920 921** d.	|	|	|	2134	|	|	2229	2229	...	|	|	...	|	|	|	2356	→	0034	|	|	0207	|	...	...
Nürnberg Hbf **920 921** a.	|	|	|	2228	|	|	2324	2324	2338	|	⊡	...	|	|	|	...	...	0125	|	|	0306	|	...	...
Augsburg Hbf **904** a.	|	|	|	|	|	|	|	|	|	|	|	...	|	|	|	...	...	...	|	|	...	0622	...	...
München Hbf **904** a.	|	|	|	2346	|	|	0041y	0041y	0049	|	|	...	|	|	|	...	...	...	|	|	...	0705	...	...
Hanau Hbf **850** d.	2135	|	|	...	|	2229	...	...	...	|	|	...	2329	2340	0001	...	...	...	0041	|	...	...	...	...
Frankfurt (Main) Hbf **850** a.	2152	2142	2142	...	2200	2244	...	...	...	2300	0021	...	2344	2356	0017	...	...	...	0058	|	...	...	...	...
Frankfurt Flughafen ✈ § a.	|	|	|	...	|	|	...	...	...	|	...	...	...	0015	0038	...	...	...	0122	|	...	...	...	...
Mannheim Hbf **912** a.	|	2228	2228	...	2242	2341	...	...	...	|	...	...	...	...	...	...	...	...	0200	|	...	...	...	...
Stuttgart Hbf **930** a.	2341	2309	2309	...	|	|	...	...	...	0044	...	...	...	...	...	...	...	...	|	|	...	...	...	...
Ulm Hbf **930** a.	...	...	...	...	|	|	...	...	...	...	...	...	...	...	...	...	...	...	|	|	...	...	...	...
Karlsruhe Hbf **912** a.	...	...	...	...	2307	0013	...	...	...	...	...	...	...	...	...	...	...	...	0238	0437	...	...	...	...
Basel SBB **912** a.	...	...	...	...	0102	...	...	...	...	...	...	...	...	...	...	...	...	...	...	0654	...	...	...	...
Zürich HB **510** a.	...	...	...	...	...	...	...	...	...	...	...	...	...	...	...	...	...	...	...	0834b	...	...	...	...

♦ – **NOTES** (LISTED BY TRAIN NUMBER)

279 – [12] and ✕ Berlin - Basel - Bern - Interlaken.
479 – ④–⑦ until Mar. 21; daily from Mar. 25. KOMET – 🛏 1, 2 cl., ▬ 2 cl., [2] and ✕ Hamburg - Zürich (Hamburg - Zürich - Brig on ⑤ Dec. 25 - Apr. 9).
491 – HANS ALBERS – 🛏 1, 2 cl., ▬ 2 cl., [2] and 🍷 Hamburg - Wien. [2] (*D* **60491**) Hamburg - Nürnberg. [R] for journeys beyond Nürnberg.
673 – [12] and ✕ Kiel - Hamburg - Karlsruhe (- Basel ♥).
1287 – PYXIS – 🛏 1, 2 cl., ▬ 2 cl., [2] (reclining) and 🍷 Hamburg - München.
2171 – ⑤–⑦ (also Dec. 23, 24, 30, 31, Apr. 1, 5, May 12, 24). WATTENMEER – [12] and 🍷 Westerland - Frankfurt.
2350 – [12] Stralsund - Berlin - Halle - Erfurt - Gemünden (a. 2332) - Würzburg.

A – To Mainz and Wiesbaden (Table **912**).
E – Also calls at Ansbach (a. 1816), Treuchtlingen (a. 1845) and Donauwörth (a. 1906).
F – From Flensburg (Table **823**).

b – 0820 on ⑥⑦ (also Dec. 25, Jan. 1, Apr. 2, 5, May 13, 24).
c – 10 minutes later from May 2.
f – Also Dec. 23, 30, Apr. 1, May 12; not Dec. 25, Jan. 1, Apr. 2, May 14.
h – Also Dec. 24, 25, 31, Jan. 1, Apr. 2, 4, May 23.
j – Ⓑ (not Dec. 24, 25, 31, May 23). Arrives 2014 Feb. 28 - May 16.
k – Also Dec. 24, 25, 31, Apr. 2, 4, May 23.
n – Not Dec. 24, 31.
p – Not Dec. 24, 25, 31, Jan. 1, Apr. 2, 4, May 23.
q – Not Dec. 24, 25, 31, Apr. 2, 4, May 23.
r – Also Dec. 23, 30, Apr. 1, 5, May 24; not Dec. 25, Apr. 2, 4, May 23.
t – Also Dec. 23, 30, Apr. 1, 5, May 12, 24; not Dec. 25, Apr. 2, 4, May 14, 23.
u – Stops to pick up only.
w – ⑦ (also Apr. 5, May 24; not Apr. 4, May 23).
y – Nürnberg - München on ⑦ (also Apr. 5, May 24; not Apr. 4, May 23).
z – On ⑥⑦ (also Dec. 25, Jan. 1, Apr. 5, May 24) departs Hamburg Altona 2010, Hamburg Hbf 2024.

♥ – Karlsruhe - Basel on ⑤⑥ (also Dec. 23, 24, 30, Apr. 1, 4; not Dec. 25, Jan. 1).
◐ – Train number **1183** on ⑤ (also Dec. 23, 30, Apr. 1, May 12; not Dec. 25, Jan. 1, Apr. 2, May 14).
⊡ – Via Gießen (Table **806**).
⚡ – *ICE* ***SPRINTER***. [R] and supplement payable.
§ – Frankfurt Flughafen Fernbahnhof.

901 Local services FRANKFURT - FULDA - KASSEL

RE / *RB* services

Other *ICE* / *IC* services: Table **850** for Bebra - Kassel Wilhelmshöhe and v.v., also Frankfurt - Fulda - Bad Hersfeld and v.v. Table **900** for Frankfurt - Fulda - Kassel Wilhelmshöhe and v.v.

km							
0	**Frankfurt** (Main) Hbf **921** d.	0526	and hourly until	2126	2226	2326	...
10	Offenbach (Main) Hbf **921** d.	0538		2138	2238	2338	...
23	Hanau Hbf **921** d.	0548		2148	2248	2348	...
104	**Fulda** a.	0648		2248	2348	0048	...

		ⒶB	†w	⚒r	ⒶB						
Fulda d.	0401	0438	0508	0516	0600	0608	0708	0808	0908	and hourly until	2308
Hanau Hbf **921** d.	0500	0539	0609	0616	0656	0709	0809	0909	1009		0009
Offenbach (Main) Hbf **921** d.	0509	0548	0617	0624	|	0717	0817	0921	1017		0017
Frankfurt (Main) Hbf **921** a.	0520	0559	0628	0636	0716	0728	0828	0932	1028		0028

km	See note ♠	Ⓐe	Ⓐe	Ⓐe	†w	⚒r	Ⓐe														Ⓒz	Ⓐe		X
0	**Fulda** d.	...	...	0548	0610	0616	0646	0719	0819	0919	1019	1119	1219	1319	1419	1519g	1619	1708h	1819	1919	2019	*2117**	2122	2222	...
42	Bad Hersfeld d.	...	*0511*	0616	0639	0644	0714	0747	0847	0947	1047	1147	1247	1347	1447	1547g	1647	1744h	1847	1947	2047	2145	2149	2250	...
56	Bebra d.	0428	0535	0627	0650	0657	0727	0758	0857	0958	1057	1158	1257	1358	1457	1558	1657	1758	1857	1958	2058	2200	2200	2301	2307
62	Rotenburg (Fulda) d.	0434	0541	0634	0656	0704	0734	0804	0903	1004	1103	1204	1303	1404	1503	1604	1703	1804	1903	2004	2104	2206	2206	...	2313
84	Melsungen d.	0453	0600	0653	0715	0723	0753	0824	0923	1024	1123	1224	1323	1424	1523	1624	1723	1824	1923	2024	2124	2225	2225	...	2331
110	**Kassel** Wilhelmshöhe **804/6** a.	0519	0617	0713	0741	0742	0812	0842	0942	1042	1142	1242	1342	1442	1542	1642	1742	1842	1942	2042	2142	2243	2243	...	2356
114	**Kassel** Hbf **804/6** a.	0525	0623	0718	0747	0748	0818	0849	0949	1049	1149	1249	1349	1449	1549	1649	1749	1849	1949	2052	2150	2252	2252	...	0006

See note ♠		ⒶB	Ⓐe	ⒶB	⚒r	Ⓒz	Ⓐe														Ⓐe	Ⓒz		⚒r	†w
Kassel Hbf **804/6** d.	...	...	...	...	0506	0606	0629	0701	0806j	0910	1010	1110	1210	1310	1410	1510	1610	1710	1810	1910	2010	2010	2105f	2309	2329
Kassel Wilhelmshöhe **804/6** d.	...	...	...	...	0510	0614	0633	0705	0814	0914	1014	1114	1214	1314	1414	1514	1614	1715	1814	1914	2014	2014	2114	2315	2334
Melsungen d.	...	...	...	...	0530	0634	0651	0731	0834	0933	1034	1133	1234	1333	1434	1533	1634	1733	1834	1933	2034	2034	2133	2343	2357
Rotenburg (Fulda) d.	...	...	...	...	0548	0652	0710	0751	0852	0951	1052	1151	1252	1351	1452	1551	1652	1751	1852	1951	2052	2052	2151	0001	0017
Bebra d.	0315	0359	0425	0522	0558	0659	0717	0800	0859	0958	1059	1158	1259	1358	1459	1558	1659	1758	1859	1958	2059	2059	2159	0007	0024
Bad Hersfeld d.	0325	0409	0437	0531	0608	0708	0726	0810	0908	1008	1108	1208	1308	1408	1508	1608	1708	1808	1908	2008	2108	2111	2209	...	...
Fulda a.	0354	0436	0506	0558	0637	0737	0755	*0854*	0937	1037	1137	1237	1337	1437	1537	1637	1737	1840	1937	2040	2137	2140	2238	...	...

B – Ⓐ (not Dec. 24, 31, June 3). [12] Bebra - Fulda - Frankfurt.
X – Runs 9–12 minutes later on ①–⑤.
e – Not Dec. 24, 31, June 3.
f – 2110 on Ⓐ (not Dec. 24, 31, June 3).
g – On ⑤ (also Dec. 23, 30, Apr. 1, May 12, June 2; not Dec. 25, Jan. 1, Apr. 2, May 14, June 4) departs Fulda 1508, Bad Hersfeld 1544.
h – On Ⓒ (also Dec. 24, 31, June 3) departs Fulda 1719, Bad Hersfeld 1747.
j – 0810 on ⚒ (not June 3).
r – Not June 3.
w – Also June 3.
z – Also Dec. 24, 31, June 3.
* – Connection by *ICE* train.
♠ – Most services are operated by CANTUS Verkehrsgesellschaft. 2nd class only.

IC services ◇ KASSEL - HANNOVER - HAMBURG 902

See Table **900** for faster *ICE* trains Karlsruhe - Frankfurt - Kassel - Göttingen - Hannover - Hamburg and v.v. See Table **903** for other regional services operated by *metronom*.

km		*IC*	*IC*	*IC*	*IC*	*IC*	*IC*	*IC*	*IC*	*IC*	*IC*	*IC*	*IC*	*IC*	*IC*	*IC*	*EC*	*IC*	*IC*	*IC*	*IC*	*IC*	*IC*	*ICE*	*ICE*	*ICE*
		2178	**2184**	**2176**	**2182**	**2182**	**2378**	**2376**	**2170**	**2170**	**2374**	**2174**	**2372**	**2082**	**2370**	**2270**	**340**	**1284**	**2276**	**2286**	**1880**	**2274**	**2274**	**580**	**292**	**272**
		①–⑤	①–⑤	①–⑤	①–⑤	①–⑥	①–⑥		⑥⑦		Y	⑤f			H	⑤⑦	Ⓑh	⑦w	①–⑥	⑦w	⑦w	⑤⑦	⑦w	⑦w	⑥k	①–⑤
		a	a O	a	a	e	e	N	L	J				B	K	r K	A	F	v		M	r		M	Z	a Z
		🍷	🍷	🍷			🍷	🍷	🍷	🍷	🍷	🍷	🍷	🍷	🍷	🍷		🍷	🍷	🍷	🍷			🍴	🍴	🍴
	Karlsruhe Hbf **911** .. d.	...	...	...	...	...	...	0702**e**	...	...	0910	0910	1110**c**	...	1310	1310	...	...	1510	1510	...	1710	1710	...	2000	2000
	Frankfurt (M) Hbf ◐ . d.	...	...	...	...	...	0649	0852	1017	...	1052	1052	1252	...	1452	1452	...	...	1652	1652	...	1852	1852	...	2113	2113
0	**Kassel** Wilhelmshöhe d.	...	...	...	0623	...	0855	1055	1159	...	1255	1255	1455	1554	1655	1655	...	1754	1857	1857	1950	2055	2055	2236	2243	2243
45	**Göttingen** d.	...	...	0548	0645	...	0917	1117	1220	...	1317	1317	1517	1614	1717	1717	...	1815	1918	1918	2012	2117	2117	2256	2306	2305
65	Northeim (Han) d.	...	...	0600	0658	...	|	|	|	...	|	|	|	|	|	|	...	|	|	|	|	|	|	|	|	|
84	Kreiensen d.	...	...	0613	0711	...	|	|	|	...	|	|	|	|	|	|	...	|	|	|	|	|	|	|	|	|
103	Alfeld (Leine) d.	...	...	0626	0724	...	|	|	|	...	|	|	|	|	|	|	...	|	|	|	|	|	|	|	|	|
120	Elze (Han) d.	...	...	0637	0737	...	|	|	|	...	|	|	|	|	|	|	...	|	|	|	|	|	|	|	|	|
153	**Hannover** Hbf a.	...	...	0656	0756	...	0956	1156	1258	...	1356	1356	1556	1654	1756	1756	...	1856	1957	1957	2051	2156	2156	2332	2341	0003
153	**Hannover** Hbf d.	0511	0555	0659	0759	0759	0959	1159	1301	1301	1359	1359	1559	1658	1759	1759	...	1859	2000	2000	2055	...	2159	2336	2344	0006
194	Celle d.	0531	0620	0720	0820	0820	1020	1220	1321	1321	1419	1419	1620	1719	1820	1820	...	1918	2020	2021	2117	...	2220	2357	|	0027
246	Uelzen d.	0555	0643	0743	0843	0843	1043	1243	1343	1343	1443	1443	1643	1743	1843	1843	1937	1942	2043	2042	2142	...	2243	0019	0027	0051
259	Bad Bevensen d.	|	|	|	0851	0851	|	|	|	|	1451	1451	1651	|	|	|	|	|	|	|	|	...	|	|	|	|
282	Lüneburg d.	0614	0700	0800	0904	0904	1100	1300	1401	1401	1502	1502	1703	1759	1900	1900	1954	1959	2100	2100	2159	...	2300	0035	0043	0107
331	**Hamburg** Hbf a.	0644	0728	0827	0931	0931	1127	1328	1428	1428	1529	1529	1730	1828	1927	1927	2021	2028	2128	2128	2225	...	2326	0103	0111	0134
338	**Hamburg** Altona a.	0659	|	0841	|	|	1141	|	...	...	1546	|	|	1842	1954	|	2038	...	2142	|	2239	...	2341	0118	0125	0148
	Rostock Hbf **830** a.	...	0932	...	1132	1132	...	1532	...	...	...	1732	1932	...	...	2132	...	...	...	2343	...	...	...	...	...	...
	Stralsund **830** a.	...	1030	...	1230	1230**j**	...	1630	...	...	...	...	2032	...	...	2230	...	...	...	...	...	...	...	...	...	...

	ICE	*IC*	*IC*	*IC*	*IC*	*EC*	*IC*	*IC*	*IC*	*IC*	*IC*	*IC*	*IC*	*IC*	*IC*	*IC*	*IC*	*IC*	*IC*	*IC*	*IC*	*IC*	*IC*	*ICE*	*ICE*
	591	**2271**	**2275**	**2179**	**2277**	**341**	**2083**	**2279**	**1879**	**2371**	**2373**	**1881**	**2375**	**2171**	**2181**	**2377**	**2173**	**2379**	**2379**	**2379**	**2175**	**2183**	**2185**	**889**	**1089**
	①–⑤	①–④	⑤f	①–⑤	①–⑥	①–⑥		①–⑥	⑤f			⑤⑦		⑤–⑦	①–④		Ⓑq		⑤⑦	⑤f	G	⑦w	⑦w	⑦w	⑤f
	a	d	S	a	e	x A	B	e		K		r M		z L	d P	O			r			O			
	🍴				🍷		🍷	🍷	🍷	🍷	🍷	🍷	🍷	🍷	🍷	🍷	🍷	🍷	🍷	🍷	🍷	🍴			
Stralsund **830** d.	...	...	...	...	...	...	...	0527	...	...	0927	...	...	...	...	1327	...	1527	1527	1527	...	1727	1927	...	...
Rostock Hbf **830** d.	...	...	...	...	...	...	...	0625	...	...	1025	...	...	...	...	1425	...	1625	1625	1625	...	1825	2025	...	...
Hamburg Altona d.	0304	...	...	0510	0609	0642	0714	|	0914	1014	|	1314	1414	...	...	|	1714	|	|	|	1914	|	|	2301	2338
Hamburg Hbf d.	0318	...	...	0524	0628	0705	0728	0828	0928	1028	1228	1328	1428	1528	1528	1628	1728	1828	1828	1828	1928	2028	2228	2314	2352
Lüneburg d.	0350	...	...	0553	0657	0734	0758	0857	0958	1057	1257	1358	1457	1557	1557	1657	1757	1857	1857	1857	1958	2057	2257	2342	0023
Bad Bevensen d.	|	...	...	0605	|	|	|	|	|	|	|	|	|	1609	1609	|	1809	|	|	|	|	|	|	|	|
Uelzen d.	0410	...	...	0614	0714	0754	0814	0914	1014	1114	1314	1414	1514	1618	1618	1714	1818	1914	1914	1914	2016	2114	2315	2359	0047
Celle d.	0439	...	...	0637	0737	...	0837	0937	1037	1137	1337	|	1537	1640	1640	1737	1841	1937	1937	1936	2040	2139	2337	0025	0116
Hannover Hbf a.	0459	...	...	0657	0757	...	0857	0957	1056	1157	1357	1453	1557	1658	1659	1757	1904	1957	1957	1956	2101	2159	2357	0044	0142
Hannover Hbf d.	0518	0600	0600	...	0800	...	0900	1000	1059	1200	1400	1456	1600	1702	1702	1800	...	...	2000	2000	...	...	...	...	...
Elze (Han) d.	|	|	|	...	|	...	|	|	|	|	|	|	|	|	1721	|	...	...	|	|	...	...	...	...	...
Alfeld (Leine) d.	|	|	|	...	|	...	|	|	|	|	|	|	|	|	1733	|	...	...	|	|	...	...	...	...	...
Kreiensen d.	|	|	|	...	|	...	|	|	|	|	|	|	|	|	1746	|	...	...	|	|	...	...	...	...	...
Northeim (Han) d.	|	|	|	...	|	...	|	|	|	|	|	|	|	|	1759	|	...	...	|	|	...	...	...	...	...
Göttingen d.	0555	0640	0640	...	0840	...	0941	1040	1140	1240	1440	1535	1640	1741	1813	1840	...	...	2038	2040	...	...	...	...	...
Kassel Wilhelmshöhe a.	0614	0701	0701	...	0901	...	1003	1101	1201	1301	1501	1557	1701	1801	...	1901	...	...	...	2101	...	...	...	...	...
Frankfurt (Main) Hbf ◐ a.	0745	0904	0904	...	1104	...	...	1304	1336	1504	1704	...	1904	1950	...	2104	...	...	...	2304	...	...	...	...	...
Karlsruhe Hbf **911** a.	...	1050	...	...	1250**n**	...	...	1450	...	1650	1850	...	2050**a**	...	...	2325**t**	...	...	...	...	...	...	...	...	...

A – WAWEL – 12 Kraków - Cottbus - Berlin - Stendal - Hamburg and v.v.
B – KÖNIGSSEE – 12 and 🍷 Berchtesgaden - München - Augsburg - Hamburg and v.v.; 12 Oberstdorf (**2084/5**) - Augsburg - Hamburg and v.v.
F – 12 and 🍷 (Dec. 20 - Apr. 5: Schwarzach -) München - Hamburg - Flensburg.
G – ①②③④⑦ (not Dec. 23, 24, 30, 31, Apr. 1, 4, May 23).
H – ①②③④⑥ (also Dec. 25, Jan. 1, Apr. 2, 4, May 14, 23; not Dec. 23, 30, Apr. 1, 5, May 12, 24).
J – Runs daily Hannover - Hamburg. Continues to Westerland (Table **821**) on ④–⑦ to Mar. 21 (also Dec. 22, 23, 29, 30; not Dec. 24, 31) and daily from Mar. 25. On ①–③ to Mar. 24 (not Dec. 22, 23, 29, 30) runs with train number **2180**.

K – From / to Konstanz (Table **916**).
L – To / from Westerland (Table **821**).
M – From / to München (Table **900**).
N – To Ostseebad Binz on ⑥ (Table **844**).
O – To / from Ostseebad Binz (Table **844**).
P – From Westerland (Table **821**) on ① to Mar. 22 and ①–④ from Mar. 29. Train number **2281** on ②–④ to Mar. 25.

S – To Stuttgart (Table **930**).
Y – ①②③④⑥⑦ (also Dec. 25, Jan. 1, Apr. 2, May 14; not Dec. 23, 30, Apr. 1, May 12).
Z – 12 and 🍴 Zürich - Basel - Hamburg.

a – ①–⑤ (not Dec. 24, 25, 31, Jan. 1, Apr. 2, 5, May 24).
c – ⑥⑦ (also Apr. 5, May 24; not Apr. 4, May 23).
d – Not Dec. 23, 24, 30, 31, Apr. 1, 5, May 12, 24.

e – ①–⑥ (not Dec. 25, 26, Jan. 1, Apr. 3, 5, May 24).
f – Also Dec. 23, 30, Apr. 1, May 12; not Dec. 25, Jan. 1, Apr. 2, May 14.
h – Not Dec. 24, 25, 30, 31, Apr. 2, 4, May 23.
j – 1249 on ⑥ from May 15 (also Mar. 27).
k – Also Dec. 24, 25, 31, Apr. 2, 4, May 23.
n – ⑥ only.
q – Not Dec. 24, 25, 31, Apr. 2, 4, May 23.
r – Also Dec. 23, 30, Apr. 1, 5, May 12, 24; not Dec. 25, Jan. 1, Apr. 2, 4, May 14, 23.
t – ⑤⑦ (also Apr. 5, May 24; not Dec. 25, Apr. 2, 4, May 23). Arrives 2251 on ⑦ (also Apr. 5, May 24).
v – Also Apr. 4, May 23; not Apr. 5, May 24.
w – Also Apr. 5, May 24; not Apr. 4, May 23.
x – Not Dec. 25, 26, 31, Jan. 1, Apr. 3, 5, May 24.
z – Also Dec. 23, 24, 30, 31, Apr. 1, 5, May 12, 24.

◇ – Also *ICE* trains making stops between Hannover and Hamburg.
◐ – See Tables **806** (via Gießen) or **900** (via Fulda).

metronom Local services GÖTTINGEN - HANNOVER - UELZEN - HAMBURG 903

Services below are operated by ***metronom***. For *ICE* services see Table **900**. For *IC* services see Table **902**.

		⚒		⚒	†m	⚒	⚒	◧	m	⊖	m⊙		⊖◇					k		n◇			k	n◇	Ⓑr	Ⓑq	⑥t
Göttingen d.	...	...	...	0407	0502	0502	...	0607	0707	0810	0907	1010	1107	1210	1307	1410	1507	1610	1707	1810	1907	...	2010	...	2107	2207	2207
Northeim (Han) d.	...	...	...	0420	0515	0515	...	0620	0720	0824	0920	1024	1120	1224	1320	1424	1520	1624	1720	1824	1920	...	2024	...	2120	2220	2220
Kreiensen d.	...	...	...	0434	0534	0534	...	0634	0734	0838	0934	1038	1134	1238	1334	1438	1534	1638	1734	1838	1934	...	2038	...	2134	2234	2234
Alfeld (Leine) d.	...	...	...	0447	0547	0547	...	0647	0747	0851	0947	1051	1147	1251	1347	1451	1547	1651	1747	1851	1947	...	2051	...	2147	2247	2247
Elze (Han) d.	...	...	...	0458	0558	0558	...	0658	0758	0903	0958	1103	1158	1303	1358	1503	1558	1703	1758	1903	1958	...	2103	...	2158	2258	2258
Hannover Hbf a.	...	...	...	0521	0623	0623	...	0723	0824	0926	1023	1126	1223	1326	1423	1526	1623	1726	1823	1927	2024	...	2126	...	2223	2323	2323
Hannover Hbf d.	...	...	...	0540	0640	...	0640	0740	0840	0940	1040	1140	1240	1340	1440	1540	1640	1740	1840	1940	2040	...	...	2140	2248	2340	2351
Celle d.	...	0506	...	0606	0706	...	0706	0806	0906	1006	1106	1206	1306	1406	1506	1606	1706	1806	1906	2006	2106	...	...	2206	2316	0006	0019
Uelzen a.	...	0536	...	0637	0737	...	0737	0837	0937	1037	1137	1237	1337	1437	1537	1637	1737	1837	1937	2037	2137	...	...	2237	...	0037	0047
	⚒	⚒	Ⓐ	d					m							k		k	w		†	⚒w					
Uelzen d.	0501	0540	0628	0702	...	...	0800	0901	1001	1100	1200	1301	1400	1502	1600	1700	1800	1900	2000	2100	2201	2201	...	2301	...	...	...
Bad Bevensen d.	0510	0549	0637	0711	...	...	0809	0909	1009	1109	1209	1309	1409	1510	1609	1709	1809	1909	2009	2109	2209	2209	...	2309	...	...	...
Lüneburg d.	0524	0604	0653	0728	...	...	0828	0928	1028	1128	1228	1328	1428	1528	1628	1728	1828	1928	2028	2128	2228	2234	...	2323	...	...	...
Hamburg Hbf a.	0556	0636	0724	0802	...	...	0902	1001	1102	1202	1302	1402	1502	1603	1702	1802	1901	2002	2102	2202	2301	2319	...	2357	...	...	...

				Ⓐ	Ⓒm	⚒			⚒	⊖◇	⚒				k⊙		k		n◇		w		k	w	n	†	⚒w
Hamburg Hbf d.	...	...	...	0544	0554**p**	0652	...	0754	0857	0957	1057	1157	1257	1357	1457	1554	1657	1757	1857	...	1957	...	2057	2158	2255	2355	2356
Lüneburg d.	...	...	...	0617	0627**p**	0722	...	0827	0933	1033	1133	1233	1333	1433	1533	1627	1733	1833	1933	...	2033	...	2133	2233	2328	0028	0041
Bad Bevensen d.	...	...	...	0632	0644	0740	...	0846	0948	1048	1150	1248	1348	1448	1548	1646	1748	1848	1948	...	2048	...	2147	2248	2343	0043	0055
Uelzen a.	...	...	...	0641	0653	0749	...	0854	0957	1057	1157	1256	1357	1456	1557	1655	1757	1856	1957	...	2057	...	2157	2256	2352	0052	0104
	⚒	⊖	m◧	Ⓐ	Ⓒ		†m		m		d						n			k	†	Ⓐw	n				
Uelzen d.	0413	0513	0609	0651	0709	0809	0809	0909	1009	1109	1209	1309	1409	1509	1609	1709	1809	1909	2009	...	2109	2128	2217	...	...	...	...
Celle d.	0447	0547	0647	0747**v**	0747	0847	0847	0947	1047	1147	1247	1347	1447	1547	1647	1747	1847	1947	2047	...	2149	2201	2251	...	...	...	...
Hannover Hbf a.	0514	0614	0714	0814	0814	0914	0914	1014	1114	1214	1314	1414	1514	1614	1714	1814	1914	2014	2114	...	2214	2226	2317	...	...	...	...
Hannover Hbf d.	0536	0636	0736	0833	0833	*0936*	0936	1033	1136	1233	1336	1433	1536	1633	1736	1833	1936**z**	2033	...	2133**y**	2236	2236	2336	...	...	...	...
Elze (Han) d.	0558	0658	0758	0855	0855	*0958*	0958	1055	1158	1255	1358	1455	1558	1655	1758	1855	1958	2055	...	2158	2258	2258	2358	...	...	...	...
Alfeld (Leine) d.	0610	0710	0810	0905	0905	*1010*	1010	1105	1210	1305	1410	1505	1610	1705	1810	1905	2010	2105	...	2210	2310	2310	0010	...	...	...	...
Kreiensen d.	0623	0723	0823	0918	0918	*1023*	1023	1118	1223	1318	1423	1518	1623	1718	1823	1918	2023	2118	...	2223	2323	2323	0023	...	...	...	...
Northeim (Han) d.	0637	0737	0837	0932	0932	*1037*	1037	1132	1237	1332	1437	1532	1637	1732	1837	1932	2037	2132	...	2237	2337	2337	0037	...	...	...	...
Göttingen d.	0649	0749	0849	0946	0946	*1049*	1049	1146	1249	1347	1449	1546	1649	1747	1849	1946	2049	2146	...	2249	2349	2349	0049	...	...	...	...

d – Runs daily from Uelzen.
k – Not Dec. 24.
m – Not Jan. 1.
n – Not Dec. 24, 31.
p – 3–4 minutes later on ⑦ (also Dec. 25, Apr. 5, May 24).
q – Not Dec. 25, 31, Jan. 1, Apr. 2, 5, May 13, 24.
r – Also Dec. 26, May 1; not Dec. 24, 31.
t – Also Dec. 25, Jan. 1, Apr. 2, 5, May 13, 24.
v – Arrives 0728.
w – Not Dec. 31.
y – 2136 on Ⓐ.
z – 1930 on ⑤ (not Dec. 25, Jan. 1, Apr. 2).
⊖ – Change trains at Hannover on ⚒.
◇ – Change trains at Uelzen on †.
◧ – Change trains at Hannover on Ⓐ.
⊙ – Change trains at Uelzen on ⚒.

904 MÜNCHEN - NÜRNBERG fast services

ICE and IC services

	ICE	ICE	ICE	ICE	ICE	ICE	ICE	ICE	ICE	ICE	ICE	ICE	ICE	ICE	ICE	ICE	ICE	ICE	ICE	ICE	ICE	ICE	ICE	ICE	ICE
	1518	1514	822	1714	684	1612	820	1126	886	728	682	1512	1610	726	882	724	680	108	1608	722	880	588	720 928 1022	1208	628
	①g	①-⑤	①g	⑥¶	①-⑤	①-⑥	①-⑤	①h						①-⑥											
		a	K		a⊖	e	aK	K		K	⊖			eK		K	⊖	B		K		⊖	K	D	K
		✕	🍷	✕	✕	✕	🍷	✕	✕	🍷	✕	✕	✕	🍷	✕	🍷	✕	✕	✕	🍷	✕	✕	🍷	✕	🍷
München Hbf ..... 930 d.	0012	0431	0448	0516	0515	0530	0551	0545y	0620	0651	0648	0719	0743	0755	0820	0855	0915	0920	0945	0955	1020	1052	1055	1119	1155
München Pasing ..... 930 d.	0022	0439	|	|	|	0538	|	|	|	|	0656	|	0751	|	|	|	|	|	0953	|	|	1101	|	|	|
Augsburg Hbf ..... 930 d.	0054	0513	|	|	|	0615	|	|	|	|	0732	|	0822	|	|	|	|	|	1024	|	|	1132	|	|	|
Donauwörth ..... d.	0112	0532	|	|	|	0634	|	|	|	|	0752	|	|	|	|	|	|	|	|	|	|	|	|	|	|
Treuchtlingen ..... d.	0132	0553	|	|	|	0653	|	|	|	|	|	|	|	|	|	|	|	|	|	|	|	|	|	|	|
Ingolstadt Hbf ..... d.	|	|	0526	0554j	0555	|	0630j	|	0659	0730j	|	0758	|	|	0859	|	|	0958	|	|	1059	|	|	1158	|
Nürnberg Hbf ..... a.	0219	0626	0554	0626	0627	0727	0657	0726	0730	0757	|	0830	0926	0857	0930	0957	1022	1030	1127	1057	1130	|	1157	1230	1257
Würzburg Hbf 900 920 ..... a.	|	|	0654	|	0727	|	0754	0825	0828	0854	0927	|	|	0954	1028	1054	1127	|	|	1154	1228	1327	1254	|	1354
Frankfurt (Main) Hbf 920 ..... a.	|	|	0805	|	|	|	0905	0936	|	1005	|	|	|	1105	|	1205	|	|	|	1305	|	|	1405	|	1505
Leipzig Hbf 851 ..... a.	0548	0946	...	0946	|	1046	...	...	|	...	|	1146	1246	...	|	...	|	1346	1446	...	|	|	...	1546	...
Berlin Hbf 851 ..... a.	...	1110	...	1110	|	1213	...	...	|	...	|	1310	1413	...	|	...	|	1510	1613	...	|	|	...	1710	...
Hamburg Hbf 900 ..... a.	...	...	...	...	1055	...	...	...	1155	...	1253	...	...	...	1353	...	1454	...	...	...	1554	1654	...	...	...

	ICE	ICE	ICE	ICE	ICE	ICE	IC	ICE	ICE	ICE	ICE	ICE	IC	ICE	ICE	ICE	ICE	ICE	ICE	ICE	ICE	ICE	ICE	ICE	ICE
	788	1606	586	626 1226	1206	1604 1704	1284	624	786	622	584 1084	1504	2206	620 926 1220	784	1602	1700	528	924	582 1082	1502	1600	526	782	980
							⑦w						Ⓑq			Ⓑq	Ⓐd	Ⓑ	⑥		n	Ⓑq	Ⓑq		⑤f
	G	R	⊖	K	D		F	K		K	E			K		V	◧	K	N				K	Y	H
	✕	✕	✕	🍷	✕	✕	🍷	🍷	✕	🍷	✕	✕	🍷	🍷	✕	✕		🍷	🍷	✕	✕	✕	🍷	✕	✕
München Hbf ..... 930 d.	1219	1225	1251	1255	1319v	1341	1345	1355	1420	1455	1514	1519	1529	1555	1616	1621	1638	1650	1650	1714	1719	1745	1755	1820	1849
München Pasing ..... 930 d.	|	|	1300	|	|	|	1353	|	|	|	|	|	1537	|	|	|	|	|	|	|	|	|	|	|	1857
Augsburg Hbf ..... 930 d.	|	|	1331	|	|	1420	1425	|	|	|	|	|	1613	|	|	|	1714	|	|	|	|	1822	|	|	1932
Donauwörth ..... d.	|	|	|	|	|	|	1444	|	|	|	|	|	1632	|	|	|	1733	|	|	|	|	1842	|	|	1952
Treuchtlingen ..... d.	|	|	|	|	|	|	1507	|	|	|	|	|	1656	|	|	|	1754	|	|	|	|	|	|	|	2012
Ingolstadt Hbf ..... d.	1258	|	|	|	1358	|	|	|	1459	|	|	1558	|	|	1658	|	|	1728	1728	|	1758	|	|	1859	|
Nürnberg Hbf ..... a.	1330	1334	|	1357	1430	1523	|	1457	1530	1557	1622	1630	1733	1657	1729	1734	1828	1757	1757	1822	1830	1929	1857	1930	|
Würzburg Hbf 900 920 ..... a.	1428	|	1527	1454	|	|	1633	1554	1628	1654	1727	|	...	1754	1828	|	...	1854	1854	1927	|	|	1954	2028	2129
Frankfurt (Main) Hbf 920 ..... a.	|	|	|	1605	|	|	|	1705	|	1805	|	|	...	1905	|	|	...	2005	2005	|	|	|	2105	|	...
Leipzig Hbf 851 ..... a.	|	1646	|	...	1746	1846n	|	...	|	...	|	1946	...	...	|	2046	...	...	...	|	2146	2250p	...	|	...
Berlin Hbf 851 ..... a.	|	1810	|	...	1910	2015n	|	...	|	...	|	2105	...	...	|	...	...	...	...	|	2256	0025p	...	|	...
Hamburg Hbf 900 ..... a.	1754	...	1853	...	...	...	2028	...	1953	...	2054	...	...	...	2154	...	...	...	...	2254	...	...	...	0007	...

	ICE	ICE	ICE	ICE	ICE	ICE	ICE	ICE	ICE	ICE	ICE
	580	524	1500	522	780	520	922	1120	920	920	1620
	⊡		n		⑦w	①-④	⑤-⑦	⑦w	Ⓑq	⑦w	⑥‡
	Q	K	J	K	A	m	k				
	✕	🍷	✕	🍷	✕	🍷	✕	✕	🍷	🍷	🍷
München Hbf ..... 930 d.	1849	1855	1919	1951	2020	2055	2055	2154	2255	2255	2255
München Pasing ..... 930 d.	1857	|	|	|	|	|	|	|	|	|	|
Augsburg Hbf ..... 930 d.	1932	|	|	|	|	|	|	|	|	|	|
Donauwörth ..... d.	1952	|	|	|	|	|	|	|	|	|	|
Treuchtlingen ..... d.	2012	|	|	|	|	|	|	|	|	|	|
Ingolstadt Hbf ..... d.	|	|	1958	2029j	2059	|	|	2233	2333	2333	2333
Nürnberg Hbf ..... a.	|	1957	2030	2057	2130	2157	2158	2304	0002	0002	0006
Würzburg Hbf 900 920 ..... a.	2129	2054	|	2154	2235	2254	2254	0001	...	0101	...
Frankfurt (Main) Hbf 920 ..... a.	|	2205	|	2305	...	...	0013	0116	...	...	...
Leipzig Hbf 851 ..... a.	|	...	2355	...	...	...	...	...	...	...	...
Berlin Hbf 851 ..... a.	|	...	0127	...	...	...	...	...	...	...	...
Hamburg Hbf 900 ..... a.	0103	...	...	...	...	...	...	...	...	...	...

	ICE	ICE	ICE	ICE	ICE	ICE	ICE	ICE	ICE
	1701	823	981	985	827	1601	1501	987	521
	Ⓐd	Ⓐd	Ⓐd	Ⓐd	Ⓐd	Ⓐd	①-⑤	⑥	
							aL	G	K
		🍷	✕	✕	🍷	✕	✕	✕	🍷
Hamburg Hbf 900 ..... d.	...	...	...	...	...	...	...	...	...
Berlin Hbf 851 ..... d.	...	...	...	...	...	...	...	...	...
Leipzig Hbf 851 ..... d.	...	...	...	...	...	...	...	...	...
Frankfurt (Main) Hbf 920 d.	...	...	...	...	...	...	...	...	0551
Würzburg Hbf 900 920 .. d.	...	...	...	...	0603	...	...	...	0705
Nürnberg Hbf ..... d.	...	0559	...	0627	0659	0618	0728	0728	0802
Ingolstadt Hbf ..... d.	...	0628	...	0701	0728	|	0801	0801	|
Treuchtlingen ..... d.	...	|	...	|	|	0652	|	|	|
Donauwörth ..... d.	...	|	0608	|	|	0712	|	|	|
Augsburg Hbf ..... 930 a.	0532	|	0627	|	|	0729	|	|	|
München Pasing ... 930 a.	0600	|	0702	|	|	0759	|	|	|
München Hbf ..... 930 a.	0610	0706	0712	0739	0806	0810	0840	0840	0906

	IC	ICE	ICE	ICE	ICE	ICE	ICE	ICE	ICE	ICE	ICE	ICE	ICE	ICE	ICE	ICE	ICE	ICE	ICE	ICE	ICE	ICE	ICE	ICE	ICE
	2201	1603	781	523 1123	581 1081	1503	525 925	1605	783	527	1505	583 1083	529	785	1607 1727	621 1121	1507 1707	585 1085	623 923	1209	1609	787	625	1509	627 927
	①-⑥	①-⑤	①-⑥	①-⑥		①-⑥		①-⑥	①-⑥	①-⑥										⑥⑦	①-⑤				
	e	a	eM	eK	⊖	e	K	eV	e	U		EG	K			K		⊖	xK	uD	aR		K		K
		✕	✕	🍷	✕	✕	🍷	✕	✕	🍷	✕	⊖✕	🍷	✕	✕	🍷	✕	✕	🍷	✕	✕	✕	🍷	✕	🍷
Hamburg Hbf 900 ..... d.	...	...	...		0457	...	...	...	0600*	...	...	0700	...	0803	...	...	...	0901	...	...	...	1001	...	...	...
Berlin Hbf 851 ..... d.	...	...	...	...	|	0441	...	...	|	...	0652	|	...	|	0752	...	0858e	|	...	0952	0952	|	...	1058	...
Leipzig Hbf 851 ..... d.	...	0458	...	...	|	|	...	0711	|	...	0816	|	...	|	0911	...	1016	|	...	1111	1111	|	...	1216	...
Frankfurt (Main) Hbf 920 ..... d.	...	|	...	0654	|	|	0754	|	|	0854	|	|	0954	|	|	1054	|	|	1154	|	|	|	1254	|	1354
Würzburg Hbf 900 920 ..... d.	...	|	0729	0805	0831	|	0905	|	0930	1005	|	1031	1105	1129	|	1205	|	1231	1305	|	|	1329	1405	|	1505
Nürnberg Hbf ..... d.	0718	0823	0827	0902	0933	0931	1002	1023	1027	1102	1128	|	1202	1227	1229	1302	1328	1332	1402	1423	1423	1427	1502	1528	1602
Ingolstadt Hbf ..... d.	|	|	0901	|	1005b	|	|	|	1101	|	1201	|	|	1301	|	|	1401z	|	|	|	|	1501	|	1601	|
Treuchtlingen ..... d.	0752	|	|	|	|	|	|	|	|	|	|	|	|	|	|	|	|	|	|	|	|	|	|	|	|
Donauwörth ..... d.	0812	|	|	|	|	|	|	|	|	|	|	|	|	|	|	|	|	|	|	|	|	|	|	|	|
Augsburg Hbf ..... 930 a.	0832	|	|	|	|	1032	|	|	|	|	|	1223	|	|	1332	|	|	|	|	|	|	|	|	|	|
München Pasing ..... 930 a.	0902	|	|	|	|	|	|	|	|	|	|	1254	|	|	|	|	|	|	|	|	|	|	|	|	|
München Hbf ..... 930 a.	0913	0948	0942	1005	1044	1122	1106	1149	1143	1205	1250	1304	1305	1339	1422	1405	1450	1444	1505	1543	1549	1543	1605	1650	1705

	ICE	ICE	ICE	ICE	ICE	ICE	ICE	ICE	ICE	ICE	ICE	ICE	ICE	ICE	ICE	ICE	ICE	ICE	ICE	ICE	ICE	ICE	ICE	ICE	ICE
	587	789	629	1611	109	589	721 921	881	1613	723	1213	681	725	883 1183	727	1615	1515	683	729	1617	885	1025	821 929	685	1517 1757
			Ⓑq						n	Ⓑq					Ⓑq	n	n			⑦w		♥		⑦w	
	⊖		K	R	B	⊖	t			K	D	⊖	K		K			⊖	K			K	⑤⑦s	⊖	n
	✕	✕	🍷	✕	✕	✕	🍷	✕	✕	🍷	✕	✕	🍷	✕	🍷	✕	✕	✕	🍷	✕	✕	✕	T🍷	✕	✕
Hamburg Hbf 900 ..... d.	1101	1201	...	...	...	1301	...	1401	...	...	...	1501	...	1603	...	...	...	1701	...	...	1801	...	...	1901	...
Berlin Hbf 851 ..... d.	|	|	...	1152	1258	|	...	|	1352	...	1458	|	...	|	...	1552	1657	|	...	1752	|	...	...	|	1850r
Leipzig Hbf 851 ..... d.	|	|	...	1311	1416	|	...	|	1511	...	1616	|	...	|	...	1711	1816	|	...	1911	|	...	...	|	2020r
Frankfurt (Main) Hbf 920 ..... d.	|	|	1454	|	|	|	1554	|	|	1654	|	|	1754	|	1854	|	|	|	1954	|	|	2018	2054	|	|
Würzburg Hbf 900 920 ..... d.	1431	1529	1605	|	|	1631	1705	1729	|	1805	|	1831	1905	1929	2005	|	|	2031	2105	|	2134	2130	2205	2229	|
Nürnberg Hbf ..... d.	|	1627	1702	1629	1728	|	1802	1827	1829	1902	1928	|	2002	2027	2102	2029	2130	|	2202	2224	2231	2235	2302	2328	2338
Ingolstadt Hbf ..... d.	|	1701	|	|	1801	|	|	1901	|	|	2001	|	|	2101	|	|	2202	|	2231	2257	2303	2310	2331	0000	0011
Treuchtlingen ..... d.	|	|	|	|	|	|	|	|	|	|	|	|	|	|	|	|	|	|	|	|	|	|	|	|	|
Donauwörth ..... d.	1608	|	|	|	|	|	|	|	1917	|	|	|	|	|	|	2116	|	|	|	|	|	|	|	|	|
Augsburg Hbf ..... 930 a.	1626	|	|	1731	|	1822	|	|	1934	|	|	2022	|	|	|	2134	|	2222	|	|	|	|	|	|	|
München Pasing ..... 930 a.	1656	|	|	1812	|	1854	|	|	|	|	|	2053	|	|	|	2215	|	2253	|	|	|	|	|	|	|
München Hbf ..... 930 a.	1707	1739	1805	1822	1838	1903	1905	1939	2023	2005	2050	2102	2105	2139	2205	2225	2251	2302	2308	2351	2346	2350	0008	0041	0059

A – To Kassel (Table **900**).
B – From / to Innsbruck via Kufstein (Table **951**).
D – From / to Innsbruck via Garmisch on dates in Table **895**.
E – From / to Lübeck on dates in Table **825**.
F – To Flensburg (Table **823**). Dec. 20 - Apr. 5 starts from Schwarzach (Tables **960** / **951**).
G – From / to Garmisch on ⑥ (Table **895**).
H – To Hannover (Table **900**).
J – (12) and ✕ München - Leipzig (- Berlin ⑦w).
K – To / from Köln, Essen or Dortmund (Tables **800** / **910**).
L – From Lichtenfels on Ⓐd (Table **851**).
M – (12) and ✕ (Hannover ①⑥c -) Fulda - München.
N – (12) and ✕ Garmisch (d. 1515) - München - Dortmund.
Q – (12) and ✕ München - Fulda (- Hamburg ⑦w).
R – To / from Warnemünde via Rostock (Table **835**).
T – From Oberhausen on ⑤ / Essen on ⑦ (Table **920**).
U – ①-⑥ (not Dec. 25, Jan. 1, Apr. 5, May 24). (12) and 🍷 Dortmund - Köln - München (- Garmisch ⑥, a. 1335).
V – To / from Dresden (Table **842**).
Y – On ⑦ arrives Hamburg 2358. Conveys (12) (*ICE* 732) (Garmisch ⑥ -) München - Hannover - Bremen.

a – Not Dec. 24, 25, 31, Jan. 1, Apr. 2, 5, May 24.
b – Not ①⑥† Feb. 6 - Apr. 4.
c – Also Dec. 24, 31, Apr. 2, 6, May 13, 25; not Dec. 26, Jan. 2, Apr. 3, 5, May 15, 24.
d – Not Dec. 24, 31, Jan. 6, June 3.
e – ①-⑥ (not Dec. 25, 26, Jan. 1, Apr. 3, 5, May 24).
f – Also Dec. 23, 30, Apr. 1, May 12, June 2; not Dec. 25, Jan. 1, Apr. 2, May 14, June 4.
g – Also Apr. 6, May 25; not Apr. 5, May 24.
h – Also Apr. 6, May 13, 22, 25 – 29, June 1 – 5; not Apr. 5, May 24.
j – Until Apr. 28.
k – Also Dec. 23, 24, 30, 31, Jan. 5, Apr. 1, 5, May 12, 24, June 2.
m – Not Dec. 23, 24, 30, 31, Jan. 5, Apr. 1, 5, May 12, 24, June 2.
n – Not Dec. 24, 31.
p – Nürnberg - Berlin on ⑤⑦ (also Dec. 23, 30, Apr. 1, 5, May 12, 24, June 2; not Dec. 25, Jan. 1, Apr. 2, 4, May 14, 23, June 4).
q – Not Dec. 24, 25, 31, Apr. 2, 4, May 23.
r – Departs Berlin 1858, Leipzig 2012 on ⑦w.
s – Also Dec. 23, 30, Apr. 1, 5, May 12, 24, June 2; not Dec. 25, Jan. 1, Apr. 2, 4, May 23.
t – Not May 14, June 4.

u – Also Dec. 24, 25, 31, Jan. 1, Apr. 2, 5, May 24.
v – 1315 on ⑦w.
w – Also Apr. 5, May 24; not Apr. 4, May 23.
x – Not Dec. 25, 26, Jan. 1, Apr. 3, 4, May 23.
y – 0614 on May 13, 22, 26 – 29, June 1 – 5.
z – Not Feb. 3 - Apr. 4.

‡ – Also Dec. 25, Apr. 2, 4, May 23.
¶ – Also Dec. 24, 31, Apr. 2; not Dec. 26, Apr. 3.
♥ – ①②③④⑥⑦ (also Dec. 25, Apr. 2, May 28, June 4; not Dec. 23, 30, Apr. 1).
⊡ – ①②③④⑦ (also Jan. 1, Apr. 2, May 14, June 4; not Dec. 23, 24, 30, 31, Apr. 1, 4, May 12, 23, June 2).
* – 0605 on ⑥ (also Apr. 2, May 13).
⊖ – Conveys (12) München - Hannover - Bremen and v.v. (Tables **900** / **813**).
◧ – Train number *IC* **2200** on ⑤ (also Dec. 23, 30, Apr. 1, May 12, June 2; not May 14, June 4).

RE / RB services — Regional services MÜNCHEN - NÜRNBERG — 905

See Table **904** for *ICE* and *IC* services

km		Ⓒz	Ⓐe		⚒r			Ⓐe		⚒r		⚒r						⚒r					⚒r		
0	**München** Hbf 930 d.	*0202*	...	...	...	0502	0537	0526	...	...	0625	...	0703	0734	0729	...	0829	*0834*	0904	0934	0928	1029	...	1104	1134
7	München Pasing 930 d.	*0209*	...	...	...	|	0543	|	...	A	|	...	|	0740	|	L	|	*0840*	|	0940	|	|	...	|	1140
62	**Augsburg** Hbf 930 d.	0327	...	...	0521	|	0628	|	...	0718	|	0721	|	0828	|	0918	|	0925	|	1028	|	|	1117	|	1224
103	Donauwörth d.	0357	...	...	0558	|	0658	|	...	0739	|	0758	|	0858	|	0939	|	0958	|	1058	|	|	1158	|	1258
	Pfaffenhofen (Ilm) d.	|	...	...	|	0527	|	0602	...	|	0702	|	0728	|	0805	|	0905	|	0929	|	1005	1105	|	1129	|
	Ingolstadt Hbf a.	|	...	...	|	0546	|	0624	...	|	0724	|	0747	|	0827	|	0927	|	0948	|	1027	1128	|	1148	|
	Ingolstadt Hbf d.	|	...	0529	|	0603	|	0627	0627	|	0726	|	0804	|	0830	|	0930	|	1004	|	1030	1130	|	1205	|
	Kinding (Altmühltal) d.	|	...	|	|	0619	|	|	|	|	|	|	0820	|	|	|	|	|	1020	|	|	|	|	1221	|
	Allersberg (Rothsee) d.	|	...	|	|	0633	|	|	|	|	|	|	0834	|	|	|	|	|	1034	|	|	|	|	1235	|
	Eichstätt Bf ★ d.	|	...	0556	|	|	|	0656	0656	|	0756	|	|	|	0856	|	0956	|	|	|	1056	1156	|	|	|
137	**Treuchtlingen** a.	0417	...	0620	0620	|	0720	0719	0719	|	0820	0820	|	0920	0919	|	1020	1020	|	1120	1119	1220	1220	|	1320
137	**Treuchtlingen** d.	0418	0513	0625j	0625	|	...	0725	0725	|	0825j	0825	|	...	0925	|	1025j	1025	|	...	1125	1225j	1225	|	...
146	Weißenburg (Bay) d.	0424	0519	0632j	0632	|	...	0732	0732	|	0832j	0832	|	...	0932	|	1032j	1032	|	...	1132	1232j	1232	|	...
199	**Nürnberg** Hbf a.	0507	0604	0717j	0717	0646	...	0817	0817	0825	0917j	0917	0849	...	1017	1025	1117j	1117	1047	...	1217	1317j	1317	1248	...

			⚒r						Ⓐe					Ⓐe	Ⓒz	Ⓐe					Ⓐe				†j
München Hbf 930 d.	1129	1229	...	1304	1334	1329	...	1429	*1434*	1504	1535	1528	1625	*1633*	1704	1706	1734	1727	...	1829	...	1904	1933	1925	...
München Pasing 930 d.	|	|	...	|	1340	|	L	|	*1440*	|	1542	|	|	*1640*	|	|	1740	|	L	|	...	|	1940	|	L
Augsburg Hbf 930 d.	|	|	1317	|	1428	|	1518	|	1525	|	1628	|	|	1725	|	|	1828	|	1918	|	1921	|	2028	|	2118
Donauwörth d.	|	|	1358	|	1458	|	1539	|	1558	|	1658	|	|	1758	|	|	1858	|	1939	|	1958	|	2058	|	2139
Pfaffenhofen (Ilm) d.	1205	1305	|	1329	|	1405	|	1505	|	1529	|	1605	1701	|	1729	1744t	|	1805	|	1905	|	1929	|	2002	|
Ingolstadt Hbf a.	1228	1328	|	1348	|	1427	|	1528	|	1548	|	1627	1724	|	1748	1803	|	1828	|	1927	|	1948	|	2025	|
Ingolstadt Hbf d.	1230	1330	|	1405	|	1430	|	1530	|	1605	|	1630	1730	|	1805	1805	|	1830	|	1930	|	2005	|	2031	|
Kinding (Altmühltal) d.	|	|	|	1421	|	|	|	|	|	1621	|	|	|	|	1821	1821	|	|	|	|	|	2021	|	|	|
Allersberg (Rothsee) d.	|	|	|	1435	|	|	|	|	|	1635	|	|	|	|	1835	1835	|	|	|	|	|	2035	|	|	|
Eichstätt Bf ★ d.	1256	1356	|	|	|	1456	|	1556	|	|	|	1656	1756	|	|	|	|	1856	|	1956	|	|	|	2056	|
Treuchtlingen a.	1319	1420	1420	|	1520	1520	|	1620	1620	|	1720	1719	1820	1820	|	|	1920	1919	|	2020	2020	|	2120	2119	|
Treuchtlingen d.	1325	1425j	1425	|	...	1525	|	1625z	1625	|	...	1725	1825z	1825	|	|	...	1925	|	2025z	2025	|	...	2125	|
Weißenburg (Bay) d.	1332	1432j	1432	|	...	1532	|	1632z	1632	|	...	1732	1832z	1832	|	|	...	1932	|	2032z	2032	|	...	2132	|
Nürnberg Hbf a.	1417	1517j	1517	1448	...	1617	1625	1717z	1717	1648	...	1817	1917z	1917	1848	1848	...	2017	2025	2117z	2117	2048	...	2217	2225

		Ⓐe							w
München Hbf 930 d.	2025	*2034*	2100	2109	2126	2202	2226	2300	2327
München Pasing 930 d.	|	*2040*	2106	|	|	2209	|	2317	|
Augsburg Hbf 930 d.	|	2125	2154	|	|	2254	|	2354	|
Donauwörth d.	|	2159	2234	|	|	2331	|	0032	|
Pfaffenhofen (Ilm) d.	2105	|	|	2134	2202	...	2302	...	0003
Ingolstadt Hbf a.	2128	|	|	2155	2224	...	2325	...	0025
Ingolstadt Hbf d.	2130	|	|	2159	2226	...	...	...	...
Kinding (Altmühltal) d.	|	|	|	2215	|	...	...	...	...
Allersberg (Rothsee) d.	|	|	|	2229	|	...	...	...	...
Eichstätt Bf ★ d.	2156	|	|	|	2253	...	...	...	...
Treuctlingen a.	2220	2220	2255	|	2317	...	...	...	...
Treuchtlingen d.	2225z	2225	...	|	2322	...	...	...	...
Weißenburg (Bay) d.	2232z	2232	...	|	2328	...	...	...	...
Nürnberg Hbf a.	2317z	2317	...	2242	0011	...	...	...	...

km	km		Ⓒz	Ⓐe		Ⓐe	Ⓒz	⚒r		Ⓐe	Ⓐe	Ⓒz
0	*0*	**Nürnberg** Hbf d.	0056	...	0511	...	...	0437	0437j	0610	0526	0538
	53	Weißenburg (Bay) d.	0138	...	|	...	...	0519	0519j	|	0608	0622
	62	**Treuchtlingen** a.	0144	...	|	...	...	0526	0526j	|	0616	0630
	62	**Treuchtlingen** d.	0145	0450	|	...	...	0527	0532	|	0631	0635
	91	Eichstätt Bf ★ d.	|	0514	|	...	...	|	0556	|	0655	0659
25		Allersberg (Rothsee) d.	|	|	0524	...	...	|	|	0623	|	|
59		Kinding (Altmühltal) d.	|	|	0539	...	...	|	|	0638	|	|
90	*118*	**Ingolstadt** Hbf a.	|	0532	0557	...	...	|	0621	0655	0720	0725
90	*118*	**Ingolstadt** Hbf d.	|	0533	0602f	...	...	|	0631	0707	0734	0734
121	*149*	Pfaffenhofen (Ilm) d.	|	0555	0620	...	...	|	0656	0727	0757	0757
		Donauwörth d.	0205	|	|	0507	0514	0603t	|	|	|	|
		Augsburg Hbf 930 a.	0227	|	|	0551	0551	0641	|	|	|	|
		München Pasing 930 a.	...	|	|	0636	0644	*0721*e	|	|	|	|
171	*199*	**München** Hbf 930 a.	...	0634	0647	0644	0652	*0729*e	0734	0754	0835	0835

			⚒r				Ⓐe		⚒r		⑥h				⚒r		Ⓒz				⚒r				
Nürnberg Hbf d.	...	0708	0630	0630j	0738	...	0835	0908	0839	0839j	0935	0939	...	1108	1038	1038j	1134	1138	...	1308	1238	1238j	1338	...	1508
Weißenburg (Bay) d.	...	|	0716	0716j	0822	...	|	|	0923	0923j	|	1023	...	|	1122	1122j	|	1222	...	|	1322	1322j	1422	...	|
Treuchtlingen a.	...	|	0723	0723j	0830	...	0905	|	0930	0930j	|	1030	...	|	1130	1130j	|	1230	...	|	1330	1330j	1430	...	|
Treuchtlingen d.	0635	|	0735	0735	0835	0835	0906	|	0935	0936	|	1035	1035	|	1135	1135	|	1240	1235	|	1335	1336	1435	1435	|
Eichstätt Bf ★ d.	|	|	|	0759	0859	|	|	|	|	1000	|	1059	|	|	|	1159	|	1303	|	|	|	1400	1459	|	|
Allersberg (Rothsee) d.	|	0721	|	|	|	|	|	0921	|	|	|	|	|	1121	|	|	|	|	|	1321	|	|	|	|	1521
Kinding (Altmühltal) d.	|	0735	|	|	|	|	|	0935	|	|	|	|	|	1135	|	|	|	|	|	1335	|	|	|	|	1535
Ingolstadt Hbf a.	|	0754	|	0825	0925	|	|	0954	|	1026	|	1125	|	1154	|	1225	|	1333	|	1354	|	1433	1525	|	1554
Ingolstadt Hbf d.	|	0806	|	0831	0931	|	|	1009	|	1032	|	1131	|	1206	|	1231	|	1334	|	1409	|	1434	1531	|	1606
Pfaffenhofen (Ilm) d.	|	0827	|	0855	0955	|	|	1030	|	1056	|	1155	|	1227	|	1255	|	1356	|	1430	|	1456	1555	|	1627
Donauwörth d.	0658	|	0758	|	|	0858	0924	|	0958	|	1021	|	1057	|	1200	|	1221	|	1257	|	1358	|	|	1457	|
Augsburg Hbf 930 a.	0727	|	0829	|	|	0929	0945	|	1030	|	1042	|	1129	|	1239	|	1242	|	1328	|	1430	|	|	1529	|
München Pasing 930 a.	0816	|	*0915*	|	|	1015	*1040*	|	*1115*	|	L	|	1215	|	...	|	L	|	1415	|	*1515*	|	|	1615	|
München Hbf 930 a.	0824	0853	*0922*	0934	1034	1022	*1048*	1053	*1122*	1135	...	1235	1222	1253	...	1335	...	1435	1422	1453	*1522*	1535	1634	1622	1654

	Ⓐe		Ⓐe				Ⓐe						Ⓐe					Ⓐe		†j			Ⓒz		
Nürnberg Hbf d.	1438	1438z	1534	1538	...	1708	1638	1638z	1734	1738	...	1908	1838	1838z	1938	...	2110	2038	2038z	2134	2139	...	...	2233	2342
Weißenburg (Bay) d.	1522	1522z	|	1622	...	|	1722	1722z	|	1822	...	|	1922	1922z	2022	...	|	2122	2122z	|	2223	...	...	|	0024
Treuchtlingen a.	1530	1530z	|	1630	...	|	1730	1730z	|	1830	...	|	1930	1930z	2030	...	|	2129	2129z	2204	2230	...	...	2304	0032
Treuchtlingen d.	1535	1535	|	1635	1635	|	1735	1735	|	1835	1835	|	1935	1935	2035	2035	|	2138	2135	2205	2235	2235	2235	2305	...
Eichstätt Bf ★ d.	|	1559	|	1659	|	|	|	1759	|	1859	|	|	|	1959	2059	|	|	|	2159	|	2259	|	|	|	...
Allersberg (Rothsee) d.	|	|	|	|	|	1721	|	|	|	|	|	1921	|	|	|	|	2123	|	|	|	|	|	|	|	...
Kinding (Altmühltal) d.	|	|	|	|	|	1735	|	|	|	|	|	1935	|	|	|	|	2137	|	|	|	|	|	|	|	...
Ingolstadt Hbf a.	|	1625	|	1725	|	1754	|	1825	|	1925	|	1954	|	2025	2125	|	2156	|	2225	|	2325	|	|	|	...
Ingolstadt Hbf d.	|	1631	|	1731	|	1806	|	1831	|	1931	|	2006	|	2031	2131	|	2207	|	2236	|	2334	|	|	|	...
Pfaffenhofen (Ilm) d.	|	1655	|	1755	|	1827	|	1855	|	1955	|	2027	|	2055	2155	|	2228	|	2259	|	2358	|	|	|	...
Donauwörth d.	1558	|	1621	|	1657	|	1800	|	1821	|	1857	|	2000	|	|	2057	|	2200	|	2223	|	2256	2258	2327	...
Augsburg Hbf 930 a.	1636	|	1641	|	1729	|	1839	|	1842	|	1929	|	2037	|	|	2129	|	2237	|	2244	|	...	2328	2348	...
München Pasing 930 a.	...	|	L	|	1815	|	...	|	L	|	2015	|	...	|	|	2218	|	...	|	K	|	...	*0019*	...	...
München Hbf 930 a.	...	1735	...	1834	1822	1853	...	1934	...	2034	2022	2053	...	2134	2234	2226	2254	...	2337	...	0037	...	*0026*	...	...

A – From Lindau (Table **935**) on Ⓐ (not Dec. 24, 31).
K – To Kempten (Table **935**).
L – From / to Lindau and Oberstdorf (Table **935**).
e – Ⓐ (not Dec. 24, 31, Jan. 6, June 3).
f – 0600 Feb. 2 - Apr. 4.
h – Also Dec. 24, 31; not Dec. 26, May 1.
j – † (also Jan. 6, June 3).
r – Not Jan. 6, June 3.
t – Arrives 13 minutes earlier.
w – Not Dec. 24.
z – Ⓒ (also Dec. 24, 31, Jan. 6, June 3).
★ – Eichstätt Bahnhof. Connecting trains operate to / from Eichstätt Stadt (*5km*, journey 9 minutes).

RB services (except train A) — TREUCHTLINGEN - WÜRZBURG — 905a

km		⚒r	Ⓒz	Ⓐe	Ⓐe	Ⓒz	Ⓐe	⑥k						Ⓐe	A										Ⓒz	Ⓐe
0	**Treuchtlingen** d.	...	0504	0512	0611	0625	*0701*	0725	0825	0925	1025	1125	1225	1305	1308	1325z	1425	1525	1625	1725	1825	1925	2025	2125	2225	2225
24	Gunzenhausen d.	...	0517	0525	0625	0639	*0716*	0739	0839	0939	1039	1139	1239	1318	1324	1339z	1439	1539	1639	1739	1839	1939	2039	2139	2239	2239
51	Ansbach a.	...	0537	0545	0645	0659	*0739*	0759	0859	0959	1059	1159	1259	1339	1342	1359z	1500	1559	1659	1759	1859	1959	2059	2200	2259	2300
51	Ansbach d.	0442	0539	0607	0702	0710	0811	0811	0910	1010	1110	1210	1310	...	1344	1410	1510	1610	1710	1810	1910	2010	2110	2207e	2300	...
83	Steinach (b Rothenb) ◐ d.	0503	0600	0628	0723	0731	0832	0832	0931	1031	1131	1231	1331	...	1404	1431	1531	1631	1731	1831	1931	2031	2131	2229e	2321	...
140	**Würzburg** Hbf a.	0549	0645	0716	0809	0816	0917	0917	1016	1116	1216	1316	1416	...	1438	1519	1615	1715	1816	1916	2016	2116	2215	2313e	0006	...

	⚒r	Ⓒz	Ⓐe	Ⓐe	Ⓒz	Ⓐe					A	Ⓒz	Ⓐe											†v	⚒m
Würzburg Hbf d.	0435	0531	0541	0632	0641	0710	0741	0841	0941	1041	1121	1141	1141	1241	1341	1441	1541	1641	1741	1841	1941	2041	2146	2241	2248
Steinach (b Rothenb) ◐ d.	0520	0615	0625	0716	0725	0755	0825	0925	1025	1125	1156	1225	1225	1326	1425	1525	1625	1725	1825	1925	2025	2125	2229	2325	2332
Ansbach a.	0541	0636	0646	0737	0746	0818	0846	0946	1046	1146	1214	1246	1246	1347	1446	1546	1646	1746	1846	1946	2046	2146	2251	2347	2354
Ansbach d.	0542	0654	0711	0754	0754	...	0854	0954	1054	1155	1216	1254	1315	1354	1454	1554	1654	1754	1854	1954	2054	2154	2254	2358	2358
Gunzenhausen d.	0601	0715	0732	0815	0815	...	0915	1015	1115	1215	1234	1315	1335	1415	1515	1615	1715	1815	1915	2015	2115	2215	2315	0018	0018
Treuchtlingen a.	0616	0730	0746	0830	0830	...	0930	1030	1130	1230	1250	1330	1349	1430	1530	1630	1730	1830	1930	2030	2130	2230	2330	0033	0033

◐ – Local trains **STEINACH** (b Rothenb) - **ROTHENBURG OB DER TAUBER** and v.v. 2nd class only *12 km* Journey time: 14 minutes.
From Steinach at 0523 ⚒**r**, 0618 Ⓒ**z**, 0630 Ⓐ**e**, 0726 Ⓐ**e**, 0734 Ⓒ**z**, 0835, 0934, 1034, 1134, 1234 Ⓒ**z**, 1245 Ⓐ**e**, 1334, 1434, 1534, 1634 Ⓒ**z**, 1645 Ⓐ**e**, 1734, 1834, 1934, 2034 and 2232.
From Rothenburg ob der Tauber at 0445 ⚒**r**, 0542 Ⓒ**z**, 0607 Ⓐ**e**, 0658 Ⓐ**e**, 0707 Ⓒ**z**, 0807, 0907, 1007, 1107, 1207, 1309, 1407, 1507, 1607, 1707, 1807, 1907, 2007 and 2211.

A – *IC* **2082/3**. KÖNIGSSEE – (12) and 🍷 Berchtesgaden - Augsburg - Hamburg and v.v.; (12) Oberstdorf (**2084/5**) - Augsburg - Hamburg and v.v.
e – Ⓐ (not Dec. 24, 31, Jan. 6, June 3).
k – Also Dec. 24, 31; not Dec. 26, May 1.
m – Not June 3.
r – Not Jan. 6, June 3.
v – Also June 3.
z – Ⓒ (also Dec. 24, 31, Jan. 6, June 3).

906 GIESSEN - KOBLENZ; LIMBURG - FRANKFURT and WIESBADEN

DB (*RE*/*RB* services); VEC★

Gießen - Limburg - Koblenz △

km												
			Ⓐe		⚒r	Ⓐe						†t
0	**Gießen** .... **807** d.	...	0518	0618	0716	0721	0823	0918		1918	2023	2118
13	Wetzlar .... **807** d.	...	0527	0630	0729	0733	0833	0929		1929	2033	2129
36	Weilburg .... d.	...	0552	0656	0743	0758	0858	0943		1943	2058	2143
65	**Limburg** (Lahn).... a.	...	0630	0733	0808	0835	0935	1008	and	2008	2135	2208
			◧	◧	|	◧	◧	|	every	|	◧	|
		⚒r	d		|	d		|	two	|	⚒y	|
65	**Limburg** (Lahn).... d.	0545	0645	0745	0810	0845	0945	1010	hours	2011	2145	2210
68	Diez .... d.	0549	0649	0749	0814	0849	0949	1014	until	2015	2149	2214
91	Nassau (Lahn)...... d.	0616	0716	0816	0831	0916	1016	1031		2032	2216	2231
99	Bad Ems............. d.	0626	0726	0826	0839	0926	1026	1039		2039	2226	2239
112	Niederlahnstein .... d.	0645	0745	0845	0852	0945	1045	1052		2052	2245	2252
117	**Koblenz** Hbf........ a.	0653	0753	0853	0858	0953	1053	1058		2059	2253	2259

	Ⓐe						n			n	n
Koblenz Hbf..... d.	0506	0656	0904		1704	1806	1904	1913	2006	2106	2317
Niederlahnstein . d.	0515	0703	0911		1711	1815	1911	1921	2015	2115	2323
Bad Ems........... d.	0533	0719	0922		1722	1833	1922	1937	2033	2133	2340
Nassau (Lahn) ... d.	0542	0728	0928	and	1728	1842	1928	1946	2042	2142	2349
Diez .... d.	0609	0746	0946	every	1746	1909	1946	2010	2109	2209	0013
Limburg (Lahn). a.	0613	0749	0949	two	1749	1913	1949	2014	2113	2213	0017
	◧	|	|	hours	|	◧	|	◧			
	⚒w	|	|	until	|	Ⓐe	|				
Limburg (Lahn). d.	0618	0750	0950		1750	1923	1950t	2023	...	...	...
Weilburg .... d.	0657	0815	1015		1815	2001	2015t	2100	...	...	...
Wetzlar ....**807** d.	0722	0833	1033		1833	2027	2033t	2127	...	...	...
Gießen ....**807** a.	0732	0843	1043		1843	2037	2043t	2137	...	...	...

Limburg - Niedernhausen - Frankfurt and Wiesbaden

km																										
		⚒r	Ⓐe	Ⓐe	⑥k	Ⓐe	Ⓐe	Ⓒz	Ⓐe	Ⓐe	Ⓐe	⚒r	Ⓐe			Ⓐe			Ⓐe		Ⓐe	Ⓒz	Ⓐe		Ⓐe	Ⓒz
0	**Limburg** (Lahn)......... d.	0418	0448	0518	0518	0555	0608	0618	0625	0638	0655	0718	0755	0818	0918	0955	1018	1118	1155	1218	1318	1318	1355	1418	1518	1518
21	Bad Camberg............ d.	0442	0512	0542	0542	0614	0633	0642	0644	0703	0714	0742	0814	0842	0942	1014	1042	1142	1214	1242	1342	1342	1414	1442	1542	1542
30	Idstein...................... d.	0451	0521	0551	0552	0621	0643	0651	0651	0713	0721	0751	0821	0851	0952	1021	1051	1152	1221	1251	1351	1352	1421	1451	1551	1552
38	Niedernhausen........‡ a.	0457	0527	0557	0559	0627	0652	0657	0657	0722	0727	0757	0827	0857	0959	1027	1057	1159	1227	1257	1357	1359	1427	1457	1557	1559
	Wiesbaden Hbf..... a.	|	*0555*	*0625*	0625	*0654*	0714	*0725*k	|	0744	|	*0825*	*0857*	*0925*	1025	|	*1125*	1225	|	*1325*	*1425*	1425	|	*1525*	*1627*	1625
70	**Frankfurt** (Main) Hbf ‡ a.	0528	0558	0628	...	0658	...	0728	0728	...	0758	0828	0858	0928	...	1058	1128	...	1258	1328	1428	...	1458	1528	1631	...

	Ⓐe		Ⓐe	Ⓐe	Ⓒz	Ⓐe					
Limburg (Lahn) .... d.	1555	1618	1655	1718	1718	1755	1818	1918	2018	2118	2218
Bad Camberg .... d.	1614	1642	1714	1742	1742	1814	1842	1942	2042	2142	2242
Idstein .... d.	1621	1651	1721	1751	1752	1821	1851	1952	2052	2152	2252
Niedernhausen ....‡ a.	1627	1657	1727	1757	1759	1827	1857	1959	2059	2158	2258
Wiesbaden Hbf...... a.	|	*1727*	*1757*	*1827*	1825	*1857*	*1925*	2025b	...	...	...
Frankfurt (Main) Hbf ‡ a.	1658	1728	1758	1828	...	1858	1928	...	...	...	...

km										
			Ⓐe	Ⓒz	Ⓐe	Ⓐe	Ⓒz	Ⓐe		Ⓐe
	Frankfurt (Main) Hbf..........‡ d.	...	0600	0630	0643	0730	...	...	0830	0857
0	**Wiesbaden** Hbf.............. d.	0531h	*0601*	*0636*k	*0650*	*0720*	0736k	0801	*0836*r	|
20	Niedernhausen..................‡ d.	0601	0631	0701	0718	0801	0801	0831	0901	0931
28	Idstein................................ d.	0608	0638	0708	0725	0808	0808	0838	0908	0938
37	Bad Camberg....................... d.	0617	0647	0717	0734	0817	0817	0847	0917	0945
58	**Limburg** (Lahn).................... a.	0640	0710	0740	0801	0840	0840	0910	0940	1003

			Ⓐe			Ⓐe	Ⓐe	Ⓒz		Ⓐe		Ⓐe	Ⓒz	Ⓐe	Ⓐe	Ⓐe	Ⓒz	Ⓐe		Ⓐe	Ⓐe	Ⓒz					
Frankfurt (Main) Hbf ‡ d.	...	1030	1100	...	1230	1300	1330	...	1430	1500	...	1600	1630	...	1700	1730	...	1800	1830	1900	1930	...	2030	...	...	...	...
Wiesbaden Hbf...... d.	0936	*1036*	|	1136	*1236*	|	*1336*	1336	*1436*	*1501*	1536	*1606*	*1636*	1636	*1706*	*1736*	1736	*1806*	*1836*	|	*1936*	1936	*2036*e	...	...	...	...
Niedernhausen ....‡ d.	1001	1101	1131	1201	1301	1331	1401	1401	1501	1531	1601	1631	1701	1701	1731	1801	1801	1831	1901	1931	2001	2001	2101	2203	2303	0003
Idstein .... d.	1008	1108	1138	1208	1308	1338	1408	1408	1508	1538	1608	1638	1708	1708	1738	1808	1808	1838	1908	1938	2008	2008	2108	2210	2310	0010
Bad Camberg .... d.	1017	1117	1145	1217	1317	1345	1417	1417	1517	1545	1617	1645	1717	1717	1745	1817	1817	1845	1917	1945	2017	2017	2117	2219	2319	0019
Limburg (Lahn) .... a.	1040	1140	1203	1240	1340	1403	1440	1440	1540	1603	1640	1703	1740	1740	1803	1840	1840	1903	1940	2003	2040	2040	2140	2242	2342	0042

b – Ⓑ (also Dec. 26, May 1; not Dec. 24, 31).
d – Runs daily Limburg - Koblenz.
e – Ⓐ (not Dec. 24, 31, June 3).
h – ⚒ (not June 3). 0536 on ⑥ (also Dec. 24, 31).
k – ⑥ (also Dec. 24, 31; not Dec. 26, May 1).
n – Not Dec. 24, 31.
r – ⚒ (not June 3).

t – † (also June 3).
w – Not June 3. Runs 3–5 minutes later on ⑥ (also Dec. 24, 31).
y – Not Dec. 24, 31, June 3.
z – Also Dec. 24, 31, June 3.
◧ – Change trains at Limburg.
△ – Additional stopping trains operate.

★ – Vectus Verkehrsgesellschaft mbH.
‡ – **Additional S-Bahn *S2* services** Frankfurt - Niedernhausen and v.v. Journey time: 35 minutes.
From Frankfurt (Main) Hbf (underground platforms): On ⚒ every 30 minutes 0522–2322; on † hourly 0522–1222, then every 30 minutes 1252–2322.
From Niedernhausen: On ⚒ every 30 minutes 0433–2303; on † hourly 0503–1203, then every 30 minutes 1233–2303.

907 GIESSEN - FULDA

RE/*RB* services

km																											
		⚒c	⑥k	Ⓐe	⑥k	Ⓐe	Ⓒz	Ⓒz	Ⓐe	Ⓒz	⑥k	Ⓐe	Ⓐe	Ⓒz	Ⓒz	Ⓐe	Ⓐe	Ⓒz	⑥k	Ⓐe	Ⓒz	Ⓒz	Ⓐe	Ⓐe	Ⓒz	Ⓐe	Ⓒz
0	**Gießen** .... d.	...	0619	0621	0743	0843	0848	0943	1043	1048	1143	1143	1241	1248	1343	1343	1443	1448	1543	1643	1648	1743	1744	1847	1848	2043	2045
23	Grünberg .... d.	...	0650	0703	0806	0906	0920	1005	1108	1120	1205	1210	1308	1322	1406	1411	1508	1520	1606	1706	1720	1806	1808	1918	1922	2110	2117
60	Alsfeld............ d.	0555	0739j	0741	0838	0937	1003	1037	1138	1204	1239	1257	1338	1405	1438	1453	1538	1604	1638	1740	1806	1839	1908j	1959	2003	2148	2155
79	Lauterbach...... d.	0613	0757	0801	0900	0951	1021	1059	1152	1223	1300	1316	1353	1424	1500	1516	1555	1623	1700	1803	1825	1854	1926	2018	2021	...	...
106	**Fulda**............. a.	0640	0825	0826	0930	1016	1056f	1130	1217	1256	1330	1348	1417	1456f	1530	1553	1620	1656	1730	1833	1852	1924	1954	2049	2049	...	...

	Ⓐe	⑥k	Ⓐe	⑥k	⑥k	Ⓐe	Ⓒz	Ⓒz	Ⓐe	⑥k	Ⓒz	Ⓐe	Ⓒz	Ⓒz	Ⓐe	⑥k	Ⓒz	Ⓐe	Ⓐe	Ⓒz	Ⓒz	Ⓐe	Ⓐe	Ⓒz	Ⓐe	Ⓐe	†w
Fulda ....d.	...	...	0457	0558	0710	0728	0832	0916	0936	1030	1116	1136	1230	1316	1320	1430	1516	1526	1605	1630	1716	1736	1819	1910	1938	2035	2125
Lauterbach ....d.	...	...	0530	0632	0738	0757	0857	0943	1005	1057	1144	1206	1257	1344	1354	1458	1544	1558	1638	1657	1744	1802	1847	1939	2019	2103	2153
Alsfeld ....d.	0457	0548	0603j	0653	0804	0813	0913	1005	1021	1113	1205	1221	1313	1406	1413	1514	1605	1617	1704	1713	1807	1819	1907	2004	2038	2122	2212
Grünberg ....d.	0535	0625	0636	0735	0847	0844	0944	1047	1050	1144	1247	1251	1346	1447	1451	1545	1647	1647	1747	1744	1849	1849	1945	2042	...	...	...
Gießen.............a.	0600	0651	0709	0805	0912	0914	1014	1112	1114	1212	1312	1314	1412	1512	1512	1612	1712	1714	1814	1812	1914	1913	2011	2109	...	...	...

c – ⚒ (not June 3). Runs 17–19 minutes later on ⑥ (also Dec. 24, 31).
e – Not Dec. 24, 31, June 3.
f – 4–8 minutes earlier on † (also June 3).
j – Arrives 11–16 minutes earlier.
k – Also Dec. 24, 31; not Dec. 26, May 1.
w – Also June 3.
z – Also Dec. 24, 31, June 3.

908 GÖTTINGEN - BEBRA

CANTUS Verkehrsgesellschaft (2nd class only)

km																				
		Ⓐe	⑥k	Ⓐe	H	⚒		Ⓐe						Ⓐe	Ⓒz		Ⓐe			
0	**Göttingen**.......... **864** d.	0443	0543	0600	0702	0814	0914	1040	1114	1240	1314	1440	1514	1614	1640	1714	1814	1914	2014	2214
20	Eichenberg......... **864** d.	0459	0558	0618	0721	0830	0930	1055	1130	1255	1330	1455	1530	1630	1655	1730	1830	1930	2030	2230
35	Bad Sooden-Allendorf d.	0509	0607	0627	0730	0839	0939	1104	1139	1304	1339	1504	1539	1639	1704	1739	1839	1939	2039	2239
49	Eschwege .... a.	0519	0618	0638	0741	0852	0951	1115	1152	1315	1351	1515	1551	1650	1715	1751	1850	1951	2050	2250
49	Eschwege ....★ d.	0524	0623	0643	0746	*0920*	*1018*	1120	*1218*	1320	*1418*	1520	*1618*	1655	1720	1756e	1855	1958e	2055	2255
87	**Bebra** ....★ a.	0553	0652	0712	0814	*0949*	*1047*	1149	*1247*	1349	*1447*	1549	*1647*	1724	1749	1824e	1924	2029e	2124	2324

	Ⓐe	⑥k	Ⓐe		⚒		Ⓐe							Ⓐe	Ⓒz	Ⓐe				F
Bebra...................★ d.	0523	0623	0633	0731	0832	0932z	1003	*1105*	1203	*1305*r	1403	*1505*	1603	1705	*1705*	1803	*1905*	2003	2103	2303
Eschwege.............★ a.	0553	0650	0700	0759	0900	1000z	1031	*1134*	1231	*1334*r	1431	*1534*	1631	1734	*1734*	1831	*1934*	2031	2131	2331
Eschwege................. d.	0558	0655	0705	0805	0905	1005	1036	1205	1236	1405	1436	1605	1636	1739	1805	1836	2005	2036	2136	2336
Bad Sooden-Allendorf d.	0609	0708	0717	0817	0917	1017	1047	1217	1247	1417	1447	1617	1647	1751	1817	1847	2017	2047	2147	2347
Eichenberg ....**865** d.	0624	0722	0732	0832	0932	1032	1059	1232	1259	1432	1500	1632	1700	1806	1832	1900	2032	2100	2206	0002
Göttingen ....**865** a.	0637	0735	0745	0845	0945	1045	1113	1245	1313	1445	1513	1645	1713	1820	1845	1913	2045	2113	2219	0015

F – From Fulda (d. 2222) and Bad Hersfeld (d. 2250).
H – To Bad Hersfeld (a. 0824) and Fulda (a. 0854).
e – Ⓐ (not Dec. 24, 31).
k – Also Dec. 24, 31; not Dec. 26, May 1.
r – 4–6 minutes later on ⑦.
z – Ⓒ (also Dec. 24, 31).
★ – Additional trains Eschwege - Bebra and v.v.: From Eschwege at 0820 Ⓒz, 1818 Ⓒz and 2018 Ⓒz. From Bebra at 0905 Ⓐe.

909 GEMÜNDEN - BAD KISSINGEN - SCHWEINFURT - WÜRZBURG

DB (*RB* services); EB ★

km																									
			Ⓐe										Ⓒz	Ⓐe				Ⓐe			Ⓐe			Ⓒz	Ⓐe
0	**Gemünden** (Main)..............d.	...	0620	0704	...	...	0904	...	...	1104	...	...	1304	1313	...	1504	...	1606	1706	...	1806	1906	...	2104	2104
28	Hammelburg ....d.	...	0657	0736	...	...	0936	...	...	1136	...	...	1336	1358	...	1536	...	1636	1737	...	1836	1936	...	2136	2203j
47	**Bad Kissingen**..................a.	...	0721	0759	...	...	0958	...	...	1158	...	...	1358	1421	...	1559	...	1658	1759	...	1858	1958	...	2158	2225
			|	|			|			|			d	d		|		d	|		d	|		|	|
47	**Bad Kissingen**.....................d.	0646	0728	0805	0826	0901	1005	1026	1101	1205	1226	1301	1405	1426	1501	1605	1626	1701	1805	1826	1901	2005	2101	2230	2230
56	Ebenhausen (Unterf)..... **870** d.	0701	0742	0817	0841	0917	1017	1041	1117	1217	1241	1317	1417	1441	1517	1617	1641	1717	1817	1841	1917	2017	2117	2241	2241
70	**Schweinfurt** Hbf... **870 876** a.	0716	0754	0829	0852	0926	1029	1052	1126	1229	1252	1326	1429	1452	1526	1629	1652	1726	1829	1852	1926	2029	2126	2253	2253
113	**Würzburg** Hbf ...... **870 876** a.	0747	*0823*	...	*0923*	0958	...	*1123*	1158	...	*1323*	1358	...	*1523*	1558	...	*1723*	1758	...	*1923*	1958	*2151*p	2158	*0016*	*0016*

			Ⓒz	Ⓐe							Ⓒz					Ⓐe							①–⑥	Ⓒz	
Würzburg Hbf....⊙ **870 876** d.	...	*0501*r	*0602*	*0624*	...	0801	*0836*	1001	*1036*	1201	*1236*	*1236*	1401	*1436*	...	*1509*	1601	*1636*	...	1801	*1836*	2001	*2036*	*2109*v	*2139*q
Schweinfurt Hbf ⊙ **870 876** d.	0458	0539	0705	0705	0730	0830	0931	1030	1131	1230	1331	1331	1430	1506	1531	1600	1630	1706	1731	1830	1931	2030	2106	2149	2224
Ebenhausen (Unter) ...... **870** d.	0518	0551	0718	0718	0744	0842	0945	1042	1145	1242	1345	1345	1442	1518	1545	1614	1642	1718	1745	1842	1945	2042	2118	2202	2240
Bad Kissingen.................... a.	0528	0602	0727	0727	0754	0853	0955	1053	1155	1253	1355	1355	1453	1527	1555	1624	1653	1727	1755	1853	1955	2053	2127	2212	2250
	|	Ⓐe		|	|		|		|	Ⓐe	|	Ⓐe		|	|	|		|	|	Ⓐe	|		|	|	
Bad Kissingen.................... d.	0544	0612	...	0732	0801z	...	1001	...	1201	1257	1401	1434	...	1532e	1601z	1631	...	1732e	1801z	1904	2001	...	2132e	2219	...
Hammelburg......................... d.	0611	0658k	...	0823j	0823z	...	1023	...	1223	1322	1423	1458	...	1558e	1623z	1658	...	1758e	1823z	1925	2023	...	2153e	2240	...
Gemünden (Main) .... a.	0647	0734	...	0854	0854z	...	1054	...	1254	1354	1454	1534	...	1635e	1654z	1734	...	1835e	1854z	...	2054	...	...	2311	...

d – Daily.
e – Ⓐ (not Dec. 24, 31, Jan. 6, June 3).
j – Arrives 26–28 minutes earlier.
k – Arrives 0639.
p – *2123* on Ⓒz.
q – *2144* on Ⓒz.
r – ⚒ (not Jan. 6, June 3).
v – † (also Jan. 6, June 3).
z – Ⓒ (also Dec. 24, 31, Jan. 6, June 3).
★ – Erfurter Bahn (2nd class only).
⊙ – Trains between Würzburg, Schweinfurt and Ebenhausen are often combined with a service to Meiningen or Erfurt. Passengers should take care to join the correct portion for their destination.

AACHEN - KÖLN - FRANKFURT via the high-speed line 910

See Tables **800**/**912** for services via Bonn and Koblenz.

km		ICE	ICE	ICE	ICE	ICE	ICE	ICE	ICE	ICE	ICE	ICE	ICE	ICE	ICE	ICE	ICE	ICE	ICE	ICE	ICE	ICE	ICE
		521	**523**	**1123**	**511**	**711**	**811**	**925**	**525**	**501**	**813**	**527**	**513**	**815**	**545**	**529**	**503**	**11**	**11**	**621**	**1121**	**121**	**515**
			①-⑤	⑥u		①-⑤	①-⑤	⑥⑦	①-⑤		①-⑤	①-⑥		①-⑥	①-⑥			①-⑥	⑦d	①-⑥	⑦j	①-⑥	
		🍷	a 🍷	🍷	🍷	a	a 🍷	c 🍷	a 🍷	🍷	a 🍷	G 🍷	M 🍷	e 🍷	e B	🍷	H 🍷	r 🍷	🍷	m 🍷	🍷	m 🍷	A 🍷
	Dortmund Hbf **800** d.	...	0406	0423	0437g	0502	...	0502	0523	0537	0600	0623	0637	0652	✕	0723c	0737	...	...	0816y	0821	...	0837
	Essen Hbf **800** d.	...	0428	0445	│	0524	...	0524	0553	│	│	0653	0659	0715	...	0753	│	...	...	0840	0853	...	│
	Amsterdam Centraal **28** ⊡ d.	...	│	│	│	│	...	│	│	│	│	│	│	│	...	│	│	...	...	│	│	0704	│
	Düsseldorf Hbf **800** d.	...	0455	0513	│	0551	...	0551	0621	│	│	0721	0727	0748	...	0821	│	...	...	0913	0923	0923	│
	Brussels Midi/Zuid **21 400** d.	...	│	│	│	│	...	│	│	│	│	│	│	│	...	│	│	0725	0725	│	│	│	│
	Aachen Hbf **802 807** d.	...	│	│	│	│	...	│	│	│	│	│	│	│	0740	│	│	0839	0839	│	│	│	│
	Köln Hbf **802 807** a.	...	│	│	0545g	│	...	│	│	0646	0709	│	0749	│	0822	│	0846	0915	0915	│	│	│	0946
0	**Köln** Hbf **802 807** d.	0422	│	│	0555	│	0620	│	│	0655	0720	│	0755	│	0826	│	0855	0928	0928	│	│	│	0955
1	**Köln** Messe/Deutz **802** d.	│	0518	0535	│	0615	│	0618	0644	│	│	0744	│	0810	0828	0844	│	│	│	0937	0945	0945	│
	Köln/Bonn Flughafen ✈ ⊖ **802** d.	│	0531	0547	│	│	│	0631	│	│	│	│	│	0821	...	│	│	│	│	│	│	│	│
25	Siegburg/Bonn 🚋 ⊖ **807** d.	0437	0542	│	0611	│	0636	0642	│	0711	0736	│	0811	0833	...	│	0911	│	│	│	│	│	1011
88	Montabaur d.	0458	0602	│	│	0646	0657	0702	│	│	0757	│	│	0857	...	│	│	│	0958	│	│	│	│
110	Limburg Süd d.	0510	0613	│	│	0657	0708	0713	│	│	0808	│	│	0908	...	│	│	│	1009	│	│	│	│
	Wiesbaden Hbf a.	│	│	│	│	0719	│	│	│	│	│	│	│	│	...	│	│	│	│	│	│	│	│
	Mainz Hbf a.	│	│	│	│	0744	│	│	│	│	│	│	│	│	...	│	│	│	│	│	│	│	│
169	**Frankfurt** Flughafen Fernbf ✈ a.	0533	0634	0634	0651	│	0726	0734	0734	0751	0826	0834	0851	0926	...	0934	0951	1016	1027	1026	1034	1034	1051
180	**Frankfurt** (Main) Hbf a.	0546	0648	0648	│	│	0741	0748	0748	│	0841	0848	│	0941	...	0948	│	1030	1041	1041	1048	1050	│
	Nürnberg Hbf **920** a.	0759	0859	0859	│	│	...	0959	0959	│	...	1059	│	...	...	1159	│	...	...	1259	1259	...	│
	Mannheim Hbf **912** a.	│	│	│	0724	0824	...	│	│	0824	...	│	0924	...	...	│	1024	...	...	│	│	...	1124
	Karlsruhe Hbf **912** a.	│	│	│	│	│	...	│	│	0858	...	│	│	...	...	│	1050	...	...	│	│	...	│
	Basel SBB **912** a.	│	│	│	│	│	...	│	│	1047	...	│	│	...	...	│	...	...	...	│	│	...	│
	Stuttgart Hbf **930** a.	│	│	│	0808	0923	...	│	│	...	...	│	1008	...	...	│	...	...	...	│	│	...	1208
	München Hbf **904 930** a.	0906	1005	1005	1033	...	...	1106	1106	...	...	1205	1233	...	...	1305	...	...	...	1405	1405	...	1433

	THA	ICE	ICE	ICE	ICE	THA	ICE	ICE	ICE	ICE	THA	ICE	ICE	ICE	ICE	ICE	ICE	ICE	ICE	ICE	ICE	ICE	THA
	9407	**923**	**623**	**105**	**625**	**9413**	**517**	**627**	**927**	**507**	**9421**	**123**	**629**	**519**	**15**	**721**	**921**	**509**	**125**	**723**	**611**	**817**	**9433**
	Y	⑦w	①-⑥	◧		⑦h		①-⑥	⑦t				Ⓑq			①-④	⑤-⑦			Ⓑq			
	[R] P	🍷	e 🍷	🍷	🍷	[R] P	🍷	e 🍷	🍷	🍷	[R] P	🍷	🍷	🍷	🍷	n 🍷	s 🍷	🍷	🍷	🍷	🍷	🍷	[R] P
Dortmund Hbf **800** d.	...	0853	...	...	1023w	...	1037	...	1100	1137t	...	...	1223w	1237	...	...	1323c	1337a	...	...	1437	...	...
Essen Hbf **800** d.	...	0917	...	...	1053	...	1059	...	│	│	...	...	1253	1259	...	...	1353	│	...	1453	1459	...	...
Amsterdam Centraal **28** ⊡ d.	...	│	...	0804v	│	...	│	...	│	│	...	1034	│	│	...	...	│	│	1234	│	│	...	...
Düsseldorf Hbf **800** d.	...	0948	...	1022v	1121	...	1127	...	│	│	...	1248	1321	1327	...	...	1421	│	1448	1521	1527	...	...
Brussels Midi/Zuid **21 400** d.	0755	│	...	│	│	0928	│	...	│	│	1128	│	│	│	1225	...	│	│	│	│	│	...	1428
Aachen Hbf **802 807** d.	0908	│	...	│	│	1039	│	...	│	│	1239	│	│	│	1339	...	│	│	│	│	│	...	1539
Köln Hbf **802 807** a.	0947	1012	...	1045v	│	1115	1149	...	1209	1246t	1315	1312	│	1349	1415	...	│	1446a	1512	│	1549	...	1615
Köln Hbf **802 807** d.	...	1019	1019	1055	│	...	1155	1219	1219	1255	...	1328	│	1355	1420	1427	│	1455	1528	│	1555	1620	...
Köln Messe/Deutz **802** d.	...	│	│	│	1144	...	│	│	│	│	...	│	1344	│	│	│	1444	│	│	1544	│	│	...
Köln/Bonn Flughafen ✈ ⊖ **802** d.	...	│	1031	│	│	...	│	│	│	│	...	│	│	│	│	1441	│	│	│	│	│	│	...
Siegburg/Bonn 🚋 ⊖ **807** d.	...	1036	1042	1111	│	...	1211	1236	1236	1311	...	│	│	1411	1436	1453	│	1511	│	│	1611	1636	...
Montabaur d.	...	1057	1102	│	│	...	│	1257	1257	│	...	│	│	│	1457	│	│	│	│	│	│	1657	...
Limburg Süd d.	...	1108	1113	│	│	...	│	1308	1308	│	...	│	│	│	1508	│	│	│	│	│	│	1708	...
Wiesbaden Hbf a.	...	│	│	│	│	...	│	│	│	│	...	│	│	│	│	│	│	│	│	│	│	│	...
Mainz Hbf a.	...	│	│	│	│	...	│	│	│	│	...	│	│	│	│	│	│	│	│	│	│	│	...
Frankfurt Flughafen Fernbf ✈ a.	...	1126	1134	1151	1234	...	1251	1326	1326	1351	...	1416	1434	1451	1526	1534	1534	1551	1616	1634	1651	1726	...
Frankfurt (Main) Hbf a.	...	1141	1148	│	1248	...	│	1344	1344	│	...	1430	1448	│	1540	1548	1548	│	1630	1648	│	1741	...
Nürnberg Hbf **920** a.	...	1359	1359	│	1459	...	│	1559	1559	│	...	...	1659	│	...	1759	1759	│	...	1859	│	...	...
Mannheim Hbf **912** a.	...	│	│	1224	│	...	1324	│	│	1424	...	...	│	1524	...	│	│	1624	...	│	1724	...	...
Karlsruhe Hbf **912** a.	...	│	│	1258	│	...	│	│	│	1450	...	...	│	│	...	│	│	1658	...	│	│	...	...
Basel SBB **912** a.	...	│	│	1447	│	...	│	│	│	...	...	...	│	│	...	│	│	1847	...	│	│	...	...
Stuttgart Hbf **930** a.	...	│	│	...	│	...	1408	│	│	...	...	...	│	1608	...	│	│	...	...	│	1808	...	...
München Hbf **904 930** a.	...	1505	1505	...	1605	...	1633	1705	1705	...	...	...	1805	1832	...	1905	1905	...	...	2005	2033	...	...

	ICE	ICE	ICE	ICE	ICE	ICE	ICE	ICE	ICE	THA	ICE	ICE	ICE	ICE	THA	ICE	ICE	ICE	ICE	ICE	THA	ICE	ICE
	725	**601**	**127**	**327**	**715**	**727**	**613**	**819**	**729**	**9441**	**603**	**129**	**821**	**929**	**9445**	**615**	**17**	**605**	**605**	**227**	**9453**	**617**	**913**
			ⒷL	⑥L	①-⑤	Ⓑq		Ⓑq					①-⑤	⑥⑦					Q				
	🍷	🍷	🍷	🍷	a 🍷	🍷	🍷	🍷	🍷	[R] P	🍷	🍷	a O	¶ 🍷	[R] P	🍷	🍷	🍷	🍷	🍷	[R] P	🍷	🍷
Dortmund Hbf **800** d.	1523w	...	...	...	...	...	1637	...	...	...	...	...	🍷	...	...	1837	...	1923	1923	...	...	2037	2137‡
Essen Hbf **800** d.	1553	...	...	...	...	1653	1659	...	1753	...	...	...	...	1840	...	1859	...	1949	1949	...	...	2059	│
Amsterdam Centraal **28** ⊡ d.	│	...	1434	1434	...	│	│	...	│	...	...	1634	...	│	...	│	...	│	│	1834	...	│	│
Düsseldorf Hbf **800** d.	1621	...	1648	1648	...	1721	1727	...	1821	...	...	1848	1908	1908	...	1927	...	2022	2022	2048	...	2127	│
Brussels Midi/Zuid **21 400** d.	│	...	│	│	...	│	│	...	│	1628	...	│	│	│	1728	│	1825	│	│	│	1928	│	│
Aachen Hbf **802 807** d.	│	...	│	│	...	│	│	...	│	1739	...	│	│	│	1839	│	1939	│	│	│	2039	│	│
Köln Hbf **802 807** a.	│	...	1712	1712	...	│	1749	...	│	1815	...	1912	│	│	1915	1949	2015	│	│	2112	2115	2149	2246‡
Köln Hbf **802 807** d.	│	1655	1720	1728	1728	│	1755	1820	│	...	1855	1920	│	│	...	1957	2028	│	│	2120	...	2155	2255
Köln Messe/Deutz **802** d.	1644	│	│	│	│	1744	│	│	1844	...	│	│	1930	1930	...	│	│	2046	2046	│	...	│	│
Köln/Bonn Flughafen ✈ ⊖ **802** d.	│	│	│	│	│	│	│	│	│	...	│	│	│	│	...	│	│	│	│	│	...	│	2308
Siegburg/Bonn 🚋 ⊖ **807** d.	│	1711	│	│	│	│	1811	1836	│	...	1911	│	1944	1944	...	2012	│	2100	2100	│	...	2211	│
Montabaur d.	│	│	│	│	1800	│	│	1857	│	...	│	│	2004	2004	...	│	│	2121	2121	│	...	│	2335
Limburg Süd d.	│	│	│	│	1811	│	│	1908	│	...	│	│	2015	2015	...	│	│	2132	2132	│	...	│	2346
Wiesbaden Hbf a.	│	│	│	│	1832	│	│	│	│	...	│	│	│	│	...	│	│	│	│	│	...	│	│
Mainz Hbf a.	│	│	│	│	1900	│	│	│	│	...	│	│	│	│	...	│	│	│	│	│	...	│	│
Frankfurt Flughafen Fernbf ✈ a.	1734	1751	1814	1816	...	1834	1851	1926	1934	...	1951	2014	2034	2034	...	2051	2116	2151	2151	2214	...	2255	0010
Frankfurt (Main) Hbf a.	1748	│	1830	1830	...	1848	│	1941	1948	...	│	2030	2048	2048	...	│	2130	│	│	2230	...	│	0023
Nürnberg Hbf **920** a.	1959	│	...	...	...	2058	│	...	2159	...	│	...	2259f	2259x	...	│	...	│	│	...	...	│	...
Mannheim Hbf **912** a.	│	1824	...	...	...	│	1924	...	│	...	2024	...	│	│	...	2124	...	2224	2224	...	...	2337	...
Karlsruhe Hbf **912** a.	│	1850	...	...	...	│	│	...	│	...	2100	...	│	│	...	│	...	2300	2300	...	...	│	...
Basel SBB **912** a.	│	...	...	...	...	│	│	...	│	...	2300z	...	│	│	...	│	...	...	0058b	...	...	│	...
Stuttgart Hbf **930** a.	│	...	...	...	...	│	2008	...	│	...	...	...	│	│	...	2208	...	...	...	...	...	0053k	...
München Hbf **904 930** a.	2105	...	...	...	...	2205	2233	...	2308	...	...	...	0008f	0008x	...	0034	...	...	...	...	...	...	...

A – From Hamburg (Table **800**).
B – To Berlin (Tables **800**, **810**). Also calls at Düren (d. 0758).
G – ①-⑥ (not Dec. 25, Jan. 1, Apr. 5, May 24). (12) and 🍷 (Hannover ① **g** -) Dortmund - München (- Garmisch ⑥).
H – From Hannover (Table **810**).
L – From Mar. 26
M – From Münster (d. 0601).
O – From Oberhausen (Table **800**).
P – From Paris (Table **20** or **21**). Special fares payable.
Q – ①②③④⑦ (not Dec. 23, 24, 30, 31, Apr. 1, 4, May 23).
Y – ①-⑥ (not Dec. 25, Jan. 1, Apr. 5, May 1, 13, 24, June 3).

a – ①-⑤ (not Dec. 24, 25, 31, Jan. 1, Apr. 2, 5, May 24).
b – Basel **Badischer Bahnhof**.
c – ⑥⑦ (also Dec. 24, 25, 31, Jan. 1, Apr. 2, 5, May 24).
d – Also Apr. 5, May 24.
e – Not Dec. 25, 26, Jan. 1, Apr. 3, 5, May 24.
f – Frankfurt - München on ⑤ (also Dec. 23, 30, Apr. 1, May 12, June 2; not Dec. 25, Jan. 1, Apr. 2).
g – ① (also Apr. 6, May 25; not Apr. 5, May 24).
h – Also Dec. 25, Jan. 1, Apr. 5, May 1, 13, 24, June 3.
j – Also Dec. 25, 26, Jan. 1, Apr. 5, May 24.
k – 0040 on the mornings of ①⑦.
m – Not Dec. 25, 26, Jan. 1, Apr. 5, May 24.
n – Not Dec. 23, 24, 30, 31, Apr. 1, 5, May 12, 24, June 2.
q – Not Dec. 24, 25, 31, Apr. 2, 4, May 23.
r – Not Apr. 5, May 24.
s – Also Dec. 23, 24, 30, 31, Apr. 1, 5, May 12, 24, June 2; not May 14, June 4.
t – ⑦ (also Dec. 25, 26, Jan. 1, Apr. 3, 5, May 24).
u – Also Dec. 24, 31, Apr. 2; not Dec. 26, Apr. 3.
v – Not Dec. 25, Jan. 1.
w – ⑦ (also Apr. 5, May 24; not Apr. 4, May 23).
x – Frankfurt - München on ⑦ **w**.
y – ⑥ (also Dec. 24, 31, Apr. 2; not Dec. 26).
z – 2253 on ⑦ **w**.
‡ – ⑥ (also Dec. 24, 25, 31, Apr. 2, 4, May 23).
¶ – Also Dec. 24, 25, 31, Apr. 2, 5, May 24; not Apr. 4, May 23.
◧ – Conveys (12) (*ICE* **505**) Köln - Basel.
⊡ – Amsterdam timings are subject to alteration on Apr. 30.
⊖ – For local connections Köln/Bonn Flughafen - Siegburg/Bonn see Tables **802** (Köln/Bonn Flughafen - Troisdorf) and **807** (Troisdorf - Siegburg/Bonn).

🚋 – Light-rail services operate Bonn Hbf - Siegburg/Bonn and v.v. Journey time: 25 minutes. Operator: Elektrische Bahnen der Stadt Bonn und des Rhein-Sieg-Kreises (SSB). See below.

Bonn Hbf → Siegburg/Bonn

On Ⓐ: 0016, 0046, 0133, 0418, 0438, 0458, 0518, 0528 and every 10–15 minutes until 2246; then 2316, 2346.

On ⑥: 0016, 0046, 0133, 0416 and every 30 minutes until 0746, 0801 and every 10–15 minutes until 2246; then 2316, 2346.

On †: 0016, 0046, 0133, 0511, 0541, 0616 and every 30 minutes until 1016, 1031 and every 15 minutes until 2246; then 2316, 2346.

Siegburg/Bonn → Bonn Hbf

On Ⓐ: 0022, 0052, 0122, 0202, 0454, 0514, 0534, 0554 and every 10–15 minutes until 2232; then 2252, 2302, 2322, 2352.

On ⑥: 0022, 0052, 0122, 0202, 0452 and every 30 minutes until 0752, 0814, 0834, 0854 and every 10–15 minutes until 2232; then 2252, 2302, 2322, 2352.

On †: 0022, 0052, 0122, 0202, 0552 and every 30 minutes until 1052, 1107 and every 15 minutes until 2222; then 2232, 2252, 2302, 2322, 2352.

910 FRANKFURT - KÖLN - AACHEN via the high-speed line

See Tables **800**/**912** for services via Koblenz and Bonn.

km		THA 9412 Y [R]P	ICE 328 ①–④ t🍷	ICE 918 ⑤z 🍷	ICE 826 🍷	THA 9416 [R]P	ICE 716 ①–⑤ a🍷	ICE 616 🍷	ICE 824 ①–⑤ aD 🍷	ICE 16 🍷	ICE 226 🍷	ICE 604 🍷	ICE 822 ①–⑥ e🍷	ICE 818 🍷	ICE 614 🍷	ICE 820 ①–⑤ a🍷	ICE 128 🍷	THA 9428 [R]P	ICE 602 🍷	ICE 728 🍷	ICE 612 🍷	ICE 726 ①–⑥ e🍷	ICE 126 J 🍷	THA 9436 ⑦h [R]P
	München Hbf **904 930** d.	...	...	...	0032g	...	...	0317		...	...	...	0448g	...	0523	0551	...	...	...	0651	0723	0755	...	...
	Stuttgart Hbf **930** d.	...	...	...	0305	...	...	0551	...	...	...	...	│	...	0751	│	...	...	...	│	0951	│	...	...
	Basel SBB **912** d.	...	...	...	│	...	...	│	...	...	...	0516b	│	...	│	│	...	...	0712e	│	│	│	...	...
	Karlsruhe Hbf **912** d.	...	...	...	│	...	...	│	...	...	...	0700	│	...	│	│	...	...	0901	│	│	│	...	...
	Mannheim Hbf **912** d.	...	...	...	0440	...	...	0635	...	...	...	0735	│	...	0835	│	...	...	0935	│	1035	│	...	...
	Nürnberg Hbf **920** d.	...	...	...	│	...	...	│	...	...	...	│	0600	...	│	0700	...	...	│	0800	│	0900	...	...
	Frankfurt (Main) Hbf d.	...	0510	0510	0544	...	...	│	0702	0729	0729	│	0810	0816	│	0910	0929	...	│	1010	│	1110	1129	...
	Frankfurt Flughafen Fernbf ✈ d.	...	0524	0524	0601	...	...	0709	0715	0743	0743	0809	0824	0832	0909	0924	0943	...	1009	1024	1109	1124	1143	...
0	**Mainz** Hbf d.	...	│	│	│	...	0609	│	│	│	│	│	│	│	│	│	│	...	│	│	│	│	│	...
10	**Wiesbaden** Hbf d.	...	│	│	│	...	0630	│	│	│	│	│	│	│	│	│	│	...	│	│	│	│	│	...
65	Limburg Süd d.	...	0544	0544	0620	...	0650	│	0734	│	│	│	│	0851	│	│	│	...	│	1044	│	│	│	...
87	Montabaur d.	...	0556	0556	0631	...	0701	│	0746	│	│	│	│	0902	│	│	│	...	│	1056	│	│	│	...
150	Siegburg/Bonn 🚊 ⊖ **807** d.	...	0618	0618	0651	...	│	0749	0808	│	│	0849	│	0923	0949	│	│	...	1049	1118	1149	│	│	...
166	Köln/Bonn Flughafen ✈ ⊖ **802** a.	...	0626	0626	│	...	0726	│	│	│	│	│	│	│	│	│	│	...	│	1126	│	│	│	...
180	**Köln** Messe/Deutz **802** a.	...	│	│	0704	...	│	│	0822	│	│	│	0914	│	│	1014	│	...	│	│	│	1212	│	...
181	**Köln** Hbf **802 807** a.	...	0639	0639	│	...	0739	0805	│	0832	0832	0905	│	0939	1005	│	1032	...	1105	1139	1205	│	1232	...
181	**Köln** Hbf **802 807** d.	0644	0646	0646	│	0744	...	0810	│	0843	0846	...	│	...	1010	│	1046	1044	1110v	...	1210	│	1246	1243
251	**Aachen** Hbf **802 807** a.	0720	│	│	│	0820	...	│	│	0915	│	...	│	...	│	│	│	1120	│	...	│	│	│	1320
	Brussels Midi/Zuid **21 400** a.	0832	│	│	│	0932	...	│	│	1035	│	...	│	...	│	│	│	1232	│	...	│	│	│	1432
	Düsseldorf Hbf **800** a.	...	0709	0709	0727	...	...	0831	0843	...	0911	...	0937	...	1031	1037	1111	...	│	...	1231	1237	1312	...
	Amsterdam Centraal **28** ⊡ a.	...	0925	│	│	...	...	│	│	...	1125	...	│	...	│	│	1325	...	│	...	│	│	1525	...
	Essen Hbf **800** a.	...	...	0736	0802	...	...	0857	0908	...	...	...	1002	...	1057	1102	...	...	│	...	1257	1302	...	...
	Dortmund Hbf **800** a.	...	...	...	0827c	...	...	0921	0936	...	...	...	...	...	1121	...	...	...	1220v	...	1321	1330r	...	...

	ICE 600 T 🍷	ICE 1008 ⑤f 🍷	ICE 724 🍷	ICE 610 🍷	ICE 722 🍷	ICE 14 🍷	ICE 124 🍷	ICE 508 🍷	THA 9448 [R]P	ICE 928 ⑥k 🍷	ICE 720 L 🍷	ICE 1022 ⑤u 🍷	ICE 518 🍷	ICE 628 🍷	ICE 816 🍷	ICE 506 🍷	ICE 806 ①–⑤ aO 🍷	ICE 1226 ⑥k 🍷	ICE 626 ⑧q 🍷	THA 9456 [R]P	ICE 122 🍷	ICE 712 ①–⑤ a🍷	ICE 516 🍷	ICE 624 🍷
München Hbf **904 930** d.	...	...	0855	0923	0955	...	...	...	...	1055	1055	1055	1123	1155	...	...		1255	1255	...	...	...	1323	1355
Stuttgart Hbf **930** d.	...	...	│	1151	│	...	...	...	...	│	│	│	1351	│	...	...	...	│	│	...	...	1434	1551	│
Basel SBB **912** d.	...	...	│	│	│	...	...	1112	...	│	│	│	│	│	...	...	...	│	│	...	...	│	│	│
Karlsruhe Hbf **912** d.	1109	1109	│	│	│	...	...	1300	...	│	│	│	│	│	...	1509	1509	│	│	...	...	│	│	│
Mannheim Hbf **912** d.	1135	1135	│	1235	│	...	...	1335	...	│	│	│	1435	│	...	1535	1535	│	│	...	...	1533	1635	│
Nürnberg Hbf **920** d.	│	│	1000	│	1100	...	...	│	...	1200	1200	1200	│	1300	...	│	│	1400	1400	...	...	│	│	1500
Frankfurt (Main) Hbf d.	│	│	1210	│	1310	1329	1329	│	...	1410	1410	1410	│	1510	1517	│	│	1610	1610	...	1629	│	│	1710
Frankfurt Flughafen Fernbf ✈ d.	1209	1209	1224	1309	1324	1343	1343	1409	...	1424	1424	1431	1509	1524	1532	1609	1609	1624	1624	...	1643	│	1709	1724
Mainz Hbf d.	│	│	│	│	│	│	│	│	...	│	│	│	│	│	│	│	│	│	│	...	│	1623	│	│
Wiesbaden Hbf d.	│	│	│	│	│	│	│	│	...	│	│	│	│	│	│	│	│	│	│	...	│	1645	│	│
Limburg Süd d.	│	│	1244	│	│	│	│	│	...	1444	1444	1450	│	│	1551	│	│	1643	1643	...	│	1706	│	│
Montabaur d.	│	│	1256	│	│	│	│	│	...	1456	1456	1501	│	│	1602	│	│	1654	1654	...	│	1717	│	│
Siegburg/Bonn 🚊 ⊖ **807** d.	1249	1249	1318	1349	│	│	│	1449	...	1518	1518	1523	1549	│	1623	1649	1649	1714	1714	...	│	1738	1749	│
Köln/Bonn Flughafen ✈ ⊖ **802** a.	│	│	1326	│	│	│	│	│	...	1526	1526	│	│	│	│	│	│	│	│	...	│	1747	│	│
Köln Messe/Deutz **802** a.	│	│	│	│	1414	│	│	│	...	1537	│	│	│	1614	│	│	│	1727	│	...	│	│	│	1814
Köln Hbf **802 807** a.	1305	1305	1339	1405	│	1432	1432	1505	...	│	1539	1539	1605	│	1639	1705	1705	│	1732	...	1739	1801	1805	│
Köln Hbf **802 807** d.	1310k	1314	...	1410	│	1443	1446	1510k	1544	│	...	...	1610	│	...	1710	1714	│	...	1744	1746	...	1810	│
Aachen Hbf **802 807** a.	│	│	...	│	│	1515	│	│	1620	│	...	...	│	│	...	│	│	│	...	1820	│	...	│	│
Brussels Midi/Zuid **21 400** a.	│	│	...	│	│	1635	│	│	1732	│	...	...	│	│	...	│	│	│	...	1932	│	...	│	│
Düsseldorf Hbf **800** a.	│	1335	...	1431	1437	...	1511	│	...	│	...	...	1631	1637	...	│	1736	1750	...	...	1811	...	│	1837
Amsterdam Centraal **28** ⊡ a.	│	│	...	│	│	...	1725	│	...	│	...	...	│	│	...	│	...	│	...	...	2025	...	│	│
Essen Hbf **800** a.	│	1406	...	1457	1502	...	...	│	...	│	...	...	1657	1702	...	│	...	1821	...	...	...	...	│	1902
Dortmund Hbf **800** a.	1420k	...	...	1521	...	...	...	1620k	...	1655	...	...	1721	...	...	1820	...	1846	...	...	...	...	1920	1929

	ICE 814 ①–⑤ a🍷	ICE 914 ①–⑤ a🍷	THA 9462 [R]P	ICE 104 ◧ 🍷	ICE 622 🍷	ICE 812 ⑧q 🍷	ICE 10 🍷	ICE 812 ⑧q 🍷	ICE 514 A🍷	ICE 1220 ⑦y H🍷	ICE 620 ①–⑤ d🍷	ICE 926 ⑥s 🍷	ICE 120 R 🍷	ICE 912 ①–③ m🍷	ICE 502 ⑧q H🍷	ICE 1002 ⑥k H🍷	ICE 528 G🍷	ICE 810 ⑧q 🍷	ICE 512 M🍷	ICE 526 ⑧q 🍷	ICE 500 🍷	ICE 524 🍷	ICE 1110 ⑦w 🍷	ICE 522 🍷
München Hbf **904 930** d.	...	...	...	...	1455	...	...	...	1523	1555	1555	1555	...	...	...	...	1650	...	1723	1755	...	1855	1923	1951
Stuttgart Hbf **930** d.	...	...	...	...	│	...	...	...	1751	│	│	│	...	...	...	...	│	...	1951	│	...	│	2151	│
Basel SBB **912** d.	...	...	...	1512	│	...	...	...	│	│	│	│	...	...	...	...	│	...	│	│	1912	│	│	│
Karlsruhe Hbf **912** d.	...	...	...	1700	│	...	...	...	│	│	│	│	...	...	1909	1909	│	...	│	│	2101	│	│	│
Mannheim Hbf **912** d.	...	...	...	1735	│	...	...	...	1835	│	│	│	...	...	1935	1935	│	...	2035	│	2135	│	2231	│
Nürnberg Hbf **920** d.	...	...	...	│	1600	...	...	...	│	1700	1700	1700	...	...	│	│	1800	...	│	1900	│	2000	│	2100
Frankfurt (Main) Hbf d.	1717	1717	...	│	1810	1816	1829	...	│	1910	1910	1910	1929	1929	│	│	2010	2016	│	2110	│	2210	│	2310
Frankfurt Flughafen Fernbf ✈ d.	1732	1732	...	1809	1824	1832	1843	...	1909	1924	1924	1924	1943	1943	2009	2009	2024	2032	2109	2124	2209	2224	2305	2329
Mainz Hbf d.	│	│	...	│	│	│	│	...	│	│	│	│	│	│	│	│	│	│	│	│	│	│	│	│
Wiesbaden Hbf d.	│	│	...	│	│	│	│	...	│	│	│	│	│	│	│	│	│	│	│	│	│	│	│	│
Limburg Süd d.	1751	1751	...	│	│	1851	│	←	│	│	1943	1944	│	│	│	│	│	2051	│	│	│	2243	│	2348
Montabaur d.	1802	1802	...	│	│	1900	│	1907	│	│	1954	1956	│	│	│	│	│	2102	│	│	│	2254	│	2359
Siegburg/Bonn 🚊 ⊖ **807** d.	1823j	1837j	...	1849	│	→	1923	1929	1949	│	2014	2018	│	│	2049	2049	│	2129	2149	│	2254	2320	2349	0025
Köln/Bonn Flughafen ✈ ⊖ **802** a.	│	│	...	│	│	...	│	1937	│	│	│	2026	│	│	│	│	│	2137	│	│	│	2328	│	│
Köln Messe/Deutz **802** a.	│	1849	...	│	1914	...	│	│	│	2014	│	│	│	│	│	│	2114	2148	│	│	│	2343	│	│
Köln Hbf **802 807** a.	1839	│	...	1905	│	...	1939	1956	2005	│	2030	2039	2039	2039	2105	2105	│	│	2205	2219	2309	│	0005	0039
Köln Hbf **802 807** d.	...	│	1911	1917n	│	...	1943	...	2010	│	...	2046	2046	2046	2110	2110	│	│	2210	2232	2314	│	...	0044
Aachen Hbf **802 807** a.	...	│	1951	│	│	...	2015	...	│	│	...	│	│	│	│	│	│	│	│	│	│	│	...	│
Brussels Midi/Zuid **21 400** a.	...	│	2103	│	│	...	2135	...	│	│	...	│	│	│	│	│	│	│	│	│	│	│	...	│
Düsseldorf Hbf **800** a.	...	1911	...	1938n	1942	...	...	...	2031	2037	...	2107	2111	2111	│	2131	2137	2209	2231	2254	2335	0005	...	0104
Amsterdam Centraal **28** ⊡ a.	...	│	...	2155n	│	...	...	...	│	│	...	│	2325	│	│	│	│	│	│	│	│	│	...	│
Essen Hbf **800** a.	...	1940	...	...	2008	...	...	...	2057	2102	...	2136	...	2136	│	2157	2202	2235	2257	2323	0005	0030	...	0134
Dortmund Hbf **800** a.	...	2003	...	...	2038	...	...	...	2121	2129	...	2159	...	2159	2220	2221	2228	2300	2321	2345	0028	0054	...	0157

A – To Hamburg (Table **800**).
D – From Darmstadt Hbf (d. 0637).
G – On ⑥ runs with train number **924** and starts from Garmisch (d. 1515).
H – To Hannover (Table **810**).
J – From Mar. 26.
L – ①②③④⑦ (not Dec. 23, 24, 30, 31, Apr. 1, 4, May 12, 23, June 2).
M – To Münster (a. 2357).
O – To Oberhausen (Table **800**).
P – [12] and 🍷 Köln - Liège - Brussels - Paris. Special fares payable.
R – ④⑤⑦ (also Dec. 23, Apr. 5, May 12, 24, June 2; not Dec. 24, 25, 31, Apr. 2, 4, May 23).
T – ①②③④⑥⑦ (also Dec. 25, Jan. 1, Apr. 2, May 14, June 4; not Dec. 23, 30, Apr. 1, May 12, June 2).
Y – ①–⑥ (not Dec. 25, Jan. 1, Apr. 5, May 1, 13, 24, June 3).

a – Not Dec. 24, 25, 31, Jan. 1, Apr. 2, 5, May 24.
b – ⑧ (not Dec. 24, 25, 31, Jan. 1, Apr. 2, 5, May 24). Basel **Badischer Bahnhof**.
c – ⑥⑦ (also Dec. 24, 25, 31, Jan. 1, Apr. 2).
d – Not Dec. 24, 25, 31, Apr. 2, 5, May 24.
e – ①–⑥ (not Dec. 25, 26, Jan. 1, Apr. 3, 5, May 24).
f – Also Dec. 23, 30, Apr. 1, May 12, June 2; not Dec. 25, Jan. 1, Apr. 2, May 14, June 4.
g – ① (also Apr. 6, May 25; not Apr. 5, May 24).

h – Also Dec. 25, Jan. 1, Apr. 5, May 1, 13, 24, June 3.
j – Arrives 1819.
k – ⑥ (also Dec. 24, 25, 31, Apr. 2, 4, May 23).
m – Not Dec. 23, Apr. 5, May 12, 24, June 2.
n – Not Dec. 24, 31.
q – Not Dec. 24, 25, 31, Apr. 2, 4, May 23.
r – ⑥ (also Dec. 24, 31, Apr. 2, 4, May 23).
s – Also Dec. 24, 25, 31, Apr. 2.
t – Not Dec. 24, Apr. 5, May 24. Terminates at Köln Hbf on May 13, June 3.
u – Also Dec. 23, 30, Apr. 1, May 12, June 2; not Dec. 25, Apr. 2.
v – ①–④ (not Dec. 23, 24, 30, 31, Apr. 1, 5, May 24).
w – Also Apr. 5, May 24; not Apr. 4, May 23.
y – Also Apr. 5, May 24.
z – Not Dec. 25, Jan. 1, Apr. 2.

◧ – Conveys [12] (*ICE* **504**) Basel - Köln.
⊡ – Amsterdam timings are subject to alteration on Apr. 30.
🚊 – Frequent light-rail services operate from / to Bonn Hbf. See page 419.
⊖ – For local connections Siegburg/Bonn - Köln/Bonn Flughafen see Tables **807** (Siegburg/Bonn - Troisdorf) and **802** (Troisdorf - Köln/Bonn Flughafen).

FRANKFURT - DARMSTADT - HEIDELBERG - KARLSRUHE 911

See Table **912** for *ICE* services via Mannheim. See Table **911a** for other local services.

km		*IC* 2099 ①–⑤ a	*IC* 2273 ①–⑥ e🍷	*EC* 113 F✕	*IC* 2271 ①–④ d	*IC* 2275 ⑤v	*IC* 2293 🍷	*IC* 2277 ⑥⑦ c🍷	*EC* 319 G🍷	*IC* 2279 🍷	*EC* 117 Ⓑq K🍷	*IC* 2299 ⑥y	*IC* 2371 N🍷	*EC* 391 L🍷	*IC* 2373 🍷	*IC* 2295 Ⓑq 🍷	*IC* 2375 Ⓑq 🍷	*IC* 2375 ①–⑤ a🍷	*IC* 1858 ⑦w R🍷	*IC* 2297 🍷	*IC* 2377 ⑦w 🍷	*IC* 2377 ⑤f 🍷	*IC* 2177 ①–④ b	*IC* 1897 ⑦w B🍷	*ICE* 775 ⑦w ✕
	Stralsund **830** d.	...	...	...	...	...	...	...	...	0527e	...	...	...	...	0927	...	...	...	...	...	1327	1327	...	...	...
	Hamburg Hbf **800 902** d.	...	...	...	...	...	...	0628k	...	0828e	...	...	1028	...	1228	...	1428	1428	...	...	1628	1628	...	...	1924
	Hannover Hbf **902** d.	...	...	...	0600	0600	...	0800k	...	1000e	...	...	1200	...	1400	...	1600	1600	...	...	1800	1800	...	1901	2041
	Kassel Wilhelmshöhe **806** d.	...	0502	...	0703	0703	...	0903	...	1103	...	...	1303	...	1503	...	1703	1703	...	...	1903	1903	...	2004	2138
0	**Frankfurt** (Main) Hbf d.	0520	0714	0820	0920	0920	1020	1120	1220	1320	1420	1420	1520	1620	1720	1820	1920	1920	1955	2020	2120	2154	2154	2158	2310
28	Darmstadt Hbf d.	0537	0731	0837	0937	0937	1037	1137	1237	1337	1437	1437	1537	1637	1737	1837	1937	1937	2012	2037	2137	2211	2211	2216	2326
50	Bensheim d.	0550	0745	0850	0950	0950	|	1150	1250	1350	1450	1450	1550	1650	1750	1850	1950	1950	2025	2050	2150	2223	2223	|	|
64	Weinheim (Bergstr) d.	0600	0758	0900	1000	1000	1056	1200	1300	1400	1500	1500	1600	1700	1800	1900	2000	2000	2036	2100	2200	2233	2233	2235	|
87	**Heidelberg** Hbf d.	0615	0814	0914	1014	1014	1110	1214	1314	1414	1514	1514	1614	1714	1814	1914	2012	2014	2052	2114	2214	2248	2248	2251	0004
120	Bruchsal **931** d.	|	0836	|	1036	|	|	1236	|	1436	|	|	1636	|	1836	|	...	2036	|	|	2236	2310	2310	|	|
	Stuttgart Hbf **930** a.	0700	|	0954	|	1112	1150	|	1354	|	1554	1554	|	1754	|	1954	...	|	2146	2154	|	|	|	2341	0044
	München Hbf **930** a.	...	|	1217	|	...	...	|	1617	|	1817	...	|	2017	|	2220	...	|	...	...	|	|	|	...	...
	Salzburg Hbf **890** a.	...	|	1409	|	...	...	|	1809	|	2009	...	|	2212	|	...	...	|	...	...	|	|	|	...	...
141	**Karlsruhe** Hbf **931** a.	...	0850	...	1050	...	...	1250	...	1450	...	...	1650	...	1850	...	...	2050	...	...	2251	2325	2325	...	...

	ICE 1092 ①–⑤ aB	*ICE* 824 ①–⑤ aD	*IC* 2278 Ⓐj	*IC* 2296 ①–⑥ e✕	*IC* 2376 ①–⑥ e🍷	*IC* 2294 ①–⑥ e🍷	*IC* 2374 ⊖ 🍷	*IC* 2290 ①–⑥ e🍷	*IC* 2290 ⑦p	*IC* 1853 ⑤ h	*IC* 2372 ⑥⑦ c🍷	*EC* 390 L🍷	*IC* 2370 J N🍷	*IC* 2270 ⑤⑦r N🍷	*EC* 318 G🍷	*IC* 2276 ①–⑥ x🍷	*IC* 2286 ⑦w S🍷	*IC* 2292 🍷	*IC* 2274 🍷	*EC* 112 F✕	*IC* 2272 ①–⑤ a🍷	*IC* 2172 ⑦w 🍷		*IC* 1876 ⑦w	*IC* 1874 ⑦w
Karlsruhe Hbf **931** d.	⚡✕	...	0615	...	0702	...	0910	...	...	1110	1110	...	1310	1310	...	1510	1510	...	1710	...	1910	...	...	...	...
Salzburg Hbf **890** d.	...	...	|	...	|	...	|	0545	...	|	|	0751e	|	|	0951	|	|	...	|	1351	|	...	...	...	...
München Hbf **930** d.	...	...	|	...	|	0516	|	0739	...	|	|	0940	|	|	1142	|	|	...	|	1541	|	...	...	...	...
Stuttgart Hbf **930** d.	...	...	|	0603	|	0805	|	1005	1005	|	|	1205	|	|	1405	|	|	1606	|	1805	|	1855	...	2009	...
Bruchsal **931** d.	...	...	0633	|	0724	|	0923	|	|	1123	1123	|	1323	1323	|	1523	1523	|	1723	|	1923	|	...	|	...
Heidelberg Hbf d.	...	...	0654	0658	0746	0846	0946	1046	1046	1146	1146	1246	1346	1346	1446	1546	1546	1646	1746	1846	1946	1946	...	2050	2124
Weinheim (Bergstr) d.	...	...	|	0714	0800	0900	1000	1100	1100	1200	1200	1300	1400	1400	1500	1600	1600	1700	1800	1900	2000	2000	...	2104	2139
Bensheim d.	...	...	m	0728	0810	0910	1010	1110	1110	1210	1210	1310	1410	1410	1510	1610	1610	1710	1810	1910	2010	2010	...	2115	2150
Darmstadt Hbf d.	0543	0637	|	0742	0824	0924	1024	1124	1124	1224	1224	1324	1424	1424	1524	1624	1624	1724	1824	1924	2024	2024	...	2127	2202
Frankfurt (Main) Hbf a.	0600	0656	0752	0800	0840	0940	1040	1140	1146	1240	1240	1340	1440	1440	1540	1640	1640	1740	1840	1940	2040	2040	...	2144	2218
Kassel Wilhelmshöhe **806** a.	...	...	...	...	1053	...	1253	...	...	...	1453	...	1653	1653	...	1855	1855	...	2053	...	2253	2253	...	...	0026
Hannover Hbf **902** a.	...	...	...	...	1156	...	1356	...	...	...	1556	...	1756	1756	...	1957	1957	...	2156r	...	...	...	...	...	...
Hamburg Hbf **902** a.	...	...	...	...	1328	...	1529	...	...	...	1730	...	1927	1927	...	2128	2128	...	2326w	...	...	...	...	...	...
Stralsund **930** a.	...	...	...	...	1630	...	...	...	...	...	2032	...	...	2230	...	...	...	...	...	...	...	...	...	...	...

B – To / from Berlin (Table **900**).
D – [12] and 🍷 Darmstadt - Köln Messe/Deutz - Dortmund.
F – [12] and ✕ Klagenfurt - Villach - Frankfurt - Siegen and v.v.; [12] Zagreb (**212/3**) - Ljubljana - Villach - Frankfurt - Siegen and v.v.
G – [12] and 🍷 Graz - Salzburg - Frankfurt and v.v.
J – ①②③④⑥ (also Dec. 25, Jan. 1, Apr. 2, 4, May 14, 23; not Dec. 23, 30, Apr. 1, 5, May 12, 24).
K – To Klagenfurt (Table **970**).
L – From / to Linz on dates in Table **950**.
N – From / to Konstanz (Table **916**).
R – From Leipzig (Table **850**).
S – To Rostock (Table **830**).

a – Not Dec. 24, 25, 31, Jan. 1, Apr. 2, 5, May 24).
b – Not Dec. 23, 24, 30, 31, Apr. 1, 5, May 12, 13, 24, June 2, 3.
c – Also Apr. 5, May 24; not Apr. 4, May 23.
d – Not Dec. 23, 24, 30, 31, Apr. 1, 5, May 12, 24.
e – ①–⑥ (not Dec. 25, 26, Jan. 1, Apr. 3, 5, May 24).
f – Not Dec. 25, Apr. 2.
h – Also Dec. 23, 30, Apr. 1; not Dec. 25, Jan. 1, Apr. 2. To Halle (Table **850**).
j – Not Dec. 24, 31, May 14, June 3, 4.
k – ⑥ (not Dec. 26, Apr. 3, 5, May 24).
m – Via Mannheim (Table **912**).
p – Also Dec. 25, 26, Jan. 1, Apr. 3, 5, May 24.
q – Not Dec. 24, 25, 31, Apr. 2, 4, May 23.

r – ⑤⑦ (also Dec. 23, 30, Apr. 1, 5, May 12, 24; not Dec. 25, Jan. 1, Apr. 2, 4, May 14, 23).
v – Also Dec. 23, 30, Apr. 1, May 12; not Dec. 25, Jan. 1, Apr. 2, May 14.
w – ⑦ (also Apr. 5, May 24; not Apr. 4, May 23).
x – Also Apr. 4, May 23; not Apr. 5, May 24.
y – Also Dec. 24, 25, 31, Apr. 2, 4, May 23.

⊖ – Train number **2174** on ⑤ (also Dec. 23, 30, Apr. 1, May 12; not Dec. 25, Jan. 1, Apr. 2, May 14).
⚡ – *ICE SPRINTER*. Ⓡ and supplement payable.

RE / RB services Local services FRANKFURT and MAINZ - MANNHEIM - HEIDELBERG - KARLSRUHE 911a

Frankfurt - Darmstadt - Heidelberg and Mannheim

	Ⓐe	Ⓐe		Ⓐe	⑦	①–⑥		Ⓐe	⑥⑦	①–⑤					Ⓐe	⑥	Ⓑ	Ⓒz	Ⓐe	A	⑦w			
Frankfurt (Main) Hbf **911/2** d.	...	0506	0606	0630	0706	0706	0806	0834	0906	0906	1006	and hourly until	1706	1806	1833	1906	1906	2006	2034	2106	2106	2206	2306	0006
Darmstadt Hbf **911** d.	0426	0530	0634	0651	0730	0734	0830	0853	0930	0930	1030		1730	1830	1853	1930	1930	2030	2053	2130	2130	2230	2330	0030
Bensheim **911** d.	0452	0557	0659	0707	0755	0757	0859	0909	0955	0959	1059		1759	1859j	1909	1955	1959	2059	2109	2155	2159	2255	2354	0055
Weinheim (Bergstr) **911** d.	0508	0610	0714	0721	0810	0811	0914	0922	1010	1014	1114		1814	1914	1922	2010	2014	2114	2122	2210	2214	2310	0010	0110
Mannheim Friedrichsfeld a.	0521	0622	0727	0732	0823	0823	0927	|	1023	1027	1127		1827	1927	|	2023	2027	2127	2131	2223	2227	2323	0023	0123
Mannheim Hbf **912** a.	*0545*	*0644*	*0743*z	0742	*0842*	*0842*	*0942*	0940	*1042*	*1042*	*1142*		*1842*	*1942*	1940	*2042*	*2042*	*2142*	*2142*	*2242*	*2242*	*2343*	|	0138
Heidelberg Hbf **911** a.	0532	0632	0737	...	0835	0833	0939	...	1035	1039	1139		1839	1939	...	2035	2039	2139	2141	2235	2239	2335	0035	...

	Ⓐe		Ⓐe		Ⓒz	Ⓐe		Ⓐe						Ⓐe			Ⓐe				A	⑦w		
Heidelberg Hbf **911** d.	0424	0525	...	0625	...	...	0724	...	0821	0921	and hourly until	1421	1525	...	1621	1724	...	1821	1921	2021	2124	2131	2221	2324
Mannheim Hbf **912** d.	|	*0516*	0602	*0612*	0716	0720	|	0820	*0816*	*0916*		*1416*	*1516*	1620	*1616*	*1716*	1820	*1816*	*1916*	*2016*	*2116*	*2116*	*2216*	*2316*
Mannheim Friedrichsfeld d.	0434	0534	|	0634	0726	0731	0735	|	0832	0932		1432	1535	|	1632	1734	|	1832	1932	2032	2135	2140	2232	2335
Weinheim (Bergstr) **911** d.	0448	0548	0620	0648	...	...	0745	0839	0845	0945		1445	1545	1639	1645	1745	1839	1845	1945	2045	2149	2150	2245	2349
Bensheim **911** d.	0503	0603	0636	0703	...	...	0800	0852	0900	1000		1500	1600	1652	1700	1800	1852	1900	2000	2100	2204	2205	2300	0004
Darmstadt Hbf **911** d.	0531	0630	0658	0730	...	...	0830	0907	0930	1030		1530	1630	1707	1730	1830	1907	1930	2030	2130	2230	2230	2330	0030
Frankfurt (Main) Hbf **911/2** a.	0550	0648	0716	0748	...	...	0848	0924	0948	1048		1548	1648	1724	1748	1848	1924	1948	2048	2148	2248	2248	2348	0048

Mainz - Worms - Mannheim

km		v		Ⓐe	⚒r	eG		⚒r		⚒r		eK				K			eK			eK			Ⓐe	zK
0	**Mainz** Hbf **912** d.	0023	...	0456	0515	0545	0552b	0621	0656	0722	0752	0813	0819e	0851	0952	1013	1051	1152	1213	1252	1351	1413	1451	1552	1613	1613
46	Worms Hbf a.	0105	...	0540	0555	0614	0633b	0706	0740	0805	0835	0839	0903e	0935	1035	1039	1135	1235	1239	1335	1435	1439	1535	1635	1639	1639
46	Worms Hbf d.	...	...	0541	0556	0615	0635	0712	0746	0818	0848	0840	0916	0948	1048	1040	1148	1249	1240	1348	1448	1440	1548	1648	1640	1640
67	Ludwigshafen Hbf a.	...	...	0557	0615	0632	0652	0730	0803	0834	0908	0855	0936	1008	1108	1055	1208	1308	1255	1408	1508	1455	1608	1708	1654	1655
70	**Mannheim** Hbf **912** a.	...	...	0603	0621	...	0658	0737	0811	0841	0914	...	0942	1014	1114	...	1214	1314	...	1414	1514	...	1614	1714	1700	...

	Ⓐe		eG		K		Ⓐe		bK	n	n	n
Mainz Hbf **912** d.	1628	1651	1719	1752	1813	1851	1922	1951	2013	2051	2152	2317
Worms Hbf a.	1716	1735	1745	1835	1839	1935	2005	2035	2039	2135	2240	0000
Worms Hbf d.	1717	1749	1746	1848	1840	1948	2018	2048	2040	2148	2241	0001
Ludwigshafen Hbf a.	1736	1808	1800	1908	1855	2008	2039	2108	2056	2208	2301	0017
Mannheim Hbf **912** a.	1742	1814	...	1914	...	2014	2046	2114	...	2214	2307	0024

	v	⚒r	⚒r	Ⓐe	⑥m	Ⓐe		⚒r	eG	
Mannheim Hbf **912** d.	0011	...	0427	0500	0527	0534	0550e	0618	...	0650
Ludwigshafen Hbf d.	0017	...	0436	0505	0533	0543	0558e	0624	0655	0659
Worms Hbf a.	0039	...	0454	0523	0551	0601	0615e	0644	0712	0718
Worms Hbf d.	...	0417	0455	0525	0553	0602	0620	0653	0713	0724
Mainz Hbf **912** a.	...	0504	0538	0608	0637	0639	0706	0736	0747	0807

	eG	Ⓒz	Ⓐe		eK	Ⓐe			K			eK			eK			K			K		n	eK	n	n
Mannheim Hbf **912** d.	...	0744	0748	0844	...	0916	0944	1044	...	1144	1244	...	1344	1444	...	1544	1644	...	1744	1844	...	1944	2044	...	2144	2248
Ludwigshafen Hbf d.	0750	0750	0755	0850	0904	0921	0950	1050	1104	1150	1250	1304	1350	1450	1504	1550	1650	1704	1750	1850	1904	1950	2050	2105	2150	2253
Worms Hbf a.	0804	0816	0816	0914	0919	0937	1014	1114	1119	1214	1311	1319	1414	1514	1519	1614	1714	1719	1814	1914	1919	2014	2114	2119	2214	2312
Worms Hbf d.	0805	0825	0825	0925	0920	0955	1025	1125	1120	1225	1324	1320	1425	1525	1520	1625	1725	1720	1825	1925	1920	2025	2125	2120	2223	2315
Mainz Hbf **912** a.	0836	0908	0908	1008	0947	1038	1108	1208	1147	1308	1408	1347	1508	1608	1547	1708	1808	1747	1908	2008	1947	2108	2208	2147	2306	0003

Mannheim - Heidelberg - Karlsruhe

S-Bahn	v	Ⓒy	Ⓐd					⊙			
Mannheim Hbf d.	0005	0535x	0544	0637t	0729h	0829	0929	and hourly until	2029	2137	2237
Heidelberg Hbf d.	0022	0558	0603	0707	0748	0848	0948		2048	2155	2255
Bruchsal d.	0048	0625	0630	0733	0817	0915	1015		2115	2221	2321
Karlsruhe Hbf a.	0106	0643	0648	0750	0832	0936	1032		2132	2235	2335

S-Bahn		Ⓒz	Ⓐe								
Karlsruhe Hbf d.	0534	0615	0620	0728f	0828	and hourly until	1928	2030	2128	2228	2328
Bruchsal d.	0558	0633	0638	0744	0844		1944	2044	2144	2244	2344
Heidelberg Hbf d.	0634	0700	0713	0813	0913		2013	2114	2214	2314	0014
Mannheim Hbf a.	0651	*0719*	0728	0829	0929		2029	2132	2232	2332	0030

A – ①–⑥ (not Apr. 5, May 24).
G – To / from Gemersheim (Table **918**).
K – To / from Karlsruhe via Germersheim (Table **918**).
b – Ⓑ (also Dec. 26, May 1; not Dec. 24, 31).
d – Not Dec. 24, 31, Jan. 6, June 3.

e – Ⓐ (not Dec. 24, 31, June 3).
f – 0726 on † (also Jan. 6, June 3).
h – Change trains at Heidelberg on Ⓒ**z**.
j – 1855 on ⑥.
m – Also Dec. 24, 31; not Dec. 26, May 1.

n – Not Dec. 24, 31.
r – Not June 3.
t – 0647 on Ⓐ**d**.
v – Not Dec. 25, Jan. 1.
w – Also Apr. 5, May 24.

x – *0537* on ⑥**m** (change trains at Heidelberg).
y – Also Dec. 24, 31, Jan. 6, June 3.
z – Ⓒ (also Dec. 24, 31, June 3).
⊙ – Karlsruhe a. 1336 (not 1332).

912 (KÖLN -) KOBLENZ - FRANKFURT - KARLSRUHE - BASEL

km	km		*ICE* 609	*CNL* 40419	*CNL* 479	*CNL* 458	*CNL* 1258	*IC* 60458	*IC* 60458	*ICE* 371	*ICE* 799	*ICE* 672	*ICE* 991	*ICE* 5	*ICE* 5	*IC* 2021	*ICE* 511	*ICE* 271	*CNL* 473	*ICE* 23	*ICE* 711	*IC* 2273	*ICE* 501	*IC* 2319	*ICE* 1597
				[R]	[R]	[R] ◧	[R] ◧	①–⑤	⑥⑦	①–⑤	⑥ p		①–⑤	①–⑥					[R]		①–⑤	①–⑥		①–⑥	
			✕ K	🍷♦	✕♦	🍷♦	✕♦	o 2	c 2	a B ✕	M ✕	♦	a M ✕	e Z ✕	Z ✕	♥	M 🍷	J ✕	🍷♦	Q ✕	a	e F 🍷	🍷	e	⊕
		Berlin Hbf **810** d.	...	...	...	...	2222	...	...		...	...			...	...	...	...	...	...	...		...	...	...
		Hamburg Hbf **800 900** d.	1946	...	1918y	...	|	...	...	...	...	...	...	0025g	...	2246	...	...	0031	...	...	...	...	...	...
		Dortmund Hbf **800** d.	2237	...	|	...	|	...	...	...	...	...	...	|	...	0152	0437g	...	|	0437v	0502	...	0537	0537	...
0		*Köln Hbf* **800 910** d.	2353	2346	|	...	|	...	...	...	...	...	...	|	...	0353	0555	...	|	0553	0615d	...	0655	0653	...
93		**Koblenz** Hbf **914** d.	0048	0043	|	...	|	...	...	...	...	...	...	|	...	0531	|	...	|	0648	|	...	|	0748	...
154		Bingen (Rhein) Hbf **914** d.	0123	|	|	...	|	...	...	...	...	...	...	|	...	0609	|	...	|	|	|	...	|	|	...
		Wiesbaden Hbf d.	|	|	|	...	|	...	...	...	0445	0500	0522	|	...	|	|	...	|	|	0732	...	|	|	...
184		**Mainz** Hbf **914** a.	0141	|	|	...	|	...	...	...	0454	0509	0536	|	...	0626	|	...	|	0738	0744	...	|	0837	...
184		**Mainz** Hbf ‡ d.	0143	|	|	...	|	...	...	...	0456	0511	0540	|	...	0628	|	...	|	0740	0746	...	|	0839	0842
	0	**Frankfurt** (Main) Hbf **930** ‡ d.	|	|	|	...	|	0402§	0402§	...	|	|	|	0538	...	|	|	0650	|	|	|	0714	|	|	|
210		**Frankfurt** Flughafen ¶ **930** ‡ a.	0202r	|	|	...	|	|	|	...	0516	0537	|	0550	...	0645	0651	|	|	0759	|	|	0751	|	0859
210		**Frankfurt** Flughafen ¶ **930** ‡ d.	0205r	|	|	...	|	|	|	...	0539	0539	|	0555	...	0648	0654	|	|	0802	|	|	0754	|	0901
221		**Frankfurt** (Main) Hbf ‡ a.	0217	|	|	...	|	|	|	...	|	0550	|	|	...	0702	|	|	|	0813	|	◐	|	|	0913
	78	**Mannheim** Hbf **930** ‡ a.	0300	|	|	0443s	0443s	0443	0443	...	0611	...	0622	0625	...	...	0724	0728	0750s	...	0824	|	0824	0921	...
	78	**Mannheim** Hbf **930** ‡ d.	0302	|	|	|	|	0445	0445	...	0613	...	0630	0627	...	...	0732	0736	|	...	0826	|	0836	0923	...
		Heidelberg Hbf **930** ‡ d.	|	|	|	0458s	0458s	0500	0500	...	|	...	|	|	...	...	|	|	|	...	0838	0814	|	0936	...
		Stuttgart Hbf **930** a.	|	|	|	|	|	|	|	...	0652	...	0708	|	...	...	0808	|	|	...	0923	|	|	1018	...
	138	**Karlsruhe** Hbf **916** ‡ d.	0347	0437s	0437s	0540s	0540s	0542	0551	0556	...	...	...	0656	0656	...	...	0800	0818s	...	...	0850	0900	...	...
	169	Baden-Baden **916** d.	0406	|	|	|	|	|	0609	0612	...	...	...	0714	0714	...	...	|	|	...	...	...	0917	...	...
	209	Offenburg **916** ★ d.	0422	0519s	0519s	0620s	0620s	0622	0629	0629	...	...	...	0730	0730	...	...	0829	0901s	...	...	...	|	...	...
	272	**Freiburg** (Brsg) Hbf ★ d.	0452	0556s	0556s	0653s	0653s	0655	0702	0702	...	...	...	0802	0802	...	...	0901	0939s	...	...	...	1002	...	...
	333	**Basel** Bad. Bf 🏛 ★ a.	0537	0644	0644	0746	0746	0746	0737	0737	...	...	...	0837	0837	...	...	0936	1027	...	...	...	1037	...	...
	338	**Basel** SBB a.	0547	0654	0654	0755	0755	0755	0747	0747	...	...	...	0847	0847	...	...	0947	1037	...	...	...	1047	...	...

	ICE 1597	*ICE* 373	*IC* 2271	*ICE* 503	*IC* 2102	*ICE* 25	*ICE* 71	*EC* 115	*EC* 7	*ICE* 1559	*ICE* 291	*ICE* 375	*IC* 119	*IC* 2277	*ICE* 105	*ICE* 27	*ICE* 73	*IC* 2005	*IC* 2007	*IC* 2015	*EC* 101	*ICE* 1651	*ICE* 871	*IC* 2013	*IC* 2279
	⑦ h		①–④								⑦ t	e		⑥⑦				⑤⑥		①–④					
	D 🍷	B ✕	♦	H 🍷	N 🍷	Q ✕	✕	✕♦	C ✕	D ✕	B ✕	B ✕	🍷♦	w ♦	🍷♦	Q ✕	✕♦	🍷♦	🍷♦	❖ E 🍷	C ✕	D ✕	✕	🍷♦	L 🍷
Berlin Hbf **810** d.	...	0432a	...	...	...	...	...	...	...	...	0549	0632	...	...	...	...	...	...	...		...	...	0832	...	...
Hamburg Hbf **800 900** d.	...	|	...	...	...	...	0618	...	0442e	...	|	|	...	0628	...	...	0824	...	...	...	0646	...	|	...	0828e
Dortmund Hbf **800** d.	...	|	...	0737	...	0636	|	...	0737	...	|	|	...	|	...	0837	|	...	0852	...	0937	...	|	0952	|
Köln Hbf **800 910** d.	...	|	...	0855	...	0753	|	0818	0853	...	|	|	0918	|	1055	0953	|	1018	1018	1018	1053	...	|	1118	|
Koblenz Hbf **914** d.	...	|	...	|	...	0848	|	0917	0948	...	◇	|	1017	|	|	1048	|	1117	1117	1117	1148	...	|	1217	|
Bingen (Rhein) Hbf **914** d.	...	|	...	|	...	|	|	0952	|	...	|	|	1052	|	|	|	|	|	|	|	|	...	|	1252	|
Wiesbaden Hbf d.	0824	|	...	|	...	|	|	|	|	1024	|	|	|	|	|	|	|	|	|	|	|	1224	|	|	|
Mainz Hbf **914** a.	0835	|	...	|	...	0938	|	1013	1037	1035	|	|	1111	|	|	1138	|	1212	1212	1212	1237	1235	|	1311	|
Mainz Hbf ‡ d.	0842	|	...	|	...	0940	|	1015	1039	1042	|	|	1113	|	|	1140	|	1217	1217	1217	1239	1242	|	1313	|
Frankfurt (Main) Hbf **930** ‡ d.	|	0850	0920	|	...	|	1005	|	|	|	1050	1050	|	1120	|	|	1205	|	|	|	|	|	1250	|	1320
Frankfurt Flughafen ¶. **930** ‡ a.	0859	|	|	0951	...	0959	|	|	|	1059	|	|	|	|	1151	1159	|	|	|	|	|	1259	|	|	|
Frankfurt Flughafen ¶. **930** ‡ d.	0901	|	|	0954	...	1002	|	|	|	1102	|	|	|	|	1154	1202	|	|	|	|	|	1302	|	|	|
Frankfurt (Main) Hbf ‡ a.	0913	|	◐	|	...	1013	|	|	|	1113	|	|	|	◐	|	1213	|	|	|	|	|	1313	|	|	◐
Mannheim Hbf **930** ‡ a.	...	0928	|	1024	...	...	1042	1101	1121	...	1128	1128	1152	|	1224	...	1242	1307	1307	1307	1321	...	1328	1352	|
Mannheim Hbf **930** ‡ d.	...	0936	|	1026	...	...	1044	1103	1123	...	1136	1136	1154	|	1236	...	1244	1309	1309	1312	1323	...	1336	1354	|
Heidelberg Hbf **930** ‡ d.	...	|	1014	|	...	...	|	|	|	...	|	|	1206	1214	|	...	|	|	|	|	|	...	|	1406	1414
Stuttgart Hbf **930** a.	...	|	|	|	...	...	|	1153	|	...	|	|	1246	|	|	...	|	|	|	1358	|	...	|	1446	|
Karlsruhe Hbf **916** ‡ d.	...	1000	1050	1050	1100	...	1108	...	1149	...	1200	1200	...	1250	1300	...	1308	1336	1336	...	1349	...	1400	...	1450
Baden-Baden **916** d.	...	|	...	...	|	...	1126	...	1207	...	|	|	...	...	|	...	1326	1356	1356	...	1407	...	|	...	...
Offenburg **916** ★ d.	...	1029	...	...	1129	...	|	...	|	...	1229	1229	...	...	1330	...	|	1415	1415	...	|	...	1429	...	...
Freiburg (Brsg) Hbf ★ d.	...	1101	...	...	1201	...	1211	...	1255	...	1301	1301	...	...	1401	...	1411	...	...	...	1455	...	1501	...	...
Basel Bad. Bf 🏛 ★ a.	...	1136	...	...	1236	...	1247	...	1329	...	1336	1336	...	...	1436	...	1447	...	...	...	1529	...	1536	...	...
Basel SBB a.	...	1147	...	...	1247	...	1255	...	1337	...	1347	1347	...	...	1447	...	1455	...	...	...	1537	...	1547	...	...

	ICE 507	*IC* 2100	*IC* 2023	*ICE* 75	*IC* 2113	*ICE* 1653	*ICE* 277	*IC* 1911	*IC* 2371	*ICE* 509	*IC* 2025	*ICE* 77	*IC* 2115	*ICE* 1655	*ICE* 279	*IC* 2011	*IC* 2011	*IC* 2246	*ICE* 601	*IC* 2373	*IC* 2104	*IC* 2027	*ICE* 79	*IC* 2311	*ICE* 1657
								⑤⑦						n		R	⑦ w	⑤							
	🍷	N 🍷	🍷	Z ✕	✕	D ✕	B ✕	x	Y 🍷	🍷		Z ✕	L ✕	✕♦	B ✕	🍷	🍷	🍷♦	🍷	L 🍷	N 🍷	✕♦	Z ✕	G ✕	✕♦
Berlin Hbf **810** d.	...	...	...	...	...	...	1032	...	...	...	...	...	...	...	1232	...	1008	...	...	...	...	...	...	...	...
Hamburg Hbf **800 900** d.	...	...	0746	1024	0846	...	|	...	1028	...	0946	1224	1046	...	|	...	|	...	...	1228	...	1146	1424	1246	...
Dortmund Hbf **800** d.	1137h	...	1036	|	1137	...	|	1152	|	1337a	1236	|	1337	...	|	...	1352	1352	...	|	...	1436	|	1537	...
Köln Hbf **800 910** d.	1255	...	1153	|	1253	...	|	1318	|	1455	1353	|	1453	...	|	1518	1518	1518	1655	|	...	1553	|	1653	...
Koblenz Hbf **914** d.	|	...	1248	|	1348	...	|	1417	|	|	1448	|	1548	...	|	1617	1617	1617	|	|	...	1648	|	1748	...
Bingen (Rhein) Hbf **914** d.	|	...	|	|	|	...	|	1452	|	|	|	|	|	...	|	1652	1652	1652	|	|	...	|	|	|	...
Wiesbaden Hbf d.	|	...	|	|	|	1424	|	|	|	|	|	|	|	1624	|	|	|	|	|	|	...	|	|	|	1824
Mainz Hbf **914** a.	|	...	1338	|	1437	1435	|	1511	|	|	1538	|	1637	1635	|	1711	1711	1711	|	|	...	1738	|	1837	1835
Mainz Hbf ‡ d.	|	...	1340	|	1439	1442	|	1513	|	|	1540	|	1638	1642	|	1713	1713	1713	|	|	...	1740	|	1839	1842
Frankfurt (Main) Hbf **930** ‡ d.	|	...	|	1405	|	|	1450	|	1520	|	|	1605	|	|	1650	|	|	|	|	1720	...	|	1805	|	|
Frankfurt Flughafen ¶. **930** ‡ a.	1351	...	1359	|	|	1500	|	|	|	1551	1559	|	|	1700	|	|	|	|	1751	|	...	1759	|	|	1859
Frankfurt Flughafen ¶. **930** ‡ d.	1354	...	1401	|	|	1503	|	|	|	1554	1602	|	|	1703	|	|	|	|	1754	|	...	1802	|	|	1902
Frankfurt (Main) Hbf ‡ a.	|	...	1412	|	|	1515	|	|	◐	|	1613	|	|	1715	|	|	|	|	|	◐	...	1813	|	|	1913
Mannheim Hbf **930** ‡ a.	1424	...	...	1442	1521	...	1528	1552	|	1624	...	1642	1721	...	1728	1752	1752	1752	1824	|	...	...	1842	1921	...
Mannheim Hbf **930** ‡ d.	1426	...	...	1444	1523	...	1536	1554	|	1636	...	1644	1723	...	1736	1754	1754	1754	1826	|	...	...	1844	1923	...
Heidelberg Hbf **930** ‡ d.	|	...	...	|	1536	...	|	1606	1614	|	...	|	1736	...	|	1806	1806	1806	|	1814	...	...	|	1936	...
Stuttgart Hbf **930** a.	|	...	...	|	1622	...	|	1646	|	|	...	|	1825	...	|	1846	1846	1846	|	|	...	...	|	2023	...
Karlsruhe Hbf **916** ‡ d.	1450	1500	...	1508	...	...	1600	...	1652	1700	...	1708	...	...	1800	...	...	...	1850	1850	1900	...	1908	...	...
Baden-Baden **916** d.	...	|	...	1526	...	...	|	...	1717	|	...	1726	...	...	|	...	...	...	...	...	|	...	1926	...	...
Offenburg **916** ★ d.	...	1529	...	|	...	...	1629	...	1733	1729	...	|	...	...	1829	...	...	...	...	...	1929	...	|	...	...
Freiburg (Brsg) Hbf ★ d.	...	1601	...	1611	...	...	1701	...	...	1801	...	1811	...	...	1901	...	...	...	...	...	2001	...	2011	...	...
Basel Bad. Bf 🏛 ★ a.	...	1636	...	1647	...	...	1736	...	...	1836	...	1847	...	...	1936	...	...	...	...	...	2036	...	2047	...	...
Basel SBB a.	...	1647	...	1655	...	...	1747	...	...	1847	...	1855	...	...	1947	...	...	...	...	...	2047	...	2055	...	...

♦ – **NOTES** (LISTED BY TRAIN NUMBER) for pages 420 and 421

73/4/6 – (12) and ✕ Kiel - Hamburg - Basel - Zürich and v.v.

105 – ICE INTERNATIONAL – (12) and 🍷 Amsterdam - Utrecht - Arnhem - Köln - Basel (starts from Köln on Dec. 25, Jan. 1); conveys (12) (*ICE* **505**) Köln - Basel.

115 – WÖRTHERSEE – (12) and ✕ Münster - München - Salzburg - Villach - Klagenfurt.

119 – (12) and 🍷 Münster - Stuttgart - Ulm - Lindau - Bregenz - Innsbruck.

360/1 – (12) and 🍷 (München ♣ -) Ulm - Stuttgart - Strasbourg and v.v.

458 – CANOPUS – 🛏 1, 2 cl., ▬ 2 cl., (2) and 🍷 Praha - Dresden - Leipzig - Zürich.

473 – AURORA – 🛏 1, 2 cl. and ▬ 2 cl. København - Basel (Hamburg d. 0011 on ⑦ from Apr. 18); 🛏 1, 2 cl. Warszawa - Basel; 🛏 1, 2 cl. Moskva / Minsk - Basel (Table **24**).

479 – ④–⑦ (daily from Mar. 25). KOMET – 🛏 1, 2 cl., ▬ 2 cl., (2) (reclining) and ✕ Hamburg - Hannover - Zürich (Hamburg - Zürich - Brig on ⑤ Dec. 25 - Apr. 9).

672 – (12) Wiesbaden - Frankfurt - Hamburg; ✕ Frankfurt - Hamburg.

1025 – ①②③④⑥⑦ (also Dec. 25, Apr. 2, May 28, June 4; not Dec. 23, 30, Apr. 1). (12) and ✕ Kiel - Köln - Nürnberg - München.

1026 – ②–⑥ to May 21 and from June 8 (not Dec. 25, 26, Jan. 1, Apr. 3, 6, May 13). (12) and ✕ Regensburg - Nürnberg - Frankfurt - Köln - Kiel.

1125 – ⑤ (also Dec. 23, 30, Apr. 1; not Dec. 25, Apr. 2, May 28, June 4). (12) and ✕ Kiel - Köln - Frankfurt - Nürnberg - Regensburg.

1126 – ①⑦ (also Dec. 25, 26, Jan. 1, Apr. 3, 6, May 13; daily May 22 - June 7). (12) and ✕ (München - Nürnberg on dates in Table **920** -) Frankfurt - Köln - Kiel.

1258 – SIRIUS – 🛏 1, 2 cl., ▬ 2 cl., (2) (reclining) and ✕ Berlin - Halle - Erfurt - Zürich.

1654 – (12) and ✕ Berlin - Leipzig - Frankfurt - Wiesbaden.

1655 – (12) and ✕ Wiesbaden - Frankfurt (- Leipzig - Berlin ⑧ **q**).

1656 – (12) and ✕ Leipzig - Frankfurt - Wiesbaden.

1657 – (12) and ✕ Wiesbaden - Frankfurt (- Leipzig ⑧ **q**) (- Dresden ⊡).

1659 – (12) and ✕ Wiesbaden - Frankfurt (- Erfurt ⑧ **q**) (- Leipzig ⊡).

1853 – ⑤ (also Dec. 23, 30, Apr. 1; not Dec. 25, Jan. 1, Apr. 2). (12) Karlsruhe - Halle.

1915 – ⑤⑦ (also Dec. 23, 30, Apr. 1, 5, May 24; not Dec. 25, Jan. 1, Apr. 2, 4, May 14, 23). (12) and 🍷 Berlin - Düsseldorf - Stuttgart (- Tübingen ⑦ **w**, a. 2150).

2004 – ⑦ (also Jan. 1, Apr. 5, May 13, 24, June 3; not Apr. 4, May 23). BODENSEE – (12) and 🍷 Konstanz - Karlsruhe - Münster - Emden.

2005 – ⑤⑥ (also Dec. 23, 24, 30, 31, Apr. 1, May 12, June 2; not Dec. 25, 26, Jan. 1, Apr. 3). BODENSEE – (12) and 🍷 Emden - Münster - Karlsruhe - Konstanz.

2006 – ⑥ (also Dec. 24, 25, 31, Apr. 2, 4, May 23). BODENSEE – (12) and 🍷 Konstanz - Karlsruhe - Dortmund.

2007 – Runs on Dec. 25, 26, Jan. 1, Apr. 3, 4, May 23 only. BODENSEE – (12) and 🍷 Dortmund - Karlsruhe - Konstanz.

2012/3 – ALLGÄU – (12) and 🍷 Oberstdorf - Ulm - Stuttgart - Köln - Dortmund - Hannover and v.v. To / from Magdeburg and Leipzig on dates in Table **810**.

2024 – (12) and ✕ Passau - Regensburg - Nürnberg - Frankfurt - Hamburg.

2027 – (12) and ✕ Hamburg - Köln - Frankfurt - Nürnberg - Passau. Train number **2327** on ⑤ (also Dec. 23, 30, Apr. 1, May 12, June 12; not Dec. 25, Jan. 1, Apr. 2, May 14).

2028/9 – (12) and 🍷 Nürnberg - Frankfurt - Köln - Hamburg and v.v.

2120/1 – (12) and ✕ Frankfurt - Köln - Hamburg (- Puttgarden from Mar. 27) and v.v. Train number **2320/1** until Mar. 26.

2246 – ⑤ (also Dec. 23, 30, Apr. 1, May 12; not Dec. 25, Jan. 1, Apr. 2, May 14). (12) and 🍷 Leipzig - Magdeburg - Hannover - Köln - Stuttgart - München.

2271 – ①–④ (not Dec. 23, 24, 30, 31, Apr. 1, 5, May 12, 24). (12) Hannover - Kassel - Gießen - Karlsruhe.

2277 – (12) and 🍷 (Hamburg ⊠ -) Kassel - Karlsruhe.

40419 – ①⑤⑥⑦ (daily fom Mar. 26). PEGASUS – 🛏 1, 2 cl., ▬ 2 cl. and (2) (reclining) Amsterdam - Zürich (Amsterdam - Zürich - Brig on ⑤ Dec. 25 - Apr. 9).

NOTES CONTINUED ON NEXT PAGE →

 See Table ***910*** *for other Köln - Frankfurt ICE services via the high-speed line*

(KÖLN -) KOBLENZ - FRANKFURT - KARLSRUHE - BASEL 912

	ICE 873	EC 360	IC 1915	IC 2375	ICE 603	ICE 603	ICE 1025	ICE 1125	ICE 671	ICE 671	ICE 603	IC 2213	ICE 1659	ICE 875	IC 1917	ICE 605	ICE 673	ICE 673	ICE 605	IC 2029	IC 2315	ICE 877	IC 2121	IC 2097	ICE 879
			⑤⑦	①–⑤	①–⑥	⑦w		⑤		⑦w	①–⑥				⑦w			⑤⑥z	♠					⑦w	⑦w
	✕	🍷♦	♦	a🍷	m🍷	🍷	✕♦	✕♦	✕	✕	m🍷	L✕	✕♦	✕	🍷	🍷	K✕	K✕	🍷	🍷♦	A✕	✕	✕♦		✕
Berlin Hbf 810 d.	1432	...	1208	...	...	...	...	...	...	...	...	...	...	1632	1358	...	...	...	...	...	...	1833	...	...	2032
Hamburg Hbf 800 900 d.	|	...	|	1428	...	...	1346	1346	1624	1624	...	1446	...	|	|	...	1824	1824	...	1546	1646	|	1746	...	|
Dortmund Hbf 800 d.	|	...	1552	|	...	...	1636	1636	|	|	...	1737	...	|	1752	1923	|	|	...	1836	1937	|	2036	...	|
Köln Hbf 800 910 d.	|	...	1718	|	1855	1855	1753	1753	|	|	...	1853	...	|	1918	2046d	|	|	...	1953	2053	|	2153	...	|
Koblenz Hbf **914** d.	|	...	1817	|	|	|	1848	1848	|	|	...	1948	...	|	2017	|	|	|	...	2048	2148	|	2248	...	|
Bingen (Rhein) Hbf **914** d.	|	...	1852	|	|	|	|	|	|	|	...	|	...	|	2052	|	|	|	...	2123	|	|	|	...	|
Wiesbaden Hbf ‡d.	|	...	|	|	|	|	|	|	|	|	...	|	2024	|	|	|	|	|	...	|	|	|	|	2324	|
Mainz Hbf **914** ‡a.	|	...	1911	|	|	|	1938	1938	|	|	...	2037	2035	|	2111	|	|	|	...	2141	2238	|	2338	2335	|
Mainz Hbf ‡d.	|	...	1913	|	|	|	1940	1940	|	|	...	2039	2042	|	2113	|	|	|	...	2143	2240	|	2340	2343	|
Frankfurt (Main) Hbf **930** ‡d.	1850	...	|	1920	|	|	|	|	2005	2005	...	|	|	2050	|	|	2205	2205	...	|	|	2300	|	|	0109
Frankfurt Flughafen ¶ **930** ‡a.	|	...	|	|	1951	1951	1959	1959	|	|	...	|	2059	|	|	2151	|	|	...	2159	2258	|	2359	|	0122
Frankfurt Flughafen ¶ **930** ‡d.	|	...	|	|	1954	1954	2002	2002	|	|	...	|	2102	|	|	2154	|	|	...	2202	2300	|	0002	|	0127
Frankfurt (Main) Hbf ‡a.	|	...	|	◐	|	|	2013	2013	|	|	...	|	2113	|	|	|	|	|	...	2213	2310	|	0013	|	|
Mannheim Hbf **930** ‡a.	1928	...	1952	|	2024	2024	...	...	2042	2042	...	2121	...	2128	2152	2224	2242	2242	...	...	...	2341	...	0036	0200
Mannheim Hbf **930** ‡d.	1936	...	1954	|	2036	2036	...	...	2044	2044	...	2123	...	2136	2158	2236	2244	2244	...	...	...	2349	...	0038	0202
Heidelberg Hbf **930** ‡d.	|	...	2006	2014	|	|	...	...	|	|	...	2136	...	|	|	|	|	|	...	...	...	|	...	0050	|
Stuttgart Hbf 930 a.	|	...	2046	|	|	|	...	...	|	|	←	2222	...	|	|	|	|	|	←	...	...	|	...	|	|
Karlsruhe Hbf **916** ‡d.	2000	2006	...	2050	2100	2102	...	...	2107	2111	2111	...	...	2200	2224	2300	2307	2311	2311	...	...	0013	...	0128	0238
Baden-Baden **916** d.	|	2022	...	...	→	2119	...	...	...	2129	2129	...	...	2218	...	→	...	2328	2330	...	...	...	...	...	...
Offenburg **916** ★ d.	2029	...	...	...	...	2135	...	...	...	2145	2145	...	...	2237	...	...	...	2345	2350	...	...	...	...	...	...
Freiburg (Brsg) Hbf ★ d.	2101	...	...	...	...	2208	...	...	...	2217	2217	...	...	2311	...	...	...	0017	0022	...	...	...	...	...	...
Basel Bad. Bf 🛃 ★ a.	2136	...	...	...	...	2243	...	...	...	2252	2252	...	...	2346	...	...	...	0053	0058	...	...	...	...	...	...
Basel SBB a.	2147	...	...	...	...	2253	...	...	...	2300	2300	...	...	2355	...	...	...	0102	...	...	...	...	...	...	...

km		IC 2120	IC 2310	ICE 874	ICE 874	IC 2278	ICE 670	ICE 670	ICE 604	ICE 604	IC 2376	IC 1114	IC 2028	ICE 676	ICE 772	IC 2010	EC 361	ICE 872	IC 2116	ICE 1656	ICE 1126	ICE 1026	ICE 78	ICE 602	ICE 602
				①g		Ⓐ▪	⑥u	①–⑥	Ⓑb		①–⑥	①–⑥		①–⑤		①–⑤				①–⑥	①⑦	②–⑥			①–⑥
		✕♦	G✕	✕	✕		✕	e⊖ ✕	🍷	🍷	eL 🍷	e⊙	🍷♦	a✕	✕	T🍷	🍷♦	✕	L✕	e♦	✕♦	✕♦	Z✕	🍷	e🍷
	Basel SBB d.	...	...	...	...	...	...	...	...	...	...	...	...	...	...	...	...	0608	...	...	...	...	0704	...	0712
	Basel Bad. Bf 🛃 ★ d.	...	...	0412	...	...	0513	...	0516	...	...	...	...	0545	...	...	...	0616	...	...	...	...	0713	...	0721
	Freiburg (Brsg) Hbf ★ d.	...	...	0447	...	...	0549	...	0552	...	...	...	...	0623	...	...	...	0652	...	...	...	...	0749	...	0756
	Offenburg **916** ★ d.	...	...	0520	...	...	|	...	0626	...	...	...	...	0657	...	...	...	0725	...	...	...	...	|	...	0828
	Baden-Baden **916** d.	...	...	0536	...	...	0633	...	0642	...	...	...	...	0714	...	...	0732	0742	...	...	...	...	0833	...	0844
	Karlsruhe Hbf **916** ‡d.	...	...	0558	0558	0615	0651	0651	0700	0700	0702	...	...	0736	...	...	0752	0800	...	...	...	...	0851	0901	0901
	Stuttgart Hbf 930 d.	...	...	|	|	|	|	|	|	|	|	0630	...	|	0727	0714	...	|	0737	...	...	...	|	|	|
	Heidelberg Hbf **930** ‡d.	...	...	|	|	0654	|	|	|	|	0746	0720	...	|	|	0755	...	|	0825	...	...	...	|	|	|
	Mannheim Hbf **930** ‡a.	...	...	0622	0622	0709	0714	0714	0723	0723	|	0731	...	0800	0804	0806	...	0822	0837	...	...	...	0914	0924	0924
0	**Mannheim** Hbf **930** ‡d.	...	...	0631	0631	0711	0716	0716	0735	0735	|	0733	...	...	0806	0808	...	0831	0839	...	...	...	0916	0935	0935
	Frankfurt (Main) Hbf ‡d.	0542	0638	|	|	|	|	|	|	|	◐	|	0742	...	|	|	...	|	|	0842	0942	0942	|	|	|
72	**Frankfurt** Flughafen ¶ **930** ‡a.	0555	0655	|	|	|	|	|	0806	0806	|	|	0755	...	0838	|	...	|	|	0857	0955	0955	|	1006	1006
	Frankfurt Flughafen ¶ **930** ‡d.	0558	0657	|	|	|	|	|	0809	0809	|	|	0758	...	0842	|	...	|	|	0858	0958	0958	|	1009	1009
	Frankfurt (Main) Hbf **930** ‡a.	|	|	0708	0708	0752	0752	0752	|	|	0840	|	|	...	0853	|	...	0908	|	|	|	|	0952	|	|
	Mainz Hbf ‡a.	0615	0715	|	|	...	|	|	|	|	|	0815	0818	...	|	0846	...	|	0918	0920	1018	1018	|	|	|
	Mainz Hbf **914** ‡d.	0617	0717	|	|	...	|	|	|	|	|	...	0820	...	|	0848	...	|	0920	0922	1020	1020	|	|	|
	Wiesbaden Hbf ‡a.	|	|	|	|	...	|	|	|	|	|	...	|	...	|	|	...	|	|	0938	|	|	|	|	|
	Bingen (Rhein) Hbf **914** d.	0634	|	|	|	...	|	|	|	|	|	...	|	...	|	0906	...	|	|	...	|	|	|	|	|
	Koblenz Hbf **914** a.	0710	0810	|	|	...	|	|	|	|	|	...	0910	...	|	0941	...	|	1010	...	1110	1110	|	|	|
	Köln Hbf 800 910 a.	0805	0905	|	|	...	|	|	0905	0905	|	...	1005	...	|	1042	...	|	1105	...	1205	1205	|	1105	1105
	Dortmund Hbf 800 a.	0921	1021	|	|	...	|	|	...	...	|	...	1121	...	|	1208f	...	|	1221	...	1321	1321	|	1220j	1220j
	Hamburg Hbf 800 900 a.	1212	1312	|	|	...	1134	1134	...	...	1328	...	1412	...	1234	|	...	|	1511	...	1612	1612	1334	...	...
	Berlin Hbf 810 a.	...	...	1125	1125	...	...	...	...	...	...	...	...	...	...	1550f	...	1325	...	...	...	...	...	...	...

	IC 2174 2374	ICE 278	IC 2114	ICE 1654	IC 2024	ICE 76	IC 2101	ICE 600	IC 1853	IC 2372	IC 1920	IC 1916	ICE 276	IC 2112	ICE 1652	IC 2006	IC 2004	IC 2014	IC 2026	ICE 74	ICE 508	IC 2270 2370	IC 2012	ICE 374	ICE 1650
				①–⑥				⊗	⑤	⑥⑦	⑦w	⑤f				⑥	⑦	①–⑤							
	🍷	B✕	✕	e♦	✕♦	✕♦	N🍷	🍷	♦	wL 🍷		S🍷	B✕	✕	D✕	🍷♦	🍷♦	●E 🍷		✕♦	🍷	Y🍷	🍷♦	J✕	D✕
Basel SBB d.	...	0812	...	...	...	0904	0912	...	...	...	...	...	1012	...	...	...	...	...	...	1104	1112	...	...	1212	...
Basel Bad. Bf 🛃 ★ d.	...	0822	...	...	...	0913	0922	...	...	...	...	...	1022	...	...	...	...	...	...	1113	1122	...	...	1222	...
Freiburg (Brsg) Hbf ★ d.	...	0857	...	...	...	0949	0957	...	...	...	...	...	1057	...	...	...	...	...	...	1149	1157	...	...	1257	...
Offenburg **916** ★ d.	...	0930	...	...	...	|	1030	...	...	...	...	...	1130	...	...	1139	1139	...	...	|	1230	1223	...	1330	...
Baden-Baden **916** d.	...	|	...	...	...	1033	|	...	...	...	...	...	|	...	...	1202	1202	...	...	1233	|	1245	...	|	...
Karlsruhe Hbf **916** ‡d.	0910	1000	...	...	...	1051	1058	1109	1110	1110	...	...	1200	...	...	1221	1221	...	...	1251	1300	1310	...	1400	...
Stuttgart Hbf 930 d.	|	|	0937	...	...	|	|	|	|	|	...	1114	|	1137	...	|	|	1209	...	|	|	|	1314	|	...
Heidelberg Hbf **930** ‡d.	0946	|	1025	...	...	|	|	|	1146	1146	...	1155	|	1225	...	|	|	|	...	|	|	1346	1355	|	...
Mannheim Hbf **930** ‡a.	|	1022	1037	...	...	1114	...	1133	|	|	...	1206	1222	1237	...	1250	1250	1256	...	1314	1323	|	1406	1422	...
Mannheim Hbf **930** ‡d.	|	1031	1039	...	...	1116	...	1135	|	|	...	1208	1231	1239	...	1258	1258	1258	...	1316	1335	|	1408	1431	...
Frankfurt (Main) Hbf ‡d.	◐	|	|	1044	1142	|	...	|	◐	◐	1215	|	|	|	1242	|	|	|	1344	|	|	◐	|	|	1442
Frankfurt Flughafen ¶ **930** ‡a.	|	|	|	1057	1155	|	...	1206	|	|	1226	|	|	|	1257	|	|	|	1355	|	1406	|	|	|	1457
Frankfurt Flughafen ¶ **930** ‡d.	|	|	|	1058	1158	|	...	1209	|	|	1228	|	|	|	1258	|	|	|	1358	|	1409	|	|	|	1458
Frankfurt (Main) Hbf **930** ‡a.	1040	1108	|	|	|	1153	...	|	1240	1240	|	|	1308	|	|	|	|	|	|	1353	|	1440	|	1508	|
Mainz Hbf ‡a.	|	|	1118	1120	1218	|	...	|	...	|	1246	1246	|	1318	1320	1340	1340	1340	1418	|	|	|	1446	|	1520
Mainz Hbf **914** ‡d.	|	|	1120	1122	1220	|	...	|	...	|	1248	1248	|	1320	1322	1342	1342	1342	1420	|	|	|	1448	|	1522
Wiesbaden Hbf ‡a.	|	|	|	1138	|	|	...	|	...	|	|	|	|	|	1338	|	|	|	|	|	|	|	|	|	1538
Bingen (Rhein) Hbf **914** d.	|	|	|	...	|	|	...	|	...	|	1306	1306	|	|	...	|	|	|	|	|	|	|	1506	|	...
Koblenz Hbf **914** a.	|	|	1210	...	1310	|	...	|	...	|	1341	1341	|	1410	...	1441	1441	1441	1510	|	|	|	1541	|	...
Köln Hbf 800 910 a.	|	|	1305	...	1405	|	...	1305	...	|	1442	1442	|	1505	...	1542	1542	1542	1605	|	1505	|	1642	|	...
Dortmund Hbf 800 a.	|	|	1421	...	1521	|	...	1420k	...	|	1608	1608	|	1621	...	1703	...	...	1721	|	1620k	|	1805	|	...
Hamburg Hbf 800 900 a.	1529	|	1712	...	1812	1534	...	...	...	1730	|	|	|	1912	...	...	...	...	2012	1734	...	1927	...	...	...
Berlin Hbf 810 a.	...	1525	...	...	...	...	...	...	...	...	1951	1951	1725	...	...	...	...	...	...	...	...	...	...	1925	...

NOTES (CONTINUED FROM PREVIOUS PAGE)

A – From Westerland (Table **821**) from Mar. 27. Train number **2215** until Mar. 26.
B – To / from Interlaken via Bern (Table **560**).
C – To Chur via Zürich (Tables **510** and **520**).
D – 🚃 Wiesbaden - Leipzig - Dresden and v.v.
E – To / from Emden (Table **812**).
F – From Kassel (Table **806**).
G – To / from Westerland (Table **821**).
H – From Hannover (Table **810**).
J – To / from Bern (Table **560**).
K – From Kiel (Table **820**).
L – From / to Stralsund (Table **830**).
M – To / from München (Table **930**).
N – 🚃 Nürnberg - Stuttgart - Basel and v.v.
Q – 🚃 Dortmund - Nürnberg - Passau - Wien and v.v.
R – ①②③④⑦ (not Dec. 23, 24, 30, 31, Apr. 1, 4, May 12, 13, 23, June 2, 3). To Tübingen Hbf (a. 1950) on ①–④ (not Apr. 5, May 24).
S – From Salzburg via München (Tables **890/930**).
T – ①–⑤ (not Dec. 24, 25, 31, Jan. 1, Apr. 2, 5, May 13, 14, 24, June 3, 4). From Tübingen Hbf (d. 0611).
Y – From / to Konstanz (Table **916**).
Z – To / from Zürich (Table **510**).

a – ①–⑤ (not Dec. 24, 25, 31, Jan. 1, Apr. 2, 5, May 24).
b – Not Dec. 24, 25, 31, Jan. 1, Apr. 2, 5, May 24.
c – Also Dec. 24, 25, 31, Jan. 1, Apr. 2, 5, May 24; not Dec. 26, Jan. 2.
d – Köln **Messe/Deutz**.
e – ①–⑥ (not Dec. 25, 26, Jan. 1, Apr. 3, 5, May 24).
f – ⑤ (also Dec. 23, 30, Apr. 1, May 12, June 2; not Dec. 25, Jan. 1, Apr. 2, May 14, June 4).
g – ① (also Apr. 6, May 25; not Apr. 5, May 24).
h – ⑦ (also Dec. 25, 26, Jan. 1, Apr. 3, 5, May 24).
j – ①–④ (not Dec. 23, 24, 30, 31, Apr. 1, 5, May 24).
k – ⑥ (also Dec. 24, 25, 31, Apr. 2, 4, May 23).
m – Also Apr. 4, May 23; not Apr. 5, May 24.
n – Not Dec. 24, 31.
o – Also Dec. 26, Jan. 2; not Dec. 24, 25, 31, Jan. 1, Apr. 2, 5, May 24.
p – Also Dec. 24, 31, Apr. 2, May 13, June 3; not Dec. 26, Apr. 3, May 15, June 5.
q – Not Dec. 24, 25, 31, Apr. 2, 4, May 23.
r – Frankfurt Flughafen Regionalbahnhof.
s – Stops to set down only.
t – Also Dec. 25, 26, Jan. 1, Apr. 3, 5, May 24.
u – Also Dec. 24, 31; not Dec. 26, Apr. 3.
v – Not Dec. 25, Jan. 1.
w – Also Apr. 5, May 24; not Apr. 4, May 23.
x – Also Dec. 23, 30, Apr. 1, 5, May 12, 24, June 2; not Dec. 25, Jan. 1, Apr. 2, 4, May 14, 23 June 4.
y – 2024 on ⑥⑦ (also Dec. 25, Jan. 1, Apr. 5, May 24).
z – Also Dec. 23, 24, 30, Apr. 1, 4; not Dec. 25, Jan. 1.

♠ – ①②③④⑦ (not Dec. 23, 24, 30, 31, Apr. 1, 4, May 23).
⊡ – ⑤⑦ (also Dec. 23, 30, Apr. 1, 5, May 24; not Dec. 25, Apr. 2, 4, May 23).
▪ – Not Dec. 24, 31, May 14, June 3, 4.
● – Not Dec. 24, 25, 31, Jan. 1, Apr. 2, 5, May 13, 24, June 3.
❖ – Not Dec. 23, 24, 30, 31, Apr. 1, 5, May 12, 24, June 2.
⊠ – ⑥ (not Dec. 26, Apr. 3, 5, May 24).
⊙ – Train number **2218** on ⑥ (also Dec. 24, Apr. 2, May 13; not May 15).
⊕ – Train number **2197** on ⑥ (also Dec. 24, Apr. 2, May 13; not Dec. 26, Apr. 3, May 15).
⊗ – Train number **1008** on ⑤ **f**.
⊖ – Train number **674** on ⑤ (also Dec. 23, 30, Apr. 1, May 12; not Apr. 2, May 14).
♥ – Also calls at Boppard (d. 0544).
♣ – To Feb. 26 and from May 17.
§ – Frankfurt (Main) **Süd**.
★ – See panel on page 422 for other local services.
◧ – On the mornings of ⑥⑦ **c** arrives Offenburg 0627, Freiburg 0700, Basel Bad. Bf 0737, Basel SBB 0747.
◐ – Via Darmstadt (Table **911**).
◇ – Via Erfurt (Table **850**).
¶ – Frankfurt Flughafen Fernbahnhof ✈.
‡ – Alternative regional services: Table **911a** for Frankfurt - Mannheim / Heidelberg and v.v., also Mainz - Mannheim - Heidleberg - Karlsruhe and v.v. Table **917a** for S-Bahn trains Frankfurt - Mainz - Wiesbaden and v.v.

912 BASEL - KARLSRUHE - FRANKFURT - KOBLENZ (- KÖLN)

	EC 100	IC 2022	ICE 72	IC 2103	ICE 506	IC 2276	ICE 712	IC 118	ICE 370	ICE 290	EC 6	ICE 1558	EC 114	ICE 70	ICE 104	IC 2274	IC 2316	ICE 26	ICE 870	IC 2318	ICE 1556	ICE 376	ICE 24	IC 2105	ICE 502
					R	2286	①–⑤		⑧q	⑥k							⑧q								◧
	✕♦	🍷	Z✕	🍷♦	🍷	🍷	a🍷	🍷♦	B✕	B✕	✕♦	D✕	✕♦	✕	🍷♦	🍷♦		Q✕	✕	♦	D✕	✕♦	Q✕	🍷❖	H🍷
Basel SBB d.	1218	...	1304	1312	...	...	...	...	1412	1412	1420	...	...	1504	1512	...	...	...	1612	...	...	1704	...	1712	...
Basel Bad. Bf 🏛 ★ d.	1227	...	1313	1322	...	...	...	...	1422	1422	1428	...	...	1513	1522	...	...	...	1621	...	...	1713	...	1721	...
Freiburg (Brsg) Hbf ★ d.	1304	...	1349	1357	...	...	...	...	1457	1457	1504	...	...	1549	1557	...	...	...	1656	...	...	1749	...	1756	...
Offenburg **916** ★ d.	|	...	|	1430	...	...	...	...	1530	1530	|	...	...	|	1630	...	...	...	1728	...	...	|	...	1828	...
Baden-Baden **916** d.	1352	...	1433	|	...	...	...	...	|	|	1552	...	...	1633	|	...	...	...	1744	...	...	1833	...	1845	...
Karlsruhe Hbf **916** ‡ d.	1412	...	1451	1458	1509	1510	...	...	1600	1600	1612	...	...	1651	1700	1710	...	...	1801	...	...	1851	...	1859	1909
Stuttgart Hbf **930** d.	|	...	|	...	|	|	1434	1512	|	|	|	...	1610	|	|	|	1636	...	|	1741	...	|	...	...	|
Heidelberg Hbf **930** ‡ d.	|	...	|	...	|	1546	1518	1555	|	|	|	...	|	|	|	1746	1720	...	|	1825	...	|	...	...	|
Mannheim Hbf **930** ‡ a.	1437	...	1514	...	1533	|	1531	1606	1622	1622	1637	...	1656	1714	1723	|	1736	...	1823	1837	...	1914	...	...	1933
Mannheim Hbf **930** ‡ d.	1439	...	1516	...	1535	|	1533	1608	1631	1631	1639	...	1658	1716	1735	|	1738	...	1831	1839	...	1916	...	...	1935
Frankfurt (Main) Hbf ‡ d.	|	1542	|	...	|	◐	|	|	|	|	|	1642	|	|	|	◐	|	1742	|	|	1842	|	1942	...	|
Frankfurt Flughafen ¶ **930** ‡ a.	|	1555	|	...	1606	|	|	|	|	|	|	1657	|	|	1806	|	|	1755	|	|	1857	|	1955	...	2006
Frankfurt Flughafen ¶ **930** ‡ d.	|	1558	|	...	1609	|	|	|	|	|	|	1658	|	|	1809	|	|	1758	|	|	1858	|	1958	...	2009
Frankfurt (Main) Hbf **930** ‡ a.	|	|	1553	...	|	1640	|	|	1708	1708	|	|	|	1753	|	1840	|	|	1908	|	|	1953	|	...	|
Mainz Hbf ‡ a.	1518	1618	|	...	|	|	1621	1646	|	|	1718	1720	1740	|	|	|	1815	1818	|	1918	1920	|	2018	...	|
Mainz Hbf **914** ‡ d.	1520	1620	|	...	|	|	1623	1648	|	|	1720	1722	1742	|	|	|	1822	1820	|	1920	1922	|	2020	...	|
Wiesbaden Hbf ‡ a.	|	|	|	...	|	|	1634	|	|	|	|	1738	|	|	|	|	1833	|	|	|	1938	|	|	...	|
Bingen (Rhein) Hbf **914** d.	|	|	|	...	|	|	|	1706	|	◇	|	...	1806	|	|	|	...	|	|	|	...	|	|	...	|
Koblenz Hbf **914** a.	1610	1710	|	...	|	|	|	1741	|	|	1810	...	1841	|	|	|	...	1910	|	2010	...	|	2110	...	|
Köln Hbf **800 910** a.	1705	1805	|	...	1705	|	1801	1842	|	|	1905	...	1942	|	1905	|	...	2005	|	2105	...	|	2205	...	2105
Dortmund Hbf **800** a.	1821	1921	|	...	1820	|	...	...	|	|	2021	...	2102	|	...	|	...	2120	|	2221q	...	|	2320	...	2221
Hamburg Hbf **800 900** a.	2112	2212	1934	...	...	2128	...	...	|	|	2315q	...	...	2137	...	2326w	...	...	|	...	...	2342f	...	...	...
Berlin Hbf **810** a.	...	...	...	...	...	...	...	...	2126	2159	...	...	...	...	...	...	...	...	2325	...	...	...	...	...	...

	IC 2272	IC 1910	ICE 272	ICE 372	IC 2110	ICE 1554	CNL 472	ICE 500	IC 2096	ICE 22	ICE 270	ICE 1110	ICE 510	ICE 522	IC 2020	IC 60459	ICE 990	ICE 990	ICE 887	ICE 1087	CNL 459	CNL 1259	CNL 478	CNL 40478	ICE 608
	①–⑤	⑦w	E	⑦w	⑧q	n	R		⑦w			⑦w	①–⑥					⑦w	①–⑥	⑦h	R	R	R	R	
	aF 🍷	M	Z✕	Z✕	✕	D✕	🍷♦	🍷		Q✕	Z✕	🍷M	⊕M	🍷	⊙	2	M✕	M✕	eG	G	🍷♦	✕♦	✕♦	🍷♦	K✕
Basel SBB d.		...	1812	1812	...	...	1804	1912	...	...	2012	...	...	...	...	2107	...	...	...	...	2107	2107	2207	2207	2326
Basel Bad. Bf 🏛 ★ d.	...	...	1822	1822	...	...	1817	1921	...	...	2022	...	...	...	...	2121	...	...	...	...	2121u	2121u	2219u	2219u	2334
Freiburg (Brsg) Hbf ★ d.	...	...	1857	1857	...	...	1904u	1956	...	...	2057	...	...	...	...	2158	...	...	...	...	2158u	2158u	2257u	2257u	0014
Offenburg **916** ★ d.	...	...	1930	1930	...	...	1937u	2028	...	...	2130	...	...	...	...	2230	...	...	...	...	2230u	2230u	2331u	2331u	0049
Baden-Baden **916** d.	...	...	|	|	...	...	|	2044	...	...	|	...	...	...	...	|	...	...	...	...	|	|	|	|	0106
Karlsruhe Hbf **916** ‡ d.	1910	...	2000	2000	...	...	2018u	2101	...	...	2200	...	...	...	...	2305	...	...	...	...	2305u	2305u	0018u	0018u	0129
Stuttgart Hbf **930** d.	|	1914	|	|	1914t	...	|	|	2035	...	|	2151	2151	...	...	|	2305	2305	...	...	|	|	|	|	|
Heidelberg Hbf **930** ‡ d.	1946	1955	|	|	2025	...	|	|	2120	...	|	|	|	...	...	2334	|	|	...	...	2334u	2334u	|	|	0210
Mannheim Hbf **930** ‡ a.	|	2006	2022	2022	2037	...	|	2124	2133	...	2222	2228	2228	...	...	2346	2342	2342	...	...	|	|	|	|	0222
Mannheim Hbf **930** ‡ d.	|	2008	2031	2031	2039	...	2116u	2135	2135	...	2235	2231	2231	...	...	...	2351	2351	...	...	2359u	2359u	|	|	0224
Frankfurt (Main) Hbf ‡ d.	◐	|	|	|	|	2042	|	|	|	2146	|	|	|	2310	2324	...	|	|	0003	0022	...	|	|	|	0315
Frankfurt Flughafen ¶ **930** ‡ a.	|	|	|	|	|	2057	|	2206	|	2157	|	2303	2303	2321	2336	...	0023	0023	0015	0038	...	|	|	|	0330r
Frankfurt Flughafen ¶ **930** ‡ d.	|	|	|	|	|	2058	|	2209	|	2159	|	2305	2313	2329	2338	...	0029	0029	0027	0042	...	|	|	|	0346r
Frankfurt (Main) Hbf **930** ‡ a.	2040	|	2108	2108	|	|	|	|	|	|	2315	|	2325	|	|	...	0042	0042	|	|	...	|	|	|	|
Mainz Hbf ‡ a.	...	2046	|	|	2118	2120	|	|	2215	2218	...	|	...	|	2359	...	...	|	0044	0059	...	|	|	|	0406
Mainz Hbf **914** ‡ d.	...	2048	|	|	2120	2122	|	|	2222	2220	...	|	...	|	0001	...	...	|	0046	0101	...	|	|	|	0408
Wiesbaden Hbf ‡ a.	...	|	|	|	|	2138	|	|	2233	|	...	|	...	|	|	...	...	|	0057	0112	...	|	|	|	|
Bingen (Rhein) Hbf **914** d.	...	|	|	|	|	...	|	|	...	|	...	|	...	|	0018	...	...	|	...	...	...	|	|	|	0425
Koblenz Hbf **914** a.	...	2141	|	|	2210	...	|	|	...	2310	...	|	...	|	0055	...	...	|	...	...	...	|	|	0446	0501
Köln Hbf **800 910** a.	...	2242	|	|	2305	...	|	2309	...	0005	...	0005	...	0039	0155	...	...	|	...	...	...	|	|	0542	0605
Dortmund Hbf **800** a.	...	2359	|	|	...	...	|	0028	...	0121v	...	...	...	0157	0329	...	...	|	...	...	...	|	|	...	0721
Hamburg Hbf **800 900** a.	...	...	0134	|	...	...	0356	...	...	...	...	...	...	...	0651	...	...	0543	...	...	...	|	0906x	...	1012
Berlin Hbf **810** a.	...	...	...	0125	...	...	...	...	...	...	...	...	...	...	...	...	...	...	...	...	...	0718	...	...	...

★ – Local services Offenburg - Basel and v.v.

	†b		Ⓐm	Ⓐn	Ⓐm		⚒y	Ⓐm	†b	⚒y															Ⓐm	
Offenburg d.	0049	...	0428	...	0525	...	0549	0634	...	0707	0807	0907	1007	1107	1204	1307	1404	1507	1607	1707	1807	1907	2007	2034	...	2244
Freiburg (Brsg) Hbf a.	0131	...	0528	...	0625	...	0649	0729	...	0756	0855	0955	1055	1155	1250	1355	1450	1555	1656	1756	1856	1955	2055	2133	...	2342
Freiburg (Brsg) Hbf d.	0132	...	0529	0607	0628	0628	0711	0734	0808	0815	0915	1015	1115	1215	1315	1415	1515	1615	1715	1815	1915	2015	...	2135	2235	2343
Basel Bad Bf a.	0220	...	0625	0702	0733	0733	0806	0813	0911	0911	1011	1111	1211	1311	1412	1511	1611	1711	1811	1911	2011	2111	...	2240	2340	0046

	Ⓐm		Ⓐm		⚒y	†b										Ⓐm		Ⓐm		Ⓒj						⑥
Basel Bad Bf d.	0519	0549	0625	0634	0748	0748	0848	0948	1048	1148	1248	1348	1448	1548	1648	1726	1748	1826	1848	1848	...	1948	...	2126	2258	2358
Freiburg (Brsg) Hbf a.	0615	0646	0718	0736	0847	0851	0944	1044	1144	1244	1344	1444	1544	1644	1744	1823	1844	1923	1944	1944	...	2044	...	2219	0003	0100
Freiburg (Brsg) Hbf d.	0626	0656	0722	0803	0903	0903	1003	1103	1203	1307	1403	1507	1603	1703	1803	1825	1907	1925	...	2003	2028	...	2125	2225	0018	...
Offenburg a.	0720	0745	0814	0851	0953	0953	1053	1153	1253	1353	1450	1553	1650	1751	1850	1921	1953	2021	...	2050	2124	...	2221	2318	0112	...

♦ – **NOTES** (LISTED BY TRAIN NUMBER)

6 – [12] and ✕ Chur - Zürich - Basel - Dortmund (- Hamburg ⑧**q**).
100 – [12] and ✕ Chur - Zürich - Dortmund - Hamburg (- Kiel ⑦**w**). Train number **102** on ⑦ (also Apr. 5, May 24; not Apr. 4, May 23).
104 – [12] and 🍷 Basel - Köln - Arnhem - Utrecht - Amsterdam (terminates at Köln on Dec. 24, 31); conveys [12] (*ICE* **504**) Basel - Köln.
114 – WÖRTHERSEE – [12] and ✕ Klagenfurt - Villach - Salzburg - München - Dortmund.
118 – [12] and 🍷 Salzburg - Innsbruck - Bregenz - Lindau - Ulm - Münster.
376 – [12] and ✕ Interlaken - Bern - Basel - Frankfurt (- Hamburg ⑤⑦**f**).
459 – CANOPUS – 🛏 1, 2 cl., ▬ 2 cl., [2] (reclining) and 🍷 Zürich - Leipzig - Dresden - Praha.
472 – AURORA – 🛏 1, 2 cl. and ▬ 2 cl. Basel - København. Conveys 🛏 1, 2 cl. Basel - Warszawa, also 🛏 1, 2 cl. Basel - Minsk / Moskva (Table **24**).
478 – ④–⑦ (daily from Mar. 25). KOMET – 🛏 1, 2 cl., ▬ 2 cl., [2] (reclining) and ✕ Zürich - Hannover - Hamburg. Starts from Brig on ⑥ Dec. 26 - Apr. 10.
1259 – SIRIUS – 🛏 1, 2 cl., ▬ 2 cl., [2] (reclining) and ✕ Zürich - Halle - Berlin.
2103 – [12] and 🍷 Basel - Stuttgart - Nürnberg.
2274 – [12] and 🍷 Karlsruhe - Kassel (- Hannover ⑤⑦**f**) (- Hamburg ⑦**w**).
2318 – [12] Stuttgart - Köln (- Dortmund ⑧**q**) (- Münster ⑦**w**).
40478 – ④–⑦ (daily from Mar. 25). PEGASUS – 🛏 1, 2 cl., ▬ 2 cl., [2] (reclining) and 🍷 Zürich - Amsterdam. Starts from Brig on ⑥ Dec. 26 - Apr. 10.

B – From Interlaken via Bern (Table **560**).
D – [12] and ✕ Dresden - Leipzig - Wiesbaden.
E – ①–⑥ (also Apr. 4, May 23; not Jan. 1, Apr. 5, May 24). On ⑥ (also Dec. 24, 25, 31, Apr. 2, 4, May 23) runs with train number **292** and arrives Hamburg Hbf 0111.
F – To Kassel (Table **806**).
G – From Hamburg (Table **900**).
H – To Hannover (Table **810**).
K – To Kiel (Table **820**).
M – From München (Table **930**).
Q – [12] and ✕ Wien - Passau - Regensburg - Nürnberg - Dortmund. Runs up to 60 minutes later May 22 - June 6.
R – On ①–⑤ **a** conveys [12] (*ICE* **806**) Karlsruhe - Köln - Oberhausen.
Z – From Zürich (Table **510**).

a – Not Dec. 24, 25, 31, Jan. 1, Apr. 2, 5, May 24.
b – Also Jan. 6, June 3.
e – Not Dec. 25, 26, Jan. 1, Apr. 3, 5, May 24.
f – ⑤⑦ (also Dec. 23, 30, Apr. 1, 5, May 12, 24; not Dec. 25, Jan. 1, Apr. 2, 4, May 14, 23).
h – Also Dec. 25, 26, Jan. 1, Apr. 3, 5, May 24.
j – Also Dec. 24, 31, Jan. 6, June 3.
k – Also Dec. 24, 25, 31, Apr. 2, 4, May 23.
m – Not Dec. 24, 31, Jan. 6, June 3.
n – Not Dec. 24, 31.
q – ⑧ (not Dec. 24, 25, 31, Apr. 2, 4, May 23).
r – Frankfurt Flughafen Regionalbahnhof.
t – 1937 on ⑤⑦ (also Apr. 5, May 24).
u – Stops to pick up only.
v – Not Dec. 25, Jan. 1.
w – ⑦ (also Apr. 5, May 24; not Apr. 4, May 23).
x – 0829 on ⑥; 0836 on ⑦ (also Dec. 25, Jan. 1, Apr. 5, May 24).
y – Not Jan. 6, June 3.
◧ – Train number **1002** on ⑥ (also Dec. 24, 25, 31, Apr. 2, 4, May 23).
⊕ – ①–⑥ (also Apr. 4, May 23; not Apr. 5, May 24). Train number **1010** on ⑤⑥ (also Dec. 23, 30, Apr. 1, 4, May 23).
❖ – To Stuttgart, Nürnberg and Passau on dates in Tables **931**, **925** and **920**.
⊙ – Also calls at Boppard Hbf (d. 0043).
◐ – Via Darmstadt (Table **911**).
◇ – Via Erfurt (Table **850**).
★ – See panel below main table for other local services.
¶ – Frankfurt Flughafen Fernbahnhof ✈.
‡ – Alternative regional services: Table **911a** for Heidelberg / Mannheim - Frankfurt, also Karlsruhe - Heidelberg - Mannheim - Mainz. Table **917a** for S-Bahn trains Wiesbaden - Mainz - Frankfurt.

913 OFFENBURG - STRASBOURG

DB / Ortenau-S-Bahn (2nd class only)

km	▷																											
			Ⓐ	Ⓒ	Ⓐ	Ⓐ		Ⓐ	Ⓒ	Ⓐ		Ⓒ		Ⓐ	Ⓐ	Ⓒ		Ⓐ		Ⓐ		Ⓐ	Ⓐ		Ⓐ			n
0	**Offenburg** d.	0632	0704	0734	0734	0804	0834	0904	1004	1034	...	1204	1234	1304	1334	1403	1434	1504	1604	1634	1704	1734	1804	1834	1904	2004	2104	2325
21	Kehl 🏛 d.	0652	0722	0752	0752	0822	0853	0922	1022	1052	...	1224	1252	1322	1356	1422	1452	1522	1622	1652	1722	1757	1822	1852	1922	2022	2122	2348
29	**Strasbourg** a.	0705	0734	0804	0805	0834	0906	0935	1034	1104	...	1237	1305	1334	1407	1434	1505	1534	1634	1704	1734	1808	1834	1904	1935	2034	2134	2400

▷																												
	v		Ⓐ		Ⓐ	Ⓐ	Ⓐ	Ⓒ		Ⓐ	Ⓒ		Ⓐ		Ⓐ	Ⓐ	Ⓒ	Ⓐ		Ⓒ	Ⓐ	Ⓐ	Ⓐ	Ⓐ	Ⓒ	Ⓒ	Ⓐ	
Strasbourg d.	0005	0622	0723	0750	0823	0853	0922	0923	1049	1252	1253	1323	1422	1453	1523	1622	1623	1653	1723	1750	1751	1823	1853	1922	1923	2022	2023	2153
Kehl 🏛 d.	0016	0634	0734	0804	0834	0904	0934	0934	1104	1304	1304	1334	1434	1504	1534	1634	1634	1704	1734	1804	1804	1834	1904	1934	1934	2034	2034	2204
Offenburg a.	0034	0652	0752	0822	0852	0922	0952	0952	1122	1322	1322	1352	1452	1522	1552	1652	1652	1722	1752	1822	1822	1852	1922	1952	1952	2052	2052	2222

n – Not Dec. 24, 31.
v – Not Dec. 25, Jan. 1.
▷ – German holiday dates apply.

RE / RB services — Local services KOBLENZ - WIESBADEN / MAINZ - FRANKFURT — 914

Koblenz - St Goarshausen - Wiesbaden - Frankfurt *(Rechte Rheinstrecke)* WARNING! SEE NOTE ✣ BELOW

km		Ⓐe	⚒r	Ⓐe	Ⓐe		Ⓐe	Ⓒd						Ⓐr			Ⓐr			Ⓐr			Ⓐr			
0	**Koblenz** Hbf ...... **906** d.	...	...	0440	0510	0555	0652	0710	0755	0910	0955	1110	1155	1225	1310	1355	1410	1510	1555	1640	1710	1755	1810	1910	2010	2210
5	Niederlahnstein .. **906** d.	...	...	0446	0516	0601	0658	0716	0801	0916	1001	1116	1201	1231	1316	1401	1416	1516	1601	1646	1716	1801	1816	1916	2016	2216
11	Braubach .... d.	...	...	0453	0523	0608	0705	0723	0808	0923	1008	1123	1208	1238	1323	1408	1423	1523	1608	1653	1723	1808	1823	1923	2023	2223
23	Kamp-Bornhofen .... d.	...	...	0504	0534	0619	0716	0734	0819	0934	1019	1134	1219	1249	1334	1419	1434	1534	1619	1704	1734	1819	1834	1934	2034	2234
35	St Goarshausen .... d.	...	...	0514	0544	0630	0727	0744	0830	0944	1030	1144	1230	1259	1344	1430	1444	1544	1630	1714	1744	1830	1844	1944	2044	2244
46	Kaub .... d.	...	...	0523	0553	0640	0737	0753	0840	0953	1040	1153	1240	1308	1353	1440	1453	1553	1640	1723	1753	1840	1853	1953	2053	2253
52	Lorch (Rhein) .... d.	...	...	0529	0559	0645	0744	0759	0845	0959	1045	1159	1245	1314	1359	1445	1459	1559	1645	1729	1759	1845	1859	1959	2059	2259
64	Rüdesheim (Rhein) .... d.	0440	0510	0540	0610	0655	0755	0810	0855	1010	1055	1210	1255	1340	1410	1455	1510	1610	1655	1740	1810	1855	1910	2010	2110	2310
94	**Wiesbaden** Hbf .... a.	0514	0544	0614	0644	0724	0824	0844	0924	1044	1124	1244	1324	1414	1444	1524	1544	1644	1724	1814	1844	1924	1944	2044	2144	2344
94	**Wiesbaden** Hbf .... d.	0520	0550	0632	0702	0732	0832	0850	0932	1050	1132	1250	1332	1432	1450	1532	1550	1650	1732	1832	1850	1932	1950	2050	2150	2350
135	**Frankfurt** (Main) Hbf .. a.	0613*	0643*	0705	0735	0805	0905	0943*	1005	1143*	1205	1343*	1405	1505	1543*	1605	1643*	1743*	1805	1905	1943*	2005	2043*	2143*	2243*	0043*

	Ⓐe	⚒r	⚒r						Ⓐe	Ⓒd	Ⓐe				Ⓐe		m	Ⓐe	Ⓐe					†w	⚒r	
Frankfurt (Main) Hbf .. d.	...	...	0517*	0617*	0753	0817*	0953	1017*	1053	1153	1153	1217*	1353	1417*	1523	1553	1621e	1653	1723	1753	1823e	1953	2017*	2117*	2117*	2247*
Wiesbaden Hbf .... a.	...	...	0607	0707	0828	0907	1028	1107	1128	1228	1228	1307	1428	1507	1558	1628	1658e	1728	1758	1828	1858e	2028	2107	2207	2207	2337
Wiesbaden Hbf .... d.	...	0521e	0612	0712	0836	0912	1036	1112	1150	1236	1236	1312	1436	1512	1612	1636	1712	1742	1812	1836	1912	2036	2112	2212	2212	2342
Rüdesheim (Rhein) ..... d.	...	0554e	0644	0744	0902	0944	1102	1144	1224	1302	1302	1344	1502	1544	1644	1702	1744	1814	1844	1902	1944	2102	2144	2244	2245	0015
Lorch (Rhein) .... d.	...	0606e	0654	0754	0910	0954	1110	1154	1236	1310	1310	1354	1510	1554	1654	1710	1754	1824	1854	1910	1954	2110	2154	2254	...	...
Kaub .... d.	0515	0615	0701	0801	0916	1001	1116	1201	1245	1316	1318	1401	1516	1601	1701	1716	1801	1831	1901	1916	2001	2116	2201	2301	...	...
St Goarshausen .... d.	0524	0624	0710	0810	0925	1010	1125	1210	1254	1325	1327	1410	1525	1610	1710	1725	1810	1840	1910	1925	2010	2125	2210	2310	...	...
Kamp-Bornhofen .... d.	0535	0635	0721	0821	0935	1021	1135	1221	1305	1335	1337	1421	1535	1621	1721	1735	1821	1851	1921	1935	2021	2135	2221	2321	...	...
Braubach .... d.	0546	0646	0732	0832	0946	1032	1146	1232	1316	1346	|	1432	1546	1632	1732	1746	1832	1902	1932	1946	2032	2146	2232	2332	...	...
Niederlahnstein .... **906** d.	0553	0653	0739	0839	0953	1039	1153	1239	1323	1353	1353	1439	1553	1639	1739	1753	1839	1912	1939	1953	2039	2153	2239	2339	...	...
Koblenz Hbf .... **906** a.	0600	0701	0746	0846	1001	1046	1201	1246	1330	1401	1401	1446	1601	1646	1746	1801	1846	1918	1946	2001	2046	2201	2246	2346	...	...

Koblenz - Bingen - Mainz - Frankfurt *(Linke Rheinstrecke)* ⊠

km		Ⓐe	⚒◧	Ⓐe		Ⓐe			Ⓐe			Ⓐe			Ⓐe			Ⓐe			Ⓐe			n	n	n
0	**Koblenz** Hbf .... d.	0502	0552	0607	0653	0707	0754	0853	0902	0954	1053	1102	1154	1253	1302	1354	1453	1502	1554	1653	1702	1754	1854	1954	2054	2154
19	Boppard Hbf .... d.	0517	0607	0621	0708	0721	0809	0908	0921	1009	1108	1121	1209	1308	1321	1409	1508	1521	1609	1708	1721	1809	1909	2009	2109	2209
24	Boppard-Bad Salzig .. d.	|	0611	|	0712	|	0813	0912	|	1013	1112	|	1213	1312	|	1413	1512	|	1613	1712	|	1813	1913	2013	2113	2213
34	St Goar .... d.	|	0619	|	0720	|	0821	0920	|	1021	1120	|	1221	1320	|	1421	1520	|	1621	1720	|	1821	1921	2021	2121	2221
41	Oberwesel .... d.	0531	0625	0635	0726	0735	0827	0926	0935	1027	1126	1135	1227	1326	1335	1427	1526	1535	1627	1726	1735	1827	1927	2027	2127	2227
47	Bacharach .... d.	|	0629	|	0730	|	0831	0930	|	1031	1130	|	1231	1330	|	1431	1530	|	1631	1730	|	1831	1931	2031	2131	2231
61	Bingen (Rhein) Hbf..... a.	0544	0642	0647	0743	0747	0844f	0943	0947	1044	1143	1147	1244	1343	1347	1444	1543	1547	1644	1743	1747	1844	1943	2044	2144	2244
61	Bingen (Rhein) Hbf..... d.	0545	0654	0648	0752	0748	0855	0955	0948	1055	1155	1148	1255	1352	1348	1455	1552	1548	1655	1752	1748	1855	1945	2056	2159	2250
62	Bingen (Rhein) Stadt .. d.	|	0657	|	0755	|	0858	0958	|	1058	1158	|	1258	1355	|	1458	1555	|	1658	1755	|	1858	1947	2059	2202	2253
73	Ingelheim .... d.	0555	0707	0656	0805	0756	0908	1008	0956	1108	1208	1156	1308	1405	1356	1508	1605	1556	1708	1805	1756	1908	1957	2109	2213	2303
91	**Mainz** Hbf .... a.	0608	0725	0708	0822	0808	0926	1026	1008	1126	1226	1208	1326	1423	1408	1526	1623	1608	1726	1823	1808	1925	2017	2126	2231	2322
119	Frankfurt Flughafen ‡ a.	0634	...	0734	...	0834	...	...	1034	...	...	1234	...	...	1434	...	...	1634	...	...	1834	...	...	...	...	...
130	**Frankfurt** (Main) Hbf.. a.	0649	...	0751	...	0849	...	...	1049	...	...	1249	...	...	1449	...	...	1649	...	...	1849	...	...	...	...	...

	⑥⑦z	⚒r		Ⓐe			Ⓐe			Ⓐe			Ⓐe			Ⓐe		Ⓐe		Ⓐe		Ⓐe			n	n
Frankfurt (Main) Hbf .. d.	...	...	...	0706	...	...	0908	...	...	1108	...	...	1308	...	...	1508	...	1608	...	1708	...	1808	...	...	...	...
Frankfurt Flughafen ‡. d.	...	...	...	0719	...	...	0923	...	...	1123	...	...	1323	...	...	1523	...	1623	...	1721	...	1823	...	...	...	...
Mainz Hbf .... d.	0007	0530e	0624	0751	0724	0830	0951	0935	1030	1151	1135	1230	1351	1330	1430	1551	1532	1652	1630	1751	1732c	1852	1830	1933c	2030	2130
Ingelheim .... d.	0025	0549e	0644	0803	0743	0849	1003	0953	1049	1203	1153	1249	1403	1347	1449	1603	1550	|	1648	1803	1753c	1904	1848	1951c	2049	2148
Bingen (Rhein) Stadt ... d.	0035	0559e	0657	|	0803	0907	|	1003	1102y	|	1203	1305	|	1402	1507	|	1601	|	1659	|	1805c	|	1903	2003c	2107	2159
Bingen (Rhein) Hbf ..... a.	0038	0602e	0700	0811	0806	0910	1011	1006	1104y	1211	1206	1308	1411	1404	1510	1611	1604	1710	1702	1811	1807c	1912	1905	2006c	2109	2201
Bingen (Rhein) Hbf ..... d.	0048	0607	0708	0811	0814	0914	1011	1015	1109	1211	1215	1309	1411	1415	1511	1611	1615	1711	1716	1811	1816	1913	1916	2011	2110	2208
Bacharach .... d.	0100	0619	0720	|	0827	0926	|	1027	1121	|	1227	1321	|	1427	1522	|	1627	|	1728	|	1828	|	1928	2023	2122	2220
Oberwesel .... d.	0104	0624	0725	0823	0832	0931	1023	1032	1126	1223	1232	1326	1423	1432	1527	1623	1632	1723	1733	1823	1833	1925	1933	2027	2127	2225
St Goar .... d.	0110	0630	0731	|	0838	0937	|	1038	1132	|	1238	1332	|	1438	1533	|	1638	|	1739	|	1839	|	1939	2033	2133	2231
Boppard-Bad Salzig ... d.	0118	0638	0739	|	0846	0945	|	1046	1140	|	1246	1340	|	1446	1541	|	1646	|	1747	|	1847	|	1947	2041	2141	2239
Boppard Hbf .... d.	0122	0642	0743	0838	0850	0949	1038	1050	1144	1238	1250	1344	1438	1450	1545	1638	1650	1738	1751	1838	1851	1940	1951	2045	2145	2243
Koblenz Hbf .... a.	0137	0659	0800	0852	0907	1005	1052	1107	1201	1252	1307	1401	1452	1507	1601	1652	1707	1751	1807	1852	1907	1954	2007	2101	2201	2300

c – Ⓒ (also Dec. 24, 31, June 3).
d – Also Dec. 24, June 3.
e – Ⓐ (not Dec. 24, 31, June 3).
f – 0848 on June 3, 10.
m – Not Dec. 24.
n – Not Dec. 24, 31.
r – Not June 3.
w – Also June 3.

y – 2 minutes earlier on ⑦ (also Apr. 5, May 24; not Apr. 4, May 23).
z – ⑥⑦ (also Apr. 2, 5, May 13, 24). Runs daily except Dec. 25, Jan. 1 Mainz Hbf - Bingen (Rhein) Hbf.

◧ – ⚒ (not June 3). Runs daily Bingen (Rhein) Hbf - Mainz Hbf.
✣ – Dec. 28 - Jan. 18 rail services are suspended between Koblenz and Wiesbaden (via St Goarshausen). A special 🚌 service operates during this period. Please enquire locally.

* – Underground platforms.
‡ – Frankfurt Flughafen Regionalbahnhof ✈.
⊠ – Stopping services Koblenz - Mainz and v.v. are operated by TransRegio Deutsche Regionalbahn GmbH.
See Table **912** for long-distance *ICE* / *IC* services.
See Table **917a** for other S-Bahn services Mainz - Frankfurt Flughafen ✈ - Frankfurt (Main) Hbf and v.v.

2009 service; KD (see shaded panel) — KÖLN - KOBLENZ - MAINZ — 914a

◐		A	A⛴	K	D	B	D	①E	A	G	L
750	**Köln** (Rheingarten) .... d.							...	...	0930	0930
1600	**Bonn** .... d.							0730	...	1230	1230
1300	Bad Godesberg .... d.							0800	...	1300	1300
900	Königswinter Fähre ...... d.							0815	...	1330	1330
750	Bad Honnef (Rhein) ..... d.	...	...	...	...	...	...	0835	...	1350	1350
400	Remagen .... d.	...	...	...	...	...	...	0910	...	1420	1420
750	Linz am Rhein .... d.	...	...	...	...	...	...	0930	...	1450	1450
1500	Bad Breisig .... d.	...	...	...	0800	...	...	1000	...	—	1520
400	Bad Hönningen .... d.	...	...	...	0805	...	...	1005	...	...	1525
1200	Andernach .... d.	...	...	...	0850	...	...	1050	...	...	...
1500	Neuwied .... d.	...	...	...	0910	...	...	1110	...	...	...
2200	**Koblenz** ⊙ .... a.	...	...	...	1040	...	...	1300	...	G	...
2200	**Koblenz** ⊙ .... d.	...	0900	0945	1100	...	...	1305	1400	1810	...
600	Winningen (Mosel) ... a.	...	|	1055	|	...	...	1420	|	|	...
800	Cochem (Mosel) ...... a.	...	|	1500	|	...	...	...	|	|	...
750	Niederlahnstein .... d.	...	0930	—	1130	...	...	...	1430	1835	...
150	Oberlahnstein .... d.	...	0940	...	1140	...	...	...	1440	1845	...
450	Braubach .... d.	...	1005	...	1205	...	...	...	1505	1910	...
400	**Boppard** .... d.	0900	1100	...	1300	...	1400	...	1600	2000	...
400	Kamp-Bornhofen .... d.	0910	1110	...	1310	...	1410	...	1610	...	...
300	Bad Salzig .... d.	0925	1125	...	1325	...	1425	...	1625	...	...
450	**St Goarshausen** ... ★ d.	1010	1210	...	1410	1410	1510	...	1710	...	...
250	**St Goar** .... ★ d.	1020	1220	...	1420	1420	1520	...	1720	...	...
450	Oberwesel .... d.	1050	1250	...	1450	1450	1550	...	1750	...	...
900	Kaub .... d.	1105	1305	...	1505	1505	1605	...	1805	...	...
600	Bacharach .... d.	1130	1330	...	1530	1530	1630	...	1830	...	...
900	Assmannshausen .... d.	1230	1430	...	1630	1630	1730	...	1930	...	...
400	**Bingen** (Rhein) .... d.	1300	1500	P	1700	1700	1800	...	2000	...	...
900	**Rüdesheim** (Rhein) ...... d.	1315	1515	1530	1715	1715	1815	...	2015	...	...
1500	Wiesbaden-Biebrich .... d.	...	...	1730	1905	1905z	2005r	...	...	...	...
1600	**Mainz** .... a.	...	...	1800	1930	1930z	2030r	...	...	...	...

A special service operates on "Rhein in Flammen" days Aug. 1, Sept. 12, 19

	A	D‡	①E	D	B	P	A	G	K	A⛴
Mainz .... d.	...	0845	...	0945r	0945z	1130	...	...	...	...
Wiesbaden-Biebrich . d.	...	0905	...	1005r	1005z	1150	...	...	...	...
Rüdesheim (Rhein) d.	0915	1015	...	1115	1115	1315	1415	1415	...	1615
Bingen (Rhein) .... d.	0930	1030	...	1130	1130	...	1430	1430	...	1630
Assmannshausen ...... d.	0945	1045	...	1145	1145	...	1445	1445	...	1645
Bacharach .... d.	1015	1115	...	1215	1215	...	1515	1515	...	1715
Kaub .... d.	1025	1125	...	1225	1225	...	1525	1525	...	1725
Oberwesel .... d.	1035	1135	...	1235	1235	...	1535	1535	...	1735
St Goar .... ★ d.	1055	1155	...	1255	1255	...	1555	1555	...	1755
St Goarshausen ★ d.	1105	1205	...	1305	1305	...	1605	1605	...	1805
Bad Salzig .... d.	1130	1230	...	1330	...	...	1630	1630	...	1830
Kamp-Bornhofen .... d.	1140	1240	...	1340	...	...	1640	1640	...	1840
Boppard .... d.	1150	1250	...	1350	...	...	1650	1650	...	1850
Braubach .... d.	1220	1320	...	...	...	...	...	1720	...	1920
Oberlahnstein .... d.	1240	1340	...	...	...	...	...	1740	...	1940
Niederlahnstein .... d.	1250	1350	...	...	...	...	...	1750	...	1950
Cochem (Mosel) .... d.	|	|	...	...	...	...	...	|	1540	|
Winningen (Mosel) d.	|	|	1600	...	...	...	...	|	1845	|
Koblenz ⊙ .... a.	1310	1410	1700	...	...	...	...	1810	2000	2010
Koblenz ⊙ .... d.	—	1430	1705	...	...	...	...	...	...	...
Neuwied .... d.	...	1520	1750	...	...	...	...	...	...	...
Andernach .... d.	...	1540	1805	...	...	...	...	...	...	...
Bad Hönningen .... d.	...	1615‡	1830	...	...	...	...	...	...	...
Bad Breisig .... d.	J	1620	1840	...	...					
Linz am Rhein .... d.	1450	1650	1905	...	...					
Remagen .... d.	1500	1700	1915	...	...					
Bad Honnef (Rhein) . d.	1525	1725	1940	...	...					
Königswinter Fähre .. d.	1540	1740	2000	...	...					
Bad Godesberg .... d.	1545	1745	2010	...	...					
Bonn .... d.	1615	1815	2030	...	...					
Köln (Rheingarten) .. a.	1800	2000	...	...	...					

Köln-Düsseldorfer Deutsche Rheinschiffahrt AG,
Frankenwerft 35,
D-50667 Köln.
✆ +49 (0) 221 20 88 319
Fax +49 (0) 221 20 88 345

A – Apr. 10 - Oct. 25.
B – Apr. 10 – 24 and Oct. 5 – 25.
D – Apr. 25 - Oct. 4.
E – ① May 25 - Sept. 28.
G – ①⑤⑥⑦ Apr. 10 – 20; daily Apr. 24 - Oct. 5; ①⑤⑥⑦ Oct. 9 – 25.
J – ①⑤⑥⑦ Apr. 10 – 20; ⑤⑥ Apr. 24 - Oct. 3; ①⑤⑥⑦ Oct. 5 – 25.

K – ①⑤⑥⑦ Apr. 25 - June 15; daily June 26 - Oct. 4.
L – ①②③④⑦ Apr. 26 - Oct. 4.
P – ①③⑥ May 4 - Oct. 17 (also Apr. 13, Oct. 21; not Aug. 8). Operated by Primus-Linie.

r – July and August only.
z – ①⑤⑥⑦ only.

⛴ – Operated by paddlesteamer *Goethe* Apr. 25 - Oct. 4.
⊙ – Koblenz (Konrad-Adenauer-Ufer).
‡ – Change ships at Bad Hönningen on ①②③④⑦.
◐ – Distance in metres from rail station to river landing stage.
★ – A passenger ferry links St Goar and St Goarshausen. Frequent trips 0600 (0800 on †) to 2100 (2300 May 1 - Sept. 30). Operator: Rheinschiffahrt Goar. ✆ + 49 (0) 6771 26 20. Fax + 49 (0) 6771 24 04.

915 KOBLENZ - TRIER - LUXEMBOURG and SAARBRÜCKEN

RE / RB services except where shown

km		⑥b	Ⓐt	Ⓐt	Ⓐt K	⚒r	N	Ⓐt K	v K	⚒r	v	⚒r				Ⓐt M	⚒r					K	*IC* 338 ①–⑥ e 🍷			
	Norddeich Mole **812** d.	...	...	...	...	...	...	...	...	...	...	...	...	...	...	...	...	...	...	...	...	...	...	...	...	...
	Emden Hbf **812** d.	...	...	...	...	...	...	...	...	...	...	...	...	...	...	...	...	...	...	...	...	...	...	...	...	...
	Köln Hbf **800 802** d.	...	...	...	...	...	...	...	...	...	...	...	...	...	...	...	...	...	...	...	...	...	...	...	...	...
0	**Koblenz** Hbf d.	...	...	...	...	...	...	...	...	...	0522r	0559	...	...	0622	...	0722	...	0740	0822	...	0924	...	0940	1022
47	Cochem (Mosel) d.	...	...	...	...	0506	...	...	...	...	0611	0635	...	...	0722	...	0758	...	0827	0858	...	0958	...	1027	1058
59	Bullay d.	...	...	...	...	0518	...	...	...	...	0621	0644	...	...	0732	...	0807	...	0838	0907	...	1008	...	1038	1107
76	Wittlich Hbf d.	...	...	...	...	0532	...	...	...	...	0637	0657	...	...	0747	...	0820	...	0854	0920	...	1023	...	1054	1120
112	**Trier** Hbf a.	...	...	...	...	0607	...	...	...	...	0712	0728	...	...	0824	...	0846	...	0935	0946	...	1049	...	1135	1146
112	**Trier** Hbf ⊙ d.	0352	0409	0522	0527	...	0620	0634	...	0701	...	0730	0730	0801r	...	0831	...	0901	...	0947	...	1056	1101	...	1148
	Luxembourg ⊙ a.	|	|	|	|	...	|	|	...	|	...	|	|	|	...	|	...	|	...	|	...	1139	|	...	|
135	Saarburg d.	0418	0429	0540	0552	...	0641	0700	...	0725	...	0748	0748	0825r	...	0849	...	0925	...	1005	...	...	1125	...	1206
161	Merzig (Saar) d.	0445	0448	0559	0621	...	0701	0729	0729	0751	...	0808	0808	0851	...	0907	...	0951	...	1023	1123	...	1151	...	1224
173	Dillingen (Saar) d.	0457	0459	0609	0632	...	0710	0738	0738	0801	...	0817	0817	0902	...	0916	...	1002	...	1031	1132	...	1202	...	1232
177	Saarlouis Hbf d.	0501	0503	0613	0635	...	0714	0741	0741	0804	...	0821	0821	0905	...	0920	...	1005	...	1035	1135	...	1205	...	1236
190	Völklingen d.	0512	0514	0624	0645	...	0722	0750	0750	0815	...	0831	0831	0916	...	0928	...	1016	...	1043	1144	...	1216	...	1245
200	**Saarbrücken** Hbf a.	0526	0526	0634	0656	...	0733	0759	0759	0827	...	0841	0841	0927	...	0938	...	1027	...	1053	1153	...	1227	...	1254

	K		K	*IC* 336 🍷				*IC* 334 🍷	L			*IC* 332 Ⓑq 🍷	Ⓐt K				*IC* 330 🍷	Ⓐt K	n	n	n	*ICE* 856 Ⓑx B	n	n	n
Norddeich Mole **812** d.	...	...	...	...	...	...	...	0953	...	...	...	1136	...	...	...	...	1354	...	...	...	...	...	...	...	...
Emden Hbf **812** d.	...	...	...	0834h	...	...	...	1034	...	...	...	1234	...	...	...	...	1434	...	...	...	...	...	...	...	...
Köln Hbf **800 802** d.	...	...	...	1218	...	...	...	1418	...	...	...	1618	...	...	...	...	1818	...	...	...	...	2018	...	...	...
Koblenz Hbf d.	1122	1222	...	1324	...	1336	1422	1524	...	1540	1622	1724	...	...	1740	1822	1924	...	...	1940	2022	2124	...	2140	2222
Cochem (Mosel) d.	1158	1258	...	1358	...	1427	1458	1558	...	1627	1658	1758	...	...	1827	1858	1958	...	...	2027	2058	2159	...	2227	2258
Bullay d.	1207	1307	...	1408	...	1438	1507	1608	...	1638	1707	1808	...	...	1838	1907	2008	...	...	2038	2107	2210	...	2238	2307
Wittlich Hbf d.	1220	1320	...	1423	...	1454	1520	1623	...	1654	1720	1823	...	...	1854	1920	2023	...	...	2054	2120	2225	...	2254	2320
Trier Hbf a.	1246	1346	...	1449	...	1535	1546	1649	...	1735	1746	1849	...	...	1935	1946	2049	...	...	2135	2146	2252	...	2335	2350
Trier Hbf ⊙ d.	1248	1348	...	1457	1501	...	1548	1657	1654	...	1748	1851	1854	1901	...	1948	2051	2054	2101	...	2148	...	2301	...	...
Luxembourg ⊙ a.	|	|	...	1539	|	...	|	1743f	|	...	|	1934	|	|	...	|	2134	|	|	...	|	...	|	...	...
Saarburg d.	1306	1406	...	...	1525	...	1606	...	1712	...	1806	...	1912	1925	...	2006	...	2112	2125	...	2206	...	2325	...	...
Merzig (Saar) d.	1325	1424	1523	...	1551	...	1624	...	1730	...	1824	...	1930	1951	...	2024	...	2130	2151	...	2224	...	2347	...	...
Dillingen (Saar) d.	1336	1432	1532	...	1602	...	1632	...	1738	...	1832	...	1938	2002	...	2032	...	2138	2202	...	2232	...	2356	...	...
Saarlouis Hbf d.	1340	1436	1535	...	1605	...	1636	...	1742	...	1836	...	1942	2005	...	2036	...	2142	2205	...	2236	...	0000	...	...
Völklingen d.	1348	1445	1544	...	1616	...	1645	...	1750	...	1845	...	1950	2016	...	2045	...	2149	2216	...	2245	...	0008	...	...
Saarbrücken Hbf a.	1358	1454	1553	...	1627	...	1654	...	1759	...	1854	...	1959	2027	...	2054	...	2200	2226	...	2254	...	0017	...	...

	Ⓐt	*ICE* 855 Ⓐt B	⚒r	Ⓐt	v	Ⓐt	Ⓒk	Ⓐt	*IC* 331§ ①–⑥ e 🍷		⚒r	*ICE* 557 ⑥p B		v	*IC* 333 🍷		K		K	*IC* 335 🍷			K		K
Saarbrücken Hbf d.	...	...	...	0434	...	0521	0534	0549	...	...	0624	...	0702	0733	...	...	0817	0904	1001	...	...	1104	1201	1304	1401
Völklingen d.	...	...	...	0441	...	0531	0541	0556	...	...	0634	...	0710	0743	...	...	0825	0911	1008	...	...	1111	1208	1311	1408
Saarlouis Hbf d.	...	...	...	0450	...	0541	0550	0607	...	...	0645	...	0718	0753	...	...	0834	0920	1016	...	...	1120	1218	1320	1416
Dillingen (Saar) d.	...	...	...	0453	...	0544	0554	0611	...	...	0648	...	0722	0757	...	...	0838	0923	1019	...	...	1123	1222	1323	1419
Merzig (Saar) d.	...	...	...	0505	...	0554	0602	0620	...	...	0659	...	0730	0807	...	...	0846	0932	1027	...	...	1132	1232	1332	1427
Saarburg d.	...	...	...	0533	...	0620	0633	0642	...	...	0726	...	0750	0833	...	...	...	0952	1046	...	...	1152	1252	1352	1446
Luxembourg ⊙ d.	...	...	...	|	...	|	|	|	0620	...	|	...	|	|	0824	...	...	|	|	1024	...	|	|	|	|
Trier Hbf ⊙ a.	...	...	...	0559	...	0647	0700	0702	0707	...	0757	...	0811	0900	0907	...	...	1011	1105	1107	...	1211	1311	1411	1505
Trier Hbf d.	0355	0500	0521	...	0613	...	...	...	0709	0721	...	0803	0813	...	0909	0921	...	1013	...	1109	1121	1213	1313	1413	...
Wittlich Hbf d.	0418	0525	0557	...	0637	...	...	...	0734	0757	...	0830	0837	...	0934	0957	...	1037	...	1134	1157	1237	1337	1437	...
Bullay d.	0431	0540	0613	...	0651	...	...	...	0749	0813	...	0845	0851	...	0949	1013	...	1051	...	1149	1213	1251	1351	1451	...
Cochem (Mosel) d.	0440	0551	0627	...	0700	...	...	...	0759	0825	...	0856	0900	...	0959	1025	...	1100	...	1159	1225	1300	1400	1500	...
Koblenz Hbf a.	0520	0629	0721	...	0738	...	...	...	0835	0918	...	0933	0938	...	1035	1118	...	1138	...	1235	1318	1340	1438	1538	...
Köln Hbf **800 802** a.	...	0742	...	...	...	...	...	...	0942	...	...	1042	...	...	1142	...	...	...	...	1342	...	...	...	...	...
Emden Hbf **812** a.	...	...	...	...	...	...	...	...	1325	...	...	...	...	...	1525	...	...	...	...	1725	...	...	...	...	...
Norddeich Mole **812** a.	...	...	...	...	...	...	...	...	1404y	...	...	...	...	...	1604	...	...	...	...	1804	...	...	...	...	...

	IC 337 🍷				Ⓐt K	*IC* 339 Ⓑq 🍷		Ⓒz K	Ⓐt M			K	Ⓑs			n	n	K	n	n	n	n	n	n	Ⓑs
Saarbrücken Hbf d.	...	...	1504	1533	1601	...	...	1601	1623	1633	1704	1801	...	...	1905	...	1933	2003	...	2033	...	2115	2234	2321	2342
Völklingen d.	...	...	1511	1543	1608	...	...	1608	1632	1643	1711	1808	...	...	1912	...	1943	2010	...	2043	...	2123	2241	2331	2353
Saarlouis Hbf d.	...	...	1520	1553	1616	...	...	1617	1643	1653	1720	1816	...	...	1921	...	1953	2020	...	2053	...	2131	2251	2341	0005
Dillingen (Saar) d.	...	...	1523	1557	1619	...	...	1620	1647	1657	1723	1819	...	...	1924	...	1957	2024	...	2057	...	2135	2254	2345	0008
Merzig (Saar) d.	...	...	1532	1607	1627	...	...	1631	1657	1709	1732	1827	...	...	1932	...	2006	2033	...	2107	...	2144	2303	2354	0020
Saarburg d.	...	...	1552	1633	1646	...	...	...	1726	1734	1752	1847	...	...	1953	...	...	2054	...	2133	...	2206	2328	...	0041
Luxembourg ⊙ d.	1424	...	|	|	|	1624	...	...	|	|	|	|	...	...	|	...	...	|	...	|	...	|	|	...	|
Trier Hbf ⊙ a.	1507	...	1611	1700	1705	1707	...	...	1753	1800	1811	1907	...	...	2012	...	...	2115	...	2200	...	2228	2400	...	0101
Trier Hbf d.	1509	1521	1613	...	...	1709	1721	...	...	...	1813	...	1913	1921	2013n	2113	...	...	2121	...	2221	...	...	...	...
Wittlich Hbf d.	1534	1557	1637	...	...	1734	1757	...	...	...	1837	...	1937	1957	2037n	2137	...	...	2157	...	2257	...	...	...	...
Bullay d.	1549	1613	1651	...	...	1749	1813	...	...	...	1851	...	1951	2013	2051n	2151	...	...	2213	...	2313	...	...	...	...
Cochem (Mosel) d.	1559	1625	1700	...	...	1759	1825	...	...	...	1900	...	2000	2025	2100n	2200	...	...	2225	...	2324	...	...	...	...
Koblenz Hbf a.	1635	1718	1738	...	...	1835	1918	...	...	...	1938	...	2038	2118n	2138n	2238	...	...	2318	...	...	...	...	...	...
Köln Hbf **800 802** a.	1742	...	...	...	...	...	...	...	...	...	...	...	...	...	...	...	...	...	...	...	...	...	...	...	...
Emden Hbf **812** a.	2125j	...	...	...	...	...	...	...	...	...	...	...	...	...	...	...	...	...	...	...	...	...	...	...	...
Norddeich Mole **812** a.	...	...	...	...	...	...	...	...	...	...	...	...	...	...	...	...	...	...	...	...	...	...	...	...	...

Complete service Trier - Luxembourg and v.v.

km	🏛 at Igel	①–⑤ a	①–⑤ a	①–⑥ d	⑦ c	①–⑤ a				①–⑥ e‡				‡		‡	①–⑤ a		Ⓑ q‡	⑥ m	n	‡	n	①–⑤ a n	n
0	**Trier** Hbf d.	0535	0624	0640	0707	0724	0752	0857	0952	1056	1152	1257	1352	1457	1552	1657	1726	1752	1851	1857	1952	2051	2152	2257	2357
51	**Luxembourg** a.	0633	0717	0745	0809	0817	0845	0942	1045	1139	1245	1345	1445	1539	1645	1743f	1814	1845	1934	1941	2041	2134	2241	2341	0041

🏛 at Wasserbillig	①–⑤ a	①–⑥ e‡	①–⑤ a		‡		‡				‡		Ⓑ q‡	⑥ m	①–⑤ a	⑥⑦ w	①–⑤ a	①–⑤ a	⑥⑦ w	①–⑤ a		n	n	①–⑤ a n	n
Luxembourg d.	0517	0620	0635	0717	0824	0917	1024	1117	1217	1317	1424	1517	1624	1624	1715	1717	1741	1815	1817	1841	1915	2017	2115	2152	2252
Trier Hbf a.	0606	0707	0734	0806	0907	1006	1107	1206	1306	1406	1507	1606	1707	1707	1804	1806	1832	1904	1904	1932	2006	2106	2206	2256	2356

B – (12) Trier - Hannover - Berlin and v.v.
K – To / from Kaiserslautern (Table **919**).
L – To Kaiserslautern on ⚒r (Table **919**).
M – To / from Mannheim (Table **919**).
N – To Mannheim on Ⓐt (Table **919**).

a – Not Dec. 25, Jan. 1, Apr. 5, May 13, 24.
b – Also Dec. 24, 31; not Dec. 26, May 1.
c – Also Dec. 25, 26, Jan. 1, Apr. 5, May 1, 13, 24.
d – Not Dec. 25, 26, Jan. 1, Apr. 5, May 1, 13, 24.
e – Not Dec. 25, 26, Jan. 1, Apr. 3, 5, May 24.
f – 1739 on ⑥⑦ (also Dec. 25, Jan. 1, Apr. 5, May 13, 24).
h – ①–⑥ to Mar. 20 (not Dec. 25, 26, Jan. 1); daily from Mar. 22.
j – Ⓑ to Mar. 19 (not Dec. 24, 25, 31); daily from Mar. 21.
k – Also Dec. 24, 31, June 3; not Dec. 25, Jan. 1.
m – Also Dec. 24, 25, 31, Apr. 2, 4, May 23; not Dec. 26, May 1.

n – Not Dec. 24, 31.
p – Also Dec. 24, 31, Apr. 2, May 13, June 3; not Dec. 26, Apr. 3, May 15, June 5.
q – Not Dec. 24, 25, 31, Apr. 2, 4, May 23.
r – ⚒ (not June 3).
s – Also Dec. 26, May 1; not Dec. 24, 31.
t – Not Dec. 24, 31, June 3.
v – Not Dec. 25, Jan. 1.
w – Also Dec. 25, Jan. 1, Apr. 5, May 13, 24.
x – Not Dec. 24, 25, 31, Apr. 2, 4, May 14, 23.
y – ①②③④⑥ to Mar. 25.
z – Also Dec. 24, 31, June 3.

⊙ – See also panel below main table.
‡ – *IC* train (see main Table).
§ – Train **231** on ①②③④⑥ to Mar. 25.

BULLAY - TRABEN-TRARBACH *13 km*

Journey time: 20 minutes.
Last services on Dec. 24, 31: From Bullay at 1717, from Traben at 1643.
From Bullay at 0655 ⚒r, 0817 and hourly until 2217.
From Traben-Trarbach at 0619 ⚒r, 0723, 0843 and hourly until 2143.

TRIER - METZ *No through services until August 2010*

km						
0	**Trier** Hbf d.	...	...	**Metz** d.	...	...
49	Apach d.	...	...	Hagondange d.	...	...
70	Thionville a.	...	...	Thionville d.	...	...
82	Hagondange a.	...	...	Apach a.	...	...
100	**Metz** a.	...	...	**Trier** Hbf a.	...	...

KARLSRUHE - OFFENBURG - KONSTANZ 916

IRE / RE services except where shown

km		⚒r	Ⓐe	⑥k	Ⓒz									IC 2005 ⑤⑥ N🍷				IC 2371 B🍷	IC 2364 ①–⑤ S				✝w	⚒r ●	⑤✝ ⊡
0	**Karlsruhe** Hbf ...... **912 943** d.	...	...	0500	...	0608	0704	0810	0910	1010	1110	1210	1310	1336	1410	1510	1610	1652	1733	1810	1910	2010	2116	2116	2221
23	Rastatt .... **943** d.	...	...	0513	...	0620	0718	0823	0923	1023	1123	1223	1323	|	1423	1523	1623	1706	1747	1823	1923	2023	2129	2129	2240
31	Baden-Baden .... **912** d.	...	...	0519	...	0626	0727	0830	0930	1030	1130	1230	1330	1356	1430	1530	1630	1717	1754	1830	1930	2030	2136	2136	2247
71	**Offenburg** .... **912 942** d.	...	0523	0554	...	0658	0759	0859	0959	1059	1159	1259	1359	1418	1459	1559	1659	1735	1813	1859	1959	2104	2205	2205	2323j
104	Hausach .... **942** d.	...	0548	0619	...	0723	0818	0921	1018	1121	1218	1321	1418	1439	1521	1618	1721	1755	...	1921	2018	2128	2228	2228	2348
114	Hornberg (Schwarzw) .... d.	...	0556	0627	...	0731	0826	0930	1026	1130	1226	1330	1426	1448	1530	1626	1730	1803	...	1930	2026	2136	2236	2236	2356
127	Triberg .... d.	...	0609	0640	...	0744	0839	0944	1039	1144	1239	1344	1439	1503	1544	1639	1744	1817	...	1944	2039	2149	2249	2249	0009
142	St Georgen (Schwarzw) .... d.	...	0625	0655	...	0759	0854	0958	1054	1158	1253	1358	1454	1520	1558	1654	1758	1832	...	1958	2054	2203	2303	2303	0023
157	Villingen (Schwarzw) ..... **938** d.	0554	0636	0705	0705	0808	0904	1009	1104	1209	1303	1409	1504	1531	1609	1704	1809	1842	...	2009	2104	2213	2312	2312	0032
171	Donaueschingen .... **938** d.	0604	0654j	0714	0714	0817	0913	1018	1113	1218	1313	1418	1513	1542	1618	1713	1818	1853	...	2018	2113	2222	2322	*2340*n	...
190	Immendingen .... **938** d.	0619	0706	0726	0726	0828	|	1029	|	1229	|	1429	|	1554	1629	|	1829	1904	...	2029	2124	2234	2334	*2353*n	...
206	Engen .... **940** d.	0633	0719	0738	0738	0841	|	1042	|	1242	|	1442	|	|	1642	|	1842	|	...	2042	|	2247	|	...	...
220	**Singen** .... **940** a.	0645	0733	0748	0748	0850	0943	1050	1143	1250	1343	1450	1543	1616	1650	1743	1850	1924	...	2050	2144	2300	2353	...	...
220	**Singen** .... **939** d.	0651	0735	0752	0752	0853	0953	1053	1153	1253	1353	1453	1553	1618	1653	1753	1853	1926	...	2053	2155b	2301	2354	...	...
230	Radolfzell .... **939** d.	0703	0746	0800	0800	0900	1000	1100	1200	1300	1400	1500	1600	1628	1700	1800	1900	1934	...	2100	2202b	2310	0001	...	...
250	**Konstanz** .... a.	0725	0810	0816	0816	0916	1016	1116	1216	1316	1416	1516	1616	1644	1716	1816	1916	1951	...	2116	2216b	2329	0016	...	...

	IC 2365 ①–⑤ S✕	⚒r	⚒r	Ⓐe	Ⓒz				IC 2006 ⑥ D🍷	IC 2004 ⑦ E🍷	IC 2370 A🍷										✝w			⑤f	m
Konstanz .... d.	...	...	0502e	0524	0551k	0638	0735	0838	0909	0909	1006	1038	1138	1238	1338	1438	1538	1638	1738	1838	1938	2038	2159	2159	2322
Radolfzell .... **939** d.	...	...	0516e	0545j	0606k	0655	0758j	0855	0923	0923	1025	1055	1158j	1255	1358j	1455	1558j	1655	1758j	1855	1958j	2055	2223	2223	2347
Singen .... **939** a.	...	...	0522e	0555	0612k	0702	0805	0902	0930	0930	1032	1102	1205	1302	1405	1502	1605	1702	1805	1902	2005	2102	2232	2232	2356
Singen .... **940** d.	...	...	0530	0557	0614	0705	0816	0905	0932	0932	1034	1105	1216	1305	1416	1505	1611	1705	1816	1905	2016	2105	2233	2233	0000
Engen .... **940** d.	...	...	0539	|	|	0715	|	0914	|	|	|	1114	|	1314	|	1514	|	1714	|	1914	|	2114	2248	2248	0013
Immendingen .... **938** d.	...	...	0552	0618	0635	0728	|	0928	0953	0953	1056	1128	|	1328	|	1528	|	1728	|	1928	|	2127	2301	2301	▬
Donaueschingen .... **938** d.	...	*0503*e	0603	0630	0645	0740	0845	0939	1005	1005	1107	1139	1245	1339	1445	1539	1645	1739	1845	1939	2045	2140	2313	2313	...
Villingen (Schwarzw) ..... **938** d.	...	0535	0612	0641	0655	0750	0855	0949	1016	1016	1117	1149	1255	1349	1455	1549	1655	1749	1855	1949	2055	2150	2323	2324	...
St Georgen (Schwarzw) .... d.	...	0544	0621	0650	0703	0759	0903	0958	1026	1026	1126	1158	1303	1358	1503	1558	1703	1758	1903	1958	2103	2158	▬	2333	...
Triberg .... d.	...	0558	0635	0705	0718	0813	0918	1012	1042	1042	1141	1212	1318	1412	1518	1612	1718	1812	1918	2012	2118	2213	...	2347	*ICE*
Hornberg (Schwarzw) .... d.	...	0612	0649	0718	0727	0828	0927	1027	1057	1057	1155	1227	1327	1427	1527	1627	1727	1827	1927	2027	2131	2226	...	0000	**608**
Hausach .... **942** d.	...	0621	0657	0727	0739	0836	0939	1035	1105	1105	1203	1235	1339	1435	1539	1635	1739	1835	1939	2035	2139	2234	...	0008	
Offenburg .... **912 942** a.	0558	0647	0718	0746	0758	0858	0958	1058	1125	1125	1221	1258	1358	1458	1558	1658	1758	1858	1958	2058	2158	2300	2323	0033	0049
Baden-Baden .... **912** a.	0617	0723	0800e	0818	0827	0927z	1027	1127	1200	1200	1240	1327	1427	1527	1627	1727	1827	1927	2027	2127	2227	...	2346	...	0104
Rastatt .... **943** a.	0624	0730	0806e	0825	0833	0933z	1033	1133	|	|	1250	1333	1433	1533	1633	1733	1833	1933	2033	2133	2233	...	2352	...	|
Karlsruhe Hbf .... **912 943** a.	0635	0748	0821e	0839	0848	0948z	1048	1148	1219	1219	1306	1348	1448	1548	1648	1748	1848	1948	2048	2148	2248	...	0005	...	0127

A – SCHWARZWALD – [12] and 🍷 Konstanz - Frankfurt - Hamburg (- Stralsund ⑤⑦t). Train number **2270** on ⑤⑦t.
B – SCHWARZWALD – [12] and 🍷 Hamburg - Frankfurt - Konstanz.
D – ⑥ (also Dec. 24, 25, 31, Apr. 2, 4, May 23). BODENSEE – [12] and 🍷 Konstanz - Dortmund.
E – ⑦ (also Jan. 1, Apr. 5, May 13, 24, June 3; not Apr. 4, May 23). BODENSEE – [12] and 🍷 Konstanz - Köln - Münster - Emden.
N – ⑤⑥ (also Dec. 23, 24, 30, 31, Apr. 1, 3, 4, May 12, 23, June 2; not Apr. 3). BODENSEE – [12] and 🍷 Emden - Münster - Köln - Konstanz. Train number **2007** on Dec. 25, 26, Jan. 1, Apr. 3, 4, May 23.

S – ①–⑤ (not Dec. 24, 25, 31, Jan. 1, Apr. 2, 5, May 24). To / from Stuttgart (Table **931**).
b – Ⓑ (also Dec. 26, May 1; not Dec. 24, 31).
e – Ⓐ (not Dec. 24, 31, Jan. 6, June 3).
f – Also Dec. 23, 30; not Dec. 25, Jan. 1, Apr. 2.
j – Arrives 7 – 10 minutes earlier.
k – ⑥ (also Dec. 24, 31; not Dec. 26, May 1).
m – Not Dec. 24, 25, 26, 31, Jan. 1.
n – Not Dec. 24, 31.

r – Not Jan. 6, June 3.
t – Also Dec. 23, 30, Apr. 1, 5, May 12, 24; not Dec. 25, Jan. 1, Apr. 2, 4, May 14, 23.
w – Also Jan. 6, June 3.
z – Ⓒ (also Dec. 24, 31, Jan. 6, June 3).

⊡ – ⑤✝ (also Jan. 6, June 3); runs daily Karlsruhe - Hausach.
● – Change trains at Offenburg on Ⓐe.

FRANKFURT - MAINZ - IDAR OBERSTEIN - SAARBRÜCKEN 917

RB / RE services

km		✝w	Ⓐe	Ⓐe	⚒r	⚒r	v										⑤f			A			n	Ⓐe	n
0	**Frankfurt** (Main) Hbf .... ‡d.	...	...	...	...	...	...	0725	0825	...	1025	...	1225	...	1425	...	1531	1625	...	1734	1825	...	2025	2225	...
11	Frankfurt Flughafen ✈ § .... ‡d.	...	...	...	...	...	...	0737	0837	...	1037	...	1237	...	1437	...	|	1637	...	|	1837	...	2037	2237	...
39	**Mainz** Hbf .... ‡d.	...	...	...	0510e	b	0655	0800	0900	1000	1100	1155	1300	1355	1500	1555	1606	1700	1755	1806	1900	1955	2100	2300	2305
80	Bad Kreuznach .... d.	...	0501	...	0542e	0632e	0737	0826	0926	1026	1126	1224	1326	1424	1526	1624	1643	1726	1824	1843	1926	2024	2126	2326	2344
102	Bad Sobernheim .... d.	...	0523	...	0603e	0654	0755	0844	0944	1044	1144	1244	1344	1444	1544	1644	1706	1744	1844	1906	1944	2044	2144	2344	0007
117	Kirn .... d.	...	0540	...	0619e	0712	0805	0854	0954	1054	1154	1254	1354	1454	1554	1654	1725	1754	1854	1925	1954	2054	2154	2354	0023
131	Idar-Oberstein .... d.	...	0558	...	0635	0729	0816	0905	1005	1105	1205	1305	1405	1505	1605	1705	1743	1805	1905	1943	2005	2105	2205	0005	0040
155	Türkismühle .... d.	0543	0628	0634	0704	0759	0837	0926	1026	1126	1226	1326	1426	1526	1626	1726	...	1826	1926	...	2026	2126	2226	0026	...
170	St Wendel .... d.	0600	...	0651	0723	0818	0850	0938	1038	1138	1238	1338	1438	1538	1638	1738	...	1838	1938	...	2038	2138	2238	0038	...
179	Ottweiler (Saar) .... d.	0608	...	0658	0733	0826	0858	0945	1045	1145	1245	1345	1445	1545	1645	1745	...	1845	1945	...	2045	2145	2245	0045	...
184	Neunkirchen (Saar) .... d.	0615	...	0705	0740	0833	0905	0952	1052	1152	1252	1352	1452	1552	1652	1752	...	1852	1952	...	2052	2152	2252	0052	...
205	**Saarbrücken** Hbf .... a.	0641	...	0722	0800	0854	0924	1011	1111	1211	1311	1412	1511	1612	1711	1812	...	1911	2012	...	2111	2212	2311	0111	...

	Ⓐe	Ⓐe	⚒r	v														n	n	n	Ⓑd	Ⓐe	n	n	n
Saarbrücken Hbf .... d.	0348	...	0446	0546	0652	0750	0852	0950	1052	1150	1252	1350	1452	1550	1652	1750	1850	1935	...	2035	2105	...	2135	2235	2335
Neunkirchen (Saar) .... d.	0404	...	0504	0602	0708	0808	0908	1008	1108	1208	1308	1408	1508	1608	1708	1808	1908	2002	...	2108	2134	...	2214	2314	0004
Ottweiler (Saar) .... d.	0410	...	0510	0608	0713	0813	0913	1013	1113	1213	1313	1413	1513	1613	1713	1813	1913	2009	...	2115	2141	...	2221	2321	0011
St Wendel .... d.	0417	...	0517	0616	0721	0821	0921	1021	1121	1221	1321	1421	1521	1621	1721	1821	1921	2020	...	2125	2151	2202	2233	2331	0025
Türkismühle .... d.	0428	...	0528	0627	0732	0832	0932	1032	1132	1232	1332	1432	1532	1632	1732	1832	1932	2037	...	2141	...	2222	2253	2347	...
Idar-Oberstein .... d.	0449	...	0549	0649	0752	0852	0952	1052	1152	1252	1352	1452	1552	1652	1752	1852	1952	2103	...	...	...	2251	...	...	...
Kirn .... d.	0500	0505	0600	0700	0803	0903	1003	1103	1203	1303	1403	1503	1603	1703	1803	1903	2003	2117	...	...	...	...	...	...	...
Bad Sobernheim .... d.	0509	0523	0610	0710	0812	0912	1012	1112	1212	1312	1412	1512	1612	1712	1812	1912	2012	2131	...	...	...	...	...	...	...
Bad Kreuznach .... d.	0529	0602	0631	0731	0831	0933	1031	1133	1231	1333	1431	1533	1631	1733	1831	1933	2033	2153	2247	...	...	...	...	...	...
Mainz Hbf .... ‡a.	0557	0639	0657	0756	0857	1004	1057	1204	1257	1404	1457	1604	1657	1804	1857	2004	2104	2220	2325	...	...	...	...	...	...
Frankfurt Flughafen ✈ § .... ‡a.	0621	|	0721	0821	0921	...	1121	...	1321	...	1521	...	1721	...	1921	...	...	...	...	...	...	...	...	...	...
Frankfurt (Main) Hbf .... ‡a.	0636	0724	0736	0836	0936	...	1136	...	1336	...	1536	...	1736	...	1936	...	...	...	...	...	...	...	...	...	...

A – ①–④ (not Dec. 24, 31, Apr. 5, May 13, 24, June 3).
b – From Bingen (Table **918**).
d – Also Dec. 26, May 1; not Dec. 24, 31.
e – Ⓐ (not Dec. 24, 31, June 3).
f – Not Dec. 25, Jan. 1, Apr. 2.
n – Not Dec. 24, 31.
r – Not June 3.
v – Not Dec. 25, Jan. 1.
w – Also June 3; not Dec. 25, Jan. 1.
‡ – See also Tables **912**, **914** and **917a**.
§ – Frankfurt Flughafen Regionalbahnhof ✈.

FRANKFURT - FRANKFURT FLUGHAFEN ✈ - MAINZ - WIESBADEN 917a

S-Bahn 8 / 9

SEE NOTE ⊠	⚒	✝	⚒	⚒		⚒		⚒	✝	⚒	⚒		✝	⚒		✝	⚒			✝	⚒		✝	⚒
Frankfurt (Main) Hbf ▽ d.	0417	0447	0447	0502	0517	0532	and at	1232	1247	1247	1302	1317	1331*	1332	1347	1401*	1402	1417	and at	2001*	2002	2017	2031*	2032
Frankfurt Flughafen ⊖ d.	0429	0459	0459	0514	0529	0544	the same	1244	1259	1259	1314	1329	1344	1344	1359	1412	1414	1429	the same	2012	2014	2029	2044	2044
Mainz Hbf .... d.	0456	|	0526	|	0556	|	minutes	|	|	1326	|	1356	|	|	1426	...	|	1456	minutes	...	|	2056	|	|
Mainz-Kastel .... d.	|	0524	|	0539	|	0609	past each	1309	1324	|	1339	|	1409	1409	|	...	1439	|	past each	...	2039	|	2109	2109
Wiesbaden Hbf .... a.	0507	0533	0537	0548	0607	0618	hour until	1318	1333	1337	1348	1407	1418	1418	1437	...	1448	1507	hour until	...	2048	2107	2118	2118

SEE NOTE ⊠										
Frankfurt (Main) Hbf ▽ d.	2047	2117	2131*	2147	2217	2231*	2247	2317	2331*	0017
Frankfurt Flughafen ⊖ d.	2059	2129	2144	2159	2229	2244	2259	2329	2344	0029
Mainz Hbf .... d.	2126	2156	|	2226	2256	|	2326	2356	|	0056
Mainz-Kastel .... d.	|	|	2209	|	|	2309	|	|	0009	|
Wiesbaden Hbf .... a.	2137	2207	2218	2237	2307	2318	2337	0007	0018	0107

SEE NOTE ⊠		⚒	✝	⚒		⚒		⚒	✝	⚒
Wiesbaden Hbf .... d.	0350	0420	0427	0441	0450	0511	and at	1120	1127	1141
Mainz-Kastel .... d.	|	|	0434	0449	|	0519	the same	|	1134	1149
Mainz Hbf .... d.	0402	0432	|	|	0502	|	minutes	1132	|	|
Frankfurt Flughafen ✈ .. ⊖ d.	0432	0502	0502	0517	0532	0547	past each	1202	1202	1217
Frankfurt (Main) Hbf .... a.	0443	0513	0513	0528	0543	0558	hour until	1213	1213	1228

SEE NOTE ⊠		⚒				⚒	✝		⚒	✝													Ⓐn	Ⓒz	
Wiesbaden Hbf .... d.	1150	1211	1220	1241	1250	1311	...	and at	1911	...	1920	1941	1950	2020	2041	2050	2120	2141	2150	2220	2241	2250	2320	2327	2350
Mainz-Kastel .... d.	|	1219	|	1249	|	1319	...	the same	1919	...	|	1949	|	|	2049	|	|	2149	|	|	2249	|	|	2334	|
Mainz Hbf .... d.	1202	|	1232	|	1302	|	...	minutes	|	...	1932	|	2002	2032	|	2102	2132	|	2202	2232	|	2302	2332	|	0002
Frankfurt Flughafen ⊖ d.	1232	1247	1302	1317	1332	1347	1347	past each	1947	1947	2002	2017	2032	2102	2117	2132	2202	2217	2232	2302	2317	2332	0002	0002	0032
Frankfurt (Main) Hbf .. a.	1243	1258	1313	1329	1343	1358	1359	hour until	1958	1959	2013	2029	2043	2113	2129	2143	2213	2229	2243	2313	2329	2343	0013	0013	0043

n – Not Dec. 24, 31.
z – Also Dec. 24, 31.
⊠ – Subject to alteration on Dec. 13. On June 3 services run as on ⑦.
▽ – From the underground platforms, except where shown by note *.
* – Departs from the main station (not underground platforms).
⊖ – Frankfurt Flughafen Regionalbahnhof ✈.

918 RHEINLAND-PFALZ LOCAL SERVICES

RB / S-Bahn services

Pirmasens - Saarbrücken

km		Ⓐe	⚒r	Ⓐe	E	⑦			n	n
0	**Pirmasens** Hbf .... d.	0515	0552	*0625*	*0732*	0732	0832	and hourly until	1932	2032
7	Pirmasens Nord .... d.	0522	0602	0641	0743	0743	0843		1943	2043
31	Zweibrücken Hbf .... d.	0552	0640	0713	0813	0813	0913		2013	2113
67	**Saarbrücken** Hbf .... a.	0636	0722	0752	0851	0851	0951		2051	2151

	⚒r	Ⓐe	⑥k	v		❖		n	n
Saarbrücken Hbf ..... d.	0602	0633	...	0704	0807	and hourly until	1907	2007	2107
Zweibrücken Hbf ..... d.	0643	0712	...	0745	0845		1945	2045	2145
Pirmasens Nord .... a.	0715	0741	0747	0816	0916		2016	2116	2215
Pirmasens Hbf .... a.	*0730*e	0753	0755	0826	0926		2026	2126	2224

Pirmasens - Landau (Pfalz) - Neustadt (Weinstr)

km		Ⓐe	⚒r	Ⓐe	v													n							
0	**Pirmasens** Hbf .... d.	0444	0544	0625	0701	0801	0901	1001	1101	1201	1301	1401	1501	1601	1701	1801	1901	2001	...	...	...	...	...	...	...
7	Pirmasens Nord .... d.	0456	0558	0639	0719	0819	0919	1019	1119	1219	1319	1419	1519	1619	1719	1819	1919	2019	...	...	...	...	...	...	...
55	**Landau** (Pfalz) Hbf ...... a.	0550	0658	0737	0818	0918	1018	1118	1218	1318	1418	1518	1618	1718	1818	1918	2018	2118	...	...	...	...	...	...	...
73	**Neustadt** (Weinstr) Hbf. a.	0618	*0723*	*0758*	*0844*	*0944*	*1044*	*1144*	*1244*	*1344*	*1444*	*1544*	*1644*	*1744*	*1844*	*1944*	*2044*	*2156*	...	...	...	...	...	...	...

	Ⓐe	Ⓐe	⚒r	⑥k	Ⓐe	†w	⑥k			†w	⚒r							Ⓒz	Ⓐe		Ⓒz	Ⓐe	n	n
Neustadt (Weinstr) Hbf .... d.	*0511*	*0554*	0616	...	0659	0703	0717	...	*0816*	0916	*0916*	*1016*	*1116*	*1216*	*1316*	*1416*	*1516*	*1616*	*1618*	*1716*	*1816*	*1818*	*1916*	*2016*
Landau (Pfalz) Hbf .... d.	0533	0618	0635	0645	0712	0722	0737	0741	0841	0941	0941	1041	1141	1241	1341	1441	1541	1641	1641	1741	1841	1841	1941	2041
Pirmasens Nord .... a.	0636	0717	...	0740	...	...	...	0840	0940	1040	1040	1140	1240	1340	1440	1540	1640	1740	1740	1840	1940	1940	2040	2140
Pirmasens Hbf .... a.	0658	0730	...	0755	...	...	...	0858	0958	1058	1058	1158	1258	1358	1458	1558	1658	1758	1758	1858	1958	1958	2058	2158

Bingen - Kaiserslautern - Pirmasens

km		Ⓐe	⚒r	⚒r	v	Ⓐ	v														†w	n	⚒d	⑤⑥f	Ⓒp
0	**Bingen** (Rhein) Hbf ..... d.	...	...	0548	...	0612	0649	0755	0855	0955	1055	1155	1255	1355	1455	1555	1655	1755	1855	1955	2102	...	2208	2208	...
16	Bad Kreuznach .... d.	...	*0506*e	0609	...	0631	0710	0816	0916	1016	1116	1216	1316	1416	1516	1616	1716	1816	1916	2016	2130	...	2228	2247	...
43	Rockenhausen .... d.	...	*0534*e	0639	...	s	0740	0855	0955	1055	1155	1255	1355	1455	1555	1655	1755	1855	1955	2055	2159	...	...	2317	...
79	**Kaiserslautern** Hbf .... a.	...	*0609*e	0717	...	...	0819	0929	1026	1126	1226	1326	1426	1526	1626	1726	1826	1926	2026	2130	2237	...	...	2349	...
79	**Kaiserslautern** Hbf .... d.	0517	0630	...	0735	...	*0835*	*0935*	*1035*	*1135*	*1235*	*1335*	*1435*	*1535*	*1635*	*1735*	*1835*	*1935*	*2035*n	...	...	2250	...	...	0030
108	Pirmasens Nord .... a.	0554	0710	...	0806	...	*0906*	*1006*	*1106*	*1206*	*1306*	*1406*	*1506*	*1606*	*1706*	*1806*	*1906*	*2006*	*2106*n	...	...	2321	...	...	0101
115	**Pirmasens** Hbf .... a.	0608	0719	...	0818	...	*0918*	*1018*	*1118*	*1218*	*1318*	*1418*	*1518*	*1618*	*1718*	*1818*	*1918*	*2018*	*2118*n	...	...	2331	...	...	0111

	Ⓒp		⚒r	⚒r	Ⓐe	Ⓐe	⚒r	v	⚒r	†w													n	n	n
Pirmasens Hbf .... d.	...	...	...	...	*0532*	0614	...	*0641*	0732	0741	...	*0841*	*0941*	*1041*	*1141*	*1241*	*1341*	*1441*	*1541*	*1641*	*1741*	*1841*	*1941*	2041	...
Pirmasens Nord .... d.	...	...	...	...	*0540*	0622	...	*0652*	0750	0750	...	*0850*	*0950*	*1050*	*1150*	*1250*	*1350*	*1450*	*1550*	*1650*	*1750*	*1850*	*1950*	2050	...
Kaiserslautern Hbf ..... a.	...	...	...	...	*0610*	0658	...	*0723*	0826	0826	...	*0926*	*1026*	*1125*	*1226*	*1326*	*1426*	*1526*	*1626*	*1726*	*1826*	*1926*	*2026*	2126	...
Kaiserslautern Hbf ..... d.	0030	...	0521	0556	0640	...	0715	0737	...	...	0832	0932	1032	1132	1232	1332	1432	1532	1638	1738	1838	1932	2032	...	2139
Rockenhausen .... d.	0104	...	0555	0636	0713	...	0750	0812	...	...	0901	1001	1101	1201	1301	1401	1501	1601	1708	1808	1908	2001	2101	...	2209
Bad Kreuznach .... d.	0135	...	0642	0717	0743	...	0822	0842	...	...	0941	1041	1141	1241	1341	1441	1541	1641	1741	1841	1941	2041	2133	...	2240
Bingen (Rhein) Hbf ...... a.	...	...	0701	0736	0802	...	...	0901	...	...	1000	1100	1200	1300	1400	1500	1600	1700	1800	1900	2000	2100	2152	...	...

Neustadt (Weinstr) - Karlsruhe and Wissembourg

km		Ⓐe	Ⓐe	Ⓐe	Ⓐe	⚒r	⚒r	⚒r	Ⓐe	Ⓒz							A	†B		A	†B			Ⓐe	Ⓒz
0	**Neustadt** (Weinstr) Hbf. d.	0428	...	0511	...	0529	0616	...	0659	0703g	0736	0809	0836	0909	0936	1009	1036	1044	1109	1136	1145	1209	1236	1307	1309
18	Landau (Pfalz) Hbf ...... d.	0447	...	0536	...	0554	0636	...	0712	0722	0758	0822	0858	0922	0958	1022	1058	1058	1122	1158	1159	1222	1258	1319	1322
31	Winden (Pfalz) .... d.	0502	0505	0551	0555	0603	0652	0658	0721	0731	0808	0831	0908	0931	1008	1031	1108	1108	1131	1208	1208	1231	1308	1331	1331
47	**Wissembourg** 🏛 ◐ a.	|	0521	|	0615	|	|	0718	|	|	0828	|	0928	|	1028	|	1128	1128	|	1228	1228	|	1328	|	|
44	Wörth (Rhein) .... d.	0518	...	0605	...	0617	0708	...	0736	0744	...	0844	...	0944	...	1044	...	...	1144	...	...	1244	...	1344	1344
58	**Karlsruhe** Hbf .... a.	0530	...	...	...	0636	0726	...	0752	0754	...	0854	...	0954	...	1054	...	...	1154	...	...	1254	...	1354	1354

					n		n	n	n	n	⑥x
Neustadt (Weinstr) Hbf .. d.	1336	1409	and at the same minutes past each hour until	1909	1936	2009	2104	*2138*	2221	2321	2321
Landau (Pfalz) Hbf .... d.	1358	1422		1922	1958	2022	2122	*2158*	2241	2341	2342
Winden (Pfalz) .... d.	1408	1431		1931	2008	2031	2131	2229	...	...	2357
Wissembourg 🏛 ◐ .a.	1428	|		|	2029	|	|	|	...	...	|
Wörth (Rhein) .... d.	...	1444		1944	...	2044	2143	2244	...	...	0013
Karlsruhe Hbf .... a.	...	1454		1954	...	2054	2154	2256	...	...	...

	Ⓐe	Ⓐe	⚒r	⚒r	Ⓒz	Ⓐe	⑥k	Ⓐe
Karlsruhe Hbf .... d.	0431	...	0558	...	0707	0714	...	...
Wörth (Rhein) .... d.	0447	...	0618	...	0716	0735	...	...
Wissembourg 🏛 ◐ .... d.	|	0527	|	0626e	|	|	0733	0733
Winden (Pfalz) .... d.	0502	0547	0630	0650	0727	0747	0753	0757
Landau (Pfalz) Hbf .... d.	0519	*0608*	0645	0702	0741	0757	0802	0806
Neustadt (Weinstr) Hbf ...... a.	0542	*0628*	0706	0723	0801	0810	0824	0826

	Ⓐe	Ⓒz						Ⓐe	Ⓒz	†B	A		†B	A						n	n	⑥x	n	n
Karlsruhe Hbf .... d.	0801	0806	...	0907	and at the same minutes past each hour until	1507	...	1601	1607	...	...	1705	...	...	1807	...	1907	...	2007	...	2106	...	2206	2315
Wörth (Rhein) .... d.	0816	0817	...	0916		1516	...	1616	1616	...	...	1716	...	...	1816	...	1916	...	2016	...	2117	...	2217	2326
Wissembourg 🏛 ◐ .d.	|	|	0833	|		|	1533	|	|	1633	1633	|	1732	1732	|	1833	|	1932	|	2033	|	2203	|	|
Winden (Pfalz) .... d.	0829	0829	0853	0929		1529	1553	1629	1629	1653	1653	1729	1753	1753	1829	1853	1929	1953	2029	2053	2129	2224	2229	2338
Landau (Pfalz) Hbf .... d.	0838	0838	0902	0938		1538	1602	1638	1638	1702	1702	1738	1802	1802	1838	1902c	1938	2002	2038	2102	2137	...	2237	2353
Neustadt (Weinstr) Hbf. a.	0851	0851	0924	0951		1551	1624	1651	1651	1714	1724	1751	1816	1824	1851	1926	1951	2024	2051	2124	2156	...	2256	0011

Wörth and Karlsruhe - Speyer - Mannheim - Heidelberg

km	km		v	Ⓐe	Ⓐe	Ⓐe	Ⓐe	⑥k	Ⓐe	Ⓐe	Ⓒz	Ⓐe	Ⓐe	Ⓒz		Ⓐe	Ⓒz	Ⓐe								
0		**Wörth** (Rhein) .... d.	...	...	...	0534	...	...	0616	...	...	...	*0651*	*0718*	...	*0736*	...	...	*0818*	...	*0918*	...	...	*1018*	...	*1118*
	0	**Karlsruhe** Hbf ⊠ ... d.	...	...	...	|	...	...	|	...	...	...	|	|	...	|	...	0808	|	...	|	...	1008	|	...	|
27	38	Germersheim .... d.	0410e	0523	0555	0605	0619	0622	0645	0704	0703	0717	0725	0749	...	0809	0813	0838	0849	0913	0949	1013	1038	1049	1113	1149
41		Speyer Hbf .... d.	0424	0539	0609	0621	0631	0635	0701	0714	0716	0727	0738	0802	0802	0823	0826	0847	0902	0926	1002	1026	1047	1102	1126	1202
61		Ludwigshafen Hbf ...... d.	0451	0607	0640	0648	0651	0659	0726	|	0741	0748	0813	0821	0821	0847	0848	0903	0921	0948	1021	1048	1103	1121	1148	1221
64		**Mannheim** Hbf ...... ⊡ a.	0456	*0621*	0645	*0658*	m	0705	...	0734	0747	m	0818	0825	0825	0853	0853	m	0926	0953	1026	1053	m	1126	1153	1226
81		**Heidelberg** Hbf ..... ⊡ a.	0514	*0639*j	0705j	*0712*j	...	0723	...	0748j	*0823*	...	...	0845	0845	*0916*	0916k	...	0944	1016t	1045	1116t	...	1145	1216t	1245

		Ⓐe					Ⓐe														Ⓐe		n	n	nL	n
Wörth (Rhein) .... d.	...	...	*1218*	...	*1318*	...	...	*1418*	...	*1518*	...	...	*1618*	...	*1718*	...	...	*1818*	...	*1918*	...	*2018*n	...	*2119*	...	...
Karlsruhe Hbf ⊠ ... d.	...	1208	|	...	|	...	1408	|	...	|	...	1608	|	...	|	...	1808	|	...	|	2008	|	...	|	...	*2225*
Germersheim .... d.	1213	1238	1249	1313	1349	1413	1438	1449	1513	1549	1613	1638	1649	1713	1749	1813	1838	1849	1913	1949	2038	2049	2120	2154	2251	2321
Speyer Hbf .... d.	1226	1247	1302	1326	1402	1426	1447	1502	1526	1602	1626	1647	1702	1727	1802	1826	1847	1902	1926	2002	2047	2102	2135	2209	2304	2334
Ludwigshafen Hbf ...... d.	1248	1303	1321	1348	1421	1448	1503	1521	1548	1621	1648	1703	1721	1751	1821	1848	1903	1921	1948	2021	2104	2121	2200	2241	2329	0000
Mannheim Hbf ...... ⊡ a.	1253	m	1326	1353	1426	1453	m	1526	1553	1626	1653	m	1726	1756	1826	1853	m	1926	1953	2026	m	2125	2206	2249	2333	0004
Heidelberg Hbf ..... ⊡ a.	1316t	...	1345	1416t	1445	1516t	...	1545	1616t	1645	1716t	...	1745	1816a	1845	1916a	...	1945	2016a	2045	...	2153	...	2313	2353	...

	Ⓐe			Ⓐe	⚒t	Ⓐe	Ⓒz	Ⓐe		⑥k	Ⓐa			Ⓐe										Ⓐe		
Heidelberg Hbf ..... ⊡ d.	0510	*0534*t	0603	...	...	...	*0634*	0644j	...	0708	0713	0743a	0813	...	0843a	0913	0943t	1013	...	1043t	1113	1143t	1213	...	1243t	1313
Mannheim Hbf ..... ⊡ d.	0530	*0554*	0622	m	...	0633	0656	0706	...	0730	0730	0804	0831	m	0904	0931	1004	1031	m	1104	1131	1204	1231	m	1304	1331
Ludwigshafen Hbf ...... d.	0536	0614	0627	0636	...	0638	0703	0713	...	0737	0737	0810	0836	0856	0910	0936	1010	1036	1056	1110	1136	1210	1236	1256	1310	1336
Speyer Hbf .... d.	0558	0639	...	0655	...	0705	0726	0737	...	0804	0804	0831	0856	0913	0931	0956	1031	1056	1113	1131	1156	1231	1256	1313	1331	1356
Germersheim .... a.	0612	0654	...	0709	0719	0719	0740	0751	0812	0818	0818	0844	0908	0921	0944	1008	1044	1108	1121	1144	1208	1244	1308	1321	1344	1408
Karlsruhe Hbf ⊠ ... a.	|	|	...	...	0754	|	...	...	|	...	...	...	|	0952	...	|	...	|	1152	...	|	...	|	1352	...	|
Wörth (Rhein) .... a.	*0647*	0724	...	...	...	0748	...	...	0840	...	...	...	*0940*	...	...	*1040*	...	*1140*	...	...	*1240*	...	*1340*	...	...	*1440*

			Ⓐe					Ⓒz	Ⓐe			Ⓐe				⑥k			⑥k		n	Ⓑh		n	n	n
Heidelberg Hbf ..... ⊡ d.	1343t	1413	...	1443t	1513	1543a	1613	...	...	1643t	1713	...	1743t	1813	...	1834	1843a	1913	1934	1943a	2013	...	2114	2144*	2214	2314*
Mannheim Hbf ..... ⊡ d.	1404	1431	m	1504	1531	1604	1631	m	*1644*	1704	1731	m	1804	1831	m	1904	1904	1931	2004	2004	2031	m	2136	2208	2240	2336
Ludwigshafen Hbf ...... d.	1410	1436	1456	1510	1536	1610	1636	1656	1659	1710	1736	1801	1810	1836	1857	1910	1910	1936	2010	2010	2036	2057	2142	2215	2246	2343
Speyer Hbf .... d.	1431	1456	1513	1531	1556	1631	1656	1714	1723	1733	1756	1818	1831	1856	1916	1931	1931	1956	2031	2031	2056	2114	2205	2243	2313	0008
Germersheim .... a.	1444	1508	1521	1544	1608	1644	1708	1721	1739	1745	1808	1830	1844	1908	1924	1944	1944	2008	2044	2044	2108	2121	2218	2256	2328	0021
Karlsruhe Hbf ⊠ ... a.	...	|	1552	...	|	...	|	1752	|	...	|	...	...	|	1953	...	...	|	...	...	|	2152	...	...	...	...
Wörth (Rhein) .... a.	...	*1540*	...	...	*1640*	...	*1740*	...	1814	...	*1840*	...	...	*1940*	...	...	...	*2040*n	...	...	*2140*	...	...	...	...	...

A – Daily until Apr. 30; ⚒ from May 3 (not June 3).
B – † from May 1 (also June 3).
E – ①–⑥ (not Dec. 25, Jan. 1).
L – Change trains at Schifferstadt (a. 2313, d. 2317).
a – Ⓐ (not Dec. 24, 31, Jan. 6, June 3).
c – 1907 on ⑥⑦ (also May 13, 24, June 3).
d – Not Dec. 24, 31, June 3.
e – Ⓐ (not Dec. 24, 31, June 3).
f – Not Dec. 25, 26, Jan. 1, Apr. 2, May 1.
g – 0709 on ⑥**k**.
h – Also Dec. 26, May 1; not Dec. 24, 31.
j – Not Jan. 6.
k – ⑥ (also Dec. 24, 31; not Dec. 26, May 1).
m – To / from Mainz (Table **911a**).
n – Not Dec. 24, 31.
p – Also June 3; not Dec. 25, 26, Jan. 1.
r – ⚒ (not June 3).
s – To Saarbrücken (Table **917**).
t – ⚒ (not Jan. 6, June 3).
v – Not Dec. 25, Jan. 1.
w – Also June 3.
x – Not Dec. 26, May 1.
z – Also Dec. 24, 31, June 3.
* – Change trains at Mannheim on Ⓑ (also Dec. 26, May 1).
⊡ – See also Tables **911a** and **923**.
⊠ – Additional connections available via Wörth (see Neustadt - Karlsruhe table above).
◐ – See Table **396** for Strasbourg connections.

RB services — WIESBADEN - MAINZ - DARMSTADT - ASCHAFFENBURG — 918a

km																									
		⚒r	Ⓐe	⚒r		Ⓐe										Ⓐe		Ⓐe							
0	**Wiesbaden** Hbf d.	...	...	0538	0638	0702	0738	0838	0938	1038	1138	1238	1338	1438	1538	1602	1638	1702	1738	1838	1938	2038	2138	2238	2338
10	**Mainz** Hbf d.	...	...	0549	0649	0716	0749	0849	0949	1049	1149	1249	1349	1449	1549	1616	1649	1716	1749	1849	1949	2049	2149	2249	2349
43	Darmstadt Hbf a.	...	...	0621	0722	0750	0821	0921	1021	1121	1221	1321	1421	1521	1621	1650	1721	1750	1821	1921	2021	2121	2221	2321	0021
43	Darmstadt Hbf d.	0452	0549	0632	0732	0800	0832r	0932	1032r	1132	1232r	1332	1432r	1532	1632r	1700	1732	1800	1832e	1932	2032e	2132e	...	...	...
87	**Aschaffenburg** Hbf a.	0535	0631	0713	0813	0841	0913r	1013	1113r	1213	1313r	1413	1513r	1613	1713r	1741	1813	1841	1913e	2013	2113e	2213e	...	...	...

	Ⓐe	Ⓐe	Ⓐe		Ⓐe		Ⓐe										Ⓐe		Ⓐe		Ⓐe				
Aschaffenburg Hbf d.	...	...	0510	0542r	0606	0640r	0716	0746	0846r	0946	1046r	1146	1246r	1346	1446r	1546	1616	1646r	1716	1746	1816	1846e	1946	2046e	...
Darmstadt Hbf a.	...	...	0552	0623r	0652	0727r	0759	0827	0927r	1027	1127r	1227	1327r	1427	1527r	1627	1659	1727r	1759	1827	1859	1927e	2027	2127e	...
Darmstadt Hbf d.	0440	0540	0610	0640	0706	0740	0810	0840	0940	1040	1140	1240	1340	1440	1540	1640	1710	1740	1810	1840	1910	1940	2040	2140	2240
Mainz Hbf d.	0513	0613	0645	0713	0743	0813	0844	0913	1013	1113	1213	1313	1413	1513	1613	1713	1745	1813	1844	1913	1944	2013	2113	2213	2313
Wiesbaden Hbf a.	0525	0625	0655	0725	0755	0825	0855	0925	1025	1125	1225	1325	1425	1525	1625	1725	1755	1825	1855	1925	1955	2025	2125	2225	2325

e – Ⓐ (not Dec. 24, 31, June 3).
r – ⚒ (not June 3).

RE / S-Bahn services except where shown — SAARBRÜCKEN - MANNHEIM (- FRANKFURT) — 919

km			*IC* 2051 ①–⑤ m	*EC* 317 G🍷		*IC* 2053 ①–⑤ m S 🍷	*ICE* 1557 ①–⑥ e D		v	Ⓐa		v		*ICE* 9551 A R✕		Ⓐa				*TGV* 9553 R🍷		⑤t		M	◇
	Paris Est **390** d.	...	...	...	...	...	...	...	...	...	...	...	...	0704	...	...	...	...	...	0909j	...	...	...	...	...
	Trier Hbf **915** d.	...	...	...	...	...	...	...	0527a	0620	...	0634a	...	|	...	0831	...	...	...	|	...	...	...	...	...
0	**Saarbrücken** Hbf d.	...	0439	0534	...	0619	0644	...	0658	0739	...	0801	...	0859	0903	0939	...	1001	...	1057	1103	...	...	1201	...
31	Homburg (Saar) Hbf d.	...	0503	0557	...	0642	0706	...	0729	0805	0754c	0828	0853	|	0927	1005	...	1028	1054	|	1128	1154	1154k	1228	1254
67	**Kaiserslautern** Hbf a.	...	0525	0620	...	0700	0727	...	0754	0825	0828c	0854	0924	0934	0954	1025	...	1054	1124	1134	1154	1224	1224k	1254	1324
		⑥⑦ b	|	|		|	|		◧	|	|	◧	|	|	◧	|		◧	|	|	◧	|	|	◧	|
67	**Kaiserslautern** Hbf d.	0516	0527	0622	0614	0702	0729	0733	0758	0826	0832	0858	0931	0936	0958	1026	1032	1058	1129	1135	1158	1225	1232	1258	1330
100	Neustadt (Weinstr) Hbf d.	0547	0552	0646	0651	0727	0751	0805	0830	0850	0905	0930	1005	|	1030	1050	1105	1130	1205	|	1230	1250	1305	1330	1405
128	Ludwigshafen Hbf **911a 918** d.	0612	0612	0705	0720	0746	|	0828	0857	|	0928	0957	1028	|	1057	|	1128	1157	1228	|	1257	|	1328	1357	1428
131	**Mannheim** Hbf **911a 918** a.	0618	0616	0709	0725	0751	0810	0834	0903	0912	0934	1003	1034	1016	1103	1112	1134	1203	1234	1214	1303	1310	1334	1403	1434
131	**Mannheim** Hbf **911a 918** ▽ d.	0637	0618	...	0729	0754	0812	0839	0907	*0929*	0939	1007	1039	1020	1107	*1129*	1139	1207	1239	1216	1307	*1329*	1339	1407	1439
	Heidelberg Hbf **911a 918** a.	0653	|	...	0744	0804	|	0853	0923	*0945*	0953	1023	1053	|	1123	*1145*	1153	1223	1253	|	1323	*1345*	1353	1423	1453
191	Darmstadt Hbf ▽ a.	...	0653	...	...	...	0845	...	...	...	...	...	...	|	...	...	...	...	...	|	...	...	...	...	...
219	**Frankfurt** (Main) Hbf ▽ a.	...	0712	...	...	...	0904	...	...	...	...	...	...	1058	...	...	...	...	...	1258	...	...	...	...	...

	IC 2055 Ⓑq H🍷	⊗		K		*ICE* 9555 R✕	⊗		M			*IC* 2057 Ⓑq 🍷		*IC* 2282 ⑥ L🍷			*ICE* 9557 Ⓑd R✕			n	*ICE* 9559 R✕		n	n	n
Paris Est **390** d.	...	...	...	...	...	1309	...	...	...	...	...	...	...	...	...	...	1709	...	...	...	1905	...	...	...	...
Trier Hbf **915** d.	...	...	...	1248	...	|	...	...	...	...	...	...	...	...	1654r	...	|	...	...	1854a	|	...	...	2054a	...
Saarbrücken Hbf d.	1248	1301	...	1401	...	1459	1503	...	1601	...	1701	1740	...	1754	1801	...	1859	1903	...	2001	2059	...	2103	2206	2301
Homburg (Saar) Hbf d.	1313	1325	1354	1428	1454	|	1525	1554	1627	1654	1727	1804	1744	1818	1828	1854	|	1928	1954	2028	|	...	2128	2233	2329
Kaiserslautern Hbf a.	1334	1350	1424	1454	1524	1534	1550	1624	1654	1724	1754	1824	1813	1841	1854	1924	1934	1954	2026	2054	2134	...	2158	2302	0002
	|	◧	|	◧	|	|	◧	|	◧	|	◧	|	|	|	◧	|	|	◧	|	◧	|	n	◧ n	▬ n	◧ v
Kaiserslautern Hbf d.	1336	1358	1432	1458	1531	1536	1558	1632	1658	1732	1758	1826	1832	1844	1858	1931	1936	1958	2032	2058	2136	2141	2232	2303	0006
Neustadt (Weinstr) Hbf d.	1401	1430	1505	1530	1605	|	1630	1705	1730	1805	1830	1850	1905	1913	1930	2005	|	2030	2105	2130	|	2210	2302	2330	0035
Ludwigshafen Hbf . **911a 918** d.	|	1457	1528	1557	1628	|	1657	1728	1757	1828	1857	|	1928	1934	1957	2028	|	2057	2128	2200	|	2241	2329	0000	0102
Mannheim Hbf ..... **911a 918** a.	1421	1503	1534	1603	1634	1616	1703	1734	1803	1834	1903	1910	1934	1939	2003	2034	2016	2103	2134	2206	2216	2249	2333	0004	0108
Mannheim Hbf . **911a 918** ▽ d.	1424	1507	1539	1607	1639	1620	1707	1739	1807	1839	1907	1912	1939	1942	2007	2037	2020	2107	2137	2207	2220	2257	2337	0005	0117
Heidelberg Hbf . **911a 918** a.	1435	1523	1553	1623	1653	|	1723	1753	1823	1853	1923	|	1953	|	2023	2053	|	2123	2153	2223	|	2313	2353	0021	0134
Darmstadt Hbf ▽ a.	...	...	...	...	...	|	...	...	...	...	...	1945	...	2022	...	...	|	...	...	...	|	...	...	...	...
Frankfurt (Main) Hbf ▽ a.	...	...	...	...	...	1658	...	...	...	...	...	2004	...	2040	...	...	2058	...	...	...	2258	...	...	...	...

	v		⚒r	*ICE* 9558 A R✕					*IC* 2058 ①–⑤ m🍷		*ICE* 9556 R✕								Ⓐa		*ICE* 9554 R✕				Ⓐa
Frankfurt (Main) Hbf ▽ d.	...	...	...	0600	...	...	...	...	0749	...	0901	...	...	...	...	...	...	...	...	...	1301	...	...	...	...
Darmstadt Hbf ▽ d.	...	...	...	|	...	...	...	...	0811	...	|	...	...	...	...	...	...	...	...	...	|	...	...	...	...
Heidelberg Hbf . **911a 918** d.	0014	...	0534r	|	0634	0704	0734	0804	|	0834	|	0904	0934	1004	1034	1104	1134	1204	*1213*	1234	|	1304	1334	1404	*1413*
Mannheim Hbf . **911a 918** ▽ a.	0030	...	0551r	0636	0651	0719	0751	0818	0846	0851	0937	0918	0951	1018	1051	1118	1151	1218	*1229*	1251	1337	1318	1351	1418	*1429*
Mannheim Hbf ..... **911a 918** d.	0031	0425	0554	0640	0656	0720	0756	0826	0848	0856	0941	0926	0956	1026	1055	1126	1156	1226	1246	1256	1341	1326	1356	1426	1446
Ludwigshafen Hbf . **911a 918** d.	0037	0432	0600	|	0703	0726	0803	0832	|	0903	|	0931	1003	1031	1103	1131	1203	1231	|	1303	|	1331	1403	1431	|
Neustadt (Weinstr) Hbf d.	0104	0506	0632	|	0732	0802	0832	0858	0910	0932	|	1004	1032	1100	1132	1200	1232	1300	1308	1332	|	1404	1432	1500	1508
Kaiserslautern Hbf a.	0132	0534	0659	0720	0759	0829	0859	0926	0931	0959	1021	1029	1059	1128	1159	1228	1259	1328	1330	1359	1421	1429	1459	1528	1530
		◧ v	◧ v M	|	▬	|	◧		|	▬ ⊖	|	|	◧ K	|	◧	|	◧	|	|	◧	|	|	◧	|	|
Kaiserslautern Hbf d.	...	0556	0703	0722	0757	0832	0903	...	0933	0957	1023	1033	1103	1133	1203	1233k	1303	1333c	1331	1403	1423	1433	1503	1533c	1531
Homburg (Saar) Hbf d.	...	0624	0745	|	0830	0904	0930	...	0953	1027	|	1104	1130	1204	1230	1304k	1330	1404c	1353	1430	|	1504	1530	1604c	1553
Saarbrücken Hbf a.	...	0657	0816	0758	0857	...	0957	...	1016	1055	1059	...	1157	...	1257	...	1357	...	1421	1455	1459	...	1557	...	1621
Trier Hbf **915** a.	...	...	...	|	...	...	1105	...	...	...	|	...	1311	...	...	...	1505	...	...	...	|	...	1705a	...	1753
Paris Est **390** a.	...	...	...	0949	...	...	...	...	...	...	1249h	...	...	...	...	...	...	...	...	...	1650	...	...	...	...

		IC 2056 ①–④ p🍷	*IC* 2196 ⑤f S		*IC* 2256 ⑦w 🍷			*IC* 2054 ①–⑤ m🍷		*TGV* 9552 R🍷				*IC* 2052 Ⓑq S🍷		*ICE* 9550 Ⓑd R✕				*EC* 316 G🍷		*ICE* 1594 Ⓑq D✕	n	*IC* 2050 ⑦w S	n
Frankfurt (Main) Hbf ▽ d.	...	...	...	...	1455	...	...	1554	...	1657	...	...	...	...	...	1901	...	...	...	...	...	2054	...	...	...
Darmstadt Hbf ▽ d.	...	...	...	...	1513	...	...	1611	...	|	...	...	...	...	...	|	...	...	...	...	...	2111	...	...	...
Heidelberg Hbf . **911a 918** d.	1434	1521	...	1504	|	1534	1604	|	1634	|	1704	1734	1804	...	1834	|	1904	1934	2004	...	2037	|	2214	2255	2314
Mannheim Hbf . **911a 918** ▽ a.	1451	1537	...	1518	1546	1551	1618	1646	1651	1740	1718	1751	1818	...	1851	1937	1918	1951	2018	...	2055	2146	2232	2306	2332
Mannheim Hbf ..... **911a 918** d.	1456	1539	1539	1526	1548	1556	1626	1648	1656	1742	1726	1756	1826	1848	1856	1941	1926	1956	2026	2050	2056	2148	2240	2308	2336
Ludwigshafen Hbf . **911a 918** d.	1503	|	|	1531	|	1603	1631	1654	1703	|	1731	1803	1831	1854	1903	|	1931	2003	2032	|	2103	|	2246	|	2343
Neustadt (Weinstr) Hbf d.	1532	1600	1600	1604*	1610	1632	1700	1712	1732	|	1805	1832	1900	1912	1932	|	2004	2032	2058	2112	2132	2210	2316	2331	0016
Kaiserslautern Hbf a.	1559	1622	1622	1630	1631	1659	1728	1733	1759	1823	1830	1859	1928	1933	1959	2021	2029	2059	2126	2133	2159	2230	2345	2354	0044
	◧	|	|	|	|	◧		|	◧	|	|	◧		|	◧ n	|	|	◧ n		|	◧ n	|	◧ v	|	
Kaiserslautern Hbf d.	1603	1624	1624	1633*	1633	1703	...	1735	1803	1825	1833	1903	...	1935	2003	2023	2032	2103	...	2135	2203	2232	0002	2356	...
Homburg (Saar) Hbf d.	1630	1644	1644	1704*	1653	1730	...	1754	1830	|	1904	1930	...	1954	2030	|	2104	2130	...	2154	2230	2253	0033	0017	...
Saarbrücken Hbf a.	1656	1707	1707	...	1716	1757	...	1819	1855	1901	...	1957	...	2019	2055	2059	...	2157	...	2218	2257	2320	0105	0039	...
Trier Hbf **915** a.	...	...	...	...	...	1907	...	...	...	|	...	2115	...	...	...	|	...	...	...	...	...	...	...	...	...
Paris Est **390** a.	...	...	...	...	...	...	...	...	...	2053	...	...	...	...	...	2249	...	...	...	...	...	...	...	...	...

A – ①–⑥ (not Dec. 25, Jan. 1, Apr. 5, May 24).
D – (12) and ✕ Saarbrücken - Frankfurt - Erfurt - Leipzig - Dresden and v.v.
G – (12) and 🍷 Graz - Salzburg - München - Stuttgart - Saarbrücken and v.v.
H – To Stuttgart on dates in Table **930**.
K – From / to Koblenz (Table **915**).
L – To Kassel (Table **806**).
M – From / to Merzig (Table **915**).
R – 🅁 for journeys to / from France.
S – To / from Stuttgart (Table **930**).

a – Ⓐ (not Dec. 24, 31, June 3).
b – Also Dec. 24, 31, Apr. 2, 5, May 24.
c – Ⓒ (also Dec. 24, 31, June 3).
d – Not Dec. 24, 31, Apr. 4, May 23.
e – Not Dec. 25, 26, Jan. 1, Apr. 3, 5, May 24.
f – Also Dec. 23, 30, Apr. 1, May 12, June 2; not Dec. 25, Jan. 1, Apr. 2, May 14, June 4.
h – 1253 on ⑦ (also Dec. 25, Jan. 1, Apr. 5, May 24).
j – 0905 on ⑦ (also Dec. 25, Jan. 1, Apr. 5, May 24).
k – ①②③④⑥⑦ (also Dec. 25, Jan. 1, Apr. 2).
m – Not Dec. 24, 25, 31, Jan. 1, Apr. 2, 5, May 24.
n – Not Dec. 24, 31.
p – Also May 14, June 4; not Dec. 23, 24, 30, 31, Apr. 1, 5, May 12, 24, June 2.
q – Not Dec. 24, 25, 31, Apr. 2, 4, May 23.
r – ⚒ (not June 3).
t – Not Dec. 25, Jan. 1, Apr. 2.

v – Not Dec. 25, Jan. 1.
w – Also Apr. 5, May 24; not Apr. 4, May 23.
z – ⚒ (not Jan. 6, June 3).

◇ – On ①–④ (not Dec. 24, 31, Apr. 5, May 13, 24, June 3) passengers from Homburg or Kaiserslautern travelling to Heidelberg should move to the front portion of the train at Mannheim.
⊗ – Not Dec. 25, Jan. 1, Apr. 2, 5, May 13, 24. On ⑥⑦ (also Dec. 24, 31, June 3) runs 3 – 4 minutes later Homburg - Kaiserslautern.
⊖ – Not Dec. 25, Jan. 1, Apr. 2, 5, May 13, 24. On ⑥⑦ (also Dec. 24, 31, June 3) departs Kaiserslautern 1003, Homburg 1030.
* – On ⑦ **w**: Neustadt d. 1600, Kaiserslautern d. 1638, Homburg a. 1709.
◧ – Change trains at Kaiserslautern.
▽ – See also Tables **912/930** (*ICE* trains) and Table **911a** (local *RE* trains).

920 FRANKFURT - NÜRNBERG - PASSAU (- WIEN)

For other regional trains see Table **921** below.

km	See note ⊠	ICE 521	ICE 21	ICE 523	ICE 1123	ICE 925	ICE 525	ICE 23	ICE 527	ICE 529	ICE 25	IC 1887	ICE 621	ICE 1121	ICE 923	ICE 623	ICE 27	ICE 625	ICE 627	ICE 927	ICE 29	ICE 629	ICE 721	ICE 921	ICE 229
			⊠	①–⑤	⑥s	⑥⑦	①–⑤	⊠	①–⑥		⊠	⑥✤	①–⑥	⑦h	⑦w	①–⑥	⊠		①–⑥	⑦r	▲	Ⓑq	①–④	⑤–⑦	●
		🍷	🍴	a🍷	🍷	z🍷	a🍷	🍴	G🍷	🍷	🍴	🍷	m🍷	🍷	🍷	e🍷	🍴	🍷	e🍷	🍷	🍴	🍷	t🍷	p🍷	🍴
	Hamburg Hbf **800 900** d.	...	...	...	...	...	...	...	...	...	...	0635	...	...	...	...	...	...	...	...	...	...	...	...	...
	Dortmund Hbf **800** d.	...	...	0406	0423	0502	0523	0437v	0623	0723c	0636	|	0816k	0821	0853	...	0837	1023w	...	1100	...	1223w	...	1323c	...
	Wuppertal Hbf **800** d.	...	...	|	|	|	|	|	|	|	0714	|	|	|	|	...	|	|	...	1137	...	|	...	|	...
	Essen Hbf **800** d.	...	...	0428	0445	0524	0553	0459v	0653	0753	|	|	0840	0853	0917	...	0859	1053	...	|	...	1253	...	1353	...
	Düsseldorf Hbf **800** d.	...	...	0455	0513	0551	0621	0527v	0721	0821	|	|	0913	0923	0948	...	0927	1121	...	|	...	1321	...	1421	...
	Köln Hbf **800 910** d.	0422	...	|	|	|	|	0553	|	|	0753	|	|	|	1019	1019	0953	|	1219	1219	...	|	1427	|	...
	Köln Messe/Deutz **910** d.	|	...	0518	0535	0618	0644	|	0744	0844	|	|	0937	0945	|	|	|	1144	|	|	...	1344	|	1444	...
	Bonn Hbf **800** d.	|	...	|	|	|	|	0614	|	|	0814	|	|	|	|	|	1014	|	|	|	...	|	|	|	...
	Koblenz Hbf **912** d.	|	...	|	|	|	|	0648	|	|	0848	|	|	|	|	|	1048	|	|	|	...	|	|	|	...
	Mainz Hbf **912** d.	|	...	|	|	|	|	0740	|	|	0940	|	|	|	|	|	1140	|	|	|	...	|	|	|	...
0	**Frankfurt** Flughafen ✈ § d.	0535	...	0637	0637	0737	0737	0802	0837	0937	1002	|	1029	1037	1129	1137	1202	1237	1329	1329	...	1437	1537	1537	...
11	**Frankfurt** (Main) Hbf d.	0551	0622	0654	0654	0754	0754	0819	0854	0954	1021	|	1054	1054	1154	1154	1221	1254	1354	1354	1416	1454	1554	1554	1621
35	Hanau Hbf d.	|	0638	|	|	|	|	0835	|	|	1038	|	|	|	|	|	1238	|	|	|	1439	|	|	|	1638
57	Aschaffenburg Hbf d.	0624	0652	0724	0724	0824	0824	|	0924	1024	|	|	1124	1124	1224	1224	|	1324	1424	1424	|	1524	1624	1624	1652
136	**Würzburg** Hbf a.	0703	0731	0803	0803	0903	0903	0924	1003	1103	1131	1116	1203	1203	1303	1303	1331	1403	1503	1503	1531	1603	1703	1703	1731
136	**Würzburg** Hbf **900** d.	0705	0735	0805	0805	0905	0905	0934	1005	1105	1134	1118	1205	1205	1305	1305	1334	1405	1505	1505	1534	1605	1705	1705	1734
238	**Nürnberg** Hbf **900** a.	0759	0828	0859	0859	0959	0959	1028	1059	1159	1228	1232	1259	1259	1359	1359	1428	1459	1559	1559	1628	1659	1759	1759	1828
238	**Nürnberg** Hbf d.	0802	0831	0902	0902	1002	1002	1031	1102	1202	1231	1235	1302	1302	1402	1402	1431	1502	1602	1602	1631	1702	1802	1802	1831
	München Hbf **904** a.	0906	|	1005	1005	1106	1106	|	1205	1305	|	|	1405	1405	1505	1505	|	1605	1705	1705	|	1805	1905	1905	|
339	**Regensburg** Hbf a.	...	0922	...	...	...	...	1122	...	...	1322	1334	...	...	...	...	1522	...	...	...	1722	...	...	...	1922
339	**Regensburg** Hbf d.	...	0924	...	...	...	...	1124	...	...	1324	1336	...	...	...	...	1524	...	...	...	1724	...	...	...	1924
379	Straubing d.	...	|	...	...	...	...	|	...	...	|	1403	...	...	...	...	|	...	...	...	|	...	...	...	|
404	Plattling **944** d.	...	1000	...	...	...	...	1200	...	...	1400	1416	...	...	...	...	1600	...	...	...	1800	...	...	...	2000
456	**Passau** Hbf 🏛 **944** a.	...	1027	...	...	...	...	1227	...	...	1427	1444	...	...	...	...	1627	...	...	...	1827	...	...	...	2027
	Linz Hbf **950** a.	...	1143	...	...	...	...	1343	...	...	1543	...	...	...	...	...	1743	...	...	...	1943	...	...	...	2143
	Wien Westbahnhof **950** a.	...	1322	...	...	...	...	1522	...	...	1722	...	...	...	...	...	1922	...	...	...	2122	...	...	...	2322

See note ⊠	ICE 723	ICE 725	IC 2027	ICE 727	ICE 729	ICE 1025	ICE 1125	IC 2105	ICE 821	ICE 929	IC 2123	IC 2029	EN 421	EN 491
	Ⓑq		¶⊠	Ⓑq		A	⑤j	⑦	⑤f	⑦w	①–④		⊡	⊡
	🍷	🍷	🍴	🍷	🍷	🍴	🍴	R🍷	O🍷	🍷	t	🍷	N Ⓡ	L Ⓡ
Hamburg Hbf **800 900** d.	...	...	1146	...	...	1346	1346	...	...	...	...	1546	...	2033
Dortmund Hbf **800** d.	...	1523w	1436	...	...	1636	1636	...	...	...	...	1836	1823	|
Wuppertal Hbf **800** d.	...	|	1514	...	...	1714	1714	...	...	...	...	1914	|	|
Essen Hbf **800** d.	1453	1553	|	1653	1753	|	|	...	...	1840	...	|	1903	|
Düsseldorf Hbf **800** d.	1521	1621	|	1721	1821	|	|	...	1908	1908	...	|	1935	|
Köln Hbf **800 910** d.	|	|	1553	|	|	1753	1753	...	|	|	...	1953	2005	|
Köln Messe/Deutz **910** d.	1544	1644	|	1744	1844	|	|	...	1930	1930	...	|	|	|
Bonn Hbf **800** d.	|	|	1614	|	|	1814	1814	...	|	|	...	2014	2034	|
Koblenz Hbf **912** d.	|	|	1648	|	|	1848	1848	...	|	|	...	2048	2115	|
Mainz Hbf **912** d.	|	|	1740	|	|	1940	1940	...	|	|	...	2143	2212	|
Frankfurt Flughafen ✈ § d.	1637	1737	1802	1837	1937	2002	2002	...	2037	2037	...	2202	|	|
Frankfurt (Main) Hbf d.	1654	1754	1818	1854	1954	2018	2018	...	2054	2054	2058	2218	2321	|
Hanau Hbf d.	|	|	1835	|	|	2035	2035	...	|	|	2115	2235	2347u	|
Aschaffenburg Hbf d.	1724	1824	1849	1924	2024	2049	2049	...	2124	2124	2129	2249	0003u	|
Würzburg Hbf a.	1803	1903	1931	2003	2103	2128	2128	...	2203	2203	2210	2341	|	0205
Würzburg Hbf **900** d.	1805	1905	1934	2005	2105	2130	2130	...	2205	2205	2212	2343	|	0207
Nürnberg Hbf **900** a.	1859	1959	2028	2058	2159	2224	2224	...	2259	2259	2306	0038	|	0306
Nürnberg Hbf d.	1902	2002	2031	2102	2202	2235	2235	2240	2302	2302	...	...	|	0324
München Hbf **904** a.	2005	2105	|	2205	2308	2350	|	|	0008	0008	...	...	|	|
Regensburg Hbf a.	...	...	2131	...	...	...	2337	2342	...	...	...	...	0427	0427
Regensburg Hbf d.	...	...	2133	...	...	...	...	2344	...	...	...	...	0430	0430
Straubing d.	...	...	2155	...	...	...	...	0008	...	...	...	...	|	|
Plattling **944** d.	...	...	2209	...	...	...	...	0022	...	...	...	...	|	|
Passau Hbf 🏛 **944** a.	...	...	2242	...	...	...	...	0055	...	...	...	...	0532	0532
Linz Hbf **950** a.	...	...	...	...	...	...	...	...	...	...	...	...	0646	0646
Wien Westbahnhof **950** a.	...	...	...	...	...	...	...	...	...	...	...	...	0904	0904

a – Not Dec. 24, 25, 31, Jan. 1, Apr. 2, 5, May 24.
c – ⑥⑦ (also Dec. 24, 25, 31, Jan. 1, Apr. 2, 5, May 24).
e – Not Dec. 25, 26, Jan. 1, Apr. 3, 5, May 24.
f – Also Dec. 23, 30, Apr. 1, May 12, June 2; not Dec. 25, Jan. 1, Apr. 2.
h – Also Dec. 25, 26, Jan. 1, Apr. 5, May 24.
j – Also Dec. 23, 30, Apr. 1; not Dec. 25, Apr. 2, May 28, June 4.
k – ⑥ (also Dec. 24, 31, Apr. 2; not Dec. 26).
m – Not Dec. 25, 26, Jan. 1, Apr. 5, May 24.
p – Also Dec. 23, 24, 30, 31, Apr. 1, 5, May 12, 24, June 2; not May 14, June 4.
q – Not Dec. 24, 25, 31, Apr. 2, 4, May 23.
r – Also Dec. 25, 26, Jan. 1, Apr. 3, 5, May 24.
s – Also Dec. 24, 31, Apr. 2; not Dec. 26, Apr. 3.
t – Not Dec. 23, 24, 30, 31, Apr. 1, 5, May 12, 24, June 2.
u – Stops to pick up only.
v – Not Dec. 25, Jan. 1.
w – ⑦ (also Apr. 5, May 24; not Apr. 4, May 23).
z – Also Dec. 24, 25, 31, Jan. 1, Apr. 2, 5, May 24.

¶ – Train number **2327** on ⑤ (also Dec. 23, 30, Apr. 1, May 12, June 12; not Dec. 25, Jan. 1, Apr. 2, May 14).
⊡ – May 22 - June 7 Regensburg a. 0509, d. 0512, Passau a. 0613, Linz a. 0733, Wien a. 0951.
● – May 22 - June 6 Frankfurt d. 1517, Hanau d. 1541, Aschaffenburg d. 1558, Würzburg a. 1636, d. 1638, Nürnberg a. 1729, d. 1732 and then as shown.
✤ – On May 22, 29, June 5 does not call at Nürnberg (timings Regensburg - Passau are up to 60 minutes later).
▲ – May 22 - June 6 runs Nürnberg - Wien only. See also note ⊠.
⊠ – May 22 - June 6 most services between Nürnberg and Regensburg are diverted via Ingolstadt. During this period timings Regensburg - Passau - Wien are up to 60 minutes later (unless shown otherwise).
§ – Frankfurt Flughafen Fernbahnhof.

A – ①②③④⑥⑦ (also Dec. 25, Apr. 2, May 28, June 4; not Dec. 23, 30, Apr. 1).
G – ①–⑥ (not Dec. 25, Jan. 1, Apr. 5, May 24). To Garmisch on ⑥ (a. 1335).
L – HANS ALBERS – 🛏 1, 2 cl., ━ 2 cl., (2) and 🍷 Hamburg - Hannover - Wien.
N – 🛏 1, 2 cl., ━ 2 cl., (2) and 🍷 (Dortmund ①–④ -) Köln - Wien. Also calls at Gelsenkirchen on ①–④ (d. 1848).
O – From Oberhausen (Table **800**).
R – ⑦ (also Apr. 5; not Apr. 4, May 23, 30, June 6). (12) and 🍷 Basel - Karlsruhe - Stuttgart - Passau.

921 Local trains FRANKFURT - WÜRZBURG - NÜRNBERG - REGENSBURG - PASSAU *RE / RB services*

For faster *ICE / IC* trains see Table **920** above.

km			Ⓒz	Ⓐe	†w	⚒r	Ⓐd	Ⓒm								Ⓒm	Ⓐd		Ⓒm	Ⓐd			†w	⚒r		⊠
0	**Frankfurt** (Main) Hbf d.	...	*0442*k	*0442*	*0530*	0634	*0726*	0730	0834	0930	1034	1130	1234	1330	1434	1530	1534	1634	1730	1734	1834	1930	2034	2034	2130	2236
4	**Frankfurt** (Main) Süd d.	...	*0448*k	*0448*	*0536*	0640	*0733*	0736	0840	0936	1040	1136	1240	1336	1440	1536	1540	1640	1736	1740	1840	1936	2040	2040	2136	2242
10	Offenbach (Main) Hbf d.	...	|	|	|	0645	*0738*	|	0845	|	1045	|	1245	|	1445	|	1545	1645	|	1745	1845	|	2045	2045	|	2248
24	Hanau Hbf d.	...	*0513*k	*0513*	*0614*	0659	0759	0759	0859	0959	1059	1159	1259	1359	1459	1559	1559	1659	1759	1759	1859	1959	2059	2059	2159	2259
46	Aschaffenburg Hbf d.	0500	0602	0604	0710	0717	0817	0817	0917	1017	1117	1217	1317	1417	1517	1617	1617	1717	1817	1817	1917	2017	2117	2133v	2221	2322
84	Lohr Bahnhof d.	0531	0633	0636	0741	0744	0844	0844	0944	1044	1144	1244	1344	1444	1544	1644	1644	1744	1844	1844	1944	2044	2144	2205	2253	2354
96	Gemünden (Main) d.	0543	0645	0655	0752	0800	0900	0900	1000	1100	1200	1300	1400	1500	1556	1700	1656	1756	1900	1858	2000	2100	2156	2217	2304	0007
109	Karlstadt (Main) d.	0554	0654	0703	0802	0808	0908	0908	1008	1108	1208	1308	1408	1508	1606	1708	1706	1806	1908	1908	2008	2108	2204	2225	2314	0016
136	**Würzburg** Hbf a.	0617	0718	0718	0824	0824	0924	0924	1024	1124	1224	1324	1424	1524	1622	1724	1722	1822	1924	1924	2024	2124	2220	2241	2336	0040

km		2	2	⚒t	Ⓐe							⑥♥									2	⊖				
0	**Würzburg** Hbf d.	...	...	0540	0606	0638	...	0740	0840	0940	1040	1118	1140	1240	1340	1440	1540	1640	1740	1840	...	1936	1946	2040	...	2255
23	Kitzingen d.	...	...	0555	0623	0654	...	0800	0900	1000	1100	|	1200	1300	1400	1500	1600	1700	1800	1900	...	|	2007	2100	...	2314
61	Neustadt (Aisch) Bf d.	0456	0544	0617	0648	0719	...	0825	0925	1025	1125	1204	1225	1325	1425	1525	1625	1725	1825	1925	2009	|	...	2125	...	2338
94	Fürth (Bay) Hbf d.	0527	0614	0644	0713	0741	...	0847	0947	1047	1147	|	1247	1347	1447	1547	1647	1747	1847	1947	2040	2113	...	2147	...	0008
102	**Nürnberg** Hbf a.	0537	0622	0652	0721	0750	...	0854	0954	1054	1154	1232	1254	1354	1454	1554	1654	1754	1854	1954	2050	2121	...	2154	...	0017

	⚒t																				L				Ⓐe
Nürnberg Hbf d.	...	0529e	0655	0736	...	...	0936	...	...	1136	...	...	1336	...	...	1536	...	1635e	1736	...	...	1936	...	...	2136	2250
Neumarkt (Oberpf) d.	0451	0554e	0719	0757	0801	0902e	0957	1001	1102e	1157	1201	1301e	1357	1401z	1501e	1557	1601	1702e	1757	1801	1902e	1957	2001	...	2157	2325
Regensburg Hbf a.	0548	0649e	0758	0839	0857	0959e	1040	1057	1159e	1239	1257	1359e	1439	1457z	1557e	1639	1657	1759e	1839	1857	1959e	2039	2057	...	2239	0015
Regensburg Hbf d.	0550	0651	0800	0844	0900	1001	1044	1059	1201	1244	1259	1401	1444	1457h	1559h	1644	1658	1800	1844	1859	2001	...	2059	2200	2244	*0021*
München Hbf **878** a.	|	|	|	1017	|	|	1217	|	|	1417	|	|	1617	|	|	1817	|	|	2017	|	|	...	|	|	0022	|
Straubing d.	0619	0721	0828	...	0928	1028	...	1128	1228	...	1328	1428	...	1528	1628	...	1729	1828	...	1929	2028	...	2128	2229	...	*0053*
Plattling a.	0636	0739	0845	...	0945	1045	...	1145	1245	...	1345	1445	...	1546	1645	...	1747	1845	...	1947	2045	...	2145	2246	...	*0111*
Plattling **944** d.	*0642*	*0800*	*0901**	...	*1005*	*1103*	...	*1205*	*1301*q	...	*1405*	*1503*	...	*1605*	*1703*	...	*1805*	*1903*	...	*2005*	*2103*	...	*2158*	*2306*	...	...
Passau Hbf **944** a.	*0718*	*0833*	*0937**	...	*1039*	*1137*	...	*1239*	*1339*q	...	*1439*	*1537*	...	*1639*	*1737*	...	*1839*	*1937*	...	*2039*	*2137*	...	*2232*	*2341*	...	...

L – To Landshut (Table **878**).
d – Not Dec. 24, 31, June 3.
e – Ⓐ (not Dec. 24, 31, Jan. 6, June 3).
h – 2 minutes later on Ⓒz.
k – ⑥ (also Dec. 24, 31; not Dec. 26, May 1).
m – Also Dec. 24, 31, June 3.

q – 8 minutes later May 22 - June 6.
r – Not June 3.
t – Not Jan. 6, June 3.
v – Arrives 2116.
w – Also June 3.
z – Ⓒ (also Dec. 24, 31, Jan. 6, June 3).

* – Through service on Ⓒ from May 1 (Plattling d. 0847, Passau a. 0918).
⊠ – Frankfurt - Aschaffenburg daily; Frankfurt - Gemünden on ①–⑥ (also Apr. 4, May 23); Frankfurt - Würzburg on ⑤⑥ (also Apr. 4, May 23).
♥ – ⑥ (not May 22, 29, June 5). *IC* **1887**: (12) and 🍷 Hamburg - Passau.
⊖ – Via Bamberg (Table **876**).

(WIEN -) PASSAU - NÜRNBERG - FRANKFURT — 920

For other regional trains see Table **921** below.

See note ⊠	IC 2122 Ⓐn	IC 2028 🍷	ICE 822 ①–⑥ e🍷	ICE 820 ①–⑤ a🍷	IC 2102 ① K🍷	ICE 1026 R ✕	ICE 1126 ①b ✕	ICE 728 🍷	ICE 726 ①–⑥ e🍷	IC 2024 ◇ ✕	ICE 724 🍷	ICE 722 🍷	ICE 228 ⊠ ✕	ICE 928 ⑥k 🍷	ICE 720 Ⓑq ¶🍷	ICE 628 🍷	IC 1886 ⑥✣ 🍷	ICE 28 ▲ ✕	ICE 626 Ⓑq 🍷	ICE 1226 ⑥k 🍷	ICE 624 🍷	ICE 26 ⊠ ✕	ICE 622 🍷	ICE 1220 ⑦c H🍷	ICE 620 ①–⑤ d🍷
Wien Westbahnhof **950** d.	...	...	...	...	...	...	...	...	...	...	...	...	0640	...	...	...	...	0840	...	...	...	1040	...	...	...
Linz Hbf **950** d.	...	...	...	...	...	...	...	...	...	...	...	...	0816	...	...	...	...	1016	...	...	...	1216	...	...	...
Passau Hbf 🏛 **944** d.	...	...	...	...	0511	...	...	...	...	0718	...	...	0929	...	...	...	1112	1129	...	...	...	1329	...	...	...
Plattling **944** d.	...	...	...	...	0544	...	...	...	...	0751	...	...	1000	...	...	...	1145	1200	...	...	...	1400	...	...	...
Straubing d.	...	...	...	...	0558	...	...	...	...	0806	...	...	|	...	...	...	1159	|	...	...	...	|	...	...	...
Regensburg Hbf a.	...	...	...	...	0620	...	...	...	...	0825	...	...	1031	...	...	...	1220	1230	...	...	...	1431	...	...	...
Regensburg Hbf d.	...	...	...	...	0622	0622	...	...	...	0827	...	...	1033	...	...	...	1223	1232	...	...	...	1433	...	...	...
München Hbf **904** d.	...	...	0448g	0551	|	|	0545y	0651	0755	|	0855	0955	|	1055	1055	1155	|	|	1255	1255	1355	|	1455	1555	1555
Nürnberg Hbf a.	...	...	0554g	0657	0721	0721	0726	0757	0857	0925	0957	1057	1124	1157	1157	1257	1320	1325	1357	1357	1457	1524	1557	1657	1657
Nürnberg Hbf **900** d.	0500	0530	0600	0700	...	0729	0729	0800	0900	0928	1000	1100	1128	1200	1200	1300	1323	1328	1400	1400	1500	1528	1600	1700	1700
Würzburg Hbf **900** a.	0554	0624	0654	0754	...	0825	0825	0854	0954	1023	1054	1154	1225	1254	1254	1354	1421	1425	1454	1454	1554	1625	1654	1754	1754
Würzburg Hbf d.	0556	0626	0656	0756	...	0827	0827	0856	0956	1025	1056	1156	1227	1256	1256	1356	1423	1427	1456	1456	1556	1627	1656	1756	1756
Aschaffenburg Hbf d.	0636	0708	0736	0836	...	|	|	0936	1036	|	1136	1236	|	1336	1336	1436	|	|	1536	1536	1636	|	1736	1836	1836
Hanau Hbf d.	|	|	|	|	...	0920	0920	|	|	1120	|	|	|	|	|	|	|	1520	|	|	|	1720	|	|	|
Frankfurt (Main) Hbf a.	0717	0736	0805	0905	...	0936	0936	1005	1105	1136	1205	1305	1340	1405	1405	1505	|	1536	1605	1605	1705	1736	1805	1905	1905
Frankfurt Flughafen ✈ § a.	...	0755	0821	0921	...	0955	0955	1020	1121	1155	1221	1321	...	1421	1421	1521	|	...	1621	1621	1721	1755	1821	1920	1921
Mainz Hbf **912** a.	...	0818	|	|	...	1018	1018	|	|	1218	|	|	...	|	|	|	|	...	|	|	|	1818	|	|	|
Koblenz Hbf **912** a.	...	0910	|	|	...	1110	1110	|	|	1310	|	|	...	|	|	|	|	...	|	|	|	1910	|	|	|
Bonn Hbf **800** a.	...	0942	|	|	...	1142	1142	|	|	1342	|	|	...	|	|	|	|	...	|	|	|	1942	|	|	|
Köln Messe/Deutz **910** a.	...	|	0914	1014	...	|	|	|	1212	|	|	1414	...	1537	|	1614	|	...	|	1727	1814	|	1914	2014	|
Köln Hbf **800 910** a.	...	1005	|	|	...	1205	1205	1139	|	1405	1339	|	...	|	1539	|	|	...	1732	|	|	2005	|	|	2030
Düsseldorf Hbf **800** a.	...	|	0937	1037	...	|	|	...	1237	|	...	1437	...	|	...	1637	|	...	...	1750	1837	|	1942	2037	...
Essen Hbf **800** a.	...	|	1002	1102	...	|	|	...	1302	|	...	1502	...	|	...	1702	|	...	...	1821	1902	|	2008	2102	...
Wuppertal Hbf **800** a.	...	1041	...	...	...	1241	1241	...	|	1441	...	...	...	1614	...	...	|	...	...	|	|	2041	|	|	...
Dortmund Hbf **800** a.	...	1121	...	...	...	1321	1321	...	1330h	1521	...	...	...	1655	...	...	|	...	...	1846	1929	2120	2038	2129	...
Hamburg Hbf **800 900** a.	...	1412	...	...	...	1612	1612	...	...	1812	...	...	...	...	...	...	1907	...	...	...	...	...	...	...	...

See note ⊠	ICE 926 ⑥t 🍷	ICE 24 ⊠ ✕	ICE 528 G🍷	ICE 526 Ⓑq 🍷	ICE 22 ⊠ ✕	ICE 524 🍷	ICE 522 🍷	ICE 20 ⊠ ✕	ICE 520 ①–④ m🍷	ICE 922 ⑤–⑦ p✕	ICE 1120 ⑦w ✕	EN 490 r L R	EN 490 Q L R	EN 420 N R
Wien Westbahnhof **950** d.	...	1240	...	...	1440	...	...	1640	...	...	...	1954	1954	1954
Linz Hbf **950** d.	...	1416	...	...	1616	...	...	1816	...	...	...	2157	2157	2157
Passau Hbf 🏛 **944** d.	...	1529	...	...	1729	...	...	1929	...	...	...	2306	2306	2306
Plattling **944** d.	...	1600	...	...	1800	...	...	2000	...	...	...	|	|	|
Straubing d.	...	|	...	...	|	...	...	|	...	...	...	|	|	|
Regensburg Hbf a.	...	1631	...	...	1831	...	...	2031	...	...	...	0012	0012	0012
Regensburg Hbf d.	...	1633	...	...	1833	...	...	2033	...	...	...	0014	0014	0014
München Hbf **904** d.	1555	|	1650	1755	|	1855	1951	|	2055	2055	2154	|	|	|
Nürnberg Hbf a.	1657	1724	1757	1857	1924	1957	2057	2124	2157	2158	2304	0113	0159	|
Nürnberg Hbf **900** d.	1700	1727	1800	1900	1927	2000	2100	2128	2201	2201	2307	0132	0218	|
Würzburg Hbf **900** a.	1754	1825	1854	1954	2025	2054	2154	2227	2254	2254	0001	0226	0311	|
Würzburg Hbf d.	1756	1827	1856	1956	2027	2056	2156	2229	...	2301	0003	0228	0313	|
Aschaffenburg Hbf d.	1836	|	1936	2036	|	2136	2236	2310	...	2343	0045	|	|	0426s
Hanau Hbf d.	|	1920	|	|	2120	|	2250	2324	...	2356	0100	|	|	0439s
Frankfurt (Main) Hbf a.	1905	1936	2005	2105	2136	2205	2305	2339	...	0013	0116	|	|	0456
Frankfurt Flughafen ✈ § a.	1921	1955	2021	2121	2157	2221	2321	...	...	...	...	|	|	|
Mainz Hbf **912** a.	|	2018	|	|	2218	|	|	...	...	...	...	|	|	0646
Koblenz Hbf **912** a.	|	2110	|	|	2310	|	|	...	...	...	...	|	|	0744
Bonn Hbf **800** a.	|	2142	|	|	2342	|	|	...	...	...	...	|	|	0817
Köln Messe/Deutz **910** a.	|	|	2114	|	|	2343	|	...	...	...	...	|	|	|
Köln Hbf **800 910** a.	2039	2205	|	2219	0005	|	0039	...	...	...	...	|	|	0842
Düsseldorf Hbf **800** a.	2107	|	2137	2254	0032v	0005	0104	...	...	...	...	|	|	0911
Essen Hbf **800** a.	2136	|	2202	2323	0057v	0030	0134	...	...	...	...	|	|	0943
Wuppertal Hbf **800** a.	|	2241	|	|	|	|	|	...	...	...	...	|	|	|
Dortmund Hbf **800** a.	2159	2320	2228	2345	0121v	0054	0157	...	...	...	...	|	|	1006
Hamburg Hbf **800 900** a.	...	...	...	...	...	...	...	...	...	...	...	0750	1003j	...

- **a** – Not Dec. 24, 25, 31, Jan. 1, Apr. 2, 5, May 24.
- **b** – Also Apr. 6, May 13, 22, 25–29, June 1–5; not Apr. 5, May 24.
- **c** – Also Apr. 5, May 24.
- **d** – Not Dec. 24, 25, 31, Apr. 2, 5, May 24.
- **e** – Not Dec. 25, 26, Jan. 1, Apr. 3, 5, May 24.
- **g** – ① (also Apr. 6, May 25; not Apr. 5, May 24).
- **h** – ⑥ (also Dec. 24, 31, Apr. 2, 4, May 23).
- **j** – 0947 on ①⑥⑦.
- **k** – Also Dec. 24, 25, 31, Apr. 2, 4, May 23.
- **m** – Not Dec. 23, 24, 30, 31, Jan. 5, Apr. 1, 5, May 12, 24, June 2.
- **n** – Not Dec. 24, 31.
- **p** – Also Dec. 23, 24, 30, 31, Jan. 5, Apr. 1, 5, May 12, 24, June 2.
- **q** – Not Dec. 24, 25, 31, Apr. 2, 4, May 23.
- **r** – Not May 21 - June 6.
- **s** – Stops to set down only.
- **t** – Also Dec. 24, 25, 31, Apr. 2.
- **v** – Not Dec. 25, Jan. 1.
- **w** – Also Apr. 5, May 24; not Apr. 4, May 23.
- **y** – 0614 on May 13, 22, 26–29, June 1–5.

- **§** – Frankfurt Flughafen Fernbahnhof.
- **¶** – Train number **1022** on ⑤ (also Dec. 23, 30, Apr. 1, May 12, June 2).
- **♣** – Köln - Dortmund on the mornings of ①–④ only (also calls at Duisburg a. 0930).
- **▲** – May 22 - June 6 runs Wien - Nürnberg (a. 1405) only.
- **✣** – On May 22, 29, June 5 Passau d. 1018, Plattling d. 1051, Straubing d. 1105, Regensburg a. 1125, d. 1127 and does not call at Nürnberg.
- **◇** – May 22 - June 6 Passau d. 0620, Plattling d. 0655, Straubing d. 0712, Regensburg a. 0745, d. 0747 and then as shown.
- **⊠** – May 22 - June 6 most services between Regensburg and Nürnberg are diverted via Ingolstadt. During this period timings Nürnberg - Würzburg - Frankfurt and beyond are up to 60 minutes later (unless otherwise shown).

- **G** – On ⑥ runs with train number **924** and starts from Garmisch (d. 1515).
- **H** – To Hannover (Table **810**).
- **K** – ① (also Apr. 6; not Apr. 5, May 24, 31). [12] and 🍷 Passau - Stuttgart - Karlsruhe - Basel.
- **L** – HANS ALBERS – 🛏 1, 2 cl., 🛌 2 cl., [2] and 🍷 Wien - Hannover - Hamburg.
- **N** – 🛏 1, 2 cl., 🛌 2 cl., [2] and 🍷 Wien - Köln (- Dortmund ♣).
- **Q** – May 21 - June 6 only.
- **R** – ②–⑥ to May 21 and from June 8 (not Dec. 25, 26, Jan. 1, Apr. 3, 6, May 13).

RE / RB services Local trains PASSAU - REGENSBURG - NÜRNBERG - WÜRZBURG - FRANKFURT — 921

For faster *ICE / IC* trains see Table **920** above.

	⚒t																				⊖					
Passau Hbf **944** d.	*0443*	*0526*	...	*0605*g	*0645*f	...	*0826*	*0917*	...	*1025*	*1117*	...	*1226*	*1316*	...	*1426*	*1516*	...	*1626*	*1716*	...	*1822*	*1916*	...	*2026*	*2128*
Plattling **944** a.	*0516*	*0559*	...	*0638*g	*0718*f	...	*0859*	*0951*	...	*1058*	*1151*	...	*1259*	*1350*	...	*1459*	*1550*	...	*1659*	*1750*	...	*1856*	*1951*	...	*2059*	*2200*
Plattling d.	0522	0625	...	0705	0730f	...	0905	1005	...	1105	1205	...	1305	1405	...	1505	1605	...	1705	1805	...	1859	2005	...	2105	2206
Straubing d.	0539	0644	...	0723	0823	...	0923	1023	...	1123	1223	...	1323	1423	...	1523	1623	...	1723	1823	...	1918	2023	...	2123	2223
München Hbf **878** d.	|	|	0544	|	|	0744	|	|	0943	|	|	1144	|	|	1344	|	|	1544	|	|	1744	|	|	1944	|	|
Regensburg Hbf a.	0611	0714	0716	0753	0851	0914	0951	1051	1114	1151	1253	1314	1352	1451	1514	1551	1652	1714	1751	1851	1915	1947	2053	2122	2152	2251
Regensburg Hbf d.	...	...	0720	0754e	0853	0919	0953e	1053	1120	1153e	1253z	1320	1353e	1453	1520	1553e	1654	1720	1753e	1853	1920	1950z	2053z	2125	...	2253
Neumarkt (Oberpf) d.	...	...	0802	0851e	0950	1002	1050e	1150	1202	1251e	1350z	1402	1450e	1550	1602	1650e	1752	1802	1850e	1950	2002	2031z	2150z	2209	...	2351
Nürnberg Hbf a.	...	...	0825	...	...	1027	...	...	1225	...	...	1425	...	...	1627	...	...	1827	...	...	2025	2053z	...	2231	...	0026

	⑥k	Ⓐe	2							x	A				x	A	Ⓐe		x	A			2		2	
Nürnberg Hbf d.	0442	0442	0543	0604	0704	0804	0904	1004	1104	1204	1204	1304	1404	1504	1604	1604	1623	1704	1804	1804	1904	...	2010	2107	2213	2335
Fürth (Bay) Hbf d.	0451	0451	0552	0612	0712	0812	0912	1012	1112	1212	1212	1312	1412	1512	1612	1612	1631	1712	1812	1812	1912	...	2019	2116	2222	2344
Neustadt (Aisch) Bf d.	0521	0526	0622	0634	0734	0834	0934	1034	1134	1234	1239	1334	1434	1534	1634	1639	1658	1734	1834	1839	1934	...	2049	2137	2252	0015
Kitzingen d.	0545	0551	...	0658	0758	0858	0958	1058	1158	1258	1302	1358	1458	1558	1658	1702	1724	1758	1858	1902	1958	2056	...	2201	...	0038
Würzburg Hbf a.	0606	0610	...	0719	0819	0919	1019	1119	1219	1319	1322	1419	1519	1619	1719	1722	1744	1819	1919	1922	2019	2116	...	2222	...	0058

	Ⓐd	Ⓐn	Ⓒs		Ⓒz	⑥k	Ⓐd								Ⓒm	Ⓐd							†w	⚒r		⊡
Würzburg Hbf d.	0424	0514	0517	...	0611	0611	0635	0735	0835	0935	1035	1135	1235	1335	1435	1435	1535	1635	1735	1835	1935	2035	2136	2139	...	2305
Karlstadt (Main) d.	0446	0536	0541	...	0633	0633	0650	0750	0850	0950	1050	1150	1250	1350	1450	1450	1550	1650	1750	1850	1950	2050	2153	2201	...	2327
Gemünden (Main) d.	0458	0547	0553	...	0645	0645	0705	0805	0905	1005	1105	1205	1305j	1405	1505	1505	1605	1705j	1805	1905j	2005	2105j	2205	2212	...	2338
Lohr Bahnhof d.	0508	0557	0603	...	0655	0655	0715	0815	0915	1015	1115	1215	1315	1415	1515	1515	1615	1715	1815	1915	2015	2115	2215	2223	...	2348
Aschaffenburg Hbf d.	0542	0640	0640	*0717*	0726	0742	0743	0843	0943	1043	1143	1243	1343	1443	1543	1543	1643	1743	1843	1943	2043	2143	2243	2256	2313	0021
Hanau Hbf d.	0604	0704	0704k	0755	...	0804	0804	0904	1003	1104	1203	1304	1403	1504	1603	1604	1704	1803	1904	2003	2104	2203	2303	...	0002v	...
Offenbach (Main) Hbf d.	0613	0713	0713k	0804	...	0813	0813	0913	|	1113	|	1313	|	1513	|	1613	1713	|	1913	|	2113	|	|	...	|	...
Frankfurt (Main) Süd a.	0616	0716	0716k	0808	...	0816	0816	0916	1025	1116	1225	1316	1425	1516	1625	1617	1716	1825	1916	2025	2116	2225	2325	...	0025	...
Frankfurt (Main) Hbf a.	0624	0724	0724k	0815	...	0824	0826	0924	1032	1124	1232	1324	1432	1524	1632	*1628*	1724	1832p	1924	2032	2124	2232	2332	...	0032	...

- **A** – May 22 - June 6 only.
- **d** – Not Dec. 24, 31, June 3.
- **e** – Ⓐ (not Dec. 24, 31, Jan. 6, June 3).
- **f** – On Ⓒz: Passau d. *0725*, Plattling a. *0758*, d. 0805.
- **g** – 22 minutes later on Ⓒz.
- **j** – 5–6 minutes earlier May 22 - June 6.
- **k** – ⑥ (also Dec. 24, 31; not Dec. 26, May 1).
- **m** – Also Dec. 24, 31, June 3.
- **n** – Not Dec. 24, 31.
- **p** – 1840 on ⑦ (also Apr. 5, May 24; not Apr. 4, May 23).
- **r** – Not June 3.
- **s** – Also Dec. 24, 31.
- **t** – Not Jan. 6, June 3.
- **v** – Arrives 2338.
- **w** – Also June 3.
- **x** – Not May 22 - June 6.
- **z** – Ⓒ (also Dec. 24, 31, Jan. 6, June 3).
- **⊖** – Runs 5–6 minutes later Plattling - Regensburg on Ⓐe.
- **⊡** – Runs 11 minutes later on ①–⑥ (also Apr. 4, May 23; not Apr. 5, May 24).

922 WÜRZBURG - HEILBRONN - STUTTGART *RE services*

km		Ⓐe	Ⓐe	Ⓐe		Ⓐe		Ⓐe					†w		Ⓑq		
0	**Würzburg** Hbf d.	...	...	...	0637	...	0837	0937	1037	1237	1437	1637	1736	1837	1936	2038	2137
43	Lauda d.	...	0532	...	0710	0718	0910	1008	1110	1310	1510	1710	1807	1910	2007	2110	2207
78	Osterburken d.	0502	0600	0609	0733	0802	0933	1032	1133	1333	1533	1733	1830	1933	2030	2133	2230
94	Möckmühl d.	0519	...	0626	0745	0819	0945	1044	1145	1345	1545	1745	1842	1945	2042	2145	2242
116	Bad Friedrichshall ⊖ d.	0544	...	0653	0801	0844	1001	1100	1201	1401	1601	1801	1858	2001	2058	2201	2258
127	**Heilbronn** Hbf **924** d.	0559	...	0712	0812	0856	1012	1110	1212	1412	1612	1812	1909	2012	2107	2210	2307
140	Lauffen (Neckar) **924** d.	0610	...	|	|	0904	|	|	|	|	|	|	|	|	2116	2218	2316
180	**Stuttgart** Hbf **924** a.	0651	...	0747	0853	0943	1053	1146	1253	1453	1653	1853	1949	2053	2155	2253	2353

	Ⓐe	†w	Ⓐe	⑥k						†w		†w	Ⓐe				⑥⑦h
Stuttgart Hbf **924** d.	0452	0456	0558	0559	0702	0907	1107	1307	1505	1605	1704	1805	1809	1907	2031	2315	2315
Lauffen (Neckar) **924** d.	0527	0532	|	0635	0739	|	|	|	|	|	|	|	|	|	2106	2352	2352
Heilbronn Hbf **924** d.	0538	0544	0641	0647	0750	0945	1145	1345	1545	1647	1745	1845	1844	1945	2117	0004	0011
Bad Friedrichshall ⊖ d.	0549	0554	0649	0657	0800	0955	1155	1355	1555	1657	1755	1855	1854	1955	2126	...	0024
Möckmühl d.	0605	0610	0713	0713	0816	1011	1211	1413	1611	1713	1811	1911	1918	2011	2142	...	0048
Osterburken d.	0616	0622	0727	0727	0828	1027	1227	1427	1627	1727	1827	1927	1930	2027	2154	...	0106
Lauda d.	0643	0650	0750	0750	0851	1050	1250	1450	1650	1750	1850	1954	1954	2050	2217	...	...
Würzburg Hbf a.	0722	0722	0822	0822	0922	1122	1322r	1522	1722t	1820	1922	2024	2024	2122	2247	...	...

e – Not Dec. 24, 31, Jan. 6, June 3.
h – ⑥⑦ (also Jan. 6, Apr. 5, May 13, 24, June 3; not Apr. 4, May 23. Change trains at Heilbronn on ⑥ (not Apr. 3)
k – Also Dec. 24, 31; not Dec. 26, May 1.
q – Also Dec. 26, May 1; not Dec. 24, 31.
r – Arrives 1357 May 22 - June 6 (change trains at Lauda).
t – Not May 22 - June 6.
w – Also Jan. 6, June 3.

⊖ – Bad Friedrichshall-Jagstfeld. See also Table **924**.

☛ Services in this table are subject to alteration from June 10.

923 MANNHEIM - EBERBACH - OSTERBURKEN *S-Bahn*

km		Ⓐe	Ⓐe	Ⓐe	⑥k	Ⓐe	Ⓐe								n	⑥t	n
0	**Mannheim** Hbf ¶ **924** d.	0422	...	0457	0537	...	0607	0637c	0729	0839		1939	2037	2137	2257	2257	2337
17	**Heidelberg** Hbf ¶ **924** d.	0442	...	0555	0555	...	0632	0655	0755	0855	and	1955	2055	2200	2315	2315	2355
28	Neckargemünd **924** d.	0456	...	0609	0609	...	0646	0709	0809	0909		2009	2109	2214	2329	2329	0009
34	Neckarsteinach d.	0502	...	0615	0615	...	0652	0715	0815	0915	hourly	2015	2115	2220	2335	2335	0015
41	Hirschhorn (Neckar) d.	0509	...	0622	0622	...	0659	0722	0822	0922		2022	2122	2227	2342	2342	0022
50	Eberbach **924** d.	0516	...	0629	0629	...	0713f	0729	0829	0929	until	2029	2129	2234	2349	2349	0029
69	Mosbach-Neckarelz **924** d.	0535	0623	0648	0648	0709	0734	0748	0848	0948		2048	2148	2258	0008	0008	0048
72	Mosbach (Baden) d.	0539	0627	0652	0652	0714	0739	0752	0852	0952		2052	2152	2302	0012	0012	0052
101	**Osterburken** a.	0612	0658	...	0723	0750	...	0823	0923	1023		2123	2223	2333	...	0043	...

	⚒v	Ⓐe	Ⓐe		Ⓐe		Ⓐe		Ⓐe	⚒v						⑥k	
Osterburken d.	...	...	0513	0536k	0606	0636z	0644	...	0706	...	0736		1836	1936	2036	2136	2236
Mosbach (Baden) d.	0435	0510	0543	0605	0635	0705	0718	...	0735	...	0805		1905	2005	2105	2205	2305
Mosbach-Neckarelz **924** d.	0440	0526g	0548	0610	0640	0710	0724	0729	0740	0740	0810	and	1910	2010	2110	2210	2310
Eberbach **924** d.	0459	0545	0607	0629	0659	0729	...	0743	0759	0759	0829		1929	2029	2129	2229	2329
Hirschhorn (Neckar) d.	0506	0552	0614	0636	0706	0736	...	|	0806	0806	0836	hourly	1936	2036	2136	2236	2336
Neckarsteinach d.	0512	0559	0620	0642	0712	0742	...	|	0812	0812	0842		1942	2042	2142	2242	2342
Neckargemünd **924** d.	0519	0605	0627	0649	0719	0749	...	|	0819	0819	0849	until	1949	2049	2149	2249	2349
Heidelberg Hbf ¶ **924** a.	0533	0619	0642	0703	0733	0803	...	0809	0833	0833	0903		2003	2103	2203	2303	0003
Mannheim Hbf ¶ **924** a.	0551	0635	0702	0719	0751	0818	...	0822	0851	0851	0918		2018	2132	2232	2332	0030

c – Ⓒ (also Dec. 24, 31, June 3; not Dec. 25, Jan. 1).
e – Not Dec. 24, 31, Jan. 6, June 3.
f – Arrives 0705.
g – Arrives 0514.
k – ⑥ (also Dec. 24, 31; not Dec. 26, May 1).
n – Not Dec. 24, 31.
t – Also Dec. 25, Jan. 5, Apr. 1, 4, 30, May 12, 23, June 2.
v – Not Jan. 6, June 3.
z – Ⓒ (also Dec. 24, 31, Jan. 6, June 3).

¶ – See also Tables **911a**, **918**, **919**.

924 MANNHEIM - HEILBRONN - STUTTGART *RE / RB services*

km	See note ⊠	Ⓐe	Ⓒz	Ⓐe	Ⓐe		Ⓐe	Ⓐe	Ⓒz			Ⓐe	Ⓒz	Ⓐe					⊙					⊙	
0	**Mannheim** Hbf ¶ **923** d.	...	...	...	...	...	...	0630	...	...	...	0707	...	0736	0807	0836	0907	...	0936	1007	1036	1107	...	1136	1207
17	**Heidelberg** Hbf ¶ **923** d.	...	...	...	...	...	...	0643	0634	...	...	0732	0734	0749	0834	0849	0934	...	0949	1034	1049	1134	...	1149	1234
29	Neckargemünd **923** d.	...	...	...	...	...	...	|	0646	...	...	0746	0746	|	0846	|	0946	...	|	1046	|	1146	...	|	1246
49	Sinsheim (Elsenz) d.	...	...	0502	...	...	...	0713	0730	...	...	0809	0813	|	0908	0914	1008	1013	|	1108	1114	1208	1213	|	1308
52	Steinsfurt d.	...	...	0507	...	...	...	0716	0734	...	...	0811	0816	|	0912	|	1012	1016	|	1112	|	1212	1216	|	1312
72	Bad Wimpfen d.	...	...	0533	...	...	...	0734	0752	...	...	0834	0834	|	▬	0935	▬	1034	|	▬	1135	▬	1234	|	▬
	Eberbach **923** d.	...	...	|	...	...	...	|	|	...	...	|	|	0814	...	|	...	|	1014f	...	|	...	|	1214f	...
	Mosbach-Neckarelz **923** d.	...	...	|	0552	0618r	0651	|	|	...	0752	|	|	0828	0854	|	0954	|	1028f	1054	|	1154	|	1228f	1254
75	Bad Friedrichshall-J. ⊖ **922** d.	...	...	0539	0612	0638r	0711	0740	0756	0801	0812	0838	0839	0841	0913	0940	1013	1038	1042f	1113	1140	1213	1238	1242f	1313
86	**Heilbronn** Hbf **922** a.	...	...	0554	0625	0651r	0724	0751	...	0810	0825	...	0852	0851	0925	0951	1025	...	1051f	1125	1151	1225	...	1251f	1325
86	**Heilbronn** Hbf **922** d.	0435	0554	0559	0627	0653	0725	0756	...	0812	0826	...	0856	0856	0926	0956e	1026	...	1056	1126	1156e	1226	...	1256	1326
99	Lauffen (Neckar) **922** d.	0445	0604	0610	0636	0704	0736	0804	...	|	0837	...	0904	0904	0937	1004e	1037	...	1104	1137	1204e	1237	...	1304	1337
139	**Stuttgart** Hbf **922** a.	0525	0643	0651	0718	0743	0815	0843	...	0853	0915	...	0943	0943	1015	1043e	1115	...	1146	1215	1243e	1315	...	1343	1415

See note ⊠			◇	⊙				Ⓒz	⊙				◇	⊙										n	
Mannheim Hbf ¶ **923** d.	1236	...	1307	1336	1407	1436	1507	...	1536	1607	1636	...	1707	1736	1807	1836	1907	...	1936	2007	2044	2107	...	2142	2250
Heidelberg Hbf ¶ **923** d.	1249	...	1334	1349	1434	1449	1534	...	1549	1634	1649	...	1734	1749	1834	1849	1934	...	1949	2034	2059	2131	...	2157	2304
Neckargemünd **923** d.	|	...	1346	|	1446	|	1546	...	|	1646	|	...	1746	|	1846	|	1946	...	|	2046	|	2146	...	|	2318
Sinsheim (Elsenz) d.	1314t	...	1408	|	1508	1514t	1608	1613	|	1708	1715t	...	1808	|	1908	1914	2008	2013	|	2108	2126	2208	2213	|	2340
Steinsfurt d.	|	...	1416	|	1512	|	1612	1616	|	1712	|	...	1816	|	1912	|	2012	2016	|	2112	|	2212	2216	|	2342
Bad Wimpfen d.	1335	...	1434	|	▬	1535	▬	1634	|	▬	1736	...	1834	|	▬	1935	▬	2034	|	▬	2144	▬	2234	|	0001
Eberbach **923** d.	|	...	|	1414f	...	|	...	|	1614f	...	|	...	|	1814f	...	|	...	|	2014f	...	|	...	|	2223	|
Mosbach-Neckarelz **923** d.	|	1354	|	1428f	1454	|	1554	|	1628f	1654	|	1754	|	1828f	1854	|	1954	|	2028f	2054	|	...	|	2237	|
Bad Friedrichshall-J. ⊖ **922** d.	1340	1413	1438	1442f	1513	1540	1613	1638	1642f	1713	1741	1813	1838	1842f	1913	1940	2013	2038	2042f	2113	2149	2201	2238	2250	0006
Heilbronn Hbf **922** a.	1351	1425	...	1451f	1525	1551	1625	...	1651f	1725	1751	1825	...	1851f	1925	1951	2025	...	2051f	2125	2200	2209	...	2300	0016
Heilbronn Hbf **922** d.	1356e	1426	...	1456	1526	1556e	1626	...	1656	1726	1754e	1826	...	1856	1926	2012	2026	...	...	2126	...	2210	...	2307	...
Lauffen (Neckar) **922** d.	1404e	1437	...	1504	1537	1604e	1637	...	1704	1737	1802e	1837	...	1904	1937	|	2037	...	...	2137	...	2218	...	2316	...
Stuttgart Hbf **922** a.	1443e	1515	...	1543	1615	1643e	1715	...	1743	1815	1839e	1915	...	1943	2015	2053	2115	...	...	2215	...	2253	...	2353	...

km	See note ⊠		Ⓐe	Ⓐe	⚒v	Ⓐe	Ⓒz	Ⓐe	⑥k					⊙					⊙					⊙	Ⓒz
0	**Stuttgart** Hbf **922** d.	0015	...	...	...	0452	...	0545	0559	...	...	0702	0745	0813	...	0845	0915e	0945	1013	...	1045	1115e	1145	1213	...
40	Lauffen (Neckar) **922** d.	0051	...	...	...	0527	...	0623	0635	0649e	...	0739	0822	0850	...	0922	0953e	1022	1050	...	1122	1153e	1223	1250	...
53	**Heilbronn** Hbf **922** a.	0102	...	...	...	0538	...	0633	0646	0659e	...	0748	0832	0901	...	0932	1001e	1032	1101	...	1132	1201e	1232	1301	...
53	**Heilbronn** Hbf **922** d.	▬	0456	0502	0529	0543	0605	0634	0647	0700	...	0806	0833	0906	...	0933	1006	1033	1106	...	1133	1206	1233	1306	...
64	Bad Friedrichshall-J. ⊖ **922** d.	...	0504	0516	0543	0554	0619	0646	0657	0710	...	0817	0847	0916	0919	0946	1017	1046	1116	1119	1146	1217	1247	1316	1319
82	Mosbach-Neckarelz **923** d.	...	0518	|	0604	|	|	0702	▬	0729	...	|	0905	0929	|	1005	|	1105	1129	|	1205	|	1305	1329	|
101	Eberbach **923** d.	...	0532	|	▬	|	|	▬	...	0743	...	|	▬	0943	|	▬	|	▬	1143	|	▬	|	▬	1343	|
	Bad Wimpfen d.	...	|	0519	...	0558	0622	...	Ⓐe	|	...	0821	...	|	0922	...	1021	...	|	1122	...	1221	...	|	1322
	Steinsfurt d.	Ⓐe	|	0538	...	0615	0641	Ⓒz	0645	|	0744	|	0845	|	0941	0945	|	1045	|	1141	1145	|	1245	|	1341
	Sinsheim (Elsenz) d.	0446	|	0544	0549	0620	0644	0649	0649b	|	0749	0839f	0849	|	0944	0949	1043	1049	|	1144	1149	1243	1249	|	1344
123	Neckargemünd **923** d.	0512	|	...	0611	|	...	0711	0715	|	0811	|	0911	|	...	1011	|	1111	|	...	1211	|	1311	|	...
135	**Heidelberg** Hbf ¶ **923** a.	0529	0556	...	0626	0648	...	0726	0728	0809	0824	0909	0924	1009	...	1024	1109	1124	1209	...	1224	1309	1324	1409	...
152	**Mannheim** Hbf ¶ **923** a.	0551	0612	...	0651	0706	...	0751	0746	0822	0851	0922	0951	1022	...	1051	1122	1151	1222	...	1251	1322	1351	1422	...

See note ⊠				Ⓐe	⊙	Ⓒz				Ⓐe	⊙	Ⓒz				n⊙					Ⓐe	Ⓒz			
Stuttgart Hbf **922** d.	1245	1315e	1345	...	1413	...	1445	1515e	1545	...	1613	...	1645	1715e	1745	1813	...	1845	1915e	1945	...	2013	...	2115	...
Lauffen (Neckar) **922** d.	1323	1353e	1422	...	1450	...	1522	1553e	1622	...	1650	...	1722	1753e	1823	1850	...	1922	1953e	2022	...	2050	...	2153	...
Heilbronn Hbf **922** a.	1333	1401e	1432	...	1501	...	1532	1601e	1632	...	1701	...	1732	1801e	1833	1901	...	1932	2001e	2032	...	2101	...	2203	...
Heilbronn Hbf **922** d.	1333	1406	1433	...	1506	...	1533	1605	1633	...	1705	...	1733	1806	1833	1906	...	1933	2006	▬	2059	2103	...	2221	...
Bad Friedrichshall-J. ⊖ **922** d.	1347	1417	1446	1450	1516	1519	1546	1617	1646	1650	1716	1719	1746	1817	1847	1916	1919	1946	2017	...	2111	2111	2115	2235	2244
Mosbach-Neckarelz **923** d.	1405	|	1505	|	1529	|	1605	|	1705	|	1729	|	1805	|	1905	1929	|	2005	|	...	2129	2129	|	2254	|
Eberbach **923** d.	▬	|	▬	|	1543	|	▬	|	▬	|	1743	|	▬	|	▬	1943	|	▬	|	...	2143	2143	|	▬	|
Bad Wimpfen d.	...	1421	...	1453	|	1522	...	1621	...	1653	|	1722	...	1821	...	|	1922	...	2021	...	|	|	2118	...	2248
Steinsfurt d.	1345	|	1445	1514	|	1541	1545	|	1645	1714	|	1741	1745	|	1845	|	1941	1945	|	2050	|	|	2141	2150	2314
Sinsheim (Elsenz) d.	1349	1443	1449	1517	|	1544	1549	1639f	1649	1717	|	1744	1749	1843	1849	|	1944	1949	2043	2100	|	|	2144	2200	2319
Neckargemünd **923** d.	1411	|	1511	1543	|	...	1611	|	1711	1743	|	...	1811	|	1911	|	...	2011	|	2125	|	|	...	2225	2341
Heidelberg Hbf ¶ **923** a.	1424	1509	1524	1556	1609	...	1624	1708	1724	1756	1809	...	1821	1909	1924	2009	...	2024	2109	2138	2206	2206	...	2240	2356
Mannheim Hbf ¶ **923** a.	1451	1522	1551	1618	1622	...	1651	1722	1751	1818	1822	...	1851	1922	1951	2022	...	2055	2122	2202j	2222	2222	...	2302	0030

b – 0654 until Mar. 19.
e – Ⓐ (not Dec. 24, 31, Jan. 6, June 3).
f – 3–4 minutes later on Ⓒz.
j – Change trains at Mannheim on Ⓐe.
k – Also Dec. 24, 31; not Dec. 26, May 1.
n – Not Dec. 24, 31.
r – ⚒ (not Jan. 6, June 3).
t – 4–5 minutes later on Ⓐe.
v – Not Jan. 6, June 3.
z – Also Dec. 24, 31, Jan. 6, June 11.
⊠ – Services in the Stuttgart area are subject to alteration from June 10.
⊖ – Bad Friedrichshall-Jagstfeld.
⊙ – Change trains at Heilbronn on Ⓐe.
◇ – Change trains at Steinsfurt on Ⓒz.
¶ – See also Tables **911a**, **918**, **919**.

925 STUTTGART - BACKNANG / AALEN - NÜRNBERG

RE services except where shown

km			IC 2061				IC 2063			IC 2065				IC 2101				IC 2069			IC 2103			IC 2163		
		Ⓐt	①–⑤ a	Ⓐt	2		🍷			🍷		Ⓒz	Ⓐt	B🍷		Ⓒz	Ⓐt	🍷			B🍷			Ⓑq 🍷		
	Karlsruhe Hbf 931 .. d.	...	...	...	...	...	0706e	...	...	0906	...	...	...	1106	...	...	...	1306	...	...	1506	...	...	1706	...	...
0	**Stuttgart** Hbf ‡ d.	0541	0605	0620	...	0641	0807	0822	0841	1007	1022	1041	1041	1207	1222	1241	1241	1407	1422	1441	1607	1619h	1641	1807	1819h	1841
31	Backnang d.	0609	|	|	...	0706	|	|	0906	|	|	1106	1106	|	|	1306	1311	|	|	1506	|	|	1706	|	|	1906
73	Schwäbisch H-H ⊡ a.	0653	|	|	...	0759	|	|	0957k	|	|	1157	1149	|	|	1357	1349	|	|	1557	|	|	1757k	|	|	1957k
73	Schwäbisch H-H ⊡ d.	0654	|	|	...	0759	|	|	0959	|	|	1159	1159	|	|	1359	1359	|	|	1559	|	|	1759	|	|	1959
	Schwäbisch Gmünd ‡ d.	|	0642	0705	...	|	0842	0905	|	1040	1105	|	|	1240	1305	|	|	1440	1505	|	1640	1705	|	1840	1905	|
	Aalen ‡ d.	|	0659	0725	0728	|	0859	0925	|	1057	1125	|	|	1257	1325	|	|	1457	1525	|	1657	1725	|	1857	1925	|
	Ellwangen d.	|	0710	...	0748	|	0910	*0948*	|	1108	*1148*	|	|	1308	*1348*	|	|	1508	*1548*	|	1708	*1748*	|	1908	*1948*	|
100	Crailsheim d.	0713	0726	...	0812	0818	0926	*1012*	1018	1125	*1212*	1218	1218	1325	*1412*	1418	1418	1525	*1612*	1618	1725	*1812*	1818	1925	*2012*	2018
146	Ansbach d.	0756j	0750	...	...	0851	0950	...	1051	1151	...	1251	1256	1350	...	1451	1456	1550	...	1651	1750	...	1851	1950	...	2051
190	**Nürnberg** Hbf a.	0841	0818	...	...	0925	1018	...	1125	1216	...	1325	1341	1416	...	1525	1541	1616	...	1725	1816	...	1925	2016	...	2125

				IC 2105			IC 2167				
	Ⓒz	Ⓒz	Ⓐt	⑤⑦f Q🍷			⑦w		Ⓒm	Ⓐt	
Karlsruhe Hbf 931 .. d.	...	...	...	1906	...	...	2106	...	...	...	...
Stuttgart Hbf ‡ d.	1945*	...	1958	2007	2022	2057	2207	2232	2245*	2258	2358
Backnang d.	2021	...	2025	|	|	2123	|	|	2325	2325	0026
Schwäbisch H-H ⊡ a.	2055	...	2102	|	|	2202	|	|	0002	0002	0102
Schwäbisch H-H ⊡ d.	...	2059	2103	|	|	2203	|	|	0003	0003	0103
Schwäbisch Gmünd ‡ d.	...	|	|	2040	2105	|	2243	2316	|	|	|
Aalen ‡ d.	...	|	|	2057	2125	|	2300	2338	|	|	|
Ellwangen d.	...	|	|	2108	*2152*	|	2311	*0004*	|	|	|
Crailsheim d.	...	2121	2121	2125	*2208*	2222	2329	*0020*	0021	0021	0121
Ansbach d.	...	...	...	2150	...	...	2354	...	...	...	...
Nürnberg Hbf a.	...	...	...	2216	...	...	0022	...	...	...	...

km						IC 2164					
		Ⓐt	Ⓐt	Ⓒz	Ⓐt	①–⑤ a🍷	Ⓐt	Ⓒz	Ⓐt	Ⓒz	Ⓐt
0	**Nürnberg** Hbf d.	...	...	...	...	0537	...	...	...	...	0614
44	Ansbach d.	...	...	...	...	0604	...	...	...	...	0707j
90	Crailsheim d.	0452	*0515*	0552	0556	0632	0635	0635	*0646*	*0651*	0742
111	Ellwangen d.	|	*0531*	|	|	0648	|	|	*0710*	*0712*	|
127	**Aalen** ‡ d.	|	0600	|	|	0701	|	|	0733	0735	|
152	Schwäbisch Gmünd ‡ d.	|	0621	|	|	0718	|	|	0752	0754	|
	Schwäbisch H-H ⊡ a.	0510	|	0610	0614	|	0653	0653	|	|	0800
	Schwäbisch H-H ⊡ d.	0511	|	0611	0618	|	0654	0702	|	|	0803
	Backnang d.	0551	|	0651	0705	|	0736	0737	|	|	0851
203	**Stuttgart** Hbf ‡ a.	0618	0714	0718	0735	0753	0803	*0815*	0843	0838	0918
	Karlsruhe Hbf 931 .. a.	...	...	...	...	0853	...	...	...	...	...

			IC 2102			IC 2160			IC 2100				IC 2066			IC 2104				IC 2062			IC 2060			IC 1868
	Ⓒz		①–⑥ e P			🍷			B🍷	Ⓐt	Ⓒz		🍷			B🍷	Ⓒz	Ⓐt		🍷			⑤⑦ f🍷		n ⊗	⑦w 🍷
Nürnberg Hbf d.	0635	...	0741	0833h	...	0941	1035	...	1141	1218	1235	...	1341	1435	...	1541	1635	1635	...	1741	1835	...	1941	2035	...	2141
Ansbach d.	0707	...	0807	0907	...	1007	1107	...	1207	1310j	1307	...	1407	1507	...	1607	1707	1707	...	1807	1907	...	2007	2107	...	2207
Crailsheim d.	0742	*0752*	0835	0942	*0952*	1035	1142	*1152*	1235	1343	1342	*1352*	1435	1543	*1552*	1635	1742	1743	*1752*	1835	1942	*1952*	2035	2142	2146	2235
Ellwangen d.	|	*0812*	0851	|	*1012*	1051	|	*1212*	1251	|	|	*1412*	1451	|	*1612*	1651	|	|	*1812*	1851	|	*2012*	2051	|	2208	2251
Aalen ‡ d.	|	0835	0903	|	1035	1103	|	1235	1303	|	|	1435	1503	|	1635	1703	|	|	1835	1903	|	2035	2103	|	2224	2303
Schwäbisch Gmünd ‡ d.	|	0854	0920	|	1054	1120	|	1254	1320	|	|	1454	1520	|	1654	1720	|	|	1854	1920	|	2054	2120	|	2243	2320
Schwäbisch H-H ⊡ a.	0800	|	|	1000	|	|	1200	|	|	1400	1400	|	|	1601	|	|	1800	1801	|	|	2000	|	|	2200	|	|
Schwäbisch H-H ⊡ d.	0803	|	|	1003	|	|	1203	|	|	1403	1403	|	|	1603	|	|	1803	1806	|	|	2003	|	|	2203	|	|
Backnang d.	0851	|	|	1051	|	|	1251	|	|	1451	1451	|	|	1651	|	|	1851	1851	|	|	2051	|	|	2251	|	|
Stuttgart Hbf ‡ a.	0918	0938	0953	1118	1138	1153	1318	1338	1353	1518	1518	1538	1553	1718	1743r	1753	1918	1918	1938	1953	2118	2138	2153	2318	2329	2355
Karlsruhe Hbf 931 .. a.	...	...	1053	...	...	1253	...	...	1453	...	...	...	1653	...	...	1853	...	...	...	2053	...	...	2253	...	...	...

B – From / to Basel (Table 912).
P – (12) and 🍷 (Passau ①g -) Nürnberg - Basel.
Q – (12) and 🍷 Basel - Nürnberg (- Passau ⑦y).

a – Not Dec. 24, 25, 31, Jan. 1, Apr. 2, 5, May 24.
e – ①–⑥ (not Dec. 25, 26, Jan. 1, Apr. 3, 5, May 24).
f – Also Dec. 23, 30, Apr. 1, 5, May 12, 24, June 2; not Dec. 25, Jan. 1, Apr. 2, 4, May 14, 23, June 4.
g – Also Apr. 6; not Apr. 5, May 24, 31.
h – 2–3 minutes later on Ⓒz.

j – Arrives 7–11 minutes earlier.
k – 7–8 minutes earlier on Ⓐt.
m – Also Dec. 31, Jan. 6, June 3.
q – Not Dec. 24, 25, 31, Apr. 2, 4, May 23.
r – 1738 on Ⓒz.
t – Not Dec. 24, 31, Jan. 6, June 3.
v – Not Dec. 25, Jan. 1.
w – Also Apr. 5, May 24; not Apr. 4, May 23.
y – Also Apr. 5; not Apr. 4, May 23, 30, June 6.
z – Also Dec. 24, 31, Jan. 6, June 3.

* – From the S-Bahn (underground) platforms.
⊗ – On Apr. 17, 23, 24, 30, May 1, 7, 8 change trains at Aalen.
⊡ – Schwäbisch Hall-Hessental.
‡ – Other *RE* trains Stuttgart - Schwäbisch Gmünd - Aalen and v.v.
From Stuttgart Hbf at 0032 v, 0507 Ⓐt, 0528 Ⓐt, 0650 Ⓐt, 0719 Ⓐt, 0722 Ⓒz, 0922, 1122, 1322, 1449 Ⓐt, 1522, 1549 Ⓐt, 1649 Ⓐt, 1719 Ⓐt, 1722 Ⓒz, 1749 Ⓐt, 1846 Ⓐt, 1922, 2122, 2332 Ⓐt and 2336 Ⓒz.
From Aalen at 0426 Ⓐt, 0503 Ⓐt, 0518 Ⓐt, 0533 Ⓐt, 0535 Ⓒz, 0627 Ⓐt, 0635 Ⓒz, 0706 Ⓐt, 0805 Ⓐt, 0935, 1135, 1335, 1535, 1605 Ⓐt, 1708 Ⓐt, 1735, 1805 Ⓐt, 1935 and 2135.

926 HEILBRONN / ASCHAFFENBURG - CRAILSHEIM and AALEN - DONAUWÖRTH / ULM

RE / RB services

Aschaffenburg - Lauda - Crailsheim ⊠

km		Ⓐt	Ⓒz							
0	**Aschaffenburg** Hbf d.	...	...	0643	0922	1122	1322	1522	1722	1922g
38	Miltenberg d.	...	...	0750j	0959	1159	1359	1559	1759	1959
69	Wertheim d.	...	...	0828j	1035	1235	1435	1635	1835	2035
93	Tauberbischofsheim d.	0547	...	0856	1056	1256	1456	1656	1856f	2100
100	**Lauda** a.	0556	...	0906	1106	1306	1506	1706	1906	2106
100	**Lauda** d.	0611	0713	0913	1113	1313	1513	1713	1913	2113n
110	Bad Mergentheim d.	0623	0725	0925	1125	1325	1525	1725	1925	2124n
169	**Crailsheim** a.	0729	0830	1028	1228	1428	1628	1828	2028	...

	Ⓒz	Ⓐt	Ⓐt								Ⓒw
Crailsheim d.	...	*0520*	...	0731	0931	1127e	1328e	1531	1731	*1931*	...
Bad Mergentheim d.	*0550*	*0643*	...	0834	1034	1234	1434	1634	1834	*2034*	...
Lauda a.	*0601*	*0654*	...	0846	1044	1244	1444	1644	1844	*2044*	...
Lauda d.	0618	0702	...	0853	1053	1253	1453	1653	1853	2110	2110
Tauberbischofsheim d.	0626	0712	...	0859	1059	1259	1459	1659	1859	2120	2120
Wertheim d.	0700	0738	0800	0921	1121	1321	1521	1721	1921	2146	2147
Miltenberg d.	0740	...	0840	0959	1159	1359	1559	1759	1959	...	2222
Aschaffenburg Hbf a.	0830	...	0930	1038	1238	1438	1638	1838	2038h	...	2306

Heilbronn - Crailsheim ⊠

km		Ⓐt	Ⓒz	Ⓐt		Ⓒz	Ⓐt	Ⓒt	Ⓐt
0	**Heilbronn** Hbf d.	*0550*	0803	0805	and every two hours until	1803	1805	2003	2005
27	Öhringen d.	0618	0825	0827		1825	1827	2025	2027
54	Schwäbisch Hall d.	0642	0851	0852		1851	1852	2051	2052
61	Schwäbisch Hall-H ⊡ a.	0649	0858	0858		1858	1858	2058	2058
88	**Crailsheim** a.	*0712*	0921	0921		1921	1921	2121	*2121*

	Ⓐt		Ⓐt	Ⓒz		Ⓐt	Ⓒz		
Crailsheim d.	*0556*	*0635*	0838	0838	and every two hours until	1838	1838	...	2038
Schwäbisch Hall-H ⊡ d.	0618	0658	0858	0900		1858	1900	...	2106
Schwäbisch Hall d.	0625	0705	0905	0906		1905	1906	...	2113
Öhringen a.	0648	0728	0928	0930		1928	1930	...	2136
Heilbronn Hbf a.	*0718*	0751	0951	0952		1951	1952	...	*2216*

Aalen - Donauwörth

km		Ⓐt	Ⓒz	Ⓐt	Ⓐt			Ⓐt	G	B	Ⓐt	G	B	Ⓐt	G	B	Ⓐt	G	B	Ⓐt	G	B	Ⓐt	G	B	x
0	**Aalen** d.	...	0531	...	0626	...	0735	0835	0935	0936	1035	1135	1136	1235	1335	1336	1435	1535	1536	1635	1735	1736	1835	1935	1936	2035
39	Nördlingen a.	...	0613	...	0706	...	0813	0913	1013	1020	1113	1219	1220	1313	1413	1420	1513	1613	1620	1713	1813	1819	1913	2013	2020	2113
39	Nördlingen d.	0527	0614	0624	0707	...	0814	0914	1014	1021	1114	1221	1221	1314	1414	1421	1514	1614	1621	1714	1814	1820	1914	2014	2021	2114
68	**Donauwörth** a.	0553	0644	0653	0733	...	0844	0944	1044	1048	1144	1248	1248	1344	1444	1448	1544	1644	1648	1744	1844	1852	1944	2048	2048	2144

	Ⓐt		Ⓐt	⚒r	Ⓒz	Ⓐt	Ⓐt	B	G	Ⓐt	B	G	Ⓐt	B	G	Ⓐt	B	G	Ⓐt	B	G	Ⓐt	B	G	Ⓐt	x
Donauwörth d.	...	...	0608	...	0704	0708	0804	0904	0904	1004	1104	1104	1204	1304	1304	1404	1504	1504	1604	1704	1704	1804	1904	1904	2004	2104
Nördlingen a.	...	...	0639	...	0731	0740	0831	0931	0931	1035	1131	1131	1236	1331	1331	1435	1531	1531	1635	1731	1731	1835	1931	1931	2035	2132
Nördlingen d.	0535	...	0639	0639	0744	0744	0844	0934	0944	1044	1134	1144	1244	1334	1344	1444	1534	1544	1644	1734	1744	1844	1934	1944	2044	2134
Aalen a.	0619	...	0721	0721	0825	0825	0925	1011	1025	1125	1211	1225	1325	1414	1425	1525	1611	1625	1725	1813	1825	1925	2011	2025	2125	2215

Aalen - Ulm ⊠

km		Ⓐt	⑥k	Ⓐt	Ⓐt	Ⓒz	Ⓐt			Ⓐt																
0	**Aalen** d.	0457	0524	0554	0625	0633	0702	0733	0833	0907	0933	1033	1107	1133	1307	1333	1507	1533	1633	1707	1733	1833	1907	1933	2039	2133
23	Heidenheim d.	0520	0547	0617	0647	0659	0725	0756e	0859	0923	0954	1059	1123	1153	1323	1353	1523	1553	1659	1723	1754	1859	1923	1953	2107	2157
73	**Ulm** Hbf a.	0608	0644	0709	0743	0743	0756	0843	0943	0954	1043	1143	1154	1243	1354	1443	1554	1643	1743	1754	1843	1943	1954	2043	2151	2247

	Ⓐt	Ⓐt	Ⓐt	Ⓒz	Ⓐt	Ⓒz	Ⓐt																			
Ulm Hbf d.	0435	0543	0553	0614	0648	0713	0803	0813	0913	1000	1013	1113	1200	1213	1313	1400	1413	1513	1600	1613	1713	1800	1813	1913	2013	2218
Heidenheim d.	0520	0630	0656	0658	0759	0759	0835	0859	1003	1032	1059	1206	1232	1259	1403	1432	1459	1603	1632	1659	1803	1832	1859	2003	2059	2314
Aalen a.	0545	0651	0721	0721	0823	0824	0851	0924	1026	1050	1124	1227	1250	1324	1426	1450	1524	1626	1650	1724	1826	1850	1924	2026	2122	2336

B – Feb. 27 - May 16.
G – To Feb. 26 and from May 17.
e – 3–4 minutes later on Ⓒz.
f – 1900 on Ⓐt.

g – 1928 on Ⓒz.
h – On Ⓐt arrive *2121* (change trains at Miltenberg).
j – On Ⓐt: Miltenberg d. 0752, Wertheim d. 0835.
k – Also Dec. 24, 31; not Dec. 26, May 1.

n – Not Dec. 24, 31.
r – Not Jan. 6, June 3.
t – Not Dec. 24, 31, Jan. 6, June 3.
w – Also Jan. 6, June 3.

x – Not Dec. 24.
z – Also Dec. 24, 31, Jan. 6, June 3.
⊠ – 2nd class only.
⊡ – Schwäbisch Hall-Hessental.

927 ROMANTISCHE STRASSE (EUROPABUS 2009) Deutsche Touring GmbH

Daily **May 2 - Oct. 19** Frankfurt → Füssen, **May 3 - Oct. 20** Füssen - Frankfurt. Reservation recommended. +49 (0)69 7903 261. Fax +49 (0)69 7003 156. www.touring.de

Frankfurt (Main) Hbf (Südseite) d. 0800 ⟶ Würzburg Hbf d. 0945 ⟶ Rothenburg ob der Tauber (Schrannenplatz) a. 1040, d. 1115 ⟶ Rothenburg ob der Tauber (Bahnhof) d. 1120 ⟶ Feuchtwangen (Marktplatz) d. 1145 ⟶ Dinkelsbühl (Schweinemarkt) a. 1205, d. 1240 ⟶ Nördlingen (Rathaus) a. 1320, d. 1335 ⟶ Augsburg Hbf d. 1435 ⟶ Augsburg (Rathaus) a. 1440, d. 1515 ⟶ **München** Hbf (Nord) d. 1625 ⟶ Oberammergau (Bahnhof) d. 1745 ⟶ Schwangau (Tourist-Info) d. 1835 ⟶ Hohenschwangau (Info Point) a. 1840 ⟶ **Füssen** (Bahnhof) a. 1900.

Füssen (Bahnhof) d. 0800 ⟶ Hohenschwangau (Info Point) d. 0820 ⟶ Schwangau (Tourist-Info) d. 0825 ⟶ Oberammergau (Bahnhof) d. 0940 ⟶ **München** Hbf (Nord) d. 1100 ⟶ Augsburg (Rathaus) a. 1205, d. 1235 ⟶ Augsburg Hbf d. 1240 ⟶ Nördlingen (Rathaus) a. 1345, d. 1400 ⟶ Dinkelsbühl (Schweinemarkt) a. 1440, d. 1510 ⟶ Feuchtwangen (Marktplatz) d. 1530 ⟶ Rothenburg ob der Tauber (Bahnhof) d. 1555 ⟶ Rothenburg ob der Tauber (Schrannenplatz) a. 1600, d. 1635 ⟶ Wüzburg Hbf a. 1730 ⟶ **Frankfurt** (Main) Hbf (Südseite) a. 1915.

20% discount available for holders of the Eurail and German Rail passes.

Operator: Deutsche Touring GmbH, Am Römerhof 17, 60486 Frankfurt (Main).

928 MÜNCHEN - BAYRISCHZELL, LENGGRIES and TEGERNSEE Bayerische Oberlandbahn GmbH

On Dec. 24, 31, Jan. 6, June 3 services run as on Ⓒ

km		Ⓒ	Ⓐ	Ⓐ	Ⓒ		ⒸA		Ⓒ		ⒸB												m		n
0	**München** Hbf ... d.	0610	0630	0703	0710	0810	0829	0910	0930	1010	1029	1110	...	1210	1310	1410	1510	1610	1710	1810	1910	2010	2110	2210	...	2350
37	Holzkirchen ... d.	0637	0701	0732	0737	0837	0858	0937	0957	1037	1058	1137	...	1237	1337	1437	1537	1637	1737	1837	1937	2037	2137	2237	...	0017
61	Schliersee ... d.	0705	0727	0805	0805	0905	0925	1005	1024	1105	1125	1205	...	1305	1405	1505	1605	1705	1805	1905	2005	2105	2205	2305	...	0045
78	**Bayrischzell** ... a.	0728	...	0828	0828	0928	...	1028	...	1128	...	1228	...	1328	1428	1528	1628	1728	1828	1928	2028	2128	2228	2328	...	0108

km		Ⓒ	Ⓐ	Ⓐ	Ⓒ		ⒸA		Ⓒ		ⒸB												m		n
0	**München** Hbf ... d.	0610	0630	0703	0710	0810	0829	0910	0930	1010	1029	1110	...	1210	1310	1410	1510	1610	1710	1810	1910	2010	2110	2210	...	2350
37	Holzkirchen ... d.	0639	0706	0735	0739	0839	0901	0939	1000	1039	1101	1139	...	1239	1339	1439	1539	1639	1739	1839	1939	2039	2139	2239	...	0019
47	Schaftlach ... d.	0651	0718	0747	0751	0851	0917	0951	1017	1051	1117	1151	...	1251	1351	1451	1551	1651	1751	1851	1951	2051	2151	2251	...	0031
57	Bad Tölz ... d.	0702	0732	0802	0802	0902	0928	1002	1028	1102	1128	1202	...	1302	1402	1502	1602	1702	1802	1902	2002	2102	2202	2302	...	0042
67	**Lenggries** ... a.	0713	0743	0813	0813	0913	0939	1013	1039	1113	1139	1213	...	1313	1413	1513	1613	1713	1813	1913	2013	2113	2213	2313	...	0053

km		Ⓒ	Ⓐ	Ⓐ	Ⓒ		ⒸA		Ⓒ		ⒸB												m		n
0	**München** Hbf ... d.	0610	0630	0703	0710	0810	0829	0910	0930	1010	1029	1110	...	1210	1310	1410	1510	1610	1710	1810	1910	2010	2110	2210	...	2350
37	Holzkirchen ... d.	0639	0706	0735	0739	0839	0901	0939	1000	1039	1101	1139	...	1239	1339	1439	1539	1639	1739	1839	1939	2039	2139	2239	...	0019
47	Schaftlach ... d.	0652	0719	0752	0752	0852	0917	0952	1017	1052	1117	1152	...	1252	1352	1452	1552	1652	1752	1852	1952	2052	2152	2252	...	0032
59	**Tegernsee** ... a.	0712	0738	0812	0812	0912	0936	1012	1036	1112	1136	1212	...	1312	1412	1512	1612	1712	1812	1912	2012	2112	2212	2312	...	0052

	Ⓐ	Ⓐ	Ⓒ	Ⓐ	Ⓒ	Ⓐ	Ⓐ						Ⓒ	Ⓐ	Ⓒ			ⒸA		Ⓒ		ⒸB			m	m
Bayrischzell ... d.	0455	...	0535	0607	0635	...	0705	0735	0835	0935	1035	1135	1235	1235	1335	1435	1535	...	1635	...	1735	...	1835	1935	2035	2135
Schliersee ... d.	0523	0558	0603	0635	0703	0704	0735	0803	0903	1003	1103	1203	1303	1303	1403	1503	1603	1640	1703	1740	1803	1840	1903	2003	2103	2203
Holzkirchen ... a.	0546	0621	0626	0659	0726	0729	0800	0826	0926	1026	1126	1226	1326	1330	1426	1526	1626	1705	1726	1805	1826	1905	1926	2026	2126	2226
München Hbf ... a.	0617	0652	0657	0732	0757	0801	0831	0857	0957	1057	1157	1257	1357	1359	1457	1557	1657	1734	1757	1836	1857	1934	1957	2057	2157	2257

	Ⓐ	Ⓐ	Ⓒ	Ⓐ	Ⓒ	Ⓐ	Ⓐ						Ⓒ	Ⓐ	Ⓒ			ⒸA		Ⓒ		ⒸB			m	m
Lenggries ... d.	0510	0549	0550	0620	0650	0650	0720	0750	0850	0950	1050	1150	1250	1250	1350	1450	1550	1625	1650	1725	1750	1825	1850	1950	2050	2150
Bad Tölz ... d.	0523	0602	0603	0633	0703	0703	0735	0803	0903	1003	1103	1203	1303	1302	1403	1503	1603	1638	1703	1738	1803	1838	1903	2003	2103	2203
Schaftlach ... d.	0539	0614	0619	0646	0719	0717	0748	0819	0919	1019	1119	1219	1319	1318	1419	1519	1619	1651	1719	1751	1819	1851	1919	2019	2119	2219
Holzkirchen ... d.	0551	0626	0631	0706	0731	0733	0803	0831	0931	1031	1131	1231	1331	1332	1431	1531	1631	1708	1731	1808	1831	1908	1931	2031	2131	2231
München Hbf ... a.	0617	0652	0657	0732	0757	0801	0831	0857	0957	1057	1157	1257	1357	1359	1457	1557	1657	1734	1757	1836	1857	1934	1957	2057	2157	2257

	Ⓐ		Ⓒ	Ⓐ	Ⓒ		Ⓐ						Ⓒ	Ⓐ	Ⓒ			ⒸA		Ⓒ		ⒸB			m	m
Tegernsee ... d.	0517	...	0557	0621	0657	...	0722	0757	0857	0957	1057	1157	1257	1255	1357	1457	1557	1626	1657	1726	1757	1826	1857	1957	2057	2157
Schaftlach ... a.	0536	...	0616	0640	0716	...	0742	0816	0916	1016	1116	1216	1316	1315	1416	1516	1616	1645	1716	1745	1816	1845	1916	2016	2116	2216
Holzkirchen ... a.	0549	...	0629	0656	0729	...	0758	0829	0929	1029	1129	1229	1329	1328	1429	1529	1629	1701	1729	1801	1829	1901	1929	2029	2129	2229
München Hbf ... a.	0617	...	0657	0732	0757	...	0831	0857	0957	1057	1157	1257	1357	1359	1457	1557	1657	1734	1757	1836	1857	1934	1957	2057	2157	2257

A – Until Mar. 27. **B** – From Mar. 28. **m** – Not Dec. 24. **n** – Not Dec. 24, 31.

929 PLATTLING - BAYERISCH EISENSTEIN - PLZEŇ DB; ČD; 2nd class only

km		v	w	Ⓐ	965 w◇	Ⓐ	Ⓐe	⑥d	⑥⑦j		967 ◇							969 ◇							971 ◇
0	**Plattling** ... d.	...	...	...	...	...	0520	0556	...	0659	...	0805	0907	...	...	1007	1107	...	1207	...	1307	1407	...	1507	...
9	Deggendorf Hbf ... d.	...	...	...	...	...	0532	0608	...	0709	...	0817	0917	...	...	1017	1117	...	1217	...	1317	1417	...	1517	...
33	Gotteszell ... d.	...	...	...	...	...	0554	0626	...	0732	...	0835	0935	...	...	1035	1135	...	1235	...	1335	1435	...	1535	...
48	Regen ... d.	...	...	...	...	...	0608	0641	...	0747	...	0849	0949	...	...	1049	1149	...	1249	...	1349	1449	...	1549	...
58	Zwiesel (Bay) ... d.	...	...	...	...	...	0617	0650	0658	0800	...	0900	1000	...	...	1100	1200	...	1300	...	1400	1500	...	1600	...
72	**Bayerisch Eisenstein** ☆ a.	...	...	...	...	...	▬	*0711*	0711	0813	...	0913	1013	...	...	1113	1213	...	1313	...	1413	1513	...	1613	...
72	**Bayerisch Eisenstein** ☆ d.	...	0410	...	...	0555	...	▬	0714	...	0845	0917	...	1045	...	1117f	1214j	1245	...	1330	1414	▬	1526	...	1645
76	Železná Ruda Město ... d.	...	0417	...	...	0602	...	...	0720	...	0852	0923	...	1052	...	1123f	1220j	1252	...	1338	1420	...	1535	...	1652
79	Špičák ... d.	...	0422	...	...	0607	...	...	0724	...	0903	0927	...	1103	...	1127f	1224j	1303	...	1344	1424	...	1544	...	1703
131	**Klatovy** ... a.	...	0518	...	...	0710	...	...	...	...	0956	...	...	1156	...	...	...	1356	...	1441	...	...	1639	...	1756
131	**Klatovy** ... d.	0358	...	0526	0606	...	0806	0846	...	...	1006	...	...	*1206*	1246	...	...	1406	...	*1446*	...	1606	1646	...	1806
141	Švihov u Klatov ... d.	0410	...	0537	0615	...	0815	0858	...	...	1015	...	...	*1215*	1258	...	...	1415	...	*1458*	...	1615	1658	...	1815
170	**Plzeň** Hlavni ... a.	0459	...	0627	0656	...	0856	0947	...	...	1056	...	...	*1256*	1347	...	...	1456	...	*1547*	...	1656	1747	...	1856
	Praha Hlavní **1120** ... a.	...	...	...	0858	...	...	...	...	...	1258	...	...	...	...	...	...	1658	...	...	...	...	...	...	2059t

		Ⓐ				n					
Plattling ... d.	1607	...	...	1707	1807	...	1907	2007	2103	2223	2310
Deggendorf Hbf ... d.	1617	...	...	1717	1817	...	1917	2017	2113	2236	2320
Gotteszell ... d.	1635	...	...	1735	1835	...	1935	2035	2130	2254	2338
Regen ... d.	1649	...	...	1749	1849	...	1949	2049	2145	2308	2352
Zwiesel (Bay) ... d.	1700	...	...	1800	1900	...	2000	2100	2153	2318	0001
Bayerisch Eisenstein ☆ a.	1713	...	...	1813	1913	...	2013	2113	...	...	...
Bayerisch Eisenstein ☆ d.	...	1730	...	1814f	...	1930	▬	...	...	...	...
Železná Ruda Město ... d.	...	1738	...	1820f	...	1938	...	...	...	...	...
Špičák ... d.	...	1744	...	1824f	...	1944	...	...	...	...	...
Klatovy ... a.	...	1841	...	...	...	2041	n	...	...	...	...
Klatovy ... d.	...	...	1846	...	...	...	2046	...	...	...	...
Švihov u Klatov ... d.	...	...	1858	...	...	...	2058	...	...	...	...
Plzeň Hlavni ... a.	...	...	1947	...	...	...	2147	...	...	...	...
Praha Hlavní **1120** ... a.	...	...	...	...	...	...	...	...	...	...	...

	⚒r	Ⓐe	Ⓒz	Ⓐe	Ⓒz				
Praha Hlavní **1120** ... d.	...	...	...	...	...	...	...	...	...
Plzeň Hlavni ... d.	...	...	...	...	...	...	...	0520	...
Švihov u Klatov ... d.	...	...	...	...	...	...	...	0615	...
Klatovy ... a.	...	...	...	...	...	...	...	0627	...
Klatovy ... d.	...	...	...	...	...	0431	...	0651	...
Špičák ... d.	...	...	...	...	...	0527	0730j	0747	...
Železná Ruda Město ... d.	...	...	...	...	...	0532	0734j	0752	...
Bayerisch Eisenstein ☆ a.	...	...	...	...	...	0537	0740j	0759	...
Bayerisch Eisenstein ☆ d.	...	...	...	...	...	...	0744	...	0844
Zwiesel (Bay) ... d.	0420	0529	0550	0622	0655	...	0759	...	0859
Regen ... d.	0429	0538	0559	0631	0705	...	0808	...	0909
Gotteszell ... d.	0444	0555	0614	0645	0720	...	0823	...	0923
Deggendorf Hbf ... d.	0502	0612	0638	0710	0738	...	0844	...	0944
Plattling ... a.	0512	0622	0649	0720	0748	...	0854	...	0954

	k				962 ◇							964 ◇		Ⓐ		n			966 ◇	n			t	968 t◇	n
Praha Hlavní **1120** ... d.	...	...	...	...	0704	...	...	...	...	...	...	1104	...	...	...	...	...	...	1504	...	...	...	...	1904	...
Plzeň Hlavni ... d.	0702	...	0810	...	0902	...	...	*1102*	...	...	1210	1302	...	*1410*	...	*1502*	...	...	1702	...	...	1810	*1910*	2102	2258
Švihov u Klatov ... d.	0743	...	0859	...	0943	...	...	*1143*	...	...	1259	1343	...	*1459*	...	*1546*	...	...	1743	...	...	1859	*1959*	2143	2346
Klatovy ... a.	0752	...	0911	...	0952	...	...	*1152*	...	...	1311	1352	...	*1511*	...	*1555*	...	...	1752	...	...	1911	*2011*	2152	2358
Klatovy ... d.	0802	...	0920	...	1002	...	...	1202	...	...	...	1402	...	1515	...	1602	...	...	...	1802	...	▬	2022	▬	...
Špičák ... d.	0902	0932	1026	...	1102	1132f	1230j	1302	...	1430	...	1502	...	1610	...	1702	...	1830f	...	1902	...	...	2116	...	...
Železná Ruda Město ... d.	0909	0936	1032	...	1109	1136f	1234j	1309	...	1434	...	1509	...	1616	...	1709	...	1834f	...	1909	...	...	2120	...	...
Bayerisch Eisenstein ☆ a.	0915	0942	1038	...	1115	1142f	1240j	1315	...	1440	...	1515	...	1622	...	1715	...	1840f	...	1915	...	...	2126	...	...
Bayerisch Eisenstein ☆ d.	...	0944	...	1044	...	1144	1244	...	1344	1444	...	...	1544	...	1644	...	1744	1844	...	...	1944	2044	...	2139	...
Zwiesel (Bay) ... d.	...	0959	...	1059	...	1159	1259	...	1359	1459	...	...	1559	...	1659	...	1759	1859	...	...	1959	2059	...	2154	...
Regen ... d.	...	1009	...	1109	...	1209	1309	...	1409	1509	...	...	1609	...	1709	...	1809	1909	...	...	2009	2109	...	2203	...
Gotteszell ... d.	...	1023	...	1123	...	1223	1323	...	1423	1523	...	...	1623	...	1723	...	1823	1923	...	...	2023	2131	...	2218	...
Deggendorf Hbf ... d.	...	1044	...	1144	...	1244	1344	...	1444	1544	...	...	1644	...	1744	...	1844	1944	...	...	2044	2149	...	2235	...
Plattling ... a.	...	1054	...	1154	...	1254	1354	...	1454	1554	...	...	1654	...	1754	...	1854	1954	...	...	2054	2159	...	2245	...

d – Also Dec. 24, 31; not Dec. 26, May 1.
e – Not Dec. 24, 31, Jan. 6, June 3.
f – Daily until Feb. 28.
j – ⑥⑦ until Feb. 28.
k – Change trains at Klatovy on Ⓐ.
n – Not Dec. 24, 31.
r – Not Jan. 6, June 3.
t – Not Dec. 24, 25, 31.
v – Not Dec. 25, Jan. 1.
w – Not Dec. 25, 26, Jan. 1.
z – Also Dec. 24, 31, Jan. 6, June 3.
☆ – Železná Ruda-Alžbětín in Czech.
◇ – Also conveys 1 Praha - Klatovy and v.v.

FRANKFURT - MANNHEIM - STUTTGART - MÜNCHEN 930

km		*ICE* 1591	*ICE* 1591	*ICE* 997	*ICE* 995	*CNL* 419	*IC* 60419	*IC* 2095	*IC* 2095	*IC* 2291	*ICE* 799	*ICE* 699	*ICE* 699	*IRE* 4219	*IRE* 4221	*IC* 2099	*ICE* 5	*ICE* 991	*EC* 317	*IRE* 4223	*ICE* 271	*ICE* 511	*IC* 2053	*EC* 361	*ICE* 591
		①–⑤	① g	⑥ j	⑦ h	[R]		① g	Ⓐ m	①–⑥	⑥ k	⑦ v	B	Ⓐ m	© ‡	①–⑤	①–⑥	①–⑤					①–⑤		
		a				🍷♦				e 🍷	A ✕	✕	✕	F	L	a	e ✕	a A ✕	🍷♦	L	✕	🍷	a R 🍷	🍷♦	✕♦
	Hamburg Hbf **800 900** d.	...	...	...	...	...	...	...	...	...	...	...	...	...	...	...	...		...	...	...	...		...	0318a
	Berlin Hbf **810** d.	...	...	...	...	...	...	...	...	...	...	...	...	...	...	...	...	...	...	...	...	...	...	...	|
	Dortmund Hbf **800** d.	...	...	...	...	...	...	...	...	...	...	...	...	...	...	...	...	...	...	...	...	0437g	...	...	|
	Köln Hbf **800 910** d.	...	...	...	...	2346	...	...	...	...	...	...	...	...	...	...	...	...	...	...	...	0555	...	...	|
	Koblenz Hbf **912** d.	...	...	...	...	0043	...	...	...	...	...	...	...	...	...	...	...	...	...	...	...	|	...	...	|
	Mainz Hbf **912** d.	...	...	...	...	|	...	...	...	...	0456	...	...	...	...	...	...	0540	...	...	...	|	...	...	|
0	**Frankfurt** (Main) Hbf **912** d.	0007	0007	0018	0018	|	...	...	...	...	|	...	...	...	...	0520	0538	|	...	...	0650	|	...	...	0750
	Frankfurt Flughafen ✈ **912** d.	0028	0028	0039	0042	|	...	...	...	...	0539	...	...	...	...	|	0555	|	...	...	|	0654	...	...	|
78	**Mannheim** Hbf **912** a.	0104	0104	0110	0112	|	...	...	...	...	0611	...	...	...	...	◐	0625	0622	...	...	0728	0724	...	...	0828
78	**Mannheim** Hbf **912** d.	0106	0106	0112	0114	|	...	...	...	...	0613	...	...	...	...	|	...	0630	0712	...	...	0732	0754	...	0830
	Heidelberg Hbf **912 931** d.	0119	0119	0125	0127	|	...	...	...	...	|	...	...	...	...	0615	...	|	|	...	...	|	0806	...	|
	Karlsruhe Hbf **931** d.	|	|	|	|	|	...	...	...	0457a	|	0607	...	...	...	|	...	|	|	...	...	|	|	0806	|
156	Vaihingen (Enz) **931** d.	0208	0208	0216	0219	|	...	...	...	0533a	|	|	...	...	...	|	...	|	|	...	...	|	|	|	|
185	**Stuttgart** Hbf **931** a.	0236	0236	0249	0251	0417	...	...	...	0549a	0652	0648	...	...	...	0700	...	0708	0754	...	...	0808	0846	0849	0908
185	**Stuttgart** Hbf **936** ⊖ d.	...	0241	0255	0255	|	0435	0503	...	0553	0656	0656	0656	0659	0702	...	...	0712	0758	0802	...	0812	...	0853	0912
207	Plochingen **936** ⊖ d.	...	|	|	|	0449s	0451	0518	...	0609	|	|	|	0713	0716	...	...	|	|	0816	...	|	...	0909	|
227	Göppingen ⊖ d.	...	|	|	|	0502s	0504	0531	...	0621	|	|	|	0725	0727	...	...	|	|	0827	...	|	...	0921	|
246	Geislingen (Steige) ⊖ d.	...	|	|	|	0517s	0519	0544	...	|	|	|	|	0736	0738	...	...	|	|	0840	...	|	...	|	|
279	**Ulm** Hbf **945** ⊖ d.	...	0337	0352	0352	0542s	0544	0609	0609	0655	0755	0755	0755	0758	0759	...	...	0808	0855	0902	...	0908	...	0955	1008c
303	Günzburg **945** ⊖ d.	...	0355	0413	0413	0559s	0601	0627	0627	0711	|	|	|	...	...	...	...	|	0911	...	...	|	...	|	|
365	**Augsburg** Hbf **904 905** ⊖ d.	...	0426	0444	0444	0633s	0636	0659	0659	0741	0839	0839	0839	...	...	...	...	0855	0942	...	...	0955	...	1038c	1055b
420	München Pasing **904 905** ⊖ a.	...	0508	0515	0515	|	|	0728	0728	0810	0908	0908	0908	...	...	...	...	0923	|	...	...	1023	...	1106c	1123b
427	**München** Hbf **904 905** ⊖ a.	...	0519	0524	0524	0716	0716	0738	0738	0819	0917	0917	0917	...	...	...	...	0933	1017	...	...	1033	...	1117c	1133b

	ICE 711	*EC* 113	*ICE* 373	*ICE* 513	*IC* 2319	*ICE* 571	*IC* 2093	*ICE* 593	*ICE* 1091	*IC* 2275	*IC* 2293	*EC* 115	*ICE* 291	*ICE* 375	*ICE* 515	*ICE* 973	*IC* 2261	*IC* 119	*ICE* 595	*EC* 319	*IRE* 4229	*IC* 2015	*ICE* 871	*ICE* 517	*ICE* 575
	①–⑤				①–⑥	①–⑥	⑤ n	⑥⑦	①–⑤	⑤ f			⑦ r	①–⑥					x			①–④			
	a	✕♦	✕	🍷♦	e	e ✕	🍷	z ✕	a ✕	♦	🍷	✕♦	✕	e ✕	🍷	✕♦	🍷	🍷♦	✕	🍷♦	L	🍷♦	✕	🍷	✕
Hamburg Hbf **800 900** d.	...	...	...	...	...	0519	...	...	...	...	...	...	...	...	0538	0724	...	...	...	...	...	...	...	...	0924
Berlin Hbf **810** d.	...	...	0432a	...	...	|	...	0531	0608*	...	...	...	0549	0632	|	|	...	...	0737	...	...	...	0832	...	|
Dortmund Hbf **800** d.	0502	...	|	0637	0537	|	...	|	|	...	...	...	|	|	0837	|	...	...	|	...	...	...	|	1037	|
Köln Hbf **800 910** d.	0615d	...	|	0755	0653	|	...	|	|	...	...	0818	|	|	0955	|	...	0918	|	...	...	1018	|	1155	|
Koblenz Hbf **912** d.	|	...	|	|	0748	|	...	|	|	...	...	0917	|	|	|	|	...	1017	|	...	...	1117	|	|	|
Mainz Hbf **912** d.	0746	...	|	|	0839	|	...	|	|	...	...	1015	|	|	|	|	...	1113	|	...	...	1217	|	|	|
Frankfurt (Main) Hbf **912** d.	|	0820	0850	|	|	0905	...	0950	0950	0920	1020	|	1050	1050	|	1105	...	|	1150	1220	...	|	1250	|	1305
Frankfurt Flughafen ✈ **912** d.	|	|	|	0854	|	0920	...	|	|	|	|	|	|	|	1054	1120	...	|	|	|	...	|	|	1254	1320
Mannheim Hbf **912** a.	0824	◐	0928	0924	0921	0953	...	1028	1028	◐	◐	1101	1128	1128	1124	1153	...	1152	1228	◐	...	1307	1328	1324	1353
Mannheim Hbf **912** d.	0826	|	▬	0932	0923	0955	...	1030	1030	|	|	1103	▬		1132	1155	...	1154	1230	|	...	1312	...	1332	1355
Heidelberg Hbf **912 931** d.	0838	0914	...	|	0936	|	...	|	|	1014	1110	|	...	...	|	|	...	1206	|	1314	...	|	...	|	|
Karlsruhe Hbf **931** d.	|	|	*IRE*	|	|	|	...	|	|	|	|	|	*IRE*	...	|	|	1206	|	|	|	...	|	...	|	|
Vaihingen (Enz) **931** d.	0905	|	**4225**	|	|	|	...	|	|	1055	|	|	**4227**	...	|	|	|	|	|	|	...	|	...	|	|
Stuttgart Hbf **931** a.	0923	0954	L	1008	1018	1034	...	1108	1108	1112	1150	1153	L	...	1208	1234	1249	1246	1308	1354	...	1358	...	1408	1434
Stuttgart Hbf **936** ⊖ d.	...	0958	1002	1012	...	...	1053	1112	1112	...	...	1158	1202	...	1212	...	1253	1257	1312	1358	1402	...	...	1412	...
Plochingen **936** ⊖ d.	...	|	1016	|	...	...	1109	|	|	...	...	|	1216	...	|	...	1309	|	|	|	1416	...	...	|	...
Göppingen ⊖ d.	...	|	1027	|	...	...	1121	|	|	...	...	|	1227	...	|	...	1321	1327	|	|	1427	...	...	|	...
Geislingen (Steige) ⊖ d.	...	|	1040	|	...	...	|	|	|	...	...	|	1240	...	|	...	|	1340	|	|	1440	...	...	|	...
Ulm Hbf **945** ⊖ d.	...	1055	1102	1108	...	...	1155	1208c	1208c	...	...	1255	1302	...	1308	...	1355	1401	1408c	1455	1502	...	...	1508	...
Günzburg **945** ⊖ d.	...	1111	...	|	...	...	|	|	|	...	...	1311	...	...	|	...	|	...	|	1511	...	...	...	|	...
Augsburg Hbf **904 905** ⊖ d.	...	1142	...	1155	...	...	1239c	1255b	1255b	...	...	1342	...	...	1355	...	1438c	...	1455b	1542	...	...	...	1555	...
München Pasing **904 905** ⊖ a.	...	|	...	1223	...	...	1306c	1323b	1323b	...	...	|	...	...	1423	...	1506c	...	1523b	|	...	...	...	1624	...
München Hbf **904 905** ⊖ a.	...	1217	...	1233	...	...	1316c	1333b	1333b	...	...	1417	...	...	1433	...	1516c	...	1533b	1617	...	...	...	1633	...

	IC 2013	*ICE* 597	*IC* 2055	*IC* 2299	*EC* 117	*ICE* 277	*ICE* 519	*IC* 2113	*ICE* 577	*IC* 1911	*IC* 2265	*IRE* 4233	*ICE* 599	*EC* 391	*ICE* 279	*ICE* 611	*IC* 2115	*ICE* 579	*IC* 2011	*IC* 2011	*IC* 2246	*IC* 2267	*IC* 2246	*ICE* 691	*ICE* 691
			⑤⑦ t	⑥ u	Ⓑ q					⑤⑦		Ⓐ m							①–④	⑦ w	⑤ f	p	⑤ f		Ⓑ ◇
	🍷♦	✕	🍷 R		🍷♦	✕	🍷	✕	✕	t	Y 🍷	L	✕	🍷♦	✕	🍷	✕♦	✕	D 🍷	🍷	🍷	🍷	🍷	✕	✕
Hamburg Hbf **800 900** d.	...	...	...	...	...	...	...	0846	1124	...	...	...	...	...	...	...	1046	1324	...	...	...	...	...	...	...
Berlin Hbf **810** d.	...	0937	...	...	...	1032	...	|	|	...	...	...	1137	...	1232	...	|	|	...	1008	...	...	...	1337	1337
Dortmund Hbf **800** d.	0952	|	...	...	...	|	1237	1137	|	1152	...	...	|	...	|	1437	1337	|	...	1352	1352	...	...	|	|
Köln Hbf **800 910** d.	1118	|	...	...	...	|	1355	1253	|	1318	...	...	|	...	|	1555	1453	|	1518	1518	1518	...	...	|	|
Koblenz Hbf **912** d.	1217	|	...	...	...	|	|	1348	|	1417	...	...	|	...	|	|	1548	|	1617	1617	1617	...	...	|	|
Mainz Hbf **912** d.	1313	|	...	...	...	|	|	1439	|	1513	...	...	|	...	|	|	1639	|	1713	1713	1713	...	...	|	|
Frankfurt (Main) Hbf **912** d.	|	1350	...	1420	1420	1450	|	|	1505	|	...	...	1550	1620	1650	|	|	1705	|	|	|	...	...	1750	1750
Frankfurt Flughafen ✈ **912** d.	|	|	...	|	|	|	1454	|	1520	|	...	...	|	|	|	1654	|	1720	|	|	|	...	...	|	|
Mannheim Hbf **912** a.	1352	1428	...	◐	◐	1528	1524	1521	1553	1552	...	...	1628	◐	1728	1724	1721	1753	1752	1752	1752	...	...	1828	1828
Mannheim Hbf **912** d.	1354	1430	1424	|	|	▬	1532	1523	1555	1554	...	...	1630	|	▬	1732	1723	1755	1754	1754	1754	...	...	1830	1831
Heidelberg Hbf **912 931** d.	1406	|	1437	1514	1514	...	|	1536	|	1606	...	...	|	1714	...	|	1736	|	1806	1806	1806	...	...	|	|
Karlsruhe Hbf **931** d.	|	|	|	|	|	*IRE*	|	|	|	|	1606	...	|	|	*IRE*	|	|	|	|	|	|	1806	...	|	|
Vaihingen (Enz) **931** d.	|	|	1505	|	|	**4231**	|	1605	|	|	|	...	|	|	**4235**	|	1808	|	|	|	|	|	...	|	|
Stuttgart Hbf **931** a.	1446	1508	1523	1554	1554	L	1608	1622	1634	1646	1649	...	1708	1754	L	1808	1825	1834	1846	1846	1846	1849	←	1908	1908
Stuttgart Hbf **936** ⊖ d.	1454	1512	...	...	1558	1602	1612	...	...	...	1653	1702	1712	1758	1802	1812	...	...	1850	...	→	1853	1858	...	1912
Plochingen **936** ⊖ d.	1509	|	...	...	|	1616	|	...	...	...	1709	1716	|	|	1816	|	...	...	1904	...	...	1909	1915	...	|
Göppingen ⊖ d.	1524	|	...	...	|	1627	|	...	...	...	1721	1727	|	|	1827	|	...	...	...	...	...	1921	|	...	|
Geislingen (Steige) ⊖ d.	|	|	...	...	|	1640	|	...	...	...	|	1740	|	|	1840	|	...	...	...	...	...	|	1938	...	|
Ulm Hbf **945** ⊖ d.	1601	1608c	...	...	1655	1702	1708	...	...	...	1755	1802	1808c	1855	1902	1908	...	...	...	...	...	1955	2002	...	2008
Günzburg **945** ⊖ d.	...	|	...	...	1711	...	|	...	...	...	|	...	|	1911	...	|	...	...	...	...	...	|	|	...	|
Augsburg Hbf **904 905** ⊖ d.	...	1655b	...	...	1742	...	1755	...	...	...	1838c	...	1855b	1942	...	1955	...	...	...	...	...	2038c	2045	...	2052
München Pasing **904 905** ⊖ a.	...	1723b	...	...	|	...	1823	...	...	...	1906c	...	1923b	|	...	2023	...	...	...	...	...	2106c	2112	...	2123
München Hbf **904 905** ⊖ a.	...	1733b	...	...	1817	...	1832	...	...	...	1916c	...	1933b	2017	...	2033	...	...	...	...	...	2116c	2123	...	2133

♦ – **NOTES** (LISTED BY TRAIN NUMBER)

113 – [12] and ✕ Siegen - Frankfurt - München - Salzburg - Villach - Klagenfurt; [12] Siegen - Frankfurt - Villach (**213**) - Ljubljana - Zagreb.

115 – WÖRTHERSEE – [12] and ✕ Münster - Köln - Bonn - München - Salzburg - Villach - Klagenfurt.

117 – [12] and 🍷 Frankfurt - München - Salzburg - Villach - Klagenfurt.

119 – [12] and 🍷 Münster - Ulm - Lindau - Bregenz - Innsbruck.

317 – [12] and 🍷 Saarbrücken - München - Salzburg - Selzthal - Graz.

319 – [12] and 🍷 Frankfurt - München - Salzburg - Selzthal - Graz.

361 – [12] and 🍷 Strasbourg - München.

391 – [12] and 🍷 Frankfurt - München - Salzburg (- Linz Ⓑ **q**).

419 – ①⑤⑥⑦ (daily fom Mar. 26). POLLUX – 🛏 1, 2 cl., ▬ 2 cl., [2] and 🍷 Amsterdam - München (Amsterdam - München - Innsbruck on ⑤ Dec. 25 - Apr. 9). Conveys 🛏 1, 2 cl., ▬ 2 cl., [2] (*CNL* **40451** – CASSIOPEIA) Paris - München / Innsbruck (Table **32**).

513 – [12] and 🍷 Münster (d. 0601) - München.

591 – Not Dec. 25. [12] and ✕ (Hamburg ①–⑤ **a** -) (Hannover ①–⑥ **y** -) Kassel - Frankfurt - München. Train number **999** on ⑦ **w**.

973 – [12] and ✕ (Kiel ①–⑥ **e** -) Hamburg - Stuttgart. Train number **573** on ⑦ (also Dec. 25, 26, Jan. 1, Apr. 3, 5, May 24).

2013 – ALLGÄU – [12] and 🍷 (Leipzig ① **g** -) (Magdeburg ①–⑥ **e** -) Hannover - Dortmund - Köln - Bonn - Ulm - Kempten - Oberstdorf.

2015 – ①–④ (not Dec. 23, 24, 30, 31, Apr. 1, 5, May 12, 24, June 2). [12] and 🍷 Emden - Münster - Stuttgart.

2115 – [12] and ✕ (Greifswald ①–⑤ **a** -) Stralsund - Hamburg - Stuttgart.

2275 – [12] Hannover - Kassel - Gießen - Frankfurt - Stuttgart.

A – From Wiesbaden (Table **912**).
B – Ⓑ to Feb. 26 and from May 16 (also Dec. 26, June 5; not Dec. 24, 31, May 23, June 3); ⑦ Feb. 28 - May 9 (not Apr. 4).
D – ①–④ (not Dec. 23, 24, 30, 31, Apr. 1, 5, May 12, 13, 24, June 2, 3). Continues to Nürtingen (a. 1917), Reutlingen Hbf (a. 1937) and Tübingen Hbf (a. 1950).
F – To Friedrichshafen (Table **933**)
L – To Lindau (Table **933**).
R – From Saarbrücken (Table **919**).
Y – To Salzburg on dates in Table **890**.
a – ①–⑤ (not Dec. 24, 25, 31, Jan. 1, Apr. 2, 5, May 24).
b – 28–37 minutes later Feb. 27 - May 16.
c – Not Feb. 27 - May 16.
d – Köln **Messe/Deutz**.
e – Not Dec. 25, 26, Jan. 1, Apr. 3, 5, May 24.
f – Also Dec. 23, 30, Apr. 1, May 12; not Dec. 25, Jan. 1, Apr. 2, May 14.
g – ① (also Apr. 6, May 25; not Apr. 5, May 24).
h – Also Apr. 5, May 24.
j – Also Dec. 24, 31, Apr. 2.
k – Also Dec. 24, 31, Apr. 2, May 13, June 3; not Dec. 26, Apr. 3, May 15, June 5.
m – Not Dec. 24, 31, Jan. 6, June 3.
n – Also Dec. 23, 30, Apr. 1, May 12, June 2; not Dec. 25, Jan. 1, Apr. 2, May 14, June 4.
p – Not Dec. 24, 25, 31, May 4, 23.
q – Not Dec. 24, 25, 31, Apr. 2, 4, May 23.
r – Also Dec. 25, 26, Jan. 1, Apr. 3, 5, May 24.
s – Stops to set down only.
t – Also Dec. 23, 30, Apr. 1, 5, May 12, 24, June 2; not Dec. 25, Jan. 1, Apr. 2, 4, May 14, 23, June 4.
u – Also Dec. 24, 25, 31, Apr. 2, 4, May 23.
v – Also May 24; not Apr. 4, May 23.
w – Also Apr. 5, May 24; not Apr. 4, May 23.
x – Terminates at Stuttgart on Dec. 25, 27, Jan. 1.
y – Also Apr. 4, May 23; not Dec. 25, Apr. 5, May 24.
z – Also Dec. 24, 25, 31, Jan. 1, Apr. 2, 5, May 24; not Dec. 26, Jan. 2.
‡ – Also Dec. 24, 31, Jan. 6, June 3.
◐ – Via Darmstadt (Table **911**).
◇ – Ⓑ (not Dec. 24, 25, 31, May 23). Feb. 28 - May 16 departs Ulm 2016, Augsburg 2100, arrives München Pasing 2129, München Hbf 2138.
***** – [R] and supplement payable for journeys from Berlin.
⊖ – See panel on page 435 for additional *RE* trains.

930 FRANKFURT - MANNHEIM - STUTTGART - MÜNCHEN

	TGV	IC	ICE	ICE	IC	ICE	IC	IC	IC	ICE	RB	IC	IC	ICE	ICE	IC	RB	ICE	ICE	ICE	RB	IC	ICE	ICE	ICE
	9575	2295	873	613	2311	771	1915	2269	2269	693	19363	1858	2297	875	615	2213	19365	773	695	1093	19367	1897	877	617	775
		Ⓑq					⑤⑦	♣	⑦¶			⑦w							⑥k	Ⓑr		⑦w			⑦w
	🍷♦	🍷	🍴	🍷	🍴♦	🍴	B			🍴		T🍷	🍷	🍴	🍷	🍴♦		🍴	🍴	🍴		🍷	🍴	🍷	🍴
Hamburg Hbf **800 900** d.	...	...	...	...	1246	1524	...	...	...	...	...	...	...	...	...	1446	...	1724	...	...	...	...	...	...	...
Berlin Hbf **810** d.	...	...	1432	...	|	|	1208	...	...	1537	...	...	...	1632	...	|	...	|	1733	1805*	...	1658p	1833	...	1924
Dortmund Hbf **800** d.	...	...	|	1637	1537	|	1552	...	...	|	...	...	...	|	1837	1737	...	|	|	|	...	|	|	2037	|
Köln Hbf **800 910** d.	...	...	|	1755	1653	|	1718	...	...	|	...	...	...	|	1957	1853	...	|	|	|	...	|	|	2155	|
Koblenz Hbf **912** d.	...	...	|	|	1748	|	1817	...	...	|	...	...	...	|	|	1948	...	|	|	|	...	|	|	|	|
Mainz Hbf **912** d.	...	...	|	|	1839	|	1913	...	...	|	...	...	...	|	|	2039	...	|	|	|	...	|	|	|	|
Frankfurt (Main) Hbf d.	...	1820	1850	|	|	1905	|	...	...	1950	...	1955	2020	2050	|	|	...	2105	2150	2150	...	2158	2300	|	2310
Frankfurt Flughafen F ✈ d.	...	|	|	1854	|	1920	|	...	...	|	...	|	|	|	2054	|	...	2120	|	|	...	|	|	2306	|
Mannheim Hbf a.	...	◐	1928	1924	1921	1953	1952	...	...	2028	...	◐	◐	2128	2124	2121	...	2153	2228	2228	...	◐	2341	2337	◐
Mannheim Hbf d.	...	|	—	1932	1923	1955	1954	...	...	2030	...	|	|	...	2132	2123	...	2156	2230	2230	...	|	...	2345	|
Heidelberg Hbf **931** d.	...	1914	*IRE*	|	1936	|	2006	...	...	|	...	2052	2114	...	|	2136	...	2210	|	|	...	2251	...	2359	0004
Karlsruhe Hbf **931** d.	1827	|	**4237**	|	|	|	|	2006	2006	|	...	|	|	...	|	|	...	|	|	|	...	|	...	|	|
Vaihingen (Enz) **931** d.	|	|		|	2005	|	|	|	|	|	...	2128	|	...	|	2205	...	|	|	|	...	2323	...	|	|
Stuttgart Hbf **931** a.	1904	1954	F	2008	2023	2034	2046	2049	2049	2108	...	2146	2154	...	2208	2222	...	2249	2309	2309	...	2341	...	0053h	0044
Stuttgart Hbf **936** ⊖ d.	1918	1958	2002	2012	...	...	2050w	2053	2053	2112	2132	...	...	...	2212	...	2232	...	...	...	2332	...	...	...	...
Plochingen **936** ⊖ d.	|	|	2016	|	...	...	2106w	2108	2108	|	2151	...	...	...	|	...	2253	...	...	...	2353	...	...	...	...
Göppingen ⊖ d.	|	|	2027	|	...	...	...	2120	2120	|	2210	...	...	...	|	...	2313	...	...	...	0013	...	...	...	...
Geislingen (Steige) ⊖ d.	|	|	2040	|	...	...	...	2133	2133	|	2232	...	...	...	|	...	2339	...	...	...	0039	...	...	...	...
Ulm Hbf **945** ⊖ d.	2016	2055	2102	2108	...	...	...	2154	2156	2208	2302	...	...	...	2308	...	0005	...	...	...	0105	...	...	...	...
Günzburg **945** ⊖ d.	|	2111	...	|	...	...	...	...	2213	|	...	...	...	...	|	...	...	...	...	...	...	...	...	...	...
Augsburg Hbf **904 905** ⊖ d.	2101	2142	...	2155	...	...	...	...	2243	2255	...	...	...	...	2356	...	...	...	...	...	...	...	...	...	...
München Pasing **904 905** ⊖ a.	|	2211	...	2223	...	...	...	...	2310	2323	...	...	...	...	0024	...	...	...	...	...	...	...	...	...	...
München Hbf **904 905** ⊖ a.	2138	2220	...	2233	...	...	...	...	2321	2333	...	...	...	...	0034	...	...	...	...	...	...	...	...	...	...

km		ICE	ICE	ICE	RB	ICE	ICE	IC	IC	RB	ICE	IC	IC	IC	ICE	IC	ICE	IRE	IRE	IC	TGV	TGV	TGV	ICE	ICE
		826	826	774	19300	616	874	2296	1114	19304	694	2268	2268	2010	772	2116	614	4222	4220	2294	9576	9576	9576	692	692
		①g		①–⑥				①–⑥	①–⑤			①n	①–⑤	①–⑤				Ⓐm	Ⓒ‡	①–⑥	E	D	⑥⑦	①–⑤	
			🍷	e🍴		🍷	🍴	e🍴	e⊡		🍴	🍷	a🍷	y♥	🍴	🍴♦	🍷	F	F	e🍷	♦	♦	t♦	a🍴	🍴
	München Hbf **904 905** ⊖ d.	0032	...	...	...	0317	...	...	...	...	...	0425	...	🍷	...	...	0523	...	...	0516	0438	0620	0620	0628	...
	München Pasing **904 905** ⊖ d.	0040	...	...	...	0325	...	...	...	...	...	0433	...	...	...	...	0531	...	...	0524	|	|	|	0636	...
	Augsburg Hbf **904 905** ⊖ d.	0112	...	...	...	0357	...	...	...	...	...	0511	...	...	...	...	0604	...	...	0556	0516	0657	0706	0708	...
	Günzburg **945** ⊖ d.	0144	...	...	...	|	...	...	...	...	...	0544	...	...	...	...	|	...	...	0629	|	|	|	|	...
	Ulm Hbf **945** ⊖ d.	0202	...	...	0411	0440	...	...	...	0449	...	0602	0602	...	...	...	0651	0654	0654	0659	|	0742	0750	0751	...
	Geislingen (Steige) ⊖ d.	|	...	...	0435	|	...	...	...	0522	...	0625	0625	...	...	...	|	0717	0717	0722	|	|	|	|	...
	Göppingen ⊖ d.	|	...	...	0457	|	...	...	...	0547	...	0639	0639	...	...		|	0729	0729	|	|	|	|	|	...
	Plochingen **936** ⊖ d.	|	...	...	0518	|	...	...	...	0607	...	0651	0651	0655	...	...	|	|	0740	0746	|	|	|	|	...
	Stuttgart Hbf **936** ⊖ a.	0300	...	...	0538	0537	...	...	...	0626	...	0707	0707	0710	...	...	0747	0756	0756	0801	0839	0839	0847	0847	...
0	**Stuttgart** Hbf **931** d.	0305	0305	0509	...	0551	...	0603	0630	...	0651	0711	0711	0714	0727	0737	0751	—	...	0805	0854	0854	0854	0851	0851
29	Vaihingen (Enz) **931** d.	0336	0336	|	...	|	...	0620	0647	...	|	|	|	|	|	0755	|	*ICE*	...	|	|	|	|	|	|
	Karlsruhe Hbf **931** a.	|	|	|	...	|	...	|	|	...	|	0753	0753	|	|	|	|	**872**	...	|	0929	0929	0929	|	|
92	**Heidelberg** Hbf **931** d.	0428	0428	0547	...	|	...	0658j	0720	...	|	...	...	0755	|	0825	|		...	0846	...	...	...	|	|
	Mannheim Hbf a.	0438	0438	0559	...	0627	...	|	0731	...	0729	...	...	0806	0804	0837	0827	🍴	...	|	...	...	...	0929	0929
	Mannheim Hbf d.	0440	0440	0605	...	0635	0631	◐	0733	...	0731	...	...	0808	0806	0839	0835	0831	...	◐	...	...	...	0931	0931
	Frankfurt Flughafen F ✈ a.	0512	0512	0638	...	0706	|	|	|	...	|	...	...	|	0838	|	0906	|	...	|	...	...	...	|	|
	Frankfurt (Main) Hbf a.	0535	0535	0652	...	|	0708	0800	|	...	0808	...	...	|	0853	|	|	0908	...	0940	...	...	...	1008	1008
	Mainz Hbf **912** a.	|	|	|	...	|	|	...	0815	...	|	...	...	0846	|	0918	|	|	...	...	...	...	...	|	|
	Koblenz Hbf **912** a.	|	|	|	...	|	|	...	...	...	|	...	...	0941	|	1010	|	|	...	...	...	...	...	|	|
	Köln Hbf **800 910** a.	0704d	0704d	|	...	0805	|	...	...	...	|	...	...	1042	|	1105	1005	|	...	...	...	...	...	|	|
	Dortmund Hbf **800** a.	...	0827z	|	...	0921	|	...	...	...	|	...	...	1208f	|	1221	1121	|	...	...	...	...	...	|	|
	Berlin Hbf **810** a.	...	...	|	...	...	1125	...	...	...	1221	...	...	1550f	|	|	...	1325	...	...	...	...	...	1421	1421
	Hamburg Hbf **800 900** a.	...	...	1035	...	...	...	...	...	...	...	...	...	...	1234	1511	...	...	...	...	...	...	...	...	...

	IC	ICE	IC	ICE	ICE	IRE	IC	IC	ICE	IC	IC	ICE	IC	ICE	ICE	IRE	EC	IC	ICE	IC	ICE	ICE	ICE	IRE	EC
	2266	770	2114	612	278	4224	2290	2290	690	2264	1916	578	2112	610	276	4218 4226	390	2014	598	2012	576	518	374	4228	318
	①–⑥						①–⑥	⑦b		A	⑤f							①–⑤							
	e🍷	🍴	🍴	🍷	🍴	L	eY		🍴	Y🍷	Y🍷	🍴	🍴	🍷	🍴	L	🍷♦	🍷♦	🍴	🍷♦	🍴	🍷	🍴	L	🍷♦
München Hbf **904 905** ⊖ d.	0641c	...	...	0723	...	...	0739	...	0824	0841c	0841c	...	...	0923	...	...	0940	...	1023	...	...	1123	...	...	1142
München Pasing **904 905** ⊖ d.	0649c	...	...	0731	...	...	|	...	0832	0849c	0849c	...	...	0931	...	...	|	...	1031	...	...	1131	...	...	|
Augsburg Hbf **904 905** ⊖ d.	0721c	...	...	0803	...	...	0816	...	0903	0921c	0921c	...	...	1003	...	...	1017	...	1103	...	...	1203	...	...	1217
Günzburg **945** ⊖ d.	|	...	...	|	...	...	0849	...	|	|	|	...	...	|	...	...	1049	...	|	...	...	|	...	...	1249
Ulm Hbf **945** ⊖ d.	0805	...	...	0851	...	0854	0905	...	0951	1005	1005	...	...	1051	...	1054	1105	...	1151	1157	...	1251	...	1254	1305
Geislingen (Steige) ⊖ d.	|	...	...	|	...	0917	|	...	|	|	|	...	...	|	...	1117	|	...	|	|	...	|	...	1317	|
Göppingen ⊖ d.	0839	...	...	|	...	0929	|	...	|	1039	1039	...	...	|	...	1129	|	...	|	1235	...	|	...	1329	|
Plochingen **936** ⊖ d.	0851	...	...	|	...	0940	|	...	|	1051	1051	...	...	|	...	1140	|	...	|	1249	...	|	...	1340	|
Stuttgart Hbf **936** ⊖ a.	0907	...	...	0947	...	0956	1001	...	1047	1107	1107	...	...	1147	...	1156	1201	...	1247	1305	...	1347	...	1356	1401
Stuttgart Hbf **931** d.	0911	0927	0937	0951	...	...	1005	1005	1051	1111	1114	1127	1137	1151	...	...	1205	1209	1251	1314	1327	1351	...	...	1405
Vaihingen (Enz) **931** d.	|	|	0955	|	...	...	|	|	|	|	|	|	1155	|	...	...	|	1226	|	|	|	|	...	...	|
Karlsruhe Hbf **931** a.	0953	|	|	|	...	...	|	|	|	1153	|	|	|	|	...	...	|	|	|	|	|	|	...	...	|
Heidelberg Hbf **931** d.	...	|	1025	|	...	...	1046	1046	|	...	1155	|	1225	|	...	...	1246	|	|	1355	|	|	...	...	1446
Mannheim Hbf a.	...	1004	1037	1027	...	...	|	|	1129	...	1206	1204	1237	1227	...	...	|	1256	1329	1406	1404	1427	...	...	|
Mannheim Hbf d.	...	1006	1039	1035	1031	...	◐	◐	1131	...	1208	1206	1239	1235	1231	...	◐	1258	1331	1408	1406	1435	1431	...	◐
Frankfurt Flughafen F ✈ a.	...	1038	|	1106	|	...	|	|	|	...	|	1238	|	1306	|	...	|	|	|	|	1438	1506	|	...	|
Frankfurt (Main) Hbf a.	...	1053	|	|	1108	...	1140	1146	1208	...	|	1253	|	|	1308	...	1340	|	1408	|	1453	|	1508	...	1540
Mainz Hbf **912** a.	...	|	1118	|	|	...	...	...	|	...	1246	|	1318	|	|	...	...	1340	|	1446	|	|	|	...	...
Koblenz Hbf **912** a.	...	|	1210	|	|	...	...	...	|	...	1341	|	1410	|	|	...	...	1441	|	1541	|	|	|	...	...
Köln Hbf **800 910** a.	...	|	1305	1205	|	...	...	...	|	...	1442	|	1505	1405	|	...	...	1542	|	1642	|	1605	|	...	...
Dortmund Hbf **800** a.	...	|	1421	1321	|	...	...	...	|	...	1608	|	1621	1521	|	...	...	...	|	1805	|	1721	|	...	...
Berlin Hbf **810** a.	...	|	|	...	1525	...	...	...	1621	...	1951	|	|	...	1725	...	...	...	1821	...	|	...	1925	...	...
Hamburg Hbf **800 900** a.	...	1435	1712	...	...	...	...	...	...	...	...	1634	1912	...	...	...	...	...	...	...	1834	...	...	...	...

♦ – **NOTES** (LISTED BY TRAIN NUMBER)

318 – [12] and 🍷 Graz - Bischofshofen - Salzburg - München - Frankfurt.
390 – [12] and 🍷 (Linz - Salzburg ①–⑥ **e** -) München - Frankfurt.
2012 – ALLGÄU – [12] and 🍷 Oberstdorf - Kempten - Ulm - Köln - Dortmund - Hannover.
2014 – ①–⑤ (not Dec. 24, 25, 31, Jan. 1, Apr. 2, 5, May 13, 24, June 3). [12] and 🍷 Stuttgart - Münster - Emden.
2116 – [12] and 🍴 Stuttgart - Hamburg - Stralsund (- Greifswald ①–⑤ **a**).
2213 – RÜGEN – [12] and 🍴 Ostseebad Binz - Hamburg - Köln - Stuttgart.
2311 – NORDFRIESLAND – [12] and 🍴 Westerland - Hamburg - Köln - Stuttgart.
9575 – [12] and 🍷 Paris - Strasbourg - München. On ⑥ Feb. 28 - May 16 does not call at Ulm, departs Augsburg 2124 and arrives München 2203. Ⓡ for international journeys.
9576 – [12] and 🍷 München - Strasbourg - Paris. Ⓡ for international journeys.

A – ①②③④⑥⑦ (also Dec. 25, Jan. 1, Apr. 2, May 14, June 4; not Dec. 23, 30, Apr. 1, May 12, June 2).
B – ⑤⑦ (also Dec. 23, 30, Apr. 1, 5, May 24; not Dec. 25, Jan. 1, Apr. 2, 4, May 14, 23). On ⑦ **w** continues to Nürtingen (a. 2118), Reutlingen Hbf (a. 2137) and Tübingen Hbf (a. 2150).
D – ①–⑤ to Feb. 26 and from May 17 (also May 13; not Dec. 24, 25, 31, Jan. 1, May 24).
E – ①–⑤ Mar. 1 - May 14 (not Apr. 2, 5, May 13).
F – To / from Friedrichshafen (Table **933**).
L – From Lindau (Table **933**).
T – From Leipzig (Table **850**).
Y – From Salzburg (Table **890**).

a – Not Dec. 24, 25, 31, Jan. 1, Apr. 2, 5, May 24.
b – Also Dec. 25, 26, Jan. 1, Apr. 3, 5, May 24.
c – Not Feb. 27 - May 16.
d – Köln **Messe/Deutz**.
e – ①–⑥ (not Dec. 25, 26, Jan. 1, Apr. 3, 5, May 24).
f – ⑤ (also Dec. 23, 30, Apr. 1, May 12, June 2; not Dec. 25, Jan. 1, Apr. 2, May 14, June 4).
g – Also Apr. 6, May 25; not Apr. 5, May 24.
h – 0040 on the mornings of ①⑦.
j – Arrives 0647.
k – Also Dec. 24, 25, 31, Jan. 1, Apr. 2, 4, May 23.
m – Not Dec. 24, 31, Jan. 6, June 3.
n – ① to Feb. 22 and from May 31 (also May 25).
p – 1708 from May 2.
q – Not Dec. 24, 25, 31, Apr. 2, 4, May 23.
r – Not Dec. 24, 25, 31, Jan. 1, Apr. 2, 4, May 23.
t – Also Dec. 24, 25, 31, Jan. 1, Apr. 2, 5, May 24.
w – ⑦ (also Apr. 5, May 24; not Apr. 4, May 23).
y – Not Dec. 24, 25, 31, Jan. 1, Apr. 2, 5, May 13, 14, 24, June 3, 4.
z – ⑥⑦ (also Dec. 24, 25, 31, Jan. 1, Apr. 2).

‡ – Also Dec. 24, 31, Jan. 6, June 3.
◐ – Via Darmstadt (Table **911**).
♣ – ①②③④⑦ (not Dec. 23, 24, 30, 31, Apr. 1, 4, May 23).
¶ – ⑦ to Feb. 21 and from May 30 (also May 24).
♥ – From Tübingen Hbf (d. 0611), Reutlingen Hbf (d. 0623) and Nürtingen (d. 0642).
⊡ – Train number **2218** on ⑥ (also Dec. 24, Apr. 2, May 13; not May 15).
⊖ – See panel on page 435 for additional *RE* services.
* – Ⓡ and supplement payable for journeys from Berlin.

MÜNCHEN - STUTTGART - MANNHEIM - FRANKFURT 930

	ICE 712	ICE 596	IC 2196	IC 118	IC 2260	ICE 974	ICE 516	ICE 290 370	IRE 4230	EC 114	IC 2292	IC 2316	ICE 1090	ICE 594	IRE 4232	IC 2362	ICE 572	IC 2318	ICE 514	ICE 870	IC 2052	IRE 4234	EC 112	ICE 592	IC 2172
	①–⑤	x	⑤f									Ⓑq	Ⓑd	⑥h	Ⓐm	⑤f					Ⓑq				⑦w
	a🍷	✕	S	🍷♦	🍷	✕♦	🍷	✕	L	✕♦	🍷	A	✕	✕		🍷	✕	N	🍷	✕	S🍷	L	✕♦	✕	K🍷
München Hbf .... **904 905** ⊖ d.	...	1223	...	...	1241c	...	1323	...	...	1340	...	...	1423	1423	...	1441c	...	...	1523	...	...	...	1541	1623	...
München Pasing **904 905** ⊖ d.	...	1231	...	...	1249c	...	1331	...	...	|	...	...	1431	1431	...	1449c	...	...	1531	...	...	...	|	1631	...
Augsburg Hbf ... **904 905** ⊖ d.	...	1303	...	...	1321c	...	1403	...	...	1417	...	...	1503	1503	...	1521c	...	...	1603	...	...	...	1617	1703	...
Günzburg .... **945** ⊖ d.	...	|	...	...	|	...	|	...	...	1449	...	...	|	|	...	|	...	...	|	...	...	...	1649	|	...
Ulm Hbf .... **945** ⊖ d.	...	1351	...	1356	1405	...	1451	...	1454	1505	...	...	1551	1551	1554	1605	...	...	1651	...	...	1654	1705	1751	...
Geislingen (Steige) .... ⊖ d.	...	|	...	1420	|	...	|	...	1517	|	...	...	|	|	1618	|	...	...	|	...	...	1717	|	|	...
Göppingen .... ⊖ d.	...	|	...	1433	|	...	|	...	1529	|	...	...	|	|	1630	|	...	...	|	...	...	1729	|	|	...
Plochingen .... **936** ⊖ d.	...	|	...	|	1449	...	|	...	1540	|	...	...	|	|	1641	1649	...	...	|	...	...	1740	|	|	...
Stuttgart Hbf .... **936** ⊖ a.	...	1447	...	1458	1504	...	1547	...	1556	1600	...	...	1647	1647	1656	1704	...	...	1747	...	...	1756	1801	1847	...
Stuttgart Hbf .... **931** d.	1434	1451	1455	1512	1508	1527	1551	...	...	1610	1606	1636	1651	1651	...	1708	1727	1741	1751	...	1756	...	1805	1851	1855
Vaihingen (Enz) .... **931** d.	1452	|	|	|	|	|	|	...	...	|	|	|	|	|	...	|	|	|	|	...	|	...	|	|	|
Karlsruhe Hbf **931** .... a.	|	|	|	|	1550	|	|	...	...	|	|	|	|	|	...	1753	|	|	|	...	|	...	|	|	|
Heidelberg Hbf .... **931** d.	1518	|	|	1555	...	|	|	...	...	|	1646	1720	|	|	...	...	|	1825	|	...	|	...	1846	|	1946
Mannheim Hbf .... a.	1531	1529	1537	1606	...	1604	1627	...	...	1656	|	1736	1729	1729	...	...	1804	1837	1827	...	1845	...	|	1929	|
Mannheim Hbf .... d.	1533	1531	...	1608	...	1606	1635	1631	...	1658	◐	1738	1731	1731	...	...	1806	1839	1835	1831	...	...	◐	1931	◐
Frankfurt Flughafen F ✈ .... a.	|	|	...	|	...	1638	1706	|	...	|	|	|	|	|	...	...	1838	|	1906	|	...	...	|	|	|
Frankfurt (Main) Hbf .... a.	|	1608	...	|	...	1653	|	1708	...	|	1740	|	1808	1808	...	...	1853	|	|	1908	...	...	1940	2008	2040
Mainz Hbf **912** .... a.	1621	|	...	1646	...	|	|	|	...	1740	...	1815	|	|	...	...	|	1918	|	|	...	...	...	|	...
Koblenz Hbf **912** .... a.	|	|	...	1741	...	|	|	|	...	1841	...	...	|	|	...	...	|	2010	|	|	...	...	...	|	...
Köln Hbf **800 910** .... a.	1801	|	...	1842	...	|	1805	|	...	1942	...	...	|	|	...	...	|	2105	2005	|	...	...	...	|	...
Dortmund Hbf **800** .... a.	...	|	...	...	...	|	1920	|	...	2102	...	...	|	|	...	...	|	2221q	2121	|	...	...	...	|	...
Berlin Hbf **810** .... a.	...	2021	...	...	...	|	...	2126r	...	...	...	...	2148*	2226	...	...	|	...	|	2325	...	...	...	0023	...
Hamburg Hbf **800 900** .... a.	...	...	...	...	...	2038	...	...	...	...	...	...	...	...	...	...	2239	...	0019	...	...	...	...	...	...

	IC 1910	EC 360	ICE 570	IC 2110	IC 2110	ICE 512	ICE 272	IRE 4236	EC 316	IC 1876	IC 2096	ICE 590	IC 2092	ICE 510	ICE 1110	ICE 270	IRE 4238	IC 2050	RB 19362	RB 19364	ICE 990	RE 19246	IC 2090	IC 60418	CNL 418
	⑦w		⑦w	①–④	⑤⑦		①–⑥			⑦w	⑦w	⊡	Ⓑq	①–⑥	⑦w		Ⓒz	⑦w	Ⓐm	Ⓒz			⑦w		Ⓡ
		🍷♦	✕	t✕	y✕	M🍷	◧✕	L	🍷♦		A	✕	🍷	◇	🍷	✕	L	S			✕		🍷		🍷♦
München Hbf .... **904 905** ⊖ d.	1612c	1643c	...	...	...	1723	...	...	1741	...	...	1823	1844	1923	1923	...	...	...	...	...	2040	...	2145c	2243	2243
München Pasing **904 905** ⊖ d.	1620c	1651c	...	...	...	1731	...	...	|	...	...	1831	|	1932	1932	...	...	...	...	...	|	...	2153c	|	|
Augsburg Hbf ... **904 905** ⊖ d.	1653c	1722c	...	...	...	1803	...	...	1818	...	...	1903	1919	2003	2003	...	...	...	...	...	2117	...	2224c	2320	2320u
Günzburg .... **945** ⊖ d.	1728c	|	...	...	...	|	...	...	1849	...	...	|	1949	|	|	...	...	...	...	...	|	...	2254c	2353	2353u
Ulm Hbf .... **945** ⊖ d.	1744	1805	...	...	...	1851	...	1854	1905	...	...	1951	2005	2051	2051	...	2054	...	2103	2110	2204	2242	2311	0010	0010u
Geislingen (Steige) .... ⊖ d.	1816	|	...	...	...	|	...	1917	|	...	...	|	|	|	|	...	2118	...	2133	2138	|	2308	|	0034	0034u
Göppingen .... ⊖ d.	1830	1839	...	...	...	|	...	1929	|	...	...	|	2039	|	|	...	2130	...	2155	2158	|	2324	2345	0048	0048u
Plochingen .... **936** ⊖ d.	|	1851	...	...	...	|	...	1940	|	...	...	|	2051	|	|	...	2141	...	2213	2215	|	2341	2357	0102	0102u
Stuttgart Hbf .... **936** ⊖ a.	1858	1907	...	...	...	1947	...	1956	2001	...	...	2047	2107	2147	2147	...	2156	...	2231	2232	2300	2400	0012	0116	|
Stuttgart Hbf .... **931** d.	1914	1911	1927	1914	1937	1951	...	━	2005	2009	2035	2051	2111	2151	2151	...	━	2209	...	...	2305	...	...	...	0125
Vaihingen (Enz) .... **931** d.	|	|	|	|	1955	|	...	*ICE*	|	|	2052	|	|	|	|	...	...	2225	...	...	|	...	...	...	|
Karlsruhe Hbf **931** .... a.	|	1953	|	|	|	|	...	**372**	|	|	|	|	2153	|	|	...	*ICE*	|	...	...	|	...	...	...	|
Heidelberg Hbf .... **931** d.	1955	...	|	2025j	2025	|	...	⑦w	|	2050	2120	|	...	|	|	...	**522**	2255	...	...	|	...	...	...	|
Mannheim Hbf .... a.	2006	...	2004	2037	2037	2027	...	✕	2048	|	2133	2129	...	2228	2228	...		2306	...	...	2342	...	...	...	|
Mannheim Hbf .... d.	2008	...	2006	2039	2039	2035	2031	2031	...	◐	2135	2131	...	2231	2231	2235	🍷	...	...	...	2351	...	...	...	|
Frankfurt Flughafen F ✈ .... a.	|	...	2038	|	|	2106	|	|	...	|	|	|	...	2303	2301	|	2329	...	...	...	0023	...	...	...	|
Frankfurt (Main) Hbf .... a.	|	...	2052	|	|	|	2108	2108	...	2144	|	2208	...	2325	|	2315	|	...	...	...	0042	...	...	...	|
Mainz Hbf **912** .... a.	2046	...	|	2118	2118	|	|	|	...	...	2215	...	...	...	|	...	|	...	...	...	...	...	...	...	|
Koblenz Hbf **912** .... a.	2141	...	|	2210	2210	|	|	|	...	...	...	...	...	...	|	...	|	...	...	...	...	...	...	...	0446
Köln Hbf **800 910** .... a.	2242	...	|	2305	2305	2205	|	|	...	...	...	...	...	...	0005	...	0039	...	...	...	...	...	...	...	0542
Dortmund Hbf **800** .... a.	2359	...	|	...	...	2321	|	|	...	...	...	...	...	...	...	...	0157	...	...	...	...	...	...	...	...
Berlin Hbf **810** .... a.	...	...	|	...	...	...	|	0125	...	...	...	...	...	...	...	...	...	...	...	...	...	...	...	...	...
Hamburg Hbf **800 900** .... a.	...	...	0037	...	...	...	0134	...	...	...	...	...	...	...	...	...	...	...	...	...	...	...	...	...	...

Other *RE* trains Stuttgart - Ulm and v.v.

	Ⓐm	Ⓒz	Ⓒz	Ⓐm			Ⓒz	Ⓐm	
Stuttgart Hbf .... d.	0608	0632	0717	0732	0832	each train runs every two hours until	1917	1932	2032
Plochingen .... d.	0630	0649	0736	0749	0849		1936	1949	2049
Göppingen .... d.	0649	0707	0754	0807	0907		1955	2007	2107
Geislingen (Steige) .... d.	0711	0723	0815	0823	0923		2016	2023	2123
Ulm Hbf .... a.	0740	0747	0844	0848	0949		2044	2047	2148

	Ⓐm	Ⓒz	Ⓐm	Ⓒz		Ⓐm	Ⓒz		Ⓐm	Ⓒz	
Ulm Hbf .... d.	0523	0601	0706	0710	0810	0910	0910	each train runs every two hours until	1910	1910	2010
Geislingen (Steige) .... d.	0555	0625	0732	0738	0833	0933	0938		1933	1938	2033
Göppingen .... d.	0609	0643	0751	0758	0850	0950	0958		1950	1958	2050
Plochingen .... d.	0623	0705	0805	0815	0908	1008	1015		2008	2015	2108
Stuttgart Hbf .... a.	0643	0724	0824	0832	0926	1026	1032		2026	2032	2126

Other *RE* trains Ulm - München and v.v. See note ♥.

	Ⓐm		Ⓐm		Ⓐm		Ⓐm																			
Ulm Hbf .... ♥ d.	...	...	0446	0524	0549	0621	0645	0724	0819	0924	1019	1124	1219	1324	1419	1524	1619	1724	1818	1924	2024	2124	2224	...	...	...
Günzburg .... d.	...	...	0504	0542	0609	0640	0704	0742	0842	0942	1042	1142	1242	1342	1442	1542	1642	1742	1842	1942	2042	2142	2242	...	...	...
Augsburg Hbf .... a.	...	...	0602	0633	0700	0733	0802	0833	0933	1033	1133	1233	1333	1433	1533	1633	1733	1833	1933	2033	2133	2233	2333	...	...	...
Augsburg Hbf .... d.	0439	0539	0606	0639	0706	0739	0806	0839	0939	1039	1139	1239	1339	1439	1539	1639	1739	1839	1939	2039	2139	2239	2339	...	...	...
München Pasing .... a.	0515	0618	0642	0715	0742	0816	0843	0915	1015	1115	1215	1315	1415	1515	1615	1715	1815	1915	2015	2118	2218	2316	0019	...	...	...
München Hbf .... a.	0522	0627	0650	0722	0750	0824	0851	0922	1022	1122	1222	1322	1422	1522	1622	1722	1822	1922	2022	2127	2226	2325	0026	...	...	...

														Ⓐm	Ⓒz					Ⓒz	Ⓐm					
München Hbf .... d.	0006	...	...	0537	0636	0734	0834	0934	1033	1134	1233	1334	1434	1535	1535	1633	1734	1833	1933	2034	2034	2100	2202	2300	...	...
München Pasing .... d.	0012	...	...	0543	0643	0740	0840	0940	1040	1140	1240	1340	1440	1542	1542	1640	1740	1840	1940	2040	2040	2106	2209	2306	...	...
Augsburg Hbf .... a.	0050	...	...	0620	0721	0817	0917	1017	1117	1217	1317	1417	1517	1619	1619	1717	1817	1917	2017	2117	2117	2147	2246	2347	...	...
Augsburg Hbf .... d.	...	...	0525	0625	0725	0825	0925	1025	1125	1222	1325	1425	1525	1625	1625	1734	1825	1925	2025	2125	2125	2152	2252	2352	...	...
Günzburg .... d.	...	...	0616	0716	0822	0921	1016	1121	1216	1321	1416	1521	1616	1716b	1721	1822	1921	2019	2121	2217	2227	2242	2342	0042	...	...
Ulm Hbf .... a.	...	...	0635	0735	0841	0939	1035	1139	1235	1339	1435	1539	1635	1734b	1739	1840	1939	2038	2139	2236	2246	2301	0001	0101	...	...

♦ – **NOTES** (LISTED BY TRAIN NUMBER)

112 – [12] and ✕ Klagenfurt - Villach - Salzburg - München - Frankfurt - Siegen;
[12] Zagreb (**212**) - Ljubljana - Villach (**112**) - Frankfurt - Siegen.

114 – WÖRTHERSEE – [12] and ✕ Klagenfurt - Villach - Salzburg - München - Köln - Dortmund.

118 – [12] and 🍷 Salzburg - Innsbruck - Bregenz - Lindau - Ulm - Münster.

316 – [12] and 🍷 Graz - Bischofshofen - Salzburg - München - Saarbrücken.

360 – [12] and 🍷 München - Karlsruhe - Strasbourg. Terminates at Karlsruhe on Mar. 6, 7.

418 – ④–⑦ to Mar. 21; daily from Mar. 25. POLLUX – 🛏 1, 2 cl., ━ 2 cl., [2] and 🍷 München - Amsterdam. Starts from Innsbruck on ⑥ Dec. 26 - Apr. 10 (Table **21**). Conveys 🛏 1, 2 cl., ━ 2 cl., [2] (*CNL* **40418** – CASSIOPEIA) Innsbruck / München - Paris (Table **32**).

974 – [12] and ✕ Stuttgart - Hamburg (- Kiel Ⓑ **q**). Train number **574** on ⑥ (also Dec. 24, 25, 31, Apr. 2, 4, May 23).

A – To Wiesbaden (Table **912**).
K – To Kassel (Table **806**).
L – From Lindau (Table **933**).
M – To Münster (Table **800**).
N – To Münster (Table **800**) on ⑦**w**.
S – To Saarbrücken (Table **919**).

a – Not Dec. 24, 25, 31, Jan. 1, Apr. 2, 5, May 24.
b – 7 minutes later Mar. 1 - May 14.
c – Not Feb. 27 - May 16.
d – Not Dec. 24, 25, 31, Jan. 1, Apr. 2, 4, May 23.
f – Also Dec. 23, 30, Apr. 1, May 12, June 2; not Dec. 25, Jan. 1, Apr. 2, May 14, June 4.
h – Also Dec. 24, 25, 31, Apr. 2, 4, May 23; not Dec. 26, Jan. 2.
j – Arrives 1959.

m – Not Dec. 24, 31, Jan. 6, June 3.
q – Ⓑ (not Dec. 24, 25, 31, Apr. 2, 4, May 23).
r – 2204 on ⑥ (also Dec. 24, 25, 31, Apr. 2, 4, May 23).
t – Not Dec. 24, 31, Apr. 5, May 24.
w – Also Apr. 5, May 24; not Apr. 4, May 23.
x – On Dec. 25, 27, Jan. 1 does not run München - Stuttgart.
y – Also Apr. 5, May 24; not Dec. 25, Apr. 2, 4, May 23.
z – Also Dec. 24, 31, Jan. 6, June 3.

◐ – Via Darmstadt (Table **911**).
◇ – ①–⑥ (also Apr. 4, May 23; not Apr. 5, May 24). Train number **1010** on ⑤⑥ (also Dec. 23, 30, Apr. 1, 4, May 23). Conveys ✕ on ①–④, 🍷 on ⑤⑥.
◧ – ①–⑥ (also Apr. 4, May 23; not Jan. 1, Apr. 5, May 24). On ⑥ (also Dec. 24, 25, 31, Apr. 2, 4, May 23) runs with train number **292** and arrives Hamburg Hbf 0111.
⊡ – Daily except Dec. 24. Continues to Kassel / Hannover on dates in Table **900**. Train number **698** on ⑤ (also Dec. 23, 30, Apr. 1, May 12, June 2; not Dec. 25, Apr. 2, May 14, June 4). Train number **992** on ⑦**w**.
* – Ⓡ and supplement payable for journeys to Berlin.
⊖ – See panel below main table for additional *RE* services.
♥ – Feb. 27 - May 16 departures from Ulm are 6–16 minutes **earlier** than shown.

931 STRASBOURG - KARLSRUHE - STUTTGART, also HEIDELBERG - STUTTGART

See Table **32** for full details of international *TGV* services from / to Paris. See Table **930** for fast trains Heidelberg - Stuttgart and v.v.

km	km		*IC* 2291 ①-⑤	*IC* 2363 ①-⑥	*ICE* 699 ⑦w	*IRE* 4901 Ⓐt	*RE* 19503 Ⓒz	*IC* 2365 ①-⑤	*IC* 2367 ①-⑤	*IC* 2063 ①-⑥	*RE* 19105 Ⓒz	*IC* 2369 Ⓐt	*ICE* 895 ⑥k	*EC* 361	*IRE* 4903	*RE* 19505	*IC* 2065	*IRE* 4905	*TGV* 9571	*RE* 19507	*IC* 2101	*IC* 2261	*IRE* 4907	*RE* 19509	*IC* 2069
			a M	h	A ✕			a O	a ✕	e N		🍷	✕	T 🍷		⊖	N 🍷		P 🍷	⊖	B 🍷	G 🍷		⊖	N 🍷
		Strasbourg .... ▲ d.	...	...	...	...	...	✕	...	...	...	...	...	0653	...	...	...	...	0945	...	...	...	...	...	...
		Karlsruhe Hbf .... a.	...	...	...	...	...	...	...	...	...	...	...	0752	...	...	...	...	1025	...	...	...	...	...	...
0		**Karlsruhe** Hbf .... d.	0457	0559	0607	0601	...	0637	0659	0706	0719	0741	0741	0806	0805	...	0906	1005	1027	...	1106	1206	1205	...	1306
26		Pforzheim .... d.	|	|	|	0624	...	|	|	0727	0743	|	|	|	0826	...	0927	1026	|	...	1127	|	1226	...	1327
	0	**Heidelberg** Hbf **930** d.	|	|	|	|	0610	|	|	|	|	|	|	|	|	0810	|	|	|	1010	|	|	|	1210	|
	33	Bruchsal .... d.	0515	0617	0621	|	0632	0654	0719	|	|	0758	0758	0819	|	0833	|	|	|	1033	|	1219	|	1233	|
39	65	Mühlacker .... d.	|	|	|	0632	0655	|	|	0737	0755	|	|	|	0834	0858	0937	1034	|	1058	1137	|	1234	1258	1337
47	73	Vaihingen (Enz) .... **930** d.	0533	|	|	0639	0705	|	|	0746	0804	|	0815	|	0841	0906	0946	1041	|	1106	1146	|	1241	1306	1346
86	112	**Stuttgart** Hbf ...... **930** a.	0549	0648	0648	0656	0738	0725	0750	0803	0837	0829	0831	0849	0858	0939	1003	1058	1104	1139	1203	1249	1258	1339	1403

	IC 2263 ⑤f	*IRE* 4909	*TGV* 9573	*RE* 19511	*IC* 2103	*IC* 2265	*IRE* 4911	*RE* 19513	*IC* 2163 Ⓑq	*IC* 2267 b	*IRE* 4913	*TGV* 9575	*RE* 19515	*IC* 2105	*IC* 2269 X	*IRE* 4915	*TGV* 9577 Ⓑy	*RE* 19517	*IC* 2167 Ⓑq	*IC* 2167 ⑦w		*IC* 1867 ⑤v	*RE* 19133		*RE* 19135
	🍷		P 🍷	⊖	B 🍷	S 🍷		⊖	N 🍷	G 🍷		R 🍷	⊖	L 🍷	H 🍷		P 🍷	⊖	🍷	N		🍷			
Strasbourg .... ▲ d.	...	...	1345	...	...	...	...	...	...	...	...	1745	...	...	...	...	1946	...	...	...	...	...	...	...	...
Karlsruhe Hbf .... a.	...	...	1425	...	...	...	...	...	...	...	...	1825	...	...	...	...	2027	...	...	...	...	...	...	...	...
Karlsruhe Hbf .... d.	1406	1405	1427	...	1506	1606	1605	...	1706	1806	1805	1827	...	1906	2006	2005	2029	...	2106	2106	...	2208	2209	...	2317
Pforzheim .... d.	|	1426	|	...	1527	|	1626	...	1727	|	1826	|	...	1927	|	2026	|	...	2127	2127	...	|	2233	...	2339
Heidelberg Hbf . **930** d.	|	|	|	1410	|	|	|	1610	|	|	|	|	1810	|	|	|	|	2010	|	|	...	|	|	...	|
Bruchsal .... d.	1419	|	|	1433	|	1619	|	1633	|	1819	|	|	1833	|	2019	|	|	2033	|	|	...	2225	|	...	|
Mühlacker .... d.	|	1434	|	1458	1537	|	1634	1658	1737	|	1834	|	1858	1937	|	2034	|	2058	2137	2137	...	|	2244	...	2351
Vaihingen (Enz) ..... **930** d.	|	1441	|	1506	1546	|	1641	1706	1746	|	1841	|	1907	1946	|	2041	|	2107	2146	2146	...	2244	2253	...	0000
Stuttgart Hbf .... **930** a.	1449	1458	1504	1539	1603	1649	1658	1739	1803	1849	1858	1904	1939	2003	2049	2058	2105	2139	2203	2203	...	2301	2325	...	0036

km		*RE* 19138			*IC* 2368 ①-⑤	*RE* 19500	*TGV* 9578 ①-⑥	*RE* 19104 Ⓐt	*IC* 2268 ①-⑤	*RE* 19106 Ⓒz	*RE* 19108 Ⓐt	*IC* 2164 ①-⑥	*RE* 19502	*TGV* 9576	*IRE* 4902	*IC* 2266 ①-⑥	*IC* 2102 ①-⑥	*RE* 19504	*IRE* 4904	*IC* 2264	*IC* 2160	*RE* 19506	*TGV* 9574	*IRE* 4906	*IC* 2262 ⑤f
◧					a	⊖	j P	⊖	a H			e N	⊖	R 🍷		e G	e J	⊖		S 🍷	N 🍷	⊖	P 🍷		🍷
0	**Stuttgart** Hbf ...... **930** d.	0019	...	...	0545	0614	0654	0638	0711	0717	0722	0800	0819	0854	0900	0911	1000	1019	1059	1111	1200	1219	1254	1259	1311
29	Vaihingen (Enz) .... **930** d.	0052	...	...	0603	0644	|	0711	|	0750	0752	0816	0850	|	0915	|	1016	1050	1115	|	1216	1250	|	1315	|
	Mühlacker .... d.	0100	...	...	0611	0700	|	0717	|	0759	0800	0823	0859	|	0921	|	1023	1059	1121	|	1223	1259	|	1321	|
66	Bruchsal .... d.	|	...	...	|	0728	|	|	0740	|	|	|	0929	|	|	0940	|	1129	|	1139	|	1329	|	|	1340
	Heidelberg Hbf **930** a.	|	...	...	|	0748	|	|	|	|	|	|	0949	|	|	|	|	1149	|	|	|	1349	|	|	|
	Pforzheim .... d.	0113	...	...	0622	...	|	0730	|	0813	0813	0834	...	|	0930	|	1034	...	1130	|	1234	...	|	1330	|
87	**Karlsruhe** Hbf .... a.	0136	...	...	0645	...	0729	0753	0753	0838	0838	0853	...	0929	0953	0953	1053	...	1153	1153	1253	...	1329	1353	1353
87	**Karlsruhe** Hbf .... d.	...	...	...	...	...	0731	...	...	...	...	...	...	0931	...	...	...	...	...	...	...	...	1331	...	...
171	**Strasbourg** .... ▲ a.	...	...	...	...	...	0813	...	...	...	...	...	...	1013	...	...	...	...	...	...	...	...	1415	...	...

	IC 2100	*RE* 19508	*IRE* 4908	*IC* 2260	*IC* 2066	*RE* 19510	*IC* 2364 ①-⑤	*TGV* 9572 ⑥⑦c	*IRE* 4910	*IC* 2362 Ⓑq	*IC* 2360 ①-⑤	*IC* 2104	*RE* 19514	*TGV* 9570 ①-⑤	*IRE* 4912	*EC* 360	*RE* 19130 Ⓒz	*RE* 19132 Ⓐt	*IC* 2062	*RE* 19516	*IRE* 4914	*IC* 2092 Ⓑq		*IC* 2060 Ⓑq	*RE* 19134 19136
	B 🍷	⊖		G 🍷	N 🍷	⊖	a O	P 🍷		G 🍷	d 🍷	B 🍷	⊖	m P		T 🍷			N 🍷	⊖		M 🍷		D 🍷	
Stuttgart Hbf .... **930** d.	1400	1419	1459	1508	1600	1617	1641	1654	1659	1708	1734	1800	1819	1854	1859	1911	1918	1919	2000	2018	2059	2111	...	2200	2217
Vaihingen (Enz) ..... **930** d.	1416	1450	1515	|	1616	1650	|	|	1715	|	|	1816	1850	|	1915	|	1950	1952	2016	2050	2115	|	...	2216	2252
Mühlacker .... d.	1423	1459	1521	|	1623	1659	|	|	1721	|	|	1823	1859	|	1921	|	1958	2000	2023	2059	2121	|	...	2223	2300
Bruchsal .... d.	|	1529	|	1537	|	1729	1712	|	|	1737	1804	|	1929	|	|	1939	|	|	|	2129	|	2140	...	|	|
Heidelberg Hbf . **930** a.	|	1549	|	|	|	1749	|	|	|	|	|	|	1949	|	|	|	|	|	|	2156	|	|	...	|	|
Pforzheim .... d.	1434	...	1530	|	1634	...	|	|	1730	|	|	1834	...	|	1930	|	2013	2013	2034	...	2130	|	...	2234	2313
Karlsruhe Hbf .... a.	1453	...	1553	1550	1653	...	1731	1729	1753	1753	1821	1853	...	1929	1953	1953	2038	2038	2053	...	2153	2153	...	2253	2338
Karlsruhe Hbf .... d.	...	...	...	...	...	...	...	1731	...	...	...	...	...	1931	...	2006	...	...	...	...	...	...	...	...	...
Strasbourg .... ▲ a.	...	...	...	...	...	...	...	1815	...	...	...	...	...	2015	...	2101	...	...	...	...	...	...	...	...	...

A – 🚆 and ✕ Karlsruhe - München. Terminates at Stuttgart on Apr. 5.
B – 🚆 and 🍷 Basel - Stuttgart - Nürnberg and v.v.
D – 🚆 and 🍷 (Nürnberg ⑤⑦r -) Stuttgart - Karlsruhe.
G – 🚆 and 🍷 Karlsruhe - Stuttgart - München and v.v. See note ⊗.
H – 🚆 and 🍷 (München ♣ -) Ulm - Karlsruhe and v.v.
J – 🚆 and 🍷 (Passau ● -) Nürnberg - Basel.
L – 🚆 and 🍷 Basel - Stuttgart (- Nürnberg ⑤⑦r) (- Passau ●).
M – 🚆 and 🍷 Karlsruhe - Stuttgart - München and v.v.
N – 🚆 and 🍷 Karlsruhe - Stuttgart - Nürnberg and v.v.
O – From / to Offenburg (Table **916**).
P – 🚆 and 🍷 Paris - Stuttgart and v.v. Ⓡ for international journeys.
R – 🚆 and 🍷 Paris - München and v.v. Ⓡ for international journeys.
S – 🚆 and 🍷 Salzburg - München - Karlsruhe and v.v. See note ⊗.
T – 🚆 and 🍷 Strasbourg - München and v.v. See notes ▲ and ⊗.
X – ①②③④⑦ (not Dec. 23, 24, 30, 31, Apr. 1, 4, May 23).

a – ①-⑤ (not Dec. 24, 25, 31, Jan. 1, Apr. 2, 5, May 24).
b – Not Dec. 24, 25, 31, May 4, 23.
c – Also Dec. 24, 25, 31, Jan. 1, Apr. 5, May 24.
d – Not Dec. 24, 25, 31, Jan. 1, Apr. 2, 5, May 14, 24, June 4.
e – Not Dec. 25, 26, Jan. 1, Apr. 3, 5, May 24.
f – Also Dec. 23, 30, Apr. 1, May 12, June 2; not Dec. 25, Jan. 1, Apr. 2, May 14, June 4.
h – Not Dec. 25, 26, Jan. 1, Apr. 3, 5, May 13, 24, June 3.
j – Not Dec. 25, Jan. 1, Apr. 5, May 24.
k – Also Dec. 24, 31, Apr. 2, June 3; not Dec. 26, Apr. 3, May 15, June 5.
m – Not Dec. 24, 25, 31, Jan. 1, Apr. 5, May 24.
q – Not Dec. 24, 25, 31, Apr. 2, 4, May 23.
r – ⑤⑦ (also Dec. 23, 30, Apr. 1, 5, May 12, 24, June 2; not Dec. 25, Jan. 1, Apr. 2, 4, May 14, 23, June 4).

t – Not Dec. 24, 31, Jan. 6, June 3.
v – Also Dec. 23, 30, Apr. 1; not Dec. 25, Jan. 1, Apr. 2.
w – Also Apr. 5, May 24; not Apr. 4, May 23.
y – Not Dec. 24, 31, Apr. 4, May 23.
z – Also Dec. 24, 31, Jan. 6, June 3.
◧ – Via high-speed line.
● – See Table **920** for days of running.
♣ – See Table **930** for days of running.
▲ – Services from / to Strasbourg are subject to alteration on Mar. 6, 7.
⊗ – Services Ulm - München and v.v. are subject to alteration Feb. 27 - May 16. See Table **930** for further details.
⊖ – Subject to alteration from June 10.

932 STUTTGART - STUTTGART FLUGHAFEN ✈

S-Bahn 2/3

20 km. Journey: 27 minutes. On Dec. 24, 31 services run as on ⑥. On Jan. 6, June 3 services run as on ⑦. Trains marked Ⓑ also run on Dec. 26, May 1. Trains marked ¶ do not run on Dec. 24.

From Stuttgart Hbf at 0455 Ⓐ, 0515 Ⓐ, 0525, 0545 Ⓑ, 0555 ⚒, 0615 Ⓐ, 0625, 0645 Ⓑ, 0655 ⚒, 0715 Ⓐ, 0725, 0745, 0755, 0815, 0825, 0845, 0855 and then at 15, 25, 45, and 55 minutes past each hour until 1815, 1825, 1845, 1855; then 1915 Ⓐ, 1925, 1945 Ⓐ, 1955, 2015 Ⓐ, 2025, 2045 Ⓐ, 2055 ¶, 2115 Ⓐ, 2125, 2155 ¶, 2225, 2255 ¶, 2325, 2355 ¶ and 0025.

From Stuttgart Flughafen ✈ at 0508, 0518 Ⓐ, 0538 ⚒, 0548 Ⓑ, 0608, 0618 Ⓐ, 0638 ⚒, 0648 Ⓑ, 0708, 0718 Ⓐ, 0738 ⚒, 0748 Ⓑ, 0808, 0818, 0838, 0848 and then at 08, 18, 38 and 48 minutes past each hour until 1808, 1818, 1838, 1848; then 1908, 1918, 1938, 1948 Ⓐ, 2008, 2018 Ⓐ, 2038, 2048 Ⓐ, 2108, 2118 Ⓐ, 2138 ¶, 2148 Ⓐ, 2208, 2238 ¶, 2308, 2338 ¶ and 0008.

933 ULM - LINDAU

IRE / RE services (except trains **C** and **D**)

km			F	B	F		B			B			B	C 🍷		B			B						2
	Stuttgart Hbf **930** .... d.	...	...	...	0659k	0802	...	...	1002	...	...	1202	...	1257	1402	...	...	1602	...	1702e	1802	...	2002	...	...
0	**Ulm** Hbf .... d.	0550	0707h	0806	0812	0912	1006	1012	1112	1206	1212	1312	1406	1411	1512	1606	1612	1712	1806	1812	1912	2012	2112	2212	2320
37	Biberach (Riß) .... d.	0618	0733h	0827	0835	0935	1027	1035	1135	1227	1235	1335	1426	1433	1535	1627	1635	1735	1827	1835	1935	2035	2139	2239	2352
62	Aulendorf .... d.	0638	0753	|	0855	0955	|	1054	1155	|	1254	1355	1442	1451	1554	1641e	1654	1754	|	1855	1955	2055	2158	2258	0012
84	Ravensburg .... d.	0651	0807	0853	0908	1008	1053	1107	1208	1253	1307	1408	1456	1505	1607	1653	1707	1807	1853	1908	2008	2108	2211	2311	0025
95	Meckenbeuren .... d.	0658	0814	|	0916	1016	|	1115	1216	|	1314	1416	|	1513	1615	|	1714	1815	|	1916	2015	2116	2218	2319	0033
99	Friedrichshafen Flughafen ✈ d.	0702	|	0902	|	|	1102	1119	|	1302	1318	|	1505	|	|	1702h	1719	|	1902	|	2020	|	2223	2323	|
103	Friedrichshafen Stadt ▲ ...... a.	0714r	0822	0908	0924	1024	1108	1124	1224	1308	1324	1424	1511	1521	1624	1708h	1724	1824	1908	1924	2026	2124	2229	2329	0043
103	Friedrichshafen Stadt ... **939** d.	*0727*	0827	...	0929	1029	...	1129	1229	...	1329	1429	...	1535	1629	...	1729	1829	...	1929	2034	2132	*2236*	*2339*	...
127	**Lindau** Hbf 🏛 .... **939** a.	*0750*	0857	...	0951	1055	...	1153	1255	...	1353	1454	...	1554	1655	...	1749	1855	...	1951	2056	2155	*2259*	*0014*	...

	Ⓒz	Ⓐe		F	F	B	F		B		D 🍷	B			B			B			B		B	2	2
Lindau Hbf 🏛 .... **939** d.	...	*0513*	0559	0703k	0802	...	0906	1004	...	1102	1202	...	1302	1406	...	1502	1605	...	1702	1804	...	1902	*2012*	*2103*	*2132*
Friedrichshafen Stadt .... **939** a.	...	*0543*	0622	0726	0824	...	0928	1026	...	1127	1219	...	1327	1427	...	1528	1626	...	1727	1826	...	1927	*2034*	*2125*	*2208*
Friedrichshafen Stadt ▲ ...... d.	0521	0549	0628	0732	0830	0850	0932	1032	1049	1132	1233	1245h	1332	1432	1450	1532	1632	1650	1732	1832	1849	1932	2046	2128	2233
Friedrichshafen Flughafen ✈ d.	|	|	0632	|	0834	0855	|	1036	1054	|	|	1250h	|	1436	1455	|	1636z	1655	|	1836	1854	|	|	|	2238
Meckenbeuren .... d.	0529	|	0637	0739	0838	|	0940	1040	|	1139	1241	|	1339	1441	|	1539	1640	|	1739	1840	|	1939	2053	2135	2242
Ravensburg .... d.	0537	0601	0645	0747	0847	0904	0948	1048	1103	1148	1250	1259h	1347	1448	1505	1548	1648	1704	1747	1848	1903	1947	2100	2142	2251
Aulendorf .... d.	0552	|	0659k	0803	0902	|	1003	1103	|	1203	1306	1314z	1403	1503	|	1603	1704	|	1803	1903	1917	2003	2113	2157	2306
Biberach (Riß) .... d.	0610	0627	0719	0820	0920	0929	1020	1121	1129	1220	1322	1330	1421	1520	1530	1620	1721	1730	1820	1920	1931	2021	2130	2212	2326
Ulm Hbf .... a.	0642	0650	0745	0845	0945	0953	1045	1145	1153	1245	1353	1345	1445	1545	1553	1645	1745	1753	1845	1945	1954	2045	2155	2237	2359
Stuttgart Hbf **930** .... a.	0756	0756	...	0956	...	...	1156	...	...	1356	1458	...	1556	...	...	1756	...	...	1956	...	2156z	...	...	...	...

B – To / from Basel Bad Bf (Table **939**).
C – *IC* **119**: 🚆 and 🍷 Münster - Köln - Stuttgart - Lindau - Bregenz - Innsbruck.
D – *IC* **118**: 🚆 and 🍷 Salzburg - Innsbruck - Bregenz - Lindau - Stuttgart - Köln - Münster.
F – Change trains at Friedrichshafen Stadt on Ⓐ**e**.

e – Ⓐ (not Dec. 24, 31, Jan. 6, June 3).
h – 3–6 minutes later on Ⓐ**e**.
k – 3–4 minutes later on Ⓒ**z**.
r – 0707 on Ⓒ**z**.

z – Ⓒ (also Dec. 24, 31, Jan. 6, June 3).
▲ – Regular services operate to / from Friedrichshafen Hafen.

RE / RB services except where shown MÜNCHEN, AUGSBURG and ULM - OBERSTDORF and LINDAU 935

For services to / from Bad Wörishofen see panel at foot of page (also on page 438)

km	km		©z	Ⓐe	ALX 🍷 ⚒K	Ⓐe	Ⓐe			Ⓐe	©z	©z	©z		Ⓐe	©z	ALX	ALX 🍷			EC 196 ♥✕					
0		**München** Hbf ⊡ d.	...	...	0452	...	...	...	...	...	...	0551	...	0619	...	...	0651	0651	...	...	0713	...	...	0752	0819	...
7		München Pasing d.	...	...	0459	...	...	...	...	...	...	0559	...	0627	...	...	0658	0658	...	...	|	...	...	0800	0827	...
42		Geltendorf d.	...	...	0521	...	...	...	...	...	...	0622	...	0651	...	...	0720	0720	...	...	|	...	...	0822	0849	...
56		Kaufering d.	...	...	0531	...	...	...	...	...	...	0631	...	0701	...	...	0731	0731	...	...	|	...	...	0832	0859	...
	0	**Augsburg** Hbf d.	...	0503	|	...	...	...	...	...	0603	|	...	|	0648	0645	|	|	...	0708v	|	...	0803t	|	|	0845
68	40	Buchloe ⊕ a.	...	0535	0539	...	...	...	...	...	0637	0640	...	0709	0712	0712	0739	0739	...	0737v	0755	...	0838t	0841	0907	0912
68	40	Buchloe ⊕ d.	...	0536	0540	...	...	...	...	...	0644	0641	...	0715e	0713	0714	0741	0741	0744	0747	0758	...	0846	0846	0908z	0913
	48	Türkheim (Bay) d.	...	0542	|	...	...	...	...	...	|	0647	...	0725e	|	|	|	|	0752	|	|	...	|	0852	|	|
88		Kaufbeuren d.	...	|	0554	0624	...	...	...	...	0658	|	...	|	0726	0726	0755	0755	|	0800	|	...	0900	|	0920z	0926
100		Marktoberdorf d.	...	|	|	0642	...	...	...	...	0714	|	...	|	|	|	|	|	|	0816	|	...	0916	|	▬	|
131		**Füssen** a.	...	|	|	0724	...	...	...	...	0755	|	...	|	|	|	|	|	|	0856	|	...	0957	|	...	|
	59	Mindelheim d.	...	0554	|	▬	...	...	...	...	...	0701	...	0732e	|	|	|	|	0801	...	|	...	▬	0901	...	|
		Ulm Hbf d.	0509	|	|	...	...	0548e	0548e	0617	...	|	0659	|	|	|	|	|	|	...	|	0758	...	|	0859	|
	86	Memmingen ⊕ a.	0555	0618	|	...	...	0649e	0649e	0710	...	0722	0734	0758e	|	|	|	|	0827	...	|	0826	...	0922	0938	|
	86	Memmingen ⊕ d.	0556	...	|	...	0630	0652e	0652e	0714	...	...	0735	...	|	|	|	|	⊖	...	|	0840	0833	...	0939	|
131		**Kempten** Hbf ⊕ a.	0622	...	0626	ALX	|	0719e	0719e	0746	...	...	0759	...	0758	0757	0823	0823	...	...	0841	0911	|	...	0959	0956
131		**Kempten** Hbf ⊕ d.	...	...	0630	🍷	|	0721	0721	...	...	...	0801	...	0804	0806	0825	0825	...	...	0843	0914	|	...	...	1003
152		Immenstadt ⊕ a.	...	...	0646	◁	|	0737	0737	...	...	...	0816	...	0820	0822	0839	0839	...	...	|	0930	|	...	...	1019
152		Immenstadt ⊕ d.	...	...	0648	0652	|	0740	0747	...	...	...	0826	...	0826	0823	0843	0853	...	...	|	0942	|	...	...	1022
		Sonthofen d.	...	...	|	0702	|	|	0757	...	...	...	0835	...	0836	|	|	0903	...	...	|	0954	|	...	...	|
		Oberstdorf a.	...	...	|	0725	|	|	0823	...	...	...	0853	...	0854	|	|	0922	...	...	|	1017	|	...	...	|
	118	Leutkirch d.	...	...	|	...	0704	|	...	...	...	...	...	...	...	|	|	...	...	...	|	...	0904	...	...	|
	129	Kißlegg 937 d.	...	...	|	...	0717	|	...	...	...	...	...	...	...	|	|	...	...	...	|	...	0920	...	...	|
	142	Wangen (Allgäu) 937 d.	...	...	|	...	0732	|	...	...	...	...	...	...	...	|	|	...	...	...	|	...	0935	...	...	|
197	148	Hergatz 937 d.	...	...	0726	...	0737	0817	...	...	...	...	...	...	...	0900	0920	...	...	...	|	...	0940	...	...	1101
220	171	**Lindau** Hbf a.	...	...	0744	...	0755	0835	...	...	...	...	...	...	...	0917	0938	...	...	...	0947	...	0956	...	...	1118

				ALX	ALX 🍷					R	R			ALX	ALX 🍷				Ⓐe	Ⓐe	©z	N ©z	N ©z	EC 194 ♥✕		
München Hbf ⊡ d.	...	...	0852	0919	0919	...	...	0951	1019	...	...	...	1051	1119	1119	...	...	1151	...	1219	1219	...	...	1234	1251	...
München Pasing d.	...	...	0859	0927	0927	...	...	0959	1027	...	...	...	1059	1127	1127	...	...	1159	...	1227	1227	...	...	|	1259	...
Geltendorf d.	...	...	0922	|	|	...	...	1022	1049	...	...	...	1122	|	|	...	...	1222	...	1249	1249	...	...	|	1322	...
Kaufering d.	...	...	0931	0956	0956	...	...	1032	1058	...	...	...	1131	1156	1156	...	...	1232	...	1258	1258	...	...	|	1331	...
Augsburg Hbf d.	0845	0903	|	0929	0929	...	1003	|	|	1044	1044	1103	|	1128	1128	...	1203	|	1233	|	|	1245	1245	|	|	1303
Buchloe ⊕ a.	0912	0936	0940	1004	1004	...	1038	1041	1105	1111	1111	1136	1140	1204	1204	...	1238	1241	1306	1306	1306	1311	1311	1316	1340	1336
Buchloe ⊕ d.	0913	0944	0944	1005	1005	...	1044	1042	1106	1112	1112	1144	1144	1205	1205	...	1244	1243	▬	1310	▬	1312	1312	1318	1344	1344
Türkheim (Bay) d.	|	0950	|	|	|	...	|	1049	|	|	|	1150	|	|	|	...	|	1250	...	|	...	|	|	|	|	1351
Kaufbeuren d.	0926	|	0957	1020	1020	...	1058	|	1119	1126	1126	|	1156	1220	1220	...	1258	|	...	1323	...	1325	1325	|	1357	|
Marktoberdorf d.	|	|	1013	|	|	...	1115	|	▬	|	|	|	1212	|	|	...	1316	|	...	|	...	|	|	|	1414	|
Füssen a.	|	|	1055	|	|	...	1155	|	...	|	|	|	1257	|	|	...	1359	|	...	|	...	|	|	|	1455	|
Mindelheim d.	|	1001	...	|	|	...	...	1101	...	|	|	1201	...	|	|	...	...	1301	...	|	...	|	|	|	...	1401
Ulm Hbf d.	|	|	...	|	|	0959	...	|	1059	|	|	|	...	|	|	1159	...	|	1259	|	...	|	|	|	...	|
Memmingen ⊕ a.	|	1027	...	|	|	1027	...	1122	1135	|	|	1227	...	|	|	1226	...	1322	1337	|	...	|	|	1344	...	1421
Memmingen ⊕ d.	|	1033	...	|	|	1041	...	...	1136	|	|	1233	...	|	|	1227	...	...	1338	|	...	|	|	1346	...	1445
Kempten Hbf ⊕ a.	0956	|	...	1047	1047	1112	...	...	1159	1156	1156	|	...	1247	1247	1252	...	...	1359	1353	...	1355	1355	|	...	|
Kempten Hbf ⊕ d.	1003	|	...	1049	1049	1115	...	...	...	1203	1203	|	...	1249	1249	1303	...	...	...	1403	Ⓐe	1403	1403	|	...	|
Immenstadt ⊕ a.	1019	|	...	1104	1104	1131	...	...	...	1219	1219	|	...	1304	1304	1319	...	...	...	1419	◁	1419	1419	|	...	|
Immenstadt ⊕ d.	1027	|	...	1108	1111	1142	...	...	...	1222	1227	|	...	1308	1317	1332	...	...	...	1422	1427	1422	1427	|	...	|
Sonthofen d.	1038	|	...	|	1120	1152	...	...	...	|	1238	|	...	|	1331	1341	...	...	...	|	1438	|	1438	|	...	|
Oberstdorf a.	1056	|	...	|	1137	1214	...	...	...	|	1256	|	...	|	1350	1403	...	...	...	|	1456	|	1456	|	...	|
Leutkirch d.	...	1107	...	|	...	...	...	...	...	|	...	1305	...	|	...	...	...	...	...	|	...	|	...	|	...	1510
Kißlegg 937 d.	...	1120	...	|	...	...	...	...	...	|	...	1325r	...	|	...	...	...	...	...	|	...	|	...	|	...	1520
Wangen (Allgäu) 937 d.	...	1135	...	|	...	...	...	...	...	|	...	1336	...	|	...	...	...	...	...	|	...	|	...	|	...	1535
Hergatz 937 d.	...	1140	...	1143	...	...	...	...	...	1300	...	1340	...	1344	...	...	...	...	...	1459	...	1459	...	|	...	1540
Lindau Hbf a.	...	...	...	1200	...	...	...	...	...	1317	...	...	...	1400	...	...	...	...	...	1517	...	1517	...	1447	...	...

	ALX	ALX 🍷	IC 2085 H										ALX	ALX 🍷	RE 2013 A 🍷				Q	Q	EC 192 ♥✕	Ⓐe	©z		ALX	ALX 🍷
München Hbf ⊡ d.	1319	1319	...	...	...	...	1351	1419	...	...	...	1451	1519	1519	...	...	1551	1619	...	...	1634	...	...	1651	1720	1720
München Pasing d.	1327	1327	...	...	...	...	1359	1427	...	...	...	1459	1527	1527	...	...	1559	1627	...	...	|	...	...	1700	1728	1728
Geltendorf d.	|	|	...	...	...	...	1422	1449	...	...	...	1522	|	|	...	...	1622	1649	...	...	|	...	...	1723	|	|
Kaufering d.	1356	1356	...	...	...	...	1432	1458	...	...	...	1531	1556	1556	...	...	1632	1658	...	...	|	...	...	1732	1759	1759
Augsburg Hbf d.	1327	1327	1356	...	...	1403	|	|	1444	1444	1503	|	1518	1518	...	1603	|	|	1644	1644	|	1703	1703	|	1729	1729
Buchloe ⊕ a.	1404	1404	|	...	...	1438	1441	1506	1511	1511	1538	1540	1604	1604	...	1638	1641	1706	1711	1711	1715	1736	1737	1740	1808	1808
Buchloe ⊕ d.	1405	1405	|	...	...	1444	1443	1507	1512	1512	1543	1543	1605	1605	...	1644	1643	1707	1712	1712	1717	1737	1744	1747	1809	1809
Türkheim (Bay) d.	|	|	|	...	...	|	1455	|	|	|	1550	|	|	|	...	|	1650	|	|	|	|	1744	1751	|	|	|
Kaufbeuren d.	1420	1420	1438	...	...	1458	|	1519	1526	1526	|	1556	1620	1620	...	1659	|	1719	1726	1726	|	|	|	1759	1823	1823
Marktoberdorf d.	|	|	|	...	...	1516	|	▬	|	|	|	1613	|	|	...	1716	|	▬	|	|	|	|	|	1815	|	|
Füssen a.	|	|	|	...	...	1558	|	...	|	|	|	1655	|	|	...	1757	|	...	|	|	|	|	|	1856	|	|
Mindelheim d.	|	|	|	...	...	...	1504	...	|	|	1601	...	|	|	...	...	1701	...	|	|	|	1754	1801	...	|	|
Ulm Hbf d.	|	|	|	1413	1413	...	|	1459	|	|	|	...	|	|	1607	...	|	1659	|	|	|	|	|	...	|	|
Memmingen ⊕ a.	|	|	|	1441	1441	...	1525	1530	|	|	1633j	...	|	|	1636	...	1722	1729	|	|	1744	1816	1822	...	|	|
Memmingen ⊕ d.	|	|	|	1443	1443	...	...	1531	|	|	1645	...	|	|	1638	...	...	1730	|	|	1746	1845	1845	...	|	|
Kempten Hbf ⊕ a.	1447	1447	1509	1512	1512	...	...	1558	1556	1556	|	...	1647	1647	1701	...	...	1757	1756	1756	|	|	|	...	1853	1853
Kempten Hbf ⊕ d.	1449	1449	1513	1517	1517	...	...	...	1603	1603	|	...	1649	1649	1706	...	...	...	1803	1803	|	|	|	...	1856	1856
Immenstadt ⊕ a.	1504	1504	1529	1533	1533	...	...	...	1619	1619	|	...	1704	1704	1721	...	...	...	1819	1819	|	|	|	...	1911	1911
Immenstadt ⊕ d.	1508	1511	1548	1536	1541	...	...	...	1622	1628	|	...	1708	1711	1736	...	...	...	1822	1827	|	|	|	...	1915	1920
Sonthofen d.	|	1521	1558	|	1550	...	...	...	|	1638	|	...	|	1720	1746	...	...	...	|	1837	|	|	|	...	|	1932
Oberstdorf a.	|	1538	1617	|	1608	...	...	...	|	1656	|	...	|	1736	1806	...	...	...	|	1856	|	|	|	...	|	1948
Leutkirch d.	|	...	...	|	...	...	...	...	|	...	1710	...	|	...	...	...	...	...	|	...	|	1910	1910	...	|	...
Kißlegg 937 d.	|	...	...	|	...	...	...	...	|	...	1720	...	|	...	...	...	...	...	|	...	|	1920	1920	...	|	...
Wangen (Allgäu) 937 d.	|	...	...	|	...	...	...	...	|	...	1732	...	|	...	...	...	...	...	|	...	|	1935	1935	...	|	...
Hergatz 937 d.	1545	...	...	1615	...	...	...	...	1659	...	1737	...	1744	...	...	...	...	...	1900	...	|	1940	1940	...	1953	...
Lindau Hbf a.	1601	...	...	1631	...	...	...	...	1717	...	...	...	1800	...	...	...	...	...	1917	...	1847	1957	1957	...	2009	...

A – ALLGÄU – (12) (*IC* **2013**) (Leipzig on dates in Table **810** -) Hannover - Dortmund - Köln - Stuttgart - Ulm (*RE* **2013**) - Oberstdorf.
H – NEBELHORN – (12) Hamburg (**2083**) - Augsburg (**2085**) - Oberstdorf. See Table **900** for timings from Hamburg.
K – ⚒ (not Jan. 6, June 3); runs daily from Kempten.
N – From Nürnberg (Table **905**).
Q – From Nürnberg (Table **905**) on Ⓐ (not Dec. 24, 31, Jan. 6, June 3).
R – From Nürnberg (Table **905**) on ⑥ (also Dec. 24, 31; not Dec. 26, May 1).

b – Change trains at Buchloe on © (also Dec. 24, 31, Jan. 6, June 3).
e – Ⓐ (not Dec. 24, 31, Jan. 6, June 3).
j – 1627 on © (also Dec. 24, 31, Jan. 6, June 3).
r – Arrives 1314.

t – On Ⓐ (not Dec. 24, 31, Jan. 6, June 3) departs Augsburg 0812, arrives Buchloe 0843.
v – On Ⓐ (not Dec. 24, 31, Jan. 6, June 3) departs Augsburg 0711, arrives Buchloe 0738.
z – © (also Dec. 24, 31, Jan. 6, June 3).

* – Change trains at Buchloe and Türkheim.
♥ – (12) and ✕ München - Bregenz - St Gallen - Zürich (Table **75**).
◁ – Detached from train in previous column at Immenstadt.
⊖ – On Ⓐ **e** continues to Lindau (0833 departure from Memmingen).
⊡ – Most trains in Table **935** use platforms 27 – 36 at München Hbf (minimum connecting time from other services is 10 minutes).
⊕ – Many services connect at Buchloe, Memmingen, Kempten and Immenstadt (connecting trains may be found in preceding columns). Minimum connectional time is 3 minutes.

ALX – *Arriva-Länderbahn-Express*. Operated by Arriva / Regentalbahn AG - Die Länderbahn.

km		Ⓐe	©z	Ⓐe	©z	Ⓐe					Ⓐe	©z										Ⓐe	©z			
0	**Augsburg** Hbf d.	0559*	0603*	0648*	0729	0733	0803b	0929	1044	1128	1203	1245	1327	1444	1518	1546	1603*	1644	1729	1803*	1845	1940	1940	2045	2147	2309*
40	Buchloe d.	0641	0641	0715	0800	0820	0851	1000	1120	1200	1253	1323	1400	1522	1600	1620	1643	1723	1800	1844	1923	2011	2020	2131	2237	2348
48	Türkheim (Bay) d.	0658	0714	0727	0812	0831	0859	1012	1127	1212	1300	1330	1412	1529	1612	1631	1702	1730	1812	1910	1930	2018	2031	2140	2246	2358
53	**Bad Wörishofen** a.	0704	0720	0733	0818	0837	0906	1018	1133	1218	1306	1336	1418	1535	1618	1637	1708	1736	1818	1916	1936	2024	2037	2147	2252	0004

935 MÜNCHEN, AUGSBURG and ULM - OBERSTDORF and LINDAU

RE / RB services except where shown

For services to / from Bad Wörishofen see panel at foot of page (also on page 437)

									EC 190			ALX										ALX				
		Ⓐe					N	N	♥✗			🍷										🍷			Q	
München Hbf ⊡ d.	...	1739	1751	...	1819	...	...	...	1834	...	1851	1919	...	...	1951	...	...	2039	...	...	...	2141	...	2251	...	2353
München Pasing d.	...	1747	1759	...	1827	...	...	...	|	...	1859	1927	...	...	1959	...	...	2047	...	...	...	2149	...	2259	...	0000
Geltendorf d.	...	|	1823	...	1849	...	...	...	|	...	1922	|	...	...	2022	...	...	2109	...	...	...	2210	...	2323	...	0023
Kaufering d.	...	1816	1832	...	1858	...	...	...	|	...	1931	1956	...	...	2032	...	...	2119	...	...	...	2219	...	2333	...	0033
Augsburg Hbf d.	...	|	|	1803	|	...	1845	1845	|	1903	|	*1940*	...	2003	|	...	2045	|	...	...	2147	|	...	|	2309	|
Buchloe ⊕ a.	...	1824	1842	1838	1906	...	1911	1911	1915	1938	1940	2004	...	2038	2041	...	2122	2128	...	...	2220	2228	...	2342	2345	0042
Buchloe ⊕ d.	...	▬	1844	1847	1907e	...	1913	1913	1918	1944	1944	2011	...	2044	2044	...	2131	2130	...	...	2237	2233	...	2348	2350	▬
Türkheim (Bay) d.	...	...	1851	|	|	...	|	|	|	1951	|	|	...	|	2051	...	2137	|	...	...	2243	|	...	2355	|	...
Kaufbeuren d.	...	...	|	1901	1920e	...	1928	1928	|	|	1956	2026	...	2058	|	...	|	2144	2149	...	|	2248	2253	|	0004	...
Marktoberdorf d.	...	...	|	1918	|	...	|	|	|	|	2012	|	...	2116	|	...	|	|	2205	...	|	|	2311	|	|	...
Füssen a.	...	...	|	1957	|	...	|	|	|	|	2055	|	...	2157	|	...	|	|	2245	...	|	|	2351	|	|	...
Mindelheim d.	...	...	1901	...	|	...	|	|	|	2001v	...	|	...	▬	2059	...	2146	|	▬	...	2251	|	▬	0003	|	...
Ulm Hbf d.	1813	1813	|	...	|	1859	|	|	|	|	...	|	2013	...	|	2059	|	|	...	2213	|	|	...	|	|	2333
Memmingen ⊕ a.	1841	1841	1923	...	|	1930	|	|	1944	2023v	...	|	2041	...	2119	2130	2207	|	...	2255	2314	|	...	0029	|	0026
Memmingen ⊕ d.	1842	1842	...	...	|	1931	|	|	1946	...	...	|	2044	2046	...	2138	...	|	...	2256	*2333*	|	...	...	|	...
Kempten Hbf ⊕ a.	1912	1912	...	...	1950e	1958	1957	1957	|	...	...	2053	2110	|	...	2204	...	2213	...	2322	|	2317	...	...	0035	...
Kempten Hbf ⊕ d.	1917	1917	...	...	...	...	2003	2003	|	...	...	2102	2113	|	...	...	...	2214	...	...	|	2327	...	...	...	...
Immenstadt ⊕ a.	1933	1933	...	...	...	...	2019	2019	|	...	...	2117	2130	|	...	...	...	2231	...	...	|	2343	...	...	...	...
Immenstadt ⊕ d.	1938	1943	...	...	...	...	2024	2030	|	...	...	2124	2136	|	...	...	...	2232	2236	...	|	2344	2347	...	...	...
Sonthofen d.	|	1952	...	...	...	...	|	2040	|	...	...	|	2145	|	...	...	...	|	2245	...	|	|	2356	...	...	...
Oberstdorf a.	|	2010	...	...	...	...	|	2103	|	...	...	|	2204	|	...	...	...	|	2304	...	|	|	0015	...	...	...
Leutkirch d.	|	...	...	...	...	...	|	...	|	...	...	|	...	2113	...	...	...	|	...	...	*0001*	|	...	...	...	...
Kißlegg 937 d.	|	...	...	...	...	...	|	...	|	...	...	|	...	2124	...	...	...	|	...	...	*0010*	|	...	...	...	...
Wangen (Allgäu) 937 d.	|	...	...	...	...	...	|	...	|	...	...	|	...	2135	...	...	...	|	...	...	...	|	...	...	...	...
Hergatz 937 d.	2015	...	...	...	...	...	2104	...	|	...	...	2202	...	2142	...	...	...	2312	...	...	...	0021	...	...	...	...
Lindau Hbf a.	2032	...	...	...	...	...	2120	...	2047	...	...	2218	...	2200	...	...	...	2329	...	...	...	0038	...	...	...	...

km																										
		ALX 🍷					N						ALX												ALX	ALX
		⚒r	Ⓐe		Ⓐe	Ⓐe	Ⓐe	Ⓐe		Ⓐe	Ⓒz	Ⓐe	🍷		Ⓐe	⑥k			N						🍷	
	Lindau Hbf d.	...	...	...	...	...	0440	...	...	...	...	...	0522	...	*0555*	0602	...	...	0640	0703t	...	...	...	0727	...	0747
	Hergatz 937 d.	...	...	...	...	...	0456	...	...	...	...	...	0540	...	0620	0619	...	...	0659	0723t	...	...	...	0744	...	0804
	Wangen (Allgäu) 937 d.	...	...	...	...	...	|	...	...	...	...	...	|	...	0625	0624	...	...	|	0728t	...	...	...	|	...	|
	Kißlegg 937 d.	...	...	...	*0516*	...	|	...	...	...	...	...	|	...	0635	0635	...	...	|	0739t	...	...	...	|	...	|
	Leutkirch d.	...	...	...	*0525*	...	|	...	...	...	...	...	|	...	0644	0644	...	...	|	0747t	...	...	...	|	...	|
0	Oberstdorf d.	...	...	...	|	0503	|	...	...	...	...	...	|	0541	|	|	...	0705	|	|	...	...	0749	|	0805	|
13	Sonthofen d.	...	...	...	|	0521	|	...	...	...	...	...	|	0559	|	|	...	0724	|	|	...	...	0807	|	0822	|
21	Immenstadt ⊕ a.	...	...	...	|	0530	0534	...	...	...	...	...	0616	0610	|	|	...	0734	0737	|	...	...	0818	0822	0835	0841
21	Immenstadt ⊕ d.	...	...	...	|	0538	0545	...	...	...	...	...	0617	0622	|	|	...	▶	0740	|	...	...	▷	0830	0851	0851
46	Kempten Hbf ⊕ a.	...	...	...	|	0554	0601	...	...	...	...	...	0632	0638	|	|	...	▬	0755	|	...	...	▬	0847	0906	0906
46	Kempten Hbf ⊕ d.	0446	...	0542	|	0556	0605	...	...	...	...	...	0648	0641	|	|	...	...	0804	|	0801	...	...	0851	0907	0907
81	Memmingen ⊕ a.	|	...	|	*0552*	0627	|	...	...	...	...	...	|	0712	0710	0710	...	...	|	0813	0827	...	...	0917	|	|
81	Memmingen ⊕ d.	|	0532	|	0600	0628	|	...	...	0622	0635	0652	|	0714	0721	...	0738	...	|	0814	0828	0838	...	0918	|	|
133	Ulm Hbf a.	|	|	|	|	0725	|	...	...	|	|	|	|	0745	0805	...	|	...	|	|	0858	|	...	0945	|	|
	Mindelheim d.	|	0554	|	0621	...	|	...	...	0645	0659	0715	|	▬	...	...	0800	...	|	0831	...	0901	...	...	|	|
	Füssen d.	|	|	|	|	...	|	...	0551	|	|	|	|	...	...	...	|	0703	|	|	...	|	0805	...	|	|
	Marktoberdorf d.	|	|	|	|	...	|	...	0638	|	|	|	|	...	...	...	|	0751	|	|	...	|	0851	...	|	|
	Kaufbeuren d.	0519	|	0616	|	...	0635	...	0652	|	|	|	0720	...	...	...	|	0805	0836	|	...	|	0905	...	0933	0933
	Türkheim (Bay) d.	|	0602	|	0631	...	|	...	|	0653	0706	0724	|	...	...	...	0809	|	|	|	...	0910	|	...	|	|
	Buchloe ⊕ a.	0530	0609	0629	0637	...	0648	...	0707	0700	0713	0730	0731	...	...	...	0816	0817	0848	0843	...	0918	0917	...	0947	0947
	Buchloe ⊕ d.	0534	0610	0631	0640	...	0649	0652	0722f	0713	0714	0735	0733	...	...	...	0823	0820	0849	0851	...	0920	0922	...	0954	0954
	Augsburg Hbf a.	*0607*e	*0647*	|	0712	...	0716	|	0757f	|	|	0811	|	...	...	...	0856	|	0916	|	...	|	0957	...	*1017*	*1017*
	Kaufering d.	0542	0618	0640	...	...	...	0700	...	0721	0723	...	0742	...	...	...	...	0828	...	0900	...	0928	...	...	1002	1002
	Geltendorf d.	|	0628	0650	...	...	...	0710	...	0731	0732	...	|	...	...	...	...	0837	...	0909	...	0937	...	...	|	|
	München Pasing a.	0610	0652	0715	...	...	...	0734	...	0756	0753	...	0811	...	...	...	...	0858	...	0933	...	0958	...	...	1033	1033
	München Hbf ⊡ a.	0618	0700	0724	...	...	...	0744	...	0804	0801	...	0819	...	...	...	...	0907	...	0941	...	1007	...	...	1041	1041

			EC 191								IC 2084	IC 2012	ALX	ALX			EC 193							ALX	ALX	
			♥✗	Ⓒz	Ⓒz	Ⓐe	Ⓐe				H	A 🍷	🍷				♥✗							🍷		
Lindau Hbf d.	0806	...	0912	...	0841	...	0841	...	...	...	...	...	...	0959	1007	...	1112	...	1041	...	...	...	...	...	1159	...
Hergatz 937 d.	0823	...	|	...	0900	...	0900	...	...	...	...	...	...	1016	1024	...	|	...	1100	...	...	...	...	...	1216	1222
Wangen (Allgäu) 937 d.	0828	...	|	...	|	...	|	...	...	...	...	...	...	|	1029	...	|	...	|	...	...	...	...	...	|	1227
Kißlegg 937 d.	0838	...	|	...	|	...	|	...	...	...	...	...	...	|	1039	...	|	...	|	...	...	...	...	...	|	1238
Leutkirch d.	0847	...	|	...	|	...	|	...	...	...	...	...	...	|	1049	...	|	...	|	...	...	...	...	...	|	1247
Oberstdorf d.	|	...	|	0900	|	0900	|	...	...	...	0931	0945	1019	|	|	...	|	1101	|	...	...	...	1145	1219	|	|
Sonthofen d.	|	...	|	0922	|	0922	|	...	...	...	0953	1007	1037	|	|	...	|	1120	|	...	...	...	1204	1238	|	|
Immenstadt ⊕ a.	|	...	|	0933	0937	0933	0937	...	...	...	1001	1015	1045	1051	|	...	|	1131	1136	...	...	...	1216	1246	1251	|
Immenstadt ⊕ d.	|	...	|	0940	0940	0940	0940	...	...	...	1016	1034	1058	1058	|	...	|	1139	1139	...	...	...	1233	1258	1258	|
Kempten Hbf ⊕ a.	|	...	|	0956	0956	0956	0956	...	...	...	1032	1050	1112	1112	|	...	|	1155	1155	...	...	...	1249	1312	1312	|
Kempten Hbf ⊕ d.	|	...	|	1004	1004	1004	1004	1004	...	...	1045	1052	1113	1113	|	...	|	1204	1204	1201	...	...	1253	1313	1313	|
Memmingen ⊕ a.	0914	...	1012	|	|	|	|	1027	...	...	|	1112	|	|	1115	...	1212	|	|	1227	...	...	1316	|	|	1313
Memmingen ⊕ d.	0934	...	1014	|	|	|	|	1028	1037	...	|	1124	|	|	1134	...	1214	|	|	1228	1240	...	1317	|	|	1331
Ulm Hbf a.	|	...	|	|	|	|	|	1058	|	...	|	1154	|	|	|	...	|	|	|	1258	|	...	1345	|	|	|
Mindelheim d.	1001	...	|	|	|	|	|	▬	1101	...	|	...	|	|	1201	...	|	|	|	▬	1301	...	...	|	|	1401
Füssen d.	|	0907	|	|	|	|	|	...	|	1005	|	...	|	|	|	1105	|	|	|	...	|	1205	...	|	|	|
Marktoberdorf d.	|	0954	|	|	|	|	|	Ⓒz	|	1050	|	...	|	|	|	1153	|	|	|	...	|	1251	...	|	|	|
Kaufbeuren d.	|	1008	|	1036	1036	1036	1036	1029	|	1104	1114	...	1139	1139	|	1207	|	1236	1236	1229	|	1305	...	1340	1340	|
Türkheim (Bay) d.	1010	|	|	|	|	|	|	|	1110	|	|	...	|	|	1210	|	|	|	|	|	1310	|	...	|	|	1410
Buchloe ⊕ a.	1017	1019	1041	1048	1048	1047	1047	1040	1117	1116	1129	...	1153	1153	1217	1218	1241	1248	1248	1240	1316	1321	...	1353	1353	1417
Buchloe ⊕ d.	1022	1020	1043	1050	1050	1052	1052	1052	1119	1121	1131	...	1154	1154	1222	1220	1243	1250	1250	1252	1325	1322	...	1354	1354	1423
Augsburg Hbf a.	1057	|	|	1116	1116	*1119*	*1119*	|	|	1155	1158	...	*1230*	*1230*	1257	|	|	1316	1316	|	|	1357	...	*1430*	*1430*	1456
Kaufering d.	...	1028	|	...	...	1100	1100	1100	1128	...	...	...	1203	1203	...	1228	|	...	...	1300	1337	...	...	1402	1402	...
Geltendorf d.	...	1037	|	...	...	1109	1109	1109	1137	...	...	...	|	|	...	1237	|	...	...	1310	1347	...	...	|	|	...
München Pasing a.	...	1058	|	...	...	1133	1133	1133	1158	...	...	...	1233	1233	...	1258	|	...	...	1333	1410	...	...	1433	1433	...
München Hbf ⊡ a.	...	1107	1128	...	...	1141	1141	1141	1207	...	...	...	1241	1241	...	1307	1328	...	...	1341	1417	...	...	1441	1441	...

A – ALLGÄU – (12) and 🍷 Oberstdorf - Ulm - Stuttgart - Köln - Dortmund - Hannover (- Leipzig on dates in Table **810**).
H – NEBELHORN – (12) Oberstdorf - Augsburg (**2082**) - Hamburg. See Table **900** for timings to Hamburg.
N – From / to Nürnberg (Table **905**).
Q – From Nürnberg (Table **905**) on † (also Jan. 6, June 3).

e – Ⓐ (not Dec. 24, 31, Jan. 6, June 3).
f – On Ⓐ (not Dec. 24, 31, Jan. 6, June 3) Buchloe d. *0710*, Augsburg a. *0744* (change trains at Buchloe).
g – *1116* on Ⓒ (also Dec. 24, 31, Jan. 6, June 3).
k – Also Dec. 24, 31; not Dec. 26, May 1.
r – Not Jan. 6, June 3.

t – 3–4 minutes later on Ⓐ (not Dec. 24, 31, Jan. 6, June 3).
v – On Ⓐ (not Dec. 24, 31, Jan. 6, June 3) Mindelheim d. 2006, Memmingen a. 2027.
z – Ⓒ (also Dec. 24, 31, Jan. 6, June 3).

***** – Change trains at Türkheim and Buchloe.
♥ – (12) and ✗ München - Bregenz - St Gallen - Zürich and v.v. (Table **75**).
▷ – Attached to train in the next column at Immenstadt.
▶ – On Ⓒ**z** attached to train in next column at Immenstadt (change trains on Ⓐ**e**).
⊡ – Most trains in Table **935** use platforms 27 – 36 at München Hbf (minimum connecting time from / to other services is 10 minutes).
⊕ – Many services connect at Buchloe, Memmingen, Kempten and Immenstadt (connecting trains may be found in preceding columns). Minimum connectional time is 3 minutes.

ALX – Arriva-Länderbahn-Express. Operated by Arriva / Regentalbahn AG - Die Länderbahn.

	Ⓐe	Ⓐe	Ⓐe	Ⓒz	Ⓐe	Ⓒz						Ⓐe	Ⓒz									Ⓒz	Ⓐe			
Bad Wörishofen d.	0544	0613	0643	0656	0711	0740	0823	0921	1023	1141	1223	1324	1341	1425	1540	1623	1651	1741	1823	1855	1941	2023	2029	2108	2208	2324
Türkheim (Bay) a.	0551	0620	0650	0703	0718	0746	0830	0928	1029	1147	1229	1330	1347	1432	1547	1629	1657	1748	1829	1902	1947	2029	2035	2115	2215	2331
Buchloe a.	*0609*	*0637*	*0700*	*0713*	*0730*	0757	0838	0935	1037	1158	1237	1337	1357	1439	1556	1637	*1717*	1758	1836	*1917*	1957	2037	2043	*2125*	*2226*	*2341*
Augsburg Hbf a.	*0647**	*0712*	*0744**	*0757**	*0811*	0830	*0916*	1017	*1119*g	1230	*1316*	1430	1430	*1516*	1630	*1716*	*1757**	1830	*1916*	*1957**	2030	*2116*	*2116*	*2214**	*2316*	*0021*

RE / RB services except where shown — LINDAU and OBERSTDORF - ULM, AUGSBURG and MÜNCHEN — 935

For services from / to Bad Wörishofen see pages 437 and 438

		N	N					ALX 🍷	ALX			EC 195 ♥✕							ALX 🍷	ALX				N Ⓐe	N	
Lindau Hbf d.	...	...	1241	...	...	...	...	...	1359	...	...	1512	...	1441	...	*1521*e	...	1539	...	1559	1608z	...	...	...	1640	...
Hergatz 937 d.	...	...	1259	...	...	...	...	...	1416	1419	...	|	...	1459	...	*1541*e	...	1555	...	1616	1619t	...	...	...	1658	...
Wangen (Allgäu) 937 d.	...	...	|	...	...	...	...	...	|	1428	...	|	...	|	...	*1546*e	...	|	...	|	1624t	...	...	...	|	...
Kißlegg 937 d.	...	...	|	...	...	...	...	...	|	1440	...	|	...	|	...	*1556*e	...	|	...	|	1640	...	...	...	|	...
Leutkirch d.	...	...	|	...	...	...	...	...	|	1450	...	|	...	|	...	*1605*e	...	|	...	|	1650	...	...	...	|	...
Oberstdorf d.	...	1301	|	...	...	...	1351	1420	|	|	...	|	1501	|	...	|	1546	|	1620	|	|	...	1659z	1659	|	...
Sonthofen d.	...	1321	|	...	...	...	1410	1437	|	|	...	|	1521	|	...	|	1616	|	1638	|	|	...	1719z	1719	|	...
Immenstadt ⊕ a.	...	1331	1336	...	...	...	1421	1446	1451	|	...	|	1531	1536	...	|	1627	1633	1646	1651	|	...	1728z	1730	1735	...
Immenstadt ⊕ d.	...	▷	1339	...	...	...	1433	1458	1458	|	...	|	1539	1539	...	|	▷	1638	1658	1658	|	...	1734z	1739	1739	...
Kempten Hbf ⊕ a.	...	▬	1355	...	...	...	1449	1512	1512	|	...	|	1555	1555	...	|	▬	1654	1712	1712	|	...	1749z	1755	1755	...
Kempten Hbf ⊕ d.	1318	...	1404	...	...	...	1452	1513	1513	|	...	|	1604	1604	1600	|	...	1702	1713	1713	|	...	1758	1804	1804	...
Memmingen ⊕ a.	1356	...	|	...	...	...	1517	|	|	1524	...	1612	|	|	1623	*1631*e	...	1727	|	|	1723	...	1819	|	|	...
Memmingen ⊕ d.	1357	...	|	...	1440	...	1531	|	|	1535	...	1614	|	|	1624	1636	...	1731	|	|	1725t	...	1820	|	|	1836
Ulm Hbf a.	1440	...	|	...	|	...	1559	|	|	|	...	|	|	|	1658	|	...	1758	|	|	|	...	1858	|	|	|
Mindelheim d.	...	...	|	...	1504	...	...	|	|	1601	...	|	|	|	▬	1701	...	...	|	|	1801	...	▬	|	|	1901
Füssen d.	...	1306	|	...	|	1405r	...	|	|	|	1507	|	|	|	...	|	1605	...	|	|	|	1705	...	|	|	|
Marktoberdorf d.	...	1355	|	...	|	1451	...	|	|	|	1554	|	|	|	...	|	1650	...	|	|	|	1751	...	|	|	|
Kaufbeuren d.	...	1408	1434	...	|	1505	...	1539	1539	|	1607	|	1636	1636	1629	|	1704	...	1739	1739	|	1805	1828	1835	1835	|
Türkheim (Bay) d.	...	|	|	...	1511	|	...	|	|	1610	|	|	|	|	|	1710	|	...	|	|	1810	|	|	|	|	1910
Buchloe ⊕ a.	...	1419	1448	...	1518	1517	...	1553	1553	1616	1618	1641	1648	1648	1640	1717	1716	...	1753	1753	1816	1817	1839	1846	1846	1917
Buchloe ⊕ d.	...	1420	1449	1452	1520	1522	...	1554	1554	1622	1619	1643	1649	1649	1651	1719	1723	...	1754	1754	1820	1819	1850	1849	1849	1919
Augsburg Hbf a.	...	|	1516	|	|	1557	...	*1630*	*1630*	1656	|	|	1716	1716	|	|	1757	...	*1830*	*1830*	1856	|	|	1916	1916	|
Kaufering d.	...	1428	...	1500	1528	...	...	1603	1603	...	1627	|	...	...	1700	1728	...	...	1803	1803	...	1827	1859	...	...	1928
Geltendorf d.	...	1437	...	1509	1537	...	...	|	|	...	1637	|	...	...	1710	1737	...	...	|	|	...	1837	1910	...	...	1937
München Pasing a.	...	1458	...	1533	1558	...	...	1633	1633	...	1658	|	...	...	1734	1758	...	...	1833	1833	...	1857	1933	...	...	1957
München Hbf ⊡ a.	...	1507	...	1541	1607	...	...	1641	1641	...	1707	1728	...	...	1742	1807	...	...	1841	1841	...	1907	1941	...	...	2007

			ALX 🍷	ALX		Ⓒz	Ⓐe	R	R	Ⓒz	Ⓐe						Ⓐe	EC 197 ♥✕		ALX 🍷	ALX					
Lindau Hbf d.	...	1728	...	1758	...	1746	...	...	1842	...	...	...	...	1933	...	2009	...	2016	...	...	2030	...	...	2135	...	...
Hergatz 937 d.	...	1745	...	1816	...	1818	1818	...	1859	...	...	...	...	1949	...	2029	...	|	...	...	2047	...	...	2151	...	...
Wangen (Allgäu) 937 d.	...	|	...	|	...	1828	1828	...	|	...	...	...	...	|	...	2034	...	|	...	...	|	...	...	|	...	...
Kißlegg 937 d.	...	|	...	|	...	1840	1840	...	|	...	...	...	...	|	...	2044	...	|	...	...	|	...	...	|	...	...
Leutkirch d.	...	|	...	|	...	1850	1850	...	|	...	...	...	...	|	...	2053	...	|	...	...	|	...	...	|	...	...
Oberstdorf d.	1741	|	1816	|	...	|	|	1904	|	...	...	...	1949	|	...	|	...	|	...	2051	|	...	2151	|	...	...
Sonthofen d.	1807	|	1838	|	...	|	|	1923	|	...	...	...	2011	|	...	|	...	|	...	2110	|	...	2214	|	...	...
Immenstadt ⊕ a.	1818	1823	1846	1851	...	|	|	1934	1937	...	...	...	2021	2027	...	|	...	|	...	2119	2123	...	2225	2229	...	...
Immenstadt ⊕ d.	▷	1830	1858	1858	...	|	|	1940	1940	...	...	...	▬	2028	...	|	2040h	|	...	2132	2132	...	▬	2233	...	...
Kempten Hbf ⊕ a.	▬	1846	1912	1912	...	|	|	1956	1956	...	...	...	...	2044	...	|	2056h	2120	...	2147	2147	...	...	2250	...	...
Kempten Hbf ⊕ d.	...	1850	1913	1913	...	|	|	2004	2004	1959	2014	...	...	2049z	2047	|	2113	2122	...	2151	2151	2207	...	*2256*	...	2259
Memmingen ⊕ a.	...	1915	|	|	...	1924	1924	|	|	2020	2039	...	...	2116z	|	2125	2137	|	...	|	|	2233	...	*2326*	...	|
Memmingen ⊕ d.	...	1931	|	|	...	1929	1945	|	|	2021	2048	2046	...	2131z	|	▬	2138	|	2143	|	|	2234	2300	*2327*	...	|
Ulm Hbf a.	...	1959	|	|	...	|	|	|	|	2058	2149	|	...	2159z	|	...	2222	|	|	|	|	2322	|	*0001*	...	|
Mindelheim d.	...	...	|	|	...	2001	2006	|	|	▬	...	2112	...	...	|	...	...	|	2211	|	|	...	2326	...	...	|
Füssen d.	1805	...	|	|	1905	|	|	|	|	...	...	|	2003	...	|	...	...	|	|	|	|	...	|	...	2222	|
Marktoberdorf d.	1850	...	|	|	1952	|	|	|	|	...	...	|	2049	...	|	...	...	|	|	|	|	...	|	...	2309	|
Kaufbeuren d.	1904	...	1939	1939	2006	|	|	2036	2036	...	...	|	2102	...	2117	...	...	|	|	2219	2219	...	|	...	2323	2331
Türkheim (Bay) d.	|	...	|	|	|	2011	2020	|	|	...	...	2119	...	...	|	...	...	|	2219	|	|	...	2334	...	...	|
Buchloe ⊕ a.	1916	...	1953	1953	2017	2017	2026	2048	2048	...	...	2125	...	...	2130	←	...	2204	2226	2232	2232	...	2341	...	...	2345
Buchloe ⊕ d.	1922	...	1954	1954	2020z	2022	2027	2049	2049	2051	...	→	...	...	2141	2134	...	2206	2241	2233	2233	...	2348	...	...	2346
Augsburg Hbf a.	1957	...	*2030*	*2030*	|	2056	2103	2116	2116	|	...	...	...	...	2214	|	...	|	2316	|	|	...	0021	...	...	|
Kaufering d.	...	...	2003	2003	2028z	...	...	...	...	2059	...	...	...	...	...	2142	...	|	...	2241	2241	...	...	...	...	2356
Geltendorf d.	...	...	|	|	2037z	...	...	...	...	2109	...	...	...	...	...	2151	...	|	...	2250	2250	...	...	...	...	0006
München Pasing a.	...	...	2033	2033	2058z	...	...	...	...	2129	...	...	...	...	...	2214	...	|	...	2312	2312	...	...	...	...	0030
München Hbf ⊡ a.	...	...	2041	2041	2107z	...	...	...	...	2137	...	...	...	...	...	2221	...	2245	...	2320	2320	...	...	...	...	0039

N – To Nürnberg (Table **905**).
R – To Nürnberg (Table **905**) on † (also Jan. 6, June 3).

e – Ⓐ (not Dec. 24, 31, Jan. 6, June 3).
h – ①–④ (not Dec. 24, 31, Jan. 6, Apr. 5, May 13, 24, June 3).
r – Change trains at Marktoberdorf on Ⓐ (not Dec. 24, 31, Jan. 6, June 3).
t – 5 minutes later on Ⓒ (also Dec. 24, 31, Jan. 6, June 3).
z – Ⓒ (also Dec. 24, 31, Jan. 6, June 3).

♥ – (12) and ✕ Zürich - St Gallen - Bregenz - München (Table **75**).
▷ – Attached to train in the next column at Immenstadt.
⊡ – Most trains in Table **935** use platforms 27 – 36 at München Hbf (minimum connecting time to other services is 10 minutes).
⊕ – Many services connect at Buchloe, Memmingen, Kempten and Immenstadt (connecting trains may be found in preceding columns). Minimum connectional time is 3 minutes.

ALX – Arriva-Länderbahn-Express. Operated by Arriva / Regentalbahn AG - Die Länderbahn.

IRE / RE services — STUTTGART - TÜBINGEN - HORB — 936

km			Ⓐe	Ⓒz	Ⓐe				
0	**Stuttgart** Hbf 930 937 d.	0048	0522	*0517*	0616	0722	0822		2322
22	Plochingen 930 d.	0107	0541	0558	0639	0742	0844	and	2344
35	Nürtingen d.	0118	0552	0609	0651	0755	0855	hourly	2355
57	Reutlingen Hbf 937 d.	0135	0608	0627	0708	0812	0912	until	0012
71	**Tübingen** Hbf 937 a.	0148	0619	0640	0720	0823	0923		0023

			Ⓒz	Ⓐe		Ⓒz	Ⓐe				
Tübingen Hbf 937 d.	0537	0625	0730	0737	0837	0932	0937	1037		2137	2236
Reutlingen Hbf 937 d.	0547	0635	0740	0748	0848	0943	0948	1048	and	2148	2250
Nürtingen d.	0604	0651	0757	0804	0904	0959	1004	1104	hourly	2204	2306
Plochingen 930 d.	0618	0701	0818	0818	0918	1018	1018	1118	until	2218	2318
Stuttgart Hbf 930 937 a.	0638	0723	0838	0838	0938	1038	1038	1138		2238	2338

TÜBINGEN Hbf - **HORB** *32 km.* 2nd class only. Journey time: 28 – 40 minutes.

From **Tübingen** Hbf at 0535 Ⓐ**e**, 0558 Ⓐ**e**, 0633 Ⓐ**e**, 0641 Ⓒ**z**, 0805, 0835 Ⓒ**z**, 1005, 1035, 1204, 1235, 1303* Ⓐ**e**, 1405, 1435, 1605, 1635, 1703 Ⓐ**e**, 1805, 1835, 1933 Ⓐ**e**, 2006, 2036, 2133 Ⓒ**z** and 2236. From **Horb** at 0455 Ⓐ**e**, 0619 Ⓐ**e**, 0640 Ⓒ**z**, 0648 Ⓐ**e**, 0730 Ⓐ**e**, 0750 Ⓒ**z**, 0848, 0924, 1048, 1124, 1248, 1324, 1417 Ⓐ**e**, 1448, 1524, 1648, 1724, 1817 Ⓐ**e**, 1848, 1924, 2048, 2124 and 2249 Ⓒ**z**.

e – Not Dec. 24, 31, Jan. 6, June 3.
z – Also Dec. 24, 31, Jan. 6, June 3.
* – Arrives Horb 1350.

DB (*IRE / RB* services); HzL — STUTTGART - TÜBINGEN - AULENDORF - HERGATZ — 937

km		2⑥k	2Ⓐe	2Ⓐe	2Ⓐe	2Ⓒz	‡Ⓐe		‡Ⓒz	‡Ⓐ		‡		‡		‡		‡◧		‡		‡	2		†v	‡
0	**Stuttgart** Hbf 936 d.	...	...	...	...	...	...	...	...	*0616*	0816	*0822*	1016	*1022*	1216	*1222*	1416	*1422*	1616	*1622*	1816	*1822*	...	2016	...	*2122*
57	Reutlingen 936 d.	...	...	...	...	...	...	...	...	*0708*	0849	*0912*	1049	*1112*	1249	*1312*	1449	*1512*	1649	*1712*	1849	*1912*	...	2049	...	*2212*
71	**Tübingen** Hbf 936 d.	...	...	...	...	...	0546	0658	0725	0727	0900	0928	1100	1128	1300	1328	1500	1528	1700	1728	1900	1928	...	2100	...	2234
96	Hechingen d.	...	...	...	...	...	0616	0717	0749	0753	0919	0952	1119	1152	1320	1352	1519	1552	1719	1752	1918	1952	...	2119	...	2257
113	Balingen (Württ) d.	...	...	...	...	...	0638	0731	0808	0808	0932	1007	1132	1206	1335	1406	1535	1607	1733	1807	1930	2010	...	2133	...	2312
131	Albstadt-Ebingen d.	...	...	...	...	...	0659	0744	0829	0829	0945	1029	1145	1229	1347	1429	1547	1631	1746	1830	1945	2030	...	2150	...	2331
158	**Sigmaringen** a.	...	...	...	...	...	0723	0809	0853	0853	1011	1054	1209	1254	1411	1454	1611	1656	1811	1854	2010	2054	...	2211	...	2355v
158	**Sigmaringen** 938 d.	...	...	0540	0645	0655	*0729*	0810	0901	0901	1012	1058	1211	1303	1411	1503	1611	1703	1812	1903	2012	...	2111	2213	2233	...
175	Herbertingen 938 d.	...	...	0555	0708	0712	*0744*	0823	0917	0917	1025	1112	1226	1318	|	1518	1624	1718	1825	1918	2025	...	2130	2230	2247	...
184	Bad Saulgau d.	...	...	0609	0724	0725	...	0832	0927	0927	1034	1127	1235	1327	1432	1527	1633	1727	1834	1927	2034	...	2138	2239	2255	...
203	**Aulendorf** d.	...	...	0625	0741	0741	...	0848	0943	0943	1050	1143	1250	1343	1447	1543	1650	1743	1850	1943	2050	...	2153	2254	2309	...
						2 d				2 d		2		2	2Ⓐe	2	2Ⓐe	2		2			2		2⑦r	
203	**Aulendorf** d.	0556	0554	...	...	0808	...	...	...	1008	...	1208	...	1408	1515	1608	1716	1808	...	2013	...	...	2208	...	2313	...
213	Bad Waldsee d.	0604	0611	...	...	0816	...	...	...	1016	...	1216	...	1416	1524	1616	1724	1816	...	2021	...	...	2216	...	2321	...
233	Kißlegg 935 a.	0620	0630	...	...	0835	...	...	...	1035	...	1235	...	1435	1549	1635	1749	1835	...	2040	...	...	2235	...	2338	...
246	Wangen (Allgäu) 935 a.	*0649*	0648	...	...	0850	...	...	...	1050	...	1250	...	1450	...	1651	...	1849	...	2056	...	...	2252	...	...	...
252	**Hergatz** 935 a.	*0655*	0653	...	...	0855	...	...	...	1056	...	1255	...	1455	...	1656	...	1855	...	2101	...	...	2257	...	...	...

d – Runs daily.
e – Not Dec. 24, 31, Jan. 6, June 3.
k – Also Dec. 24, 31; not Dec. 26, May 1.
r – Also Dec. 26, Jan. 6, Apr. 5, May 13, 24, June 3; not Apr. 4, May 23.
v – † (also Jan. 6, June 3).
z – Also Dec. 24, 31, Jan. 6, June 3.
◧ – Change trains at Sigmaringen on Ⓐ**e**.
‡ – Operated by Hohenzollerischen Landesbahnen (HzL) Tübingen - Sigmaringen and v.v. 2nd class only.

937 HERGATZ - AULENDORF - TÜBINGEN - STUTTGART

DB (*IRE* / *RB* services); HzL

	Ⓐe	‡Ⓐe	‡Ⓒz	2Ⓐe		2			2		2		2		2	Ⓐe		2		2⑤¶	2			2		
Hergatz 935 d.	...	...	...	*0526*	*0619*k	0659	...	...	0902	...	1102	...	1302	...	1502	*1619*	...	1702	...	*1818*	1902	...	...	2106	...	...
Wangen (Allgäu) 935 d.	...	...	...	*0531*	*0624*k	0704	...	...	0907	...	1107	...	1307	...	1507	*1624*	...	1707	...	*1828*	1907	...	...	2111	...	...
Kißlegg 935 d.	...	0517	...	0552	0637k	0719	...	...	0922	...	1122	...	1324	...	1522	1637	...	1722	...	1841	1922	...	...	2126	...	...
Bad Waldsee d.	...	0535	...	0614	0653k	0737	...	...	0940	...	1140	...	1342	...	1540	1653	...	1740	...	1857	1940	...	...	2144	...	...
Aulendorf a.	...	0543	...	0622	0700k	0745	...	...	0948	...	1148	...	1350	...	1548	1701	...	1748	...	1905	1948	...	...	2151	...	...
		|		|	|	2	‡		‡		‡		‡		‡◧	|		‡		▬	2	‡	2	2Ⓐe	2†w	2
Aulendorf d.	...	0553	...	0633	0707	0812	...	0907	1012	1107	1212	1307	1412	1507	1612	1706	1706	1812	1907	...	2012	...	2118	2201	2201	2313
Bad Saulgau d.	...	0608	...	0650	0723	0832	...	0926	1034	1123	1235	1327	1433	1527	1633	1727	1727	1834	1927	...	2034	...	2139	2218	2218	2330
Herbertingen 938 d.	...	0616	...	0702	0732	0840	...	0937	1044	1132	1244	1337	1444	1537	1643	1737	1737	1844	1937	...	2044	...	2148	2230	2230	2339
Sigmaringen 938 a.	...	0630	...	0719	0748	0856	...	0949	1057	1146	1258	1348	1458	1548	1657	1749	1749	1858	1948	...	2100	...	2205	2247	2253	2355
Sigmaringen d.	0545	0634	0657	...	0749	...	0900	0950	1100	1148	1303	1350	1500	1550	1701	1750	1750	1910	1949	...	...	2106	...	...	...	...
Albstadt-Ebingen d.	0608	0703	0722	...	0808	...	0924	1010	1124	1210	1327	1410	1528	1609	1725	1811	1811	1934	2009	...	...	2130	...	...	...	...
Balingen (Württ) d.	0620	0734	0746	...	0825	...	0949	1027	1149	1227	1350	1427	1553	1625	1751	1827	1827	1954	2025	...	...	2149	...	...	...	...
Hechingen d.	0634	0752	0804	...	0837	...	1007	1039	1207	1239	1407	1439	1607	1637	1807	1840	1840	2009	2038	...	...	2205	...	...	...	...
Tübingen Hbf 936 a.	0653	0815	0828	...	0857	...	1030	1057	1230	1257	1430	1457	1630	1657	1830	1857	1857	2032	2059	2137	...	2229	...	...	...	...
Reutlingen 936 a.	0707	*0847*	*0847*	...	0908	...	*1047*	1108	*1247*	1308	*1447*	1508	*1647*	1708	*1847*	1908	1908	*2047*	2108f	2147	...	*2249*	...	...	...	...
Stuttgart Hbf 936 a.	0743	*0938*	*0938*	...	0943	...	*1138*	1143	*1338*	1343	*1538*	1543	*1738*	1743	*1938*	1943	1943	*2138*	2143f	2238	...	*2338*	...	...	...	...

e – Not Dec. 24, 31, Jan. 6, June 3.
f – ⑤⑥† (also Dec. 24, 31, Jan. 6, June 3).
k – ⑥ (also Dec. 24, 31; not Dec. 26, May 1).
w – Also Jan. 6, June 3.
z – Also Dec. 24, 31, Jan. 6, June 3.
¶ – Also Dec. 23, 30, Jan. 5, Apr. 1, May 12, June 2; not Dec. 25, Jan. 1, Apr. 2.
◧ – Change trains at Sigmaringen on Ⓐ Dec. 23 - Jan. 8, Ⓐ Apr. 1–9 and Ⓐ May 25 - June 4.
‡ – Operated by Hohenzollerischen Landesbahnen (HzL) Tübingen - Sigmaringen and v.v. 2nd class only.

938 ULM and ROTTWEIL - NEUSTADT (Schwarzw) - FREIBURG

DB (*RE* / *RB* services); HzL

km		Ⓒz	Ⓐe	‡Ⓐe	2Ⓐe		Ⓐe	Ⓒz			2		2		2		2		2		2		‡Ⓐe	2†w	2⚒r
0	**Ulm** Hbf d.	...	...	...	...	...	0552	0605	...	0810	0915	1015	1115	1215	1315	1415	1515	1615	1715	1815	1915	2024	...	2113	2113
16	Blaubeuren d.	...	...	...	...	...	0608	0618	...	0822	0930	1026	1127	1226	1330	1426	1530	1626	1730	1826	1931	2036	...	2129	2131
34	Ehingen (Donau) d.	...	...	...	...	...	0628	0634	...	0834	0942	1039	1142	1239	1343	1439	1543	1639	1742	1839	1945	2053	...	2146	2149
76	Herbertingen 937 d.	...	...	...	...	...	0708	0701	...	0907	1012	1112j	1215	1306	1411	1506	1612	1706	1812	1906	2013	2128	...	2214	2219
93	**Sigmaringen** 937 a.	...	...	...	...	...	0723	0716	...	0922	1028	1125	1229	1322	1428	1522	1628	1722	1828	1922	2029	2142	...	2231	2236
93	**Sigmaringen** d.	...	...	...	...	...	0733	0717	...	0930	▬	1130	▬	1330	▬	1530	▬	1730	▬	1930	▬	▬	...	2239	▬
135	Tuttlingen a.	...	...	...	...	...	0814	0750	...	1010	...	1210	...	1410	...	1610	...	1810	...	2010	...	...	...	2313	...
135	Tuttlingen d.	...	...	...	...	...	0816	0816	...	1016	...	1216	...	1416	...	1616	...	1816	...	2016	...	...	...	2314	...
145	Immendingen 916 d.	...	...	...	...	...	0824	0824	...	1024	...	1224	...	1424	...	1624	...	1824	...	2024	‡	...	...	2323	‡Ⓒw
	Rottweil d.	...	...	0557	0700	0705z	|	|	0911	|	1111	|	1311	|	1511	|	1711	|	1911	|	2119	...	2157	|	2253
	Trossingen Bahnhof ▲ d.	...	...	0607	0713	0716z	|	|	0920	|	1120	|	1320	|	1520	|	1720	|	1920	|	2129	...	2208	|	2303
	Villingen (Schwarzw) 916 d.	0605	0620	0628	0733	0738	|	|	0938	|	1138	|	1338	|	1538	|	1738	|	1938	|	2145	2213	2245f	|	2322
164	Donaueschingen 916 a.	0615	0640	*0645*	...	0749	0839	0839	0949	1039	1149	1239	1349	1439	1549	1639	1749	1839	1949	2039	...	2221	2302	2336	2339
164	Donaueschingen d.	0616	0642	...	...	0750	0848	0848	0950	1048	1150	1248	1350	1448	1550	1648	1750	1848	1950	2048	...	...	...	...	...
204	**Neustadt** (Schwarzw) a.	0656	0726	...	...	0826	0926	0926	1026	1126	1226	1326	1426	1526	1626	1726	1826	1926	2026	2126	...	...	...	...	...

km		2⑥k	‡⑥k	‡Ⓐe	Ⓐe	‡Ⓒz	Ⓒz	Ⓐe														⚒r	2†w	‡Ⓒw	
0	**Neustadt** (Schwarzw) d.	...	...	...	...	...	...	*0626*	0732	0832	0932	1032	1132	1232	1330	1432	1532	1632	1732	1832	1932	2032	2032	...	2202
40	Donaueschingen a.	...	...	...	...	...	...	*0705*	0809	0910	1009	1110	1209	1310	1409	1510	1609	1710	1809	1910	2009	2107	2109	...	2240
40	Donaueschingen 916 d.	...	0458	0503	0518	0715	0720	0719	0810	0919	1010	1119	1210	1319	1410	1519	1610	1719	1810	1919	2010	2108	2119	2122	2241
54	Villingen (Schwarzw) 916 d.	...	0517	0522	|	0736	|	|	0822	|	1022	|	1222	|	1422	|	1622	|	1822	|	2022	2118	|	2146j	2259
69	Trossingen Bahnhof ▲ d.	...	0546h	0538	|	0752	|	|	0835	|	1035	|	1235	|	1435	|	1635	|	1835	|	2035	*2143*e	|	2201	...
81	**Rottweil** a.	...	0556	0549	|	0802	|	|	0844	|	1044	|	1244	|	1444	|	1644	|	1844	|	2044	*2153*e	|	2211	...
	Immendingen 916 d.	...	▬	▬	0532	▬	0734	0740j	▬	0934	▬	1134	▬	1334	▬	1534	▬	1734	▬	1934	...	...	2134	...	...
	Tuttlingen a.	...	...	...	0539	...	0741	0748	...	0941	...	1141	...	1342	...	1541	...	1741	...	1941	...	...	2141	...	...
	Tuttlingen d.	...	...	...	0542	...	0751	0751	...	0947	...	1147	...	1347	...	1547	...	1747	...	1947	...	...	2156	...	...
	Sigmaringen a.	...	2Ⓐe	2Ⓒz	0622	2	0825	0825	2	1022	2	1222	2	1422	2	1622	2	1822	2	2022	...	...	2231	...	...
	Sigmaringen 937 d.	0520	0534	0611	0633	0729	0835	0835	0924	1030	1128	1230	1323	1430	1524	1629	1724	1830	1924	2030	...	...	2233	...	...
	Herbertingen 937 d.	0533	0548	0626	0646	0744	0851	0851	0938	1045	1143	1246	1338	1445	1538	1645	1738	1845	1938	2046	...	...	2247	...	...
	Ehingen (Donau) d.	0602	0617	0702	0715	0815	0918	0918	1011	1118	1211	1317	1411	1518	1611	1718	1811	1919	2013	2112	...	...	...	...	...
	Blaubeuren d.	0619	0633	0720	0732	0833	0930	0930	1027	1130	1227	1330	1427	1530	1627	1730	1827	1931	2025	2131	...	...	...	...	...
	Ulm Hbf a.	0637	0644	0740	0744	0844	0942	0942	1039	1142	1239	1342	1439	1542	1639	1742	1839	1942	2042	2143	...	...	...	...	...

km		Ⓐe	Ⓐe	⚒r	Ⓐe	Ⓐe	Ⓐe	Ⓐe	Ⓒy	Ⓒz	Ⓐe	Ⓑm										n🚌		n
0	**Neustadt** (Schwarzw) d.	🚌	0529	0558	0608	🚌	0631	...	0701	0708	...	0731	0801	...	0831	...	and at the same minutes past each hour until	...	2031	...	...	2040	2131	2223
	Seebrugg d.	0459	|	|	|	0601	|	0641	|	|	0705	|	|	...	|	0839		1939	|	...	2021	|	|	|
5	Titisee d.	0531	0536	0605	0614	0633	0638	0708	0708	0715	0731	0738	0808	...	0838	0908		2008	2038	...	2048	2055	2138	2230
36	**Freiburg** (Brsg) Hbf a.	...	0615	0643	...	...	0719	0748	0748	...	...	0818	0848	...	0918	0948		2048	2118	...	...	2148	2218	2313

km		Ⓐe	Ⓐe	⑥k	Ⓐe	Ⓐe	Ⓒz	Ⓒz	Ⓐe	Ⓐe										n🚌				n
0	**Freiburg** (Brsg) Hbf d.	...	0538	🚌	...	0640	0640	...	0710	...	0742	...	0810	0840	and at the same minutes past each hour until	1910	1940	...	2010	...	...	2110	2225	2325
31	Titisee d.	0608	0615	0628	0630	0719	0722	0724	0749	0752	0819	...	0849	0919		1949	2019	...	2049	2053	2058	2149	2301	0001
50	**Seebrugg** a.	0633	|	0701	0658	|	0748	|	|	0818	|	...	0916	|		2016	|	...	|	2126	|	|	|	|
	Neustadt (Schwarzw) a.	...	0621	...	...	0725	...	0730	0755	...	0825	...	...	0925		...	2025	...	2055	...	2104	2155	2307	0007

e – Ⓐ (not Dec. 24, 31, Jan. 6, June 3).
f – Arrives 2224.
h – Arrives 0532.
j – Arrives 7 minutes earlier.
k – Also Dec. 24, 31; not Dec. 26, May 1.
m – Also Dec. 26, May 1; not Dec. 24, 31.
n – Not Dec. 24, 31.
r – Not Jan. 6, June 3.
w – Also Jan. 6, June 3.
y – Also Dec. 24, 31, Jan. 6, June 3; not Dec. 25.
z – Ⓒ (also Dec. 24, 31, Jan. 6, June 3).
‡ – Operated by Hohenzollerischen Landesbahnen (HzL). 2nd class only.
▲ – Regular services operate to / from Trossingen Stadt (operated by HzL). Journey time: 5 minutes.

939 LINDAU - SCHAFFHAUSEN - BASEL

IRE / *RB* services

km			v	Ⓐe	Ⓒz	2Ⓐ	2Ⓒz	U	2	U	2	U	2	U	⑥⑦k	2	U	2	U	2	2	2†w	2⚒r	2†w	2
0	**Lindau** Hbf 933 d.	...	...	0637	0647	0703	*0706*	*0834*	*0906*	*1034*	*1102*	*1234*	*1302*	*1434*	...	*1502*	*1635*	*1702*	*1834*	*1902*	2012	2012	*2103*	*2103*	*2132*
24	**Friedrichshafen** Stadt 933 d.	0436e	...	0704	0713	0732	0732	0914	0938	1114	1138	1313	1338	1513	1525	1538	1714	1740	1915	1933	2035	2035	2130	2130	2240
58	Überlingen d.	0514e	...	0730	0733	0807	0807	0934	1012	1134	1212	1334	1412	1534	1600	1612	1734	1814	1934	2010	2113	2113	2155	2155	2317
83	Radolfzell 916 d.	0540e	0637	0753	0753	0843	0843	0953	1043	1153	1243	1353	1443	1553	1631	1643	1753	1843	1953	2043	2140	2141	2213	2212	2343
93	**Singen** 916 a.	0547e	0647	0800	0800	*0856*	*0856*	1000	*1056*	1200	*1256*	1400	*1456*	1600	1640	*1656*	1800	*1856*	2000	*2056*	...	2149	2222	*2232*	2350
		|	Ⓐn	|	|	Ⓐn		|	Ⓐn	|	Ⓐn	|	Ⓑm	|	|	Ⓐn	|	Ⓑm	|	2		2d	▬	2d	
93	**Singen** 🏛 940 d.	0552	0651	0802	0802	0902	...	1002	1102	1202	1302	1402	1502	1602	1643	1702	1802	1902	2002	2106	...	2206	2	2306	...
112	**Schaffhausen** 🏛 940 d.	0611	0710	0815	0815	0915	...	1015	1115	1215	1315	1415	1515	1615	1658	1715	1815	1915	2015	2126	...	2224	2302	0002t	...
131	Erzingen (Baden) 🏛 d.	0625	0729	0829	0829	0929	...	1029	1129	1229	1329	1429	1529	1629	1714	1729	1829	1929	2029	2142	...	...	2324	0024	...
151	Waldshut d.	0640	0742	0842	0842	0942	...	1042	1142	1242	1344	1442	1542	1642	1733	1742	1842	1942	2042	2157	...	...	2342	...	...
174	Bad Säckingen d.	0654	0755	0855	0855	0955	...	1055	1155	1255	1356	1455	1555	1655	1752	1755	1855	1955	2055	2218	...	...	...	...	...
191	Rheinfelden (Baden) d.	0704	0805	0905	0905	1005	...	1105	1205	1305	1405	1505	1605	1705	1805	1805	1905	2005	2105	2234	...	...	...	...	...
206	**Basel** Bad Bf a.	0715	0816	0916	0916	1016	...	1116	1216	1316	1416	1516	1616	1716	1816	1816	1916	2016	2116	2250	...	...	...	...	...

		2⚒	2Ⓐe	2Ⓐe	2Ⓒz	U	Ⓐn	U	Ⓐn	⑥⑦k	U			Ⓐn	U	Ⓐn	U	Ⓐn	U	Ⓑm	U		Ⓐn		n2
Basel Bad Bf d.	...	...	...	0456	...	0638	0743	0843	0943	0925	1043	...	...	1143	1243	1343	1443	1543	1643	1743	1843	1943	2043	2143	2258
Rheinfelden (Baden) d.	...	...	...	0512	...	0647	0751	0851	0951	0940	1051	...	...	1151	1251	1351	1451	1551	1651	1751	1851	1951	2051	2151	2312
Bad Säckingen d.	...	...	...	0530	...	0658	0801	0901	1001	0953	1101	...	...	1201	1301	1401	1501	1601	1701	1801	1901	2001	2101	2201	2328
Waldshut d.	...	...	...	0556	0602	0712	0815	0915	1015	1015	1115	...	...	1215	1315	1415	1515	1615	1715	1815	1915	2015	2115	2215	2350
Erzingen (Baden) 🏛 d.	...	...	*0531*	0625	0632	0729	0829	0929	1029	1029	1129	...	...	1229	1329	1429	1529	1629	1729	1829	1929	2029	2128	2231	...
Schaffhausen 🏛 940 d.	...	0527	0556	0644	0700	0742	0842	0942	1042	1044	1142	...	...	1242	1342	1442	1542	1642	1742	1842	1942	2042	2146	2244	...
Singen 🏛 940 a.	...	0547	0617	0702	0717	0756	0856	0956	1056	1058	1156	...	...	1256	1356	1456	1556	1656	1756	1856	1956	2056	2202	2259	...
	2Ⓐe	2Ⓒz	|	d	v	|	2d	|	2d	|	|	2Ⓒz		2d	|	2d	|	2d	|	2d	|	2d	2d	|	
Singen 916 d.	0538	0610	0619	0709	0723	0758	*0902*	0958	*1102*	1109	1158	...	...	*1302*	1358	*1502*	1558	*1702*	1758	*1902*	1958	*2102*	*2212*	2307	...
Radolfzell 916 d.	0546	0618	0627	0718	0732	0806	0914	1006	1114	1127q	1206	...	...	1314	1406	1514	1606	1714	1806	1918	2006	2118	2228	2317	...
Überlingen d.	0610	0642	0654	...	...	0824	0942	1024	1142	1154	1224	...	...	1342	1424	1542	1624	1742	1824	1955	2025	2141	2251	2345	...
Friedrichshafen Stadt 933 a.	0648	0724	0744	...	...	0843	1026	1043	1222	1226	1243	1254	1329	1422	1443	1622	1643	1827	1843	2030	2044	2219	2326	0026	...
Lindau Hbf 933 a.	*0737*	0750	0827	...	...	*0907*	*1055*	*1124*	*1255*	*1255*	...	1324	1353	*1454*	*1524*	*1655*	*1724*	...	*1924*	*2056*	*2126*	2259	*0014*	...	...

U – From / to Ulm (Table **933**).
d – Daily.
e – Ⓐ (not Dec. 24, 31, Jan. 6, June 3).
k – Also Apr. 2, 5, May 13, 24.
m – Also Dec. 26, May 1; not Dec. 24, 31.
n – Not Dec. 24, 31.
q – Arrives 1117.
r – Not Jan. 6, June 3.
t – Arrives 2327.
v – Not Dec. 25, 26, Jan. 1.
w – Also Jan. 6, June 3.
z – Also Dec. 24, 31, Jan. 6, June 3.

STUTTGART - SINGEN - SCHAFFHAUSEN - ZÜRICH 940

km																										
									ICE 181			ICE 183		ICE 185		ICE 187		ICE 281		ICE 283			ICE 285			
					‡ Ⓐe	Ⓒz		Ⓐe	✕			✕		✥		✕		✕		✕			⊖			⊠
0	**Stuttgart** Hbf ..... **942** d.	...	...	...	0518	0618	...	0618	0758	0818	0918	0955	1018	1153	1218	1355	1418	1553	1618	1755	1818	1918	1958	2018	2118	2225
26	Böblingen .... **942** d.	...	...	...	0538	0638	...	0638	|	0838	0938	|	1038	|	1238	|	1440	|	1638	|	1838	1938	|	2038	2138	2245
42	Herrenberg .... **942** d.	...	...	...	0547	0650	...	0650	|	0850	0948	|	1050	|	1250	|	1450	|	1650	|	1850	1948	|	2050	2147	2259
57	Eutingen im Gäu **942** d.	...	...	...	0600	0705	...	0705	|	0907	1004	|	1107	|	1307	|	1507	|	1707	|	1907	2004	|	2105	2203	2314
67	Horb .... d.	...	...	...	0608	0714	...	0717	0841	0917	1012	1040	1117	1240	1317	1440	1517	1640	1717	1840	1917	2012	2041	2117	2213	2322
110	Rottweil .... d.	...	...	...	0641	0744	...	0751	0910	0951	1047	1110	1151	1310	1351	1510	1551	1710	1751	1910	1951	2047	2110	2149	2249z	2353
138	Tuttlingen .... d.	...	...	...	0720	0805	...	0818j	0927	1014	...	1127	1214	1327	1414	1527	1614	1727	1814	1927	2014	...	2127	2220	▬	0014
157	Engen .... **916** d.	...	...	...	0736	0822	...	0835	|	1030	...	|	1230	|	1430	|	1630	|	1830	|	2030	...	|	▬	...	0029
172	**Singen** .... **916** a.	...	...	...	0746	0833	...	0844	0949	1040	...	1149	1240	1349	1440	1549	1639	1749	1840	1949	2040	...	2149	...	...	0040
																										⑥⑦c
172	**Singen** .... **939** d.	0552	0631	0734	0751	...	0834r	0906	0954	1034	...	1154	1234	1354	1434	1554	1634	1754	1834	1954	2006	...	2156	2206	2306	0046
191	**Schaffhausen** ▦ **939** a.	0604	0652	0753	0806	...	0853	0924	1007	1053	...	1207	1253	1407	1453	1607	1653	1807	1853	2007	2024	...	2209	2224	2327	0102
191	**Schaffhausen** ▦ ...... d.	0607	0707	0754	...	0809	0909	...	1009	1109	...	1209	1309	1409	1509	1609	1709	1809	1909	2009	2109	...	2211	2309	0009	0103
219	Bülach .... d.	0630	0730	0826	...	0830	0930	...	1030	1130	...	1230	1330	1430	1530	1630	1730	1830	1930	2030	2130	...	2231	2330	0031	0132
239	**Zürich** HB .... a.	0648	0748	...	...	0848	0948	...	1048	1148	...	1248	1348	1448	1548	1648	1748	1848	1948	2048	2148	...	2248	2348	0048	0156

							ICE 284			ICE 282		ICE 280		ICE 186		ICE 184			ICE 182		ICE 180					
			2⚒				⊡			✕		✕		✕		△			✕		✕					
Zürich HB .... d.	0017	...	...	...	0504	0610	0710	...	0810	0910	1010	1110	1210	1310	1410	1510	1610	1705	1710	1810	1910	...	2010	2110	2210	2310
Bülach .... d.	0040	...	...	...	0531	0631	0731	...	0831	0931	1031	1131	1231	1331	1431	1531	1631	1725	1731	1831	1931	...	2031	2131	2231	2331
Schaffhausen ▦....... a.	0107	...	...	...	0610	0657	0750	...	0852	0950	1052	1150	1252	1350	1452	1550	1654	1749	1751	1854	1951	...	2052	2152	2252	2352
Schaffhausen ▦ **939** d.	0110c	...	0527	...	0630	0710	0752	...	0904	0952	1104	1152	1304	1352	1504	1552	1704	...	1752	1904	1953	...	2104	2204v	▬	0004c
Singen ....**939** a.	0130c	...	0547	...	0649	0729	0805	...	0924	1005	1124	1205	1324	1405	1524	1605	1724	...	1805	1924	2005	...	2126	2224v	...	0024c
			Ⓐe																				Ⓒz¶			
Singen ....**916** d.	...	...	0551	...	0714k	...	0809	...	0919	1009	1119	1209	1319	1409	1519	1609	1719	...	1809	1919	2009	...	2130	...	...	...
Engen ....**916** d.	...	...	0600	...	0724k	...	|	...	0928	|	1128	|	1328	|	1528	|	1728	...	|	1928	|	...	2139	...	...	...
Tuttlingen .... d.	Ⓐe	...	0614	...	0739k	...	0832	...	0945	1032	1145	1232	1345	1432	1545	1632	1745	...	1832	1945	2032	...	2153	...	...	...
Rottweil .... d.	0505	0603	0639	0700t	0810	...	0849	0909	1010	1049	1210	1249	1410	1449	1610	1649	1811	...	1849	2010	2049	...	2215	...	...	...
Horb .... d.	0539	0642	0710	0743	0846	...	0921	0943	1046	1121	1246	1321	1446	1521	1646	1721	1846	...	1921	2046	2121	2146	2246	Ⓐe	...	...
Eutingen im Gäu..**942** d.	0554	0655	|	0756	0857	...	|	0956	1057	|	1257	|	1457	|	1657	|	1857	...	|	2057	|	2159	2256	2257	...	...
Herrenberg ....**942** d.	0611	0711	0726	0811	0912	...	|	1010	1111	|	1311	|	1511	|	1711	|	1911	...	|	2111	|	2212	2310	2311	2317	...
Böblingen ....**942** d.	0622	0722	0736	0822	0922	...	|	1021	1122	|	1322	|	1522	|	1722	|	1922	...	|	2122	|	2230	2322	...	2330	...
Stuttgart Hbf.......**942** a.	0642	0743	0757	0842	0942	...	1006	1042	1142	1202	1342	1406	1542	1602	1742	1806	1942	...	2007	2142	2206	2255	2343	...	2355	...

c – ⑥⑦ (also Jan. 1, Apr. 2, 5, May 13, 14, 24).
e – Not Dec. 24, 31, Jan. 6, June 3.
j – Arrives 0811.
k – On Ⓒz departs Singen 0722, Engen 0731, Tuttlingen 0745.
r – 0838 on Ⓒ (also Dec. 24, 31).
t – 0703 on Ⓐe.
v – ⑥⑦ (also Dec. 24, 25, 31, Jan. 1, Apr. 2, 5, May 13, 24).
z – Ⓒ (also Dec. 24, 31, Jan. 6, June 3).
⊠ – Change trains at Horb on Ⓒ until Mar. 21 (also Dec. 24, 31, Jan. 6; not Dec. 19).
¶ – Change trains at Horb until Mar. 21 (except on Dec. 19).
△ – Runs as *IC* **486** on ①–④. Conveys ✕ on ⑤–⑦.
✥ – Runs as *IC* **487** on ①–④. Conveys ✕ on ⑤–⑦.
⊡ – Runs as *IC* **488** on ②–④. Conveys ✕ on ①⑤⑥⑦.
⊖ – Runs as *IC* **489** on ①–③. Conveys ✕ on ④–⑦.
‡ – Operated by Hohenzollerischen Landesbahnen Rottweil - Singen.

PFORZHEIM - HORB and BAD WILDBAD 941

RB services (2nd class only)

km																										
		Ⓐe	⑥k	Ⓐe	Ⓐe	Ⓐe	Ⓒz	Ⓒz	Ⓐe								Ⓐe		Ⓐe		Ⓐe		n	Ⓐe	Ⓒz	n
0	**Horb** .... d.	0453	0540	0548	0616	0649	0653	0751	0753	0853	0953	1053	1153	1253	1353	1453	...	1553	...	1653	...	1753	1853	1927	1953	...
15	Hochdorf (b. Horb)..... d.	0504	0551	0559	0627	0700	0704	0802	0803	0904	1004	1104	1204	1304	1404	1504	...	1604	...	1704	...	1804	1904	1955h	2004	2216
25	Nagold .... d.	0518	0601	0609	0637	0710	0714	0814	0814	0914	1014	1114	1214	1314	1414	1514	1544	1614	1644	1714	1744	1813	1914	2014j	2014	2229
34	Wildberg (Württ)........ d.	0526	0609	0617	0645	0718	0722	0822	0822	0922	1022	1122	1222	1322	1422	1522	1551	1622	1651	1722	1751	1822	1922	2022	2022	2237
45	Calw .... d.	0537	0620	0628	0657	0731	0736	0835	0835	0935	1035	1135	1235	1333	1432	1532	1603	1633	1703	1732	1803	1835	1935	2035	2035	2248
52	Bad Liebenzell .... d.	0545	0629	0643j	0705	0744	0744	0842	0842	0943	1043	1143	1243	1344	1444	1544	1614	1644	1714	1744	1814	1843	1943	2043	2043	2255
71	**Pforzheim** Hbf.......... a.	0607	0651	0706	0726	0808	0808	0907	0907	1007	1107	1207	1307	1407	1507	1607	1637	1707	1737	1807	1836	1907	2007	2107	2107	2318

	Ⓐe	Ⓐe	v					Ⓐe		Ⓐe		Ⓐe		Ⓐe		Ⓐe		Ⓐe		Ⓐe			n		n	⑤f
Pforzheim Hbf........... d.	0443	0638	0749	0849	0949	1049	1149	1219	1249	1319	1349	1419	1449	1519	1549	1619	1649	1719	1749	1837	1849	1949	2049	2139	2349	2349
Bad Liebenzell .... d.	0505	0707j	0815	0915	1015	1115	1215	1245	1315	1345	1415	1445	1515	1545	1615	1645	1715	1745	1815	1859	1915	2015	2111	2201	0010	0010
Calw .... d.	0512	0717	0822	0922	1022	1122	1222	1252	1322	1352	1422	1452	1522	1552	1622	1652	1722	1752	1822	1907	1922	2022	2118	2208	0018	0018
Wildberg (Württ) .... d.	0527	0733	0835	0935	1035	1135	1235	1305	1335	1405	1435	1505	1535	1605	1635	1705	1735	1805	1835	1922	1935	2035	2129	2220	0030	0030
Nagold.......................... d.	0537	0743	0843	0943	1043	1143	1243	1313	1343	1413	1443	1513	1543	1613	1643	1713	1743	1814	1843	1930	1943	2043	2138	2230	0037	0038
Hochdorf (b. Horb)...... d.	0548	0753	0853	0953	1053	1153	1253	...	1353	...	1453	...	1553	...	1653	...	1753	1824	1853	1940	1953	2053	2148	2252j	...	0048
Horb............................ a.	0600	0805	0905	1005	1105	1205	1305	...	1405	...	1505	...	1605	...	1705	...	1805	1835	1905	1951	2005	2105	...	2304	...	0100

S-Bahn service **S6 Pforzheim** Hbf - **Bad Wildbad** Bf. *23 km.* Journey time: 26 – 34 minutes. Trains continue to / start from Bad Wildbad Kurpark (additional journey time: 3 – 4 minutes).
From Pforzheim Hbf at 0017, 0517 Ⓐe, 0612 Ⓐe, 0647 ⚒r, 0705 Ⓐe, 0747, 0847, 0947, 1047, 1147, 1227 Ⓐe, 1247, 1317 Ⓐe, 1347, 1447, 1547, 1617 Ⓐe, 1647, 1717 Ⓐe, 1747, 1817 Ⓐe, 1847, 1917 Ⓐe, 1947, 2047, 2147, 2217 and 2317. **From Bad Wildbad** Bf at 0509 Ⓐe, 0536 Ⓐe, 0605 Ⓐe, 0639 ⚒r, 0701 Ⓐe, 0739, 0809 Ⓐe, 0839, 0909 Ⓐe, 0939, 1039, 1139, 1219 Ⓐe, 1239 Ⓒz, 1309 Ⓐe, 1339, 1439, 1539, 1609 Ⓐe, 1639, 1709 Ⓐe, 1739, 1809 Ⓐe, 1839, 1939, 2039, 2139, 2255 and 2355.

e – Not Dec. 24, 31, Jan. 6, June 3.
f – Also Dec. 23, 30; not Dec. 25, Apr. 30.
h – Arrives 1938.
j – Arrives 7 – 13 minutes earlier.
k – Also Dec. 24, 31; not Dec. 26, May 1.
n – Not Dec. 24, 31.
r – Not Jan. 6, June 3.
v – Not Dec. 25, Jan. 1.
z – Also Dec. 24, 31, Jan. 6, June 3.

STUTTGART - FREUDENSTADT - OFFENBURG 942

DB (*RE*/*RB* services); OSB ★; 2nd class only

km																									
					Ⓐe																		n	Ⓒk	Ⓐe
0	**Stuttgart** Hbf........ **940** d.	...	...	...	0518	0618	0718	0818	0918	1018	...	1118	1218	1318	1418	1518	1618	1718	1818	1918	...	2018	2118	2225	2235u
26	Böblingen .... **940** d.	...	...	...	0538	0638	0738	0838	0938	1038	...	1138	1238	1338	1440	1538	1638	1738	1838	1938	...	2038	2138	2245	2259
42	Herrenberg .... **940** d.	...	...	...	0547	0650	0748	0850	0948	1050	...	1148	1250	1348	1450	1548	1650	1748	1850	1948	...	2050	2147	2259	2317
57	Eutingen im Gäu.. **940** d.	...	...	...	0635	0708	0808	0908	1008	1108	...	1208	1308	1408	1508	1608	1708	1808	1908	2008	...	2108	2208	2318	2334
62	Hochdorf (b. Horb) ...... d.	...	...	...	0643	0713	0812	0913	1012	1113	...	1212	1313	1412	1513	1612	1713	1812	1913	2012	...	2113	2212	2323	2338
87	**Freudenstadt** Hbf ...... a.	...	...	...	0711	0740	0840	0940	1040	1140	...	1240	1340	1440	1540	1640	1740	1840	1940	2040	...	2140	2240	2348	0003
	Change trains	Ⓐe	Ⓐe	⑥k							Ⓐj	Ⓒb									⑤f	Ⓐe			
87	**Freudenstadt** Hbf .. ★ d.	0533	0640	0643	...	0743	0843	0943	1043	1143	1220	1243	1343	1443	1543	1643	1743	1843	1943	2043	...	2143	...	...	...
103	Alpirsbach.............. ★ d.	0550	0657	0700	...	0800	0900	1000	1100	1200	1237	1300	1400	1500	1600	1700	1800	1900	2000	2100	...	2200	...	...	...
112	Schiltach................ ★ d.	0601	0708	0711	...	0811	0911	1011	1111	1211	1254	1311	1411	1511	1611	1711	1811	1911	2011	2111	...	2211	...	...	...
122	Wolfach .... ★ d.	0612	0719	0722	...	0822	0922	1022	1122	1222	1305	1322	1422	1522	1622	1722	1822	1922	2022	2122	...	2222	...	...	...
126	Hausach **916** .... ★ a.	0616	0723	0726	...	0826	0926	1026	1126	1226	1309	1326	1426	1526	1626	1726	1826	1926	2026	2126	2139	2226	...	...	...
159	**Offenburg 916** .... ★ a.	0647	0746	0754	...	0854	0954	1054	1154	1254	1340	1354	1454	1554	1654	1754	1854	1954	2054	2158q	2204	2300	...	...	...

		Ⓐe		Ⓐe	Ⓐe	Ⓒz					Ⓐe	Ⓒz								Ⓐe					n
Offenburg 916 .... ★ d.	...	0446	...	0558	0701	0704	0804	0904	1004	1104	1159	1204	1304	1404	1504	1604	1704	1804	1904	2004	...	...	...	...	2226
Hausach **916** .... ★ d.	...	0521	...	0627	0730	0731	0831	0931	1031	1131	1231	1231	1331	1431	1531	1631	1731	1831	1931	2031	...	...	...	...	2253
Wolfach .... ★ d.	...	0526	...	0632	0735	0736	0836	0936	1036	1136	1236	1236	1336	1436	1536	1636	1736	1836	1936	2036	...	...	...	...	2258
Schiltach.................. ★ d.	...	0537	...	0643	0747	0747	0847	0947	1047	1147	1248	1248	1347	1447	1547	1647	1747	1847	1947	2047	...	...	...	...	2309
Alpirsbach................ ★ d.	...	0550	...	0700	0800	0800	0900	1000	1100	1200	1300	1300	1400	1500	1600	1700	1800	1900	2000	2100	...	...	...	...	2321
Freudenstadt Hbf ... ★ a.	...	0607	...	0717	0817	0817	0917	1017	1117	1217	1317	1317	1417	1517	1617	1717	1817	1917	2017	2117	...	...	...	...	2338
Change trains	Ⓐe	Ⓐe	Ⓒz	d		d						d									n		Ⓒz	Ⓐe	
Freudenstadt Hbf ....d.	0514	0615	0619	0719	...	0819	0919	1019	1119	1219	...	1319	1419	1519	1619	1719	1819	1919	2019	...	2119	...	2219	2219	...
Hochdorf (b. Horb)........d.	0539	0641	0644	0744	...	0845	0944	1045	1144	1245	...	1344	1445	1544	1645	1744	1845	1944	2045	...	2151	...	2248	2248	...
Eutingen im Gäu...**940** a.	0543	0646	0649	0749	...	0849	0949	1049	1149	1249	...	1349	1449	1549	1649	1749	1849	1949	2049	...	2155	...	2252	2252	...
Herrenberg ....**940** a.	0610	0710	0710	0810	...	0911	1009	1110	1210	1310	...	1410	1510	1610	1710	1810	1910	2010	2110	...	2212	2217	2310	2311	...
Böblingen ....**940** a.	0621	0721	0721	0821	...	0922	1020	1121	1221	1321	...	1421	1521	1621	1721	1821	1921	2021	2121	...	...	2230	2321	2330	...
Stuttgart Hbf.........**940** a.	0642	0743	0743	0842	...	0942	1042	1142	1242	1342	...	1442	1542	1642	1742	1842	1942	2042	2142	...	...	2255	2343	2355	...

b – Runs daily Dec. 23 - Jan. 10, Apr. 1 – 11 and May 22 - June 6.
d – Runs daily from Freudenstadt.
e – Not Dec. 24, 31, Jan. 6, June 3.
f – Also Dec. 23, 30; not Dec. 25, Jan. 1, Apr. 2.
j – Not Dec. 23 - Jan. 8, Apr. 1 – 9, May 24 - June 4.
k – Also Dec. 24, 31; not Dec. 26, May 1.
n – Not Dec. 24, 31.
q – † (also Jan. 6, June 3).
u – Departs from the underground platforms.
z – Also Dec. 24, 31, Jan. 6, June 3.
★ – Freudenstadt - Offenburg operated by Ortenau-S-Bahn GmbH.

943 KARLSRUHE - FREUDENSTADT

S-Bahn (2nd class only)

km		Ⓐe	Ⓐe	⑥k	Ⓐe	Ⓒz	Ⓐe	Ⓐe	Ⓒz	†w			B	A	A					Ⓒz	Ⓐe		n	
	Karlsruhe Bahnhofsvorplatz d.	0433	0508	0513	0538	0613	...	...	0713	...	0813	0913	...	1013	1113	Train A	...	1813	1913	2013	2013	2113	2213	2315
0	**Karlsruhe Hbf** 916 d.	|	|	|	|	|	0611	0707	|	0806	|	|	1010	|	|	runs	1810	|	|	|	|	|	|	|
24	Rastatt 916 d.	0500	0533	0538	0609	0638	0634	0738	0738	0829	0838	0938	1029	1038	1138	hourly	1829	1838	1938	2038	2038	2138	2238	2340
40	Gernsbach Bf d.	0519	0601	0600	0640	0700	0701	0800	0800	0844	0900	1000	1044	1100	1200	and	1844	1900	2000	2100	2100	2200	2300	0000
51	Forbach (Schwarzw) d.	0551	0626	0618	0659	0718	0718	0818	0818	0900	0918	1018	1100	1118	1218	train B	1900	1918	2018	2118	2118	2218	2318	0018
61	Schönmünzach d.	0604	0638	0631	0710	0731	0733	0831	0831	0911	0931	1031	1111	1131	1231	runs every	1911	1931	2031	2131	2131	2231	2331	0033
74	Baiersbronn Bf d.	0620	0654	0648	0725	0748	0752	0848	0848	0922	0948	1048	1122	1148	1248	two hours	1922	1948	2048	2145	2148	2245	2345	0046
79	**Freudenstadt** Stadt a.	0627	0701	0656	0732	0756	0759	0856	0856	0929	0956	1056	1129	1156	1256	until	1929	1956	2056	2152	2156	2252	2352	0054
82	**Freudenstadt** Hbf a.	0633	0707	0707	0738	0807	0809	0907	0907	0937	1007	1112	1137	1207	1307		1937	2007	2107	2158	2207	2257	2357	0059

	Ⓐe	Ⓐe	Ⓒz	Ⓐe	Ⓒz	Ⓐe	Ⓐe		✕r	A	A	B							†w					
Freudenstadt Hbf d.	0444	0533	0602	0617	0653	0653	0720	0745t	0823	0853	0953	1023	Train A	1453	1553	1623	1653	1753	1823	1853	1953	2053	2153	2302
Freudenstadt Stadt d.	0451	0540	0607	0633	0703	0705	0733	0803	0830	0903	1003	1030	runs	1503	1603	1630	1703	1803	1830	1903	2003	2103	2203	2308
Baiersbronn Bf d.	0459	0547	0615	0641	0710	0713	0740	0810	0837	0910	1010	1037	hourly	1510	1610	1637	1710	1810	1837	1910	2010	2110	2210	2316
Schönmünzach d.	0519	0605	0630	0658	0728	0729	0751	0828	0849	0928	1028	1049	and	1528	1628	1649	1728	1828	1849	1928	2028	2128	2228	2330
Forbach (Schwarzw) d.	0529	0620	0640	0710	0740	0740	0801	0840	0901	0940	1040	1101	train B	1540	1640	1701	1740	1840	1901	1940	2040	2140	2240	2342
Gernsbach Bf d.	0546	0640	0700	0730	0800	0800	0816	0900	0916	1000	1100	1116	runs every	1600	1700	1716	1800	1900	1916	2000	2100	2200	2300	0000
Rastatt 916 d.	0604	0706	0722	0754	0822	0822	0830	0922	0931	1022	1122	1131	two hours	1622	1722	1731	1822	1922	1931	2022	2122	2222	2322	0022
Karlsruhe Hbf 916 a.	0622	0727	|	0816	|	|	0849	|	0949	|	|	1149	until	|	|	1749	|	|	1949	|	|	|	|	|
Karlsruhe Bahnhofsvorplatz a.	...	...	0747	...	0847	0847	...	0947	...	1047	1147	...		1647	1747	...	1847	1947	...	2047	2147	2247	2347	0047

A – Train runs hourly.
B – Train runs every **two** hours.
e – Not Dec. 24, 31, Jan. 6, June 3.
k – Also Dec. 24, 31; not Dec. 26, May 1.
n – Not Dec. 24.
r – Not Jan. 6, June 3.
t – 0753 on Ⓒz.
w – Also Jan. 6, June 3.
z – Also Dec. 24, 31, Jan. 6, June 3.

944 MÜNCHEN - PASSAU

RE services

km		✕r	Ⓐe	Ⓐe	Ⓒz											Ⓐe							Ⓒz	Ⓐe
0	**München** Hbf 878 d.	*0455*	0525	0604	0624	0723	0824	0925	1024	1125	1224	1325	1423	1525	1621	*1642*	1724	1823	1925	2024	2124	...	2326	2326
42	Freising 878 d.	*0519*	0549	0628	0651	0748	0848	0949	1048	1149	1248	1349	1448	1549	1648	*1708*	1749	1848	1949	2048	2148	...	2349	2349
76	Landshut (Bay) Hbf 878 d.	0544	0614	0650	0715	0809	0909	1014	1109	1213	1312	1414	1510	1614	1710	1736	1816	1910	2014	2111	2212	...	0014	0029
121	Landau (Isar) d.	0625	0701t	0737	0744	0845	0944	1050	1144	1244	1343	1450	1544	1650	1744	1814	1850	1943	2045	2145	2248	...	0043	0101
139	Plattling a.	0640	0714	0750	0757	0857	0954	1101	1154	1256	1354	1501	1554	1701	1754	1826	1901	1954	2057	2156	2304	...	0055	0114
139	Plattling 920 d.	0642	0725	0800	0800	0901	1005	1103	1205	1301y	1405	1503	1605	1703	1805	1828	1903	2005	2103	2158	2306	...	0056	0115
191	**Passau** Hbf 920 a.	0718	0800	0833	0833	0937	1039	1137	1239	1339y	1439	1537	1639	1737	1839	1900	1937	2039	2137	2232	2341	...	0130	0149

	✕r		Ⓐe	Ⓒz	Ⓐe																			
Passau Hbf 920 d.	0443	0526	0605	0627	0645	...	0725	0826	0917	1025	1117	1226	1316	1426	1516	1626	1716	1822	1916	2026	2128	...	2210	...
Plattling 920 a.	0516	0559	0638	0700	0718	...	0758	0859	0951	1058	1151	1259	1350	1459	1550	1659	1750	1856	1951	2059	2200	...	2244	...
Plattling d.	0519	0601	0640	0702	0723	...	0800	0902	1003	1102	1203	1302	1403	1502	1603	1702	1803	1902	2003	2102	2202	...	2248	...
Landau (Isar) d.	0532	0613	0653	0714	0735	...	0813	0914	1013	1114	1213	1314	1413	1515	1613	1715	1813	1915	2013	2114	2215	...	2301	...
Landshut (Bay) Hbf 878 d.	0607	0647	0727	0749	0807	...	0849	0947	1048	1147	1249	1350	1448	1547	1648	1750	1850	1950	2049	2147	2248	...	2329	2335
Freising 878 a.	0628	0709	0746	0809	0828	...	0909	1008	1109	1208	1309	1410	1509	1608	1709	1810	1910	2010	2110	2208	2309	...	...	2355
München Hbf 878 a.	0655	0736	0815	0835	0856	...	0936	1035	1135	1235	1335	1436	1535	1635	1735	1836	1936	2036	2136	2235	2335	...	...	0022

e – Not Dec. 24, 31, Jan. 6, June 3.
r – Not Jan. 6, June 3.
t – Arrives 0649.
y – 8 minutes later May 22 - June 6.
z – Also Dec. 24, 31, Jan. 6, June 3.

945 REGENSBURG - DONAUWÖRTH - ULM

RB services (2nd class only)

SERVICE UNTIL APRIL 28. See Table **930** for other connecting trains Günzburg - Ulm and v.v. On Dec. 24, 31, Jan. 6 services run as on Ⓒ.

km		Ⓐ	¶	Ⓐ	Ⓐ	Ⓒ◇	Ⓐ	Ⓒ◇	Ⓐ	Ⓐ	Ⓒ◇	Ⓐ	Ⓐ	Ⓒ◇	Ⓐ	Ⓐ	Ⓒ◇	Ⓐ	Ⓐ	Ⓒ◇	Ⓐ	Ⓐ	Ⓒn	Ⓐ	Ⓐ	n
0	**Regensburg** Hbf d.	...	...	*0511*	*0615*	0644	0745	0845	0845	0944	1045	1045	1144	1244	1244	1344	1444	1444	1544	1644	1644	1744	1844	1844	1944	2044
46	Neustadt (Donau) d.	...	...	*0556*	*0655*	0731	0831	0931	0931	1031	1131	1131	1230	1331	1331	1431	1531	1531	1631	1731	1731	1831	1931	1931	2031	2131
74	**Ingolstadt** Hbf a.	...	...	*0621*	*0719*	0751	0851	0951	0951	1051	1151	1151	1251	1351	1351	1451	1551	1551	1651	1751	1751	1851	1951	1951	2051	2151
74	**Ingolstadt** Hbf d.	0500	0604	0700	0808	0807	0907	1007	1007	1107	1207	1207	1308	1407	1407	1507	1607	1607	1707	1807	1807	1907	2007	2007	*2105*	*2207*c
95	Neuburg (Donau) d.	0518	0624	0718	0825	0825	0925	1025	1025	1125	1225	1225	1326	1425	1425	1525	1625	1625	1725	1825	1825	1925	2025	2025	*2128*	*2225*c
127	**Donauwörth** a.	0547	0652	0753	0852	0852	0952	1052	1052	1152	1252	1252	1353	1452	1452	1552	1652	1652	1752	1852	1852	1953	2052	2052	*2154*	*2252*c
127	**Donauwörth** d.	0606	0702r	0802	0902	0902	1002	1102	1102	1202	1302	1302	1402	1502	1502	1602	1702	1702	1802	1902	1902	2002	*2102*	2102	...	...
153	Dillingen (Donau) d.	0640	0725	0824	0931	0925	1024	1125	1131	1224	1325	1331	1424	1525	1537	1624	1725	1731	1824	1925	1933	2024	*2126*	2133	...	...
176	Günzburg 930 a.	0658	0743	0841	0948	0944	1041	1144	1148	1241	1344	1348	1441	1544	1555	1640	1744	1748	1841	1944	1953	2041	*2145*	2152	...	...
200	**Ulm** Hbf 930 a.	0716	0816v	...	1017f	1009f	...	1209f	1216f	1316f	1409f	1416f	...	1609f	1616f	1716f	1809f	1822f	...	2009f	2016f	...	*2211*f	...	...	...

	Ⓐ	Ⓒ	Ⓐ	Ⓐ	Ⓒ	Ⓐ	Ⓐ	Ⓒ◇	Ⓐ	Ⓐ	Ⓒ◇	Ⓐ	Ⓐ	Ⓒ◇	Ⓐ	Ⓐ	Ⓒ◇	Ⓐ	Ⓐ	Ⓒ◇	Ⓐ	Ⓐ◧	Ⓒ◇	Ⓐ	Ⓐ	Ⓒ◇
Ulm Hbf 930 ‡ d.	...	...	...	...	...	...	0744f	0748f	...	0944f	0948f	...	1144f	1148f	1244f	1344f	1348f	...	1544f	1548f	1644f	1744f	1748f	...	1944f	1948f
Günzburg 930 ‡ d.	...	...	0510	*0557*	0615	0653	0804	0804	0914	1004	1004	1114	1204	1204	1314	1404	1404	1514	1603	1604	1714	1804	1804	1914	2004	2004
Dillingen ‡ d.	...	...	0529	*0614*	0633	0710	0827	0822	0931	1027	1022	1131	1227	1222	1331	1427	1422	1531	1627	1622	1731	1824*	1822	1931	2027	2022
Donauwörth ‡ a.	...	...	0553	*0638*	0653	0737	0850	0847	0953	1052	1047	1153	1252	1247	1353	1452	1447	1553	1651	1647	1753	1847*	1847	1953	2052	2047
Donauwörth d.	0459	0510	0601	0704	0702	0803	0903	0902	1003	1103	1103	1203	1303	1303	1403	1503	1503	1603	1703	1703	1803	1903	1902	2003	2101	2102n
Neuburg (Donau) d.	0530	0534	0635	0736	0736	0837	0937	0937	1037	1137	1137	1237	1337	1337	1437	1537	1537	1637	1736	1736	1836	1937	1937	2037	2127	2128n
Ingolstadt Hbf a.	0549	0553	0653	0754	0754	0854	0954	0954	1054	1154	1154	1254	1354	1354	1454	1554	1554	1654	1754	1754	1854	1954	1954	2054	2145	2145n
Ingolstadt Hbf d.	*0600*	0605	0705	0805	0805	0905	1005	1005	1105	1205	1205	1306	1405	1405	1505	1605	1605	1705	1805	1805	1905	2005	2005	...	...	...
Neustadt (Donau) d.	*0620*	0627	0730	0831	0831	0931	1031	1031	1131	1231	1231	1331	1431	1431	1531	1631	1631	1731	1831	1831	1931	2031	2031	...	...	...
Regensburg Hbf a.	*0707*	0712	0812	0912	0912	1012	1112	1112	1212	1312	1312	1412	1512	1512	1612	1712	1712	1812	1912	1912	2012	2112	2112	...	...	...

c – Ⓒ only.
f – Until Feb. 26.
n – Not Dec. 24.
r – 0705 on Ⓐ.
v – Until Feb. 26. 0809 on Ⓒ.
* – Until Feb. 26 Dillingen 1827, Donauwörth 1852.
◇ – Change trains at Donauwörth until Feb. 21.
¶ – Change trains at Donauwörth on Ⓒ until Feb. 21.
◧ – Change trains at Ingolstadt from Mar. 1.
‡ – **Additional trains**. On Ⓐ: Günzburg d. 2114 → Dillingen d. 2131 → Donauwörth a. 2153.
On Ⓐ: Günzburg d. 2245 → Dillingen d. 2301 → Donauwörth a. 2322.
On Ⓒ**n**: Ulm Hbf d. 2200**f** → Günzburg d. 2220 → Dillingen d. 2238 → Donauwörth a. 2302.

946 KÖLN - GEROLSTEIN - TRIER

RE | *RB* services

km		Ⓐe	✕r			†w	✕r	†w	✕r									Ⓒz	Ⓐe			⑤⑥	†w	✕r	Ⓐe	
0	**Köln** M/Deutz § d.	...	...	...	0605	0705	0715	0805	0815	0915	1015	1115	1215	1315	1415	1515	1615	1715	1715	1815	1915	1915	2005	2015	2015	2205
1	**Köln** Hbf d.	...	...	...	0611	0711	0721	0811	0821	0921	1021	1121	1221	1321	1421	1521	1621	1721	1721	1821	1921	1921	2011	2027	2027	2211
41	Euskirchen d.	...	...	...	0700	0800	0800	0900	0900	1000	1100	1200	1300	1400	1500	1600	1700	1800	1800	1900	2000	2000	2100	2110	2110	2300
56	Mechernich d.	...	...	...	0711	0811	0811	0911	0910	1011	1110	1211	1310	1411	1510	1611	1710	1811	1811	1910	2011	2011	2111	2121	2121	2311
65	Kall d.	...	...	...	0720	0820	0820	0920	0918	1020	1118	1220	1318	1420	1518	1620	1718	1820	1820	1918	2020	2020	2120	2130	2130	2320
81	Blankenheim d.	...	...	...	0737	0836	0836	0937	0934	1036	1134	1236	1334	1436	1534	1636	1734	1836	1836	1934	2036	2036	2137	2147	2147	2337
94	Jünkerath d.	...	...	0654e	0751	0848	0848	0951	0948	1048	1148	1248	1348	1448	1548	1648	1748	1848	1848	1948	2048	2048	2151	2201	2201	2351
113	**Gerolstein** a.	...	...	0711e	0808	0903	0903	1008	1007	1103	1207	1303	1407	1503	1607	1703	1807	1903	1903	2007	2103	2103	2208	2218	2218	0008
113	**Gerolstein** d.	0446	0600	0712	0817	0904	0904	1017	1017	1104	1217	1304	1417	1504	1617	1704	1817	1904	*1912*	2017n	...	2104	2222	...	2222	...
143	Bitburg-Erdorf d.	0519	0633	0745	0859	0934	0934	1059	1059	1132	1259	1332	1459	1532	1659	1734	1859	1932	*1945*	2050b	...	2136	2259	...	2259	...
182	**Trier** Hbf a.	0603	0719	0839	0940	1008	1009	1140	1140	1208	1340	1409	1540	1609	1740	1809	1940	2008	*2039*	2140n	...	2211	2340	...	2340	...

	✕r	⑥k	Ⓐe	✕r	⑥k	✕r	†w	Ⓐe	⑥k		g									Ⓑm	⑥k		†w	✕d	◧	⑤⑥
Trier Hbf d.	...	...	...	...	0532	...	0544v	0556	0608	0759	0816	0959	1016	1159	1216	1332t	1416	1559	1616	1759	1759	1816	1959	2028	2216	2328
Bitburg-Erdorf d.	...	...	...	...	0606	...	0619v	0658	0653	0834	0859	1033	1058	1234	1258	1433	1458	1634	1658	1833	1833	1858	2034	2112	2258	0012
Gerolstein a.	...	...	...	...	0643	...	0649v	0732	0730	0859	0932	1059	1132	1259	1332	1459	1532	1659	1732	1859	1859	1932	2059	2159	2332	0049
Gerolstein d.	0445	0549	0555	0619	0644	0644	0650	0737	0746	0900	0946	1100	1146	1300	1346	1500	1546	1700	1746	1900	1900	1945	2100	2151	...	...
Jünkerath d.	0502	0606	0612	0636	0709	0709	0709	0811	0811	0915	1011	1115	1211	1315	1411	1515	1611	1715	1811	1915	1915	2007	2115	2207	...	...
Blankenheim d.	0516	0620	0623	0650	0725	0725	0725	0825	0825	0927	1025	1127	1225	1327	1425	1527	1625	1727	1825	1927	1927	2022	2127	2222	...	...
Kall d.	0533	0637	0639	0706	0742	0742	0742	0841	0841	0942	1041	1142	1241	1342	1441	1542	1641	1742	1841	1942	1942	2039	2142	2239	...	...
Mechernich d.	0541	0645	0646	0715	0749	0749	0751	0848	0848	0949	1048	1149	1248	1349	1448	1549	1648	1749	1848	1949	1949	2048	2149	2248	...	...
Euskirchen d.	0557	0700	0657	0730	0802	0802	0807	0902	0902	1002	1102	1202	1300	1400	1502	1602	1702	1802	1902	2002	2007	2107	2207	2307	...	...
Köln Hbf a.	0639	0739	0739	0812	0839	0839	0851	0939	0939	1039	1139	1239	1339	1439	1539	1639	1739	1839	1939	2039	2051	2151	2251	2351	...	...
Köln M/Deutz § a.	0646	0744	0744	0817	0845	0845	0857	0944	0944	1044	1144	1244	1344	1444	1544	1644	1744	1844	1944	2044	2057	2157	2257	2357	...	...

b – Not Dec. 24, 31. 2059 on †**w**.
d – Not Dec. 24, 31, June 3.
e – Ⓐ (not Dec. 24, 31, June 3).
g – Change trains at Gerolstein on Ⓐ**e**.
k – Also Dec. 24, 31; not Dec. 26, May 1.
m – Also Dec. 26, May 1; not Dec. 24, 31.
n – Not Dec. 24, 31.
r – Not June 3.
t – 1359 on Ⓒ**z**.
v – Not Dec. 25, Jan. 1.
w – Also June 3.
z – Also Dec. 24, 31, June 3.
◧ – ①②③④⑦ (not Dec. 24, 31).
§ – Köln Messe/Deutz.

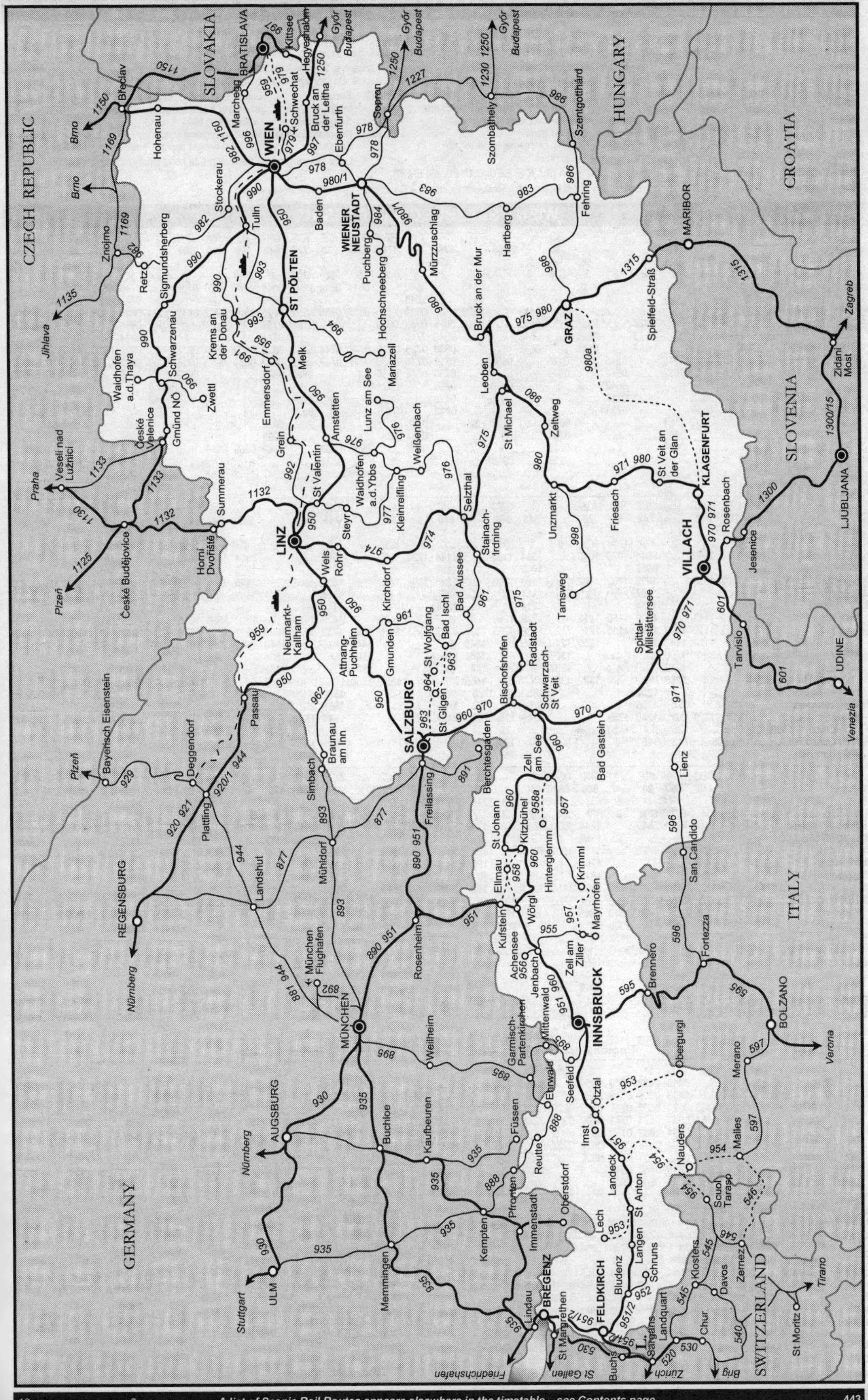

A list of Scenic Rail Routes appears elsewhere in the timetable – see Contents page

AUSTRIA

Operator: Except where otherwise stated, rail services are operated by Österreichische Bundesbahnen (**ÖBB**).

Timings: Valid **December 13, 2009 - June 12, 2010** unless stated otherwise in individual tables. See page 2 for public holiday dates.

Services: Trains convey both first- and second-class seating unless footnotes show otherwise or there is a '2' in the train column. Overnight sleeping car (🛏) or couchette (▬) trains do not necessarily convey seating accommodation - refer to individual footnotes for details. Descriptions of sleeping and couchette cars appear on page 8.

Train categories:

RJ	**Railjet**	Austrian high-speed train. Conveys first and economy (2nd) class. *Premium class* also available to first class ticket holders (supplement payable).
ICE	**InterCity Express**	German high-speed train.
ÖEC	**ÖBB-EuroCity**	Quality international or internal express train.
ÖIC	**ÖBB-InterCity**	Quality internal express train.
EC	**EuroCity**	Quality international express train.
IC	**InterCity**	Internal or international express train.
D	**Schnellzug**	Ordinary fast train.
REX	**Regional Express**	Semi-fast regional train.
EN	**EuroNight**	Quality overnight express train. Special fares payable.

Local stopping trains are shown with no category / train number.

Reservations: Seats may be reserved on all express trains (*RJ, ICE, ÖEC, ÖIC, EC, IC, EN, D*).

Catering: Three types of catering are indicated in the tables: ✕ – Restaurant car; ⊗ – Bordbistro; 🍷 – At seat trolley service.

950 WIEN - SALZBURG and PASSAU

km ♣			*REX*				*EC*		*D*		*REX*	*ÖIC*	*REX*	*ICE*	*ICE*	*ICE*	*ÖIC*	*RJ*	*RJ*	*ÖIC*		*ÖEC*	*RJ*	*ICE*	*ÖIC*	*REX*
			5885				**390**		**966**		**1780**	**540**	**1782**	**660**	**260**	**228**	**542**	**160**	**560**	**860**		**740**	**262**	**28**	**690**	**5914**
		⚒	⚒			⚒	①–⑥	⚒		Ⓐ	Ⓐ		©													P
		2	2	2	2	2	⊗♦	2		2	2	🍷	2	✕	✕	G✕	🍷	Z⊗	⊗	🍷	2	✕	⊗	G✕	V🍷	2
0	**Wien** Westbahnhof ... d.	...	...	...	...	...	...	...	...	0415	...	0540	...	0614	0614	0640	0644	0720	0720	0736	...	0740	0820	0840	0844	...
6	**Wien** Hütteldorf ● .... d.	...	...	...	...	...	...	...	...	0423	...	0548	...	|	|	|	0652	|	|	|	...	0748	|	|	0852	...
61	**St Pölten** Hbf .... d.	...	...	...	...	...	...	0433	...	0529	...	0624	...	0655	0655	0722	0728	0802	0802	0819	...	0825	0902	0922	0928	0908
121	Amstetten .... d.	...	...	*0428*	...	0455	...	0535	...	0616	0621	0653	0624	|	|	|	0757	|	|	|	...	0855	|	|	0957	1002
158	St Valentin .... 977 d.	...	...	0513	...	0526	...	0613	...	...	0640	0710	0701	|	|	|	0814	|	|	|	...	0914	|	|	1014	1025
183	**Linz** Hbf .... 977 a.	...	...	0538	...	0546	...	0638	...	...	0656	0725	0719	0744	0744	0813	0829	0850	0850	0913	...	0929	0950	1013	1029	1042
183	**Linz** Hbf .... ‡ d.	*0456*	0510	...	0545	...	0625	...	0653	...	0713	0728	0736	0747	0747	0816	0832	0853	0853	0916	0920	0932	0953	1016	1032	1045
208	**Wels** Hbf .... ‡ d.	0522	0527	...	0612	...	0640	...	0714	...	0730	0742	0755	|	|	0830	0845	|	|	0929	0940	0945	|	1030	1045	1102
	Neumarkt-Kallham. ‡ d.	0550	|	...	0642	...	|	...	0738	...	0758	|	0821	|	|	|	|	|	|	|	1008	|	|	|	|	1129
	Schärding .... d.	0623	|	...	0717	...	|	...	|	...	0828	|	0851	|	|	|	|	|	|	|	1042	|	|	|	|	1156
	Passau Hbf ▦ ...... a.	0636	|	...	0731	...	|	...	|	...	0843	|	0906	|	|	0922	|	|	|	|	1057	|	|	1122	|	1210
238	Attnang-Puchheim..... d.	...	0551	...	...	...	0658	...	⊙	...	...	0758	...	|	|	...	0902	|	|	|	...	1002	|	...	1102	...
243	Vöcklabruck .... d.	...	0556	...	...	...	0704	...	|	...	...	0804	...	|	|	...	0908	|	|	|	...	1008	|	...	1108	...
308	**Salzburg** Hbf........... a.	...	0649	...	...	...	0749	...	|	...	...	0848	...	0853	0853	...	0949	0959	0959	1029	...	1049	1059	...	1149	...
	München Hbf **890** .. a.	...	...	...	...	...	0933	...	0948	...	...	...	...	|	1030	...	|	|	|	...	...	|	1230	...	...	...
	Innsbruck Hbf **951**.. a.	...	...	...	...	...	...	...	...	...	...	...	...	1046	...	...	1347	1151	1151	...	...	1252	...	...	...	...
	Bregenz **951** .... a.	...	...	...	...	...	...	...	...	...	...	...	...	1313	...	...	...	...	1417	...	...	1547	...	...	...	...

	ÖEC	*ÖIC*		*ÖEC*	*RJ*	*ICE*		*ÖIC*	*ÖEC*		*ÖIC*	*RJ*	*ICE*		*ÖIC*	*ÖEC*		*ÖIC*	*RJ*	*ICE*			*ÖEC*		*ÖEC*	*IC*
	162	**862**		**742**	**60**	**26**		**548**	**564**		**640**	**62**	**24**		**746**	**566**		**642**	**64**	**22**			**692**		**568**	**868**
														Ⓐ								©		Ⓐ		
	Z✕	🍷	2	T✕	B⊗	H✕	2	🍷	✕	2	🍷	B⊗	H✕	2	🍷	✕	2	🍷	B⊗	H✕	2	2	K✕	2	✕	🍷
Wien Westbahnhof .... d.	0920	0940	...	0944	1020	1040	...	1044	1120	...	1144	1220	1240	...	1244	1320	...	1344	1420	1440	...	...	1444	...	1520	1540
Wien Hütteldorf ● ..... d.	|	|	...	0952	|	|	...	1052	|	...	1152	|	|	...	1252	|	...	1352	|	|	...	...	1452	...	|	|
St Pölten Hbf............ d.	1002	1022	...	1028	1102	1122	...	1128	1202	...	1228	1302	1322	...	1328	1402	...	1428	|	1522	...	...	1528	...	1602	1622
Amstetten .... d.	|	|	...	1057	|	|	...	1157	|	...	1257	|	|	...	1357	|	...	1457	|	|	...	...	1557	...	|	|
St Valentin........... 977 d.	|	|	...	1114	|	|	...	1214	|	...	1314	|	|	...	1414	|	...	1514	|	|	...	...	1614	...	|	|
Linz Hbf .... 977 a.	1050	1113	...	1129	1150	1213	...	1229	1250	...	1329	1350	1413	...	1429	1450	...	1529	1550	1613	...	...	1629	...	1650	1713
Linz Hbf .... ‡ d.	1053	1116	1120	1132	1153	1216	1220	1232	1253	1320	1332	1353	1416	1420	1432	1453	1520	1532	1553	1616	1620	1620	1632	1636	1653	1716
Wels Hbf .... ‡ d.	|	1129	1140	1145	|	1230	1240	1245	|	1340	1345	|	1430	1440	1445	|	1540	1545	|	1630	1640	1640	1645	1654	|	1729
Neumarkt-Kallham ‡ d.	|	|	1208	|	|	|	1305	|	|	1408	|	|	|	1505	|	|	1608	|	|	|	1705	1705	|	1715	|	|
Schärding............... d.	|	|	1242	|	|	|	1337	|	|	1442	|	|	|	1537	|	|	1642	|	|	|	1738	1745	|	1745	|	|
Passau Hbf ▦ .... a.	|	|	1255	|	|	1322	1350	|	|	1455	|	|	1522	1550	|	|	1655	|	|	1722	...	1758	|	1758	|	|
Attnang-Puchheim...... d.	|	|	...	1202	|	...	...	1302	|	...	1402	|	...	...	1502	|	...	1602	|	...	...	...	1702	...	|	|
Vöcklabruck............... d.	|	|	...	1208	|	...	...	1308	|	...	1408	|	...	...	1508	|	...	1608	|	...	...	...	1708	...	|	|
Salzburg Hbf............ a.	1159	1229	...	1249	1259	...	...	1349	1359	...	1449	1459	...	...	1549	1559	...	1649	1659	...	...	...	1749	...	1759	1829
München Hbf **890** ... a.	|	...	...	|	1430	...	...	...	|	...	...	...	...	...	...	|	...	...	1833	...	...	...	...	...	|	...
Innsbruck Hbf **951** .. a.	1351	...	...	1452	...	...	...	...	1606	...	...	...	...	...	...	1806	...	...	...	...	...	...	...	...	2006	...
Bregenz **951**........... a.	...	...	...	...	...	...	...	...	1847	...	...	...	...	...	...	2043	...	...	...	...	...	...	...	...	2247	...

		ÖEC	*RJ*	*ICE*		*ÖIC*	*ÖEC*	*IC*		*ÖIC*	*RJ*	*RJ*	*ÖIC*		*ÖEC*	*ÖIC*	*EN*	*RJ*	*IC*	*EN*	*D*		*ÖIC*	*EN*	*EN*	*EN*
		748	**66**	**20**		**646**	**662**	**840**		**648**	**68**	**762**	**940**		**764**	**942**	**490**	**42**	**744**	**237**	**207**		**766**	**466**	**246**	**462**
					Ⓐ		¶	Ⓑ				Ⓑt								🅁		⚒				
	2	✕	B⊗	G✕	2	🍷	✕	🍷	2	🍷	B⊗	⊗	N🍷	2	✕	🍷	♦	B⊗		♦	♦	2	🍷	♦	△	♦
Wien Westbahnhof .... d.	...	1544	1620	1640	...	1644	1720	1740	...	1744	1820	1820	1844	...	1920	1944	1954	2020	2040	2040	...	...	2120	2225	2244	...
Wien Hütteldorf ● ..... d.	...	1552	|	|	...	1652	|	|	...	1752	|	|	1852	...	|	1952	2003	|	2048	2048	...	...	|	|	|	0009
St Pölten Hbf............ d.	...	1628	|	1722	...	1728	1802	1822	...	1828	|	|	1928	...	2002	2028	2041	2102	2125	2125	...	...	2202	2309	2329	0052
Amstetten .... d.	...	1657	|	|	...	1757	|	|	...	1857	|	|	1957	...	|	2057	2111	|	2155	2155	...	...	|	|	0004	|
St Valentin........... 977 d.	...	1714	|	|	...	1814	|	|	...	1914	|	|	2014	...	|	2114	2130	|	2214	2214	...	...	|	|	0025	|
Linz Hbf .... 977 a.	...	1729	1750	1813	...	1829	1850	1913	...	1929	1950	1950	2029	...	2050	2129	2145	2150	2229	2229	...	...	2250	0007	0041	0158
Linz Hbf .... ‡ d.	1720	1732	1753	1816	1820	1832	1853	...	1920	1932	1953	1953	2032	2026r	2053	2132	2157	2153	2232	2232	2246	...	...	0010	0044	0201
Wels Hbf .... ‡ d.	1740	1745	|	1830	1840	1845	|	...	1938	1945	|	|	2045	2048	|	2145	2212	|	2246	2246	2303	2306	...	0025	0101	0218
Neumarkt-Kallham ‡ d.	1808	|	|	|	1908	|	|	...	2006	|	|	|	|	2116	|	|	|	|	|	|	|	2335	...	|	|	|
Schärding............... d.	1842	|	|	|	1952	|	|	...	2039	|	|	|	|	2150	|	|	2252	|	|	|	|	0009	...	|	|	|
Passau Hbf ▦ .... a.	1855	|	|	1922	2005	|	|	...	2052	|	|	|	|	2203	|	|	2304	|	|	|	|	...	...	|	|	|
Attnang-Puchheim...... d.	...	1802	|	...	...	1902	|	...	...	2002	|	|	2102	...	|	2202	...	|	2305	2305	2323	...	...	|	0120	0238
Vöcklabruck............... d.	...	1808	|	...	...	1908	|	...	...	2008	|	|	2108	...	|	2208	...	|	2311	2311	2328	...	...	|	|	|
Salzburg Hbf............ a.	...	1849	1859	...	...	1949	1959	...	...	2049	2059	2059	2149	...	2159	2249	...	2259	2352	2352	0014	...	...	0126	0208	0326
München Hbf **890** ... a.	...	|	2034	...	...	...	|	...	...	...	2230	|	...	...	|	...	...	...	...	...	...	...	...	|	|	0615
Innsbruck Hbf **951** .. a.	...	2051	...	...	...	...	2151	...	...	...	...	2300	...	...	2354	...	...	...	...	...	...	...	...	0338	0434	...
Bregenz **951**........... a.	...	...	...	...	...	...	0012	...	...	...	...	...	...	...	...	...	...	...	...	...	...	...	...	...	0808	...

Regional trains WIEN - MELK - AMSTETTEN - LINZ (2nd class only)

km		⚒	ⒶL	⚒		S	⚒	P									◧									n
0	**Wien** Westbahnhof ... d.	...	0415	*0452*	0610	0654	...	*0746*c	0914	...	1014	1114	...	1214	1314	...	1414	1514	...	1614	1714	...	1814	1914	2129	2350
6	**Wien** Hütteldorf ● .... d.	...	0423	*0500*	0619	0701	...	*0755*c	0922	...	1022	1122	...	1222	1322	...	1422	1522	...	1622	1722	...	1822	1922	2136	2358
61	**St Pölten** Hbf .... d.	0433	0529	0602	0718	0750	0839	0908	1014	1039	1114	1214	1239	1314	1414	1439	1514	1614	1633	1714	1814	1833	1914	2014	2223	0047
85	Melk........................ d.	0457	0547	0626	0743	0809	0903	0929	1033	1103	1133	1233	1303	1333	1433	1503	1533	1633	1658	1733	1833	1858	1933	2033	2241	0105
94	Pöchlarn .... d.	0504	0554	0633	0750	0815	0909	0936	1039	1109	1139	1239	1309	1339	1439	1509	1539	1639	1706	1739	1839	1906	1939	2039	2247	0112
107	Ybbs an der Donau... d.	0517	0601	0646	0800	0824	0922	0949	1049	1122	1149	1249	1322	1349	1449	1522	1549	1649	1720	1749	1849	1920	1949	2049	2256	0121
124	Amstetten .... a.	0533	0616	0701	0813	0836	0937	1000	1101	1137	1201	1301	1337	1401	1501	1537	1601	1701	1735	1801	1901	1935	2001	2101	2308	0134
163	St Valentin .... 977 a.	0611	*0639*	0740	0840	...	...	1023	1139	...	1238r	1339	...	1439r	1538	...	1640r	1739	...	1839r	1939	...	2039r	*2139*	...	...
188	**Linz** Hbf .... 977 a.	0638	*0656*	*0808*	*0908*	...	...	1042	*1208*	...	*1308*r	*1408*	...	*1508*r	*1608*	...	*1708*r	*1808*	...	*1908*a	*2008*	...	*2108*r	...	...	...

♦ – **NOTES** (LISTED BY TRAIN NUMBER)

207 – MATTHIAS BRAUN – [12] Praha - Summerau ▦ - Salzburg; 🛏 1, 2 cl. and ▬ 2 cl. Praha - Salzburg (**466**) - Zürich; 🛏 1, 2 cl. Praha - Salzburg (**499**) - Zagreb.

237 – ALLEGRO DON GIOVANNI – 🛏 1, 2 cl., ▬ 2 cl. and [2] Wien - Villach - Tarvisio ▦ - Udine - Venezia (Table **88**).

390 – ①–⑥ (not Dec. 25, 26, Jan. 1, Apr. 3, 5, May 24). [12] Linz - Stuttgart - Frankfurt.

462 – KÁLMÁN IMRE – 🛏 1, 2 cl., ▬ 2 cl. and [2] Budapest - München. Conveys Dec. 13 - Jan. 9 (from Bucureşti) 🛏 1, 2 cl. Bucureşti - Budapest - München.

466 – WIENER WALZER – ▬ 2 cl. and [2] Budapest - Wien - Zürich; 🛏 1, 2 cl., ▬ 2 cl. and [2] Wien - Zürich. 🅁 for journeys to Switzerland.

490 – HANS ALBERS – 🛏 1, 2 cl., ▬ 2 cl. and [2] Wien - Nürnberg - Hamburg; 🛏 1, 2 cl., ▬ 2 cl. and [2] (*EN* **420**) Wien - Nürnberg - Frankfurt - Köln. 🅁 for journeys to Germany.

B – From Budapest (Table **1250**).

G – [12] and ✕ Wien - Nürnberg - Frankfurt.

H – [12] and ✕ Wien - Nürnberg - Frankfurt - Köln - Dortmund.

K – To Klagenfurt (Table **970**).

L – To Kleinreifling (Table **976**).

N – Conveys [12] Wien - Salzburg (**1516**) - Saalfelden (see Table **960**).

P – From Apr. 3. [2] Wien Franz-Josefs-Bf (d. 0729) - St Pölten - Passau.

S – On © continues to Schladming via Selzthal (Tables **975** and **977**).

T – Conveys [12] Wien - Attnang-Puchheim - Stainach-Irdning (Table **961**).

V – To Villach (Table **970**).

Z – To Zürich (Table **520**).

a – Ⓐ only.

c – © only.

n – Not Dec. 24, 31.

r – ⚒ only.

t – Not Dec. 24, 25, 31, Jan. 1, 5, Apr. 4, May 23.

△ – Conveys 🛏 1, 2 cl., ▬ 2 cl. and [2].

◧ – Change trains at Amstetten on Ⓐ.

⊙ – Via Simbach (Tables **893/962**).

● – See note on page 445.

♣ – Via high-speed alignments.

‡ – See also Table **965**.

¶ – Train category *RJ* from Apr. 11.

PASSAU and SALZBURG - WIEN 950

km		EN 463	ÖIC 841	EN 247			IC 843	EN 467	D 206		IC 745	EN 236	EN 491	REX 1657	RJ 767		ÖIC 541			REX 1663	RJ 43		ÖIC 543	ÖEC 765	ÖIC 545	
					⚒	Ⓐ	①–⑥					🅁		⚒				⚒	Ⓐn		①–⑥	⚒			⊖	
		♦	🍷	△	2	2	🍷	♦	♦	2		♦	♦	2	⊗	2	🍷	2	2	2	N⊗	2	🍷	✕	🍷	2
	Bregenz **951** d.	...	...	2146	...	...	...	...	...	...	...	...	...	...	...	...	...	...	...	...	...	...	...	...	...	...
	Innsbruck Hbf **951** d.	...	...	0114	...	...	...	0217	...	...	...	...	...	...	...	...	...	...	...	...	0503	...	...	0606	...	...
	München Hbf **890** d.	2340	...	|	...	...	...	|	...	...	...	...	...	...	...	...	...	...	...	...	|	...	...	|	...	...
	Salzburg Hbf d.	0217	...	0345	...	...	...	0424	0439	...	0500	0500	...	0510	0600	...	0607	...	...	...	0702	...	0710	0802	0810	...
	Vöcklabruck d.	|	...	|	...	...	...	|	|	...	0545	0545	...	0612	|	...	0654	...	...	0704	|	...	0754	|	0854	...
	Attnang-Puchheim d.	0306	0420	0435	...	...	...	|	0526	...	0551	0551	...	0623	0644	...	0700	...	...	0712	|	...	0800	|	0900	...
0	**Passau** Hbf 🏛 d.	|	|	|	...	0410	...	|	|	0430c	|	|	0535	|	|	0546	|	0603	0632	|	|	0646	|	|	|	0805
14	Schärding d.	|	|	|	0401	0424	...	|	|	0444	|	|	0549	|	|	0600	|	0618	0645	|	|	0700	|	|	|	0818
52	Neumarkt-Kallham ‡ d.	|	|	|	0435	0452	...	|	|	0520	|	|	|	|	|	0636	|	0647	0712	|	|	0736	|	|	|	0854
81	**Wels** Hbf ‡ d.	0325	0438	0454	0503	0517	...	0526	0545	0550	0613	0613	0631	0647	|	0706	0716	0719	0735	0737	|	0806	0816	|	0916	0923
106	**Linz** Hbf ‡ a.	0340	0452	0509	0524	0533	...	0540	0600	0614	0627	0627	0646	0703	0707	0722	0728	0744	0753	0759	0807	0822	0828	0907	0928	0939
106	**Linz** Hbf **977** d.	0342	0455	0512	...	...	0538	0543	...	...	0630	0630	0649	...	0710	...	0731	...	...	...	0810	...	0831	0910	0931	...
131	St Valentin **977** d.	0402	0513	0531	...	...	0554	|	...	...	0648	0648	0711	...	|	...	0748	...	...	...	|	...	0848	|	0948	...
168	Amstetten d.	0425	0532	0552	...	...	0611	0617	...	...	0707	0707	0739	...	|	...	0805	...	...	...	|	...	0905	|	1005	...
228	**St Pölten** Hbf d.	0500	0605	0626	...	...	0644	0650	...	...	0739	0739	0819	...	|	...	0834	...	...	...	|	...	0934	1000	1034	...
283	**Wien** Hütteldorf ● a.	0545	0647	0707	...	...	0723	0727	...	...	0819	0819	0855	...	|	...	0909	...	...	...	|	...	1009	|	1109	...
289	**Wien** Westbahnhof a.	...	0658	0716	...	...	0732	0736	...	...	0828	0828	0904	...	0840	...	0918	...	...	...	0940	...	1018	1040	1118	...

	RJ 61	ÖEC 741	ÖEC 663	ÖEC 693		ICE 21	RJ 63	ÖIC 549	ÖEC 561	ÖIC 641		ICE 23	RJ 65	ÖEC 743		ÖIC 863	ÖEC 163	ÖIC 643		ICE 25	RJ 67	ÖIC 645		ÖIC 865	ÖEC 565	ÖIC 691
			¶			✣						✣								✣			Ⓐ			
	B⊗	✕	✕	K✕	2	G✕	B⊗	🍷	✕	🍷	2	H✕	B⊗	✕	2	🍷	Z✕	🍷	2	H✕	B⊗	🍷	2	🍷	✕	K🍷
Bregenz **951** d.	...	...	0547	...	...	...	...	...	0713	...	...	...	...	0809	...	...	...	...	...	...	...	...	...	...	1116	...
Innsbruck Hbf **951** d.	...	0707	0809	...	...	...	...	...	0954	...	...	...	...	1106	...	...	1209	...	...	...	...	...	...	...	1354	...
München Hbf **890** d.	0727	|	|	...	...	...	0927	...	|	...	...	...	1127	|	...	...	|	...	...	...	1327	...	...	...	|	...
Salzburg Hbf d.	0902	0910	1002	1010	...	...	1102	1110	1202	1210	...	...	1302	1310	...	1332	1402	1410	...	...	1502	1510	...	1532	1602	1610
Vöcklabruck d.	|	0954	|	1054	...	...	|	1154	|	1254	...	...	|	1354	...	|	|	1454	...	...	|	1554	...	|	|	1654
Attnang-Puchheim d.	|	1000	|	1100	...	...	|	1200	|	1300	...	...	|	1400	...	|	|	1500	...	...	|	1600	...	|	|	1700
Passau Hbf 🏛 d.	|	|	|	|	1005	1033	|	|	|	|	1205	1233	|	|	1311	|	|	|	1405	1433	|	|	1511	|	|	|
Schärding d.	|	|	|	|	1018	|	|	|	|	|	1218	|	|	|	1325	|	|	|	1418	|	|	|	1525	|	|	|
Neumarkt-Kallham ‡ d.	|	|	|	|	1054	|	|	|	|	|	1254	|	|	|	1357	|	|	|	1454	|	|	|	1557	|	|	|
Wels Hbf ‡ d.	|	1016	|	1116	1123	1130	|	1216	|	1316	1323	1330	|	1416	1423	1431	|	1516	1523	1530	|	1616	1623	1631	|	1716
Linz Hbf ‡ a.	1007	1028	1107	1128	1139	1143	1207	1228	1307	1328	1339	1343	1407	1428	1439	1443	1507	1528	1539	1543	1607	1628	1639	1643	1707	1728
Linz Hbf **977** d.	1010	1031	1110	1131	...	1146	1210	1231	1310	1331	...	1346	1410	1431	...	1446	1510	1531	...	1546	1610	1631	...	1646	1710	1731
St Valentin **977** d.	|	1048	|	1148	...	|	|	1248	|	1348	...	|	|	1448	...	|	|	1548	...	|	|	1648	...	|	|	1748
Amstetten d.	|	1105	|	1205	...	|	|	1305	|	1405	...	|	|	1507	...	1514	|	1605	...	|	|	1705	...	|	|	1805
St Pölten Hbf d.	1100	1134	1200	1234	...	1239	1300	1334	1400	1434	...	1439	1500	1539	...	1543	1600	1634	...	1639	1700	1734	...	1739	1800	1834
Wien Hütteldorf ● a.	|	1209	|	1309	...	|	|	1409	|	1509	...	|	|	1614	...	1618	|	1709	...	|	|	1809	...	|	|	1909
Wien Westbahnhof a.	1140	1218	1240	1318	...	1322	1340	1418	1440	1518	...	1522	1540	1624	...	1628	1640	1718	...	1722	1740	1818	...	1822	1840	1918

		ICE 27	RJ 69	IC 849	ÖIC 647	ÖIC 15647		REX 5927	ÖEC 567	REX 5927	ÖIC 649	ICE 29	ICE 261		ÖEC 747	D 963	RJ 569	RJ 169	ÖIC 845	ICE 229	ICE 661		ÖIC 847		EC 391	
		✣		⑦t	M	⑦t		P		P		✣												Ⓒ	Ⓑ	⑤⑥
	2	H✕	B⊗	🍷	T🍷	🍷	2	2	✕	2	🍷	G✕	✕	2	✕		⊗	Z⊗	🍷	G✕	✕	2	🍷	J 2	⊗♦	v 2
Bregenz **951** d.	...	...	...	...	...	...	...	...	1316	...	...	...	...	...	...	...	1541	...	...	...	1636	...	...	...	...	...
Innsbruck Hbf **951** d.	...	...	...	...	...	...	...	...	1554	...	1413	...	...	...	1706	...	1809	1809	...	...	1906	...	...	...	...	...
München Hbf **890** d.	...	...	1527	...	...	...	...	...	|	...	|	...	1723	...	|	1748	|	|	...	...	|	...	...	...	2024	...
Salzburg Hbf d.	...	...	1700	...	1705	1710	...	...	1802	...	1810	...	1902	...	1910	|	2002	2002	2010	...	2102	...	2110	...	2215	2322
Vöcklabruck d.	...	...	|	...	1749	1754	...	...	|	...	1854	...	|	...	1954	|	|	|	2054	...	|	...	2154	...	2301	0034
Attnang-Puchheim d.	...	...	|	1755	1800	1800	...	...	|	...	1900	...	|	...	2000	⊙	|	|	2100	...	|	...	2200	2203	2307	0039
Passau Hbf 🏛 d.	1605	1633	|	|	|	|	1711	1719	|	...	|	1833	|	1846	|	|	|	|	|	2033	|	2057	|	|	|	...
Schärding d.	1618	|	|	|	|	|	1725	1734	|	...	|	|	|	1901	|	|	|	|	|	|	|	2110	|	|	|	...
Neumarkt-Kallham ‡ d.	1654	|	|	|	|	|	1757	1803	|	...	|	|	|	1935	|	2013	|	|	|	|	|	2145	|	|	|	...
Wels Hbf ‡ d.	1723	1730	|	1811	1816	1816	1823	1833	|	...	1916	1930	|	2002	2016	2037	|	|	2116	2130	|	2211	2216	2225	2325	...
Linz Hbf ‡ a.	1739	1743	1807	1823	1828	1828	1839	1851	1907	...	1928	1943	2007	...	2028	2057	2107	2107	2128	2143	2207	...	2228	2240	2342	...
Linz Hbf **977** d.	...	1746	1810	1826	1831	1831	...	1857	1910	←	1931	1946	2010	...	2031	...	2110	2110	2131	2146	2210	...	2231	...	...	...
St Valentin **977** d.	...	|	|	1843	1848	1848	...	1922	|	1924	1948	|	|	...	2048	...	|	|	2148	|	|	...	2248	...	...	...
Amstetten d.	...	|	|	1900	1905	1905	...	→	|	1948	2005	|	|	...	2105	...	|	|	2205	|	|	...	2305	...	...	...
St Pölten Hbf d.	...	1839	1900	1929	1934	1934	...	...	2000	2051	2034	2039	2100	...	2134	...	2200	2200	2234	2239	2300	...	2334	...	...	...
Wien Hütteldorf ● a.	...	|	|	2004	2009	2009	...	...	|	...	2109	|	|	...	2209	...	|	|	2309	|	|	...	0009	...	...	...
Wien Westbahnhof a.	...	1922	1940	2013	2018	2018	...	...	2040	...	2118	2122	2140	...	2218	...	2240	2240	2318	2322	2340	...	0018	...	...	...

Regional trains LINZ - AMSTETTEN - MELK - WIEN (2nd class only)

		⚒	⚒			L													◧		ⒸS	⚒	†	P		
Linz Hbf **977** d.	...	*0441*	...	...	0700r	...	*0853*a	...	*0953*a	...	...	*1150*r	*1253*	...	*1353*r	*1450*	...	*1553*r	*1650*	...	...	*1753*	*1753*	1857	...	...
St Valentin **977** d.	...	0510	0534	0611	0721r	*0818*r	0921a	...	1021a	1121c	...	1219r	1321	...	1421r	1519	...	1621r	1720	...	...	1821	1821	1924	...	...
Amstetten d.	0415	0539	0614	0651	0758	0858	0958	1020	1058	1158	1220	1256	1358	1420	1458	1556	1620	1658	1758	1820	1852	1908j	1914j	1948	2020	2217
Ybbs an der Donau d.	0428	0552	0630	0706	0811	0910	1011	1035	1111	1211	1235	1309	1411	1435	1511	1609	1635	1711	1811	1835	1905	1921	1927	2003	2035	2229
Pöchlarn d.	0435	0559	0639	0719	0820	0919	1020	1048	1120	1220	1248	1318	1420	1448	1520	1618	1648	1720	1820	1848	1915	1931	1936	2018	2048	2238
Melk d.	0442	0606	0646	0726	0826	0925	1026	1055	1126	1226	1255	1324	1426	1455	1526	1624	1655	1726	1826	1855	1922	1937	1943	2030	2055	2244
St Pölten Hbf d.	0505	0630	0709	0749	0846	0946	1046	1118	1146	1246	1318	1344	1446	1518	1546	1644	1718	1746	1846	1918	1942	1955	2003	2051	2118	2305
Wien Hütteldorf ● a.	0551	0718	0753	...	0932	1031	1132	...	1232	1332	...	1432	1532	...	1632	1732	...	1832	1932	...	2026	...	2048	*2213*r	...	2352
Wien Westbahnhof a.	0600	0728	0802	...	0944	1044	1144	...	1244	1344	...	1444	1544	...	1644	1744	...	1844	1944	...	2034	...	2100	*2222*r	...	0001

♦ – **NOTES** (LISTED BY TRAIN NUMBER)

206 – MATTHIAS BRAUN – [12] Salzburg - Linz - Summerau 🏛 - Praha; 🛏 1, 2 cl. and ▬ 2 cl. Zürich (**467**) - Salzburg (**206**) - Praha; 🛏 1, 2 cl. Zagreb (**498**) - Salzburg (**206**) - Praha.

236 – ALLEGRO DON GIOVANNI – 🛏 1, 2 cl., ▬ 2 cl. and [2] Venezia - Udine - Tarvisio 🏛 - Villach - Salzburg - Wien (Table **88**).

391 – Ⓑ (not Dec. 24, 25, 31, Apr. 2, 4, May 23). [12] Frankfurt - Stuttgart - München - Linz.

463 – KÁLMÁN IMRE – 🛏 1, 2 cl., ▬ 2 cl. and [2] München - Budapest. Conveys Dec. 13 - Jan. 11 🛏 1, 2 cl. München - Budapest - Bucureşti.

467 – WIENER WALZER – ▬ 2 cl. and [2] Zürich - Wien - Budapest; 🛏 1, 2 cl., ▬ 2 cl. and [2] Zürich - Wien. 🅁 for journeys from Switzerland.

491 – HANS ALBERS – 🛏 1, 2 cl., ▬ 2 cl. and [2] Hamburg - Hannover - Nürnberg - Wien. 🛏 1, 2 cl., ▬ 2 cl. and [2] (*EN* **421**) Köln - Frankfurt - Nürnberg - Wien. 🅁 for journeys from Germany. May 22 - June 7 Passau d. 0622, Schärding d. 0636, Wels d. 0718, Linz a. 0733, d. 0735, St Valentin d. 0758, Amstetten d. 0826, St Pölten d. 0906, Wien Hütteldorf a. 0942, Wien Westbahnhof a. 0951.

B – To Budapest (Table **1250**).
G – [12] and ✕ Frankfurt - Nürnberg - Regensburg - Passau 🏛 - Wien.
H – [12] and ✕ Dortmund - Köln - Frankfurt - Nürnberg - Regensburg - Passau 🏛 - Wien.
J – From Stainach-Irdning (Table **961**).
K – From Klagenfurt (Table **970**).
L – From Kleinreifling (Table **976**).
M – ①–⑥ (also Jan. 3, Apr. 4, May 23; not Jan. 6, Apr. 5, May 24).
N – ①–⑥ (not Dec. 25, 26, Jan. 1, 2, 6, Apr. 5, May 24). [12] and 🍷 Innsbruck - Wien - Hegyeshalom 🏛 - Györ - Budapest.
P – Fom Apr. 3. [2] Passau - St Pölten - Wien Franz-Josefs-Bahnhof (a. 2209).
S – From Schladming via Selzthal (Tables **975** and **977**).
T – Conveys [12] Stainach-Irdning - Attnang-Puchheim - Wien (Table **961**).
Z – From Zürich (Table **520**).

a – Ⓐ only.
c – Ⓒ only.
j – Arrives 1856.
n – Not Dec. 24, 31.

r – ⚒ only.
t – Also Jan. 6, Apr. 5, May 24; not Jan. 3, Apr. 4, May 23.
v – Also Dec. 24, 25, 31, Jan. 5, Apr. 4, 30, May 12, 23, June 2.

◧ – Change trains at Amstetten on Ⓐ.
⊖ – Conveys [12] Saalfelden (**1501**) - Salzburg - Wien. See Table **960**.
△ – Conveys 🛏 1, 2 cl., ▬ 2 cl. and [2].
⊙ – Via Simbach (Tables **893**/**962**).
¶ – Train category *RJ* from Apr. 11.
‡ – See also Table **965**.
✣ – 60 minutes later May 22 - June 6.
● – S-Bahn trains operate every 10 – 15 minutes to / from Wien Heiligenstadt (journey time: 21 minutes). See panel below for Wien S-Bahn links to / from other Wien stations (connections to / from Wien Flughafen ✈ are available at Rennweg – see Table **979**).

WIEN S-Bahn	Ⓐn		Ⓐn	Ⓐn	Ⓐn				
Hütteldorf d.	0554	0622	0649	0722	0749	0821	and hourly until	2321	2351
Meidling **981/2** a.	0605	0634	0702	0734	0802	0832		2332	0002
Südbahnhof **981/2** a.	0613	0643	0710	0743	0810	0840		2340	0010
Rennweg a.	0616	0646	0713	0746	0813	0843		2343	0013
Mitte **981/2** a.	0618	0648	0715	0748	0815	0845		2345	0015
Praterstern **981/2** a.	0622	0652	0719	0752	0819	0849		2349	0019
Floridsdorf **981/2** a.	0631	0701	0728	0801	0828	0858		2358	0028

WIEN S-Bahn		Ⓐn	Ⓐn		Ⓐn				
Floridsdorf **981/2** d.	0502	0532	0632	0702	0732	0802	and hourly until	2202	2302
Praterstern **981/2** d.	0510	0540	0640	0710	0740	0810		2210	2310
Mitte **981/2** d.	0514	0544	0644	0714	0744	0814		2214	2314
Rennweg d.	0516	0546	0646	0716	0746	0816		2216	2316
Südbahnhof **981/2** d.	0520	0550	0650	0720	0750	0820		2220	2320
Meidling **981/2** d.	0528	0558	0658	0728	0758	0828		2228	2328
Hütteldorf a.	0539	0609	0709	0739	0814	0839		2239	2339

951 SALZBURG and MÜNCHEN - INNSBRUCK - BREGENZ - LINDAU

km		EN 466		D 15464	EN 464	EN 246		EC 760			RJ 362		IC 118	EC 81					ICE 660	EC 85		RJ 160	RJ 560			ÖEC 740
							⚒					⊙		R	Ⓐ	†				R				⊙		
		♦	2	♦	♦	△	2	✕	2	2	⊗	2	⊗♦	✕♦	2	2	2	2 J	✕	✕♦	2	⊗	⊗	2	2	✕
	Wien Westbf **950** ... d.	2225	...	...	...	2244	...	...	...	...	...	...	...	...	...	...	...	...	0614	...	...	0720	0720	...	...	0740
	Linz Hbf **950** .... d.	0010	...	...	...	0044	...	...	...	...	...	...	...	...	...	...	...	...	0747	...	...	0853	0853	...	...	0932
0	**Salzburg** Hbf........... d.	0140	...	...	...	0210	...	...	...	...	0602	...	0653	...	...	...	...	...	0857	...	...	1002	1002	...	...	1053
	München Hbf. **890** d.	|	...	...	...	|	...	...	...	...	|	...	|	0731	...	...	...	...	|	0931	...	|	|	...	...	|
	München Ost. **890** d.	|	...	...	...	|	...	...	...	...	|	...	|	0740	...	...	...	...	|	0940	...	|	|	...	...	|
	Rosenheim . **890** ☆ d.	|	...	...	...	|	...	...	...	*0610r*	|	...	|	0812	...	...	*0835*	...	|	1012	...	|	|	...	*1035*	|
120	Kufstein 🏛 ....☆ d.	|	...	...	...	|	0452	...	0514	0649	|	...	0808	0836	0849	...	0917	...	|	1036	1053	|	|	...	1117	1208
134	Wörgl Hbf .... **960** d.	|	...	0252	...	|	0506	...	0536	0700	|	...	0818	0846	0900	...	0936	1000	|	1046	1104	|	|	...	1136	1218
159	Jenbach............. **960** d.	|	...	|	...	|	0528	...	0558	0720	|	...	0832	0902	0920	...	0958	1015	|	1102	1120	|	|	...	1158	1232
193	**Innsbruck** Hbf... **960** a.	0338	...	0333	...	0434	0602	...	0632	0747	0751	...	0851	0923	0947	...	1032	1042	1046	1123	1147	1151	1151	...	1232	1252
193	**Innsbruck** Hbf.......... d.	0340	...	0356	0455	0521	▬	0621	0637	...	0754	0757	0856	▬	0957	0957	...	...	1048	...	...	1154	1154	1157	...	1256
239	Ötztal......................... d.	|	...	|	|	0546	...	0645	0732	...	|	0831	0924	...	1031	1037	...	...	|	...	...	|	|	1231	...	1324
248	Imst-Pitztal.................. d.	|	...	|	|	0556	...	0654	0747	...	|	0841	0934	...	1041	1047	...	...	|	...	...	|	|	1241	...	1334
265	Landeck - Zams .... d.	|	...	0454	0546	0611	...	0708	0802	...	0837	0856	0951	...	1056	1107	...	...	1130	...	...	1237	1237	1256	...	1348
293	St Anton am Arlberg.. d.	|	...	0519	0613	0636	...	0734	▬	...	0901	▬	1018	...	...	...	...	...	1154	...	...	1301	1301	...	...	1412
304	Langen am Arlberg ... d.	|	...	0530	0625	0648	...	0744	...	...	|	...	1028	...	...	...	...	...	1204	...	...	|	|	...	...	1422
329	Bludenz .... **952** d.	0526	0539	0614	0706	0721	①–⑤	0813	...	...	0935	...	1100	...	...	...	...	...	1236	...	...	1335	1335	...	...	1451
350	**Feldkirch**........... **952** a.	0540	0559	0635	0721	0736	w 2	0825	2	...	0946	2	1111	2	...	...	...	...	1247	...	...	1346	1346	...	...	1505
350	**Feldkirch**........... **952** d.	0545	0600	0738	0738	0742	0751	0827	0842	...	0948	0950	1113	1145	...	...	...	...	1249	...	...	1350	1353	...	...	1513
369	**Buchs** 🏛 .... **952** a.	0601	|	0753	0753	|	0812	|	0904	...	1006	|	|	1202	...	...	...	...	|	...	...	1406	|	...	...	|
	Zürich HB **520** .... a.	0720	|	0920	0920	|	...	|	...	...	1120	|	|	...	...	...	...	...	|	...	...	1520	|	...	...	|
375	Dornbirn............. **952** d.	...	0629	...	...	0800	...	0841	...	...	...	1010	1134	...	...	...	...	...	1305	...	...	...	1407	...	...	1535
387	**Bregenz** 🏛........ **952** a.	...	0644	...	...	0808	...	0849	...	...	...	1017	1142	...	...	...	...	...	1313	...	...	...	1417	...	...	1547
397	**Lindau** Hbf 🏛.... **952** a.	...	...	...	...	*0831*	...	*0905*	...	...	...	1030	1153	...	...	...	...	...	*1340*	...	...	...	*1456*	...	...	...

	EC 87	ÖEC 162			ÖEC 742	D 968	EC 89	ÖEC 564	IC 1281	IC 960	EC 83	ÖEC 566		EC 189		ÖEC 568	ICE 109	ÖEC 748		ÖEC 662			CNL 485	RJ 762		ÖEC 764
	R		⊙			Ⓒ	R		⑥	Ⓐ	R		①–⑤		⊙					¶	⚒		R	Ⓑt		
	✕♦	✕	2	2	✕	2	♦	✕	♦	🍷	♦	✕	e	✕	2	✕	✕♦	✕	2	✕	2	2	✕♦	⊗	2	✕
Wien Westbf **950**.... d.	...	0920	...	...	0944	...	...	1120	...	...	...	1320	...	...	...	1520	...	1544	...	1720	...	...	...	1820	...	1920
Linz Hbf **950**........... d.	...	1053	...	...	1132	...	...	1253	...	...	...	1453	...	...	...	1653	...	1732	...	1853	...	...	...	1953	...	2053
Salzburg Hbf.............. d.	...	1202	...	...	1253	...	...	1402	...	...	...	1602	...	...	...	1802	...	1853	...	2002	...	...	...	2106	...	2202
München Hbf...**890** d.	1131	|	...	...	|	...	1331	|	1511	...	1531	|	1700	1731	...	|	1841	|	...	|	...	...	2103	|	...	|
München Ost...**890** d.	1140	|	...	...	|	...	1340	|	|	...	1540	|	1708	1741	...	|	|	|	...	|	...	...	|	|	...	|
Rosenheim.. **890** ☆ d.	1212	|	...	*1234*	|	...	1412	|	1548	...	1612	|	1744	1812	...	|	|	|	...	|	*2035*	*2035*	2143	|	...	|
Kufstein 🏛............☆ d.	1236	|	...	1317	1408	...	1436	1520	1623	...	1636	1720	1813	1836	...	1917	1938	2008	2017	|	2117	2117	2209	|	2222	|
Wörgl Hbf............**960** d.	1246	|	...	1336	1418	...	1446	1532	1633	...	1646	1732	*1831*	1846	...	1927	1948	2018	2036	|	2136	2136	2220	2229	*2236*	2323
Jenbach...............**960** d.	1302	|	...	1358	1432	...	1502	1547	▬	...	1702	1747	*1852*	1902	...	1945	2002	2032	2058	|	2158	2158	2236	|	*2258*	|
Innsbruck Hbf.....**960** a.	1323	1351	...	1432	1452	...	1523	1606	...	...	1723	1806	▬	1923	...	2006	2023	2051	2132	2151	2232	2232	2256	2300	*2332*	2354
Innsbruck Hbf........... d.	...	1354	1357	...	...	1503	▬	1612	...	1657	...	1812	...	...	1928	2012	...	...	...	2154	2235	...	...	...	2349	...
Ötztal......................... d.	...	|	1431	...	...	1530	...	1638	...	1724	...	1838	...	...	2002	2038	...	...	...	|	2315	...	...	...	0038	...
Imst-Pitztal.................. d.	...	|	1441	...	...	1539	...	1647	...	1736	...	1847	...	...	2012	2047	...	...	...	|	2325	...	...	...	0048	...
Landeck - Zams.......... d.	...	1437	1456	...	...	1554	...	1701	...	1754	...	1901	...	...	2027	2101	...	...	...	2238	2340	...	...	...	0103	...
St Anton am Arlberg .. d.	...	1500	▬	...	...	1618	...	1730	...	1820	...	1925	...	...	...	2124	...	...	...	2302	...	...	...	...	...	...
Langen am Arlberg .... d.	...	|	...	...	...	1627	...	1741	...	1831	...	1936	*IC*	...	...	2135	...	...	...	|	...	...	...	...	...	...
Bludenz ....**952** d.	...	1534	...	...	...	1700	...	1807	...	1905	...	2003	**166**	...	...	2202	...	...	...	2336	...	...	...	...	...	...
Feldkirch ....**952** a.	...	1545	2	...	...	1715	2	1818	2	1916	...	2016	...	...	...	2213	...	...	...	2347	...	...	...	...	...	...
Feldkirch ....**952** d.	...	1548	1550	...	...	1717	1734	1820	1834	1918	...	2018	2021	...	...	2218	...	...	...	2349	...	...	...	...	...	...
Buchs 🏛 ....**952** a.	...	1606	|	...	...	|	1752	|	1852	|	...	|	2036	...	...	|	...	...	...	|	...	...	...	...	...	...
Zürich HB **520**........ a.	...	1720	|	...	...	|	...	|	...	|	...	|	2224	...	...	|	...	...	...	|	...	...	...	...	...	...
Dornbirn ....**952** d.	...	...	1610	...	...	1739	...	1836	...	1939	...	2035	...	...	...	2235	...	...	...	0004	...	...	...	...	...	...
Bregenz 🏛..........**952** a.	...	...	1617	...	...	1748	...	1847	...	1947	...	2043	...	...	...	2247	...	...	...	0012	...	...	...	...	...	...
Lindau Hbf 🏛 .....**952** a.	...	...	1630	...	...	1759	...	*1927*	...	*2005*	...	*2059*	...	...	...	*2304*	...	...	...	...	...	...	...	...	...	...

km		CNL 484	RJ 43			ÖEC 765		ÖEC 741	ICE 108		ÖEC 663			IC 961		ÖEC 561	EC 82		ÖEC 743	IC 1284			ÖEC 163		IC 165	ÖEC 565
		R	①–⑥		⚒					⊡	¶	⚒	①–⑤				R	①–⑤		⑦						
		✕♦	v B ⊗	2	2	✕	2	✕	✕♦	2	✕	2	w 2	🍷	2	✕	♦	w 2	✕	♦	2	2	✕	2		✕
	Lindau Hbf 🏛.... **952** d.	...	...	...	...	...	...	...	...	...	...	...	...	...	...	*0654*	...	...	*0754*	...	...	0928	...	...	...	*1059*
	Bregenz 🏛........ **952** d.	...	...	...	...	...	...	...	...	...	0547	...	...	0611	...	0713	...	...	0809	...	...	0941	...	...	...	1116
	Dornbirn............. **952** d.	...	...	...	...	...	...	...	...	...	0556	...	...	0619	...	0724	...	...	0819	...	...	0950	...	...	...	1126
	Zürich HB **520** .... d.	...	...	...	...	...	...	...	...	...	|	...	...	|	...	|	...	...	|	...	...	|	0840	...	1006	|
	Buchs 🏛 .... **952** d.	...	...	...	...	...	...	...	...	...	|	...	0603	|	0716	|	...	0817	|	...	...	|	0954	...	1122	|
	Feldkirch........... **952** a.	...	...	...	...	...	...	...	...	...	0610	...	0625	0640	0737	0741	...	0835	0839	...	...	1009	1009	...	1137	1140
	Feldkirch........... **952** d.	...	...	...	...	...	...	...	...	...	0612	...	▬	0642	▬	0743	...	...	0849	...	...	▬	1013	...	▬	1142
	Bludenz .... **952** d.	...	...	...	...	...	...	...	...	...	0626	...	...	0656	...	0757	...	...	0903	...	...	...	1026	...	...	1156
	Langen am Arlberg ... d.	...	...	...	...	...	...	...	...	...	|	...	...	0721	...	0822	...	...	0932	...	...	...	1050	...	...	1221
	St Anton am Arlberg.. d.	...	...	...	...	...	...	...	...	...	0659	...	...	0733	...	0834	...	...	0943	...	...	2	1101	...	...	1232
	Landeck - Zams .... d.	...	...	0404	0434	...	0512	0611a	...	0701	0724	...	...	0756	...	0900	...	...	1007	...	...	1052	1124	...	*EC*	1300
	Imst-Pitztal................. d.	...	...	0426	0451	...	0528	0624a	...	0717	|	...	...	0810	...	0913	...	...	1021	...	...	1107	|	...	**88**	1313
	Ötztal......................... d.	...	...	0437	0504	...	0539	0635a	...	0727	|	...	...	0826	*IC*	0923	...	...	1032	...	...	1127z	|	...	**R**	1323
	Innsbruck Hbf.......... a.	...	...	0526	0553	...	0610	0702a	...	0801	0806	...	2	0857	**1280**	0948	...	...	1056	...	...	1201	1206	...	♦	1348
0	**Innsbruck** Hbf... **960** d.	0436	0503	0528	▬	0606	0612	0707	0736	...	0809	0813	0828	...	⑥	0954	1036	...	1106	...	1128	...	1209	1213	1236	1354
34	Jenbach............. **960** d.	0500	|	0602	①–⑤	|	0640	0727	0757	...	|	0840	0902	...	♦	1014	1058	...	1126	...	1202	...	|	1240	1258	1414
59	Wörgl Hbf .... **960** d.	0518	0536	0630	e	0639	0700	0742	0812	...	|	0855	0930	...	1023	1030	1114	...	1141	1206	1230	...	|	1300	1314	1430
73	Kufstein 🏛............☆ d.	0530	|	0643	0700	|	0713	0751	0821	...	|	0905	0943	...	1034	1045	1124	...	1151	1220	1243	...	|	1310	1324	1445
107	Rosenheim . **890** ☆ a.	0551	|	...	0730	|	...	|	|	...	|	...	*1023*	...	1110	|	1143	...	|	1240	*1324*	...	...	...	1343	|
162	**München** Ost. **890** a.	|	|	...	0809	|	...	|	|	...	|	...	...	...	|	|	1214	...	|	|	...	...	|	...	1414	|
172	**München** Hbf. **890** a.	0630	|	...	0819	|	...	|	0915	...	|	...	...	...	1150	|	1225	...	|	1322	...	...	|	...	1425	|
	Salzburg Hbf........... a.	...	0658	...	...	0800	...	0907	...	...	0959	...	...	...	...	1158	...	...	1307	...	...	...	1359	...	...	1558
	Linz Hbf **950** .... a.	...	0807	...	...	0907	...	1028	...	...	1107	...	...	...	...	1307	...	...	1428	...	...	...	1507	...	...	1707
	Wien Westbf **950** ... a.	...	0940	...	...	1040	...	1218	...	...	1240	...	...	...	...	1440	...	...	1624	...	...	...	1640	...	...	1840

♦ – **NOTES** (LISTED BY TRAIN NUMBER)

81 – VAL GARDENA / GRÖDNERTAL – [12] and ✕ München - Brennero 🏛 - Bolzano/Bozen.
82/3 – GARDA – [12] Verona - Bolzano/Bozen - Brennero 🏛 - München and v.v.
85 – MICHELANGELO – [12] and ✕ München - Brennero 🏛 - Bolzano/Bozen - Verona - Bologna.
87 – TIEPOLO – [12] and ✕ München - Brennero 🏛 - Bolzano/Bozen - Verona.
88/9 – LEONARDO DA VINCI – [12] Milano - Verona - Bolzano/Bozen - Brennero 🏛 - München and v.v.
108/9 – [12] and ✕ Innsbruck - München - Nürnberg - Leipzig - Berlin and v.v.
118 – [12] and ⊗ Salzburg - Lindau - Ulm - Stuttgart - Köln - Münster.
484/5 – LUPUS – 🛏 1, 2 cl., ▬ 2 cl., [2] and ✕ Roma - Verona - Brennero 🏛 - München and v.v.; 🛏 1, 2 cl., ▬ 2 cl. and [2] (**40484/5** – PICTOR) Venezia - Verona - München and v.v.
464 – ZÜRICHSEE – 🛏 1, 2 cl., ▬ 2 cl. and [2] Graz - Bruck a. d. Mur - Selzthal - Schwarzach - Zürich. Conveys from Schwarzach (except when train **15464** runs) 🛏 1, 2 cl.*, ▬ 2 cl.* and [2] Beograd (**414**) - Zagreb - Ljubljana - Villach - Schwarzach (**464**) - Zürich.
466 – WIENER WALZER – ▬ 2 cl. and [2] Budapest - Hegyeshalom 🏛 - Wien - Zürich; 🛏 1, 2 cl., ▬ 2 cl. and [2] Wien - Zürich; 🛏 1, 2 cl. and ▬ 2 cl. Praha (**207**) - Salzburg - Zürich and v.v. Ⓡ for journeys to Switzerland.
1280 – ⑥ Dec. 26 - Apr. 10 (also Jan. 6). GROSSGLOCKNER – [12] Zell am See - Wörgl - München.
1281 – ⑥ Dec. 19 - Apr. 3 (also Dec. 23). GROSSGLOCKNER – [12] München - Wörgl - Schwarzach.
1284 ⑦ Dec. 20 - Mar. 28 (also Apr. 5). GROSSGLOCKNER – [12] Schwarzach - Wörgl - München - Hamburg - Flensburg.
15464 – From Wörgl daily to Jan. 7 and Mar. 26 - Apr. 7 (also Feb. 13, 14, 20, 21); ①⑥⑦ from Apr. 10 (also May 13, 14, 25, June 3, 4). 🛏 1, 2 cl.*, ▬ 2 cl.* and [2] Beograd (**414**) - Zagreb - Ljubljana - Villach - Schwarzach (**15464**) - Feldkirch (**464**) - Zürich.

B – To Budapest (Table **1250**).
J – From St Johann in Tirol (Table **960**).
R – Ⓡ for journeys to / from Italy.

a – Ⓐ only.
e – Not Dec. 24, 25, 31, Jan. 1, 6, Apr. 2, 5, May 13, 24, June 3.
n – Not Dec. 24.
r – ①–⑥ (not Dec. 25, 26, Jan. 1, 6, Apr. 2, 5, May 1, 13, 24, June 3).
t – Not Dec. 24, 25, 31, Jan. 1, 5, Apr. 4, May 23.
v – Not Dec. 25, 26, Jan. 1, 2, 6, Apr. 5, May 24.
w – Not Dec. 25, Jan. 1, Apr. 5, May 13, 24.
z – 1122 on †.

* – 🛏 1, 2 cl. and ▬ 2 cl. from / to Zagreb.
△ – Conveys 🛏 1, 2 cl., ▬ 2 cl. and [2].
¶ – Train category *RJ* from Apr. 11.
⊙ – 6 minutes later at Ötztal, Imst-Pitztal and Landeck-Zams on †.
⊡ – 5–9 minutes **earlier** at Landeck-Zams, Imst-Pitztal and Ötztal on †.
☆ – Additional local trains **Rosenheim - Kufstein** and v.v. (journey time 27–30 minutes): **From Rosenheim** at 0734, 0935, 1135, 1334, 1436, 1535, 1634, 1835, 1935, 2135, 2235 **n** and 2334 **n**.
From Kufstein at 0634 ①–⑥ **r**, 0754, 0854 and hourly to 1754; then 1855, 1954, 2054, 2154 and 2254 **n**.

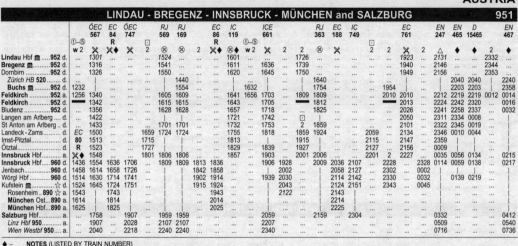

LINDAU - BREGENZ - INNSBRUCK - MÜNCHEN and SALZBURG 951

		ÖEC	EC	ÖEC		RJ	RJ		EC	IC		ICE			RJ	EC	IC			EC		EN	EN	D		EN
		567	**84**	**747**		**569**	**169**		**86**	**119**		**661**			**363**	**188**	**749**			**761**		**247**	**465**	**15465**		**467**
	①–⑤		R		⊡				R		①–⑤							⊡								
	w 2	✕	✕♦	✕	2	⊗	⊗	2	✕♦	⊗♦	w 2	✕	2	2	⊗	✕		2	2	✕	2	△	♦	♦	2	♦
Lindau Hbf 🏛 .....**952** d.	...	*1301*	...	...	...	*1524*	...	...	...	1601	...	...	...	1726	...	...	...	...	...	*1923*	...	*2131*	...	...	2332	...
Bregenz 🏛 ....**952** d.	...	1316	...	...	...	1541	...	...	...	1611	...	1636	...	1739	...	...	...	...	...	1940	...	2146	...	...	2344	...
Dornbirn ....**952** d.	...	1326	...	...	...	1550	...	...	...	1620	...	1645	...	1750	...	...	...	...	...	1949	...	2156	...	...	2353	...
Zürich HB **520** .... d.	...	|	...	...	...	|	1440	...	...	|	...	|	...	|	1640	...	...	...	...	|	...	|	2040	2040	|	2240
Buchs 🏛 ....**952** d.	1232	|	...	...	...	|	1554	...	...	|	1632	|	...	|	1754	...	...	...	1954	|	...	|	2203	2203	|	2358
Feldkirch ....**952** a.	1256	1340	...	...	...	1605	1609	...	...	1641	1656	1703	...	1809	1809	...	...	...	2010	2010	...	2212	2219	2219	0012	0014
Feldkirch ....**952** d.	▬	1342	...	...	...	1615	1615	...	...	1643	...	1705	...	▬	1812	...	...	...	▬	2013	...	2224	2242	2320	...	0016
Bludenz ....**952** d.	...	1356	...	...	...	1628	1628	...	...	1657	...	1718	...	...	1825	...	...	...	...	2026	...	2241	2258	2337	...	0032
Langen am Arlberg .... d.	...	1422	...	...	...	|	|	...	...	1721	...	1742	...	⊡	|	...	...	...	...	2050	...	2311	2334	0008	...	|
St Anton am Arlberg .. d.	...	1433	...	...	...	1701	1701	...	...	1732	...	1753	...	2	1859	...	...	...	...	2101	...	2322	2345	0019	...	|
Landeck - Zams.......... d.	*EC*	1500	...	...	1659	1724	1724	...	...	1755	...	1818	...	1859	1924	...	...	2059	...	2134	...	2346	0010	0044	...	|
Imst-Pitztal................. d.	**80**	1513	...	...	1715	|	|	...	...	1813	...	|	...	1915	|	...	...	2115	...	2147	...	2359	|	|	...	|
Ötztal.......................... d.	**R**	1523	...	...	1727	|	|	...	...	1829	...	1839	...	1927	|	...	...	2127	...	2156	...	0009	|	|	...	|
Innsbruck Hbf........... a.	✕♦	1548	...	...	1801	1806	1806	...	...	1857	...	1903	...	2001	2006	...	...	2201	2	2227	...	0035	0056	0134	...	0215
Innsbruck Hbf.....**960** d.	1436	1554	1636	1706	...	1809	1809	1813	1836	...	...	1906	1928	...	2009	2036	2107	...	2228	...	2328	0114	0059	0138	...	0217
Jenbach...............**960** d.	1458	1614	1658	1726	...	|	|	1842	1858	...	...	|	2002	...	|	2058	2127	...	2302	...	0002	|	|	|	...	|
Wörgl Hbf ....**960** d.	1514	1630	1714	1741	...	|	|	1902	1914	...	...	1939	2030	...	|	2114	2142	...	2330	...	0032	|	0139	0219	...	|
Kufstein 🏛............☆ d.	1524	1645	1724	1751	...	|	|	1915	1924	...	...	|	2043	...	|	2124	2151	...	2343	...	0045	|	...	...	...	|
Rosenheim .. **890** ☆ a.	1543	|	1743	|	...	|	|	...	1943	...	...	|	*2122*	...	|	2143	|	...	...	...	...	|	...	...	...	|
München Ost...**890** a.	1614	|	1814	|	...	|	|	...	2014	...	...	|	...	...	|	2214	|	...	...	...	...	|	...	...	...	|
München Hbf...**890** a.	1625	|	1825	|	...	|	|	...	2025	...	...	|	...	...	|	2225	|	...	...	...	...	|	...	...	...	|
Salzburg Hbf............ a.	...	1758	...	1907	...	1959	1959	...	...	...	...	2059	...	...	2159	...	2304	...	...	...	...	0332	...	...	...	0412
Linz Hbf **950**........... a.	...	1907	...	2028	...	2107	2107	...	...	...	...	2207	...	...	...	...	...	...	...	...	...	0509	...	...	...	0540
Wien Westbf **950**.... a.	...	2040	...	2218	...	2240	2240	...	...	...	...	2340	...	...	...	...	...	...	...	...	...	0716	...	...	...	0736

♦ – **NOTES** (LISTED BY TRAIN NUMBER)

80 – VAL GARDENA / GRÖDNERTAL – [12] and ✕ Bolzano/Bozen - Brennero 🏛 - München.

84 – MICHELANGELO – [12] and ✕ Bologna - Verona - Bolzano/Bozen - Brennero 🏛 - München.

86 – TIEPOLO – [12] and ✕ Verona - Bolzano/Bozen - Brennero 🏛 - München.

119 – [12] and ⊗ Münster - Köln - Stuttgart - Ulm - Lindau - Innsbruck.

465 – ZÜRICHSEE – 🛏 1, 2 cl., ▬ 2 cl. and [2] Zürich - Schwarzach - Selzthal - Bruck a. d. Mur - Graz. Conveys (except when train **15465** runs) 🛏 1, 2 cl.*, ▬ 2 cl.* and [2] Zürich - Schwarzach (**415**) - Villach - Ljubljana - Zagreb - Beograd.

467 – WIENER WALZER – ▬ 2 cl. and [2] Zürich - Wien - Hegyeshalom 🏛 - Budapest; 🛏 1, 2 cl., ▬ 2 cl. and [2] Zürich - Wien; 🛏 1, 2 cl. and ▬ 2 cl. Zürich - Salzburg (**206**) - Praha. Ⓡ for journeys to / from Switzerland.

15465 – Daily to Jan. 6 and Mar. 25 - Apr. 6 (also Feb. 12, 13, 19, 20); ⑤–⑦ from Apr. 9 (also May 12, 13, 24, June 2, 3). 🛏 1, 2 cl.*, ▬ 2 cl.* and [2] Zürich (**465**) - Feldkirch (**15465**) - Schwarzach (**415**) - Villach - Ljubljana - Zagreb - Beograd.

R – Ⓡ for journeys from Italy.

w – Not Dec. 25, Jan. 1, Apr. 5, May 13, 24.

⊡ – 3 – 5 minutes **earlier** at Landeck-Zams, Imst-Pitztal and Ötztal on †.

△ – Conveys 🛏 1, 2 cl., ▬ 2 cl. and [2].

☆ – See note on page 446 for additional local trains.

VORARLBERG LOCAL SERVICES 952

2nd class only (except where shown)

(Schruns ⊡ -) Bludenz - Bregenz - Lindau ⊖

		Ⓐz							Ⓐ										Ⓐ								
Schruns.... ⊡ d.	...	...	...	...	0703v	...	...	...	...	...	...	...	1307	...	...	1507	...	1603	...	...	...	...	...	...	...	...	...
Bludenz ...... ⊡ d.	...	0509	0605	0656	0731	0802	0839	0939	1009	1109	1139	1300	1339	1430	1439	1539	1600	1630	1700	1730	1809	1909	2039	2139	2239	2339	0039
Feldkirch ....d.	0500	0530	0618	0713	0747	0830	0900	1000	1030	1130	1200	1317	1400	1447	1500	1600	1617	1647	1717	1747	1830	1930	2100	2200	2300	0000	0100
Dornbirn ....d.	0529	0559	0639	0735	0809	0859	0929	1029	1059	1159	1229	1339	1429	1509	1529	1629	1639	1709	1739	1809	1859	1959	2129	2229	2329	0029	0129
Bregenz 🏛........d.	0545	0615	0650	0747	0819	0915	0945	1045	1115	1215	1245	1349	1445	1519	1545	1645	1648	1719	1749	1819	1915	2015	2147	2244	2344	0044	0144
Lindau Hbf 🏛 ..a.	0556	0627	0659	0758	0831	0927	0957	1057	1127	1227	1257	1401	1456	1531	1557	1657	...	1731	1801	1831	1927	2027	2159	*2304*	...	...	...

						Ⓐ			Ⓐ			Ⓐ								Ⓐ							
Lindau Hbf 🏛 ..d.	...	...	0631	0716	0754	0831	0901	0958	1031	...	1157	1227	1327	1427	...	1524	1631	1701	1757	1827	1901	1957	2031	2101	2227	...	...
Bregenz 🏛........d.	0514	0614	0644	0729	0814	0844	0914	1010	1044	1114	1210	1240	1340	1440	1510	1544	1644	1714	1810	1840	1914	2010	2044	2114	2240	2314	0014
Dornbirn ....d.	0530	0630	0700	0743	0830	0900	0930	1021	1100	1130	1221	1251	1351	1451	1521	1600	1700	1730	1821	1851	1930	2021	2100	2130	2251	2330	0030
Feldkirch ....d.	0601	0701	0731	0810	0901	0931	1001	1044	1131	1201	1244	1314	1414	1514	1544	1631	1731	1801	1844	1914	2001	2044	2130	2201	2314	0001	0101
Bludenz ...... ⊡ a.	0621	0721	0751	0825	0921	0951	1021	1059	1151	1221	1259	1329	1429	1529	1559	1651	1751	1821	1859	1929	2021	2059	...	2221	2329	0021	0121
Schruns.... ⊡ a.	0650v	...	...	...	...	...	...	...	...	1257	...	...	1457	1557	...	...	...	...	...	...	...	...	...	...	...	...	...

St Margrethen - Bregenz - Lindau △

km																										
						EC 191			*EC* 193					*EC* 195								*EC* 197				
			Ⓐ			Z			Z					Z					Ⓐ			Z				
0	St Margrethen 🏛 ...... d.	0624	0654	0724	0811	0842	0911	...	1042	1155	...	1311	1355	1442	...	1555	1624	1655	1724	1755	1855	1942	2055	2154	2235	2354
12	**Bregenz** 🏛.............. a.	0640	0710	0740	0827	0853	0927	...	1053	1210	...	1327	1410	1453	...	1610	1640	1710	1740	1810	1910	1953	2110	2211	2251	0010
22	**Lindau** Hbf 🏛.......... a.	*0659*	*0727*	*0758*	*0857*	0905	*0957*	...	1105	*1227*	...	1340	*1427*	1505	...	*1630*	*1657*	*1731*	*1801*	*1831*	*1927*	2005	*2159*	...	2304	...

							EC 196								*EC* 194							*EC* 192			*EC* 190	
		Ⓐ					Z		Ⓐ					Z				Ⓐ			Z			Z		
Lindau Hbf 🏛 .... d.	...	...	*0631*	*0716*	*0831*	...	0954	1059	1129	...	*1227*	...	1357	1454	*1524*	1605	*1631*	*1701*	*1726*	...	1855	*1923*	*2031*	2055	*2131*	*2227*
Bregenz 🏛................ d.	0541	0618	0648	0748	0852	...	1006	1110	1141	1206	1248	...	1410	1506	1548	1618	1648	1718	1748	...	1906	1949	2048	2106	2148	2252
St Margrethen 🏛 .... a.	0557	0633	0703	0803	0903	...	1018	1125	...	1222	1304	...	1425	1518	1603	1634	1703	1734	1803	...	1918	2004	2103	2118	2204	2308

Feldkirch - Buchs ⊖

km		A	A	A					A			
0	**Feldkirch**........ d.	0533	0634	0714	0751	0842	1145	1634	1704	1734	1834	...
16	Schaan-Vaduz d.	0552	0653	0733	0809	0901	1158	1649	1719	1749	1849	...
19	**Buchs** 🏛........ a.	0555	0656	0736	0812	0904	1202	1652	1722	1752	1852	...

	A		A	A		A		A			
Buchs 🏛.............. d.	0603	0716	0817	1232	...	1632	1702	1732	1804	1904	1954
Schaan-Vaduz .... d.	0606	0719	0820	1235	...	1635	1705	1735	1807	1907	1957
Feldkirch.............. a.	0625	0737	0835	1256	...	1656	1726	1756	1826	1926	2010

A – ①–⑤ (not Dec. 25, Jan. 1, Apr. 5, May 13, 24).

Z – [12] and ✕ Zürich - St Gallen - Lindau - München and v.v. See also Table **75**.

v – ⚒ only.

z – Runs daily Bregenz - Lindau.

△ – Austrian holiday dates apply.

⊖ – See also Table **951**.

⊡ – Complete service **BLUDENZ - SCHRUNS** and v.v. (*12 km*, journey 20 minutes). Operated by Montafonerbahn AG ✆ +43 (0) 5556 9000.
From Bludenz at 0540 Ⓐ, 0630 ⚒, 0703, 0733, 0807, 0833, 0937, 1033, 1130, 1207 ⚒, 1237, 1307 ⚒, 1337, 1437, 1537, 1603, 1633, 1703, 1737, 1810, 1835, 1935, 2035, 2135, 2233.
From Schruns at 0510 Ⓐ, 0540 ⚒, 0630, 0703, 0733, 0807, 0903, 1003, 1103, 1130 ⚒, 1207, 1237 ⚒, 1307, 1407, 1507, 1537, 1603, 1633, 1703, 1737, 1810, 1903, 2003, 2103, 2203.

🚌 IMST - ÖTZTAL - OBERGURGL and ST ANTON - LECH 953

ÖBB-Postbus

km	🚌 Route **4194**																						
																Ⓐ							
0	**Imst** (Postamt).............................d.	0605	0635	...	0805	0905	1010	1110	1155	1235	1325	...	1505	1610	1645	...	...	1810	1900	...	...	...	...
13	**Ötztal** (Bahnhof) ....a.	0619	0649	...	0819	0919	1024	1124	1209	1249	1339	...	1519	1624	1659	...	...	1824	1914	...	...	...	...
13	**Ötztal** (Bahnhof) ....d.	0620	0700	...	0835	0930	1035	1135	1215	1300	1345	...	1530	1630	1705	1730	...	1840	1915	...	...	...	...
21	Oetz (Posthotel Kassel)....................d.	0634	0714	...	0849	0944	1049	1149	1229	1314	1359	...	1544	1644	1719	1744	...	1854	1929	...	...	...	...
54	Sölden (Postamt).............................d.	0722	0802	...	0937	1032	1137	1237	1317	1402	1447	...	1632	1732	1807	1832	...	1942	2017	...	...	...	...
58	Zwieselstein (Gh Neue Post) ....d.	0730	0810	...	0945	1040	1145	1245	1325	1410	1455	...	1640	1740	1815	1840	...	1950	2025	...	...	...	...
68	**Obergurgl** (Zentrum) ....a.	0745	0825	...	1000	1055	1200	1300	1340	1425	1510	...	1655	1755	1830	...	...	2005	2040	...	...	...	...

🚌 Route **4194**																							
	Ⓐ																						
Obergurgl (Zentrum) ....d.	...	...	...	0655	0745	0845	...	1010	1110	1205	1300	1345	...	1515	1555	1655	1755	1855	...	...	...	...	...
Zwieselstein (Gh Neue Post) ....d.	0520	0555	...	0710	0800	0900	...	1025	1125	1220	1315	1400	...	1530	1610	1710	1810	1910	...	...	...	...	...
Sölden (Postamt)...............................d.	0530	0605	...	0720	0810	0910	...	1035	1135	1230	1325	1410	...	1540	1620	1720	1820	1920	...	...	...	...	...
Oetz (Posthotel Kassel).....................d.	0615	0650	...	0810	0900	1000	...	1125	1225	1320	1415	1500	...	1630	1710	1810	1910	2010	...	...	...	...	...
Ötztal (Bahnhof) ....a.	0627	0702	...	0822	0912	1012	...	1137	1237	1332	1427	1512	...	1642	1722	1822	1922	2022	...	...	...	...	...
Ötztal (Bahnhof) ....d.	...	0705	...	0825	0915	1015	...	1140	1240	1335	1430	1515	...	1645	1730	1825	1925	2025	...	...	...	...	...
Imst (Postamt)..................................a.	...	0720	...	0840	0930	1030	...	1155	1255	1350	1445	1530	...	1700	1745	1840	1940	2040	...	...	...	...	...

🚌 Route **4248**: **ST ANTON AM ARLBERG - LECH** *20 km* Journey time: 38 – 48 minutes

From St Anton am Arlberg Bahnhof at 0755, 0905, 0955, 1055, 1225, 1325 ◇, 1505, 1705 ◇, 1732 and 1755 ◇.

From Lech Postamt at 0819 ◇, 0849, 1049, 1249 ◇, 1349, 1649, 1749 ◇ and 1819.

Winter service: **Valid Dec. 13 - Apr. 25.**

☛ All services call at St Christoph am Arlberg and Zürs.

Services marked ◇ operate until Apr. 11 only.

954 LANDECK - NAUDERS - SCUOL and MALLES

				Ⓐ				
Landeck - Zams (Bahnhof) **951** d.	0650	0805	1005	1105	1205	and	1805	1905
Ried im Oberinntal (Postamt) d.	0718	0833	1033	1133	1233	hourly	1833	1933
Nauders (Postamt) a.	0758	0913	1113	1213	1313	until	1913	2013
Nauders (Mühle) a.	0800	0915	1115	1215	1315		1915	2017

					Ⓐ				
Nauders (Postamt) d.	0605	0845	0945	1145	1245	1345	and	1645	1755
Nauders (Mühle) d.	0607	0847	0947	1147	1247	1347	hourly	1647	1757
Ried im Oberinntal (Postamt) d.	0648	0928	1028	1228	1328	1428	until	1728	1838
Landeck - Zams (Bahnhof) **951** a.	0713	0953	1053	1253	1353	1453		1753	1903

Nauders (Mühle) d.	0847	0947	1147	1347	1547	1747	1947	...
Martina (posta) 🏛 d.	0901	1001	1201	1401	1601	1801	2001	...
Scuol Tarasp (Staziun) **546** a.	0928	1028	1228	1428	1628	1828	2028	...

Scuol Tarasp (Staziun) **546** d.	0730	0830	1030	1230	1430	1630	1830	...	...
Martina (posta) 🏛 d.	0800	0900	1100	1300	1500	1700	1900	...	...
Nauder (Mühle) a.	0811	0911	1111	1311	1511	1711	1911	...	...

	⚒	⚒	⚒					⚒
Nauders (Postamt) d.	...	0717	0817	0917	and hourly		1917	2017
Reschenpass / Passo di Resia 🏛 d.	0623	0723	0823	0923	on ⚒ (every		1923	2023
Resia d.	0627	0727	0827	0927	**two** hours		1927	2027
Malles Stazione **597** a.	0658	0758	0858	0958	on †) until		1958	2058

	⚒	⚒		⚒	✣		⚒	⚒
Malles Stazione **597** d.	0605	0705	0802	0902	and hourly	1802	1902	2002
Resia d.	0636	0736	0833	0933	on ⚒ (every	1833	1933	2033
Passo di Resia / Reschenpass 🏛 d.	0640	0740	0837	0937	**two** hours	1837	1937	2037
Nauders (Postamt) a.	0646	0746	0843	0943	on †) until	1843	1943	...

✣ – The 1202 from Malles runs 30 minutes later on Ⓑ.

Operators: Landeck - Nauders - Scuol-Tarasp: Bundesbus, Postautostelle, A-6500 Landeck: ✆ +43 (0) 5442 64 422.
Auto da posta, Agentura Scuol, CH-7550 Scuol: ✆ +41 (0) 81 86 41 683, Fax +41 (0) 81 86 49 148.
Nauders - Malles: SAD – Servizi Autobus Dolomiti, Via Conciapelli 60, I-39100 Bolzano: ✆ +39 0471 97 12 59, Fax +39 0471 97 00 42.

955 JENBACH - MAYRHOFEN

2nd class only Narrow gauge Zillertalbahn *

km														A	B	
0	**Jenbach** Zillertalbahnhof § d.	0630	0652	...	0725	0755		1755	1825	...	1925	...		1035	1535	...
11	Fügen-Hart △ d.	0644	0709	...	0743	0813	and every	1813	1843	...	1941	...		1104	1604	...
13	Uderns d.	0648	0713	...	0748	0818		1818	1848	...	1946	...	also	1110	1610	...
17	Kaltenbach-Stumm d.	0655	0720	...	0755	0825	30 minutes	1825	1855	...	1953	...		1128	1628	...
21	Aschau im Zillertal △ d.	0703	0727	...	0803	0833		1833	1903	...	2001	...		1137	1637	...
25	**Zell am Ziller** d.	0712	0736	...	0812	0842	until	1842	1912	...	2010	...		1147	1647	...
32	**Mayrhofen** a.	0724	0748	...	0824	0854		1854	1924	...	2022	...		1205	1705	...

													A	B	
Mayrhofen d.	0537	0637	...	0737	0807		1807	1837	...	1937	...		1254	1724	...
Zell am Ziller d.	0549	0648	...	0748	0818	and every	1818	1848	...	1947	...		1311	1741	...
Aschau im Zillertal △ d.	0556	0656	...	0756	0826		1826	1856	...	1954	...	also	1320	1750	...
Kaltenbach-Stumm d.	0602	0702	...	0802	0832	30 minutes	1832	1902	...	2000	...		1337	1807	...
Uderns d.	0608	0712	...	0809	0839		1839	1909	...	2007	...		1347	1817	...
Fügen-Hart △ d.	0613	0718	...	0815	0845	until	1845	1915	...	2012	...		1355	1825	...
Jenbach Zillertalbahnhof § a.	0630	0735	...	0835	0905		1905	1935	...	2027	...		1420	1850	...

A – Daily Dec. 25 - Jan. 6, Apr. 2–5 and from May 1 (also ③ Jan. 13 - Mar. 17).
B – Daily from May 29.

– Steam train. Special fares apply.
§ – Adjacent to ÖBB station.

* – Zillertaler Vehrkehrsbetriebe, Austraße, A-6200 Jenbach. ✆ +43 (0) 5244 606 0.

956 JENBACH - ACHENSEE

Achenseebahn 2nd class only

Narrow gauge rack railway operated by steam locomotives. Special fares apply. **Service May 29 - October 3, 2010** *.

km									
0	**Jenbach** Achensee-Bahnhof § d.	0840	1015	1055	1215	1345	1500	1645	...
5	Maurach d.	0915	1050	1130	1250	1420	1535	1720	...
7	**Achensee** Seespitz-Bahnstation a.	0925	1100	1140	1300	1430	1545	1730	...

Achensee Seespitz-Bahnstation d.	0930	1110	1230	1400	1515	1600	...	1736
Maurach d.	0937	1117	1237	1407	1522	1607	...	1742
Jenbach Achensee-Bahnhof § a.	1010	1150	1310	1440	1555	1640	...	1815

§ – Adjacent to ÖBB station.

Operator: Achenseebahn AG, A-6200 Jenbach: ✆ +43 (0) 5244 62243, Fax +43 (0) 5244 622435.

* – Service May 1–28 and October 4–24: **Jenbach** → **Achensee** at 1105, 1305 and 1505; **Achensee** → **Jenbach** at 1200, 1400 and 1600.

957 MAYRHOFEN - (🚌) - KRIMML - ZELL AM SEE

2nd class only

km	🚌 *Routes* **4094** and **670** *Valid June 6 - Oct. 4, 2009*		A		A ①–⑤	A ⑥⑦			A ◇	
0	**Mayrhofen** Bahnhof d.	0830	...	...	...	...	...	...	...	1830
8	Zell am Ziller Bahnhof d.	0852	...	1052	...	...	1322	1552	...	1847
28	**Gerlos** Gasthaus Oberwirt d.	0927	...	1127	...	...	1357	1627	...	1920
37	Königsleiten Sessellift d.	0934r	0944r	1140	1400	1400	1410	1636r	1644r	...
50	Krimml Wasserfälle a.	...	1004	...	1424	1424	...	...	1704	...
53	**Krimml** Bahnhof a.	...	*1014*	...	1434	*1436*	...	...	1714	...

🚌 *Routes* **670** and **4094** *Valid June 6 - Oct. 4, 2009*		A ⊖				A		A	
Krimml Bahnhof d.	...	0834	...	...	...	*1318*	...	*1538*	...
Krimml Wasserfälle d.	...	0841	...	...	...	1327	...	1547	...
Königsleiten Sessellift d.	...	0907	0950	...	1155	1353	1450	1613	1720
Gerlos Gasthaus Oberwirt d.	0700	...	1003	...	1208	...	1503	...	1733
Zell am Ziller Bf a.	0734	...	1036	...	1241	...	1536	...	1806
Mayrhofen Bahnhof a.	0748	...	...	...	...	...	...	...	1819

Train (narrow gauge) / 🚌 : KRIMML - ZELL AM SEE ⊡

km		©🚌		Ⓐ	Ⓐ		🚌		🚌			🚌			🚌			🚌			🚌		🚌	
	Krimml Wasserfälle d.	0523	...	...	...	...	0823	...	0923	...	...	1123	...	...	1323	...	...	1523	...	...	1723	...	1823	...
0	**Krimml** Bahnhof d.	0529	...	...	...	...	0829	...	0929	...	...	1129	...	...	1329	...	...	1529	...	...	1729	...	1829	...
14	Bramberg d.	0550	0552	0622	0702	0752	0850	0852	0950	0952	1052	1150	1152	1252	1350	1352	1452	1550	1552	1652	1750	1752	1850	1852
24	Mittersill Bahnhof d.	...	0608	0638	0724	0808	...	0908	...	1008	1108	...	1208	1308	...	1408	1508	...	1608	1708	...	1808	...	1908
53	**Zell am See** Lokalbahn a.	...	0656	0726	0806	0856	...	0956	...	1056	1156	...	1256	1356	...	1456	1556	...	1656	1756	...	1856	...	1956

		🚌				🚌			🚌			🚌			🚌			🚌		🚌		©🚌	Ⓐ🚌	
Zell am See Lokalbahn d.	0630	...	...	0800	0900	...	1000	1100	...	1200	1300	...	1400	1500	...	1600	1700	...	1800	...	1900	...	...	2000
Mittersill d.	0718	...	...	0848	0948	...	1048	1148	...	1248	1348	...	1448	1548	...	1648	1748	...	1848	...	1948	...	...	2048
Bramberg a.	0734	0736	...	0904	1004	1006	1104	1204	1206	1304	1404	1406	1504	1604	1606	1704	1804	1806	1904	1906	2004	2006	2010	2104
Krimml Bahnhof a.	...	0756	...	...	...	1026	...	...	1226	...	...	1426	...	...	1626	...	...	1826	...	1926	...	2029	2030	...
Krimml Wasserfälle a.	...	0803	...	...	...	1033	...	...	1233	...	...	1433	...	...	1633	...	...	1833	...	1933	...	2038	2037	...

A – July 4 - Sept. 13, 2009.
r – Königsleiten Abzw Gerlospass.

◇ – Change at Krimml Wasserfälle on Ⓑ.
⊖ – Change at Krimml Wasserfälle on ①–⑤.

⊡ – Runs year round. Train call at Mittersill on request only. All trains are currently replaced by 🚌 between Krimml and Bramberg. **Operator**: Pinzgauer Lokalbahn.

958 🚌 WÖRGL - ELLMAU - KITZBÜHEL and ST JOHANN

ÖBB-Postbus routes **4006**, **4060**, **4902**

	Ⓐ	Ⓐ	⑥h	⚒	⚒	⚒	⚒			⚒		Ⓐ	⚒	Ⓑm	⚒		⚒		†	⚒	Ⓐ	⚒	⚒	Ⓐ	Ⓑm
Wörgl Bahnhof d.	0550	...	...	0640	0745	...	0845	...	...	1120	...	1210	1210	...	...	...	1405	...	...	1615	...	1725	...	1835	...
Kufstein Bahnhof ▲ d.	*0545*	...	*0545*	|	*0735*	...	|	*0842*	1108	|	1208	|	|	...	...	1345	|	1520	...	*1620*	...	*1715*	1800	|	*1828*
Söll (Dorf) d.	0610	...	0612	0700	0805	...	0917	0917	1136	1140	1240	1240	1240	1240	...	1414	1435	1545	1545	1645	...	1755	1828	1905	1905
Scheffau ★ d.	0617	...	0619	...	0812	...	0924	0924	...	1147	...	1247	1247	1247	...	...	1444	...	1552	1653	...	1805	...	1913	1913
Ellmau (Dorf) d.	0626	0626	0628	...	0821	0900	0940	0940	...	1203	...	1303	1303	1303	1315	...	1501	...	1604	1706	1715	1820	...	1924	1924
Kitzbühel Bahnhof a.	|	0650	|	...	|	0924	|	|	...	|	...	|	...	|	1345	...	|	...	|	|	1745	|	...	|	|
St Johann in Tirol Bahnhof a.	0644	...	0646	...	0839	...	1000	1000	...	1223	...	1323	...	1323	...	...	1521	...	1627	1730	...	1840	...	1940	1940

	⚒	Ⓐ	⚒	†	⚒	⚒			⚒		⚒	Ⓐ	⑥h		⚒		⚒	Ⓐ	Ⓑ	Ⓐ	⚒	⚒	Ⓐ	Ⓐ	Ⓐ
St Johann in Tirol Bahnhof d.	0535	0535	0725	0750	...	0840	...	1055	1055	...	...	1230	...	1330	1330	...	1550	...	1700	1700	...	1740	...	...	1850
Kitzbühel Bahnhof d.	|	|	|	|	0800	|	...	|	|	...	1215	|	...	|	|	...	|	1620	|	|	...	|	...	1815	|
Ellmau (Dorf) d.	0552	0552	0743	0812	0830	0902	...	1117	1117	...	1245	1257	1303	1352	1352	...	1612	1650	1722	1722	...	1759	...	1845	1909
Scheffau ★ d.	0559	0559	0750	0818	...	0908	...	1123	1123	...	...	1303	1309	1358	1358	...	1618	...	1728	1728	...	1805	...	...	1915
Söll (Dorf) d.	0612	0615	0805	0832	...	0925	0925	1137	1140	1240	...	1320	1323	1412	1415	1550	1635	...	1742	1745	1745	1817	1855	...	1925
Kufstein Bahnhof ▲ a.	*0640*	|	*0830*	...	...	|	0950	*1205*	|	1308	...	*1357*	|	*1447*	|	1622	*1710*	...	...	*1820*	|	*1853*	|	...	*1945*
Wörgl Bahnhof a.	...	0645	0835	...	...	0955	...	...	1210	...	...	1350	1350	...	1445	...	1705	...	...	1808	1808	...	1915	...	1945

h – Not Dec. 26, May 1.
m – Also Dec. 26, May 1.

▲ – Timings Kufstein - Söll and v.v. are subject to confirmation.
★ – Scheffau Gh zum Wilder Kaiser.

ZELL AM SEE - HINTERGLEMM 958a

ÖBB-Postbus Route **680**

km		⚒	E	E		E		E		A		A		A	
0	**Zell am See** Bahnhof d.	0610p	0655	0820	0920	1020	1120	1220	1320	1420	1520	1620	1720	1820	1920
20	Saalbach Schattberg a.	0637	0725	0852	0952	1052	1152	1252	1352	1452	1552	1652	1752	1852	1952
23	**Hinterglemm** Ellmauweg a.	0643	0731	0858	0958	1058	1158	1258	1358	1458	1558	1658	1758	1858	1958

	⚒	E		E		E		E		A		A		A	
Hinterglemm Ellmauweg d.	0621	0657	0755	0920	1020	1120	1220	1320	1420	1520	1620	1720	1820	1915	...
Saalbach Schattberg d.	0628	0703	0805	0930	1030	1130	1230	1330	1430	1530	1630	1730	1830	1921	...
Zell am See Bahnhof a.	0700	0735	0839	1004	1104	1204	1304	1404	1504	1604	1704	1804	1904	1951p	...

A – Daily to Apr. 9; Ⓐ from Apr. 12.
E – Daily to Apr. 10; ⚒ from Apr. 12.

p – Zell am See Postplatz (not Bahnhof).

Information: ✆ +43 (0) 6542 5444-18

Danube shipping: BUDAPEST - BRATISLAVA - WIEN - LINZ - PASSAU 959

2009 service

Hydrofoil services. 🍷.	V	W	B	R	V	V	P	Y	T
	[R]♠	[R]♠	[R]◇	⊙	[R]♠	[R]♠	⊙	⊙	[R]♠
Wien Reichsbrücke ▲ d.	...	...	0900	0945	...	...	1700	1730	...
Wien Schwedenplatz ▲ d.	0830	0900	|	|	1230	1630	|	|	1900
Bratislava d.	0945	1015	1030u	1115	1345	1745	1830	1900	2015
Budapest § a.	...	...	1430	...	...	...	...	...	...

	Z	V	B	V	W	R	V		T
	⊙	[R]♠	[R]◇	[R]♠	[R]♠	⊙	[R]♠		[R]♠
Budapest § d.	...	...	0900	...	...	...	...	...	...
Bratislava d.	0900	1030	1330s	1430	1700	1730	1830	...	2230
Wien Schwedenplatz a.	|	1200	|	1600	1830	|	2000	...	2400
Wien Reichsbrücke ▲ a.	1045	...	1530	...	...	1915	...	...	...

All sailings convey ✗	④A	J	C	⑦N	D	⑦E	K	D	D
	⊖	⊡	◐	⊖	◐	[R]◐	⊡	◐	◐
Wien Reichsbrücke ▲ d.	...	...	...	0730n	...	0830	...	...	...
Tulln d.	...	...	...	0950n	...	1120	...	...	...
Krems an der Donau d.	0830	1010	1015	1220	1300	1355	1540	1545	...
Dürnstein d.	0900	1040	1050	1250	1330	1430	1610	1620	...
Spitz an der Donau d.	0955	1140	1145	1345	1420	...	1705	1715	1725
Melk a.	1120	1300	1315	1510	1540	...	1820	...	1840
Grein d.	1430	...	...	1820	...	...	...	...	...
Linz Nibelungenbrücke a.	1830	...	...	2220	...	...	...	...	...

	K	D	C	J	⑥N	③A	⑦F	D	D
	⊡	◐	◐	⊡	⊖	⊖	[R]◐	◐	◐
Linz Nibelungenbrücke d.	...	...	...	...	0900	0900	...	...	...
Grein d.	...	...	...	...	1200	1200	...	...	...
Melk d.	0825	1100	1350	1350	1440	1440	...	1615	...
Spitz an der Donau d.	0915	1150	1440	1445	1520	1520	...	1705	1720
Dürnstein d.	0940	1210	1510	1515	1600	1600	1640	...	1740
Krems an der Donau d.	1005	1240	1530	1535	1620	1620	1700	...	1800
Tulln d.	...	...	...	...	1820q	...	1855	...	...
Wien Reichsbrücke ▲ a.	...	...	...	...	2030q	...	2100	...	...

All sailings convey ✗	G	M	L
	⊖	⊖	⊖
Linz Nibelungenbrücke d.	...	0930r	1420
Schlögen d.	...	1425	1755
Obernzell d.	1435	1615	1935
Passau Liegestelle 11 🚌 d.	1545	1715	2040
Deggendorf a.	2035	...	...

	L	M	G
	⊖	⊖	⊖
Deggendorf d.	...	...	0945
Passau Liegestelle 11 🚌 d.	0900	1200	1345
Obernzell d.	0945	1245	1435
Schlögen a.	1105	1410	...
Linz Nibelungenbrücke a.	1405	1750r	...

A – July 1 - Aug. 27.
B – Daily May 1 - Sept. 27.
C – Daily Apr. 5 - Oct. 26.
D – Daily Apr. 18 - Sept. 28.
E – ⑦ May 10 - Sept. 20 (also June 20; not June 7, 21, July 5, 19, Aug. 2, 9, Sept. 6).
F – ⑦ May 10 - Sept. 20 (not June 7, July 5, 19, Aug. 2, 9, Sept. 6).
G – ①②③④⑥⑦ Apr. 25 - Oct. 11.
J – Daily Apr. 11 - Oct. 26.
K – Daily May 1 - Oct. 4.
L – ②–⑦ Apr. 24 - Oct. 4 (also ⑥⑦ Oct. 10 – 25).
M – Apr. 25 - Oct. 11.
N – Apr. 25 - Oct. 4.
P – ⑤⑥ Sept. 4 – 26.
R – ③–⑦ Apr. 29 - Sept. 27.
T – ④–⑦ May 1 - Sept. 27.
V – Daily Apr. 4 - Nov. 1.
W – © Apr. 4 – 26; daily May 1 - Sept. 27; ⑥⑦ Oct. 3 - Nov. 1.
Y – ⑤⑥ May 1 – 23; ③–⑦ May 27 - Aug. 30.
Z – ⑤⑥ May 1 – 23; ③–⑦ May 27 - Aug. 30; ⑤⑥ Sept. 4 – 26.

n – Not June 21.
q – Not June 20.
r – ②–⑦ only. Change ships at Schlögen.
s – Calls to set down only.
u – Calls to pick up only.

§ – Nemzetközi hajóállomás (International shipping terminal).

▲ – DDSG operates Wien sightseeing cruises Schwedenplatz - Reichsbrücke and v.v. Daily Apr. 3 - Oct. 31.
From Schwedenplatz (duration 1 hr 55 m) at 1030 and 1400 (also 1130 and 1500 Apr. 25 - Sept. 27).
From Reichsbrücke (duration 1 hr 20 m) at 1230 and 1600 (also 1330 and 1700 Apr. 25 - Sept. 27).

Operators:
⊡ – Brandner Schiffahrt GmbH, Ufer 50, A-3313 Wallsee. ✆ +43 (0) 7433 25 90 21, Fax +43 (0) 7433 25 90 25.
◐ – DDSG Blue Danube Schiffahrt GmbH, Handelskai 265, A-1020 Wien. ✆ +43 (0) 1 588 80, Fax +43 (0) 1 588 80 440.
⊖ – Wurm und Köck, Höllgasse 26, D-94032 Passau. ✆ +49 (0) 851 929292, Fax +49 (0) 851 35518.
⊙ – SPaP - LOD – Slovenská Plavba a Prístavy - Lodná Osobná Doprava a.s., Fajnorovo nábrežie 2, 811 02 Bratislava. Reservation recommended. Check-in 15 minutes before departure. Bratislava: ✆ +421 2 529 32 226, Fax +421 2 529 32 231.
◇ – Operator: MAHART PassNave, H-1056 Budapest, Belgrád rakpart. Check-in 60 minutes before departure. Budapest: ✆ +36 1 4844 005, Fax +36 1 266 4201.
♠ – *Twin City Liner*. Central Danube GmbH, Handelskai 265, A-1020 Wien. Check-in 30 minutes before departure. ✆ +43 (0) 1 588 80. Internet booking: www.twincityliner.com

SALZBURG - SCHWARZACH - INNSBRUCK 960

km		D 15464		D 499	EN 464						ÖEC 590				IC 1280			ÖIC 592		IC 1284		ÖIC 542		
							⚒	⚒		Ⓐ		Ⓐ	⚒		⑥G		⚒		Ⓐ	⑦M				
		B	2	L	A	2	2	2	2	2	✗	2	2	2		2	2	🍷	2		2	🍷	2	2
	Wien Westbahnhof 950 d.	...	...	...	...	...	...	...	...	...	...	...	...	...	...	...	...	...	...	...	...	0644	...	...
0	**Salzburg** Hbf 951 970/5 ‡ d.	...	0019	0134	...	...	...	...	0435	...	0612	...	...	...	...	0710	...	0812	...	...	0910	1015	...	1110
29	Golling-Abtenau 970 ‡ d.	...	0057	|	...	...	...	...	0506	...	0633	...	...	...	...	0734	...	0833	...	...	0934	1040	...	1134
	Graz Hbf 975 d.	...	|	|	2228	...	...	...	|	...	|	...	...	...	...	|	...	|	...	...	|	|	...	|
53	**Bischofshofen** 970/5 ‡ d.	...	0122	|	0158	...	...	...	0531	...	0654	...	...	...	...	0756	...	0854	...	...	0956	1104	...	1156
61	St Johann im Pongau 970 ‡ d.	...	0132	|	|	...	...	...	0541	...	0703	...	...	...	...	0805	...	0903	...	...	1005	1113	...	1205
67	**Schwarzach - St Veit** 970 ‡ a.	...	0137	0223	0211	...	...	...	0546	...	0709	...	...	...	...	0810	...	0909	...	...	1010	1119	...	1210
67	**Schwarzach - St Veit** d.	0113	...	...	0235	...	...	...	0547	...	...	0713	...	...	...	0813	...	...	0913	0950	1013	1121	...	1213
99	**Zell am See** d.	|	...	...	|	...	...	...	0623	...	...	0747	...	...	0839	0847	...	...	0947	1020	1047	1150	...	1247
113	Saalfelden d.	|	...	...	|	0413	...	0559	0636	...	...	0759	0759	...	0850	0859	...	...	0957	1031	1059	1200	...	1259
131	Hochfilzen d.	|	...	...	|	0430	0549	0616	0653	...	...	0816	0816	...	0906	0916	1016	...	...	1047	1116	1215	...	1316
148	St Johann in Tirol d.	|	...	...	|	0445	0604	0634	0709	0759	...	0834	0834	0918	0923	0934	1034	...	...	1103	1134	1231	1318	1334
157	**Kitzbühel** d.	|	...	...	|	0453	0612	0643	0717	0808	...	0843	0843	0926	0931	0943	1043	...	...	1112	1143	1239	1326	1343
166	Kirchberg in Tirol d.	|	...	...	|	0502	0623	0654	0726	0819	...	0854	0854	0934	0943	0954	1054	...	...	1124	1154	1247	1334	1354
192	Wörgl Hbf 951 a.	0250	...	...	|	0529	0648	0723	0751	0848	...	0923	0923	0959	1011	1023	1123	...	...	1152	1223	1309	1359	1423
217	Jenbach 951 a.	|	...	...	|	0549	*0708*r	*0749*a	0811	*0919*	...	*0957*	*0957*	1014	...	*1052*	*1157*	...	...	*1230*	*1252*	1324	1419	*1452*
251	**Innsbruck** Hbf 951 a.	0333	...	...	0450	0619	*0736*r	*0817*a	0839	*0947*	...	*1032*	*1032*	1042	...	*1132*	*1232*	...	...	*1252*	*1332*	1347	1447	*1532*

		ÖIC 690					ÖEC 113					EC 115	IC 518				ÖEC 692					EC 117		REX 1516
	Ⓐ		Ⓐ	⚒	Ⓐ			Ⓐ	⚒	Ⓐ						Ⓐ		Ⓑz	⑥k	Ⓐ		Ⓑw		¶
	2	🍷	2	2	2	2	E✗	2	2	2	2	D✗	🍷	2	2	2	✗	2	2	2	2	F⊗	2	
Wien Westbahnhof 950 d.	...	0844	...	...	...	...	...	...	...	...	...	...	...	...	...	...	1444	...	...	...	...	...	...	1844
Salzburg Hbf 951 970/5 ‡ d.	...	1212	...	...	...	1310	1412	...	...	...	1510	1612	...	...	1709	1744	1812	...	...	...	1910	2012	...	2210
Golling-Abtenau 970 ‡ d.	...	1233	...	...	...	1334	1433	...	...	...	1534	1633	...	...	1733	1811	1833	...	...	...	1934	2033	...	2234
Graz Hbf 975 d.	...	|	...	...	...	|	|	...	...	...	|	|	1338	...	|	|	|	...	...	...	|	|	...	|
Bischofshofen 970/5 ‡ d.	...	1254	...	...	...	1356	1454	...	...	...	1556	1654	1649	...	1756	1836	1854	...	...	...	1956	2054	...	2256
St Johann im Pongau 970 ‡ d.	...	1303	...	...	...	1405	1503	...	...	...	1605	1703	1658	...	1804	1846	1903	...	...	...	2005	2103	...	2305
Schwarzach - St Veit 970 ‡ a.	...	1309	...	...	...	1410	1509	...	...	...	1610	1709	1704	...	1810	1851	1909	...	...	...	2010	2109	...	2311
Schwarzach - St Veit d.	...	...	1313	...	...	1413	...	1513	...	...	1613	...	1712	...	1813	1854	...	1913	1913	...	2013	...	2113	2313
Zell am See d.	...	...	1347	...	...	1447	...	1547	...	...	1647	...	1743	...	1847	1931	...	1947	1949	...	2047	...	2149	2348
Saalfelden d.	...	...	1359	...	...	1459	...	1559	1559	...	1659	...	1753	...	1859	1943	...	1959	2001	...	2059	...	2201	2359
Hochfilzen d.	...	...	1416	1416	...	1516	...	1616	1616	1703	1716	...	|	1903	1916	...	...	2016	...	2103	2116	...	...	...
St Johann in Tirol d.	1404	...	1434	1434	1518	1534	...	1634	1634	1718	1734	...	1820	1918	1934	...	...	2034	...	2118	2134	...	...	...
Kitzbühel d.	1413	...	1443	1443	1526	1543	...	1643	1643	1726	1743	...	1828	1926	1943	...	...	2043	...	2126	2143	...	...	...
Kirchberg in Tirol d.	1424	...	1454	1454	1534	1554	...	1654	1654	1734	1754	...	1836	1934	1954	...	...	2054	...	2134	2154	...	...	...
Wörgl Hbf 951 a.	1453	...	1523	1523	1559	1623	...	1723	1723	1759	1823	...	1858	1959	2023	...	...	2123	...	2159	2223	...	...	...
Jenbach 951 a.	*1519*	...	*1545*	*1545*	1619	*1652*	...	*1745*	*1745*	1819	*1852*	...	1913	2019	*2057*	...	...	*2157*	...	2219	*2257*	...	...	...
Innsbruck Hbf 951 a.	*1547*	...	*1606*	*1606*	1647	*1732*	...	*1806*	*1806*	1847	*1932*	...	1936	2047	*2132*	...	...	*2232*	...	2247	*2332*	...	...	...

A – ZÜRICHSEE – 🛏 1, 2 cl., ▬ 2 cl. and (2) Graz - Feldkirch - Buchs 🚌 - Zürich. Conveys from Schwarzach (except when train **B** runs) 🛏 1, 2 cl.*, ▬ 2 cl.* and (2) Beograd (**414**) - Zagreb - Ljubljana - Villach - Schwarzach (**464**) - Zürich.
B – From Schwarzach daily to Jan. 7 and Mar. 26 - Apr. 7 (also Feb. 13, 14, 20, 21); ①⑥⑦ from Apr. 10 (also May 13, 14, 25, June 3, 4). 🛏 1, 2 cl.*, ▬ 2 cl.* and (2) Beograd (**414**) - Zagreb - Ljubljana - Villach - Schwarzach (**15464**) - Feldkirch (**464**) - Buchs 🚌 - Zürich.
D – WÖRTHERSEE – (12) and ✗ Münster - Köln - Stuttgart - München - Klagenfurt.
E – (12) and ✗ Siegen - Frankfurt - Stuttgart - München - Klagenfurt.
F – (12) and 🍷 Frankfurt - Stuttgart - München - Klagenfurt.
G – ⑥ Dec. 26 - Apr. 10 (also Jan. 6). GROSSGLOCKNER. To München (Table **951**).
L – LISINSKI – 🛏 1, 2 cl., ▬ 2 cl. and (2) München - Villach - Ljubljana - Zagreb.
M – ⑦ Dec. 20 - Mar. 28 (also Apr. 5). GROSSGLOCKNER – (12) and 🍷 Schwarzach - München - Hamburg - Flensburg.

a – Ⓐ only.
k – Also Dec. 24, 25, 31, Jan. 5, Apr. 4, 30, May 12, 23, June 2.
r – 11 minutes later on ⑥.
w – Not Dec. 24, 25, 31, Apr. 2, 4, May 23.
z – Not Dec. 24, 25, 31, Jan. 5, Apr. 4, 30, May 12, 23, June 2.
* – 🛏 1, 2 cl. and ▬ 2 cl. from Zagreb.
¶ – Train *ÖIC* **940** Wien - Salzburg.
‡ – See panel on page 450 for additional local stopping trains.

960 SALZBURG - SCHWARZACH - INNSBRUCK

	EN 465	D 15465			REX 1501							ÖEC 693			IC 515	EC 114			ÖEC 112					
			⚒		¶	⚒		Ⓐ		⚒	Ⓐ							Ⓐ		⚒			⚒	Ⓐ
	G	F	2	2		2	2	2	2	2	2	✕	2	2	🍷	D ✕	2	2	H ✕	2	2	2	2	2
Innsbruck Hbf ... 951 d.	0059	0138	...	...	...	0436	...	0513	...	0528	0528	...	0628	0713	0824	...	0852	...	...	0954	1028	1113	1128	1128
Jenbach ... 951 d.	|	|	...	...	...	0500	...	0540	...	0602	0602	...	0702	0742	0846	...	0919	...	...	1014	1107	1140	1202	1202
Wörgl Hbf ... 951 d.	0140	0220	...	...	...	0541	...	0601	...	0630	0630	...	0737	0802	0902	...	0937	...	...	1037	1137	1200	1237	1237
Kirchberg in Tirol ... d.	|	|	...	...	...	0607	...	0631	...	0700	0700	...	0807	0828	0924	...	1007	...	...	1107	1207	1226	1307	1307
Kitzbühel ... d.	|	|	...	...	...	0618	...	0642	...	0711	0711	...	0818	0836	0932	...	1018	...	...	1118	1218	1234	1318	1318
St Johann in Tirol ... d.	|	|	...	...	...	0627	...	0651	...	0720	0720	...	0827	0843	0940	...	1027	...	...	1127	1227	1241	1327	1327
Hochfilzen ... d.	|	|	...	...	...	0645	...	0709	...	0738	0745	...	0845	...	|	...	1045	...	...	1145	1245	...	1345	1345
Saalfelden ... d.	|	|	...	0458v	0556	0705	0705	0726	0733	...	0805	...	0905	...	1008	...	1105	1205	...	...	1305	...	1402	1405
Zell am See ... d.	|	|	...	0508v	0606	0715	0715	...	0746	...	0815	...	0915	...	1019	...	1115	1215	...	...	1315	...	...	1415
Schwarzach - St Veit ... a.	0319	0359	...	0541v	0640	0748	0748	...	0821	...	0848	...	0948	...	1048	...	1148	1248	...	...	1348	...	...	1448
Schwarzach - St Veit ... 970 ‡ d.	0324	...	0452	0542	0642	0750	0750	...	0822	...	...	0851	0950	...	1056	1051	1150	...	1251	...	1350	...	...	...
St Johann im Pongau .. 970 ‡ d.	|	...	0457	0548	0648	0756	0756	...	0827	...	...	0857	0956	...	1102	1057	1156	...	1257	...	1356	...	...	...
Bischofshofen ... 970/5 ‡ d.	0338	...	0508	0558	0658	0806	0806	...	0838	...	...	0908	1006	...	1113	1108	1206	...	1308	...	1406	...	...	...
Graz Hbf 975 ... a.	0700	...	|	|	|	|	|	...	|	...	...	|	|	...	1422	|	|	...	|	...	|	...	...	...
Golling-Abtenau ... 970 ‡ d.	...	...	0532	0620	0720	0827	0827	...	0902	...	...	0928	1027	...	...	1128	1227	...	1328	...	1427	...	...	...
Salzburg Hbf ... 951 970/5 ‡ a.	...	...	0609	0645	0745	0849	0849	...	0939	...	...	0948	1049	...	...	1148	1249	...	1348	...	1449	...	...	...
Wien Westbahnhof 950 ... a.	...	...	...	...	1118	...	...	...	...	...	...	1318	...	...	...	...	...	...	...	...	...	...	...	...

	ÖIC 691			ÖIC 649				ÖEC 110	IC 1281						ÖEC 593					IC 899				
			Ⓐ			Ⓐ	Ⓐ		⑥E	Ⓐ				⚒		⚒	Ⓐ	Ⓒ	Ⓐ				①–⑤	
	🍷	2	2	🍷	2	2	2	M ✕	🍷	2	2	2	2	2	✕	2	2	2	2		2	2	z 2	2
Innsbruck Hbf ... 951 d.	...	1228	1313	1413	1428	1513	1554	...	...	1613	1628	1713	1743a	1743a	...	1828	1913	1928	1952	...	2128	2328	2328	...
Jenbach ... 951 d.	...	1307	1340	1434	1507	1540	1614	...	...	1642	1707	1742	1810a	1810a	...	1907	1940	2002	2017	...	2202	0002	0002	...
Wörgl Hbf ... 951 d.	...	1337	1400	1449	1537	1600	1637	...	1645	1707	1737	1802	1837	1837	...	1936	2000	2037	2046	...	2237	0029	0029	...
Kirchberg in Tirol ... d.	...	1407	1426	1511	1607	1626	1707	...	1717	1737	1807	1828	1907	1907	...	2006	2026	2107	2112	...	2307	...	0056	0056
Kitzbühel ... d.	...	1418	1434	1520	1618	1634	1718	...	1728	1748	1818	1836	1918	1918	...	2017	2034	2118	2121	...	2318	...	0104	0104
St Johann in Tirol ... d.	...	1427	1441	1528	1627	1642	1727	...	1736	1757	1827	1844	1927	1927	...	2027	2042	2127	2129	...	2327	...	0112	0112
Hochfilzen ... d.	...	1445	...	1544	1645	1656	1745	...	1757	1815	1845	1858	1945	1945	...	2044	2056	2145	2145	...	2345	...	0127	0127
Saalfelden ... d.	...	1505	...	1600	1705	...	1805	...	1812	...	1905	▬	2002	2005	...	...	...	2205	2205	...	0002	...	0143	0143
Zell am See ... d.	...	1515	...	1610	1715	...	1815	...	1824	...	1916	...	...	2015	...	...	...	2215	2215	...	...	...	...	...
Schwarzach - St Veit ... a.	...	1548	...	1639	1748	...	1848	...	1854	...	1950	S 2	...	2048	...	...	...	2248	2248	...	...	...	...	...
Schwarzach - St Veit ... 970 ‡ d.	1451	1550	...	1641	1750	...	...	1851	...	...	1951	2022	...	2057	2051	...	...	...	...	2251	...	...	...	...
St Johann im Pongau .. 970 ‡ d.	1457	1556	...	1647	1756	...	...	1857	...	...	1957	2027	...	2102	2057	...	...	...	...	2257	...	...	...	...
Bischofshofen ... 970/5 ‡ d.	1508	1606	...	1657	1806	...	...	1908	...	...	2007	2036	...	2111	2108	...	...	...	...	2308	...	...	...	...
Graz Hbf 975 ... a.	|	|	...	|	|	...	...	|	...	...	|	...	...	...	|	...	...	...	...	|	...	...	...	...
Golling-Abtenau ... 970 ‡ d.	1528	1627	...	1719	1827	...	...	1928	...	...	2028	...	...	...	2128	...	...	...	...	2328	...	...	...	...
Salzburg Hbf ... 951 970/5 ‡ a.	1548	1649	...	1744	1849	...	...	1948	...	...	2053	...	...	...	2148	...	...	...	...	2350	...	...	...	...
Wien Westbahnhof 950 ... a.	1918	...	...	2118	...	...	...	...	...	...	...	...	...	...	...	...	...	...	...	...	...	...	...	...

D – WÖRTHERSEE – ⊂12⊃ and ✕ Klagenfurt - München - Stuttgart - Köln - Dortmund.
E – ⑥ Dec. 19 - Apr. 3 (also Dec. 23). GROSSGLOCKNER. From München (Table **951**).
F – From Zürich daily to Jan. 6 and Mar. 25 - Apr. 6 (also Feb. 12, 13, 19, 20); ⑤–⑦ from Apr. 9 (also May 12, 13, 24, June 2, 3). 🛏 1, 2 cl.*, ▬ 2 cl.* and ⊂2⊃ Zürich (**465**) - Buchs 🛃 - Feldkirch (**15465**) - Schwarzach (**415**) - Villach - Ljubljana - Zagreb - Beograd.
G – ZÜRICHSEE – 🛏 1, 2 cl., ▬ 2 cl. and ⊂2⊃ Zürich - Buchs 🛃 - Feldkirch - Graz. Conveys Zürich - Schwarzach (except when train **F** runs) 🛏 1, 2 cl.*, ▬ 2 cl.* and ⊂2⊃ Zürich (**465**) - Schwarzach (**415**) - Villach - Ljubljana - Zagreb - Beograd.
H – ⊂12⊃ and ✕ Klagenfurt - München - Stuttgart - Frankfurt - Siegen.
M – ⊂12⊃ and ✕ Klagenfurt - München.
S – To Schladming (Table **975**).

a – Ⓐ only.
v – ⚒ only.
z – Not Dec. 24, 25, 31, Jan. 1, 5, 6, Apr. 5, 30, May 12, 13, 24, June 2, 3.

* – 🛏 1, 2 cl. and ▬ 2 cl. to Zagreb.
¶ – Train ÖIC **545** Salzburg - Wien.
❖ – Change trains at Bischofshofen on the 2022 from Schwarzach.
‡ – See panel for other local stopping trains.

Salzburg Hbf ... d.	0619		2219
Golling-Abtenau ... d.	0657	and	2257
Bischofshofen ... d.	0722	hourly	2322
St Johann im Pongau ... d.	0732	until	2332
Schwarzach - St Veit ... a.	0737		2337
			❖
Schwarzach - St Veit ... d.	0522		2222
St Johann im Pongau ... d.	0527	and	2227
Bischofshofen ... d.	0538	hourly	2238
Golling-Abtenau ... d.	0602	until	2302
Salzburg Hbf ... a.	0639		2339

961 ATTNANG-PUCHHEIM - STAINACH-IRDNING

2nd class only

km																			
		⚒								A									
0	**Attnang-Puchheim** ... d.	...	...	0605	0713	0813	0913	1013	1113	1213	1313	1413	1513	1613	1713	1813	1913	2006	2106
12	**Gmunden** ... d.	...	...	0623	0734	0828	0934	1028	1134	1228	1334	1428	1534	1628	1734	1828	1935	2025	2124
17	Altmünster am Traunsee ... d.	...	...	0629	0740	0834	0940	1034	1140	1234	1340	1434	1540	1634	1740	1834	1941	2030	2130
22	Traunkirchen ... d.	...	...	0635	0746	0840	0946	1040	1146	1240	1346	1440	1546	1640	1746	1840	1947	2036	2136
27	Ebensee Landungsplatz ... d.	...	...	0643	0754	0846	0954	1046	1154	1246	1354	1446	1554	1646	1754	1846	1955	2044	2143
44	**Bad Ischl** ... d.	...	...	0706	0820	0905	1020	1105	1220	1305	1420	1505	1620	1705	1820	1905	2020	2105	2207
54	Bad Goisern ... d.	...	...	0721	0834	0916	1034	1116	1234	1316	1434	1516	1634	1716	1834	1916	2034	2118	...
64	Hallstatt ⊡ ... d.	...	...	0733	0849	0927	1049	1127	1249	1327	1449	1527	1649	1727	1849	|	|	|	...
67	Obertraun-Dachsteinhöhlen . d.	...	...	0737	0852	0930	1052	1131	1252	1330	1452	1531	1652	1730	1852	1930	2052	2133	...
78	**Bad Aussee** ... d.	0501	0632	0750	...	0942	...	1143	...	1342	...	1543	...	1742	...	1942	2104	2145	...
93	Bad Mitterndorf ... d.	0519	0651	0805	...	1001	...	1200	...	1401	...	1600	...	1801	...	2001	...	...	...
108	**Stainach-Irdning** ... a.	0536	0708	0819	...	1017	...	1217	...	1417	...	1617	...	1817	...	2017	...	...	...

			⚒										B				ⒸL	Ⓐ	
Stainach-Irdning ... d.	...	...	...	0611v	0714	...	0942	...	1142	...	1342	...	1542	...	1742	...	1942	1942	2050
Bad Mitterndorf ... d.	...	...	...	0628v	0731	...	1000	...	1159	...	1400	...	1559	...	1800	...	2000	2000	2107
Bad Aussee ... d.	...	0458	0601	0651	0810r	...	1017	...	1217	...	1417	...	1617	...	1817	...	2016	2018	2125
Obertraun-Dachsteinhöhlen .. d.	...	0510	0613	0704	0824	0907	1029	1107	1229	1307	1429	1507	1629	1707	1829	1907	2028	...	...
Hallstatt ⊡ ... d.	...	|	|	0708	0827	0911	1032	1111	1232	1311	1432	1511	1632	1711	1832	|	|	...	...
Bad Goisern ... d.	...	0525	0629	0722	0842	0925	1043	1125	1244	1325	1443	1525	1644	1725	1843	1925	2043	...	...
Bad Ischl ... d.	0438	0539	0643	0736	0853	0938	1054	1138	1254	1338	1454	1538	1654	1743t	1854	1938	2054	...	...
Ebensee Landungsplatz ... d.	0501	0602	0709	0800	0915	1003	1115	1203	1315	1403	1515	1603	1715	1803	1917	2003	2117	...	...
Traunkirchen ... d.	0509	0610	0718	0808	0921	1011	1122	1211	1322	1411	1522	1611	1722	1811	1923	2011	2123	...	...
Altmünster am Traunsee ... d.	0515	0616	0724	0815	0927	1018	1127	1218	1327	1418	1527	1618	1727	1818	1929	2018	2131	...	...
Gmunden ... d.	0521	0622	0730	0828	0933	1028	1133	1228	1333	1428	1533	1628	1733	1828	1935	2025	2137	...	...
Attnang-Puchheim ... a.	0538	0639	0747	0846	0947	1045	1147	1245	1347	1445	1547	1645	1747	1845	1948	2042	2153	...	...

A – Conveys ⊂12⊃ Wien (**742**) - Attnang-Puchheim - Stainach.
B – Conveys ⊂12⊃ Stainach - Attnang-Puchheim (**647**) - Wien on ①–⑥ (also Jan. 3, Apr. 4, May 23; not Jan. 6, Apr. 5, May 24).
L – To Linz (Table **950**).

r – Arrives 0749.
t – 1738 on Ⓒ (also Dec. 24, 31).
v – ⚒ only.

⊡ – Connecting ⛴ services operate Hallstatt Bahnhof - Hallstatt Zentrum and v.v. **Operator**: Hallstättersee-Schifffahrt Hemetsberger KG ✆ +43 (0) 6134 8228.

962 LINZ - BRAUNAU - SIMBACH

2nd class only

km																									
		⚒	Ⓐ	†	⚒	Ⓐ	G	Ⓐ	Ⓒ		Ⓐ		Ⓒ	⚒	Ⓐ		Ⓐ		Ⓒz	Ⓐn	Ⓐ		B		
0	**Linz** Hbf ... 950 d.	0456	...	0545	0555	0555	0653	0713	0736	0920	1016	1120	1120	1220	1220	1320	1420	1520	1520	1620	1640	1720	1810	1920	2132
25	**Wels** Hbf ... 950 d.	0522	...	0621	0621	0621	0714	0730	0755	0940	1040	1140	1140	1240	1240	1340	1440	1540	1540	1640	1701	1740	1833	1938	2148
54	Neumarkt-Kallham. 950 d.	0549	0553	0651	0651	0651	0738	0810	0831	1010	1110	1210	1210	1310	1310	1410	1510	1610	1610	1707	1734	1810	1856	2013	2217
76	Ried im Innkreis ... d.	...	0614	0712	0712	0712	0754	0831	0854	1031	1131	1231	1231	1331	1331	1431	1531	1631	1631	1728	1754	1831	1913	2034	2237
113	**Braunau** am Inn ... a.	...	...	0741	0741	0741	0819	0910	0930	1110	1210	1310	1310	1410	1410	1510	1610	1710	1710	1810	1823	1908	1944	2112	...
115	**Simbach** (Inn) 🛃 ... a.	...	...	...	...	0745	0823	0914	0934	1116	...	...	1314	...	1416	1516	...	...	1714	1814	...	...	1949	...	...

	⚒	Ⓐ	⑥k	†		⚒	†	ⒶA		ⒸD	Ⓐ				⚒	Ⓐ			Ⓐn	†	⑥z	Ⓐn		M	
Simbach (Inn) 🛃 ... d.	...	...	...	...	...	...	...	0719	...	0815	...	0948	...	1148	...	1448	1523	...	...	1748	1748	1827	...	1924	...
Braunau am Inn ... d.	...	0510	0510	...	...	0629	0629	0724	0750	0820	0852	0952	...	1152	1252	1452	1526	1552	1714	1752	1752	1831	...	1929	1955
Ried im Innkreis ... d.	0455	0550	0550	0611	...	0712	0712	0754	0831	0854	0931	1031	...	1231	1331	1531	...	1631	1807	1831	1831	1913	...	1955	2034
Neumarkt-Kallham 950 a.	0514	0612	0612	0630	0636	0731	0731	0809	0850	0909	0950	1050	...	1250	1350	1550	...	1650	1828	1850	1850	1931	1935	2012	2052
Wels Hbf ... 950 a.	0548	0637	0637	...	0704	0804	0804	0832	0920	0932	1021	1120	...	1320	1421	1621	...	1720	1859	1921	...	...	2002	2035	2123
Linz Hbf ... 950 a.	0614	0655	0703	...	0722	0822	0828	0850	0939	0950	1056	1139	...	1339	1439	1639	...	1739	1928	1943	...	...	2028	2057	2143

A – From Mühldorf (Table **893**).
B – ⊂12⊃ Linz - Mühldorf (- München Ⓐ). See also Table **893**.
D – ⊂12⊃ München - Mühldorf - Linz. See also Table **893**.

G – *D* **966**. ⊂12⊃ (Kleinreifling ⚒ -) Garsten - Linz - Simbach - München. See also Table **893**.
M – *D* **963**. ⊂12⊃ München - Simbach - Linz. See also Table **893**.

k – Not Dec. 26, May 1.
n – Not Dec. 24, 31.
z – Also Dec. 24, 31.

SALZBURG and ST WOLFGANG - STROBL - BAD ISCHL — 963

Routes 150, 2560

km	Route 150	⚒		Ⓐn	⑥k		⚒		⑥k	Ⓐn	Ⓒz	Ⓐn	⑥k	Ⓐn	Ⓒz	Ⓐn	Ⓐn	Ⓒz	Ⓐn	Ⓐn	Ⓒz	Ⓐn		†	⚒
0	**Salzburg** Hbf △ d.	0555	...	*0625*	0645	0815	0915	1015	1115	1115	1215	1220	1315	1320	1415	1420	1520	1615	1625	1725	1815	1820	1915	2115	2230
32	St Gilgen (Busbahnhof) d.	0645	0645	0735	0735	0910	1010	1110	1210	1220	1310	1315	1410	1410	1510	1510	1610	1710	1710	1810	1910	1910	2005	2158	2313
45	Strobl (Busbahnhof) d.	0703	0703	0753	0753	0928	1028	1128	1228	1238	1328	1333	1428	1428	1528	1528	1628	1728	1728	1828	1928	1928	2021	2213	2328
57	**Bad Ischl** Bahnhof a.	0725	0725	0815	0815	0950	1050	1150	1250	1300	1350	1355	1450	1450	1550	1550	1650	1750	1750	1850	1950	1950	2040	2230	2345

Route 150	Ⓐn	⚒	Ⓐn	Ⓐn	⑥k		⚒					⑥k	Ⓐn	Ⓒz	Ⓐn	⑥k	Ⓐn		⚒		Ⓐn		Ⓐn	
Bad Ischl Bahnhof d.	...	0502	...	...	...	0611	0645	0745	...	0923	1023	1123	1123	1223	1223	1323	1333	1423	1523	1623	1723	1823	1923	2023
Strobl (Busbahnhof) d.	...	0518	0548	0615	...	0631	0707	0807	...	0945	1045	1145	1145	1245	1245	1345	1355	1445	1545	1645	1745	1845	1945	2045
St Gilgen (Busbahnhof) d.	0515	0535	0605	0630	0635	0646	0727	0827	...	1005	1105	1205	1220	1305	1315	1405	1415	1505	1605	1705	1805	1905	2005	2101
Salzburg Hbf △ a.	0553	0619	0649	0719	0719	0730	0819	0919	...	1057	1157	1257	1307	1357	1407	1457	1507	1557	1657	1757	1853	1953	2053	...

km	Route 2560	Ⓐn	⚒	⚒	Ⓒz	†	Ⓐn	Ⓐn	Ⓐn	♣	Ⓒz	Ⓐn	Ⓐn		Ⓐn			Ⓐn			Ⓐn	●			
0	**St Wolfgang** ⊡ ‡... ♥ d.	0500	0600	0648	0740	0740	0743	0753	0903	0913	1010	1013	1103	1210	1318	1410	1513	1513	1610	1713	1713	1813	1813	1913	2003
7	Strobl (Busbahnhof) ♥ d.	0513	0613	0700	0752	0753	|	0805	|	0927	1025	|	|	1225	1333	1425	1527	1528	1625	1727	1728	1827	|	1927	2017
19	**Bad Ischl** Bahnhof a.	0535	0640	...	...	0815	0815	...	0935	...	1052	1045	1135	1252	1400	1452	...	1555	1652	...	1755	...	1845	...	...

Route 2560	Ⓐn	⚒	⚒		Ⓐn	Ⓐn	Ⓒz	Ⓐn			⚒			Ⓐn			Ⓐn			Ⓐn				
Bad Ischl Bahnhof d.	0605	0645	...	0823	0913	...	0913	1023	...	1113	1215	...	1333	1423	...	1518	1623	...	1713	1815	...	1913	...	...
Strobl (Busbahnhof) d.	0632	0708	0810	|	|	0930	0935	1045	1045	1135	1245	1245	1355	1445	1445	1540	1645	1645.	1735	1845	1845	|	1930	2045
St Wolfgang ⊡ ‡ a.	0645	0723	0825	0855	0945	0945	0950	1100	1100	1150	1300	1300	1410	1500	1500	1555	1700	1700	1750	1900	1900	1945	1945	2100

k – Also Dec. 24, 31; not Dec. 26, May 1.
n – Not Dec. 24, 31.
z – Also Dec. 24, 31.

♥ – Additional services St Wolfgang - Strobl: 1028 Ⓐ **n**, 1113 Ⓒ **z** and 1313 Ⓒ **z**.
⊡ – St Wolfgang Schafbergbahnhof. All services also call at St Wolfgang Markt.
△ – All services also call at Mirabellplatz.

♣ – From Dec. 25. Runs 15 minutes later from May 15.
● – Runs 15 minutes later on Ⓒ (also Dec. 24, 31).
‡ – The **Schafbergbahn** narrow-gauge steam rack railway operates **St Wolfgang** - **Schafbergspitze** (*6 km*). Services operate subject to demand (minimum 20 passengers) and weather conditions **May 1 - Oct. 26**. 2nd class only. Special fares payable. **Journey time**: 45 minutes each way. ✆ +43 (0) 6138 2232.

STROBL - ST GILGEN (WOLFGANGSEE) — 964

WINTER TIMETABLE: Feb. 7 - Apr. 25 *

	A	†d	A	†d	A	A	†d	A	A
Strobl Schiffstation ⊡ d.	1000	...	1130	...	1300	1430	...	1600	1730
St Wolfgang Markt d.	1030	1100	1205	1300	1330	1500	1500	1630	1800
St Wolfgang Schafbergbahnhof d.	1038	1110	1155	1310	1338	1508	1510	1638	1808
St Gilgen Schiffstation ● a.	1115	1145	1245	1345	1415	1545	1545	1715	...

	A	A	†d	A	†d	A	†d	A	A
St Gilgen Schiffstation ● d.	1000	1130	1200	1300	1400	1430	1600	1600	1730
St Wolfgang Schafbergbahnhof d.	1035	1205	1235	1335	1435	1505	1635	1635	1805
St Wolfgang Markt d.	1045	1215	1245	1345	1445	1515	1645	1645	1815
Strobl Schiffstation ⊡ a.	1115	1245	...	1415	...	1545	...	1715	...

A – Apr. 1 – 5 only.
d – Also Mar. 27, 29, 30, 31; not Apr. 2, 4, 5.
* – Subject to lake conditions.
⊡ – Approximately 400 metres from Strobl Busbahnhof.
● – Approximately 500 metres from St Gilgen Busbahnhof.

TAUERN TUNNEL CAR - CARRYING TRAINS — 969

BÖCKSTEIN - MALLNITZ-OBERVELLACH and v.v. *11 km*. Transit time: 11 minutes. Passengers without cars are also conveyed. ✆ 05-1717. E-mail: autoschleuse.tauernbahn@pv.oebb.at

From Böckstein at 0620, 0720, 0750 **B**, 0820, 0850 **C** and at 20 and 50 **C** minutes past each hour until 1620, 1650 **C**, then 1720, 1750 **D**, 1820, 1850 **D**, 1920, 2020, 2120 and 2220.

From Mallnitz-Obervellach at 0550, 0650, 0720 **B**, 0750, 0820 **C**, 0850 and at 20 **C** and 50 minutes past each hour until 1620 **C**, 1650, then 1720 **D**, 1750, 1820 **D**, 1850, 1950, 2050 and 2150.

B – ⑥ until Apr. 3 (also Dec. 25, Jan. 6, May 13, 22, June 3, 5, 12).
C – ⑥ until Apr. 3 (also Dec. 25, Jan. 6, Apr. 5, May 13, 16, 22, 24, June 3, 5, 6, 12).
D – Jan. 6, Apr. 5, May 16, 24, June 6 only.

SALZBURG - VILLACH - KLAGENFURT — 970

km		*D* **499** ♦	*EN* **237** 🅁 ♦	*EN* **234** 2		*D* **415** ♦	2		⚒ 2	*REX* **1563** 2	*ÖEC* **590** ✕	*ÖIC* **592** 🍷	*ÖEC* **111** ✕♦	*ÖIC* **690** 🍷	2	*ÖEC* **113** ✕♦	Ⓐ 2	*EC* **115** ✕♦	*ÖEC* **692** ✕	*EC* **117** Ⓑ ⊗♦			
	Wien Westbahnhof **950** d.	...	2040	...	...	...	...	...	...	...	...	...	...	0844	...	...	...	...	1444	...	...	...	...
	München Hbf **890** d.	2340	|	...	...	...	...	...	...	...	...	...	0827	|	...	1227	...	1427	|	1827	...	...	...
0	**Salzburg** Hbf **960 975** d.	0134	0134	...	...	...	...	...	...	...	0612	0812	1012	1212	...	1412	...	1612	1812	2012	...	...	...
29	Golling-Abtenau **960** d.	|	|	...	...	...	...	...	...	...	0633	0833	1033	1233	...	1433	...	1633	1833	2033	...	...	...
53	**Bischofshofen** **960 975** d.	|	|	...	...	...	...	...	...	...	0654	0854	1054	1254	...	1454	...	1654	1854	2054	...	...	...
61	St Johann im Pongau **960** d.	|	|	...	...	...	...	...	...	...	0703	0903	1103	1303	...	1503	...	1703	1903	2103	...	...	...
67	**Schwarzach - St Veit** **960** d.	0226	0226	...	...	0430	...	...	...	...	0711	0911	1111	1311	...	1511	...	1711	1911	2111	...	...	...
86	Bad Hofgastein d.	|	|	...	...	0447	...	...	...	...	0729	0929	1129	1329	...	1529	...	1729	1929	2129	...	...	...
97	Bad Gastein d.	|	|	...	...	0503	...	...	...	...	0742	0942	1142	1342	...	1542	...	1742	1942	2142	...	...	...
113	Mallnitz-Obervellach d.	|	|	...	...	0518	...	...	0646	...	0756	0956	1156	1356	...	1556	1740	1756	1956	2156	...	...	...
146	Spittal-Millstättersee **971** d.	|	|	...	...	0545	...	...	0717	0723	0821	1021	1221	1421	...	1621	1811	1821	2021	2221	...	...	...
182	**Villach** Hbf **971** a.	0351	0351	...	...	0608	...	...	...	0748	0843	1043	1243	1443	...	1643	...	1843	2043	2245	...	...	...
182	**Villach** Hbf **971** d.	...	...	0417	...	...	0620	...	...	0750	0846	1046	1248	...	1450	1648	...	1848	2046	2248	...	...	...
198	Velden am Wörthersee **971** d.	...	...	|	...	...	0635	...	...	0801	0857	1057	1259	...	1505	1659	...	1859	2057	2259	...	...	...
207	Pörtschach am Wörthersee **971** d.	...	...	|	...	...	0643	...	...	|	0903	1103	1305	...	1513	1705	...	1905	2103	2305	...	...	...
220	**Klagenfurt** Hbf **971** a.	...	...	0438	...	...	0656	...	...	0816	0912	1112	1317	...	1526	1717	...	1917	2112	2317	...	...	...

	D **498** ♦	*EN* **236** 🅁 ♦		⚒ 2		*ÖEC* **693** ✕	*EC* **114** ✕♦	*ÖEC* **112** ✕♦	*ÖIC* **691** 🍷	2	*ÖIC* **591** 🍷	*REX* **1747** Ⓐ 2	*ÖEC* **110** ✕♦	*ÖEC* **593** ✕	*IC* **899**		2	*D* **414** ♦					
Klagenfurt Hbf **971** d.	...	...	...	...	...	0646	0843	1031	1246	1432	...	1538	1631	1846	2046	...	2146	...	...	...	...	...	...
Pörtschach am Wörthersee **971** d.	...	...	...	...	...	0655	0855	1043	1255	1446	...	1549	1643	1855	2055	...	2158	...	...	...	...	...	...
Velden am Wörthersee **971** d.	...	...	...	...	...	0702	0902	1050	1302	1454	...	1555	1650	1902	2102	...	2204	...	...	...	...	...	...
Villach Hbf **971** a.	...	...	...	...	...	0713	0913	1101	1313	1509	...	1609	1703	1913	2113	...	2220	...	...	...	...	...	...
Villach Hbf **971** d.	0146	0146	...	0528	...	0716	0916	1116	1316	...	1516	1610	1718	1916	2116	...	...	2300	...	...	...	...	...
Spittal-Millstättersee **971** d.	|	|	...	0603	...	0739	0939	1139	1339	...	1539	1636	1741	1939	2139	...	...	2325	...	...	...	...	...
Mallnitz-Obervellach d.	|	|	...	0633	...	0806	1006	1206	1406	...	1606	1707	1806	2006	2206	...	...	2357	...	...	...	...	...
Bad Gastein d.	|	|	...	...	...	0819	1019	1219	1419	...	1619	...	1819	2019	2219	...	...	0014	...	...	...	...	...
Bad Hofgastein d.	|	|	...	...	...	0831	1031	1231	1431	...	1631	...	1831	2031	2231	...	...	0026	...	...	...	...	...
Schwarzach - St Veit **960** d.	0320	0320	...	...	...	0851	1051	1251	1451	...	1651	...	1851	2051	2251	...	...	0042	...	...	...	...	...
St Johann im Pongau **960** d.	|	|	...	...	...	0857	1057	1257	1457	...	1657	...	1857	2057	2257	...	...	...	...	...	...	...	...
Bischofshofen **960 975** d.	|	|	...	...	...	0908	1108	1308	1508	...	1708	...	1908	2108	2308	...	...	...	...	...	...	...	...
Golling-Abtenau **960** d.	|	|	...	...	...	0928	1128	1328	1528	...	1728	...	1928	2128	2328	...	...	...	...	...	...	...	...
Salzburg Hbf **960 975** a.	0409	0409	...	...	...	0948	1148	1348	1548	...	1748	...	1948	2148	2350	...	...	...	...	...	...	...	...
München Hbf **890** a.	0615	|	...	...	...	|	1333	1533	|	...	...	...	2133	...	...	...	...	...	...	...	...	...	...
Wien Westbahnhof **950** a.	...	0828	...	...	...	1318	...	...	1918	...	...	...	...	...	...	...	...	...	...	...	...	...	...

♦ – **NOTES** (LISTED BY TRAIN NUMBER)

110 – [12] and ✕ Klagenfurt - München; [12] Beograd (**210**) - Zagreb - Ljubljana - Villach (**110**) - München.
111 – [12] and ✕ München - Klagenfurt; [12] München - Villach (**211**) - Ljubljana - Zagreb - Beograd.
112 – [12] and ✕ Klagenfurt - München - Stuttgart - Frankfurt - Siegen; [12] Zagreb (**212**) - Ljubljana - Villach (**112**) - München - Stuttgart - Frankfurt - Siegen.
113 – [12] and ✕ Siegen - Frankfurt - Stuttgart - München - Klagenfurt; [12] Siegen - Frankfurt - Stuttgart - München - Villach (**213**) - Ljubljana - Zagreb.
114 – WÖRTHERSEE – [12] and ✕ Klagenfurt - München - Stuttgart - Köln - Dortmund.
115 – WÖRTHERSEE – [12] and ✕ Münster - Köln - Stuttgart - München - Klagenfurt.
117 – Ⓑ (not Dec. 24, 25, 31, Apr. 2, 4, May 23). [12] and ⊗ Frankfurt - Stuttgart - München - Klagenfurt.
236/7 – ALLEGRO DON GIOVANNI – 🛏 1, 2 cl., ▬ 2 cl. and [2] Venezia - Udine - Tarvisio - Villach - Salzburg - Wien and v.v.
414 – [2] Beograd - Zagreb - Ljubljana - Villach - Schwarzach (**464/15464**) - Innsbruck - Feldkirch (**464**) - Zürich; 🛏 1, 2 cl. and ▬ 2 cl. Zagreb - Ljubljana - Villach - Schwarzach (**464/15464**) - Innsbruck - Feldkirch (**464**) - Zürich.
415 – [2] Zürich (**465**) - Feldkirch (**465/15465**) - Innsbruck - Schwarzach (**415**) - Villach - Ljubljana - Zagreb - Beograd; 🛏 1, 2 cl. and ▬ 2 cl. Zürich (**465**) - Feldkirch (**465/15465**) - Innsbruck - Schwarzach (**415**) - Villach - Ljubljana - Zagreb.
498 – LISINSKI – 🛏 1, 2 cl., ▬ 2 cl. and [2] Zagreb - Ljubljana - Villach - München; [2] Beograd (**414**) - Zagreb (**498**) - München; 🛏 1, 2 cl. Zagreb - Salzburg (**206**) - Praha. Mar. 27 - Sept. 18 (from Rijeka) conveys ▬ 2 cl. (also 🛏 1, 2 cl. Apr. 29 - Sept. 18) Rijeka (**480**) - Ljubljana (**296**) - München.
499 – LISINSKI – 🛏 1, 2 cl., ▬ 2 cl. and [2] München - Villach - Ljubljana - Zagreb; [2] München - Zagreb (**415**) - Beograd; 🛏 1, 2 cl. Praha (**207**) - Salzburg (**499**) - Zagreb. Mar. 28 - Sept. 19 (from München) conveys ▬ 2 cl. (also 🛏 1, 2 cl. Apr. 30 - Sept. 19) München - Ljubljana (**481**) - Rijeka.

971 LIENZ - VILLACH - KLAGENFURT - FRIESACH (- WIEN)

			EC 172								ÖIC 534	ÖIC 534					EC 102				ÖIC 538	ÖIC 538			
	⚒ 2	⚒ 2	✕	Ⓐ 2	B 2	2	Ⓐ 2	⚒ 2	Ⓐ 2	Ⓒ 2	①–⑤		B 2	2	Ⓐ 2	2	✕	B 2	Ⓐ 2	2	⑥ 🍷	🍷	B 2	2	⚒ 2
Lienz d.	...	...	...	...	...	...	...	...	0526	0526	0547	...	...	0623	...	0728	...	...	0832	0925	0950	...	...	...	...
Spittal-Millstättersee a.	...	...	...	...	...	...	...	...	0627	0627	0633	...	...	0722	...	0827	...	...	0929	1027	1038	...	...	...	...
Spittal-Millstättersee 970 d.	...	0448	...	←	0535a	...	0602	0602	0630	0631*	0637	...	0641a	0723	...	0831	...	...	0931	1031	1044	...	...	...	...
Villach Hbf 970 a.	...	0521	...	0521	0603a	...	0635	0635	0655	0704*	0701	...	0715a	0748	...	0904	...	...	1004	1104	1108	...	...	...	...
		→		|	|		|	d 2	|		|		|	|					|	▬ 2	|				
Villach Hbf 970 d.	0500	...	0527	0530	0605	0620	0641	0645	0659	...	0716	0716	0720	0750	0820	...	0914	0920	1020	1050	1116	1116	1120	1150	1220
Velden am Wörthersee 970 d.	0515	...	|	0545	|	0635	0654	0700	0711	...	|	|	0735	0801	0833	...	0925	0935	1035	1105	|	|	1135	1205	1235
Pörtschach am W'see 970 d.	0523	...	|	0553	|	0643	0700	0708	|	...	|	|	0743	|	0839	...	|	0943	1043	1113	|	|	1143	1213	1243
Klagenfurt Hbf 970 a.	0536	...	0548	0606	0626	0656	0710	0721	0726	...	0737	0737	0756	0816	0849	...	0937	0956	1056	1126	1137	1137	1156	1226	1256
Klagenfurt Hbf 980 d.	...	...	0550	0608	0628	0704	...	...	...	...	0739	0739	0804	...	0851	...	0939	1004	1104	...	1139	1139	1204	...	1310
St Veit an der Glan 980 d.	...	...	0603	0628	0641	0724	...	...	...	...	0753	0753	0824	...	0903	...	0953	1024	1124	...	1153	1153	1224	...	1330
Friesach 980 a.	...	...	|	0700	0705	0756	...	...	...	...	|	|	0856	...	...	...	1015	1056	1156	...	|	|	1256	...	1402
Wien Meidling 980 a.	...	...	0928	...	...	...	...	...	...	...	1128	1128	...	...	...	...	1328	...	...	...	1528	1528	...	...	...

		ÖIC 732					ÖEC 630					ÖEC 530					ÖEC 730			IC 738				EC 117	
	2	🍷	B 2	2	⚒ 2	2	✕	B 2	Ⓐ 2	⚒ 2	2	✕	B 2	2	⚒ 2	2	✕	2	Ⓑ 2	⑦z 🍷	⚒ 2	2	⚒ 2	Ⓑw	2
Lienz d.	1125	...	...	...	1225	1325	...	...	...	1425	1525	1550	...	...	1625	1725	...	...	...	...	1825	1925	2025	...	...
Spittal-Millstättersee a.	1227	...	...	...	1327	1427	...	...	...	1527	1627	1638	...	...	1726	1828	...	...	...	...	1927	2027	2126	...	...
Spittal-Millstättersee 970 d.	1236	...	...	...	1331	1431	...	...	...	1531	1631	1644	...	...	1732	1831	...	...	...	...	1931	2031	2131	2221	...
Villach Hbf 970 a.	1309	...	...	...	1404	1504	...	...	...	1604	1704	1708	...	...	1805	1904	...	...	...	...	2004	2104	2204	2245	...
	▬ 2				|	▬ 2				Ⓐ 2	▬ 2	|			⚒ 2	▬ 2					d 2	2		|	
Villach Hbf 970 d.	1250	1316	1320	1350	1420	1450	1514	1520	1550	1630	1650	1714	1730	1750	1820	1850	1916	1920	1950	2020	2055	2150	...	2248	2350
Velden am Wörthersee 970 d.	1305	|	1335	1405	1435	1505	1525	1535	1605	1645	1705	|	1745	1805	1835	1905	|	1935	2005	|	2110	2205	...	2259	0005
Pörtschach am W'see 970 d.	1313	|	1343	1413	1443	1513	|	1543	1613	1653	1713	1729	1753	1813	1843	1913	|	1943	2013	|	2118	2213	...	2305	0013
Klagenfurt Hbf 970 a.	1326	1337	1356	1426	1456	1526	1537	1556	1626	1706	1726	1737	1806	1826	1856	1926	1937	1956	2026	2041	2131	2226	...	2317	0026
Klagenfurt Hbf 980 d.	...	1339	1404	...	1504	...	1539	1604	1628	1710	...	1739	1808	...	1904	...	1939	2004	...	2043	2133	2228	...	...	0028
St Veit an der Glan 980 d.	...	1353	1424	...	1524	...	1553	1624	1647	1730	...	1753	1833	...	1924	...	1953	2024	...	2057	2152	2248	...	...	0047
Friesach 980 a.	...	1415	1456	...	1556	...	|	1656	...	1802	...	1815	1905	...	1956	...	|	2056	...	|	...	2320	...	...	...
Wien Meidling 980 a.	...	1728	...	...	...	...	1928	...	...	...	...	2128	...	...	...	...	2328	...	...	0028	...	...	...	...	...

km															ÖEC 731	ÖEC 112				ÖEC 531				
		⚒ 2	2	⚒ 2	⚒ 2	2	Ⓐ 2	⚒ 2	2	⚒ U 2	Ⓐ 2	Ⓐ 2	2	2	B 2	✕	✕	2	2	B 2	✕	⚒ 2	2	Ⓐ 2	2
	Wien Meidling 980 d.	...	...	...	...	...	...	...	...	...	...	...	...	...	...	0630	...	...	...	...	0830	...	...	...	...
0	Friesach 980 d.	...	...	...	...	0522	0522	0545	0611v	0644	0706	...	...	0807	0907	|	...	...	...	1107	1145	...	...	1207	...
33	St Veit an der Glan 980 d.	...	...	...	...	0556	0556	0616	0645	0720	0740	...	...	0840	0940	1009	...	...	...	1140	1209	...	...	1240	...
53	**Klagenfurt** Hbf 980 a.	...	...	...	...	0615	0615	0631	0704	0740	0759	...	...	0859	0959	1021	...	...	...	1159	1221	...	...	1259	...
53	**Klagenfurt** Hbf 970 d.	...	...	0530	0602	0622	0622	0633	0710	0742	0802	0817	0832	0902	1002	1023	1031	...	1132	1202	1223	...	1232	1302	1332
66	Pörtschach am W'see 970 d.	...	...	0543	0616	0636	0636	0646	0721	0754	0816	|	0846	0916	1016	|	1043	...	1146	1216	1232	...	1246	1316	1346
75	Velden am Wörthersee 970 d.	...	...	0550	0624	0644	0644	0653	0727	0801	0824	0832	0854	0924	1024	|	1050	...	1154	1224	|	...	1254	1324	1354
91	**Villach** Hbf 970 a.	...	...	0606	0639	0659	0659	0710	0743	0817	0839	0846	0909	0939	1039	1044	1101	...	1209	1239	1246	...	1309	1339	1409
					d 2		|		2			⚒ 2		2		⚒ 2	|				|			d 2	
91	**Villach** Hbf 970 d.	0528	...	...	0656	...	0709	...	0756	...	...	0856	...	0956	...	1056	1116	1156	...	...	1253	1257	...	1356	...
127	Spittal-Millstättersee 970 a.	0601	...	...	0729	...	0734	...	0829	...	...	0929	...	1029	...	1129	1138	1229	...	...	1316	1330	...	1429	...
127	Spittal-Millstättersee d.	...	0626	...	...	...	0736	...	0831	...	...	0931	...	1031	...	1131	...	1231	...	...	1319	1331	...	1431	...
195	**Lienz** a.	...	0725	...	...	...	0827	...	0934	...	...	1030	...	1134	...	1234	...	1334	...	...	1409	1434	...	1534	...

		ÖEC 533				ÖIC 733	ÖIC 733		ÖEC 110				EC 103					ÖIC 537						EC 173	
	B 2	✕	2	⚒ 2	B 2	🍷	Ⓑ 🍷	⚒ 2	✕	⚒ 2	B 2	Ⓐ 2	✕	2	Ⓐ 2	2	B 2	🍷	⚒ 2	2	⚒ 2	Ⓑ 2	B 2	✕	⚒ 2
Wien Meidling 980 d.	...	1030	...	...	...	1230	1230	...	...	...	...	...	1430	...	...	...	...	1630	...	...	...	...	...	1830	...
Friesach 980 d.	1307	|	...	1407	1507	1545	1545	...	...	1607	1653	...	|	...	1807	...	1907	1945	...	...	2007	...	2053	|	...
St Veit an der Glan 980 d.	1340	1409	...	1440	1540	1609	1609	...	...	1640	1722	1740	1809	...	1840	...	1940	2009	...	...	2040	...	2126	2159	...
Klagenfurt Hbf 980 a.	1359	1421	...	1459	1559	1621	1621	...	...	1659	1734	1759	1821	...	1859	...	1959	2021	...	...	2059	...	2145	2211	...
Klagenfurt Hbf 970 d.	1402	1423	1432	1502	1602	1623	1623	...	1631	1702	1736	1802	1823	1832	1902	1932	2002	2023	...	2032	2102	...	2146	2214	2218
Pörtschach am W'see 970 d.	1416	|	1446	1516	1616	|	|	...	1643	1716	1749	1816	|	1846	1916	1946	2016	|	...	2046	2116	...	2158	|	2232
Velden am Wörthersee 970 d.	1424	1436	1454	1524	1624	|	|	...	1650	1724	1755	1824	|	1854	1924	1954	2024	2036	...	2054	2124	...	2204	|	2240
Villach Hbf 970 a.	1439	1446	1509	1539	1639	1644	1644	...	1703	1739	1809	1839	1844	1909	1939	2009	2039	2046	...	2109	2139	...	2220	2235	2255
		⚒ 2		d 2			|		|	d 2	|		⚒ 2		d 2										
Villach Hbf 970 d.	...	1456	...	1556	...	...	1652	1656	1718	1756	1810b	...	1856	...	1956	...	...	...	2057	...	...	2145	...	...	...
Spittal-Millstättersee 970 a.	...	1529	...	1629	...	...	1716	1729	1740	1829	1835b	...	1929	...	2029	...	...	...	2130	...	...	2218	...	...	...
Spittal-Millstättersee d.	...	1531	...	1640	...	...	1719	1731	...	1831	...	...	1931	...	2031	...	...	...	2131	...	...	...	...	...	...
Lienz a.	...	1634	...	1739	...	...	1810	1834	...	1934	...	...	2034	...	2128	...	...	...	2228	...	...	...	...	...	...

B – To / from Bruck a. d. Mur (Table **980**).
U – From Unzmarkt (Table **980**).
a – Ⓐ only.
b – Ⓑ only.
d – Daily.
v – ⚒ only.
w – Not Dec. 24, 25, 31, Apr. 2, 4, May 23.
z – Also Jan. 6, Apr. 5, May 24; not Dec. 27, Jan. 3, Apr. 4, May 23.
* – On Dec. 25, Jan. 1, 6, Apr. 5, May 13, 24, June 3 Spittal-Millstättersee d. *0630*, Villach a. *0655* (change trains at Spittal-Millstättersee).

974 LINZ - SELZTHAL

2nd class only (except *IC* trains)

km				IC 501																IC 601						
		⚒	Ⓐ						⚒							Ⓐ			Ⓐn		Ⓐn			Ⓐn		
0	**Linz** Hbf d.	0506	0536	0610	0632	0736	0836	0858	0936	1058	1136	1258	1355	1436	1536	1558	1658	1736	1756	1810	...	1858	1936	2036	2136	2306
28	Rohr - Bad Hall d.	0540	0609	|	0709	0809	0909	0921	1010	1121	1209	1321	1421	1509	1609	1621	1721	1809	1819	|	...	1921	2009	2109	2209	2339
32	Kremsmünster d.	0545	0615	|	0715	0814	0914	0927	1015	1125	1214	1325	1426	1514	1614	1625	1726	1814	1823	|	←	1925	2014	2114	2214	2344
51	Kirchdorf a. d. Krems d.	0603	0633	0646	0740	0833	0933	0940	1033	1140	1232	1340	1447	1540	1632	1640	1740	1833	1838	1846	1853	1940	2033	2133	2232	0002
68	Hinterstoder d.	0625	...	|	0801	0859	...	1001	...	1201	...	1401	1508	1601	...	1705	1802	...	→	|	1913	2001	2058	...	...	...
82	Windischgarsten d.	0639	...	0715	0815	0913	...	1015	...	1215	...	1415	1522	1615	...	1719	1816	...	...	1915	1927	2015	2112	...	...	...
87	Spital am Pyhrn d.	0646	...	|	0821	0918	...	1021	...	1221	...	1421	1528	1621	...	1733	1822	...	...	|	1933	2021	2119	...	...	...
104	**Selzthal** 975 a.	0702	...	0735	0839	...	...	1038	...	1239	...	1439	...	1639	...	1751	1840	...	...	1935	...	2039	2135	...	...	...
	Graz Hbf 975 a.	...	...	0905	|	...	...	...	...	|	...	|	...	|	...	...	...	...	...	2105	...	...	...	...	...	...
111	Liezen 975 a.	...	...	...	0851a	...	...	...	...	1251a	...	1451a	...	1651a	...	...	...	...	...	...	...	...	...	...	...	...

										IC 502															IC 602	
	⚒	Ⓐ		⚒		⚒	Ⓐ	Ⓒ											Ⓐn					Ⓐn		
Liezen 975 d.	...	...	...	...	...	...	...	...	...	...	...	0905a	...	...	...	1305a	...	1505a	...	...	1705a	...	...	...	...	...
Graz Hbf 975 d.	...	...	...	...	...	...	...	...	...	0652	...	|	...	...	...	|	...	|	...	...	|	...	...	...	1855	...
Selzthal 975 d.	...	0428	...	...	...	0547	0615	0615	0721	0826	...	0921	...	1121	...	1321	...	1521	...	...	1717	...	1921	...	2026	...
Spital am Pyhrn d.	...	0445	...	...	...	0604	0631	0631	0739	|	...	0939	1045	1138	...	1338	...	1537	...	1643	1733	...	1938	2025	|	...
Windischgarsten d.	...	0452	...	...	...	0610	0639	0639	0745	0846	...	0945	1051	1145	...	1345	...	1545	...	1650	1739	...	1946	2034	2046	...
Hinterstoder d.	...	0505	...	...	...	0624	0654	0654	0800	|	...	1000	1105	1200	...	1400	...	1600	...	1705	1753	...	2000	2047	|	...
Kirchdorf a. d. Krems d.	0428	0526	0526	0556	0626	0646	0721	0726	0821	0915	0946	1021	1126	1221	1326	1421	1526	1626	1656	1726	1813	1926	2021	2107	2115	2126
Kremsmünster d.	0445	0546	0546	0615	0645	0702	0736	0744	0836	|	1005	1036	1145	1236	1346	1436	1545	1646	1715	1746	1832	1946	2036	...	|	2145
Rohr - Bad Hall d.	0449	0550	0550	0619	0650	0708	0740	0749	0840	|	1010	1040	1149	1240	1350	1440	1549	1650	1721	1750	1837	1950	2040	...	|	2149
Linz Hbf a.	0524	0624	0624	0654	0728k	0735	0804	0824	0904	0948	1045	1104	1224	1304	1424	1504	1624	1724	1754	1824	1901	2024	2104	...	2148	2224

a – Ⓐ only.
k – 0724 on Ⓒ.
n – Not Dec. 24, 31.

SALZBURG - BISCHOFSHOFEN - SELZTHAL - GRAZ 975

km		⚒ 2	EN 465 A	⚒ 2	⚒ 2	Ⓐ 2	2	IC 501	2	IC 719 ⊗	ÖIC 534	2	IC 513 🍷	EC 102 ✕	2	IC 515 C🍷	ÖIC 538 🍷	2	EC 317 S⊗	ÖIC 732 🍷	Ⓑ 2	REX 3295 Ⓒ T 2	IC 519 🍷	ÖEC 630 ✕	2
0	**Salzburg** Hbf ... 960 970 d.	...	...	...	...	...	...	...	...	0615	...	...	0815	...	...	*1015*	...	...	1215	...	...	...	1415	...	...
53	**Bischofshofen** ... 960 970 a.	...	...	...	...	...	...	...	...	0702	...	...	0902	...	...	*1102*	...	...	1302	...	...	...	1502	...	...
53	**Bischofshofen** ... d.	...	0338	...	...	...	...	...	...	0713	...	0740v	0913	...	...	1113	...	...	1313	...	...	...	1513	...	...
77	Radstadt ... d.	...	|	...	...	...	0610	...	...	0736	...	0809	0936	...	...	1136	...	...	1336	...	...	...	1536	...	1609
94	Schladming ... d.	...	0416	0500	...	...	0629	...	...	0752	...	0831	0952	...	1031	1152	...	1231	1352	...	1431	1511	1552	...	1631
133	**Stainach-Irdning** ... d.	0427	0447	0541	...	...	0710	...	...	0822	...	0912	1022	...	1112	1222	...	1312	1422	...	1512	1553	1622	...	1712
145	Liezen ... d.	0438	|	0553	...	...	0726	...	...	0833	...	0926	1033	...	1126	1233	...	1326	1433	...	1526	1605	1633	...	1726
	Linz Hbf **974** ... d.	|	|	|	...	...	|	0610	...	|	...	|	|	...	|	|	...	|	|	...	|	|	|	...	|
152	**Selzthal** ... a.	0444	0504	0559	...	...	0732	0735	←	0840	...	0932	1040	...	1132	1240	...	1332	1440	...	1532	1612	1640	...	1732
152	**Selzthal** ... d.	0451	0513	0606	...	0714	→	0738	0742	0846	...	0939	1048	...	1139	1248	...	1339	1446	...	1539	...	1648	...	1739
158	Stadt Rottenmann ... d.	0458	|	0613	...	0720	...	0744	0748	0852	...	0945	|	...	1145	|	...	1345	1452	...	1545	...	|	...	1745
169	Trieben ... d.	0506	|	0621	...	0728	...	|	0756	|	...	0953	|	...	1153	|	...	1353	|	...	1553	...	|	...	1753
215	St Michael ... a.	0540	0550	0655	...	0802	...	|	0830	0921	...	1028	1121	...	1228	1321	...	1428	1521	...	1628	...	1721	...	1828
215	St Michael ... 980 d.	0541	0551	0701	0707	0803	...	|	0843	0922	...	1033	1122	...	1233	1322	...	1433	1522	...	1633	...	1722	...	1833
225	Leoben Hbf ... 980 a.	0549	0559	0708	0714	0810	...	0820	0850	0929	...	1040	1129	...	1240	1329	...	1440	1529	...	1640	...	1729	...	1840
225	Leoben Hbf ... 980 d.	0551	0601	0709	0716	0811	...	0822	0851	0938	0934	1041	1138	1134	1241	1338	1334	1441	1538	1534	1641	...	1738	1734	1841
	Bruck a. d. Mur ... 980 a.	|	0612	|	0729	0824	...	|	0903	|	0944	1053	|	1144	1253	|	1344	1453	|	1544	1653	...	|	1744	1853
	Wien Meidling **980** ... a.	|	|	|	...	...	...	|	|	|	1128	|	|	1328	|	|	1528	|	|	1728	|	...	|	1928	|
293	**Graz** Hbf ... 980 a.	0645	0700	0801	...	...	...	0905	*0956*	1022	...	*1133*	1222	...	*1333*	1422	...	*1533*	1622	...	*1733*	...	1822	...	*1933*

	IC 611 🍷	Ⓐ 2	2	IC 601	2	2	EC 319 F⊗	ÖEC 730 ✕	Ⓑ ◧ 2	E 2	Ⓑ 2
Salzburg Hbf ... 960 970 d.	1615	1644	...	...	...	...	1815	...	...	*1919*	...
Bischofshofen ... 960 970 a.	1702	1734	...	...	...	...	1902	...	...	*2020*	...
Bischofshofen ... d.	1713	1738	...	...	...	...	1913	...	...	2037	...
Radstadt ... d.	1736	1806	1809	...	...	...	1936	...	...	2109	...
Schladming ... d.	1752	▬	1831	...	...	...	1952	...	2031	2128	2135
Stainach-Irdning ... d.	1822	...	1912	...	...	...	2022	...	2112	...	2214
Liezen ... d.	1833	...	1926	...	...	...	2033	...	2126	...	...
Linz Hbf **974** ... d.	|	...	|	1810	...	...	|	...	|	...	...
Selzthal ... a.	1840	...	1932	1935	←	...	2040	...	2132	...	...
Selzthal ... d.	1848	...	→	1938	1942	...	2046	...	2142	...	...
Stadt Rottenmann ... d.	|	...	...	1944	1948	...	2052	...	2148	...	...
Trieben ... d.	|	ÖEC	...	|	1956	...	|	...	2156	...	...
St Michael ... a.	1921	530	...	|	2030	...	2121	...	2230	...	...
St Michael ... 980 d.	1922		...	|	...	2035	2122	...	2235	...	...
Leoben Hbf ... 980 a.	1929	✕	...	2020	...	2042	2129	...	2242	...	...
Leoben Hbf ... 980 d.	1938	1934	...	2022	...	2043	2138	2134	2243	...	...
Bruck a. d. Mur ... 980 a.	|	1944	...	|	...	2055	|	2144	2255	...	...
Wien Meidling **980** ... a.	|	2128	...	|	...	|	|	2328	|	...	...
Graz Hbf ... 980 a.	2022	...	...	2105	...	*2133*	2222	...	*2333*	...	...

	⚒ 2	⚒ 2	2	Ⓐ 2	⚒ 2	EC 318 F⊗	△2	IC 502	ÖEC 731 ✕
Graz Hbf ... 980 d.	...	...	...	...	...	0545	*0626*z	0652	...
Wien Meidling **980** ... d.	...	...	...	...	...	|	|	|	0630
Bruck a. d. Mur ... 980 d.	...	...	...	...	0613	|	0708	|	0815
Leoben Hbf ... 980 a.	...	...	...	...	0625	0629	0720	0739	0825
Leoben Hbf ... 980 d.	...	...	...	...	...	0631	0721	0741	...
St Michael ... 980 a.	...	...	...	...	...	0637	0728	|	...
St Michael ... d.	...	...	...	0600	...	0638	0730	|	...
Trieben ... d.	...	...	...	0636	...	|	0805	|	...
Stadt Rottenmann ... d.	...	...	...	0644	...	0708	0812	0817	...
Selzthal ... a.	...	...	...	0650	...	0713	0818	0823	...
Selzthal ... d.	...	0544	...	...	...	0719	0824	0826	...
Linz Hbf **974** ... a.	...	|	...	...	...	|	|	0948	...
Liezen ... d.	...	0552	...	...	...	0726	0832	...	...
Stainach-Irdning ... d.	...	0604	2	...	...	0737	0845	...	...
Schladming ... d.	0506	0648	0648	...	...	0810	0928	...	...
Radstadt ... d.	0525	0706	0706	...	...	0826	...	...	...
Bischofshofen ... a.	0554	0735	0735	...	...	0848	...	...	...
Bischofshofen .. 960 970 d.	*0558*	*0738*	*0738*	...	...	0857	...	...	...
Salzburg Hbf ... 960 970 a.	*0645*	*0839*	*0839*	...	...	0944	...	...	...

	IC 512 🍷	△2	ÖEC 531 ✕	IC 514 🍷	REX 3294 Ⓒ T 2	Ⓑ △2	ÖEC 533 ✕	EC 316 S⊗	△2	ÖIC 733 🍷	IC 518 C🍷	△2	⚒ 2	EC 103 ✕	IC 610 🍷	Ⓐ 2	⚒ 2	Ⓑ △2	⚒ 2	ÖIC 537 🍷	IC 718	△2	IC 602	△2	EN 464 A
Graz Hbf ... 980 d.	0738	*0826*	...	0938	...	*1026*	...	1138	*1226*	...	1338	*1426*	1500	...	1538	...	...	*1626*	*1700*	...	1738	*1826*	1855	*2026*	2228
Wien Meidling **980** ... d.	|	|	0830	|	...	|	1030	|	|	1230	|	|	|	1430	|	...	...	|	|	1630	|	|	|	|	|
Bruck a. d. Mur ... 980 d.	|	0908	1015	|	...	1108	1215	|	1308	1415	|	1508	|	1615	|	...	...	1708	|	1815	|	1908	|	2108	2317
Leoben Hbf ... 980 a.	0822	0920	1025	1022	...	1120	1225	1222	1320	1425	1422	1520	1554	1625	1622	...	...	1720	*1754*	1825	1822	1920	1939	2120	2328
Leoben Hbf ... 980 d.	0831	0921	...	1031	...	1121	...	1231	1321	...	1431	1521	1556	...	1631	...	...	1721	1801	...	1831	1921	1941	2121	2330
St Michael ... 980 a.	0837	0928	...	1037	...	1128	...	1237	1328	...	1437	1528	1605	...	1637	...	...	1728	1809	...	1837	1928	|	2128	2338
St Michael ... d.	0838	0930	...	1038	...	1130	...	1238	1330	...	1438	1530	1608	...	1638	...	...	1730	1810	...	1838	1930	|	2130	2340
Trieben ... d.	|	1005	...	|	...	1205	...	|	1405	...	|	1605	1644	...	|	...	...	1805	1846	...	|	2005	|	2205	|
Stadt Rottenmann ... d.	|	1012	...	|	...	1212	...	1308	1412	...	|	1612	1652	...	|	...	...	1812	1854	...	1908	2012	2017	2212	|
Selzthal ... a.	0911	1018	...	1111	...	1218	...	1313	1418	...	1511	1618	1658	...	1711	...	...	1818	1900	...	1913	2018	2023	2218	0017
Selzthal ... d.	0919	1024	...	1119	1135	1224	...	1319	1424	...	1519	1624	...	...	1719	...	1735	1824	...	...	1919	2024	2026	2224	0029
Linz Hbf **974** ... a.	|	|	...	|	|	|	...	|	|	...	|	|	...	...	|	...	|	|	...	...	|	|	2148	|	|
Liezen ... d.	0926	1032	...	1126	1144	1232	...	1326	1432	...	1526	1632	...	...	1726	...	1743	1832	...	...	1926	2032	...	2231	|
Stainach-Irdning ... d.	0937	1045	...	1137	1157	1245	...	1337	1445	...	1537	1645	...	...	1737	...	1755	1845	...	...	1937	2045	...	2243	0046
Schladming ... d.	1010	1128	...	1210	1248	1328	...	1410	1529	...	1610	1729	...	...	1810	...	1848	1928	...	...	2010	2128	...	2330	0118
Radstadt ... d.	1026	...	...	1226	...	...	...	1426	1552	...	1626	1752	...	...	1826	1920	...	...	...	...	2026	...	...	2350	|
Bischofshofen ... a.	1048	...	...	1248	...	...	...	1448	...	...	1648	...	...	...	1848	1950	...	...	...	...	2048	...	...	...	0156
Bischofshofen ... 960 970 d.	1057	...	...	1257	...	...	...	1457	...	...	*1657*	...	...	...	1857	*2007*	...	...	...	...	2057	...	...	...	...
Salzburg Hbf ... 960 970 a.	1144	...	...	1344	...	...	...	1544	...	...	*1744*	...	...	...	1944	*2053*	...	...	...	...	2144	...	...	...	...

A – ZÜRICHSEE – 🛏 1, 2 cl., ▬ 2 cl. and (2) Graz - Innsbruck - Buchs 🏛 - Zürich and v.v.
C – (12) and 🍷 Innsbruck - Schwarzach - Bischofshofen - Graz and v.v.
E – From Schwarzach (Table **960**).
F – (12) and ⊗ Graz - München - Stuttgart - Frankfurt and v.v.
S – (12) and ⊗ Graz - München - Stuttgart - Saarbrücken and v.v.

T – (2) Wien - Amstetten - Selzthal - Schladming and v.v. See also Tables **950** and **976**.

v – ⚒ only.
z – *0611* on †.

◧ – Change trains at St Michael on ⑤⑦.
△ – Between Bruck a. d. Mur and St Michael combined with a service on the Klagenfurt route (Table **980**) – passengers should take care to join the correct portion for their destination.

AMSTETTEN - KLEINREIFLING - SELZTHAL 976

2nd class only

km		⚒	ⒶL	Ⓐ	W	ⒶL	⑥e	Ⓐ	Ⓒ	ⒸG	⚒	Ⓐ			Ⓐ	Ⓐ	n	Ⓐ	ⒶL	n	⑥e	Ⓐ	Ⓒ	Ⓐn	Ⓑm	
0	**Amstetten** ... d.	0449	...	0541	0626	...	0659	0718	0759	0838	0859	0959	1059	1159	...	1259	1359	1459	...	1558r	...	1707	1759	1807	1907	1959
23	Waidhofen a. d. Ybbs. d.	0520	...	0608	0710f	...	0731	0749	0829	0907	0928	1027	1129	1230	...	1329	1430	1530	...	1633	...	1733	1826	1833	1933	2027
41	Weyer ... d.	0544	...	...	0729	...	...	...	0851	0927	0946	...	1146	1249	...	1346	1449	1549	...	1652	...	1752	1845	1852	1952	...
47	**Kleinreifling** ... a.	0552	...	...	0737	...	...	...	0859	0935	0954	...	1154	1257	...	1354	1457	*1610*	...	1700	...	1800	1852	1900	2000	...
47	**Kleinreifling** ... d.	...	0646	...	...	0850	...	...	...	0948	...	...	...	1258c	1300	...	1458c	...	1615	...	1749	...	1853t	1901	...	...
61	Weißenbach-St Gallen d.	...	0700	...	...	0904	...	...	...	1002	...	...	...	1312c	1314	...	1512c	...	1629	...	1803	...	1908t	1915	...	...
119	**Selzthal** ... a.	...	...	...	...	...	...	...	...	1107	...	...	...	...	...	...	...	...	...	...	...	...	...	...	...	...

	⚒	Ⓐ		ⒶL		⑥e	Ⓐ	W	Ⓐ	ⒶS		⚒		Ⓐ	ⒶS		Ⓐn	Ⓐ		Ⓐn	ⒶL	ⒸG	Ⓐ	†	Ⓑm	n
Selzthal ... d.	...	...	...	...	...	...	...	...	...	...	...	...	...	...	...	...	...	...	...	...	...	1628	...	...	...	...
Weißenbach-St Gallen. d.	...	...	...	0600	...	...	0706	...	...	0940	...	...	...	...	1339	1343c	...	...	1550c	...	1659	1732	...	...	...	1948
Kleinreifling ... a.	...	...	...	0614	...	...	0720	...	...	0954	...	...	...	...	1354	1358c	...	...	1604c	...	1714	1747	...	...	...	2002
Kleinreifling ... d.	...	0511	0603e	...	0635	...	0721	0801	...	...	0959	1102e	1159	1302	...	1359	1502	1546	1605c	1704	...	1754	1804	1905	...	2003
Weyer ... d.	...	0524	0612e	...	0647	...	0728	0809	...	...	1011	1110e	1210	1310	...	1410	1510	1553	1613	1715	...	1804	1815	1913	...	2011
Waidhofen a. d. Ybbs.. d.	0455	0545	0634	...	0708	0746	...	0828	0931	...	1031	1131	1231	1331	...	1431	1530	...	1633	1733	...	1825	1833	1933	1933	2031
Amstetten ... a.	0524	0614	0701	...	0736	0814	...	0856	0959	...	1059	1159	1259	1359	...	1459	1559	...	1700	1800	...	1850	1900	2000	2000	2058

Waidhofen a. d. Ybbs - Lunz am See ❖

km	*Narrow gauge*	ⒸJ	Ⓒ	Ⓐ				Ⓐ		Ⓒ	
0	Waidhofen a. d. Ybbs. d.	0710	0909	0932	...	1432	...	1635	...	1835	...
6	Gstadt ... a.	0724	0921	0944	...	1444	...	1647	...	1847	...
54	Lunz am See ... ❖ a.	*0828*	*1025*	*1049*	...	*1548*	...	*1751*	...	*1951*	...

Narrow gauge	Ⓐy	ⒸJ	ⒸK	Ⓐw	ⒸJ				Ⓒ	Ⓐ
Lunz am See ... ❖ d.	0600	*0708*	*0747*	*0808*	*1010*	...	*1310*	...	*1705*	*1710*
Gstadt ... d.	0659	0812	0851	0912	1114	...	1415	...	1809	1817
Waidhofen a. d. Ybbs ... a.	0715	0824	0904	0925	1126	...	1428	...	1822	1829

G – (2) Wien - Selzthal - Schladming and v.v.
J – From May 1.
K – Until Apr. 25.
L – From / to Linz (Table **977**).
S – To St Valentin (Table **977**).

W – From / to Wien (Table **950**).

c – Ⓒ only.
e – ⑥ (not Dec. 26, May 1).
f – Arrives 0657.

m – Also Dec. 26, May 1.
n – Not Dec. 24, 31.
r – 1607 on Ⓐ.
t – † only.

w – Not Dec. 24 - Jan. 6, Mar. 29 - Apr. 6, May 25.
y – Ⓐ (not Dec. 24 - Jan. 6, Feb. 1 – 5, Mar. 29 - Apr. 6, May 25). By 🚌 throughout.

❖ – All services Gstadt - Lunz and v.v. are operated by 🚌.

977 LINZ - KLEINREIFLING

2nd class only

km		⚒w	⚒		w			⚒		Ⓐ	Ⓐ		Ⓐ			Ⓐw		Ⓐn		Ⓐ		Ⓐn					
0	**Linz** Hbf ...**950** d.	0441	0517	0618	0653	0750	*0831*	0853	0953	*1031*	*1131*	1150	1223	1253	1353	1423	1450	*1531*	1553	1623	1650	*1731*	1753	*1853*	1953	2153	2255
25	St Valentin **950** d.	0511	0544	0649	0722	0820	0852	0920	1020	1052	1152	1220	1252	1320	1420	1452	1520	1552	1620	1653	1717	1752	1820	1923	2020	2220	2322
45	Steyr.............. d.	0535	0608	0715	0748	0848	0913	0947	1047	1113	1213	1247	1313	1347	1447	1518	1547	1616	1647	1715	1747	1813	1850	1948	2046	2245	2347
47	Garsten........... a.	0537	0611	0718	0751	0851	0915	0950	1050	1115	1215	1250	1315	1350	1450	1520	1550	1619	1650	1718	1750	1815	1853	1951	2049	2248	2349
91	**Kleinreifling**... a.	0645	...	...	0849	0944c	1008a	...	1146c	1208	...	1348c	1408	1452a	1546c	1614	...	1713	1745c	1813	1846a	...	1948	...	2143	...	...

		Ⓐ	m	⚒	⚒	w			Ⓐ	Ⓒ	Ⓐw		⚒	Ⓐ			Ⓐw				Ⓐ	Ⓐw	Ⓒ	Ⓐn			
Kleinreifling.....d.	...	0436	0515r	...	...	0615	...	0750	...	...	0955	1014c	...	1155	1213c	...	1355	1413c	...	1615	...	1715	...	...	1818	...	2024
Garsten ....d.	0437	0530	0605	0612	0637	0710	0809	0843	0909	0928	1043	1109	1208	1243	1309	1409	1443	1509	1609	1709	1743	1809	1809	1843	1910	2009	2118
Steyr.................d.	0442	0535	0610	0616	0641	0715	0814	0847	0914	0932	1047	1114	1213	1247	1314	1414	1447	1514	1614	1714	1747	1814	1814	1847	1914	2014	2122
St Valentin . **950** a.	0505	0600	|	0640	0705	0741	0838	0906	0938	0955	1107	1140	1240	1306	1338	1440	1506	1540	1640	1740	1806	1840	1840	1906	1940	2039	2144
Linz Hbf .... **950** a.	0538	0622	0643	0700	0738	0808	0908	*0929*	1008	1023	*1129*	1208	1308	*1329*	1408	1508	*1529*	1608	1708	1808	*1829*	1908	*1929*	*1929*	2008	2108	2211

a – Ⓐ only.
c – Ⓒ only.
m – To München via Simbach (Tables **962**/**893**).
n – Not Dec. 24, 31.
r – ⚒ only.
w – To / from Weißenbach on Ⓐ (Table **976**).

978 WIEN and WIENER NEUSTADT - SOPRON

ÖBB / GySEV★ (2nd class only except where shown)

km		Ⓐn			Ⓐ		D⁄		Ⓐ	B⁄	Ⓐ			Ⓐ		Ⓐ			Ⓐ	Ⓐn	Ⓐn				Ⓐn
0	**Wien** Meidling ● ....d.	0533	...	*0547a*	*0630*	0634	0703	*0730c*	0737	0800	*0830*	0838	*0930*	0938	...	*1030*	1038	*1130*	1138	*1203*	*1230*	1238	...	*1330*	1338
	Wiener Neustadt Hbf......d.	|	0607	0632	0706	|	0734	0807	|	0832	0907	|	1007	|	1032	1107	|	1207	|	1237	1307	|	1332	1407	|
	Mattersburg ....d.	|	0631	0647	0731	|	|	0831	|	0847	0931	|	1031	|	1047	1131	|	1231	|	1259	1331	|	1347	1431	|
38	Ebenfurth..........................d.	0613	|	|	|	0710	|	|	0810	|	|	0910	|	1010	|	|	1110	|	1210	|	|	1310	|	|	1410
70	**Sopron** 🛃 ....a.	0647	0648	0659	0747	0748	0758	0847	0848	0859	0947	0948	1047	1048	1059	1147	1148	1247	1248	1314	1347	1348	1359	1447	1448

	Ⓐn	S	Ⓐn		Ⓐn	S		Ⓐn	Ⓐn	Ⓐn				Ⓐn	Ⓐn	Ⓐn				Ⓐn		Ⓐn			
Wien Meidling ● .... d.	...	*1403*	*1433*	1438	*1447*	*1503*	*1530*	1538	1600	*1633*	1638	1700	*1730*	1738	1800	*1830*	1838	*1900a*	*1930*	1938	*2000a*	...	2038	...	*2135*
Wiener Neustadt Hbf....... d.	1432	1437	1507	|	1532	1537	1607	|	1632	1707	|	1732	1807	|	1832	1907	|	1932	2007	|	2032	2107	|	2132	2232
Mattersburg...................... d.	1447	1459	1531	|	1547	1559	1631	|	1647	1731	|	1747	1831	|	1847	1931	|	1947	2031	|	2047	2131	|	2147	2256
Ebenfurth........................... d.	|	|	|	1510	|	|	|	1610	|	|	1710	|	|	1810	|	|	1910	|	|	2010	|	|	2110	|	|
Sopron 🛃 .... a.	1459	1514	1547	1548	1559	1614	1647	1648	1659	1747	1748	1759	1847	1848	1859	1947	1948	1959	2047	2048	2059	2147	2148	2159	2311

km		Ⓐn	Ⓐn	Ⓐn	Ⓐn	Ⓐ	Ⓐ	Ⓐ		Ⓐn		Ⓐn				S	Ⓐ			Ⓐ	Ⓐ		S		Ⓐ
0	**Sopron** 🛃 ....d.	0412	0415	0442	0501	0512	0515	0542	0544	0601	0613	0615	0701	0713	0715	0800	0813	0815	0913	0915	1013	1015	1101	1113	1115
	Ebenfurth..........................d.	0455	|	0525	|	0555	|	0626	|	|	0655	|	|	0755	|	|	0855	|	0955	|	1055	|	|	1155	|
17	Mattersburg ....d.	|	0431	|	0515	|	0531	|	0601	0615	|	0631	0715	|	0731	0814	|	0831	|	0931	|	1031	1114	|	1131
33	**Wiener Neustadt** Hbf......a.	|	0453	|	0528	|	0553	|	0623	0628	|	0653	0728	|	0754	0827	|	0853	|	0953	|	1053	1127	|	1153
77	**Wien** Meidling ● ....a.	0525	*0531*	0555	0600	0626	*0630*	0655	...	0700	0725	*0730*	0800	0825	*0834*	*0858r*	0925	*0928*	1025	*1028*	1125	*1128*	*1158*	1225	*1228*

	Ⓐ				Ⓐn	Ⓐn				Ⓐn	Ⓐn			Ⓐn	Ⓐn				Ⓐn			E⁄	Ⓐn	A⁄	
Sopron 🛃 .... d.	1213	1215	1301	1313	1315	1413	1415	1501	1513	1515	1613	1615	1713	1715	1813	1815	1901	1913	1915	2001	2015	2033	2115	2201	2240
Ebenfurth........................... d.	1255	|	|	1355	|	1455	|	|	1555	|	1655	|	1755	|	1855	|	|	1955	|	|	|	|	|	|	|
Mattersburg...................... d.	|	1231	1314	|	1331	|	1431	1514	|	1531	|	1631	|	1731	|	1831	1914	|	1931	2014	2031	|	2131	2214	2256
Wiener Neustadt Hbf....... a.	|	1253	1327	|	1353	|	1453	1527	|	1553	|	1653	|	1753	|	1853	1927	|	1953	2027	2053	2059	2153	2227	2317
Wien Meidling ● .... a.	1325	*1328*	*1358*	1425	*1428*	1525	*1528*	*1558*	1625	*1628*	1725	*1728*	1825	*1828*	1925	*1928*	*1958*	2025	*2043*	*2058*	...	2125	...	2255	*2358*

A – Conveys [12] Budapest (*IC* **918**) - Csorna (*IC* **938**) - Sopron (**9951**) - Wien. See also Table **1250**.
B – Conveys [12] Wien - Sopron (*IC* **937**) - Csorna (*IC* **917**) - Budapest. See also Table **1250**.
D – *IC* **285**: ZAGREB – [12] Wien - Sopron - Szombathely - Nagykanizsa - Gyékényes - Zagreb; [2] Wien - Gyékényes (**891**) - Pécs
E – *IC* **284**: ZAGREB – [12] Zagreb - Gyékényes - Nagykanizsa - Szombathely - Sopron - Wien; [2] Pécs (**892**)- Gyékényes (**284**) - Wien.
S – To / from Szombathely (Table **1227**).

a – Ⓐ (not Dec. 24, 31).
c – Ⓒ only.
n – Not Dec. 24, 31.
r – ⚒ only.
● – See note ● on page 455.
★ – GySEV / ROeEE: Györ-Sopron-Ebenfurti Vasút / Raab-Oedenburg-Ebenfurter Eisenbahn.
⁄ – Supplement payable in Hungary. 🅁 for journeys from Hungary.

979 FLUGHAFEN WIEN ✈ Schwechat

CAT ★: S-Bahn (2nd class only)

km		★	★	★		★	★														
0	**Wien** Praterstern ....d.	*CAT*	...	...	and	...	...	S-Bahn	0428	0452	0504	0552	0613	0643	0713	0743	0813	0843	and at	2213	2243	2343
2	**Wien** Mitte.................d.	→	0538	0608	every	2238	2308	→	0432	0456	0508	0556	0617	0647	0717	0747	0817	0847	the same	2217	2247	2347
	Wien Meidling ▲.....d.		|	|	30	|	|		|	*0442*	*0448*	*0542*	*0600*	*0636*	*0703*	*0727*	*0803*	*0833*	minutes	*2203*	*2233*	*2333*
3	**Wien** Rennweg...........d.		|	|	minutes	|	|		0434	0458	0510	0558	0619	0649	0719	0749	0819	0849	past each	2219	2249	2349
21	**Flughafen Wien** ✈ ....a.		0554	0624	until	2254	2324		0456	0520	0533	0620	0642	0712	0742	0812	0842	0912	hour until	2242	2312	0012

km		★	★	★		★	★														
0	**Flughafen Wien** ✈ ....d.	*CAT*	0605	0635	and	2305	2335	S-Bahn	0539	0609	0639	0709	0721	0739	0809	0845	0918	0948	and at	2248	2318	0018
18	**Wien** Rennweg...........a.	→	|	|	every	|	|	→	0600	0630	0700	0730	0742	0800	0830	0906	0939	1009	the same	2309	2339	0039
24	**Wien** Meidling ▲.....a.		|	|	30	|	|		*0618*	*0648*	*0718*	*0748*	*0757*	*0818*	*0845*	*0927*	*0957*	*1027*	minutes	*2327*	*2357*	*0103*
	Wien Mitte..................a.		0621	0651	minutes	2321	2351		0603	0633	0703	0733	0745	0803	0833	0909	0942	1012	past each	2312	2342	0042
	Wien Praterstern ....a.		...	...	until	...	...		0607	0637	0707	0737	0749	0807	0837	0913	0946	1016	hour until	2316	2346	0046

★ – *City Airport Train (CAT)*. Non-stop service with special fares.
▲ – Change trains at Rennweg (cross platform).

🚌 *Vienna Airport Lines*: Wien Westbahnhof (Felberstraße) – Wien Meidling (Dörfelstraße) – Flughafen Wien ✈ and v.v.
🚌 From **Wien Westbahnhof**: 0500 and every 20 minutes until 1900, then every 30 minutes until 2300. Journey time: 45 minutes (from Westbahnhof), 30 minutes (from Meidling).
🚌 From **Flughafen Wien** ✈: 0600 and every 20 minutes until 2000, then every 30 minutes until 2330, also 2359. Journey time: 30 minutes (to Meidling), 45 minutes (to Westbahnhof).

🚌 ÖBB-Bahn Bus / SAD Bratislava: **Bratislava**, AS Mlynské nivy (bus station) – **Flughafen Wien** ✈ and v.v. 🅁 (✆ +43 (0)810 222 333-6). Journey time: 60 minutes.
Only a limited service operates on Dec. 24, 25, 26, 31, Jan. 1, Apr. 4, 5.
🚌 From **Bratislava** AS Mlynské nivy at 0530, 0600, 0700, 0730 ①–⑤, 0800, 0830, 0900, 0930 ①–⑤, 1000, 1100 ⚒, 1105 †, 1200, 1300 and hourly until 2000.
🚌 From **Flughafen Wien** ✈ at 0815, 0830, 0940, 1030, 1130, 1230, 1300 ①–⑤, 1330, 1430, 1500 ①–⑤, 1530, 1630 and hourly until 2330.

980 WIEN - GRAZ, KLAGENFURT and VILLACH

km							ÖIC 551	IC 512	ÖEC 731		IC 553		ÖEC 151 s	IC 514	ÖEC 531	ÖIC 555 §		ÖEC 255	EC 316	ÖEC 533	ÖIC 559		ÖIC 257	IC 518	ÖIC 733
		⚒ 2	⚒ 2	⚒ 2	2	△2	🍷	🍷	✖	2	🍷	△2	✖♦	🍷	✖♦	🍷	△2	M✖	⊗	✖	🍷	△2	M🍷	🍷	🍷♦
	Břeclav **982** ....d.	...	...	...	...	...	...	...	...	...	...	...	...	...	...	...	...	...	...	...	...	...	...	...	...
0	**Wien** Meidling ● .... **981** d.	...	...	...	...	...	0603	...	0630	...	0703	...	0803	...	0830	0903	...	1003	...	1030	1103	...	1203	...	1230
45	**Wiener Neustadt** Hbf .. **981** a.	...	...	...	...	...	0628	...	0655	...	0728	...	0828	...	0855	0928	...	1028	...	1055	1128	...	1228	...	1255
45	**Wiener Neustadt** Hbf .. **981** d.	...	...	...	...	...	0632	...	0657	...	0732	...	0832	...	0857	0932	...	1032	...	1057	1132	...	1232	...	1257
113	Mürzzuschlag.............. **981** d.	...	0525	...	0620	...	0730	...	|	...	0830	...	0930	...	|	1030	...	1130	...	|	1230	...	1330	...	|
	Graz Hbf .... **975 980a** d.	*0345a*	|	*0508a*	|	*0611*	|	0738	|	...	|	*0826*	|	0938	|	|	*1026*	|	1138	|	|	*1226*	|	1338	|
154	**Bruck** an der Mur ....a.	*0431a*	0607	*0554a*	0702	*0657*	0756	|	0813	...	0856	*0901*	0956	|	1013	1056	*1101*	1156	|	1213	1256	*1301*	1356	|	1413
154	**Bruck** an der Mur .... **975** d.	0438	0609	0613	0709	0708	0758	|	0815	...	0858	0908	0958	|	1015	1058	1108	1158	|	1215	1258	1308	1358	|	1415
208	**Graz** Hbf ....a.	|	0656	|	0756	|	0833	|	|	...	0933	|	1033	|	|	1133	|	1233	|	|	1333	|	1433	|	|
170	Leoben Hbf.................. **975** d.	0452	▬	0626	...	0721	...	0822	0827	0835	...	0921	...	1022	1027	...	1121	...	1222	1227	...	1321	...	1422	1427
◧	St Michael .... **975** a.	0500	...	|	...	0728	...	...	|	|	...	0928	...	...	|	...	1128	...	...	|	...	1328	...	...	|
◧	St Michael ....d.	0507	...	|	...	0733	...	...	|	|	...	0933	...	...	|	...	1133	...	...	|	...	1333	...	...	|
201	Knittelfeld..........................d.	0527	...	0648	...	0749	...	...	0846	0858	...	0949	...	...	1046	...	1149	...	...	1246	...	1349	...	...	1446
209	Zeltweg..............................d.	0536	⚒	0655	...	0756	...	...	|	0906	...	0956	...	...	|	...	1156	...	...	|	...	1356	...	...	|
216	Judenburg...........................d.	0544	2	0703	...	0804	...	...	0900	0914	...	1004	...	...	1100	...	1204	...	...	1300	...	1404	...	...	1500
235	Unzmarkt ....d.	0600	0608	0718	...	0818	...	...	0914	0930	...	1018	...	...	1114	...	1218	...	...	1314	...	1420	...	...	1514
272	Friesach..................... **971** a.	...	0643	...	...	0852	...	...	|	...	...	1052	...	...	1144	...	1252	...	...	|	...	1454	...	...	1544
305	St Veit an der Glan ...... **971** a.	...	0718	...	...	0939	...	...	1007	...	...	1139	...	...	1207	...	1339	...	...	1407	...	1539	...	...	1607
325	**Klagenfurt** Hbf .**970/1 980a** a.	...	0740	...	...	0959	...	...	1021	...	...	1159	...	...	1221	...	1359	...	...	1421	...	1559	...	...	1621
363	**Villach** Hbf .... **970/1** a.	...	0817	...	...	1039	...	...	1044	...	...	1239	...	...	1246	...	1439	...	...	1446	...	1639	...	...	1644

FOR NOTES SEE NEXT PAGE →

WIEN - GRAZ, KLAGENFURT and VILLACH — 980

	ÖEC 653		ÖIC 259	IC 610	EC 103	IC 657		REX 1763	EC 159	IC 718	ÖIC 537	ÖIC 659		REX 1765	ÖIC 751	ÖEC 150	EC 173		ÖEC 753		EN 235	IC 755	EN 1237	ÖEC 757	
								⚒						Ⓐ							R		R		⑤–⑦
	✕	△2	M🍷	🍷	✕♦	🍷	△2	2	✕♦		🍷	🍷	△2	2	🍷	✕	✕♦	2	✕	△2	♦	🍷	♦	✕	2
Břeclav **982** d.	...	...	...	...	1302	...	...	...	...	...	...	...	...	...	...	...	1702	...	...	...	...	...	...	...	...
Wien Meidling ● **981** d.	1303	...	1403	...	1430	1503	...	...	1603	...	1630	1703	...	...	1803	...	1830	...	1903	...	1930	2003	2030	2103	...
Wiener Neustadt Hbf **981** a.	1328	...	1428	...	1455	1528	...	...	1628	...	1655	1728	...	...	1828	...	1855	...	1928	...	1955	2028	2055	2128	...
Wiener Neustadt Hbf **981** d.	1332	...	1432	...	1457	1532	...	...	1632	...	1657	1730	...	...	1832	...	1857	...	1932	...	1957	2032	2057	2132	...
Mürzzuschlag **981** d.	1430	...	1530	...	|	1630	...	...	1730	...	|	1830	...	...	1930	...	|	...	2030	...	|	2130	|	2230	...
Graz Hbf **975 980a** d.	|	*1426*	|	1538	|	|	*1626*	1700	|	1738	|	|	*1826*	1900	|	1926	|	...	|	*2026*	|	|	|	|	*2228*
Bruck an der Mur a.	1456	*1501*	1556	|	1613	1656	*1701*	|	1756	|	1813	1856	*1901*	|	1956	2001	2013	...	2056	*2101*	2123	2156	2220	2256	*2305*
Bruck an der Mur **975** d.	1458	1508	1558	|	1615	1658	1708	|	1758	|	1815	1858	1908	|	1958	...	2015	...	2058	2108	2125	2158	2222	2258	2310
Graz Hbf a.	1533	|	1633	|	|	1733	|	|	1833	|	|	1933	|	|	2033	...	|	...	2133	|	|	2233	|	2333	|
Leoben Hbf **975** d.	...	1521	...	1622	1627	...	1721	1757	...	1822	1827	...	1921	1955	...	...	2027	2033	...	2121	2140	...	2235	...	2322
St Michael **975** a.	...	1528	...	...	|	...	1728	|	...	...	|	...	1928	|	...	...	|	|	...	2128	|	...	|	...	|
St Michael d.	...	1533	...	...	|	...	1733	|	...	...	|	...	1933	|	...	...	|	|	...	2133	|	...	|	...	|
Knittelfeld d.	...	1549	...	...	1646	...	1749	1817	...	...	1846	...	1949	2015	...	...	|	2056	...	2149	2203	...	|	...	2345
Zeltweg d.	...	1556	...	...	|	...	1756	1823	...	...	|	...	1956	2021	...	...	|	2104	...	2156	|	...	|	...	2353
Judenburg d.	...	1604	...	...	1700	...	1804	1831	...	...	1900	...	2004	2029	...	...	|	2112	...	2204	|	...	|	...	0001
Unzmarkt d.	...	1618	...	...	1714	...	1818	1844	...	...	1914	...	2018	2042	...	...	|	2128	...	2218	|	...	|	...	0016
Friesach **971** a.	...	1652	...	...	|	...	1852	...	...	...	1944	...	2052	...	...	...	|	...	...	2252	2300	...	|	...	...
St Veit an der Glan **971** a.	...	1720	...	...	1807	...	1939	...	...	...	2007	...	2125	...	...	...	2158	...	...	...	|	...	|	...	...
Klagenfurt Hbf **970/1 980a** a.	...	1734	...	...	1821	...	1959	...	...	...	2021	...	2145	...	...	...	2211	...	...	...	2336	...	0019	...	...
Villach Hbf **970/1** a.	...	1809	...	...	1844	...	2039	...	...	...	2046	...	2220	...	...	...	2235	...	...	...	0001	...	0043	...	...

		ÖEC 78	EN 1236	REX 1750	EN 234		ÖIC 552		EC 172	ÖIC 551		ÖIC 250		ÖIC 556	ÖIC 534	IC 719	ÖEC 252		IC 650	EC 102	IC 513	EC 158		ÖIC 652	ÖIC 538
	Ⓐ		R	⚒	R	⚒	⚒	⚒																	
	2	✕♦	♦	2	♦	2	🍷	2	✕♦	🍷	2	M🍷	2	🍷	♦	⊗	M✕	2	🍷	✕♦	🍷	✕♦	2	🍷	🍷♦
Villach Hbf **970/1** d.	...	...	0344	...	0417	...	...	...	0527	...	...	...	0605	...	0716	...	...	0720	...	0914	...	...	0920	...	1116
Klagenfurt Hbf **970/1 980a** d.	...	...	0409	...	0439	...	...	...	0550	...	...	...	0628	...	0739	...	...	0804	...	0939	...	...	1004	...	1139
St Veit an der Glan **971** d.	...	...	|	...	|	...	...	*0501*	0603	...	...	...	0641	...	0753	...	...	0824	...	0953	...	...	1024	...	1153
Friesach **971** d.	...	...	|	0451	|	...	...	*0527*	|	...	...	...	0706	...	|	...	...	0905	...	1016	...	...	1105	...	|
Unzmarkt d.	0444	...	|	0526	|	0548	...	0607	|	...	0656	...	0740	...	0847	...	...	0939	...	1047	...	...	1139	...	1247
Judenburg d.	0500	...	|	0543	|	0604	...	0623	|	...	0712	...	0755	...	0901	...	...	0954	...	1101	...	...	1154	...	1301
Zeltweg d.	0508	...	|	0551	|	0612	...	0631	|	...	0720	...	0804	...	|	...	...	1003	...	|	...	...	1203	...	|
Knittelfeld d.	0516	...	|	0559	|	0621	...	0639	|	...	0728	...	0811	...	0914	...	...	1010	...	1114	...	...	1210	...	1314
St Michael a.	0535	...	|	|	|	|	...	0658	|	...	|	...	0827	...	|	...	...	1026	...	|	...	...	1226	...	|
St Michael **975** d.	0546	...	|	|	|	|	...	0707	|	...	|	...	0833	...	|	...	...	1033	...	|	...	...	1233	...	|
Leoben Hbf **975** d.	0554	...	0610	0623	0628	0645	...	0716	0734	...	0747	...	0841	...	0934	0938	...	1041	...	1134	1138	...	1241	...	1334
Graz Hbf d.	|	0540	|	|	|	|	0626	|	|	...	|	0726	|	0826	|	|	0926	|	1026	|	|	1126	|	1226	|
Bruck an der Mur **975** a.	0608	0615	0622	|	0639	0657	0701	0729	0744	...	0758	0801	0853	0901	0944	|	1001	1053	1101	1144	|	1201	1253	1301	1344
Bruck an der Mur d.	...	0617	0625	|	0641	*0709*	0703	*0735*	0746	0758	*0809*r	0803	*0858*	0903	0946	|	1003	*1058*	1103	1146	|	1203	*1258*	1303	1346
Graz Hbf **975 980a** a.	...	|	|	0715	|	*0756*	|	*0815*	|	0833	*0856*r	|	*0933*	|	|	1022	|	*1133*	|	|	1222	|	*1333*	|	|
Mürzzuschlag **981** d.	...	0646	|	...	0708	...	0732	...	|	...	...	0832	...	0932	|	...	1032	...	1132	|	...	1232	...	1332	|
Wiener Neustadt Hbf **981** a.	...	0745	0751	...	0802	...	0828	...	0902	...	...	0928	...	1028	1102	...	1128	...	1228	1302	...	1328	...	1428	1502
Wiener Neustadt Hbf **981** d.	...	0747	0755	...	0804	...	0833	...	0904	...	...	0833	...	1033	1104	...	1133	...	1233	1304	...	1333	...	1433	1504
Wien Meidling ● **981** a.	...	0816	0855	...	0834	...	0858	...	0928	...	...	0958	...	1058	1128	...	1158	...	1258	1328	...	1358	...	1458	1528
Břeclav **982** a.	...	0953	...	...	...	...	...	...	1053	...	...	...	...	...	...	...	...	...	...	1453	...	...	...	...	...

	IC 515	ÖIC 254		IC 656	ÖIC 732	EC 317	ÖEC 256		ÖEC 750	ÖEC 630	IC 519	ÖIC 258		IC 752	ÖEC 530	IC 611	ÖEC 150		ÖIC 754	ÖEC 730	EC 319	IC 756			IC 738
							t		¶														⑦	⑤⑥	⑦z
	🍷	M🍷	2		🍷	⊗	M✕	2	✕	✕	🍷	M🍷	2	🍷	✕♦	🍷	✕♦	2	🍷	✕	⊗	🍷	2	2	🍷
Villach Hbf **970/1** d.	...	...	1120	...	1316	...	...	1320	...	1514	...	...	1520	...	1714	...	...	1730	...	1916	...	...	...	...	2020
Klagenfurt Hbf **970/1 980a** d.	...	...	1204	...	1339	...	...	1404	...	1539	...	...	1604	...	1739	...	...	1808	...	1939	...	...	...	...	2043
St Veit an der Glan **971** d.	...	...	1224	...	1353	...	...	1424	...	1553	...	...	1624	...	1753	...	...	1833	...	1953	...	...	...	...	2057
Friesach **971** d.	...	...	1305	...	1416	...	...	1505	...	|	...	...	1705	...	1816	...	...	1906	...	|	...	...	2102	...	|
Unzmarkt d.	...	...	1339	...	1447	...	...	1539	...	1647	...	...	1739	...	1847	...	...	1940	...	2047	...	...	2136	2140	|
Judenburg d.	...	...	1354	...	1501	...	...	1554	...	1701	...	...	1754	...	1901	...	...	1955	...	2101	...	...	2151	2155	2201
Zeltweg d.	...	...	1403	...	|	...	...	1603	...	|	...	...	1803	...	|	...	...	2004	...	|	...	...	2200	2204	|
Knittelfeld d.	...	...	1410	...	1514	...	...	1610	...	1714	...	...	1810	...	1914	...	...	2011	...	2114	...	...	2207	2211	2214
St Michael a.	...	...	1426	...	|	...	...	1626	...	|	...	...	1826	...	|	...	...	2027	...	|	...	...	2223	2227	|
St Michael **975** d.	...	...	1433	...	|	...	...	1633	...	|	...	...	1833	...	|	...	...	2035	...	|	...	...	2235	2235	|
Leoben Hbf **975** d.	1338	...	1441	...	1534	1538	...	1641	...	1734	1738	...	1841	...	1934	1938	...	2043	...	2134	2138	...	2243	2243	2234
Graz Hbf d.	|	1326	|	1426	|	|	1526	|	1626	|	|	1726	|	1826	|	|	1926	|	2026	|	|	2126	|	|	|
Bruck an der Mur **975** a.	|	1401	1453	1501	1544	|	1601	1653	1701	1744	|	1801	1853	1901	1944	|	2001	2055	2101	2144	|	2201	2255	2255	2244
Bruck an der Mur d.	|	1403	*1458*	1503	1546	|	1603	*1658*	1703	1746	|	1803	*1858*	1903	1946	|	2003	*2058*	2103	2146	|	2203	*2258*	*2258*	2246
Graz Hbf **975 980a** a.	1422	|	*1533*	|	|	1622	|	*1733*	|	|	1822	|	*1933*	|	|	2022	|	*2133*	|	|	2222	|	*2333*	*2333*	|
Mürzzuschlag **981** d.	...	1432	...	1532	|	...	1632	...	1732	|	...	1832	...	1932	|	...	2032	...	2132	|	...	2232	...	...	|
Wiener Neustadt Hbf **981** a.	...	1528	...	1628	1702	...	1728	...	1828	1902	...	1928	...	2028	2102	...	2128	...	2228	2302	...	2328	...	...	0002
Wiener Neustadt Hbf **981** d.	...	1533	...	1633	1704	...	1733	...	1833	1904	...	1933	...	2033	2104	...	2133	...	2233	2304	...	2333	...	...	0004
Wien Meidling ● **981** a.	...	1558	...	1658	1728	...	1758	...	1858	1928	...	1958	...	2058	2128	...	2158	...	2258	2328	...	2358	...	...	0028
Břeclav **982** a.	...	...	...	...	...	...	...	...	...	...	...	...	...	...	...	...	...	...	...	...	...	...	...	...	...

♦ – **NOTES** (CONTINUED FROM PREVIOUS PAGE)

78 – GUSTAV KLIMT – 🚃12 and ✕ Graz - Wien - Břeclav 🏛 - Praha.

102/3 – POLONIA – 🚃12 and ✕ Villach - Wien - Břeclav 🏛 - Ostrava - Warszawa and v.v.

150/1 – EMONA – 🚃12 and ✕ Ljubljana - Maribor - Spielfeld-Straß 🏛 - Graz - Wien and v.v.; 🚃2 Rijeka (**482/3**) - Ljubljana - Wien and v.v.

158/9 – CROATIA – 🚃12 and ✕ Zagreb - Maribor - Spielfeld-Straß 🏛 - Graz - Wien and v.v.

172/3 – VINDOBONA – 🚃12 and ✕ Villach - Wien - Břeclav 🏛 - Praha - Dresden - Berlin - Hamburg and v.v.

234/5 – ALLEGRO TOSCA – 🛏 1, 2 cl., ▬ 2 cl. and 🚃2 Roma - Venezia - Wien and v.v. Conveys (subject to confirmation) 🛏 1, 2 cl. and ▬ 2 cl. Milano - Venezia - Wien and v.v.

530/1 – 🚃12 and ✕ Lienz - Villach - Wien and v.v.

534 – 🚃12 (Lienz ①–⑤ -) Villach - Wien.

538 – 🚃12 and 🍷 (Lienz ⑥ -) Villach - Wien.

733 – 🚃12 and 🍷 Wien - Villach (- Lienz Ⓑ).

1236 – Fom Villach on ⑦ from Mar. 28 (also Dec. 30, 31, Jan. 2–7, Apr. 6, May 14, 25, June 4); previous night from Firenze. ALLEGRO ROSSINI – 🛏 1, 2 cl., ▬ 2 cl. and 🚃2 Firenze - Venezia - Wien. Train number **1238** on Dec. 30, 31, Jan. 2–7, Apr. 6, May 14, 25, June 4.

1237 – ⑤ from Mar. 26 (also Dec. 28, 29, 30, Jan. 1–5, Apr. 4, May 12, 23, June 2). ALLEGRO ROSSINI – 🛏 1, 2 cl., ▬ 2 cl. and 🚃2 Wien - Venezia - Firenze. Train number **1239** on Dec. 28, 29, 30, Jan. 1–5, Apr. 4, May 12, 23, June 2.

M – To / from Maribor (Table **1315**).

R – Ⓡ for journeys from / to Italy.

a – Ⓐ only.

r – ⚒ only.

s – Also calls at Semmering (d. 0915).

t – Also calls at Semmering (d. 1645).

z – Also Jan. 6, Apr. 5, May 24; not Dec. 27, Jan. 3, Apr. 4, May 23.

¶ – On © runs with train number **15750** and also calls at Semmering (d. 1745).

§ – On © runs with train number **15555** and also calls at Semmering (d. 1015).

◧ – Leoben - St Michael is *10 km*. St Michael - Knittelfeld is *22 km*.

△ – Between Bruck a. d. Mur and St Michael combined with a service on the Selzthal route (Table **975**) – passengers should take care to join the correct portion for their destination.

● – See Tables **981/2** for S-Bahn trains to / from Wien Südbahnhof, Mitte, Praterstern and Floridsdorf. See Table **979** for S-Bahn connections to / from Wien Flughafen ✈. See panel on page 445 for S-Bahn trains from / to Wien Hütteldorf. U-bahn line **U6** provides a direct link Wien Meidling - Westbahnhof - Spittelau - Floridsdorf and v.v.

🚌 GRAZ - KLAGENFURT — 980a

ÖBB *Intercitybus*. Rail tickets valid. 1st and 2nd class. 🍷 in first class. Number of seats limited so reservation is recommended.

	851	853		855	857	859		951	953	
	🚌	🚌		🚌	🚌	🚌		🚌	🚌	
Graz Hbf d.	0639	0824	...	1039	1239	1424	...	1639	1839	...
Klagenfurt Hbf a.	0839	1024	...	1239	1439	1624	...	1839	2039	...

	850	852	854	856		858	950		952	954
	M🚌	🚌	🚌	🚌		🚌	🚌		🚌	🚌
Klagenfurt Hbf d.	0620	0720	0920	1120	...	1325	1525	...	1725	1925
Graz Hbf a.	0820	0920	1120	1320	...	1525	1725	...	1925	2125

M – ① (not Apr. 5, May 1).

981 Local trains WIEN - WIENER NEUSTADT - MÜRZZUSCHLAG

2nd class only

WIEN - WIENER NEUSTADT

km					⚒n	⚒n						©B									M		P		
0	**Wien** Praterstern .... **980/2** d.	0046	...	...	0439	0516	0546	0616	0646	0716	0746	...	...	0816	0846		2146	2216	...	2246	2249	2346	2349	...
2	**Wien** Mitte .... **980/2** d.	0050	...	...	0443	0520	0550	0620	0650	0720	0750	...	...	0820	0850		2150	2220	...	2250	2253	2350	2353	...
5	**Wien** Südbahnhof ..... **980/2** d.	0056	...	...	0449	0526	0556	0626	0656	0726	0756	...	...	0826	0856	and every	2156	2226	...	2256	2259	2356	2359	...
9	**Wien** Meidling ● ...... **980/2** d.	0104	...	...	0458	0535	0605	0635	0705	0735	0805	0812	...	0835	0905	30 minutes	2205	2235	...	2304	2308	0004	0008	...
21	Mödling .... d.	0113	...	...	0510	0547	0617	0647	0717	0747	0817	|	...	0847	0917	until	2217	2247	...	|	2325	|	0025	...
32	Baden .... d.	0120	...	...	0518	0555	0625	0655	0725	0755	0825	0835	...	0855	0925		2225	2255	...	2317	2337	0017	0037	...
54	**Wiener Neustadt** Hbf . **980/2** a.	0136	...	...	0538	0615	0645	0715	0745	0815	0845	0849	...	0915	0945		2245	2315	...	2329	0002	0029	0108	...

	ⒶnM	⚒n	Ⓐn		M									©B									⚒n	
Wiener Neustadt ...... **980/2** d.	0502	0504	0534	0604	0617	0634	0704	0734	0810	0840		1710	1740	1807	1810	1840	1910	1940	2010	2040	2110	2140	2240	2342
Baden .... d.	|	0524	0554	0624	|	0654	0724	0754	0831	0901		1731	1801	1822	1831	1901	1931	2001	2031	2101	2131	2201	2301	0008
Mödling .... d.	|	0531	0601	0631	|	0701	0731	0801	0838	0908	and every	1738	1808	|	1838	1908	1938	2008	2038	2108	2138	2208	2308	0033
Wien Meidling ● .... **980/2** a.	0531	0543	0613	0643	0646	0713	0743	0813	0852	0922	30 minutes	1752	1822	1843	1852	1922	1952	2022	2052	2122	2152	2222	2322	0049
Wien Südbahnhof .... **980/2** a.	0542	0551	0621	0651	0703	0721	0751	0821	0900	0930	until	1800	1830	...	1900	1930	2000	2030	2100	2130	2200	2230	2330	0057
Wien Mitte .... **980/2** a.	0548	0557	0627	0657	0709	0727	0757	0827	0906	0936		1806	1836	...	1906	1936	2006	2036	2106	2136	2206	2236	2336	0103
Wien Praterstern .... **980/2** a.	0552	0601	0631	0701	0713	0731	0801	0831	0910	0940		1810	1840	...	1910	1940	2010	2040	2110	2140	2210	2240	2340	0107

WIENER NEUSTADT - SEMMERING - MÜRZZUSCHLAG

km		Ⓐn	⚒n	⚒n	n	¶	©B	©¶				Ⓐn			Ⓐn			Ⓐn			Ⓐn			M	P
0	**Wiener Neustadt** Hbf .. **980** d.	...	0540	0640	0800	0832	0850	0932	1000	1200	1300	...	1400	1500	...	1600	1700	...	1800	1900	...	2000	2100	2331	0031
27	Gloggnitz .... d.	...	0602	0701	0822	|	0916	|	1022	1222	1322	...	1422	1522	...	1622	1722	...	1822	1922	...	2022	2124	2353	0053
34	Payerbach-Reichenau .... d.	0514	0634	0719	0834	|	0923	|	1034	1234	1330	1334	1434	1530	1534	1634	1730	1734	1834	1930	1934	2030	2134	0001	0101
55	Semmering .... d.	0542	0702	0746	0902	0915	0948	1015	1102	1302	...	1402	1502	...	1602	1702	...	1802	1902	...	2002	...	2202	0026	...
69	**Mürzzuschlag** .... **980** a.	0559	0719	0803	0919	0929	1007	1029	1119	1319	...	1419	1519	...	1619	1719	...	1819	1919	...	2019	...	2219	0040	...

	ⒶnM	Ⓐn	©M	ⒶM	⚒n		⚒n				Ⓐn			Ⓐn			¶	Ⓐn		©B	©¶		Ⓐn		
Mürzzuschlag .... **980** d.	0349	0419	0511	0516	0537	...	0608	0737	0935	1135	1235	...	1335	1435	...	1535	1632	1635	...	1645	1732	1735	1835	...	1935
Semmering .... d.	0403	0436	0526	|	0554	...	0625	0754	0952	1152	1252	...	1352	1452	...	1552	1645	1652	...	1703	1745	1752	1852	...	1952
Payerbach-Reichenau .... d.	0430	0505	0552	0552	0623	0627	0654	0821	1021	1221	1321	1324	1421	1521	1524	1621	|	1721	1724	1730	|	1821	1921	1924	2022
Gloggnitz .... d.	0439	0524	0600	0600	...	0637	0708	0833	1033	1233	...	1333	1433	...	1533	1633	|	...	1733	1739	|	1833	...	1933	2031
Wiener Neustadt Hbf ... **980** a.	0500	0545	0615	0615	...	0659	0729	0854	1054	1254	...	1354	1454	...	1554	1654	1728	...	1754	1800	1828	1854	...	1954	2054

B – © until Apr. 5. (2) Bratislava - Wiener Neustadt - Mürzzuschlag and v.v.
M – (2) Wien - Wiener Neustadt - Mürzzuschlag and v.v.
P – (2) Břeclav - Wien - Wiener Neustadt - Payerbach-Reichenau.

n – Not Dec. 24, 31.
¶ – *EC*/*IC* train (see Table **980**).

● – See panel on page 445 for S-Bahn trains from/to Wien Hütteldorf. U-bahn line **U6** provides a direct link Wien Spittelau - Westbahnhof - Meidling and v.v.

982 WIEN - BŘECLAV and ZNOJMO

2nd class only

WIEN - BŘECLAV (see Table **1150** for full details of international express trains).

km			378		104		78	172				70		102		72		74			76				
		⚒n	★		♠		★	★		⚒n		★	⚒n	♠		★		★	Ⓐn		★	Ⓑz			
	Wiener Neustadt Hbf **980/1** d.	...	...	0520a	...	0720v	0747	0904	0910	1010	1110	1204	1210	1304	1310	1404	1510	1604	1610	1710	1804	1810	1910	2010	2140
0	**Wien** Meidling .... **980/1** d.	0500	...	0600	0733	0800	0825	0932	0954	1054	1154	1233	1254	1333	1354	1433	1554	1633	1654	1754	1833	1854	1954	2054	2224
	Wien Simmering .... d.	|	...	|	0759	|	0857	0946	|	|	|	1257	|	1357	|	1457	|	1657	|	|	1857	|	|	|	|
4	**Wien** Südbahnhof .... **981** d.	0507	...	0607	|	0807	|	|	1001	1101	1201	|	1301	|	1401	|	1601	|	1701	1801	|	1901	2001	2101	2231
7	**Wien** Mitte .... **981** d.	0513	...	0613	|	0813	|	|	1007	1107	1207	|	1307	|	1407	|	1607	|	1707	1807	|	1907	2007	2107	2237
9	**Wien** Praterstern .... **981** d.	0517	0550	0617	|	0817	|	|	1011	1111	1211	|	1311	|	1411	|	1611	|	1711	1811	|	1911	2011	2111	2241
14	**Wien** Floridsdorf ⊡ .... d.	0526	0600	0626	|	0826	|	|	1020	1120	1220	|	1320	|	1420	|	1620	|	1720	1820	|	1920	2020	2120	2250
40	Gänserndorf .... d.	0549	|	0649	|	0849	|	|	1043	1143	1243	|	1343	|	1443	|	1643	|	1743	1843	|	1943	2043	2143	2313
74	Hohenau 🏛 .... a.	0621	|	0721	|	0921	|	|	1115	1215	1315	|	1415	|	1515	|	1715	|	1815	1915	|	2015	2115	2215	2345
92	**Břeclav** 🏛 .... a.	0637	0653	0737	0853	0937	0953	1053	1131	...	1331	1353	...	1453	1531	1553	1731	1753	...	1931	1953	...	2131r	...	...

					71		73		75		103		77				173		79		105			177	
	Ⓐn			⚒n	★		★		★		♠	⚒n	★		⚒n		★	Ⓐn	★		♠	Ⓐn		★	
Břeclav 🏛 .... d.	...	0525	0625	0655	0802	0825	1002	1025	1202	1225	1302	...	1402	1425	...	1625	1702	...	1802	1825	1902	...	2025	2102	2225r
Hohenau 🏛 .... d.	0442	0542	0642	0712	|	0842	|	1042	|	1242	|	1342	|	1442	1542	1642	|	1742	|	1842	|	1942	2042	|	2242
Gänserndorf .... d.	0514	0614	0714	0744	|	0914	|	1114	|	1314	|	1414	|	1514	1614	1714	|	1814	|	1914	|	2014	2114	|	2314
Wien Floridsdorf ⊡ .... d.	0538	0638	0738	0808	|	0938	|	1138	|	1338	|	1438	|	1538	1638	1738	|	1838	|	1938	|	2038	2138	2159	2338
Wien Praterstern .... **981** a.	0545	0645	0745	0815	|	0945	|	1145	|	1345	|	1445	|	1545	1645	1745	|	1845	|	1945	|	2045	2145	2204	2345
Wien Mitte .... **981** a.	0549	0649	0749	0819	|	0949	|	1149	|	1349	|	1449	|	1549	1649	1749	|	1849	|	1949	|	2049	2149	...	2349
Wien Südbahnhof .... **981** a.	0555	0655	0755	0825	|	0955	|	1155	|	1355	|	1455	|	1555	1655	1755	|	1855	|	1955	|	2055	2155	...	2355
Wien Simmering .... a.	|	|	|	|	0906	|	1058	|	1258	|	1358	|	1458	|	|	|	1758	|	1910	|	1958	|	|	...	|
Wien Meidling .... **980/1** a.	0603	0703	0803	0833	0923	1003	1123	1203	1323	1403	1423	1503	1523	1603	1703	1803	1823	1903	1929	2003	2020	2103	2203	...	0003
Wiener Neustadt Hbf **980/1** a.	0645	0745	0845	0915	0955	1045	1155	1245	1355	1445	1455	1545	1555	1645	1745	1845	1855	1945	...	2045	...	2145	2245	...	0029

WIEN - RETZ - ZNOJMO △

km		⚒n		E		⚒n		⚒n	†t	⚒n	⚒n		Ⓐn		⚒n		Ⓐn		
0	**Wien** Meidling .... **989** d.	0545	0645	0745	0816	0945	1045	1145	1242	1245	1345	1445	1545	1645	1745	1845	1945	2045	2306
4	**Wien** Südbahnhof ..... d.	0552	0652	0752	0825	0952	1052	1152	1249	1252	1352	1452	1552	1652	1752	1852	1952	2052	2313
7	**Wien** Mitte .... **989** d.	0558	0658	0758	0831	0958	1058	1158	1255	1258	1358	1458	1558	1658	1758	1858	1958	2058	2319
9	**Wien** Praterstern **989** d.	0602	0702	0802	0835	1002	1102	1202	1259	1302	1402	1502	1602	1702	1802	1902	2002	2102	2323
14	**Wien** Floridsdorf ⊡ ... d.	0611	0711	0811	0844	1011	1111	1211	1311	1311	1411	1511	1611	1711	1811	1911	2011	2111	2332
34	Stockerau .... **989** d.	0628	0728	0828	0915	1028	1128	1228	1328	1328	1428	1528	1628	1728	1828	1928	2028	2127	2348
60	Hollabrunn .... d.	0645	0745	0845	0941	1045	1145	1245	1345	1345	1445	1545	1645	1745	1845	1945	2045	2153	0009
90	**Retz** 🏛 .... d.	0715	0815	0912	...	1112	1215	1312	1415	1415	1512	1615	1712	1815	1912	2015	2112	2220	0036
96	Šatov 🏛 .... d.	0723	0823	...	...	...	1223	...	1423	1423	...	1623	...	1823r	...	2023r	...	...	...
107	**Znojmo** .... a.	0734	0834	...	...	...	1234	...	1434	1434	...	1634	...	1834r	...	2034r	...	...	...

	Ⓐn	⚒n	⚒n		⚒n		⚒n		⚒n	⚒n	Ⓐn	©t	⚒n		⚒n		Ⓐn		
Znojmo .... d.	...	...	...	...	...	0653	0753	0857	...	...	1257	1257	...	1457	...	1657r	...	1857r	...
Šatov 🏛 .... d.	...	...	...	...	...	0704	0804	0908	...	...	1308	1308	...	1508	...	1708r	...	1908r	...
Retz 🏛 .... d.	0418	0512	0530	0552	0636	0715	0818	0918	1018	1218	1318	1318	1418	1518	1618	1718	1818	1918	2018
Hollabrunn .... d.	0446	0539	0559	0621	0706	0746	0846	0946	1046	1246	1346	1346	1446	1546	1646	1746	1846	1946	2046
Stockerau .... **989** d.	0503	0558	0628	0642	0728	0803	0903	1003	1103	1303	1403	1403	1503	1603	1703	1803	1903	2003	2103
Wien Floridsdorf ⊡ .... d.	0520	0620	0650	0705	0750	0820	0920	1020	1120	1320	1420	1418	1520	1620	1720	1820	1920	2020	2120
Wien Praterstern .**989** a.	0527	0627	0657	0712	0757	0827	0927	1027	1127	1327	1427	1430	1527	1627	1727	1827	1927	2027	2127
Wien Mitte .... **989** a.	0531	0631	0701	0716	0801	0831	0931	1031	1131	1331	1431	1434	1531	1631	1731	1831	1931	2031	2131
Wien Südbahnhof ...... a.	0537	0637	0707	0725	0807	0837	0937	1037	1137	1337	1437	1440	1537	1637	1737	1837	1937	2037	2137
Wien Meidling ...... **989** a.	0545	0645	0715	0733	0815	0845	0945	1045	1145	1345	1445	1448	1545	1645	1745	1845	1945	2045	2145

E – ⚒ to Apr. 24 (not Dec. 24, 31); daily from Apr. 26.

a – Ⓐ (not Dec. 24, 31).
n – Not Dec. 24, 31.
r – Not Dec. 24, 25, 31.
t – Also Dec. 24, 31.
v – ⚒ (not Dec. 24, 31).
z – Not Dec. 24, 25, 31, Apr. 4, May 23.

★ – *EC* train to/from Praha (see Table **1150** for further details).
♠ – *EC* train to/from Warszawa (see Table 99 for further details).
△ – Austrian holiday dates apply.
⊡ – U-Bahn line **U6** provides a direct link Wien Westbahnhof - Spittelau - Floridsdorf and v.v.

983 (WIEN -) WIENER NEUSTADT - FEHRING

2nd class only

km		⚒G	Ⓐ		Ⓐ	©		Ⓐ			†	Ⓐn		Ⓐ		⚒	Ⓑn	
0	**Wien** Meidling .... **980/1** d.	...	0458n	...	0717n	0730	0930	0930	1130	1330	1330	1433	1530	1630	1730	1830	1930	2103
44	**Wiener Neustadt** Hbf. **980/1** d.	...	0600	...	0800	0800	1000	1000	1200	1400	1400	1500	1600	1700	1800	1900	2003	2137
99	Friedberg .... d.	...	0718z	...	0854	0854	1102k	1102k	1300k	1502e	1502e	1553	1653	1755	1902e	1954	2059	2251
126	Hartberg .... d.	0615	0756	...	0927	0927	1136	1137	1347v	1536	1556	...	1727	1826	1936	2028	2135	...
157	Fürstenfeld .... d.	0653	0834	...	1006	1006	...	1214	1425	...	1634	...	1805	...	2014	...	...	...
177	**Fehring** .... a.	0722	0903	...	1035	1035	...	1243	1454	...	1702	...	1834	...	2043	...	...	...

	Ⓐn	⚒n	Ⓐ		⚒n	⚒					†		©	Ⓐ	†	Ⓐ	Ⓐ	
Fehring .... d.	...	...	0500	...	...	0607	...	0920	...	1302	1511	...	1720	1720	...	1929	...	2128
Fürstenfeld .... d.	...	...	0529	...	...	0636	0740	0949	...	1331	1540	...	1749	1749	...	1958	...	2157
Hartberg .... d.	0427	0527	0607	...	...	0721k	0819	1027	1221	1427t	1618	1618	1827	1827	...	2036	2048	...
Friedberg .... d.	0506	0606	0643	0643	0710	0802k	0902e	1102	1302k	1502	1702e	1702e	1902	1902	1945	...	2122	...
Wiener Neustadt Hbf.. **980/1** a.	0559	0659	0742	0742	0758	0857	0959	1155	1355	1555	1758	1758	1958	1958	2029	...	...	...
Wien Meidling .... **980/1** a.	0630	0730	0816	0816	0830	0928	1028	1228	1428	1628	1828	1828	2028	2043n	2055	...	...	...

G – To Graz (Table **986**).

e – Arrives 9–10 minutes earlier.
k – Arrives 6–7 minutes earlier.
n – Not Dec. 24, 31.
t – Arrives 1409.
v – Arrives 1334.
z – Arrives 0702.

2nd class only — WIENER NEUSTADT - PUCHBERG am Schneeberg - HOCHSCHNEEBERG — 984

WIENER NEUSTADT - PUCHBERG am Schneeberg *28 km.* Journey time: 44–46 minutes.
From Wiener Neustadt at 0038 † **m**, 0737, 0837 **A**, 0937, 1037 **E**, 1137, 1237 **E**, 1337, 1437 **E**, 1537, 1637, 1737, 1837 Ⓑ **w**, 1937, 2037 Ⓑ **w**, 2137.
From Puchberg at 0455 Ⓐ **n**, 0525 Ⓐ **n**, 0555 ⚒, 0624 Ⓐ **n**, 0638 Ⓒ **k**, 0647 Ⓐ **n**, 0738, 0837, 0938 Ⓒ **G**, 1038, 1138 **E**, 1238, 1338 **E**, 1438, 1538 **E**, 1638, 1738, 1838, 1938 Ⓑ **w**, 2038 ⑤⑥ **r**.

PUCHBERG am Schneeberg - **HOCHSCHNEEBERG** *Schneebergbahn* (narrow-gauge rack railway). *9 km* Journey time: ± 50 minutes.
Services run **Apr. 24 - Nov. 1, 2010** subject to demand and weather conditions. **Operator**: NÖ Schneebergbahn GmbH, Bahnhofplatz 1, A-2734 Puchberg. ✆ +43 (0) 2636 3661 20.
From Puchberg at 0900, 1100, 1330 and 1530. **From Hochschneeberg** at 1000, 1200, 1430 and 1630. Additional trains operate when there is sufficient demand.

A – Ⓐ (daily from Apr. 19).
E – ⚒ (daily from Apr. 19).
G – From Apr. 24.
k – Also Dec. 24, 31.
m – Not Dec. 25.
n – Not Dec. 24, 31.
r – Also Dec. 24, 25, 31, Jan. 5, Apr. 4, 30, May 12, 23, June 2.
w – Not Dec. 23, 24, 25, 30, 31, Apr. 4, May 23.

ÖBB, GySEV ●; 2nd class only — GRAZ - SZENTGOTTHÁRD - SZOMBATHELY — 986

km				A✗						⚒			Ⓑ	†	⚒				⚒	Ⓐ		Ⓑ	Ⓐ		
0	**Graz** Hbf d.	...	...	0610	...	0807e	1007	...	1144	1236	1330	1519	1604	1604	1632	1743	1803	...	1841	1921	2011	2011	2115	2204	0004
29	Gleisdorf d.	...	...	0649	...	0845	1044	...	1220	1309	1405	1551	1639	1639	1705	1815	1843	...	1914	1959	2047	2047	2153	2239	0039
53	Feldbach d.	...	...	0715	...	0907	1108	...	1245	1335	1427	1611	1703	1703	1724	1834	1909	...	1933	2022	2111	2111	2216	2301	0101
62	Fehring d.	...	...	0725	...	0919	1122	...	1257	1350	1439	1623	1714	1735	1735	1843	1920	...	1942	2033	2122	2123	2226	2311	0111
82	Szentgotthárd 🏛 a.	...	...	0743	...	0942	1143	...	1323	1412	1502	1645	...	1758	1758	*1908*a	1941	...	...	...	...	2146	*2252*	...	...
				|																					
										d					d		d	n				n			
82	Szentgotthárd 🏛 d.	0408	0535	0754	0845	0955	1145	1225	1339	1430	1613	1703	...	...	1819	...	1943	2054	...	...	...	2220	...	...	...
110	Körmend d.	0444	0611	0827	0921	1032	1220	1303	1418	1508	1650	1739	...	...	1855	...	2020	2130	...	...	...	2257	...	...	...
146	**Szombathely** a.	0518	0645	0856	0956	1106	1254	1338	1454	1542	1724	1813	...	...	1931	...	2054	2205	...	...	...	2331	...	...	...

				⚒		⚒H														Ⓐ		B✗		n	n
Szombathely d.	...	...	...	0408	0454	...	0620	...	0716	0934	...	1017	...	1145	1315	...	1431	1551	1639	...	1818	1910	2029	2140	2245
Körmend d.	...	...	...	0445	0531	...	0704	...	0749	1008	...	1055	...	1222	1350	...	1505	1626	1714	...	1856	1941	2106	2218	2319
Szentgotthárd 🏛 a.	...	...	...	0520	0606	...	0737	...	0825	1043	...	1131	...	1257	1426	...	1540	1701	1750	...	1931	2014	2141	2252	2353
	⚒	Ⓐ		⚒								Ⓑ		⚒	Ⓑ				Ⓐ			|			
Szentgotthárd 🏛 d.	...	0401	...	0530	0619	...	0745	...	...	1059	1059c	1148	1148j	1301	1437	1536	...	1711	1817	...	1946	2040	...	...	...
Fehring d.	0345	0428	0450	0556	0642	0730	0808	0920	...	1121	1124	1207	1210	1323	1500	1600	...	1735	1839	1859	2010	2101	...	...	...
Feldbach d.	0356	0438	0501	0606	0654	0740	0819	0930	...	...	1134	...	1221	1335	1511	1612	...	1746	...	1912	2022	2111	...	...	...
Gleisdorf d.	0420	0455	0531	0626	0713	0759	0846	0953	...	...	1155	...	1244	1405	1529	1639	...	1815	...	1935	2047	2129	...	...	...
Graz Hbf a.	0456	0533	0607	0702	0748	0833	0921	1021	...	...	1230	...	1321	1441	1603	1721	...	1854	...	2009	2121	2203	...	...	...

A – 2 Graz (**4760**) - Szentgotthárd (*IC* **917**) Györ - Budapest.
B – 2 Budapest (*IC* **916**) - Györ - Szentgotthárd (**4761**) - Graz.
H – From Hartberg (Table **983**).
a – Ⓐ only.
c – Ⓒ only.
d – Daily.
e – 0809 on †.
j – † only.
n – Not Dec. 24, 31.
✗ – Ⓡ and supplement payable in Hungary.
● – GySEV: Györ-Sopron-Ebenfurti Vasút.

2nd class only — WIEN - GMÜND and KREMS an der Donau — 990

km		Ⓐ	⚒	⚒	†				P		ⒸE	Ⓐ				Ⓐ		n			Ⓐ			
0	**Wien** Franz-Josefs-Bf d.	...	0459	0553	0616	0622	0651	0725	0729	0751	0754	0825	0923	0951	1029	...	1051	1124	1151	1229	...	1251	1326	1351
1	Wien Spittelau ● d.	...	0501	0556	0619	0625	0654	0728	|	0754	0757	0827	0926	0954	1032	...	1054	1127	1154	1232	...	1254	1329	1354
3	Wien Heiligenstadt △ d.	...	0505	0559	0622	0628	0657	0731	0735	0757	0800	0831	0930	0957	1035	...	1057	1130	1157	1235	...	1257	1333	1357
33	Tulln d.	...	0537	0621	0644	0650	0723	0752	0801	0819	0827	0857	0955	1019	1056	...	1119	1155	1219	1256	...	1319	1358	1419
44	Absdorf-Hippersdorf d.	...	0549j	0632	0656	0700	0732	0803	...	0828	0836	0906	1007	1029	1106	...	1129	1207	1229	1306	...	1329	1407	1429
76	**Krems** an der Donau a.	...	0638	0714	0722	|	0803	|	...	0855	0904	0936	|	1054	|	...	1154	|	1254	|	...	1354	|	1454
79	Eggenburg d.	...	▬	...	...	0727	...	0833	...	...	...	▬	1043	...	1136	...	...	1244	...	1336	...	...	1444	...
89	**Sigmundsherberg** d.	0615	...	...	...	0735	...	0841	...	...	...	...	1052	...	1144	...	...	1253	...	1344	...	...	1454	...
121	Göpfritz d.	0641	Ⓐ🚌	...	...	0800	...	0906	...	...	...	⚒	...	...	1210	...	...	...	...	1410	...	...	...	...
138	Schwarzenau ⊡ d.	0655	0658	...	...	0814	...	0922	...	...	...	1136	...	...	1225	1305	...	...	...	1425	1538	...	...	...
162	**Gmünd** NÖ a.	...	0740	...	...	0837	...	0944	...	...	...	1158	...	...	1247	1328	...	...	...	1447	1600	...	...	...

					Ⓐ				Ⓐ			⚒	Ⓐ	Ⓐ	Ⓐ							Ⓑz		
Wien Franz-Josefs-Bf d.	1429	1451	1522	1551	1555	1624	1651	1658	1716	1719	1750	1755	1755	1820	1826	1851	1857	1921	1951	2029	2051	2058	2151	2302
Wien Spittelau ● d.	1432	1454	1525	1554	1558	1628	1654	1701	1719	1723	1753	1759	1759	1823	1830	1854	1900	1923	1954	2032	2054	2101	2154	2304
Wien Heiligenstadt △ d.	1435	1457	1528	1557	1601	1631	1657	1705	1723	1727	1757	1802	1802	1826	1833	1857	1903	1927	1957	2035	2057	2104	2157	2308
Tulln d.	1456	1519	1551	1619	1624	1654	1719	|	|	1752	1819	1824	1824	|	1856	1919	|	1952	2019	2056	2119	2129	2219	2345
Absdorf-Hippersdorf d.	1506	1529	1604	1629	|	1706	1728	|	|	1805	1829	1833	1833	1904	1906	1929	|	2005	2029	2111	2129	2139	2229	...
Krems an der Donau a.	|	1554	|	1654	|	|	1759	|	1818	|	1855	|	|	|	1938	1954	|	|	2055	|	2204	|	2256	...
Eggenburg d.	1536	...	1639	...	|	1736	...	1756	...	1847	...	1903	1903	1934	...	...	2003	2043	...	2140	...	2206	...	...
Sigmundsherberg d.	1544	...	1647	...	1702	1744	...	1805	...	1856	...	1910	1911	1942	...	...	2011	2053	...	2149	...	2214	...	...
Göpfritz d.	1610	...	...	...	1727	1812	...	1830	...	...	...	...	1937	...	...	...	2041	...	...	2214	...	...	...	...
Schwarzenau ⊡ d.	1625	...	...	...	1742	1827	...	1844	...	...	...	...	1952	...	...	...	2055	...	...	2228	...	...	...	...
Gmünd NÖ a.	1647	...	...	...	1805	1850	...	1906	...	...	...	...	2014	...	...	...	2117	...	...	2250	...	...	...	...

	Ⓐ	Ⓐ	⚒	⚒	Ⓐ	†	Ⓐ	⚒n		Ⓐ		Ⓒ	Ⓐ	⚒	⚒		Ⓐ🚌		⚒			Ⓑz		
Gmünd NÖ d.	...	...	0346	...	...	...	0420	...	...	...	...	0513	0531	...	...	0616	0741	...	...	...	...	...	0913	...
Schwarzenau ⊡ d.	...	...	0408	...	...	...	0441	...	...	0526	...	0535	0553	...	...	0639	0810	...	...	...	...	...	0937	...
Göpfritz d.	...	...	0422	...	...	...	0457	...	...	0540	...	0550	0606	...	...	0653	▬	...	...	...	...	...	0952	...
Sigmundsherberg d.	...	0410	0447	...	...	0505	0522	0528	...	0606	0616	0616	0630	...	0642	0718	...	...	0805	...	0907	...	1017	...
Eggenburg d.	...	0421	0456	...	...	0514	|	0537	...	...	0625	0625	|	...	0652	0727	...	...	0815	...	0917	...	1025	...
Krems a. d. Donau d.	0425	|	|	0452	0521	|	|	|	0614	...	|	|	|	0644	|	|	0726	0815	|	0903	|	1003	|	1103
Absdorf-Hippersdorf d.	0456	0502	|	0530	|	0549	|	0608	0648	...	0654	0654	|	0721	0729	0755	0759	0852	0857	0928	0955	1028	1054	1128
Tulln d.	0506	0511	0534	0539	|	0558	|	0617	0658	...	0703	0703	|	0730	0738	0804	0809	0901	0906	0937	1004	1037	1103	1137
Wien Heiligenstadt △ a.	0526	0535	0554	0605	0614	0622	0619	0643	0719	...	0724	0724	0729	0755	0758	0824	0829	0921	0930	0957	1028	1057	1124	1157
Wien Spittelau ● a.	0530	0538	0558	0609	0618	0626	0623	0647	0723	...	0727	0727	0732	0758	0802	0828	0832	0925	0934	1001	1032	1101	1127	1201
Wien Franz-Josefs-Bf a.	0533	0541	0601	0612	0621	0629	0626	0650	0727	...	0731	0731	0735	0801	0805	0831	0835	0928	0937	1004	1035	1104	1131	1204

				⚒		n			Ⓐ					Ⓐ						ⒸE			P	
Gmünd NÖ d.	...	...	1114	1202	...	...	...	1314	1340	...	...	...	1514	1617	...	...	...	1735	...	...	...	1929	...	...
Schwarzenau ⊡ d.	...	...	1137	1223	...	...	...	1337	1402	...	...	...	1537	1640	...	...	...	1757	...	...	...	1952	...	...
Göpfritz d.	...	...	1151	...	...	...	...	1351	...	...	...	...	1551	...	...	...	...	1812	...	...	...	2006	...	...
Sigmundsherberg d.	1108	...	1217	...	...	1308	...	1417	...	...	1508	...	1615	...	...	1707	...	1837	...	...	...	2032	...	...
Eggenburg d.	1118	...	1226	...	...	1318	...	1426	...	...	1518	...	1624	...	...	1717	...	1846	...	...	...	2043	...	...
Krems a. d. Donau d.	|	1201	|	...	1303	|	1400	|	...	1503	|	1601	|	...	1703	|	1803	|	1903	1951	2001	|	...	2103
Absdorf-Hippersdorf d.	1155	1228	1256	...	1328	1355	1428	1456	...	1528	1555	1628	1657	...	1728	1759	1828	1921	1928	2019	2028	2111	...	2128
Tulln d.	1203	1237	1304	...	1337	1403	1437	1504	...	1537	1604	1637	1706	...	1737	1807	1837	1930	1937	2029	2037	2121	2133	2137
Wien Heiligenstadt △ a.	1227	1257	1325	...	1357	1427	1457	1526	...	1557	1628	1657	1726	...	1757	1831	1857	1950	1957	2054	2057	2142	2204	2157
Wien Spittelau ● a.	1231	1301	1329	...	1401	1431	1501	1529	...	1601	1632	1701	1730	...	1801	1835	1901	1954	2001	2058	2101	2146	|	2201
Wien Franz-Josefs-Bf a.	1234	1304	1332	...	1404	1434	1504	1533	...	1604	1635	1704	1733	...	1804	1838	1904	1957	2004	2101	2104	2149	2209	2204

E – Ⓒ from Mar. 27. 2 Wien - Krems - Emmersdorf and v.v.
P – From Apr. 3. 2 Wien - St Pölten - Passau and v.v.
b – Runs to / from Zwettl bus station.
j – 0553 on ⑥.
n – Not Dec. 24, 31.
w – Not Dec. 26, May 1.
z – Also Dec. 26, May 1.
△ – S-Bahn trains run every 15–20 minutes from / to Wien Hütteldorf (journey time: 21 minutes).
● – Direct U-bahn links: Line **U4** – Wien Mitte - Spittelau.
Line **U6** – Wien Meidling - Westbahnhof - Spittelau - Floridsdorf.

⊡ – Local trains **Schwarzenau** to **Waidhofen** a. d. Thaya (*10 km*, journey 17 minutes) and **Schwarzenau** to **Zwettl** (*22 km*, journey 30–32 minutes).
Schwarzenau to **Waidhofen** at 0512 Ⓐ, 0554 ⚒, 0700, 0816, 0938, 1226, 1427, 1538, 1626, 1800, 1847 and 1955 Ⓐ.
Waidhofen to **Schwarzenau** at 0533 Ⓐ, 0620 ⚒, 0754, 0901, 1116, 1316 Ⓒ, 1340 Ⓐ, 1517, 1605, 1721 Ⓐ, 1736 Ⓒ, 1824, 1931 and 2035 Ⓐ.
Schwarzenau to **Zwettl** at 0523 ⑥ **w**, 0658 Ⓐ 🚌 **b**, 0815 Ⓒ, 0816 Ⓐ 🚌, 0938, 1226 Ⓒ, 1426, 1626 Ⓒ, 1644 Ⓐ and 1845.
Zwettl to **Schwarzenau** at 0553 Ⓐ 🚌, 0606 ⑥ **w**, 0736 Ⓐ 🚌 **b**, 0849 Ⓒ, 1103, 1303 Ⓒ, 1503, 1723 and 1919.

991 KREMS - SPITZ - EMMERSDORF

2nd class only

km		Ⓐ	⚒		⚒	D		ⒸG		🚌	D		🚌	Ⓐ	E		A	🚌	Ⓐ		A	Ⓐ		
	Wien Franz-Josefs-Bf **990** . d.	...	...	...	...	...	...	0754	...	...	...	...	...	...	...	...	...	...	...	...	...	...	...	...
0	**Krems** an der Donau ... d.	0421	0454	...	0649	0805	0902	0918	1100	...	1200	1300	...	1333	1400	1500	1600	...	1636	1700	1801	1831	1900	2000
7	Dürnstein-Oberloiben ... d.	0431	0507	...	0705	0815	0914	0930	1111	...	1211	1311	...	1346	1411	1511	1611	...	1647	1711	1812	1847	1911	2011
13	Weißenkirchen ... d.	0438	0514	...	0712	0822	0921	0942	1118	...	1218	1318	...	1353	1418	1519	1618	...	1654	1718	1819	1854	1919	2018
18	**Spitz** an der Donau ... a.	0445	0522	...	0720	0829	0929	0949	1126	1132	1226	1326	1332	1401	1426	1526	1626	1632	1702	1726	1827	1902	1926	2026
26	Aggsbach Markt ... a.	...	0550	...	...	...	...	1017	...	1142*	...	...	1342*	1428	...	...	...	1642*	...	...	...	...	...	...
34	Emmersdorf an der Donau ... a.	...	0604	...	...	...	...	1033	...	1150*	...	...	1350*	...	...	...	...	1650*	...	...	...	...	...	...

	Ⓐ	Ⓐ	⚒	⚒	⚒	D		🚌		D	🚌		E	Ⓐ		🚌	A		A	Ⓐ	ⒸG			
Emmersdorf an der Donau ... d.	...	...	...	0608	...	...	...	1107*	...	...	1307*	...	...	...	...	1607*	...	...	...	...	1824	...	...	...
Aggsbach Markt ... d.	...	...	...	0623	...	...	...	1115*	...	...	1315*	...	...	1442	...	1615*	...	...	...	...	1840	...	...	...
Spitz an der Donau ... d.	0451	0528	0608	0649	0728	0833	0933	1125	1130	1230	1325	1330	1430	1508	1530	1625	1630	1730	1831	1908	1909	1930	...	2030
Weißenkirchen ... d.	0459	0536	0616	0658	0736	0841	0942	...	1138	1238	...	1338	1438	1519	1538	...	1638	1738	1839	1919	1919	1938	...	2038
Dürnstein-Oberloiben ... d.	0507	0543	0623	0705	0743	0848	0949	...	1145	1245	...	1346	1445	1526	1545	...	1647	1745	1837	1926	1926	1945	...	2045
Krems an der Donau ... a.	0518	0554	0635	0717	0755	0858	1000	...	1156	1256	...	1356	1456	1537	1556	...	1656	1756	1856	1937	1937	1956	...	2056
Wien Franz-Josefs-Bf **990** .. a.	...	...	...	...	...	...	...	...	...	...	...	...	...	...	...	...	...	...	...	...	2101	...	...	...

A – Ⓐ to Mar. 26; daily from Mar. 29. D – ⚒ to Mar. 26; daily from Mar. 29. E – ⚒ to Mar. 27; daily from Mar. 29. G – From Mar. 27. * – Town centre.

992 SARMINGSTEIN - GREIN - ST VALENTIN and LINZ

2nd class only

km		Ⓐ	Ⓐ	Ⓐ	⚒	Ⓐ	†			Ⓐ	⚒		⚒		⚒		⚒		Ⓐ		Ⓐ	Ⓐ		Ⓐ		Ⓑ
0	Sarmingstein ... d.	...	...	0510	0521	...	0554	...	0626	...	...	...	...	...	...	...	...	...	...	...	...	...	...	1858	...	...
3	St Nikola-Struden ... d.	...	...	0515	0526	...	0559	...	0631	0659	...	0802	0903	1003	1103	1203	1303	1403	1503	1603	...	1703	1803	1903	...	1934
8	Grein Stadt ... d.	0402	...	0523	0534	...	0607	...	0639	0707	...	0810	0911	1011	1111	1211	1311	1411	1511	1611	...	1711	1811	1911	1911	1942
10	Grein-Bad Kreuzen ... d.	0406	0442	0527	0538	0601	0611	0611	0643	0711	0711	0814	0915	1015	1115	1215	1315	1415	1515	1615	1646	1715	1815	1915	1915	1947
31	Perg ... d.	0435	0511	0555	0611	0630	0641	0641	0713	0743	0743	0844	0945	1045	1145	1245	1345	1445	1546	1645	1715	1745	1846	1945	1945	2016
	St Valentin ... a.	0458	|	|	0634	|	0705	0705	|	0806	0806	|	1009	|	1209	|	1409	|	1609	|	1738	1809	|	2009	2009	2038
65	**Linz** Hbf ... a.	*0538*	0551	0632	*0700*	0705	*0725*	*0725*	0754	*0829*	*0829*	0925	*1029*	1125	*1229*	1325	*1429*	1525	*1629*	1725	*1808*	*1829*	1925	*2029*	*2029*	*2108*

km		Ⓐ	Ⓐ	⚒				⚒		⚒		⚒		Ⓐ	⚒	Ⓐ	Ⓐ		Ⓐ	⚒	Ⓑ		Ⓐ		Ⓐ	Ⓒ
	Linz Hbf ... d.	...	0526	*0618*	*0649**	...	0835	*0931*	1035	*1131*	1235	*1331*	1435	*1450*	*1531*	*1531*	1602	1635	1702	*1731*	*1753*	1835	1935	...	*2031*	2035
0	**St Valentin** ... d.	0503	|	0648	0719	...	|	0952	|	1152	|	1352	|	1522	1552	1552	|	|	|	1752	1823	|	|	...	2052	|
18	Perg ... d.	0527	0610	0712	0742	...	0915	1015	1115	1215	1315	1415	1516	1545	1615	1615	1645	1715	1745	1815	1845	1915	2016	...	2115	2115
39	Grein-Bad Kreuzen ... d.	0600	0644	0743	0814	...	0947	1047	1147	1247	1347	1447	1547	1614	1646	1647	1714	1747	1816	1847	1916	1947	2046	...	2144	2144
41	Grein Stadt ... d.	0603	0647	0746	0817	...	0950	1050	1150	1250	1350	1450	1550	...	...	1650	...	1750	1819	1850	1919	1950	2049	...	...	...
46	St Nikola-Struden ... a.	0610	0654	0753	0824	...	0957	1057	1157	1257	1357	1457	1557	...	...	1657	...	1757	1826	1857k	1926	1957	2056	...	...	...
49	Sarmingstein ... a.	0615	...	...	...	...	...	...	...	...	...	...	...	...	...	...	...	...	1831	...	...	2002	2101	...	...	...

k – ⑥ (not Dec. 26, May 1). * – *0630* May 22 - June 7.

993 ST PÖLTEN - KREMS and TULLN

2nd class only

km		Ⓐ	⚒	Ⓐ	Ⓐ	⚒	⚒	⚒	⚒		†		🚌			🚌			🚌			🚌	Ⓐ		Ⓐ🚌	
0	**St Pölten** Hbf ... d.	0450	0530	0550	0556	0613	0633	0708	0742	...	0744	0810	0910	0943	1037	1110	1143	1237	1310	1343	1437	1510	1517	1543	1610	1637
11	Herzogenburg ... d.	0506	0544	0605	0611	0635	0647	0728	0755	0756	0756	0819	0940	0952	1047	1140	1152	1247	1340	1352	1447	1540	1526	1552	|	1647
	Tulln ... a.	|	0626	0659	|	0733	|	|	0839	|	|	|	1055	|	|	1255	|	|	1455	|	|	1655	|	|	1728	|
30	**Krems** a. d. Donau ... a.	0537	...	...	0639	...	0718	0756	...	0826	0826	0843	...	1024	1111	...	1224	1311	...	1424	1511	...	1555	1624	...	1712

	Ⓐ🚌	🚌	Ⓐ		Ⓐ🚌		🚌			P	
St Pölten Hbf ... d.	1710	1710	1717	1743	1810	1837	1935	1943	2040	2056	2139
Herzogenburg ... d.	|	1740	1726	1752	|	1847	2005	1952	2101	2106	2152
Tulln ... a.	1828	1855	|	|	1928	|	2120	|	|	2130	|
Krems a. d. Donau ... a.	...	...	1755	1824	...	1911	...	2028	2131	...	2219

	Ⓐn	Ⓐ	Ⓐn	⚒	⚒		⚒	⚒	⚒	⚒
Krems a. d. Donau ... d.	0435	0455	...	0539	0603	0614	...	0640	...	0720
Tulln ... d.	|	|	0459	|	|	|	0620	|	0700	|
Herzogenburg ... d.	0506	0528	0546	0611	0632	0647	0708	0713	0743	0755
St Pölten Hbf ... a.	0524	0542	0604	0627	0642	0703	0717	0722	0752	0810

	†	Q		🚌			🚌			🚌			🚌		Ⓐ🚌		🚌	Ⓐ🚌		Ⓐ🚌		🚌			🚌	Ⓑ
Krems a. d. Donau ... d.	0724	...	0834	...	0947	1035	...	1147	1235	...	1347	1435	...	1547	...	1636	...	...	1747	...	1836	...	1945	2020	...	2051
Tulln ... d.	|	0810	|	0815	|	|	1002	|	|	1202	|	|	1402	|	1601	|	1602	1701	|	1801	|	1802	|	|	2002	|
Herzogenburg ... d.	0755	0855	0906	0931	1013	1107	1118	1213	1307	1318	1413	1507	1518	1613	1659	1708	1718	1759	1813	1859	1915	1918	2014	2045	2118	2123
St Pölten Hbf ... a.	0810	0903	0915	1002	1022	1116	1149	1222	1316	1349	1422	1516	1549	1622	...	1716	1749	...	1822	...	1923	1949	2022	2055	2149	2132

P – From Apr. 3. [2] Passau - Wien Franz-Josefs-Bahnhof (a. 2209). Q – From Apr. 3. [2] Wien Franz-Josefs-Bahnhof (d. 0729) - Passau. n – Not Dec. 24, 31.

994 ST PÖLTEN - MARIAZELL

Narrow gauge 2nd class only

km			¶	ⒶH	Ⓒ				⚒	Ⓐ	Ⓒ
0	**St Pölten** Hbf ... d.	0734	0834	1034	1034	...	1334	1641	1736	2008	2108
12	Ober Grafendorf ... d.	0756	0856	1053	1054	...	1353	1701	1759	2028	2127
31	Kirchberg a. d. Pielach . d.	0831	0932	1128	1127	...	1433	1736	1836	2102	2202
43	Frankenfels ... d.	0851	0953	1148x	1147	...	1453	1757	1857	2123	2223
48	Laubenbachmühle ... d.	0900	1004	1157	1157	...	1503	1807	1907	2132	2232
57	Winterbach ... ● d.	0916	1022	1212	1212	...	1519	1823	...	...	...
67	Gösing ... d.	0936	1041	1228	1229	1417	1536	1840	...	...	...
80	Mitterbach ... ● d.	1001	1106	1253	1253	1443	1600	1904	...	...	...
84	**Mariazell** ... a.	1008	1113	1259	1300	1450	1607	1911	...	...	...

				ⒶH		Ⓒ	Ⓐ¶	Ⓒ¶	Ⓐ	Ⓒ
Mariazell ... d.	...	0755	1151	1302	1336	1500	1501	1656	1658	1807
Mitterbach ... ● d.	...	0801	1157	1308	1342	1507	1507	1703	1704	1813
Gösing ... d.	...	0827	1230	1333	1409	1537	1537	1731	1731	1841
Winterbach ... ● d.	...	0842	1246	1348	...	1552	1552	1746	1746	1856
Laubenbachmühle ... d.	0649	0901	1302	1404	...	1609	1609	1807	1807	1912
Frankenfels ... d.	0659	0911	1311	1413	...	1618	1617x	1815x	1816x	1922
Kirchberg a. d. Pielach d.	0720	0933	1332	1432	...	1638	1638	1836	1836	1942
Ober Grafendorf ... d.	0756	1007	1407	1509	...	1714	1714	1909	1908	2017
St Pölten Hbf ... a.	0816	1025	1431	1529	...	1735	1736	1930	1926	2036

H – From May 3. x – Stops on request. ¶ – Also conveys [1]. Conveys ✕ on Ⓒ from May 1. ● – Trains stop on request.

996 WIEN - BRATISLAVA via Marchegg

2nd class only

km																
0	**Wien** Südbahnhof △ ... d.	0525	0725	0825	0925	1025	1125	1225	1325	1425	1525	1625	1725	1825	2025	2225
4	**Wien** Simmering ⊖ ... d.	0532	0732	0831	0932	1031	1132	1231	1332	1431	1532	1631	1732	1831	2031	2231
47	Marchegg 🏛 ... d.	0617	0817	0905	1017	1105	1217	1305	1417	1505	1617	1705	1817	1905	2105	2308
53	Devínska Nová Ves 🏛 ... d.	0624	0824	0912	1024	1112	1224	1312	1424	1512	1624	1712	1824	1912	2112	2315
66	**Bratislava** Hlavná ... a.	0637	0837	0925	1037	1125	1237	1325	1437	1525	1637	1725	1837	1925	2125	2328

Bratislava Hlavná ... d.	0551	0701	0751	0901	0951	1101	1151	1301	1351	1501	1551	1701	1751	1901	2101	2245
Devínska Nová Ves 🏛 ... d.	0604	0714	0804	0914	1004	1114	1204	1314	1404	1514	1604	1714	1804	1914	2114	2258
Marchegg 🏛 ... d.	0613	0722	0813	0922	1013	1122	1213	1322	1413	1522	1613	1722	1813	1922	2122	2307
Wien Simmering ⊖ ... d.	0652	0754	0852	0954	1052	1154	1252	1354	1452	1554	1652	1754	1852	1954	2154	2340
Wien Südbahnhof △ ... a.	0657	0759	0857	0959	1057	1159	1257	1359	1457	1559	1657	1759	1857	1959	2159	2345

⊖ – For U-Bahn connections (line U3) from / to Wien Mitte and Wien Westbahnhof.
△ – **Wien** Südbahnhof (Ostbahn). Temporary platforms located at Schweizer-Garten-Straße.

997 WIEN - BRATISLAVA via Bruck an der Leitha

2nd class only

km						Ⓐn		Ⓐn		Ⓐn		Ⓐn		Ⓐn		Ⓐn		Ⓐn	ⒸM		Ⓐn			
0	**Wien** Südbahnhof △ ... **1250** d.	0049	...	...	0505	0611	0705	0805	0911	1005	1111	1205	1311	1405	1511	1605	1711	1805	...	1911	2005	2111	...	2311
	Wien Meidling ... d.	|	...	...	|	|	|	|	|	|	|	|	|	|	|	|	|	|	1844	|	|	|	...	|
41	Bruck an der Leitha ... **1250** d.	0129	...	...	0532	0638	0732	0832	0938	1032	1138	1232	1338	1432	1538	1632	1738	1832	1929	1938	2032	2138	...	2338
69	Kittsee 🏛 ... d.	0154	...	...	0557	0705	0757	0857	1003	1057	1203	1257	1403	1457	1603	1657	1803	1857	1947	2003	2057	2203	...	0003
74	**Bratislava** - Petržalka 🏛 ... a.	0159	...	...	0602	0710	0802	0902	1008	1102	1208	1302	1408	1502	1608	1702	1808	1902	1953	2008	2102	2208	...	0008

km		Ⓒt	Ⓐn	Ⓐn		Ⓐn	ⒸM	Ⓐn	Ⓐn		Ⓐn		Ⓐn		Ⓐn		Ⓐn		Ⓐn		Ⓐn		Ⓐn	
0	**Bratislava** - Petržalka 🏛 ... d.	0428	*0428*	0456	0603	0641	0656	0700	0734	0834	0941	1034	1141	1234	1341	1434	1541	1634	1741	1834	1941	2034	2141	2241
5	Kittsee 🏛 ... d.	0433	*0433*	0501	0608	0646	0703	0705	0739	0839	0946	1039	1146	1239	1346	1439	1546	1639	1746	1839	1946	2039	2146	2246
33	Bruck an der Leitha ... **1250** d.	0458	0505	0531	0632	0711	0723	0724	0804	0904	1011	1104	1211	1304	1411	1508	1611	1704	1811	1904	2011	2104	2211	2311
71	**Wien** Meidling ... a.	|	|	|	|	|	0809	|	|	|	|	|	|	|	|	|	|	|	|	|	|	|	|	|
	Wien Südbahnhof △ ... **1250** a.	0525	0531	0559	0659	0737	...	0753	0831	0931	1037	1131	1237	1331	1437	1535	1637	1731	1837	1931	2037	2131	2237	2337

M – Ⓒ until Apr. 5. [2] and ✕ Bratislava - Mürzzuschlag and v.v. See also Table **981**.
n – Not Dec. 24, 31.
t – Also Dec. 24, 31.
△ – **Wien** Südbahnhof (Ostbahn). Temporary platforms located at Schweizer-Garten-Straße.

2nd class only; Narrow gauge *Murtalbahn*

UNZMARKT - TAMSWEG 998

km		Ⓐe	Ⓐ		Ⓐ		Ⓐ		Ⓒ	Ⓐ		Ⓐ	†	
0	**Unzmarkt** ... d.	...	0719	0918	1118	1318	1518	...	*1718*	1718	...	1918	2049	...
27	Murau-Stolzalpe ... d.	0628	0800	1000	1200	1400	1600	...	1800	1812	...	1958	2125	...
34	St Lorenzen ... d.	0640	0810	1010	1210	1410	1610	...	1810	1822	...	...	2135	...
44	Stadl an der Mur ... d.	0658	0824	1024	1224	1424	1624	...	1824	1836	...	...	2149	...
65	**Tamsweg** ... a.	0731	0855	1055	1255	1455	1655	...	1855	1907	...	...	2220	...

	Ⓐ	Ⓐ		Ⓒ	Ⓐe	Ⓐ		D	Ⓐ	Ⓐe		Ⓐ	†	
Tamsweg ... d.	...	0655	...	0705	0752	0905	1105	1305	...	1352	1505	1710	1905	...
Stadl an der Mur ... d.	...	0726	...	0735	0824	0935	1135	1335	...	1424	1535x	1740	1935	...
St Lorenzen ... d.	...	0741	...	0749	0838	0949	1149	1349	...	1438	1549	1754	1949	...
Murau-Stolzalpe ... d.	0615	0800	0800	0800	0850	1002	1202	1402	1402	1450	1602	1808	2000	...
Unzmarkt ... a.	0653	0840	0840	...	...	1040	1240	1440	1440	...	1640	1842	2038	...

D – Ⓐ Dec. 24 - Jan. 5, Ⓐ Feb. 15 – 19, Ⓐ Mar. 29 - Apr. 6 (also Mar. 19, May 14, 25, June 4).

e – Not Dec. 24 - Jan. 5, Feb. 15 – 19, Mar. 19, Mar. 29 - Apr. 6, May 14, 25, June 4.

x – Stops on request.

Operator: Steiermärkische Landesbahnen. ✆ +43 (0) 3532 2233.

POLAND

Operator: Polskie Koleje Państwowe (PKP).

Services: All trains convey first and second class seating, **except** where shown otherwise in footnotes or by '2' in the train column, or where the footnote shows sleeping and/or couchette cars only. Descriptions of sleeping (🛏) and couchette (▬) cars appear on page 8. As shown in the individual tables, Russian/Ukrainian sleeping car services cannot be used for journeys in or between Poland and Germany unless seating cars are also conveyed. Note that train numbers often change en route by one or two digits. In station names, Gł. is short for Główny or Główna, meaning main station.

Timings: Valid **December 13, 2009** until further notice, incorporating ongoing amendments. Further changes are expected in June, 2010. Many trains, including long-distance and express services, do not run over the Christmas and Easter periods. A number of long-distance trains running only in high summer (particularly to coastal resorts) are not shown due to lack of space.

Tickets: A higher fare is payable for travel by all *EC*, *IC*, *Ex*, and *IR* trains. Special fares are payable on *TLK* (Tanie Linie Kolejowe / cheap railway lines) trains, also Ⓡ.

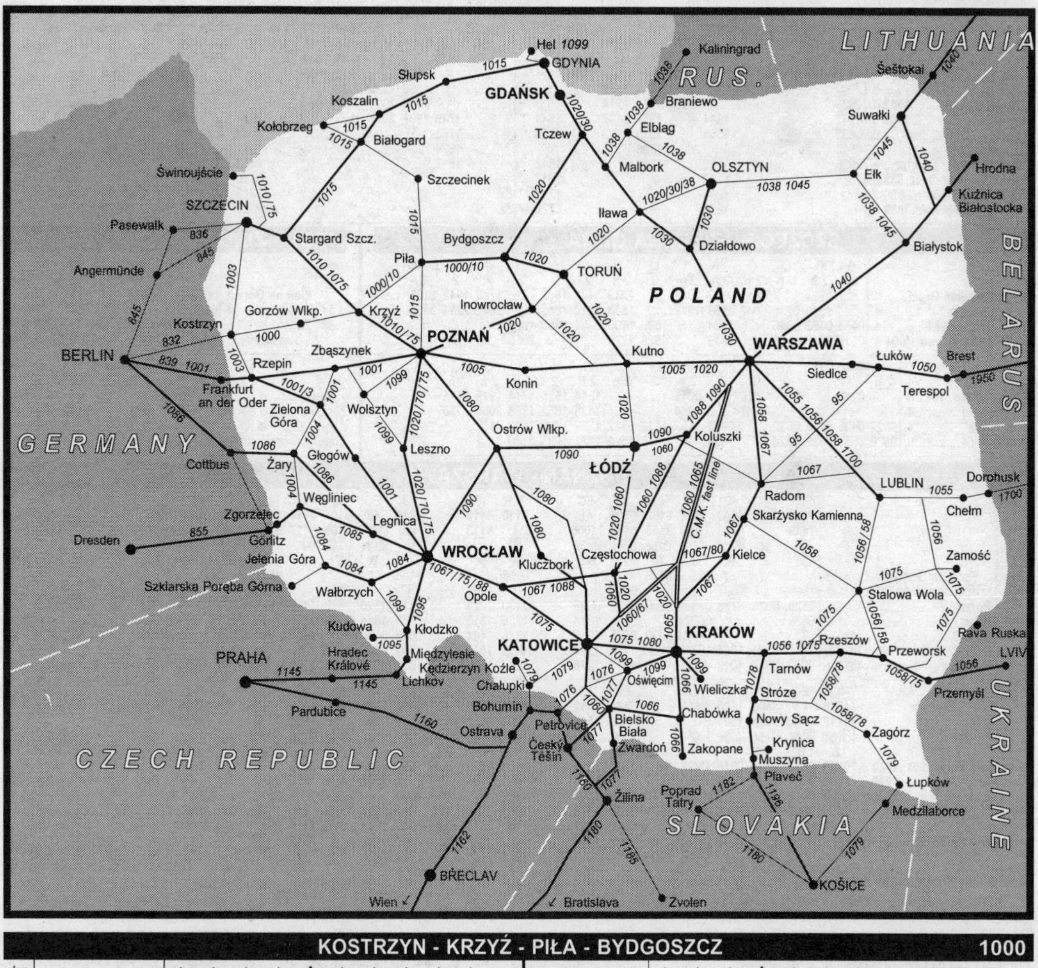

KOSTRZYN - KRZYŻ - PIŁA - BYDGOSZCZ 1000

km		◇	◇	◇ w	◇	A 88100	◇	◇	◇	◇ q	◇	
0	**Kostrzyn** ... d.	0550	0900	...	1100	0702	1320	1621	1825	...	1952	...
43	Gorzów Wlkp. ... d.	0630	0942	...	1144	0748	1401	1714	1908	...	2036	...
103	Krzyż ... a.	0723	1033	...	1306	0838	1454	1754	1955	...	2125	...
103	Krzyż **1010** ... d.	...	...	1040	*1433*	0853	*1635*	...	...	2005	...	...
161	**Piła 1010** ... a.	...	...	1131	*1524*	0955	*1726*	...	...	2056	...	...
248	**Bydgoszcz** ... **1010** a.	...	...	...	...	1117	...	...	...	...	...	...
	Warszawa ▲ ... a.	...	...	...	...	1510	...	...	...	...	...	...

	◇	◇ q	◇	A 38104	◇	◇ w	◇	◇ q	◇	◇	◇	
Warszawa ▲ ... d.	...	...	...	1240	...	...	...	...	...	...	...	...
Bydgoszcz. **1010** d.	...	...	...	1637	...	...	...	...	...	...	...	...
Piła 1010 ... d.	...	0608	*0920*	1758	...	1445	...	1720	...	...	...	...
Krzyż **1010** ... a.	...	0710	*1003*	1855	...	1536	...	1821	...	...	...	...
Krzyż ... d.	0516	...	1103	1906	1435	...	1615	...	1805	2100	...	...
Gorzów Wlkp. ... d.	0610	...	1156	1959	1540	...	1713	...	1910	2155	2310	...
Kostrzyn ... a.	0650	...	...	2043	1611	...	1750	...	1939	2311	2350	...

A – *TLK* 🚃12 Kostrzyn - Krzyż (**83104**/**88101**) - Bydgoszcz - Warszawa - Lublin - Przemyśl and v.v. Conveys 🚃12 Szczecin - Krzyż - Lublin - Przemyśl and v.v.

q – To / from Chojnice.

w – Not Dec. 25, 26, Jan. 1, Apr. 4, 5.

◇ – Stopping train. 2nd class only.

▲ – Warszawa Centralna (Table **1020**).

1001 BERLIN - POZNAŃ and WROCŁAW

See Table **56** for train **441/440** Berlin - Moskva / St Petersburg and train **1248/440 441/1249** Berlin - Saratov (these are not available for journeys Germany - Poland or v.v.)

km		TLK		2	2	IC	EN [R]		EC	TLK			TLK	EC		EC	78243	◇	TLK			EC				
		7310		◇	◇	7100/1	447	67431	41	75102		5881	75104	341	◇	45	◇	2	7116	5883	◇	47	5885			
		7311	2	①–⑤	①–⑥	[R] ✕	71008	◇	71006	75103	◇	◇	75105	[R] ✕	2	71002	2	①–⑤	✕ [R]	2	2	71000	2	◇		
		F	◇	C	H	Z	J	2	Bq	D	2	2	D	M	b	B		C	Z	◇	b	B	◇	2		
	Berlin Hauptbahnhof .. **839** d.	...	...	...	...	...	0423	...	0629	...	...	...	...	0941e	...	1229	...	...	...	...	...	1629	...	...	...	...
0	**Berlin** Ostbahnhof ...... **839** d.	...	...	...	...	...	0447	...	0640	...	...	...	...	0951x	...	1240	...	...	...	...	...	1640	...	...	...	...
82	Frankfurt an der Oder. **839** a.	...	...	...	...	...	|	...	0730	...	...	...	...	|	...	1330	...	...	...	...	...	1730	...	...	...	...
82	Frankfurt an der Oder 🏛 ... d.	...	...	...	...	...	|	...	0733	...	...	0919	...	◐	...	1333	...	...	...	1519	...	1733	1846	...	...	...
93	Kunowice 🏛 .... d.	...	...	...	...	...	|	...	|	...	...	0932	...	|	...	|	...	...	...	1533	...	|	1859	...	...	...
105	Rzepin .... a.	...	...	...	...	...	|	...	0754	...	...	0943	...	|	...	1354	...	...	...	1544	...	1754	1910	...	...	...
105	Rzepin .... **1003** d.	...	0445	...	...	...	0604s	...	0807	...	0800	0956	...	|	1154	1407	...	*1448*	...	1558	1600	1807	1924	...	...	...
176	**Zielona Góra** .... **1003** d.	0635	0613	...	...	...	|	...	|	...	0928	|	...	|	1319	*1526a*	...	|	...	|	1727	|	2050	...	...	...
229	Glogów .... d.	0804	0740	...	...	...	|	0454	|	...	1045	|	...	|	1435	|	...	|	...	|	1845	|	...	...	...	...
**	**Zielona Góra** .... d.	|	|	...	...	0423	|	0615	|	0737	|	|	1207	|	|	|	1350	|	1505	|	|	|	...	1850	...	...
180	Zbąszynek .... **1099** d.	|	|	0402	0502	0537	|	0737	|	0854	|	1053	1322	|	|	1445	1510	1602	1624	1655	|	|	...	1959	...	...
186	Zbąszyń .... **1099** d.	|	|	0406	0509	|	|	0742	|	0902	|	...	1328	|	|	|	1516	1610	1631	1701	|	|	...	2005	...	...
261	**Poznań** Gł. .... a.	|	|	0515	0615	0625	0732	0845	0925	0951	|	...	1420	|	|	1525	1615	1715	1725	1805	|	1925	...	2115	...	...
329*	**Wrocław** Gł. .... a.	0953	0938	...	...	|	|	...	|	...	1303	...	...	1518	1816	|	...	...	|	...	2103	|	...	...	...	...
	Katowice **1075** .... a.	1225	...	...	...	|	|	...	|	...	...	...	...	1754	...	|	...	...	|	...	...	|	...	...	...	...
	Kraków **1075** .... a.	1419	...	...	...	|	|	...	|	...	...	...	...	1935	...	|	...	...	|	...	...	|	...	...	...	...
	Warszawa Centralna **1005**. a.	...	...	...	...	0904	1024	...	1206	...	...	...	...	...	...	1806	...	...	2050	...	...	2206	...	...	...	...
	Warszawa Wschodnia **1005**. a.	...	...	...	...	0917	1037	...	1218	...	...	...	...	...	...	1818	...	...	2102	...	...	2218	...	...	...	...

			TLK	◇	EC		5882		TLK	EC	EC						TLK	77231	EC			IC	EN [R]	TLK		
	5880	77241	1717	2	46		77021	◇	57104	44	340	77227	5884	◇		7635	57102	◇	40	77233		1700/1	446	3710		
	◇	◇	[R] ✕	①–⑥	17001	◇	◇	2	57105	17003	[R] ✕	◇	◇	2	◇	◇	57103	2	17007	◇	◇	[R] ✕	17009	3711		
	2	2	Z	f	B	2	2	b	D	B	M	2	2	b	2	2	D	k	Bg	2	2	Z	J	F		
Warszawa Wschodnia **1005** d.	...	...	0548	...	0623	...	...	...	...	1123	...	...	...	...	...	...	...	...	1624	...	...	1723	1753	...	...	...
Warszawa Centralna **1005** d.	...	...	0600	...	0635	...	...	...	...	1135	...	...	...	...	...	...	...	...	1635	...	...	1735	1810u	...	...	...
Kraków **1075** .... d.	...	...	|	...	|	...	...	...	...	|	0724	...	...	...	...	...	...	...	|	...	...	|	|	1347	...	...
Katowice **1075** .... d.	...	...	|	...	|	...	...	...	...	|	0907	...	...	...	...	...	...	...	|	...	...	|	|	1534	...	...
Wrocław Gł. .... d.	...	...	|	0539	|	0550	...	0950	...	|	1148	...	...	1350	1550	...	...	...	|	...	1750	|	|	1834	...	...
Poznań Gł. .... d.	...	0740	0938	|	0923	|	1045	|	1408	1423	|	1440	...	|	|	1640	1739	1740	1923	1940	|	2026	2118u	|	...	...
Zbąszyń .... **1099** d.	...	0850	1029	|	|	|	1151	|	1511	|	|	1550	...	|	|	1754	1831	1848	|	2047	|	|	|	|	...	...
Zbąszynek .... **1099** d.	...	0859	1037	|	|	|	1158	|	1519	1503	|	1555	1645	|	|	1801	1839	1855	|	2055	|	2113	|	|	...	...
Zielona Góra .... a.	...	0953	1154	|	|	|	|	|	1648	|	|	...	|	|	|	1912	1956	...	|	...	|	2228	|	|	...	...
Glogów .... d.	...	...	...	0748	|	0758	|	1158	...	|	|	...	|	1558	1759	2003	...	...	|	...	1958	...	|	2026	...	...
Zielona Góra .... **1003** d.	0620	...	...	0911	|	0918	|	1314	...	|	|	...	|	1714	1911	...	...	...	|	...	2114	...	|	2149	...	...
Rzepin .... **1003** a.	0747	...	...	...	1041	1054	1257	1437	...	1541	|	...	1743	1837	2034	...	...	...	2041	...	2238	...	|	...	...	...
Rzepin .... d.	0802	...	...	...	1053	...	1315	...	...	1553	|	...	1753	...	...	...	...	...	2043	...	...	...	2249u	...	...	...
Kunowice 🏛 .... d.	0813	...	...	...	|	...	1328	...	...	|	|	...	1804	...	...	...	...	...	|	...	...	...	|	...	...	...
Frankfurt an der Oder 🏛 ... a.	0826	...	...	...	1112	...	1341	...	...	1612	◐	...	1817	...	...	...	...	...	2112	...	...	...	|	...	...	...
Frankfurt an der Oder **839** d.	...	...	...	...	1117	...	...	...	...	1617	|	...	...	...	...	...	...	...	2115	...	...	...	|	...	...	...
Berlin Ostbahnhof ...... **839** a.	...	...	...	...	1205	...	...	...	...	1715	1718x	...	...	...	...	...	...	...	2215	...	...	...	0001	...	...	...
Berlin Hauptbahnhof ... **839** a.	...	...	...	...	1216	...	...	...	...	1726	1733z	...	...	...	...	...	...	...	2227	...	...	...	0029	...	...	...

1003 SZCZECIN - ZIELONA GÓRA

km		◇	◇	◇	◇	◇	◇	◇	◇	◇	◇	◇	◇	◇	84500	
		2 h	2 h	2 h	2 p	2 h	2 p	2	2 h	2	2	2	2	2	E	
0	**Szczecin** Gł. .... d.	...	...	...	0612	0812	1042	...	1242	1442	1542	...	1742	1942	2133	...
104	Kostrzyn .... d.	...	0510	0715	0842	1059	1312	...	1513	1712	1813	...	2012	2214	2355	...
136	Rzepin **1001** .... d.	0453	0553	0800	...	1154	...	1400	1600	...	1855	1924	...	...	|	...
207	**Zielona Góra** . **1001** a.	0619	0717	0926	...	1318	...	1526	1726	...	...	2050	...	...	0145	...

	◇	48501	◇	◇	◇	◇	◇	◇	◇	◇	◇	◇	◇	◇		
	2 p	Q	2	2	2	2	2 h	2	2 p	2 h	2	2 h	2 h	2 h		
Zielona Góra .. **1001** d.	...	0215	...	...	0620	...	0918	...	...	1314	1525	1714	1919	2114	...	...
Rzepin **1001** .... d.	...	|	...	...	0747	0800	1054	...	...	1438	1652	1838	2055	2238	...	...
Kostrzyn .... d.	0322	0406	0422	0622	...	0842	...	1122	1322	1522	1735	1922	2137	...	...	...
Szczecin Gł. .... a.	0520	0553	0625	0820	...	1038	...	1320	1520	1721	1935	2120	...	...	...	...

1004 ZIELONA GÓRA - ŻAGAŃ

km		w	m	w		w	m	
		2 ◇	2 ◇	2 ◇	2 ◇	2 ◇	2 ◇	2 ◇
0	**Zielona Góra** d.	0622	...	1021	...	1536	...	...
54	Żary .... d.	0732	0800	1133	1318	1640	1808	1853
67	Żagań .... a.	|	0814	|	1332	|	1822	|
	Węgliniec .. a.	0825	...	1226	...	1733	...	1949

			w	m	w	m	w	w
	2 ◇	2 ◇	2 ◇	2 ◇	2 ◇	2 ◇	2 ◇	2 ◇
Węgliniec ... d.	...	...	0742	...	1309	...	1602	2045
Żagań .... d.	0451	0811	|	1117	|	1539	|	|
Żary .... d.	0504	0826	0843	1129	1404	1552	1700	2140
Zielona Góra a.	0614	...	0953	...	1520	...	1805	...

1005 POZNAŃ - WARSZAWA

For other trains Warszawa - Wrocław and v.v. see Table 1090

km		TLK	IC	IC	EN	IC	IC	EC		TLK	IC		TLK	EC	IC	TLK	IC	EC		TLK				
		7118	7100	6103	447	8102	6105	41		8110	6112		8210	45	6101	7116	8100	47		81200				
		7119	[R]	6102	71008	8103	6104	71006		81412	6113		[R]	71002	6100	7117	8101	71000		81201				
		[R]	✕	[R] ✕	[R]	[R] ✕	[R] ✕	[R] ✕		[R]	[R]		🍷	[R] ✕	[R] ✕	[R] 🍷	[R] 🍷	[R] ✕						
		✕	Z	R	J	R	R	Bq		✕	✕		§	B	⑧ r	Z	⑧	B		G				
	Szczecin Gł. **1010** .... d.	...	...	...	...	0538	...	...	...	0858	...	...	1148	...	...	...	1557	...	...	2320	...	...	...	...
	Wrocław Gł. **1070** .... d.	...	...	0507	...	|	0607	...	...	|	1007	...	|	...	1407	...	|	...	...	|	...	...	...	...
0	**Poznań** Gł. .... d.	0528	0628	0728	0732s	0800	0828	0928	...	1130	1228	...	1428	1528	1628	1728	1828	1928	...	0225	...	...	...	...
100	Konin .... d.	0636	|	|	0822s	|	|	1014	...	1230	1316	...	1533	1614	|	1831	|	2014	...	0354	...	...	...	...
179	Kutno .... **1020** d.	0725	|	|	0907s	0926	0955	1057	...	1316	1401	...	1625	1657	|	1925	1956	2056	...	0447	...	...	...	...
306	**Warszawa** Centralna ... **1020** a.	0848	0904	1007	1024s	1037	1106	1206	...	1435	1514	...	1750	1806	1905	2050	2108	2206	...	0615	...	...	...	...
311	**Warszawa** Wschodnia . **1020** a.	0902	0917	1019	1037	1052	1117	1218	...	1447	1526	...	1802	1818	1917	2102	2122	2218	...	0627	...	...	...	...

	TLK	EC	IC	IC	TLK		EC	IC		IC	IC	EC	IC	IC	EN	IC	TLK		TLK					
	1716	46	1800	1600	2811		44	1612		1810	1603	40	1802	1701	446	1605	1719		18201					
	1717	17001	1801	1601	[R]		17003	1613		18410	1602	17007	[R]	[R]	17009	1604	1718		18200					
	[R] ✕	[R] ✕	[R] ✕	[R] ✕	🍷		[R] ✕	[R]		[R]	[R] ✕	[R] ✕	✕	✕	[R] ✕	[R] ✕	[R]							
	Z	B	①–⑥		§		B	✕		✕	⑧ j	Bg	⑧ j	Z	J	⑧ j	✕		G					
Warszawa Wschodnia . **1020** d.	0548	0623	0720	0818	0927	...	1123	1218	...	1418	1523	1624	1648	1723	1753	1818	1848	...	2252	...	...	...	...	...
Warszawa Centralna ... **1020** d.	0600	0635	0735	0835	0940	...	1135	1235	...	1435	1535	1635	1700	1735	1810u	1835	1900	...	2315	...	...	...	...	...
Kutno .... **1020** d.	0732	0757	0857	|	1113	...	1257	1357	...	1602	|	1757	1820	|	1939u	1956	2035	...	0051	...	...	...	...	...
Konin .... d.	0820	0836	|	|	1201	...	1336	1438	...	1647	|	1836	|	|	2025u	|	2123	...	0147	...	...	...	...	...
Poznań Gł. .... a.	0932	0920	1022	1118	1310	...	1420	1527	...	1748	1817	1920	1942	2021	2118u	2118	2232	...	0310	...	...	...	...	...
Wrocław Gł. **1070** .... a.	...	...	|	1338	|	...	...	1749	...	|	2034	...	|	...	...	2339	...	...	|	...	...	...	...	...
Szczecin Gł. **1010** .... a.	...	...	1252	...	1548	...	...	...	...	2021	...	...	2204	...	...	...	...	...	0557	...	...	...	...	...

NOTES FOR TABLES 1001 - 1005

B – BERLIN WARSZAWA EXPRESS – (12) and ✕ [R], Berlin - Warszawa and v.v. Special fares apply.
C – ①–⑤ (not Dec. 24, 25, 31, Jan. 1, Apr. 5, May 3, June 3, 4).
D – (12) Zielona Góra - Poznań - Bydgoszcz - Gdynia and v.v.
E – June 20 - Aug. 31: (12) Świnoujście - Szczecin - Katowice - Bielsko Biała.
F – (12) Zielona Góra - Wrocław - Przemyśl and v.v.
G – 🛏 1, 2 cl., ▬ 2 cl. and (2) Szczecin - Poznań - Warszawa - Lublin and v.v. 🛏 1, 2 cl., and (12) Szczecin - Poznań - Warszawa - Terespol and v.v.
H – ①–⑥ (not Dec. 25, Jan. 1, Apr. 5, May 3, June 3).
J – JAN KIEPURA – 🛏 1, 2 cl. Amsterdam / Basel / München - Warszawa - Moskva and v.v. (journey 2 nights). 🛏 1, 2 cl., ▬ 2 cl., (2) and 🍷 Amsterdam - Köln - Warszawa and v.v.; see Table **24**.
K – ⑧ Dec. 13 - June 20 and Sept. 1 - Dec. 12.
L – ⑧ Dec. 13 - June 26 and Aug. 30 - Dec. 12.
M – WAWEL – (12) and ✕ (Hamburg ♣) - Berlin - Wrocław - Katowice - Kraków and v.v.
P – ①–⑥ Dec. 13 - June 27 and Aug. 31 - Dec. 12.
Q – June 19 - Aug. 30: (12) Bielsko Biała - Katowice - Szczecin - Świnoujście.
R – ①–⑥ (not Dec. 25, 26, Jan. 1, 2, Apr. 5).
S – 🛏 1, 2 cl. and ▬ 2 cl. Świnoujście - Szczecin - Warszawa and v.v.
Z – (12) and ✕ Zielona Góra - Poznań - Warszawa and v.v.

a – Arrival time.
b – From / to Szczecin (Table **1010**).
c – Not Dec. 24, 25, Apr. 4.
e – 0935 May 3 - Dec. 10.
f – Not Dec. 26, Jan. 2, May 1, June 5.
g – Not Dec. 24.
h – To / from Wrocław Gł (Table **1001**).
j – Not Dec. 24, 25, 31, Jan. 1, Apr. 4.
k – Not Dec. 24, 25, 31, Jan. 1, Apr. 4, May 2.
m – To / from Legnica (Table **1086**).
p – Not Dec. 25, Jan. 1.
q – Not Dec. 25.

r – Also Apr. 3; not Dec. 25, 31, Apr. 4, 5.
s – Stops to set down only.
u – Stops to pick up only.
w – To / from Jelenia Góra. (Table **1084**).
x – Not May 3 - Dec. 10.
y – Berlin **Lichtenberg**.
z – 1740 May 3 - Dec. 10.

◇ – Stopping train.
* – Via Zielona Góra.
§ – To / from Lublin (Table **1055**) and Białystok (Table **1040**).
♣ – For dates of running see Table **56**.
** – Zielona Góra - Zbąszynek: *58 km*.
◐ – 🏛 between Berlin and Wrocław is Forst / Zasieki; ticketing point is Forst.

SZCZECIN - POZNAŃ 1010

km		2 ◇ ①–⑥	83106 83107 G	*IC* 8102 🅁✕ R	*TLK* 83100 83101 P	*TLK* 83104 83105 T	*IR* 87142 2	2 ◇ q	*TLK* 8110 81412 🅁✕	*TLK* 83110 83111	*Ex* 8110 81410 🅁✕	*TLK* 8310 83410 🅁✕	*TLK* 8210 🅁✕ h k	*IR* 87144 2	*TLK* 81100 L	2 ◇	*IC* 8100 81402 ⑧	87102 87500	83500 83501 D	2 ◇	83510 83200 B	*TLK* 83706 83706 K	83706 81010 C	81200 81201 A	
	Świnoujście d.	...	...	...	...	...	...	...	0713x	...	0918x	1011z	...	...	...	...	1413c	...	...	...	1755j	2043	2043	...	...
0	**Szczecin** Gł. **1015** d.	...	...	0538	0655	0705	0722	...	0858	1049	1057	1150	1148	1317	1458	...	1557	1630	1655	1755	1955	2235	2235	2320	...
15	Szczecin Dąbie **1015** d.	...	...	0551	0704	0720	0737	...	0912	1103	1111	1204	1203	1332	1513	...	1611	1645	1711	1813	2011	2215	2253	2333	...
40	Stargard Szczeciński **1015** d.	...	...	0608	0727	0738	0755	...	0930	1122	1128	1221	1221	1349	1531	...	1629	1706	1734	1839	2035	2314	2314	2352	...
130	Krzyż **1000** d.	0515	0628	0658	0827	0853	0856	1040	1025	1228	1224	1317	1321	1450	1630	1630	1724	1814	1841	2004	2139	0049	0128	0051	...
	Piła **1000** d.	0606	|	|	|	1005	|	1131	|	|	|	|	|	|	|	1721	|	|	|	*2056*	|	|	0302	|	...
	Bydgoszcz **1000** a.	...	|	|	|	1117	|	*1310*	|	|	|	|	|	|	|	*1910*	|	|	|	|	|	|	0413	|	...
213	**Poznań** Gł. a.	...	0730	0749	0923	|	0955	...	1121	1326	1318	1411	1416	1552	1732	...	1819	1915	1945	2120	2243	0146	|	0149	...
	Wrocław Gł. **1070** a.	...	1020	|	1203	|	...	...	|	1603	|	|	|	...	...	...	|	2220	...	...	0135	0432	|	|	...
	Warszawa Cent. **1005** a.	...	|	1037	|	1510	...	...	1435	|	1625	|	1750	...	...	...	2108	...	...	...	|	|	0810	0605	...
	Kraków Gł **1075, 1080** a.	...	1519	...	1710	...	...	...	...	2048	...	2125	...	...	...	...	...	...	...	...	0657	0918	...	...	...

	2 ◇	38500 38501 E	65101 78101	2 ◇	*IC* 1800 1801 ①–⑥	*IR* 78133 2	*TLK* 18101 L	*TLK* 3811 38411 🅁✕	*TLK* 2811 🅁✕ h k	*TLK* 38110 38111	2 ◇	*IR* 78135 2	78243 2 ◇	2 ◇	*Ex* 1811 18411 🅁✕	*TLK* 38104 38105 T	*TLK* 38100 38101 P	*IC* 1803 🅁✕ ⑧g	38106 38107 G	18010 38705 C	*TLK* 38704 38705 K	*TLK* 18200 18201 A	38201 38512 B		
Kraków Gł. **1075, 1080** d.	...	...	...	...	...	...	...	0535	...	0740	...	...	...	...	...	...	1135	...	1247	...	1945	...	2150	...	...
Warszawa Cent. **1005** d.	...	...	...	...	0735	...	...	|	0955	|	...	...	...	...	1435	1240	|	1700	|	2130	|	2315	|	...	...
Wrocław Gł. **1070** d.	...	...	0530	...	|	...	...	|	|	1235	...	...	...	...	|	|	1635	|	1735	|	0024	|	0312	...	...
Poznań Gł. d.	0641	0700	0838	...	1031	1007	1038	1236	1325	1508	...	1630	1641	...	1747	|	1908	1951	2030	|	0305	0330	0600	...	...
Bydgoszcz **1000** d.	|	|	|	*0751*	|	|	|	|	|	|	...	|	|	*1541*	|	1637	|	|	|	0134	|	|	|	...	...
Piła **1000** d.	|	|	|	0920	|	|	|	|	|	|	1550	|	|	1720	|	1758	|	|	|	0301	|	|	|	...	...
Krzyż **1000** d.	0754	0815	0938	1011	1127	1106	1137	1330	1420	1607	1641	1732	1752	1811	1854	1920	2007	2043	2129	0451	0451	0427	0703	...	...
Stargard Szczeciński **1015** d.	0915	0925	1038	...	1219	1206	1234	1428	1514	1703	...	1834	1915	...	1948	2016	2103	2132	...	0555	0555	0524	0807	...	...
Szczecin Dąbie **1015** a.	0937	0943	1055	...	1237	1222	1252	1445	1532	1720	...	1851	1937	...	2005	2037	2122	2149	...	0614	0614	0542	0825	...	...
Szczecin Gł. **1015** a.	0958	0959	1113	...	1252	1238	1307	1500	1548	1737	...	1908	1958	...	2021	2053	2137	2204	...	0631	0631	0557	0843	...	...
Świnoujście a.	...	...	...	...	1445x	...	...	1640t	...	...	...	...	...	...	2207v	...	...	...	...	0818	0818	...	1054j	...	...

km		◇ 2 Q	◇ 2	◇ 2		◇ 2		◇ 2 S	◇ 2	◇ 2	◇ 2	
0	**Świnoujście** d.	0528	0640	0821	...	1150	...	1407	1528	1711	1940	...
101	Szczecin Dąbie a.	0708	0812	1000	...	1317	...	1548	1707	1846	2120	...
116	**Szczecin** Gł. a.	0727	0830	1017	...	1335	...	1606	1729	1904	2138	...

	◇ 2	◇ 2	◇ 2		◇ 2		◇ 2 S	◇ 2		◇ 2	◇ 2
Szczecin Gł. d.	0415	0512	0828	...	1143	...	1433	1543	...	1843	2043
Szczecin Dąbie d.	0431	0527	0845	...	1159	...	1448	1601	...	1858	2059
Świnoujście a.	0611	0710	1041	...	1329	...	1619	1743	...	2038	2229

A – 🛏 1, 2 cl., ▬ 2 cl. and [2] Szczecin - Poznań - Warszawa - Lublin and v.v. 🛏 1, 2 cl., and [12] Szczecin - Poznań - Warszawa - Terespol and v.v.
B – 🛏 1, 2 cl., ▬ 2 cl. and [12] Szczecin - Poznań - Kraków - Przemyśl and v.v.; From Świnoujście to Przemyśl Apr. 9 - Sept. 27; from Przemyśl to Świnoujście Apr. 8 - Sept. 26.
C – 🛏 1, 2 cl., ▬ 2 cl. and [2] Świnoujście - Szczecin - Warszawa and v.v.
D – June 19 - Aug. 30: 🛏 1, 2 cl., ▬ 2 cl. and [12] Szczecin - Zakopane.
E – June 20 - Aug. 31: 🛏 1, 2 cl., ▬ 2 cl. and [12] Zakopane - Szczecin.
G – [12] Gorzów Wlkp - Krzyż - Poznań - Kraków - Rzeszów and v.v.
K – 🛏 1, 2 cl., ▬ 2 cl., [2] and ✕ Świnoujście - Kraków and v.v.
L – [12] Szczecin - Poznań - Ostrów Wlkp - Łódź and v.v.
P – [12] Szczecin - Poznań - Kraków - Przemyśl and v.v.
Q – Dec. 13 - June 20 and Sept. 1 - Dec. 12.
R – ①–⑥ (not Dec. 25, 26, Jan. 1, 2, Apr. 5).
S – ①–⑤ (not Dec. 25, Jan, 1).
T – [12] Szczecin / Gorzów Wlkp. - Lublin and v.v.
b – ⑥ June 19 - Aug. 28.
c – ⑦ June 20 - Aug. 29.
f – From Zielona Góra (Table **1001**).
g – Not Dec. 24, 25, 31, Jan. 1, Apr. 4.
h – To / from Białystok (Table **1040**).
j – Apr. 9 - Sept. 27.
k – To / from Lublin (Table **1055**).
t – June 20 - Aug. 30.
v – June 19 - Aug. 31.
x – ⑥ June 19 - Aug. 28.
z – June 21 - Aug. 31.
◇ – Stopping train.

SZCZECIN - KOSZALIN - GDYNIA - GDAŃSK 1015

km		*Ex* 81414 🅁✕ O	48201 48503 C	◇	*TLK* 85102 85103 G	*TLK* 8316 🅁✕ Q	2 ◇	*Ex* 83414 🅁✕ J q	◇ 2	*TLK* 81104 81113 E	48101 H	2 ◇	*TLK* 85100 85101 G	2 ◇ w	38103 38102 M	2 ◇	2 ◇	*TLK* 85104 85105	*TLK* 83702 🅁✕ D	82500 83202 F	2 ◇	38108 38109 L	*IR* 78137 78136 2	2 ◇	81502 81503 A
0	**Szczecin** Gł. § d.	...	...	...	0610	...	...	...	0735	1032	...	1235	1403	...	...	1535	...	1738	...	...	...	...	...	1933	2010
15	Szczecin Dąbie § d.	...	...	...	0625	...	...	...	0755	1047	...	1253	1418	...	...	1553	...	1753	...	...	...	...	...	1953	2024
40	Stargard Szczeciński § d.	...	...	0455	0644	...	...	...	0821	1105	...	1319	1436	...	...	1619	...	1812	...	...	...	...	...	2019	2042
*231	**Poznań** Gł. d.	...	0121	|	|	...	0520	...	|	|	1125	|	|	1212	1322	|	1445	|	...	...	1650	1723	1820	|	|
*135	Piła d.	...	0325	|	|	...	0730	...	|	|	1311	|	|	1418	1515	|	1647	|	...	...	1836	1916	1954	|	|
*64	Szczecinek d.	...	0421	|	|	...	0839	...	|	|	1406	|	|	1534	1616	|	1756	|	...	...	1935	2016	2044	|	|
151	Białogard a.	...	0512	0630	0806	...	0940	...	1002	1224	1458	1457	1553	1634	1708	1809	1859	1930	...	...	2034	2108	2135	2157	2207
151	Białogard ▶ d.	...	0514	0646	0807	...	0941	...	1003	1226	1500	1510	1557	1636	1710	1811	1910	1932	...	...	2036	2106	2135	2158	2209
187	Kołobrzeg ▶ a.	...	0543	|	|	...	1017	...	|	|	1529	|	|	1711	1740	|	1945	|	...	...	|	2137	|	|	|
**43	Kołobrzeg d.	0311	...	|	|	0835	...	0925	|	|	...	|	|	...	...	|	...	|	1855	1940	|	...	|	|	|
175	**Koszalin** d.	0353	...	0708	0823	0920	...	1011	1027	1244	...	1535	1617	...	...	1835	...	1949	1951	2034	2053	...	2152	2220	2231
242	Słupsk d.	0439	...	...	0919	1015	...	1058	1120	1331	...	1640	1708	...	...	1934	...	2037	2048	2132	...	...	2236	...	2322
294	Lębork d.	0514	...	...	0954	1049	...	1156	...	1404	...	...	1741	...	...	...	...	2113	2131	2218	...	...	...	...	2358
353	**Gdynia** Gł. ... **1020, 1030** a.	0555	...	...	1040	1138	...	1238	...	1449	...	...	1843	...	...	...	...	2158	2228	2305	...	...	...	...	0042
353	**Gdynia** Gł. ... **1020, 1030** d.	0559	...	...	1054	1144	...	1252	...	1455	...	...	1847	...	...	...	...	2202	2252	2325	...	...	...	...	0104
362	Sopot **1020** a.	0610	...	...	1104	1155	...	1302	...	1505	...	...	1857	...	...	...	...	2212	2303	2334	...	...	...	...	0113
374	**Gdańsk** Gł. **1020, 1030** a.	0630	...	...	1121	1214	...	1321	...	1524	...	...	1916	...	...	...	...	2228	2319	2352	...	...	...	...	0129
	Warszawa C. **1030** a.	1035	...	...	...	1645	...	1806	...	...	...	...	...	...	...	...	...	...	...	0455	...	...	...	...	...

	2 ◇	2 ◇	2 ◇	83108 83109 L	*IR* 87134 87135 2	2 ◇ w	38203 28501 F	*TLK* 58105	*TLK* 38703 ✕ D	83102 83103 M	*TLK* 58101 58102 G	84100 H	2 ◇	2 ◇	2 ◇	2 ◇	*TLK* 18105 18104 E	2 ◇	*TLK* 3816 🅁✕ Q	*TLK* 58103 58102 G	*Ex* 38415 🅁✕ K p	84200 84502 C	*Ex* 18414 🅁✕ P	18503 18502 B	
Warszawa C. **1030** d.	...	...	...	...	...	...	2220	...	...	...	...	...	...	...	...	...	...	...	1050	...	1300	...	1550	...	...
Gdańsk Gł. .. **1020, 1030** d.	...	...	...	...	...	...	0315	0601	0756	...	0916	...	...	...	...	...	1402	...	1519	1631	1745	...	1947	0219	...
Sopot **1020** d.	...	...	...	...	...	...	0332	0616	0812	...	0933	...	...	...	...	...	1420	...	1536	1648	1800	...	2004	0234	...
Gdynia Gł. ... **1020, 1030** a.	...	...	...	...	...	...	0342	0627	0823	...	0945	...	...	...	...	...	1431	...	1549	1700	1813	...	2016	0244	...
Gdynia Gł. ... **1020, 1030** d.	...	...	...	...	...	...	0403	0630	0852	...	0956	...	...	...	...	...	1437	...	1604	1708	1828	...	2020	0306	...
Lębork d.	...	...	...	...	...	...	0504	0725	0954	...	1050	...	...	...	...	...	1525	...	1658	1803	1915	...	2112	0400	...
Słupsk d.	...	...	0511	...	0730	...	0548	0800	1059	...	1126	...	1227	...	1417f	...	1600	1737	1800	1838	1955	...	2147	0447	...
Koszalin d.	0434	...	0612	...	0824	...	0655	0845	1159	...	1212	...	1329	...	1534	1650	1645	1837	1855	1923	2057	...	2246	0545	...
Kołobrzeg a.	|	...	|	...	|	...	0750	|	1247	...	|	...	|	...	|	|	|	|	1947	|	2144	...	2330	|	...
Kołobrzeg ▶ d.	|	...	|	0605	|	0820	...	|	...	0950	|	1250	|	1415	|	|	|	|	...	|	...	2230	...	|	...
Białogard ▶ a.	0452	...	0633	0639	0842	0856	...	0901	...	1026	1245	1326	1352	1453	1557	1708	1700	1900	...	1944	...	2300	...	0608	...
Białogard d.	0453	0530	0636	0644	0843	0857	...	0903	...	1028	1248	1328	1400	1503	1558	1712	1703	1908	...	1953	...	2304	...	0609	...
Szczecinek d.	|	0630	|	0736	0942	1007	...	|	...	1124	|	1429	|	1617	|	1826	|	|	...	|	...	2359	...	|	...
Piła d.	|	0736	|	0832	1034	1119	...	|	...	1222	|	1529	|	1727	|	1946	|	|	...	|	...	0056	...	|	...
Poznań Gł. a.	|	0927	|	1025	1216	1326	...	|	...	1420	|	1718	|	1927	|	2134	|	|	...	|	...	0251	...	|	...
Stargard Szczeciński § d.	0640	...	0815	...	...	...	...	1028	...	...	1410	...	1545	...	1745	...	1824	2055	...	2114	...	...	...	0740	...
Szczecin Dąbie § a.	0703	...	0837	...	...	...	...	1045	...	...	1428	...	1607	...	1809	...	1843	2117	...	2132	...	...	...	0800	...
Szczecin Gł. § a.	0720	...	0855	...	...	...	...	1101	...	...	1444	...	1623	...	1827	...	1900	2135	...	2148	...	...	...	0817	...

A – June 20 - Aug. 31: ▬ 2 cl. and [12] Szczecin - Białystok.
B – June 19 - Aug. 30: ▬ 2 cl. and [12] Białystok - Szczecin.
C – Apr. 8 - Sept. 26 from Katowice; Apr. 9 - Sept. 27 from Kołobrzeg: 🛏 1, 2 cl., ▬ 2 cl. and [12] Katowice - Kołobrzeg and v.v.
D – From Kołobrzeg June 20 - Aug. 30: Kołobrzeg - Warszawa - Katowice (arrive 0947) - Kraków (1148); from Kraków June 19 - Aug. 29: Kraków (depart 1914) - Katowice (depart 2117) - Warszawa - Kołobrzeg: 🛏 1, 2 cl., ▬ 2 cl., [2] and ✕.
E – [12] Szczecin - Gdańsk - Białystok and v.v.
F – 🛏 1, 2 cl., ▬ 2 cl. and [12] Kołobrzeg - Kielce - Kraków and v.v.
G – [12] Szczecin - Gdańsk - Olsztyn and v.v.
H – [12] Katowice - Wrocław - Poznań - Kołobrzeg and v.v.
J – June 27 - Aug. 31.
K – June 26 - Aug. 30.
L – [12] Przemyśl - Poznań - Kołobrzeg and v.v.
M – [12] Kraków - Poznań - Kołobrzeg and v.v.
O – ①⑥ (also Apr. 6; not Apr. 5).
P – ⑤⑦ (also Apr. 5, not Apr. 4).
Q – [12] Kołobrzeg - Kraków / Lublin and v.v.
f – ①–⑤ (not Dec. 25, Jan, 1).
j – Not Dec. 25, Jan. 1.
w – From / to Wrocław (Table **1070**).
* – Distance from Białogard.
** – Distance from Koszalin.
§ – See also Table **1010**.
◇ – Stopping train.

▶ – Other local trains: From Białogard to Kołobrzeg: 0550, 0640 j, 0941, 1242, 1415 f, 1532, 1636, 2115. From Kołobrzeg to Białogard: 0550 j, 0641 f, 1200, 1531, 1625, 1830, 2024.

1020 GDYNIA - BYDGOSZCZ - ŁÓDŹ, POZNAŃ, KATOWICE and KRAKÓW

km		*TLK*	*TLK*	*TLK*	*TLK*	*TLK*	*TLK*	**56104**	*IR*	*TLK*	*TLK*	*TLK*	*TLK*	*TLK*	*IR*	**57102**	*TLK*	*TLK*	*TLK*	**16112**	*TLK*	*TLK*	*TLK*	*IR*	**57100**	**54502**	**56510**
		81010	**52104**	**54110**	**5112**	**51108**	**56102**	**56105**	**51132**	**52102**	**54102**	**54102**	**57104**	**83104**	**57124**	**57103**	**52108**	**54100**	**52100**	**16113**	**51106**	**56100**	**51102**	**57126**	**57101**	**54503**	**56200**
			52105	**54111**	🄡 ✕	**51109**	**56103**		**51133**	**52103**	**54103**	**43103**	**57105**	**83104**	**57125**		**53109**	**54101**	**52101**		**51107**	**56101**	**51103**	**57127**			
		D	P		Q	M			2 R	P			G	B	2	G	⑧ f k		P	z			j	2 U	J	C	A
0	**Gdynia** Gł. ... **1030** d.	...	...	...	...	...	0524	...	...	...	0648	0648	0914	...	...	1244	...	1046	...	...	...	1501	1531	...	1746	1851	2207
9	Sopot ... **1030** d.	...	...	...	...	...	0534	...	...	...	0658	0658	0924	...	...	1254	...	1056	...	...	...	1511	1541	...	1756	1901	2218
21	**Gdańsk** Gł. ... **1030** d.	...	...	...	...	...	0555	...	...	...	0717	0717	0943	...	...	1313	...	1115	...	...	...	1530	1602	...	1815	1921	2237
53	Tczew ... **1030** d.	...	...	...	...	...	0625	...	...	...	0744	0744	1009	...	...	1341	...	1142	...	...	...	1603	1638	...	1841	1949	2314
181	**Bydgoszcz** Gł. ... d.	0421	0514	0550	0605	0711	0815	...	0840	0910	0943	0943	1154	1122	...	1523	1305	1342	1500	...	1644	1750	1835	...	2026	2152	0101
	Olsztyn ... d.	|	|	|	|	|	|	0624	|	|	|	|	|	|	1145	|	|	|	|	1324	|	|	|	1655	|	|	|
	Iława ... d.	|	|	|	|	|	|	0720	|	|	|	|	|	|	1239	|	|	|	|	1422	|	|	|	1749	|	|	|
232	**Toruń** Gł. ... d.	0520	0618	0654	0709	0815	|	0906	0935	1011	1048	1048	|	1227	1418	|	1408	1446	1604	1609	1746	|	1939	1929	|	2258	|
287	Włocławek ... d.	0602	0658	0733	0748	0854	|	|	1014	1051	1127	1127	|	1308	|	|	1448	1527	1644	|	1825	|	2017	|	|	2342	|
227	Inowrocław ... d.	|	|	|	|	|	0901	0955	|	|	|	|	1237	|	1455	1607	|	|	|	1653	|	1837	|	2005	2109	|	0145
342	Kutno ... d.	0639	0734	0808	0824	0931	|	|	1052	1126	1202	1202	|	1344	|	|	1524	1604	1722	|	1900	|	2101	|	|	0021	|
410	**Łódź** Kaliska ... a.	|	|	0931	|	|	|	|	|	|	1327	1327	|	|	|	|	|	1737	|	|	|	|	2226	|	|	0140	|
469	**Warszawa** Cent ... a.	0810	0856	|	0947	1055	|	|	1215	1250	|	|	|	1510	|	|	1650	|	1850	|	2025	|	...	|	|	|	|
474	**Warszawa** Wsch ... a.	0827	0922	|	0958	1112	|	|	1227	1302	|	|	|	1522	|	|	1702	|	1902	|	2037	|	...	|	|	|	|
283	Gniezno ... d.	...	...	|	...	...	0949	1044	...	...	|	|	1324	...	1544	1654	...	|	...	1745	...	1928	...	2055	2201	|	0232
334	**Poznań** Gł. ... a.	...	...	|	...	...	1030	1133	...	...	|	|	1405	...	1629	1735	...	|	...	1830	...	2010	...	2146	2247	|	0315
	Wrocław **1070** ... a.	...	...	|	...	...	1305	1420	...	...	|	|	...	...	...	...	...	|	...	2119	...	2259	...	...	...	|	0540
483	**Częstochowa Os.** ⊠ ▲ d.	...	...	1141	...	...	...	...	...	...	1536	1610	...	...	...	...	...	1943	...	...	...	...	...	...	...	0404	...
526	Zawiercie ... ▲ d.	...	...	1217	...	...	...	...	...	...	1623	1646	...	...	...	...	...	2026	...	...	...	...	...	...	...	0447	...
561	Sosnowiec Gł. ... ▲ d.	...	...	1244	...	...	...	...	...	...	1654	|	...	...	...	...	...	2053	...	...	...	...	...	...	...	0523	...
569	**Katowice** ... ▲ a.	...	...	1255	...	...	...	...	...	...	1706	|	...	...	...	...	...	2105	...	...	...	...	...	...	...	0535	...
615	**Kraków** Gł. ... a.	...	...	...	...	...	...	...	...	...	...	1854	...	...	...	...	...	...	...	...	...	...	...	...	...	...	...

	75100	*IR*	*TLK*	*TLK*	*TLK*	*TLK*	*TLK*	**61113**	*TLK*	*TLK*	*IR*	*TLK*	*TLK*	*TLK*	*TLK*	*TLK*	**65105**	*TLK*	**65102**	*TLK*	*TLK*	*IR*	*TLK*	*TLK*	**65201**	**45503**	
	75101	**75114**	**15102**	**15106**	**65101**	**25101**	**45100**	**61112**	**75102**	**25108**	**75116**	**38104**	**75104**	**34102**	**45102**	**25102**	**65104**	**1512**	**65103**	**15108**	**45110**	**15130**	**25104**	**18011**	**65200**	**45502**	
		75115	**15103**	**15107**	**65100**	**28511**	**45101**		**75103**	**25109**	**75117**	**38105**	**75105**	**45103**	**45103**	**25103**		**1513**		**15109**	**45111**	**15131**	**25105**				
	K	2 T	j			P		z	G	Q k	2	B	G			P		⑧ f		M		2 S	P	D	A	C	
Kraków Gł. ... d.	...	...	...	...	...	...	...	...	...	...	...	...	...	1015	...	...	...	...	...	...	...	...	...	...	...	...	...
Katowice ... ▲ d.	...	...	...	...	...	...	0657	...	...	...	...	...	...	|	1127	...	...	...	...	...	1551	...	...	...	...	2245	...
Sosnowiec Gł. ... ▲ d.	...	...	...	...	...	...	0709	...	...	...	...	...	...	|	1137	...	...	...	...	...	1602	...	...	...	...	2257	...
Zawiercie ... ▲ d.	...	...	...	...	...	...	0749	...	...	...	...	...	...	1158	1204	...	...	...	...	...	1638	...	...	...	...	2328	...
Częstochowa Os. ⊠ ▲ d.	...	...	...	...	...	...	0824	...	...	...	...	...	...	1249	1249	...	...	...	...	...	1712	...	...	...	...	0007	...
Wrocław **1070** ... d.	...	...	...	...	0535	...	|	0635	...	...	...	...	...	|	|	...	1335	...	1535	...	|	...	...	...	2340	|	...
Poznań Gł. ... d.	0523	0611	...	...	0822	...	|	0936	1002	...	1200	...	1442	|	|	...	1618	...	1810	...	|	...	...	...	0300	|	...
Gniezno ... d.	0601	0655	...	...	0856	...	|	1017	1034	...	1238	...	1516	|	|	...	1656	...	1849	...	|	...	...	...	0335	|	...
Warszawa Wsch ... d.	|	|	...	0628	|	0813	|	|	|	1013	|	1213	|	|	|	1413	|	1525	|	1628	|	1733	1838	2118	|	|	...
Warszawa Cent ... d.	|	|	...	0640	|	0840	|	|	|	1040	|	1240	|	|	|	1440	|	1540	|	1640	|	1810	1855	2130	|	|	...
Łódź Kaliska ... d.	|	|	0602	|	|	|	1036	|	|	|	|	|	|	1507	1507	|	|	|	|	|	1923	|	|	|	|	0227	...
Kutno ... d.	|	|	0720	0814	|	1019	1154	|	|	1215	|	1414	|	1633	1633	1614	|	1713	|	1810	2041	1945	2028	2303	|	0346	...
Inowrocław ... d.	0654	0749	|	|	0951	|	|	1109	1129	|	1331	|	1609	|	|	|	1748	|	1943	|	|	|	|	|	0430	|	...
Włocławek ... d.	|	|	0756	0849	|	1054	1229	|	|	1250	|	1449	|	1708	1708	1649	|	1748	|	1846	2115	2021	2103	2339	|	0422	...
Toruń Gł. ... d.	|	0831	0840	0931	|	1138	1309	1152	|	1332	1408	1534	|	1754	1754	1735	1830	1830	|	1934	2156	2101	2143	0021	|	0507	...
Iława ... d.	|	0945	|	|	|	|	|	1317	|	|	1522	|	|	|	|	|	1950	|	|	|	|	|	|	|	|	|	...
Olsztyn ... a.	|	1038	|	|	|	|	|	1415	|	|	1614	|	|	|	|	|	2049	|	|	|	|	|	|	|	|	|	...
Bydgoszcz Gł. ... d.	0753	...	0949	1027	1029	1235	1426	...	1209	1429	...	1633	1649	1905	1905	1832	...	1926	2040	2031	2252	2154	2241	0116	0507	0627	...
Tczew ... **1030** d.	1026	...	1236	...	1316	...	1714	...	1458	...	...	...	1937	2153	2153	...	...	...	2316	...	...	...	...	...	0804	0903	...
Gdańsk Gł. ... **1030** a.	1052	...	1303	...	1342	...	1740	...	1526	...	...	...	2003	2219	2219	...	...	...	2342	...	...	...	...	...	0828	0929	...
Sopot ... **1030** a.	1108	...	1321	...	1359	...	1757	...	1544	...	...	...	2021	2236	2236	...	...	...	0001	...	...	...	...	...	0845	0948	...
Gdynia Gł. ... **1030** a.	1119	...	1336	...	1411	...	1809	...	1555	...	...	...	2032	2249	2249	...	...	...	0012	...	...	...	...	...	0857	0959	...

A – 🛏 1, 2 cl., ▬ 2 cl. and (12) Gdynia - Wrocław and v.v.
B – (12) Szczecin / Kostrzyn - Lublin - Przemyśl and v.v.
C – ⑤⑦ (daily June 20 - Aug. 31): 🛏 1, 2 cl., ▬ 2 cl. and (12) Gdynia - Katowice - Bielsko Biała and v.v.
D – 🛏 1, 2 cl., ▬ 2 cl. and (2) Świnoujście - Warszawa and v.v.
E – (12) Bydgoszcz - Warszawa - Lublin - Przemyśl and v.v.
G – (12) Gdynia - Poznań - Zielona Góra and v.v.
J – ⑧ (daily June 20 - Aug. 29).
K – ①–⑥ (daily June 21 - Aug. 30).

M – To / from Białystok (Table **1040**).
P – To / from Lublin (Table **1055**).
Q – ①–⑥ (not Dec. 25, 26, Jan. 1, 2, Apr. 5).
R – ①–⑤ (not Dec. 25, Jan. 1).
S – ⑧ (not Dec. 25, Jan. 1).
T – ①–⑥ (not Dec. 25, 31, Jan. 1).
U – ⑧ (not Dec. 25, 31, Jan. 1).

e – Łódź **Widzew**.

f – Not Dec. 24, 25, 31, Jan. 1, Apr. 4.
j – From / to Hel June 20 - Aug. 31.
k – To / from Chełm (Table **1055**).
x – June 20 - Aug. 31.
z – From / to Ełk and Suwałki (Table **1045**).

⊠ – Full name is Częstochowa Osobowa.
▲ – For additional trains see Table **1060**.

1030 GDYNIA - GDAŃSK - WARSZAWA

km		*TLK*	*TLK*	*IC*	**53100**	*Ex* 🄡	**5302**	**54112**	**7**	*Ex*		*TLK*	*Ex*		*IC*			*IC*	*Ex*	*TLK*		**83202**	
		52106	**56110**	**5306**	**53101**	**5114**	**53400**	**54113**	**55000**	**5310**		**8316**	**5312**		**5300**	**51100**	**51530**	**5100**	**51410**	**53202**		**53502**	
		52107	**56111**	🄡 ✕		**81414**	🄡 ✕			🄡 ✕		🄡 ✕	**83414**		🄡		2	🄡	🄡 ✕	🄡			
		①–⑥	U w	E		q			A	H		Q	🄡 t		✕		D	✕	D f	C		B	
0	**Gdynia** Gł. ... **1038** ▲ d.	...	0501	0531	...	0559	0725	...	0807	0923	...	1144	1325	...	1523	...	1623	1657	1812	1854	...	2325	...
9	Sopot ... **1038** ▲ d.	...	0511	0540	...	0610	0735	...	0816	0934	...	1155	1335	...	1533	...	1632	1707	1823	1904	...	2335	...
21	**Gdańsk** Gł. ... **1038** ▲ d.	...	0530	0600	...	0630	0755	...	0834	0955	...	1214	1355	...	1555	...	1649	1730	1840	1924	...	2355	...
53	Tczew ... **1038** d.	...	0556	|	...	0702	0828	...	0908	1027	...	1240	1428	...	|	...	1721	1802	|	1951	...	0024	...
72	Malbork ... **1038** d.	...	0617	|	...	0722	0849	...	0930	1048	...	1300	1449	...	1649	...	1740	1824	|	2012	...	0043	...
**	**Olsztyn** ... **1020 1038** d.	0520	|	|	0640	|	|	0837	...	|	...	|	|	...	|	1705	|	|	|	|	...	|	...
141	Iława ... **1020 1038** d.	|	0710	|	|	0807	0932	0934	...	1132	...	1351	1533	...	1733	|	1831	1909	2006	2056	...	0135	...
201	Działdowo ... d.	0641	0748	|	0819	0846	|	1016	...	1212	...	1434	1614	...	|	1819	1915	|	2047	2137	...	0220	...
251	Ciechanów ... d.	0717	0822	|	0851	|	|	1050	...	|	...	1514	|	...	|	1853	1952	|	|	2219	...	0301	...
345	**Warszawa** Wschodnia ... a.	0831	0933	0949	1040	1024	1149	1238	...	1355	...	1628	1754	...	1950	2039	2141	2130	2300	2230	...	0445	...
350	**Warszawa** Centralna ... a.	0840	0942	1006	1050	1035	1205	1257	...	1410	...	1645	1810	...	2005	2050	2150	2140	2310	2340	...	0455	...
	Katowice **1060** ... a.	...	...	|	|	...	|	1654	...	|	...	|	|	...	|	...	...	...	...	0408	...	|	...
	Kraków Gł. **1065** ... a.	...	...	1244	1620	...	1444	...	...	1647	...	2202	2045	...	2244	...	...	...	...	...	...	1034	...

	IC	*TLK*	*Ex*		*IC*	*TLK*		*Ex*		*Ex*	**45112**	*Ex* 🄡	*IC*	**8**	**35100**	*TLK*	*IC*	**25106**		**38203**		*TLK*	
	1501	**15101**	**15411**	**15531**	**3500**	**3817**		**3512**		**3510**	**45113**	**1514**	**3506**	**55002**	**35101**	**65110**	**3502**	**25107**		**35503**		**35202**	
	1500		🄡 ✕	2	**3501**	🄡 ✕		**38414**		🄡 ✕		**18414**	🄡 ✕			**65111**	**35400**					🄡	
	🄡 ✕		D f	D	🄡 ✕	Q		🄡 p		H		q	⑧	A		U w	🄡	⑧		B		C	
Kraków Gł. **1065** ... d.	...	...	...	...	0600	0450	...	1000	...	1200	...	...	1400	...	1210	...	...	...	...	1710	...	...	...
Katowice **1060** ... d.	...	...	...	...	|	|	...	|	...	|	1047	...	|	...	|	...	...	...	...	|	...	0047	...
Warszawa Centralna ... d.	0650	0710	0800	0815	0850	1040	...	1250	...	1450	1522	1550	1650	...	1732	1800	1850	1938	...	2220	...	0445	...
Warszawa Wschodnia ... d.	0659	0719	0810	0823	0905	1112	...	1317	...	1505	1533	1600	1705	...	1748	1809	1905	1947	...	2230	...	0454	...
Ciechanów ... d.	|	0830	|	1010	|	1224	...	|	...	|	1705	|	|	...	2014	1924	|	2204	...	0015	...	0604	...
Działdowo ... d.	|	0909	1020	1047	|	1304	...	1457	...	1643	1806	1736	|	...	2056	2002	|	2239	...	0051	...	0647	...
Iława ... **1020 1038** d.	0910	|	|	1131	1119	1341	...	1535	...	1721	1829	1813	|	...	|	2040	2116	|	...	0137	...	0727	...
Olsztyn ... **1020 1038** a.	|	1022	|	|	|	|	...	|	...	|	1942	|	|	...	2209	|	|	2349	...	|	...	|	...
Malbork ... **1038** d.	0957	...	1143	1223	1206	1432	...	1621	...	1808	...	1859	|	2118	...	2126	2203	...	...	0228	...	0815	...
Tczew ... **1038** d.	1019	...	|	1242	|	1453	...	1645	...	1830	...	1921	|	2144	...	2145	2224	...	...	0246	...	0837	...
Gdańsk Gł. ... **1038** ▲ a.	1048	...	1227	1307	1256	1519	...	1716	...	1902	...	1947	2049	2210	...	2212	2255	...	...	0312	...	0907	...
Sopot ... **1038** ▲ a.	1106	...	1240	1321	1314	1532	...	1734	...	1920	...	2004	2108	2227	...	2229	2313	...	...	0331	...	0925	...
Gdynia Gł. ... **1038** ▲ a.	1122	...	1252	1332	1331	1549	...	1750	...	1935	...	2016	2123	2238	...	2240	2329	...	...	0342	...	0938	...

A – (2) Gdynia - Malbork - Kaliningrad and v.v.
B – Dec. 13 - June 18 and Aug. 31 - Dec. 11 to Kołobrzeg; June 19 - Aug. 30 to Hel. Dec. 13 - June 19 and Sept. 1 - Dec. 11 from Kołobrzeg; June 20 - Aug. 31 from Hel: 🛏 1, 2 cl., ▬ 2 cl., (12) and ✕ Kołobrzeg / Hel - Gdynia - Warszawa - Kielce - Kraków and v.v.
C – 🛏 1, 2 cl., ▬ 2 cl. and (2) Gdynia - Zakopane and v.v.
D – June 20 - Aug. 31.
E – ①–⑥ (not Dec. 25, 26, Jan. 1, Apr. 5).
H – To / from Przemyśl (Tables **1058** / **1075**).
Q – (12) Kołobrzeg - Kraków / Lublin and v.v.

U – ①–⑥ (not Dec. 25, 26, Jan. 1, 2, Apr. 5).

b – To / from Lublin (Table **1055**).
e – From / To Kołobrzeg (Table **1015**).
f – To / from Hel (Table **1099**).
k – To / from Kielce (Table **1067**).
p – June 20 - Aug. 30 to Kołobrzeg (Table **1015**).
q – From / to Kołobrzeg on dates in Table **1015**.
t – June 21 - Aug. 31 from Kołobrzeg (Table **1015**).
w – To / from Wrocław (Table **1090**).

y – To / from Bielsko Biała (Table **1060**).

** – Olsztyn - Działdowo: *84 km.*
▲ – Frequent local trains run between **Gdynia** and **Gdańsk**.

GDYNIA - GDAŃSK - OLSZTYN and KALININGRAD 1038

km		70140 70141 w	51104 51105	55000 7 2		TLK 85102 85103	70142 70143 2	TLK 81104 81105	85100 85101	81502 81503 C	
	Szczecin Gł. **1015** d.	...	...	...	...	0610	...	1032	1403	2010	...
0	**Gdynia** Gł. **1030** d.	0539	0724	0758	...	1054	1226	1455	1847	0104	...
9	Sopot **1030** d.	0548	0734	0807	...	1104	1235	1505	1857	0114	...
21	**Gdańsk** Gł. **1030** d.	0604	0753	0825	...	1121	1251	1524	1916	0132	...
53	Tczew **1030** d.	0634	0822	0908	...	1148	1324	1552	1942	0200	...
72	Malbork **1030** ▲ d.	0652	0842	0931	...	1212	1343	1613	2003	0221	...
101	Elbląg ▲ d.	|	0906	0959	...	1237	|	1641	2029	0246	...
156	Braniewo ⊞ a.	|	|	1048	...	|	|	|	|	|	...
219	**Kaliningrad** § a.	|	|	1535	...	|	|	|	|	|	...
	Iława d.	0752	|	...	...	|	1441	|	|	|	...
200	**Olsztyn** a.	0846	1033	...	...	1405	1545	1822	2158	0408	...
471	*Białystok* **1045** a.	...	1508	...	...	...	...	2258	...	0840	...

	58101 58100	70120 70121	18105 18104		TLK 58103 58102	15105 15104	55002 8 2	70122 70123 m	18503 18502 D	
Białystok **1045** d.	...	...	0648	...	...	1240	...	...	1910	...
Olsztyn d.	0632	0820	1122	...	1336	1706	...	1953	2344	...
Iława d.	|	0928	|	...	|	|	...	2053	|	...
Kaliningrad § d.	|	|	|	...	|	|	1823	|	|	...
Braniewo ⊞ d.	|	|	|	...	|	|	1950	|	|	...
Elbląg ▲ d.	0801	|	1252	...	1513	1839	2039	|	0111	...
Malbork **1030** ▲ d.	0825	1022	1316	...	1536	1905	2108	2146	0136	...
Tczew **1030** d.	0847	1043	1336	...	1558	1924	2148	2205	0156	...
Gdańsk Gł. **1030** a.	0913	1111	1402	...	1631	1950	2213	2233	0220	...
Sopot **1030** a.	0933	1125	1420	...	1648	2007	2230	2247	0236	...
Gdynia Gł. **1030** a.	0945	1135	1431	...	1700	2020	2241	2257	0247	...
Szczecin Gł. **1015** a.	1444	...	1900	...	2148	...	...	...	0815	...

C – June 20 - Aug. 31: ▬ 2 cl. and [12] Szczecin - Białystok.
D – June 19 - Aug. 30: ▬ 2 cl. and [12] Białystok - Szczecin.
m – Not Dec. 25, Jan. 1.
w – Not Dec. 24, 31.
§ – Moskva time (2 hours ahead of Polish time, 1 hour ahead of Kaliningrad time).
▲ – Additional local trains run Malbork - Elbląg and v.v. Journey 30 minutes.

WARSZAWA - BIAŁYSTOK - VILNIUS and HRODNA 1040

PKP, BCh, LG

km		79821 2	77641 2	138 2	77621 2 ①–⑤	41500 41501 L	11201	77623 ⑥⑦ 2	10011 910	394 91001 2	41103 ①–⑥ g	79825 2 Ⓑ	TLK 51108 b	77625 2	134 2		61105 61104 S	77627 2	31106 31107 N	77103 V	77105	79827 2	77645 2	TLK 8210 T	41100 41101 P	140 19021 2	2 IR 77119 ⑤⑦	🚌 99928 A [R]
0	**Warszawa** Centralna d.	...	...	...	...	0405	0615	...	0725	...	0925	...	1105	...	...	...	1325	...	1525	1625	1725	...	...	1755	1925	...	2025	2300
5	**Warszawa** Wschodnia d.	...	...	...	...	0414	0625	...	0734	...	0940	...	1114	...	...	...	1334	...	1534	1634	1734	...	...	1824	1934	...	2034	|
184	**Białystok** a.	...	...	...	...	0645	0845	...	1000	...	1155	...	1340	...	...	...	1555	...	1755	1855	1955	...	...	2043	2155	...	2255	|
184	**Białystok** d.	0509	...	...	0633	0700	...	0900	1010	...	...	1205	1406c	1444	...	...	...	1655	1810	...	...	2005	...	...	...	2222	...	0140
225	Sokółka d.	0555	0627	...	0734	0752	...	0946	1053	...	...	1245	1449c	1531	...	...	...	1745	1855	...	...	2045	2050	...	...	2308	...	|
324	**Suwałki** d.	0727	|	...	|	0941	...	|	1244	...	...	1417	1634c	|	...	...	...	|	2035	...	...	2217	|	...	...	|	...	|
377	Šeštokai ⊞ ◐ § a.	...	|	...	|	...	...	|	1448	1503	...	...	...	|	...	...	...	|	...	...	...	...	|	...	...	|	...	|
471	**Kaunas** **1810** § a.	...	|	...	|	...	...	|	...	1633	...	...	...	|	...	...	...	|	...	...	...	...	|	...	...	|	...	0610
575	**Vilnius** § a.	...	|	...	|	...	...	|	...	1750	...	...	...	|	...	...	...	|	...	...	...	...	|	...	...	|	...	0750
241	Kuźnica Białostocka a.	...	0643	...	0750	...	...	1002	...	...	...	...	...	1548	...	...	...	1801	...	...	...	...	2106	...	...	2325	...	...
241	Kuźnica Białostocka ⊞ d.	...	...	0715	...	...	...	...	...	...	...	...	...	...	1635	...	...	...	...	...	...	...	...	...	...	0025	...	...
268	Hrodna ⊞ ‡ a.	...	...	0910	...	...	...	...	...	...	...	...	...	...	1830	...	...	...	...	...	...	...	...	...	...	0220	...	...

	77110 V	14100 14101 P	77622 2	TLK 2810 T	139 2	77640 2	79820 2	77108	77624 2	13106 13107 N	137 2	79822 2 Ⓑ	16104 16105 S	TLK 15108 b	14103 Ⓑg	2 IR 77118 ⑤⑦		77628 2	77644 2	393 10012 2	910 10012	79824 2	11200	133 19026 2	14500 14501 L		🚌 99927 B [R]	
Hrodna ⊞ ‡ d.	...	...	...	...	0535	...	...	...	...	...	1005	...	...	...	...	...	...	...	...	...	...	...	...	1950	...	...	...	...
Kuźnica Białostocka ⊞ a.	...	...	...	...	0530	...	...	...	...	...	1000	...	...	...	...	...	...	...	...	...	...	...	...	1945	...	...	...	...
Kuźnica Białostocka d.	...	...	0520	...	...	0605	...	...	0715	...	...	...	...	...	...	...	...	1459	1643	...	...	...	...	2025	...	...	...	...
Vilnius § d.	...	...	|	...	...	|	...	...	|	...	...	...	...	...	...	...	...	|	|	1200	...	...	...	|	...	...	2230	...
Kaunas **1810** § d.	...	...	|	...	...	|	...	...	|	...	...	...	...	...	...	...	...	|	|	1317	...	...	...	|	...	...	0005	...
Šeštokai ⊞ ◐ § d.	...	...	|	...	...	|	...	...	|	...	...	...	...	...	...	...	...	|	|	1448	1508	...	...	|	...	...	|	...
Suwałki d.	...	...	|	...	...	|	0501	...	|	0730	...	0925	...	1058e	...	...	...	|	|	...	1529	1720	...	|	2048	...	|	...
Sokółka d.	...	...	0537	...	...	0621	0638	...	0732	0904	...	1058	...	1303e	...	...	...	1515	1659	...	1705	1857	...	2048	2227	...	|	...
Białystok a.	...	...	0620	...	...	...	0720	...	0821	0945	...	1136	...	1345e	...	...	...	1556	...	...	1746	1935	...	2132	2305	...	0230	...
Białystok d.	0500	0600	...	0700	...	...	...	0800	...	1000	...	...	1200	1400	1600	1655	...	...	...	...	1800	...	2000	...	2320	...	|	...
Warszawa Wschodnia a.	0720	0820	...	0916	...	...	...	1020	...	1220	...	...	1421	1620	1812	1920	...	...	...	...	2021	...	2217	...	0148	...	|	...
Warszawa Centralna a.	0734	0830	...	0935	...	...	...	1030	...	1230	...	...	1431	1635	1840	1940	...	...	...	...	2030	...	2226	...	0200	...	0500	...

A – ①③⑤ (also Dec. 20, 22, 27, 29, May 1, 8, 15, 22, 29, June 5, 12; not Dec. 21, 23, 28, 30) 🚌 run by PKP InterCity. [R].
B – ②④⑥ (also Dec. 21, 23, 28, 30, May 2, 9, 16, 23, 30, June 6, 13; not Dec. 22, 24, 29, 31) 🚌 run by PKP InterCity. [R].
L – From Bielsko Biała June 19 - Aug. 30; from Suwałki June 20 - Aug. 31: [12] Bielsko Biała - Warszawa - Suwałki and v.v.
N – [12] Kraków - Warszawa - Białystok - Suwałki and v.v.
P – [12] Katowice - Warszawa - Białystok and v.v.
S – [12] Wrocław - Częstochowa - Warszawa - Białystok and v.v.
T – [12] Szczecin - Poznań - Warszawa - Białystok and v.v.
V – ①–⑤ (not Dec. 25, Jan. 1).
W – To/from Ełk (Table **1045**).
b – From/to Bydgoszcz (Table **1020**).
c – June 19 - Aug. 30.
e – June 20 - Aug. 31.
g – From/to Częstochowa (Table **1088**).
§ – Lithuanian time (Polish time +1 hour).
‡ – Belarus time (Polish time +1 hour).
◧ – ⊞ at Szypliszki (Poland) / Kalvarija (Lithuania).
◐ – ⊞ at Trakiszki / Mockava; ticketing point is Mockava.

OLSZTYN - EŁK - BIAŁYSTOK 1045

km		◇ 2	51106 🚌	81502 Z	◇ 2		◇ 2	◇ 2	51104 W	◇2 C	◇ 2	61113 A	◇ 2	81104 B	
0	**Olsztyn** d.	...	...	0411	...	...	0850	0943	1041	...	...	1425	1552	1827	...
120	Giżycko d.	...	...	0614	...	...	1116	|	1246	...	...	1637	|	2028	...
167	Ełk a.	...	...	0703	...	...	1205	1314	1332	...	...	1723	1920	2124	...
167	Ełk d.	0541	0540	0715	0756	...	...	...	1344	1413	1620	1735	...	2136	...
	Suwałki a.	|	|	|	|	...	...	...	|	|	|	1930	...	|	...
271	**Białystok** a.	0721	0740	0840	0941	...	...	...	1508	1548	1755	...	...	2258	...

	◇ 2	◇ 2	18105 B	16112 A		15105 W	◇ 2	◇ 2	◇2 C	◇ 2	18503 Z	15107 🚌		
Białystok d.	0526	...	0648	...	...	1240	1415	...	1700	1805	1910	2015	...	...
Suwałki d.	|	...	|	0820	...	|	|	...	|	|	|	|	...	...
Ełk a.	0706	...	0812	1013	...	1410	1601	...	1840	1942	2031	2210	...	...
Ełk d.	...	0747	0824	1028	...	1422	...	1625	...	...	2052	...	...	...
Giżycko d.	...	|	0919	1116	...	1509	...	1718	...	...	2149	...	...	...
Olsztyn a.	...	1110	1117	1316	...	1700	...	1926	...	...	2339	...	...	...

A – [12] Wrocław - Poznań - Olsztyn - Ełk - Suwałki and v.v.
B – [12] and ✕ Szczecin - Olsztyn - Ełk - Białystok and v.v.
C – ①–⑤ (not Dec. 25, Jan. 1).
W – From/to Gdynia (Table **1038**).
Z – From/to Szczecin on dates in Table **1038**.
◇ – Stopping train.

WARSZAWA - BREST 1050

km		◇2 C	◇ 2		81201 B	◇ 2	◇ 2	◇ 2	◇2 C	409 A	◇ 2	61110 w	12 ⊗	◇ 2	◇ 2	◇ D 2	◇ 2	10 ⊗	10101 G	10105 q	◇ 2	◇	◇ 2	◇ 2	116 ⊗	◇ 2	◇ 2	441
0	**Warszawa** Centralna d.	...	...	...	0610	...	...	0804r	...	...	...	1130	...	...	1255r	...	...	1555	1630	1730	...	1750	...	1857r	2100	2057r	2257r	2300
5	**Warszawa** Wschodnia d.	...	...	...	0630	...	...	0813	...	...	...	1139	1300	...	1304	...	...	1605	1640	1739	...	1801	...	1906	2110	2106	2306	2353
93	Siedlce d.	...	...	...	0732	...	...	0948	...	...	...	1244	1400	...	1427	*1442*	...	1705	1740	1838	...	1937	...	2029	2216	2229	0029	⊗
121	Łuków d.	0530	0630	...	0752	0830	...	1019	1030	1115	1230	1303	|	1430	...	1530	1630	1727	1800	1858	...	2008	2030	...	2217	...	...	0122
173	Biała Podlaska d.	0622	0722	...	0837	0922	...	...	1122	|	1322	1338	|	1522	...	1622	1722	|	1845	1945	...	...	2122	...	2321	...	...	|
210	Terespol ⊞ a.	0709	0809	...	0925	1009	1123	...	1209	1235	1409	1415	1525	1609	...	1708	1809	1842	1932	2035	2200	...	...	...	0003	...	...	0238
217	**Brest** ⊞ ‡ a.	...	...	...	...	...	1244	...	...	1504	...	...	1741	...	...	...	...	2058	...	...	2318	...	...	...	0222	...	...	0516
	Moskva **1950** a.	...	...	...	...	...	...	...	...	0805	...	...	1033	...	...	...	...	1145	...	...	...	...	...	...	1954	...	...	2035

	440	◇ 2	115 ⊗	◇ 2	◇ 2	10106 G	9 ⊗	◇ 2	◇ 2	◇ 2	◇ 2	10102 C	◇ 2	◇2 C	11 ⊗	408 A	16110 w	◇ 2	10502 ⑦	◇ 2	◇ 2	◇ 2	18200 B	◇ 2	◇2 C	◇ 2	◇ 2	
Moskva **1950** d.	0800	...	1027	...	...	...	1650	...	...	...	...	...	...	...	2109	2344	...	...	...	...	...	...	...	...	...	...	...	...
Brest ⊞ ‡ d.	2115	...	0240	...	...	...	0532	...	...	0750	...	...	...	...	1223	1440	...	...	..	...	...	...	...	1833	...	...	...	...
Terespol ⊞ d.	2113	...	0238	...	...	0415	0530	0652	...	0708	0847	0915	...	1152	1248	1438	1500	1542	1620	1752	...	...	1905	1751	1952	...	...	...
Biała Podlaska d.	|	...	0318	...	...	0500	0605	0740	...	...	0932	1001	...	1240	|	|	1537	1630	1704	1840	...	...	1953	...	2040	...	...	...
Łuków d.	2225	...	0403	...	0457	0553	0646	0840	0858	...	1032	1054	...	1340	|	1602	1618	1730	1756	1940	1952	...	2048	...	2140	2200	...	...
Siedlce d.	⊗	0339	0426	0451	0530	0613	0709	...	0931	...	...	1113	1341	...	1418	...	1637	...	1819	...	2024	2045	2112	...	...	2232	2240	...
Warszawa Wschodnia a.	2338	0502	0534	0613	0641	0716	0814	...	1104	...	...	1210	1503	...	1514	...	1741	...	1926	...	...	2208	2212	...	...	...	0009	...
Warszawa Centralna a.	0101	0512r	0546	0622r	0650	0724	0835	...	1113r	...	...	1229	1512r	...	...	...	1750	...	1935	...	...	2217r	2240	...	...	...	0018r	...

A – VLTAVA – 🛏 1, 2 cl. Moskva - Praha and v.v. [2] Terespol - Łuków - Katowice and v.v. (for additional cars see Table **95**).
B – [12] Szczecin/Zielona Góra - Poznań - Warszawa - Terespol and v.v.
C – ①–⑥ (not Dec. 25, Jan. 1).
D – ①–⑤ (not Dec. 25, Jan. 1).
G – ①–⑤ (not Dec. 24, 25, Jan. 1).
p – [12] Kraków - Warszawa - Terespol.
q – Not Dec. 25, Jan. 1.
r – Warszawa **Śródmieście** (adjacent to Centralna).
w – From/to Wrocław (Table **1090**).
◇ – Stopping train.
‡ – Belarus time (Polish time +1 hour).
⊗ – Conveys only sleeping car passengers to/from Brest and points east thereof. For composition and days of running see **International** section (Tables **24/56/94**).

1055 WARSZAWA - LUBLIN - CHEŁM

For Warszawa - Lublin - Yahodyn - Kyïv sleeping car services, see Table **1700**

km		TLK	TLK	TLK	TLK	TLK	83104	TLK	52108	TLK	TLK	
		81200	13109	52104	12101	52102	83105	8316	52109	8210/1	52100	
		12201	22109	52105		52103		1217	Ⓑ	[R]✕	52101	
		H	C	b	J	b	K	p	F	R	b	
0	**Warszawa** Centralna d.	0620	0655	0915	1100	1255	1515	...	1655	1755	1855	...
5	**Warszawa** Wschodnia d.	0655	0704	0924	1109	1305	1524	1649	1705	1815	1904	...
125	Puławy Miasto d.	0832	0844	1105	1250	1451	1703	1822	1853	1944	2055	...
175	**Lublin** a.	0907	0920	1140	1325	1526	1738	1856	1930	2020	2130	...
175	**Lublin** d.	...	0940	...	*1458*	*1558*	*1758*f	*1858*	1933	...	*2306*	...
249	Chełm a.	...	1035	...	*1611*	*1711*	*1912*f	*2011*	2029	...	*0019*	...

	TLK	TLK	TLK	25108	38104	TLK	TLK	TLK	TLK	TLK	
	21100	25100	2810/1	25109	38105	28102	21102	25104	22108	21200	
		25101	[R]✕	①–⑥		28103	[R]✕	25105	31108	18200	
	J	b	R	F	K	b	Ⓑt	b	C	H	
Chełm d.	...	*0400*j	...	0654	...	*1050*	*1220*	...	1648	...	...
Lublin a.	...	*0512*j	...	0751	...	*1202*	*1332*	...	1743	...	...
Lublin d.	0505	0545	0700	0755	0950	1200	1350	1625	1800	2005	...
Puławy Miasto d.	0541	0622	0735	0831	1027	1236	1426	1701	1836	2040	...
Warszawa Wschodnia a.	0714	0811	0912	1011	1211	1411	1612	1836	2011	2230	...
Warszawa Centralna a.	0723	0820	0935	1020	1220	1420	1621	1845	2020	2300	...

FOR NOTES SEE TABLE 1058

1056 PRZEMYŚL - LVIV / WARSZAWA - RAVA RUSKA - LVIV

km			13109	7310	7310	83102
			52/107	52/107	52	35
			C	B	D	M
	Warszawa C. **1058** d.	...	0645	...	...	...
	Kraków Gł. **1075** d.	...	|	1301	1301	2234
0	**Przemyśl** d.	...	1917	1917	1917	0247
13	Medyka 🏛 d.	...	|	|	|	|
20	Mostiska II 🏛 ‡ d.	...	2222	2222	2222	0451
98	**Lviv** ‡ a.	...	2344	2344	2344	0603
	Chernivtsi **1720** a.	...	|	|	|	...
	Kyïv **1750** a.	...	|	|	1018	...
	Odesa **1750** a.	...	1331	1331	...	...

	108/5	2108/51	51	36	
	31108	37102	37102	38102	
	C	B	D	M	
Odesa **1750** d.	1813	1813	...	...	...
Kyïv **1750** d.	|	|	2042	...	...
Chernivtsi **1720** d.	|	|	|	...	...
Lviv ‡ d.	0719	0719	0719	2359	...
Mostiska II 🏛 ‡ d.	0937	0937	0937	0145	...
Medyka 🏛 d.	|	|	|	|	...
Przemyśl a.	0933	0933	0933	0117	...
Kraków Gł. **1075** a.	|	1527	1527	0514	...
Warszawa C. **1058** a.	2029	...	...	...	...

		52108
	13109	52109
	Q	F V
		Ⓑ
Warszawa Cent. d.	0655	1655
Warszawa Wsch. d.	0704	1705
Lublin a.	0920	1930
Lublin d.	0940	1933
Rejowiec a.	1019	2012
Rejowiec d.	*1100*	*2100*
Zamość a.	*1155*	*2155*
Zawada a.	*1210*	*2215*

	25108	
	25109	31108
	F V	Q
	①–⑥	
Zawada d.	*0555*	*1535*
Zamość d.	*0615*	*1550*
Rejowiec a.	*0715*	*1645*
Rejowiec d.	0711	1704
Lublin a.	0751	1743
Lublin d.	0755	1800
Warszawa Wsch. a.	1011	2011
Warszawa Cent. a.	1020	2020

FOR NOTES SEE TABLE 1058

1058 WARSZAWA and LUBLIN - PRZEMYŚL

km		13109		Ex		83104		IC	13511	
		13108		5310		83105		1309		
		C		[R]A		K		[R]P	W	
0	**Warszawa** Centralna d.	0655	...	...	...	1515	...	...	2245	...
5	**Warszawa** Wschodnia d.	0704	...	1403	...	1524	...	1703	2254	...
	Warszawa Centralna d.	|	...	1415	...	|	...	1715	|	...
175	**Lublin** d.	0932	...	|	...	1750	...	|	0133	...
278	Stalowa Wola Rozwadów d.	1129	...	**k**	...	1946	...	**k**	0337	...
	Rzeszów **1075** d.	|	...	1922	...	|	...	2222	|	...
353	Przeworsk **1075** d.	1256	...	2007	...	2115	...	2305	|	...
	Rzeszów **1075** a.	|	...	|	...	|	...	|	0555	...
	Zagórz **1078** a.	|	...	|	...	|	...	|	1030	...
368	Jarosław **1075** d.	1311	...	2022	...	2134	...	2320	...	...
403	**Przemyśl** **1075** a.	1343	...	2055	...	2204	...	2352	...	...

	IC	38104		Ex		31108		31510	
	3108	38104		3510		31109			
	[R]S	K		[R]A		C		X	
Przemyśl **1075** d.	0411	0522	...	0823	...	1335	...	...	...
Jarosław **1075** d.	0440	0547	...	0852	...	1406	...	...	...
Zagórz **1078** d.	|	|	...	|	...	|	...	1735	...
Rzeszów **1075** d.	|	|	...	|	...	|	...	2151	...
Przeworsk **1075** d.	0453	0610	...	0905	...	1420	...	|	...
Rzeszów **1075** d.	0533	|	...	0946	...	|	...	|	...
Stalowa Wola Rozwadów d.	**k**	0754	...	**k**	...	1602	...	0027	...
Lublin d.	|	0950	...	|	...	1800	...	0248	...
Warszawa Centralna a.	1055	|	...	1455	...	|	...	|	...
Warszawa Wschodnia a.	1107	1211	...	1507	...	2011	...	0506	...
Warszawa Centralna a.	...	1220	...	...	...	2020	...	0515	...

A – [12] and ✕ Gdynia - Warszawa - Kraków - Przemyśl and v.v.
B – From Wrocław Dec. 25, 26, Jan. 1 - 9, June 25 - Aug. 28; from Odesa Dec. 26, 27, Jan. 2 - 10; June 26 - Aug. 28: ▬ 2 cl. Wrocław - Kraków - Odesa and v.v.
C – [12] Warszawa - Przemyśl / Chełm and v.v. 🛏 2 cl. Warszawa - Odesa and v.v.
D – *TLK* 🛏 2 cl. Wrocław - Kraków - Przemyśl - Kyïv and v.v. Conveys 🛏 1, 2 cl. Praha / Wien - Kyïv on dates in Table **96**.
F – *TLK* [12] Bydgoszcz - Lublin - Rejowiec - Chełm and v.v.
H – 🛏 1, 2 cl., ▬ 2 cl. and [2] Lublin - Warszawa - Poznan - Szczecin and v.v.
J – ①–⑤ (not Dec. 24 - Jan. 1, Apr. 5, May 3).
K – *TLK* [12] Szczecin / Kostrzyn - Bydgoszcz - Warszawa - Przemyśl and v.v.
M – 🛏 2 cl. Wrocław - Kraków - Lviv and v.v.

P – ⑤⑦: [12] and ✕ Warszawa - Kraków - Przemyśl.
Q – 🚌 Lublin - Zawada and v.v.
R – From / to Szczecin (Table **1010**).
S – ①⑥: [12] and ✕ Przemyśl - Kraków - Warszawa.
T – 🛏 2 cl. Wrocław - Kraków - Lviv and v.v.
V – 🚌 Rejowiec - Zawada and v.v.
W – June 19 - Aug. 30.
X – June 20 - Aug. 31.

b – From / to Bydgoszcz (Table **1020**).
f – ①–⑤ (not Dec. 25, Jan. 1).
h – Not Dec. 25, Jan. 1.
j – ①–⑥ (not Dec. 25, Jan. 1).
k – Via Kraków (Tables **1065** / **1075**).
p – From / to Kołobrzeg.
q – Not Dec. 25, Jan. 1.
t – Not Dec. 24, 25, 31, Jan. 1, Apr. 4.
‡ – Ukrainian (East European) time.

1060 WARSZAWA - KATOWICE - GLIWICE and BIELSKO BIAŁA

km		54502	EC103	IC		13101	IC	14100	EC110	54110	TLK	EC105	IR	54112	IC	54100	54101	IC	IC		IC	IC	54102	407	TLK	
		54503	14001	1607	13101	44101	1410	14101	14005	54111	1412	14003	14123	54113	1611	54101	43103	1401	1609	14109	1415	1403	54103	14011	53202	
			[R]✕	[R]			1411		[R]✕		[R]✕	[R]✕	14122		[R]✕			[R]✕	[R]		[R]✕	[R]✕			[R]	
		A	H	P	①–⑥	①–⑥	[R]✕	p	J	b	Ⓑj	E	k	q				Ⓑy	✕					C	B	
	Gdynia Gł. **1030** d.	2050	...	...	...	...	...	...	...	...	...	...	...	...	...	0732	0732	...	...	...	...	...	1134	...	1854	...
0	**Warszawa** Wschodnia § d.	|	0633	0708	...	...	0808	0822	0923	...	1008	1233	1323	1233	1408	|	|	1513	1610	1633	1713	1913	|	2057	2332	...
5	**Warszawa** Centralna § d.	◐	0645	0725	...	...	0825	0850	0945	...	1025	1245	1335	1250	1425	◐	◐	1525	1625	1650	1725	1925	◐	2110	2345	...
*194	**Łódź** Fabryczna d.	0348r	|	|	0615	0615	|	|	|	0940r	|	|	|	|	|	1417r	1417r	|	|	|	|	|	1819r	|	|	...
*167	Koluszki § d.	|	|	|	|	|	|	1006	|	|	|	|	|	1404	|	|	|	|	|	1801	|	|	|	|	|	...
*128	Piotrków Trybunalski § d.	0500	|	|	0710	0710	|	1036	|	1050	|	|	|	1435	|	1526	1526	|	|	1833	|	|	1926	|	|	...
*43	**Częstch Ob** ¶ **1020** § d.	0612	|	|	0826	0841	|	1139	|	1150	|	|	|	1539	|	1637	1647	|	|	1939	|	|	2029	|	|	...
259	Zawiercie **1020** d.	0653	|	0917	0900	0914	1020	1214	|	1225	1227	|	1608	1614	1616	1712	1721	1716	1817	2014	1920	2128	2104	|	0328	...
294	Sosnowiec Gł. **1020** a.	0728	0859	0943	|	0942	1044	1243	1159	1254	1254	1457	1635	1643	1640	1739	|	1742	1843	2042	1943	2148	2132	2340	0357	...
302	**Katowice** **1020** a.	0740	0911	0954	|	0952	1054	1254	1211	1306	1305	1508	1645	1654	1651	1751	|	1754	1854	2054	1954	2159	2144	2352	0408	...
	Kraków Gł. a.	|	...	|	1055	...	|	...	...	|	...	...	...	...	|	...	1919	|	|	...	...	|	...	...	|	...
	Gliwice **1075** a.	|	...	1025	...	...	|	...	...	|	...	...	...	...	1723	...	...	|	1926	...	...	|	...	...	|	...
	Wrocław Gł. **1075** a.	|	...	1230	...	...	|	...	...	|	...	...	...	...	1925	...	...	|	2130	...	...	|	...	...	|	...
357	**Bielsko Biała** **1077** a.	0856	...	...	...	...	1200	...	...	1415	...	...	...	...	...	...	...	1900	...	...	...	2305	...	...	0532	...

	406	IC	45100	IC		IC	Ex	IR	34102	45102	45112	IC	EC104	45110	41100	TLK	EC115	IC		44100	EC102	IC	45502	TLK		
	41010	4102	45101	6108	41108	4100	4114	41120	45102	45103	45113	6110	41002	45111	41101	4112	41004	4110	31100	31100	41000	6106	45503	35702		
		[R]✕		[R]		[R]	[R]✕	41121				[R]	[R]✕			[R]✕	[R]✕	[R]	🍷	🍷	[R]✕	[R]✕		[R]		
	C	Q		✕		✕		k			q	✕	E	b	p	Ⓑy	J	🍷	Ⓑ	Ⓑ	H		A	B		
Bielsko Biała **1077** d.	...	0507	...	...	...	0707	...	...	...	...	...	...	...	1451	...	...	...	1707	...	...	...	...	2155	...	...	...
Wrocław Gł. **1075** d.	...	|	...	0439	...	|	...	...	...	...	...	0839	...	|	...	...	...	|	...	...	...	1739	|	...	...	...
Gliwice **1075** d.	...	|	...	0636	...	|	...	...	...	...	...	1035	...	|	...	...	...	|	...	...	...	1936	|	...	...	...
Kraków Gł. d.	...	|	...	|	...	|	...	...	0905	...	...	|	...	|	...	...	...	|	1715	...	...	|	|	2244	...	...
Katowice **1020** d.	0420	0609	0613	0709	0647	0809	0909	0925	|	1010	1047	1109	1300	1555	1447	1500	1600	1809	|	1810	1900	2009	2255	0047	...	...
Sosnowiec Gł. **1020** d.	0431	0619	0625	0719	0658	0819	0919	0935	|	1022	1058	1119	1310	1616	1458	1511	1610	1819	|	1820	1910	2019	2302	0059	...	...
Zawiercie **1020** d.	|	0643	0656	0743	0729	0842	0943	1001	1046	1052	1129	1143	|	1646	1529	1540	|	1843	1856	1848	|	2044	2331	|	...	...
Częstch Ob ¶ **1020** § d.	|	|	0734	|	0804	|	|	|	1140	1140	1204	|	|	1724	1604	|	|	|	1940	1940	|	|	0007	0158	...	...
Piotrków Trybunalski § d.	|	|	0849	|	0916	|	|	|	1252	1252	1314	|	|	1836	1715	|	|	|	2050	2050	|	|	0118	|	...	...
Koluszki § d.	|	|	|	|	0944	|	|	|	|	|	1344	|	|	|	1743	|	|	|	|	|	|	|	|	|	...	...
Łódź Fabryczna a.	|	|	0950r	|	|	|	|	|	1354r	1354r	|	|	|	1940r	|	|	|	|	2142	2142	|	|	0225r	|	...	...
Warszawa Centralna § a.	0710	0838	◐	0938	1100	1034	1140	1229	◐	◐	1500	1338	1522	...	1900	1740	1824	2040	...	...	2124	2238	◐	0440	...	...
Warszawa Wschodnia § a.	0722	0850	|	0949	1112	1047	1152	1243	|	|	1517	1350	1534	...	1932	1752	1837	2052	...	...	2142	2250	|	0452	...	...
Gdynia Gł. **1030** a.	...	...	1724	...	...	...	...	...	2135	2135	...	...	...	...	...	...	...	...	...	...	...	...	0959	1006	...	...

A – ⑤⑦ (daily June 19 - Aug. 31): 🛏 1, 2 cl., ▬ 2 cl. and [12] Gdynia - Katowice - Bielsko Biała and v.v.
B – 🛏 1, 2 cl., ▬ 2 cl. and [2] Gdynia - Katowice - Bielsko Biała and v.v.
C – CHOPIN – 🛏 1, 2 cl., ▬ 2 cl. and [2] Warszawa - Bratislava / Budapest / Praha / Wien and v.v.
E – SOBIESKI – [12] and ✕ Warszawa - Zebrzydowice 🏛 - Wien and v.v.
H – POLONIA – [12] and ✕ Warszawa - Zebrzydowice 🏛 - Wien - Villach and v.v.
J – PRAHA – [12] and ✕ Warszawa - Zebrzydowice 🏛 - Praha and v.v.
L – ①–⑥ (not Dec. 25, Jan. 1).
P – ①–⑥ (not Dec. 25, Jan. 1, Apr. 5).
Q – ①–⑥ (not Dec. 25, 26, Jan. 1, 2, Apr. 5).

b – To / from Bydgoszcz (Table **1020**).
j – Also Dec. 26; not Dec. 24, 25, 31, Apr. 4.
k – Not Dec. 25, 26, 27, Jan. 1, 2, 3, Apr. 4, 5, May 1, 2, 3, June 3, 4, 5, 6.

p – From / to Białystok (Table **1040**).
q – From / to Olsztyn (Table **1030**).
r – Łódź **Kaliska**.
y – Not Dec. 24, 25, 31, Jan. 1, Apr. 4.

* – Distance from Zawiercie.
◐ – Via Bydgoszcz (Table **1020**).
¶ – Full name is Częstochowa Osobowa.
§ – For Warszawa - Częstochowa see Table **1088**.

WARSZAWA - KRAKÓW 1065

Via CMK high-speed line ▲

km	For trains via Kielce (including night trains) see Table **1067**	Ex	IC	IR	Ex	IC	IC	IR		IC	Ex	IR	Ex	Ex	IR	IC	Ex	Ex	IR	IC	IC		
		1311	**1301**	**13120**	**1313**	**1307**	**5307**	**13122**	**1317**	**5303**	**53401**	**13126**	**5311**	**1315**	**13128**	**1303**	**1309**	**5313**	**13124**	**1319**	**5301**		
		13411		**13121**	**13413**		**13407**	**13123**				**13127**	**5310**	**13415**	**13129**			**83415**	**13125**	**13001**	**5300**		
		🅁✕	🅁✕	🍷2	🅁✕	🅁✕	🅁✕	🍷2	🅁✕	🅁✕	🅁✕	🍷2	🅁✕	🅁✕	🍷2	🅁✕	🅁✕	🅁✕	🍷2	🅁✕	🅁✕		
		K		y	Z	A	m	y	⑤f	⑧k	⑥wz	y	E	G Z	r y		g	q	y	F			
	Gdynia Gł. **1030** d.	...	...	...	...	...	0531j	...	...	0725	0725	...	0923	...	...	...	...	1325	...	...	1523	...	...
0	**Warszawa** Wschodnia d.	0603	0658	0712	0758	0903	0953	1018	1103	1157	1157	1248	1403	1503	1518	1602	1703	1802	1758	1918	1958	...	...
5	**Warszawa** Centralna d.	0615	0715	0730	0815	0915	1015	1030	1115	1215	1215	1300	1415	1515	1530	1615	1715	1815	1830	1930	2015	...	...
297	**Kraków** Gł. a.	0847	0943	1029	1045	1145	1244	1333	1344	1444	1444	1608	1647	1745	1823	1842	1945	2045	2139	2229	2244	...	...

	IC	IC	IR	IC	Ex	IR	Ex	Ex	IR	Ex	IC	Ex	Ex	IR	Ex	IC	IC	IC	IR	Ex	Ex		
	3118	**3500**	**31120**	**3102**	**3108**	**31126**	**3114**	**3512**	**31122**	**3510**	**3506**	**3116**	**31414**	**31124**	**35400**	**3502**	**3100**	**3106**	**31128**	**3112**	**3110**		
	31000	**3501**	**31121**			**31127**		**38414**	**31123**	**3511**	**31406**			**31125**					**31129**	**31412**	**31410**		
	🅁✕	🅁✕	🍷2	🅁✕	🅁✕	🍷2	🅁✕	🅁✕	🍷2	🅁✕	🅁✕	🅁✕	🅁✕	🍷2	🅁✕	🅁✕	🅁✕	🅁✕	🍷2	🅁✕	🅁✕		
	F		y		h	r y	B	q	y	E	m	⑤f	⑦b	y	⑦pz	A		⑧k	y	Z	K		
Kraków Gł. d.	0521	0614	0625	0714	0814	0825	0914	1014	1120	1214	1414	1511	1514	1523	1614	1614	1714	1800	1824	1914	2014	...	...
Warszawa Centralna a.	0825	0848	0935	0946	1055	1125	1150	1250	1430	1451	1647	1750	1750	1840	1850	1850	1947	2050	2140	2151	2250	...	...
Warszawa Wschodnia a.	0832	0855	0942	0953	1102	1132	1157	1257	1436	1458	1654	1757	1757	1847	1857	1857	1954	2057	2147	2158	2257	...	...
Gdynia Gł. **1030** a.	...	1331	...	...	...	...	...	1750	...	1935	2123t	...	...	...	2329	2329	...	...	...	...	...	...	...

A – ①–⑥ (not Dec. 25, Jan. 1, Apr. 5, May 1, June 4).
B – ②–⑤ (not Dec. 25, Jan. 1, Apr. 6, June 3, 4).
E – [12] and ✕ Gdynia - Kraków - Przemyśl and v.v.
F – ①–⑤ (not Dec. 24, 25, 28, 29, 30, 31, Jan. 1, Apr. 5, May 3, June 3, 4).
G – ①–⑤ (also Jan. 2, not Dec. 24, Jan. 1, Apr. 5, June 3).
K – Conveys [12] Warszawa - Krynica and v.v. on dates in Table **1078**.
Z – Conveys [12] Warszawa - Kraków - Zakopane and v.v.; for dates of running see Table **1066**.

b – Also Jan. 1, Apr. 5, May 3, June 3; not Apr. 4, May 2.
f – Not Dec. 25, Jan. 1, Apr. 30, June 4.
g – To Przemyśl on ⑤⑦ (also Dec. 23, 30, Apr. 5, May 3, June 2; not Dec. 25, Jan. 1, Apr. 4, May 2, June 4).
h – From Przemyśl on ①⑥ (also Dec. 24, 31, Apr. 6, May 4, June 3; not Dec. 26, Jan. 2, Apr. 5, May 3, June 5).
j – ①–⑥ (not Dec. 25, 26, Jan. 1, Apr. 5).
k – Not Dec. 25, 31, Apr. 4, 30, June 3.
m – Not Dec. 25.
p – Also Jan. 1, Apr. 5, June 4; not Apr. 4.

q – From / to Kołobrzeg on dates in Table **1015**.
r – To / from Rzeszów.
t – ⑧ (not Dec. 24, 25, 31, Apr. 4).
w – Also Dec. 31, Apr. 30, June 3; not May 1.
y – Not Dec. 25, Apr. 4.
z – To / from Zakopane on dates in Table **1066**.

▲ – Ticketing route is via Idzikowice.

KRAKÓW and KATOWICE - ZAKOPANE 1066

Ex trains convey ✕

km		**13500**	◇	**83500**	◇	*TLK*	◇	🚂		*IC*✕	◇	*IR*	**13105**	**7311**	◇	*IC*	◇	*TLK*✕		◇		
		13501	2	**83501**	2	**53702**	2	A		**13413**	2	**63128**	**13505**	**33411**	2	**53401**	2	**13415**		2		
		L		C		🅁F		❖		🅁K		2 P	L	⑥p		🅁G		🅁⑤f				
	Warszawa Cent **1065 1067** d.	2140	...	...	...	0030	...	...	...	0815	...	...	0655	...	...	1215	...	1515	...	...	...	...
	Katowice **1060** d.	|	...	0213	...	0435	...	...	...	|	...	1018	|	1130	...	|	...	|	...	...	...	...
0	**Kraków** Gł. d.	0312	...	|	0528	0650	0725	...	...	1049	1131	1157	1228	1329	1444	1453	1620	1750	...	2226	...	...
5	Kraków Płaszów d.	0332	...	|	0541	0718	0738	...	...	1107	1145	1210	1251	1354	1457	1515	1643	1821	...	2239	...	...
68	Sucha Beskidzka d.	0446	0516	0615	0711	0840	0901	...	...	1210	1308	1322	1414	1517	1622	1623	1821	1924	...	2359	...	...
103	Chabówka a.	0528	0601	0657	0752	0919	0940	...	...	1255	1349	1407	1454	1556	1713	1720	...	2009	...	...	...	...
103	Chabówka d.	0541	0615	0707	0806	0929	0954	1009	...	1305	1403	1419	1507	1606	1727	1732	...	2019	...	...	...	...
126	Nowy Targ d.	0610	0647	0737	0836	1002	1028	|	...	1332	1432	1445	1543	1654	1757	1808	...	2051	...	...	...	...
147	**Zakopane** a.	0632	0711	0804	0900	1028	1052	1136	...	1352	1459	1512	1616	1713	1825	1830	...	2112	...	...	...	...

	◇	◇	◇		◇	*TLK*✕	*Ex*✕	**33410**	**35400**	*IC*	**31504**	◇	🚂	◇	*IR*	*IC*		◇	**38500**	*TLK*	**31500**	
	2	2	2		2	**31414**	**31414**	**3710**	🅁	**35400**	**31104**	2	A	2	**36130**	**31412**		2	**38501**	**35702**	**31501**	
						🅁⑦q	🅁⑦q	⑦p	H	🅁H	L		❖		2 Q	🅁K			D	🅁F	L	
Zakopane d.	...	...	0405	...	0940	1111	1117	1147	1201	1229	1220	1238	1339	1432	1441	1609	...	1746	1805	1845	2118	...
Nowy Targ d.	...	...	0437	...	0959	1131	1137	1207	1221	1249	1244	1259	|	1455	1509	1629	...	1807	1835	1915	2151	...
Chabówka a.	...	...	0457	...	1029	1153	1203	1233	1256	1319	1310	1330	1505	1524	1541	1654	...	1836	1909	1941	2217	...
Chabówka d.	...	...	0511	...	1051	1207	1216	1243	1306	1329	1327	1351	...	1538	1559	1704	...	1848	1920	1953	2227	...
Sucha Beskidzka d.	0451	0610	0610	...	1134	1321	1312	1356	1410	1439	1423	1436	...	1625	1650	1749	...	1933	2019	2052	2321	...
Kraków Płaszów a.	0607	0735	0730	...	1305	1425	1427	1507	1524	1546	1532	1553	...	1741	1754	1852	...	2048	|	2157	0030	...
Kraków Gł. a.	0620	0754	0746	...	1318	1459	1455	1538	1552	1608	1556	1605	...	1754	1806	1909	...	2101	|	2229	0053	...
Katowice **1060** a.	...	...	...	...	...	|	|	1729	|	|	|	...	...	...	1943	|	...	...	0010	0025	|	...
Warszawa Cent **1065 1067** a.	...	...	...	...	...	1750	1755	...	1855	1850	2105	...	...	...	...	2151	...	...	...	0440	0556	...

A – July 12, 19, Aug. 9, 16, 23, 30 (subject to confirmation).
C – June 19 - Aug. 30: 🛏 1, 2 cl., ▬ 2 cl. and [12] Szczecin - Zakopane (Tables **1010**, **1080**).
D – June 20 - Aug. 31: 🛏 1, 2 cl., ▬ 2 cl. and [12] Zakopane - Szczecin (Tables **1010**, **1080**).
F – 🛏 1, 2 cl., ▬ 2 cl. and [2] Gdynia - Warszawa - Katowice - Kraków - Zakopane and v.v.
G – ⑥: [12] Gdynia Gł. - Warszawa - Kraków - Zakopane.
H – ⑦ (also Jan. 1, Apr. 5, June 4; not Apr. 4): [12] Zakopane - Kraków - Warszawa - Gdynia Gł.
L – For dates of running see Table **1067**.
K – ⑥⑦ Dec. 13 - Mar. 31, daily Apr. 1 – 6; ⑥⑦ Apr. 7 – 29, daily Apr. 1 – 6; ⑥⑦ May 5 - June 2; daily June 3 - Oct. 4.

P – ①–⑥ June 26 - Aug. 29: [2] Wrocław (depart 0735) Kraków - Zakopane.
Q – ⑧ June 26 - Aug. 30: [2] Zakopane - Kraków - Wrocław (arrive 2233).

f – Also Dec. 31, Jan. 2, June 2; not Jan. 1.
p – From / to Poznań (Table **1075**).
q – Also Jan. 1, Apr. 5, May 3, June 3; not Apr. 4, May 2.

❖ – Subject to confirmation.
🚂 – Normally hauled by steam locomotive (not guaranteed).

WARSZAWA and LUBLIN - KIELCE - KRAKÓW 1067

km	*For fast trains to Kraków see Table* **1065**			**83203**	*TLK*	*TLK*	*TLK*		**52106**	**53100**		*TLK*	**13106**			*TLK*	**23102**			**13102**	**12112**	**13500**	*TLK*	**26500**		
				53503	**23100**	**23100**	**12104**		**52107**	**53101**		**26100**	**13107**		**12111**	**8316**	**23103**	◇		**13103**	**12113**	**13501**	**53702**	**26501**		
		◇	◇		**23101**	**24101**	**12105**	◇	⑥q		◇	**26101**		◇	①–⑤	**8317**		2	◇				🅁			
		2	2	A			H	2	w	M	2		y	2		E		⑧	2	f		B	G	C		
0	**Warszawa** Wschodnia d.	...	...	0447	...	...	0618	...	0858	1043	...	...	1222	...	1442	1638	...	1628	...	1657	1842	2122	0017	...	...	...
5	**Warszawa** Centralna d.	...	...	0500	...	...	0630	...	0910	1055	...	...	1255	...	1455	1650	...	1640	...	1710	1855	2140	0030	...	...	...
	Lublin d.	...	...	|	0612	0612	|	...	|	|	...	1225	|	...	|	|	1645	|	...	|	|	|	|	2100	...	...
108	Radom d.	...	...	0657	0748	0748	0847	...	1108	1248	...	1358	1451	...	1700	1853	1825	1840	...	1906	2057	2334	|	2234	...	...
149	Skarżysko Kamienna d.	...	...	0747	0841	0841	0939	...	1156	1336	...	1448	1539	...	1750	1944	1913	1936	1940	1955	2146	0023	|	2322	...	...
193	Kielce d.	0535	0718	0831	0927	0940	1019	1220	1237	1422	1431	1544	1625	1814	1830	2025	2003	...	2027	2038	2226	0106	|	0015	...	...
	Katowice a.	0902	|	|	|	1143	...	1552	...	|	1802	|	|	|	...	|	|	...	...	|	...	|	0420	|	...	...
	Częstochowa Stradom d.	...	|	|	...	...	...	...	...	|	...	1748	|	|	...	|	|	...	...	|	...	|	|	0225	...	...
	Wrocław Gł. a.	...	|	|	|	...	...	...	...	|	...	2056	|	|	...	|	|	...	...	|	...	|	|	0534	...	...
325	**Kraków** Gł. a.	...	0930	1034	1104	...	...	...	...	1620	...	...	1824	2033	...	2202	2200	...	...	2238	...	0309	0626	...	...	...
	Zakopane **1066** a.	...	...	...	...	...	...	...	...	...	...	...	...	...	...	...	...	...	...	...	...	0632	1028	...	...	...

		21112	*TLK*	**31102**	**32100**	**31106**	*TLK*	**35100**		**25106**			*TLK*	**38202**	*TLK*	*TLK*		*TLK*	**31500**	**62500**						
		21113	**3816**	**31103**	**32101**	**31107**	**62100**	**35101**		**25107**			**21104**	**35502**	**42100**	**32100**	◇	**35702**	**31501**	**62501**						
	◇		**3817**				**62101**		◇	⑧	◇	◇	**21105**		**32101**	**32101**	2	🅁								
	2		E	f		y		M	2	w	2	2	⑧j	A				G	B	C						
Zakopane **1066** d.	...	...	...	...	...	...	...	...	...	...	...	...	...	...	...	...	...	1845	2118	...	...	...	...	...	...	...
Kraków Gł. d.	...	...	0550	0610	0735	1010	...	1210	...	...	1437	...	...	1710	...	1623	1910	2244	0056	...	...	...	...	...	...	...
Wrocław Gł. d.	...	...	|	|	|	|	0800	|	...	...	|	...	...	|	...	|	|	|	|	2255	...	...	...	...	...	...
Częstochowa Stradom d.	...	...	|	|	|	|	1037	|	...	...	|	...	...	|	...	|	|	|	|	0141	...	...	...	...	...	...
Katowice d.	...	...	|	|	|	*0748*	|	|	1140	...	|	...	...	|	1528	|	|	0047	|	|	...	...	...	...	...	...
Kielce d.	...	0540	0728	0804	0945	1203	1303	1404	1454	1610	1657	1712	1752	1906	1813	1813	2121	|	0252	0404	...	...	...	...	...	...
Skarżysko Kamienna d.	0510	0622	0805	0843	1025	1241	1342	1443	...	1648	...	1756	1828	1947	1849	1849	...	|	0331	0441	...	...	...	...	...	...
Radom d.	0545	0701	0849	0919	1102	1317	1424	1519	...	1724	...	...	1910	2031	1938	1938	...	|	0410	0517	...	...	...	...	...	...
Lublin a.	|	|	|	|	1236	|	1555	|	...	|	...	...	|	|	2114	2114	...	|	|	0645	...	...	...	...	...	...
Warszawa Centralna a.	0735	0845	1042	1105	...	1510	...	1705	...	1915	...	...	2104	2215	...	...	...	0440	0556	...	...	...	...	...	...	...
Warszawa Wschodnia a.	0757	0857	1057	1122	...	1532	...	1717	...	1927	...	...	2117	2227	...	...	...	0452	0622	...	...	...	...	...	...	...

A – From Kołobrzeg until June 19 and from Sept. 1; From Hel June 20 - Aug. 31; To Kołobrzeg until June 18 and from Aug. 31; To Hel June 19 - Aug. 30: 🛏 1, 2 cl. and [12] Kołobrzeg / Hel - Warszawa - Kraków and v.v.
B – From Warszawa June 19 - Aug. 30; from Zakopane June 20 - Aug. 31: [12] Warszawa - Zakopane and v.v.
C – ⑤⑦ (daily June 20 - Aug. 31; also Apr. 5).
E – [12] Kołobrzeg - Warszawa - Kraków and v.v.
G – 🛏 1, 2 cl., ▬ 2 cl. and [2] Gdynia - Warszawa - Katowice - Kraków - Zakopane and v.v.
H – ①–⑥ (not Dec. 25, 26, Jan. 1, 2, Apr. 5).
M – [12] Olsztyn - Warszawa - Kraków and v.v.

f – From / to Terespol (Table **1050**).
j – Not Dec. 24, 25, 31, Jan. 1, Apr. 4.
q – Also Apr. 5.
x – June 20 - Aug. 31.
w – From / to Olsztyn (Table **1030**).
y – From / to Suwałki (Train **1067**).

◇ – Stopping train.

1070 POZNAŃ - WROCŁAW

FOR NOTES SEE TABLE 1075

km					TLK		TLK	TLK				IC						IC			IC			IC	
		449	56200		7310	2	7610	83100	56100	2	83108	1601	56104	83104	2	83102	2	1612	2	84100	1603	16112	56102	1605	83201
		83706	56201		[R] ✕	◇		83101		◇	83109	1600	56105	83105	◇	83103	◇	1613	◇	84510	1602	16113	56103	1604	83510
		D Y	E		Z	h	J	m	n		F	V	q	m p	j	B	h w	[R] V		G	D V	e	m n	D V	S
0	Poznań Gł. d.	0202	0307	...	0547	0645	0725	0935	0940	1000	1035	1121	1140	1235	1346	1435	1512	1530	1615	1735	1820	1835	1945	2121	2252
69	Leszno d.	0300	0408	...	0648	0747	0822	1034	1040	1100	1139	1215	1243	1339	1501	1538	1633	1624	1722	1837	1914	1937	2046	2215	2356
165	Wrocław Gł. a.	0432	0540	...	0820	0919	0950	1203	1220	1255	1320	1338	1420	1518	1650	1720	1808	1749	1856	2020	2034	2119	2220	2339	0135

		IC		IC					IC					IC								TLK			
	38200	6103	65101	6105	61113	2	48100	2	6113	38102	2	38104	65105	6101	38108	65103	2	38100	38106		2	3711	65201	38704	
	38511	6102	65100	6104	61112	◇	48101	◇	6112	38103	◇	38105	65104	6100	38109	65102	◇	38101	38107		◇	[R] ✕	65200	448	
	S	M V	m n	M V	e		G	j	V	B	h w	m	q	V Q	F	n	h w	m	A		h	Z	E	D Y	
Wrocław Gł. d.	0312	0507	0535	0607	0635	0741	0835	0854	1007	1040	1135	1238	1335	1407	1435	1535	1554	1635	1735	...	1935	2035	2340	0024	...
Leszno d.	0452	0628	0707	0728	0811	0913	1010	1039	1128	1212	1312	1411	1509	1528	1612	1707	1740	1813	1911	...	2107	2206	0112	0153	...
Poznań Gł. a.	0555	0725	0812	0825	0912	1032	1111	1155	1225	1312	1422	1512	1613	1625	1715	1807	1857	1915	2011	...	2214	2307	0214	0255	...

1075 WROCŁAW - KATOWICE - KRAKÓW - PRZEMYŚL

km		IR	TLK	TLK	🚌	IR 2	TLK	IR 2	TLK	🚌	IR 2	TLK	Ex	TLK	EC 341	IC	IR 2	TLK	IR 2	TLK	IR 2	TLK	TLK	TLK		
		43120	43100	63100	32111	63120	73102	63136	7310	32106	73124	83100	5311	53108	73000	1309	63128	83110	83120	83102	63136	63200	83200	83206		
		43121	43101	63101		63121	[R] ✕	63137	7311		73125	83101	[R] ✕	53109	[R] 🍷	[R] ✕	63129	83111	83121	83103	63137	63500	83512	449		
		L 2	H			f	Z	f	J		f		K	C	W	T	y		y	35 P	f	N	S	Y		
	Świnoujście 1010 d.	...	...	...	...	...	...	...	...	...	...	...	...	...	...	...	...	...	...	...	...	...	1755c	2043	...	...
	Szczecin Gł. 1010 d.	...	...	...	...	...	...	...	...	...	...	0655	...	...	...	...	...	0915	1050	...	...	...	1955	2235	...	...
	Poznań Gł. 1070 d.	...	...	...	...	...	0512	...	...	...	...	0935	...	...	...	...	...	1200	1335	...	1500	...	2252	0225	...	...
0	**Wrocław** Gł. 1088 d.	...	...	0608	...	0735	0808	0928	1008	...	1135	1208	...	1333	1521	...	1530	1608	1630	1720	1755	2235	0110	0508	...	...
42	Brzeg 1088 d.	...	...	0641	...	0808	0841	1002	1040	...	1207	1241	...	1405	|	...	1602	1640	1703	1753	1825	2310	0149	0539	...	...
82	Opole Gł. 1088 d.	...	...	0707	...	0840	0908	1031	1107	...	1237	1307	...	1432	1614	...	1635	1708	1734	1836	1855	2340	0226	0607	...	...
162	Gliwice 1060 d.	0614	...	0818	...	0946	1018	1138	1218	...	1346	1418	...	1618	1723	...	1742	1818	1842	1948	2002	0052	0345	0718	...	...
190	**Katowice** 1060 a.	0646	...	0850	...	1013	1050	1213	1250	...	1408	1450	...	1650	1754	...	1813	1850	1913	2020	2038	0121	0416	0750	...	...
190	**Katowice** ▲ d.	0653	0720	0905	...	1015	1055	1215	1255	...	1415	1455	...	1655	1757	...	1815	1855	1915	2025	2040	0125	0431	0755	...	...
268	**Kraków** Gł. ▲ a.	0835	0919	1058	...	1200	1248	1356	1448	...	1555	1648	...	1848	1935	...	1955	2048	2100	2218	2224	0316	0629	0948	...	...
268	**Kraków** Gł. 1078 d.	0842	0924	1103	...	1202	1301	1403	1500	...	1612	1702	1720	1853	...	1955	2000x	2057	...	2234	...	0321	0634	...	...	...
273	Kraków Płaszów 1078 d.	0849	0933	1113	...	1211	1310	1408	1510	...	1622	1711	1729	1904	...	2004	2009x	2105	...	|	...	0339	0656	...	...	...
346	Tarnów 1078 d.	0946	1033	1213	...	1258	1412	1510	1611	...	1710	1811	1822	2004	...	2109	2114x	...	...	2334	...	0443	0757	...	...	...
379	Dębica d.	1010	1102	1241	...	1322	1441	1534	1640	1725	1734	1841	1848	2033	...	2137	2142x	...	...	0002	...	0512	0833	...	...	...
426	Rzeszów 1058 d.	1051	1151	1332	...	1417	1532	1618	1731	|	1818	1933	1929	2123	...	2222	2230x	...	...	0048	...	0558	0909	...	...	...
463	Przeworsk 1058 d.	1134	1235	1417	...	...	1615	1702	1815	|	1902	2017	2017	2208	...	2305	...	...	...	|	...	0651	1001	...	...	...
478	Jarosław 1058 d.	1147	1251	1435	1520	...	1631	1716	1831	|	1916	2032	2032	2223	...	2320	...	...	...	|	...	0707	1016	...	...	...
* *	Zamość a.	|	|	|	1910	...	|	|	|	2245	|	|	|	|	...	|	...	...	...	|	...	|	|	...	...	...
513	**Przemyśl** 1058 a.	1224	1325	1509	...	...	1705	1747	1904	...	1947	2106	2104	2257	...	2352	...	...	...	0207	...	0741	1059	...	...	...

		36	IR 2	EC 340	TLK	IC	IR 2	TLK	TLK	Ex	🚌	IR 2	TLK	IR 2	TLK	IR 2	🚌	TLK	IR 2	TLK	TLK	IR	TLK	TLK		
	48101	38102	36120	37001	38110	3108	36122	35108	38100	3510	23106	37126	3710	36128	37102	36132	23110	36100	36134	34100	38204	34120	38200	36501		
		38103	36121	[R] 🍷	38111	[R] ✕	36123	35109	38101	[R] ✕		37127	3711	36129	[R] ✕	36133		36101	36136	34101	448	34121	38510	36200		
	G	P	y	W		U	f	F	k	K		f	J	f	Z	f			⑤⑦y	H	Y	D 2	S	N		
Przemyśl 1058 d.	...	0154	...	...	...	0411	...	0542	0743	0823	...	0916	0931	1135	1138	1335	...	1342	...	1542	...	1630	1733	2213	...	...
Zamość d.	...	|	...	...	...	|	...	|	|	|	0515	|	|	|	|	|	0850	|	...	|	...	|	|	|	...	...
Jarosław 1058 d.	...	|	...	...	...	0440	...	0614	0814	0852	|	0947	1003	1207	1211	1407	1240	1414	...	1614	...	1702	1804	2246	...	...
Przeworsk 1058 d.	...	|	...	...	...	0453	...	0627	0827	0905	|	1005	1015	1220	1224	1420	...	1427	...	1627	...	1715	1817	2300	...	...
Rzeszów 1058 d.	...	0307	...	...	...	0533	0700z	0709	0908	0946	|	1041	1056	1301	1305	1500	...	1506	...	1708	...	1755	1858	2345	...	...
Dębica d.	...	0350	...	...	...	0616	0738z	0755	0954	1030	1045	1127	1142	1339	1351	1538	...	1554	...	1755	...	1834	1944	0031	...	...
Tarnów 1078 d.	...	0416	...	...	...	0653	0804z	0823	1022	1058	...	1155	1210	1405	1419	1604	...	1622	...	1822	...	1902	2012	0100	...	...
Kraków Płaszów 1078 d.	...	|	...	...	0708	0752	0855z	0923	1123	1157	...	1255	1311	1457	1520	1655	...	1723	...	1923	...	1953	2133	0221	...	...
Kraków Gł. 1078 a.	...	0514	...	...	0716	0759	0903z	0930	1130	1204	...	1303	1319	1503	1527	1703	...	1730	...	1930	...	1959	2141	0230	...	...
Kraków Gł. ▲ d.	...	0532	0605	0724	0740	...	0905	0935	1135	...	...	1305	1335	1505	1535	1705	...	1735	1805	1942	1935	2005	2154	0233	...	...
Katowice ▲ a.	...	0725	0748	0904	0932	...	1047	1127	1326	...	...	1447	1527	1652	1727	1847	...	1926	1947	2132	2125	2148	2347	0427	...	...
Katowice 1060 d.	0534	0730	0750	0907	0937	...	1049	1130	1330	...	...	1449	1530	1700	1730	1849	...	1930	1957	...	2130	2150	0002	0430	...	...
Gliwice 1060 d.	0607	0801	0827	0936	1007	...	1119	1201	1401	...	...	1519	1601	1730	1801	1919	...	2001	2025	...	2201	2219	0037	0507	...	...
Opole Gł. 1088 d.	0721	0918	0941	1048	1123	...	1234	1318	1518	...	...	1634	1719	1841	1918	2034	...	2118	2135	...	2319	...	0210	0621	...	...
Brzeg 1088 d.	0749	0946	1010	|	1149	...	1301	1346	1546	...	...	1701	1746	1907	1945	2101	...	2146	2204	...	2346	...	0239	0648	...	...
Wroclaw Gł. 1088 a.	0826	1025	1045	1143	1214	...	1335	1423	1625	...	...	1735	1821	1942	2022	2135	...	2222	2238	...	0021	...	0315	0726	...	...
Poznań Gł. 1070 a.	1111	...	...	...	1510	...	...	1715	1915	...	...	2015	...	...	2307	...	...	...	...	...	0248	...	0605	...	...	...
Szczecin Gł. 1010 a.	...	...	...	...	1750	...	...	...	2157	...	...	...	...	...	...	...	...	...	...	...	0631	...	0843	...	...	...
Świnoujście 1010 a.	...	...	...	...	...	...	...	...	...	...	...	...	...	...	...	...	...	...	...	...	0818	...	1054c	...	...	...

NOTES FOR TABLES 1070 and 1075

- B – (12) Kołobrzeg - Poznań - Kraków and v.v.
- C – (12) Jelenia Góra - Węgliniec - Zgorzelec - Wrocław - Przemyśl and v.v.
- D – ⑧ (not Dec. 24, 25, 31, Jan. 1, Apr. 4).
- E – 🛏 1, 2 cl., ▬ 2 cl. and (12) Gdynia - Wrocław and v.v.
- F – (12) Kołobrzeg - Poznań - Wrocław - Przemyśl and v.v.
- G – (12) Kołobrzeg - Poznań - Wrocław - Katowice and v.v.
- H – Also conveys (12) Katowice - Rzeszów - Zagórz and v.v.
- J – (12) Zielona Góra / Poznań - Wrocław - Przemyśl and v.v.
- K – (12) and ✕ Gdynia - Warszawa - Kraków - Przemyśl and v.v. (Table **1030**).
- L – ①–⑥ (not Dec. 25, 26, Jan. 1, Apr. 5).
- M – ①–⑥ (not Dec. 25, 26, Jan. 1, 2, Apr. 5).
- N – (12) Wrocław - Przemyśl and v.v.
- P – 🛏 2 cl. Wrocław - Kraków - Lviv and v.v.
- Q – ⑧ (also Apr. 3; not Dec. 25, 31, Apr. 4, 5).
- S – (12) Szczecin - Poznań - Kraków - Przemyśl and v.v.
- T – ⑤⑦: (12) and ✕ Warszawa - Kraków - Przemyśl.
- U – ①⑥: (12) and ✕ Przemyśl - Kraków - Warszawa.
- V – (12) and ✕ [R] Warszawa - Poznań - Wrocław and v.v.
- W – WAWEL – (12) and ✕ Berlin - Wrocław - Kraków and v.v. For dates from / to Hamburg see Table **56**.
- X – ①–⑤.
- Y – 🛏 1, 2 cl., ▬ 2 cl., (2) and ✕ Świnoujście - Szczecin - Poznań - Wrocław - Katowice - Kraków and v.v.
- Z – (12) Poznań - Wrocław - Przemyśl and v.v. 🛏 2 cl. Wrocław - Kraków - Przemyśl - Kyïv and v.v. Conveys (12) Poznań - Kraków - Zakopane on dates in Table **1066**. Conveys ▬ 2 cl. Wrocław - Kraków - Odesa and v.v. on dates in Table **1056**. Conveys 🛏 1, 2 cl. Praha / Wien - Kyïv on dates in Table **96**.
- c – Apr. 9 - Sept. 27.
- e – From / to Ełk and Suwałki (Table **1045**).
- f – Not Dec. 25, Apr. 4.
- g – From Wałbrzych Gł. (Table **1084**).
- h – To / from Szklarska Poręba Górna (Table **1084**).
- j – From / to Kołobrzeg (Table **1015**).
- k – Not Dec. 25, 26, Jan. 1, 2, Apr. 4.
- m – From / to Szczecin (Table **1010**).
- n – From / to Bydgoszcz and Gdynia (Table **1020**).
- p – To / from Rzeszów (Table **1075**).
- q – To / from Toruń and Olsztyn (Table **1020**).
- s – Arrival time, stops to set down only.
- u – Departure time, stops to pick up only.
- w – To / from Kudowa Zdrój (Table **1095**).
- x – ⑧ (not Dec. 24, 25, 31, Jan. 1, Apr. 4).
- y – Also Dec. 23, Mar. 31, Apr. 6, May 3, June 2; not Dec. 25, 27, Jan. 1, Apr. 2, 4, May 2, June 4.
- z – ①–⑥ (not Dec. 25, 26, Jan. 1, 2, Apr. 5).
- ◇ – Stopping train.
- * * – *179 km* from Jarosław, *207 km* from Dębica.
- ▲ – Additional trains run Katowice - Kraków and v.v. (Journey time: 80–106 minutes).

1076 KATOWICE and KRAKÓW - OSTRAVA

km		EC	EC	EC		400			407	
		103	110	105	408	407	400	407	400	
		✕⁄	✕⁄	✕⁄						
		P §	§	§	V	K	W	C	S	
	Warszawa Cent. 1060 d.	0645	0945	1245	...	...	...	2110	2110	...
0	**Katowice** d.	0913	1214	1511	2210	...	...	2357	2347	...
∆116	**Kraków** Gł. 1099 d.	|	|	|	|	2211	2211	|	|	...
∆51	Oświecim 1099 d.	|	|	|	|	2339	2339	|	|	...
74	Zebrzydowice 🏛 d.	1015	1315	1613	2330	0049	0049	0105	0105	...
94	Bohumín 🏛 1160 a.	1033	1331	1633	2348	0107	0107	0128	0128	...
94	Bohumín 🏛 1160 d.	1045	1340	1645	0042	0217	0210	0210	0210	...
102	**Ostrava** Hlavní 1160 a.	1052	1346	1652	0050	0224	0218	0218	0218	...
	Praha Hlavní 1160 a.	|	1751	|	0505	|	0651	|	0651	...
	Wien Westbf 1150 a.	1423y	...	2044z	...	0622z	...	0622z	...	...

	401			406		EC	EC	EC	
	406	401	406	401	409	104	111	102	
						✕⁄	✕⁄	✕⁄	
	S	W	C	K	V	§	§	P §	
Wien Westbf 1150 d.	...	...	2208x	2208x	...	0712x	...	1333y	...
Praha Hlavní 1160 d.	2132	2132	|	|	2300	|	1011	|	...
Ostrava Hlavní 1160 d.	0211	0211	0159	0208	0302	1105	1405	1705	...
Bohumín 🏛 1160 a.	0218	0218	0206	0206	0309	1112	1411	1712	...
Bohumín 🏛 1160 d.	0254	0307	0254	0307	0329	1126	1426	1726	...
Zebrzydowice 🏛 d.	0314	0327	0314	0327	0350	1145	1445	1745	...
Oświecim 1099 a.	|	0436	|	0436	|	|	|	|	...
Kraków Gł. 1099 a.	|	0624	|	0624	|	|	|	|	...
Katowice a.	0417	...	0417	...	0457	1250	1550	1850	...
Warszawa Cent. 1060 a.	0710	...	0710	...	...	1522	1824	2124	...

- C – CHOPIN – 🛏 1, 2 cl., ▬ 2 cl. and (2) Warszawa - Wien and v.v. Conveys 🛏 1, 2 cl., ▬ 2 cl. and (2) Warszawa - Bratislava - Budapest and v.v. Conveys 🛏 1, 2 cl. Moskva - Wien / Budapest and v.v.
- K – 🛏 1, 2 cl. (also ▬ 2 cl. Apr. 29 - Sept. 27 from Kraków; Apr. 30 - Sept. 28 from Wien) Kraków - Wien and v.v. 🛏 1, 2 cl. and ▬ 2 cl. Kraków - Bratislava - Budapest and v.v.
- P – POLONIA – (12) and ✕ Warszawa - Wien - Villach and v.v.
- S – 🛏 1, 2 cl., ▬ 2 cl. and (2) Warszawa - Praha and v.v.
- V – VLTAVA – 🛏 1, 2 cl. Moskva - Terespol - Katowice - Praha and v.v. For additional cars see Table **95**.
- W – SILESIA – 🛏 1, 2 cl., ▬ 2 cl. and (12) Kraków - Praha and v.v.
- x – Calls at Wien **Meidling** 15–21 minutes later.
- y – Wien **Meidling**.
- z – Calls at Wien **Meidling** 14–22 minutes earlier.
- ⁄ – Supplement payable.
- § – [R] in Poland.
- ∆ – Distance from Zebrzydowice.

TRAIN NAMES:

EC **104 / 105** SOBIESKI
EC **110 / 111** PRAHA

KATOWICE and KRAKÓW - ŽILINA 1077

km		4105	413	401	2221	415	335	4109	4107	721	
		◇ 2	◇ 2	◇ 2 B	◇	◇ 2 A	34009 y	◇ 2	333 p	◇ 2	
	Kraków Gł. ....**1099** d.	...	...	...	...	...	0735	...	...	...	...
	Oświecim ....**1099** d.	...	...	...	...	...	|	...	...	...	...
0	**Katowice** ....**1060** d.	0410	0504	0650	0658	0716	0922	1225	1528	1816	...
	Bielsko Biała..........**1060** d.	0525	0622	0758	|	0842	1025	1340	1628	1934	...
	Zywiec .... d.	0555	0658	0836	|	0914	1051	1419	1654	2006	...
	Zwardoń 🏛 .... d.	0702	0805	0932	|	1013	1151	1546	1756	2113	...
87	Cieszyn 🏛...................... d.	|	...	...	0903	...	|	|	|	...	...
89	Český Těšín 🏛........**1160** d.	|	...	...	0908	...	|	|	|	...	...
127	Čadca 🏛.................**1160** d.	0833	...	...	...	...	1233	1635	1833	...	...
158	**Žilina** ....**1160** a.	0915	...	...	...	...	1315	1717	1915	...	...

km		414	4104	332	424	2224	4108	334	428		
		◇ 2	◇ 2	4106 q	◇ 2	◇	◇ 2	43008 y	◇ 2		
0	**Žilina** ....**1160** d.	...	0525	0952	...	...	1348	1557	...	...	...
31	Čadca 🏛.................**1160** d.	...	0628	1034	...	...	1434	1635	...	...	...
	Český Těšín 🏛........**1160** d.	...	|	|	...	1610	|	|	...	...	...
	Cieszyn 🏛...................... d.	...	|	|	...	1621	|	|	...	...	...
52	Zwardoń 🏛 .... d.	0434	0733	1115	1436	|	1545	1726	1945	...	...
89	Zywiec .... d.	0534	0835	1213	1538	|	1656	1825	2046	...	...
110	**Bielsko Biała**..........**1060** d.	0613	0910	1248	1611	|	1736	1855	2121	...	...
	Katowice ....**1060** a.	0725	1020	1344	1721	1830	1845	1946	2229	...	...
	Oświecim ....**1099** a.	...	...	...	...	...	...	|	...	...	...
	Kraków Gł. ....**1099** a.	...	...	...	...	...	...	2139	...	...	...

A – ①–⑤ (not Dec. 25, Jan. 1, Apr. 5, May 3, June 3).
B – ⑥⑦ (also Dec. 25, Jan. 1, Apr. 5, May 3, June 3).
p – Not Dec. 24, 25, Apr. 3, 4.
q – Not Dec. 25, 26, Apr. 4, 5.
y – Not Dec. 25, Jan. 1, Apr. 4.
◇ – Stopping train.

TRAIN NAMES **333/332** GORAL **335/334** SKALNICA

KRAKÓW - ZAGÓRZ and KRYNICA 1078

km								53512 53513	53513 33513	621	13501 33501	13511	623	33101			*TLK* 13411	43101 33511	66131	625				627	
		2 ◇	2 ◇ ①–⑤ j	2 ◇	2 ◇	2 ◇	V	P	H	2 ◇	F	A	2 ◇ ①–⑤ j	◇	2 ◇	2 ◇ ①–⑤ j	Ⓡ ✗ G	V	2 ◇	2 ◇	V	2 ◇	2 ◇	2 ◇	2 ◇ j
	Warszawa Cent. **1065** .....d.	...	...	...	...	...	...	...	...	...	2140	2245	...	...	...	...	0615	...	...	...	...	...	...	...	...
	Katowice **1075**...............d.	...	...	...	...	...	...	...	...	...	|	|	...	...	...	...	|	0720	...	...	...	...	...	...	...
0	**Kraków** Gł................ **1075** d.	...	...	...	...	...	...	0326	0326	...	0312	|	...	0622	...	...	0857	0928	1040	...	...	...	...	...	...
5	Kraków Płaszów......... **1075** d.	...	...	...	...	...	...	|	|	...	0348	|	...	0630	...	...	0906	0937	1048	...	...	...	...	...	...
78	Tarnów .... **1075** d.	...	...	...	...	...	...	0443	0443	0435	0455	|	0531	0747	...	...	1003	1036	1204	...	...	...	...	1442	...
136	Stróze..............................d.	...	...	0433y	...	...	...	0614	0623	0551	0624	|	0648	0905	...	...	1104	|	1322	1443	...	...	...	1559	...
**	Rzeszów ....d.	...	...	|	0443	...	...	|	|	|	|	0607	|	|	...	...	|	1157	|	|	...	...	...	|	1531
182	Jasło ....d.	0441	0541	|	0630	0646	...	|	0740	|	|	0820	|	|	1255	1349	|	1407	|	|	...	1450	1548	|	1724
205	Krosno.............................d.	0525	0631	|	...	0730	...	|	0831	|	|	0904	|	|	1340	1440	|	1500	|	|	...	1542	1638	|	...
244	Sanok...............................d.	0641	0745	|	...	0841	...	|	0942	|	|	1015	|	|	1452	1603	|	1629	|	|	...	1703	1752	|	...
251	**Zagórz** ....a.	0653	0758	|	...	0854	...	|	0956	|	|	1030	|	|	1505	1617	|	1643	|	|	...	1716	1806	|	...
167	**Nowy Sącz**.....................d.	...	...	0513	...	...	...	0657	...	0630	0716	...	0731	0947	...	...	1141	...	1403	1524	...	...	...	1639	...
	Krynica..........................d.	...	...	|	...	...	0758	|	...	...	|	...	...	|	...	...	|	...	|	|	1721	...	...	...	...
217	Muszyna ....d.	...	...	0626	...	...	0815	0816z	...	...	0835x	...	...	1058	...	...	1243x	...	1512	1640	1738	...	...	...	...
228	**Krynica**..........................a.	...	...	0643	...	...	|	0834	...	...	0853	...	...	1116	...	...	1310	...	1529	1657	|	...	...	...	...
231	**Plaveč** 🏛 ....a.	...	...	...	...	...	0838	...	...	...	...	...	...	...	...	...	...	...	...	...	1801	...	...	...	...
	Košice **1196** ....a.	...	...	...	...	...	...	...	...	...	...	...	...	...	...	...	...	...	...	...	...	...	...	...	...

	73101	629	2221	66133	66135		*Ex* Ⓡ 1309 3309	33001 1381		
		2 ◇		2 ◇	2 ◇		⑤⑦	🍷 C		
Warszawa Cent. **1065** ...... d.	...	...	...	...	...	...	1715	...	...	...
Katowice **1075**.................. d.	1230	...	...	...	...	...	|	...	...	...
Kraków Gł.................. **1075** d.	1422	...	1630	1745	1938	...	2020	2245	...	...
Kraków Płaszów .... **1075** d.	1431	...	1639	1753	1946	...	2029	2254	...	...
Tarnów .... **1075** d.	1530	1552	1735	1910	2110	...	2139	2350	...	...
Stróze.................................. d.	...	1714	1847	2022	2222	...	2240	0055	...	...
Rzeszów........................ d.	...	|	|	|	...	...	|	|	...	...
Jasło .... d.	...	|	|	|	...	...	|	|	...	...
Krosno .... d.	...	|	|	|	...	...	|	|	...	...
Sanok .... d.	...	|	|	|	...	...	|	|	...	...
Zagórz............................ a.	...	|	|	|	...	...	|	|	...	...
Nowy Sącz .... d.	...	1755	1926	2102	...	...	2316	0136	...	...
Krynica........................... d.	...	|	...	...	...	...	...	|	...	...
Muszyna .... d.	...	1913	...	...	...	...	...	0304	...	...
Krynica........................... a.	...	1930	...	...	...	...	...	|	...	...
Plaveč 🏛 .... a.	...	...	...	...	...	...	...	0325	...	...
Košice **1196** .... a.	...	...	...	...	...	...	...	0500	...	...

	6022		*Ex* Ⓡ 3308 3108	2222	66120		38108 38109	6024		
	2 ◇	2 ◇	①⑥		2 ◇	2 ◇ j		2 ◇	2 ◇	2 ◇
Košice **1196** .... d.	...	...	...	...	...	...	...	...	...	...
Plaveč 🏛 .... d.	...	...	...	...	...	...	...	...	...	...
Krynica........................... d.	...	...	...	...	0443	...	...	0608	...	...
Muszyna .... d.	...	...	...	...	0504	...	...	0630	...	...
Krynica........................... a.	...	...	...	...	|	...	...	|	...	...
Nowy Sącz........................ d.	0412	...	0451	0541	0616	...	...	0740	...	...
Zagórz .... d.	|	...	|	|	|	...	...	|	...	0353
Sanok................................. d.	|	...	|	|	|	...	...	|	...	0406
Krosno............................... d.	|	...	|	|	|	...	...	|	...	0527
Jasło .... d.	|	...	|	|	|	0442	...	|	...	0616
Rzeszów .... d.	|	0455	|	|	|	0640	0720	|	...	...
Stróze................................. d.	0451	|	0526	0618	0657	...	|	0819	...	...
Tarnów .... **1075** d.	0609	0612	0643	0727	0807	...	0831	0930	0933	...
Kraków Płaszów ..... **1075** a.	...	0717	0741	0828	0919	...	0933	...	1046	...
Kraków Gł. .... **1075** a.	...	0726	0750	0837	0928	...	0942	...	1055	...
Katowice **1075**............. a.	...	...	|	...	...	...	1129	...	...	...
Warszawa Cent. **1065** .. a.	...	...	1055	...	...	...	...	...	...	...

				6026			66122	6030	33514 34100	33102	*Ex* 31410						6032		31510		33516 35512	35512 35513	33506 31500	33000 1380	
	2 ◇ ①–⑤ j	2 ◇	V	2 ◇	2 ◇	2 ◇	2 ◇ ①–⑤ j	2 ◇	W	◇	Ⓡ ✗ G	2 ◇	2 ◇	2 ◇	2 ◇ ①–⑤ j	2 ◇	2 ◇	2 ◇	B	V	K	Q	J	🍷 D	
Košice **1196** .... d.	...	...	...	...	...	...	...	...	...	...	...	...	...	...	...	...	...	...	...	...	...	...	...	2304	...
Plaveč 🏛 .... d.	...	...	0903	...	...	...	...	...	...	...	...	...	...	...	...	...	...	...	...	1811	...	...	...	0104	...
Krynica............................ d.	...	...	|	1008	...	...	...	...	...	1454	1556	...	...	...	...	...	1745	...	...	|	...	1909	1956	|	...
Muszyna .... d.	...	...	0927	1030	...	...	...	...	...	1516	1622x	...	...	...	...	...	1807	...	...	1836	...	1940x	2022x	0135	...
Krynica............................ a.	...	...	0944	|	...	...	...	...	...	|	|	...	...	...	...	...	|	...	...	1852	...	|	|	|	...
Nowy Sącz .... d.	...	...	...	1141	...	...	1425	1525	...	1627	1724	...	...	...	...	...	1915	...	...	...	...	2049	2130	0245	...
Zagórz............................. d.	0443	0548	...	|	...	1033	|	|	1117	|	|	1259	...	...	1357	1510	|	...	1735	...	1755	|	|	|	...
Sanok .... d.	0456	0601	...	|	...	1045	|	|	1131	|	|	1312	...	...	1410	1523	|	...	1754	...	1815	|	|	|	...
Krosno .... d.	0629	0732	...	|	...	1158	|	|	1242	|	|	1436	...	...	1538	1641	|	...	1904	...	1925	|	|	|	...
Jasło .... d.	0719	0818	...	|	...	1241	|	|	1349	|	|	1525	1535	...	1624	1725	|	...	1955	...	2008	|	|	|	...
Rzeszów......................... d.	...	...	...	|	...	...	|	|	1610	|	|	...	1728	1820	...	...	|	...	2151	...	|	|	|	|	...
Stróze.................................. d.	...	...	...	1218	...	...	1504	1604	|	1704	1758	...	...	|	...	...	1953	...	|	...	2139	2139	2208	0321	...
Tarnów .... **1075** d.	...	...	...	1330	1339	...	1621	1717	1723	1818	1859	...	...	1939	...	...	2104	2107	|	...	2302	2302	2320	0423	...
Kraków Płaszów .... **1075** a.	...	...	...	...	1452	...	1737	...	1828	1931	1956	...	...	2056	...	...	...	2224	|	...	|	|	0022	0521	...
Kraków Gł.................. **1075** a.	...	...	...	...	1500	...	1746	...	1837	1940	2004	...	...	2105	...	...	...	2233	|	...	0009	0009	0053	0529	...
Katowice **1075**.................. a.	...	...	...	...	...	...	...	...	2029	...	|	...	...	...	...	...	...	...	|	...	...	...	|	...	...
Warszawa Cent. **1065** ...... a.	...	...	...	...	...	...	...	...	...	...	2245	...	...	...	...	...	...	...	0515	...	...	...	0556	...	...

A – June 19 - Aug. 30: [12] Warszawa - Zagórz.
B – June 20 - Aug. 31: [12] Zagórz - Warszawa.
C – CRACOVIA – June 18 - Aug. 30: [2] Kraków - Košice - Lökösháza; June 20 - Aug. 30: 🛏 2 cl. and [2] Kraków - Bucureşti. June 18 - Aug. 30: 🛏 2 cl. and [2] Kraków - Košice - Budapest - Keszthely. For additional cars to Varna and Burgas see Table **99**.
D – CRACOVIA – June 19 - Aug. 31: [2] Lökösháza - Košice - Kraków; June 19 - Aug. 29: 🛏 2 cl. and [2] Bucureşti - Kraków. June 19 - Aug. 31: 🛏 2 cl. and [2] Keszthely - Budapest - Košice - Kraków. For additional cars from Varna and Burgas see Table **99**.
F – June 19 - Aug. 30: 🛏 2 cl. and [12] Warszawa - Kraków - Krynica.
G – ⑥⑦ (also Dec. 25, 28, 29, 30, 31, Jan. 1, Apr. 1, 2, 5, 6, 30, May 3, June 3, 4).
H – June 19 - Aug. 30 from Gdynia: [12] Gdynia (depart 1451) - Kraków - Zagórz.
J – June 20 - Aug. 31: 🛏 2 cl. and [12] Krynica - Kraków - Warszawa.
K – June 20 - Aug. 31: [12] Zagórz - Kraków - Gdynia (arrive 1230).
P – June 19 - Aug. 30 from Gdynia: 🛌 1, 2 cl. and [12] Gdynia (depart 1451) - Krynica.
Q – June 20 - Aug. 31: 🛌 1, 2 cl. and [12] Krynica - Gdynia (arrive 1344).
V – June 20 - Aug. 30.
W – June 21 - Aug. 31.
j – Not Dec. 25, Jan. 1.
x – Arrive 10 minutes earlier.
y – ①–⑥.
z – Arrive 0732.
◇ – Stopping train.
** – Rzeszów - Jasło: *71 km.*

ZAGÓRZ - ŁUPKÓW - MEDZILABORCE - HUMENNÉ 1079

km		A	A		A	A	
		2 ◇	2 ◇	2 ◇	2 ◇	2 ◇	2 ◇
0	**Zagórz**.. d.	0657	...	...	1509	...	...
48	Łupków 🏛.. d.	0838	0843	...	1650	1707	...
63	Medzilaborce Mesto 🏛...................**1194** d.	...	0902	0957	...	1726	1834
65	Medzilaborce..................................**1194** d.	...	0905	1010	...	1729	1840
106	Humenné ....**1194** a.	...	...	1119	...	...	1943

		A	A		A	A
	2 ◇	2 ◇	2 ◇	2 ◇	2 ◇	2 ◇
Humenné ....**1194** d.	0626	...	...	1437	...	...
Medzilaborce...............................**1194** d.	0734	0808	...	1558	1632	...
Medzilaborce Mesto 🏛 ....**1194** d.	...	0812	...	1601	1636	...
Łupków 🏛.. d.	...	0832	0848	...	1656	1709
Zagórz... a.	...	...	1029	...	...	1850

A – ⑤⑥⑦ June 19 - Aug. 29.
◇ – Stopping train.

OSTRAVA - **BOHUMÍN** 🏛 - **KATOWICE**. *89 km.* Daily.
Ostrava Hlavní dep. 1609, Bohumín 🏛 1622, Chałupki 1633, Rybnik 1725, **Katowice** arr. 1825.
Katowice dep. 0508, Rybnik 0623, Chałupki 0720, Bohumín 🏛 0729, **Ostrava Hlavní** arr. 0739.

OSTRAVA - **BOHUMÍN** 🏛 - **KĘDZIERZYN KOŹLE**. *66 km.* Daily (not Dec. 25, Apr. 4).
Ostrava Hlavní dep. 1035, Bohumín 🏛 1043, Chałupki 1050, Kędzierzyn Koźle arr. 1154.
Kędzierzyn Koźle dep. 1405, Chałupki 1530, Bohumín 🏛 1536, **Ostrava Hlavní** arr. 1538.

1080 POZNAŃ - OSTRÓW - KATOWICE - KRAKÓW

For other trains Poznań - Katowice - Kraków (via Wrocław) see Table **1075**

km													
				◇	◇	◇	◇	*TLK*	◇	*TLK*		**83500**	**84200**
		◇	◇	2	2	2	2	**8310**	2	**81100**	◇	**83501**	**84502**
		2	2	j		f	T	**83412**		p	2	A	Q
	Szczecin Gł. **1010** .. d.	...	...	...	...	...	...	1150	...	1450	...	1655	...
0	**Poznań** Gł. d.	...	0630	...	1050	1250	...	1414	1520x	1735	1850	1950	0254
67	Jarocin d.	...	0740	...	1156	1354	...	1504	1619x	1825	1953	2054	0353
114	Ostrów Wlkp ⊠ **1090** d.	0605	0820	...	1241	1435	1455	1539	1700	1901	2040	2135	0432
160	Kępno d.	0647	0910	...	1317	...	1528	1615	1747	...	2121	2211	0510
201	Kluczbork a.	0725	0945	...	1400	...	1615	|	1825	...	...	2256	0545
		▬					◇	|				|	|
		◇	◇		◇		2	|	◇			|	|
		2	2		2		j	|	2			|	|
201	Kluczbork d.	...	1031	1231	1428	...	1631	|	1831	...	...	2258	0547
252	Lubliniec d.	0840	1134	1334	1537	...	1734	|	1932	...	...	0000	0650
302	Bytom d.	1014	1309	1509	1709	...	1909	1910	2108	...	...	0133	0821
320	**Katowice** a.	1042	1337	1537	1737	...	1937	1938	2137	...	...	0201	0850
398	**Kraków** Gł. a.	...	...	...	...	...	...	2125	...	...	...	...	...

		TLK	◇	◇	*TLK*		◇			◇	**48201**	**38500**
	◇	**18101**	2	2	**3810**	◇	2	◇	◇	2	**48503**	**38501**
	2	p			**38410**	2	j	2	2	j	P	B
Kraków Gł. d.	...	...	...	...	0521	...	...	...	...	...	...	...
Katowice d.	...	...	...	0543	0713	0743	0943	1143	1343	1743	1919	0022
Bytom d.	...	...	...	0612	0742	0812	1012	1212	1412	1812	1952	0051
Lubliniec d.	...	...	...	0737	|	0937	1137	1337	1539	1937	2114	0211
Kluczbork a.	...	...	...	0831x	|	1028	1228	1428	1629	2028	2206	0302
					|				▬		|	|
					|		◇	◇	◇ 2		|	|
					|		2	2			|	|
Kluczbork d.	...	...	0754	...	|	...	1254	1454	...	...	2208	0304
Kępno d.	0541	...	0839	...	1014	...	1337	1536	...	...	2252	0407
Ostrów Wlkp. ⊠**1090** d.	0620	0845	0921	...	1049	...	1441	1623	1635	...	2330	0459
Jarocin d.	0712	0922	1015	...	1134	...	1535	...	1724	...	0010	0546
Poznań Gł. a.	0814	1020	1124	...	1233	...	1614	...	1817	...	0118	0650
Szczecin Gł. **1010** .. a.	...	1352	...	...	1500	...	...	...	...	...	...	0959

A – June 19 - Aug. 30: 🛏 1, 2 cl., ▬ 2 cl. and (12) Szczecin - Zakopane.
B – June 20 - Aug. 31: 🛏 1, 2 cl., ▬ 2 cl. and (12) Zakopane - Szczecin.
P – Apr. 8 - Sept. 26: 🛏 1, 2 cl., ▬ 2 cl. and (12) Katowice - Poznań - Kołobrzeg.
Q – Apr. 9 - Sept. 27: 🛏 1, 2 cl., ▬ 2 cl. and (12) Kołobrzeg - Poznań - Katowice.
T – ①–⑤ (not Dec. 24, 25, Jan. 1, Apr. 5, May 3, 4, June 4).
f – Not Dec. 24, 25, 26, 31, Apr. 4, May 1, 2.
j – Not Dec. 25–27, Jan. 1, Apr. 4, 5, May 1–3, June 3.
p – To / from Łódź (Table **1090**).
x – ①–⑤ (not Dec. 24, 25, Jan. 1, Apr. 5, May 3, June 3, 4).
⊠ – Full name is Ostrów Wielkopolski.
◇ – Stopping train.

1084 WĘGLINIEC - JELENIA GÓRA - WAŁBRZYCH - WROCŁAW

km																								
		◇	◇ 2	◇ 2	◇ 2	◇	◇ 2	**60510**	◇ 2	◇	◇	◇ 2	◇ 2	◇ 2	◇ 2	◇ 2	**38109**	◇	**63500**	◇ 2	**65502**	◇ 2		
		2	f	j	P	2	w	E	m	2	2			g	p	⑦b	P	2	Jq	g	C	g		
0	Węgliniec d.	...	...	...	...	0535	...	...	...	...	0858	...	...	1227	...	...	1644	...	...	1734	...	2046	...	...
**	Szklarska Poręba Górna d.	...	...	...	...	|	...	...	0838	...	|	...	1244x	|	1438	...	|	...	...	|	...	|	...	...
74	**Jelenia Góra** d.	...	...	...	0547	0723	0753	0928	0941	0947	1050	1251	1349	1410	1549	1658	1820	1744	1843	1942	1931	2219	...	...
121	Wałbrzych Gł. d.	...	0511	0611	0710	...	0919	1057	...	1119	...	1411	1519	...	1719	1823	...	1919	2009	...	2058	...	...	...
151	Jaworzyna Śląska d.	0511	0610	0710	0807	...	1010	1155	...	1210	...	1507	1616	...	1815	1915	...	2010	2107	...	2156	...	...	...
200	**Wrocław** Gł. a.	0624	0716	0815	0916	...	1118	1256	...	1316	...	1621	1727	...	1922	2018	...	2118	2214	...	2305	...	...	...

	◇ 2	◇ 2	**56503**	◇	**60100**	◇	**36501**	◇	◇	◇ 2	◇ 2	◇ 2	◇	◇ 2	◇ 2	**60501**	◇	◇	◇ 2	◇ 2	◇ 2	◇	◇ 2	
	g	R	B	2	**83108**	2	Jq	2	2	p	g	f	2	c	h	F	2	2		p	y	2	k	
Wrocław Gł. d.	...	...	0439	0542	P	0644	0749	...	...	0942	...	1136	...	1357	...	1428	1446	1539	1646	1749	1903	2046	2236	...
Jaworzyna Śląska d.	...	...	0540	0640	...	0739	0856	...	...	1038	...	1239	...	1457	...	1525	1539	1639	1739	1841	2003	2146	2352	...
Wałbrzych Gł. d.	...	0547	0630	0727	...	0827	0943	...	...	1127	...	1327	...	1552	...	1614	1627	1727	1850	1927	2100	2241	0031	...
Jelenia Góra a.	0602	0723	0800	0858	0920	1007	1108	1119	1153	1256	1417	1500	1610	...	1913	1744	1809	1901	...	2059	...	...	...	...
Szklarska Poręba Górna a.	|	*0830*	...	1002x	|	...	...	|	|	1402	|	...	|	...	|	...	...	...	...	2230	...	...	...	...
Węgliniec a.	0740	...	...	...	1058	...	...	1309	1339	...	1540	...	1758	...	2044	...	...	...	...	...	...	...	...	...

B – June 19 - Aug. 30: ▬ 2 cl. and (12) Gdynia (depart 1943) - Wrocław - Jelenia Góra.
C – June 20 - Aug. 31: ▬ 2 cl. and (12) - Jelenia Góra - Wrocław - Gdynia (arrive 0923).
E – June 21 - Sept. 27: (12) Jelenia Góra - Wrocław - Warszawa.
F – June 20 - Sept. 26: (12) Warszawa - Wrocław - Jelenia Góra.
J – June 20 - Aug. 31.
P – ①–⑥ (not Dec. 25, 26, Jan. 1, 2, Apr. 5, May 3, June 4, 5).
R – ①–⑤ (not Dec. 25, 26, Jan. 1, Apr. 5, May 3, June 4).
b – Also May 3; not Dec. 27, Apr. 4, May 2.
c – Not Apr. 4, 5, May 1.
f – Not Dec. 25, 26.
g – From / to Zielona Góra (Table **1004**).
h – To Zary (Table **1004**).
j – Not Dec. 25 – 27, Jan. 1 – 3, Apr. 4, 5, May 2, 3, June 4 – 6.
k – Not Dec. 24, 31.
m – Not Dec. 25.
p – To / from Poznań (Table **1070**).
q – To / from Przemyśl (Table **1075**).
w – Not Dec. 19 – 24, 28 – 31, Jan. 3, 4, 16, 23, May 1, June 3.
x – ⑥⑦ (also Apr. 5).
y – Not Dec. 24 – 24, Dec. 31 - Jan. 2, Apr. 4, 5, May 1, 2, June 3 – 5.
** – Szklarska Poręba Górna - Jelenia Góra: *32 km.*
◇ – Stopping train.

1085 GÖRLITZ - WROCŁAW

km												
		◇	◇	**61102**	**17041**		**60100**	◇	**17043**			**17045**
		2	2	**61103**	**60002**	◇	**83108**	2	**60004**	◇	◇	**60006**
		A	⑦f	z		2	Px	x		2	2	
	Dresden Hbf. **855** . d.	...	...	...	0727	...	...	...	1328	...	...	1728
0	**Görlitz** 🏛 d.	...	...	...	0845	...	...	...	1445	...	...	1845
2	Zgorzelec 🏛 d.	...	...	0652	0852	...	...	...	1452	...	...	1852
30	Węgliniec d.	0521	0610	0728	0911	1240	1114	1346	1511	1558	1804	1911
55	Bolesławiec d.	0541	0631	0743	0928	1301	1129	1407	1528	1619	1825	1928
99	Legnica d.	0622	0712	0809	0955	1342	1156	1448	1555	1700	1905	1955
165	**Wrocław** Gł. a.	0747	0835	0923	1102	1507	1309	1622	1701	1818	2030	2102
	Warszawa C. **1090** a.	...	...	1600	...	...	...	...	...	...	...	...

	17040			**17042**		**38109**	◇		**17044**	**16103**	
	60001	◇	◇	**60003**	◇	**66101**	2	◇	**60005**	**16102**	
		2	2		2	Px	y	2		z	
Warszawa C. **1090** .. d.	...	...	...	...	...	...	...	...	...	1320	...
Wrocław Gł. d.	0705	0837	1053	1305	1323	1455	1532	1632	1805	2016	...
Legnica d.	0807	0951	1208	1407	1440	1553	1650	1800	1907	2121	...
Bolesławiec d.	0835	1030	1247	1435	1520	1618	1729	1839	1935	2150	...
Węgliniec d.	0854	1053	1311	1454	1544	1635	1752	1902	1954	2219	...
Zgorzelec 🏛 d.	0913	...	...	1513	...	...	...	...	2013	2248	...
Görlitz 🏛 a.	0919	...	...	1519	...	...	...	...	2019	...	...
Dresden Hbf. **855** .. a.	1030	...	...	1630	...	...	...	...	2130	...	...

A – ①–⑥ (not Dec. 25, 26, Jan. 1, 2, Apr. 5, May 3).
P – Conveys (12) Jelenia Góra - Zgorzelec - Wrocław - Przemyśl and v.v.
f – Not Dec. 25, 26, Jan. 1, 2, Apr. 5, May 3.
x – Not Dec. 25, 26, Jan. 1, 2, Apr. 4.
y – Not Dec. 24, 25, 26, 31, Jan. 1, 2, Apr. 4.
z – Not Dec. 24, 25, 31, Jan. 1, Apr. 4.
◇ – Stopping train.

1086 COTTBUS - FORST - WROCŁAW

km														
							EC			◇				
		◇	◇	◇	◇		**341**	◇	◇	2	◇	◇		◇
		2	2	2	2	B	A	2	2	C	2	2	B	2
	Berlin Hbf. **838** .... d.	...	...	...	...	...	0941	...	...	...	...	...	...	...
0	**Cottbus** d.	...	0607	...	...	...	1121	...	...	...	1625	...	...	...
22	Forst 🏛 d.	...	0627	0632	...	...	1142	...	...	...	1655	...	...	1933
36	Tuplice d.	...	▬	0649	...	...	|	1256j	...	1607	1713	...	...	1949
57	Żary d.	0510	◇	0714	0810	...	1225	1324	1615	1631	1738	1814	...	2012
70	Zagań d.	0522	2	0731	0824	...	1245	1333	1629	...	1755	1829	...	2027
144	Legnica d.	0658	0737	...	0947	0956	1424	1509	1800	...	...	1950	1956	...
210	**Wrocław** Gł. a.	...	0856	...	...	1100	1537	...	...	...	...	...	2100	...
	Katowice **1075** .... a.	...	...	...	...	...	1820	...	...	...	...	...	...	...
	Kraków Gł. **1075** . a.	...	...	...	...	...	1956	...	...	...	...	...	...	...

							EC					
	◇	◇	◇	◇	◇	◇	**340**	◇	◇	◇	◇	◇
	2	2	2	2	2	2	A	2	2	2	2	2
Kraków Gł. **1075** d.	...	...	...	...	...	...	0723	...	...	...	...	...
Katowice **1075** . d.	...	...	...	...	...	...	0854	...	...	...	...	...
Wrocław Gł. d.	...	...	...	...	0732	...	1132	*1232*	*1431*	...	...	...
Legnica d.	...	...	0558	...	0850	0958	1257	1412	1559	...	...	2007
Zagań d.	0513	...	0720	0811	...	1119	1424	1535	1729	...	...	2125
Żary d.	0528	...	0732	0826	...	1133	1442	1545	1732	1846	...	2140
Tuplice d.	0553	...	...	0851	...	1154j	|	...	...	1909	...	...
Forst 🏛 d.	0610	0633	...	0910	...	...	1528	...	...	1925	1933	...
Cottbus a.	...	0652	...	0932	...	...	1546	...	...	...	1952	...
Berlin Hbf. **838** . a.	...	...	...	...	...	...	1730	...	...	...	...	...

A – WAWEL – (12) and 🍷 Berlin - Wrocław - Kraków and v.v. Ⓡ ✗. For dates from / to Hamburg see Table **56**.
B – (12) Dresden - Legnica - Wrocław.
C – ①–⑤ (not Dec. 25, Jan. 1).
j – ⑥⑦ (also Dec. 24, Apr. 4).
✗ – Supplement payable.
◇ – Stopping train.

1088 WARSZAWA - CZĘSTOCHOWA - WROCŁAW

§ – For other trains Warszawa - Wrocław (via Łódź) and additional trains Warszawa - Skierniewice - Koluszki see Table **1090**

km										
		Ex Ⓡ	**16107**	**14100**	*IR* 2	**54112**	**16104**	**14109**	**14102**	**16200**
		16411	**16106**	**14101**	**13122**	**54113**	**16105**	**54506**	**14103**	**16201**
		⑥		T	C	p	B		⑥b	A
0	**Warszawa** Wschodnia § d.	0548	0632	0822	1228	1233	1423	1633	1832	2227
5	**Warszawa** Centralna § d.	0605	0650	0850	1240	1250	1450	1650	1850	2250
71	Skierniewice § d.	|	0740	0940	1327	1340	1540	1738	1940	2346
111	Koluszki **1060** § d.	|	0804	1006	1359	1404	1604	1801	2004	0012
150	Piotrków Trybunalski **1060** d.	0734	0835	1036	1426	1435	1636	1833	2035	0045
235	Częstochowa Osobowa **1060** d.	0836	0940	1137	1525	1537	1742	1937	2137	0203
275	Lubliniec d.	|	1037	*1330*	...	*1652*	1843	...	...	0303
330	Opole Gł. **1075** d.	1026	1137	...	...	...	2005	...	...	0413
370	Brzeg **1075** d.	|	1205	...	...	...	2036	...	...	0443
412	**Wrocław** Gł. **1075** a.	1120	1239	...	...	...	2113	...	...	0521

	41102	**41108**	**61104**	**45112**	**41100**	**61106**	*Ex* Ⓡ	**61200**	
	①–⑥	**45504**	**61105**	**45113**	**41101**	**61107**	**61411**	**61201**	
	b		B	p	T		⑦	A	
Wrocław Gł. **1075** d.	...	...	0715	...	...	1505	1740	2335	...
Brzeg **1075** d.	...	...	0749	...	...	1537	|	0013	...
Opole Gł. **1075** d.	...	...	0823	...	...	1607	1839	0057	...
Lubliniec d.	...	*0637*	0924	...	*1429*	1721	|	0205	...
Częstochowa Osobowa **1060** d.	0604	0804	1004	1204	1604	1802	2008	0256	...
Piotrków Trybunalski **1060** d.	0716	0916	1113	1314	1715	1912	2115	0408	...
Koluszki **1060** § d.	0746	0944	1142	1344	1743	1942	|	0439	...
Skierniewice § d.	0811	1007	1207	1408	1807	2006	|	0504	...
Warszawa Centralna § a.	0905	1100	1300	1500	1900	2100	2243	0600	...
Warszawa Wschodnia § a.	0932	1112	1332	1517	1932	2117	2253	0612	...

A – 🛏 1, 2 cl. and (12) Warszawa - Wrocław and v.v.
B – (12) Białystok - Warszawa - Wrocław and v.v.
C – ①–⑥ (not Dec. 25, Jan. 1).
T – (12) Białystok - Warszawa - Częstochowa - Katowice - Bielsko Biała and v.v.
b – From / to Białystok (Table **1040**).
p – From / to Olsztyn (Table **1030**).

WARSZAWA - ŁÓDŹ - WROCŁAW 1090

See Table **1005** for the through trains Warszawa - Wrocław via Poznań (also Łódź - Poznań via Kutno).

km		*IR*	*IR*	*IR*	*IR*	*IR*	*IR*	*IR*	*IR*	*IR*	*IR*	*IR*	*IR*	*IR*	*IR*	*IR*	*IR*	*IR*	*IR*	*IR*	
		19100	**19102**	**19500**	**19104**	**19502**	**19106**	**19504**	**19108**	**19506**	**19110**	**19508**	**19510**	**19512**	**1910**	**19112**	**19514**	**19114**	**19516**	**19116**	
		19101	**19103**	**19501**	**19105**	**19503**	**19107**	**19505**	**19109**	**19507**	**19111**	**19509**	**19511**	**19513**	**1911**	**19113**	**19515**	**19115**	**19517**	**19117**	
				B		**C**		**B**		**B**		**B**	**y**	**D**	**B**		**B**		**B**		
0	**Warszawa** Wschodnia .... **1088** d.	0608	0703	0803	0908	1003	1108	1202	1308	1358	1508	1538	1558	1606	1658	1708	1808	1908	2008	2108	...
5	**Warszawa** Centralna .... **1088** d.	0620	0720	0820	0920	1020	1120	1220	1320	1420	1520	1550	1610	1620	1710	1720	1820	1920	2020	2120	...
71	Skierniewice .... **1088** d.	0704	0806	0904	1006	1104	1206	1304	1404	1504	1606	1634	1702	1707	|	1806	1904	2006	2104	2204	...
111	Koluszki............................ **1088** d.	0725	0829	0925	1029	1125	1229	1325	1425	1525	1629	1657	1723	1729	|	1829	1925	2029	2125	2225	...
132	Łódź Widzew..............................d.	0739	0844	0939	1044	1139	1244	1339	1439	1539	1644	1711	1738	1744	1824	1844	1939	2044	2142	2239	...
138	**Łódź** Fabryczna ....a.	0747	0852	0947	1052	1147	1252	1347	1447	1547	1652	1719	1745	1752	1832	1852	1947	2052	2150	2247	...

	IR	*IR*	*IR*	*IR*	*IR*	*IR*	*IR*	*IR*	*IR*	*IR*	*IR*	*IR*	*IR*	*IR*	*IR*	*IR*	*IR*	*IR*	*IR*		
	91501	**91503**	**91101**	**91505**	**9111**	**91103**	**91507**	**91105**	**91509**	**91107**	**91511**	**91109**	**91513**	**91111**	**91515**	**91113**	**91517**	**91115**	**91117**		
	91500	**91502**	**91100**	**91504**	**9110**	**91102**	**91506**	**91104**	**91508**	**91106**	**91510**	**91108**	**91512**	**91110**	**91514**	**91112**	**91516**	**91114**	**91116**		
	E	**B**	**y**	**E**	**B**		**B**		**B**		**B**		**B**		**B**		**⑧h**				
Łódź Fabryczna ....d.	0454	0531	0554	0614	0634	0654	0754	0854	1001	1054	1201	1254	1401	1454	1601	1654	1801	1901	2101	...	...
Łódź Widzew...................................d.	0502	0538	0602	0621	0641	0702	0802	0902	1008	1102	1208	1302	1408	1502	1608	1702	1808	1908	2108	...	...
Koluszki................................ **1088** d.	0518	0552	0618	0640	|	0718	0817	0918	1022	1118	1222	1318	1422	1518	1622	1718	1822	1922	2122	...	...
Skierniewice .... **1088** d.	0541	0614	0640	0704	|	0741	0839	0941	1044	1141	1244	1341	1444	1541	1644	1741	1844	1944	2144	...	...
Warszawa Centralna .... **1088** a.	0630	0700	0730	0755	0800	0830	0925	1030	1130	1230	1330	1430	1530	1630	1730	1830	1929	2030	2230	...	...
Warszawa Wschodnia......... **1088** a.	0642	0712	0742	0807	0812	0842	0937	1042	1142	1242	1342	1442	1542	1642	1747	1842	1940	2042	2242	...	...

km		*TLK*	*TLK*	*TLK*	*TLK*	*TLK*		
		18101	**16100**	**56110**	**16102**	**16110**		
			16101	**56111**	**16103**	**16111**		
		A		**g**		**⑧ft**		
0	**Warszawa** Wschodnia .... **1088** d.	...	0533	0935	1335	1743	...	...
5	**Warszawa** Centralna .... **1088** d.	...	0545	0950	1350	1755	...	...
71	Skierniewice........................ **1088** d.	...	0636	1037	1437	1842	...	...
111	Koluszki .... **1088** d.	...	0659	1101	1502	1906	...	...
132	Łódź Widzew ....d.	...	0716	1116	1521	1921	...	...
147	**Łódź** Kaliska................................d.	0618	0750	1148	1553	1952	...	...
260	Kalisz...d.	0806	0939	1337	1745	2141	...	...
284	Ostrów Wielkopolski .... **1080** d.	0826	1002	1358	1807	2202	...	...
390	**Wrocław** Gł. ....a.	...	1155	1552	1958	2353	...	...

	TLK	*TLK*	*TLK*	*TLK*	*TLK*		
	61110	**61103**	**65110**	**61100**	**81100**		
	61111	**61102**	**65111**	**61101**			
	Gt		**g**		**A**		
Wrocław Gł. ....d.	0448	0943	1146	1540	...	...	...
Ostrów Wielkopolski .... **1080** d.	0650	1145	1341	1740	1920	...	...
Kalisz...d.	0711	1206	1402	1800	1941	...	...
Łódź Kaliska...............................d.	0913	1406	1602	2002	2127	...	...
Łódź Widzew ....d.	0932	1424	1620	2024	...	...	...
Koluszki .... **1088** d.	0948	1440	1637	2043	...	...	...
Skierniewice.......................... **1088** d.	1011	1506	1703	2106	...	...	...
Warszawa Centralna......... **1088** a.	1100	1600	1755	2155	...	...	...
Warszawa Wschodnia .... **1088** a.	1137	1617	1807	2207	...	...	...

A – (1,2) Łódź Kaliska - Ostrów Wlkp. - Poznań - Szczecin and v.v.
B – ①–⑤ (not Dec. 24 - Jan. 1, Apr. 5, May 3, June 3, 4).
C – ①–⑤ (not Dec. 24, 25, 28, 29, 30, Jan. 1, Apr. 5, May 3, June 3, 4).
D – ①–⑥ (not Dec. 25, 26, Jan. 1, 2, Apr. 5).
E – ①–⑤ (not Apr. 5, May 3, June 3, 4).
G – ①–⑥ (not Dec. 25, Jan. 1, Apr. 5).
f – Not Dec. 24, 31, Apr. 4.
g – From / to Gdynia (Table **1030**).
h – Not Dec. 24, 25, 31, Jan. 1, Apr. 4.
t – From / to Terespol (Table **1050**).
y – Not Dec. 25, Jan. 1.

WROCŁAW - KŁODZKO - LICHKOV 1095

km		**16201**	**252**	2	2	2	2	2	2	2	2	2
		66511	**66001**	◇	◇	◇	◇	◇	◇	◇	◇	◇
		A	**B**		**j**						**p**	
	Warszawa C. **1090**...d.	2250	...	...	...	...	...	...	...	...	...	...
0	**Wrocław** Gł.....................d.	0559	0602	0635	...	0943	1035	1235	1435	1635	1745	1906
72	Kamieniec Ząbkowicki..d.	0727	0728	0803	...	1104	1203	1403	1606	1806	1907	2035
94	Kłodzko Gł.......................a.	0749	0751	0831	...	1129	1231	1431	1631	1831	1932	2100
94	Kłodzko Gł.......................d.	...	0752	0847	...	1130	1247	1447	1632	1832	1958	2101
138	**Kudowa Zdrój** ....a.	...	|	|	...	1354	|	|	|	|	2230	|
130	Międzylesie......................a.	...	0834	0918	...	...	1321	1511	1720	1953	...	2149
130	Międzylesie ▦ ....d.	...	0837	*0948*t	1048	...	...	*1629*f	*1844*f	...	...	...
139	**Lichkov** ▦ ....a.	...	0845	*0957*t	1057	...	...	*1638*f	*1853*f	...	...	...
	Pardubice **1145**........a.	...	1012	...	...	...	...	...	...	...	...	...

	2	2	2	2	2	2	2	2	2	**253**	**66510**
	◇	◇	◇	◇	◇	◇	◇	◇	◇	**66002**	**61200**
			t	**p**						**B**	**A**
Pardubice **1145**..... d.	...	...	...	...	...	...	...	...	...	1744	...
Lichkov ▦ ....d.	...	...	0821	...	*1010*j	...	*1520*f	...	*1814*f	1911	...
Międzylesie ▦ ....a.	...	...	0830	...	*1019*j	...	*1529*f	...	*1823*f	1920	...
Międzylesie ....d.	0531	0659	...	...	1037	1334	1533	...	1830	1923	...
Kudowa Zdrój...... d.	|	|	...	0657	|	|	|	1441	|	|	...
Kłodzko Gł. .... a.	0610	0741	...	0823	1110	1410	1610	1659	1910	2002	...
Kłodzko Gł. .... d.	0611	0742	...	0825	1111	1411	1611	1722	1911	2003	2135
Kamieniec Ząbkowicki d.	0644	0819	...	0900	1144	1444	1644	1746	1944	2027	2201
Wrocław Gł............. a.	0814	0935	...	1030	1316	1618	1816	1916	2116	2151	2319
Warszawa C. **1090**. a.	...	...	...	...	...	...	...	...	...	...	0600

A – From Warszawa June 19 - Sept. 26; from Kudowa Zdrój June 20 - Sept. 27: ━ 2 cl. and (1,2) Warszawa - Wrocław - Kudowa Zdrój and v.v.
B – (1,2) Wrocław - Lichkov - Pardubice and v.v.
p – From / to Poznań (Table **1070**).
f – Not Dec. 24, 25, 31.
j – ⑥⑦ (not Dec. 26, Apr. 4).
t – Not Dec. 25, 26, Jan. 1, Apr. 4, 5.
◇ – Stopping train.

2nd class only POLISH LOCAL RAILWAYS 1099

Certain trains Wolsztyn - Poznań and Wolsztyn - Leszno are hauled by steam locomotive - for details see www.parowozy.com.pl

km		①–⑥	①–⑤		🚂			①–⑤		🚂	
		A	**F**		**W**	**w**		**F**		**J**	
0	Zbąszynek .... d.	...	...	0645	...	0840	...	1245	1515	...	1855
6	Zbąszyń..................... d.	...	...	0651	...	0846	...	1241	1521	...	1906
28	Wolsztyn.................... d.	0510	0600	0730	0800	0911	...	1313	1602	1750	1934
75	**Leszno**..................... a.	0605	0710	0821	0853	1008	...	1413	1653	1855	2023

		🚂		①–⑤		⑧		🚂	⑧	
		H	**w**	**F**		**C**		**X**	**C**	
Leszno .... d.	0611	0958	1020	1220	1420	1530	1733	2030	2120	...
Wolsztyn .... d.	0714	1051	1116	1311	1518	1625	1828	2124	2215	...
Zbąszyń....................... a.	0739	...	1141	1336	1542	...	1852	...	...	...
Zbąszynek .... a.	0753	...	1148	1352	1548	...	1908	...	...	...

km		①–⑤	**77325**				**77333**				
		G	🚂				🚂 **w**				
0	**Wolsztyn** .... d.	0430	0511	0728	...	1130	1400	1600	...	1943	...
81	**Poznań** Gł.................. a.	0609	0708	0923	...	1309	1557	1745	...	2129	...

	①–⑤		**77324**				**77332**			
	G		🚂 **w**				🚂			
Poznań Gł. .... d.	0545	0635	0855	...	1333	1555	1715	1935	...	...
Wolsztyn...................... a.	0722	0830	1046	...	1509	1733	1906	2115	...	...

KRAKÓW - TRZEBINIA - OŚWIĘCIM (for Auschwitz). *65 km.* Journey time: 77–90 mins (from Kraków), 90–111 mins (from Oświęcim). Additional services by changing at Trzebinia.
From **Kraków Główny**: 0615, 0653 (*EC* **118**), 0705, 0845, 1105, 1445, 1539, 1841, 2142 ⑧, 2215 (*D* **200**).
From **Oświęcim**: 0356 ①–⑥, 0427, 0445 (*D* **201**), 0501, 0655, 0815, 1115, 1634 ⑦, 2008 (*EC* **119**), 2021.

KRAKÓW - SKAWINA - OŚWIĘCIM (for Auschwitz). *70 km.* Journey time: 106–110 mins (from Kraków), 111–118 mins (from Oświęcim).
From **Kraków Główny**: 0441, 0545 **F**, 1430, 1520, 1758.
From **Oświęcim**: 0350, 0535, 1318 **F**, 1536, 1738.

KATOWICE - OŚWIĘCIM. *33 km.* Journey time: 56–62 mins. From **Katowice**: 0540 **F**, 0650, 1435, 1534, 1855. From **Oświęcim**: 0517 **F**, 0632, 0818, 1550, 1830.

KRAKÓW - WIELICZKA (for Salt Mine). *15 km.* Journey time: 26 mins.
From **Kraków Główny**: 0503, 0554 **F**, 0630, 0736, 0835, 0935, 1135, 1335, 1435, 1535, 1635 **F**, 1736, 1835, 2038.
From **Wieliczka Rynek**: 0533, 0624 **F**, 0707, 0806, 0908, 1006, 1206, 1406, 1506, 1606, 1706 **F**, 1806, 1906, 2108.

WAŁBRZYCH - KŁODZKO. *51 km.*
From Wałbrzych Główny: 0614, 1154, 1554, 1941.
From Kłodzko Główne: 0441, 0941, 1341, 1741.

KRAKÓW - WADOWICE (Birth place of Pope John Paul II). *62 km.* Journey time 79 – 98 (minutes. Special fares payable. From **Kraków**: 1323. From **Wadowice**: 0744.

GDYNIA - HEL. *77 km.* Local services only.

Dec. 14 - June 19 and Sept. 1 - Dec. 12. Journey time 96–109 mins.
From **Gdynia Gł.**: 0537, 0704, 1034, 1232, 1346, 1516, 1632, 1902, 2035.
From **Hel**: 0431, 0620, 0745, 0946, 1233, 1430, 1632, 1834.

June 20 - Aug. 31. Journey time 114–147 mins
From **Gdynia Gł.**: 0310, 0347, 0405 **h**, 0539, 0703, 0828, 0928, 0954, 1123, 1217, 1316, 1346, 1516, 1627, 1803 ⑧ **x**, 1943, 2149.
From **Hel**: 0402, 0627, 0834, 1048, 1130, 1300, 1425, 1507, 1607, 1642, 1732, 1852, 2011, 2058 **h**, 2126, 2214.

A – ①–⑥ (not Dec. 25, 26, Jan. 1, 2, Apr. 5, May 3, June 4, 5).
C – ⑧ (not Dec. 24, 25, 31, Jan. 1, Apr. 4, May 2, June 3, 4).
F – ①–⑤ (not Dec. 24, 25, 31, Jan. 1, Apr. 5, May 3, June 3, 4).
G – ①–⑤ (not Dec. 25, Jan. 1, Apr. 5, May 3, June 3).
H – HEFAJSTOS – May 2, Sept. 19: 🚂, (1,2) and ✕ Wrocław (depart 0806) - Lesno - Wolsztyn.
J – HEFAJSTOS – May 2, Sept. 19: 🚂, (1,2) and ✕ Wolsztyn - Lesno - Wrocław (arrive 2035).
W – THE WOLSZTYN EXPERIENCE – Feb. 14, Apr. 11, July 4, Aug. 28, Oct. 31 (dates subject to confirmation): 🚂, (1,2) and ✕ Wolsztyn - Lesno - Wrocław (arrive 1106).
X – THE WOLSZTYN EXPERIENCE – Feb. 14, Apr. 11, July 4, Aug. 28, Oct. 31 (dates subject to confirmation): 🚂, (1,2) and ✕ Wrocław (depart 1821) - Lesno - Wolsztyn.
h – From / to Warszawa and Kraków. Table **1030**.
x – ⑧ (not Dec. 25, 26, Jan. 1, Apr. 4, 5).
w – Not Dec. 25, 26, Jan. 1, Apr. 4, 5.
🚂 – Normally hauled by steam locomotive (not guaranteed), except July / August.
⊠ – Operated on behalf of The Wolsztyn Experience. Special fares payable.

Christmas / New Year cancellations – see page 539

CZECH REPUBLIC

Services: Operator: České Dráhy (ČD); railway infrastructure and timetables is the responsibility of Správa železniční dopravní cesty (SŽDC). All daytime trains convey first and second classes of travel unless otherwise shown by '2' at the top of the column or by a note (which may be in the table heading).

Timings: Valid **December 13, 2009 - December 11, 2010**. Amendments are likely from **March 7** and **June 13**. A reduced service runs on the evening of Dec. 24, 31 and morning of Dec. 25, Jan. 1. For further details of Christmas and New Year cancellations see page 539.

Reservations: It is possible to reserve seats on most Express trains.

Supplements: SuperCity (*SC*) trains are operated by tilting *Pendolino* units and have a compulsory reservation fee of 200 CZK or €7.00.

Station names: hlavní = main; západ = west; východ = east; horní = upper; dolní = lower; starý = old; město = town; předměstí = suburban; nádraží = station.

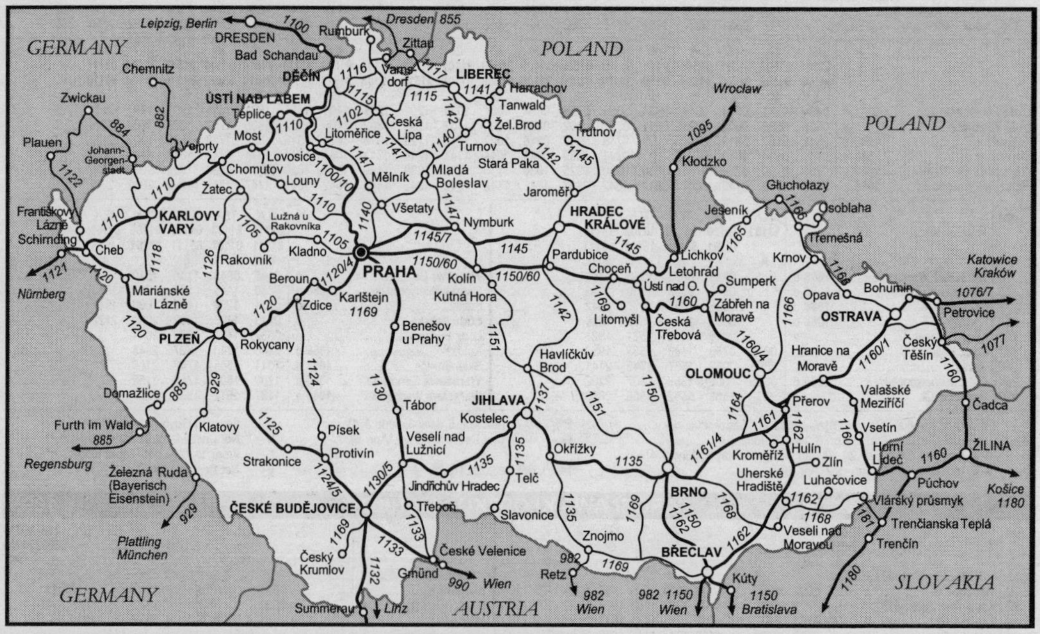

1100 PRAHA - ÚSTÍ NAD LABEM - DĚČÍN - DRESDEN

km	Praha - Ústí : see also **1110**	*EN*			*EC*		*EC*		*EC*		*EC*		*EC*				*EC*			*EN**				
		476	**440**		**178**	**770**	**176**	**772**	**378**	**774**	**174**	**776**	**172**	**778**	**976**	**1165**	**170**	**780**	**782**	**456**	**784**	**978**	**786**	**788**
				2	✕		✕		✕		✕		✕			2	✕					2		
		♦	♦		♦		♦		♦		♦		♦		Ⓐ		♦		Ⓐ	**CP**		Ⓐ		
0	**Praha** hlavní ▷ d.	0333	0518	...	0631	0650	0831	0850	1031	1050	1231	1250	1431	1450	1550	...	1631	1650	1750	1831	1850	1950	2050	2329
3	**Praha** Holešovice ▷ d.	|	0529	...	0640	0659	0840	0859	1040	1059	1240	1259	1440	1459	1559	...	1640	1659	1759	1840	1859	1959	2059	2338
27	Kralupy nad Vltavou d.	|	0550	...	|	0719	|	0919	|	1119	|	1319	|	1519	1619	...	|	1719	1819	|	1919	2019	2119	2359
66	Roudnice nad Labem d.	|	0612	...	|	0743	|	0943	|	1143	|	1343	|	1543	1643	...	|	1743	1843	|	1943	2043	2143	0022
84	Lovosice d.	|	0624	...	|	0758	|	0958	|	1158	|	1358	|	1558	1658	...	|	1758	1858	|	1958	2058	2158	0035
106	**Ústí nad Labem** hlavní ▷ a.	0442	0640	...	0742	0813	0942	1013	1142	1213	1342	1413	1542	1613	1713	...	1742	1813	1913	1942	2013	2113	2213	0050
106	**Ústí nad Labem** hlavní ▶ d.	0443	...	0700	0743	0815	0943	1015	1143	1215	1343	1415	1543	1615	...	1727	1743	1815	1915	1943	2015	*2117*	2215	0051
129	**Děčín** ▶ a.	0500	...	0728	0800	0832	1000	1032	1200	1232	1400	1432	1600	1632	...	1743	1800	1832	1932	2000	2032	*2133*	2232	0107
129	**Děčín** 🏛 ⊖ d.	0502	...	...	0802	...	1002	...	1202	...	1402	...	1602	...	...	...	1802	...	...	2002	...	...	...	...
151	Bad Schandau 🏛 ⊖ **857** d.	|	...	...	0820	...	1020	...	1220	...	1420	...	1620	...	...	...	1820	...	...	2019	...	...	...	...
191	**Dresden** Hbf **857** a.	0546	...	...	0846	...	1046	...	1246	...	1446	...	1646	...	...	...	1846	...	...	2047	...	...	...	...

					*EN**			*EN**		*EC*		*EC*		*EC*		*EC*		*EC*		*EC*			*EN*	
	771	**773**	**775**	**777**	**457**	**1156**	**975**	**459**	**779**	**171**	**781**	**173**	**783**	**175**	**785**	**177**	**787**	**379**	**789**	**179**		**441**	**477**	
						2	2			✕		✕		✕		✕		✕		✕	2			
			Ⓐ		**P**		Ⓐ	**C**		♦		♦		♦		♦		♦		♦		♦	♦	
Dresden Hbf **857** d.	...	...	...	...	0710	...	...	0816	...	0910	...	1110	...	1310	...	1510	...	1710	...	1910	...	...	2210	...
Bad Schandau 🏛 ⊖ **857** d.	...	...	...	...	0739	...	...	0857	...	0939	...	1139	...	1339	...	1539	...	1739	...	1939	...	...	|	...
Děčín 🏛 ⊖ a.	...	...	...	...	0755	...	...	0915	...	0955	...	1155	...	1355	...	1555	...	1755	...	1955	...	...	2255	...
Děčín ▶ d.	0424	0524	0624	0724	0757	0816	...	0917	0924	0957	1124	1157	1324	1357	1524	1557	1724	1757	1924	1957	2037	...	2257	...
Ústí nad Labem hlavní ▶ a.	0438	0538	0638	0738	0811	0832	...	0931	0938	1011	1138	1211	1338	1411	1538	1611	1738	1811	1938	2011	2105	...	2311	...
Ústí nad Labem hlavní ▷ d.	0440	0540	0640	0740	0813	...	0839	0933	0940	1013	1140	1213	1340	1413	1540	1613	1740	1813	1940	2013	...	2113	2313	...
Lovosice d.	0458	0558	0658	0758	|	...	0858	|	0958	|	1158	|	1358	|	1558	|	1758	|	1958	|	...	2131	|	...
Roudnice nad Labem d.	0512	0612	0712	0812	|	...	0912	|	1012	|	1212	|	1412	|	1613	|	1812	|	2012	|	...	2144	|	...
Kralupy nad Vltavou d.	0538	0638	0738	0838	|	...	0938	|	1038	|	1238	|	1438	|	1638	|	1838	|	2038	|	...	2209	|	...
Praha Holešovice ▷ a.	0558	0658	0758	0858	0916	...	0958	1037	1058	1116	1258	1316	1458	1516	1658	1716	1858	1916	2058	2116	...	2228	0016	...
Praha hlavní ▷ a.	0609	0709	0809	0909	0927	...	1009	1051	1109	1127	1309	1327	1509	1527	1709	1727	1909	1927	2109	2127	...	2239	0027	...

ADDITIONAL LOCAL TRAINS DĚČÍN - DRESDEN AND V.V.

2nd class

						Sn			
Děčín 🏛 ⊖ d.	0640	0900	1100	1300	1500	1610	1700	1900	...
Bad Schandau a.	0703	0933	1133	1333	1533	1629	1733	1933	...
Bad Schandau **857** d.	*0711*	*0941*	*1141*	*1341*	*1541*	1630	*1741*	*1941*	...
Dresden Hbf **857** a.	*0758*	*1029*	*1229*	*1429*	*1629*	1705	*1829*	*2028*	...

		Su							
Dresden Hbf **857** d.	*0630*	0825	*0900*	*1100*	*1300*	*1500*	*1700*	*1900*	...
Bad Schandau **857** a.	*0716*	0900	*0946*	*1146*	*1346*	*1546*	*1746*	*1946*	...
Bad Schandau d.	0720	0901	0952	1152	1352	1552	1752	1952	...
Děčín 🏛 ⊖ a.	0752	0921	1024	1224	1424	1624	1824	2024	...

♦ – **NOTES** (LISTED BY TRAIN NUMBERS)

170/1 – HUNGARIA – 12 ✕ Budapest - Bratislava - Praha - Dresden - Berlin and v.v.
172/3 – VINDOBONA – 12 ✕ Villach - Wien - Praha - Dresden - Berlin - Hamburg and v.v.
174/5 – JAN JESENIUS – 12 ✕ Budapest - Bratislava - Praha - Dresden - Berlin - Hamburg and v.v.
176 – ALOIS NEGRELLI – 12 ✕ Brno - Praha - Dresden - Berlin - Hamburg.
177 – JOHANNES BRAHMS – 12 ✕ Berlin - Dresden - Praha - Brno - Wien Praterstern.
178 – JOHANNES BRAHMS – 12 ✕ Praha - Dresden - Berlin.
179 – ALOIS NEGRELLI – 12 ✕ Berlin - Dresden - Praha.
378 – CARL MARIA VON WEBER – 12 ✕ Wien - Praha - Dresden - Berlin - Stralsund - (Binz ◐).
379 – CARL MARIA VON WEBER – 12 ✕ (Binz ◐) - Stralsund - Berlin - Dresden - Praha - Brno.
440/1 – EXCELSIOR – 🛏 1, 2 cl., ▬ 2 cl. §, 12 Cheb - Karlovy Vary - Praha - Žilina - Košice and v.v.; 🛏 1, 2 cl. Cheb - Praha (**477/6**) - Bratislava (**811/0**) - Zvolen - Banská Bystrica and v.v.
476/7 – METROPOL – 🛏 1, 2 cl., ▬ 2 cl., 2 Budapest - Bratislava - Brno - Praha - Dresden - Berlin and v.v.; 🛏 1, 2 cl., ▬ 2 cl., 2 Wien Westbf - Brno - Praha - Dresden - Berlin and v.v.

C – CANOPUS – 2 (Ⓡ $) Praha - Dresden - Leipzig - Erfurt and v.v.; 🛏 1, 2 cl., ▬ 2 cl., 2 (Ⓡ) Praha - Leipzig - Erfurt - Frankfurt Sud - Basel - Zürich and v.v. See Table **54**.

P – PHOENIX – 2 (Ⓡ $) Praha - Dresden - Berlin and v.v.; 🛏 1, 2 cl., ▬ 2 cl., 2 (Ⓡ) Praha - Dresden - Berlin - Hannover - Amsterdam and v.v. See Table **54**.
S – ⑥⑦ Apr. 3 - Oct. 31, also Apr. 2 - 5, May 13, 24.
n – From Litoměřice město (d. 1507), Ústí nad Labem hlavní (d. 1548).
u – To Ústí nad Labem hlavní (a. 0943), Litoměřice město (a. 1020).
◐ – Extended to / from Binz on dates in Table **844**.
▶ – Ústí nad Labem - Děčín: see also Table **1115** and foot of Table **1110**.
▷ – For other non-stop trains Praha - Ústí nad Labem and v.v. see Table **1110**.
⊖ – Routeing point for international tickets: Schöna.

§ – ▬ : not Dec. 24 - Jan. 1 from Cheb, not Dec. 23 - 31 from Košice.
$ – Includes 2 - 3 carriages without Ⓡ.
* – *CNL* in Germany.

Other local services:

Praha Masarykovo - Lovosice: every 1 - 2 hours.

Lovosice - Ústí nad Labem: hourly.

LOVOSICE - LITOMĚŘICE - ČESKÁ LIPA — 1102

Local trains, 2nd class

km										
0	**Lovosice 1100** d.	0600	0801	1001	1201	1401	1601	1801	2001	2213
8	Litoměřice horní d.	0615	0816	1016	1216	1416	1616	1816	2016	2225
50	**Česká Lípa** a.	0725	0925	1125	1325	1525	1725	1925	2125	...

		Ⓐ									
Česká Lípa d.	...	0440	0634	0834	1034	1234	1434	1634	1834	2034	...
Litoměřice horní d.	0019	0559	0740	0940	1140	1340	1540	1740	1940	2141	2212
Lovosice 1100 a.	0031	0614	0753	0953	1153	1353	1553	1753	1953	2154	2228

Also: Lovosice - Litoměřice horní: 0500, 0638 Ⓐ, 0702 Ⓐ, 0737, 0836, 0936, 1029, 1136, 1229, 1301Ⓐ, 1336, 1436, 1501Ⓐ, 1536, 1636, 1701Ⓐ, 1736, 1836, 1901Ⓐ, 1936, 2029, 2137, 2308.
Litoměřice horní - Lovosice: 0440Ⓐ, 0529, 0637Ⓐ, 0700Ⓐ, 0759, 0840Ⓐ, 0911, 0959, 1111, 1159, 1259, 1359, 1440Ⓐ, 1459, 1559, 1640Ⓐ, 1700, 1759, 1840Ⓐ, 1859, 1959, 2113.

PRAHA - RAKOVNIK - CHOMUTOV - JIRKOV — 1105

km		**1284**	**1286**	**1880**	**1882**	**1290**	**1292**	**1890**	**1294**	**1296**	**1298**
				2	2			2Ⓐ			Ⓑh
0	**Praha** Masarykovo d.	0702	0902	1002	1202	1302	1502	1617	1702	1902	2102
31	Kladno a.	0741	0941	1041	1241	1341	1541	1708	1741	1943	2143
64	Lužná u Rakovnika a.	0821	1021	*1130*	*1330*	1421	1621	1751	1821	2021	2221
73	**Rakovník** a.	0834	1034	*1148*	*1348*	1434	1634	1804	1834	2034	2234

	1285	**1883**	**1287**	**1289**	**1889**	**1891**	**1293**	**1295**	**1297**	**1299**
	⚒n	2			2	2				
Rakovník d.	0513	0618	0721	0921	*1007*	*1207*	1321	1521	1721	1921
Lužná u Rakovnika d.	0526	0632	0734	0934	*1022*	*1222*	1334	1534	1734	1934
Kladno d.	0608	0714	0815	1015	1115	1315	1415	1615	1815	2015
Praha Masarykovo a.	0646	0753	0852	1052	1252	1352	1452	1652	1852	2052

km	*2nd class*										
0	**Rakovník** d.	0605	0807	*1007*	...	*1408*	*1607*	...	*1807*	...	...
9	Lužná u Rakovnika d.	0624	0824	1024	...	1424	1624	...	1824	...	...
50	Žatec **1126** d.	0712	0910	1110	...	1511	1710	...	1910	...	...
75	**Chomutov** **1126** a.	0742	0942	1142	...	1543	1742	...	1942	...	...
81	Jirkov a.	0756	...	1156	...	1556	1756	...	1956	...	...

Jirkov d.	...	...	0600	0800	...	...	1200	1400	1600	1800
Chomutov **1126** d.	...	...	0616	0812	...	...	1212	1414	1612	1812
Žatec **1126** d.	...	...	0644	0843	...	...	1243	1443	1643	1843
Lužná u Rakovnika a.	...	...	0730	0927	...	...	1327	1529	1727	1927
Rakovník a.	...	...	0748	*0948*	...	...	*1348*	*1548*	*1748*	1948

h – Not Dec. 24, 25, 31, Jan. 1, Apr. 4, July 4, 5.
n – ①–⑥ (not Dec. 25, 26, Jan. 1, 2, Apr. 5, July 5, 6).

Change at Lužná u Rakovnika for connections to / from Chomutov (lower table).
Fast trains run hourly Praha - Kladno.

PRAHA - ÚSTI NAD LABEM - CHOMUTOV - KARLOVY VARY - CHEB — 1110

km		**1688**	◇	**1690**	**440**	**606**	◇	**608**	◇	◇	**610**	**1694**	◇	**612**	◇	**1696**	**614**	◇	**1698**	**616**	◇	**618**	◇	◇
		2		2Ⓐ	E	m	Ⓐ			Ⓐ		2Ⓐ	Ⓐ			2Ⓐ			Ⓐ					
0	**Praha** hlavní ▶ d.	...	...	...	0518	0731	...	0931	...	...	1131	...	...	1331	...	...	1531	...	...	1731	...	1931	...	...
3	**Praha** Holešovice ▶ d.	...	...	...	0529	0740	...	0940	...	...	1140	...	...	1340	...	...	1540	...	...	1740	...	1940	...	...
106	**Ústí nad Labem** hlavní ▶ a.	...	...	...	0640	0842	...	1042	...	...	1242	...	...	1442	...	...	1642	...	...	1842	...	2042	...	...
106	**Ústí nad Labem** hlavní d.	0055	...	0441	0648	0848	...	1048	...	...	1248	1347	...	1448	...	1547	1648	...	1747	1848	...	2048	...	*2224*
123	Teplice v Čechách d.	0116	...	0502	0706	0906	...	1106	...	...	1306	1407	...	1506	...	1607	1706	...	1807	1906	...	2106	...	*2244*
152	**Most** d.	0145	...	0531	0733	0933	...	1133	...	...	1333	1434	...	1533	*1612*	1634	1733	*1808*	1839	1933	...	2133	...	2320
177	**Chomutov** d.	0205	0529	0553	0755	0955	...	1155	...	...	1355	1454	...	1555	*1634*	1654	1755	*1834*	1859	1955	...	2153	*2156*	2340
196	Klášterec nad Ohři d.	▬	0544	▬	0810	1010	...	1210	1217	...	1410	▬	1534	1610	1657	...	1810	1857	...	2010	...	▬	2220	...
236	**Karlovy Vary** ⊙ a.	Ⓐ◇	0629	◇	0847	1047	...	1247	1302	...	1447	◇	1619	1647	1742	...	1847	1942	...	2047	...	◇	2303	...
236	**Karlovy Vary** ⊙ d.	0536	0631	0742	0849	1049	1200	1249	1318	1413	1449	1516	1630	1649	1744	...	1849	2000	...	2049	2115	2226	...	...
262	Sokolov d.	0603	0700	0816	0913	1113	1227	1313	1345	1441	1513	1544	1659	1713	1813	...	1913	2029r	...	2113	2141	2251	...	...
291	**Cheb** a.	0638	0735	0851	0942	1142	1302	1342	1420	1516	1542	1619	1734	1742	1848	...	1942	2104r	...	2142	2216	2325	...	...

	1689	**605**		**619**	**1695**	◇	**611**	◇	**613**	**615**	◇	**617**	◇	◇	**609**	◇	◇	**607**	◇	**441**	◇	◇	◇	◇
	2	Ⓐ			Ⓐ								Ⓐ	Ⓒ		Ⓐ		m		E	Ⓐ			
Cheb d.	...	...	0333	...	...	0542	0612	0708	0812	1012	1107	1212	1236	1317	1412	1434	1543	1612	1714	1812	...	...	2005	2233
Sokolov d.	...	...	0405	...	...	0618	0640	0750	0840	1040	1143	1240	1312	1352	1440	1511	1619	1640	1752	1840	...	...	2041	2308
Karlovy Vary ⊙ a.	...	...	0432	...	...	0645	0704	0817	0904	1104	1210	1304	1339	1419	1504	1537	1645	1704	1819	1904	...	...	2107	2332
Karlovy Vary ⊙ d.	...	...	0446	...	...	0649	0706	...	0906	1106	1221	1306	...	1421	1506	1538	1649	1706	*1821*	1906	2023	...	▬	*2334*
Klášterec nad Ohři d.	...	...	0533	...	...	0734	0743	...	0943	1143	1304	1343	...	1504	1543	1622	1734	1743	*1904*	1943	2106	2109	Ⓐ	*0017*
Chomutov d.	0323	0457	0550	0600	0700	...	0800	...	1000	1200	*1326*	1400	...	*1526*	1600	...	...	1800	...	2000	...	2132	2239	*0035*
Most d.	0344	0522	...	0622	0721	...	0822	...	1022	1222	*1349*	1422	...	*1549*	1622	...	...	1822	...	2022	...	2204	2300	...
Teplice v Čechách d.	0413	0550	...	0650	0748	...	0850	...	1050	1250	...	1450	...	...	1650	...	...	1850	...	2050	...	2237	...	...
Ústí nad Labem hlavní a.	0435	0607	...	0707	0810	...	0907	...	1107	1307	...	1507	...	...	1707	...	...	1907	...	2107	...	2258	...	...
Ústí nad Labem hlavní ▶ d.	...	0613	...	0713	...	...	0913	...	1113	1313	...	1513	...	...	1713	...	...	1913	...	2113	...	...	...	...
Praha Holešovice ▶ a.	...	0716	...	0816	...	...	1016	...	1216	1416	...	1616	...	...	1816	...	...	2016	...	2228	...	...	...	...
Praha hlavní ▶ a.	...	0727	...	0827	...	...	1027	...	1227	1427	...	1627	...	...	1827	...	...	2027	...	2239	...	...	...	...

km	*via Louny (2 cl.)*	Ⓒ	Ⓑh
0	**Praha** Masarykovo d.	0656	1626
47	Slaný d.	0756	1731
90	Louny d.	0842	1825
115	**Most** a.	0910	...

via Louny (2 cl.)	⚒n	Ⓒ
Most d.	...	1644
Louny d.	0532	1716
Slaný d.	0623	1801
Praha Masarykovo a.	0730	1900

Local trains (2 cl.)				
Děčín d.	0528	and	1928	2037
Ústí nad Labem hlavní d.	0557	hourly	1957	2117
Teplice v Čechách d.	0617	⊡	2017	2137
Most a.	0650	until	2050	2210

Local trains (2 cl.)			
Most d.	0504	and	2004
Teplice v Čechách d.	0537	hourly	2037
Ústí nad Labem hlavní d.	0600	⊖	2100
Děčín a.	0628	until	2128

E – EXCELSIOR – 🛏 1, 2 cl., ▬ 2 cl. §, (12) Cheb - Karlovy Vary - Praha - Žilina - Košice and v.v.; 🛏 1, 2 cl. Cheb - Praha (**477/6**) - Bratislava (**811/0**) - Zvolen - Banská Bystrica and v.v.
h – Not Dec. 24, 25, 31, Jan. 1, Apr. 4, July 4, 5.
m – Conveys 🛏 1, 2 cl. Cheb - Karlovy Vary - Praha (**409/8**) - Moskva and v.v.
n – ①–⑥ (not Dec. 25, 26, Jan. 1, 2, Apr. 5, July 5, 6).
r – On Ⓒ Sokolov d. 2042, Cheb a. 2117.
▶ – For other non-stop trains see Table **1100**.
⊙ – Known locally as Karlovy Vary horní (upper).
◇ – Stopping train. 2nd class only.
⊡ – Also Děčín - Ústí at 0454, 2228.
⊖ – Also Ústí - Děčín at 0450, 0521, 2230.
§ – ▬: not Dec. 24 - Jan. 1 from Cheb, not Dec. 23 - 31 from Košice.

ÚSTÍ NAD LABEM - DĚČÍN - ČESKÁ LIPA - LIBEREC — 1115

2nd class

km		**1995**	**1155**	◇	**1157**	**1159**	**1161**	**1163**	**1165**	**1167**	**1169**
				◧							Ⓑh
0	**Ústí nad Labem** hl. § d.	...	0727	...	0927	1127	1327	1527	1727	1927	2117
23	**Děčín** § a.	...	0743	...	0943	1143	1343	1543	1743	1943	2133
23	**Děčín** d.	0521	0745	0841	0945	1145	1345	1545	1745	1945	2138
54	Česká Lipa a.	0607	0821	0926	1021	1221	1421	1621	1821	2021	2214
54	Česká Lipa d.	0609	0827	*0940*	1027	1227	1427	1627	1827	2023	...
113	**Liberec** a.	0731	0941	*1111*	1141	1341	1541	1741	1941	2130	...

	1154	**1156**	**1158**	**1160**	◇	**1162**	**1164**	**1166**	**1168**	◇
	⚒n				◐					
Liberec d.	...	0627	0827	1027	1044	1227	1427	1627	1827	2040
Česká Lipa a.	...	0733	0933	1133	1220	1333	1533	1733	1933	2210
Česká Lipa d.	0610	0739	0939	1139	*1230*	1339	1539	1739	1939	*2226*
Děčín a.	0645	0814	1014	1214	*1314*	1414	1614	1814	2014	*2311*
Děčín § d.	0647	0816	1016	1216	...	1416	1616	1816	2016	...
Ústí nad Labem hl. § a.	0704	0832	1032	1232	...	1432	1632	1832	2032	...

h – Not Dec. 24, 25, 31, Jan. 1, Apr. 4, July 4, 5.
n – ①–⑥ (not Dec. 25, 26, Jan. 1, 2, Apr. 5, July 5, 6).
§ – See also Table **1100** and foot of Table **1110**.
◧ – Every 2 hours 0841 - 1841 (also at 2041 to Ceská Lipa).
◐ – Every 2 hours 1044 - 1844.
◇ – Stopping train. 2nd class.

DĚČÍN - VARNSDORF / RUMBURK — 1116

Local trains, 2nd class

km											
0	**Děčín** d.	0615	0815	...	1015	1215	1415	1615	1815	2015	2236
50	Rybniště a.	0726	0926	1030	1126	1326	1526	1726	1926	2122	2347
61	Varnsdorf a.	*0747*	|	1047	|	*1347*	*1547*	*1747*	*1947*	*2143*	|
61	**Rumburk** a.	0740	0940	...	1140	1340	1540	1740	1940	2136	2400

	Ⓐ										
Rumburk d.	0417	0616	0816	1016	1216	1416	1616	1816	...	2016	...
Varnsdorf d.	|	*0603*	*0803*	|	*1203*	*1405*	*1603*	*1803*	1950	|	...
Rybniště d.	0429	0629	0829	1029	1229	1429	1629	1829	2007	2029	...
Děčín a.	0533	0744	0944	1144	1344	1544	1744	1944	...	2147	...

VARNSDORF - ZITTAU - LIBEREC — 1117

Local trains, 2nd class

km		u	d▽		d			⊖Ⓐ	d▽			d
0	**Varnsdorf** d.	0616	...	1055	...	1255	1455	*1525*	...	1629	1855	...
27	Zittau 🚌 ▷ d.	0636	0843	1115	1243	1315	1515	1551	1643	1718	1915	2043
45	**Liberec** ▷ a.	0728	0918	1156	1318	1356	1557	1627	1718	1756	1957	2118

	c	Ⓐ⊖	d		d▽	Ⓐ⊖	⑥⑦			d		d▽
Liberec ▷ d.	0626	0702	0838	1027	1238	1330	1330	1501	1603	1638	1828	2035
Zittau 🚌 ▷ a.	0700	0736	0910	1103	1310	1403	1403	1540	1640	1710	1904	2110
Varnsdorf a.	0721	*0800*	*0941*	1126	...	*1426*	1424	1601	1701	...	1926	*2148*

c – On Ⓐ Liberec d. 0631, Zittau a. 0709, Varnsdorf a. 0735.
d – To / from Dresden (Table **855**).
u – On Ⓐ Zittau d. 0644.
▽ – To / from Tanwald on Ⓒ (Table **1141**).
▷ – Additional trains: Zittau - Liberec 0433 Ⓐ, 0620 Ⓐ ⊖, 0915 Ⓐ ⊖, 0915 ⑥⑦, 1222 Ⓐ ⊖; Liberec - Zittau 0446 Ⓐ, 0803 ⑥⑦, 1130 Ⓐ ⊖, 1730 Ⓐ ⊖.
⊖ – Operator: Railtrans.

KARLOVY VARY - MARIÁNSKÉ LÁZNĚ — 1118

Operator: Viamont. 2nd class

km										
0	**Karlovy Vary** dolní (lower) d.	0620	0900	1100	1300	1500	1700	1910	2100	...
33	Bečov nad Teplou d.	0650	0932	1134	1332	1532	1732	1941	2134	...
53	**Mariánské Lázně** a.	0737	1019	1221	1419	1619	1819	2028	2221	...

Mariánské Lázně d.	0600	0827	1045	1227	1427	1627	1850	2045	...
Bečov nad Teplou d.	0650	0917	1133	1315	1515	1715	1941	2133	...
Karlovy Vary dolní (lower) a.	0722	0949	1205	1349	1549	1749	2013	2205	...

Christmas/New Year cancellations – see page 539

1120 PRAHA - PLZEŇ - MARIÁNSKÉ LÁZNĚ - CHEB

km		750	350	752	962	754	354	756		964	758	352	760	966		762	356	764	968		766	766	970	960
		⊡	N		z		M			z		N		k			M		k		Ⓑ h	h		Ⓑ h
0	**Praha** hlavní 1124 d.	0404	0504	0604	0704	0804	0904	1004	...	1104	1204	1304	1404	1504	...	1604	1704	1804	1904	...	2004	2004	2104	2334
4	Praha Smíchov 1124 d.	0412	0512	0612	0712	0812	0912	1012	...	1112	1212	1312	1412	1512	...	1612	1712	1812	1912	...	2012	2012	2112	2342
43	Beroun 1124 d.	0441	0541	0641	0741	0841	0941	1041	...	1141	1241	1341	1441	1541	...	1641	1741	1841	1941	...	2041	2041	2141	0011
52	Zdice 1124 d.	0449	|	0649	|	0849	|	1049	...	|	1249	|	1449	|	...	1649	|	1849	|	...	2049	2049	|	|
91	Rokycany d.	0531	0631	0731	0831	0931	1031	1131	...	1231	1331	1431	1531	1631	...	1731	1831	1931	2031	...	2131	2131	2231	0058
114	**Plzeň** hlavní a.	0550	0650	0750	0850	0950	1050	1150	...	1250	1350	1450	1550	1650	...	1750	1850	1950	2050	...	2150	2150	2250	0118
114	**Plzeň** hlavní d.	0606	0700	0806	...	1006	1100	1206	...	...	1406	1500	1606	...	...	1806	1900	2006	...	...	2206	...	...	...
	Furth im Wald 🚌 **885** a.	|	0810	|	...	|	1210	|	...	...	|	1610	|	...	...	|	2012	|	...	...	|	...	...	...
147	Stříbro d.	0631	...	0831	...	1031	...	1231	...	...	1431	...	1631	...	...	1831	...	2031	...	...	2231	...	...	...
190	Mariánské Lázně d.	0721	...	0921	...	1121	...	1321	...	...	1521	...	1721	...	...	1921	...	2121	...	...	2321	...	...	...
220	**Cheb** a.	0747	...	0947	...	1147	...	1347	...	...	1547	...	1747	...	...	1947	...	2147	...	...	2347	...	...	...

	961	963	751	751	965	753	351		755	967	757	355		759	969	761	353		763	971	765	357	767	
	①–⑥ n			①–⑥ n	k		N			z		M			z		N			z		M	⊡	
Cheb d.	...	...	...	0410	...	0610	...	...	0810	...	1010	...	...	1210	...	1410	...	...	1610	...	1810	...	2010	...
Mariánské Lázně d.	...	...	...	0437	...	0637	...	...	0837	...	1037	...	...	1237	...	1437	...	...	1637	...	1837	...	2037	...
Stříbro d.	...	...	...	0529	...	0729	...	...	0929	...	1129	...	...	1329	...	1529	...	...	1729	...	1929	...	2129	...
Furth im Wald 🚌 **885** d.	...	...	...	|	...	|	0750	...	|	...	|	1150	...	|	...	|	1550	...	|	...	|	1952	|	...
Plzeň hlavní a.	...	...	...	0552	...	0752	0857	...	0952	...	1152	1257	...	1352	...	1552	1657	...	1752	...	1952	2059	2152	...
Plzeň hlavní d.	0410	0510	0610	0610	0710	0810	0910	...	1010	1110	1210	1310	...	1410	1510	1610	1710	...	1810	1910	2010	2110	2210	...
Rokycany d.	0431	0531	0631	0631	0731	0831	0931	...	1031	1131	1231	1331	...	1431	1531	1631	1731	...	1831	1931	2031	2131	2231	...
Zdice 1124 d.	0512	0612	0712	0712	|	0912	|	...	1112	|	1312	|	...	1512	|	1712	|	...	1912	|	2112	|	2312	...
Beroun 1124 d.	0521	0621	0721	0721	0821	0921	1021	...	1121	1221	1321	1421	...	1521	1621	1721	1821	...	1921	2021	2121	2221	2321	...
Praha Smíchov 1124 a.	0550	0650	0750	0750	0850	0950	1050	...	1150	1250	1350	1450	...	1550	1650	1750	1850	...	1950	2050	2150	2250	2350	...
Praha hlavní 1124 a.	0558	0658	0758	0758	0858	0958	1058	...	1158	1258	1358	1458	...	1558	1658	1758	1858	...	1958	2058	2158	2258	2358	...

M – [12] Praha - Furth im Wald - Regensburg - München and v.v. (Table **57**).
N – [12] Praha - Schwandorf - Nürnberg and v.v. (Table **57**).
h – Not Dec. 24, 25, 31, Jan. 1, Apr. 4, July 4, 5.
k – To/from Klatovy (Table **929**).

n – Not Dec. 25, 26, Jan. 1, 2, Apr. 5, July 5, 6.
z – To/from Klatovy, Železná Ruda (Table **929**).
⊡ – Conveys 🛏 1, 2 cl., ▬ 2 cl. § Plzeň - Praha (**440/1**) - Žilina - Košice and v.v.; [2] Cheb - Plzeň - Praha (**440/1**) - Žilina - Košice and v.v.

§ – ▬: not Dec. 24 - Jan. 1 from Plzeň, not Dec. 23 - 31 from Košice.

TRAIN NAMES: **350/3** KAREL ČAPEK, **351/2** JAN HUS, **354/7** FRANZ KAFKA, **355/6** ALBERT EINSTEIN.

1121 CHEB - MARKTREDWITZ - NÜRNBERG

27 km *												
	⊖	⊖	⊖		⊖	⊖		⊖	⊖	⊖		⊖
	C	A		C			d					
Cheb d.	0622	0651	0822	0915	1022	1222	1302	1422	1622	1822	1915	2022
Schirnding 🚌 d.	0636	0705	0836	0929	1036	1240	1316	1436	1636	1840	1929	2036
Marktredwitz a.	0648	0717	0852	0942	1048	1252	1329	1448	1648	1852	1942	2048
Nürnberg **880** a.	*0817*	*0915*	*1018*	1115	*1218*	*1415*	1515	*1618*	*1818*	*2018*	2124	*2218*

	⊖		⊖	⊖		⊖	⊖	⊖		⊖	⊖
		C									
Nürnberg **880** d.	*0545*	0648	*0748*	*0948*	1048	*1148*	*1348*	*1548*	1648	*1748*	*1948*
Marktredwitz d.	0710r	0828	0910v	1110	1228	1310v	1510	1710	1828	1913	2110
Schirnding 🚌 d.	0723r	0840	0923v	1123	1240	1326v	1523	1723	1840	1932	2123
Cheb a.	0736r	0854	0936v	1136	1254	1339v	1536	1736	1854	1945	2136

A – ①–⑤ (not Dec. 24, 25, 31, Jan. 1, 6, Apr. 2 - 5, May 13, 24, June 3, Nov. 1).
C – ⑥⑦ (also Dec. 24, 25, 31, Jan. 1, 6, Apr. 2 - 5, May 13, 24, June 3, Nov. 1).
d – Runs 13 minutes later to Marktredwitz on dates in note **C**.
r – On dates in note **A** runs 24 - 26 minutes later.
v – On dates in note **C** runs 3 - 9 minutes later.
⊖ – Operator: Vogtlandbahn (Arriva).
* – Cheb - Schirnding = 13 km; Cheb - Marktredwitz = 27 km.

1122 CHEB - FRANTIŠKOVY LÁZNĚ - PLAUEN - ZWICKAU

Local trains 2nd class

km										
0	**Cheb** ▶ d.	0607	0807	1007	1207	1407	1607	1807	2007	...
9	**Františkovy Lázně** ▶ d.	0615	0815	1015	1215	1415	1615	1815	2015	...
27	Bad Brambach 🚌 **881** d.	0638	0838	1038	1238	1438	1638	1838	2038	...
76	**Plauen** **880/1** a.	0746	0946	1146	1346	1546	1746	1946	2146	...
101	Reichenbach (Vogtl) ... **880/1** a.	0826	1026	1226	1426	1626	1826	2026	2213	...
124	**Zwickau** (Sachs) **880/1** a.	0850	1051	1250	1450	1650	1850	2050	2237	...

								c	
Zwickau (Sachs) **880/1** d.	...	0708	0906	1106	1306	1506	1706	1912	...
Reichenbach (Vogtl) **880/1** d.	0520	0733	0933	1133	1333	1533	1733	1934	...
Plauen **880/1** d.	0611	0811	1011	1211	1411	1611	1811	2011	...
Bad Brambach 🚌 **881** d.	0721	0921	1121	1321	1521	1721	1921	2121	...
Františkovy Lázně ▶ d.	0743	0943	1143	1343	1543	1743	1943	2143	...
Cheb 1110 ▶ a.	0750	0950	1150	1350	1550	1750	1950	2150	...

c – Change at Weischlitz (2022/2028).
Operator: Vogtlandbahn (Arriva).

▶ – Additional local trains Cheb - Františkovy Lázně and v.v. (operated by ČD):
From Cheb: 0506 Ⓐ, 0556, 0647 Ⓐ, 0816, 1016, 1216, 1423, 1526 Ⓑ, 1616, 1827, 2016, 2235.
From Františkovy Lázně: 0516, 0631 Ⓐ, 0722, 0826 Ⓐ, 0934, 1134, 1325, 1536 Ⓑ, 1734, 1934, 2125.

1124 PRAHA - BEROUN - PŘÍBRAM - PISEK - ČESKÉ BUDĚJOVICE

2nd class

km		1242	1242	1244	1246	1248	1250	1252	1254	1256
			Ⓐ		Ⓒ	⚒n				
0	**Praha** hlavní 1120 d.	...	0534	0734z	0934	1134	1334	1534	1734	1934
4	Praha Smíchov 1120 d.	...	0542	0742	0942	1142	1342	1542	1742	1942
43	Beroun 1120 d.	...	0611	0811	1011	1211	1411	1611	1811	2011
52	Zdice 1120 d.	...	0622	0822	1022	1222	1422	1622	1822	2022
82	Příbram d.	...	0700	0900	1100	1300	1500	1700	1900	2100
100	Březnice d.	0717	0717	0917	1117	1317	1517	1717	1917	2116
142	Písek d.	0759	0759	0959	1159	1359	1559	1759	1959	*2218*
155	Protivín 1125 d.	0815	0815	1015	1215	1415	1615	1815	2015	...
192	**České Budějovice** 1125 a.	0846	0846	1046	1246	1446	1646	1846	2046	...

	1241	1243	1245	1247	1249	1251	1253	1255	1257
	Ⓐ			⑥v					
České Budějovice 1125 d.	...	0507a	0707	0907	1107	1307	1507	1707	1907
Protivín 1125 d.	...	0543	0743	0943	1143	1343	1543	1743	1943
Písek d.	...	0558	0758	0958	1158	1358	1558	1758	1956
Březnice d.	0552	0642	0842	1042	1242	1442	1642	1842	...
Příbram d.	0610	0701	0901	1101	1301	1501	1701	1901	...
Zdice 1120 d.	0641	0739	0939	1139	1339	1539	1739	1939	...
Beroun 1120 d.	0651	0751	0951	1151	1351	1551	1751	1951	...
Praha Smíchov 1120 a.	0720	0820	1020	1220	1420	1620	1820	2020	...
Praha hlavní 1120 a.	*0733*	0828	1028	1228	1428	1628	1828	2028	...

a – Ⓐ only.
n – ①–⑥ (not Dec. 25, 26, Jan. 1, 2, Apr. 5, July 5, 6).
v – Also Dec. 24, Sept. 28, Oct. 28, Nov. 17; not Dec. 26 - Jan. 2.
z – Ⓒ only (on Ⓐ connection departs *0724*).

1125 PLZEŇ - ČESKÉ BUDĚJOVICE

km		929	667	669	665	663	661	925	923	921
		⚒n						h		
0	**Plzeň** hlavní d.	...	0603	0803	1003	1203	1403	1603	1803	2003
34	Nepomuk d.	...	0632	0832	1032	1232	1432	1632	1832	2032
59	Horažďovice předměstí d.	...	0652	0852	1052	1252	1452	1652	1852	2052
76	Strakonice d.	0507	0707	0907	1107	1307	1507	1707	1907	2107
99	Protivín 1124 d.	0526	0726	0926	1126	1326	1526	1726	1926	2126
136	**České Budějovice** 1124 a.	0559	0759	0959	1159	1359	1559	1759	1959	2159
	Jihlava **1135** a.	0833	1033	1233z	1433	1633	1833	2031	...	...
	Brno **1135** a.	1037	1237	1437z	1637	1837	2037	...	...	...

	920	922	924	660	662	664	666	668	
			h						2
Brno **1135** d.	...	...	...	0720	0920z	1120	1320	1520	...
Jihlava **1135** d.	...	0525a	0725	0925	1125z	1325	1525	1725	...
České Budějovice 1124 d.	0601	0801	1001	1201	1401	1601	1801	2001	2240
Protivín 1124 d.	0633	0833	1033	1233	1433	1633	1833	2033	2322
Strakonice d.	0652	0852	1052	1252	1452	1652	1852	2052	2345
Horažďovice předměstí d.	0710	0910	1110	1310	1510	1710	1910	2110	...
Nepomuk d.	0730	0930	1130	1330	1530	1730	1930	2130	...
Plzeň hlavní a.	0758	0958	1158	1358	1558	1758	1958	2158	...

a – Ⓐ only.
h – To/from Havlíčkův Brod (Table **1137**).
n – ①–⑥ (not Dec. 25, 26, Jan. 1, 2, Apr. 5, July 5, 6).
z – ⑤⑥⑦ (daily June 12 - Sept. 11), also Dec. 24, Apr. 5, Sept. 28, Oct. 28, Nov. 17.

1126 PLZEŇ - CHOMUTOV - MOST

2nd class

km		1190		1192	1194	1196		1990		1490	
								Ⓑh		⑦e	
0	**Plzeň** hlavní d.	0605	...	1005	1405	1605	...	1805	...	2005	...
59	Blatno u Jesenice d.	0710	...	1110	1510	1710	...	1910	...	2110	...
107	Žatec 1105 d.	0802	...	1202	1602	1802	...	1957z	...	2202	...
130	Chomutov 1110 a.	0827	...	1227	1627	1827	...	2022	...	2227	...
155	**Most** 1110 a.	0850	...	1250	1650	1850	...	2045	...	2250	...

	1991		1191	1193		1195	1197		1491	
	⚒n								⑦e	
Most 1110 d.	0502	...	0705	0905	...	1305	1705	...	1905	...
Chomutov 1110 d.	0525	...	0728	0928	...	1328	1728	...	1928	...
Žatec 1105 d.	0551z	...	0753	0953	...	1353	1753	...	1953	...
Blatno u Jesenice d.	0646	...	0846	1046	...	1446	1846	...	2046	...
Plzeň hlavní a.	0755	...	0954	1154	...	1554	1954	...	2154	...

e – Also Apr. 5, July 6, Sept. 28; not Apr. 4, July 4, Sept. 26.
h – Not Dec. 24, 25, 31, Jan. 1, Apr. 4, July 4, 5.
n – ①–⑥ (not Dec. 25, 26, Jan. 1, 2, Apr. 5, July 5, 6).
z – Žatec **západ**.

PRAHA - TÁBOR - ČESKÉ BUDĚJOVICE — 1130

km		631	892	*IC* 101	633	635	639	641	643	645	647	649	207	651	653	655	657
		Ⓐ	⊡k	L									B				
0	**Praha** hlavní .... d.	0516	0616	0716	0816	0916	1116	1216	1316	1416	1516	1616	1716	1816	1916	2016	2216
49	Benešov u Prahy .... d.	0559	0659	0759	0859	0959	1159	1259	1359	1459	1559	1659	1759	1859	1959	2059	2259
103	**Tábor** .... d.	0656	0756	0856	0956	1056	1256	1356	1456	1556	1656	1756	1856	1956	2056	2152	2352
130	Veselí nad Lužnicí .... ▷ d.	0720	0820	0920	1020	1120	1320	1420	1520	1620	1720	1820	1920	2020	2120	2215	0015
169	**České Budějovice** ... ▷ a.	0755	0855	0955	1055	1155	1355	1455	1555	1655	1755	1855	1955	2055	2155	2250	0050

	630	632	634	636	638	206	640	644	646	648	650	652	654	*IC* 100	890	656	
	Ⓐ					B								L	⊙k		2
České Budějovice ... ▷ d.	0404	0504	0604	0704	0804	0904	1004	1204	1304	1404	1504	1604	1704	1804	1904	2004	*2235*
Veselí nad Lužnicí .... ▷ d.	0437	0537	0637	0737	0837	0937	1037	1237	1337	1437	1537	1637	1737	1837	1937	2037	2328
Tábor .... d.	0504	0604	0704	0804	0904	1004	1104	1304	1404	1504	1604	1704	1804	1904	2004	2104	2359
Benešov u Prahy .... d.	0558	0658	0758	0858	0958	1058	1158	1358	1458	1558	1658	1758	1858	1958	2058	2158	...
Praha hlavní .... a.	0640	0740	0840	0940	1040	1140	1240	1440	1540	1640	1740	1840	1940	2040	2140	2240	...

B – MATTHIAS BRAUN – (2) Praha - České Budějovice and v.v.; (2) Praha - Linz - Salzburg and v.v. For 🛏 / ▬ see Table **1132**.

L – ANTON BRUCKNER – to / from Linz.

k – Conveys 🛏 1, 2 cl. České Budějovice - Praha (**440/1**) - Žilina - Košice and v.v.

▷ – See also Table **1135**.

⊡ – On June 13 - Sept. 12 continues to Český Krumlov (a. 1006), Nové Údolí (a. 1152).

⊙ – On June 13 - Sept. 12 from Nové Údolí (d. 1613), Český Krumlov (d. 1801).

ČESKÉ BUDĚJOVICE - LINZ — 1132

2nd class (except train **B**)

km			1931	*IC* 101	1933	1935			1939	207
				L			Ⓑh			B
	Praha hlavní **1130** .... d.	...	...	0716	...	...	...	...	...	1716
0	**České Budějovice** .... d.	0533	0804	1006	1218	1417	1607	...	1810	2037
50	Rybnik .... d.	0649	0855	1052	1315	1514	1721	...	1908	2122
64	Summerau 🏛 .... a.	0705	0910	1110	1331	1528	1741	...	1924	2138
64	Summerau .... d.	*0715*	0912	1113	1336	1533	...	1810	1933	2147
73	Freistadt .... d.	*0724*	0921	1122	1345	1541	...	1819	1941	2156
126	**Linz** Hbf .... a.	*0825*	1024	1215	1443	1641	...	1924	2046	2244

	206	1930		1932	1934	*IC* 100			1938
	B					L		Ⓑh	
Linz Hbf .... d.	0614	0721	...	1112	1308	1535	1735	...	1935
Freistadt .... d.	0705	0821	...	1218	1405	1624	1840	...	2042
Summerau .... a.	0714	0830	...	1226	1414	1633	1848	...	2050
Summerau 🏛 .... d.	0715	0837	...	1236	1434	1636	...	1852	2056
Rybnik .... d.	0733	0856	1101	1252	1451	1656	...	1859	2123
České Budějovice .... a.	0821	0954	1155	1351	1550	1742	...	1956	2221
Praha hlavní **1130** .... a.	1140	...	...	...	...	2040	...	...	...

B – MATTHIAS BRAUN – (2) Praha - Linz - Salzburg and v.v.; 🛏 1, 2 cl., ▬ 2 cl. Praha - Salzburg - Innsbruck - Zürich and v.v. (Table **52**). Conveys May 1 - Sept. 11 🛏 1, 2 cl. Praha - Salzburg (**498/9**) - Ljubljana - Zagreb and v.v., returning May 2 - Sept. 12.

L – ANTON BRUCKNER – (12) Praha - Linz and v.v. Classified *EC* in Austria.

h – Also Dec. 19, 26; not Jan. 1, Apr. 4, July 4, 5.

ČESKÉ BUDĚJOVICE - ČESKÉ VELENICE - GMÜND — 1133

2nd class only

Service to June 12 △

km			Ⓐ	Ⓐ	Ⓐ	Ⓐz		C			B						B	D					Ⓐ		
0	**České Budějovice** ..... d.	...	0505	0620	...	...	0712	...	...	...	1004	...	...	1334	...	...	1506	...	1620	...	1819	...	2101	...	2240
*55	Veselí nad Lužnicí ... d.	0453	|	|	0622	0645	|	0740	...	0950	|	1150	...	|	1350	...	|	1550	|	1750	|	1945	|	2146	|
*34	Třeboň .... d.	0516	|	|	0650	0720	|	0803	...	1013	|	1213	...	|	1413	...	|	1613	|	1813	|	2008	|	2209	|
50	České Velenice .... a.	0557	0603	0719	0736	0759	0812	0844	...	1054	1102	1254	...	1435	1454	...	1608	1654	1724	1854	1920	2047	2202	2248	2337
50	České Velenice 🏛 ...... d.	...	...	0724	...	...	0814	...	...	...	1106	...	...	1437	...	...	1610	...	1726	...	1922	...	...	...	...
52	**Gmünd NÖ** 🏛 .... a.	...	...	0728	...	...	0818	...	...	...	1110	...	...	1441	...	...	1614	...	1730	...	1925	...	...	...	...
	Wien FJB **990** .... a.	...	...	...	...	...	*1131*	...	...	...	*1332*	...	...	*1733*	...	...	...	...	*1957*	...	*2149*	...	...	...	...

	Ⓐ			Ⓐ	Ⓐ	Ⓐz		C						B		⑤f	B			D	E	G			t
Wien FJB **990** .... d.	...	...	...	...	...	...	...	...	...	*0622*	...	...	...	...	...	*1029*	*1229*	...	*1429*	...	...	...	*1658*	*1857*	...
Gmünd NÖ 🏛 .... d.	...	...	...	...	...	...	...	...	0733	0847	...	...	...	1219	...	1303	1450	...	1650	...	...	...	1928	2128	...
České Velenice 🏛 .... a.	...	...	...	...	...	...	...	...	0737	0851	...	...	...	1223	...	1307	1454	...	1654	...	...	...	1932	2132	...
České Velenice .... d.	0359	0455	0503	0606	0609	0636	...	0656	0742	0853	0907	...	1107	1225	1310	1326	1457	1507	1657	1707	1905	1926	1933	2133	2207
Třeboň .... d.	|	|	0546	0649	|	0718	0741	0741	|	|	0951	...	1151	|	1351	|	|	1551	|	1751	1946	2009	|	|	2249
Veselí nad Lužnicí .... a.	|	|	0611	0713	|	...	0806	0806	|	|	1016	...	1216	|	1416	|	|	1616	|	1816	2011	2032	|	|	2312
České Budějovice ...... a.	0456	0553	...	...	0709	...	...	...	0842	0945	...	...	...	1321	...	1423	1556	...	1756	...	...	...	2031	2230	...

B – Daily Dec. 13 - 31, Ⓐ Jan. 4 - June 11.

C – Ⓒ (daily July 1 - Aug. 31), also Dec. 23 - 31, Jan. 29, Apr. 1, 2, Oct. 27 - 29.

D – Daily Dec. 13 - June 30; Ⓒ July 3 - Aug. 29; daily Sept. 1 - Dec. 11.

E – Ⓒ to June 12; daily from June 13.

G – Ⓐ Dec. 14 - June 11.

f – Also Dec. 23, 30; not Dec. 25, Jan. 1.

t – To Tábor, arrive 2359.

z – Not Dec. 23 - 31, Jan. 29, Apr. 1, 2, July 1 - Aug. 31, Oct. 27 - 29.

* – Distance from České Velenice.

△ – **From June 13, 2010** timings České Budějovice - Wien will be as follows (change at České Velenice): depart České Budějovice 0509 Ⓐ, 0809, 1009, 1209 Ⓐ, 1409, 1609 Ⓐ, 1809; depart Wien FJB 0622, 0725 Ⓐ, 1029, 1229 Ⓐ, 1429, 1624 Ⓐ, 1857.

ČESKÉ BUDĚJOVICE - JIHLAVA - BRNO — 1135

km		1661	927	929	667	669	665	663	661	2	925
		2Ⓐ	E			F					k
	Plzeň **1125** .... d.	...	...	...	0603	0803	1003	1203	1403	...	1603
0	**České Budějovice** ...... d.	...	0410	0610	0810	1010	1210	1410	1610	...	1810
39	Veselí nad Lužnicí ... ▷ d.	...	0445	0643	0843	1043	1243	1443	1643	...	1843
65	Jindřichův Hradec .... ▷ d.	...	0516	0716	0916	1116	1316	1516	1716	...	1916
117	Kostelec u Jihlavy .... d.	...	0615	0815	1015	1215	1415	1615	1815	...	2014
132	**Jihlava** .... a.	...	0633	0833	1033	1233	1433	1633	1833	...	2031
132	**Jihlava** .... d.	0531	0639	0839	1039	1239	1439	1639	1839	1930	...
161	Okříšky .... d.	0604	0707	0907	1107	1307	1507	1707	1907	2019	...
173	Trebíč .... d.	0620	0723	0923	1123	1323	1523	1723	1923	2044	...
236	**Brno** hlavní .... a.	0737	0837	1037	1237	1437	1637	1837	2037	2210	...

	1837	922	924	660	662	664	666	668	926	928
	Ⓐ	Ⓐ	k		F					Ⓑh
Brno hlavní .... d.	...	...	...	0720	0920	1120	1320	1520	1720	1920
Trebíč .... d.	...	...	...	0831	1031	1231	1431	1631	1831	2037
Okříšky .... d.	...	...	...	0845	1045	1245	1445	1645	1845	2052
Jihlava .... a.	...	...	...	0919	1119	1319	1519	1719	1919	2119
Jihlava .... d.	...	0525	0725	0925	1125	1325	1525	1725	1934	...
Kostelec u Jihlavy .... d.	...	0543	0743	0943	1143	1343	1543	1743	1953	...
Jindřichův Hradec ... ▷ d.	0548	0645	0845	1045	1245	1445	1645	1845	2056	...
Veselí nad Lužnicí ... ▷ d.	0621	0716	0916	1116	1316	1516	1716	1916	2129	...
České Budějovice ..... a.	0701	0749	0949	1149	1349	1549	1749	1949	2202	...
Plzeň **1125** .... a.	...	0958	1158	1358	1558	1758	1958	2158	...	...

CONNECTIONS OKŘÍŠKY - ZNOJMO

km		Ⓐ			Ⓐ	Ⓒ	Ⓐ	⑦e	Ⓐ		
0	Okříšky .... d.	0607	0710	0920	1120	1316	1416	1520	1616	1720	1920
32	Moravské Budějovice ... a.	0644	0745	0955	1155	1351	1451	1555	1656	1758	2000
70	Znojmo .... a.	0732	0847	1047	1247	1449	*1549*	*1647*	1751	1847	...

	Ⓐ	Ⓐ	⚒u			⑦e	Ⓐ			z
Znojmo .... d.	0424	*0534*	0704	...	1104	*1304*	1359	1459	1704	1904
Moravské Budějovice .. d.	0524	0625	0747	0804	1158	1404	1454	1602	1804	1944
Okříšky .... a.	0558	0704	...	0839	1233	1438	1533	1641	1839	2016

JIHLAVA - KOSTELEC U JIHLAVY - TELČ - SLAVONICE §

			Ⓐ	Ⓐ	Ⓒ	Ⓐ	Ⓒ	Ⓐ		Ⓐ	⑦e	Ⓐ
Jihlava .... d.	*0733*	*0925*	1045	*1224*	*1243*	*1350*	*1444*	*1456*	*1645*	*1841*	*1934*	*2047*
Kostelec u J.. a.	*0759*	*0943*	1106	*1247*	*1307*	*1410*	*1504*	*1518*	*1705*	*1902*	*1952*	*2107*
Kostelec u J.. d.	0820	1023	1111	1311	1311	1420	1515	1525	1711	1911	2019	2113
Telč .... a.	0856	1059	1147	1347	1347	1502	1550	1601	1746	1947	2056	2150
Slavonice ...... a.	0954c	1206c	1250	1448	1448	1605	1648	...	1848r	2048	...	...

	Ⓐ	Ⓒ	Ⓐ		Ⓐ	Ⓒ	Ⓐ		⑦e	⚒	⑦e	Ⓐ
Slavonice ...... d.	0703	0810	0842	1105	...	1305	...	1505	...	1705	1810	*1905*
Telč .... d.	0805	0902	0935	1204	1324	1404	1441	1604	1657	1804	1910	2028
Kostelec u J .. a.	0846	0938	1011	1240	1404	1440	1517	1640	1736	1840	1947	2105
Kostelec u J .. d.	0853	*0955*	*1015*	*1249*	*1415*	*1444*	*1521*	*1645*	*1815*	*1903*	*2014*	*2110*
Jihlava .... a.	0913	*1016*	*1033*	*1309*	*1433*	*1514*	*1548*	*1714*	*1833*	*1923*	*2031*	*2130*

E – Ⓐ from České Budějovice; ①–⑥ (not Dec. 25, 26, Jan. 1, 2, Apr. 5, July 5, 6) from Jihlava.

F – ⑤⑥⑦ (daily June 12 - Sept. 11), also Dec. 24, Apr. 5, Sept. 28, Oct. 28, Nov. 17.

c – Ⓒ only.

e – Also Apr. 5, July 6, Sept. 28; not Apr. 4, July 4, Sept. 26.

h – Not Dec. 24, 25, 31, Jan. 1, Apr. 4, July 4, 5.

k – To / from Havlíčkův Brod (Table **1137**).

r – ⚒ only.

u – On Ⓐ to June 30 / from Sept. 1 d. 0644, a. 0735.

z – To Jihlava on Ⓐ (arrive 2106).

▷ – Additional trains: from Veselí nad Lužnicí 0717, 0940, 1140 Ⓐ, 1340, 1540, 1741, 1940 Ⓐ, 2140, 2328 Ⓐ; from Jindřichův Hradec 0517 Ⓒ, 0730, 0942, 1142, 1342 Ⓐ, 1542, 1739, 1942, 2222 Ⓐ. Journey 35 minutes.

§ – Kostelec - Telc *23 km*, Kostelec - Slavonice *53 km*.

HAVLÍČKŮV BROD - JIHLAVA — 1137

2nd class

km					924		1183										1181			915				
			Ⓐ		▽		△					Ⓐ			Ⓐ		△	Ⓐ		P		Ⓐ		
0	Havlíčkův Brod .... d.	0448	0603	0647	0658	0805	0854	...	1005	1205	...	1312	1405	...	1511	1605	1650	1712	1805	1901	...	2005	2105	...
27	Jihlava .... a.	0517	0633	0718	0722	0835	0917	...	1035	1235	...	1344	1435	...	1545	1636	1718	1744	1835	1924	...	2034	2134	...

		914						1180										1182					925	
		Q	Ⓐ	Ⓒ	Ⓐ			△				Ⓐ		Ⓐ		Ⓐ		△		Ⓐ			▽	
Jihlava .... d.	0519	0530	0605	0654	0726	0729	...	0844	0923	...	1122	1236	1322	1436	1522	1614	...	1648	1722	1813	...	1925	2035	...
Havlíčkův Brod .... a.	0548	0554	0643	0734	0752	0752	...	0912	0953	...	1152	1305	1352	1505	1552	1644	...	1711	1752	1844	...	1953	2058	...

P – Ⓑ (not Dec. 24, 25, 31, Jan. 1, Apr. 4, July 4, 5). From Praha (Table **1151**).

Q – ①–⑥ (not Dec. 25, 26, Jan. 1, 2, Apr. 5, July 5, 6). To Praha (Table **1151**).

△ – To / from Pardubice (Table **1142**).

▽ – To / from České Budějovice and Plzeň (Table **1135**).

1140 PRAHA - MLADÁ BOLESLAV - TURNOV - LIBEREC / TANWALD

2nd class only

km			1138	1140		1144	1146	1148	1940		®r
0	**Praha** hlavní	d.	0547	0725	0925	1147	1325	1525	1725	1925	2106	2106
34	Neratovice	d.	0632	0800	1000	1232	1400	1600	1800	2000	2149	2149
40	Všetaty	d.	0643	0807	1007	1243	1407	1607	1807	2007	2157	2157
72	**Mladá Boleslav**	a.	0718	0835	1035	1321	1435	1635	1835	2035	2232	2232
72	**Mladá Boleslav**	d.	▬	0838	1038	1347	1438	1638	1838	2038	...	2240
88	Mnichovo Hradiště	d.	...	0858	1058	1409	1458	1658	1858	2058	...	2259
102	**Turnov**	a.	...	0912	1112	1428	1512	1712	1912	2116	...	2315
	Turnov **1142**	d.	...	0921	1121	...	1521	1721	1921	2121	...	2318
	Liberec **1142**	a.	...	0958	1158	...	1558	1758	1958	2158	...	2356
102	**Turnov**	d.	...	0919	1119	...	1519	1719r	1919	...	...	...
116	Železný Brod	a.	0701	0935	1135	...	1535	1735r	1935	...	...	...
133	**Tanwald**	a.	0727	1004	1204	...	1604	1804r	2004	...	...	...

		1941 Ⓐ	1137	1139		1143	1145	1147	1149		©
Tanwald	d.	...	0549n	0752	...	1146	1346	1546c	1746	2025	...
Železný Brod	d.	...	0626n	0820	...	1220	1420	1620c	1820	2052	...
Turnov	a.	...	0642n	0836	...	1236	1436	1636c	1836	▬	...
Liberec **1142**	d.	0400	0602	0802	...	1202	1402	1602	1802	...	2031
Turnov **1142**	a.	0438	0639	0839	...	1239	1439	1639	1839	...	2112
Turnov	d.	0441	0644	0844	0922	1244	1444	1644	1844	...	2122
Mnichovo Hradiště	d.	0459	0658	0858	0940	1258	1458	1658	1858	...	2140
Mladá Boleslav	a.	0519	0715	0915	1000	1315	1515	1715	1915	...	2200
Mladá Boleslav	d.	0521	0723	0924	1037	1324	1524	1724	1924	2037	2206
Všetaty	d.	0551	0753	0953	1121	1353	1553	1753	1953	2121	2248
Neratovice	d.	0600	0800	1000	1130	1400	1600	1800	2000	2130	2257
Praha hlavní	a.	0638	0838	1038	1212	1438	1638	1838	2038	2212	2335

c – © only.

n – ①–⑥ (not Dec. 25, 26, Jan. 1, 2, Apr. 5, July 5, 6).

r – ® (not Dec. 24, 25, 31, Jan. 1, Apr. 4, July 4, 5).

1141 LIBEREC - TANWALD - HARRACHOV

km						Ⓐ	©d					©d	⑤⑥
0	**Liberec**	▷ d.	0720	0800	0840	0920	0920	1000	1118	1320	1520	1720	1920
12	Jablonec §	▷ d.	0739	0819	0859	0939	0939	1019	1137	1339	1539	1739	1939
27	Tanwald	▷ a.	0813	0853	0933	1013	1013	1053	1213	1413	1613	1813	2013
27	Tanwald	d.	0822r	0854r	0936c	1022	1022	1056c	1221	1421	1621	1821	2021
39	**Harrachov**	a.	0850r	0920r	1005c	1052	1052	1125c	1249	1449	1649	1849	2049

					z	d					©	d
Harrachov	d.	...	0901r	0946r	1106	...	1150c	1256	1456	1656	1905	...
Tanwald	a.	...	0934r	1018r	1140	...	1217c	1323	1523	1723	1930	...
Tanwald	▷ d.	0820	0940	1020	...	1142	1220	1340	1540	1740	...	1938
Jablonec §	▷ d.	0900	1020	1057	...	1218	1300	1420	1620	1820	...	2013
Liberec	▷ a.	0919	1039	1116	...	1236	1319	1450	1639	1839	...	2032

c – © only.
d – To / from Dresden on © (Table **1117** / **855**).

r – © (daily Dec. 13 - Mar. 28, May 29 - Sept. 28).
z – Change at Kořenov (1112 / 1120).

§ – Jablonec nad Nisou.
▷ – Trains run approx every 40 mins Liberec - Tanwald and v.v.

1142 LIBEREC - TURNOV - HRADEC KRÁLOVÉ - PARDUBICE

2nd class

km			625 v	981	983	985	987	989	991	993	995	997
0	**Liberec**	d.	...	0400	0602	0802	1002	1202	1402	1602	1802	2002
38	Turnov	d.	...	0439	0643	0842	1042	1242	1442	1642	1842	2042
52	Železný Brod	d.	...	0456	0700	0900	1100	1300	1500	1700	1900	2100
76	Stará Paka	d.	...	0525	0727	0927	1127	1327	1527	1727	1927	2127
107	Dvůr Králové n. L.	d.	...	0600	0800	1000	1200	1400	1600	1800	2000	2200
122	Jaroměř **1145**	d.	...	0621	0821	1021	1221	1421	1621	1821	2021	2221
139	**Hradec Králové** **1145**	a.	...	0635	0835	1035	1235	1435	1635	1835	2035	2237
139	**Hradec Králové** ►	d.	0540	0642	0842	1042	1242	1442	1642	1842	2042	2242
159	Pardubice-Rosice	a.	0556	0658	0858	1058	1258	1458	1658	1858	2058	2300
161	**Pardubice** ►	a.	0600	0702	0902	1102	1302	1502	1702	1902	2102	2304

		980	982	984	986	988	990	992	994	996
Pardubice ►	d.	0455	0655	0855	1055	1255	1455	1655	1855	2055
Pardubice-Rosice	d.	0459	0700	0900	1100	1300	1500	1700	1900	2100
Hradec Králové ►	a.	0518	0718	0918	1118	1318	1518	1718	1918	2118
Hradec Králové **1145**	d.	0523	0723	0923	1123	1323	1523	1723	1923	2123
Jaroměř **1145**	d.	0542	0742	0942	1142	1342	1542	1742	1942	2143
Dvůr Králové n. L.	d.	0559	0759	0959	1159	1359	1559	1759	1959	2159
Stará Paka	d.	0631	0831	1031	1231	1431	1631	1831	2031	2234
Železný Brod	d.	0700	0900	1100	1300	1500	1700	1900	2100	2301
Turnov	d.	0721	0921	1121	1321	1521	1721	1921	2121	2318
Liberec	a.	0758	0958	1158	1358	1558	1758	1958	2158	2356

km			1183			1181	
0	**Pardubice**	d.	0655	0925	1125	1455	1725
2	Pardubice-Rosice	d.	0702	0930	1132	1502	1732
11	Chrudim	d.	0720	0943	1150	1519	1745
92	**Havlíčkův Brod**	a.	0852	1153	1354	1648	1920
	Jihlava **1137**	a.	0917	...	...	1718	...

			1180			1182
Jihlava **1137**	d.	...	0844	...	...	1648
Havlíčkův Brod	d.	0646	0915	1212	1410	1716
Chrudim	d.	0838	1041	1404	1638	1841
Pardubice-Rosice	a.	0855	1054	1424	1655	1854
Pardubice	a.	0911	1107	1438	1708	1907

v – To Olomouc and Vsetin (Table **1160**).

► – Additional trains **Hradec Kralové - Pardubice** and v.v. Journey 25 - 30 minutes. *Subject to alteration Dec. 23 - Jan. 1.*
From Hradec Kralové: 0104, 0523 Ⓐ, 0602, 0705, 0742 ⚒, 0805 and hourly to 2105, 2211.
From Pardubice: 0026, 0522, 0603 Ⓐ, 0625 and hourly to 2125, 2240 (also 0755 ⚒, 1355 Ⓐ, 1555 ®, 1755 ®).

1145 PRAHA - HRADEC KRÁLOVÉ - TRUTNOV / LETOHRAD

km			943 ⚒n	849	945	851	947	853	949	855	793	857	791	859	951	953	955	957	959
0	**Praha** hlavní	d.	0510	0610	0710	0810	0910	1010	1110	1210	1310	1410	1510	1610	1710	1810	1910	2010	2210
35	Lysá nad Labem **1147**	d.	0543	0643	0743	0843	0943	1043	1143	1243	1343	1443	1543	1643	1743	1843	1943	2043	2243
50	Nymburk **1147**	d.	0556	0656	0756	0856	0956	1056	1156	1256	1356	1456	1556	1656	1756	1856	1956	2056	2256
57	Poděbrady **1147**	d.	0602	0702	0802	0902	1002	1102	1202	1302	1402	1502	1602	1702	1802	1902	2002	2102	2302
116	**Hradec Králové**	a.	0651	0751	0851	0951	1051	1151	1251	1351	1451	1551	1651	1751	1851	1951	2051	2151	2348
116	**Hradec Králové** **1142**	d.	0705	0804	0905	1004	1105	1204	1305	1404	1505	1604	1705	1804	1905	2002	...	...	...
133	Jaroměř **1142**	d.	|	0821	|	1021	|	1221	|	1421	|	1621	|	1821	|	2021	...	...	...
185	**Trutnov**	a.	|	0920	|	1120	|	1320	|	1520	|	1720	|	1920	|	2120	...	...	...
137	Týniště nad Orlicí	a.	0728	...	0928	...	1128	...	1328	...	1528	...	1728	...	1928	...	...	...	...
148	Kostelec nad Orlici město	a.	0745	...	0945	...	1145	...	1345	...	1545	...	1744	...	1945	...	...	...	...
178	**Letohrad**	a.	...	...	...	...	...	...	...	...	...	...	1828	...	...	...	...	...	...

		946 ⚒n	948	790	846	950	848	952	850	954	852	956	854	792	856	958	858	2	2
Letohrad	d.	...	...	0531	...	...	...	...	...	...	...	...	...	...	...	1736	...	...	...
Kostelec nad Orlici město	d.	...	...	0614	...	0815	...	1015	...	1215	...	1415	...	1615	...	1815	...	...	...
Týniště nad Orlicí	d.	...	...	0630	...	0832	...	1032	...	1232	...	1432	...	1632	...	1832	...	...	...
Trutnov	d.	...	...	|	0640	|	0841	|	1041	|	1241	|	1440	|	1640	|	1840	...	...
Jaroměř **1142**	d.	...	...	|	0741	|	0941	|	1141	|	1341	|	1541	|	1741	|	1941	...	...
Hradec Králové **1142**	a.	...	...	0653	0755	0854	0955	1054	1155	1254	1355	1454	1555	1654	1755	1854	1955	...	...
Hradec Králové	d.	0508	0608	0708	0808	0908	1008	1108	1208	1308	1408	1508	1608	1708	1808	1908	2008	...	...
Poděbrady **1147**	d.	0554	0654	0754	0854	0954	1054	1154	1254	1354	1454	1554	1654	1754	1854	1954	2054	2147	...
Nymburk **1147**	d.	0602	0702	0802	0902	1002	1102	1202	1302	1402	1502	1602	1702	1802	1902	2002	2102	2206	2301
Lysá nad Labem **1147**	d.	0614	0714	0814	0914	1014	1114	1214	1314	1414	1514	1614	1714	1814	1914	2014	2114	2225	2325
Praha hlavní	a.	0647	0747	0847	0947	1047	1147	1247	1347	1447	1547	1647	1747	1847	1947	2047	2147	2302	0002

PARDUBICE - WROCLAW

		253 b
Praha hlavní **1150**	d.	1639
Pardubice	d.	1744
Ústí nad Orlicí	d.	1830
Letohrad	d.	1848
Lichkov 🏛	a.	1909
Wroclaw Gl **1095**	a.	2151

		252 d
Wroclaw Gl **1095**	d.	0602
Lichkov 🏛	d.	0847
Letohrad	d.	0910
Ústí nad Orlicí	d.	0926
Pardubice	a.	1012
Praha hlavní **1150**	a.	1121

b – Not Dec. 24, 25, 31, Apr. 3, 4.
d – Not Dec. 25, 26, Jan. 1, Apr. 4, 5.
n – ①–⑥ (not Dec. 25, 26, Jan. 1, 2, Apr. 5, July 5, 6).

1147 DĚČÍN - ÚSTÍ NAD LABEM - MĚLNÍK - KOLÍN

Dečin - Ústí : see Table 1100

km			2Ⓐ	2	2		2	2	2	2	
0	**Děčín** hlavní	d.	0424	0600	0802	...	1202	1402	1602	1802	...
28	**Ústí n. Labem** Střekov	a.	0503	0640	0844	...	1244	1444	1644	1844	...

		2Ⓐ	2	2		2	2	2	2		
Ústí n. Labem Střekov	d.	0516	0655	0913	...	1313	1513	1713	1913	...	...
Děčín hlavní	a.	0555	0735	0955	...	1355	1555	1755	1955	...	...

km			711 ⚒n	713	715	717	719	721	723	725	2
0	**Ústí n. Labem** západ	d.	0447	0647	0847	1047	1247	1447	1647	1847	2003
2	**Ústí n. Labem** Střekov	d.	0452	0652	0852	1052	1252	1452	1652	1852	2008
27	Litoměřice město	d.	0512	0712	0912	1112	1312	1512	1712	1912	2031
63	**Mělník**	d.	0539	0739	0939	1139	1339	1539	1739	1939	2104
73	Všetaty	d.	0547	0747	0947	1147	1347	1547	1747	1947	2114
85	Stará Boleslav	d.	0556	0756	0956	1156	1356	1556	1756	1956	2126
96	Lysá nad Labem **1145**	d.	0606	0806	1006	1206	1406	1606	1806	2006	2137
111	Nymburk **1145**	d.	0619	0819	1019	1219	1419	1619	1819	2019	...
118	Poděbrady **1145**	d.	0627	0827	1027	1227	1427	1627	1827	2027	...
134	**Kolín**	d.	0642	0842	1042	1242	1442	1642	1842	2042	...

		2Ⓐ	2y	710	712	714	716	718	720	722	724 ®h
Kolín	d.	...	...	0715	0915	1115	1315	1515	1715	1915	2115
Poděbrady **1145**	d.	...	...	0730	0930	1130	1330	1530	1730	1930	2130
Nymburk **1145**	d.	...	...	0740	0940	1140	1340	1540	1740	1940	2140
Lysá nad Labem **1145**	d.	0418	0558	0752	0952	1152	1352	1552	1752	1952	2152
Stará Boleslav	d.	0428	0608	0759	0959	1159	1359	1559	1759	1959	2159
Všetaty	d.	0442	0621	0809	1009	1209	1409	1609	1809	2009	2209
Mělník	d.	0451	0630	0817	1017	1217	1417	1617	1817	2017	2217
Litoměřice město	d.	0526	0706	0846	1046	1246	1446	1646	1846	2046	2246
Ústí n. Labem Střekov	a.	0547	0728	0904	1104	1304	1504	1704	1904	2104	2304
Ústí n. Labem západ	a.	0552	0733	0909	1109	1309	1509	1709	1909	2109	2309

km			Ⓐ								F
0	**Rumburk**	d.	0458	...	0712	...	1112	1312c	1512	1712	1712
45	Česka Lípá	d.	0624	0624	0824	...	1224	1424	1624	1810	1824
99	Mladá Boleslav	d.	0722	0722	0922	...	1322	1522	1722	...	1922
129	Nymburk **1145**	a.	0748	0748	0948	...	1348	1548	1748	...	1948
136	Poděbrady **1145**	d.	0756	0756	0956	...	1356	1556	1756	...	1956
152	**Kolín**	a.	0810	0810	1010	...	1410	1610	1810	...	2010

			2Ⓐ							F	
Kolín	d.	...	...	0746	0946	...	1346	1546	1746	1946	...
Poděbrady **1145**	d.	...	...	0800	1000	...	1400	1600	1800	2000	...
Nymburk **1145**	d.	...	...	0808	1008	...	1408	1608	1808	2008	...
Mladá Boleslav	d.	...	...	0833	1033	...	1433	1633	1833	2033	...
Česka Lípá	a.	...	0513	0935	1135	...	1535	1735	1935	2135	...
Rumburk	a.	...	0611	1041	1241c	...	1641	1841	2041	...	...

F – ⑤⑥⑦ (daily June 12 - Sept. 11).
c – ⑤⑥⑦ (also holidays).

h – Not Dec. 24, 25, 31, Jan. 1, Apr. 4, July 4, 5.
n – ①–⑥ (not Dec. 25, 26, Jan. 1, 2, Apr. 5, July 5, 6).

y – On © runs 20 minutes later.

PRAHA - PARDUBICE - BRNO - BŘECLAV - WIEN/BRATISLAVA 1150

km						EC	EC	EC	SC*	EC	EC	EC	EC	EC	EC	IC	EC	EC	EC	EC	EC	IC	EC	EC
		371	1662	373	375	71	71	345	73	273	75	275	103	77	171	571	173	137	79	175	105	573	177	277
		2		2	2	✕	✕	✕	R 🍷	✕	✕	✕	✕	✕	✕	✕	✕	✕	✕	✕	✕	✕	✕	✕
		Ⓐk	Ⓐ	⚒r	⚒r	⚒n	§	♦	§		§		♦	§	♦		♦	♦		♦	♦		♦	S
0	**Praha** hlavní ▷ d.	...	...	...	...	0439	...	0539	0639	0739	0839	0939	...	1039	1139	1239	1339	...	1439	1539	...	1639	1739	1739
62	Kolín ▷ d.	...	...	...	...	|	...	0619	|	0819	|	1019	...	|	1219	|	1419	...	|	1619	...	|	1819	1819
104	**Pardubice** ▷ d.	...	...	...	...	0541	...	0641	0741	0841	0941	1041	...	1141	1241	1341	1441	...	1541	1641	...	1741	1841	1841
164	Česká Třebová ▷ d.	...	...	...	...	0618	...	0718	|	|	1018	|	...	1218	|	1418	|	...	1618	|	...	1818	|	|
255	**Brno** hlavní a.	...	...	...	...	0722	...	0822	0922	1022	1122	1222	...	1322	1422	1522	1622	...	1722	1822	...	1922	2022	2022
255	**Brno** hlavní **1162** d.	*0416*	0504	...	*0523*	0724	0724	0824	0924	1024	1124	1224	...	1324	1424	1524	1624	...	1724	1824	...	...	2024	2024
314	**Břeclav** **1162** a.	*0521*	0551	...	*0622*	0757	0757	0857	0957	1057	1157	1257	...	1357	1457	1557	1657	...	1757	1857	...	...	2057	2057
314	**Břeclav** d.	0526	...	0600	0700	0802	0802	0900	1002	1100	1202	1300	1302	1402	1500	...	1702	1700	1802	1900	1902	...	2102	2111
	Wien Meidling **982** a.	|	...	|	|	0923	0923	|	1123	|	1323	|	1423	1523	|	...	1823	|	1929	|	2020	...	2204p	|
332	Kúty 🏛 d.	0544	...	0617	0717	...	...	0914	...	1114	...	1314	...	...	1514	...	...	1714	...	1914	...	...	...	2125
396	**Bratislava** hlavná a.	0627	...	0700	0800	...	...	0951	...	1151	...	1351	...	...	1551	...	...	1751	...	1951	...	...	...	2202
	Budapest Keleti **1175** a.	...	...	...	...	...	...	1232	...	1432	...	...	...	...	1832	...	...	...	...	2232	...	...	...	...

	IC	EC	Ex			471		EN	EN
	575	379	577		471	477	471	477	477
	✕	✕	Ⓑ						
		♦	h		Y	X	W	♦	V
Praha hlavní ▷ d.	1839	1939	2039	...	2311	2311	2311	0037	0037
Kolín ▷ d.	|	2019	|	...	2356	2356	2356	|	|
Pardubice ▷ d.	1941	2041	2141	...	0023	0023	0023	|	|
Česká Třebová ▷ d.	2018	2118	2218	...	0117	0117	0117	|	|
Brno hlavní a.	2123	2222	2330	...	0224	0224	0224	0322	0322
Brno hlavní **1162** d.	...	...	...	...	0244	0244	0244	0324	0324
Břeclav **1162** a.	...	...	...	...	0322	0322	0322	0357	0357
Břeclav d.	...	...	...	...	0335	0447	0459	0447	0459
Wien Meidling **982** a.	...	...	...	...	|	|	0608	|	0608
Kúty 🏛 d.	...	...	...	...	0350	0501	...	0501	...
Bratislava hlavná a.	...	...	...	...	0433	0540	...	0540	...
Budapest Keleti **1175** a.	...	...	...	...	0820	0832	...	0832	...

	Ex	EC	IC	EC	EC		IC	EC	EC
	576	176	574	278	378		572	104	174
		✕	✕	✕	✕		✕	✕	✕
	⚒n	♦	⚒n	T	♦			♦	♦
Budapest Keleti **1175** d.	...	...	...	...	...	...	...	...	0528
Bratislava hlavná d.	...	...	...	0605	...	...	...	...	0808
Kúty 🏛 d.	...	...	...	0643	...	...	...	...	0847
Wien Meidling **982** d.	...	...	...	|	0550p	...	...	0733	|
Břeclav a.	...	...	...	0655	0653	...	...	0853	0859
Břeclav **1162** d.	...	...	...	0702	0702	...	...	...	0902
Brno hlavní **1162** a.	...	...	...	0733	0733	...	...	...	0933
Brno hlavní d.	0429	0535	0635	0735	0735	...	0835	...	0935
Česká Třebová ▷ d.	0539	0639	0739	|	|	...	0939	...	|
Pardubice ▷ d.	0616	0716	0816	0916	0916	...	1016	...	1116
Kolín ▷ d.	|	0738	|	0938	0938	...	|	...	1138
Praha hlavní ▷ a.	0720	0821	0921	1021	1021	...	1121	...	1221

	EC	EC	EC	IC	EC	EC	EC	EC		SC*	EC		EC	EC		EC		EN	EN			476		
	78	136	172	570	170	70	102	274	370	72	272	372	74	344	374	76		476	476		470	470	470	
	✕	✕	✕	✕	✕	✕	✕	✕	2	R 🍷	✕	2	✕	✕	2	✕								
	♦	♦	♦		♦	§	♦		Ⓐk	§		Ⓑs	§	♦	Ⓑs	§		♦	V		W	X	Y	
Budapest Keleti **1175** d.	...	...	...	...	0928	...	...	...	...	...	1328	...	...	1528	...	...	...	1958	...	...	...	1958	1938	...
Bratislava hlavná d.	...	1008	...	...	1208	...	...	1408	1454	...	1608	1654	...	1808	1854	...	...	2250	...	...	...	2250	2355	...
Kúty 🏛 d.	...	1047	...	...	1247	...	...	1447	1539	...	1647	1739	...	1847	1939	...	...	2330	...	...	...	2330	0040	...
Wien Meidling **982** d.	0825	|	0932	...	|	1233	1333	|	|	1433	|	|	1633	|	|	1833	...	|	2223	...	2223	|	|	...
Břeclav a.	0953	1059	1053	...	1259	1353	1453	1459	1554	1553	1659	1754	1753	1859	1954	1953	...	2343	2333	...	2333	2343	0053	...
Břeclav **1162** d.	1002	...	1102	1202	1302	1402	...	1502	...	1602	1702	...	1802	1902	...	2002	...	0005	0005	...	0200	0200	0200	...
Brno hlavní **1162** a.	1033	...	1133	1233	1333	1433	...	1533	...	1633	1733	...	1833	1933	...	2033	...	0036	0036	...	0237	0237	0237	...
Brno hlavní d.	1035	...	1135	1235	1335	1435	...	1535	...	1635	1735	...	1835	1935	...	2035	...	0038	0038	...	0259	0259	0259	...
Česká Třebová ▷ d.	1139	...	|	1339	|	1539	...	|	...	|	|	...	1939	|	...	2139	...	|	|	...	0413	0413	0413	...
Pardubice ▷ d.	1216	...	1316	1416	1516	1616	...	1716	...	1816	1916	...	2016	2116	...	2216	...	|	|	...	0458	0458	0458	...
Kolín ▷ d.	|	...	1338	|	1538	|	...	1738	...	|	1938	...	|	2138	...	|	...	|	|	...	0526	0526	0526	...
Praha hlavní ▷ a.	1321	...	1421	1521	1621	1721	...	1821	...	1921	2021	...	2121	2221	...	2321	...	0322	0322	...	0615	0615	0615	...

SLOWER TRAINS PRAHA - ČESKÁ TŘEBOVÁ - BRNO

km		1975	867	869	871	873	1979	875	877	879	865	577
		Ⓐ	Ⓐu				Ⓐ					Ⓑh
0	**Praha** hlavní ▷ d.	...	0544	0744	0944	1144	*1244*	1344	1544	1744	1944	2039
62	Kolín ▷ d.	...	0632	0832	1032	1232	*1332*	1432	1632	1832	2032	|
104	**Pardubice** ▷ d.	...	0706	0906	1106	1306	*1401*	1506	1706	1906	2106	2141
139	Choceň ▷ d.	...	0727	0927	1127	1329	*1420*	1527	1729	1927	2127	|
154	Ústí nad Orlicí ▷ d.	...	0741	0941	1141	1343	*1435*	1541	1743	1941	2141	|
164	**Česká Třebová** ▷ a.	...	0752	0952	1152	1354	*1446*	1552	1754	1952	2152	2217
164	**Česká Třebová** d.	0653	0757	0957	1157	1357	1453	1557	1757	1957	...	2218
181	Svitavy d.	0705	0811	1011	1211	1411	1505	1611	1811	2011	...	2229
208	Letovice d.	0733	0833	1033	1233	1433	1533	1633	1833	2033	...	2249
233	Blansko d.	0753	0854	1054	1254	1454	1554	1654	1854	2054	...	2309
255	**Brno** hlavní a.	0815	0915	1115	1315	1515	1615	1715	1915	2115	...	2330

	864	576	866	868	870	872	874	876	878	938
	Ⓐ	⚒n					△	△		Ⓑh
Brno hlavní d.	...	0429	0647	0847	1047	1247	1444	1644	1847	2047
Blansko d.	...	0450	0710	0910	1110	1310	1510	1710	1910	2110
Letovice d.	...	0508	0729	0929	1129	1329	1529	1729	1929	2129
Svitavy d.	0449	0527	0749	0949	1149	1349	1549	1749	1951	2149
Česká Třebová a.	0500	0538	0800	1000	1200	1400	1600	1800	2002	2200
Česká Třebová ▷ d.	0503	0539	0803	1003	1203	1403	1603	1803	2003	...
Ústí nad Orlicí ▷ d.	0514	|	0814	1014	1214	1414	1614	1814	2014	...
Choceň ▷ d.	0529	|	0829	1029	1229	1429	1629	1829	2029	...
Pardubice ▷ d.	0556	0616	0856	1056	1256	1456	1656	1856	2056	...
Kolín ▷ d.	0626	|	0926	1126	1326	1526	1726	1926	2126	...
Praha hlavní ▷ a.	0715	0720	1015	1215	1415	1615	1815	2015	2215	...

♦ – **NOTES** (LISTED BY TRAIN NUMBERS)

78 – GUSTAV KLIMT – [12] ✕ Graz - Wien - Brno - Praha.

102/3 – POLONIA – [12] ✕ Warszawa - Ostrava - Břeclav - Wien - Villach and v.v.

104/5 – SOBIESKI – [12] ✕ Warszawa - Ostrava - Břeclav - Wien Meidling - Wien Westbf and v.v. (arrive Wien Westbf 2044, depart 0712).

136 – MORAVIA – [12] Bratislava - Břeclav - Ostrava - Bohumín.

137 – MORAVIA – [12] Bohumín - Ostrava - Břeclav - Bratislava - Novy Zámky.

170/1 – HUNGARIA – [12] ✕ Berlin - Dresden - Praha - Budapest and v.v.

172/3 – VINDOBONA – [12] ✕ Hamburg - Berlin - Praha - Wien - Villach and v.v.

174/5 – JÁN JESENIUS – [12] ✕ Hamburg - Berlin - Praha - Budapest and v.v.

176 – ALOIS NEGRELLI – [12] ✕ Brno - Praha - Dresden - Berlin - Hamburg.

177 – JOHANNES BRAHMS – [12] ✕ Berlin - Dresden - Praha - Wien.

344/5 – AVALA – [12] ✕ Praha - Bratislava - Budapest - Beograd and v.v. For ▬ 2 cl. Praha - Bar/Thessaloniki and v.v. (summer only) see Table **1360**.

378 – CARL MARIA VON WEBER – [12] ✕ Wien - Praha - Berlin - Stralsund - Binz ◐.

379 – CARL MARIA VON WEBER – [12] ✕ Binz ◐ - Stralsund - Berlin - Praha - Brno.

476/7 – METROPOL – 🛏 1, 2 cl., ▬ 2 cl., [2] Berlin - Dresden - Praha - Brno - Bratislava - Budapest and v.v.; 🛏 1, 2 cl. Cheb (**441/0**) - Karlovy Vary - Praha (**477/6**) - Bratislava (**811/0**) - Zvolen - Banská Bystrica and v.v. For other cars conveyed between Břeclav and Budapest see Tables **95** and **99**.

S – SLOVENSKA STRELA – [12] Praha (**177**) - Břeclav (**277**) - Bratislava; [2] Berlin (**177**) - Praha - Břeclav (**277**) - Bratislava.

T – SLOVENSKA STRELA – [12] Bratislava (**278**) - Břeclav (**378**) - Praha; [2] Bratislava (**278**) - Břeclav (**378**) - Praha - Berlin - Stralsund - Binz ◐.

V – 🛏 1, 2 cl., ▬ 2 cl., [2] Berlin - Dresden - Praha - Brno - Břeclav (**407/6**) - Wien Westbf and v.v. (arrive 0622, depart 2208).

W – AMICUS – 🛏 1, 2 cl. Praha - Brno - Břeclav (**407/6**) - Wien Westbf and v.v. (arrive 0622, depart 2208). Also conveys [2] (change at Břeclav).

X – AMICUS – 🛏 1, 2 cl., [2] Praha (**470/1**) - Brno - Břeclav (**476/7**) - Budapest and v.v.; conveys (except when train **Y** runs) [12] Praha - Brno and v.v.

Y – AMICUS – May 27 - Sept. 27 from Praha, May 28 - Sept. 28 from Budapest. [12] Praha - Brno - Bratislava - Györ - Budapest and v.v.; 🛏 1, 2 cl., ▬ 2 cl., [2] Praha - Budapest - Lökösháza and v.v. Conveys on dates in Table **60** (summer only) 🛏 1, 2 cl., ▬ 2 cl. Praha - Burgas/Varna and v.v.

e – ⑦ (also Apr. 5, July 6, Sept. 28; not Apr. 4, July 4, Sept. 26).

h – Not Dec. 24, 25, 31, Jan. 1, Apr. 4, July 4, 5.

k – ①–⑤ (not Dec. 24, 25, Jan. 1, 6, Apr. 2 - 5, July 5, Sept. 1, 15, Nov. 1, 17).

n – ①–⑥ (not Dec. 25, 26, Jan. 1, 2, Apr. 5, July 5, 6).

p – Wien **Praterstern** (see Table **982**).

r – ①–⑥, not Dec. 25, 26, Jan. 2, Apr. 3 - 5, July 5, Nov. 1.

s – Not Dec. 24, 25, Jan. 1, Apr. 2 - 4, July 4, Oct. 31.

u – Daily Česká Třebová - Brno.

x – Runs on ①–⑥ **n** from Havlíčkův Brod.

◐ – Runs Stralsund - Binz and v.v. on dates in Table **844**.

▷ – See also Table **1160**.

△ – Other trains Brno - Česká Třebová: 1344 Ⓐ, 1544 Ⓐ, 1744 Ⓐ.

§ – To/from Wiener Neustadt.

* – Pendolino tilting train. Classified *EC* in Austria.

OTHER TRAIN NAMES:

70/71 – GUSTAV MAHLER
72/73 – SMETANA
74/75 – FRANZ SCHUBERT
76/77 – ANTONÍN DVOŘÁK
79 – GUSTAV KLIMT
272/3 – JAROSLAV HAŠEK
274/5 – SLOVAN

PRAHA - HAVLIČKŮV BROD - BRNO 1151

For faster trains see Table **1150**

km		675	677	679	681	683	685	687	915	689	691	913
		⚒n					Ⓐ		Ⓑh		Ⓑh	
0	**Praha** hlavní d.	0600	0800	1000	1200	1400	1500	1600	1700	1800	1900	2000
62	Kolín d.	0650	0850	1050	1250	1450	1550	1650	1750	1850	1950	2050
73	Kutná Hora d.	0700	0900	1100	1300	1500	1600	1700	1800	1900	2000	2100
82	Čáslav d.	0709	0909	1109	1309	1509	1609	1709	1809	1909	2009	2109
136	**Havlíčkův Brod** d.	0802	1002	1202	1402	1602	1702	1802	1901	2002	2102	2200
	Jihlava **1137** a.	|	|	|	|	|	|	|	1924	|	|	...
169	Ždár nad Sázavou d.	0831	1031	1231	1431	1631	1731	1831	...	2031	2131e	...
257	**Brno** hlavní a.	0942	1142	1342	1542	1742	1842	1942	...	2142	2233e	...

	914	670	672	674	676	678	680	682	684	688
		Ⓐx						Ⓑh		
Brno hlavní d.	...	0522	0622	0822	1022	1222	1422	1522	1622	1822
Ždár nad Sázavou d.	...	0632	0732	0932	1132	1332	1532	1632	1732	1932
Jihlava **1137** d.	0530n	|	|	|	|	|	|	|	|	|
Havlíčkův Brod d.	0558	0658	0758	0958	1158	1358	1558	1658	1758	1958
Čáslav d.	0651	0751	0851	1051	1251	1451	1651	1751	1851	2051
Kutná Hora d.	0701	0801	0901	1101	1301	1501	1701	1801	1901	2101
Kolín d.	0712	0812	0912	1112	1312	1512	1712	1812	1912	2112
Praha hlavní a.	0805	0905	1005	1205	1405	1605	1805	1905	2005	2205

FOR NOTES SEE TABLE 1150 ABOVE

ADDITIONAL TRAINS Havlíčkův Brod - Brno: 0602 (**671**), 0702 Ⓐ (**673**), 0802 (**675**).
Brno - Havlíčkův Brod: 1522 ⑥ (**682**), 1722 Ⓐ (**686**).

1160 PRAHA - OLOMOUC - OSTRAVA - ŽILINA

FASTEST TRAINS (calling only at points shown). See below for other services. *SC* (*SuperCity*) trains are named *SC PENDOLINO* and are operated by tilting trains.

km		*SC* 501	*SC* 503	*SC* 505	*SC* 507	*SC* 509	*SC* 511	*SC* 513	*SC* 515	*SC* 517
		R 🍷 Ⓐ	R 🍷	R 🍷 ⑧h	R 🍷	R 🍷	R 🍷 ⑤f	R 🍷	R 🍷 ⑧h	R 🍷 ⑦e
0	**Praha** hlavní △ d.	0526	0926	1126	1326	1526	1626	1726	1926	2026
104	Pardubice △ d.	0623	1023	1223	1423	1623	|	1823	2023	2123
252	**Olomouc** d.	0734	1134	1334	1534	1734	|	1934	2134	2234
353	Ostrava Svinov ♥ a.	0822	1222	1422	1622	1822	1922	2022	2222	2322
358	**Ostrava** hlavní ♥ a.	0830	1230	1430	1630	1830	1930	2030	2230	2330
366	Bohumín ♥ a.	...	...	...	...	1839	1939	2039	2239	2339

	SC 500	*SC* 502	*SC* 504	*SC* 506	*SC* 508	*SC* 510	*SC* 512	*SC* 514
	R 🍷 Ⓐ	R 🍷 ⚒n	R 🍷	R 🍷	R 🍷	R 🍷 ⑧h	R 🍷	R 🍷 ⑤⑦r
Bohumín ♥ d.	0419	0519	0719	0919c	...	...	...	1919
Ostrava hlavní ♥ d.	0427	0527	0727	0927	1327	1527	1727	1927
Ostrava Svinov ♥ d.	0435	0535	0735	0935	1335	1535	1735	1935
Olomouc d.	0523	0623	0823	1023	1423	1623	1823	2023
Pardubice △ d.	0634	0734	0934	1134	1534	1734	1934	2134
Praha hlavní △ a.	0731	0831	1031	1231	1631	1831	2031	2231

OTHER TRAINS. *SEE ABOVE FOR FASTEST TRAINS PRAHA - OSTRAVA*

km		441	*Ex* 141	625	*Ex* 527	*EC* 143	705	*EC* 127	*EC* 145	627	*Ex* 529	*EC* 111	*EC* 231	707	*EC* 121	*EC* 147	629	*Ex* 525	*IC* 543	703	*EC* 129	*EC* 149	623	*Ex* 523	
		♦		⊡	L	✕ ‡	L	✕ ‡	✕ ‡		✕ L	✕ ♦	D‡	L	✕	✕ ‡q		✕ L	✕	V	‡	‡		✕ Y	2
	Praha Smíchov d.	...	...	...	...	...	0631c	...	...	0831	...	...	...	1026	...	...	1226	...	...	1426	...	...	1626	...	...
0	**Praha** hlavní △ d.	0024	0411	...	0511	0611	0644	0711	0811	0844	0911	1011	1011	1044	1111	1211	1244	1311	1411	1444	1511	1611	1644	1711	...
62	Kolín △ d.	0108	0457	...	0557	0657	0732	0757	0857	0932	0957	1057	1057	1132	1157	1257	1332	1357	1457	1532	1557	1657	1732	1757	...
104	**Pardubice** △ d.	0134	0521	0602	0626	0721	0801	0821	0921	1001	1026	1121	1121	1201	1226	1321	1401	1426	1521	1601	1626	1721	1801	1826	...
139	Choceň △ d.	|	|	0620	|	|	0820	|	|	1020	|	|	|	1220	|	|	1420	|	|	1620	|	|	1820	|	...
154	Ústí nad Orlicí △ d.	|	|	0635	|	|	0835	|	|	1035	|	|	|	1235	|	|	1435	|	|	1635	|	|	1835	|	...
164	Česká Třebová △ d.	0216	0601	0648	0705	0801	0848	0901	1001	1048	1105	1201	1201	1248	1305	1401	1448	1505	1601	1648	1705	1801	1848	1905	...
206	Zábřeh na Moravé d.	|	0625	0716	|	0825	0916	|	1025	1116	|	1225	1225	1316	|	1425	1516	|	1625	1716	|	1825	1916	|	...
252	**Olomouc** a.	0302	0651	0748	0751	0851	0948	0951	1051	1148	1151	1251	1251	1348	1351	1451	1548	1551	1651	1748	1751	1851	1948	1951	...
252	**Olomouc** d.	0305	0654	0805	0754	0854	0957	0954	1054	1157	1154	1254	1254	1357	1354	1454	1557	1554	1654	1757	1754	1854	1957	1954	...
274	Přerov a.	0320	|	|	0809	|	1012	|	|	|	1209	|	|	1412	|	|	|	1609	|	1812	|	|	|	2009	...
274	Přerov ▷ d.	0334	|	|	...	|	*1026*	|	|	|	*1226*	|	|	*1426*	|	|	|	*1626*	|	*1826*	|	|	|	*2026*	...
303	Hranice na Moravě ▷ d.	0353	0724	0847	...	0924	*1044*	1025	1124	1239	*1244*	1324	1324	*1444*	1425	1524	1639	*1644*	1724	*1844*	1825	1924	2039	*2044*	...
353	Ostrava Svinov ▷ d.	0424	0754	|	...	0954	*1120*	|	1154	|	*1320*	1356	1410	*1520*	|	1554	|	*1720*	1754	*1920*	|	1954	|	*2120*	...
358	**Ostrava** hlavní ▷ d.	0433	0803	|	...	1003	*1129*	|	1203	|	*1329*	1405	|	*1529*	|	1603	|	*1729*	1803	*1929*	|	2003	|	*2129*	...
366	Bohumín ▷ a.	0440	0810	|	...	1010	*1136*	|	1210	|	*1336*	1411	|	*1536*	|	1610	|	*1736*	1810	*1936*	|	2010	|	*2136*	...
366	Bohumín d.	0441	0821	|	...	1021	...	|	1221	|	...	1426	|	...	|	1621	|	...	...	...	|	2021	|	...	2143
	Katowice **1076** a.	|	|	|	...	|	...	|	|	|	...	1550	|	...	|	|	|	...	...	...	|	|	|	...	|
381	Karviná hlavní d.	0452	0832	|	...	1032	...	|	1232	|	...	...	|	...	|	1632	|	...	...	...	|	2032	|	...	2158
397	Český Těšín **1077** d.	0511	0851	|	...	1051	...	|	1251	|	...	...	1451	...	|	1651	|	...	...	...	|	2051	|	...	2221
435	Čadca 🏛 **1077** d.	0605	0945	|	...	1145	...	|	1345	|	...	...	1545	...	|	1745	|	...	...	...	|	2145	|	...	2319
329	Valašské Meziříčí d.	|	|	0912	...	|	...	1049	|	1304	...	...	|	...	1449	|	1704	...	...	...	1849	|	2104	...	|
348	**Vsetín** d.	|	|	0928	...	|	...	1108	|	1320	...	...	|	...	1508	|	1720	...	...	...	1908	|	2120	...	|
366	Horní Lideč 🏛 d.	|	|	...	...	|	...	|	|	...	...	...	|	...	|	|	...	...	...	...	|	|	...	...	|
394	Púchov **1180** d.	|	|	...	...	|	...	1148	|	...	...	...	|	...	1548	|	...	...	...	...	1948	|	...	...	|
Δ439	**Žilina** **1180** a.	0635	1015	...	...	1215	...	1225	1415	...	...	...	1615	...	1625	1815	...	...	...	...	2025	2215	...	...	*0007*z
	Košice **1180** a.	1002	...	...	...	...	...	...	...	...	...	...	...	...	1918	...	...	...	...	...	...	...	...	...	...

	IC 581	621	*IC* 545	443	401		*EN* 425	447	409	
	✕		✕	♦	♦		⊠ ♦	E ♦	⊠ ♦	
Praha Smíchov d.	...	1826	...	...	...	...	...	...	...	...
Praha hlavní △ d.	1811	1844	2011	2111	2132	...	2200	2232	2300	...
Kolín △ d.	1857	1932	2057	2157	2220	...	2253	2320	2347	...
Pardubice △ d.	1921	2001	2121	2222	2252	...	2320	2346	0014	...
Choceň △ d.	|	2020	|	|	2313	...	|	|	|	...
Ústí nad Orlicí △ d.	|	2035	|	|	2329	...	|	|	|	...
Česká Třebová △ d.	2001	2048	2201	2303	2342	...	|	|	|	...
Zábřeh na Moravé d.	2025	2116	2225	|	0007	...	|	|	|	...
Olomouc a.	2051	2148	2251	2350	0034	...	0045	0115	0149	...
Olomouc d.	2054	2151	2254	2353	0037	...	0048	0118	0152	...
Přerov a.	|	|	|	0008	0053	...	|	|	|	...
Přerov ▷ d.	|	|	|	0035	0116	...	|	|	|	...
Hranice na Moravě ▷ d.	2124	2226	2324	|	|	...	|	|	|	...
Ostrava Svinov ▷ d.	2200	|	0000	0123	0202	...	|	0218	0253	...
Ostrava hlavní ▷ d.	2208	|	0009	0132	0211	...	|	0227	0302	...
Bohumín ▷ a.	|	|	0015	0139	0218	...	|	0234	0309	...
Bohumín d.	|	|	...	0141	0307	...	|	0241	0329	...
Katowice **1076** a.	|	|	...	|	0417	...	|	|	0457	...
Karviná hlavní d.	|	|	...	0152	...	...	|	|	...	...
Český Těšín **1077** d.	2247	|	...	0211	...	...	|	0311	...	...
Čadca 🏛 **1077** d.	...	|	...	0305	...	...	|	0405	...	...
Valašské Meziříčí d.	...	2252	...	|	...	...	|	|	...	...
Vsetín d.	...	2308	...	|	...	...	|	|	...	...
Horní Lideč 🏛 d.	...	...	...	|	...	...	|	|	...	...
Púchov **1180** d.	...	...	...	|	...	...	|	|	...	...
Žilina **1180** a.	...	...	...	0335	...	...	0329	0435	...	...
Košice **1180** a.	...	...	...	0707	...	...	0727	0802	...	...

	408	446	*EN* 424		400	*IC* 544	442	*Ex* 522	620	*IC* 580
	⊠ ♦	F ♦	⊠ ♦		♦	✕	♦	✕ Z		✕
Košice **1180** d.	...	2005	2105	...	...	...	2205	...	...	...
Žilina **1180** d.	...	2332	0055	...	...	...	0132	...	...	...
Púchov **1180** d.	...	|	|	...	...	...	|	...	...	...
Horní Lideč 🏛 d.	...	|	|	...	...	...	|	...	...	...
Vsetín d.	...	|	|	...	...	...	|	...	0446	...
Valašské Meziříčí d.	...	|	|	...	...	...	|	...	0504	...
Čadca 🏛 **1077** d.	...	0005	|	...	...	...	0205	...	|	...
Český Těšín **1077** d.	...	0057	|	...	...	...	0257	...	|	0512
Karviná hlavní d.	...	|	|	...	...	...	0313	...	|	|
Katowice **1076** d.	2210	|	|	...	2357	...	|	...	|	|
Bohumín a.	2348	0124	|	...	0107	...	0324	...	|	|
Bohumín ▷ d.	0042	0130	|	...	0210	0342	0329	...	|	|
Ostrava hlavní ▷ d.	0052	0138	|	...	0220	0351	0338	...	|	0553
Ostrava Svinov ▷ d.	0101	0146	|	...	0229	0401	0348	...	|	0604
Hranice na Moravě ▷ d.	|	|	|	...	|	0433	|	...	0531	0636
Přerov ▷ a.	|	|	|	...	0313	|	0433	...	|	|
Přerov d.	|	|	|	...	0336	|	0453	0549	|	|
Olomouc a.	0202	0243	0345	...	0352	0502	0508	0605	0602	0705
Olomouc d.	0205	0246	0348	...	0355	0505	0511	0608	0611	0708
Zábřeh na Moravé d.	|	|	|	...	0422	0530	0546	|	0646	0734
Česká Třebová △ d.	|	|	|	...	0448	0553	0611	0653	0711	0758
Ústí nad Orlicí △ d.	|	|	|	...	|	|	0622	|	0722	|
Choceň △ d.	|	|	|	...	0510	|	0636	|	0736	|
Pardubice △ d.	0344	0416	0520	...	0532	0637	0658	0737	0758	0837
Kolín △ d.	0417	0444	0553	...	0600	0702	0726	0802	0826	0902
Praha hlavní △ a.	0505	0532	0700	...	0651	0751	0815	0851	0915	0951
Praha Smíchov a.	...	...	...	...	...	...	...	...	0931	...

	Ex 524	622	*EC* 148	*EC* 128	702	*Ex* 146	*IC* 542	*Ex* 526	624	*EC* 144	*EC* 120	704	*EC* 230	*EC* 110	*Ex* 528	626	*EC* 142	*EC* 126	706	*IC* 540	628	*Ex* 140			440
	✕ W		‡	‡	L	s	✕	L		✕ D‡	✕	L	‡	✕ ♦	✕ L		✕ ‡	✕ ‡	L	✕		p	2 d	2	♦
Košice **1180** d.	...	...	...	...	...	...	...	...	...	...	0839	...	...	...	...	...	...	...	...	...	...	...	...	...	1805
Žilina **1180** d.	...	*0451*	0542	0736	...	0742	...	...	...	0942	1136	...	1142	...	...	...	1342	1536	...	...	...	1742	...	*1954*x	2132
Púchov **1180** d.	...	*0549*	|	0813	...	|	...	...	...	|	1213	...	|	...	...	...	|	1613	...	...	...	|	*2013*	|	|
Horní Lideč 🏛 d.	...	0628	|	|	...	|	...	...	...	|	|	...	|	...	...	...	|	|	...	...	...	|	2100	|	|
Vsetín d.	...	0646	|	0853	...	|	...	...	1046	|	1253	...	|	...	...	1446	|	1653	...	...	1846	|	2125	|	|
Valašské Meziříčí d.	...	0704	|	0911	...	|	...	...	1104	|	1311	...	|	...	...	1504	|	1711	...	...	1904	|	2203	|	|
Čadca 🏛 **1077** d.	...	|	0615	|	...	0815	...	...	|	1015	|	...	1215	...	...	|	1415	|	...	...	|	1815	|	2042	2205
Český Těšín **1077** d.	...	|	0707	|	...	0907	...	...	|	1107	|	...	1307	...	...	|	1507	|	...	...	|	1907	|	2147	2257
Karviná hlavní d.	...	|	0724	|	...	0924	...	...	|	1124	|	...	|	...	...	|	1524	|	...	...	|	1924	|	2207	2313
Katowice **1076** d.	...	|	|	|	...	|	...	...	|	|	|	...	|	1214	...	|	|	|	...	...	|	|	|	|	|
Bohumín a.	...	|	0736	|	...	0936	...	...	|	1136	|	...	|	1331	...	|	1536	|	...	...	|	1936	|	2221	2324
Bohumín ▷ d.	*0630*	|	0750	|	*0830*	...	0950	*1030*	|	1150	|	*1230*	|	1340	*1430*	|	1550	|	*1630*	1745	|	1950	|	*2225*	2325
Ostrava hlavní ▷ d.	*0638*	|	0759	|	*0838*	...	0959	*1038*	|	1159	|	*1238*	|	1348	*1438*	|	1559	|	*1638*	1754	|	1959	|	*2233*	2333
Ostrava Svinov ▷ d.	*0647*	|	0809	|	*0847*	...	1009	*1047*	|	1209	|	*1247*	1409*	1409	*1447*	|	1609	|	*1647*	1804	|	2009	|	*2240*	2343
Hranice na Moravě ▷ d.	*0719*	0731	0836	0936	*0919*	...	1036	*1119*	1131	1236	1336	*1319*	1436	1436	*1519*	1531	1636	1736	*1719*	1836	1931	2036	2238	...	0012
Přerov ▷ a.	*0737*	|	|	|	*0937*	...	|	*1137*	|	|	|	*1337*	|	|	*1537*	|	|	|	*1737*	|	|	|	2302	...	0030
Přerov d.	0749	|	|	|	0947	...	|	1149	|	|	|	1347	|	|	1549	|	|	|	1747	|	|	|	...	...	0040
Olomouc a.	0805	0802	0905	1005	1002	...	1105	1205	1202	1305	1405	1402	1505	1505	1605	1602	1705	1805	1802	1905	2002	2105	...	...	0055
Olomouc d.	0808	0811	0908	1008	1011	...	1108	1208	1211	1308	1408	1411	1508	1508	1608	1611	1708	1808	1811	1908	2011	2108	...	...	0058
Zábřeh na Moravé d.	|	0846	0934	|	1046	...	1134	|	1246	1334	|	1446	1534	1534	|	1646	1734	|	1846	1934	2046	2134	...	...	|
Česká Třebová △ d.	0853	0911	0958	1053	1111	...	1158	1253	1311	1358	1453	1511	1558	1558	1653	1711	1758	1853	1911	1958	2111	2158	...	...	0146
Ústí nad Orlicí △ d.	|	0922	|	|	1122	...	|	|	1322	|	|	1522	|	|	|	1722	|	|	1922	|	2122	|	...	...	|
Choceň △ d.	|	0936	|	|	1136	...	|	|	1336	|	|	1536	|	|	|	1736	|	|	1936	|	2136	|	...	...	|
Pardubice △ d.	0937	0958	1037	1137	1158	...	1237	1337	1358	1437	1537	1558	1637	1637	1737	1758	1837	1937	1958	2037	2158	2237	...	...	0227
Kolín △ d.	1002	1026	1102	1202	1226	...	1302	1402	1426	1502	1602	1626	1702	1702	1802	1826	1902	2002	2026	2102	2226	2302	...	...	0252
Praha hlavní △ a.	1051	1115	1151	1251	1315	...	1351	1451	1515	1551	1651	1715	1751	1751	1851	1915	1951	2051	2115	2151	2315	2351	...	...	0337
Praha Smíchov a.	...	1131	...	...	1326	...	...	...	1536	...	...	1726	...	...	...	...	...	...	2131	...	2331	...	...	...	...

FOR NOTES SEE FOOT OF NEXT PAGE *Connections may be available at Olomouc with train in previous column* *FOR FASTEST TRAINS SEE TOP OF PAGE*

BRNO - PŘEROV - OSTRAVA - BOHUMÍN 1161

km	*For notes see foot of page*	406	731	831	*IC* 533	733	*EC* 104	735	*EC* 136	737	837	739	839	*EC* 102	741	841	743	843	*IC* 531	745	1539	747	
		♦	Ⓐ	⚒n	✕		♦		♦					♦					✕		⑦e	k	
0	**Brno** hlavní **1164** d.	...	0502	0602	...	0702	...	0902	...	1102	1202	1302	1402	...	1502	1602	1702	1802	...	1902	2002	2102	...
45	Vyškov na Moravě **1164** d.	...	0543	0643	...	0743	...	0943	...	1143	1243	1343	1443	...	1543	1643	1743	1843	...	1943	2043	2141	...
71	Kojetin d.	...	0609	0709	...	0809	...	1009	...	1209	1309	1409	1509	...	1609	1709	1809	1909	...	2009	2109	2209	...
	Wien Meidling **1150** d.	2223	|	|	...	|	0733	|	...	|	|	|	|	1333	|	|	|	|	...	|	|	|	...
	Břeclav **1162** d.	0010	|	|	0708	|	0908	|	1108	|	|	|	|	1508	|	|	|	|	1908	|	|	|	...
88	**Přerov** ▽ d.	0105	0626	0726	0811	0826	1011	1026	1211	1226	1326	1426	1526	1611	1626	1726	1826	1926	2011	2026	2126	2226	...
117	Hranice na Moravě ▽ d.	|	0644	0744	|	0844	|	1044	|	1244	1344	1444	1544	|	1644	1744	1844	1944	|	2044	2144	2244	...
167	Ostrava Svinov ▽ a.	0148	0717	0811	0853	0917	1053	1117	1253	1317	1411	1517	1611	1653	1717	1811	1917	2011	2053	2117	2211	2317	...
172	**Ostrava** hlavní ▽ a.	0157	0727	0821	0903	0927	1103	1127	1303	1327	1421	1527	1621	1703	1727	1821	1927	2021	2103	2127	2221	2327	...
180	Bohumín ▽ a.	0206	0736	0830	0912	0936	1112	1136	1312	1336	1430	1536	1630	1712	1736	1830	1936	2030	2112	2136	2230	2336	...

	407		730	830	732	*IC* 530	832	734	736	*EC* 103	738	838	740	*EC* 137	840	742	*EC* 105	842	744	*IC* 532	1538	746	
	♦		Ⓐk	⚒n		✕				♦				♦			♦			✕	⑦e		
Bohumín ▽ d.	0218	...	0430	0535	0630	0645	0735	0830	1030	1045	1230	1335	1430	1445	1535	1630	1645	1735	1830	1845	1935	2030	...
Ostrava hlavní ▽ d.	0226	...	0438	0543	0638	0654	0743	0838	1038	1054	1238	1343	1438	1454	1543	1638	1654	1743	1838	1854	1943	2038	...
Ostrava Svinov ▽ d.	0235	...	0447	0552	0647	0704	0752	0847	1047	1104	1247	1352	1447	1504	1552	1647	1704	1752	1847	1904	1952	2047	...
Hranice na Moravě ▽ d.	|	...	0519	0619	0719	|	0819	0919	1119	|	1319	1419	1519	|	1619	1719	|	1819	1919	|	2019	2119	...
Přerov ▽ d.	0319	...	0539	0639	0739	0747	0839	0939	1139	1147	1339	1439	1539	1547	1639	1739	1747	1839	1939	1947	2039	2139	...
Břeclav **1162** a.	0413	...	|	|	|	0851	|	|	|	1251	|	|	|	1651	|	|	1851	|	|	2051	|	|	...
Wien Meidling **1150** a.	0608	...	|	|	|	...	|	|	|	1423	|	|	|	...	|	|	2020	|	|	...	|	|	...
Kojetin d.	...	...	0555	0655	0755	...	0855	0955	1155	...	1355	1455	1555	...	1655	1755	...	1855	1955	...	2055	2155	...
Vyškov na Moravě **1164** d.	...	...	0618	0718	0818	...	0918	1018	1218	...	1418	1518	1618	...	1718	1818	...	1918	2018	...	2118	2218	...
Brno hlavní **1164** d.	...	...	0658	0757	0857	...	0957	1057	1257	...	1457	1557	1657	...	1757	1857	...	1957	2055	...	2157	2255	...

OLOMOUC - UHERSKÉ HRADIŠTĚ - BŘECLAV - BRNO 1162

For direct services Olomouc - Brno see Table **1164**. Train **406/7** runs non-stop Přerov - Břeclav and v.v. (see Table **1161**)

km	*For notes see foot of page*	800	709	802	*IC* 530	*Ex* 527	804	705	806	*EC* 103	*Ex* 529	808	707	810	*EC* 137	*Ex* 525	812	*EC* 105	703	814	*IC* 532	*Ex* 523	816	
		⚒n	⚒n		✕					♦					♦			♦	V			Y	Ⓑh	
	Praha hlavní **1160** d.	...	...	...	...	0511	...	0644	...	...	0911	...	1044	...	...	1311	...	...	1444	...	...	1711	...	...
0	**Olomouc** ▽ d.	...	0557	0706	...	0754	0906	0957	1106	...	1154	1306	1357	1506	...	1554	1706	...	1757	1906	...	1954	2106	...
	Ostrava hlavní **1161** d.	...	|	|	0654	|	|	|	|	1054	|	|	|	|	1454	|	|	1654	|	|	1854	|	|	...
22	Přerov ▽ d.	...	0615	0723	0747	0815	0923	1015	1123	1147	1215	1323	1415	1523	1547	1615	1723	1747	1815	1923	1947	2012	2123	...
37	Hulín d.	...	0628	0734	|	0828	0934	1028	1134	|	1228	1334	1429	1534	|	1629	1734	|	1828	1935	|	2024	2134	...
50	Otrokovice ★ d.	...	0639	0744	0805	0839	0944	1039	1144	1205	1239	1344	1439	1544	1605	1639	1744	1805	1839	1944	2005	2033	2144	...
68	Staré Město u Uh. Hradiště d.	...	0659	0755	0817	0859	0955	1059	1155	1217	1259	1355	1459	1555	1617	1659	1755	1817	1859	1955	2017	...	2155	...
73	Uherské Hradiště ⊖ d.	...	0707	|	|	0906	|	1106	|	|	1306	|	1506	|	|	1706	|	|	1905	|	|	...	|	...
90	Uherský Brod d.	...	0725	|	|	0924	|	1124	|	|	1324	|	1524	|	|	1724	|	|	...	|	|	...	|	...
104	**Luhačovice** a.	...	0743	|	|	0942	|	1142	|	|	1342	|	1542	|	|	1742	|	|	...	|	|	...	|	...
102	Hodonin d.	0616	...	0817	0837	...	1017	...	1217	1237	...	1417	...	1617	1637	...	1817	1837	...	2017	2037	...	2217	...
122	**Břeclav** a.	0631	...	0831	0851	...	1031	...	1231	1251	...	1431	...	1631	1651	...	1831	1851	...	2031	2051	...	2231	...
122	**Břeclav** **1150** d.	0638	...	0838	*0902*	...	1038	...	1238	*1302*	...	1438	...	1638	*1702*	...	1838	*1902*	...	2038	...	...	...	...
181	**Brno** hlavní **1150** a.	0724	...	0924	*0933*	...	1124	...	1324	*1333*	...	1524	...	1724	*1733*	...	1924	*1933*	...	2124	...	...	...	...

	700 442	*Ex* 522	801	*Ex* 524	*IC* 533	803	702	*EC* 104	805	*Ex* 526	*EC* 136	807	704	809	*Ex* 528	*EC* 102	811	706	813	708	*IC* 531	815		817
	2Ⓐ	Z	⚒n	W				♦			♦					♦					✕		2	Ⓑh
Brno hlavní **1150** d.	...	...	...	...	...	0636	...	*0824*	0836	...	*1024*	1036	...	1236	...	*1424*	1436	...	1636	...	*1824*	1836	...	2036
Břeclav **1150** a.	...	...	...	...	...	0721	...	*0857*	0921	...	*1057*	1121	...	1321	...	*1457*	1521	...	1721	...	*1857*	1921	...	2121
Břeclav d.	...	...	0528	...	0708	0728	...	0908	0928	...	1108	1128	...	1328	...	1508	1528	...	1728	...	1908	1928	2035	2128
Hodonin d.	...	...	0542	...	0723	0742	...	0923	0942	...	1123	1142	...	1342	...	1523	1542	...	1742	...	1923	1942	2056	2142
Luhačovice d.	...	...	|	...	|	|	0814n	|	|	1014	|	|	1214	|	1414	|	|	1615	|	1814	|	|	|	▬
Uherský Brod d.	...	...	|	...	|	|	0834n	|	|	1034	|	|	1234	|	1434	|	|	1634	|	1834	|	|	|	...
Uherské Hradiště ⊖ d.	...	...	|	0652	|	|	0852	|	|	1052	|	|	1252	|	1452	|	|	1652	|	1852	|	|	|	...
Staré Město u Uh. Hradiště d.	0408	...	0603	0712	0742	0803	0912	0942	1003	1112	1142	1203	1312	1403	1512	1542	1603	1712	1803	1912	1942	2003	2132	2
Otrokovice ★ d.	0420	0524	0615	0724	0753	0815	0924	0953	1015	1124	1153	1215	1324	1415	1524	1553	1615	1724	1815	1924	1953	2015	2147	2213
Hulín d.	0429	0534	0624	0734	|	0824	0934	|	1024	1134	|	1224	1334	1424	1534	|	1624	1734	1824	1934	|	2024	...	2225
Přerov ▽ a.	0441	0545	0635	0745	0809	0835	0945	1009	1035	1145	1209	1235	1345	1435	1545	1609	1635	1745	1835	1945	2009	2035	...	2240
Ostrava hlavní **1161** a.	|	|	|	|	0903	|	|	1103	|	|	1303	|	|	|	|	1703	|	|	|	|	2103	|	...	|
Olomouc ▽ a.	0508	0605	0652	0805	...	0852	1002	...	1052	1205	...	1252	1402	1452	1605	...	1652	1802	1852	2005	...	2052	...	2302
Praha hlavní **1160** a.	0815	0851	...	1051	...	...	1315	...	...	1451	...	...	1715	...	1851	...	...	2115	...	...	...	...	...	...

BRNO - PROSTĚJOV - OLOMOUC - ŠUMPERK 1164

km		1647	1403	903	931	933	901	935	937	939
		Ⓐ	Ⓒb							
0	**Brno** hlavní **1161** d.	0514	0613	0718	0918	1118	1318	1518	1718	1918
45	Vyškov na Moravé **1161** d.	0600	0700	0800	1000	1200	1400	1600	1800	2000
61	Nezamyslice d.	0619	0719	0819	1019	1219	1419	1619	1819	2019
80	Prostějov d.	0635	0735	0835	1035	1235	1435	1635	1835	2035
100	**Olomouc** a.	0651	0753	0851	1051	1251	1451	1651	1851	2051
100	**Olomouc** **1160** d.	0657	0755	0857	...	1257	1457	1657	1857	2057
146	Zábřeh na Moravé **1160** d.	0735	0831	0940	...	1335	1540	1735	1935	2135
159	**Šumperk** a.	0751	|	|	...	1348	|	1751	1951	2150
	Jesenik **1165** a.	...	1009	1113	...	...	1713	...	...	...

	1646	930	900	932	934	902	936	1400	938
	Ⓐ							Ⓒb	
Jesenik **1165** d.	...	...	0640	...	...	1240	...	1539	...
Šumperk d.	0455	0608	|	1015	...	|	1615	|	1815
Zábřeh na Moravé **1160** d.	0514	0631	0831	1031	...	1431	1631	1731	1831
Olomouc **1160** a.	0552	0702	0902	1102	...	1502	1702	1802	1902
Olomouc d.	0558	0707	0907	1107	1307	1507	1707	1807	1907
Prostějov d.	0615	0725	0925	1125	1325	1525	1725	1825	1925
Nezamyslice d.	0637	0739	0939	1139	1339	1539	1739	1841	1939
Vyškov na Moravé **1161** d.	0659	0801	1001	1201	1401	1601	1801	1901	2001
Brno hlavní **1161** a.	0743	0838	1038	1238	1438	1638	1838	1938	2038

♦ – **NOTES FOR TABLES 1160 / 1161 / 1162 / 1164** (LISTED BY TRAIN NUMBER)

102/3 – POLONIA – [12] ✕ Villach - Wien - Břeclav - Ostrava - Katowice - Warszawa and v.v.

104/5 – SOBIESKI – [12] ✕ Wien Westbf (d. 0712 / a. 2044) - Břeclav - Ostrava - Katowice - Warszawa and v.v.

110/1 – PRAHA – [12] ✕ Praha - Ostrava - Katowice - Warszawa and v.v.

136 – MORAVIA – [12] Bratislava - Břeclav - Ostrava - Bohumín.

137 – MORAVIA – [12] Bohumin - Ostrava - Břeclav - Bratislava - Nové Zámky.

400/1 – SILESIA – 🛏 1, 2 cl., ▬ 2 cl. [12] Praha - Kraków and v.v.; 🛏 1, 2 cl., ▬ 2 cl. [2] Praha - Bohumín (**406/7**) - Warszawa and v.v.; [2] Praha - Ostrava - Bohumín and v.v.; 🛏 1, 2 cl. Praha - Kraków - Przemysl - Lviv - Kyïv and v.v. Conveys on days in Table **96** 🛏 1, 2 cl. Praha - Kraków - Lviv - Odesa and v.v.

406/7 – CHOPIN – 🛏 1, 2 cl., ▬ 2 cl., [2] Wien Westbf ◐ - Bohumín - Warszawa and v.v.; 🛏 1, 2 cl. Wien - Bohumín (**400/1**) - Kraków and v.v. (also ▬ 2 cl. on dates in Table **99**); 🛏 1, 2 cl. Wien - Bohumín (**408/9**) - Minsk - Moskva and v.v.; 🛏 1, 2 cl., ▬ 2 cl., [2] Budapest (**476/7**) - Bratislava - Břeclav (**406/7**) - Warszawa and v.v.; 🛏 1, 2 cl., ▬ 2 cl. Budapest (**476/7**) - Bratislava - Břeclav (**406/7**) - Bohumín (**400/1**) - Kraków and v.v.; 🛏 1, 2 cl. Budapest (**476/7**) - Bratislava - Břeclav (**406/7**) - Bohumín (**408/9**) - Moskva and v.v. Conveys on dates in Table **96** 🛏 1, 2 cl. Wien - Kyïv and v.v.

408/9 – VLTAVA – 🛏 1, 2 cl. Praha - Bohumín - Minsk - Moskva and v.v. (also Praha - Minsk on ②④⑦, Minsk - Praha on ①③⑥); 🛏 1, 2 cl. Cheb (**607/6**) - Karlovy Vary - Praha (**409/8**) - Moskva and v.v. Conveys on dates in Table **95**, 🛏 1, 2 cl. Praha - Brest - Orsha - St Peterburg and v.v.

424/5 – SLOVAKIA – 🛏 1, 2 cl., ▬ 2 cl. and [2] Praha - Poprad Tatry - Košice and v.v.; 🛏 1, 2 cl. Praha - Žilina (**1846/7/9**) - Banská Bystrica - Zvolen and v.v.

440/1 – EXCELSIOR – 🛏 1, 2 cl., ▬ 2 cl. §, [12] Cheb - Karlovy Vary - Praha - Žilina - Košice and v.v.; 🛏 1, 2 cl., ▬ 2 cl. § Plzeň (**767/750**) - Praha (**441/0**) - Žilina - Košice and v.v.; [2] Cheb (**767/750**) - Plzeň - Praha (**441/0**) - Žilina - Košice and v.v.; 🛏 1, 2 cl. České Budějovice (**890/2**) - Praha (**441/0**) - Žilina - Košice and v.v.

442/3 – ŠIRAVA – 🛏 1, 2 cl., ▬ 2 cl., [12] Praha - Košice - Humenné and v.v. Conveys 🛏 1, 2 cl. Brno (**747/730** or **732**) - Bohumín (**443/2**) - Košice and v.v.

446/7 – VIHORLAT – [12] Praha - Košice and v.v.

D – DETVAN – [12] Praha - Žilina - Zvolen and v.v.
E – Dec. 22, Apr. 2, June 30, Aug. 30, Oct. 27 only.
F – Jan. 3, Apr. 5, July 6, Aug. 31, Oct. 31 only.
L – To / from Luhacovice (Table **1162**).
V – To Veseli nad Moravou (arrive 1923).
W – From Veseli nad Moravou (depart 0637). Runs on ①–⑥ **n** Veseli - Olomouc, daily Olomouc - Praha.
Y – [12] Praha - Přerov - Zlín střed (arrive 2055).
Z – [12] Zlín střed (depart 0457) - Přerov - Praha.
b – Ⓒ Dec. 25 - Mar. 14; Ⓒ June 12 - Sept. 12.
c – Ⓒ only.
d – Change at Valašské Meziříčí.
e – Also Apr. 5, July 6, Sept. 28; not Apr. 4, July 4, Sept. 26.
f – Also Dec. 22, 23, June 30, Aug. 31, Oct. 27; not Dec. 25, Jan. 1, Oct. 29. To Karvina (a. 1955), Český Těšín (a. 2013), Třinec (2023).
h – Not Dec. 24, 25, 31, Jan. 1, Apr. 4, July 4, 5.
k – Conveys 🛏 1, 2 cl. Brno - Bohumín (**443/2**) - Košice and v.v. Arrives Brno in train **732** on Ⓒ.
n – ①–⑥ (not Dec. 25, 26, Jan. 1, 2, Apr. 5, July 5, 6).
p – Conveys [12] Banská Bystrica (**1844**) - Žilina - Praha.
q – Conveys [12] Praha - Žilina (**1845**) - Zvolen.
r – Also Dec. 22, 23, Apr. 5, June 30, July 6, Aug. 31, Sept. 28, Oct. 27; not Dec. 25, Jan. 1, Apr. 4, July 4, Sept. 26, Oct. 29.
s – Conveys [12] Zvolen (**1840**) - Žilina - Bohumín.
u – ①–⑥ **n** from Bohumín.

x – ④⑤⑦ (also Dec. 23, Apr. 5, June 30, Oct. 30, Nov. 1; not Dec. 24 - Jan. 2, Apr. 2 - 4).
z – Not night of Dec. 24 - 26, 31, Apr. 3, 4.

★ – Connection to **Zlín** by local train (1 - 2 per hour) or trolleybus (every 10 minutes), *11 km*.
♥ – *SC* trains do not carry passengers locally on the section Ostrava Svinov - Bohumín.
◐ – Depart 2208 / arrive 0622.
⊖ – Connecting trains run to / from Staré Město u Uherské Hradiště (journey 7 mins).
△ – See also Table **1150**.
▷ – See also Table **1161**.
▽ – See also Table **1160**.
⊡ – From Hradec Králové (0540).
⊠ – International journeys only.
▵ – *466 km* via Ostrava.
‡ – Classified *Ex* in Slovakia.
§ – ▬ : not Dec. 23 - Jan. 1.
* – Arrive 1345.

OTHER TRAIN NAMES
120/1 KOŠIČAN

Christmas / New Year cancellations – see page 539

1165 OLOMOUC - ZÁBŘEH NA MORAVÉ - JESENIK

km		1401	1631	1403	903	1701	1703	901	1633	1635	
		2Ⓒ	Ⓐ	Ⓒb		2	2		2	2	
	Brno 1164 d.	...	...	0613	0718	...	1118	1318	...	...	...
0	**Olomouc** ▷ d.	0657	...	0755	0857	1056	1257	1457	1629	...	...
46	Zábřeh na Moravé ▷ d.	0740	...	0831	0940	1140	1340	1540	|	...	...
	Šumperk d.	|	0738	|	|	|	|	|	1738	1938	2047
71	Hanušovice d.	0810	0810	0905	1010	1210	1412	1610	1811	2014	2125
107	**Jesenik** a.	0913	0913	1009	1113	1313	1513	1713	1915	2116	2229

	1632	900	1700	1702	902	1704	1706	1400	1708	1402
	2		2	2		2	Ⓒd	Ⓒb	2	2Ⓒ
Jesenik d.	0451	0640	0840	1040	1240	1440	1539	1539	1640	1749
Hanušovice d.	0551	0746	0946	1146	1346	1546	1653	1653	1746	1856
Šumperk a.	0622	|	|	|	|	|	|	|	|	|
Zábřeh na Moravé ▷ a.	|	0815	1015	1215	1415	1615	1719	1719	1815	1929
Olomouc ▷ a.	0732	0902	1102	1257	1502	1702	1800	1800	1902	2003b
Brno 1164 a.	...	1038	1238	...	1638	1838	...	1938	2038	...

b – Ⓒ Dec. 25 - Mar. 14; Ⓒ June 12 - Sept. 12.
d – Ⓒ (except when train **1400** runs).
▷ – See also Table **1160**.

1166 OLOMOUC / JESENIK - OPAVA - OSTRAVA

2nd class only

km		881	819	1627	883	821	823	885	825	827	887	829
		⚒r										
0	**Olomouc** d.	...	0707r	0859	...	1107	1307	...	1507	1707	...	1907
64	Bruntál d.	...	0832r	1032	...	1232	1432	...	1632	1832	...	2032
•58	**Jesenik** d.	0534	|	|	0934	1116*	|	1334	1516*	|	1734	|
•17	Tremešná ve Slez. △ d.	0641	|	|	1041	1239*	|	1441	1633*	|	1841	|
87	Krnov d.	0706	0906	1057	1106	1306	1506	1506	1706	1857	1906	2057
116	Opava východ ▶ d.	0743	0943	...	1143	1343	1543	1543	1743	...	1943	2137
144	**Ostrava** Svinov ▶ a.	0804	1004	...	1204	1404	1604	1604	1805	...	2004	...

	880	820	822	882	1626	824	884	826	828	886
	⚒r									
Ostrava Svinov ▶ d.	0606	...	0806	1006	...	1206	1406	...	1606	1806
Opava východ ▶ d.	0630	...	0830	1030	...	1230	1430	...	1630	1830
Krnov d.	0705	0709	0909	1105	1109	1309	1505	1509	1709	1905
Tremešná ve Slez. △ a.	0721	|	0929*	1121	|	1329*	1521	|	1729*	1921
Jesenik a.	0828	|	1053*	1235	|	1453*	1634	|	1853*	2036
Bruntál d.	...	0739	0937	...	1137	1337	...	1537	1737	...
Olomouc a.	...	0852	1052	...	1253	1452	...	1652	1852	...

r – ①–⑥ (not Dec. 25, 26, Jan. 1, 2, Apr. 5, July 5, 6).
• – Distance from Krnov.
△ – Station for narrow gauge line to Osoblaha (journey 46 mins, *20 km*): depart Tremešná 1125, 1525, 1925; depart Osoblaha 0950, 1350, 1750.
▶ – Fast trains **Opava** východ - **Ostrava** Svinov - **Ostrava** hlavní (journey 35 minutes): From Opava východ: every 2 hours 0709 - 1909. From Ostrava hlavní: every 2 hours 0657 - 1857. Local trains run approx hourly Opava východ - Ostrava Svinov.
* – Local train, change at Krnov.

1168 BRNO - UHERSKÉ HRADIŠTĚ - BYLNICE - VLÁRSKÝ PRŮSMYK

2nd class only

km										
0	**Brno** hlavní d.	0735	0928	1128	1328	1528	1728	1928	2128	...
67	Kyjov d.	0837	1032	1232	1432	1632	1832	2032	2232	...
90	Veselí nad Moravou d.	0902	1101	1301	1501	1701	1901	2058	2258	...
108	Uherské Hradiště ▷ a.	0919	1118	1318	1519	1718	1921	...	...	...
113	**Staré Město u Uh. H** ▷ a.	0927	1126	1326	1527	1726	1928	...	...	...

Staré Město u Uh. H. ▷ d.	...	...	0833	1033	1233	1433	1633	1833	2018	...
Uherské Hradiště ▷ d.	...	...	0840	1040	1240	1440	1640	1840	2040	...
Veselí nad Moravou d.	0601	0701	0901	1101	1301	1501	1701	1901	2101	...
Kyjov d.	0628	0728	0928	1128	1328	1528	1728	1928	2128	...
Brno hlavní a.	0733	0833	1033	1233	1433	1633	1833	2033	2233	...

km						Ⓐ	d			b
0	**Staré Město u Uh. H** ▷ d.	0533r	0818	1006	1218	1259	1406	1618	1833	2058
5	Uherské Hradiště ▷ d.	0541	0825	1023	1225	1323	1423	1625	1842	2112
7	Kunovice d.	0547	0828	1027	1228	1327	1428	1628	1848	2118
22	Uherský Brod ▷ d.	0622	0852	1052	1252	1352	1452	1652	1908	2138
35	Bojkovice a.	0646	0914	1114	1314	1417	1514	1714	1925	2157
63	Bylnice ▶ a.	0730	0956	1156	1356	1518	1556	1756	...	2234
68	**Vlárský průsmyk** 🏛 ▶ a.	0737	...	1206	...	1526	...	...	...	...

	Ⓐ			Ⓐ			Ⓐ		d	Ⓐ
Vlárský průsmyk 🏛 ▶ d.	0526	0754	...	...	...	...	...	...	...	...
Bylnice ▶ d.	0542	0802	1002	...	1202	1402	...	1602	1802	2042
Bojkovice d.	0632	0845	1045	1145	1245	1445	1545	1645	1845	2116
Uherský Brod ▷ d.	0652	0908	1108	1208	1308	1508	1608	1708	1906	2139
Kunovice a.	0710	0927	1127	1227	1327	1527	1627	1727	1924	2157
Uherské Hradiště ▷ a.	0716	0932	1132	1232	1332	1532	1632	1732	1930	2201
Staré Město u Uh. H ▷ a.	0724	0939	1139	1259	1349	1539	1647	1749	1937	...

b – From Brno (depart 1928).
d – Change at Kunovice on certain dates.
r – ⚒ only.
▷ – See also Table **1162**.
▶ – See Table **1181** for connections to Slovakia.

1169 OTHER LOCAL SERVICES

2nd class

BŘECLAV - ZNOJMO *69 km* Journey 90 minutes

From Břeclav: every 2 hours 0931 - 1931, also 0650**c**, 1233Ⓐ, 1433Ⓐ, 1633Ⓐ, 2131Ⓐ.
From Znojmo: every 2 hours 0855 - 1855, also 0658, 1155Ⓐ, 1355Ⓐ, 1555Ⓐ, 1755Ⓐ.

BRNO - ZNOJMO *89 km* Journey 2 hours Change at Miroslav and Hrušovany

From Brno: 0651, 0851, 1051, 1251, 1451, 1651, 1851Ⓒ.
From Znojmo: 0658, 0855, 1055, 1255, 1455, 1655, 1900Ⓒ.

ČESKÉ BUDĚJOVICE - ČESKÝ KRUMLOV *31 km* Journey 60 - 65 mins

To June 12 / from Sept. 13:
From České Budějovice: 0525, 0714, 0907, 1109, 1304, 1504, 1708, 1904, 2242.
From Český Krumlov: 0431Ⓐ, 0603, 0833, 1003Ⓒ, 1149, 1400, 1602, 1747, 1941.

June 13 - Sept. 12:
From České Budějovice: 0525, 0707, 0916*, 1109, 1321, 1504, 1704, 1904, 2242.
From Český Krumlov 0431Ⓐ, 0603, 0823, 1006, 1147, 1602, 1801*, 2001.

* – Praha (d. 0616) - Nové Údolí (a. 1152) and Nové Údolí (d. 1613) - Praha (a. 2140).

CHOCEŇ - LITOMYŠL *24 km* Journey 55 minutes ★

From Choceň: 0513Ⓐ, 0630Ⓐ, 0639Ⓒ, 0840Ⓒ, 1040, 1239, 1431Ⓐ, 1440Ⓒ, 1544, 1640, 1838, 2040Ⓒ, 2140Ⓐ.
From Litomyšl: 0529Ⓒ, 0537Ⓐ, 0623Ⓐ, 0729Ⓒ, 0824Ⓐ, 1024Ⓒ, 1222, 1329Ⓒ, 1406Ⓐ, 1530, 1637, 1821, 1928.

HULIN - KROMĚŘÍŽ *8 km* Journey 8 minutes

1 - 2 trains per hour, connecting with trains in Table **1162**.

KOJETIN - KROMĚŘÍŽ *9 km* Journey 12 minutes

From Kojetin: 0508Ⓐ, 0623, 0723, 0812, 0922, 1212, 1322, 1422Ⓐ, 1522, 1622, 1722, 1822, 1922Ⓐ, 2012, 2112⑦**e**, 2212, 2253Ⓑ**h**.
From Kroměříž: 0420Ⓐ, 0449Ⓐ, 0549, 0639⚒, 0739, 0839, 1139, 1249, 1339, 1439, 1539, 1639, 1739, 1804⑦**e**, 1839, 1939, 2004⑦**e**, 2139, 2235Ⓑ**h**.

PRAHA - KARLŠTEJN *33 km* Journey 42 minutes

From Praha hlavní: hourly 0509 - 2309 (every 30 minutes 1109 - 2009). From Karlštejn: hourly 0509 - 2309 (every 30 mins 1209 - 2109). Trains continue to / from Beroun (10 mins to Beroun).

c – 0731 on Ⓒ (daily July 1 - Aug. 31).
e – Also Apr. 5, July 6, Sept. 28; not Apr. 4, July 4, Sept. 26.
h – Not Dec. 24, 25, 31, Jan. 1, Apr. 4, July 4, 5.
★ – Change at Vysoké Myto město on certain journeys.

SLOVAKIA

Operator: National railway company is Železničná spoločnosť Slovensko (ŽSSK) on the network of Železnice Slovenskej Republiky (ŽSR).

Services: All trains convey first and second class seating, **except** where shown otherwise in footnotes or by '2' in the train column, or where the footnote shows sleeping and/or couchette cars only. Descriptions of sleeping (🛏) and couchette (━) cars appear on page 8.

Timings: Valid from **December 13**, 2009. Amendments are expected from **March 7** and **June 13**. Holiday variations are shown where possible (but see page 539 for additional Christmas and New Year cancellations). Certain local trains may be cancelled during the period **Dec. 24 - Jan. 1** and these cancellations may not be shown in the tables.

Reservations: It is possible to reserve seats on most Express trains.

Supplements: A higher level of fares applies to travel by *EC* and *IC* trains.

1170 BRATISLAVA - LEVICE - ZVOLEN

km		◇	811	831	833	833 933	835	◇	Ex 531	837	801
		Ⓐ v	H			2			Ⓑ	2u	Ⓑ P
0	**Bratislava** hlavná 1175 d.	...	0615	1015	1215	1215	1415	...	1559	1815	2351
49	Galanta 1175 d.	...	0649	1049	1249	1249	1449	...	|	1849	0026
*10	Nové Zámky 1175 ▶ d.	0500	|	1102a	1253	1253	1444	1600	1637	1902	|
89	Šurany ▶ d.	0513	0720	1119	1320	1320	1520	1617	1656	1920	0058
131	Levice d.	0613	0806	1157	1402	1402	1603	1740	1734	2014	0136
198	Hronská Dúbrava 1185 d.	0805	0910	1259	1506	1506	1708	1905	|	2122	|
209	**Zvolen** osob. 1185 a.	0816	0920	1308	1516	1516	1718	1915	1839	2132	0250
	Banská Bystrica 1185 a.	...	0947	1336	1544	|	1750	...	1901	2200	|
	Košice 1190 a.	...	1348	...	...	1858	...	...	...	...	0643
	Prešov 1196 a.	...	...	...	...	1942	...	...	...	...	0733

	820	Ex 530	830	930 830	832	932 832	834	1530 2	810	800
	① 2g	①–⑥		2		2		⑦ d	H	Ⓑ P
Prešov 1196 d.	...	...	...	...	...	0814	...	...	...	2209
Košice 1190 d.	...	...	...	0604c	...	0902	...	...	1458	2253
Banská Bystrica 1185 d.	0348	0533	0840	|	1141	|	1454	1726	1902	|
Zvolen osob. 1185 d.	0414	0553	0925	0925	1225	1225	1520	1755	1929	0244
Hronská Dúbrava 1185 d.	|	|	0936	0936	1236	1236	1531	1805	1940	|
Levice d.	0528	0657	1038	1038	1339	1339	1643	1912	2042	0402
Šurany ▶ d.	0609	0734	1121	1121	1428	1428	1729	1956	2122	0445
Nové Zámky 1175 ▶ a.	0622	0817	|	|	1534r	1534r	1833	|	2135a	0459
Galanta 1175 d.	0644	0802	1152	1152	1459	1459	1802	2026	2153	0517
Bratislava hlavná 1175 a.	0723	0832	1226	1226	1533	1533	1835	2101	2226	0551

H – HOREHRONEC – (12) Bratislava - Banská Bystrica - Košice and v.v. Conveys 🛏 1, 2 cl. Cheb (**441/0**) - Karlovy Vary - Praha (**477/6**) - Bratislava (**811/0**) - Banská Bystrica and v.v.
P – POĽANA – 🛏 1, 2 cl. and (12) Bratislava - Prešov and v.v.; (12) Bratislava - Zvolen and v.v. Will not run on Dec. 24, 25, 31, Jan. 1, Apr. 2, 4, July 4, Oct. 31.
a – Ⓐ only.
c – ①–⑥ (not Dec. 25, 26, Jan. 1, Apr. 3, 5).
d – Also Jan. 6, Apr. 5, July 5, Sept. 1, Nov. 1; not Dec. 27, Apr. 4, July 4, Oct. 31.
g – Also Jan. 7, Apr. 6, July 6, Sept. 2, Nov. 2; not Apr. 5, July 5, Nov. 1. Runs on Ⓐ Levice - Bratislava.
r – ⚒ only.
u – Not Apr. 2 - 4.
v – Daily Nové Zámky - Levice.
▶ – Local trains run 10 - 12 times per day.
◇ – Stopping train. 2nd class only.
* – Distance from Šurany.

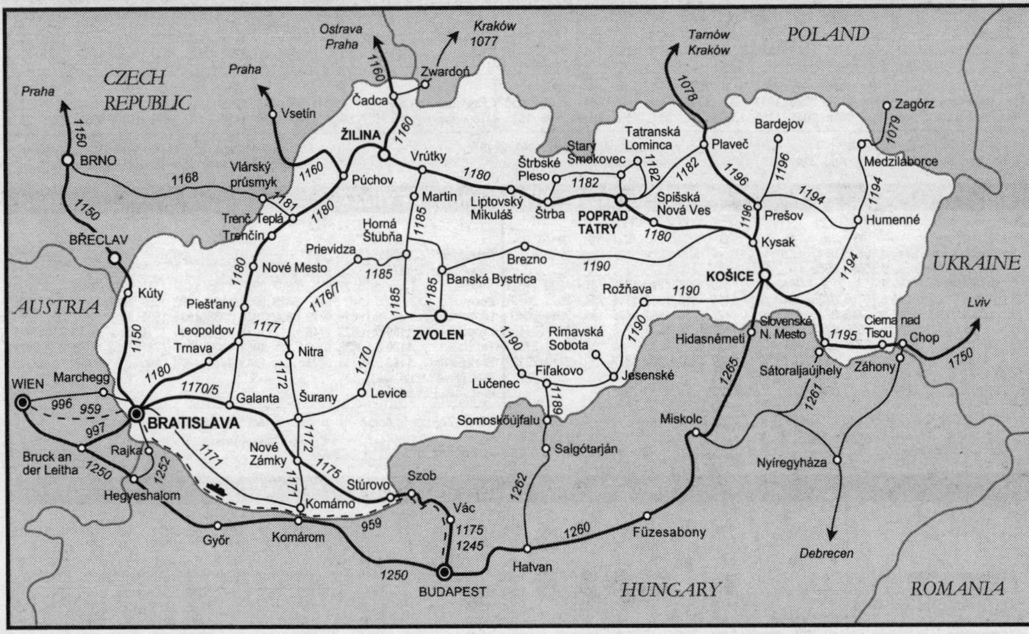

BRATISLAVA - KOMÁRNO — 1171

2nd class

km		△		Ⓐ		Ⓐ	Ⓐ	Ⓒ	Ⓐ		
	Bratislava hl. **1175** ... d.	...	...	...	...	...	1515	...	...	...	...
0	Nové Zamky ... d.	0828	1128	1328	1442	1542	1632	1632	1751	1837	2052
29	Komárno ... a.	0855	1202	1356	1511	1610	1703	1703	1822	1905	2123

	Ⓐ		Ⓐ			Ⓐ		Ⓐ		▽	
Komárno ... d.	0549	0633	0737	1028	1258	1402	1454	1536	1630	1807	2011
Nové Zamky ... a.	0619	0707	0810	1057	1326	1430	1527	1613	1702	1835	2040
Bratislava hl. **1175** ... a.	0734	...	...	...	...	...	...	...	...	...	...

km					Ⓐ	Ⓐ	Ⓒ	Ⓐ	Ⓐ		
0	**Bratislava** hlavná ... d.	0606	1040	1303	1400	1452	1530	1556	1633	1737	2109
5	Bratislava Nové Mesto d.	0629	1050	1314	1418	1501	1538	1605	1648	1747	2120
42	Dunajská Streda ... d.	0735	1148	1417	1518	1545	1654	1654	1747	1853	2221
94	**Komárno** ... a.	0842	1254	1524	1627	...	1804	1804	1854	2008	2328

	Ⓐ	Ⓐ				Ⓐ	Ⓒ	Ⓐ		⑦d	
Komárno ... d.	0415	0501	0626	0859	...	1308	1452	1529	1707	1848	1908
Dunajská Streda ... d.	0527	0631	0734	1005	1212	1416	1616	1640	1826	1943	2020
Bratislava Nové Mesto . a.	0612	0730	0834	1110	1310	1519	1722	...	1931	2029	2119
Bratislava hlavná ... a.	0622	0740	0844	1120	1321	1529	1731	...	1943	2039	2128

d – Also Jan. 6, Apr. 5, Nov. 1; not Dec. 27, Jan. 3, Apr. 4, July 1 - Aug. 31, Oct. 31.

△ – Additional journeys: 0504, 0548 Ⓐ, 0650, 0740 Ⓐ.
▽ – Additional journey: 1910 Ⓐ.

Subject to alteration Dec. 24 - Jan. 6.

NOVÉ ZAMKY - NITRA — 1172

2nd class

km		Ⓐ	Ⓒ		Ⓒd	Ⓐ			Ⓐ			△
0	**Nové Zamky** ... d.	0634	0700	0749	0847	1102	1253	1444	1540	1637	1743	1841
10	Šurany ... d.	0647	0722	0806	0900	1123	1309	1456	1552	1659	1756	1853
36	**Nitra** ... a.	0727	0751	0841	0940	1157	1342	1531	1631	1736	1835	1935

				Ⓐb	⚒			Ⓐ		Ⓑ	Ⓐ§
Nitra ... d.	0634	0850	1203	1318	1440	1541	1643	1744	1843	1953	2042
Šurany ... a.	0710	0923	1236	1402	1517	1615	1722	1819	1917	2026	2116
Nové Zamky . a.	0725	0936	1251	1416	1534	1627	1742	1840	1933	2040	2135

b – Not Dec. 24 - Jan. 6, July 1 - Aug. 31.
d – Daily Dec. 24 - Jan. 6, July 1 - Aug. 31.
n – Not Dec. 24 - 27, Jan. 1, Apr. 4, 5.
v – Not Dec. 24 - 26, 31, Apr. 3, 4.
△ – Additional journeys: 2107 **n**, 2247 **v**.
§ – Additional journey: 2226 **n**.

BRATISLAVA - ŠTÚROVO - BUDAPEST — 1175

km		2137	471	471 477	*EN* 477	2135	*EC* 345	*EC* 273	*EC* 171	*EC* 137	*EC* 175
		2				2	✕	✕	✕		✕
			C	B	M		A	R	H	N	J
	Praha hlavní **1150** .. d.	...	2311	2311	0037	...	0539	0739	1139	...	1539
	Brno hlavní **1150** ... d.	...	0244	0244	0324	...	0824	1024	1424	...	1824
	Břeclav **1150** ... d.	...	0335	0447	0447	...	0900	1100	1500	1700	1900
0	**Bratislava** hlavná ... d.	...	0455	0553	0553	...	0954	1154	1554	1754	1954
91	Nové Zámky ... d.	*0536*	|	0649	0649	...	1047	1247	1647	1845	2047
135	Štúrovo ... a.	*0617*	|	0715	0715	...	1112	1312	1712	▬	2112
135	Štúrovo 🏛 ... d.	0643	|	0718	0718	0943	1115	1315	1715	1843	2115
150	Szob 🏛 ... ▷ d.	0657	◐	|	|	0957	|	|	|	1857	|
180	Nagymaros-Visegrád ▷ d.	0711	|	|	|	1011	1136	1336	1736	1911	2136
197	Vác ... ▷ d.	0728	|	0750	0750	1028	1150	1350	1750	1928	2150
214	**Budapest** Nyugati . ▷ a.	0754	|	|	|	1054	|	|	|	1954	|
214	**Budapest** Keleti ... a.	...	0820	0832	0832	...	1232	1432	1832	...	2232

	◇	*EC* 174	2112	*EC* 170	*EC* 272	*EC* 344	2136	*EN* 476	476 470	470
		✕	2	✕	✕	✕	2			
		J		H	R	A		M	B	C
Budapest Keleti ... d.	...	0528	...	0928	1328	1528	...	1958	1958	1938
Budapest Nyugati .. ▷ d.	0441	|	0807	|	|	|	1707	|	|	|
Vác ... ▷ d.	0527	0610	0834	1010	1410	1610	1734	2037	2037	|
Nagymaros-Visegrád ▷ d.	0542	0623	0849	1023	1423	1623	1749	|	|	|
Szob 🏛 ... ▷ d.	0557	|	0904	|	|	|	1804	|	|	◐
Štúrovo 🏛 ... a.	0610	0644	0917	1044	1444	1644	1817	2109	2109	|
Štúrovo ... d.	...	0647	...	1047	1447	1647	*1836*	2112	2112	|
Nové Zámky ... d.	...	0714	...	1114	1514	1714	*1919*	2140	2140	|
Bratislava hlavná ... a.	...	0805	...	1205	1605	1805	...	2234	2234	2320
Břeclav **1150** ... a.	...	0859	...	1259	1659	1859	...	2343	2343	0053
Brno hlavní **1150** ... a.	...	0933	...	1333	1733	1933	...	0036	0237	0237
Praha hlavní **1150** ... a.	...	1221	...	1621	2021	2221	...	0322	0615	0615

2nd class — **ADDITIONAL TRAINS BRATISLAVA - NOVÉ ZAMKY - STÚROVO** — See also Table **1170**

				877			871	875	873		
				u			Ⓐk	Ⓐ			
Bratislava hlavná ... d.	0631**n**	0727	1039	1315	1338	1435	1515	1615	1715	1835	2102
Galanta ... d.	0728	0837	1135	1352	1434	1529	1549	1654	1757	1932	2157
Nové Zámky ... a.	0813	0922	1220	1431	1518	1613	1616	1725	1825	2018	2240
Nové Zámky ... d.	*0831***a**	*0953*	...	...	1537	1623	...	*1735*	*1848*	...	2245
Štúrovo ... a.	*0913***a**	*1042*	...	...	1620	1707	...	*1818*	*1927*	...	2327

	874	872	870		876						
	Ⓐ		Ⓐk		u						
Štúrovo ... d.	...	0455	...	0535	*0736*	*0927***a**	...	1248	1453	1651	...
Nové Zámky ... a.	...	0528	...	0617	*0818*	*1017***a**	...	1337	1535	1733	...
Nové Zámky ... d.	0415	0530	0625	0631	0829	1026	1141	1344	1544	1747**r**	2007
Galanta ... d.	0447	0600	0655	0721	0905	1115	1226	1430	1629	1844	2051
Bratislava hlavná .. a.	0526	0635	0734	0823	0941	1218**n**	1321	1525	1724	1944	2148

A – AVALA – [12] ✕ Praha - Bratislava - Budapest - Beograd and v.v. Conveys on summer dates in Table **60**, ▬ 2 cl. Praha / Bratislava - Beograd - Thessaloniki and v.v. Conveys on dates in Table **1360** ▬ / 🛏 Praha / Bratislava - Subotica - Bar and v.v.

B – AMICUS – 🛏 1, 2 cl., [2] Praha (**471/0**) - Břeclav (**477/6**) - Budapest and v.v.

C – AMICUS – May 27 - Sept. 27 from Praha, May 28 - Sept. 28 from Budapest. 🛏 1, 2 cl., ▬ 2 cl., [12] Praha - Győr - Budapest and v.v.; 🛏 1, 2 cl., [2] Praha - Budapest - Lökösháza and v.v. Conveys on summer dates in Table **60** 🛏 2 cl., ▬ 2 cl. Praha / Bratislava - Burgas / Varna and v.v.

H – HUNGARIA – [12] ✕ Berlin - Dresden - Praha - Bratislava - Budapest and v.v.

J – JÁN JESENIUS – [12] ✕ Hamburg - Berlin - Dresden - Praha - Budapest and v.v.

M – METROPOL – 🛏 1, 2 cl., ▬ 2 cl., [2] Berlin Hbf - Dresden - Praha - Bratislava - Budapest and v.v.; 🛏 1, 2 cl., ▬ 2 cl., [2] Warszawa (**407/6**) - Břeclav - Budapest and v.v.; 🛏 1, 2 cl., ▬ 2 cl. Kraków (**400/1**) - Bohumín (**407/6**) - Břeclav - Budapest and v.v.; 🛏 1, 2 cl. Moskva - Katowice - Břeclav - Budapest and v.v. Conveys on summer dates in Table **95** 🛏 1, 2 cl. St Peterburg - Katowice - Břeclav - Budapest - Zagreb and v.v.

N – MORAVIA – [12] Bohumin - Ostrava - Břeclav - Bratislava - Nové Zámky.

R – JAROSLAV HAŠEK – [12] ✕ Praha - Budapest and v.v.

a – Ⓐ only.
k – To / from Komárno (Table **1171**). Will not run Dec. 24 - Jan. 6.
n – Bratislava **Nové Mesto**.
r – 1755 on Ⓒ.
u – Not Dec. 24 - Jan. 6, Apr. 2 - 5, May 1, 8, July 5, Aug. 29, Sept. 1, 15, Nov. 1, 17.
◐ – Via Rajka 🏛 and Győr (Table **1250**).
▷ – For local trains see Table **1245**.

Christmas / New Year cancellations – see page 539

1176 NITRA - TOPOL'ČANY - PRIEVIDZA

2nd class

km												
			Ⓐ	©	⚒	⑦	Ⓐ		Ⓐ		c	
0	Nitra d.	0643	0810	0947	1238	1345	1450	1533	1649	1846	1956	2225
33	Topoľčany a.	0737	0915	1039	1334	1443	1544	1637	1756	1938	2047	2318

		Ⓐ							Ⓑ	⑦	⚒
Topoľčany d.	0522	0615	0744	...	1107	1422	1546	1700	1845	2006	2025
Nitra a.	0615	0710	0836	...	1201	1527	1641	1803	1951	2102	2130

km												
		Ⓐ	©	Ⓐ	⑥	Ⓐd	Ⓐ		Ⓐ	©	Ⓐ	△
0	Topoľčany ▷ d.	0644	0740	0920	1041	1203	1244	1342	1440	1448	1545	1658
44	Prievidza ▷ a.	0802	0845	1031	1155	1320	1410	1505	1550	1608	1705	1815

		Ⓐ			Ⓐd	Ⓐ	©	Ⓐ		▽	⚒
Prievidza ▷ d.	0555	0653	0956	1216	1255	1343	1427	1438	1544	1841	2228
Topoľčany ▷ a.	0717	0802	1106	1318	1414	1512	1529	1617	1655	2005	2334

c – Not Dec. 24, 25, 31, Apr. 2-4.
d – Not Dec. 24 - Jan. 6, July 1 - Aug. 31.

△ – Additional journeys: 1941, 2219 ⚒.
▽ – Additional journey: 1708 ⑦.

▷ – For fast trains see Table **1176**. Certain trains continue to / from Nitra (upper panel) or Nové Zamky (Table **1172**).

1177 BRATISLAVA - NITRA and PRIEVIDZA

2nd class

km		1735	721			725	1733		723			
		G	F	⚒		G	Ⓐ		Ⓑh	⑥	⚒u	⑦
•	Bratislava Petržalka d.	0636	0642	...	...	...	...	...	...	...	...	...
	Brat. Nové Mesto d.	0653	0659	...	...	...	...	...	...	...	...	...
0	**Bratislava** hl. **1180** d.	|	|	*0810*	*1017*	1340	1538	*1610*	1638	*1810*	*1929*	*1957*
46	Trnava **1180** d.	0736	0736	*0842*	*1110*	1415	1614	*1642*	1714	*1842*	*2021*	*2029*
63	Leopoldov **1180** a.	0748	0748	*0853*	*1124*	1427	1628	*1653*	1728	*1853*	*2034*	*2040*
63	Leopoldov d.	0800	0758	0919	1129	1437	1638	1659	1738	1859	2047	2119
87	Zbehy a.	0828	0820	0951	1202	1459	|	1739	1804	1929	2119	2155
98	**Nitra** a.	0848	*0848*	1012	1223	*1527***c**	1720	1803**c**	*1827*	1951	2140	2212
114	Topoľčany **1176** a.	...	0845	...	...	1525	...	...	1833	...	...	...
158	**Prievidza** **1176** a.	...	0943	...	...	1623	...	...	1940	...	...	...

	1732	722						720		1520	
	Ⓐ	⚒	F	G	Ⓐ	Ⓐ				⑦d	
Prievidza **1176** d.	...	0546	...	...	...	...	...	1640	...	1820	...
Topoľčany **1176** d.	...	0641	...	...	...	...	...	1735	...	1924	...
Nitra d.	0527	|	0801	0928	1135	1429	1543	*1739*	*1846***c**	|	2036
Zbehy d.	|	0707	0823	0955	1205	1502	1558	1807	1910	|	2058
Leopoldov a.	0610	0729	0850	1028	1239	1536	1635	1830	1950	2012	2137
Leopoldov **1180** d.	0623	0740	...	1038	*1316*	*1620*	*1716*	1842	*1955*	2014	*2215*
Trnava **1180** a.	0638	0752	...	1052	*1328*	*1632*	*1728*	1852	*2010*	2029	*2233*
Bratislava hl. **1180** a.	0715	0828	...	1143	*1400*	*1704*	*1800*	|	*2105*	|	*2331*
Brat. Nové Mesto a.	...	...	...	...	...	...	...	1927	...	2112	...
Bratislava Petržalka a.	...	...	...	...	...	...	...	1942	...	2127	...

F – © (daily Dec. 24 - Jan. 6, July 1 - Aug. 31).
G – Ⓐ (not Dec. 24 - Jan. 6, July 1 - Aug. 31).
c – Change at Lužianky.

d – Also Jan. 6, Apr. 5, Nov. 1; not Dec. 27, Jan. 3, Apr. 4, July 1 - Aug. 31, Oct. 31.
h – Also Oct. 30, Nov. 1; not holidays or Dec. 27.

u – ①–⑥ (not Dec. 25, 26, Jan. 1, Apr. 3-5).
• – Petržalka - Trnava: *51 km*.

1180 BRATISLAVA - ŽILINA - KOŠICE

km		443	*EN* 425	763	701	441	*IC* 501	601	603	*IC* 505	605	607	*IC* 511	*EC* 121	609	1507	703	611	*IC* 503	705	1705	707	1707	1615	615
				2			✕🅁	✕	✕	✕🅁	✕	✕	✕🅁	✕	✕	2🅁		✕	✕🅁		✕		2	2	
		♦Y	♦	R	P	♦	b				♦		Ⓐu		⊖△	⑤f	Ⓐ		n	E	⑤f	Y		⑤B	♦
0	**Bratislava** hlavná **1177** d.	...	...	...	...	...	0535	0610	0810	0935	1010	1210	1335	...	1410	1500	1510	1610	1735	1810	1810	1957	2110	2210	2310
46	Trnava **1177** d.	...	...	...	0416	...	0605	0642	0842	1005	1042	1242	|	...	1442	1532	1542	1642	|	1842	1842	2029	2147	2242	2342
64	Leopoldov **1177** d.	...	...	...	0429	...	|	0655	0855	|	1055	1255	|	...	1455	|	1555	1655	|	1855	1855	2042	2203	2255	2355
81	Piešťany d.	...	...	...	0441	...	|	0707	0907	|	1107	1307	|	...	1507	|	1607	1707	|	1907	1907	2054	2215	2307	0007
99	Nové Mesto nad Váhom d.	...	...	...	0454	...	|	0720	0920	|	1120	1320	|	...	1520	|	1620	1720	|	1920	1920	2107	2229	2320	0020
123	**Trenčín** d.	...	...	...	0514	...	0652	0740	0940	1052	1140	1340	1446	...	1540	1619	1640	1740	|	1940	1940	2126	▬	2340	0040
131	Trenčianska Teplá d.	...	...	...	0522	...	|	0748	0948	|	1148	1348	|	...	1548	|	1648	1748	|	1948	1948	2133	...	2348	0048
	Praha hlavní **1160** d.	2111	2200	...	|	0024	|	|	|	|	|	|	|	1111	|	|	|	|	|	|	|	|	...	|	|
158	Púchov **1160** d.	|	|	...	0548	|	|	0809	1009	|	1209	1409	|	1548	1609	|	1714	1809	|	2012	2012	2156	...	0009	0109
203	**Žilina** **1160** a.	0335	0329	...	0628	0635	0749	0847	1047	1149	1247	1447	1541	1625	1646	1715	1751	1847	1938	2051	2051	2235	...	0047	0147
203	**Žilina** **1185** d.	0353	0344	0453	...	0653	0752	0853	1053	1152	1253	1453	1544	1628	1654	1727	...	1853	1941	2055	2055	...	2	0059	0157
224	Vrútky **1185** d.	0412	|	0512	...	0712	|	0912	1112	|	1312	1512	|	|	1713	|	...	1912	|	2112	2117	...	2115	0117	0216
242	Kraľovany d.	0427	|	0527	...	0727	|	0927	1127	|	1327	1527	|	|	1727	|	...	1927	|	m	2131	...	2138	|	0231
260	Ružomberok d.	0444	0432	0544	...	0744	|	0944	1144	|	1344	1544	|	|	1744	1810	...	1944	|	▬	2147	...	2202	0145	0248
286	Liptovský Mikuláš d.	0503	0451	0603	...	0803	0849	1003	1203	1249	1403	1603	1642	1725	1803	1830	...	2003	2038	...	2205	...	2227	0204	0307
325	Štrba d.	0532	|	0632	...	0832	|	1032	1232	|	1432	1632	|	1753	1832	|	...	2032	|	2	|	...	2306r	|	0336
344	**Poprad-Tatry** d.	0552	0600c	0647	...	0847	0930	1047	1247	1330	1447	1647	1723	1808	1847	1913	...	2047	2119	2239	2247	...	2325r	0246	0352
370	Spišská Nová Ves d.	0612	0624	0707	...	0907	|	1107	1307	|	1507	1707	1743	1828	1907	1933	...	2107	|	2309	2306	...	...	0306	0412
410	Margecany d.	0639	|	0734	...	0934	|	1134	1334	|	1534	1734	|	|	1934	|	...	2134	|	2353	|	...	...	0333	0439
429	Kysak § **1196** a.	0653	0712	0748	...	0948	1024	1148	1348	1424	1548	1748	1822	1905	1948	2011	...	2148	2213	...	|	...	...	|	0453
445	**Košice** **1196** a.	0707	0727	0802	...	1002	1036	1202	1402	1436	1602	1802	1834	1918	2002	2024	...	2202	2225	...	2354	...	...	|	0507
	Prešov **1196** a.	|	...	...	...	...	...	...	...	...	|	...	...	...	...	...	...	...	...	...	...	...	...	0402	|
	Humenné **1194** a.	0913	...	...	...	...	...	...	...	...	1820	...	...	...	...	...	...	...	...	...	...	...	...	0547	0725

	702	704	706	706	600	*IC* 502	602	604	*EC* 120	606	708	608	*IC* 504	610	1506	760	612	*IC* 500	440	446	*EN* 424	442	1614	700	614
			①	Ⓐ	✕	✕🅁	✕	✕	✕	✕	2	✕	✕🅁	✕	2	2	✕	✕🅁				⊖	2	⊖	
	Ⓐ		g		Q	n		♦△			Ⓑh				⑦e	Ⓐ		d	♦	♦	♦	♦Z	⑦D	Z	♦
Humenné **1194** d.	...	...	...	...	...	...	...	0526	...	...	...	...	...	...	...	...	...	...	...	...	...	2000	2141	...	2155
Prešov **1196** d.	...	...	...	...	...	...	...	|	...	...	...	...	...	...	...	...	...	...	...	...	...	|	2308	...	|
Košice **1196** d.	...	...	...	...	0405	0531	0605	0805	0839	1005	...	1205	1331	1405	1520	1511	1605	1731	1805	2005	2105	2205	|	...	0005
Kysak **1196** d.	...	...	...	...	0419	0545	0619	0819	0853	1019	...	1219	1345	1419	1534	1525	1619	1745	1819	2019	2119	2219	|	...	0019
Margecany d.	...	...	...	...	0434	|	0634	0834	|	1034	...	1234	|	1434	|	1540	1634	|	1834	2034	|	2234	2340	...	0034
Spišska Nová Ves d.	...	...	...	...	0502	|	0702	0902	0933	1102	...	1302	|	1502	1613	1615	1702	|	1902	2103	2159	2302	0008	...	0102
Poprad-Tatry d.	...	...	...	...	0523	0641	0724	0924	0953	1124	...	1324	1441	1524	1633	1632	1724	1841	1924	2125	2238	2324	0029	...	0124
Štrba d.	...	...	...	...	0539	|	0741	0941	1008	1141	...	1341	|	1541	|	▬	1741	|	1941	2141	|	2341	|	...	0141
Liptovský Mikuláš d.	...	...	0510	...	0609	0723	0809	1009	1036	1209	...	1409	1523	1609	1714	...	1809	1923	2009	2211	2328	0009	0111	...	0209
Ružomberok d.	...	...	0531	...	0629	|	0829	1029	|	1229	...	1429	|	1629	1734	...	1829	|	2029	2231	2352	0029	0131	...	0229
Kraľovany d.	...	m	0548	...	0646	|	0846	1046	|	1246	...	1446	|	1646	|	**1508**	1846	|	2046	2247	|	0046	|	...	0246
Vrútky **1185** d.	...	0456	0604	...	0701	|	0901	1101	|	1301	...	1501	|	1701	|	⑦	1901	|	2101	2303	|	0103	0159	...	0301
Žilina **1185** a.	...	0519	0620	...	0717	0820	0917	1117	1133	1317	...	1517	1620	1717	1814	**k**	1917	2020	2117	2319	0039	0119	0215	...	0317
Žilina **1160** d.	...	0523	0623	0623	0723	0823	0923	1123	1136	1323	1423	1523	1623	1723	1826	1831	1923	2023	2132	2332	0055	0132	0227	0240	0323
Púchov **1160** d.	...	0602	0702	0702	0802	|	1002	1202	1212	1402	1503	1602	|	1802	|	1910	2002	|	|	|	|	|	0302	0317	0402
Praha hlavní **1160** a.	...	|	|	|	|	|	|	|	1651	|	|	|	|	|	|	|	|	|	0337	0532	0700	0815	|	|	|
Trenčianska Teplá d.	...	0622	0722	0722	0821	|	1021	1221	...	1421	1524	1621	|	1821	|	1935	2021	|	▬	...	...	...	0321	0337	0421
Trenčín d.	0528	0629	0729	0729	0828	|	1028	1228	...	1428	1532	1628	1718	1828	1922	1943	2028	2118	...	...	...	...	0328	0344	0428
Nové Mesto nad Váhom d.	0549	0649	0749	0749	0849	|	1049	1249	...	1449	1553	1649	|	1849	|	2006	2049	|	...	...	...	...	0349	0404	0449
Piešťany d.	0602	0702	0802	0802	0902	|	1102	1302	...	1502	1606	1702	|	1902	|	2018	2102	|	2	...	...	...	0402	0417	0502
Leopoldov **1177** d.	0616	0716	0816	0816	0916	|	1116	1316	...	1516	1620	1716	|	1916	|	2031	2116	|	2215	...	...	...	0416	0431	0516
Trnava **1177** d.	0630	0730	0830	0830	0930	|	1130	1330	...	1530	1634	1730	1806	1930	2010	2045	2130	2205*	2241	...	...	...	0430	0445	0530
Bratislava hlavná **1177** a.	0700	0800	0900	0900	1000	1027	1200	1400	...	1600	1704	1800	1833	2000	2040	2120	2200	2233	2331	...	...	...	0500	0515	0600

♦ – **NOTES** (LISTED BY TRAIN NUMBERS)

424/5 – SLOVAKIA – 🛏 1, 2 cl., ▬ 2 cl., (2) Praha - Žilina - Košice and v.v.; 🛏 1, 2 cl. Praha - Žilina - Banská Bystrica - Zvolen and v.v.

440/1 – EXCELSIOR – 🛏 1, 2 cl., ▬ 2 cl., (12) Cheb - Karlovy Vary - Praha - Žilina - Košice and v.v.; 🛏 1, 2 cl., ▬ 2 cl. Plzeň (**767/750**) - Praha (**441/0**) - Žilina - Košice and v.v. (also (2) from / to Cheb); 🛏 1, 2 cl. České Budějovice (**890/2**) - Praha (**441/0**) - Košice and v.v.

442/3 – ŠÍRAVA – 🛏 1, 2 cl., ▬ 2 cl., (12) Praha - Žilina - Košice - Humenné and v.v. Conveys 🛏 1, 2 cl. Brno (**747/730** or **732**) - Žilina - Košice and v.v.

446 – VIHORLAT – Jan. 3, Apr. 5, July 6, Aug. 31, Oct. 31 only. (12) Košice - Žilina - Praha.

604/5 – (12) and ✕ Bratislava - Košice (**1902/3**) - Humenné and v.v.; (2) Bratislava - Košice - Čierna nad Tisou and v.v.

614/5 – ZEMPLÍN – 🛏 1, 2 cl., ▬ 2 cl., (12) Bratislava - Košice - Humenné and v.v. Not Dec. 24, 31 from Bratislava and Humenné.

B – ⑤ Dec. 18 - June 25 (also Dec. 23, Apr. 1; not Dec. 25, Jan. 1, Apr. 2).
D – ⑦ Dec. 13 - June 27 (also Apr. 5; not Dec. 27, Apr. 4).
E – Daily except ⑤ (also runs Jan. 1, Apr. 2; not Dec. 23, 24, 31, Apr. 1).
P – ①–⑥ (not Dec. 25 - Jan. 6, Apr. 3, 5).

Q – ①–⑥ (not Dec. 24-26, 28-31, Jan. 1, 6, Apr. 2, 5, July 5, Sept. 1, 15, Nov. 17).
R – Ⓐ (daily May 1 - Oct. 10). On Dec. 22, Apr. 2, June 30, Aug. 30, Oct. 27 (from Praha) is train **447**, (12) Praha (d. 2232) - Žilina - Košice.
Y – Also conveys 🛏 1, 2 cl. Bratislava (**707**) - Žilina (**443**) - Košice.
Z – Also conveys 🛏 1, 2 cl. Košice (**442**) - Žilina (**700**) - Bratislava.
b – Not Dec. 25 - Jan. 2, Apr. 3-5.
c – Arrive 0530.
d – Not Dec. 24 - Jan. 1, Apr. 2-4.
e – Also Jan. 6, Apr. 5, July 5, Nov. 1; not Dec. 27, Jan. 3, Apr. 4, July 4, Oct. 31.
f – Also Dec. 23, Apr. 1; not Dec. 25, Jan. 1, Apr. 2.
g – Also Apr. 7, Sept. Nov. 2; not Dec. 21, 28, Jan. 4, Apr. 5, July 1 - Aug. 30, Nov. 1.
h – Not Dec. 24 - Jan. 5, Apr. 2, 4.
k – Also Jan. 6, Apr. 5, 6, Nov. 1; not Dec. 27, Jan. 3, Apr. 4, July 1 - Aug. 31, Oct. 31.
m – To / from Martin (Table **1185**).
n – Not Dec. 24, 25, 31, Jan. 1.
r – ⚒ only.
u – Also Nov. 1; not Dec. 28-31.

⊖ – Also conveys 🛏 1, 2 cl. Bratislava - Košice - Chop - Lviv and v.v. (extended to / from Kyïv on dates in Table **96**).
△ – Conveys 🛏 1, 2 cl. Žilina - Košice - Čierna nad Tisou - Chop - Moskva and v.v. (journey 2 nights).
§ – Many trains call to set down only.
* – Calls to set down only.

OTHER TRAIN NAMES:
120/1 – KOŠICAN
500/1 – ZELMER
502/3 – ŠARIŠ
511 – GORENJE

2nd class — TRENČIN - VLÁRSKÝ PRŮSMYK - BYLNICE — 1181

km		P	Q		R		S		⑦	
0	Trenčin ... 1180 d.	*0610*	...	...	*1250*	...	1453	...	1713	...
8	Trenčianska Teplá ... 1180 d.	0626	0726	...	1325	...	1508	...	1725	...
22	Vlárský průsmyk 🏛 ... 1168 d.	0643	0743	...	1346	...	1535	...	1744	...
27	Bylnice ... 1168 a.	...	...	...	1352	...	1541	...	1750	...

		P	Q		R		S		⑦
Bylnice ... 1168 d.	...	...	...	...	1436	...	1602	...	1906
Vlárský průsmyk 🏛 ... 1168 d.	...	0648	0746	...	1443	...	1614	...	1913
Trenčianska Teplá ... 1180 a.	...	0705	0803	...	1500	...	1635	...	1930
Trenčin ... 1180 a.	...	*0719*	*0815*	...	*1515*	...	...	...	...

P – ①–⑤ (not Dec. 24 - Jan. 1, Apr. 5, July 5, 6, Sept. 28, Oct. 28, Nov. 17).
Q – ⑥⑦ (also Dec. 24, 25, Jan. 1, Apr. 5, July 5, 6, Sept. 28, Oct. 28, Nov. 17).
R – ⑥⑦ (also Dec. 24, 25, Jan. 1, 6, Apr. 2, 5, July 5, Sept. 1, 15, Nov. 1, 17).
S – ①–⑤ (not Dec. 24, 25, Jan. 1, 6, Apr. 2, 5, July 5, Sept. 1, 15, Nov. 1, 17).

2nd class — LOCAL LINES IN POPRAD TATRY AREA — 1182

km			Ⓐ				Ⓐ					
0	**Poprad Tatry** .. d.	0455	0548	0725	1002	1126	1407	1456	1539	1739	1902	2139
8	Studený Potok . d.	0507	0559	0738	1017	1137	1420	1508	1556	1750	1914	2152
14	Kežmarok ... d.	0520	0617	0748	1025	1147	1434	1518	1607	1759	1924	2202
44	Stará Lubovňa . d.	0602	0658	0830	1107	1229	1529	1607	1724**r**	...	2007	2247
60	**Plaveč** ... a.	0621	0716	0848**c**	1125	1247	...	1626	1743	...	2025	2304

		Ⓐ					Ⓐ			Ⓑ	
Plaveč ... d.	0414	*0507*	0737	0904	1140	1438	...	1700	...	1913	2144
Stará Lubovňa d.	0432	0529	0756	0925	1157	1456	1535	1719	...	1933	2210
Kežmarok ... d.	0518	0615	0845	1006	1242	1543	1637	1802	1844	2019	2258
Studený Potok d.	0528	0625	0854	1015	1251	1553	1648	1812	1857	2029	2306
Poprad Tatry . a.	0541	0637	0907	1028	1304	1606	1701	1825	1920	2042	2318

km		Ⓒ	Ⓐ	Ⓐ							N	Ⓒ	Ⓐ	Ⓐ										
0	**Poprad Tatry** ... d.	0447	...	0548	...	0739	...	1002	...	1126	...	...	1407	...	1456	...	1539	...	1727	1739	...	2049	2139	...
8	Studený Potok ... d.	0458	0458	0559	0600	0751	0855	1013	1021	1137	1142	1300	1419	1421	1508	1514	1551	1600	1739	1750	1813	2100	2151	2153
17	**Tatranská Lomnica** ... a.	0511	0511	...	0613	0805	0908	...	1034	...	1155	1313	...	1434	...	1527	...	1613	1752	...	1826	2113	...	2206

								N	Ⓒ		Ⓐ													
Tatranská Lomnica ... d.	0515	...	0628	0838	...	0955	...	1124	1237	...	1336	...	1455	1539	...	1617	1757	...	1843	...	...	2137	2210	...
Studený Potok ... a.	0527	0528	0641	0850	0854	1007	1015	1136	1249	1251	1348	...	1507	1551	1553	1630	1809	1812	1855	1857	...	2149	2222	...
Poprad Tatry ... a.	...	0541	0653	...	0907	...	1028	...	...	1304	...	...	...	...	1606	1643	...	1825	...	1920	...	...	2234	...

Poprad Tatry - Starý Smokovec (journey 25 minutes, *13* km, narrow gauge): 0415 **S**, 0507, 0604, 0627 Ⓐ, 0727, 0827 **N**, 0927, 1004, 1127 **S**, 1227, 1327, 1404, 1427, 1504, 1527, 1627, 1727, 1827, 1927, 2004, 2104 **N**, 2204, 2304. Most continue to Štrbské Pleso (see below).

Starý Smokovec - Štrbské Pleso (journey 40 - 45 minutes, *16* km, narrow gauge): 0534, 0631, 0701 Ⓐ, 0801, 0901 **N**, 1001, 1031, 1201 **S**, 1301, 1401, 1431, 1501, 1531, 1601, 1701, 1801, 1901, 2001, 2031, 2131 **N**, 2231. Most journeys start from Poprad Tatry (see above).

Starý Smokovec - Tatranská Lomnica (14 mins, *6* km, nar. gauge): 0456, 0538, 0656, 0802, 0902 **N**, 1002, 1102, 1202 **S**, 1302, 1402, 1502, 1602, 1702, 1802, 1902, 2035, 2135 **a**.

Štrbské Pleso - Štrba (journey 17 - 18 minutes, *5* km, rack railway): 0509, 0614, 0714, 0809, 0903, 1003 **N**, 1103, 1203, 1257 **N**, 1403, 1444, 1544, 1623, 1703, 1812, 1903, 2003, 2235.

Starý Smokovec - Poprad Tatry (journey 25 minutes, *13* km, narrow gauge): 0443, 0534, 0655, 0732 Ⓐ, 0755, 0855 **N**, 0955, 1055, 1155 **S**, 1255, 1355, 1455, 1555, 1655, 1755, 1832, 1855, 1955, 2032, 2135 **b**, 2232, 2332 **N**. Most start from Štrbské Pleso (see below).

Štrbské Pleso - Starý Smokovec (journey 40 - 45 minutes, *16* km, narrow gauge): 0456, 0613, 0643 Ⓐ, 0713, 0813 **N**, 0913, 1013, 1113 **S**, 1213, 1313, 1413, 1513, 1613, 1713, 1743, 1813, 1913, 1943, 2043, 2143, 2243 **N**. Most journeys continue to Poprad Tatry (see above).

Tatranská Lomnica - Starý Smokovec (14 mins, *6* km, nar. gauge): 0517, 0614, 0714 **z**, 0835, 0935 **N**, 1035, 1135 **S**, 1235, 1335, 1435, 1535, 1635, 1735, 1835, 1935, 2114, 2214.

Štrba - Štrbské Pleso (journey 15 minutes, *5* km, rack railway): 0439, 0556, 0645, 0751, 0845, 0945 **N**, 1045, 1145, 1239 **N**, 1345, 1425, 1520, 1605, 1645, 1755, 1845, 1945, 2045.

N – Dec. 13 - Apr. 6, June 1 - Sept. 30.
S – June 1 - Sept. 30.
a – Štrbské Pleso - Tatranská Lomnica.
b – Tatranská Lomnica - Poprad Tatry.
c – Ⓒ (daily July 1 - Aug. 31).
r – Arrive 1655.
z – 0735 on Ⓒ (also Dec. 21 - Jan. 6, Feb. 1, 15 - 19, July 1 - Aug. 31).

2nd class ❖ — ŽILINA - VRÚTKY - MARTIN - BANSKÁ BYSTRICA - ZVOLEN — 1185

km			1847		1849	1855							1841			1843			*Ex* 231				1845		1857	705
			①–⑥	Ⓐ	⑦	①–⑥	Ⓒ	Ⓒ	Ⓐ	Ⓒ	Ⓐ	Ⓐ			Ⓐ	Ⓐ		Ⓐ							⑦	◇
			P		**P**	**S**						**u**		**x**					**D**				**d**		**e**	**B**
0	**Žilina 1180** ... d.	0443	0548	*0622*	0713	0713	*0653*	*0853*	*0853*	*1053*	*1053*	...	1320	*1253*	*1408*	1500	...	*1549*	1633	*1654*	...	*1757*a	1901	...	2000	2055
21	Vrútky **1180** ... a.	0506	0608	*0646*	0730	0730	*0710*	*0910*	*0910*	*1110*	*1110*	...	1337	*1310*	*1424*	1518	...	*1605*	1650	*1711*	...	*1821*a	1918	...	2021	2112
21	Vrútky ... d.	0510	0610	0652	0732	0732	0715	0913	0942	1117	1117	...	1339	1319	1429	1520	1526	1611	1651	1719	...	1825	1920	1927	2023	2113
28	**Martin** ... d.	0519	0618	0701	0740	0740	0724	0922	0951	1126	1126	...	1346	1327	1438	1528	1536	1621	1658	1728	...	1834	1928	1937	2031	2120
51	Diviaky ... d.	0547	|	0730	0757	0757	0809	0948	1019	1154	1154	1205	1402	1417	1507	|	1605	1651	|	1757	1843	1903	|	2005	|	...
52	Turčianske Teplice ... d.	0550	0636	0734	0800	0800	0812	0951	1022	1157	1157	1208	1404	1420	1511	1546	1608	1655	1716	1800	1846	1906	1946	2008	2048	...
61	Horná Štubňa ... a.	0601	|	0745	|	0809	0823	|	1033	1209	|	1218	|	1430	1522	|	1619	|	|	|	1857	1918	|	2019	|	...
99	**Prievidza** ... a.	*0715*	|	*0848*	|	|	0931	|	*1137*	*1315*	|	*1315*	|	1542	*1635*	|	*1747*	|	|	|	1955	...	|	*2116*	|	...
61	Horná Štubňa ... d.	0602	|	...	|	0810	...	|	...	1220	|	1220	|	...	...	|	1638	|	|	|	...	...	|	2020	|	...
80	Kremnica ... d.	0627	|	...	|	0834	...	|	...	1246	|	1246	|	...	...	|	1704	|	|	|	...	...	|	2046	|	...
106	Hronská Dúbrava § d.	0704	|	...	|	0903	...	|	...	1319	|	1319	|	...	...	|	1739	|	|	|	...	...	|	2119	|	...
97	**Banská Bystrica** ... a.	|	0725	...	0852	|	...	1038	...	|	1251	|	1449	...	...	1635	|	1746	1756	1855	...	...	2034	|	2128	...
97	**Banská Bystrica** .. ▶ d.	|	0727	...	0854	|	...	*1041*	...	|	1256	|	*1454*	...	...	1637	|	...	1757	*1902*	...	...	2037	|	*2134*	...
*118	**Zvolen** osob. ... ▶ a.	0714	0755	...	0918	0913	...	*1111*	...	1329	1328	1329	*1518*	...	...	1708	1749	...	1818	*1926*	...	...	2102	2129	*2210*	...

	704			1840			*Ex* 144		1854							1842			1844						1846
			Ⓐ		Ⓐ	Ⓒ				Ⓐ	Ⓐ	Ⓐ	Ⓒ	Ⓐ	Ⓒ		Ⓐ								
	C			**b**			**D**	**x**	**S**		**x**								**c**						**P**
Zvolen osob. ... ▶ d.	...	...	0427	0513	0613	0613	0726	...	0919	1021	...	1036	1054	...	...	*1310*	...	1424	*1521*	1527	...	1605	*1819*	1854	1907
Banská Bystrica .... ▶ a.	...	...	|	0543	|	|	0746	...	|	|	...	1106	|	...	...	*1336*	...	|	*1544*	|	...	1635	*1851*	|	1939
Banská Bystrica ... d.	...	...	|	0544	|	|	0748	...	|	|	...	1108	|	...	...	1350	...	|	1547	|	...	1645	1856	|	1943
Hronská Dúbrava § ... d.	...	...	0438	|	0623	0623	|	...	0929	1031	...	|	1104	...	...	|	...	1435	|	1537	...	|	|	1905	|
Kremnica ... d.	...	...	0519	|	0658	0717	|	...	0958	1106	...	|	1140	...	...	|	...	1511	|	1611	...	|	|	1939	|
Horná Štubňa ... a.	...	...	0549	|	0723	0742	|	...	1020	1131	...	|	1205	...	...	|	...	1536	|	1636	...	|	|	2003	|
Prievidza ... d.	...	...	*0435*	|	*0611*	*0643*	|	0859	|	|	1035	|	*1104*	...	1243	|	*1338*	*1436*z	|	*1510*	1645	|	|	*1849*	|
Horná Štubňa ... d.	...	0506	0550	|	0724	0753	|	0955	1021	1131	1138	|	1206	1245	1351	|	1436	1536	|	1636	1743	|	|	2004	|
Turčianske Teplice ... d.	...	0517	0600	0626	0734	0803	0829	1005	1029	...	1148	1200	1217	1255	1401	1430	1447	1547	1626	1647	1752	1743	1949	2014	2027
Diviaky ... d.	...	0520	0603	|	0737	0807	|	1008	|	...	1150	1203	1220	1259	1404	|	1450	1550	|	1650	1754	1759	1952	2017	|
Martin ... d.	0446	0548	0631	0643	0804	0835	0845	1036	1049	...	...	1231	1247	1328	1432	1447	1519	1619	1643	1718	...	1828	...	2043	2048
Vrútky ... a.	0454	0556	0641	0651	0814	0844	0852	1044	1056	...	...	1240	1256	1337	1441	1454	1528	1627	1650	1727	...	1838	...	2052	2056
Vrútky **1180** ... d.	0456	*0607*	*0644*	0653	0815	...	0854	*1049*	1107	...	...	*1301*	*1301*	*1359*	*1501*	1504	*1553*	*1641*	1653	1729	...	*1901*	...	*2101*	2105
Žilina 1180 ... a.	0519	*0627*	*0706*	0710	0837	...	0911	*1109*	1124	...	...	*1317*	*1317*	*1419*	*1517*	1530	*1614*	*1703*	1709	1752	...	*1917*	...	*2117*	2127

▶ – *Full service :* ⊖	1840					*Ex* 144		811			831				833				835		*Ex* 531	1846		837	
			Ⓐ		Ⓐ	**D**			Ⓐ				Ⓐ			Ⓐ					Ⓑ			**v**	
Zvolen ... d.	0513	0556	0615	0639	0707	0726	0831	0923	1036	1219	1310	1351	1415	1459	1521	1536	1605	1649	1723	1819	1843	1907	2019	2134	2225
Banská Bystrica ... a.	0543	0625	0652	0709	0740	0746	0905	0947	1106	1252	1336	1421	1451	1535	1544	1608	1635	1723	1750	1851	1901	1939	2050	2200	2257

	Ex 530				1847		830	1849				832			834						*Ex* 231		810	1845	
	①–⑥		Ⓐ		①–⑥			⑦	Ⓐ		Ⓐ			Ⓐ					Ⓐ		**D**				
Banská Bystrica ... d.	0533	0600	0627	0657	0727	0816	0840	0854	0926	1040	1114	1141	1256	1338	1424	1454	1520	1611	1637	1725	1757	1826	1902	2037	2134
Zvolen ... a.	0551	0633	0658	0725	0755	0849	0906	0918	0955	1111	1146	1207	1328	1408	1455	1518	1555	1642	1708	1758	1818	1859	1926	2103	2210

– [12] Bratislava - Žilina - Martin. On ⑤ change at Vrutky (depart Vrutky 2128, arrive Martin 2135).
– [12] Martin - Žilina - Bratislava.
– DETVAN – [12] and ✕ Praha - Ostrava Svinov - Zvolen and v.v.
– Conveys 🛏 1, 2 cl. Praha (**424/5**) - Zvolen and v.v.
– July 1 - Aug. 31.
– Ⓐ only.
– Conveys [12] Zvolen - Žilina (**146**) - Bohumín.

c – Conveys [12] Banská Bystrica - Žilina (**140**) - Praha.
d – Conveys [12] Praha (**147**) - Žilina - Zvolen.
e – Also Jan. 6, Apr. 5, Sept. 1, Nov. 1; not Dec. 27, Jan. 3, Apr. 4, July 1 - Aug. 31, Oct. 31.
u – Change at Horná Štubňa.
v – Not Dec. 24 - 26, Jan. 1, Apr. 2 - 4.
x – Not Dec. 24 - Jan. 6.
z – Not ⑥.
▶ – For complete service see panel below main table.

❖ – 2nd class only, except trains **B**, **C**, **D**.
⊖ – Also from Zvolen 0434; from Banská Bystrica 0442, 0516, 1941, 2232. Certain trains run to / from Bratislava (Table **1170**).
◇ – Additional trains Vrútky - Horná Štubňa: 2121 ⑦, 2220 ①–⑥ (not Dec. 25, 26, Jan. 1, Apr. 3 - 5).
* – *117* km via Kremnica.
§ – Junction for Banská Štiavnica (5 - 6 trains per day, journey 30 minutes). See also Table **1170**.

2nd class — FIL'AKOVO - SOMOSKÖÚJFALU — 1189

km						⑦		Ⓒ	Ⓐ	
0	Fil'akovo **1190** ... d.	0552	...	0951	...	1501	...	1737	1857	...
14	Somosköújfalu 🏛 **1262** ... a.	0611	...	1010	...	1520	...	1755	1916	...

					⑦		Ⓒ	Ⓐ	
Somosköújfalu 🏛 **1262** ... d.	0620	...	1052	...	1537	...	1758	1922	...
Fil'akovo **1190** ... a.	0638	...	1110	...	1556	...	1816	1941	...

Christmas/New Year cancellations – see page 539

1190 ZVOLEN/BANSKÁ BYSTRICA - KOŠICE

2nd class ★

km		931			1931			933		935	801
		Ⓐ			Ⓒ			△		Ⓑs	Ⓑ P
	Bratislava hlavná **1170** d.	...	...	...	...	...	...	1215	...	...	2351
0	**Zvolen** osob. d.	0557	*0602*	*0818*	0926	*1000*a	1333	1533	1725	1845	0311
54	Lučenec d.	0650	*0716*	0929	1015	1114	1439	1623	1837	1932	0402
70	Fil'akovo a.	0702	*0735*	0947	1027	1137	1456	1635	1856	1944	0415
70	Fil'akovo d.	0705	0822	...	1028	1147	*1458*	1636	...	1945	0417
98	Jesenské d.	0733	0902	...	1054	1227	*1539*	1703	...	2011	0444
109	Rimavská Sobota a.	*0810*	0921	...	*1112*r	1246	*1559*x	*1742*	...	*2031*	*0530*a
161	Rožňava d.	0824	...	...	1145	...	...	1801	...	2103	0541
233	**Košice** a.	0918	...	...	1238	...	...	1858	...	2157	0643
	Prešov **1196** a.	...	...	...	1326**z**	...	...	1942	...	...	0733

		930	932					934		800
	Ⓐk	▷ R	△		Ⓐk				Ⓐ	Ⓑ P
Prešov **1196** d.	...	...	0814	...	...	...	...	1452**z**	...	2209
Košice d.	...	0604	0902	...	...	...	...	1530	...	2253
Rožňava d.	...	0701	0956	...	...	...	...	1624	...	2355
Rimavská Sobota d.	*0551*	*0707*	*1008*	*1307*	...	1435**a**	1520	*1638*	...	|
Jesenské d.	*0610*	0750	1048	1330	...	1455**a**	1538	1719	...	0049
Fil'akovo a.	*0646*	0815	1113	1408	...	1535**a**	1617	1744	...	0115
Fil'akovo d.	*0650*	0816	1114	...	1418	1604	...	1745	2031	0116
Lučenec d.	0717	0829	1127	...	1439	1624	...	1800	2049	0130
Zvolen osob. a.	0826	0914	1214	...	1550	1734	...	1848	2152	0228
Bratislava hlavná **1170** a.	...	1226	1533	...	...	...	...	...	...	0551

km				811							
				H		F	Ⓐ	E			
0	**Zvolen** **1185** d.	0556	...	0923	*1219*	...	*1415*	...	1605	...	...
21	**Banská Bystrica** **1185** d.	0628	...	1000	*1259*	...	*1517*	...	1635	*1652*	...
64	Brezno a.	0723	...	1046	*1401*	...	*1618*	...	...	*1801*	...
64	Brezno d.	0724	...	1047	1404	...	1621	...	...	1830	...
107	Červená Skala a.	0820	...	1135	1517	...	1715	...	...	1924	...
107	Červená Skala d.	...	0822	1136	...	1605	...	1723	...	...	1926
135	Dedinky d.	...	0858*	1206	...	1635*	...	1758	...	...	1956*
192	Gelnica d.	...	1018	1305	...	1804	...	1919	...	...	2110
200	Margecany a.	...	1030	1314	...	1817	...	1931	...	...	2121
200	Margecany **1180** d.	...	*1134*	1322	...	*1856*	...	*1934*	...	...	*2134*
219	Kysak **1180** a.	...	*1148*	1336	...	*1917*	...	*1948*	...	...	*2148*
235	**Košice** **1180** a.	...	*1202*	1348	...	*1936*	...	*2002*	...	...	*2202*

						810	760			
				Ⓐ		H	Ⓐ	F	Ⓑ	
Košice **1180** d.	...	...	*0805*	...	...	1458	1511	...	...	*1805*
Kysak **1180** d.	...	...	*0819*	...	...	1512	1525	...	...	*1819*
Margecany **1180** a.	...	...	*0833*	...	...	1526	1538	...	...	*1833*
Margecany d.	0519	...	0836	...	...	1535	...	1606	...	1857
Gelnica d.	0531	...	0848	...	...	1544	...	1618	...	1922
Dedinky d.	0707	...	1006*	...	...	1648	...	1750	...	2100**u**
Červená Skala a.	0738	...	1036	...	...	1717	...	1821	...	...
Červená Skala d.	...	0825	...	1038	1257	1718	...	...	1824	...
Brezno a.	...	0921	...	1136	1352	1803	...	...	1922	...
Brezno d.	...	0922	...	*1221*	*1412*	1804	...	...	*1951*	...
Banská Bystrica **1185** a.	...	1028	...	*1329*	*1515*	1849	...	...	*2047*	...
Zvolen **1185** a.	...	1111	...	...	*1555*	1926	...	...	...	...

E – Ⓒ (daily July 1 - Aug. 31).
F – Ⓐ (not July 1 - Aug. 31).
H – HOREHRONEC – (12) Bratislava - Zvolen - Brezno - Košice and v.v.
P – POL'ANA – 🛏 1, 2 cl. and (2) Bratislava - Prešov and v.v. Runs on Ⓑ (not Dec. 24, 25, 31, Jan. 1, Apr. 2, 4, July 4, Oct. 31) from Bratislava and Prešov.
R – ①–⑥ (not Dec. 25, 26, Jan. 1, Apr. 3, 5).
a – Ⓐ only.
k – Not Dec. 24 - Jan. 6.
r – Not ⑥.
s – Not Dec. 24, 25, 31, Apr. 2, 4.
u – Ⓑ (not Dec. 24, 25, 31, Apr. 2, 4, July 4).
x – Change at Jesenské.
z – ⑦ (also Jan. 6, Apr. 5, July 5, Sept. 1, Nov. 1; not Dec. 27, Apr. 4, July 4, Oct. 31).
★ – Except trains **H** and **P**.
△ – (2) Bratislava (**833/2**) - Zvolen (**933/2**) - Košice - Prešov and v.v.
▷ – (2) Košice - Zvolen (**830**) - Bratislava.
* – Request stop.

1194 KOŠICE/PREŠOV - HUMENNÉ - MEDZILABORCE

2nd class

km			615	443	8907	8909	1901	1903	1905	1907	
			Z	S	u		Ⓐ	B	v		
	Bratislava hl **1180** d.	...	2310	...	...	...	...	1010	...	...	...
0	**Košice** d.	...	0535	0725	1040	1440	1540	1640	1840	2230	...
68	Trebišov d.	...	0623	0811	1129	1526	1633	1728	1927	2314	...
88	Michalovce d.	...	0656	0844	1202	1602	1705	1758	1957	2345	...
112	**Humenné** a.	...	0725	0913	1234	1633	1738	1820	2021	0006	...

	1900	1902	8904	8906	8908	1904	1906	442	614
	P	B	u			v	⑦b	S	Z
Humenné d.	0338	0526	0618	0940	1131	1540	1840	2000	2155
Michalovce d.	0357	0549	0657	1009	1203	1601	1901	2024	2220
Trebišov d.	0428	0621	0731	1044	1239	1632	1942	2059	2255
Košice a.	0514	0709	0816	1130	1323	1716	2027	2143	2346
Bratislava hl **1180** a.	...	1400	...	...	...	...	...	...	0600

km							Ⓐr				
0	Prešov d.	0332	0544	0833	...	1141	1440	1516	1637	2024	...
70	Humenné a.	0516	0733	1003	...	1311	1558	1700	1828	2218	...

Humenné d.	0407	0539	0739	1119	1426	...	1637	1757	...
Prešov a.	0538	0714	0914	1250	1604**x**	...	1816	1937	...

km											
0	Humenné d.	0422	0614	0822	1018	1315	1437	1636	1823	2027	2227
41	Medzilaborce ▷ a.	0541	0731	0931	1136	1419	1602	1801	1939	2141	2335
43	Medzilaborce mesto ▷ a.	0547	0737**a**	0937	1142	...	1608	1806	1945	2146	...

Medzilaborce mesto ▷ d.	0406	0552	0750**a**	0954	1146	1428	1621	1838	2011
Medzilaborce ▷ d.	0411	0559	0804	1006	1158	1436	1628	1844	2017
Humenné a.	0521	0719	0920	1116	1305	1536	1735	1947	2119

B – Conveys (12) and ✕ Bratislava (**604/5**) - Žilina - Košice - Humenné and v.v.
P – ①–⑥ (not Dec. 24-26, Jan. 1, 6, Apr. 2-5).
S – ŠIRAVA – 🛏 1, 2 cl., ▬ 2 cl. and (12) Praha - Humenné and v.v.
Z – ZEMPLÍN – 🛏 1, 2 cl., ▬ 2 cl., (12) Bratislava - Košice - Humenné and v.v. Not Dec. 24, 31 from Bratislava and Humenné.
a – Ⓐ only.
b – ⑦ (also Jan. 6, Apr. 5, 6; not Dec. 27, Jan. 3, Apr. 4, July 1 - Aug. 31).
r – Ⓐ (not July 1 - Aug. 31).
u – Not Dec. 24-26, Jan. 1, Apr. 4, 5.
v – Not Dec. 24-26, 31, Apr. 2-4.
x – 1536 on ⑦ (also Apr. 5, Nov. 1; not Dec. 27, Jan. 3, Apr. 4, July 1 - Aug. 31, Oct. 31).
▷ – For connections to Poland (summer only) see Table **1079**.

1195 KOŠICE - ČIERNA NAD TISOU - CHOP

2nd class

km								605		8815	
				①–⑥ n				B		⊖△	
0	**Košice** d.	0511	0745	1006	1206	1445	1545	1625	1845	2045	2245
62	Slovenské Nové Mesto d.	0619	0852	1112	1310	1551	1653	1715	1953	2150	2359
95	Čierna nad Tisou a.	0657	0930	1149	1347	1630	1730	1750	2030	2227	0035
95	Čierna nad Tisou 🛃 d.	...	...	...	*1401*	...	...	...	...	*2304*	...
105	**Chop** 🛃 ⊕ a.	...	...	...	*1547*	...	...	...	...	*0050*	...

			604							8814
			B △			⑦ u	①–⑥ n			⊖
Chop 🛃 ⊕ d.	...	...	*0510*	...	...	...	...	...	...	*1820*
Čierna nad Tisou 🛃 a.	...	...	*0516*	...	...	...	...	...	...	*1826*
Čierna nad Tisou d.	0407	0510	0617	0710	1005	1253	1410	1527	1829	1952
Slovenské Nové Mesto d.	0444	0547	0647	0746	1041	1332	1449	1606	1906	2029
Košice a.	0550	0650	0731	0850	1146	1437	1555	1711	2010	2130

B – (2) Bratislava (**604/5**) - Košice - Čierna nad Tisou and v.v.
n – Not Dec. 25, 26, Jan. 1, Apr. 5, July 5.
u – Also Dec. 25, 26, Jan. 1, Apr. 5, July 5.
⊕ – East European time (one hour ahead).
⊖ – Conveys 🛏 1, 2 cl. Bratislava (**609/700**) - Košice - Chop - Lviv and v.v. (extended to/from Kyïv on dates in Table **96**)
△ – Conveys 🛏 1, 2 cl. Žilina (**609/4**) - Košice - Chop (**15/6**) - Moskva and v.v.

1196 KOŠICE - PREŠOV - PLAVEČ

2nd class ★

km					801					1910			1931								933						1380
				Ⓐ	①–⑥ Pu	①–⑥ u	⑦ d					Ⓐ	⑦ z§		b			Ⓑ h			⊖		⑤ f				V
0	**Košice** **1180** d.	0454	...	0536	0704	0640	0654	0830	1010	1151	...	1240	1242	1350	...	1447	1554	...	1654	1810	1913	1940	...	...	2213	2254	2329
16	Kysak **1180** d.	0512	...	0554	0717	0701	0715	0848	1028	1207	...	1258	1257	1412	1441	1506	1612	...	1712	1828	1926	1958	2018	2203	2230	2311	2342
33	**Prešov** a.	0537	...	0620	0733	0723	0737	0910	1050	1223	...	1325	1326	1437	1458	1528	1634	...	1737	1852	1942	2020	2041	2230	2252	2333	2358
33	**Prešov** d.	0545	...	0636	...	0746	0746	...	1052	*1316*r	...	...	...	...	...	1534	1640	...	...	1854	...	...	...	...	2254	...	0001
65	Lipany a.	0626	0646	0714	...	0824	0824	...	1130	*1354*r	1357	...	...	...	...	1618	1718	1721	...	1931	...	...	...	...	2332	...	0025
88	**Plaveč** 🛃 ▷ a.	...	0718	...	...	...	...	...	...	...	1429	...	...	....	...	1651	...	1753	...	2004	...	...	...	...	...	...	0055

		1381					932							934										800	
		V			Ⓐ		⊖						Ⓐ	⑦ z			Ⓑ h	Ⓑ h					Ⓑ h		Ⓑ Pv	⑦ e
Plaveč 🛃 ▷ d.	...	0320	...	0431	...	*0607*	...	...	...	1146	...	...	...	...	...	...	1540	...	...	...	1830	...	...	...	...	...
Lipany d.	...	0348	0435	0503	...	0645	...	0903r	1101r	1217	1222	...	...	...	1454	...	1611	1620	...	1748	1902	...	2100	...	...	...
Prešov a.	...	0413	0513	0541	...	0726	...	0941r	1138r	...	1300	...	...	...	1531	...	...	1701	...	1825	1941	...	2137	...	...	...
Prešov d.	0343	0414	0515	0543	0635	0745	0814	0945	1140	...	1302	1345	1438	1452	1533	1713	...	1713	1751	1827	1945	2045	2139	2139	2209	2359
Kysak **1180** a.	0406	0429	0540	0608	0659	0811	0831	1008	1203	...	1325	1408	1504	1509	1556	1739	...	1739	1815	1855	2012	2108	2202	2202	2225	0015
Košice **1180** a.	0423	0443	0555	0626	0717	0828	0844	1026	1221	...	1343	1429	1522	1525	1614	1757	...	1757	...	1910	2030	2126	2220	2220	2237	...

P – POL'ANA – 🛏 1, 2 cl. and (2) Bratislava - Košice - Prešov and v.v. (Table **1170**).
V – VARSÓVIA – from Warszawa June 17 - Sept. 3; from Keszthely June 18 - Sept. 4. ▬ 2 cl. and (12) Warszawa - Kraków - Košice - Budapest - Keszthely and v.v. Also runs on Sept. 5 with (12) Košice - Keszthely and v.v. Conveys 🛏 1, 2 cl. Warszawa - Burgas/Varna and v.v. (also ▬ 2 cl. Košice - Burgas/Varna and v.v.) on summer dates in Table **99**.
b – On ⑦**z** depart 1432, arrive 1449.
d – Also Dec. 25, 26, Jan. 1, 2, Apr. 3, 5, July 5, Nov. 1.
e – Also Jan. 6, Apr. 5, July 5, Nov. 1; not Apr. 4, July 4, Oct. 31.
f – Also Dec. 23, Apr. 1; not Dec. 25, Jan. 1, Apr. 2.
h – Not Dec. 24, 25, 31, Apr. 2, 4, July 4.
r – Ⓐ only.
u – ①–⑥ (also Dec. 25, 26, Jan. 1, 2, Apr. 3, 5, July 5, Nov. 1).
v – Not Dec. 24, 25, 31, Jan. 1, Apr. 2, 4, July 4, Oct. 31.
z – Also Jan. 6, Apr. 5, July 5, Sept. 1, Nov. 1; not Dec. 27, Apr. 4, July 4, Oct. 31.
⊖ – To/from Bratislava via Zvolen (Table **1170**).
▷ – For connections to Poland see Table **1078**.
§ – To/from Zvolen (Table **1190**).
★ – Except trains **C** and **P**.

PREŠOV - BARDEJOV *45* km, 70-75 mins.
From Prešov: 0332, 0544, 0747, 1141, 1516, 1637, 1902, 2024, 2258 Ⓑ **h**.
From Bardejov: 0506, 0557 Ⓐ, 0709, 1154, 1426, 1647, 1825, 2033 Ⓑ **h**, 2222.

HUNGARY

Operator: MÁV-START, running on the network of MÁV, except the lines from Sopron to Györ and Szombathely which are operated by Györ - Sopron - Ebenfurthi Vasút (GySEV).

Services: All trains convey first and second class seating, **except** where shown otherwise in footnotes or by '2' in the train column, or where the footnote shows sleeping- and / or couchette cars only. Descriptions of sleeping- (🛏) and couchette (▬) cars appear on page 8. Certain international services, as indicated in the tables, cannot be used for internal journeys in Hungary, whilst others generally convey dedicated carriages for internal journeys, which may be made without reservation.

Timings: Valid from **December 13, 2009.** Amendments are made at various dates during the year and will be shown when information is received. Certain trains will not run at Christmas, notably on the evening of Dec. 24, 31 or on Dec. 25, Jan. 1 - see page 539 for further details.

Reservations: Most **Domestic** InterCity (*IC*) trains have **compulsory** reservation, as shown by 🄁 in the tables. *IC* trains require a supplement of 540 HUF which includes the reservation fee. The price of the supplement may be reduced on certain journeys or on certain dates. Passengers having passes which include the supplement (e.g. Eurail) have to pay only the reservation fee of 140 HUF. For domestic journeys on **International** *EC / IC / EN* trains, the supplement is 400 HUF, but seat reservation is not possible. For international journeys on these trains the supplement does not apply (unless shown) but seat reservation is possible (and is **compulsory** on certain trains where shown).

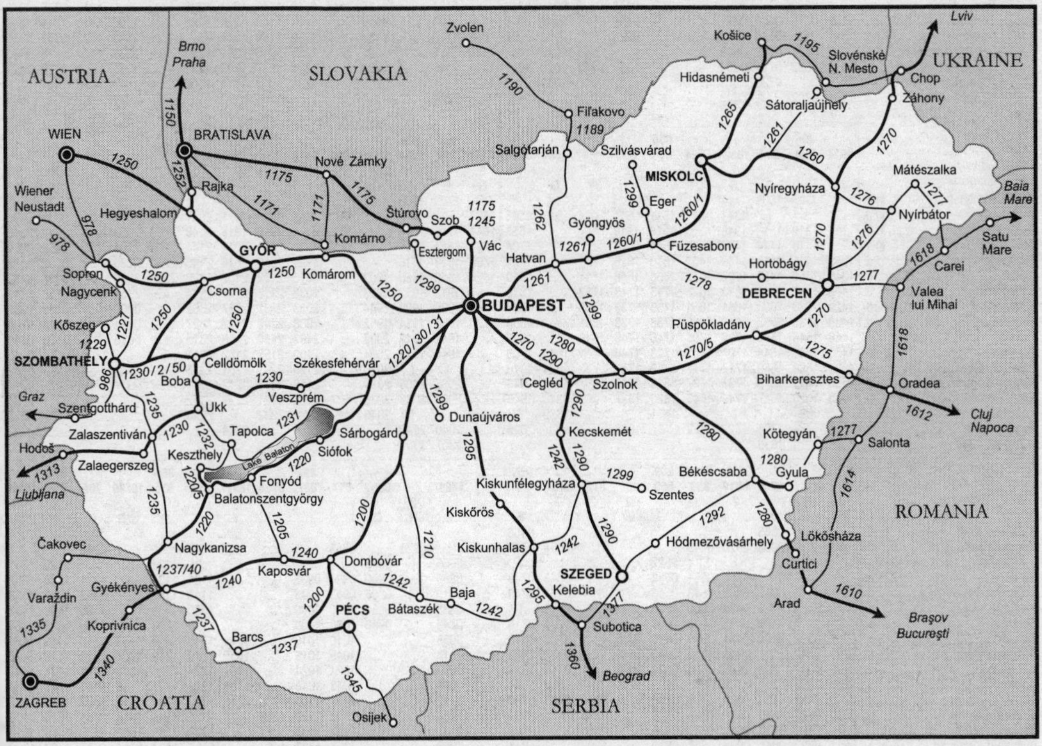

BUDAPEST - DOMBÓVÁR - PÉCS 1200

km		*IC* 800 🄁✕	8012	*IC* 802 🄁✕	*IC* 537 ✕ D	*IC* 804 🄁✕	1824 ⑤f	8024	*IC* 814 🄁✕	8016	*IC* 806 🄁✕	*IC* 818 🄁✕	*IC* 828 🄁✕ n	8026	*IC* 816 🄁✕	*IC* 808 🄁✕
0	**Budapest** Keleti .... d.	0545	...	0745	0945	1145	...	...	1345	...	1545	...	...	...	1745	1945
*	**Budapest** Déli .... d.	|	0716	|	|	|	1241	1316	|	1516	|	1646	1646	1716	|	|
13	Budapest Kelenföld ...... d.	0600	0723	0800	1000	1200	1248	1323	1400	1523	1600	1653	1653	1723	1800	2000
93	Sárbogárd .... d.	0701	0831	0901	1101	1301	1358	1431	1501	1631	1701	1804	1804	1831	1901	2101
173	Dombóvár .... a.	0750	0955	0950	1150	1350	1511	1555	1550	1755	1750	1905	1905	1955	1950	2150
173	Dombóvár .... d.	0751	1006	0951	1151	1351	...	1606	1551	1806	1751	1909	...	2006	1951	2151
218	Szentlőrinc .... d.	0823	1053	1023	1223	1423	...	1653	1623	1853	1823	1951	...	2053	2023	2223
237	**Pécs** .... a.	0836	1116	1036	1236	1436	...	1711	1636	1911	1836	2004	...	2111	2036	2236

	IC 809 🄁✕	*IC* 819 🄁	*IC* 829 🄁 n	*IC* 807 🄁✕	*IC* 817 🄁✕	8027	*IC* 805 🄁✕	8015	*IC* 815 🄁✕	*IC* 536 ✕ D	*IC* 1823 🄁✕ ⑦e	8013	*IC* 813 🄁✕	*IC* 801 🄁✕	2	2 ⑧
Pécs .... d.	0523	0559	...	0723	0923	1043	1123	1242	1323	1523	...	1643	1723	1919	2043	2241
Szentlőrinc .... d.	0537	0617	...	0737	0937	1106	1137	1306	1337	1537	...	1706	1737	1933	2106	2300
Dombóvár .... a.	0607	0651	...	0810	1010	1153	1210	1353	1410	1610	...	1753	1810	2010	2153	2349
Dombóvár .... d.	0611	0701	0701	0811	1011	1157	1211	1357	1411	1611	1642	1757	1811	2011	...	...
Sárbogárd .... d.	0701	0756	0756	0901	1101	1329	1301	1529	1501	1701	1746	1929	1901	2101	...	...
Budapest Kelenföld .... a.	0759	0857	0857	0959	1159	1432	1359	1632	1559	1759	1857	2032	1959	2159	...	...
Budapest Déli .... a.	|	0905	0905	|	|	1440	|	1640	|	|	1905	2040	|	|	...	...
Budapest Keleti .... a.	0814	...	...	1014	1214	...	1414	...	1614	1814	...	...	2014	2214	...	...

D – DRÁVA – 🚃12 ✕ Košice - Budapest - Pécs and v.v.; 🚃12 Budapest - Sarajevo and v.v. (Table **92**).

e – Not June 19 - Aug. 29. From Kaposvár (Table **1240**).

f – Not June 19 - Aug. 29. To Nagykanizsa (Table **1240**).

n – To / from Nagykanizsa (Table **1240**).

* – Budapest Déli - Kelenföld: *4 km.*

FONYÓD - PÉCS 1205

km		8807 Q		8801 P
	Keszthely **1220** .... d.	0848	...	1700
0	**Fonyód** .... ▶ d.	0954	...	1825
53	Kaposvár .... ▶ a.	1122	...	1952
82	Dombóvár alsó .... d.	...	...	2044
129	Szentlőrinc .... d.	...	...	2125
148	**Pécs** .... a.	...	...	2141

		8802 P		8806 Q
Pécs .... d.	...	0730	...	...
Szentlőrinc .... d.	...	0749	...	...
Dombóvár alsó .... d.	...	0844	...	...
Kaposvár .... ▶ d.	...	0925	...	1647
Fonyód .... ▶ a.	...	1036	...	1805
Keszthely **1220** .... a.	...	1121	...	1859

P – 🚃12 Pécs - Keszthely - Tapolca - Celldömölk and v.v.

Q – 🚃12 Kaposvár - Fonyód - Keszthely - Tapolca - Celldömölk - Szombathely and v.v.

▶ – **Additional trains Fonyód - Kaposvár**
Journey 80 - 90 minutes, *53 km.*
From Fonyód 0346 ⚒, 0539, 0730, 1154, 1306, 1514, 1623, 2026.
From Kaposvár 0400, 0603, 0743, 1123 Ⓐ, 1330, 1441, 1843, 2248 Ⓑ.

BUDAPEST - SÁRBOGÁRD - SZEKSZÁRD - BAJA 1210

2nd class

km							836		Ⓐ	838	
0	**Budapest** Déli .... ▷ d.	...	...	...	...	...	1341r	...	...	1741	...
4	Budapest Kelenföld . ▷ d.	...	...	...	...	...	1348r	...	...	1748	...
84	**Sárbogárd** .... ▷ d.	0550	0706	0910	1110	1310	1510	1710	1810	1910	2110
149	Szekszárd.................. a.	0651	0811	1011	1211	1411	1611	1811	1925	2011	2211
168	Bátaszék .... **1242** a.	0747	0846	1046	1246	1446	1646	1846	2022	2046	2304
188	**Baja** .... **1242** a.	0818	0905	1105	1305	1505	1705	1905	...	2105	2324

		839						Ⓐ	8303	
Baja .... **1242** d.	0437	0603	0649	0845	1045	1245	1445	...	1645	1845
Bátaszék .... **1242** d.	0456	0622	0708	0908	1108	1308	1508	...	1708	1908
Szekszárd .... d.	0539	0701	0743	0943	1143	1343	1543	1634	1743	1943
Sárbogárd .... ▷ a.	0653	0802	0853	1053	1253	1453	1653	1748	1853	2053
Budapest Kelenföld. ▷ a.	...	0917	...	...	...	...	...	...	2012c	...
Budapest Déli ...... ▷ a.	...	0925	...	...	...	...	...	...	2020c	...

c – ⑦ (not June 19 - Aug. 29).

r – ⑤ (not June 19 - Aug. 29).

▷ – See also Table **1200**.

1220 BUDAPEST - SZÉKESFEHÉRVÁR - FONYÓD - KESZTHELY / NAGYKANIZSA

km		8530 2	8612 2	8510 2	8710 2	2 ⒶT	18500 2 S	*IC* 200 F	850 860	850	8802 P	18502 Z	8722	5609 ⊕ S	18702 ⒸS	852 862	852	16809 △ S	1381 B	*Ex* 1787 2[R] ⒸS	2 ⒶT	5209 M	854 874	854
•	**Budapest** Keleti ◧ d.	...	...	...	...	...	...	0630	...	...	...	...	...	...	...	...	...	...	0930	...	...	1015	...	...
0	**Budapest** Déli ◧ d.	...	...	0336	0436	...	0541	|	0711	0711	...	0741	0746	...	0841	0911	0911	...	|	⊡	...	|	1111	1111
4	Budapest Kelenföld ◧ d.	...	...	0343	0443	...	0548	0645	0718	0718	...	0748	0753	0836	0848	0918	0918	0932	0945	1003	...	1029	1118	1118
67	**Székesfehérvár** ◧ a.	...	...	0459	0559	...	0648	0744	0814	0814	...	0848	0904	0937	0949	1014	1014	1033	1043	1109	...	1128	1214	1214
67	**Székesfehérvár** d.	...	...	0533	0633	...	0650	0746	0816	0816	...	0850	0920	0941	0953	1016	1016	1035	1048	1113	...	1130	1216	1216
115	Siófok d.	0435	...	0625	0728	0744	0744	0829	0858	0858	...	0947	1012	1026	1041	1058	1058	1128	1138	1156	...	1212	1258	1258
130	Balatonföldvár d.	0455	...	0648	...	0807	0807	0850	0913	0913	...	1014	...	1048	1105	1113	1113	1147	1153	1210	...	1228	1313	1313
146	Balatonlelle d.	0517	...	0709	...	0833	0833	0907	0933	0933	...	1042	...	1109	1126	1133	1133	1206	1211	1229	...	1253	1333	1333
149	Balatonboglár d.	0523	...	0714	...	0839	0839	0912	0938	0938	...	1054	...	1115	1131	1138	1138	1211	1218	1235	...	1304	1338	1338
157	**Fonyód** a.	0533	...	0723	...	0848	0848	0920	0946	0946	...	1104	...	1125	1141	1146	1146	1232	1226	1243	...	1313	1346	1346
157	**Fonyód** d.	0546	0640	0731	...	...	0850	0922	0948	0948	1040	1107	...	1128	...	1148	1148	1234	1228	...	1300	1315	1348	1348
165	Balatonfenyves d.	0559	0649	0741	...	...	0925	|	0959	0959	1051	1118	...	1137	...	1159	1159	1243	|	...	1311	1323	1359	1359
181	Balatonszentgyörgy a.	0621	0712	0803	...	...	...	0943	1015	1015	1110	1139	...	1201	...	1215	1215	1301	1250	...	1332	1342	1415	1415
181	Balatonszentgyörgy **1225** d.	0622	0714	0809	...	...	...	0947	1020	1027	1111	1145	...	1202	...	1220	1227	1303	1251	...	1335	1353r	1420	1427
	Keszthely **1225** a.	|	0726	|	...	...	...	|	1031	|	1121	|	...	1213	...	1231	|	1314	1302	...	1347	1404r	1431	|
221	**Nagykanizsa** a.	0702	...	0849	...	...	...	1021	...	1106	...	1224	...	...	...	...	1306	...	...	...	...	...	...	1506
352	*Zagreb* **1340** a.	...	...	...	...	...	...	1259	...	...	...	...	...	...	...	...	...	...	...	...	...	...	...	...

	8514 2	204 864	204 D	18504 2 S	8524 2 ⒷT	856 866	856	Y	8806 Q	8516 2	18606 2 G	*EN* 240 E	240 1204 A	18606 2 G	908	8518 2	858 868	858	1868 R	2	2 R		2 U	2 V
Budapest Keleti ◧ d.	...	1305	1305	...	...	...	...	...	...	...	...	1700	1700	...	...	...	...	...	...	...	...	...	...	...
Budapest Déli ◧ d.	...	|	|	1341	...	1511	1511	...	...	1546	1631	|	|	...	1811	...	1911	1911	2041	*2046*	2046	...	2236	2336
Budapest Kelenföld ◧ d.	...	1318	1318	1348	...	1518	1518	...	...	1553	1641	1718	1718	...	1818	...	1918	1918	2048	*2053*	2053	...	2243	2343
Székesfehérvár ◧ a.	...	1414	1414	1449	...	1614	1614	...	...	1704	1747	1814	1814	...	1914	...	2014	2014	2144	*2204*	2204	...	2359	0059
Székesfehérvár d.	1245	1416	1416	1450	1450	1616	1616	...	...	1721	1750	1816	1816	←	...	1921	2016	2016	2146	2230	2230	...	0002	0103
Siófok d.	1345	1458	1458	1602*	1602*	1658	1658	1711	...	1810	1851	1858	1858	1902	...	2010	2102	2102	2228	2324	2330	...	0058	0152
Balatonföldvár d.	1406	1513	1513	1623	1623	1713	1713	1732	...	1830	→	1912	1912	1923	...	2033	2117	2117	2244	...	2351	...	0118	0211
Balatonlelle d.	1429	1533	1533	1651	1651	1733	1733	1755	...	1851	...	1929	1929	1944	...	2053	2137	2137	2302	...	0009	...	0139	0235
Balatonboglár d.	1438	1538	1538	1656	1656	1738	1738	1801	...	1856	...	1934	1934	1952	...	2058	2142	2142	2307	...	0014	...	0144	0240
Fonyód a.	1448	1546	1546	1705	1705	1746	1746	1810	...	1905	...	1942	1942	2002	...	2107	2150	2150	2315	...	0023	...	0153	0249
Fonyód d.	1453	1548	1548	1707	1707	1748	1748	...	1814	1906	...	1944	1944	2004	...	2109	2152	2152	2317	...	...	...	...	0252
Balatonfenyves d.	1503	1559	1559	1717	1717	1759	1759	...	1824	1916	...	|	|	2015	...	2120	2201	2201	2326	...	...	...	...	0302
Balatonszentgyörgy a.	1530	1615	1615	1737	1737	1815	1815	...	1846	1943	...	2005	2005	2034	...	2140	2217	2217	2341	...	...	...	...	0322
Balatonszentgyörgy **1225** d.	1535	1620	1627	*1743*	1743	1820	1827	...	1848	1945	...	2006	2006	2035	...	2151	2221	2229	2342	...	...	...	...	0324
Keszthely **1225** a.	|	1631	|	|	|	1831	|	...	1859	|	...	|	|	2046	...	|	2232	|	2353	...	...	...	...	0335
Nagykanizsa a.	1613	...	1706	*1822*	1822	...	1906	...	...	2025	...	2040	2040	...	...	2230	...	2308	...	...	...	...	...	...
Zagreb **1340** a.	...	...	1936	...	...	...	...	...	...	...	...	2307	2307	...	...	...	...	...	...	...	...	...	...	...

	2 W	2 L	1205 A	8519 2	859	869 859	2 Ⓐ	8727 2	8529 2	*EN* 241 E		18607 L	2 H	8807 Q	857	867 857	8725 2	18517 2 Y	855	865 855	18705 2 ⒸS	205 D	875 205	16806 ▽ S
Zagreb **1340** d.	...	...	0055	...	...	...	...	...	...	0456	...	...	...	...	...	...	...	...	...	...	...	1000	...	...
Nagykanizsa d.	...	...	0308	0320	0449	...	...	...	0558	0713	...	...	0820	...	0853	...	...	...	1049	...	...	1249	...	...
Keszthely **1225** d.	...	...	|	|	|	0522	...	...	|	|	...	0755	|	0848	|	0922	...	...	|	1122	...	|	1322	1341
Balatonszentgyörgy **1225** a.	...	...	0341	0358	0531	0533	...	...	0643	0748	...	0806	0902	0900	0931	0933	...	...	1131	1133	...	1331	1333	1352
Balatonszentgyörgy d.	...	...	0342	0404	0543	0543	...	...	0654	0749	...	0815	...	0905	0943	0943	...	...	1143	1143	...	1343	1343	1353
Balatonfenyves d.	...	...	|	0424	0600	0600	...	...	0715	|	...	0836	...	0930	1000	1000	...	...	1200	1200	...	1400	1400	1417
Fonyód a.	...	...	0403	0433	0608	0608	...	...	0724	0810	...	0845	...	0940	1008	1008	...	...	1208	1208	...	1408	1408	1425
Fonyód d.	0203	0332	0405	0434	0610	0610	0635	...	0727	0813	...	0858	...	...	1010	1010	...	1045	1210	1210	1253	1410	1410	1428
Balatonboglár d.	0213	0342	|	0443	0619	0619	0644	...	0737	0822	...	0913	...	...	1019	1019	...	1055	1219	1219	1304	1419	1419	1438
Balatonlelle d.	0218	0347	|	0448	0624	0624	0649	...	0742	0827	...	0920	...	...	1024	1024	...	1100	1224	1224	1310	1424	1424	1443
Balatonföldvár d.	0239	0408	|	0509	0643	0643	0712	...	0802	0844	...	0949	...	...	1043	1043	...	1136	1243	1243	1338	1443	1443	1503
Siófok d.	0259	0429	0451	0532	0700	0700	0732	0740	0823	0900	...	1012	...	...	1100	1100	1138	1211	1300	1300	1410	1500	1500	1527
Székesfehérvár a.	0350	0520	0530	0627	0738	0738	...	0834	...	0939	...	1059	...	...	1138	1138	1233	...	1338	1338	1500	1538	1538	1610
Székesfehérvár ◧ d.	0354	0521	0532	0651	0739	0739	...	0851	...	0942	...	1107	...	...	1139	1139	1251	...	1339	1339	1505	1539	1539	1613
Budapest Kelenföld ◧ a.	0511	0637	0641	0807	0837	0837	...	1007	...	1041	...	1213	...	...	1237	1237	1407	...	1437	1437	1614	1637	1637	1722
Budapest Déli ◧ a.	0520	0645	|	0815	0845	0845	...	1015	...	|	...	1225	...	...	1245	1245	1415	...	1445	1445	1625	|	|	...
Budapest Keleti ◧ a.	...	...	0659	...	...	...	...	...	...	1059	...	...	...	...	...	...	...	...	...	...	...	1654	1654	...

	8615 2 T	2 ⒶS	18603 S	1380 B	5608 ⊕ S	853	863 853	*Ex* 1786 2[R] ⒸS	5008 N	2	18503 2 Z	18601 2 ⑦S	8801 P	851	861 851	8721 2	971	18701 2 X	*IC* 201 F	8511 2		1861 R	8531 2	2 V
Zagreb **1340** d.	...	...	...	...	...	...	...	...	...	...	...	...	...	...	...	...	...	...	1545	...	...	...	...	...
Nagykanizsa d.	...	...	...	...	...	1449	...	...	...	1528	1528	...	...	1649	...	...	...	...	1830	1823	...	...	2105	...
Keszthely **1225** d.	1407	1407	...	1432	1501	|	1522	...	1539c	|	|	...	1700	|	1722	...	...	...	|	|	...	2000	|	2310
Balatonszentgyörgy **1225** a.	1418	1418	...	1443	1512	1531	1533	...	1550c	1613	1613	...	1712	1731	1733	...	...	...	1915	1908	...	2011	2143	2321
Balatonszentgyörgy d.	1420	...	1420	1444	1513	1543	1543	...	1555	1625	1625	...	1714	1743	1743	...	...	1825	1917	1923	...	2012	2158	2322
Balatonfenyves d.	1442	...	1442	|	1533	1600	1600	...	1617	1647	1647	...	1739	1800	1800	...	...	1851	|	1952	...	2034	2220	2348
Fonyód a.	1452	...	1452	1510	1543	1608	1608	...	1624	1658	1658	...	1748	1808	1808	...	...	1901	1942	2001	...	2042	2229	2357
Fonyód d.	1456	...	1456	1511	1550	1610	1610	1615	1627	1707	1707	1748	...	1810	1810	...	...	1905	1944	2005	...	2045	2231	0001
Balatonboglár d.	1507	...	1507	1520	1601	1619	1619	1625	1637	1718	1718	1800	...	1819	1819	...	...	1915	1953	2015	...	2057	2240	0013
Balatonlelle d.	1512	...	1512	1525	1607	1624	1624	1630	1642	1723	1723	1805	...	1824	1824	...	...	1920	1958	2020	...	2102	2244	0018
Balatonföldvár d.	1536	...	1536	1546	1635	1643	1643	1653	1704	1748	1748	1822	...	1843	1843	...	...	1945	2015	2044	...	2128	2306	0038
Siófok d.	1608	...	1608	1602	1702	1700	1700	1713	1732	1808	1810	1854	...	1900	1900	1920	...	2009	2030	2103	...	2145	2325	0100
Székesfehérvár a.	1705	...	1702	1645	1743	1738	1738	1752	1822	...	1903	1943	...	1938	1938	2015	...	2100	2111	2151	...	2228	...	0149
Székesfehérvár ◧ d.	...	...	1705	1647	1744	1739	1739	1756	1824	...	1907	1945	...	1939	1939	...	2028	2105	2113	2154	...	2231	...	0151
Budapest Kelenföld ◧ a.	...	...	1814	1752	1845	1837	1837	1852	1925	...	2015	2043	...	2037	2037	...	2132	2221	2211	2311	...	2331	...	0307
Budapest Déli ◧ a.	...	...	1825	|	...	1845	1845	⊙	|	...	2025	2050	...	2045	2045	...	2140	2230	|	2320	...	2340	...	0315
Budapest Keleti ◧ a.	...	...	...	1809	...	...	...	...	1944	...	...	...	...	...	...	...	...	...	2229	...	...	...	...	...

A – ADRIA – from Budapest ②⑤ June 18 - Aug. 27, from Split ③⑥ June 19 - Aug. 28 (next day from Zagreb). 🛏 1, 2 cl., 🛏 2 cl., (2) and 🍸 Budapest - Zagreb - Split and v.v.

B – VARSÓVIA – from Warszawa June 17 - Sept. 3 (next day from Košice); from Keszthely June 18 - Sept. 4. 🛏 2 cl. and (12) Warszawa - Kraków - Košice - Budapest - Keszthely and v.v. Also runs on Sept. 5 with (12) Košice - Keszthely and v.v.

D – MAESTRAL – (12) Budapest - Murakeresztúr - Zagreb and v.v. Conveys on dates in Table **97**, 🛏 1, 2 cl. Moskva / Kyïv (**15 / 6**) - Budapest - Zagreb and v.v. Conveys on dates in Table **95**, 🛏 1, 2 cl. St Peterburg - Budapest - Zagreb and v.v.

E – VENEZIA – 🛏 1, 2 cl., 🛏 2 cl., (2) ✕ Budapest - Zagreb - Ljubljana - Venezia and v.v.; (12) Budapest - Nagykanizsa - Gyékényes and v.v. Conveys 🛏 Moskva - Budapest - Venezia once weekly (see Table **97**).

F – KVARNER – (12) Budapest - Zagreb and v.v.

G – ⑤ Apr. 30 - June 11; daily June 18 - Aug. 29; ⑤ Sept. 3 - 24.

H – © May 1 - June 13; daily June 19 - Aug. 29.

L – June 19 - Aug. 30.

M – ⑥ (daily May 1 - Sept. 26). From Sátoraljaújhely and Miskolc (Table **1261**).

N – ⑦ (daily May 1 - Sept. 26). To Miskolc (Table **1261**).

P – (12) Pécs - Fonyód - Keszthely - Tapolca - Celldömölk and v.v. (see Table **1205**).

Q – (12) Kaposvár - Fonyód - Keszthely - Tapolca - Celldömölk - Szombathely and v.v. (Table **1205**).

R – June 18 - Aug. 29.

S – June 19 - Aug. 29.

T – Dec. 13 - June 18, Aug. 30 - Dec. 11.

U – ⑤⑥ June 18 - Aug. 28 (also ④ July 1 - Aug. 26).

V – ④⑤⑥ June 18 - Aug. 28.

W – ⑥⑦ June 19 - Aug. 29 (also ⑤ July 2 - Aug. 27).

X – ⑦ May 2 - June 13; daily June 19 - Aug. 29; ⑦ Sept. 5 - 26.

Y – © Apr. 3 - June 13; daily June 19 - Aug. 29; © Sept. 4 - Nov. 1.

Z – © Apr. 3 - 25; daily May 1 - Aug. 29; © Sept. 4 - Nov. 1.

c – ⑦ (runs on © May 1 - Sept. 26).

r – ⑥ (runs on © May 1 - Sept. 26).

⊕ – From / to Miskolc (**5609** departs Miskolc 0555, **5608** arrives Miskolc 2127).

⊡ – From Szeged (d. 0723), Kecskemét (d. 0834), Köbánya-Kispest (d. 0948).

⊙ – To Köbánya-Kispest (d. 1912), Kecskemét (a. 2020), Szeged (a. 2128).

△ – From Nyíregyháza (d. 0517), Debrecen (d. 0613), Köbánya-Kispest (0915).

▽ – To Köbánya-Kispest (d. 1741), Debrecen (a. 2031), Nyíregyháza (a. 2119).

◧ – See also Tables **1230 / 31**.

• – Keleti - Kelenföld: *13 km*.

* – Arrive 1544.

BALATONSZENTGYÖRGY - KESZTHELY - TAPOLCA 1225

km				8612			860	8802		862	16809		874		864		19804	866	8806					868
		2	2	2	2	2	△		2	△			△	2	△	2	2	△		2	2	2	2	△
								P			S	ⒶT					W		Q					
0	**Balatonszentgyörgy** ▶ d.	0401	0545	0714	0808	0948	1020	1111	1145	1220	1303	1335	1420	1540**a**	1620	1743	...	1820	1848	1917	2012	...	2150	2221
10	Keszthely ▶ a.	0413	0556	0726	0819	1000	1031	1121	1157	1231	1314	1347	1431	1551**a**	1631	1755	...	1831	1859	1928	2024	...	2202	2232
10	Keszthely d.	0414	0615	...	0821	...	*1037*	1124	...	*1235*	*1330*	*1349*	*1449*	1557	*1705*	...	1758	*1837*	1930	...	2025	2115	...	*2238*
35	**Tapolca** a.	0442	0645	...	0849	...	*1108*	1157	...	*1305*	*1400*	*1420*	*1520*	1627	*1737*	...	1824	*1907*	2002	...	2054	2145	...	*2307*

		869			8807	867				19807	865		875		1380	863		8801	861					
	2	△	2	2		△	2	2	2	2	△	2	△	2		△	2		△	2	2	2	2	2
					Q		S			W				T	S			P						S
Tapolca d.	...	*0446*	0535	0650	0808	...	0905	...	1020	1046	...	1240	...	*1329*	*1336*	*1430*	1523	1628	...	...	1804	1914	2057	2220
Keszthely a.	...	*0518*	0608	0724	0839	...	0942	...	1057	1114	...	1319	...	*1405*	*1414*	*1506*	1555	1659	...	...	1836	1946	2133	2255
Keszthely ▶ d.	0345	0522	0609	0733	0848	0922	...	1002	...	...	1122	...	1322	1407	1432	1522	1600	1700	1722	1805	1900	1947	2134	...
Balatonszentgyörgy ▶ a.	0357	0533	0621	0745	0900	0933	...	1013	...	...	1133	...	1333	1418	1443	1533	1612	1712	1733	1818	1913	1958	2145	...

P – (12) Pécs - Fonyód - Tapolca - Celldömölk and v.v.
Q – (12) Kaposvár - Fonyód - Tapolca - Celldömölk - Szombathely and v.v.
S – June 19 - Aug. 29.
T – Dec. 13 - June 18, Aug. 30 - Dec. 11.
W – Ⓒ (daily June 19 - Aug. 29). (2) Keszthely - Szombathely and v.v.
a – Ⓐ only.
△ – To / from Budapest (Table **1220**).
▶ – For additional summer trains see Table **1220**.

Several trains continue beyond Tapolca to Ukk and beyond – see Table 1232.

SOPRON - SZOMBATHELY 1227

Operated by GySEV

km			*IC* 285									
		2	Z	2s	2	2s	2s	2	2	2	2	2
	Wien Meidling **978** d.	...	0703	...	...	...	...	...	...	...	...	...
	W. Neustadt **978** d.	...	0734	...	...	...	...	1437	1537	...	...	...
0	**Sopron** d.	0700	0814	0854	1137	1318	1428	1530	1643	1745	1933	2225
38	Bük d.	0746	0850	0937	1226	1401	1518	1612	1731	1827	2017	2309
62	**Szombathely** a.	0808	0909	0958	1248	1421	1542	1633	1752	1849	2039	2331

										IC 284
	2	2s	2	2s	2	2	2s	2	2	Z
Szombathely d.	0618	0720	0936	1128	1308	1423	1516	1635	1825	1928
Bük d.	0642	0746	1000	1150	1330	1445	1541	1659	1850	1948
Sopron a.	0729	0837	1045	1235	1425	1526	1629	1744	1933	2026
W. Neustadt **978** a.	0827	...	1127	...	...	...	...	...	...	2059
Wien Meidling **978** a.	...	...	...	...	...	...	...	...	...	2125

Z – ZÁGRÁB / ZAGREB – (12) Wien - Zagreb and v.v. (Table **92**); (2) Wien - Pécs and v.v.; (12) Sopron - Pécs and v.v.
s – To / from Szentgotthárd (Table **986**).

Additional trains: Sopron - Szombathely 0334, 0430, 0601. Szombathely - Sopron 0416, 0521, 2105, 2245.

SZOMBATHELY - KOSZEG 1229

2nd class

From **Szombathely**: 0508 ⚒, 0605, 0708, 0805, 0908, 1005, 1108, 1205 Ⓐ, 1308, 1405 Ⓐ, 1508, 1605, 1708, 1805, 1908, 2108, 2247 Ⓑ.
From **Köszeg**: 0430 ⚒, 0537, 0630, 0737, 0830, 0937, 1030, 1137 Ⓐ, 1230, 1337 Ⓐ, 1430, 1537, 1630, 1737, 1830, 2030, 2218.

18 km, journey time 25 - 30 minutes

BUDAPEST - SZÉKESFEHÉRVÁR - ZALAEGERSZEG and SZOMBATHELY 1230

For faster trains Budapest - Szombathely (via Györ) see Table **1250**

km			900	902	904	9006	246	246 9004	906	908	9058
		2					C				2
0	**Budapest** Déli ▶ d.	...	0611	0811	1011	1211	1411	1411	1611	1811	1846
4	B'pest Kelenföld ▶ d.	...	0618	0818	1018	1218	1418	1418	1618	1818	1853
67	**Székesfehérvár** ▶ a.	...	0714	0914	1114	1314	1514	1514	1714	1914	2004
67	**Székesfehérvár** d.	...	0715	0915	1115	1315	1515	1515	1715	1915	2018
90	Várpalota d.	...	0732	0932	1132	1332	1532	1532	1732	1932	2049
112	Veszprém d.	0555	0801	1001	1201	1401	1601	1601	1801	2001	2134
148	Ajka d.	0635	0830	1030	1230	1430	1630	1630	1830	2030	2225
181	Boba a.	0710	0856	1056	1256	1456	1656	1656	1856	2056	2258
	Zalaegerszeg ◐ a.	|	0957**z**	1157**z**	1357**z**	1557**z**	1757	|	1956**z**	2201**z**	|
181	Boba d.	0711	0900	1100	1300	1500	...	1659	1900	2100	2259
191	Celldömölk d.	0724	0909	1109	1309	1509	...	1709	1909	2111	2310
236	**Szombathely** a.	0806	0943	1143	1343	1543	...	1743	1943	2145	...

		909	907	905	9003 247	247	9005	903	901	9021
	2					C				2
Szombathely d.	...	0605	0805	1005	1205	...	1400	1605	1805	1958
Celldömölk d.	0422	0641	0841	1041	1241	...	1441	1641	1841	2041
Boba a.	0433	0649	0849	1049	1249	...	1449	1649	1849	2052
Zalaegerszeg ◐ d.	|	0600**z**	0800**z**	1000**z**	|	1202	1400**z**	1600**z**	1800**z**	|
Boba d.	0434	0700	0900	1100	1300	1300	1500	1700	1900	2056
Ajka d.	0508	0727	0927	1127	1327	1327	1527	1727	1927	2130
Veszprém d.	0547	0800	1000	1200	1400	1400	1600	1800	2000	2211
Várpalota d.	0615	0822	1022	1222	1422	1422	1622	1822	2022	...
Székesfehérvár a.	0638	0838	1038	1238	1438	1438	1638	1838	2038	...
Székesfehérvár ▶ d.	0640	0839	1039	1239	1439	1439	1639	1839	2039	...
B'pest Kelenföld ▶ a.	0748	0938	1138	1338	1538	1538	1738	1938	2138	...
Budapest Déli ▶ a.	0755	0945	1145	1345	1545	1545	1745	1945	2145	...

See also note △

CELLDÖMÖLK - BOBA - UKK - ZALAEGERSZEG

km			959		957		955	9005		246	9501	951
		2	B	2	B	2	B	B	2	C	B	B
0	**Celldömölk** .. **1232** d.	0812	...	1001	*1041*	1150	*1241*	*1441*	1605	*1641*	*1841*	*2041*
10	Boba **1232** a.	0824	...	1013	*1049*	1159	*1249*	*1449*	1614	*1649*	*1849*	*2052*
10	Boba **1232** d.	0825	0907	1014	1107	1200	1307	1507	1615	1707	1907	2107
28	Ukk **1232** d.	0847	0924	1038	1124	1218	1324	1524	1638	1724	1924	2124
59	Zalaszentiván a.	0923	0948	1118	1148	1258	1348	1548	1717	1748	1947	2148
59	Zalaszentiván ▷ d.	0924	0949	1119	1149	1259	1349	1549	1723	1749	1948	2153
68	**Zalaegerszeg** ▷ a.	0934	0957	1128	1157	1309	1357	1557	1732	1757	1956	2201

	950	952	9504		247	954		956	958		
	B	B	B	2	C	B	2	B	B	2	2
Zalaegerszeg .. ▷ d.	0600	0800	1000	1032	1202	1400	1432	1600	1800	1832	2037
Zalaszentiván ▷ a.	0608	0808	1008	1040	1210	1408	1441	1608	1808	1840	2045
Zalaszentiván d.	0609	0809	1009	1041	1211	1409	1442	1609	1809	1841	2046
Ukk **1232** d.	0634	0834	1034	1124	1234	1434	1524	1634	1834	1924	2126
Boba **1232** a.	0650	0850	1050	1143	1250	1450	1545	1650	1850	1942	2144
Boba **1232** d.	*0704*	*0900*	*1100*	1144	*1300*	*1500*	1546	*1659*	*1900*	1943	2145
Celldömölk **1232** a.	*0716*	*0908*	*1108*	1157	*1308*	*1508*	1558	*1707*	*1908*	1954	2158

B – Conveys (12) Budapest - Boba - Zalaegerszeg and v.v. (see upper table).
C – CITADELLA – (12) Budapest - Hodoš - Ljubljana and v.v.
z – (12) Budapest - Boba - Zalaegerszeg and v.v. (train splits / joins at Boba).
◐ – See lower table.
▶ – See also Tables **1220** and **1231**.
△ – Additional local trains: from Celldömölk 0603, 1401, 1804, 2005, 2200 Ⓑ; from Zalaegerszeg 0432, 0640, 0838, 1235, 1633.
▷ – See also Table **1235**.

BUDAPEST - SZÉKESFEHÉRVÁR - BALATONFÜRED - TAPOLCA 1231

km		9710	9720	970	9712	9712	19702	9722	9722	1974	16907	9714		9704	9724	1976	9716	19708	9718	9718	978	9728	9738	
		2	2		2	2		2	2		△	2			2		2		2	2		2	2	
					E		S	T	S	S	S	T				V		S	T	S			F	
0	**Budapest** Déli ▶ d.	...	*0336*	0616	0651	*0711*	0816	*0911*	*0911*	1016	...	*1111*	...	1216	...	1416	1501	1616	...	...	1816	...	*2046*	...
4	B'pest Kelenföld ▶ d.	...	*0343*	0623	0700	*0718*	0823	*0918*	*0918*	1023	1044	*1118*	...	1223	...	1423	1508	1623	...	...	1823	...	*2053*	...
67	**Székesfehérvár** ▶ a.	...	*0459*	0726	0809	*0814*	0926	*1014*	*1014*	1122	1147	*1214*	...	1326	...	1526	1609	1726	...	...	1926	...	*2204*	...
67	**Székesfehérvár** d.	0423**z**	0535	0740	0822	0822	0940	1021	1021	1140	1221	1221	...	1340	1421	1540	1621	1740	1821	1821	1940	1948	2240	...
117	Balalatonalmádi d.	0531**z**	0642	0836	0923	0923	1035	1123	1123	1235	1323	1323	...	1435	1523	1635	1723	1835	1923	1923	2035	2101	2347	...
132	**Balatonfüred** d.	0553	0706	0901	0949	0949	1101	1155	1143	1300	1350	1350	...	1506	1615	1700	1750	1906	1950	1943	2100	2128	0007	...
157	Révfülöp d.	0635	0745	0928	1035	1035	1140	1236	...	1327	1434	1434	...	1548	1701	1727	1834	1948	2032	...	2127	2217	...	...
168	Badacsonytomaj d.	0650	0803	0940	1050	1050	1159	1249	...	1339	1449	1449	...	1603	1716	1739	1849	2003	2047	...	2139	2231	...	...
170	Badacsony d.	0653	0806	0944	1053	1053	1202	1252	...	1343	1452	1452	...	1606	1719	1743	1852	2006	2050	...	2143	2234	...	...
184	**Tapolca** a.	0712	0825	0958	1112	1112	1221	1310	...	1357	1511	1511	...	1625	1738	1757	1911	2025	2109	...	2157	2253	...	...

	9739	9719	9729	979	9729	19707	9717	19607	1975	9715		9705	16906	9725	1973	9713	16701	9723	9723	971	9711	9711	9721	
	2	2	2		2		2	2		2			▽	2		2		2	2		2	2	2	
	Ⓐ					S		S	S			T	S		W	T	S		S		⑦S			
Tapolca d.	...	0444	0530	0606	...	0741	0850	0850	1006	...	...	1138	1138	1245	1403	1445	1540	1647	1647	1806	1845	1845	2113	...
Badacsony d.	...	0501	0549	0621	...	0800	0909	0909	1021	...	...	1156	1156	1306	1418	1507	1558	1707	1707	1821	1907	1907	2132	...
Badacsonytomaj d.	...	0504	0552	0625	...	0803	0912	0912	1025	...	...	1159	1159	1309	1422	1510	1602	1710	1710	1825	1910	1910	2138	...
Révfülöp d.	...	0517	0607	0635	←	0818	0928	0928	1035	...	...	1214	1214	1326	1433	1525	1617	1727	1727	1835	1925	1925	2153	...
Balatonfüred d.	0410	0552	0648	0702	0719	0902	1010	1010	1102	1210	...	1302	1302	1410	1502	1610	1702	1810	1810	1902	2010	2010	2231	...
Balalatonalmádi d.	0430	0612	→	0722	0740	0922	1034	1034	1122	1234	...	1322	1322	1434	1522	1634	1722	1834	1834	1922	2034	2034	2252**r**	...
Székesfehérvár a.	0533	0718	...	0815	0845	1015	1134	1134	1215	1334	...	1415	1415	1534	1615	1734	1815	1934	1934	2015	2134	2134	2356**r**	...
Székesfehérvár ▶ d.	*0537*	0732	...	0828	*0851*	1028	*1139*	1207	1228	*1339*	...	1428	1428	...	1628	*1739*	1828	*1939*	2006	2028	2148	*2154*	...	...
B'pest Kelenföld ▶ a.	*0645*	0845	...	0932	*1007*	1132	*1237*	1313	1332	*1437*	...	1532	1533	...	1732	*1837*	1932	*2037*	2112	2132	2257	*2311*	...	...
Budapest Déli ▶ a.	*0655*	0855	...	0940	*1015*	1140	*1245*	1325	1340	*1445*	...	1540	...	...	1740	*1845*	1940	*2045*	2120	2140	2305	*2320*	...	...

E – Apr. 3 - Nov. 1.
F – Ⓑ (daily June 19 - Aug. 29).
S – June 19 - Aug. 29.
T – Dec. 13 - June 18, Aug. 30 - Dec. 11.
V – ⑤ Apr. 30 - June 18; daily June 19 - Aug. 29.
W – ⑦ May 2 - June 13; daily June 19 - Aug. 29.
r – Ⓑ (daily June 19 - Aug. 29).
z – ⚒ (daily June 19 - Aug. 29).
▶ – See also Tables **1220** and **1230**.
△ – From Záhony (d. 0510), Nyiregyháza (d. 0641), Debrecen (d. 0729), Köbánya-Kispest (d. 1023).
▽ – To Köbánya-Kispest (d. 1611), Debrecen (a. 1847), Nyiregyháza (a. 1936), Záhony (a. 2048).

1232 SZOMBATHELY - UKK - TAPOLCA - KESZTHELY

km		8807	19607	9627	19807		9615	9613	8801	9623	9611	9621
		k	S	2	E	2	2	2	n	2	2	2
0	**Szombathely** d.	0625	0707	...	0915		1205	1305	1400	...	...	...
45	Celldömölk a.	0706	0751	...	0953	...	1239	1345	1440	...	...	...
45	Celldömölk ... **1230** d.	0707	0752	...	0954	1001	1310	1415	1506	...	1804	1948
55	Boba **1230** d.	0717	|	0907	|	1014	1325	1426	1520	1707	1814	2000
73	Ukk **1230** a.	0739	0819	0923	|	1032	1344	1447	1540	1723	1832	2016
73	Ukk d.	0740	0820	0927	|	1100	1345	1448	1541	1727	1835	2017
81	Sümeg d.	0749	0828	0938	1026	1112	1356	1459	1556	1739	1847	2028
101	Tapolca ▷ a.	0807	0845	1001	1044	1135	1419	1522	1620	1802	1910	2050
126	**Keszthely** ▷ a.	0839	...	1057	1114	...	1506	1555	1659	1836	1946	2133
	B'zentgyörgy ▷ a.	0900	...	...	...	...	...	1612	1712	1913	1958	2145
	Fonyód **1220** a.	0940	...	...	...	...	...	...	1748	...	...	...

		9622	8802	9614	9616	9616	9636	19804	19606	8806	9618
	2§	2	n	2	2	2	2	E	S	k	2⊡
Fonyód **1220** d.	...	...	1040	...	...	...	...	...	...	1814	...
B'zentgyörgy ▷ d.	0808	...	1111	...	...	1540**a**	...	...	...	1848	2012
Keszthely ▷ d.	0821	0925**z**	1124	1349**v**	1449	1557	1705	1758	1837	1930	2025
Tapolca ▷ d.	0850	1002	1202	1430	1530	1635	1750	1826	1913	2004	2055
Sümeg d.	0910	1025	1228	1501	1556	1659	1816	1846	1931	2028	2114
Ukk a.	0919	1036	1242	1515	1607	1711	1827	|	1940	2036	2122
Ukk **1230** d.	0924	1045	1243	1524	1615	1725	1834	|	1941	2037	2126
Boba **1230** d.	0943	1104	1306	1546	1639	1746	1850	|	2000	2054	2145
Celldömölk ... **1230** a.	0953	1114	1320	1558	1651	1756	...	1915	2011	2104	2158
Celldömölk d.	...	...	1348	...	1709	...	...	1917	2015	2114	...
Szombathely a.	...	...	1429	...	1743	...	...	1951	2058	2155	...

E – © (daily June 19 - Aug. 29).
S – June 19 - Aug. 29. To / from Budapest (Table **1231**).
a – Ⓐ only.
k – To / from Kaposvár (Table **1205**).
n – To / from Pécs (Table **1205**).
v – Ⓐ (not June 21 - Aug. 27).
z – June 19 - Aug. 29.
▷ – For additional trains see Table **1225**.
⊡ – Additional train on Ⓑ: Keszthely 2115, Tapolca 2200, Sümeg 2221, Ukk 2231, Boba 2249, Celldömölk 2259.
§ – Additional train: B'zentgyörgy 0545, Keszthely 0615, Tapolca 0646, Sümeg 0709, Ukk 0720.

1235 SZOMBATHELY - ZALASZENTIVÁN - NAGYKANIZSA

2nd class ★

km			8900						IC 285			8904						8906						
									Z													Ⓑ		
0	**Szombathely** d.	...	0535	...	...	0609	0707	...	0910	1050	...	1313	1345	...	1430	...	1623	1705	...	1815	1934	...	2233	...
49	Zalaszentiván a.	...	0616	...	...	0707	0805	...	0955	1145	...	1354	1443	...	1530	...	1720	1746	...	1918	2032	...	2328	...
49	Zalaszentiván ▷ d.	...	|	...	...	0710	0808	...	1013	1149	...	1410	1503	...	1549	...	1723	1749	...	1922	2046	...	2340	...
58	**Zalaegerszeg** ▷ a.	...	|	...	...	0719	0817	...	1023	1157	...	1419	1513	...	1557	...	1732	1757	...	1931	2056	...	2350	...
	Zalaegerszeg ▷ d.	0342	0600	...	0605	...	0800	...	0939	1137	...	1325**a**	...	1437	1535	...	1702	1738	...	1832	...	2230	...	...
	Zalaszentiván ▷ a.	0351	0608	...	0614	...	0808	...	0949	1147	...	1333**a**	...	1446	1544	...	1711	1747	...	1840	...	2239	...	...
49	Zalaszentiván d.	0355	0617	...	0624	...	0814	...	0956	1154	...	1355	...	1457	1552	...	1721	1750	...	1921	...	2240	...	...
102	**Nagykanizsa** a.	0458	0706	...	0731	...	0921	...	1039	1258	...	1444	...	1603	1700	...	1825	1842	...	2031	...	2345	...	...
	Pécs **1237** a.	...	0955	...	...	...	...	...	...	...	...	1745	...	...	...	...	...	2127	...	...	...	...	...	...

								8909					8905					IC 284					8901	
	⚒	⚒																Z						
Pécs **1237** d.	...	...	...	...	...	...	...	0516	...	...	...	...	1053	...	...	...	...	...	...	...	...	...	1812	...
Nagykanizsa d.	...	0340	...	...	0551	0640	...	0751	...	...	1135	...	1335	...	1445	...	1615	1803	...	1843	...	2007	2102	2209
Zalaszentiván a.	...	0442	...	...	0657	0747	...	0841	...	...	1240	...	1427	...	1547	...	1717	1847	...	1946	...	2109	2150	2311
Zalaszentiván ▷ d.	...	0444	...	...	0659	0749	...	0847	...	...	1244	...	1503	...	1549	...	1723	1850	...	1948	...	2111	2153	2316
Zalaegerszeg ▷ a.	...	0453	...	...	0709	0758	...	0856	...	...	1254	...	1513	...	1557	...	1732	1859	...	1956	...	2121	2201	2326
Zalaegerszeg ▷ d.	...	...	0432	0535	...	...	0730	0838	...	1137	...	...	1400	1437	1535	...	1702	1832	...	1939	...	...	|	...
Zalaszentiván ▷ a.	...	...	0440	0545	...	...	0739	0846	...	1147	...	...	1408	1446	1544	...	1711	1840	...	1948	...	...	|	...
Zalaszentiván d.	0400	...	0456	0558	...	...	0750	0849	...	1200	...	...	1428	1455	1552	...	1724	1848	1900	1953	...	...	2151	...
Szombathely a.	0455	...	0556	0657	...	...	0845	0931	...	1255	...	...	1510	1550	1647	...	1839	1927	1956	2052	...	...	2233	...

Z – ZÁGRÁB / ZAGREB – 12 Wien - Zagreb and v.v. (Table **92**). For Wien - Sopron - Pécs portion see Table **1237**.
a – Ⓐ (not Dec. 21 - Jan. 1, June 16 - Aug. 31).
★ – Except where train number shown.
▷ – Timings in *italics*: change at Zalaszentiván. For additional trains see Table **1230**.

1237 NAGYKANIZSA - PÉCS

km			8900	IC 285	IC 891			8904		8906
		2		Z	Y	2	2Ⓑ		2	
	Wien Meidling **1227** d.	...	...	0703	0703	...	...	...	...	...
	Szombathely **1235** d.	...	0535	0910	0910	...	...	1313	...	1705
0	**Nagykanizsa** **1240** d.	0418	0710	1040	1040	1048	...	1455	...	1843
29	Gyékényes **1240** d.	0452	0741	1125	1108	1151	...	1521	...	1909
	Zagreb **1340** a.	|	|	1259	|	|	...	|	...	|
84	Barcs d.	0619	0848	...	1201	1305	1400	1632	1857	2025
114	Szigetvár d.	0704	0919	...	1229	...	1447	1710	1941	2056
129	Szentlőrinc d.	0724	0938	...	1243	...	1512	1724	2002	2110
148	**Pécs** a.	0745	0955	...	1257	...	1543	1745	2025	2127

		8909	8905		IC 284	IC 892	8901		
	2			2	Z	Y		2	2
Pécs d.	...	0516	1053	1400	...	1530	1812	2011	2152
Szentlőrinc d.	...	0533	1112	1425	...	1547	1833	2034	2225
Szigetvár d.	...	0547	1126	1445	...	1601	1847	2057	2245
Barcs d.	0503	0618	1202	1524	...	1631	1921	2135	2325
Zagreb **1340** d.	|	|	|	|	1545	|	|	...	...
Gyékényes **1240** a.	0609	0724	1308	1638	1714	1723	2027	...	...
Nagykanizsa **1240** a.	0656	0750	1334	...	1802	1802	2100	...	...
Szombathely **1235** a.	...	0931	1510	...	1927	1927	2233	...	...
Wien Meidling **1227** a.	...	...	...	...	2125	2125	...	...	...

Y – 2 Wien - Nagykanizsa - Pécs and v.v.; 12 Sopron - Nagykanizsa - Pécs and v.v.
Z – ZÁGRÁB / ZAGREB – 12 Wien - Nagykanizsa - Zagreb and v.v. (Table **92**).

1240 NAGYKANIZSA - KAPOSVÁR - DOMBÓVAR

km			1829		IC 829		8219	8217		8227		8215		8225	IC 1823		8213		8223					
		⚒	Ⓑ	2Ⓐ	🄱b	2			2		2		2		🄱⑦	2		2		2	2	2Ⓑ	2⑥	2Ⓑ
0	**Nagykanizsa** **1237** d.	...	...	...	0418	...	0500	0710	...	0855	...	1048	...	...	b	...	1438	...	1655	...	1843	...	...	2108
29	Gyékényes **1237** d.	0310	...	0402	0441	...	0539	0743	...	0935	...	1135	...	1345	...	...	1535	...	1732	...	1925	2048	2048	2145
59	Somogyszob d.	0353	...	0450	0523	...	0625	0826	...	1023	...	1223	...	1431	...	...	1618	...	1817	...	2016	2145	2145	...
99	**Kaposvár** a.	0449	...	0546	0607	...	0721	0922	...	1119	...	1319	...	1527	...	...	1719	...	1913	...	2117	2246	2246	...
99	**Kaposvár** d.	0450	0525	...	0608	0642	0725	0925	1045	1125	1245	1325	1445	1528	1602	1645	1725	1845	1923	2045	...	2257	...	...
130	**Dombóvár** a.	0540	0600	...	0643	0732	0800	1000	1135	1200	1335	1400	1539	1603	1641	1735	1800	1942	2003	2135	...	2347	...	...

				8200		8202		8204		8224			1824	8206			8226		IC 828	8208		8228		
	2	2	2		2		2		2		2	2	⑤b		2			2	🄱b		2	Ⓑ	2	
Dombóvár d.	...	0425	0614	0805	...	1005	1020	1205	1220	1402	1420	...	1513	1605	1618	...	1805	1820	1916	2005	2020	2200	2205	...
Kaposvár a.	...	0518	0710	0840	...	1040	1113	1240	1313	1438	1513	...	1552	1640	1713	...	1840	1913	1951	2040	2113	2235	2255	...
Kaposvár d.	...	0519	0725	...	0925	...	1125	...	1335	1439	...	1553	1553	...	1721	...	1844	...	2000	...	2120	2248	...	...
Somogyszob d.	...	0626	0827	...	1022	...	1222	...	1432	1548	...	1650	1650	...	1818	...	1946	...	2045	...	2217	2345	...	...
Gyékényes **1237** a.	0610	0708	0909	...	1104	...	1304	...	1514	1635	...	1731	1731	...	1900	...	2028	...	2126	...	2259	0027	...	...
Nagykanizsa **1237** a.	0656	0750	...	...	...	...	1334	...	1600	...	...	1813	1813	...	1950	...	2100	...	2150	...	...	...	...	...

b – To / from Budapest (Table **1200**).

1242 DOMBÓVAR - BAJA - KISKUNFÉLEGYHÁZA - KECSKEMÉT

2nd class

km		780	7800	782	7802	784	7804	786	7806	788	
130	**Dombóvár** d.	...	...	0620	0820	1020	1220	1420	1620	1820	2020
190	Bátaszék **1210** d.	...	0525	0735	0935	1135	1335	1535	1735	1935	2139
210	**Baja** **1210** a.	...	0545	0755	0955	1155	1355	1555	1755	1955	...
210	**Baja** d.	0409	0609	0809	1009	1209	1409	1609	1809	2009	...
286	Kiskunhalas a.	0520	0720	0920	1120	1320	1520	1720	1920	2120	...
286	Kiskunhalas d.	0532	0732	0932	1132	1332	1532	1732	1932	...	...
332	Kiskunfélegyháza **1290** a.	0615	0815	1015	1215	1415	1615	1815	2014	...	...
357	**Kecskemét** **1290** a.	0636	0836	1036	1236	1436	1636	1836	...	...	...

	789	7809	787	7807	785	783		7803	781	7801
							Ⓐ			
Kecskemét **1290** d.	...	0520	0722	0922	1122	1322	...	1522	1722	1922
Kiskunfélegyháza **1290** d.	...	0545	0745	0945	1145	1345	1438	1545	1745	1945
Kiskunhalas a.	...	0625	0825	1025	1225	1425	1518	1625	1825	2025
Kiskunhalas d.	0437	0637	0837	1037	1237	1437	1528	1637	1837	2037
Baja a.	0542	0742	0942	1142	1342	1542	1638	1742	1942	2142
Baja **1210** d.	0550	0758	0958	1158	1358	1558	...	1758	1958	...
Bátaszék **1210** d.	0620	0820	1020	1220	1420	1620	...	1820	2028	...
Dombóvár a.	0739	0939	1139	1339	1539	1739	...	1939	2141	...

1245 BUDAPEST - VÁC - SZOB

2nd class

km										
0	**Budapest** Nyugati d.	0041	0441	0541	0707	then	2107	2141	2241	2341
34	Vác d.	0127	0527	0627	0734	hourly	2134	2227	2327	0027
51	Nagymaros-Visegrád ¶ d.	0142	0542	0642	0749	until	2149	2242	2342	0042
64	**Szob** a.	0156	0556	0656	0803		2203	2256	2356	0056

		©							
Szob d.	0457	0557	0657	then	1857	2004	2104	2204	2304
Nagymaros-Visegrád ¶ d.	0511	0611	0711	hourly	1911	2018	2118	2218	2318
Vác d.	0528	0628	0728	until	1928	2034	2134	2234	2334
Budapest Nyugati a.	0554	0654	0754		1954	2116	2216	2316	0016

¶ – A ferry operates across the river to Visegrád.

Certain trains extend to / from Štúrovo (Table **1175**). For *EC* trains see Table **1175**.

BUDAPEST - GYÖR - SOPRON / SZOMBATHELY / WIEN 1250

km	*FAST TRAINS*		*IC* 910	*IC*	*RJ*	*RJ*	*IC* 922	*IC*	*RJ*		*RJ*	*IC* 924	*IC*	*RJ*	*IC* 916	*IC*		*RJ*	*RJ*	*EN*	*IC* 918	*IC*	*EN*	
		346	*IC* 930	**910**	**60**	**62**	*IC* 932	**922**	**64**		**66**	*IC* 934	**924**	**68**	*IC* 936	**916**		**42**	**40**	**466**	*IC* 938	**918**	**462**	
		✕	R	R ✕	🍷	🍷	R	R ✕	🍷		🍷	R	R ✕	🍷	R	R ✕		🍷	🍷	✕	R	R ✕		
		D			**M**	**S**			**M**		**M**			**M**	**n**	**G**		**S**		**W**	⊙		**K**	
0	**Budapest** Keleti d.	0600	0610	0610	0710	0910	1010	1010	1110	...	1310	1410	1410	1510	1610	1610	...	1710	1810	1905	1910	1910	2105	...
13	Budapest Kelenföld d.	0614	0624	0624	0724	0924	1024	1024	1124	...	1324	1424	1424	1524	1624	1624	...	1724	1824	1919	1924	1924	2119	...
75	Tatabánya d.	|	0658	0658	0758	0958	1058	1058	1158	...	1358	1458	1458	1558	1658	1658	...	1758	1858	|	1958	1958	|	...
141	**Györ** a.	0726	0738	0738	0834	1034	1138	1138	1234	...	1434	1538	1538	1634	1738	1738	...	1834	1934	2031	2038	2038	2231	...
141	**Györ** d.	0727	0739	0739	0835	1035	1139	1139	1235	...	1435	1539	1539	1635	1739	1739	...	1835	1935	2032	2039	2039	2232	...
172	Csorna d.	|	0802	0810	|	|	1202	1210	|	...	|	1602	1610	|	1802	1810	...	|	|	|	2102	2110	|	...
226	**Sopron** 🏛 a.	|	0841	|	|	|	1241	|	|	...	|	1641	|	|	1841	|	...	|	|	|	2141	|	|	...
244	**Szombathely** ▷ a.	|	...	0901	|	|	...	1301	|	...	|	...	1701	|	...	1901	...	|	|	|	...	2201	|	...
	Graz **986** a.	|	...	...	|	|	...	...	|	...	|	...	...	|	...	2203	...	|	|	|	...	...	|	...
177	Mosonmagyaróvár d.	0746	...	...	0854	1054	...	...	1254	...	1454	...	...	1654	...	...	...	1854	1954	|	...	...	|	...
188	Hegyeshalom 🏛 d.	0758	...	...	0906	1106	...	...	1306	...	1506	...	...	1706	...	...	...	1906	2006	2103	...	...	2301	...
219	Bruck an der Leitha d.	0817	...	...	|	|	...	...	|	...	|	...	...	|	...	...	...	|	|	2122	...	...	2321	...
261	Wien Meidling a.	|	...	...	0954	1154	...	...	1354	...	1554	...	...	1754	...	...	...	1954	2054	|	...	...	2354	...
272	**Wien** Westbahnhof a.	0858	...	...	1008	1208	...	...	1408	...	1608	...	...	1808	...	...	...	2008	2108	2201	...	...	...	...

FAST TRAINS	*EN*	*IC* 939	*IC*	*RJ*		*EN*	*IC* 937	*IC*	*RJ*		*RJ*	*IC* 935	*IC*	*RJ*	*IC* 933	*IC*	*RJ*		*RJ*	*IC* 931	*IC*		*RJ*	
	463	*IC* 919	**919**	**41**		**467**	*IC* 917	**917**	**43**		**61**	*IC* 915	**915**	**63**	*IC* 913	**913**	**65**		**67**	*IC* 911	**911**	**347**	**69**	
		R ✕	R ✕	🍷		✕	R	R	🍷		🍷	R	R ✕	🍷	R	R ✕	🍷		🍷	R	R ✕	✕	🍷	
	K					**W**	⊙	**G**	**S**		**M**			**M**			**M**		**M**			**D**	**M**	
Wien Westbahnhof d.	...	...	...	0650	...	0758	...	...	0950	...	1150	...	...	1350	...	...	1550	...	1750	...	...	1850	1950	...
Wien Meidling d.	0600	...	...	0705	...	|	...	...	1005	...	1205	...	...	1405	...	...	1605	...	1805	...	...	|	2005	...
Bruck an der Leitha d.	0634	...	...	|	...	|	...	...	|	...	|	...	...	|	...	...	|	...	|	...	...	1933	|	...
Hegyeshalom 🏛 d.	0655	...	...	0757	...	0857	...	...	1057	...	1257	...	...	1457	...	...	1657	...	1857	...	...	1957	2057	...
Mosonmagyaróvár d.	0702	...	...	0804	...	0904	...	...	1104	...	1304	...	...	1504	...	...	1704	...	1904	...	...	2006	2104	...
Graz **986** d.	|	...	...	|	...	|	...	0610	|	...	|	...	...	|	...	...	|	...	|	...	...	|	|	...
Szombathely ▷ d.	|	...	0606	|	...	|	...	0900	|	...	|	...	1300	|	...	1500	|	...	|	...	1900	|	|	...
Sopron 🏛 d.	|	0615	|	|	...	|	0910	|	|	...	|	1310	|	|	1510	|	|	...	|	1910	|	|	|	...
Csorna d.	|	0706	0706	|	...	|	1001	1001	|	...	|	1401	1401	|	1601	1601	|	...	|	2001	2001	|	|	...
Györ a.	0720	0725	0725	0821	...	0921	1020	1020	1121	...	1321	1420	1420	1521	1620	1620	1721	...	1921	2020	2020	2029	2121	...
Györ d.	0721	0726	0726	0822	...	0922	1021	1021	1122	...	1322	1421	1421	1522	1621	1621	1722	...	1922	2021	2021	2031	2122	...
Tatabánya d.	|	0805	0805	0855	...	|	1100	1100	1155	...	1355	1500	1500	1555	1700	1700	1755	...	1955	2100	2100	2124	2155	...
Budapest Kelenföld a.	0833	0842	0842	0932	...	1033	1137	1137	1232	...	1432	1537	1537	1633	1737	1737	1832	...	2032	2137	2137	2204	2232	...
Budapest Keleti a.	0849	0859	0859	0949	...	1049	1154	1154	1249	...	1449	1554	1554	1649	1754	1754	1849	...	2049	2154	2154	2220	2249	...

SLOWER SERVICES BUDAPEST - GYÖR - SZOMBATHELY / SOPRON

See above for faster services

km								9202						9204					9406						☆	☆
				9200	**990**	**9302**		**9202**	**992**			**9304**		**9204**	**996**	**9404**	**9206**		**998**	**9208**	**470**	**9408**				
		2	2⚒				2			2Y	2Ⓐ		2					2			**A**	**B**	2	2	2	2
0	**Budapest** Keleti d.	...	...	0638	...	0838	...	1038	1038	...	...	1238	...	1438	1438	1538	1638	...	1738	1838	1938	1938	...	2121**d**	2221**d**	2321**d**
13	Budapest Kelenföld d.	...	...	0652	...	0852	...	1052	1052	...	...	1252	...	1452	1452	1552	1652	...	1752	1852	1952	1952	...	2128	2228	2328
75	Tatabánya ☆ d.	...	...	0731	...	0931	...	1131	1131	...	...	1331	...	1531	1531	1631	1731	...	1831	1931	2031	2031	...	2213	2313	0013
84	Tata ☆ d.	...	...	0739	...	0939	...	1139	1139	...	...	1339	...	1539	1539	1639	1739	...	1839	1939	2039	2039	...	2224	2324	0024
104	Komárom ☆ d.	...	...	0753	...	0953	...	1153	1153	...	...	1353	...	1553	1553	1653	1753	...	1853	1953	2053	2053	...	2244	2344	0044
141	**Györ** a.	...	...	0823	...	1023	...	1223	1223	...	...	1423	...	1623	1623	1723	1823	...	1923	2023	2123	2123	...	2323	...	...
141	**Györ** d.	0555	0645	0840	0835	...	1045	1240	1235	1325	1405	...	1445	1640	1635	...	1840	1845	1935	2040	...	...	2240	...	...	...
213	Celldömölk a.	|	|	0945	|	...	|	1345	|	|	|	...	|	1745	|	...	1945	|	|	2147	...	...	|	...	...	...
258	**Szombathely** ▷ a.	|	|	1045	|	...	|	...	|	|	|	...	|	1845	|	...	...	|	|	...	...	...	|	...	...	...
172	Csorna d.	0626	0721	...	0902	...	1120	...	1302	1357	1443	...	1520	...	1703	...	...	1920	2001	...	...	...	2311	...	...	...
226	**Sopron** 🏛 a.	0717	0810	...	0945	...	1210	...	1345	1448	1535	...	1610	...	1745	...	...	2010	2043	...	...	...	2359	...	...	...

						999				997					995					991				△	
		9409		**471**	**9407**	**9209**	**9209**		**9307**	**9207**	**9207**		**9305**	**9303**	**9205**	**9205**			**9203**	**9201**	**9201**	**347**			
	2		2⚒	**A**	**B**			2				2					2	2				**D**	2	2	2
Sopron 🏛 d.	0352	...	0452	...	...	0555	...	0752	...	0955	...	1152	...	...	1355	...	1430	1552	...	1755	...	...	1952	...	2230
Csorna d.	0441	...	0543	...	...	0641	...	0845	...	1041	...	1245	...	...	1441	...	1521	1645	...	1841	...	...	2041	...	2326
Szombathely ▷ d.	|	...	|	...	...	|	0519	|	...	|	0905	|	...	...	|	1305	|	|	1505	|	1705	...	|	...	|
Celldömölk d.	|	...	|	...	...	|	0605	|	...	|	1006	|	...	...	|	1406	|	|	1606	|	1806	...	|	...	|
Györ a.	0510	...	0612	...	...	0705	0716	0915	...	1105	1111	1315	...	...	1505	1511	1553	1715	1715	1905	1915	...	2112	...	2355
Györ d.	...	0547	...	0631	0631	0731	0731	...	0931	1131	1131	...	1331	1431	1531	1531	...	...	1731	1931	1931	2033	...	2131	...
Komárom △ d.	...	0613	...	0700	0700	0800	0800	...	1000	1200	1200	...	1400	1500	1600	1600	...	...	1800	2000	2000	2102	...	2210	...
Tata △ d.	...	0627	...	0714	0714	0814	0814	...	1014	1214	1214	...	1414	1514	1614	1614	...	...	1814	2014	2014	2116	...	2229	...
Tatabánya △ d.	...	0636	...	0724	0724	0824	0824	...	1024	1224	1224	...	1424	1524	1624	1624	...	...	1824	2024	2024	2126	...	2241	...
Budapest Kelenföld a.	...	0716	...	0804	0804	0904	0904	...	1104	1304	1304	...	1504	1604	1704	1704	...	...	1904	2104	2104	2203	...	2327	...
Budapest Keleti a.	...	0731	...	0820	0820	0920	0920	...	1120	1320	1320	...	1520	1620	1720	1720	...	...	1920	2120	2120	2219	...	2335**d**	...

LOCAL TRAINS GYÖR - WIEN

2nd class

Györ d.	0448	0548	0748	0948	1148	1348	1548	1748	1948	...
Mosonmagyaróvár d.	0514	0614	0814	1014	1214	1414	1614	1814	2014	...
Hegyeshalom a.	0524	0624	0824	1024	1224	1424	1624	1824	2024	...
Hegyeshalom 🏛 d.	0530	0630	0836	1036	1236	1436	1636	1836	2036	...
Bruck an der Leitha d.	0554	0654	0900	1100	1300	1500	1700	1900	2100	...
Wien Südbahnhof ◐ a.	0623	0723	0927	1127	1327	1527	1727	1927	2127	...

Wien Südbahnhof ◐ d.	0633	0833	1033	1233	1433	1633	1833	2033	2133	...
Bruck an der Leitha d.	0701	0901	1101	1301	1501	1701	1901	2101	2201	...
Hegyeshalom 🏛 a.	0725	0926	1126	1326	1526	1726	1926	2126	2226	...
Hegyeshalom d.	0736	0936	1136	1336	1536	1736	1936	2136	2236	...
Mosonmagyaróvár d.	0744	0944	1144	1344	1544	1744	1944	2144	2244	...
Györ a.	0810	1010	1210	1410	1610	1810	2010	2210	2310	...

A – AMICUS – May 27 - Sept. 27 from Praha (next day from Bratislava), May 28 - Sept. 28 from Budapest. (12) Praha - Brno - Bratislava - Györ - Budapest and v.v.; 🛏 1, 2 cl., ▬ 2 cl., (2) Praha - Budapest - Lökösháza and v.v. Conveys on dates in Table **60** (summer only) 🛏 1, 2 cl. and ▬ 2 cl. Praha - Burgas / Varna and v.v.
B – Daily except when train **A** runs.
D – DACIA – 🛏 1, 2 cl., ▬ 2 cl., (12) Wien - Budapest - Bucureşti and v.v.; 🛏 1, 2 cl., ▬ 2 cl. Wien - Budapest - Beograd and v.v.; 🛏 1, 2 cl. Wien - Budapest - Beograd - Sofiya and v.v.
G – HALÁSZBÁSTYA – (12) and ✕ Budapest - Szombathely - Graz and v.v.
K – KÁLMÁN IMRE – 🛏 1, 2 cl., ▬ 2 cl., (2) München - Wien - Budapest and v.v. Conveys Dec. 13 - Jan. 11, June 17 - Sept. 17, 🛏 1, 2 cl. München - Wien - Budapest - Arad - Bucureşti, returning Dec. 13 - Jan. 9, June 15 - Sept. 15.
M – (12) and 🍷 München - Salzburg - Wien - Budapest and v.v. (Table **65**).
S – (12) and 🍷 Salzburg - Wien - Budapest and v.v. (Table **65**).
W – WIENER WALZER – (12) ✕ Wien - Budapest and v.v.; 🛏 1, 2 cl., ▬ 2 cl., (2) Zürich - Wien - Budapest and v.v.

Y – Ⓐ June 18 - Aug. 30.
d – Budapest **Déli**.
n – To Wiener Neustadt, arrive 1927.
◐ – Wien Südbahnhof (Ostbahn). Temporary platforms located at Schweizer-Garten-Straße.
⊙ – To / from Wien Meidling (Table **978**).
☆ – Local trains run hourly 0421 - 2321 Budapest Déli - Komárom.
△ – Local trains run hourly 0710 - 2210 Komárom - Budapest Déli.
▷ – For services Budapest - Szombathely via Székesfehérvár see Table **1230**.
§ – See also Table **1250**.
RJ – *Railjet* service, first and economy (2nd) class. *Premium class* also available to first class ticket holders (supplement payable). Classified *EC* in Hungary.

GYÖR - BRATISLAVA 1252

km		2	2	2	2	2	2	2	**470** A	**9408** B	2
	Budapest Keleti **1250** d.	...	...	...	...	...	...	...	1938	1938	...
0	**Györ** § d.	0848	1048	1248	1448	1648	1848	2048	2125	2125	2248
36	Mosonmagyaróvár § d.	0914	1114	1314	1514	1714	1914	2114	2146	2146	2314
47	Hegyeshalom § d.	0924	1124	1324	1524	1724	1924	2124	2155	2155	2324
60	Rajka a.	...	...	...	...	...	...	...	2209	...	...
60	Rajka 🏛 d.	...	...	...	...	...	...	...	2235	...	...
79	Bratislava Petržalka a.	...	...	...	...	...	...	...	2256	...	...
96	**Bratislava** hlavná a.	...	...	...	...	...	...	...	2320	...	...

	9409	**471** A	**9407** B	2	2	2	2	2	2	2
Bratislava hlavná d.	...	0455	...	...	...	...	...	...	...	...
Bratislava Petržalka d.	...	0517	...	...	...	...	...	...	...	...
Rajka 🏛 a.	...	0537	...	...	...	...	...	...	...	...
Rajka d.	...	0548	...	...	...	...	...	...	...	...
Hegyeshalom § d.	0506	0602	0602	0836	1036	1236	1436	1636	1836	2036
Mosonmagyaróvár § d.	0514	0609	0609	0844	1044	1244	1444	1644	1844	2044
Györ § a.	0540	0630	0630	0910	1110	1310	1510	1710	1910	2110
Budapest Keleti **1250** a.	0731	0820	0820	...	...	...	...	...	...	...

OR NOTES SEE TABLE 1250 ABOVE

1260 BUDAPEST - MISKOLC - NYÍREGYHÁZA
Fast trai

For slower trains Budapest - Miskolc see Table **1261**. Most *IC* trains continue beyond Debrecen to/from Budapest Nyugati. For trains Budapest - Debrecen - Nyiregyháza see Table **127**

km		*IC* 560 [R] ⚒	*IC* 659 [R]	*IC* 532 R	2	*IC* 657 [R]	*IC* 502 [R] Ⓐ	2	*IC* 564 [R]	*IC* 512 [R] Ⓑ	2	*IC* 655 [R]	*IC* 504 [R] ⚒	2	*IC* 566 [R]	*IC* 514 [R] Ⓑ	2	*IC* 653 [R]	*IC* 506 [R]	2	*IC* 568 [R]	*IC* 536 ✗ H	2	*IC* 508 [R] Ⓑ	2	2
0	**Budapest** Keleti . ▶ d.	...	...	0633	...	0733	0833	...	0933	1033	...	1133	1233	...	1333	1433	...	1533	1633	...	1733	1833	...	1933	...	.
126	Füzesabony .... ▶ d.	...	...	0755	...	0855	0955	...	1055	1155	...	1255	1355	...	1455	1555	...	1655	1755	...	1855	1955	...	2055	...	.
183	**Miskolc** .... ▶ a.	...	...	0832	...	0932	1032	...	1132	1232	...	1332	1432	...	1532	1632	...	1732	1832	...	1932	2032	...	2132	...	.
183	**Miskolc** .... d.	0630	0734	...	*0837*	0934	...	*1037*	1134	...	*1237*	1334	...	*1437*	1534	...	*1637*	1734	...	*1837*	1934	...	*2037*	...	2137	23
221	Szerencs .... d.	0655	0759	...	0915	0959	...	1115	1159	...	1315	1359	...	1515	1559	...	1715	1759	...	1915	1959	...	2115	...	2215	23
239	Tokaj .... d.	0707	0811	...	0936	1011	...	1136	1211	...	1336	1411	...	1536	1611	...	1736	1811	...	1936	2011	...	2136	...	2236	23
271	**Nyíregyháza** .... a.	0733	0834	...	1017	1034	...	1217	1234	...	1417	1434	...	1617	1634	...	1817	1834	...	2017	2034	...	2217	...	2317	00
	Debrecen **1270** .... a.	0806	0906	...	...	1106	...	...	1306	...	...	1506	...	...	1706	...	...	1906	...	...	2106	...	...	...	...	.

	529	*IC* 519 [R]	2	*IC* 537 ✗ H	*IC* 569 [R]	2	*IC* 517 [R] ⚒	*IC* 650 [R]	2	*IC* 515 [R] Ⓐ	*IC* 567 [R]	2	*IC* 505 [R] Ⓑ	*IC* 652 [R]	2	*IC* 513 [R] Ⓑ	*IC* 565 [R]	2	*IC* 503 [R] Ⓑ	*IC* 654 [R]	2	*IC* 533 R	*IC* 563 [R]	2	2	2
Debrecen **1270** ..... d.	...	...	...	...	0654	...	...	0854	...	...	1054	...	...	1254	...	...	1454	...	...	1654	...	...	1854	...	...	.
Nyíregyháza .... d.	*0343*	0526	0543	...	0726	0743	...	0926	0943	...	1126	1143	...	1326	1343	...	1526	1543	...	1726	1743	...	1926	1943	2043	22
Tokaj .... d.	*0418*	0550	0618	...	0750	0823	...	0950	1023	...	1150	1223	...	1350	1423	...	1550	1623	...	1750	1823	...	1950	2023	2123	23
Szerencs .... d.	0445	0602	0638	...	0802	0840	...	1002	1040	...	1202	1240	...	1402	1440	...	1602	1640	...	1802	1840	...	2002	2040	2215z	23
Miskolc .... a.	0519	0625	*0719*	...	0825	*0919*	...	1025	*1119*	...	1225	*1319*	...	1425	*1519*	...	1625	*1719*	...	1825	*1919*	...	2025	*2121*	2249	..
Miskolc .... ▶ d.	0534	0628	...	0728	0828	...	0928	1028	...	1128	1228	...	1328	1428	...	1528	1628	...	1728	1828	...	1928	...	...	...	..
Füzesabony .... ▶ d.	0617	0705	...	0805	0905	...	1005	1105	...	1205	1305	...	1405	1505	...	1605	1705	...	1805	1905	...	2005	...	...	...	..
Budapest Keleti .. ▶ a.	0757	0827	...	0927	1027	...	1127	1227	...	1327	1427	...	1527	1627	...	1727	1827	...	1927	2027	...	2127	...	...	..	..

H – DRAVA-HERNÁD – [12] and ✗ Pécs - Budapest - Miskolc - Košice and v.v.
R – RÁKÓCZI – [12] Budapest - Miskolc - Košice and v.v.; [2] Budapest - Košice - Humenné and v.v.

z – Arrive 2140.
▶ – For slower services see Table **1261**.

1261 BUDAPEST - MISKOLC - SÁTORALJAÚJHELY
Slower trai

For fast trains Budapest - Miskolc - Szerencs see Table **1260**. For faster journeys use *IC* train (Table **1260**) and change at Füzesabony (for Eger) or Szerencs (for Sátoraljaújhely)

km		2	2	2	5500	5200	5510	520	5502	522	5512	524	5504	526	5506	528	5516	*IC* 1528 ⑤E	5208	1380 C	5508	5008 k	5108	2
0	**Budapest** Keleti .... ▶ d.	...	...	...	0503	0603	0703	0803	0903	1003	1103	1203	1303	1403	1503	1603	1703	1758	1803	1828	1903	2003	2203	22
67	Hatvan .... d.	...	...	*0505*	0558	0658	0758	0858	0958	1058	1158	1258	1358	1458	1558	1658	1758	|	1858	1947	1958	2058	2258	23
87	Vámosgyörk ⊡ .... d.	...	...	*0521*	0613	0711	0813	0911	1013	1111	1213	1311	1413	1511	1613	1711	1813	|	1911	2000	2013	2111	2311	00
126	Füzesabony .... ▶ a.	...	...	*0557*	0649	0737	0849	0937	1049	1137	1249	1337	1449	1537	1649	1737	1849	1923	1937	2024	2049	2137	2337	00
126	Füzesabony .... ▶ d.	...	...	0602	0706	0739	0906	0939	1106	1139	1306	1339	1506	1539	1706	1739	1906	1925	1939	2026	2106	2139	2339	..
143	**Eger** ⊙ .... a.	...	...	|	0724	|	0924	|	1124	|	1324	|	1524	|	1724	|	1924	|	|	|	2124	|	|	..
139	Mezőkövesd .... d.	...	...	0614	▬	0749	...	0949	▬	1149	▬	1349	▬	1549	▬	1749	▬	|	1949	2035	▬	2149	2349	..
183	**Miskolc** .... ▶ a.	...	...	0652	2	0820	...	1020	2	1220	2	1420	2	1620	2	1820	2	2003	2020	2108	2	2220	0020	..
183	**Miskolc** .... ▶ d.	*0537*	*0637*	...	*0737*	0837	...	1037	*1137*	1237	*1337*	1437	*1537*	1637	*1737*	1837	*1937*	2016	2037	...	*2137*	...	...	..
221	Szerencs .... ▶ d.	0613	0713	...	0813	0913	...	1113	1213	1313	1413	1513	1613	1713	1813	1913	2013	2045	2113	...	2224	...	...	..
257	Sárospatak .... a.	0700	0800	...	0900	1000	...	1200	1300	1400	1500	1600	1700	1800	1900	2000	2100	2131	2200	...	2305	...	...	..
267	**Sátoraljaújhely** .... a.	0709	0809	...	0909	1009	...	1209	1309	1409	1509	1609	1709	1809	1909	2009	2109	2140	2209	...	2314	...	...	..

	5009	5509	529	5519	1381 C	5209 k	*IC* 1527 ⑥F	2	527	5517	525	2	5205	2	523	2	521	*IC* 1521 ⑦G	2	5201	2	2	2	2
Sátoraljaújhely .... d.	...	...	0351	...	...	0547	0620	0647	0747	...	0947	1047	1147	1247	1347	1447	1547	1621	1647	1747	1847	1947	...	*204*
Sárospatak .... d.	...	...	0401	...	...	0601	0631	0701	0801	...	1001	1101	1201	1301	1401	1501	1601	1632	1701	1801	1901	2001	...	*21*
Szerencs .... ▶ d.	...	...	0445	...	...	0645	0712	0743	0845	...	1045	1143	1245	1343	1445	1543	1645	1717	1743	1845	1943	2047	...	*22*
Miskolc .... ▶ a.	...	...	0519	...	...	0719	0738	*0819*	0919	...	1119	*1219*	1319	*1419*	1519	*1619*	1719	1743	*1819*	1919	*2019*	2121	...	*22*
Miskolc .... ▶ d.	0329	...	0534	...	0632	0734	0753	▬	0934	...	1134	▬	1334	▬	1534	▬	1734	1753	▬	1934	...	...	2204	23
Mezőkövesd .... d.	0407	...	0606	...	|	0806	|	...	1006	...	1206	...	1406	...	1606	...	1806	|	...	2006	...	...	2242	23
Eger ⊙ .... d.	|	0434	|	0634	|	|	|	0834	|	1034	|	1234	|	1434	|	1634	|	|	1834	|	...	...	|	|
Füzesabony .... ▶ a.	0418	0452	0615	0652	0708	0815	0831	0852	1015	1052	1215	1252	1415	1452	1615	1652	1815	1831	1852	2015	...	...	2254	23
Füzesabony .... ▶ d.	0419	0503	0617	0709	0709	0817	0832	0909	1017	1109	1217	1309	1417	1509	1617	1709	1817	1832	1909	2017	...	...	...	...
Vámosgyörk ⊡ .... d.	0454	0539	0645	0745	|	0845	|	0945	1045	1145	1245	1345	1445	1545	1645	1745	1845	|	1945	2045	...	...	...	...
Hatvan .... d.	0511	0557	0702	0802	0757	0902	|	1002	1102	1202	1302	1402	1502	1602	1702	1802	1902	|	2002	2102	...	...	...	...
Budapest Keleti .... ▶ a.	0617	0712	0757	0857	0912	0957	1002	1057	1157	1257	1357	1457	1557	1657	1757	1857	1957	2002	2057	2157	...	...	...	...

C – VARSOVIA – from Warszawa June 17 - Sept. 3 (next day from Miskolc); from Keszthely June 18 - Sept. 4. For composition see Table **1265.**
E – ⑤ Jan. 8 - June 11; ⑤ Sept. 3 - Dec. 10. *IC* train, [R].
F – ⑥ Jan. 9 - June 12, ⑥ Sept. 4 - Dec. 11. *IC* train, [R].
G – ⑦ Jan. 10 - June 13, ⑥ Sept. 5 - Dec. 5. *IC* train, [R].
c – Change at Szerencs.
k – To/from Balatonszentgyörgy or Keszthely on dates in Table **1220**.

▶ – For faster trains see Table **1260**.
⊡ – Connecting trains **Vámosgyörk - Gyöngyös** and v.v. (journey 16 mins):
From Vámosgyörk : 0455 Ⓐ, 0533, 0617 and hourly to 1917 (not 1017).
From Gyöngyös : 0514 Ⓐ, 0554, 0652 and hourly to 1952 (not 1052).
⊙ – Full service **Füzesabony - Eger** and v.v. (journey 18 minutes):
From Füzesabony : 0420, 0506, 0606, 0634, 0706 and hourly to 2306.
From Eger : 0334 and hourly to 2234.

1262 HATVAN - SALGÓTARJÁN - SOMOSKÖÚJFALU
2nd clas

km								Ⓐ		n	
0	Hatvan .... d.	0610	0810	1010	1210	1410	1610	1710	1810	2010	2210
59	Salgótarján .... a.	0739	0939	1139	1339	1539	1739	1839	1939	2139	2339
65	Somosköújfalu 🛃 .... a.	0749	0949	1149	1349	1549	1749	1849	1949	2149	2349

						⑦b				
Somosköújfalu 🛃 ...... d.	0619	0819	1019	1219	1419	1600	1619	1819	2019	221
Salgótarján .... d.	0630	0830	1030	1230	1430	1611	1630	1830	2030	223
Hatvan .... a.	0750	0950	1150	1350	1550	1728	1750	1950	2150	235

b – To Budapest Keleti, arrive 1837.
n – On ⑦ starts from Budapest Keleti (depart 1908).

Additional journeys:
From Hatvan to Somosköújfalu: 0410, 0710Ⓐ, 1310Ⓐ, 1510Ⓐ, 1910Ⓐ, 2110Ⓐ (also 0510Ⓐ, 1110Ⓐ to Salgótarján).
From Somosköújfalu: 0219, 0319, 0419, 0519Ⓐ, 1119Ⓐ, 1519Ⓐ, 1719Ⓐ, 1919Ⓐ, 2119Ⓐ (also 0730Ⓐ, 1330Ⓐ from Salgótarjár

1265 MISKOLC - KOŠICE

km		2	*IC* 532 R	2	2	2	2	2	*IC* 536 ✗ H	1380 C
	Budapest Keleti **1260/1** ..... d.	...	0633	...	...	...	...	...	1833	1828
	Füzesabony **1260/1** .... d.	0502	0755	0802	1002	1202	1402	1602	1955	2026
0	**Miskolc** .... d.	0607	0834	0907	1107	1307	1507	1707	2034	2134
61	Hidasnémeti .... a.	0713	0926	1013	1213	1413	1613	1813	2126	2230
61	Hidasnémeti 🛃 .... d.	...	0929	...	...	...	...	...	2129	2245
87	**Košice** .... a.	...	0950	...	...	...	...	...	2150	2305

	1381 C	*IC* 537 ✗ H	2	2	2	2	2	*IC* 533 R	2
Košice .... d.	0502	0613	...	...	...	...	...	1813	...
Hidasnémeti 🛃 .... a.	0522	0633	...	...	...	...	...	1833	...
Hidasnémeti .... d.	0532	0636	0947	1147	1347	1547	1647	1836	214
Miskolc .... a.	0630	0726	1053	1253	1453	1653	1753	1926	225
Füzesabony **1260/1** .... a.	0708	0804	...	1354	1554	1754	1854	2004	235
Budapest Keleti **1260/1** ... a.	0912	0927	...	...	...	...	...	2127	...

C – VARSOVIA – from Warszawa June 17 - Sept. 3 (next day from Košice); from Keszthely June 18 - Sept. 4. 🛏 2 cl. and [12] Warszawa - Kraków - Košice - Budapest - Keszthely and v.v. Also runs on Sept. 5 with [12] Košice - Keszthely and v.v. Conveys 🛏 1, 2 cl. Warszawa - Burgas/Varna and v.v. (also 🛏 2 cl. Košice - Burgas/Varna and v.v.) on summer dates in Table **99**.

H – HERNÁD – [12] and ✗ Pécs - Budapest - Miskolc - Košice and v.v.
R – RÁKÓCZI – [12] Budapest - Miskolc - Košice and v.v.; [2] Budapest - Košice (**890** **1904**) - Humenné and v.v.

Other local trains run Miskolc - Hidasnémeti.

BUDAPEST - DEBRECEN - NYÍREGYHÁZA - ZÁHONY - CHOP 1270

For trains to/from Romania see Table **1275**

km		*IC* 569 R ✕ ◇	*IC* 650 R ✕ ◇	*IC* 622 R ✕ ⚒	*IC* 567 R ✕ ◇	*IC* 612 R ✕ ⚒	*IC* 652 R ✕ ◇	*IC* 604 R ✕ ⚒	*IC* 565 R ✕ ◇	*IC* 614 R ✕ ⚒	*IC* 654 R ✕ ◇	*IC* 624 R ✕	*IC* 563 R ✕ ◇	*IC* 626 R ✕ Ⓑ	*IC* 616 R ✕	16 T	*IC* 608 R ✕ Ⓑ
0	**Budapest** Nyugati ◧ d.	...	0623	0723	0823	0923	1023	1123	1223	1323	1423	1523	1623	1723	1823	1843**k**	1923
11	Köbánya Kispest ◧ d.	...	0637	0737	0837	0937	1037	1137	1237	1337	1437	1537	1637	1737	1837	|	1937
18	Ferihegy ✈ ◧ d.	...	0643	0743	0843	0943	1043	1143	1243	1343	1443	1543	1643	1743	1843	|	1943
73	Cegléd ◧ d.	...	0718	0818	0918	1018	1118	1218	1318	1418	1518	1618	1718	1818	1918	|	2018
100	**Szolnok** ◧ d.	...	0738	0838	0938	1038	1138	1238	1338	1438	1538	1638	1738	1838	1938	2004	2038
177	Püspökladány d.	...	0824	0924	1024	1124	1224	1324	1424	1524	1624	1724	1824	1924	2024	2103	2124
201	Hajdúszoboszló d.	...	0839	0939	1039	1139	1239	1339	1439	1539	1639	1739	1839	1939	2039	2121	2139
221	**Debrecen** a.	...	0852	0952	1052	1152	1252	1352	1452	1552	1652	1752	1852	1952	2052	2135	2152
221	**Debrecen** d.	0654	0854	0954	1054	1154	1254	1354	1454	1554	1654	1757	1854	1954	2054	2136	2154
270	**Nyíregyháza** a.	0724	0924	1024	1124	1224	1324	1424	1524	1624	1724	1827	1924	2024	2124	2208	2224
270	**Nyíregyháza** d.	*0737*	...	1029	...	...	...	...	...	...	...	1829	...	2026	...	2209	...
313	Kisvárda d.	*0822*	...	1107	...	...	...	...	...	...	...	1900	...	2053	...	2240	...
335	Záhony ▦ ▶ a.	*0848*	...	1128	...	...	...	...	...	...	...	1918	...	2111	...	2258	...
341	**Chop** ▦ ⊙ ▶ a.	...	...	...	...	...	...	...	...	...	...	...	...	...	...	0113	...

Debrecen - Záhony runs approx hourly *(connections available from IC at Nyíregyháza).*

Budapest Nyugati d.	S	...	0503	0628	E	1628	1828	2028	2228
Köbánya Kispest d.	L	...	0517	0642	V	1642	1842	2042	2242
Ferihegy d.	O	...	0526	0648	E	1648	1848	2048	2248
Cegléd d.	W	...	0624	0724	R	1724	1924	2124	2324
Szolnok d.	E	...	0650	0750	Y	1750	1950	2150	2346
Püspökladány d.	R	0657	0757	0857		1857	2057	2257	0048
Hajdúszoboszló d.		0716	0816	0916	2	1916	2116	2316	...
Debrecen a.	T	0731	0831	0931		1931	2131	2331	...
Debrecen d.	R	0737	0837	0937	H	1937	2139	...	...
Nyíregyháza a.	A	0819	0919	1019	O	2019	2219	...	...
Nyíregyháza d.	I	0837	0937	1037	U	2037	2252	...	...
Kisvárda d.	N	0922	1022	1122	R	2122	2337	...	...
Záhony a.	S	0948	1048	1148	S	2148	0003	...	...
Chop a.		...	...	...		...	...	...	...

	IC 609 R ✕ ⚒	*IC* 627 R ✕	*IC* 560 R ✕ ⚒◇	15 T	*IC* 659 R ✕ ◇	*IC* 607 R ✕ ⚒	*IC* 657 R ✕ ◇	*IC* 605 R ✕	*IC* 564 R ✕ ◇	*IC* 615 R ✕ Ⓑ	*IC* 655 R ✕ ◇	*IC* 623 R ✕ Ⓑ	*IC* 566 R ✕ ◇	*IC* 621 R ✕ Ⓑ	*IC* 621 R ✕ ⑦	*IC* 653 R ✕ ◇	*IC* 568 R ✕ ◇
Chop ▦ ⊙ ▶ d.	...	...	...	0540	...	...	...	...	...	...	...	...	...	...	...	...	...
Záhony ▦ ▶ d.	...	0540	...	0630	...	...	...	...	...	...	...	1431	...	...	1631	...	...
Kisvárda d.	...	0559	...	0650	...	...	...	...	...	...	...	1451	...	...	1651	...	...
Nyíregyháza a.	...	0626	...	0723	...	...	...	...	...	...	...	1520	...	...	1720	...	...
Nyíregyháza d.	0536	0628	0736	0728	0836	0936	1036	1136	1236	1336	1436	1536	1636	1736	1736	1836	2036
Debrecen a.	0606	0658	0806	0801	0906	1006	1106	1206	1306	1406	1506	1606	1706	1806	1806	1906	2106
Debrecen d.	0608	0708	0808	0813	0908	1008	1108	1208	1308	1408	1508	1608	1708	1808	1808	1908	...
Hajdúszoboszló d.	0621	0721	0821	0828	0921	1021	1121	1221	1321	1421	1521	1621	1721	1821	1821	1921	...
Püspökladány d.	0636	0736	0836	0846	0936	1036	1136	1236	1336	1436	1536	1636	1736	1836	1836	1936	...
Szolnok ◧ d.	0722	0822	0922	0957	1022	1122	1222	1322	1422	1522	1622	1722	1822	1922	1922	2022	...
Cegléd ◧ d.	0743	0843	0943	|	1043	1143	1243	1343	1443	1543	1643	1743	1843	1943	1943	2043	...
Ferihegy ✈ ◧ d.	0817	0917	1017	|	1117	1217	1317	1417	1517	1617	1717	1817	1917	2017	2017	2117	...
Köbánya Kispest ◧ a.	0822	0922	1022	|	1122	1222	1322	1422	1522	1622	1722	1822	1922	2022	2022	2122	...
Budapest Nyugati ◧ a.	0837	0937	1037	1117**k**	1137	1237	1337	1437	1537	1637	1737	1837	1937	2037	2037	2137	...

Záhony - Debrecen runs approx hourly *(connections available into IC at Nyíregyháza).*

Chop d.	S	...	...	...	...		...	...	...
Záhony d.	L	...	...	*0602*	0812	E	1612	1712	2012
Kisvárda d.	O	...	...	*0629*	0839	V	1639	1739	2039
Nyíregyháza a.	W	...	...	*0713*	0923	E	1723	1823	2123
Nyíregyháza d.	E	...	0541	0741	0941	R	1741	1841	2141
Debrecen a.	R	...	0623	0823	1023	Y	1823	1923	2223
Debrecen d.		0423	0629	0829	1029		1829	1929	—
Hajdúszoboszló d.	T	0440	0645	0845	1045	2	1845	1945	...
Püspökladány d.	R	0459	0708	0908	1108		1908	2008	2
Szolnok d.	A	0603	0815	1015	1215	H	2015	2124	2224
Cegléd d.	I	0628	0838	1038	1238	O	2038	2148	2248
Ferihegy d.	N	0717	0912	1112	1312	U	2112	2244	2344
Köbánya Kispest a.	S	0722	0917	1117	1317	R	2117	2252	2352
Budapest Nyugati a.		0737	0932	1132	1332	S	2132	2307	0007

T – TISZA – 12 Budapest - Záhony and v.v.; 2 Záhony - Chop and v.v. 2 cl. Budapest - Lviv/Kyïv/Moskva and v.v. (Table **97**); 2 cl. Beograd - Budapest - Kyïv/Moskva and v.v. (Table **97**). Conveys 2 cl. Venezia/Zagreb - Moskva and Zagreb - Kyïv on dates in Table **97** (also Thessaloniki - Moskva in summer). Conveys 2 cl. Bar - Beograd - Budapest - Moskva on dates in Table **1360**.

k – Budapest **Keleti**.

◧ – Also **1290** Budapest - Cegléd; **1280** Budapest - Szolnok.

▶ – Full service Záhony - Chop (2nd class):

						T
Záhony ... d.	0630	0805	1138	1536	2010	2358
Chop .. ⊙ a.	0747	0922	1255	1653	2127	0113

	T					
Chop . ⊙ d.	0540	0832	1035	1415	1740	2230
Záhony ... a.	0458	0749	0952	1332	1657	2147

⊙ – Ukrainian (East European) time, one hour ahead of Hungarian time.

◇ – To/from Miskolc (Table **1260**).

BUDAPEST - BIHARKERESZTES - ORADEA 1275

km		6430 2	*IC** 367 B ⊖	2	*IC** 363 ⊖	2	*IC** 365 ⊖	2	2	407 C ⊖
0	**Budapest Keleti** ▷ d.	...	0643	...	0943	...	1343	...	...	1743
100	Szolnok ▷ d.	...	0805	...	1105	...	1505	...	...	1903
177	Püspökladány ▷ d.	0635	0910	1110	1210	1410	1610	1710	1810	2010
228	Biharkeresztes a.	0726	1003	1204	1256	1457	1656	1800	1903	2056
228	Biharkeresztes ▦ d.	0741	1018	...	1313	...	1713	...	...	2113
241	Episcopia Bihor ▦ ⊙ a.	0856	1133	...	1428	...	1828	...	...	2228
241	Episcopia Bihor ⊙ d.	0919	1151	...	1443	...	1849	...	...	2243
247	**Oradea** ⊙ a.	0927	1159	...	1451	...	1857	...	...	2251
	Cluj Napoca **1612** ⊙ a.	...	1447	...	1731	...	2149	...	...	0140

	406 C ⊖	2	*IC** 364 ⊖	6415 2	*IC** 366 B ⊖	2	2	*IC** 362 ⊖	2
Cluj Napoca **1612** ⊙ d.	0217	...	0621	...	1022	...	...	1512	...
Oradea ⊙ d.	0501	...	0910	1111	1310	...	...	1808	...
Episcopia Bihor ⊙ a.	0511	...	0918	1119	1318	...	...	1816	...
Episcopia Bihor ▦ ⊙ d.	0533	...	0933	1134	1333	...	...	1833	...
Biharkeresztes ▦ a.	0448	...	0848	1049	1248	...	...	1748	...
Biharkeresztes d.	0504	0607	0904	1104	1304	1503	1700	1804	1905
Püspökladány ▷ a.	0550	0654	0950	1150	1350	1550	1747	1850	1952
Szolnok ▷ a.	0657	...	1057	...	1457	...	...	1957	...
Budapest Keleti ▷ a.	0817	...	1217	...	1617	...	...	2117	...

B – HARGITA – 12 and ✕ Budapest - Cluj Napoca - Braşov and v.v.

C – CORONA – 1, 2 cl., 2 cl., 12 and ✕ Budapest - Cluj Napoca - Deda - Braşov and v.v.

⊙ – Romanian (East European) time.

⊖ – R for international journeys.

▷ – For connections Budapest **Nyugati** - Püspökladány see Table **1270**.

* – Classified *IC* in Hungary.

OTHER TRAIN NAMES:

362/3 – BIHAR/BIHARIA
364/5 – ADY ENDRE

2nd class DEBRECEN and NYÍREGYHÁZA - MÁTÉSZALKA 1276

km									△			Ⓑ
0	**Debrecen** d.	0505	0715	0915	1115	1315	1515	1715	1807	1915	2115	2245
58	Nyírbátor d.	0633	0833	1033	1233	1433	1636	1833	1908	2036	2233	0002
78	**Mátészalka** a.	0657	0857	1057	1257	1457	1700	1857	1927	2100	2257	0025

			▽								
Mátészalka d.	0414	0455	0532	0703	0903	1103	1303	1503	1703	1902	2103
Nyírbátor d.	0438	0520	0552	0727	0927	1127	1327	1527	1727	1931	2127
Debrecen a.	0555	0639	0652	0844	1044	1244	1444	1644	1850	2046	2244

km		⚒				⑦	⚒				Ⓑ	
0	**Nyíregyháza** d.	0534	0829	1029	1229	1429	1429	1629	1829	2042	*2242*	...
38	Nyírbátor d.	0703	1000	1200	1400	1553	1600	1753	1953	2159	0002	...
58	**Mátészalka** a.	0730	1023	1222	1423	1615	1624	1816	2015	2228	0025	...

		▽						⑦	⚒		Ⓑ
Mátészalka d.	0440	0532	...	0734	0934	1134	1334	1527	1534	1722	1950
Nyírbátor d.	0504	0551	0555	0759	0959	1159	1359	1559	1559	1759	2016
Nyíregyháza a.	0620	...	0711	0916	1116	1316	1516	1716	1716	1916	2132

△ – *IC* **624/638** from Budapest Nyugati, depart 1523, R.

▽ – *IC* **639/627** to Budapest Nyugati, arrive 0937, R.

2nd class DEBRECEN - ORADEA and BAIA MARE and other cross-border services 1277

km		6812	6814	6816
0	**Debrecen** d.	0712	1112	1512
30	Nyirábrány ▦ a.	0751	1151	1551
39	Valea lui Mihai ▦ ⊙ a.	0927	1327	1727
39	Valea lui Mihai ⊙ d.	...	1347	1752
105	**Oradea** ⊙ a.	...	1503	|
70	Carei **1618** ⊙ a.	...	...	1838
106	Satu Mare **1618** ⊙ a.	...	...	1926
165	**Baia Mare** **1616** ⊙ a.	...	...	2127

	6817	6827	6811
Baia Mare **1616** ⊙ d.	0358	...	...
Satu Mare **1618** ⊙ d.	0619	...	...
Carei **1618** ⊙ d.	0714	...	...
Oradea ⊙ d.	|	...	1645
Valea lui Mihai ⊙ a.	0748	...	1811
Valea lui Mihai ▦ ⊙ d.	0837	1037	1837
Nyirábrány ▦ d.	0809	1009	1809
Debrecen a.	0848	1048	1848

km				
0	**Békéscsaba** **1280** d.	0653	1253	1653
16	Gyula **1280** d.	0715	1315	1715
36	Kötegyán ▦ a.	0739	1339	1739
50	**Salonta** ▦ ⊙ a.	0909	1509	1909

Salonta ▦ ⊙ d.	0950	1550	1950
Kötegyán ▦ d.	0921	1521	1921
Gyula **1280** d.	0953	1553	1953
Békéscsaba **1280** a.	1013	1613	2013

km				
0	**Mátészalka** d.	0535	1235	...
18	Tiborszállás ▦ a.	0607	1307	...
18	Tiborszállás ▦ d.	0625	1320	...
33	**Carei** ⊙ a.	0751	1446	...

Carei ⊙ d.	0924	1639	...
Tiborszállás ▦ a.	0850	1605	...
Tiborszállás ▦ d.	0905	1620	...
Mátészalka a.	0950	1652	...

⊙ – Romanian (East European) time, one hour ahead of Hungarian time.

2nd class DEBRECEN - FÜZESABONY 1278

km									Ⓑ		
0	**Debrecen** d.	0526	0726	0926	1126	1326	1526	1726	1926	2045	2240
42	Hortobágy d.	0618	0815	1015	1215	1415	1615	1815	2014	2136	2330
73	Tiszafüred d.	0659	0859	1059	1259	1459	1659	1859	2058	2211	0004
103	**Füzesabony** a.	0732	0932	1132	1332	1532	1732	1932	2131	2252	...

									Ⓑ	
Füzesabony d.	0422	0610	0822	1022	1222	1422	1622	1822	2022	2200
Tiszafüred d.	0501	0701	0901	1101	1301	1501	1701	1901	2056	2235
Hortobágy d.	0536	0736	0936	1136	1336	1536	1736	1936	2139	...
Debrecen a.	0631	0831	1031	1231	1431	1631	1831	2029	2225	...

1280 BUDAPEST - BÉKÉSCSABA - LÖKÖSHÁZA - ARAD

km		7310	7400	IC 75	1373	IC 375	IC 373	7304	IC 377	1822	7306	IC 79	7308	IC 379	7408	EN 473	17308	EN 347
		2		⊖	[R] U	⊖ P	⊖ T		⊖	Y		⊖		⊖ n		⊖ W	⑤⑦	⊖ D
0	**Budapest** Keleti **1270** d.	...	0613	0713	0848	0913	1113	1213	1313	...	1413	1513	1613	1713	1813	1913	2013	2313
100	Szolnok **1270** d.	...	0734	0834	1027	1034	1234	1334	1434	...	1534	1634	1734	1834	1934	2034	2134	0034
141	Mezőtúr d.	*0527*	0800	0900	|	1100	1300	1400	1500	...	1600	1700	1800	1900	2000	2100	2200	|
159	Gyoma d.	*0546*	0813	0913	|	1113	1313	1413	1513	...	1613	1713	1813	1913	2013	2113	2213	|
196	**Békéscsaba** a.	*0618*	0838	0938	1127	1138	1338	1438	1538	...	1638	1738	1838	1938	2038	2138	2238	0132
196	**Békéscsaba** d.	0640	...	0943	1129	1143	1343	1443	1543	...	1643	1743	1843	1943	...	2143	2243	0135
225	Lökösháza a.	0712	...	1010	1149	1210	1410	1505	1610	...	1705	1810	1910	2005	...	2203	2305	0155
225	Lökösháza 🏛 d.	0738	...	1025	1245	1225	1425	...	1625	...	...	1825	...	2025	...	2218	...	0210
236	Curtici 🏛 ⊙ d.	0910	...	1152	1357	1352	1552	...	1752	...	...	1952	...	2152	...	2345	...	0337
253	**Arad** ⊙ a.	0927	...	1214	1452	1414	1614	...	1814	1900	...	2014	...	2214	...	0007	...	0359
	Timişoara **1614** ⊙ a.	...	...	1303	...	|	...	...	|	|	...	2103	...	...	...	|	...	|
	Târgu Mureş **1610** ⊙ a.	...	...	...	...	|	...	...	2342	|	...	...	...	...	...	|	...	|
	Braşov **1600** ⊙ a.	...	...	...	...	2117	...	...	...	|	...	...	...	...	...	0726	...	1110
	Bucureşti Nord **1600** ⊙ a.	...	...	...	...	0035**z**	...	...	...	0515	...	...	...	...	...	1034	...	1407

	EN 346	7309	EN 472	7307	IC 78	IC 378	1821	IC 376	7305	IC 372	7403	IC 374	1372	7301	IC 74	17301		7311
	⊖ D		⊖ W		⊖	⊖ n	Y	⊖		⊖ T		⊖ P	[R] U		⊖	⑤⑦	2	2
Bucureşti Nord **1600** ⊙ d.	1600	...	1910	...	...	...	2345	...	...	...	...	0530**z**	...	...	...	...	...	...
Braşov **1600** ⊙ d.	1856	...	2216	...	...	...	|	...	...	...	...	0832	...	...	...	...	...	...
Târgu Mureş **1610** ⊙ d.	|	...	|	...	...	...	|	0610	...	...	...	|	...	...	...	...	...	...
Timişoara **1614** ⊙ d.	|	...	|	...	0654	...	|	|	...	...	...	|	...	...	1654	...	...	...
Arad ⊙ d.	0204	...	0549	...	0743	0947	0959	1149	...	1342	...	1549	1440	...	1743	...	...	2035
Curtici 🏛 ⊙ a.	0223	...	0608	...	0802	1006	...	1208	...	1401	...	1608	1459	...	1802	...	...	2054
Lökösháza 🏛 a.	0150	...	0535	...	0735	0935	...	1135	...	1335	...	1535	1455	...	1735	...	...	2023
Lökösháza d.	0213	0455	0555	0652	0750	0950	...	1150	1250	1350	...	1550	1530	1643	1750	1850	...	2050
Békéscsaba a.	0233	0517	0615	0714	0812	1012	...	1212	1312	1412	...	1612	1556	1708	1812	1912	...	2112
Békéscsaba d.	0253	0525	0618	0718	0818	1018	...	1218	1318	1418	1518	1618	1613	1718	1818	1918	2038	...
Gyoma d.	|	0559	0646	0746	0846	1046	...	1246	1346	1446	1546	1646	|	1746	1846	1946	2118	...
Mezőtúr d.	|	0614	0659	0759	0859	1059	...	1259	1359	1459	1559	1659	|	1759	1859	1959	2133	...
Szolnok **1270** d.	0355	0649	0727	0827	0927	1127	...	1327	1427	1527	1627	1727	1752	1827	1927	2027	...	...
Budapest Keleti **1270** a.	0517	0812	0847	0947	1047	1247	...	1447	1547	1647	1747	1847	1912	1947	2047	2147	...	...

BÉKÉSCSABA - GYULA

Journey 20 minutes

From **Békéscsaba**: 0526, 0601, 0653, 0753, 0853, 0953, 1053, 1153, 1253, 1353, 1435, 1553, 1620**s**, 1653, 1753, 1853, 1953, 2053, 2230.

From **Gyula**: 0504, 0544, 0620**s**, 0653, 0753, 0853, 0953, 1053, 1153, 1253, 1353, 1453, 1553, 1653, 1720**s**, 1753, 1853, 1953, 2053.

NOTES (continued from below):

n – To / from Simeria (Table **1610**).
s – To / from Szeged (Table **1292**).
v – From Simeria, depart 0720.
z – Runs Braşov - Bucureşti and v.v. on Dec. 13 - Feb. 28, May 31 - Sept. 19 only.
⊙ – Romanian (East European) time.
⊖ – [R] for international journeys (and domestic journeys in Romania).

OTHER TRAIN NAMES:

74 / 75 – TRAIANUS
78 / 79 – KÖRÖS / CRIŞ
376 / 377 – MAROS / MUREŞ
378 / 379 – ZARÁND

D – DACIA – 🛏 1, 2 cl., ▬ 2 cl., (2) Wien - Budapest - Bucureşti and v.v.; (12) Budapest - Bucureşti and v.v.

P – PANNONIA – (12) and ✕ Budapest - Braşov (- Bucureşti on dates in note **z**) and v.v. Conveys Dec. 13 - Jan. 11, June 17 - Sept. 17, 🛏 1, 2 cl. München - Wien - Budapest - Bucureşti, returning Dec. 13 - Jan. 9, June 15 - Sept. 15. Conveys May 27 - Sept. 27 🛏 1, 2 cl., ▬ 2 cl., (2) Praha (**471/0**) - Budapest - Lökösháza, returning May 28 - Sept. 28 (conveyed in train **U** when that train runs).

T – TRANSILVANIA – (12) and ✕ Budapest - Arad - Sibiu and v.v.

U – NESEBAR – from Budapest to Varna ⑥ June 13 - Sept. 5, returning next day. From Budapest to Burgas ③⑤⑦ June 18 - Sept. 19, returning next day. 🛏 1, 2 cl. Budapest - Varna / Burgas and v.v.; 🛏 1, 2 cl., ▬ 2 cl. Praha - Budapest - Varna / Burgas and v.v. For portion from Warszawa / Košice see summer Table **99**.

W – ISTER – 🛏 1, 2 cl., ▬ 1, 2 cl., (2) and ✕ Budapest - Bucureşti and v.v.; (12) Budapest - Lökösháza and v.v.

Y – 🛏 1, 2 cl., ▬ 2 cl. and (12) Arad - Craiova - Bucureşti - Constanţa and v.v.

FOR OTHER NOTES SEE ABOVE

1290 BUDAPEST - KECSKEMÉT - SZEGED

km			IC 710	IC 760	IC 702		IC 756	IC 766	7008	7108
		2	[R]	[R]	[R]		[R]	[R]		
0	**Budapest** Nyugati § d.	0403	0553	0653	0753	and	1753	1853	1953	2053
11	Kőbánya Kispest § d.	0417	0607	0707	0807	hourly	1807	1907	2007	2107
18	Ferihegy ✈ § d.	0426	0613	0713	0813	✣	1813	1913	2013	2113
73	Cegléd § d.	0530	0648	0748	0848	until	1848	1948	2048	2203
106	**Kecskemét** d.	0606	0711	0811	0911		1911	2011	2113	2225
131	Kiskunfélegyháza d.	0631	0731	0831	0931		1931	2031	2131	2241
191	**Szeged** a.	0715	0815	0915	1015		2015	2115	2215	2325

	7009	IC 709	IC 719	IC 707		IC 753	IC 763	7001	17101
		[R]	[R]	[R]		[R]	[R]		⑦
Szeged d.	0436	0547	0645	0745		1745	1845	1945	2045
Kiskunfélegyháza d.	0523	0631	0731	0831	and	1831	1931	2031	2131
Kecskemét d.	0539	0647	0747	0847	hourly	1847	1947	2047	2147
Cegléd § d.	0608	0713	0813	0913	✣	1913	2013	2117	2218
Ferihegy ✈ § d.	0657	0747	0847	0947	until	1947	2047	2152	2252
Kőbánya Kispest § a.	0702	0752	0852	0952		1952	2052	2157	2257
Budapest Nyugati § a.	0717	0807	0907	1007		2007	2107	2212	2312

✣ – 0953 from Budapest and 1045 from Szeged run on ⑤–⑦ and holidays only.

§ – For additional trains see Table **1270**.

Note: on this line only, all *IC* trains have designated carriages for the use of passengers without seat reservations.

1292 SZEGED - BÉKÉSCSABA

2nd class

km								z				
0	**Szeged** d.	0520	0620	0720	0920	1120	1320	1420	1520	1620	1720	1920
31	Hódmezővásárhely d.	0559	0703	0759	0959	1159	1359	1503	1559	1703	1759	1959
62	Orosháza d.	0629	0728	0829	1029	1229	1429	1528	1629	1728	1829	2029
97	**Békéscsaba** a.	0711	0807	0912	1109	1309	1509	1607	1709	1807	1909	2109

	z								z	
Békéscsaba d.	0645	0745	0945	1145	1345	1443	1545	1643	1745	1945
Orosháza d.	0730	0830	1030	1230	1430	1530	1630	1730	1830	2030
Hódmezővásárhely d.	0800	0900	1100	1300	1500	1600	1700	1800	1900	2100
Szeged a.	0833	0937	1137	1337	1537	1637	1737	1837	1937	2137

z – To / from Gyula (Table **1280**).

Additional trains: from Szeged 1820⑤⑦, from Békéscsaba 0545, 1845⑤⑦.

1295 BUDAPEST - KISKUNHALAS - KELEBIA

km			790	792	343	IC 345	7904	796	798		341
		2Ⓐ	2	2	N	A	2	2	2	2	B
0	**Budapest Keleti** d.	...	...	...	1005	1300	...	...	...	...	2300
0	Kőbánya Kispest d.	0445	0604	0804	|	|	1404	1604	1804	1932	|
61	Kunszentmiklós-Tass d.	0558	0709	0909	1109	1401	1509	1709	1909	2050	|
107	Kiskőrös d.	0649	0801	1001	1201	1450	1601	1801	2001	2138	0034
134	Kiskunhalas a.	0721	0833	1033	1233	1520	1633	1833	2033	2209	0102
163	**Kelebia** 🏛 a.	...	0911	1111	1311	1550	1711	1911	2111	...	0142
	Beograd **1360** a.	...	...	...	1750	2036	...	...	...	...	0629

	340	799	797	7907	795	IC 344	342	791	7901
	B	2	2	2	2	A◇	N	2	2s
Beograd **1360** d.	2125	...	...	...	...	0720	1000	...	...
Kelebia 🏛 d.	0215	0448	0646	0846	1046	1210	1446	1646	1846
Kiskunhalas d.	0249	0524	0724	0924	1124	1241	1524	1724	1924
Kiskőrös d.	0317	0600	0800	1000	1200	1310	1600	1800	2000
Kunszentmiklós-Tass d.	|	0649	0850	1050	1250	1400	1650	1850	2050
Kőbánya Kispest a.	|	0755	0951	1151	1351	|	|	1951	2149
Budapest Keleti a.	0504	...	...	...	...	1455	1804	...	...

A – AVALA – (12) and ✕ Praha - Budapest - Beograd and v.v. For other cars see Table **1360**.

B – BEOGRAD – 🛏 1, 2 cl. and ▬ 2 cl. Wien - Budapest - Beograd and v.v.; (2) Budapest - Beograd and v.v.; 🛏 1, 2 cl. Wien - Budapest - Beograd - Sofiya and v.v.

N – IVO ANDRIC – (12) Budapest - Beograd and v.v.

◇ – [R] from Beograd.

1299 OTHER LOCAL SERVICES

Most trains 2nd class only

BUDAPEST - DUNAÚJVÁROS — *80 km*, journey 85 minutes

From **Budapest** Déli: 0456, 0556, 0656, 0856, 1056, 1256, 1356, 1456, 1556, 1656, 1856, 2056.

From **Dunaújváros**: 0331, 0431, 0531, 0631, 0731, 0831, 1037, 1231, 1437, 1537, 1637, 1731, 1837, 2031, 2237.

BUDAPEST - ESZTERGOM — *53 km*, journey 95 - 105 minutes

From **Budapest** Nyugati: 0610, 0721, 0820, 0852Ⓐ, 0921 and hourly to 2321 (also on Ⓐ at 1352, 1452, 1552, 1652, 1752, 1852).

From **Esztergom**: 0333, 0416, 0456, 0532Ⓐ, 0549Ⓐ, 0605, 0637Ⓐ, 0704, 0728Ⓐ, 0809 and hourly to 2209 (also at 1233Ⓐ).

BUDAPEST - VASÚTMÚZEUM (Railway Museum) — *5 km*, journey time 8 minutes

②-⑦ Mar. 16 - Dec. 5, 2010. Trains continue to / from Esztergom.

From Budapest Nyugati: 1021, 1121, 1321. From Vasútmúzeum: 1029, 1329, 1629.

BUDAPEST - SZENTENDRE — *21 km*, journey time 38 minutes

HÉV suburban trains from Budapest Batthyány tér, every 10 - 20 minutes (30 - 40 evenings).

EGER - SZILVÁSVÁRAD — *34 km*, journey time 65 minutes

From **Eger**: 0446, 0746, 0946, 1346, 1446, 1746, 1946.

From **Szilvásvárad**: 0410, 0610, 0910, 1110, 1510, 1710, 1805⑦, 1910.

Via Szilvásvárad-Szalajkavölgy (for the forest railway), 6 minutes from Szilvásvárad.

HATVAN - SZOLNOK — *68 km*, journey 71 - 73 minutes

From **Hatvan**: Ⓐ: hourly 0515 - 2215 (not 0915). Ⓒ: every 2 hours 0615 - 2215.

From **Szolnok**: Ⓐ: hourly 0433 - 2133 (not 0933). Ⓒ: every 2 hours 0433 - 2033, also 2133.

KISKUNFÉLEGYHÁZA - CSONGRÁD - SZENTES — *39 km*, journey time 55 minutes

From **Kiskunfélegyháza**: 0534Ⓐ, 0734, 0934, 1234, 1434, 1634, 1834, 2042⑦, 2134.

From **Szentes**: 0633, 0833, 1133, 1333, 1533, 1733, 1933⑦ (calls Csongrád 17 mins later).

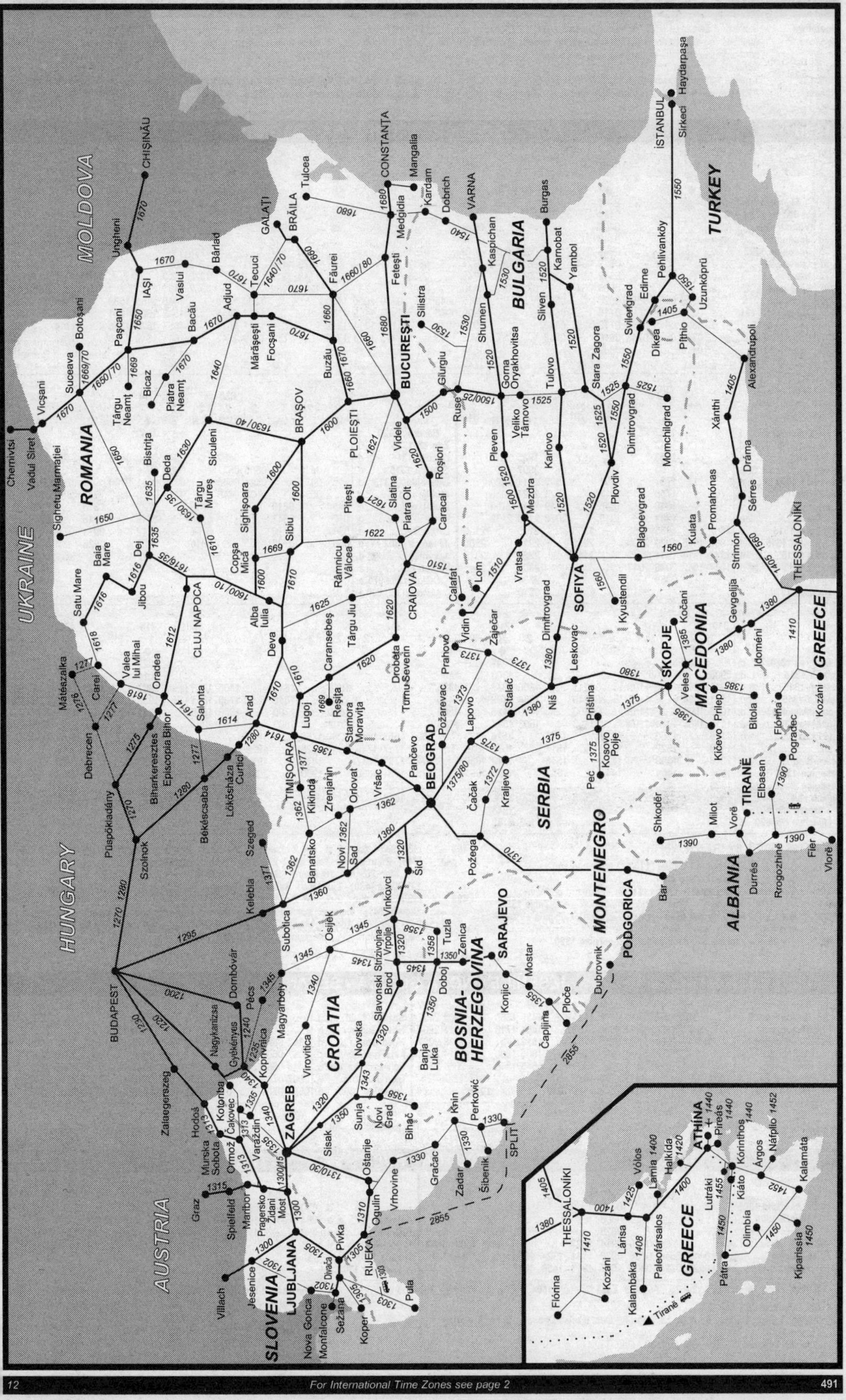
UKRAINE
MOLDOVA
ROMANIA
HUNGARY
AUSTRIA
SLOVENIA
CROATIA
BOSNIA-HERZEGOVINA
SERBIA
MONTENEGRO
ALBANIA
MACEDONIA
BULGARIA
GREECE
TURKEY
CHIŞINĂU
Ungheni
IAŞI
Paşcani
Suceava
Botoşani
Vicşani
Chernivtsi
Vadul Siret
Sighetu Marmaţiei
Baia Mare
Satu Mare
Jibou
Dej
Bistriţa
Deda
Târgu Mureş
Sighişoara
CLUJ NAPOCA
Oradea
Valea lui Mihai
Carei
Mátészalka
Debrecen
Püspökladány
Szolnok
BUDAPEST
Kelebia
Szeged
Békéscsaba
Lökösháza
Curtici
Arad
Salonta
Biharkeresztes
Episcopia Bihor
Deva
Alba Iulia
Copşa Mică
Sibiu
BRAŞOV
Siculeni
Bacău
Adjud
Mărăşeşti
Focşani
Tecuci
GALAŢI
BRĂILA
Tulcea
Făurei
Buzău
PLOIEŞTI
BUCUREŞTI
CONSTANŢA
Mangalia
Medgidia
Feteşti
Giurgiu
Ruse
Videle
Roşiori
Caracal
Piatra Olt
Slatina
Piteşti
Râmnicu Vâlcea
CRAIOVA
Calafat
Vidin
Lom
Târgu Jiu
Drobeta Turnu Severin
Caransebeş
Reşiţa
Lugoj
TIMIŞOARA
Stamora Moraviţa
Vršac
Pančevo
BEOGRAD
Zrenjanin
Kikinda
Novi Sad
Subotica
Šid
Vinkovci
Osijek
Strizivojna-Vrpolje
Slavonski Brod
Doboj
Tuzla
Zenica
SARAJEVO
Mostar
Konjic
Ploče
Čapljina
Dubrovnik
Banja Luka
Novska
ZAGREB
Sisak
Sunja
Novi Grad
Bihać
Knin
Perković
SPLIT
Šibenik
Zadar
Gračac
Oštarije
Ogulin
Vrhovine
RIJEKA
Pula
Koper
Sežana
Divača
Pivka
LJUBLJANA
Jesenice
Villach
Nova Gorica
Monfalcone
Zidani Most
Pragersko
Maribor
Spielfeld
Graz
Murska Sobota
Hodoš
Ormož
Čakovec
Kotoriba
Varaždin
Koprivnica
Gyékényes
Nagykanizsa
Zalaegerszeg
Pécs
Dombóvár
Magyarboly
Virovitica
Požega
Čačak
Kraljevo
Lapovo
Požarevac
Stalać
Niš
Zaječar
Prahovo
Priština
Kosovo Polje
Peć
PODGORICA
Bar
Shkodër
Milot
Vorë
TIRANË
Durrës
Rrogozhinë
Elbasan
Pogradec
Fier
Vlorë
SKOPJE
Veles
Kičevo
Prilep
Bitola
Kočani
Gevgelija
Idoméni
Flórina
Kozáni
THESSALONÍKI
Strimón
Kulata
Promahónas
Sérres
Dráma
Xánthi
Alexandroúpoli
Pýthio
Dikea
Uzunköprü
Pehlivanköy
Edirne
Svilengrad
Dimitrovgrad
Momchilgrad
Plovdiv
Stara Zagora
Tulovo
Karlovo
SOFIYA
Kyustendil
Blagoevgrad
Mezdra
Vratsa
Pleven
Gorna Oryakhovitsa
Veliko Târnovo
Shumen
Kaspichan
VARNA
Dobrich
Kardam
Silistra
Burgas
Karnobat
Yambol
Sliven
ISTANBUL
Sirkeci
Haydarpaşa
Leskovac
Dimitrovgrad
Lárisa
Kalambáka
Paleofársalos
Lamía
Vólos
Halkída
ATHÍNA
Pireás
Kórinthos
Árgos
Náfplio
Kalamáta
Kiparissía
Olimbía
Pátra
Kiáto
Lutráki
Tiranë

SLOVENIA, CROATIA and BOSNIA-HERZEGOVINA

Operators: Slovenske Železnice (SŽ); Hrvatske Željeznice (HŽ); Željeznice Federacije Bosne i Hercegovine (ŽFBH) and Željeznice Republike Srpske (ŽRS).
Services: All trains convey first and second class seating, **except** where shown otherwise in footnotes or by '2' in the train column, or where the footnote shows sleeping and / or couchette cars only. Descriptions of sleeping (🛏) and couchette (▬) cars appear on page 10. Travel on *ICS* trains in Slovenia requires compulsory reservation and payment of a special fare.
Timings: Timings valid from **December 13, 2009** except where indicated otherwise. Readers should note that some local trains, particularly in Bosnia, are subject to alteration.
Tickets: A supplement is payable for travel by internal express trains. Reservation of seats is possible on most express trains.

1300 VILLACH - JESENICE - LJUBLJANA - ZAGREB — SŽ, HŽ, ÖBB

km		*EN* 241 🅁 ♦	2 Ⓐ	2	499 ♦	2	2	2 Ⓐ	2 Ⓐ	415 ♦	2 Ⓐ	2 ⑥	2 Ⓐ	2	2 Ⓐ	2 Ⓐ	*IC* 313	2 ⚒	2 Ⓐ	2 Ⓐ	*EC* 211 ✕ ♦	2 Ⓐ	631 2	2	2	2 Ⓐ	*IC* 311
	München Hbf **890** d.	...	...	...	2340	...	...	...	...	...	...	...	...	...	...	...	...	...	...	...	0827	...	...	...	...	...	...
	Salzburg Hbf **970** d.	...	...	...	0134	...	...	...	...	...	...	...	...	...	...	...	...	...	...	...	1012	...	...	...	...	...	...
0	**Villach** Hbf d.	...	...	...	0407	...	...	...	...	0626	...	...	...	...	...	...	1052	...	...	...	1253	...	...	...	...	...	1452
38	**Jesenice** 🏛 a.	...	...	...	0448	...	...	...	...	0707	...	...	...	...	...	...	1132	...	...	...	1333	...	...	...	...	...	1532
38	**Jesenice 1302** d.	...	...	...	0509	0531	...	0605	0626	0712	...	0751	...	...	...	1109	1137	...	...	1235	1337	...	...	1418	...	1527	1536
51	Lesce-Bled d.	...	...	...	0522	0547	...	0620	0640	0727	...	0812	...	...	...	1123	1150	...	...	1249	1350	...	...	1435	...	1542	1548
74	Kranj d.	...	...	...	0542	0613	...	0647	0708	0749	...	0836	...	...	...	1148	1211	...	...	1322	1410	...	...	1459	...	1616	1613
102	**Ljubljana** a.	...	...	...	0603	0644	...	0720	0741	0810	...	0907	...	...	...	1220	1232	...	...	1352	1431	...	...	1531	...	1650	1633
102	**Ljubljana 1315** d.	0159	0450	0550	0620	...	0655	...	...	0815	0845	...	0950	*1050*	1150	...	...	*1250*	*1350*	...	1448	1455	1530	...	1545	...	1635
166	Zidani Most **1315** d.	0253	0600	0655	0715	...	0800	...	...	0909	0955	...	1055	1155	1301	...	...	1402	1455	...	1542	1601	1631	...	1655	...	1729
182	Sevnica **1315** d.	0308	0619	0715	0730	...	0819	...	...	0924	1014	...	1114	1214	1319	...	...	1421	1514	...	1557	1620	1646	...	1714	...	1745
215	Dobova **1315** 🏛 d.	0349	0647	0743	0810	...	0848	...	...	1005	1043	...	1143	1243	1348	...	...	1449	1542	...	1641	1649	1718	...	1742	...	1827
245	**Zagreb 1315** a.	0418	...	...	0839	...	...	...	...	1034	...	...	...	...	...	...	...	...	...	...	1710	...	...	...	...	...	1856
	Beograd **1320** a.	...	...	...	...	...	...	...	...	1720	...	...	...	...	...	...	...	...	...	...	2327	...	...	...	...	...	...

	2 Ⓑ	2	*EC* 213 ♦	2	2	2 Ⓐ	2	315 ♦	2 ⚒N	2 Ⓐ
München Hbf **890** d.	...	...	1227	...	...	...	...	...	...	...
Salzburg Hbf **970** d.	...	...	1412	...	...	...	...	...	...	...
Villach Hbf. d.	...	...	1653	...	...	...	...	1925	...	...
Jesenice 🏛 a.	...	...	1733	...	...	...	...	2007	...	...
Jesenice 1302 d.	...	...	1737	...	1801	...	1909	2011	2020	...
Lesce-Bled d.	...	...	1750	...	1817	...	1923	2024	2035	...
Kranj d.	...	...	1810	...	1845	...	1949	2044	2100	...
Ljubljana a.	...	...	1831	...	1915	...	2020	2110	2132	...
Ljubljana 1315 d.	1655	1750	1835	1855	...	1950	...	2115	...	2155
Zidani Most **1315** d.	1800	1855	1929	2000	...	2055	...	2210	...	2258
Sevnica **1315** d.	1819	1914	1944	2019	...	2113	...	2225	...	2316
Dobova **1315** 🏛 d.	1847	1942	2026	2047	...	...	...	2305	...	2345
Zagreb 1315 a.	...	...	2055	...	...	...	...	2334	...	...
Beograd **1320** a.	...	...	...	...	...	...	...	0619	...	...

	2 Ⓐ	2	2 Ⓐ	2	630 2 ①–⑥	2 ⑥N	632 2 Ⓐ	314 ♦	2	2 Ⓐ	2	*EC* 212 ♦	2
Beograd **1320** d.	...	...	...	...	...	...	...	2140	...	...	...	...	...
Zagreb 1315 d.	...	...	...	...	...	...	...	0500	...	...	...	0700	...
Dobova **1315** 🏛 d.	...	...	...	...	0452	...	0540	0550	0600	...	0705	0745	...
Sevnica **1315** d.	...	0413	...	0505	0527	...	0608	0616	0631	...	0735	0809	...
Zidani Most **1315** d.	...	0431	...	0524	0548	...	0625	0631	0700	...	0754	0826	...
Ljubljana 1315 a.	...	0534	...	0630	0646	...	0718	0723	0803	...	0859	0917	...
Ljubljana d.	0450	...	0610	...	...	0650	...	0727	...	0818	...	0927	0945
Kranj d.	0521	...	0647	...	...	0720	...	0749	...	0848	...	0949	1017
Lesce-Bled d.	0547	...	0710	...	...	0752	...	0812	...	0911	...	1009	1040
Jesenice 1302 a.	0601	...	0722	...	...	0810	...	0823	...	0925	...	1020	1054
Jesenice 🏛 d.	...	...	...	...	...	...	...	0827	...	...	...	1024	...
Villach Hbf. a.	...	...	...	...	...	...	...	0908	...	...	...	1104	...
Salzburg Hbf **970** a.	...	...	...	...	...	...	...	...	...	...	...	1348	...
München Hbf **890** a.	...	...	...	...	...	...	...	...	...	...	...	1533	...

	IC 310	2 Ⓐ	2	2	2 Ⓐ	2 Ⓐ	2	2	*EC* 210 ✕ ♦	2	2 Ⓐ	2 Ⓐ	*IC* 312	2 Ⓐ	2	2	2	2 Ⓑ	2 Ⓐ	2	2 Ⓐ	414 ♦	2 Ⓑ	2 Ⓑ	498 ♦	2 Ⓑ	*EN* 240 🅁 ♦
Beograd **1320** d.	...	...	...	...	...	...	...	...	0545	...	...	...	...	...	...	...	...	...	...	...	...	1020	...	...	...	...	...
Zagreb 1315 d.	0900	...	...	...	...	...	...	...	1300	...	...	...	...	...	...	...	...	...	...	...	...	1814	...	...	2115	...	2335
Dobova **1315** 🏛 d.	0945	1005	...	1105	...	1211	...	1305	1345	...	1405	...	...	...	1511	...	1611	...	1705	1805	...	1907	1911	2005	2220	2211	0040
Sevnica **1315** d.	1011	1034	...	1135	...	1240	...	1334	1409	...	1435	...	...	...	1540	...	1640	...	1735	1835	...	1931	1940	2035	2227	2241	0104
Zidani Most **1315** d.	1026	1053	...	1155	...	1300	...	1400	1425	...	1500	...	...	...	1600	...	1700	...	1800	1855	...	1947	2000	2100	2242	2300	0119
Ljubljana 1315 a.	1119	1156	...	1303	...	1403	...	1503	1517	...	1603	...	...	...	1703	...	1803	...	1903	2003	...	2039	2103	2203	2333	0003	0210
Ljubljana d.	1126	...	1250	...	1333	...	1441	...	1525	1533	...	1627	1655	1713	...	1750	...	1855	...	...	2025	2048	...	...	2350	...	...
Kranj d.	1148	...	1322	...	1410	...	1517	...	1552	1616	...	1700	1717	1746	...	1825	...	1929	...	...	2101	2117	...	...	0012	...	...
Lesce-Bled d.	1213	...	1350	...	1434	...	1548	...	1612	1639	...	1723	1737	1817	...	1848	...	1954	...	...	2125	2137	...	...	0032	...	...
Jesenice 1302 a.	1224	...	1404	...	1448	...	1602	...	1623	1651	...	1735	1754	1830	...	1900	...	2008	...	...	2139	2148	...	...	0043	...	...
Jesenice 🏛 d.	1228	...	...	...	...	...	...	...	1627	...	...	...	1758	...	...	...	...	...	...	...	...	2153	...	...	0049	...	...
Villach Hbf. a.	1308	...	...	...	...	...	...	...	1706	...	...	...	1838	...	...	...	...	...	...	...	...	2232	...	...	0131	...	...
Salzburg Hbf **970** a.	...	...	...	...	...	...	...	...	1948	...	...	...	...	...	...	...	...	...	...	...	...	...	...	...	0409	...	...
München Hbf **890** a.	...	...	...	...	...	...	...	...	2133	...	...	...	...	...	...	...	...	...	...	...	...	...	...	...	0615	...	...

♦ – **NOTES** (LISTED BY TRAIN NUMBER)

210/1 – SAVA – [12] Beograd - Villach (**110/1**) - München and v.v.; ✕ Beograd - Jesenice and v.v.
212/3 – MIMARA – [12] Zagreb - Villach (**112/3**) - Frankfurt and v.v.
240/1 – VENEZIA – For days of running and composition – see Table **1305**.
314/5 – 🛏 1, 2 cl., ▬ 2 cl. and [12] Beograd - Zagreb - Ljubljana - Villach and v.v.
414/5 – For days of running and composition – see Table **1320**.
498 – LISINSKI – 🛏 1, 2 cl., ▬ 2 cl. and [2] Zagreb - Salzburg (**462/3**) - München; [2] Vinkovci (**748**) - Zagreb - München; 🛏 1, 2 cl. Zagreb - Salzburg (**206**) - Praha. Conveys Dec. 14 - 18, Jan. 1 - 6, Mar. 26 - Apr. 16, May 2 - Sept. 18 (from Rijeka): ▬ 2 cl. (also 🛏 1, 2 cl. June 20 - Sept. 19) Rijeka (**480**) - Ljubljana - Salzburg - München.
499 – LISINSKI – 🛏 1, 2 cl., ▬ 2 cl. and [2] München (**463**) - Salzburg - Zagreb; [2] München - Zagreb (**741**) - Vinkovci; 🛏 1, 2 cl. Praha (**207**) - Salzburg - Zagreb. Conveys Dec. 14 - 19, Jan. 2 - 7, Mar. 27 - Apr. 17, May 3 - Sept. 19 (from München): ▬ 2 cl. (also 🛏 1, 2 cl. June 21 - Sept. 20) München - Salzburg - Ljubljana (**481**) - Rijeka.
N – Conveys on ⑥: [2] Nova Gorica - Jesenice - Ljubljana and v.v.

1302 Subject to alteration — JESENICE - NOVA GORICA - SEŽANA — 2nd class only SŽ

km		Ⓐ	m	j	Ⓐ	⚒N		Ⓐ	Ⓐ		Ⓑ		ⒷW
0	**Jesenice 1300** d.	...	0407	0407	0611	0818	1115	...	1435	1655	...	1901	2152
10	Bled Jezero d.	...	0423	0423	0627	0834	1130	...	1451	1710	...	1917	2204
28	Bohinjska Bistrica d.	...	0444	0444	0654	0902	1151	...	1513	1731	...	1938	2227
56	Most na Soči d.	...	0521	0521	0731	0939	1228	...	1605	1806	...	2014	2301
89	Nova Gorica a.	...	0608	0608	0815	1022	1309	...	1645	1845	...	2054	2336
89	Nova Gorica d.	0455	0612	...	0913	...	*1410*	1530	...	...	1847	...	...
130	**Sežana 1305** a.	0557	0715	...	1013	...	*1510*	1630	...	...	1946	...	...

	Ⓐ		Ⓐ	⚒	⚒	Ⓐ	⚒		⑥N	Ⓑ	h	Ⓑ
Sežana 1305 d.	...	...	0517	0634a	1018a	...	1430a	1635	...	...	2000	2050
Nova Gorica a.	...	...	0610	0726a	1110a	...	1522a	1727	...	...	2051	2142
Nova Gorica d.	0317	0528	...	0735	1115	1414	1524	...	1808	1933	2100	...
Most na Soči d.	0357	0609	...	0817	1158	1456	1603	...	1854	2016	2141	...
Bohinjska Bistrica d.	0446	0652	...	0900	1248	1540	1643	...	1939	2058	2225	...
Bled Jezero d.	0507	0713	...	0922	1310	1600	1712	...	1959	2119	2247	...
Jesenice 1300 a.	0524	0729	...	0939	1327	1616	1728	...	2014	2135	2303	...

N – Conveys on ⑥: [2] Ljubljana - Jesenice - Nova Gorica and v.v.
W – Runs 22–28 minutes later on Ⓐ.
a – Ⓐ only.
h – ⑥ June 12 - Aug. 28.
j – ⑥ (not June 12 - Aug. 28).
m – Ⓐ (also ⑥ June 12 - Aug. 28).

1303 DIVAČA - PULA — 2nd class only HŽ, SŽ

km		Ⓐ	Ⓐ	q	1472 A		Ⓐz	Ⓐ	Ⓐ	Ⓐ	
	Ljubljana **1305** d.	...	...	...	0633	...	...	...	...	...	...
0	**Divača 1305** d.	...	...	...	0806	...	...	...	1505	...	...
12	Hrpelje-Kozina d.	...	...	...	0828	...	...	...	1520	...	...
48	Buzet 🏛 d.	...	0520q	0710	0914	1122	...	...	1554	1600	1956r
61	Lupoglav ▲ d.	0445	0540	0730	0928	1141	1324	1508	...	1619	2015
135	**Pula** a.	0620	0725	0907	1047	1313	1458	1647	...	1752	2146

	q	Ⓐz		Ⓐz	Ⓐ	Ⓐ		Ⓐ	Ⓐ	1473 A	
Pula d.	0505	0655	0920	...	1320	...	1427	1530	1720	1818	1935
Lupoglav ▲ a.	0641	0832	1056	1240	1500t	...	1609	1717	1902	1938	2114
Buzet 🏛 d.	0703	...	1115	1258	1528	1605	...	...	1922	2003	2133r
Hrpelje-Kozina d.	...	...	...	...	...	1644	...	...	...	2100	...
Divača 1305 a.	...	...	...	...	...	1658	...	...	...	2112	...
Ljubljana **1305** a.	...	...	...	...	...	...	...	...	...	2240	...

A – ISTRA – Apr. 24 - May 2, June 25 - Aug. 29: [2] Maribor (**1604/5**) - Hrpelje-Kozina - Pula and v.v.
q – ⚒ (daily June 19 - Aug. 27).
r – ⑦ Jan. 3 - Apr. 18, May 9 - June 13, Sept. 5 - Dec. 5 (also Dec. 13, 20; not Apr. 4).
t – Depart 1510.
z – Dec. 13-24, Jan. 11 - June 18, Aug. 30 - Dec. 11.

▲ – 🚌 service **Lupoglav - Rijeka and v.v.**: Journey 40 minutes. *Subject to alteration.*
From Lupoglav: 0645, 1100, 1610, 2110.
From Rijeka: 0600, 1015, 1425Ⓐ, 1520Ⓒ, 1920.

SŽ, HŽ — LJUBLJANA (- RIJEKA, KOPER) - SEŽANA - MONFALCONE — 1305

km		EN 240					481	1605	ICS 1011			IC 503								483		652			IC 509				
		♦⊖	2Ⓐ	2Ⓐp	2	2	♦	♦	♦[R]	2Ⓐ	2Ⓐ	♦	2	2Ⓐ	2Ⓐ	2Ⓐ	2	2Ⓐ	2Ⓐ	♦	2	2Ⓑ	2Ⓐ	2Ⓑ		2	2Ⓐ	2	2Ⓐ
	Maribor **1315** d.	...	...	...	...	...	...	0340	0540	...	...	0650	...	...	...	...	...	...	...	...	...	...	...	...	...	...	...	...	...
0	**Ljubljana** d.	0228	0425	...	0553	...	0620	0633	0740	0808	...	0933	...	1042	...	1210	1320	...	1433	1453	1540	1610	1653	...	1810	1854	1940	2040	2226
67	Postojna d.	0324	0530	...	0658	...	0718	0731	0830	0914	...	1028	...	1149	...	1316	1426	1454	1539	1554	1646	1708	1759	...	1911	2000	2047	2145	2331
80	Pivka d.	0336	0543	...	0712	...	0731	0743	0841	0927	0935	1040	...	1202	1206	1330	1439	1507	1552	1608	1659	1720	1812	1820	1923	2013	2100	2158	2343
	Ilirska Bistrica 🏛 d.	|	|	...	|	...	0758	|	|	|	0951	|	...	|	1222	|	|	1523	|	1632	|	|	|	1836	|	|	|	|	...
	Šapjane 🏛 d.	|	|	...	|	...	0825	|	|	|	...	|	...	|	...	|	|	...	|	1656	|	|	|	1857	|	|	|	|	...
	Rijeka 1310 a.	|	|	...	|	...	0854	|	|	|	...	|	...	|	...	|	|	...	|	1725	|	|	|	*1945*	|	|	|	|	...
104	Divača **1303** d.	0359	0608	0615	0736	0747	...	0806	0903	0951	...	1103	1108	1226	...	1354	1503	...	1616	...	1723	1742	1836	...	1947	2037	2124	2222	...
116	Hrpelje-Kozina ⊡ d.	|	|	0630	|	0800	...	0824	0914	|	...	1116	|	|	...	|	|	...	|	...	1736	|	|	...	1959	|	|	|	...
153	**Koper** ⊡ a.	|	|	0705	|	0836	...	0858	0945	|	...	1152	|	|	...	|	|	...	|	...	1811	|	|	...	2033	|	|	|	...
113	**Sežana** ▲ 🏛 a.	0408	0618	...	0746	...	...	...	...	1001	...	...	1118	1236	...	1404	1513	...	1626	...	...	1751	1847	...	...	2047	2134	2232	...
117	Villa Opicina ⊗ 🏛 a.	0426	...	...	...	...	...	...	...	...	...	...	...	...	...	...	...	...	...	...	...	...	...	...	...	...	...	...	...
150	**Monfalcone 605/6** a.	0542	...	...	...	...	...	...	...	...	...	...	...	...	...	...	...	...	...	...	...	...	...	...	...	...	...	...	...
	Venezia SL **605** a.	0716	...	...	...	...	...	...	...	...	...	...	...	...	...	...	...	...	...	...	...	...	...	...	...	...	...	...	...

km					IC 508							482					IC 502		ICS 1024		653					1604	480		EN 241
		2Ⓐ	2Ⓐ	2		2Ⓐ	2	2Ⓐ	2	2	2Ⓐ	♦	2Ⓐp	2Ⓐ	2Ⓐ	2	♦	2Ⓐ	♦[R]	2	2Ⓑ	2	2	2Ⓑ	2	♦	♦		♦⊖
	Venezia SL **605** d.	...	...	...	...	...	...	...	...	...	...	...	...	...	...	...	...	...	...	...	...	...	...	...	...	...	...	...	2120
	Monfalcone 605/6 d.	...	...	...	...	...	...	...	...	...	...	...	...	...	...	...	...	...	...	...	...	...	...	...	...	...	...	...	2259
	Villa Opicina ⊗ 🏛 d.	...	...	...	...	...	...	...	...	...	...	...	...	...	...	...	...	...	...	...	...	...	...	...	...	...	...	...	2348
	Sežana ▲ 🏛 d.	0440	0515	0600	...	...	0720	0923	1044	...	1248	...	...	...	1425	1520	...	1652	...	1732	1833	1950	...	...	...	...	...	...	0005
	Koper ⊡ d.	|	|	|	0523	...	|	|	|	1003	|	...	1328	...	|	|	1445	|	1639	|	|	|	...	...	1912	2010	...	...	|
	Hrpelje-Kozina ⊡ d.	|	|	|	0559	...	|	|	|	1036	|	...	1415	...	|	|	1520	|	1710	|	|	|	...	...	1947	2100	...	...	|
	Divača **1303** d.	0450	0526	0610	0612	...	0731	0934	1054	1101	1259	...	1428	...	1436	1530	1532	1703	1722	1743	1842	2000	...	...	2009	2112	...	...	|
0	**Rijeka 1310** d.	|	|	...	|	...	|	|	...	|	|	1250	...	...	|	...	|	|	|	|	|	...	1815	...	|	|	2045	...	|
28	Šapjane 🏛 d.	|	|	...	|	...	|	|	...	|	|	1333	...	...	|	...	|	|	|	|	|	...	1851	1921	|	|	2130	...	|
40	Ilirska Bistrica 🏛 d.	|	|	...	|	0632	|	|	...	|	|	1354	...	1418	|	...	|	|	|	|	|	...	...	1942	|	|	2200	...	|
56	Pivka d.	0514	0550	...	0636	0650	0754	0958	...	1125	1324	1410	...	1435	1500	...	1555	1727	1742	1807	1905	...	...	1958	2033	2134	2216	...	0035
	Postojna d.	0528	0603	...	0649	0702	|	1011	...	1138	1337	1422	...	1446	1513	...	1610	1740	1753	1820	1917	...	...	...	2046	2146	2228	...	0047
	Ljubljana a.	0634	0707	...	0748	0806	0910	1114	...	1242	1440	1518	...	...	1616	...	1704	1843	1843	1924	2017	...	...	...	2150	2240	2322	...	0140
	Maribor **1315** a.	...	...	...	...	...	...	...	...	...	...	...	...	...	...	...	1952	...	2043	...	...	...	...	...	...	0126	...	...	...

♦ – **NOTES** (LISTED BY TRAIN NUMBER)

240/1 – VENEZIA – 🛏 1,2 cl., 🛌 2 cl., [2] and ✖ Budapest - Zagreb - Ljubljana - Venezia and v.v.; 🛌 2 cl. Beograd (**412/3**) - Zagreb - Venezia and v.v. Conveys on dates in Table **97**: 🛏 1, 2 cl. Moskva / Kyïv (**15/6**) - Budapest - Venezia and v.v. Train **240** conveys ②⑤ June 18 - Aug. 27: 🛏 1, 2 cl., 🛌 2 cl. and [12] Budapest - Zagreb (**1204**) - Split.

480/1 – OPATIJA – [12] Rijeka - Ljubljana and v.v. Conveys Dec. 14 - 18, Jan. 1 - 6, Mar. 26 - Apr. 16, May 2 - Sept. 18 (from Rijeka, one day later from München): 🛌 2 cl. (also 🛏 1, 2 cl. June 20 - Sept. 19 from Rijeka, one day later from München) Rijeka - Ljubljana (**498/9**) - Salzburg (**462/3**) - München and v.v.

482/3 – LJUBLJANA – [12] Rijeka - Ljubljana and v.v.; [2] Rijeka - Ljubljana (**150/1**) - Wien and v.v.

502/3 – POHORJE – [12] and ✖ Koper - Maribor and v.v.; [12] Koper - Pragersko (**516/7**) - Hodoš and v.v.

1011/24 – ⑥ June 13 - Aug. 29: [12] and 🍷 Maribor - Koper and v.v.

1604/5 – Apr. 24 - May 2, June 25 - Aug. 29: [2] and ✖ Maribor - Koper; [2] Maribor - Hrpelje-Kozina (**1472/3**) - Pula and v.v.

m – Ⓐ (daily June 20 - Aug. 31).

p – Not Dec. 28 - 31, Feb. 22 - 26, Apr. 28 - 30, June 28 - Aug. 31, Oct. 25 - 29.

⊖ – [R] and special fares payable for journeys to / from Italy.

⊡ – 🚌 service (hourly 0630 – 1930) on ⚒ Koper - Trieste and v.v. An irregular 🚌 service also operates Trieste - Hrpelje-Kozina and v.v.

⊗ – 🚋 service (every 20 minutes, approximately 0700 – 2000) Villa Opicina (Stazione Trenovia) - Trieste (Piazza Oberdan) and v.v. Operator: Trieste Trasporti S.p.A. Villa Opicina tram terminus is ±20 minutes walk from railway station.

▲ – 🚌 service **Sežana - Trieste and v.v.**: Journey 28 minutes.
From **Sežana**: 0800◧, 0930◧, 1100◧, 1630♣, 1800♣, 1930♣.
From **Trieste** Autostazione: 0845◧, 1015◧, 1145◧, 1545♣, 1715♣, 1845♣.
Service subject to alteration. No service on ⑥⑦, Slovenian and Italian holidays.
Operators: ◧ – Avrigo D.D., Nova Gorica; ♣ – Trieste Trasporti S.p.A.

HŽ 2nd class only except where shown — RIJEKA - ZAGREB — 1310

km		1901		703				IC 501		701	
								[R] 🍷			
		L		T	⚒			R			
0	**Rijeka 1305** d.	0020	...	0545	...	*0735*	...	1200	1340	1710	...
61	Delnice d.	0129	...	0654	...	*0851*	...	1306	1454	1818	...
90	Moravice d.	0211	0625	0735	0802	0950	1128	1350	1551	1906	1937
120	Ogulin **1330** d.	0248	0702	0805	0838	1025	1202	1419	1626	1936	2010
176	Karlovac **1330** d.	0345	0810	0900	0947	1124	1316	1508	1741	2026	2112
229	**Zagreb 1330/40** a.	0425	0909	0938	1044	1216	1408	1551	1830	2105	2207
	Osijek **1340** a.	1119	...	1429	...	...	...	...	...	...	...

	1984		IC 500		700				702	
			[R] 🍷							
	M		R				Ⓐ		T	
Osijek **1340** d.	1932	...	...	...	...	...	...	...	1202	...
Zagreb 1330/40 d.	0108	0640	0635	0817	1231	1323	1426	1524	1650	1721
Karlovac **1330** d.	0151	0740	0715	0922	1314	1427	1532	1630	1728	1816
Ogulin **1330** d.	0245	0905	0806	1026	1402	1540	1640	1734	1816	1919
Moravice d.	0328	0936	0850	1110	1455	1610	1710	1804	1900	1955
Delnice d.	0357	...	0919	1143	1525	...	...	...	1931	...
Rijeka 1305 a.	0503	...	1022	1300	1628	...	...	...	2034	...

L – June 20 - Aug. 29: [2] Rijeka - Zagreb (**413**) - Vinkovci; [2] Rijeka - Zagreb (**783**) - Osijek; 🛌 2 cl. Rijeka - Zagreb (**241**) - Budapest.

M – June 18 - Aug. 27 (from Osijek, one day later from Zagreb): [2] Osijek - Zagreb - Rijeka; [2] Vinkovci (**412**) - Zagreb - Rijeka; 🛌 2 cl. Budapest (**240**) - Zagreb - Rijeka.

R – RIJEKA – [12] and 🍷 Zagreb - Rijeka and v.v.

T – [12] Osijek - Zagreb - Rijeka and v.v.

SŽ, MÁV 2nd class only except where shown — MARIBOR - ČAKOVEC, MURSKA SOBOTA and ZALAEGERSZEG — 1313

km										IC 247							640				1642	IC 518			IC 516		
		Ⓐ	Ⓐ	Ⓐ	Ⓐ	Ⓐ	Ⓐ	⑥	Ⓐ	C	Ⓐ	Ⓐ	g	Ⓐ	Ⓐ	Ⓐ	2	Ⓐ			y	P		Ⓐ	M	Ⓐ	Ⓐ
	Ljubljana **1315** d.	...	...	...	...	...	...	...	...	0650	...	...	...	...	...	...	...	...	...	...	1345	1515	...	...	1725	...	...
0	**Maribor 1315** d.	...	...	...	...	...	0700	0700	...	|	...	1034	1225	1225	1325	1440	...	...	1525	...	|	|	...	1827	|	...	2205
19	Pragersko **1315** d.	...	...	...	...	0617	|	0731	...	0907	...	1108	1257	1257	|	|	1450	...	|	...	1604	1722	...	|	1940	...	2236
37	Ptuj d.	...	...	...	...	0646	0746	0756	...	0921	...	1133	1320	1324	1407	1522	1504	...	1612	...	1634	1737	...	1915	1954	...	2302
59	Ormož d.	...	...	0449	0531	0709	0810	0819	0815	0940	1055	1157	1345	1349	1433	1544	1523	1548	1636	1640	1702	1755	1800	1941	2015	2024	2326
	Središče 🏛 d.	...	...	0503	|	▬	|	|	0826	|	|	▬	|	|	1444	▬	|	1559	|	1654	|	|	1811	...	|	2035	...
	Čakovec 1335 a.	...	...	0513	|	...	|	|	▬	|	|	...	|	|	▬	Ⓐ	|	...	|	1704	|	|	▬	...	|	...	...
98	**Murska Sobota** d.	0310	0510	▬	0624	...	0857	0906	...	1020	1141	...	1432	1435	...	1500	1607	...	1722	...	1751	1833	...	...	2105	...	...
127	Hodoš a.	0339	0545	...	...	...	...	...	...	1047	...	...	1459	...	...	1530	1634	...	...	...	...	1900	...	...	2139	...	...
127	Hodoš 🏛 d.	*0340*	*0600*	0813	...	1017	...	...	1151	1114	...	1406	...	...	1537	...	...	...	...	...	...	...	1910	...	...	...	...
174	**Zalaegerszeg** a.	*0500*	*0701*	0909	...	1117	...	...	1347	1151	...	1506	...	...	1639	...	...	...	...	...	...	...	2009	...	...	...	...
	Budapest D **1230** a.	...	...	...	...	...	...	...	...	1545	...	...	...	...	...	...	...	...	...	...	...	...	...	...	...	...	...

km			IC 519			IC 517																1641			IC 246		
			P	Ⓐ	Ⓐ	M	Ⓐ			Ⓐ	Ⓐ		Ⓐ	Ⓐ	Ⓐ	g	Ⓐ	Ⓐ		Ⓐ		g			C		Ⓐ
	Budapest D **1230** d.	...	...	...	...	...	...	...	...	...	...	...	...	...	...	...	...	...	...	...	...	...	...	...	1411	...	...
	Zalaegerszeg d.	...	...	...	...	...	...	0523	0730	1030	...	1131	...	...	...	...	...	...	1402	...	1535	...	...	1734	1812	2023	...
	Hodoš 🏛 a.	...	...	...	...	...	...	0621	0830	1130	...	1238	...	...	...	...	...	...	1500	...	1630	...	...	1827	1851	2122	...
	Hodoš d.	...	0420	...	...	0505	0557	▬	...	▬	...	▬	...	...	...	...	...	...	▬	1555	...	1700	...	▬	1910	...	2220
	Murska Sobota d.	...	0449	...	...	0540	0628	...	...	...	*0935*	...	1210	...	1455	1455	...	...	...	1630	...	1726	...	1755	1934	...	2248
0	**Čakovec 1335** d.	...	|	0525	...	|	|	...	...	Ⓐ	|	...	|	...	|	|	...	...	1713	...	...	|	...	|	|	...	...
12	Središče 🏛 d.	0430	|	0538	...	|	|	Ⓐ	...	1030	|	Ⓐ	|	1510	|	|	1607	...	1726	...	...	|	1827	|	|	...	...
22	Ormož d.	0442	0526	0550	0553	0627	0715	0718	...	1041	1045	1205	1258	1521	1547	1547	1618	1710	1738	...	...	1812	1838	1847	2012	...	...
	Ptuj d.	0507	0542	...	0618	0645	...	0746	...	...	1110	1229	1322	...	1614	1614	...	1736	...	...	...	1836	...	1912	2030	...	...
	Pragersko **1315** d.	0539	0609	...	0655	0717	...	0818	...	...	1144	1301	1359	...	1645	1645	...	1758	...	...	...	1909	...	1952	2102	...	...
	Maribor 1315 a.	0602	|	...	0717	|	...	0840	...	...	1207	1324	1422	...	1710	1710	...	...	...	...	...	|	...	2014	|	...	...
	Ljubljana **1315** a.	...	0810	...	...	0928	...	...	...	...	...	...	...	...	...	...	...	...	...	...	...	2112	...	...	2305	...	...

C – CITADELLA – [12] Budapest - Ljubljana and v.v.

M – MURA – [12] Koper (**502/3**) - Pragersko - Hodoš and v.v.

P – PTUJ – Ⓐ: [2] Ljubljana - Hodoš and v.v.

g – ⑦ Dec. 13 - June 20, Sept. 5 - Dec. 5 (also Feb. 8, Apr. 5, Nov. 1; not Dec. 27, Feb. 7, Apr. 4, 25, Oct. 31).

j – Arrive 1541.

y – ⑤ Dec. 14 - June 18, Sept. 3 - Dec. 12 (also Dec. 24; not Dec. 25, Jan. 1).

1315 LJUBLJANA and ZAGREB - MARIBOR - GRAZ

SŽ, HŽ, ÖBB

km		IC	ICS	IC	IC	ICS	EC		ICS	EC	IC		IC		ICS	IC		EC	ICS	IC	ICS	ICS	ICS			
		250	12	252	247	14	158		18	256	506		258	1642	20	518		150	22	502	1124	1024	26		604	1604
		🍷	[R]	🍷		[R]	🍴	2	[R]	🍴		2			[R]	2		🍴	[R]	🍴	[R]	[R]	[R]	2		
					◆		◆							y		◆		◆	Ⓐ	◆	t	◆			w	◆
	Rijeka **1305** d.	...	...	...	...	...	...	...	...	...	...	...	...	...	...	...	...	1250	...	...	...	...	...	...	...	...
0	**Ljubljana 1300** d.	...	0545	...	0650	0805	...	1050	1213	...	1235	1250	...	1345	1445	1515	...	1600	1650	1725	1850	1850	1945	2050	2225	2255
*	**Zagreb 1300** d.	...	|	...	|	|	0725	|	|	...	|	|	...	|	|	|	...	|	|	|	|	|	|	|	|	|
	Dobova **1300** 🛃 d.	...	|	...	|	|	0813	|	|	...	|	|	...	|	|	|	...	|	|	|	|	|	|	|	|	|
	Sevnica **1300** d.	...	|	...	|	|	0839	|	|	...	|	|	...	|	|	|	...	|	|	|	|	|	|	|	|	|
64	Zidani Most **1300** d.	...	0630	...	0747	0850	|	1200	1259	...	1331	1400	...	1442	1531	1608	...	1654	1735	1825	1935	1935	2030	2153	2334	2357
89	Celje d.	...	0650	...	0815	0910	0918	1225	1319	...	1358	1428	...	1510	1550	1638	...	1719	1756	1851	1956	1956	2050	2219	0001	0025
137	Pragersko **1313** d.	...	0722	...	0857	0941	0959	1311	1354	...	1444	1516	...	1551	1624	1719	...	1758	1830	1936	2030	2030	2124	2308	0045	0109
156	**Maribor 1313** a.	...	0736	...	...	0953	1014	1331	1406	...	1502	1541	...	...	1635	...	...	1814	1843	1952	2043	2043	2138	2327	0102	0126
156	**Maribor** d.	0619	...	0821	...	...	1022	...	...	1422	...	...	1621	...	...	...	...	1821	...	...	...	...	...	...	...	...
172	Spielfeld-Straß 🛃 a.	0637	...	0839	...	...	1039	...	...	1439	...	...	1639	...	...	...	...	1839	...	...	...	...	...	...	...	...
172	Spielfeld-Straß 🛃 d.	0649	...	0851	...	...	1051	...	...	1451	...	...	1651	...	...	...	...	1851	...	...	...	...	...	...	...	...
219	**Graz Hbf** a.	0723	...	0923	...	...	1123	...	...	1523	...	...	1723	...	...	...	...	1923	...	...	...	...	...	...	...	...
	Wien Meidling **980** a.	0958	...	1158	...	...	1358	...	...	1758	...	...	1958	...	...	...	...	2158	...	...	...	...	...	...	...	...

				ICS	ICS	IC	IC	IC	ICS		EC	ICS	EC		IC	ICS		IC	ICS			ICS	EC		IC
	605	1605		607	11	1011	519	503	251	13		151	17	255		257	19	1611	259	21	1615	1641	23	159	1613	246
			2	2	[R]	[R]	2		🍴	[R]	2	🍴	[R]	🍴	2		[R]	2		[R]	2	2	[R]	🍴	2	
	w	◆		Ⓐ	x	◆	◆	◆				◆						g		Ⓐ	g	g		◆	g	◆
Wien Meidling **980** d.	...	...	...	...	...	...	...	...	...	...	...	0803	...	1003	...	1203	...	...	1403	...	...	...	...	1603	...	...
Graz Hbf d.	...	...	...	...	...	...	...	...	0634	...	...	1036	...	1236	...	1436	...	...	1638	...	...	...	...	1838	...	...
Spielfeld-Straß 🛃 a.	...	...	...	...	...	...	...	...	0709	...	...	1109	...	1309	...	1509	...	...	1709	...	...	...	...	1909	...	...
Spielfeld-Straß 🛃 d.	...	...	...	...	...	...	...	...	0721	...	...	1121	...	1321	...	1521	...	...	1721	...	...	...	...	1921	...	...
Maribor a.	...	...	...	...	...	...	...	...	0739	...	...	1138	...	1338	...	1538	...	...	1739	...	...	...	...	1938	...	...
Maribor 1313 d.	0340	0340	0515	0440	0540	0540	...	0650	...	0817	1015	1146	1245	...	1520	...	1545	1620	...	1650	1800	...	1945	1955	2005	...
Pragersko **1313** d.	0357	0357	0535	0457	0555	0555	0609	0717	...	0831	1035	1202	1259	...	1539	...	1559	1639	...	1703	1817	1909	1959	2011	2021	2102
Celje d.	0441	0441	0621	0545	0633	0633	0652	0759	...	0906	1123	1241	1335	...	1623	...	1635	1724	...	1735	1859	1950	2035	2049	2102	2142
Zidani Most **1300** d.	0507	0507	0645	0611	0654	0654	0718	0829	...	0925	1147	1308	1354	...	1647	...	1654	1750	...	1754	1926	2015	2054	|	2128	2206
Sevnica **1300** d.	|	|	...	|	|	|	|	|	...	|	...	|	|	...	...	...	|	|	...	|	|	|	|	2127	|	|
Dobova **1300** 🛃 d.	|	|	...	|	|	|	|	|	...	|	...	|	|	...	...	...	|	|	...	|	|	|	|	2205	|	|
Zagreb 1300 a.	|	|	...	|	|	|	|	|	...	|	...	|	|	...	...	...	|	|	...	|	|	|	|	2234	|	|
Ljubljana 1300 a.	0607	0607	...	0713	0738	0738	0810	0928	...	1009	...	1406	1438	...	...	...	1738	1843	...	1838	2022	2112	2138	...	2222	2305
Rijeka **1305** a.	...	...	...	...	...	...	...	...	...	...	...	1725	...	...	...	...	...	...	...	...	...	...	...	...	...	...

ADDITIONAL SERVICES MARIBOR - ZIDANI MOST and v.v.: 2nd class only

	Ⓐ	Ⓐ	Ⓐ	Ⓐ	Ⓐ	Ⓐ		Ⓐ		Ⓐ	Ⓐ		Ⓑ	
Maribor d.	0615	0715	0755	1120	1215	1315	1415	1615	1715	1815	1920	2015	2100	2220
Pragersko d.	0635	0735	0814	1140	1235	1335	1435	1635	1735	1835	1938	2035	2119	2240
Celje d.	0723	0823	0910	1228	1323	1422	1523	1723	1823	1923	2023	2123	2207	2326
Zidani Most d.	0747	0847	0934	1252	1347	1447	1547	1747	1847	1947	2047	2147	2232	...

	Ⓐ		Ⓐ	Ⓐ	Ⓐ	Ⓐ	Ⓐ	Ⓐ			Ⓐ			Ⓐ
Zidani Most d.	0557	0700	0800	0918	1000	1100	1304	1500	1600	1700	1800	1900	2000	2100
Celje d.	0622	0725	0825	0943	1025	1125	1329	1525	1625	1725	1825	1925	2025	2125
Pragersko d.	0710	0811	0912	1030	1109	1209	1415	1612	1712	1812	1912	2012	2112	2212
Maribor a.	0730	0831	0933	1050	1128	1228	1436	1633	1733	1833	1933	2033	2133	2233

◆ – **NOTES** (LISTED BY TRAIN NUMBER)

150/1 – EMONA – [12] and 🍴 Ljubljana - Wien and v.v.; [2] Rijeka (**482/3**) - Ljubljana - Wien and v.v.
158/9 – CROATIA – [12] and 🍴 Zagreb - Wien and v.v.
246/7 – CITADELLA – [12] Budapest - Ljubljana and v.v.
502/3 – POHORJE – [12] and 🍴 Koper - Maribor and v.v.; [12] Koper - Pragersko (**516/7**) - Hodoš and v.v.
518/9 – PTUJ – Ⓐ: [2] Ljubljana - Hodoš and v.v.
1011/24 – ⑥ June 13 - Aug. 29: [12] and 🍷 Maribor - Koper and v.v.
1604/5 – ISTRA – Apr. 24 - May 2, June 25 - Aug. 29: [2] and 🍴 Maribor - Koper; [2] Maribor - Hrpelje-Kozina (**1472/3**) - Pula and v.v.

g – ⑦ Dec. 13 - June 20, Sept. 5 - Dec. 5 (also Feb. 8, Apr. 5, Nov. 1; not Dec. 27, Feb. 7, Apr. 4, 25, Oct. 31).
t – ⑦ Dec. 14 - June 6, Sept. 5 - Dec. 11 (also Feb. 8, Apr. 5, Nov. 1; not Feb. 7, Apr. 4, 25, Oct. 31).
w – Dec. 14 - Apr. 23, May 3 - June 24, Aug. 30 - Dec. 11.

x – Not ⑥ June 13 - Aug. 29.
y – ⑤ Dec. 14 - June 18, Sept. 3 - Dec. 12 (also Dec. 24; not Dec. 25, Jan. 1).
***** – Zagreb - Celje: *104 km*.

1320 ZAGREB - VINKOVCI - BEOGRAD

SŽ, HŽ, ŽS

km								EC	IC		
		413	741	415	743	450	745	211	551	747	315
		🍴		🍴	🍷			🍴	[R] 🍷		
		◆	◆	◆		◆		◆			◆
	Ljubljana **1300** d.	...	...	0815	...	...	...	1448	...	...	2115
0	**Zagreb** d.	0603	0900	1058	1321	...	1515	1725	1820	2112	2355
105	Novska d.	0740	1033	1237	1458	...	1654	1858	|	2244	0128
191	Slavonski Brod d.	0839	1131	1335	1556	...	1752	1955	2035	2349	0227
224	Strizivojna-Vrpolje **1345** d.	0856	1149	1353	1614	1657	1809	2012	2052	0011	0246
	Osijek **1345** a.	|	|	|	|	|	|	|	2142	|	|
256	**Vinkovci** d.	0931	1209	1423	1634	1723	1829	2042	...	0035	0321
288	Šid 🛃 d.	1036	...	1533	...	1830	...	2144	...	...	0433
407	**Beograd** a.	1218	...	1720	...	2018	...	2327	...	...	0619

			IC			EC					
	314	740	550	742	744	210	451	746	414	748	412
			[R] 🍷			🍴			🍴	🍷	🍴
	◆					◆	◆		◆	◆	◆
Beograd d.	2140	...	...	...	...	0545	0815	...	1020	...	1525
Šid 🛃 d.	0058	...	...	...	...	0853	1118	...	1338	...	1833
Vinkovci d.	0144	0304	...	0603	0740	0945	1205	1248	1445	1724	1930
Osijek **1345** d.	|	|	0522	|	|	|	|	|	|	|	|
Strizivojna-Vrpolje **1345** d.	0204	0329	0614	0623	0800	1005	1225	1308	1505	1749	1950
Slavonski Brod d.	0221	0352	0632	0641	0817	1023	...	1325	1522	1811	2008
Novska d.	0320	0458	|	0743	0915	1121	...	1424	1618	1914	2105
Zagreb a.	0453	0639	0846	0918	1052	1254	...	1600	1755	2051	2244
Ljubljana **1300** a.	0723	...	...	...	...	1517	...	...	2039	...	...

◆ – **NOTES** (LISTED BY TRAIN NUMBER)

210/1 – SAVA – [12] Beograd - Villach (**110/1**) - München and v.v.; 🍴 Beograd - Jesenice and v.v.
314/5 – 🛏 1, 2 cl., ▬ 2 cl. and [12] Beograd - Zagreb - Ljubljana - Villach and v.v.
412 – NIKOLA TESLA – [12] and 🍴 Beograd - Zagreb; ▬ 2 cl. Beograd - Zagreb (**240**) - Venezia. Conveys June 18 - Aug. 27: [2] Vinkovci - Zagreb (**1984**) - Rijeka.
413 – NIKOLA TESLA – [12] and 🍴 Zagreb - Beograd; ▬ 2 cl. Venezia (**241**) - Zagreb - Beograd. Conveys June 19 - Sept. 4 (from Split and Zadar, following day from Zagreb): [2] Split (**1822**) - Zagreb - Vinkovci; [2] Zadar (**1920**) - Knin (**1822**) - Zagreb - Vinkovci. Also conveys June 20 - Aug. 29 (from Rijeka and Zagreb): [2] Rijeka (**1901**) - Zagreb - Vinkovci.
414 – [2] Beograd - Schwarzach-St Veit (**464**) - Zürich; 🛏 1, 2 cl. and ▬ 2 cl. Zagreb - Schwarzach-St Veit - Zürich; [2] Beograd - Zagreb (**498**) - Salzburg (**462**) - München; [12] and 🍴 Beograd - Ljubljana - Villach.
415 – [2] Zürich (**465**) - Schwarzach-St Veit - Beograd; 🛏 1, 2 cl. and ▬ 2 cl. Zürich (**465**) - Schwarzach-St Veit - Zagreb; [2] München (**463**) - Salzburg (**499**) - Zagreb - Beograd; [12] and 🍴 Villach - Ljubljana - Beograd.
450/1 – ▬ 2 cl., [2] and 🍷 Beograd - Sarajevo and v.v.
741 – [12] Zagreb - Vinkovci; [2] München (**463**) - Salzburg (**499**) - Zagreb - Vinkovci.
748 – [12] and 🍷 Vinkovci - Zagreb; [2] Vinkovci - Zagreb (**498**) - Salzburg (**462**) - München. Conveys June 18 - Sept. 3: [2] Vinkovci - Zagreb (**1823**) - Split; [2] Vinkovci - Zagreb (**1823**) - Knin (**1921**) - Zadar.

1322 Subject to alteration — LOCAL SERVICES in Croatia

2nd class only HŽ

ZAGREB - SISAK CAPRAG and v.v.: Journey 60–75 minutes. All services call at Sisak (6 minutes from Sisak Caprag).
From Zagreb: 0543, 0648, 0748Ⓐ, 1048, 1146Ⓐ, 1349, 1448Ⓐ, 1548, 1647Ⓐ, 1748Ⓐ, 1842, 1948, 2046Ⓐ, 2249.
From Sisak Caprag: 0411⚒, 0513, 0617, 0718, 0818Ⓐ, 1018Ⓐ, 1217, 1418Ⓐ, 1518, 1618Ⓐ, 1718, 1818Ⓐ, 1919, 2116.

SISAK CAPRAG - SUNJA and v.v.: Journey 25 minutes.
From Sisak Caprag: 0342, 0722, 0803, 1218, 1456, 1659, 1920Ⓐ, 1957.
From Sunja: 0449, 0553, 0654, 1153, 1255, 1635, 1855, 2052, 2133Ⓐ.

SUNJA - NOVSKA and v.v.: Journey 70 minutes.
From Sunja: 0827, 1242Ⓐ**q**, 1530, 2031.
From Novska: 0443, 0544, 1043, 1403Ⓐ**q**, 1731.

q – Not June 13 - Aug. 30.

HŽ 2nd class only except where shown ZAGREB - ZADAR, ŠIBENIK and SPLIT 1330

km						ICN				ICN				ICN														
						521				1523				525				1823	1823				825		825			1204
																		1921							5831			
						[R] 🍷				[R] 🍷				[R] 🍷														
					Ⓐ q	S		Ⓐ		S w				S			x	A	♦				♦	x	C	h		♦
0	**Zagreb 1310** .. d.	...	...	...	...	0750	...	...	...	1115	...	...	...	1519	...	...	...	2133	2133	...	...	...	2250	...	2250	...	...	2332
53	Karlovac **1310** d.	...	...	...	...	0826	...	...	...	1155	...	...	...	1600	...	...	...	2213	2213	...	...	...	2329	...	2339	...	...	│
109	**Ogulin 1310**... d.	...	...	...	...	0916	...	...	...	│	...	...	...	│	...	...	...	2310	2310	...	...	...	0026	...	0026	...	...	0107
225	Gospić .... d.	...	...	...	...	1055	...	...	...	1355	...	...	...	1801	...	...	...	0130	0130	...	...	...	0250	...	0250	...	...	│
269	Gračac .... d.	...	...	...	...	1129	...	...	...	│	...	...	...	1835	...	...	...	0213	0213	...	...	...	0328	...	0328	...	...	│
333	Knin .... a.	...	...	...	...	1221	...	...	...	1516	...	...	...	1926	...	...	...	0326	0326	...	...	...	0441	...	0441	...	...	0531
333	Knin .... d.	0728	...	1117	...	1222	...	1249	...	1517	1539	...	1645	1927	1951	...	...	0339	0338	0406	0417	...	0442	...	0442	...	0525	0533
	Zadar .. ⊡ a.	│	...	1331	...	│	...	1510	...	│	│	...	1859	│	│	...	...	0540	│	│	0632	...	│	...	│	...	0745	│
387	Perković ...... a.	0834	...	...	...	1306	...	...	...	1604	1658	...	...	2010	2058	...	...	...	0440	0512	...	...	0545	...	0545	...	▬	0644
387	Perković .... d.	0835	0839	...	1223	1307	1310	...	1500	1605	1700	1720	...	2011	2103	2104	2325	...	0444	...	...	0526	0556	0548	0600	0600	0710	0646
	Šibenik... ⊡ a.	0903	│	...	│	│	1338	...	1528	│	1728	│	...	│	2131	│	2349	...	│	...	...	│	│	0616	0628	0628	0738	│
435	**Split**.......... ⊡ a.	...	0941	...	1330	1349	...	...	...	1651	...	1825	...	2052	...	2213	...	...	0549	...	...	0631	0656	...	...	...	...	0746

							ICN			ICN				ICN														
							520			1522				524				1205				1920	1822			5826	824	
																						1822				824		
							[R] 🍷			[R] 🍷				[R] 🍷														
			x				S		Ⓐ q	S w				S			Ⓐ	♦	z			B	♦	y		D	♦	
Split .... ⊡ d.	0400	...	...	...	0653	...	0755	...	0955	1053	...	...	...	1500	...	1520	...	1609	...	1940	...	...	2047	...	...	...	2207	...
Šibenik... ⊡ d.	│	0431	0626	...	│	0756	│	1010	│	│	1418	...	...	│	1537	│	...	│	...	│	2015	...	│	...	2235	2235	│	...
Perković ....a.	0505	0504	0700	...	0804	0831	0837	1044	1100	1133	1450	...	...	1542	1612	1623	...	1717	...	2052	2050	...	2156	...	2308	2308	2317	...
Perković ....d.	...	0514	...	...	...	0850	0838	...	...	1134	...	...	...	1543	1625	...	...	1718	...	...	2100	...	2157	...	...	2328	2328	...
Zadar .. ⊡ d.	...	│	...	0643	...	│	│	...	...	│	...	1014	1407	│	│	...	1542	│	1950	...	│	2045	│	2117	...	│	│	...
Knin...............a.	...	0627	...	0900	...	0958	0923	...	...	1218	...	1231	1626	1628	1732	...	1800	1820	2202	...	2209	2242	2303	2330	...	0034	0034	...
Knin...............d.	...	...	...	...	...	...	0924	...	...	1223	...	...	...	1629	...	...	...	1822	...	...	...	2314	2314	...	...	0035	0035	...
Gračac............d.	...	...	...	...	...	...	1020	...	...	│	...	...	...	1724	...	...	...	│	...	...	...	0048	0048	...	...	0210	0210	...
Gospić.............d.	...	...	...	...	...	...	1053	...	...	1356	...	...	...	1802	...	...	...	│	...	...	...	0133	0133	...	...	0249	0249	...
Ogulin 1310....d.	...	...	...	...	...	...	1231	...	...	│	...	...	...	│	...	...	...	2311	...	...	...	0409	0409	...	...	0502	0502	...
Karlovac **1310**..d.	...	...	...	...	...	...	1313	...	...	1604	...	...	...	2006	...	...	...	│	...	...	...	0459	0459	...	...	0553	0553	...
Zagreb 1310 ...a.	...	...	...	...	...	...	1348	...	...	1649	...	...	...	2042	...	...	...	0044	...	...	...	0538	0538	...	...	0631	0631	...

FOR NOTES SEE BELOW TABLE 1340

HŽ, MÁV 2nd class only except where shown ZAGREB - VARAŽDIN - NAGYKANIZSA 1335

km					992								994	790		IC 590									
				⚒							Ⓐ	Ⓐ		⚒		[R] Z			Ⓐ					⚒	⑦
0	**Zagreb** .... d.	...	...	0431	0716	...	0927	...	...	1121	...	1313	1410	1512	1525	1624	...	...	1623	...	1800	1913	2101	2223	...
38	Zabok .... d.	...	...	0546	0807	...	1036	...	...	1220	...	1420	1512	1604	1630	k	←	...	1732	...	1918	2020	2207	2319	...
104	**Varaždin** .... ▲ d.	0554	...	0744	0941	1023	1210	1307	...	1423f	1521	1601	1640	1719	1807	1819	1906	...	1929	2003	2055	2214p	2334	0046	0051
115	Čakovec **1313**........... d.	0606	...	0758	0953	1034	...	1319	...	1439	1538	...	1652	1737	→	1829	1919	...	...	2016	2105	2225	...	...	0101
145	Kotoriba .... 🛃 d.	0645	...	0832	1026	1107	...	1353	...	1519	1614	...	1729	1807	...	...	1959	2056	...	2051	...	2257	...	...	...
151	Murakeresztúr....... 🛃 d.	*0654*	0740	...	...	...	...	...	1545	...	...	...	...	...	...	...	...	2103	...	...	...	...	...	...	...
165	**Nagykanizsa**............ a.	...	0750	...	...	...	...	...	1600	...	...	...	...	...	...	...	...	...	...	...	...	...	...	...	...

				991	IC 591		791													995		997			
			⚒		[R] Z		⚒		⚒		Ⓐ	⚒			Ⓐ	⚒	⚒			K					
Nagykanizsa............. d.	...	...	...	...	...	...	...	...	...	...	...	...	1048	...	...	...	...	...	...	...	...	...	1843	...	...
Murakeresztúr........ 🛃 d.	...	...	...	...	...	...	...	*0729*	...	...	...	...	1103	...	...	...	...	...	...	...	...	...	1853	*2113*	...
Kotoriba .... 🛃 d.	...	...	...	0442	...	0553d	0650	0742	...	...	1110	1158	...	1239	...	...	1403a	1450	...	1700	1815a	1907	...	2121	2210
Čakovec **1313**........... d.	...	...	...	0519	0531	0634d	0727	0822	1005	...	1151	1234	...	1320	1404	...	1437	1534	...	1736	1853	1950	...	2155	2249
Varaždin .... ▲ d.	0258	0348	0431	0535	0543	0647	0743	0832	1015	1035	1213	1244	...	1330	1414	1420	1447	1544	1547	1753	1914	2004	...	2205	2259
Zabok ....d.	0432	0519	0630	0700	k	0835	0904	...	...	1221	1351	...	...	...	...	1605	...	...	1731	1917	2051	2130	...	...	...
Zagreb ....a.	0529	0622	0729	0758	0736	0931	0952	...	...	1320	1455	...	...	...	...	1706	...	...	1833	2013	2149	2220	...	...	...

▲ – **VARAŽDIN - KOPRIVNICA and v.v.** 2nd class only except where shown:

km			Z			Ⓐ			⑦Q			
0	Varaždin............d.	0440	0543	0650	1029	1253	1417	1609	1702	1907	2220	...
42	Koprivnica..........a.	0530	0617	0735	1117	1343	1504	1656	1752	1954	2306	...

	⚒					Ⓐ			Z	⑦Q			
Koprivnica ....d.	0444	0534	0840	1150	1256	1413	1517	1706	1742	1815	1906	2004	2155
Varaždin..........a.	0532	0633	0927	1237	1343	1505	1605	1750	1817	1900	1954	2049	2248

FOR NOTES SEE BELOW TABLE 1340

HŽ, MÁV ZAGREB - KOPRIVNICA - NAGYKANIZSA and OSIJEK 1340

km			EN					IC	IC	IC	IC		
		1205	241	783	205	703	981	201	284	590	581	971	995
		♦	V	♦	♦	🍷	2	♦	♦	[R] Z	[R] 🍷	2	K
	Rijeka **1310** ....d.	...	...	0020d	...	0545	...	...	...	...	...	...	...
0	**Zagreb** ....d.	0055	0456	0656	1000	1000	1300	1545	1545	1624	1701	1825	2015
57	Križevci ....d.	0135	0537	0740	1043	1043	1355	1625	1625	1703	1739	1918	2114
88	Koprivnica **1335**..........d.	0206	0611	0818	1121	1122	1442	1700	1700	1732	1821	1959	2151
103	Gyékényes .... 🛃 d.	0241	0645	│	1210	│	│	1756	1737	...	│	...	...
132	**Nagykanizsa** ....a.	0305	0714	│	1220	│	│	1820	1802	...	│	...	...
	Budapest K **1220** ......a.	0659	1059	│	1609	│	│	2229	...	...	│	...	...
153	Virovitica.....................d.	...	...	0923	...	1225	1601	...	...	...	1920	...	...
225	Našice ....d.	...	...	1037	...	1346	1737	...	...	...	2030	...	...
275	**Osijek 1345** ....a.	...	...	1119	...	1429	1830	...	...	...	2111	...	...

		IC	IC	IC	IC				EN	
	980	591	580	200	285	702	204	782	240	1984
	2	[R] Z	[R] 🍷	♦	♦	🍷	♦	♦	V	♦
Osijek 1345 .... d.	0005	...	0525	...	...	1202	...	1620	...	1932
Našice......................... d.	0053	...	0607	...	...	1246	...	1705	...	2032
Virovitica .... d.	0215	...	0718	...	...	1401	...	1820	...	2207
Budapest K **1220** ... d.	│	...	│	0630	...	│	1305	│	1700	│
Nagykanizsa .... d.	│	...	│	1025	1040	│	1707	│	2042	│
Gyékényes........ 🛃 d.	│	...	│	1125	1125	│	1758	│	2134	│
Koprivnica **1335** .... d.	0331	0625	0827	1145	1145	1508	1816	1944	2152	2330
Križevci .... d.	0410	0655	0857	1216	1216	1538	1846	2014	2223	0012
Zagreb..................... a.	0505	0736	0936	1259	1259	1622	1936	2056	2307	0053
Rijeka **1310** .... a.	...	...	...	...	...	2034	...	...	...	0503

♦ – **NOTES FOR TABLES 1330/35/40** (LISTED BY TRAIN NUMBER)

200/1 – KVARNER – [12] and ✕ Zagreb - Budapest; [12] Zagreb - Nagykanizsa (**284/5**) - Wien and v.v.
204/5 – MAESTRAL – [12] Budapest - Gyékényes - Zagreb and v.v. Conveys on dates in Table **97**: 🛏 1, 2 cl. Moskva / Kyïv / St Peterburg - Budapest - Zagreb and v.v.
284 – ZAGREB – [12] Zagreb (**200/1**) - Nagykanizsa - Wien and v.v.
782 – [12] and 🍷 Osijek - Zagreb. Conveys June 18 - Sept. 3: [2] Osijek - Zagreb (**1823**) - Split.
783 – [12] and 🍷 Zagreb - Osijek. Conveys June 19 - Sept. 4 (from Split, one day later from Zagreb): [2] Split (**1822**) - Zagreb - Osijek.
824/5 – 🛏 1, 2 cl. and [2] Split - Zagreb and v.v.
1204 – ADRIA – ②⑤ June 18 - Aug. 27 (from Zagreb): 🛏 1, 2 cl., ▬ 2 cl. and [12] Budapest (**240**) - Zagreb - Split.
1205 – ADRIA – ③⑥ June 19 - Aug. 28 (from Split): 🛏 1, 2 cl., ▬ 2 cl. and [12] Split - Zagreb - Budapest.
1822 – June 19 - Sept. 4: 🛏 1, 2 cl. and [2] Split - Zagreb; [2] Split - Zagreb (**413**) - Vinkovci; [2] Split - Zagreb (**783**) - Osijek; 🛏 1, 2 cl., ▬ 2 cl. and [2] Split - Zagreb (**783**) - Koprivnica (**1474**) - Bratislava - Praha.
1823 – June 18 - Sept. 3: 🛏 1, 2 cl. and [2] Zagreb - Split; [2] Vinkovci (**748**) - Zagreb - Split; [2] Osijek (**782**) - Zagreb - Split; 🛏 1, 2 cl., ▬ 2 cl. and [2] Praha (**1475**) - Bratislava - Zagreb - Split.
1984 – June 18 - Aug. 27: [2] Osijek - Zagreb - Rijeka.

A – June 18 - Sept. 3 (from Vinkovci and Zagreb, one day later from Knin): [2] Vinkovci (**748**) - Zagreb (**1823**) - Knin (**1921**) - Zadar.
B – June 19 - Sept. 4: [2] Zadar (**1920**) - Knin (**1822**) - Zagreb (**413**) - Vinkovci.
C – June 18 - Sept. 3: [2] Zagreb (**825**) - Perković (**5831**) - Šibenik.
D – June 19 - Sept. 4: [2] Šibenik (**5828**) - Perković (**824**) - Zagreb.
K – [2] Kotoriba - Zagreb - Koprivnica.
Q – Also Apr. 5, Nov. 1; not Apr. 4, Oct. 31.
S – [12] and 🍷 Zagreb - Split and v.v. [R].
V – VENEZIA – For days of running and composition – see Table **1305**.
Z – Ⓐ: [2] Čakovec - Zagreb and v.v. [R].

a – Ⓐ only.
d – ⚒ only.
f – Arrive 1349.
h – June 5 - Sept. 4.
k – Via Koprivnica.
p – Arrive 2156.
q – Not June 19 - Aug. 29.
w – June 11 - Sept. 12.
x – Not June 5 - Sept. 4.
y – Not June 19 - Sept. 4.
z – June 19 - Sept. 4.

⊡ – Frequent 🚌 services operate Zadar - Šibenik - Split and v.v.; some continue to Ploče and Dubrovnik. Bus station locations: Zadar, Split and Ploče are adjacent to rail station, Šibenik approximately 10 minutes walk.

1345 PÉCS - OSIJEK - DOBOJ

2nd class only except where shown HŽ, MÁV, ŽRS

km							8110				451				259					8114				
				Ⓐ							A	⚒			B									
	Budapest K **1200** d.	...	...	...	...	...	...	...	...	...	...	...	...	...	0945	...	...	...	...	...	...	...	...	...
0	**Pécs** d.	...	...	...	...	...	0640	...	...	...	...	...	...	...	1300	...	...	...	...	1652	...	...	...	...
43	Magyarbóly 🛃 d.	...	...	...	...	...	0755	...	...	...	...	...	...	...	1402	...	...	...	...	1810	...	...	...	...
54	Beli Manastir 🛃 d.	0421	...	0543	0703	...	0807	0820	...	1053	...	1224	...	1410	1430	...	...	1606	...	1822	1843	...	2005	2230
82	**Osijek 1340** a.	0453	...	0615	0735	...	...	0852	...	1125	...	1256	...	1442	1457	...	...	1639	...	...	1915	...	2038	2302
82	**Osijek 1340** d.	...	...	...	...	0749	...	...	...	...	...	...	1415	...	1458	...	1628	...	...	...	...	1940	...	...
	Vinkovci a.	...	...	...	...	0833	...	...	...	...	1205	...	1459	...	|	...	1712	...	...	...	...	2024	...	...
130	Strizivojna-Vrpolje **1320** d.	...	...	...	...	...	...	...	...	...	1226	...	...	...	1550	...	...	...	...	...	...	...	...	...
150	Slavonski Šamac 🛃 d.	...	...	...	...	...	...	...	...	...	1300	...	...	...	1630	...	...	...	...	...	...	...	...	...
154	Šamac 🛃 d.	...	0454	...	...	...	...	...	1016	...	1321	...	...	...	1659	...	...	...	...	...	...	...	...	...
226	**Doboj 1350** a.	...	0625	...	...	...	...	...	1206	...	1430	...	...	...	1800	...	...	...	...	...	...	...	...	...

km								8117				258		450						8111				
		Ⓐ		⚒						⚒		B		A										
	Doboj 1350 d.	...	...	...	0732	...	...	...	...	...	...	1005	...	1440	...	...	...	1537	...	...	...	...	1950	...
	Šamac 🛃 d.	...	...	...	0903	...	...	...	...	...	...	1122	...	1606	...	...	...	1748	...	...	...	...	2127	...
	Slavonski Šamac 🛃 d.	...	...	...	...	...	...	...	...	...	...	1145	...	1640	...	...	...	...	...	...	...	...	...	...
	Strizivojna-Vrpolje **1320** d.	...	...	...	...	...	...	...	...	...	...	1203	...	1657	...	...	...	...	...	...	...	...	...	...
0	Vinkovci d.	...	...	0537	...	0641	...	...	...	...	1156	|	...	1717	...	...	1510	...	...	...	1730	...	...	...
35	**Osijek 1340** a.	...	...	0621	...	0725	...	...	...	...	1240	1252	...	...	...	...	1554	...	...	...	1814	...	...	...
	Osijek 1340 d.	0503	0624	...	...	...	0741	...	1010	1144	...	1259	...	...	1320	1527	...	...	1802	...	...	1924	...	2150
	Beli Manastir 🛃 d.	0534	0655	...	...	...	0812	0848	1041	1215	...	1343	...	...	1351	1558	...	...	1833	1900	...	1955	...	2221
	Magyarbóly 🛃 d.	...	...	...	...	...	...	0916	...	...	...	1417	...	...	...	...	...	...	...	1932	...	...	...	...
	Pécs d.	...	...	...	...	...	...	1019	...	...	...	1457	...	...	...	...	...	...	...	2039	...	...	...	...
	Budapest K **1200** d.	...	...	...	...	...	...	...	...	...	...	1814	...	...	...	...	...	...	...	...	...	...	...	...

A – 🛏 2 cl., (2) and 🍷 Beograd - Sarajevo and v.v.
B – DRAVA – (12) Budapest - Pécs - Osijek - Sarajevo and v.v.

1350 ZAGREB - DOBOJ - SARAJEVO

2nd class only except where shown HŽ, ŽFBH, ŽRS

km														451	397						259				399
														A	Z						B				S
0	**Zagreb 1322** d.	...	...	...	...	...	...	...	...	...	...	...	...	...	0853	...	...	...	...	...	...	...	...	...	2126
72	Sunja **1322** ⊡ d.	...	...	...	...	...	...	...	...	...	...	...	...	...	1015	...	...	...	...	...	...	...	...	...	2248
112	Novi Grad **1358** ⊡ d.	...	...	...	...	...	...	...	...	...	...	...	...	...	1144	...	...	...	...	...	...	...	...	...	0011
214	Banja Luka d.	...	...	...	...	0421	...	...	...	0730	...	0955	...	...	1315	...	...	...	...	1532	...	...	1930	...	0143
324	**Doboj 1345** a.	...	...	...	...	0637	...	...	...	0957	...	1218	...	...	1503	...	...	...	...	1810	...	...	2213	...	0335
324	**Doboj 1345** d.	...	0423	...	...	...	0725	...	...	...	...	...	1322	1442	1512	1542	...	...	...	...	1814	1925	...	...	0345
347	Maglaj d.	...	0450	0500	...	...	0801	0940	...	...	...	...	1358	1509	1539	1618	...	1700	...	...	1842	2001	...	...	0413
370	Zavidovici d.	...	...	0526	...	...	...	1008	...	...	...	...	...	1530	1600	...	...	1728	...	...	1903	...	...	...	0434
419	Zenica d.	0452	...	0626	0750	...	...	1106	1129	...	1530	...	...	1617	1647	...	...	1826	1922	...	1948	...	...	...	0521
447	Kakanj d.	0525	...	...	0827	...	...	...	1207	...	1603	...	...	1643	1713	...	1737	...	1955	...	2017	...	...	...	0547
465	Visoko d.	0546	...	...	0848	...	...	...	1228	...	1623	...	...	1700	1730	...	1803	...	2016	...	2034	...	...	...	0604
472	Podlugovi d.	0554	...	...	0856	...	...	...	1236	...	...	...	...	1707	1737	...	1811	...	2024	...	2041	...	...	...	0611
496	**Sarajevo 1355** a.	0628	...	...	0930	...	...	...	1310	...	...	...	...	1735	1805	...	1845	...	2058	...	2109	...	...	...	0639

						258				396	450													398
						B				Z	A													S
Sarajevo 1355 d.	...	...	...	0436	...	0702	...	0721	...	1027	1135	1142	...	...	...	1543	...	...	...	...	1906	...	...	2120
Podlugovi d.	...	...	...	0511	...	0731	...	0756	...	1056	1204	1217	...	...	...	1618	...	...	...	...	1941	...	...	2149
Visoko d.	...	...	...	0519	...	0738	...	0804	...	1103	1211	1230	...	...	...	1626	...	...	1736	...	1949	...	...	2156
Kakanj d.	...	...	...	0548	...	0755	...	0830	...	1120	1228	1251	...	...	...	1646	...	...	1757	...	2019	...	...	2213
Zenica d.	...	...	...	0620	0725	0822	...	0902	...	1147	1255	1323	...	...	1523	...	...	...	1829	1925	2051	...	...	2240
Zavidovici d.	...	...	...	...	0824	0908	...	...	...	1233	1341	...	...	...	1622	...	...	...	...	2024	...	...	...	2326
Maglaj d.	...	0554	...	...	0851	0929	...	...	1128	1254	1402	...	1432	...	1649	...	1734	...	...	2051	...	2107	...	2347
Doboj 1345 a.	...	0630	...	...	...	0955	...	...	1204	1320	1428	...	1508	...	...	...	1810	...	...	...	...	2143	...	0013
Doboj 1345 d.	0359	...	0718	...	...	...	1107	...	...	1329	...	...	...	1525	...	...	...	1920	...	...	...	...	...	0029
Banja Luka d.	0619	...	0935	...	...	...	1330	...	...	1529	...	...	...	1742	...	...	...	2137	...	...	...	...	...	0221
Novi Grad **1358** ⊡ d.	...	...	...	...	...	...	...	...	...	1657	...	...	...	...	...	...	...	...	...	...	...	...	...	0348
Sunja **1322** ⊡ d.	...	...	...	...	...	...	...	...	...	1844	...	...	...	...	...	...	...	...	...	...	...	...	...	0522
Zagreb 1322 a.	...	...	...	...	...	...	...	...	...	2005	...	...	...	...	...	...	...	...	...	...	...	...	...	0643

A – 🛏 2 cl., (2) and 🍷 Beograd - Sarajevo and v.v.
B – DRAVA – (12) Budapest - Pécs - Osijek - Sarajevo and v.v.
S – (2) Zagreb - Sarajevo and v.v.
Z – (12) Zagreb - Sarajevo - Pločë and v.v.

⊡ – 🛃 at Volinja (Croatia) / Dobrljin (Bosnia-Herzegovina).

1355 SARAJEVO - PLOČE

Most services 2nd class only HŽ, ŽFBH

km				391						397	
				P					⚒q	Z	
	Zagreb **1350** d.	...	...	...	...	...	...	...	...	0855	...
0	**Sarajevo 1350** d.	...	...	0705	0715	...	1540	...	...	1818	1910
67	Konjic d.	...	...	0818	0841	...	1706	...	...	1931	2044
129	Mostar d.	...	...	0926	...	...	...	...	...	2043	...
149	Žitomislići d.	...	...	0946	...	...	...	...	...	2103	...
163	Čapljina 🛃 d.	...	...	1017	...	...	...	...	...	2134	...
173	Metković d.	0715	...	1042	...	1325	...	1727	1854	2200	...
194	**Ploče** a.	0740	...	1100	...	1350	...	1752	1920	2218	...

		396						390		
		Z						P		⚒q
Ploče d.	...	0620	0605	1247	...	1410	...	1700	...	1810
Metković d.	...	0653	0631	1313	...	1436	...	1734	...	1836
Čapljina 🛃 d.	...	0721	...	...	...	...	...	1802	...	...
Žitomislići d.	...	0715	...	...	...	...	...	1819	...	...
Mostar d.	...	0736	...	...	...	...	...	1840	...	...
Konjic d.	0514	0848	...	...	1124	...	1718	1947	...	...
Sarajevo 1352 a.	0640	1000	...	...	1250	...	1852	2059	...	...
Zagreb **1350** a.	...	1945	...	...	...	...	...	...	...	...

P – (12) (also 🍷 June 13 - Sept. 6) Ploče - Sarajevo and v.v.
Z – (12) Zagreb - Sarajevo - Pločë and v.v.

q – Not June 20 - Aug. 29.

1358 LOCAL SERVICES in Bosnia

2nd class only HŽ, ŽFBH, ŽRS

VINKOVCI - TUZLA and v.v. :

km				⊗			⊗	⚒
0	Vinkovci d.	0348	0920	...	...	1511	...	1932
46	Drenovci 🛃 d.	0443	1016	1050	...	1607	...	2027
55	Brčko d.	...	...	1120	...	...	1730	...
127	Tuzla a.	...	...	1325	...	...	1935	...

		⊗				⊗	⚒
Tuzla d.	...	0722	...	...	...	1514	...
Brčko d.	...	0941	...	...	...	1719	...
Drenovci 🛃 d.	0504	0954	1041	...	1626	...	2048
Vinkovci a.	0559	...	1136	...	1720	...	2143

TUZLA - DOBOJ and v.v. :

km								
0	Tuzla d.	...	1036	...	...	1709	...	...
32	Petrovo Novo d.	0540	1120	1402	...	1753	2100	...
60	Doboj a.	0628	1208	1450	...	1841	2148	...

Doboj d.	0442	0728	...	1305	1528	1930	...
Petrovo Novo d.	0530	0817	...	1353	1617	2018	...
Tuzla a.	...	0900	...	...	1700	...	...

NOVI GRAD - BIHAĆ and v.v. :

km			Ⓐ⊗	⊗		⊗	
0	Novi Grad d.	0512	...	1155	1315	1715	1800
20	Blatna d.	0535	0540	1219	1338	1739	1823
78	Bihać a.	...	0707	1346	...	1906	...

	Ⓐ⊗		⊗		⊗	
Bihać d.	0356	...	0944	...	1459	...
Blatna d.	0523	0617	1112	1400	1627	1832
Novi Grad a.	...	0640	1135	1423	1650	1855

⊗ – Not during 'heating' season (nominally until Apr. 15 or May 1).

SERBIA, MONTENEGRO and FYRO MACEDONIA

MAP PAGE 491

Operators: **ŽS**: Železnice Srbije (Железнице Србије). **ŽCG**: Železnice Crne Gore (Железнице Црне Горе). **MŽ**: Makedonski Železnici (Македонски Железници). Services in Kosovo are overseen by the United Nations Interim Administration Mission in Kosovo (UNMIK), operating as **KŽ** Kosovske Železnice / **HK** Hekurudhat e Kosovës.

Services: All trains convey first- and second-class seating, except where shown otherwise in footnotes, by a '2' in the train column, or where the footnote shows that the train conveys sleeping- (🛏) and / or couchette (▬) cars only. Descriptions of sleeping- and couchette cars are given on page 8.

Timings: Valid from **December 13, 2009** except where indicated otherwise. Readers should note, however, that only partial information was available at press date and consequently local services are subject to alteration.
Services may be amended or cancelled at short notice and passengers are strongly advised to check locally before travelling.

Tickets: A supplement is payable for travel by internal express trains. Reservation of seats is possible on most express trains.

Visas: Most nationals do not require a visa to enter Serbia and Montenegro, but must obtain an entry stamp in their passport, sight of which will be required by officials on leaving the country. These must be obtained at an authorised border point recognised by the government - this excludes Kosovo's external borders with Montenegro, Former Yugoslav Republic Of Macedonia (FYROM) and Albania. Note also that the authorities in Serbia and Montenegro do not consider entry points from Kosovo to be official border crossing points. Visas are not required for entry into FYROM for most nationals.

Currency: Visitors to FYROM must declare all foreign currency on arrival. In Serbia and Montenegro this applies only to large amounts (currently €2000). A certificate issued by the customs officer must be presented on departure, otherwise any funds held may be confiscated.

Security: Following the declaration of independence by Kosovo (which has not been recognised by Serbia) caution should be exercised when travelling, particularly in southern Serbia and northern Kosovo. Caution is also advised in the northern and western border regions of the Former Yugoslav Republic Of Macedonia.

ŽS (BUDAPEST -) KELEBIA - SUBOTICA - BEOGRAD 1360

km		341			541					343				345		1139				437				
		◐		2	🄡 🍷	2		2	2		2	2		⚡		🍷		2		🍷	2	2	2	
		B												A		G				P				
	Budapest K **1295** d.	2300	...	...	...	...	...	...	...	1005	...	...	...	1300	...	...	...	...	...	...	...	...	...	...
0	**Kelebia** 🏛 d.	0212	...	...	...	...	...	...	...	1341	...	...	...	1620	...	...	...	...	...	...	...	...	...	...
10	**Subotica 1362** 🏛 a.	0223	...	...	...	...	...	...	...	1352	...	...	...	1631	...	...	...	...	...	...	...	...	...	...
10	**Subotica** d.	0253	...	0433	0545	0720	...	1029	1300	1425	1548	...	...	1706	...	...	...	...	...	1840	...	...	...	...
108	Novi Sad **1362** a.	0456	...	0654	0742	0930	...	1253	1518	1621	1804	...	...	1904	...	...	...	...	...	2042	1921	...	2222	...
108	Novi Sad d.	0502	...	0728	0749	0945	...	1300	...	1625	...	1810	...	1912	...	1937	...	1949	...	2108	2128	2246	0034	...
181	Novi Beograd d.	0620	...	0902	0909	1119	...	1428	...	1741	...	1939	...	2027	...	2106	...	2130	...	2227	...	0014	...	...
186	**Beograd** a.	0629	...	0911	0918	1128	...	1437	...	1750	...	1948	...	2036	...	...	...	2139	...	...	...	0023	...	...

		436	1138			344				342						542				340				
	2	🍷	🍷	2		⚡		2			2	2		2	2	🄡 🍷		2	2	◐		2		
		P	G			A														B				
Beograd d.	...	...	...	...	...	0720	...	0825	...	1000	1105	1325	...	1636	...	1835	...	2035	...	2125	...	2255	...	...
Novi Beograd d.	...	0450	0605	...	...	|	...	0836	...	1011	1116	1336	...	1646	...	1846	...	2046	...	|	...	2306	...	...
Novi Sad **1362** a.	...	0617	0738	...	...	0846	...	1007	...	1128	1249	1510	...	1829	...	2011	...	2218	...	2249	...	0038	...	...
Novi Sad d.	0433	0653	...	0738	...	0856	...	1010	...	1135	1305	1525	...	...	1915	2019	...	...	2220	2254	...	...	...	...
Subotica 1362 a.	0642	0858	...	0949	...	1053	...	1216	...	1330	1517	1755	...	...	2126	2218	...	...	0025	0050	...	...	...	...
Subotica 🏛 d.	...	...	...	...	...	1129	...	...	...	1401	...	...	...	...	...	...	...	...	...	0125	...	...	...	...
Kelebia 🏛 a.	...	...	...	...	...	1140	...	...	...	1412	...	...	...	...	...	...	...	...	...	0136	...	...	...	...
Budapest K **1295** a.	...	...	...	...	...	1455	...	...	...	1804	...	...	...	...	...	...	...	...	...	0504	...	...	...	...

A – AVALA – ⟨12⟩ and ✕ Praha - Budapest - Beograd and v.v. Also conveys: June 11 - Sept. 19 (from Praha and Budapest) ▬ 2 cl. Praha - Budapest - Beograd (**335**) - Thessaloníki; June 12 - Sept. 20 (from Thessaloníki) ▬ 2 cl. Thessaloníki - Beograd (**334**) - Budapest - Praha; ① June 14 - Sept. 20 (from Bratislava, one day later from Thessaloníki) ▬ 2 cl. Bratislava - Thessaloníki and v.v.; June 9 - Sept. 17 (from Kyïv / Moskva) 🛏 2 cl. Kyïv ③ / Moskva ⑤ - Thessaloníki; June 11 - Sept. 20 (from Thessaloníki) 🛏 2 cl. Thessaloníki ① - Moskva, 🛏 2 cl. Thessaloníki ⑤ - Kyïv. Also conveys Kyïv / Moskva / Praha / Bratislava - Bar cars (see note **P**).

B – BEOGRAD – ⟨2⟩ Budapest - Beograd and v.v.; 🛏 1, 2 cl. and ▬ 2 cl. Wien - Budapest - Beograd and v.v.; 🛏 1, 2 cl. Wien - Beograd (**490/1**) - Sofija and v.v.

G – FRUŠKA GORA – June 18 - Aug. 30 (from Novi Sad, one day later from Bar): 🛏 1, 2 cl., ▬ 1, 2 cl., ⟨2⟩ and 🍷 Novi Sad - Bar and v.v.

P – PANONIJA – 🛏 1, 2 cl., ▬ 1, 2 cl., ⟨2⟩ and 🍷 Subotica - Novi Beograd - Bar and v.v. Also conveys: June 11 - Sept. 20 (from Praha), June 12 - Sept. 21 (from Bar) ▬ 2 cl. Praha - Budapest (**344/5**) - Subotica - Bar and v.v.; ⑤ June 11 - Sept. 17 (from Bratislava, one day later from Bar) ▬ 2 cl. Bratislava - Subotica - Bar and v.v.; ② June 15 - Sept. 14 (from Moskva) 🛏 2 cl. Moskva - Bar; ⑤ June 18 - Sept. 17 (from Bar) 🛏 2 cl. Bar - Moskva.

◐ – Supplement payable for travel in Serbia.
⚡ – Supplement payable for travel in Hungary and Serbia.
⊗ – Service reported to be suspended.

ŽS 2nd class only SUBOTICA - KIKINDA, ZRENJANIN, NOVI SAD and PANČEVO 1362

km											
	Subotica 1360 d.	0150	...	...	0725	...	1310	...	1544	...	2115
	Senta d.	0309	...	...	0842	...	1417	...	1659	...	2224
	Banatsko Miloševo d.	0401	...	...	0933	...	▬	...	1749	...	▬
0	**Kikinda 1377** d.	0418	0430	...	0950	1130	...	...	1806	1810	...
19	Banatsko Miloševo d.	▬	0450	...	...	1148	...	...	...	1828	...
71	**Zrenjanin** d.	0330	0640	1035	...	1331	1510	...	...	2011	2035
96	Orlovat stajalište d.	0426	0735	1134	...	...	1605	1653	...	...	2132
	Novi Sad **1360** a.	0633	|	1335	...	...	|	1852	...	...	|
145	**Pančevo** glavna **1365** a.	...	0845	...	...	...	1715	...	...	...	2242

Pančevo glavna **1365** d.	...	...	...	...	...	1155	...	1810	...	...	2300
Novi Sad **1360** d.	...	...	...	0710	...	|	1434	|	...	1920	|
Orlovat stajalište d.	0544	...	...	0915	...	1306	1634	1921	...	2134j	0010
Zrenjanin d.	0637	0700	...	1010	...	1410	▬	2016	2025	2229	0103
Banatsko Miloševo a.	▬	0844	...	...	...	1553	...	...	2209	▬	...
Kikinda 1377 a.	0430	0901	1000	...	...	1611	1830	...	2226	...	...
Banatsko Miloševo d.	0457	...	1024	...	...	...	1857	...	...	...	...
Senta d.	0549	...	1115	...	1427	...	1949	...	...	2236	...
Subotica 1360 a.	0656	...	1222	...	1534	...	2058	...	...	2345	...

j – Arrive 2122.

ŽS, CFR 2nd class only except where shown BEOGRAD - VRŠAC - TIMIŞOARA 1365

km								361				
								B				
0	**Beograd** d.	...	...	...	...	...	...	1550	...	...	...	...
	Beograd centar ▶ d.	0530	...	1030	...	1427	...	|	1850	...	2216	...
19	Pančevo glavna **1362** ▶ d.	0609	0636	1109	1130	1500	1520	1637	1925	1935	2252	2335
87	Vršac a.	...	0813	...	1301	...	1651	1756	...	2106	...	0106
87	Vršac 🏛 d.	...	...	...	...	...	...	1820	...	...	...	...
107	Stamora Moraviţa 🏛 ... § a.	...	...	...	...	...	...	1942	...	...	...	...
107	Stamora Moraviţa § d.	...	...	...	...	...	...	2002	...	...	...	...
163	**Timişoara** Nord § a.	...	...	...	...	...	...	2057	...	...	...	...
	Bucureşti N **1620** a.	...	...	...	...	...	...	0537	...	...	...	...

			360								
			B								
Bucureşti N **1620** d.	...	...	2105	...	...	...	...	...	...	...	...
Timişoara Nord § d.	...	...	0545	...	...	...	...	...	...	...	...
Stamora Moraviţa § a.	...	...	0640	...	...	...	...	...	...	...	...
Stamora Moraviţa 🏛 ... § d.	...	...	0707	...	...	...	...	...	...	...	...
Vršac 🏛 a.	...	...	0629	...	...	...	...	...	...	...	...
Vršac d.	0440	...	0654	0905	...	1330	...	1715	...	2145	...
Pančevo glavna **1362** ▷ d.	0604	0651	0813	1030	1051	1455	1537	1856	2006	2310	2329
Beograd centar ▷ a.	...	0724	|	...	1126	...	1617	...	2043	...	2359
Beograd a.	...	...	0854	...	...	...	...	...	...	...	...

B – BUCUREŞTI – 🛏 1, 2 cl., ▬ 2 cl. and ⟨12⟩ Beograd - Timişoara - Bucureşti and v.v.

▶ – Beograd centar - Pančevo glavna: approximately hourly 0336 – 2216.
▷ – Pančevo glavna - Beograd centar: approximately hourly 0451 – 2329.

§ – Romanian (East European) time.

1370 BEOGRAD - PODGORICA - BAR ŽCG, ŽS

km			1141							431	897				433	781		513			1139		435	437	1343
		2		2	2	2	2	2	2	🍷		2	2		✖	⊗	2	2	2	2	🍷			🍷	
			◆							B	◆					K					G		L	P	A
0	**Beograd** d.	...	...	...	0315	...	0705	...	...	1010	...	...	1135	...	1310	1515	1545	1725	...	1925	2109**n**	...	2210	2229**n**	2310
93	Valjevo d.	...	...	...	0523	...	0914	...	...	1142	...	...	1323	...	1442	1644	1737	1900	...	2128	2229	...	2343	0008	|
	Kraljevo **1372/5** d.	...	0223	...	|	...	|	...	...	|	1130	...	|	...	|	1848**p**	|	|	...	|	|	...	|	|	|
159	Požega **1372** d.	...	|	...	0701	...	1030	...	...	1302	1302	...	1434	...	1543	1751	1851	2000	...	2242	2328	...	0048	0115	0145
185	Užice d.	...	0347	...	0738	...	1110	...	...	1332	1332	...	1508	...	1618	...	1932	2042	...	2310	2358	...	0122	0205	0223
288	Prijepolje d.	...	0539	...	0853	...	1301	...	...	1453	1453	...	1654	...	1739	...	2111	2155	...	...	0150	...	0253	0333	|
338	Bijelo Polje d.	0635	0719	...	0922	...	...	...	...	1633	1633	1745	...	...	1918	...	...	...	...	...	0337	...	0423	0508	0602
468	**Podgorica** d.	0914	0959	1013	...	1310	...	1443	1730	1903	1903	2030	...	...	2159	...	...	...	0530	...	0607	...	0659	0748	0835
524	**Bar** a.	1021	1052	1113	...	1414	...	1544	1826	2009	2009	2127	...	...	2257	...	...	...	0629	...	0714	...	0802	0841	0928

	512	780				430	896					432					1140		436			1138	434		1342
	2	⊗	2	2	2	🍷		2	2	2	2	✖	2	2	2	2			🍷	2	2	🍷			
		K				B	◆										◆		P			G	L		A
Bar d.	...	...	...	...	0533	0600	0600	0647	...	...	1135	1220	1300	1450	1610	...	1800	...	1855	1920	...	2015	2105	...	2205
Podgorica d.	...	...	...	...	0640	0705	0705	0744	...	...	1231	1320	1356	1546	1713	...	1905	...	2000	2019	...	2115	2210	...	2310
Bijelo Polje d.	...	...	...	...	0915	0950	0950	...	...	...	...	1605	...	...	...	...	2154	...	2250	...	...	0016	0057	...	0153
Prijepolje d.	0330	...	0400	0736	...	1101	1101	...	1205	1530	...	1716	...	...	...	2007	2306	...	0002	...	...	0127	0204	...	|
Užice d.	0504	...	0602	0925	...	1234	1234	...	1400	1728	...	1848	...	...	...	2156	0025	...	0146	...	0220	0304	0331	...	0438
Požega **1372** d.	0528	0550	0631	0955	...	1313	1320	...	1435	1758	...	1911	...	...	...	...	|	...	0208	...	0250	0332	0357	...	0513
Kraljevo **1372/5** a.	|	0450**p**	|	|	...	|	1415	...	|	|	...	|	...	...	...	...	0138	...	|	...	|	|	|	...	|
Valjevo d.	0627	0649	0747	1115	...	1413	...	...	1550	1915	...	2012	...	...	...	...	...	...	0309	...	0406	0429	0457	...	|
Beograd a.	0756	0816	0941	1319	...	1557	...	...	1750	2111	...	2143	...	...	...	...	...	...	0446**n**	...	0601	0603**n**	0626	...	0731

A – AUTO-VOZ – June 11 - Sept. 11 (from Beograd, one day later from Bar): 🛌 1, 2 cl. and 🛏 1, 2 cl. Beograd - Bar and v.v.
B – TARA – [12] and 🍷 Beograd - Bar and v.v. Conveys Dec. 13 - June 10, Sept. 5 - Dec. 10 (from Skopje); Dec. 14 - June 11, Sept. 6 - Dec. 11 (from Bar): 🛏 2 cl. Niš - Bar and v.v.
G – FRUŠKA GORA – June 18 - Aug. 30 (from Novi Sad, one day later from Bar): 🛌 1, 2 cl., 🛏 1, 2 cl., [2] and 🍷 Novi Sad - Bar and v.v.
K – [12] and 🍷 Beograd - Kraljevo and v.v.
L – LOVĆEN – 🛌 1, 2 cl., 🛏 1, 2 cl. and [2] Beograd - Bar and v.v.
P – PANONIJA – 🛌 1, 2 cl., 🛏 2 cl., [2] and 🍷 Subotica - Novi Beograd - Bar and v.v. Also conveys Moskva / Praha / Bratislava - Bar cars (see Table **1360**, note **P**).

n – **Novi Beograd**.
p – Via Požega.
w – May 28 - Sept. 26.
y – May 29 - Sept. 27.
z – Not May 28 - Sept. 27.

◆ – For days of running and composition – see Table **1380**.
⊗ – Service reported to be suspended.

1372 POŽEGA - KRALJEVO 2nd class only except where shown ŽS

tariff km		1140							896	781		
		◆							◆	⊗K		
0	**Požega 1370** d.	...	...	0715	...	1255	1630	...	1320	1754	...	2135
45	Čačak d.	0112	...	0753	...	1332	1709	...	1349	1822	...	2213
83	**Kraljevo 1370/5** a.	0138	...	0837	...	1414	1753	...	1415	1848	...	2257
	Lapovo **1375/80** a.	0429	...	...	...	...	...	...	1648	...	...	...
	Niš **1373/80** a.	0654	...	...	...	...	...	...	1913	...	...	...

	780					897					1141
	⊗K					◆					◆
Niš **1373/80** d.	...	...	...	...	...	0645	...	...	...	...	2055
Lapovo **1375/80** d.	...	...	...	...	...	0905	...	...	...	...	2310
Kraljevo 1370/5 d.	0450	...	0530	...	1045	1130	...	1500	2000	...	0223
Čačak d.	0519	...	0615	...	1130	1158	...	1544	2045	...	0249
Požega 1370 a.	0546	...	0652	...	1207	1225	...	1620	2122	...	...

K – [12] and 🍷 Beograd - Požega - Kraljevo and v.v.
◆ – For days of running and composition – see Table **1380**.
⊗ – Service reported to be suspended.

1373 BEOGRAD - ZAJEČAR - NIŠ 2nd class only except where shown ŽS

tariff km													971	
													Z	
0	**Beograd** d.	...	...	...	...	...	0735	...	...	...	...	...	1620	1910
98	Požarevac d.	...	...	...	...	...	0944	...	...	...	...	...	1830	2112
199	Majdanpek d.	...	0405	...	...	0950	▬	...	...	1635	...	...	2120	...
★	Prahovo p d.	...	|	0420	0910	|	...	...	1730	|	...	2200	|	...
296	**Zaječar** d.	0340	0620	0625**f**	1059	1205	1210	1505	1930	1850	2010	2349	2314	...
343	Knjaževac d.	0441	...	0725	...	...	1322	1608	...	...	2112	...	...	...
420	**Niš 1372/80** a.	0619	...	0907	...	...	1502	1753	...	...	2249	...	...	...

		970											
		Z											
Niš 1372/80 d.	...	...	0255	...	...	0710	1100	...	...	1555	...	...	1928
Knjaževac d.	...	...	0446	...	...	0852	1241	...	...	1736	...	...	2117
Zaječar d.	...	0200	0548	0630	0645	0952	1341	1405	1515	1838	1905	1950	2219
Prahovo p a.	...	|	...	0817	|	...	▬	|	1702	...	|	2137	...
Majdanpek d.	...	0353	...	...	0858	...	...	1616	...	...	2116	...	...
Požarevac d.	0425	0700	...	...	...	...	1630	...	...	...	...	...	...
Beograd a.	0625	0837	...	...	...	...	1826	...	...	...	...	...	...

Z – [2] Beograd - Zaječar and v.v.
f – Arrive 0608.
★ – Prahovo - Zaječar: *81 km*.

1375 LAPOVO and PRIŠTINA - KOSOVO POLJE - SKOPJE 2nd class only except where shown ŽS, KŽ

km		881			891		⊗		761		⊗		
					⊠	⊠	⊠		⊠		⊠		
	Beograd **1380** d.	2250	...	...	...	...	...	...	...	...	...	...	...
0	**Lapovo 1380** d.	0127	0405	...	...	...	...	1135	...	...	...	1655	...
28	**Kragujevac** d.	0208	0505	...	...	...	...	1226	...	...	...	1746	...
82	Kraljevo **1370/2** d.	0403	0635	0710	...	...	...	1355	...	1445	...	1925	2330
163	Raška d.	0534	...	0845	...	...	...	▬	...	1622	...	▬	0104
180	Lešak d.	0610	...	0912	...	...	0955	...	...	1649	1650	...	...
210	Zvečan d.	0707	...	1015	...	...	1052	**893**	...	1750	1747	...	...
214	Kosovska Mitrovica d.	...	...	▬	...	...	1058	⊠	...	...	1753	...	...
	Priština d.	...	...	⊠	0624	0740	|	1250	1730	...	|	⊠	...
247	**Kosovo Polje** d.	...	...	0425	0636	0751	1159	1330	1740	...	1854	1900	...
*	Peć a.	...	...	|	|	0940	...	|	1906	...	...	|	...
276	Uroševac d.	...	...	0502	0709	...	...	1413	...	...	...	1946	...
304	Deneral Janković 🛃 a.	...	...	0540	0747	...	...	1455	...	...	...	2027	...
331	**Skopje 1380/5** a.	...	...	...	0901	...	...	...	...	...	...	...	...

	760		880	⊗	890			⊗	892		
	⊠	⊠		⊠	⊠		⊠	⊠	⊠		⊠
Skopje 1380/5 d.	...	...	...	...	...	...	...	...	1613	...	...
Deneral Janković 🛃 d.	...	0557§	...	...	1058§	...	...	...	1730	...	2045§
Uroševac d.	...	0643	...	...	1146	...	...	...	1814	...	2129
Peć d.	0550	|	...	...	|	...	1120	...	|	...	|
Kosovo Polje d.	0722	0730	...	0735	1225	...	1321	1415	1857**j**	...	2209
Priština a.	0730	▬	...	|	1235§	...	1330	|	1908	...	...
Kosovska Mitrovica d.	▬	...	...	0837	...	...	▬	1517	▬	...	...
Zvečan d.	...	...	0805	0844	...	1045	...	1524	1810	...	...
Lešak d.	...	...	0915	0940	...	1148	...	1620	1914	...	...
Raška d.	0415	...	0943	...	...	1218	...	...	1943	...	...
Kraljevo **1370/2** d.	0600	0715	1135	...	...	1351	1425	...	2118	2200	...
Kragujevac d.	...	0851	1328	...	...	...	1557	...	...	2345	...
Lapovo 1380 a.	...	0943	1408	...	...	...	1640	...	...	0029	...
Beograd **1380** a.	...	...	1706	...	...	...	...	...	...	...	...

j – Arrive 1843.
⊗ – Currently suspended.
§ – Subject to confirmation.
⊠ – Service operated by KŽ (see country heading).
* – Kosovo Polje - Peć: *82 km*.

1377 MINOR BORDER CROSSINGS 2nd class only ŽS, MÁV, CFR

SUBOTICA - SZEGED and v.v. :

km								
0	Subotica d.	0850	1018	*1435*	Szeged d.	0650	1230	1415
24	Horgoš 🛃 d.	0952	1122	1537	Röszke 🛃 d.	0719	1300	1455
31	Röszke 🛃 d.	1022	1153	1610	Horgoš 🛃 d.	0752	1333	1513
43	Szeged a.	1037	1208	1625	Subotica a.	0840	1420	*1737*

KIKINDA - TIMIŞOARA and v.v. :

km															
0	Kikinda **1362** d.	...	...	0930	...	...	1630	...	Timişoara § d.	0618	0800	...	1328	1605	...	1930
19	Jimbolia 🛃 § d.	0510	0910	1049	1237	1440	1749	1950	Jimbolia 🛃 § d.	0732	0848	1120	1416	1652	1820	2036
58	Timişoara § a.	0600	0959	...	1325	1529	...	2047	Kikinda **1362** a.	...	...	1039	...	...	1739	...

§ – East European time, one hour ahead of Central European time.

ŹS, MŻ, BDŽ — BEOGRAD - NIŠ - SOFIYA, SKOPJE and THESSALONÍKI — 1380

km					1140	1193			337	491						391			591		896			293	335
		2	2	2	N	2	2	2	Q	F	2	2	2	2	2	♀	2	2	♀		M	2	2	Z	H
0	**Beograd 1375** d.	...	...	...	...	...	0340	0720	0750	0750	...	...	1025	...	...	1405	...	1530	1650	...	...	...	1935	2115	2150
110	Lapovo **1372/5** d.	0325	...	...	0455	...	0627	0948	1007	1007	...	...	1302	...	1532	1552	...	1757	1837	...	1715	...	2211	2331	0006
135	Jagodina d.	0349	...	...	0512	...	0657	1013	1024	1024	...	...	1326	...	1557	1610	...	1822	1855	...	1732	...	2240	2348	0023
155	Paraćin d.	0412	...	...	0532	...	0722	1035	1044	1044	...	...	...	...	1619	1630	...	1844	1917	...	1752	...	2302	0008	0043
176	Stalać **1372** d.	0435	...	...	0551	...	0747	1057	1103	1103	...	...	...	...	1642	1649	...	1906	1937	...	1810	...	2324	0027	0102
244	**Niš 1372/3** a.	0606	...	...	0654	...	0913	1224	1200	1200	...	...	...	...	1810	1745	...	2040	2034	...	1913	...	0053	0124	0159
244	**Niš** d.	...	...	0720	0835	0835	...	...	1215	1235	...	1550	...	...	...	1800	1935	...	...	...	...	...	...	0222	0220
	Dimitrovgrad 🏛 d.	...	...	|	|	|	...	...	|	1517	...	|	...	...	...	|	|	...	...	...	...	...	...	0452	|
	Dragoman 🏛 § d.	...	...	|	|	|	...	...	|	1649	...	|	...	...	...	|	|	...	...	...	...	...	...	0625	|
	Sofiya § a.	...	...	|	|	|	...	...	|	1730	...	|	...	...	...	|	|	...	...	...	...	...	...	0715	|
288	Leskovac d.	...	...	0822	0916	0916	...	...	1259	...	...	1650	...	...	...	1841	2035	...	...	...	...	...	...	...	0302
392	Preševo 🏛 d.	...	...	1102	1203	1203	...	...	1540	...	...	...	...	...	...	2128	2329	...	...	...	...	...	...	...	0545
401	Tabanovci 🏛 d.	...	0723	...	1235	1235	...	...	1620	...	...	...	...	1955	...	2210	...	...	...	...	...	0505	...	...	0625
462	**Skopje** a.	...	0820	...	1330	1330	...	...	1659	...	...	...	...	2051	...	2250	...	...	...	...	...	0600	...	...	0706
462	**Skopje 1375/85** d.	...	...	...	...	...	...	...	1730	...	1942	...	...	...	...	...	...	...	...	...	...	0609	...	...	0740
524	Veles **1385** d.	...	...	...	...	...	...	...	1813	...	2041	...	...	...	...	...	...	...	...	...	...	0705	...	...	0827
651	Gevgelija a.	...	...	...	...	...	...	...	1947	...	2224	...	...	...	...	...	...	...	...	...	...	0848	...	...	0955
651	Gevgelija 🏛 d.	...	...	...	...	...	...	...	2010	...	...	...	...	...	...	...	...	...	...	...	...	...	...	...	1025
654	Idoméni 🏛 a.	...	...	...	...	...	...	...	2115	...	...	...	...	...	...	...	...	...	...	...	...	...	...	...	1130
654	Idoméni d.	...	...	...	...	...	...	...	2150	...	...	...	...	...	...	...	...	...	...	...	...	...	...	...	1205
730	**Thessaloníki 1400** § a.	...	...	...	...	...	...	...	2237	...	...	...	...	...	...	...	...	...	...	...	...	...	...	...	1254

km				590	897						490				336			1141	1192			292		334	
		2	2	♀	M	2	2	2	2	2	F	2	2	2	Q	2		N	2	2	2	Z		H	
	Thessaloníki 1400 § d.	...	...	...	...	...	...	...	...	...	...	...	...	...	0557	...	...	...	...	...	...	...	...	1705	...
	Idoméni a.	...	...	...	...	...	...	...	...	...	...	...	...	...	0646	...	...	...	...	...	...	...	...	1754	...
	Idoméni 🏛 d.	...	...	...	...	...	...	...	...	...	...	...	...	...	0712	...	...	...	...	...	...	...	...	1830	...
	Gevgelija 🏛 a.	...	...	...	...	...	...	...	...	...	...	...	...	...	0617	...	...	...	...	...	...	...	...	1735	...
	Gevgelija d.	...	...	...	...	...	...	...	0459	...	...	...	...	...	0637	...	...	...	...	...	1552	...	...	1804	...
	Veles **1385** d.	...	...	...	...	...	...	...	0642	...	...	...	...	...	0806	...	...	...	...	...	1735	...	...	1936	...
	Skopje 1375/85 a.	...	...	...	...	...	...	...	0739	...	...	...	...	...	0847	...	...	...	...	...	1829	...	...	2017	...
	Skopje d.	...	...	...	...	0610	...	...	...	...	...	...	...	...	0900	...	...	1435	1435	...	1840	...	...	2045	...
	Tabanovci 🏛 a.	...	...	...	...	0707	...	...	...	...	...	...	...	...	1002	...	...	1555	1555	...	1934	...	...	2155	...
	Preševo 🏛 d.	...	0215	...	...	...	...	...	...	...	...	...	1147	...	1035	...	...	1630	1630	...	...	...	...	2236	...
	Leskovac d.	...	0503	...	...	...	...	...	...	...	...	...	1434	1710	1258	...	...	1856	1856	...	...	...	...	0053	...
0	**Sofiya** § d.	...	|	...	...	...	...	...	...	...	1140	...	|	|	|	...	...	|	|	...	...	2040	...	|	...
42	Dragoman 🏛 § d.	...	|	...	...	...	...	...	...	...	1223	...	|	|	|	...	...	|	|	...	...	2130	...	|	...
63	Dimitrovgrad 🏛 d.	...	|	...	...	...	...	...	...	...	1230	...	|	|	|	...	...	|	|	...	...	2140	...	|	...
161	**Niš 1372/3** a.	...	0559	...	...	...	...	...	...	...	1447	...	1529	1817	1336	...	...	1934	1934	...	...	2343	...	0131	...
	Niš d.	0326	...	0600	0645	...	0730	1020	...	...	1515	1535	...	...	1400	1915	...	2055	...	2317	...	0010	...	0152	...
	Stalać **1372** d.	0454	...	0658	0743	...	0901	1151	...	...	1613	1717	...	...	1458	2046	...	2153	...	0050	...	0118	...	0250	...
	Paraćin d.	0515	...	0718	0802	...	0922	1212	...	...	1632	1738	...	...	1517	2107	...	2212	...	0111	...	0137	...	0309	...
	Jagodina d.	0539	...	0738	0822	...	0951	1236	...	1449	1653	1802	...	...	1537	2131	...	2232	...	0135	...	0117	...	0330	...
	Lapovo **1372/5** d.	0620	...	0758	0840	...	1025	1301	...	1524	1713	1838	...	...	1557	2206	...	2250	...	0200	...	0217	...	0350	...
	Beograd 1375 a.	0851	...	0957	...	...	1252	...	...	1757	1921	2100	...	...	1806	0049	...	...	...	...	...	0425	...	0559	...

F – BALKAN – [2] Beograd - Sofiya and v.v.; [sleeper] 1, 2 cl. Wien (**346/7**) - Budapest (**340/1**) - Beograd - Sofiya and v.v. Also conveys: [sleeper] 1, 2 cl. Beograd - Sofiya - İstanbul and v.v.

H – HELLAS EXPRESS – [sleeper] 1, 2 cl., [couchette] 2 cl. and [12] Beograd - Skopje - Thessaloníki and v.v. Conveys ⑤ June 25 - Sept. 3 (from Skopje), ⑦ June 27 - Sept. 5 (from Sofiya): [couchette] 2 cl. Skopje (**334/5**) - Niš - Sofiya and v.v. Also conveys: June 11 - Sept. 19 (from Praha and Budapest) [couchette] 2 cl. Praha - Budapest (**345**) - Beograd - Thessaloníki; June 12 - Sept. 20 (from Thessaloníki) [couchette] 2 cl. Thessaloníki - Beograd (**344**) - Budapest - Praha; ① June 14 - Sept. 20 (from Bratislava, one day later from Thessaloníki) [couchette] 2 cl. Bratislava - Thessaloníki and v.v.; June 9 - Sept. 17 (from Kyïv/Moskva) [sleeper] 2 cl. Kyïv ③ / Moskva ⑤ - Thessaloníki; June 11 - Sept. 20 (from Thessaloníki) [sleeper] 2 cl. Thessaloníki ① - Moskva, [sleeper] 2 cl. Thessaloníki ⑤ - Kyïv.

M – Dec. 13 - June 10, Sept. 5 - Dec. 10 (from Niš, one day later from Bar): [2] Niš - Požega (**430/1**) - Bar and v.v.

N – NIŠAVA – June 11 - Sept. 4 (from Niš, one day later from Bar): [sleeper] 1, 2 cl., [couchette] 2 cl. and [2] Niš - Bar and v.v. Conveys June 26 - Aug. 28 (from Skopje, one day later from Bar): [sleeper] 1, 2 cl. Skopje (**1192/93**) - Niš - Bar and v.v.

Q – OLYMPUS – [12] and ♀ Beograd - Thessaloníki and v.v.

Z – [sleeper] 1, 2 cl., [couchette] 2 cl. and [12] Beograd - Sofiya and v.v. Conveys ⑤ June 25 - Sept. 3 (from Skopje), ⑦ June 27 - Sept. 5 (from Sofiya): [couchette] 2 cl. Skopje (**334/5**) - Niš - Sofiya and v.v.

* – Estimated time.

§ – East European time.

MŽ 2nd class only — BRANCH LINES in FYRO Macedonia — 1385

SKOPJE - KOČANI and BITOLA and v.v. :

km												
0	Skopje **1380** d.	0222	0646	1430	1530	1815	Bitola d.	0333	...	1242	...	1843
62	Veles **1380** d.	0310	0739	1522	1621	1912	Prilep d.	0414	...	1332	...	1932
★	Kočani a.	0501	|	|	1811	|	Kočani d.	|	0521	|	1827	|
170	Prilep d.	...	0929	1707	...	2107	Veles **1380** d.	0555	0714	1523	2021	2116
228	Bitola a.	...	1017	1755	...	2145	Skopje **1380** a.	0644	0814	1620	2108	2205

SKOPJE - KIČEVO and v.v. :

km								
0	Skopje d.	0250	0800	1630	Kičevo d.	0510	1215	1854
86	Tetovo d.	0347	0905	1735	Tetovo d.	0613	1319	1958
163	Kičevo a.	0445	1007	1837	Skopje a.	0715	1422	2059

★ – Veles - Kočani: *110 km.*

ALBANIA

SEE MAP PAGE 491

Operator: **HSH**: Hekurudha Shqiptarë.

Timings: Valid from **November 5, 2008**

Services: Trains convey one class of accommodation only. Tickets are not sold in advance, only for the next available departure.

Security: Most visits to Albania are now reported to be trouble free, but travellers are advised to avoid the north-east of the country.

HSH One class only — ALBANIAN RAILWAYS — 1390

Times for Milot, Vorë, Rrogozhinë, Lushnjë and Fier are subject to minor variation

km											
0	Shkodër a.	...	0555	...	...	...	...	...	...	...	...
47	Milot d.	...	0731*	...	...	...	...	...	...	...	...
	Tiranë d.	0555	|	0830	...	...	1410	1445	...	1615	2000
82	Vorë a.	0617*	0845	0852*	←	...	1432*	1507*	...	1637*	2022*
82	Vorë d.	0618	→	0854	0857	...	1438	1508	...	1641	2023
98	**Tiranë** a.	|	...	|	0921	...	|	|	...	|	|
102	**Durrës** a.	0653	...	0928	...	...	1507	1542	...	1712	2057
102	**Durrës** d.	0707	...	...	...	...	1525	1600	...	...	...
	Durrës Plazh a.	|	...	...	...	...	|	|	...	...	...
138	Rrogozhinë d.	0818*	...	...	...	...	1638*	1712*	...	...	...
179	Elbasan a.	0938	...	...	...	...	1755	|	...	...	...
255	Pogradec a.	1232	...	...	...	...	...	|	...	...	...
155	Lushnjë a.	...	...	...	...	...	...	1745*	...	...	...
187	Fier a.	...	...	...	...	...	...	1843*	...	...	...
221	Vlorë a.	...	...	...	...	...	...	1952	...	...	...

Vlorë d.	...	...	0540	...	...	...	...	...	...	...
Fier d.	...	...	0650*	...	...	...	...	...	...	...
Lushnjë d.	...	...	0748*	...	...	...	...	...	...	...
Pogradec d.	...	...	|	...	...	...	...	...	1250	...
Elbasan d.	...	0600	|	...	...	...	...	...	1555	...
Rrogozhinë d.	...	0713*	0822*	...	...	...	...	...	1712*	...
Durrës Plazh d.	...	|	|	...	...	...	...	...	|	...
Durrës a.	...	0828	0935	...	...	...	...	...	1820	...
Durrës d.	0610	0845	0950	...	1300	...	...	1730	1835	...
Tiranë d.	|	|	|	...	|	1315	...	|	|	...
Vorë a.	0645*	0921	1024	...	1335*	1340*	...	1805*	1909	...
Vorë d.	0647	0922	1025	...	1337	1345*	...	1807*	1911	...
Tiranë a.	0710	0946	1049	...	1401	|	...	1830	1935	...
Milot d.	...	...	...	...	...	1502*	...	...	...	...
Shkodër a.	...	...	...	...	...	1642	...	...	...	...

* – Estimated time.

GREECE

SEE MAP PAGE 491

Operator: ΤΡΑΙΝΟΣΕ Α.Ε. - TRAINOSE S.A.

Services: All trains convey first and second class seating except where shown otherwise in footnotes or by '2' in the train column, or where the footnote shows sleeping and/or couchette cars only. Descriptions of sleeping (🛏) and couchette (▬) cars appear on page 8. Services that convey catering may vary from day to day.

Timings: Timings have been compiled from the latest information received. However, readers should be aware that a substantial amount of engineering work is taking place throughout the country and timetable amendments may come into effect at short notice.

Tickets: Reservation of seats is possible (and recommended) on most express trains. *IC* trains carry a supplement which varies depending upon distance travelled. Break of journey is only permitted when tickets are so endorsed before travel with the station quoted.

1400 ATHÍNA - LÁRISA - THESSALONÍKI

km		883 592		*IC* 70	*IC* 50		884	500		*IC* 52	1520		*IC* 54		502	*IC* 40		1522	*IC* 56	*IC* 74		504	604	
				✕⟋	✕◇			🍷		✕⟋	2		✕⟋		🍷	🍷⟋		2	✕◇	✕⟋		[R] ♦	🍷 ♦	
0	**Athína** Lárisa **1420/40** d.	...	...	0650	0753	...	0821	0921	...	1051	1219	...	1321	...	1453	1553	...	1753	1928	2039	...	2255	2359	...
61	Inói **1420** d.	...	...	0734	|	...	0912	1010	...	1135	1317	...	1405	...	1542	1637	...	1846	|	2123	...	2350	0054	...
89	Thíva d.	...	...	0750	|	...	0929	1028	...	1151	1337	...	1422	...	1602	1654	...	1906	|	2140	...	0012	0115	...
129	Levadiá d.	...	...	0808	|	...	0950	1053	...	1209	1403	...	1440	...	1626	1714	...	1931	|	2159	...	|	0141	...
154	Tithoréa d.	...	...	|	|	...	1001	1106	...	|	1421	...	1451	...	1642	1725	...	1951	|	|	...	|	0156	...
169	Amfíklia d.	...	...	|	|	...	1017	|	...	|	1433	...	1506	...	1654	|	...	2003	|	|	...	|	|	...
210	Lianokládi d.	...	...	0902	0948	...	1059	1157	...	1304	1524	...	1546	...	1739	1813	...	2105	2123	2256	...	0147	0303	...
	Lamia a.	...	...	|	|	...	|	|	...	|	1537	...	|	...	|	|	...	2114	|	|	...	|	|	...
291	Paleofársalos **1408** d.	...	...	1009	|	...	1216	1307	...	1407	...	...	1652	...	1854	1918	...	...	|	|	...	|	0434	...
	Kalambáka **1408** a.	0744	...	|	|	...	1303	|	...	|	...	...	|	...	|	|	...	...	|	|	...	|	|	...
333	**Lárisa 1425** ▲ d.	0857	...	1030	1111	...	...	1342	...	1428	...	...	1713	...	1931	1938	...	...	2246	0030	...	0358	0515	...
	Vólos **1425** a.	|	...	|	|	...	...	|	...	|	...	...	|	...	|	2031	...	...	|	|	...	|	|	...
417	Kateríni ▲ d.	0948	...	1111	|	...	...	1420	...	1506	...	...	1751	...	2009	...	...	...	|	0106	...	0446	0609	...
465	Platí **1410** ▲ d.	1013	...	1132	|	...	...	1441	...	1528	...	...	1811	...	2030	...	...	...	|	0128	...	0511	0637	...
502	**Thessaloníki 1410** ▲ a.	1039	...	1152	1220	...	...	1502	...	1548	...	...	1831	...	2051	...	...	...	2355	0148	...	0536	0700	...
	Alexandrúpoli Port **1405** a.	...	...	1716	...	...	...	...	...	...	...	...	...	...	...	...	...	...	...	0653	...	...	1315	...

km		1521	*IC* 41	*IC* 51		*IC* 53	*IC* 71		501		*IC* 55	1523		885	503		591 886	*IC* 57		605	505		*IC* 75	
		2	🍷⟋	✕◇		✕⟋	✕⟋		🍷		✕⟋	2			🍷			✕◇		🍷 ♦	[R] ♦		✕⟋	
	Alexandrúpoli Port **1405** a.	...	...	...	...	...	0642	...	...	...	...	...	...	...	...	...	...	...	...	1522	...	...	2032	...
	Thessaloníki 1410 ▲ d.	...	...	0713	...	1013	1140	...	1242	...	1454	...	...	...	1633	...	1759	1850	...	2259	2333	...	0141	...
	Platí **1410** ▲ d.	...	...	|	...	1034	1201	...	1304	...	1515	...	...	...	1655	...	1824	|	...	2323	2359	...	0202	...
	Kateríni ▲ d.	...	...	|	...	1054	1222	...	1326	...	1536	...	...	...	1717	...	1849	|	...	2351	0025	...	0224	...
0	Vólos **1425** d.	...	0615	|	...	|	|	...	|	...	|	...	...	...	|	...	|	|	...	|	|	...	|	...
61	**Lárisa 1425** ▲ d.	...	0711	0834	...	1136	1300	...	1418	...	1614	...	...	...	1809	...	1941	2011	...	0058	0126	...	0311	...
—	Kalambáka **1408** d.	...	|	|	...	|	|	...	|	...	|	...	...	1736	|	...	2051	|	...	|	|	...	|	...
	Paleofársalos **1408** d.	...	0730	|	...	1157	1321	...	1439	...	1635	...	...	1824	|	...	...	|	...	0125	|	...	|	...
0	Lamia d.	0628	|	|	...	|	|	...	|	...	|	1815	...	|	|	...	...	|	...	|	|	...	|	...
6	Lianokládi d.	0648	0838	0947	...	1305	1430	...	1551	...	1738	1835	...	1940	2009	...	...	2124	...	0250	0324	...	0434	...
—	Amfíklia d.	0730	0924	|	...	|	|	...	|	...	|	1922	...	2019	2053	...	...	|	...	|	|	...	|	...
	Tithoréa d.	0742	0936	|	...	1350	|	...	1638	...	|	1934	...	2031	2105	...	...	|	...	0345	|	...	|	...
	Levadiá d.	0801	0951	|	...	1402	1525	...	1651	...	1832	1954	...	2042	2118	...	...	|	...	0402	|	...	0528	...
	Thíva d.	0828	1011	|	...	1421	1543	...	1714	...	1850	2020	...	2102	2141	...	...	|	...	0430	0456	...	0546	...
	Inói **1420** d.	0848	1032	|	...	1437	1559	...	1730	...	1906	2042	...	2118	2158	...	...	|	...	0451	0518	...	0602	...
	Athína Lárisa **1420/40** a.	0945	1115	1140	...	1521	1643	...	1818	...	1950	2136	...	2208	2246	...	...	2317	...	0546	0612	...	0646	...

▲ – Local service Thessaloníki - Litóhoro - Lárisa and v.v.:

Thessaloníki d.	0608	0808	0945	1215	1320	1410	1600	1734	1945	2105	...
Platí d.	0634	0834	1011	1241	1346	1436	1626	1800	2011	2131	...
Kateríni d.	0657	0857	1034	1304	1409	1459	1649	1823	2034	2155	...
Litóhoro ⛰ d.	0705	0905	1042	1312	1417	1507	1657	1831	2042	2202	...
Lárisa a.	0741	0941	1118	1348	1453	1543	1733	1907	2118	2238	...

Lárisa d.	0650	0800	1002	1200	1400	1510	1553	1756	2000	2130	...
Litóhoro ⛰ d.	0727	0837	1039	1237	1437	1547	1630	1833	2037	2207	...
Kateríni d.	0735	0845	1047	1245	1445	1555	1638	1841	2045	2215	...
Platí d.	0758	0908	1110	1308	1508	1618	1701	1904	2108	2238	...
Thessaloníki a.	0823	0933	1135	1333	1533	1643	1726	1929	2133	2303	...

FOR NOTES SEE TABLE 1405

1405 THESSALONÍKI - ALEXANDRÚPOLI - DÍKEA

OSE, BDZh

km		*IC* 74	1680	1682	604	1684	*IC* 70	614		*IC* 92	444
		✕⟋	2	2	♦🍷	2	✕⟋	🍷		✕⟋	♦[R]
	Athína **1400** d.	2039	...	...	2359	...	0650	...	...	...	...
0	**Thessaloníki** d.	0201	...	...	0718	...	1221	1417	...	1825	1938
42	Kilkís d.	0227	...	...	0752	...	1250	1446	...	1850	2004
97	Rodópoli d.	0259	...	...	0832	...	1322	1524	...	1923	|
130	Strimón d.	|	...	...	0900	...	|	1548	...	|	|
162	Sérres d.	0337	...	...	0926	...	1400	1610	...	2001	2116
232	Dráma d.	0421	...	...	1021	...	1444	1701	...	2051	2205
327	Xánthi d.	0535	...	...	1144	...	1557	1821	...	2212	2325
374	Komotiní d.	0602	...	...	1217	...	1624	1850	...	2239	2353
443	**Alexandrúpoli** d.	0653	0714	1034	1315	1414	1716	1947	...	2331	0039
556	Píthio d.	...	0859	1221	...	1601	...	...	...	...	0252
*	*İstanbul Sirkeci* **1550** a.	...	|	|	...	|	...	...	...	...	0807
574	Néa Orestiáda d.	...	0919	1241	...	1621	...	...	...	...	...
611	Díkea a.	...	0951	1313	...	1653	...	...	...	...	...

	445	*IC* 71	613		1681	605	1683	*IC* 91	*IC* 75	1685
	♦[R]	✕⟋	🍷		2	♦🍷	2	✕⟋	✕⟋	2
Díkea d.	...	...	...	...	1125	...	1505	...	...	1741
Néa Orestiáda d.	...	...	...	...	1157	...	1537	...	...	1813
İstanbul Sirkeci **1550** d.	2100	...	...	...	|	...	|	...	...	|
Píthio d.	0250	...	...	...	1220	...	1600	...	...	1834
Alexandrúpoli d.	0415	0642	0829	...	1405	1522	1745	1755	2032	2041
Komotiní d.	0507	0735	0929	...	...	1625	...	1849	2125	...
Xánthi d.	0536	0803	1001	...	...	1701	...	1917	2153	...
Dráma d.	0649	0913	1124	...	...	1828	...	2031	2308	...
Sérres d.	0735	0957	1213	...	...	1919	...	2125	2353	...
Strimón d.	|	|	1234	...	...	1942	...	|	|	...
Rodópoli d.	|	1033	1259	...	...	2010	...	2205	0029	...
Kilkís d.	0854	1105	1341	...	...	2055	...	2240	0104	...
Thessaloníki a.	0920	1130	1410	...	...	2128	...	2304	0130	...
Athína **1400** a.	...	1643	...	...	...	0546	...	...	0646	...

♦ – **NOTES FOR TABLES 1400 / 1405** (LISTED BY TRAIN NUMBER)

444/5 – FILÍA - DOSTLUK EXPRESS – 🛏 1, 2 cl. Thessaloníki - İstanbul and v.v.
504/5 – 🛏 1, 2 cl. Athína - Thessaloníki and v.v.; 🛏 1, 2 cl. Athína - Thessaloníki (**360/3**) - Sofiya and v.v.
604 – [12] and 🍷 Athína - Thessaloníki - Alexandrúpoli; ▬ 2 cl. Athína - Thessaloníki.
605 – [12] and 🍷 Alexandrúpoli - Thessaloníki - Athína; ▬ 2 cl. Thessaloníki - Athína.

⟋ – [R] with supplement payable. *Icity* train.
◇ – [R] with supplement payable. *IcityE* train.
⛰ – Station for Mount Ólimbos.
* – Píthio - İstanbul: *268 km*.

1408 LÁRISA - PALEOFÁRSALOS - KALAMBÁKA

km					884						886
		2	2			2		2	2		
	Thessaloníki **1400** d.	...	...	...	...	...	...	...	...	...	1759
	Athína **1400** d.	...	...	...	0821	...	...	...	...	...	|
	Lárisa 1400 d.	0500	0626	...	|	...	...	1743	...	...	1941
0	Paleofársalos **1400** d.	0527	0650	...	1216	1444	...	1807	1922	...	2004
31	Kardítsa d.	0546	0706	...	1232	1500	...	...	1941	...	2020
60	Tríkala d.	0604	0723	...	1249	1517	...	...	1959	...	2037
82	**Kalambáka 1400** ⊡ a.	0619	0737	...	1303	1531	...	...	2014	...	2051

		883				885				
	2			2				2	2	
Kalambáka 1400 ⊡ d.	0630	0744	...	1331	...	1736	...	2100	2150	...
Tríkala d.	0646	0759	...	1346	...	1751	...	2115	2206	...
Kardítsa d.	0707	0816	...	1403	...	1808	...	2132	2225	...
Paleofársalos **1400** a.	0725	0832	...	1418	...	1823	...	2147	2241	...
Lárisa 1400 a.	0756	0856	...	...	...	|	...	2211	2310	...
Athína **1400** a.	...	|	...	...	...	2208	...	...	...	...
Thessaloníki **1400** a.	...	1039	...	...	...	...	...	...	...	...

⊡ – An infrequent bus service operates Kalambáka - Igumenítsa and v.v. (approximately *250 km*).

THESSALONÍKI - ÉDESSA - KOZÁNI and FLÓRINA 1410

km																									
		Ⓐ						Ⓐ					Ⓐ					Ⓐ					Ⓐ		
0	**Thessaloníki 1400** ..... d.	0448	...	0618	0618	...	0701	0838	0958	...	1112	...	1231	1400	...	1511	...	1646	1751	...	1911	...	2017	2216	...
38	Platí **1400** .... d.	0512	...	0644	0644	...	0728	0905	1025	...	1139	...	1259	1428	...	1537	...	1715	1818	...	1939	...	2046	2243	...
69	Véria .... d.	0537	...	0716	0716	...	0803	0936	1054	...	1212	...	1330	1500	...	1610	...	1748	1850	...	2010	...	2118	2316	...
97	Skídra .... d.	0556	...	0738	0738	...	0824	0957	1116	...	1234	...	1352	1523	...	1632	...	1809	1912	...	2031	...	2139	2337	...
112	**Édessa** .... d.	0608	...	0751	0751	...	0836	1010	1128	...	1247	...	1404	1535	...	1645	...	1821	1924	...	2045	...	2151	2349	...
162	Amíndeo .... d.	...	...	0838	0839	...	...	1059	...	...	1337	...	...	...	...	1733	...	...	...	...	2133	...	...	...	...
	Kozáni .... a.	...	...	0920	|	...	...	|	...	...	|	...	...	...	...	|	...	...	...	...	|	...	...	...	...
196	**Flórina** .... a.	...	...	...	0904	...	...	1124	...	...	1402	...	...	...	...	1758	...	...	...	...	2158	...	...	...	...
km			Ⓐ										Ⓐ		Ⓐ				Ⓐ					Ⓐ	
	Flórina .... d.	...	...	...	0608	...	...	...	0941	...	...	...	1219	...	...	1501	...	...	...	...	...	1926	...	...	...
0	Kozáni .... d.	...	...	...	|	...	...	0926	|	...	...	...	|	...	...	|	...	...	...	...	...	|	...	...	...
60	Amíndeo .... d.	...	...	...	0638	...	...	1011	1011	...	...	...	1249	...	...	1531	...	...	...	...	...	1956	...	...	...
	Édessa .... d.	0500	0640	...	0725	0917	...	1100	1100	...	1152	...	1337	...	1444	1617	...	1712	1830	1935	...	2044	...	2156	...
	Skídra .... d.	0513	0653	...	0739	0930	...	1114	1114	...	1205	...	1351	...	1457	1631	...	1725	1843	1948	...	2057	...	2209	...
	Véria .... d.	0535	0715	...	0802	0953	...	1133	1133	...	1228	...	1412	...	1519	1650	...	1747	1906	2011	...	2118	...	2230	...
	Platí **1400** .... d.	0606	0746	...	0833	1026	...	1157	1157	...	1300	...	1445	...	1553	1714	...	1820	1938	2044	...	2149	...	2300	...
	Thessaloníki 1400 ..... a.	0633	0812	...	0859	1052	...	1230	1230	...	1326	...	1515	...	1619	1740	...	1846	2004	2110	...	2215	...	2326	...

ATHÍNA - INÓI - HALKÍDA 1420

Local rail service. 2nd class. *83 km.* Journey: 70–90 minutes.
All trains call at Inói (± 60 minutes from Athína).

From **Athína** Lárisa: 0433Ⓐ, 0528, 0622, 0720, 0840, 1019, 1142, 1330, 1425Ⓐ, 1522, 1642, 1835, 1953, 2139, 2320.
From **Halkída**: 0508Ⓐ, 0603, 0701, 0758, 0900, 1058, 1200, 1320, 1502, 1559Ⓐ, 1711, 1815, 1910Ⓐ, 2025, 2216, 2338.

LÁRISA - VÓLOS 1425

Local rail service. Journey: ± 60 minutes.
See Table **1400** for *IC* services from / to Athína.

From **Lárisa**: 0710, 1106, 1352, 1602, 1841, 2143.
From **Vólos**: 0928, 1227, 1457, 1710, 2033, 2244.

PIREÁS, ATHÍNA and ATHÍNA AIRPORT ✈ - KÓRINTHOS - KIÁTO 1440

2nd class

km																										
0	Pireás .... ▲ d.	0436	...	...	0544	...	...	...	...	...	0644	...	...	and	...	...	2144	...	...	...	...	...	2244	...	...	...
10	**Athína** Lárisa **1400** .. ▲ d.	0457	...	...	0606	...	...	...	...	...	0706	...	...	at the	...	...	2206	...	...	...	...	...	2306	...	...	...
	Athína Airport ✈ .. ▲ d.	|	0531	0545	|	0600	0614	...	0631	0645	|	0700	0714	same	2131	2145	|	2200	2214	...	2231	2245	|	2300	2314	2331
	Neratziótissa .... ▲ d.	|	0553	0607	|	0622	0636	...	0653	0707	|	0722	0736	minutes	2153	2207	|	2222	2236	...	2253	2307	|	2322	2336	2353
20	Ano Liosia .... ▲ d.	0510	0602	0616	0619	0631	0645	...	0702	0716	0719	0731	0745	past each	2202	2216	2219	2231	2245	...	2302	2316	2319	2331	2345	0002
90	**Kórinthos** (new station) d.	0604	...	...	0713	...	...	...	...	...	0813	...	...	hour	...	...	2313	...	...	...	...	...	0013	...	...	...
111	**Kiáto 1450** .... a.	0618	...	...	0727	...	...	...	...	...	0827	...	...	until	...	...	2327	...	...	...	...	...	0027	...	...	...

km																										
	Kiáto 1450 .... d.	...	...	...	0536	...	...	...	...	...	0636	...	and	...	...	...	2136	...	...	...	...	...	2236	...	...	...
	Kórinthos (new station) d.	...	...	...	0551	...	...	...	...	...	0651	...	at the	...	...	...	2151	...	...	...	...	...	2251	...	...	...
0	Ano Liosia .... ▲ d.	0606	0621	0635	0647	0650	...	0706	0721	0735	0747	0750	same	2206	2221	2235	2247	2250	...	2306	2321	2335	2347	2350	...	0006
9	Neratziótissa .... ▲ d.	0616	0631	0645	|	0700	...	0716	0731	0745	|	0800	minutes	2216	2231	2245	|	2300	...	2316	2331	2345	|	0000	...	0016
34	Athína Airport ✈ .. ▲ a.	0637	0652	0706	|	0721	...	0737	0752	0806	|	0821	past each	2237	2252	2306	|	2321	...	2337	2352	0006	|	0021	...	0037
	Athína Lárisa **1400** .. ▲ d.	...	...	...	0704	...	...	...	...	...	0804	...	hour	...	...	...	2304	...	...	...	...	...	0004	...	...	...
	Pireás .... ▲ a.	...	...	...	0722	...	...	...	...	...	0822	...	until	...	...	...	2322	...	...	...	...	...	0022	...	...	...

▲ – Frequent Metro services operate as follows:
Line 1: Pireás - Monastiraki - Omónia - Attiki - Neratziótissa (journey time: ± 45 minutes).
Line 2: Syntagma - Omónia - Athína Lárisa (for **Athína** mainline station) - Attiki (journey time: ± 7 minutes).
Line 3: Monastiraki - Syntagma - Athína Airport ✈ (journey time: ± 37 minutes).
Operators: ISAP Line 1; Attiko Metro Lines 2 and 3.

Allow sufficient time for connecting shipping services at Pireás as the port is very large.

KIÁTO - PÁTRA - KALAMÁTA 1450

Narrow gauge. 2nd class only (except *IC* trains)

km		**1350**	*IC* **20**		*IC* **22**	**1352**	**300**	**304**		*IC* **12**	
			Ⲯ✗		Ⲯ✗					Ⲯ✗	
0	**Kiáto 1440** .... d.	...	0737	...	0955	...	1237	1745	...	1945	...
13	Xilókastro .... d.	...	0749	...	1007	...	1251	1802	...	1957	...
56	Diakoftó .... d.	...	0840	...	1055	...	1347	1858	...	2045	...
109	**Pátra** .... a.	...	0931	...	1146	...	1444	1955	...	2139	...
109	**Pátra** .... d.	0617	0934	...	1149	...	...	...	...	...	...
186	Amaliáda .... d.	0745	1052	...	1307	...	...	...	...	...	...
209	**Pírgos** .... d.	0813	1111	...	1324	...	...	...	...	...	...
	Kiparissía .... d.	|	|	...	...	1508	...	...	...	...	...
266	Kaloneró .... d.	0917	1205	...	...	1519	...	...	...	...	...
272	Kiparissía .... a.	|	|	...	...	|	...	...	...	...	...
339	**Kalamáta 1452** .... a.	1040	1321	...	...	1645	...	...	...	...	...

	IC **11**	**301**		**303**		*IC* **21**	**1351**	*IC* **23**		**1353**
	Ⲯ✗					Ⲯ✗		Ⲯ✗		
Kalamáta 1452 .... d.	...	...	...	...	...	...	1325	1632	...	1739
Kiparissía .... d.	...	...	...	...	...	...	|	|	...	|
Kaloneró .... d.	...	...	...	...	...	...	1455	1749	...	1905
Kiparissía .... a.	...	...	...	...	...	...	1502	|	...	|
Pírgos .... d.	...	...	...	...	...	1444	...	1844	...	2010
Amaliáda .... d.	...	...	...	...	...	1502	...	1902	...	2037
Pátra .... a.	...	...	...	...	...	1619	...	2019	...	2204
Pátra .... d.	0734	0956	...	1503	...	1622	...	2022	...	...
Diakoftó .... d.	0825	1056	...	1601	...	1713	...	2116	...	...
Xilókastro .... d.	0917	1153	...	1658	...	1804	...	2204	...	...
Kiáto 1440 .... a.	0928	1206	...	1711	...	1815	...	2215	...	...

✗ – Ⓡ with supplement payable.

KÓRINTHOS - ÁRGOS - KALAMÁTA 1452

Narrow gauge. 2nd class only

Trípoli - Kalamáta and v.v. currently closed for reconstruction

Kórinthos (new) 1440 ...... d.	1023	1023	...	1423	1423	...	1823	1823	...	2223	...
Árgos .... a.	1128	1128	...	1528	1528	...	1928	1928	...	2328	...
Náfplio .... a.	|	1149	...	|	1549	...	|	1949	...	2346	2351
Árgos .... d.	1130	...	...	1530	...	...	1930	...	...	...	0012
Trípoli .... d.	1250	...	...	1650	...	...	2046	...	...	...	0128
Kalamáta 1450 .... a.	...	...	...	...	...	...	...	...	...	...	...

Kalamáta 1450 .... d.	...	...	...	...	...	...	...	...	...	...	...
Trípoli .... d.	0530	...	0724	...	1111	...	...	1511	...	...	...
Árgos .... a.	0646	...	0840	...	1231	...	...	1631	...	...	...
Náfplio .... d.	0707	0717	|	...	|	1216	...	|	1616	...	2017
Árgos .... d.	...	0735	0841	...	1235	1235	...	1635	1635	...	2035
Kórinthos (new) 1440 .. a.	...	0840	0946	...	1340	1340	...	1740	1740	...	2140

PELOPÓNNISOS narrow-gauge branches 1455

Athína – Lutráki *Service currently suspended* 2nd class only

km		⑥⑦	
0	**Athína** Ágii Anárgiri ◇ ... d.	0710	1600
79	Isthmós .... d.	0840	1730
85	**Lutráki** .... a.	0851	1741

	⑥⑦	
Lutráki .... d.	0909	1809
Isthmós .... d.	0921	1821
Athína Ágii Anárgiri ◇ .... a.	1050	1950

Diakoftó – Kalávrita 2nd class only, rack railway

km				Ⓐ		Ⓐ
0	**Diakoftó** ... d.	0810	1115	1233	1412	1532
23	**Kalávrita** .. a.	0917	1222	1343	1522	1642

			Ⓐ		Ⓐ
Kalávrita d.	0928	1227	1410	1530	1650
Diakoftó a.	1035	1337	1520	1640	1757

Katákolo – Pírgos – Olimbía 2nd class only

km			Ⓐ		Ⓐ			Ⓐ		Ⓐ		
0	Katákolo .... d.	...	0836	...	1017	1111	...	1253	...	1447	1648	...
12	Pírgos .... a.	0655	0856	...	1039	1135	...	1317	...	1511	1710	...
33	Olimbía .... a.	0724	0918	...	...	1201	...	1347	...	1538	...	...

	Ⓐ				Ⓐ	Ⓐ					
Olimbía .... d.	0730	...	0922	...	...	1205	...	1351	...	1542	...
Pírgos .... d.	0801	...	0950	...	1044	1230	...	1420	...	1612	...
Katákolo .... a.	0823	...	1012	...	1106	1248	...	1442	...	1634	...

◇ – Ágii Anárgiri is situated 5 km north of Athína Lárisa station.

BULGARIA and TURKEY IN EUROPE

SEE MAP PAGE 491

Operator: Български Държавни Железници – Bâlgarski Dârzhavni Zheleznitsi (БДЖ - BDZh); Türkiye Cumhuryeti Devlet Demiryolları (TCDD).

Services: All trains convey first and second class seating, except where shown otherwise in footnotes or by '2' in the train column, or where the footnote shows sleeping and/or couchette cars only. Descriptions of sleeping (🛏) and couchette (▬) cars appear on page 8. Reservation of seats is possible on most express trains. Services covering Turkey in Asia and beyond are given in the **Thomas Cook Overseas Timetable**.

Timings: BDŽ schedules are valid **December 13, 2009 - December 11, 2010**. Timetable amendments are possible at short notice so please confirm timings locally before travelling. TCDD schedules are the latest available. Please refer to Tables **60**, **98** and **99** for international through cars to / from Burgas and Varna (summer only).

1500 BUCUREŞTI - RUSE - SOFIYA

km		4611	2610	2612	2614	463/5	463	40115	2654	383
						[R]	[R]	2		[R]
			🍷	🍷		T	R			B
0	**Bucureşti** Nord .... **1600** d.	...	...	...	...	1224	1224	...	...	2002
51	Videle .... **1600** d.	...	...	...	...	1314	1314	...	...	|
114	Giurgiu Nord .... a.	...	...	...	...	1410	1410	...	...	2150
114	Giurgiu Nord 🏛 .... d.	...	...	...	...	1425	1425	...	...	2205
131	**Ruse** 🏛 .... a.	...	...	...	...	1450	1450	...	...	2230
131	**Ruse** .... **1525** d.	0600	*0802*	*1116*	*1309*	1527	1527	1758	...	2330
242	Gorna Oryakhovitsa .. **1520/5** d.	0815	1056	1427	1609	1726	1733	2026	2042	0140
342	Pleven .... **1520** d.	0932	1204	1543	1724	...	1844	...	2155	0257
448	Mezdra .... **1520** d.	1051	1320	1710	1845	...	1954	...	...	0414
536	**Sofiya** .... **1520** a.	1230	1453	1848	2024	...	2130	...	...	0555

	2611	464/2	462	2613	40114	40116	4612	382
		[R]	[R]		2	2		[R]
	🍷	T	R	🍷				B
Sofiya .... **1520** d.	0705	...	0905	1005	...	...	1540	1940
Mezdra .... **1520** d.	0835	...	1036	1137	...	...	1713	2114
Pleven .... **1520** d.	0946	...	1155	1300	...	...	1830	2235
Gorna Oryakhovitsa .... **1520/5** d.	1051	1325	1325	1412	1506	1655	1956	2359
Ruse .... **1525** a.	*1337*	1525	1525	...	1737	1930	2155	0205
Ruse 🏛 .... d.	...	1600	1600	...	...	...	...	0315
Giurgiu Nord 🏛 .... a.	...	1625	1625	...	...	...	...	0340
Giurgiu Nord .... d.	...	1640	1640	...	...	...	...	0355
Videle .... **1600** a.	...	1739	1739	...	...	...	...	|
Bucureşti Nord .... **1600** a.	...	1830	1830	...	...	...	...	0544

B – BULGARIA EXPRESS – 🛏 1, 2 cl. and (12) Bucureşti - Sofiya and v.v.; 🛏 1, 2 cl.* Moskva - Kyïv - Sofiya and v.v. Conveys on dates in Table **98**: 🛏 2 cl.* Minsk - Kyïv - Sofiya and v.v., 🛏 2 cl.* Lviv - Sofiya and v.v.

R – ROMANIA – (2) Sofiya - Bucureşti and v.v.; 🛏 1, 2 cl. and ▬ 1, 2 cl. Thessaloníki - Sofiya - Bucureşti and v.v.; 🛏 1, 2 cl. Sofiya - Bucureşti (**370/1**) - Budapest and v.v.;

T – BOSPHOR – 🛏 1, 2 cl. and ▬ 2 cl. Bucureşti - Svilengrad 🏛 - Kapıkule 🏛 - İstanbul and v.v.; (2) Bucureşti - Dimitrovgrad and v.v.

* – Only available for journeys from / to Russia, Belarus or Ukraine.

1510 SOFIYA - VIDIN - CALAFAT - CRAIOVA

km		70102	7620	1620	7622	7624	7630	70242
		2		P				2
0	**Sofiya** ... **1520** d.	...	0715	0925	1225	1625	1910	...
88	Mezdra .. **1520** d.	0536	|	|	1412	|	2055	...
106	Vratsa .... d.	0559	0904	1104	1430	1804	2111	...
182	Brusartsi ..... ⊖ d.	0738	1026	...	1557	1918	2231	2234
204	Lom .... ⊖ a.	|	|	...	|	|	2257	|
269	**Vidin** 🏛 ★ ..... a.	0930	1205	...	1740	2050	...	0022

	7631	7621	1623	7623	70103	7625
			P		2	
Vidin 🏛 ★ .... d.	...	0605	...	1245	1355	1608
Lom .... ⊖ d.	0535	|	...	|	|	|
Brusartsi .... ⊖ d.	0606	0737	...	1426	1553	1800
Vratsa .... d.	0734	0850	1335	1550	1722	1927
Mezdra .... **1520** a.	0750	|	|	1605	1741	|
Sofiya .... **1520** a.	0948	1035	1522	1755	2010	2115

km								
		E			G ▲			
0	**Calafat** 🏛 ★ .. d.	0335	0600	...	1200	...	1510	...
107	**Craiova 1620** . a.	0650	0927	...	1531	...	1837	...

			⑧ r			⑧
Craiova 1620 .... d.	0812	...	1420	1645	...	2005
Calafat 🏛 ★ .... a.	1132	...	1745	2005	...	2317

E – ①–⑥ (not Dec. 25, 26, Jan. 1, 2, Apr. 5, May 1, 24, Dec. 1).

G – ①–⑥ only.

P – (2) Plovdiv - Sofia - Vratsa and v.v.

r – Not Dec. 24, 25, 31, Jan. 1, Apr. 4, 30, May 23, Nov. 30.

⊖ – Additional journeys Brusartsi - Lom and v.v. Journey time: 26–30 minutes. **From Brusartsi** at 0620, 0750, 1040, 1430, 1610, 1801, 1921 and 2006. **From Lom** at 0704, 0830, 0950, 1335, 1520, 1705, 1845 and 2130.

▲ – During engineering work: Calafat 1315, Craiova 1639.

★ – An infrequent vehicle / passenger ⛴ service operates Vidin - Calafat and v.v. (the ferry terminal at Vidin is approx. 5 km north of the railway station). Only operates with a full load of vehicles so a long wait may be possible. Journey time: 20 minutes.

1520 SOFIYA - PLOVDIV - BURGAS and VARNA

km	km					2655	8631	8611	2611		3621	2613	8613	8613 8661	2615	8615	4612	4640	3623	8641	2641	2637	8637	3637	8627	2627
																							△	▲	△	△
			⊙	⊙	⊙			🍷	🍷	⊙		🍷					R		🍷			B				
0	0	**Sofiya** .... **1500 1510** ▫ d.	...	...	...	...	...	0630	0705	...	0720	1005	1045	1045	1320	1345	1540	...	1605	1630	1730	2125	...	2225	2240	2325
	119	Pazardzhik .... ▫ d.	...	...	...	...	...	0808	|	...	|	|	1240	1240	|	1542	|	...	|	1809	|	|	...	|	0035	|
	156	**Plovdiv** .... ▫ a.	...	...	...	...	...	0830	|	...	|	|	1308	1308	|	1610	|	...	|	1833	|	|	...	|	0104	|
	156	**Plovdiv** .... d.	...	...	...	...	0655	0833	|	...	|	|	1318	1318	|	1615	|	1410	|	1840	|	|	2310	|	0110	|
	262	Stara Zagora .... d.	...	...	...	...	0841	1008	|	...	|	|	1502	1502	|	1807**v**	|	1613	|	2031	|	|	0056	|	0324**z**	|
	340	Yambol .... d.	...	0652	0845	...	0944	1109	|	...	|	|	1605	1605	|	1920	|	|	|	2130	|	|	0208**v**	|	0428	|
		Karlovo .... d.	...	|	|	...	|	|	|	0600	0945	|	|	|	|	|	|	|	1822	...	|	|	|	0050	|	|
		Tulovo .... d.	...	|	|	...	|	|	|	0758**z**	1111**t**	|	|	|	|	|	|	1659	1928	...	|	|	|	0211**v**	|	|
		Sliven .... d.	0545	|	|	...	|	|	|	0920	1217	|	|	|	|	|	|	|	2031	...	|	|	|	0320	|	|
	389	Karnobat .... **1530** d.	0645	0742	0938	...	1031	1147	|	▬	1304	|	1655	1710	|	2005	|	|	2114	...	|	|	0253	0409	0513	|
	450	**Burgas** .... **1530** a.	0803	0850	1047	...	|	1229	|	...	1350	|	|	1754	|	2052	|	◐	2200	...	|	|	|	|	0559	|
88		Mezdra .... **1500 1510** d.	▬	...	...	...	|	...	0835	...	...	1137	|	...	1458	...	1713	|	...	...	1859	2304	|	|	...	0128
194		Pleven .... **1500** d.	...	...	...	0655	|	...	0946	...	...	1300	|	...	1617	...	1830	|	...	...	2011	0027	|	|	...	0248
294		Gorna Oryakhovitsa .. **1500** a.	...	...	...	0807	|	...	1051	...	...	1412	|	...	1728	...	1942	1943	...	...	2120	0137	|	|	...	0404
294		Gorna Oryakhovitsa .... d.	⊙	...	...	0814	|	...	1056	⊙	...	1422	|	...	1740	...	...	1955	...	...	...	0142	|	|	...	0414
435		Shumen .... **1530** d.	0745	...	...	1003	|	...	1240	1310	...	1611	|	...	1930	...	...	2158	...	...	...	0333	|	|	...	0611
459		Kaspichan .... **1530** d.	0812	...	...	1020	|	...	|	1338	...	1629	|	...	1949	...	...	...	...	...	...	0352	|	|	...	0631
518		Povelyanovo .... **1530** d.	0911	...	...	1109	|	...	|	1444	...	1715	1856	...	2035	...	...	...	...	...	...	...	0459	0608	...	0722
543	546	**Varna** .... **1530** a.	0942	...	...	1135	1242	...	1359	1518	...	1740	1918	...	2100	...	...	...	...	...	...	...	0525	0634	...	0747

km		2640	8640	3620	4641	4611	8610			2610	8660 8612	8612	2612	2614	3622		8614	8632	2654			8626	3636	2626	8636	2636
																						△	▲	△	△	
				🍷	A	R		⊙	⊙	🍷			🍷			⊙	🍷			⊙	⊙					C
	Varna .... **1530** d.	...	...	...	...	...	...	...	0630	0745	...	0925	1056	1240	...	1410	...	1510	1720	...	1945	...	2145	2230	2305	...
	Povelyanovo .... **1530** d.	...	...	...	...	...	...	...	0702	0805	...	0948	|	1303	...	1444	...	1531	|	...	2017	...	2208	2253	2328	...
	Kaspichan .... **1530** d.	...	...	...	...	...	...	...	0806	|	...	|	1205	1350	...	1550	...	|	1829	...	2121	...	|	2341	|	0035
	Shumen .... **1530** d.	...	...	...	0555	...	...	...	0830	0905	...	|	1225	1409	...	1616	...	|	1848	...	2146	...	|	0001	|	0055
	Gorna Oryakhovitsa .... a.	...	...	...	0804	...	...	...	▬	1051	...	|	1417	1559	...	▬	...	|	2037	...	▬	...	|	0151	|	0244
	Gorna Oryakhovitsa .. **1500** d.	0500	...	...	0820	0815	...	...	...	1056	...	|	1427	1609	...	...	...	|	2042	...	...	...	|	0159	|	0249
	Pleven .... **1500** d.	0611	...	...	|	0932	...	...	...	1204	...	|	1543	1724	...	...	...	|	2155	...	...	...	|	0318	|	0406
	Mezdra .... **1500 1510** d.	0725	...	...	|	1051	...	...	...	1320	...	|	1710	1845	...	...	...	|	...	...	⊙	...	|	0437	|	0532
0	**Burgas** .... **1530** d.	|	...	0535	◐	|	0655	0714	...	|	1052	|	|	|	1430	...	1540	|	...	1758	1945	2216	|	|	|	|
61	Karnobat .... **1530** d.	|	...	0622	|	|	0745	0829	⊙	|	1156**t**	1156**v**	|	|	1515	⊙	1624	1722	...	1911	2100	2305	0011	|	0121	|
119	Sliven .... d.	|	...	0704	|	|	|	0923	*0945*	|	|	|	|	|	1558	1736	|	|	...	2014	|	|	0101	|	|	|
195	Tulovo .... d.	|	...	0807	1115	|	|	...	1125	|	|	|	|	|	1720**t**	1944**r**	|	|	...	...	|	|	0228**t**	|	|	|
269	Karlovo .... d.	|	...	0917	|	|	|	...	1254	|	|	|	|	|	1843	2112	|	|	...	...	|	|	0345	|	|	|
	Yambol .... d.	|	0515	|	|	|	0831	...	...	|	1242	1242	|	|	|	...	1702	1802	...	...	2148	2350	|	|	0207	|
	Stara Zagora .... d.	|	0620	|	1201	|	0943	...	...	|	1352	1352	|	|	|	...	1806	1906	...	...	...	0100	|	|	0326**t**	|
	Plovdiv .... a.	|	0756	|	1341	|	1128	...	...	|	1544	1544	|	|	|	...	1937	2044	...	...	...	0238	|	|	0513	|
	Plovdiv .... ▫ d.	|	0800	|	...	|	1135	...	...	|	1550	1550	|	|	|	...	1942	...	...	...	...	0245	|	|	...	|
	Pazardzhik .... ▫ d.	|	0829	|	...	|	1209	...	...	|	1624	1624	|	|	|	...	2010	...	...	...	...	0319	|	|	...	|
418	**Sofiya** .... **1500 1510** ▫ a.	0900	1020	1130	...	1230	1411	...	...	1453	1835	1835	1848	2024	2101	...	2158	...	...	...	...	0521	0611	0618	...	0715

	8611		1621	8613	8615		1623	8641	1625	1627	8627
	🍷	⊙				⊙	F				
Sofiya .... d.	0630	0645	0830	1045	1345	1410	1530	1630	1730	1830	2240
Pazardzhik .... d.	0808	0909	1024	1240	1542	1628	1708	1809	1926	2024	0035
Plovdiv .... a.	0830	0948	1051	1308	1610	1703	1730	1833	1954	2050	0104

	8626	1650	1620	8640	8610		1622		8612		1624	8614
		D	F			⊙		⊙		⊙		🍷
Plovdiv .... d.	0245	0600	0700	0800	1135	1210	1255	1405	1550	1732	1810	1942
Pazardzhik .... d.	0319	0633	0729	0829	1209	1249	1328	1450	1624	1812	1843	2010
Sofiya .... a.	0521	0836	0920	1020	1411	1512	1530	1722	1835	2034	2046	2158

B – 🛏 1, 2 cl. and (12) Sofiya - Dobrich - Kardam (Table **1540**). Conveys 🛏 1, 2 cl. and (12) Sofiya - Kaspichan (**9636**) - Samuil - Silistra (Table **1530**).

C – 🛏 1, 2 cl. and (12) Kardam - Dobrich - Sofiya (Table **1540**). Conveys 🛏 1, 2 cl. and (12) Silistra (**9637**) - Samuil - Kaspichan (**2636**) - Sofiya (Table **1530**).

D – From Dimitrovgrad (Table **1550**).

F – (2) Plovdiv - Sofiya - Vratsa and v.v.

R – To / from Ruse (Table **1500**).

r – Arrives 1901.

t – Arrives 15 – 20 minutes earlier.

v – Arrives 9 – 11 minutes earlier.

z – Arrives 24 – 26 minutes earlier.

⊙ – Local stopping train. 2nd class only.

△ – Conveys 🛏 1, 2 cl. and (12).

▲ – Conveys ▬ 2 cl. and (12).

▫ – See panel below main table for complete service Sofia - Plovdiv and v.v.

◐ – Via Veliko Târnovo (Table **1525**).

RUSE - STARA ZAGORA - MOMCHILGRAD and PLOVDIV 1525

km					4641				463/5	4647	8636
		⊙	⊙	⊙m	S	⊙	⊙	⊙	[R]B		
0	**Ruse** 1500 d.	...	...	...	*0600*	0802	1116	1309	1527	2157	...
111	Gorna Oryakhovitsa 1500 a.	...	...	...	*0808*	1035	1355	1541	1726	2356	...
111	Gorna Oryakhovitsa d.	...	0505	...	0820	*1120*	1431	1620	1748	0001	...
125	Veliko Târnovo d.	...	0527	...	0837	*1145*	1452	1644	1806	0018	...
226	Tulovo d.	...	0819	...	1115t	▬	1716	1937	2009	0224	...
253	Stara Zagora a.	...	0859	...	1151	...	1754	2016	2045	0300	...
253	Stara Zagora 1520 d.	0500	...	1016	1201	...	...	▬	2048	0316	0326
359	**Plovdiv** 1520 a.	|	...	|	1341	...	...	...	|	|	0513
310	Dimitrovgrad a.	0628	...	1151	...	⊙	...	⊙	2202	0436	...
310	Dimitrovgrad d.	...	...	...	...	1455	...	2035	...	*0555*	...
411	**Momchilgrad** a.	...	...	...	...	1739	...	2325	...	*0849*	...

			464/2			4640			8637	4646
	⊙	⊙	[R]B	⊙	⊙r	S	⊙	⊙		
Momchilgrad d.	...	...	...	0615	...	...	...	*1650*	...	*1945*
Dimitrovgrad a.	...	...	...	0905	...	...	...	*1946*	...	*2243*
Dimitrovgrad d.	...	...	0650	▬	1307	...	...	2002	...	2325
Plovdiv 1520 d.	...	...	|	...	|	1410	...	|	2310	|
Stara Zagora 1520 a.	...	...	0806	⊙	1459	1601	...	2126	0051	0041
Stara Zagora d.	...	0705	0816	1021	...	1613	1840	...	...	0105
Tulovo d.	...	0746	0915t	1102	...	1659v	1940t	...	...	0201t
Veliko Târnovo d.	0635	1025	1123	1329	...	1925	2224	...	...	0424
Gorna Oryakhovitsa a.	0656	1044	1140	1347	...	1943	2245	...	...	0440
Gorna Oryakhovitsa 1500 d.	0713	1116	1325	*1506*	...	*1956*	...	...	...	0445
Ruse 1500 a.	0940	1337	1525	*1737*	...	*2155*	...	...	...	0652

B – BOSPHOR – (2) Bucureşti - Dimitrovgrad and v.v.; conveys 🛏 1, 2 cl. and ▬ 2 cl. Bucureşti - Ruse - İstanbul and v.v.
S – To / from Shumen (Table **1520**).
m – Change trains at Mikhailovo (a. 1040, d. 1050).
r – Change trains at Mikhailovo (a. 1409, d. 1440).
t – Arrives 17 – 21 minutes earlier.
v – Arrives 1650.
⊙ – Local stopping train. 2nd class only.

RUSE - SILISTRA, VARNA and BURGAS 1530

km		9636	9621	3660*			8661	9623			9637
		K	🍷	2	⊙	⊙			⊙	⊙	L
0	**Ruse** d.	...	0610	0610	0730	...	...	1615	1739	...	...
71	Razgrad d.	...	0738	0738	0914	...	...	1734	1920	...	...
93	Samuil d.	0504	0801	0801	0936	0940	...	1755	1940	2020	2321
206	**Silistra** a.	0722	|	|	|	1220	...	|	...	2310	|
142	Kaspichan a.	...	0903	0903	1047	▬	...	1900	...	...	0024
142	Kaspichan 1520 d.	...	0909	0925	*1055*	⊙	...	1905	...	...	...
166	Shumen 1520 d.	...	|	0942	*1118*	*1350*	...	|	...	...	...
216	Komunari d.	...	|	1051	...	1524	...	|	...	...	...
299	Karnobat 1520 a.	...	|	1209	...	1700	1710	|	...	...	...
360	**Burgas** 1520 a.	...	|	1306	...	...	1754	|	...	...	...
201	Povelyanovo 1520 d.	...	|	...	...	...	...	1953	...	...	...
226	**Varna** 1520 a.	...	1022	...	...	...	...	2018	...	...	...

	9636				9620	8631				3661	9622	9637
	K	⊙	⊙	⊙			⊙	⊙	⊙	2	🍷	L
Varna 1520 d.	...	...	...	...	0915	...	...	...	...	...	1735	...
Povelyanovo 1520 d.	...	...	...	...	0938	...	...	...	...	...	1758	...
Burgas 1520 d.	...	...	...	...	|	*0855*	...	...	...	1504	|	...
Karnobat 1520 d.	...	...	...	...	|	1031	...	...	...	1602	|	...
Komunari d.	...	...	...	...	|	1139	1210	...	...	1722	|	...
Shumen 1520 d.	...	...	...	*0611*	|	...	1322	...	*1611*	1833	|	...
Kaspichan 1520 a.	...	...	...	*0630*	1024	...	▬	...	*1628*	1849	1854	...
Kaspichan d.	0400	...	...	0638	1026	...	...	...	1642	1908	1908	...
Silistra d.	|	...	0505	|	|	...	⊙	1500	|	|	|	2055
Samuil d.	0454	0555	0756	0802	1122	...	1552	1743	1758	2010	2010	2311
Razgrad d.	...	0616	...	0824	1141	...	1613	...	1822	2031	2031	...
Ruse a.	...	0759	...	0952	1255	...	1757	...	2001	2150	2150	...

K – 🛏 1, 2 cl. and (12) Sofiya (**2637**) - Kaspichan (**9636**) - Samuil - Silistra.
L – 🛏 1, 2 cl. and (12) Silistra - Samuil - Kaspichan (**2636**) - Sofiya.
* – Train **9621** Ruse - Kaspichan.
⊙ – Local stopping train. 2nd class only.

VARNA and SOFIYA - DOBRICH - KARDAM 1540

km		2637	2627				2615		
		△	△	2	2	2		2	
0	**Varna** 1520 1530 d.	...	...	0705	1105	1432	...	2030	...
	Sofiya 1520 d.	2125	2325	|	|	|	1320	|	...
25	Povelyanovo 1520 1530 d.	|	0721	0736	1137	1503	2034	2101	...
93	**Dobrich** a.	0620	...	0907	1304	1623	...	2230	...
131	Kardam a.	0737	...	1013	...	1730	...	...	...

		2610		2614			2636
	2	🍷	2		2	2	△
Kardam d.	...	...	1030	...	...	1742	2040
Dobrich d.	0640	...	1136	...	1355	1850	2204
Povelyanovo 1520 1530 a.	0800	0805	1255	1303	1524	2008	|
Sofiya 1520 a.	|	1453	|	2024	|	|	0715
Varna 1520 1530 a.	0838	...	1329	...	1603	2041	...

△ – Conveys 🛏 1, 2 cl. and (12).

BDŽ; TCDD (SOFIYA -) PLOVDIV - İSTANBUL 1550

km	Bulgarian/Greek train number					1641		444	491	463/5
	Turkish train number			81721				81021	81031	81031
		2	2		2	2		[R]T	[R]R	[R]B
	Bucureşti 1500 d.	...	...	...	...	...	...	...	...	1224
	Beograd 1380 d.	...	...	...	...	...	...	...	0750	|
0	*Sofiya* 1540 d.	...	*0630*	...	...	*1630*	*1730*	...	1910	|
156	**Plovdiv** d.	0540	0920	...	1804	1855	2015	...	2148	|
234	Dimitrovgrad d.	0740	1110	...	2005	2028	2207	...	2354	2354
299	Svilengrad a.	0904	▬	...	2135	▬	▬	...	0105	0105
299	Svilengrad 🏛 d.	▬	...	...	▬	**81731**	...	...	0120	0120
318	Kapıkule 🏛 a.	...	...	...	...		...	...	0145	0145
318	Kapıkule d.	...	...	0700	...	1535	...	...	0330	0330
338	Edirne d.	...	...	0733	**82901**	1603	...	...	0355	0355
	Thessaloníki 1405 d.	...	**82861**	|	2	|	**81741**	1938	|	|
	Píthio 🏛 d.	...	2	|	1530	|		0251	|	|
	Uzunköprü 🏛 d.	...	0750	|	1601	|	1640	0400	|	|
385	Pehlivanköy d.	**81601**	0815	0828	...	1658	1702	0421	|	|
406	Alpullu d.		0837	0852	...	1717	1732	0448	0502	0502
506	Çerkezköy d.	0700	...	1036	...	...	1919	0606	0621	0621
593	Halkalı d.	0837	...	1221	...	...	2103	0727	0743	0743
621	**İstanbul** Sirkeci a.	0924	...	1304	...	...	2133	0807	0825	0825

km	Turkish train number	81742	81732	82902	81722	82864	81602	81022	81032	81032
	Bulgarian/Greek train number							445	490	464/2
				2		2		[R]T	[R]R	[R]B
0	**İstanbul** Sirkeci d.	0830	...	...	1550	...	1800	2100	2200	2200
28	Halkalı d.	0916	...	...	1635	...	1839	2136	2238	2238
115	Çerkezköy d.	1101	...	...	1819	...	2020	2259	0002	0002
215	Alpullu d.	1258k	1250	...	2005	2015	▬	0026	0124	0124
237	Pehlivanköy d.	1319	1311	...	2026	2038	...	0045	|	|
258	Uzunköprü 🏛 d.	1339	|	1410	|	2059	...	0140	|	|
268	Píthio 🏛 a.	▬	|	1438	|	...	...	0208	|	|
	Thessaloníki 1405 a.	...	|	▬	|	...	...	0920	|	|
	Edirne d.	...	1405	...	2118	...	...	▬	0230	0230
	Kapıkule a.	...	1432	...	2145	...	...	...	0252	0252
	Kapıkule 🏛 d.	...	▬	...	▬	...	...	...	0405	0405
	Svilengrad 🏛 a.	2	...	...	2	...	**1650**	**1640**	0430	0430
	Svilengrad d.	0540	2	2	1808	...		2	0508	0508
	Dimitrovgrad d.	0706	0938	1725	1958f	...	0430	0600	0641	0650
	Plovdiv a.	0903	1115	1910	2140	...	0548	0728	0801	|
	Sofiya 1540 a.	...	*1411*	*2158*	...	...	0836	*1020*	1035	|
	Beograd 1380 a.	...	...	...	...	...	...	...	1918	|
	Bucureşti 1500 a.	...	...	...	...	...	...	...	...	1830

B – BOSPHOR – 🛏 1, 2 cl. and ▬ 2 cl. Bucureşti - İstanbul and v.v.
R – BALKAN EXPRESS – 🛏 1, 2 cl. Beograd - Sofiya - İstanbul and v.v. Conveys June 2 - Oct. 30 (from Sofia), June 3 - Oct. 31 (from İstanbul) ▬ 2 cl. Sofia - İstanbul and v.v.
T – FILIA - DOSTLUK EXPRESS – 🛏 1, 2 cl. Thessaloníki - İstanbul and v.v.
f – Arrives 1936.
k – Arrives 1243.

IDO BOSPHORUS FERRIES 1555

Ferry service **İstanbul Karaköy - Haydarpaşa** (for Asian rail services) and v.v. *2 km*. Journey time: 15 – 35 minutes. **Operator**: IDO – İstanbul Deniz Otobüsleri.

From İstanbul Karaköy: On Ⓐ at 0610, 0630, 0700, 0725, 0740, 0810, 0845, 0915, 0930, 0950, 1020, 1040, 1100 and every 20 minutes until 1620; then 1645, 1700, 1715, 1730, 1800, 1815, 1830, 1845, 1900, 1915, 1930, 1940, 2000, 2030, 2100, 2130, 2200, 2230 and 2300. On ⑥ at 0630, 0700, 0730, 0750, 0810 and every 20 minutes until 1930; then 2000, 2030, 2100, 2130, 2200, 2230 and 2300. On † at 0630 and every 30 minutes until 2300.

From Haydarpaşa: On Ⓐ at 0620, 0635, 0705, 0720, 0735, 0750, 0805, 0820, 0835, 0905, 0920, 0935, 1035, 1055, 1115, 1120, 1140, 1200 and every 20 minutes until 1700; then 1715, 1730, 1745, 1815, 1830, 1845, 1900, 1915, 1930, 2005, 2035, 2105, 2135, 2205, 2235 and 2305. On ⑥ at 0635, 0705, 0725, 0750, 0810, 0830 and every 20 minutes until 1930; then 2005, 2035, 2105, 2135, 2205, 2235 and 2305. On † at 0635, 0705, 0735, 0750, 0820 and every 30 minutes until 1920; then 2005, 2035, 2105, 2135, 2205, 2235, 2305.

BDŽ, OSE SOFIYA - KULATA - THESSALONÍKI 1560

km		361	5621	6621	5611	6623	5623	363	363	6625	5625	463
		◇	2	2	2	2	2	◇	V[R]	2		T[R]
0	**Sofiya** d.	0700	0740	0810	1205	1440	1530	1705	1705	1740	1955	2230
33	Pernik d.	|	0836	0904	1308	1533	1632	|	|	1830	2045	2328
48	Radomir d.	|	0859	0926	1330	1555	1654	|	|	1855	2108	2349
102	**Kyustendil** a.	|	|	1048	|	1715	|	|	|	2015	|	|
91	Dupnitsa d.	|	0957	...	1414	...	1747	|	|	...	2157	0033
123	**Blagoevgrad** d.	0902	1044	...	1444	...	1821	1906	1906	...	2235	0103
186	Sandanski d.	1001	1150	...	1549	...	1928	2006	2006	...	...	0203
210	Kulata a.	1020	1223	...	1620	...	2000	2025	2025	...	...	0225
210	Kulata 🏛 d.	1045	...	...	...	...	...	2045	2045	...	...	0315
211	Promahónas 🏛 a.	1050	...	...	...	...	...	2050	2050	...	...	0319
211	Promahónas d.	1111	...	...	...	...	...	2110	2110	...	...	0348
225	Strimón 1405 d.	1134	...	...	...	...	...	2134	2134	...	...	0413
354	**Thessaloníki** 1405 a.	1250	...	...	...	...	...	2252	2252	...	...	0539
	Athína 1400 a.	...	...	...	...	...	...	...	0612	...	...	...

	462	5620	6620	5622	360	360	6622	5624	6624	5610	362
	T[R]		2	2	Z[R]	◇	2	2	2	2	◇
Athína 1400 d.	...	...	...	...	2255	...	...	...	...	...	...
Thessaloníki 1405 d.	0030	...	...	...	0640	0640	...	...	...	...	1736
Strimón 1405 d.	0208	...	...	...	0811	0811	...	...	...	...	1903
Promahónas a.	0221	...	...	...	0823	0823	...	...	...	...	1915
Promahónas 🏛 d.	0254	...	...	...	0843	0843	...	...	...	...	1935
Kulata 🏛 a.	0300	...	...	...	0848	0848	...	...	...	...	1940
Kulata d.	0350	...	...	0605	0914	0914	...	1430	...	1705	2004
Sandanski d.	0412	...	...	0644	0933	0933	...	1508	...	1743	2028
Blagoevgrad d.	0516	0610	...	0758	1034	1034	...	1620	...	1907	2129
Dupnitsa d.	0545	0650	...	0836	|	|	...	1650	...	1941	|
Kyustendil d.	|	|	0715	|	|	|	1155	|	1730	|	|
Radomir d.	0628	0741	0839	0922	|	|	1320	1734	1856	2024	|
Pernik d.	0648	0800	0905	0942	|	|	1338	1800	1918	2044	|
Sofiya a.	0805	0904	0956	1031	1232	1232	1431	1854	2004	2130	2325

T – ROMANIA – 🛏 1, 2 cl. and ▬ 1, 2 cl. Bucureşti - Thessaloníki and v.v.; 🛏 1, 2 cl. and (2) Sofiya - Thessaloniki and v.v.
V – 🛏 1, 2 cl. Sofiya - Thessaloníki (**505**) - Athína.
Z – 🛏 1, 2 cl. Athína (**504**) - Thessaloníki - Sofiya.
◇ – Not available for internal Bulgarian journeys. Subject to confirmation.

ROMANIA

SEE MAP PAGE 491

Operator: CFR – Societatea Naţională de Transport Feroviar de Călători (CFR Călători).

Services: Trains convey 1st- and 2nd-class seating accommodation unless otherwise indicated. Sleeping- (🛏) and couchette (▬) cars are described on page 8. Russian-type sleeping-cars, as used in trains to and from destinations in Belarus, Moldova, Russia and Ukraine, are described on page 515; these cars are not accessible to passengers making journeys wholly within Romania or between Romania and Bulgaria.

Timings: Valid **December 13, 2009 - June 12, 2010** unless stated otherwise. Summer dates refer to last years schedules.

Tickets: Reservation is obligatory for travel by all services for which a train number is shown in the tables, and passengers boarding without a prior reservation are surcharged. Supplements are payable for travel by **Intercity** (*IC*) and most other fast trains. Trains shown without numbers are slow stopping-services calling at all, or most, stations.

1600 BUCUREŞTI - BRAŞOV - SIBIU and CLUJ NAPOCA

km								*IC*						*IC*	*IC*							*EN*	**472**				
				1633		**935**	**1737**	**374**	**1745**	**831**	**1621**	**11621**		**531**	**525**	**827**	**11833**	**346**	**1735**	**1643**	**1741**	**472**	**741**	**1631**	**11631**	**1635**	**1641**
		⊗	♣	⚒	⊗	Z	Ⓐ	P				⊙	⊗	✕	✕			D		B	N	J	M		⊗	W⊙	N
	Constanţa **1680** ....d.	...	...	...	...	2152	...	...	...	...	...	...	...	...	...	...	...	...	...	...	...	...	...	1538	...	1538	...
0	**Bucureşti** Nord ....d.	...	...	...	...	|	0500	0530z	0730	0830	0950	0950	...	1300	1300	1515	...	1600	1644	1740	1810	1910	1910	2008	...	2008	2040
59	Ploieşti Vest ....d.	...	...	...	...	0326p	0548	0612z	0813	0912	1032	1032	...	1342	1342	1559	...	1641	1742	1826	1855	1951	1951	2051	...	2051	2124
92	Câmpina ....d.	...	...	...	...	|	0617	|	0835	0937	1102	1102	...	|	|	1624	...	1704	1807	1850	1918	2014	2014	2114	...	2114	2151
121	Sinaia.......................d.	...	...	...	...	0508	▬	0716z	0937	1026	1150	1150	...	1447	1447	1717	...	1748	▬	1943	2010	2058	2058	2158	...	2158	2240
140	Predeal ....d.	...	...	...	...	0540	...	0751z	1014	1101	1228	1228	...	1521	1521	1754	...	1818	...	2021	2053	2136	2136	2237	...	2237	2312
166	**Braşov**....................a.	...	...	...	...	0610	♣	0822z	1046	1132	1258	1258	...	1551	1551	1825	...	1848	...	2051	2123	2206	2206	2307	...	2307	2342
166	**Braşov**....................d.	...	0300	0400	0616	0624	0730	0832	1058	...	1310	1310	1406	1604	1604	1833	1849	1856	⊗	...	2135	2216	2216	2317	2330	2330	2354
231	Făgăraş ....d.	0345	0428	|	0808	|	0905	|	|	...	|	1422	1546	|	|	|	2001	|	2013	...	|	|	|	|	0042	0042	|
293	Podu Olt ...... **1622** d.	0506	|	|	0937	|	|	|	|	...	|	|	1742	|	|	|	|	|	2148	...	|	|	|	|	|	|	|
315	**Sibiu** .... **1622** a.	0544	0551	|	1015	|	1028	|	|	...	1711v	1544	1822	|	|	|	2121	|	2228	...	|	|	|	|	0206	0206	|
	Timişoara **1610**..a.	...	1251	|	...	|	...	|	|	...	|	2239	...	|	|	|	...	|	...	...	|	|	|	|	...	...	|
294	**Sighişoara**...............d.	...	...	0604	...	0832	...	1037	1310	...	1517	...	...	1813	1813	2037	...	2100	...	...	2341	0020	0020	0121	...	...	|
333	Mediaş ....d.	...	...	0638	...	0907	...	1111	1348	...	1551	...	...	1847	1847	2110	...	2133	...	...	0018	|	|	0155	...	...	|
344	Copşa Mică ....d.	...	...	0651	...	0921	...	|	1401	...	1623	...	...	|	|	2130	...	|	...	...	0031	|	|	0217	...	...	|
374	Blaj ....d.	...	...	0720	...	0951	...	1151	1431	...	...	...	...	1927	1927	2200	...	2212	...	...	0101	|	|	0247	...	...	◐
395	Teiuş.....................△ d.	...	...	0744	...	1015	...	|	1455	...	...	...	...	1958	2003	2229	...	|	...	...	0125	0214	0157	0311	...	...	|
408	Aiud ....△ d.	...	...	0755	...	1027	...	|	1506	...	...	...	...	|	|	2240	...	|	...	...	0137	|	|	0323	...	...	|
429	Războieni ....△ d.	...	...	0816	...	1100	...	|	1527	...	...	...	...	2028	|	2301	...	|	...	...	0158	|	|	0344	...	...	|
446	Câmpia Turzii.......△ d.	...	...	0832	...	1117	...	|	1544	...	...	...	...	2044	|	2317	...	|	...	...	0215	|	|	0401	...	...	|
497	**Cluj Napoca** ....△ a.	...	...	0929	...	1211	...	|	1641	...	...	...	...	2141	|	0014	...	|	...	...	0312	|	|	0456	...	...	|
	Oradea **1612** .....a.	...	...	...	...	1540	...	|	|	...	...	...	...	0038	|	...	...	|	...	...	0637	|	|	0755	...	...	|
	Baia Mare **1616**.a.	...	...	...	...	...	...	|	2032	...	...	...	...	...	|	...	...	|	...	...	|	|	0627	...	...	...	0946
	Satu Mare **1616**.a.	...	...	...	...	...	...	|	2233	...	...	...	...	...	|	...	...	|	...	...	0909	|	0819	...	...	...	...
	Arad **1610**..............a.	...	...	...	...	...	...	1543	...	...	...	...	...	...	2340	...	...	0202	...	...	...	0547	...	...	...	...	...
	Budapest K **1280** ..a.	...	...	...	...	...	...	1847	...	...	...	...	...	...	...	...	...	0517	...	...	...	0847	...	...	...	...	...

			EN												*IC*	*IC*	*IC*										
			742	**473**	**11836**	**826**	**347**	**832**	**1746**			**11622**	**1622**		**532**	**526**	**375**	**1634**		**1642**	**936**	**1742**	**1644**	**1738**	**1632**	**11634**	**1636**
		⊗	M	J	⊗		D			⊗	♣	⊙		⊗	✕	✕	P	Ⓑ	♣	N	Y	N	B	Ⓐ		⊗	W⊙
	Budapest Keleti **1280** ......d.	...	...	1913	...	...	2313	...	...	...	...	...	...	...	...	...	0913	...	...	...	...	...	...	...	...	...	...
	Arad **1610** ....d.	...	...	0009	...	...	0401	...	...	...	...	...	...	...	...	1200	1416	...	...	...	...	...	...	...	...	...	...
	Satu Mare **1616** ....d.	...	2111	|	...	...	|	...	0418	...	...	...	...	...	...	|	|	...	...	...	...	1620	...	...	...	...	...
	Baia Mare **1616** ....d.	...	2242	|	...	...	|	...	0604	...	...	...	...	...	...	|	|	...	...	1655	...	|	...	...	...	...	...
	Oradea **1612**...............d.	...	|	|	...	...	|	...	|	...	...	...	...	...	1058	|	|	...	...	|	1654	1843	...	...	2017	...	...
	Cluj Napoca..................△ d.	...	|	|	...	0246	|	...	0950	...	...	...	...	...	1353	|	|	1711	...	|	2019	2151	...	...	2313	...	...
	Câmpia Turzii ....△ d.	...	|	|	...	0344	|	...	1048	...	...	...	...	...	1450	|	|	1810	...	|	2118	2248	...	...	0011	...	...
	Războieni ....△ d.	...	|	|	...	0401	|	...	1105	...	...	...	...	...	1508	|	|	1827	...	|	2154	2305	...	...	0029	...	...
	Aiud.................................△ d.	...	|	|	...	0419	|	...	1124	...	...	...	...	...	|	|	|	1846	...	|	2212	2323	...	...	0047	...	...
	Teiuş ....△ d.	...	0351	0351	...	0442	|	...	1143	...	...	...	...	...	1551	1551	|	1904	...	|	2230	2341	...	...	0105	...	...
	Blaj.......................................d.	...	|	|	...	0507	0749	...	1208	...	...	...	...	...	1616	1616	1800	1930	...	◐	2256	0006	...	...	0131	...	...
	Copşa Mică ....d.	...	|	|	...	0556	|	...	1238	...	...	...	1442	...	|	|	|	2000	...	|	2327	0036	...	...	0202	...	...
	Mediaş....................................d.	...	|	|	...	0609	0830	...	1251	...	...	...	1455	...	1656	1656	1840	2013	...	|	2340	0052	...	...	0215	...	...
	Sighişoara............................d.	...	0533	0533	...	0653	0915	...	1337	...	...	...	1539	...	1740	1740	1924	2057	...	|	0024	0138	...	...	0259	...	...
	Timişoara **1610** ....d.	...	|	|	...	|	|	...	|	...	...	0811	|	...	|	|	|	|	1352	|	|	|	...	...	|	...	...
	Sibiu..................... **1622** d.	0442	|	|	0557	|	|	...	|	1157	1312	1454	1340v	1437	|	|	|	|	2037	|	|	|	...	...	|	0220	0220
	Podu Olt.................. **1622** d.	0527	|	|	|	|	|	...	|	1238	|	|	|	1530	|	|	|	|	|	|	|	|	...	...	|	|	|
	Făgăraş.....................................d.	0702	|	|	0721	|	|	...	|	1421	1505	1621	|	1709	|	|	|	|	2217	|	|	|	...	...	|	0348	0348
	Braşov....................................a.	...	0726	0726	0838	0848	1110	...	1536	1559	1622	1731	1732	1848	1933	1933	2117	2250	2327	0213	0221	0333	...	...	0453	0459	0459
	Braşov....................................d.	...	0738	0738	...	0858	1120	1405	1550	...	...	1744	1744	...	1947	1947	2129z	...	...	0305	0239	0344	0359	...	0521	...	0521
	Predeal......................................d.	...	0815	0815	...	0931	1149	1436	1626	...	...	1819	1819	...	2024	2024	2207z	...	...	0343	0316	0419	0435	...	0557	...	0557
	Sinaia..d.	...	0843	0843	...	1005	1215	1510	1657	...	...	1850	1850	...	2057	2057	2239z	...	...	0409	0343	0448	0507	...	0627	...	0627
	Câmpina......................................d.	...	0928	0928	...	1103	1303	1555	1753	...	...	2001	2001	...	|	|	|	...	...	0454	|	0540	0556	0645	0717	...	0717
	Ploieşti Vest...............................d.	...	0954	0954	...	1128	1327	1620	1818	...	...	2029	2029	...	2214	2214	2355z	...	...	0518	0451	0604	0624	0714	0742	...	0742
	Bucureşti Nord ....a.	...	1034	1034	...	1210	1407	1702	1900	...	...	2112	2112	...	2255	2255	0035z	...	...	0600	|	0647	0706	0802	0825	...	0825
	Constanţa **1680**.......................a.	...	...	...	...	...	...	...	...	...	...	...	...	...	...	...	...	...	...	...	1040	...	...	...	1311	...	1311

FOR NOTES SEE TABLE 1610 ON NEXT PAGE

1610 CLUJ NAPOCA and SIBIU - DEVA - ARAD and TIMISOARA

km			*IC*			*IC*	*IC*			*IC*									*IC*						*EN*
		1811	**378**	**1821**	**1837**	**376**	**372**	**1825**		**374**			**1832**	**1623**	**1828**		**1815**	**1813**	**525**	**1818**	**346**		**1924**	**1765**	**472**
		⚒		A	K	T				P			C		R	2	Ⓑ	Ⓑ	V	Ⓑ	D	2	S	L	J
0	**Cluj Napoca**................▷ d.	...	...	...	0432	...	...	0912	...	...	...	1212	1456	...	1600	...	...	...	...	1749	...	1958	2224	0050	...
52	Câmpia Turzii...............▷ d.	...	...	...	0531	...	...	1010	...	...	...	1325	1555	...	1656	...	...	...	...	1850	...	2109	2323	0148	...
	Târgu Mureş............... d.	...	...	...	|	0610	...	|	...	...	...	|	|	...	|	1542	1642	...	...	|	...	|	|	|	...
	Luduş .... d.	...	...	...	|	0650	...	|	...	...	...	|	|	...	|	1645	1724	...	...	|	...	|	|	|	...
69	Războieni.....................▷ d.	...	...	...	0550	0725	...	1027	...	...	...	1346	1613	...	1713	1717	|	...	...	1907	...	2129	2340	0205	...
90	Aiud..............................▷ d.	...	...	...	0609	0744	...	1045	...	...	...	1411	1631	...	1731	1743	|	...	...	1925	...	2154	2359	0223	...
103	Teiuş ....▷ d.	...	...	...	0632	0802	...	1101	...	...	...	1428	1654	...	1747	1758	1828	...	...	1942	...	2208	0017	0240	...
	Bucuresti Nord **1600**..... d.	...	...	2345	|	|	...	|	...	0530z	...	|	|	...	|	|	|	...	1300	|	1600	▬	|	|	1910
	Braşov **1600** .... d.	...	...	|	|	|	...	|	...	0832	...	|	|	...	|	|	|	...	1604	|	1856	...	|	|	2216
•83	**Sibiu**............................ d.	0320	...	|	|	|	0840	|	...	|	...	|	|	1554	|	|	|	1723	|	|	|	...	|	|	|
•9	Sebeş Alba.................... d.	0455	...	▽	|	|	1011	|	...	|	...	|	|	1725	|	|	|	1849	|	|	|	...	|	|	|
122	**Alba Iulia** .... d.	|	...	|	0656	0826	|	1125	...	1228	...	1502	1717	|	1810	1833	1852	|	2003	2005	2248	...	0041	0304	0240
132	Vinţu de Jos..................... d.	0511	...	|	0708	0837	1035	1136	...	|	...	1512	1727	1743	1821	1844	1903	1921	2039	2015	|	Q	0052	0315	|
176	Simeria .... **1625** d.	0605	0720	0738	0815	0926	1124	1230	1232	1331	1535	...	...	1838	1915	...	...	2018	2127	...	2350	0248	0215	0408	|
185	Deva..................... **1625** d.	0616	0732	0750	0826	0938	1137	...	1245	1342	1548	...	...	1850	1925	...	...	2030	2139	...	0001	0301	0227	0419	0346
208	Ilia .... d.	0640	0759	0817	0852	|	|	...	1319	|	1622	...	...	1917	...	...	...	2054	|	...	|	0327	0252	0445	|
298	Radna .... d.	|	0907	0927	|	|	|	...	1505	|	1808	...	...	|	...	...	...	|	|	...	|	0500	0400	0556	|
333	**Arad** .... a.	|	0940	0959	|	1139	1337	...	1557	1543	1852	...	...	|	...	...	...	|	2340	...	0202	0537	0432	0642n	0547
	Budapest Keleti **1280**.... a.	|	1247	1447	|	1447	1647	...	...	1847	...	...	...	|	...	...	...	|	...	...	0517	|	|	|	0847
291	Lugoj .... **1620** a.	0809	...	...	1045	...	...	...	...	...	...	...	...	2105	...	...	...	2223	...	...	...	|	|	|	...
355	**Timişoara** Nord .... **1620** a.	0953	...	...	1219	...	...	...	...	...	...	...	...	2239	...	...	...	2356	...	...	...	0727	0539	0742	...

ADDITIONAL TRAINS TÂRGU MUREŞ - RĂZBOIENI

km								**949**		
		⚒		2Ⓐ	2	2		Y	Ⓑ	
0	**Târgu Mureş** ....d.	0328	0740	1206	1427	1542	1936	2022	2223	...
40	Luduş ....d.	0443	0845	1312	1533	1645	2038	2110	2333	...
59	**Războieni**..............................a.	0512	0912	1341	1602	1714	2107	2131	0002	...

				948					
	2⚒		2⚒	Z		2Ⓐ	2	2	
Războieni.............................d.	0405	0437	0719	1123	1205	1528	1716	2007	...
Luduş ....d.	0434	0514	0743	1144	1234	1608	1748	2039	...
Târgu Mureş ....a.	0541	0630	0845	1226	1343	1734	1851	2141	...

CONTINUED ON NEXT PAGE

TIMIŞOARA and ARAD - DEVA - SIBIU and CLUJ NAPOCA 1610

	1826	1923 S	1817 ⚒	1829 R	347 D	1816 ⚒	1812 ⚒	1831 C		
Timişoara Nord ... **1620** d.	...	2310	...	...	...	...	0509	...	...	...
Lugoj ... **1620** d.	...	|	...	...	...	...	0642	...	...	...
Budapest Keleti **1280** ... d.	...	|	...	...	2313	...	|	...	...	...
Arad ... d.	...	0014	...	...	0401	...	|	...	0618	0750
Radna ... d.	...	0044	...	...	|	...	|	...	0657	0830
Ilia ... d.	...	0155	...	...	|	...	0824	...	0846	1020
Deva ... **1625** d.	...	0220	...	0520	0557	...	0848	...	0918	1050
Simeria ... **1625** d.	0147	0233	...	0534	0617	...	0900	...	0931	1103
Vinţu de Jos ... d.	0240	0325	...	0623	|	0950	0952	1028	...	...
Alba Iulia ... d.	0253	0337	...	0635	0711	1002	|	1039	...	...
Sebeş Alba ... d.	|	|	...	|	|	|	1005	|	...	...
Sibiu ... a.	|	|	...	|	|	|	1136	|	...	...
Braşov **1600** ... a.	|	|	...	|	1110	|	...	|	...	...
Bucureşti Nord **1600** ... a.	|	|	...	|	1407	|	...	|	...	...
Teiuş ... ▷ d.	0319	0401	...	0712	...	1025	...	1107	...	...
Aiud ... ▷ d.	0331	0413	...	0724	...	1036	...	1118	...	...
Războieni ... ▷ d.	0352	0434	0636	0744	...	1058	...	1139	...	...
Luduş ... d.	|	|	|	|	...	1118	...	|	...	...
Târgu Mureş ... a.	|	|	|	|	...	1201	...	|	...	...
Câmpia Turzii ... ▷ d.	0408	0450	0652	0801	...	...	...	1155	...	...
Cluj Napoca ... ▷ a.	0504	0546	0751	0854	...	...	...	1252	...	...

	1624	*IC* 526 V		*IC* 375 P	Q	*IC* 373	1766 L	1814 Ⓑ		*IC* 377 T	1822 A	1838 K	*IC* 379	*EN* 473 J
Timişoara Nord ... **1620** d.	0811	...	...	...	1347	...	1500	1550	...	...	...	1738	...	...
Lugoj ... **1620** d.	0945	...	...	...	|	...	|	1721	...	...	...	1911	...	...
Budapest Keleti **1280** ... d.	|	...	...	0913	|	1113	|	|	...	1313	1313	|	1713	1913
Arad ... d.	|	1200	...	1416	1520	1616	1547**n**	|	1745	1824	1900	|	2216	0009
Radna ... d.	|	|	...	|	1552	|	1626	|	1824	|	1932	|	2245	|
Ilia ... d.	1121	|	...	|	1709	|	1737	1853	2029	|	2045	2052	2353	|
Deva ... **1625** d.	1146	1358	...	1611	1733	1813	1802	1917	2103	2021	2111	2118	0017	|
Simeria ... **1625** d.	1159	1411	...	1630	1744	1827	1815	1929	2116	2035	2125	2144	0028	|
Vinţu de Jos ... d.	1256	1455	1540	|	...	1931	1907	2029	...	2120	|	2235	...	|
Alba Iulia ... d.	|	1506	1552	1723	...	|	1919	|	...	2132	|	2249	...	0306
Sebeş Alba ... d.	1309	|	|	|	...	1945	|	2041	...	|	▽	|	...	|
Sibiu ... a.	1443	|	|	|	...	2116	|	2212	...	|	|	|	...	|
Braşov **1600** ... a.	...	1933	|	2117	...	...	|	...	...	|	|	|	...	0726
Bucureşti Nord **1600** ... a.	...	2255	|	0035**z**	...	...	|	...	...	|	0515	|	...	1034
Teiuş ... ▷ d.	...	...	1625	...	...	...	1942	...	...	2156	...	2315	...	...
Aiud ... ▷ d.	...	...	1638	...	...	...	1954	...	...	2207	...	2327	...	...
Războieni ... ▷ d.	...	...	1708	...	...	...	2017	...	...	2240	...	2349	...	...
Luduş ... d.	...	...	|	...	...	...	|	...	...	2301	...	|	...	...
Târgu Mureş ... a.	...	...	|	...	...	...	|	...	...	2342	...	|	...	...
Câmpia Turzii ... ▷ d.	...	...	1728	...	...	...	2035	...	...	...	...	0006	...	...
Cluj Napoca ... ▷ a.	...	...	1846	...	...	...	2132	...	...	...	...	0103	...	...

NOTES FOR TABLES 1600 AND 1610

A – 🛏 1, 2 cl., ━ 2 cl., [12] Constanţa - Bucureşti - Craiova - Arad and v.v.
B – 🛏 1, 2 cl., ━ 2 cl., [12] Bucureşti - Braşov - Miercurea Ciuc - Sighetu and v.v.
C – [12] Cluj Napoca - Târgu Jiu - Craiova and v.v. (Table **1625**).
D – DACIA – [12] Bucureşti - Budapest and v.v.; 🛏 1, 2 cl., ━ 2 cl. and [2] Bucureşti - Budapest - Wien and v.v.
J – ISTER – 🛏 1, 2 cl., ━ 1, 2 cl., [2] and ✕ Bucureşti - Budapest and v.v. Train **473** conveys 🛏 1, 2 cl. Budapest - Bucureşti (**463**) - Thessaloníki.
K – ━ 2 cl. and [12] Iaşi - Cluj Napoca - Timişoara and v.v.
L – [12] Iaşi - Cluj Napoca - Timişoara and v.v.
M – MARAMUREŞ – 🛏 1, 2 cl., ━ 2 cl. and [2] Bucureşti - Satu Mare and v.v.
N – Conveys 🛏 1, 2 cl., ━ 2 cl., [12].
P – PANNONIA – [12] and ✕ Budapest - Braşov (- Bucureşti on dates in note **z**) and v.v. Conveys Dec. 13 - Jan. 11, June 17 - Sept. 17: 🛏 1, 2 cl. München - Wien - Budapest - Bucureşti, returning Dec. 13 - Jan. 9, June 15 - Sept. 15. Conveys May 27 - Sept. 27: 🛏 1, 2 cl., ━ 2 cl., [2] Praha (**471/0**) - Budapest - Lökösháza, returning May 28 - Sept. 28.
Q – [12] Timişoara - Arad - Târgu Jiu and v.v.
R – [12] Cluj Napoca - Deva - Târgu Jiu and v.v. (Table **1625**).
S – [12] Sighetu - Cluj Napoca - Timişoara and v.v.
T – MUREŞ – [12] Târgu Mures - Lökosháza - Budapest and v.v.
V – AUREL VLAICU – [12] and ✕ Bucureşti - Teius (**531/2**) - Arad and v.v.
W – [12] Constanţa - Bucureşti - Sibiu and v.v.
Y – June 19 - Sept. 12. [12] Oradea / Cluj Napoca - Constanţa - Mangalia. Conveys [12] Târgu Mureş (train **949**, depart 2022) - Războieni - Constanţa - Mangalia.
Z – June 20 - Sept. 13. [12] Mangalia - Constanţa - Cluj Napoca / Oradea. Conveys [12] Mangalia - Constanţa - Războieni (**948**) - Târgu Mureş (arrive 1226).

n – Aradu Nou.
p – Ploieşti Sud.
v – Via Copşa Mică.
z – Runs Braşov - Bucureşti and v.v. on Dec. 13 - Feb. 28, May 31 - Sept. 19 only.
♣ – Operated by Regiotrans. Special tickets required.
⊗ – Runs as required (dates not advised).
⊙ – Summer only. Dates to be confirmed.

△ – For additional trains see Table **1610**.
▷ – For additional trains see Table **1600**.
▽ – Via Craiova and Târgu Jiu (Table **1625**).
◐ – Via Miercurea Ciuc (Table **1630**).
• – Distance from Vinţu de Jos.

OTHER TRAIN NAMES:
IC **372/3** TRANSILVANIA
IC **378/9** ZARAND

CLUJ NAPOCA - ORADEA 1612

km		406 C	1741 N	1631	364	731 2t	366	1935	362	1833 J	733 2t	1937 Ⓑ	*IC* 531 ✕
	Bucureşti N **1600** ... d.	...	1810	2008	...	...	...	...	...	...	...	...	1300
	Braşov **1600** ... d.	1849	2135	2317	...	...	0248	...	...	...	...	...	1604
0	**Cluj Napoca** ... d.	0217	0332	0515	0621	0712	1022	1356	1512	1512	1712	1937	2157
50	Huedin ... d.	0312	0435	0611	0716	0803	1116	1450	1612	1612	1804	2032	2252
153	**Oradea** ... a.	0455	0637	0755	0902	0945	1307	1642	1758	1758	1952	2232	0038
	Budapest K **1275** ... a.	0817	...	...	1217	...	1617	...	2117	...	...	...	...

	1936 ⚒	732 2t	1834 J	*IC* 532 ✕	367	363	1938	365	1742 N	734 2t	1632	407 C
Budapest K **1275** d.	...	...	...	...	0643	0943	...	1343	...	...	...	1743
Oradea ... d.	0550	0847	0942	1058	1204	1453	1654	1904	1843	2055	2017	2254
Huedin ... d.	0739	1037	1133	1244	1352	1636	1855	2054	2037	2239	2204	0046
Cluj Napoca ... a.	0836	1130	1230	1337	1447	1731	1954	2149	2133	2332	2258	0140
Braşov **1600** ... a.	...	...	...	1933	2231	...	...	...	0333	...	0453	0919
Bucureşti N **1600** a.	...	...	...	2255	...	...	...	...	0647	...	0825	...

C – CORONA – 🛏 1, 2 cl., ━ 2 cl. and [12] Budapest - Cluj Napoca - Deda - Braşov and v.v.
J – [12] Timişoara - Oradea - Cluj Napoca - Iaşi and v.v.
N – 🛏 1, 2 cl., ━ 2 cl., [12].
t – To / from Timişoara (Table **1614**).

ORADEA - ARAD - TIMIŞOARA 1614

km		1924 S	1744 M	1946 ⚒	731 2	*IC* 75 T		1948		1833 J	*IC* 79 C	733 2
	Cluj Napoca **1612** .. d.	2224	...	...	0712	...	...	...	...	1512	...	1712
0	**Oradea** ... d.	|	0442	0620	0947	...	...	1647	1541	1820	...	1957
39	Salonta ... d.	|	0519	0656	1027	...	...	1731	1648	1858	...	2036
121	**Arad** ... a.	0432	0640	0830	1145	...	...	1912	1854	2040	...	2155
121	**Arad** ... ▶ d.	0449	0650	0833	...	1216	1428	1920	1906	2055	2016	2200
178	**Timişoara** Nord ... ▶ a.	0539	0750	0925	...	1303	1546	2014	2025	2145	2103	2247

	732 2	1834 J	*IC* 78 C	1945	1947 Ⓑ		1743 M	*IC* 74 T	734 2		1923 S
Timişoara Nord ... ▶ d.	0550	0623	0654	0730	1250	1305	1610	1654	...	1942	2310
Arad ... ▶ a.	0638	0718	0741	0832	1346	1415	1701	1741	...	2109	2359
Arad ... d.	0642	0733	...	0836	1350	*1427*	1706	...	1846	...	0014
Salonta ... d.	0807	0900	...	1004	1524	*1613*	1832	...	2010	...	|
Oradea ... a.	0844	0938	...	1043	1604	*1708*	1915	...	2052	...	|
Cluj Napoca **1612** .. a.	1130	1230	...	...	...	...	...	...	2332	...	0546

C – CRIŞ – [12] Timişoara - Arad - Budapest and v.v.
J – [12] Timişoara - Oradea - Cluj Napoca - Iaşi and v.v.
M – [12] Timişoara - Oradea - Satu Mare - Baia Mare and v.v.
S – [12] Sighetu - Cluj - Timişoara and v.v. (Table **1650**).
T – TRAIANUS – [12] Timişoara - Arad - Budapest and v.v.
▶ – Additional local trains (journey 70 - 75 mins): From Arad: 0434, 0555, 0752, 1328, 1748. From Timişoara: 0433, 0525, 1347, 1601, 1741.

CLUJ NAPOCA - BAIA MARE - SATU MARE 1616

km		1744 T	D	1741 N	741 M	941 R	844	1641 N	1745	846 Ⓑ
	Bucureşti Nord **1600** ... d.	...	...	1810	1910	...	...	2040	0730	...
	Braşov **1600** ... d.	...	...	2135	2216	...	...	2354	1058	...
	Constanţa **1680** ... d.	...	...	|	|	1429	...	|	|	...
0	**Cluj Napoca** ... d.	...	...	0332	|	|	0642	▽	1657	1833
59	Dej Călători ... d.	...	...	|	0421	0636	0746	0657	1814	1936
135	Jibou ... d.	...	...	△	0533	0800	0904	0835	1932	2046
193	**Baia Mare** ... a.	...	...	|	0642	0907	1012	0946	2032	2140
193	**Baia Mare** ... ▷ d.	0108	0358	|	0700	0922	1015	...	2046	2147
252	**Satu Mare** ... ▷ a.	0224	0551	0909	0819	1047	1136	...	2233	2317

	1746	843 ⚒	942 Q	1642 N	1742 N	845	D	742 M	1743 T
Satu Mare ... ▷ d.	0418	0729	1330	...	1620	1750	1930	2111	2142
Baia Mare ... ▷ a.	0550	0901	1455	...	|	1904	2127	2228	2316
Baia Mare ... d.	0604	0909	1510	1655	|	1909	...	2242	...
Jibou ... d.	0709	1007	1611	1816	△	2011	...	2336	...
Dej Călători ... d.	0838	1109	1748	1943	|	2124	...	0056	...
Cluj Napoca ... a.	0938	1205	|	▽	2151	2218	...	|	...
Constanţa **1680** ... a.	|	...	0931	|	|	...	...	|	...
Braşov **1600** ... a.	1536	...	...	0245	0333	...	...	0726	...
Bucureşti Nord **1600** ... a.	1900	...	...	0600	0647	...	...	1034	...

D – From / to Debrecen (Table **1277**).
M – MARAMUREŞ – 🛏 1, 2 cl., ━ 2 cl., [2] Bucureşti - Satu Mare and v.v.
N – Conveys 🛏 1, 2 cl., ━ 2 cl. and [12].
Q – June 19 - Sept. 12. [12] Satu Mare - Baia Mare - Constanţa - Mangalia.
R – June 20 - Sept. 13. [12] Mangalia - Constanţa - Baia Mare - Satu Mare.
T – [12] Baia Mare - Satu Mare - Arad - Timişoara and v.v. (Table **1618**).
△ – Via Oradea (Tables **1612 / 1618**).
▽ – Via Miercurea Ciuc (Table **1630**).
▷ – See also panel below main table.

LOCAL TRAINS BAIA MARE - SATU MARE

				⚒					⚒
Baia Mare d.	0731	1146	1546	1930	Satu Mare d.	0444	0758	1145	1615
Satu Mare a.	0938	1339	1739	2134	Baia Mare a.	0626	0950	1326	1756

ORADEA - CAREI - SATU MARE 1618

km			1741 B				Ⓐ	D	D	1743	
	Timişoara **1614** ... d.	...	...	...	...	...	...	...	...	1610	...
0	**Oradea** ... d.	0301	0655	0806	...	1453	1544	...	1645	1922	1940
66	Valea lui Mihai ... d.	0445	0807	0931	1215	1614	1706	1752	1837	2029	2106
97	Carei ... d.	0522	0835	...	1252	1725	...	1838	...	2057	2143
133	**Satu Mare** ... a.	0613	0909	...	1343	1813	...	1926	...	2131	2230
	Baia Mare **1616** ... a.	...	...	...	...	...	...	2127	...	2316	...

	1744		Ⓐ	D		D			1742 B	
Baia Mare **1616** ... d.	0108	...	...	0358	...	...	...	...	...	...
Satu Mare ... d.	0229	0324	...	0619	0740	...	1430	1536	1620	2002
Carei ... d.	0304	0407	...	0714	0839	...	1521	1628	1655	2102
Valea lui Mihai ... d.	0330	0441	0535	0837	0939	1347	...	1735	1721	2154
Oradea ... a.	0437	0612	0703	...	1108	1503	...	1910	1828	2321
Timişoara **1614** ... a.	0750	...	...	...	...	...	...	...	...	...

B – 🛏 1, 2 cl., ━ 2 cl. and [12] Bucureşti - Cluj Napoca - Oradea - Satu Mare and v.v.
D – From / to Debrecen (Table **1277**).

1620 BUCUREŞTI - CRAIOVA - TIMIŞOARA

km		1762 2b	991 N	2	791	IC 591 ✗		821 R		2Ⓑ	1691 ✗		693	1721 S	1725 T		IC 593 ✗	795	1823 T	1723 R	1693		360 B	695 V	1821 A
0	**Bucureşti** Nord d.	...	0005n	...	0545	0645	...	0945	...	...	1045	...	1245	1345	1445	...	1545	1645	1745	1845	1945	...	2105	2245	2345
51	Videle d.	...	|	...	0631	0731	...	1030	...	...	1132	...	1331	1432	1532	...	1631	1732	1831	1930	2031	...	2150	2332	0029
100	Roşiori Nord d.	...	0148	...	0722	0822	...	1120	...	...	1223	...	1429	1524	1622	...	1722	1822	1922	2025	2122	...	2240	0025	0120
155	Caracal d.	...	0232	...	0805	0905	...	1203	...	...	1309	...	1512	1609	1708	...	1805	1908	2008	2110	2208	...	2322	0110	0205
209	**Craiova** a.	...	0315	...	0848	0948	...	...	...	...	1352	...	1555	...	1751	...	1848	1951	2051	...	2251	...	0005	0155	0248
209	**Craiova** 1625 d.	...	0325	0330	0850	0954	...	...	...	1240	1400	...	1602	...	1754	...	1855	...	2101	...	2300	...	0015	0205	0300
245	Filiaşi 1625 d.	...	0352	0418	0914	|	...	...	...	1330	1424	...	1626	...	1816	...	|	...	2123	...	2325	...	0038	|	0323
323	Drobeta Turnu Severin d.	...	0517	0618	1035	1130	...	...	...	1525	1549	...	1744	...	...	1835	2040	...	...	...	0051	...	0200	0346	...
347	Orşova d.	...	0548	0658	...	|	...	...	1302	...	1618	...	1811	...	...	1920	|	...	...	...	0118	...	0228	|	...
364	Băile Herculane d.	...	0611	...	...	1217	...	...	1328	...	1645	...	1837	...	...	1947	2126	...	...	...	0144	...	0249	0434	...
435	Caransebeş d.	0652	0812	...	...	1340	...	...	1555	...	1813	...	2001	...	...	2207	2248	...	...	...	0310	...	0412	0607	...
474	Lugoj 1610 d.	0728	0842	...	...	1409	...	...	1706	...	1843	...	2031	...	...	2246	2317	...	...	...	0340	...	0441	0636	...
533	**Timişoara** Nord 1610 a.	0810	0925	...	...	1451	...	...	1820	...	1925	...	2113	...	...	2346	2359	...	...	...	0421	...	0523	0725	...
	Beograd 1365 a.	...	...	...	...	...	...	...	...	...	...	...	...	...	...	...	...	...	...	...	...	...	0854	...	...

	794 Ⓐ	1722 S	1724 T	1692		IC 592 ✗	798 Ⓒ	822 R	792	1824 T	2	694	2	1730 R	Ⓑ	IC 594 ✗	Ⓑ	1761 2d		992 M	1694	1822 A	361 B		696 V
Beograd 1365 d.	...	...	...	...	...	...	...	...	...	...	...	...	...	...	...	...	...	...	...	...	...	...	1550	...	...
Timişoara Nord 1610 d.	...	...	...	0505	...	0630	...	...	...	...	...	1345	...	...	1418	1600	...	1656	...	1826	2005	...	2115	...	2240
Lugoj 1610 d.	...	...	...	0557	...	0714	...	...	...	...	...	1436	...	...	1535	1644	...	1741	...	1921	2058	...	2159	...	2333
Caransebeş d.	...	...	...	0628	...	0743	...	...	...	...	...	1505	...	...	1635	1713	←	1808	...	2014	2128	...	2228	...	0018
Băile Herculane d.	...	...	...	0751	...	0905	...	...	...	...	...	1628	...	...	1908	1836	1908	...	...	2154	2301	...	2359	...	0142
Orşova d.	...	...	...	0813	...	0927	...	...	...	...	1547	1649	←	...	→	|	1939	...	...	2217	2322	...	0021	...	|
Drobeta Turnu Severin d.	...	...	...	0845	...	0958	...	...	1422	...	1630	1720	1632	...	...	1924	2026	...	...	2257	2353	...	0052	...	0248
Filiaşi 1625 d.	...	...	0635	1010	...	1117	...	...	1540	1704	→	1842	1850	...	...	|	...	...	...	0034	0110	0133	0203	...	|
Craiova 1625 a.	...	...	0700	1035	...	1142	...	...	1605	1730	...	1907	1947	...	...	2055	...	...	...	0100	0135	0158	0228	...	0433
Craiova d.	0510	...	0705	1042	...	1148	1310	...	1610	1740	...	1915	...	...	...	2101	...	...	...	0115	0142	0210	0240	...	0442
Caracal d.	0549	0700	0744	1121	...	1226	1350	1620	1650	1819	...	1954	...	2100	...	2140	...	...	...	0155	0221	0249	0318	...	0520
Roşiori Nord d.	0636	0745	0830	1206	...	1308	1436	1704	1735	1905	...	2036	...	2145	...	2222	...	...	...	0238	0307	0335	0400	...	0601
Videle d.	0727	0837	0921	1257	...	1358	1527	1754	1828	1958	...	2127	...	2243	...	|	...	...	...	|	0358	0427	0450	...	0652
Bucureşti Nord a.	0814	0921	1008	1344	...	1445	1614	1839	1917	2045	...	2214	...	2330	...	2358	...	...	...	0422n	0445	0515	0537	...	0740

A – 🛏 1, 2 cl., ▬ 2 cl. and (12) Constanţa - Bucureşti - Craiova - Târgu Jiu - Arad and v.v.
B – BUCUREŞTI – 🛏 1, 2 cl., ▬ 2 cl. and (12) Bucureşti - Beograd and v.v. Train **360** conveys 🛏 1, 2 cl. Thessaloníki (**462**) - Bucureşti - Timişoara (**78**) - Budapest.
M – June 19 - Sept. 12. (12) Timişoara (also Reşiţa Sud, d. 1914) - Constanţa - Mangalia.
N – June 20 - Sept. 13. (12) Mangalia - Constanţa - Timişoara (also Reşiţa Sud a. 0832).
R – To / from Râmnicu Vâlcea (Table **1622**).
S – To / from Sibiu (Table **1622**).
T – To / from Târgu Jiu (Table **1625**).
V – VALAHIA – 🛏 1, 2 cl., ▬ 2 cl. and (12) Bucureşti - Timişoara and v.v.; 🛏 1, 2 cl. and (12) Bucureşti - Caransebeş (**698/9**) - Reşiţa Sud and v.v. (arrive 0729; depart 2238).
b – From Reşiţa Sud (depart 0552). Ⓡ.
d – To Reşiţa Sud (arrive 1910). Ⓡ.
n – Bucureşti Băneasa.

1621 BUCUREŞTI - PITEŞTI - CRAIOVA

km		1891	1789	1791	1893		1793	1795	1895	1797	
0	**Bucureşti** Nord d.	0520	0720	0920	1120	...	1320	1520	1720	1920	...
108	Piteşti d.	0716	0900	1103	1307	...	1507	1710	1918	2100	...
189	Slatina d.	0830	...	...	1425	...	...	1835	2037	...	...
206	Piatra Olt 1622 d.	0850	...	...	1445	...	...	1853	2105	...	...
250	**Craiova** 1622 a.	0934	...	...	1543	...	...	...	2148	...	...

	1788 Ⓐ	1892	1790	1792	1794	1894	1796	1896	1798	
Craiova 1622 d.	...	0445	...	...	...	1240	...	1640	...	...
Piatra Olt 1622 d.	...	0528	...	...	...	1325	...	1725	1925	...
Slatina d.	...	0546	...	...	...	1344	...	1744	1944	...
Piteşti d.	0545	0715	0915	1115	1315	1515	1715	1915	2115	...
Bucureşti Nord a.	0733	0857	1056	1304	1458	1650	1905	2105	2300	...

1622 SIBIU - RÂMNICU VÂLCEA - CRAIOVA

km		1722		⚒	1727		2⚒	822	2	1730		1720 Ⓑ	2
0	**Sibiu** 1600 d.	0315	0325	...	0625	0800	...	...	...	...	1546	1725	...
	Braşov 1600 d.	|	|	...	|	|	...	...	...	...	|	|	...
22	Podu Olt 1600 d.	|	0405	...	|	0841	...	...	1255	...	1265	|	2008
83	Călimăneşti d.	|	0551	0630	|	1047	...	1420	1445	...	1827	|	2146
99	**Râmnicu Vâlcea** d.	0520	0619	0705	0822	1115	1240	1440	1516	1900	1910	1946	2212
186	Piatra Olt ▶ d.	0627	0835	0928	0942	...	1520	1548	1739	2020	2144	2105	...
	Caracal ▶ a.	0658	...	...	|	...	...	1617	...	2054	...	|	...
	Bucureşti N 1620 a.	0921	...	...	|	...	...	1839	...	2330	...	|	...
230	**Craiova** ⊡ a.	...	...	...	1025	...	...	...	...	...	...	2148	...

		2		1726 ⚒	821	2⚒		2	1728	1721	1723
Craiova ⊡ d.	...	...	...	0720	...	...	...	...	1500	...	...
Bucureşti N 1620 d.	...	...	...	|	0945	...	...	...	|	1345	1846
Caracal ▶ d.	...	...	...	|	1205	...	...	...	|	1619	2112
Piatra Olt ▶ d.	0030	0400	0628	0805	1236	1247	...	...	1549	1650	2146
Râmnicu Vâlcea d.	0258	0642	0904	0917	1349	1501	1547	1650	1702	1816	2258
Călimăneşti d.	0323	0709	0942	|	1405	...	1615	1724	|	|	...
Podu Olt 1600 a.	0551	0924	1202	|	...	...	1809	1928	|	|	...
Braşov 1600 a.	|	...	|	|	...	...	|	...	|	|	...
Sibiu 1600 a.	0633	...	1243	1114	...	...	1852	...	1859	2010	...

⊡ – For additional trains Piatra Olt - Craiova see Table **1621**.

▶ – Additional local trains Piatra Olt - Caracal (journey 45 minutes): From Piatra Olt: 0538Ⓐ, 0807, 1315, 1610Ⓑ; from Caracal: 0535⚒, 0715⚒, 1332Ⓐ, 1742.

1625 CRAIOVA - TÂRGU JIU - DEVA

km		1829	1821 A	995 N	1831		1695	2	2		1823	Q
	Bucureşti N 1620 d.	...	2345	0005n	...	...	...	...	...	...	1745	...
0	**Craiova** 1620 d.	...	0300	0325	0515	...	0856	1405	1548	1940	2101	...
36	**Filiaşi** 1620 d.	...	0325	0411	0540	...	0919	1506	1642	2034	2124	...
107	**Târgu Jiu** d.	0155	0435	0546	0648	...	1024	1650	1830	2216	2232	2240f
157	Petroşani a.	0304	0545	0656	0758	...	▬	1828	2009	...	2348	0024f
157	Petroşani d.	0307	0548	0659	0800	1110	1520	*1845*	...	...	2351	0027
237	Simeria 1610 d.	0450	0738	0839	|	1357	1757	*2120*	...	...	0131	0248
246	**Deva** 1610 a.	0500	0748	0851	|	1408	1809	*2133*	...	...	...	0259
	Cluj Napoca 1610 a.	0846	|	...	1252	...	...	...	...	...	...	|
	Arad 1610 a.	...	0959	...	...	...	...	...	...	...	...	0537

		1696	2	1824	2	Q	1832	1828	996 M	1822 A	
Arad 1610 d.	...	...	...	1010	...	1520	...	...	...	1900	...
Cluj Napoca 1610 d.	...	...	...	|	...	|	1456	1600	...	|	...
Deva 1610 d.	*0425*	...	...	1218	*1540*	1733	|	1943	1930	2111	...
Simeria 1610 d.	*0440*	...	*1010*	1252	*1605*	1752	|	1915z	1943	2125	...
Petroşani a.	*0721*	...	*1250*	1437	*1844*	1952	2005	2140	2130	2310	...
Petroşani d.	0755	...	1410	1440	1910	1955f	2010	2145	2135	2313	...
Târgu Jiu d.	0932	1358	1610	1555	2052	2141f	2128	2305	2258	0026	...
Filiaşi 1620 a.	1113	1503	1802	1702	2252	...	2243	...	0023	0132	...
Craiova 1620 a.	1214	1530	1900	1755	2345	...	2310	...	0100	0158	...
Bucureşti N 1620 a.	...	...	...	2100	...	...	...	...	0422n	0515	...

A – 🛏 1, 2 cl., ▬ 2 cl. and (12) Constanţa - Bucureşti - Craiova - Târgu Jiu - Arad and v.v.
M – June 19 - Sept. 12. (12) Deva - Constanţa - Mangalia.
N – June 20 - Sept. 13. (12) Mangalia - Constanţa - Deva.
Q – (12) Târgu Jiu - Arad - Timişoara and v.v.
f – ⑤⑦ only.
n – Bucureşti Băneasa.
z – Via Deva.

1630 BRAŞOV - MIERCUREA CIUC - DEDA - TÂRGU MUREŞ

km		941 R	1641 Z	366 H		1972			IC 549		406 C	1643 S
	Bucureşti N 1600 d.	...	2040	...	...	...	...	...	1300*	...	...	1740
0	**Braşov** △ d.	...	2354	0248	0404	...	1140	...	1600	1612	1849	2105
32	Sfântu Gheorghe △ d.	...	0023	0322	0458	...	1223	...	1630	1656	1921	2136
95	**Miercurea Ciuc** △ d.	...	0127	0430	0631	...	1347	1545	1739	1833	2028	2251
	Galaţi 1640 d.	...	|	|	|	0540	|	|	|	|	|	|
103	Siculeni △ d.	0120	0140	0445	0643	1142	1359	1559	1751	1914	2040	2303
150	Gheorghieni d.	0215	0242	0529	0746	1230	1509	1736	1834	2027	2127	0000
184	Topliţa d.	0250	0320	0607	0831	1308	1610	1827	1910	2117	2203	0036
228	Deda a.	0401	0432	0726	0954	1428	1742	...	2023	...	2315	0148
228	Deda 1635 d.	*0414*d	0455	...	*1026*c	1442	1756	...	2035	...	...	...
250	Reghin 1635 d.	*0454*d	0538	...	*1108*c	1514	1833	...	2103	...	...	...
282	**Târgu Mureş** 1635 a.	*0550*d	0635	...	*1203*c	1600	1929	...	2148	...	...	...

	407 C		1973	IC 540		Ⓐ	367 H	942 Q	1642 Z	1644 S	
Târgu Mureş 1635 d.	...	1015	1229	1324	1420	1541	...	...	2007	...	*2220*b
Reghin 1635 d.	...	1106	1313	1407	1515	1640	...	...	2104	...	*2312*b
Deda 1635 a.	...	1154	1347	1440	1557	1723	...	...	2145	...	*2355*b
Deda d.	0439	1206	1401	1456	1618	...	1755	2001	2206	2322	0227
Topliţa d.	0547	1337	1521	1607	1745	...	1911	2125	2323	0037	0412
Gheorghieni d.	0633	1421	1558	1643	1835	...	1949	2208	2359	0113	0458
Siculeni △ d.	0732	1529	1705	1730	1947	...	2041	2257	0051	0204	0617
Galaţi 1640 a.	|	|	2319	|	|	...	|	...	|	|	|
Miercurea Ciuc △ d.	0743	1538	...	1740	1957	...	2052	...	0101	0214	0628
Sfântu Gheorghe △ d.	0851	1720	...	1849	2142	...	2201	...	0217	0321	0811
Braşov △ a.	0919	1801	...	1923	2225	...	2231	...	0245	0347	0855
Bucureşti N 1600 a.	...	...	...	2255	...	...	...	...	0600	0706	...

FOR NOTES SEE TABLE 1635

TÂRGU MUREŞ and BISTRIŢA - DEJ - CLUJ NAPOCA 1635

For Târgu Mureş - Cluj Napoca via Războieni see Table **1610**

km		941 R	1949 Ⓐ	1641 Y		366 H			1844	406 C	1643 S
	Bucureşti Nord **1600** d.	...	...	2040	...	...	...	...	...	...	1740
	Braşov **1630** d.	...	...	2354	...	0248	...	...	...	1849	2105
0	**Târgu Mureş** **1630** d.	...	...	|	...	|	0713	...	2007	|	|
33	Reghin **1630** d.	...	...	|	...	|	0811	...	2104	|	|
55	Deda **1630** a.	...	...	0432	...	0726	0854	...	2145	2315	0148
55	Deda d.	0407	...	0444	...	0727	▬	...	...	2318	0149
•	**Bistriţa** Nord d.	|	0506	|	0728	|	1535	1918	...	|	|
102	Sărăţel d.	0512	0518	0552	0746	0818	1553	1935	...	0010	0242
127	Beclean pe Someş ▷ d.	0559	0544	0618	0821	0842	1630	2010	...	0034	0306
152	Dej Călători ▷ d.	0636	0612	0657	0917	0911	1714	2050	...	0105	...
	Baia Mare **1616** a.	0907	|	0946	|	|	|	...	...	|	...
211	**Cluj Napoca** ▷ a.	...	0739	...	1045	1010	1840	...	...	0205	...
	Budapest Keleti **1275** a.	...	...	...	...	1617	...	...	...	0817	...

			1940 Ⓐ		367 H	942 Q	1642 Y	1644 S		407 C
Budapest Keleti **1275** d.	...	...	...	...	0643	...	...	...	...	1743
Cluj Napoca ▷ d.	...	1120	1530	...	1501	...	...	...	1947	0152
Baia Mare **1616** d.	...	|	|	...	|	1510	1655	...	|	|
Dej Călători ▷ d.	0434	1246	1645	1720	1611	1748	1943	...	2125	0259
Beclean pe Someş ▷ d.	0513	1321	1714	1758	1637	1837	2008	2200	2206	0323
Sărăţel d.	0612	1357	1739	1834	1702	1903	2057	2226	2243	0347
Bistriţa Nord a.	0632	1416	1752	1853	|	|	|	|	2303	|
Deda a.	▬	...	▬	...	1753	1953	2148	2317	...	0438
Deda **1630** d.	1132a	...	1559	...	1755	...	2206	2322	...	0439
Reghin **1630** a.	1211a	...	1642	...	|	...	|	|	...	|
Târgu Mureş **1630** a.	1313a	...	1739	...	|	...	|	|	...	|
Braşov **1630** a.	...	...	...	...	2231	...	0245	0347	...	0919
Bucureşti Nord **1600** a.	...	...	...	...	...	...	0600	0706	...	...

				Ⓑ
Bistriţa Nord d.	0745	1212	1523	1940
Sărăţel d.	0819	1229	1557	2016
Deda a.	0929	...	1706	2126

	⚒			
Deda d.	0450	...	1238	1727
Sărăţel d.	0619	0920	1407	1857
Bistriţa Nord a.	0639	0936	1425	1916

C – CORONA – [sleeper] 1,2 cl., [couchette] 2 cl., [12] and ✕ Braşov - Cluj - Budapest and v.v.
H – HARGHITA – [12] and ✕ Braşov - Cluj - Budapest and v.v.
Q – June 19 - Sept. 12. [12] Satu Mare / Sighetu Marmaţiei - Constanţa - Mangalia.
R – June 20 - Sept. 13. [12] Mangalia - Constanţa - Sighetu Marmaţiei / Satu Mare.
S – [sleeper] 1,2 cl., [couchette] 2 cl. and [12] Bucureşti - Sighetu Marmaţiei and v.v.
Y – [sleeper] 1,2 cl., [couchette] 2 cl. and [12] Bucureşti - Baia Mare and v.v. [12] Bucureşti - Sărăţel - Bistriţa and v.v. (arrive 0550 / depart 2009).
Z – [12] Bucureşti - Deda (**1843/4**) - Târgu Mureş and v.v. (see also Table **1635** note **Y**).

a – Ⓐ only.
b – Ⓑ only.
c – Ⓒ only.
d – ⚒ only.

• – *10 km* from Sărăţel.
△ – Additional trains: see Table **1640**.
▷ – Additional trains: see Table **1650** (also **1616** Cluj - Dej).
* – Combined with *IC* **525** and *IC* **531** Bucuresti - Braşov.

BRAŞOV- MIERCUREA CIUC - ADJUD - GALAŢI 1640

km		1751 S	1768 B⚒			1975		1973		1977		942 Q
0	**Braşov** ▷ d.	2300	...	0404	...	0941	...	...	...	1450	...	...
32	Sfântu Gheorghe ▷ d.	2330	...	0458	...	1011	...	...	...	1520	...	...
95	**Miercurea Ciuc** ▷ d.	0036	...	0631	0704	1120	...	...	1540	1629	1938	...
	Târgu Mureş **1630** d.	|	...	|	|	|	...	1229	|	|	|	...
103	Siculeni ▷ d.	0049	...	0641	0720	1130	...	1705	1550	1639	1947	2309
144	Ghimeş d.	0159	...	...	0849	▬	1320	1824	1835	1706	2109	0026
179	Comăneşti d.	0241	0350	...	0941	1250	1411	1908	1933	...	2158	0119
216	Oneşti d.	0331	0438	...	...	1351	1520	1958	2050	...	2325	0216
254	**Adjud** **1670** d.	0430	0519	...	...	1451	1640	2043	2149	...	0030	0302
279	Mărăşeşti **1670** a.	0453	0541	...	...	1524	1715	2105	2224	...	0105	0327
279	Mărăşeşti d.	0501	...	...	...	...	...	2106	...	...	...	...
	Iaşi **1670** a.	0823	...	...	...	...	...	|	...	...	...	...
298	Tecuci **1670** a.	...	...	...	...	...	...	2129	...	...	...	...
383	**Galaţi** **1670** a.	...	...	...	...	...	...	2319	...	...	...	...

		1974	1972		1752 S	1976			Ⓐ	1767 B Ⓑ			941 R
Galaţi **1670** d.	...	...	0540	*0732*	...	...	...	...	1522	...	...	1725	...
Tecuci **1670** d.	...	...	0730	*1003*	...	...	...	...	1743	...	...	1953	...
Iaşi **1670** d.	...	...	|	|	1028	...	...	...	|	...	...	|	...
Mărăşeşti a.	...	...	0753	*1030*	1340	...	...	...	1808	...	...	2020	...
Mărăşeşti **1670** d.	0415	...	0754	1217	1346	...	1415	1718	...	1850	1905	...	2026
Adjud **1670** d.	0501	...	0827	1254	1436	...	1500	1808	...	1923	1950	...	2115
Oneşti d.	0552	...	0901	1350	1517	...	1552	1904	...	2000	2052	...	2154
Comăneşti d.	0708	...	0953	1453	1606	...	1658	2015	...	2047	2152	...	2308
Ghimeş d.	0805	...	1035	1542	1647	...	1750	2104	...	...	...	...	2351
Siculeni ▷ d.	0943	1139	1132	...	1756	1820	1908	...	...	...	...	...	0107
Târgu Mureş **1630** a.	|	|	1600	...	|	|	|	...	...	...	...	...	...
Miercurea Ciuc ▷ d.	0951	1151	...	...	1806	1832	1916	...	...	...	...	...	...
Sfântu Gheorghe ▷ d.	...	1308	...	...	1922	2005	...	...	...	...	...	...	...
Braşov ▷ a.	...	1335	...	...	1950	2032	...	...	...	...	...	...	...

B – [12] Comăneşti - Adjud - Bucureşti and v.v.
Q – June 19 - Sept. 12. [12] Satu Mare / Sighetu Marmaţiei - Constanţa - Mangalia.
R – June 20 - Sept. 13. [12] Mangalia - Constanţa - Sighetu Marmaţiei / Satu Mare.
S – [12] Iaşi (train **1664/5**) - Adjud - Braşov and v.v.; [12] Suceava - Adjud - Braşov and v.v.
▷ – For additional trains see Table **1630**.

IAŞI - SUCEAVA - DEJ - CLUJ NAPOCA 1650

km		1653 B	1942	1833	1859 ⑤–⑦	943 Q	1931 ⑤–⑦	1924	1644 A	1765	1837 J
0	**Iaşi** d.	...	...	0606	0834	...	1056	...	...	1533	1917
76	Paşcani **1670** d.	0308	...	0715	0943	...	1207	...	...	1642	2026
122	Vereşti **1670** d.	0344	...	0749	|	...	1242	...	...	1716	2100
137	**Suceava** **1670** d.	0412	...	0811	1027	...	1304	...	...	1729	2121
140	Suceava Nord **1670** a.	|	...	|	|	...	|	...	...	1737	|
140	Suceava Nord d.	|	...	|	|	...	|	...	...	1802	|
187	Gura Humorului Oraş d.	0500	...	0859	1114	...	1352	...	...	1850	2209
219	Câmpulung Moldovenesc d.	0545	...	0942	1155	...	1440	...	...	1935	2254
257	Vatra Dornei Băi d.	0651	...	1048	1259	...	1547	...	...	2042	0004
351	Năsăud d.	...	...	1240	...	...	1752	...	...	2231	0206
*118	**Sighetu Marmaţiei** d.	...	0050	|	...	1300	|	1620	1715	|	|
*61	Vişeu de Jos d.	...	0304	|	...	1445	|	1814	1912	|	|
357	Salva d.	...	0526	1250	...	1635	1803	2013	2121	2242	0216
379	Beclean pe Someş **1635** d.	...	0551	1317	...	1700	1833	2040	2146	2309	0242
402	Dej Călători **1635** d.	...	0639	1346	...	...	1903	2110	...	2339	0314
460	**Cluj Napoca** **1635** a.	...	0739	1446	...	...	2002	2209	...	0038	0414
	Oradea **1612** a.	...	...	1758	...	...	...	|	...	|	|
	Timişoara N **1610 / 14** a.	...	...	2145	...	...	...	0539	...	0742	1219

	1838 J	1643 A	944 R	1923	1932 ⑤–⑦	1858 ⑤–⑦	1834	1654 B	1943	1766
Timişoara N **1610 / 14** d.	1738	...	...	2310	...	...	0623	...	...	1500
Oradea **1612** d.	|	...	...	|	...	...	0942	...	...	|
Cluj Napoca **1635** d.	0115	...	...	0601	0848	...	1243	...	1530	2144
Dej Călători **1635** d.	0221	...	...	0708	0955	...	1349	...	1700	2250
Beclean pe Someş **1635** d.	0245	0327	0600	0733	1020	...	1414	...	1725	2315
Salva d.	0308	0413	0625	0815	1043	...	1437	...	1804	2338
Vişeu de Jos d.	|	0603	0806	1006	|	...	|	...	2040	|
Sighetu Marmaţiei a.	|	0754	1002	1157	|	...	|	...	2240	|
Năsăud d.	0316	...	...	...	1052	...	1446	...	...	2346
Vatra Dornei Băi d.	0507	...	...	...	1247	1609	1637	2148	...	0132
Câmpulung Moldovenesc d.	0614	...	...	...	1355	1703	1746	2255	...	0240
Gura Humorului Oraş d.	0656	...	...	...	1437	1740	1830	2338	...	0323
Suceava Nord a.	|	...	...	...	|	|	|	|	...	0411
Suceava Nord **1670** d.	|	...	...	...	|	|	|	|	...	0433
Suceava **1670** d.	0800	...	...	...	1532	1838	1934	0040	...	0441
Vereşti **1670** d.	0811	...	...	...	1544	|	1945	0052	...	0452
Paşcani **1670** d.	0852	...	...	...	1624	1924	2027	0144	...	0534
Iaşi a.	0957	...	...	...	1729	2028	2132	...	...	0639

A – [sleeper] 1,2 cl., [couchette] 2 cl. and [12] Sighetu - Bucureşti and v.v.
B – [sleeper] 1,2 cl., [couchette] 2 cl. and [12] Bucureşti - Vatra Dornei Băi and v.v.
J – [couchette] 2 cl. and [12] Iaşi - Timişoara and v.v.
Q – June 19 - Sept. 12. [12] Satu Mare / Sighetu Marmaţiei - Constanţa - Mangalia.
R – June 20 - Sept. 13. [12] Mangalia - Constanţa - Sighetu Marmaţiei / Satu Mare.
* – Distance from Salva.

BUCUREŞTI - GALAŢI 1660

km		C	871		11671 q	1671 p	1675 ⑤	1673	*IC* 575 Ⓐ	1871 C⊙	873	11731 ⊙
0	**Bucureşti** Nord ▷ d.	...	0610	...	0850	0910	1230	1352	1540	...	1852	...
	Ploieşti Sud ▷ d.	...	|	...	0935	|	1318	|	1624	...	|	1923
**	Buzău ▷ d.	0428	|	...	1044	|	1428	|	1733	...	|	2032
71	Urziceni d.	|	0733	...	|	1028	|	1451	|	...	1958	|
•	Feteşti d.	|	|	0709	|	|	|	|	|	1827	|	|
138	Făurei d.	0539	0845	0942	1141	1141	1527	1601	1829	|	2107	2128
198	Brăila d.	0639	0927	1043	1226	1226	1609	1643	1906	2053	2145	2209
229	**Galaţi** a.	0728	1002	1130	1304	1304	1647	1721	1940	2130	2219	2246

	IC 572 Ⓐ	1872 C⊙	11732 ⊙	876	1672	11672 q	1676 ⑦	1674 p	11674 q	C	872	
Galaţi d.	0510	0550	0640	0700	0935	0935	1134	1440	1440	1652	1735	1945
Brăila d.	0545	0627	0717	0735	1016	1016	1211	1519	1519	1740	1810	2033
Făurei d.	0626	|	0759	0816	1104	1103	1256	1603	1602	1928	1851	2135
Feteşti a.	|	0821	|	|	|	|	|	|	|	2106	|	|
Urziceni d.	|	...	|	|	1221	|	|	1717	|	...	2000	|
Buzău ▷ d.	|	...	0857	0914	|	1201	1355	|	1700	...	|	2250
Ploieşti Sud ▷ d.	|	...	1001	1021	|	1309	1505	|	1806	...	|	...
Bucureşti Nord ▷ a.	0852	...	...	1102	1326	1353	1549	1829	1850	...	2109	...

C – [12] Galaţi - Constanţa and v.v.
p – Not Apr. 5 - Oct. 3.
q – Apr. 5 - Oct. 3.
** – Buzău - Făurei: *40 km*.
• – Feteşti - Făurei: *89 km*.
▷ – For additional trains see Table **1670**.
⊙ – Summer only. Dates to be confirmed.

OTHER SERVICES 1669

Local trains, 2nd class

PAŞCANI - TÂRGU NEAMT Journey: ± 45 minutes
From Paşcani: 0334Ⓐ, 0720, 1648, 2030Ⓑ.
From Târgu Neamt: 0500Ⓐ, 0957, 1800, 2139Ⓑ.

REŞIŢA - CARANSEBEŞ Journey: ± 80 minutes
From Reşiţa Sud: 0421, 0613, 1227, 1302, 1519, 1730, 2053.
From Caransebeş: 0433, 0747, 1101, 1345, 1550, 1912, 2258.
For long-distance trains see Table **1620**.

SIBIU - COPSA MICĂ Journey: ± 80 minutes
From Sibiu: 0450Ⓐ, 0735, 1215, 1558, 1927, 2310Ⓑ.
From Copsa Mică: 0437⚒, 0620Ⓐ, 0736, 1253, 1548, 1922.

SIMERIA - HUNEDOARA Journey: ± 30 minutes
From Simeria: 0452, 0715, 1030, 1440, 1627, 1941.
From Hunedoara: 0531, 0803, 1115, 1530, 1714, 2027.

VEREŞTI - BOTOŞANI: Journey: ± 65 minutes
From Vereşti: 0508[R], 0635**b**, 0824, 1631, 1743[R], 2103.
From Botoşani: 0519, 1009, 1230[R], 1614[R], 1804, 2220**b**.

b – To / from Bucureşti (Table **1670**) [R]. Conveys [sleeper] 1, 2 cl.

LONG DISTANCE TRAINS OPERATED BY REGIOTRANS:

Selected services and stations only. Regiotrans tickets required. See also Table **1600**.

Braşov (0638) - Bucureşti N (0947 / 1005 §) - Constanţa (1354 §).
Constanţa (1716 §) - Bucureşti N (2113 § / 2120) - Braşov (0034).

Braşov (d. 0638) - Ploieşti Vest (a. 0853 / d. 0916) - Iaşi (1522).
Iaşi (d. 1547) - Ploieşti Vest (a. 2158 / d. 2221) - Braşov (0034).

Braşov (d. 0300) - Sibiu (a. 0551 / d. 0605) - Timişoara (a. 1251).
Timişoara (d. 1352) - Sibiu (a. 2025 / d. 2037) - Braşov (a. 2327).

Sighisoara (d. 0730 / 1554) - Copsa Mică - Sibiu (a. 0929 / 1804).
Sibiu (d. 0950 / 1815) - Copsa Mică - Sighisoara (a. 1200 / 2028).

§ – Operates Braşov - Bucureşti and v.v. only until May 13.

1670 BUCUREŞTI - BUZĂU - BACĂU - IAŞI and SUCEAVA

km						IC	IC	⊠			IC						IC			IC	IC		⊠				
		1751	1851	1665	936	551	564	382	1655	1964	555	751	661	1966	651	1861	557	1661	1552	553	561	941	402	1653		663	753
		V	H	W	C	✕	✕	A	✕	⑤–⑦	✕				F	J	T			✕		M	P	N	2	de	d
0	**Bucureşti** Nord .... **1660** d.	...	...	...	...	0600	0600	0625	0701	...	0900	1100	1200	...	1400	...	1500	1610	...	1700	1700	...	1950	2102	...	2300	2340
59	Ploieşti Sud .... **1660** d.	...	...	...	0459	0643	0643	0716	0746	...	0944	1143	1244	...	1445	...	1545	1655	...	1743	1743	...	2042	2147	...	2344	0023
128	**Buzău** .... **1660/80** d.	...	0148	...	0603	0748	0748	0822	0856	...	1054	1252	1353	...	1554	...	1651	1804	...	1849	1849	...	2157	2256	...	0050	0132
161	Râmnicu Sărat .... d.	...	0223	...	▬	0822	0822	|	0931	...	1128	1326	1427	...	1628	...	1727	1838	...	|	|	1929	|	2331	...	|	|
199	Focşani .... d.	...	0304	...	...	0859	0859	0933	1009	...	1207	1404	1504	...	1707	...	1808	1918	...	1957	1957	2008	2309	0011	...	0156	0245
219	Mărăşeşti .... **1640** d.	...	0338	...	...	|	|	|	1040	...	1237	1435	|	...	|	...	1841	|	...	2034	2040	2048	|	0044	...	|	0329
244	Adjud .... **1640** d.	0439	0402	0430	...	0951	0951	|	1105	...	1303	1459	|	...	1801	...	1907	|	2105	2058	|	2112	|	0110	...	|	0341
303	**Bacău** .... d.	0530	0445	|	**1962**	1033	1033	1111	1145	...	1343	1541	|	...	1854	...	1948	|	2154	2140	|	...	0049	0153	...	|	0424
346	Roman .... d.	0602	0517	|		1105	1105	|	▬	...	...	1612	|	...	1925	...	...	|	2205	2211	|	...	0124	0225	...	|	0456
	Galaţi .... **1640** d.	|	|	|	0600	|	|	|	...	1150	...	|	|	1617	|	...	...	|	|	|	|	...	|	|	...	|	|
	Făurei .... **1680** d.	|	|	|	|	|	|	|	...	|	...	|	|	|	|	1647	...	|	|	|	|	...	|	|	...	|	|
	Tecuci .... **1640** d.	|	|	|	0744	|	|	|	...	1329	...	|	1606	1759	|	1848	...	2021	|	|	|	...	|	|	...	0259	|
	Bârlad .... d.	|	|	0607	0829	|	|	|	...	1405	...	|	1650	1842	|	1932	...	2104	|	|	2142	...	|	|	...	0343	|
	Vaslui .... d.	|	|	0711	0922	|	|	|	...	1459	...	|	1747	1937	|	2034	...	2201	|	|	2233	...	|	|	...	0440	|
	Iaşi .... a.	|	|	0823	1021	|	1246	|	2	1606	...	|	1855	2036	|	2148	...	2314	2359	|	2330	...	0301	|	...	0548	|
	Iaşi .... ‡ RO d.	|	|	...	...	|	...	|	1300	...	...	|	...	...	|	...	...	...	...	|	...	...	0306	|	0450	...	|
	Ungheni **1730** ▣ MD a.	|	|	...	...	|	...	|	1450	...	...	|	...	...	|	...	...	...	...	|	...	...	0524	|	0638	...	|
	Chişinău 1730 .... a.	|	|	...	...	|	...	|	...	...	...	|	...	...	|	...	...	...	...	|	...	...	0852	|	...	...	|
387	Paşcani .... ▷ d.	0635	0550	...	...	1140	...	1226	...	...	...	1652	...	...	1958	...	...	...	...	2246	...	...	...	0308	...	...	0536
432	Vereşti .... ▷ a.	0708	0633	...	...	|	...	|	...	...	...	1728	...	...	2031	...	...	...	...	|	...	...	...	0344	...	...	0613
476	Botoşani **1669** .... a.	|	0804	...	...	|	...	|	...	...	...	1852	...	...	|	...	...	...	...	|	...	...	...	|	...	...	0737
448	**Suceava** .... ▷ a.	0724	0644**p**	...	...	1220	...	1324	...	...	...	1750**p**	...	...	2043	...	...	...	...	2326	...	...	...	0357	...	...	0635**p**
450	**Suceava** Nord .... § RO a.	...	0654**p**	...	...	...	...	|	...	...	...	...	...	...	2053	...	...	...	...	...	...	...	...	...	...	...	...
539	Chernivtsi .... § UA a.	...	...	...	...	...	...	1816	...	...	...	...	...	...	...	...	...	...	...	...	...	...	...	...	...	...	...

km*				IC		IC							⊠	IC				IC	IC						⊠		
		1654		552	1551	562	1662	1963	652	1664	1965	1752	383	556	754		662	554	563	1967	1862	1852	664	752	401	942	
		N	2	✕					G	W	⑤–⑦	V	B			2		✕			J	H	de	d	P	M	
	Chernivtsi .... § UA d.	...	...	...	...	...	...	...	...	...	...	...	0705	...	...	...	...	...	...	...	...	...	...	...	...	...	...
	Suceava Nord .... § RO d.	...	...	...	...	...	...	...	0745	...	...	...	|	...	...	...	...	...	...	...	...	2130	...	...	...	...	...
	Suceava .... ▷ d.	0040	...	0512	...	...	...	...	0752	...	...	1115	1232	...	1313**q**	...	...	1637	...	...	...	2137	...	2304**q**	...	...	...
	Botoşani **1669** .... d.	|	...	|	...	...	...	...	|	...	...	|	|	...	1230	...	...	|	...	...	...	|	...	2220	...	...	...
	Vereşti .... ▷ d.	0052	...	|	...	...	...	...	0803	...	...	1126	|	...	1346	...	...	|	...	...	...	2149	...	2337	...	...	...
	Paşcani .... ▷ d.	0144	...	0559	...	...	...	...	0845	...	...	1208	1332	...	1436	...	...	1734	...	...	...	2233	...	0027	...	...	...
0	**Chişinău 1730** .... d.	|	...	|	...	...	...	...	|	...	...	|	|	...	|	...	...	|	...	...	...	|	...	|	1710	...	...
107	Ungheni **1730** ▣ MD d.	|	0755	|	...	...	...	...	|	...	...	|	|	...	|	1740	...	|	...	...	...	|	...	|	2110	...	...
128	**Iaşi** .... ‡ RO a.	|	0921	|	...	...	...	...	|	...	...	|	|	...	|	1907	...	|	...	...	...	|	...	|	2324	...	...
128	**Iaşi** .... d.	|	▬	|	0501	0515	0557	0658	|	1028	1100	|	|	...	|	▬	1455	|	1612	1812	2245	|	2331	|	2331	...	...
196	Vaslui .... d.	|	...	|	|	0615	0710	0756	|	1139	1200	|	|	...	|	...	1606	|	|	1915	0010	|	0041	|	|	...	...
248	Bârlad .... d.	|	...	|	|	0700	0800	0842	|	1230	1247	|	|	...	|	...	1655	|	|	2001	0104	|	0130	|	|	...	...
297	Tecuci .... **1640** d.	|	...	|	|	|	0853	0918	|	|	1330	|	|	...	|	...	1750	|	|	2043	0149	|	0226	|	|	...	...
	Făurei .... **1680** a.	|	*IC*	|	|	|	|	|	|	|	|	|	|	...	|	...	|	|	|	|	0345	|	|	|	|	...	...
382	**Galaţi** .... **1640** a.	|	**558**	|	|	|	|	1100	|	|	1511	|	|	...	|	**1656**	|	|	|	2226	▬	|	|	|	|	...	...
	Roman .... d.	0214	**T**	0625	0635	|	|	...	0912	|	...	1235	|	...	1506		|	1801	1801	...	...	2301	|	0057	0109	...	...
	Bacău .... d.	0250	0523	0701	0717	|	|	...	1001	|	...	1317	1439	1500	1542	1615	|	1836	1836	...	...	2338	|	0133	0149	...	...
	Adjud .... **1640** d.	0337	0609	0745	0801	|	|	...	1047	1408	...	1402	|	1550	1628	1701	|	1921	1921	...	...	0026	|	0219	|	0302	...
	Mărăşeşti .... **1640** d.	0401	0633	0823	...	0803	|	...	|	...	...	...	|	1615	1652	1726	|	|	|	...	...	0050	|	|	|	0339	...
	Focşani .... d.	0433	0703	0853	...	...	0946	...	1140	...	...	...	1618	1646	1724	1757	1838	2013	2013	...	**935**	0121	|	0317	0332	0412	...
	Râmnicu Sărat .... d.	0515	|	|	...	...	1028	...	1222	...	...	...	|	1724	1805	1836	1919	2051	2051	...	**C**	0202	|	0400	|	0455	...
	Buzău .... **1660/80** d.	0551	0813	1003	...	...	1105	...	1258	...	...	...	1733	1800	1841	1911	1957	2129	2129	...	0219	0234	0427	0435	0457	...	...
	Ploieşti Sud .... **1660** d.	0702	0918	1106	...	...	1215	...	1409	...	...	...	1839	1905	1948	2017	2059	2232	2232	...	0325	...	0534	0541	0608	...	...
	Bucureşti Nord .... **1660** a.	0746	1000	1147	...	...	1258	...	1452	...	...	...	1930	1946	2031	2059	2141	2313	2313	...	...	...	0617	0625	0659	...	...

BACĂU - PIATRA NEAMŢ - BICAZ

km			①–⑤						F	*IC* 557	⑧
0	**Bacău** .... d.	0406	0546	0859	...	1407	1655	...	1910	2004	2049
60	Piatra Neamţ .... a.	0539	0724	1036	...	1535	1839	...	2019	2111	2225
86	**Bicaz** .... a.	0627	...	...	...	1623	1927	...	...	2145	...

	IC 558	⚒			G		①–⑤			
Bicaz .... d.	0330	...	...	0650	...	...	...	...	1644	1950
Piatra Neamţ .... d.	0402	0454	...	0730	0826	...	1420	1609	1724	2031
Bacău .... a.	0511	0627	...	0857	0934	...	1556	1736	1851	2204

A – BULGARIA EXPRES – 🛏 1,2 cl. Sofiya (**382**) - Ruse - Vadul Siret (**60**) - Kyïv - Moskva; 🛏 2 cl. Sofiya - Kyïv. ◇
B – BULGARIA EXPRES – 🛏 1,2 cl. Moskva (**59**) - Kyïv - Vadul Siret (**383**) - Ruse - Sofiya; 🛏 2 cl. Kyïv - Sofiya. ◇
C – June 19 - Sept. 12 (from Cluj Napoca / Târgu Mures, one day later from Mangalia): (12) Cluj Napoca / Târgu Mureş - Constanţa - Mangalia and v.v.
F – Conveys (12) Bucureşti - Bacău (**657**) - Piatra Neamţ.
G – Conveys (12) Piatra Neamţ (**658**) - Bacău - Bucureşti.
H – (12) Suceava - Constanţa (- Mangalia, summer only) and v.v.
J – (12) Iaşi - Constanţa (- Mangalia, summer only) and v.v.
M – June 19 - Sept. 12 (from Satu Mare / Sighetu Marmaţiei, one day later from Mangalia): (12) Satu Mare / Sighetu Marmaţiei - Baia Mare - Constanţa - Mangalia and v.v.

N – 🛏 1,2 cl., ▬ 2 cl. and (12) Bucureşti - Vatra Dornei Băi and v.v.
P – PRIETENIA – uneven dates from Bucureşti, even dates from Chişinău. 🛏 2 cl. Bucureşti - Ungheni (**106/5**) - Chişinău and v.v. *Subject to confirmation.*
T – (12) Bucureşti - Bicaz / Comăneşti and v.v.
V – (12) Suceava - Adjud - Braşov and v.v.
W – (12) Iaşi - Adjud (**1751/2**) - Braşov and v.v.
d – Also conveys 🛏 1,2 cl.
e – Also conveys ▬ 2 cl.
p – Portion detached from main train at Vereşti.
q – Portion attached to main train at Vereşti.

◇ – See also Table **98**.
⊠ – For international journeys only.
▷ – For additional trains see Table **1650**.
‡ – ▣ : Nicolina (RO).
§ – ▣ : Vicşani (RO) / Vadul Siret (UA).
* – Other distances: Tecuci - Făurei: *92 km*; Tecuci Nord - Focşani: *35 km*; Iaşi - Roman: *114 km*.
MD – Moldova. RO – Romania.
UA – Ukraine.

1680 BUCUREŞTI - CONSTANŢA - MANGALIA

Engineering work may affect services between Bucureşti and Constanţa

km				1852	1862				1822	689	689		1636					681			1981			685
		2		H	J	2	2	2	A	①–⑤	h		S	2		2	2	✕	2	2	⑧		G	
0	**Bucureşti** Nord .... d.	...	...	...	...	...	...	...	0542	0735	0735	...	0919	...	...	...	...	1400	1329**o**	...	1505	...	...	1937
	Buzău .... **1670** d.	...	...	0304	...	...	...	...	|	|	|	0702	|	...	...	...	...	|	|	...	|	1520	...	|
	Făurei .... **1670** d.	...	...	0400	0410	...	...	...	|	|	|	0821	|	...	...	...	...	|	|	...	|	1639	...	|
146	Feteşti .... d.	...	0441	0518	0535	...	...	0708	0840	1028	1028	1019	1159	...	...	...	...	1636	1653	...	1823	1829	2108	2231
190	Medgidia .... d.	...	0541	0602	0618	...	0720	0804	0926	1109	1109	1122	1244	...	...	...	1635	1721	1753	...	1922	1941	2151	2315
334	**Tulcea** Oraş .... a.	...	|	|	|	...	1031	|	|	|	|	|	|	...	...	...	1945	|	|	...	2158	|	|	|
225	**Constanţa** .... a.	...	0638	0629	0648	...	...	0850	1000	1136	1136	1211	1311	...	...	...	...	1747	1842	...	...	2028	2226	2341
225	**Constanţa** .... d.	0615	...	0644**h**	0707**h**	0740	...	...	1028**h**	...	1200	...	...	1400	...	1615	...	1802**h**	...	1910	...	...	...	...
239	Eforie Nord .... d.	0639	...	0704**h**	0729**h**	0807	...	...	1051**h**	...	1221	...	...	1424	...	1642	...	1823**h**	...	1934	...	...	...	...
268	**Mangalia** .... a.	0728	...	0800**h**	0838**h**	0906	...	...	1148**h**	...	1317	...	...	1516	...	1734	...	1918**h**	...	2023	...	...	...	...

km			680			684	1982				1861			1631	686	686				1821			1851	
		G		2		✕	⚒	2	2		J		2	S	①–⑤	h	2		2	A	2		H	
0	**Mangalia** .... d.	...	...	0525	...	0605**h**	...	...	0803	...	1129**h**	...	1355	...	...	1454	1557	...	...	1722**h**	1820	...	1941**h**	...
29	Eforie Nord .... d.	...	...	0616	...	0705**h**	...	...	0857	...	1242**h**	...	1443	...	...	1558	1657	...	...	1824**h**	1911	...	2037**h**	...
43	**Constanţa** .... a.	...	...	0640	...	0728**h**	...	...	0924	...	1305**h**	...	1510	...	...	1622	1721	...	...	1847**h**	1935	...	2101**h**	...
43	**Constanţa** .... d.	0542	0611	...	0727	0748	...	...	...	1147	1330	1440	...	1538	1639	1639	...	1749	...	1902	...	1942	2116	...
	Tulcea Oraş .... d.	|	|	...	|	|	0600	0718	...	|	|	|	...	|	|	|	...	|	1610	|	...	|	|	...
78	Medgidia .... d.	0619	0642	...	0823	0815	0841	1028	...	1236	1359	1536	...	1607	1708	1708	...	1837	1914	1930	...	2032	2145	...
122	Feteşti .... d.	0709	0725	...	0920	0859	0924	...	...	1336	1443	1658	...	1654	1749	1749	...	1936	...	2014	...	2129	2230	...
211	Făurei .... **1670** d.	0917	|	...	1131	|	|	...	...	|	1633	1905	...	|	|	|	...	...	...	|	...	...	0023	...
251	Buzău .... **1670** a.	...	|	...	1245	|	|	...	...	|	...	2019	...	|	|	|	...	...	...	|	...	...	0118	...
268	**Bucureşti** Nord .... a.	...	0959	...	...	1156	1230	...	...	1707**o**	...	...	...	1927	2028	2028	...	...	...	2305	...	...	...	...

A – 🛏 1,2 cl., ▬ 2 cl., (12) Constanţa - Bucureşti - Craiova - Arad and v.v.
G – From / to Galaţi. See Table **1660**.
H – From / to Suceava. See Table **1670**.
J – From / to Iaşi. See Table **1670**.
S – From / to Sibiu / Oradea. See Table **1600**.
h – Summer only – dates to be confirmed.
o – Bucureşti Obor.

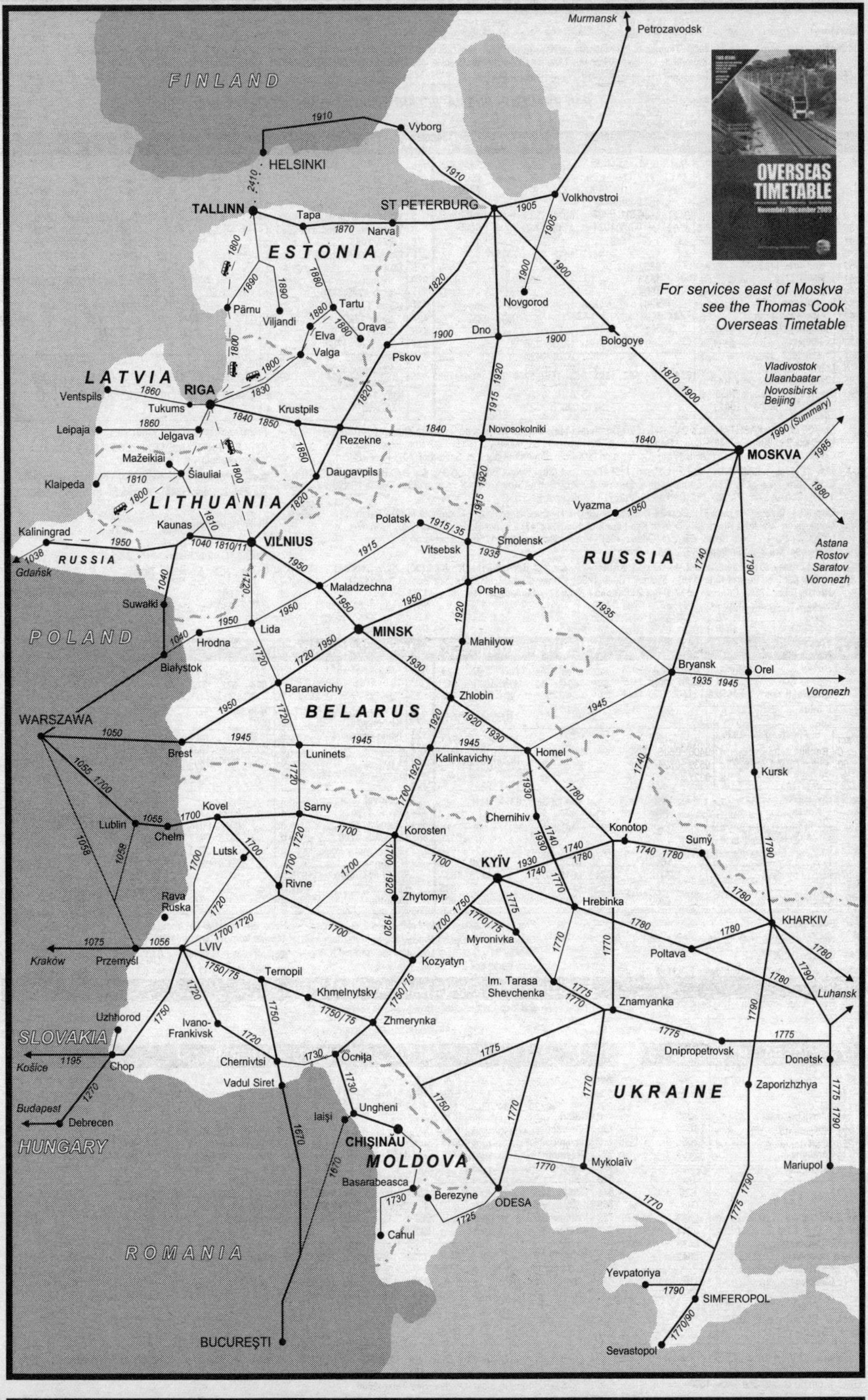
FINLAND
Murmansk
Petrozavodsk
OVERSEAS TIMETABLE
Vyborg
HELSINKI
TALLINN
ST PETERBURG
Volkhovstroi
Tapa
Narva
ESTONIA
Novgorod
For services east of Moskva see the Thomas Cook Overseas Timetable
Pärnu
Viljandi
Tartu
Orava
Elva
Valga
Dno
Bologoye
Pskov
LATVIA
Ventspils
RIGA
Tukums
Leipaja
Jelgava
Krustpils
Rezekne
Novosokolniki
Vladivostok
Ulaanbaatar
Novosibirsk
Beijing
MOSKVA
Mažeikiai
Šiauliai
Klaipeda
Daugavpils
LITHUANIA
Vyazma
Kaliningrad
Kaunas
VILNIUS
Polatsk
Vitsebsk
Smolensk
Astana
Rostov
Saratov
Voronezh
RUSSIA
Gdańsk
Maladzechna
Orsha
Suwałki
POLAND
Lida
Hrodna
MINSK
Mahilyow
Białystok
Bryansk
Orel
Baranavichy
Zhlobin
WARSZAWA
BELARUS
Brest
Luninets
Kalinkavichy
Homel
Kovel
Sarny
Chernihiv
Lublin
Chełm
Lutsk
Korosten
Konotop
Sumy
KYÏV
Rivne
Zhytomyr
Hrebinka
Rava Ruska
KHARKIV
Myronivka
Kraków
Przemyśl
LVIV
Kozyatyn
Poltava
Ternopil
Im. Tarasa Shevchenka
Khmelnytsky
Luhansk
Znamyanka
Uzhhorod
Zhmerynka
SLOVAKIA
Ivano-Frankivsk
Košice
Chop
Chernivtsi
Ocniţa
Dnipropetrovsk
Donetsk
Vadul Siret
Zaporizhzhya
Budapest
Iaşi
Ungheni
UKRAINE
Debrecen
HUNGARY
CHIŞINĂU
MOLDOVA
Mykolaïv
Mariupol
Basarabeasca
Berezyne
ODESA
Cahul
ROMANIA
Yevpatoriya
SIMFEROPOL
BUCUREŞTI
Sevastopol

UKRAINE and MOLDOVA

SEE MAP PAGE 509

Operators : UZ: Ukrzaliznytsya (УЗ: Укрзалізниця). **CFM**: Calea Ferată din Moldova. Other operators as indicated in the table headings and notes.

Timings : Valid from **May 31, 2009**. Timings of international services to and from non-CIS countries should be verified from the international tables at the front of this book. Local time is used throughout: i.e. East European Time for Ukraine and Moldova – for other countries, see the time comparison chart on page **2**.

Tickets : Prior reservation is necessary except for travel by purely local trains.

SEE ALSO THE PANEL ***RAIL TRAVEL IN RUSSIA, BELARUS, UKRAINE, and MOLDOVA*** ON PAGE 515

1700 KYÏV - KOVEL - WARSZAWA — UZ, PKP

km		*Sko* **111** H	*Fir* **77**	*Sko* **55** Y	*Sko* **29** A	*Sko* **29** C	*Sko* **67** K	*Pas* **659**	*Fir* **43** F	*Fir* **363**
	Moskva Kiyevskaya **1740** d.	...	1638	1908	...	...	...	...	...	...
0	**Kyïv 1750** d.	0421	0546	0720	0924	0924	1533	1604	1916	2115
156	Korosten **1920** d.	0650	|	1004	1148	1148	1743	1900	2133	|
241	Zhytomyr **1920** a.	|	|	1140	|	|	|	|	|	|
311	Sarny **1720** d.	|	|	...	1412	1412	|	2315	|	|
159	Kozyatyn **1750** d.	|	0832	...	|	|	|	|	|	2352
391	Rivne **1720** d.	|	1330	...	|	|	2130	|	|	0458
469	Lutsk **1720** d.	|	1509	...	|	|	|	|	|	0647
453	**Kovel 1720** d.	|	1701	...	1638	1638	0008	0217	|	0858
652	**Lviv 1720 1750** a.	1445	...	...	|	|	|	0643	0352	...
512	Yahodyn 🏛 UA d.	...	...	...	1932	1932	0317	...	...	...
520	Dorohusk 🏛 PL a.	...	...	...	1850	1850	0238	...	...	...
541	Chełm **1055** a.	...	...	...	2022	2022	0426	...	...	...
615	Lublin **1055** a.	...	...	...	2111	2111	0523	...	...	...
785	Warszawa Wschodnia **1055** a.	...	...	...	2326	2326	0811	...	...	...
790	**Warszawa** Centralna **1055** a.	...	...	...	2345	0101	0820	...	...	...
	Berlin Lichtenberg **1001** a.	...	...	...	0712	0900h	...	...	...	...

km		*Sko* **112** H	*Fir* **44** F	*Fir* **364**	*Pas* **660**	*Sko* **68** K	*Fir* **78**	*Sko* **30** D	*Sko* **30** B	*Pas* **344** Z
	Berlin Lichtenberg **1001** d.	...	...	...	...	...	...	1515h	2147	...
0	**Warszawa** Centralna **1055** d.	...	...	...	...	1645	...	2300	0440	...
5	Warszawa Wschodnia **1055** d.	...	...	...	...	1654	...	2357	0502	...
175	Lublin **1055** d.	...	...	...	...	1938	...	0225	0727	...
249	Chełm **1055** d.	...	...	...	...	2034	...	0346	0819	...
270	Dorohusk 🏛 PL d.	...	...	...	...	2143	...	0448	0930	...
278	Yahodyn 🏛 UA d.	...	...	...	...	0110	...	0818	1248	...
	Lviv 1720 1750 d.	1705	2130	...	1927	|	...	|	|	...
337	**Kovel 1720** d.	|	|	1820	0049	0222	0928	0937	1400	...
421	Lutsk **1720** d.	|	|	2041	|	|	1145	|	|	...
499	Rivne **1720** d.	|	|	2227	|	0425	1311	|	|	...
731	Kozyatyn **1750** d.	|	|	|	|	|	1806	|	|	...
	Sarny **1720** d.	|	|	|	0351	|	|	1145	1606	...
	Zhytomyr **1920** d.	|	|	|	|	|	|	|	|	1714
	Korosten **1920** d.	0037	0353	|	0758	0812	|	1442	1905	1932
	Kyïv 1750 a.	0248	0620	0607	1034	1027	2017	1648	2112	2145
	Moskva Kiyevskaya **1740** a.	...	...	...	...	...	1130	...	...	1432

A – May 30 - Oct. 2: KASHTAN – 🛏 2 cl. Kyïv (**29**) - Dorohusk (**444**) - Berlin. Conveys on ②⑤ from Kharkiv (③⑥ from Kyïv) 🛏 2 cl. Kharkiv (**343**) - Kyïv - Berlin (Table **1780**). Conveys on ①②③④⑥ (②③④⑤⑦ from Kovel) 🛏 2 cl. Odesa (**84**) - Kovel - Berlin (Table **1750**). Conveys on ③⑦ from Simferopol 🛏 2 cl. Simferpol (**40**) - Kyïv - Berlin.

B – May 31 - Oct. 3: KASHTAN – 🛏 2 cl. Berlin (**445**) - Dorohusk (**30**) - Kyïv. Conveys on ④⑦ 🛏 2 cl. Berlin - Kyïv (**344**) - Kharkiv (Table **1780**). Conveys on ①③④⑤⑥ 🛏 2 cl. Berlin - Kovel (**84**) - Kozyatyn (**83**) - Odesa (Table **1750**). Conveys on ②⑤ 🛏 2 cl. Berlin - Kyïv (**282**) - Simferopol.

C – Dec. 13 - May 29 (not Dec. 31); Oct. 3 - Dec. 11: KASHTAN – 🛏 2 cl. Kyïv (**29**) - Dorohusk (**440**) - Berlin. Conveys on ②⑤ from Kharkiv (③⑥ from Kyïv) 🛏 2 cl. Kharkiv (**343**) - Kyïv - Berlin (Table **1780**). Conveys on ①②③⑥ (②③④⑦ from Kovel) 🛏 2 cl. Odesa (**106**) - Kovel - Berlin (Table **1750**). Conveys on ④⑦ from Simferopol 🛏 2 cl. Simferpol (**40**) - Kyïv - Berlin.

D – Dec. 12 - May 30 (not Jan. 1); Oct. 4 - Dec. 11: KASHTAN – 🛏 2 cl. Berlin (**441**) - Dorohusk (**30**) - Kyïv. Conveys on ④⑦ 🛏 2 cl. Berlin - Kyïv (**118**) - Kharkiv (Table **1780**). Conveys on ①③④⑤ 🛏 2 cl. Berlin - Kyïv (**123**) - Odesa (Table **1750**). Conveys on ②⑥ 🛏 2 cl. Berlin - Kyïv (**12**) - Simferopol.

F – To / from Ivano-Frankivsk (Table **1720**).

H – From / to Kharkiv (Table **1780**).

K – KYÏV EKSPRES / KIEV EXPRESS – 🛏 1, 2 cl. Kyïv - Warszawa and v.v.

Y – 🛏 2 cl. Moskva (**55**) - Kyïv (**343**) - Korosten - Zhytomyr.

Z – 🛏 2 cl. Zhytomyr (**344**) - Korosten - Kyïv (**56**) - Moskva.

h – Berlin **Hauptbahnhof**.

PL – Poland (Central European Time).

UA – Ukraine (East European Time).

1720 VILNIUS and MINSK - LVIV - CHERNIVTSI — LDZ, LG, BCh, UZ

km		*Pas* **47** J	*Pas* **608**		*Pas* **668** P	*Pas* **604** ◇	*Fir* **43**	*Pas* **371** A	*Pas* **371** B	*Sko* **141** M
0	**Vilnius** § LT d.	...	...	...	...	...	...	...	...	...
95	Lida § BY d.	...	...	...	...	...	...	...	...	...
	St Peterburg Vit. **1920** d.	1245	...	...	...	...	...	...	...	...
	Minsk d.	0153	...	...	...	...	...	1549	1549	...
200	Baranavichy Polesskiye d.	0412	...	...	...	...	...	1820	1820	...
316	Luninets **1700** ‡ BY d.	0616	...	...	...	...	...	2022	2022	...
422	Sarny **1700** ‡ UA d.	0947	...	...	...	...	...	2331	2331	...
509	Rivne **1700** d.	1131	...	...	...	...	...	0114	0114	...
	Kovel d.	|	...	...	1559	...	...	|	|	...
	Lutsk d.	|	...	...	1821	...	...	|	|	...
	Kyïv **1700 1750** d.	|	...	...	|	...	1916	|	|	0120
716	**Lviv** a.	1519	...	...	2255	...	0352	0454	0454	1013
716	**Lviv** d.	...	1645	...	2335	2130	0417	...	0520	1040
857	Ivano-Frankivsk d.	...	2012	...	0240	0518	0702	...	1115	1334
912	Kolomyya d.	...	2125	...	0358	0642	...	...	...	1446
983	**Chernivtsi** a.	...	2300	...	0530	0843	...	...	...	1607

km		*Sko* **608**	*Pas* **372** C	*Pas* **372** D	*Fir* **44**	*Sko* **48** K	*Pas* **668**	*Pas* **134** Q	*Pas* **604** ◇	*Sko* **142** M
0	**Chernivtsi** d.	0735	...	...	...	...	1517	...	2016	2212
71	Kolomyya d.	0907	...	...	...	...	1713	...	2240	2341
126	Ivano-Frankivsk d.	1025	...	1304	1815	...	1850	...	0035	0114
267	**Lviv** a.	1259	...	1837	2105	...	2159	...	0804	0400
267	**Lviv** d.	...	1900	1900	2130	2312	2230	0108	...	0420
	Kyïv **1700 1750** a.	...	|	|	0620	|	|	|	...	1322
443	Lutsk a.	...	|	|	...	|	0256	0825	...	...
527	**Kovel** a.	...	|	|	...	|	0520	1020	...	...
474	Rivne **1700** d.	...	2303	2303	...	0305	...	...	...	...
561	Sarny **1700** ‡ UA d.	...	0048	0048	...	0445	...	...	...	...
667	Luninets **1700** ‡ BY d.	...	0422	0422	...	0815	...	...	...	...
783	Baranavichy Polesskiye d.	...	0703	0703	...	1032	...	...	...	...
923	**Minsk** a.	...	0900	0900	...	1222	...	...	...	...
	St Peterburg Vit. **1920** a.	...	...	...	...	0525	...	...	...	...
	Lida § BY d.	...	...	...	...	...	...	...	...	...
	Vilnius § LT a.	...	...	...	...	...	...	...	...	...

A – Even dates.

B – June 2 - Sept. 6, even dates.

C – Uneven dates [... *31, 3* ...].

D – June 3 - Sept. 7, uneven dates [... *31, 3* ...].

J – Even dates [... *30, 1, 4* ...] (daily May 14 - Sept. 30).

K – Even dates (daily May 12 - Sept. 28).

M – From / to Moskva (Table **1750**).

P – Conveys on ① Dec. 13 - May 30; ⑥ May 31 - Oct. 3; ① Oct. 4 - Dec. 11 from Berlin 🛏 2 cl. Berlin - Kovel - Lviv.

Q – Conveys on ⑦ Dec. 13 - May 29; ⑤ May 30 - Oct. 2; ⑦ Oct. 3 - Dec. 12 🛏 2 cl. Lviv - Kovel - Berlin.

◇ – Runs via Stry (*105 km* from Lviv, *108 km* from Ivano-Frankivsk).

▮ – 🏛 : Joniškis (LT) / Meitene (LV).

§ – 🏛 : Benyakoni (BY) / Stasylos (LT).

‡ – 🏛 : Horyn (BY) / Udrytsk (UA).

BY – Belarus.

LT – Lithuania.

LV – Latvia.

UA – Ukraine.

1725 ODESA - BEREZYNE — UZ

km		*Pas* **686** y	
0	**Odesa** Holovna d.	1545	...
84	Bilhorod-Dnistrovsky d.	1820	...
174	Artsyz d.	2035	...
209	**Berezyne** a.	2303	...

		Pas **686** y	
Berezyne d.	...	2323	...
Artsyz d.	...	0244	...
Bilhorod-Dnistrovsky d.	...	0438	...
Odesa Holovna a.	...	0642	...

y – May 25 - Oct. 10.

1730 CAHUL - CHIŞINĂU - CHERNIVTSI — UZ, CFM

km		*Pas* **645** d	*Pas* **609** d	*Sko* **47** M		*Sko* **61** S	*Sko* **341** M
0	**Cahul** d.	1616	...	...	...	...	...
136	Basarabeasca a.	0227	...	...	...	...	...
136	Basarabeasca d.	0313	...	...	...	...	...
331	**Chişinău 1670** d.	0715	...	1150	...	1928	2000
438	Ungheni **1670** d.	...	...	|	...	2211	2308
516	Bălţi Oraş d.	...	...	1513	...	2352	0050
614	Ocniţa 🏛 MD d.	...	1425	1719	...	0253	0401
768	**Zhmerynka** ‡ UA a.	...	|	2202	...	0745	0919
729	Mamalyha 🏛 UA a.	...	1804	...	...	...	...
787	**Chernivtsi** a.	...	1942	...	...	...	...

	Pas **646** d	*Sko* **341** M	*Pas* **610** d	*Sko* **47** M		*Sko* **61** S
Chernivtsi d.	...	...	0848	...	...	...
Mamalyha 🏛 UA d.	...	...	1030	...	...	...
Zhmerynka ‡ UA d.	...	0646	|	1247	...	1903
Ocniţa 🏛 MD d.	...	1209	1400	1736	...	0031
Bălţi Oraş d.	...	1446	...	1926	...	0300
Ungheni **1670** d.	...	1659	...	|	...	0515
Chişinău 1670 d.	1905	2015	...	2248	...	0727
Basarabeasca a.	0331	...	...	...	...	...
Basarabeasca d.	0516	...	...	...	...	...
Cahul a.	1139	...	...	...	...	...

M – To / from Moskva (Table **1750**).

S – To / from St Peterburg (Table **1750**).

d – [4] only.

‡ – 🏛 : Mohyliv-Podilski (UA).

MD – Moldova.

UA – Ukraine.

RZhD, UZ — MOSKVA - BRYANSK - SUMY, CHERNIHIV and KYÏV — 1740

km		Sko 59 Ad	Sko 33 U	Sko 141	Sko 341	Sko 89 Z	Sko 73	Sko 41	Sko 41 V	Fir 77 K	Sko 55 LX	Sko 117	Sko 47	Fir 5	Fir 23	Sko 15 S	Fir 1 F	Fir 3	Fir 3 Ac	Sko 21 g
0	**Moskva** Kiyevskaya d.	0025	1048	1235	1243	1343	1546	1646	1646	1638	1908	1801	1937	2023	2120	2213	2323	2129	2129	2250
387	Bryansk Orlovski d.	0642	1705	1900	1919	1948	2200	2349	2349	2326	0114	0025	0216	0252	0323	0426	|	0357	0357	0454
504	Suzemka RU d.	|	|	|	|	2146	|	|	|	0125	|	0240	|	|	|	|	0457	0556	0556	|
519	Zernove UA d.	|	|	2016	|	|	|	|	|	|	|	0228	|	|	|	|	|	|	|	0610
651	Konotop **1780** d.	0943	1958	2221	2233	2300	0118	0217	0217	0258	0340	0440	0530	0523	0555	0757	|	0721	0725	0802
780	**Sumy 1780** d.	|	|	|	|	|	|	|	|	|	|	0732	|	|	|	|	|	|	|	|
829	**Chernihiv** a.	|	|	|	|	|	|	|	0456	|	|	...	|	|	|	|	|	|	|	|
872	**Kyïv** a.	1308	|	0104	0140	0122	0353	0510	...	0529	0624	...	0820	0750	0834	1042	0800	0958	0958	1108
	Odesa Holovna **1750 1770** a.	|	1156	|	|	...	|	...	...	...	...	...	|	...	1909	|	...	...	|	...
	Chişinău **1750** a.	|	...	|	2015	...	|	...	...	...	...	...	2248	...	...	|	...	...	|	...
	Lviv **1750** a.	|	...	1013	...	...	1357	...	...	...	...	...	...	...	...	2052	...	...	|	...
	Chernivtsi **1750** a.	0620	...	1607	...	...	...	...	...	...	...	...	...	...	...	...	...	...	0620	...

	Sko 56 LY	Fir 24	Sko 47	Sko 34 G	Sko 60 Ba	Sko 142 Bb	Sko 341	Sko 658 W	Sko 42	Sko 22 h	Fir 2 F	Fir 6	Sko 74	Sko 117	Sko 90 Z	Sko 16 T	Fir 78 K	Fir 4
Chernivtsi **1750** d.	...	...	...	...	1859	2212	...	...	...	...	...	...	...	...	...	...	...	...
Lviv **17507** d.	...	...	...	...	|	0420	...	...	...	...	...	...	0837	...	...	1057	...	...
Chişinău **1750** d.	...	...	1150	...	|	|	2000	...	...	...	...	...	|	...	...	|	...	...
Odesa Holovna **1750 1770** d.	...	1504	|	1800	|	|	|	...	...	...	...	...	|	...	...	|	...	...
Kyïv d.	0023	0121	0218	|	0958	1342	1348	...	1435	1704	2009	1905	1847	...	2015	2036	2042	2117
Chernihiv d.	|	|	|	|	|	|	|	1447	|	|	|	|	|	...	|	|	|	|
Sumy 1780 d.	|	|	|	|	|	|	|	|	|	|	|	|	|	1913	|	|	|	|
Konotop **1780** d.	0308	0357	0506	0953	1252	1644	1654	1821	1821	2002	|	2149	2121	2238	2304	2330	2339	0008
Zernove UA d.	|	|	|	|	|	1919	|	|	|	|	|	|	|	0105	|	|	0154	|
Suzemka RU d.	0628	0720	|	|	1617	2103	|	|	|	|	0135	|	|	|	0242	|	0338	|
Bryansk Orlovski d.	0815	0910	1044	1507	1732‡	2245	2304	2335	2335	0050	|	0233	0256	0408	|	0427	0523	0445
Moskva Kiyevskaya a.	1432	1516	1623	2118	2236	0452	0518	0533	0533	0619	0639	0902	0910	1004	0931	0959	1130	1058

FOR NOTES, SEE TABLE **1750** BELOW.

UZ, CFM — KYÏV - ODESA, CHERNIVTSI and LVIV / ODESA - CHERNIVTSI and LVIV — 1750

km		Sko 141	Sko 89	Sko 341	Sko 73	Sko 111	Sko 55	Sko 47	Fir 23	Sko 15	Sko 15 D	Sko 15 S	Sko 59 A	Sko 61	Sko 115	Fir 43 N	Sko 13	Fir 108 R	Sko 51 P	Fir 26	Fir 123 M	Fir 91	Fir 83 M	Sko 19 H	Sko 7 E
	Moskva Kiyevskaya **1740** d.	1235	1343	1243	1546	...	1908	1937	2120	2213	2213	2213	2129e	...	...	...	...	...	...	...	...	...	...	...	...
	Kharkiv **1780** d.	|	|	|	|	1911	|	|	|	|	|	|	|	...	0712	...	1101	...	...	...	...	...	...	...	...
0	**Kyïv 1700** d.	0120	0152	0204	0408	0421	0646	0837	0902	1110	1110	1110	1540k	...	1659	1916	2012	...	2042	...	1821	2215	...	...	2358
	St Peterburg Vitebski **1920** d.	|	|	|	|	|	|	|	|	|	|	|	|	1620r	|	|	|	...	|	...	|	|	...	2355q	|
159	Kozyatyn **1700** d.	|	0423	0433	0629	|	0856	1047	1112	1329	1329	1329	1622	1700	1921	|	|	...	2311	...	2035	|	0141	0159	0221
221	Vinnytsya d.	|	0519	0534	0726	|	0951	1141	1208	1424	1424	1424	1740	1754	2019	|	|	...	0006	...	2140	|	0238	0255	0322
	Odesa Holovna d.	|	|	|	|	|	|	|	|	|	|	|	|	|	|	|	|	1813	|	1900	|	|	|	|	|
268	Zhmerynka **1775** d.	|	0610	0646	|	|	|	1247	1317	|	|	|	|	1903	2129	|	|	0015	0113	0122	2255	|	0345	0410	|
654	**Odesa** Holovna a.	|	...	|	|	◧	|	|	1909	|	|	|	|	|	|	◧	|	|	|	|	0541	|	0957	1018	|
	Chişinău **1730** a.	|	...	2015	|	|	|	2248	...	|	|	|	|	0727	|	|	|	|	|	|	...	|	...	...	|
367	Khmelnytsky **1775** d.	|	...	...	0939	|	1147	...	...	1624	1624	1624	2012	...	2315	|	|	0142	0242	0251	...	|	...	...	0545
486	Ternopil **1775** d.	|	...	...	1139	|	...	...	...	1837	1837	1837	2350	...	0117	|	|	0342	0437	0450	...	|	...	...	0744
594	**Chernivtsi** a.	1607j	...	...	|	|	...	...	...	|	|	|	0620	...	|	|	|	|	|	|	...	|	...	...	|
	Bucureşti Nord **1670** a.	|	...	...	|	|	...	...	...	|	|	|	1930	...	|	|	|	|	|	|	...	|	...	...	|
	Sofiya **1500** a.	|	...	...	|	|	...	...	...	|	|	|	0555	...	|	|	|	|	|	|	...	|	...	...	|
627	**Lviv 1775** a.	1013	...	...	1357	1445	...	...	...	2052	2052	2052	...	...	0331	0352	0537	0557	0651	0710	...	0633	...	...	0959
627	**Lviv** d.	...	...	...	...	...	...	...	...	2120	2120	2120	...	...	...	...	0604	0623	...	...	...	...	...	...	1026
852	Mukacheve d.	...	...	...	...	...	...	...	...	0155	0155	0155	...	...	...	...	1039	1110	...	...	...	...	...	...	1459
893	**Chop** a.	...	...	...	...	...	...	...	...	0245	0245	0245	...	...	...	...	1132	1214	...	...	...	...	...	...	1547
	Košice **1195** a.	...	...	...	...	...	...	...	...	|	0731	|	...	...	...	...	|	|	...	...	...	...	...	...	2130
	Budapest Keleti **1270** a.	...	...	...	...	...	...	...	...	|	...	1117	...	...	...	...	|	|	...	...	...	...	...	...	...
915	**Uzhhorod** a.	...	...	...	...	...	...	...	...	0403	...	...	...	...	...	...	1235	1316	...	...	...	...	...	...	...

	Sko 52 Q	Fir 107 R	Sko 8	Sko 61	Sko 142	Sko 341	Sko 74	Sko 14	Sko 90	Sko 16 DE	Sko 16 T	Sko 16	Sko 116	Sko 56	Fir 24	Sko 47	Sko 112	Fir 84 M	Sko 20 J	Fir 26	Fir 44 N	Fir 92	Fir 106 M	Sko 60 B
Uzhhorod d.	...	1805	...	...	...	...	...	2145	...	...	...	0135	...	...	...	...	...	...	...	...	...	...	...	...
Budapest Keleti **1270** d.	...	|	...	...	...	...	...	|	...	...	1843	|	...	...	...	...	...	...	...	...	...	...	...	...
Košice **1195** d.	...	|	...	...	...	...	...	|	...	2045	|	|	...	...	...	...	...	...	...	...	...	...	...	...
Chop d.	...	1855	2026	...	...	...	...	2243	...	0434	0434	0434	...	...	...	...	...	...	...	...	...	...	...	...
Mukacheve d.	...	2003	2138	...	...	...	...	2357	...	0538	0538	0538	...	...	...	...	...	...	...	...	...	...	...	...
Lviv a.	...	0057	0223	...	...	...	...	0450	...	1031	1031	1031	...	...	...	...	...	...	...	...	...	...	...	...
Lviv 1775 d.	0011	0140	0246	...	0420	...	0837	0516	...	1057	1057	1057	1240	...	...	...	1705	...	...	1943	2130	2247	...	...
Sofiya **1500** d.	|	|	|	...	|	...	|	|	...	|	|	|	|	...	...	...	|	...	...	|	|	|	...	1940
Bucureşti Nord **1670** d.	|	|	|	...	|	...	|	|	...	|	|	|	|	...	...	...	|	...	...	|	|	|	...	0620
Chernivtsi d.	|	|	|	...	2212j	...	|	|	...	|	|	|	|	...	...	...	|	...	...	|	|	|	...	1859
Ternopil **1775** d.	0228	0355	0503	...	|	...	1059	|	...	1307	1307	1307	1504	...	...	...	|	...	...	2203	|	|	...	0142
Khmelnytsky **1775** d.	0437	0601	0712	...	|	...	1315	|	...	1511	1511	1511	1745	1904	...	...	|	...	...	0009	|	|	...	0352
Chişinău **1730** d.	|	|	|	1928	|	2000	|	|	...	|	|	|	|	|	...	1150	|	...	...	|	|	|	...	|
Odesa Holovna d.	|	|	|	|	|	|	|	|	...	|	|	|	|	|	1504	|	◧	1822	1832	|	◧	|	2257	|
Zhmerynka **1775** d.	0626	0745	|	0810	|	0938	|	|	1526	|	|	|	1942	|	2119	2224	|	0031	0050	0156	|	|	0357	|
Odesa Holovna a.	|	1331	|	|	|	|	|	|	|	|	|	|	|	|	|	|	|	|	|	0750	|	|	|	|
Vinnytsya d.	0713	...	0913	0901	|	1025	1516	|	1621	1706	1706	1706	2034	2104	2204	2308	|	0117	0138	...	|	|	0437	0555
Kozyatyn **1700** d.	0807	...	1012	1020	|	1121	1616	|	1735	1759	1759	1759	2150	2200	2258	0001	|	0209	0252	...	|	|	0523	0704
St Peterburg Vitebski **1920** a.	|	...	|	1243z	|	|	|	|	|	|	|	|	|	|	|	|	|	...	0615z	...	|	|	...	|
Kyïv 1700 a.	1021	...	1222	...	1322	1330	1827	1433	1946	2001	2001	2001	0010	0003	0101	0208	0248	...	...	...	0620	0726	...	0919
Kharkiv **1780** a.	...	...	...	...	|	|	|	2253	|	|	|	|	1020	|	|	|	1145	...	...	...	...	...	...	|
Moskva Kiyevskaya **1740** a.	...	...	...	...	0452	0518	0910	...	0931	0956	0956	0956	...	1432	1516	1623	...	...	...	...	...	...	...	0452f

A – BOLGARIYA EKSPRESS – 🛏 1, 2 cl. Moskva (**3** ▽) - Kyïv - Vadul Siret (**383**) - Sofiya. Conveys on ⑥ (also ② June 12 - Aug. 31) 🛏 2 cl. Minsk (**86**) - Kyïv - Sofiya. Conveys (on dates shown in Table **98**) 🛏 2 cl. Moskva - Ruse - Varna and Burgas.
B – BOLGARIYA EKSPRES – 🛏 1, 2 cl. Sofiya (**382**) - Vadul Siret (**60**) - Kyïv (**142** △) - Moskva. Conveys on ② (also ⑤ June 15 - Sept. 3) 🛏 2 cl. Sofiya - Kyïv - Minsk. Conveys (on dates shown in Table **98**) 🛏 2 cl. Varna and Burgas - Ruse - Moskva.
D – 🛏 1, 2 cl. Moskva - Chop - Košice - Žilina and v.v.
E – Conveys (on dates shown in Table **96**) 🛏 1, 2 cl. Kyïv / Lviv - Chop - Bratislava and v.v.
F – Uneven dates in Aug., Nov., Dec. Even dates in June, July, Sept., Oct.
G – Even dates (daily June 2 - Sept. 14, Dec. 26 - 31).
H – From St Peterburg ①③⑤ (daily June 1 - Oct. 16).
J – ③⑤⑦ (daily May 30 - Oct. 18).
K – To / from Kovel (Table **1700**).
L – To / from Khmelnytsky (Table **1750**).
M – Conveys (on dates shown in Table **56**) 🛏 2 cl. Berlin - Odesa and v.v.
N – To / from Ivano-Frankivsk (Table **1720**).

P – To Przemyśl (Table **1056**). Conveys 🛏 1, 2 cl. Kyïv - Praha; 🛏 2 cl. Kyïv - Wrocław (Table **96**).
Q – From Przemyśl (Table **1056**). Conveys 🛏 1, 2 cl. Praha - Kyïv; 🛏 2 cl. Wrocław - Kyïv (Table **96**).
R – Conveys 🛏 2 cl. Odesa - Lviv - Przemyśl - Warszawa and v.v. (Table **1056**). Conveys (on dates shown in Table **96**) 🛏 1, 2 cl. Odesa - Praha and v.v.
S – TISSA – 🛏 2 cl. Moskva - Kyïv - Záhony (**629**) - Budapest (**794**) - Kelebia (**345**) - Beograd. Conveys (on dates shown in Table **97**) 🛏 1, 2 cl. Moskva - Budapest - Zagreb / Venezia; 🛏 2 cl. Kyïv - Budapest - Zagreb.
T – TISSA – 🛏 2 cl. Beograd (**344**) - Kelebia (**793**) - Budapest (**628**) - Záhony - Kyïv - Moskva. Conveys (on dates shown in Table **97**) 🛏 1, 2 cl. Venezia / Zagreb (**205**) - Budapest - Moskva; 🛏 2 cl. Zagreb - Budapest - Kyïv.
U – Uneven dates [... *29, 1* ...]; daily June 1 - Sept. 13, Dec. 25 - 30.
V – Moskva - Nizhyn (**58**) - Chernihiv.
W – Chernihiv - Nizhyn (**42**) - Moskva.
X – Conveys 🛏 2 cl. Moskva - Kyïv (**343**) - Korosten - Zhytomyr, (Table **1700**).
Y – Conveys 🛏 2 cl. Zhytomyr (**344**) - Korosten - Kyïv (**56**) - Moskva, (Table **1700**).
Z – To / from Zhmerynka (Table **1750**).

a – June 16 - Sept. 6 (previous day from Chernivtsi).
b – Until June 16 and from Sept. 7 (previous day from Chernivtsi).
c – Until June 12 and from Sept. 3.
d – June 13 - Sept. 3.
e – 0025 June 13 - Sept. 3.
f – 2236 June 16 - Sept. 6.
g – May 31 - Oct. 2, Dec. 24 - 30.
h – June 1 - Oct. 3, Dec. 25 - 31.
j – Via Lviv.
k – 1357 June 13 - Sept. 3.
q – Two days earlier.
r – Previous day.
z – Next day.

▽ – Train **59** June 13 - Sept. 3.
△ – Train **60** June 15 - Sept. 5.
RU – Russia (Moskva Time).
UA – Ukraine (East European Time).
◧ – Via Korosten (Table **1700**).
‡ – Bryansk Lgovski.

1770 KYÏV and ODESA - SEVASTOPOL — UZ

km		Fir 23 Z	Fir 40	Sko 250 E	Fir 12 S h	Fir 28	Fir 650 H	Fir 121	Pas 382 A	Sko 33 C
	Moskva Kiyevskaya **1740** .. d.	2120	...	...	...	...	...	...	...	1048
0	Konotop d.	0555	...	...	...	...	...	...	...	1958
414	Znamyanka d.	|	...	...	...	...	...	...	...	0454
	Kyïv 1775 d.	0902	1252	...	1751	2021	...	1904	...	|
	Myronivka **1775** d.	|	1424	...	|	|	...	2202	...	|
	Minsk **1930** d.	|	|	...	|	|	...	|	0948	|
	Chernihiv d.	|	|	1205	|	|	...	|	1856	|
	Hrebinka d.	|	|	1605	|	|	...	|	2340	|
	Cherkasy d.	|	|	1742	|	|	...	|	0115	|
	Im. T. Shevchenka **1775** ... d.	|	1606	1859	2055	2317	...	0001	0219	|
826	**Odesa** Holovna a.	1909	|	|	|	|	2329	|	|	1156
	Mykolaïv d.	...	d	0043	d	0448	0425	0553	d	...
	Kherson d.	...	|	0220	|	0600	0527	...	|	...
	Simferopol **1775 1790** a.	...	0415	0736	0850	1106	1155	...	1546	...
	Sevastopol 1775 1790 a.	...	0616	...	...	1306	...	...	...	...

km		Sko 250 F	Fir 122	Fir 40 h	Fir 12 S	Fir 28	Fir 650 G	Fir 24 Z	Pas 382 B	Sko 34 D
0	**Sevastopol 1775 1790** d.	...	...	1324	...	1452	...	...	...	...
78	Simferopol **1775 1790** d.	1014	...	1537	1626	1710	1925	...	2154	...
360	Kherson d.	1536	...	|	|	2212	0202	...	|	...
415	Mykolaïv d.	1637	1923	d	d	2334	0338	...	d	...
	Odesa Holovna d.	|	|	|	|	|	0810	1504	|	1800
726	Im. T. Shevchenka **1775** ... d.	2227	0120	0433	0443	0526	...	|	1301	|
756	Cherkasy d.	2308	|	|	|	|	...	|	1357	|
848	Hrebinka d.	0129	|	|	|	|	...	|	1552	|
1054	**Chernihiv** a.	0534	|	|	|	|	...	|	1950	|
	Minsk **1930** a.	...	|	|	|	|	...	|	0529	|
835	Myronivka **1775** d.	...	0301	|	|	|	...	|	...	|
942	**Kyïv 1775** a.	...	0530	0738	0742	0845	...	0101	...	|
	Znamyanka d.	...	...	...	...	...	...	|	...	0040
	Konotop a.	...	...	...	...	...	...	0337	...	0919
	Moskva Kiyevskaya **1740** .. a.	...	...	...	...	...	...	1516	...	2118

A – 6, 10, 14, 18, 22, 26, 30 of each month Jan. - May and Oct. - Dec.; even dates [... *30, 1, 4* ...] June - Sept.
B – 4, 8, 12, 16, 20, 24, 28 of each month Jan. - May and Oct. - Dec.; even dates June - Sept.
C – Uneven dates (daily June 1 - Sept. 13, Dec. 25 - 30).
D – Even dates (daily June 2 - Sept. 14, Dec. 26 - 31).
E – Even dates June 20 - Aug. 30.
F – Uneven dates June 21 - Aug. 31.
G – June 2 - Aug. 31 (also May 31).
H – June 1 - Aug. 30.
S – SLAVUTICH.
Z – Via Zhmerynka (Table **1750**).
d – Via Dnipropetrovsk (Table **1775**).
h – Conveys (on dates shown in Table **56**) 2 cl. Berlin - Kyïv - Simferpol and v.v.

1775 LVIV and KYÏV - MARIUPOL and SEVASTOPOL — UZ

km		Fir 40	Fir 84 Y	Fir 84 Z	Fir 12 A h	Sko 86	Fir 38 D	Fir 72	Fir 80 N	Pas 282 P h	Sko 22 T	Sko 70 E
0	**Lviv 1750** d.	...	...	...	...	0944	...	...	...	...	1623	1747
141	Ternopil **1750** d.	...	...	...	...	1202	...	...	...	...	1844	2010
260	Khmelnytsky **1750** d.	...	...	...	...	1400	...	...	...	...	2100	2220
359	Zhmerynka **1750** d.	...	...	...	...	1545	...	...	...	...	2247	0005
468	Kozyatyn **1750** d.	...	...	...	...	1742	...	...	...	...	|	0204
	Kyïv 1770 d.	1252	1505	1636	1751	|	1923	2027	2312	2249	|	|
663	Myronivka **1770** d.	1424	1633	1808	|	2019	|	2150	0028	|	|	0449
772	Im. T. Shevchenka **1770** .. d.	1606	1821	2018	2055	2154	2218	2336	0200	0135	|	0640
864	Znamyanka d.	1727	1947	2150	2210	2314	2334	0051	0317	0248	0800	0800
973	Pyatykhatky d.	|	2141	2341	|	0107	|	0246	0510	|	0959	0959
1052	Dniprodzerzhynsk d.	|	2247	0043	|	0208	|	0352	0613	|	1114	1114
1088	**Dnipropetrovsk** Holovny . d.	2114	0015	0136	0146	0259	0306	0445	0657	0638	1214	1214
1357	Donetsk a.	|	0504	0600	|	|	0710	|	...	|	1650	1650
1489	**Mariupol** a.	|	0807	0847	|	|	...	|	...	|	...	2000
1214	Zaporizhzhya **I 1790** d.	2312	...	...	0350	0453	...	0642	...	0841	...	...
1326	Melitopol **1790** d.	0103	...	...	0532	0637	...	...	...	1035	...	...
1570	Simferopol **1770 1790** a.	0415	...	...	0850	0950	...	...	...	1330	...	...
1648	**Sevastopol 1770 1790** a.	0616	...	...	...	...	...	...	...	...	...	...

	Sko 70 U	Sko 21 E	Sko 86	Fir 72	Fir 79 N	Fir 37 D	Fir 40 h	Fir 12 A	Fir 84	
Sevastopol 1770 1790 d.	...	...	...	...	...	...	1324	...	...	...
Simferopol **1770 1790** d.	...	...	1312	...	...	...	1537	1626	...	...
Melitopol **1790** d.	...	...	1645	...	...	...	1858	1954	...	...
Zaporizhzhya **I 1790** d.	...	...	1814	1925	...	...	2030	2133	...	...
Mariupol d.	1007	...	|	|	...	...	|	|	1649	...
Donetsk d.	1349	1349	|	|	...	1920	|	|	2003	...
Dnipropetrovsk Holovny d.	1830	1830	2025	2157	2245	2322	2330	2357	0030	...
Dniprodzerzhynsk d.	1906	1906	2101	2235	2323	|	|	|	0115	...
Pyatykhatky d.	2018	2018	2210	2348	0038	|	|	|	0232	...
Znamyanka d.	2215	2232	0008	0141	0240	0256	0309	0319	0434	...
Im. T. Shevchenka **1770** d.	2347	|	0137	0304	0408	0416	0433	0443	0643	...
Myronivka **1770** d.	0129	|	0312	0437	0536	|	|	|	0825	...
Kyïv 1770 a.	|	|	|	0556	0654	0701	0738	0742	1004	...
Kozyatyn **1750** d.	0441	|	0619	...	...	...	...	...	...	...
Zhmerynka **1750** d.	0654	0835	0826	...	...	...	...	...	...	...
Khmelnytsky **1750** d.	0828	1012	0955	...	...	...	...	...	...	...
Ternopil **1750** d.	1040	1217	1150	...	...	...	...	...	...	...
Lviv 1750 a.	1307	1433	1409	...	...	...	...	...	...	...

A – SLAVUTICH.
D – DONBAS.
E – Even dates.
N – DNIPRO.
P – May 31 - Oct. 19.
T – Uneven dates [... *31, 3* ...].
U – Uneven dates [... *29, 1* ...].
Y – Daily May 31 - Sept. 30.
Z – Daily Oct. 1 - May 30.
h – Conveys (on dates shown in Table **56**) 2 cl. Berlin - Kyïv - Simferpol and v.v.

1780 KYÏV and HOMEL - KHARKIV and LUHANSK — BCh, UZ

km **		Sko 112	Fir 164 S	Pas 312 W	Fir 20	Pas 606	Sko 14	Sko 100 R	Sko 118 H	Fir 344 J	Pas 116
	Uzhhorod **1750** d.	...	...	...	...	...	2145	...	...	...	...
	Lviv **1750** d.	1705	...	...	...	...	0516	...	...	...	1240
0	**Kyïv** d.	0313	0633	...	1840	...	1453	...	1948	2235	0042
148	Hrebinka d.	0527	|	...	2035	...	1654	...	2200	|	|
333	**Poltava** Kyïvska d.	0905	1035	...	2328	...	2017	...	0139	|	|
	Kaliningrad **1950** .. d.	|	|	1403	|	...	|	...	|	|	|
	Minsk **1930** d.	|	|	0057	|	...	|	0825	|	|	|
	Homel § BY d.	|	|	0635	|	...	|	1404	|	|	|
	Konotop **1740** § UA d.	|	|	1236	|	...	|	1932	|	0200	0349
	Sumy **1740** d.	|	|	1530	|	1650	|	2206	|	0506	0623
491	**Kharkiv** a.	1145	1228	1921	|	2120	2253	0121	0417	0944	1020
	Simferopol **1790** ... a.	...	...	...	|	|	...	1055	...	...	...
814	**Luhansk** a.	...	...	...	0947	1022	...	...	...	...	...

	Fir 20	Pas 311 U	Pas 606	Sko 115	Sko 13	Fir 163 S	Sko 111	Pas 343 K	Fir 63	Sko 100 Q
Luhansk d.	1649	...	1803	...	...	...	...	...	...	...
Simferopol **1790** .... d.	|	...	|	...	...	...	...	...	...	1335
Kharkiv d.	|	0050	0636	0712	1101	1627	1911	1835	2255	2314
Sumy **1740** d.	|	0442	1200	1109	|	|	|	2320	|	0238
Konotop **1740** § UA d.	|	0733	...	1353	|	|	|	0247	|	0510
Homel § BY a.	|	1339	...	|	|	|	|	|	|	1038
Minsk **1930** a.	|	1917	...	|	|	|	|	|	|	1612
Kaliningrad **1950** ... a.	|	0856	...	|	|	|	|	|	|	...
Poltava Kyïvska d.	0327	...	...	|	1415	1840	2233	|	0148	...
Hrebinka d.	0620	...	...	|	1758	|	0158	|	0455	...
Kyïv a.	0806	...	...	1639	1952	2217	0401	0613	0715	...
Lviv **1750** a.	...	...	...	0331	0537	...	1445	...	...	...
Uzhhorod **1750** a.	...	...	...	...	1235	...	...	...	...	...

H – On ④⑦ Dec. 12 - May 30; Oct. 4 - Dec. 11 from Berlin – conveys 2 cl. Berlin (**441**) - Kyïv - Kharkiv.
J – On ④⑦ May 31 - Oct. 3 from Berlin – conveys 2 cl. Berlin (**445**) - Kyïv - Kharkiv.
K – On ②⑤ conveys 2 cl. Kharkiv - Kyïv (**440** / **444**) - Berlin.
Q – Even dates (daily June 2 - Oct. 2).
R – Uneven dates [... *29, 1* ...] (daily June 1 - Oct. 1).
S – STOLICHNY EKSPRES.
U – Uneven dates [... *29, 1* ...].
W – Even dates.
§ – : Terekowka (BY) / Khorobychi (UA).
** – Homel - Konotop: *222 km.* Sumy - Kharkiv: *195 km.* Kharkiv - Luhansk: *439 km.*
BY – Belarus.
UA – Ukraine.

1790 MOSKVA - KHARKIV - MARIUPOL and SEVASTOPOL — RZhD, UZ

km		Sko 7 S	Sko 25 y	Fir 29 z	Sko 17	Sko 100 R	Sko 9	Fir 15	Sko 67 K x	Sko 77
0	**Moskva** Kurskaya d.	0403	0824	0944	1032	...	1440	1449	1611	1629
194	Tula **I** d.	0645	1130	1226	1319	...	1726	1734	1951	2007
383	Orel d.	0932	1420	1506	1555	...	2007	2015	2227	2259
537	Kursk d.	1159	1635	1717	1825	...	2230	2243	0030	0100
697	Belgorod § RU d.	1551	2008	2039	2148	...	0140	0156	0341	0413
	Kyïv **1780** d.	|	|	|	|	...	|	|	|	|
	Minsk **1780** d.	|	|	|	|	0825	|	|	|	|
781	**Kharkiv** § UA a.	1655	2036	2149	2245	0121	0205	0246	0402	0510
781	**Kharkiv** d.	1728	2116	2209	2310	0139	0244	0313	0445	0530
1098	Donetsk a.	|	|	|	|	|	0833	|	|	1230
1230	**Mariupol** a.	|	|	|	|	|	...	|	|	1505
1081	Dnipropetrovsk Holovny a.	|	|	|	|	|	...	0741	|	...
1108	Zaporizhzhya **I 1775** d.	2225	0134	0220	0332	0600	...	...	0926	...
1220	Melitopol **1775** d.	0007	0314	0351	0517	0733	...	...	1135	...
1464	Simferopol **1770 1775** a.	0310	|	0648	0840	1055	...	...	1440	...
1543	Yevpatoriya a.	|	0716	...	|	...	...	...	...	...
1542	**Sevastopol 1770 1775** a.	0505	...	...	1045	...	...	...	...	...

	Fir 16	Sko 10	Sko 78	Sko 68 K z	Sko 100 Q	Fir 30 w	Sko 18	Sko 26 v	Sko 8 S
Sevastopol 1770 1775 d.	...	...	...	...	...	...	1705	...	2215
Yevpatoriya d.	...	...	...	...	...	...	|	1929	|
Simferopol **1770 1775** d.	...	...	...	1212	1335	1445	1936	|	0050
Melitopol **1775** d.	...	...	...	1526	1652	1743	2255	2341	0407
Zaporizhzhya **I 1775** d.	...	...	...	1704	1836	1911	0024	0108	0550
Dnipropetrovsk Holovny d.	1415	...	...	|	|	|	|	|	|
Mariupol d.	|	...	1050	|	|	|	|	|	|
Donetsk d.	|	1444	1332	|	|	|	|	|	|
Kharkiv a.	1848	2043	2049	2130	2254	2355	0454	0547	1026
Kharkiv § UA d.	1928	2115	2109	2203	2314	0034	0514	0601	1056
Minsk **1780** a.	|	|	|	|	1612	|	|	|	|
Kyïv **1780** a.	|	|	|	|	...	|	|	|	|
Belgorod § RU d.	2223	0011	0037	0100	...	0330	0847	0928	1352
Kursk d.	0116	0250	0333	0343	...	0653	1142	1225	1720
Orel d.	0317	0500	0537	0547	...	0852	1350	1430	1957
Tula **I** d.	0535	0743	0815	0823	...	1134	1629	1656	2228
Moskva Kurskaya a.	0906	1036	1109	1115	...	1444	1934	2014	0110

K – KRYM.
Q – Even dates (daily June 2 - Oct. 2).
R – Uneven dates [... *29, 1* ...] (daily June 1 - Oct. 1).
S – From / to St Peterburg (Table **1900**).
v – May 25 - Oct. 1.
w – May 26 - Oct. 3.
x – May 25 - Oct. 3.
y – May 27 - Oct. 3.
z – May 24 - Oct. 1.
RU – Russia (Moskva Time).
UA – Ukraine (East European Time).
§ – : Krasny Khutor (RU) / Kozacha Lopan (UA).

For services Moskva - Kharkiv - Rostov and beyond, see the *Thomas Cook Overseas Timetable.*

LITHUANIA, LATVIA and ESTONIA

SEE MAP PAGE 509

Operators: Lithuania: **LG** (Lietuvos Geležinkeliai). Latvia: **LDz** (Latvijas Dzelzceļš). Estonia: **Edelaraudtee** (except for international trains, which are operated by **GoRail**).

Services: Trains convey first- and second-class seating unless indicated otherwise. International trains to and from CIS countries (Belarus, Russia, Ukraine) are composed of Russian-style sleeping-cars (for details of train types and classes of travel in the CIS, see the panel on page **515**).

Timings: Valid from **May 31, 2009**. Timings are expressed in local time at the station concerned (time comparison chart: page **2**).

Reservations: Reservation is compulsory for travel by long-distance and international services – *i.e.* all those for which a train number is shown.

🚌 KALININGRAD and VILNIUS - RIGA - TARTU and TALLINN — 1800

Operators:	A	E	E	E	E	E	E	E	E	E	E	
Kaliningrad d.	2100	...	...	...	...	...	...	...	...	...	...	...
Vilnius d.	|	...	...	...	0700	...	...	...	...	...	2100	...
Riga d.	0600	0700	0830	1000	1130	1230	1530	1830	1845	2100	0125	...
Valga d.	...	|	1115	|	...	|	|	|	2120	|	|	...
Tartu a.	...	|	1235	|	...	|	|	|	2240	|	|	...
Pärnu d.	...	0935	...	1230	...	1500	1800	2105	...	2330	0420	...
Tallinn harbour a.	...	|	...	|	...	|	|	|	...	|	0620	...
Tallinn bus station a.	...	1125	...	1425	...	1655	2000	2255	...	0115	0630	...

Operators:	E	E	E	E	E	E	E	A	E	E	E	E
Tallinn bus station d.	...	0700	...	1000	1230	1545	...	...	1830	2100	0030	...
Tallinn harbour d.	...	|	...	1010	|	|	...	...	|	|	|	...
Pärnu d.	...	0850	...	1205	|	1740	...	...	2020	2300	0220	...
Tartu d.	0645	|	...	|	|	|	1745	...	|	|	|	...
Valga d.	0805	|	...	|	|	|	1905	...	|	|	|	...
Riga a.	1050	1125	1230	1430	1655	2010	2150	2210	2255	0150	0510	0700
Vilnius a.	...	...	1700	...	...	...	...	|	...	0620	...	1055
Kaliningrad a.	...	...	...	...	...	...	...	0710	...	...	...	...

A – Also on ①④⑥ Kaliningrad dep. 0920, arrive Riga 1820; on ②⑤⑦ depart Riga 1000, arrive Kaliningrad 1900.
E – Mootor Reisi (www.eurolines.ee).
T – Toks or BAL (www.eurolines.lt).
☛ Also: 🚌 Vilnius - Riga at 0930 (E), 1300 (T), 1330 (E), 1600 (T), 1830 (E); 🚌 Riga - Vilnius at 0700 (E), 0800 (E), 1530 (E), 1800 (T), 1845 (E).

LG — VILNIUS - KLAIPEDA — 1810

km			17		19			21		
		c		2		2	c		2	
0	**Vilnius 1040, 1811** d.	...	0630	...	0900	...	...	1730	...	...
192	Radviliškis d.	0607	0844	...	1122	1430	1503	1946	...	...
212	Šiauliai d.	0630	0906	0920	1142	1504	1536	2008	2030	...
***	Mažeikiai a.	|	|	1036	|	1620	|	|	2146	...
376	**Klaipeda** a.	0918	1103	...	1351	...	1826	2203	...	...

		18			20			22	
	2		c	2		c	2		
Klaipeda d.	...	0625	0812	...	1139	1504	...	1700	...
Mažeikiai d.	0649	|	|	1149	|	|	1714	|	...
Šiauliai d.	0804	0833	1101	1306	1341	1751	1829	1905	...
Radviliškis d.	...	0851	1133	1338	1359	1826	...	1923	...
Vilnius 1040, 1811 a.	...	1108	...	...	1614	...	...	2140	...

c – 3rd class only. *** *78 km* Šiauliai - Mažeikiai.

LG 3rd class — VILNIUS - KAUNAS — 1811

km		①–⑤	①–⑤		①–⑤				x					
0	Vilnius **1040** d.	0508	0528	0640	0730	0836	1020	1110	1200	1400	1630	1725	1827	1920
104	Kaunas **1040** a.	0609	0708	0748	0848	1016	1129	1223	1315	1510	1731	1830	2004	2031

	①–⑤		①–⑤							x			
Kaunas **1040** d.	0457	0537	0625	0822	0907	1057	1157	1337	1530	1635	1750	1937	2052
Vilnius **1040** a.	0633	0722	0736	0934	1052	1242	1309	1521	1642	1750	1902	2049	2206

x – From / to Šeštokai (Table **1040**).

LG, LDz, RZhD — VILNIUS - ST PETERBURG — 1820

km		c	c	*Pas* 92	c	*Fir* 38 B		
0	**Vilnius** d.	0520	1500	1820	1849	...	...	...
147	Turmantas ▦ LT a.	0751	1737	|	2124	...	...	...
173	Daugavpils ▦ LV a.	...	...	2027	...	...	...	...
173	Daugavpils d.	...	...	2047	...	...	...	...
	Riga **1840** d.	...	...	|	...	1930	...	...
260	Rezekne I d.	...	...	2202	...	2250r	...	...
304	Karsava ▦ LV d.	...	...	2325	...	0018	...	...
337	Pytalovo ▦ RU d.	...	...	0148	...	0243	...	...
431	Pskov d.	...	...	0347	...	0428	...	...
715	**St Peterburg** Vitebski a.	...	...	0821	...	0908	...	...

	c	*Pas* 91	c	*Fir* 37 B	c		
St Peterburg Vitebski d.	...	2030	...	2208	...	...	...
Pskov d.	...	0110	...	0246	...	...	...
Pytalovo ▦ RU d.	...	0334	...	0507	...	...	...
Karsava ▦ LV d.	...	0352	...	0525	...	...	...
Rezekne I d.	...	0436	...	0635r	...	...	...
Riga **1840** a.	...	|	...	0935	...	...	...
Daugavpils a.	...	0547	...	...	...	...	...
Daugavpils ▦ LV d.	...	0607	...	...	...	...	...
Turmantas ▦ LT d.	0355	|	0813	...	1806	...	...
Vilnius a.	0625	0815	1039	...	2044	...	...

B – BALTIYA – 🛏 1,2 cl., ▬ 3 cl. and 🚗 (not Dec. 31).
c – 3rd class only.
r – Rezekne II.
LT – Lithuania.
LV – Latvia (East European Time).
RU – Russia (Moskva Time).

LDz — RIGA - CESIS - VALGA — 1830

km												①–⑤		
0	**Riga** d.	0558	0635	0752	0907	1042	1151	1354	1540	1724	1805	1900	2100	...
53	Sigulda d.	0712	0740	0906	1021	1150	1305	1502	1654	1838	1858	2014	2212	...
93	Cesis d.	...	0822	...	...	1237	...	1545	...	...	1941	...	2254	...
121	Valmiera d.	...	0854	...	...	1308	...	1617	...	...	2013	...	2325	...
164	Lugaži ▦ LV a.	...	0941	...	...	...	...	1705	...	...	2101	...	...	...
168	**Valga** ▦ EE a.	...	0948	...	...	...	...	1711	...	...	2107	...	...	...

	①–⑤										⑧		
Valga ▦ EE d.	...	...	0525	...	...	...	1027	...	...	...	...	1729	
Lugaži ▦ LV d.	...	...	0533	...	...	...	1035	...	...	...	...	1737	...
Valmiera d.	...	0523	0618	...	...	...	1120	...	1426	...	...	1822	...
Cesis d.	...	0550	0649	...	...	...	1153	...	1459	...	...	1854	...
Sigulda d.	0556	0629	0731	0817	0957	1114	1232	1350	1541	1707	1852	1937	2131
Riga a.	0704	0740	0840	0931	1110	1227	1339	1503	1652	1820	2005	2039	2244

EE – Estonia. LV – Latvia.

LDz, RZhD — RIGA - REZEKNE - MOSKVA — 1840

km			*Pas* 662 N		*Fir* 2 L P		*Fir* 4 J w	*Fir* 38 B w	
0	**Riga 1850** d.	1015	...	...	1620	1645	1810	1930	...
129	Krustpils (Jekabpils) **1850** d.	1233	...	...	1812	1901	2008	2113	...
224	**Rezekne** II d.	1412	...	...	1937	2039	2129	2250	...
	St Peterburg Vitebski **1820** a.	|	...	...	|	|	|	0908	...
279	Zilupe ▦ LV d.	1514	...	...	2113	2141	2304	...	...
305	Sebezh ▦ RU d.	...	1537	...	2336	...	0127	...	...
416	Novosokolniki d.	...	1820	...	|	...	0305	...	...
445	**Velikiye Luki** a.	...	1913	...	0135	...	0338	...	...
445	**Velikiye Luki** d.	...	2045	...	0200	...	0400	...	...
686	Rzhev d.	...	0213	...	0536	...	0747	...	...
921	**Moskva** Rizhskaya a.	...	0642	...	0941	...	1216	...	...

		Fir 37 B w	*Fir* 1 L Q	*Fir* 3 J w	*Pas* 661 N			
Moskva Rizhskaya d.	...	...	1910	2102	2008	...	...	...
Rzhev d.	...	...	2301	0100	0039	...	...	...
Velikiye Luki a.	...	...	0224	0424	0650	...	...	...
Velikiye Luki d.	...	...	0250	0445	0850	...	...	...
Novosokolniki d.	...	...	|	0519	1006	...	...	...
Sebezh ▦ RU d.	...	...	0558	0755	1225	...	...	...
Zilupe ▦ LV d.	0335	...	0610	0807	...	1550	...	...
St Peterburg Vitebski **1820** d.	|	2208	|	|	...	|	...	...
Rezekne II d.	0439	0635	0705	0902	...	1655	...	...
Krustpils (Jekabpils) **1850** d.	0617	0752	0822	1019	...	1840	...	...
Riga 1850 a.	0830	0935	1010	1205	...	2040	...	...

B – BALTIJA – 🛏 1,2 cl. and ▬ 3 cl.
J – JURMALA – 🛏 1,2 cl.
L – LATVIJAS EKSPRESIS – 🛏 1,2 cl.
N – 🛏 2 cl. and ▬ 3 cl.
P – Dec. 24 - Jan. 9 and from May 30.
Q – Dec. 25 - Jan. 10 and from May 31.
w – Not Dec. 31.
LV – Latvia (East European Time).
RU – Russia (Moskva Time).

LDz, BCh — RIGA - DAUGAVPILS - POLATSK — 1850

km			✣				D			
0	**Riga 1840** d.	0710	0845	1015	...	1500	1610	1645	1725	2052
129	Krustpils (Jekabpils) **1840** d.	0931	1113	1233	...	1750	1759	2141	1937	2331
218	Daugavpils § LV d.	1053	...	...	...	...	1903	...	2103	...
379	**Polatsk** § BY a.	...	...	...	...	...	...	...	...	...

			D		✣				
Polatsk § BY d.	...	...	...	...	...	...	...	...	...
Daugavpils § LV d.	...	...	0614	0724	...	...	...	...	1800
Krustpils (Jekabpils) **1840** d.	0500	0617	0722	0851	1154	...	1811	1840	1940
Riga 1840 a.	0729	0830	0906	1114	1420	...	2031	2040	2152

D – DINABURGA express service: special fares payable. BY – Belarus. LV – Latvia. ✣ – Subject to confirmation. § – ▦: Indra (LV) / Bihosava (BY).

LDz — RIGA AREA local trains — 1860

RIGA - JELGAVA and v.v. *43 km*
1–2 trains per hour. Journey ± 49 minutes.

RIGA - VENTSPILS and v.v. Daily. *176 km*.
Riga depart 1815, Ventspils arrive 2058.
Ventspils depart 0620, Riga arrive 0905.

RIGA - LIELVARDE and v.v. *51 km*
1–2 trains per hour. Journey ± 60 minutes. Certain of these trains continue to / start from **Aizkraukle** *82 km* ± 86 minutes.

RIGA - SAULKRASTI and v.v. *48 km*
1–2 trains per hour. Journey ± 60 minutes. Certain of these trains continue to / start from **Skulte** *56 km* ± 70 minutes.

RIGA - SLOKA (JURMALA) and v.v. *35 km*
1–2 trains per hour. Journey ± 52 minutes. Certain of these trains continue to / start from **Tukums** *65 km* ± 84 minutes.

RIGA – LIEPAJA and v.v. daily. *223 km*. Riga depart 1830, Liepaja arrive 2135; Liepaja depart 0600, Riga arrive 0910.

1870 TALLINN - ST PETERBURG and MOSKVA

Edelaraudtee, GoRail, RZhD

km		(bus) ①–⑤	(bus)	(bus)	(bus)	(bus)	222 B	34 A	224 B	(bus)	(bus)
0	**Tallinn 1880** d.	0600	0700	1015	1100	1430	1605	1720	1820	2300	2359
77	Tapa **1880** d.	|	|	|	|	|	1738	1838	1955	|	|
104	Rakvere d.	|	|	1145	1230	|	1802	1903	2018	|	0130
163	Jõhvi d.	|	0920	1305	1350	1650	1900	1955	...	|	0240
209	Narva (customs) EE d.	0830	1020	1400	1455	1750	1946	2118	...	0200	0335
380	**St Peterburg** Baltiski RU a.	1300	1530	1845	2015	2250	...	|	...	0705	0830
633	Bologoye **1900** RU a.	...	...	...	...	...	...	0548	...	...	...
797	Tver **1900** a.	...	...	...	...	...	...	0734	...	...	...
964	**Moskva** Oktyabrskaya **1900** a.	...	...	...	...	...	...	0920	...	...	...

	221 B	34 A	223 B	(bus)	(bus)	(bus) ⑧	(bus) ⑧	(bus)	(bus)	(bus)
Moskva Oktyabrskaya **1900** d.	...	1805	...	...	...	...	...	...	...	...
Tver **1900** d.	...	2034	...	...	...	...	...	...	...	...
Bologoye **1900** RU d.	...	2232	...	...	...	...	...	...	...	...
St Peterburg Baltiski RU d.	...	|	...	0715	1115	1400	1645	1800	2300	2345
Narva (customs) EE d.	...	0505	0627	1025	1425	1710	1955	|	0150	0255
Jõhvi d.	...	0551	0714	1120	1525	1805	2050	|	0315	0355
Rakvere d.	0543	0653	0812	|	1645	|	|	|	0435	0515
Tapa **1880** d.	0607	0718	0836	|	|	|	|	|	|	|
Tallinn 1880 a.	0735	0827	1002	1335	1810	2020	2305	2320	0600	0640

A – *Firmenny*. (sleeper) 1, 2 cl. Ⓡ.
B – (T) (*tavaklassi*; general class).
EE – Estonia (East European Time).
RU – Russia (Moskva Time).
(bus) – Operated by Eurolines Estonia. Timings apply to bus, not rail, stations except for St Peterburg Baltiski rail station.

1880 TALLINN - TARTU - ORAVA and VALGA

Edelaraudtee

km		✣		✣	A	①–⑤ ◇	✣	⑤⑦ ◇		⑧	✣	◇	⑤⑦ ◇
0	**Tallinn 1870** d.	...	0640	...	...	0746	...	1355	1442	...	...	1645	1959
77	Tapa **1870** d.	...	0814	...	...	0900	...	1509	1612	...	...	1759	2113
142	Jõgeva d.	...	0910	...	...	0944	...	1553	1714	...	...	1848	2157
190	**Tartu** a.	...	0950	...	...	1015	...	1624	1756	...	...	1919	2228
190	**Tartu** d.	0457	...	1019	1024	...	1130	...	...	1814	1910	...	...
233	Põlva d.	|	...	|	1119	...	|	...	...	1909	|	...	...
262	**Orava** a.	|	...	|	1148	...	|	...	...	1938	|	...	...
215	Elva d.	0546	...	1103	...	...	1219	...	...	...	2000	...	...
273	**Valga** a.	...	...	...	...	...	...	...	...	...	...	...	...

	①–⑥ ◇	✣	①–⑥		✣	⑤⑦ ◇	A	⑧ ◇	✣		✣	⑤⑦ ◇
Valga d.	...	...	...	...	...	...	...	...	...	...	...	...
Elva d.	...	0632	...	...	1229	...	...	...	1718	...	1811	...
Orava d.	...	|	0553	...	|	...	1548	...	|	...	|	...
Põlva d.	...	|	0625	...	|	...	1620	...	|	...	|	...
Tartu a.	...	0720	0720	...	1317	...	1715	...	1803	...	1859	...
Tartu d.	0639	...	...	0734	...	1405	...	1723	...	1804	...	1954
Jõgeva d.	0711	...	...	0813	...	1437	...	1755	...	1847	...	2026
Tapa **1870** d.	0756	...	...	0918	...	1526	...	1841	...	1946	...	2112
Tallinn 1870 a.	0859	...	...	1047	...	1629	...	1944	...	2115	...	2215

A – May 31 - Sept. 30.
✣ – Subject to confirmation.
◇ – Conveys (12) (and 🍷 in 1st class). All other trains convey (T) (*tavaklass*; general class).
☛ Express (bus) services operate Tallinn - Tartu and v.v. 20+ times daily (journey: 2½ hrs).

1890 TALLINN - PÄRNU and VILJANDI

Edelaraudtee

km						⑤⑥⑦						
0	**Tallinn** d.	0658	0750	0837	1035	1334	1422	1635	1725	1825	1920	2125
54	Rapla d.	0812	0846	0951	1146	1429	1535	1728	1835	1940	2033	2235
72	Lelle d.	0832	0901	...	...	1445	1550	1743	1852	...	2049	2250
136	**Pärnu** a.	0943	|	...	...	|	...	|	2001	...	|	|
98	Türi d.	...	0924	...	...	1506	...	1806	...	...	2113	2314
151	**Viljandi** a.	...	1018	...	...	1603	...	1902	...	...	...	...

	①–⑤				⑥⑦			⑤⑥⑦				
Viljandi d.	...	...	0639	...	...	...	...	1324	...	1622	...	...
Türi d.	0526	0620	0735	...	0930	...	...	1420	...	1718	...	...
Pärnu d.	|	|	|	0717	|	...	...	|	...	|	1709	...
Lelle d.	0550	0645	0757	0829	0954	...	...	1443	1615	1741	1819	...
Rapla d.	0606	0700	0811	0845	1009	1040	1222	1457	1632	1755	1835	1949
Tallinn a.	0715	0807	0908	0954	1105	1148	1330	1552	1742	1848	1948	2103

☛ All trains convey (T) (*tavaklass*; general class).

RUSSIA and BELARUS

SEE MAP PAGE 509

Operators: **RZhD**: Rossiskiye Zheleznye Dorogi (РЖД: Российские Железные Дороги). **BCh**: Belaruskaya Chyhunka (БЧ: Беларуская Чыгунка).

Timings: Valid from **May 31, 2009**. Moskva Time is used for all Russian stations (including Kaliningrad, where local time is one hour behind Moskva Time). The timings of international services to and from non-CIS countries should be verified from the international tables at the front of this book.

Tickets: Except for travel by purely local trains, prior reservation is necessary and passports and visas must be presented when purchasing tickets.

See also the panel ***RAIL TRAVEL IN RUSSIA, BELARUS, UKRAINE, and MOLDOVA*** on page **517**.

1900 MOSKVA - ST PETERBURG

RZhD

km		*Fir* 38	*Sko* 16	*Sko* 30 A	*Sko* 8	*Sko* 802	♥ 152 p	*Fir* 24 △	♥ 156	*Sko* 814	*Fir* 160 △	*Sko* 18	♥ 158 q	*Fir* 166 ①–⑥	*Fir* 10	*Sko* 56	*Fir* 28 D	*Sko* 66 F
	Sevastopol **1790** d.	...	...	...	2215	...	...	...	...	...	...	...	...	...	...	...	...	...
0	**Moskva** Oktyabrskaya § **1870** d.	0030	0050	0105	0125k	...	0645	1230	1300	1530	1630	1825	1900	1900	1923	2020	2130	2130
167	Tver **1870** d.	0226	0240	0301	0334	...	|	1416	1406	1722	1754	2045	|	|	2155	2305	2352	2352
331	Bologoye **1870** d.	0410	0436	0510	0527	...	|	1611	1512	1925	1921	2232	|	|	0030	0124	0150	0150
588	Dno d.	|	|	|	|	...	|	|	|	|	|	|	|	|	0543	|	|	|
687	**Pskov** a.	|	|	|	|	...	|	|	|	|	|	|	|	|	0730	|	|	|
606	Novgorod na Volkhove d.	|	|	|	|	0805	|	|	|	|	|	|	|	|	...	|	|	|
650	**St Peterburg** Glavny ‡ a.	0848	0838c	0946	1008	1120	1030	1952	1715	2309	2200	|	2245	2330	...	0500	0528	0528
	Helsinki **1910** a.	...	|	...	...	...	...	...	...	...	...	|	...	...	...	...	...	...
	Petrozavodsk **1905** a.	...	1628	...	...	...	...	...	...	...	...	0850	...	...	...	...	...	...
	Murmansk **1905** a.	...	1157	...	...	...	...	...	...	...	...	...	...	...	...	...	...	...

	Sko 42	*Fir* 32	*Fir* 26	*Fir* 12 P	*Fir* 54 ⊠	*Fir* 2	*Fir* 4
Sevastopol **1790** d.	...	...	...	...	...	...	...
Moskva Oktyabrskaya § **1870** d.	2150	2250	2300	2330	2340	2355	2359
Tver **1870** d.	0021	0054	0117	|	|	|	|
Bologoye **1870** d.	0219	|	|	|	|	|	|
Dno d.	|	|	|	|	|	|	|
Pskov a.	|	|	|	|	|	|	|
Novgorod na Volkhove d.	0610	|	|	|	|	|	|
St Peterburg Glavny ‡ a.	...	0602c	0645	0740	0835	0755	0800
Helsinki **1910** a.	...	1206	...	...	...	...	...
Petrozavodsk **1905** a.	...	...	...	...	...	...	...
Murmansk **1905** a.	...	...	...	...	...	...	...

	Fir 31	*Sko* 17	*Sko* 55	♥ 151 p	♥ 155	*Fir* 23 △	*Fir* 159 △	*Sko* 813	*Sko* 801
Murmansk **1905** d.	...	...	...	...	...	...	...	...	...
Petrozavodsk **1905** d.	...	1900	...	...	...	...	...	...	...
Helsinki **1910** d.	1752	|	...	...	...	...	...	...	...
St Peterburg Glavny ‡ d.	0149c	|	0040	0645	1300	1305	1600	1505	1718
Novgorod na Volkhove d.	|	|	|	|	|	|	|	|	2024
Pskov d.	|	|	|	|	|	|	|	|	...
Dno d.	|	|	|	|	|	|	|	|	...
Bologoye **1870** d.	|	0447	0510	|	1459	1706	1842	1849	...
Tver **1870** d.	0628	0651	0719	|	1604	1855	1959	2031	...
Moskva Oktyabrskaya § **1870** a.	0825	0857	0953	1030	1715	2055	2130	2213	...
Sevastopol **1790** a.	...	...	...	...	...	...	...	...	...

km		*Fir* 165 ⑧	♥ 157 q	*Sko* 7	*Sko* 42	*Sko* 29 B	*Fir* 37	*Fir* 27 E	*Sko* 65 D	*Fir* 10	*Sko* 15	*Fir* 25	*Fir* 11 Q	*Fir* 53 ⊠	*Fir* 1	*Fir* 3
	Murmansk **1905** d.	...	...	...	...	...	...	...	...	...	1941	...	...	...	...	...
	Petrozavodsk **1905** d.	...	...	...	...	...	...	...	...	...	1517	...	...	...	...	...
	Helsinki **1910** d.	...	...	...	...	...	...	...	...	...	|	...	...	...	...	...
0	**St Peterburg** Glavny ‡ d.	1830	1900	2000	...	2201	2220	2237	2237	...	2251c	2300	2330	2340	2355	2359
192	Novgorod na Volkhove d.	|	|	|	2120	|	|	|	|	...	|	|	|	|	|	|
	Pskov d.	|	|	|	|	|	|	|	|	1800	|	|	|	|	|	|
	Dno d.	|	|	|	|	|	|	|	|	2017	|	|	|	|	|	|
319	Bologoye **1870** d.	|	|	0007	0112	0155	0207	0219	0219	0213	0247	|	|	|	|	|
483	Tver **1870** d.	|	|	0150	0330	0337	0351	0407	0407	0358	0443	0450	|	|	|	|
650	**Moskva** Oktyabrskaya § **1870** a.	2300	2245	0348k	0532	0550	0602	0556	0556	0625	0654	0700	0710	0835	0755	0800
	Sevastopol **1790** a.	...	...	0505	...	...	...	...	...	...	...	...	...	...	...	...

Named trains:

1/2	KRASNAYA STRELA
3/4	EKSPRESS
5/6	NIKOLAYEVSKI EKSPRESS
7/8	NEVA
11/12	ALEXANDER NEVSKY
17/18	KARELIYA
25/26	SMENA
31/32	LEV TOLSTOI
37/38	AFANASI NIKITIN
42	ILMEN
159/160	AVRORA

A – ①–⑥ (daily May 31 - Sept. 5).
B – ⑧ (daily May 30 - Sept. 4).
D – Uneven dates [... *31*, *3* ...].
E – Even dates.
F – Even dates [... *30*, *1*, *4* ...].
P – ①③⑤. Luxury train.
Q – ②④⑦. Luxury train.
c – St Peterburg Ladozhski.
k – Moskva Kurskaya.
p – Not Jan. 1.
q – Not Dec. 31, Jan. 1.
△ – Conveys (Sd) seating.
§ – Also known as *Leningradski vokzal*.
‡ – Also known as *Moskovski vokzal*.
⊠ – *Grand Express* (sleeper) 1, cl. with ensuite, shower, sofa, air conditioning, TV, DVD and wi-fi.
♥ – From Dec. 18: *Sapsan* high-speed train, special fares payable. ✕ Ⓡ ⚡.

RZhD (MOSKVA and) ST PETERBURG - PETROZAVODSK - MURMANSK 1905

km		Sko 18 K	Sko 382	Sko 16	Sko 12 C	Sko 212 A		Sko 22	Pas 658
	Moskva Oktyabrskaya **1900** .. d.	1825	2045	0050	...	0117	...	...	...
0	**St Peterburg** Ladozhski .... d.	|	|	0856	0934	1102	...	1720	2202
* 114	Volkhovstroi I .... d.	0350	|	1115	1145	1321	...	1939	0033
394	**Petrozavodsk** .... d.	0850	1145	1645	1703	1832	...	0057	0650
773	Belomorsk .... d.	...	2110	2340	0015	0219	...	0758	...
1161	Kandalaksha .... d.	...	0451	0640	0731	0910	...	1502	...
1438	**Murmansk** .... a.	...	1108	1157	1308	1444	...	2019	...

	Sko 11 D	Sko 21		Sko 211 B	Sko 15	Sko 17 K	Sko 381	Pas 657
Murmansk .... d.	0154	0905	...	1741	1941	...	1844	...
Kandalaksha .... d.	0713	1429	...	2303	0107	...	0152	...
Belomorsk .... d.	1419	2130	...	0559	0755	...	0937	...
Petrozavodsk .... d.	2200	0446	...	1309	1517	1900	1957	2300
Volkhovstroi I .... d.	0256	1006	...	1816	2025	0039	0101	0505
St Peterburg Ladozhski .... a.	0500	1211	...	2030	2231	|	|	0707
Moskva Oktyabrskaya **1900** .. a.	...	...	...	0418	0654	0857	1115	...

A – May 31 - Sept. 6.
B – June 1 - Sept. 7.
C – July 18 - Sept. 6.
D – July 19 - Sept. 5.
K – KARELIYA.
* – Moskva - Vokhovstroi: *641 km*.

RZhD, VR ST PETERBURG - HELSINKI 1910

km		Fir 32 T	Fir 34 R	Sko 36 S	
	Moskva Okt. **1900** . d.	2250	...	...	...
***	**St Peterburg** Lad. ◧ d.	0607	...	...	...
0	**St Peterburg** Finl. § a.	|	0717	1630	...
129	Vyborg .... a.	0759	0857	1820	...
129	Vyborg .... ⊞ RU d.	0834	0927	1850	...
159	Vainikkala ...... ⊞ FI a.	0845	0932	1854	...
159	Vainikkala .... d.	0905	0952	1914	...
250	**Kouvola 797** .... a.	1004	1047	2006	...
312	Lahti **797** .... a.	1047	1125	2043	...
400	Tikkurila **797** .... a.	1142	1218	2132	...
413	Pasila **797** .... a.	1153	1229	2142	...
416	**Helsinki 797** .... a.	1200	1235	2148	...

	Sko 35 S	Fir 33 R	Fir 31 T
Helsinki 797 .... d.	0723	1523	1823
Pasila **797** .... d.	0729	1529	1829
Tikkurila **797** .... d.	0739	1540	1840
Lahti **797** .... d.	0825	1633	1933
Kouvola 797 .... d.	0900	1711	2014
Vainikkala .... a.	0951	1806	2114
Vainikkala ..... ⊞ FI d.	1011	1826	2134
Vyborg .... ⊞ RU a.	1155	2023	2318
Vyborg .... d.	1225	2053	2353
St Peterburg Finl. § a.	1415	2251	|
St Peterburg Lad. ◧ a.	...	...	0144
Moskva Okt. **1900**. a.	...	...	0825

RZhD, BCh ST PETERBURG - MALADZECHNA 1915

km		Sko 79 E
0	**St Peterburg** Vit. **1920** ...... d.	1815
245	Dno **1920** .... d.	2222
421	Novosokolniki **1920** ..... ‡ RU d.	0147
568	Vitsebsk **1920** .... d.	0354
670	Polatsk .... ‡ BY d.	0552
868	**Maladzechna** .... a.	0858
	Vilnius **1950** .... a.	1242
	Kaliningrad **1950** .... a.	2029

	Sko 80 C
Kaliningrad **1950** .... d.	0950
Vilnius **1950** .... d.	1548
Maladzechna .... d.	1913
Polatsk .... ‡ BY d.	2253
Vitsebsk **1920** .... d.	0043
Novosokolniki **1920** .. ‡ RU d.	0447
Dno **1920** .... d.	0731
St Peterburg Vit. **1920** ... a.	1110

NOTES FOR TABLES 1910 AND 1915

C – Uneven dates [... *29, 1* ...] (daily June 5 - Sept. 5).
E – Even dates (daily June 6 - Sept. 6).
R – REPIN – (12) and ✕ Ⓡ St Peterburg - Helsinki and v.v.
S – SIBELIUS – (1) meeting room, (12) and ✕ Ⓡ. St Peterburg - Helsinki and v.v.
T – LEV TOLSTOI – 🛏 1, 2 cl. and ✕ Moskva - Helsinki and v.v.

*** *143 km* St Peterburg Ladozhski - Vyborg.
‡ – ⊞: Yezyaryshcha (BY) / Zaverezhye (RU).
§ – Finlyandski vokzal.
◧ – Ladozhski vokzal.

BY – Belarus (East European Time).
FI – Finland (East European Time).
RU – Russia (Moskva Time).

RZhD, BCh, UZ ST PETERBURG - HOMEL and KOZYATYN 1920

km		Sko 47 D	Sko 49 A	Sko 53	Sko 61	Fir 55	Sko 83 K	Fir 51	Sko 19 BR
0	**St Peterburg** Vitebski **1915** ...... d.	1245	1500	1558	1620	...	1747	1908	2355
245	Dno **1915** .... d.	1630	1903	1955	2008	...	2136	2306	0357
421	Novosokolniki **1915** .... § RU d.	1934	2200	2300	2340	...	0044	0222	0725
568	Vitsebsk .... § BY d.	2116	2351	0038	0119	...	0306	0408	0921
	Moskva Belorusskaya **1950** .... d.	|	|	|	|	2119	|	|	|
652	**Orsha** Tsentralnaya .... a.	2238	0107	0200	0239	0325	0425	0540	1047
652	**Orsha** Tsentralnaya .... d.	2259	0127	0217	0259	0344	0441	0600	1111
	Minsk Passazhirski **1950** .... a.	0140	0355	|	|	|	|	0851	|
	Lviv **1720** .... a.	1519	|	|	|	|	|	...	|
	Brest Tsentralny **1950** .... a.	...	0911	|	|	|	|	...	|
726	Mahilyow I .... d.	...	...	0356	0437	0548	0626	...	1257
853	Zhlobin **1930** .... d.	...	...	0621	0709	0805	0857	...	1608
	Homel 1930 .... a.	...	...	0740	|	0932	1027	...	|
	Kyïv Passazhirski **1930** .... a.	...	...	1440	|	...	...	...	|
954	Kalinkavichy **1700** .... ‡ BY d.	...	...	...	0850	...	...	...	1811
1109	Korosten **1700** .... ‡ UA d.	...	...	...	1308	...	...	...	2218
1191	Zhytomyr **1700** .... d.	...	...	...	1501	...	...	...	2358
1267	**Kozyatyn** .... a.	...	...	...	1640	...	...	...	0136
	Odesa Holovna **1750** .... a.	...	...	...	|	...	...	...	1018
	Chişinău **1750** .... a.	...	...	...	0727	...	...	...	...

	Sko 48 E	Sko 20 BS	Fir 52	Sko 50	Sko 54	Sko 83 L	Sko 61 A	Fir 55
Chişinău **1750** .... d.	...	...	...	...	...	...	1928	...
Odesa Holovna **1750** .... d.	...	1832	...	...	...	...	|	...
Kozyatyn .... d.	...	0252	...	...	...	...	1020	...
Zhytomyr **1700** .... d.	...	0432	...	...	...	...	1207	...
Korosten **1700** .... ‡ UA d.	...	0626	...	...	...	...	1355	...
Kalinkavichy **1700** .... ‡ BY d.	...	1028	...	...	...	...	1745	...
Kyïv Passazhirski **1930** .... d.	...	|	...	...	1030	...	|	...
Homel 1930 .... d.	...	|	...	...	1655	1818	|	1936
Zhlobin **1930** .... d.	...	1215	...	...	1817	1945	1935	2104
Mahilyow I .... d.	...	1454	...	...	2048	2204	2255	2347
Brest Tsentralny **1950** .... d.	...	|	...	1405	|	|	|	|
Lviv **1720** .... d.	2312	|	...	|	|	|	|	|
Minsk Passazhirski **1950** .... d.	1240	|	1740	1848	|	|	|	|
Orsha Tsentralnaya .... a.	1536	1611	2013	2119	2210	2327	0041	0112
Orsha Tsentralnaya .... d.	1556	1637	2030	2135	2233	2345	0103	0134
Moskva Belorusskaya **1950** .... a.	|	|	|	|	|	|	|	0955
Vitsebsk .... § BY d.	1751	1831	2214	2315	0006	0140	0234	...
Novosokolniki **1915** .... § RU d.	2158	2254	0206	0316	0402	0524	0624	...
Dno **1915** .... d.	0125	0220	0512	0601	0702	0835	0905	...
St Peterburg Vitebski **1915** ...... a.	0525	0615	0853	0940	1044	1204	1243	...

A – Conveys (on dates shown in Table **95**) 🛏 1, 2 cl. St Peterburg - Orsha - Brest - Praha and v.v.
B – Conveys (on dates shown in Table **56**) 🛏 1, 2 cl. St Peterburg - Orsha - Berlin and v.v.
D – Even dates [... *30, 1, 4* ...] (daily May 14 - Sept. 30).
E – Even dates (daily May 12 - Sept. 28).
K – Uneven dates [... *31, 3* ...].
L – Even dates.
R – ①③⑤ (daily June 1 - Oct. 16).
S – ③⑤⑦ (daily May 30 - Oct. 18).

BY – Belarus (East European Time).
RU – Russia (Moskva Time).
UA – Ukraine.

§ – ⊞: Yezyaryshcha (BY) / Zaverezhye (RU).
‡ – ⊞: Slovechno (BY) / Berezhest (UA).

Named trains:
51/52 ZVYAZDA
53/54 LYBID
55/56 SOZH

BCh, UZ MINSK - HOMEL - KYÏV 1930

km		Pas 312 E	Pas 134 B	Sko 53 L	Sko 100 H	Pas 382 S	Sko 94 F		Sko 86 A
	Kaliningrad **1950** .... d.	1403	2011	...	...	...	...	...	...
	Vilnius **1950** .... d.	2000	0204	...	...	...	...	...	...
0	**Minsk** Passazhirski .... d.	0057	0648	...	0825	0948	1131	...	2050
	St Peterburg Vitebski **1920** .... d.	|	|	1558	|	|	|	...	|
214	Zhlobin **1920** .... d.	0430	1021	0621	1217	1327	1513	...	0036
304	**Homel 1920** .... a.	0600	1149	0740	1344	1447	1636	...	0156
304	**Homel** .... ‡ BY d.	0635	...	0803	1404	1512	1701	...	0221
	Kharkiv Passazhirski **1780** ..... a.	1921	...	|	0121	|	|	...	|
415	Chernihiv .... ‡ UA d.	...	...	1141	|	1856	2052	...	0604
	Simferopol **1775 1790** .... a.	...	...	|	1055	1546	|	...	|
624	**Kyïv** Passazhirski **1700 1720** .... a.	...	...	1440	...	...	0003	...	0851
	Odesa **1750** .... a.	...	...	...	...	...	1027	...	...

	Sko 94 G	Sko 100 J	Pas 311 C	Sko 54 L	Pas 133 E	Sko 54 A	Pas 382 T	Sko 86
Odesa **1750** .... d.	1430	...	...	...	...	...	...	...
Kyïv Passazhirski **1700 1720** .... d.	0052	...	...	1030	...	1030	...	1822
Simferopol **1775 1790** .... d.	|	1335	...	|	...	|	2154	|
Chernihiv .... ‡ UA d.	0415	|	...	1324	...	1324	2010	2133
Kharkiv Passazhirski **1780** ..... d.	|	2314	0050	|	...	|	|	|
Homel .... ‡ BY a.	0734	1038	1339	1625	...	1625	2337	0051
Homel 1920 .... d.	0813	1111	1402	1655	1705	1828x	2358	0115
Zhlobin **1920** .... d.	0933	1238	1543	1817	1833	1948	0145	0239
St Peterburg Vitebski **1920** .... a.	|	|	|	1044	|	|	|	|
Minsk Passazhirski .... a.	1250	1612	1917	...	2206	2310	0529	0558
Vilnius **1950** .... a.	...	...	0055	...	0255	...	...	...
Kaliningrad **1950** .... a.	...	...	0856	...	1032	...	...	...

A – Conveys (on dates shown in Table **98**) 🛏 2 cl. Minsk - Kyïv - Sofiya and v.v.
B – Uneven dates [... *31, 3* ...].
C – Uneven dates [... *29, 1* ...].
E – Even dates.
F – Even dates (daily June 12 - Sept. 30).
G – Uneven dates [... *31, 3* ...] (daily June 13 - Oct. 1).
H – Uneven dates [... *29, 1* ...] (daily June 1 - Oct. 1).
J – Even dates (daily June 2 - Oct. 2).
L – LYBID.
T – 4, 8, 12, 16, 20, 24, 28 of each month Jan. - May and Oct. - Dec.; even dates June - Sept.
S – 6, 10, 14, 18, 22, 26, 30 of each month Jan. - May and Oct. - Dec.; even dates [... *30, 1, 4* ...] June - Sept.
x – Train **615** Homel - Minsk.
‡ – ⊞: Teryukha (BY) / Hornostayivka (UA).

BY – Belarus.
UA – Ukraine.

1935 VORONEZH - POLATSK RZhD, BCh

km		Pas 468 A	Fir 39 D
0	**Voronezh** d.	0250	...
246	Kursk d.	1110	...
324	Lgov d.	1300	...
541	Bryansk Orlovski a.	1824	...
541	Bryansk Orlovski d.	1854	...
	Moskva Beloruss. **1950** d.	|	2144
796	Smolensk a.	0145	0329
796	Smolensk d.	...	0356
937	Vitsebsk § RU d.	...	0555
1039	**Polatsk** § BY a.	...	0738

	Pas 467 B	Fir 39 D
Polatsk § BY d.	...	1758
Vitsebsk § RU d.	...	2007
Smolensk a.	...	2325
Smolensk d.	0702	2355
Moskva Beloruss. **1950** a.	|	0549
Bryansk Orlovski a.	1306	...
Bryansk Orlovski d.	1336	...
Lgov a.	1755	...
Kursk a.	1945	...
Voronezh a.	0200	...

1945 VORONEZH - HOMEL - BREST RZhD, BCh

km		Sko 75	Pas 376 Y	Pas 663
0	**Voronezh** d.	...	1800	...
**	Moskva Beloruss. d.	1553	|	...
548	Bryansk Orlovski d.	0045	0738	...
776	Zlynka ⊞ RU d.	0503	1226	...
802	Dobrush ⊞ BY d.	0436	1151	...
827	**Homel** a.	0502	1218	...
827	**Homel** d.	0522	...	2055
956	Kalinkavichy **1700** d.	0753	...	2340
1133	Luninets **1700** d.	1118	...	0325
1361	**Brest** Tsentr. **1700** a.	1548	...	0743

	Pas 376 Z	Sko 76	Pas 664
Brest Tsentr. **1700** d.	...	1014	1934
Luninets **1700** d.	...	1429	0008
Kalinkavichy **1700** d.	...	1740	0351
Homel a.	...	1941	0625
Homel d.	1739	2010	...
Dobrush ⊞ BY d.	1810	2044	...
Zlynka ⊞ RU d.	1936	2211	...
Bryansk Orlovski a.	0010	0240	...
Moskva Beloruss. a.	|	1140	...
Voronezh a.	1145	...	...

NOTES FOR TABLES **1935** and **1945**:

A – June 23 - Sept. 27. Uneven dates [... *31, 3* ...].
B – June 21 - Sept. 25. Uneven dates [... *29, 1* ...].
D – DVINA.
Y – Uneven dates [... *31, 2, 5* ...].
Z – Uneven dates [... *31, 3* ...].
** – Moskva - Bryansk: *485 km.*
§ – ⊞: Zavolsha (BY) / Rudnya (RU).
BY – Belarus (East European Time).
RU – Russia (Moskva Time).

1950 MOSKVA - MINSK, VILNIUS, KALININGRAD and BREST RZhD, BCh, LG

km		Sko **113** BB	Fir **105**	Sko **69** S	Sko **19** B	Sko **13** M	Pas **301**	Pas **311** K	Sko **19** U	Sko **25**	Sko **103**		Pas **133** GY	Fir **29**	Sko **27**	Sko **47** H	Sko **9** P	Fir **77**	Sko **5**	Sko **49** J	Sko **147** F	Sko **11** A	Pas **395**	Fir **55** X
0	**Moskva** Belorusskaya d.	...	...	...	...	0800	...	...	...	1027	...	...	...	1357	1543	...	1650	1700	1855	...	1855	2109	1937	2119
243	Vyazma d.	0454	...	0745	...	1036	...	...	...	1402	...	...	...	1740	1915	...	1945	2051	2223	...	2250	0035	2344	0046
419	Smolensk § RU d.	0752	...	1117	...	1220	...	...	...	1620	...	...	...	2000	2139	...	2132	2307	0016	...	0116	0231	0238	0300
	St Peterburg Vitebski ▲ d.	|	...	|	2355	|	...	...	2355	|	...	...	...	|	|	1245	|	|	|	1500	|	|	|	|
538	Orsha Tsentralnaya § BY a.	0824	...	1157	1047	1235	...	...	1503	1653	...	...	...	2029	2208	2238	2143	2331	0034	0107	0145	0257	0309	0325
538	Orsha Tsentralnaya d.	0826	...	1213	1250	1250	...	...	1707	1707	...	...	...	2044	2221	2259	2153	2344	0047	0127	0200	0311	0322	...
750	**Minsk** a.	1201	...	1445	1504	1504	...	...	2006	2006	...	...	...	2321	0053	0140	0009	0210	0311	0355	0456	0549	0635	...
750	**Minsk** d.	1203	1333	1503	1529	1529	1813	1945	2040	...	2040	...	2226	2346	0110	0153	0019	0232	0333	0408	0515	0619	0649	...
828	Maladzechna ‡ BY d.	|	|	|	|	|	1924	2119	|	...	|	...	2345	0103	|	|	|	0344	0444	|	0644	|	|	...
956	Lida d.	|	|	|	|	|	|	|	|	...	|	...	|	|	|	|	|	0624	|	|	|	|	|	...
1088	Hrodna a.	|	|	|	|	|	|	|	|	...	|	...	|	|	|	|	|	0839	|	|	|	|	|	...
944	**Vilnius** ‡ LT a.	|	|	|	|	|	2205	0055	|	...	|	...	0255	0421	|	|	|	...	0800	|	1014	|	|	...
944	**Vilnius** ¶ LT d.	|	|	|	|	|	...	0115	|	...	|	...	0315	0441	|	|	|	...	...	|	1034	|	|	...
1286	**Kaliningrad** ¶ Ka a.	|	|	|	|	|	...	0856	|	...	|	...	1032	1157	|	|	|	...	...	|	1807	|	|	...
892	Baranavichy Tsentralnye d.	|	1522	1653	|	|	...	...	2224	...	2224	...	...	...	0300	0412p	|	...	...	0556	...	0804	0918p	...
	Lviv **1720** a.	|	|	|	|	|	...	...	|	...	|	...	...	...	|	1519	|	...	...	|	...	|	|	...
1094	**Brest** Tsentralny a.	1732	1756	1855	1855	1855	...	...	0029x	...	0029x	...	...	...	0535	...	0342	...	...	0911	...	1011	1218	...
	Warszawa Wschodnia **1050** a.	2338	...	2338	2338	2338	...	...	0549	...	0549	...	...	...	...	...	0830	...	...	...	...	1534	...	...

	Fir **39** D	Fir **3** Y	Fir **7** R	Pas **305**	Fir **1**	Sko **131**	Sko **21** V	Sko **79** L	Fir **51**
Moskva Belorusskaya d.	2144	2334	2334	...	2225	2334	2344	...	...
Vyazma d.	0124	0204	0204	...	0207	0253	0309	...	...
Smolensk § RU d.	0329	|	|	...	0420	0455	0505	...	...
St Peterburg Vitebski ▲ d.	...	|	|	...	|	|	|	1815	1908
Orsha Tsentralnaya § BY a.	...	0342	0342	...	0443	0520	0528	|	0540
Orsha Tsentralnaya d.	...	0352	0352	...	0456	0533	0542	|	0600
Minsk a.	...	0606	0606	...	0729	0824	0807	|	0851
Minsk d.	...	...	...	0630	...	0838	0825	|	...
Maladzechna ‡ BY d.	...	...	...	0754	...	|	|	0915	...
Lida d.	...	...	...	|	...	|	|	|	...
Hrodna a.	...	...	...	|	...	|	|	|	...
Vilnius ‡ LT a.	...	...	...	1108	...	|	|	1242	...
Vilnius ¶ LT d.	...	...	...	...	...	|	|	1300	...
Kaliningrad ¶ Ka a.	...	...	...	...	...	|	|	2029	...
Baranavichy Tsentralnye d.	...	...	...	...	...	1027	1014	...	...
Lviv **1720** a.	...	...	...	...	...	|	|	...	...
Brest Tsentralny a.	...	...	...	...	...	1242	1226	...	...
Warszawa Wschodnia **1050** a.	...	...	...	...	...	...	...	...	...

	Sko **104**	Sko **104** **132**	Fir **106**	Pas **302**	Sko **14** W	Sko **14** M	Sko **14** Q	Sko **70** T	Sko **64** AA
Warszawa Wschodnia **1050** d.	2100	2100	...	...	2100	2353	2353	2353	2353
Brest Tsentralny d.	0410z	0430z	0620	...	0720z	0720	0720	0720	0720
Lviv **1720** d.	|	|	|	...	|	|	|	|	|
Baranavichy Tsentralnye d.	0618	0657	0855	...	|	|	|	0928	0928
Kaliningrad ¶ Ka d.	|	|	|	...	|	|	|	|	|
Vilnius 1850 ¶ LT a.	|	|	|	...	|	|	|	|	|
Vilnius ‡ LT d.	|	|	|	0640	|	|	|	|	|
Hrodna d.	|	|	|	|	|	|	|	|	|
Lida d.	|	|	|	|	|	|	|	|	|
Maladzechna ‡ BY d.	|	|	|	0920	|	|	|	|	|
Minsk a.	0804	0837	1037	1040	1046	1046	1046	1114	1114
Minsk d.	...	0852	...	...	1111	1111	1111	1127	1127
Orsha Tsentralnaya a.	...	1136	...	...	1332	1332	1332	1408	1408
Orsha Tsentralnaya § BY d.	...	1150	...	...	1637	1348	1637	1426	1925
St Peterburg Vitebski ▲ a.	...	|	...	...	0615	|	0615	|	|
Smolensk § RU d.	...	1413	...	...	...	1604	...	1655	2148
Vyazma d.	...	1639	...	...	...	1805	...	1937	0037
Moskva Belorusskaya a.	...	1954	...	...	...	2035	...	...	...

	Sko **48** E	Fir **52**	Fir **39** D	Sko **50**	Sko **26**	Pas **306**	Sko **80** C	Sko **22** V	Sko **22** Jd	Fir **4** R	Fir **8** Y	Fir **2**	Sko **6**	Sko **28**	Fir **30**	Fir **56** X	Fir **78**	Sko **12** A	Pas **312** K	Sko **10** P	Sko **148** L	Pas **396**		Pas **134** GZ
Warszawa Wschodnia **1050** d.	...	...	...	...	...	...	...	...	...	...	...	...	...	...	...	...	...	1300	...	1540	...	...	...	...
Brest Tsentralny d.	...	...	...	1405	...	...	...	1707	1707	...	...	...	...	1740	...	...	...	1950	...	2230	...	2144	...	...
Lviv **1720** d.	2312	...	...	|	...	...	...	|	|	...	...	...	...	|	...	...	...	|	...	|	...	|	...	...
Baranavichy Tsentralnye d.	1032p	...	...	1646	...	...	...	1921	1921	...	...	...	...	2014	...	...	...	2156	...	|	...	0117p	...	...
Kaliningrad ¶ Ka d.	|	...	...	|	...	...	0950	|	|	...	...	...	...	|	1202	...	...	|	1403	|	1627	|	...	2011
Vilnius 1850 ¶ LT a.	|	...	...	|	...	...	1531	|	|	...	...	...	...	|	1731	...	...	|	1940	|	2222	|	...	0144
Vilnius ‡ LT d.	|	...	...	|	...	1416	1548	|	|	...	...	...	1700	|	1748	...	...	|	2000	|	2239	|	...	0204
Hrodna d.	|	...	...	|	...	|	|	|	|	...	...	...	|	|	|	...	1722	|	|	|	|	|	...	|
Lida d.	|	...	...	|	...	|	|	|	|	...	...	...	|	|	|	...	1935	|	|	|	|	|	...	|
Maladzechna ‡ BY d.	|	...	...	|	...	1728	1913	|	|	...	...	...	2010	|	2057	...	2157	|	2313	|	0145	|	...	0515
Minsk a.	1222	...	...	1828	...	1846	|	2102	2102	...	...	...	2140	2203	2216	...	2312	2346	0030	0158	0258	0316	...	0629
Minsk d.	1240	1740	...	1848	1826	...	|	2118	2118	2147	2147	2155	2203	2218	2237	...	2332	0011	...	0211	0324	0340	...	...
Orsha Tsentralnaya a.	1536	2013	...	2119	2131	...	|	2344	2344	0002	0002	0018	0032	0050	0103	...	0206	0234	...	0424	0605	0632	...	...
Orsha Tsentralnaya § BY d.	1556	2030	...	2135	2145	...	|	2359	0103	0014	0014	0031	0051	0103	0119	0134	0221	0247	...	0434	0623	0646	...	...
St Peterburg Vitebski ▲ a.	0534	0853	...	0940	|	...	1110	|	1243	|	|	|	|	|	|	|	|	|	...	|	|	|	...	...
Smolensk § RU d.	...	...	2355	...	0012	...	...	0229	...	|	|	0300	0313	0334	0342	0355	0446	0507	...	0648	0856	0935	...	...
Vyazma d.	...	...	0235	...	0244	...	...	0443	...	0412	0412	0522	0530	0555	0603	0620	0714	0723	...	0852	1151	1232	...	...
Moskva Belorusskaya a.	...	...	0549	...	0556	...	...	0805	...	0625	0625	0846	0858	0920	0927	0955	1026	1033	...	1145	1548	1623	...	...

A – VOSTOK-ZAPAD EKSPRESS – 🛏 1, 2 cl. Moskva - Warszawa - Amsterdam, Basel and München and v.v. See Table **24**.
B – 🛏 2 cl. St Peterburg - Orsha (**13**) - Berlin. For days of running, see Table **56**.
C – Uneven dates [... *29, 1* ...] (daily June 5 - Sept. 5).
D – DVINA – to / from Polatsk (Table **1935**).
E – Even dates (daily May 24 - Sept. 28).
F – Uneven dates [... *31, 3* ...] (daily June 7 - Sept. 7).
G – 🛏 2 cl. and ▬ 3 cl. Homel - Kaliningrad and v.v.
H – Even dates [... *30, 1, 4* ...] daily May 25 - Sept. 30.
J – Conveys (on dates shown in Table **95**) 🛏 2 cl. St Peterburg - Praha and Zagreb and v.v.
K – Uneven dates [... *29, 1* ...] from Kharkiv; even dates from Kaliningrad. 🛏 2 cl., ▬ 3 cl. Kharkiv - Kaliningrad and v.v.
L – Even dates (daily June 6 - Sept. 6).
M – MOSKVA EKSPRESS – 🛏 1, 2 cl. Moskva (**13**) - Terespol (**442**) - Warszawa (**440**) - Berlin, and Berlin (**441**) - Warszawa (**443**) - Brest ⊞ (**14**) - Moskva. For days of running, see Table **56**. Conveys 🛏 1, 2 cl. Moskva - Paris and v.v.; for days of running, Table **24**.
P – POLONEZ – 🛏 1, 2 cl., 🛏 1, 2 cl. (Lux) and 🍷 Warszawa - Moskva and v.v. ✕ Brest - Moskva and v.v.
Q – 🛏 2 cl. Berlin (**441**) - Orsha (**20**) - St Peterburg. For days of running, see Table **56**.
R – Uneven dates [... *29, 1* ...].
S – ④ (④⑥ May 29 - Sept. 30) from Saratov; ⑤ (⑤⑦ May 30 - Sept. 26) from Vyazma). 🛏 1, 2 cl. (1, 2, 4 berth) Saratov - Vyazma - Berlin. For other through coaches, see Tables **1980** and **1985**.
T – ⑥ (①⑥ May 31 - Oct. 2): 🛏 1, 2 cl. (1, 2, 4 berth) Berlin - Vyazma - Saratov. For other through coaches, see Tables **1980** and **1985**.
V – VLTAVA – 🛏 1, 2 cl. Moskva - Cheb, Budapest, Praha and Wien and v.v. ✕ Moskva - Brest. See Table **95**.
U – ①②③⑤⑦ May 31 - Oct. 16; ③⑤ Oct. 21 - Dec. 12: 🛏 2 cl. St Peterburg (**19**) - Orsha (**25**) - Brest (**103**) - Warszawa (journey 2 nights).
W – ②③④⑤⑦ June 2 - Oct. 18; ⑤⑦ Oct. 23 - Dec. 12: 🛏 2 cl. Warszawa (**104**) - Brest (**14**) - Orsha (**20**) - St Peterburg (journey 2 nights).
X – SOZH – to / from Homel (Table **1920**).
Y – Even dates.
Z – Uneven dates [... *31, 3* ...].
AA – 🛏 2 cl. ⑥: Berlin - Orsha (**64**) - Novosibirsk.
BB – 🛏 2 cl. ②: Novosibirsk (**113**) - Brest (**1248**) - Berlin.

d – Train **61** from Orsha.

p – Baranavichy Polesskiye.
x – Depart 0240.
z – Arrive 0222.

§ – ⊞: Osinovka (BY) / Krasnoye (RU).
‡ – ⊞: Hudahai (BY) / Kena (LT).
¶ – ⊞: Kybartai (LT) / Nesterov (Ka).
BY – Belarus (East European Time).
Ka – Kaliningrad region of Russia (Moskva Time).
LT – Lithuania (East European Time).
RU – Russia (Moskva Time).
▲ – See Tables **1915** and **1920**.

Other named trains:

1/2 BELORUSSIYA / BELARUS
3/4 MINSK
7/8 SLAVYANSKI EKSPRESS
29/30 YANTAR
77/78 NEMAN / NYOMAN
103/104 SUZORYE
105/106 BUH

RZhD, KTZh VYAZMA - ADLER and ASTANA 1980

km		Sko 70 A	Sko 70 C
	Berlin Hbf **56** d.	1515 ⑥	1515 ⑥
	Warszawa W. **1050** d.	2353 :	2353 :
	Brest Tsentr. **1950** d.	0720 ⑦	0720 ⑦
	Minsk **1950** d.	1127 :	1127 :
0	**Vyazma** d.	2000 :	2000 :
470	Ryazan d.	0327 ①	0327 ①
680	Michurinsk a.	0623 :	0623 :
680	Michurinsk d.	0703 :	0724 :
1058	Rossosh a.	|	1347 :
1498	**Rostov na Donu** a.	|	2237 :
2032	**Adler** a.	|	1012 ②
753	Tambov d.	0824 :	...
1133	**Saratov** a.	1516 :	...
1133	**Saratov** d.	2325 :	...
3315	**Astana** ‡ a.	2237 ③	...

	Sko 69 D	Sko 69 B
Astana ‡ d.	...	1115 ②
Saratov a.	...	0619 ④
Saratov d.	...	1129 :
Tambov d.	...	1807 :
Adler d.	1512 ③	| :
Rostov na Donu d.	0255 ④	| :
Rossosh d.	1121 :	| :
Michurinsk a.	1812 :	1932 :
Michurinsk d.	2004 :	2004 :
Ryazan d.	2332 :	2332 :
Vyazma a.	0722 ⑤	0722 ⑤
Minsk **1950** a.	1445 :	1445 :
Brest Tsentr. **1950** a.	1855 :	1855 :
Warszawa W. **1050** a.	2338 ⑥	2338 ⑥
Berlin Hbf **56** a.	0900 :	0900 :

BCh, RZhD MINSK - NOVOSIBIRSK 1985

km		Sko 70 N
	Berlin Hbf **56** d.	1515 ⑥
	Warszawa W. **1050** d.	2353 :
	Brest Tsentr. **1950** d.	0720 ⑦
0	**Minsk 1950** d.	1127 :
212	Orsha **1950** § BY d.	1925 :
331	Smolensk **1950** § RU d.	2148 :
507	Vyazma **1950** d.	0056 ①
1346	Sergach a.	1643 :
1615	**Kazan** a.	2047 :
1919	Agryz a.	0131 ②
2265	Krasnoufimsk a.	0726 :
2490	**Yekaterinburg** (Sverdlovsk) a.	1131 :
2816	Tyumen a.	1729 :
3388	Omsk a.	0208 ③
4015	**Novosibirsk** a.	1052 :

	Sko 113 P
Novosibirsk d.	1858 ②
Omsk d.	0401 ③
Tyumen d.	1205 :
Yekaterinburg (Sverdlovsk) d.	1757 :
Krasnoufimsk d.	2138 :
Agryz d.	0317 ④
Kazan d.	0845 :
Sergach d.	1332 :
Vyazma **1950** a.	0454 ⑤
Smolensk **1950** § RU a.	0752 :
Orsha **1950** § BY a.	0824 :
Minsk 1950 a.	1201 :
Brest Tsentr. **1950** a.	1732 :
Warszawa W. **1050** a.	2338 ⑥
Berlin Hbf **56** a.	0900 :

NOTES FOR TABLES 1980 and 1985:

A – ⑥ (①⑥ May 31 - Oct. 2): 🛏 1, 2 cl. (1, 2, 4 berth) Berlin - Saratov. 🛏 2 cl. Warszawa - Saratov (**108**) - Astana.
B – ④ (④⑥ May 29 - Sept. 30): 🛏 1, 2 cl. (1, 2, 4 berth) Saratov - Berlin. 🛏 2 cl. Astana (**107**) - Saratov (**69**) - Warszawa.
C – ⑥: 🛏 1, 2 cl. Berlin (**1249**) - Brest (**70**) - Michurinsk (**87**) - Adler.
D – ③: 🛏 1, 2 cl. Adler (**88**) - Michurinsk (**69**) - Terespol (**1249**) - Berlin.

N – 🛏 2 cl. ⑥: Berlin - Orsha (**64**) - Novosibirsk.
P – 🛏 2 cl. ②: Novosibirsk - Brest (**69**) - Berlin.
‡ – Kazak Eastern Time (= Moskva Time + 3 hrs).

§ – 🛃: Osinovka (BY) / Krasnoye (RU).
BY – Belarus (East European Time).
RU – Russia (Moskva Time).

RZhD, MTZ, CR TRANS-SIBERIAN RAILWAY (Summary Table) 1990

For full details of this and other services east of Moskva, see the Thomas Cook Overseas Timetable in the blue cover

km	*All timings in Russia are in Moskva Time*	Sko 4 ②		Fir 2 Ra		Sko 20 ⑤	
0	**Moskva** Yaroslavskaya d.	2135	*1st day*	2125	*1st day*	2355	*1st day*
461	Nizhni-Novgorod (Gorki) d.	0349	*2nd day*	0339	*2nd day*	0623	*2nd day*
917	Vyatka (Kirov) d.	1008	*2nd day*	0958	*2nd day*	1241	*2nd day*
1397	Perm d.	1752	*2nd day*	1742	*2nd day*	2037	*2nd day*
1778	**Yekaterinburg** (Sverdlovsk) d.	2353	*2nd day*	2343	*2nd day*	0224	*3rd day*
2676	Omsk d.	1142	*3rd day*	1132	*3rd day*	1526	*3rd day*
3303	**Novosibirsk** d.	1918	*3rd day*	1933	*3rd day*	2312	*3rd day*
4065	Krasnoyarsk d.	0709	*4th day*	0745	*4th day*	1102	*4th day*
5153	**Irkutsk** d.	0013	*5th day*	0133	*5th day*	0432	*5th day*
5609	Ulan-Ude d.	0830	*5th day*	0910	*5th day*	1135	*5th day*
6266	Ulaanbaatar ‡ a.	0730	*6th day*	|	|	|	|
6166	Chita d.	|	|	1839	*5th day*	2112	*5th day*
7573	**Harbin** § a.	|	|	|	|	1250	*7th day*
8120	Shenyang § a.	|	|	|	|	1918	*7th day*
****	**Beijing** § a.	1404	*7th day*	|	|	0531	*8th day*
8493	Khabarovsk a.	...	...	1100	*7th day*	...	...
9259	**Vladivostok** a.	...	...	2348	*7th day*	...	...

All timings in Russia are in Moskva Time	Sko 3 ③		Fir 1 Rb		Sko 19 ⑥	
Vladivostok d.	...	...	1500	*1st day*	...	...
Khabarovsk d.	...	...	0345	*2nd day*	...	...
Beijing § d.	0745	*1st day*	|	|	2256	*1st day*
Shenyang § d.	|	|	|	|	0850	*2nd day*
Harbin § d.	|	|	|	|	1510	*2nd day*
Chita d.	|	|	2006	*3rd day*	2102	*3rd day*
Ulaanbaatar ‡ d.	1350	*2nd day*	|	|	|	|
Ulan-Ude d.	0340	*3rd day*	0531	*4th day*	0634	*4th day*
Irkutsk d.	1105	*3rd day*	1249	*4th day*	1345	*4th day*
Krasnoyarsk d.	0407	*4th day*	0652	*5th day*	0713	*5th day*
Novosibirsk d.	1617	*4th day*	1906	*5th day*	2005	*5th day*
Omsk d.	2356	*4th day*	0316	*6th day*	0307	*6th day*
Yekaterinburg (Sverdlovsk) d.	1208	*5th day*	1551	*6th day*	1608	*6th day*
Perm d.	1745	*5th day*	2129	*6th day*	2145	*6th day*
Vyatka (Kirov) d.	0101	*6th day*	0447	*7th day*	0501	*7th day*
Nizhni-Novgorod (Gorki) d.	0650	*6th day*	1046	*7th day*	1058	*7th day*
Moskva Yaroslavskaya a.	1428	*6th day*	1758	*7th day*	1813	*7th day*

R – ROSSIYA – 🛏 1, 2 cl. and ▬ 3 cl. Moskva - Vladivostok and v.v.
a – From Moskva on uneven dates [... 29, 1 ...].
b – From Vladivostok on even dates (also on the 1st, 3rd and 5th – not the 2nd, 4th or 6th – of Jan., Feb., Apr., June, Aug., Sept., Nov.).

**** *7622 km* via Ulaanbaatar (Trans-Mongolian Railway). *8961 km* via Harbin (Trans-Manchurian Railway).

‡ – Mongolian Time.
§ – Chinese Time.

RAIL TRAVEL IN RUSSIA, BELARUS, UKRAINE, and MOLDOVA

CARRIAGE TYPES

As trains generally operate over very long distances, most accommodation is designed for overnight as well as day use. Carriage types (with their Russian names) are:

Spálny vagón СВ (🛏 1 cl. in the tables) – 2-berth compartments (9 per carriage)
Kupéiny К (🛏 2 cl. in the tables) – 4-berth compartments (9 per carriage)
Platskártny ПЛ (▬ 3 cl. in the tables) – Dormitory-style carriage with 54 bunks
Óbshchi О (4 in the tables) – 4th-class hard seating (81 places per carriage) ★
★ Not recommended for long-distance travel and not normally indicated in the tables.

A few day trains convey more comfortable *Sidyáchi* (seating) accommodation with 54–62 places per carriage (shown as Sid in the tables).

TRAIN TYPES

Ordinary long-distance trains are classified *Passazhírsky* (shown as *Pas* in the tables): they normally convey at least ▬ 3 cl. and 🛏 2 cl.

Faster long-distance trains are classified *Skóry* (shown as *Sko* in the tables): they normally convey at least ▬ 3 cl. and 🛏 2 cl. and often also 🛏 1 cl.

The top grade of fast long-distance trains are classified *Firménny* (shown as *Fir* in the tables). They are composed of higher-quality carriages dedicated to a particular, and usually named, service. They normally convey 🛏 2 cl. and 🛏 1 cl. carriages.

International services to, from and via Poland, Slovakia, Hungary and Romania convey through sleeping cars of the normal European ('RIC') types, with single and double compartments in first class, and 3- or 4-berth compartments in second class. The railways of the former Soviet Union being of broad gauge (1520mm), the bogies (trucks) of these through cars are changed at the frontier with these countries.

DAYS OF RUNNING

Many trains run on alternate days only: even dates or uneven dates. The examples below illustrate the system used to indicate exceptions to the pattern of even or uneven dates at the end of a month with 31 days and at the beginning of the month following:

e.g. "Uneven dates [... 29, 1 ...]" means that the train does not run on the 31st of a month with 31 days.
e.g. "Even dates [... 30, 1, 4 ...]" means that the train, **following a month with 31 days**, runs exceptionally on the 1st, but not the 2nd, of the month.

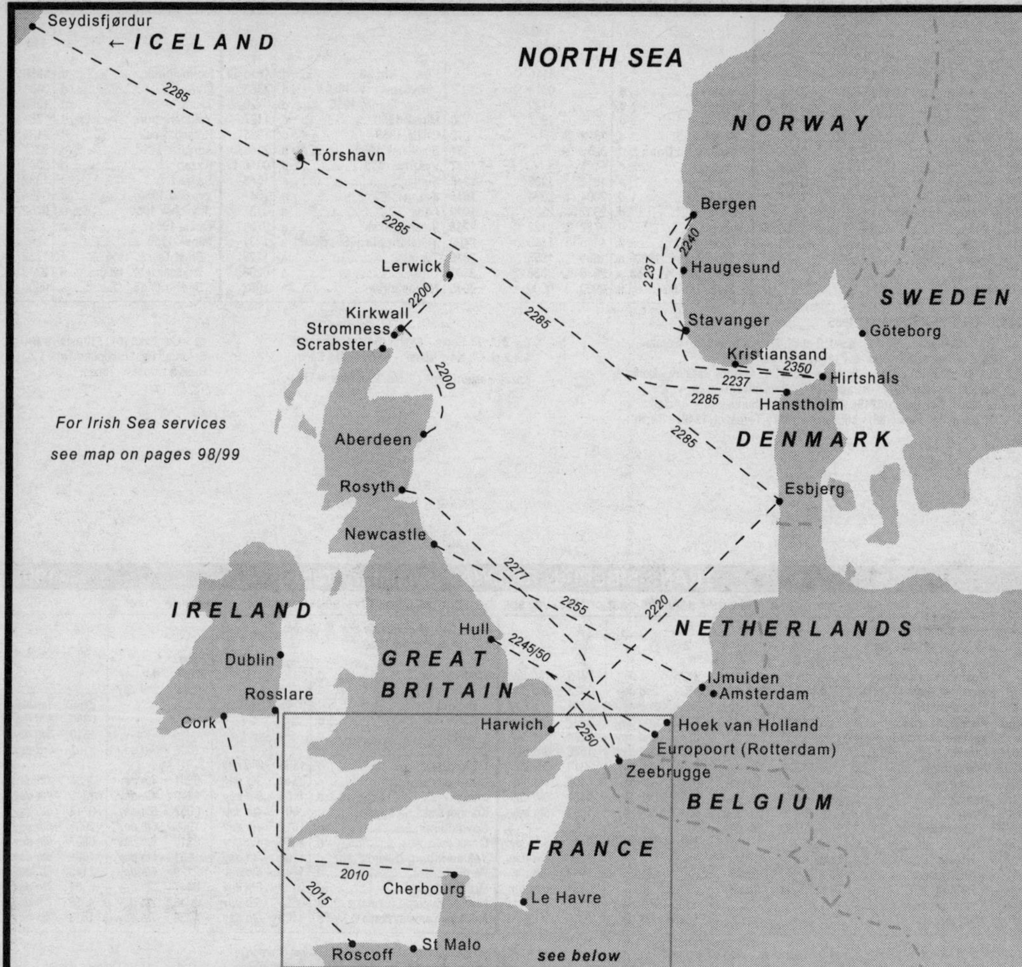

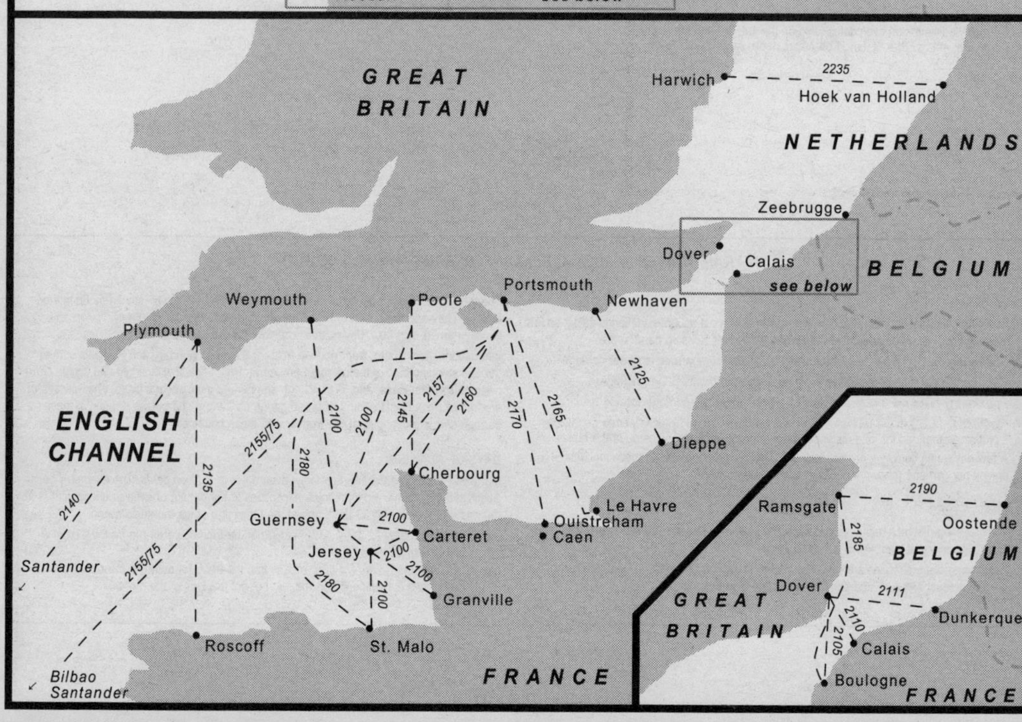

For domestic shipping routes please see relevant country maps

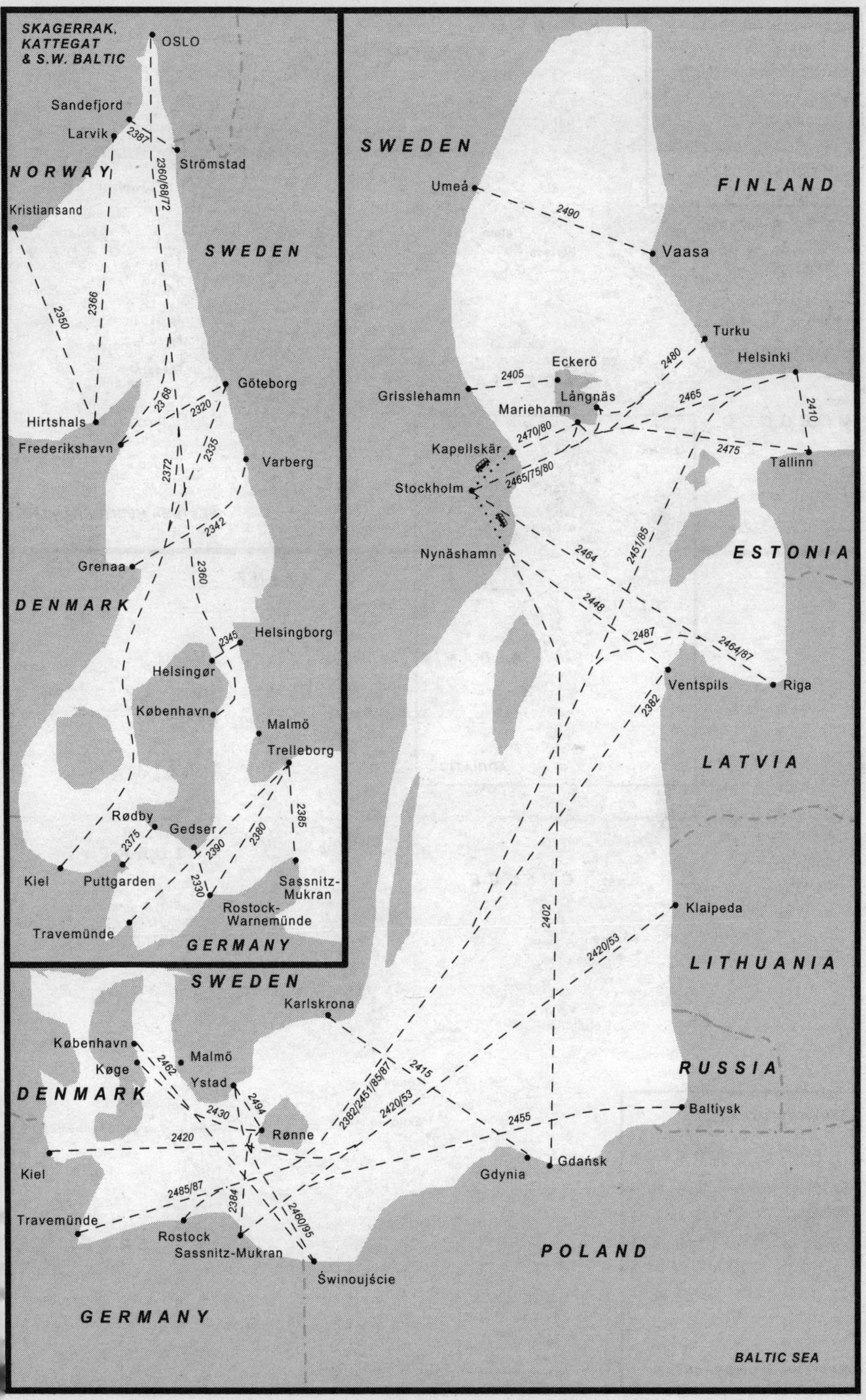
SKAGERRAK, KATTEGAT & S.W. BALTIC
OSLO
Sandefjord
Larvik
2387
Strömstad
2360/68/72
NORWAY
Kristiansand
SWEDEN
2350
2366
Göteborg
Hirtshals
23 68
2320
Frederikshavn
2335
Varberg
2372
2342
Grenaa
2360
DENMARK
Helsingborg
2345
Helsingør
København
Malmö
Trelleborg
Rødby
2375
Gedser
2390
2380
2385
Kiel
Puttgarden
2330
Sassnitz-Mukran
Rostock-Warnemünde
Travemünde
GERMANY
SWEDEN
Umeå
2490
FINLAND
Vaasa
Turku
Eckerö
2405
2480
Helsinki
Grisslehamn
Långnäs
2465
Mariehamn
2410
2470/80
Kapellskär
2475
Tallinn
2465/75/80
Stockholm
2451/85
Nynäshamn
2464
ESTONIA
2448
2487
2464/87
Ventspils
Riga
2382
LATVIA
2402
Klaipeda
2420/53
LITHUANIA
SWEDEN
Karlskrona
København
Malmö
Køge
2462
Ystad
2415
RUSSIA
DENMARK
2430
2494
2382/2451/85/87
2420/53
Rønne
2455
Baltiysk
2420
Kiel
Gdynia
Gdańsk
2485/87
2384
2460/95
Travemünde
Rostock
Sassnitz-Mukran
POLAND
Świnoujście
GERMANY
BALTIC SEA

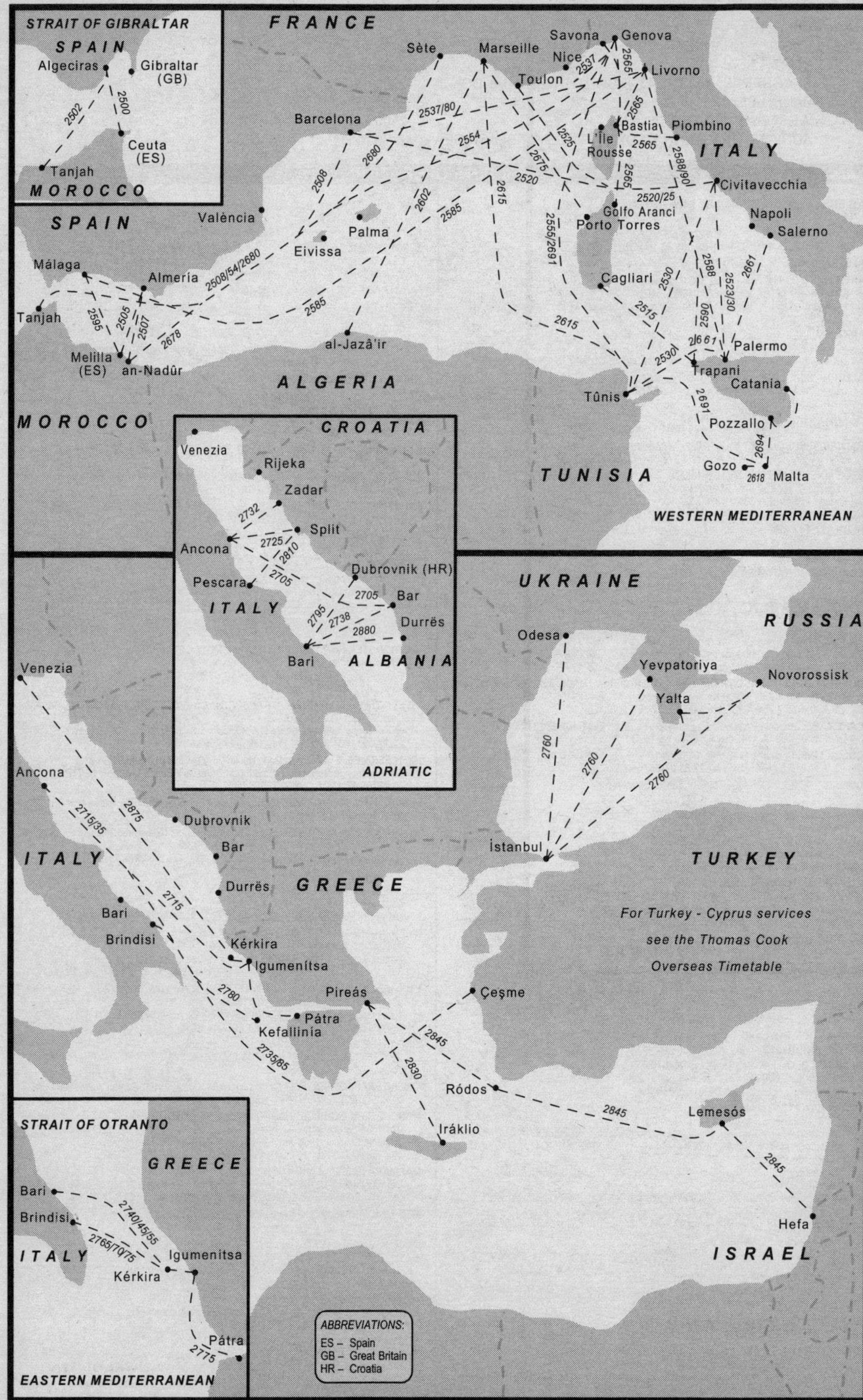
STRAIT OF GIBRALTAR
SPAIN
Algeciras
Gibraltar (GB)
2502
2500
Ceuta (ES)
Tanjah
MOROCCO
FRANCE
Sète
Marseille
Savona
Genova
Nice
Livorno
Toulon
Barcelona
2537/80
2554
Bastia
Piombino
L'Île Rousse
2565
ITALY
2520
2520/25
Civitavecchia
València
Palma
Eivissa
Golfo Aranci
Porto Torres
Napoli
Salerno
SPAIN
Málaga
Almería
Tanjah
Cagliari
2508/54/2680
2585
2615
2515
2530
Melilla (ES)
an-Nadûr
al-Jazâ'ir
Palermo
Trapani
ALGERIA
Tûnis
Catania
MOROCCO
Pozzallo
Gozo
Malta
TUNISIA
WESTERN MEDITERRANEAN
CROATIA
Venezia
Rijeka
Zadar
Split
Ancona
Pescara
Dubrovnik (HR)
Bar
Durrës
Bari
ITALY
ALBANIA
ADRIATIC
UKRAINE
RUSSIA
Odesa
Yevpatoriya
Novorossisk
Yalta
2760
Venezia
Ancona
Dubrovnik
Bar
Durrës
İstanbul
TURKEY
ITALY
GREECE
Bari
Brindisi
Kérkira
Igumenítsa
Pireás
Çeşme
Pátra
Kefallinía
For Turkey - Cyprus services see the Thomas Cook Overseas Timetable
2715/35
2875
2715
2780
2735/85
2845
2830
Ródos
Iráklio
Lemesós
Hefa
ISRAEL
STRAIT OF OTRANTO
GREECE
Bari
Brindisi
2740/45/55
2765/70/75
ITALY
Igumenitsa
Kérkira
Pátra
2775
EASTERN MEDITERRANEAN
ABBREVIATIONS:
ES – Spain
GB – Great Britain
HR – Croatia

SHIPPING CONTENTS

SHIPPING OPERATORS

A G EMS: Postfach 11 54, 26691 Emden-Außenhafen.
✆ +49 (0)1805 180 182, fax +49 21 / 89 07 405.

ALILAURO: Via Caracciolo 11, 80122 Napoli.
✆ +39 081 76 14 909, fax +39 081 76 14 250.

ALSTRAFIKKEN: ✆ +45 70 23 15 15.

ANEK LINES: 32 Akti Possidonos, 185 31 Pireás.
✆ +30 210 4118611, fax +30 210 4115465.
UK agent: Viamare, Suite 3, 447 Kenton Road, Harrow, HA3 0XY. ✆ 020 8206 3420, fax 020 8206 1332.

ARKADIA LINES: Kifissias Ave 215, 15124 Maroussi, Greece.
✆ +30 210 6123402, fax +30 210 6126206.
UK agent: Viamare (see Anek Lines) ✆ 020 8206 3420, fax 020 8206 1332.

AZZURRA LINE: Old Bakery Street, Valletta, Malta.
Italy agent: Pier Paola Santelia, Stazione marittima, Bari ✆ +39 080 52 31 824, fax +39 080 52 30 287.
Croatia agent: Elite Shipping Agency, Gruska obala 1, 20000 Dubrovnik, Croatia.
✆ +385 (20) 31 31 78, fax +385 (20) 31 31 80.

BALEÀRIA (EUROLÍNIES MARÍTIMES): Estació Marítima, 03700 Dénia.
✆ +34 902 160 180, fax +34 (96) 578 76 06.

BLUE LINE: Postboks 36, Englandsvej 370, DK 2770 Kastrup, Denmark.
Italy agent: ✆ +39 071 20 40 41, fax +39 071 20 26 18.
Croatia agent: ✆ +385 21 352 533, fax +385 21 352 482.
UK agent: Viamare (see Anek Lines) ✆ 020 8206 3420, fax 020 8206 1332.

BLUE STAR FERRIES: 26, Akti Posidonos, 185 31 Pireás.
✆ +30 210 422 5000, fax +30 210 422 5265.
UK agent: Viamare (see Anek Lines) ✆ 020 8206 3420, fax 020 8206 1332.

BORNHOLMSTRAFIKKEN: Havnen, 3700 Rønne.
✆ +45 56 95 18 66, fax +45 56 91 07 66.

BRITTANY FERRIES: Reservations: ✆ 0871 244 0744.
Millbay, Plymouth, PL1 3EW. ✆ 0871 244 1401.
Wharf Road, Portsmouth, PO2 8RU. ✆ 0871 244 1402.
Ringaskiddy, Cork. ✆ +353 (0)21 437 8401.
Gare Maritime, Port du Bloscon, 29688 Roscoff. ✆ +33 (0)2 98 29 28 13.
Estación Maritima, 39002 Santander. ✆ +34 9 42 36 06 11.

BUMERANG SHIPPING COMPANY TOURISM TRAVEL & TRADE S.A.: Rihtim Cad. Veli Alemdar Han Kat. 6, 80030 Karaköy - Istanbul.
✆ +90 (0)212 251 7373, fax +90 (0)212 251 1472.

CAREMAR: Campania Regionale Marittima S.p.A., Molo Beverello, 80133 Napoli.
✆ +39 081 58 05 111, fax +39 081 55 14 551.

COLOR LINE: Postboks 1422 Vika, 0115 Oslo.
✆ +47 810 00 811, fax +47 22 83 07 76.

COMARIT: 7 Rue du Mexique, Tanjah (Tangiers), Morocco.
✆ + 212 (0)9 32 00 32, fax + 212 (0)9 32 59 00.

COMPAGNIE MAROCAINE DE NAVIGATION (COMANAV):
7 Boulevard de la Résistance, Casablanca 05.
✆ +212 (0)2 30 30 12, fax +212 (0)2 30 84 55.
U.K. Agent: Southern Ferries, 30 Churton Street, Victoria, London SW1V 2LP.
✆ 0844 815 7785, fax 0844 815 7795.

COMPAGNIE TUNISIENNE DE NAVIGATION: Dag Hammarskjoeld Avenue 5, Tûnis.
✆ +216 (1) 341777, fax +216 (1) 335714.
UK agent: Southern Ferries (see Comanav). ✆ 0844 815 7785, fax 0844 815 7795.
France agent: SNCM, Marseille. ✆ +33 (0)4 91 56 30 10, fax +33 (0)4 91 56 31 00.

CONDOR FERRIES LTD.: New Harbour Rd. South, Hamworthy, Poole, BH15 4AJ.
✆ 01202 207 216, Reservations: ✆ 0845 609 1024.
The Quay, Weymouth, Dorset DT4 8DX. ✆ 01305 761 551, fax 01305 760 776.
Jersey: ✆ 01534 872 240. Guernsey 12023 (local calls only).
Reservations: ✆ 0870 243 5140.

CORSICA FERRIES: (including SARDINIA FERRIES), 5 bis, Rue Chanoine Leschi, 20296 Bastia. ✆ +33 (0)4 95 32 95 95, fax +33 (0)4 95 32 14 71.

DESTINATION GOTLAND: PO Box 1234, 621 23 Visby, Gotland, Sweden.
✆ +46 (0)498 20 10 20, fax +46 (0)498 20 18 90.

DFDS LISCO: Ostuferhafen 15, 24149, Kiel.
✆ +49 (0)431 20976 420, fax +49 (0)431 20976 102.
Reservations: ✆ +370 46 393616.

DFDS SEAWAYS: Scandinavia House, Parkeston Quay, Harwich CO12 4QG.
✆ 0871 522 9955.
International Ferry Terminal, Royal Quays, North Shields, NE29 6EE.
Axelborg Vesterbrogade 4A, 1620 København V. ✆ +45 33 156341, fax +45 33 936330.
Skandiahamnen, P.O. Box 8895, 402 72 Göteborg. ✆ +46 (0)31 65 06 00, fax +46 (0)31 54 3925.
Van-den-Smissen Strasse 4, 2000 Hamburg 50. ✆ +49 (0)40 389 0371, fax +49 (0)40 389 03120.
P.O. Box 548, 1970 BA, IJmuiden. ✆ +31 (0)255 534 546, fax +31 (0)255 535 349.

ECKERÖ LINJEN: Keskuskatu 1, 00100 Helsinki.
✆ +358 (0)9 22 88 544, fax (0)9 22 88 5222.
Torggatan 2, Box 158, 22101 Mariehamn.
✆ +358 (0)18 28 000, fax +358 (0)18 28 380.
Grisslehamn: ✆ +46 (0)175 30 920, fax +46 (0)175 30 820.
Eckerö: ✆ +358 (0)18 28 300, fax +358 (0)18 38 230.

EIMSKIP: Iceland Steamship Company Ltd, P.O. Box 220, 121 Reykjavík.
✆ +354 525 7000, fax +354 525 7179.

ENDEAVOR LINES: Posidonos Av 35, 183 44 Moschato, Athína.
✆ +30 210 9405 222, fax +30 210 9405 066.
Reservations: Nautilus Shipping Agencies, 72 Othonos Amalias Av, 26221 Patras.
✆ +30 2610 620061 / 622676, fax +30 2610 620031.
Brindisi: +39 0831 548116, fax +39 0831 548118.

E N T M V: Enterprise Nationale de Transport Maritime de Voyageurs, Gare Maritime, Quai d'Ajaccio, al-Jazâ'ir. ✆ +213 (021) 42 30 48.
Alacant: ✆ +34 965 14 90 10, fax +34 965 20 82 90.

EUROFERRIES: Ferry Terminal, Royal Harbour, Ramsgate, CT11 9FT.
Gare Maritime, Place de la République, 62200 Boulogne-sur-Mer.
✆ +44 (0)844 414 5355, www.euroferries.co.uk

FANØTRAFIKKEN: ✆ +45 70 23 15 15.

FERRIMAROC: Muelle de Ribera s/n, 04002 Almería.
✆ +34 (50) 27 48 00, fax +34 (50) 27 63 66.
UK agent: Wasteels London. ✆ 020 7834 7066, fax 020 7630 7628.

FERRYS RAPIDOS DEL SUR (FRS): C/ Alcade Juan Núñez 10, Edificio Santa Catalina, Bloque 2, Bajo A, 11380 Tarifa - Cádiz. ✆ +34 956 68 18 30, fax +34 956 62 71 80.

FINNLINES DEUTSCHLAND AG: Finnlines Passagierdienst, Einsiedelstrasse 45, 23554 Lübeck. ✆ +49 (0)451 1507 443, fax +49 (0)451 1507 444.
Finland agent: Nordic Ferry Center, Itämerenkatu 21, 5th floor, 00180 Helsinki.
✆ +358 (0)9 2510 200, fax +358 (0)9 2510 2022.
Finnlines UK Ltd., 8 Heron Quay, London. ✆ (0)207 519 7300, fax (0)207 536 0255.

FJORD LINE: Rosenkrantzgt 3, Postboks 4008 Dreggen, 5023 Bergen.
✆ +47 815 33 500, fax +47 55 31 88 00.

FLAGGRUTEN: Partrederiet Flagruten ANS, Postboks 2005 Nordnes, 5024 Bergen.
✆ +47 55 23 87 00, +47 55 23 87 01.

FÖRDE REEDEREI SEETOURISTIK: Norderhofenden 19-20, D 24937 Flensburg.
✆ +49 (0)461 864 0, fax +49 (0)461 864 30.

GOZO CHANNEL: Hay Wharf, Sa Maison, Malta.
✆ +356 21 243964.

GRANDI NAVI VELOCI: Via Fieschi 17, 16121 Genova.
✆ +39 010 58 93 31, fax +39 010 55 09 225.
UK agent: Viamare (see Anek Lines) ✆ 020 8206 3420, fax 020 8206 1332.

GRIMALDI FERRIES: Via M. Campodisola 13, Napoli.
✆ +39 081 496 444, fax +39 081 551 7716.
UK agent: Viamare (see Anek Lines) ✆ 020 8206 3420, fax 020 8206 1332.

HURTIGRUTEN (NORWEGIAN COASTAL VOYAGE):
Havnegata 2, N-8501 Narvik. ✆ +47 76 96 76 00.
Booking ✆ +47 810 30000, +47 76 11 82 45.
Kirkegata 1, N-9291 Tromsø.

INTERNATIONAL MARITIME TRANSPORT CORPORATION (I M T C): 122 Bd Anfa, Casablanca. ✆ +212 (0)2 299 209, fax +212 (0)2 299 202.
Spain agent: Vapores Suardiaz Andalucia S.A. (VS), Avda. Del Puerto 1-6, 11006 Cádiz. ✆ +34 956 282 111, fax +34 956 282 846.

IRISH FERRIES: 2-4 Merrion Row, Dublin 2. ✆ +353 (0)1 890 31 31 31.
Corn Exchange Building, Ground Floor, Brunswick Street, Liverpool L2 7TP.
✆ 08705 17 17 17, fax 0151 236 0562.

ISLE OF MAN STEAM PACKET CO.: Imperial Buildings, Douglas, Isle of Man IM1 2BY.
✆ 08705 523 523, fax 01624 645697.

ISLES OF SCILLY STEAMSHIP CO.: The Weighbridge, Quay Street, Penzance, Cornwall, TR18 4BZ. ✆ 0845 710 5555, fax 01736 51223.

ITALIAN RAILWAYS: Piazza della Croce Rossa, 00161 Roma.
✆ +39 06 884 0724, fax +39 06 883 1108.

JADROLINIJA: Riva 16, 51000 Rijeka, Croatia.
✆ +385 (51) 66 61 11, fax +385 (51) 21 31 16.
UK agent: Viamare (see Anek Lines) ✆ 020 8206 3420, fax 020 8206 1332.

KYSTLINK: Kongshavn 8, 3970 Langesund, Norway.
✆ +47 35 96 68 00, fax +47 35 96 68 01.
Denmark: ✆ +45 96 56 00 68, fax +45 96 56 00 69.
Sweden: ✆ +46 526 14 000, fax +46 526 14 125.

L D LINES: Continental Ferry Port, Wharf Road, Portsmouth, PO2 8QW.
✆ 0844 576 8836, fax 01235 84 56 08.
Terminal de la Citadelle, BP 90746, F-76060 Le Havre. ✆ 0825 304 304.
Outside UK and France ✆ +33 (0)2 32 14 52 09.

LINDA LINE OY: Makasiiniterminaali, 00140 Helsinki.
✆ +358 (0)9 668 9700, fax +358 (0)9 668 97070.
Tallinn: ✆ +372 -6 412 412.

LINEAS FRED. OLSEN: Polígono Industrial de Añaza, 38109 Santa Cruz de Tenerife.
✆ +34 (902) 10 01 07, fax +34 (922) 62 82 32.

MANCHE ÎLES EXPRESS: Albert Quay, St Helier, Jersey.
✆ 01534 880 756, fax 01534 880 314.
Terminal Building, New Jetty, White Rock, St Peter Port, Guernsey
✆ 01481 701 316, fax 01481 701 319.

MARMARA LINES:
Germany agent: RECA Handels GmbH, Neckarstrasse 37, 71065 Sindelfingen.
✆ +49 (0)7031 86 60 10, fax +49 (0)7031 87 65 68.

MED LINK LINES: 49 Corso Garibaldi Str., 72100 Brindisi.
✆ +39 0831 52 76 67, fax +39 0831 56 40 70.

MEDMAR LINEE LAURO: Piazza Municipo 88, 80133 Napoli. ✆ +39 081 551 33 52, fax +39 081 552 43 29.
UK agent: Viamare (see Anek Lines) ✆ 020 8206 3420, fax 020 8206 1332.

MINOAN LINES: 2 Vassileos Konstantinou Ave. (Stadion), 116 35 Athína.
✆ +30 210 7512356, fax +30 210 7520540.
UK agent: Magnum Travel, 747 Green Lanes, Winchmore Hill, London N21 3SA.
✆ 020 8360 5353, fax 020 8360 1056.

MOBY LINES: Via Ninci 1, 57037 Portoferraio, Italy.
✆ +39 0565 91 81 01, fax +39 0565 91 67 58.
UK agent: SMS, London. ✆ 020 7244 8422, fax 020 7244 9829.

MOLS-LINIEN: Færgehavnen, 8400 Ebeltoft.
✆ +45 89 52 52 52, fax +45 89 52 52 92.

MONTENEGRO LINES: Barska Plovidba, Obala 13 jula bb, 85000 Bar.
✆ +381 85 312-366/312-809/311-465, fax +381 85 311-652.

NAUTAS FERRY:
✆ +34 902 161 181, fax +34 (96) 578 76 06.

NAVIERA ARMAS: Juan Rejón 32-5y6, 35008 Las Palmas de Gran Canaria, España.
✆ +34 (928) 22 72 82, fax +34 (928) 46 99 91.

NAVIGAZIONE LIBERA del GOLFO: Molo Beverello, 80133 Napoli.
✆ +39 081 55 20 763, fax +39 081 55 25 589.

NORDIC JET LINE: Kanavaterminaali, 00161 Helsinki.
✆ +358 (0)9 681 770, fax +358 (0)9 681 77 111.

NORDIC FERRY SERVICES: www.nordic-ferry.com

NORDLANDSEKSPRESSEN: OVDS, Bodø.
✆ +47 75 52 10 20, fax +47 75 52 08 35.

NORFOLK LINE: Kranenburgweg 180, 2583 ER The Hague, Netherlands.
✆ + 31 70 35 27 400, fax +31 70 35 27 435.
Reservations: Dover - Dunkerque ✆ 0844 847 5042;
Rosyth - Zeebrugge ✆ 0844 499 0007; Irish Sea ✆ +44 (0)8 44 499 0007.

NORTHLINK FERRIES: Kiln Corner, Ayre Road, Kirkwall, Orkney KW15 1QX.
✆ 01856 851 144, fax 01856 851 155.
Reservations: ✆ 0845 6000 449.

P & O FERRIES:

United Kingdom:	Channel House, Channel View Road, Dover, CT17 9TJ. King George Dock, Hedon Road, Hull HU9 5QA. Peninsular House, Wharf Road, Portsmouth PO2 8TA. ✆ 08716 645 645.
Belgium:	Leopold II Dam 13, Kaaien 106-108, 8380, Zeebrugge. ✆ +32 070 70 77 71.
France:	41 Place d'Armes, BP 888, 62225, Calais. Gare Maritime Transmanche, BP 46, 50652, Cherbourg. Terminal de la Citadelle, BP 439, 76057, Le Havre. ✆ +33 0825 12 01 56.
Netherlands:	Europoort Beneluxhaven, Havennummer 5805, Rotterdam/ Europoort, Postbus 1123, 3180 AC, Rozenburg. ✆ +31 020 200 8333.
Spain:	Cosme Echevarrieta 1, 48009, Bilbao. ✆ +34 902 02 04 61.

P & O IRISH SEA: Larne Harbour, Larne BT40 1AQ.
✆ 0870 24 24 777.

POLFERRIES: Polish Baltic Shipping Co., ul. Portowa 41, 78 100 Kolobrzeg.
✆ +48 (0)965 252 11, fax +48 (0)965 266 12.

POSEIDON LINES: 32 Alkyonidon Avenue, 166 73 Voula, Athína.
✆ +30 210 965 8300, fax +30 210 965 8310.
UK agent: Viamare (see Anek Lines) ✆ 020 8206 3420, fax 020 8206 1332.

REEDEREI CASSEN EILS: Bei der Alten Liebe 12, 27472 Cuxhaven.
✆ +49 (0)4721 35082, fax +49 (0)4721 31161.

R G LINE: Satamaterminaali, Vaskiluoto, 65170 Vaasa.
Bookings: ✆ 0207 716 810, fax 0207 716 820.

SALAMIS LINES: 28th October Avenue, P.O. Box 531, Limassol, Cyprus.
✆ +357 (0)5 35 55 55, fax +357 (0)5 36 44 10.
Greece agent: Salamis Lines (Hellas), 9 Filellinon Str., 18536 Pireás.
✆ +30 210 429 4325, fax +30 210 429 4557.
Salamis Cruise Lines: ✆ +357 2586 0000, fax +357 2537 4437.

SAMSØTRAFIKKEN: Strandbakkevej 2, Kolby Kås, DK-8305 Samsø, Denmark.
✆ +45 70 10 17 44.

SARDINIA FERRIES: see Corsica Ferries.

SCANDLINES: DSB Kunde, Vester Farimagsgade 3, København.
✆ +45 33 151515, fax +45 33 151020.
Gedser: ✆ +45 54 160 055, fax +45 54 160 0533.
Helsingborg: ✆ +46 (0)42 186 100, fax +46 (0)42 187 410.
Helsingør: ✆ +45 49 258 892, fax +45 49 258 895.
Rødby: ✆ +45 54 605 166, fax +45 54 605 834.
Rønne: ✆ +45 56 951 069, fax +45 56 958 910.
Trelleborg: ✆ +46 410 65000, fax +46 410 13386.

SCANDLINES DEUTSCHLAND GmbH: Am Warnowkai 8, 18147 Rostock Seehafen.
✆ +49 (0)381 673 12 92, fax +49 (0)381 673 12 99.
Puttgarden: ✆ +49 (0)4371 86 51 61, fax +49 (0)4371 86 51 62.
Sassnitz: ✆ +49 (0)38392 644 20, fax +49 (0)38392 644 29.
Klaipeda: ✆ +370 6 314 376, fax +370 6 311 121.

SCANDLINES EUROSEABRIDGE: Uberseehafen, 18147 Rostock.
✆ +49 (0)381 458 4448, fax +49 (0)381 458 4442.

SEA CONTAINERS FINLAND: Makasiiniterminaali M4, Eteläsatama, 00140 Helsinki.
✆ +358 9 180 4678, fax ✆ +358 9 180 4699.
Reservations: ✆ +372 610 0000, fax +372 610 0011.

SEAFRANCE: Eastern Docks, Dover, Kent CT16 1JA. ✆ 0871 423 7119.

SILJA LINE: Mannerheimintie 2, 00100 Helsinki.
✆ +358 (0)9 180 4422, fax +358 (0)9 180 4279.
Reservations: ✆ +358 600 174 552.

SIREMAR: Sicilia Regionale Marittima, Via Principe di Belmonte 1/c, 90139 Palermo.
✆ +39 091 58 26 88, fax +39 091 58 22 67.

SMYRIL LINE: Jonas Broncksgøta 37, Postboks 370, 110 Tórshavn.
✆ +298 315 900, fax +298 315 707.

SNAV FERRIES: Via Giordano Bruno 84, 80122 Napoli.
✆ +39 081 428 5555, fax +39 081 428 5259.
UK agent: Viamare (see Anek Lines) ✆ 020 8206 3420, fax 020 8206 1332.

S N C M: Société Nationale Maritime Corse Mediterranée, 61, Boulevard des Dames, 13002 Marseille. ✆ +33 (0)4 91 56 30 10, fax +33 (0)4 91 56 31 00.
UK agent: Southern Ferries (see Comanav). ✆ 0844 815 7785, fax 0844 815 7795.

SPLIT TOURS: ✆ +385 (0)21 352 533.

STENA LINE: Stena House, Station Approach, Holyhead, LL65 1DQ. ✆ 08705 70 70 70.
Prince's Dock, 14 Clarendon Road, Belfast, BT1 3GB. ✆ 08705 204 204.
The Ferry Terminal, Dun Laoghaire, Co. Dublin. ✆ 01 204 7777.
Masthuggskajen, 405 19 Göteborg. ✆ +46 (0)31 704 00 00, fax +46 (0)31 85 85 95.
Trafikhavn, 9900 Frederikshavn. ✆ +45 98 424366, fax +45 98 422750.
Box 94, 432 22, Varberg. ✆ +46 (0)340 690 900, fax +46 (0)340 851 25.
Box 150 8500, Grenaa. ✆ +45 87 58 75 00, fax +45 86 32 01 18.
Box 104 371 22, Karlskrona. ✆ +46 (0)455 665 50, fax +46 (0)455 220 99.

SUPERFAST FERRIES: 157 C. Karamanli Av., 166 73 Voula, Athína.
✆ +30 210 969 1100, fax +30 210 969 1190.
Reservations: ✆ +30 210 89 19 130, fax +30 210 89 19 139.
United Kingdom: The Terminal Building, Port of Rosyth, Fife, KY11 2XP.
✆ 0870 234 0870, fax 0138 360 8020.
UK agent: Viamare (see Anek Lines) ✆ 020 8206 3420, fax 020 8206 1332.
Germany: ✆ +49 451 88 00 61 66, fax +49 451 88 00 61 29.

SWANSEA CORK FERRIES: 52 South Mall, Cork, Ireland.
✆ +353 (0)21 271166, fax +353 (0)21 275061.
Swansea: ✆ 01792 456116, fax 01792 644356.

TALLINK: Erottajankatu 19, 00130 Helsinki.
✆ +358 (0)9 2282 1211, fax +358 (0)9 635311.

TIRRENIA: Rione Sirignano 2, Casella Postale 438, 80121 Napoli.
✆ +39 081 720 11 11, fax +39 081 720 14 41.
UK agent: S.M.S. Travel & Tourism, 40/42 Kenway Road, London SW5 0RA.
✆ 020 7373 6548, fax 020 7244 9829.

TOREMAR: Via Calafati 6, Casella Postale 482, 57123 Livorno.
✆ +39 0586 22 45 11, fax +39 0586 22 46 24.

TRANSEUROPA FERRIES: Slijkensesteenweg 2, B-8400 Oostende.
✆ +32 (0)59 340 260, fax +32 (0)59 340 261.
Ferry Terminal, New Port, Ramsgate CT11 9FT. ✆ 01843 595522.

TRANSMANCHE FERRIES: Harbour, Newhaven, BN9 0BG. ✆ 0800 917 12 01.
Quai Gaston Lalitte, 76200 Dieppe. ✆ +33 (0)800 650 100, fax +33 (0)2 32 14 52 00.

TRASMEDITERRANEA: Obenque 4, Alameda de Osuna, 28042 Madrid.
✆ +34 (91) 322 91 00, fax +34 (91) 322 91 10.
UK agent: Southern Ferries (see Comanav). ✆ 0844 815 7785, fax 0844 815 7795.

TT-LINE: Mattentwiete 8, 20457 Hamburg.
✆ +49 (0)40 3601 442 446, fax +49 (0)40 3601 407.

UKRFERRY SHIPPING COMPANY: 4a Sabanskiy lane, Odesa, 65014, Ukraine.
✆ +380 (482) 344 059, fax +380 (482) 348 297, 348 108.

UNITY LINE: Plac Rodła 8, 70419, Szczecin, Poland.
✆ +48 (0)91 35 95 592, fax +48 (0)91 35 95 673.
Sweden agent: Pol-Line AB, Färjeterminalen, 27139 Ystad.
✆ +46 (0)411 55 69 00, fax +46 (0)411 55 69 53.

USTICA LINES: Via A. Staita 23, 91100 Trapani, Sicily.
✆ +39 092 322 200, fax + 39 092 323 289.
Reservations: ✆ +39 0923 873 813, fax +39 0923 593 200.

VENTOURIS FERRIES: 91 Pireos Avenue, 185 41 Pireás.
✆ +30 210 4825815, fax +30 210 4832919.

VIKING LINE: P.O. Box 35, 22101 Mariehamn.
✆ +358 (0)18 26011, fax +358 (0)18 15811.
UK agent: Emagine UK Ltd, Leigh, WN7 1AZ. ✆ 01942 262662, fax 01942 606500.

VIRTU FERRIES LTD: Sea Passenger Terminal, Pinto Road, Valletta, Malta.
Reservations: ✆ +356 21 228777, fax +356 21 235435.

CAIRNRYAN - LARNE 2005

P & O Irish Sea **by ship** Journey 1 hour 45 minutes **2009 service**

January 1 - March 12 and October 6 - December 31

Depart Cairnryan: 0415①②③④⑤⑥, 0730, 1030①②③④⑤⑥, 1300⑦, 1330①②③④⑤⑥, 1630, 2000, 2300⑦, 2359①②③④⑤.

Depart Larne: 0415①②③④⑤⑥, 0730, 1030①②③④⑤⑥, 1300⑦, 1330①②③④⑤⑥, 1630, 2000, 2300⑦, 2359①②③④⑤.

March 13 - October 5

Depart Cairnryan: 0415①②③④⑤⑥, 0730, 1030, 1300⑦, 1330①②③④⑤⑥, 1630, 2000, 2300⑦, 2359①②③④⑤.

Depart Larne: 0415①②③④⑤⑥, 0730, 1030①②③④⑤⑥, 1300⑦, 1330①②③④⑤⑥, 1630, 2000, 2300⑦, 2359①②③④⑤.

Subject to alteration during Xmas/New Year period.

P & O Irish Sea **by fast ferry** **March 13 - October 5, 2009** **(No winter service)**

Cairnryan		Larne	Larne		Cairnryan
1500	→	1600	1255	→	1355

CHERBOURG - ROSSLARE 2010

Celtic Link Ferries **by ship** **Service to December 20, 2009**

Sailings from Portsmouth Continental Ferry Port and Cherbourg.

Cherbourg		Rosslare	Rosslare		Cherbourg
1900⑦	→	1230①	1800⑥	→	1330⑦
2000⑤	→	1330⑥	2000②④	→	1530③⑤
2100③	→	1430④			

No foot passengers conveyed on weekday sailings

Irish Ferries **Service to December 21, 2009**

Cherbourg		Rosslare	
1800	→	1130	June 1, 3, 9, 15, 17, 23, 29, July 1, 7, 13, 15, 19, 21, 27, 29, Aug. 2, 4, 8, 10, 12, 16, 18, 20, 24, 26, 30, Sept. 1, 3, 7, 9, 13, 15, 21, 23, 27, 29.
2000	→	1400	② Oct. 6 - Dec. 15 (also Dec. 21).
2130	→	1430	⑥ Oct. 3 - Dec. 19.
2130	→	1530	④ Oct. 1 - Dec. 17.
Rosslare		**Cherbourg**	
1530	→	1100	May 17, 19, 25, 31, June 2, 8, 14, 16, 22, 28, 30, July 6, 12, 14, 18, 20, 26, 28, Aug. 1, 3, 7, 9, 11, 15, 17, 19, 23, 25, 29, 31, Sept. 2, 6, 8, 12, 14, 20, 22, 26, 28, 30.
1800	→	1400	⑦ Feb. 1 - May 10, Oct. 4 - Dec. 20.
2300	→	1830	③⑤ Feb. 4 - May 13, Oct. 2 - Dec. 18.

CORK - ROSCOFF 2015

Brittany Ferries **Service to October 31, 2009**

Sailings from Cork (Ringaskiddy) and Roscoff. **(No winter service)**

Cork		Roscoff		Roscoff		Cork	
1600	→	0700	⑥ Apr. 4 - Oct. 31.	2130	→	1030	⑤ Apr. 3 - Oct. 30.

Departure times may vary owing to tidal conditions.

DOUGLAS - BELFAST 2020

Isle Of Man Steam Packet Co. **by SEACAT catamaran** **2009 service**

Sailings from Belfast Albert Quay. **(No winter service)**

Douglas		Belfast		Belfast		Douglas	
0600	→	0855	Aug. 23, 30 only.	1045	→	1340	See note **E**.
0700§	→	0955	See note **E**.	1100	→	1355	Aug. 23, 30 only.
1000	→	1255	See note **H**.	1400	→	1655	See note **H**.
1200	→	1455	Sept. 13, 27 only.	1600	→	1855	Sept. 13, 27 only.
1345	→	1640	See note **F**.	1815	→	2110	See note **J**.
				1900	→	2155	May 27, 29 only.

E – Apr. 5, 8, 12, 16, 19, 30, May 5, 14, 17, 21, July 12, 17, Sept. 6, 10, 24.
F – May 27, 29, July 5, 20, 26, Aug. 2, 9, 16.
H – July 2, 8, 23, 30, Aug. 6, 13, 20, 25, Sept. 3.
J – July 5, 20, 26, Aug. 2, 9, 16.
§ – July 17 depart 0630.

A special service will operate during the TT Race period (May 30 - June 28)

DOUGLAS - DUBLIN 2025

Isle Of Man Steam Packet Co. **by SEACAT catamaran** **2009 service**

Sailings from Dublin North Wall. **(No winter service)**

Douglas		Dublin		Dublin		Douglas	
0700	→	0955	Apr. 13 only.	1045	→	1340	Apr. 13 only.
1000	→	1255	See note **A**.	1400	→	1655	See note **E**.
1345	→	1640	See note **B**.	1815	→	2110	See note **C**.
1530	→	1825	Apr. 10 only.	1915	→	2210	See note **D**.
1800	→	2055	Sept. 4 only.	2130	→	0025	Sept. 4 only.

A – May 24, July 3, 6, 10, 16, 19, 24, 31, Aug. 7, 14, 21, 24, 27, 31, Sept. 7.
B – May 28, July 13, 27, Aug. 3, 10, 17.
C – July 6, 13, 19, 27, Aug. 3, 10, 17, 31.
D – Apr. 10, May 28.
E – July 3, 10, 16, 24, 31, Aug. 7, 14, 21, 24, 27, Sept. 7.

A special service will operate during the TT Race period (May 30 - June 28)

FISHGUARD - ROSSLARE 2030

Stena Line **by ship** **2009 service** **(No service Dec. 25, 26)**

Fishguard		Rosslare		Rosslare		Fishguard	
0245	→	0615		0900	→	1230	
1430	→	1800	Not Dec. 24.	2115	→	0030	Not Dec. 24.

Stena Line **by *LYNX* catamaran** **May 14 - September 12, 2009** **(No winter service)**

Fishguard		Rosslare	Rosslare		Fishguard
1130	→	1330	0800	→	1000
1830	→	2030	1500	→	1700

FLEETWOOD - LARNE 2032

Stena Line **by ship** Journey 8 hours **2009 service**

Conveys passengers with vehicles only

Departure times vary – contact operator for details

HEYSHAM - DOUGLAS 2035

Isle Of Man Steam Packet Co. **by ship** **Service to January 5, 2010** **(No service Dec. 25)**

Heysham		Douglas	
0215	→	0545	Daily June 17 - Dec. 19, Dec. 21 - 24, 27, Dec. 29 - 31, Jan. 2 - 5 (not June 4 - 6, 21, July 5, Aug. 16, Sept. 13, Oct. 4, Nov. 1, Dec. 6).
0300	→	0630	June 4 - 6 only.
1415	→	1745	Daily June 17 - Nov. 6; ①②③④⑤ Nov. 9 - Jan. 5.
Douglas		**Heysham**	
0815	→	1145	Aug. 20 - 22, 28, 29 only.
0845	→	1215	Daily June 17 - Nov. 6; ①②③④⑤ Nov. 9 - Jan. 5 (not Aug. 20 - 22, 28, 29).
1945	→	2315	①②③④⑤⑦ June 17 - Jan. 5 (not Dec. 24, 27, 31).
2000	→	2330	⑥ June 27 - Jan. 2 (not July 4, Aug. 15, Sept. 12, Oct. 3, Dec. 5, 19).

A special service will operate during the TT Race period (May 30 - June 16)

HOLYHEAD - DUBLIN 2040

Irish Ferries **by ship** **2009 service**

Sailings from Holyhead and Dublin Ferryport. **(No service Dec. 25, 26)**

Holyhead		Dublin	Dublin		Holyhead
0240	→	0555	0805	→	1130
1410	→	1725	2055	→	0020

Sailing times may vary owing to tidal conditions.

Dublin Ferryport - Dublin Busaras (Central Bus Station).

Irish Ferries **by fast ferry** Journey 1 hour 55 minutes **2009 service**

Sailings from Holyhead and Dublin Ferryport. **(No service Dec. 25, 26)**

Depart Holyhead: 1200**A**, 1715. Depart Dublin: 0845**A**, 1430.

Dublin Ferryport - Dublin Busaras (Central Bus Station).

A – Daily Apr. 3 - 19; ⑤⑥⑦ Apr. 20 - May 14; daily May 15 - Oct. 4; ⑤⑥⑦ Oct. 5 - Nov. 1.

Stena Line **2009 service**

Sailings from Holyhead and Dublin Ferryport. **(No service Dec. 25, 26)**

Holyhead		Dublin		Dublin		Holyhead	
0230	→	0545		0820	→	1135	
1350	→	1705		1600	→	1915	See note **A**.
2130	→	0045	See note **A**.	2115	→	0030	

A – ①②③④⑤⑥ Jan. 6 - Mar. 1, Mar. 15 - Dec. 31.

Subject to alteration during Xmas/New Year period

HOLYHEAD - DUN LAOGHAIRE 2045

Stena Line **by *HSS* fast ferry** **2009 service**

Sailings from Holyhead and Dun Laoghaire. **(No service Dec. 25, 26)**

Holyhead		Dun Laoghaire	Dun Laoghaire		Holyhead
1025	→	1225	1330	→	1530

Dun Laoghaire - Dublin Busaras (Central Bus Station).

BIRKENHEAD (LIVERPOOL) - DUBLIN 2049

Norfolk Line **2009 service**

Sailings from Birkenhead Twelve Quays Terminal and Dublin Port Passenger Terminal.

Birkenhead		Dublin		Dublin		Birkenhead	
1000	→	1700	②③④⑤⑥	1000	→	1700	②③④⑤⑥
2200	→	0500		2200	→	0500	

BIRKENHEAD (LIVERPOOL) - BELFAST 2050

Norfolk Line **2009 service**

Sailings from Birkenhead Twelve Quays Terminal and Belfast Victoria Terminal.

Birkenhead		Belfast		Belfast		Birkenhead	
1030	→	1830	②③④⑤⑥⑦	1030	→	1830	②③④⑤⑥⑦
2200	→	0600	①	2200	→	0600	①
2230	→	0630	②③④⑤⑥⑦	2230	→	0630	②③④⑤⑥⑦

LIVERPOOL - DUBLIN 2052

P & O Irish Sea **2009 service**

Conveys passengers with vehicles only

Liverpool		Dublin		Dublin		Liverpool	
1000	→	1800	②③④⑤⑥	1000	→	1800	②③④⑤⑥
2200	→	0600		2200	→	0600	

Subject to alteration during holiday periods

LIVERPOOL - DOUGLAS 2053

Isle Of Man Steam Packet Co. **by *SeaCat*** **Service to January 5, 2010**

Liverpool		Douglas	
1130	→	1400	Daily June 17 - Sept. 5; ①⑤⑥ Sept. 7 - Oct. 3.
1600	→	1830	Aug. 29, Sept. 5, 6 only.
1930	→	2200	Daily June 17 - Aug. 26, Sept. 8 - Oct. 18, Oct. 21 - 26, Oct. 29 - Nov. 1 (not Aug. 23).
2030	→	2300	Daily Aug. 27 - Sept. 7 (also Aug. 23).
Douglas		**Liverpool**	
0600	→	0830	Aug. 28, 29 only.
0730	→	1000	Daily June 17 - Sept. 5; ①⑤⑥ Sept. 7 - Oct. 3 (not Aug. 28, 29).
1000	→	1230	⑥ Oct. 10 - 31.
1100	→	1330	Aug. 29, Sept. 5, 6 only.
1530	→	1800	Daily June 17 - Aug. 31, Sept. 8 - Oct. 9, Oct. 11 - 16; ①④⑤⑦ Oct. 18 - Nov. 1 (also May 31).
1630	→	1900	Daily Sept. 1 - 7.

Additional sailings by ferry ⑥⑦ Nov. 7 - Jan. 3: Liverpool depart 1400; Douglas depart 0800.

A special service will operate during the TT Race period (May 30 - June 16)

2055 PEMBROKE - ROSSLARE

Irish Ferries **2009 service (No service Dec. 25, 26)**

Pembroke		Rosslare	Rosslare		Pembroke
0245	→	0630	0845	→	1230
1430	→	1815	2100	→	0045

Sailing times may vary owing to tidal conditions

2065 ROSSLARE - ROSCOFF

Irish Ferries **2009 service (No winter service)**

Rosslare		Roscoff	
1600	→	1030	May 21, 23, 27, 29, June 4, 6, 10, 12, 18, 20, 24, 26, July 2, 4, 8, 10, 16, 22, 24, 30, Aug. 5, 13, 21, 27, Sept. 4, 10, 16, 18, 24.
1730	→	1100	May 15 only.
Roscoff		**Rosslare**	
1800	→	1100	May 16, 22, 24, 28, 30, June 5, 7, 11, 13, 19, 21, 25, 27, July 3, 5, 9, 11, 17, 23, 25, 31, Aug. 6, 14, 22, 28, Sept. 5, 11, 17, 19, 25.

2070 STRANRAER - BELFAST

Stena Line **by *HSS* fast ferry** **Service to January 5, 2010**
Sailings from Stranraer and Belfast. **(No service Dec. 25, 26)**

Stranraer		Belfast	Belfast		Stranraer
0440	→	0700	0725	→	0925
0950	→	1150	1215	→	1415
1440	→	1640	1705	→	1925
1950	→	2200	2235	→	0055

Subject to alteration during Xmas / New Year period

Stena Line **by ship** **Service to January 5, 2010**
Sailings from Stranraer and Belfast. **(No service Dec. 25, 26)**

Stranraer		Belfast		Belfast		Stranraer	
0710§	→	1010§	②③④⑤⑥	0320§	→	0610§	②③④⑤⑥
1515§	→	1815§	⑤ May 1 - Sept. 30.	1100§	→	1350§	See note **S**.
1550§	→	1850§	See note **T**.	1920§	→	2210§	①②③④⑤
2320§	→	0220§	①②③④⑤	2000	→	2250	⑥⑦
2359	→	0300	⑥⑦				

S – ⑤⑦ May 1 - Sept. 30 (also ⑥ July 1 - Aug. 31).
T – ⑦ May 1 - June 30; ⑥⑦ July 1 - Aug. 31; ⑦ Sept. 1-30.
§ – No foot passengers conveyed.

Subject to alteration during Xmas / New Year period

2080 TROON - LARNE

P & O Irish Sea **by fast ferry** **March 13 - October 5, 2009**
(No winter service)

Troon		Larne	Larne		Troon
1005	→	1155	0715	→	0905
2020	→	2210	1730	→	1920

ENGLISH CHANNEL

2100 CHANNEL ISLAND SERVICES

POOLE and WEYMOUTH - GUERNSEY - JERSEY by fast ferry

Condor Ferries **2009 service**
Sailings from St Helier Elizabeth Terminal and St Peter Port.

Weymouth - Guernsey - Jersey: Jan. - Mar.: 1–3 sailings per week; Apr. - Sept.: 5–6 sailings per week (daily July 15 - Sept. 7); Oct.: daily; Nov. - Dec.: 1–3 sailings per week. Journey time 2 hours 10 minutes (Guernsey), 3 hours 25 minutes (Jersey).

Poole - Guernsey: Apr. - Sept.: 2–5 sailings per week (daily July 18 - Sept. 1); Oct.: occasional sailings. Journey time 2 hours 40 minutes.
Poole - Jersey (most services via Guernsey): Apr. - Sept.: 2–5 sailings per week (daily July 30 - Sept. 2); Oct.: occasional sailings. Journey time 3 hours.

Departure times vary owing to tidal conditions.

POOLE and WEYMOUTH - GUERNSEY - JERSEY - ST MALO by fast ferry

Condor Ferries **2009 service**
Sailings by catamaran from St Helier Elizabeth Terminal or Albert Quay, St Malo Gare Maritime de la Bourse and St Peter Port.

Weymouth - St Malo: 1–2 sailings per week (5–7 sailings Apr. 2 - Sept. 30, daily in Oct.). Journey 5 hours 15 minutes. A change of vessel may be necessary in either Guernsey or Jersey in summer (extended journey time).

Poole - St Malo (via Guernsey or Jersey): up to 6 sailings per week May 6 - Sept. 26; journey 4 hours 35 minutes.

OTHER SERVICES:

Manche iles Express operate catamaran services in summer from Jersey to Carteret, Granville, Sark and Guernsey, and from Alderney to Diélette and Guernsey.

2105 DOVER - BOULOGNE

L D Lines **by fast ferry** **2009 service**

Dover		Boulogne		Boulogne		Dover	
				Until November 10			
0415§	→	0615§	①②③④⑤	0700♣	→	0700	①②③④⑤
0745	→	0945		1045§♣	→	1100§	
1230§	→	1430§		1700	→	1700	
1900	→	2100		2230§	→	2245§	
				From November 11			
0700	→	0945		0500§	→	0545§	①②③④⑤⑥
1230§	→	1515§		1045	→	1130	
1800	→	2045		1615	→	1700	
2330§	→	0215§	①②③④⑤⑦	2200§	→	2245§	

§ – No foot passengers conveyed on this service.
♣ – From October foot passengers will be conveyed on 1045 sailing (not 0700).

2110 DOVER - CALAIS

P & O Ferries Journey 75-90 minutes **2009 service**
Sailings from Dover Eastern Docks and Calais Maritime. **(No service Dec. 25)**
Conveys passengers with vehicles only on night services.

Depart Dover: 0115, 0320, 0425, 0530, 0640, 0830, 0925, 1020, 1110, 1300, 1355, 1450, 1540, 1730, 1825, 1920, 2015, 2215, 2315, 2355.
Depart Calais: 0130, 0235, 0340, 0440, 0645, 0750, 0855, 0950, 1140, 1235, 1330, 1420, 1610, 1705, 1800, 1850, 2040, 2135, 2235, 2335.

Minor schedule changes are possible.
A reduced service will operate on Dec. 24, 26 (no service Dec. 25)

connections:
Dover Eastern Docks - Dover Priory station: from Dover Eastern Docks on arrival of ship; from Dover Priory station approximately every 20 minutes 0715–1930.
Calais Port - Calais Ville station 1100–1915; Calais Ville station - Calais Port 1030–1930.

SeaFrance *Conveys passengers with vehicles only* **2009 service**
Sailings from Dover Eastern Docks and Calais Maritime. Journey 70-100 minutes

Depart Dover: 0050, 0200, 0600, 0810, 1000, 1220, 1400, 1625, 1800, 2035, 2200.
Depart Calais: 0100, 0500, 0700, 0900, 1115, 1300, 1515, 1700, 1925, 2100, 2340.

§ – Conveys passengers with vehicles only.

connections:
Dover Eastern Docks - Dover Priory station: from Dover Eastern Docks on arrival of ship; from Dover Priory station approximately every 20 minutes 0715–1930.
Calais Port - Calais Ville station 1100–1915; Calais Ville station - Calais Port 1030–1930.

2111 DOVER - DUNKERQUE

Norfolk Line **by ship** *Conveys passengers with vehicles only* **2009 service**
Sailings from Dover Eastern Docks and Dunkerque. Journey 1 hour 45 minutes

Depart Dover: 0200①②③④⑤⑥, 0400①②③④⑤⑥, 0600②③④⑤⑥, 0800, 1000, 1200, 1400, 1600, 1800, 2000①②③④⑤⑦, 2200, 2359①②③④⑤⑦.
Depart Dunkerque: 0200①②③④⑤⑥, 0400②③④⑤⑥, 0600, 0800, 1000, 1200, 1400, 1600, 1800①②③④⑤⑦, 2000, 2200①②③④⑤⑦, 2359①②③④⑤⑦.

2125 NEWHAVEN - DIEPPE

Transmanche Ferries **by ship** **2009 service**
Sailings from Newhaven and Dieppe. **(No service Dec. 25)**

Newhaven		Dieppe		Dieppe		Newhaven	
0800	→	1300	⑦	0500	→	0800	①②③④⑤⑥
0930	→	1430	①②③④⑤⑥	1800	→	2100	①②③④⑤⑦
2230	→	0330	①②③④⑤⑦	2000	→	2300	⑥

Departure times may vary owing to tidal conditions.

2130 PENZANCE - ST. MARY'S

Isles Of Scilly Steamship Co. **2009 service ▲**
Sailings from Penzance Lighthouse Pier and St Mary's. **(No winter service)**

Penzance		St Mary's		St Mary's		Penzance	
0630	→	0910	⑥ May 18-30.	0945	→	1225	⑥ May 18-30.
0915	→	1155	See note **A**.	1500	→	1740	⑥ July 20 - Aug. 29.
1030	→	1310	⑥ July 20 - Aug. 29.	1630♣	→	1910♣	See note **A**.
1345	→	1625	⑥ May 18-30.	1700	→	1940	⑥ May 18-30.

A – ①③⑤⑥ Mar. 30 - Apr. 11; ①②③④⑤⑥ Apr. 13 - May 16; ①②③④⑤ May 18-30; ①②③④⑤⑥ June 1 - July 18; ①②③④⑤ July 20 - Aug. 29; ①②③④⑤⑥ Aug. 31 - Oct. 3; ①③⑤⑥ Oct. 5-31.
♣ – June 3 depart 1415 (Penzance a. 1655).
▲ – Subject to alteration Apr. 30 - May 4.

Departure times may vary owing to tidal conditions.

 For international shipping maps – see pages 518 - 520

PLYMOUTH - ROSCOFF 2135

Brittany Ferries — **Service to March 15, 2010**

Sailings from Plymouth Millbay, Roscoff and St Malo Terminal Ferry du Naye.

From Plymouth and Roscoff: up to 4 sailings per week (no service Dec. 23 - Feb. 11).

PLYMOUTH - SANTANDER 2140

Brittany Ferries — **Service to March 15, 2010**

Sailings from Plymouth Millbay and Santander. **(No service Dec. 22 - Feb. 13)**

Plymouth		Santander	
1200⑦	→	1300①	Nov. 8 - Dec. 20, Feb. 14 - Mar. 7.
1600⑦	→	1230①	Nov. 1 only.
Santander		**Plymouth**	
1600④	→	1500⑤	Nov. 5 only.
1900①	→	1800②	Nov. 9 - Dec. 21, Feb. 15 - Mar. 8.

POOLE - CHERBOURG 2145

Brittany Ferries by ship — **Service to March 31, 2010**
(No service Dec. 25, Jan. 1, Jan. 5 - 31)

Poole		Cherbourg		Cherbourg		Poole	
November 1 - January 4							
1230	→	1745	②③④⑤⑥⑦	0800	→	1115	See note **Q**.
2345	→	0630	See note **P**.	1900	→	2230	Not Dec. 24, 31.
2345	→	0730	⑦				
February 1 - March 31							
1230	→	1745	②③④⑤⑥⑦	0800	→	1115	②③④⑤⑥⑦
2345	→	0630	①②③④⑤⑥	1900	→	2230	Daily.
2345	→	0730	⑦				

P – ①②③④⑤⑥ (not Dec. 24, 31). **Q** – ②③④⑤⑥⑦ (not Jan. 4).

🚌 Cherbourg Port - Cherbourg station (operated by Zéphir).

Brittany Ferries by fast ferry — **May 18 - September 27, 2009**
(No winter service)

Poole		Cherbourg	Cherbourg		Poole
0730	→	1045	1130	→	1245

PORTSMOUTH - BILBAO 2155

P & O Ferries — **2009 service**

Sailings from Portsmouth Continental Ferry Port and Bilbao (Santurtzi).
Santurtzi is located approximately 13 km to the north west of Bilbao city centre.

Portsmouth		Bilbao		Bilbao		Portsmouth	
2000	→	0800§	See note **M**.	1230	→	1715¶	See note **R**.
2115	→	0800§	See note **P**.	1315	→	1715¶	See note **S**.

M – Feb. 4, 7, 11, 14, 18, 21, 25, 28, Mar. 4, 7, 11, 14, 18, 21, 25, 28, Apr. 1, 4, 8, 11, 15, 18, 22, 25, 29, May 2, 6, 9, 13, 16, 20, 23, Sept. 26, 30, Oct. 3, 7, 10, 14, 17, 21, 24, 28, 31, Nov. 4, 7, 11, 14, 18, 21, 25, 28, Dec. 2, 5, 9, 12, 16.

P – May 26, 29, June 1, 4, 7, 10, 13, 16, 19, 22, 25, 28, June 1, 4, 7, 10, 13, 16, 19, 22, 25, 28, July 1, 4, 7, 10, 13, 16, 19, 22, 25, 28, 31, Aug. 3, 6, 9, 12, 15, 18, 21, 24, 27, 30, Sept. 2, 5, 8, 11, 14, 17, 20, 23.

R – Feb. 6, 9, 13, 16, 20, 23, 27, Mar. 2, 6, 9, 13, 16, 20, 23, 27, 30, Apr. 3, 6, 10, 13, 17, 20, 24, 27, May 1, 4, 8, 11, 15, 18, 22, 25, Sept. 25, 28, Oct. 2, 5, 9, 12, 16, 19, 23, 26, 30, Nov. 2, 6, 9, 13, 16, 20, 23, 27, 30, Dec. 4, 7, 11, 14, 18.

§ – Approximate time (two days later). ¶ – Approximate time (following day).

PORTSMOUTH - CHANNEL ISLANDS 2157

Condor Ferries — **2009 service**
(No service Dec. 24 - 26, 31, Jan. 1)

Sailings from Portsmouth Continental Ferry Port, St Helier and St Peter Port.

Portsmouth		St Peter Port		St Peter Port		St Helier		St Helier		Portsmouth
0900 **A**	→	1600 **A**	→	1730 **A**	→	1930 **A**	→	2100 **A**	→	0630 **B**

A – ①②③④⑤⑥. **B** – ②③④⑤⑥⑦.

Departure times may vary owing to tidal conditions.

PORTSMOUTH - CHERBOURG 2160

Brittany Ferries by fast ferry — **Service to March 15, 2010**
(No winter service)

Sailings from Portsmouth Continental Ferry Port and Cherbourg.

Portsmouth		Cherbourg		Cherbourg		Portsmouth	
0800	→	1200	Nov. 1, 2 only.	1730	→	1930	Nov. 1 only.

Additional sailings by ship from Portsmouth Jan. 11 - 14, Mar. 8;
from Cherbourg Dec. 26, Jan. 2, 8, 11 - 15.

🚌 Cherbourg Port - Cherbourg station (operated by Zéphir).

Celtic Link Ferries by ship — **2009 service (No service Dec. 25, 26)**

Sailings from Portsmouth Continental Ferry Port and Cherbourg.

Portsmouth		Cherbourg	Cherbourg		Portsmouth
0900⑦	→	1430⑦	2330⑦	→	0300①
1400⑤⑥	→	1930⑤⑥	2330⑤⑥	→	0300⑥⑦
1600①②③④	→	2130①②③④	2330①②③④	→	0300②③④⑤

No foot passengers conveyed on weekend sailings

Condor Ferries by ship — **2009 service (No winter service)**

Sailings from Portsmouth Continental Ferry Port and Cherbourg.

Portsmouth		Cherbourg		Cherbourg		Portsmouth	
0930	→	1430	⑦ May 24 - Sept. 6.	1700	→	2200	⑦ May 24 - Sept. 6.

PORTSMOUTH - LE HAVRE 2165

L D Lines — **2009 service**

Sailings from Portsmouth Continental Ferry Port and Le Havre Quai de Southampton.

Portsmouth		Le Havre		Le Havre		Portsmouth	
1015	→	1645	⑤ Oct. 2 - 30.	1600	→	2045	See note **E**.
1115	→	1745	⑥	1700	→	2130	See note **F**.
1200	→	1830	See note **C**.	2300	→	0615	①②③④⑤
2300	→	0800		2300	→	0700	⑦

C – ①②③④⑤ (not ⑤ Oct. 2 - 30).
E – ⑤⑦ Oct. 2 - Nov. 1; daily Nov. 12 - Dec. 11.
F – Daily except dates in note **E**.
G – ①②③④ (also May 31, June 14, 28, July 12, 26, Aug. 9, 23, Sept. 6).

PORTSMOUTH - OUISTREHAM (CAEN) 2170

Brittany Ferries by ship — **Service to March 15, 2010**
(No service Dec. 25, Jan. 1)

Sailings from Portsmouth Continental Ferry Port and Ouistreham.

Portsmouth		Ouistreham		Ouistreham		Portsmouth	
0730	→	1430	Nov. 1, 5 - 8.	0800	→	1300	See note **D**.
0815	→	1500	See note **C**.	0815	→	1315	Mar. 9, 10.
0830	→	1530	Nov. 2, 3, 9 - 12.	0830	→	1315	See note **G**.
1230	→	1930	Nov. 4 only.	1600	→	2100	Nov. 1, 4 - 8.
1430	→	2130	See note **D**.	1630	→	2115	See note **H**.
1445	→	2130	See note **E**.	1700	→	2200	Nov. 2, 3, 9 - 12.
2245	→	0630	Nov. 1, 4 - 8, Jan. 2.	2300	→	0600	Nov. 4 - 7.
2245	→	0645	See note **F**.	2300	→	0630	See note **J**.
2330	→	0630	Nov. 2, 9 - 11.	2300	→	0700	Nov. 1 - 3, 8 - 11.
2330	→	0645	Nov. 12.				
2330	→	0800	Nov. 3.				

C – ①②③④⑥⑦ Nov. 14 - Mar. 15 (also Jan. 8; not Dec. 24, 26, 31, Jan. 2, 11 - 15, Mar. 8).
D – Nov. 1 - 12 (not Nov. 4).
E – Nov. 13 - Mar. 15 (not Jan. 11 - 14, 31, Mar. 14).
F – Nov. 13 - Mar. 15 (not Dec. 24, 31, Jan. 2, 11 - 14, 31).
G – ①②③④⑥⑦ Nov. 14 - Mar. 15 (not Dec. 26, Jan. 2, 12 - 15, Mar. 9, 10).
H – Nov. 13 - Mar. 15 (not Dec. 24, 31, Jan. 11 - 15, 31).
J – Nov. 12 - Mar. 15 (not Dec. 24, 31, Jan. 11 - 14).

🚌 Ouistreham - Caen station (journey 45 minutes) to connect with most sailings.

Brittany Ferries by fast ferry — **April 1 - September 27, 2009**

Sailings from Portsmouth Continental Ferry Port and Ouistreham. **(No winter service)**

Portsmouth		Ouistreham		Ouistreham		Portsmouth	
0700	→	1145	⑤⑥⑦	1230	→	1500	⑤⑥⑦

PORTSMOUTH - SANTANDER 2175

Brittany Ferries — **Service to March 15, 2010 (No service Nov. 5 - Mar. 14)**

Sailings from Portsmouth Continental Ferry Port and Santander.

Portsmouth		Santander	
1100③	→	1200④	Nov. 4 only.
Santander		**Portsmouth**	
1600①	→	1700②	Nov. 2 only.
1630①	→	1700②	Mar. 15 only.

PORTSMOUTH - ST MALO 2180

Brittany Ferries — **Service to March 15, 2010**

Sailings from Portsmouth Continental Ferry Port and St. Malo Terminal Ferry du Naye.

Portsmouth		St. Malo		St. Malo		Portsmouth	
2030	→	0815	See note **A**.	1030	→	1815	See note **B**.

A – ①②③④⑤⑦ (not Dec. 23 - 26, 30, 31).
B – ①②③④⑤⑥ (not Dec. 24 - 27, 30).

Times may vary owing to tidal conditions.

RAMSGATE - BOULOGNE 2185

Euroferries — **November 14, 2009 - April 30, 2010**

Ramsgate		Boulogne	Boulogne		Ramsgate
0835	→	1050	0730	→	0745
1245	→	1500	1140	→	1155
1655	→	1910	1550	→	1605
2105	→	2320	2000	→	2015

RAMSGATE - OOSTENDE 2190

Transeuropa Ferries — **2009 service**

Conveys passengers with vehicles only

Ramsgate		Oostende		Oostende		Ramsgate	
0700	→	1200	⑥⑦	0800	→	1100	
0800	→	1300	①②③④⑤	1330	→	1630	
1200	→	1700	⑥⑦	1800	→	2100	⑥
1330	→	1830	①②③④⑤	2100	→	2359	①②③④⑤
1830	→	2330		2130	→	0030	⑦

2200 ABERDEEN - KIRKWALL - LERWICK

NorthLink Ferries **2009 service**

Aberdeen		Kirkwall		Kirkwall		Lerwick
January 1 - March 31 and November 1 - December 31						
1700④⑥⑦	→	2300④⑥⑦	→	2345④⑥⑦	→	0730⑤⑦①
1900①②③⑤	→	→	→	→	→	0730②③④⑥
April 1 - October 31						
1700②④⑥⑦	→	2300②④⑥⑦	→	2345②④⑥⑦	→	0730③⑤⑦①
1900①③⑤	→	→	→	→	→	0730②④⑥

Lerwick		Kirkwall		Kirkwall		Aberdeen
January 1 - March 31 and November 1 - December 31						
1730③⑤	→	2300③⑤	→	2345③⑤	→	0700④⑥
1900①②④⑥⑦	→	→	→	→	→	0700②③⑤⑦①
April 1 - October 31						
1730①③⑤	→	2300①③⑤	→	2345①③⑤	→	0700②④⑥
1900②④⑥⑦	→	→	→	→	→	0700③⑤⑦①

Subject to alteration February - April during ship maintenance

A 🚌 transfer service is available Kirkwall - Stromness and v.v. in conjunction with evening sailings.

2220 HARWICH - ESBJERG

DFDS Seaways **2009 service**

Sailings from Harwich International Port and Esbjerg Englandskajen.

Harwich		Esbjerg	
1745	→	1300	③⑤⑦ until May 17; uneven dates May 19 - 31; even dates June 2 - July 30; uneven dates Aug. 1 - 31; even dates Sept. 2 - 20; ③⑤⑦ Sept. 23 - Dec. 20 (also Dec. 22, 28, 30).

Esbjerg		Harwich	
1845	→	1200	②④⑥ until May 16; even dates May 18 - 30; uneven dates June 1 - July 31; even dates Aug. 2 - 30; uneven dates Sept. 1 - 19; ②④⑥ Sept. 22 - Dec. 19 (also Dec. 21, 27, 29).

For rail services from / to London – see Table **204**

2235 HARWICH - HOEK VAN HOLLAND

Stena Line by ship **Service to December 23, 2009 (No service Dec. 24, 25)**

Sailings from Harwich International Port and Hoek van Holland.

Harwich		Hoek		Hoek		Harwich	
0900	→	1630	See note **H**.	1430	→	2000	See note **K**.
1100	→	1815	Jan. 1 only.	2200	→	0630	Not Dec. 31, Mar. 7.
2345	→	0745	See note **J**.				

H – Not Dec. 26, Jan. 1, Mar. 8.
J – Not Dec. 31, Mar. 21 - 24.
K – Not Dec. 26, Mar. 21 - 24.

See Table **15a** for connecting rail services London - Harwich and v.v. and Hoek van Holland - Amsterdam and v.v.

Subject to alteration during Xmas / New Year period

2237 HIRTSHALS - STAVANGER - BERGEN

Fjord Line **Service to December 20, 2009**

Hirtshals		Stavanger		Bergen	Bergen	Stavanger	Hirtshals
0800⑥	→	1930⑥		...	1000⑤	1800⑤	0600⑥
1230④⑦	→	0015⑤①	→	0800⑤①	1230①③	2030①③	0800②④
1430②	→	0200③	→	1000③	...	2100⑥	0830⑦

Subject to alteration during Xmas / New Year period

2240 NORWEGIAN COASTAL SERVICES

Flaggruten **2009 service**

BERGEN - HAUGESUND - KOPERVIK - STAVANGER

Sailings from Bergen Strandkaiterminalen, Haugesund Hurtigbåtterminalen, Kopervik and Stavanger Hurtigbåtterminalen.

Bergen		Haugesund		Kopervik		Stavanger	
...		0640	→	0700	→	0800	①②③④⑤
0730	→	1040	→	1100	→	1200	①②③④⑤
1010	→	1325	→	1350	→	1445	⑥
...		1500	→	1520	→	1620	①②③④⑤
1240	→	1535	→	1600	→	1655	⑦
1615	→	1920	→	1940	→	2040	①②③④⑤
1630	→	1920	→	1945	→	2040	⑦

Stavanger		Kopervik		Haugesund		Bergen	
0720	→	0815	→	0835	→	1130	①②③④⑤
0950	→	1045	→	1110	→	1410	⑥
1200	→	1255	→	1320	→	1605	⑦
1330		1425		1450		...	①②③④⑤
1645	→	1740	→	1805	→	2110	①②③④⑤
1715	→	1810	→	1835	→	2120	⑦
2045	→	2140	→	2210		...	①②③④⑤

Hurtigruten **2009 service**

BERGEN - TRONDHEIM - TROMSØ - KIRKENES

WINTER SERVICE – **January 1 - April 14 and September 15 - December 31**

NORTHBOUND	*arrive*	*depart*	*day*	SOUTHBOUND	*arrive*	*depart*	*day*
Bergen ♣	...	2230	A	Kirkenes	...	1245	A
Florø		0445	B	Vadsø		|	A
Måløy		0730	B	Vardø	1600	1700	A
Ålesund	1200	1500	B	Honningsvåg		0615	B
Molde		1830	B	Hammerfest	1115	1245	B
Kristiansund		2300	B	Tromsø	2345	0130	B/C
Trondheim	0600	1200	C	Finnsnes		0445	C
Rørvik		2115	C	Harstad	0800	0830	C
Brønnøysund		0100	D	Stokmarknes		1515	C
Sandnessjøen		0415	D	Svolvaer	1830	2000	C
Bodø	1230	1500	D	Stamsund		2200	C
Stamsund		1930	D	Bodø	0200	0400	D
Svolvaer	2100	2200	D	Sandnessjøen		1330	D
Stokmarknes		0100	E	Brønnøysund		1700	D
Harstad	0645	0800	E	Rørvik		2130	D
Finnsnes		1145	E	Trondheim	0630	1000	E
Tromsø	1430	1830	E	Kristiansund		1700	E
Hammerfest	0515	0645	F	Molde		2130	E
Honningsvåg	1145	1515	F	Ålesund	2359	0045	E/F
Vardø	0400	0415	G	Måløy		0545	F
Vadsø		0800	G	Florø		0815	F
Kirkenes	0945	...	G	Bergen ♣	1430	...	F

SUMMER SERVICE – **April 15 - September 14**

NORTHBOUND	*arrive*	*depart*	*day*	SOUTHBOUND	*arrive*	*depart*	*day*
Bergen ♣	...	2000	A	Kirkenes	...	1245	A
Florø		0215	B	Vadsø		|	A
Måløy		0430	B	Vardø	1600	1700	A
Ålesund	0845	0930	B	Honningsvåg		0615	B
Geiranger ▲		1330	B	Hammerfest	1115	1245	B
Ålesund		1845	B	Tromsø	2345	0130	B/C
Molde		2200	B	Finnsnes		0445	C
Kristiansund		0145	C	Harstad	0800	0830	C
Trondheim	0815	1200	C	Stokmarknes		1515	C
Rørvik		2115	C	Svolvaer	1830	2000	C
Brønnøysund		0100	D	Stamsund		2200	C
Sandnessjøen		0415	D	Bodø	0200	0400	D
Bodø	1230	1500	D	Sandnessjøen		1330	D
Stamsund		1930	D	Brønnøysund		1700	D
Svolvaer	2100	2200	D	Rørvik		2130	D
Stokmarknes		0100	E	Trondheim	0630	1000	E
Harstad	0645	0800	E	Kristiansund		1700	E
Finnsnes		1145	E	Molde		2130	E
Tromsø	1430	1830	E	Ålesund		|	E
Hammerfest	0515	0645	F	Geiranger		|	E
Honningsvåg	1145	1515	F	Ålesund	2359	0045	E/F
Vardø	0400	0415	G	Måløy		0545	F
Vadsø		0800	G	Florø		0815	F
Kirkenes	0945	...	G	Bergen ♣	1430	...	F

A – 1st day. .... **G** – 7th day.
♣ – Sailings from Bergen Frilenesset.
▲ – Embarkation and disembarkation take place by tender - passengers are required to be at the quay 30 minutes before departure.

Other ports served: Torvik, Nesna, Ørnes, Sortland, Risøyhamn, Skjervøy, Øksfjord, Havøysund, Kjøllefjord, Mehamn, Berlevåg, Båtsfjord.

Nordlandsekspressen **Service to April 5, 2010**

BODØ - SVOLVÆR

Bodø		Svolvær		Svolvær		Bodø	
1715	→	2050	①②③④⑥	0630	→	1000	①②③④⑤⑥
1800	→	2135	⑤	1600	→	1930	⑦
2030	→	2330	⑦				

HELGOLAND (Germany) services 2242

The following services operate:

Route:		Operator:
BÜSUM - HELGOLAND	Summer only	**Reederei Cassen Eils**
CUXHAVEN - HELGOLAND	Summer service	**Förde Reederei Seetouristik**
	Winter service	**Reederei Cassen Eils**
HAMBURG - HELGOLAND	Summer service	**Förde Reederei Seetouristik**
WILHELMSHAVEN - HELGOLAND	Summer only	**A G Ems**

HULL - ROTTERDAM 2245

P & O Ferries **2009 service**

(No service Jan. 1, Dec. 25, 26, Dec. 31)

Sailings from Hull King George Dock and Rotterdam Europoort.

Hull		Rotterdam	Rotterdam		Hull
2100	→	0815	2100	→	0800

🚌 connections (reservation recommended):
Hull railway station (depart 1715) - King George Dock and v.v.
Rotterdam Centraal Station (depart 1700) - Europoort and v.v.
Amsterdam Centraal Station (depart 1700) - Europoort and v.v.

HULL - ZEEBRUGGE 2250

P & O Ferries **2009 service**

(No service Dec. 25, 26, 31)

Sailings from Hull King George Dock and Zeebrugge Leopold II Dam.

Hull		Zeebrugge		Zeebrugge		Hull	
1800	→	0845§	See note **L**.	1800	→	0815◇	See note **N**.
1900	→	0845§	See note **M**.	1900	→	0815◇	See note **P**.

L – Jan. 23, 25, 26, 28, 30, Feb. 1, 3, 5, 7, 9.
M – Not Jan. 22, 24, 27, 29, 31, Feb. 2, 4, 6, 8, 10.
N – Jan. 22, 24, 25, 27, 29, 31, Feb. 2, 4, 6, 8.
P – Not Jan. 21, 23, 26, 28, 30, Feb. 1, 3, 5, 7, 9.
§ – On ⑥⑦ arrive 0930. ◇ – On ⑥⑦ arrive 0900.

🚌 connections (reservation recommended):
Hull railway station (depart 1715) - King George Dock and v.v.
Brugge Station (depart 1730) - Zeebrugge and v.v.

NEWCASTLE - IJMUIDEN (AMSTERDAM) 2255

DFDS Seaways **2009 service**

Sailings from Newcastle International Ferry Terminal, Royal Quays and IJmuiden Felison Terminal.

Newcastle		IJmuiden		IJmuiden		Newcastle	
1700	→	0930	Not Dec. 24, 25, 31.	1730	→	0900	Not Dec. 24, 25, 30.

🚌 connections:
Newcastle rail station - International Ferry Terminal (North Shields) and v.v.
(depart Newcastle station 2½ and 1¼ hours before sailing; depart Ferry Terminal following arrival of ship).
Victoria Hotel Amsterdam (near Centraal station) - IJmuiden and v.v.
(depart hotel every 10 minutes 1530 - 1630; depart Ferry Terminal following arrival of ship).

ROSYTH - ZEEBRUGGE 2277

Norfolk Line **2009 service**

Rosyth		Zeebrugge	Zeebrugge		Rosyth
1700②④⑥	→	1400③⑤⑦	1800①③⑤	→	1300②④⑥

A 🚌 connection operates Rosyth ferry terminal - Inverkeithing railway station and v.v.

SCRABSTER - STROMNESS 2280

NorthLink Ferries **2009 service**

Scrabster		Stromness		Stromness		Scrabster	
0845	→	1015	See note **A**.	0630	→	0800	See note **A**.
1200	→	1330	⑥⑦	0900	→	1030	⑥⑦
1315	→	1445	See note **A**.	1100	→	1230	See note **A**.
1900	→	2030	Daily.	1645	→	1815	Daily.

A – ①②③④⑤ (also ⑥ June 13 - Aug. 15).

ICELAND and the FAEROE ISLANDS 2285

Smyril Line **2009 service**

	arrive	*depart*
	June 13 - August 28	
Hanstholm	1400⑥	1800⑥
Tórshavn	2330⑦	0200①
Hanstholm	0800②	1100②
Tórshavn	1630③	1800③
Seydisfjördur	1000④	1300④
Tórshavn	0430⑤	0730⑤
	August 29 - October 2	
Esbjerg	0900⑥§	1500⑥
Tórshavn	0500①	1400①
Seydisfjördur	0900②	2000③
Tórshavn	1500④	2100④
	October 3 - December 21	
Esbjerg	0900⑥	1500⑥
Tórshavn	0500①	2100④

§ – Arrive 1300 on Aug. 29.

SKAGERRAK, KATTEGAT & SOUTH WEST BALTIC

ÅRHUS - KALUNDBORG 2300

Mols-Linien **by ship** Journey 2 hours 40 minutes **Service to March 26, 2010**

August 31 - October 10

Depart Århus: 0300①②③④⑤, 0700②③④⑤, 0900⑥, 1000⑦, 1100①②③④⑤, 1230 (June 20, Oct. 10 only), 1400⑦, 1500①②③④⑤, 1900①②③④⑤⑦, 2300①②③④⑤⑦.
Depart Kalundborg: 0300②③④⑤, 0700①②③④⑤, 0900 (June 20, Oct. 10 only), 1000⑦, 1100①②③④⑤, 1230⑥, 1400⑦, 1500①②③④⑤, 1900①②③④⑤⑦, 2300①②③④⑤⑦.

October 11 - March 26

Depart Århus: 0300②③④⑤ (also Oct. 12), 0700②③④⑤, 0900 (Oct. 17 only), 1100①②③④⑤ (also Oct. 11, 18), 1500①②③④⑤, 1900①②③④⑤ (also Oct. 11, 18), 2130⑦ (not Oct. 11, 18), 2300①②③④⑤.
Depart Kalundborg: 0300②③④⑤, 0700②③④⑤ (also Oct. 12), 1100①②③④⑤, 1230 (Oct. 17 only), 1500①②③④⑤ (also Oct. 11, 18), 1700⑦ (not Oct. 11, 18), 1900①②③④⑤, 2300①②③④⑤ (also Oct. 11, 18).

Subject to alteration Dec. 21 - Jan. 3, and during other holiday periods

BØJDEN - FYNSHAV 2304

Alstrafikken (Nordic Ferry Services) Journey 50 minutes **2009 service**

Depart Bøjden: 0500 **A**, 0700, 0900, 1000 **S**, 1100, 1200 **S**, 1300, 1400 **S**, 1500, 1600 **S**, 1700, 1900, 2100 **B**.
Depart Fynshav: 0600 **A**, 0800, 1000, 1100 **S**, 1200, 1300 **S**, 1400, 1500 **S**, 1600, 1700 **S**, 1800, 2000, 2200 **B**.

A – ①②③④⑤⑥.
B – ⑦ (daily June 1 - Aug. 31).
S – June 1 - Aug. 31.

Subject to alteration on and around holidays

EBELTOFT - SJÆLLANDS ODDE 2310

Mols-Linien **by catamaran** Journey 65 minutes **2009 service**

Ebeltoft - Sjællands Odde and v.v.: 6 - 13 sailings daily in summer; 5 - 9 in winter.

Subject to alteration during holiday periods

ESBJERG - FANØ 2312

Fanøtrafikken (Nordic Ferry Services) Journey 12 minutes **2009 service**

Departures every 40 minutes (0630 - 1950 from Esbjerg, 0650 - 2010 from Fanø).

Subject to alteration on and around holidays

FREDERIKSHAVN - GÖTEBORG 2320

Stena Line **by ship** **2009 service**

Sailings from Frederikshavn Trafikhavn and Göteborg.

Frederikshavn		Göteborg		Göteborg		Frederikshavn	
			June 29 - August 9				
0345	→	0715		0800	→	1115	Not July 7, 21.
1150	→	1515	Not July 7, 21.	0930	→	1255	
1330	→	1655	See note **S**.	1100	→	1400	See note **S**.
1430	→	1745	See note **S**.	1600	→	1915	
1430	→	1755	See note **T**.	1845	→	2200	
2000	→	2315		2355	→	0315	
2245	→	0215					
			August 10 - 30				
0345	→	0715	Aug. 10 - 15 only.	0800	→	1115	See note **V**.
1150	→	1515	See note **V**.	0930	→	1255	See note **W**.
1430	→	1755	See note **W**.	1600	→	1915	
2000	→	2315		1845	→	2200	①②③④⑤⑦
2245	→	0215	①②③④⑤⑦.	2355	→	0315	Aug. 10 - 14 only.
2245	→	0215					
			August 31 - December 20				
0715	→	1030	⑦	0800	→	1115	See note **R**.
0815	→	1130	Dec. 15 only.	0900	→	1215	See note **Z**.
1150	→	1505	See note **Y**.	1600	→	1915	Not Dec. 14.
1400	→	1715	See note **Z**.	1830	→	2145	①②③④⑤⑦
2000	→	2315	Not Dec. 14.	2355	→	0400	①②③④⑤
2230	→	0200	①②③④⑤⑦.				

R – ⑦ (also Sept. 14, Oct. 19, Nov. 23, Dec. 15).
S – July 4, 11, 18, 20, 25, Aug. 1 only. **T** – Not July 4, 11, 18, 20, 25, Aug. 1.
V – ②③④⑤⑥⑦ (also Aug. 10; not Aug. 11).
W – ①③④⑤⑥⑦ (also Aug. 11).
Y – Sept. 14, Oct. 19, Nov. 23, Dec. 15 only.
Z – Not Sept. 14, Oct. 19, Nov. 23, Dec. 15.

Stena Line **by *HSS* fast ferry** Journey 2 hours **2009 service**

Sailings from Frederikshavn Trafikhavn and Göteborg. **(no winter service)**

June 29 - August 9

Depart Frederikshavn: 0945, 1515 **N**, 1730 **P**, 2030 **N**.
Depart Göteborg: 0700, 1230 **N**, 1500 **P**, 1800 **N**.

August 10 - 30

Depart Frederikshavn: 1000 **L**, 1730 **K**.
Depart Göteborg: 0730 **L**, 1500 **K**,

K – Not Aug. 17 - 20, 24 - 27. **L** – Not Aug. 23, 30.
N – ④⑤⑥⑦ (also July 20 - 22, 27 - 29).
P – June 29 - July 1, July 6 - 8, 13 - 15, Aug. 3 - 5.

2330 GEDSER - ROSTOCK

Scandlines Deutschland — **2009 service**

Sailings from Rostock Überseehafen and Gedser.

Journey 1 hour 45 minutes

Depart Gedser: 0200 **D**, 0230 **D**, 0345 **D**, 0700, 0900, 1100, 1300, 1500, 1700, 1900, 2100, 2315 **D**, 2345 **D**.

Depart Rostock: 0130 **D**, 0215 **D**, 0400 **D**, 0430 **D**, 0600, 0900, 1100, 1300, 1500, 1700, 1900, 2100, 2345 **D**.

D – Not daily – contact operator for details.

Subject to alteration on and around holidays

2335 GÖTEBORG - KIEL

Stena Line — **2009 service**

Sailings from Kiel Schwedenkai and Göteborg. **(No service Dec. 24, 25)**

Göteborg		Kiel	Kiel		Göteborg
1900	→	0900	1900	→	0900

2342 GRENAA - VARBERG

Stena Line Journey 4 - 5½ hours — **2009 service**

Grenaa		Varberg		Varberg		Grenaa	
Until May 17 and September 21 - December 23							
0100	→	0615	①②③④⑤	0900	→	1315	See note **E**.
1425	→	1840	①②③④⑤⑦	1945	→	2400	See note **F**.
May 18 - June 25							
0100	→	0615	Not May 24, 31.	0900	→	1315	
1425	→	1840		1945	→	2400	Not May 23, 30.
June 26 - August 9							
0100	→	0615	June 26 only.	0800	→	1215	
1315	→	1730		1830	→	2245	
2345	→	0415					
August 10 - September 20							
0100	→	0615	See note **G**.	0900	→	1315	Not Sept. 13, 20.
1425	→	1840		1945	→	2400	

E – ①②③④⑤ (also Apr. 12).
F – ①②③④⑤⑦ (not Apr. 10, Dec. 23).
G – Not Aug. 10, Sept. 13, 20.

2345 HELSINGØR - HELSINGBORG

Scandlines Journey 20 minutes — **2009 service**

From Helsingør and Helsingborg: Sailings every 20 minutes 0640 - 2140 (every 30 minutes at other times).

Subject to alteration on and around holidays

2350 HIRTSHALS - KRISTIANSAND

Color Line **by ship** — **2009 service**

Hirtshals		Kristiansand		Kristiansand		Hirtshals	
March 1 - April 13, April 22 - June 25 and August 10 - December 23							
1215	→	1530	See note **H**.	0800	→	1115	See note **H**.
2045	→	2400		1630	→	1945	
April 14 - 21							
2115	→	0030		0800	→	1115	
June 26 - August 9							
0445	→	0800	⑥	0045	→	0400	⑥
0530	→	0845	⑦	0130	→	0445	⑦
0630	→	0945	①	0230	→	0545	①
1215	→	1530	②③④⑤	0800	→	1115	②③④⑤
1315	→	1630	⑥	0900	→	1215	⑥
1415	→	1730	⑦	1000	→	1315	⑦
1445	→	1800	①	1030	→	1345	①
2045	→	2400	②③④⑤ (not July 8).	1630	→	1945	②③④⑤ (not July 8).
2130	→	0045	⑥	1730	→	2045	⑥
2230	→	0145	⑦	1830	→	2145	⑦
2315	→	0230	①	1900	→	2230	①

H – Not Mar. 2, 30, Apr. 27, May 11, 25, June 8, 22, Aug. 17, 31, Sept. 14, 28, Oct. 12, 26, Nov. 9, 23, Dec. 7, 21.

2355 KALUNDBORG - SAMSØ

Samsøtrafikken (Nordic Ferry Services) — **2009 service**

Journey 1 hour 50 minutes

Depart Kalundborg: 0955, 1800, 2225⑦.

Depart Kolby Kås (Samsø): 0740, 1540, 2015⑦.

Subject to alteration during holiday periods

2360 KØBENHAVN - OSLO

DFDS Seaways — **2009 service**

Sailings from København Dampfærgevej and Oslo Vippetangen (Utstikker 2).

København		Oslo	Oslo		København
1700	→	0930	1700	→	0930

2366 LARVIK - HIRTSHALS

Color Line — **2009 service** **(no service Sept. 7 - 10)**

Larvik		Hirtshals		Hirtshals		Larvik	
March 1 - 29							
0800		1145	②③④⑤	0200		0600	⑤
1245		1630	⑥⑦	0800		1145	⑥⑦
1730		2115	①②③④	1245		1630	①②③④⑤
1900	→	2245	⑤	1730	→	2115	⑥⑦
2215		0200	⑥⑦	2215		0200	①②③
March 30 - April 13 and April 22 - December 23							
0800	→	1145	See note **L**.	1245	→	1630	See note **L**.
1730	→	2115	Not July 1.	2215	→	0200	Not July 1.
April 14 - 21							
1645	→	2030		1215	→	1600	

L – ②③④⑤⑥⑦ (also ① June 22 - Aug. 3; Apr. 13, June 1).

2368 OSLO - FREDERIKSHAVN

Stena Line — **2009 service**

Sailings from Oslo Vippetangen and Frederikshavn.

Oslo		Frederikshavn		Frederikshavn		Oslo	
1930	→	0730	See note **F**.	0930	→	1830	See note **J**.
				1000	→	1830	See note **G**.
				1830	→	0730	See note **H**.

F – ②③④⑤⑥⑦ (daily June 19 - Aug. 23).
G – ③④⑤⑥⑦ Jan. 1 - June 18; daily June 19 - Aug. 23.
H – ① Jan. 1 - June 19, Aug. 24 - Dec. 31.
J – ③④⑤⑥⑦ Aug. 24 - Dec. 31.

Subject to alteration during Xmas / New Year period

2372 OSLO - KIEL

Color Line — **2009 service**

Sailings from Oslo Color Line Terminalen, Hjortnes and Kiel Oslo-Kai.

Oslo		Kiel		Kiel		Oslo	
1400	→	1000	See note **K**.	1400	→	1000	See note **L**.

K – Not Apr. 13, 15, 17, 19, 21, May 10, 12.
L – Not Apr. 14, 16, 18, 20, 22, May 11, 13.

🚌 Oslo Color Line Terminal - Oslo Sentral rail station.
Kiel Oslo-Kai - Hamburg ZOB (Central Bus Station).

2375 PUTTGARDEN - RØDBY

Scandlines Deutschland Journey 45 minutes — **2009 service**

Departures every 30 minutes (40 minutes 2215 ⑥⑦ - 0615 ⑦①).

Subject to alteration on and around holidays

2380 ROSTOCK - TRELLEBORG

Scandlines Deutschland — **2009 service**

Sailings from Rostock Überseehafen and Trelleborg.

Journey 5 hours 45 minutes (§ – 7½ hours)

Depart Rostock: 0745②③④⑥⑦, 1500, 2245 §.

Depart Trelleborg: 0730②③④⑥⑦, 1500, 2245 §.

Subject to alteration on and around holidays

TT Line **by ship** — **2009 service**

Sailings from Rostock Überseehafen and Trelleborg.

Rostock		Trelleborg		Trelleborg		Rostock	
0800	→	1345		0800	→	1345	②③④⑤⑥⑦
1530	→	2100	②③④⑤⑥⑦	1530	→	2100	①②③④⑤⑥
2130	→	0530	⑦	1530	→	2200	⑦
2300	→	0600	①②③④⑤⑥	2300	→	0630	
2330	→	0630	⑦				

Subject to alteration during holiday periods

For international shipping maps – see pages 518 - 520

SKAGERRAK, KATTEGAT & SOUTH WEST BALTIC continued

ROSTOCK - VENTSPILS 2382

Scandlines Deutschland — **Service to December 21, 2009**

Sailings from Rostock Überseehafen and Ventspils.
Journey 26 hours

Depart Rostock: 1730②③⑤⑥. Depart Ventspils: 0400②④⑤⑦.

Subject to alteration on and around holidays

SASSNITZ-MUKRAN - RØNNE 2384

Bornholmstrafikken (Nordic Ferry Services) — **2009 service**

Up to 3 sailings per week (daily in summer), journey 3 hours 30 minutes.

SASSNITZ-MUKRAN - TRELLEBORG 2385

Scandlines Deutschland Journey 4 hours — **2009 service**

Sailings from Trelleborg and Fährhafen Sassnitz-Mukran.

Depart Sassnitz-Mukran: 0215, 0745, 1245, 1745, 2230 **A**.
Depart Trelleborg: 0300 **B**, 0745, 1245, 1745, 2230②③④⑤⑥⑦.

A – ⑦ (also ⑤⑥ June 1 - Sept. 6). B – ① (also ⑥⑦ June 1 - Sept. 6).

Subject to alteration on and around holidays

STRÖMSTAD - SANDEFJORD 2387

Color Line Journey 2½ hours — **2009 service**

January 23 - June 18 and August 17 - December 23

Depart Strømstad: 1000 **S**, 1300, 1630 **S**, 1930, 2230②③④⑤⑥⑦ **S**.
Depart Sandefjord: 0700 **S**, 1000, 1300 **S**, 1630, 1930②③④⑤⑥⑦ **S**.

June 19 - August 16

Depart Strømstad: 1000, 1330, 1700, 2000, 2300 (not July 6).
Depart Sandefjord: 0700, 1000, 1330, 1700, 2000 (not July 6).

December 24 - 31

Depart Strømstad: 1000 **T**, 1300 **V**, 1630 **W**, 1930 **W**, 2230 **X**.
Depart Sandefjord: 0700 **T**, 1000 **V**, 1300 **W**, 1630 **W**, 1930 **X**.

S – Not Mar. 30, 31, Apr. 14.
T – Not Dec. 25, 31.
V – Not Dec. 24, 25.
W – Not Dec. 24, 31.
X – Not Dec. 24, 25, 28, 31.

TRAVEMÜNDE - TRELLEBORG 2390

TT Line — **2009 service**

Sailings from Travemünde Skandinavienkai and Trelleborg.

Travemünde		Trelleborg		Trelleborg		Travemünde	
0300	→	1045	②③④⑤⑥	0230	→	1045	②③④⑤
0330	→	1100	①	0630	→	1500	①
1000	→	1715		1000	→	1830	①②③
1430	→	2200	⑤	1000	→	1830 §	④⑤⑥⑦
1645	→	0015	①②③④	1345	→	2100	⑥
2200	→	0730		1715	→	0015	①②③
2300	→	0630	⑥	1715	→	0045	④⑤⑦
				2200	→	0730	

§ – Arrive 1715 June 13 - Aug. 30.

Subject to alteration during holiday periods

🚌 connection available Trelleborg - Malmö railway station and v.v. for certain sailings.

BALTIC SEA

GDAŃSK - NYNÄSHAMN 2402

Polferries — **Service to January 10, 2010**

Gdańsk		Nynäshamn		Nynäshamn		Gdańsk	
1800	→	1200	See note **A**.	1800	→	1200	See note **C**.
1800	→	1300	See note **B**.	1800	→	1300	See note **D**.

A – ①③⑤ Mar. 2 - 13; ①③⑤ Mar. 30 - June 12; uneven dates June 15 - July 31; even dates Aug. 2 - 28; ①③⑤ Aug. 31 - Dec. 11; uneven dates Dec. 13 - 29; even dates Jan. 2 - 10 (not Apr. 10, 13, Dec. 23, 25).
B – ②④⑦ Mar. 1 - June 18; even dates June 20 - July 30; uneven dates Aug. 1 - 27; ②④⑦ Aug. 30 - Dec. 3; even dates Dec. 6 - 20; uneven dates Jan. 5 - 11 (not Apr. 12).
C – ②④⑦ Mar. 1 - 15; ②④⑦ Mar. 31 - June 14; even dates June 16 - July 30; uneven dates Aug. 1 - 27; ②④⑦ Aug. 30 - Dec. 3; even dates Dec. 6 - 30; uneven dates Dec. 3 - 11 (not Apr. 12, 14, Dec. 24, 26).
D – ①③⑤ Mar. 2 - June 19; uneven dates June 21 - July 31; even dates Aug. 2 - 28; ①③⑤ Aug. 31 - Dec. 4; uneven dates Dec. 7 - 21; even dates Jan. 6 - 10 (not Apr. 13).

GRISSLEHAMN - ECKERÖ 2405

Eckerö Linjen Journey 2 hours — **Service to January 10, 2010** **(No service Dec. 24,25)**

May 1 - August 30

Depart Grisslehamn: 1000, 1500, 2000.
Depart Eckerö: 0830, 1330, 1830.

August 31 - January 10

Depart Grisslehamn: 1000 (not Jan. 1), 1500, 2000④⑤⑥⑦ (not Dec. 31).
Depart Eckerö: 0830①⑤⑥⑦ (not Jan. 1), 1330, 1830.

🚌 connections: Stockholm Cityterminalen (near Central station) - Grisslehamn and v.v. (departing 2 hours before ship departure).
Eckerö - Mariehamn and v.v. (departing 1 hour before ship departure).

HELSINKI - TALLINN 2410

Eckerö Line by ship — **2009 service** **(No service Dec. 24, 25, 31)**

Sailings from Helsinki Länsiterminaali and Tallinn A-terminal.

Helsinki		Tallinn		Tallinn		Helsinki	
0800	→	1100	①②③④⑤	1600	→	1930	⑦
0800	→	1130	⑥	1700	→	2030	①②③④⑤⑥
1030	→	1330	⑦				

Linda Line Oy by hydrofoil — **April 2 - September 27, 2009**

Linda Line Express Journey 1 hour 30 minutes
Sailings from Helsinki Makasiiniterminaali and Tallinn Linnahalli.

April 2 - June 24 and August 17 - September 27

Depart Helsinki: 0800①②③④⑤⑥, 1000, 1200, 1500⑤⑦, 1700, 1900, 2100⑤⑦.
Depart Tallinn: 0800①②③④⑤⑥, 1000①②③④⑤⑥, 1200⑤⑥⑦, 1500①②③④⑤⑦, 1700, 1900, 2100⑤⑥⑦.

June 25 - August 16

Depart Helsinki: 0800①②③④⑤⑥, 1000, 1200, 1400①②③④⑤⑥, 1500⑦, 1700, 1900, 2100.
Depart Tallinn: 0800①②③④⑤⑥, 1000, 1200①②③④⑤⑥, 1300⑦, 1500, 1700, 1900, 2100.

Services operate during the ice-free period only (generally from mid-April to November/December)

continued

Tallink by ship — **Service to December 23, 2009**

Sailings from Helsinki Länsiterminaali and Tallinn D-terminal.

Helsinki		Tallinn	Notes	Tallinn		Helsinki	Notes
0730	→	0930	①②③④⑤	0730	→	0930	See note **V**.
0830	→	1030	⑥	1100	→	1300	①②③④⑤⑦
1030	→	1230		1130	→	1330	⑥
1430	→	1630	Not Aug. 4.	1300	→	1630	See note **T**.
1730	→	1930	Not Aug. 4.	1400	→	1600	
1830	→	2200	See note **W**.	1730	→	1930	
2200	→	2400		2100	→	2300	Not Aug. 4.

T – Not June 7, 8, July 25, 26, Aug. 4, 5, Sept. 5, 15, 27.
V – ①②③④⑤⑥ (not Aug. 5).
W – Not June 6,7, July 24 - 26, Aug. 4.

Subject to alteration during Xmas/New Year period

Viking Line by ship Journey 2½ hours — **2009 service**

Sailings from Helsinki Katajanokka terminal and Tallinn A-terminal.

Depart Helsinki: 1130, 2000⑦, 2130①②③④⑤⑥.
Depart Tallinn: 0800, 1630⑦, 1800①②③④⑤⑥.

Variations: last departure before Xmas 1800 from Tallinn Dec. 23;
first departure after Xmas 1130 from Helsinki Dec. 26.

KARLSKRONA - GDYNIA 2415

Stena Line — **2009 service**

Karlskrona		Gdynia		Gdynia		Karlskrona	
Until June 21 and August 31 - December 13							
0900	→	1930	②③④⑥⑦	0900	→	1930	②③④⑥⑦
1930	→	0730	⑤	1930	→	0730	①
2030	→	0730	⑥	2000	→	0730	⑤
2030	→	0830	⑦	2100	→	0730	②③⑥⑦
2100	→	0730	①②③④	2100	→	0900	④
June 22 - August 30							
0900	→	1930		0900	→	1930	
2100	→	0730		2100	→	0730	

Subject to alteration Apr. 6 - 13

KIEL - KLAIPEDA 2420

DFDS Lisco — **Service to December 21, 2009**

Sailings from Kiel Ostuferhafen and Klaipeda International Ferry Port.

Kiel		Klaipeda	Klaipeda		Kiel
1400①	→	1200②	1500①	→	1100②
1600②	→	1400③	1700②	→	1300③
1800③	→	1600④	1900③	→	1500④
2000④	→	1800⑤	2100④	→	1700⑤
2200⑤	→	2000⑥	2300⑤	→	1900⑥
2300⑥	→	2100⑦	0100⑦	→	2100⑦

Subject to alteration during Xmas/New Year period

2430 KØGE - RØNNE

Bornholmstrafikken (Nordic Ferry Services) — **Service to January 4, 2010**

Køge		Rønne		Rønne		Køge	
0800	→	1345	See note **K**.	1430	→	2030	See note **K**.
2330	→	0600		2330	→	0600	

K – ① June 15 - 22; ①⑥⑦ June 27 - Aug. 16; ① Aug. 17 - Sept. 7 (also Apr. 2, 8, 16, 23, 30, May 7, 14, 20, 28; not June 27, 28, Aug. 15, 16).

2445 NYNÄSHAMN - VISBY

Destination Gotland — **Service to January 11, 2010**

Nynäshamn		Visby		Visby		Nynäshamn	
			August 25 - October 12				
0900	→	1220	①	0705	→	1025	①②③④⑤⑥
1105	→	1425	①②③④⑤⑥	0805	→	1120	⑦
1200	→	1515	⑦	1255	→	1555	⑤
1630	→	1930	⑤	1600	→	1915	⑤⑥⑦
2005	→	2320	⑤⑥⑦	1645	→	2000	①②③④
2105	→	0020	①②③④	1920	→	2235	⑦
			October 13 - November 5				
1105	→	1425	See note **V**.	0705	→	1025	①②③④⑤⑥
1200	→	1515	⑦	0805	→	1120	⑦
2005	→	2320	See note **W**.	1600	→	1915	⑤⑦ (not Nov. 1).
2105	→	0020	See note **X**.	1645	→	2000	①②③④ (also Nov. 1).
			November 6 - January 11				
1105	→	1425	See note **Y**.	0705	→	1025	See note **P**.
1200	→	1515	⑦ (also Jan. 1, 6).	0805	→	1120	See note **N**.
2005	→	2320	See note **Z**.	1600	→	1915	⑤⑦ (also Jan. 6).
2105	→	0020	See note **Q**.	1645	→	2000	See note **Q**.

N – ⑦ (also Dec. 26, Jan. 1, 6)
P – ①③④⑤⑥ (not Dec. 24 - 26, 31, Jan. 1, 6).
Q – ①②③④ (not Dec. 24, 31, Jan. 6).
V – ①②③④⑤ (also Oct. 31).
W – ⑤⑥⑦ (not Oct. 31, Nov. 1).
X – ①②③④ (also Nov. 1).
Y – ①③④⑤ (also Dec. 12; not Dec. 24, 25, 31, Jan. 1, 6).
Z – ⑤⑥⑦ (also Jan. 6; not Dec. 12).

Subject to alteration during Easter and Xmas / New Year periods

🚌 service Stockholm Cityterminalen - Nynäshamn connects with most sailings.

2448 NYNÄSHAMN - VENTSPILS

Scandlines — **Service to December 21, 2009**

Journey 11 hours

Depart Nynäshamn: 0830⑦, 1030①, 1900②, 2200⑤, 2230③.
Depart Ventspils: 0030②, 0930③, 1800⑥, 2030④, 2330⑦.

2450 OSKARSHAMN - VISBY

Destination Gotland — **Service to January 11, 2010**

Oskarshamn		Visby		Visby		Oskarshamn	
			August 23 - October 12				
1100	→	1400	③	0720	→	1020	③⑥
1540	→	1835	⑦	1200	→	1455	⑦
1910	→	2210	⑥	1705	→	2000	①②③④⑤
2110	→	2350	⑦	1735	→	2015	⑦
2110	→	0005	①②④⑤				
2115	→	0010	③				
			October 13 - January 11				
1100	→	1400	See note **B**.	0720	→	1020	See note **A**.
1910	→	2210	See note **C**.	1705	→	2000	See note **E**.
2110	→	0005	See note **D**.				
2115	→	0010	③				

A – ③ (also Oct. 17, 24, Dec. 19, 26, Jan. 2, 9; not Dec. 23, Jan. 6).
B – ③ (also Oct. 31; not Dec. 23, Jan. 6).
C – Oct. 17, 24, Dec. 19, 26, Jan. 2, 9.
D – ①②④⑤⑦ (not Dec. 24, 31).
E – ①②③④⑤⑦ (not Dec. 24, 31).

Subject to alteration during Easter and Xmas / New Year periods

2451 ROSTOCK - HELSINKI

Tallink Journey 23 - 24 hours — **2009 service**

Sailings from Rostock Überseehafen and Helsinki Vuosaari▲.

Rostock		Helsinki	Helsinki		Rostock
0500③④⑥⑦	→	0800④⑤⑦①	2100①②④⑤	→	2300②③⑤⑥

No departures from Helsinki Dec. 24, 25; from Rostock Dec. 26, 27.

▲ – 🚌 connection (number 90 B) from Tallink terminal to Helsinki Vuosaari metro station for onward journeys to Helsinki centre (Rautatientori metro station).

2453 SASSNITZ-MUKRAN - KLAIPEDA

DFDS Lisco — **Service to December 20, 2009**

Sailings from Sassnitz Fahrhafen and Klaipeda International Ferry Port.

Sassnitz-Mukran		Klaipeda	Klaipeda		Sassnitz-Mukran
1600⑥	→	1100⑦	1600⑦	→	1000①

2455 SASSNITZ-MUKRAN - BALTISK

DFDS Lisco — **Service to September 30, 2009**

Sailings from Sassnitz Fahrhafen and Baltisk Ferry Terminal.

Sassnitz-Mukran		Baltisk	Baltisk		Sassnitz-Mukran
1700③	→	1000④	1800④	→	1000⑤

2460 ŚWINOUJŚCIE - RØNNE

Polferries — **July 4 - August 29, 2009 (No winter service)**

Świnoujście		Rønne	Rønne		Świnoujście
1000⑥	→	1515⑥	1730⑥	→	2245⑥

2462 ŚWINOUJŚCIE - KØBENHAVN

Polferries — **Service to January 11, 2010**

Świnoujście		København	København		Świnoujście
		March 1 - June 24 and August 20 - January 11			
2000②④⑥§	→	0800③⑤⑦	1000⑦	→	1900⑦
2100⑦	→	0800①	2000①③⑤	→	0800②④⑥
		June 25 - August 19			
1000④⑤	→	1900④⑤	1000⑦	→	1900⑦
2000②	→	0800③	2000①③	→	0800②④
2100⑦	→	0800①	2100④⑤	→	0800⑤⑥
2330⑥	→	0830⑦			

§ – Depart 2330 Aug. 22, 29.

No departure from Świnoujście Apr. 11, Dec. 24, 26, 31; from København Apr. 12, Dec. 25, 27, Jan. 1

2464 STOCKHOLM - RIGA

Tallink — **2009 service**

Sailings from Stockholm Frihamnterminalen and Riga passenger port.

Stockholm		Riga	Riga		Stockholm
1700	→	1100	1730	→	0930

2465 STOCKHOLM - MARIEHAMN - HELSINKI

Silja Line — **2009 service**

Sailings from Stockholm Värtahamnen and Helsinki Olympiaterminaali.

Stockholm		Mariehamn		Helsinki		Helsinki		Mariehamn		Stockholm	
1600	→	2355	→	1400	Dec. 24.	1600	→	0425	→	1200	Dec. 24.
1700	→	2355	→	0955	Note **B**.	1700	→	0400	→	0900	May 29.
1700	→	2355	→	1100	Dec. 25.	1700	→	0425	→	0930	Note **A**.
2100	→	0355	→	1330	May 30.						

A – Not Not Dec. 24, May 29.
B – Not Dec. 24, 25, May 30.

🚌 Stockholm Värtahamnen - Ropsten metro station (for Stockholm Centralen).

Viking Line — **2009 service (No service Dec. 24, 25)**

Sailings from Stockholm Stadsgården and Helsinki Katajanokka.

Stockholm		Mariehamn		Helsinki		Helsinki		Mariehamn		Stockholm	
1645	→	2345	→	0945	Note **A**.	1730	→	0435	→	0940	Note **B**.

A – Not Sept. 7, 9, 11, 13, 15, 17. **B** – Not Sept. 6, 8, 10, 12, 14, 16.

Connections:
🚌 Stockholm Cityterminalen (near Central station) - Slussen metro station - Viking Line terminal. Tram no. 4T runs daily from Helsinki city centre to the Viking Line Terminal.

2470 (STOCKHOLM -) KAPELLSKÄR - MARIEHAMN

Viking Line Sailings from Kapellskär and Mariehamn. — **2009 service (No service Dec. 24 - 26)**

Stockholm (*by* 🚌)		Kapellskär		Mariehamn		Mariehamn		Kapellskär		Stockholm (*by* 🚌)	
				June 1 - August 30							
0710♦	→	0900	→	1200	Note **K**.	0730	→	0830	→	*1000*♦	Note **K**.
1310♦	→	1500	→	1800		1245	→	1400	→	*1530*♦	
1810♦	→	2000	→	2300	Note **L**.	1830	→	1930	→	*2100*♦	Note **L**.
				August 31 - December 31							
0710♦	→	0900	→	1200	⑤⑥	0730	→	0830	→	*1000*♦	⑤⑥
1010♦	→	1200	→	1530	①②③④	0800	→	0915	→	*1045*♦	①②③④
1210♦	→	1400	→	1730	⑦	1200	→	1315	→	*1445*♦	⑦
1310♦	→	1500	→	1800	⑤⑥	1245	→	1400	→	*1530*♦	⑤⑥
1710♦	→	1900	→	2200	①②③④	1600	→	1730	→	*1900*♦	①②③④
1810♦	→	2000	→	2300	⑤⑥⑦	1830	→	1930	→	*2100*♦	⑤⑥⑦

K – Not June 20. **L** – Not June 19.

Variations: no service Dec. 24, 25, 26. Last sailing before Xmas 1900 on Dec. 23.

♦ – Connecting 🚌 service from / to Stockholm Cityterminalen (near Central station).

2475 STOCKHOLM - TALLINN

Tallink — **2009 service**

Sailings from Stockholm Värtahamnen and Tallinn D-terminal.

Stockholm		Mariehamn		Tallinn	Tallinn		Mariehamn		Stockholm
1745	→	0100	→	1000	1800	→	0500	→	1000

For international shipping maps – see pages 518 - 520

BALTIC SEA continued

STOCKHOLM - TURKU via Mariehamn / Långnäs — 2480

Silja Line — **2009 service**

Sailings from Stockholm Värtahamnen and Turku.

Stockholm		Mariehamn ⊡		Långnäs §		Turku	
0710	→	1345	→	→	→	1915	See note **A**.
1930	→	→	→	0255	→	0700	See note **B**.

Turku		Långnäs §		Mariehamn		Stockholm	
0815	→	→	→	1345	→	1815	See note **C**.
2015	→	0045	→	→	→	0610	See note **D**.

A – Not Sept. 21 - 27, Dec. 24 - 26, 31, Jan. 1, 2.
B – Not Oct. 6, Dec. 23 - 25.
C – Not Oct. 6, Dec. 24 - 26.
D – Not Sept. 20 - 26, Dec. 23 - 25, 31, Jan. 1.

§ – Långnäs is 28km from Mariehamn. ⊡ – No sailings May 28 - June 5.

Nearest metro station to Stockholm Värtahamnen is Gärdet (for Stockholm Centralen).

Viking Line — **2009 service**

Sailings from Stockholm Stadsgården and Turku Linnansatama. **(No service Dec. 24, 25)**

Stockholm		Mariehamn		Långnäs §		Turku	
0745	→	1425	→	→	→	1950	Not Sept. 22 - 24.
2010	→	→	→	0330	→	0735	Not Sept. 22 - 24.

Turku		Långnäs §		Mariehamn		Stockholm	
0845	→	→	→	1425	→	1855	Not Sept. 22 - 24.
2100	→	0110	→	→	→	0630	Not Sept. 21 - 23.

§ – Långnäs is 28km from Mariehamn.

🚌 connections: Stockholm Cityterminalen (near Central station) - Slussen metro station - Viking Line terminal; Turku city centre - harbour (bus no. 1).

TRAVEMÜNDE - HELSINKI — 2485

Finnlines Deutschland — **2009 service**

Sailings from Travemünde Skandinavienkai and Helsinki Hansaterminaali.

Travemünde		Helsinki	Helsinki		Travemünde
0300②③④⑤⑦	→	0645③④⑤⑥①	1500⑦	→	0700②
0300⑥	→	0700⑦	1800①②③④⑤⑥	→	2000②③④⑤⑥⑦
1500⑦	→	0645②	2200②⑤	→	0700④⑦
1900③	→	0645⑤			
1900⑤	→	0700⑦			

TRAVEMÜNDE - RIGA — 2487

DFDS Lisco — **2009 service**

Sailings from Travemünde Skandinavienkai and Riga Vecmilgravis.

Travemünde		Riga	Riga		Travemünde
2100③	→	0800⑤	0200②	→	1100③
1000⑦	→	2100①	2100⑤	→	0600⑦

VAASA - UMEÅ (HOLMSUND) — 2490

R G Line — **Service to December 23, 2009**

Vaasa		Umeå		Umeå		Vaasa	
0800	→	1130	⑦	0800	→	1330	③
0900	→	1230	④⑤ (not Oct. 16).	0900	→	1430	①②
1500	→	1830	③	1300	→	1830	⑦
2000	→	2330	①②⑦	1800	→	2330	④⑤ (not Oct. 16).
				2000	→	0130	③

Subject to alteration during Xmas / New Year and Easter periods

YSTAD - RØNNE — 2494

Bornholmstrafikken (Nordic Ferry Services) by fast ferry — **2009 service**

Up to 5 sailings daily, journey 75 minutes.

See Table **727** for rail connections Ystad - København and v.v.

Bornholmstrafikken (Nordic Ferry Services) by ship — **2009 service**

Up to 3 sailings daily, journey 2 hours 30 minutes.

See Table **727** for rail connections Ystad - København and v.v.

YSTAD - ŚWINOUJŚCIE — 2495

Polferries — **Service to January 11, 2010** **(No service Dec. 24, 25, 31, Jan. 1)**

Ystad		Świnoujście		Świnoujście		Ystad	
1400	→	2030	Not Apr. 11, 12, Dec. 26, Jan. 2.	2330	→	0630	Not Apr. 10, 11, Dec. 23, 30.

Unity Line — **2009 service** **(No service Dec. 24, 25, 31)**

Ystad		Świnoujście	Świnoujście		Ystad
1330	→	2000	1300	→	1945
2200	→	0700	2300	→	0700

A connecting 🚌 service operates Świnoujście terminal - Szczecin Hotel Radisson SAS and v.v.: Świnoujście depart 0730, Szczecin arrive 0900. Return journey Szczecin depart 1000, Świnoujście arrive 1130.

WESTERN MEDITERRANEAN

ALGECIRAS - CEUTA — 2500

Baleària (Eurolínies Marítimes) by fast ferry — **Service to November 2, 2009**

Journey 30 minutes

Depart Algeciras: 0700, 1000, 1300, 1600, 1900, 2200.
Depart Ceuta: 0830, 1130, 1430, 1730, 2030, 2330.

Trasmediterranea by fast ferry Journey 45 mins. — **2009 service**

Subject to alteration at Easter and Christmas

Depart Algeciras: 0600, 0800, 0900, 1100, 1200, 1400, 1500, 1700, 1800, 2000, 2100.
Depart Ceuta: 0730, 0930, 1030, 1230, 1330, 1530, 1630, 1830, 1930, 2130, 2230.

ALGECIRAS - TANJAH (TANGIERS) — 2502

Nautas Ferry Journey 90 minutes — **2009 service**

From Algeciras: 0900, 1330, 1730. From Tanjah: 1030, 1430, 1830.

Trasmediterranea (& associated operators) Journey 2½ hours — **2009 service**

From Algeciras and Tanjah: Up to 4 departures daily in winter (additional services in summer). Also 2 – 4 sailings by hydrofoil.

ALMERÍA - MELILLA — 2505

Trasmediterranea Journey 6 - 8 hours — **2009 service**

Until October 31

Depart Almería: 1630①, 2359②③④⑤⑥⑦.
Depart Melilla: 0900①, 1200②③④⑥⑦, 1430⑤.

November 1 - December 31

Depart Almería: 1630①, 2359②③④⑤⑥⑦.
Depart Melilla: 0900①, 1430②③④⑤⑥⑦

Additional sailings by fast ferry in summer (journey 3 hours)

Subject to alteration during Easter and Xmas / New Year periods

ALMERÍA - AN-NADÛR (NADOR) — 2507

Ferrimaroc / Trasmediterranea Journey 5 - 10 hours — **2009 service**

From Almería and an-Nadûr: 1 – 3 sailings daily, departure times vary.

BARCELONA - TANJAH (TANGIERS) — 2508

Grandi Navi Veloci — **2009 service**

Barcelona		Tanjah	Tanjah		Barcelona
1400⑦	→	1430①	2355①	→	0830③

BALEARIC ISLANDS (see map page 317) — 2510

Trasmediterranea — **2009 service**

BARCELONA - EIVISSA (IBIZA) by ship Journey 8 - 9 hours

Depart Barcelona: **until Sept. 13**: 0930④⑦, 1200⑥, 2230②; **Sept. 15 - Oct. 10** 2300②④⑤⑥; **Oct. 13 - 31**: 2230②④, 2300⑤⑥; **Nov. 3 - Dec. 19**: 2300②④⑤⑥.
Depart Eivissa: **until Sept. 13**: 1030③, 1900④⑦, 2200⑥; **Sept. 16 - Dec. 20**: 1030③⑤, 1900⑥⑦.

BARCELONA - MAÓ (MAHÓN) by ship Journey 8 - 9 hours

Depart Barcelona: **June 15 - Sept. 13**: 2230①③④⑤⑥⑦; **Sept. 14 - Oct. 9**: 2300①③⑤; **Oct. 12 - 28**: 2230①③; **Nov. 2 - Dec. 18**: 2300①③⑤.
Depart Maó: **June 16 - Sept. 13**: 1100①②④⑤⑥⑦; **Sept. 15 - Oct. 10**: 1130②④⑥; **Oct. 13 - 29**: 1100②④; **Nov. 3 - Dec. 19**: 1130②④⑥.

BARCELONA - PALMA by ship Journey 6½ - 8½ hours

Depart Barcelona: **Apr. 14 - Dec. 20**: 2300.
Depart Palma: **Apr. 14 - Sept. 13**: 1230⑥, 2330①②③④⑤⑦; **Sept. 14 - Dec. 20**: 1230①②③④⑤, 2330⑥⑦.

PALMA - EIVISSA (IBIZA) by ship Journey 4 - 5 hours

Depart Palma: **Sept. 19 - Dec. 20**: 0900⑥⑦, 1045⑥.
Depart Eivissa: **until Sept. 13**: 1900④⑦; **Sept. 19 - Dec. 20**: 1900⑥⑦.

PALMA - MAÓ (MAHÓN) by ship Journey 5½ hours

Depart Palma: **Sept. 6 - Dec. 20**: 0800⑦.
Depart Maó: **Sept. 6 - Dec. 20**: 1730⑦.

VALÈNCIA - MAÓ (MAHÓN) via Palma by ship Journey 14 - 15 hours

Depart València: **Sept. 5 - Dec. 19**: 2300⑥.
Depart Maó: **Sept. 6 - Dec. 20**: 1730⑦.

VALÈNCIA - PALMA by ship Journey 8 hours

Depart València: **Sept. 12 - Dec. 19**: 2300①②③④⑤⑥.
Depart Palma: **June 15 - Sept. 13**: 1145②③④⑤⑥, 2359⑦; **Sept. 15 - Dec. 20**: 1045⑥, 1145②③④⑤, 2359⑦.

VALÈNCIA - SANT ANTONI (IBIZA) by catamaran Journey 3 - 3½ hours

Depart València: **until Sept. 13**: 1530⑤⑦.
Depart Sant Antoni: **until Sept. 13**: 1030⑤⑦.

continued

Baleària (Eurolínies Marítimes) — Service to January 12, 2010

DÉNIA - EIVISSA (IBIZA) - PALMA by fast ferry

Dénia		Eivissa		Palma		Palma		Eivissa		Dénia	
1700	→	1900/2000	→	2200	Note A.	0800	→	1000/1100	→	1300	Note A.
2100	→	0115/0200	→	0700	Note B.	0930	→	1345/1500	→	1915	Note C.
...		0245	→	0645	Note D.	1000	→	1400		...	Note D.

A – Daily until Jan. 11 (not Nov. 3 - Dec. 3).
B – ①②③④⑥ until Jan. 12. C – ②③④⑤⑦ until Jan. 12.
D – ①⑥ until Jan. 12.

OTHER SERVICES:

Dénia - Sant Antoni and v.v.: 1–2 sailings daily, journey 4 hours.
València - Palma and v.v.: 1 sailing daily except ②, journey 6½ hours by fast ferry (some services via Eivissa).

2512 CANARY ISLANDS

Lineas Fred. Olsen — 2009 services

CORRALEJO (FUERTEVENTURA) - PLAYA BLANCA (LANZAROTE) Journey 30 mins.
Depart Corralejo: 0745①②③④⑤, 0900, 1100, 1330①②③④⑤, 1500, 1700, 1900.
Depart Playa Blanca: 0710①②③④⑤, 0830, 1000, 1230①②③④⑤, 1400, 1600, 1800.

LOS CRISTIANOS (TENERIFE) - SANTA CRUZ (PALMA) Journey 5 hours
Depart Los Cristianos: 1930①②③④⑤⑦. Depart Santa Cruz: 0600①②③④⑤⑥.

LOS CRISTIANOS (TENERIFE) - VALVERDE (EL HIERRO)
Depart Los Cristianos: 1200②⑤⑦. Depart Valverde: 1500②⑤⑦.

SAN SEBASTIÁN (GOMERA) - LOS CRISTIANOS (TENERIFE) Journey 30 mins.
Depart San Sebastián: 0730, 0800, 1030②⑤⑥⑦, 1130, 1230①③④, 1650, 1700.
Depart Los Cristianos: 0830, 0900, 1200②⑤⑦, 1330①③④⑥, 1400, 1830, 1930.

SANTA CRUZ (TENERIFE) - AGAETE (GRAN CANARIA) Journey 60 minutes
Departures from Santa Cruz and Agaete: 0700①②③④⑤, 0900, 1300①②③④⑤, 1600, 1800, 1930.

Naviera Armas — 2009 services

Corralejo (Fuerteventura) - Playa Blanca (Lanzarote) and v.v.	5-7 sailings daily.
Las Palmas (Gran Canaria) - Arrecife (Lanzarote) and v.v.	5 sailings per week.
Las Palmas (Gran Canaria) - Morro Jable (Fuerteventura) and v.v.	1 sailing daily.
Las Palmas (G. Canaria) - Puerto del Rosario (Fuerteventura) and v.v.	3 sailings per week.
Las Palmas (Gran Canaria) - Santa Cruz (La Palma) and v.v.	2 sailings per week.
Las Palmas (Gran Canaria) - Santa Cruz (Tenerife) and v.v.	1-3 sailings daily.
Los Cristianos - San Sebastián Gomera and v.v.	1-3 sailings daily.
Santa Cruz (La Palma) - Arrecife (Lanzarote) and v.v.	1 sailing per week.
Santa Cruz (Tenerife) - Arrecife (Lanzarote) and v.v.	5 sailings per week.
Santa Cruz (Tenerife) - Santa Cruz (La Palma) and v.v.	3 sailings per week.
Santa Cruz (Tenerife) - Valverde and v.v.	3 sailings per week.

Other inter-Island services operate

Trasmediterranea — Service to December 18, 2009

CÁDIZ - GRAN CANARIA - TENERIFE - PALMA - LANZAROTE - CÁDIZ

	arrive	*depart*
Cádiz	1000①	1700②
Lanzarote (Arrecife)	2300③	0130④
Gran Canaria (Las Palmas)	0800④	1400④
Tenerife (Santa Cruz)	1800④	2330④
Palma (Santa Cruz)	0800⑤	1800⑤
Tenerife (Santa Cruz)	2330⑤	1100⑥
Gran Canaria (Las Palmas)	1430⑥	1630⑥
Lanzarote (Arrecife)	2300⑥	0005⑦

OTHER SUMMER SERVICES:

Las Palmas - Morro Jable and v.v.	2-7 sailings per week by hydrofoil.
Santa Cruz Tenerife - Morro Jable and v.v.	2-7 sailings per week by hydrofoil.
San Sebastián Gomera - Los Cristianos and v.v.	3-4 sailings daily by hydrofoil, 1-2 sailings daily by ferry.
Valverde - Los Cristianos and v.v.	1-6 sailings per week.
Santa Cruz Tenerife - Las Palmas and v.v.	up to 3 sailings daily.
Santa Cruz Tenerife - Santa Cruz Palma and v.v.	1 sailing per week.

2520 CIVITAVECCHIA - BARCELONA

Grimaldi Lines — 2009 service

Civitavecchia		Barcelona		Barcelona		Civitavecchia	
2215	→	1715	See note X.	2215	→	1715	See note X.

X – ①②③④⑤⑥ (daily July 20 - Sept. 5).

2523 CIVITAVECCHIA - PALERMO

SNAV — May 27 - September 12, 2009 (No winter service)

Civitavecchia		Palermo	Palermo		Civitavecchia
1900	→	0900	1900	→	0800

2525 CIVITAVECCHIA - TOULON

Grimaldi Lines — 2009 service

Civitavecchia		Toulon		Toulon		Civitavecchia	
2100	→	1230	①③⑤	1800	→	0930	⑥
				2100	→	1230	②④

2530 CIVITAVECCHIA - PALERMO - TÛNIS

Grimaldi Navi Veloci — 2009 service

Civitavecchia		Palermo		Tûnis		Palermo		Civitavecchia
2000①③	→	0800②④		...		2000②④	→	0800③⑤
2000⑤	→	0800/1100⑥	→	2000/2300⑥	→	1000/2000⑦	→	0800①

Grimaldi Ferries — 2009 service

Civitavecchia		Tûnis	Tûnis		Civitavecchia
2359③	→	1500④	2130②	→	1600③

2537 GENOVA - BARCELONA

Grandi Navi Veloci — 2009 service

Genova		Barcelona		Barcelona		Genova	
1800	→	1200	⑥	1500	→	0900	③
2000	→	1400	See note G.	2000	→	1400	See note J.
2115	→	1515	See note H.	2115	→	1515	②④ (not Dec. 24).
				2355	→	1755	⑥ (not May 23).

G – ④ Apr. 30 - May 14, Nov. 5 - Dec. 17.
H – ①③⑤ (not May 22, Dec. 25).
J – ⑤ Apr. 24 - May 15, Nov. 6 - Dec. 18.

2547 GENOVA - PALERMO

Grandi Navi Veloci — 2009 service (No service Dec. 24, 25)

Genova		Palermo		Palermo		Genova	
2100	→	1700	See note P.	2100	→	1700	See note P.
2200	→	1800	See note Q.	2200	→	1800	See note Q.

P – June 15 - Sept. 12; ①②③④⑤⑥ Sept. 14 - Oct. 3 (not June 21, Aug. 16).
Q – ①②③④⑤⑥ Apr. 27 - June 13, Oct. 5 - Dec. 30.

2554 GENOVA - TANJAH (TANGIERS)

Grandi Navi Veloci — 2009 service

Genova		Tanjah	Tanjah		Genova
1800⑥	→	1430①	2355①	→	0830④

All sailings via Barcelona (see Table **2508**)

2555 GENOVA - TÛNIS

Compagnie Tunisienne de Navigation / S N C M — 2009 service

Departure times vary. Journey 20-24 hours

From Genova: Apr. 4, 11, 18, 25, May 2, 9, 16, 23, 30, June 6, 13, 18, 20, 22, 23, 25, 27, 30, July 2, 3, 4, 8, 11, 12, 15, 16, 18, 20, 21, 25, 27, 30, 31, Aug. 1, 3, 6, 8, 11, 14, 15, 16, 19, 22, 26, 29, 30, Sept. 2, 4, 5, 7, 10, 12, 13, 16, 19, 26, 28, Oct. 3, 10, 17, 24, 31, Nov. 7, 14, 21, 24, 28, Dec. 5, 12, 19, 21, 26, 28.

From Tûnis: Apr. 3, 10, 17, 24, May 1, 8, 15, 22, 29, June 5, 12, 17, 19, 20, 22, 24, 26, 29, July 1, 3, 7, 10, 11, 14, 16, 17, 20, 24, 26, 29, 31, Aug. 2, 7, 10, 12, 14, 15, 18, 21, 24, 25, 28, 29, Sept. 1, 3, 4, 6, 9, 11, 12, 15, 18, 25, 27, Oct. 2, 9, 16, 23, 30, Nov. 6, 13, 20, 23, 27, Dec. 4, 11, 17, 18, 20, 25, 27.

Grandi Navi Veloci — 2009 service

Departure times vary. Journey 24 hours

From Genova: ③⑥ Apr. 29 - June 24; ①③⑤⑥ June 26 - Aug. 8; ②⑤⑦ Aug. 11 - Sept. 20; ③⑥ Sept. 23 - Dec. 26.

From Tûnis: ④⑦ Apr. 30 - June 25; ②④⑦ June 28 - Aug. 9; ①③⑥⑦ Aug. 12 - Sept. 21; ④⑦ Sept. 24 - Dec. 27.

2560 GULF OF NAPOLI (including Gulf of Salerno and Ponziane Islands)

Alilauro — 2009 services (subject to confirmation)

Napoli Mergellina or Beverello - Capri: 5-11 sailings daily.
Napoli Mergellina - Forio: 5 sailings daily (summer only).
Napoli Beverello - Ischia: 2-6 sailings daily by ship, 4-8 sailings daily by catamaran.
Napoli Mergellina - Ischia: 4-7 sailings daily.
Napoli Mergellina or Beverello - Sorrento: 5-9 sailings daily.
Napoli - Sorrento - Positano - Amalfi: summer only, infrequent sailings.
Pozzuoli - Ischia: frequent service by ship.
Sorrento - Capri: 7-16 sailings daily by catamaran, also 1-6 sailings by ship.
Salerno - Amalfi - Positano - Capri: summer only, infrequent sailings by catamaran.

Additional infrequent services to Capri operate (summer only) from Ischia, Castellammare di Stábia, Torre Annunziata, Positano and Amalfi.

Caremar — 2009 services

Napoli - Capri: 6 sailings daily by catamaran, 3 sailings by ship.
Napoli - Ischia: 9 sailings daily by catamaran, 5 sailings by ship.
Napoli - Procida: 8 sailings daily by catamaran, 5 sailings by ship.
Pozzuoli - Procida - Ischia: 2 sailings daily by catamaran, 2 sailings by ship.
Sorrento - Capri: 4 sailings daily by catamaran.

Additional infrequent services operate between Procida and Ischia, Formia and Ventotene, Formia and Ponza, Anzio and Ponza.

Medmar — 2009 services

Napoli - Ischia: up to 7 sailings daily.
Ischia - Pozzuoli: up to 10 sailings daily.

Additional infrequent services operate between Pozzuoli, Procida and Ischia.

Navigazione Libera del Golfo by *Linea Jet* — 2009 services

Napoli (Molo Beverello) - Capri: 4 sailings daily (9-10 in summer). Journey 40 minutes.
Sorrento - Capri: 6-8 sailings daily (19-20 in summer). Journey 25 minutes.

Additional services operate (summer only) between Castellammare di Stábia and Capri.

SNAV Journey 40 minutes — 2009 service

Napoli (Beverello) - Capri: 0710⚒, 0930, 1135, 1440, 1735.
Capri - Napoli (Beverello): 0815⚒, 1035, 1335, 1630, 1835.

For international shipping maps – see pages 518 - 520

CORSICA 2565

Sailings from mainland FRANCE

MARSEILLE - AJACCIO 2009 service

S N C M Journey 9 - 12 hours

From Marseille and Ajaccio: Feb. - Oct.: up to 2 sailings daily; Nov. - Jan.: daily sailings. Most sailings overnight, departure times vary.

MARSEILLE - BASTIA 2009 service

S N C M Journey 10 - 13 hours

From Marseille and Bastia: Feb. - Oct.: up to 2 sailings daily; Nov. - Jan.: daily sailings. Most sailings overnight, departure times vary.

MARSEILLE - L'ÎLE ROUSSE 2009 service

S N C M Journey 8 - 11½ hours

From Marseille and L'Île Rousse: Apr. - Oct.: 13 – 17 sailings per month; Nov. - Mar.: up to 3 sailings per week.
All sailings overnight, departure times vary.

MARSEILLE - PORTO VECCHIO 2009 service

S N C M Journey 14 hours

From Marseille and Porto Vecchio: Apr. - Oct.: 13 – 18 sailings per month; Nov. - Mar.: up to 3 sailings per week.
All sailings overnight, departure times vary.

MARSEILLE - PROPRIANO 2009 service

S N C M Journey 9½ - 12½ hours.

From Marseille and Propriano: Mar. - Oct.: 13 – 18 sailings per month; Nov. - Feb.: up to 3 sailings per week.
Most sailings overnight, departure times vary.

NICE - AJACCIO 2009 service

Corsica Ferries Journey 4½ - 9 hours

From Nice and Ajaccio: Apr. - June: 11 – 14 sailings per month; July - Aug.: 21 – 29 sailings per month; Sept. - Oct.: 14 sailings per month.
Most sailings by day, departure times vary.

NICE - BASTIA 2009 service

Corsica Ferries Journey 5 - 6 hours

From Nice and Bastia: Apr. - Nov.: 5 – 6 sailings per week (daily mid-June - mid-Sept.).
All sailings by day, departure times vary.

S N C M Journey 5 hours

From Nice and Bastia: Apr. - Sept.: up to 11 sailings per month.
All sailings by day, departure times vary.

NICE - CALVI 2009 service

Corsica Ferries Journey 4 - 5½ hours

From Nice and Calvi: Apr. - May: 2 – 3 sailings per week; June - July: 6 – 7 sailings per week; Aug. - mid-Sept.: 5 – 6 sailings per week; mid-Sept. - Oct.: 2 – 3 sailings per week.
All sailings by day, departure times vary.

S N C M Departure times vary (all day sailings). Journey 3 - 4 hours

From Nice and Calvi: Apr. - Sept.: up to 20 sailings per month.
All sailings by day, departure times vary.

NICE - L'ÎLE ROUSSE 2009 service

Corsica Ferries Journey 5 - 5½ hours

From Nice and L'Île Rousse: 2 – 3 sailings per week (July and Aug. only).
All sailings by day, departure times vary.

S N C M Journey 3 - 6½ hours (night = 12 hours)

From Nice and L'Île Rousse: 1 sailing per week (up to 20 sailings per month in peak summer).
Departure times vary.

TOULON - AJACCIO 2009 service

Corsica Ferries Journey 6 - 10 hours

From Toulon and Ajaccio: Apr. - Oct: up to 2 sailings daily (1 – 2 sailings daily July - Aug).
Departure times vary.

TOULON - BASTIA 2009 service

Corsica Ferries Journey 9 - 10 hours

From Toulon and Bastia: Daily Apr. 1 - Nov. 6.
Departure times vary.

TOULON - L'ÎLE ROUSSE 2009 service

Corsica Ferries Journey 6 - 7 hours

From Toulon and L'Île Rousse: May - June: up to 2 sailings per week; July - early-Sept.: 3 – 5 sailings per week.
All sailings by day, departure times vary.

Sailings from ITALY

GENOVA - BASTIA 2009 service

Moby Lines

Genova		Bastia	Bastia		Genova	
0900	→	1345	1445	→	1930	Daily May 28 - Sept. 13; ⑥⑦ Sept. 19 - 27.

LIVORNO - BASTIA 2009 service

Corsica Ferries Journey 4 hours (night = 7½ hours)

From Livorno and Bastia: Apr. - May: 1 – 2 sailings daily; June - mid-Sept: 1 – 3 sailings daily; mid-Sept. - Oct.: 6 sailings per week.
Most sailings by day, departure times vary.
Additional sailings by fast ferry late-July - mid-Sept.

Moby Lines Journey 4 hours (night = 8½ hours)

From Livorno and Bastia: May: 4 sailings per week; June - Sept.: 1 – 3 sailings daily; Oct. - Dec.: 3 sailings per week.
Departure times vary.

PIOMBINO - BASTIA 2009 service

Corsica Ferries Journey 2 hours

From Piombino and Bastia: late-July - early-Sept.: 3 – 5 sailings per week.
All sailings by day, departure times vary.

SAVONA - BASTIA 2009 service

Corsica Ferries Journey 6 - 10 hours

From Savona and Bastia: Apr. - May: 3 – 5 sailings per week; June: 1 – 2 sailings daily; July - Aug.: 2 sailings daily; Sept.: up to 2 sailings daily; Oct.: 4 – 5 sailings per week.
Departure times vary.

CORSICA - SARDINIA

BONIFACIO - SANTA TERESA DI GALLURA 2009 services

Moby Lines Journey 50 minutes **Apr. 9 - Sept. 20 only**

From Bonifacio: 0830, 1300, 1700, 2030.
From Santa Teresa di Gallura: 0700, 1000, 1510, 1900.

Saremar Journey 1 hour

Up to 3 sailings per day.

2570 ITALIAN COASTAL SERVICES (including Egadi and Eolian Islands)

Alilauro **2009 services**

Napoli Mergellina - Stromboli - Panarea - Salina - Vulcano - Lipari and v.v.: 3 sailings per week (daily late July – late Aug.).

Siremar **2009 services**

NAPOLI - MILAZZO via Stromboli, Ginostra, Panarea, Lipari and Vulcano.
Also serves Rinella and S.M. Salina on certain days. Journey 16 - 20 hours.
Sailings from Napoli: 2000②⑤. Sailings from Milazzo: 1500①④.

OTHER SERVICES by ship:
Milazzo - Vulcano - Lipari: 2 – 3 sailings per day; journey 2 hours.
Milazzo - Vulcano - Lipari - Panarea - Ginostra - Stromboli: 1 – 3 sailings per week; journey 6 hours.
Milazzo - Vulcano - Lipari - S. M. Salina - Filicudi - Alicudi: 4 – 5 sailings per week; journey 6 hours.
Trapani - Favignana - Levanzo - Marettimo: 6 – 7 sailings per week; journey 3 hours.
Palermo - Ustica: 5 – 7 sailings per week; journey 2½ hours.
Trapani - Pantelleria: 6 – 7 sailings per week; journey 4½ - 5½ hours.
Porto Empedocle (Agrigento) - Linosa - Lampedusa: 6 – 7 sailings per week; journey 8 hours.

OTHER SERVICES by hydrofoil 2 – 6 sailings per day:
Lipari - Panarea - Ginostra - Stromboli.
Lipari - S. M. Salina - Rinella.
Milazzo - Vulcano - Lipari.
Milazzo - Vulcano - Lipari - Rinella - Filicudi - Alicudi.
Milazzo - Vulcano - Lipari - S. M. Salina.
Palermo - Ustica.
Trapani - Levanzo - Favignana - Marettimo.

Ustica Lines by hydrofoil **2009 services** (subject to alteration)

EGADI & EOLIAN ISLANDS

The Sicilian ports of Cefalù, Messina, Milazzo, Palermo and Trapani are linked by island-hopping services serving Alicudi, Favignana, Filicudi, Levanzo, Lipari, Marettimo, Panarea, Salina Rinella, Salina S. M., Stromboli and Vulcano.

Services operate to differing frequencies (additional sailings in summer).

LAMPEDUSA - LINOSA by hydrofoil Journey 1 hour

Depart Lampedusa: 0730①③④⑤⑥⑦**D**▲, 0900**B**, 0930**F**, 1315③⑥**A**▲, 1635**B**, 1715**F**.
Depart Linosa: 1015**C**, 1045**F**, 1115③⑥**A**▲, 1735①③④⑤⑥⑦**E**▲, 1740**C**, 1815①③④⑤⑥⑦**F**▲, 1830**F**.

A – Jan. 1 - Apr. 30, Nov. 1 - Dec. 31. **B** – Apr. 1 - 30, Sept. 16 - Oct. 31.
C – Apr. 1 - 30, Sept. 16 - Nov. 4. **D** – May 1 - Oct. 31.
E – Sept. 16 - Oct. 31. **F** – May 1 - Sept. 15.
▲ – From / to Porto Empedocle (for Agrigento); additional journey time 3 – 3¼ hours.

MILAZZO - VULCANO by hydrofoil Journey 45 minutes

Jan. 1 - May 31, Sept. 17 - Dec. 31: 6 – 7 departures daily; June 1 - Sept. 16: 8 daily.

PALERMO - MILAZZO - CEFALÙ - PALERMO by hydrofoil

Palermo		Cefalù		Milazzo		Cefalù		Palermo	
...		...		0620	→	→	→	1135	June 1 - Sept. 16.
...		...		0630	→	1110	→	1220	①⑤⑦ until May 31 and from Sept. 17.
...		...		1510		2010	→	2105	June 1 - Sept. 16.
0655	→	0805	→	1245		...		...	June 1 - Sept. 16.
1400	→	→	→	1920		...		...	June 1 - Sept. 16.
1400	→	1510	→	2000		...		...	①⑤⑦ until May 31 and from Sept. 17.

TRAPANI - PANTELLERIA by hydrofoil June 10 - Oct. 10 only Journey 2½ hours

Depart Trapani: 1800. Depart Pantelleria: 0830.

2580 LIVORNO - BARCELONA

Grimaldi Lines **2009 service**

Livorno		Barcelona	Barcelona		Livorno
2330①③⑤	→	2200②④⑥	2359②④⑥	→	1930③⑤⑦

2585 LIVORNO - MÁLAGA

Ustica Lines **2009 service**

Livorno		Málaga	Málaga		Livorno
1900②	→	0800⑤	1700⑤	→	2200①

2588 LIVORNO - PALERMO

Grandi Navi Veloci **2009 service**

Livorno		Palermo	Palermo		Livorno
2359①③⑤	→	1900②④⑥	2359②④⑥	→	1900③⑤⑦

2590 LIVORNO - TRAPANI

Ustica Lines **2009 service**

Livorno		Trapani	Trapani		Livorno
0200③⑦	→	0700④①	1930①⑤	→	2100②⑥

2595 MÁLAGA - MELILLA

Trasmediterranea Journey 7 - 8 hours **2009 service**

Depart Málaga and Melilla: 1 – 2 sailings daily. Also daily sailings by fast ferry in summer (journey 4 hours).

Subject to alteration during Easter and Xmas / New Year periods

2602 MARSEILLE - AL-JAZÂ'IR (ALGIERS)

S N C M / E N T M V Journey 20 hours **2009 service**

Departures from Marseille: Sept. 2, 3, 5, 6 - 10, 12, 13, 15, 16, 21 - 24, 26, 27, 29, Oct. 3, 5, 6, 10, 13, 14, 17, 19, 20, 22, 24, 27, 28, 31, Nov. 3, 5, 10, 17, 24, 26, Dec. 1, 8, 15, 22, 29.
Departures from al-Jazâ'ir: Sept. 1, 3, 4, 6, 7 - 11, 13, 14, 16, 21 - 25, 27, 28, 30, Oct. 1, 5, 7, 10, 12, 14, 15, 19, 21, 23, 24, 26, 28, 29, Nov. 4, 6, 11, 18, 25, 27, Dec. 2, 9, 16, 23, 30.

Departure times vary

Other services operate from Marseille to Annâbah, Bijâyah, Sakîkdah, Wâhran (Oran) and v.v.

2615 MARSEILLE - TÛNIS

Compagnie Tunisienne de Navigation / S N C M **2009 service**

Departure times vary. Journey 20 - 24 hours

Departures from Marseille: Apr. 2, 4, 9, 11, 16, 18, 20, 23, 25, 30, May 2, 4, 7, 9, 14, 16, 21, 23, 28, 30, June 4, 6, 11, 13, 18, 20 - 23, 25, 27 - 30, July 2, 3, 5 - 7, July 9 - Aug. 14, Aug. 16 - 19, 21 - 25, 27, 28, 30, 31, Sept. 2 - 4, 6, 7, 9, 10, 12 - 14, 16, 17, 19, 24, 26, Oct. 1, 3, 8, 10, 15, 17, 22, 24, 29, 31, Nov. 5, 7, 12, 14, 19, 21, 26, 28, Dec. 3, 5, 10, 12, 17, 19, 22, 24, 26, 29, 30.
Departures from Tûnis: Apr. 1, 5, 8, 12, 15, 19, 22, 26, 29, May 3, 5, 10, 13, 17, 20, 24, 27, 31, June 3, 7, 10, 14, 17, 19, 21, 23 - 26, 28, 29, July 1, 4 - 8, 10, 11, 13 - 23, 25, 27, 29, 31, Aug. 1 - 5, 7 - 12, 14 - 23, 25, 26, 29 - 31, Sept. 1 - 9, 11, 13, 15, 16, 20, 23, 27, 30, Oct. 4, 7, 11, 14, 18, 21, 25, 28, Nov. 1, 4, 8, 11, 15, 18, 22, 25, 29, Dec. 2, 6, 9, 13, 16, 20, 21, 23, 27 - 29.

2618 MGARR (Gozo) - CIRKEWWA (Malta)

Gozo Channel Co. Journey 25 minutes **2009 service**

Departures from Mgarr and Cirkewwa: every 30 - 45 minutes 0600 - 1930 (less frequent at other times).

2621 NAPOLI - MILAZZO

Ustica Lines by hydrofoil **2009 service** **(No winter service)**

SERVICE DISCONTINUED

See Table 2570 for alternative sailings Napoli - Milazzo and v.v. (all year).

2625 NAPOLI - PALERMO

Tirrenia **2009 service**

Napoli		Palermo		Napoli	
2015	→	0630 / 2015	→	0800	Even dates Oct. 2 - 30; uneven dates Nov. 1 - Dec. 31.
2015	→	0800 / 2000	→	0630	Uneven dates Oct. 1 - 31; even dates Nov. 2 - Dec. 30.

SNAV **2009 service**

Napoli		Palermo		Palermo		Napoli	
0900	→	1900	Aug. 1 - 30.	0900	→	1900	Aug. 1 - 30.
2000	→	0630		2000	→	0630	
2100	→	0730	Aug. 1 - 30.	2100	→	0730	Aug. 1 - 30.

2630 NAPOLI - TRAPANI

Ustica Lines by hydrofoil **Service to September 30, 2009** **(No winter service)**

①④⑥▲: Napoli 1500 → Ustica 1900 / 1915 → Favignana 2115 / 2130 → Trapani 2205.
①④⑥▲: Trapani 0630 → Favignana 0650 / 0655 → Ustica 0900 / 0915 → Napoli 1315.
▲ – Also ⑤ July 1 - Aug. 31.

2650 PORTIMÃO - FUNCHAL - CANARY ISLANDS

Naviera Armas **2009 service**

Portimão		Funchal (Madeira)		Santa Cruz (Tenerife)		Las Palmas (Gran Canaria)
1200⑦	→	0900 / 1900①	→	0800②	→	1030②

Santa Cruz (Tenerife)		Las Palmas (Gran Canaria)		Funchal (Madeira)		Portimão
1600⑤	→	1930⑤	→	0800 / 1030⑥	→	0730⑦

2660 REGGIO DI CALABRIA - MESSINA

Ustica Lines by hydrofoil Journey 15 minutes **2009 service**

From Reggio di Calabria and Messina: 3 sailings in summer, 2 in winter.

2661 SALERNO - PALERMO - TÛNIS

Grimaldi Ferries **2009 service**

Salerno		Palermo		Tûnis		Palermo		Salerno
1900①	→	0600② / 1000②	→	2030② / 2330④	→	0930⑤ / 1200⑤	→	2100⑤
0500⑥	→	1600⑥ / 2000⑥	→	0830⑦ / 1100⑦	→	2200⑦ / 0100①	→	1000①

SARDINIA 2675

Sailings from FRANCE

MARSEILLE - PORTO TORRES — 2009 service

S N C M — Journey 16 - 19 hours

From Marseille and Porto Torres: Feb. - Oct.: 7 – 16 sailings per month; Nov. - Jan.: 1 sailing per week.
Most sailings overnight, departure times vary.

Sailings from mainland ITALY

CIVITAVECCHIA - ARBATAX — 2009 service

Tirrenia

Civitavecchia		Arbatax	
1830	→	0500	③⑤ Sept. 16 - Dec. 30.
Arbatax		**Civitavecchia**	
2359	→	1030	③⑦ Sept. 16 - Dec. 30.

CIVITAVECCHIA - CAGLIARI — 2009 service

Tirrenia

Civitavecchia		Cagliari	
1830	→	0900	Daily **except** when service below sails.
1830	→	1115	③⑤ Sept. 16 - Dec. 30 (via Arbatax).
Cagliari		**Civitavecchia**	
1800	→	0830	Daily **except** when service below sails.
1800	→	1030	③⑦ Sept. 16 - Dec. 30 (via Arbatax).

CIVITAVECCHIA - GOLFO ARANCI — 2009 service

Sardinia Ferries — Journey 5 - 10 hours.

From Civitavecchia and Golfo Aranci: Apr. - May: occasional sailings; June - Sept.: up to 6 sailings per week.
Most sailings by day, departure times vary.

CIVITAVECCHIA - OLBIA — 2009 service

Moby Lines

Civitavecchia		Olbia		Olbia		Civitavecchia	
0900	→	1645	Aug. 18 - Sept. 20.	0900	→	1345	June 1 - Sept. 27.
1500	→	1945	June 1 - Sept. 27.	1200	→	1900	June 1 - Aug. 16.
2200	→	0800	June 1 - Aug. 16.	2200	→	0800	Aug. 17 - Sept. 20.

Tirrenia

Civitavecchia		Olbia	
2230	→	0530	Apr. 1 - July 30, Sept. 1 - Dec. 31.
2359	→	0630	July 31 - Aug. 31.
Olbia		**Civitavecchia**	
2230	→	0530	Apr. 1 - July 30, Sept. 1 - Dec. 31.
2359	→	0630	July 31 - Aug. 31.

Additional sailings available June - mid-Sept.

GENOVA - ARBATAX — 2009 service

Tirrenia

Genova		Arbatax	
1800	→	1200	①⑤ Oct. 19 - Nov. 30.
1930	→	1200	①⑤ Oct. 2 - 16, Dec. 4 - 28.
Arbatax		**Genova**	
1400	→	0715	②⑥ Oct. 3 - Dec. 29.

GENOVA - OLBIA — 2009 service

Grandi Navi Veloci

Genova		Olbia		Olbia		Genova	
1000	→	1900	See note **D**.	1000	→	1900	See note **F**.
2130	→	0730	See note **E**.	2130	→	0730	See note **G**.

D – Aug. 17 - Oct. 10 (June 2).
E – May 22, 23, 29 - 31, June 3 - 6, June 8 - Aug. 15.
F – May 23, 30, 31, June 4 - 6, June 9 - Aug. 15.
G – Aug. 16 - Oct. 10 (also May 24, June 1, 2, 7).

Moby Lines

Genova		Olbia		Olbia		Genova	
2200	→	0730	May 22 - Oct. 10.	2200	→	0730	May 21 - Oct. 10.

Tirrenia — Journey 9 - 13 hours

From Genova and Olbia: 3 sailings per week (additional sailings in Aug.).
Departure times vary.

GENOVA - PORTO TORRES — 2009 service

Grandi Navi Veloci — Journey 11 hours — Departure times vary.

From Genova: ①③⑤⑦ Apr. 6 - May 13; daily May 15 - Aug. 15; ①②③④⑤⑦ Aug. 17 - Sept. 25; ①③④⑤ Sept. 28 - Oct. 30; ①③⑤ Nov. 2 - Dec. 30 (also Apr. 30).

From Porto Torres: ②④⑥⑦ Apr. 7 - May 14; daily May 16 - Sept. 26; ②④⑤⑥ Sept. 29 - Oct. 31; ②④⑥ Nov. 3 - Dec. 29 (also May 1).

Moby Lines

Genova		Porto Torres		Porto Torres		Genova	
1000	→	2000	See note **P**.	1000	→	2000	See note **S**.
2200	→	0800	See note **R**.	2200	→	0800	See note **T**.

P – ①④⑤⑥⑦ Aug. 17 - Sept. 27.
R – ①③④⑤⑥⑦ May 28 - Aug. 15; ② Aug. 18 - Sept. 22.
S – ①④⑤⑥⑦ May 29 - Aug. 15.
T – ② June 2 - Aug. 11; ①③④⑤⑥⑦ Aug. 16 - Sept. 27.

Tirrenia

Genova		Porto Torres	Porto Torres		Genova	
2030	→	0630	2030	→	0630	Daily Sept. 1 - Dec. 31.

LIVORNO - GOLFO ARANCI — 2009 service

Sardinia Ferries — Journey 6½ - 10 hours.

From Livorno and Golfo Aranci: Apr. - May: up to 2 sailings daily; June - Sept.: 2 sailings daily; Oct.: 1 sailing daily.
Departure times vary.

LIVORNO - OLBIA — 2009 service

Moby Lines

From Livorno and Olbia: Jan. - Mar.: 1 sailing daily; Apr. - May: 1 – 2 sailings daily; June - Sept.: 2 – 3 sailings daily; Oct. - Dec. 1 sailing daily.
Departure times vary.

NAPOLI - CAGLIARI — 2009 service

Tirrenia

Napoli		Cagliari	
1915	→	1130	④ Sept. 17 - Dec. 31.
Cagliari		**Napoli**	
1830	→	1045	③ Sept. 16 - Dec. 30.

PIOMBINO - OLBIA — 2009 service

Moby Lines

From Piombino and Olbia: May - June: 5 sailings per week; June - July: 1 – 2 sailings daily; Aug.: 6 sailings per week; Sept. - Dec.: 5 sailings per week.
Departure times vary.

Sailings from SICILY

PALERMO - CAGLIARI — 2009 service

Tirrenia

Palermo		Cagliari		Cagliari		Palermo	
1700⑥	→	0630⑦	Apr. 4 - Dec. 26.	1900⑤	→	0930⑥	Apr. 3 - Dec. 25.

TRAPANI - CAGLIARI — 2009 service

Tirrenia

Cagliari		Trapani	
1000	→	2000	⑦ Apr. 5 - Dec. 27.
1900	→	0600	① Oct. 5 - Dec. 28.
Trapani		**Cagliari**	
2100	→	0830	② Oct. 6 - Dec. 29.
2359	→	1000	⑦ Apr. 5 - Dec. 27.

SÈTE - AN-NADÛR (NADOR) 2678

Cie. Marocaine de Navigation (Comanav) — 2009 service

Depart 1900 from Sète, 2100 from an-Nadûr. Sailings arrive 2 days later.
Departures from Sète: June - Oct.: up to 6 – 8 sailings per month.
Departures from an-Nadûr: June - Oct.: up to 6 – 8 sailings per month.

SÈTE - TANJAH (TANGIERS) 2680

Cie. Marocaine de Navigation (Comanav) — 2009 service

Depart 1900 from Sète, 1800 from Tanjah. Sailings arrive 2 days later.
Departures from Sète: June - Oct.: up to 6 – 8 sailings per month.
Departures from Tanjah: June - Oct.: up to 6 – 8 sailings per month.

VALLETTA - CATANIA 2690

Virtu Ferries by catamaran — 2009 service

Valletta		Catania	
0500	→	0800	⑥ Apr. 4 - 25; ②⑥ May 2 - Sept. 29; ⑥ Oct. 3 - Dec. 26.
Catania		**Valletta**	
1930	→	2230	⑥ Apr. 4 - 25.
2000	→	2300	②⑥ May 2 - Sept. 29; ⑥ Oct. 3 - Dec. 26.

VALLETTA - GENOVA 2691

Grandi Navi Veloci — 2009 service

Valletta		Genova	Genova		Valletta
1500①	→	2030②	1800⑥	→	0830①

Departure times may vary

VALLETTA - POZZALLO 2694

Virtu Ferries by catamaran — Journey 1½ hours — 2009 service

1 – 2 sailings daily on ①③④⑤⑦ only; departure times vary.

For shipping operator details – see pages 521/522

2695 VILLA S. GIOVANNI - MESSINA

Italian Railways Journey 35 minutes **Service to December 12, 2009**

From Villa S.G.: 0135, 0235, 0415, 0515, 0655, 0755, 0935, 1035, 1215, 1315, 1455, 1555, 1735, 1835, 2015, 2115, 2255, 2355.

From Messina: 0010, 0115, 0250, 0350, 0525, 0630, 0815, 0910, 1050, 1150, 1330, 1430, 1610, 1710, 1850, 1950, 2130, 2230.

2699 OTHER SERVICES

Moby Lines **2009 services**

Piombino - Portoferraio (Elba): 7 sailings daily in winter, 13 - 16 sailings in summer, journey 1 hour (no service on Dec. 25).

Toremar **2009 services**

Services operate from Piombino to Cavo, Pianosa, Portoferraio and Rio Marina; from Livorno to Capraia and Gorgona; and from Porto Santo Stefano to Isola del Giglio.

ADRIATIC / EASTERN MEDITERRANEAN / BLACK SEA

2705 ANCONA - BAR

Montenegro Lines **2009 service (No winter service)**

Ancona		Bar	
1600	→	0700	④⑥ July 4 - Sept. 5 (also Aug. 24, 31).
Bar		**Ancona**	
1600 §	→	0700 §	③⑤ July 3 - Sept. 4 (also Aug. 23, 30).

§ – Sails 4 hours later on ③ Aug. 19, 26, Sept. 2.

2715 ANCONA - PÁTRA via Igumenítsa

Anek Lines **Service to January 10, 2010**

February 17 - March 29 and November 3 - January 10
(from Pátra, following day from Ancona)

Ancona		Igumenítsa		Pátra
1600①③④⑤⑥⑦	→	0830②④⑤⑥⑦①	→	1400②④⑤⑥⑦①
Pátra		**Igumenítsa**		**Ancona**
1700②③④⑤⑥⑦	→	2230②③④⑤⑥⑦	→	1300③④⑤⑥⑦①

March 31 - November 1 ▲
(from Pátra, following day from Ancona)

Ancona		Igumenítsa		Pátra	Pátra		Igumenítsa		Ancona
1600	→	0800	→	1330	1700	→	2230	→	1230

▲ – No sailings from Pátra (following day from Ancona): Apr. 13, 27, May 11, June 1, 8, 22, July 27, Sept. 14, 28, Oct. 12, 26.

🚌 connection Pátra - Pireás - Athína and v.v. operates most days in summer.

Minoan Lines **Service to October 31, 2009**

Ancona		Igumenítsa		Pátra	Pátra		Igumenítsa		Ancona
1700	→	0900	→	1500	1800	→	2330	→	1400

No sailings from Pátra: Mar. 4, 11, 18, 25, Apr. 1, 8, 15, 22, 29, May 6, 13, 20, 27, June 3, 10, 17, July 15, Aug. 12, Sept. 9, 16, 23, 30, Oct. 7, 14, 21, 28 (one day later from Ancona).

Superfast Ferries **2009 service**

Ancona		Igumenítsa		Pátra		Pátra		Igumenítsa		Ancona	
1330	→	0530	→	1130		1430	→	2000	→	1030	
1800	→	1000	→	1600	②④⑥	1900	→	2359	→	1500	①③⑤

Subject to alteration during ship maintenance periods

🚌 connection Pátra - Pireás - Athína and v.v.

Tickets available on-board ship and from 30 Amalías av., Síndagma, Athína.

2725 ANCONA - SPLIT

Blue Line Journey 9 hours **2009 service**

March 29 - July 23 and September 6 - October 31
Depart Ancona: 2030①②③④⑤⑥. Depart Split: 2030①②③④⑤⑦.

July 24 - August 27
Depart Ancona: 1030 **A**, 2030. Depart Split: 1030 **A**, 2030.

August 28 - September 5
Depart Ancona: 2030. Depart Split: 2030 (not Sept. 5).

November 1 - December 20
Depart Ancona: 2030①③⑤. Depart Split: 2030②④⑦.

A – ⑤⑥⑦ July 31 - Aug. 9; ①⑥⑦ Aug. 10 - 27.

Jadrolinija **2009 service**

Ancona		Split		Split		Ancona	
2100	→	0700	See note **V**.	2100	→	0700	See note **W**.

V – ①③⑤ (not Dec 25, Jan. 1).
W – ②④⑦ (not Dec. 24, 31).

SNAV by catamaran *Croazia Jet* **June 13 - September 6, 2009 (No winter service)**
Journey 4½ hours

Ancona		Split	Split		Ancona
1100	→	1530	1700	→	2130

2732 ANCONA - ZADAR

Jadrolinija **2009 service**

Ancona		Zadar		Zadar		Ancona	
September 2 - 30							
2200	→	0700	②④⑥	1200	→	1800	⑤⑥
				2200	→	0700	①③
October 1 - December 31							
2200	→	0700	See note **X**.	2200	→	0700	See note **Y**.

X – ②④⑥ (not Dec. 24, 26, 31).
Y – ①③⑤ (not Dec. Dec. 23, 25, 30).

2735 ANCONA - ÇEŞME

Marmara Lines **2009 service (No winter service)**

Ancona		Çeşme	
2230⑥	→	0630②	May 2 - June 27, Aug. 15 - Oct. 24.
2230⑥	→	2330①	July 4 - Aug. 8.
Çeşme		**Ancona**	
1100④	→	1800⑥	Apr. 30 - July 30, Sept. 17 - Oct. 22.
1430④	→	1800⑥	Aug. 6 - Sept. 10.

2738 BARI - BAR

Azzurra Line Journey 8½ – 10 hours **2009 service (No winter service)**

Departure times vary.

From Bari: Apr. 21, 28, May 5, 6, 12, 19, 26, June 9, 13, 16, 20, 27, July 2, 9, 16, 23, Aug. 3, 6, 13, 20, 27, Sept. 5, 12.

From Bar: Apr. 22, 29, May 13, 20, 27, June 10, 14, 17, 21, 28, July 3, 10, 17, 24, Aug. 4, 7, 14, 21, 28, Sept. 6, 13.

Montenegro Lines **2009 service**

Bari		Bar		Bar		Bari	
1000	→	1900	③ Aug. 19 - Sept. 2.	1200	→	2100	See note **C**.
1200	→	2100	See note **B**.	2200	→	0800	See note **D**.
2200	→	0800	See note **A**.				

A – ①③⑤ Jan. 1 - June 30; ①③⑤⑥ July 1 - 11; ①③⑤⑥⑦ July 13 - 26; daily July 27 - Aug. 12; ② Aug. 18 - Sept. 1; ①③⑤ Sept. 7 - Dec. 19 (also June 27, Aug. 16, 17, Dec. 19, 21, 22, 23, 28, 30).
B – Aug. 14, 15, 20 - 24, 27 - 31, Sept. 3 - 6, 13.
C – ⑥ July 4 - 11; ⑥⑦ July 18 - 26; ④⑤⑥⑦ July 30 - Aug. 9 (also June 27, Dec. 19, 22, 23).
D – ②④⑦ Jan. 1 - July 26; ①②⑦ July 27 - Aug. 11; daily Aug. 13 - Sept. 6; ②④⑦ Sept. 8 - Dec. 19 (also Sept. 12, Dec. 20, 27, 29).

2740 BARI - KÉRKIRA (CORFU)

Ventouris Ferries **Service to September 30, 2009**

From Bari and Kérkira: 1 - 2 per week (6 - 7 per week in summer). Departure times vary.

2745 BARI - IGUMENÍTSA

Ventouris Ferries Journey 12½ hours **Service to September 30, 2009**

From Bari and Igumenítsa: Up to 6 sailings per week (1 - 2 per day in summer). Departure times vary.

2755 BARI - PÁTRA via Kérkira and Igumenítsa

Blue Star Ferries / Superfast Ferries **2009 service**

Bari		Kérkira		Igumenítsa		Pátra
1200⑦	→	2100⑦	→	2230⑦	→	0600①
2000①–⑥	→	0500②–⑦§	→	0630②–⑦	→	1230②–⑦
Pátra		**Igumenítsa**		**Kérkira**		**Bari**
1800	→	2359	→	0130⊡	→	0830

§ – Kérkira sailings operate ⑤⑥ July 24 - Aug. 29 only.
⊡ – Kérkira sailings operate ⑥⑦ Aug. 1 - Sept. 6 only.

Subject to alteration during ship maintenance periods

🚌 connection Pátra - Pireás - Athína and v.v.

Tickets available on-board ship and from 30 Amalías av., Síndagma, Athína.

2760 BLACK SEA services

Bumerang Shipping Company Tourism Travel & Trade S.A.

İSTANBUL - YALTA - NOVOROSSISK Irregular sailings, journey 30 hours

İSTANBUL - YEVPATORIYA Journey 24 hours

Ukrferry **2009 service**

İSTANBUL - ODESA

İstanbul		Odesa	Odesa		İstanbul
2359④	→	1300⑥	2100①	→	0800③

Schedules subject to change at short notice

BRINDISI - IGUMENÍTSA 2765

Endeavor Lines **2009 service**

From Brindisi: Daily May 1 - Dec. 31 (not Dec. 5, 25 - 27).
From Igumenítsa: Daily May 1 - Nov. 30, Dec. 2, 4 - 6, 8, 10, 12 - 14, 16, 18 - 20, 22, 24, 28, 30 (not Nov. 1). Additional sailing Sept. 1 - 6, Dec. 2, 4 - 6, 8, 10, 12, 14, 16, 18 - 20, 22, 28, 30.

Departure times vary

BRINDISI - KÉRKIRA (CORFU) 2770

Endeavor Lines **2009 service (No winter service)**

Brindisi		Kérkira		Kérkira		Brindisi	
1800	→	0845	See note **A**.	0915	→	1445	See note **B**.

A – May 28, 29, June 4, 5, 10, 12, 13, 18, 19, 24, 26, 27, July 2 - 8, 10 - 15, 17 - 29, 31, Aug. 1 - 5, 7 - 12, 15 - 19, 21 - 26, 28 - 31, Sept. 1, 2, 4, 5, 11 - 13.
B – May 4, June 3, 5, 6, 11, 13, 14, 19, 20, 25, 27, 28, July 3 - 9, 11 - 16, 18 - 30, Aug. 1 - 6, 8 - 13, 16 - 20, 22 - 27, 29 - 31, Sept. 1 - 3, 5, 6, 12 - 14.

Times may vary

BRINDISI - PÁTRA 2775

Endeavor Lines **2009 service**

Brindisi		Pátra		Pátra		Brindisi	
1830	→	1030	See note **M**.	1730	→	0830	See note **N**.

M – Not Nov. 1, Dec. 1, 25 - 27.
N – Not Oct. 31, Dec. 24 - 26, 31.

Times may vary

BRINDISI - SÁMI (Kefallinía) 2780

Endeavor Lines **2009 service (No winter service)**

Brindisi		Sámi		Sámi		Brindisi	
1830	→	0645	See note **K**.	2045	→	0830	See note **L**.

K – June 5, 6, 10, 12 - 14, 19, 20, 24, 26 - 28; daily July 2 - Sept. 6.
L – June 7, 10, 12 - 14, 19 - 21, 24, 26 - 28, 30; daily July 3 - Sept. 13 (also Sept. 19, 20).

Sailings also operate from Brindisi to Zákinthos (Zante); June 1 - Sept. 30.

BRINDISI - ÇEŞME 2785

Marmara Lines

Brindisi	Çeşme	Çeşme	Brindisi

NO SERVICE

DUBROVNIK - BARI 2795

Azzurra Line Journey 9 – 10 hours **2009 service (No winter service)**

Departure times vary.
From Dubrovnik: Apr. 11, 14, May 1, 3, 30, June 2, 13, 20, 24, 27, July 4, 11, 18, 25, 28, 31, Aug. 1, 8, 11, 12, 15, 18, 19, 22, 25, 26, 29, Sept. 1, 8.
From Bari: Apr. 10, 14, 30 May 3, 29, June 2, 12, 19, 23, 26, July 3, 10, 17, 24, 27, 30, 31, Aug. 7, 10, 11, 14, 17, 18, 21, 24, 25, 28, 31, Sept. 7.

Jadrolinija **2009 service**

Dubrovnik		Bari	
1130	→	1930	⑤ June 5 - Sept. 25.
1230	→	2000	⑦ June 7 - Sept. 27.
1530	→	2130	⑥ Apr. 11 - May 30, Oct. 2 - 23.
1600	→	2200	⑥ June 5 - Sept. 25.
2300	→	0800	② Feb. 3 - May 26; ①②③ June 1 - Sept. 28; ② Oct. 5 - Dec. 28.
Bari		**Dubrovnik**	
2200	→	0700	③ Feb. 4 - May 27; ②③④⑤⑦ June 2 - Sept. 30; ③ Oct. 7 - Dec. 30.
2230	→	0700	⑥ Apr. 11 - May 30, Oct. 3 - 24.
2359	→	0700	⑥ June 6 - Sept. 26.

GREEK ISLANDS 2800

Summary table of regular ⛴ services to the Greek Islands.

Each route is operated by various shipping companies to differing schedules.
Further details are given in the **Thomas Cook Guide to Greek Island Hopping**.
Additional inter-island routes are operated at less regular intervals.

Pireás to Égina, Póros, Ídra, Spétses, Kíthira, Andikíthira.
Pireás to Sérifos, Sífnos, Mílos, Folégandros.
Pireás to Páros, Íos, Thíra (Santoríni), Iráklio.
Pireás to Náxos, Amorgós, Astipálea.
Pireás to Pátmos, Léros, Kálimnos, Kos, Nísiros, Tílos, Sími, Ródos, Kárpathos, Kásos.
Pireás to Ikaría, Sámos, Híos, Lésvos.
Pireás and **Rafína** to Síros, Dílos, Míkonos, Tínos, Ándros.
Pátra to Zákinthos (Zante), Kefallinía, Itháki, Kérkira (Corfu), Igumenítsa.
Vólos, Ágios Konstantínos and **Kími** to Skíathos, Skópelos, Alónissos, Skíros.
Kavála to Thásos, Samothráki, Límnos.

PESCARA - SPLIT 2810

SNAV **by catamaran** *Croazia Jet* **June 13 - September 6, 2009 (No winter service)**

Pescara		Split	Split		Pescara
1030	→	1615	1700	→	2330

PIREÁS - IRÁKLIO 2830

Superfast Ferries **2009 service**

Pireás		Iráklio	Iráklio		Pireás
1530	→	2200	2345	→	0615

PIREÁS - LEMESÓS (LIMASSOL) - HEFA 2845

Salamis Lines **2009 service**

Salamis Cruise Lines operate 2/3 day cruises Apr. - Oct. – contact operator for details.

RIJEKA - SPLIT - DUBROVNIK 2855

Jadrolinija **2009 service**

June 1 - September 30

Rijeka	Split	Stari Grad	Korčula	Dubrovnik	
...	...	...	1800① →	2150①	
2000① →	0700② →	0900② →	1300② →	1615②	
...	...	...	1800③ →	2150③	Not Sept. 30.
2000⑤ →	0630⑥ →	0815⑥ →	1130⑥ →	1430⑥	
...	1800⑥ →	→ →	2200⑥	...	June 27 - Sept. 5.
...	...	...	0700⑦ →	1050⑦	
Dubrovnik	**Korčula**	**Stari Grad**	**Split**	**Rijeka**	
0830① →	1240①	...	...	...	
0830③ →	1240③	...	...	...	
1000④ →	1330④ →	1700④ →	2000④ →	0700⑤	
0830⑥ →	1240⑥	...	...	...	
...	1330⑥ →	→ →	1730⑥	...	June 27 - Sept. 5.
1000⑦ →	1330⑦ →	1700⑦ →	2000⑦ →	0700①	

October 1 - December 31

Rijeka	Split	Stari Grad	Korčula	Dubrovnik	
1900① →	0700② →	0900② →	1300② →	1615②	From Oct. 27.
2000① →	0700② →	0900② →	1300② →	1615②	Until Oct. 26.
1900⑤ →	0700⑥ →	0900⑥ →	1300⑥ →	1615⑥	From Oct. 30.
2000⑤ →	0630⑥ →	0815⑥ →	1130⑥ →	1430⑥	Until Oct. 23.
Dubrovnik	**Korčula**	**Stari Grad**	**Split**	**Rijeka**	
0900④ →	1235④ →	1630④ →	1930④ →	0700⑤	
0900⑦ →	1235⑦ →	1630⑦ →	1930⑦ →	0700①	

VENEZIA - PÁTRA via Igumenítsa and Kérkira (Corfu) 2875

Anek Lines **Service to January 8, 2010**

January 8 - April 6 and October 8 - January 8
(from Pátra, 2 days later from Venezia)

Venezia	Igumenítsa	Kérkira	Pátra	Pátra	Kérkira	Igumenítsa	Venezia
1900② →	2100③ →	2300③ →	0600④	2359① →	→	→ 0800② →	0730③
1900③ →	2100④ →	→	→ 0600⑤	2359④ →	→	→ 0800⑤ →	0730⑥
1200⑥ →	1400⑦ →	→	→ 2100⑦	2359⑤ →	0615⑥ →	0800⑥ →	0730⑦
1200⑦ →	1400① →	→	→ 2100①	2359⑦ →	→	→ 0800① →	0730②

April 9 - October 5
(from Pátra, 2 days later from Venezia)

Venezia	Igumenítsa	Kérkira	Pátra	Pátra	Kérkira	Igumenítsa	Venezia
1900② →	2030③ →	2230③ →	0600④	2359① →	0630② →	0830② →	0730③
1900③ →	2030④ →	2230④ →	0600⑤	2359④ →	0630⑤ →	0830⑤ →	0730⑥
1200⑥ →	1300⑦ →	1430⑦ →	2100⑦	2359⑤ →	0630⑥ →	0830⑥ →	0730⑦
1200⑦ →	1300① →	1430① →	2100①	2359⑦ →	0630① →	0830① →	0730②

Minoan Lines **2009 service**

January 26 - March 31
(from Pátra, 2 days later from Venezia)

Venezia	Kérkira	Igumenítsa	Pátra	Pátra	Kérkira	Igumenítsa	Venezia
1700① →	→	→ 2015② →	0500③	2359① →	0700② →	0900② →	0800③
1400③ →	1115④ →	1230④ →	1930④	2359③ →	→	→ 0900④ →	0800⑤
1400⑤ →	→	→ 1300⑥ →	1930⑥	2359④ →	0700⑤ →	0900⑤ →	0800⑥
1700⑥ →	1900⑦ →	2015⑦ →	0500①	2359⑥ →	→	→ 0900⑦ →	0800①

April 1 - October 31
(from Pátra, 2 days later from Venezia)

Venezia	Igumenítsa	Kérkira	Pátra	Pátra	Kérkira	Igumenítsa	Venezia
1700① →	2000② →	2130② →	0500③	2359① →	0700② →	0900② →	0800③
1400③ →	1200④ →	1330④ →	2000④	2359③ →	0700④ →	0900④ →	0800⑤
1400⑤ →	1200⑥ →	1330⑥ →	2000⑥	2359④ →	0700⑤ →	0900⑤ →	0800⑥
1700⑥ →	2000⑦ →	2130⑦ →	0500①	2359⑥ →	0700⑦ →	0900⑦ →	0800①

Subject to alteration during Xmas/New Year period

BARI - DURRËS 2880

Tirrenia **2009 service**

Bari		Durrës		Durrës		Bari	
1200	→	1900	Dec. 19, 24 only.	1200	→	1900	Dec. 19, 24 only.
2300	→	0800		2300	→	0800	

Ventouris Ferries Journey 10 hours **2009 service**

March 1 - May 31
From Bari and Durrës: 4 – 5 sailings per week (most departures overnight).
June 1 - September 30
From Bari and Durrës: 1 – 3 sailings per day (most departures overnight).

OTHER SERVICES 2899

Jadrolinija **2009 services**

Many local services operate to the Islands along the Croatian coast.

Split Tours **2009 services**

Many local Island services operated from Split.

Venezia Lines **2009 services**

Summer services from Venezia to Mali Lošinj, Piran, Poreč, Pula, Rabac and Rovinj.

Scenic Rail Routes of Europe

The following is a list of some of the most scenic rail routes of Europe, detailed timings for most of which can be found within the timetable. Routes marked * are the Editor's personal choice. This list does not include specialised mountain and tourist railways.

Many more scenic lines are clearly marked on the Thomas Cook New Rail Map of Europe - see the back of this book for details.

Types of scenery : C-Coastline, F-Forest, G-Gorge, L-Lake, M-Mountain, R-River.

ALBANIA

Elbasan - Pogradec	ML G R

AUSTRIA

Bruck an der Mur - Villach	R
Gmunden - Stainach Irdning*	ML
Innsbruck - Brennero	M
Innsbruck - Garmisch Partenkirchen*	M
Innsbruck - Schwarzach-St Veit	M G
Klagenfurt - Unzmarkt	M
Landeck - Bludenz*	M
Linz - Krems	R
St Pölten - Mariazell*	M
Salzburg - Villach*	M G
Selzthal - Hieflau - Steyr	M G R
Wiener Neustadt - Semmering - Graz	M

BELGIUM and LUXEMBOURG

Liège - Luxembourg*	R
Liège - Marloie	R
Namur - Dinant	R

BULGARIA

Septemvri - Dobriniste	M
Sofija - Burgas	M
Tulova - Gorna Orjahovitza	M

CROATIA and BOSNIA

Rijeka - Ogulin	M
Ogulin - Split	M
Sarajevo - Ploče	M G R

CZECH REPUBLIC

Karlovy Vary - Mariánské Lázně	R F
Karlovy Vary - Chomutov	R
Praha - Děčín	R

DENMARK

Struer - Thisted	C

FINLAND

Kouvola - Joensuu	L F

Many other lines run through scenic areas.

FRANCE

Aurillac - Neussargues	M G
Bastia - Ajaccio	M
Chambéry - Bourg St Maurice	M
Chambéry - Modane	ML
Chamonix - Martigny*	M G
Clermont Ferrand - Béziers	M G
Clermont Ferrand - Nîmes*	M G R
Gap - Briançon	ML
Genève - Aix les Bains	M R
Grenoble - Veynes - Marseille	M
Marseille - Ventimiglia	C
Mouchard - Besançon - Montbéliard	R
Nice - Digne	M
Nice / Ventimiglia - Cuneo*	M G
Perpignan - Latour de Carol*	M G
Portbou - Perpignan	C
Sarlat - Bergerac	R
Toulouse - Latour de Carol	M
Valence - Veynes	M

GERMANY

Arnstadt - Meiningen	M
Bonn - Siegen	R
Dresden - Děčín	G R
Freiburg - Donaueschingen	G F
Garmisch Partenkirchen - Kempten	M
Heidelberg - Neckarelz	R
Koblenz - Mainz*	G R
München - Lindau	M
Murnau - Oberammergau	ML
Naumburg - Saalfeld	R

GERMANY - continued

Niebüll - Westerland	C
Nürnberg - Pegnitz	G R
Offenburg - Konstanz	M F
Pforzheim - Nagold / Wildbad	F
Plattling - Bayerisch Eisenstein	F
Rosenheim - Freilassing - Berchtesgaden	ML
Rosenheim - Wörgl	M
Stuttgart - Singen	F
Titisee - Seebrugg	L F
Trier - Koblenz - Giessen	R
Ulm - Göppingen	M
Ulm - Tuttlingen	R

GREAT BRITAIN and IRELAND

Alnmouth - Dunbar	C
Barrow in Furness - Maryport	C
Coleraine - Londonderry	C
Dun Laoghaire - Wicklow	C
Edinburgh - Aberdeen	C
Exeter - Newton Abbot	C
Glasgow - Oban / Mallaig*	ML
Inverness - Kyle of Lochalsh*	M C
Liskeard - Looe	R
Llanelli - Craven Arms	M
Machynlleth - Pwllheli	M C
Perth - Inverness	M
Plymouth - Gunnislake	R
Rosslare - Waterford	C R
St Erth - St Ives	C
Sheffield - New Mills	M
Shrewsbury - Aberystwyth	M R
Skipton - Settle - Carlisle	M R

GREECE

Korinthos - Patras	C
Diakoptó - Kalávrita	M G

HUNGARY

Budapest - Szob	R
Eger - Szilvásvárad	M
Székesfehérvár - Balatonszentgyörgy	L
Székesfehérvár - Tapolca	L

ITALY

Bologna - Pistoia	M
Bolzano - Merano	M
Brennero - Verona*	M
Brig - Arona	ML
Domodossola - Locarno*	M G
Firenze - Viareggio	M
Fortezza - San Candido	M
Genova - Pisa	C
Genova - Ventimiglia	C
Lecco - Tirano	ML
Messina - Palermo	C
Napoli - Sorrento	C
Roma - Pescara	M
Salerno - Reggio Calabria	C
Taranto - Reggio Calabria	C
Torino - Aosta	M

NORWAY

Bergen - Oslo*	ML
Bodø - Trondheim	ML
Dombås - Åndalsnes	M
Drammen - Larvik	C
Lillestrom - Kongsvinger	R
Myrdal - Flåm*	M C
Oslo / Røros - Trondheim	ML
Stavanger - Kristiansand	M

POLAND

Jelenia Góra - Walbrzych	M
Kraków - Zakopane	M
Olsztyn - Elk	L
Olsztyn - Morag	L
Tarnów - Krynica	M

PORTUGAL

Guarda - Entroncamento	M R
Pampilhosa - Guarda	M
Porto - Coimbra	C R
Porto - Pocinho*	R
Porto - Valença	M C
Regua - Vila Real	M G
Tua - Mirandela*	M G R

ROMANIA

Braşov - Ploeşti	M
Caransebeş - Craiova	M G R
Feteşti - Constanţa	R
Oradea - Cluj Napoca	R

SERBIA and MONTENEGRO

Priboj - Bar	ML

SLOVAKIA

Banská Bystrica - Brezno - Košice	M
Žilina - Poprad Tatry	M

SLOVENIA

Jesenice - Sežana	M R
Maribor - Zidani Most	M
Trieste - Ljubljana - Zagreb	G R

SPAIN

Algeciras - Ronda	M R
Barcelona - Latour de Carol	M
Bilbao - San Sebastián	M
Bilbao - Santander	M
Ferrol - Gijón*	C
Granada - Almería	M
Huesca - Canfranc	M G R
León - Monforte de Lemos	M
León - Oviedo	M
Lleida - La Pobla de Segur	ML
Madrid - Aranda - Burgos	ML
Málaga - Bobadilla	G
Santander - Oviedo	M C
Zaragoza - València	M R

SWEDEN

Bollnäs - Ånge - Sundsvall	ML
Borlänge - Mora	ML F
Borlänge - Ludvika - Frövi	ML F
Narvik - Kiruna	M F
Östersund - Storlien	L F

Many other lines run through scenic areas.

SWITZERLAND

Andermatt - Göschenen	G
Basel - Delémont - Moutier	M R
Chur - Arosa	M G
Chur - Brig - Zermatt*	M
Chur - St Moritz*	M G
Davos - Filisur	M G
Davos - Landquart	M
Interlaken Ost - Jungfraujoch*	M
Interlaken Ost - Luzern	ML
Interlaken West - Spiez	L
Lausanne - Brig	ML R
Lausanne - Neuchâtel - Biel	ML
Montreux - Zweisimmen - Lenk	ML G
Rorschach - Kreuzlingen	L
St Moritz - Scuol Tarasp	M
St Moritz - Tirano*	M
Spiez - Zweisimmen	G
Thun - Brig*	ML
Zürich / Luzern - Chiasso	ML
Zürich - Chur	ML

Many other lines run through scenic areas.

CHRISTMAS AND NEW YEAR CANCELLATIONS

This year we are experimenting with showing more details of Christmas and New Year cancellations in the Czech Republic, Slovakia and Hungary. These may be shown by footnotes in relevant tables, but further cancellations of mainline trains are shown below. The list may not be comprehensive.

It is not possible to show cancellations of local trains. Many of these do not run on the evening of Dec. 24 or Dec. 31, or on the morning of Dec. 25, Jan. 1, and some local trains may be cancelled throughout the Christmas / New Year holiday period.

CZECH REPUBLIC

The following trains (shown by train number) will not run on the dates shown:

DECEMBER 24:

Ex140 (terminates at Olomouc), SC512, SC513, Ex523, IC545, Ex577, IC581 (terminates at Ostrava hlavní), 618, 621 (terminates at Olomouc), 653, 655, 656, 657, 661 (terminates at České Budějovice), 668 (terminates at České Budějovice), 682, 688, 722, 725, 744, 745, 746, 747, 764 (terminates at Plzeň), 766, 767, 786, 788, 789, 792 (terminates at Hradec Králové), 799 (terminates at Týniště nad Orlicí), 816, 817, 829, 856, 858, 865, 878, 886, 890, 913, 915, 921, 925 (terminates at České Budějovice), 926, 940, 955, 959, 968, 970, 971, 995, 996, 997, 1167, 1168, 1196, 1197, 1256, 1257, 1633, 1635, 1734, 1737, 1738, 1940.

DECEMBER 25:

Ex141 (starts from Olomouc), SC512, SC513, Ex522, IC544, IC545, Ex577, IC580 (starts from Ostrava hlavní), 618, 619, 620 (starts from Olomouc), 634, 657, 667 (starts from České Budějovice), 671, 675, 700, 746, 747, 750, 751, 753 (starts from Plzeň), 767, 771, 788, 789, 790 (starts from Týniště nad Orlicí), 791 (starts from Hradec Králové), 800, 801, 816, 817, 830, 831, 849 (starts from Hradec Králové), 864, 865, 867, 881, 890, 892, 912, 914, 920, 924 (starts at České Budějovice), 960, 961, 963, 968, 970, 971, 980, 995, 996, 997, 1167, 1168, 1242, 1243, 1632, 1688, 1689, 1737, 1738, 1995

DECEMBER 26:

IC544, Ex577, 619, 700, 750, 800, 801, 864, 960, 961, 963, 980, 1688, 1689.

DECEMBER 31:

Ex140 (terminates at Olomouc), SC512, SC513, Ex523, IC545, Ex577, IC581 (terminates at Ostrava hlavní), 618, 621 (terminates at Olomouc), 653, 655, 656, 657, 661 (terminates at České Budějovice), 668 (terminates at České Budějovice), 682, 688, 722, 725, 744, 745, 746, 747, 764 (terminates at Plzeň), 766, 767, 786, 788, 789, 792 (terminates at Hradec Králové), 799 (terminates at Týniště nad Orlicí), 816, 817, 829, 856, 858, 865, 878, 886, 890, 913, 915, 921, 925 (terminates at České Budějovice), 926, 940, 955, 959, 968, 970, 971, 995, 996, 997, 1167, 1168, 1196, 1197, 1256, 1257, 1633, 1635, 1737, 1738, 1940, 1979.

JANUARY 1:

Ex141 (starts from Olomouc), Ex522, IC544, Ex577, IC580 (starts from Ostrava hlavní), 619, 620 (starts from Olomouc), 634, 667 (starts from České Budějovice), 671, 675, 700, 750, 751, 753 (starts from Plzeň), 771, 790 (starts from Týniště nad Orlicí), 791 (starts from Hradec Králové), 800, 801, 830, 831, 849 (starts from Hradec Králové), 864, 867, 881, 892, 912, 914, 920, 924 (starts at České Budějovice), 960, 961, 963, 980, 1242, 1243, 1632, 1688, 1689, 1995.

SLEEPERS AND COUCHETTES:

The following cancellations are additional to those shown in the tables:

1, 2 cl. České Budějovice - Košice in train **890 / 441** will not run Dec. 24 - 26, 31. 1, 2 cl. Košice - České Budějovice in train **440 / 892** will not run Dec. 23 - 25, 31.

1, 2 cl. Brno - Košice in train **747 / 443** will not run Dec. 24 - 26, 31. 1, 2 cl. Košice - Brno in train **442 / 730** or **732** will not run Dec. 23 - 25, 31.

2 cl. Cheb - Košice and v.v. in train **441 / 440** will not run Dec. 24 - Jan. 1 from Cheb, Dec. 23 - 31 from Košice.

2 cl. Plzeň - Košice and v.v. in train **441 / 440** will not run Dec. 24 - Jan. 1 from Plzeň, Dec. 23 - 31 from Košice.

SLOVAKIA

In addition to cancellations shown in relevant tables, the following trains (shown by train number) will not run on the dates shown:

DECEMBER 24:

Ex531, 837, 873, 1907.

DECEMBER 25:

Ex530, Ex531, 704, 831, 834, 837, 872, 1842.

DECEMBER 26:

Ex530, 704, 722, 831, 834, 837, 1842.

DECEMBER 31:

873, 1907.

JANUARY 1:

Ex530, Ex531, 704, 837, 872

HUNGARY

In addition to cancellations shown in relevant tables, the following trains (shown by train number) will not run on the dates shown:

DECEMBER 24:

IC503, 521 (terminates at Miskolc), IC563 (terminates at Nyiregyháza), IC616, IC624 (terminates at Nyiregyháza), IC653 (terminates at Nyiregyháza), IC753, IC756, IC763, IC766, 781 (terminates at Baja), 798, IC801, IC808, IC818, IC828, 858, 868, 901, 908, IC918, IC938, 951, 958, 5108, 5201, 7008, 7108, 7800, 7801, 7806 (terminates at Kiskunhalas), 7901, 8223 (terminates at Kaposvar).

DECEMBER 25:

IC650 (starts at Nyiregyháza), 780 (starts from Kiskunhalas), IC819, IC829, 5509, 7009.

DECEMBER 31:

IC503, IC506, 521 (terminates at Miskolc), IC563 (terminates at Nyiregyháza), IC616, IC653 (terminates at Nyiregyháza), 781 (terminates at Baja), IC801, IC808, IC818, IC828, 901, 908, IC918, IC938, 951, 958, 5108, 5201, 7800, 7801, 8223 (terminates at Kaposvar).

JANUARY 1:

IC650 (starts at Nyiregyháza), IC819, IC829, 5509.